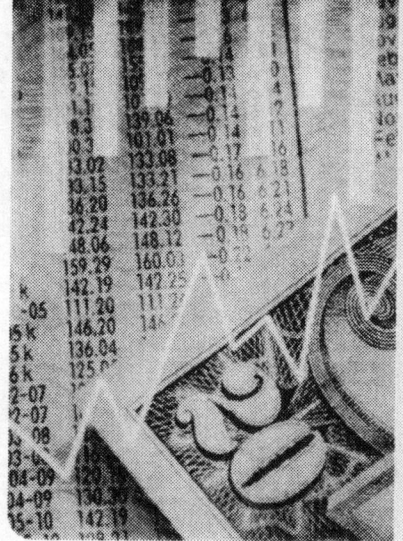

Hoover's Handbook of

American Business

2021

HOOVERS™

A D&B COMPANY

Austin, Texas

Hoover's Handbook of American Business 2021 is intended to provide readers with accurate and authoritative information about the enterprises covered in it. Hoover's researched all companies and organizations profiled, and in many cases contacted them directly so that companies represented could provide information. The information contained herein is as accurate as we could reasonably make it. In many cases we have relied on third-party material that we believe to be trustworthy, but were unable to independently verify. We do not warrant that the book is absolutely accurate or without error. Readers should not rely on any information contained herein in instances where such reliance might cause financial loss. The publisher, the editors, and their data suppliers specifically disclaim all warranties, including the implied warranties of merchantability and fitness for a specific purpose. This book is sold with the understanding that neither the publisher, the editors, nor any content contributors are engaged in providing investment, financial, accounting, legal, or other professional advice.

The financial data (Historical Financials sections) in this book are from a variety of sources. Mergent Inc., provided selected data for the Historical Financials sections of publicly traded companies. For private companies and for historical information on public companies prior to their becoming public, we obtained information directly from the companies or from trade sources deemed to be reliable. Hoover's, Inc., is solely responsible for the presentation of all data.

Many of the names of products and services mentioned in this book are the trademarks or service marks of the companies manufacturing or selling them and are subject to protection under US law. Space has not permitted us to indicate which names are subject to such protection, and readers are advised to consult with the owners of such marks regarding their use. Hoover's is a trademark of Hoover's, Inc.

A D&B COMPANY

10 9 8 7 6 5 4 3 2 1

Publishers Cataloging-in-Publication Data

Hoover's Handbook of American Business 2021

    Includes indexes.

    ISBN: 978-1-64972-056-6

    ISSN 1055-7202

    1. Business enterprises — Directories. 2. Corporations — Directories.

HF3010 338.7

U.S. AND WORLD BOOK SALES

Mergent Inc.

580 Kingsley Park Drive

Fort Mill, SC

29715

Phone: 704-559-6961

e-mail: skardon@ftserussell.com

Web: www.mergentbusinesspress.com

Mergent Inc.

Executive Managing Director: John Pedernales

Publisher and Managing Director of Print Products : Thomas Wecera

Director of Print Products: Charlot Volny

Quality Assurance Editor: Wayne Arnold

Production Research Assistant: Davie Christna

Data Manager: Jason Horvat

MERGENT CUSTOMER SUPPORT FOR PRINT
Support and Fulfillment Manager: Stpehanie Kardon 704-559-6961

ABOUT MERGENT INC.

For over 100 years, Mergent, Inc. has been a leading provider of business and financial information on public and private companies globally. Mergent is known to be a trusted partner to corporate and financial institutions, as well as to academic and public libraries. Today we continue to build on a century of experience by transforming data into knowledge and combining our expertise with the latest technology to create new global data and analytical solutions for our clients. With advanced data collection services, cloud-based applications, desktop analytics and print products, Mergent and its subsidiaries provide solutions from top down economic and demographic information, to detailed equity and debt fundamental analysis. We incorporate value added tools such as quantitative Smart Beta equity research and tools for portfolio building and measurement. Based in the U.S., Mergent maintains a strong global presence, with offices in New York, Charlotte, San Diego, London, Tokyo, Kuching and Melbourne. Mergent, Inc. is a member of the London Stock Exchange plc group of companies. The Mergent business forms part of LSEG's Information Services Division, which includes FTSE Russell, a global leader in indexes.

MERGENT
BUSINESS PRESS
by FTSE Russell

Abbreviations

AFL-CIO – American Federation of Labor and Congress of Industrial Organizations
AMA – American Medical Association
AMEX – American Stock Exchange
ARM – adjustable-rate mortgage
ASP – application services provider
ATM – asynchronous transfer mode
ATM – automated teller machine
CAD/CAM – computer-aided design/computer-aided manufacturing
CD-ROM – compact disc – read-only memory
CD-R – CD-recordable
CEO – chief executive officer
CFO – chief financial officer
CMOS – complementary metal oxide silicon
COO – chief operating officer
DAT – digital audiotape
DOD – Department of Defense
DOE – Department of Energy
DOS – disk operating system
DOT – Department of Transportation
DRAM – dynamic random-access memory
DSL – digital subscriber line
DVD – digital versatile disc/digital video disc
DVD-R – DVD-recordable
EPA – Environmental Protection Agency
EPROM – erasable programmable read-only memory
EPS – earnings per share
ESOP – employee stock ownership plan
EU – European Union
EVP – executive vice president
FCC – Federal Communications Commission
FDA – Food and Drug Administration
FDIC – Federal Deposit Insurance Corporation

FTC – Federal Trade Commission
FTP – file transfer protocol
GATT – General Agreement on Tariffs and Trade
GDP – gross domestic product
HMO – health maintenance organization
HR – human resources
HTML – hypertext markup language
ICC – Interstate Commerce Commission
IPO – initial public offering
IRS – Internal Revenue Service
ISP – Internet service provider
kWh – kilowatt-hour
LAN – local-area network
LBO – leveraged buyout
LCD – liquid crystal display
LNG – liquefied natural gas
LP – limited partnership
Ltd. – limited
mips – millions of instructions per second
MW – megawatt
NAFTA – North American Free Trade Agreement
NASA – National Aeronautics and Space Administration
NASDAQ – National Association of Securities Dealers Automated Quotations
NATO – North Atlantic Treaty Organization
NYSE – New York Stock Exchange
OCR – optical character recognition
OECD – Organization for Economic Cooperation and Development
OEM – original equipment manufacturer
OPEC – Organization of Petroleum Exporting Countries
OS – operating system
OSHA – Occupational Safety and Health Administration

OTC – over-the-counter
PBX – private branch exchange
PCMCIA – Personal Computer Memory Card International Association
P/E – price to earnings ratio
RAID – redundant array of independent disks
RAM – random-access memory
R&D – research and development
RBOC – regional Bell operating company
RISC – reduced instruction set computer
REIT – real estate investment trust
ROA – return on assets
ROE – return on equity
ROI – return on investment
ROM – read-only memory
S&L – savings and loan
SCSI – Small Computer System Interface
SEC – Securities and Exchange Commission
SEVP – senior executive vice president
SIC – Standard Industrial Classification
SOC – system on a chip
SVP – senior vice president
USB – universal serial bus
VAR – value-added reseller
VAT – value-added tax
VC – venture capitalist
VoIP – Voice over Internet Protocol
VP – vice president
WAN – wide-area network
WWW – World Wide Web

Contents

List of Lists

HOOVER'S RANKINGS

Companies Profiled

Companies Profiled (continued)

Companies Profiled (continued)

Companies Profiled (continued)

Companies Profiled (continued)

About Hoover's Handbook of American Business 2021

In these tough economic times, it pays to have all the facts, whether you're making business, financial, or employment decisions. When you need information about companies, *Hoover's Handbook of American Business* is the place to turn for answers. Throughout its history, it has stood as one of America's respected sources of business information, packed with the information you need.

We at Hoover's Business Press pledge we will continue our work to add more value to this already valuable resource. So search away for the business information you need to make the important decisions facing you. Leave the fact-finding and digging and the sorting and sifting to the editors at Hoover's.

Hoover's Handbook of American Business is the first of our four-title series of handbooks that covers, literally, the world of business. The series is available as an indexed set, and also includes *Hoover's Handbook of World Business*, *Hoover's Handbook of Private Companies*, and *Hoover's Handbook of Emerging Companies*. This series brings you information on the biggest, fastest-growing, and most influential enterprises in the world.

HOOVER'S ARCHIVES FOR BUSINESS NEEDS

In addition to the 2,550 companies featured in our handbooks, comprehensive coverage of more than 6 years of Hoovers Books are published in the Hoovers Archives.. Our goal is to provide one site that offers authoritative, updated intelligence on US and global companies, industries, and the people who shape them. Stay with the Hoovers famaily of products and History and package the books with the archives products.

We welcome the recognition we have received as a provider of high-quality company information — online, electronically, and in print — and continue to look for ways to make our products more available and more useful to you.

We believe that anyone who buys from, sells to, invests in, lends to, competes with, interviews with, or works for a company should know all there is to know about that enterprise. Taken together, this book and the other Hoover's products and resources represent the most complete source of basic corporate information readily available to the general public.

This latest version of *Hoover's Handbook of American Business* contains, as always, profiles of the largest and most influential companies in the United States. Each of the companies profiled here was chosen because of its important role in American business. For more details on how these companies were selected, see the section titled "Using Hoover's Handbooks."

HOW TO USE THIS BOOK

This book has four sections:

1. "Using Hoover's Handbooks" describes the contents of our profiles and explains the ways in which we gather and compile our data.

2. "A List-Lover's Compendium" contains lists of the largest, smallest, best, most, and other superlatives related to companies involved in American business.

3. The company profiles section makes up the largest and most important part of the book — 750 profiles of major US enterprises.

4. Three indexes complete the book. The first sorts companies by industry groups, the second by headquarters location. The third index is a list of all the executives found in the Executives section of each company profile.

Using Hoover's Handbooks

SELECTION OF THE COMPANIES PROFILED

The 750 enterprises profiled in this book include the largest and most influential companies in America. Among them are:

- more than 710 publicly held companies, from 3M to Zions Bancorporation
- more than 30 large private enterprises (such as Cargill and Mars)
- several mutual and cooperative organizations (such as State Farm and Ace Hardware)
- a selection of other enterprises (such as Kaiser Foundation Health Plan, the US Postal Service, and the Tennessee Valley Authority) that we believe are sufficiently large and influential enough to warrant inclusion.

In selecting these companies, our foremost question was "What companies will our readers be most interested in?" Our goal was to answer as many questions as we could in one book — in effect, trying to anticipate your curiosity. This approach resulted in four general selection criteria for including companies in the book:

1. Size. The 500 or so largest American companies, measured by sales and by number of employees, are included in the book. In general, these companies have sales in excess of $2 billion, and they are the ones you will have heard of and the ones you will want to know about. These are the companies at the top of the *FORTUNE*, *Forbes*, and *Business Week* lists. We have made sure to include the top private companies in this number.

2. Growth. We believe that relatively few readers will be going to work for, or investing in, the railroad industry. Therefore, only a few railroads are in the book. On the other hand, we have included a number of technology firms, as well as companies that provide medical products and services — pharmaceutical and biotech companies, health care insurers, and medical device makers.

3. Visibility. Most readers will have heard of the Hilton Worldwide and Harley-Davidson companies. Their service or consumer natures make them household names, even though they are not among the corporate giants in terms of sales and employment.

4. Breadth of coverage. To show the diversity of economic activity, we've included, among others, a professional sports team, one ranch, the Big Four accounting firms, and one of the largest law firms in the US. We feel that these businesses are important enough to enjoy at least "token" representation. While we might not emphasize certain industries, the industry leaders are present.

ORGANIZATION

The profiles are presented in alphabetical order. This alphabetization is generally word by word, which means that Legg Mason precedes Leggett & Platt. You will find the commonly used name of the enterprise at the beginning of the profile; the full, legal name is found in the Locations section. If a company name is also a person's name, like Walt Disney, it will be alphabetized under the first name; if the company name starts with initials, like J. C. Penney or H.J. Heinz, look for it under the combined initials (in the above examples, JC and HJ, respectively). Basic financial data is listed under the heading Historical Financials; also included is the exchange on which the company's stock is traded if it is public, the ticker symbol used by the stock exchange, and the company's fiscal year-end.

The annual financial information contained in the profiles is current through fiscal year-ends occurring as late as May 2014. We have included certain nonfinancial developments, such as officer changes, through September 2014.

OVERVIEW

In the first section of the profile, we have tried to give a thumbnail description of the company and what it does. The description will usually include information on the company's strategy, reputation, and ownership. We recommend that you read this section first.

HISTORY

This extended section, included for almost all companies in the book, reflects our belief that every enterprise is the sum of its history and that you have to know where you came from in order to know where you are going. While some companies have limited historical awareness, we think the vast majority of the enterprises in this book have colorful backgrounds. We have tried to focus on the people who made the enterprises what they are today. We have found these histories to be full of twists and ironies; they make fascinating reading.

EXECUTIVES

Here we list the names of the people who run the company, insofar as space allows. In the case of public companies, we have shown the ages and total compensation of key officers. In some cases the published data is for the previous year although the company has announced promotions or retirements since year-end. Total compensation is the sum of salary, bonus, and the value of any other benefits, such as stock options or deferred compensation.

Although companies are free to structure their management titles any way they please, most modern corporations follow standard practices. The ultimate power in any corporation lies with the shareholders, who elect a board of directors, usually including officers or "insiders" as well as individuals from outside the company. The chief officer, the person on whose desk the buck stops, is usually called the chief executive officer (CEO). Often, he or she is also the chairman of the board.

As corporate management has become more complex, it is common for the CEO to have a "right-hand person" who oversees the day-to-day operations of the company, allowing the CEO plenty of time to focus on strategy and long-term issues. This right-hand person is usually designated the chief operating officer (COO) and is often the president of the company. In other cases one person is both chairman and president.

A multitude of other titles exists, including chief financial officer (CFO), chief administrative officer, and vice chairman. We have always tried to include the CFO, the chief legal officer, and the chief human resources or personnel officer. Our best advice is that officers' pay levels are clear indicators of who the board of directors thinks are the most important members of the management team.

The people named in the Executives section are indexed at the back of the book.

The Executives section also includes the name of the company's auditing (accounting) firm, where available.

LOCATIONS

Here we include the company's full legal name and its headquarters, street address, telephone and fax numbers, and Web site, as available. The back of the book includes an index of companies by headquarters locations.

In some cases we have also included information on the geographic distribution of the company's business, including sales and profit data. Note that these profit numbers, like those in the Products/Operations section below, are usually operating or pretax profits rather than net profits. Operating profits are generally those before financing costs (interest income and payments) and before taxes, which are considered costs attributable to the whole company rather than to one division or part of the world. For this reason the net income figures (in the Historical Financials section) are usually much lower, since they are after interest and taxes. Pretax profits are after interest but before taxes.

Headquarters for companies that are incorporated in Bermuda, but whose operational headquarters are in the US, are listed under their US address.

PRODUCTS/OPERATIONS

This section lists as many of the company's products, services, brand names, divisions, subsidiaries, and joint ventures as we could fit. We have tried to include all its major lines and all familiar brand names. The nature of this section varies by company and the amount of information available. If the company publishes sales and profit information by type of business, we have included it.

COMPETITORS

In this section we have listed companies that compete with the profiled company. This feature is included as a quick way to locate similar companies and compare them. The universe of competitors includes all public companies and all private companies with sales in excess of $500 million. In a few instances we have identified smaller private companies as key competitors.

HISTORICAL FINANCIALS

Here we have tried to present as much data about each enterprise's financial performance as we could compile in the allocated space. The information varies somewhat from industry to industry and is less complete in the case of private companies that do not release data (although we have always tried to provide annual sales and employment). There are a few industries, venture capital and investment banking, for example, for which revenue numbers are unavailable as a rule.

The following information is generally present.
A 5-year table, with relevant annualized compound growth rates, covers:
- Sales — fiscal year sales (year-end assets for most financial companies)
- Net income — fiscal year net income (before accounting changes)
- Net profit margin — fiscal year net income as a percent of sales (as a percent of assets for most financial firms)
- Employees — fiscal year-end or average number of employees
- Stock price — the fiscal year close
- P/E — high and low price/earnings ratio
- Earnings per share — fiscal year earnings per share (EPS)
- Dividends per share — fiscal year dividends per share
- Book value per share — fiscal year-end book value (common shareholders' equity per share)

The information on the number of employees is intended to aid the reader interested in knowing whether a company has a long-term trend of increasing or decreasing employment. As far as we know, we are the only company that publishes this information in print format.

The numbers on the left in each row of the Historical Financials section give the month and the year in which the company's fiscal year actually ends. Thus, a company with a March 31, 2020, year-end is shown as 3/20.

In addition, we have provided in graph form a stock price history for most public companies. The graphs, covering up to five years, show the range of trading between the high and the low price, as well as the closing price for each fiscal year. Generally, for private companies, we have graphed net income, or, if that is unavailable, sales.

Key year-end statistics in this section generally show the financial strength of the enterprise, including:
- Debt ratio (long-term debt as a percent of shareholders' equity)
- Return on equity (net income divided by the average of beginning and ending common shareholders' equity)
- Cash and cash equivalents
- Current ratio (ratio of current assets to current liabilities)
- Total long-term debt (including capital lease obligations
- Number of shares of common stock outstanding
- Dividend yield (fiscal year dividends per share divided by the fiscal year-end closing stock price)
- Dividend payout (fiscal year dividends divided by fiscal year EPS)
- Market value at fiscal year-end (fiscal year-end closing stock price multiplied by fiscal year-end number of shares outstanding)

Per share data has been adjusted for stock splits. The data for public companies has been provided to us by Mergent Inc. Other public company information was compiled by Hoover's, which takes full responsibility for the content of this section.

In the case of private companies that do not publicly disclose financial information, we usually did not have access to such standardized data. We have gathered estimates of sales and other statistics from numerous sources.

Hoover's Handbook of

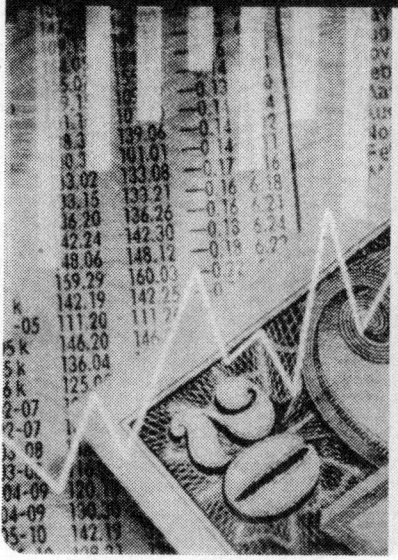

American Business

A List-Lover's Compendium

The 300 Largest U.S. Public Companies by Sales in
Hoover's Handbook of American Business 2021

Rank	Company	Sales ($ mil.)	Rank	Company	Sales ($ mil.)	Rank	Company	Sales ($ mil.)
1	Walmart Inc	$523,964	60	StoneX Group Inc	$54,036	119	Duke Energy Corp	$25,079
2	Amazon.com Inc	$386,064	61	Energy Transfer Operating LP	$54,032	120	Netflix Inc	$24,996
3	Apple Inc	$274,515	62	Goldman Sachs Group Inc	$53,922	121	Kraft Heinz Co (The)	$24,977
4	Exxon Mobil Corp	$264,938	63	Morgan Stanley	$53,823	122	SYNNEX Corp	$24,676
5	CVS Health Corp	$256,776	64	Caterpillar Inc.	$53,800	123	Tesla Inc	$24,578
6	Berkshire Hathaway Inc	$254,616	65	Sysco Corp	$52,893	124	PBF Energy Inc	$24,508
7	UnitedHealth Group Inc	$242,155	66	Pfizer Inc	$51,750	125	CBRE Group Inc	$23,894
8	McKesson Corp	$231,051	67	HCA Healthcare Inc	$51,336	126	Broadcom Inc (DE)	$23,888
9	AmerisourceBergen Corp.	$189,894	68	American International Group Inc	$49,746	127	Baker Hughes Company	$23,838
10	Alphabet Inc	$182,527	69	Cisco Systems Inc	$49,301	128	Dollar Tree Inc	$23,611
11	AT&T Inc	$181,193	70	Charter Communicati Inc (New)	$48,097	129	Cummins, Inc.	$23,571
12	Costco Wholesale Corp	$166,761	71	American Express Co.	$47,020	130	Qualcomm Inc	$23,531
13	Cigna Corp (New)	$153,566	72	Delta Air Lines Inc (DE)	$47,007	131	Starbucks Corp.	$23,518
14	Cardinal Health, Inc.	$152,922	73	Merck & Co Inc	$46,840	132	Amgen Inc	$23,362
15	Chevron Corporation	$146,516	74	American Airlines Group Inc	$45,768	133	Penske Automotive Group Inc	$23,179
16	Microsoft Corporation	$143,015	75	T-Mobile US Inc	$44,998	134	Nucor Corp.	$22,589
17	JPMorgan Chase & Co	$142,422	76	Allstate Corp	$44,675	135	Lennar Corp	$22,489
18	Walgreens Boots Alliance Inc	$139,537	77	Best Buy Inc	$43,638	136	Gilead Sciences Inc	$22,449
19	General Motors Co	$137,237	78	United Airlines Holdings Inc	$43,259	137	Southwest Airlines Co	$22,428
20	Verizon Communications Inc	$131,868	79	Tyson Foods Inc	$43,185	138	Lumen Technologies Inc	$22,401
21	Ford Motor Co. (DE)	$127,144	80	TJX Companies, Inc.	$41,717	139	International Paper Co	$22,376
22	Marathon Petroleum Corp.	$124,813	81	General Dynamics Corp	$39,350	140	Eli Lilly & Co	$22,320
23	Kroger Co (The)	$122,286	82	Oracle Corp	$39,068	141	AFLAC Inc.	$22,307
24	Fannie Mae	$120,304	83	Progressive Corp. (OH)	$39,022	142	Rite Aid Corp.	$21,928
25	Bank of America Corp	$113,589	84	Dow Inc	$38,542	143	Visa Inc	$21,846
26	Home Depot Inc	$110,225	85	Publix Super Markets, Inc..	$38,463	144	PNC Financial Services Group	$21,624
27	Phillips 66	$109,559	86	NIKE Inc	$37,403	145	DuPont de Nemours Inc	$21,512
28	Valero Energy Corp	$108,324	87	Coca-Cola Co (The)	$37,266	146	PayPal Holdings Inc	$21,454
29	Anthem Inc	$104,213	88	World Fuel Services Corp.	$36,819	147	Micron Technology Inc.	$21,435
30	Wells Fargo & Co (New)	$103,915	89	Northrop Grumman Corp	$36,799	148	Southern Co.	$21,419
31	Federal Reserve System	$103,846	90	Honeywell International Inc	$36,709	149	AutoNation, Inc.	$21,336
32	Comcast Corp	$103,564	91	ConocoPhillips	$36,670	150	Occidental Petroleum Corp	$21,232
33	Citigroup Inc	$103,449	92	Deere & Co.	$35,540	151	McDonald's Corp	$21,077
34	General Electric Co	$95,214	93	Exelon Corp	$34,438	152	Marriott International, Inc.	$20,972
35	Dell Technologies Inc	$92,154	94	Capital One Financial Corp	$33,766	153	ManpowerGroup	$20,864
36	Facebook Inc	$85,965	95	Plains GP Holdings LP	$33,669	154	Bank of New York Mellon Corp	$20,822
37	Johnson & Johnson	$82,059	96	Plains All American Pipeline LP	$33,669	155	Hartford Financial Services	$20,740
38	Target Corp	$78,112	97	AbbVie Inc	$33,266	156	Whirlpool Corp	$20,419
39	Intel Corp	$77,867	98	Enterprise Products Partners L.P.	$32,789	157	Carmax Inc.	$20,320
40	International Business Ma. Corp.	$77,147	99	3M Co	$32,184	158	DR Horton Inc	$20,311
41	Raytheon Technologies Corp	$77,046	100	Abbott Laboratories	$31,904	159	Kohl's Corp.	$19,974
42	Freddie Mac	$75,125	101	Travelers Companies Inc (The	$31,581	160	Lear Corp.	$19,810
43	Centene Corp	$74,639	102	Philip Morris International Inc	$29,805	161	DXC Technology Co	$19,577
44	United Parcel Service Inc	$74,094	103	Arrow Electronics, Inc.	$28,917	162	Union Pacific Corp	$19,533
45	Lowe's Companies Inc	$72,148	104	CHS Inc	$28,406	163	Synchrony Financial	$19,461
46	Procter & Gamble Co (The)	$70,950	105	ViacomCBS Inc	$27,812	164	Genuine Parts Co.	$19,392
47	MetLife Inc	$69,620	106	Dollar General Corp	$27,754	165	NextEra Energy Inc	$19,204
48	FedEx Corp	$69,217	107	U.S. Bancorp (DE)	$27,325	166	Exelon Generation Co LLC	$18,924
49	PepsiCo Inc	$67,161	108	Jabil Inc	$27,266	167	Carrier Global Corp	$18,608
50	Lockheed Martin Corp	$65,398	109	Hewlett Packard Enterprise Co	$26,982	168	Tenet Healthcare Corp.	$18,479
51	Disney (Walt) Co. (The)	$65,388	110	Mondelez International Inc	$26,581	169	Kimberly-Clark Corp.	$18,450
52	Humana, Inc.	$64,888	111	United Natural Foods Inc.	$26,514	170	CDW Corp	$18,032
53	Prudential Financial Inc	$64,807	112	Bristol Myers Squibb Co.	$26,145	171	Jones Lang LaSalle Inc	$17,983
54	Archer Daniels Midland Co.	$64,656	113	US Foods Holding Corp	$25,939	172	Danaher Corp	$17,911
55	Albertsons Companies Inc	$62,455	114	Paccar Inc.	$25,600	173	Sherwin-Williams Co (The)	$17,901
56	Boeing Co.	$58,158	115	Thermo Fisher Scientific Inc	$25,542	174	Avnet Inc	$17,634
57	HP Inc	$56,639	116	Macy's Inc	$25,331	175	General Mills Inc	$17,627
58	Federal Reserve Bank Of New Y	$56,535	117	Altria Group Inc	$25,110	176	WestRock Co	$17,579
59	Energy Transfer LP	$54,213	118	Performance Food Group Co	$25,086	177	HollyFrontier Corp	$17,487
						178	Tenneco Inc	$17,450

SOURCE: MERGENT INC., DATABASE, FEBRUARY 2021

The 300 Largest U.S. Public Companies by Sales in
Hoover's Handbook of American Business 2021 (continued)

Rank	Company	Sales ($ mil.)	Rank	Company	Sales ($ mil.)	Rank	Company	Sales ($ mil.)
179	EOG Resources, Inc.	$17,380	220	Howmet Aerospace Inc	$14,192	261	CSX Corp	$11,937
180	Lincoln National Corp.	$17,258	221	Uber Technologies Inc	$14,147	262	Vistra Corp	$11,809
181	Applied Materials, Inc.	$17,202	222	Illinois Tool Works, Inc.	$14,109	263	Charles Schwab Corp	$11,785
182	PG&E Corp (Holding Co)	$17,129	223	Murphy USA Inc	$14,035	264	Berry Global Group Inc	$11,709
183	Becton Dickinson And Co	$17,117	224	Discover Financial Services	$13,989	265	Kinder Morgan Inc.	$11,700
184	Salesforce.Com Inc	$17,098	225	Parker-Hannifin Corp	$13,696	266	Crown Holdings Inc	$11,665
185	Mastercard Inc	$16,883	226	Textron Inc	$13,630	267	Ally Financial Inc	$11,618
186	Molina Healthcare Inc	$16,829	227	Kellogg Co	$13,578	268	LabCorp	$11,555
187	Emerson Electric Co.	$16,785	228	Jacobs Engineering Group, Inc.	$13,567	269	Live Nation Entertainment In	$11,548
188	Cognizant Technology Solutio	$16,783	229	Qurate Retail Inc	$13,458	270	Xcel Energy Inc	$11,529
189	Western Digital Corp	$16,736	230	Biogen Inc	$13,445	271	Corning Inc	$11,503
190	Core Mark Holding Co Inc	$16,671	231	Toyota Motor Credit Corp.	$13,284	272	Grainger (W.W.), Inc.	$11,486
191	Marsh & McLennan Companies I	$16,652	232	AECOM	$13,240	273	Ball Corp	$11,474
192	XPO Logistics, Inc.	$16,648	233	Community Health Systems, In	$13,210	274	Pilgrims Pride Corp.	$11,409
193	Sunoco LP	$16,596	234	BJs Wholesale Club Holdings Inc	$13,191	275	DaVita Inc	$11,388
194	Dominion Energy Inc (New)	$16,572	235	State Street Corp.	$13,131	276	Universal Health Services, Inc.	$11,378
195	Gap Inc	$16,383	236	Otis Worldwide Corp	$13,118	277	Baxter International Inc	$11,362
196	Principal Financial Group In	$16,222	237	Global Partners LP	$13,082	278	Bed, Bath & Beyond, Inc.	$11,159
197	Ross Stores Inc	$16,039	238	Ameriprise Financial Inc	$12,967	279	Discovery Inc	$11,144
198	Colgate-Palmolive Co.	$15,693	239	United States Steel Corp.	$12,937	280	Keurig Dr Pepper Inc	$11,120
199	American Electric Power Co I	$15,561	240	L Brands, Inc	$12,914	281	Leidos Holdings Inc	$11,094
200	Nordstrom, Inc.	$15,524	241	MGM Resorts International	$12,900	282	IQVIA Holdings Inc	$11,088
201	Waste Management, Inc. (DE)	$15,455	242	Adobe Inc	$12,868	283	Conagra Brands Inc	$11,054
202	Robinson (C.H.) Worldwide, I	$15,310	243	Aramark	$12,830	284	PulteGroup Inc	$11,036
203	PPG Industries Inc	$15,146	244	DISH Network Corp	$12,808	285	FirstEnergy Corp	$11,035
204	Booking Holdings Inc	$15,066	245	Lithia Motors Inc	$12,673	286	Reliance Steel & Aluminum Co	$10,974
205	Omnicom Group, Inc.	$14,954	246	DTE Energy Co	$12,669	287	NVIDIA Corp	$10,918
206	Loews Corp.	$14,931	247	AutoZone, Inc.	$12,632	288	Entergy Corp. (New)	$10,879
207	Ecolab Inc	$14,906	248	Consolidated Edison Inc	$12,574	289	Sempra Energy	$10,829
208	Stryker Corp	$14,884	249	LKQ Corp	$12,506	290	Consolidated Edison Co. of N	$10,821
209	Goodyear Tire & Rubber Co.	$14,745	250	Santander Holdings USA Inc.	$12,379	291	VMware Inc	$10,811
210	Automatic Data Processing Inc.	$14,590	251	Edison International	$12,347	292	CNA Financial Corp	$10,767
211	BlackRock Inc	$14,539	252	Southern California Edison C	$12,306	293	Boston Scientific Corp.	$10,735
212	Texas Instruments, Inc.	$14,461	253	Fox Corp	$12,303	294	ODP Corp (The)	$10,647
213	Halliburton Company	$14,445	254	CenterPoint Energy, Inc	$12,301	295	Molson Coors Beverage Co	$10,579
214	Stanley Black & Decker Inc	$14,442	255	Florida Power & Light Co.	$12,192	296	VF Corp.	$10,489
215	Truist Financial Corp	$14,424	256	Federal Reserve Bank of San F	$12,188	297	Steel Dynamics Inc.	$10,465
216	Freeport-McMoRan Inc	$14,402	257	Quanta Services, Inc.	$12,112	298	Sonic Automotive, Inc.	$10,454
217	Fluor Corp.	$14,348	258	Expedia Group Inc	$12,067	299	Alcoa Corporation	$10,433
218	Reinsura Group of America, Inc.	$14,300	259	Group 1 Automotive, Inc.	$12,044	300	Fidelity National Informatio Inc	$10,333
219	Lauder (Estee) Cos., Inc. (The)	$14,294	260	Unum Group	$11,999			

The 300 Most Profitable Public U.S. Companies
Hoover's Handbook of American Business 2021

Rank	Company	Net Income ($ mil.)	Rank	Company	Net Income ($ mil.)	Rank	Company	Net Income ($ mil.)
1	Berkshire Hathaway Inc	$81,417	60	Viatris Inc	$4,917	119	EOG Resources, Inc.	$2,735
2	Apple Inc	$57,411	61	Booking Holdings Inc	$4,865	120	Humana, Inc.	$2,707
3	Microsoft Corporation	$44,281	62	Allstate Corp	$4,847	121	Micron Technology Inc.	$2,687
4	Alphabet Inc	$40,269	63	Anthem Inc	$4,807	122	Marathon Petroleum Corp.	$2,637
5	JPMorgan Chase & Co	$36,431	64	Delta Air Lines Inc (DE)	$4,767	123	Travelers Companies Inc (The	$2,622
6	Facebook Inc	$29,146	65	Southern Co.	$4,754	124	NIKE Inc	$2,539
7	Bank of America Corp	$27,430	66	Boston Scientific Corp.	$4,700	125	Illinois Tool Works, Inc.	$2,521
8	Amazon.com Inc	$21,331	67	Dell Technologies Inc	$4,616	126	Fifth Third Bancorp (Cincinn	$2,512
9	Intel Corp	$20,899	68	Enterprise Products Partners L.P.	$4,591	127	Advanced Micro Devices Inc	$2,490
10	Wells Fargo & Co (New)	$19,549	69	BlackRock Inc	$4,476	128	Automatic Data Processing Inc.	$2,467
11	Citigroup Inc	$19,401	70	Bank of New York Mellon Corp	$4,441	129	Lennar Corp	$2,465
12	Verizon Communications Inc	$19,265	71	United Parcel Service Inc	$4,440	130	Valero Energy Corp	$2,422
13	Pfizer Inc	$16,273	72	NRG Energy Inc	$4,438	131	Alexion Pharmaceuticals Inc.	$2,404
14	Johnson & Johnson	$15,119	73	Lowe's Companies Inc	$4,281	132	Paccar Inc.	$2,388
15	Walmart Inc	$14,881	74	PayPal Holdings Inc	$4,202	133	DR Horton Inc	$2,374
16	Exxon Mobil Corp	$14,340	75	Prudential Financial Inc	$4,186	134	Colgate-Palmolive Co.	$2,367
17	Fannie Mae	$14,160	76	Energy Transfer Operating LP	$4,084	135	Florida Power & Light Co.	$2,334
18	AT&T Inc	$13,903	77	Costco Wholesale Corp	$4,002	136	Southwest Airlines Co	$2,300
19	UnitedHealth Group Inc	$13,839	78	Biogen Inc	$4,001	137	Cummins, Inc.	$2,260
20	Procter & Gamble Co (The)	$13,027	79	Progressive Corp. (OH)	$3,970	138	Lam Research Corp	$2,252
21	Home Depot Inc	$11,242	80	NortonLifeLock Inc	$3,887	139	State Street Corp.	$2,242
22	Cisco Systems Inc	$11,214	81	NextEra Energy Inc	$3,769	140	Ford Motor Credit Company LLC	$2,228
23	Visa Inc	$10,866	82	Duke Energy Corp	$3,748	141	Sempra Energy	$2,198
24	Comcast Corp	$10,534	83	Synchrony Financial	$3,747	142	General Mills Inc	$2,181
25	Oracle Corp	$10,135	84	Charles Schwab Corp	$3,704	143	Plains All American Pipeline LP	$2,171
26	Merck & Co Inc	$9,843	85	Thermo Fisher Scientific Inc	$3,696	144	Kimberly-Clark Corp.	$2,157
27	International Business Ma Corp.	$9,431	86	Abbott Laboratories	$3,687	145	Tyson Foods Inc	$2,140
28	Morgan Stanley	$9,042	87	Applied Materials, Inc.	$3,619	146	T Rowe Price Group, Inc.	$2,131
29	Coca-Cola Co (The)	$8,920	88	Energy Transfer LP	$3,592	147	S&P Global Inc	$2,123
30	Goldman Sachs Group Inc	$8,466	89	Mondelez International Inc	$3,555	148	CME Group Inc	$2,117
31	Eli Lilly & Co	$8,318	90	HCA Healthcare Inc	$3,505	149	Carrier Global Corp	$2,116
32	Mastercard Inc	$8,118	91	General Dynamics Corp	$3,484	150	Regeneron Pharmaceuticals, Inc.	$2,116
33	AbbVie Inc	$7,882	92	T-Mobile US Inc	$3,468	151	Simon Property Group, Inc.	$2,102
34	Amgen Inc	$7,842	93	Bristol Myers Squibb Co.	$3,439	152	Intercontinental Exchange Inc	$2,089
35	PepsiCo Inc	$7,314	94	Vornado Realty L.P.	$3,359	153	Hartford Financial Services	$2,085
36	Freddie Mac	$7,214	95	American International Group Inc	$3,348	154	Stryker Corp	$2,083
37	ConocoPhillips	$7,189	96	CSX Corp	$3,331	155	Discovery Inc	$2,069
38	Philip Morris International Inc	$7,185	97	ViacomCBS Inc	$3,308	156	Blackstone Group Inc (The)	$2,050
39	U.S. Bancorp (DE)	$6,914	98	AFLAC Inc.	$3,304	157	MGM Resorts International	$2,049
40	Lockheed Martin Corp	$6,833	99	Target Corp	$3,281	158	Norfolk Southern Corp	$2,013
41	American Express Co.	$6,759	100	TJX Companies, Inc.	$3,272	159	KKR & Co Inc	$2,005
42	General Motors Co	$6,732	101	Truist Financial Corp	$3,224	160	Cincinnati Financial Corp.	$1,997
43	CVS Health Corp	$6,634	102	Charter Communications Inc (New)	$3,222	161	Emerson Electric Co.	$1,965
44	VMware Inc	$6,412	103	Northrop Grumman Corp	$3,189	162	Kraft Heinz Co (The)	$1,935
45	Honeywell International Inc	$6,143	104	Vornado Realty Trust	$3,148	163	M & T Bank Corp	$1,929
46	Caterpillar Inc.	$6,093	105	Phillips 66	$3,076	164	American Electric Power Co I	$1,921
47	McDonald's Corp	$6,025	106	Electronic Arts	$3,039	165	Ameriprise Financial Inc	$1,893
48	MetLife Inc	$5,899	107	United Airlines Holdings Inc	$3,009	166	American Tower Corp (New)	$1,888
49	eBay Inc	$5,667	108	Danaher Corp	$3,008	167	Air Products & Chemicals Inc	$1,887
50	Texas Instruments, Inc.	$5,595	109	Publix Super Markets, Inc.	$3,005	168	Cognizant Technology Solutio	$1,842
51	Capital One Financial Corp	$5,546	110	Broadcom Inc (DE)	$2,960	169	Qwest Corp	$1,827
52	Raytheon Technologies Corp	$5,537	111	Discover Financial Services	$2,957	170	Intuit Inc	$1,826
53	Gilead Sciences Inc	$5,386	112	Exelon Corp	$2,936	171	Citizens Financial Group Inc	$1,791
54	3M Co	$5,384	113	Chevron Corporation	$2,924	172	Markel Corp (Holding Co)	$1,790
55	PNC Financial Services Group	$5,369	114	HP Inc	$2,844	173	Roper Technologies Inc	$1,768
56	Union Pacific Corp	$5,349	115	Newmont Corp	$2,805	174	Bio-Rad Laboratories Inc	$1,759
57	Adobe Inc	$5,260	116	NVIDIA Corp	$2,796	175	PPL Corp	$1,746
58	Qualcomm Inc	$5,198	117	Netflix Inc	$2,761	176	Marsh & McLennan Companies I	$1,742
59	Cigna Corp (New)	$5,104	118	Deere & Co.	$2,751	177	AutoZone, Inc.	$1,733

SOURCE: MERGENT INC., DATABASE, FEBRUARY 2021

Rank	Company	Net Income ($ mil.)	Rank	Company	Net Income ($ mil.)	Rank	Company	Net Income ($ mil.)
178	Georgia Power Co	$1,720	219	FedEx Corp	$1,286	260	Edwards Lifesciences Corp	$1,047
179	KeyCorp	$1,717	220	Edison International	$1,284	261	Rockwell Automation, Inc.	$1,023
180	Ally Financial Inc	$1,715	221	CBRE Group Inc	$1,282	262	Magellan Midstream Partners	$1,021
181	Dollar General Corp	$1,713	222	ONEOK Inc	$1,279	263	ERP Operating L.P.	$1,006
182	Public Service Enterprise Gr	$1,693	223	Marriott International, Inc.	$1,273	264	Illumina Inc	$1,002
183	American Airlines Group Inc	$1,686	224	Nucor Corp.	$1,271	265	Baxter International Inc	$1,001
184	Waste Management, Inc. (DE)	$1,670	225	Entergy Corp. (New)	$1,258	266	CNA Financial Corp	$1,000
185	Ross Stores Inc	$1,661	226	Keurig Dr Pepper Inc	$1,254	267	Fox Corp	$999
186	Kroger Co (The)	$1,659	227	Consolidated Edison Co. of N	$1,250	268	Santander Consumer USA Holdi	$994
187	Campbell Soup Co	$1,628	228	PPG Industries Inc	$1,243	269	Cadence Design Systems Inc	$989
188	Prologis LP	$1,620	229	Welltower Inc	$1,232	270	Equity Residential	$970
189	Regions Financial Corp	$1,582	230	Dow Inc	$1,225	271	Kellogg Co	$960
190	Prologis Inc	$1,573	231	International Paper Co	$1,225	272	Corning Inc	$960
191	Ecolab Inc	$1,559	232	Analog Devices Inc	$1,221	273	Stanley Black & Decker Inc	$956
192	Sherwin-Williams Co (The)	$1,541	233	KLA Corp	$1,217	274	Clorox Co (The)	$939
193	Best Buy Inc	$1,541	234	Parker-Hannifin Corp	$1,206	275	Laureate Education Inc	$938
194	Southern California Edison C	$1,530	235	Comerica, Inc.	$1,198	276	Masco Corp.	$935
195	Public Storage	$1,521	236	Whirlpool Corp	$1,184	277	Loews Corp.	$932
196	Activision Blizzard, Inc.	$1,503	237	Vertex Pharmaceuticals, Inc.	$1,177	278	First Republic Bank (San Fr CA)	$930
197	Zoetis Inc	$1,500	238	Cheniere Energy Partners L P	$1,175	279	Starbucks Corp.	$928
198	Northern Trust Corp	$1,492	239	DTE Energy Co	$1,169	280	Vistra Corp	$928
199	Southern Copper Corp	$1,486	240	Amphenol Corp.	$1,155	281	Phillips 66 Partners LP	$923
200	Twitter Inc	$1,466	241	Murphy Oil Corp	$1,150	282	Host Hotels & Resorts Inc	$920
201	MPLX LP	$1,434	242	Hershey Company (The)	$1,150	283	Toyota Motor Credit Corp.	$913
202	Moody's Corp.	$1,422	243	Virginia Electric & Power Co	$1,149	284	FirstEnergy Corp	$912
203	Huntington Bancshares Inc	$1,411	244	SVB Financial Group	$1,137	285	Eversource Energy	$909
204	PulteGroup Inc	$1,407	245	WEC Energy Group Inc	$1,135	286	Hormel Foods Corp.	$908
205	Duke Energy Carolinas LLC	$1,403	246	Zimmer Biomet Holdings Inc	$1,132	287	McKesson Corp	$900
206	DISH Network Corp	$1,400	247	Exelon Generation Co LLC	$1,125	288	American Financial Group Inc	$897
207	Principal Financial Group In	$1,394	248	Otis Worldwide Corp	$1,116	289	FleetCor Technologies Inc	$895
208	O'Reilly Automotive, Inc.	$1,391	249	Hologic Inc	$1,115	290	Rocket Companies Inc	$894
209	Intuitive Surgical Inc	$1,379	250	Monster Beverage Corp (New)	$1,108	291	Fiserv Inc	$893
210	Archer Daniels Midland Co.	$1,379	251	Unum Group	$1,100	292	Southwestern Energy Co	$891
211	Xcel Energy Inc	$1,372	252	Paychex Inc	$1,098	293	United Rentals Inc	$890
212	Dominion Energy Inc (New)	$1,358	253	Jones Financial Companies LL	$1,092	294	Carmax Inc.	$888
213	Xerox Holdings Corp	$1,353	254	CoBank, ACB	$1,091	295	Lincoln National Corp.	$886
214	Tennessee Valley Authority	$1,352	255	Alabama Power Co	$1,085	296	Hilton Worldwide Holdings In	$881
215	Consolidated Edison Inc	$1,343	256	Republic Services Inc	$1,073	297	NVR Inc.	$879
216	Omnicom Group, Inc.	$1,339	257	Fidelity National Financial Inc	$1,062	298	Cintas Corp	$876
217	Centene Corp	$1,321	258	Western Union Co	$1,058	299	Becton Dickinson And Co	$874
218	Yum! Brands Inc	$1,294	259	Old Republic International C	$1,056	300	Reinsurance Group of America, Inc.	$870

The 300 Largest U.S. Public Employers in
Hoover's Handbook of American Business 2021

Rank	Company	Employees	Rank	Company	Employees	Rank	Company	Employees
1	Walmart Inc	2,200,000	60	Macy's Inc	123,000	119	LabCorp	65,000
2	Amazon.com Inc	1,298,000	61	Kohl's Corp.	122,000	120	DaVita Inc	65,000
3	United Parcel Service Inc	495,000	62	Lockheed Martin Corp	114,000	121	Autoliv Inc	65,000
4	Yum China Holdings Inc	450,000	63	ABM Industries, Inc.	114,000	122	Brinks Co (The)	64,600
5	Kelly Services, Inc.	446,700	64	Tenet Healthcare Corp.	113,600	123	American Express Co.	64,500
6	Kroger Co (The)	435,000	65	Honeywell International Inc	113,000	124	Western Digital Corp	63,800
7	Home Depot Inc	415,700	66	Intel Corp	110,600	125	Goodyear Tire & Rubber Co.	63,000
8	Berkshire Hathaway Inc	391,500	67	Abbott Laboratories	107,000	126	HanesBrands Inc	63,000
9	International Business Machine	383,800	68	General Dynamics Corp	102,900	127	Brinker International, Inc.	62,200
10	Target Corp	368,000	69	Caterpillar Inc.	102,300	128	Cummins, Inc.	61,615
11	Starbucks Corp.	349,000	70	CBRE Group Inc	100,000	129	Sherwin-Williams Co (The)	61,111
12	Walgreens Boots Alliance Inc	331,000	71	XPO Logistics, Inc.	100,000	130	Marathon Petroleum Corp.	60,910
13	UnitedHealth Group Inc	325,000	72	AutoZone, Inc.	100,000	131	Southwest Airlines Co	60,800
14	Lowe's Companies Inc	320,000	73	Procter & Gamble Co (The)	99,000	132	Morgan Stanley	60,431
15	Cognizant Technology Solutio	292,500	74	Northrop Grumman Corp	97,000	133	Danaher Corp	60,000
16	CVS Health Corp	290,000	75	Charter Communications Inc (New)	96,100	134	Stanley Black & Decker Inc	59,438
17	TJX Companies, Inc.	286,000	76	United Airlines Holdings Inc	96,000	135	Hewlett Packard Enterprise Co	59,400
18	HCA Healthcare Inc	280,000	77	3M Co	95,000	136	Truist Financial Corp	59,000
19	SYNNEX Corp	277,900	78	L Brands, Inc	94,400	137	Facebook Inc	58,601
20	Costco Wholesale Corp	273,000	79	Bloomin' Brands Inc	94,000	138	Brookdale Senior Living Inc	58,400
21	Albertsons Companies Inc	270,000	80	Jones Lang LaSalle Inc	93,400	139	Automatic Data Processing Inc.	58,000
22	PepsiCo Inc	267,000	81	Ross Stores Inc	92,500	140	Sysco Corp	57,000
23	Wells Fargo & Co (New)	260,000	82	Delta Air Lines Inc (DE)	91,224	141	Centene Corp	56,600
24	JPMorgan Chase & Co	256,981	83	Universal Health Services, Inc.	90,400	142	GameStop Corp	56,000
25	Concentrix Corp	250,000	84	Pfizer Inc	88,300	143	Genuine Parts Co.	55,000
26	Aramark	247,900	85	Coca-Cola Co (The)	86,200	144	Jacobs Engineering Group, Inc.	55,000
27	AT&T Inc	246,000	86	Emerson Electric Co.	83,500	145	Bed, Bath & Beyond, Inc.	55,000
28	FedEx Corp	245,000	87	Chipotle Mexican Grill Inc	83,000	146	Fidelity National Information Servi	55,000
29	Raytheon Technologies Corp	243,200	88	O'Reilly Automotive, Inc.	82,167	147	Hyatt Hotels Corp	55,000
30	Jabil Inc	240,000	89	McKesson Corp	80,000	148	Genesis Healthcare Inc	55,000
31	Bank of America Corp	208,000	90	Community Health Systems, In	80,000	149	Cracker Barrel Old Country Store.	55,000
32	Publix Super Markets, Inc.	207,000	91	Mondelez International Inc	79,000	150	Sykes Enterprises. Inc.	54,900
33	General Electric Co	205,000	92	Tenneco Inc	78,000	151	Interpublic Group of Compani	54,300
34	McDonald's Corp	205,000	93	Cisco Systems Inc	77,500	152	AECOM	54,000
35	Disney (Walt) Co. (The)	203,000	94	Whirlpool Corp	77,000	153	Pilgrims Pride Corp.	53,100
36	Citigroup Inc	200,000	95	Marsh & McLennan Companies I	76,000	154	HP Inc	53,000
37	Dollar Tree Inc	193,100	96	NIKE Inc	75,400	155	T-Mobile US Inc	53,000
38	Ford Motor Co. (DE)	186,000	97	Thermo Fisher Scientific Inc	75,000	156	Carrier Global Corp	52,635
39	Darden Restaurants, Inc. (Unif	177,895	98	Exxon Mobil Corp	74,900	157	PNC Financial Services Group	51,918
40	Marriott International, Inc.	174,000	99	Amphenol Corp.	74,000	158	Capital One Financial Corp	51,900
41	Hilton Worldwide Holdings In	173,000	100	Cigna Corp (New)	73,700	159	Prudential Financial Inc	51,511
42	Comcast Corp	168,000	101	Philip Morris International Inc	73,500	160	Cedar Fair LP	51,200
43	Dell Technologies Inc	165,000	102	Becton Dickinson And Co	72,000	161	International Paper Co	51,000
44	Lear Corp.	164,100	103	Merck & Co Inc	71,000	162	LKQ Corp	51,000
45	General Motors Co	164,000	104	Anthem Inc	70,600	163	Healthcare Services Group In	51,000
46	Microsoft Corporation	163,000	105	Omnicom Group, Inc.	70,000	164	Foot Locker, Inc.	50,999
47	Apple Inc	147,000	106	MGM Resorts International	70,000	165	Parker-Hannifin Corp	50,520
48	Dollar General Corp	143,000	107	U.S. Bancorp (DE)	69,651	166	Six Flags Entertainment Corp	50,450
49	Boeing Co.	141,000	108	Deere & Co.	69,634	167	Ecolab Inc	50,200
50	Tyson Foods Inc	139,000	109	Otis Worldwide Corp	69,000	168	Fluor Corp.	50,182
51	DXC Technology Co	138,000	110	Freeport-McMoRan Inc	68,100	169	Rite Aid Corp.	50,000
52	Alphabet Inc	135,301	111	Baker Hughes Company	68,000	170	Baxter International Inc	50,000
53	Verizon Communications Inc	135,000	112	Nordstrom, Inc.	68,000	171	L3Harris Technologies Inc	50,000
54	Oracle Corp	135,000	113	Texas Roadhouse Inc	67,900	172	Laureate Education Inc	50,000
55	American Airlines Group Inc	133,700	114	ASGN Inc	67,700	173	Select Medical Holdings Corp	49,900
56	Johnson & Johnson	132,200	115	HireQuest Inc	67,050	174	Corning Inc	49,500
57	Gap Inc	129,000	116	IQVIA Holdings Inc	67,000	175	TTEC Holdings Inc	49,500
58	Barrett Business Services, I	127,085	117	Advance Auto Parts Inc	67,000	176	WestRock Co	49,300
59	Best Buy Inc	125,000	118	Conduent Inc	67,000	177	MetLife Inc	49,000

SOURCE: MERGENT INC., DATABASE, FEBRUARY 2021

Rank	Company	Employees	Rank	Company	Employees	Rank	Company	Employees
178	Salesforce.Com Inc	49,000	219	State Street Corp.	39,103	260	Travelers Companies Inc (The	30,800
179	Jones Financial Companies LL	49,000	220	AMC Entertainment Holdings I	38,862	261	LHC Group Inc	30,399
180	Bank of New York Mellon Corp	48,400	221	Goldman Sachs Group Inc	38,300	262	Wynn Resorts Ltd	30,200
181	Chevron Corporation	48,200	222	Archer Daniels Midland Co.	38,100	263	Cardinal Health, Inc.	30,000
182	Tesla Inc	48,016	223	Hertz Global Holdings Inc (New)	38,000	264	AbbVie Inc	30,000
183	Lauder (Estee) Cos., Inc. (The)	48,000	224	Dillard's Inc.	38,000	265	Bristol Myers Squibb Co.	30,000
184	VF Corp.	48,000	225	Kraft Heinz Co (The)	37,000	266	Texas Instruments, Inc.	30,000
185	Humana, Inc.	47,200	226	Sanmina Corp	37,000	267	Newell Brands Inc	30,000
186	Berry Global Group Inc	47,000	227	Epam Systems, Inc.	36,739	268	Avis Budget Group Inc	30,000
187	Quest Diagnostics, Inc.	47,000	228	RR Donnelley & Sons Company	36,400	269	CommScope Holding Co Inc	30,000
188	Burlington Stores Inc	47,000	229	Dana Inc	36,300	270	Avery Dennison Corp	30,000
189	StarTek, Inc.	47,000	230	Boston Scientific Corp.	36,000	271	Sprouts Farmers Market Inc	30,000
190	Allstate Corp	46,290	231	Republic Services Inc	36,000	272	AMERCO	30,000
191	Cheesecake Factory Inc. (The)	46,250	232	EMCOR Group, Inc.	36,000	273	Sally Beauty Holdings Inc	30,000
192	American International Group Inc	46,000	233	NCR Corp.	36,000	274	Amkor Technology Inc.	29,650
193	American Eagle Outfitters, Inc.	46,000	234	Dow Inc	35,700	275	BGSF Inc	29,430
194	Las Vegas Sands Corp	46,000	235	NOV Inc	35,479	276	Hunt (J.B.) Transport Servic	29,056
195	Illinois Tool Works, Inc.	45,000	236	DuPont de Nemours Inc	35,000	277	BorgWarner Inc	29,000
196	Waste Management, Inc. (DE)	44,900	237	General Mills Inc	35,000	278	Yellow Corp (New)	29,000
197	Fiserv Inc	44,000	238	Textron Inc	35,000	279	Duke Energy Corp	28,793
198	Ulta Beauty Inc	44,000	239	Ascena Retail Group Inc	35,000	280	Red Robin Gourmet Burgers In	28,586
199	Michaels Companies Inc	44,000	240	ON Semiconductor Corp	34,800	281	ViacomCBS Inc	28,570
200	Abercrombie & Fitch Co	44,000	241	Colgate-Palmolive Co.	34,300	282	United Natural Foods Inc.	28,300
201	Vail Resorts Inc	43,500	242	MAXIMUS Inc.	34,300	283	Penn National Gaming Inc	28,300
202	Acadia Healthcare Company In	42,800	243	Leidos Holdings Inc	34,000	284	Icahn Enterprises LP	28,033
203	Lumen Technologies Inc	42,500	244	Yum! Brands Inc	34,000	285	US Foods Holding Corp	28,000
204	Huntington Ingalls Industrie	42,000	245	Big Lots, Inc.	34,000	286	ManpowerGroup	28,000
205	Mohawk Industries, Inc.	41,800	246	Bright Horizons Family Solutions.	33,800	287	KBR Inc	28,000
206	Howmet Aerospace Inc	41,700	247	Eli Lilly & Co	33,625	288	Cooper-Standard Holdings Inc	28,000
207	Dick's Sporting Goods, Inc	41,600	248	Gallagher (Arthur J.) & Co.	33,300	289	Southern Co.	27,943
208	Progressive Corp. (OH)	41,571	249	Addus HomeCare Corp	33,238	290	PPG Industries Inc	27,700
209	Qualcomm Inc	41,000	250	Crown Holdings Inc	33,000	291	United States Steel Corp.	27,500
210	Quanta Services, Inc.	40,300	251	Exelon Corp	32,713	292	Wabtec Corp.	27,500
211	Micron Technology Inc.	40,000	252	Tractor Supply Co.	32,000	293	O-I Glass Inc	27,500
212	Kimberly-Clark Corp.	40,000	253	ExlService Holdings Inc	31,700	294	Cerner Corp.	27,400
213	Stryker Corp	40,000	254	Newmont Corp	31,600	295	BJs Wholesale Club Holdings Inc	27,231
214	Halliburton Company	40,000	255	Encompass Health Corp	31,570	296	Booz Allen Hamilton Holding Corp.	27,200
215	ODP Corp (The)	40,000	256	Carrols Restaurant Group Inc	31,500	297	Carmax Inc.	27,050
216	PVH Corp	40,000	257	Kellogg Co	31,000	298	Paccar Inc.	27,000
217	Cintas Corp	40,000	258	VMware Inc	31,000	299	Penske Automotive Group Inc	27,000
218	Ryder System, Inc.	39,900	259	Union Pacific Corp	30,960	300	Xerox Holdings Corp	27,000

The **Mergent** 500 Largest Global Corporations (By Revenues)

Rank	Company	Sales ($ mil.)	Rank	Company	Sales ($ mil.)	Rank	Company	Sales ($ mil.)
1	Walmart Inc	$523,964	68	Comcast Corp	$103,564	135	Lloyds Banking Group Plc	$66,539
2	China Petroleum & Chemical C	$426,286	69	Citigroup Inc	$103,449	136	Roche Holding AG	$65,947
3	Amazon.com Inc	$386,064	70	ITOCHU Corp (Japan)	$101,179	137	Lockheed Martin Corp	$65,398
4	PetroChina Co Ltd	$358,163	71	HSBC Holdings Plc	$101,027	138	Disney (Walt) Co. (The)	$65,388
5	Royal Dutch Shell Plc	$352,106	72	Nestle SA	$96,064	139	Japan Post Insurance Co Ltd	$65,292
6	Volkswagen AG	$283,647	73	General Electric Co	$95,214	140	Imperial Brands PLC	$65,072
7	BP PLC	$282,423	74	CITIC Ltd	$94,189	141	Humana, Inc.	$64,888
8	Toyota Motor Corp	$275,725	75	Eneos Holdings Inc	$92,232	142	Prudential Financial Inc	$64,807
9	Apple Inc	$274,515	76	Dell Technologies Inc	$92,154	143	Archer Daniels Midland Co.	$64,656
10	Exxon Mobil Corp	$264,938	77	Hyundai Motor Co., Ltd.	$91,586	144	Tata Motors Ltd	$64,622
11	Cementos Bio-Bio S.A. (Chile)	$263,182	78	Nissan Motor Co., Ltd.	$91,007	145	Equinor ASA	$64,358
12	CVS Health Corp	$256,776	79	Deutsche Telekom AG	$90,417	146	AUDI AG	$62,516
13	Berkshire Hathaway Inc	$254,616	80	Enel SpA	$90,188	147	Albertsons Companies Inc	$62,455
14	UnitedHealth Group Inc	$242,155	81	Hitachi. Ltd.	$88,398	148	Renault S.A. (France)	$62,355
15	McKesson Corp	$231,051	82	Legal & General Group PLC (U	$88,195	149	Toyota Tsusho Corp	$61,668
16	Glencore PLC	$215,111	83	BNP Paribas (France)	$87,744	150	Shanghai Jinfeng Investment C	$61,522
17	Samsung Electronics Co Ltd	$199,548	84	Facebook Inc	$85,965	151	Korea Electric Power Corp KE	$59,447
18	Daimler AG	$193,952	85	Reliance Industries Ltd	$85,217	152	Unilever Plc (United Kingdom)	$58,361
19	AmerisourceBergen Corp.	$189,894	86	LVMH Moet Hennessy Louis Vuit	$84,499	153	Boeing Co.	$58,158
20	Industrial and Commercial Ba	$184,033	87	Tesco PLC	$83,354	154	Dai-ichi Life Holdings Inc	$57,965
21	Alphabet Inc	$182,527	88	Carrefour S.A.	$83,244	155	Tokyo Electric Power Company	$57,498
22	AT&T Inc	$181,193	89	JD.com, Inc.	$82,907	156	HP Inc	$56,639
23	Hon.Hai Precision Industry C	$178,459	90	Johnson & Johnson	$82,059	157	Federal Reserve Bank Of New Y	$56,535
24	Total SE	$176,249	91	Manulife Financial Corp	$80,573	158	Societe Generale	$56,518
25	Costco Wholesale Corp	$166,761	92	ENI S.p.A.	$79,762	159	POSCO (South Korea)	$56,110
26	Exor NV	$161,403	93	China Communicat C Group Ltd	$79,732	160	Idemitsu Kosan Co Ltd	$55,696
27	China Construction Bank Corp	$157,301	94	Aeon Co Ltd	$79,146	161	Repsol S.A.	$55,396
28	Cigna Corp (New)	$153,566	95	Airbus SE	$79,130	162	Vinci SA	$55,197
29	Cardinal Health. Inc.	$152,922	96	Grupo Financiero Galicia SA	$79,061	163	China Pacific Insurance (Gro	$54,997
30	Honda Motor Co Ltd	$150,546	97	Target Corp	$78,112	164	Nippon Steel Corp (New)	$54,551
31	Mitsubishi Corp	$149,021	98	Intel Corp	$77,867	165	Telefonica SA	$54,367
32	Chevron Corporation	$146,516	99	International Business Machines	$77,147	166	Tencent Holdings Ltd.	$54,222
33	Microsoft Corporation	$143,015	100	Raytheon Technologies Corp	$77,046	167	Energy Transfer LP	$54,213
34	JPMorgan Chase & Co	$142,422	101	Petroleo Brasileiro SA	$76,589	168	Alimentation Couche-Tard Inc	$54,132
35	AXA SA	$140,272	102	Sony Corp	$76,093	169	StoneX Group Inc	$54,036
36	Walgreens Boots Alliance Inc	$139,537	103	Freddie Mac	$75,125	170	Energy Transfer Operating LP	$54,032
37	Rosneft Oil Co OJSC (Moscow)	$139,403	104	Telecom Argentina SA	$74,959	171	China Telecom Corp Ltd	$53,999
38	General Motors Co	$137,237	105	Centene Corp	$74,639	172	LG Electronics Inc	$53,963
39	Verizon Communications Inc	$131,868	106	PTT Public Co Ltd	$74,519	173	Goldman Sachs Group Inc	$53,922
40	Ford Motor Co. (DE)	$127,144	107	Nippon Life Insurance Co.	$74,447	174	Morgan Stanley	$53,823
41	PJSC Lukoil	$125,991	108	Mexican Petroleum	$74,101	175	Caterpillar Inc.	$53,800
42	Banco Santander SA	$125,750	109	United Parcel Service Inc	$74,094	176	America Movil SAB de CV	$53,244
43	Itau Unibanco Holding S.A.	$125,516	110	Koninklijke Ahold Delhaize N	$73,854	177	Sysco Corp	$52,893
44	Marathon Petroleum Corp.	$124,813	111	Alibaba Group Holding Ltd	$72,536	178	China Vanke Co Ltd	$52,872
45	Prudential Plc	$124,308	112	Lowe's Companies Inc	$72,148	179	KDDI Corp	$52,806
46	PJSC Gazprom	$122,672	113	Zurich Insurance Group AG	$71,792	180	Anheuser Busch InBev SA/NV	$52,329
47	Kroger Co (The)	$122,286	114	Deutsche Post AG	$71,117	181	Denso Corp. (Japan)	$51,961
48	China Railway Group Ltd	$122,285	115	Procter & Gamble Co (The)	$70,950	182	Pfizer Inc	$51,750
49	Stellantis NV	$121,469	116	ArcelorMittal SA	$70,615	183	Zhejiang Material Industrial	$51,582
50	SAIC Motor Corp Ltd	$121,198	117	Munich Re Group	$70,449	184	Banco BBVA Argentina SA	$51,582
51	Fannie Mae	$120,304	118	Country Garden Holdings Co L	$69,832	185	HCA Healthcare Inc	$51,336
52	China Railway Construction Cor	$119,348	119	MetLife Inc	$69,620	186	JBS S.A.	$50,880
53	Allianz SE	$118,041	120	Mitsui & Co., Ltd.	$69,420	187	Mitsubishi UFJ Financial Gro	$50,830
54	Bayerische Motoren Werke AG	$117,003	121	FedEx Corp	$69,217	188	George Weston Ltd	$50,741
55	Bank of America Corp	$113,589	122	AEGON NV	$69,135	189	Lenovo Group Ltd	$50,716
56	Electricite de France	$112,224	123	Panasonic Corp	$69,006	190	Sberbank Russia	$50,229
57	Home Depot Inc	$110,225	124	Marubeni Corp.	$68,842	191	Continental AG (Germany, Fed	$49,939
58	Japan Post Holdings Co Ltd	$110,089	125	Banco Bilbao Vizcaya Argenta	$68,713	192	Novartis AG Basel	$49,898
59	Nippon Telegraph & Telephone	$109,621	126	China Evergrande Group	$68,633	193	American International Group Inc	$49,746
60	Phillips 66	$109,559	127	Brookfield Asset Management Inc	$67,826	194	Tokio Marine Holdings Inc	$49,634
61	Valero Energy Corp	$108,324	128	GlaxoSmithKline Plc	$67,454	195	Swiss Re AG	$49,314
62	China Mobile Limited	$107,199	129	Engie SA	$67,431	196	Cisco Systems Inc	$49,301
63	Credit Agricole SA	$105,429	130	PepsiCo Inc	$67,161	197	Vodafone Group Plc	$49,270
64	Anthem Inc	$104,213	131	Seven & i Holdings Co. Ltd.	$66,994	198	State Bank Of India	$49,113
65	Assicurazioni Generali S.p.A	$104,204	132	Siemens AG (Germany)	$66,902	199	Bayer AG	$48,891
66	Wells Fargo & Co (New)	$103,915	133	Surgutneftegas PJSC	$66,705	200	Sumitomo Corp.	$48,824
67	Federal Reserve System	$103,846	134	BASF SE	$66,598			

The Mergent 500 Largest Global Corporations (By Revenues)

Rank	Company	Sales ($ mil.)	Rank	Company	Sales ($ mil.)	Rank	Company	Sales ($ mil.)
201	Metallurgical Corp China Ltd	$48,667	267	Fujitsu Ltd	$38,897	334	Xiamen International Trade Gr	$31,337
202	Xiamen C & D Inc	$48,466	268	A.P. Moller – Maersk A/S	$38,890	335	Industria De Diseno Textil I	$31,222
203	Charter Communications Inc	$48,097	269	Deutsche Bank AG	$38,806	336	Subaru Corp	$30,807
204	Compagnie de Saint-Gobain	$47,826	270	Suning.com Co Ltd	$38,692	337	Royal Philips NV	$30,657
205	Orange	$47,432	271	Dow Inc	$38,542	338	Air France-KLM	$30,527
206	AIA Group Ltd.	$47,234	272	Phoenix Group Holdings PLC	$38,513	339	Schneider Electric SE	$30,492
207	American Express Co.	$47,020	273	Publix Super Markets, Inc.	$38,463	340	Sun Life Financial Inc	$30,471
208	Tianjin Tianhai Investment C	$47,017	274	Enbridge Inc	$38,450	341	Takeda Pharmaceutical Co Ltd	$30,320
209	Delta Air Lines Inc (DE)	$47,007	275	CK Hutchison Holdings Ltd	$38,401	342	Sumitomo Life Insurance Co.	$30,217
210	Merck & Co Inc	$46,840	276	Ericsson	$38,024	343	Medipal Holdings Corp	$29,969
211	E.ON SE	$46,443	277	J.Sainsbury PLC	$37,734	344	Centrica Plc	$29,942
212	Volvo AB	$46,437	278	Power Corp. of Canada	$37,670	345	Anglo American Plc (United K	$29,870
213	Royal Bank of Canada (Montre	$46,029	279	innogy SE	$37,652	346	Philip Morris International Inc	$29,805
214	ThyssenKrupp AG	$45,812	280	Vale SA	$37,570	347	East Japan Railway Co.	$29,710
215	American Airlines Group Inc	$45,768	281	NIKE Inc	$37,403	348	Safran	$29,697
216	Hongkong And Shanghai Bankin	$45,692	282	ICICI Bank Ltd (India)	$37,311	349	Xiaomi Corp	$29,582
217	T-Mobile US Inc	$44,998	283	Coca-Cola Co (The)	$37,266	350	Metro AG (New)	$29,543
218	SoftBank Corp (New)	$44,783	284	Saudi Basic Industries Corp –	$37,263	351	Shanghai Construction Group	$29,533
219	Allstate Corp	$44,675	285	Mitsubishi Heavy Industries	$37,230	352	Wistron Corp	$29,335
220	Accenture plc	$44,327	286	OMV AG (Austria)	$36,918	353	Kansai Electric Power Co., I	$29,334
221	ACS Actividades de Construcc	$44,210	287	World Fuel Services Corp.	$36,819	354	Arrow Electronics, Inc.	$28,917
222	Woolworths Group Ltd	$43,769	288	Northrop Grumman Corp	$36,799	355	Medtronic PLC	$28,913
223	Best Buy Inc	$43,638	289	Honeywell International Inc	$36,709	356	Haier Smart Home Co Ltd	$28,852
224	SAP SE	$43,357	290	Loblaw Companies Ltd	$36,688	357	Yanzhou Coal Mining Co Ltd	$28,836
225	United Airlines Holdings Inc	$43,259	291	ConocoPhillips	$36,670	358	Gree Electric Appliances Inc	$28,816
226	Tyson Foods Inc	$43,185	292	Canon Inc	$36,230	359	International Consolidated A	$28,637
227	Rio Tinto Ltd	$43,165	293	Meiji Yasuda Life Insurance	$35,810	360	Sumitomo Electric Industries	$28,623
228	Rio Tinto Plc (United Kingdo	$43,165	294	Taiwan Semiconductor Manufac	$35,740	361	NEC Corp	$28,514
229	Brookfield Business Partners	$43,032	295	Deere & Co.	$35,540	362	EDENOR	$28,445
230	BHP Group Plc	$42,931	296	Mitsubishi Chemical Holdings	$35,428	363	Lloyds Bank plc	$28,409
231	BHP Group Ltd	$42,931	297	HDFC Bank Ltd	$35,128	364	CHS Inc	$28,406
232	Veolia Environnement	$42,784	298	Aisin Seiki Co Ltd	$34,865	365	Danone	$28,391
233	Bouygues S.A.	$42,676	299	China Shenhua Energy Co., Lt	$34,760	366	SUEZ	$28,349
234	Wilmar International Ltd	$42,641	300	LyondellBasell Industries NV	$34,727	367	BT Group Plc	$28,296
235	MS&AD Insurance Group Holdin	$42,602	301	Mazda Motor Corp. (Japan)	$34,587	368	Unicredit SpA	$28,253
236	M&G plc	$42,428	302	Jiangxi Copper Co., Ltd.	$34,543	369	Chubu Electric Power Co Inc	$28,245
237	Sanofi	$42,251	303	Imperial Oil Ltd	$34,531	370	Linde plc	$28,228
238	Talanx AG	$42,033	304	Exelon Corp	$34,438	371	CRH Plc	$28,214
239	Baoshan Iron & Steel Co Ltd	$41,973	305	JFE Holdings Inc	$34,359	372	CNH Industrial NV	$28,079
240	China Unicom (Hong Kong) Ltd	$41,751	306	Great-West Lifeco Inc	$34,325	373	ABB Ltd	$27,978
241	China United Network Communi	$41,751	307	Wal-Mart de Mexico S.A.B. de	$34,189	374	Financiere De L Odet SA (Fra	$27,919
242	TJX Companies, Inc.	$41,717	308	Chubb Ltd	$34,186	375	X5 Retail Group NV	$27,867
243	Lufthansa AG (Germany, Fed.	$41,665	309	British American Tobacco Plc	$34,172	376	ViacomCBS Inc	$27,812
244	UBS Group AG	$41,562	310	Sompo Holdings Inc	$34,116	377	Dollar General Corp	$27,754
245	Toronto Dominion Bank	$41,207	311	Poly Real Estate Group Co.,	$33,914	378	LafargeHolcim	$27,643
246	Bunge Ltd.	$41,140	312	Capital One Financial Corp	$33,766	379	U.S. Bancorp (DE)	$27,325
247	Mitsubishi Electric Corp	$41,110	313	Plains GP Holdings LP	$33,669	380	Aluminum Corp of China Ltd.	$27,316
248	Jardine Matheson Holdings Lt	$40,922	314	Plains All American Pipeline LP	$33,669	381	KB Financial Group, Inc.	$27,278
249	Iberdrola SA	$40,911	315	L'Oreal S.A.	$33,541	382	Jabil Inc	$27,266
250	Intesa Sanpaolo S.P.A.	$40,653	316	Cnooc Ltd.	$33,514	383	Cie Generale des Etablisseme	$27,098
251	Sumitomo Mitsui Financial Gr	$40,557	317	AbbVie Inc	$33,266	384	Empire Co Ltd	$27,066
252	Daiwa House Industry Co Ltd	$40,352	318	CRRC Corp Ltd	$32,912	385	Hewlett Packard Enterprise Co	$26,982
253	Gazprom Neft PJSC	$39,933	319	Bank Nova Scotia Halifax	$32,872	386	Coles Group Ltd (New)	$26,949
254	Compass Group PLC (United Ki	$39,848	320	Enterprise Products Partners L.P.	$32,789	387	Heineken Holding NV (Netherl	$26,912
255	Barclays PLC	$39,767	321	Compal Electronics Inc	$32,749	388	Heineken NV (Netherlands)	$26,912
256	Fresenius SE & Co KGaA	$39,756	322	AKBANK	$32,709	389	Shanghai Pharmaceuticals Hol	$26,812
257	Casino Guichard Perrachon S.	$39,645	323	Jardine Strategic Holdings L	$32,665	390	Ferguson PLC (New)	$26,798
258	Banco Bradesco SA	$39,580	324	Westpac Banking Corp	$32,621	391	Fomento Economico Mexicano,	$26,782
259	Suncor Energy Inc	$39,480	325	Danske Bank A/S	$32,533	392	Samsung C&T Corp (New)	$26,642
260	Cresud SA Comercial Industrial Financiera Y Agropecuaria Cres	$39,449	326	Bridgestone Corp. (Japan)	$32,473	393	Randstad NV	$26,583
261	Magna International Inc	$39,431	327	3M Co	$32,184	394	Mondelez International Inc	$26,581
262	General Dynamics Corp	$39,350	328	Suzuki Motor Corp.	$32,137	395	Adidas AG	$26,542
263	Xiamen Xiangyu Co Ltd	$39,150	329	Abbott Laboratories	$31,904	396	United Natural Foods Inc.	$26,514
264	Oracle Corp	$39,068	330	ING Groep NV	$31,779	397	Adecco Group AG	$26,303
265	Progressive Corp. (OH)	$39,022	331	China Taiping Insurance Hold	$31,629	398	China Resources Pharmaceutic	$26,256
266	Hennes & Mauritz AB	$38,951	332	Travelers Companies Inc (The	$31,581	399	Nokia Corp	$26,177
			333	Toshiba Corp	$31,542	400	Bristol Myers Squibb Co.	$26,145

Rank	Company	Sales ($ mil.)	Rank	Company	Sales ($ mil.)	Rank	Company	Sales ($ mil.)
401	Bank of Montreal (Quebec)	$25,958	435	Sodexo	$24,235	469	Nucor Corp.	$22,589
402	US Foods Holding Corp	$25,939	436	Flex Ltd	$24,210	470	Henkel AG & Co KGAA	$22,583
403	Naturgy Energy Group SA	$25,863	437	BAE Systems Plc	$24,173	471	Anhui Conch Cement Co Ltd	$22,568
404	Koc Holdings AS	$25,798	438	WH Group Ltd	$24,103	472	Lennar Corp	$22,489
405	Reckitt Benckiser Group Plc	$25,671	439	Hannover Rueck SE	$24,047	473	Gilead Sciences Inc	$22,449
406	Paccar Inc.	$25,600	440	Shinhan Financial Group Co.	$23,961	474	Sumitomo Chemical Co., Ltd.	$22,442
407	Thermo Fisher Scientific Inc	$25,542	441	CBRE Group Inc	$23,894	475	Southwest Airlines Co	$22,428
408	Oversea-Chinese Banking Corp	$25,495	442	Broadcom Inc (DE)	$23,888	476	Lumen Technologies Inc	$22,401
409	Macy's Inc	$25,331	443	Schlumberger Ltd	$23,868	477	International Paper Co	$22,376
410	Cosmo Energy Holdings Co Ltd	$25,223	444	Baker Hughes Company	$23,838	478	Eli Lilly & Co	$22,320
411	Standard Chartered Plc	$25,188	445	LG Display Co Ltd	$23,828	479	Johnson Controls International	$22,317
412	Swiss Life Holding AG	$25,158	446	McKesson Europe AG	$23,782	480	AFLAC Inc.	$22,307
413	Mapfre SA	$25,156	447	Ageas NV	$23,760	481	JSC VTB Bank	$22,305
414	Altria Group Inc	$25,110	448	AntarChile S.A. (Chile)	$23,716	482	Ultrapar Participacoes SA	$22,215
415	New China Life Insurance Co	$25,088	449	Empresas COPEC SA	$23,716	483	China Southern Airlines Co L	$22,178
416	Performance Food Group Co	$25,086	450	Dollar Tree Inc	$23,611	484	Sekisui House, Ltd. (Japan)	$22,172
417	Duke Energy Corp	$25,079	451	Cummins, Inc.	$23,571	485	Telenor ASA	$22,168
418	Weichai Power Co Ltd	$25,058	452	Qualcomm Inc	$23,531	486	Recruit Holdings Co Ltd	$22,105
419	Netflix Inc	$24,996	453	China Overseas Land & Invest	$23,519	487	Magnit PJSC	$21,992
420	Kraft Heinz Co (The)	$24,977	454	Starbucks Corp.	$23,518	488	Rite Aid Corp.	$21,928
421	Huaneng Power International	$24,932	455	Daikin Industries Ltd	$23,494	489	Rolls Royce Holdings Plc	$21,904
422	Alfresa Holdings Corp Tokyo	$24,860	456	Diageo Plc	$23,485	490	Visa Inc	$21,846
423	L'Air Liquide S.A.	$24,837	457	Ceconomy AG	$23,405	491	Telecom Italia SpA	$21,831
424	SYNNEX Corp	$24,676	458	China Life Insurance Co Ltd	$23,386	492	Kuehne & Nagel International	$21,821
425	Komatsu Ltd	$24,651	459	Amgen Inc	$23,362	493	Ecopetrol SA	$21,765
426	Tesla Inc	$24,578	460	NN Group NV (Netherlands)	$23,329	494	COSCO Shipping Holdings Co L	$21,709
427	Olam International Ltd.	$24,568	461	Credit Suisse Group AG	$23,259	495	Longfor Group Holdings Ltd	$21,705
428	PBF Energy Inc	$24,508	462	Penske Automotive Group Inc	$23,179	496	Leonardo SpA	$21,691
429	China Grand Automotive Servi	$24,497	463	Morrison (Wm.) Supermarkets	$23,015	497	PNC Financial Services Group	$21,624
430	Mitsubishi Shokuhin Co., Ltd	$24,456	464	Nippon Steel Trading Corp	$22,849	498	Bank of Japan	$21,612
431	AstraZeneca Plc	$24,384	465	Banco Santander Brasil SA	$22,842	499	Valeo	$21,602
432	NatWest Group PLC	$24,337	466	Swire (John) & Sons Ltd. (Unit	$22,782	500	KT Corp (Korea)	$21,565
433	Sunac China Holdings Ltd	$24,333	467	National Australia Bank Ltd.	$22,686			
434	Commonwealth Bank of Austral	$24,312	468	Endesa S.A.	$22,633			

Hoover's Handbook of

American Business

The Companies

1st Source Corp

Need a bank? Don't give it a 2nd thought. Contact 1st Source Corporation parent of 1st Source Bank which provides commercial and consumer banking services through some 80 branches in northern Indiana and southwestern Michigan. The bank offers deposit accounts; business agricultural and consumer loans; residential and commercial mortgages; credit cards; and trust services. Its specialty finance group provides financing for aircraft automobile fleets trucks and construction and environmental equipment through about two-dozen offices nationwide; such loans account for nearly half of 1st Source's portfolio.

Operations

1st Source Bank subsidiary Specialty Finance Group offers specialized financing for new and used private and cargo aircraft automobiles and light trucks for leasing and rental agencies medium and heavy duty trucks and construction and environmental equipment. Another subsidiary 1st Source Insurance provides commercial and retail property/casualty coverage and life and health coverage. 1st Source Corporation Investment Advisors serves trust and investment clients of 1st Source Bank as well as the investment advisor of Wasatch Mutual Funds.

Geographic Reach

Indiana-based 1st Source serves customers across around 20 counties in Michigan and its home state.

Sales and Marketing

1st Source offers commercial and agricultural loans and leases to the transportation construction and real estate sectors. It offers retail loans to individuals.

Financial Performance

1st Source Corporation's revenues have been climbing for the past five years. Similarly net income has been on an upward trajectory.

In 2017 revenue increased 10% to a record $284.3 million as both interest and non-interest income rose. Net interest income grew 9% while non-interest income (including equipment rentals trust and wealth advisory fees and gains on investment securities) grew 11%.

Thanks to the higher revenue net income rose 18% to $68.1 million in 2017.

The company ended 2017 with $78 million in cash and cash equivalents a 28% decline from what it had at the end of 2016. Operating activities provided some $113 million and financing activities provided another $315 million but investment activities used $462 million that year.

Strategy

1st Source has been investing in its technology to better serve its customers. It invested $1.3 million on a new customer relationship management system during 2017 and it expects to continue development and implementation of that project. It also spent $2.2 million on cyber security initiatives that year. Additionally the company is increasing the bandwidth at its branches.

When it believes it can serve a new customer base the bank adds new branches to its network. In 2018 it opened a location on the campus of Indiana University South Bend. However like all banking companies 1st Source has seen a decline in transactions at its branches as customers embrace mobile banking. During 2017 the company consolidated three locations.

To improve its mobile experience 1st Source offers live customer support via Facebook Messenger.

EXECUTIVES

Chairman And Ceo, Christopher J. (Chris) Murphy, age 73, $726,923 total compensation
Evp Administration Secretary And General Counsel, John B. Griffith, age 62, $328,429 total compensation
Evp Cfo And Treasurer, Andrea G. Short, age 57, $275,769 total compensation
President 1st Source Bank, James R. Seitz, age 67, $325,010 total compensation
Svp And Chief Credit Officer 1st Source Bank, Jeffrey L. Buhr, $226,565 total compensation
President 1st Source Insurance, John Ball
Vice President, Sean Brady
Vice President Of Sales Officer, Scott Carter
Assistant Vice President, Amy Wagoner
Vice President, Rick Michalski
Vice President, John Lutz
Vice President Marketing, Melissa Collins
Vice President, Luke Squires
Assistant Vice President, Adam Hamilton
Asstant Vice President Small Business Banking, Julie Herring
Assistant Vice President, Michele Miller
Asst Vp Talent Acquisition, Janet Hughes
Vice President Andamp; Controller Loan Accounting, Dave Crim
Vice President And Trust Officer, Alberta Barker
Vice President, David Silvers
Vice President, Denise Myers
Vice President Trust Tax Manager, Pam Stearns
Vice President And Chief Auditor, Michael Niezgodski
Assistant Vice President, Bryan Byers
Vice President And Retirement Services Manager, Steven Perlewitz
Assistant Vice President Infrastructure And Networks, Steven Moore
Vice President And Trust Officer, Michael Evans
Vice President, Richard Curran
Vice President, Shelli Alexander
Assistant Vice President, Mark Taylor
Vice President, Robert Jamieson
Assistant Vice President Branch Manager, Patricia Lahey
Auditors: BKD, LLP

LOCATIONS

HQ: 1st Source Corp
100 North Michigan Street, South Bend, IN 46601
Phone: 574 235-2000
Web: www.1stsource.com

PRODUCTS/OPERATIONS

2017 Sales

	$ mil.	% of total
Interest		
Loans & leases	194	62
Taxable investment securities	13	4
Tax-exempt investment securities	2	1
Other	1	.
Interest expenses		
Non-interest		
Equipment rentals	30	10
Trust fees	21	7
Debit card income	11	4
Service charges on deposit accounts	9	3
Insurance commissions	5	2
Mortgage banking	4	2
Gains on investment securities available-for-sale	4	1
Other	10	4
Total	**284**	**100**

Selected Subsidiaries

1st Source Bank
  1st Source Capitol Corporation
  1st Source Corporation Investment Advisors Inc.
  1st Source Insurance Inc.
  1st Source Solar 1 LLC
  1st Source Specialty Finance Inc.

Michigan Transportation Finance Corporation
SFG Aircraft Inc.
SFG Commercial Aircraft Leasing
SFG Equipment Leasing Corporation I
Washington and Michigan Insurance Inc.
1st Source Funding LLC
1st Source Intermediate Holding LLC
1st Source Master Trust
Trustcorp Mortgage Company

COMPETITORS

Bank of America	Old National Bancorp
Fifth Third	PNC Financial
Huntington Bancshares	U.S. Bancorp
JPMorgan Chase	Wells Fargo
KeyCorp	

HISTORICAL FINANCIALS

Company Type: Public

Income Statement

FYE: December 31

	ASSETS ($ mil.)	NET INCOME ($ mil.)	INCOME AS % OF ASSETS	EMPLOYEES
12/19	6,622	91	1.4%	1,175
12/18	6,293	82	1.3%	1,150
12/17	5,887	68	1.2%	1,125
12/16	5,486	57	1.1%	1,150
12/15	5,187	57	1.1%	1,150
Annual Growth	6.3%	12.5%	—	0.5%

2019 Year-End Financials

Debt ratio: 1.28%	No. of shares (mil.): 25
Return on equity: 11.56%	Dividends
Cash ($ mil.): 83	Yield: 2.1%
Current ratio: —	Payout: 30.9%
Long-term debt ($ mil.): —	Market value ($ mil.): 1,323

	STOCK PRICE ($) FY Close	P/E High/Low		PER SHARE ($) Earnings	Dividends	Book Value
12/19	51.88	15	12	3.57	1.10	32.47
12/18	40.34	19	12	3.16	0.96	29.56
12/17	49.45	20	16	2.60	0.76	27.70
12/16	44.66	20	12	2.22	0.72	26.00
12/15	30.87	16	13	2.17	0.67	24.75
Annual Growth	13.9%	—	—	13.3%	13.2%	7.0%

3M Co

Loath to be stuck in one industry 3M makes everything from tape to high-tech security gear. The diversified company's products fall under four segment categories: Safety & Industrial Transportation & Electronics Health Care and Consumer. 3M boasts some of the world's most recognizable consumer brands including Post-it notes Scotch tapes Scotchgard fabric protectors Scotch-Brite scouring pads Filtrete home air filters and ACE bandages. 3M sells products directly to users and through numerous wholesalers retailers distributors and dealers worldwide. The company generates about 60% of its sales outside the US. 3M was founded in 1902 as a small mining venture in Northern Minnesota called Minnesota Mining and Manufacturing Company.

HISTORY

Five businessmen in Two Harbors Minnesota founded Minnesota Mining and Manufacturing (3M) in 1902 to sell corundum to grinding-wheel manufacturers. The company soon needed to raise working capital. Co-founder John Dwan offered his friend Edgar Ober 60% of 3M's stock. Ober persuaded Lucius Ordway VP of a plumbing business to help underwrite 3M. In 1905 the two took over the company and moved it to Duluth.

In 1907 future CEO William McKnight joined 3M as a bookkeeper. Three years later the plant moved to St. Paul. The board of directors declared a dividend to shareholders in the last quarter of 1916 and 3M hasn't missed a dividend since. The next two products 3M developed — Scotch-brand masking tape (1925) and Scotch-brand cellophane tape (1930) — assured its future

McKnight introduced one of the first employee pension plans in 1931 and in the late 1940s he implemented a vertical management structure. 3M introduced the first commercially viable magnetic recording tape in 1947.

In 1950 after a decade of work and $1 million in development costs 3M employee Carl Miller completed the Thermo-Fax copying machine which was the foundation of 3M's duplicating division.

Products in the 1960s included 3M's dry-silver microfilm photographic products carbonless papers overhead projection systems and medical and dental products. The company moved into pharmaceuticals radiology energy control and office markets in the 1970s and 1980s.

A 3M scientist developed Post-it Notes (1980) because he wanted to attach page markers to his church hymnal. Recalling that a colleague had developed an adhesive that wasn't very sticky he brushed some on paper and began a product line that now generates hundreds of millions of dollars each year.

In 1990 the company bought sponge maker O-Cel-O. But not all of its inventions have brought 3M good news. In 1995 along with fellow silicone breast-implant makers Baxter International and Bristol-Myers Squibb it agreed to settle thousands of personal-injury claims related to implants. The companies paid an average of $26000 per claim.

3M spun off its low-profit imaging and data-storage businesses in 1996 as Imation Corp. and closed its audiotape and videotape businesses. The next year 3M sold its National Advertising billboard business to Infinity Outdoor for $1 billion and its Media Network unit (a printer of advertising inserts) to Time Warner.

The company created the 3M Nexcare brand for its line of first-aid and home health products in 1998. To regain earnings growth 3M closed about 10% of its plants in the US and abroad; it also discontinued unprofitable product lines. The next year 3M sold its heart-surgery-equipment health care unit to Japan's Terumo and its Eastern Heights Bank subsidiary to Norwest Bank of Minnesota. It also bought out Hoechst AG's 46% stake in Dyneon LLC a fluorine elastomer joint venture between the two companies.

3M bought Polaroid's Technical Polarizer and Display Films business and a controlling stake in Germany-based Quante AG (telecom systems) in 2000. In addition the company decided to halt the manufacture of many of its Scotchgard-brand repellent products due to research revealing that one of the compounds (perfluorooctane sulfonate) used in the manufacturing process is "persistent and pervasive" in the environment and in people's bloodstreams. As 2000 drew to a close 3M named GE executive James McNerney to succeed L. D. DeSimone as its chairman and CEO. With the sale of Eastern Heights and several health care businesses (including its cardiovascular systems unit) 3M was rewarded with its second-best financial performance in 14 years.

3M then bought Robinson Nugent (electronic connectors) and MicroTouch Systems (touch screens) in 2001. It also announced plans to cut 6000 jobs and authorized a stock buy-back program of up to $2.5 billion.

The company changed its legal name from Minnesota Mining and Manufacturing Company to 3M Company that year. Also in 2002 3M restructured its business segments around end uses rather than products or raw materials. So the Health Care segment encompassed everything from transdermal skin patches to software for hospital coding and classification. Similarly the Consumer and Office Business unit became responsible for Post-its O-Cel-O sponges wood-finishing materials and air conditioner filters. By the end of that year the company had cut more than 8500 jobs 11% of its total workforce.

Nevertheless a strong year in 2003 emboldened the company to look to expand. 3M closed a deal to buy fellow Minnesota resident HighJump Software a maker of supply chain software for businesses in February 2004. CEO McNerney left 3M in 2005 to join Boeing in the same capacity and was replaced by George Buckley formerly of the Brunswick Corporation.

That year the company made a billion-dollar acquisition of liquid filtration producer CUNO. 3M's own filtration products business — primarily air filters — amounted to more than $1 billion in annual sales before the deal and the deal added nearly half that. (3M eventually changed CUNO's name to 3M Purification.)

The company signaled a new strategic direction in 2006 when it broke up its pharmaceutical unit along geographic lines and sold it in pieces. In total 3M got $2.1 billion for the sale of its pharmaceutical operations. The next year it sold HighJump Software. High-tech venture capital firm Battery Ventures bought HighJump to set it up as a stand-alone company.

The company then ran through another string of acquisitions in 2007 buying companies such as Unifam Lingualcare Innovative Paper Technologies and Diamond Productions.

Its 2008 acquisition of protection products maker Aearo Technologies helped 3M's sales growth in the area of safety security and protection services. It added to the unit with the purchase (through its 3M Canada subsidiary) of Toronto-based MTI PolyFab which makes thermal and acoustic insulation for aerospace products. 3M also capitalized on its purchase of Beiersdorf subsidiary Futuro which makes medical products such as wraps elastic bandages and compression hosiery.

3M made two moves into the high-tech security field in 2010. The company acquired Cogent Inc. for $943 million. Known as Cogent Systems the firm provides finger palm face and iris biometric systems for governments law enforcement agencies and commercial enterprises. 3M also acquired Attenti Ltd. an Israeli manufacturer of people-tracking technology for $230 million. Attenti makes remote monitoring devices to track people awaiting trial or on probation as well as for eldercare facilities to monitor patient safety.

The company expanded its consumer and office business line in 2010 by acquiring a majority stake in Japanese company A-One the top office label brand in Asia and the second-largest label business worldwide. It also acquired Alpha Beta Enterprise a manufacturer of box sealing tape and masking tape headquartered in Taiwan. Both acquisitions will expand 3M's presence in the global packaging market.

Also in 2010 3M acquired J.R. Phoenix Ltd. a manufacturer of hand hygiene and skin care products for health care and professional use. The majority of J.R. Phoenix products are sold under the Laura Line brand in Canada. The deal expanded 3M's line of hand hygiene skin care products to the healthcare market in Canada. The company also acquired UK-based Dailys Ltd. a global supplier of non-woven disposable chemical protective coveralls for industrial use.

The company made several acquisitions in 2010 including Minnesota-based Arizant which manufactures forced-air warming garments designed to prevent hypothermia in surgical settings a growing international market estimated at some $1 billion per year.

3M completed nine acquisitions in 2011 that totaled $649 million including the do-it-yourself unit and professional division of France's GPI Group a manufacturer and marketer of home improvement products such as tapes hooks insulation and floor protection products. The deal boosts 3M's presence in Western Europe. It also added to its growing Industrial and Transportation segment by acquiring a majority stake in Switzerland-based Winterthur Technology Group an international supplier of precision grinding technologies that makes grinding tools used in the aircraft automotive industrial and steel industries.

Back in the US it acquired Florida-based Nida-Core a manufacturer of structural honeycomb core and fiber-reinforced foam core materials and Nida-Core's French affiliate Structiso SARL. The acquisition allows 3M's Engineered Products and Solutions department to build on its composite and engineered materials product portfolio.

In a related deal in 2012 3M acquired Maryland-based CodeRyte which provides clinical natural language processing (NLP) technology and computer-assisted coding for healthcare outpatient providers. Terms of the sale were not disclosed. 3M will apply CodeRyte's NLP technology to its new 3M 360 Encompass system used by its 3M Health Information Systems division for clinical documentation and coding workflows. More than 5000 hospitals worldwide use 3M's coding for patient data for measurement and reimbursement purposes. The 3M system also addresses data problems resulting from health care reform requirements.

In an effort to broaden its global presence in office education and consumer products in 2012 3M acquired the Office and Consumer Products business of Avery Dennison Corp. for $550 million.

Continuing a quest for technology buys on 2012 3M acquired the Federal Signal Technologies Group (FSTech) from Federal Signal Corp. for $110 million in cash. FSTech focuses on hardware and software services for the $3 billion electronic tolling industry. The business also complements offerings from 3M's Traffic Safety Systems Division.

Growing its ceramics portfolio in 2012 it also bought advanced technical ceramics producer Ceradyne for $860 million. The deal adds Ceradyne's advanced ceramics technologies portfolio to its own diversified product line.

In 2014 3M formed partnership with US-China Clean Energy Research Center Building Energy Efficiency Consortium under which 3M participates in research on building efficiency strategies tools and practices in areas such as building envelope technologies and integration of new construction materials for increasing energy efficiency.

In a move aimed at bringing greater economic efficiencies to Premier's more than 100000 health care provider members in 2014 the company reached a group purchasing agreement with health care alliance company Premier Inc. for multiple catheter securement and stability products. The new agreement allows them to take advantage of special pricing and terms pre-negotiated by Premier.

In 2013 the company and China-based Hunan Reshine New Material Company signed a patent license agreement to expand the use of nickel manganese and cobalt in lithium ion batteries (in growing demand in consumer electronics automotive and other markets).

That year in order to expand its manufacturing assets in Asia 3M Company invested in plants in China and Singapore to support the growing window film business.

It also signed a patent license agreement with Korea-based ECOPRO to further expand the use of nickel-manganese-cobalt (NMC) cathode materials in lithium ion batteries.

EXECUTIVES

Evp Safety And Graphics, Frank R. Little, age 59
Chairman President And Ceo, Inge G. Thulin, age 67, $1,483,929 total compensation
Evp Consumer, Joaquin Delgado, age 60, $629,074 total compensation
Vice Chair And Evp, Hak Cheol (H.C.) Shin, age 63, $765,496 total compensation
Evp International Operations, Julie L. Bushman, age 58, $599,029 total compensation
Evp Industrial Business Group, James L. (Jim) Bauman, age 60
Evp And Coo, Michael F. Roman, age 60, $747,022 total compensation
Svp And Cfo, Nicholas C. Gangestad, age 55, $681,551 total compensation
Evp Health Care, Michael G. Vale, age 54, $633,302 total compensation
Evp Electronics And Energy Business Group, Ashish K. Khandpur, age 52
Svp Business Development And Marketing And Sales, Jon T. Lindekugel, age 56
Svp Business Transformation And Information Technology, Eric Hammes
National Sales Manager, Jim Stevens
National Sales Manager, Daryl Charton
Vp Information Technology, David Drew
Vice President Research And Development 3m Infection Prevention Division, Ann Meitz
Information Technology Sales Vice President, Dave Herington
Vice President Finance And Treasurer, Sarah Grauze
Vice President, Jerome Hamilton
Vice President, Tom Simpson
National Account Manager, Rick Bennett
Vice President Global Supply Chain, Val Young
Vice President And Associate General Counsel, Ann M Hanrahan
Vp Of Marketing, Douglas Michael
National Account Manager, Pat Kinate
Vice President Business And Marketing, Ingrid Blair
Vice President Engineering, Hector Dalton
Vice President Mobile Interactive Solutions Division, Mark Colin
Vice President, Patrick Moran
Vice President Of Marketing, Sharon Cohen
Vice President And General Manager 3m Construction And Home Improvement Markets Division, Jeffrey Lavers
National Sales Manager, Corey Willson
Vice President And General Manager Corrosion Protection Products, Paiul Acito
Vice President, Janice Angell
Vice President, Jamie Meilahn
Vice President And Chief Sustainability Officer 3m Research And Development, Gayle Schueller
Vice President, Martyn Tiplady
Vp And Gm Traffic Safety And Security Division 3m Safety And Graphics Business, John Riccardi
National Sales Manager, Scott Helterbrand
Vice President Implementations, George Moon
National Sales Manager, Steve Shogren
National Sales Manager, Chris Decolli
Vice President Environmental Health And Safety Operations, Jean Sweeney
National Sales Manager, Scott McConnell

Vice President Global Marketing 3m Unitek Orthodontic Products, Marcello Napol
Vice President Of Sales And Marketing, Harlan Brown
Senior Vice President Human Resources, Marlene McGrath
Senior Vice President Human Resources, Kay Grenz
Vice President Engineering And Manufacturing, Billy Roberts
National Sales Manager, Casey Nolden
National Account Manager, David Radliff
Vice President Cio, Ernie Park
Vice President 3m Government Markets, Rory Yanchek
Senior Vice President General Counsel And Secretary, Ivan Fong
Vice President, Corrado Dugo
Vice President, John Huberty
Vice President Of Sales And Marketing, Robert Sidney
Vice President Research And Development, Thomas Isberg
Vice President, Janette Shimanski
Vice President And General Manager Automotive Afte, Laino Richard
Global Vice President Of Research And Development, David Segal
Global Medical Director, Oyebode Taiwo
National Account Manager, MIKE ZIELINSKI
National Sales Manager, Jd Sobol
Vice President Biometrics Solutions, Ramsey Billups
Vice President And General Manager, Erik Aunan
Vice President Global Human Resources Business Operations, Jonathan Ruppel
National Sales Manager, Andrew Petrone
National Sales Manager, Ed Weksner
Vice President, Walter Rossini
Vice President, Tammy Le
Vice President, Carlos Morin
Vice President, Steven Osero
Corporate Treasurer And Vice President Investor Relations, Matt Ginter
Treasurer, Jan Angell
Board Member, Herbert Henkel
Treasurer, William Schmoll
Secretary, Irene Mccallum
Assistant Secretary, Michael Dai
Board Member, Gregory Page
Sec Treas, Dorothy Gorecki
Treasurer, Tara Lindsay
Auditors: PricewaterhouseCoopers LLP

LOCATIONS

HQ: 3M Co
3M Center, St. Paul, MN 55144-1000
Phone: 651 733-1110   **Fax:** 651 733-9973
Web: www.3M.com

2018 Sales

	$ mil.	% of total
United States	12,840	39
Asia Pacific	10,254	31
Europe Middle East and Africa	6,654	21
Latin America and Canada	3,024	9
Other Unallocated	(7)	-
Total	**32,765**	**100**

PRODUCTS/OPERATIONS

2018 Sales

	$ mil.	% of total
Industrial	12,267	35
Safety and Graphics	6,827	19
Health Care	6,021	17
Electronics and Energy	5,472	15
Consumer	4,796	14
Corporate and unallocated	50	-
Eliminations	(2668)	-
Total	**32,765**	**100**

Selected Segments and Products

Industrial and Transportation
  Automotive aftermarket products
  Automotive products
  Closures for disposable diapers
  Coated and nonwoven abrasives
  Films
  Filtration products
  Specialty adhesives
  Tapes
Health Care
  Dental products
  Drug delivery systems
  Health information systems
  Infection prevention
  Medical and surgical supplies
  Microbiology products
  Skin health products
Safety Security and Protection
  Commercial cleaning products
  Consumer safety products
  Corrosion protection products
  Floor matting
  Occupational health and safety products
  Safety and security products
  Track and trace products
Consumer and Office
  Carpet and fabric protectors
  Commercial cleaning products
  Fabric protectors (Scotchgard)
  High-performance cloth (Scotch-Brite)
  Home-improvement products
  Repositionable notes (Post-it)
  Scour pads (Scotch-Brite)
  Sponges (O-Cel-O)
  Tape (Scotch)
Display and Graphics
  Commercial graphics systems
  Optical films for electronic display
  Specialty film and media products
  Traffic control materials
Electro and Communications
  Insulating and splicing products for electronics telecommunications and electrical industries
  Packaging and interconnection devices

Selected Mergers and Acquisitions

COMPETITORS

ACCO Brands	Henkel
BASF SE	Honeywell
Bayer AG	International
Beiersdorf	Illinois Tool Works
Bostik	Johnson & Johnson
Bridgestone	Kimberly-Clark
Carlisle Companies	RPM International
Corning	Ricoh Company
Danaher	S.C. Johnson
GE	Sealed Air Corp.
H.B. Fuller	Sika

HISTORICAL FINANCIALS

Company Type: Public

Income Statement
FYE: December 31

	REVENUE ($ mil.)	NET INCOME ($ mil.)	NET PROFIT MARGIN	EMPLOYEES
12/20	32,184	5,384	16.7%	95,000
12/19	32,136	4,570	14.2%	96,163
12/18	32,765	5,349	16.3%	93,516
12/17	31,657	4,858	15.3%	91,536
12/16	30,109	5,050	16.8%	91,584
Annual Growth	**1.7%**	**1.6%**	**—**	**0.9%**

2020 Year-End Financials

Debt ratio: 39.90%   No. of shares (mil.): 577
Return on equity: 46.83%   Dividends
Cash ($ mil.): 4,634   Yield: 3.3%
Current ratio: 1.89   Payout: 68.9%
Long-term debt ($ mil.): 18,082   Market value ($ mil.): 100,985

| STOCK PRICE ($) | | P/E | PER SHARE ($) | | |
FY Close		High/Low	Earnings	Dividends	Book Value
12/20	174.79	19 13	9.25	5.88	22.27
12/19	176.42	28 19	7.81	5.76	17.50
12/18	190.54	28 20	8.89	5.44	16.99
12/17	235.37	30 21	7.93	4.70	19.44
12/16	178.57	22 16	8.16	4.44	17.26
Annual Growth	(0.5%)	— —	3.2%	7.3%	6.6%

Abbott Laboratories

With activities ranging from filling baby bottles to making generic medications and cardiovascular devices Abbott Laboratories is a diverse health care products manufacturer. Its cardiovascular and neuromodulation segment makes products for cardiac rhythm management electrophysiology and other areas of cardiovascular care. Abbott's diagnostics division makes laboratory testing systems and point-of-care tests. The nutritional products division makes such well-known brands as Similac infant formula and Ensure supplements. Abbott also sells branded generic medicines (including gastroenterology and women's health products) in emerging markets and makes the FreeStyle diabetes care line.

Operations

Abbott operates in four reportable segments: Medical Devices Nutritional Products Diagnostic Products and Established Pharmaceutical Products.

A global leader in cardiovascular product sales Medical Devices segment is Abbott's largest bringing in about 40% of total sales. It researches and manufactures devices in the areas of cardiac rhythm management heart failure electrophysiology vascular disease and structural repair as well as neuromodulation devices to treat movement and chronic pain disorders. Products include Assurity and Endurity pacemakers MitraClip valve repair systems XIENCE drug-eluting stents and TactiCath and FlexAbility ablation catheters.

The Diagnostics segment (about 25% of total sales) makes laboratory systems that screen and diagnose for cancer cardiovascular disease fertility and infectious diseases among others. It also makes rapid diagnostics systems for infectious diseases and other conditions; point-of-care testing systems; molecular diagnostics for genetic (DNA and RNA) and genomic testing; and laboratory informatics and automation tools.

The Nutritional Products segment (25% of revenue) sells pediatric and adult formulations around the world. Brands include Similac Ensure Isomil Glucerna PediaSure and Zone Perfect. The segment also provides nutritional products used for enteral feeding in health care facilities.

Abbott's Established Pharmaceutical Products (some 15% of sales) are branded generics marketed in emerging markets. These include gastroenterology drugs (such as Creon Duspatel and Heptral) women's health products (Duphaston and Femoston) cardiovascular and metabolic offerings (Lipanthyl Teveten and Synthroid among others) pain and central nervous system medications (Serc Brufen and Sevedol) and respiratory drugs and vaccines (Influvac Biaxin Klacid and Klacirid).

Geographic Reach

Abbott Park Illinois-based Abbott has more than 90 manufacturing plants as well as R&D facilities in countries around the globe including Brazil Canada China Colombia Germany India Ireland the Netherlands Pakistan Russia Spain Singapore the UK and the US.

The company's products are sold in more than 160 countries allowing the company to reduce dependence on any specific market. Abbott earns about 35% of its revenues in the US. Other major markets include China Germany India Japan Switzerland and the Netherlands each accounting for around 5% of sales.

Sales and Marketing

Abbott conducts distribution operations both from its own distribution centers and through third-party partners. Established pharmaceutical and nutritional customers include health care organizations wholesalers pharmacies retailers government agencies consumers and third-party distribution entities. Diagnostic and cardiovascular and neuromodulation products are sold to blood banks hospitals surgery centers physicians medical labs plasma protein therapeutic companies government agencies alternative testing sites and commercial laboratories.

Financial Performance

Abbott's revenue has been rising for the last five years. It has an overall growth of 56% between 2015 and 2019. Net income declined until 2017 but redeemed itself in 2018 and 2019.

Revenue increased 4% from $30.6 billion in 2018 to $31.9 billion in 2019. This was due to the increase in sales in all of the company's segments.

The company's net earnings totaled $3.7 billion in 2019 compared to $2.4 billion in 2018.

Cash at the end of 2019 was $3.9 billion. Operating activities generated $6.1 billion while investing and financing activities used $1.8 billion and $4.3 billion respectively.

Strategy

Over the last several years Abbott proactively shaped the company with the strategic intent to deliver sustainable growth in all of its businesses. Significant steps over the last three years included:

In January 2017 Abbott acquired St. Jude Medical Inc. (St. Jude Medical) a global medical device manufacturer for approximately $23.6 billion. As part of the acquisition Abbott also assumed repaid or refinanced approximately $5.9 billion of St. Jude Medical's debt. The acquisition provided expanded opportunities for future growth and is an important part of the company's effort to develop a strong diverse portfolio.

In October 2017 Abbott acquired Alere Inc. (Alere) a diagnostic device and service provider for approximately $4.5 billion. As part of the acquisition Abbott also tendered for Alere's preferred shares for a total value of approximately $0.7 billion and assumed and subsequently repaid approximately $3.0 billion of Alere's debt. The acquisition established Abbott as a leader in point of care testing expanded Abbott's global diagnostics presence and provided access to new products channels and geographies.

In February 2017 Abbott completed the sale of Abbott Medical Optics (AMO) its vision care business to Johnson & Johnson for $4.325 billion in cash and recognized an after-tax gain of $728 million.

Company Background

Dr. Wallace Abbott started making his dosimetric granule (a pill that supplied uniform quantities of drugs) at his home outside Chicago in 1888. The company was incorporated as Abbott Alkaloidal Company in 1894 and changed its name to Abbott Laboratories in 1915.

During WWI Abbott scientists synthesized anesthetics previously available only from Germany. Abbott expanded its research capacity products and sales force and went public in 1929. International operations began in the mid-1930s with branches in Argentina Brazil Cuba Mexico and the UK. Abbott contributed to the WWII effort by ratcheting up US production of penicillin. It later developed antibiotic erythromycin. Consumer infant and nutritional products joined the roster in the 1960s diagnostic equipment followed in the 1970s.

The company spun off its proprietary pharmaceutical products division including top-selling autoimmune drug Humira (the first fully-human monoclonal antibody drug approved by the FDA in 2002) into AbbVie in 2013.

To focus on cardiovascular and diagnostic operations Abbott sold its Abbott Medical Optics subsidiary to Johnson & Johnson for $4.3 billion in early 2017.

HISTORY

Dr. Wallace Abbott started making his dosimetric granule (a pill that supplied uniform quantities of drugs) at his home outside Chicago in 1888. Aggressive marketing earned Abbott the American Medical Association's criticism though much of the medical profession supported him.

During WWI Abbott scientists synthesized anesthetics previously available only from Germany. Abbott improved its research capacity in 1922 by buying Dermatological Research Laboratories; in 1928 it bought John T. Milliken and its well-trained sales force. Abbott went public in 1929.

International operations began in the mid-1930s with branches in Argentina Brazil Cuba Mexico and the UK.

Abbott was integral to the WWII effort; the US made only 28 pounds of penicillin in 1943 before the company began to ratchet up production. Consumer infant and nutritional products (such as Selsun Blue shampoo Murine eye drops and Similac formula) joined the roster in the 1960s. The FDA banned Abbott's artificial sweetener Sucaryl in 1970 saying it might be carcinogenic and in 1971 millions of intravenous solutions were recalled following contamination deaths.

EXECUTIVES

Svp And Chief Marketing And External Affairs Officer, Elaine R. Leavenworth, age 62
Vice President Diagnostic Commercial Operations Europe Africa And Middle East, Jaime Contreras
Vp Licensing And Acquisitions, William Chase
Chairman And Ceo, Miles D. White, age 64, $1,900,000 total compensation
Evp Human Resources, Stephen R. (Steve) Fussell, age 63, $454,689 total compensation
Evp Ventures, John M. Capek, age 58, $675,000 total compensation
Evp Nutritional Products, Heather L. Mason, age 60
Svp And Group President Cardiovascular And Neuromodulation, Eric S. Fain, age 59
Evp Medical Devices, Robert B. Ford, age 46
Evp Diagnostic Products, Brian J. Blaser, age 55, $692,057 total compensation
Evp General Counsel And Secretary, Hubert L. Allen, age 54, $650,000 total compensation
Svp Finance And Cfo, Brian B. Yoor, age 50, $584,231 total compensation
Svp U.s. Nutrition, Roger M. Bird, age 63
Svp Abbott Vascular, Deepak Nath, age 47
Svp Established Pharmaceuticals Latin America, Daniel Salvadori, age 41
Svp Diabetes Care, Jared L. Watkin, age 52
Evp Established Pharmaceuticals Emerging Markets, Andrew H. Lane, age 49
President Cardiovascular And Neuromodulation, Michael T. (Mike) Rousseau, age 64
Svp International Nutrition, Joseph (Joe) Manning, age 51

Senior Non It Management Chief Executive Officer Chief Financial Officer Vice President Directo, Randi Pickens
Senior Vice President, Ann Long
Vice President Sales, Scott Calus
Vp Of Internal Audit, David Mark
Executive Vice President Human Resources, Mary Moreland
Vp Of Intellectual Property Strategy, Andy Brookes
Medical Director, Thomas Podsadecki
Senior Vice President Central Region, Pamela Switalski
Evp Corporate Development, Richard W Ashley, age 78
Divisional Vice President, Brian Wentworth
Senior Vice President, Maureen Snider
Vice President Sales Training And Development, Randee Stelman
Division Vice President Pediatric Commercial Operations, Rich Schaefer
Vice President Marketing And Human Resources, Jennifer Pestikas
Medical Director, Roger Trinh
Medical Director, Gwendolyn Janssen
Vice President, Thomas Brown
Vice President Commercial Services, Danielle Virant
Divisional Vice President Quality Assurance Abbott P, Julio Salwen
Divisonal Vp Of Infrastructure Services, Paul Hennenfent
Svp Of Developed Markets Of Established Pharma, Jean-yves Pavee
Regional Vice President Public Relations, Natalie Christensen
Vice President Software Development, Samir Shah
Senior Vice President Abbott Vascular, Chuck Brynelsen
Svp Established Pharmaceuticals Emerging Markets, Sean Shrimpton
Senior Vice President Established Pharmaceuticals Latin America, Alejandro Wellisch
Area Vice President Heart Failure Management, Roger Graham
Divisional Vp Operations, Brad Roberts
Vice President, Terry Preston
Area Treasurer, Quintin Noble
Board Member, Phebe Novakovic
Board Member, Sally Blount
Board Member, Samuel Scott
Board Member, Roxanne Austin
Board Member, William Osborn
Auditors: Ernst & Young LLP

LOCATIONS
HQ: Abbott Laboratories
100 Abbott Park Road, Abbott Park, IL 60064-6400
Phone: 224 667-6100
Web: www.abbottinvestor.com

2017 Sales

	$ mil.	% of total
US	9,673	35
China	2,146	8
Germany	1,366	5
Japan	1,255	5
India	1,237	4
Netherlands	929	3
Switzerland	841	3
Russia	664	2
France	628	2
Brazil	541	2
Italy	507	2
UK	498	2
Colombia	494	2
Canada	443	2
Vietnam	427	2
Other countries	5,741	21
Total	**27,390**	**100**

PRODUCTS/OPERATIONS

2017 Sales by Segment

	$ mil.	% of total
Cardiovascular and Neuromodulation	8,911	33
Nutritionals	6,925	25
Diagnostics	5,616	20
Established Pharmaceuticals	4,287	16
Other	1,651	6
Total	**27,390**	**100**

Selected Products
Nutritional
  Alimentum (infant formula)
  EAS nutritional brands
  AdvantEdge (nutritional supplements)
  Myoplex (nutritional supplements)
  Ensure (adult nutrition)
  Freego (enteral pump)
  Glucerna (nutritional beverage for diabetics)
  Isomil (soy-based infant formula)
  Jevity (liquid food for enteral feeding)
  NeoSure (infant formula)
  Osmolite
  Pedialyte (pediatric electrolyte solution)
  PediaSure (children's nutrition)
  Similac (infant formula)
  Zone Perfect (nutritional bars)
Established Pharmaceuticals (branded generics)
  Creon (pancreatic enzyme replacement therapy)
  Duphaston (progesterone deficiency)
  Klacid (macrolide antibiotic)
Diagnostic
  Abbott PRISM (high-volume blood-screening system)
  ARCHITECT (clinical chemistry system)
  Cell-Dyn (hematology systems and reagents)
  Diagnostic and screening assays
  Informatics and automation solutions for lab use
  i-STAT (blood analyzer)
  m2000 (instrument that detects and measures infectious agents)
  Vysis (genomic-based tests)
Medical Devices
  Acculink/Accunet (carotid stent)
  Hi-Torque Balance Middleweight (coronary guidewire licensed from Asahi Intecc)
  MitraClip (valve repair)
  Multi-Link 8 Multi-Link Mini Vision and Multi-Link Vision (coronary metallic stents)
  Perclose (vessel closure)
  StarClose (vessel closure)
  Trek (balloon dilation)
  Xience V Xience nano and Xience Prime (drug-eluting stents)

COMPETITORS

Allergan plc	Mannatech
Bard	Mead Johnson
Baxter International	Mylan
Becton Dickinson	Nestlé
Boston Scientific	Perrigo
Cordis	Roche Holding
Danone	Sandoz International
Dr. Reddy's	GmbH
GNC	Schiff Nutrition
Heinz	International
Herbalife Ltd.	Sun Pharmaceutical
Johnson & Johnson	Teva
LifeScan	

HISTORICAL FINANCIALS
Company Type: Public

Income Statement   FYE: December 31

	REVENUE ($ mil.)	NET INCOME ($ mil.)	NET PROFIT MARGIN	EMPLOYEES
12/19	31,904	3,687	11.6%	107,000
12/18	30,578	2,368	7.7%	103,000
12/17	27,390	477	1.7%	99,000
12/16	20,853	1,400	6.7%	75,000
12/15	20,405	4,423	21.7%	74,000
Annual Growth	**11.8%**	**(4.4%)**	**—**	**9.7%**

2019 Year-End Financials
Debt ratio: 26.72%
Return on equity: 11.97%
Cash ($ mil.): 3,860
Current ratio: 1.44
Long-term debt ($ mil.): 16,661
No. of shares (mil.): 1,762
Dividends
  Yield: 1.4%
  Payout: 62.1%
Market value ($ mil.): 153,091

	STOCK PRICE ($) FY Close	P/E High/Low	PER SHARE ($) Earnings	Dividends	Book Value
12/19	86.86	43 32	2.06	1.28	17.64
12/18	72.33	55 42	1.33	1.12	17.39
12/17	57.07	213 145	0.27	1.06	17.72
12/16	38.41	48 39	0.94	1.04	13.94
12/15	44.91	17 13	2.92	0.96	14.40
Annual Growth	**17.9%**	**— —**	**(8.4%)**	**7.5%**	**5.2%**

AbbVie Inc

AbbVie is vying for dominance in the world of medications. The firm develops and commercializes biopharmaceutical and small molecule drugs with a focus on immunology oncology virology and neuroscience. Its primary product is Humira best known as a rheumatoid arthritis drug; it accounts for some 60% of sales and is the world's top-selling prescription drug. Other key products include cancer treatment Imbruvica and hepatitis C drug Mavyret. Products are sold globally but the US is AbbVie's largest market. With the pending expiration of Humira's patent protection AbbVie is looking for the next big thing. The company tie-up with Allergan for $63 billion in 2019. The US generates about 70% of total sales.

Operations

AbbVie focuses on treating conditions such as chronic autoimmune diseases (including rheumatoid arthritis psoriasis and Crohn's disease) cancers and viral conditions (including hepatitis C and HIV). It also has products that address metabolic or hormonal conditions endocrinology ailments and neurological disorders (including Parkinson's disease).

Top product Humira is a biologic therapy that treats several autoimmune conditions and generates nearly $20 billion in sales or about 60% of total revenue. Leukemia and lymphoma drug Imbruvica accounts for 15% of sales and hepatitis C medication Mavyret each account for 10% of sales. Other major offerings include Creon (enzyme insufficiency) Lupron (endometriosis) Synthroid (hyperthyroidism) and Synagis (respiratory syncytial virus).

The company has a pipeline of medications in clinical development that covers such areas as oncology neurology immunology cystic fibrosis and women's health. It has a number of partnerships with other pharma firms to develop new treatments including Alector (Alzheimer's disease) and Calico Life Sciences (age-related diseases).

Geographic Reach

AbbVie collects about 70% of sales from the US. Key foreign markets include Japan Germany Canada and France.

The Chicago-based company has six primary manufacturing facilities in the US (in Illinois Puerto Rico Massachusetts and Michigan) and five key international plants (in Italy Ireland Germany Singapore). It operates seven US R&D facilities in Illinois California and Massachusetts as well as one R&D center in Germany.

Sales and Marketing

AbbVie uses a combination of direct and third-party resources to market and sell its products worldwide. In the US AbbVie markets directly to physicians consumers managed care providers insurers pharmacy benefit managers (PBMs) hospitals and government agencies (including the US Department of Veterans Affairs and the Department of Defense). Products are primarily distributed through independent wholesalers; some sales are made directly to pharmacies and patients. Internationally AbbVie principally markets to payers physicians and regulatory bodies and sells products directly and through distributors.

Three wholesale distributors – McKesson Cardinal Health and AmerisourceBergen ?account for nearly all of US sales. No individual wholesaler accounted for greater than 40% of AbbVie's 2019 gross revenues in the US. Its products are generally sold worldwide directly to wholesalers distributors government agencies health care facilities specialty pharmacies and independent retailers from AbbVie-owned distribution centers and public warehouses. AbbVie's advertising expenses were $1.1 billion in 2019 $1.1 billion in 2018 and $846 million in 2017 respectively.

Financial Performance

AbbVie has seen steady revenue growth the last five years. For this period revenue posted a 46% increase since 2015. Except in 2017 when net income showed a 11% drop earnings generally enjoyed upward trend.

In 2019 revenue grew 2% to $33.3 billion primarily driven by revenue growth related to IMBRUVICA and VENCLEXTA as well as the continued strength of HUMIRA in the U.S. and newly launched immunology assets SKYRIZI and RINVOQ offset by international HUMIRA biosimilar competition.

Net income rose 39% in 2019 to $7.9 billion primarily due to reduced operating costs and expenses.

AbbVie ended 2019 with $40 billion in cash an increase of $32.6 billion from 2019. Operating activities contributed $13.3 billion while investing activities provided another $596 million (primarily from sales and maturities of investment securities) and financing activities also contributed $18.7 billion mostly proceeds from issuance of long-term debt.

Strategy

AbbVie may pursue acquisitions technology licensing arrangements and strategic alliances or dispose of some of its assets as part of its business strategy.

The company intends to continue to advance its mission in a number of ways including: (i) growing revenues by diversifying revenue streams ensuring strong commercial execution of new product launches and driving late-stage pipeline assets to the market; (ii) continuing to invest and expand its pipeline in support of opportunities in immunology oncology and neuroscience with additional targeted investment in cystic fibrosis and women's health as well as continued investment in key on-market products; (iii) expanding operating margins; and (iv) returning cash to shareholders via a strong and growing dividend while also reducing incremental debt.

For 2020 AbbVie expects to achieve its strategic objectives through: Completion and successful integration of the proposed Allergan acquisition; Hematologic oncology revenue growth from both IMBRUVICA and VENCLEXTA; Immunology revenue growth driven by successful commercial launches of SKYRIZI and RINVOQ as well as HUMIRA U.S. sales growth; Effective management of HUMIRA international biosimilar erosion; and the favorable impact of pipeline products and indications recently approved or currently under regulatory review where approval is expected in 2020.

Mergers and Acquisitions

In early 2020 AbbVie tied-up with a fellow drugmaker Allergan for $63 billion. The purchase will boost the company's revenue as it looks for a Humira replacement. Allergan will add new product lines including beauty medications (such as Botox) and eye care treatments (such as Restasis) as well as offerings that compliment AbbVie's offerings in neurology digestive diseases women's health and other fields.

Company Background

Biopharmaceutical research company AbbVie was formed in 2012 by former parent Abbott Labs which spun off AbbVie into a separate publicly-traded company in 2013. As the company faced the patent expirations of many of its top sellers in the following years (including Aluvia TriCor Niaspan and Humira) it focused on expanding its R&D operations.

After a failed attempt to purchase Irish rare-disease medication manufacturer Shire for $54 billion in 2014 AbbVie instead pumped up its oncology pipeline by acquiring Pharmacyclics for $20.8 billion in 2015 and Stemcentrx for $5.8 billion in 2016.

EXECUTIVES

Chairman And Ceo, Richard A. (Rick) Gonzalez, age 66, $1,600,000 total compensation

Evp External Affairs General Counsel And Corporate Secretary, Laura J. Schumacher, age 57, $979,369 total compensation

Evp Commercial Operations, Carlos Alban, age 57, $888,461 total compensation

Evp And Cfo, William J. Chase, age 52, $979,369 total compensation

President Pharmacyclics, Wulff-Erik von Borcke

Svp Operations, Azita Saleki-Gerhardt, age 57

Evp Research And Development And Chief Scientific Officer, Michael E. Severino, age 54, $960,969 total compensation

Evp And Chief Strategy Officer, Henry O. Gosebruch, $894,523 total compensation

Vp And Chief Ethics And Compliance Officer, Karen Hale

Group Medical Director, Aileen Pangan

Vice President, Sean Mcewen

Vice President Human Resources And Operations, Leanna Walther

Medical Director, Hana Florian

Divisional Vice President Global Pharmaceutical Sciences, Juergen Zeidler

Vice President, Sharon Greenlees

Vice President, Clement Pimor

Senior Vice President, Jeffrey R Stewart

Vice President Finance, Kevin Buckbee

Associate Medical Director Physician Professional Development Program, Christopher Ocampo

Associate Medical Director Infectious Diseases Develop, Susan Rhee

Vice President Pharmacy Immunology And Neurology Supply Chain, Chris Mlynek

Senior Medical Director, Nasser Khan

Vice President, Tiffany Cincotta

Divisional Vice President, Katie Rielly-gauvin

Medical Director, Melissa Wigderson

Medical Director, Bruce Barger

Dvp Immunology Research, Lisa Olson

Vice President Immunology Global Commercial Development, Nisha Burns

Vice President Quality Assurance, Marilyn Frontz

Vice President And General Manager Abbvie Germany, Patrick Horber

Senior Medical Director, Earle Bain

National Sales Manager, Randee Stelman

Senior Medical Director, Dilek Arikan

Medical Director, Yan Luo

Vice President, Perry Siatis

Vice President, Russell Garich

Senior Medical Director, Mayra Ballina

Medical Director, David Carter

Senior Medical Director, Kristof Chwalisz

National Sales Manager, Cheryl Lawrence-tarr

Divisional Vice President, Tracie Haas

Vice President Business Human Resources Global Commercial Operations, Heather Lowe

Group Medical Director, Margaret Burroughs

Vice President Regional Manufacturing Operations Europe, Thomas Scheidmeir

Vice President Tax, Scott Reents

Vice President Licensing And Aqcuisitions Immunology, Suzanne Lebold

Medical Director, Kevin Douglas

Vice President Corporate Strategy Office, Scott Brun

Vice President Controller Operations, Joe Karich

Medical Director, Daniel Cohen

Medical Director, Gwen Levy

Vice President Assistant Treasurer, Tabetha Skarbek

Vice President And Assistant Corporate Controller, Ross Berman

Vice President And Treasurer, Amarendra Duvvur

Vice President, Chris Turek

Vice President Us Operations Oncology, Byran Litton

Vice President Corporate Strategy Group, Leah Bloom

Medical Director, Manuel Uribe

Vice President, Davidsen Steve

Vice President Corporate Contoller, Brian Durkin

Vice President Heor Virology Endocrinology Renal, Vipan Sood

Medical Director Oncology Early Development, Greg Vosganian

Vice President Device Solutions Combination Product Development, Ramakrishna Venugopalan

Board Member, Rebecca Roberts

Auditors: Ernst & Young LLP

LOCATIONS

HQ: AbbVie Inc
1 North Waukegan Road, North Chicago, IL 60064-6400
Phone: 847 932-7900
Web: www.abbvie.com

2017 Sales

	$ mil.	% of total
US	18,251	65
Germany	1,157	4
UK	807	3
Japan	764	3
France	730	3
Canada	659	2
Spain	521	2
Italy	475	2
Brazil	410	1
The Netherlands	362	1
Other	4,080	14
Total	**28,216**	**100**

PRODUCTS/OPERATIONS

2017 Sales

	$ mil.	% of total
Humira	18,427	65
Imbruvica	2,573	9
Hepatitis C products	1,274	5
Creon	831	3
Lupron	829	3
Synthroid	781	3
Synagis	738	3
AndroGel	577	2
Kaletra	423	1
Sevoflurane	410	1
Duodopa	355	1
Other	998	4
Total	**28,216**	**100**

COMPETITORS

Amgen	Merck
AstraZeneca	Novartis
Bayer AG	Pfizer
Bristol-Myers Squibb	Roche Holding
Eli Lilly	Sanofi
GlaxoSmithKline	Teva
Johnson & Johnson	

HISTORICAL FINANCIALS

Company Type: Public

Income Statement   FYE: December 31

	REVENUE ($ mil.)	NET INCOME ($ mil.)	NET PROFIT MARGIN	EMPLOYEES
12/19	33,266	7,882	23.7%	30,000
12/18	32,753	5,687	17.4%	30,000
12/17	28,216	5,309	18.8%	29,000
12/16	25,638	5,953	23.2%	30,000
12/15	22,859	5,144	22.5%	28,000
Annual Growth	9.8%	11.3%	—	1.7%

2019 Year-End Financials

Debt ratio: 74.88%	No. of shares (mil.): 1,478
Return on equity: —	Dividends
Cash ($ mil.): 39,924	Yield: 4.8%
Current ratio: 3.18	Payout: 81.0%
Long-term debt ($ mil.): 62,975	Market value ($ mil.): 130,943

	STOCK PRICE ($) FY Close	P/E High/Low	PER SHARE ($) Earnings	Dividends	Book Value
12/19	88.54	17 12	5.28	4.28	(5.53)
12/18	92.19	34 21	3.66	3.59	(5.71)
12/17	96.71	30 18	3.30	2.56	3.20
12/16	62.62	18 14	3.63	2.28	2.91
12/15	59.24	23 15	3.13	2.02	2.45
Annual Growth	10.6%	— —	14.0%	20.6%	—

Adobe Inc

Adobe Systems makes software that helps customers create distribute and manage digital content from the cloud. One of the top publishing software providers it has been known for brands such as Acrobat Photoshop and Marketing Cloud. Adobe serves customers such as content creators and web application developers with its digital media products and marketers advertisers publishers and others with its digital marketing business. A long-time publisher of traditional software packages Adobe is moving its products to cloud-based versions. Subscriptions account for about 90% of revenue.

Operations

Adobe's business is organized into three reportable segments: Digital Media Digital Experience and Publishing.

Adobe's Digital Media segment about 70% of revenue includes products such as Photoshop and Illustrator under the umbrella of the Adobe Creative Cloud a subscription service.

Its Digital Experience segment about 30% of revenue includes tools for creating managing and measuring digital advertising and marketing initiatives. Elements within the segment are Adobe Advertising Cloud Adobe Analytics Cloud Adobe Marketing Cloud and Magento Commerce Cloud.

The Publishing unit less than 5% of revenue includes legacy products and services that address diverse market opportunities including eLearning solutions technical document publishing web conferencing document and forms platform web application development and high-end printing.

Geographic Reach

The US is Adobe's largest market representing more than 50% of revenue; other North American countries contribute about 5%. The EMEA (Europe Middle East and Africa) region generates more than 25% of revenue and the Asia-Pacific region led by Japan contributes about 15%.

Headquartered in San Jose California Adobe has field offices in about 30 countries across the Americas Asia and Europe.

Sales and Marketing

Adobe sells directly and through distributors resellers systems integrators and retailers. In addition it licenses its technology to hardware manufacturers for integration into their products.

Financial Performance

Adobe Systems' revenue more than doubled from 2015-2019 propelled by its digital offerings and higher sales through subscriptions.

Revenue rose 24% to $11 billion in 2019 (ended September) an increase of $2.1 billion from than 2018. Sales from Creative revenue grew 21% while subscription revenue jumped 26% year-to-year. Their success in driving growth in Annualized Recurring Revenue has positively affected their revenue growth.

Net income was no slouch for Adobe in 2019 increasing more than 14% to about $3 billion in 2019 from 2018 due to increase in revenue and offset in part by the increase in operating expense and cost of revenue.

Cash and cash equivalents stood at $2.7 billion at the end of 2019 compared to $1.6 billion at the close of 2018. Operations generated about $4.4 billion in cash in 2019 while investing activities used $455 million and financing activities used $2.9 billion.

Adobe's indebtedness rose to $4.14 billion in 2019 from $4.129 billion in 2018 doubling its debt-to-equity ratio. A higher level of debt could affect it how the responds to changing economic conditions and reduce cash flow for other expenses.

Strategy

Adobe Systems' charge into the cloud and a subscription-based business model has paid off for the company. It has reported rising revenue and net income for the past five years and driven its profit margin to about 28% in 2018 from about 7% in 2014.

The company's goal is to be the leading provider of cloud-based solutions for delivering digital experiences and enabling digital transformation. The Adobe Experience Cloud applications services and platform are designed to manage customer journeys enable shoppable experiences and deliver intelligence for business of any size in any industry.

A key component of Adobe's strategy is developing a large partner ecosystem to expand reach and breadth of Adobe solutions in the global marketplace. In order to assist partners in building their respective digital practices Adobe Global Services provides a comprehensive set of deliverables through Adobe's Solution Partner Program.

Adobe's strategy with Creative Cloud is designed to enable them to increase their revenue with users attract more new customers and grow their recurring and predictable revenue stream that is recognized ratably.

Mergers and Acquisitions

In 2019 Adobe Systems bought Allegorithmic the maker of Substance a tool for creating 3D textures and materials in game and video post-production. Adobe intends to combine Allegorithmic's Substance 3D design tools with Creative Cloud's imaging video and motion graphics tools for video game creators visual effects artists in film and tel-

evision designers and marketers. The acquisition price accounts for approximate $106.2 million.

Company Background

When Charles Geschke hired John Warnock as chief scientist for Xerox's new graphics and imaging lab he set the stage for one of the world's largest software makers. While at the Xerox lab the pair developed the PostScript computer language which tells printers how to reproduce digitized images on paper. When Xerox refused to market it the duo left that company and started Adobe (named after a creek near their homes in San Jose California) in 1982.

HISTORY

When Charles Geschke hired John Warnock as chief scientist for Xerox's new graphics and imaging lab he set the stage for one of the world's largest software makers. While at the Xerox lab the pair developed the PostScript computer language which tells printers how to reproduce digitized images on paper. When Xerox refused to market it the duo left that company and started Adobe (named after a creek near their homes in San Jose California) in 1982.

EXECUTIVES

Svp Product Marketing Professional Publishing Solutions, Bryan Lamkin, age 59, $568,590 total compensation

Evp And Chief Marketing Officer, Ann Lewnes, age 58

Evp General Counsel And Corporate Secretary, Michael A. (Mike) Dillon, age 61

Evp And Cfo, Mark S. Garrett, age 62, $698,977 total compensation

Chairman President And Ceo, Shantanu Narayen, age 56, $1,010,260 total compensation

Evp Customer And Employee Experience, Donna Morris, age 52

Evp Worldwide Field Operations, Matthew A. (Matt) Thompson, age 62, $673,720 total compensation

Svp And General Manager Digital Marketing, Bradley (Brad) Rencher, age 46, $573,514 total compensation

Evp And Cto, Abhay Parasnis, age 45, $183,583 total compensation

Vice President Licensing And Associate General Counsel, Joe Ramirez

Vice President Tax, Barry Slivinsky

Vice President Corporate Responsibility, Holly Campbell

Vice President Of Engineering And Information Technology, Kevin M Davis

Vice President Corporate Development, Taylor Barada

Assistant Vice President Southeast Regio, Gregory Rains

Senior Vice President Worldwide Sales And Field Operations, Matt Thompson

Vice President Customer Care, Lambert Walsh

Vice President, Steven Plous

Vice President Product Development, Govind Balakrishnan

Vice President Manager Director, Angelica Pina

Vice President And Chief Security Officer, Brad Arkin

Vice President Product Management, Bill Ingram

Senior Vice President Engineering, Bob Wulff

Vice President Worldwide Sales Operations, Adil Munshi

Vice President Of Architecture, Anjul Bhambhri

Assistant Vice President Sales Adobe Mar, Allen Jeffries

Vice President Licensing And Associate General Counsel, Joseph Ramirez

Vp Strategy And Operations Cloud Technology, Kira Dales

Vice President Chief Accounting Officer And Corporate Controller, Mark Garfield
Board Member, John Warnock
Auditors: KPMG LLP

LOCATIONS

HQ: Adobe Inc
345 Park Avenue, San Jose, CA 95110-2704
Phone: 408 536-6000
Web: www.adobe.com

2018 Sales

	$ mil.	% of total
Americas:		
United States	4,632	53
Other	484	5
Europe Middle East & Africa	2,550	28
APAC:		
Japan	609	8
Other	753	6
Total	**9,030**	**100**

PRODUCTS/OPERATIONS

2018 Sales

By Segment	$ mil.	% of total
Digital Media	6,325	70
Digital Experience	2,443	27
Publishing	261	3
Total	**9,030**	**100**

2018 Sales

	$ mil.	% of total
Subscription	7,992	88
Products	622	7
Services and support	485	5
Total	**9,030**	**100**

ProductsCreativity and Design

Creative Cloud
Photoshop
Lightroom
Dreamweaver
InDesign
Illustrator (graphic artwork creation)
Adobe XD
Adobe Premiere Pro
After Effects
Dimension
Acrobat Pro
Animate
Adobe Audition1
Bridge
Media Encoder
InCopy
Prelude
Fuse
Marketing and Analytics
Analytics
Advertising Cloud
Audience Manager
Campaign
Experience Cloud
Experience Manager
Media Optimizer
Primetime
Target
PDF and E-Signature
Acrobat Pro DC
Acrobat Pro 2017
Acrobat Standard DC
Adobe DC for teams
Adobe DC for enterprise
Document Cloud
Export PDF
Fill & Sign for Mobile

COMPETITORS

Apple Inc.	Getty Images
Autodesk	Google
Avid Technology	IBM
Box Inc.	Microsoft
Canon	Quark
Citrix Systems	SAS Institute
Dropbox	Shutterstock

HISTORICAL FINANCIALS

Company Type: Public

Income Statement

FYE: November 27

	REVENUE ($ mil.)	NET INCOME ($ mil.)	NET PROFIT MARGIN	EMPLOYEES
11/20	12,868	5,260	40.9%	22,516
11/19	11,171	2,951	26.4%	22,634
11/18*	9,030	2,590	28.7%	21,357
12/17	7,301	1,693	23.2%	17,973
12/16	5,854	1,168	20.0%	15,706
Annual Growth	**21.8%**	**45.7%**	**—**	**9.4%**

*Fiscal year change

2020 Year-End Financials

Debt ratio: 16.95%
Return on equity: 44.33%
Cash ($ mil.): 4,478
Current ratio: 1.48
Long-term debt ($ mil.): 4,117

No. of shares (mil.): 479
Dividends
  Yield: —
  Payout: —
Market value ($ mil.): 228,497

	STOCK PRICE ($) FY Close	P/E High/Low	PER SHARE ($) Earnings	Dividends	Book Value
11/20	477.03	49 26	10.83	0.00	27.69
11/19	309.53	51 34	6.00	0.00	21.83
11/18*	250.89	52 32	5.20	0.00	19.20
12/17	179.52	54 30	3.38	0.00	17.22
12/16	99.73	47 31	2.32	0.00	15.02
Annual Growth	**47.9%**	**—**	**47.0%**	**—**	**16.5%**

*Fiscal year change

Advance Auto Parts Inc

Advance Auto Parts (AAP) has taken the lead in the race to become the #1 provider of automotive aftermarket parts in North America. Serving both the do-it-yourself (DIY) and professional installer markets AAP operates more than 4875 stores under the Advance Auto Parts Autopart International (AI) Carquest and Worldpac banners in the US and Canada. Its stores carry brand-name and private-label replacement parts batteries maintenance items and automotive chemicals for individual car and truck owners. AAP's Carquest AI and Worldpac stores cater to commercial customers including garages service stations and auto dealers.

Operations

Parts and batteries account for more than 65% of Advance Auto Parts' total product sales; the rest comes from accessories and chemicals (about 20%) engine maintenance (around 10%) and other products. It carries a wide range of national and private label brands including Bosch Castrol Moog and Prestone as well as Autocraft Tough One Wearever and Carquest.

The company's namesake banner is the largest and includes over 4300 stores that serve both the professional and DIY markets with some 21000 stock keeping units. Carquest which has about 385 locations focuses more heavily on the professional market and also serves about 1250 independently owned stores that operate under the Carquest name. The Autopart International and Worldpac banners (with some 180 stores and about 160 stores respectively) target the professional market offering imported aftermarket and OEM products and private-label parts.

Geographic Reach

North Carolina-based Advance Auto Parts has stores across the US as well as Puerto Rico the US Virgin Islands and Canada. The company also have another corporate office in Roanoke Virginia.

It has distribution centers in more than 30 US states and four Canadian provinces.

Sales and Marketing

Advance Auto Parts serves professional customers (garages service stations auto dealers) as well as DIY consumers. The professional market accounts for about 60% of total sales.

The company builds its marketing and advertising campaigns around radio television direct marketing mobile and social media sponsorships store events and in-store marketing. It is focused on creating an omnichannel experience where customers can buy online and pick up in stores. In addition its "Speed Perks" customer loyalty campaign targets core DIY customers and emphasizes service. The company's advertising expenses ranges from $100 to $120 million annually.

Financial Performance

Advance Auto Parts' revenue had been on a steady decline for three years since 2015. It did jump back slightly in 2018 however. Net income has been a little more sporadic see-sawing between $425 million and $500 million over the past five years.

In 2019 the company reported revenue of $9.7 billion up 1% from the prior year. It saw an overall improvement in its comparable store sales growth of 1% driven by improvements in their Professional business and increased sales in several product categories including parts and batteries and accessories and chemicals.

Net income increased to $487 million in 2019 up by 15% from 2018 driven by the $6.7 million decrease in interest expense due to the early redemption of the company's 2020 senior unsecured notes.

Cash at the end of 2019 was $419 million a decrease of $478 million from the prior year. Cash from operations contributed $867 million to the coffers while investing activities used $463 million mainly for the purchases of property and equipment. Financing activities used another $882.1 million for dividends to stockholders and a stock repurchase program.

Strategy

To generate DIY customer traffic and appeal to their Professional customers the company focuses on their merchandising strategy that carries a broad selection of high quality reputable brand name automotive parts and accessories. They also negotiate agreements to purchase merchandise over a specified period of time along with other provisions including pricing volume and payment terms. In 2019 they have purchased merchandise from over 1100 vendors with no single vendor accounting for more than 10% of purchases.

The company is focused on improving customer experience and driving consistent execution for both Professional and DIY customers. To be able to achieve these improvements the company planned strategic initiatives that includes development of a demand-based assortment advancement towards optimizing their footprint by market continued roll out of Speed Perks 2.0 program development of a more efficient end-to-end supply chain enhancement of their DIY omni-channel business including eCommerce performance continued success of the roll-out of their partnership with Walmart.com and the purchase of the DieHard.

Advance Auto Parts Inc. intend to continue to expand the markets they serve as part of their growth strategy which may include opening new stores or branches as well as expansion of their online business. The company may also grow their business through strategic acquisitions.

Company Background

Founded as Advance Stores Company in 1929 AAP was a general merchandise retailer until the

1980s. From there the company shifted its focus to automotive parts retailing targeting DIY customers. It initiated a professionald delivery program in 1996.

In 2014 AAP acquired General Parts International (GPI) for about $2.1 billion — creating the largest automotive aftermarket parts provider in North America with $9 billion-plus in annual sales. GPI a privately-held distributor and supplier of original equipment and aftermarket replacement parts to commercial markets owned the CARQUEST and WORLDPAC brands. The deal added 1233 Carquest stores 103 Worldpac branches in 45 states and Canada and the business of nearly 1400 independently-owned Carquest stores to AAP's network.

EXECUTIVES

President And Ceo, Thomas R. (Tom) Greco, age 61, $803,852 total compensation
Svp E-commerce, Scott Bauhofer
President Â– Northern Division, Maria Ayres
President Southern Division, David McCartney
President Western Division, Mike Pack
President Autopart International, Michael Creedon
Evp Commercial, Robert B. (Bob) Cushing, age 66, $453,910 total compensation
President Carquest Canada, Steve Gushie
Evp General Counsel And Secretary, Tammy M. Finley, age 53, $400,005 total compensation
Svp And Cio, James A. (Andy) Paisley
Svp And Chief Marketing Officer, Walter Scott
Evp And Cfo, Thomas B. (Tom) Okray, age 57, $86,540 total compensation
Svp Supply Chain, Todd Greener
Evp Supply Chain Strategy And Transformation, Leslie Keating
Svp Professional Business, Al Wheeler
Assistant Vice President Strategic Store Systems, Craig Anderman
National Sales Manager, Chad Schnitz
Regional Vice President, Ernesto Valderrama
Vice President, Warren Shatzer
Vice President Of Human Resources, Kathy Gillis
Vice President Store Development, Jim Germann
Senior Vice President General Counsel And Corporate Secretary, Sarah Powell
Senior Vice President Finance, James Doran
Vice President Commercial Marketing, John Hanighen
Vp Of It Applications Development, Ben Jorgensen
Svp Marketing Insights And Analytics, Yogi Jashnani
Senior Vice President Communications And Investor Relations, Elisabeth Eisleben
Senior Vice President Chief Accounting Officer Controller, Andrew Page
Chairman, Jeffrey C. Smith
Auditors: DELOITTE & TOUCHE LLP

LOCATIONS

HQ: Advance Auto Parts Inc
2635 East Millbrook Road, Raleigh, NC 27604
Phone: 540 362-4911
Web: www.AdvanceAutoParts.com

PRODUCTS/OPERATIONS

2018 Sales

	% of total
Parts & Batteries	66
Accessories & Chemicals	20
Engine Maintenance	13
Other	1
Total	**100**

Selected Products

Parts & Batteries
 Batteries and battery accessories
 Belts and hoses
 Brakes and brake pads
 Chassis parts
 Climate control parts
 Clutches and drive shafts
 Engines and engine parts
 Exhaust systems and parts
 Hub assemblies
 Ignition components and wire
 Radiators and cooling parts
 Starters and alternators
 Steering and alignment parts
Accessories & Chemicals
 AC chemicals and accessories
 Air fresheners
 Antifreeze and washer fluid
 Electrical wire and fuses
 Electronics
 Floor mats seat covers and interior accessories
 Hand and specialty tools
 Lighting
 Performance parts
 Sealants adhesives and compounds
 Tire repair accessories
 Vent shades mirrors and exterior accessories
 Washes waxes and cleaning supplies
 Wiper blades
Engine Maintenance
 Air filters
 Fuel and oil additives
 Fuel filters
 Grease and lubricants
 Motor Oil
 Oil filters
 Part cleaners and treatments
 Transmission fluid

Selected Brands

Bosch
Castrol
Dayco
Denso
Gates
Monroe
Moog
Prestone
Purolator
Trico
Wagner

COMPETITORS

Amazon.com	Replacement Parts
AutoZone	Somerset Tire Service
Fisher Auto Parts	TBC Retail
Genuine Parts	U.S. Auto Parts
Keystone Automotive Operations	Uni-Select
	VIP
O'Reilly Automotive	Wal-Mart
Pep Boys	

HISTORICAL FINANCIALS

Company Type: Public

Income Statement   FYE: December 28

	REVENUE ($ mil.)	NET INCOME ($ mil.)	NET PROFIT MARGIN	EMPLOYEES
12/19	9,709	486	5.0%	67,000
12/18	9,580	423	4.4%	71,000
12/17	9,373	475	5.1%	71,000
12/16*	9,567	459	4.8%	74,000
01/16	9,737	473	4.9%	73,000
Annual Growth	**(0.1%)**	**0.7%**	**—**	**(2.1%)**

*Fiscal year change

2019 Year-End Financials

Debt ratio: 6.64%
Return on equity: 13.75%
Cash ($ mil.): 418
Current ratio: 1.27
Long-term debt ($ mil.): 747

No. of shares (mil.): 69
Dividends
 Yield: 0.0%
 Payout: 3.5%
Market value ($ mil.): 10,963

	STOCK PRICE ($) FY Close	P/E High/Low	PER SHARE ($) Earnings	Dividends	Book Value
12/19	158.35	26 20	6.84	0.24	51.26
12/18	155.46	32 18	5.73	0.24	49.00
12/17	99.69	27 12	6.42	0.24	46.19
12/16*	169.12	28 22	6.20	0.24	39.54
01/16	150.51	31 22	6.40	0.24	33.56
Annual Growth	**1.3%**	**— —**	**1.7%**	**(0.0%)**	**11.2%**

*Fiscal year change

Advanced Micro Devices Inc

Advanced Micro Devices (AMD) makes a range of microprocessors that power a wide range of devices from PCs to industrial machinery. The company produces microprocessors that power PCs servers and game consoles and embedded processors that control functions in machines used in industrial control and automation as well as medical imaging and telecommunications. Besides processors AMD makes graphics cards and systems-on-a-chip. In recent years the company has armed itself with new product families: Radeon for graphics and Ryzen for computing to strengthen its position against longtime rival and market leader Intel. Majority of AMD's sales comes from international customers.

Operations

AMD operates through two segments: Computing and Graphics and Enterprise Embedded and Semi-custom. Computing and Graphics products accounting for around 70% of sales include AMD's Ryzen chips for PCs and Radeon graphic processors for game systems and other devices. The products from the Enterprise Embedded and Semi-custom segment approximately 30% of sales are used in data centers kiosks machine-to-machine applications and security and storage systems.

AMD outsources manufacturing of its products to third-party foundries including GLOBALFOUNDRIES and Taiwan Semiconductor Manufacturing Company. AMD performs assembly test and packaging of its microprocessors and embedded processors.

Geographic Reach

Accounting for over 25% of sales the US and China (including Hong Kong) are the AMD's largest geographic markets. Europe Taiwan and Japan each generate more than 10% of AMD's sales while Singapore accounts for almost 10%.

AMD's corporate headquarters is in Santa Clara California but most of its US operations are conducted at its Austin Texas facilities. Overall the company has about 40 locations in about 25 countries with about 20 in the Asia/Pacific region (where it has assembly test and packaging facilities). In addition AMD has research and development facilities in the US and design and development engineering teams in China Canada India Singapore and Taiwan.

Sales and Marketing

AMD markets its products through a direct sales force as well as through a network of independent distributors and sales representatives. The company's major customer Sony Interactive Entertainment LLC accounts for more than 10% of the total revenue. Its marketing and advertising expenses totaled approximately $217 million $176 million and \$156 million for the years 2019 2018 and 2017 respectively.

Financial Performance

AMD's revenue has increased by a leap and a bound in the past two years rising at around 15% rate as manufacturers have increasingly adopted its newer chips.

Net revenue for 2019 was \$6.7 billion an increase of 4% compared to 2018 net revenue of \$6.5 billion. Computing and Graphics net revenue of \$4.7 billion in 2019 increased by 14% compared to \$4.1 billion in 2018 primarily as a result of a 22% increase in average selling price and a 4% increase in unit shipments.

Net income for 2019 improved to \$341 million compared to \$337 million in the prior year. The increase was primarily due to having lower cost of sales and higher revenue.

AMD had about \$1.5 billion in cash and equivalents in 2019 about \$387 million more than 2018. In 2019 operations generated \$493 million investing activities used \$149 million and financing activities provided \$43 million.

Strategy

AMD follows a documented strategic sourcing process which helps ensure a solid fit between a project's requirements and a supplier's capabilities. As a result of thorough up-front analysis this process also significantly improves the odds of long-term success for all members of a project team.

AMD Ventures is looking for innovative software and application companies who strategically align with their technologies and serve large and growing markets across high-performance client server and embedded.

Company Background

Founded in 1969 AMD has survived and sometimes thrived during the ups and downs of the age of the microprocessor. The company has constantly battled Intel the business's big kahuna trying to find an edge in price and performance.

EXECUTIVES

Svp And Cfo, Devinder Kumar, age 65, \$530,005 total compensation
President And Ceo, Lisa Su, age 51, \$886,340 total compensation
Svp Global Operations, Chekib Akrout, age 62
Svp And Cto, Mark D. Papermaster, age 59, \$549,994 total compensation
Svp And General Manager Enterprise Embedded And Semi-custom Business Group, Forrest E. Norrod, age 54, \$530,005 total compensation
Svp And General Manager Computing And Graphics Business Group, James R. (Jim) Anderson, age 48, \$499,990 total compensation
Vice President Information Technology And Chief Information Officer, Frederick Mapp
Corporate Vice President Engineering And Gm Research And Development China, Alan Lee
Corporate Vice President Of Investor Relations, Ruth Cotter
Corporate Vice President Alliances, Roy Taylor
Corporate Vice President Finance, Gary Lloyd
Svp General Counsel And Corporate Secretary, Harry Wolin
Vice President Finance And Sales Operations, Denise Gourlay
Vice President, Mike Rayfield
Executive Vice President Computing And Graphics Business Group, Sandeep Chennakeshu
Senior Vice President Global Operations, Keivan Keshvari
Corporate Vice President Finance, Pearly Teh
Corporate Vice President, Martin Ashton
Chairman, John E. Caldwell, age 70
Board Member, Mike Inglis
Auditors: Ernst & Young LLP

LOCATIONS

HQ: Advanced Micro Devices Inc
2485 Augustine Drive, Santa Clara, CA 95054
Phone: 408 749-4000
Web: www.amd.com

2018 Sales

	$ mil.	% of total
China	2,516	39
US	1,327	21
Japan	1,225	19
Singapore	728	11
Europe	470	7
Other regions	209	3
Total	**6,475**	**100**

PRODUCTS/OPERATIONS

2018 Sales

	$ mil.	% of total
Computing and Graphics	4,125	64
Enterprise Embedded and Semi-Custom	2,350	36
Total	**6,475**	**100**

Selected Products

Computing
  Accelerated processing units (APUs; Fusion combines central processing and graphics processing units on a single chip)
  Microprocessors (Ryzen Athlon Opteron Phenom Sempron and Turion lines)
  Motherboard reference design kits and chipsets
Graphics
  Embedded graphics processing units
  Macintosh notebook and desktop PC graphics processors (Radeon)
  Motherboard chipsets (for AMD and Intel processors)
  Server and workstation graphics processing units
Personal connectivity
  Embedded processors
  Networking chips

COMPETITORS

ARM Holdings	NVIDIA
Analog Devices	NXP Semiconductors
Atmel	STMicroelectronics
Hitachi	Samsung Electronics
Infineon Technologies	Silicon Integrated Systems
Intel	Texas Instruments
Marvell Technology	VIA Technologies
Matrox Electronic Systems	

HISTORICAL FINANCIALS

Company Type: Public

Income Statement   FYE: December 26

	REVENUE ($ mil.)	NET INCOME ($ mil.)	NET PROFIT MARGIN	EMPLOYEES
12/20	9,763	2,490	25.5%	12,600
12/19	6,731	341	5.1%	11,400
12/18	6,475	337	5.2%	10,100
12/17	5,329	43	0.8%	8,900
12/16	4,272	(497)	—	8,200
Annual Growth	**23.0%**	**—**		**11.3%**

2020 Year-End Financials

Debt ratio: 3.68%	No. of shares (mil.): 1,211
Return on equity: 57.64%	Dividends
Cash ($ mil.): 1,595	Yield: —
Current ratio: 2.54	Payout: —
Long-term debt ($ mil.): 330	Market value ($ mil.): 111,182

	STOCK PRICE ($) FY Close	P/E High/Low	PER SHARE ($) Earnings	Dividends	Book Value
12/20	91.81	46 18	2.06	0.00	4.82
12/19	46.18	150 55	0.30	0.00	2.42
12/18	17.82	96 28	0.32	0.00	1.26
12/17	10.28	380244	0.04	0.00	0.63
12/16	11.34	—	(0.60)	0.00	0.44
Annual Growth	**68.7%**	**—**	**—**		**81.4%**

ADVENTIST HEALTH SYSTEM SUNBELT HEALTHCARE CORPORATION

EXECUTIVES

Pres-Ceo, Terry Shaw
Cfo, Paul Rathdun
Asst SEC, Louis Mark Block
Coordinator, Pennie Moore
Regional Laboratory Administra, Dhobie Wong
Information Security, Teresa Majors
Admin Director Strategic Plann, Belinda Grant
Podiatrist, Tara Fussell
Administrator, Adnan Chowdhury
Erp It Security Analyst, Aubrey Alleyne
Senior Telecommunications Anal, Becky Beranek
Auditors: ERNST & YOUNG LLP ORLANDO FL

LOCATIONS

HQ: ADVENTIST HEALTH SYSTEM SUNBELT HEALTHCARE CORPORATION
900 HOPE WAY, ALTAMONTE SPRINGS, FL 327141502
Phone: 407 357-1000
Web: WWW.ADVENTHEALTH.COM

HISTORICAL FINANCIALS

Company Type: Private

Income Statement   FYE: December 31

	REVENUE ($ mil.)	NET INCOME ($ mil.)	NET PROFIT MARGIN	EMPLOYEES
12/18	10,974	635	5.8%	78,000
12/17	10,083	1,167	11.6%	—
12/16	9,651	806	8.4%	—
12/14	519	26	5.1%	—
Annual Growth	**114.4%**	**121.7%**	**—**	**—**

ADVENTIST HEALTH SYSTEM/SUNBELT, INC.

Adventist Health System/Sunbelt one of the country's largest faith-based hospital systems runs about 45 hospitals 15 nursing homes 25 home health care agencies and approximately 40 Centra Care-branded urgent care centers in about 10 states (mostly in the Southeast). The not-for-profit system's acute care hospitals have some 8100 beds combined; its long-term care facilities offer around 1900 beds. The company's Florida division includes about two dozen hospitals as well as home health agencies and nursing homes. Adventist Health is sponsored by the Seventh-Day Adventist Church as part of that denomination's legacy of providing health care.

Geographic Reach

Adventist Health operates in 10 states: Colorado Florida Georgia Illinois Kansas Kentucky North Carolina Tennessee Texas and Wisconsin. Its largest market is Orlando.

Strategy

Adventist Health strives to provide "whole person" care combining medical spiritual and social services to its communities. The system has launched a number of initiatives to help it meet federal standards as the US government encourages hospital systems to improve health care quality safety and expenses. Among the new types of offerings it has embraced are telemetry monitoring of at-risk patients and art therapy for cancer patients.

Adventist improves its existing facilities through expansion and renovation projects. In 2018 the company broke ground on a new 76-bed patient tower at its Florida Hospital Celebration Health facility. The previous year it completed the $3.2 million renovation of its cancer unit at the Florida Hospital for Children in Orlando.

Furthermore the company increases its already hefty size through acquisitions and through affiliation agreements (particularly in markets where it doesn't have a major presence). For example in mid-2018 the company acquired Munroe Regional Medical Center in West Florida adding more than 400 beds to its portfolio. Earlier that year it acquired Bayfront Health Dade City Hospital from Community Health Systems; it renamed the hospital Florida Hospital Dade City. In Texas Adventist Health partners with St. David's Healthcare at Adventist Health's Central Texas Medical Center and the system has a separate agreement with Scott & White Healthcare to grow medical services at Adventist Health's Metroplex Health System. Adventist is also partnering with Texas Health Resources to build a $150 million hospital campus in Mansfield Texas.

Mergers and Acquisitions

Adventist Health adds to its portfolio through regular acquisitions. In mid-2018 the company acquired Munroe Regional Medical Center in West Florida adding more than 400 beds to its holdings. Earlier that year it acquired Bayfront Health Dade City Hospital from Community Health Systems; it renamed that hospital Florida Hospital Dade City.

EXECUTIVES

Senior Vice President, Jeffrey Bromme
Cio And Director, Brent G. Snyder
President And Ceo Mid-america Region; President And Ceo Shawnee Mission Medical Center, Samuel H. (Sam) Turner
Executive Vice President President/ceo Multi-state Division, Richard K. (Rich) Reiner
Executive Vice President President/ceo Florida Division, Lars D. Houmann
Evp Florida Division; Evp Florida Hospital, Des D. Cummings
President And Ceo Appalachia Region; President And Ceo Park Ridge Hospital, Jimm A. Bunch
Evp Florida Division; President And Ceo Florida Region, Michael H. Schultz
President And Ceo Metroplex Health System, Carlyle Walton

President Ceo, Kenneth A. (Ken) Finch
President And Ceo Takoma Regional Hospital, Daniel Wolcott
President And Ceo Midwest Region; President And Ceo Adventist Midwest Health, David L. Crane
Cfo, David W. Evans
Chief Technology Officer, Michael Emmons
Vice President And Chief Nursing Officer, Ellen Lenkevich
Medical Director, Steven Dukes
Vice President Marketing And Brand Strategy, Kevin Edgerton
Vice President Managed Care, John Brownlow
Senior Vice President Chief Strategy Officer Florida Hospital, Josef Ghosn
I:iadvenlist Vice President Medical Mission, Ted Hamilton
Senior Vice President And Chief Clinical Officer, Carlene Jamerson
Assistant Vice President Materiel Management, Lowell Church
Assistant Vice President, Harry Janke
Vice President Facilities And Construction, Jody Barry
Senior Vice President, Mark Martin
Vice President Of Population Health And Care Innovation Information Technology Solutions, Jennifer Jackson
Vice President, Russ Weaver
Vice President Of Regional Operations, Cary Smith
Director Of Nursing, Angela Jacobson
Vice President Finance And Chief Officer, Andrew Jahn
Associate Vice President Of Human Resources, Jeni Hasselbrac
Vice President Of Treasury, Jeff Graff
Corporate Vice President And Chief Information Officer, Alan Soderblom
Assistant Vice President Public Relations, Jacobs Lanell
Physical Therapy Director, RAY OWENS
Head Nurse, Madelyn Smith
Medical Records Director, KEVIN CARPENTER
Dir Of Home Healthcare Srv, CHRISTINA HARWOOD
Medical Director, Pamela Huang
Vpres, Ryan Small
Medical Director, Dipti Mehta
Vp Operations, Kathy Roberts
Director Of Nursing, Janet Redhi
Health Care Director, Richelle Cheek
Health Care Director, Beth Rowe
Director Of Radiology, John Mckissack
Operating Room Dir, Carolyn Hopper
Vice President, Pamela Hodges
Auditors: ERNEST & YOUNG LLP ORLANDO

LOCATIONS

HQ: ADVENTIST HEALTH SYSTEM/SUNBELT, INC. 900 HOPE WAY, ALTAMONTE SPRINGS, FL 327141502
Phone: 407 357-1000
Web: WWW.ADVENTISTHEALTHSYSTEM.COM

Selected Facilities

Colorado
Avista Adventist Hospital (Louisville)
Littleton Adventist Hospital
Parker Adventist Hospital
Porter Adventist Hospital (Denver)
Florida
Florida Hospital Altamonte (Altamonte Springs)
Florida Hospital Apopka
Florida Hospital Carrollwood (Tampa)
Florida Hospital Celebration Health (Celebration)
Florida Hospital DeLand
Florida Hospital East Orlando
Florida Hospital Fish Memorial (Orange City)
Florida Hospital Flagler (Palm Coast)
Florida Hospital Heartland Medical Center (Sebring)

Florida Hospital Kissimmee
Florida Hospital Lake Placid
Florida Hospital Memorial Medical Center (Daytona Beach)
Florida Hospital North Pinellas (Tarpon Springs)
Florida Hospital Oceanside (Ormond Beach)
Florida Hospital Orlando
Florida Hospital Pepin Heart Institute (Tampa)
Florida Hospital Tampa
Florida Hospital Waterman (Tavares)
Florida Hospital Wauchula
Florida Hospital Winter Park Memorial Hospital
Florida Hospital Zephyrhills
Georgia
Gordon Hospital (Calhoun)
Emory-Adventist Hospital (Smyrna)
Illinois
Adventist Bolingbrook Hospital
Adventist GlenOaks Hospital (Glendale Heights)
Adventist Hinsdale Hospital
Adventist La Grange Memorial Hospital
Kansas
Shawnee Mission Medical Center
Kentucky
Manchester Memorial Hospital
North Carolina
Park Ridge Hospital (Fletcher)
Tennessee
Jellico Community Hospital
Takoma Regional Hospital (Greeneville)
Texas
Central Texas Medical Center (San Marcos)
Huguley Memorial Medical Center (Fort Worth)
Metroplex Adventist Hospital (Killeen)
Rollins Brook Community Hospital (Lampasas)
Wisconsin
Chippewa Valley Hospital (Durand)

PRODUCTS/OPERATIONS

Selected Products
Behavioral Health
Cardiovascular
Diabetes
Digestive Health
Emergency
Eye Care Center
Family Practice
Home Health/Home Care
Imaging Services
Mammography/Breast Center/Breast Care
Minimally Invasive/Robotic Surgery
Neurology
Neurosurgery
NICU
OB/Birth Care
Oncology/Cancer
Orthopedics
Outpatient Surgery
Pain Medicine
Pediatrics
Psychology
Rehab
Senior Care
Sleep Center
Stroke Care/Stroke Center
Surgery
Therapy Services
Urology
Wellness Center
Women's Services
Wound Care

COMPETITORS

Ascension Health
BayCare Health System
CHRISTUS Health
Catholic Health Initiatives
Community Health Systems
Encompass Health

HCA
Kindred Healthcare
Mount Sinai Medical Center of Florida
Orlando Health
Tenet Healthcare
Universal Health Services

HISTORICAL FINANCIALS

Company Type: Private

Income Statement   FYE: December 31

	REVENUE ($ mil.)	NET INCOME ($ mil.)	NET PROFIT MARGIN	EMPLOYEES
12/19	11,892	1,607	13.5%	46,960
12/09*	0	0	—	—
10/08	145	(8)	—	—
Annual Growth	49.2%	—	—	—

*Fiscal year change

AECOM

AECOM is one of the world's top engineering and design groups. The company provides planning consulting architectural and engineering design services for civil and infrastructure construction to public and private clients. The company also offers other services including logistics and consulting in a range of end markets that include energy and environmental construction. Some of AECOM's major projects include the Heathrow Terminal 2 Hudson Yards Melbourne Metro Tunnel and Inglewood Basketball & Entertainment Center in California. AECOM generates more than 75% of sales in the Americas region.

Operations

AECOM operates through three business segments: Americas (more than 75% of total sales) International (nearly 15%) and AECOM Capital (ACAP) which invests primarily in real estate projects.

AECOM's Americas and International segments comprise a broad array of services generally provided on a fee-for-service basis. These services include planning consulting architectural and engineering design program management and construction management for industrial commercial institutional and government clients worldwide. For each of these services its technical expertise includes civil structural process mechanical geotechnical systems and electrical engineering architectural landscape and interior design urban and regional planning project economics cost consulting and environmental health and safety work. Its Americas segment provides services generally in the US Canada and Latin America. Its International segment provides similar services generally in Europe the Middle East and Africa and Asia-Pacific regions.

Geographic Reach

Based in Los Angeles California the company generates around 75% of its sales from the Americas about 10% from Europe Middle East and Africa while another some 10% from Asia Pacific.

It has primary office locations in the US as well as in Australia Hong Kong Singapore the United Arab Emirates India and the UK.

Sales and Marketing

AECOM serves several sectors such as transportation facilities environmental energy water and government.

Nearly 60% of its revenue derived from private entities. US federal government agencies (Departments of Defense Energy Justice and Homeland Security) US states and local governments and non-US governments accounts for more than 40%.

Financial Performance

AECOM's revenue has gradually declined in the past years falling 25% between 2016 and 2020.

The company's net income has also followed a similar trajectory significantly falling to a loss in recent years following volatility.

AECOM's revenue for the year ended 2020 decreased $402.5 million to $13.2 billion as compared to $13.6 billion for the corresponding period last year. The decrease in revenue for the year was primarily due to decreases in its Americas segment of $251.1 million and in its International segment of $150 million.

The company recorded a loss of $186.4 million in 2020 a slight improvement from its reported net loss of $261.1 million the year prior. The company incurred a $188.3 million restructuring expense for the year however its general and administrative expenses declined. AECOM also did not repeat its impairment loss of $24.9 million from the year prior during the current fiscal year.

AECOM added $737.9 million to its cash stores in 2020 to $1.8 billion compared to $1.1 billion in 2019. Cash provided by operations was $329.6 million while cash from investing activities contributed another $2 billion from the sale of discontinued operations. Financing activities used $1.6 billion mainly for borrowings repayments unsecured senior notes redemptions and repurchases of common stock.

Strategy

AECOM's strategy is focused on setting a new standard of excellence in the professional services industry. First its recently simplified operating structure promotes greater connectivity and collaboration across its seven regions and five global business lines. The company drives growth by prioritizing its core markets leaning into its greatest strengths and ensuring its best talent and resources are focused on nurturing client relationships. The company is transforming the way it delivers work through technology and digital platforms improving the client experience and increasing efficiency. Lastly AECOM is building upon its position as a leading ESG company unified by its purpose to deliver a better world.

In early 2021 AECOM completed the sale of the Civil construction business to Oroco Capital. The sale of its Civil construction which the company announced in late 2020 together with the sale of its Power construction business in October represents a significant milestone in advancing its strategy and focusing its efforts on its higher-margin and lower-risk Professional Services businesses. With the completion of these sales AECOM has now exited substantially all of its self-perform at-risk construction businesses.

AECOM also advanced the next stage of its strategy in late 2020 with the integration its Design & Consulting Services (DCS) businesses into one global organization. This initiative further simplified the operating structure of the company and enabled greater connectivity and collaboration across the enterprise.

Company Background

AECOM formed in 1990 through the merger of five subsidiaries of Ashland Inc. Since then more than 50 companies have joined AECOM. The company completed its initial public offering in 2007.

EXECUTIVES

Associate Vice President Network Architect, Michael Bradvica

Vice President Communications, Frank Pollare

Vice President Leasing, David B Kilpatrick

Chief Executive Aecom Capital, John T. Livingston

President Major Pursuits, Frederick W. (Fred) Werner, age 67, $661,540 total compensation

Svp And Chief Marketing And Communications Officer, Heather Rim

Chairman And Ceo, Michael S. (Mike) Burke, age 56, $1,276,928 total compensation

Group President Construction Services, Daniel P. McQuade, age 60

Evp And General Counsel, Carla J. Christofferson, age 52

Chief Executive Europe The Middle East India And Africa (emia), Steve Morriss

President Technical And Operational Services, Randall A. (Randy) Wotring, age 63, $705,389 total compensation

Evp And Cfo, W. Troy Rudd, age 56, $528,851 total compensation

Evp And Chief Human Resources Officer, Mary E. Finch, age 50

Chief Executive Australia-new Zealand, Lara Poloni

Senior Vice President, Stephen Polechronis

Vice President, Herbert Higginbotham

Associate Vice President, Atma Sookram

Vice President, Mark Kelley

Vice President, John S Prizner

Associate Vice President, Samuel Pickard

Associate Vice President, John Bachmann

Vice President Energy, Shawn Kelly

Associate Vice President, Rudy Schmidtke

Vice President, Rod Mccrary

Vice President, Brian Sands

Associate Vice President, Robert Humbert

Assistant Vice President Casu, Andy Shepard

Svp Mergers And Acquisitions, Matt Clark

Associate Vice President, George Sholy

Northeast Executive Vice President, Ira A Levy

Vice President Global Tax, Donna Cote

Vice President, Will Wright

Vice President, Juli Binaco

Senior Vice President, Dale Sands

Group Associate Vice President Contracts Compliance And Internal Audit, Edward Condoleo

Vice President, Mark Griffiths

Vice President, Ron Osborne

Assistant Vice President Techn, Richard Silos

Associate Vice President, Robert Joseph

Associate Vice President, Dean Simpson

Vice President, Michael Girman

Assoc. Vice President, James Fillis

First Vice President, Ryan Mahoney

Vice President Investor Relations, Paul Cyril

Senior Vice President, Diana Mendes

Associate Vice President, Chris Mcguire

Vice President Principal Civil Engineer, Robert Murphy

Associate Vice President, David Plotkin

Evp Americas Transportation, Matthew Cummings

First Vice President, Tom Parsons

Executive Vice President, Bill Endres

Associate Vice President, Dawn Swider

Associate Vp, Dennis Struecker

Associate Vp, Wendy Thu

Senior Vice President Corporate Finance, Roger Willard

Vice President Technical Services, Jeff Brier

Executive Vice President Mid Atlantic Region Tishman Construction, John Barron

Senior Vice President Assistant General Counsel Head Of Litigation, Laura Abrahamson

Vice President Project Manager, Randy Kirschner

Associate Vice President Project Management, Jeff Endersby

Vice President Transportation, Michael Andersen

Senior Vice President Operations Finance, Charles Thuss

Vice President Of Operations Support, Richard Blagg

Vice President Corporate Development And Mergers And Acquisitions, Stan Lin

Evp And General Manager Federal Construction Services, Vern Kuehn

Evp, Vahid Ownjazayeri

Senior Vice President Strategic Planning And Technical Services, Mark Morris
Vice President Operations And, Brad White
Associate Vice President, John Holmes
Vice President, Dan Shumaker
Executive Vice President, Rebecca Nolan
Senior Vice President Pacific Region Business Line Lead, Sujan Punyamurthula
Vice President Marketing And Business Development, Carol Papillo
Vice President Strategic Captures Managementservices Group, Matt Einseln
Regional Vice President, Kevin Jeansonne
Vice President Purchasing, Marty Adelman
Senior Vice President Operations, Steve Richards
Vice President, Michael House
Vice President Senior Project Manager, Karen Maestas
Senior Vice President Talent Management, Susan Dumond
Vice President, Richard Romig
Associate Vice President, Alastair Macgregor
Vice President, Wesley Ishizu
Vice President Pmcm Transit Business Line, Bill Wilkerson
Senior Vice President Chicago Metro Area Executive, Denise Casalino
Vice President, James Karl
Associate Vice President, Brent Miyazaki
Vice President Director Of Healthcare Facilities Business Line Infrastructure Environment, Joe Greenan
Executive Vice President Cyber Strategy, Dean Fox
Vice President, Juan Alfonso
Vice President, Garry Lay
Vice President Transportation, Daniel Faust
Vice President, Carlos Garcia
Associate Vice President, Jerry Farhat
Vice President, Ivan Kuncheff
Vice President Principal Geologist, Robert Macwilliams
Senior Vice President, Russel Rudden
Vice President Business Development, Don Dracon
Senior Vice President, Chris Ward
Vice President, Jason Majzoub
District Vice President, Lee Grant
Senior Vice President Engineering And Om Oil Gas, Ken Martinez
Vice President, Thomas Elsroth
Associate Vice President, James Sullivan
Vice President Water Resources, Richard Millet
Vice President, Melad Hanna
Vice President Regional Managing Principal Buildings Places, Bob Lavey
Vice President Transportation, Liam Dalton
Vice President, Bill Rohrer
Vice President, Alex Houseal
Senior Vice President, Michael Steer
Vice President Of Human Resources, Ramesh Patel
Vice President, Steve Wilcox
Vice President Grand Rapids Buildings Places Practice Leader, Thomas Vanhattum
Vice President Pbr Program Manager, John Heinicke
Vice President And Chief Engineer, Feury John
Vice President Of Operations, Dave Sampson
Vice President Emerging Technology, Seth Finkel
Vice President, Jose De Almagro
Vice President Operations Em Spectrum And Information Assurance, Marshall Denney
Vice President Global Talent And Leadership Development, Julie Holbein
Vice President, Paul Boddie
Senior Vice President Operations, Leo Sain
Senior Vice President, Luigi Sciabarrasi
Senior Vice President Operations, Michael Terry
Vice President, Rishit Patel
Associate Vice President, Rodney Croslen
Executive Vice President Marketing And Business Development, Tom Wrenn

Corporate Vice Presidentstrategy, Fernanda Philbrick
Vice President Principal Seismologist, Hong Thio
Group Senior Vice President, Jim Earley
Vice President Water Resources, Kenneth Myers
Vice President Water Resourc, Joseph Ehasz
Senior Vice President Operations, Bob Mcquinn
Vice Chairman, Daniel R. (Dan) Tishman, age 65
Advisory Board Member, Antonio Santoro
Secretary, Annis Catherine
Auditors: Ernst & Young LLP

LOCATIONS

HQ: AECOM
300 South Grand Avenue, 9th Floor, Los Angeles, CA 90071
Phone: 213 593-8000
Web: www.aecom.com

2018 Sales

	$ mil.	% of total
US	14,753	73
Europe	1,984	10
Asia/Pacific	1,440	7
Canada	1,212	6
Other foreign countries	765	4
Total	**20,155**	**100**

PRODUCTS/OPERATIONS

Selected Services

Architecture & Design
Construction
Decommissioning & Closure
Engineering
Environmental Services
International Development
IT & Cybersecurity
Operations & Maintenance
Planning & Consulting
Program Management/Construction Management
Risk Management & Resilience
Specialized Services
  Cities Solutions
  Equity Investment
  Fabrication
  Process Technologies
  Public/Private Partnerships
Technical Services

2018 Sales

	$ mil.	% of total
Design and Consulting Services	8,223	41
Construction Services	8,238	41
Management Services	3,693	18
Total	**20,155**	**100**

COMPETITORS

Amec Foster Wheeler	MWH Global
Bechtel	Parsons Brinckerhoff
Black & Veatch	Parsons Corporation
EMCOR	STV
Fluor	Skidmore Owings
Henkels & McCoy	Stantec
Jacobs Engineering	Terracon
KBR	Tetra Tech
Louis Berger	Tutor Perini

HISTORICAL FINANCIALS

Company Type: Public

Income Statement

FYE: September 30

	REVENUE ($ mil.)	NET INCOME ($ mil.)	NET PROFIT MARGIN	EMPLOYEES
09/20	13,239	(186)	—	54,000
09/19	20,173	(261)	—	86,000
09/18	20,155	136	0.7%	87,000
09/17	18,203	339	1.9%	87,000
09/16	17,410	96	0.6%	87,000
Annual Growth	**(6.6%)**	**—**	**—**	**(11.2%)**

2020 Year-End Financials

Debt ratio: 15.86%	No. of shares (mil.): 157
Return on equity: (-5.32%)	Dividends
Cash ($ mil.): 1,708	Yield: —
Current ratio: 1.24	Payout: —
Long-term debt ($ mil.): 2,041	Market value ($ mil.): 6,571

	STOCK PRICE ($) FY Close	P/E High/Low		PER SHARE ($) Earnings	Dividends	Book Value
09/20	41.84	—	—	(1.16)	0.00	20.97
09/19	37.56	—	—	(1.66)	0.00	23.43
09/18	32.66	46	37	0.84	0.00	26.07
09/17	36.81	18	12	2.13	0.00	25.37
09/16	29.73	58	37	0.62	0.00	21.88
Annual Growth	**8.9%**	**—**	**—**	**—**	**—**	**(1.1%)**

AES Corp.

The AES Corp. is a world power producer. The US-based company has about 110 generation facilities in nearly 15 countries throughout the Americas(NorthCentralSouth) Asia and Europe. AES sells electricity to utilities industrial users and intermediaries. The company also sells power directly to end-users such as homes and businesses mainly in Latin America and the US. Non regulated generates the biggest share of electricity while regulated generate about 30%. The US supplies more than 30% of AES' revenue. Overall AES provides power to about 2.5 million customers.

HISTORY

Applied Energy Services (AES) was founded in 1981 three years after passage of the Public Utilities Regulation Policies Act which enabled small power firms to enter electric generation markets formerly dominated by utility monopolies. Cofounders Roger Sant and Dennis Bakke who had served in President Nixon's Federal Energy Administration saw that an independent power producer (IPP) could make money by generating cheap power in large volumes to sell to large power consumers and utilities.

AES set about building massive cogeneration plants (producing both steam and electricity) in 1983. The first plant Deepwater went into operation near Houston in 1986. By 1989 AES had three plants on line and it then opened plants in Connecticut and Oklahoma. In 1991 the company formally renamed AES went public but one plant's falsified emissions reports caused AES's stock to plummet in 1992.

Facing environmental groups' opposition to new power plant construction and an overall glut in the US power market AES bought interests in two Northern Ireland plants in 1992 and began expanding into Latin America in 1993. Also in 1993 AES set up a separately traded subsidiary AES China Generating Co. to focus on Chinese development projects. AES won a plant development contract with the Puerto Rico Electric Power Authority (1994) and a bid to privatize an Argentine hydrothermal company (1995).

In 1996 AES began adding stakes in electric utility and distribution companies to its portfolio including interests in formerly state-owned Brazilian electric utilities Light-Servi Sos de Eletricidade (1996) and CEMIG (1997); one Brazilian and two Argentine distribution companies (1997); and a distribution company in El Salvador (1998).

AES almost doubled its revenues after buying Destec Energy's international operations from NGC (now Dynegy) in 1997. By the next year prospects in international markets were dimming so AES turned to the US market again. It bought three California plants from Edison International and arranged for The Williams Companies to supply natural gas to the facilities and market the electricity generated. AES also won a bid to buy six plants from New York State Electric & Gas (now Energy East) affiliate NGE.

Also in 1998 despite black days in many world markets AES bought 90% of Argentine electric distribution company Edelap and a 45% stake in state-owned Orissa Power Generation in India. Its moves paid off: AES posted a 70% gain in sales that year.

It bought CILCORP an Illinois utility holding company in an $886 million deal in 1999. Boosting its presence in the UK AES bought the Drax power station a 3960-MW coal-fired plant from National Power. It also bought a majority stake in Brazilian data transmission company Eletronet from Brazil's government-owned utility ELETROBR S. In 2000 AES increased its interests in Brazilian power distributors. It also gained a 73% stake (later expanded to 87%) in Venezuelan electric utility Grupo EDC in a $1.5 billion hostile takeover.

The next year AES bought IPALCO the parent of Indianapolis Power & Light in a $3 billion deal. Also in 2001 AES acquired the outstanding shares of Chilean generation company Gener in which it previously held a 60% stake.

That year AES moved to take control of CANTV Venezuela's #1 telecom company. Through Grupo EDC which already owned 6.9% of CANTV AES offered to buy 43.2% of the company. But AES withdrew the offer after the CANTV board rejected it. (AES sold Grupo EDC's stake in CANTV the following year.) AES also sold some generation assets in Argentina to TOTAL FINA ELF (now TOTAL) for about $370 million.

In 2002 AES sold its 24% interest in Light Servi os de Eletricidade (Light) to Electricit de France (EDF) in exchange for a 20% stake in Brazilian utility Eletropaulo (increasing its stake in Eletropaulo to 70%). In that same year the company sold its retail energy marketing unit (AES NewEnergy) to Constellation Energy Group for $240 million and its CILCORP subsidiary which holds utility Central Illinois Light to Ameren.

In 2007 the company acquired two 230 MW petroleum coke-fired power generation facilities in Tamuin Mexico for $611 million. It also bought a 51% stake in Turkish power generator IC ICTAS Energy Group.

AES has faced controversy in Brazil where an unstable power market has caused the company to default on debts incurred from its purchases of stakes in local utilities (as well as bankrupt telecom firm Eletronet) in recent years. To restructure its debt with Banco Nacional de Desenvolvimento Economico e Social (BNDES) AES completed a deal in 2007 in which the firm's interests in AES Eletropaulo AES Uruguaiana AES Tiete and AES Sul was placed into a new holding company (Brasiliana Energia). AES owns 50.1% of that company while BNDES holds 49.9%.

To raise cash in 2008 and 2009 AES sold the AES Ekibastuz power plant and Maikuben coal mine in Kazakhstan to Kazakhmys (renamed KAZ Minerals) for $1.1 billion.

In 2008 the company boosted it assets in the Philippines acquiring the 660 MW Masinloc coal-fired power plant in Barangay Bula for $930 million.

EXECUTIVES

Evp And Cfo, Thomas M. (Tom) O'Flynn, $683,000 total compensation
Ceo, Andrés R. Gluski, $1,165,000 total compensation
Evp General Counsel And Corporate Secretary, Brian A. Miller, $585,000 total compensation
President Brazil Strategic Business Unit (sbu), Julian Nebreda
Svp Technology And Services And Cio, Elizabeth Hackenson, $433,000 total compensation
Svp And Coo, Bernerd Da Santos, $456,000 total compensation
President Asia Strategic Business Unit (sbu), Marty Crotty
President Europe Strategic Business Unit (sbu), Mark Green
President Mexico Central America And The Caribbean (mcac) Strategic Business Unit (sbu), Manuel Pérez Dubuc
President Us Strategic Business Unit (sbu), Ken Zagzebski
President And Coo, Patrick Moran
Vp Global Network And Ciso, Scott Goodhart
Vice President Of Human Resources, James Valdez
Vice President Of Information Systems, Ramon Eulacio
Vice President (human Resources), Paritosh Mishra
Vice President Finanzas, Rosa Alvarado
Vice President De Geraasao E Gestao De Energia, Arturo Gris
Svp Global Engineering And Construction, Mike Chilton
Vice President Of Sales And Marketing, Hacker Todd
Chairman, Charles O. Rossotti
Board Director, Kevin Walker
Board Member, Tarun Khanna
Board Member, Kristina Johnson
Board Member, John Morse
Auditors: Ernst & Young LLP

LOCATIONS

HQ: AES Corp.
    4300 Wilson Boulevard, Arlington, VA 22203
Phone: 703 522-1315   **Fax:** 703 528-4510
Web: www.aes.com

2018 Sales

	$ mil.	% of total
United States	3,462	36
Chile	2,087	19
Dominican Republic	884	8
El Salvador	768	7
Brazil	527	5
Argentina	487	4
Panama	438	4
Colombia	428	4
Bulgaria	426	4
Mexico	399	3
United Kingdom	390	3
Vietnam	245	2
Jordan	95	1
Philippines	93	-
Kazakhstan	- -	-
Other non-US	76	-
Total	**10,736**	**100**

PRODUCTS/OPERATIONS

2018 Sales

	$ mil.	% of total
Regulated	2,939	27
Non-Regulated	7,797	73
Total	**10,736**	**100**

Selected Electric Utilities and Distribution Companies

AES CLESA (electric utility El Salvador)
AES Edelap (electric utility Argentina)
AES Eden (electric utility Argentina)
AES Edes (electric utility Argentina)
AES Gener (electric generation Chile)

AES India Private Ltd.
AES SeaWest Inc.
Brasiliana Energia
    AES Sul Distribuidora Gaucha de Energia SA (AES Sul electric utility Brazil)
    AES Tiete (power generation Brazil)
    AES Uruguaiana (power generation Brazil)
    Eletropaulo Metropolitana Eletricidade de São Paulo S.A. (AES Electropaulo electric distribution Brazil)
CAESS (electric utility El Salvador)
Companhia Energé;tica de Minas Gerais (CEMIG Brazil)
DPL (electric utility US)
EEO (electric utility El Salvador)
IC ICTAS Energy Group (power generation Turkey)
IPALCO Enterprises Inc. (holding company)

COMPETITORS

CPFL Energia	Exelon
Calpine	IBERDROLA
CenterPoint Energy	International Power
Duke Energy	NextEra Energy
E.ON UK	PG&E Corporation
Edison International	Public Service
Endesa S.A.	Enterprise Group
Enersis	Sempra Energy

HISTORICAL FINANCIALS

Company Type: Public

Income Statement

FYE: December 31

	REVENUE ($ mil.)	NET INCOME ($ mil.)	NET PROFIT MARGIN	EMPLOYEES
12/19	10,189	303	3.0%	—
12/18	10,736	1,203	11.2%	9,000
12/17	10,530	(1,161)	—	10,500
12/16	13,586	(1,130)	—	19,000
12/15	14,963	306	2.0%	21,000
Annual Growth	**(9.2%)**	**(0.2%)**	**—**	**—**

2019 Year-End Financials

Debt ratio: 59.75%	No. of shares (mil.): 663
Return on equity: 7.60%	Dividends
Cash ($ mil.): 1,029	Yield: 2.7%
Current ratio: 1.03	Payout: 71.8%
Long-term debt ($ mil.): 18,238	Market value ($ mil.): 13,213

	STOCK PRICE ($) FY Close	P/E High/Low		PER SHARE ($) Earnings	Dividends	Book Value
12/19	19.90	44	31	0.45	0.55	5.85
12/18	14.46	9	6	1.81	0.52	6.17
12/17	10.83	—	—	(1.76)	0.48	5.00
12/16	11.62	—	—	(1.71)	0.44	5.42
12/15	9.57	31	20	0.44	0.40	5.53
Annual Growth	**20.1%**	**—**	**—**	**0.6%**	**8.1%**	**1.4%**

AFLAC Inc

To soften the financial stresses during periods of disability or illness Aflac sells supplemental health and life insurance products including coverage for cancer accidents short-term disability critical illness hospital indemnity dental vision and in US aas well as third sector insurance (cancer medical and income support) and first sector insurance (protection and savings type) in Japan. It is a leading supplier of supplemental insurance in the US and is an industry leader in Japan's life and cancer insurance markets. Aflac which is marketed through — and is an acronym for — American Family Life Assurance Company sells policies that pay cash benefits to more than 50 million people worldwide.

Operations

Aflac operates through two reportable segments – Aflac Japan and Aflac US. The Japan segment accounts for about 70% of total revenue while the US accounts for the remainder. Aflac Japan became a subsidiary of its parent to better fit the importance of that market.

The firm's primary line of business is voluntary supplemental and life insurance. Aflac US markets and administers group products through Continental American Insurance Company (dba Aflac Group Insurance).

In addition to accident term and whole life and cancer coverage Aflac offers short-term disability critical illness hospital indemnity dental and vision products. Aflac individual and group insurance help provide protection to more than 50 million people.

Geographic Reach

Despite its US roots Columbus Georgia- based Aflac relies heavily on Japan where it makes about 70% of its insurance sales and where its policies fill in gaps not covered by the national health insurance system. Aflac has a presence in all 50 US states Puerto Rico and the District of Columbia.

Sales and Marketing

In Japan Aflac primarily sells through independent corporate agencies individual agencies and affiliated corporate agencies. Aflac Japan was represented by more than 9000 sales agencies with more than 109000 licensed sales associates are employed via this model.

Japanese banks and postal offices sell insurance. Aflac has agreements with some 90% of Japan's banks and offers cancer insurance in more than 20000 postal outlets providing a key outlet.

In the US Aflac is focusing on group insurance with larger customers. Here the company provides supplemental coverage to major medical plans. The Aflac US sales force includes about 8200 agents and brokers

The company spent $219 million $218 million and $210 million on advertising expense for the years 2019 2018 and 2017 respectively.

Financial Performance

Aflac's revenues grew by about 7% in the last five years despite fluctuating figures in the years between 2016 and 2018. Its net premiums and net investment income has shifted accordingly with the trend. Its profits have also been inconsistent with $4.6 billion at its height in 2017. It has since risen in 2019 following a slight drop the year before.

Revenues were up 3% to $22.3 billion in 2019 compared with $21.8 billion in 2018 due to an increase in net premiums that year. There was also an increase in its net investment income and a significant decrease from its realized investment losses by about 69%.

Net earnings were $3.3 billion a $384 million increase compared with $2.9 billion the prior year. This was partly due to an increase in revenues and pretax earnings despite a slight increase in benefits and expenses from the prior year.

Cash at the end of 2019 was $4.9 billion a $559 increase from $4.3 billion in 2018. Cash from operations generated $5.5 billion. Investing activities used $3.2 billion mostly for securities and commercial mortgage and other loans. Financing activities used another $1.7 billion for treasury stock purchases and dividends paid to stockholders.

Strategy

Aflac's strategy for growth in the U.S. and Japan has remained straightforward and consistent for many years. The company develops relevant supplemental insurance products and sells it through expanded distribution channels. To help promote its insurance products the company's marketing campaigns feature the Aflac Duck.

Its long-term growth strategy involves sales of relevant products sold through expansive distribution in order to reach its customers. Its products are protecting against rising co-pays high deductibles and other out-of-pocket expenses arising from a medical event which is then sold through agents brokers partnerships or directly. With this Aflac insures more than 50 million people in the United States and Japan.

Additionally the company also pursues growth through product development distribution expansion and digital advancements to improve the customer experience. Its objectives in 2020 are to maintain strong pre-tax margins in its Aflac Japan and Aflac U.S. segments through disciplined product pricing stable investment returns and leveraging a period of favorable benefit ratios to invest in its platform for future growth and efficiency.

The company believes that its efforts will support its prudent strategies for capital deployment in the form of dividends share repurchases and opportunistic investments that enhance the company's business with a focus on digital distribution and leveraging the company's brand distribution and scale.

Mergers and Acquisitions

In 2020 Aflac Incorporated's insurance subsidiaries American Family Life Assurance Company of Columbus (Aflac of Columbus) and American Family Life Assurance Company of New York (Aflac of New York) entered into a definitive agreement to acquire Zurich North America's U.S. Corporate Life and Pensions (Group Benefits) business which consists of group life disability and absence management products. The acquisition will expand Aflac's value proposition and enhances position on the first page of the employee benefits enrollment. Terms of this transaction were not disclosed.

In late 2019 Aflac Incorporated completed its acquisition of Florida-based Argus Holdings LLC and its subsidiary Argus Dental & Vision Inc. a premier benefits organization and national network dental and vision company. Argus has joined forces with Aflac to advance its vision of being the number one distributor of benefit solutions to the US workforce. Terms were not disclosed.

HISTORY

American Family Life Assurance Company (AFLAC) was founded in Columbus Georgia in 1955 by brothers John Paul and William Amos to sell life health and accident insurance. Competition was fierce and the little company did poorly. With AFLAC nearing bankruptcy the brothers looked for a niche.

The polio scares of the 1940s and 1950s had spawned insurance coverage written especially against that disease; the Amos brothers (whose father was a cancer victim) took a cue from that concept and decided to sell cancer insurance. In 1958 they introduced the world's first cancer-expense policy. It was a hit and by 1959 the company had written nearly a million dollars in premiums and expanded across state lines.

The enterprise grew quickly during the 1960s especially after developing its cluster-selling approach in the workplace where employers were usually willing to make payroll deductions for premiums. By 1971 the company was operating in 42 states.

While visiting the World's Fair in Osaka in 1970 John Amos decided to market supplemental cancer coverage to the Japanese whose national health care plan left them exposed to considerable expense from cancer treatment. After four years the company finally won approval to sell in Japan since the policies did not threaten existing markets and because the Amoses found notable backers in the insurance and medical industries. AFLAC became one of the first US insurance companies to enter the Japanese market and it enjoyed an eight-year monopoly on the cancer market. Back in the US in 1973 AFLAC organized a holding company and began buying television stations in the South and Midwest.

The 1980s were marked by US and state government inquiries into dread disease insurance. Critics said such policies were a poor value because they were relatively expensive and covered only one disease. However the inquiries led nowhere and demand for such insurance increased bringing new competition. In the 1980s AFLAC's scales tilted: US growth slowed while business grew in Japan which soon accounted for most of the company's sales.

EXECUTIVES

Evp Treasurer And Head Of Corporate Finance And Development, Kenneth S. (Ken) Janke, age 62

President, Kriss Cloninger, age 72, $975,000 total compensation

Chairman And Ceo, Daniel P. (Dan) Amos, age 68, $1,441,100 total compensation

Evp And Cfo, Frederick J. (Fred) Crawford, age 56, $700,000 total compensation

President Aflac International; Chairman Aflac Japan, Charles D. Lake, age 59, $333,333 total compensation

Evp And General Counsel, Audrey Boone Tillman, age 55

President Aflac, Paul S. Amos, age 45, $700,000 total compensation

President Aflac U.s., Teresa L. White, age 54

Svp And Chief Marketing Officer, Gail A. Galuppo, age 56

Svp Business Services; President And Ceo Communicorp, Eric B. Seldon

Evp And Global Chief Investment Officer, Eric M. Kirsch, age 59, $593,800 total compensation

Managing Director And Global Head Of Credit Global Investments, Bradley E. Dyslin

Svp And Cio, Julia K. Davis

Managing Director And Head Of Global Investments And Corporate It, J. Pete Kelso

Evp Global Chief Risk Officer And Chief Actuary, J. Todd Daniels, age 49

Senior Managing Director And Global Head Macro Investment Strategy Quantitative Research And Trading Global Investments, Timothy (Chip) Stevens

Managing Director And Chief Investment Officer Global Investments, Teresa Q. McTague

President Aflac Corporate Ventures, Nadeem G. Khan

Vice President, Darlene Porter

Vice President Controller Financial Reporting And Regulatory Compliance, Michael Bruder

Executive Vice President And Chief Financial Officer, Rob Moran

Vp Transformation, Jamie Lee

Vice President Trade Operations, Evan Philippopoulos

Second Vice President Financial And Information Technology Audits, Ellsworth Quinton

Assistant Vice President Marketing, James Wardrup

Vice President, Douglas Brown

Second Vice President, Kevin Dunlap

Second Vice President Travel Meetingsand Incentives, Heidi Carlisle

Second Vice President, Marty Pearson

Vice President U.s. Internal Audit, Lamar Barnett

Vice President Sales, Peter Crahan

Second Vice President, Gary Allen

Seconv Vice President Event Productions, Oz Roberts

2nd Vice President, Newton Walker

Vice President, Michael Fisher

Senior Vice President Chief Compliance Officer U.s., Thomas L McDaniel

Second Vice President Customer Service, Tammy Briggs

Vice President Of Finance, Nick Bettin

Avp Senior Risk Analyst, Alexander Lin

Vice President Product Innovation And Marketing, Stephanie Shields

Vice President Government Relations, John Laughbaum

Vice President, Jamie Rizzo

Regional Vice President Aflac Broker Channel, Jay Hutchins

Svp Financial Services And Chief Accounting Officer, June Howard

Senior Vice President Chief Esg And Communications Officer, Catherine Hernandez-blades

Senior Vice President Head Of Financial Planning And Analysis, Steven Beaver

Senior Vice President Global Risk And Corporate Reinsurance Officer, Michel G Perreault

Senior Vice President Of Internal Operations, Virgil R Miller

Second Vice President Shareholder Services, Patricia A Bell

Seconv Vice President Event Productions, Oz R Roberts

Executive Vice President, Kenneth S Janke

Assistant Vice President Senior Tech And Desktop Supp, Jack Chong

Vice President Innovation Technology, Joe Parsons

Vice President Human Resources And Chief People Officer, Brenda Mullins

Assistant Vice President Trade Operations, Rama Kolluri

Vice President And Counsel Federal Affairs, Bradley Knox

Senior Vice President Global Security Chief Information Security Officer, Timothy Callahan

Senior Vp, Ron Sanders

Vice President Regulatory Compliance, Ronda Tranter

Avp Compliance Manager, Victor Charles

Svp And Chief Digital Information Officer, Richard L Gilbert

Assistant Vice President, Albert Wong

Vice President Credit Union Services Sales Director, Jimmy Hill

Board Member, Jeromy Song

Board Member, Jim Aiken

Board Member, Barbara Rimer

Board Member, Melvin Stith

Board Member, Douglas Johnson

Board Member, David Bowers

Board Member, Toshihiko Fukuzawa

Vice Chairman Of Aflac Life Insurance Japan, Hiroshi Yamaguchi

Board Member, Aaron Kenny

Board Member, Bob Johnson

Auditors: KPMG LLP

LOCATIONS

HQ: AFLAC Inc
 1932 Wynnton Road, Columbus, GA 31999
Phone: 706 323-3431 **Fax:** 706 596-3488
Web: www.aflac.com

PRODUCTS/OPERATIONS

2017 Sales

	$ mil.	% of total
Aflac Japan	15,028	69
Aflac U.S.	6,289	29
Corporate	210	1
Other	140	1
Total	**21,667**	**100**

2017 Sales

	$ mil.	% of total
Net premiums	18,531	85
Net investment income	3,220	15
Other	67	-
Adjustments	(151)	-
Total	**21,667**	**100**

COMPETITORS

American Fidelity Assurance Company	Meiji Yasuda Life
American National Insurance	MetLife
Asahi Mutual Life	Nippon Life Insurance
CNO Financial	Taiyo Life
Colonial Life & Accident	Torchmark
	Unum Group

HISTORICAL FINANCIALS
Company Type: Public

Income Statement				FYE: December 31
	ASSETS ($ mil.)	NET INCOME ($ mil.)	INCOME AS % OF ASSETS	EMPLOYEES
12/19	152,768	3,304	2.2%	11,729
12/18	140,406	2,920	2.1%	11,390
12/17	137,217	4,604	3.4%	11,318
12/16	129,819	2,659	2.0%	10,212
12/15	118,296	2,533	2.1%	9,915
Annual Growth	6.6%	6.9%	—	4.3%

2019 Year-End Financials

Debt ratio: 4.20%
Return on equity: 12.61%
Cash ($ mil.): 4,896
Current ratio: —
Long-term debt ($ mil.): —

No. of shares (mil.): 726
Dividends
 Yield: 2.0%
 Payout: 26.6%
Market value ($ mil.): 38,447

	STOCK PRICE ($) FY Close	P/E High/Low	Earnings	Dividends	Book Value
12/19	52.90	13 10	4.43	1.08	39.84
12/18	45.56	24 11	3.77	1.04	31.06
12/17	87.78	15 12	5.77	0.87	31.50
12/16	69.60	23 17	3.21	0.83	25.24
12/15	59.90	22 19	2.93	0.79	20.86
Annual Growth	(3.1%)	— —	10.9%	8.1%	17.6%

AG Mortgage Investment Trust Inc

AG Mortgage Investment Trust invests in acquires and manages a diverse portfolio of residential mortgage assets as well as other real estate-related securities and financial assets. Residential mortgage-backed securities backed by US government agencies including Fannie Mae Freddie Mac and Ginnie Mae known as "Agency RMBS" make up more than 50% of the mortgage real estate investment trust's (REIT) portfolio. Credit assets including RMBS not issued or backed by the government account for most of the rest. Formed in 2011 by executives of investment adviser Angelo Gordon looking to profit from a recovery in the US mortgage bond market the mortgage REIT is managed by a subsidiary of Angelo Gordon.

Operations

The company conducted its business through the following segments: Securities and Loans and Single-Family Rental Properties. It sold its portfolio of single-family rental properties and no longer separate its business into segments.

It manages a diversified risk-adjusted portfolio of Agency RMBS and Credit Investments which include Residential Investments and Commercial Investments.

Geographic Reach

Its principal office is located in New York.

Financial Performance

AG Mortgage's total net interest income has gradually declined over the years falling 26% between 2015 and 2019. Despite this decline the REIT's profits have grown fivefold in the same five-year period.

Net interest income declined $4.4 million to $81.6 million in 2019 from $86 million the year prior. Interest income increased due to an increase in the weighted average cost of its GAAP investment portfolio and U.S. Treasury securities offset by an increase in interest expense.

Net income increased $91.4 million to $92.9 million in 2019 from $1.6 million in 2018. The increase was mainly due to the $83.8 million unrealized gain on real estate securities and loans in 2019 compared to the $20.9 million loss the year prior.

Cash and cash equivalents at the end of the year were $125.4 million a $41 million increase from the year prior. Operating activities generated $65.2 million in 2019 while financing activities provided another $722.7 million from borrowings under financing arrangements. Investing activities used $747.0 million mainly for purchase of real estate securities and residential mortgage loans.

Strategy

AG Mortgage invests in a diversified pool of residential and commercial mortgage assets and financial assets to generate attractive risk-adjusted returns for its investors over the long-term through a combination of dividends and capital appreciation. It continues to optimize its capital allocation across its target assets using leverage to increase potential returns for its stockholders.

AG Mortgage generates income principally from the yields earned on its investment portfolio and to the extent that leverages its deployed on the difference between the yields earned on its investments and the sum of its borrowing and hedging costs. It uses leverage to increase potential returns to its stockholders and to fund the acquisition of its assets. AG Mortgage may use a number of sources to finance its investments. It currently finances the acquisition of certain assets within its portfolio with repurchase agreements and financing facilities. It may also utilize derivative instruments in an effort to hedge the interest rate risk associated with the financing of its portfolio.

AG Mortgage's overall portfolio strategy is designed to generate attractive returns through various phases of the economic cycle. It believes that its broad approach within the real estate market which considers all major categories of real estate assets allows it to invest in a variety of attractive investment opportunities and helps insulate its portfolio from some of the risks that arise from investing in a single collateral type.

EXECUTIVES

Cfo Principal Accounting Officer And Treasurer, Brian C. Sigman, age 42, $150,000 total compensation

Chairman And Ceo, David N. Roberts, age 58

President And Chief Investment Officer, Jonathan Lieberman, age 57

General Counsel And Secretary, Raul E. Moreno, age 39, $28,493 total compensation

Auditors: PricewaterhouseCoopers LLP

HQ: AG Mortgage Investment Trust Inc
245 Park Avenue, 26th Floor, New York, NY 10167
Phone: 212 692-2000
Web: www.agmit.com

COMPETITORS

ARMOUR Residential REIT	Hatteras Financial
Annaly Capital Management	MFA Financial
	MFResidential
Bimini Capital Management	PIMCO REIT
	PennyMac Mortgage
Capstead Mortgage	Provident Mortgage Capital
Galiot Capital	

HISTORICAL FINANCIALS

Company Type: Public

Income Statement				FYE: December 31
	ASSETS ($ mil.)	NET INCOME ($ mil.)	INCOME AS % OF ASSETS	EMPLOYEES
12/19	4,347	92	2.1%	—
12/18	3,548	1	0.0%	—
12/17	3,789	118	3.1%	—
12/16	2,628	63	2.4%	—
12/15	3,164	13	0.4%	—
Annual Growth	8.3%	61.0%		

2019 Year-End Financials

Debt ratio: 5.16%	No. of shares (mil.): 32
Return on equity: 12.35%	Dividends
Cash ($ mil.): 81	Yield: 12.3%
Current ratio: —	Payout: 6,333.3%
Long-term debt ($ mil.): —	Market value ($ mil.): 505

	STOCK PRICE ($) FY Close	P/E High/Low		PER SHARE ($) Earnings	Dividends	Book Value
12/19	15.42	8	6	2.39	1.90	25.93
12/18	15.93	—	—	(0.42)	1.98	22.82
12/17	19.01	5	5	3.77	2.00	25.34
12/16	17.11	10	6	1.80	1.90	23.68
12/15	12.84	1952	1258	0.01	2.28	23.58
Annual Growth	4.7%			—293.2%	(4.4%)	2.4%

AGCO Corp.

This company has been plowing the furrow of premium agricultural equipment since 1990. AGCO makes tractors combines hay and forage tools sprayers grain storage and protein production systems seeding and tillage implements and replacement parts for agricultural end uses. It sells through a global network of almost 3300 dealers and distributors spanning about 140 countries. It also builds diesel engines gears and generators through its power engines unit. Core brands include Massey Ferguson GSI Challenger Valtra (Finland-based) and Fendt (Germany). AGCO Finance offers financing services to retail customers and dealers via a venture with Rabobank a Dutch bank specializing in agricultural loans. Europe accounts for nearly 60% of AGCO's sales.

Operations

Tractors account for more than 55% of AGCO's sales and replacement parts around 15%. Grain storage and protein production systems account for over 10% and other machinery products account for over 15%.

Geographic Reach

Georgia-based AGCO has manufacturing locations in the US France Italy Finland Germany Austria Hungary Denmark Brazil and China. It manufactures and assembles its products in around 45 locations worldwide including four locations where the company operates joint ventures. Europe is its largest market representing about 60% of net sales followed by North America at around a quarter of sales.

Sales and Marketing

AGCO distributes its products primarily through a network of nearly 3300 independent dealers and distributors who are responsible for retail sales to the equipment's end user in addition to after-sales service and support of the equipment. Distributors also sell its products through a network of dealers supported by the distributor. Sales are not dependent on any specific dealer distributor or group of dealers. AGCO also sources machinery and parts from third parties to control costs inventory and supply.

Financial Performance

AGCO's revenue is closely linked to shifts in the agricultural industry. Sales of its equipment are affected by among other things changes in net cash farm income farm land values weather conditions the demand for agricultural commodities commodity prices and general economic conditions. As a result AGCO's revenue has been fluctuating in the last five years but overall rising about 21% between 2015 and 2019.

Sales in 2019 decreased 3% to $9 billion compared to $9.4 billion in 2018 primarily as a result of sales declines in its South American and APA regions partially offset by sales growth in our North American and EME regions on a constant currency basis.

Net income decreased 56% to $125.2 million in 2019 compared to 2018.

Cash at the end of 2019 was $432.8 million an increase of $107 million from the prior year. Cash from operations contributed $695.9 million to the coffers while investing activities used $271.6 million mainly for purchases of property plant and equipment. Financing activities used $313.4 million primarily for debt repayment.

Strategy

AGCO's long-term strategy includes establishing a greater manufacturing and supply-chain and/or marketing presence in emerging markets such as India China and Africa.

The company has made significant investments in smart farming technology that leverages data collected from machinery to increase productivity. AGCO now offers a full line of smart farming equipment that serve the needs of a farm's entire operations from soil preparation and planting spraying and harvesting to grain storage and protein production. The company's IDEAL combine launched in 2019 has more than 80 onboard computers and sensors that provide data visualization of the machinery's operation.

AGCO further boosted its smart ag offerings in 2019 with the announcement of a strategic partnership with Solinftec a provider of digital agriculture solutions. The deal allows AGCO customers access to Solinftec's digital offerings including onboard computers soil sensors and algorithms that enable real-time insights that improve agricultural efficiency.

Solinftec's solutions launched in Brazil in early 2019 for producers of sugarcane soybeans cotton and corn and will be available to US soybean and corn producers in 2020.

The market downturn had the additional effect of prompting AGCO to improve its operational efficiency in search of margin growth amid low revenue. The company targeted purchasing factory productivity and product development. AGCO also balanced reductions in sales and administrative and fixed manufacturing costs with focused spending.

HISTORY

In 1861 American Edward Allis purchased the bankrupt Reliance Works a leading Milwaukee-based manufacturer of sawmills and flour-milling equipment. Under shrewd management The Reliance Works of Edward P. Allis & Co. weathered financial troubles - bankruptcy in the Panic of 1873 — but managed to renegotiate its debt and recover. By the time Allis died in 1889 Reliance Works employed some 1500 workers.

The company branched into different areas of manufacturing in the late 19th century and by the 20th century the Edward P. Allis Co. (as it was then known) was the world leader in steam engines. In 1901 the company merged with another manufacturing giant Fraser & Chalmers to form the Allis-Chalmers Company. In the 1920s and 1930s Allis-Chalmers entered the farm equipment market.

Although overshadowed by John Deere and International Harvester (IH) Allis-Chalmers made key contributions to the industry — the first rubber-tired tractor (1932) and the All-Crop harvester. Allis-Chalmers spun off its farm equipment business in the 1950s and phased out several unrelated products. The company with its orange-colored tractors expanded and prospered from the 1940s through the early 1970s. Then the chafing farm economy of the late 1970s and early 1980s hurt Allis-Chalmers' sales.

After layoffs and a plant shutdown in 1984 the company was purchased in 1985 by German machinery maker Klockner-Humbolt-Deutz (KHD) who moved the company (renamed Deutz-Allis) to Georgia. In the mid-1980s low food prices hurt farmers and low demand hurt the equipment market. KHD was never able to bring profits up to a satisfactory level and in 1990 the German firm sold the unit to the US management in a buyout led by Robert Ratliff. Ratliff believed the company could succeed by acquiring belly-up equipment makers turning them around and competing on price. It was renamed AGCO in 1991.

EXECUTIVES

Svp And Cfo, Andrew H. (Andy) Beck, age 56, $530,000 total compensation
Svp; General Manager Asia/pacific And Africa, Gary L. Collar, age 63, $480,000 total compensation
Chairman President And Ceo, Martin H. Richenhagen, age 67, $1,345,575 total compensation
Svp; General Manager Americas, Robert B. Crain, age 60, $306,667 total compensation
Svp And Chief Supply Chain Officer, Hans-Bernd Veltmaat, age 65, $575,000 total compensation
Svp; General Manager Europe And Middle East, Rob Smith, age 54, $566,512 total compensation
Vice President General Counsel, Debra Kuper
National Sales Manager, Martin Mills
South America Financial Vp, Julio Escossi
Senior Vice President Human Resources, Lucinda Smith
Vice President, Hans Lehmann
Vice President Finance, Frederic Devienne
Vice President Distribution Development, Alistair Mclelland
Senior Vice President Engineering, Helmut Endres
Vice President Sales And Marketing, Steven Clarke
Vice President Global Purchasing Materials Logistics And 3rd Party, Mike Clem
Vice President Sales And Program Management, Joshua Harrison
Vp Sales And Marketing, Santos Werner
Vice President, Gary Pulliam
Assistant Secretary, Lynnette Schoenfeld
Assistant Treasurer, Chris Smither
Auditors: KPMG LLP

LOCATIONS

HQ: AGCO Corp.
  4205 River Green Parkway, Duluth, GA 30096
Phone: 770 813-9200
Web: www.agcocorp.com

2017 Sales

	$ mil.	% of total
Europe/Africa/Middle East	4,614	57
North America	1,876	24
South America	1,063	12
Asia/Pacific	752	7
Total	**8,306**	**100**

2016 Sales

	% of total
United States	19
Other Europe	15
Germany	12
South America	12
France	10
Finland and Scandinavia	9
United Kingdom and Ireland	6
Canada	4
Middle East and Algeria	4
Asia	4
Australia and New Zealand	3
Mexico Central America and Caribbean	2
Africa	2
Total	**100**

PRODUCTS/OPERATIONS

2017 Sales

	$ mil.	% of total
Tractors	4,785	57
Replacement parts	1,305	16
Grain storage and protein production systems	1,049	13
Other machinery	582	7
Combines	349	4
Application equipment	235	3
Total	**8,306**	**100**

Selected Products

Application equipment
Combine Harvesters
Grounds care
Hay and forage
Implements attachments and material handling
Power generation
Seeding and tillage
Tractors

COMPETITORS

Buhler Industries	Komatsu
CNH Industrial	Kubota
Caterpillar	Mahindra
Deere	Toro Company

HISTORICAL FINANCIALS

Company Type: Public

Income Statement   FYE: December 31

	REVENUE ($ mil.)	NET INCOME ($ mil.)	NET PROFIT MARGIN	EMPLOYEES
12/19	9,041	125	1.4%	21,000
12/18	9,352	285	3.1%	21,200
12/17	8,306	186	2.2%	20,500
12/16	7,410	160	2.2%	19,800
12/15	7,467	266	3.6%	19,600
Annual Growth	**4.9%**	**(17.2%)**	**—**	**1.7%**

2019 Year-End Financials

Debt ratio: 17.34%	No. of shares (mil.): 75
Return on equity: 4.33%	Dividends
Cash ($ mil.): 432	Yield: 0.8%
Current ratio: 1.29	Payout: 38.6%
Long-term debt ($ mil.): 1,191	Market value ($ mil.): 5,830

	STOCK PRICE ($) FY Close	P/E High/Low	PER SHARE ($) Earnings	PER SHARE ($) Dividends	PER SHARE ($) Book Value
12/19	77.25	49 33	1.63	0.63	37.81
12/18	55.67	20 14	3.58	0.60	38.32
12/17	71.43	32 25	2.32	0.56	38.08
12/16	57.86	31 22	1.96	0.52	34.93
12/15	45.39	19 14	3.06	0.48	33.86
Annual Growth	**14.2%**	**— —**	**(14.6%)**	**7.0%**	**2.8%**

AGFIRST FARM CREDIT BANK

The expenses involved in equipping and operating a farm add up quickly which is where AgFirst Farm Credit Bank comes in. AgFirst is one of a half-dozen members of the Farm Credit System a federally chartered network of agricultural and rural lending cooperatives. Boasting $30 billion in assets the bank provides financing to 19 farmer-owned agricultural credit associations. The associations in turn offer mortgages and loans to some 80000 farmers agribusinesses and rural home-owners through 280 branches in 15 eastern states and Puerto Rico. They also offer crop insurance credit-related life insurance and financial planning services. Instead of accepting deposits AgFirst raises money by selling bonds and notes on the capital markets.

Operations

AgFirst's capital markets arm arranges participates in and sells loan syndications for agribusinesses. Its correspondent lending unit buys sells and services agricultural and rural home loans throughout the US. About 68% of the bank's loan portfolio consisted of direct notes in 2014 while purchased participations/syndications made up another 19% of loan assets. The rest of the portfolio consisted of correspondent lending (12%) and loans to OFIs (less than 1%).

The bank makes almost all of its money from interest income. About 79% of its total revenue came from loan interest in 2014 with another 18% of revenue coming from interest on investment securities and other assets. The remainder of its revenue mostly came from loan fees.

Geographic Reach

Columbia South Carolina-based AgFirst serves 15 eastern US states and Puerto Rico. Its largest markets are in Florida North Carolina Georgia Virginia and Pennsylvania. The bank is also active in Alabama Delaware the District of Columbia Kentucky Louisiana Maryland Mississippi Ohio South Carolina Tennessee West Virginia and Puerto Rico.

Financial Performance

AgFirst Farm Credit Bank has struggled to grow its annual revenues and profits over the past several years as its loan assets have not increased and as interest margins continue to be squeezed in the low-interest environment.

The bank's revenue fell 7% to $703.8 million during 2014 as its loan assets barely grew to $20.9 billion or about the same levels as they've been since 2010.

Revenue declines in 2014 coupled with a rise in insurance fund premiums and salaries caused AgFirst's net income to shrink 17% to $380.3 million for the year. The bank's operating cash levels fell sharply to $370.9 million on lower cash earnings and unfavorable working capital changes mostly related to changes in accounts receivables balances.

Strategy

AgFirst has focused on maintaining strong personal relationships with its local customer base. It's also been investing more in security-based IT investments to protect its customers from security breaches. In 2015 it built a modern Data Center to accommodate the bank's growth with 1 Petabyte of data.

Company Background

The Farm Credit System was established by Congress in 1916 to provide a reliable source of credit for US farmers and ranchers.

EXECUTIVES

Ceo, Leon T. (Timmy) Amerson
Svp And Cfo, Charl L. Butler
Svp And Cio, Benjamin F. Blakewood
Senior Vice President, David Bridges
Vice President Executive Account Manager, Michael Mancini
Vice President Capital Markets, Neda Beal
Vice President Capital Mkts, John Burnside
Vice President Human Resources, Jeffery Payne
Vice President Chief Audit Officer, William Beckham
Executive Vice President, Larry Doyle
Senior Vice President And General Counsel, Isvara Wilson
Vice President, Steven Oshea
Vice President, Katie Hane
Vice President Finance, Steve Mcclam
Vice President Of Investments And Funding, Richard Wilkins
Vice President: Marketing Customer Support Corpo, Ann Lamar Tuten
Vice Chairman, Dale R. Hershey
Chairman, Robert H. Spiers
Board Member, Robert Holden
Auditors: PRICEWATERHOUSECOOPERS LLP MI

LOCATIONS

HQ: AGFIRST FARM CREDIT BANK
  1901 MAIN ST.,COLUMBIA, SC 292012443
Phone: 803 799-5000
Web: WWW.AGFIRST.COM

PRODUCTS/OPERATIONS

2014 Sales

	$ mil.	% of total
Interest		
Loans	566	79
Investment securities & other	127	18
Non-interest		
Loan fees	8	2
Building lease income	3	-
Net other-temporary impairment losses	(1.4)	-
Gains (losses) on called debt	(7.7)	-
Gains (losses) on investments net	0	-
Gains (losses) on other transactions	0	-
Other	7	1
Total	**703**	**100**

COMPETITORS

AgriBank	Farm Family Holdings
Bank of America	First National of
COUNTRY Financial	Nebraska
Cat Financial	Rabo AgriFinance

Company Type: Private

Income Statement FYE: December 31

	ASSETS ($ mil.)	NET INCOME ($ mil.)	INCOME AS % OF ASSETS	EMPLOYEES
12/17	32,487	344	1.1%	530
12/15	30,620	336	1.1%	—
Annual Growth	3.0%	1.2%	—	—

AGNC Investment Corp

AGNC Investment (formerly American Capital Agency) is taking on the rocky real estate market. The real estate investment trust (REIT) was created in 2008 to invest in securities backed by single-family residential mortgages and collateralized mortgage obligations guaranteed by government agencies Fannie Mae Freddie Mac and Ginnie Mae. The Maryland-based REIT is externally managed and advised by American Capital AGNC Management a subsidiary of US publicly traded alternative asset manager American Capital which spun off American Capital Agency in 2008 but retained about a 33% stake in the REIT.

Operations

American Capital Agency generates income from investing in leveraged agency mortgage-backed securities (agency MBS) which consist of residential mortgage pass-through securities and collateralized mortgage obligations (CMOs) backed by federal agencies. About 97% of its total revenue came from interest income in 2014 while the remainder came from gains on agency securities sales. It may also collect gains on derivative instruments and other securities.

Its leverage was 5.3 times its stockholders' equity in 2014 (down from 7.3 times in 2013).

Financial Performance

American Capital Agency's revenue and profits had been trending higher over the past few years as the security valuations rose with the strengthening housing market leading to higher interest income.

The REIT's revenues and profits fell steeply in 2014 mostly as it lost $1.24 billion on derivative instruments and other securities (compared to a gain of $1.2 billion in 2013). Additionally its investment portfolio value declined by 29% after shifting its investments from MBS repo funded assets to TBA dollar roll funded assets which led to 33% less interest income.

American Capital Agency's operating cash levels fell by 35% to $1.62 billion in 2014 due to lower cash earnings.

Strategy

Set up as an investment vehicle American Capital Agency's chief goal is to preserve its net asset value (NAV) and generate risk-adjusted returns for shareholders through regular monthly dividends and net realized gains from its investments and hedging activities.

The REIT's investment strategy as it reiterated in 2015 is designed to: manage a portfolio of agency securities and similar assets with attractive risk-adjusted returns; take advantage of undervalued agency securities in the market; manage financing interest rate prepayment and extension risks; preserve its net book value; and continue providing regular monthly distributions to its shareholders as a REIT.

Company Background

American Capital Agency raised some $300 million from its 2008 IPO. The REIT used the proceeds from the offering to build and develop its investment portfolio.

EXECUTIVES

CIO-Ceo, Gary D Kain
Chb, Prue B Larocca
Pres-Coo, Peter J Federico
Exec V Pres Agency Portfolio I, Christopher J Kuehl
Sr V Pres-Cfo, Bernice E Bell
Sr V Pres, Aaron J Pas
Sr V Pres-Gen Counsel-Cco-Sec, Kenneth L Pollack
Auditors: Ernst & Young LLP

LOCATIONS

HQ: AGNC Investment Corp
2 Bethesda Metro Center, 12th Floor, Bethesda, MD 20814
Phone: 301 968-9315   **Fax:** 301 968-9301
Web: www.agnc.com

COMPETITORS

ARMOUR Residential REIT	CIFC
Annaly Capital Management	Capstead Mortgage
	Chimera
Anworth Mortgage Asset	Hatteras Financial
Bimini Capital Management	JAVELIN Mortgage
	MFA Financial
	Redwood Trust

HISTORICAL FINANCIALS

Company Type: Public

Income Statement FYE: December 31

	ASSETS ($ mil.)	NET INCOME ($ mil.)	INCOME AS % OF ASSETS	EMPLOYEES
12/19	113,082	688	0.6%	51
12/18	109,241	129	0.1%	56
12/17	70,376	771	1.1%	56
12/16	56,880	623	1.1%	54
12/15	57,021	215	0.4%	3
Annual Growth	18.7%	33.7%	—	103.1%

2019 Year-End Financials

Debt ratio: 0.20%	No. of shares (mil.): 540
Return on equity: 6.57%	Dividends
Cash ($ mil.): 831	Yield: 11.3%
Current ratio: —	Payout: 172.4%
Long-term debt ($ mil.): —	Market value ($ mil.): 9,563

	STOCK PRICE ($) FY Close	P/E High/Low	PER SHARE ($) Earnings	Dividends	Book Value
12/19	17.68	16 13	1.16	2.00	20.41
12/18	17.54	95 82	0.21	2.16	18.47
12/17	20.19	11 9	2.04	2.16	22.37
12/16	18.13	11 9	1.79	2.30	22.22
12/15	17.34	41 31	0.54	2.48	23.62
Annual Growth	0.5%	—	21.1%	(5.2%)	(3.6%)

Air Products & Chemicals Inc

Air Products and Chemicals has built a solid business out of gasses and liquids. The company produces and distributes atmospheric process and specialty gases in the US and across the world. It is a leading hydrogen supplier as well as helium and liquefied natural gas (LNG) process technology and equipment. Air Products and Chemicals which generates more than 60% revenue outside the US also provides related equipment and services (air separation hydrocarbon recovery natural gas liquefaction etc.) to customers in the refining gasification electronics chemicals metals manufacturing and food and beverage industries.

HISTORY

In the early 1900s Leonard Pool the son of a boilermaker began selling oxygen to industrial users. By the time he was 30 he was district manager for Compressed Industrial Gases. In the late 1930s Pool hired engineer Frank Pavlis to help him design a cheaper more efficient oxygen generator. In 1940 they had the design and Pool established Air Products in Detroit (initially sharing space with the cadavers collected by his brother who was starting a mortuary science college). The company was based on a simple breakthrough concept: the provision of on-site gases. Instead of delivering oxygen in cylinders Pool proposed to build oxygen-generating facilities near large-volume gas users and then lease them reducing distribution costs.

Although industrialists encouraged Pool to pursue his ideas few orders were forthcoming and the company faced financial crisis. The outbreak of WWII got the company out of difficulty as the US military became a major customer. During the war the company moved to Chattanooga Tennessee for the available labor.

The end of the war brought with it another downturn as demand dried up. By waiting at the Weirton Steel plant until a contract was signed Pool won a contract for three on-site generators. Weirton was nearly the company's only customer. Pool relocated the company to Allentown Pennsylvania to be closer to the Northeast's industrial market where he could secure more contracts with steel companies.

The Cold War and the launching of the Sputnik satellite in 1957 propelled the company's growth. Convinced that Soviet rockets were powered by liquid hydrogen the US government asked Air Products to supply it with the volatile fuel. The company entered the overseas market that year through a joint venture with Butterley (UK) to which it licensed its cryogenic processes and equipment. The company went public in 1961 and formed a subsidiary in Belgium in 1964.

Air Products diversified into chemicals when it bought Houdry Process (chemicals and chemical-plant maintenance 1962) and Airco's chemicals and plastics operations in the 1970s. The company continued to diversify in the mid-1980s as it built large-scale plants for its environmental- and energy-systems business and added Anchor Chemical and the industrial chemicals unit of Abbott Labs.

In 1995 and 1996 Air Products expanded into China and other countries by winning 20 contracts with semiconductor makers. It bought Carburos Metálicos Spain's #1 industrial gas supplier in 1996. To focus on its core gas and chemical lines the company shed most of its environmental- and energy-systems business.

Expanding further in Europe Air Products bought the methylamines and derivatives unit of UK-based Imperial Chemical Industries (ICI) in 1997. The company sold its remaining interest in American Ref-Fuel (a waste-to-energy US operation).

In 1998 Air Products bought Solkatronic Chemicals and opened a methylamines plant in Florida to complement its ICI purchase. To further target semiconductor makers it formed Air Products Electronic Chemicals and allied with AlliedSignal Chemical (now part of Honeywell International).

The next year Air Products and France's L'Air Liquide agreed to buy and break up BOC Group. European Union regulators initially approved the deal but in 2000 the companies shelved the plan when other regulatory issues arose. Also in 2000 Air Products sold its polyvinyl alcohol business to Celanese for about $326 million. The company boosted its European presence in 2001 with the acquisition of Messer Griesheim's (Germany) respiratory home-care business and 50% of AGA's Netherlands industrial gases operations.

Air Products was hurt by the slowdown in manufacturing primarily in the electronics and steel industries which are major customers for gases. Its chemical revenues also were hurt by pressure on pricing. To improve profits the company initiated cost cuts including job cuts (about 10% of its employees) and divestitures such as its US packaged gas business.

The company broadened its health care operations in late 2002 by acquiring American Homecare Supply. It appeared briefly that Air Products wanted to devote a great deal of attention to the health care business. The company had created its Air Products Healthcare unit in 1999 and expanded it greatly three years later with the acquisition of American Homecare Supply. Air Products proceeded to add to the division through subsequent acquisitions; however the US portion of the business never performed to the company's expectations and Air Products sold the domestic operations of the health care unit in 2008 and 2009.

It also decided to divest its chemicals operations in the latter half of the decade. Those operations included the production of catalysts surfactants and intermediates derived from vinyl acetate monomer (VAM) all of which it sold in 2008. Air Products had sold its amines business to chemical company Taminco in 2006. The company's polymers operations which were run through a joint venture with Wacker-Chemie called Air Products Polymers were divested in 2008. The company sold most of its holdings in the JV to Wacker for $265 million though two facilities that had belonged to the joint venture were sold to Ashland Performance Materials.

In 2007 Air Products made a small but strategic move into Eastern Europe. The company took advantage of Linde's selloff of some BOC assets after the German company bought BOC in 2006. Air Products acquired the Polish Gazy SP for just under $500 million with the hopes of moving into the Central and Eastern European markets to take advantage of the migration of manufacturing to the region.

In 2010 the company made a major bid to buy rival Airgas but it was rejected. The Airgas board considered the $5.1 billion offer too low. Air Products extended its tender offer to Airgas stockholders several times making its "best and final offer" of $70 a share in December 2010. Airgas also rejected that offer.

In late 2012 Air Products opened an advanced gas applications laboratory in Shanghai to support the increasing needs in high-growth markets in China across Asia.

In addition to growing organically the company has been divesting operations to focus on its higher growth operations and to pursue strategic acquisitions. By early 2012 the company began divesting units to focus on more profitable operations. It sold its homecare business in continental Europe (which supplied oxygen and infusion treatments in Belgium France Germany Portugal and Spain) to Germany's Linde for $750 million. The company also began evaluating its homecare assets in Argentina Brazil Ireland and the UK.

With more money in its coffers from divestments in 2012 the company acquired Germany-based ROVI Cosmetics International which develops delivery systems for the personal care industry in Europe. The unit is now part of the company's Performance Materials division. To extend its Latin American footprint Air Products in 2012 acquired a 67% stake in Indura S.A. an industrial gas company in Chile for $884 million.

Expanding its portfolio of industrial gases offerings in North America to include liquid carbon dioxide in 2013 Air Products acquired EPCO Carbon Dioxide Products Inc. a privately-held Louisiana-based producer and marketer of liquid carbon dioxide.

EXECUTIVES

Chairman President And Ceo, Seifi Ghasemi, age 74, $1,200,000 total compensation
Evp Industrial Gases, Corning F. Painter, age 59, $573,077 total compensation
President Industrial Gases Europe And Africa, Ivo Bols
President Industrial Gases Asia, Wilbur W. Mok, age 60
President Industrial Gases Middle East India Egypt And Turkey, Richard Boocock
Svp And Cfo, M. Scott Crocco, age 57, $581,923 total compensation
President Industrial Gases Americas, Marie Ffolkes
Evp Materials Technologies, Guillermo Novo, age 59, $465,000 total compensation
President China Industrial Gases, Choon Seong Saw
Vp And Cio, Alyssa A. Budraitis
President Air Products Korea, Kyo Yung (K Y) Kim
President Air Products San Fu, Eugene Y. C. Lu
President Southeast Asia Industrial Gases, Alex Tan
Manager Government Relations, Robert Episcopo
Svp And Chro, Jennifer Grant
Vice President Environment Health Safety And Quality And Corporate Chief Engineer, Joseph Pietrantonio
Vice President Chief Audit Executive, Melissa Schaeffer
Board Member, Matthew Paull
Auditors: KPMG LLP

LOCATIONS

HQ: Air Products & Chemicals Inc
7201 Hamilton Boulevard, Allentown, PA 18195-1501
Phone: 610 481-4911   **Fax:** 610 481-5900
Web: www.airproducts.com

2018 Sales

	$ mil.	% of total
US	3,149	35
Europe/Middle East	2,292	26
Asia (Excluding China & India)	904	10
China	1,585	18
Other (Canada Latin America India)	998	11
Total	**8,930**	**100**

PRODUCTS/OPERATIONS

2018 Sales

	$ mil.	% of total
Industrial Gases- Americas	3,758	42
Industrial Gases- EMEA	2,193	24
Industrial Gases- Asia	2,458	28
Industrial Gases- Global	436	5
Corporate and other	84	1
Total	**8,930**	**100**

Selected Products and Services

Industrial Gases
  Argon
  Carbon dioxide
  Carbon monoxide
  Helium
  Hydrogen
  Nitrogen
  Oxygen
  Synthesis gas
Equipment and Services
  Air-pollution control systems
  Air-separation equipment
  Hydrogen-purification equipment
  Natural gas-liquefaction equipment

COMPETITORS

Airgas	Messer Group
Iwatani International	Praxair
L'Air Liquide	Taiyo Nippon Sanso
Matheson Tri-Gas	The Linde Group

HISTORICAL FINANCIALS

Company Type: Public

Income Statement

FYE: September 30

	REVENUE ($ mil.)	NET INCOME ($ mil.)	NET PROFIT MARGIN	EMPLOYEES
09/20	8,856	1,886	21.3%	19,275
09/19	8,918	1,760	19.7%	17,700
09/18	8,930	1,497	16.8%	16,300
09/17	8,187	3,000	36.6%	15,300
09/16	9,524	631	6.6%	18,600
Annual Growth	(1.8%)	31.5%	—	0.9%

2020 Year-End Financials

Debt ratio: 31.42%	No. of shares (mil.): 221
Return on equity: 16.27%	Dividends
Cash ($ mil.): 5,253	Yield: 1.7%
Current ratio: 3.59	Payout: 60.5%
Long-term debt ($ mil.): 7,430	Market value ($ mil.): 65,832

	STOCK PRICE ($) FY Close	P/E High/Low		PER SHARE ($) Earnings	Dividends	Book Value
09/20	297.86	36	21	8.49	5.18	54.66
09/19	221.86	29	19	7.94	4.58	50.15
09/18	167.05	25	22	6.78	5.20	49.46
09/17	151.22	11	10	13.65	3.62	46.19
09/16	150.34	54	40	2.89	3.34	32.57
Annual Growth	18.6%	—	—	30.9%	11.6%	13.8%

Alaska Air Group, Inc.

The fifth-largest airline in the US Alaska Air Group ferries more than 46 million passengers each year to nearly 120 destinations through its two carrier brands Alaska Airlines and Horizon Air. It completes an average of 1300 flights per day from the US Canada Costa Rica and Mexico. In 2019 passengers to and from Seattle Portland and the Bay Area accounted for more than three-quarters of our total guests. Alaska Airlines' fleet comprises over 165 Boeing 737 more than 735 jet aircrafts and more than 70 Airbus A320.

Operations

Alaska Air comprises three reportable segments Mainline Regional and Horizon.

The Mainline segment accounts for some 80% of Alaska Air's sales and offers long-haul flights from the western US particularly Seattle Portland and the Bay Area throughout the US Canada Mexico and Costa Rica on its 166 Boeing 737s and 71 Airbus A320s. It also includes cargo services mainly to and within Alaska.

Alaska Air's Regional business consists of shorter-haul flights operated by Horizon SkyWest and PenAir (collectively Air Group) which together carry over 10 million passengers annually in Washington Oregon Idaho and California. Horizon's fleet which carries some 70% of Air Group's regional passengers comprises 30 E175 jets and over 30 Bombardier Q400 turboprops. The regional fleet operated by SkyWest consisted of more than 30 E175 aircraft. The Regional segment generates roughly 15% of Alaska Air's sales.

The Horizon segment brings in the remaining 5% or so of sales. It consists of capacity sold to Alaska under capacity purchase agreements.

Geographic Reach

Delaware-based Alaska Air Group serves around 115 destinations through an expansive network in Alaska US Hawaii Canada Costa Rica and Mexico. The company leases operations training and data facilities in Portland and Spokane as well as line maintenance stations in Boise Bellingham San Jose Redmond Seattle and Spokane. It also leases call center facilities in Phoenix and Boise.

Sales and Marketing

Alaska Air's airline tickets are distributed through the airline's website and through traditional and online travel agencies. The travel agencies use global distribution systems to obtain fare and inventory data from airlines and reservation call centers located in Phoenix; Kent Washington; and Boise Idaho.

As its name implies Alaska Air Group transports more passengers between Alaska and the US mainland than any other airline. Besides its own flights the regional segment provides passenger service through contracts with SkyWest Airlines Horizon and Peninsula Airways.

Advertising expense was $72 million $79 million and $91 million during the years ended December 31 2019 2018 and 2017.

Financial Performance

Alaska Air's revenue has achieved lift-off in the last five years with an overall growth of 57%.

In 2019 the company's sales grew 6% to $8.8 billion due to the growth on all segments.

Net income rose 76% from $437 million in 2018 to $769 million in 2019.

Alaska Air's cash on hand ended the year at $232 million. The company's operations generated $1.7 billion while its investing activities used $791 million and its financing activities used $813 million. Alaska Air's main cash uses were aircraft and other flight equipment purchases capital expenditures net payments of long-term debt and dividends.

Strategy

Alaska Air strives toward maintaining and improving competitive cost structure by setting aggressive unit cost-reduction goals.

The company's strategy includes being the premier carrier for people living on the West Coast. This results in a high concentration of our business in key West Coast markets. Alaska Air believes that concentrating their service offerings in this way allows them to maximize investment in personnel aircraft and ground facilities as well as to gain greater advantage from sales and marketing

efforts in those regions. As a result The company remains highly dependent on our key markets.

The company routinely engages in analysis and discussions regarding their strategic position including alliances codeshare arrangements interline arrangements and frequent flyer program enhancements and will continue to have future discussions with other airlines regarding similar activities.

HISTORY

Pilot Mac McGee started McGee Airways in 1932 to fly cargo between Anchorage and Bristol Bay Alaska. He joined other local operators in 1937 to form Star Air Lines which began airmail service between Fairbanks and Bethel in 1938. In 1944 a year after buying three small airlines Star adopted the name Alaska Airlines.

The company expanded to include freight service to Africa and Australia in 1950. This expansion coupled with the seasonal nature of the airline's business caused losses in the early 1970s. Developer Bruce Kennedy gained control of the board turning the firm around by the end of 1973. But the Civil Aeronautics Board forced the carrier to drop service to northwestern Alaska in 1975 and by 1978 it served only 10 Alaskan cities and Seattle.

Kennedy became CEO the next year. The 1978 Airline Deregulation Act allowed Alaska Air to move into new areas as well as regain the routes it had lost. By 1982 it was the largest airline flying between Alaska and the lower 48 states.

In 1985 the airline reorganized forming Alaska Air Group as its holding company. The next year Alaska Air Group bought Jet America Airlines (expanding its routes eastward to Chicago St. Louis and Dallas) and Seattle-based Horizon Air Industries (which served 30 Northwest cities). When competition in the East and Midwest cut profits in 1987 Kennedy shut down Jet America to focus on West Coast operations.

To counterbalance summer traffic to Alaska the airline began service to two Mexican resorts in 1988. Fuel prices and sluggish traffic hurt 1990 earnings but Alaska Air Group stayed in the black unlike many other carriers. Kennedy retired as chairman and CEO in 1991.

That year the airline began service to Canada and seasonal flights to two Russian cities. Neil Bergt's MarkAir airline declared war cutting fares and horning in on Alaska Air Group's territory. Alaska Air Group's profits were slashed and MarkAir went into bankruptcy.

Alaska Air extended Russian flights to year-round in 1994. The airline began service to Vancouver in 1996. That year it became the first major US carrier to use the GPS satellite navigation system. In 1997 it added service to more than a dozen new cities but halted service to Russia because of that country's economic woes in 1998.

Alaska Air Group and Dutch airline KLM agreed to a marketing alliance in 1998 that included reciprocal frequent-flier programs and code-sharing and in 1999 it added code-sharing agreements with several major airlines including American and Continental. Alaska Airlines developed an online check-in system a first among US carriers.

In 2000 an Alaska Airlines MD-83 crashed into the Pacific Ocean near Los Angeles killing all 88 people on board. A federal investigation of Alaska Airlines' maintenance practices found deficiencies but the FAA eventually accepted the airline's plan to tighten safety standards.

Like most carriers in the latter part of 2001 Alaska Airlines cut back its flights as a result of reduced demand after the September 11 terrorist attacks. As demand slowly returned in 2002 Alaska Airlines began to add new destinations and

increase the number of flights on some established routes.

In its biggest deal ever Alaska Air Group in late 2016 acquired Virgin America for $2.6 billion.

EXECUTIVES

Vice President Information And Technology Alaska Airlines, Kris Kutchera

Chairman President And Ceo Alaska Air Group Inc. Chairman And Ceo Alaska Airlines Inc. And Chairman Virgin America And Horizon Air Industries Inc., Bradley D. (Brad) Tilden, age 59, $487,600 total compensation

President And Ceo Horizon Air Industries Inc., Gary L. Beck

Svp Communications And External Affairs, Joseph A. (Joe) Sprague, $303,846 total compensation

Evp Finance And Cfo, Brandon S. Pedersen, age 53, $390,769 total compensation

Evp And Chief Commercial Officer Alaska Airlines, Andrew R. Harrison, age 49, $383,077 total compensation

President And Coo Alaska Airlines, Benito (Ben) Minicucci, age 53, $426,923 total compensation

Coo Horizon Air Industries Inc., Constance Von Muehlen

Vice President Of Operation, Bill Mackay

Vice President Maintenance And Engineering Alaska Airlines, Kurt Kinder

Vice President Of Marketing, Jimmy Johnson

Vice President Airport Operations And Customer Service Alaska Airlines, Wayne Newton

Vice President Strategic Sourcing And Supply Chain Management, Ann Ardizzone

Regional Vice President Alas Ka, Marilyn Romano

Vice President Marketing Alaska Airlines, Sangita Woerner

Vice President Marketing, Gwen Bacon

Vice President Revenue Management, Kevin Ger

Vice President Bay Area Alaska Airlines, Annabel Chang

Vice President Flight Operations, John Ladner

Vice President Of Customer Service, Renee Spicer

Vice President External Relations, Diana Birkett Rakow

Senior Vice President Purchasing Officer, Erik Null Davies

Senior Vice President Maintenance And Engineering, Constance Vonmuehlen

Vice President Sales, David Oppenheim

Senior Vice President, Jim Johnson

Vice President Finance And Treasurer Alaska Airlines, Mark Eliasen

Board Member, Susan Li

Auditors: KPMG LLP

LOCATIONS

HQ: Alaska Air Group, Inc.
  19300 International Boulevard, Seattle, WA 98188
Phone: 206 392-5040
Web: www.alaskaair.com

PRODUCTS/OPERATIONS

2018 Sales

	$ mil.	% of total
Passenger Revenue	7,632	92
Mileage Plan other revenue	434	5
Cargo and other	198	3
Total	**8,264**	**100**

2018 Sales

	$ mil.	% of total
Alaska		
Mainline	7,063	80
Regional	1,197	14
Horizon	512	6
Consolidating	(508)	-
Total	**8,264**	**100**

Selected Products and Services

Accessible services
Baggage
Book a Shipment
Children traveling alone
Customer of size
Delayed baggage
Emergency exit row
General Air Freight
GoldStreak®; Package Express
Infants and children
Price a Shipment
Priority Air Freight
Rate charts and surcharges
Ticket receipt
Track a Shipment
Traveling with pets

COMPETITORS

Aeromexico	JetBlue
Air Canada	Mesa Air
Allegiant Travel	SkyWest
American Airlines	Southwest Airlines
Group	United Continental
Delta Air Lines	WestJet
Hawaiian Holdings	

HISTORICAL FINANCIALS

Company Type: Public

Income Statement FYE: December 31

	REVENUE ($ mil.)	NET INCOME ($ mil.)	NET PROFIT MARGIN	EMPLOYEES
12/19	8,781	769	8.8%	24,134
12/18	8,264	437	5.3%	23,376
12/17	7,933	1,034	13.0%	23,156
12/16	5,931	814	13.7%	19,112
12/15	5,598	848	15.1%	15,143
Annual Growth	11.9%	(2.4%)	—	12.4%

2019 Year-End Financials

Debt ratio: 11.54%	No. of shares (mil.): 123
Return on equity: 19.03%	Dividends
Cash ($ mil.): 221	Yield: 2.0%
Current ratio: 0.64	Payout: 22.6%
Long-term debt ($ mil.): 1,264	Market value ($ mil.): 8,333

	STOCK PRICE ($) FY Close	P/E High/Low		PER SHARE ($) Earnings	Dividends	Book Value
12/19	67.75	12	9	6.19	1.40	35.21
12/18	60.85	21	16	3.52	1.28	30.45
12/17	73.51	12	7	8.35	1.20	30.24
12/16	88.73	14	8	6.54	1.10	23.77
12/15	80.51	13	9	6.56	0.80	19.26
Annual Growth	(4.2%)	—		(1.4%)	15.0%	16.3%

ALASKA HOUSING FINANCE CORP

EXECUTIVES

Chb, Frank Roppel
Ceo, Daniel R Fauske
Cfo, Joseph M Dubler
Coordinator, Tammie Robertson
Human Resources Director, Elaine Hodl
Accounting Staff, Joanne McClure
Rural, John Anderson
Personnel Technician, Jill Smart
Compliance Officer, Kim Coy
Planner, Andy Petroni
Senior Programmer Analyst, Colin Coker

LOCATIONS

HQ: ALASKA HOUSING FINANCE CORP
4300 BONIFACE PKWY # 130, ANCHORAGE, AK 995044387
Phone: 907 338-6100
Web: WWW.AHFC.US

HISTORICAL FINANCIALS

Company Type: Private

Income Statement FYE: June 30

	ASSETS ($ mil.)	NET INCOME ($ mil.)	INCOME AS % OF ASSETS	EMPLOYEES
06/20	4,609	35	0.8%	152
06/19	4,322	32	0.8%	—
06/06	5,229	306	5.9%	—
06/05	4,762	(23)	—	—
Annual Growth	(0.2%)			

ALASKA PERMANENT FUND CORPORATION

EXECUTIVES

Ceo, Angela Rodell
Coo*, Marcus Frampton
Chief Financial Officer*, Valerie Mertz
Information Specialist, Andrew Loney
Principal, Chris Poag
Communications Manager, Paulyn Swanson
Portfolio Manager, Timothy Andreyka
Human Resources Director, Chad Brown
Investment Officer Real Estate, Christi Grussendorf
Senior Associate Private Marke, Jared Brimberry
Senior Associate, Maria Skuratovskaya
Auditors: KPMG LLP ANCHORAGE AK

LOCATIONS

HQ: ALASKA PERMANENT FUND CORPORATION
801 W 10TH ST STE 302, JUNEAU, AK 998011878
Phone: 907 796-1500
Web: WWW.APFC.ORG

HISTORICAL FINANCIALS

Company Type: Private

Income Statement FYE: June 30

	ASSETS ($ mil.)	NET INCOME ($ mil.)	INCOME AS % OF ASSETS	EMPLOYEES
06/19	70,049	1,405	2.0%	50
06/18	67,671	5,109	7.6%	—
06/17	61,824	6,675	10.8%	—
06/16	55,346	(30)	—	—
Annual Growth	8.2%			

Albertsons Companies Inc

LOCATIONS

HQ: Albertsons Companies Inc
250 Parkcenter Blvd., Boise, ID 83706
Phone: 208 395-6200
Web: www.AlbertsonsCompanies.com

HISTORICAL FINANCIALS

Company Type: Public

Income Statement FYE: February 29

	REVENUE ($ mil.)	NET INCOME ($ mil.)	NET PROFIT MARGIN	EMPLOYEES
02/20	62,455	466	0.7%	270,000
02/19	60,534	131	0.2%	267,000
02/18	59,924	46	0.1%	275,000
02/17	59,678	(373)	—	—
02/16	58,734	(502)	—	—
Annual Growth	1.5%	—	—	—

2020 Year-End Financials

Debt ratio: 36.48%	No. of shares (mil.): 279
Return on equity: 24.61%	Dividends
Cash ($ mil.): 470	Yield: —
Current ratio: 0.97	Payout: —
Long-term debt ($ mil.): 8,493	Market value ($ mil.): —

ALBERTSONS COMPANIES, INC.

Albertsons Companies is one of the biggest supermarket retailers in the US with nearly 2250 stores in some 35 states and the District of Columbia. In addition to traditional grocery items many of the stores offer pharmacies and coffee shops and over 400 include adjacent gas stations. The company operates under some 20 banners including Albertsons Vons Pavilions Randalls Tom Thumb Carrs Jewel-Osco Shaw's/Star Market Safeway Market Street Haggen and United. It also owns meal kit company Plated. Albertsons Companies which traces its roots to 1939 is owned by Cerberus Capital Management which has been looking to take the company public for quite some time. In 2018 the retailer called off its pending acquisition of the Rite Aid pharmacy chain amid investor pushback.

HISTORY

J. A. "Joe" Albertson Leonard Skaggs (whose family ran Safeway) and Tom Cuthbert founded Albertson's Food Center in Boise Idaho in 1939. Albertson who left his position as district manager for Safeway to run the store thought big from the start. The 10000-sq.-ft. store was not only eight times the size of the average competitor it also offered an in-store butcher shop and bakery one of the country's first magazine racks and homemade "Big Joe" ice-cream cones. The men ended their partnership in 1945 the year Albertson's was incorporated and by 1947 it operated six stores in Idaho.

The company opened its first combination food store and drugstore a 60000-sq.-ft. superstore in 1951 and began locating stores in growing suburban areas. Albertson's went public to raise expansion capital in 1959 and by 1960 had 62 stores in Idaho Oregon Utah and Washington. The food retailer acquired Greater All American Markets (1964) a grocery chain based in Downey California and Semrau & Sons (1965) of Oakland which aided the company's thrust into the California market.

Albertson's and the Skaggs chain (by this time run by L. S. Skaggs Jr.) reunited temporarily in 1969 financing six Skaggs-Albertson's food-and-drug-combination stores. (The partnership dissolved in 1977 with each side taking half of the units.) By 1986 the company had reached $5 billion in sales a fivefold increase over 1975.

The company purchased 74 Jewel Osco combination food stores and drugstores (mostly in Arkansas Florida Oklahoma and Texas) from American Stores in 1992. Co-founder Albertson died in 1993 at age 86.

In 1997 the United Food and Commercial Workers union which represents supermarket employees sued Albertson's alleging the company forced employees to work overtime without pay. (It was settled in 1999 resulting in a $22 million charge.) Also in 1997 Albertson's began selling gasoline at a few stores. Acquisitions the next year (including Buttrey Food and Drug Stores) added stores and states. That year the company began serving online customers in the Dallas-Fort Worth area.

In 1999 the grocer revisited its roots when it acquired American Stores (Skaggs' successor) which operated more than 1550 stores in 26 states. To obtain regulatory approval for the $12 billion deal Albertson's sold 145 stores in overlapping markets in three states (most were in California).

In 2001 Larry Johnston former CEO of GE Appliances took over as chairman and CEO of Albertson's. Facing increasing competition (especially from Wal-Mart) Johnston announced in March 2002 aggressive restructuring plans that included job cuts and closing 95 stores in under-performing markets specifically Memphis and Nashville Tennessee and Houston and San Antonio Texas.

Already allowing customers to order drugs online (from its online drugstore Savon.com) and groceries in Seattle Albertson's expanded its online operations to San Diego in 2001 and in early 2002 to Los Angeles San Francisco and parts of Oregon and Washington. Albertson's exited the New England drugstore market in 2002 when it sold 80 New England Osco stores to Brooks Pharmacy.

In February 2004 Albertson's launched its "Blue Ribbon" brand of beef a private-label line of roasts and steaks. Also in February the company consolidated its Southwest Intermountain Northwest and Rocky Mountain divisions to form a new Intermountain West Division and combined the Acme and Florida divisions into a new Eastern Division.

A four-and-a-half month strike by grocery workers in Southern California ended in March 2004. The dispute pitted workers' demands for continued generous health care coverage vs. management's call for cost cuts to remain profitable in the face of Wal-Mart's entry into the Southern California grocery market. In April Albertson's completed the acquisition of JS USA Holdings which runs Shaw's and Star Markets stores in New England from UK grocer J Sainsbury. The deal to buy Shaw's was worth about $2.4 billion (cash and leases). In September Albertson's gained a toehold in the gourmet-food market with the purchase of Bristol Farms the operator of about a dozen upscale food markets in Southern California. In October Albertson's combined its Northern and Southern California food divisions into a single business unit the newly formed California Food Division. In an effort to improve efficiency Albertson's reorganized its supply chain food operations and Six Sigma Quality functions in May 2005.

In June 2006 Albertson's was sold to a consortium that included SUPERVALU CVS Cerberus Capital Management and Kimco for about $9.7 billion. Following the acquisition and the divvying up of Albertson's assets the surviving company went private and changed its name to Albertsons LLC. Concurrently Johnston left Albertsons and was succeeded by Robert Miller chairman of drugstore chain Rite Aid and the former head of Fred Meyer for eight years in the 1990s. Of the company's 27 price-impact Super Saver stores 25 closed their doors in mid-2006. Also in June the company put about 45 stores on the auction block. (It was announced in late 2006 that discount apparel retailer Ross Stores would acquire these stores.) In July the company shut down its online shopping service Albertsons.com.

In February 2007 Albertsons sold 132 grocery stores and two distribution centers in Northern California and Nevada to Save Mart Supermarkets for an undisclosed amount. Other recent closings include stores in Texas in the Dallas-Fort Worth Austin and Longview markets; Colorado; and Oklahoma.

Albertsons also sold eight of its stores in Wyoming to SUPERVALU in January 2008. The divestments continued in September with the sale of 49 supermarkets in Florida to Publix Super Markets for about $500 million. Also in 2008 Albertsons sold about 100 of its Express fuel centers in Arizona Colorado Florida Louisiana and Texas to Valero Energy and Reb Oil.

EXECUTIVES

Evp And General Counsel, Robert A. (Bob) Gordon
Coo, Wayne A. Denningham
Chief Marketing & Merchandising Officer, Shane Sampson
President Jewel Osco, Mike Withers
President Seattle Division, Karl Schroeder
President Houston Division, Sidney Hopper
Chairman And Ceo, Robert G. (Bob) Miller
Chief Administrative Officer, Justin Dye
President Southwest Division, Shane Dorcheus
President United, Robert Taylor
Evp And Cio, Anuj Dhanda
President Portland Division, Greg McNiff
President Southern Division, Dennis Bassler
Evp East Operations, Susan Morris
President Shaws, Paul Gossett
President Southern California Division, Lori Raya
President Acme Markets Division, Dan Croce
Evp And Cfo, Bob Dimond
Evp West Region Operations, Jim Perkins
Evp Human Resources Labor Relations Public Affairs And Government Relations, Andrew (Andy) Scoggin
Evp Corporate Development And Real Estate, Justin Ewing
President Eastern Division, Dan Valenzuela
President Northern California Division, Tom Schwilke
President Denver Division, Todd Broderick
President Intermountain Division, Brad Street
Svp Merchandising, Dennis Clark
Senior Vice President Digital And Ecommerce, Narayan Iyengar
Evp And Chief Data And Analytics Officer, Gautam Kotwal
Vice President Merchandising Strategy, Merritt Mccoy
Pharmacy Manager, Jim Mayes
Group Vice President Corporate Law, Laura Donald
Auditors: DELOITTE & TOUCHE LLP BOISE

LOCATIONS

HQ: ALBERTSONS COMPANIES, INC.
   250 E PARKCENTER BLVD, BOISE, ID 837063999
Phone: 208 395-6200
Web: WWW.ALBERTSONSCOMPANIES.COM

PRODUCTS/OPERATIONS

2018 Sales

	$ mil.	% of total
Non-perishables	26,372	44
Perishables	24,921	41
Pharmacy	4,987	8
Fuel	3,456	6
Other	799	1
Total	**60,535**	**100**

COMPETITORS

ALDI	Quality Food
Amazon.com	Roundy's
Costco Wholesale	Stater Bros.
Fry's Food	Target Corporation
H-E-B	Wal-Mart
Kroger	Wegmans
Lidl	Winn-Dixie
Publix	

HISTORICAL FINANCIALS

Company Type: Private

Income Statement

FYE: February 29

	REVENUE ($ mil.)	NET INCOME ($ mil.)	NET PROFIT MARGIN	EMPLOYEES
02/20	62,455	466	0.7%	270,000
02/19	60,534	131	0.2%	—
02/18	59,924	46	0.1%	—
Annual Growth	2.1%	217.4%		

Alcoa Corporation

Auditors: PricewaterhouseCoopers LLP

LOCATIONS

HQ: Alcoa Corporation
   201 Isabella Street, Suite 500, Pittsburgh, PA 15212-5858
Phone: 412 315-2900
Web: www.alcoa.com

HISTORICAL FINANCIALS

Company Type: Public

Income Statement

FYE: December 31

	REVENUE ($ mil.)	NET INCOME ($ mil.)	NET PROFIT MARGIN	EMPLOYEES
12/19	10,433	(1,125)	—	13,800
12/18	13,403	227	1.7%	14,000
12/17	11,652	217	1.9%	14,600
12/16	9,318	(400)	—	14,000
12/15	11,199	(863)	—	16,000
Annual Growth	(1.8%)	—		(3.6%)

2019 Year-End Financials

Debt ratio: 12.30%	No. of shares (mil.): 185
Return on equity: (-23.68%)	Dividends
Cash ($ mil.): 879	Yield: —
Current ratio: 1.38	Payout: —
Long-term debt ($ mil.): 1,799	Market value ($ mil.): 3,992

	STOCK PRICE ($) FY Close	P/E High/Low		PER SHARE ($) Earnings	Dividends	Book Value
12/19	21.51	—	—	(6.07)	0.00	22.16
12/18	26.58	49	21	1.20	0.00	29.17
12/17	53.87	46	24	1.16	0.00	24.42
12/16	28.08	—	—	(2.19)	0.00	30.91
Annual Growth	(6.4%)	—	—	—	—	(8.0%)

Alerus Financial Corp

EXECUTIVES

President; Chief Executive Officer Chairman Director, Randy Newman
Regional President Twin Cities, Sara Ausman
Vice President Commercial Relationship Manager, Robert Hartzell
Vice President, Kim Kaus
Board Member, Sally Smith
Board Member, Lloyd Case
Board Member, Karen Bohn
Board Of Directors, Dan Coughlin
Board Of Directors, Kevin Lemke
Auditors: CliftonLarsonAllen LLP

LOCATIONS

HQ: Alerus Financial Corp
401 Demers Avenue, Grand Forks, ND 58201
Phone: 701 795-3200   **Fax:** 701 795-3378
Web: www.alerus.com

HISTORICAL FINANCIALS

Company Type: Public

Income Statement   FYE: December 31

	ASSETS ($ mil.)	NET INCOME ($ mil.)	INCOME AS % OF ASSETS	EMPLOYEES
12/19	2,356	29	1.3%	789
12/18	2,179	25	1.2%	—
12/17	2,137	15	0.7%	—
12/16	2,050	14	0.7%	—
12/15	1,744	16	0.9%	—
Annual Growth	7.8%	15.7%	—	—

2019 Year-End Financials

Debt ratio: 2.49%	No. of shares (mil.): 17
Return on equity: 12.24%	Dividends
Cash ($ mil.): 144	Yield: 2.4%
Current ratio: —	Payout: 31.4%
Long-term debt ($ mil.): —	Market value ($ mil.): 390

	STOCK PRICE ($) FY Close	P/E High/Low		PER SHARE ($) Earnings	Dividends	Book Value
12/19	22.85	12	10	1.91	0.57	16.76
12/18	19.25	14	10	1.84	0.53	14.30
12/17	20.45	18	15	1.10	0.48	13.18
12/16	17.00	19	16	1.00	0.44	12.47
12/15	18.90	17	15	1.17	0.42	13.61
Annual Growth	4.9%	—	—	13.0%	7.9%	5.3%

Alleghany Corp.

Alleghany is a holding company with a focus on property/casualty reinsurance and insurance. Its subsidiaries include Transatlantic Holdings (TransRe) which offers property/casualty reinsurance globally through Transatlantic Reinsurance. The group also issues specialty property/casualty insurance policies through RSUI Group and CapSpecialty. Targeting small and midsized US firms CapSpecialty underwrites specialty lines of property and casualty insurance and professional lines of business. Alleghany's offerings are marketed in the US and abroad.

HISTORY

Alleghany was formed in 1929 by Clevelanders Mantis and Oris Van Sweringen as a pyramid railroad holding company. It collapsed in 1934 and after passing through several hands it was bought in 1937 by speculator Robert Young with backing from Woolworth heir Allan Kirby.

Young resurrected the company's Chesapeake and Ohio railroad but another holding Missouri Pacific Railroad (Mo-Pac) failed to thrive and Young embarked on a 40-year struggle to maximize Mo-Pac's value. Young focused on railroads even as the industry declined but he also made other investments including a chunk of IDS (which became the US's largest mutual fund company) and real estate. He also trimmed company holdings from nearly 70 to about 10. By the time Young committed suicide in 1958 Alleghany was in trouble and Kirby who had always kept to the shadows took over.

In his first three years at the helm Kirby fought a takeover attempt by Abraham Sonnabend and a proxy fight with investors John and Clint Murchison. After being ousted briefly in 1961 Kirby reemerged in control of the company. Allan suffered a stroke in 1965 and his son Fred Morgan "F. M." Kirby II took over.

In 1966 the company sold its interest in the New York Central railroad (bought in 1945) and eight years later finally emerged from the Mo-Pac mess with about $42 million in cash and some stock. Alleghany used the cash to buy metal fabricating company MSL Industries and the rest of IDS.

Fred Kirby's mantra was flexibility and in 1984 he sold IDS to American Express for a then-flabbergasting $800 million including a pile of stock. Kirby used these proceeds to buy Chicago Title & Trust the same year. Two years later he liquidated the old Alleghany and reincorporated Alleghany Financial CT&T's parent as Alleghany Corporation.

Kirby used the cash from the American Express deal to buy and then spin off a construction company. Other purchases followed in the 1990s including more title operations a California thrift and in 1991 Celite which produced filtration materials. This line was expanded the next year with the purchase of Harborlite. After several purchases in direct insurance (quickly flipped for a profit) in 1993 Alleghany bought Underwriters Re.

In 1994 and 1995 the company bought up shares of Burlington Northern Railroad which merged with Santa Fe in 1995.

In the 1990s CT&T lost market share through industry consolidation so in 1998 Alleghany spun off CT&T's title operations (later acquired by Fidelity National Financial). The next year hit by a down market in reinsurance Alleghany agreed to sell Underwriters Re to Swiss Reinsurance keeping its hand in the market via Alleghany Underwriting Holdings Ltd. (AUL).

In 1999 the company bulked up its asset management operations through acquisitions and in 2000 its industrial fastener business Heads & Threads International bought Acktion's Reynold's Fasteners unit. In 2001 Alleghany sold Lloyd's reinsurer Alleghany Underwriting to Bermuda-based Talbot Holdings and Dutch bank ABN Amro bought the company's asset management business.

The company built up its insurance operations with the purchase of Resurgens Specialty Underwriting (RSUI Group) a subsidiary of British insurance powerhouse Royal & Sun Alliance. It also expanded insurance operations with the 2004 acquisitions of Capitol Transamerica and Darwin National Assurance Company (formerly known as U.S. AEGIS Energy Insurance Company) later renamed as Darwin Professional Underwriters. In early 2006 it took Darwin through an initial public offering and used the funds to reduce its equity interest while retaining majority ownership. (Alleghany's 55% stake in Darwin was sold to Allied World Assurance in 2008.)

While Alleghany collected insurance firms it shed other operations. The company sold Heads & Threads to a management-led investors group in 2004. In 2005 it sold its World Minerals subsidiary (diatomite production) to the US branch of Imerys in a deal valued at about $217 million.

Hurricane Katrina took a serious bite out of profits in 2005. In response Alleghany Insurance Holdings created AIHL Re a reinsurance subsidiary to provide reinsurance directly to RSUI while RSUI worked to reduce its exposure and increased its prices on property insurance. Once the reinsurance market settled down AIHL Re was allowed to go dormant in 2008.

During the quieter 2006 and 2007 hurricane seasons Alleghany found it still had an appetite for insurance providers. The company plunked down $120 million in cash to purchase 33% of monoline homeowners insurance provider Homesite Group in 2006 and spent $198 million to acquire Employers Direct in 2007.

Alleghany held 55% of Darwin Professional Underwriters a specialty property/casualty insurance writer but in 2008 sold it to Allied World Assurance for approximately $300 million.

F. M. Kirby retired as chairman at the end of 2006. His brother Allan Kirby retired from the board in 2010 leaving Jefferson Kirby F. M.'s son as the last family member on the board as directors. F. M. died at the age of 91 in early 2011.

Transatlantic Holdings caught Alleghany's eye and in early 2012 the company paid some $3.4 billion for the long-tail reinsurer. The deal's announcement in late 2011 ended a months-long buyout battle for Transatlantic.

EXECUTIVES

Vice President Of Finance And Accounting, Jerry Borrelli
Chairman And Ceo Capspecialty Inc. (f/k/a Capitol Transamerica Corporation), Stephen J. Sills, age 71
Chairman Alleghany Capital Corporation, Udi Toledano, age 70
President And Ceo, Weston M. Hicks, age 64, $1,000,000 total compensation
President And Ceo Alleghany Properties, David J. Bugatto, age 55
President And Ceo Transatlantic Holdings Inc., Michael C. (Mike) Sapnar, age 53
Chairman President And Ceo Pacific Compensation Corporation, Janet D. (Jan) Frank, age 69
Svp Head Of Fixed Income And Treasurer, Roger B. Gorham, age 57, $600,000 total compensation

Svp General Counsel And Secretary, Christopher K. Dalrymple, age 52, $650,000 total compensation
Chairman And Ceo Rsui Group Inc., David E. (Dave) Leonard
Svp And Cfo, John L. (Jack) Sennott, age 54, $650,000 total compensation
Evp, Joseph P. Brandon, age 61, $825,000 total compensation
President And Ceo Alleghany Capital Corporation, David Van Geyzel
Vp Finance And Chief Risk Officer, Kerry J. Jacobs
Vice President, Jeff Kirby
Vice President And Tax Director, John Carr
Assistant Vice President, Gloria Seigler
Vice President Property Treaty, Valerie Sotomayor
Chairman, Jefferson W. Kirby, age 58
Auditors: Ernst & Young LLP

LOCATIONS

HQ: Alleghany Corp.
1411 Broadway, 34th Floor, New York, NY 10018
Phone: 212 752-1356
Web: www.alleghany.com

PRODUCTS/OPERATIONS

2017 Sales

	$ mil.	% of total
Reinsurance		
Casualty & other	2,626	41
Property	1,181	18
Insurance		
RSUI Group	721	11
Cap Specialty	260	4
PacificComp	163	3
Net investment income	451	7
Net realized capital gains	107	2
Other	928	14
Adjustments	(16.9)	
Total	**6,424**	**100**

2017 Sales

	$ mil.	% of total
Net premiums earned	4,955	77
Net investment income	451	7
Net realized capital gains	107	2
Other	928	14
Adjustments	(16.9)	-
Total	**6,424**	**100**

Selected Subsidiaries

Alleghany Capital Corporation
Alleghany Properties LLC
CapSpecialty Inc.
Roundwood Asset Management LLC
RSUI Group Inc.
Transatlantic Holdings Inc.

COMPETITORS

AIG	OdysseyRe
CNA Surety	PartnerRe
California Casualty	Reinsurance Group of
Everest Re	America
General Re	RenaissanceRe
Hannover Re	State Farm
Liberty Mutual Agency	Swiss Re
Munich Re Group	Travelers Companies
Nationwide	

HISTORICAL FINANCIALS

Company Type: Public

Income Statement

	ASSETS ($ mil.)	NET INCOME ($ mil.)	INCOME AS % OF ASSETS	EMPLOYEES
				FYE: December 31
12/19	26,931	857	3.2%	10,786
12/18	25,344	39	0.2%	9,300
12/17	25,384	90	0.4%	4,402
12/16	23,756	456	1.9%	3,420
12/15	22,846	560	2.5%	3,135
Annual Growth	**4.2%**	**11.2%**	**—**	**36.2%**

2019 Year-End Financials

Debt ratio: 6.50%
Return on equity: 10.42%
Cash ($ mil.): 1,179
Current ratio: —
Long-term debt ($ mil.): —
No. of shares (mil.): 14
Dividends
  Yield: —
  Payout: —
Market value ($ mil.): 11,486

	STOCK PRICE ($) FY Close	P/E High/Low	Earnings	PER SHARE ($) Dividends	Book Value
12/19	799.57	13 10	59.39	0.00	611.00
12/18	623.32	250 215	2.62	10.00	527.75
12/17	596.09	112 89	5.85	0.00	553.20
12/16	608.12	21 15	29.59	0.00	515.24
12/15	477.93	15 13	35.13	0.00	486.02
Annual Growth	**13.7%**	**— —**	**14.0%**	**—**	**5.9%**

Allegiance Bancshares Inc

LOCATIONS

HQ: Allegiance Bancshares Inc
8847 West Sam Houston Parkway N., Suite 200, Houston, TX 77040
Phone: 281 894-3200
Web: www.allegiancebank.com

HISTORICAL FINANCIALS

Company Type: Public

Income Statement

	ASSETS ($ mil.)	NET INCOME ($ mil.)	INCOME AS % OF ASSETS	EMPLOYEES
				FYE: December 31
12/19	4,992	52	1.1%	588
12/18	4,655	37	0.8%	569
12/17	2,860	17	0.6%	375
12/16	2,450	22	0.9%	327
12/15	2,084	15	0.8%	310
Annual Growth	**24.4%**	**35.3%**	**—**	**17.4%**

2019 Year-End Financials

Debt ratio: 3.67%
Return on equity: 7.50%
Cash ($ mil.): 346
Current ratio: —
Long-term debt ($ mil.): —
No. of shares (mil.): 20
Dividends
  Yield: —
  Payout: —
Market value ($ mil.): 772

	STOCK PRICE ($) FY Close	P/E High/Low	Earnings	PER SHARE ($) Dividends	Book Value
12/19	37.60	16 12	2.47	0.00	34.59
12/18	32.37	19 12	2.37	0.00	32.04
12/17	37.65	30 23	1.31	0.00	23.20
12/16	36.15	21 9	1.75	0.00	21.59
12/15	23.65	18 15	1.43	0.00	20.17
Annual Growth	**12.3%**	**— —**	**14.6%**	**—**	**14.4%**

ALLEGIS GROUP, INC.

Allegis Group is one of the world's largest staffing and recruitment firms. Among its group of staffing companies are Aerotek (engineering automotive and scientific professionals) Aston Carter (recruitment for accounting finance and professional skills) and TEKsystems (information technology staffing and consulting). Other Allegis Group units include sales support outsourcer MarketSource. Allegis Group operates through more than 500 locations worldwide. Chairman Jim Davis helped found the company (originally known as Aerotek) in 1983 to provide contract engineering personnel to two clients in the aerospace industry.

Operations

Operating through a group of about 10 companies Allegis Group serves businesses and organizations from the engineering automotive finance IT life sciences and other industries. The company also serves government agencies and subcontractors. Aerotek and TEKsystems are among the group's largest and most established companies; other Allegis companies provide niche services including disability recruitment through its Getting Hired unit and legal recruitment though Major Lindsey & Africa.

Allegis Group's core services include staffing and recruitment (screening onboarding and retention) search (CEO and board member services) talent advisory (executive report data file and segment analysis) managed delivery and workforce management.

Geographic Reach

Hanover Maryland-based Allegis Group operates in more than 500 locations around the globe including offices throughout the US the UK and Europe as well as in the Middle East Asia and Asia Pacific region.

Sales and Marketing

Allegis Group has served approximately 20000 clients.

Company Background

In 1983 Stephen Bisciotti and Jim Davis founded the company (originally known as Aerotek) in Maryland. At the time the founders' firm matched job seekers with aeronautics engineering and light industrial positions. In the late 1980s the company expanded into the IT application markets.

Aerotek extended its reach into commercial environmental and energy industries through its 2001 acquisition of Onsite Companies. The company later changed its name to Allegis Group while the other divisions remained separate companies until eventually consolidating under the Allegis Group banner.

EXECUTIVES

It Vice President Of Finance, Celeste Slifer
Cfo, Paul J. Bowie
President, Andy Hilger

Senior Vice President, Mary Pat Smith
Vice President National Account Director At Allegis Rpo, John Markey
Vice President Human Resources, Tanya Axenson
Chairman, James C. (Jim) Davis
Auditors: PRICEWATERHOUSECOOPERS LLP B

LOCATIONS

HQ: ALLEGIS GROUP, INC.
7301 PARKWAY DR, HANOVER, MD 210761159
Phone: 410 579-3000
Web: WWW.ALLEGISGROUP.COM

PRODUCTS/OPERATIONS

Selected Subsidiaries

Aerotek
Aerotek Aviation LLC
Aerotek Canada
Aerotek Scientific LLC
Allegis Group Canada
Allegis Group India
Major Lindsey & Africa
MarketSource Inc
Stephen James Associates
TEKsystems
TEKsystems Canada
TEKsystems Netherlands
TEKsystems United Kingdom

COMPETITORS

ASG Renaissance	Kelly Services
Adecco	Korn/Ferry
CDI	ManpowerGroup
Curran Partners	RDL Corporation
ExecuNet	Randstad Holding
Heidrick & Struggles	Robert Half
Horton International	Snelling Staffing
Innovative Management Solutions Group	Volt Information

HISTORICAL FINANCIALS

Company Type: Private

Income Statement				FYE: December 31
	REVENUE ($ mil.)	NET INCOME ($ mil.)	NET PROFIT MARGIN	EMPLOYEES
12/19	13,583	0	—	85,000
12/18	13,402	0	—	—
12/17	12,296	0	—	—
12/16	11,502	0	—	—
Annual Growth	5.7%	—	—	—

ALLIED UNIVERSAL HOLDCO LLC

EXECUTIVES

Ceo, Steve Jones
Regional Vice President, Craig Demartini
Client Manager, Anders Siverling
Site Supervisor, Bryan Overton
Supervisor, Dustin Rost
Operations Manager, Eric Hartley
Branch Manager, Herbert Morency
Human Resources Coordinator, Jill English
Director of Security, John Lopez
Site Supervisor Raytheon Sas O, Jose Rincon
Account Manager (security Spec, Joseph Nelson

LOCATIONS

HQ: ALLIED UNIVERSAL HOLDCO LLC
1551 N TUSTIN AVE STE 650, SANTA ANA, CA 927058664
Phone: 866 877-1965
Web: WWW.AUS.COM

HISTORICAL FINANCIALS

Company Type: Private

Income Statement				FYE: December 31
	ASSETS ($ mil.)	NET INCOME ($ mil.)	INCOME AS % OF ASSETS	EMPLOYEES
12/19	6,432	(381)	—	88,000
12/17	4,451	(69)	—	—
Annual Growth	20.2%	—	—	—

Allstate Corp

Ya gotta hand it to Allstate: The "good hands" company has managed to work its way towards the top of the property/casualty insurance pile. Serving more than 145 million policies in force the company is one of the top overall property/casualty insurers. Its Allstate Protection segment sells auto homeowners and other property/casualty insurance products in Canada and the US. Other divisions provide life insurance voluntary benefits such as short-term disability and critical illness policies and consumer protection plans.

Operations

Allstate operates through seven segments: Allstate Protection Service Businesses Allstate Life Allstate Benefits Allstate Annuities Discontinued Lines and Coverages and Corporate and Other. The company has more than 145 million policies in force including around 35 million Property-Liability policies.

Allstate's property and liability operations – consisting of the Allstate Protection and Discontinued Lines and Coverages segments – account for more than 85% of Allstate's total revenue.

Most of the Allstate Protection's sales come from traditional personal auto and homeowners policies. It also sells specialty products including coverage for motorcycle and boat owners renters and landlords and mobile home dwellers. The segment includes subsidiaries Esurance (auto insurance) Encompass (package policies) and Answer Financial (agency sales). Commercial products are geared towards small business owners.

The Discontinued Lines and Coverages segment includes results from property/casualty policies written prior to the 1980s that are in runoff.

The Allstate Life segment accounting for about 5% of sales offers term whole and variable life insurance products through subsidiaries including Allstate Life Insurance and American Heritage Life. The unit also sells retirement products offered by third parties.

The Service Businesses segment (another 5%) includes consumer protection plan provider Allstate Protection Plans Allstate Dealer Services telematics unit Arity Allstate Roadside Services Arity and Allstate Identity Protection. InfoArmor offers identity protection via employers.

Allstate Benefits provides voluntary benefits policies such as life accident short-term disability and critical illness policies for employer groups. Allstate Annuities comprises the run-off annuity business.

About 5% combined generates from both of this segment.

Geographic Reach

Allstate's largest property/casualty markets are California Florida New York and Texas. The Service Businesses operate in the US Puerto Rico Europe and Canada. Allstate has some 450 administrative claims data and other facilities in North America. It also has offices in Ireland India and London. The company is headquartered in Northbrook Illinois.

Sales and Marketing

The Allstate Protection segment maintains a network of approximately 10800 exclusive agencies which sell its insurance products through approximately 27100 licensed sales professionals and 1000 financial specialists. It also offers these products and Encompass-branded products through some 3400 independent agencies that are primarily located in rural areas of the US. Esurance and Answer Financial products are distributed online and via contact centers.

The Allstate Life offerings are sold through exclusive agents while Allstate Benefits offerings are sold through exclusive and independent agents.

The Services Businesses segment distributes through retail stores auto dealerships affinity groups wholesale partners and exclusive agencies.

Allstate spent $7 million $8.7 million and $8.3 million on advertising for FY 2019 2018 and 2017 respectively.

Financial Performance

Allstate's revenue has grown steadily over the past five years with the company reporting a 22% rise in sales between 2015 and 2019 driven by organic and acquisitive growth. Net income has fluctuated in the $1.7 billion to $3.4 billion range however with profits only rising significantly in the last year.

Revenue rose 12% in 2019 to some $44.7 billion. Insurance premiums – the largest contributor to revenue – increased 6% but growth was offset by lower investment income.

Net income also increased significantly by 133% to some $4.7 billion in 2019 primarily due to net realized capital gains in 2019 compared to losses in 2018 from increased valuations on equity investments and higher underwriting income in Allstate Protection.

The company ended 2019 with $338 million in cash down $161 million from 2018. Operating activities contributed $5.1 billion while investing activities used $2.8 billion (on securities partnership and mortgage loan investments) and financing activities used $2.5 billion via treasury stock purchases contractholder fund withdrawals and dividends.

Strategy

Allstate is focused on increasing market share in its core auto and homeowners markets as well as in other business lines. It creates shareholder value through customer satisfaction unit growth attractive returns on capital sustainable profitability and a diversified business platform.

Allstate has implemented a multi-year Transformative Growth Plan that leverages the Allstate brand people and technology. The Transformative Growth Plan enables it to better serve customers in a changing world with its three components: expand customer access; improve customer value; and increase investments in marketing and technology.

Allstate also regularly introduces new product offerings to meet shifting customer needs. For example Allstate Benefits launched an enhanced critical illness insurance offering in Canada in 2019 and has also acquired iCracked in the same year to offer consumer protection plans and tech support. Allstate has also agreed to acquire National General Holdings Corporation in 2020 with the closing expected in early 2021 which increases Allstate's market share in personal property-liability and significantly expands its independent agent distribution.

At the same time Allstate is working to reduce its operational costs through modernization efforts such as the adoption of data analytics capabilities to improve pricing and underwriting processes. It continues to invest in auto telematics (wireless devices that track drivers' habits) which allow for more accurate policy pricing. It has also made claims settlement processes more efficient by adding digital imaging capabilities.

Catastrophe management is also a key part of the company's stability. To limit its exposure to catastrophic claims in the face of increasing severe weather events in recent years Allstate limits its activities in geographies that are vulnerable to hurricanes fires and earthquakes such as California and Florida.

Mergers and Acquisitions

In 2019 the company acquired iCracked Inc. for $1.4 billion which offers on-site on-demand repair services for smartphones and tablets in North America supporting Allstate Protection Plans' (formerly known as SquareTrade) operations. iCracked is a privately held San Francisco-based company.

Company Background

The Allstate Corporation was founded in 1992 to hold the assets of Allstate Insurance Company which dates back to 1931. Allstate Insurance was originally formed by retail firm Sears to sell car insurance. It added homeowners and other property/casualty lines as well as life insurance in the 1950s. Sears divested a 20% stake in 1993 when Allstate went public and sold off the rest of its shares in Allstate in 1995. The company formed the Allstate Federal Savings Bank subsidiary to expand its financial services in 1998.

Acquisitions have included CNA Personal Insurance (now Encompass 1999) American Heritage Life Investment (workplace offerings 1999) Sterling Collision (2001) and SquareTrade (consumer protection 2017).

HISTORY

Allstate traces its origins to a friendly game of bridge played in 1930 on a Chicago-area commuter train by Sears president Robert Wood and a friend insurance broker Carl Odell. The insurance man suggested Sears sell auto insurance through the mail. Wood liked the idea financed the company and in 1931 put Odell in charge (that hand of bridge must have shown Wood that Odell was no dummy). The company was named Allstate after one of Sears' tire brands. Allstate was born just as Sears was beginning its push into retailing and Allstate went with it selling insurance out of all the new Sears stores.

Growth was slow during the Depression and WWII but the postwar boom was a gold mine for both Sears and Allstate. Suburban development made cars a necessity; 1950s prudence necessitated car insurance; and Sears made it easy to buy the insurance at their stores and increasingly at freestanding agencies.

In the late 1950s Allstate added home and other property/casualty insurance lines. It also went into life insurance — in-force policies zoomed from zero to $1 billion in six years the industry's fastest growth ever.

Sears formed Allstate Enterprises in 1960 as an umbrella for all its noninsurance operations. In 1970 that firm bought its first savings and loan (S&L). The insurer continued to acquire other S&Ls and to add subsidiaries throughout the 1970s and 1980s.

This strategy dovetailed with Sears' strategy which was to become a diversified financial services company. In 1985 Sears introduced the Discover Card through Allstate's Greenwood Trust Company. However by the late 1980s it was obvious Sears would never be a financial services giant. Moreover it was losing so much in retailing that by 1987 Allstate was the major contributor to corporate net income. Sears began to dismantle its financial empire in the 1990s.

Allstate also suffered from a backlash against high insurance rates. When Massachusetts instituted no-fault insurance in 1989 Allstate stopped writing new auto insurance there. Later the company had to refund $110 million to customers to settle a suit with California over rate rollbacks required by 1988's Proposition 103.

The Allstate Corporation was founded in 1992 to hold the assets of Allstate Insurance Company. Allstate went public in 1993 when Sears sold about 20% of its stake. That year Allstate began reducing its operations in Florida to protect itself against high losses from hurricanes. Two years later Sears sold its remaining interest to its shareholders. Also in 1995 Allstate sold 70% of PMI its mortgage insurance unit to the public.

EXECUTIVES

Vice President, Sari Macrie
Svp Corporate Relations, Victoria Dinges
Chairman President And Ceo The Allstate Corporation And Allstate Insurance Company, Thomas J. Wilson, age 62, $1,200,000 total compensation
Vice President Finance, Norma Gorman
Senior Vice President, Bryan Anderson
Evp Marketing Innovation And Corporate Relations Allstate Insurance, Sanjay Gupta, age 52
President Allstate Financial, Mary Jane B. Fortin, $632,752 total compensation
President Service Businesses, Don Civgin, age 59, $776,885 total compensation
Evp Product Integration And Management, W. Guy Hill
Evp Product Operations Allstate Insurance, Steven P. Sorenson, age 56
Evp Brand Operations Allstate Insurance, Thomas M. Troy
Evp Technology And Strategic Ventures, Suren Gupta, age 58, $537,404 total compensation
President West Territory Allstate Personal Lines, Thomas F. Clarkson
President East Territory, David Prendergast
President Allstate Personal Lines, Glenn T. Shapiro
Evp Allstate Brand Distribution Allstate Insurance Company (aic), Katherine (Kathy) Mabe
Vice Chairman The Allstate Corporation And Allstate Insurance Company, Steven E. (Steve) Shebik, age 63, $770,673 total compensation
Evp General Counsel And Secretary Allstate Corp And Allstate Insurance Company (aic), Susan L. Lees, age 62
Evp Allstate Personal Lines Business Transformation, Brian R. Bohaty
Evp Human Resources, Harriet K. Harty, age 53
Evp And Chief Investment Officer; President Allstate Investments, John Dugenske
Evp And Cfo The Allstate Corporation And Allstate Insurance Company, Mario Rizzo
Seniorvp Pmotechnologyandoperations, Linda Honour
Vice President Of Technology, Patricia Coffey
Vice President Corporate Strategy, Ron Chadha
Assistant Vice President, Steve King
Assistant Vice President, Terrance Ray
Senior Vice President Corporate Relations, Stacy Sharpe
Svp Chief Risk Officer, Mike Demetre

Vice President Integrated Marketing Communications, Pam Hollander
Vice President, Darin Reeser
Senior Vice President Agency Operations, Jeanine Raquet
Vice President Human Resources, Kelly Noll
Vice President Human Resources, Joseph Testor
Senior Vice President Marketing, Lisa Cochrane
Assistant Vice President, Jeffrey Deigl
Vice President Human Resources, Amy Mills
West Central Region Field Senior Vice President, Jeff Thompson
Assistant Vice President Hr, Iris Chester
Vice President, Alex Schwab
Vice President Investor Relations, Robert Block
Field Senior Vice President, Troy Hawkes
Vice President Director Manager, Carl Majeski
Vice President, Bob Transon
Vice President Of Analytics, Mia Boom-ibes
Vice President Manager, Steve Hallmark
Vice President Product Technology, Daniel Butch Necastro
Assistant Vice President Claims, Pam Overton
Assistant Vice President, James Haidu
Vice President Insurance Reserves, Shantelle Thomas
Senior Vice President Call Center, Dan Murray
Vice President Customer Experience, Christina Metzger
Vice President, Alan Eifert
Vice President Of National Account Management, Kerry Flack
Senior Vice President E Business And Direct Marketing, Robert Wasserman
Vice President Finance, Tom McDonnell
Field Vice President, Roger Odle
Assistant Vice President, Daniel Brown
Vice President, Heather Vangrevenhof
Vice President And Senior Key Account Manager, Stephen Lipker
Assistant Vice President Strategic Initiatives Management Office, Kimberly Purdy
Vice President, Antoinette Bussetti
Product Vice President, Laura Bartlett
Assistant Vice President Allstate Marketing Customer Communication Division, Richard Heneberry
Vice President Director Manager, Beth Drinan
Vice President Talent Acquisition, Cathy Winn
Senior Vice President Vehicle Product Management, Julie Parsons
Senior Vice President And Group Chief Information Officer, Peter Logothetis
Vice President Business Development, Jerry Lamparski
Field Vice President, Andy Garza
Senior Vice President, Kellie Rakes
Vice President, Elizabeth Smith
Assistant Vice President Finance, Kevin Corbett
Vice President Risk Assesment, Bob Roberts
Vp Internal Audit, Kathy Swain
Vice President Sales And Marketing, Alita Collier
Vice President Regional Sales Manager, Rebecca Bates
Vice President, Angela Booles
Vice President, Steve Miller
Vice President Manager Director, Bob Halter
Vice President Director Manager, Howard Gurvitz
Senior Vice President Human Resources, Joan Crockett
Senior Vice President Agency Sales And Regional Marketing, Patty VanLammeren
Assistant Vice President Claims, Sharon Broome
Vice President, Shane O'Brien
Floridian Executive Vice President, George Grawe
Vice President Claims, Dale Sherman
Vice President Product Operations Allstate, Guy W Hill
Executive Vice President Human Resources, Liz Oppenhuis

Field Senior Vice President, Alice Byrne
Vice President Policy Administ, Lori Rutten
Vice President Of Coiled Tubing And Cementing, Katie R Jones
Vice President Finance, Michael Kasper
Afvp, Brian Walsh
Vice President Finance, Joy Ann Sweet
Vice President Tax, Karen Gardner
Executive Vice President, Larry Dahl
Vice President, Debbie Parker
Vice President, Ralph Eureste
Vice President Infrastructure Engineering And Operations, Joe Skala
Vice President Of Sales Emerging Businesses Affinity Solutions, Rob Gamble Rob Gamble
Vice President Field, Armond Bechard
Senior Vice President, Robert Apatoff
Assistant Vice President Compliance, Diane Ierna
Senior Vice President Of North American Sales, Joseph R Eckert
Vice President Procurement, Lori Yellvington
Vice President Human Resources, Joan Naughton-Gerdes
Vice President Sales And Marketing Encompass At Allstate, Dan Maloney
Vice President Regional Sales Manager, Andrea Barfield-bolger
Vice President Investor Relations, Cindy Guenther
Vice President Information Technology Group, James Baum
Vice President Marketing, Christian Lopez
Vice President, Katherine Smith
Vice President Natural Resources Group, James Carney
Senior Vice President Policy Administration, Shawn Anderson
Vice President, Amy Hsu
Assistant Vice President, Bob Aubrey
Vice President, Beverly Peryea-labarge
Vice President Of Lending, Brent Wylam
Vice President Pennsylvania, David Kozak
Senior Vice President, Denniston Kinkead
Executive Vice President, Dean Atteberry
Vice President And Operations Officer, Jeffrey Burke
Assistant Vice President Finance, Jeffrey Hernandez
Assistant Vice President, John Cicero
Vice President Special Program And Products, Joseph Bindner
Vice President Benefits Practice, Luca Magistro
Vice President Regional Sales Manager, Michael Jasuta
Senior Vice President And Chief Marketing Officer, Nate Son
Vice President Claims, Michael Zelinsky
Senior Vice President Director Fiduciary Risk Manager, Patrick Thimmes
Vice President, Ramon Vasquez
Senior Vice President, Rhonda Decker
Vice President Commercial Banker, Ricardo Estrada
Vice President And Senior Actuary Global Financial Solutions, Philip Fusz
Assistant Vice President Contract Surety, Rennel Rodarmel
Vice President Customer Insights And Experience Manager, Rick Flora
Senior Vice President Willis, Shawn Burns
Vice President, Steve Kretschmar
Second Vice President Treasury, Suzanne Nitzberg
Assistant Vice President Contract Surety, Thomas Rohan
Vice President, Aaron Shealy
Vice President Strategic Planning And Execution, Andrew Schatz
Vice President, Andrew Leach
Vice President Head Of Accident And Health For Latin America, David Chiang
Senior Vice President, Hugo Valdes

Managing Vice President Customer Service And Loss Mitigation At Capital One Auto Finance, Jesse Fernandez
Vice President Surety Claims, Joe Hayden
Vice President Money, Michael Paluch
Vice President And Investment Officer, Pamela Sharp
National Sales Manager, Rhonda Tyner
Auditors: Deloitte & Touche LLP

LOCATIONS

HQ: Allstate Corp
2775 Sanders Road, Northbrook, IL 60062
Phone: 847 402-5000
Web: www.allstate.com

PRODUCTS/OPERATIONS

2017 Sales

	$ mil.	% of total
Property/liability		
Auto	21,878	57
Homeowners	7,310	19
Other personal lines	1,750	5
Commercial lines	495	1
Other business lines	883	2
Others	1,879	5
Allstate Financial	4,294	11
Corporate & other	35	-
Total	**38,524**	**1,010**

Selected Subsidiaries

Allstate Insurance Company of Canada
Allstate Life Insurance Company
Allstate Motor Club
American Heritage Life Insurance Company
Encompass Insurance Company
Esurance Insurance Company
Kennett Capital Inc.
Northbrook Indemnity Company
Pafco Insurance Company (Canada)

COMPETITORS

Farmers Group	Prudential
GEICO	State Farm
Hanover Insurance	The Hartford
Liberty Mutual	Torchmark
MetLife	Travelers Companies
Nationwide	USAA
Progressive Corporation	

HISTORICAL FINANCIALS

Company Type: Public

Income Statement

				FYE: December 31
	ASSETS ($ mil.)	NET INCOME ($ mil.)	INCOME AS % OF ASSETS	EMPLOYEES
12/19	119,950	4,847	4.0%	46,290
12/18	112,249	2,252	2.0%	45,700
12/17	112,422	3,189	2.8%	42,900
12/16	108,610	1,877	1.7%	43,500
12/15	104,656	2,171	2.1%	41,600
Annual Growth	**3.5%**	**22.2%**	**—**	**2.7%**

2019 Year-End Financials

Debt ratio: 5.53%
Return on equity: 20.49%
Cash ($ mil.): 338
Current ratio: —
Long-term debt ($ mil.): —

No. of shares (mil.): 319
Dividends
 Yield: 1.7%
 Payout: 14.2%
Market value ($ mil.): 35,872

	STOCK PRICE ($) FY Close	P/E High/Low		PER SHARE ($) Earnings	Dividends	Book Value
12/19	112.45	8	6	14.03	2.00	81.50
12/18	82.63	17	13	5.96	1.84	64.19
12/17	104.71	12	9	8.36	1.48	63.52
12/16	74.12	16	12	4.67	1.32	56.21
12/15	62.09	14	11	5.05	1.20	52.56
Annual Growth	**16.0%**		**—**	**29.1%**	**13.6%**	**11.6%**

ALLY BANK

Ally Bank is on your side when it comes to banking. Formerly known as GMAC Bank Ally Bank (which is a subsidiary of government-backed Ally Financial)Â offers savings and money market accounts as well as traditionalÂ and no-penalty CDs. The online bank also offers interest checking accounts. The bankÂ offers its services online and over the phone; it operates no physical branch locations. Clients also can use any ATM in the US and Ally will reimburse any fees charged by other banks. Ally Bank was revamped and renamed in 2009 in the midst of GM's (very public) financial difficulties. Predecessor GMAC Bank had been in operation since 2001.

EXECUTIVES

Chb-Pres-Ceo, Diane E Morais
Exec V Pres, Jeffrey J Brown
Cfo, James N Young
SEC, Cathy L Quenneville
Director of Remarketing Sales, Mark Juday
Area Sales Manager, Anthony Stoothoff
CRA Officer, Jan Bergeson
Senior Credit Manager, Anthony Zimmer
Bank Compliance Manager, Brett Hoskin

LOCATIONS

HQ: ALLY BANK
6985 S UNION PARK CTR # 435, MIDVALE, UT 840474177
Phone: 801 790-5005
Web: WWW.ALLY.COM

COMPETITORS

Bank of America	Citibank
BofI	E*TRADE Bank
Charles Schwab	State Farm

HISTORICAL FINANCIALS

Company Type: Private

Income Statement

				FYE: December 31
	ASSETS ($ mil.)	NET INCOME ($ mil.)	INCOME AS % OF ASSETS	EMPLOYEES
12/16	123,547	1,273	1.0%	42
12/07*	28,472	291	1.0%	—
06/06	3,586	0	0.0%	—
Annual Growth	**38.0%**	**114.3%**	**—**	**—**

*Fiscal year change

Ally Financial Inc

Ally Financial wants to be your friend in the financing business. One of the leading online banks in the US Ally operates branchless online-only retail bank Ally Bank which offers deposit mortgage (through Ally Home) auto and investing products. Ally also provides auto financing for over 19000 auto dealerships (mostly GM and Chrysler) and their customers. The company sells both consumer finance protection and insurance products to automotive dealers and commercial insurance products directly to dealers. Additionally the company offers securities-brokerage and investment-advisory services through Ally Invest. Ally's robust corporate-finance business offers capital for equity sponsors and middle-market companies.

Operations

Ally Financial carries over $180 billion in assets. The company operates four business segments: Automotive Finance Insurance Mortgage Finance and Corporate Finance with the remaining activity reported in Corporate and Other.

Automotive Finance is Ally's biggest earner at some 70% of sales. The segment provides auto financing to consumers auto dealers companies and municipalities.

Insurance the next biggest at over 20% of sales offers consumer finance protection and insurance products through its automotive dealer channel. It also sells commercial insurance directly to dealers.

The Mortgage Finance segment accounting for about 5% manages a held-for-investment consumer mortgage portfolio and bulk purchases high-quality jumbo loans. The segment also offers direct-to-consumer mortgages under Ally Home consisting of a variety of jumbo and conforming fixed- and adjustable-rate mortgage products.

Corporate Finance offers senior secured leveraged cash flow and asset-based loans to US-based middle market companies; it accounts for nearly 5% of Ally's total revenue.

Corporate and Other primarily consists of centralized corporate treasury activities such as management of the cash and corporate investment securities and loan portfolios short- and long-term debt retail and brokered deposit liabilities derivative instruments original issue discount and the residual impacts of our corporate funds-transfer pricing (FTP) and treasury asset liability management (ALM) activities.

Geographic Reach

Ally Financial focuses almost entirely on the US. It has corporate offices in Detroit Michiganand Charlotte North Carolina. As an online-only bank Ally has no physical branch network. Its services are available in most US states with California and Texas having the highest concentrations of consumer loans (at around 25% each).

Sales and Marketing

Ally Financial and its subsidiaries serve some 4 million consumers and nearly 18000 auto dealers. Some of its top clients include General Motors and Chrysler.

Ally sells its consumer financial and insurance products primarily through the automotive dealer channel. It sells commercial insurance products directly to dealers. As a direct bank Ally Bank raises deposit funds via its internet telephone mobile and mail channels.

Financial Performance

Ally Financial has been declining since 2015 but redeemed itself in 2019.

Revenue increased to $7.1 billion in 2019 an approximately 8% growth from the year prior.

Net income was $1.7 billion in 2019 an increase from $1.3 billion in 2018. Results were favorably impacted by higher net financing revenue primarily driven by higher yields and growth in earning assets.

Cash provided by operating activities was $4.1 billion in 2019 while investing activities used $3.8 billion. Financing activities used another $1.5 billion. The company ended fiscal 2019 with $4.3 billion in cash and cash equivalents.

Strategy

Ally is always looking for ways to develop and innovate on its products and services. Its strategic focus is centered around differentiating its company as a relentless ally for the financial well-being of its customers ongoing optimization of its market lending automotive and insurance business lines sustained growth in customers and optimization of its deposit funding profile expanding consumer product offerings efficient capital deployment and disciplined risk management and ensuring that its culture remains aligned with a relentless focus on its customers communities associates and stockholders.

Ally has invested in expanding its digital product offerings. Ally Financial acquired Charlotte North Carolina-based Health Credit Services in October 2019. The tech-driven patient financing company is expected to help Ally expand its digital point-of-sale lending products. The company also invested in and partnered with Better.com a digital mortgage company to better position itself with consumers in the digital financial space.

Mergers and Acquisitions

In 2020 Ally Financial Inc. entered a definitive agreement to acquire CardWorks in a transaction valued at approximately $2.65 billion. Cardworks is a privately held company with $4.7 billion in assets and $2.9 billion in deposits. Under the terms of the agreement Merrick Bank a wholly owned subsidiary of CardWorks Inc. will merge into Ally Bank.

Ally Financial acquired Charlotte North Carolina-based Health Credit Services in October 2019. The tech-driven patient financing company which will operate as an indirect subsidiary of Ally is expected to help Ally expand its digital product offerings.

Company Background

Ally Financial was founded as a subsidiary of General Motors in 1919. It was owned by GM until 2006 when the automaker sold a 51% stake in the company to the Cerberus Capital Management investment group for some $7 billion. Formerly known as GMAC the company was bailed out by the US government following the global financial crisis after which it took its current name.

EXECUTIVES

President Auto Finance, Timothy M. (Tim) Russi, age 57, $541,800 total compensation
Cio, Michael Baresich
Ceo And Director, Jeffrey J. (JB) Brown, age 46, $1,000,000 total compensation
President And Ceo Ally Commercial Finance Llc, William (Bill) Hall
President Consumer And Commercial Banking Products, Diane Morais, age 54, $550,000 total compensation
Cfo, Christopher A. Halmy, age 51, $600,000 total compensation
President Ally Insurance, Douglas Timmerman
Chief Risk Officer, David Shevsky, age 58, $500,000 total compensation
Executive Vice President Organizational Effectiveness, Renee Otjen
Chairman, Franklin W. (Fritz) Hobbs, age 72
Treasurer, Bradley Brown
Auditors: DELOITTE & TOUCHE LLP

LOCATIONS

HQ: Ally Financial Inc
Ally Detroit Center, 500 Woodward Ave., Floor 10, Detroit, MI 48226
Phone: 866 710-4623
Web: www.ally.com

PRODUCTS/OPERATIONS

2017 sales

	$ mil.	% of total
Financing revenue and other interest income	8,322	84
Insurance premiums and service revenue earned	973	10
Gain on mortgage and automotive loans net	68	1
Other gain on investments net	102	1
Other income	408	4
Loss on extinguishment of debt	(7)	-
Total	**9,866**	**100**

2017 Sales

	% of total
Automotive Finance	71
Insurance	19
Corporate Finance	2
Mortgage Finance	4
Corporate and Other	4
Total	**100**

Selected Products and Services

Bank
Online Savings
Interest Checking
Money Market
Credit Card
Ally CashBack Credit Card
Auto
Personal
Business
RVs
Home Loans
Buy a Home
Refinance
Invest
Self-Directed Trading
Managed Portfolios
Forex & Futures
Research & Tools
Ally Invest API

COMPETITORS

Bank of America
Citigroup
Ford Motor Credit
Mercedes-Benz Credit
Mercedes-Benz Financial Services USA
Mitsubishi Motors Credit of America
Toyota Motor Credit
Volkswagen Financial Services

HISTORICAL FINANCIALS

Company Type: Public

Income Statement				FYE: December 31
	ASSETS ($ mil.)	NET INCOME ($ mil.)	INCOME AS % OF ASSETS	EMPLOYEES
12/19	180,644	1,715	0.9%	8,700
12/18	178,869	1,263	0.7%	8,200
12/17	167,148	929	0.6%	7,900
12/16	163,728	1,067	0.7%	7,600
12/15	158,581	1,289	0.8%	7,100
Annual Growth	3.3%	7.4%	—	5.2%

2019 Year-End Financials

Debt ratio: 20.27%
Return on equity: 12.39%
Cash ($ mil.): 3,555
Current ratio: —
Long-term debt ($ mil.): —
No. of shares (mil.): 374
Dividends
  Yield: 2.2%
  Payout: 16.7%
Market value ($ mil.): 11,440

STOCK PRICE ($)		P/E		PER SHARE ($)		
	FY Close	High/Low		Earnings	Dividends	Book Value
12/19	30.56	8	5	4.34	0.68	38.51
12/18	22.66	10	7	2.95	0.56	32.77
12/17	29.16	14	9	2.04	0.40	30.87
12/16	19.02	9	7	2.15	0.16	28.52
12/15	18.64	—	—	(2.66)	0.00	27.88
Annual Growth	13.2%	—	—	—	—	8.4%

Alphabet Inc

Google is a search engine. Core to Google's business is its ubiquitous Search product; other key products and platforms include Android Chrome Gmail Google Drive Google Maps Google Play and YouTube. The firm generates revenue through ad sales in two categories: Performance Advertising creates and delivers relevant ads that users click on and Brand Advertising lets businesses run ad campaigns to promote brand awareness. In addition Google Display Network allows advertisers to build a custom network of sites utilizing a wide range of targeting technologies. Google is owned by Alphabet Inc. a holding company that also includes emerging businesses such as Calico and about life sciences. The Google story begins in 1995 at Stanford University.

Operations
Since its founding as a search engine the company has branched out to provide a wide range of popular services such as Webmail (Gmail) interactive maps (Google Maps) Web browsing (Google Chrome) voice search (Google Assistant) presentations (Google Drive) Business (Adsense) and video and music (YouTube). In addition the organization of photos contacts and notes are offered as well.

The company's Android operating system is a platform for mobile products. Google hardware includes Pixel phones Chromebook laptops Google Nest the Google Home Hub smart display Android Auto and OS. The company sells digital content such as apps music and movies through Google Play Store. It also offers a suite of cloud computing services through Google Cloud.

Beyond its advertising business which accounts for the majority of revenue (less than 85%) the firm generates a smaller share of revenue (about 15%) from apps movies music and other digital content purchased through Google Play; the sale of Google hardware devices; and Google Cloud offerings. Parent company Alphabet's non-Google offerings which fall under the "Other Bets" business unit account for less than half a percent of the holding company's revenue.

Geographic Reach
The Mountain View California-based Google operates from more than 70 offices in 50 countries. International domains include Google.ba Google.dm Google.nr Google.co.jp and Google.ca and the Google interface is available in almost 110 languages.

The US accounts for over 45% of Alphabet's revenue and Google is responsible for nearly all of Alphabet's revenue. Europe Middle East and Africa account for the next largest share of business (more than 30%) followed by the Asia/Pacific region (nearly 20%) and Other Americas (more than 5%).

Sales and Marketing
The customers generally purchase advertising inventory through Google Ads Google Ad Manager as part of the Authorized Buyers marketplace and Google Marketing Platform among others.

Certain customers receive cash-based incentives or credits which are accounted for as variable consideration.

The company's performance advertising creates and delivers relevant ads that users will click on leading to direct engagement with advertisers. Most of its performance advertisers pays when a user engages in their ads. Performance advertising lets advertisers connect with users while driving measurable results. Brand advertising helps enhance users' awareness of and affinity with advertisers' products and services through videos text images and other interactive ads that run across various devices.

Strategy
Google continues to make significant R&D investments in areas of strategic focus such as advertising cloud machine learning and search as well as in new products and services. In addition its capital expenditures have grown over the last several years. Google expects this trend to continue in the long term as it invests heavily in land and buildings for data centers and offices and information technology infrastructure which includes servers and network equipment.

A key part of Google's strategy is to deepen enhance and further the integration of its Google Cloud Platform. It also focused on continually improving the quality and applicability of its voice and translation services strengthening security rolling out machine-learning and natural language processing and enhancing its G Suite of communication tools (Gmail Docs Drive Calendar and Hangouts). Its Chrome Enterprise is an integrated back-end solution that provides the tools needed to run a business.

Meanwhile as consumers increasingly use smart phones to access the internet more people are looking at Google's ads more often. However the company's growth – while still positive – may be showing signs of a slowdown. Mobile ad views have increased substantially but these ads cost less than ads viewed on desktop computers so the price Google can command for mobile ads is less.

Despite massive and rapid growth (or perhaps because of it) Google faces its fair share of challenges. Critics of the company have alleged it engages in anti-competitive practices privacy violations and data leaks among other transgressions. Another concern for the company is rising costs. Google is spending more to acquire content for YouTube market new hardware products and build new data centers.

Mergers and Acquisitions
Google struck a deal to acquire wearable fitness products company Fitbit late in 2019 for about $2.1 billion. Buying Fitbit supports Google's efforts to expand its hardware offerings while positioning it to compete against Apple and Samsung Electronics in the growing smartwatch space.

Google bought CloudSimple a software firm that helps run computing workloads based on VMware's virtualization technology in 2019. Terms were not disclosed. The acquisition makes it easier for Google cloud customers to use VMware software.

That same year Google agreed to buy Looker a developer of software for analyzing big data for $2.4 billion in cash. Looker would become part of the Google Cloud unit providing the unit's customers with business intelligence. Google also agreed to acquire Alooma a company that helps companies move data from multiple locations to one data warehouse to accelerate growth of its cloud operations. In Google's case that single data warehouse would be its Google Cloud service.

Company Background
Google is the product of two computer science grad students Sergey Brin and Larry Page who met in 1995 at Stanford University where they studied methods of searching and organizing large datasets. They discovered a formula to rank the order of random search results by relevancy and in 1997 they adopted the name Google to their findings. In 1998 the two presented their discovery at the World Wide Web Conference and by 1999 they had raised almost $30 million in funding from private investors venture capital firms and Stanford University. Later that year the Google site was launched.

In 2014 the once highly secretive company went public in one of the most anticipated IPOs ever raising $1.6 billion. Alphabet was launched the following as the holding company for Google and other subsidiaries. The corporate restructure was designed to provide some separation between Google's core search business and its increasingly diverse side projects. Alphabet replaced Google as the publicly-traded entity.

HISTORY

Google is the product of two computer science grad students Sergey Brin and Larry Page who met in 1995 at Stanford University where they studied methods of searching and organizing large datasets. They discovered a formula to rank the order of random search results by relevancy and in 1997 they adopted the name Google to their findings. In 1998 the two presented their discovery at the World Wide Web Conference and by 1999 they had raised almost $30 million in funding from private investors venture capital firms and Stanford University. Later that year the Google site was launched.

Brin and Page hired tech industry veteran Eric Schmidt (former CTO at Sun Microsystems and former CEO of Novell) in 2001 as Google's CEO. Brin previously the company's chairman adopted the role of president of technology and Page previously CEO of Google became president of product. Also in 2001 Google launched AdWords its search-based advertising service. The following year the company launched another advertising service the context-based AdSense.

In 2004 the company entered the social networking sphere with the launch of its Orkut product which allows users (by invitation only) to search and connect with one another through online networks of friends. Later that year the once highly secretive company went public in one of the most anticipated IPOs ever raising $1.6 billion.

In October 2015 Google became a subsidiary of Alphabet Inc.

EXECUTIVES

Ceo, Sundar Pichai, age 48
Svp And Cfo Alphabet Inc. And Google Inc., Ruth M. Porat, age 63
President Enterprise Sales, Tariq M. Shaukat, age 47
Vp And Ceo Google Israel, Meir Brand
Vice President Google Creative Lab, Robert Wong
Vice President Of Worldwide Operations, Jim Miller
Vice President Finance, Tom Hutchinson
Board Member, Marc Ellenbogen
Auditors: Ernst & Young LLP

LOCATIONS

HQ: Alphabet Inc
1600 Amphitheatre Parkway, Mountain View, CA 94043
Phone: 650 253-0000
Web: www.abc.xyz

PRODUCTS/OPERATIONS

Selected Products & Advertising Platforms

AdWords
DoubleClick Digital Marketing
Google Analytics
Google Consumer Surveys
Google Display Network
Google for Retail
Google+ for Brands
YouTube

COMPETITORS

AOL	MSN
Apple Inc.	Myspace
Ask.com	NetEase
Baidu	SINA
Blucora	Shopping.com
CityGrid Media	Shopzilla
Conversant	Sohu.com
Daum Communications	Spotify
Facebook	Twitter
LiveJournal	Yahoo!
LookSmart	craigslist

HISTORICAL FINANCIALS

Company Type: Public

Income Statement   FYE: December 31

	REVENUE ($ mil.)	NET INCOME ($ mil.)	NET PROFIT MARGIN	EMPLOYEES
12/20	182,527	40,269	22.1%	135,301
12/19	161,857	34,343	21.2%	118,899
12/18	136,819	30,736	22.5%	98,771
12/17	110,855	12,662	11.4%	80,110
12/16	90,272	19,478	21.6%	72,053
Annual Growth	19.2%	19.9%		17.1%

2020 Year-End Financials

Debt ratio: 4.36%	No. of shares (mil.): 675
Return on equity: 18.94%	Dividends
Cash ($ mil.): 26,465	Yield: —
Current ratio: 3.07	Payout: —
Long-term debt ($ mil.): 13,932	Market value ($ mil.): 1,183,421

	STOCK PRICE ($) FY Close	P/E High/Low		Earnings	PER SHARE ($) Dividends	Book Value
12/20	1,752.64	31	18	58.61	0.00	329.59
12/19	1,339.39	27	21	49.16	0.00	292.65
12/18	1,044.96	29	22	43.70	0.00	255.38
12/17	1,053.40	59	44	18.00	0.00	219.50
12/16	792.45	30	24	27.85	0.00	201.12
Annual Growth	21.9%	—	—	20.4%	—	13.1%

Altabancorp

Auditors: Moss Adams LLP

LOCATIONS

HQ: Altabancorp
1 East Main Street, American Fork, UT 84003
Phone: 801 642-3998
Web: www.peoplesutah.com

HISTORICAL FINANCIALS

Company Type: Public

Income Statement   FYE: December 31

	ASSETS ($ mil.)	NET INCOME ($ mil.)	INCOME AS % OF ASSETS	EMPLOYEES
12/19	2,406	44	1.8%	490
12/18	2,184	40	1.9%	459
12/17	2,123	19	0.9%	483
12/16	1,665	23	1.4%	430
12/15	1,555	19	1.3%	414
Annual Growth	11.5%	22.6%		4.3%

2019 Year-End Financials

Debt ratio: —	No. of shares (mil.): 18
Return on equity: 14.24%	Dividends
Cash ($ mil.): 210	Yield: 0.0%
Current ratio: —	Payout: 21.0%
Long-term debt ($ mil.): —	Market value ($ mil.): 568

	STOCK PRICE ($) FY Close	P/E High/Low		Earnings	PER SHARE ($) Dividends	Book Value
12/19	30.12	14	11	2.33	0.49	17.61
12/18	30.15	18	13	2.14	0.41	15.49
12/17	30.30	30	22	1.08	0.34	13.91
12/16	26.85	21	11	1.30	0.29	12.82
12/15	17.21	15	13	1.17	0.18	11.92
Annual Growth	15.0%	—	—	18.8%	28.4%	10.3%

Altice USA Inc

Auditors: KPMG LLP

LOCATIONS

HQ: Altice USA Inc
1 Court Square West, Long Island City, NY 11101
Phone: 516 803-2300
Web: www.alticeusa.com

HISTORICAL FINANCIALS

Company Type: Public

Income Statement   FYE: December 31

	REVENUE ($ mil.)	NET INCOME ($ mil.)	NET PROFIT MARGIN	EMPLOYEES
12/19	9,760	138	1.4%	10,700
12/18	9,566	18	0.2%	12,185
12/17	9,326	1,520	16.3%	9,414
12/16	6,017	(832)	—	15,300
Annual Growth	17.5%	—		(11.2%)

2019 Year-End Financials

Debt ratio: 71.60%	No. of shares (mil.): 633
Return on equity: 4.50%	Dividends
Cash ($ mil.): 701	Yield: —
Current ratio: 0.70	Payout: —
Long-term debt ($ mil.): 24,249	Market value ($ mil.): 17,306

	STOCK PRICE ($) FY Close	P/E High/Low		Earnings	PER SHARE ($) Dividends	Book Value
12/19	27.34	151	82	0.21	0.00	3.76
12/18	16.52	776	487	0.03	2.04	5.36
12/17	21.23	16	8	2.18	1.29	7.77
12/16	0.00	—	—	(8,320.00)	0.00	3.23
Annual Growth	—	—	—	—	—	5.2%

ALTICOR INC.

Where there's a will (and an army of independent sales representatives) there's Amway. Operated through holding company Alticor Amway is the world's top direct-selling company with millions of individual ABOs (Amway Business Owners) pitching everything from air filters to vitamins. The company makes some 450 unique products across the categories of nutrition (which generates about half of sales) beauty and personal care and home. It is active in more than 100 countries across the globe with Asia (led by China) its largest market. Alticor is controlled by the families of Rich DeVos and Jay Van Andel who founded Amway in 1959.

Operations

Nutrition products (supplements skin care products weight management programs) account for about 50% of total Amway sales. Beauty and personal care items (makeup shampoo toothpaste) generate about a quarter of sales and home products (water and air filters cookware cleaners) contribute about 20%. The company's top products include Nutrilite supplements Artistry color cosmetics eSpring water treatment systems and XS energy drinks.

Geographic Reach

Based in Ada Michigan Amway operates in more than 100 countries. Its top markets by sales are China the US and South Korea; other leading markets include India Japan Malaysia Russia Taiwan and Thailand.

The company has manufacturing facilities farms and warehouses in Brazil China Hungary India Japan Mexico the Netherlands Poland Russia South Korea Taiwan Thailand Vietnam and the US.

Sales and Marketing

Amway's 450-plus products are marketing worldwide by more than 3 million independent distributors who purchase the products and resell them. The company provides a host of support services including personal mentors brand centers online learning tools and call centers.

Financial Performance

While privately-owned Alticor doesn't report full results Amway reported global sales of $8.6 billion in 2017 down from $8.8 billion in 2016.The company points to a challenging Chinese market for its revenue decline over the past few years

Strategy

Amway's strategy is pretty straight-forward: continue to enhance and expand its line of products to serve more markets and appeal to more customers and create tools that make selling those products easier for the 3+ million ABOs (Amway Business Owners).

In 2017 Amway introduced a new formula for its Nutrilife Double X product one of the best-selling supplements in the world that includes a phytonutrient blend designed to help the body fight free radicals. Other additions to the company's product portfolio that year include a reformulated

Essentials by Artistry skincare line and its first in-car air filtration system Atmosphere Drive. Amway also pushed its XS brand of energy drinks into new countries in 2017 including China and India with more launches planned for 2018. The company has more than 800 patents worldwide and another 250 pending applications.

Direct selling of course looks a lot different in the age of Amazon than it did some 60 years ago when Amway was founded. The company has been making significant investment in tools and technologies in recent years to enable its ABOs to better compete. It has spent some $70 million in mobile apps for ABOs including the flagship Amway MyBiz app which provides back office data and analytics. In addition Amway has boosted its own customer service capabilities with instant messaging bots and other technologies to help it handle the more than 12 million annual customer requests. Other recent initiatives include a content sharing app for ABOs in the Philippines a beauty app for customers in South Korea and a one-stop product education and purchase portal in for ABOs in China.

EXECUTIVES

President And Director; President Amway; And President Quixtar, Doug DeVos
Vice President Information Service, Richard Holwill
Executive Vice President Of Sales Amway Regions, Jim Payne
General Vice President Attorney, Scott Balfour
Vice President Regulatory Affairs And Quality Assurance, John Coyle
Vice President Internal Audit, Nick Thole
Vp Human Resources, Kelly Savage
Vice President, Louis Huey
Chairman, Steve Van Andel
Treasurer, William G Roth
Tres, Jeffery C Tuori

LOCATIONS

HQ: ALTICOR INC.
   7575 FULTON ST E, ADA, MI 493550001
Phone: 616 787-1000
Web: WWW.AMWAY.COM

PRODUCTS/OPERATIONS

2017 Sales

	% of total
Nutrition	50
Beauty & personal care	26
Home	21
Other	3
Total	**100**

Selected Brands

Nutrition
   Nutrilite
Beauty & personal care
   Artistry
   G&H
   Glister
   Satinique
Home
   Amway Home
   Atmosphere Sky
   eSpring
   iCook
Other
   XS

COMPETITORS

Avon	Melaleuca
Bath & Body Works	New Avon
Bluestem Brands	Newell Brands
Colgate-Palmolive	Nikken
Estée Lauder	Nu Skin
Forever Living	Procter & Gamble
GNC	Revlon
Herbalife Ltd.	Shaklee
Johnson & Johnson	Tupperware Brands
L'Oréal	Unilever PLC
Mary Kay	

HISTORICAL FINANCIALS

Company Type: Private

Income Statement

FYE: December 31

	REVENUE ($ mil.)	NET INCOME ($ mil.)	NET PROFIT MARGIN	EMPLOYEES
12/15	9,459	0	—	14,000
12/14	10,804	0	—	
12/13	11,754	0	—	
Annual Growth	**(10.3%)**	—	—	

Altria Group Inc

The house the Marlboro Man built Altria Group owns the largest cigarette company in the US. Altria operates through subsidiary Philip Morris USA which sells Marlboro — the world's #1-selling cigarette brand. Controlling about half of the US tobacco market Altria manufactures cigarettes under the Parliament Virginia Slims and Basic brands among many others. Altria however has diversified from solely a cigarette maker to a purveyor of cigars and pipe tobacco through John Middleton Co. and Nat Sherman; smokeless tobacco products through UST; and wine through Ste. Michelle Wine Estates. The company also owns a 10% stake in brewing giant AB InBev.

HISTORY

Philip Morris opened his London tobacco store in 1847 and by 1854 was making his own cigarettes. Morris died in 1873 and his heirs sold the firm to William Thomson just before the turn of the century. Thomson introduced his company's cigarettes to the US in 1902. American investors bought the rights to leading Philip Morris brands in 1919 and in 1925 the new company Philip Morris & Co. introduced Marlboro which targeted women smokers and produced modest sales.

When the firm's larger competitors raised their prices in 1930 Philip Morris Companies countered by introducing inexpensive cigarettes that caught on with Depression-weary consumers. By 1936 it was the fourth-biggest cigarette maker.

The firm acquired Benson & Hedges in 1954. It signed ad agency Leo Burnett which promptly initiated the Marlboro Man campaign. Under Joseph Cullman (who became president in 1957) Philip Morris experienced tremendous growth overseas. After dipping to sixth place among US tobacco companies in 1960 it rebounded at home thanks to Marlboro's growing popularity among men (Marlboro became the #1 cigarette brand in the world in 1972).

In 1970 Philip Morris bought the nation's seventh-largest brewer Miller Brewing and with aggressive marketing it vaulted to #2 among US beer makers by 1980. To protect itself against a shrinking US tobacco market in 1985 Philip Morris paid $5.6 billion for General Foods (Kool-Aid Post Stove Top). In 1988 it bought Kraft (Miracle Whip Velveeta). The next year Philip Morris joined Kraft with General Foods.

In 1994 Australian Geoffrey Bible became CEO. By late 1998 the company and its rivals had settled tobacco litigation with most states agreeing to pay about $250 billion over 25 years to receive protection from further state suits.

In 1999 Philip Morris bought three cigarette brands (L&M Chesterfield and Lark) from the Brooke Group. The US government filed a massive lawsuit against Big Tobacco and Philip Morris admitted — no kidding — that smoking increases the risk of getting cancer and other illnesses.

In 2000 Philip Morris vowed to appeal after a state court awarded $74 billion in punitive damages to Florida smokers. The court later ruled that Philip Morris Lorillard and the Liggett Group would pay at least $709 million in the case regardless of the outcome but would not have to pay damages until after the appeals are resolved. A Los Angeles jury awarded Richard Boeken $3 billion in punitive damages. The company appealed even after Boeken later agreed to reduced damages of $100 million. (Boeken died in 2002.)

In December 2000 Philip Morris completed its purchase of Nabisco Holdings for $18.9 billion. In June 2001 Philip Morris spun off Kraft Foods in what was the second-largest IPO in US history; it retained an 84% stake in the company and 97% of the voting rights.

In April 2002 CFO Louis Camilleri succeeded Bible as CEO; in September Camilleri became chairman upon Bible's retirement. In July 2002 Philip Morris sold Miller Brewing to South African Breweries for $5.6 billion ($3.6 billion in SAB stock and the assumption of $2 billion in Miller debt) in July 2002.

In the ongoing saga of tobacco-related litigation Philip Morris said it would appeal an October 2002 verdict by a California jury that ordered the company to pay $28 billion in punitive damages the most ever in an individual tobacco liability lawsuit (later reduced to $28 million). In January 2003 Philip Morris changed its name to Altria Group in an effort to distance itself from its tobacco litigation. In April a Florida appeals court threw out the state's multibillion-dollar judgment (made in 2000) against Philip Morris USA and four other US tobacco companies stating that thousands of Florida smokers could not lump their complaints together in a single case.

In March 2003 Philip Morris USA lost an Illinois lawsuit which claimed the company's use of the word "light" was misleading and violated Illinois consumer fraud laws. The judge ordered Philip Morris USA to pay damages of $10 billion and post a $12 billion bond. The Illinois Supreme Court has lowered the bond to $7 billion and agreed to hear Philip Morris USA's appeal of the original verdict.

In 2005 Altria purchased a $4.8 billion stake in Indonesia's third-largest tobacco firm PT Hanjaya Mandala Sampoerna which makes kreteks or clove cigarettes. Also in 2005 the company formed a long-term alliance with China National Tobacco Corp.

In mid-2006 Altria unseated Roger Deromedi from Kraft's top spot and appointed Irene Rosenfeld to head the company. The executive realignment was part of Altria's plan to spin off Kraft. Deromedi a 28-year Kraft veteran had been under fire for the unit's stale sales since taking over as sole CEO in 2003. Rosenfeld spent more than 20 years at Kraft and exited the firm in mid-2003 as president of Kraft Foods North America. The former chairman and CEO of Frito-Lay Rosenfeld is known for her integration expertise as well as restructuring and turning around companies.

In March 2007 Altria completed the spinoff of Kraft Foods to Altria shareholders. Also in 2007 Altria bought US cigar maker John Middleton from privately held Bradford Holdings. Based in Pennsylvania John Middleton specializes in machine-made cigars — most notably the Black & Mild brand. The deal was valued at $2.2 billion. A year later in March 2008 Altria spun off its Philip Morris International arm also to shareholders and moved its headquarters from New York City's Park Avenue to Richmond Virginia to be closer to its bread and butter operations. (As part of the move Altria in late 2007 agreed to sell the headquarters that has housed the firm since 1982 to a unit of privately held Global Holdings for some $525 million. Altria relocated about 100 of its about 500 employees in the move from New York City to Richmond.)

In January 2009 the company purchased smokeless tobacco maker UST as well as its wine business. The $11 billion deal gave Altria a significant foothold in the US smokeless tobacco market garnering popular brands Copenhagen and Skoal into Altria's fold. Following the acquisition Altria consolidated the sales forces of UST's U.S. Smokeless Tobacco brands and Philip Morris USA and relocated U.S. Smokeless Tobacco Company to Richmond Virginia. Altria has since launched a new versions of certain brands designed to compete with value-priced brands such as Reynolds American's Grizzly and Swedish Match AB's Timber Wolf.

In June 2009 the passage of the Family Smoking and Tobacco Control Act by the US Congress gave the U.S. Food and Drug Administration unprecedented authority to regulate tobacco products including the authority to regulate marketing ban candy flavorings and reduce nicotine in tobacco products.

EXECUTIVES

Evp And Chief Compliance And Administrative Officer, Martin J. (Marty) Barrington, $1,408,333 total compensation
President And Ceo Ste. Michelle Wine Estates, Theodor P. (Ted) Baseler
Svp Research Development And Regulatory Affairs And Chief Innovation Officer, James E. (Jim) Dillard, $530,833 total compensation
President And Ceo Altria Group Distribution, Craig A. Johnson, $901,667 total compensation
Coo, Howard A. Willard, $833,333 total compensation
President And Ceo U.s. Smokeless Tobacco, Brian W. Quigley
Cfo, William F. (Billy) Gifford, $640,833 total compensation
Evp And General Counsel, Denise F. Keane, $938,500 total compensation
Vp Investor Relations Altria Client Services, Clifford B. (Cliff) Fleet
President Nu Mark, Jody L. Begley
Vp And Cio, Daniel C. Cornell
Vp Finance And Controller Philip Morris Capital, John Spera
Svp Corporate Citizenship Altria Client Services, Jennifer Hunter
Vice President State Government Affairs, Henry Turner
Vice President Human Resources, Rodger Rolland
Vp Human Resources Ste. Michelle Wine Estates, Kelly Gamble
Svp Communications And Corporate Affairs Ste. Michelle Wine Estates, Kari Leitch
Senior Vice President Compliance Officer, Elizabeth Escalera
Svp Research Development And Sciences; Chief Innovation Officer, James Dillard Iii
Vice President And General Manager Marlboro, Kevin Crosthwaite
Vice President, Nicole Bielawski
Auditors: PricewaterhouseCoopers LLP

LOCATIONS

HQ: Altria Group Inc
6601 West Broad Street, Richmond, VA 23230
Phone: 804 274-2200
Web: www.altria.com

PRODUCTS/OPERATIONS

2018 Sales

	$ mil.	% of total
Smokeable products	22,297	88
Smokeless products	2,262	9
Wine	691	3
All Other	114	
Total	**25,364**	**100**

COMPETITORS

Altadis U.S.A.	Loews
British American Tobacco	North Atlantic Trading
	Ravenswood Winery
Constellation Brands	Reynolds American
E. & J. Gallo	Sebastiani Vineyards
Imperial Brands	Swedish Match
Japan Tobacco	Treasury Wine Estates

HISTORICAL FINANCIALS

Company Type: Public

Income Statement

FYE: December 31

	REVENUE ($ mil.)	NET INCOME ($ mil.)	NET PROFIT MARGIN	EMPLOYEES
12/19	25,110	(1,293)	—	7,300
12/18	25,364	6,963	27.5%	8,300
12/17	25,576	10,222	40.0%	8,300
12/16	25,744	14,239	55.3%	8,300
12/15	25,434	5,241	20.6%	8,800
Annual Growth	(0.3%)	—		(4.6%)

2019 Year-End Financials

Debt ratio: 56.91%
Return on equity: (-12.31%)
Cash ($ mil.): 2,117
Current ratio: 0.59
Long-term debt ($ mil.): 27,042

No. of shares (mil.): 1,857
Dividends
Yield: 6.5%
Payout: 348.9%
Market value ($ mil.): 92,732

	STOCK PRICE ($) FY Close	P/E High/Low		PER SHARE ($) Earnings	Dividends	Book Value
12/19	49.91	—	—	(0.70)	3.28	3.35
12/18	49.39	19	13	3.68	3.00	7.89
12/17	71.41	15	12	5.31	2.54	8.09
12/16	67.62	10	8	7.28	2.35	6.57
12/15	58.21	23	18	2.67	2.17	1.47
Annual Growth	(3.8%)	—	—	—	10.9%	22.9%

Amazon.com Inc

Amazon.com began as a bookstore and becomes a store for almost all products. Its website still offers millions of books as well as other media home furnishings clothing pet supplies office products health and beauty jewelry consumer electronics software lawn and patio grocery automotive products and hundreds of other product categories. In terms of electronics Amazon manufactures and sells electronic devices including Kindle Fire tablet Fire TV Echo Ring and other devices and develops and produces media content. The company is also the dominant cloud services provider (through Amazon Web Services or AWS)

an influential entertainment company through its video streaming operations a force to be reckoned with in grocery with its ownership of natural foods chain Whole Foods and a leader in digital personal assistant devices with Alexa and its Echo product line. Amazon.com Inc. was incorporated in 1994 in the state of Washington and reincorporated in 1996 in the state of Delaware.

HISTORY

Jeff Bezos was researching the Internet in the early 1990s for hedge fund D.E. Shaw. He realized that book sales would be a perfect fit with e-commerce because book distributors already kept meticulous electronic lists. Bezos who as a teen had dreamed of entrepreneurship in outer space took the idea to Shaw. The company passed on the idea but Bezos ran with it trekking cross country to Seattle (close to a facility owned by major book distributor Ingram) and typing up a business plan along the way.

Bezos founded Amazon.com in 1994. After months of preparation he launched a website in July 1995 (Douglas Hofstadter's Fluid Concepts and Creative Analogies was its first sale); it had sales of $20000 a week by September. Bezos and his team kept working with the site pioneering features that now seem mundane such as one-click shopping customer reviews and e-mail order verification.

Amazon went public in 1997. Moves to cement the Amazon.com brand included becoming the sole book retailer on AOL's website and Netscape's commercial channel.

In 1998 the company launched its online music and video stores and it began to sell toys and electronics. Amazon also expanded its European reach with the purchases of online booksellers in the UK and Germany and it acquired the Internet Movie Database. Bezos also expanded the company's base of online services buying Junglee (comparison shopping) and PlanetAll (address book calendar reminders).

By midyear Amazon.com had attracted so much attention that its market capitalization equaled the combined values of profitable bricks-and-mortar rivals Barnes & Noble and Borders Group even though their combined sales were far greater than the upstart's. Late that year Amazon formed a promotional link with Hoover's publisher of this profile.

After raising $1.25 billion in a bond offering early in 1999 Amazon.com began a spending spree with deals to buy all or part of several dot-coms. However some have since been sold (HomeGrocer.com) and others have gone out of business or bankrupt — Pets.com living.com (furniture). It also bought the catalog businesses of Back to Basics and Tool Crib of the North.

Amazon.com began conducting online auctions in early 1999 and partnered with venerable auction house Sotheby's. Also that year Amazon added distribution facilities including one each in England and Germany.

In 2000 the company inked a 10-year deal with Toysrus.com to set up a co-branded toy and video game store. (The partnership came to a bitter end in 2006 after Toys "R" Us sued Amazon.com when it began selling toys from other companies.) Also that year Amazon.com added foreign-language sites for France and Japan.

In 2001 Amazon cut 15% of its workforce as part of a restructuring plan that also forced a $150 million charge. That year the company also made a deal with Borders to provide inventory fulfillment content and customer service for borders.com. As part of a deal to expand their marketing partnership AOL invested $100 million in Amazon.com in 2001. Later that year Amazon purchased some assets from Egghead.com (which filed for Chapter 11 in August) and relaunched the site.

In 2002 the firm introduced clothing sales featuring hundreds of retailers including names such as The Gap Nordstrom and Lands' End. Amazon.com received accreditation from ICANN (the Internet Corporation for Assigned Names and Numbers) as an Internet domain name registrar becoming one of about 160 entities permitted to register Internet addresses.

The company launched its Search Inside the Book feature in 2003. The tool allows customers to search the text inside books for more relevant search returns. At launch the search feature covered more than 120000 books from over 190 publishers. Amazon expanded into China in 2004 with the purchase of Joyo.com. (It renamed the unit Joyo Amazon in 2007.)

In 2005 Amazon launched Amazon Prime a two-day shipping service for an annual fee of $79.

Amazon.com began testing the online dry grocery waters in 2006. It launched the Amazon Fresh delivery service for the Seattle area a year later to include perishables.

The company acquired shopping site Shopbop.com in 2006 boosting its apparel offerings. Also that year IBM filed a pair of patent infringement lawsuits alleging that Amazon.com has been violating at least five of its patents — including technologies that govern how the online retailer handles product recommendations and displays advertising — for about four years. In 2007 the two companies settled the litigation and signed a long-term patent cross-license agreement.

The Internet bookseller in November 2007 introduced the Kindle an electronic portable book reader. The launch Amazon's first foray into the tech hardware market is aimed at kindling demand for electronic books.

Also in 2007 Amazon launched Endless.com which sells shoes and accessories; Askville.com where users can solicit answers from others on the site; and the Amazon MP3 site which offers digital music free of copyright restrictions. In addition Amazon acquired audiobook publisher Brilliance Audio.

Amazon stayed focused on entertainment in 2008. The company launched Amazon Video On Demand a service that gives customers the option to stream or download ad-free digital movies and TV shows on Macs or PCs. It also purchased AbeBooks an online retailer of more than 110 million primarily used rare and out-of-print books as well as Shelfari a social-networking site for booklovers. Additionally Amazon.com sold its UK and German online DVD rental services to Internet movie-rental company LOVEFiLM International in exchange for stock. The deal gave Amazon about a 40% stake in LOVEFiLM.

Shopping was also at the top of Amazon's list in 2008. In May the company invested in The Talk Market a user-generated TV Shopping Channel. In June Amazon launched an online office supplies store and sewed up the acquisition of the online fabrics retailer Fabrics.com.

In June 2009 Amazon agreed to pay Toys "R" Us $51 million to settle a dispute dating back to 2004. The settlement was related to a partnership that gave the toy seller exclusive rights to supply some of the toys on Amazon's site. In November Amazon completed its $888 million acquisition of shoe e-tailer Zappos.com — the #1 online shoe and apparel retailer. (Besides footwear and clothing Zappos also sells handbags housewares and beauty products.) The purchase allowed Amazon to boost its sales and expand its products portfolio by leveraging Zappos' widely recognized customer service expertise.

In mid-2010 Amazon acquired Woot Inc. a pioneer in the deal-of-the-day genre of online retailing.

While neither Amazon or Woot would disclose the selling price reports valued the deal at about $110 million in cash.

In January 2011 Amazon completed its move to a new corporate headquarters in Seattle's South Lake Union neighborhood. Amazon also made several acquisitions that year. The company acquired the remaining shares it didn't already own in LOVEFiLM International. It purchased a pair of UK companies: online book seller The Book Depository and digital agency Pushbutton (later folding the operation into its Amazon Development Centre in London). The behemoth also picked up voice-to-text startup Yap based in Charlotte North Carolina that year.

Kiva Systems which Amazon bought in 2012 was purchased to provide the firm with a boost in automation capabilities. Amazon picked up some former talent including Amazon ex Dave Schappell when it bought online education marketplace Teachstreet and shuttered the site in 2012. Acquiring England's Evi and its namesake cloud-based Artificial Intelligence expertise in 2012 offered Amazon a leg up in answer engine technology.

To extend the reach of its Kindle range Amazon in 2013 acquired Poland's IVONA Software. Months after being bought by Amazon in 2013 social cataloging company Goodreads announced it had amassed some 20 million members. In 2013 Amazon also purchased electrowetting display panel expert Liquavista from Samsung Electronics which had held the company for fewer than three years.

Investments in 2014 include acquiring the .buy domain for nearly $4.6 million. Besides the domain purchase Amazon has been focused on games. It acquired Silent Hill: Homecoming video game developer Double Helix Games based in Irvine California. Its newest release Strider is available on five platforms. Amazon also bought cloud-based digital comics platform ComiXology in 2014. In late 2014 Amazon purchased game-streaming site Twitch which boasted 55 million monthly active users after talks with Google turned to anti-trust concerns.

EXECUTIVES

Ceo Worldwide Consumer Business, Jeffrey A. (Jeff) Wilke, age 54, $175,000 total compensation
Chairman President And Ceo, Jeffrey P. (Jeff) Bezos, age 57, $81,840 total compensation
Ceo Amazon Web Services, Andrew R. (Andy) Jassy, age 53, $175,000 total compensation
Svp And Cfo, Brian T. Olsavsky, $160,000 total compensation
Vice President, Sharon Chiarella
Vice President Home Improvements, John Witham
Vice President, Seth Dallaire
Vice President, David Criscione
Vice President Worldwide Discovery, Kim Rachmeler
Vice President E Commerce Platform Services, Gene Pope
Vice President Information Technology, Kathryn Giorgianni
Vice President Corporate Sales Development, Robert Saltzman
National Account Manager, Cherie Ponselle
Vice President Logistics, Michael Indresano
Vice President Global Inventory Platform, Jason Murray
Vice President Finance Softlines, Rebecca Hollingsworth
Vice President, Adrian Cockcroft
Senior Vice President, Steve Kessel
Vice President Commerce Platform, Diane Gonzalez

Treasurer, Kenneth Helton
Auditors: Ernst & Young LLP

LOCATIONS

HQ: Amazon.com Inc
410 Terry Avenue North, Seattle, WA 98109-5210
Phone: 206 266-1000   **Fax:** 206 266-1821
Web: www.amazon.com

2018 Sales

	$ mil.	% of total
North America	141,366	61
International	65,866	28
AWS	25,655	11
Total	**232,887**	**100**

2018 Sales

	$ mil.	% of total
US	160,146	69
Germany	19,881	9
UK	14,524	6
Japan	13,829	6
Other countries	24,507	10
Total	**232,887**	**100**

PRODUCTS/OPERATIONS

2018 Sales

	$ mil.	% of total
Online stores	122,987	53
Third-party seller services	42,745	18
AWS	25,655	11
Physical stores	17,224	8
Subscription services	14,168	6
Other	10,108	4
Total	**232,887**	**100**

Selected Departments

Apparel shoes and jewelry
Books
  Books
  Kindle e-books
  Textbooks
  Magazines
Computers and office
  Computers and accessories
  Computer components
  Office products and supplies
  PC games
  Software
Digital downloads
  Amazon shorts
  Game downloads
  Kindle Store
  MP3 downloads
Electronics
  Audio TV and home theater
  Camera photo and video
  Car electronics and GPS
  Cell phones and service
  Home appliances
  MP3 and media players
  Musical instruments
  Video games
Grocery health and beauty
  Beauty
  Diapers
  Gourmet food
  Grocery
  Health and personal care
  Natural and organic
Home and garden
  Bedding and bath
  Furniture and decor
  Home appliances
  Home improvement
  Kitchen and dining
  Patio lawn and garden
  Pet supplies
  Sewing craft and hobby
  Vacuums and storage
Kindle
  Books
  Blogs
  Magazines
  Newspapers
Movies music and games

Blu-ray
Movies and TV
Music
Musical instruments
Video games
Video On Demand
Sports and outdoors
Action sports
Camping and hiking
Cycling
Exercise and fitness
Fan gear
Golf
Team sports
Tools auto and industrial
Automotive
Home improvement
Industrial and scientific
Lighting and electrical
Motorcycle and ATV
Outdoor power equipment
Plumbing fixtures
Power and hand tools
Toys kids and baby
Apparel (kids and baby)
Baby
Books
Movies
Music
Software
Toys and games
Video games

Selected Operations

A9.com (search technology development)
Amazon.ca (Canada)
Amazon.cn (China)
Amazon.de (Germany)
Amazon.fr (France)
Amazon.co.jp (Japan)
Amazon.co.uk (UK)
Audible (audiobooks and other recorded content)
Endless (shoes and handbags)
Internet Movie Database (IMDb)
IVONA Software
Joyo (China)
LOVEFiLM International Ltd.
Whole Foods Market (grocery stores)
Woot.com (US)
Zappos.com (US)

COMPETITORS

Alibaba Group	Netflix
Costco Wholesale	Overstock.com
Google	Sprouts
HSN	Target Corporation
Home Depot	Wal-Mart
Kroger	Wayfair
Lowe's	eBay
Microsoft	

HISTORICAL FINANCIALS

Company Type: Public

Income Statement   FYE: December 31

	REVENUE ($ mil.)	NET INCOME ($ mil.)	NET PROFIT MARGIN	EMPLOYEES
12/20	386,064	21,331	5.5%	1,298,000
12/19	280,522	11,588	4.1%	798,000
12/18	232,887	10,073	4.3%	647,500
12/17	177,866	3,033	1.7%	566,000
12/16	135,987	2,371	1.7%	341,400
Annual Growth	29.8%	73.2%	—	39.6%

2020 Year-End Financials

Debt ratio: 9.91%	No. of shares (mil.): 503
Return on equity: 27.37%	Dividends
Cash ($ mil.): 84,396	Yield: —
Current ratio: 1.05	Payout: —
Long-term debt ($ mil.): 31,816	Market value ($ mil.): 1,638,236

	STOCK PRICE ($) FY Close	P/E High/Low	PER SHARE ($) Earnings	Dividends	Book Value
12/20	3,256.93	83 39	41.83	0.00	185.69
12/19	1,847.84	86 64	23.01	0.00	124.62
12/18	1,501.97	99 57	20.14	0.00	88.69
12/17	1,169.47	189 119	6.15	0.00	57.25
12/16	749.87	169 96	4.90	0.00	40.43
Annual Growth	44.4%	— —	70.9%	—	46.4%

Ambac Financial Group, Inc.

Ambac has scaled back in a major way. Holding company Ambac Financial operates through subsidiaries including its flagship unit Ambac Assurance Everspan Financial Guarantee and Ambac Assurance UK. The businesses offered financial guarantees and related services to customers around the world. Ambac Assurance guaranteed public finance structured finance and international finance obligations. Its US account is the highest premiums which accounts for about 75%.

Operations

In addition to its core financial guarantee offerings in better days Ambac also insured infrastructure and utility finance deals internationally. Its Ambac Financial Services unit offered interest rate swaps credit swaps and investment management primarily to states and municipal authorities tied to their bond financing.

Public finance is its highest premiums which accounts for 40% followed by International finance which accounts for about 30% and the remaining accounts for accelerated earnings and structured finance.

About 45% of sales were generated from net premiums around over 40% came from total net investment income and net investment gains and income on variable interest entities account for the rest.

Geographic Reach

Ambac's run-off operations primarily bring in revenues from the US market which accounts for about 75% of revenues. The company also has international operations (also in runoff) in markets including the UK (some 25% of revenues) France Austria Germany and Italy.

Its corporate headquarters is located in New York and also maintains an office in London England.

Financial Performance

Ambac's revenue in 2019 amounted to $496 million a 3% increase from $511 million in 2018.

The company recorded a net loss of $216 million in 2019 as opposed to a net income of $267 million in the previous year.

Cash and cash equivalents at the end of the year were $81 million $2 million less than the previous year. Cash used by operating activities was $311 million. Investing activities provided $1 billion primarily from sales of bonds while financing activities used $691 million primarily for payments of consolidated VIE liabilities.

Strategy

Ambac has been focused on and continues to progress all key strategic priorities specifically active runoff of Ambac Assurance and its subsidiaries through transaction terminations policy commutations reinsurance settlements and restructurings

with a focus on its watch list credits and known and potential future adversely classified credits that will improve risk profile and maximizing the risk-adjusted return on invested assets; ongoing rationalization of Ambac's capital and liability structures; loss recovery through active litigation management and exercise of contractual and legal rights; ongoing review and adjustments focused on improving the effectiveness and efficiency of Ambac's operating platform; and evaluation of opportunities in certain business sectors that meet acceptable criteria that will generate long-term stockholder value with attractive risk-adjusted returns.

HISTORY

Mortgage Guaranty Insurance Corporation (MGIC) in 1971 founded American Municipal Bond Assurance Corporation (Ambac Indemnity) in Milwaukee. That year Ambac wrote the very first municipal bond insurance policy — for a bond to fund a medical building and a sewage treatment facility in Juneau Alaska. New York City's 1975 moratorium on debt payments helped make the new product more attractive. The company wrote the first insurance policies for mutual funds (1977) and secondary market municipal bonds (1983). In 1981 Ambac moved to New York; four years later it became a Citibank subsidiary. It went public in 1991.

In 1995 Ambac and rival MBIA allied to offer bond insurance overseas. Two years later the company formed a UK subsidiary to serve Europe. In recognition of the growing market the joint venture was amended in 2000 to provide for individual operations by the two partners in Europe though they continued to reinsure each other there and to work jointly in Japan. Ambac went on a buying spree in 1996 and 1997 buying the investment advisory and broker dealer operations of Cadre and Construction Loan Insurance (renamed Connie Lee Holdings) a guarantor of college bonds and hospital infrastructure bonds.

In 1998 as Ambac lost share in the US municipal bond market because it declined to cut premiums the company began concentrating on asset-backed securities and international bonds. Two years later Ambac entered the Japanese market through a joint venture with Yasuda Fire & Marine.

In late 2010 after missing a scheduled interest payment and failing to reach an agreement for a prepackaged bankruptcy proceeding with its creditors the company voluntarily filed for Chapter 11 bankruptcy protection. Through the filing Ambac hoped to restructure more than $1.6 billion in outstanding debt. The company also haggled with the IRS over $700 million in allegedly improper tax refunds received between 2003 and 2008.

The bankruptcy court approved a plan of reorganization for Ambac in 2012 and the plan went into effect the following year.

EXECUTIVES

Senior Managing Director Chief Accounting Officer And Controller, Robert B. Eisman, age 52, $500,000 total compensation

President And Ceo Ambac Financial Group And Ambac Assurance Corporation, Claude L. LeBlanc, age 55

Senior Managing Director Cfo And Treasurer, David Trick, age 49, $770,000 total compensation

President Ceo And Director, Nader Tavakoli, age 61, $1,800,000 total compensation

Senior Managing Director And General Counsel, Stephen M. Ksenak, age 54, $525,000 total compensation

Senior Managing Director Restructuring And Corporate Development, David Barranco, age 49

Senior Managing Director Cio And Chief
  Administrative Office, Michael Reilly, age 63
Assistant Vice President Business Applications
  And Support, Sarbah Arthur
Vice President Automation Support, Alexandre
  Duarte
Assistant Vice President And Closing Coordinator,
  Yolanda Ortiz
Vice President, Valerie Anderson
Assistant Vice President, John Osmanzai
First Vp Housing Group, Kelly Wimmer
Vice President, Gary Stein
First Vice President, Sunil Rao
Vice President Of Technology, Scott Brown
Assistant Vice President Risk Operations, Pranay
  Nadkarni
Vice President Of Finance, Michael Klaassens
Assistant Vice President Finance, Chris Dudonis
Vice President Of Technology, Charu Kanbur
Avp In Technology, Venka Korsapati
Assistant Vice President Payroll, Yanira Vergara
First Vice President Credit Risk Management,
  Robert Bose
Vice President Of Finance, David Harris
Vice President, Regina Watkins
First Vice President, Sulexan Chery
Vice President, Alice Wong
First Vice President, Roza Dimitrova
Vice President, Veronica Prasad
First Vice President, David Park
Chairman, Jeffrey S. Stein
Board Member, Ian Haft
Member Board Of Directors, Alexander Greene
Auditors: KPMG LLP

LOCATIONS

HQ: Ambac Financial Group, Inc.
  One World Trade Center, New York, NY 10007
Phone: 212 658-7470   Fax: 212 208 3414
Web: www.ambac.com

2015 Permiums by Geographic

	$ mil.	% of total
United States	229	73
United Kingdom	68	22
Other international	14	5
Total	312	100

PRODUCTS/OPERATIONS

2015 Net Premiums

	$ mil.	% of total
Accelerated earnings	137	44
Public Finance	97	31
International Finance	43	14
Structured Finance	34	11
Total	312	100

2015 Sales

	$ mil.	% of total
Net premiums earned	312	44
Total net investment income	266	37
Net realized investment gains	53	8
Net change in fair value of credit derivatives	41	6
Income (loss) on variable interest entities	31	4
Other income	7	1
Net other-than-temporary impairment losses recognized in earnings	(25.6)	-
Derivative products	(42.5)	-
Total	644	100

Selected Services

Adversely Classified Credit
Amendment Waiver and Consen
Credit Risk Management (CRM)
International Finance Insured Portfolio
U.S. Public Finance Insured Portfolio
U.S. Structured Finance

COMPETITORS

Assured Guaranty   MBIA
FGIC

HISTORICAL FINANCIALS

Company Type: Public

Income Statement

	ASSETS ($ mil.)	NET INCOME ($ mil.)	INCOME AS % OF ASSETS	EMPLOYEES
				FYE: December 31
12/19	13,320	(216)	—	104
12/18	14,588	267	1.8%	113
12/17	23,192	(328)	—	124
12/16	22,635	74	0.3%	154
12/15	23,728	493	2.1%	171
Annual Growth	(13.4%)	—	—	(11.7%)

2019 Year-End Financials

Debt ratio: 55.38%   No. of shares (mil.): 45
Return on equity: (-14.08%)   Dividends
Cash ($ mil.): 24   Yield: —
Current ratio: —   Payout: —
Long-term debt ($ mil.): —   Market value ($ mil.): 983

	STOCK PRICE ($) FY Close	P/E High/Low	Earnings	Dividends	Book Value
12/19	21.57	— —	(4.69)	0.00	32.42
12/18	17.24	5 3	3.99	0.00	35.12
12/17	15.98	— —	(7.25)	0.00	30.52
12/16	22.50	16 7	1.64	0.00	37.94
12/15	14.09	3 1	10.72	0.00	37.41
Annual Growth	11.2%	— —	—	—	(3.5%)

AMCAP FUND INC

EXECUTIVES

President, Marry Clemeson
Treas, Mary C Hall
Sr V Pres, Gordon Crawford
Sr V Pres, Paul G Haaga Jr
SEC, Julie Williams
Principal, Walter Stern

LOCATIONS

HQ: AMCAP FUND INC
  333 S HOPE ST STE LEVB, LOS ANGELES, CA
  900713003
Phone: 213 486-9200
Web: WWW.CAPITALGROUP.COM

HISTORICAL FINANCIALS

Company Type: Private

Income Statement

	ASSETS ($ mil.)	NET INCOME ($ mil.)	INCOME AS % OF ASSETS	EMPLOYEES
				FYE: February 28
02/19	65,322	1,248	1.9%	300
02/18	64,019	9,994	15.6%	—
02/16	44,148	(2)	—	—
Annual Growth	14.0%	—	—	—

Amerant Bancorp Inc

Auditors: RSM US LLP

LOCATIONS

HQ: Amerant Bancorp Inc
  220 Alhambra Circle, Coral Gables, FL 33134
Phone: 305 460-4038
Web: www.mercantilbank.com

HISTORICAL FINANCIALS

Company Type: Public

Income Statement

	ASSETS ($ mil.)	NET INCOME ($ mil.)	INCOME AS % OF ASSETS	EMPLOYEES
				FYE: December 31
12/19	7,985	51	0.6%	829
12/18	8,124	45	0.6%	911
12/17	8,436	43	0.5%	939
12/16	8,434	23	0.3%	
12/15	0	15		
Annual Growth	—	35.9%	—	—

2019 Year-End Financials

Debt ratio: 16.62%   No. of shares (mil.): 43
Return on equity: 6.49%   Dividends
Cash ($ mil.): 121   Yield: —
Current ratio: —   Payout: —
Long-term debt ($ mil.): —   Market value ($ mil.): 940

	STOCK PRICE ($) FY Close	P/E High/Low	Earnings	Dividends	Book Value
12/19	21.79	19 11	1.20	0.00	19.35
12/18	13.01	54 6	1.08	0.94	16.76
Annual Growth	13.8%	— —	2.7%	—	3.7%

American Airlines Group Inc

American Airlines Group (AAG) is the largest airline in the US and one of the largest in the world. The company's mainline carriers provide scheduled air transportation along with its group of regional subsidiaries and third-party regional carriers operating as American Eagle. It also offers freight and mail services through its cargo division. In all American operates an average of 6800 flights daily to more than 365 destinations in more than 60 countries. It operates more than 940 mainline aircraft and approximately 605 regional aircraft. American Airlines Group is also a founding member of oneworld alliance where member carriers share airport lounge facilities and offer interconnected loyalty programs. About quarter of passenger sales of American Airlines Group is generated from the US.

Operations

American Airlines Group are managed as a single business unit that provides scheduled air transportation for passenger and cargo through its mainline carrier network as well as through regional carriers. Its passenger segment accounts for more than 90% of total sales and operates more than 940 aircraft. Regional operations provide services under the "American Eagle" brand. American Eagle carriers include wholly-owned subsidiaries Envoy PSA and Piedmont. Third-party regional carriers including Republic Mesa Compass and SkyWest.

The company's Cargo segment (accounts for more than 1% of total sales) also provides a wide range of freight and mail services with facilities and interline connections available across the globe.

Other operating revenue associated with American Airlines Group airport clubs and loyalty program generate more than 5% of sales.

Geographic Reach

Headquartered in Fort Worth TX American Airlines Group flies to more than 365 destinations in more than 60 countries. Its hubs are located in Charlotte Chicago Dallas/Fort Worth Los Angeles Miami New York Philadelphia Phoenix and Washington DC with international services to Canada Central and South America Asia Europe Australia and New Zealand. About 75% of sales on passenger sales are generated in the US. More than 10% are generated in Latin America exceeding 10% are generated in Atlantic and about 5% in the Pacific.

Sales and Marketing

American Airlines Group sells its tickets through several distribution channels including its website (www.aa.com) reservations centers and third-party distribution channels. Its loyalty program offers rewards to travelers for their continued patronage. Advertising expense was $129 million $128 million and $135 million for the years ended December 31 2019 2018 and 2017 respectively.

Financial Performance

Except in 2016 American Airline's revenue has been soaring higher every year. 2019 revenue is 12% higher than 2015.

In 2019 the company's revenue rose 3% ($1.2 billion) from $44.5 billion to $45.8 billion. This was primarily due to the $1.3 billion increase in passenger segment which was offset by the cargo segment.

Net income rose from $1.4 billion in 2018 to $1.78 billion in 2019.

Cash at the end of fiscal 2019 was $290 million an increase of $4 million from the prior year. Cash from operations contributed $3.8 billion to the coffers while investing activities used $2.2 billion mainly for capital expenditures. Financing activities used another $1.6 billion for dividends to stockholders and the company's stock repurchase program.

Strategy

An important part of our strategy to expand our network has been to expand our commercial relationships with other airlines such as by entering into global alliance joint business and codeshare relationships and in one recent instance involving China Southern Airlines Company Limited (China Southern Airlines) by making a significant equity investment in another airline in connection with initiating such a commercial relationship. We may explore similar non-controlling investments in and joint ventures and strategic alliances with other carriers as part of our global business strategy.

Company Background

In 2011 American Airlines' parent company AMR Corporation filed for bankruptcy. It emerged from Chapter 11 in late 2013 and at the same time merged with rival US Airways in a mega deal worth $11 billion. The milestone transaction created the world's largest airline. The combined entity formed the American Airlines Group and is led by former US Airways CEO Doug Parker.

HISTORY

In 1929 Sherman Fairchild created a New York City holding company called the Aviation Corporation (AVCO) combining some 85 small airlines in 1930 to create American Airways. In 1934 the company had its first dose of financial trouble after the government suspended private airmail for months. Corporate raider E. L. Cord took over and named the company American Airlines.

EXECUTIVES

Evp Corporate Affairs, Stephen L. (Steve) Johnson, age 63, $600,936 total compensation

Chairman And Ceo, W. Douglas (Doug) Parker, age 58, $1 total compensation

Evp People And Communications, Elise R. Eberwein, age 54

Evp And Cfo, Derek J. Kerr, age 55, $600,936 total compensation

President, Robert D. Isom, age 56, $641,306 total compensation

Evp And Cio, Maya Leibman, age 55, $600,936 total compensation

Evp And Chief Integration Officer, Beverly K. Goulet, age 65

Vice President People Services, Jocelyn Moore

Auditors: KPMG LLP

LOCATIONS

HQ: American Airlines Group Inc
 1 Skyview Drive, Fort Worth, TX 76155
Phone: 817 963-1234   **Fax:** 817 967-9641
Web: www.aa.com

2017 Sales

	$ mil.	% of total
DOT Domestic	29,612	70
DOT Latin America	5,422	13
DOT Atlantic	5,059	12
DOT Pacific	2,114	5
Total	**42,207**	**100**

Selected Hub Locations

Charlotte
Chicago
Dallas/Fort Worth (DFW)
Los Angeles
Miami
New York City
Philadelphia
Phoenix
Washington DC

PRODUCTS/OPERATIONS

2017 Sales

	$ mil.	% of total
Mainline passenger	29,238	69
Regional passenger	6,895	16
Cargo	800	2
Other	5,274	13
Total	**42,207**	**100**

Selected Carriers

Regional Subsidiaries
 Envoy
 PSA
 Piedmont
Regional Third-Party Carriers
 Republic
 Mesa
 Compass
 ExpressJet
 SkyWest
 Trans States

COMPETITORS

Air France-KLM	Hawaiian Holdings
Alaska Air	JetBlue
Delta Air Lines	Lufthansa
Echo Global	Southwest Airlines
FedEx	Spirit Airlines
Frontier Airlines	UPS
Greyhound	

HISTORICAL FINANCIALS

Company Type: Public

Income Statement

FYE: December 31

	REVENUE ($ mil.)	NET INCOME ($ mil.)	NET PROFIT MARGIN	EMPLOYEES
12/19	45,768	1,686	3.7%	133,700
12/18	44,541	1,412	3.2%	128,900
12/17	42,207	1,919	4.5%	126,600
12/16	40,180	2,676	6.7%	122,300
12/15	40,990	7,610	18.6%	118,500
Annual Growth	**2.8%**	**(31.4%)**	**—**	**3.1%**

2019 Year-End Financials

Debt ratio: 40.53%	No. of shares (mil.): 428
Return on equity: —	Dividends
Cash ($ mil.): 438	Yield: 1.3%
Current ratio: 0.45	Payout: 11.2%
Long-term debt ($ mil.): 21,454	Market value ($ mil.): 12,281

	STOCK PRICE ($) FY Close	P/E High/Low		Earnings	PER SHARE ($) Dividends	Book Value
12/19	28.68	10	6	3.79	0.40	(0.28)
12/18	32.11	19	10	3.03	0.40	(0.37)
12/17	52.03	14	10	3.90	0.40	8.26
12/16	46.69	10	5	4.81	0.40	7.46
12/15	42.35	5	3	11.07	0.40	9.02
Annual Growth	**(9.3%)**	—	—	**(23.5%)**	**(0.0%)**	—

AMERICAN ASSETS TRUST, INC.

American Assets Trust is a self-administered real estate investment trust (REIT) that owns develops and operates upscale retail office and residential property mostly in Northern and Southern California but also in Oregon Washington Texas and Hawaii. Its approximately 3.1 million square foot portfolio includes more than 10 shopping centers about 10l of office buildings a 369-room hotel and retail complex and more than five multi-family residential properties. Its tenants include SalesForce Autodesk the Veterans Benefits Administration and well-known retailers such as Kmart Lowe's Sports Authority Old Navy and Vons. Formed in 1967 as American Assets the firm went public in 2011.

Operations

The REIT leases retail office and multifamily properties as well as hotels. Its retail portfolio which made up of about 30% of its revenue during 2019 spans about 3 million rentable square feet while its office holdings (about 40% of revenue) measure about 3.4 million square feet.

In addition American Assets Trust mixed-use property (more than 15% of revenue) the Embassy Suites at Waikiki Beach Walk in Honolulu is a 369-room-all-suite hotel with approximately 97000 square feet of accompanying retail space. The

REIT generates the rest of its revenue from its more than 2100 multifamily units in San Diego and Imperial Beach California.

Geographic Reach

San Diego-based American Assets Trust's primary markets include San Diego; the San Francisco Bay area; Portland Oregon; Bellevue Washington; and Oahu Hawaii. More than 60% of its property by square footage was located in Southern and Northern California at the end of 2019 while about 15% of its property space was in Oregon. The rest of its properties were in Hawaii (nearly 10% of square footage) Texas (about 10%) and Washington state (more than 5%).

Sales and Marketing

The REIT's largest anchored tenants by revenue in 2019 included: Lowe's Nordstrom Rack Sprouts Farmers Market.

Financial Performance

America Assets Trusts' annual revenues have risen 33% since 2015 as its property valuations have appreciated and have commanded higher rental rates. Net income declined for the same period but bounced back in 2019.

The REIT's revenue climbed 11% to $366.7 million in 2019 thanks to property revenue increasing by $35.9 million and rental revenue increasing by $34.3 million.

Net income increased by $26 million in 2019 mainly due to higher revenue.

Cash at the end of 2019 was $109.5 million. Net cash provided by operating activities was $153.8 million and cash provided by financing activities was $497.5 million. Investing activities used $599.2 million for acquisition of real estate and capital expenditures.

Strategy

The company's primary business objectives are to increase operating cash flows generate long-term growth and maximize stockholder value. Specifically it pursues the following strategies to achieve these objectives:

Capitalizing on acquisition opportunities in high-barrier-to-entry markets by focusing on markets that generally are characterized by strong supply and demand characteristics including high barriers to entry and diverse industry bases that appeal to institutional investors;

Repositioning/redevelopment and development of office retail and multifamily properties by pursuing ground-up development of undeveloped land where it believes it can generate attractive risk-adjusted returns;

Disciplined capital recycling strategy by pursuing an efficient asset allocation strategy that maximizes the value of its investments by selectively disposing of properties whose returns appear to have been maximized and redeploying capital into acquisition repositioning redevelopment and development opportunities with higher return prospects in each case in a manner that is consistent with its qualification as a REIT; and

Proactive asset and property management by actively manage its properties employ targeted leasing strategies leverage its existing tenant relationships and focus on reducing operating expenses to increase occupancy rates at its properties attract high-quality tenants and increase property cash flows thereby enhancing the value of its properties.

Mergers and Acquisitions

In 2019 American Assets Trust has successfully closed on the acquisition of La Jolla Commons consisting of two trophy office towers an entitled development parcel and two parking structures located in the preeminent University Town Center submarket of San Diego California. The purchase price of $525 million less a seller credit of approximately $11.5 million was paid with a combination of cash on hand and funds drawn against the Company's existing credit facility.

Company Background

American Assets Trust went public in January 2011 with an offering valued at about $564 million. (About $4 million of that figure went to chairman Ernest Rady who controlled the company prior to its IPO.) The IPO proceeds were used to repay debt and to purchase and renovate property.

EXECUTIVES

Chairman President And Ceo, Ernest S. Rady, $259,616 total compensation
Ceo And President, John W. Chamberlain
Evp And Cfo, Robert F. Barton, $373,846 total compensation
Vp Construction And Development, Jerry Gammieri, $186,923 total compensation
Vp Retail Properties, Chris Sullivan
Vp Office Properties, Jim Durfey
Vp And Regional Manager Portland, Wade Lange
Auditors: ERNST & YOUNG LLP SAN DIEGO

LOCATIONS

HQ: AMERICAN ASSETS TRUST, INC.
 11455 EL CMINO REAL STE 2, SAN DIEGO, CA 92130
Phone: 858 350-2600
Web: WWW.AMERICANASSETSTRUST.COM

2015 Properties

	No.
Southern California	7
Northern California	4
Hawaii	3
Oregon	2
Texas	1
Washington	1
Total	**18**

PRODUCTS/OPERATIONS

2015 Sales

	$ mil.	% of total
Rental Income		
Retail	97	35
Office	92	34
Mixed-Use	53	19
Multifamily	18	7
Other Property Income	13	5
Total	**275**	**100**

Selected Tenants

Alliant International University
Autodesk Inc.
California Bank & Trust
Caradigm USA LLC
Drug Enforcement Administration
Foodland Super Market
HDR Engineering
Inome Inc.
Insurance Company of the West
Integra Telecom Holdings
Kmart
Lowe's
Marshalls
McDermott Will & Emery
Nordstrom Rack
Officemax
Old Navy
Portland Energy Conservation
Quiksilver
salesforce.com inc.
Sports Authority
Sprouts Farmers Market
Treasury Call Center
Veterans Benefits Administration
Vons

Selected Properties

Retail
 Alamo Quarry
 Carmel County Plaza
 Carmel Mountain Plaza
 Del Monte Shopping Center
 Lomas Sante Fe Plaza
 Rancho Carmel Plaza
 Solana Beach Towne Centre
 South Bay Market Place
 The Shops at Kalakaua
 Waikele Center
Mixed-use
 Waikiki Beach Walk - Hotel
 Waikiki Beach Walk - Retail
Multi-family
 Imperial Beach Gardens
 Loma Palisades
 Mariner's Point
 Santa Fe Park RV Resort
Office
 Fireman's Fund Headquarters
 Solana Beach Corporate Centre
 The Landmark at One Market
 Torrey Reserve Campus
 Valencia Corporate Center

COMPETITORS

CBL & Associates	Macerich
Properties	Simon Property Group
GGP	Taubman Centers
Hersha Hospitality	

HISTORICAL FINANCIALS

Company Type: Private

Income Statement

	ASSETS ($ mil.)	NET INCOME ($ mil.)	INCOME AS % OF ASSETS	EMPLOYEES
12/17	2,259	40	1.8%	113
12/16	1,986	45	2.3%	—
12/15	1,978	53	2.7%	—
12/14	1,941	31	1.6%	—
Annual Growth	5.2%	8.8%	—	—

FYE: December 31

AMERICAN BALANCED FUND, INC.

EXECUTIVES

Chb-Ceo, Robert G O'Donnell
Pres, Paul G Haaga Jr
V Pres, Hilda L Applbaum
Sr V Pres, Abner Goldstine
Sr V Pres, John H Smet
V Pres, J Dale Harvey
V Pres, Jeffrey T Lager
Asst Treas, R Marcia Gould
SEC, Patrick F Quan
Auditors: DELOITTE & TOUCHE LLP COSTA M

LOCATIONS

HQ: AMERICAN BALANCED FUND, INC.
 1 MARKET, SAN FRANCISCO, CA 941051596
Phone: 707 864-3945

HISTORICAL FINANCIALS

Company Type: Private

Company Type: Private

Income Statement   FYE: December 31

	ASSETS ($ mil.)	NET INCOME ($ mil.)	INCOME AS % OF ASSETS	EMPLOYEES
12/18	129,090	2,254	1.7%	9
12/17	128,462	23,932	18.6%	—
12/15	87,394	4,903	5.6%	—
12/00	6,203	832	13.4%	—
Annual Growth	18.4%	5.7%	—	—

American Electric Power Co Inc

Serving markets in Ohio Michigan Indiana and other midwestern states American Electric Power (AEP) is one of the largest power generators and distributors in the US. The holding company owns the nation's largest electricity transmission system and distribution lines comprising a network of more than 227000 miles. AEP's electric utilities boasts 5.4 million customers in about 10 states and has about 21100 megawatts of largely coal-fired generating capacity although it is adding renewable sources to its generation portfolio. AEP is also a top wholesale energy company.

HISTORY

In 1906 Richard Breed Sidney Mitchell and Henry Doherty set up American Gas & Electric (AG&E) in New York to buy 23 utilities from Philadelphia's Electric Company of America. With properties in seven northeastern US states AG&E began acquiring and merging small electric properties creating the predecessors of Ohio Power (1911) Kentucky Power (1919) and Appalachian Power (1926). AG&E also bought the predecessor of Indiana Michigan Power (1925).

By 1926 the company was operating in Indiana Kentucky Michigan Ohio Virginia and West Virginia. In 1935 AG&E engineer Philip Sporn later known as the Henry Ford of power introduced his high-voltage high-velocity circuit breaker. AG&E picked up Kingsport Power in 1938.

Becoming president in 1947 Sporn began an ambitious building program that continued through the 1960s. Plants designed by AG&E (renamed American Electric Power in 1958) were among the world's most efficient and electric rates stayed 25%-38% below the national average.

AEP bought Michigan Power in 1967 six years after Donald Cook succeeded Sporn as president. Cook who refused to attach scrubbers to the smokestacks of coal-fired plants was criticized in the early 1970s by environmental protesters. AEP's first nuclear plant named in Cook's honor went on line in Michigan in 1975. He retired in 1976.

The firm moved from New York to Columbus Ohio in 1980 after buying what is now Columbus Southern Power (formed in 1883). It set up AEP Generating in 1982 to provide power to its electric utilities.

AEP began converting its second nuke Zimmer to coal in 1984. In 1992 AEP finally began installing scrubbers at its coal-fired Gavin plant in Ohio after being ordered to comply with the Clean Air Act. It also cleaned up its image by planting millions of trees in 1996.

The company formed AEP Communications after Congress passed the Telecommunications Act of 1996. The next year AEP jumped into the UK's deregulated electric market; AEP and New Century Energies (now Xcel Energy) bought Yorkshire Electricity (later Yorkshire Power Group) for $2.8 billion. However a $109 million UK windfall tax on the transaction — and increased wholesale competition — hurt AEP's bottom line.

As the normally staid electric industry succumbed to merger mania AEP agreed in 1997 to buy Central and South West (CSW) of Texas in a $6.6 billion deal. AEP's sales would nearly double and CSW was to bring its own UK utility SEEBOARD and other overseas holdings.

In 1998 AEP bought a 20% stake in Pacific Hydro an Australian power producer and CitiPower an Australian electric distribution company. AEP also bought Equitable Resources' Louisiana natural gas midstream operations including an intrastate pipeline. In 1999 China's Pushan Power Plant (70%-owned by AEP) began operations. Environmental concerns resurfaced that year when the EPA sued the utility alleging its old coal-powered plants which had been grandfathered from the Clean Air Act had been quietly upgraded to extend their lives.

Regulators approved the company's acquisition of CSW in 2000 but AEP had to agree to relinquish control of its 22000 miles of transmission lines to an independent operator. The CSW deal closed later that year. (However the SEC's approval of the deal was challenged by a federal appeals court in 2002.)

AEP sold its 50% stake in Yorkshire Power Group to Innogy (now RWE npower) in 2001; it also purchased Houston Pipe Line Co. (which it later sold in early 2005) from Enron for $727 million. AEP became one of the largest US barge operators that year when it bought MEMCO Barge Line from Progress Energy. It also purchased two UK coal-fired power plants (4000 MW) from Edison Mission Energy a subsidiary of Edison International in a $960 million deal.

In 2002 AEP sold its UK utility SEEBOARD to Electricité de France in a $2.2 billion deal; it also sold its Australian utility CitiPower to a consortium led by Cheung Kong Infrastructure and Hongkong Electric for $855 million. The following year the company sold two of its competitive Texas retail electric providers (WTU Retail Energy and CPL Retail Energy) to UK utility Centrica. It also divested its power plant development subsidiary AEP Pro Serv and its stakes in telecom firms C3 Communications and AFN.

The company sold two UK power plants to Scottish and Southern Energy for $456 million in 2004 and it sold a 50% stake in a third UK plant to Scottish Power in a $210 million deal. AEP also sold four independent power plants in Florida and Colorado to Bear Stearns for $156 million that year.

In 2006 the company sold its Plaquemine cogeneration plant to Dow Chemical for $64 million. Also that year it formed a joint venture company with MidAmerican Energy Holdings to build and own new electric transmission assets within the Electric Reliability Council of Texas.

AEP settled an eight-year lawsuit with the US government in 2007 and agreed to pay more than $4.6 billion to reduce hazardous air pollution from 16 coal-burning power plants.

In 2011 the company reached a $425 million settlement covering all claims with BOA and Enron related to their purchase of Houston Pipeline Company from Enron in 2001.

Growing its retail business in the US in 2012 AEP acquired Chicago-based Blue Star Energy and its independent retail electric supplier BlueStar Energy Solutions. The company has about 23000 customer accounts. The deal also gives AEP the opportunity to hedge the output of its soon-to-be unregulated Ohio power generation.

By the end of 2012 AEP was operating 310 MW of wind power facilities and had about 180 MW of long-term purchase power agreements for wind power.

In 2013 AEP received the regulatory go-ahead to separate its AEP Ohio-owned generation assets from its Ohio distribution and transmission operations and complete transfer of that generation to AEP's competitive generation company (AEP Generation Resources) and regulated affiliates Appalachian Power and Kentucky Power.

To create a more customer friendly service in 2013 AEP launched a new enhanced version of its website at aepenergy.com. optimized for mobile devices.

EXECUTIVES

Svp And Chief Administrative Officer, Lana L. Hillebrand, age 60, $490,680 total compensation

Executive Vice President Sales And Marketing, John Powers

Vice Chairman, Robert P. (Bob) Powers, age 66, $723,773 total compensation

President And Coo Southwestern Electric Power, Venita McCellon-Allen, age 61, $410,919 total compensation

Vice President Transmission Engineering And Project Services, Scott Moore

Vp Corporate Communications; President American Electric Power Foundation, Dale E. Heydlauff, age 60

Evp External Affairs, Charles R. Patton, age 61

Svp Portfolio Management And Optimization, Charles E. (Chuck) Zebula, age 60, $446,310 total compensation

President And Coo Aep Ohio, Julie Sloat, age 47

Evp And Cfo, Brian X. Tierney, age 53, $730,800 total compensation

President And Coo Public Service Company Of Oklahoma, J. Stuart Solomon, age 58

Chairman President And Ceo, Nicholas K. (Nick) Akins, age 60, $1,325,077 total compensation

Evp General Counsel And Secretary, David M. Feinberg, age 51, $615,354 total compensation

Evp Generation, Mark C. McCullough, age 60

Evp Utilities, Paul Chodak, age 56

Evp Aep Transmission And President And Coo Aep Transmission Holding Company (aepthco), Lisa M. Barton, age 54, $532,039 total compensation

President And Coo Kentucky Power, Matthew J. Satterwhite, age 47

President And Coo Indiana Michigan Power, Toby L. Thomas

President And Coo Appalachian Power, Chris T. Beam

President And Coo Aep Texas, Judith Talavera

Vice President, Thomas Householder

Senior Vice President Engineering Projects And Filed Services, William L Sigmon

Vice President Of Human Resources, Vicki Zeiger

Vice President Of Human Resources, Mark Dobbins

Vice President And Director, John Keane

Vice President Business Logistics, John Harper

Vice President, Lance Sogan

Vice President Energy Marketing Asset Investments And Renewables, Kevin Brady

Senior Vice President Commercial Operations, Todd Busby

Vice President, Andy Reis

Vice President Governmental Affairs American Elec, Anthony Kavanagh

Vice President And Chief Security Officer, Stan Partlow

Vice President Customer Services Marketing And Distribution Servi, Craig Rhoades
Senior Vice President, Jeffrey Cross
Senior Vice President Governmental Affairs, Tony Kavanagh
Senior Vice President Of Marketing, Brian Neville
Vice President Information Technology, Brian Bueter
Vice President Marketing Operations, Bob Bradish
Senior Vice President Grid Development, A Wade Smith
Svp Fossil And Hydro Generation, Daniel Lee
National Account Manager, James B Clark
Chief Sales Officer, Blake Tucker
Vice President Trading, John Sniffen
National Account Manager, James Clark
Vice President Fuel Procurement, Mark Leskowitz
Vice President Cng Services, Larry Gearhart
Vp And Chief Digital Officer, Derek Kramer
Vice President Of Government Affairs, Greg Clark
Board Member, Thomas Hoaglin
Assistant Secretary, Thomas Berkemeyer
Secretary, Timothy King
Board Member, Sara Tucker
Board Member, Steve Rasmussen
Secretary, Robert Mckinney
Auditors: PricewaterhouseCoopers LLP

LOCATIONS

HQ: American Electric Power Co Inc
1 Riverside Plaza, Columbus, OH 43215-2373
Phone: 614 716-1000   Fax: 614 223-1823
Web: www.aep.com

PRODUCTS/OPERATIONS

2018 Sales

	$ mil.	% of total
Vertically Integrated Utilities	9,645	60
Transmission and Distribution Utilities	4,653	29
Generation and Marketing	1,940	11
Other Revenue and adjustments	(43.2)	-
Total	**16,195**	**100**

Selected Subsidiaries

AEP Energy Services Inc. (energy marketing and trading)
AEP Generating Co. (electricity generator marketer)
AEP Retail Energy (retail energy marketing in deregulated territories)
AEP Texas Central Company (formerly Central Power and Light electric utility)
AEP Texas North Company (formerly West Texas Utilities electric utility)
AEP Towers (wireless communications towers)
Appalachian Power Company (electric utility)
Columbus Southern Power Company (electric utility)
Indiana Michigan Power Company (electric utility)
Kentucky Power Company (electric utility)
Kingsport Power Company (electric utility)
Ohio Power Company (electric utility)
Public Service Company of Oklahoma (electric utility)
Southwestern Electric Power Company (electric utility)
Wheeling Power Company (electric utility)
Utility Distribution/Customer Service Divisions
AEP Ohio (handles distribution customer service and external affairs functions for Columbus Southern Power Company Ohio Power Company and Wheeling Power Company)
AEP Texas (handles distribution customer service and external affairs functions for AEP Texas Central Company and AEP Texas North Company)
Appalachian Power (handles distribution customer service and external affairs functions for Appalachian Power Company and Kingsport Power Company)
Indiana Michigan Power (handles distribution customer service and external affairs functions for Indiana Michigan Power Company)
Kentucky Power (handles distribution customer service and external affairs functions for Kentucky Power Company)
Public Service Company of Oklahoma (handles distribution customer service and external affairs functions for Public Service Company of Oklahoma)
Southwestern Electric Power Company (handles distribution customer service and external affairs functions for Southwestern Electric Power Company)

COMPETITORS

BP	Entergy
CMS Energy	Exelon
CenterPoint Energy	FirstEnergy
Constellation Energy Group	PG&E Corporation
DTE	Sempra Energy
Dominion Energy	Southern Company
Duke Energy	TVA
	Xcel Energy

HISTORICAL FINANCIALS

Company Type: Public

Income Statement

FYE: December 31

	REVENUE ($ mil.)	NET INCOME ($ mil.)	NET PROFIT MARGIN	EMPLOYEES
12/19	15,561	1,921	12.3%	17,408
12/18	16,195	1,923	11.9%	17,582
12/17	15,424	1,912	12.4%	17,666
12/16	16,380	610	3.7%	17,634
12/15	16,453	2,047	12.4%	17,405
Annual Growth	(1.4%)	(1.6%)	—	0.0%

2019 Year-End Financials

Debt ratio: 38.95%
Return on equity: 9.92%
Cash ($ mil.): 509
Current ratio: 0.40
Long-term debt ($ mil.): 25,126

No. of shares (mil.): 494
Dividends
Yield: 2.8%
Payout: 69.8%
Market value ($ mil.): 46,704

	STOCK PRICE ($) FY Close	P/E High/Low	PER SHARE ($) Earnings	Dividends	Book Value
12/19	94.51	25 19	3.88	2.71	39.81
12/18	74.74	21 16	3.90	2.53	38.66
12/17	73.57	20 16	3.88	2.39	37.19
12/16	62.96	57 46	1.24	2.27	35.38
12/15	58.27	15 13	4.17	2.15	36.44
Annual Growth	12.9%	— —	(1.8%)	6.0%	2.2%

American Equity Investment Life Holding Co

American Equity Investment Life Holding (American Equity Life) helps middle-income investors plan for a cushier retirement. The company issues and administers fixed-rate and indexed annuities through subsidiaries American Equity Investment Life Insurance Eagle Life Insurance Company and American Equity Investment Life Insurance Company of New York. Licensed in 50 states and the District of Columbia the company sells its products through various channels including about 21000 independent agents and over 40 national marketing associations. American Equity Life also offers a variety of universal life insurance products. The company targets individuals between the ages of 45 and 75.

Operations

The company has one business segment which represents its core business comprised of the sale of fixed index and fixed rate annuities.

Geographic Reach

West Des Moines Iowa-based American Equity Life is licensed in all fifty US states but five states bring in a large portion of its business. Florida Texas California Pennsylvania and Illinois together account for about one-third of American Equity Life's direct premiums.

Sales and Marketing

American Equity Life distributes its products through independent agents brokers/agents banks registered investment advisors and other channels.

The company's target market includes the group of individuals ages 45-75 who are seeking to accumulate tax-deferred savings or create guaranteed lifetime income.

Financial Performance

American Equity Life's revenue has been rising over the past few years: It rose in 2016 and 2017 declined in 2018 and rebounded in 2019.

In 2019 revenue rose 124% to $3.4 billion largely due to gains related to changes in fair values of derivatives.

Net income declined by 46% in 2019 from $458 million in 2018 to $246 million. Net income for the year ended December 31 2019 was negatively impacted by net realized investment losses of $11.7 million of which $18.7 million was recognized as OTTI partially offset by $7.0 million of net realized gains.

The company ended 2019 with $2.2 billion $1.9 billion more than it had at the end of 2018. Financing activities provided $1.7 billion in net cash and operating activities provided $3.4 billion while investing activities used $3.1 billion.

Strategy

As the company's target demographic — US individuals between the ages of 45 and 75 — continues to expand American Equity Life hopes to take advantage of the resulting demand for fixed index annuity products. It has several strategies in place to encourage growth including expanding and enhancing its distribution network; continuing to introduce innovative and competitive products; use its expertise to Achieve Targeted Spreads on Annuity Products; Maintain our Profitability Focus and Improve Operating Efficiency; Take Advantage of the Growing Popularity of Index Products; Focus on High Quality Service to Agents and Policyholders; and Be Proactive in the Changing Regulatory Environment.

American Equity Life is also working to increase sales by introducing innovative and competitive new products. With its focus on fixed index and fixed rate annuities the company has launched a number of first-of-its-kind policy riders. It uses its expertise as well as technological advances to both improve its investment management activities and operate more efficiently. The company's 2018 sales were boosted by new products in the guaranteed lifetime income benefit market and the strength of its accumulation products.

Exceptional customer experience is another area of focus.

Ongoing low interest rates have challenged the company's efforts to hit its target rate for investment spread. Additionally certain index strategies have had higher options costs which has raised the firm's aggregate cost of money. And although American Equity remains a leader in the fixed index annuity space new competition has decreased the company's overall market share.

Company Background

David Noble founded American Equity Life in 1995. The company went public in 2003.

EXECUTIVES

Chairman President And Ceo, John M. Matovina, age 65, $727,500 total compensation

President American Equity Life Insurance Co.,
Ronald J. (Ron) Grensteiner, age 57, $510,000 total compensation

Evp And Chief Investment Officer, Jeffrey D. (Jeff) Lorenzen, age 54, $445,000 total compensation

Cfo And Treasurer, Ted M. Johnson, age 50, $500,000 total compensation

Evp And Coo, Bruce D. Cheek

Evp General Counsel And Corporate Secretary, Renee D. Montz, age 48, $356,250 total compensation

Vice President: Information Management, Ted Hughes

Assistant Vice President Andndash; Technical Services, Kevin Seuferer

Assistant Vice President, Janelle Leatherman

Vice President Financial Reporting And Tax, Aaron Boushek

Assistant Vice President, Young Dennis

Assistant Vice President Product Development, Samuel Richeson

Vice President Investor Relations, Steven Schwartz

Vice President Information Technology, Ann Cannavo

Vice President Of Process Improvement, David Hammond

Auditors: Ernst & Young LLP

LOCATIONS

HQ: American Equity Investment Life Holding Co
6000 Westown Parkway, West Des Moines, IA 50266
Phone: 515 221-0002
Web: www.american-equity.com

PRODUCTS/OPERATIONS

2018 Sales

	$ mil.	% of total
Net investment income	2,722	92
Fees & commissions	224	7
Total premiums earned	26	1
Adjustments	(37.2)	-
Total	**2,936**	**100**

COMPETITORS

Allianz Life	National Western
Aviva	Northwestern Mutual
Great American Life	Prudential
Integrity Life	Sammons Financial

HISTORICAL FINANCIALS

Company Type: Public

Income Statement   FYE: December 31

	ASSETS ($ mil.)	NET INCOME ($ mil.)	INCOME AS % OF ASSETS	EMPLOYEES
12/19	69,696	246	0.4%	608
12/18	61,625	458	0.7%	554
12/17	62,030	174	0.3%	515
12/16	56,053	83	0.1%	530
12/15	49,041	219	0.4%	490
Annual Growth	**9.2%**	**2.9%**	**—**	**5.5%**

2019 Year-End Financials

Debt ratio: 0.94%	No. of shares (mil.): 91
Return on equity: 7.06%	Dividends
Cash ($ mil.): 2,293	Yield: 1.0%
Current ratio: —	Payout: 34.4%
Long-term debt ($ mil.): —	Market value ($ mil.): 2,727

	STOCK PRICE ($) FY Close	P/E High/Low		PER SHARE ($) Earnings	Dividends	Book Value
12/19	29.93	12	8	2.68	0.30	50.16
12/18	27.94	7	5	5.01	0.28	26.55
12/17	30.73	16	11	1.93	0.26	31.91
12/16	22.54	25	13	0.97	0.24	26.04
12/15	24.03	11	8	2.72	0.22	23.90
Annual Growth	**5.6%**	**—**		**(0.4%)**	**8.1%**	**20.4%**

American Express Co.

American Express makes money even if you do leave home without it. Best known for its charge cards and revolving credit cards the company is also one of the world's largest providers of travel services. And yes the company still issues traveler's checks. Its Travelers Cheque Group is the world's largest issuer of traveler's checks. Still the company's charge and credit cards are its bread and butter; American Express boasts about $200 million in assets and about $1.1 billion in annual billed business and has about 70 million proprietary cards-in-force worldwide. About three-quarters of company's total sales comes from US.

HISTORY

In 1850 Henry Wells and his two main competitors combined their delivery services to form American Express. When directors refused to expand to California in 1852 Wells and executive William Fargo formed Wells Fargo while remaining at American Express.

American Express merged with Merchants Union Express in 1868 and developed a money order to compete with the government's postal money order. Fargo's difficulty in cashing letters of credit in Europe led to the offering of Travelers Cheques in 1891.

In WWI the US government nationalized and consolidated all express delivery services compensating the owners. After the war American Express incorporated as an overseas freight and financial services and exchange provider (the freight operation was sold in 1970). In 1958 the company introduced the American Express charge card. It bought Fireman's Fund American Insurance (sold gradually between 1985 and 1989) and Equitable Securities in 1968.

James Robinson CEO from 1977 to 1993 hoped to turn American Express into a financial services supermarket. The company bought brokerage Shearson Loeb Rhoades in 1981 and investment banker Lehman Brothers in 1984 among others. In 1987 it introduced Optima a revolving credit card to compete with MasterCard and Visa. It had no experience in underwriting credit cards though and was badly burned by losses.

Most of the financial units were combined as Shearson Lehman Brothers. But the financial services supermarket never came to fruition and losses in this area brought a steep drop in earnings in the early 1990s. Harvey Golub was brought in as CEO in 1993 to restore stability.

The company sold its brokerage operations as Shearson (to Travelers now Citigroup) and spun off investment banking as Lehman Brothers in 1994. In late 1996 it teamed with Advanta Corp. to allow Advanta Visa and MasterCard holders to earn points in the American Express Membership Rewards program. The move sparked a lawsuit from Visa and MasterCard which prohibit their member banks from doing business with American Express. That set off a spate of lawsuits culminating in the US Justice Department filing an antitrust suit against Visa and MasterCard. A federal judge sided with the Justice Department in 2001 but Visa and MasterCard appealed.

In 1997 Kenneth Chenault became president and COO putting him in line to succeed Golub.

Online banking service Membership B@nking was launched in 1999. That year American Express invested in Ticketmaster (the ticketing giant that merged with Live Nation Entertainment in 2010). In 2000 the company established a headquarters in Beijing to develop business in China. Also that year American Express bought more than 4500 ATMs from Electronic Data Systems (now HP Enterprise Services) making it a leading US operator of ATMs.

In 2001 Chenault replaced Golub as chairman and CEO. American Express was hit hard that year by bad investments in below-investment grade bonds by its money-management unit which shaved about $1 billion from earnings. Adding to its woes the company's employees at its New York City headquarters across the street from the World Trade Center were displaced by the 2001 terrorist attacks; its headquarters reopened in May 2002.

To grow its corporate travel management business Amex acquired Rosenbluth International a leading global travel management company with corporate travel operations in 15 countries in 2003. When Rosenbluth became fully integrated into the organization in mid-2004 American Express announced a relaunch of its corporate travel organization renamed American Express Business Travel.

American Express underwent a mild shakeup in late 2004 when it cut 2.5% of its workforce in a restructuring that included the company's business travel operations. The restructuring also included the sale of the company's banking operations in Bangladesh Egypt Luxembourg and Pakistan and the relocation of some finance operations. On a brighter note the company that year announced a milestone agreement with Industrial and Commercial Bank of China (ICBC) one of the biggest banks in China to issue the first American Express-branded credit cards in that country.

To focus on its travel and credit card operations the company in 2005 spun off Ameriprise Financial (formerly American Express Financial Advisors) a provider of insurance mutual funds investment advice and brokerage and asset management services. Toward that same end American Express sold its Tax and Business Services division to H&R Block and its UK-based American Express Financial Services Europe to TD Waterhouse (now part of TD AMERITRADE). Also in 2005 the company sold its equipment leasing business to Key Equipment Finance.

In 2007 the company's business travel division bought the rest of Farrington American Express Travel Services Limited it didn't already own. The travel management company had been a joint venture with Farrington Travel. The move was part of American Express's global expansion push especially in the Asia-Pacific region.

The company discontinued its Travelers Cheque card that year after determining that customers preferred paper travelers checks over a stored-value card. However sales of the travelers checks continued to decline in 2007 affected by the rising use of ATMs among other factors.

Also in 2007 American Express reached a $2.5 billion settlement with Visa and other defendants including JPMorgan Chase Capital One U.S. Bancorp and Wells Fargo dropping them from the lawsuit that alleged the companies conspired to block American Express from the bank-issued card business in the US. The following year it reached a $1.8 billion settlement with Mastercard the final remaining defendant in the suit.

American Express sold the international operations of American Express Bank to Stanchart in 2008.

American Express became a banking holding company in 2009. As a result it received some $3.4 billion from the Troubled Asset Relief Fund (TARP) early that year; it repaid the debt within months.

EXECUTIVES

Evp And Cio, Marc D. Gordon, age 59
Evp And Cfo, Jeffrey C. (Jeff) Campbell, age 59, $1,000,000 total compensation
Chairman And Ceo, Stephen J. (Steve) Squeri, age 61, $1,350,000 total compensation
Evp And General Counsel, Laureen E. Seeger, age 58, $800,000 total compensation
Group President Global Consumer Services, Douglas E. Buckminster, age 60, $700,000 total compensation
President Global Risk Banking & Compliance And Chief Risk Officer, Denise Pickett
Group President Global Merchant & Network Services, Anré Williams, age 54
President Global Services Group, Paul D. Fabara, age 54
Chief Corporate Affairs Officer, Michael J. OÁ'Neill, age 66
Chief Strategy Officer, Mohammed Badi
President Global Commercial Services, Anna Marrs
Chief Marketing Officer, Elizabeth Rutledge
Vice President Human Resources, Christine Anderson
Vice President Of Sales And Marketing, David Bonalle
Vice President Of Marketing, Kathleen King
Vice President Business Development Regional Sales Central Region Global Corporate Payments, Lewis Scott
Evp Global Infrastructure And Digital Workplace, Brian Saluzzo
Vice President, Liwen Liang
Vice President Architecture And Strategy, Howard Johnson
Vice President Operations, Nicole Samuels
Vice President, Leslie Morris
Vice President Capabilities Planning And Enablement, Jaime Hullinger
Vice President Technologies, Jennifer Weber
Vice President Technologies, Amy Heydon
Vice President Online Commerce Marketing, Carl Barkey
Vice President And General Manager Client Solutions, Howard Fulton
Vice President Human Resources Business Partner, Connie Schan
Svp Risk Management, Shen Chang
Vice President, Shreya Patel
Senior Vice President And Marketing Us Middle Market Global Corporate Payments, Pablo Ribas
Svp Global Security Group Global Corporate Services, Mic Chandrani
Vice President Client Management, Larry Restiano
Vice President, David Carroll
Vice President, Trang Dinh
Vice President International Analytics Data Analytics And Capabilities, Kathleen Haggerty
Vice President Of Human Resour, John Apollo
Vice President Of Customer Marketing Development, Eddie Alvarez
Vice President, Sanjay Khanna
Director Of Nursing, Karen Diprofio
Executive Vice President Human Resources, Manu Narang
Vice President Of Marketing, Greg Keeley
Vice President Strategy, Sabra Mannan

Vice President Small Merchant Acquisition, Mickey Hansen
Vp Consumer Lending Underwriting, Guillermo Rabiela
Vice President Public Affairs And Communications, Charlotte Fuller
Vice President Social Marketing Innovation, Phil Wilson
Vice President Global Business And Market Development, David Wolf
Senior Vice President Global Strategy And Capabilities, Priscilla Kam
Vice President, Bruce Krarup
Vice President, Ravi Varma
Vice President Of Content, Lou Paskalis
Vice President Direct Marketing Acquisitions And N, Tina Eide
Vice President Customer Service, Laurie Farquhar
Vice President Of Finance, Stefano Rosic
Vice President Finance Manda Controller, Dylan Haverty-Stacke
And Enterprise Fraud Capabilities, Chad Gonzales
Vice President Risk Management, Sanjay Gwalani
Vice President And Senior Counsel, Emily Goodman Binick
Vice President Operational Excellence Finance And Global Business Services, Rita Magann
Vice President Web Engineering Platform Security And Advanced Frameworks, Deepak Arora
Vice President Compliance And Ethics, Glenn Jarvis
Vice President Global Loyalty Solutions, Sarah Sugarman
Vice President Demand Management, Colleen Doyle
Vice President, Jen Humpal
Vice President Learning And Development Global Servicing Network, Emma Hanman
Evp Enterprise Risk Management, Alex Weldon
Vice President Operational Risk Governance Group, Felipe Toro
Vice President Delivery Transformation, Randy Brokaw
Vice President And Senior Counsel, Michelle Visiedo
Vice President, Victor Gold
Vice President, Atul Dalmia
Vice President, Katie Naylor
Vice President Engineering, Phil Lundrigan
Vice President Capacity Management, Richard Glynn
Senior Vice President Of Intl Risk Management, David Nigro
Vice President, Brady Fife
Vice President And General Manager Global Merchant Services, Verity Jansson
Senior Vice President Of Global Human Resources, Gabriella Giglio
Vice President Digital Acquisition, John Dotto
Senior Vice President Finance, Christina Wong
Vice President Of Advertising, Allison Silver
Vice President Fraud, Nancy Yee
Vice President Government Relations, Sean Peterson
Vice President Global Operations And Financial Management, Paul Garvey
General Auditor Senior Vice President, Julie Scammahorn
Vice President Enterprise Personalization And Mobile, Wissam Magazachi
Vice President Us Benefits, Tammy Yee
Vice President, Leo Gardina
Senior Vice President Global Head Of Tax Chief Tax Officer, Joe Gagliano
Vice President Of Human Resources, Kim Seymour
Vice President Risk Management, Lei Chen
Vice President Business Development, Franki Schmidt
Vice President Technologies Communications, Gerilyn Cammaroto

Vice President Global Credit And Fraud Risk Management Capabilities, Lynn Almoro
Vice President Of Credit Operations, Todd Schemm
Vice President Of Consumer And Small Business Services Technologies, Miles Farrel
Foreign Exchange Vice President, Helen Grace
Vice President Small Merchant Marketing, Sangeeta Naik
Vice President World Service Global New Accounts, Donna Visco
Vice President Engineering, Anchal Gupta
Vice President End User Computing, Gary Kensey
Vice President Global Risk Oversight, Wenbiao Zhao
Vice President State Government Affairs, Steve Lemson
Vice President Strategic Communications, Frank Vaccaro
Vice President Of Finance, Julie Bush
Vice President, Linda Marshall
Vice President David Jones Strategic Alliance, Kylea Boward
Vice President National Client Group, Greg Hybl
Vice President Lfo Finance, Jessica Lieberman
Senior Vice President And General Manager Head Of Service Delivery Emea American Express Business T, Suzan Kereere
Vice President International Finance, Jason Brown
Vice President Digital Product Engineering And Data Analytics, Vivek Tripathi
Vice President Technologies Finance, Phil Konort
Vice President Of International, Tom Young
Vice President, Tom Taris
Vice President Business Development, Lisa L Rankin
Vice President Consumer Engagement Strategy And Marketing, Robin Neviaser
Vp Finance, Phyllis Mccormick
Senior Vice President Employee And Shareholder Communications, Pat Locke
Vice President, John Standring
Vice President, Eduardo Gomez Garcia
Svp Enterprise Digital Group, Luke Gebb
Senior Vice President Global Brand Integration And Insights, Mary Reilly
Vice President Finance, Kirstie Myers
Vice President Global Account Dev, Chris Yule
Vice President Lfo Open Finance, Rob Pereless
Vice President Global Commercial Card Ri, Ray Didonato
Vice President Lfo Technologies, Michael Ullrich
Vice President, Cheryl Daniels
Vice President Custoemr Expericence, Holly Hamilton
Vice President Service Delivery, Jacinthe Ladouceur
Vice President, Linda Presti
Vice President Uk Small Merchants, John Lemonius
Vice President, Jeffrey Irvine
Vice President Consumer Card Customer Strategy, Kelly Stevens
Vice President Executive Compensation, Anil Agarwal
Vice President Mandamp;a Controllership, Cory Vieira
Vice President Open Digital Strategy And Services Development, Scott Belous
Vice President Human Resources East Asia, Sonia Cargan
Vice President Customer Marketing Analytics, Mahasweta Dhawan
Vice President Global Media American Express, Joseph Bihlmier
Vice President Global Business Development, Steve Murphy
Vice President Retail Travel Network, Ellen Bettridge
Executive Vice President Principal Accounting Officer Corporate Controller, Richard Petrino

Senior Vice President And Country Manager
France, Nicolas Sireyjol
Vice President International Lending Product
Development, Jennifer Hawkins
Senior Vice President Of Business Development,
Thomas Tierney
Vice President Global Card Issuance And World
Service Tech Investment Strategy, Deborah Craft
Vice President Information Technology, Alex
Palacio
Auditors: PricewaterhouseCoopers LLP

LOCATIONS

HQ: American Express Co.
200 Vesey Street, New York, NY 10285
Phone: 212 640-2000   Fax: 212 640-0404
Web: www.americanexpress.com

2016 Sales

	% of total
United States	74
Europe the Middle East and Africa (EMEA)	10
Japan Asia/Pacific and Australia (JAPA)	9
Latin America Canada and the Caribbean (LACC)	7
Total	**100**

PRODUCTS/OPERATIONS

2016 Sales

	$ mil.	% of total
Non-interest		
Discount revenue	18,680	56
Net card fees	2,886	9
Other commissions & fees	2,753	8
Other	2,029	6
Interest		
Loans including fees	7,205	21
Interest & dividends on investment securities	131	—
Deposits with banks & other	139	—
Total	**33,823**	**100**

2016 Sales by Segment

	% of total
U.S. Consumer Services (USCS)	39
Global Commercial Services (GCS)	30
International Consumer and Network Services (ICNS)	17
Global Merchant Services (GMS)	14
Total	**100**

COMPETITORS

BCD Travel	JPMorgan Chase
Bank of America	JTB Corp.
Barclays	MasterCard
Capital One	Ovation Travel Group
Citibank	PayPal
Discover	Visa Inc
Expedia	Western Union
HSBC	

HISTORICAL FINANCIALS

Company Type: Public

Income Statement

FYE: December 31

	ASSETS ($ mil.)	NET INCOME ($ mil.)	INCOME AS % OF ASSETS	EMPLOYEES
12/19	198,321	6,759	3.4%	64,500
12/18	188,602	6,921	3.7%	59,000
12/17	181,159	2,736	1.5%	55,000
12/16	158,893	5,408	3.4%	56,400
12/15	161,184	5,163	3.2%	54,800
Annual Growth	**5.3%**	**7.0%**	**—**	**4.2%**

2019 Year-End Financials

Debt ratio: 29.16%
Return on equity: 29.80%
Cash ($ mil.): 23,932
Current ratio: —
Long-term debt ($ mil.): —
No. of shares (mil.): 810
Dividends
  Yield: 1.2%
  Payout: 19.3%
Market value ($ mil.): 100,837

	STOCK PRICE ($)	P/E		PER SHARE ($)		
	FY Close	High/Low	Earnings	Dividends	Book Value
12/19	124.49	16 12	7.99	1.60	28.48
12/18	95.32	14 11	7.91	1.44	26.32
12/17	99.31	33 25	2.97	1.31	21.22
12/16	74.08	13 9	5.65	1.19	22.68
12/15	69.55	18 13	5.05	1.10	21.33
Annual Growth	**15.7%**	**— —**	**12.2%**	**9.8%**	**7.5%**

American Financial Group Inc

American Financial Group (AFG) insures American businessmen in pursuit of the Great American Dream. Through the operations of Great American Insurance Company AFG offers commercial property/casualty insurance and in the sale of traditional fixed and indexed annuities in the retail financial institutions broker-dealer and registered investment advisor markets. The company also provides surety and fidelity coverage and risk management services. For individuals and employers AFG provides a wide range of annuity policies through its Great American Financial Resources Inc. (GAFRI) subsidiary.

Operations
AFG operates through two primary segments: Property and Casualty Insurance and Annuity.

The Property and Casualty Insurance segment is the largest accounting for about 70% of AFG's annual revenue. Focusing on commercial policies its operations are divided into more than 30 businesses grouped under the specialty casualty (professional excess and surplus workers' compensation targeted programs and general liabilities) property and transportation (marine crops and commercial auto) and specialty financial (fidelity and surety lend/lease risk management) categories.

In the Annuities segment (making up about a quarter of sales) focused on the sale of fixed and indexed annuities in the retail financial institutions broker-dealer and registered investment advisor through independent producers and through direct relationships with certain financial institutions.

Geographic Reach
Headquartered in Cincinnati Ohio AFG has more than 120 locations throughout North America and Europe. The company's largest markets include California Florida Texas New York and Illinois.

Sales and Marketing
AFG primarily markets its insurance policies through a nationwide network of independent agents and brokers; a small number are written through employee agents. Annuity products are marketed through a retail network of approximately 60 national marketing organizations and managing general agents; it also sells retail policies through financial institution partners including Wells Fargo BB&T PNC Financial Services LPL Financial and Regions Financial. Education market annuities are sold through national and regional agencies.

Financial Performance
AFG has reported steadily increasing revenue over the past five years showing 34% growth between 2015 and 2019. Profits also increased over

the past five years rising a total of 155% over the five-year period.

Revenue rose 15% in 2019 to $8.2 billion primarily due to growth in property/casualty net written premiums driven by specialty casualty policy sales. Revenue from the annuity segment also rose on increased investment income. Growth was partly offset by realized losses on securities that year.

Net income increased 69% to some $869 million in 2019 due to lower income tax provisions despite higher operating expenses.

The company ended 2019 with $2.3 billion in cash up $799 million from 2018. Operating activities contributed $2.5 billion while investing activities used $3.1 billion (mostly fixed maturity purchases) and financing activities contributed $1.4 billion via annuity reciepts.

Strategy
Like all property/casualty insurers AFG seeks to balance out calm and catastrophe by operating on long-term income cycles where years of profits balance out years of increased claims. The company sees opportunity in such specialty areas as niche professional coverage and it has worked to build its operations both organically and through acquisitions.

In terms of annuities AFG is focused on fixed and indexed products and has steered away from offering variable annuities and other types of offerings where it doesn't have a competitive advantage. The company introduces product enhancements to meet evolving demographic needs and to adapt to shifts in financial markets.

To help prepare against larger-than-usual claims volumes in a given year which can be triggered by high catastrophe losses and other factors insurers must monitor pricing carefully and make sure they set aside sufficient claims reserves. AFG is investing in predictive analytics capabilities to improve claims processes and underwriting effectiveness.

In 2019 AFG announces the newly formed Accident & Health division. This division will build upon Great American's existing array of Accident & Health Insurance coverages focusing on customized coverages for organizations and educational institutions. In the same year AFG initiated plans to exit the Lloyd's of London property and casualty market in 2020.

Mergers and Acquisitions
In 2019 National Interstate a property and casualty insurance subsidiary of AFG entered into an agreement with Atlas Financial Holdings (AFH) to become the exclusive underwriter of AFH's paratransit book of business. In connection with the transaction AFG was granted a five-year warrant to acquire approximately 2.4 million shares of AFH (20% at the acquisition date). The estimated fair value of the warrant was approximately $1 million at the date it was received.

Company Background
The company traces its roots to 1959 when Carl Lindner Jr. branched his ice-cream chain operations into real estate and banking. His United Dairy Farmers business launched in the 1930s became American Financial Corp. in 1960 and went public in 1961. It acquired United Liberty Life Insurance in 1963 and National General parent of Great American Insurance Group (founded 1872) in the 1970s. The company entered and exited a number of business lines over the years including construction and publishing. Its banking operations were spun off in 1980 and the company went private in 1981.

Lindner created American Financial Group in 1995 to merge AFC with Premier Underwriters. It exited some commercial lines in 1998 to focus on property/casualty and life and annuities; it also exited some medical insurance operations in the 2000s while growing its specialty property/casualty operations. In 2016 it sold its struggling Neon (formerly Marketform) medical malpractice operations which provided coverage in 30 countries (primarily in Australia Italy and the UK).

HISTORY

When his father became ill in the mid-1930s Carl Lindner Jr. dropped out of high school to take over his family's dairy business. He built it into a large ice-cream store chain called United Dairy Farmers. Lindner branched out in 1955 with Henthy Realty and in 1959 he bought three savings and loans. The next year Lindner changed the company's name to American Financial Corp. (AFC). He took it public in 1961 using the proceeds to buy United Liberty Life Insurance (1963) and Provident Bank (1966).

Lindner also formed the American Financial Leasing & Services Company in 1968 to lease airplanes computers and other equipment. In 1969 the company acquired Phoenix developer Rubenstein Construction and renamed it American Continental. AFC bought several life casualty and mortgage insurance firms in the 1970s including National General parent of Great American Insurance Group (founded 1872) later the core of AFC's insurance segment. The company also moved into publishing by buying 95% of the Cincinnati Enquirer paperback publisher Bantam Books and hardback publisher Grosset & Dunlap.

But the publishing interests soon went back on the block as Lindner concentrated on insurance which was then suffering from an industry-wide slowdown. In addition to selling the Enquirer AFC spun off American Continental in 1976. American Continental's president was Charles Keating who had joined AFC in 1972 and whose brother published the Enquirer. Keating (who was later jailed released then eventually pleaded guilty in connection with the failure of Lincoln Savings) underwent an SEC investigation during part of his time at AFC for alleged improprieties at Provident Bank. The bank was spun off in 1980.

Lindner took AFC private in 1981. That year following a strategy of bottom-feeding the firm began building its interest in the non-railroad assets of Penn Central the former railroad that had emerged from bankruptcy as an industrial manufacturer. Later that decade AFC increased its ownership in United Brands (later renamed Chiquita Brands International) from 29% to 45%. Lindner installed himself as CEO and reversed that company's losses. In 1987 AFC acquired a TV company Taft Communications (renamed Great American Communications) entailing a heavy debt load. To reduce its debt AFC trimmed its holdings including Circle K Hunter S&L and an interest in Scripps Howard Broadcasting.

Great American Communications went bankrupt in 1992 and emerged the next year as Citicasters Inc. (sold 1996). In 1995 Lindner created American Financial Group to effect the merger of AFC and Premier Underwriters of which he owned 42%. The result was American Financial Group (AFG).

AFG's results in the 1990s were uneven and it typically did not make an underwriting profit. In 2003 the insurer kept operating expenses down (partly by merging two of its holding company subsidiaries into AFG) and swung to a profit even though premium revenue was down.

The company shed some commercial lines to concentrate on its property/casualty and life and annuities businesses. To refine its mix AFG transferred Atlanta Casualty Company Infinity Insurance Company Leader Insurance Company and Windsor Insurance Company into 40%-owned Infinity Property and Casualty which went public in 2003. In 2004 the business exchanged its stake in

Provident Financial Group for a holding in National City Corporation.

Founder and chairman Carl Lindner retired as CEO in 2005 and died in 2011. No one was named to replace him as chairman but two of his sons Carl Lindner III and Craig Lindner carried on as co-CEOs.

The company sold its Medicare supplement and critical illness insurance operations in 2012 and its long-term care unit in 2015. In mid-2016 the company acquired the rest of transportation-focused National Interstate Corporation it didn't already own for $320 million.

EXECUTIVES

Co-president Co-ceo And Director, S. Craig Lindner, age 65, $1,150,000 total compensation
Co-president Co-ceo And Director, Carl H. Lindner, age 67, $1,150,000 total compensation
Evp And Cfo, Joseph E. (Jeff) Consolino, age 53, $868,269 total compensation
Svp And Chief Administrative Officer, Michelle A. (Shelly) Gillis, age 51, $332,315 total compensation
Svp And General Counsel, Vito C. Peraino, age 64, $565,962 total compensation
Divisional Senior Vice President Product Management Property And Inland Marine Division Gaic, Julie Kadnar
Divisional Senior Vice President Great American Professional Risk Insurance Services, Robert Nagaishi
Associate Vice President Infrastructure And Operations, James Niehaus
Assistant Vice President, John Fronduti
Vp And Assistant General Counsel, Mark Weiss
Divisional Vice President Development And Reinsurance Crop Insurance Division Gaic, Dean Clarke
Vice President, Howard Baird
Senior Vice President Underwriting Republic Indemnity, David Harkins
Senior Vice President, David Meyer
Vice President Underwriting Executive Liability Division, Bob Rubin
Assistant Vice President Marketing And Sales, Douglas Grebe
Vice President, Robert Dobbs
Senior Vice President Financial Mid Continent Group Gaic, Gregg Jones
Divisional Senior Vice President Bonds North California Office Gaic, Francis Plante
Divisional Vp Marketing Executive Liability Division Great American Insurance Group, Jonathan Starck
Divisional Vice President Claims Specialty Human Services Division Gaic, Doug Svenkerud
Divisional Vice President Loss Prevention Ocean Marine Division Gaic, Edward Wilmot
Divisional Senior Vice President Specialty Excess And Surplus Division Great American Insurance Group, Brian Sloan
Divisional Vice President Dallas Excess Liability Division Gaic, Kathleen Zale
Divisional Vice President Marketing Trucking Division Gaic, Tim Clinton
Divisional Senior Vice President Ocean Marine East Regional Office Gaic, Forrest Downing
Divisional Vice President Underwriting Environmental Division Great American Insurance Group, Sara Brothers
Divisional Vice President San Francisco Excess Liability Division Great American Insurance Group, Marcus Lampley
Divisional Vp Claims And Cincinnati Operations Financial Insitution Services Great American Insurance Group, Pat Sinnard
Avp And Actuary Gafri, Richard Sutton

Divisional Vice President Fidelity And Crime Division New York Great American Insurance Group, George Pierce Jr
Vice President, Rhonda Royals
Divisional Vice President And Actuary, Rebecca Schriml
Vice President Claims, Brad Fisher
Assistant Vice President And Senior Corporate Counsel, Freeman Durham
Vice President Of Claims, Steve Winborn
Board Member, Gregory Joseph
Board Member, Kenneth Ambrecht
Auditors: Ernst & Young LLP

LOCATIONS

HQ: American Financial Group Inc
301 East Fourth Street, Cincinnati, OH 45202
Phone: 513 579-2121
Web: www.afginc.com

PRODUCTS/OPERATIONS

2017 Sales

	$ mil.	% of total
Net earned insurance premiums	4,601	67
Net investment income	1,831	27
Income of managed investment entities	222	3
Realized gains on securities	5	-
Other	206	3
Total	**6,865**	**100**

COMPETITORS

AIG	MetLife
Allianz	Pacific Life
Arch Capital	RLI
CNA Financial	The Hartford
Chubb Limited	Tokio Marine
Cincinnati Financial	Travelers Companies
HCC Insurance	W. R. Berkley
Jackson National Life	XL Group plc
Liberty Mutual	Zurich Insurance Group
Markel	

HISTORICAL FINANCIALS

Company Type: Public

Income Statement

FYE: December 31

	ASSETS ($ mil.)	NET INCOME ($ mil.)	INCOME AS % OF ASSETS	EMPLOYEES
12/19	70,130	897	1.3%	7,700
12/18	63,456	530	0.8%	7,600
12/17	60,658	475	0.8%	600
12/16	55,072	649	1.2%	400
12/15	49,859	352	0.7%	400
Annual Growth	**8.9%**	**26.3%**	**—**	**109.5%**

2019 Year-End Financials

Debt ratio: 2.10%	No. of shares (mil.): 90
Return on equity: 15.96%	Dividends
Cash ($ mil.): 2,314	Yield: 4.5%
Current ratio: —	Payout: 50.2%
Long-term debt ($ mil.): —	Market value ($ mil.): 9,902

	STOCK PRICE ($) FY Close	P/E High/Low		PER SHARE ($) Earnings	Dividends	Book Value
12/19	109.65	11	9	9.85	4.95	69.42
12/18	90.53	20	14	5.85	4.45	55.66
12/17	108.54	20	16	5.28	4.79	60.38
12/16	88.12	12	9	7.33	2.15	56.55
12/15	72.08	19	14	3.94	2.03	52.50
Annual Growth	**11.1%**		**—**	**25.7%**	**25.0%**	**7.2%**

AMERICAN HIGH INCOME TRUST

EXECUTIVES

President, Larry Clemmenson
V Pres-Treas, Mary C Cremin
V Pres, Michael J Downer
SEC, Julie F Williams
Auditors: DELOITTE & TOUCHE LLP COSTA M

LOCATIONS

HQ: AMERICAN HIGH INCOME TRUST
  333 S HOPE ST STE 5200, LOS ANGELES, CA
  900713061
Phone: 949 766-6305
Web: WWW.CAPITALGROUP.COM

HISTORICAL FINANCIALS

Company Type: Private

Income Statement				FYE: September 30
	ASSETS ($ mil.)	NET INCOME ($ mil.)	INCOME AS % OF ASSETS	EMPLOYEES
09/19	16,645	25	0.2%	1
09/18	16,817	577	3.4%	—
09/16	17,336	1,555	9.0%	—
Annual Growth	(1.3%)	(74.7%)	—	—

AMERICAN HONDA FINANCE CORPORATION

If you're fonda the idea of driving a Honda you might want to call on American Honda Finance. Operating as Honda Financial Services the company provides retail financing in the US for Honda and Acura automobiles motorcycles all-terrain vehicles power equipment and outboard motors. Its American Honda Service division administers service contracts while Honda Lease Trust offers leases on new and used vehicles. Honda Financial Services also offers dealer financing and related dealer services. Ancillary services include servicing loans and securitizing and selling loans into the secondary market. A subsidiary of American Honda Motor the company began as a wholesale motorcycle finance provider in 1980.

Operations

American Honda Finance (AHF) acquires retail installment contracts and closed-end vehicle lease contracts from purchasers and lessees and authorized Honda and Acura dealers. It also provides these authorized dealers with wholesale flooring and commercial loans.

AHF also acquires used auto loans of non-Honda and non-Acura vehicles and provides these third-party dealers iwth wholesale loans. Additionally the company offers vehicle service contracts services underwriting and pricing of consumer financing services and incentive financing programs for Honda and Acura products.

Geographic Reach

The company is headquartered in Torrance California and operates nine regional offices that support all authorized Honda and Acura dealers across North America.

Financial Performance

While full financials of the subsidiary were not available American Honda Finance's (AHF) revenue has been on the uptrend as auto sales continue to strengthen along with the US economy. Revenue in fiscal 2014 (ended March 31 2014) grew by 22% to Â 5.97 trillion ($58.1 billion) thanks to larger revenues from its parent company's auto business and positive foreign currency exchange rates.

Despite higher selling general and administrative expenses and R&D expenses AHF's operating income also increased 39% to Â 290.9 billion ($2.83 billion) in 2014 after the company continued its cost reduction measures.

Strategy

American Honda Finance Corp. (AHFC) exists to provide stability to support sales of new and used Honda and Acura vehicles throughout North America Honda Motor's largest market. To that end AHFC seeks to preserve funding diversity balanced liquidity and maintain a prudent maturity profile. To spur growth of its US business in 2012 the company opened its ninth regional office a 25000-square-foot facility in Charlotte North Carolina to serve Honda buyers in the Carolinas Maryland Tennessee Virginia and West Virginia.

EXECUTIVES

Ceo, Hideo Tamaka
Sr V Pres*, Stephan Smith
V Pres-Cfo*, John Weisickle
Information Specialist, Hung Le
Information Technology Directo, David Newallis
Information Technology Directo, John Thompson
Export Territory Manager, Dave Huerta
Dealer Relations Manager, Paul Arbios
Regional Manager, Dean Hardesty
Marine OEM Sales Manager, Dennis Ashley
General Manager, Glenn Yamamoto
Auditors: KPMG LLP LOS ANGELES CALIFO

LOCATIONS

HQ: AMERICAN HONDA FINANCE CORPORATION
  1919 TORRANCE BLVD, TORRANCE. CA 905012722
Phone: 310 972-2239
Web: WWW.HONDAFINANCIALSERVICES.COM

Selected Offices
Alpharetta GA
Charlotte NC
Cypress CA
Elgin IL
Holyoke MA
Irving TX
San Ramon CA
Torrance CA
Wilmington DE

COMPETITORS

Ally Financial
Automotive Finance Corporation
Bank of America
Credit Acceptance
Ford Motor Credit
Mercedes-Benz Financial Services USA
Mitsubishi Motors Credit of America
Toyota Motor Credit

HISTORICAL FINANCIALS

Company Type: Private

Income Statement				FYE: March 31
	ASSETS ($ mil.)	NET INCOME ($ mil.)	INCOME AS % OF ASSETS	EMPLOYEES
03/17	69,854	753	1.1%	1,000
03/16	66,653	910	1.4%	—
03/08	50,526	(45)	—	—
03/07	41,431	394	1.0%	—
Annual Growth	5.4%	6.7%	—	—

American International Group Inc

EXECUTIVES

Pres, Salvatore De Fini
V Pres*, David Walsh
Chief of Infrastructure Transf, Al Stuart
Accounting Staff, Ian Galloway
Financial Planner, Rose Thomas
Director, Ira Feingold
Auditors: PricewaterhouseCoopers LLP

LOCATIONS

HQ: American International Group Inc
  175 Water Street, New York, NY 10038
Phone: 212 770-7000
Web: www.aig.com

HISTORICAL FINANCIALS

Company Type: Public

Income Statement				FYE: December 31
	ASSETS ($ mil.)	NET INCOME ($ mil.)	INCOME AS % OF ASSETS	EMPLOYEES
12/19	525,064	3,348	0.6%	46,000
12/18	491,984	(6)	—	49,600
12/17	498,301	(6,084)	—	49,800
12/16	498,264	(849)	—	56,400
12/15	496,943	2,196	0.4%	66,400
Annual Growth	1.4%	11.1%	—	(8.8%)

2019 Year-End Financials

Debt ratio: 6.73%
Return on equity: 5.49%
Cash ($ mil.): 2,856
Current ratio: —
Long-term debt ($ mil.): —

No. of shares (mil.): 870
Dividends
  Yield: 2.4%
  Payout: 63.0%
Market value ($ mil.): 44,657

	STOCK PRICE ($) FY Close	P/E High/Low	PER SHARE ($)		
			Earnings	Dividends	Book Value
12/19	51.33	15 10	3.74	1.28	75.49
12/18	39.41	— —	(0.01)	1.28	65.04
12/17	59.58	— —	(6.54)	1.28	72.49
12/16	65.31	— —	(0.78)	1.28	76.66
12/15	61.97	38 29	1.65	0.81	75.10
Annual Growth	(4.6%)	— —	22.7%	12.1%	0.1%

AMERICAN MUTUAL FUND

EXECUTIVES

Chb, Jonathan B Lovelace Jr
Chb-Ceo*, James K Dunton
V Chb*, James W Ratzlaff
Pres*, Robert G O'Donnell
V Pres*, Joyce Gordon
V Pres*, Joanna F Jonsson
SEC*, Vince Carti
Treas*, Mary C Hall
Treasurer, Mary Hall
Auditors: DELOITTE & TOUCHE LLP COSTA M

LOCATIONS

HQ: AMERICAN MUTUAL FUND
333 S HOPE ST FL 51, LOS ANGELES, CA 900711420
Phone: 213 486-9200
Web: WWW.CAPITALGROUP.COM

HISTORICAL FINANCIALS

Company Type: Private

Income Statement				FYE: October 31
	ASSETS ($ mil.)	NET INCOME ($ mil.)	INCOME AS % OF ASSETS	EMPLOYEES
10/19	60,172	9,524	15.8%	200
10/18	50,526	3,375	6.7%	—
Annual Growth	19.1%	182.2%		

American National Bankshares, Inc. (Danville, VA)

American National Bankshares with total assets of around $2.5 billion is the holding company for American National Bank and Trust. Founded in 1909 the bank operates some 30 branches that serve southern and central Virginia and north central North Carolina. Operating through two segments — Community Banking and Trust and Investment Services — it offers checking and savings accounts CDs IRAs and insurance. Lending activities primarily consist of real estate loans: Commercial mortgages account for about 40% of its loan portfolio while residential mortgages bring in another 20%. American National Bankshares' trust and investment services division manages nearly $610 million in assets.

Operations

American National Bankshares operates through two segments: Community Banking which accounts for more than 80% of the company's total revenue and offers deposit accounts and loans to individuals and small and middle-market businesses; and Trust and Investment Services which provides estate planning trust account administration investment management and retail brokerage services.

The bank makes more than 80% of its revenue from interest income. About 68% of its total revenue came from loan interest during 2015 while another 13% came from interest income on investment securities. The rest of its revenue came from trust fees (6% of revenue) deposit account service charges (3%) mortgage banking income (2%) brokerage fees (1%) and other miscellaneous income sources.

Geographic Reach

Danville Virginia-based American National Bankshares has 25 branches mostly in southern Virginia and in North Carolina (including in Alamance and Guilford Counties). It also has two loan production offices in Roanoke Virginia and Raleigh North Carolina.

Sales and Marketing

American National Bankshares has been cutting back on its advertising and marketing spend in recent years. It spent $356000 on advertising and marketing in 2015 up from $453000 and $607000 in 2014 and 2013 respectively.

Financial Performance

The bank group has struggled to consistently grow its revenues and profits over the past several years despite steadily increasing loan business mostly due to shrinking interest margins on loans stemming from the low-interest environment.

American National had a breakthrough year in 2015 however as its revenue jumped 17% to $68.46 million almost entirely thanks to its acquisition of MainStreet BankShares which boosted its loan and other interest-earning assets by double digits and increased its non-interest income by 19% with newly acquired deposit and other fee related income.

Double-digit revenue growth in 2015 drove the group's net income up 18% to $15.04 million. The bank's operating cash levels climbed 16% to $19.26 million for the year thanks to the boost in cash-denominated earnings.

Strategy

American National Bankshares grows its branch reach as well as its loan and deposit business by opening new branch locations or by buying other branches or banks.

The bank continues to have the largest deposit market share in the Dannville Virginia metro area boasting a 32.8% market share in the region as of mid-2015. It also had the second-largest market share in Pittsylvania County Virginia with a 21.1% share.

Mergers and Acquisitions

In 2019 American National Bankshares acquired Roanoke Virginia-based Hometown Bankshares for about $85 million. The acquisition expands American National's network to around 30 branches. The combined company has about $2.5 billion in assets.

Company Background

In 2011 American National acquired bank holding company MidCarolina Financial expanding its presence in North Carolina specifically in both Alamance and Guilford counties.

EXECUTIVES

Evp And Cfo, William W. Traynham, age 63, $211,232 total compensation
President And Ceo, Jeffrey V. Haley, age 59, $240,000 total compensation
Evp; Evp And Chief Administrative Officer American National Bank And Trust, Dabney T. P. (Dexter) Gilliam, age 64, $124,544 total compensation
Evp; Evp And Chief Credit Officer American National Bank And Trust, R. Helm Dobbins, age 68, $139,570 total compensation
Executive Vice President President - Alamance Region, Charles T. Canaday, age 59

Evp; Evp And Chief Banking Officer American National Bank And Trust, H. Gregg Strader
Vice President Of Retail Banking, Michelle Gaydica
Senior Vice President, Debra Carlson
Sr Vice President, Troy Woodard
Vice President, Lee Burris
Assistant Vice President, Terri Claar
Executive Vice President And Regional President, Rhonda Joyce
Vice President Retail Banking Manager, Barry Jarrett
Assistant Vice President, Derwin Hall
Vice President, Bill Via
Executive Vice President, Kevin Meade
Senior Vice President, Gray Goldsmith
Senior Vice President, Andy Agee
Senior Vice President, Allen Clark
Vice President Commercial Relationship Manager, Mike Gee
Assistant Vice President Mortgage Loan Officer, Amy Lowman
Senior Vice President, Craig Patterson
Chairman, Charles H. (Charlie) Majors, age 74
Board Member, Rhonda Owen
Board Of Directors, Michael Haley
Board Member, Joel Shepherd
Auditors: Yount, Hyde & Barbour, P.C.

LOCATIONS

HQ: American National Bankshares, Inc. (Danville, VA)
628 Main Street, Danville, VA 24541
Phone: 434 792-5111
Web: www.amnb.com

PRODUCTS/OPERATIONS

2015 Sales

	$ mil.	% of total
Interest and Dividend Income		
Interest and fees on loans	46	69
Taxable	4	6
Tax-exempt	3	5
Other	0	1
Non-interest income		
Trust fees	3	7
Service charges on deposit accounts	2	3
Other fees and commissions	2	3
Other	4	6
Total	68	100

Selected Subsidiaries

American National Bank and Trust Company
AMNB Statutory Trust I A Delaware Statutory Trust
MidCarolina Trust I A Delaware Statutory Trust
MidCarolina Trust II A Delaware Statutory Trust

Selected Services

Business Banking
  Cash Management
  Checking
  Loans
  Savings
Personal Banking
  Checking
  Loans
  Savings
Insurance
  Business
  Personal

COMPETITORS

BB&T	First Citizens
Bank of America	BancShares
First Century	NewBridge Bancorp
Bankshares	

HISTORICAL FINANCIALS

Company Type: Public

Income Statement

FYE: December 31

	ASSETS ($ mil.)	NET INCOME ($ mil.)	INCOME AS % OF ASSETS	EMPLOYEES
12/19	2,478	20	0.8%	355
12/18	1,862	22	1.2%	305
12/17	1,816	15	0.8%	328
12/16	1,678	16	1.0%	320
12/15	1,547	15	1.0%	303
Annual Growth	12.5%	8.6%	—	4.0%

2019 Year-End Financials

Debt ratio: 1.43%
Return on equity: 7.70%
Cash ($ mil.): 79
Current ratio: —
Long-term debt ($ mil.): —

No. of shares (mil.): 11
Dividends
Yield: 2.6%
Payout: 53.8%
Market value ($ mil.): 438

	STOCK PRICE ($) FY Close	P/E High/Low		PER SHARE ($) Earnings	Dividends	Book Value
12/19	39.57	20	15	1.98	1.04	28.93
12/18	29.31	16	11	2.59	1.00	25.52
12/17	38.30	24	20	1.76	0.97	24.13
12/16	34.80	19	12	1.89	0.96	23.37
12/15	25.61	15	12	1.73	0.93	22.95
Annual Growth	11.5%	—	—	3.4%	2.8%	6.0%

American National Group Inc

True to its name American National Insurance Company offers agricultural commercial and personal property/casualty insurance as well as life insurance annuities limited health and other types of insurance throughout the US Puerto Rico and other territories. Its subsidiaries include Garden State Life Insurance Standard Life and Accident Insurance and Farm Family Casualty Insurance Company. Also known as American National the company markets its products through independent insurance agents broker-dealers employee benefit firms financial institutions and large marketing organizations.

Operations

American National operates in five segments: Property/Casualty (personal and commercial coverage) Life (including whole term universal indexed credit life and variable life insurance) Annuity (deferred indexed single premium immediate and variable annuity products) Health (Medicare Supplement stop-loss credit disability insurance) and Corporate and Other (income from investments not related to the insurance segments as well as non-insurance operations).

While the company considers its Life and Annuity segments its main areas of focus it earns more of its premiums from Property/Casualty insurance. In fact the Property/Casualty segment brings in more than 35% of the company's total revenues. Altogether premiums account for almost 55% of revenues. Investment income accounts for around 25%.

American National has more than $118 billion in life insurance in-force.

Geographic Reach

The Texas-based American National is licensed to conduct business in all 50 states including the District of Columbia and Puerto Rico. The company has three buildings in League City Texas used by its Life Health and Corporate and Other segments four in Springfield Missouri and another one in Glenmont New York both used primarily by its Property and Casualty segment.

Sales and Marketing

American National markets life insurance and annuities through its diversified distribution network to satisfy the needs of its markets. Independent Marketing Group (IMG) markets policies through financial institutions employee benefits organizations broker-dealers marketing organizations and independent agents and brokers. The company's Career Sales and Service Division primarily serves the middle-income market (life annuities and health coverage) though exclusive employee agents. Multiple Line agents serves individuals families farmers ranchers and other agricultural clients and small business owners across the country. Specialty Market Group (SMG) offers both credit life products as well as certain property and casualty related products through independent managing general agents and managing general underwriters.

The group's Health segment serves middle-income seniors self-insured employers and individuals and performs marketing through independent agents and managing general underwriters.

The company serves about 6 million customers.

Financial Performance

American National's revenues have hovered around $3 billion for the past five years before finally reaching the $4 billion mark in 2019. Overall its revenues have grown 35% between 2015 and 2019. Its net income however has fluctuated in the same period struggling to maintain consistent growth over the years before achieving its peak figure of $620 million in 2019.

In 2019 revenue rose 22% to $4.1 billion. This increase was driven largely by net investment income other policy revenues and a recovery of $422.5 million in gains on equity securities. This was partially offset by a 2% decrease in premiums.

Net income rose 22% to $620 million in 2019 from $159 million in the year prior. That was primarily due to higher realized investment earnings and lower policyholder benefits.

American National's cash at the end of 2019 was $452 million $183.8 million higher from the prior year. Cash from operations generated $506.4 million while financing activities contributed another $201.1 million largely from changes in notes payable. Investing activities used $523.7 million mostly for short-term investments additions to property and equipment and security purchases.

Strategy

In its quest to be a leading financial products and services company American National aims to maintain the conservative business practices it has upheld for more than a century including controlling risk factors in its growth and investment strategies. The company looks to maintain strong finances through profitable growth primarily by investing in its distribution channels expanding into new geographic markets attracting and training employees and enhancing marketing programs.

Another key strategy is improving its use of technology to improve its operating efficiencies and the services it offers its customers. In 2019 American National launched its newly redesigned website AmericanNational.com. The site has been designed to create a more manageable and easy-to-use experience for clients and visitors with a new modernized look and more relevant content.

American National also executed a holding company reorganization in July 2020 which it announced in February earlier that year. Pursuant to such reorganization American National is now the parent company of ANICO and has replaced it as the publicly held corporation.

Company Background

American National was founded by Galveston businessman W. L. Moody in 1905. The Moody Foundation a charitable trust controlled by W L. Moody descendant Robert Moody and his family and the Moody National Bank together own about 70% of the company.

Based in hurricane-prone Galveston Texas American National knows first-hand the importance of property/casualty insurance and how to evaluate risk. The company withdrew from writing some policies along the Atlantic and Gulf coasts in 2005 and in 2008 it moved its claims processing facilities further inland to San Antonio.

American National launched the American National Life Insurance Company of New York in 2010.

EXECUTIVES

Evp Independent Marketing Group, David A. Behrens, age 57, $532,569 total compensation
Chairman President And Ceo, James E. Pozzi, age 69, $918,847 total compensation
Evp Cfo Treasurer And Multiple Line (ml) And Property And Casualty (p&c) Operations, Timothy A. Walsh, age 58, $400,400 total compensation
Evp Career Sales And Service Division, Hoyt J. Strickland, age 63, $375,353 total compensation
Assistant Vice President National Business Development Executive, Emerson Unger
Vice President Health Administration, Tracy Milina
Vice President Application Development, Toya Harper
Vice President, Wayne Smith
Evp Health Insurance Operations, James Stelling
Vice President Broker Dealer Marketing, Steven Dobbe
National Sales Manager, Mike Sawdey
Vice President Of Sales, Craig Klenk
Assistant Vice President Life Insurance, Sharon Garner
Vice President Special Markets, Mark Walker
National Sales Manager, Kendra Kelly
Vice President, Kara Phillips
Assistant Vice President Advanced Sales And Priority Markets, Walter Rudecki
National Sales Manager, Michael Kresl
Vice President Life Policy Administration, Bruce Pavelka
Assistant Vice President, Wayne Cucco
Assistant Vice President And Assistant Actuary, Michael Shumate
Associate Medical Director, Kim Mlcak
National Sales Manager, J Taylor
Svp Application Development And Support, Meredith Mitchell
Senior Vice President Securities Investments, Gordon Dixon
Vice President Human Resources, Olivia Smith
Vice President Marketing, Debie Knowles
Assistant Vice President Data Communications Messaging (its), Jimmy Watson
National Sales Manager, Jason Weaver
Assistant Vice President And Director Telecommunications, James McEniry
Senior Vice President Actuary, Frank Broll
Vice President Fixed Income, Anne Lemire
Vice President, Bob Schefft
Assistant Vice President And Associate Medical Director, John White
Assistant Vice President Director Life Marketing Sales Director, Clu Jon O'Neal

Svp Independent Marketing Group Operations, Lee Ferrell
National Sales Manager, Thomas Granata
Assistant Vice President Of Claims, Brittany Newsom
National Sales Manager, Alice Pitts
Svp And Chief Marketing Officer Multiple Line, Scott Campbell
Senior Vice President Computing Services, Brian Bright
Vice President, Trish Boudreaux
National Sales Manager, Brooke ChFC
Vice President Sales, Dan Safriet
Vice President Commercial Services, Iris Gillies
Vice President Information Technology, Jeff Mills
Vice President Chief Life, Byrd Matthew
Vice President Life New Business, Chairez Philip
Avp Financial Marketing Credit Insurance Division, Eddie Waters
National Sales Manager, David Mcelroy
Assistant Vice President Of Claims, Thomas Legrand
National Sales Manager, James Tadeo
Vice President And Controller, Michelle Gage
Vice President Sales, Gretta Bassett
Vice President Mortgage Loan Production, Denny Fisher
Vice President Direct Marketing And Sales, Richard Katz
Vice President And Health Actuary, Bill Watson
Vice President, Ryan Novak
Vice President Acquisitions, Lasneske Cheryl
Secretary, Mark Flippin
Auditors: DELOITTE & TOUCHE LLP

LOCATIONS

HQ: American National Group Inc
One Moody Plaza, Galveston, TX 77550-7999
Phone: 409 763-4661
Web: www.anico.com

PRODUCTS/OPERATIONS

2017 Sales

	$ mil.	% of total
Premiums		
Property/Casualty	1,360	40
Life	328	10
Annuity	222	6
Accident & Health	156	5
Net investment income	966	28
Other policy revenue	248	7
Realized investment gains	104	3
Other	37	1
Adjustments	(13.3)	-
Total	**3,411**	**100**

Selected Subsidiaries

American National Life Insurance Company of Texas (ANTEX)
American National Life Insurance Company of New York
American National Property and Casualty Company (ANPAC)
ANICO Financial Services Inc.
Garden State Life Insurance Company
Pacific Property and Casualty Company
Standard Life and Accident Insurance Company
United Farm Family Insurance Company

COMPETITORS

Allstate
American Financial Group
CNO Financial
Farmers Group
HCI Group
Mutual of Omaha
National Western
Nationwide
New York Life
Penn Mutual
Prudential
State Farm
Torchmark
USAA

HISTORICAL FINANCIALS

Company Type: Public

Income Statement   FYE: December 31

	ASSETS ($ mil.)	NET INCOME ($ mil.)	INCOME AS % OF ASSETS	EMPLOYEES
12/19	28,597	620	2.2%	—
12/18	26,912	159	0.6%	4,640
12/17	26,386	493	1.9%	4,621
12/16	24,533	181	0.7%	4,597
12/15	23,746	242	1.0%	4,736
Annual Growth	**4.8%**	**26.4%**	**—**	**—**

2019 Year-End Financials

Debt ratio: 0.55%
Return on equity: 11.03%
Cash ($ mil.): 452
Current ratio: —
Long-term debt ($ mil.): —
No. of shares (mil.): 26
Dividends
Yield: 0.0%
Payout: 14.2%
Market value ($ mil.): 3,164

	STOCK PRICE ($) FY Close	P/E High/Low	Earnings	PER SHARE ($) Dividends	Book Value
12/19	117.68	7 5	23.07	3.28	222.77
12/18	127.24	22 19	5.91	3.28	195.54
12/17	128.25	7 6	18.31	3.28	194.82
12/16	124.61	19 14	6.71	3.26	172.85
12/15	102.27	13 10	9.02	3.14	165.55
Annual Growth	**3.6%**	**—**	**26.5%**	**1.1%**	**7.7%**

American Tower Corp (New)

Growth in wireless communications is taking American Tower to new heights. The company rents space on towers and rooftop antenna systems to wireless carriers and radio and TV broadcasters who use the infrastructure to enable their services. It owned about 25000 towers in the US nearly 75000 in India and nearly 60000 throughout the rest of the world. Its portfolio additionally includes approximately 1775 Distributed Antenna System networks. American Tower also offers tower-related services such as site acquisition structural analysis to determine support for additional equipment and zoning and permitting management services.

Operations

American Tower's primary business is the leasing of antenna space on multi-tenant communications sites. It provides the service to wireless providers radio and television broadcast companies wireless data providers government agencies and municipalities and tenants from several other industries.

The company operates six business segments mostly based in regions where it leases its properties. The US Property segment is its largest and accounts for some 55% of revenue. The other geographic segments are: Latin America Property about 20 % of revenue; Asia Property more than 15% of revenue; Africa property with nearly 10%; and Europe with less than 5%. The Services segment which generates the remaining revenue acquires sites and offers zoning and permitting services and structural analysis to support its site leasing businesses.

Geographic ReachBoston MA-headquartered American Tower operates its corporate functions in the US and runs distributed operations in its international markets. The company produces most of its revenue in the US. More than 15% of revenue comes from India about 10% originates in Brazil and more than 5% comes from Mexico. The communications firm also operates in a variety of countries in Europe and Africa (Germany France Ghana Kenya Nigeria South Africa and Uganda) and in Latin America (Argentina Chile Colombia Costa Rica Mexico Paraguay and Peru).

Sales and MarketingAmerican Tower's top three tenants generate most of its total revenue: more than 20% from AT&T Mobility some 15% from Verizon Wireless and about 10% from T-Mobile. Other top tenants include Sprint Airtel Telefonica MTN Group Limited and Vodafone.

Financial Performance

In 2019 revenue rose 2% year-over-year to $7.6 billion. U.S. property segment revenue growth of $366.6 million was attributable to tenant billings growth of $276.5 million.

Net income jumped 52% to $1.9 billion in 2019 compared to 2018's $1.3 billion. The increase in net income was primarily due to an increase in their operating profit a decrease in other operating expenses primarily related to a decrease in impairment charges of $299.8 million and a decrease in stock-based compensation expense.

Cash grew by about $273.1 million in 2019 to end the year with $1.6 billion in the coffers. Cash provided by operations and financing activities were $3.8 billion and $521.7 million respectively. Cash used for investing activities was $4.0 billion.

Strategy

As the use of wireless services on handsets tablets and other advanced mobile devices grows and evolves there is a corresponding increase in demand for the communications infrastructure required to deploy current and future generations of wireless communications technologies. To capture this demand the company's primary operational focus is to increase the occupancy of their existing communications real estate portfolio to support global connectivity invest in and selectively grow their communications real estate portfolio further improve their operational performance and efficiency including through innovation initiatives and maintain a strong balance sheet. American Tower believe these efforts to meet their tenants' needs will support and enhance their ability to capitalize on the growth in demand for wireless infrastructure. In addition the company expect to explore new opportunities to enhance or extend their shared communications infrastructure businesses including those that may make their assets incrementally more attractive to new tenants or to existing tenants for new uses and those that increase their operational efficiency.

Mergers and Acquisitions

In early 2020 American Tower has completed its previously announced acquisition of London-based Eaton Towers Holdings Limited adding approximately 5700 communications sites to its African portfolio. The transaction cost was approximately $1.85 billion including the assumption of existing Eaton Towers' debt.

In addition to early 2020 transaction the company has also reached an agreement with MTN Group Limited to acquire MTN's minority stakes in each of the company's joint ventures in Ghana and Uganda for total consideration of approximately $523 million. The transaction is expected to close in the first quarter of 2020 and will result in a one-time impact for American Tower of approximately $65 million in 2020 from the payment of previously deferred cash interest related to joint venture debt.

Company Background

In 1995 American Tower starts off as a subsidiary of American Radio and begins to grow through acquisitions. American Tower parent company – American Radio – is sold to CBS/Viacom and American Tower is spun off into a separate company. The company goes public under the New York Stock Exchange (NYSE) as AMT in 1998.

American Tower shifts operational focus from acquiring and developing towers to improving operations. This leads to the sale of the American Tower ancillary businesses in 2003 and the sale of the construction services unit in 2004. American Tower acquires XCEL in 2009 an Indian company that owns and operates approximately 1700 tower sites. In the US the company focuses its efforts on enhancing operations and customer service and in 2018 acquires over 700 towers from Telkom Kenya.

EXECUTIVES

Evp And Cfo, Thomas A. (Tom) Bartlett, age 61, $750,000 total compensation

Chairman President And Ceo, James D. (Jim) Taiclet, age 59, $1,100,000 total compensation

Evp International Operations; President Latin America And Emea, William H. (Hal) Hess, age 57, $650,000 total compensation

Evp And President Us Tower, Steven C. Marshall, age 59, $650,000 total compensation

Evp; President Asia, Amit Sharma, age 60

Evp Chief Administrative Officer General Counsel And Secretary, Edmund (Ed) DiSanto, age 68, $600,000 total compensation

Ceo Europe Middle East And Africa, Leah C. Stearns

Chairman Atc Europe, Stephen Harris

Senior Vice President Corporate Legal, Ruth Dowling

Senior Vice President Finance Latam, Alejandro Messmacher

Senior Vice President Information Technology And Pe Ust, James Blestowe

Chief Sales Officer, Vivek Garg

Vice President Compensation And Benefits, Michelle Freeman

Auditors: DELOITTE & TOUCHE LLP

LOCATIONS

HQ: American Tower Corp (New)
116 Huntington Avenue, Boston, MA 02116
Phone: 617 375-7500
Web: www.americantower.com

2017 Sales

	$ mil.	% of total
U.S.	3,703	56
India	1,164	17
France	59	1
Germany	63	1
Ghana	122	2
Nigeria	213	3
South Africa	106	2
Uganda	60	1
Argentina	15	-
Brazil	620	10
Chile	40	1
Colombia	89	1
Costa Rica	19	-
Mexico	364	5
Paraguay	2	-
Peru	17	-
Total	**6,663**	**100**

PRODUCTS/OPERATIONS

2017 Sales

	$ mil.	% of total
Property	6,566	99
Services	98	1
Total	**6,664**	**100**

COMPETITORS

Crown Castle International	SBA Communications
LCC International	VelociTel
Microwave Transmission Systems	

HISTORICAL FINANCIALS

Company Type: Public

Income Statement   FYE: December 31

	REVENUE ($ mil.)	NET INCOME ($ mil.)	NET PROFIT MARGIN	EMPLOYEES
12/19	7,580	1,887	24.9%	5,454
12/18	7,440	1,236	16.6%	5,026
12/17	6,663	1,238	18.6%	4,752
12/16	5,785	956	16.5%	4,507
12/15	4,771	685	14.4%	3,371
Annual Growth	**12.3%**	**28.8%**		**12.8%**

2019 Year-End Financials

Debt ratio: 56.20%	No. of shares (mil.): 442
Return on equity: 36.33%	Dividends
Cash ($ mil.): 1,501	Yield: 1.6%
Current ratio: 0.47	Payout: 105.2%
Long-term debt ($ mil.): 21,127	Market value ($ mil.): 101,785

	STOCK PRICE ($) FY Close	P/E High/Low	PER SHARE ($) Earnings	Dividends	Book Value
12/19	229.82	56 37	4.24	3.78	11.41
12/18	158.19	60 48	2.77	3.15	12.10
12/17	142.67	57 38	2.67	2.62	14.56
12/16	105.68	59 42	1.98	2.17	15.84
12/15	96.95	73 61	1.41	1.81	15.69
Annual Growth	**24.1%**	—	**31.7%**	**20.2%**	**(7.6%)**

Ameriprise Financial Inc

Ameriprise Financial provides solutions to help clients confidently achieve their financial objectives.It does so through its various brands and affiliates — which include Ameriprise Financial Services Columbia Threadneedle and RiverSource. Ameriprise manages some $973 billion in assets for individual and institutional clients. It markets and administers its products primarily through a network of over 4000 financial advisors. Founded in 1894 Ameriprise Financial was spun off from American Express in 2005.

Operations

Ameriprise operates four main segments: Advice & Wealth Management Asset Management Annuities Corporate and other and Protection.

Its Advice & Wealth Management segment includes over 2000 employee advisors and approximately 7800 independent franchises. Together they provide financial planning advice and brokerage services primarily to the firm's US retail clients. The segment generates about 40% of revenue.

Asset Management (nearly 25% of revenue) offers investment management and products to retail high-net-worth and institutional clients globally. It does so through Columbia Management in the US and Threadneedle internationally. Columbia manages about 150 funds (mutual funds ETFs etc.) and about 70 variable insurance trust funds (VIT

Funds) in the US while Threadneedle manages about 155 funds outside the US.

The Annuities segment provides variable and fixed annuity products to individual clients via Ameriprise's RiverSource subsidiary. It also brings in more than 15% of revenue.

The Corporate & Other segment which accounts for about 10% of sales consists of the long term care business and net investment income or loss on corporate level assets including excess capital held in our subsidiaries and other unallocated equity and other revenues as well as unallocated corporate expenses.

The Protection segment offers Ameriprise clients insurance products including life disability income and property/casualty. It represents nearly 10% of sales.

Geographic Reach

Ameriprise Financial and its affiliates are headquartered in Minneapolis Minnesota. Other primary offices are in New York City Boston London and India. The US is by far its largest market generating more than 90% of profits. Ameriprise's non-US presence is mostly through its Columbia Threadneedle brand which has activities in the US UK and Europe in addition to an early-stage presence in the other major continents.

Sales and Marketing

Ameriprise's customers are varied ranging from individuals to universities to institutional clients The company's primary retail clients come from the 'mass affluent consumer' segment which controls more than $100000 all investable assets in the US. The firm markets to them through its financial advisor network and its website. Ameriprise tends to the non-retail segment (institutional & high-net-worth individuals) by nurturing direct relationships with entities such as employee savings plan endowments pension plans sovereign wealth funds corporations banks trusts and governmental entities.

Financial Performance

Net revenues increased $132 million or 1% to $13.0 billion for the year ended December 31 2019 compared to $12.8 billion for the prior year. Management and financial advice fees increased $239 million or 4% to $7.0 billion for the year ended December 31 2019 compared to $6.8 billion for the prior year primarily due to higher average equity markets wrap account net inflows and a $57 million increase in performance fees partially offset by asset management net outflows and a $27 million negative foreign currency translation impact.

Net income fell 10% to $1.9 billion due to higher banking and deposit interest expense and overall expenses.

Ameriprise's cash balance grew by $330 million to $6.2 billion during 2019. Operations generated $2.3 billion while investing activities used $3.2 billion and financing provided $1.2 billion.

Strategy

Ameriprise uses strategic marketing alliances local marketing programs for their advisors and on-site workshops through its Business Alliances group to generate new clients for financial planning and other financial services. An important aspect of the company's strategy is creating alliances that help them generate new financial services clients within their target market segment - the mass affluent and affluent and increasingly those with $500000 to $5000000 in investable assets. Ameriprise's alliance arrangements are generally for a limited duration of one to five years with an option to renew. Additionally these types of marketing arrangements typically provide that either party may terminate the agreements on short notice usually about sixty days. The company compensate their alliance partners for providing opportunities to market to their clients.

On October 1 2019 the company completed the sale of their Ameriprise Auto & Home Insurance business ("AAH") to American Family Insurance Mutual Holding Company (American Family Insurance).

EXECUTIVES

Chairman And Ceo, James M. (Jim) Cracchiolo, age 61, $1,025,000 total compensation
Ceo Global Asset Management, William F. (Ted) Truscott, age 59, $675,000 total compensation
Evp And Cfo, Walter S. Berman, age 78, $675,000 total compensation
Evp Human Resources, Kelli A. Hunter, age 59
President Advice And Wealth Management Products And Service Delivery, Joseph E. (Joe) Sweeney, age 59, $550,000 total compensation
Chief Strategy Officer; President Insurance And Annuities, John R. Woerner, age 51
Evp Marketing Corporate Communications And Community Relations, Deirdre D. McGraw, age 50
Coo; President Advice & Wealth Management Business Development, Neal Maglaque
Evp And Cio, Randy Kupper
Evp And Global Chief Investment Officer, Colin Moore, $475,000 total compensation
Evp Ameriprise Franchise Group, Bill Williams
Evp Ameriprise Advisor Group, Pat O'Connell
Evp And General Counsel, Karen Wilson Thissen
Vice President Operations, George Tsafaridis
Vice President, William Emptage
Vice President Of Marketing, Heather Melloh
Vice President Human Resources, Karen Dekker
Vice President Technology Operations, Heather Null Hanscom
Field Vice President, Homer Smith
Vice President Corporate Communications And Community Relations, Sharon Hughes
Vice President Head Of Fixed Income Capital Markets Trading, Pete Sirbu
Vp Compensation, John Cronin
Vice President Financial Applications Support Controllership, John Mead
Vice President Appointed Actuary, Stephen Blaske
Vice President And General Manager, Sandeep Sugavanam
Regional Vice President, Tara Eisenbeis
Vice President Wholesaling Operations, Mike Kirchner
Vp Controller, Michael Mattox
Senior Vice President Investor Relations, Alicia Charity
Vice President, Gregory Blockhus
Vice President Managed Accounts, Eric Paluck
Vice President Marketing, Linda Moriarty
Vice President P1 Business Development, Craig Wallenta
Financial Advisor And Vp Brehm And Murray, Jay Murray
Associate Vice President, Jeffrey Hess
Vice President Human Resources Business Partner, Melanie Demont
Vice President Compliance, Stephanie Rustad
Vice President And Group Counsel, Daniel Moakley
Field Vice President, Todd Orton
Vice President Business Development And National, Lynn Abbott
Vice President Human Resources Services, Jay Rasula
Vice President And Group Counsel, David Fogel
Vice President Risk Management Owned Assets, David Berger
Vice President, Paul Major
Svp Corporate Tax, Richard Bush
Vice President=clr Project Management Office, Mike Greene
Vice President, Chip Pierron
Franchise Field Vice President, Brad Sabol

Vice President General Manager Managed Products, Greg Nordmeyer
Vice President Clearing Operations, Dan McAskin
Vice President Architecture, Tom Esselman
Financial Advisor Vice President, Barry Craine
Senior Vice President Treasurer, Jim Hamalainen
Senior Franchise Field Vice President, Dean Mcgill
Vice President Trading Brokerage Clearing, Gregory Carr
Franchise Field Vice President, Matthew Roesser
Vice President Information Technology, Clarissa C Ramos
Vice President Product Management, Sarah Arnold
Assistant Vice President, Stacia Murray
Vice President Portfolio Manager, Nic Pifer
Senior Vice President Corp Comm And Community Relations Ameriprise Financial Inc., Deirdre Davey
Vice President, Erika Perrault
Vice President And Group Counsel, Kurt Johansen
Region Vice President, Matthew Miller
Regional Vice President, John Leahy
Vice President Finance, Jennifer Seifriz
Vice President Finance, Rob Bardot
Vp Head Of Advice Wealth Management Ops, Manish Ganatra
Vice President Training And Development, Lamont Boykins
Vice President Of Technical Department, Jacqueline Glockner
Vice President Field Strategy And Implement, Mark Traut
Vice President Human Capital Projects, Carol Hondlik
Vice President, Nancy Anderson
Vice President Clearing Operations, Michael Pszybylski
Executive Vice President Ameriprise Advisor Group, Patrick O'connell
Vice President Treasury, Shweta Jhanji
Avp Financial Advisor, Michael Geary
Senior Regional Vice President Insurance West, Bj Seastone
Vice President, Amanda Schneider
Vice President Broker Dealer Operations Recruiting And Finance Compliance Oversight, Brett Flansburg
Vp Hr Communications And Human Capital Strategies, Kristin Kooda-chizek
Vice President And India Head Of Technology, Rajeev Sethi
Vice President And Financial Advisor, Edward Moran
Vice President Financial Advisor, Jeffrey Greenwald
Vice President, Kurtis Larson
Vice President Strategic Transformation, Michael Jordan
Associate Vice President Financial Advisor, Jeffrey Lynn
Vice President Investment Management Annuity Products, Kevin St John
Vice President Derivative And Product Risk, Manuel Balsera
Vice President Complex Product Management Wmps, Steven Williamson
Vice President, Gary Farthing
Vice President Alternative Investments, Paul Mumma
Regional Vice President Retirement Wealth Strateg, Joseph Peppe
Division Vice President Riversource Annuities, Doug Brewers
Vp Diversity And Inclusion, Rudy Rodriguez
Vice President Financial Advisor, Nathan Foret
V.p. Sales, Andrew Wright
Vice President Marketing Strategy Retail Retirement, Abu Arif
Senior Vice President Arris Financial Group, Marcus Hall

Vice President Planning And Administration, Matt Haglund
Vice President Risk Management, Jennifer Zwach
Divisional Vice President, Michael J DeLorenzo
Associate Vice President Of Finance, Brian Mccabe
Associate Vice President, Bob Dennis
Vice President, Pradeep Gokhale
Associate Vice President Investments, John Stella
Associate Vice President, Karen Hartley
Vice President, Christopher Grella
Regional Vice President, Rob Elstad
Vice President Diversity And Inclusion Ameriprise Financial, Rodolfo Rodriguez
Financial Advisor: Vice President, Amy Boyle
Vice President Treasury, Mike Pollei
Vice President And Investment Officer, Josh Waterman
Vice President Finance, Dawn Brockman
Vice President Finance, Dave Melander
Vice President Finance (columbia Threadneedle Investments), Brian Engelking
Vice President Annuity Product Development, Steve Wolfrath
Vice President Editorial Planning And Governance, Tracey Domke
Franchise Region Vice President, Barry Stockdale
Vice President, James J Obrien
Vice President Flight Operations And Chief Pilot, Steve Kozlow
Associate Vice President, Daniel Shontere
Regional Vice President, Tim McClurg
Vice President Federal Government Affairs, Elizabeth Varley
Regional Vice President, John Berg
Vice President Investments, Jack Boone
Vice President Financial Advisor, Mark Masson
Associate Vice President, Mark Silbert
Franchise Field Vice President Pacific Northwest, George Varones
Vice President I And A Pmo, Abir Roy
Vice President And Group Counsel, Edward Walton
Evp Finance, Brian N McGrane
Franchise Field Vice President Assistant, Deborah Gable
Associate Vice President Financial Advisor, Clare Hiatt
Vice President Financial Advisor, James Motteler
Vice President, James Obrien
Vice President, Jason Reiling
Vice President Compensation, Luke Malloy
Vice President Finance, Margulis Michael
Associate Vice President, Gardner Quin
Vice President Financial Advisor, Rath Colin
Vice President, Hagenbach Scott
Vice President, Lomsdalen Stephen
Vice President Wealth Management Solutions National Sales Manager, David Lieberman
Vice President And Chief Counsel, David Andrew
Regional Vice President Annuities New England, Doug Lawrence
Auditors: PricewaterhouseCoopers LLP

LOCATIONS

HQ: Ameriprise Financial Inc
1099 Ameriprise Financial Center, Minneapolis, MN 55474
Phone: 612 671-3131
Web: www.ameriprise.com

PRODUCTS/OPERATIONS

2018 Sales

	$ mil.	% of total
Advice & Wealth Management	5,237	41
Asset Management	2,961	23
Protection	2,145	17
Annuities	2,120	16
Corporate and other	231	2
Non-operating revenue	141	1
Total	**12,835**	**100**

2018 Sales

	$ mil.	% of total
Management & financial advice fees	6,776	52
Distribution fees	1,877	15
Net investment income	1,596	12
Premiums	1,426	11
Other revenues	1,249	10
Banking & deposit interest expense	(89)	-
Total	**12,835**	**100**

PRODUCTS & SERVICES
Cash Cards & Lending
Financial Planning
Insurance & Annuities
Investments
Personal Trust Services

Selected Subsidiaries and Affiliates

American Enterprise Investment Services Inc.
Ameriprise Financial Services Inc.
Ameriprise Certificate Company
Ameriprise Trust Company
Columbia Management Investment Advisers LLC
Columbia Management Investment Distributors Inc.
IDS Property Casualty Insurance Company
J. & W. Seligman & Co. Incorporated
RiverSource Distributors Inc.
RiverSource Life Insurance Co. of New York
Threadneedle Asset Management Holdings

Selected Brands

Ameriprise Financial®;
Columbia Management®;
RiverSource®;

COMPETITORS

AXA Financial	MassMutual
Allstate	Merrill Lynch
Bank of America	MetLife
Bank of New York Mellon	Nationwide Financial
Calamos Asset Management	New York Life
	Northwestern Mutual
Capital Group	PNC Financial
Charles Schwab	Primerica
Citigroup	Principal Financial
FMR	Prudential
First Eagle Investment Mangement	Regions Financial
	State Street
John Hancock Financial Services	TIAA
	U.S. Bancorp
Lincoln Financial Group	

HISTORICAL FINANCIALS

Company Type: Public

Income Statement   FYE: December 31

	REVENUE ($ mil.)	NET INCOME ($ mil.)	NET PROFIT MARGIN	EMPLOYEES
12/19	12,967	1,893	14.6%	12,500
12/18	12,835	2,098	16.3%	14,000
12/17	12,027	1,480	12.3%	13,000
12/16	11,696	1,314	11.2%	13,000
12/15	12,170	1,562	12.8%	13,000
Annual Growth	1.6%	4.9%	—	(1.0%)

2019 Year-End Financials

Debt ratio: 3.24%	No. of shares (mil.): 123
Return on equity: 33.45%	Dividends
Cash ($ mil.): 3,827	Yield: 2.2%
Current ratio: 0.67	Payout: 26.8%
Long-term debt ($ mil.): 4,725	Market value ($ mil.): 20,646

	STOCK PRICE ($) FY Close	P/E High/Low		PER SHARE ($) Earnings	Dividends	Book Value
12/19	166.58	12	7	13.92	3.81	46.22
12/18	104.37	13	7	14.20	3.53	40.99
12/17	169.47	18	12	9.44	3.24	40.90
12/16	110.94	15	10	7.81	2.92	40.66
12/15	106.42	16	12	8.48	2.59	42.20
Annual Growth	11.9%	—	—	13.2%	10.1%	2.3%

Ameris Bancorp

Ameris Bancorp enjoys the financial climate of the Deep South. It is the holding company of Ameris Bank which holds roughly $3.6 billion in assets and serves retail and consumer customers through more than 75 full-service and mortgage branches in Alabama Georgia South Carolina and northern Florida. In addition to its standard banking products and services the bank also provides treasury services mortgage and refinancing solutions and investment services through an agreement with Raymond James Financial. Loans secured by commercial real estate accounted for approximately 45% of the company's loan portfolio while 1-4 family residential and construction & land development mortgages accounted for nearly a quarter and about 10% respectively.

Operations
Like most banks Ameris earns the vast majority of its recurring revenue (71.5%) from interest income from loans. Nearly 80% of these loans are made up of commercial real estate 1-4 family residential and construction & land development loans. The remaining 20% are from a mix of commercial multi-family residential and consumer loans (home improvement home equity personal lines of credit auto loans and student loans).

Traditional banking products (deposit accounts) and services along with investment products and services (which primarily earn income from fees and commissions) made up about 28% of the bank's annual sales in fiscal 2013.

Sales and Marketing
Through an acquisition-oriented growth strategy Ameris seeks to grow its brand and presence in the markets it currently serves in Georgia Alabama Florida and South Carolina as well as in neighboring communities. In addition the bank expects its community-oriented philosophy will help strengthen existing customer relations and attract new customers.

The company spent $1.62 million on advertising and public relations in Fiscal Year 2013 just under the $1.622 million it spent in 2012 and more than double the $722000 it spent in 2011. The company increased its advertising spending by $900000 during 2012 to support its revenue and growth- strategies during the year.

Financial Performance
Ameris carried $3.67 billion in total assets as of December 31 2013. Loans made up $2.5 billion (approximately 68.9% of total assets). The bank also reported carrying $3 billion in deposits.

Ameris' net revenue dipped in fiscal 2013 declining 5% to $163 million from its high of $172 million in 2012 mostly from an $11.3 million dip in non-interest revenue. But this dip in non-interest revenue is primarily because the bank recorded a large gain of $20 million from acquisitions in 2012. When excluding this acquisition gain from 2012's revenues and thanks to $6.1 million revenue increase in mortgage banking activity management reports that total non-interest income actually increased $8.7 million in 2013 compared to 2012. A decline in interest-earning loan assets from $2.47 billion in 2013 compared to $2.5 billion in 2012 also played a role in the dip in net revenues.

Thanks to aggressive acquisitions and despite revenue decreasing net income jumped a whopping 43% to $20 million in 2013 from $14 million in 2012. This is only slightly below the bank's net income high of $21 million in 2011. It's most notable acquisition of Prosperity Bank increased Ameris' total assets by $744.9 million and added $449.7 million in loans to its interest-earning loan portfolio. Adding to the extra income from new

loans Ameris collected higher net interest margins on all of its loans which increased to 4.74% in 2013 from 4.60% in 2012.

Strategy
Ameris plans to continue using its community banking philosophy to lessen its risk and identify prime local lending markets. Management reports that by encouraging a personalized service experience and building deeper customer relationships the bank has already grown a "substantial" base of low-cost core deposits (which pad the bank's reserves and lessen financial risk). And between its bench of experienced decision makers and lenders operating in a "decentralized" structure (which differentiates Ameris from mega banks) and its deep familiarity with local markets management believes the bank can better identify prime growth markets (for lending and bank services) with managed risk in the years ahead.

Mergers and Acquisitions
Integral to the bank's growth strategy Ameris has aggressively acquired banks to broaden its reach into its primary southern markets.

In 2019 the company's shareholders voted to acquire Fidelity Southern the holding company for Fidelity Bank. The combined company will have $16.2 billion in assets. Following the transaction Ameris will have more than 70 branches and some $4.7 billion in deposits in the Atlanta metropolitan area and about 25 branches and roughly $1.8 billion in deposits in the Jacksonville metropolitan area.

Ameris Bancorp purchased Jacksonville Bancorp and its eight branches more than doubling its branch network in Jacksonville Illinois to 14 branches.

Company Background
In addition to acquiring several troubled and failing banks with help from the FDIC Ameris merged with Prosperity Bank in 2013 which broadened its reach into Florida through Prosperity's branches in St. Augustine Jacksonville Panama City Lynn Haven Palatka and Ormand Beach.

Georgia's economy was one of the hardest hit in the US during the recession and Ameris has taken advantage of the plethora of banks seized by regulators in the state. Since 2009 the company has acquired about 10 failed banks in Georgia though FDIC-assisted transactions adding some 20 branches to its network. Ameris also snagged the failed First Bank of Jacksonville in Florida which had two locations.

EXECUTIVES

Chief Banking Executive Ameris Bancorp And Ameris Bank, Andrew B. (Andy) Cheney, age 70, $400,000 total compensation

Evp And Chief Credit Officer, Jon S. Edwards, age 58, $260,000 total compensation

Evp Chief Administrative Officer And Corporate Secretary, Cindi H. Lewis, age 66, $90,333 total compensation

President And Ceo, Edwin W. (Ed) Hortman, age 66, $625,000 total compensation

Evp And Chief Banking Officer Georgia And Alabama, Lawton E. Bassett

Evp Cfo And Coo, Dennis J. Zember, age 50, $320,000 total compensation

Evp And Chief Risk Officer, Stephen A. Melton, $275,000 total compensation

Evp And Chief Banking Officer, James A. LaHaise

Exec V Pres-cio, Thomas Limerick

Assistant Vice President, Ann Dunn

Vice President Branch Manager, Colleen Cline

Vice President, Thomas Luther

Senior Vice President, Rob Kowkabany

Vice President Special Assets Division, Leo Story

Vice President Residential Mortgage, Greg
Seabaugh
Senior Vice President Division President
Construction, Chap Bennett
Vice President Commercial Lender, Greg Marini
Senior Vice President, Karen Cross
Assistant Vice President Commercial Banker,
Jason Glas
Assistant Vice President Branch Manager, Ruth
Myrick
Senior Vice President, Jw Dukes
Vice President Sba Business Development
Officer, Jordan Samsel
Vice President Coastal Sales Manager, Jason Fralix
Vice President Senior Treasury Services Advisor,
Lori Putnam
Vice President Accounting Manager P. O. Box
3668, Marsha Dotson
Vice President, Connie Romay
Vice President Mortgage Sales Manager, Marlene
Buhler
Assistant Vice President And Office Manager, Erin
Scott
Vice President Business Banker, Robbie Nichols
Senior Vice President Commercial Banking,
Gerald Lockhart
Senior Vice President, Frank Cox
Senior Vice President Commercial Lending,
Jennifer Ccim
Avp Regional Compliance Officer, Sybrena Jacobs
Vice President, Vicki Beaudry
Vice President, Mark Mathews
Chairman, Daniel B. Jeter, age 68
Board Member, William Bowen
Auditors: Crowe LLP

LOCATIONS

HQ: Ameris Bancorp
3490 Piedmont Rd N.E., Suite 1550, Atlanta, GA 30305
Phone: 404 639-6500
Web: www.amerisbank.com

PRODUCTS/OPERATIONS

2016 sales chart

	$ mil.	% of total
Interest income:		
Interest and fees on loans	218	64
Interest on taxable securities	17	5
Interest on nontaxable securities	1	.
Interest on deposits in other banks	0	.
Interest on federal funds sold	- -	
Non Interest income:		
Service charges on deposit accounts	42	13
Mortgage banking activity	48	14
Other service charges commissions and fees	3	1
Net gains on sales of securities	- -	
Gain on sale of SBA loans	3	1
Other noninterest income	7	2
Total	**344**	**100**

2016 sales chart

	% of total
Banking Division	91
Retail Mortgage Division	5
Warehouse Lending Division	3
SBA Division	1
Total	**100**

Selected Acquisitions

American United Bank
Central Bank of Georgia
Darby Bank & Trust
First Bank of Jacksonville
High Trust Bank
Montgomery Bank & Trust
One Georgia Bank
Satilla Community Bank
Tifton Banking Company
United Security Bank

COMPETITORS

BBVA Compass
Bancshares
Bank of America
Capital City Bank
Colony Bankcorp
Community Capital
Bancshares

First South Bancorp
(NC)
Regions Financial
Southwest Georgia
Financial
SunTrust
Thomasville Bancshares

HISTORICAL FINANCIALS

Company Type: Public

Income Statement

FYE: December 31

	ASSETS ($ mil.)	NET INCOME ($ mil.)	INCOME AS % OF ASSETS	EMPLOYEES
12/19	18,242	161	0.9%	2,722
12/18	11,443	121	1.1%	1,804
12/17	7,856	73	0.9%	1,460
12/16	6,892	72	1.0%	1,298
12/15	5,588	40	0.7%	1,304
Annual Growth	**34.4%**	**41.0%**	—	**20.2%**

2019 Year-End Financials

Debt ratio: 2.18%
Return on equity: 8.22%
Cash ($ mil.): 597
Current ratio: —
Long-term debt ($ mil.): —

No. of shares (mil.): 69
Dividends
Yield: 1.1%
Payout: 17.1%
Market value ($ mil.): 2,957

	STOCK PRICE ($) FY Close	P/E High/Low	PER SHARE ($) Earnings	Dividends	Book Value
12/19	42.54	16 12	2.75	0.50	35.53
12/18	31.67	21 11	2.80	0.40	30.66
12/17	48.20	26 21	1.98	0.40	21.59
12/16	43.60	23 12	2.08	0.30	18.51
12/15	33.99	27 18	1.27	0.20	15.98
Annual Growth	**5.8%**	—	— **21.3%**	**25.7%**	**22.1%**

AmerisourceBergen Corp.

AmerisourceBergen is the source for many of
North America's pharmacies and health care
providers. The distribution company serves as a
go-between for drug makers and the pharmacies
doctors' offices hospitals and other health care
providers that dispense drugs. Operating primarily
in the US it distributes generic branded and over-
the-counter pharmaceuticals as well as some medical supplies and other products using its network
of facilities. Its specialty distribution unit focuses
on sensitive and complex biopharmaceuticals.
Other operations include pharmaceutical packaging commercialization and consulting services and
animal health product distribution.

Operations

AmerisourceBergen operates through an alphabet soup of subsidiaries. Its main operating segment — Pharmaceutical Distribution Services —
distributes drugs specialty drugs over-the-counter
health care products including equipment and outsourced compounded sterile preparations. Customers include hospitals health systems pharmacies clinics and long-term care facilities. It delivers
specialty drugs for particular diseases (especially
cancer) directly to the doctors who administer
them. The segment also distributes plasma and
other blood products injectable pharmaceuticals

and vaccines. Pharmaceutical Distribution Services
brings in around 95% of the group's total annual
revenue.

Other operations are engaged in global commercialization services and animal health.
AmerisourceBergen Consulting Services (ABCS)
provides integrated manufacturing services including clinical trial support and post-approval commercialization support. Another unit World
Courier provides specialty logistics and transportation for the biopharmaceutical sector in more than
50 countries. MWI distributes animal health pharmaceuticals vaccines parasiticides micro-feed ingredients and other products to the companion
animal and production animal markets in the US
and the UK. These operations combined bring in
less than 5% of the group's total revenue.

Geographic Reach

AmerisourceBergen's Pharmaceutical Distribution Services segment owns distribution facilities
in Alabama California Illinois Massachusetts Michigan Missouri Ohio Pennsylvania Texas and Virginia. The company also have significant facilities
located in Puerto Rico plus the following states:
Arizona Colorado Florida Georgia Hawaii Indiana
Kentucky Minnesota Mississippi New York North
Carolina Utah and Washington.

ABCS is headquartered in South Carolina and
internationally in Canada.

World Courier is headquartered in London and
has locations in more than 50 countries around
the world.

MWI is active in the US and the UK. It is headquartered in Idaho and owns facilities in Alabama
Idaho Texas and Virginia as well as in the UK. It
leases locations in California Colorado Florida
Idaho Indiana Kansas Massachusetts Minnesota
North Carolina Pennsylvania Texas Washington
and the UK.

Sales and Marketing

AmerisourceBergen serves customers including
hospitals and health systems retail and mail order
pharmacies medical clinics and long-term care facilities throughout North America. The company's
two largest customers Walgreens Boots Alliance
and Express Scripts account for approximately
35% and approximately 15% of total revenue respectively. Its top 10 customers account for some
two-thirds of revenue.

Each of the company's businesses have independent sales and marketing personnel who specialize in their respective offerings.

AmerisourceBergen also has a corporate marketing group for branding and broad-scale initiatives.

Financial Performance

In 2019 revenue increased by 6.9% from the
prior fiscal year primarily due to the revenue
growth of their Pharmaceutical Distribution Services segment. The Pharmaceutical Distribution
Services segment grew its revenue by 6.9% from
the prior fiscal year primarily due to the growth of
some of its largest customers continued strong
specialty product sales and overall market growth.
Revenue in Other increased 8.5% from the prior
fiscal year primarily due to ABCS's growth in its
Canadian operations growth at MWI growth at
World Courier and the January 2018 consolidation
of the specialty joint venture in Brazil.

Net income fell 47% to $854.1 million in fiscal
2019. That fall was due to the $325.5 fall in their
income tax expense.

The company ended fiscal 2019 with $3.4 billion
in net cash $887.7 million more than it had at the
end of fiscal 2018. Operating activities provided
$2.3 billion in cash while investing activities used
$375.8 million and financing activities used an-
other $1.1 billion.

Strategy

The company's business strategy is focused on the global pharmaceutical supply channel where they provide value-added distribution and global commercialization services to healthcare providers and pharmaceutical manufacturers that improve channel efficiencies and patient outcomes. Implementing this disciplined and focused strategy in a seamless and unified way has allowed them to significantly expand their business and they believe they are well positioned to grow revenue and increase operating income through the execution of the following key element of their business strategy: optimize and grow their pharmaceutical distribution and strategic global sourcing businesses; optimize and grow their global commercialization services and animal health businesses; acquisitions and divestures.

Company Background

AmerisourceBergen traces its roots back to 1871 when Lucien Napoleon Brunswig partnered with wholesale drug firm Wheelock-Finlay. In the 1900s the company began focusing exclusively on wholesale drug distribution.

HISTORY

In 1977 Cleveland millionaire and horse racing enthusiast Tinkham Veale went into the drug wholesaling business. His company Alco Standard (now IKON Office Solutions) already owned chemical electrical metallurgical and mining companies but by the late 1970s the company was pursuing a strategy of zeroing in on various types of distribution businesses.

Alco's first drug wholesaler purchase was The Drug House (Delaware and Pennsylvania); the next was Duff Brothers (Tennessee). The company then bought further wholesalers in the South East and Midwest. Its modus operandi was to buy small well-run companies for cash and Alco stock and leave the incumbent management in charge.

By the early 1980s Alco was the US's third-largest wholesale drug distributor and growing quickly (28% between 1983 and 1988) at a time of mass consolidation in the industry (the number of wholesalers dropped by half between 1980 and 1992). In 1985 Alco Standard spun off its drug distribution operations as Alco Health Services retaining 60% ownership.

Alco Health boosted its sales above $1 billion mostly via acquisitions and expanded product lines. The company offered marketing and promotional help to its independent pharmacy customers (which were beleaguered by the growth of national discounters) and also targeted hospitals nursing homes and clinics.

The US was in the midst of its LBO frenzy in 1988 but an Alco management group failed in its attempt. Rival McKesson then tried to acquire Alco Health but that deal fell through for antitrust reasons. Later in 1988 management turned for backing to Citicorp Venture Capital in another buyout attempt. This time the move succeeded and a new holding company Alco Health Distribution was formed.

In 1993 Alco Health was named as a defendant in suits by independent pharmacies charging discriminatory pricing policies; a ruling the next year limited its liability. To move away from a reliance on independent drugstores Alco Health began targeting government entities and others.

Alco Health went public as AmeriSource Health in 1995. Throughout the next year AmeriSource made a series of acquisitions to move into related areas including inventory management technology drugstore pharmaceutical supplies and disease-management services for pharmacies.

In 1997 AmeriSource acquired Alabama-based Walker Drug for $140 million adding 1500 independent and chain drugstores in the Southeast to its customer list. That year McKesson once again made an offer to buy AmeriSource this time for $2.4 billion while two other major wholesale distributors Cardinal Health and Bergen Brunswig reached a similar pact. The deals were scrapped in 1998 when the Federal Trade Commission voted against both pacts and a federal judge supported that decision.

Later that year AmeriSource signed a five-year deal to become the exclusive pharmaceutical supplier to not-for-profit Sutter Health; in 1999 it renewed similar contracts with the US Department of Veterans Affairs and Pharmacy Provider Services Corporation. That year AmeriSource bought Midwest distributor C.D. Smith Healthcare.

In 2001 AmeriSource bought Bergen Brunswig and the combined company renamed itself AmerisourceBergen.

Its AmerisourceBergen Packaging Group (ABPG) was taken apart in 2012 and its American Health Packaging and AndersonBrecon businesses were moved into other divisions. In 2013 the company sold its AndersonBrecon division which provided contract packaging services to an investor group led by Frazier Healthcare for some $308 million. It also sold its AmerisourceBergen Canada Corporation (ABCC) pharma distribution business that year while retaining its Canadian specialty distribution operations.

In 2012 its biggest customer Medco Health Solutions (17% of revenues) merged with Express Scripts which contracted with one of Amerisource-Bergen's competitors; however following the merger Express Scripts alleviated concerns when it signed a new supply agreement with AmerisourceBergen.

In 2013 AmerisourceBergen signed a 10-year agreement to supply Walgreen Boots Alliance.

EXECUTIVES

Vice President, Stan Byrum
Chairman President And Ceo, Steven H. Collis, age 59, $1,234,231 total compensation
Evp And Cfo, Tim G. Guttman, age 61, $706,539 total compensation
Evp And Chief Marketing Officer, Gina K. Clark, age 63
Evp And Chief Legal & Business Officer, John G. Chou, age 64, $621,231 total compensation
Group President Pharmaceutical Distribution And Strategic Global Sourcing, James F. (Jim) Cleary, age 57
Evp And President Health Systems Physician Practices And Strategic Health Solutions, Peyton R. Howell, age 53
Evp And Cio, Dale Danilewitz, age 58
Evp; President Amerisourcebergen Drug, Robert P. Mauch, age 53, $593,077 total compensation
Evp And Chief Human Resources Officer, Kathy H. Gaddes, age 57
Evp Strategy And Development, Sun Park, age 44
Vice President Strategic Accounts, Kent Rischar
Vp Integration, Frank Napoli
Vice President Gerneric Rx Product Development, Brian Jones
Vice President Information Systems, Dennis Hone
Vice President Operations, Joe Williamson
Vice President Professional Services, Kathryn Uchida
Vice President Operations West, Bill Wilson
Vice President Health Systems Business Developmen, Matthew Glucksmann
Senior Vice President, George P Rafferty
Vice President Of Sales, Greg Arnold
Vice President, Derek Idalski
Vice President Strategic Accounts, Susan Bertot
Human Resource Vice President Director Manager, Matijasich Richard
Vice President Sales, Lianne Chung
Vice President Information Technology, Michael Wondrasch
Vice President Of Strategic Accounts, Matt Johnson
Gvp Business Development, Bruce Bennett
Vice President Financial Planning And Analysis, Jeannine Altrogge
Vice President Community Pharmacy Buying Groups, Rich Hazinski
Segment Vice President, Jeff Sharkey
Vice President Human Resources, Jay Webster
Vice President Contracts Chargebacks, Linda Ewald
Vice President Finance, Nik Kristic
Vice President Global Sourcing Operations, Barbara Miller
Group Vice President, Derek Redcross
Vice President National Accounts Ltc Gpo's, Rick Miller
Vice President Of Information Technology, Sandy Piscitello
Vice President Business Operations, Terry Forrest
Pharmacy Manager, Troy Rebert
Vice President Health Sys Solutions, Rick Lang
Vice President Health Systems Sales, Michael Haddad
Vice President Integration Management Business Architect, Emily D Lightfoot
Vice President Financial Processes, Brian Mangiaracina
Vice President Customer Solutions, Jeff Wilkinson
Vice President Generics Sales, Russell Procopio
Lead Vice President Sales, Scott Snyder
Senior Vice President, Joe Short
Vice President Supply Chain Solutions, Wesley Jones
Executive Assistant To Senior Vice President Chief Human Resources Officer And Chief Information Officer, Kelly Jakeman
Vice President Tax, Daniel Hirst
Senior Vice President Strategic Accounts, Steve Iampietro
Vice President Infrastructure And Technology, John Demartino
Vice President Global Technology Sourcing And Vendor Management, Kate Schutzler
Chief Financeancial Officer Senior Vice President, Mike Dicandilo
Senior Vice President Of Marketing, Thomas Connolly
Vice President Marketing, Michael Clarke
Vice President Operations, Michael Rathburn
Vice President Market Development, Vicki Cooney
Sales Vice President, Catherine Carminati
Vice President Nephrology, William Venus
Vice President Communications, Gabriel Weissman
Vice President Human Resources, Rosalyn Wesley
Vice President Procurement, Lindell Denny
Vice President, Blake Jarrell
Vice President Policy, Stacie Heller
Vice President Accounts Payable, Judi Schmidt
Senior Vice President Corporate Controller, Lazarus Krikorian
Vice President Supply Chain Solutions, Michael Kody
Vice President Specialty Client Strategies, Erin K Rausch
Vice President Engineering, John Shook
Senior Vice President Government Affairs, Rita Norton
Vice President Of Pricing Global Sourcing And Manufacturer Relations, Alexander Kugler
Vice President Consumer Products Strategic Global Sourcing, Doug Trueman
Vice President Relationship Manager, Matthew Winter
Eits Vice President Distribution Services, Andy Johnson

Vice President Health Systems Solutions, Steve Miller

Vice President Global Animal Health Sourcing And Inventory Management, Kevin Price

Vice President Tax Planning And Research, Melissa Haskin

Vice President Of Infrastructure Services, Ty Mallard

Vice President Marketing And Business Development, Jeff Nordquist

Group Vice President Health Systems, Andrew Moore

Vice President Strategic Accounts, Joseph Cappello

Vice President And Controller Western Financial Center, Mark Krikorian

Vice President Health Systems Solutions, Dave Bartel

Board Member, Henry W McGee

Board Member, Douglas Conant

Board Member, Lon R Greenberg

Auditors: Ernst & Young LLP

LOCATIONS

HQ: AmerisourceBergen Corp.
 1300 Morris Drive, Chesterbrook, PA 19087-5594
Phone: 610 727-7000   Fax: 610 647-0141
Web: www.amerisourcebergen.com

PRODUCTS/OPERATIONS

2018 Sales by Segment

	$ mil.	% of total
Pharmaceutical Distribution Services	161,699	96
Other	6,332	4
Adjustments	(92.4)	-
Total	**167,939**	**100**

COMPETITORS

Cardinal Health	Medline Industries
Express Scripts	Owens & Minor
FFF Enterprises	Quality King
Henry Schein	UPS
McKesson	

HISTORICAL FINANCIALS

Company Type: Public

Income Statement				FYE: September 30
	REVENUE ($ mil.)	NET INCOME ($ mil.)	NET PROFIT MARGIN	EMPLOYEES
09/20	189,893	(3,408)	—	22,000
09/19	179,589	855	0.5%	22,000
09/18	167,939	1,658	1.0%	21,000
09/17	153,143	364	0.2%	20,000
09/16	146,849	1,427	1.0%	19,000
Annual Growth	**6.6%**	—	—	**3.7%**

2020 Year-End Financials

Debt ratio: 9.30%
Return on equity: (-365.53%)
Cash ($ mil.): 4,597
Current ratio: 0.98
Long-term debt ($ mil.): 3,618
No. of shares (mil.): 204
Dividends
 Yield: 1.7%
 Payout: 21.9%
Market value ($ mil.): 19,794

	STOCK PRICE ($) FY Close	P/E High/Low		PER SHARE ($) Earnings	Dividends	Book Value
09/20	96.92	—	—	(16.65)	1.66	(4.99)
09/19	82.33	23	17	4.04	1.60	13.92
09/18	92.22	14	10	7.53	1.52	13.76
09/17	82.75	58	41	1.64	1.46	9.47
09/16	80.78	16	11	6.32	1.36	9.68
Annual Growth	**4.7%**	—	—	—	—	**5.1%**

Amgen Inc

Amgen is among the biggest of the biotechs. The company uses cellular biology and medicinal chemistry to target cancers kidney ailments inflammatory disorders and other diseases. Their top protein-based therapeutic products include Enbrel (rheumatoid arthritis) Neulasta (anti-infective for cancer patients) Prolia and XGEVA (osteoporosis and bone metastases) and Aranesp and Epogen (used to fight anemia in chronic kidney disease and cancer patients). In addition Amgen has extensive drug research and development programs. Amgen's products are marketed in about 100 countries; the US market accounts for almost 75% of sales.

HISTORY

Amgen was formed as Applied Molecular Genetics in 1980 by a group of scientists and venture capitalists to develop health care products based on molecular biology. George Rathmann a VP at Abbott Laboratories and researcher at UCLA became the company's CEO and first employee. Rathmann decided to develop a few potentially profitable products rather than conduct research. The company initially raised $19 million.

Amgen operated close to bankruptcy until 1983 when company scientist Fu-Kuen Lin cloned the human protein erythropoietin (EPO) which stimulates the body's red blood cell production. Amgen went public that year. It formed a joint venture with Kirin Brewery in 1984 to develop and market EPO. The two firms also collaborated on recombinant human granulocyte colony stimulating factor (G-CSF later called Neupogen) a protein that stimulates the immune system.

Amgen joined Johnson & Johnson subsidiary Ortho Pharmaceutical (later Ortho-McNeil Pharmaceutical) in a marketing alliance in 1985 and created a tie with Roche in 1988. Fortunes soared in 1989 when the FDA approved Epogen (the brand name of EPO) for anemia. (It is most commonly used to counter side effects of kidney dialysis.)

In 1991 Amgen received approval to market Neupogen to chemotherapy patients. A federal court ruling also gave it a US monopoly for EPO. The following year Amgen won another dispute forcing a competitor to renounce its US patents for G-CSF.

As the company grew it needed to transform itself from startup to going concern; to do so Amgen hired MCI veteran Kevin Sharer as president in 1992. Neupogen's usage was expanded in 1993 to include treatment of severe chronic neutropenia (low white-blood-cell count).

In 1993 Amgen became the first American biotech to gain a foothold in China through an agreement with Kirin Pharmaceuticals to sell Neupogen (under the name Gran) and Epogen there. The purchase of Synergen in 1994 added another research facility accelerating the pace of and increasing the number of products in research and clinical trials.

Although Amgen had two proven sellers in Epogen and Neupogen its growth lay in its pipeline. In 1997 Amgen and partner Regeneron Pharmaceuticals reported the failure of human trials for a drug to treat Lou Gehrig's disease. Still its new drug Stemgen for breast cancer patients undergoing chemotherapy was recommended for approval by an FDA advisory committee in 1998. Amgen had to swallow a couple of tough legal pills in 1998. First a dispute with J&J over Amgen's 1985 licensing agreement with Ortho Pharmaceutical ended when an arbiter ordered Amgen to pay about $200 million. Later that year however Amgen won a legal battle with J&J over the rights to a promising anemia drug.

Work on its product pipeline continued in 1999: Amgen ended development of obesity and Parkinson's disease drugs after clinical trials produced discouraging results while it began human tests with partner Guilford Pharmaceuticals on a drug designed to regenerate damaged nerve cells in the brains of Parkinson's disease patients. (Guildford and Amgen ended the collaboration in 2001.)

In 2000 the firm resumed its battle to keep its stranglehold on the Epogen market: It sued Transkaryotic Therapies and Aventis (later Sanofi-Aventis) for alleged patent violations over its Epogen product in both the US and the UK. Although it initially won its case in the UK that verdict was overturned in 2002 making Amgen vulnerable to competition before Epogen's patents expire in 2004. That year it won EU and US approval for Aranesp an updated version of Epogen; Amgen in 2002 teamed with former J&J marketing partner Fresenius to sell Aranesp in Germany and take some market share away from J&J. Meanwhile an arbitration committee found J&J had breached its contract with Amgen when it sold Procrit to the dialysis market which Amgen had reserved for itself in their 1985 licensing deal.

In 2003 the company bought leukemia and rheumatoid arthritis drugs maker Immunex. As part of the FTC's blessing on the $10.3 billion union Amgen and Immunex licensed some technologies to encourage competition. Merck Serono gained access to Enbrel data and Regeneron Pharmaceuticals licensed some interleukin inhibitor rights.

The next year Amgen spent $1.3 billion to purchase the remaining 79% of cancer treatment technology maker Tularik that it did not already own.

Additional drug approvals included Neulasta (2002) Sensipar (2004) Vectibix (2006) Nplate (2008) Prolia and XGEVA (2010).

In the 2010s Amgen worked to extend its reach in international markets. In addition to extending its product offerings into high-growth regions such as Japan China Russia and Africa the firm made select international acquisitions.

The firm entered the biosimilar market in 2011. It acquired deCODE Genetics (genome analysis) and Micromet (BLINCYTO developer) in 2012 and Onyx Pharmaceuticals (Kyprolis developer) in 2013. Additional drugs Corlanor IMLYGIC and Repatha were launched in 2015.

EXECUTIVES

Svp Us Commercial Operations, Laura Hamill

Evp Full Potential Initiatives, Brian M. McNamee, age 64

Svp Global Marketing And Commercial Development, Suzanne Blaug

Evp Global Commercial Operations, Anthony C. (Tony) Hooper, age 65, $1,031,788 total compensation

Svp General Counsel And Secretary, Jonathan P. Graham, age 59, $916,789 total compensation

Evp And Cfo, David W. Meline, age 62, $946,733 total compensation

Svp Global Business Services, Michael A. Kelly, age 63, $511,757 total compensation

Evp Research And Development, Sean E. Harper, age 57, $946,246 total compensation

Chairman And Ceo, Robert A. (Bob) Bradway, age 58, $1,531,731 total compensation

Svp Global Regulatory Affairs And Safety, Paul R. Eisenberg

Svp And Head European Region, Corinne Le Goff

Svp Manufacturing, Esteban Santos

Vice President, Brian Kotzin

Medical Director, Lucy Yan
Vp Human Resources, John Oakes
Medical Director Medical Sciences, Jane Parnes
Medical Director International Development
Amgen International, Georg Kreuzbauer
Vice President Market Access And Payer Strategy,
Tom Rice
Vice President Of Global Archi, Kyle Cribbs
Vp Operations, Jesse Daignault
Vp Supply Chain, Rayne Waller
Vice President Business Development, David
Piacquad
Vp Human Resources, Edda Colon
Medical Director, Vladimir Hanes
Vice President Finance And Treasurer, Mary
Lehmann
Vice President General Manager Germany, Roland
Wandeler
National Sales Manager, Mike Ellis
Vice President Corporate Accounts, Aston William
Vice President Of Pre Clinical Research, David
Balaban
Vice President General Manager Us Bone Health
Bu, Ken Keller
Administrative Coordinate Government Relations,
Janice Vasquez
Vice President, Rob Lenz
Vice President Sales, Jeff Ludwig
Vice President Investor Relations, Arvind Sood
Vice President Global Development, Richard
Markus
Vice President Information Technology, Betty
Endres
Executive Medical Director, Primal Kaur
Senior Executive Assistant To Kurt Gustafson
Vice President Operations Finance Commercial
Manufacturing, Heidi Katz
National Sales Manager, Garvan Byrne
Vp Of Marketing, Dave Marek
Vice President, Karen Laureano
Senior Vice President Global Business Services
And Finance, Judy Gawlik Brown
Executive Vice President Global Commercial
Operations, Tony Hooper
Vice President Global Scientific Affairs, Rosh Dias
Vice President Global Product General Manager,
Simon Clowes
Vice President Oncology And Inflammation
Discovery Rese, Flavius Martin
Medical Director Global Development, Jyotsna
Reddy
Executive Medical Director, Cesar Cerezoolmos
Senior Vice President Business Development,
Dave Piacquad
Medical Director Global Development.
Neuroscience, Hernan Picard
Vice President Of Information Technology,
Christina Sarff
Evp Global Commercial Operations, Murdo Gordon
Medical Director Medical Affairs Cardiovascular,
Kiran Philip
Vp Us Medical Affairs, Robert Cuddihy
Senior Vice President Finance, Joe Peter
National Sales Manager, Alan Ng
Treasurer, Loretta Joseph
Auditors: Ernst & Young LLP

LOCATIONS

HQ: Amgen Inc
One Amgen Center Drive, Thousand Oaks, CA 91320-
- 1799
Phone: 805 447-1000   Fax: 805 447-1010
Web: www.amgen.com

2017 Sales

	$ mil.	% of total
U.S.	18,029	79
Rest of the world	4,820	21
Total	**22,849**	**100**

Selected Locations

Algeria
Australia
Austria
Belgium
Brazil
Bulgaria
Canada
China
Colombia
Croatia
Czech Republic
Denmark
Egypt
Estonia Japan
Finland
France
Germany
Greece
Hong Kong
Hungary
Iceland
India
Ireland
Italy
Latvia
Lithuania
Luxembourg
Mexico
Netherlands
Norway
Poland
Portugal
Romania
Russia
Saudi Arabia
Slovakia
Slovenia
South Africa
Spain
Sweden
Switzerland
Turkey
United Arab Emirates
United Kingdom
United States

PRODUCTS/OPERATIONS

2017 Sales

	$ mil.	% of total
Product sales	21,795	95
Other revenues	1,054	5
Total	**22,849**	**100**

2017 Sales

	$ mil.	% of total
ENBREL	5,433	24
Neulasta	4,534	20
Aranesp	2,053	9
Prolia	1,968	9
Sensipar/Mimpara	1,718	8
XGEVA	1,575	7
EPOGEN	1,096	5
NEUPOGEN	835	4
KYPROLIS	642	3
Vectibix	642	3
Nplate	549	2
Repatha	319	1
BLINCYTO	175	0
Other	256	1
Other revenues	1,054	4
Total	**22,849**	**100**

Top Selling Products

Neupogen/Neulasta (chemotherapy-induced neutropenia
- low white blood cells and cancer-related infections)
Enbrel (rheumatoid arthritis psoriasis)
Aranesp (chemotherapy-induced anemia and chronic
renal failure anemia sustained duration Epogen)
Epogen (anemia in chronic renal failure)
Sensipar/Mimpara (also known as Mimpara chronic
kidney disease)
Xgeva (to prevent bone fractures)
Vectibix (monoclonal antibody for colorectal cancer)
Nplate (romiplostim for autoimmune bleeding disorder
ITP or immune thrombocytopenic purpura)
Prolia (postmenopausal osteoporosis)

COMPETITORS

AbbVie	Merck
AstraZeneca	Merck KGaA
Bayer HealthCare	Millennium: The Takeda
Pharmaceuticals Inc.	Oncology Company
Celgene	Nektar Therapeutics
Chugai	Regeneron
Eli Lilly	Pharmaceuticals
Genentech	Sanofi
GlaxoSmithKline	Teva
Hospira	UCB
Janssen Biotech	

HISTORICAL FINANCIALS

Company Type: Public

Income Statement   FYE: December 31

	REVENUE ($ mil.)	NET INCOME ($ mil.)	NET PROFIT MARGIN	EMPLOYEES
12/19	23,362	7,842	33.6%	23,400
12/18	23,747	8,394	35.3%	21,500
12/17	22,849	1,979	8.7%	20,800
12/16	22,991	7,722	33.6%	19,200
12/15	21,662	6,939	32.0%	17,900
Annual Growth	**1.9%**	**3.1%**	**—**	**6.9%**

2019 Year-End Financials

Debt ratio: 50.08%   No. of shares (mil.): 591
Return on equity: 70.73%   Dividends
Cash ($ mil.): 6,037   Yield: 2.4%
Current ratio: 1.44   Payout: 45.0%
Long-term debt ($ mil.): 26,950   Market value ($ mil.): 142,569

	STOCK PRICE ($) FY Close	P/E High/Low		PER SHARE ($) Earnings	Dividends	Book Value
12/19	241.07	19	13	12.88	5.80	16.36
12/18	194.67	16	13	12.62	5.28	19.85
12/17	173.90	70	56	2.69	4.60	34.95
12/16	146.21	17	13	10.24	4.00	40.47
12/15	162.33	19	14	9.06	3.16	37.25
Annual Growth	**10.4%**	**—**	**—**	**9.2%**	**16.4%**	**(18.6%)**

Amphenol Corp.

A connected world needs connections at the
basic level: from component to component and
from device to device. That's where Amphenol
Corp. comes in. The company is a manufacturer
of connector and interconnect products for the
communications industrial automotive aerospace
military mobile networks and devices. In addition
it designs manufactures and markets electrical
electronic and fiber optic connectors and interconnect systems antennas sensors and sensor-based
products and coaxial and high-speed specialty
cable. It is also used for electrical and optical signals in computers wired and wireless communications networking equipment vehicles aircraft and
spacecraft and energy applications. Amphenol also
makes high-speed and specialized coaxial cable.
Nearly 70% of its sales come from outside the US.
Certain predecessor businesses of the company
were founded in 1932.

Operations

The company operates through two reporting
segments: Interconnect Products and Assemblies
and Cable Products and Solutions.

Amphenol's Interconnect Products and Assemblies segment accounts for about 95% of sales.
This primarily designs manufactures and markets
a broad range of connector and connector systems
value-add products and other products including

antennas and sensors used in a broad range of applications in a diverse set of end markets.

The Cable Products and Solutions segment accounts for 5% of revenue from sales of cables and components for the broadband communications and information technology markets.

In terms of markets information technology and data communications industrial and automotive each account for about 20% of revenue. Mobile devices account for about 15% of revenue; military accounts for more than 10% and mobile networks supplies about 10% and broadband communications and commercial aerospace about 5% each.

Geographic Reach

Amphenol based in Wallingford Connecticut has broad geographic coverage with some 475 locations — manufacturing facilities warehouses and offices — in more than 30 countries around the world. The company handles its own manufacturing with facilities in low-cost manufacturing areas and near customers. The US accounts for about 30% of Amphenol's sales and the China provides about 30% with other countries supplying the rest.

The company designs manufactures and assembles its products at facilities in the Americas Europe Asia Australia and Africa.

Sales and Marketing

Amphenol's customers include many of the leaders in their respective industries. Its products are sold directly to original equipment manufacturers (OEMs) electronic manufacturing services (EMS) firms original design manufacturers (ODMs) cable system operators and IT companies. The company sells its products through its own global sales force independent representatives and a global network of electronics distributors. The Company's sales to distributors represented approximately 15% of the company's net sales in 2019.

The company's sales are heavily weighted in the communications industry. The combination of sales to information technology and data communication mobile device mobile network and broadband communications companies adds up to about half of its revenue.

Financial Performance

In 2019 the company reported net sales of $8.2 billion which was flat compared to 2018 along with operating income and net income attributable to Amphenol Corporation of $1.6 billion and $1.2 billion respectively both representing a decrease of 4% from 2018. Net income was primarily impacted by excess tax benefits related to a stock-based compensation.

In 2019 Amphenol had $891.2 million in cash in its coffers about $388.1 million less than in 2018. Operations generated $1.5 billion in 2019 while investing and financing activities used $1.2 billion and $648.4 million respectively.

Strategy

Amphenol's overall strategy is to provide its customers with comprehensive design capabilities a broad selection of products and a high level of service on a worldwide basis while maintaining continuing programs of productivity improvement and cost control. Specifically its business strategy is as follows:

Pursuing broad diversification. The company constantly drives to increase the diversity of its markets customers applications and products. Due to the tremendous variety of opportunities in the electronics industry management believes that it is important to ensure participation wherever significant growth opportunities are available.

Developing high technology performance-enhancing interconnect solutions. The company seeks to expand the scope and number of its preferred supplier relationships. Amphenol works closely with its customers at the design stage to create and manufacture innovative solutions.

Expanding global presence. The company intends to further expand its global manufacturing engineering sales and service operations to better serve its existing customer base penetrate developing markets and establish new customer relationships.

Controlling costs. Amphenol recognizes the importance in today's global marketplace of maintaining a competitive cost structure.

Pursuing strategic acquisitions and investments. The company believes that the industry in which it operates is highly fragmented and continues to provide significant opportunities for strategic acquisitions. Accordingly it continues to pursue acquisitions of high-growth potential companies with strong management teams that complement existing business while further expanding its product lines technological capabilities and geographic presence.

Fostering collaborative entrepreneurial management. Amphenol's management system is designed to provide clear income statement and balance sheet responsibility in a flat organizational structure. Each general manager is incented to grow and develop his or her business and to think entrepreneurially in providing innovative timely and cost-effective solutions to customer needs.

Mergers and Acquisitions

In 2019 the company acquired SSI Controls Technologies ("SSI") the sensor manufacturing division of SSI Technologies Inc. for approximately $400 net of cash acquired plus a performance-related contingent payment. SSI which is headquartered in the state of Wisconsin in the United States is a leading designer and manufacturer of sensors and sensing solutions for the global automotive and industrial markets.

During 2019 the company completed nine acquisitions (including SSI) for $937.4 net of cash acquired. All but one of the acquisitions are included in the Interconnect Products and Assemblies segment.

Company Background

Amphenol was founded in 1932 to make sockets to plug vacuum tubes into radios. Its first customer was RCA. Amphenol was founded by entrepreneur Arthur J. Schmitt in the Chicago area.

EXECUTIVES

Svp And Group General Manager It And Communications Products Division, Richard E. (Rick) Schneider, age 62, $490,000 total compensation
President Ceo And Director, Richard A. (Adam) Norwitt, age 51, $1,061,000 total compensation
Svp And Group General Manager Military And Aerospace Operations Group, Luc Walter, age 61, $560,000 total compensation
Svp And Cfo, Craig A. Lampo, age 50, $450,000 total compensation
Svp And Group General Manager Worldwide Rf And Microwave Products, Zachary W. Raley, age 51, $500,000 total compensation
Vp And Group General Manager Global Interconnect Systems Group, Jean-Luc Gavelle, age 60
Vp And Group General Manager Automotive And Sensor Products Division, John Treanor, age 62
Vp And Group General Manager Industrial Products Group, Martin W. Booker, age 61
Vp And Group General Manager It Communications Products Group, William J. Doherty, age 61
Vp And General Manager Mobile Consumer Products Group, Yaobin (Richard) Gu
Vice President Tax, Tom Meotti
Board Member, Stanley Clark
Chairman, Martin H. Loeffler, age 76
Auditors: DELOITTE & TOUCHE LLP

LOCATIONS

HQ: Amphenol Corp.
358 Hall Avenue, Wallingford, CT 06492
Phone: 203 265-8900   **Fax:** 203 265-8746
Web: www.amphenol.com

2018 Sales

	$ mil.	% of total
China	2,594	32
US	2,241	27
Other countries	3,366	41
Total	**8,202**	**100**

PRODUCTS/OPERATIONS

2018 Sales

	$ mil.	% of total
Interconnect products & assemblies	7,781	95
Cable products	420	5
Total	**8,202**	**100**

Selected Products

Interconnect products
  Fiber Optic
  Harsh Environment
  High-speed
  Power Busbars and Distribution Systems
  Radio Frequency
  Antennas
Cable Products   Coaxial
  Power
  Specialty
Others Antennas
  Flexible and Rigid Printed Circuit Boards
  Switches

COMPETITORS

3M	Huber + Suhner Inc.
Belden	Japan Aviation
Carlisle Companies	Electronics Industry
CommScope	Molex
Delphi Automotive	Panduit
Systems	Radiall
Esterline	Sensata
Hirose Electric	TE Connectivity
Hon Hai	Yazaki

HISTORICAL FINANCIALS

Company Type: Public

Income Statement
FYE: December 31

	REVENUE ($ mil.)	NET INCOME ($ mil.)	NET PROFIT MARGIN	EMPLOYEES
12/19	8,225	1,155	14.0%	74,000
12/18	8,202	1,205	14.7%	73,600
12/17	7,011	650	9.3%	70,000
12/16	6,286	822	13.1%	62,000
12/15	5,568	763	13.7%	50,700
Annual Growth	**10.2%**	**10.9%**	**—**	**9.9%**

2019 Year-End Financials

Debt ratio: 33.35%	No. of shares (mil.): 297
Return on equity: 27.03%	Dividends
Cash ($ mil.): 891	Yield: 0.8%
Current ratio: 1.97	Payout: 25.6%
Long-term debt ($ mil.): 3,203	Market value ($ mil.): 32,242

	STOCK PRICE ($) FY Close	P/E High/Low	PER SHARE ($) Earnings	Dividends	Book Value
12/19	108.23	28 19	3.75	0.96	15.21
12/18	81.02	24 19	3.85	0.88	13.46
12/17	87.80	43 31	2.06	0.70	13.05
12/16	67.20	26 17	2.61	0.58	11.92
12/15	52.23	24 20	2.41	0.53	10.51
Annual Growth	**20.0%**	**— —**	**11.7%**	**16.0%**	**9.7%**

Andersons Inc

Agribusiness giant The Andersons operates in a variety of areas including trade ethanol and plant nutrients and rail. It generates about half its sales from grain trading – primarily corn soybeans and wheat – via grain elevators located in the midwestern US. The company purchases and sells ethanol offers facility operations risk management and ethanol and corn oil marketing services to the ethanol plants it invests in and operates. The Anderson's Plant Nutrient Group makes and sells fertilizers crop protection chemicals and related products and the company leases repairs and sells railcars locomotives and barges through its Rail Group. It operates primarily in the US where nearly 80% of the company's total revenue is generated from.

Operations

The Andersons operates through four business segments: Trade Group (nearly 80% of sales) Ethanol Group (more than 10%) Plant Nutrient Group (nearly 10%) and Rail Group (generates the remaining).

It operates grain elevators and ethanol plants in Ohio Indiana Michigan and other US states through which customers buy and sell grain – primarily corn soybeans and wheat – and ethanol. The company also provides customers with marketing operations support and other services related to its grain and ethanol businesses.

The Andersons also sells a host of lawn plant and crop care products such as liquid and pelleted fertilizers and golf course and turf applications as well as corncob-based animal bedding and cat litter materials. In addition it leases repairs and sells new and used boxcars gondolas tank cars locomotives and barges and offers fleet management services.

Geographic Reach

Based in Ohio The Andersons' agricultural and Ethanol operations are spread across some 15 US states as well as Puerto Rico and Canada. Its railcar operations which include about two dozen repair facilities and a fabrication shop are primarily in the southern western and midwestern US. The US generates about 80% of the company's total sales.

Sales and Marketing

The Andersons distributes its products through its distributors and retailers. Most of the company's exported commodity sales are made through intermediaries while some commodities are shipped directly to foreign countries mainly Canada. The company ships grain from its facilities by rail truck or boat. Rail shipments are made primarily to grain processors and feeders with some rail shipments made to exporters on the Gulf of Mexico or east coast. Boat shipments are from the Port of Toledo or the Port of Houston. In addition commodities are transported via truck for direct ship transactions in which producers sell grain to the Company but delivered directly to the end user.

The Company does not have any customers who represent 10% or more of total revenues.

Advertising expense of $2.5 million in 2019 $1.9 million in 2018 and $2.5 million in 2017 respectively.

Financial Performance

After a rise in revenue in 2015 it slid down for three consecutive years until a sudden surge in 2019. Net income fluctuated for the same period.

In 2019 the company reported revenue of $8.2 billion a jump of 168% from the prior year. The change was a result of huge increases in sales of the trade segment.

Net income slid down 56% that year to $18.3 million as operating administrative and general expenses increased 69% from previous year.

Cash at the end of 2019 was $54.9 million an increase of $32.3 million from the prior year. Cash provided by operations was $348.6 million while investing activities used $325 million mainly for acquisitions and purchase of assets. Financing activities added $8.7 million to the coffers.

Strategy

The Andersons is looking to profit from macroeconomic trends including world population growth escalating demand for protein and increasing North American crop production. Its diverse agribusiness and industrial based activities are all exposed to these trends in one way or another from handling bulk commodities to using its rail cars and logistics assets to move them.

To capitalize on some of those trends the company is focused on growing its food ingredients and specialty grains business within the Grain Group while revamping the division with divestitures (four grain elevators in Tennessee) and acquisitions (Lansing Trade Group and its Canadian joint venture with Lansing Thompsons Limited). It expects to achieve some $10 million in productivity synergies from the Lansing purchase by the end of 2020.

The company continuously look for opportunities to enhance its existing businesses through strategic acquisitions and trade group will focus on growth of originations risk management services and the food ingredient business while monitoring macroeconomic events which could cause more volatility in the market.

Mergers and Acquisitions

In 2019 The Andersons took full ownership of Kansas-based Lansing Trade Group (it previously owned nearly a third) for some $324 million. The purchase which will be merged into the Grain Group to create The Andersons Trade Group enhances the company's position in the broader US agricultural marketplace.

Company Background

The Andersons grain terminal was founded in Maumee Ohio in 1947. It expanded into other areas of agriculture (fertilizer blending ear corn and cob milling lawn products) over the next two decades.

The company goes public in 1996 the same decade sales reach $1 billion. The Andersons enters the ethanol business the following decade.

EXECUTIVES

Svp Of General Counsel And Corporate Secretary, Naran Burchinow
President Retail Group, Daniel T. Anderson, $211,998 total compensation
President And Ceo, Patrick E. (Pat) Bowe, $900,000 total compensation
President Rail Group, Joseph E. McNeely
Cfo, John J. Granato, $403,846 total compensation
President Grain Group, Corbett J. (Corey) Jorgenson, $287,500 total compensation
Vp And General Manager Ethanol Group, Michael S. Irmen
Cio, Anthony Lombardi
President Plant Nutrient Group, Jeffrey C. Blair
Vice President Finance And Treasurer, James Burmeister
Vice President Of Manufacturing Manager, Naveed Ahmed
Vice President Marketing, Philip Couch
Svp And Cfo, Brian Valentine
Vice President General Manager Ethanol, James Pirolli
Vice President, Greg Logue
Chairman, Michael J. (Mike) Anderson
Board Member, Ross Manire
Board Member, Catherine Kilbane
Board Member, John Stout
Board Member, Patrick Mullin
Board Member, Gerard Anderson
Treasurer, Dana Anderson
Secretary, Elizabeth Moyer
Secretary, Sondra Anderson
Auditors: DELOITTE & TOUCHE LLP

LOCATIONS

HQ: Andersons Inc
1947 Briarfield Boulevard, Maumee, OH 43537
Phone: 419 893-5050
Web: www.andersonsinc.com

PRODUCTS/OPERATIONS

2018 Sales

	$ mil.	% of total
Grain Group	1,437	47
Ethanol Group	743	24
Plant Nutrient Group	690	23
Rail Group	174	6
Total	**3,045**	**100**

COMPETITORS

ADM	GROWMARK
Ag Processing Inc.	Gavilon Group
Bartlett and Company	Louis Dreyfus Group
Bunge Limited	Scoular
CHS	Southern States
Cargill	Wilbur-Ellis

HISTORICAL FINANCIALS

Company Type: Public

Income Statement   FYE: December 31

	REVENUE ($ mil.)	NET INCOME ($ mil.)	NET PROFIT MARGIN	EMPLOYEES
12/19	8,170	18	0.2%	2,320
12/18	3,045	41	1.4%	1,858
12/17	3,686	42	1.2%	1,843
12/16	3,924	11	0.3%	2,998
12/15	4,198	(13)	—	3,443
Annual Growth	18.1%	—		(9.4%)

2019 Year-End Financials

Debt ratio: 31.43%	No. of shares (mil.): 33
Return on equity: 2.03%	Dividends
Cash ($ mil.): 54	Yield: 2.7%
Current ratio: 1.35	Payout: 57.5%
Long-term debt ($ mil.): 1,016	Market value ($ mil.): 843

	STOCK PRICE ($) FY Close	P/E High/Low		PER SHARE ($) Earnings	Dividends	Book Value
12/19	25.28	67	32	0.55	0.69	29.20
12/18	29.89	28	19	1.46	0.67	29.14
12/17	31.15	29	20	1.50	0.65	28.74
12/16	44.70	109	59	0.41	0.63	27.43
12/15	31.63	—	—	(0.46)	0.58	27.34
Annual Growth	(5.4%)	—	—	—	4.5%	1.7%

Annaly Capital Management Inc

A real estate investment trust (REIT) Annaly Capital Management invests in and finances residential and commercial assets. It primarily manages a portfolio of mortgage-backed securities including mortgage pass-through certificates collateralized mortgage obligations and agency callable debentures. Commencing operations in 1997 the firm typically invests in high-quality securities issued or guaranteed by the likes of Freddie Mac Fannie Mae and Ginnie Mae and backed by single-family residential mortgages. More than 90% of Annaly's assets are agency mortgage-backed securities which carry an implied AAA rating. The firm is externally managed by Annaly Management Company LLC. In late 2019 Glenn Votek will serve as Chief Executive Officer and President on an interim basis as Kevin Keyes' departure from the company.

Operations

Annaly invests through four primary groups: Agency Residential Credit Commercial Real Estate and Middle Market Lending. The Agency group primarily invests in agency mortgage-backed securities and related derivatives. The Residential Credit group invests in non-agency residential mortgage-backed assets within securitized products and residential mortgage loan markets. Commercial Real Estate writes and invests in commercial mortgage loans securities and related assets and Middle Market Lending provides customized debt financing to middle-market businesses.

Annaly Agency Group is the largest portfolio generating about 95% while Residential Credit Group Commercial Real Estate Group and Middle Market Lending Group generates the remaining.

Geographic Reach

Headquartered in New York New York Annaly's residential mortgage loans primarily operates in California New York and Florida. Commercial trusts operates primarily in California Texas and New York while residential trusts primarily operates in California Texas Illinois and Washington.

Financial Performance

Annaly's net interest income had been steadily decreasing in five consecutive years; fell about 41% between 2015 and 2019.

The company's net loss in 2019 was $2.2 billion.

The company recorded an increase about $115 to $1.9 billion in 2019 compared to $1.7 billion in 2018. Operating activities used $1.2 billion while investing activities used $20.6 billion. Financing activities provided $22 billion. Annaly's main cash was used primarily in payments on purchases of Residential Securities payments on reverse repurchase agreements and dividends paid.

Strategy

In support of its diversification strategy its operating platform has expanded and has included investments in systems infrastructure and personnel. Its technology investments have led to the development of proprietary portfolio analytics financial and capital allocation modeling and other risk and reporting tools which coupled with cutting-edge digital transformation applications support the diversification and operating efficiency of the company's business. Its operating platform supports its investments in Agency assets as well as residential credit assets commercial real estate assets residential mortgage loans mortgage servicing rights and corporate loans. The diversity of its investment alternatives provides the company the flexibility to adapt to changes in market conditions and to take advantage of potential opportunities.

In mid-2019 the company announced that its Board of Directors has authorized the repurchase of up to $1.5 billion of its outstanding shares of common stock through late 2020.

In late 2019 Annaly and Curium jointly announced that Annaly has successfully implemented CuriumEDM as part of its multi-phased technology initiative focused on driving operational efficiencies and promoting transparency across its diversified operating platform.

In early 2019 Annaly and Capital Impact announced the launch of a new joint venture (Venture) with a $25 million commitment to support affordable housing and other community development projects in Washington D.C. (D.C.). This Venture represents Annaly's second impact investing partnership since 2017 with Capital Impact a national mission-driven non-profit community development financial institution.

EXECUTIVES

Cfo, Glenn A. Votek, age 61, $91,346 total compensation
Chairman President And Ceo, Kevin G. Keyes, age 52, $375,000 total compensation
Chief Legal Officer, Anthony C. Green
Chief Investment Officer, David L. Finkelstein, age 47
Chief Credit Officer, Timothy P. Coffey, age 46
Senior Vice President, Sarah Fowlkes
Vp It, Christopher Sullivan
Vice President, George Varghese
Vice President, Tom Brethour
Vp Business Development, David Burgess
Auditors: Ernst & Young LLP

LOCATIONS

HQ: Annaly Capital Management Inc
1211 Avenue of the Americas, New York, NY 10036
Phone: 212 696-0100   **Fax:** 212 696-9809
Web: www.annaly.com

COMPETITORS

AG Mortgage Investment Trust	Institutional Financial Markets
Capstead Mortgage	JAVELIN Mortgage
Drive Shack	MFA Financial
Impac Mortgage Holdings	Redwood Trust
	iStar Financial Inc

HISTORICAL FINANCIALS

Company Type: Public

Income Statement   FYE: December 31

	ASSETS ($ mil.)	NET INCOME ($ mil.)	INCOME AS % OF ASSETS	EMPLOYEES
12/19	130,295	(2,162)	—	175
12/18	105,787	54	0.1%	170
12/17	101,760	1,569	1.5%	152
12/16	87,905	1,433	1.6%	189
12/15	75,190	466	0.6%	149
Annual Growth	14.7%	—	—	4.1%

2019 Year-End Financials

Debt ratio: 8.11%	No. of shares (mil.): 1,430
Return on equity: (-14.47%)	Dividends
Cash ($ mil.): 1,850	Yield: 11.1%
Current ratio: —	Payout: —
Long-term debt ($ mil.): —	Market value ($ mil.): 13,472

	STOCK PRICE ($) FY Close	P/E High/Low		PER SHARE ($) Earnings	Dividends	Book Value
12/19	9.42	—	—	(1.60)	1.05	11.04
12/18	9.82	—	—	(0.06)	1.20	10.74
12/17	11.89	9	7	1.37	2.49	12.82
12/16	9.97	8	6	1.39	3.17	12.33
12/15	9.38	26	22	0.42	1.20	12.71
Annual Growth	0.1%			—	(3.3%)	(3.5%)

Anthem Inc

Health benefits provider Anthem through a number of subsidiaries provides health coverage to approximately 41 million members in the US. One of the nation's largest health insurers Anthem is a Blue Cross and Blue Shield Association licensee in more than a dozen states (where it operates as Anthem Empire and BCBS) and provides non-BCBS plans under the Unicare Amerigroup CareMore Simply Healthcare HealthSun HealthLink and other brands in more than 25 states. Plans include PPO HMO POS indemnity and hybrid plans offered to employers individuals and Medicare and Medicaid recipients. Anthem also provides administrative services to self-insured groups as well as specialty insurance.

Operations

Anthem operates through three segments: Government Business Commercial and Specialty Business and Other.

The Government Business segment accounting for about 60% of Anthem's total revenue provides Medicare Advantage Medicare Part D supplemental special needs and dual-eligibility plans as well as Medicaid and Children's Health Insurance Programs (CHIP) coverage. The segment's National Government Services unit acts as a Medicare contractor in some regions. The segment also includes services related to the Federal Employee Program.

The Commercial and Specialty Business segment accounting for about 35% of sales provides BCBS and non-BCBS health plans for employer groups and individuals; managed care services such as claims processing and underwriting for self-funded groups; and specialty products including dental vision life and disability coverage. The remaining revenue comes from the others segment.

Through several of its subsidiaries Anthem also performs claims processing stop loss insurance benefits management and other administrative tasks for government-run Medicare plans other insurance firms and employer groups.

Altogether the company serves more than 79 million customers.

Geographic Reach

Anthem is headquartered in Indianapolis Indiana and its subsidiaries are licensed to conduct insurance operations in about 50 states. It serves BCBS customers in more than a dozen states including California New York and Virginia and serves non-BCBS customers in more than 25 other states under UniCare Amerigroup Simply Healthcare and other brand names.

The firm has its largest concentration of customers in California Florida Georgia Indiana New York Ohio Texas and Virginia.

Sales and Marketing

Anthem markets most of its products through a network of independent agents and brokers. The exception is the company's national account and large employer-focused products which are sold by an in-house sales force customer-hired consultants and independent brokers.

The company uses print broadcast and other modes of advertising to promote itself. Advertising expenses totaled $467 million $385 million and $338 million for 2019 2018 and 2017 respectively.

Altogether the company serves more than 79 million people including approximately 41 million health plan members.

Financial Performance

The company's revenue increased 13% to $104.2 billion in 2019 compared to $92.1 billion in the prior year. The increase in operating revenue was primarily from higher premiums and to a lesser extent increased administrative fees and other revenue.

Net income for the year ended December 31 2019 was $4.8 billion an increase of $1.1 billion or 28% from the year ended December 31 2018. The increase in net income was due to higher operating results in both our Commercial & Specialty Business and Government Business segments in part due to the benefits realized from the launch of IngenioRx in 2019 net realized gains on financial instruments and lower income tax expense.

Cash held by the company in 2019 was $4.9 billion compared to $3.9 billion in the prior year. Cash provided by operations was $6.1 billion while cash used for investing and financing activities were $2.8 billion and $2.3 billion respectively.

Strategy

The company intend to retain the responsibilities for IngenioRx's clinical and formulary strategy and development member and employer experiences operations sales marketing account management and retail network strategy. From December 2009 through December 2019 we delegated certain PBM functions and administrative services to Express Scripts Inc. or Express Scripts pursuant their PBM agreement with Express Scripts or the ESI PBM Agreement.

The future results of their operations will also be impacted by certain external forces and resulting changes in the company's business model and strategy. The continuing growth in their government-sponsored business exposes them to increased regulatory oversight.

Anthem's strategy has been and will continue to be to only participate in rating regions where they have an appropriate level of confidence that these markets are on a path toward sustainability including but not limited to factors such as expected financial performance regulatory environment and underlying market characteristics.

Mergers and Acquisitions

In 2020 Anthem completed acquiring Beacon Health Options a Boston-based behavioral company as part of its strategy to diversify into health services. The firm aims to provide integrated and personalized care delivery models for people with complex and chronic conditions. Terms were not disclosed.

In 2020 Anthem Inc. announced that it has completed its acquisition of Medicaid plans in Missouri and Nebraska following the recent regulatory approval of WellCare's merger with Centene Corporation.

This acquisition expands Anthem's footprint to serve Medicaid beneficiaries in 23 states and the District of Columbia. The Missouri and Nebraska health plans will become wholly owned subsidiaries under the Government Business Division of Anthem Inc.

Company Background

Anthem traces its roots back to the formation of Blue Cross of Indiana and Blue Shield of Indiana in 1944 and 1946. The company changed its name to WellPoint after merging with WellPoint Health Networks in 2004; WellPoint Health Networks was formed by Blue Cross of California in 1992. The company changed its name from WellPoint back to Anthem in 2014.

In 2017 a federal judge blocked the planned $48 billion merger between Anthem and rival Cigna. The combined health insurance behemoth would have served some 53 million customers and generated sales of about $115 billion. The merger was blocked just weeks after a similar planned merger between Aetna and Humana was halted.

Recent acquisitions have included HealthSun (Medicare Advantage in Florida 2017) and Simply Healthcare (2015).

HISTORY

Anthem's earliest predecessor prepaid hospital plan Blue Cross of Indiana was founded in 1944. Unlike other Blues Blue Cross of Indiana never received tax advantages or mandated discounts so it competed as a private insurer. Within two years it had 100000 members; by 1970 there were nearly 2 million.

Blue Shield of Indiana another Anthem precursor also grew rapidly after its 1946 formation as a mutual insurance company to cover doctors' services. The two organizations shared expenses and jointly managed the state's Medicare and Medicaid programs.

The 1970s and early 1980s were difficult as Indiana's economy stagnated and health insurance competition increased. In 1982 the joint operation restructured adding new management and service policies to improve its performance.

Following the 1982 merger of the national Blue Cross and Blue Shield organizations the Indiana Blues merged in 1985 as Associated Insurance Companies. The next year the company moved outside Indiana began diversifying to help insulate itself from such industry changes as the shift to managed care and renamed itself Associated Group to reflect a broader focus.

By 1990 Associated Group had more than 25 operating units with nationwide offerings including health insurance HMO services life insurance insurance brokerage financial services and software and services for the insurance industry.

The group grew throughout the mid-1990s buying health insurer Southeastern Mutual Insurance (including Kentucky Blue Cross and Blue Shield) in 1992 diversified insurer Federal Kemper (a Kemper Corporation subsidiary) in 1993 and Seattle-based property/casualty brokerage Pettit-Morry in 1994. That year it entered the health care delivery market with the creation of American Health Network.

In 1995 the company merged with Ohio Blues licensee Community Mutual and took the Anthem name. Merger-related charges caused a loss that year.

Anthem bounced back the next year thanks to cost-cutting and customers switching to its more profitable managed care plans. Anthem divested its individual life insurance and annuity business and its Anthem Financial subsidiaries. Its 1996 deal to buy Blue Cross and Blue Shield of New Jersey fell apart in 1997 because of New Jersey Blue's charitable status. Anthem did manage to buy Blue Cross and Blue Shield of Connecticut that year.

Anthem in 1997 sold four property/casualty insurance subsidiaries to Vesta Insurance Group. It bought the remainder of its Acordia property/casualty unit (workers' compensation) then sold Acordia's brokerage operations. That year Anthem was involved in court battles regarding the Blue mergers in Kentucky as well as in Connecticut where litigants feared a rise in their premiums. Expenses related to merging Blues organizations contributed to a loss that year.

Anthem shed the rest of its noncore operations in 1998 selling subsidiary Anthem Health and Life Insurance Company to Canadian insurer Great-West Life Assurance. Its proposed purchase of Blue Cross and Blue Shield of Maine (which it acquired in 2000) and merger with the Blues in Rhode Island were met with outcries similar to those that dogged earlier pairings.

Larry Glasscock was appointed president and CEO of the company in 1999. Under Glasscock's leadership Anthem aggressively expanded through mergers and acquisitions. It bought Blues plans in Colorado Nevada and New Hampshire in 1999

and finalized the acquisition of Maine's Blue plan in 2000.

In 2001 it became a publicly traded company and sold its military insurance business to Humana. In the next couple of years it snapped up Virginia-based Trigon Healthcare and a Wisconsin Blue plan.

And in 2004 Anthem made its biggest leap yet merging with WellPoint Health Networks in a deal that made it the nation's largest health insurer. After the merger — which added Blue plans in California Georgia Missouri and Wisconsin — Anthem changed its name to WellPoint. The company changed its name back to Anthem in 2014.

EXECUTIVES

Evp And Chief Administrative Officer, Gloria M. McCarthy, age 67, $699,999 total compensation

President Ceo And Director, Gail K. Boudreaux

Evp And Cfo, John E. Gallina, age 60, $623,918 total compensation

Evp And President Government Business, Peter D. Haytaian, age 50, $740,371 total compensation

Evp And General Counsel, Thomas C. Zielinski, age 69

Evp And President Commercial And Specialty Business, Brian T. Griffin, age 61, $740,368 total compensation

Evp And Chief Clinical Officer, Craig E. Samitt, age 55

President Medicare East Region, Tomas Orozco

President Life And Disability, Greg Poulakos

President Specialty, Nicholas L. Brecker

Senior Vice President; President And Chief Executive Officer Anthem National Accounts, John Langenus

Vice President Information Technology, Sean Keneally

Vice President And Chief Information Security Officer, Roy Mellinger

Vice President Interplan And Plng National Account, Jai Bills

Assistant Vice President Information Technology Project Management Office, Sheri Coyner

Regional Vice President Sales National Accounts, Salem Shunnarah

Regional Vice President And Medical Director, Tony Linares

Regional Vice President, Julie Theodore

Vice President Commercial Claims, Jennifer Wade

Vice President Health Services, Ruth Hollenback

Svp And Cio, Tim Skeen

Vice President Pharmacy Sales And Account Management, Kelly McNulty

Vice President, Renee Hunter

Vice President Corporate Accounting And Reporting, Ryan Judy

Executive Vice President And President And Chief Executive Officer Commercial And Specialty Busines, Ken Goulet

Senior Vice President Provider Alignment Solutions, Colin Drozdowski

Medical Director And State, Kimberly L Roop

Vice President Marketing, James Jackson

Vp Analtics Strategy And Integrations, Tanya Rylee

Senior Vice President Public Affairs, Julie Goon

Vice President Information Technology, James Marshall

Svp Corporate Communications, Bonnie Jacobs

Vice President Comm Operations Insightsandanalytics, Katy Berry

Vice President Strategy Planningandexecution, Manan Shah

Regional Vice President Ca Small Group Sales, Colin Havert

Staff Vice President Business Continuation, Steve Labrique

Staff Vice President Systems Migration, Tracy Tutson

Vice President And Counsel, Ronald Odom
Senior Vice President And Chief Compliance
  Officer, Edward Stubbers
Vice President Care Management Operational
  Solutions, Lisa Ledford-Crissey
Vice President Provider Alignment Solutions,
  Hongmai Pham
Director Of Government Relations, Nick DeJong
Vice President Tax, Christopher LaFollette
Vice President Marketing, Erin Miller
Vice President And Chief Security Officer, Greg
  Wurm
Regional Vice President Finance And Medicare,
  Kevin Wirges
Vice President Medical And Clinical Pharmacy
  Policy, John Whitney
Vice President Public Policy Institute, Jennifer
  Kowalski
Regional Vice President Of Federal Government
  Relations, Samuel Marchio
Vice President And Counsel, Jason Wagner
Assistant Vice President Enterprise Pmo, Vanslyke
  Carol
Staff Vice President Contracting Admin, Jim Taske
Staff Vice President Strategic Initiatives
  Accountable Care Solutions, Ryan Schoettle
Regional Vice President Senior Clinical Officer,
  Maureen Dempsey
Medical Director, Lisa Hadley
Medical Director Medicare Care Management,
  Michelle Overfelt
Vice President, Ashwini Hassija
Medical Director, Jo Nishimoto
Senior Vice President Anthem National Accounts,
  Kenneth Goulet
Vice President And General Manager Key
  Accounts And Small Group, Joe Greenberg
Staff Vp Marketing, Angela Cherland
Vice President Federal Affairs, Elizabeth P Hall
National Account Manager, Cheryl Cervar
Regional Vice President Of Underwriting, Carter
  Browning
Medical Director, Maureen Prowse
Medical Director, Edward Margules
Vice President Public Policy, Anthony Mader
Medical Director Provider Group Partnerships
  And Clinical Performance, Demetria Malloy
Staff Vice President Medical Policy Development,
  John Yao
Vice President Health Care Analytics Data
  Integration And Clinical Information, Chuck
  Martel
Vice President It, Nitin Gotmare
Assistant Vice President It, Chuck Bennett
Vice President, Kari Conners
Board Member, Robert L Dixon
Chairman, Joseph R. Swedish, age 68
Board Member, Ramiro G Peru
Board Member, Ashley Clark
Board Member, Bessie Clark
Auditors: Ernst & Young LLP

LOCATIONS

HQ: Anthem Inc
  220 Virginia Avenue, Indianapolis, IN 46204
Phone: 800 331-1476
Web: www.antheminc.com

PRODUCTS/OPERATIONS

2017 Sales

	$ mil.	% of total
Premiums	83,647	93
Administrative fees	5,380	6
Net investment income	866	1
Net realized gains on financial instruments	144	-
Other	33	-
Adjustments	(33.1)	-
Total	90,039	100

2017 Premiums

	% of total
Government Business	54
Commercial and Specialty Business	46
Other	
Total	100

Selected Operations

Blue-licensed subsidiaries
  Anthem Blue Cross (California)
  Anthem Blue Cross and Blue Shield (Colorado
  Connecticut Kentucky Indiana Maine Missouri Nevada
  New Hampshire Ohio Virginia Wisconsin)
  Blue Cross Blue Shield of Georgia
  Empire Blue Cross Blue Shield (New York)
Non-Blue Cross Subsidiaries and Affiliates
  AIM Specialty Health (benefits management)
  American Imaging Management (Diagnostic imaging)
  Anthem Life Insurance (life and accident)
  Anthem Workers' Compensation
  CareMore (Medicare Advantage and special needs
  plans)
  DeCare Dental (Dental benefit management)
  HealthLink (Administrative services)
  Golden West Dental & Vision (Dental/vision California)
  Meridian Resource Company (Cost containment)
  National Government Services (Administration of
  government contracts)
  Resolution Health (Cost containment)
  TrustSolutions (Fraud prevention)
  UniCare (Health care plans)

COMPETITORS

Aetna	Kaiser Foundation
CIGNA	Health Plan
Centene	Medical Mutual
Delta Dental Plans	Molina Healthcare
EmblemHealth	UnitedHealth Group
Humana	WellCare Health Plans

HISTORICAL FINANCIALS

Company Type: Public

Income Statement				FYE: December 31
	REVENUE ($ mil.)	NET INCOME ($ mil.)	NET PROFIT MARGIN	EMPLOYEES
12/19	104,213	4,807	4.6%	70,600
12/18	92,105	3,750	4.1%	63,900
12/17	90,039	3,842	4.3%	56,000
12/16	84,863	2,469	2.9%	53,000
12/15	79,156	2,560	3.2%	53,000
Annual Growth	7.1%	17.1%	—	7.4%

2019 Year-End Financials

Debt ratio: 25.93%
Return on equity: 15.95%
Cash ($ mil.): 4,937
Current ratio: 1.65
Long-term debt ($ mil.): 17,787

No. of shares (mil.): 252
Dividends
  Yield: 1.0%
  Payout: 17.3%
Market value ($ mil.): 76,390

	STOCK PRICE ($) FY Close	P/E High/Low		PER SHARE ($) Earnings	Dividends	Book Value
12/19	302.03	17	12	18.47	3.20	125.45
12/18	262.63	20	15	14.19	3.00	110.88
12/17	225.01	16	10	14.35	2.70	103.49
12/16	143.77	16	12	9.21	2.60	95.17
12/15	139.44	18	13	9.38	2.50	88.21
Annual Growth	21.3%	—	—	18.5%	6.4%	9.2%

Anworth Mortgage Asset Corp.

What's an Anworth? Depends on the mortgage market. An externally managed real estate investment trust (REIT) Anworth Mortgage invests in finances and manages residential mortgage-related assets primarily mortgage-backed securities (MBS) guaranteed by the US government or federally sponsored entities Fannie Mae Freddie Mac and Ginnie Mae. As a REIT the trust is exempt from paying federal income tax so long as it distributes dividends back to shareholders. Anworth were incorporated in Maryland in 1997.

Operations

Anworth Mortgage has three types of investments including Agency mortgage-backed securities non-agency mortgage-backed securities and residential mortgage loans.

Agency MBS which include residential mortgage pass-through certificates and collateralized mortgage obligations or CMOs which are securities representing interests in pools of mortgage loans secured by residential property and accounts for about 75% of loans.

Non-Agency MBS (more than 10%) which are securities issued by companies that are not guaranteed by federally sponsored enterprises and that are secured primarily by first-lien residential mortgage loans. The rest accounts for residential mortgage loans.

The company's interest income accounts all of the company's total sales.

Geographic Reach

Its corporate headquarters is located in Santa Monica California.

Financial Performance

Anworth Mortgage's net income has been fluctuating for the last five years with the company even recording net losses in 2018 and 2019.

The company recorded a net loss of $55.4 million in 2019 88% more than $6.5 million in the previous year.

Cash and cash equivalents at the end of the year were $112.9 million 238% higher compared to $33.5 million in 2018. Cash provided by operating activities was $64.7 million. Investing activities provided $108.4 million to the coffers primarily from proceeds from sales. Financing activities used $93.6 million primarily for repayments on purchase agreements.

Strategy

Anworth Mortgage's investment objective is to provide attractive risk-adjusted total returns to its stockholders over the long-term primarily through dividends and secondarily through capital appreciation. Its strategy is to invest in residential MBS (both Agency MBS and Non-Agency MBS) residential mortgage loans and residential rental properties.

The company seeks to acquire assets that will produce competitive returns after considering the amount and nature of the investment's anticipated returns its ability to pledge the investment to secure collateralized borrowings and the costs associated with financing managing and reserving for these investments.

Its primary financing source for its Agency MBS and Non-Agency MBS portfolios is repurchase agreements. We have acquired residential mortgage loans that are being held-for-securitization. These loans are financed by a warehouse line of credit which is a short-term revolving credit facility extended by the financial institution for loans that are being held pending securitization.

The company also invests in the subordinate classes of newly formed securitization trusts which allows it to consolidate all of the loans of these trusts. These residential mortgage loans are financed through ABS issued by the securitization trusts. The ABS which are held by unaffiliated third parties are non-recourse financing. The difference in the amount of the loans and the amount of the ABS represents the company's retained net interest in the loans held in the securitization trusts.

EXECUTIVES

President And Chief Investment Officer, Joseph E. McAdams, age 51, $700,000 total compensation
Evp, Heather U. Baines, age 78, $50,495 total compensation
Chairman And Ceo, Joseph Lloyd McAdams, age 74
Svp And Portfolio Manager, Bistra Pashamova, age 49, $275,000 total compensation
Cfo Treasurer And Secretary, Charles J. Siegel, age 70, $250,000 total compensation
Board Member, Robert Davis
Auditors: RSM US LLP

LOCATIONS

HQ: Anworth Mortgage Asset Corp.
1299 Ocean Avenue, 2nd Floor, Santa Monica, CA 90401
Phone: 310 255-4493　　　**Fax:** 310 434-0070
Web: www.anworth.com

COMPETITORS

AG Mortgage Investment Trust	Hatteras Financial
ARMOUR Residential REIT	Huntington Preferred Capital
American Capital Agency Corp.	MFA Financial
Annaly Capital Management	Redwood Trust
Capstead Mortgage	Two Harbors
	Webster Preferred Capital

HISTORICAL FINANCIALS

Company Type: Public

Income Statement　　　　　　　　　FYE: December 31

	ASSETS ($ mil.)	NET INCOME ($ mil.)	INCOME AS % OF ASSETS	EMPLOYEES
12/19	4,938	(55)	—	—
12/18	5,037	(6)	—	—
12/17	5,765	54	0.9%	—
12/16	5,395	22	0.4%	—
12/15	6,636	14	0.2%	—
Annual Growth	(7.1%)	—	—	—

2019 Year-End Financials

Debt ratio: 3.49%	No. of shares (mil.): 98
Return on equity: (-9.61%)	Dividends
Cash ($ mil.): 8	Yield: 12.2%
Current ratio: —	Payout: —
Long-term debt ($ mil.): —	Market value ($ mil.): 348

	STOCK PRICE ($) FY Close	P/E High/Low	PER SHARE ($) Earnings	Dividends	Book Value
12/19	3.52	— —	(0.65)	0.43	5.79
12/18	4.04	— —	(0.16)	0.56	5.90
12/17	5.44	13 11	0.47	0.60	7.11
12/16	5.17	32 23	0.17	0.60	6.84
12/15	4.35	67 54	0.08	0.60	7.10
Annual Growth	(5.2%)		—	(8.0%)	(5.0%)

Apple Inc

Ask Siri to name the most successful company in the world and it might respond: Apple. And it's not just out of familial pride. Apple consistently ranks highly in profit revenue market capitalization and consumer cachet and it was the first reach a trillion dollar market cap. The iPhone in its 12th year has been the company's golden goose generating tens of billions in revenue and profit. Other Apple products and services include Mac computers and iPad tablets as well as the App Store Apple Music the Apple Watch and other wearable devices. Apple has entered entertainment with the Apple TV+ streaming service. The company has inked alliances with corporations to deepen its penetration of the enterprise market. 45% of Apple's revenue comes from outside the Americas.

HISTORY

College dropouts Steve Jobs (1955-2011) and Steve Wozniak founded Apple in 1976 in California's Santa Clara Valley. After Jobs' first sales call brought an order for 50 units the duo built the Apple I in his garage and sold it without a monitor keyboard or casing. Demand convinced Jobs there was a distinct market for small computers and the company's name (a reference to Jobs' stint on an Oregon farm) and the computer's user-friendly look and feel set it apart from others.

By 1977 Wozniak added a keyboard color monitor and eight peripheral device slots (which gave the machine considerable versatility and inspired numerous third-party add-on devices and software). Sales jumped from $7.8 million in 1978 to $117 million in 1980 the year Apple went public. In 1983 Wozniak left the firm and Jobs hired PepsiCo's John Sculley as president. Apple rebounded from failed product introductions that year by unveiling the Macintosh in 1984. After tumultuous struggles with Sculley Jobs left in 1985 and founded NeXT a designer of applications for developing software. That year Sculley ignored Microsoft founder Bill Gates' appeal for Apple to license its products and make the Microsoft platform an industry standard.

Apple blazed the desktop publishing trail in 1986 with its Mac Plus and LaserWriter printers. The following year it formed the software firm that later became Claris (and ultimately FileMaker). The late 1980s brought new competition from Microsoft whose Windows operating system (OS) featured a graphical interface akin to Apple's. Apple sued but lost its claim to copyright protection in 1992.

In 1993 Apple unveiled the Newton handheld computer but sales were slow. Earnings fell drastically so the company trimmed its workforce. (Sculley was among the departed.) In 1994 Apple cried "uncle" and began licensing clones of its OS hoping a flurry of cheaper Mac-alikes would encourage software developers. By 1996 struggling Apple realized Mac clones were stealing sales. That year it hired Gilbert Amelio formerly of National Semiconductor as CEO.

The company bought NeXT in 1997 but sales kept dropping and it subsequently cut about 30% of its workforce canceled projects and trimmed research costs. Meanwhile Apple's board ousted Amelio and Jobs took the position back on an interim basis. The CEO forged a surprising alliance with Microsoft which included releasing a Mac version of Microsoft's popular office software. To protect market share Jobs also stripped the cloning license from chief imitator Power Computing and put it out of business.

In 1998 Apple jumped back into the race with its colorful cocktail of iMacs and its first server software the Mac OS X. That year the company also revamped its profitable Claris unit (by cutting 300 employees shifting most operations to Apple and renaming it FileMaker) and stopped making its Newton handheld device and printer products.

Apple in 1999 opened a new chapter in portable computing with the introduction of its iBook laptop and (taking a cue from Dell) began selling built-to-order systems online. In 2000 after two and a half years as the semipermanent executive in charge Jobs took the "interim" out of his title and revamped the company's Web site and unveiled a suite of consumer Internet services. Jobs unveiled overhauled desktop lines later that year including an eight-inch cube-shaped G4. The company ended 2000 on a sour note as an industrywide slowdown and poor response to the G4 cube resulted in Apple's first unprofitable quarter in years.

Apple opened 2001 with another round of product upgrades including faster processors components such as CD and DVD burners and an ultra-slim version of its PowerBook called Titanium. The company also made a move to reclaim some of its slipping share in the education market purchasing software maker PowerSchool. Soon Apple confirmed a long-rumored plan to open a chain of retail stores in the US. The company then acquired DVD authoring software maker Spruce Technologies. In line with its strategy to market Macs as "digital hubs" for devices such as cameras and other peripherals Apple closed the year with the introduction of a digital music player called the iPod.

In 2002 Apple introduced a new look for its iMac line; featuring a half-dome base and a flat-panel display supported by a pivoting arm the redesign was the first departure from the original (and at the time radical) all-in-one design since iMac's debut in 1998. Looking to reclaim market share in the education sector Apple then introduced the eMac — a computer similar to the iMac to be sold only to students and educators (Apple later introduced a retail version). It continued its product push that year with the announcement that it would begin offering a rack-mount server called Xserve. In 2004 Apple debuted a streamlined iMac design powered by its G5 processor.

Apple announced it would begin incorporating Intel processors into its PC lines in 2005 ending more than a decade of using PowerPC microprocessors; the transition was completed the following year. Also that year Apple Motorola and Cingular Wireless (now AT&T Mobility) announced the debut of a mobile phone with iTunes functionality. Apple also unveiled the iPod nano an updated (and even smaller) version of its miniature iPod model as well as an iPod capable of playing video. In 2006 Apple reached a settlement in a dispute with Creative Technology over technology used in digital music players; Apple agreed to pay the company $100 million in exchange for a license to use Creative's patent related to navigation and organization.

The company also launched an online movie service in 2006 and previewed a device called iTV for watching downloaded content on televisions. (Apple announced availability of its television device redubbed Apple TV early the following year.)

Apple unveiled a mobile phone offering called the iPhone in 2007. To reflect the growing breadth of its product portfolio the company announced it would change its name from Apple Computer to simply Apple. The company kicked off 2008 with the release of an updated Apple TV device in conjunction with an iTunes movie rental service.

Looking toward the continued development of its mobile devices Apple purchased P.A. Semi a developer of low-power processors in 2008. In another move intended to bring more of its chip design in-house Apple bought Intrinsity a provider of chip design software in 2010.

After beginning 2011 with a leave of absence and then stepping down as CEO Steve Jobs died on October 5 2011. COO Tim Cook had been named CEO after Jobs' resignation though Jobs retained the chairman title until his death.

EXECUTIVES

Vice President Worldwide Developer Relations, Ron Okamoto

Svp Worldwide Marketing, Philip W. Schiller, age 60, $494,942 total compensation

Svp Software Engineering, Craig Federighi, age 51

Svp General Counsel And Secretary, D. Bruce Sewell, age 62, $1,000,000 total compensation

Svp Retail And Online Stores, Angela Ahrendts, age 59, $1,000,000 total compensation

Svp Internet Software And Services, Eduardo H. (Eddy) Cue, age 56, $1,000,000 total compensation

Chief Design Officer, Jonathan Ive

Svp And Cfo, Luca Maestri, age 57, $1,000,000 compensation

Coo, Jeffrey E. (Jeff) Williams, age 56, $947,596 total compensation

Svp Hardware Engineering, Daniel (Dan) Riccio, age 58, $1,000,000 total compensation

Svp Hardware Technologies, Johny Srouji

Vice President Corporate Development, Adrian Perica

Vice President, Celia Vigil

National Account Manager, Jed Bludworth

V P, Antonia Fuentes

Vice President Engineering, Lucy Chen

Senior Vice President Of Design Apple, Jony Ive

Vp Systems, Oconnor Niall

First Vice President Of Human Resources, Ann Bowers

Vice President Of Product Design, Doug Field

Senior Vice President, Jan Larson

Vice President, Jasmine Mele

Vice President Of Corporate Information Security, George Stathakopoulos

Vice President Negotiation Apple Content, Pete Distad

Vice President Product Integrity, Steve Kenner

Svp Retail And People, Deirdre O'brien

Vice President Hardware Engineering, Kate Bergeron

Vice President, Jennifer Bailey

Vice President Of Marketing, Bob Jones

Vice President Of Marketing, Nancy Macintosh

Vice President Cloud Services, Peter Stern

Vice President Platform Architecture, Tim Millet

Vice President Display Engineering, Wei Chen

National Account Manager, Luke Hagekyriakou

Managing Director Latin America Csac, Jorge Velez

Vice President Enterprise And Government, John Solomon

Executive Vice President, Noreen Krall

Vice President Visi. Hardware Engineering, Bob Mansfield

National Sales Manager, Eric Dubois

Vice President App Store, Matt Fischer

Vp Sales, Andrew Liao

Vice President, Siobhan Murphy

Vice President Of Marketing, Peggy Ann

Senior Vice President Internet Software And Services, Ted Cui

Senior Vice President Worldwide Marketing, David Schiller

Ea For Vice President Health, Stefani Ouzounian

Director, Arthur D. (Art) Levinson, age 70

Vice President And Treasurer, Gary Wipfler

Auditors: Ernst & Young LLP

LOCATIONS

HQ: Apple Inc
  One Apple Park Way, Cupertino, CA 95014
Phone: 408 996-1010   **Fax:** 408 974-2483
Web: www.apple.com

2019 Sales

	$ mil.	% of total
Americas	116,914	45
Europe	60,288	23
Asia/Pacific		
Greater China	43,678	17
Japan	21,506	8
Rest of Asia/Pacific	17,788	7
Total	**260,174**	**100**

PRODUCTS/OPERATIONS

2019 Sales

	$ mil.	% of total
iPhone	142,381	55
Services	46,291	18
Mac	25,740	10
Wearables Home and Accessories	24,482	8
iPad	21,280	7
Total	**260,174**	**100**

Selected Products

Hardware
  Desktop computers (iMac Mac mini Mac Pro)
  Displays (Cinema Thunderbolt)
  External hard drives (Airport Time Capsule)
  Keyboards
  Media devices (Apple TV)
  Mice (Magic Mouse)
  Mobile phones (iPhone)
  Portable computers (MacBook MacBook Air MacBook Pro)
  Portable digital music player (iPod touch)
  Tablet computers (iPad)
  Wearable technology (Apple Watch)
  Webcams (iSight)
  Wireless networking systems (AirPort)
Software
  MultimediaDVD Studio Pro FinalCut GarageBand iDVD iLife suite iMovie Photo iTunes Quicktime Soundtrack)
  Networking (Apple Remote Desktop AppleShare IP)
  Operating systems (macOS iOS watchOS tvOS)
  Personal productivity (AppleWorks FileMaker iWork Keynote Pages)
  Server (Mac OS X Server)
  Web browser (Safari)
Online Services
  Applications for iPad iPhone iPod touch (App Store)
  Applications for Mac (Mac App Store)
  Music Streaming (Apple Music)
  Cloud service (iCloud)
  E-books (iBooks)
  Electronic greeting cards (iCard)
  E-mail (Webmail)
  Online multimedia store (iTunes)
  Personal Web page creation (HomePage)
  Remote network storage (iDisk)
  Software (antivirus backup)
  Technical support (AppleCare)

COMPETITORS

AT&T	Google
Acer	HP
Adobe Systems	HTC Corporation
Alphabet Inc.	LG Electronics
Amazon.com	Lenovo
Best Buy	Microsoft
Bose	Netflix
CASIO COMPUTER	Nokia
Cisco Systems	PayPal
Comcast	Philips Electronics
Ericsson	Samsung Electronics
Facebook	Sony
Fitbit	Spotify
Garmin	Wal-Mart

HISTORICAL FINANCIALS

Company Type: Public

Income Statement

FYE: September 26

	REVENUE ($ mil.)	NET INCOME ($ mil.)	NET PROFIT MARGIN	EMPLOYEES
09/20	274,515	57,411	20.9%	147,000
09/19	260,174	55,256	21.2%	137,000
09/18	265,595	59,531	22.4%	132,000
09/17	229,234	48,351	21.1%	123,000
09/16	215,639	45,687	21.2%	116,000
Annual Growth	**6.2%**	**5.9%**	**—**	**6.1%**

2020 Year-End Financials

Debt ratio: 34.71%—
Return on equity: 73.89%
Cash ($ mil.): 38,016
Current ratio: 1.36
Long-term debt ($ mil.): 98,667

Dividends
  Yield: 0.0%
  Payout: 24.2%
  Market value ($ mil.): —

	STOCK PRICE ($) FY Close	P/E High/Low	PER SHARE ($) Earnings	Dividends	Book Value
09/20	112.28	153 32	3.28	0.80	3.85
09/19	218.82	78 48	2.97	0.75	5.09
09/18	225.74	76 51	2.98	0.68	5.63
09/17	154.12	71 46	2.30	0.60	6.54
09/16	112.71	59 43	2.08	0.55	6.01
Annual Growth	**(0.1%)**	**— —**	**12.1%**	**9.9%**	**(10.5%)**

Applied Materials, Inc.

Applied Materials is the leading producer of the machines that make computer chips flat panel TVs and solar energy devices. The company's equipment handles the complex processes of making chips from laying down patterns on silicon at the beginning to packaging them for shipment at the end. Its display business produces equipment for manufacturing organic light-emitting diodes (OLEDs) and other display technologies for TVs personal computers and smart phones. The services business offers manufacturing consulting and automation software. Based in California Applied has factories around the world. Asian customers account for about 80% of revenue.

Operations

Applied operates in three segments: Semiconductor Systems Applied Global Services and Display.

Semiconductor Systems more than 60% of revenue makes a wide range of manufacturing equipment used to fabricate integrated circuits including patterning systems transistor and interconnect products metrology inspection and review systems and packaging technologies. Key products are the Vantage the Radiance and Centura Systems VIISta Systems the Raider and Nokota Platforms and the Centura RP Epi.

Applied Global Services around a quarter of revenue provides products that improve equipment and fab performance and productivity including spares upgrades services and factory automation software for semiconductor display and other products.

The Display and Adjacent Markets segment about 10% of revenue engineers products for making liquid crystal displays (LCDs) organic light-emitting diodes (OLEDs) and other display technologies for TVs personal computers tablets smart phones and other consumer-oriented devices as well as equipment for flexible substrates.

Geographic Reach

Applied has operations in the US Asia/Pacific and Europe. Customers in China account for about 30% of revenue. Customers in Taiwan account for about 20% of revenue and those in the US Korea and Japan each supply about 10% of Applied's revenue.

Products in Semiconductor Systems are manufactured in Santa Clara California; Austin Texas; Gloucester Massachusetts; Kalispell Montana; Rehovot Israel; and Singapore. Products in the Display and Adjacent Markets segment are manufactured in Alzenau Germany and Tainan Taiwan. Other products are manufactured in Treviso Italy.

The company's headquarter offices are in Santa Clara California. The company also have offices plants and warehouse in many locations throughout the world including Europe Japan North America (principally the United States) Israel China India Korea Southeast Asia and Taiwan.

Sales and Marketing

Due to the highly technical nature of its products Applied's direct sales force does most of the company's marketing and selling worldwide. Applied's biggest customers for chip-making equipment are three of the biggest chipmakers: Samsung Electronics Taiwan Semiconductor Manufacturing Company and Intel each accounting for at least 10% of revenue.

Financial Performance

Applied Materials has manufactured strong revenue gains in the past years except in 2019.

Applied's 2019 (ended October) revenue decreased by 13% to $14.6 billion from 2018 on stronger sales across its businesses. Semiconductor sales decreased by 15% as customers added production capacity and moved to new technologies while Display and Adjacent Markets revenue decreased by 28% on increased demand for equipment used in making TVs and mobile devices.

Net income receded to $2.7 billion in 2019 from $3 billion. Income before taxes was about $563 million in 2019.

Applied's coffers held $3.1 billion in cash and equivalent in 2019 compared to $3.4 billion in 2018. Cash from operations was about $3.2 billion in 2019 while investing activities used $443 million and financing activities used $3.1 billion

Strategy

Applied Materials sees growth in semiconductors driven by the expansion of the internet of things big data and artificial intelligence and technologies such as augmented and virtual reality. In displays the company forecasts continuing demand for big and small screens. It is investing in research development and engineering to help its customers make more chips and with fewer defects.

Applied Materials slightly increased its R&D spending in 2019 remaining in the $2 billion mark and increasing it by $20 million higher than 2018. R&D in the Semiconductor Systems and Display and Adjacent Markets segments address etch e-beam inspection and material engineering. In etch R&D Applied focuses on supporting the adoption of precision etch technology for the growing use of 3D logic and memory chips.

Besides R&D the company pumped more capital into improving plants and property for new ones. Capital spending fell to $441 million in 2019 decrease from 2018.

Applied has moved into other areas of technology to reduce its exposure to the volatility of the semiconductor business. While it's grown quickly the Display and Adjacent Markets depends on four customers for almost 70% of sales with each customers accounted for at least 10% of the segment's sales.

Mergers and Acquisitions

Applied agreed to acquire Kokusai Electronics which provides high-productivity batch processing systems and services for memory foundry and logic customers for $2.2 billion in 2019. The seller was investment firm KKR. Kokusai's systems complement Applied's portfolio in single-wafer processing systems and could enhance Applied's position with customers in Japan and Asia. With completion of the deal Kokusai would become part of Applied's Semiconductor Products Group and continue to be based in Tokyo. The transaction was expected to close in 2020.

Company Background

The leading maker of computer chip-making equipment Applied Materials has helped drive the technology revolution of the past 50 years. The company was founded in 1967 in Mountain View California as a maker of chemical vapor deposition systems for fabricating semiconductors. After years of rapid growth the company went public in 1972. It has added the manufacturing of equipment for solar technology and displays to its portfolio to help temper the ups and downs of the cyclical semiconductor industry.

HISTORY

Applied Materials was founded in 1967 in Mountain View California as a maker of chemical vapor deposition systems for fabricating semiconductors. After years of rapid growth the company went public in 1972. Two years later it purchased wafer maker Galamar Industries.

In 1975 Applied Materials suffered a 45% drop in sales as the semiconductor industry (and the US economy) contracted. Financial and managerial problems plagued the company following the recession so in 1976 James Morgan a former division manager for conglomerate Textron was chosen to replace founder Michael McNeilly as CEO. Two years later Morgan also became chairman.

After selling Galamar (1977) and other non-core units and extending the company's line of credit Morgan announced a plan to move into Japan. The company's first joint venture Applied Materials Japan was set up in 1979.

Applied got into the ion implanter market in 1980 through its acquisition of the UK's Lintott Engineering.

EXECUTIVES

Vice President, Erix Yu

Svp Engineering, Gino Addiego, age 60, $457,692 total compensation

Group Vp; General Manager Transistor And Interconnect Group, Steve Ghanayem

Svp General Counsel And Secretary, Thomas F. Larkins, $489,231 total compensation

Group Vp; General Manager Imaging And Process Control Group, Robert J. Perlmutter, age 63

Svp And Cto; President Applied Ventures, Omkaram (Om) Nalamasu, age 61, $468,846 total compensation

Group Vp And Cio, Jay Kerley

Svp And Cfo, Daniel (Dan) Durn, age 53

President And Ceo, Gary E. Dickerson, age 62, $1,019,231 total compensation

Svp; General Manager New Markets And Service Group, Ali Salehpour, age 58, $560,577 total compensation

Group Vp; General Manager Patterning And Packaging Group, Prabu G. Raja

Regional President, Russell Tham

Vice President Human Resources, Blake Wolfe

Corporate Vp Applied Materials Fellow Engineering And Product Technology Development Display And Flexible Technology Business Group, John White

Corporate Vp Applied Materials Fellow And Gm Dielectric Cvd Products Dielectric Deposition Products Semiconductor Products Group, Hari Ponnekanti

Vice President And Treasurer, Robert Friess

Corporate Vice President And General Manager Of Display Business Group, Brian Shieh

Vice President Global Internal Audit, Jean Chun

Vice President, Aninda Moitra

Vice President Marketing, Shayne Bennett

Vice President, Ramesh Viswanathan

Vice President And General Manager Of Front End Products Division, Sundar Ramamurthy

Vice President, Mike Parcella

Svp Worldwide Operations And Supply Chain, Joseph Flanagan

Vice President And General Manager Service And Spares Applied Global Services, Seehack Foo

Vice President Technology Development, Cheri Lamotte

Vice President, Brent Bloom

Vice President Intellectual Property, James Wilson

Corporate Vice President, Mehdi Vaez-iravani

Vice President And General Manager, Mukund Srinivasan

Corporate Vice President, Hussein Fawaz

Vice President Marketing And Business Development, Lior Engel

Vice President Non Semi Operations, Robert Davis

Vice President General Management, Ta Won Kim

Vice President Marketing And Business Development, Lee Fang Chew

Vice President Engineering, Sanjay Natarajan

Vice President, Michael Parcella

Vice President Marketing And Business Development, Terrance Lee

Chairman, Thomas J. (Tom) Iannotti, age 64

Board Member, Alexander Karsner

Assistant Treasurer, Randy Webb

Assistant Treasurer Customer, Brad Mccurrie

Assistant Treasurer, Avi Cohen-Hillel

Auditors: KPMG LLP

LOCATIONS

HQ: Applied Materials, Inc.
3050 Bowers Avenue, P.O. Box 58039, Santa Clara, CA 95052-8039
Phone: 408 727-5555
Web: www.appliedmaterials.com

2018 Sales

	$ mil.	% of total
Asia/Pacific		
China	5,113	29
Korea	3,603	21
Taiwan	2,732	16
Japan	2,405	14
Southeast Asia	802	5
US	1,532	9
Europe	1,066	6
Total	**17,253**	**100**

PRODUCTS/OPERATIONS

2018 Sales

	$ mil.	% of total
Semiconductor Systems	10,903	63
Applied Global Services	3,754	22
Display and Adjacent Markets	2,498	14
Corporate & Other	98	1
Total	**17,253**	**100**

Products and Technologies

Semiconductor
Display
Solar
Roll to Roll WEB Coating
Emerging Technologies and Products
Automation Software
Product Library

Selected Products

Chemical mechanical polishing/planarization systems (wafer polishing)
Deposition systems (deposit layers of conducting and insulating material on wafers)
  Dielectric deposition (chemical vapor deposition or CVD)
  Metal (CVD electroplating or physical vapor deposition)
  Silicon and thermal deposition
  Sputtering (physical vapor deposition) for solar cells
  Thin-film silicon solar cells
  Web coating for flexible solar cells
Etch systems (remove portions of a wafer surface for circuit construction)
Inspection systems (defect review for reticles — patterned plates which hold precise images of chip circuit patterns — and wafers)
Ion implant systems (implant ions into wafer surface to change conductive properties)
Manufacturing process optimization software
Metrology systems
  CD-SEM (scanning electron microscope system)
Optical monitoring systems (for glass or web coating systems)
Rapid thermal processing systems (heat wafers to change electrical characteristics)

COMPETITORS

AIXTRON	Micronic Laser Systems
ASM International	Nikon
Ebara	Sumitomo Heavy
Hitachi	Industries
Hitachi Kokusai	Tokyo Electron
Electric	ULVAC
KLA-Tencor	Veeco Instruments
Lam Research	

HISTORICAL FINANCIALS

Company Type: Public

Income Statement

FYE: October 25

	REVENUE ($ mil.)	NET INCOME ($ mil.)	NET PROFIT MARGIN	EMPLOYEES
10/20	17,202	3,619	21.0%	24,000
10/19	14,608	2,706	18.5%	22,000
10/18	17,253	3,313	19.2%	21,000
10/17	14,537	3,434	23.6%	18,400
10/16	10,825	1,721	15.9%	16,700
Annual Growth	12.3%	20.4%	—	9.5%

2020 Year-End Financials

Debt ratio: 24.37%	No. of shares (mil.): 914
Return on equity: 38.62%	Dividends
Cash ($ mil.): 5,351	Yield: 0.0%
Current ratio: 3.00	Payout: 21.9%
Long-term debt ($ mil.): 5,448	Market value ($ mil.): 55,708

	STOCK PRICE ($) FY Close	P/E High/Low		PER SHARE ($) Earnings	Dividends	Book Value
10/20	60.95	17	10	3.92	0.86	11.57
10/19	55.72	19	10	2.86	0.82	8.97
10/18	32.36	19	10	3.23	0.60	7.07
10/17	56.69	18	9	3.17	0.40	8.82
10/16	28.66	20	10	1.54	0.40	6.69
Annual Growth	20.8%	—	—	26.3%	21.1%	14.7%

Aramark

Keeping employees fed and clothed is a mark of this company. ARAMARK is one of the leading contract foodservice providers in the world and a high-ranking uniform supplier in the US. The company offers corporate dining services and operates concessions at sports arenas and other entertainment venues. The firm also provides facilities management services. Through ARAMARK Uniform and Career Apparel the company supplies uniforms for healthcare public safety and technology workers. US customers generate about three-quarters of the company's revenue.

HISTORY

Davre Davidson began his career in foodservice by selling peanuts from the backseat of his car in the 1930s. He landed his first vending contract with Douglas Aircraft (later McDonnell Douglas now part of Boeing) in 1935. Through that relationship Davidson met William Fishman of Chicago who had vending operations in the Midwest. Davidson and Fishman merged their companies in 1959 to form Automatic Retailers of America (ARA). Davidson became chairman and CEO of the new company; Fishman served as president.

Focusing on candy beverage and cigarette machines ARA became the leading vending machine company in the US by 1961 with operations in 38 states. Despite slimmer profit margins ARA moved into food vending in the early 1960s. It acquired 150 foodservice businesses between 1959 and 1963 quickly becoming a leader in the operation of cafeterias at colleges hospitals and work sites. The company (which changed its name to ARA Services in 1966) grew so rapidly that the FTC stepped in; ARA agreed to restrict future food vending acquisitions.

ARA provided foodservices at the 1968 Summer Olympics in Mexico City beginning a long-term relationship with the amateur sports event. The company also diversified into publication distribution that year and in 1970 it expanded into janitorial and maintenance services. A foray into residential care for the elderly began in 1973 (and ended in 1993 with the sale of the subsidiary). ARA also entered into emergency room staffing services (sold 1997). The company expanded into child care (National Child Care Centers) in 1980.

CFO Joseph Neubauer became CEO in 1983 and was named chairman in 1984. To avoid a hostile takeover shortly thereafter he led a $1.2 billion leveraged buyout. After the buyout ARA began refining its core operations. It acquired Szabo (correctional foodservices) in 1986 Children's World Learning Centers in 1987 and Coordinated Health Services (medical billing services) in 1993.

ARA changed its name to ARAMARK in 1994 as part of an effort to raise its profile with its ultimate customers the public. The company's concession operations suffered from long work stoppages in baseball (1994) and hockey (1995). ARAMARK acquired Galls (North America's #1 supplier of public safety equipment) in 1996 and in 1997 announced plans to become 100% employee-owned.

The following year ARAMARK entered into a joint venture with privately held Anderson News Company exchanging its magazine distribution operations for a minority stake in the new business. In 2000 the company was on hand to supply foodservices to the Olympic Games in Sydney.

With the new millennium the company was focused on expansion buying the food and beverage concessions business of conglomerate Ogden Corp. for $236 million. The company penned a 10-year deal with Boeing in 2000 to supply foodservices to about 100 locations one of the biggest foodservice contracts ever. It also bought the Correctional Foodservice Management division of G4S Secure Solutions (USA) then named The Wackenhut Corporation.

ARAMARK continued its expansion with the purchase of ServiceMaster's management services division in 2001 for about $800 million — opening doors in nonfood management groundskeeping and custodial services. However the company lost a bid to cater the 2002 Olympic Games in Salt Lake City to rival Compass Group. In late 2001 ARAMARK went public.

The company bought Hilton's 14 Harrison Conference Centers and university lodgings for about $49 million in 2002. Also it paid $100 million for Premier Inc.'s Clinical Technology Services which maintains and repairs clinical equipment in about 170 hospitals and healthcare facilities in the US. ARAMARK also completed its acquisition of Fine Host Corporation which added approximately 900 client locations for about $100 million.

In 2003 ARAMARK exited the child care business when it sold its Educational Resources unit (operator of Children's World Learning Centers) to Michael Milken's Knowledge Learning Corporation for $225 million. ARAMARK later bought Restauraci "n Colectiva and Rescot a foodservice company based in Zaragoza Spain. Longtime executive Bill Leonard was named president and CEO that year with Neubauer taking on the title of executive chairman.

Expanding its Canadian presence in cleanroom services in 2004 ARAMARK acquired Toronto-based Cleanroom Garments a supplier of apparel and accessories for Canadian manufacturers in pharmaceutical aerospace and automotive industries. The company's Healthcare Management Services group meanwhile signed a 10-year agreement with Evanston Northwestern Healthcare to provide managed services to three Chicago-area hospitals. That year ARAMARK made its first foray into China by acquiring a 90% stake in Bright China Service Industries a facilities services firm. After a brief reign Leonard resigned that year and Neubauer returned to being CEO of the company.

In 2007 Neubauer with the backing of such investment firms as CCMP Capital Thomas H. Lee Partners and Warburg Pincus took ARAMARK private for $8.3 billion including the assumption of $2 billion in debt.

The company provided catering and other foodservices for the 2008 Olympic Games in Beijing. That year ARAMARK also acquired The Patman Group expanding its reach into India.

In 2011 ARAMARK sold its ownership stake in SeamlessWeb to Spectrum Equity Investors for $50 million. SeamlessWeb provides online and mobile food ordering.

EXECUTIVES

Chairman President And Ceo, Eric J. Foss, age 62, $1,622,625 total compensation
Evp Human Resources, Lynn B. McKee, age 64, $666,475 total compensation
Svp Controller And Chief Accounting Officer, Joseph M. (Joe) Munnelly, age 56, $384,503 total compensation
Coo Uniform And Refreshment Services, Brad C. Drummond
Coo International, Brent J. Franks
Evp And Cfo, Stephen P. (Steve) Bramlage, age 49, $300,000 total compensation
Coo Europe, Harrald F. Kroeker, age 62
Coo Healthcare Education And Facilities, Victor L. Crawford, age 59
Coo Sports Leisure Corrections And Business Dining, Marc Bruno
Evp General Counsel And Secretary, Stephen R. (Steve) Reynolds, age 62, $517,650 total compensation
Coo Emerging Markets, Marty Welch
Senior Vice President Finance, Christina Morrison
Vice President Strategic Partnerships, Brian Drew
Vice President Finance, Barbara Ratliff

Associate Vice President Of Marketing, Karen Parker
Regional Vice President, Patrick Liebler
Vice President Global Operational Excellence, Autumn Bayles
Assistant Vice President, Ray Verlinghieri
Vice President Finance, Eric Brown
Vice President Of Sales, Betsy Kline
Vp And Chief Diversity Officer, Ash Hanson
Vice President Of Global Business Servic, Brian Gabbard
Vice President Of Operations, Mark Peden
Vice President Of Tax, Robert Deitz
Assistant Vice President Decision Support, Brannon Transue
Regional Vice President, Alicia Kent
Vice President Of Business Development, Hans Lindh
Vice President Of Business Development, Timothy Grant
Associate Vice President Investments, Philip Desilva
Regional Vice President Aramark Business Dining, Prentiss Hall
Vice President Compensation And Benefits, Scott Haverlock
Vice President Global Security, Edward Hanko
National Account Manager, Sarah Crandell
Vice President Sales South Region, Karen Mitchal
National Account Manager, Hilarie Hionis
Senior Vice President, John Hanner
Vice President Pricing Strategy, Yogesh Bhardwaj
Associate Vice President Consumer Insights, Jill Marchick
Vice President Strategic Development Aramark Healthcare, Mike Morgioni
Regional Vice President, Anthony Barber
Regional Vice President, Stephen Cantrell
Associate Vice President, Michelle Clark
National Account Manager, Steve Kennedy
Vp Of It, Brendan O'malley
Avp Financial Controls, Daniel Ross
Investor Relations Vice President, Kate Pearlman
Assistant Vice President Sales Effectiveness, Christopher Lindberg
Auditors: DELOITTE & TOUCHE LLP

LOCATIONS

HQ: Aramark
2400 Market Street, Philadelphia, PA 19103
Phone: 215 238-3000
Web: www.aramark.com

2018 Sales

	$ mil.	% of total
United States	11,795	75
International	3,994	25
Total	**15,789**	**100**

PRODUCTS/OPERATIONS

2018 Sales

	$ mil.	% of total
FSS United States	10,137	64
FSS International	3,655	23
Uniform	1,996	13
Total	**15,789**	**100**

Brands
Brands
WearGuard
Crest
Aramark

Services
Food hospitality and facilities
Rental sale and maintenance of uniform apparel and other items

Selected Operations
Food and support services
 ARAMARK Colleges and Universities
 ARAMARK Conference Centers
 ARAMARK Convention Centers
 ARAMARK Correctional Services
 ARAMARK Cultural Attractions
 ARAMARK Facility Services
 ARAMARK Food Services
 ARAMARK Healthcare
 ARAMARK Higher Education
 ARAMARK Innovative Dining Solutions
 ARAMARK Parks and Resorts
 ARAMARK Refreshment Services (vending services)
 ARAMARK Senior Living
 ARAMARK Sports and Entertainment
Uniform and career apparel
 ARAMARK Cleanroom Services
 ARAMARK Uniform & Career Apparel
 Galls (tactical equipment and apparel)

COMPETITORS

ABM Industries	G&K Services
Autogrill	Healthcare Services
Centerplate	ISS A/S
Cintas	SSP
Compass Group	Serco
Delaware North	Sodexo
Elior	UniFirst

HISTORICAL FINANCIALS
Company Type: Public

Income Statement
FYE: October 2

	REVENUE ($ mil.)	NET INCOME ($ mil.)	NET PROFIT MARGIN	EMPLOYEES
10/20*	12,829	(461)	—	247,900
09/19	16,227	448	2.8%	283,500
09/18	15,789	567	3.6%	274,400
09/17	14,604	373	2.6%	260,500
09/16	14,415	287	2.0%	266,500
Annual Growth	**(2.9%)**	—		**(1.8%)**

*Fiscal year change

2020 Year-End Financials

Debt ratio: 59.05%
Return on equity: (-15.00%)
Cash ($ mil.): 2,509
Current ratio: 1.99
Long-term debt ($ mil.): 9,178

No. of shares (mil.): 253
Dividends
 Yield: 1.6%
 Payout: —
Market value ($ mil.): 6,971

	STOCK PRICE ($) FY Close	P/E High/Low	PER SHARE ($) Earnings	Dividends	Book Value
10/20*	27.55	— —	(1.83)	0.44	10.81
09/19	43.02	24 15	1.78	0.44	13.40
09/18	43.02	20 16	2.24	0.42	12.28
09/17	40.61	27 22	1.49	0.41	10.01
09/16	38.03	32 25	1.16	0.38	8.83
Annual Growth	**(7.7%)**	— —	—	**3.7%**	**5.2%**

*Fiscal year change

Archer Daniels Midland Co.

Archer-Daniels-Midland (ADM) forges every link in the food chain from field to processing to store. One of the world's largest processors of agricultural commodities the company converts corn oilseeds and wheat into products for food animal feed industrial and energy uses at nearly 350 pro-cessing plants worldwide. The company is also a leading manufacturer of protein meal vegetable oil corn sweeteners flour biodiesel ethanol and other value-added food and feed ingredients. ADM operates an extensive US grain elevator and global transportation network that buys stores transports and resells feed commodities for the agricultural processing industry connecting crops with markets on six continents.

Operations
Archer-Daniels-Midland (ADM) conducts its business through three operating segments: Ag Services and Oilseeds Carbohydrate Solutions and Nutrition.

Ag Services and Oilseeds accounts for approximately three quarters of ADM's revenue and buys stores cleans and transports agricultural commodities such as oilseeds corn wheat milo oats rice and barley. It resells them as food and feed ingredients and as raw materials for the agriculture processing industry. Oilseeds products produced and marketed by the segment include ingredients for food feed energy and industrial customers.

The Carbohydrate Solutions segment accounts for 15% of sales is engaged in corn and wheat wet and dry milling and other activities. It carries out corn wet and dry milling to convert corn into sweeteners starches syrups glucose dextrose and bioproducts. It also ferments dextrose to produce alcohol and other food and animal feed ingredients

Nutrition segment brings in the remaining revenue and produces natural flavor ingredients flavor systems natural colors proteins emulsifiers and soluble fiber among other specialty products. Additionally it buys processes and sells edible beans and soy proteins.

A big part of ADM's business is getting products from one place to another. It has developed a comprehensive transportation network that moves commodities and processed products around the world. It owns or leases approximately 1900 barges 11900 rail cars 330 trucks 1300 trailers 90 boats and seven oceangoing vessels; and leases under operating leases approximately 610 barges 16900 rail cars 320 trucks 280 trailers 40 boats and nearly 20 oceangoing vessels.

Geographic Reach
The US is Archer-Daniels-Midlands's largest market accounting for more than 40% of total sales. Switzerland accounts for around 20% Cayman Islands more than 5% Brazil Germany and other countries accounts the remainder. The company connecting crops and markets in more than 190 countries. ADM currently owns or leases nearly 350 processing plants and more than 480 procurement facilities nearly 45% of which are located outside of the US.

In total ADM has nearly 350 owned or leased US or non-US processing plants and more than 480 owned or leased US or non-US procurement facilities. The company also has 230 warehouses and terminals primarily used as bulk storage facilities and 55 innovation centers.

Overall ADM has plants and facilities in North and South America Europe Africa and Asia.

Sales and Marketing
Archer-Daniels-Midland's products are distributed mainly in bulk from processing plants or storage facilities directly to customers' facilities. ADM has developed transportation capability to move both commodities and processed products virtually anywhere in the world.

Financial Performance
Archer-Daniels-Midland's revenue rose after the consecutive decreases in 2015 2016 and 2017. In 2019 revenues increased $315 million to $64.7 billion due to overall higher sales volumes ($3.2 billion) partially offset by lower sales prices ($2.9 billion). The increase in sales volumes was due

principally to soybeans wheat cotton and higher sales volumes of feed ingredients related to acquisitions.

In 2019 Net income fell 24% to $1.4 billion from $1.8 billion the previous year.

Cash at the end of 2019 totaled $3 billion an $853 million decrease from the previous year. Operating activities used $5.5 billion while investing activities generated $5.3 billion. Financing activities used another $660 million.

Strategy

The company's strategy involves expanding the volume and diversity of crops that it merchandises and processes expanding the global reach of its core model and expanding its value-added product portfolio. One of ADM's strategies is to expand the global reach of its core model may include expanding or developing its business in emerging market areas such as Asia Eastern Europe the Middle East and Africa. As the company adds new products to its portfolio it is keeps an eye on operations that fail to meet expectations.

One of the Company's strategies is to expand the global reach of its core model which may include expanding or developing its business in emerging market areas. Both developed and emerging market areas are subject to impacts of economic downturns including decreased demand for the Company's products and reduced availability of credit or declining credit quality of the Company's suppliers customers and other counterparties.

The Company's strategy also involves expanding the volume and diversity of crops it merchandises and processes expanding the global reach of its core model and expanding its value-added product portfolio. Government policies including but not limited to antitrust and competition law trade restrictions food safety regulations sustainability requirements and traceability can impact the Company's ability to execute this strategy successfully.

Mergers and Acquisitions

In early 2020 ADM acquired Yerbalatina Phytoactives (Yerbalatina) a natural plant-based extracts and ingredients manufacturer based in Brazil. This acquisition e xpands ADM's already significant 6000-person-strong business in Brazil.

HISTORY

John Daniels began crushing flaxseed to make linseed oil in 1878 and in 1902 he formed Daniels Linseed Company in Minneapolis. George Archer another flaxseed crusher joined the company the following year. In 1923 the company bought Midland Linseed Products and became Archer Daniels Midland (ADM). ADM kept buying oil processing companies in the Midwest during the 1920s. It also started to research the chemical composition of linseed oil.

ADM entered the flour milling business in 1930 when it bought Commander-Larabee (then the #3 flour miller in the US). In the 1930s the company discovered a method for extracting lecithin (an emulsifier food additive used in candy and other products) from soybean oil significantly lowering its price.

The enterprise grew rapidly following WWII. By 1949 it was the leading processor of linseed oil and soybeans in the US and was fourth in flour milling. During the early 1950s ADM began foreign expansion in earnest.

In 1966 the company's leadership passed to Dwayne Andreas a former Cargill executive who had purchased a block of Archer family stock. Andreas focused ADM on soybeans including the production of textured vegetable protein a cheap soybean by-product used in foodstuffs.

EXECUTIVES

Svp Chief Risk Officer And President North America, Mark A. Bemis, age 59
Svp Agricultural Services Business Unit; President Europe, Joseph D. (Joe) Taets, age 54, $700,008 total compensation
Evp And Cfo, Ray G. Young, age 59, $825,048 total compensation
Svp General Counsel And Secretary, D. Cameron Findlay, age 61, $700,000 total compensation
Svp Chief Strategy Officer And Chief Sustainability Officer, Ismael Roig, age 53
Svp And President Corn Processing, Christopher M. (Chris) Cuddy, age 46
Chairman And Ceo, Juan R. Luciano, age 58, $1,283,340 total compensation
President Adm Europe Middle East And Africa (emea), Pierre-Christophe Duprat, age 52
Svp And Cto, Todd A. Werpy, age 57
Svp And President Oilseeds Processing Business Unit, Gregory A. (Greg) Morris, age 48, $650,004 total compensation
Svp And President Wild Flavors And Specialty Ingredients, Vince F. Macciocchi, age 54
President North Asia, Donald Chen, age 57
President Southeast Asia Australia And New Zealand And Global Destination Marketing, Ian Pinner, age 47
President Global Trade, Gary McGuigan
Vice President, Brent Flickinger
Vice President Global Security, Jeffrey Larner
Vice President Of Research And Development, Leif Solheim
Executive Vice President And Chief Risk Officer, Roger Hoffman
Vice President Bio Products, John Hansen
Vice President Human Resources Canada And Cost Management, Crocifissa Mandraccia
Vice President Environmental, Mark E Calmes
Vice President Of Insurance And Risk Management, Brendan Gardiner
National Account Manager, Thomas Frangione
Vice President Human Resources And Global Rewards, Robert Cabanelas
Vice President Compliance, Angie Shaw
Board Member, Patrick Moore
Board Member, Debra Sandler
Board Member, Donald Felsinger
Board Member, Terrell Crews
Board Member, Pierre Dufour
Board Member, Francisco Sanchez
Auditors: Ernst & Young LLP

LOCATIONS

HQ: Archer Daniels Midland Co.
77 West Wacker Drive, Suite 4600, Chicago, IL 60601
Phone: 312 634-8100
Web: www.adm.com

2015 Sales

	$ mil.	% of total
US	31,828	47
Switzerland	11,681	17
Germany	3,436	5
Other countries	20,757	31
Total	**67,702**	**100**

PRODUCTS/OPERATIONS

2015 Sales

	$ mil.	% of total
Agricultural services	33,658	44
Oilseeds processing	29,393	39
Corn processing	10,051	13
Wild Flavors and Specialty Ingredients	2,423	3
Other	634	1
Intersegment Elimination	(8457)	-
Total	**67,702**	**100**

Selected Commodities
Barley
Corn
Milo (sorghum)
Oats
Oilseeds
Rice
Rye
Wheat

Selected Brands
Consumer food
  Casa (canned refried beans)
  Commander (wheat flour)
  Five Roses (wheat flour)
  Gigantic (wheat flour)
  Midland Harvest (rice)
  Novasoy (soy supplement)
  Top King (wheat flour)
  VegeFull (cooked ground beans)
Industrial food
  Ambrosia (chocolate)
  CardioAid (plant sterol)
  EnviroStrip (dry-stripping)
  Evolution Chemicals (sustainable alternative chemical)
  NovaLipid (fats and oils)
  NovaSoy (isoflavones)
  VegeFull (dried bean-based food ingredient)

Selected Products
Agricultural
  Fertilizer
Feed ingredients
  Animal nutrition
  Corn co-products
  Milling products
  Oils/energy products
  Premixes
  Specialty feed ingredients
Food
  Acidulants
  Beverage alcohol
  Edible beans and bean ingredients
  Fiber
  Flour and whole grains
  Lecithin
  Natural-source vitamin E
  Oils
  Plant sterols
  Polyols and gums
  Proteins
  Rice
  Soy isoflavones
  Starches
  Sweeteners
Fuel
  Biodiesel
  Ethanol
Industrials
  Acidulants
  De-icers
  Dispersants
  Dust control products
  Emulsifiers and thickeners
  Fermentation nutrients
  Fertilizers
  Industrial oils
  Polyols
  Propylene glycol
  Solvents
  Starches
  Superabsorbents

Selected Services
Agriculture
  Grain merchandising
  Grain milling
  Grain processing
Information
  Billing and invoicing
  Inventory
  Logistics
  Payment
  Product search
Transportation
  Land
  Rail
  Truck
  Water
  Ocean
  River

Selected Subsidiaries Joint Ventures and Other Holdings

Almidones Mexicanos S.A. (50% wet corn milling plant Mexico)

Alfred C. Toepfer International (80% agricultural commodities trading and processed products Germany)

Compagnie Industrielle et Financiere des Produits Amylaces SA (Luxembourg) (42% joint venture investments in food feed ingredients and bioenergy)

Eaststarch C.V. (50% wet corn milling plants Netherlands)

Edible Oils Limited (50% procure package sell edible oils UK)

Golden Peanut LLC (100% peanut hulls oil meal and seed)

Gruma S.A.B. de C.V (23% corn flour and corn tortilla manufacturer Mexico)

Kalama Export Company (45% grain export elevator)

Red Star Yeast LLC (40% joint venture fresh and dry yeast manufacturer US and Canada)

Stratas Foods LLC (50% procure package sell edible oils North America)

Telles LLC (50% market sell corn-based bioplastic)

COMPETITORS

AGRI Industries	Ingredion
Abengoa Bioenergy	Liberty Vegetable Oil
Ag Processing Inc.	LifeLine
Ajinomoto	Little Sioux Corn
Andersons	Processors
Barry Callebaut	Louis Dreyfus Group
Bartlett and Company	MGP Ingredients
Bayer CropScience	Malt Products
Brenntag North America	Corporation
Bunge Limited	Nestlé
CHS	Nisshin Oillio
CP Kelco	Northern Growers
Cargill	Omega Protein
Cosun	Pacific Ethanol
Danisco A/S	Pioneer Hi-Bred
Dow AgroSciences	Renewable Energy Group
DuPont Agriculture	Riceland Foods
General Mills	Scoular
Green Brick Partners	Syngenta
Green Plains	S dzucker
Hain Celestial	Tate & Lyle
Hershey	

HISTORICAL FINANCIALS

Company Type: Public

Income Statement — FYE: December 31

	REVENUE ($ mil.)	NET INCOME ($ mil.)	NET PROFIT MARGIN	EMPLOYEES
12/19	64,656	1,379	2.1%	38,100
12/18	64,341	1,810	2.8%	31,600
12/17	60,828	1,595	2.6%	31,300
12/16	62,346	1,279	2.1%	31,800
12/15	67,702	1,849	2.7%	32,300
Annual Growth	(1.1%)	(7.1%)	—	4.2%

2019 Year-End Financials

Debt ratio: 20.19%
Return on equity: 7.22%
Cash ($ mil.): 852
Current ratio: 1.55
Long-term debt ($ mil.): 7,672

No. of shares (mil.): 557
Dividends
Yield: 3.0%
Payout: 66.6%
Market value ($ mil.): 25,817

	STOCK PRICE ($) FY Close	P/E High/Low		PER SHARE ($) Earnings	Dividends	Book Value
12/19	46.35	19	15	2.44	1.40	34.48
12/18	40.97	16	12	3.19	1.34	33.96
12/17	40.08	17	14	2.79	1.28	32.88
12/16	45.65	22	14	2.16	1.20	29.97
12/15	36.68	18	11	2.98	1.12	30.08
Annual Growth	6.0%		—	(4.9%)	5.7%	3.5%

Arconic Corp

LOCATIONS

HQ: Arconic Corp
201 Isabella Street, Pittsburgh, PA 15212-5872
Phone: 412 992-2500
Web: www.arconic.com

HISTORICAL FINANCIALS

Company Type: Public

Income Statement — FYE: December 31

	REVENUE ($ mil.)	NET INCOME ($ mil.)	NET PROFIT MARGIN	EMPLOYEES
12/19	7,277	225	3.1%	15,400
12/18	7,442	170	2.3%	15,300
12/17	6,824	209	3.1%	—
Annual Growth	3.3%	3.8%	—	—

2019 Year-End Financials

Debt ratio: 5.27%
Return on equity: —
Cash ($ mil.): 72
Current ratio: 1.07
Long-term debt ($ mil.): 250

No. of shares (mil.): 109
Dividends
Yield: —
Payout: —
Market value ($ mil.): —

	STOCK PRICE ($) FY Close	P/E High/Low		PER SHARE ($) Earnings	Dividends	Book Value
12/19	0.00	—	—	(0.00)	0.00	24.89
12/18	0.00	—	—	(0.00)	0.00	(0.00)
Annual Growth	—		—	—	—	—

ARMOUR Residential REIT Inc.

ARMOUR Residential hopes to protect its investments with the strength of the US government. A real estate investment trust or REIT ARMOUR Residential invests in single-family residential mortgage-backed securities issued or guaranteed by Fannie Mae Freddie Mac and Ginnie Mae. The company's investments include fixed-rate adjustable-rate and hybrid adjustable-rate mortgages (hybrid mortgages start off with fixed rates that may eventually increase as the loan matures). To a lesser extent the company also invests in government-issued bonds unsecured notes and other debt. Formed in 2008 ARMOUR Residential is externally managed by ARMOUR Residential Management LLC.

Operations
ARMOUR Residential's has net loss in year 2019 due to the increase in derivatives.
Geographic Reach
The REIT is based in Vero Beach Florida.
Sales and Marketing
ARMOUR trades its securities and derivatives with banks brokers dealers or principal counter parties (originators GSEs and other investors).
Financial Performance
The company's net loss further increase by $143.9 million to a net loss of $249.9 million in 2019. The main factor for the difference in net loss for 2019 compared to 2018 was the increase in losses on its derivatives in 2019 compared to 2018.

Cash held by the company at the end of 2019 increased by $41.0 million to $273.2 million compared from $232.2 million in the prior year. Cash provided by financing activities was $4.5 billion while cash used for operations and investing activities were $40.7 million and $4.4 billion respectively. Main use for cash was purchases of agency securities.
Strategy
The company seeks to create shareholder value through thoughtful investment and risk management that produces current yield and superior risk adjusted returns over the long term. Armour focuses on residential real estate finance supports home ownership for a broad and diverse spectrum of Americans by bringing private capital into the mortgage markets. The company is deeply committed to implementing sustainable environmental responsible social and prudent governance practices that improve its work and its world.Armour invest in mortgage backed securities ("MBS"). Some MBS are issued or guaranteed by a United States ("U.S.") Government-sponsored entity ("GSE") such as the Federal National Mortgage Association ("Fannie Mae") the Federal Home Loan Mortgage Corporation ("Freddie Mac") or a government agency such as Government National Mortgage Administration ("Ginnie Mae") (collectively "Agency Securities"). The company's Agency securities consist primarily of fixed rate loans. The remaining Agency Securities are either backed by hybrid adjustable rate or adjustable rate loans.

EXECUTIVES

Vice Chairman Co-ceo And President, Jeffrey J. Zimmer, age 63, $871,904 total compensation
Co-vice Chairman Co-ceo Cio And Head Risk Management, Scott J. Ulm, age 61, $871,904 total compensation
Cfo, James R. Mountain, $80,425 total compensation
Coo, Mark Gruber, $104,699 total compensation
Chairman, Daniel C. Staton
Auditors: Deloitte & Touche LLP

LOCATIONS

HQ: ARMOUR Residential REIT Inc.
3001 Ocean Drive, Suite 201, Vero Beach, FL 32963
Phone: 772 617-4340
Web: www.armourreit.com

COMPETITORS

AG Mortgage Investment Trust	Capstead Mortgage
American Capital Agency Corp.	Hatteras Financial
	MFA Financial
Annaly Capital Management	Orchid Island Capital
	Provident Mortgage Capital
Anworth Mortgage Asset	TMAC Mortgage
Apollo Residential Mortgage	

HISTORICAL FINANCIALS

Company Type: Public

Income Statement — FYE: December 31

	ASSETS ($ mil.)	NET INCOME ($ mil.)	INCOME AS % OF ASSETS	EMPLOYEES
12/19	13,272	(249)	—	—
12/18	8,464	(105)	—	—
12/17	8,928	181	2.0%	—
12/16	7,978	(45)	—	—
12/15	13,055	(31)	—	19
Annual Growth	0.4%	—	—	—

Debt ratio: —	No. of shares (mil.): 58
Return on equity: (-19.51%)	Dividends
Cash ($ mil.): 181	Yield: 12.0%
Current ratio: —	Payout: —
Long-term debt ($ mil.): —	Market value ($ mil.): 1,052

	STOCK PRICE ($) FY Close	P/E High/Low		PER SHARE ($) Earnings	Dividends	Book Value
12/19	17.87	—	—	(4.59)	2.16	24.40
12/18	20.50	—	—	(2.92)	2.28	25.75
12/17	25.72	7	5	4.17	2.28	31.67
12/16	21.69	—	—	(1.67)	3.02	29.74
12/15	21.76	—	—	(1.09)	1.65	33.40
Annual Growth	(4.8%)	—	—	—	7.0%	(7.5%)

Arrow Electronics, Inc.

Arrow Electronics hits its target markets with a quiver of thousands of electronic products. The company is a global distributor of electronic components and enterprise computing solutions. It sells semiconductors passive components interconnect products computing and memory and computer peripherals to more than 175000 equipment and contract manufacturers resellers and other commercial customers. The company's Global ECS' portfolio of computing solutions includes data-center cloud security and analytics solutions. Arrow Electronics which generates more than 55% of revenue outside the US operates from more than 335 locations across the globe.

Operations

Arrow Electronics operates in two segments — Global Components and Global Enterprise Computing Solutions (ECS).

Global Components accounts some 70% of sales. Its offerings consist of semiconductor passive electro-mechanical and interconnect products (capacitors resistors potentiometers power supplies relays switches and connectors) as well as computing and memory products. More than 70% of the unit's sales are from semiconductor products and related services making the company highly dependent on that industry's boom-and-bust cycle.

Arrow Electronics' Global ECS business (some 30%) sells software storage and servers to value-added resellers and managed service providers. ECS has expanded its offerings software-defined architectures hybrid and public cloud unified computing and managed services. Software is the unit's biggest seller accounting around 40% of revenue.

Geographic Reach

Arrow Electronics based in Centennial Colorado has 295 sales facilities and more than 40 distribution and value-added centers serving over 90 countries. Both business segments have operations in each of the three largest electronics markets: Americas; Europe; the Middle East and Africa (EMEA); and the Asia-Pacific region The company leases six major warehouses and logistics centers located in Reno Nevada Phoenix Arizona Solon Ohio Venlo Netherlands Hong Kong and Shenzhen China. The company also has some 35 smaller distribution centers located throughout the Americas EMEA and Asia-Pacific regions.

The company generates about 45% of sales from the Americas (mostly the US) with EMEA accounting for more than 30% and the Asia-Pacific region contributing over 25%.

Sales and Marketing

Arrow Electronics serves more than 175000 OEMs and contract manufacturers through its components business segment and value-added resellers through its ECS business segment. Most of its sales are made on an order-by-order basis rather than through long-term sales contracts.

The company's customers are in the telecommunications automotive and transportation aerospace and defense medical professional services and alternative energy industries among others.

Financial Performance

For four years since 2015 Arrow Electronics achieved meaningful revenue growth. However sales in 2019 dropped. Net income for the same period fluctuated.For four years since 2015 Arrow Electronics achieved meaningful revenue growth. However sales in 2019 dropped. Net income for the same period fluctuated.

In 2019 the company reported a revenue of $28.9 billion a drop of 3% from the prior year. The decrease was driven by a 2.9% decrease in the global components business segment sales and a 1.7% decrease in global ECS business segment sales.

Net income suffered a loss of $204.1 million. The loss was impacted by goodwill and other impairments of $623.8 million and digital inventory write-downs net of $22.3 million among others.

Cash at the end of 2019 was $300.1 million a decrease of $209.2 million from the prior year. Operating activities contributed $858 million to the coffers while investing activities used $173.6 million mainly for acquisitions and capital expenditures. Financing activities used another $906.3 million for stock repurchases.

Strategy

The company's financial objectives are to grow sales faster than the market increase the markets served grow profits faster than sales and increase return on invested capital. To achieve its objectives the company seeks to capture significant opportunities to grow across products markets and geographies. To supplement its organic growth strategy the company continually evaluates strategic acquisitions to broaden its product and value-added service offerings increase its market penetration and expand its geographic reach.

Over the past three years the global components business segment completed four strategic acquisitions to broaden its digital capabilities to meet the evolving needs of customers and suppliers. These acquisitions also expanded the global components business segment's portfolio of products and services offerings at every phase of technology deployment including custom hardware and software and new Internet of Things based business models.

Over that same span the global ECS business segment completed one strategic acquisition to further expand its portfolio of products. Aligned with the vision of guiding innovation forward in the IT channel the company is investing in emerging and adjacent markets such as managed services software-defined architectures hybrid and public cloud and unified computing within the ECS business.

Company Background

Arrow Radio began in 1935 in New York City as an outlet for used radio equipment. By 1977 it had become the US's fourth-largest electronics distributor. In 1979 Arrow bought the #2 US distributor Cramer Electronics and went public.

EXECUTIVES

Chairman President And Ceo, Michael J. (Mike) Long, age 62, $1,150,000 total compensation
Svp And Chro, Gretchen Zech

Vp And Cio, Vincent P. (Vin) Melvin, age 56
President Global Components, Andrew D. (Andy) King, age 56, $500,000 total compensation
Svp And Chief Strategy Officer, M. Catherine (Cathy) Morris, age 61, $475,000 total compensation
President Global Enterprise Computing Solutions, Sean J. Kerins, age 57, $550,000 total compensation
Svp And Cfo, Christopher D. (Chris) Stansbury, age 54, $452,308 total compensation
Vp Global Communications, John Hourigan
Vice President Semiconductor Marketing, Murdoch Fitzgerald
Vice President And Treasurer, Michael Taunton
Senior Vice President Human Resources, John McMahon
Vice President Enterprise Services, Mark Endry
Vp Legal Affairs, Martin Hillery
Vice President Global Supply Chain, Timothy Kolbus
Vp Corporate Marketing And Communications, Richard Kylberg
Vice President Business Development, Steve Maser
Vice President Digital Marketing And General Manager Verical, Darryl Shaper
Svp And Chief Strategy Officer, M Catherine Morris
Vice President Business Transformation A, Cedric Doignie
Auditors: Ernst & Young LLP

LOCATIONS

HQ: Arrow Electronics, Inc.
9201 East Dry Creek Road, Centennial, CO 80112
Phone: 303 824-4000
Web: www.arrow.com

2018 Sales

	$ mil.	% of total
Americas	13,559	45
Europe Middle East & Africa	8,810	30
Asia/Pacific	7,307	25
Total	**29,676**	**100**

PRODUCTS/OPERATIONS

2018 Sales

	$ mil.	% of total
Global Components	20,856	70
Global Enterprise Computing Solutions (ECS)	8,819	30
Total	**29,676**	**100**

Selected Products and Services

Computer Products
    Communication control equipment
    Controllers
    Design systems
    Desktop computers
    Flat-panel displays
    Microcomputer boards and systems
    Monitors
    Printers
    Servers
    Software
    Storage products
    System chassis and enclosures
    Workstations
Electronic Components
    Capacitors
    Connectors
    Potentiometers
    Power supplies
    Relays
    Resistors
    Switches

Services

    Analysis implementation and support
    Component design
    Contract manufacturing
    Forecast and order management
    Inventory management

COMPETITORS

Avnet	Richardson Electronics
Digi-Key	SYNNEX
Future Electronics	TTI Inc.
Heilind Electronics	Tech Data
Ingram Micro	WPG Holdings
N.F. Smith	Yosun
Newark Corporation	ePlus

HISTORICAL FINANCIALS

Company Type: Public

Income Statement
FYE: December 31

	REVENUE ($ mil.)	NET INCOME ($ mil.)	NET PROFIT MARGIN	EMPLOYEES
12/19	28,916	(204)	—	19,300
12/18	29,676	716	2.4%	20,100
12/17	26,812	401	1.5%	18,800
12/16	23,825	522	2.2%	18,700
12/15	23,282	497	2.1%	18,500
Annual Growth	5.6%	—	—	1.1%

2019 Year-End Financials

Debt ratio: 18.12%
Return on equity: (-4.03%)
Cash ($ mil.): 300
Current ratio: 1.52
Long-term debt ($ mil.): 2,640

No. of shares (mil.): 80
Dividends
  Yield: —
  Payout: —
Market value ($ mil.): 6,832

	STOCK PRICE ($) FY Close	P/E High/Low		PER SHARE ($) Earnings	Dividends	Book Value
12/19	84.74	—	—	(2.44)	0.00	59.69
12/18	68.95	11	8	8.10	0.00	62.51
12/17	80.41	19	15	4.48	0.00	56.47
12/16	71.30	13	8	5.68	0.00	49.64
12/15	54.18	12	10	5.20	0.00	45.56
Annual Growth	11.8%	—	—	—	—	7.0%

Arrow Financial Corp.

Arrow Financial has more than one shaft in its quiver. It's the holding company for two banks: $2 billion-asset Glens Falls National Bank operates 30 branches in eastern upstate New York while $400 million-asset Saratoga National Bank and Trust Company has around 10 branches in Saratoga County. Serving local individuals and businesses the banks offer standard deposit and loan products as well as retirement trust and estate planning services and employee benefit plan administration. Its subsidiaries include: McPhillips Insurance Agency and Upstate Agency which offer property and casualty insurance; Capital Financial Group which sells group health plans; and North Country Investment Advisors which provides financial planning services.

Operations

Arrow Financial's loan portfolio consisted of residential real estate mortgages and home equity loans (40% of loan assets) commercial and commercial real estate loans (31%) and indirect auto loans (29%) at the end of 2015.

The banking group makes more than 70% of its revenue from interest income. About 58% of Arrow Financial's total revenue came from loan interest (including fees) during 2015 while another 14% came from interest on taxable and tax-exempt investment securities. The rest of its revenue came from insurance commissions (9% of revenue) customer service fees (9%) fiduciary activity income (8%) and other miscellaneous income sources.

Geographic Reach

Glens Falls National Bank has 30 branches in eastern upstate New York (in Warren Washington Saratoga Essex and Clinton Counties). Saratoga Springs-based Saratoga National Bank operates nine branches in Saratoga Albany and Rensselaer Counties.

Financial Performance

Arrow Financial Corporation's revenues and profits have been slowly rising since 2013 mostly as steady — and more creditworthy — loan growth has spurred more interest income.

The group's revenue climbed 4% to $98.86 million during 2015 mostly as 7%-plus growth in loan and other interest-earning assets continued to spur additional interest income.

Revenue growth in 2015 pushed Arrow Financial's net income up 6% to $24.66 million. The banking group's operating cash levels dipped 6% to $28.93 million despite earnings growth mostly due to unfavorable working capital changes.

Strategy

Arrow Financial has been working its loan portfolio quality by implementing smarter lending strategies with stronger underwriting and collateral control procedures and credit review systems.

It's also slowly expanding its business and branch network in the Capital District of New York which has been a key market for the bnak's growth. In September 2015 its Saratoga National Bank subsidiary opened its ninth branch in Troy. In June 2014 it opened a new branch in Colonie after opening two new branches in Queensbury and Clifton Park in 2013.

EXECUTIVES

Evp Bank Card Business Development And Marketing Glen Falls National Bank And Trust, David S. (Dave) DeMarco, $178,500 total compensation
Director Arrow Financial Corporation And Chairman Saratoga National Bank And Trust, Raymond F. (Ray) O'Conor, $178,500 total compensation
President And Ceo, Thomas J. (Tom) Murphy, age 62, $300,000 total compensation
Svp And Cfo Arrow Financial Corporation And Evp And Cfo Glens Falls National Bank And Trust Company, Edward J. Campanella, age 52
Assistant Vice President, Suzanna Bernd
Vice President, Jim Brown
Vice President Trust Officer, Laura Vamvalis
Vice President, Peter Capozzola
Executive Vice President Marketing, Dennis Martinez
Chairman, Thomas L. Hoy, age 71
Board Member, David Kruczlnicki
Vice Chair, Leslie D'angelico
Board Member, Michael B Clarke
Board Member, Colin Read
Board Member, Tenee Casaccio
Board Member, Mark Behan
Board Member, Elizabeth Miller
Auditors: KPMG LLP

LOCATIONS

HQ: Arrow Financial Corp.
250 Glen Street, Glens Falls, NY 12801
Phone: 518 745-1000
Web: www.arrowfinancial.com

PRODUCTS/OPERATIONS

2015 Sales

	$ mil.	% of total
Interest and dividend income		
Interest and Fees on Loans	56	58
Fully Taxable	8	8
Exempt from Federal Taxes	5	6
Non-interest income		
Fees for Other Services to Customers	9	9
Insurance Commissions	9	9
Income From Fiduciary Activities	7	8
Other	2	2
Total	98	100

Selected Subsidiaries

Glens Falls National Bank and Trust Company
  Arrow Properties Inc. (real estate investment trust)
  Capital Financial Group Inc.
  Glens Falls National Community Development Corporation
  Glens Falls National Insurance Agencies LLC (dba McPhillips Agency)
  Loomis & LaPann Inc.
  NC Financial Services Inc.
  North Country Investment Advisers Inc.
  Upstate Agency LLC
Saratoga National Bank and Trust Company

COMPETITORS

Ballston Spa Bancorp	Community Bank System
Bank of America	KeyCorp
Citizens Financial Group	NBT Bancorp
	TrustCo Bank Corp NY

HISTORICAL FINANCIALS

Company Type: Public

Income Statement
FYE: December 31

	ASSETS ($ mil.)	NET INCOME ($ mil.)	INCOME AS % OF ASSETS	EMPLOYEES
12/19	3,184	37	1.2%	520
12/18	2,988	36	1.2%	516
12/17	2,760	29	1.1%	533
12/16	2,605	26	1.0%	524
12/15	2,446	24	1.0%	511
Annual Growth	6.8%	11.0%	—	0.4%

2019 Year-End Financials

Debt ratio: 0.79%
Return on equity: 13.12%
Cash ($ mil.): 70
Current ratio: —
Long-term debt ($ mil.): —

No. of shares (mil.): 15
Dividends
  Yield: 2.7%
  Payout: 41.9%
Market value ($ mil.): 584

	STOCK PRICE ($) FY Close	P/E High/Low		PER SHARE ($) Earnings	Dividends	Book Value
12/19	37.80	16	13	2.43	1.02	19.53
12/18	32.02	17	13	2.36	0.97	17.55
12/17	33.95	21	16	1.92	0.90	16.39
12/16	40.50	24	15	1.75	0.87	15.32
12/15	27.17	18	16	1.65	0.88	14.20
Annual Growth	8.6%	—	—	10.2%	3.8%	8.3%

Asbury Automotive Group Inc

Car dealership giant Asbury Automotive Group oversees more than 105 new vehicle franchises representing about 90 dealership locations in about 10 states including the Carolinas Florida Texas and Virginia. The dealerships sell more than 30 different brands of US-made and imported new and used vehicles. Asbury also offer parts servicing and collision repair from about 25 repair centers as well as financing insurance and warranty and service contracts. The auto dealer has grown by acquiring large locally branded dealership groups as well as smaller groups and individually owned dealerships throughout the US. Honda vehicles account for about 20% of Asbury's new car sales.

Operations

Asbury sells more than 105000 new vehicles each year representing around 55% of its revenue. Used car sales bring in 30%. The company also operates a parts and services division (more than 10% of revenue) and a finance and insurance division (about 5%).

Approximately 80% of Asbury's sales come from import brands. Honda and its luxury brand Acura account for more than 20% of new vehicle revenue while Toyota accounts for 20% and Nissan supplies over 10%. Ford is Asbury's top-selling US-based brand accounting for 10% of new car sales. Mercedes-Benz USA and BMW of North America accounts more than 5% each of new vehicle revenue.

Geographic Reach

Duluth Georgia-based Asbury operates dealerships in more than 15 metropolitan markets mostly in the southeastern US. Aside from the Carolinas Florida Texas and Virginia Asbury has dealerships in Indiana Georgia Mississippi and Missouri.

The company's operations encompassed about 90 franchised dealership locations throughout ten states and 25 collision repair centers.

Sales and Marketing

The company have discipline-specific executives who focus on increasing the penetration of current services and expanding the breadth of their offerings to customers through the implementation of best practices and continuous training on their technology solutions throughout their dealership network. In addition they have marketing initiatives designed to attract customers to their online channels and mobile applications.

Advertising expense from continuing operations totaled $34.4 million for the fiscal year 2019.

Financial Performance

Despite the fell of revenue from the previous years Asbury's spiked and caught up its sales performance from 2018 (up 6%) to 2019 (up 5%).

Revenue rose to $7.2 billion in 2019 a 5% increase from $6.9 billion in 2019 driven by stronger sales in all its categories: new vehicle revenue (up 2%) used vehicle revenue (up 8%) parts and service revenue (up 10%) and finance and insurance revenue (up 8%).

Net income followed revenue's lead and came in at $184.4 million an increase of 10% compared to $168.0 million in 2019 on higher sales and lower taxes year-over-year.

Asbury had $3.5 million in cash and equivalents in 2019 compared to $8.3 million the year before. Operations produced $349.8 million investing activities used $227.6 million and financing activities used another $127.0 million.

The company had total debt of $943.3 million in 2019. The amount of debt could impede its ability to borrow more money for acquisitions or capital expenditures and limit its flexibility to respond to market and industry conditions.

Strategy

The company seek to create long-term value for their stockholders by striving to drive operational excellence and deploy capital to its highest risk adjusted returns. To achieve these objectives they employ the strategies described as following: Invest in and attract top talent to improve backend operations and front-line service; Implement best practices and improve productivity; Provide an exceptional customer experience; Centralize streamline and automate processes; Leverage their scale and cost structure to improve their operating efficiencies; Successfully integrate Park Place and maximize the benefits of this transformational Acquisition; Deploy capital to highest risk adjusted returns; Continue to invest in their business; and Evaluate opportunities to refine their dealership portfolio.

Asbury's believe that the automotive retailing industry is a mature industry whose sales are significantly impacted by the prevailing economic climate both nationally and in local markets. Accordingly they believe that their future growth depends in part on their ability to manage expansion control costs in their operations and acquire and effectively integrate acquired dealerships into their organization. When seeking to acquire other dealerships they often compete with several other national regional and local dealership groups and other strategic and financial buyers some of which may have greater financial resources than them. Competition for attractive acquisition targets may result in fewer acquisition opportunities for them and they may have to forgo acquisition opportunities to the extent they cannot negotiate such acquisitions on acceptable terms.

Mergers and Acquisitions

n late-2019 Asbury Automotive Group announces the acquisition of the Park Place Dealerships one of the country's largest and most prominent luxury dealer groups for $1 billion in an all-cash transaction excluding vehicle inventory.

EXECUTIVES

Svp Corporate Development And Real Estate, George C. Karolis, age 45, $397,728 total compensation

President And Ceo, David W. Hult, age 54, $745,182 total compensation

Vp And Cio, Barry Cohen

Svp And Cfo, Sean D. Goodman, age 55

Senior Vice President General Counsel And Secretary, George Villasana

Vice President Manufacturer Relations, Matthew Mees

Senior Vice President Operations, John Hartman

Chairman, Thomas C. DeLoach, age 73

Vice Chairman, Craig T. Monaghan, age 63

Board Member, Tom Reddin

Auditors: Ernst & Young LLP

LOCATIONS

HQ: Asbury Automotive Group Inc
2905 Premiere Parkway N.W., Suite 300, Duluth, GA 30097
Phone: 770 418-8200
Web: www.asburyauto.com

PRODUCTS/OPERATIONS

2018 Sales

	$ mil.	% of total
New vehicles	3,788	55
Used vehicles	1,972	29
Parts & services	821	12
Finance & insurance	292	4
Total	**6,874**	**100**

2018 Sales

	% of total
Imports	47
Luxury	33
Domestic	20
Total	**100**

Selected Brands

Coggin Automotive Group
Courtesy Autogroup
David McDavid Auto Group
Gray-Daniels Auto Family
Nalley Automotive Group
Plaza Motor Company

COMPETITORS

AutoNation	Penske Automotive
Buchanan Automotive	Group
CarMax	Ron Tonkin Family of
Ferman Automotive	Dealerships
Group 1 Automotive	Scott-McRae
Hendrick Automotive	Sonic Automotive
Island Lincoln-Mercury	

HISTORICAL FINANCIALS

Company Type: Public

Income Statement

FYE: December 31

	REVENUE ($ mil.)	NET INCOME ($ mil.)	NET PROFIT MARGIN	EMPLOYEES
12/19	7,210	184	2.6%	8,500
12/18	6,874	168	2.4%	8,200
12/17	6,456	139	2.2%	8,000
12/16	6,527	167	2.6%	7,900
12/15	6,588	169	2.6%	8,600
Annual Growth	2.3%	2.2%	—	(0.3%)

2019 Year-End Financials

Debt ratio: 59.33%
Return on equity: 32.94%
Cash ($ mil.): 3
Current ratio: 1.29
Long-term debt ($ mil.): 907

No. of shares (mil.): 19
Dividends
  Yield: —
  Payout: —
Market value ($ mil.): 2,155

	STOCK PRICE ($) FY Close	P/E High/Low		PER SHARE ($) Earnings	Dividends	Book Value
12/19	111.79	13	7	9.55	0.00	33.52
12/18	66.66	9	7	8.28	0.00	24.46
12/17	64.00	10	7	6.62	0.00	18.94
12/16	61.70	9	6	7.40	0.00	13.16
12/15	67.44	15	10	6.41	0.00	12.68
Annual Growth	13.5%	—	—	10.5%	—	27.5%

ASCENSION HEALTH ALLIANCE

EXECUTIVES

Pres-Ceo, Joseph Impicciche
Pres-Ceo, Joseph R Impicciche
Sr Exec Advsr, Sister Bernice Coreil DC

Evp, John D Doyle
Evp, Robert J Henkel
Evp, Susan Nestor Levy
Evp, Sister Maureen McGuire DC
Evp, David B Pryor
Executive Administrative Assis, Teresa Hatton
Regional Director, Andrew Gwin
Cco Clinical & Network Svs, Richard Fogel
Auditors: ERNST & YOUNG LLP ST LOUIS

LOCATIONS

HQ: ASCENSION HEALTH ALLIANCE
101 S HANLEY RD STE 450, SAINT LOUIS, MO
631053463
Phone: 314 733-8000
Web: WWW.ASCENSION.ORG

HISTORICAL FINANCIALS

Company Type: Private

Income Statement   FYE: June 30

	ASSETS ($ mil.)	NET INCOME ($ mil.)	INCOME AS % OF ASSETS	EMPLOYEES
06/17	34,320	1,638	4.8%	111,719
06/16	32,469	(339)	—	—
06/15	30,963	(42)	—	—
Annual Growth	5.3%	—	—	—

Associated Banc-Corp

A lot of Midwesterners are associated with Associated Banc-Corp the holding company for Associated Bank. One of the largest banks based in Wisconsin the bank operates about 200 branches in that state as well as in Illinois and Minnesota. Catering to consumers and local businesses it offers deposit accounts loans mortgage banking credit and debit cards and leasing. The bank's wealth management division offers investments trust services brokerage insurance and employee group benefits plans. Commercial loans including agricultural construction and real estate loans make up more than 60% of bank's loan portfolio. The bank also writes residential mortgages consumer loans and home equity loans.

Operations

Associated Banc-Corp boasts total assets of more than $27 billion making it one of the 50 largest publicly traded US bank holding companies. More than 70% of revenue comes from interest income mostly from loans. Roughly 60% of Associated Banc-Corp's $18 billion loan portfolio consists of commercial and industrial real estate construction commercial real estate loans and lease financing.

Nearly 30% of the company's income is from non-interest sources including: trust service fees service charges insurance commissions brokerage and annuity commissions and mortgage banking income among others. It also offers benefits consulting services through its Associated Financial Group subsidiary.

Geographic Reach

The company offers a full range of financial products and services in more than 200 banking locations serving more than 100 communities throughout Wisconsin Illinois and Minnesota and commercial financial services in Indiana Michigan Missouri Ohio and Texas.

Sales and Marketing

Associated Banc-Corp spent $26.1 million on business development and advertising in 2014 compared to $23.3 million in 2013 and $21.3 million in 2012.

Financial Performance

Associated Banc-Corp's revenue has remained flat for the past several years at just above $1 billion. Revenue in 2014 inched up by less than 1% to $1.03 billion mostly thanks to higher interest income as loan assets grew by 11% and as interest and dividends on investment securities also grew by double digits. Offsetting much of this growth the company's net mortgage banking income shrunk by $28 million (56%) driven by lower gains on sales and related income as secondary mortgage production declined.

Profit levels have been steadily rising over the past several years since losses in 2009 and 2010 with net income in 2014 rising by 1% to $190.51 million. Higher revenue combined with lower interest expenses on deposits and lower personnel costs all helped to boost the company's bottom line.

Despite higher earnings cash from operations fell 56% to $212.74 million primarily as the company made fewer net proceeds from the sale of its mortgage loans held for sale. The company's total loans grew by 11% to $17.6 billion in 2014 while total deposits rose by 9% to $18.77 billion.

Strategy

The company intends to continue pursuing a profitable growth strategy by carefully screening its prospective customers in light of the risks expenses and difficulties frequently encountered by companies in significant growth stages of development. Associated Banc-Corp hopes to keep its momentum going via organic growth including increasing its fee income and commercial deposits among other measures. It is also remodeling or relocating many of its branches.

Associated Banc-Corp also plans to continue strong loan business growth. For 2015 the company expects high single-digit annual average loan growth after posting loan double-digit loan growth across most categories in 2014.

Mergers and Acquisitions

Associated purchased BankMutual a Wisconsin-based bank in 2018.

In early 2015 subsidiary Associated Financial Group agreed to buy Minnesota-based Ahmann & Martin Co a risk and benefits consulting firm to gain new clients and expand its financial risk and insurance product and service lines.

Company Background

Hampered by one of the worst economic environments in recent history the bank saw an increase in nonperforming loans (particularly business- and housing-related loans) and more than tripled its provision for loan losses from 2008 to 2009. The company cut its losses in 2010 and nearly turned a profit as it concentrated on improving its credit quality. It moved away from construction lending and its nonperforming loans and its provisions for loan losses decreased. Even though 2011 revenues were down Associated Banc-Corp returned to profitability as credit quality continued to improve.

EXECUTIVES

Evp And Chief Risk Officer, Arthur G. (Art) Heise, age 62
President And Ceo, Philip B. (Phil) Flynn, age 62, $1,250,000 total compensation
Evp General Counsel And Corporate Secretary, Randall J. Erickson, age 61, $406,667 total compensation
Evp And Head Retail Banking, David L. Stein, age 56, $545,849 total compensation
Evp And Chief Human Resources Officer, Judith M. Docter, age 59
Evp And Chief Credit Officer, Scott S. Hickey, age 64, $644,531 total compensation
Evp And Chief Strategy Officer, Oliver Buechse, age 51
Evp And Head Commercial Real Estate, Breck F. Hanson
Evp And Head Corporate Banking, Donna N. Smith
Evp And Head Specialized Industries And Commercial Financial Services, John A. Utz, $348,417 total compensation
Evp And Head Community Markets, Timothy J. Lau
Evp And Cfo, Christopher J. Del Moral-Niles, $477,500 total compensation
Evp And Chief Audit Executive, Patrick J. Derpinghaus
Evp Cio And Coo, James Yee, $458,333 total compensation
Evp And Head Private Client And Institutional Services, William M. Bohn
President Southern Illinois, Phillip Hickman
Senior Vice President Investme, Sara Walker
Vice President Information Security Engineer, Patrick Pirwitz
Assistant Vice President Insured Risk Manager, Jean Ehren
Svp Segment Executive, Lou Banach
Vice President Customer Care Program And Operations Manager, Wendy Kumm
Senior Vice President Specialized Financial Services Insurance Industry, Peter Bulandr
Senior Vice President Commercial Lending, Jon Hein
Senior Vice President, Ron Murphy
Vice President Atm Channel Manager, Deanna Helminiak
Vice President Mortgage Underwriting Manager, Tammy Kurey
Vice President Digital Solutions Manager, Justin Chapman
Vice President Treasury Management Officer, Shelly Lapoint
Vice President Foreign Exchange, Jessie Bushmaker
Assistant Vice President Senior Bank Manager, Kim Klinkner
Vp Digital Solutions Manager Service Delivery, William Vogel
Vice President, Paul Schmerse
Vice President, Diana Michel
Vice President And Relationship Manager, Viktor Gottlieb
Senior Vice President, John Halechko
Senior Vice President, Angela O'neill
Assistant Vice President Residential Loan Officer, Kim Anders
Senior Vice President, Diane Gantner
Executive Vice President And Director Human Resources, Judy Docter
Assistant Vice President Senior Branch Manager, Ernesto Guillen
Assistant Vice President Underwriting, Jodi Sowinski
Vice President Senior Project Manager, Brooke Kusch
Sr. Branch Manager Avp, Jake Nyen
Avp Digital Solutions Sr Analyst, John Krueger
Vp Business Analyst Manager, Brad Abts
Vice President Field Exams, Jeff Kohr
Vice President, Thomas Kneesel
Senior Vice President Director Of Customer Experience, Irene Hogan
Vice President International Banking, Paul Eversman
Senior Vice President Regional Manager, Gregory T Warsek

Vice President Public Relations Senior Manager, Jennifer Kaminski

Senior Vice President Human Resources Di, Harlan Knuth

Svp Standardized Services Manager Commercial Support Services, Jason Wilson

Vice President Of Operation Management, Caryn Levey

Svp And Business Solutions Director It Shared Services, Bob Kapla

Vice President, Nate Selk

Vice President Trust Officer, John Duffy

Vice President Commercial Banking Relationship Manager, Scott Hoerth

Vice President Investments, Brad Hanna

Vice President Market Manager, Kenneth Alburg

Porfolio Manager Vice President, Mark Buechler

Vice President Senior Contract Management, Jeremy Allen

Senior Vice President, Larry Bickelhaupt

Assistant Vice President Administrative Analyst Project Administrator, Nata Nash

Avp Trade Capital Markets Back Office Specialist, Ellen Muench

Vice President And Portfolio Manager, Liliana Huerta

Vice President Manager, Kate Wesolowski

Vice President, Tracy Session

Vice President, Ryun Van Cuyk

Vice President, John Adams

Senior Vice President Director Of Treasury Management Product And Strategy, Michael Dacko

Vice President Design And Construction Services, Anthony Ferro

Vice President Senior Systems Analyst, Steven Weber

Executive Vice President Chief Credit Officer, John Hankerd

Business Development Officer Vice President, Stan Kroll

Senior Vice President, Farhan Iqbal

Vice President, Adam Demont

Vice President Market Manager, Charles Cafazza

Vice President Senior Project Manager, Melissa Birling

Svp Texas Market Manager, Dean Rosencrans

Vice President, Dave Bolwerk

Vice President Relationship Manager Government Banking, Joseph Hockers

Senior Vice President Regional Sales Manager, Tim Damato

Vice President Relationship Manager For The Commercial Real Estate Team, Krista Casper

Vice President Commercial Banking, Josh Dooley

Vice President, David Brookfield

Svp Director Hr Applications, Bob Simmons

Vice President Portfolio Manager, John Lotzer

Avp Talent Acquisition Consultant, Ashley Koepke

Vp Community Accountability Officer, William Kopka

Vice President Experiential Marketing Manager, Jenny Strachota

Vice President And Multicultural And Affordable Sales Integration Manager, LaDonna Reed

Vp Process Consultant, Mary Thornton

Vice President Information Technology Business Solutions, Tony Miller

Senior Vice President Special Loan Group Team Lead, Mike Waltz

Vice President Senior Program Manager, Marck Simson

Senior Vice President Capital Markets, Frank Barbaro

Vice President, Jiri Mikl

Vice President Relationship Manager, Daniel Barrins

Vice President Human Resource Business Partner, Lynn Smits

Assistant Vice President, Kimberly Mccann

Senior Vice President Market Manager Commercial Real Estate, Jim Vitt

Assistant Vice President, John Johnson

Vice President Of Private Banking, Welter Douglas

Senior Vice President Director Of Quantitative Modelin, David Greenwold

Svp Private Banking Credit Manager, Daniel Bishop

Vice President Private Banker, Gene Williams

Vp Sr Project Manager Commercial Banking, Kristi Hatcher

Vice President Portfolio Manager, Kyle Rabine

Senior Vp, Brian Maurice

Vice President Telecommunications Services Lead, Don Cross

Avp And Senior Records Management Analyst, Adam Mcvey

Vice President Private Banking Manager, Tracy Stansbury

Vice President Operations Senior Unit Manager, Teriann Van Sistine

Senior Vice President, Kathy Bozek

Vice President, Matthew Rotter

Vice President Residential Underwriting Manager, Anita Fehler

Senior Vice President, Daniel Holzhauer

Vp Risk And Controls Manager Operations And Technology, Kevin Ress

Vice President Senior Financial Consultant, Adam Dalke

Vice President Information Technology, Kathleen Wenzel

Vice President Portfolio Management, John Shaw

Vice President Senior Benefits Consultant, Dustin Rossow

Vice President Leadership Development Program Manager, Heidi Smith

Senior Vice President Segment Leader, Rod Murray

Vp And Sr Relationship Manager Retirement Plan Services, Scott Hoene

Vice President Special Loans Group, Michael Stevens

Vice President Portfolio Manager, Mick Tiffany

Vice President Portfolio Manager, Steven Berglund

Vice President, Judith Wood

Assistant Vice President, Jim Larchrid

Avp Senior Auditor, Kurt Kuschel

Senior Vice President, Randy Stille

Vice President, Nick Bickler

Vp Sr System Analyst, Steve Weber

Vp Mortgage Warehouse Group, Joseph Souza

Vice President, Jon Gluckman

Svp Commercial Banking Team Leader, Andrew Shallow

Assistant Vice President, Jeffrey Schaefer

Assistant Vice President Residential Loan Officer, Tammy Niemann

Bank Manager Assistant Vice President, Lynn Lusch

Vice President And Senior Relationship Manager Trust Officer, Chad Borns

Vice President, Sonia Schneider

Vp Portfolio Manager, Sarah Crosby

Senior Vice President, Daniel Thompson

Vice President, Rory Dunn

Auditors: KPMG LLP

LOCATIONS

HQ: Associated Banc-Corp
433 Main Street, Green Bay, WI 54301
Phone: 920 491-7500
Web: www.associatedbank.com

PRODUCTS/OPERATIONS

2016 Sales

	$ mil.	% of total
Interest		
Loans including fees	659	58
Investment securities including dividends and Interest	127	11
Other	4	0
Noninterest		
Insurance Commissions	80	7
Service charges on deposit accounts	66	6
Card-based & other nondeposit fees	50	4
Trust Service fees	46	4
Other	108	10
Total	1,144	100

2016 Sales

	% of total
Community Consumer and Business	59
Corporate and Commercial Specialty	36
Risk Management and Shared Services	5
Total	100

COMPETITORS

Bank Mutual	Northern Trust
Harris	TCF Financial
KeyCorp	U.S. Bancorp

HISTORICAL FINANCIALS

Company Type: Public

Income Statement

FYE: December 31

	ASSETS ($ mil.)	NET INCOME ($ mil.)	INCOME AS % OF ASSETS	EMPLOYEES
12/19	32,386	326	1.0%	4,669
12/18	33,647	333	1.0%	4,655
12/17	30,483	229	0.8%	4,388
12/16	29,139	200	0.7%	4,441
12/15	27,715	188	0.7%	4,383
Annual Growth	4.0%	14.8%	—	1.6%

2019 Year-End Financials

Debt ratio: 1.70%	No. of shares (mil.): 157
Return on equity: 8.48%	Dividends
Cash ($ mil.): 581	Yield: 3.1%
Current ratio: —	Payout: 34.6%
Long-term debt ($ mil.): —	Market value ($ mil.): 3,464

	STOCK PRICE ($) FY Close	P/E High/Low		Earnings	Dividends	Book Value
12/19	22.04	12	10	1.91	0.69	24.95
12/18	19.79	15	10	1.89	0.62	22.99
12/17	25.40	18	15	1.42	0.50	21.18
12/16	24.70	20	12	1.26	0.45	20.32
12/15	18.75	17	14	1.19	0.41	19.42
Annual Growth	4.1%	—	—	12.6%	13.9%	6.5%

ASSOCIATED WHOLESALE GROCERS, INC.

Associated Wholesale Grocers (AWG) knows its customers can't live on bread and milk alone. The second-largest retailer-owned distribution cooperative in the US (behind Wakefern Food Corporation) AWG supplies more than 3800 grocery retail outlets in more than half of the US states from 10 distribution centers which collectively have some 7 million square feet of space. In addition to its wholesale grocery operation AWG offers a variety of business services to its members including marketing and merchandising programs retail accounting supermarket development and access to low-cost merchandise through its Value Merchandisers subsidiary. AWG was founded by a group of independent grocers in 1924.

Geographic Reach
Kansas City-headquartered Associated Wholesale Grocers began in Missouri and its operations are generally centered on that state. It operates ten wholesale divisions in Missouri Nebraska Kansas Oklahoma Louisiana Alabama Tennessee and Wisconsin. Its distribution activities extend into another 25 states.

AWG's Valu Merchandisers subsidiary is gaining a foothold in non-US regions such as the Caribbean Central & South America and the Middle East.

Sales and Marketing
As a cooperative AWG serves the needs of its members who collectively determine how best to utilize the co-ops operations. Its board of directors is made up of nearly 20 people each a key executive at a grocer retail chain which receives products from AWG.

AWG serves up several private label brands to stores. They include Superior Selections Clearly Organic Best Choice Always Save and IGA.

Financial Performance
Associated Wholesale Grocers (AWG) has grown net sales in recent years from $7.8 billion in 2016 to more recent results exceeding $9.0 billion. Net income has trended positively over the same period from $175 million in 2012 to a spiked of more than $225 million in 2014 to a current result near $190 million.

For the year 2016 net sales grew 3% to $9.2 billion. Product price deflation pushed sales lower as did the loss of Albertsons' membership in the distribution co-op. AWG gained 800 new member stores in conjunction with its unification with Affiliated Foods Midwest which increased sales sufficiently to overcome the negative influencers.

Net income for the year was $190 million 4% lower than the prior year due to a corresponding increase in the co-op's general and administrative expenses.

Strategy
As a supplier to primarily independent and non-national grocers the co-op must retain size in order to compete with larger corporate firms. Years 2016 and 2017 saw its size shrink in Texas particularly in the hotly contested Dallas-Fort Worth market. Associated Wholesale Grocers lost two key members Albertsons (owner of Tom Thumb's and Safeway) and WinCo. It countered this by uniting with Affiliated Foods Midwest a distribution co-op with some 800 retail stores but the loss of such notable members is expected influence AWG's posturing within the North Texas area.

AWG continues to build sales of its billion-dollar private-label products line which includes the Best Choice IGA and Always Save brands. In addition to marketing the products as lower-cost alternatives to brand-name products the co-op has been investing in efforts to make sure the quality of its private-label items matches competing national brands. The company also owns and operates the Value Merchandisers Company (VMC) which offers some 22000 nonfood items to its members including health and beauty care general merchandise and seasonal and promotional products.

Operating in a fragmented business AWG competes with a large number of local and regional suppliers as well as distributors of specialty items. The food wholesale business also has its share of national giants including C & S Wholesale Nash-Finch and wholesale grocery and retail company SUPERVALU.

EXECUTIVES

Svp And Division Manager Nashville, Mike Danes
Evp And Chief Marketing Officer, Steve Arnold
Svp And Division Manager Memphis, Gary Jennings
Svp Finance, David Carl
Svp Distribution, Richard Kearns
Svp And Cio, Jon Payne
Svp And Division Manager Fort Worth, Linda Lawson
Svp Springfield, Tim Bellanti
Evp Division Operations, David Smith
Svp And Division Manager Oklahoma City, Danny Lane
Svp Grocery Products, Dan Funk
Svp Perishables, Jerry Edney
Svp And Division Manager Gulf Coast, Bob Durand
President Valu Merchandisers Company (vmc), Dave Sutton
President Always Fresh, Michael Schumacher
Vp Sales And Merchandising Memphis Division, David Gates
Senior Vice President, Maurice Henry
Vice President Of Sales Great Lakes, Sonny Leon
Vice President Of Fresh Merchandising Bakery Deli And Food Service, Daniel Koch
Vice President Of Corporate Distribution, Mark Wilson
Director, Bob Hufford
Vice Chairman, Don Woods

LOCATIONS
HQ: ASSOCIATED WHOLESALE GROCERS, INC.
5000 KANSAS AVE, KANSAS CITY, KS 661061135
Phone: 913 288-1000
Web: WWW.AWGINC.COM

COMPETITORS

Affiliated Foods	GSC Enterprises
Affiliated Foods Midwest	H. T. Hackney
	McLane
Albertsons	SUPERVALU
Alex Lee	SpartanNash
C&S Wholesale	Wakefern Food
Central Grocers	Wal-Mart
Dearborn Wholesale Grocers	WinCo Foods

HISTORICAL FINANCIALS
Company Type: Private

Income Statement
FYE: December 31

	REVENUE ($ mil.)	NET INCOME ($ mil.)	NET PROFIT MARGIN	EMPLOYEES
12/17	9,703	199	2.1%	5,500
12/15	8,935	198	2.2%	—
12/14	8,934	226	2.5%	—
12/13	8,380	192	2.3%	—
Annual Growth	3.7%	0.8%	—	—

Assurant Inc

From appliance protection to trailer park coverage Assurant aims to give its customers peace of mind. The company provides a diverse range of specialty insurance products such as extended service contracts for electronics appliances and vehicles; mobile device protection; manufactured home coverage; renters insurance; creditor-placed homeowners insurance; and pre-need funeral policies. Assurant's products are distributed through sales offices and independent agents across North America and in Latin America Europe and the Asia/Pacific region. The US accounts for about 80% of sales.

Operations
Assurant operates through three primary segments: Global Lifestyle Global Housing and Global Preneed.

The Global Lifestyle segment accounting for about three-quarters of the company's total revenue provides mobile device protection extended warranties for consumer electronics and appliances vehicle warranty protection and credit insurance. The division operates primarily in North America but also in Latin America Europe and the Asia/Pacific region.

The Global Housing segment bringing in about 20% of sales offers lender-placed homeowners insurance and multi-family housing products (renters insurance and related offerings) primarily in the US. Other products include voluntary homeowners flood and manufactured housing insurance.

The Global Preneed segment accounting for some 5% of revenue offers pre-funded funeral insurance which provides whole life or annuity death benefits for funeral costs in the US and Canada.

Geographic Reach
Roughly 80% of New York City-based Assurant's sales are in the US but the company also operates in Canada Latin America Europe and the Asia/Pacific region.

Sales and Marketing
Assurant sells its products through mobile carriers independent brokers agents financial institution representatives and third-party marketing organizations as well as through retail outlets including mortgage loan offices funeral homes and retailers. It markets multi-family housing products through property management firms and affinity marketing partners.

Financial Performance
The company reported declining revenue in 2017 and 2016due to divestitures and difficult market conditions. The company returned to modest growth in 2018 but reported an overall revenue decline of 2% between 2015 and 2019. Net income grew 170% during the five-year period.

Revenue increased 25% in 2019 to nearly $10.1 billion. The Global Lifestyle segment reported a 37% jump in sales that year driven by full year contribution from the TWG along with organic mobile device and auto program growth. Revenue in the Global Housing segment declined 2% due to the sale of the mortgage solutions business while the Global Preneed unit grew 4% mainly because of growth in the US business.

Net income increased 52% to $363.9 million in 2019 due to higher policyholder payouts acquisition costs and other expenses.

The company ended 2019 with nearly $1.9 billion in cash up $613.1 million from 2018. Operating activities contributed $1.4 billion while investing activities used $619.8 million (mostly on consolidated investment purchases) and financing activities used another $179.2 million primarily for acquisition of common stocks and dividends paid..

Strategy
Assurant works to develop innovative niche products within the lifestyle and housing markets. Its target areas for growth are connected living (mobile device electronics and appliance protection) multi-family housing (renters insurance) and global automotive (vehicle protection) services. The firm is also looking to expand its risk management offerings.

Assurant typically expands by pursuing a conservative acquisition strategy investing in purchases that neatly complement its existing offerings. For example it purchased The Warranty Group to boost its vehicle and lifestyle product portfolio in 2018 and two mobile device repair companies in 2019. The company has also grown through organic measures including launching new product offerings in fields such as cybersecurity and ecommerce protection plans.

In addition Assurant partners with other companies to expand its reach. To grow its lifestyle operations the company has established partnerships with firms including AppleCare Services Darty KDDI and Fair. It has also teamed up with cybersecurity firms DigitalShield SnoopWall and GamaSec.

To focus on key markets Assurant has exited some noncore businesses in recent years including its health insurance and employee benefits businesses. In 2018 the company sold its mortgage solutions operations to Dallas-based Xome Holdings for $36.7 million. It also sold its Time Insurance subsidiary part of the runoff Assurant Health unit to Haven Holdings for $30.9 million in 2018.

Mergers and Acquisitions

Bolting on to that acquisition the firm acquired MMI-CPR which franchises more than 700 Cell Phone Repair shops (mostly in the US) in late 2019. Assurant acquired CPR from a subsidiary of investment firm Merrymeeting Group and a third party. Financial terms of the transaction were not disclosed.

Assurant acquired Canadian mobile device repair outfit All Tech-Neek Electronics (ATNE) in 2019. The addition of ATNE which operates in Ontario broadened Assurant's presence in Canada.

Company Background

Assurant traces its roots to the LaCrosse Mutual Aid Association which was founded in 1892 to provide disability insurance in Wisconsin. The company formerly known as Fortis Inc. was spun off by the Fortis group (now known as Ageas) in 2004 and became publicly traded.

With a wary eye on US health care reform Assurant sold assets of its underperforming Assurant Health (small employer and individual health plans) unit to National General Holdings in 2016 and shuttered the rest of the business. It also sold Assurant Employee Benefits to Sun Life Financial in a deal valued at some $975 million.

In 2017 Assurant bought Green Tree Insurance Agency (homeowners and manufactured housing policies) from Walter Investment Management for $125 million plus additional performance-based payouts.

EXECUTIVES

Evp Chief Legal Officer And Secretary, Bart R. Schwartz, age 67, $595,000 total compensation
President Global Home, Michael P. Campbell
Evp And Chief Communication And Marketing Officer, Francesca Luthi
President And Ceo, Alan B. Colberg, age 58, $955,000 total compensation
Evp And Chief Risk Officer, Christopher J. Pagano, age 56, $639,583 total compensation
Evp Cfo And Treasurer, Richard S. Dziadzio, age 57, $283,205 total compensation
President And Ceo Assurant Specialty Property, Gene E. Mergelmeyer, age 61, $657,500 total compensation
Evp And Cto, Ajay Waghray, age 58, $338,335 total compensation
Evp And Chief Human Resources Officer, Robyn Price Stonehill, age 48
President Global Lifestyle, Keith W. Demmings
Evp And Chief Strategy Officer, Robert A. Lonergan
Senior Vice President Human Resources, Cynthia Lowden
Vice President Information Technology Transformation And Innovation, Norbert Monfort

Senior Vice President, Lynn Gelsomin
Senior Vice President Global Sales And Business Development, Allen Tuthill
Senior Vice President And Chief Compliance Officer, Doris Vigo
Senior Vice President Head Investments, Paul Koenig
Senior Vice President Chief Accounting Officer And Controller, Daniel Pacicco
Executive Vice President Valuations, Jennifer Sells
Senior Vice President Portfolio Manager, Matthew Sosland
Vice President Application Development, Stuart Saunders
Vice President, Dan Barone
Vice President Client Relations, Brandon Fox
Vice President, John Sheehan
Vp Brand And Marketing Strategy, Krystl Black
Vp Business Unit And International Marketing, Margaret Nagle
Svp Corporate Development, Joe Pehota
Senior Vice President Global Head Of Risk, R David Conner
Vice President Us Business Development, Dave Ronis
Vps Resident, Hall Absher
Vice President Human Resources, Sam Medina
Senior Vice President, Gregory Giammario
Chair, Elaine D. Rosen, age 67
Board Member, Debra Perry
Auditors: PricewaterhouseCoopers LLP

LOCATIONS

HQ: Assurant Inc
28 Liberty Street, 41st Floor, New York, NY 10005
Phone: 212 859-7000
Web: www.assurant.com

2017 Sales

	$ mil.	% of total
US	4,980	78
Other countries	1,434	22
Total	**6,415**	**100**

PRODUCTS/OPERATIONS

2017 Sales by Segment

	$ mil.	% of total
Lifestyle	3,510	55
Housing	2,250	35
Preneed	443	7
Corporate & other	210	3
Total	**6,415**	**100**

COMPETITORS

Allstate	Home Buyers Warranty
AmTrust Financial	Homesteaders Life
American Home Shield	Maiden Holdings
Americo	Monumental Life
Asurion	NGL Insurance
Bankers Financial	Nationwide
First American	State Farm
Great American Insurance Company	Warrantech

HISTORICAL FINANCIALS

Company Type: Public

Income Statement | | | | FYE: December 31

	ASSETS ($ mil.)	NET INCOME ($ mil.)	INCOME AS % OF ASSETS	EMPLOYEES
12/19	44,291	382	0.9%	14,200
12/18	41,089	251	0.6%	14,750
12/17	31,843	519	1.6%	14,750
12/16	29,709	565	1.9%	14,700
12/15	30,043	141	0.5%	16,700
Annual Growth	**10.2%**	**28.2%**	**—**	**(4.0%)**

2019 Year-End Financials

Debt ratio: 4.53%	No. of shares (mil.): 59	
Return on equity: 7.11%	Dividends	
Cash ($ mil.): 1,867	Yield: 1.8%	
Current ratio: —	Payout: 60.3%	
Long-term debt ($ mil.): —	Market value ($ mil.): 7,858	

	STOCK PRICE ($) FY Close	P/E High/Low		PER SHARE ($) Earnings	Dividends	Book Value
12/19	131.08	23	15	5.84	2.43	94.30
12/18	89.44	28	21	3.98	2.28	82.57
12/17	100.84	11	9	9.39	2.15	81.47
12/16	92.86	10	7	9.13	2.03	73.26
12/15	80.54	42	29	2.05	1.37	68.70
Annual Growth	**12.9%**	**—**	**—**	**29.9%**	**15.4%**	**8.2%**

AT&T Inc

If there's a way to communicate there's a good chance AT&T Inc. provides it. The company offers wireless wireline satellite WiFi IP network Virtual Private Network and fiber optic cable services. It is one of the biggest wireline and wireless providers in the US with more than 165 million subscribers. It offers digital TV voice and internet service through its U-verse brand and satellite Pay-TV through DIRECTV. AT&T acquired Time Warner Inc. in 2018 after winning a court challenge by the US government. The deal added Time Warner's content such as HBO and CNN to AT&T's distribution capabilities. The US supplies the majority of the company's revenue.

Operations

AT&T have four reportable segments: Communications WarnerMedia Latin America and Xandr.

Communications segment is its biggest segment generating more than 75% of revenue. The unit provides wireless and wireline telecom video and broadband services to consumers in the US and businesses in the US and around the world. Parts of the Communications segment are: the Entertainment Group which provides video internet interactive and targeted advertising and voice services to residential customers in the US; Mobility which serves business governmental wholesale customers and individual subscribers who purchase wireless services through employers; and the Business Wireline segment which provides advanced IP-based services as well as traditional voice and data services to business customers.

The WarnerMedia Segment (almost 20% of revenue) develops produces and distributes feature films television gaming and other content in various physical and digital formats globally. This segment includes Turner HBO and Warner Bros.

The company's Latin America segment nearly 5% of revenue provides entertainment and wireless services outside the US. This segment contains the Vrio and Mexico businesses.

AT&T operates an advertising service called Xandr which utilize data insights to develop and deliver targeted advertising across video and digital platfroms.

Overall AT&T generates about 90 % of revenue from service and approximately 10% from equipments.

Geographic Reach

Dallas Texas-based AT&T has nearly 5800 store in the US. The company has tried to increase its international telecommunications operations but still gets about 90% of revenue from the US. Europe and all other Latin America are two of its biggest international markets accounting for approximately 5% of revenue combined. The remaining revenues are generated in Mexico Brazil Asia/Pacific Rim and other.

Sales and Marketing

AT&T is nothing if not ubiquitous. The company is a big advertiser to businesses and consumers with presence on TV networks other networks and digital properties print radio and other media. The company operates its own retail stores where it offers smartphones from major manufacturers such as Apple and Samsung. The company spends $6.1 billion $5.1 billion and $3.7 billion on advertising for the years 2019 2018 and 2017 respectively.

Financial Performance

AT&T's revenue has risen at a 6% annual rate for the past five years which includes a year of lower revenue (2017).

Operating revenues increased in from $170.8 billion in 2018 to $181.2 billion in 2019 primarily due to including a full year's worth of Time Warner results which was acquired in June 2018. Partially offsetting the increase were declines in the Communications segment driven by continued pressure in legacy and video services and lower wireless equipment upgrades that were offset by growth in advanced data and wireless services.

Net income dropped about $5.5 billion from 2018 to $13.9 billion in 2019.

AT&T's cash holdings rose to $12.3 billion in 2019 from $5.4 billion in 2018. Operations generated $48.7 billion in 2019 while investing activities used $16.7 billion and financing activities used $25.1 billion.

Strategy

As the US wireless phone market becomes saturated (AT&T and Verizon count more than 280 million subscribers between them) carriers are looking for ways to generate more traffic on their networks to generate revenue. AT&T Inc. bought a content carrier DIRECTV in 2015.

One concern is whether HBO can maintain its cultural cache built on series such as The Sopranos and Game of Thrones that were developed under Hollywood-oriented leadership under the telecommunications-focused AT&T.

As of June 2020 AT&T's 5G network is available for consumers in 28 additional markets across the country and covers 179 million people. AT&T now offers access to 5G on its best unlimited wireless plans for consumers and businesses in a total of 355 markets in the U.S.

AT&T agreed to sell more than 1000 wireless communication towers to Peppertree Capital Management a private equity firm for about $680 million. AT&T will lease capacity from Peppertree. The sale is part of AT&T's plan to sell non-strategic assets to pay down debt.

In 2018 AT&T began work on FirstNet a government funded nationwide network for first-responders and public agencies. A possible bonus AT&T would be excess wireless capacity that it could use for its paying customers.

EXECUTIVES

Ceo Business Solutions And International, F. Thaddeus Arroyo, age 56
President And Ceo Sbc Southwest, William A. (Bill) Blase, age 65
Sevp And Cfo, John J. Stephens, age 61, $870,833 total compensation
Chairman And Ceo, Randall L. Stephenson, age 60, $1,791,667 total compensation
Ceo At&t Entertainment And Internet Services At&t Services Inc., John T. Stankey, age 58, $965,833 total compensation

Sevp And Global Marketing Officer, Lori M. Lee, age 54
President Public Sector And Wholesale Solutions, Xavier Williams
Ceo At&t Communications, John M. Donovan, age 59, $858,833 total compensation
Sevp External And Legislative Affairs At&t Services Inc., Robert W. (Bob) Quinn, age 59
Sevp And General Counsel, David R. McAtee, age 51
Sevp And Chief Compliance Officer, David S. Huntley, age 61
Ceo New Advertising & Analytics Company, Brian Lesser
President Business Operations At&t Business, Sorabh Saxena
Assistant Vice President Growth Platforms, Marcus Owenby
Vice President, Judy Phillips
Vice President Shared Services, Kevin Jeffries
Senior Vice President Of Emerging Devices, Chris Penrose
Assistant Vice President, Guy Bevente
Sales Vice President Premier Client Group, Sean Murphy
Area Vice President Government Solutions Group, Tim Walsh
Senior Vice President Finance, David Muro
Assistant Vice President C And E Osp, James Keown
Vice President Of Workforce Development And Diversity, Belinda Grant-anderson
Vice President Access Management, John Nolan
Regional Vice President, Craig Warbinton
Sales Vice President Wholesale Wireline North, Maryann Allen
Assistant Vice President Wi Fi Services, Josh Goodell
Vice President Wholesale Wireline Sales, Joan Jambor
Assistant Vice President Life Cycle Management, Armond Suraci
Assistant Vice President Sales Operations, Sandra Galst
Assistant Vice President Ran Engineering, Rajive Beri
Regional Vice President Business Integrated Solutions At At And T Mobility, Maurice Styles
Assistant Vice President Sales, Erin Miller
Vice President Customer Service, Glenn Riggin
Vice President Financial Planning, George Goeke
Senior Vice President Corporate Strategy, Steve McGaw
Vice President Of Acquisitions, James Bielar
Rvp, Meredith Caram
Assistant Vice President Network Services, Ron Royster
Associate Vice President, Tara Colon
Assistant Vice President Network Services, Raymond Perkins
Vice President Fleet Operations, Jerome Webber
Assistant Vice President Firstnet, Doug Clark
Information Technology Vice President, John Monday
Senior Vice President Global Solutions And Sales Operations, Alex Parker
Assistant Vice President Network Contracting, Roland Tunez
Vice President Human Resources, Gary Oliver
Vice President Information Technology Operations, Robert Gamiel
Assistant Vice President Business Advertising, Kelly Thengvall
Svp Assistant General Counsel, Tim Leahy
Vice President And General Manager, Gary Lackhouse
Associate Vice President Risk Management, Wayne Johnson
Sales Vice President, Steve Williams
Regional Vice President, Angela Rutherford

Vice President Operations Royal Dutch Shell, John Walton
Assistant Vice President Sales Operations, Suzanne Galvanek
Assistant Vice President Communications, Sarah Donohue
Regional Vice President Global Access Management, Bob Flappan
Vice President, Michele Smith
Svp Corporate Real Estate Atandt Operations, J Schleyer
Assistant Vice President Information Technology, Kristi Dryden
Assistant Vice President Radio Access Network Engineering, Joel Barone
Vice President Project Managment, Maria Dillard
Director Of Government Relations, Jane Sosebee
Regional Vice President Public Affairs, Sage Rhodes
Vice President Of Chemical Development, Damon Holzer
Vice President U Verse Product Managemetn, G W Shaw
Vice President Area, Larry Lelah
Att Ravpn Contact, Sam Tuffaha
Vice President Head Product And Business Development At&t Adworks, Matthew Van Houten
Director Evpn, Gregory Feenstra
Rvp Business Integrated Solutions, Martha K Wells
Vice President, Michael Flanagan
Vice President Small Business Product Management, Tom Hughes
Regional Vice President, Stephen Vergine
Sales Center Vice President, Vicky Santangelo
Executive Vice President Wholesale And Gem Solutio, Sherry Morse
Assistant Vice President Project Program Management, William Schutts
Assistant Vice President (assistant Vice President) Accounting, Lonnie Shirey
Vice President Of Project Development, Jeff Lewis
Vice President Of Engineering, Polly Bessel
National Account Manager, Kevin Moore
Sales Vice President, Michael Dechiara
National Account Manager, Dean Ramsey
Sales Center Vice President, Steve D'Lugos
Vice President, John Potter
Avp Customer Experience, Nicole Rafferty
Sales Vice President, Dan Roche
Vice President, Steve Mitchell
Customer Network Operations Vice President, Marvonia Walker
Client Executive Vice President, Knute A Olson
Vice President Audit Services, Gerry Chicoine
Assistant Vice President, John Blinkiewicz
Vice President Broadband And Narrowband Operations, Diane Young
Vice President And Senior Counsel, Diana Fellure
Assistant Vice President Corporate Communications, Nathan Melihercik
National Account Manager, Edward Hale
Vice President Business Development At And T Government Solutions, Robert Caffrey
Assistant Vice President Life Cycle Management Global Customer Service, Judy Miller
Senior Vice President Labor Relations Sbc Services, Michael Rodriguez
Assistant To Assistant Vice President Product Advertising, Pam Krueger
Vice President Antenna Solutions, Chad Townes
Executive Vice President Historian, Olga De La Vega
National Sales Manager Small Business Solutions, Jeff Ketler
Senior Vice President Signature Global Client Groups, John Finnegan
Assistant Vice President Technical Project Management Antenna Solutions Group, Stephen McNamara

Vice President Supply Chain Operations, Jim McGuire
Vice President Corporate Strategy, Christopher Sambar
Vice President Platforms And Enablers, Brad Mohs
Senior Vice President Advanced Solutions, Abhi Ingle
Architecture And Vendor Vice President, Ron Fowinkle
Assistant Vice President Billing Operations, Wesley Carpenter
Vice President Market Insights, Helen McGrath
Vice President Service Platforms, Pari Bajpay
Vice President Premier Client Group, Trish Renz
Area Vice President Sales, Marcus Cathey
Vice President General Manager, Bob Holliday
Vice President Glbl Managed Services And Outsourcing, Constance Diehl-boyle
Vice President, Jack Duffy
Assistant Vice President Digital Care Strategy, Kim Keating
Solution Implementation Manager At And T Vpn Tunneling Services, Brian Congleton
Senior Vice President Managed Services, Robin Young
Assistant Vice President National Security Network Regulatory, Brooks Fitzsimmons
Vice President At&t University, Nate Edwards
First Vice President Membership, Barry Winkler
Senior Vice President Employee Communications And Corporate Sponsorships, Gail Torreano
Vice President Sales, Kevin McKeand
Vice President Of U Verse Media Sales, Chris Monteferrante
Assistant Vice President External Affairs Operations, Gloria Corey
Vice President, Randy Cook
Senior Vice President Of Customer Experience, Carmen P Nava
Assistant Vice President Information Technology, Joseph Green
Intellectual Property Vice President, Ronald Sherman
Assistant Vice President Regulatory And External Affairs, Pat Wingo
Area Vice President Silicon Valley Growth Markets, Thomas McDonough
Vice President Platform Strategy And Solutions, Richard Batelaan
Sale Vice President, Jeffrey Hefflinger
Vice Presdient, Trudy Vankirk
Regional Vice President Public Relations, Robert Schauer
Assistant Vice President Network Services, Robert Spieler
Regional Vice President Southeast, Ivan Somavilla-castro
Vice President Civil, Mike Leff
Area Vice President, Karime Bavrica
Vice President Benefits, Susan Colburn
Assistant To Assistant Vice President Information Technology, Kathleen Wiegand
National Sales Manager, David Plante
National Account Manager, Dom Cimmino
Auditors: Ernst & Young LLP

LOCATIONS

HQ: AT&T Inc
208 S. Akard St., Dallas, TX 75202
Phone: 210 821-4105
Web: www.att.com

2018 Sales

	$ mil.	% of total
United States	154,795	91
Europe	4,073	2
Mexico	3,100	2
Brazil	2,420	2
Asia/Pacific Rim	2,215	1
Latin America Other	3,055	2
Total	170,756	100

PRODUCTS/OPERATIONS

2018 Sales

	$ mil.	% of total
Service	152,345	89
Equipment	18,411	11
Total	170,756	100

2018 Sales

	$ mil.	% of total
Communications	144,631	83
WarnerMedia	18,941	11
Latin America	7,652	4
Xandr	1,740	1
Corporate and Other	1,191	1
Certain Significant Items	(3,399)	-
Total	170,756	100

Selected Services

Voice
 Local
 Long-distance
 Wholesale
Data
 Application management
 Data equipment sales
 Data storage
 Database management
 Dedicated Internet service
 Digital television
 Directory and operator assistance
 Disaster recovery
 Enterprise networking
 Hardware and operating system management
 Internet access and network integration
 Managed Web hosting
 Network design
 Network implementation
 Network installation
 Network integration
 Network management
 Outsourcing
 Packet services
 Private lines
 Satellite video
 Switched and dedicated transport
 Voice-over-IP networks
 Wholesale networking
 WiFi

COMPETITORS

Altice USA	Equinix
América MOvil	Frontier
CenturyLink	Communications
Charter Communications	Sprint Communications
Comcast	T-Mobile USA
Consolidated	TelefOnica
Communications	U.S. Cellular
Cox Communications	Verizon
DISH Network	

HISTORICAL FINANCIALS

Company Type: Public

Income Statement   FYE: December 31

	REVENUE ($ mil.)	NET INCOME ($ mil.)	NET PROFIT MARGIN	EMPLOYEES
12/19	181,193	13,903	7.7%	246,000
12/18	170,756	19,370	11.3%	268,000
12/17	160,546	29,450	18.3%	252,000
12/16	163,786	12,976	7.9%	268,000
12/15	146,801	13,345	9.1%	281,450
Annual Growth	5.4%	1.0%	—	(3.3%)

2019 Year-End Financials

Debt ratio: 29.57%—
Return on equity: 7.55%
Cash ($ mil.): 12,130
Current ratio: 0.79
Long-term debt ($ mil.): 151,309

Dividends
 Yield: 5.2%
 Payout: 91.4%
 Market value ($ mil.): —

	STOCK PRICE ($) FY Close	P/E High/Low	PER SHARE ($) Earnings	Dividends	Book Value
12/19	39.08	21 15	1.89	2.04	25.39
12/18	28.54	14 10	2.85	2.00	25.28
12/17	38.88	9 7	4.76	1.96	22.94
12/16	42.53	21 16	2.10	1.92	20.06
12/15	34.41	15 13	2.37	1.88	19.96
Annual Growth	3.2%	— —	(5.5%)	2.1%	6.2%

ATHENE ANNUITY & LIFE ASSURANCE COMPANY

EXECUTIVES

Ceo, James R Belardi
Pres, Chip Smith
V Pres Fin, Cfo, David Attaway
Evp, Matthew Easley
Pres, Guy H Smith
Exec V Pres, Christopher Grady
Sr V Pres, Rod Mims

LOCATIONS

HQ: ATHENE ANNUITY & LIFE ASSURANCE COMPANY
2000 WADE HAMPTON BLVD, GREENVILLE, SC 296151037
Phone: 864 609-1000
Web: WWW.ATHENE.COM

HISTORICAL FINANCIALS

Company Type: Private

Income Statement   FYE: December 31

	ASSETS ($ mil.)	NET INCOME ($ mil.)	INCOME AS % OF ASSETS	EMPLOYEES
12/13	11,775	49	0.4%	120
12/12	10,481	11	0.1%	—
Annual Growth	12.3%	330.4%	—	—

Atlantic Capital Bancshares Inc

Auditors: Ernst & Young LLP

LOCATIONS

HQ: Atlantic Capital Bancshares Inc
945 East Paces Ferry Road N.E., Suite 1600, Atlanta, GA 30326
Phone: 404 995-6050
Web: www.atlanticcapitalbank.com

HISTORICAL FINANCIALS

Company Type: Public

Income Statement

FYE: December 31

	ASSETS ($ mil.)	NET INCOME ($ mil.)	INCOME AS % OF ASSETS	EMPLOYEES
12/19	2,910	49	1.7%	204
12/18	2,955	28	1.0%	340
12/17	2,891	(3)	—	353
12/16	2,727	13	0.5%	347
12/15	2,638	(1)	—	361
Annual Growth	2.5%	—	—	(13.3%)

2019 Year-End Financials

Debt ratio: 1.71%
Return on equity: 15.34%
Cash ($ mil.): 466
Current ratio: —
Long-term debt ($ mil.): —

No. of shares (mil.): 21
Dividends
  Yield: —
  Payout: —
Market value ($ mil.): 399

	STOCK PRICE ($) FY Close	P/E High/Low		PER SHARE ($) Earnings	Dividends	Book Value
12/19	18.35	9	7	2.12	0.00	15.01
12/18	16.37	19	13	1.09	0.00	12.80
12/17	17.60	—	—	(0.15)	0.00	11.99
12/16	19.00	35	22	0.53	0.00	12.10
12/15	14.98	—	—	(0.09)	0.00	11.79
Annual Growth	5.2%	—	—	—	—	6.2%

Atlantic Union Bankshares Corp

Union Bankshares (formerly Union First Market Bankshares) is the holding company for Union Bank & Trust which operates approximately 100 branches in central northern and coastal portions of Virginia. The bank offers standard services such as checking and savings accounts credit cards and certificates of deposit. Union Bank & Trust maintains a loan portfolio heavily weighted towards real estate: Commercial real estate loans make up more than 30% while one- to four-family residential mortgages and construction loans account for approximately 15% and 20% respectively. The bank also originates personal and business loans.

EXECUTIVES

Evp And Director Of Mortgage And Wealth Management, Jeffrey W. Farrar, age 59
Evp Union Bankshares And Chief Retail Officer Union Bank & Trust, Elizabeth M. Bentley, age 59, $268,491 total compensation
Evp And Chief Risk Officer, David G. (Dave) Bilko, age 60
President And Ceo Union Bankshares Corporation And Ceo Union Bank & Trust, John C. Asbury, age 55
Evp And Cfo, Robert M. (Rob) Gorman, age 61, $351,167 total compensation
Evp Union Bankshares And Chief Banking Officer Union Bank & Trust, D. Anthony (Tony) Peay, age 60, $348,997 total compensation
Evp And Cio, M. Dean Brown, age 55, $259,625 total compensation
Svp And Chief Marketing Officer, L. Duane Smith, age 53
Evp And Chief Human Resource Officer, Loreen A. LaGatta, age 51
Evp And President Union Bank & Trust, John G. Stallings, age 53

Senior Vice President, Chris Lumpkin
Vice President Business Banking Relationship Manager, Ann Hillsman
Vice President Business Banking Relationship Manager, Scott Jenkins
Senior Vice President And Trust Advisor Union Wealth Management, Jack Catlett
Senior Vice President, Michael Horan
Vice President And Trust Advisor Union Wealth Management, Sharon Barcalow
Assistant Vice President Commercial Real Estate, Diana Allen
Vice President And Senior Branch Manager, Terri Hirst
Assistant Vice President Branch Manager, Jody Hardy
Assistant Vice President Branch Manager, Diane Collier
Senior Vice President Private Banking Services And Client Advisor Rjfs, Norfleet Stallings
Senior Vice President And Director Of Bank Operations, Barbara Fischer
Senior Vice President, Mike Walsh
Vice President Uis Financial Advisor, Chris Rinehart
Senior Vice President, John Scott
Vice President And Senior Market Manager, Cheryl Kirby
Evp And President Union Bank And Trust, Maria P Tedesco
Senior Vice President Union Bank And Trust Company, Jay Baldwin
Vice President Uis Financial Advisor, Mike Whitmore
Vice President And Trust Advisor, Barbara Dickinson
Vice President Private Banking Services And Client Advisor Rjfs, Brian Adams
Vice President Uis And Financial Advisor Rjfs, John Faith
Vice President Uis And Financial Advisor Rjfs, Mason Garner
Vice President Uis And Financial Advisor Rjfs, Michael Johnson
Vice President Uis And Financial Advisor Rjfs, Preston Wall
Vice President Uis And Financial Advisor Rjfs, John Tekavec
Vice President And Portfolio Manager Union Wealth Management, Michael Snow
Senior Vice President Private Banking Services And Client Advisor Rjfs, Ben Mason
Senior Vice President Uis; Financial Advisor, Randy Vaughan
Svp, Michael D'aiutolo
Assistant Vice President Human Resources Business Partner, Saswati Khandat
Vp Director Community Engagement, Kat Costello
Vp Svp Portfolio Manager, Chris O'brien
Vice President Talent Acquisition, Tatyana Manelis
Vice President Commercial Banking, Timothy Schwan
Vice President, Thomas Moore
Senior Vice President Commercial Banking, T Ricky Frantz
Vice President Mortgage Division, Robert Racer
Vice Chairman Union Bankshares Corporation And Union Bank & Trust, G. William (Billy) Beale, age 70
Chairman, Raymond D. (Ray) Smoot, age 73
Auditors: Ernst & Young LLP

LOCATIONS

HQ: Atlantic Union Bankshares Corp
1051 East Cary Street, Suite 1200, Richmond, VA 23219
Phone: 804 633-5031
Web: www.bankatunion.com

PRODUCTS/OPERATIONS

2015 Sales

	$ mil.	% of total
Interest		
Loans including fees	247	72
Other	29	9
Noninterest		
Other service charges commission and fees	15	5
Service charges on deposit accounts	18	5
others	30	9
Adjustments	(0.3)	-
Total	341	100

Selected Subsidiaries

Union First Market Bank
Union Insurance Group LLC
Union Investment Services Inc.
Union Mortgage Group Inc.

COMPETITORS

BB&T
Bank of America
C&F Financial
Eastern Virginia Bankshares
JPMorgan Chase
PNC Financial
Regions Financial
SunTrust
TowneBank
Wells Fargo

HISTORICAL FINANCIALS

Company Type: Public

Income Statement

FYE: December 31

	ASSETS ($ mil.)	NET INCOME ($ mil.)	INCOME AS % OF ASSETS	EMPLOYEES
12/19	17,562	193	1.1%	1,989
12/18	13,765	146	1.1%	1,609
12/17	9,315	72	0.8%	1,149
12/16	8,426	77	0.9%	1,416
12/15	7,693	67	0.9%	1,422
Annual Growth	22.9%	30.3%	—	8.8%

2019 Year-End Financials

Debt ratio: 6.14%
Return on equity: 8.72%
Cash ($ mil.): 397
Current ratio: —
Long-term debt ($ mil.): —

No. of shares (mil.): 80
Dividends
  Yield: 2.5%
  Payout: 40.3%
Market value ($ mil.): 3,004

	STOCK PRICE ($) FY Close	P/E High/Low		PER SHARE ($) Earnings	Dividends	Book Value
12/19	37.55	16	12	2.41	0.96	31.41
12/18	28.23	19	12	2.22	0.88	29.17
12/17	36.17	23	18	1.67	0.81	23.92
12/16	35.74	21	12	1.77	0.77	22.95
12/15	25.24	18	13	1.49	0.68	22.23
Annual Growth	10.4%	—	—	12.8%	9.0%	9.0%

ATRIUM HEALTH FOUNDATION

The Â medical facilities under the watchful eye of the Â Charlotte-Mecklenburg Hospital Authority Â care for the injured and infirmed. Â As the largest health care system in the Carolinas the organization Â operating as Â Carolinas HealthCare System (CHS) Â owns Â or manages Â more than Â 30Â affiliated hospitals. Â It also operates long-term care facilities research centers rehabilitation facilities Â surgery centers Â home health agencies radiation therapy facilities and other health care operations.Â Collectively CHSÂ facilities have more than 6400 beds and affiliated physician practices employ more than 1700 doctors. The network's flagship facility is the 875-bedÂ Carolinas Medical Center in Charlotte North Carolina.

EXECUTIVES

Assistant Vice President, Luann Bailey
Group Vice President Levine Childrens Atrium Health Medical, Jennifer Terry
Assistant Vice President Of Human Resources, Dana Burnette
Assistant Vice President, Melissa Snuggs
Director Of Pharmacy, Chris Barringer
Executive Vice President And Chief Strategy Officer, Rasu Shrestha
Assistant Vice President Of Human Resources, Nehemie Owen
Vice President Diversity And Inclusion, Kinneil Coltman
Auditors: KPMG LLP CHARLOTTE NORTH CAR

LOCATIONS

HQ: ATRIUM HEALTH FOUNDATION
1000 BLYTHE BLVD, CHARLOTTE, NC 282035812
Phone: 704 355-2000
Web: WWW.CAROLINASHEALTHCARE.ORG

PRODUCTS/OPERATIONS

2010 Revenue

	% of total
Tertiary & acute care services	72
Physicians' services	16
Post-acute care services	3
Specialty services	2
Other services & non-operating activities	7
Total	**100**

Selected Hospitals and Health Care Pavilions

AnMed Health Medical Center
AnMed Health Rehabilitation Hospital
AnMed Health Women's and Children's Hospital
Anson Community Hospital
Bon Secours/St. Francis Hospital
Cannon Memorial Hospital
Carolinas Medical Center
Carolinas Medical Center - Kannapolis (health care pavilion)
Carolinas Medical Center - Lincoln
Carolinas Medical Center - Mercy
Carolinas Medical Center - NorthEast
Carolinas Medical Center - Pineville
Carolinas Medical Center - Steele Creek (health care pavilion)
Carolinas Medical Center - Union
Carolinas Medical Center - University
Carolinas Medical Center - Waxhaw (health care pavilion)
Carolinas Rehabilitation
Carolinas Rehabilitation - Mount Holly
Cleveland Regional Medical Center
CMC - Randolph
Columbus Regional Healthcare System
Crawley Memorial Hospital
Grace Hospital
Kings Mountain Hospital
Levine Children's Hospital
MedWest - Harris
MedWest - Haywood
MedWest - Swain
Roper Hospital
Roper St. Francis - Mount Pleasant Hospital
Scotland Memorial Hospital
Stanly Regional Medical Center
St. Luke's Hospital
Valdese Hospital
Wallace Thomson Hospital
Wilkes Regional Medical Center

COMPETITORS

Alamance Regional Medical Center
CaroMont
Community Health Systems
Cone Health
Conway Medical Center
Cumberland County Hospital System
Davis Regional Medical Center
Duke University Health System
FirstHealth of the Carolinas
Georgetown Hospital System
Grand Strand Regional Medical Center
HCA

Haywood Regional
High Point Regional Health System
McLeod Health
Mission Hospitals
Morehead Memorial Hospital
New Hanover Regional Medical Center
Novant Health
Palmetto Health
Presbyterian Healthcare
Rex Healthcare
Soliant Health
Tenet Healthcare
UNC Hospitals
Upstate Affiliate
Vidant Health
WakeMed

HISTORICAL FINANCIALS

Company Type: Private

Income Statement   FYE: December 31

	REVENUE ($ mil.)	NET INCOME ($ mil.)	NET PROFIT MARGIN	EMPLOYEES
12/19	7,510	1,223	16.3%	62,000
12/18	6,228	(69)	—	—
12/17	5,991	829	13.9%	—
12/16	5,676	493	8.7%	—
Annual Growth	**9.8%**	**35.3%**	**—**	**—**

Autoliv Inc

Autoliv is a leading supplier of automotive safety systems. Its lineup includes components and modules for passive safety systems such as seat belts frontal- and side-impact airbag systems steering wheels inflator systems pedestrian protection systems and battery cable cutters. Autoliv's customers include all of the world's largest automakers and the company has around 65 manufacturing facilities in 25 countries. Together the Renault/Nissan/Mitsubishi alliance and Volkswagen account for about 15% of sales. About 75% of sales comes from outside of US.

Operations

Autoliv's passive safety systems comprise a single reportable segment but airbag products account for about two-thirds of sales while seatbelt products make up remaining third.

Geographic Reach

Autoliv has nearly 15 technical centers and crash test tracks in 10 countries and around 65 production facilities in 25 countries. Regionally Asia is the company's largest market accounting for more than 35% of sales. The Americas and Europe generate about 30% and about 35% respectively.

Autoliv is based in Stockholm Sweden.

Sales and Marketing

Autoliv is dependent on a small number of global automakers. Autoliv's top five customers account for more than half of company sales and the ten largest nearly 80%. Its largest customers are the Renault/Nissan/Mitsubishi alliance Volkswagen Hyundai/Kia Ford Honda and Fiat Chrysler. Other customers include Toyota Daimler General Motors and BMW.

Financial Performance

Between 2015 and 2019 sales increased by about 12%.

Sales in 2019 decreased nearly 2% to $8.5 billion compared to $8.7 billion in 2018. Airbag sales grew organically by 2% mainly driven by strong performance for steering wheels particularly in Americas with slight net growth contribution coming from airbags as a result of growth in Americas and China and a decline in Europe. Seatbelt sales declined organically by 0.2% with main growth contributors being China and to a lesser degree Americas offset by a decline in Europe. The trend of higher sales of more advanced and higher value-added seatbelt systems continued.

Net income decreased 142% to $461.5 million in 2019 compared to 2018 primarily due to the increase on their operating income and decrease on their income tax expense.

Cash at the end of 2019 was $444.7 million a decrease of $171.1 million from the prior year. Cash from operations contributed $640.7 million to the coffers while investing activities used $476.1 million mainly for capital expenditures. Financing activities used $338.1 million.

Strategy

The company's growth has been enhanced through opportunities including acquisitions of businesses products and technologies and joint venture agreements that they believe will complement their business. Autoliv regularly evaluate acquisition opportunities frequently engage in acquisition discussions conduct due to diligence activities in connection with the possible acquisitions and where appropriate engage in acquisition negotiations.

The company's productivity improvement target is to achieve at least 5% savings per year. To meet this target Autoliv has developed a set of strategies to reduce costs in manufacturing:

Autoliv production system (APS) is based on lean manufacturing methodology which aims to continuously increase output with less resources. APS provides the target conditions and tools to achieve the delivery of goods and services at the right time in the right amount at the required quality and at the lowest cost possible to all our customers.

One Product One Process (1P1P) strategy focuses on product and process standardization and reducing cost and complexity. The 1P1P strategy combined with initiatives to reduce costs for components from external suppliers ensures that they continuously optimize their supply base footprint consolidate purchase volumes to fewer suppliers improve productivity in our supply chain standardize components and redesign their products.

Strategic Initiatives including Automation Digitalization Supply Chain Management Effectiveness and RD&E Effectiveness.

Company Background

Autoliv traces its origins back to 1956 when Autoliv AB a Swedish corporation pioneered automotive seat belt technology. By 1967 the company had invented the retractor belt. Granges Weda AB another maker of seat belt retractors acquired the company in 1975. Electrolux bought the Granges Group (later renamed SAPA) in 1989 and changed its name to Electrolux Autoliv. Throughout the 1980s and 1990s the company continued to grow through acquisitions buying seat belt manufacturing operations primarily in Europe but also in Australia and New Zealand. In 1994 the company changed its name to Autoliv AB and went public with Electrolux selling all its shares during the offering.

HISTORY

Autoliv traces its origins back to 1956 when Autoliv AB a Swedish corporation pioneered automotive seat belt technology. By 1967 the company had invented the retractor belt. Granges

Weda AB another maker of seat belt retractors acquired the company in 1975. Electrolux bought the Granges Group (later renamed SAPA) in 1989 and changed its name to Electrolux Autoliv. Throughout the 1980s and 1990s the company continued to grow through acquisitions buying seat belt manufacturing operations primarily in Europe but also in Australia and New Zealand. In 1994 the company changed its name to Autoliv AB and went public with Electrolux selling all its shares during the offering.

EXECUTIVES

Chairman President And Ceo, Jan Carlson, age 60, $1,376,766 total compensation
Cto, Steven (Steve) Fredin, age 58, $578,240 total compensation
President Passive Safety, Mikael Bratt, age 53
Group Vp Research And Development And Cto, Johan L ¶fvenholm, age 51
Group Vp Finance And Cfo, Mats Backman, age 52, $381,074 total compensation
China Vice President Quality, Jesse Crookston
Vice President Global Business Unit, Walter Guertler
Group Vice President Human Resources, Karin Eliasson
Vice President North America Operations, Jorge Loyo
Vice President Manufacturing, Shigetoh Masashi
Vp Passive Safety, Stephanie Jett
Treasurer, Thomas Williams
Auditors: Ernst & Young AB

LOCATIONS

HQ: Autoliv Inc
Klarabergsviadukten 70, Section B7, Box 70381, Stockholm SE-107 24
Phone: (46) 8 587 20 600
Web: www.autoliv.com

2016 Sales

	$ mil.	% of total
Asia		
China	1,766	18
Japan	949	9
Rest of Asia	901	9
Americas	3,380	34
Europe	3,075	30
Total	**10,073**	**100**

PRODUCTS/OPERATIONS

2017 Sales

	$ mil.	% of total
Passive Safety	8,134	78
Electronics	2,322	22
Corporate and other	5	-
Inter-segment sales	(66.6)	-
Total	**10,382**	**100**

2017 Sales

	$ mil.	% of total
Asia		
China	1,839	18
Japan	1,040	10
Rest of Asia	965	9
Americas	3,247	31
Europe	3,290	32
Total	**10,382**	**100**

Selected Products

Anti-whiplash seats
Child restraints
Electronics
Frontal airbags
Inflators
Leg airbags
Seat belts
Side-impact airbags
Steering wheels

Selected Subsidiaries and Affiliates

Airbags International Ltd (UK)
Autoflator AB
Autoliv AB
Autoliv Argentina SA
Autoliv ASP BV (The Netherlands)
Autoliv ASP Inc. (US)
Autoliv Australia Proprietary Ltd
Autoliv Autosicherheitstechnik GmbH (Germany)
Autoliv BKI SA (Spain)
Autoliv BV (The Netherlands)
Autoliv Canada Inc
Autoliv Cankor Otomotiv Emniyet Sistemleri Sanayi Ve (Turkey)
Autoliv China Electronics Co. Ltd
Autoliv do Brasil Ltda.
Autoliv East Europe AB
Autoliv Electronics AB
Autoliv Electronics SAS (France)
Autoliv France SNC
Autoliv Holding BV (The Netherlands)
Autoliv Holding Inc. (US)
Autoliv Holding Ltd. (UK)
Autoliv Italia S.P.A.
Autoliv Japan Ltd
Autoliv KFT (Hungary)
Autoliv KLE SAU (Spain)
Autoliv Ltd (UK)
Autoliv Nichiyo Co. (Japan)
Autoliv Overseas BV (The Netherlands)
Autoliv Poland Sp zoo
Autoliv Romania SA
Autoliv Safety Technology Inc. (US)
Autoliv Sicherheitstechnik GmbH (Germany)
Autoliv Southern Africa Pty Ltd
Autoliv Stakupress GmbH (Germany)
Autoliv Sverige AB
Autoliv Thailand Ltd
Autoliv UK Holding Ltd
Marling BV (The Netherlands)
Mei-An Autoliv Co. (59% Taiwan)
Nanjing Hongguang Autoliv Vehicle Safety Co. Ltd. (50% China)
NSK Safety Technology (Thailand) Co. Ltd.
OEA Inc. (US)
Svensk Airbag AB
Van Oerle Alberton BV (The Netherlands)
Van Oerle Alberton Holding BV (The Netherlands)
Van Oerle Webco Pty Ltd (Australia)

COMPETITORS

AISIN World Corp.	Key Safety Systems
ASHIMORI INDUSTRY CO. LTD.	Kongsberg Automotive
	Magna International
Autocam	Mitsubishi Electric
Bosch Corp.	NFA
CASCO Products	Neaton Auto Products
DENSO	Nihon Plast
Delphi Automotive Systems	Nippon Kayaku
Ensign-Bickford	Sequa
Gentex	Special Devices
Hella	Toyoda Gosei
Honeywell International	Toyota Boshoku
International Textile Group	Valeo

HISTORICAL FINANCIALS

Company Type: Public

Income Statement

FYE: December 31

	REVENUE ($ mil.)	NET INCOME ($ mil.)	NET PROFIT MARGIN	EMPLOYEES
12/19	8,547	461	5.4%	65,000
12/18	8,678	190	2.2%	67,000
12/17	10,382	427	4.1%	72,000
12/16	10,073	567	5.6%	70,300
12/15	9,169	456	5.0%	64,100
Annual Growth	**(1.7%)**	**0.3%**	**—**	**0.3%**

2019 Year-End Financials

Debt ratio: 30.93%
Return on equity: 23.12%
Cash ($ mil.): 444
Current ratio: 1.25
Long-term debt ($ mil.): 1,726
No. of shares (mil.): 87
Dividends
Yield: 2.9%
Payout: 100.8%
Market value ($ mil.): 7,364

	STOCK PRICE ($) FY Close	P/E High/Low		Earnings	PER SHARE ($) Dividends	Book Value
12/19	84.41	16	12	5.29	2.48	24.18
12/18	70.23	73	32	2.18	2.46	21.62
12/17	127.08	27	20	4.87	2.38	46.39
12/16	113.15	20	15	6.42	2.30	41.68
12/15	124.77	25	19	5.17	2.22	39.22
Annual Growth	**(9.3%)**	**—**	**—**	**0.6%**	**2.8%**	**(11.4%)**

Automatic Data Processing Inc.

Automatic Data Processing (ADP) is one of the largest payroll and tax filing processors in the world serving over 860000 clients. Employer services (payroll processing tax and benefits administration services) account for the majority of the company's sales and its PEO (Professional Employer Organization) services are provided through ADP TotalSource. Other offerings include accounting auto collision estimates for insurers employment background checks and business development training services. The US accounts for more than 85% of the company's revenue.

Operations

ADP operates two business segments Employer Services accounting for nearly 70% of total revenue and Professional Employer Organization (PEO) Services which brings in over 30% of revenue.

Employer Services offers a range of business outsourcing and HCM (Human Capital Management) services in more than 140 countries. Products and services offered to employers include payroll and tax management systems tailored to small to medium-size business and large enterprises. Certain offerings including multi-currency payroll systems cater to companies that operate internationally. Beyond payroll and tax products ADP provides systems for time and attendance management 401(K) and other retirement services recruiting and HR and tax compliance.

PEO Services provides employment administration outsourcing services through a co-employment relationship in which employees who work at a client's location are co-employed by ADP and its client. The segment operates as ADP TotalSource.

Geographic Reach

Headquartered in Roseland New Jersey ADP provides its payroll tax compliance and other employer services in more than 140 countries. PEO Services however operates exclusively in the US.

The US is ADP's biggest market accounting for more than 85% of total revenue. Sales in Europe account for about 10% while Canada accounts for less than 5%.

Sales and Marketing

ADP serves more than 860000 clients. The company markets its solutions primarily through its direct sales force. The company also markets HCM Solutions Global Solutions and HRO Solutions (other than PEO) through indirect sales channels such as marketing relationships with certified public accountants and banks among others. None of the company's major business units has a single homogeneous client base or market.

Financial Performance

ADP has achieved unprecedented growth over the last several years with revenue trending up each year during the five-year period between 2016 and 2020.

In fiscal 2020 revenue climbed 2% to $14.6 billion from $14.1 billion the previous year. The revenue growth was due to new business started from New Business Bookings partially offset by business losses and a decrease in interest earned on funds held for clients.

Profits rose 8% from $2.3 billion in 2019 to $2.5 billion in 2020.

Cash at the end of the fiscal year sat at $7.1 billion $257.4 million more than at the end of fiscal 2019. Cash from operations added $3 billion investing activities generated $3.2 billion and financing used $5.9 billion.

Strategy

ADP's business strategy is based on three strategic pillars which are designed to position it as the global market leader in HCM technology and services:

Grow a complete suite of cloud-based HCM solutions (HCM Solutions). ADP develops cloud-based software and offer comprehensive solutions that assist employers of all types and sizes in managing the entire worker spectrum and employment cycle – from full-time to freelancer and from hire to retire.

Grow and scale its market-leading HR Outsourcing solutions (HRO Solutions). The company offers comprehensive HRO solutions in which it provides complete management solutions for HR administration payroll administration talent management employee benefits benefits administration employer liability management and other HCM and employee benefits functions.

Leverage the company's global presence to offer clients HCM solutions wherever it does business (Global Solutions). ADP is expanding its international HCM and HRO businesses comprised of its established local in-country software solutions and its market-leading cloud-based multi-country solutions.

Company Background

In 1949 22-year-old Henry Taub started Automatic Payrolls a manual payroll preparation service in Paterson New Jersey. Taub's eight accounts created gross revenue of around $2000 that year. In 1952 his brother Joe joined the company and a childhood friend Frank Lautenberg took a pay cut to become its first salesman. Automatic Payrolls grew steadily during the 1950s. In 1961 the company went public and changed its name to Automatic Data Processing (ADP).

EXECUTIVES

President And Ceo, Carlos A. Rodriguez, $1,000,000 total compensation
Vp And Cfo, Jan Siegmund, $650,000 total compensation
Evp Worldwide Sales And Marketing, Edward B. (Ed) Flynn, $525,000 total compensation
President Small Business Services Retirement Services And Insurance Services, John C. Ayala
President Added Value Services, Douglas W. (Doug) Politi
President Employer Services - Totalsource, Maria Black
Vp Global Product And Technology, Stuart Sackman
President Major Account Services And Adp Canada, Tom Perrotti

Vice President Global Procurement, Steve Verderano
Vice President Of Sales Operations And Training, Art Baumann
Vice President Human Resources, Deb Hughes
Corporate Medical Director, Daniela Weinberger
Vice President Of Sales Minneapolis, Randy Nixon
Vice President, Randy Terbush
Vice President Client Services, Linda Reisner
Vice President Inside Sales, Mike Keim
Vice President Corporate, Michael Lindemann
Vice President Of Information Technology, Bill Washkau
Vice President Finance, David Bataille
Vice President Comprehensive Services Hcm Solutions, Cheryl Mulvehill
Vice President Of Field Operations, Nick Maniaci
Vice President, Huyen Tran
Vice President Product And Field Operations, Johnathan Fiore
Vice President Technical Services, Jennifer Marasovich
Divisional Vice President, Laci Buzzelli
Vice President, Mitch Kleiman
Staff Vice President Corporate Development, David Garfinkel
Vice President Sales Sbs, Anthony D Miskowiec
Vice President Information Technology Business Security, Josh Sowers
Vice President Business Development, Jason Rusnak
Senior Vice President And Chief Security Officer, Roland Cloutier
Corporate Vice President Global Product And Technology, Don Weinstein
Vice President Sales, Tim McGowan
Vice President Technical Services, Gary Resh
Division Vice President Of Sales South Central Usa, Reagan Dailey
Vice President Of Sales Houston, Stefani Pady
Vp Operations, Suthakar Maharajan
Division Vice President Sales And Operations, Diana Harrington
Vice President And Chief Ip Counsel, Neal Feivelson
Vice President, Chris Hollander
Vice President Service Centers, Rob Longshore
Vice President, Kimberly Hooven
Dvp Rgm National Accounts, Jay Little
Vice President Public Relation, Ravi Marrapu
Vice President Sales, Venkatachalam Subramaniam
Vice President Of Sales, Max Pearlstein
Vice President, Kurt Weber
Vice President, Jaclyn Schweiger
Vice President Of Inside Sales, Frank Fusco
Vice President Of Sales Automatic Data Processing Insurance Agency Inc., Darrick Edison
Vice President Of Sales, Joe Weishaar
Vice President Service Technology, Paul Przysiecki
Vice President Of Sales, Erron Stark
Vice President Of Sales Learning, David Farhi
Vice President Implementation, Lynne Tholen
Major Accounts Vice President Of Sales, Chris Olson
Division Vice President Strategy And Business Development, Chris Rush
Vice President Of Sales, John Hohman
Vice President, Paul Ordonez
Vice President Investor Relations, Christian Greyenbuhl
Vice President Of Production, Marissa Olson
Vice President Client Services, Kristen Appleman
Vice President Sales, Christine Talcott
Vice President Storage Administration, Jim Sanandres
Vice President, Tricia Russo
Vice President Marketing, Rick Weber
Vice President Corporate Benefits, Zafer Datoo
Vice President Sales, Brad Kaluzna
Vice President Of Sales, John Marzilli

National Sales Manager, C J Donnelly
Vice President Of Sales, John Goglia
Vice President Of Sales And Marketing, Mark Konecke
Div. Vice President Sales, Dave Piromalli
Vice President Of Implementation Regnl Implementation Executive Ts, Courtney Orlowski
Vice President Of Sales, Stephanie Karasiak
Dvp Business Transformation, Jill Vitali
Vice President Implementation Ma, Terence Crowe
Vice President Sales, Vanessa Calderon
Vice President Sales Europe, Tim Johnson
Vice President, Dana Fox
Vice President Technical Services, Don Speer
Sbs Central Dvp, Michele Tomassetti
Vice President Of Marketing, Mark Villoresi
National Account Manager, Elizabeth Bardwell
Vice President Hcm Specialized Services, Jennifer Crowley
Vice President, Matt Aufiero
Vice President Compensation, Val Stubbins
Vice President National Accounts Of Canada, Stefan Sarazen
Vice President Of Sales, Aaryn Kerkis
Vice President Marketing, Amy Selich
Area Vice President Of Sales, John Piscioniere
Senior Division Vp Of Sales, Dave Greenberg
Vice President Operations, Tim Seymour
Senior Vice President Government Services, Deborah Sage
Vice President, Terri Sampson
Vice President, Nick Smith
Vice President Sales, Daina Bowler
Vice President Call Center, Jill Sterling
Vice President Sales, Adrian Spires
Vice President Fp And A Sales Finance, Donna Lukasko
Vice President Implementation, Chris Bacon
Vice President Of Global Consulting, Christine Stanowski
Vice President And General Manager, Laurn Rice
Dvp Human Resources, Jill Altana
Vice President, Chris Backer
Vice President, Kristin Andreski
Vice President Human Resources Shared Services, Peggy Jude
Vice President Managing Counsel, Lisse Kravetz
Vice President Strategic Client Partnership, April Glonek
Vice President Of Data Quality, Paulo Barbieri
Adp Vice President Of Implementation, Greg Flach
Division Vice President General Manager Comprehensive Outsourcing Services, Glenn Pettigrew
Senior Vice President Human Resources Employer Services Group, Yvonne Surowiec
National Sales Manager, Vince Scotto
Vice President And Director Internet Media, Grace Luongo
Vice President Executive Deferred Compensation, Rosemary Murphy-harris
Vice President Managing Counsel, Kevin Isom
Vice President And General Manager Field Services Engineering, Doug Karlson
Vice President Sales, Gerald Nealon
National Sales Manager, Bill Cordes
Corporate Vp, Michael C Eberhard
Vice President, Brad Walters
Vice President, Bob Buckley
Vice President Of Sales, Pj Villani
National Sales Manager, David Weiss
Vice President Of Sales, Rich Weidmyer
Vice President Of Sales, Michael Wallington
National Sales Manager, Randy Jackman
Vice President Of Sales, Jason Whiffen
Vice President Systems Technology, Tammy Griffin
Vice President Of Professional Services, Ed Davis
Division Vice President, George Michaels
Vice President Managing Counsel Comprehensive Services, Elizabeth J Mazza

Vice President Of Sales, Bob Sprague
Vice President Counsel, Ann Hammenecker
Regional Vice President Of Sales, Laura Jansen
Vice President Sales, Jason Ortwerth
Senior Business Intelligence Developer, Marsha French
Vice President South Florida, Gary Peters
Senior Vice President Global Business Solutions, Tina Tromiczak
Vice President Of Service, Dave Leshovsky
Vice President Human Resources, Caron Cone
Div. Vice President Sales, Chris Luongo
Vp Operations, John Sheehy
Vice President Client Service, Ryan Heidenthal
Vice President Client Experience, Lydia Schulz
Vp Service Strategy, Shannon Mcginness
National Account Manager, Jorge Catarino
Vice President Adp Innovation Lab, Jerome Gouvernel
Vice President Telesales Marketing, Elizabeth Gelb-O'Connor
Vice President Client Services, Amber Eccleston
Auditors: DELOITTE & TOUCHE LLP

LOCATIONS

HQ: Automatic Data Processing Inc.
One ADP Boulevard, Roseland, NJ 07068
Phone: 973 974-5000 **Fax:** 973 974-5390
Web: www.adp.com

2018 Sales

	$ mil.	% of total
US	11,486	86
Europe	1,245	10
Canada	322	2
Other	271	2
Total	**13,325**	**100**

PRODUCTS/OPERATIONS

2018 Sales

	% of total
Employer Services	72
PEO Services	28
Total	**100**

Selected Services

Dealer Services
  Business management
  Computer systems sales
  Employee productivity training
  Hardware maintenance
  Manufacturer and dealer data communications networks
  Software licensing and support
  Vehicle registration services
Employer Services
  401(k) record keeping and reporting
  Benefits administration and outsourcing
  Employment screening and background checks
  Human resource record keeping and reporting
  Payroll processing
  Tax filing
  Unemployment compensation management

COMPETITORS

CBIZ	Intuit
Ceridian	Paychex
Computer Sciences Corp.	TriNet Group
Insperity	Ultimate Software

Company Type: Public

Income Statement   FYE: June 30

	REVENUE ($ mil.)	NET INCOME ($ mil.)	NET PROFIT MARGIN	EMPLOYEES
06/20	14,589	2,466	16.9%	58,000
06/19	14,175	2,292	16.2%	58,000
06/18	13,325	1,620	12.2%	57,000
06/17	12,379	1,733	14.0%	58,000
06/16	11,667	1,492	12.8%	57,000
Annual Growth	5.7%	13.4%	—	0.4%

2020 Year-End Financials

Debt ratio: 5.12%
Return on equity: 44.11%
Cash ($ mil.): 1,908
Current ratio: 1.05
Long-term debt ($ mil.): 1,002

No. of shares (mil.): 429
Dividends
Yield: 2.3%
Payout: 60.3%
Market value ($ mil.): 64,008

	STOCK PRICE ($) FY Close	P/E High/Low	PER SHARE ($) Earnings	Dividends	Book Value
06/20	148.89	32 19	5.70	3.52	13.38
06/19	165.33	32 23	5.24	3.06	12.44
06/18	134.14	38 28	3.66	2.52	7.88
06/17	102.46	27 22	3.85	2.24	8.94
06/16	91.87	28 22	3.25	2.08	9.83
Annual Growth	12.8%	— —	15.1%	14.1%	8.0%

AutoNation, Inc.

AutoNation wants to instill patriotic fervor in the fickle car-buying public. The brainchild of entrepreneur Wayne Huizenga (Waste Management Blockbuster) AutoNation is the #1 auto dealer in the US ahead of Penske Automotive Group. It owns over 315 new-vehicle franchises in about more than 15 states and conducts online sales through AutoNation.com and individual dealer websites. The company sells more than 30 brands of new vehicles. In addition to auto sales AutoNation provides maintenance and repair services (it owns more than 80 AutoNation-branded collision centers) sells auto parts and finances and insures vehicles.

Operations

More than 50% of AutoNation's total revenue comes from new vehicle sales; used vehicle sales generate over 25%. Parts and service and finance and insurance account for beyond 15% and 5% of revenue respectively.

The company divides the vehicle market into three segments — Domestic Import and Premium Luxury — each of which generates around a third of AutoNation's sales. Their Domestic segment is comprised of retail automotive franchises that sell new vehicles manufactured by General Motors Ford and FCA US. The Import segment is comprised of retail automotive franchises that sell new vehicles manufactured primarily by Toyota Honda and Nissan. Their Premium Luxury segment is comprised of retail automotive franchises that sell new vehicles manufactured primarily by Mercedes-Benz BMW Audi Lexus and Jaguar Land Rover. The franchises in each segment also sell used vehicles parts and automotive repair and maintenance services and automotive finance and insurance products.

Geographic Reach

AutoNation has over 315 new-vehicle franchises in more than 15 US states. Florida Texas and California are its largest markets together accounting for more than 60% of revenue.

The company is headquartered in Fort Lauderdale Florida. The company also owns or leases numerous facilities relating to its operations under each operating segment. These facilities are located in the following states: Alabama Arizona California Colorado Florida Georgia Illinois Maryland Minnesota Nevada New York Ohio Tennessee Texas Virginia and Washington.

Sales and Marketing

AutoNation sells vehicles through its online website and its stores.

Advertising expense net of manufacturer advertising reimbursements was $187.8 million in 2019 $197.8 million in 2018 and $192.8 million in 2017.

Financial Performance

In the beginning of the past five years the revenue increased for about 5% until it drops little bit by bit in the later years from 2017 to 2019.

In 2019 the company reported revenue of $21.3 billion down less than a percent from the prior year. New vehicle sales fell primarily due to a decrease in same store unit volume partially offset by an increase in revenue PVR.

Net income in 2019 raised 14% to $450 million the increase was primarily due to continuing operations.

Cash at the end of 2019 was $42.5 million a decrease of $6.9 million from the prior year. Cash from operations contributed $769.2 million to the coffers while investing activities used $115.8 million mainly for purchases of property and equipment. Financing activities used another $660.3 million primarily for payments of commercial paper.

Strategy

AutoNation seeks to create long-term value for stockholders by being the best-run most profitable automotive retailer in the United States. The company believes that the significant scale of its operations and the quality of its managerial talent allow it to achieve efficiencies in key markets. To achieve and sustain operational excellence the company is pursuing the following strategies: Creating an industry-leading automotive retail customer experience in stores and through digital channels; Continuing to invest in the AutoNation retail brand to enhance strong customer satisfaction and expand market share; Leveraging significant scale and cost structure to improve operating efficiency; and Continuing to invest in strategic partnerships to evolve with the changing automotive retail industry and to widen access to new and expanding sales channels for vehicles parts and service.

The company continues to build upon its comprehensive customer-focused brand extension strategy which includes AutoNation-branded parts and accessories AutoNation-branded Customer Financial Services products (including extended service and maintenance contracts and other vehicle protection products) AutoNation-branded collision centers AutoNation-branded automotive auctions AutoNation USA stand-alone used vehicle sales and service centers and their parts distribution network. The company also continues to evaluate potential strategic investment and partnership opportunities that will further enhance its ability to adapt to changing customer behavior and expectations such as its minority investment in Vroom Inc. and its partnership with Waymo.

Company Background

AutoNation started in 1980 as Republic Resources which brokered petroleum leases did exploration and production and blended lubricants. In 1989 after oil prices crashed and a stockholder group tried to force Republic into liquidation Browning-Ferris Industries (BFI) founder Thomas Fatjo gained control of the company and refocused it on a field he knew well — solid waste. He renamed the firm Republic Waste.

Republic moved into hazardous waste in 1992 just before the industry nosedived due to stringent new environmental rules. In 1994 Republic spun off its hazardous-waste operations as Republic Environmental Systems and Republic's stock began rising immediately.

That attracted the attention of Wayne Huizenga who had founded Waste Management and Blockbuster Video. To him Republic was not merely a midsized solid-waste firm. No Huizenga saw Republic as a publicly traded vehicle that could allow him to tap into the stock market to fund his latest project: an integrated nationwide auto dealer — a first for the highly fragmented and localized industry.

By 1996 Huizenga's still-separate auto concept AutoNation was operational with 55 automobile franchises and seven used-car stores. Republic bought Alamo Rent A Car and National Car Rental System and in 1997 AutoNation was bought by Republic.

Republic became AutoNation in 1999.

HISTORY

AutoNation started in 1980 as Republic Resources which brokered petroleum leases did exploration and production and blended lubricants. In 1989 after oil prices crashed and a stockholder group tried to force Republic into liquidation Browning-Ferris Industries (BFI) founder Thomas Fatjo gained control of the company and refocused it on a field he knew well — solid waste. He renamed the firm Republic Waste.

Michael DeGroote founder of BFI rival Laidlaw bought into Republic in 1990. (Fatjo left the next year.) DeGroote's investment funded more acquisitions. Republic moved into hazardous waste in 1992 just before the industry nosedived due to stringent new environmental rules. In 1994 Republic spun off its hazardous-waste operations as Republic Environmental Systems and Republic's stock began rising immediately.

That attracted the attention of Wayne Huizenga who had founded Waste Management and Blockbuster Video. To him Republic was not merely a midsized solid-waste firm. No Huizenga saw Republic as a publicly traded vehicle that could allow him to tap into the stock market to fund his latest project: an integrated nationwide auto dealer — a first for the highly fragmented and localized industry.

In 1995 Republic bought Hudson Management a trash business owned by Huizenga's brother-in-law and Huizenga bought a large interest in Republic. As a result Huizenga took control of Republic's board. The firm became Republic Industries and DeGroote stepped back from active management.

Huizenga's investment helped Republic acquire more waste businesses and his name brought a flood of new investors. The firm diversified with electronic security acquisitions but growth in this field faltered with a failed bid to buy market leader ADT in 1996. (Republic sold its security division to Ameritech in 1997.)

By 1996 Huizenga's still-separate auto concept AutoNation was operational with 55 automobile franchises and seven used-car stores. Republic bought Alamo Rent A Car and National Car Rental System and in 1997 AutoNation was bought by Republic. The combined company continued buying dealerships and car rental firms at a sizzling rate.

Republic spun off its solid-waste operations to the public in 1998 as Republic Services. That year Republic bought or agreed to buy 181 new-car franchises opened nine AutoNation USA dealerships and opened 62 CarTemps USA insurance-replacement locations.

Republic became AutoNation in 1999.

Having survived a market downturn in the late 2000s in 2013 the company began marketing its domestic and import stores under the AutoNation retail brand in local markets. The re-branding of the stores which previously operated under various local market retail brands (including Mike Shad in Jacksonville Florida and GO in Colorado) was completed that year. (The exception is the company's luxury dealership business which will continue to operate under their existing retail brands.) Using its website store signage and media presence the car dealer is working to increase consumer awareness of the AutoNation brand.

In 2013 the company acquired 12 franchises.

EXECUTIVES

Executive Vice President Secretary And General Counsel, Jonathan Ferrando

Chairman And Ceo, Michael J. (Mike) Jackson, age 72, $1,250,000 total compensation

Evp And Chief Marketing Officer, Marc Cannon, age 58

Evp And Cfo, Cheryl Miller, age 47, $596,875 total compensation

Evp Franchise Operations Mergers & Acquisitions And Corporate Real Estate, Donna Parlapiano, age 55, $532,084 total compensation

Evp General Counsel And Corporate Secretary, Coleman Edmunds

President Eastern Region, Jim Bender

Evp And Cto, Thomas M. (Tom) Conophy, age 59

President Western Region, Lance Iserman

President Central Region, Ron Ardisonne

Svp, Scott Arnold

Board Member, Kaveh Khosrowshahi

Board Member, Tomago Collins

Auditors: KPMG LLP

LOCATIONS

HQ: AutoNation, Inc.
200 SW 1st Avenue, Fort Lauderdale, FL 33301
Phone: 954 769-6000
Web: www.autonation.com

2018 Stores

	No.
Florida	50
Texas	42
California	39
Georgia	16
Colorado	15
Washington	15
Arizona	14
Nevada	11
Tennessee	8
Maryland	7
Illinois	7
Alabama	4
Ohio	4
New York	4
Virginia	2
Minnesota	1
Total	**239**

PRODUCTS/OPERATIONS

2018 Sales

	$ mil.	% of total
New vehicle	11,751	55
Used vehicle	5,123	24
Parts & services	3,447	16
Finance & insurance	981	5
Other	108	
Total	**21,412**	**100**

2018 Sales

	$ mil.	% of total
Domestic	7,134	33
Import	6,786	32
Premium Luxury	7,010	33
Corporate & other	481	2
Total	**21,412**	**100**

COMPETITORS

Asbury Automotive
Brown Automotive
CarMax
Ed Morse Auto Group 1 Automotive
Hendrick Automotive
Holman Enterprises
JM Family Enterprises
Lithia Motors
Penske Automotive Group
Potamkin Automotive
Sonic Automotive

HISTORICAL FINANCIALS

Company Type: Public

Income Statement

FYE: December 31

	REVENUE ($ mil.)	NET INCOME ($ mil.)	NET PROFIT MARGIN	EMPLOYEES
12/19	21,335	450	2.1%	25,000
12/18	21,412	396	1.8%	26,000
12/17	21,534	434	2.0%	26,000
12/16	21,609	430	2.0%	26,000
12/15	20,862	442	2.1%	26,000
Annual Growth	0.6%	0.4%	—	(1.0%)

2019 Year-End Financials

Debt ratio: 19.96%
Return on equity: 15.31%
Cash ($ mil.): 42
Current ratio: 0.86
Long-term debt ($ mil.): 1,578
No. of shares (mil.): 89
Dividends
Yield: —
Payout: —
Market value ($ mil.): 4,345

	STOCK PRICE ($) FY Close	P/E High/Low		Earnings	Dividends	Book Value
12/19	48.63	11	7	4.97	0.00	35.39
12/18	35.70	14	8	4.34	0.00	30.17
12/17	51.33	13	9	4.43	0.00	25.88
12/16	48.65	14	10	4.15	0.00	22.95
12/15	59.66	17	14	3.89	0.00	21.20
Annual Growth	(5.0%)	—	—	6.3%	—	13.7%

AutoZone, Inc.

With 5885 stores in the US AutoZone is one of the nation's leading auto parts chains. It also has more than 620 stores in Mexico and about 35 in Brazil. AutoZone stores sell failure parts (alternators engines batteries) maintenance items (oil antifreeze) and discretionary merchandise and accessories (car stereos floor mats) under brand names and private labels. AutoZone's commercial sales program provides credit and distributes parts and other products to garages dealerships and other businesses. The company operates an electronic parts catalog Z-net that provides a wide range of information on parts for employees and customers. AutoZone was founded in 1979.

Operations

AutoZone operates through one primary segment Auto Parts Stores which accounts for the majority of revenue. Leveraging a consistent store format each AutoZone store boasts between 90% and 100% of selling space — up to 40% to 50% of which is dedicated to hard parts inventory. Stores are outfitted with Z-net AutoZone's proprietary electronic catalog that gives employees advice and information for customers' vehicles down to the year make model and engine type. In-house brands including the popular Duralast and the family of Duralast brands ProElite ShopPro SureBilt TruGrade and Valucraft.

Product-wise failure (or hard) parts account for nearly half of sales; these include batteries belts engines mufflers radiators and water pumps among other merchandise. Maintenance items (fluids pads spark plugs windshield wipers) and discretionary items (floor mats protectants and cleaners stereos) generate about 35% and over 15% of sales respectively.

Other revenue is generated by e-commerce operations and diagnostic and other software (provided through the company's ALLDATA business) used in automotive repair. The company also has a smartphone app through which customers can find and buy parts.

Geographic Reach

Based in Tennessee AutoZone operates about 6550 AutoZone stores in some 55 US states Puerto Rico and Saint Thomas. Texas California Florida Ohio and Illinois are the company's largest markets and together account for more than 35 of locations.

AutoZone has a dozen distribution centers in the US (Arizona California Florida Georgia Illinois Ohio Pennsylvania Tennessee Texas and Washington and two in Mexico); store support centers are in Tennessee as well as Mexico and Brazil. In addition the company has operations in China that support the sourcing efforts in Asia.

Sales and Marketing

AutoZone sells to do-it-yourself (DIY) consumers as well as commercial sales program that provides commercial credit and prompt delivery of parts and other products to local regional and national repair garages dealers service stations and public sector accounts.

The company relies on targeted advertising and promotions to build its brand utilize advertising direct marketing loyalty programs and promotions primarily to highlight its great value the availability of high quality parts and develop a relationship with an expanding base of customers. Broadcast and digital media are its primary advertising methods of driving retail traffic to its stores while leveraging a dedicated sales force and its ProVantage loyalty program to drive commercial sales.

Advertising expense for the company was $77.6 million in 2020 $87.5 million in 2019 and $95.2 million in 2018.

Financial Performance

Annual revenue growth is driven by the opening of new stores the development of new commercial programs and increases in same store sales. Autozone's revenue has been rising in the last few years with an overall growth of 19% between 2016 and 2020. Net income grew by 40% in the same period.

For the fiscal year 2020 (ended August) the company reported net sales of $12.6 billion compared with $11.9 billion for 2019 (ended August) a 7% increase from fiscal 2019 (ended August). This growth was driven primarily by a domestic same store sales increase of 7% and net sales of $244.7 million from new stores.

Net income for fiscal 2020 (ended August) increased by 7% to $1.7 billion and diluted earnings per share increased 13% to $71.9 from $63.4 in fiscal 2019. Net income and diluted earnings per share for fiscal 2019 benefitted from an additional week of sales.

The company's cash at the end of 2020 was $1.8 billion a $1.6 billion growth from the previous year. Operating activities generated $2.7 million while investing activities used $497.9 million mainly for capital expenditures. Financing activities

used another $643.6 million mainly for Net payments of commercial paper and purchases of treasury stock.

Strategy

AutoZone's marketing and merchandising strategy's key elements consists of:

Customer Service - Customer service is the most important element in its marketing and merchandising strategy which is based upon consumer marketing research. The company emphasizes that its AutoZoners (employees) should always put customers first by providing prompt courteous service and trustworthy advice;

Merchandising - AutoZone believes that customer satisfaction is often impacted by its ability to promptly provide specific automotive products as requested. Each store carries the same basic products but the company tailors its hard parts inventory to the makes and models of the vehicles in each store's trade area and its sales floor products are tailored to the local store's demographics;

Pricing - For many of its products AutoZone offers multiple value choices in a good/better/best assortment with appropriate price and quality differences from the "good" products to the "better" and "best" products;

Brand Marketing: Marketing and Loyalty - The company utilizes advertising direct marketing loyalty programs and promotions primarily to highlight great value the availability of high quality parts and develop a relationship with an expanding base of customers. Broadcast and digital media are its primary advertising methods of driving retail traffic to stores while AutoZone leverages a dedicated sales force and its ProVantage loyalty program to drive commercial sales.

Store Design Visual Merchandising and Promotional Execution - The company's typical store utilizes colorful exterior and interior signage exposed beams and ductwork and brightly lit interiors. Maintenance products accessories and non-automotive items are attractively displayed for easy browsing by customers.

Company Background

Joseph "Pitt" Hyde took over the family grocery wholesale business Malone & Hyde (established 1907) in 1968. He expanded into specialty retailing opening drugstores sporting goods stores and supermarkets but his fortunes began to accelerate on Independence Day 1979 when he opened his first Auto Shack auto parts store in Forrest City Arkansas.

Using retailing behemoth Wal-Mart as a model Hyde concentrated on smaller markets in the South and Southeast emphasizing everyday low prices and centralized distribution operations. He stressed customer service to provide his do-it-yourself customers with expert advice on choosing parts. While a number of retailers have tried to copy Wal-Mart's successful model Hyde had an inside track: Before starting Auto Shack he served on Wal-Mart's board for seven years.

Auto Shack had expanded into seven states by 1980 and by 1983 it had 129 stores in 10 states. The next year Malone & Hyde's senior management with investment firm Kohlberg Kravis Roberts (KKR) took the company private in an LBO. Auto Shack continued to expand reaching 192 stores in 1984. The company was spun off to Malone & Hyde's shareholders in 1987 and Malone & Hyde's other operations were sold. The company changed its name to AutoZone in 1987 in part to settle a lawsuit with RadioShack.

HISTORY

Joseph "Pitt" Hyde took over the family grocery wholesale business Malone & Hyde (established 1907) in 1968. He expanded into specialty retailing opening drugstores sporting goods stores and su-

permarkets but his fortunes began to race on Independence Day 1979 when he opened his first Auto Shack auto parts store in Forrest City Arkansas.

Using retailing behemoth Wal-Mart as a model Hyde concentrated on smaller markets in the South and Southeast emphasizing everyday low prices and centralized distribution operations. He stressed customer service to provide his do-it-yourself customers with expert advice on choosing parts. While a number of retailers have tried to copy Wal-Mart's successful model Hyde had an inside track: Before starting Auto Shack he served on Wal-Mart's board for seven years.

Auto Shack had expanded into seven states by 1980 and by 1983 it had 129 stores in 10 states. The next year Malone & Hyde's senior management with investment firm Kohlberg Kravis Roberts (KKR) took the company private in an LBO. Auto Shack continued to expand reaching 192 stores in 1984. The company was spun off to Malone & Hyde's shareholders in 1987 and Malone & Hyde's other operations were sold. The company changed its name to AutoZone in 1987 in part to settle a lawsuit with RadioShack.

To build its online presence AutoZone in 2013 acquired AutoAnything an online retailer of specialized automotive products.

EXECUTIVES

Evp Finance Information Technology And Alldata And Cfo, William T. (Bill) Giles, age 61, $560,539 total compensation

Chairman President And Ceo, William C. (Bill) Rhodes, age 55, $1,000,000 total compensation

Svp Commercial, Larry M. Roesel, age 63, $425,308 total compensation

Svp Merchandising And Store Development, Mark A. Finestone, age 59, $430,154 total compensation

Evp Mexico Brazil Imc And Store Development, William W. Graves, age 60, $430,154 total compensation

Vp Operations, Thomas B. Newbern, age 58, $430,154 total compensation

Svp And Cio, Ronald B. (Ron) Griffin, age 67, $407,692 total compensation

Svp Marketing And E-commerce, Albert (Al) Saltiel, age 57

Vice President Merchandising, William Hackney

Svp General Counsel And Secretary, Kristen Wright

Vice President Merchandising, Bill Edwards

National Account Manager, Lee Fitts

Vice President Merchandising, John Lammers

Vice President Of Ecommerce, Jamey Maki

Auditors: Ernst & Young LLP

LOCATIONS

HQ: AutoZone, Inc.
123 South Front Street, Memphis, TN 38103
Phone: 901 495-6500
Web: www.autozone.com

2019 Stores

	No.
US	5,772
Mexico	604
Brazil	35
Total	**6,411**

PRODUCTS/OPERATIONS

2019 Sales

	$ mil.	% of total
Auto Parts Locations		
Failure	5,728	48
Maintenance	4,141	35
Discretionary	1,776	15
Other	218	2
Total	**11,863**	**100**

Selected Merchandise

Accessories
  Car stereos
  Floor mats
  Lights
  Mirrors
Hard Parts
  Alternators
  Batteries
  Brake shoes and pads
  Carburetors
  Clutches
  Engines
  Spark plugs
  Starters
  Struts
  Water pumps
Maintenance Items
  Antifreeze
  Brake fluid
  Engine additives
  Oil
  Power steering fluid
  Transmission fluid
  Waxes
  Windshield wipers
Other
  Air fresheners
  Dent filler
  Hand cleaner
  Paint
  Repair manuals
  Tools

Selected Brands

ALLDATA
AutoZone
Duralast
Duralast Gold
ProElite
SureBilt
Valucraft

COMPETITORS

Advance Auto Parts	Goodyear Tire & Rubber
Amazon.com	O'Reilly Automotive
CARQUEST	Pep Boys
Costco Wholesale	Sears Holdings
Fisher Auto Parts	Target Corporation
Genuine Parts	Wal-Mart

HISTORICAL FINANCIALS

Company Type: Public

Income Statement

FYE: August 29

	REVENUE ($ mil.)	NET INCOME ($ mil.)	NET PROFIT MARGIN	EMPLOYEES
08/20	12,631	1,732	13.7%	100,000
08/19	11,863	1,617	13.6%	96,000
08/18	11,221	1,337	11.9%	90,000
08/17	10,888	1,280	11.8%	87,000
08/16	10,635	1,241	11.7%	84,000
Annual Growth	4.4%	8.7%	—	4.5%

2020 Year-End Financials

Debt ratio: 38.69%	No. of shares (mil.): 23
Return on equity: —	Dividends
Cash ($ mil.): 1,750	Yield: —
Current ratio: 1.08	Payout: —
Long-term debt ($ mil.): 5,513	Market value ($ mil.): 27,797

	STOCK PRICE ($) FY Close	P/E High/Low		PER SHARE ($) Earnings	Dividends	Book Value
08/20	1,189.12	17	10	71.93	0.00	(37.56)
08/19	1,101.69	18	11	63.43	0.00	(71.30)
08/18	770.52	16	11	48.77	0.00	(59.06)
08/17	528.95	18	11	44.07	0.00	(51.32)
08/16	753.47	20	17	40.70	0.00	(61.39)
Annual Growth	12.1%		—	15.3%	—	—

Avery Dennison Corp

Avery Dennison has worked out how to make the most of a sticky situation. The company is a world-leader in sticky labels used by businesses to add their branding to products such as drinks food personal care items and pharmaceuticals. It also makes RFID tags for individual products. Its adhesives extend to vinyl wraps and specialty materials designed for digital imaging screen printing and sign-cutting applications. Under the Avery Dennison and Fasson brands it makes papers films and foils coated with adhesive. It also makes retail branding and security tags printer systems and fasteners as well as medical adhesive products. The California-based company gets 75% of its revenue from international customers.

Operations

Avery Dennison has three operating segments: Label and Graphic Materials (LGM) the largest at more than 65% of sales; Retail Branding and Information Solutions (RBIS) which accounts for nearly 25% of sales; and Industrial and Healthcare Materials (IHM) about 10% of sales.

The LGM segment makes pressure-sensitive adhesives (PSAs) which are sticky labels that are applied via pressure rather than heat or other means. Through the Fasson JAC and Avery Dennison brands the segment makes papers plastic films metal foils fabrics and specially coated backing papers and films. It sold in roll or sheet form with either solid or patterned adhesive coatings in a wide range of face materials sizes thickness and adhesive properties.

The RBIS segment designs manufactures and sells a variety of branding and information products and services. Branding items include creative services brand embellishments graphic tickets tags and labels and sustainable packaging. Among the RBIS products are item-level RFID tags; visibility and loss prevention solutions price ticketing and marking care content and country of origin compliance solutions and brand protection and security solutions.

The IHM segment sells branded tapes and fasteners pressure-sensitive medical devices and performance polymers.

Geographic Reach

Avery Dennison has wide geographic reach throughout its operations with about 180 manufacturing and distribution facilities in more than 50 countries and even geographic distribution of sales. The US is the company's biggest single-nation market accounting for nearly 25% of revenue. Asia is its largest regional market accounting for around 35% of revenue while Europe brings in more than 30%.

Based in Glendale California Avery Dennison has divisional offices located in Mentor Ohio; Hong Kong and Kunshan China; and Oegstgeest the Netherlands.

Sales and Marketing

Avery Dennison's major customers include advertising agencies distributors designers government agencies graphics vendors label converters architecture and building electronics and electrical package designers packaging engineers and manufacturers printers and sign manufacturers.

Label and packaging materials are sold worldwide to label converters for labeling decorating and specialty applications in the home and personal care beer and beverage durables pharmaceutical wine and spirits and food market segments.

Avery Dennison also sells durable cast and reflective films to the construction automotive and fleet transportation market segments and reflective films for traffic and safety applications.

The company also sells directly and via third-party distributors and retailers.

Financial Performance

Building on two years of sales gains Avery Dennison'a revenue punched over the $7 billion mark(a company high) in 2018. The company's net income has fluctuated in recent years but it jumped to a company record in 2018.

The company's sales declined by 1% to $7.1 billion in 2019 compared to its prior year. The LGM segment fell about 2%The RBIS segment's sales were up about 26% boosted by strength from RFID products and external embellishments. The IHM business posted a 3% sales decrease in 2019 from 2018.

Avery Dennison net income declined about $304 million in 2019compared to $467 million in 2018. This was due to higher employee-related costs pension plan settlement charges and impact of foreign currency translation primarily offset by benefits from productivity initiatives. Including savings from restructuring actions and tax benefit from discrete foreign structuring transaction.

The company's cash holdings were $253.7 million in 2019 compared to $232 million in 2018. Operations produced about $746.5 million in 2019 while investing activities used $251 million and financing activities used $470.3 million. Avery Dennison's main cash uses were purchases of property plant and equipment stock repurchases and dividends paid.

Strategy

Avery Dennison's growth strategy is based on expanding its presence in high-value and emerging markets.

It also aims to return the IHM segment to growth and profitability by rebuilding customer relationships strengthening product pipeline and driving aggressive productivity improvements. It launched two new wound care technologies CHG (an antimicrobial agent) and TASA (Thin Absorbent Skin Adhesive).

The company's focus on emerging markets has helped drive sales in Asia particularly China. But Avery Dennison's performance in China could be affected by local economic conditions which had a negative impact as well as US tariffs placed on goods made in China. In addition due to COVID-19 Pandemic many of its manufacturing and other operations in China experienced limited production and/or closure in early 2020. In addition many of its employees in the region have been unable to travel within and outside of the region. This outbreak of contagious disease as well as any other adverse public health developments – particularly in Asia where approximately 60% of its employees are located and a significant portion of our sales are generated – could have a material adverse effect on its business as well as sales to customers in China (including Hong Kong) were approximately 20% of its net sales in 2019.

However acquisitions and heavy investments has presented the company with limited cash to fund new opportunities in the market or meet its short term debt obligations. Moreover Avery Dennison might be affected by a rapidly changing industry as customers move away from plastics and reduce waste in a more sustainable fashion. The company looks to build on its portfolio of sustainable products through research.

Mergers and Acquisitions

In 2019 Avery Dennison acquired Smartrac's Transponder (RFID Inlay) Division for the purchase price of ?225 million. The division is a leader in the development and manufacture of RFID products with 2019 estimated global revenue of approximately ?125 million or approximately $140 million. Said Mitch Butier Avery Dennison chairman president and CEO. "Smartrac's Transponder Division represents an excellent strategic fit for us accelerating our strategy to expand our Intelligent Labels platform across a variety of end markets and customers within the industrial and retail segments and extending our reach to new channels."

Company Background

Ray Stanton ("Stan") Avery invented the world's first self-adhesive label as a way to merchandise objects. In 1935 he founded Avery Adhesives in downtown Los Angeles and in 1990 the company merged with Dennison Manufacturing to form Avery Dennison.

In 1969 Avery obtained listing on the New York Stock Exchange. In the photo Stan Avery Russ Smith and the president of the New York Stock Exchange watch as the company's symbol appears on the electronic board of the NYSE for the first time.

HISTORY

Avery Dennison was created in 1990 by the merger of Avery International and Dennison Manufacturing. In 1935 Stanton Avery founded Kum-Kleen Products which would become Avery International. After a fire destroyed the plant's equipment in 1938 Avery who had renamed the company Avery Adhesives improved the machinery used in making the labels.

During and after WWII Avery Adhesives shifted toward the industrial market for self-adhesives. The company incorporated in 1946. At that time Avery Adhesives sold 80% of its production consisting of industrial labels to manufacturers that labeled their own products. The company lost its patent rights for self-adhesive labels in 1952 transforming the firm and the entire industry. As a result a new division was created — the Avery Paper Company (later renamed Fasson) — to produce and market self-adhesive base materials. Avery Adhesives went public in 1961.

Dennison was started in 1844 by the father-and-son team of Andrew and Aaron Dennison to produce jewelry boxes. By 1849 Aaron's younger brother Eliphalet Whorf (E.W.) was running the business and expanding it into tags labels and tissue paper. Dennison was incorporated in 1878 with $150000 in capital.

EXECUTIVES

Svp And Chief Human Resources Officer, Anne Hill, age 61, $512,787 total compensation
President Materials Group, Georges Gravanis, age 63, $523,775 total compensation
President And Ceo, Mitchell R. Butier, age 49, $988,333 total compensation
Svp And Cfo, Gregory S. (Greg) Lovins, age 47
Vp And Gm Global Commercial Retail Branding And Information Solutions, Michael Barton
Vice President Global Finance, Garrett Gabel
Vice President Corporate Development, Stephen Keller
Vp And Assistant General Counsel Label And Graphic Materials Materials Group Graphic Solutions, Ken Schwartz
Vice President Strategy And Corporate Development, Danny Allouche
National Account Manager, Jay Siedel
Market Vice President, Gregoire Pastour
Vice President And General Manager Label And Graphic Materials Europe, Jeroen Diderich
Vice President And General Manager Global Graphics And Reflective Solutions And Vice President Glo, Hassan Rmaile
Vice President And General Manager Emea And South Asia Region Retail Branding And Information Solut, Elif Kagitcibasi

Vice President Communications Label And Graphic Materials, Amy White
Vice President Sourcing And Supply Chain, Michael Colarossi
Vice President Strategy And Mergers And Acquisitions, Henrik Kajueter
Global Vp Hr, Anne Ceruti
Chairman, Dean A. Scarborough, age 65
Board Member, David Pyott
Board Member, Bradley Alford
Board Member, Julia Stewart
Board Member, Martha Sullivan
Board Member, Anthony Anderson
Board Member, Kenneth Hicks
Board Member, Patrick Siewert
Auditors: PricewaterhouseCoopers LLP

LOCATIONS

HQ: Avery Dennison Corp
  207 Goode Avenue, Glendale, CA 91203
Phone: 626 304-2000
Web: www.averydennison.com

2018 Sales

	$ mil.	% of total
Asia	2,473	35
Europe	2,251	31
US	1,625	23
Latin America	490	7
Other regions	319	4
Total	**7,159**	**100**

PRODUCTS/OPERATIONS

2018 Sales

	$ mil.	% of total
Label and Graphic Materials	4,851	68
Retail Branding and Information Solutions	1,613	22
Industrial and Healthcare Materials	694	10
Total	**7,159**	**100**

Selected Brands

Avery
Avery Dennison
Avery Graphics
Fasson

COMPETITORS

3M	LINTEC CORPORATION
Bostik	Newell Brands
Brady Corporation	Nitto Denko
Checkpoint Systems	

HISTORICAL FINANCIALS

Company Type: Public

Income Statement   FYE: December 28

	REVENUE ($ mil.)	NET INCOME ($ mil.)	NET PROFIT MARGIN	EMPLOYEES
12/19	7,070	303	4.3%	30,000
12/18	7,159	467	6.5%	30,000
12/17	6,613	281	4.3%	30,000
12/16*	6,086	320	5.3%	—
01/16	5,966	274	4.6%	—
Annual Growth	**4.3%**	**2.6%**		

*Fiscal year change

2019 Year-End Financials

Debt ratio: 35.34%
Return on equity: 28.20%
Cash ($ mil.): 253
Current ratio: 1.04
Long-term debt ($ mil.): 1,499
No. of shares (mil.): 83
Dividends
  Yield: 0.0%
  Payout: 63.3%
Market value ($ mil.): 10,972

	STOCK PRICE ($) FY Close	P/E High/Low		PER SHARE ($) Earnings	Dividends	Book Value
12/19	131.61	37	24	3.57	2.26	14.44
12/18	88.83	23	16	5.28	2.01	11.27
12/17	114.86	37	22	3.13	1.76	11.89
12/16*	70.22	22	16	3.54	1.60	10.48
01/16	62.66	22	17	2.95	1.46	10.73
Annual Growth	**20.4%**	—		**4.9%**	**11.5%**	**7.7%**

*Fiscal year change

Avis Budget Group Inc

Avis Budget Group (ABG) has a car rental brand for you. The company's core brands include: Avis Rent A Car which targets corporate and leisure travelers at the high end of the market; Budget Rent A Car and Payless Car Rental both marketed to those on a budget; and Zipcar a car-sharing service. The company and their licensees operate their brands in approximately 180 countries in North America Europe Australia and New Zealand. Their rental fleet totaled approximately 660000 vehicles in 2019 and they completed more than 41 million vehicle rental transactions worldwide. Their brands and mobility solutions have an extended global reach with more than 11000 rental locations including approximately 4300 locations operated by their licensees. The company generates nearly 70% of its revenue from its on-airport locations. Avis's Budget Truck is one of the leading truck rental businesses in the US.

HISTORY

Cendant began life through the 1997 merger of CUC International and HFS. A giant in hospitality HFS was cobbled together as Hospitality Franchise Systems by LBO specialist Blackstone Group in 1992. With brands including Days Inn Ramada and Howard Johnson HFS went public that year. In 1995 HFS bought real estate firm Century 21. The next year it added Electronic Realty Associates (ERA) and Coldwell Banker. Also in 1996 HFS acquired the Super 8 Motels brand as well as car-rental firm Avis (founded by Warren Avis in 1946 it went through a succession of owners until acquired by HFS). The next year HFS sold 75% of Avis' #1 franchisee to the public and later bought relocation service firm PHH.

In an attempt to leverage the power of his brands HFS CEO Henry Silverman began looking at direct marketing giant CUC International. CUC was founded in 1973 as Comp-U-Card America by Walter Forbes and other investors envisioning a computer-based home shopping network. During the 1980s CUC developed as a discount direct marketer and catalog-based shopping club. It went public in 1983 with 100000 members. CUC saw explosive growth as it signed up 7.6 million members between 1989 and 1993. In 1996 CUC acquired Rent Net an online apartment rental service and later bought entertainment software publishers Davidson & Associates and Sierra On-Line. In 1997 CUC bought software maker Knowledge Adventure and launched online shopping site Net-Market.

CUC and HFS completed their $14.1 billion merger in December 1997 with Silverman as CEO and Forbes as chairman. While the name Cendant was derived from "ascendant" the marriage quickly headed in the opposite direction. Accounting irregularities from before the merger that had inflated CUC's revenue and pretax profit by about $500 million were revealed in 1998. Cendant's stock price tumbled taking a $14 billion hit in one day. Forbes resigned that summer. Silverman quickly took action and began to sell off operations. Cendant Software National Leisure Group (now World Travel Holdings) National Library of Poetry and Match.com all were sold that year for a total of about $1.4 billion. The company also acquired Jackson Hewitt the US's #2 tax-preparation firm and UK-based National Parking.

Through 1999 the company continued to sell assets. Cendant sold its fleet business — including PHH Vehicle Management Services — to Avis Rent A Car for $5 billion and sold its Entertainment Publications unit the world's largest coupon book marketer and publisher to The Carlyle Group. Cendant later paid $2.8 billion in one of the largest shareholder class action lawsuit settlements. (Accounting firm Ernst & Young also settled with Cendant shareholders for $335 million.)

In 2000 Cendant introduced Move.com a relocation and real estate Internet portal. Also that year the company launched Cendant Internet Group to help cement its presence on the Web and bought the brand name and franchising rights of AmeriHost Inns from AmeriHost Properties. Later in 2000 cable programming company Liberty Media (now Liberty Interactive) invested $400 million in Cendant. The next year the company began licensing and outsourcing its Incentives and Marketing Services business (practically all of the businesses that made up the former CUC International) to Trilegiant a new company formed by the units' management.

In 2001 after selling Move.com to Homestore (later called Move) for $761 million Cendant sought to expand its travel holdings with a slew of acquisitions. Its purchases included timeshare resort firm Fairfield Communities ($690 million); travel services firm Galileo International ($2.4 billion); online travel reservation service Cheap Tickets ($425 million); and vacation timeshare marketer Equivest Finance ($100 million). In late 2001 Cendant cut some 6000 jobs to improve its bottom line and announced that during the next year or so it would cut an additional 10000 jobs and eliminate about 7% of its franchised hotels.

In 2002 the company sold its UK-based National Car Park unit which accounted for 3% of sales as part of its strategy to sell off noncore businesses. In June Cendant bought TRUST International from Bertelsmann and later that year purchased car-rental company Budget Rent A Car for about $110 million then slashed costs by closing facilities and laying off more than 450 employees. The company also purchased Novasol AS which rented out private vacation homes in Northern Europe.

Cendant terminated its licensing and services agreements with Trilegiant in January 2004 and in February Sotheby's Holdings sold its 15 Sotheby's International Realty offices (along with the brand's licensing rights) to the company for about $100 million. In March Cendant's Jackson Hewitt subsidiary filed for its IPO. In May the company purchased Dutch vacation rental company Landal Green Parks (LGP) for about $150 million. Also that month former chairman Walter Forbes and former vice chairman E. Kirk Shelton went on trial for federal fraud and conspiracy stemming from the pre-merger accounting irregularities. (Shelton was found guilty of multiple counts of fraud in early 2005.) In October CFO Ronald Nelson was named president taking over for Henry Silverman who remained chairman and CEO.

In 2004 Cendant acquired online travel firm Orbitz in a deal valued at about $1.25 billion. Quick on the heels of the Orbitz deal the company Cendant also purchased ebookers (a European online travel site now called Flightbookers) in a deal worth about $400 million and acquired two travel groups collectively known as Gullivers for about $1.1 billion.

As 2004 wound to a close Cendant completed the acquisition of the Ramada International Hotels & Resorts brand and franchising operations from Marriott International. Cendant already owned the rights to the brand and franchising operations in the US and Canada which included some 820 US properties and about 70 Canadian properties. In 2005 Cendant acquired the Wyndham hotel brand from Wyndham International Inc. for $101 million. The deal included the franchise agreements for 82 hotels and the management contracts for another 29 hotels but not the actual properties which were located in the US Mexico and the Caribbean. The next year Cendant acquired the Baymont Inn & Suites brand of limited-service midscale lodging from Blackstone's La Quinta Corporation (now LQ Management). The Baymont Inn & Suites brand covered 115 franchised properties; the properties themselves were not included in the deal.

Cendant in 2005 spun off its mortgage operations PHH Mortgage (formerly Cendant Mortgage) and fleet management (PHH Arval) businesses under the PHH Corporation umbrella. Also that year Cendant spun off Wright Express (payment processing and information services for fleet management) in an IPO and sold its marketing services division to Apollo Management for about $1.8 billion.

The divestitures that began in 2005 culminated in the unwinding of the Cendant conglomerate the next year. The company spun off its hotel and real estate operations and sold its travel services division in 2006 reconfiguring itself around its rental car businesses and renaming itself Avis Budget Group. Silverman became chairman and CEO of the company's real estate business Realogy and Nelson took over as chairman and CEO of the slimmed-down Avis Budget Group which took on its new name in September 2006.

Warren Avis the founder of Avis Rent A Car died in April 2007 at the age of 92. In October the company acquired a 48% stake in chauffeured transportation company Carey International for $60 million. (In 2009 due to losses at Carey it wrote down its investment in the company to zero.)

Avis Budget Group acquired Avis Europe plc in October 2011. The purchase followed ABG's withdrawal from its battle with rival Hertz to acquire Dollar Thrifty Automotive Group (DTG). Instead the company turned to Europe for growth by reuniting with Avis Europe which was legally separated from Avis in 1986. The deal created what ABG says is the largest publicly traded rental car business in the world.

In 2012 in continuing to bulk up its global operations after its purchase of Avis Europe ABG in 2012 acquired New Zealand's largest independently-owned car rental company Apex Car Rentals. The purchase added more than 4000 rental cars and strengthened Avis's position in New Zealand and Australia.

EXECUTIVES

President International, Mark J. Servodidio, age 55, $596,538 total compensation
Interim Cfo, Martyn R. Smith, age 65
Evp And Chief Marketing Officer, W. Scott Deaver, age 69
Ceo And Coo, Larry D. De Shon, age 61, $1,000,000 total compensation
Svp And Cio, Gerard Insall
Evp General Counsel And Chief Compliance Officer, Michael K. Tucker, age 62
Svp North America Operations, Joseph A. (Joe) Ferraro, age 63, $623,269 total compensation
Svp And Chief Human Resources Officer, Edward P. (Ned) Linnen, age 50
Evp And Chief Innovation Officer, Arthur Orduna
Vice President Enterprise Applications, Steve Hoffman
Vice President International Controller, Gerard Monusky
Vice President Technical Operations Real Estate In, Jennifer Smith
Vice President Fleet Control, Neil Schamus
Vice President Human Resources, April Scavone
Vice President Tax, Izzy Martins
Vice President Information Technology, John Page
Senior Vice President, Joseph Siino
Vice President Area, Jeff Eisenbarth
Executive Vice President Strategy And Pricing, Scott Deaver
Vice President And Associate General Counsel, Rosalie Shoeman
Vice President, John Barrows
Vice President Of Engineering, Jennifer Rodean
Vice President Human Resources, Roger Deverman
Vice President Ecommerce, Joseph Kirrane
Vice President Financial Planning And Analysis, David Crowther
Executive Vice President Of Division, Angel Burton
Senior Vice President Global Digital Customer Experience, Neil Zamore
Vice President, Tom Whittaker
Vice President Supply Chain Americas, Mark Haeussler
Senior Vice President Management Information Services, Suzzane Wetherington
Vice President, Kurt Freudenberg
Vice President Fleet Services, Gregg Nierenberg
Svp Global Digital Customer Experience, Neal Zamore
Vice President Of Information Technology, Paul Tomlin
Vice President, John Damrell
Senior Vice President Of Marketing, Mark Sotir
Chairman, Ronald L. (Ron) Nelson, age 68
Board Member, Eduardo Mestre
Board Member, Robert Salerno
Board Member, Jeffrey Fox
Secretary And Treasurer, Chris Barnhardt
Auditors: DELOITTE & TOUCHE LLP

LOCATIONS

HQ: Avis Budget Group Inc
6 Sylvan Way, Parsippany, NJ 07054
Phone: 973 496-4700
Web: www.avisbudgetgroup.com

2016 Locations

	$ mil.	% of total
AvisBudget		
Americas		
Company-operated	1,550	1,400
Licensees	700	650
International		
Company-operated	1,200	650
Licensees	2,050	1,350
Total	**5,550**	**4,050**

2016 Sales

	$ mil.	% of total
United States	5,674	66
All other countries	2,985	34
Total	**8,659**	**100**

2016 Sales

	$ mil.	% of total
Americas	6,121	71
International	2,538	29
Total	**8,659**	**100**

2016 Car Rental Sales

	% of total
On-Airport	70
Off-airport	30
Total	**100**

PRODUCTS/OPERATIONS

2016 Sales

	$ mil.	% of total
Vehicle rental	6,081	70
Others	2,578	30
Total	**8,659**	**100**

COMPETITORS

AMERCO
Enterprise Rent-A-Car
Europcar
Herc Holdings
Penske Truck Leasing
Ryder System
Sixt

HISTORICAL FINANCIALS

Company Type: Public

Income Statement   FYE: December 31

	REVENUE ($ mil.)	NET INCOME ($ mil.)	NET PROFIT MARGIN	EMPLOYEES
12/19	9,172	302	3.3%	30,000
12/18	9,124	165	1.8%	30,000
12/17	8,848	361	4.1%	31,000
12/16	8,659	163	1.9%	30,000
12/15	8,502	313	3.7%	30,000
Annual Growth	**1.9%**	**(0.9%)**	**—**	**0.0%**

2019 Year-End Financials

Debt ratio: 62.71%	No. of shares (mil.): 73
Return on equity: 56.45%	Dividends
Cash ($ mil.): 686	Yield: —
Current ratio: 0.96	Payout: —
Long-term debt ($ mil.): 14,484	Market value ($ mil.): 2,383

	STOCK PRICE ($) FY Close	P/E High	P/E Low	PER SHARE ($) Earnings	PER SHARE ($) Dividends	PER SHARE ($) Book Value
12/19	32.24	9	5	3.98	0.00	8.88
12/18	22.48	24	11	2.06	0.00	5.48
12/17	43.88	11	5	4.25	0.00	7.07
12/16	36.68	23	12	1.75	0.00	2.57
12/15	36.29	22	11	2.98	0.00	4.48
Annual Growth	**(2.9%)**	**—**	**—**	**7.5%**	**—**	**18.6%**

Avnet Inc

If you need an electronic component Avnet probably has it. The company is one of the world's top distributors of electronic components (including connectors and semiconductors) Inductors and storage products and software with competitors Arrow Electronics and World Peace Group. It works with more than 1400 suppliers to provide some 2.1 million customers with parts and services. Customers include startups small and mid-sized businesses and big companies that produce electronics. Avnet has about 115 locations around the world and makes most of its sales to international customers with Asia/Pacific generating roughly 40% of revenue. Semiconductors and related products comprise about three quarters of Avnet's revenue.

Operations

Avnet is composed of two segments Electronic Components (EC) and Farnell.

Electronic Components generates about 95% of revenue selling semiconductors and interconnect passive and electromechanical devices (IP&E). EC also offers design tools and engineering services to support product design as well as supply chain services to OEMs.

The Farnell unit accounts for more than 5% of revenue from distributing kits tools electronic components and industrial automation components as well as test and measurement products.

Additionally Avnet provides aftermarket services — from technical design integration and assembly through a business unit called Avnet Integrated and it offers supply chain services including warehousing distribution solutions and transportation solutions through a unit called Avnet Logistics.

Avnet works with about 1400 suppliers; products from Texas Instruments have accounted for about 10% of Avnet's billings.

Overall Avnet generate more than three quarters of its revenue in semiconductors followed by IP&E with about 20% and the rest comes from computers and other products with more than 5% combined.

Geographic Reach

Avnet has a fairly even geographic spread of sales with each region contributing between 25% to 40% of revenue. Customers in Asia account for about 40% of revenue with customers in EMEA providing about 35% and those in the Americas supplying more than 25%.

Headquartered in Phoenix Arizona the company has warehousing integration operations and offices in Arizona and South Carolina in the US and overseas in Belgium Germany the UK and China.

Sales and Marketing

Avnet's customers include original equipment manufacturers electronic manufacturing services providers and original design manufacturers.

Financial Performance

From 2016 until 2019 the company revenue was on an upswing but declined in 2020.

In 2020 (ended June) revenue fell to $17.6 billion down by about $1.9 billion from 2019. Sales in constant currency decreased by 8.7% year over year. The year-over-year sales decline which occurred in both operating groups and across all three regions was primarily due to lower demand resulting from the continuation of the global industry-wide slowdown that started in the second half of fiscal 2019 and impacts on demand from the COVID-19 pandemic.

Avnet reported a net loss of $31.1 million in 2020. The loss was due to lower sales and high operating expenses.

Avnet's coffers held $477 million in cash and equivalents in 2020 compared to $546.1 million the previous year. Operations generated $730.2 million while investing activities used $135 million and financing activities used another $644.6 million. Main cash uses were for repayment of public notes and repurchases of stocks.

Strategy

Avnet announced in September 2020 the availability of the Avnet mmWave Radio Development Kit for Xilinx Zynq UltraScale+ RFSoC Gen-3.

The new Radio Development Kit enables system architects to explore the entire signal chain from the RF in millimeter wave spectrum to digital by harnessing the integration of Xilinx RFSoC Gen-3 for direct-RF sampling at intermediate frequencies up to 6 GHz. The kit combines the DTRX2 mmWave Radio daughtercard – jointly developed by Otava and Avnet – with the Zynq UltraScale+ RFSoC ZCU208 Evaluation Kit from Xilinx Inc. Using MATLAB and Simulink from MathWorks the kit enables users to quickly develop wideband mmWave wireless systems across a range of applications including 5G NR in the FR2 bands K and Ka-band Satcom radar and aerospace and defense uses.

The Zynq UltraScale+ RFSoC solve system-level challenges by integrating more of the RF signal chain providing lower power smaller footprint and better performance than discrete solutions. Avnet's kit continues that strategy by solving system-level challenges for prototype and deployment.

Mergers and Acquisitions

Avnet has a strong history of using acquisitions to grow its geographic footprint across the globe. That practice continues to be a key part of its strategy today with Avnet seeking to acquire primarily smaller businesses in markets where it is trying to expand its presence or increase its scale.

In late 2019 Avent agreed to acquire Witekio formerly known as Adeneo Embedded a privately held company with expertise in software and embedded devices for an undisclosed amount. Witekio strengthens Avnet's portfolio for the Internet of Things.

Company Background

Avnet got its start in 1921 and was incorporated in 1955. Avnet sold parts for the new technology of the day radio. Over the years Avnet has adjusted with the times buying companies to address new markets while selling parts of the company to exit other markets.

EXECUTIVES

Vp And President Avnet Technology Solutions Emea, Graeme A. Watt

Senior Vice President Of Marketing, Alex Iuorio

Ceo, William J. (Bill) Amelio

Svp Chief Human Resources Officer And Global Marketing And Communications, MaryAnn G. Miller, $540,000 total compensation

Svp And President Avnet Technology Solutions Global, Patrick Zammit, $488,400 total compensation

Vp And President Avnet Technology Solutions Americas, Jeff Bawol

President Avnet Electronics Marketing Americas, Chuck Delph

Cio, Kevin V. Summers

Svp And President Avnet Electronics Marketing Global, Gerald W. (Gerry) Fay, $600,000 total compensation

Svp And Chief Global Logistics And Operations Officer, Michael D. (Mike) Buseman

Vp And President Avnet Technology Solutions Asia Pacific, William Chu

Cfo, Thomas (Tom) Liguori

Vp And President Avnet Electronics Marketing Emea, Miguel Fernandez

Acting President Avnet Electronics Marketing Asia And Japan, Frederick Fu

Vice President Of Human Resources Ts Americas, Kaylene Moss

Senior Vice President And Chief People Officer, Ken Arnold

Vice President Sales, Brad Johnson

Vice President And Director Cable Assembly And Value Added Services, Jim Mooney

Vice President And General Counsel, Cheree Mcalpine

Regional Vice President Of South Europe For Silica, Mario Orlandi

Senior Vice President, Dennis Losik

Vice President Of Marketing, Ivan Ho

Vice President Human Resources, Aaron Dean

Vice President Sales, Peter Rzonca

Vice President Global Operations, Derinda Ehrlich

Vice President, Ray Ramey

Vp Operations, Rich Fitzgerald

Vice President Global Program Management Office, Ellen Owens

Vice President Logistics Operations And
Transportation, Lisa Kelley
Vice President Sales, Arbi Baghdasarian
Vice President Digital Marketing, Jessica Daughetee
Vice President Global Infrastructure, Bonnie Bauer
Senior Vice President Global Programming
Operations, Douglas Adams
Vice President Director Of Investorrelations,
Vince Keenan
Vice President Global Trade Compliance, Robert
Bowen
Vice President Information Systems, Bob Laurie
Senior Vice President Chief Human Resources
Officer And Corporate Marketing And
Communications, Maryann G Miller
Vice President Global Procurement And
Administrative Services, James Azzinaro
Vice President Global Supply Chain Operations,
Susan Cunningham
Vice President Engineering And Technology, Jim
Beneke
Vice President Of Global Technical Marketing,
Vivian — Han
Vice President Global Contracts And Security, Joel
Legin
Vice President Operations, Tim Blevins
Chairman, William H. (Bill) Schumann
Board Member, Mike Bradley
Auditors: KPMG LLP

LOCATIONS

HQ: Avnet Inc
2211 South 47th Street, Phoenix, AZ 85034
Phone: 480 643-2000
Web: www.avnet.com

2019 Sales

	$ mil.	% of total
Asia/Pacific	7,619	39
Europe Middle East and Africa	6,762	35
Americas	5,135	26
Total	**19,518**	**100**

PRODUCTS/OPERATIONS

2019 Sales by Operating Group

	$ mil.	% of total
Electronic Components	18,060	93
Premier Farnell	1,458	7
Total	**19,518**	**100**

2019 Sales by Product Category

	$ mil.	% of total
Semiconductors	14,973	77
Interconnect passive & electromechanical	3,516	18
Computers	533	2
Other	496	2
Total	**19,036**	**100**

Selected Products

Amplifiers
Analog Switch Multiplexer
Batteries
Capacitor
Circuit Protection
Communication
Data Conversion
Discrete
Displays
DSP
Embedded Boards
Enclosures Racks & Cabinets
Filter
Inductor
Interconnect
Interface
Kits And Tools
Lighting
Logic And Timing
Memory
Microcontrollers
Miscellaneous
Motors

Optoelectronics
Peripherals
Power Management
Power Supplies
Processor
Programmable Logic
Resistor
RF And Microwave
Sensors And Transducers
Software
Storage
Switches And Relays
Systems
Test & Measurement
Thermal Management
Transformer

COMPETITORS

Allied Electronics	N.F. Smith
Arrow Electronics	Plexus
Digi-Key	SYNNEX
Future Electronics	TTI Inc.
Heilind Electronics	Tech Data
Ingram Micro	WPG Holdings

HISTORICAL FINANCIALS
Company Type: Public

Income Statement
FYE: June 27

	REVENUE ($ mil.)	NET INCOME ($ mil.)	NET PROFIT MARGIN	EMPLOYEES
06/20	17,634	(31)	—	14,600
06/19	19,518	176	0.9%	15,500
06/18*	19,036	(156)	—	15,400
07/17	17,439	525	3.0%	15,700
07/16	26,219	506	1.9%	17,700
Annual Growth	(9.4%)	—	—	(4.7%)

*Fiscal year change

2020 Year-End Financials

Debt ratio: 17.58%
Return on equity: (-0.79%)
Cash ($ mil.): 477
Current ratio: 2.78
Long-term debt ($ mil.): 1,424

No. of shares (mil.): 98
Dividends
  Yield: 0.0%
  Payout: —
Market value ($ mil.): 2,573

	STOCK PRICE ($) FY Close	P/E High/Low		PER SHARE ($) Earnings	Dividends	Book Value
06/20	26.04	—	—	(0.31)	0.84	37.72
06/19	45.27	31	21	1.59	0.80	39.80
06/18*	42.89	—	—	(1.30)	0.74	40.45
07/17	38.88	12	9	4.08	0.70	42.10
07/16	40.27	12	10	3.80	0.68	36.84
Annual Growth	(10.3%)	—	—	—	5.4%	0.6%

*Fiscal year change

AXOS BANK

EXECUTIVES

Ceo, Greg Garrabants
Sr V Pres-Cfo, Andrew Micheletti
Evp-Chief Credit Offr-Chief RE, Tom Constantine
Gen Counsel, Eshel Bar-Adon
Exec V Pres, Brian Swanson
Executive Vice-President, Adriaan Van Zyl
Assistant Vice-President, Joel Kodish
Human Resources Manager, Maria Dews
Assistant Vice-President, Danielle Austin
Vice President, Gilbert Gomez
Underwriter, Jessica Montoya

LOCATIONS

HQ: AXOS BANK
4350 LA JOLLA VILLAGE DR, SAN DIEGO, CA
921221243
Phone: 858 350-6200
Web: WWW.AXOSBANK.COM

HISTORICAL FINANCIALS
Company Type: Private

Income Statement
FYE: December 31

	ASSETS ($ mil.)	NET INCOME ($ mil.)	INCOME AS % OF ASSETS	EMPLOYEES
12/17	8,908	150	1.7%	102
12/16	8,162	137	1.7%	—
12/15	6,656	104	1.6%	—
12/14	5,190	71	1.4%	—
Annual Growth	19.7%	28.1%	—	—

Axos Financial Inc

Formerly Bofl Holding Axos Financial is the
holding company for Axos Bank which provides
consumers and businesses a variety of deposit and
loan products via the internet. It conducts its business without any physical bank branches supporting its customers through a comprehensive online
banking platform and the occasional physical retail
locations of its partners. Most of its business originates in its home state of California though its
operations attract customers from every US state.
Founded in 2000 the company holds some $10.9
billion in assets more than $8.6 billion in deposits
and a total portfolio of net loans and leases of
about $9.1 billion.

Operations

Axos Financial operates through two segments:
Banking Business and Securities Business.

The holding company's Banking Business division provides nearly all its revenue houses its online and concierge banking prepaid card mortgage
vehicle and unsecured lending services. The Banking Business addresses consumers and small businesses through its online platform and over the
phone. The segment also offers software products
and consulting services for Chapter 7 bankruptcy
and non-Chapter 7 trustees and fiduciaries cash
management and commercial and industrial real
estate loans.

Axos' Securities Business accounts for about
2% of revenue and provides broker-dealer and registered investment advisor services to its own
clients and Banking Business clients.

More than 80% of Axos' revenue is generated
by net interest income; non-interest income is derived mostly from banking and service fees. The
bank's net loan and lease portfolio is dominated
by single-family real estate: nearly 50% of its value
is represented by mortgages; almost 10% comprises commercial specialty lender finance and construction loans secured by single-family real estate
and warehouses. Some 20% is secured by multi-
family real estate and another roughly 15% is
made up of commercial and real estate loans.

Geographic Reach

San Diego California-based Axos Financial holds
deposits from customers in every US state with
large sources of balances in Florida and the Mid-
Atlantic states. Around 70% of its mortgage portfolio is secured by real estate in California. Its next
largest geographic segments by loan principal are

New York and Florida each of which comprises less than 10%.

Sales and Marketing

Because the bank is branchless the traditional means of attracting customers?such as local advertising a physical bank presence community charity sponsorship?are not used. Rather the bank creates brand awareness through direct mail email digital marketing personal sales and print advertising. It also garners deposits through financial advisory companies and affinity partnerships.

Financial Performance

In recent years Axos Financial has experienced strong annual increases in revenue and in net income: each has added more than 170% since fiscal 2014. Net interest income?the company's greatest source of income?was boosted by its growing loan and lease portfolio particularly in residential real estate.

Axos posted revenue of $439.4 million in 2018 a 15% increase from 2017. A rise in the bank's net interest margin and a larger loan portfolio accounted for most of the gain. Banking and service fees pushed up non-interest income marginally. Net income rose 13% to $152.4 million on the strength of revenue.

The holding company depleted $20.6 million of its cash to end the year with $622.9 million. Operations generated $167.9 million and financing activities added $837.4 million entirely due to increased deposits. Axos used $1 Billion on investments?principally loans held for investment.

Strategy

Axos Financial's strategy is simply to grow its loan portfolio?and therefore its interest income?through new products expanded distribution channels leveraged data mining and acquisitions.

In 2018 the bank introduced two new products: factoring?in which a company sells its accounts receivable at a discount often to meet short term cash requirements?and its Universal Digital Bank online banking platform. The platform expands the bank's analytics and personalization capabilities enabling greater product cross-selling. It also facilitates development of in-house and third-party apps.

Axos is also growing through a spate of recent acquisitions. In 2019 the company received regulatory approval to acquire about $170 million in deposits from MWABank. That year the company also acquired financial advisor WiseBanyan Holdings gaining its digital wealth management platform and about $150 million in assets under management. Furthermore it expanded its service offerings and added about $35 million in yearly fee income through its purchase of clearing firm COR Clearing. In 2018 it bought Nationwide Building Society's banking and lending business?including $0.7 billion in checking savings and money market accounts and $1.7 billion in time deposit accounts. It also acquired the trustee and fiduciary services business of Epiq Systems which encompasses its software and consulting services for Chapter 7 and non-Chapter 7 trustees and fiduciaries.

Mergers and Acquisitions

In 2019 Axos Financial took a step toward growing its deposit base when it received regulatory approval to acquire about $170 million in deposits from MWABank. That year the company also acquired financial advisor WiseBanyan Holdings gaining its digital wealth management platform and about $150 million in assets under management. Furthermore it expanded its service offerings and added about $35 million in yearly fee income through its purchase of clearing firm COR Clearing.

Axos bought Nationwide Building Society's banking and lending business?including $0.7 bil-

lion in checking savings and money market accounts and $1.7 billion in time deposit accounts?in 2018. It also acquired the trustee and fiduciary services business of Epiq Systems encompassing its software and consulting services for Chapter 7 and non-Chapter 7 trustees and fiduciaries.

Company Background

Axos Financial launched in 2000 as Bank of Internet USA as a digital bank offering checking accounts. The company went public in 2005 as BofI Holding. In 2018 after launching its Universal Digital Bank Platform BofI changed its name to Axos Financial in tandem with a listing on the NYSE.

EXECUTIVES

Evp And Cfo Bofi Holding Inc. And Bofi Federal Bank, Andrew J. Micheletti, age 63, $231,000 total compensation
President And Ceo Bofi Holding Inc. And Bofi Federal Bank, Gregory Garrabrants, age 49, $375,000 total compensation
Evp Specialty Finance And Chief Legal Officer Bofi Federal Bank, Eshel Bar-Adon, age 65, $250,000 total compensation
Evp And Chief Credit Officer Bofi Federal Bank, Thomas Constantine, age 58, $235,000 total compensation
Evp And Chief Lending Officer Bofi Federal Bank, Brian Swanson, age 40, $235,000 total compensation
Evp Chief Of Staff And Chief Performance Officer Bofi Federal Bank, Jan Durrans
Evp Chief Deposit Officer And Chief Marketing Officer Bofi Federal Bank, Eduardo Urdapilleta
Senior Vice President, Jason Kenoyer
Vice President Director Of Financial Reporting, Pete Bauer
First Vice President And Compliance Management, Sandy Hill
Vice President Construction Loan Manager, David Thomas
Assistant Vice President Product Delivery, Bryan Iv Hugh
Executive Vice President Director Of Deposits Development, Lane Elliott
Vice President Marketing, Dana Berry
Senior Vice President, Lance Soloway
Assistant Vice President Commercial Relationship Manager, Aap Bleiman
Chairman, Paul J. Grinberg, age 59
Vice Chairman, Nicholas A. Mosich
Board Member, Edward Ratinoff
Board Member, James Argalas
Secretary, Angela Lopez
Auditors: BDO USA, LLP

LOCATIONS

HQ: Axos Financial Inc
9205 West Russell Road, STE 400, Las Vegas, NV 89148
Phone: 858 649-2218
Web: www.bofiholding.com

PRODUCTS/OPERATIONS

2018 Sales

	$ mil.	% of total
Interest and dividend income:		
Loans and leases including fees	447	79
Investments	28	5
Interest expense	(106.6)	-
Non-interest income:		
Banking and service fees	47	11
Mortgage banking income	13	3
Gain on sale - other	5	1
Prepayment penalty fee income	3	1
Gain (loss) on sale of securities	(0.2)	-
Total	455	100

COMPETITORS

Ally Bank	ISN Bank
California Bank & Trust	MUFG Americas Holdings
Discover	PacWest Bancorp
E*TRADE Bank	San Diego County Credit Union
First IB	Scottrade
HSBC USA	

HISTORICAL FINANCIALS

Company Type: Public

Income Statement				FYE: June 30
	ASSETS ($ mil.)	NET INCOME ($ mil.)	INCOME AS % OF ASSETS	EMPLOYEES
06/20	13,851	183	1.3%	1,099
06/19	11,220	155	1.4%	1,007
06/18	9,539	152	1.6%	801
06/17	8,501	134	1.6%	681
06/16	7,601	119	1.6%	647
Annual Growth	16.2%	11.4%		14.2%

2020 Year-End Financials

Debt ratio: 1.70%
Return on equity: 15.88%
Cash ($ mil.): 1,950
Current ratio: —
Long-term debt ($ mil.): —
No. of shares (mil.): 59
Dividends
  Yield: —
  Payout: —
Market value ($ mil.): 1,316

	STOCK PRICE ($) FY Close	P/E High/Low		PER SHARE ($) Earnings	Dividends	Book Value
06/20	22.08	10	5	2.98	0.00	20.65
06/19	27.25	17	10	2.48	0.00	17.55
06/18	40.91	19	10	2.37	0.00	15.32
06/17	23.72	16	7	2.07	0.00	13.13
06/16	17.71	77	7	1.85	0.00	10.81
Annual Growth	5.7%	—		12.7%	—	17.6%

Baker Hughes Company

Auditors: KPMG LLP

LOCATIONS

HQ: Baker Hughes Company
17021 Aldine Westfield Road, Houston, TX 77073-5101
Phone: 713 439-8600
Web: www.bakerhughes.com

HISTORICAL FINANCIALS

Company Type: Public

Income Statement				FYE: December 31
	REVENUE ($ mil.)	NET INCOME ($ mil.)	NET PROFIT MARGIN	EMPLOYEES
12/19	23,838	128	0.5%	68,000
12/18	22,877	195	0.9%	66,000
12/17	17,259	(73)		64,000
12/16	13,269	403	3.0%	34,000
12/15	16,688	(606)	—	—
Annual Growth	9.3%	—		—

2019 Year-End Financials

Debt ratio: 11.90%	No. of shares (mil.): 1,027
Return on equity: 0.65%	Dividends
Cash ($ mil.): 3,249	Yield: 2.8%
Current ratio: 1.52	Payout: 313.0%
Long-term debt ($ mil.): 6,301	Market value ($ mil.): 26,335

	STOCK PRICE ($) FY Close	P/E High/Low	PER SHARE ($) Earnings	Dividends	Book Value
12/19	25.63	124 90	0.23	0.72	21.34
12/18	21.50	81 45	0.45	0.72	16.88
12/17	31.64	— —	(0.17)	0.35	13.03
Annual Growth	(5.1%)	— —	—	19.8%	13.1%

Ball Corp

The Ball Corporation produces sustainable aluminum beverage packaging and aerospace products. Ball's packaging revenue (about 90% of its net sales) is derived from a relatively few major beverage-producing companies and brands such as Coca-Cola and Anheuser-Busch InBev. Additionally its aerospace segment provides an array of aerospace systems and services (such as spacecraft instruments and sensors radio frequency systems and components data exploitation solutions); about 15% of these sales are to the US government. Ball Corporation operates about 70 locations in about 40 countries with the US its largest market at approximately 50% of the total sales.

Operations

Ball Corporation divides its operations between four business segments. Its three beverage packaging segments – North and Central America (more than 40% of total revenue) Europe (more than 20%) and South America (approximately 15%) – are all the leading provider of aluminum cans for soft drinks energy drinks beer and other beverages in their respective markets.

The company's aerospace segment (about 15%) makes and sells aerospace and related products for the civil commercial and national security aerospace markets.

Geographic Reach

The company operates about 75 facilities spanning Asia Europe North America and South America. The US accounts for half of total revenues and more than 10% of sales come from Brazil.

Ball Corporation's headquarters as well as its aerospace segment offices are located in Broomfield CO. Regional offices for Europe are in Wakefield UK; Middle East and Asia operations are in Cairo Manisa and Mumbai respectively; and South American offices are in Rio de Janeiro. Ball's R&D facilities are primarily located in Westminster Colorado.

Sales and Marketing

Ball's packaging revenue is derived primarily from long-term contracts with a relatively few customers. Anheuser-Busch InBev and affiliates contributes about 15% of net sales. Other large accounts include Coca-Cola (about 10% of revenue) and the US government (about 15%).

Financial Performance

Except for a dip in 2015 Ball's revenue has seen steady growth the last five years rising about 45% between 2015 and 2019. Higher beverage packaging volumes across most geographies.

Sales in 2019 decreased by 1% to $11.4 billion or $161 million compared to $11.6 billion in 2018 primarily as a result of selling the U.S. and Argentine steel food and steel aerosol businesses selling our China beverage packaging business the pass through of lower aluminum prices the conclusion of the South America segment's end sales associated with the Rexam acquisition and unfavorable exchange rates for our Europe segment partially offset by higher beverage can unit volumes and higher pricing in our Europe and North and Central America segments and increased sales in the aerospace segment.

Net income increased 25% to $566 million in 2019 compared to 2018 primarily due to higher beverage can unit volumes and prices increased sales in the aerospace segment lower selling general and administrative expenses and lower income tax expense partially offset by the conclusion of our South America segment's end sales agreement associated with the Rexam acquisition higher interest expense higher business consolidation and other costs unfavorable U.S. aluminum scrap rates and manufacturing inefficiencies experienced in our North and Central America segment.

Cash at the end of 2019 was $1.8 billion an increase of $1.1 billion from the prior year. Cash from operations contributed $1.5 billion to the coffers while investing activities used $422 million mainly for capital expenditures. Financing activities used $46 million primarily for repayment of long-term borrowings.

Strategy

Ball is continuing its "Drive for 10" vision – a 10-year initiative established in 2011 which is focused on key levers underpinning its corporate strategy. Ball is focused on growing its existing business while also adding new products to its portfolio.

The company is streamlining processes and systems and increasing the sustainability of its beverage cans. In 2018 it is continuing with its global finance transformation projects by opening shared service centers in Belgrade Serbia and Querétaro Mexico. To tighten its beverage and food can operations it closed several plants in the US and one in Germany.

In late 2019 the company sold its Argentina steel aerosol packaging business which included facilities in Garin and San Luis Argentina and recorded a loss on disposal of $52 million which included the write-off of cumulative translation adjustments of $45 million related to the Argentina business that had been previously recorded in accumulated other comprehensive income. The company completed the sale of its metal beverage packaging business in China for upfront consideration of approximately $213 million Earlier in 2018 Ball divested its US steel food and steel aerosol packaging business to form a new joint venture named Ball Metalpack. Ball holds a 49% stake in Ball Metalpack; JV partner Platinum Equity controls 51%.

As consumer awareness about the environmental impacts of plastic packaging continues to increase Ball is well-positioned to offer aluminum container alternatives to plastic cartons and glass. More beverages – including sparkling waters wine and coffee ?- are making the move to cans. The Ball Aluminum Cups business was launched during 2019 to serve the growing demand for innovative sustainable beverage packaging among customers and consumers. In late 2019 the company announced that it will begin construction on its first dedicated aluminum cups manufacturing facility to serve the growing demand for innovative sustainable beverage packaging for U.S. customers and consumers. The new aluminum cups manufacturing facility will be adjacent to Ball's existing aluminum beverage can manufacturing plant in Rome Georgia and is expected to ramp up production in the fourth quarter of 2020. Ball plans to hire approximately 145 new employees for the cups facility to support the multi-year investment of approximately $200 million.

On the aerospace side Ball increased its contracted backlog $2.5 billion in 2019. That year NASA selected Ball to design and develop the Wide Field Instrument which will contribute to the WFIRST space mission that aims to explore areas including dark matter exoplanets and infrared astrophysics.

Mergers and Acquisitions

In early 2020 the company entered into a purchase agreement to acquire Tubex Industria E Comercio de Embalagens Ltda an aluminum aerosol packaging business with a plant near Sao Paolo Brazil along with associated contracts and other related assets for $80 million plus a potential earn out.

Company Background

The Ball Corporation began in 1880 when Frank Ball and his four brothers started making wood-jacket tin cans to store and transport kerosene and other materials. In 1884 the company switched to tin-jacketed glass containers for kerosene lamps. The lamps however were soon displaced by Thomas Edison's electric light bulb.

The Ball brothers then learned that the patent to the original sealed-glass storage container (the Mason jar) had expired. By 1886 the brothers had entered the sealed-jar business and imprinted their jars with the Ball name.

The company began diversifying but a 1947 antitrust ruling prohibited it from buying additional glass subsidiaries. Ball decided to take advantage of the space race by buying Control Cells (aerospace science research) in 1957; that operation became Ball Brothers Research Corporation (later Ball Aerospace Systems Division).

Ball established its metal beverage-container business in 1969 when it bought Jeffco Manufacturing of Colorado. The operation soon won contracts to supply two-piece cans to Budweiser Coca-Cola Dr Pepper Pepsi and Stroh's Beer. Ball went public in 1973.

HISTORY

The Ball Corporation began in 1880 when Frank Ball and his four brothers started making wood-jacket tin cans to store and transport kerosene and other materials. In 1884 the company switched to tin-jacketed glass containers for kerosene lamps. The lamps however were soon displaced by Thomas Edison's electric light bulb.

The Ball brothers then learned that the patent to the original sealed-glass storage container (the Mason jar) had expired. By 1886 the brothers had entered the sealed-jar business and imprinted their jars with the Ball name. In their first year they made 12500 jars and sparked a patent war with the two reigning jar producers who asserted that they controlled the correct patents and threatened to sue. The Ball lawyers proved that the patents had expired and the jar remained Ball's mainstay for many years.

The company began diversifying but a 1947 antitrust ruling prohibited it from buying additional glass subsidiaries. Ball decided to take advantage of the space race by buying Control Cells (aerospace science research) in 1957; that operation became Ball Brothers Research Corporation (later Ball Aerospace Systems Division). The Soviets launched Sputnik that year igniting a massive US scientific effort in 1958 and Ball won federal contracts to make equipment for the US space program.

Ball established its metal beverage-container business in 1969 when it bought Jeffco Manufacturing of Colorado. The operation soon won contracts to supply two-piece cans to Budweiser Coca-Cola Dr Pepper Pepsi and Stroh's Beer.

EXECUTIVES

Svp And Cfo, Scott C. Morrison, age 57, $666,728 total compensation

Chairman President And Ceo, John A. Hayes, age 54, $1,238,615 total compensation

Svp Human Resources And Administration, Lisa A. Pauley, age 58, $464,443 total compensation

Svp And Coo Global Beverage Packaging, Daniel W. Fisher, age 47

Vp Technology, M. Andrew (Drew) Crouch

Vp General Counsel And Corporate Secretary, Charles E. Baker, age 62, $492,871 total compensation

Svp; President Ball Aerospace And Technologies, Robert D. (Rob) Strain, age 63

Svp And Coo Food And Aerosol Packaging, James N. Peterson, age 51

Vice President Investor Relations, Ann Scott

Director Progam Development Chief Sales Officer, Jim Good

Vice President Business Services, Gary Bybee

Vice President Sales, Bruce Doelling

Vice President, Art Morrissey

Vp Human Resources Metal Beverage Americas, John Olson

Vice President Manufacturing, Steve Marcontell

Vice President, Roy Nelson

Vice President, Shelley B Petroy

Vice President Finance N.a. Metal Beverage Packaging Division, Rob Kim

Vp Finance, Douglas Bradford

Vice President, Jason Myers

Senior Vice President Of International Sales, David Fredericks

Vice President Sales Telecomm Products, Tom Messler

Vice President Manufacturing, John Skubala

Vice President And General Manager Of National Security Space, Fred Doyle

Programming Vice President, Alan Gans

Vice President Communications And Corporate Relat, Kathleen Pitre

Vice President Supply Chain, Tom Schranz

Vice President Global Business Services, Brian Gabbard

Vice President Information Technology And Services, Cheryl Martin

Vice President, Bob Hall

Vice President, Vikki Schiff

Vice President North American Supply Chain, James Strasser

Svp Commercial Global Beverage, Thomas Haensch

Vp Of Engineering, Larry Wetzel

Vice President And General Manager Civil Space, Makenzie Lystrup

Vice President And General Manager, Debra D Facktor

Vice President, Leon Petersen

Board Member, Michael Cave

Board Member, David R Hoover

Board Member, Daniel Heinrich

Board Member, Cathy Ross

Board Member, Stuart Taylor

Board Member, Dan Heinrich

Auditors: PricewaterhouseCoopers LLP

LOCATIONS

HQ: Ball Corp
  9200 West 108th Circle, Westminster, CO 80021
Phone: 303 469-3131
Web: www.ball.com

2017 Sales

	$ mil.	% of total
US	5,496	50
Brazil	1,427	13
Other	4,060	37
Total	**10,983**	**100**

PRODUCTS/OPERATIONS

2017 Sales

	$ mil.	% of total
Beverage packaging North and Central America	4,178	38
Beverage packaging Europe	2,360	22
Beverage packaging South America	1,692	15
Food and aerosol packaging	1,138	10
Aerospace	991	9
Other	624	6
Total	**10,983**	**100**

Selected Products

Packaging
  Aluminum beverage cans
  Metal food containers and ends
  Steel aerosol containers
  Extruded aluminum aerosol containers
  Aluminum slugs
  Paint and general line cans
Aerospace and technologies
  Aerospace hardware and components
  Antennas and video tactical systems
  Satellites and spacecraft
  Space-based instruments and sensors
  Radio frequency systems
  Technical services

COMPETITORS

Amcor	Saint-Gobain
Arconic	Containers
Ardagh Group	Sequa
Crown Holdings	Silgan
Reynolds Food	Teledyne Technologies
Packaging	Tetra Laval
Rio Tinto Alcan	

HISTORICAL FINANCIALS

Company Type: Public

Income Statement
FYE: December 31

	REVENUE ($ mil.)	NET INCOME ($ mil.)	NET PROFIT MARGIN	EMPLOYEES
12/19	11,474	566	4.9%	18,300
12/18	11,635	454	3.9%	17,500
12/17	10,983	374	3.4%	18,300
12/16	9,061	263	2.9%	18,450
12/15	7,997	280	3.5%	15,200
Annual Growth	9.4%	19.1%		4.7%

2019 Year-End Financials

Debt ratio: 45.03%	No. of shares (mil.): 324
Return on equity: 17.67%	Dividends
Cash ($ mil.): 1,798	Yield: 0.8%
Current ratio: 0.88	Payout: 33.9%
Long-term debt ($ mil.): 6,337	Market value ($ mil.): 20,994

	STOCK PRICE ($) FY Close	P/E High/Low	Earnings	Dividends	Book Value
12/19	64.67	47 26	1.66	0.55	9.08
12/18	45.98	38 27	1.29	0.40	10.31
12/17	37.85	76 35	1.05	0.37	11.26
12/16	75.07	99 77	0.82	0.26	9.82
12/15	72.73	75 59	1.00	0.26	4.40
Annual Growth	(2.9%)	— —	13.7%	20.6%	19.9%

Banc Of California Inc

Banc of California offers deposit and loan services at 35 branches in Southern California's Los Angeles Orange County and San Diego. Customers enjoy checking savings and money market accounts as well as mobile online and card payment services telephone banking automated bill payment safe deposit boxes direct deposit and wire transfers. Customers can also access their accounts through a nationwide network of 55000 surcharge-free ATMs. In addition to its branches the $9 billion-asset Banc of California operates around 70 mortgage loan production offices in California Arizona Oregon Indiana Idaho Nevada and Virginia.

Operations

Banc of California operates three core segments: Commercial Banking which offers commercial consumer and real estate secured loans as well as deposit accounts; Mortgage Banking which originates conforming SFR loans and sells the loans in the secondary market; and the Financial Advisory segment which purchases sells and manages SFR mortgage loans.

Unlike most retail banks Banc of California's income streams are less dependent on interest rates. The bank made 50% of its revenue from loan interest (including fees) during 2015 and another 5% from interest on investments. But it also made 29% of its revenue from its mortgage banking business while the rest came from other non-interest income sources.

Geographic Reach

The Irvine California-based bank has 90-plus banking locations in California including 35 branches in San Diego Orange Santa Barbara and Los Angeles Counties (as of mid-2016). It has 68 loan production offices in California Arizona Oregon Virginia Indiana Maryland Colorado Idaho and Nevada.

Sales and Marketing

The bank spent $6.2 million on advertising during 2015 or 23% more than in the prior year due to higher overall marketing costs tied to the bank's continued expansion.

Financial Performance

Banc of California's revenue has risen sevenfold since 2011 as a slew of bank acquisitions and organic growth have driven its loan and deposit business as well as its mortgage banking business.

The bank's revenue jumped 46% to $486.5 million during 2015 thanks to a 34% spike in loan interest income on more loan origination and loan and lease purchase activity; and thanks to a 52% rise in mortgage banking income as the bank originated and sold nearly twice as many mortgage loans on the secondary market than in 2014.

Strong revenue growth in 2015 caused Banc of California's net income to double to $62 million despite an uptick in salary and benefits cost that stemmed from additional hiring and commercial banking and mortgage banking expansion. The bank's operations used $45.24 million during the year or less than one-tenth as much cash as in 2014 mostly after adjusting its earnings for non-cash items related to proceeds of mortgage banking loans held-for-sale and proceeds from other loans held-for-sale.

Strategy

With its eye on becoming "California's Bank" Banc of California sometimes acquires smaller banks or bank branch networks to boost its loan and deposit business while expanding its branch network (mostly around California).

From 2010 through 2015 the bank has made seven acquisitions including three bank acquisitions (Gateway Bancorp Beach Business Bank and The Private Bank of California) and three other specialty financial firm acquisitions (Palisades Group which it divested in 2016; CS Financial; and Renovation Ready.)

Mergers and Acquisitions

In November 2014 the bank bought 20 branches in Southern California from Banco Popular North America (BPNA) along with $1.07 billion in loans and $1.08 billion in deposits for a total price of $24 million.

In January 2014 Banc of California purchased service contracts and intellectual property of RenovationReady a specialized loan services provider that served financial institutions and mortgage bankers that originated agency-eligible residential renovation and construction loan products.

Company Background

In 2012 it paid $15.5 million for Gateway Business Bank and $37 million for Beach Business Bank. The next year it took over The Private Bank of California for $25 million and bought The Palisades Group a residential mortgage investment advisory firm and specialty finance company CS Financial. In 2014 it announced plans to buy 20 branches of Banco Popular North America to reach California's Hispanic community.

In 2013 it sold eight branches to AmericanWest Bank in order to reshape its retail branch network to focus on servicing small - to midsized businesses and high net worth families.

EXECUTIVES

Evp Division General Counsel Lending, John F. Madden, age 59

Evp Enterprise Risk Analytics, Gilda Youdeem

Managing Director Institutional Banking And Fiduciary Services, Steven C. (Steve) Canup

Evp And Cfo Banc Of California Inc. And Banc Of California N.a., John A. Bogler

Evp And General Counsel Banking, Angelee J. Harris, age 50

Chief Investment Officer, Brian P. Kuelbs, age 57

Managing Director Community Banking, Gaylin D. Anderson

Vice Chairman And Evp, Jeffrey T. Seabold, age 53, $750,000 total compensation

President And Ceo, Douglas H. (Doug) Bowers, age 62

Chief Risk Officer, Hugh F. Boyle, age 60, $599,679 total compensation

Managing Director Warehouse Lending, Zoila Price

Evp And Chief Compliance Officer, Diane M. Summers

Evp Community Development, Gary S. Dunn

Evp And Cio, Ken Plummer

Evp Division General Counsel Banking, Manisha K. Merchant

Managing Director Construction Lending, Jim Fraser

Managing Director Cre Lending, Thomas Senske

Managing Director Sba Lending, Heather Endresen

Managing Director Commercial Banking, David Park

Chief Credit Officer, Paul Simmons

Managing Director Portfolio Lending, Julie Duong

Svp Operations, Robert Villaneda

Svp Marketing, Samantha Haugh

Managing Director Payment Solutions, Ben Kessler

Evp General Counsel And Secretary, John C. Grosvenor, age 70, $501,378 total compensation

Evp Private Banking, Jay D. Sanders

Vice President Client Service Officer, Christina Beltran

Vice President Credit Administration, Edward Massey

Executive Vice President, Chang Liu

Vice President, Warren Paez

Assistant Vice President Private Banking Officer, Joyce Jicka

Senior Vice President, Jerry Konzen

Vice President Information Technology Infrastructure, Len Tateyama

Assistant Vice President Credit Portfolio Manager, Aida Rodriguez

Vice President Deposit Operations Manager, Elizabeth Sevesind

Vice President, Justin Coleman

Vice President Information Technology, Curtis Yamasaki

Executive Vice President, Rita Dailey

Senior Vice President National Sales Manager, Adam Liebross

Senior Vice President Client Management, Todd Evett

Vice President Commercial Banking, John Treiber

Senior Vice President Commercial Lending, John Maclean

Executive Vice President, Jim Wiegandt

Vice President Payroll Manager, Dana King

Vp Consumer Credit Administrator Portfolio Manager, Nathan Hennigan

Evp Ciso, Chris Forbes

Senior Vice President Associate General Counsel, Brian Farrell

Svp Relationship And Manager Commercial Real Estate Lending, Warren Ramsey

Svp Business Manager Commercial Banking, Brian Ledermann

Senior Business Intelligence Developer, Dabao Rinna

Svp Portfolio Operations, Amber Mandir

Vice President Treasury Relationship Manager Deposits And Treasury Management, Francine Acuna

Vice President Senior Relationship Manager Business Banking, Dan Oriskovich

Senior Vice President Market Manager Business Banking, Timothy Nguyen

Vice President Relationship Manager Business Banking, Edward Bernabeo

Chairman, Robert D. Sznewajs, age 73

Board Member, Halle J Benett

Board Member, Bonnie G Hill

Board Member, Mary A Curran

Auditors: Ernst & Young LLP

LOCATIONS

HQ: Banc Of California Inc
3 MacArthur Place, Santa Ana, CA 92707
Phone: 855 361-2262
Web: www.bancofcal.com

PRODUCTS/OPERATIONS

2013 Sales

	$ mil.	% of total
Interest and dividend income		
Loans including fees	116	53
Securities and others	3	2
Noninterest income		
Net gain on mortgage banking activities	68	31
Gain on sale of branches	12	6
Net gain on sale of loans	8	4
Loan servicing income	2	1
Customer service fees	1	1
Others	4	2
Total	**217**	**100**

COMPETITORS

American Business Bank	East West Bancorp
Bank of America	JPMorgan Chase
Bank of the West	MUFG Americas Holdings
BofI	PacWest Bancorp
California Bank & Trust	Pacific Mercantile
	Pacific Premier
City National	Simplicity Bancorp
Comerica	U.S. Bancorp

HISTORICAL FINANCIALS

Company Type: Public.

Income Statement   FYE: December 31

	ASSETS ($ mil.)	NET INCOME ($ mil.)	INCOME AS % OF ASSETS	EMPLOYEES
12/19	7,828	23	0.3%	660
12/18	10,630	45	0.4%	741
12/17	10,327	57	0.6%	738
12/16	11,029	115	1.0%	1,797
12/15	8,235	62	0.8%	1,710
Annual Growth	(1.3%)	(21.3%)	—	(21.2%)

2019 Year-End Financials

Debt ratio: 2.22%	No. of shares (mil.): 50
Return on equity: 2.56%	Dividends
Cash ($ mil.): 373	Yield: 1.8%
Current ratio: —	Payout: 620.0%
Long-term debt ($ mil.): —	Market value ($ mil.): 874

	STOCK PRICE ($) FY Close	P/E High/Low		PER SHARE ($) Earnings	Dividends	Book Value
12/19	17.18	350	265	0.05	0.31	17.83
12/18	13.31	48	28	0.45	0.52	18.67
12/17	20.65	32	20	0.71	0.52	20.01
12/16	17.35	12	6	1.94	0.49	19.65
12/15	14.62	11	8	1.34	0.48	17.15
Annual Growth	4.1%	—	—	(56.0%)	(10.4%)	1.0%

BancFirst Corp. (Oklahoma City, Okla)

This Oklahoma bank wants to be more than OK. It wants to be super . BancFirst Corporation is the holding company for BancFirst a super-community bank that emphasizes decentralized management and centralized support. BancFirst operates more than 100 branches in more than 50 Oklahoma communities. It serves individuals and small to midsized businesses offering traditional deposit products such as checking and savings accounts CDs and IRAs. Commercial real estate lending (including farmland and multifamily residential loans) makes up more than a third of the bank's loan portfolio while one-to-four family residential mortgages represent about 20%. The bank also issues business construction and consumer loans.

Operations

The company operates three core units: metropolitan banks community banks and other financial service. Metropolitan and community banks offer traditional banking products such as commercial and retail lending and a full line of deposit accounts in the metropolitan Oklahoma City and Tulsa areas. Community banks consist of banking locations in communities throughout Oklahoma. Other financial services are specialty product business units including guaranteed small business lending residential mortgage lending trust services securities brokerage electronic banking and insurance.

The company's BancFirst Insurance Services arm sells property/casualty coverage while the bank's trust and investment management division oversees some $1.21 billion of assets on behalf of clients. Bank subsidiaries Council Oak Investment Corporation and Council Oak Real Estate focus on small business and property investments respectively.

Like other retail banks BancFirst makes the bulk of its money from interest income. More than 60% of its total revenue came from loan interest (including fees) during 2015 while another 2% came from interest on taxable securities. The rest of its revenue came from service charges on deposits (19% of revenue) insurance commissions (5%) trust revenue (3%) securities transactions (3%) and loan sales (1%).

Geographic Reach

BancFirst has 95 banking locations serving more than 52 communities across Oklahoma.

Sales and Marketing

The bank customers are generally small to medium-sized businesses engaged in light manufacturing local wholesale and retail trade commercial and residential real estate development and construction services agriculture and the energy industry.

BancFirst spent about $6.9 million for advertising and promotion during 2015 compared to $6.6 million in each of 2014 and 2013.

Financial Performance

BancFirst's annual revenues have risen 20% since 2011 thanks to continued loan asset and deposit growth (partly thanks to branch expansion). The company's annual profits have grown more than 40% over the same period as it's kept a lid on operating expenses and loan loss provisions.

BancFirst's revenue climbed 6% to $306.85 million during 2015 thanks to a combination of loan asset growth and gains on the sales of some of its securities.

Revenue growth in 2015 drove the company's net income up nearly 4% to $66.17 million. The bank's operating cash levels increased by almost 2% to $78.1 million with the rise in cash-based earnings.

Strategy

BancFirst's strategy focuses on providing a full range of commercial banking services to retail customers and small to medium-sized businesses in both the non-metropolitan trade centers and cities in the metropolitan statistical areas of Oklahoma. It operates as a 'super community bank' managing its community banking offices on a decentralized basis which permits them to be responsive to local customer needs. Underwriting funding customer service and pricing decisions are made by presidents in each market within the company's strategic parameters.

Mergers and Acquisitions

In October 2015 BancFirst purchased $196 million-asset CSB Banchsares and its Bank of Commerce branches in Yukon Mustang and El Reno in Oklahoma. The deal also added $148 million in new loan business and $170 million in deposits.

Company Background

The company has been buying smaller banks to expand in Oklahoma. In 2011 it acquired FBC Financial Corporation and its subsidiary bank 1st Bank Oklahoma with about five branches throughout the state. In 2010 BancFirst acquired Union Bank of Chandler Okemah National Bank and Exchange National Bank of Moore adding about another five branches. It acquired First State Bank Jones in 2009 to expand in eastern Oklahoma.

President and CEO David Rainbolt owns some 40% of BancFirst .

EXECUTIVES

Evp Investments Bancfirst, Robert M. Neville, age 64

Evp Financial Services Bancfirst, D. Jay Hannah, age 64

Evp Interim Cfo And Chief Risk Officer, Randy P. Foraker, age 64, $174,423 total compensation

Evp Human Resources Bancfirst, J. Michael Rogers, age 76

Evp And Head Operions Bancfirst, Scott Copeland, age 55

Sevp And Chairman Executive Committee, Dennis L. Brand, age 72, $525,000 total compensation

Vice Chairman And Ceo Council Oak Investment Corporation And Council Oak Real Estate Inc., William O. Johnstone, age 72, $200,000 total compensation

Evp And Chief Credit Officer Bancfirst, Roy C. Ferguson, age 73

Regional Executive Bancfirst, Karen James, age 64

President And Ceo Bancfirst, Darryl Schmidt, age 58, $350,000 total compensation

Regional Executive Bancfirst, David M. Seat, age 69

Evp And Cto Bancfirst, David Westman, age 64

Ceo, David R. Harlow, age 57, $325,000 total compensation

Regional Executive Bancfirst, Harvey G. Robinson, age 61

Evp Cfo And Treasurer, Kevin Lawrence, age 41, $214,231 total compensation

President Bancfirst Frederick, Jason McQueen

Evp And Chief Internal Auditor, Paul Fleming, age 69

Regional Executive Bancfirst, John Anderson, age 64

Executive Vice President, Debbie Kuykendall

Vice President, Tyler Smith

Senior Vice President, Patrick A Lippmann

Senior Vice President General Manager, Michael Kernan

Senior Vice President, Blane Allen

Senior Vice President Chief In, Scott Lewis

Senior Vice President Treasury Sales Director, Ashlea Briggs

Senior Vice President, Denise Duffle

Senior Vice President, Brian Renz

Vp Global Services, Michele Braselton

Vice President Lockbox Manager, Jennifer Seargent

Assistant Vice President, Tamara Reed

Assistant Vice President, Ben Purkeypile

Assistant Vice President Network Services, Dian Joysizemore

Vice President Marketing, Ben Harrington

Vice President Treasury Management Ctp, Luis Castillo

Executive Vice President, Sean Shadid

Vice President Consumer Lending, Shirley Myers

Senior Vice President Investments, Bob Neville

Senior Vice President, Kevin Calabrese

Senior Vice President, David Vinall

Svp, Greg Hoog

Executive Vice President, Janet W Gotwals

Senior Vice President, Kevin J Calabrese

Executive Vice President, Bob Winchester

Vice President, Delynn Rains

Assistant Vice President And Consumer Loan Officer, Jenny Gifford

Assistant Vice President, Dauna Dines

Assistant Vice President, Scott Hofmann

Assistant Vice President Commercial Loan Officer, Mary Johnston

Senior Vice President Corporate Banking, Matt Crew

Las Vice President, Teresa Richardson

Vice President Customer Service Officer, Karen Wilson

Senior Vice President, Mark C Demos

Senior Vice President, Trent Cronk

Vice Chairman, James R. Daniel, age 80

Vice Chairman, K. Gordon Greer, age 83

Chairman, David E. Rainbolt, age 64

Board Member, Ronald Norick

Board Member, Frank Keating

Auditors: BKD, LLP

LOCATIONS

HQ: BancFirst Corp. (Oklahoma City, Okla)
101 N. Broadway, Oklahoma City, OK 73102-8405
Phone: 405 270-1086   **Fax:** 405 270-1089
Web: www.bancfirst.com

PRODUCTS/OPERATIONS

2015 Sales

	$ mil.	% of total
Interest		
Loans including fees	190	63
Securities	6	2
Interest-bearing deposit	4	1
Noninterest		
Service charges on deposits	57	18
Insurance commissions	14	5
Security transactions	9	3
Trust revenue	9	3
Income from sale of loans	2	1
Cash management	7	2
Other	5	2
Total	**306**	**100**

Selected Subsidiaries

BancFirst
  BancFirst Agency Inc. (credit life insurance)
  BancFirst Community Development Corporation
  Council Oak Investment Corporation (small business investments)
  Council Oak Real Estate Inc. (real estate investments)
Council Oak Partners LLC
BancFirst Insurance Services Inc.

COMPETITORS

Arvest Bank	Midland Financial
BOK Financial	Southwest Bancorp
Bank of America	UMB Financial
International Bancshares	Wells Fargo

HISTORICAL FINANCIALS

Company Type: Public

Income Statement   FYE: December 31

	ASSETS ($ mil.)	NET INCOME ($ mil.)	INCOME AS % OF ASSETS	EMPLOYEES
12/19	8,565	134	1.6%	1,948
12/18	7,574	125	1.7%	1,906
12/17	7,253	86	1.2%	1,782
12/16	7,018	70	1.0%	1,773
12/15	6,692	66	1.0%	1,744
Annual Growth	6.4%	19.5%	—	2.8%

2019 Year-End Financials

Debt ratio: 0.31%
Return on equity: 14.14%
Cash ($ mil.): 1,868
Current ratio: —
Long-term debt ($ mil.): —
No. of shares (mil.): 32
Dividends
  Yield: 1.9%
  Payout: 31.3%
Market value ($ mil.): 2,041

	STOCK PRICE ($) FY Close	P/E High/Low		PER SHARE ($) Earnings	Dividends	Book Value
12/19	62.44	15	12	4.05	1.24	30.74
12/18	49.90	17	13	3.76	1.02	27.69
12/17	51.15	40	18	2.65	0.80	24.32
12/16	93.05	42	23	2.22	0.74	22.49
12/15	58.62	32	26	2.09	0.70	21.01
Annual Growth	1.6%	—	—	18.0%	15.4%	10.0%

BancorpSouth Bank (Tupelo, MS)

Like Elvis Presley BancorpSouth has grown beyond its Tupelo roots. It's the holding company for BancorpSouth Bank which operates some 290 branches in nine southern and midwestern states. Catering to consumers and small and midsized businesses the bank offers checking and savings accounts loans credit cards and commercial banking services. BancorpSouth also sells insurance and provides brokerage investment advisory and asset management services throughout most of its market area. Real estate loans including consumer and commercial mortgages and home equity construction and agricultural loans comprise approximately three-quarters of its loan portfolio. BancorpSouth has assets of $13 billion.

Geographic Reach

Mississippi-based BancorpSouth Bank operates in Alabama Arkansas Florida Illinois Louisiana Mississippi Missouri Tennessee and Texas. BancorpSouth's insurance and financial advisory businesses also operate in Illinois and Florida respectively.

Financial Performance

BancorpSouth reported net income of $94.1 million in 2013 an increase of 12% versus 2012. The decreased provision for credit losses was the primary factor contributing to the rise. Net interest revenue — the bank's primary source of revenue — fell 4% year over year to $$398.9 million the fourth consecutive year of decline. Net interest revenue declined because the decrease in interest expense was more than offset by the decrease in interest revenue as the yield on earning assets declined by a greater amount than that of interest-bearing liabilities. Noninterest income also declined on lower mortgage origination revenue in 2013 versus 2012.

Strategy

The regional bank has grown via the acquisition of other banks and insurance agencies and by opening new branches most recently in Texas and Louisiana. To reduce its reliance on interest-related revenue BancorpSouth hopes to diversify its revenue stream by increasing the amount it generates from mortgage lending insurance brokerage and securities activities. To this end subsidiary BancorpSouth Insurance Services has acquired small insurance agencies in Arkansas Missouri and Texas.

Mergers and Acquisitions

In 2014 BancorpSouth agreed to acquire Central Community Corp. the holding company for First State Bank Central Texas headquartered in Austin Texas. First State Bank operates 31 branches in Austin Round Rock Killeen and several other Central Texas communities. BancorpSouth has also agreed to purchase Ouachita Bancshares Corp. with a dozen branches in Louisiana. Both deals were announced in January 2014 and were expected to close promptly. However they've been delayed because BancorpSouth needs more time to get regulatory approvals and to meet "closing conditions necessary to complete" the mergers.

EXECUTIVES

Sevp Cfo And Treasurer, John G. Copeland, age 67
Evp And Corporate Secretary Bancorpsouth And Bancorpsouth Bank, Cathy S. Freeman, age 55
Chairman And Ceo Bancorpsouth Inc. And Bancorpsouth Bank, James D. (Dan) Rollins, age 61, $840,000 total compensation
Evp Bancorpsouth Inc. And Vice Chairman And Chief Lending Officer Bancorpsouth Bank, James R. Hodges, $382,500 total compensation
President And Coo, Chris A. Bagley, $495,000 total compensation
President Equipment Finance And Leasing, Kyle Gilliam
Sevp And General Counsel, Chuck Pignuolo, age 64
Executive Vice President, Clyde Guyse
Auditors: BKD, LLP

LOCATIONS

HQ: BancorpSouth Bank (Tupelo, MS)
One Mississippi Plaza, 201 South Spring Street, Tupelo, MS 38804
Phone: 662 680-2000
Web: www.bancorpsouth.com

PRODUCTS/OPERATIONS

2016 Sales

	$ mil.	% of total
Interest		
Loans & leases	440	58
Securities	41	5
Deposits with other banks	1	-
Noninterest		
Insurance commissions	115	15
Deposit service charges	43	6
Mortgage lending	41	5
Credit card debit card and merchant fees	37	5
Wealth management	21	3
Other	19	3
Total	**762**	**100**

Selected Subsidiaries

BancorpSouth Bank
  BancorpSouth Insurance Services Inc.
  BancorpSouth Investment Services Inc.
  BancorpSouth Municipal Development Corporation
  Century Credit Life Insurance Company
  Personal Finance Corporation

COMPETITORS

BBVA Compass Bancshares
Capital One
First Horizon
Great Southern Bancorp
Hancock Holding
Regions Financial
Renasant
SunTrust
Trustmark

HISTORICAL FINANCIALS

Company Type: Public

Income Statement   FYE: December 31

	ASSETS ($ mil.)	NET INCOME ($ mil.)	INCOME AS % OF ASSETS	EMPLOYEES
12/19	21,052	234	1.1%	4,693
12/18	18,001	221	1.2%	4,445
12/17	15,298	153	1.0%	3,947
12/16	14,724	132	0.9%	3,998
12/15	13,798	127	0.9%	4,002
Annual Growth	**11.1%**	**16.4%**	**—**	**4.1%**

2019 Year-End Financials

Debt ratio: 1.43%
Return on equity: 9.58%
Cash ($ mil.): 333
Current ratio: —
Long-term debt ($ mil.): —
No. of shares (mil.): 104
Dividends
  Yield: 2.2%
  Payout: 33.0%
Market value ($ mil.): 3,283

	STOCK PRICE ($) FY Close	P/E High/Low	PER SHARE ($) Earnings	Dividends	Book Value
12/19	31.41	14 11	2.30	0.71	25.69
12/18	26.14	16 11	2.23	0.62	22.10
12/17	31.45	20 16	1.67	0.14	18.97
12/16	31.05	22 13	1.41	0.45	18.40
12/15	23.99	20 15	1.33	0.35	17.58
Annual Growth	**7.0%**	**— —**	**14.7%**	**19.3%**	**9.9%**

Bank First Corp

EXECUTIVES

Chb, Robert S Weinert
Vice President, Bill Bradley
Vice President Of Business Banking, Brandon Suemnicht
Vp Of Agricultural Lending, Brad Rahmlow
Auditors: Dixon Hughes Goodman LLP

LOCATIONS

HQ: Bank First Corp
402 North 8th Street, Manitowoc, WI 54220
Phone: 920 652-3100   **Fax:** 920 652-3182
Web: www.bankfirstnational.com

HISTORICAL FINANCIALS

Company Type: Public

Income Statement   FYE: December 31

	ASSETS ($ mil.)	NET INCOME ($ mil.)	INCOME AS % OF ASSETS	EMPLOYEES
12/19	2,210	26	1.2%	284
12/18	1,793	25	1.4%	253
12/17	1,753	15	0.9%	249
12/16	1,316	14	1.1%	173
12/15	1,237	13	1.1%	—
Annual Growth	**15.6%**	**18.8%**	**—**	**—**

2019 Year-End Financials

Debt ratio: 3.10%
Return on equity: 13.20%
Cash ($ mil.): 53
Current ratio: —
Long-term debt ($ mil.): —
No. of shares (mil.): 7
Dividends
  Yield: 1.1%
  Payout: 21.3%
Market value ($ mil.): 496

	STOCK PRICE ($) FY Close	P/E High/Low	PER SHARE ($) Earnings	Dividends	Book Value
12/19	70.01	19 12	3.87	0.80	32.49
12/18	46.60	15 11	3.81	0.68	26.37
12/17	44.70	18 14	2.44	0.64	23.76
12/16	33.33	14 11	2.40	0.59	20.53
12/15	28.25	13 10	2.13	0.51	18.97
Annual Growth	**25.5%**	**— —**	**16.1%**	**11.9%**	**14.4%**

Bank of America Corp

Among the United States' largest banks by assets (alongside JPMorgan Chase and Citigroup) ubiquitous Bank of America Corporation operates one of the country's most extensive branch networks with nearly 4500 locations and roughly 17,000 ATMs. The bank's core services include consumer and small and middle-market businesses institutional investors large corporations and governments with a full range of banking investing asset management and other financial and risk management products and services. Its online banking operation counts nearly 40 million active users and about 30 million mobile users. Bank of America acquired Merrill Lynch in 2009 making it one of the world's leading wealth managers with about $2.5 trillion assets under management and boasting a beefed up trading and international businesses. Its US operations account for the vast majority of sales.

HISTORY

Bank of America predecessor NationsBank was formed as the Commercial National Bank in 1874 by citizens of Charlotte North Carolina. In 1901 George Stephens and Word Wood formed what became American Trust Co. The banks merged in 1957 to become American Commercial Bank which in 1960 merged with Security National to form North Carolina National Bank.

In 1968 the bank formed holding company NCNB which by 1980 was the largest bank in North Carolina. Under the leadership of Hugh McColl who became chairman in 1983 NCNB became the first southern bank to span six states.

NCNB profited from the savings and loan crisis of the late 1980s by managing assets and buying defunct thrifts at fire-sale prices. The company nearly doubled its assets in 1988 when the FDIC chose it to manage the shuttered First Republicbank then Texas' largest bank. The company renamed itself NationsBank in 1991.

In 1993 the company bought Chicago Research & Trading a government securities dealer and provider of oil and gas financing. A 1993 joint venture with Dean Witter and Discover to open securities brokerages in banks led to complaints that customers were not fully informed of the risks of some investments and that brokers were paying rebates to banking personnel for customer referrals. Dean Witter withdrew from the arrangement in 1994 and SEC investigations and a class-action lawsuit ensued. NationsBank settled the lawsuit for about $30 million the next year. (The company agreed to pay nearly $7 million to settle similar charges in 1998.)

NationsBank scooped up St. Louis-based Boatmen's Bancshares and Montgomery Securities (now Banc of America Securities) in 1997. The next year it bought Barnett Banks Florida's #1 bank.

Enter BankAmerica. Founded in 1904 as Bank of Italy BankAmerica had once been the US's largest bank but had fallen behind as competitors consolidated. The company's board of directors was pondering ways to become more competitive and in 1998 decided a merger was the best way. With the ink barely dry on its Barnett Banks deal NationsBank obliged.

After the merger the combined firm announced it would write down a billion-dollar bad loan to D.E. Shaw & Co. which followed the same Russian-investment-paved path of descent as Long-Term Capital Management. David Coulter (head of the old BankAmerica which made the loan) took the fall for the loss resigning as president; the balance of power shifted to the NationsBank side in 1999 when Kenneth Lewis took the post.

The Russian debacle and merger hiccups led the firm in early 1999 to reorganize and reduce overseas operations; it sold its private banking operations in Europe and Asia to UBS. Also that year it bought the recreational-vehicle financing unit of Associates First Capital (now part of Citigroup) 50% of Denver-based mutual fund firm Marsico Capital Management (it bought the rest in 2001) and BA Merchant Services. The bank also changed its name to Bank of America and began offering online banking through America Online. To avoid a court battle the bank settled charges that it retained proceeds from unclaimed bonds in California.

In 1999 the company earned the ire of labor officials for a program in which employees were recruited to maintain ATMs without being paid or provided supplies. EVP Frank Gentry who crafted the NationsBank/BankAmerica deal retired in 2000 signaling an end to the company's buying spree. Its focus turned inward as it set about the difficult integration of the two firms.

McColl retired as chairman in 2001. Later that year the company announced it would cease its subprime lending and car leasing operations.

In 2003 Bank of America's mutual fund chief Robert Gordon was among several employees who left the firm amidst a New York attorney general's investigation into hedge fund client Canary Capital Partners which allegedly had access to Bank of America's trading platform to make illegal after-hours trades of the company's erstwhile Nations Funds. Bank of America also paid $10 million for failing to provide documents to the SEC during its investigation of the scandal the largest-ever fine levied by the regulatory body for such an infraction.

The company sold its securities clearing and broker/dealer services units to ADP in 2004. In early 2005 the company struck a deal with regulators to implement tighter controls cut fees charged to investors exit the mutual fund clearing business and pay more than $500 million in fines including $140 million to settle complaints against FleetBoston. Also that year Bank of America remitted about another $460 million to settle investor claims that it did not adequately conduct due diligence when underwriting bonds of doomed telecom firm WorldCom in 2001 and 2002. (The claim involved 17 other investment banks as well; Citigroup paid more than $2.2 billion to clear itself of similar charges in late 2004).

Bank of America previously fattened up by purchasing northeastern banking behemoth FleetBoston for some $50 billion in 2004 and credit card giant MBNA for approximately $35 billion in cash and stock in early 2006. The latter deal roughly doubled the bank's credit card customer base (as well as its income from credit card fees) and gave the bank access to some 5000 organizations and institutions with which MBNA had affinity marketing relationships.

In early 2007 the company shed its venture capital arm BA Venture Partners (now Scale Venture Partners) to focus on middle-market private equity investments carried out by its BA Capital Investors unit.

In 2007 Bank of America bought U.S. Trust from Charles Schwab for more than $3 billion and acquired Chicago-based LaSalle Bank from Netherlands-based ABN AMRO for some $21 billion. Following the acquisition of U.S. Trust Bank of America merged the asset manager with its private banking and wealth management business to form U.S. Trust Bank of America Private Wealth Management. Prior acquisitions include credit card giant MBNA in 2006 a deal that doubled the bank's credit card customer base and its income from credit card fees.

In an effort to boost the economy and stimulate lending the US government in 2008 bought some $250 billion worth of preferred shares in the country's top banks. Approximately $45 billion of that was slated for Bank of America ($20 billion more than the original investment total). As a result of the government intervention US Treasury official (and so-called "pay czar") ordered then-CEO Lewis to receive no salary in 2009 and slashed compensation for other highly paid employees. Bank of America finished paying back the debt in late 2009.

As the global economy reeled from a credit freeze and subsequent recession in 2008 Bank of America added to its coffers by buying up troubled mortgage lender Countrywide Financial and investment bank Merrill Lynch. Countrywide had fallen on hard times as one of the hardest-hit victims of the subprime mortgage crisis. The deal was initially for $4 billion in stock but was finalized at around $2.5 billion as the economic climate sunk.

The Countrywide purchase made Bank of America the largest residential mortgage lender and servicer in the US. The company also settled a lawsuit contending that Countrywide engaged in deceptive lending practices. Bank of America agreed to pay more than $8 billion toward reductions on interest rates and principals of some 400000 troubled mortgage accounts. To avoid the stigma of the subprime loan crisis Countrywide was renamed Bank of America Home Loans in 2009.

Bank of America paid some $50 billion in stock to buy Merrill Lynch which had been crippled by the global credit crisis. Hoping to increase its up-front account fee revenues Bank of America began making a concerted push to cross-promote Merrill Lynch's wealth management business to the bank's affluent clients.

However the Merrill Lynch deal also brought its fair share of headaches. With the approval of Bank of America leadership the failed investment bank gave early bonuses worth billions to its executives prompting angry Bank of America shareholders and lawmakers to cry foul. The Securities and Exchange Commission slapped Bank of America with a $33 million fine for misleading shareholders about the bonuses. That fine was rejected by a federal judge in 2009 and the matter was ordered to go to trial. Bank of America ultimately agreed to pay $150 million in a settlement. In another Merrill Lynch-related settlement Bank of America agreed to pay $315 million in 2011 for claims that Merrill Lynch made false and misleading statements about its mortgage-backed securities sold to investors.

Then-CEO Ken Lewis in particular came under fire for not disclosing how bleak Merrill Lynch's financial condition was prior to the purchase; Lewis in turn said he had been implicitly pressured by the government to keep the troubles under wraps to prevent the deal from collapsing. A push to oust Lewis at the company's annual meeting in 2009 didn't pass but shareholders split the chairman and CEO positions to provide more accountability to the public. Director Walter Massey was named chairman and Lewis stepped down at the end of the year. Brian Moynihan the head of consumer and small business banking succeeded Lewis as CEO. Longtime Dupont CEO Charles Holliday took over as chairman in 2010 replacing the retiring Massey.

EXECUTIVES

Chairman And Ceo, Brian T. Moynihan, age 60, $1,500,000 total compensation

Chief Operations And Technology Officer, Catherine P. (Cathy) Bessant, age 59

Coo, Thomas K. (Tom) Montag, age 64, $1,000,000 total compensation

President Preferred And Small Business Banking And Co-head Consumer Banking, Dean C. Athanasia, age 53

President Retail Banking And Co-head Consumer Banking, Thong M. Nguyen, age 61

Vice Chairman And Head Global Wealth And Investment Management, Terence P. (Terry) Laughlin, age 65, $850,000 total compensation

Chief Risk Officer, Geoffrey S. Greener, age 55, $850,000 total compensation

Cfo, Paul M. Donofrio, age 59, $850,000 total compensation

Head Of Merrill Lynch Wealth Management, John Thiel

Head Merrill Lynch Wealth Management, Andy Sieg

Global Sponsorship Marketing Vice President, Tim Brant

Vice President, Michael Young

Vice President, Victor Ward

Svp Consumer Information Security, Brian Metzner

Vice President;gwim Senior Credit Underwriter, Teri Berry

Information Technology Team Manager Assistant Vice President, Leo Kaplin

Vice President, Paul Mccormac

Vice President Operations Project Consultant, Carol Rogers

Vice President Financial Governance, Rob Edwards

Vp Senior Technical Manager, John Syper

Vice President Human Resources Manager, Michelle John

Senior Vice President, Richard H Vitale

Vice President Small Business Banker, Carlos Gonzalez

Senir Vice President Enterprise Business And Community Events, Lori Rianda

Vice President Senior Technology Manager Applications Programming, John Kwok

Vice President Technology Project Manager, Bruce Mills

Vice President Business Enablement, Amanda Hite

Vice President, Debbie Kirk

Vice President;gwim Senior Credit Underwriter, Erin H Grow

Svp Mortgage Servicing Executive Svp Vendor Operations Executive, Aaron Menne

Svp Corporate Investments, Benjamin Tyner

Senior Vice President Leadership Development Executive, Stephanie Asbury

Vice President, Deborah Watson

Vice President, Myra Wardwell

Vice President Client Manager, Angela Meadows

Vice President, Teresa A Bednarski

Assistant Vice President;loan Administration Specialist, Annette Palmer

Vice President, John Waccard

Senior Vice President Business Executive Consumer Technology And Operations, Sudheer Omanakuttan

Senior Vice President Life Events Services, Sandra Agusti

Assistant Vice President Technology Audit Consultant, Marcela Sanchez

Vice President Head Of Business Lending, Marc Deville

Vice President Of Information Technology, Parthasarathi Bhattacharya

Vice President, Prasad Pedireddi

Vice President Senior Technology Manager, Janice Stlaurent

Vice President Banking Center Manager, Peter Ackermann

Assistant Vice President;gwim Document Administrator, Kimberly Lewis

Senior Vice President Channel Strategy And Dev Man, Colleen Sims

Vice President Of Customer, Scott Prince

Senior Vice President, Michael Hewlett

Vice President, Cynthia White

Vice President, Clay Walker

Vice President, Gene Werner

Vice President Human Resources, Stacey Moninski

Senior Vice President Business Control Manager Business Controls And Quality Assurance, Dan Peril

Vp Senior Client Manager Commercial Real Estate Banking Cdb Bank Of America Merrill Lynch, Valerie Williams

Vice President Operations Manager, Lauren Glad

Vice President Senior Tech Manager Gwim Branch Delivery Services, Joe Divita

Senior Vice President, Erin De Avila

Vice President Supplier Diversity Development Manager, Ed Franklin

Vice President Program Manager Centralized Sales, Victor Shetti

Senior Vice President, Tim Gauvin

Senior Vice President Senior Project Manager, Terry Lomas

Vice President Senior Technology Manager Systems Engineer Anly, Albert Hansen

Assistant Vice President, William Pagano

Assistant Vice President;gwim Loan Monitoring Specialist, Jacquelyn Capers

Senior Vice President Business Development, Alfred Hamilton

Senior Vice President, Robert Maloney

Senior Vice President, Thomas Gluckman

Senior Vice President;compliance Program Executive, Paige Brockmann

Senior Vice President, Stacey Ware

Vice President Senior Audit Consultant Corporate Audit Global Technology, Romelle K Parsons

Senior Vice President, Roy Woodham

Vice President Of Information Technology, Peter Montano

Vice President Infrastructure, Chris Ritchie

Vice President; Supplier Manager, Vonshe Jenkins

Vice President Enterprise Data Services, Giovanni Simeone

Vice President Sales Process Integration, Jason Marsilio

Senior Vice President Senior Credit Products Officer, Bill Franey

Senior Vice President, John Lenckos

Senior Vice President Quality And Reporting Manager, Belinda Eaton

Vice President Technology Architecture And Operations, Jim Drake

Vice President Small Business Card Services, Erin McCullen

Vice President Technology Manager, Steve Plair

Vice President Risk Technology, Lilian Okai

Senior Vice President Market Manager Pennsylvania Corporate Social Responsibility, Deborah O'brien

Vice President Marketing, Michele Ekarius

Vice President Ecommerce Channel Consultant, Jennifer Deisinger

Vice President, Susan Davis

Vice President Of Credit, Michael Boggess

Group Vice President, Robert Brown

Vice President Existing Customer Marketing Strategies, Alex Wisniewski Alex Wisniewski

Srvp Echannels Atm Channels, Ron Schnittman

Vice President Senior Technology Manager Apps Prog Erm Technology Group, Kalpesh Salot

Vice President, Pushpanjali Kottapalli

Vice President Commercial Information Officer, Julie Smith

Senior Vice President, Joyce Taylor

Vice President, Amy Larch

Avp Assistant Manager, Corey Schissler

Vice President Leveraged Finance, Michael Tynan

Vice President Unit Manager Corporation, Brian Greene

Vp; North Texas Project Manager, Wendy Morales

Assistant Vice President, Nikhil Nangia

Senior Vice President Portfolio Manager, Craig Murlless

Vice President, Alex Zhu

Senior Vice President Information Architecture Technolo, Michelle Boston

Assistant Vice President Intermediate Financial Analyst, Ryan Murtos

Vp Network Services Operations Governance, Steve Johnston

Vice President National Remarketing Manager, Jeannie Chiaromonte

Assistant Vice President, Christopher Hopkins

Vice President Small Business Banking, Mary Morris

Svp Core Checking Product Manager, Kelly Dinda

Vice President Product Delivery Senior Officer Credit, Stuart Dudley

Vice President; Operations Project Consultant Transportation Services Commercial Services, Dina Scott

Vice President, Bill Onisick

Vice President Campus Recruiter, Marisa Witherspoon

Assistant Vice President Quantitative Operations Associate, Ankit Tanwar

Senior Card Account Manager Vice President, Janet Jernigan

Vice President Tech Project Solutions Cnslt (tdm), Lynn Solowski

Vice President; Operations Project Consultant, Charles Martinez

Vice President Consultant System Engineer, Prajwal Shetty Prajwal Shetty

Vice President; Team Manager Systems Engineering Doss Utility Platform Management, Ed Chaconas

Vice President Senior Operations Consultant, Sylvia Coats

Vice President, Manish Bhargava

Assistant Vice President Senior Marketing Programs Development Manager I, Marcia Carneiro

Vice President Competitive Research, Himani Bahl

Vice President, Shontell Knox

Vice President Global Information Security, Benjamin Tweel

Vice President Learning Performance Solutions, Jennifer Banker

Vice President Operations, Beth Law

Assistant Vice President Process Design Consultant, Jennifer Montgomery

Vice President, Julie Wallis

Vice President, Allyson Webster

Process Design Consultant Vice President, Grisel Wallace

Senior Vice President Corporate Communications, Sharon Wilkerson

Assistant Vice President; Senior Credit Support Associate, Gayle Sellitto

Senior Vice President, Laurin Titus

Vice President, Torivia Whiten

Vice President, Terrie Wilkerson

Vice President, Karla Wargo

Vice President, Mary Wahlin

Vice President, Wanda White

Vice President, Eileen Webb

Vice President, Christopher Walford

Vice President, Marry Wanchik

Vice President, Beth Watson

Senior Vice President Of Organizational Development, Cynthia Bowman

Vice President Of Operations, Sethu Iyer

Assistant Vice President Business Support, Shannon Hart

Vice President Business Support Manager Strategic Portfolio Management (operational Risk), Brad Birkenholtz

Auditors: PricewaterhouseCoopers LLP

LOCATIONS

HQ: Bank of America Corp
Bank of America Corporate Center, 100 N. Tryon Street, Charlotte, NC 28255
Phone: 704 386-5681
Web: www.bankofamerica.com

2017 Sales by Region

	$ mil.	% of total
US	74,380	86
EMEA	7,907	9
Asia	3,405	4
Latin America	1,210	1
Total	**87,352**	**100**

PRODUCTS/OPERATIONS

2017 Sales

	$ mil.	% of total
Interest income	44,667	51
Non-interest income	42,685	49
Total	**87,352**	**100**

	% of total
Consumer Banking	39
Global Banking	22
Global Wealth & Investment Management	21
Global Markets	18
Total	**100**

Selected Products & Services

Capital raising and advisory
Card solutions
Equipment finance/leasing
Fraud prevention
Interest rate currency and commodity risk management
Investment solutions and management
Lending and financing
Liquidity management
Merchant services
Mergers and acquisitions
Payments/receivables management
Philanthropic management
Retirement and benefit plan services
Trade services

COMPETITORS

BB&T	JPMorgan Chase
Bank of New York Mellon	KeyCorp
	MUFG Americas Holdings
Capital One	Morgan Stanley
Citigroup	PNC Financial
Citizens Financial Group	RBC Financial Group
	State Street
Goldman Sachs	SunTrust
HSBC	U.S. Bancorp
HSBC USA	Wells Fargo

HISTORICAL FINANCIALS

Company Type: Public

Income Statement   FYE: December 31

	ASSETS ($ mil.)	NET INCOME ($ mil.)	INCOME AS % OF ASSETS	EMPLOYEES
12/19	2,434,079	27,430	1.1%	208,000
12/18	2,354,507	28,147	1.2%	204,000
12/17	2,281,234	18,232	0.8%	209,000
12/16	2,187,702	17,906	0.8%	208,000
12/15	2,144,316	15,888	0.7%	213,000
Annual Growth	**3.2%**	**14.6%**	—	**(0.6%)**

2019 Year-End Financials

Debt ratio: 9.79%
Return on equity: 10.35%
Cash ($ mil.): 161,560
Current ratio: —
Long-term debt ($ mil.): —

Dividends
Yield: 1.8%
Payout: 24.0%
Market value ($ mil.): —

	STOCK PRICE ($) FY Close	P/E High/Low	PER SHARE ($) Earnings	Dividends	Book Value
12/19	35.22	13 9	2.75	0.66	29.97
12/18	24.64	12 9	2.61	0.54	27.44
12/17	29.52	18 14	1.56	0.39	25.97
12/16	22.10	15 7	1.50	0.25	26.54
12/15	16.83	13 11	1.31	0.20	24.68
Annual Growth	**20.3%**	— —	**20.4%**	**34.8%**	**5.0%**

Bank of Hawaii Corp

Bank of Hawaii Corporation is the holding company for Bank of Hawaii (familiarly known as Bankoh) which has about 70 branches and 380-plus ATMs in its home state plus an additional dozen in American Samoa Guam Palau and Saipan. Founded in 1897 the bank operates through four business segments: retail banking for consumers and small businesses in Hawaii; commercial banking including property/casualty insurance for middle-market and large corporations (this segment also includes the bank's activities beyond the state); investment services such as trust asset management and private banking; and treasury which performs corporate asset and liability management services.

Operations

Bank of Hawaii operates through four segments including retail banking and commercial banking (which together account for about 85% of total net income) and investment services and treasury. The retail banking and commercial baking segments offer a range of financial products and services to consumers and small businesses and middle-market and large enterprises respectively. The company's investment services include private banking trust services and investment advisory services while the treasury segment includes corporate asset and liability management activities.

Bank of Hawaii generates nearly 60% of total revenue from interest and fees on loans. About 60% of its loan portfolio is made up of consumer loans (residential mortgage is the largest) with commercial loans accounting for the rest (commercial mortgage is the largest).

Geographic Reach

Bank of Hawaii provides a broad range of financial services and products to customers not only Hawaii but in Guam and other Pacific islands. Its principal offices are located in Honolulu.

Sales and Marketing

Bank of Hawaii spent about $6 million on advertising in 2017 and 2016 compared to $5.3 million in 2015.

Financial Performance

As Hawaii's real estate market continues to set records (in median sales prices for Oahu homes among other areas) Bank of Hawaii has seen consistent growth over the past five years with revenue up more than 15% since 2013. Net income has been on a similar trajectory rising just more than 20% during that time.

In 2017 the company reported revenue of $642.7 million which is up 5% from the prior year. The increase was powered by growth in the commercial and consumer lending portfolios as well as higher net interest margin; it was somewhat offset by a decline in noninterest income led by a nearly $7 million drop in mortgage banking income.

Net income rose 2% to $184.7 million in 2017 on the increase in revenue. The retail and commercial baking segments together account for 85% of total net income.

Cash at the end of fiscal 2017 was $447.8 million a decrease of $431.8 million from the prior year. Cash from operations contributed $175.1 million to the coffers while investing activities used $1 billion mainly because of net change in loans and leases and purchases of investment securities held-to-maturity. Financing activities provided another $415 million on a net change in deposits.

Strategy

A primary focus for Bank of Hawaii along with many other regional banks is modernizing and digitizing its business. It continues to renovate branches into what it calls the Branch of Tomorrow which includes updated technology interactive and private meeting spaces and more. In addition the company has introduced easy-deposit ATMs a Cardless Cash feature and enhancements to its mobile banking app.

Company Background

Bank of Hawaii traces its history to 1897 when businessman Peter Cushman Jones and friends Joseph Ballard Atherton and Charles Montague Cooke established a bank to serve the Hawaiian Islands. It was the first chartered and incorporated bank to do business in the Republic of Hawaii.

The company had branches on every major island in the archipelago by 1930. In 1971 it reorganized as a bank holding company.

EXECUTIVES

Sevp And Cfo, Dean Y. Shigemura
Evp Hawaii Commercial Group Bank Of Hawaii, Peter S. Ho, age 56, $776,077 total compensation
Vice Chairman And Chief Risk Officer, Mary E. Sellers, age 64, $427,565 total compensation
Vice Chairman Client Solutions Group, Sharon M. Crofts
Vice Chairman And Chief Administrative Officer, Mark A. Rossi, age 71, $433,776 total compensation
Vice Chairman; Chief Commercial Officer, Wayne Y. Hamano, $355,170 total compensation
Vice Chairman; Residential And Consumer Lending Group Manager, Derek J. Norris, age 70, $224,615 total compensation
Executive Vice President, Betty Brow
Senior Vice President, Galen Nakamura
Vice President, Rowell Comia
Vice President Of Operations, Andrew Boyles
Assistant Vice President And Operations Manager, Chris Onzuka
Senior Vice President, Lani Fernandez
Vice President Loan And Deposit Operations, Linda Bernal
Senior Vice President, Kevin Baptist
Vice President And Talent Acquisition Manager, Greg Chilson
Vice President Manager, John Hulihee
Vice President Of Cash Management, Bernie Alama
Vice President, Jonna Wickesser
Assistant Vice President And Grants Administrator, Paula Boyce
Vice President And Manager Product, Jennifer Lam
Senior Vice President And Contact Center Manager Operations, Doree J Ohelo
Vice President Of Lending, Cindy Okamura
Assistant Vice President Dealer Marketing Relationship Officer, Craig Ito
Vice President And Audit Consultant, Irene E B Kwan
Senior Vice President And Senior Audit Manager, James P Garcia
Vice President Commercial Credit Manager, Rita Jugo
Vice President, Tom Guinan
Vice President And Commercial Banking Officer, Jenny Kajioka
Senior Vice President, Terri Okada
Vice President, Kathleen Bryan
Assistant Vice President, Gil Farias
Svp And Manager, Mark Tokito
Vice President And Service Manager, Susan Marciel
Vice President, Toshiya Matsumoto
Vice President Audit Manager, Domingo Grace
Vice President, Dean Uyeda
Vice President And West Oahu Isb Area Manager Of Bank Of Hawaii, Charleen Deuprey
Vice President, Edison Kobayashi
Executive Vice President Human Resources, Lester Stiefel
Vice President, Miki Ikeda
Assistant Vice President And Customer Service Manager, Randi Yoshikawa
Vice President And Sales And Marketing And Client Development Manager, Dale Tanimoto
Senior Vice President, Brent Flygar
Senior Vice President, Ellen Mulholland
Vice President, Mario Subia
Vice President, Brian Watase
Senior Vice President Retail Deposits, Matt Emerson
Vice President, Malcom Lau

Financial Consultant And Vice President, Christopher Otto

Vice President And Manager Palau Island, Christina Michelsen

Senior Vice President, Shanae Souza

Senior Vice President, Kevin Sakamoo

Senior Vice President Director Of Corporate Security, Brian Ishikawa

Vice President, Randy Matsumoto

Vice President Private Client Services, Annalena Zanolini

Vice President, Rudy Alvior

Vice President, Helen Chang

Vice President Administration, Nelson Dang

Vice President, Paul Ramelb

Senior Vice President, Leilani Williams

Vice President, Natalie Fogle

Vice President Wealth Advisor, Helen Kim

Assistant Vice President And Senior Auditor, Jason Smith

Executive Vice President, Cynthia Wyrick

Vice President And Senior Portfolio Manager, David Okamoto

Vice President, Sharon Pati

Vice President Business Banking, Gregory Knue

Vice President Corporate Communications, Melissa Torres-laing

Senior Vice President Commercial Banking, Robert Mancini

Vice President And Private Wealth Advisor, Lisa Goo

Vice President Senior Portfolio Manager, Stephanie Nomura

Vice President, Janelle Higa

Vice President, Corey Shimabuku

Vice President, Jennifer Gershman

Vice President And Service Manager, Lisa Revilla

Vice President, Ryan Kitamura

Vice President, Amy Honda

Assistant Vice President Senior Consumer Loan Officer Dealer Indirect Lending Bank Of Hawaii, Cheryl Kaohi

Vice President Commercial Banking, Vincent Perez

Vp And Corporate Counsel, Val Ito

Vice President, Rosemarie Aquino

Assistant Vice President And Senior Auditor, Daniel Li

Vice President, Joseph Jaquay

Vice President And Lease Marketing Manager, Mark Carkin

Assistant Vice President Service Manager, Kimberly Holani

Vice President Commercial Banking Officer, Christopher Frost

Vice President, Gunjan Doshi

Vice President Strategy And Analytics Manager, Thanh T Tran

Vice President, Helene B Davis

Vice President, Holly Araki

Vice President And Manager Corporate Sourcing And Accounts Payable Department, Calla Oda

Senior Vice President, William Carpenter

Senior Vice President, Joel Tolentino

Vice President, Kawika Fiddler

Assistant Vice President, Ian Emberson

Senior Vice President, Lee Asuncion-yacapin

Vice President Commercial Banking Officer, Alison Lee

Vice President And Trust Officer, Eddie Quan

Vp It Server Administration, Christine Hirano

Vice President, Joshua Miller

Vice President Corporate Counsel, Steven Johnson

Vice President And Financial Advisor, Naalei Keaunui

Executive Vice President, Sheila Haunani Gomes

Vice President And Relationship Manager, Marissa Machida

Vice President Institutional Services, Keith Sato

Vice President Wealth Advisor, Helen Curlow

Vice President And Real Estate Manager Corporate Facilities, Michael Taylor

Executive Vice President, Jody Stange

Vice President And Senior Portfolio Manager, Ly Warren

Vice Chairman And Chief Strategy Officer, Kent T. Lucien, age 66

Vice Chairman, Donna A. Tanoue, age 66

Vice Chairman Consumer Banking Group, James C. (Jim) Polk

Secretary, Jill Rotolo

Secretary, SHERRY SERRANO

Board Member, Pamela Moy

Board Member, ROBERT WO

Board Member, ROB NICHOLS

Board Member, Robert Huret

Board Member, Barbara Tanabe

Board Member, Mark Burak

Board Member, Clinton Churchill

Board Member, Victor Nichols

Board Member, Raymond Vara

Board Member, Haunani Apoliona

Auditors: Ernst & Young LLP

LOCATIONS

HQ: Bank of Hawaii Corp
130 Merchant Street, Honolulu, HI 96813
Phone: 888 643-3888
Web: www.boh.com

PRODUCTS/OPERATIONS

2017 Sales

	$ mil.	% of total
Net Interest Income		
Interest and Fees on Loans and Leases	370	48
Income on Investment Securities	128	21
Other	4	-
Interest Expense	(46.5)	-
Non-interest Income		
Trust and Asset Management	45	8
Mortgage Banking	13	2
Service Charges on Deposit Accounts	32	6
Fees Exchange and Other Service Charges	54	9
Investment Securities Gains Net	10	2
Annuity and Insurance	6	1
Bank-Owned Life Insurance	6	1
Other	15	2
Total	**642**	**100**

Selected Products/Services

Personal
Banking Products
Checking
Savings
Special Packages
Loans & Lines
Mortgages
Credit Cards
Debit Cards
Online & Mobile Banking
IRAs
Small Business
Banking Products
Checking
Savings
Special Packages
Credit Card
Debit Card
Loans & Leasing
Trade & International
Business Services
Online Banking
Corporate & Commercial
Checking
Savings
Cash Management
Loans & Leasing
International Trade Services
Business Needs

COMPETITORS

American Savings Bank
Australia and New Zealand Banking
Bank of America
Central Pacific Financial
First Hawaiian
HSBC
Territorial Bancorp
Westpac Banking

HISTORICAL FINANCIALS

Company Type: Public

Income Statement

FYE: December 31

	ASSETS ($ mil.)	NET INCOME ($ mil.)	INCOME AS % OF ASSETS	EMPLOYEES
12/19	18,095	225	1.2%	2,124
12/18	17,143	219	1.3%	2,122
12/17	17,089	184	1.1%	2,132
12/16	16,492	181	1.1%	2,122
12/15	15,455	160	1.0%	2,200
Annual Growth	4.0%	8.9%	—	(0.9%)

2019 Year-End Financials

Debt ratio: 0.06%
Return on equity: 17.68%
Cash ($ mil.): 304
Current ratio: —
Long-term debt ($ mil.): —

No. of shares (mil.): 40
Dividends
  Yield: 2.7%
  Payout: 46.5%
Market value ($ mil.): 3,810

	STOCK PRICE ($) FY Close	P/E High/Low		PER SHARE ($) Earnings	Dividends	Book Value
12/19	95.16	17	12	5.56	2.59	32.14
12/18	67.32	17	12	5.23	2.34	30.56
12/17	85.70	21	17	4.33	2.04	29.05
12/16	88.69	21	13	4.23	1.89	27.24
12/15	62.90	19	15	3.70	1.80	25.79
Annual Growth	10.9%	—	—	10.7%	9.5%	5.7%

Bank of Marin Bancorp

Bank of Marin supports the wealthy enclave of Marin County north of San Francisco. The bank operates more than 20 branches in the posh California counties of Marin Sonoma and Napa as well as in San Francisco and Alameda counties. Targeting area residents and small to midsized businesses the bank offers standard retail products as checking and savings accounts CDs credit cards and loans. It also provides private banking and wealth management services to high net-worth clients. Commercial mortgages account for the largest portion of the company's loan portfolio followed by business construction and home equity loans.

Geographic Reach

Bank of Marin has branches in Alameda Corte Madera Emeryville Greenbrae Mill Valley Napa Novato Oakland Petaluma San Francisco San Rafael Santa Rosa Sausalito Sonoma and Tiburon.

Sales and Marketing

Its customer base is made up of individuals small to midsize businesses professionals and not-for-profit organizations.

Financial Performance

The bank makes its money through interest income and non-interest income such as service charges and fees. Interest income accounts for almost 90% of overall revenues. The bank has seen its revenue levels fluctuate over the years and in 2013 revenues fell 5% to $68 million due to lower yields on investments and new loans with lower interest rates.

Mergers and Acquisitions

In 2013 the bank gained a branch in Alameda with the purchase of NorCal Community Bancorp the holding company of the Bank of Alameda.

EXECUTIVES

President Ceo And Director Bank Of Marin Bancorp And Bank Of Marin, Russell A. (Russ) Colombo, age 67, $400,355 total compensation

Evp Retail Banking Bank Of Marin, Peter Pelham, age 63, $214,725 total compensation

Evp And Cfo, Tani Girton, age 60, $239,500 total compensation

Evp And Chief Credit Officer Bank Of Marin, Elizabeth Reizman, age 61, $221,250 total compensation

Evp Commercial Banking Bank Of Marin, Timothy D. (Tim) Myers, age 49, $215,000 total compensation

Evp And Cio, James T. Burke, age 65

Chairman Bank Of Marin Bancorp And Bank Of Marin, Brian M. Sobel, age 65

Auditors: Moss Adams LLP

LOCATIONS

HQ: Bank of Marin Bancorp
504 Redwood Boulevard, Suite 100, Novato, CA 94947
Phone: 415 763-4520
Web: www.bankofmarin.com

PRODUCTS/OPERATIONS

2015 Sales

Interest income	$ mil.	% of total
Interest and fees on loan	61	78
Interest on investment securities	7	10
Non-Interest income		
Wealth management & trust services	2	3
Service charges on deposit accounts	2	3
Debit card interchange fees	1	2
Others	3	4
Total	**78**	**100**

Selected Services
Business checking
Cash management
Credit cards
Floating home loans
Home equity lines
Lending
Online and mobile
Personal checking
Personal savings

COMPETITORS

Bank of America	MUFG Americas Holdings
Bank of the West	Patelco Credit Union
Citibank	SVB Financial
Community Bank of the Bay	U.S. Bancorp
	Wells Fargo
FNB Bancorp (CA)	Westamerica
First Republic (CA)	

HISTORICAL FINANCIALS

Company Type: Public

Income Statement				FYE: December 31
	ASSETS ($ mil.)	NET INCOME ($ mil.)	INCOME AS % OF ASSETS	EMPLOYEES
12/19	2,707	34	1.3%	306
12/18	2,520	32	1.3%	305
12/17	2,468	15	0.6%	313
12/16	2,023	23	1.1%	262
12/15	2,031	18	0.9%	274
Annual Growth	7.4%	16.7%	—	2.8%

2019 Year-End Financials

Debt ratio: 0.11%	No. of shares (mil.): 13
Return on equity: 10.48%	Dividends
Cash ($ mil.): 183	Yield: 1.7%
Current ratio: —	Payout: 31.6%
Long-term debt ($ mil.): —	Market value ($ mil.): 612

	STOCK PRICE ($) FY Close	P/E High/Low	PER SHARE ($) Earnings	Dividends	Book Value
12/19	45.05	19 16	2.48	0.80	24.81
12/18	41.24	38 16	2.33	1.27	22.85
12/17	68.00	57 46	1.28	0.56	21.46
12/16	69.75	39 25	1.89	0.51	18.81
12/15	53.40	36 30	1.52	0.90	17.67
Annual Growth	(4.2%)	— —	13.0%	(2.9%)	8.8%

Bank of New York Mellon Corp

The Bank of New York Mellon (BNY Mellon) is a New York state-chartered bank which houses the Investment Services businesses including Asset Servicing Issuer Services Treasury Services Clearance and Collateral Management as well as the bank-advised business of Asset. The firm boasts $37.1 trillion in assets under custody and administration and some $1.9 trillion in assets under management. BNY Mellon N.A. also offers wealth management services. Alexander Hamilton a founding father of the US and icon of the US $10 bill helped establish in 1784. The Bank of New York which merged in 2007 with Pittsburgh's Mellon Financial to form BNY Mellon.

HISTORY

In 1784 Alexander Hamilton (at 27 already a Revolutionary War hero and economic theorist) and a group of New York merchants and lawyers founded New York City's first bank The Bank of New York (BNY). Hamilton saw a need for a credit system to finance the nation's growth and to establish credibility for the new nation's chaotic monetary system.

Hamilton became US secretary of the treasury in 1789 and soon negotiated the new US government's first loan — for $200000 — from BNY. The bank later helped finance the War of 1812 by raising $16 million and the Civil War by loaning the government $150 million. In 1878 BNY became a US Treasury depository for the sale of government bonds.

The bank's conservative fiscal policies and emphasis on commercial banking enabled it to weather economic turbulence in the 19th century. In 1922 it merged with New York Life Insurance and Trust (formed in 1830 by many of BNY's directors) to form Bank of New York and Trust. The bank survived the crash of 1929 and remained profitable paying dividends throughout the Depression. In 1938 it reclaimed its Bank of New York name.

During the mid-20th century BNY expanded its operations and its reach through acquisitions including Fifth Avenue Bank (trust services 1948) and Empire Trust (serving developing industries 1966). In 1968 the bank created holding company The Bank of New York Company to expand statewide with purchases such as Empire National Bank (1980).

BNY relaxed its lending policies in the 1980s and began to build its fee-for-service side boosting its American Depositary Receipts business by directly soliciting European companies and seeking government securities business. The bank bought New York rival Irving Trust in a 1989 hostile takeover and in 1990 began buying other banks' credit card portfolios.

As the economy cooled in the early 1990s BNY's book of highly leveraged transactions and nonperforming loans suffered so the company sold many of those loans.

In the mid-1990s BNY bought processing and trust businesses and continued to build its retail business in the suburbs. It pared noncore operations selling its mortgage banking unit (and in 1998 moved its remaining mortgage operations into a joint venture with Alliance Mortgage); credit card business (1998); and factoring and asset-based lending operations (1999). In late 1997 and again in 1998 the bank tried to woo Mellon Bank (now Mellon Financial) into a merger but was rejected; it had better luck in 2006.

The growth of the firm's custody services accelerated in the late 1990s. In 1997 BNY bought operations from Wells Fargo Signet Bank (later part of First Union) and NationsBank (now Bank of America). By 1998 BNY had bought some two dozen corporate trust businesses. Two years later it acquired the trust operations of Royal Bank of Scotland and Barclays Bank.

During this period BNY also built its other operations largely through purchases. It bought the Bank of Montreal's UK-based fiscal agency business (1998) and Eastbrook Capital Management which manages assets for businesses and wealthy individuals (1999).

Scandal rocked the firm in 1999 when the US began investigating the possible flow of money related to Russian organized crime; the following year a former bank executive admitted to having laundered about $7 billion through BNY. The bank reached a non-prosecution agreement in the US in 2005 and four years later agreed to a $14 million settlement with Russia.

In 2000 BNY bought the corporate trust business of Dai-Ichi Kangyo Bank (now part of Mizuho Financial) and Harris Trust and Savings Bank. It also purchased a trio of securities clearing and processing firms in addition to hedge fund manager Ivy Asset Management. The next year BNY bought the corporate trust operations of U.S. Trust.

Purchases in 2002 included equity research firm Jaywalk institutional trader Francis P. Maglio & Co. and a pair of Boston-area asset managers for high-net-worth individuals Gannet Welsh & Kotler and Beacon Fiduciary Advisors. BNY bought Pershing from Credit Suisse First Boston in 2003.

Fallout from the money laundering scandal lingered. In 2006 the Federal Reserve accused the bank of not tightening its own controls to prevent a recurrence of illegal activity. But there were apparently no hard feelings between BNY and the federal government who tapped the company in 2008 to act as custodian for the US Treasury's $700 million Troubled Asset Relief Program (TARP) meant to provide liquidity to banks.

The Bank of New York jettisoned much of its traditional banking services for more lucrative fee-based securities and financial services swapping virtually all its retail branches in metropolitan New York for JPMorgan Chase's corporate trust business in 2006. Both units were valued at more than $2 billion each and JPMorgan Chase paid an additional $150 million in cash to make up the difference.

In 2007 Bank of New York merged with Mellon Financial to create BNY Mellon). It was the New York company's third attempt to acquire the Pittsburgh-based firm. The deal cemented the company's status as one of the largest securities servicing companies in the world and augmented its other areas of focus including asset management and corporate trust and treasury services.

The company followed that transaction with the sale of Mellon 1st Business Bank to U.S. Bancorp in 2008.

In 2009 the company acquired Insight Investment Management which specializes in liability-driven investment services fixed income products and alternative investments from Lloyds Bank for some $387 million. Also that year BNY Mellon bought analytics firm Portsmouth Financial Systems. The acquisition offered customers more transparency in structured credit portfolios.

In 2010 BNY Mellon sold one of the last remnants of Mellon Financial's banking operations the Florida-based Mellon United National Bank to Banco de Sabadell. Mellon had previously sold most of its retail business to Royal Bank of Scotland's US banking arm Citizens Financial Group in 2001. In 2015 looking to bolster its Investment Management business BNY bought New York-based Cutwater Asset Management which boasts some $23 billion in assets. The acquired company works closely with one of BNY Mellon's premier investment firms and leading European asset manager Insight Investment.In 2016 BNY Mellon bought California-based Atherton Lane Advisors one of the Menlo Park region's investment managers as well as its $2.5 billion in assets under management and 700 high net worth clients. The deal moved BNY into a key wealth market for a national and global expansion strategy.

EXECUTIVES

Chairman And Ceo, Gerald L. Hassell, age 68, $1,000,000 total compensation
Ceo Clearing Markets And Client Management, Thomas P. (Todd) Gibbons, age 63, $650,000 total compensation
Ceo Investment Management, Mitchell E. Harris, $625,000 total compensation
Sevp And General Counsel, J. Kevin McCarthy, age 56
Ceo Pershing, Lisa Dolly
Ceo Global Asset Servicing And Chairman Europe Middle East And Africa (emea), Hani Kablawi
Sevp And Chief Human Resources Officer, Monique R. Herena
Sevp And Head Client Service Delivery, Doug Shulman
Sevp And Chief Risk Officer, James S. (Jim) Wiener
Ceo Exchange Traded Funds, Jeff McCarthy
Chairman Asia Pacific, J. David Cruikshank
Ceo Issuer Services, Francis J. (Frank) La Salla
Ceo Alternative Investment Services (ais) And Structured Products, Chandresh Iyer
Sevp And Cio, Bridget E. Engle
Cfo, Michael P. Santomassimo
Ceo Bny Mellon Markets, Michelle M. Neal
Senior Vice President, John Weisenhorn
Assistant Vice President Systems And Technology, Rebecca Stalker
Vice President Relationship Manager, Mary Snyder
Vice President Director Of Sales, Donna Nemecek
Vice President, Robert Dawson
Assistant Vice President Systems, Kenneth Kenneth Newman Newman
Vice President Information Technology Manager, James Milella
Vice President Messaging Engineering, Anwar Ahmed
Vice President Information Technology, Joseph Aboulafia
Vice President, Keith Koble
Vice President Of Human Resources Business Partner, Louise Lisi

Senior Vice President And Director Of Employee Benefits, Robert Perego
Vice President, Patricia Gallagher
Vice President Business Analysis Quality, Lynn Leshe
Vice President Global Trade Finance Servs Div, Andrea Ratay
Vice President, Randolph Medrano
Vice President, Cary Jones
Vice President, Ellie Whalen
Vice President, Raymond Connery
Assistant Vice President, Jeffrey Roe
Vice President, Joseph Schnorr
Senior Vice President Legal Affairs, Bill Robinson
Vice President Of Information Technology, Gopinath Tatachar
Financial Analyst Vice President Corporate Trust, Evelina Lotte
Assistant Vice President Investments, Remy Quito
Vice President, Edward Dougherty
Assistant Vice President, John Rushmore
Vice President, David Sunderwirth
Assistant Vice President, Ann Lynch
Vice President, Gordon Wong
Vice President, Mary Milner
Vice President Customer Technology Solutions Delivery, Carl Hagelin
Vice President, Charles Baker
Vice President, Justin Verdesca
Vice President, Brian Stern
Assistant Vice President Information Security, Sam Dekay
Assistant Vice President, Panagiota Bouboulis
Vice President And Relationship Manager, Mark Hochgesang
Vice President, Brian Weddington
Vice President, Melinda Valentine
Assistant Vice President Business Services Group, Danny Wong
Vice President, Paul Angotta
Vice President, Elizabeth Wagner
Vice President, Claudia Leslie
Vice President, Brenda Stone
Vice President North American Banks Division, Joseph Barnes
Vice President, Reyne Macadaeg
Vice President Application Development, Brian Burton
Assistant Vice President, Glenn Obando
Vice President, Peter Helt
Assistant Vice President, Kerri Shenkin
Vice President, Paul Meskiewicz
Vice President, Rebecca Newman
Vice President, Derrick Cornelious
Vice President Relationship Manager Long Island Queens Brooklyn Regional Commercial Banking, Gail Rnian-bivona
Senior Vice President Customer Care, Bruce Falkin
Vice President, Larisa Turetsky
Vice President, Peter Holland
Executive Vice President, John Moore
Vice President Information Risk Management, Michael Lam
Vice President Of Information Solutions, Peter Farrell
Vice President Marketing Communications, Geraldine Lutzel
Vice President, David Cook
Vice President U S Corporate Banking, Mark O'Connor
Vice President, Lawrence Timmins
Vice President, Ron Giromonte
Vice President, Irene Kugel
Vice President, Carol Turi
Vice President, Joseph Sierra
Vice President Of Information Technology, Jola Shirinian
Vice President Of Sales, Sarah Foster
Vice President Human Resources, Susan McFarlan

Vice President Of Information Technology Learning, Michael Dermody
Assistant Vice President Internal Audit, Maria Dolinski
Vice President Benefits Disbursements, Steve Coates
Vice President It Procurement Bank Of New York Mellon, Rich Castman
Assistant Vice President; Critical System Engineer, Dan Gaffney
Senior Vice President, Douglas Owen
Vice President Global Corporate Trust, Mike Maio
Vice President, Timothy Fitzgerald
Vice President, Wayne Ross
Assistant Vice President, Clarence Burleigh
Assistant Vice President, Karen O'Donohoe
Assistant Vice President Technology Global Markets And Ecommerce, Vadim Kazakevich
Assistant Vice President, Neil Grill
Assistant Vice President, Jeff Charmatz
Senior Vice President Chief Information Officer, Kurt Wetzel
Senior Vice President, James McTiernan
Assistant Vice President Corporate General Services, Patrick Koziol
Executive Vice President The Bank Of New York, John R Mohr
Executive Vice President The Bank Of New York, Thomas V Ford
Assistant Vice President Enterprise Bi Architect, Ron Van Der Laan
First Vice President Operations Strategy Group, Mary Hannon
Vice President, Jeffrey Wolf
Vp Alternative Investment Services, Thomas Ryder
Vice President, Karen Manning
Executive Vice President The Bank Of New York, William Kerr
Vice President, Larnie Richardson
Vice President, Hussain Shaik
Vp Markets Technology, Christopher Simons
Assistant Vice President Project Manager, Richard Ludwig
Vice President, Kristine Gullo
Vice President Information Technology Asset, Karen Saxton
Middle Office Manager Vice President, Christopher Hart
Vice President, Sean Grace
Middleware Specialist Iii Vice President, Mark Barnett
Vice President Corporate Events, Kat Fleming
Vice President, John Sabatino
Vice President Unix Specialist Systems Engineer, Shannon Hughes
Vice President Ais, Mit Desai
Vice President, Andre Schneider
Vice President Treasury Risk Management Within The Enterprise Audit Function, Francis Feola
Vice President Internal Communications Manager Corporate Communications, Michael Soloway
Vice President Sec And Shareholder Reporting, Basel Masry
Vice President Information Security, Donald Lorenz
Vice President Team Leader Financial Reporting, Suzanne Jordan
Vice President, William Ewing
Vice President, Stacey Swentkowsky
Vice President, Heather Hinojosa
Vice President, Housto Earl Cockrell
Vice President And Cao, Joshua Tkalcevic
Vice President, Carolyn Lauro
Vice President Global Institutional Accounting, Dena Dojcak
Vice President Information Technology Project Manager, Steve Capizzi
Vice President Itcollaborationservices, Courtney Kane

Vice President Intelligent Process Automation (rpa Ai MI), Sidney Prescott
Vp Risk Technology, Tina Rojtas
Board Member, Thomas J Mastro
Assistant Treasurer, Wendy Havener
Assistant Treasurer Of Information Security, Nicholas Aromando
Assistant Treasurer, Cheryl Baye
Assistant Treasurer, David Rocco
Assistant Treasurer, Daniel Giles
Assistant Treasurer, Nina Cheung
Assistant Treasurer, Denise Freytas
Auditors: KPMG LLP

LOCATIONS

HQ: Bank of New York Mellon Corp
240 Greenwich Street, New York, NY 10286
Phone: 212 495-1784
Web: www.bnymellon.com

PRODUCTS/OPERATIONS

2016 Revenue

	$ mil.	% of total
Investment servicing fees		
Asset servicing	4,244	27
Clearing services	1,404	9
Issuer services	1,026	7
Treasury services	547	3
Interest net	3,138	22
Investment management & performance fees	3,350	23
Foreign exchange & other trading revenue	701	4
Investment & other income	341	2
Financing-related fees	219	1
Distribution & servicing	166	1
Net securities gains	75	1
Income from consolidated investment management funds	26	-
Total	**15,237**	**100**

Selected Subsidiaries and Business Lines

BNY Capital Funding LLC - State of Organization: Delaware
BNY Capital Markets Holdings Inc. - State of Incorporation: New York
BNY Capital Resources Corporation - State of Incorporation: New York
BNY International Financing Corporation - Incorporation: United States
BNY Mellon Capital Markets LLC - State of Organization: Delaware
BNY Mellon Fund Managers Limited - Incorporation: England
BNY Mellon Global Management Limited - Incorporation: Ireland
BNY Mellon International Asset Management Group Limited - Incorporation: England
BNY Mellon International Asset Management (Holdings) Limited - Incorporation: England and Wales
BNY Mellon International Asset Management (Holdings) No. 1 Limited - Incorporation: England and Wales
BNY Mellon Investment Management Cayman Ltd. - Incorporation: Cayman Islands
BNY Mellon Investment Management EMEA Limited - Incorporation: England
BNY Mellon Investment Management Europe Holdings Limited - Incorporation: England
BNY Mellon Investment Management (Europe) Limited - Incorporation: England
BNY Mellon Investment Management (Jersey) Limited - Incorporation: Jersey
BNY Mellon Investment Servicing (US) Inc. - State of Incorporation: Massachusetts
BNY Mellon National Association - Incorporation: United States
BNY Mellon Securities Services (Ireland) Limited - Incorporation: Ireland
BNY Mellon Trust Company (Ireland) Limited - Incorporation: Ireland
BNYM GIS Funding I LLC - State of Organization: Delaware
BNYM GIS Funding III LLC - State of Organization: Delaware
BNYM GIS (UK) Funding II LLC - State of Organization: Delaware
Insight Investment Funds Management Limited - Incorporation: England
Insight Investment Management (Global) Limited - Incorporation: England
Insight Investment Management Limited - Incorporation: England
MAM (MA) Holding Trust - State of Incorporation: Massachusetts
MBC Investments Corporation - State of Incorporation: Delaware
Mellon Canada Holding Company - Incorporation: Canada
Mellon Overseas Investment Corporation - Incorporation: United States
Pershing Group LLC - State of Organization: Delaware
Pershing Holdings (UK) Limited - Incorporation: England
Pershing Limited - Incorporation: England
Pershing LLC - State of Organization: Delaware
Pershing Securities Limited - Incorporation: England
Standish Mellon Asset Management Company LLC - State of Organization: Delaware
The Bank of New York Mellon - State of Organization: New York
The Bank of New York Mellon (International) Limited - Incorporation: England
The Bank of New York Mellon (Luxembourg) S.A. - Incorporation: Luxembourg
The Bank of New York Mellon SA/NV - Incorporation: Belgium
The Dreyfus Corporation - State of Incorporation: New York
Walter Scott & Partners Limited - Incorporation: Scotland

COMPETITORS

Bank of America	JPMorgan Chase
Barclays	Morgan Stanley
BlackRock	Northern Trust
Charles Schwab	PNC Financial
Citigroup	Prudential
Credit Suisse (USA)	State Street
Deutsche Bank	U.S. Bancorp
Franklin Templeton	Wells Fargo
HSBC	

HISTORICAL FINANCIALS

Company Type: Public

Income Statement   FYE: December 31

	ASSETS ($ mil.)	NET INCOME ($ mil.)	INCOME AS % OF ASSETS	EMPLOYEES
12/19	381,508	4,441	1.2%	48,400
12/18	362,873	4,266	1.2%	51,300
12/17	371,758	4,090	1.1%	52,500
12/16	333,469	3,547	1.1%	52,000
12/15	393,780	3,158	0.8%	51,200
Annual Growth	(0.8%)	8.9%	—	(1.4%)

2019 Year-End Financials

Debt ratio: 7.21%
Return on equity: 10.82%
Cash ($ mil.): 114,683
Current ratio: —
Long-term debt ($ mil.): —

No. of shares (mil.): 900
Dividends
  Yield: 2.3%
  Payout: 30.5%
Market value ($ mil.): 45,331

	STOCK PRICE ($) FY Close	P/E High/Low		PER SHARE ($) Earnings	Dividends	Book Value
12/19	50.33	12	9	4.51	1.18	46.06
12/18	47.07	14	11	4.04	1.04	42.31
12/17	53.86	15	12	3.72	0.86	40.70
12/16	47.38	16	10	3.15	0.72	37.05
12/15	41.22	17	13	2.71	0.68	35.05
Annual Growth	5.1%	—	—	13.6%	14.8%	7.1%

Bank OZK

Bank of the Ozarks is the holding company for the bank of the same name which has about 260 branches in Alabama Arkansas California the Carolinas Florida Georgia New York and Texas. Focusing on individuals and small to midsized businesses the $12-billion bank offers traditional deposit and loan services in addition to personal and commercial trust services retirement and financial planning and investment management. Commercial real estate and construction and land development loans make up the largest portion of Bank of the Ozarks' loan portfolio followed by residential mortgage business and agricultural loans. Bank of the Ozarks grows its loan and deposit business by acquiring smaller banks and opening branches across the US.

Operations

The bank makes three-fourths of its total revenue from interest income while the rest comes from fee-based sources. About 43% of Bank of the Ozark's total revenue came from non-purchased loan interest in 2014 while another 26% came from interest on purchased loans and a further 8% came from interest on its investment securities. The rest of its revenue came from service charges on deposit accounts (8% of revenue) mortgage lending income (1%) trust income (1%) and other non-recurring sources.

Geographic Reach

Bank of the Ozarks had 174 branches in eight states at the end of 2014 with 81 of them in Alabama and another 75 branches split among Georgia North Carolina and Texas. It has two loan offices in Houston and Manhattan that serve as an extension of the bank's Dallas-based Real Estate Specialties Group.

Sales and Marketing

The bank spent $3.03 million on advertising and public relations expenses in 2014 compared to $2.2 million and $4.09 million in 2013 and 2012 respectively.

Financial Performance

Bank of the Ozarks' annual revenues and profits have doubled since 2010 mostly as its loan assets have doubled from recent bank acquisitions spawning higher interest income.

The bank's revenue jumped 31% to $376 million during 2014 mostly thanks to strong purchased and non-purchased loan asset growth during the year from recent bank acquisitions. Its non-interest income grew 12% thanks to a 20% increase in deposit account service charges stemming from newly acquired deposit customers.

Strong revenue growth in 2014 boosted Bank of the Ozarks' net income by 30% to $119 million for the year. Its operating cash levels jumped 22% to $61 million during the year mostly thanks to higher cash earnings.

Strategy

Bank of the Ozarks continues its strategy of loan and deposit volume growth by acquiring smaller banks in new and existing geographic markets. It has also opened new branches and loan offices sparingly. During 2014 for example the bank opened retail branches in Bradenton Florida; Cornelius North Carolina; and Hilton Head Island South Carolina along with a new loan production office in Asheville North Carolina.

Mergers and Acquisitions

In July 2016 Bank of the Ozarks acquired Georgia-based Community & Southern Holdings and its Community & Southern Bank subsidiary. Adding some 45 branch locations in Georgia plus another in Florida it was the company's largest acquisition to-date.

Also in July 2016 the bank purchased C1 Financial along with its 32 CI Bank branches on the west coast of Florida and in Miami-Dade and Orange Counties. The deal added $1.7 billion in total assets $1.4 billion in loans and $1.3 billion in deposits. This transaction was the bank's fifteenth acquisition in the past six years.

In August 2015 the bank purchased Bank of the Carolinas Corporation (BCAR) — and its eight Bank of the Carolinas branches in North Carolina $345 million in total assets $277 million in loans and $296 million in deposits — for a total price of $65.4 million.

In February 2015 Bank of the Ozarks bought Intervest Bancshares Corporation and its seven Intervest National Bank branches in (five in Clearwater Florida and two more in New York City and Pasadena Florida) for $238.5 million. The deal added $1.5 billion in assets including $1.1 billion in loans and $1.2 billion in deposits.

In May 2014 it bought Arkansas-based Summit Bancorp Inc. and its 23 Summit Bank branches across Arkansas for $42.5 million though it closed more than a handful of them later in the year.

In March 2014 the company acquired Houston-based Bancshares Inc. and its subsidiary Omnibank N.A. for $21.5 million adding three branches in Houston Texas and a branch each in Austin Cedar Park Lockhart and San Antonio.

Company Background

The expansion strategy of Bank of the Ozarks - which had a mere five branches in Arkansas 20 years ago — centered on opening new locations in smaller communities in Arkansas. But with the financial crash the bank was able to expand to more states through a series of FDIC-assisted transactions to take over failed banks. It bought Chestatee State Bank First Choice Community Bank Horizon Bank Oglethorpe Bank Park Avenue Bank Unity National and Woodlands Bank.

Chairman and CEO George Gleason initially bought the bank more than three decades ago at age 25.

EXECUTIVES

Chief Credit Officer Bank Of The Ozarks, Darrel Russell, age 66, $252,308 total compensation
Chairman; Chief Executive Officer Of The Company And The Bank, George G. Gleason, age 66, $1,730,769 total compensation
President Leasing Division Bank Of The Ozarks, Scott Hastings, age 62, $181,925 total compensation
President Mortgage Division Bank Of The Ozarks, Gene Holman, age 72, $150,042 total compensation
President Trust And Wealth Management Division Bank Of The Ozarks, Rex Kyle, age 63, $241,674 total compensation
President Real Estate Specialties Group Bank Of The Ozarks, Dan Thomas, age 57, $1,242,308 total compensation
Evp And Controller, Greg McKinney, age 52, $368,077 total compensation
Chief Operating Officer And Chief Banking Officer Of The Company And The Bank, Tyler Vance, age 45, $366,923 total compensation
President Western Division, Don Keesee
Senior Vice President Market Leader, Russell Hewatt
Senior Vice President Of Information Systems, Malcolm Hicks
Vice President Payment Systems, Paula Shaw
Senior Vice President, Chris Bragg
Senior Vice President Retail Banking Manager, Bob Moore
Vice President Regional Manager, Lisa Amato
Vice President Commercial Loan Officer, Austin Simpson
Vice President Lending, Erik Larson

Assistant Vice President Community Development Officer, Kimberly L Marshall
Vice President Marketing, Mark Greenhaw
Senior Vice President Treasury Management, Steve Woodruff
Assistant Vice President Branch Operations Manager, Fabian Garantiva
Senior Vice President Commercial Lender, Jeni Chokron
Vice President, Eric Teague
Senior Vice President, Ryan Tanner
Assistant Vice President Branch Manager, Pam Toney
Assistant Vice President Branch Manager, Derek Labrosse
Assistant Vice President Community Development Officer, Joann Smith
Executive Vice President, David Sarner
Executive Vice President, Martin Ball
Senior Vice President, Aram Zakian
Vice President Loan Officer, Dawn Speas
Vice President Treasury Management Wire Manager, Mona Kalchik
Auditors: PricewaterhouseCoopers LLP

LOCATIONS

HQ: Bank OZK
18000 Cantrell Road, Little Rock, AR 72223
Phone: 501 978-2265   **Fax:** 501 978-2224
Web: www.bankozarks.com

PRODUCTS/OPERATIONS

2014 Sales

	$ mil.	% of total
Interest income		
Non-purchased loans and leases	162	43
Purchased loans	98	26
Investment securities	30	8
Non-interest income		
Service charges on deposit accounts	26	8
Other income from purchased loans net	14	4
Others	43	11
Total	**376**	**100**

Selected Services

Personal Banking
Apple PayChecking AccountsCredit CardsFree Bill PayFREE Debit CardsCustom Debit Card CardsMobile BankingMortgage LoansM KeeperOnline BankingOverdraft Prote LoansReloadable Spending CardsRetir   .nt PlanningReorder ChecksSafe
Business Banking
Business ProductsApple Pay for BusinessDebit CardEMV Chip CardsBusiness Credit CardsChecking & Money MarketCommercial LoansExpress DepositMerchant ProcessingOnline BankingOverdraft ProtectionReorder ChecksTreasury Management Services
Online & Mobile Banking
Online BankingMobile BankingMobile DepositOnline Bill Pay
Wealth Management Services
Investment ProgramsFinancial PlanningCustomer Service

COMPETITORS

Arvest Bank	IBERIABANK
BOK Financial	JPMorgan Chase
BancorpSouth	Regions Financial
Bank of America	Simmons First
Bear State Financial	SunTrust
Cullen/Frost Bankers	Wells Fargo
Home BancShares	

HISTORICAL FINANCIALS

Company Type: Public

Income Statement

FYE: December 31

	ASSETS ($ mil.)	NET INCOME ($ mil.)	INCOME AS % OF ASSETS	EMPLOYEES
12/19	23,555	425	1.8%	2,774
12/18	22,388	417	1.9%	2,563
12/17	21,275	421	2.0%	2,400
12/16	18,890	269	1.4%	2,315
12/15	9,879	182	1.8%	1,642
Annual Growth	24.3%	23.6%	—	14.0%

2019 Year-End Financials

Debt ratio: 2.95%
Return on equity: 10.75%
Cash ($ mil.): 1,495
Current ratio: —
Long-term debt ($ mil.): —

No. of shares (mil.): 128
Dividends
  Yield: 3.0%
  Payout: 29.4%
Market value ($ mil.): 3,934

	STOCK PRICE ($) FY Close	P/E High/Low	PER SHARE ($) Earnings	Dividends	Book Value
12/19	30.51	10 7	3.30	0.94	32.19
12/18	22.83	16 7	3.24	0.80	29.32
12/17	48.45	17 12	3.35	0.37	26.98
12/16	52.59	21 13	2.58	0.63	23.02
12/15	49.46	26 15	2.09	0.55	16.19
Annual Growth	(11.4%)	— —	12.1%	14.3%	18.7%

BankUnited Inc.

BankUnited is uniting the north and south again. It's the bank holding company for BankUnited N.A. which provides standard banking services to individuals and businesses through nearly 90 banking centers in about 15 Florida counties and five banking centers in the New York metro area. Deposit offerings include checking and savings accounts treasury management services and certificates of deposit. Commercial loans including multi-family residential mortgages account for some 80% of the bank's lending portfolio. In 2018 the company launched BankUnitedDirect an online division offering money market and CD accounts nationwide. BankUnited does not offer investment banking or wealth management services.

Sales and Marketing

BankUnited serves individuals growing companies and established middle-market companies. It markets its products through local television and radio ads digital and print ads and direct mail campaigns.

Financial Performance

BankUnited's revenue has been growing steadily for the last five years. Profits were relatively static until 2017 when they more than doubled. Cash flow has been somewhat volatile.

In 2017 revenue increased 14% to $1.1 billion as both interest and non-interest income grew. Interest on loans and securities rose while gains of sales of loans boosted non-interest income.

Net income rose 172% to $591 million that year. Part of that gain was due to a $327.9 million income tax benefit received.

The company ended 2017 with some $195 million in cash versus $448 million held at the end of 2016. Financing activities provided $1.9 billion in cash and operating activities provided $319 million. Investing activities used $2.5 billion in 2017 (the fifth straight year investments have used more than $2 billion).

Strategy

BankUnited has placed its bets on two large and growing markets — the Miami metro area and the Tri-State area of New York New Jersey and Connecticut. Because those geographic markets are so attractive though competition is fierce.

The company is also open to making strategic acquisitions of other financial firms or companies in complementary businesses.

Company Background

BankUnited was formed in 2009 following the demise of the former BankUnited FSB which collapsed under the weight of bad mortgages. A team of private investors bought BankUnited from the FDIC injected $900 million in fresh capital and in 2011 took the company public via an initial public offering (IPO); it was the first IPO of a rescued bank during the economic crisis.

In February 2012 BankUnited acquired Herald National Bank for $65 million in cash and stock. At the time of the purchase BankUnited converted to a bank holding company. It also converted the charter of subsidiary BankUnited from a thrift to a national commercial bank. Herald National was merged into BankUnited in mid-2012.

EXECUTIVES

President New York Region, Joseph (Joe) Roberto, age 63, $300,000 total compensation

Chief Risk Officer, Mark P. Bagnoli, age 68

President And Ceo, Rajinder P. (Raj) Singh, age 49, $500,000 total compensation

Cfo, Leslie N. Lunak, age 63, $400,000 total compensation

Coo, Thomas M. Cornish, age 62, $500,000 total compensation

Cio, Julio Jogaib

Vice President Information Technology, William Hynes

Senior Vice President Commercial Real Estate, Robert Hummel

Assistant Vice President Portfolio Manager, Tracey Snow

Senior Vice President, Steven Hart

Vice President, Kenneth Lipke

Senior Vice President Commercial Private Banking, Corey Prinz

Executive Vice President, Cristina Di Mauro

Vice President, Laura Lowy

Vice President, Bill Williams

Vice President, Peter Dumelle

Senior Vice President, Elizabeth Claisse

Assistant Vice President, Pedro Garcia

Vice President, Susan Kay

Vice President Project Management Office, Janet Marotta

Senior Vice President Associate General Counsel, Alina Pastiu

Vice President Assistant Banking Center Manager, Sarah Townsend

Vice President Credit Officer, Patrick Rigney

Vice President Community Development Outreach, Naima Oyo

Vice President Treasury Management Relationship Manager Treasury Management, Mark Stevens

Vice President, Carol Hammond

Vice President, Sabine Bouchereau

Senior Vice President Corporate Finance, Cristina Frias

Senior Vice President Community Development Officer, Claire Raley

Vice President Banking Center Assistant Manager, Theresa Schuman

Vice President Electronic Banking, Juliana Tancrati

Vice President Commercial Banker, Jaime Fimiani

Vice President Accounting Department, Dorrett Boothe

Vice President Portfolio Analytics Manager, Matthew Crawford

Senior Vice President Bsa Officer, Scott Nathan

Vp Busines Banker, Nicholas Marrone

Senior Vice President Enterprise Stress Testing, Filippo Ghia

Senior Vice President Marketing And Public Relations, Mary Harris

Vice President Financial Center Manager, John Hernandez

Senior Vice President Corporate Banking, Joseph Disanti

Vice President Corporate Banking, Justin Allbright

Vice President And Business Banking, Jose Alonso

Vice President Relationship Manager, Patricia Lubian

Vice President Human Resources And Employee Relations, Ellen Gioia

Assistant Vice President Business Banking, Artesa Purellku

Vice President Senior Relationship Manager, Daniel Vaccaro

Vice President Business Banking, Jason Costello

Vice President Commercial Banking, Ted Kunkel

Assistant Vice President Corporate Real Estate, Kristin Maresca

Vice President Banking Center Manager, Paige Homan

Vice President Commercial Real Estate, Jeremy Romine

Senior Vice President Corporate Lending, Gerry Mcpartland

Senior Vice President, Michael Del Rocco

Vice President, Oleg Kochanov

Vice President, Wendy Spears

Senior Vice President Senior Credit Officer Commercial Real Estate, John Kenyon

Vice President Underwriter, Alexandra Tovar

Vice President Branch Manager, Renea Austin

Senior Vice President, Henry Ngai

Assistant Vice President, Gloria Persaud

Vice President Commercial And Consumer Loan Servic, Rebecca Thrasher

Vice President Corporate Portfolio Manager, Jeff Landroche

Vice President Business Banker, Timothy Byrnes

Vice President, Christopher Demeter

Senior Vice President Environmental Risk Manager, Michael Tartanella

Senior Vice President Corporate Lending, Craig Kincade

Senior Vice President Business Banking Sales Manager, Gregory Milford

Vice President Banking Center Manager, Pat Kelly

Vice President Branch Sales Leader, Milton Price

Vice President Credit Review, Nicholas Cross

Vice President, Monica Antongeorgi

Vice President Corporate Portfolio Manager, Thomas Mcgregor

Vice President Corporate Banking Division, Milciades Herrera

Senior Vice President, Tyson Carballo

Svp Commercial Real Estate Lender, Ellen Hoey

Executive Vice President, Gardner Semet

Vice President Corporate Portfolio Manager, Bradley Hendren

Senior Vice President, Larry Crowley

Vice President Operations Manager, Jose Alvarado

Vice President Corporate Banking, Jennifer Garcia-Barbon

Vice President Commercial Private Banker, Mike Smith

Vice President Business Development Officer, Marissa Ames

Vice President Private Client Team Lead, Thomas Pla

Vice President Commercial Underwriter Bankunited, Gregory O'Brien

Vice President Business Banking Lead Underwriter, Alexanders Saenz

Senior Vice President Corporate Team Leader, Christine Gerula

Assistant Vice President Financial Reporting, Niurka Hiott

Vice President, Guillermo Doria

Vice President, Brenda Greenberg

Senior Vice President, Karen Gladding

Senior Vice President Senior Commercial Credit Officer, Maria Arguello

Vice President Corporate Portfolio Manager, Jeanne Klimschot

Avp Corporate Banking Portfolio Manager, Anthony Fulchi

Assistant Vice President, Shannie DeFreitas

Executive Vice President Mortgage Services, Ray Barbone

Vice President Doral Branch Sales Leader, Ralph Vasallo

Vice President Branch Sales Leader, Monica Ribeiro

Vice President Business Development Officer, Stephen Speer

Senior Vice President Team Leader, Thomas Riele

Senior Executive Vice President, Nick Bustle

Senior Vice President, Elizabeth Martone

Vice President, Dianne Brodie

Assistant Vice President Sba Loan Closer, Muni Chum

Vice President; Business Banking, Jairo Cardona

Vice President Market Manager, Jeff Fusco

Senior Vice President, Brett Shulick

Vice President Relationship Manager, Marshall Fulton

Avp Sba Loan Closer, Leslie Giannantoni

Executive Vice President Director Of Business Banking, Brian Clay

Svp Credit Review Group Manager, Nancy Lanzoni

Vice President Commercial Credit Review Officer Iii, Elizabeth Nader

Vice President Retail And Small Business Banking, Sean Chaderton

Senior Vice President Senior Cre Credit Officer Florida Region, Raul Llanes

Vp Electronic Banking Manager, Daniel Cox

Vice President Business Banking Lead Underwriter, Larry Candelario

Senior Vice President, Candy Dugan

Senior Vice President Commercial Private Banking, Kelly Sleece

Vice President Relationship Manager, Larry Marchini

Assistant Vice President Branch Manager, Darlene Curti

Vice President Business Development Officer, Alan Hice

Senior Vice President, Benjamin Fisher

Senior Vice President And Head, Elliot Leibowitz

Senior Vice President Corporate Banking, Jackson Young

Vice President Business Banking, Richard Rippy

Vice President Business Development Officer, Jared Johnson

Vice President Branch Sales Leader, Pablo Estepe

Vice President Business Banking, Ryan Shirley

Senior Vice President Corporate Finance, Jorge Ray

Vp Operational Risk, Kavitha Singh

Senior Vice President, Luis Garcia

Assistant Vice President Mortgage Warehouse Lending, Rosemarie Loparrino

Vice President Sba Underwriter, Scott Meckes

Executive Vice President New York, Ben Stacks

Vice President Sba Underwriter, Amy Luce

Vice President Senior Analyst Business Development Officer, Will Tinsley

Vice President, Lon Gopie

Vice President, Peter Hughes

Senior Vice President Of Government Institutional Banking Gib Team Leader For Private Client Svc, Emsley Hylton

Vice President Branch Manager, Sebastian Cannata

Senior Vice President, Steven Markowski
Vice President, Kevin Karstens
Svp Commercial Private Banking, Theonie Golden
Vice President Business Banker, Jeffrey Goldstein
Vice President Portfolio Manager, Noel Lassise
Vice President Credit Officer, Ward Burns
Executive Vice President, Michael Wilcox
Vice President Treasury Management Product Management, Dana Heffernan
Assistant Vice President Sba Loan Closer, Pannah Hem
Vice President Sba Loan Administration Supervisor Production Support, Stephanie Byerly
Avp Portfolio Manager, Zahra Holness
Senior Vice President Corporate Security, Edward Hausdorf
Auditors: KPMG LLP

LOCATIONS

HQ: BankUnited Inc.
14817 Oak Lane, Miami Lakes, FL 33016
Phone: 305 569-2000
Web: www.bankunited.com

COMPETITORS

BB&T	Ocean Bankshares
Bank of America	PNC Financial
Capital One	Regions Financial
Citibank	Signature Bank
Great Florida Bank	SunTrust
JPMorgan Chase	TD Bank USA
M&T Bank	Valley National
New York Community	Bancorp
Bancorp	Wells Fargo

HISTORICAL FINANCIALS

Company Type: Public

Income Statement				FYE: December 31
	ASSETS ($ mil.)	NET INCOME ($ mil.)	INCOME AS % OF ASSETS	EMPLOYEES
12/19	32,871	313	1.0%	1,511
12/18	32,164	324	1.0%	1,790
12/17	30,346	614	2.0%	1,763
12/16	27,880	225	0.8%	1,706
12/15	23,883	251	1.1%	1,741
Annual Growth	8.3%	5.6%	—	(3.5%)

2019 Year-End Financials

Debt ratio: 1.31%
Return on equity: 10.61%
Cash ($ mil.): 214
Current ratio: —
Long-term debt ($ mil.): —
No. of shares (mil.): 95
Dividends
  Yield: 2.3%
  Payout: 30.7%
Market value ($ mil.): 3,478

	STOCK PRICE ($) FY Close	P/E High/Low		PER SHARE ($) Earnings	Dividends	Book Value
12/19	36.56	12	10	3.13	0.84	31.33
12/18	29.94	15	9	2.99	0.84	29.49
12/17	40.72	7	5	5.58	0.84	28.32
12/16	37.69	18	13	2.09	0.84	23.22
12/15	36.06	17	11	2.35	0.84	21.65
Annual Growth	0.3%	—	—	7.4%	(0.0%)	9.7%

Banner Corp.

Flagging bank accounts? See Banner Corporation. Banner is the holding company for Banner Bank which serves the Pacific Northwest through about 100 branches and 10 loan production offices in Washington Oregon and Idaho. The company also owns Islanders Bank which operates three branches in Washington's San Juan Islands. The banks offer standard products such as deposit accounts credit cards and business and consumer loans. Commercial loans including business agriculture construction and multifamily mortgage loans account for about 90% of the company's portfolio. Bank subsidiary Community Financial writes residential mortgage and construction loans.

Geographic Reach

Washington-based Banner Bank is focused on five primary markets in the Northwest: the Puget Sound region of Washington; the greater Portland Oregon market; Boise Idaho; and Spokane Washington. The fifth is the bank's historical base in the agricultural communities in the Columbia Basin region of Washington and Oregon.

Sales and Marketing

Banner Corp. reported advertising and marketing expenses of $6.9 million in 2013 versus $7.2 million in 2012. Banner Bank launched a redesigned website and new ad campaign in Boise Seattle and Portland and on social media in fall 2014.

Financial Performance

The regional bank holding company reported revenue of $223 million in 2013 an increase of 4% versus 2012. The rise in revenue was due to increased operating income as a result of gains on the sale of securities and a fee received from the termination of the bank's proposed acquisition of Home Federal Bancorp. The bank's growing customer base led to increased income from deposit fees and other service charges of $1.3 billion (5%) in 2013 versus the prior year. Net income declined 28% in 2013 versus 2012 to $46.6 million primarily due to higher provision for income tax expenses. After three consecutive years of losses (2008 thru 2010) the bank returned to profitability in 2011 and has remained profitable.

Banner Corp. has total consolidated assets of about $4.5 billion.

Strategy

Historically Banner Corp. has grown by acquisition. Since going public (in 1995) Banner has acquired about 10 commercial banks. Islanders Bank was acquired in 2007 the same year Banner acquired F&M Bank and NCW Community Bank of Wenatchee both also based in Washington. After the spate of acquisitions the company focused on opening branches. The company continues to look for acquisition opportunities with an eye on banks shut down by regulators.

In 2013 however a plan to merge with Home Federal Bancorp was terminated when that bank received a better offer from Cascade Bancorp. Also the company abandoned plans to buy Idaho Banking Company out of bankruptcy after being outbid.

Mergers and Acquisitions

In August 2014 Banner Bank acquired Siuslaw Financial Group the holding company for Siuslaw Bank the operator of 10 branches along the coast of Oregon. In June 2014 Banner Bank purchased six branches in Oregon from Sterling Savings Bank.

EXECUTIVES

Evp And Cfo Banner Corporation, Lloyd W. Baker, age 71, $260,724 total compensation
Evp Retail Banking And Administration, Cynthia D. (Cindy) Purcell, age 62, $289,038 total compensation
Evp And Chief Lending Officer Banner Corporation And Banner Bank, Richard B. Barton, age 76, $264,895 total compensation
President And Ceo, Mark J. Grescovich, age 55, $716,415 total compensation
Evp Real Estate Lending Operations, Douglas M. Bennett, age 67, $236,174 total compensation
Evp And Cio, Steven W. (Steve) Rust, age 72
Evp Retail Products And Services, Gary W. Wagers, age 59
Evp And Commercial Executive East Region, M. Kirk Quillin, age 57
Evp And Commercial Executive West Region, James T. (Jim) Reed, age 57
Evp And Cfo Banner Bank, Peter J. Conner, age 54
Evp Human Resources, Kayleen Kohler
Evp And Mortgage Banking Director, Kenneth A. (Ken) Larsen, age 50
Evp And General Counsel Banner Bank, Craig Miller
Evp And Chief Risk Officer Banner Bank, Judy Steiner
Evp And Commercial Executive (south Region), Keith A. Western, age 64
Senior Vice President And Sba Manager, Walter Mclaughlin
Vice President Sr. Commercial Relationship Manager, Jeanne Walker
Vice President Senior Relationship Manager, Scott A Cordell
Assistant Vice President Branch Manager, Azar Ghiasvand
Vice President And Manager, Charlie Martinez
Vice Chairman Banner Corporation And Banner Bank, Jesse G. Foster, age 82
Chairman Banner Corporation And Banner Bank, Gary L. Sirmon, age 77
Auditors: Moss Adams LLP

LOCATIONS

HQ: Banner Corp.
10 South First Avenue, Walla Walla, WA 99362
Phone: 509 527-3636
Web: www.bannerbank.com

PRODUCTS/OPERATIONS

2016 Sales

	% of total
INTEREST INCOME:	
Loans receivable	75
Mortgage-backed securities	4
Securities and cash equivalents	3
NON-INTEREST INCOME:	
Deposit fees and other service charges	10
Mortgage banking operations	6
BOLI	1
Miscellaneous	1
Total	100

COMPETITORS

Bank of America	Sound Financial
Cascade Bancorp	U.S. Bancorp
Columbia Banking	Umpqua Holdings
FCA	Washington Federal
Glacier Bancorp	Wells Fargo
KeyCorp	

HISTORICAL FINANCIALS

Company Type: Public

Income Statement				FYE: December 31
	ASSETS ($ mil.)	NET INCOME ($ mil.)	INCOME AS % OF ASSETS	EMPLOYEES
12/19	12,604	146	1.2%	2,198
12/18	11,871	136	1.2%	2,187
12/17	9,763	60	0.6%	2,128
12/16	9,793	85	0.9%	2,137
12/15	9,796	45	0.5%	2,143
Annual Growth	6.5%	34.1%	—	0.6%

2019 Year-End Financials

Debt ratio: 1.89%	No. of shares (mil.): 35
Return on equity: 9.52%	Dividends
Cash ($ mil.): 307	Yield: 2.8%
Current ratio: —	Payout: 37.1%
Long-term debt ($ mil.): —	Market value ($ mil.): 2,023

	STOCK PRICE ($) FY Close	P/E High/Low	PER SHARE ($) Earnings	Dividends	Book Value
12/19	56.59	15 12	4.18	1.61	44.59
12/18	53.48	16 12	4.15	1.83	42.03
12/17	55.12	34 28	1.84	1.98	38.89
12/16	55.81	22 15	2.52	0.65	39.34
12/15	45.86	28 21	1.89	0.72	37.97
Annual Growth	5.4%	—	21.9%	22.3%	4.1%

Bar Harbor Bankshares

Bar Harbor Bankshares which holds Bar Harbor Bank & Trust is a Maine -stay. Boasting $1.6 billion in assets the bank offers traditional deposit and retirement products trust services and a variety of loans to individuals and businesses through 15 branches in the state's Hancock Knox and Washington counties. Commercial real estate and residential mortgages loans make up nearly 80% of the bank's loan portfolio though it also originates business construction agricultural home equity and other consumer loans. About 10% of its loans are to the tourist industry which is associated with nearby Acadia National Park. Subsidiary Bar Harbor Trust Services offers trust and estate planning services.

Operations

Around 80% of the bank's loan assets are tied to real estate. About 41% of its loan portfolio was made up of residential real estate mortgages at the end of 2015 while another 37% was made up of commercial real estate mortgages. The rest of the portfolio was tied to commercial and industrial loans (8% of loan assets) home equity loans (5%) agricultural and farming loans (3%) commercial construction (3%) and other consumer loans (1%).

More than 80% of Bar Harbor's revenue comes from interest income. About 61% of its total revenue came from loan interest (including fees) during 2015 while another 25% came from interest income on investment securities. The remainder of its revenue came from trust and other financial services (6% of revenue) debit card service charges and fees (3%) deposit account service charges (1%) and other miscellaneous income sources.

Geographic Reach

The Bar Harbor Maine-based group operates 15 branches across the downeast midcoast and central regions of Maine more specifically in Bar Harbor Northeast Harbor Southwest Harbor Somesville Deer Isle Blue Hill Ellsworth Rockland Topsham South China Augusta Winter Harbor Milbridge Machias and Lubec.

Sales and Marketing

Bar Harbor serves individuals and retirees nonprofits municipalities as well as businesses that are vital to Maine's coastal economy including retailers restaurants seasonal lodging bio research laboratories.

Financial Performance

The group's annual revenues have risen more than 10% since 2011 as its loan assets have swelled over 35% to $990 million. Its profits have grown more than 30% over the same period as

Bar Harbor has kept a lid on rising operating costs and as it's enjoyed low interest rates.

Bar Harbor's revenue climbed 4% to $64.2 million during 2015 mostly as its loan and other interest earning assets grew by more than 7%.

Revenue growth in 2015 drove the bank's net income up 4% to $15.15 million. Bar Harbor's operating cash levels spiked 31% to $20.33 million for the year mainly thanks to favorable working capital changes related to changes in other assets.

Strategy

Bar Harbor Bankshares looks to grow its loan and deposit business organically and through strategic bank acquisitions targeting the downeast midcoast and central Maine markets. It also continued in 2016 to focus on managing its operating expenses building upon its strong efficient ratio of 56.3% in 2015.

EXECUTIVES

Evp Business Banking Bar Harbor Bank & Trust, Gregory W. Dalton, age 60, $203,000 total compensation

Evp Retail Banking, Stephen M. Leackfeldt, age 63, $225,000 total compensation

Evp And Chief Risk Officer, Richard B. Maltz, $255,000 total compensation

Evp Cfo And Treasurer, Josephine Iannelli, age 48

President And Ceo Bar Harbor Bankshares And Bar Harbor Bank & Trust, Curtis C. Simard, age 49, $438,000 total compensation

Senior Vice President, Steve Gurin

Senior Vice President Internal Audit, Johanne Lapointe

Executive Vice President Regional President Of Nh Vt Of Bhbt, William Mciver

Vice President Mortgage Loan Originator, Teri Minelli

Vice President Residential Lending Manager, Sarah Sachs

Chairman, David B. Woodside, age 68

Board Member, David Colter

Auditors: RSM US LLP

LOCATIONS

HQ: Bar Harbor Bankshares
P.O. Box 400, 82 Main Street, Bar Harbor, ME 04609-0400
Phone: 207 288-3314
Web: www.bhbt.com

PRODUCTS/OPERATIONS

2015 sales

	$ mil.	% of total
Interest and dividend income		
Interest and fees on loans	39	61
Interest on securities	15	24
Dividends on FHLB stock	0	1
Non-interest income		
Trust and other financial services	3	6
Debit card service charges and fees	1	3
Net securities gains	1	2
Other operating income	1	2
Service charges on deposit accounts	0	1
Total	**64**	**100**

Selected Services

Retail Products and Services
Retail Brokerage Services
Electronic Banking Services
Commercial Products and Services

COMPETITORS

Bangor Savings Bank	TD Bank USA
Bank of America	The First Bancorp
Camden National	
People's United Financial	

HISTORICAL FINANCIALS

Company Type: Public

Income Statement

FYE: December 31

	ASSETS ($ mil.)	NET INCOME ($ mil.)	INCOME AS % OF ASSETS	EMPLOYEES
12/19	3,669	22	0.6%	460
12/18	3,608	32	0.9%	445
12/17	3,565	25	0.7%	423
12/16	1,755	14	0.9%	186
12/15	1,580	15	1.0%	221
Annual Growth	23.4%	10.5%	—	20.1%

2019 Year-End Financials

Debt ratio: 1.63%	No. of shares (mil.): 15
Return on equity: 5.90%	Dividends
Cash ($ mil.): 56	Yield: 3.3%
Current ratio: —	Payout: 51.5%
Long-term debt ($ mil.): —	Market value ($ mil.): 395

	STOCK PRICE ($) FY Close	P/E High/Low	PER SHARE ($) Earnings	Dividends	Book Value
12/19	25.39	19 15	1.45	0.86	25.48
12/18	22.43	14 10	2.12	0.79	23.87
12/17	27.01	28 15	1.70	0.75	22.96
12/16	47.33	30 18	1.63	0.73	17.19
12/15	34.42	22 18	1.67	0.67	17.10
Annual Growth	(7.3%)	—	(3.4%)	6.3%	10.5%

BARCLAYS BANK DELAWARE

Spending money is a rewarding experience for holders of Barclays Bank Delaware cards. With co-branded credit cards from Barclays Bank Delaware (aka Barclays US) customers accumulate points that can be redeemed for air travel hotel stays and other perks. The company a division of Barclays issues Visa and MasterCard credit cards in addition to co-branded credit cards through partnerships with over 25 top companies including Priceline Choice Privileges Carnival World and JetBlue. Founded as Juniper Financial in 2000; it became a part of Barclays in 2004.

Operations

The company creates customized co-branded credit card programs for some of the country's most successful travel entertainment retail cashback business expenses and financial institutions. Barclays also offer personal loans by invitation to some customers.

Geographic Reach

Barclays US is headquartered in Wilmington Delaware and has customers and clients across 40 countries.

Sales and Marketing

Barclays US collaborates with over 25 top companies to deliver an array of consumer and small business credit card programs uses partnerships to expand its business. Some of its major partners include Barnes & Noble Frontier Airlines Priceline.com Wyndham Holland America and Diamond Resorts World.

Strategy

Barclays US has been growing in recent years as the global economy improves and it continues to play a pivotal role in furthering innovation and shared growth for all as it evolves the future of banking.

Barclays US continues to focus on next-generation payment technology and digital safety for its customers. Its website and mobile app now utilize a new simplified log-in process to verify one's identity. It added a verification method a SecurPass code to help customers confirm their identity when they attempt to log in on an unknown device as well as Fraud Text Alerts that help protect customers' card in real time.

Company Background

In 1966 Barclays launches Barclaycard the first credit card in the UK. Following that year it introduces the world's first ATM. Barclays acquires Juniper Bank a credit card company formed in 2000 and creating Barclaycard US in 2004. In 2009 Barclaycard becomes a top-10 credit card issuer in the U.S. It launches the first mobile app for card members in 2011. In 2018 Barclaycard rebrands to Barclays in the U.S. offering a range of personal banking products to U.S. consumers.

EXECUTIVES

Managing Director Corporate Communications, Kevin M. Sullivan
Ceo, Amer Sajed
Cfo, Gerald (Jerry) Pavelich
Chief Credit Officer, Michael Mayer
Assistant Vp Strategic Cost Management, Glenn Watson
Vp Data Science And Advanced Analytics, Vishal Morde

LOCATIONS

HQ: BARCLAYS BANK DELAWARE
100 S WEST ST, WILMINGTON, DE 198015015
Phone: 302 255-8000
Web: WWW.BARCLAYCARDUS.COM

PRODUCTS/OPERATIONS

Selected Card Partnerships

Ameriprise
Bank Atlantic
Barnes & Noble
BJ's
Frontier
L.L. Bean
US Airways
Best Western
Priceline.com
Payless
Travelocity
Virgin America

COMPETITORS

Alliance Data Systems	Citibank
American Express	Discover
Bank of America	JPMorgan Chase
Capital One	

HISTORICAL FINANCIALS

Company Type: Private

Income Statement
FYE: December 31

	ASSETS ($ mil.)	NET INCOME ($ mil.)	INCOME AS % OF ASSETS	EMPLOYEES
12/14	25,012	239	1.0%	349
12/13	19,055	331	1.7%	—
12/08	12,418	20	0.2%	—
12/07	7,470	0	—	—
Annual Growth	18.8%	—	—	—

Baxter International Inc

Medical products manufacturer Baxter International is a leading producer of intravenous (IV) fluids and systems. The company makes a range of sterile IV solutions generic injectable pharmaceuticals and parenteral nutritional products along with IV administration sets infusion systems and devices. The company also makes dialyzers and other products like peritoneal dialysis (PD) hemodialysis (HD) and additional dialysis. Its biological sealants and inhaled anesthetics are used in surgical and acute therapy environments. Baxter's products are sold in more than 100 countries; the company generates more than 40% of sales in the US.

HISTORY

Idaho surgeon Ralph Falk his brother Harry and California physician Donald Baxter formed Don Baxter Intravenous Products in 1931 to distribute the IV solutions Baxter made in Los Angeles. Two years later the company opened its first plant located outside Chicago. Ralph Falk bought Baxter's interest in 1935 and began R&D efforts leading to the first sterilized vacuum-type blood collection device (1939) which could store blood for weeks instead of hours. Product demand during WWII spurred sales above $1.5 million by 1945.

In 1949 the company created Travenol Laboratories to make and sell drugs. Baxter went public in 1951 and began an acquisition program the next year. In 1953 failing health caused both Falks to give control to William Graham a manager since 1945. Under Graham's leadership Baxter absorbed Wallerstein (1957); Fenwal Labs (1959); Flint Eaton (1959); and Dayton Flexible Products (1967).

In 1975 Baxter's headquarters moved to Deerfield Illinois. In 1978 the company debuted the first portable dialysis machine and had $1 billion in sales. Vernon Loucks Jr. became CEO two years later. Baxter claimed the title of the world's leading hospital supplier in 1985 when it bought American Hospital Supply (a Baxter distributor from 1932 to 1962). Offering more than 120000 products and an electronic system that connected customers with some 1500 vendors Baxter captured nearly 25% of the US hospital supply market in 1988. That year it became Baxter International.

In 1992 Baxter spun off Caremark (home infusion therapy and mail-order drugs) but kept a division that controlled 75% of the world's dialysis machine market.

In 1993 Baxter pleaded guilty (and was temporarily suspended from selling to the Veterans Administration) to bribing Syria to remove Baxter from a blacklist for trading in Israel.

The company entered the US cardiovascular perfusion services market in 1995 with the purchases of PSICOR and SETA. Baxter along with two other silicone breast-implant makers agreed to settle thousands of claims (at an average of $26000 each) from women suffering side-effects from the implants. The next year Baxter spun off its cost management and hospital supply business as Allegiance (sold to Cardinal Health in 1999).

Buys in 1997 boosted Baxter's presence in Europe and its share of the open-heart-surgery devices market. That year it agreed to pay about 20% of a $670 million legal settlement in a suit relating to hemophiliacs infected with HIV from blood products.

In response to concerns posed by shareholders Baxter in 1999 said it would phase out the use of PVC (polyvinyl chloride) in some products by

2010. In 2000 the firm spun off its underperforming cardiovascular unit as Edwards Lifesciences. To strengthen core operations it lined up a number of purchases including North American Vaccine.

Purchases in 2001 included the cancer treatment unit of chemicals firm Degussa. Also that year Baxter withdrew dialysis equipment from Spain and Croatia after patients who used its products died. It also ended production of two types of dialyzers that were sold there. As the number of deaths mounted to more than 50 in seven countries Baxter began facing lawsuits; it later settled with the families of many of the patients. In September 2002 the FDA issued a warning when several patients died after using Baxter's Meridian dialysis machines. The same year Baxter bought Fusion Medical to expand its BioScience unit.

Robert L. Parkinson Jr. took over as chairman and CEO in April 2004. Parkinson succeeded Harry M. Jansen Kraemer Jr. William Graham who remained on the Baxter board of directors as honorary chairman emeritus after his official retirement in 1996 died in 2006.

In 2005 the FDA seized Baxter's existing inventories of previously recalled 6000 Colleague Volumetric Infusion Pumps and nearly 1000 Syndeo PCA Syringe Pumps; the federal agency resorted to these measures after the company did not fix production and design problems with the pumps in a suitable amount of time after batches of the product had been recalled earlier that year.

Baxter's product troubles didn't end there. In 2008 Baxter halted production of heparin after hundreds of bad reactions (including several deaths) occurred in patients using the drug. Subsequent investigations focused on raw heparin supplied to Baxter by a Chinese factory which apparently added a cheaper ingredient into the drug which contaminated it. Heparin-related litigation continued for Baxter in following years.

In 2009 the company acquired the hemofiltration (renal replacement therapy) product line of Edwards Lifesciences in a $65 million deal.

To meet increasing demand Baxter also expanded its infusion systems portfolio that year by entering an agreement to distribute medical device maker SIGMA's Spectrum large volume infusion pumps domestically and internationally. The deal also gave Baxter a 40% stake in the company (with the option to buy the rest) as well as access to future products under development. In 2012 Baxter exercised its right to buy and paid $90 million in cash for the remaining 60% of the company.

The addition of the Spectrum system was especially helpful when the FDA ordered the company to recall all of its Colleague infusion pumps in the US market in 2010. Patients were given the option of receiving Spectrum pumps to replace the Colleague systems.

As part of restructuring efforts in 2010 the company sold its noncore US generic injectables business to Hikma Pharmaceuticals for about $112 million. Baxter divested the business to focus on its proprietary injectable formulation and packaging operations. The sale also included Baxter's manufacturing facility in New Jersey and a warehouse and distribution center in Tennessee.

The company grew its BioScience operations in 2010 by acquiring all of the hemophilia-related assets from privately-held Archemix in a deal worth up to $315 million. Archemix has products under development including a synthetic hemophilia treatment to improve the body's blood clotting capabilities. Then to jump into the bone grafting market the company spent some $330 million to acquire UK-based ApaTech which sells bone grafting materials in the US and Europe; the deal gave Baxter manufacturing and research facilities in Germany the UK and the US.

In 2015 Baxter split its operations into two companies — one focused on biopharmaceuticals (Baxalta) and the other on medical products (Baxter).

EXECUTIVES

Vice President Information Technology, Martin McBride
Corporate Vp And Cio, Paul E. Martin
Chairman And Ceo, José E. (Joe) Almeida, age 58, $1,300,000 total compensation
Corporate Vp Human Resources, Jeanne K. Mason, age 64, $540,192 total compensation
Corporate Vp And Cfo, James K. Saccaro, age 47, $644,415 total compensation
Corporate Vp And President Hospital Products, Brik V. Eyre, age 56, $618,533 total compensation
Corporate Vp And Chief Scientific Officer, Marcus Schabacker, age 56
Corporate Vp And President International, Paul Vibert, age 60
Corporate Vp And President Renal, Giuseppe Accogli, age 49, $514,028 total compensation
Vice President, Michael Baughman
Vice President Of Manufacturing, Manuel Domenech
Vice President Product Quality, Mahesh Chaubal
Vice President Bioscience, Paul Grozier
Vice President Engineering, Ernest Shepard
Vice President Project Management Office (research And Development), Karen Marks
Vice President Manufacturing Strategy, Kathleen Warren
Global Vice President Application Services, Michael Hamill
Senior Vice President Of Business Development, Claude Knopf
Vice President Marketing, Cindy Huey
Senior Vice President Treasurer And Head Of Global Planning, Scott Bohaboy
Vice President Marketing User Services Hospital Products, Omar Khalil
Vice President, Darin Buser
Vice President Global Operations, Phil Batchelor
Vice President Of Integration, Cathy Skala
Medical Director, Mary Gellens
Associate Medical Director, Carol Schermer
Vice President Of Human Resources, Brian Smith
National Sales Manager Inside Sales, Valarie Taulien
Vice President, Laurie Hernandez
Vice President Human Resources, Mike Edicola
Vice President Talent Management, Irina Konstantinovsky
Vice President Sales, Mike Canzoneri
Corporate Vice President And Chief Scientific Officer, Norbert Riedel
Vice President Of Global Research And Development, Noel Barrett
Vice President Sales, Joe Pudlo
Vice President Corporate Audit, John Mccoy
Corporate Vice President And Cio, Karenann Terrell
Vice President Finance, Patrick Marschall
Human Resources Vice President Latin America, Paulo Bolgar
Vice President Employee Services, Faye Katt
Vice President Biosurgery Research And Development, Russ Holscher
Vice President Manufacturing Strategy, Kathy Warren
Vp Pharmacy, Susan Camberis
Vice President Planning And Deployment, Prabir Sen-Gupta
Senior Vice President Of Human Resources, Mike Tucker
Pharmacy Manager, Bruce Hastie
Vice President Human Resources, Paulohenrique Bolgar
Svp And Controller, Caroline Karp

Corporate Vice President Human Resources, Jeannie K Mason
Vice President Research And Development And Quality Information Technology, Andrew Worley
Vice President Global Business Development, Doerr David
Vice President, Robert Felicelli
Vice President Quality, Katherine Azuara
Vice President Global Marketing Research And Development, George Bowen
Vice President Head Global Business Development, Nicholas Manusos
Vice President Corporate Audit, Kim Roll-Wallace
Senior Vice President And Corporate Secretary, Ellen Mcintosh
Senior Vice President General Counsel, Sean Martin
Corporate Vice President Associate General Counsel And Corporate Secretary, Stephanie Shinn
Medical Director, Maggie Gellens
Vice President Of Digital Innovation, Jonathan Handler
Vice President Global Medical Affairs Hospital Products, Dheerendra Kommala
Vice President Meeting Programming And Design, Stasia L Ogden
Vice President Strategy Hospital Products, David H Roman
Vice President Of Engineering, Greg Kamykowski
Vice President Global Engineering (baxter Global Operations), Bass William
Senior Vice President And President Emea, Cristiano Franzi
Senior Vice President Chief Science And Technology Officer, Sumant Ramachandra
Senior Vice President And President Apac, Andrew Frye
Senior Vp Business Development And Licensing, Dennis Crowley
Vice President Commercial Training, Ashley Bentley
Vice President Supply Chain, Tyler Vassar
Vice President Strategic Initiatives And Business Development, Jay Saccaro
Vice President Manufacturing Operations, Jon Rushford
Medical Director, Keith Friend
Vice President, Sarah Creviston
Senior Vice President Chief Accounting Officer, Brian Stevens
Corporate Vice President And Chief Information Off, Paul E Martin
Vice President, Philippe Reale
Assistant Vice President Idn, Maryjo Fernald
Vice President Operations Ecm, Arthur Fiocco
Vice President Global Businesses, Hiranda Donoghue
Vice President, George Guerra
Vice President Corporate Audit, Kim Roll Wallace
Vice President, John Jewell
Executive Vice President, Greg Schulte
Vice President Global Regulatory Affairs, Lynn Pawelski
Board Member, Peter S Hellman
Board Member, Albert Stroucken
Board Member, Michael Mahoney
Board Member, Alexander Chen
Assistant Treasurer, Jeff Schaible
Board Member, Munib Islam
Treasurer, John Carlson
Treasurer, Michael Kelley
Auditors: PricewaterhouseCoopers LLP

LOCATIONS

HQ: Baxter International Inc
One Baxter Parkway, Deerfield, IL 60015
Phone: 224 948-2000   **Fax:** 847 948-2964
Web: www.baxter.com

2017 Sales

	$ mil.	% of total
US	4,510	42
Europe	2,731	26
Asia/Pacific	2,110	20
Latin America & Canada	1,210	12
Total	**10,561**	**100**

PRODUCTS/OPERATIONS

2017 Sales

	$ mil.	% of total
Renal	3,480	33
Medical delivery	2,698	26
Pharmaceuticals	1,883	18
Nutrition	882	8
Advanced surgery	707	7
Acute therapies	456	4
Others	455	4
Total	**10,561**	**100**

COMPETITORS

Becton Dickinson	Genzyme
CSL	Grifols
CSL Behring	Hospira
CareFusion	Kimberly-Clark Health
Fresenius Medical Care	Terumo

HISTORICAL FINANCIALS

Company Type: Public

Income Statement				FYE: December 31
	REVENUE ($ mil.)	NET INCOME ($ mil.)	NET PROFIT MARGIN	EMPLOYEES
12/19	11,362	1,001	8.8%	50,000
12/18	11,127	1,624	14.6%	50,000
12/17	10,561	717	6.8%	47,000
12/16	10,163	4,965	48.9%	48,000
12/15	9,968	968	9.7%	50,000
Annual Growth	3.3%	0.8%	—	0.0%

2019 Year-End Financials

Debt ratio: 29.41%	No. of shares (mil.): 506
Return on equity: 12.77%	Dividends
Cash ($ mil.): 3,335	Yield: 1.0%
Current ratio: 2.32	Payout: 28.7%
Long-term debt ($ mil.): 4,809	Market value ($ mil.): 42,325

	STOCK PRICE ($) FY Close	P/E High/Low	PER SHARE ($) Earnings	Dividends	Book Value
12/19	83.62	46 33	1.93	0.85	15.57
12/18	65.82	26 20	2.97	0.73	15.19
12/17	64.64	50 34	1.29	0.61	16.85
12/16	44.34	5 4	9.01	0.51	15.36
12/15	38.15	41 18	1.76	1.27	16.15
Annual Growth	21.7%	— —	2.3%	(9.6%)	(0.9%)

BAYLOR SCOTT & WHITE HOLDINGS

EXECUTIVES

Ceo, Jim Hinton
ADM, Jared Kastriner
Auditors: PRICEWATERHOUSECOOPERS LLP DA

LOCATIONS

HQ: BAYLOR SCOTT & WHITE HOLDINGS
301 N WASHINGTON AVE, DALLAS, TX 752461754
Phone: 214 820-3151
Web: WWW.BSWHEALTH.COM

HISTORICAL FINANCIALS

Company Type: Private

Income Statement

FYE: June 30

	REVENUE ($ mil.)	NET INCOME ($ mil.)	NET PROFIT MARGIN	EMPLOYEES
06/17	9,084	630	6.9%	1
06/15	7,535	356	4.7%	—
Annual Growth	9.8%	33.0%	—	—

2019 Year-End Financials

Debt ratio: 1.27%
Return on equity: 9.57%
Cash ($ mil.): 550
Current ratio: —
Long-term debt ($ mil.): —

No. of shares (mil.): 17
Dividends
 Yield: 4.0%
 Payout: 45.1%
Market value ($ mil.): 242

	STOCK PRICE ($) FY Close	P/E High/Low	PER SHARE ($) Earnings	Dividends	Book Value
12/19	13.79	12 9	1.20	0.56	13.67
12/18	10.47	16 10	1.01	0.56	12.60
12/17	14.50	22 16	0.75	0.56	11.73
12/16	13.00	21 16	0.63	0.56	11.63
12/15	10.40	18 14	0.69	0.56	11.91
Annual Growth	7.3%	— —	14.8%	(0.0%)	3.5%

BCB Bancorp Inc

BCB Bancorp be the holding company for BCB Community Bank which opened its doors in late 2000. The independent bank serves Hudson County and the surrounding area from about 15 offices in New Jersey's Bayonne Hoboken Jersey City and Monroe. The bank offers traditional deposit products and services including savings accounts money market accounts CDs and IRAs. Funds from deposits are used to originate mortgages and loans primarily commercial real estate and multi-family property loans (which together account for more than half of the bank's loan portfolio). BCB agreed to acquire IA Bancorp in a $20 million deal in 2017.

EXECUTIVES

Pres-Ceo, Thomas M Coughlin
Chb, Mark D Hogan
V Chb, Joseph J Brogan
Cfo, Thomas P Keating
V Pres-General Counsel, John J Brogan
Chief Appraiser, Anthony Diodato
Auditors: Wolf & Company, P.C.

LOCATIONS

HQ: BCB Bancorp Inc
104-110 Avenue C, Bayonne, NJ 07002
Phone: 201 823-0700
Web: www.bcb.bank

COMPETITORS

Bank of America
City National Bancshares
Hudson City Bancorp
Meridian Capital Group
New York Community Bancorp

PNC Financial
Provident Financial Services
Sterling Bank
Stewardship Financial

HISTORICAL FINANCIALS

Company Type: Public

Income Statement

FYE: December 31

	ASSETS ($ mil.)	NET INCOME ($ mil.)	INCOME AS % OF ASSETS	EMPLOYEES
12/19	2,907	21	0.7%	365
12/18	2,674	16	0.6%	365
12/17	1,942	9	0.5%	314
12/16	1,708	8	0.5%	353
12/15	1,618	7	0.4%	331
Annual Growth	15.8%	31.5%	—	2.5%

Becton, Dickinson & Co

Don't worry you'll only feel a slight prick if Becton Dickinson (BD) is at work. The company's BD Medical segment is one of the top global manufacturers of syringes and other injection and infusion devices. BD Medical also makes IV catheters and syringes pre-fillable drug delivery systems self-injection devices for diabetes patients and related supplies such as anesthesia trays and sharps disposal systems. The BD Life Sciences segment makes products for the safe collection and transportation of diagnostic specimens; it also makes instruments and reagent systems that detect cancers infectious diseases and health care associated infections (HAIs). BD Interventional provides vascular urology oncology and surgical specialty products. The company's domestic operations accounts for around 55% of the total revenue.

Operations

BD operates through three reportable segments: BD Medical (more than half of total revenue) BD Life Sciences (around 25% of revenue) and BD Interventional (some 25% of revenue).

BD Medical specializes in the manufacturing of syringes catheters and injection devices. Other products include pre-filled syringes and diabetic pen needles. The segment is divided in four key areas: Medication Delivery Solutions Medication Management Solutions Diabetes Care and Pharmaceutical Systems.

BD Life Sciences operates in three key areas: pre-analytical systems diagnostic systems and biosciences. Its products include safety-engineered equipment for the collection of blood automated diagnostic platforms and cell analysis equipment.

BD Interventional also operates in three key areas: surgery peripheral intervention and urology and critical care. That segment's products include catheters stents and grafts.

Geographic Reach

BD has manufacturing marketing and warehousing operations in the US; Europe the Middle East and Africa (EMEA); Greater Asia; Latin America; and Canada. The company's executive offices are located at New Jersey.

Though the company is working to increase international sales (especially in emerging markets) the US remains its largest segment accounting for about 55% of sales. The Europe is BD's second-largest operating region accounting for about 20% of revenue. Asia brings in some 15% of revenue.

Sales and Marketing

BD's customers include entities in health care (including hospitals and pharmacies) drug development medical research (including academic and government labs) clinical research (such as reference labs and blood banks) and agricultural or food analysis. The company uses a direct sales force and independent representatives to market and distribute its products in the US and abroad. In the US products are sold primarily to distributors who then resell to end-users.

Financial Performance

Worldwide revenues in 2019 of $17.3 billion increased 8% from the prior-year period. The increase reflected a favorable impact of approximately 6% resulting from the inclusion of revenues from their acquisition of Bard in the first quarter of fiscal year 2019 but not in the first quarter of the prior-year period as operating activities of the business which was acquired on December 29 2017 were not included in their consolidated results of operations until January 1 2018.

The company's net income increased by $923 million to $1.1 billion compared to $159 million in the prior year. The rise was due to the increase on their revenue while maintaining a lower expenses and having an income tax benefits.

Cash held by the company decreased by $646 million to $590 million compared to $1.2 billion in the prior year. Cash provided by operations was $3.3 billion while cash used by investing and financing activities were $741 million and $3.2 billion respectively.

Strategy

A significant element of their strategy is to increase revenue growth by focusing on innovation and new product development. New product development requires significant investment in research and development clinical trials and regulatory approvals. The results of the company' product development efforts may be affected by a number of factors including their ability to anticipate customer needs innovate and develop new products and technologies successfully complete clinical trials obtain regulatory approvals and reimbursement in the United States and abroad manufacture products in a cost-effective manner obtain appropriate intellectual property protection for their products and gain and maintain market acceptance of their products.

BD remains focused on delivering sustainable growth and shareholder value while making appropriate investments for the future. BD management operates the business consistent with the following core strategies: To increase revenue growth by focusing on their core products services and solutions that deliver greater benefits to patients healthcare workers and researchers; To supplement their internal growth through strategic acquisitions; To continue investment in research and development for platform extensions and innovative new products; To make investments in growing their operations in emerging markets; To improve operating effectiveness and balance sheet productivity; and To drive an efficient capital structure and strong shareholder returns.

Company Background

Maxwell Becton and Fairleigh Dickinson established medical supply firm Becton Dickinson and Company in New York in 1897. In 1907 the company moved to New Jersey and became one of the first US firms to make hypodermic needles.

During WWI Becton Dickinson (BD) made all-glass syringes and introduced the cotton elastic bandage. After the war its researchers designed an improved stethoscope and created specialized hypodermic needles.

After the deaths of Dickinson (1948) and Becton (1951) their respective sons Fairleigh Jr. and Henry took over. BD went public in 1963 to raise money for new expansion.

HISTORY

Maxwell Becton and Fairleigh Dickinson established a medical supply firm in New York in 1897. In 1907 the company moved to New Jersey and became one of the first US firms to make hypodermic needles.

During WWI Becton Dickinson (BD) made all-glass syringes and introduced the cotton elastic bandage. After the war its researchers designed an improved stethoscope and created specialized hypodermic needles. The company supplied medical equipment to the armed forces during WWII. Becton and Dickinson helped establish Fairleigh Dickinson Junior College (now Fairleigh Dickinson University) in 1942. The company continued to develop products such as the Vacutainer blood-collection apparatus its first medical laboratory aid.

After the deaths of Dickinson (1948) and Becton (1951) their respective sons Fairleigh Jr. and Henry took over. The company introduced disposable hypodermic syringes in 1961. BD went public in 1963 to raise money for new expansion. In the 1960s the company opened plants in Brazil Canada France and Ireland and climbed aboard the conglomeration bandwagon by diversifying into such businesses as industrial gloves (Edmont 1966) and computer systems (Spear 1968). BD also went on a major acquisition spree in its core fields during the 1960s and 1970s buying more than 25 medical supply testing and lab companies by 1980.

Wesley Howe successor to Fairleigh Dickinson Jr. expanded the company's foreign sales in the 1970s. Howe thwarted a takeover by the diversifying oil giant Sun Company (now Sunoco) in 1978 and began to sell BD's non-medical businesses in 1983 ending with the 1989 sale of Edmont. Acquisitions including Deseret Medical (IV catheters surgical gloves and masks; 1986) sharpened BD's focus on medical and surgical supplies.

In the 1990s BD formed a number of alliances and ventures including a 1991 agreement to make and market Baxter International's InterLink needleless injection system which reduces the risk of accidental needle sticks and a 1993 joint venture with NeXagen (now part of Gilead Sciences) to make and market in vitro diagnostics. As tuberculosis reemerged in the US as a serious health threat the firm improved its TB-detection and drug-resistance test systems which cut testing time from as much as seven weeks to less than two.

In 1996 BD introduced GlucoWatch (a glucose monitoring device developed by Cygnus) and acquired the diagnostic business and brand name of MicroProbe (now Epoch Pharmaceuticals).

Previously known on Wall Street as a homely company that focused on cutting costs BD changed its image with a string of acquisitions beginning in 1997. The firm acquired PharMingen (biomedical research reagents) and Difco Laboratories (microbiology media) which broadened its product lines. BD also collaborated with Nanogen on diagnosis products for infectious disease.

EXECUTIVES

Chairman And Ceo, Vincent A. (Vince) Forlenza, age 67, $1,105,000 total compensation
Evp And President Global Health, Gary M. Cohen, age 62, $605,700 total compensation
Evp And General Counsel, Jeffrey S. Sherman, age 65, $560,333 total compensation
Evp Integrated Supply Chain Officer, Stephen (Steve) Sichak, age 62
Evp Cfo And Chief Administrative Officer, Christopher R. (Chris) Reidy, age 63, $746,568 total compensation
Evp Strategic Planning And Chief Marketing Officer, Nabil Shabshab, age 54

Evp And Chief Human Resource Officer, Linda M. Tharby, age 52
President, Thomas E. Polen, age 47, $651,000 total compensation
Evp; President Greater Asia, James Lim, age 55
President Pharmaceutical Systems, Alexandre Conroy, age 56, $530,334 total compensation
Evp And Chief Quality Officer, Pierre Boisier
Evp And President Life Sciences Segment, Alberto Mas, age 58
Evp Research And Development And Chief Medical Officer, Ellen R. Strahlman, age 62, $664,427 total compensation
Evp And Chief Regulatory Officer, Richard J. Naples
Vice President Global Supply Chain, Larry Smith
Svp Corporate Finance Controller And Treasurer, John Gallagher
Senior Vice President Chief Intellectual Property Counsel And Assistant Secretary, David Highet
Svp Corporate Secretary And Associate General Counsel, Gary M Defazio
Vice President Finance, Jim Clark
Vice President Strategic Initiatives, Ben Verwer
Executive Vice President Global Operations Chief Supply Chain Officer, James Borzi
Vice President, J Natale
Worldwide Vp Medical Affairs Diabetes Care, Larry Hirsch
Vice President Human Resources World Wide Businesses, Thomas Ruddy
Vp Hr Strategy And Service Delivery, Michael Tindall
Senior Vice President Taxes, Antionette Segreto
Vice President Quality, Keith Alderman
Vice President Information Technology Global Operations, Robert Shannon
Evp And General Counsel, Samrat Khichi
Evp And Chief Medical Officer, William Sigmund
Vice President Corporate Marketing, Carol Stone
Group Vice President, Sharon Luboff
Assistant Secretary, Patricia Walesiewicz
Assistant Secretary, David Singer
Assistant Secretary, Robert Thibeault
Board Member, Claire Fraser-liggett
Board Member, Willard Overlock
Auditors: Ernst & Young LLP

LOCATIONS

HQ: Becton, Dickinson & Co
1 Becton Drive, Franklin Lakes, NJ 07417-1880
Phone: 201 847-6800
Web: www.bd.com

2018 Sales

	$ mil.	% of total
US	8,769	55
EMEA	3,298	21
Greater Asia	2,460	15
Other	1,457	9
Total	**15,983**	**100**

PRODUCTS/OPERATIONS

2018 Sales by Segment

	$ mil.	% of total
Medical	8,616	54
Life Sciences	4,330	27
Interventional	3,037	19
Total	**15,983**	**100**

Selected Products

Medical
  Anesthesia needles and trays
  Hypodermic needles and syringes
  Intravenous catheters
  Insulin syringes and pen needles
  Prefillable drug-delivery systems
  Prefillable IV flush syringes
  Safety needles and syringes
  Sharps disposal systems
Diagnostics

Bar-code systems for patient identification and data capture
Blood culturing systems
Cytology systems (for cervical cancer screening)
Drug susceptibility systems
Immunodiagnostic test kits
Microorganism identification systems
Molecular diagnostics (for infectious disease and hospital infection testing)
Plated media
Rapid diagnostic assays
Safety-engineered blood collection devices
Sample collection products
Specimen management systems
Biosciences
  Cell culture media
  Cell sorters and analyzers
  Cell growth and screening products
  Cellular imaging systems
  Clinical and research laboratory software
  Diagnostic assays
  Labware (tubes pipettes Petri dishes etc.)
  Molecular biology reagents (for study of genes)
  Monoclonal antibodies (for biomedical research)
  Other research reagents

COMPETITORS

Abbott Labs	Hospira
B. Braun Melsungen	Johnson & Johnson
Baxter International	Novo Nordisk
Boston Scientific	Roche Diagnostics
Dako	Terumo
Fresenius	Thermo Fisher
Gen-Probe	Scientific
Hologic	bioMérieux

HISTORICAL FINANCIALS

Company Type: Public

Income Statement

FYE: September 30

	REVENUE ($ mil.)	NET INCOME ($ mil.)	NET PROFIT MARGIN	EMPLOYEES
09/20	17,117	874	5.1%	72,000
09/19	17,290	1,233	7.1%	70,093
09/18	15,983	311	1.9%	76,032
09/17	12,093	1,100	9.1%	41,933
09/16	12,483	976	7.8%	50,928
Annual Growth	**8.2%**	**(2.7%)**	**—**	**9.0%**

2020 Year-End Financials

Debt ratio: 33.20%	No. of shares (mil.): 290
Return on equity: 3.89%	Dividends
Cash ($ mil.): 2,825	Yield: 1.3%
Current ratio: 1.54	Payout: 116.6%
Long-term debt ($ mil.): 17,224	Market value ($ mil.): 67,481

	STOCK PRICE ($) FY Close	P/E High/Low		PER SHARE ($) Earnings	Dividends	Book Value
09/20	232.68	104	73	2.71	3.16	81.94
09/19	252.96	66	52	3.94	3.08	77.95
09/18	261.00	423	312	0.60	3.00	78.27
09/17	195.95	44	35	4.60	2.92	56.82
09/16	179.73	40	29	4.49	2.64	35.79
Annual Growth	**6.7%**	**—**	**—**	**(11.9%)**	**4.6%**	**23.0%**

Bed, Bath & Beyond, Inc.

Bed Bath & Beyond (BBB) is one of the nation's superstore domestics retailer with about 975 BBB stores throughout the US Puerto Rico and Canada.

The stores' floor-to-ceiling shelves stock better-quality (brand-name and private-label) goods in two main categories: domestics (bed linens bathroom and kitchen items) and home furnishings (cookware and cutlery small household appliances picture frames and more). BBB also operates around 260 Cost Plus and World Market stores and four smaller specialty chains: about 125 buybuy Baby stores about 80 Christmas Tree Shops nearly 55 Harmon discount health and beauty shops and three One Kings Lane stores. California and Texas are its largest markets accounting for about 20% of its total stores.

Operations

BBB sells a wide assortment of domestics merchandise and home furnishings. Sales of home furnishings generate about 65% of the retailer's total revenue while domestic merchandise makes up about 35% of total revenue each year.

Domestics merchandise includes categories such as bed linens and related items bath items and kitchen textiles while home furnishings include categories such as kitchen and tabletop items fine tabletop basic housewares general home furnishings (including furniture and wall décor) consumables and certain juvenile products.

Some of the company's proprietary brands include Bee & Willow Home Wamsutta Olivia & Oliver SALT and Artisanal Kitchen Supply.

BBB purchases substantially all of its merchandise in the US while the rest are purchased from importers. It also purchases a small amount of its merchandise directly from overseas sources. It has approximately 10600 suppliers with the ten largest accounting for nearly 20% of total purchases.

Geographic Reach

Nearly all of the New Jersey-based BBB's about 1430 stores are in the US though around 70 of its stores are located across nine Canadian provinces while three are in Puerto Rico. Nearly 40% of the company's stores are in five US states: California Texas Florida New York and New Jersey.

In Mexico BBB also has a joint venture where it currently operates some ten stores under the BBB banner.

Sales and Marketing

BBB prefers to locate its stores in strip malls and power strip shopping centers in suburban areas of medium and large-sized cities. It also places its stores near major off-price and conventional malls.

The company's marketing efforts include email mobile SMS social search digital display content and influencer marketing online affiliate programs and public relations efforts as well as traditional print media such as postcards newspaper inserts circulars and catalogs all of which sometimes include coupon offers.

BBB spent $478.5 million $463.2 million and $444.4 million in advertising for FY 2019 2018 and 2017 respectively.

Financial Performance

After three straight years of revenue growth since 2016 the company took a downturn after that. Net income decreased drastically until the company took losses in the last two years.

Revenue decreased to $11.2 billion in fiscal 2020 an approximately 7% drop from the year prior. The decrease was due to a decrease in the number of transactions in stores partially offset by an increase in the average transaction amount.

The company net loss increased to $613.8 million in fiscal 2020 due to unfavorable impact from goodwill and other impairments an incremental charge for markdowns severance costs shareholder activity costs and a loss from a sale-lease-back transaction including transaction costs.

Cash on hand at the end of fiscal 2020 was $1 billion. Cash provided by operating activities was $590.9 million while investing activities provided

another $91.4 million. Financing activities used $182.8 million for the repurchase of stocks and payment of dividends.

Strategy

The company's strategic growth plans are grounded in five key pillars: Product Price Promise Place and People and focused on a singular purpose to make it easy to feel at home. With these five pillars as its framework the company is embracing a commitment to build and manage a modern durable business model. The company remains focused on accelerating its extensive transformation efforts and driving against the following near-term priorities: stabilizing sales and driving top-line growth; resetting the cost structure; reviewing and optimizing the company's asset base including its portfolio of retail banners; and refining the company's organization structure.

The company plans to invest in and clarify compelling value through its pricing strategy to sharpen its value-for-quality proposition and to acquire regain and retain customers. It is also adapting its physical channels to further integrate its omnichannel capabilities to enhance the in-store customer experience by bringing products services and solutions as well as the company's brand to life. This includes services such as reserve online and pickup in-store purchase online and return in-store and online appointment scheduling for one of the company's various registry services. Beginning in April 2020 in some locations customers can buy online and pick up in store or pick up orders curbside.

Company Background

In 1971 Bed Bath & Beyond was founded by Warren Eisenberg and Leonard Feinstein who originally called it Bed 'n Bath and opened the first store in New Jersey. As per the name it initially only sold items for the bedroom and bathroom. By 1985 it had expanded to 17 operate in New York New Jersey Connecticut and California and the first superstore is opened. In 1987 the company's name is changed to Bed Bath & Beyond.

In 1991 BBB's sales reach $134 million and following that year the firm goes public. By 1994 electric appliances are added the store's product offerings. In 1999 sales exceed $1 billion. By 2000 the firm grows to 311 stores in 43 states.

HISTORY

Warren Eisenberg and Leonard Feinstein both employed by a discounter called Arlan's brainstormed an idea in 1971 for a chain of stores offering only home goods. They were betting that customers were in Feinstein's words interested in a "designer approach to linens and housewares." The two men started two small linens stores (about 2000 sq. ft) named bed n bath one in New York and one in New Jersey.

Expansion came at a fairly slow pace as the company moved only into California and Connecticut by 1985. By then the time was right for such a specialty retailer: Department stores were cutting back on their houseware lines to focus on the more profitable apparel segment and baby boomers were spending more leisure time at their homes (and more money on spiffing them up). Eisenberg and Feinstein opened a 20000-sq.-ft. superstore in 1985 that offered a full line of home furnishings. The firm changed its name to Bed Bath & Beyond (BBB) two years later in order to reflect its new offerings.

With the successful superstore format the company built all new stores in the larger design. BBB grew rapidly; square footage quadrupled between 1992 and 1996. The company went public in 1992. That year it eclipsed the size of its previous stores when it opened a 50000-sq.-ft. store in Man-

hattan. (It later enlarged this store to 80000 sq. ft.; the company's stores now average 42000 sq. ft.)

BBB's management has attributed its success in part to the leeway it gives its store managers who monitor inventory and have the freedom to try new products and layouts. One example often cited by the company is the case of a manager who decided to sell glasses by the piece instead of in sets. Sales increased 30% and the whole chain incorporated the practice.

The retailer opened 28 new stores in 1996 33 in 1997 (its first-ever billion-dollar sales year) and 45 in 1998.

In 1999 the company dipped a toe into the waters of e-commerce by agreeing to buy a stake in Internet Gift Registries which operates the WeddingNetwork website. The company later began offering online sales and bridal registry services. Keeping up its rapid expansion pace the company opened 70 stores in 1999 85 in 2000 and 95 in 2001.

In 2002 BBB acquired Harmon Stores a health and beauty aid retailer with 29 stores in three states. It acquired Christmas Tree Shops a giftware and household items retailer with 23 stores in six states for $200 million in 2003.

In March 2007 BBB acquired buybuy BABY which operates eight stores on the East Coast for $67 million. The retailer opened its first Canadian location in Ontario north of Toronto in December. In 2008 BBB added three more stores in Canada and its first locations in Mexico via a joint venture there under the Home & More banner.

In June 2012 the company bought Cost Plus which operates nearly 260 stores in 30 states under the World Market Cost Plus World Market and Cost Plus Imports banners for $495 million in cash.

In 2015 BBB acquired Of a Kind an e-commerce website that features specially commissioned limited edition items from emerging fashion and home designers.

In 2016 the company acquired online home goods retailer One Kings Lane Inc. in an all-cash deal. The deal the value of which was undisclosed bolstered BBB's furniture and home décor offerings in the online space. One Kings offers an extensive collection of designer and vintage furniture rugs kitchenware lighting and other décor for homes.

Also in 2016 the company acquired PersonalizationMall.com a online seller of personalized gifts for $190 in cash.In early 2017 it acquired Decorist an online interior design platform that provides personalized home design services. Decorist also offers photorealistic 3-D renderings of how items will look in their actual homes and offers additional online services.

EXECUTIVES

Vice President, Jim Brendle
Vice President, William Plate
Vice President Real Estate, Seth Geldzahler
Vice President Stores Midwest Region, Dana Pelan
Vice President, Patrick M Kelley
Vice President, Francis Garrity
Vice President Supply Chain Logistics, Jeffrey Macak
Vice President Of Human Resources Operations, Tina Suojanen
Vice President, Eugene Castagna
Vice President Brands And Merchant Cross Concept Integration, Jean Lindsley
Vice President Of Transportation, Doug Hanley
Vice President, Hiten Shroff
Vice President, John Mariani
Vice President Information Technology, Guy Miller
Vice President Customer Service, Hank Rinehardt

Vice President, Edward Kopil

Vice President Of Design And Development, Robert Caruso

Vice President Corporate Purchasing, Teresa Miller

Senior Vice President Of Sales, Josh Lighty

Vice President Ecom Merchandising, Nancy Oconnor

Vice President Information Technology Infrastructure And Security, David Ortiz

Vice President Digital Marketing And Crm, Tom Kuypers

Vice President Visual Merchandising, Cindy Davis

Vice President Of Information Technology, Louis Sepe

Vice President Human Resources, Concetta Van Dyke

Vice President Finance, Jason Quint

Vice President Merchandise Planning Al, Nika Markus

Vp And Corporate Counsel, Michael Callahan

Vp Payroll, Paula Barone

Regional Vice President, Bill Onksen

Senior Business Intelligence Developer, Jaskiran Singh

Vice President, Robert Roe

Executive Vice President Supply Chain, Jason Pankowski

Vp Gmm, Steve Mcgee

Vice President, Lisa Cavanagh

Vice President, Chris Jackey

Vice President Store Operations, Christine Pirog

Vice President Information Technology, Bob Roe

Vice President Of Information Technology, Timothy Kirchner

Vice President Of Supply Chain, Jeff Macak

Vice President Financial Management, Laura Crossen

Vice President, Bill Plate

Regional Vice President Southeast, Sal Dimino

Vice President Sales And Marketing, Eric Roth

Vp, Matt Mffiorilli

Department Head, Morgan Biggs

Vice President Pmo, Andrea Arrowsmith

Vp Pricing, Barrie Carmel

Vice President Portfolio Management, Jinny Uppal

Vp Risk Management, Manuel Homem

Vice President Digital And Ecommerce, Corey Bergstrom

Board Member, Jordan Heller

Board Member, Victoria Morrison

Board Member, Klaus Eppler

Board Member, Dean S Adler

Board Member, Adam Heller

Auditors: KPMG LLP

LOCATIONS

HQ: Bed, Bath & Beyond, Inc.
650 Liberty Avenue, Union, NJ 07083
Phone: 908 688-0888   **Fax:** 908 810-8813
Web: www.bedbathandbeyond.com

2017 Stores

	No.
California	184
Texas	119
New York	101
Florida	96
New Jersey	91
Illinois	55
Ohio	49
Virginia	46
Massachusetts	44
Michigan	44
Pennsylvania	44
North Carolina	43
Arizona	42
Georgia	39
Washington	37
Colorado	35
Tennessee	29
Connecticut	25
Ontario Canada	25
Alabama	24

	No.
South Carolina	24
Indiana	23
Maryland	23
Missouri	23
Louisiana	20
Oregon	17
Utah	16
Wisconsin	16
Minnesota	15
Nevada	15
New Hampshire	14
Kansas	12
Alberta Canada	12
British Columbia Canada	12
Iowa	11
Kentucky	11
Idaho	10
New Mexico	10
Other	90
Total	**1,546**

PRODUCTS/OPERATIONS

2017 Stores

	No.
Bed Bath & Beyond	1,023
Cost Plus World Market	276
BABY Stores	113
Christmas Tree Shops	80
Harmon stores	54
Total	**1,546**

COMPETITORS

Amazon.com	Macy's
Art.com	Pier 1 Imports
Babies "R" Us	Ross Stores
Burlington Coat Factory	Sensational Beginnings
Children's Place	TJX Companies
Container Store	Target Corporation
Dillard's	Tuesday Morning Corporation
Euromarket Designs	Wal-Mart
Garden Ridge	Wayfair
Gymboree	Williams-Sonoma
Kmart	

HISTORICAL FINANCIALS

Company Type: Public

Income Statement

FYE: February 29

	REVENUE ($ mil.)	NET INCOME ($ mil.)	NET PROFIT MARGIN	EMPLOYEES
02/20*	11,158	(613)	—	55,000
03/19	12,028	(137)	—	62,000
03/18	12,349	424	3.4%	65,000
02/17	12,215	685	5.6%	65,000
02/16	12,103	841	7.0%	62,000
Annual Growth	(2.0%)	—		(3.0%)

*Fiscal year change

2020 Year-End Financials

Debt ratio: 19.11%
Return on equity: (-28.46%)
Cash ($ mil.): 1,000
Current ratio: 1.55
Long-term debt ($ mil.): 1,488

No. of shares (mil.): 126
Dividends
  Yield: 0.0%
  Payout: —
Market value ($ mil.): 1,368

	STOCK PRICE ($) FY Close	P/E High/Low		Earnings	PER SHARE ($) Dividends	Book Value
02/20*	10.81	—	—	(4.94)	0.67	13.95
03/19	16.69	—	—	(1.02)	0.63	19.36
03/18	21.83	14	6	3.04	0.58	20.56
02/17	41.04	11	8	4.58	0.38	18.59
02/16	48.99	15	8	5.10	0.00	16.34
Annual Growth	(31.5%)	—	—	—	—	(3.9%)

*Fiscal year change

Berkley (WR) Corp

Holding company W. R. Berkley offers an assortment of niche commercial property/casualty insurance across two segments – Insurance and Reinsurance. The Insurance segment comprising more than 50 operating companies underwrites commercial insurance coverage including excess and surplus lines and admitted lines. It also develops self-insuring programs aimed at employers and employer groups. The Reinsurance segment allows insurance companies to pool their risks in order to reduce their liability. Berkley serves customers in 60 countries in the Americas Europe and the Asia/Pacific region.

Operations

Berkley's Insurance segment accounts for more than 80% of the company's total revenue while the Reinsurance segment accounts for about 10%. The remainder is brought in by other operations.

In addition to insurance products Berkley offers a variety of fee-based services such as claims administrative and consulting services.

Geographic Reach

Headquartered in Greenwich Ct Berkley offers insurance and reinsurance through more than 50 operating units in more than 60 nations in North America South America Europe Africa and the Asia/Pacific region.

Sales and Marketing

Berkley primarily serves small to midsized business customers. The insurer sells its high-risk coverage products directly and through retail and wholesale agents brokers and managing general agents to a wide variety of clients. The regional products business' offerings are sold through a network of brokers and commission-based independent agents.

Financial Performance

Berkley's revenue have been continuously increasing over the past five years. Between 2015 and 2019 the company's revenue increased by 9% to $7.9 billion.

In 2019 revenue rose to roughly 3% to $7.9 billion compared from $7.7 billion in 2018. The increase was primarily due to an increase in Insurance and Reinsurance & Monoline Excess revenue in the present year. Net income increased 6% to $681.9 million in 2019.

The increase in net income was primarily due to an after-tax increase in underwriting income an increase in income from minority interest an after-tax decrease in interest expense an increase in after-tax foreign currency gains a decrease in tax expense an after-tax increase in other income partially offset by a decrease in after-tax net investment gains an after-tax decrease in net investment income mainly driven by investment funds an after-tax increase in corporate expenses an after-tax reduction in insurance service fee income of $6 million and an after-tax decrease in income from non-insurance businesses.

The company ended 2019 with $1.0 billion in net cash about $206.1 million higher than it had at the end of 2018. Operating activities provided $1.1 billion while investing activities used $424.9 million and financing activities used $513.2 million. Berkley's main cash was primarily used to purchase fixed maturity securities payment of senior notes and other debt and cash dividends to common stockholders.

Strategy

Strategically Berkley's decentralized structure promotes the development of specialized expertise in a range of areas and enables the company to adapt to cyclical market conditions and insulate itself from great risk. While the company has made a handful of acquisitions through the years it prefers to expand by forming new operating units after identifying needs in specific areas. In 2018 the company launched Berkley Healthcare which specializes in services and products for health care providers. In mid-2019 Berkley formed Berkley Prime Transportation which will focus on providing primary commercial transportation insurance products countrywide for standard and preferred risks. The new division will focus on leveraging analytics and technology to develop new methods of providing quality and responsive service to agents and customers.

Other recent additions include firms specializing in cybersecurity and health care. In 2018 subsidiary Berkley One established a partnership with data defense services provider CyberScout to offer a suite of cyber solutions covering identity theft cyber bullying and system compromise. That same unit is also rolling out its platform serving high-net-worth customers in certain states; it is now active in about a dozen states.

The company focuses on growing world markets including Scandinavia South America Australia and the Asia-Pacific region. Additionally Berkley exits insurance lines as demand diminishes.

With the insurance market being so fragmented and new competitors entering the fray Berkley is under pressure to keep its prices down. This has led to a slowdown in premium growth for the company.

Company Background

Bill Berkley and a partner established investment management firm Berkley Dean & Company in 1967. The company went public as W.R. Berkley Corporation in 1973. Over the years it expanded through the formation of new companies as well as acquisitions.

EXECUTIVES

Evp Investments, James G. Shiel, age 60, $650,000 total compensation
Senior Vice President Insurance Risk Management, Robert Gosselink
Senior Vice President, Peter Kamford
Senior Vice President Underwriting, Michele Fleckenstein
Evp, C. Fred Madsen
Evp And Secretary, Ira S. Lederman, age 67, $650,000 total compensation
Evp, Eugene G. Ballard, age 67, $650,000 total compensation
President And Ceo, W. Robert (Rob) Berkley, age 47, $993,769 total compensation
Evp, Robert C. Hewitt, age 59
Evp, Philip S. Welt, age 61
Evp, Robert D. Stone, age 56
Evp, John K. Goldwater
Evp, William M. Rohde
Evp, Jeffrey M. (Jeff) Hafter
Evp, Lucille T. Sgaglione
Svp Cfo And Treasurer, Richard M. Baio, $497,981 total compensation
Evp, Kathleen M. Tierney
Vp And Chief Marketing Officer, Jonathan M. Levine
Svp And Cio, Richard M. Lowery
Evp, James P. Bronner
Svp And Chief Project Officer, Mir Mazhar
Evp, Kenneth P. Sroka
Executive Vice President, James Gilbert
Assistant Vice President And Corporate Actuary, Gene Zhang
Vice President Analytics, Robert McPherson
Assistant Vice President Of Application Developmen, Jim Leonardis
Vice President, Marie Gwin

Vice President And Head Corporate Catastrophe Analysis, Robert Sabio
Executive Vice President, Ricardo Gonzalez
Vice President Actuarial And Data Analysis, Debbie Savoie
Executive Vice President, Steven Walsh
Senior Vice President Information Technology, Kevin H Ebers
Vice President Corporate Actuary, Jessica Somerfeld
Senior Vice President, C Madsen
Senior Vice President Underwriting, Joseph Walsh
Senior Vice President Chief Corporate Actuary, Paul Hancock
Senior Vice President Human Resources, Carol La Punzina
Svp, Steven Taylor
Vice President Claims, Brian Yoshikuni
Vice President, Beena Gadgil
Senior Vice President Enterprise Risk Management, Gillian James
Vice President And Senior Counsel, John Littzi
Vice President Marketing, John Bowen
Assistant Vice President Actuarial Analysis, Scott Jensen
Vice President And Corporate Controller, Andrea Kanefsky
Vice President Real Estate Operations, Jesse Faneuil
Senior Vice President Corporate Strategy And Development, Jared Abbey
Vice President Insurance Risk Management, Laura Goodall
Vice President Enterprise Risk Management, Trish Conway
Senior Vice President Marketing, Christoph Ritterson
Senior Vice President Customer Experience Berkley One, Susan Vella
Senior Vice President Insurance Risk Management, Melissa Emmendorfer
Vice President Actuary, Dustin J Turner
Vice President Team Infrastructure, Mike Chang
Vice President Actuary, Dustin Turner
Vice President And Chief Information Security Officer, Keith Wilson
Evp, Michael Maloney
Vp Marketing And Distribution Manager, Ryan Reeves
Senior Vice President, Tod Bolden
Vp International Network Manager, Brenda Menichillo
Vice President Underwriting, Tom Ravn
Chairman, William R. (Bill) Berkley, age 74
Assistant Secretary Human Resources, Donna Syko
Assistant Treasurer, George Richardson
Auditors: KPMG LLP

LOCATIONS

HQ: Berkley (WR) Corp
475 Steamboat Road, Greenwich, CT 06830
Phone: 203 629-3000
Web: www.wrberkley.com

PRODUCTS/OPERATIONS

2018 Sales

	$ mil.	% of total
Insurance	6,456	84
Reinsurance	1,600	8
Net investment gains	480	6
Corporate & other	154	2
Total	**7,718**	**100**

2018 Sales

	$ mil.	% of total
Net premiums earned	6,371	82
Net investment income	674	9
Revenue from non-insurance businesses	373	5
Net realized and unrealized gains on investments	154	2
Insurance service fees	117	2
Other	0	
Total	**7,718**	**100**

Selected Property/Casualty Segments

Specialty (includes excess and surplus lines and admitted specialty lines)
Regional (commercial lines property/casualty)
Alternative markets (includes excess workers' compensation monoline workers' compensation accident and health and insurance services)
Reinsurance (facultative or treaty basis; participates in business written through Lloyd's of London)
International business (global underwriting)

COMPETITORS

AIG	Munich Re America
Allied World Assurance	Nationwide
American Financial Group	Swiss Re
	Transatlantic
Arch Capital	Reinsurance
Berkshire Hathaway	Travelers Companies
CNA Financial	White Mountains
Everest Re	Insurance Group

HISTORICAL FINANCIALS

Company Type: Public

Income Statement — FYE: December 31

	ASSETS ($ mil.)	NET INCOME ($ mil.)	INCOME AS % OF ASSETS	EMPLOYEES
12/19	26,643	681	2.6%	7,493
12/18	24,895	640	2.6%	7,448
12/17	24,299	549	2.3%	7,722
12/16	23,364	601	2.6%	7,683
12/15	21,730	503	2.3%	7,621
Annual Growth	**5.2%**	**7.9%**	**—**	**(0.4%)**

2019 Year-End Financials

Debt ratio: 9.86%
Return on equity: 11.85%
Cash ($ mil.): 1,023
Current ratio: —
Long-term debt ($ mil.): —
No. of shares (mil.): 183
Dividends
Yield: 2.4%
Payout: 46.6%
Market value ($ mil.): 12,674

	STOCK PRICE ($) FY Close	P/E High/Low		Earnings	PER SHARE ($) Dividends	Book Value
12/19	69.10	24	16	3.52	1.68	33.12
12/18	73.91	24	20	3.33	1.39	29.72
12/17	71.65	25	21	2.84	1.03	29.69
12/16	66.51	20	15	3.12	1.01	27.76
12/15	54.75	22	18	2.58	0.31	24.87
Annual Growth	**6.0%**			**8.1%**	**52.2%**	**7.4%**

Berkshire Hathaway Inc

Berkshire Hathaway is the holding company where Warren Buffett one of the world's richest men makes his money and spreads his risk. The company invests in a variety of industries. The most important of these are insurance businesses conducted on both a primary basis and a reinsurance basis a freight rail transportation business and a group of utility and energy generation and distribution businesses.. Its core insurance subsidiaries include GEICO National Indemnity and reinsurance giant General Re. The company's other large holdings include Marmon Group McLane Company MidAmerican Energy and Shaw Industries.

Operations

Berkshire Hathaway operates as a holding company with a highly decentralized structure without integrated business functions (such as sales marketing purchasing legal and human resources). Practicing a minimal day-to-day management leadership style the firm owns a diverse group of companies from a variety of industries with its core subsidiaries being insurance reinsurance freight rail transportation utilities and energy generation companies.

The insurance businesses constitute some 65% of total revenue and are conducted through numerous domestic and foreign-based insurance entities. Berkshire's insurance businesses provide insurance and reinsurance of property and casualty and life accident and health risks worldwide. Its most recognizable holding is GEICO (auto insurance). Sales and service revenues make up around 40% of the insurance business revenue while about 20% comes from insurance premiums. Nearly 15% of Berkshire Hathaway revenue comes from its railroad utilities and energy subsidiaries.

Lesser known to most are the company's investment in industries outside of energy and insurance. Such holdings include a railroad transportation company (Burlington Northern Santa Fe) a carpet manufacturer (Shaw Industries) a wholesale distributor of consumer goods (McLane) a manufacturer of clay bricks (Acme Brick) a battery company (Duracell) and a specialty chemicals producer (Lubrizol).

Berkshire also holds investment stakes in American Express ($18.9 billion) Apple ($73.7 billion) Bank of America ($33.4 billion) Coca-Cola ($22.1 billion) and Wells Fargo ($18.6 billion).

Geographic Reach

Omaha Nebraska-headquartered Berkshire Hathaway operates primarily in the US though it provides insurance (and reinsurance) to clients in the Asia/Pacific Canada and Europe regions.

Financial Performance

Buffett's famed investment vehicle has enjoyed mostly upward trends in revenue and profits highlighting the investors' knack for choosing financially successful companies over the long term. It grew revenue from $200 billion in 2015 to almost $255 billion in 2019. Net income expanded from $24 billion in 2015 to a peak of $81 billion in 2019.

In 2019 Berkshire recorded $254.6 billion in revenues across its collection of businesses up from $247.8 billion in 2018. Huge gains from interest from dividend and other investment income drove increase in total revenues.

Berkshire reported a net income of $81.4 billion in 2019 compared to $4 billion in 2018. The big jump was because of huge gain in investment and derivative incomes.

Berkshire ended 2019 with approximately $64.6 billion in cash and cash equivalents. While operating activities provided $38.7 billion and financing activities also generated $730 million investing activities used more than $5.6 billion mainly for purchases of treasury bills and securities.

Strategy

Equity securities represent a significant portion of Berkshire Hathaway's investment portfolio. Strategically it strives to invest in businesses that possess excellent economics and able and honest management and it prefers to invest a meaningful amount in each investee. Consequently equity investments are concentrated in relatively few issuers. In 2019 approximately 67% of the total fair value of equity securities was concentrated in five issuers.

The company often hold its equity investments for long periods and short-term price volatility has occurred in the past and will occur in the future. It also strives to maintain significant levels of shareholder capital and ample liquidity to provide a margin of safety against short-term price volatility.

It also invests in bonds loans or other interest rate sensitive instruments. The company strategy is to acquire or originate such instruments at prices considered appropriate relative to the perceived credit risk. It also issues debt in the ordinary course of business to fund business operations business acquisitions and for other general purposes. It also attempts to maintain high credit ratings in order to minimize the cost of own debt. It infrequently utilize derivative products such as interest rate swaps to manage interest rate risks.

Company Background

Chairman and CEO Warren Buffett along with associates slowly accumulated a majority of shares in the Berkshire Hathaway textile company in the early 1960s. To stabilize revenues and reduce financial risks Buffett diversified the company with a purchase of Indemnity and National Fire & Marine Insurance Company in 1967. Thus began the long prosperous road towards profitability and dozens of acquisitions. Buffett still owns about 20% of Berkshire Hathaway's shares.

HISTORY

Warren Buffett bought his first stock — three shares of Cities Service — at age 11. In the 1950s he studied at Columbia University under famed investor Benjamin Graham. Graham's axioms: Use quantitative analysis to discover companies whose intrinsic worth exceeds their stock prices; popularity is irrelevant; the market will vindicate the patient investor.

In 1956 Buffett then 25 founded Buffett Partnership. Its $105000 in initial assets multiplied as the company bought Berkshire Hathaway (textiles 1965) and National Indemnity (insurance 1967). When Buffett nixed the partnership in 1969 because he believed stocks were overvalued value per share had risen 30-fold.

In late 2012 the firm also acquired Omaha-based online party supplier Oriental Trading Company.

Berkshire Hathaway's $28-billion purchase of ketchup giant H.J. Heinz in 2013 is also a textbook example of the firm's investment strategy as the firm and its investment partner Brazil's 3G Capital took the ketchup maker private to speed its transformation into a global food business.

EXECUTIVES

Chairman Bnsf Railway., Matthew K. (Matt) Rose, age 61

Svp And Cfo, Marc D. Hamburg, age 70, $1,550,000 total compensation

Chairman And Ceo, Warren E. Buffett, age 90, $100,000 total compensation

Head Of Reinsurance, Ajit Jain, age 68

Head Of Berkshire Hathaway Energy, Greg Abel

Vice President Human Resources And Administration, Jennifer Johnson

Vice Chairman, Charles T. (Charlie) Munger, age 96

Board Member, Thomas Murphy

Treasurer And Controller, Janet Saar

Auditors: DELOITTE & TOUCHE LLP

LOCATIONS

HQ: Berkshire Hathaway Inc
  3555 Farnam Street, Omaha, NE 68131
Phone: 402 346-1400
Web: www.berkshirehathaway.com

PRODUCTS/OPERATIONS

2016 sales

	$ mil.	% of total
Insurance and Other		
Sales and service revenues	119,489	53
Insurance premiums earned	45,881	21
Investment gains	5,128	2
Interest dividend and other investment income	4,725	2
Railroad Utilities and Energy	37,542	17
Finance and Financial Products		
Sales and service revenues	6,208	3
Investment gains	2,425	1
Interest dividend and other investment income	1,455	1
Derivative gains	751	0
Total	**223,604**	**100**

Subsidiaries and Selected Holdings

Acme Brick Company (bricks)
Applied Underwriters (workers' compensation)
Ben Bridge Jeweler (jewelry retailer)
Benjamin Moore (architectural and industrial paint)
Berkshire Hathaway Automotive
Berkshire Hathaway Energy Company
Berkshire Hathaway GUARD Insurance Companies
Berkshire Hathaway Homestate Companies
Berkshire Hathaway Life Insurance Company of
  Nebraska
BH Media Group (digital marketing publishing)
Boat U.S. (insurance)
Borsheim Jewelry Company (jewelry retailer)
Brooks (shoes)
The Buffalo News (newspaper)
Burlington Northern Santa Fe (railroad)
Business Wire Inc. (news service)
Central States Indemnity Co. of Omaha (credit and
  disability insurance)
Clayton Homes (manufactured housing and financing)
CORT Business Services Corp. (provider of rental
  furniture accessories and related services)
CTB International (manufacturer of equipment and
  systems for poultry hog and egg production)
The Fechheimer Brothers (uniforms and accessories)
FlightSafety International (high technology training to
  operators of aircraft and ships)
Forest River (recreational vehicles)
Fruit of the Loom (apparel)
Garan Inc. (apparel)
GEICO (property/casualty insurance)
General Re Corporation (property/casualty reinsurance)
H.H. Brown Shoe Company
Helzberg's Diamond Shops (jewelry retailer)
HomeServices of America (real estate services)
International Dairy Queen Inc. (licensing and servicing
  Dairy Queen Stores)
Johns Manville (building and equipment insulation)
Jordan's Furniture (retailing home furnishings)
Justin Brands (western footwear and apparel)
Kraft Heinz
Larson-Juhl
LiquidPower Speciality Products
Lubrizol (specialty chemicals)
Marmon Holdings (manufacturing and service)
McLane Company (wholesale distribution of groceries
  and non-food items)
MedPro Group (Med Pro; professional liability insurer)
MidAmerican Energy Holdings Company
  HomeServices of America Inc. (residential real estate
    brokerage)
  Kern River Gas Transmission Company
  Northern Electric
  Northern Natural Gas
  Pacific Power
  Rocky Mountain Power
  Yorkshire Electricity
MiTek (building components)
National Indemnity Company (specialty insurance)
Nebraska Furniture Mart (retailing home furnishings)
NetJets Inc. (fractional ownership programs for general
  aviation aircraft)
Oriental Trading Company (party supplies)
Pampered Chef Ltd. (kitchenware and housewares)
Precision Castparts Corp (aerospace parts manufacturer)
Precision Steel Warehouse (steel service center)
R.C. Willey Home Furnishings (home furnishings
  retailer)
Richline Group (jewelry manufacturer)
Scott Fetzer Company (manufacture and distribution of
  diversified products)

See's Candies (boxed chocolates and other confectionery
   products)
Shaw Industries (carpets and rugs)
Star Furniture Co. (home furnishings retailer)
TTI Inc. (electronics distribution)
United States Liability Insurance Group
XTRA Corporation (transportation equipment)

COMPETITORS

AEA Investors	Lincoln Financial
Allstate	Group
Apollo Global	Progressive
Management	Corporation
Bain Capital	State Farm
BlackRock	TPG
Blackstone Group	The Carlyle Group
CNA Financial	The Hartford
KKR	

HISTORICAL FINANCIALS

Company Type: Public

Income Statement   FYE: December 31

	ASSETS ($ mil.)	NET INCOME ($ mil.)	INCOME AS % OF ASSETS	EMPLOYEES
12/19	817,729	81,417	10.0%	391,500
12/18	707,794	4,021	0.6%	389,000
12/17	702,095	44,940	6.4%	377,000
12/16	620,854	24,074	3.9%	367,700
12/15	552,257	24,083	4.4%	331,000
Annual Growth	10.3%	35.6%	—	4.3%

2019 Year-End Financials

Debt ratio: 12.64%
Return on equity: 21.05%
Cash ($ mil.): 127,997
Current ratio: —
Long-term debt ($ mil.): —

No. of shares (mil.): 1
Dividends
   Yield: —
   Payout: —
Market value ($ mil.): 551,819

	STOCK PRICE ($) FY Close	P/E High/Low	PER SHARE ($) Earnings	Dividends	Book Value
12/19	339,590.00 261,416.60	7	649,828.00	0.00	
12/18	306,000.00 212,503.41	1371	152,446.00	0.00	
12/17	297,600.00 211,749.91	11	927,326.00	0.00	
12/16	244,121.00 172,108.12	17	1314,645.00	0.00	
12/15	197,800.00 155,501.45	15	1314,656.00	0.00	
Annual Growth	14.5%	— —	35.8%	—	13.9%

Berkshire Hills Bancorp Inc

Berkshire Hills Bancorp is the holding company
for Berkshire Bank which serves individuals and
small businesses through some 90 branches in
Massachusetts New York Connecticut and Vermont. Established in 1846 the bank provides standard deposit products such as savings checking
and money market accounts CDs and IRAs in addition to credit cards investments private banking
wealth management and lending services. Real estate mortgages make up nearly three-quarters of
Berkshire Hills Bancorp's loan portfolio which also
includes business and consumer loans. In addition
to its banking activities the company also owns insurance agency Berkshire Insurance Group.

Geographic Reach

Berkshire Hills Bancorp also is eyeing further
expansion into Connecticut and other parts of New
England and New York by opening new branches
and through acquisitions.

Financial Performance

Berkshire Hills Bancorp's revenue increased in
fiscal 2013 compared to the prior year. It reported
$262 million in revenue for fiscal 2013 up from
$230 million in fiscal 2012. Net income also went
up to $58 million in fiscal 2013 compared to the
$47 million Berkshire Hills Bancorp reported for
net income in fiscal 2012.

The company's cash on hand increased by more
than $100 million in fiscal 2013 compared to fiscal
2012 levels.

Strategy

Berkshire Hills Bancorp which was established
in 1846 believes one of its competitive advantages
is the regional niche it serves which has been relatively unscathed by the recession compared to
other parts of the country.

The bank's performance has been boosted by
an increase in business development in the company's market area in addition to growth in its
asset-based lending and private banking businesses. The bank also has grown its loans and deposits and has plans to grow its insurance and
wealth management operations as well.

In 2016 the company completed the $150 mil-
lion acquisition of New Jersey-based First Choice
Bank. That deal which add eight bank branches
and introduce Berkshire Hills to the greater
Philadelphia area will bring the bank's network to
more than 100 branches.

EXECUTIVES

President And Ceo, Michael P. Daly, $575,000 total
   compensation
Sevp Human Resources, Linda A. Johnston
Coo Berkshire Bank, Sean A. Gray, $350,000 total
   compensation
Evp Commercial Banking, George F. Bacigalupo,
   $229,554 total compensation
President Berkshire Bank, Richard M. Marotta,
   $350,000 total compensation
Evp, Glenn S. Welch
**Sevp And Cfo Berkshire Hills Bancorp Inc. And
   Berkshire Bank,** James M. (Jamie) Moses
**Vice President Information Technology
   Infrastructure,** John O White
Vice President Relationship Manager, Justin Priddle
Avp Collections Officer, Melanie Asta
Senior Vice President, Mary Cologero
First Vice President, Philip Martin
Assistant Vice President, Gregory S Kay
Vice President Loan Closing Manager, Dana Neas
Vice President Global Management, Eric Navarra
Svp Team Leader Business Banking, Robert
   Romprey
Chairman, William J. (Bill) Ryan
Treasurer, Mike Macy
Auditors: Crowe LLP

LOCATIONS

HQ: Berkshire Hills Bancorp Inc
   60 State Street, Boston, MA 02109
Phone: 800 773-5601
Web: www.berkshirebank.com

PRODUCTS/OPERATIONS

2015 Sales

	mil$ mil.	% of total
Interest and dividend income		
Loans	211	70
Securities and other	35	12
Non-interest income		
Loan related income	8	3
Mortgage banking income	4	1
Deposit related fees	25	8
Insurance commissions and fees	10	3
Wealth management fees	9	3
Other	(5.3)	-
Gain on securities net	2	-
Total	301	100

COMPETITORS

Bank of America	KeyCorp
Citizens Financial	Pathfinder Bancorp
Group	Sovereign Bank
Hudson City Bancorp	TD Bank USA

HISTORICAL FINANCIALS

Company Type: Public

Income Statement   FYE: December 31

	ASSETS ($ mil.)	NET INCOME ($ mil.)	INCOME AS % OF ASSETS	EMPLOYEES
12/19	13,215	97	0.7%	1,550
12/18	12,212	105	0.9%	1,917
12/17	11,570	55	0.5%	1,992
12/16	9,162	58	0.6%	1,731
12/15	7,831	49	0.6%	1,221
Annual Growth	14.0%	18.4%	—	6.1%

2019 Year-End Financials

Debt ratio: 0.82%
Return on equity: 5.89%
Cash ($ mil.): 579
Current ratio: —
Long-term debt ($ mil.): —

No. of shares (mil.): 49
Dividends
   Yield: 2.8%
   Payout: 46.7%
Market value ($ mil.): 1,630

	STOCK PRICE ($) FY Close	P/E High/Low	PER SHARE ($) Earnings	Dividends	Book Value
12/19	32.88	17 13	1.97	0.92	35.47
12/18	26.97	19 11	2.29	0.88	34.19
12/17	36.60	28 24	1.39	0.84	33.04
12/16	36.85	20 13	1.88	0.80	30.65
12/15	29.11	17 14	1.73	0.76	28.64
Annual Growth	3.1%	— —	3.3%	4.9%	5.5%

Berry Global Group Inc

With a portfolio that includes tapes tubes and
trash bags Berry Global is one of the top maker of
plastic products and engineered materials for customers across a broad range of industries. Its products include shrink wrap and other packaging films
cloth and foil tapes plastic cups and lids components for diapers and other personal care items
and prescription bottles. Key markets include the
healthcare personal care and food and beverage
industries. Berry Global operates worldwide but
North America is by far its largest market. In 2019
Berry Global completed the acquisition of plastic
packaging company RPC Group for $6.5 billion.

Operations

Berry Global reports four operating segments:
Consumer Packaging North America; Health Hy-

giene & Specialties; Engineered Materials; and Consumer Packaging International.

Consumer Packaging North America segment manufacture containers and pails lightweight polypropylene cups and lids for hot and cold beverages and laminated tubes. The segment accounts for some a 30% of total revenue.

The Health Hygiene and Specialties segment primarily consists of nonwoven specialty materials and films used in hygiene infection prevention personal care industrial construction and filtration applications. The segment accounts for about a 30% of total revenue.

Engineered Materials generate about 30% of total revenue it manufactures tapes and adhesives polyethylene-based film products can liners printed films and laminated products.

The Consumer Packaging International segment primarily consists of bottles canister containers closure and dispensing systems polythene films and pharmaceutical devices and packaging. The segment accounts for some 15% of total revenue.

Geographic Reach

Headquartered in Evansville Indiana Berry Global has some 300 manufacturing facilities throughout North America Europe Middle East India Africa South America and Asia Pacific.

North America represents about a three-quarters of the company's sales.

Sales and Marketing

Berry Global sells its products to a very diverse customer base through a direct sales force and strategic distributors. Since many products are customized the sales team creates partnership with customers. The company's top ten customers account for 20% of total revenue.

Financial Performance

Berry Global's revenue has seen upward mobility increasing more than $2 billion in the last five years thanks to a string of acquisitions. In fiscal 2019 (ended September) the company reported net sales of $8.9 billion up 13% from the previous year. Acquisitions claimed the lion's share of revenue increase ($1.5 billion) partially offset by prior period divestiture sales of $20 million and favorable impact of currency exchange ($48 million).

Berry has been profitable for five years straight but has enjoyed a sharp spike in the last couple of years. Profits fell about 20% to $404 million in fiscal 2019 primarily due to a net income tax benefit of $86 million (compared to $19 million in expenses the prior year).

Cash holdings were at $750 million at the end of 2019 (ended September). Operations provided $1.2 billion offset by $6.3 billion going towards investment (mostly in acquisitions). Financial activities brought in $5.4 billion.

Strategy

Enjoying half a decade of growing revenue and profits Berry Global is looking to turn competition up a notch. To that end the company is focusing on continuing strategic acquisitions on one hand and company restructuring to save money on the other.

Berry Global acquisition strategy is focused on improving its long-term financial performance enhancing its market positions and expanding its existing and complementary product lines. In 2018-19 period Berry has shelled out $6.8 billion to acquire Laddawn Clopay RPC plastic businesses. A major area of focus has been to expand its custom bag film and flexible packaging products as well as adhesive tapes.

in 2019 the company sells its Seal for Life business to Arsenal Capital. Divesting SFL was made part of Berry Global ongoing portfolio analysis and decision to provide resources to further focus its efforts to deliver growth in targeted markets and advantaged products.

Berry's continued growth is even more impressive due to an already-crowded competitive landscape dominated by big producers including Silgan Aptar Reynolds 3M and Fitesa. The company's large and diverse customer base its scale and common customers across segments enables the company to minimize sales and marketing costs. However with current levels of healthy cash flow and reasonably costs of plastic resin the company will focus on paying down its considerable debts ($11.4 billion in long-term debt).

Mergers and Acquisitions

In 2019 Berry Global acquired RPC for $6.5 billion. Through the acquisition Berry and RPC creates a leading global supplier of valued-added protective solutions and one of the world's largest plastic packaging companies.

In 2018 Berry Global acquired Laddawn a manufacturer of blown polyethylene bags and films with a unique-to-industry e-commerce sales platform for $241 million. The combined Laddawn and Berry custom film product portfolio will provide a vast range of product offerings to thousands of valued customers further strengthening its core films business

The company also completed its acquisition of Clopay for $475 million in early 2018. The acquisition is expected to bring $40 million in cost synergies while expanding Berry's reach in the elastic films and laminates business.

Company Background

Berry Global was established in 1967 under the name of Imperial Plastics. In 1972 the injection molding company entered the container market and in 1983 Imperial plastics was purchased by Jerry Berry Sr. and renamed Berry Plastics. In 1988 it acquired some 40 companies. It began trading on the NYSE in 2012. In 2017 the company changed its name from Berry Plastics Group Inc. to Berry Global Inc.

EXECUTIVES

Vp Global Purchasing, Scott Farmer
Evp Strategic Corporate Development, Brett C. Bauer
Evp Operations, Rodgers K. Greenwalt
Cfo, Mark W. Miles, age 48, $453,380 total compensation
Chairman And Ceo, Thomas E. (Tom) Salmon, age 57, $499,617 total compensation
Evp Supply Chain, Terri Pitcher
Evp Human Resources, Ed Stratton
Evp General Counsel And Secretary, Jason K. Greene, age 49
President Engineered Materials, Curt L. Begle, age 44, $420,288 total compensation
President Flexible Packaging, Lawrence A. (Larry) Goldstein, age 57
Evp International, Jeffrey D. (Jeff) Thompson, age 48
Cio, Mark Freeman
President North America Avintiv, Scott Tracey, age 52
President Consumer Packaging, Jean-Marc Galvez
Auditors: Ernst & Young LLP

LOCATIONS

HQ: Berry Global Group Inc
  101 Oakley Street, Evansville, IN 47710
Phone: 812 424-2904
Web: www.berryplastics.com

2018 Sales

	$ mil.	% of total
North America	6,474	82
Europe	807	11
South America	332	4
Asia	256	3
Total	**7,896**	**100**

PRODUCTS/OPERATIONS

2018 Sales

	$ mil.	% of total
Consumer Packaging	2,463	31
Health Hygiene & Specialties	2,734	35
Engineered Materials	2,672	34
Total	**7,869**	**100**

Selected Products

Rigid Plastics
  Bottles
  Containers
  Closures
  Foodservice items
  Housewares
  Overcaps
  Prescription vials
  Tubes
Engineered Materials
  Can liners
  Corrosion protection
  Polyethylene-based film products
  Specialty tapes and adhesives
Flexible packaging
  Custom films
  Flexible packaging products
  Printed bags
  Pouches

Selected Brands

Versalite
Color Scents
Ruffies
Polyken
Nashua
Reemay
Stopaq
Qubic

COMPETITORS

3M	Reynolds Food
AptarGroup	Packaging
Bemis	Silgan Plastics
Intertape Polymer	Tredegar

HISTORICAL FINANCIALS

Company Type: Public

Income Statement

FYE: September 26

	REVENUE ($ mil.)	NET INCOME ($ mil.)	NET PROFIT MARGIN	EMPLOYEES
09/20	11,709	559	4.8%	47,000
09/19	8,878	404	4.6%	48,000
09/18	7,869	496	6.3%	24,000
09/17*	7,095	340	4.8%	23,000
10/16	6,489	236	3.6%	21,000
Annual Growth	**15.9%**	**24.1%**	**—**	**22.3%**

*Fiscal year change

2020 Year-End Financials

Debt ratio: 61.30%
Return on equity: 30.22%
Cash ($ mil.): 750
Current ratio: 1.75
Long-term debt ($ mil.): 10,162

No. of shares (mil.): 133
Dividends
  Yield: —
  Payout: —
Market value ($ mil.): 6,337

	STOCK PRICE ($) FY Close	P/E High/Low		PER SHARE ($) Earnings	Dividends	Book Value
09/20	47.43	13	6	4.14	0.00	15.66
09/19	39.32	19	12	3.00	0.00	12.23
09/18	48.39	16	12	3.67	0.00	10.89
09/17*	56.65	22	16	2.56	0.00	7.73
10/16	43.85	24	15	1.89	0.00	1.79
Annual Growth	**2.0%**	**—**	**—**	**21.7%**	**—**	**72.1%**

*Fiscal year change

Best Buy Inc

Electronics giant Best Buy is preparing to outlast the competition with a compelling mix of products and services. The multinational retailer sells both products and services through more than 1230 stores in the US Canada and Mexico under the Best Buy Best Buy Business Best Buy Express Best Buy Mobile Best Buy Health CST Geek Squad GreatCall Lively Magnolia and Pacific Kitchen and Home Sales banners. Its stores sell a variety of electronic gadgets and wearables tablets movies music computers mobile phones and appliances. On the services side it offers installation and maintenance delivery design in-home consultations memberships protection plans repair set-up technical support and health-related services. With 2.3 million staff members Best Buy's Geek Squad provides support for customers' technology products in a variety of ways online on the phone at customers' homes and at Best Buy store locations. The company also provides health and safety technology solutions to aging customers through its GreatCall provider.

HISTORY

Tired of working for a father who ignored his ideas on how to improve the business (electronics distribution) Dick Schulze quit. In 1966 with a partner he founded Sound of Music a Minnesota home/car stereo store. Schulze bought out his partner in 1971 and began to expand the chain. While chairing a school board Schulze saw declining enrollment and realized his target customer group 15- to 18-year-old males was shrinking. In the early 1980s he broadened his product line and targeted older more affluent customers by offering appliances and VCRs.

After a 1981 tornado destroyed his best store (but not its inventory) Schulze spent his entire marketing budget to advertise a huge parking-lot sale. The successful sale taught him the benefits of strong advertising and wide selection combined with low prices. In 1983 Schulze changed the company's name to Best Buy and began to open larger superstores. The firm went public two years later.

Buoyed by the format change and the fast-rising popularity of the VCR Best Buy grew rapidly. Between 1984 and 1987 it expanded from eight stores to 24 and sales jumped from $29 million to $240 million. In 1988 another 16 stores opened and sales jumped by 84%. But Best Buy began to butt heads with many expanding consumer electronics retailers and profits took a beating.

To set Best Buy apart from its competitors in 1989 Schulze introduced the Concept II warehouse-like store format. Thinking that customers could buy products without much help Schulze cut payroll by taking sales staff off commission and reducing the number of employees per store by about a third. The concept proved to be such a hit in the company's home territory Minneapolis/St. Paul that it drove major competitor Highland Appliance to bankruptcy. Customers were happy but many of Best Buy's suppliers believing sales help was needed to sell products pulled their products from Best Buy stores. The losses didn't seem to hurt Best Buy; it took on Sears and Montgomery Ward in the Chicago market in 1989 and continued expanding.

In 1994 the company debuted Concept III an even larger store format. Best Buy opened 47 new stores in 1995 but found itself swimming in debt. Earnings plummeted in fiscal 1997 partly due to a huge PC inventory made obsolete by Intel's newer product. Best Buy started selling CDs on its website in 1997. That year it realized it had overextended itself with its expansion super-sized stores and financing promotions. Best Buy underwent a speedy massive makeover by scaling back expansion and doing away with its policy of "no money down no monthly payments no interest" (and next-to-no profits).

In 1999 Best Buy began to enter new markets (including New England) and introduced its Concept IV stores which highlighted digital products and featured stations for computer software and DVD demonstrations. Also in 1999 Best Buy formed a separate subsidiary for its online operations (BestBuy.com Inc.) and invested $10 million in consumer electronics information website etown.com (etown.com closed down in February 2001).

In 2000 Best Buy agreed to pay $88 million for Seattle-based Magnolia Hi-Fi a privately held chain of 13 high-end audio and video stores. In early 2001 Best Buy bought The Musicland Group (at the time operator of more than 1300 Sam Goody Suncoast On Cue and Media Play music stores) for about $425 million. The company began its international expansion in November 2002 with its $377 million acquisition of Future Shop Canada's leading consumer electronics retailer. Over the next year Best Buy opened eight of its own Best Buy stores in Ontario Canada.

In June 2002 Schulze turned over his responsibilities as CEO to vice chairman Brad Anderson; Schulze remained as chairman of the board. Best Buy acquired Geek Squad a computer support provider for $3 million the same year.

Best Buy shut down more than 100 Musicland stores (90 Sam Goody music stores and 20 Suncoast video stores) and laid off about 700 employees in January 2003; in June it sold the entire Musicland subsidiary (then about 1100 stores) to an affiliate of investment firm Sun Capital Partners. Three years later Best Buy purchased Pacific Sales Kitchen and Bath Centers which sells appliances and offers assistance on residential remodeling for $410 million.

Philip Schoonover a top executive in charge of customer segments defected to rival Circuit City in 2004. The company also dismissed Ernst & Young as its independent auditor after a former board member disclosed personal business dealings with the firm.

In 2006 the chain acquired home appliance and remodeling retailer Pacific Sales Kitchen and Bath Centers for about $410 million.

To facilitate its expansion in China Best Buy purchased a 75% stake in Jiangsu Five Star Appliance Co. in May 2006 and later opened the first Best Buy store in China in Shanghai.

To enhance its technology product offering for small businesses Best Buy in fiscal 2008 acquired Seattle-based Speakeasy a provider of broadband voice data and IT services. The deal valued at some $97 million made Speakeasy a wholly owned subsidiary that operates through the Best Buy for Business unit. Speakeasy CEO Bruce Chatterley as well as his management team was retained to run the Speakeasy operation once the deal closed. In a bid to add digital music downloads to its playlist Best Buy acquired a majority stake in Napster for about $127 million. The retailer's 2008 purchase of the music-swapping service included Napster's approximately 700000 digital entertainment subscribers.

In June 2008 Best Buy acquired a 50% stake in Carphone Warehouse's European and US retail interests for about $2.2 billion. In late October the company acquired digital music pioneer Napster for about $127 million via a tender offer for the firm's shares.

In early 2009 the retailer acquired the 25% of China's Jiangsu Five Star Appliance that it didn't already own. It also entered the Mexican market with its first store there.

CEO Brad Anderson retired in mid-2009 and COO and longtime employee Brian Dunn took over as CEO. Dunn's stint as chief executive lasted about three years. The 28-year company veteran stepped down in April 2012 handing his CEO title in the interim to board director Mike Mikan. In September 2012 the company named turnaround expert and Frenchman Hubert Joly to the position of CEO. Previously Joly served as head of T.G.I. Friday's and Radisson parent Carlson. In 2019 longtime Best Buy executive Corie Barry took over the company as CEO.

EXECUTIVES

Chairman And Ceo, Hubert Joly, age 61, $1,175,000 total compensation
Sevp And Chief Merchandising And Marketing Officer, R. Michael (Mike) Mohan, age 52, $833,654 total compensation
Sevp And President Multichannel Retail, Shari L. Ballard, age 53, $800,000 total compensation
President And Coo Best Buy Canada, Ron Wilson
Evp General Counsel And Secretary, Keith J. Nelsen, age 56, $650,000 total compensation
President Services, Trish Walker, age 53
Cfo, Corie S. Barry, age 45, $713,462 total compensation
Vice President Sales Operations, Chris Schmidt
Senior Vice President Loyalty And Membership And President Financial Services, Mark Williams
Chief Strategic Growth Officer Executive Vice President, Asheesh Saksena
Senior Vice President Information Technology And Cio, Colleen Dunn
Svp Chief Administrative Officer Best Buy Canada, Philippe Arrata
Svp Merchandising Canada, Tony Sandhu
Vice President Marketing, Jennie Weber
Vice President, John Schmidt
Vice President Pricing And Merchandising Strategy Analytics, Nicole Nelson
Senior Vice President Retail And Geek Squad Services Canada, Mat Povse
Vice President Returns Damages And Recommerce, Jeremy Witte
Senior Vice President Workforce Design, Damien Harmon
Secretary Treasurer, Vicki Fulmer
Board Member, Karen Mcloughlin
Board Of Directors, Cindy Kent
Auditors: DELOITTE & TOUCHE LLP

LOCATIONS

HQ: Best Buy Inc
7601 Penn Avenue South, Richfield, MN 55423
Phone: 612 291-1000
Web: www.investors.bestbuy.com

2017 Sales

	$ mil.	% of total
Domestic	36,248	92
International	3,155	8
Total	**39,403**	**100**

PRODUCTS/OPERATIONS

2018 U.S. Stores by Brand

	No.
Best Buy	
U.S. Best Buy	1,008
Mobile Stand-Alone Stores	257
Pacific Sales	28
Total	**1,293**

2018 Sales

	$ mil.	% of total
Domestic	38 662.9	92
International	3 498.8	8
Total	**42,151**	**100**

2018 International Stores by Brand

	No.
Canada	
Best Buy	134
Best Buy Mobile	51
Mexico	
Best Buy	25
Express	6
Total	**216**

2018 Sales by Domestic Category

	% of total
Products	
Consumer Electronics	33
Computing & Mobile Phones	45
Entertainment	8
Appliances	10
Services	4
Total	**100**

2018 Sales by International Category

	% of total
Products	
Computing & mobile phones	46
Consumer electronics	32
Entertainment	7
Appliance	8
Services	5
Other	2
Total	**100**

Selected Brands

Domestic
  Best Buy
  Best Buy Mobile
  Geek Squad
  Magnolia Audio Video
  Pacific Sales
International
  Canada
  Best Buy
  Cell Shop
  Connect Pro
  Future Shop
  Geek Squad
  China
  Five Star
  Europe
  The Carphone Warehouse
  The Phone House
  Geek Squad
  Mexico
  Best Buy
  Geek Squad

Selected Products

Consumer Electronics
  Audio
  Car stereos
  Home theater audio systems
  MP3 players
  Satellite radio systems
  Video
  Digital cameras and camcorders
  DVD players
  Televisions
Computing and mobile phones
  Computers
  Networking equipment
  Office furniture
  Printers
  Scanners
  Supplies
  Telephones
Entertainment
  CDs
  Computer software
  DVDs
  Subscription plans
  Video game hardware and software
Appliances
  Dishwashers
  Microwave ovens
  Refrigerators
  Stoves and ranges
  Vacuum cleaners
  Washers and dryers

COMPETITORS

ARTISTdirect
Amazon.com
Apple Inc.
Audible Inc.
Barnes & Noble
Brilliant Digital
  Entertainment
Brookstone
Buy.com
Buzz Media
Conn's
Costco Wholesale
Dell
Fry's Electronics
Gateway Inc.
HMV Retail
Hastings Entertainment
Home Depot
Lowe's

METRO AG
MSN
MediaNet Digital
Myspace
Office Depot
OfficeMax
RadioShack
RealNetworks
Sears Holdings
Sony Music
Staples
Systemax
Target Corporation
Trans World
  Entertainment
Wal-Mart
Yahoo!
eMusic.com

HISTORICAL FINANCIALS

Company Type: Public

Income Statement

FYE: February 1

	REVENUE ($ mil.)	NET INCOME ($ mil.)	NET PROFIT MARGIN	EMPLOYEES
02/20	43,638	1,541	3.5%	125,000
02/19	42,879	1,464	3.4%	125,000
02/18*	42,151	1,000	2.4%	125,000
01/17	39,403	1,228	3.1%	125,000
01/16	39,528	897	2.3%	125,000
Annual Growth	**2.5%**	**14.5%**	**—**	**0.0%**

*Fiscal year change

2020 Year-End Financials

Debt ratio: 8.15%
Return on equity: 45.55%
Cash ($ mil.): 2,229
Current ratio: 1.10
Long-term debt ($ mil.): 1,257

No. of shares (mil.): 256
Dividends
  Yield: 0.0%
  Payout: 34.7%
Market value ($ mil.): 21,722

	STOCK PRICE ($) FY Close	P/E High/Low		PER SHARE ($) Earnings	Dividends	Book Value
02/20	84.69	16	10	5.75	2.00	13.56
02/19	58.47	16	9	5.20	1.80	12.44
02/18*	71.24	23	13	3.26	1.36	12.76
01/17	43.47	13	7	3.81	1.57	15.14
01/16	27.93	16	10	2.56	1.43	13.52
Annual Growth	**32.0%**	**—**	**—**	**22.4%**	**8.7%**	**0.1%**

*Fiscal year change

Biogen Inc

With its pipeline full of biotech drugs Biogen aims to meet the unmet needs of patients around the world. The biotech giant is focused on developing treatments in the areas of multiple sclerosis and neuroimmunology. Its product roster includes best-selling drugs Tecfidera and Avonex for the treatment of relapsing multiple sclerosis (MS); Tysabri a drug treatment for MS and Crohn's disease; and Fampyra which improves walking in adults with MS. Other products include Plegridy for RMS. Biogen which serves customers around the world gets majority of its revenue from the US.

Operations

Biogen's top-selling drug Tecfidera is sold in markets around the globe and accounts for more than 30% of annual revenue. It's an oral therapy marketed in the US for the treatment of patients with relapsing forms of MS and for patients with relapsing-remitting MS (RRMS).

The firm's next-best seller Interferon which accounts for approximately 15% of revenue includes Avonex and Pledgridy. A treatment to improve walking in adults with MS the Avonex pen is a single-use auto-injector version of the drug for once-weekly dosing. Plegridy is given by injection to treat relapsing forms of MS and effective in people under 18 and over 65 years of age.

Another top-selling global drug is Spinraza also bringing in about 15% of revenue. It is given as an injection for the treatment of Spinal Muscular Atrophy (SMA).

Anti-CD20 therapeutic program sales conducted through a partnership with Genentech account for over 15% of sales. In addition to non-Hodgkin's lymphoma and rheumatoid arthritis Rituxan included in anti-CD20 is approved to treat leukemia follicular lymphoma and vasculitis.

Another drug MS treatment Fampyra (also known as Ampyra) is sold in partnership with Acorda Therapeutics. Biogen is also co-marketing Zinbryta another MS treatment in the US with AbbVie.

In addition to gaining revenue from the development and sales of its products (both directly and through partnerships) Biogen receives royalties on some patents it has licensed to other companies.

Geographic Reach

Biogen headquartered in Massachusetts has offices in the US Australia Canada Japan and several European countries. The US is Biogen's largest market bringing in more than 45% of revenue. The remaining revenues are generated from the rest of the world.

Sales and Marketing

Biogen primarily distributes its products in the US through wholesale pharmaceutical distributors mail-order specialty distributors and shipping service providers. Two wholesale distributors AmerisourceBergen and McKesson each bring in more than 10% of the firm's total revenue. Outside of the US distribution varies but includes wholesale pharmaceutical distributors and third-party distribution partners.

Biogen's direct sales force focuses on specialist physicians in private and at major medical centers. The company also handles global marketing efforts for Tysabri. Roche Group and its sublicenses handles sales and marketing duties for Rituxan while marketing duties for Fampyra are split with Acorda. (Biogen sells the drug in Europe.)

Financial Performance

Biogen's revenue and profits have steadily risen over the years as it has introduced new products. It has an overall growth of 35% between 2015 and 2019.

Total revenues were $14.4 billion for 2019 representing an increase of 7% over $13.5 billion in 2018.

Net income attributable to Biogen Inc. was favorably impacted by a decrease in The Company's effective tax rate to 16% for the year ended December 31 2019 from 24% for 2018 due in part to an internal reorganization of certain intellectual property rights the impact of Swiss Tax Reform and the 2018 unfavorable impacts of U.S. Tax Reform.

Biogen held about $2.9 billion in cash and equivalents in 2019 compared to $1.2 billion the year before. In 2019 operations generated $7.1 billion. Investing activities provided $470.5 million while financing activities used $5.9 billion.

Strategy

Biogen is the industry leader in multiple sclerosis treatments and it has a strong biosimilars business in Europe where it sells Benepali a biosimilar version of Enbrel and Flixabi a biosimilar of Remicade. In 2019 Biogen released Vumerity an oral therapy for relapsing MS. The treatment was developed in collaboration with Alkermes.

Biogen's researchers leverage their expertise in MS to work in remyelination and repair and neuroprotection with potential applications in Alzheimer's Disease Parkinson's disease ALS stroke and pain. The company spent $20 million $18 million and $12 million for research and development in 2019 2018 and 2017 respectively.

Additionally Biogen invested $1 billion in a 10-year exclusive agreement with Ionis in 2018 gaining access to Ionis' antisense platform across a broad range of neurological diseases to develop antisense oligonucleotide (ASOs) candidates. A previous collaboration with Ionis resulted in Spinraza the first treatment for spinal muscular atrophy (SMA). The drug posted more than $2 billion in sales in 2019 with strong growth in the US and internationally.

The company has had its share of setbacks. In early 2019 it halted studies of its lead Alzheimer's treatment aducanumab when independent experts assessed that it wouldn't make the grade. However the company with its partner Eisai pursue regulatory approval to continue the studies of aducanumab in the US in late 2019.

Mergers and Acquisitions

Biogen has expanded its operations through purchases of drug development firms as well as by purchasing commercialized and development-stage drugs.

In early 2020 Biogen entered into an agreement to acquire Pfizer Inc. for $75 million. Pfizer is a New York-based company that develops potential treatment of patients with behavioral and neurological symptoms across various psychiatric and neurological diseases. The company plans to further develop the treatment that is highly complementary to its existing pipeline of potential disease-modifying therapies such as Alzheimer's and Parkinson's disease.

In early 2019 the company struck a deal to buy London-based gene therapy startup Nightstar Therapeutics for $800 million. Nightstar is focused on treatments for inherited retinal disorders. Biogen is increasingly investing in the ophthalmology field.

Company Background

One of the world's first global biotechnology companies Biogen was founded in 1978 by Charles Weissmann Heinz Schaller Kenneth Murray and Nobel Prize winners Walter Gilbert and Phillip Sharp. It has the leading portfolio of medicines to treat multiple sclerosis introduced the first approved treatment for spinal muscular atrophy and commercializes biosimilars of advanced biologics.

HISTORY

Biogen Idec was formed out of the 2003 merger of IDEC Pharmaceuticals and Biogen.

The company began experiencing troubles with its lead product — Tysabri developed with partner Elan— soon after its formation. Sales were temporarily halted in 2005 after several patients died from a rare neurological condition. The companies were allowed to reintroduce Tysabri in 2006 (when it was also launched in Europe) under a strict risk management plan that insures sufficient doctor and patient education about risks and proper usage.

Activist investor Carl Icahn held a minority stake in the company for several years and kept a watchful eye over his investment. In 2007 he bullied the company to put itself up for sale but no buyer came through. Then he began a series of proxy battles in an attempt to stack the board with his own nominees to gain further control. By 2010 he had secured three seats on the board filled with his own representatives and resumed talks of seeing Biogen Idec broken into parts and/or sold to a larger pharmaceutical company.

Ichan's persistence might have contributed to the retirement of Biogen Idec's long-time CEO James Mullen in mid-2010 with George Scangos (former CEO of Exelixis) stepping in as Mullen's replacement. Scangos implemented sharp changes in late 2010 launching a reorganization plan aimed at reducing operational costs and increasing efficiencies. The plan included a 13% workforce reduction and a streamlining of R&D programs to focus primarily on neurological disease. Biogen Idec halted or licensed out its oncology and cardiovascular development programs and consolidated a number of US sites. As a sign that he was pleased with Mullen's work in early 2011 Icahn reduced his ownership stake and did not seek to gain control of more board seats; he sold his remaining interests in the firm in mid-2011.

EXECUTIVES

Evp Chief Legal Officer And Corporate Secretary, Susan H. Alexander, age 63, $697,721 total compensation
Evp And Cfo, Jeffrey D. (Jeff) Capello, age 55
Evp Human Resources, Kenneth A. (Ken) DiPietro, age 62, $648,023 total compensation
Ceo And Director, Michel Vounatsos, $519,231 total compensation
Evp And Head Of Research And Development, Michael D. (Mike) Ehlers, $491,827 total compensation
Evp Neurology Discovery And Development Center Neurodegeneration Therapeutic Area And Chief Medical Officer, Alfred W. Sandrock, age 62, $564,596 total compensation
Evp Pharmaceutical Operations And Technology, Paul McKenzie
Vp And Chief Accounting Officer And Interim Principal Financial Officer, Greg Covino, age 54
Evp And Head Of Global Marketing Market Access And Customer Innovation, Chirfi Guindo
Vice President Global Public Affairs, Katja Buller
Vice President Head Of Us Neurology Marketing, Dell Faulkingham
Vice President Customer Support, Janis Meyer
Vice President, Adam Adamson
Medical Director, Martha Fournier
Senior Vice President Translational Medicine And Technology, Timothy Harris
Vice President Sales And Field Operations, Todd Nichols
Medical Director Clinical Development, Mark Beatty
Vice President Of Quality, Sid Senroy
Senior Vice President Program Management, Johnathan Palmer
Vice President Global Commercial Strategy, Adrian Gottschalk
Vice President Treasurer, Michael Dambach
Executive Vice President Human Resources, Scott Handren
Executive Vice President Of Human Resources, Kenneth Dipetrio
Vice President Of Global Medical Affairs Biogen Idec's Avonex, Thorsten Eickenhorst
Vice President Managing Director, Simon Jordan
Vice President Research And Development Technology, Andrew Allen
Vice President Executive Director Biogen Idec Innovation Incubator, Rainer Fuchs
Vice President Medical Research, Bradley Maroni
Vice President Human Resources Worldwide Medical And Us Organization, Lauren Duprey
Associate Medical Director, Satish Eraly
Vice President Alzheimers Disease, Samantha Haeberlein
Associate Medical Director Clinical Development, Christian Hehn
Senior Vice President Research And Early Development, Anirvan Ghosh
Vice President Legal Chief Employment Counsel, Jo A Taormina
Vp Neurology Research, Chris Henderson
Vice President And Ciso, Bob Litterer
Associate Medical Director, Monroe Butler
Senior Medical Director, Donna Masterman
Vice President Heor Global Market Access, Christopher Leibman
Director, Stelios Papadopoulos, age 72
Abm, Karmon Warren
Abm, Don Benson
Auditors: PricewaterhouseCoopers LLP

LOCATIONS

HQ: Biogen Inc
225 Binney Street, Cambridge, MA 02142
Phone: 617 679-2000
Web: www.biogen.com

2018 Sales

	$ mil.	% of total
US	6,800	51
Rest of World	4,086	30
Anti-CE therapeutic programs	1,980	15
Other revenue	585	4
Total	**13,452**	**100**

PRODUCTS/OPERATIONS

2018 Sales

	$ mil.	% of total
Products		
Tecfidera	4,274	32
Interferon	2,663	17
Tysabri	1,864	14
Spinraza	1,724	13
Benepali	485	4
Fampyra	92	1
Flixabi	43	
Fumaderm	22	-
Imraldi	16	-
Zynbryta	1	-
Anti-CD therapeutic programs	1,980	15
Other	585	4
Total	**13,452**	**100**

Selected Products

Approved
  Avonex (multiple sclerosis)
  Fampyra (multiple sclerosis with Acorda Therapeutics)
  Fumaderm (severe psoriasis in Germany only)
  Rituxan (non-Hodgkin's lymphoma chronic lymphocytic leukemia follicular lymphoma rheumatoid arthritis vasculitis)
  Tecfidera (multiple sclerosis)
  Tysabri (multiple sclerosis Crohn's disease; with Elan Pharmaceuticals)
In development
  GA101 (chronic lymphocytic leukemia non-Hodgkin's lymphoma)
  Plegridy (PEGylated interferon beta 1a relapsing forms of multiple sclerosis)
  Tysabri (secondary-progressive MS)

COMPETITORS

AbbVie	Johnson & Johnson
Abbott Labs	Merck KGaA
Amgen	Novartis
Bayer HealthCare	Pfizer
Pharmaceuticals	Roche Holding
Bristol-Myers Squibb	Sanofi
Genentech	Teva
GlaxoSmithKline	UCB

HISTORICAL FINANCIALS

Company Type: Public

Income Statement

FYE: December 31

	REVENUE ($ mil.)	NET INCOME ($ mil.)	NET PROFIT MARGIN	EMPLOYEES
12/20	13,444	4,000	29.8%	9,100
12/19	14,377	5,888	41.0%	7,400
12/18	13,452	4,430	32.9%	7,800
12/17	12,273	2,539	20.7%	7,300
12/16	11,448	3,702	32.3%	7,400
Annual Growth	4.1%	2.0%	—	5.3%

2020 Year-End Financials

Debt ratio: 30.16%
Return on equity: 33.19%
Cash ($ mil.): 1,331
Current ratio: 1.84
Long-term debt ($ mil.): 7,426

No. of shares (mil.): 152
Dividends
Yield: —
Payout: —
Market value ($ mil.): 37,317

	STOCK PRICE ($) FY Close	P/E High/Low		PER SHARE ($) Earnings	Dividends	Book Value
12/20	244.86	14	10	24.80	0.00	70.21
12/19	296.73	11	7	31.42	0.00	76.60
12/18	300.92	18	12	21.58	0.00	66.12
12/17	318.57	29	21	11.92	0.00	59.63
12/16	283.58	19	13	16.93	0.00	56.23
Annual Growth	(3.6%)	—	—	10.0%	—	5.7%

BJ's Wholesale Club Holdings Inc

Auditors: PricewaterhouseCoopers LLP

LOCATIONS

HQ: BJ's Wholesale Club Holdings Inc
25 Research Drive, Westborough, MA 01581
Phone: 774 512-7400
Web: www.bjs.com

HISTORICAL FINANCIALS

Company Type: Public

Income Statement

FYE: February 1

	REVENUE ($ mil.)	NET INCOME ($ mil.)	NET PROFIT MARGIN	EMPLOYEES
02/20	13,190	187	1.4%	27,231
02/19	13,007	127	1.0%	26,383
02/18*	12,754	50	0.4%	26,520
01/17	12,350	44	0.4%	—
01/16	12,467	24	0.2%	—
Annual Growth	1.4%	66.9%	—	—

*Fiscal year change

2020 Year-End Financials

Debt ratio: 32.18%
Return on equity: —
Cash ($ mil.): 30
Current ratio: 0.75
Long-term debt ($ mil.): 1,352

No. of shares (mil.): 137
Dividends
Yield: —
Payout: —
Market value ($ mil.): 2,817

	STOCK PRICE ($) FY Close	P/E High/Low		PER SHARE ($) Earnings	Dividends	Book Value
02/20	20.52	21	15	1.35	0.00	(0.40)
02/19	26.47	29	18	1.05	0.00	(1.47)
Annual Growth	(6.2%)	—	—	6.5%	—	—

BlackRock Inc

With about $7 trillion in assets under management BlackRock is the world's largest public investment management firm. It specializes in equity and fixed income products as well as alternative and money market instruments which it invests in on behalf of institutional and retail investors worldwide. Clients include pension plans governments insurance companies financial institutions endowments foundations charities third party fund sponsors and retail investors. BlackRock also provides technology products and services through its Aladdin Aladdin Wealth eFront Cache Matrix and Future Advisors systems. The firm has offices in more than 30 countries. The company's largest geographical market is the Americas with more than 65% of the total revenue.

Operations

BlackRock manages about $7 trillion in assets under management (AUM) through over 100 investment teams across the globe.

The BlackRock Solutions division provides risk management advisory and enterprise investment system services. iShares one of BlackRock's brands is a leading provider of exchange-traded funds (ETFs). BlackRock's iShares is the world's largest ETF in the world with nearly $2 trillion in assets under management. Product offerings include single- and multi-asset portfolios investing in equities fixed income alternatives and money market instruments.

BlackRock also offers technology products and services including Aladdin Aladdin Wealth eFront Cache matrix and Future Advisors as well as advisory services and solutions to a broad base of institutional and wealth management clients.

BlackRock's Asset Liability And Debt and Derivative Investment Network or Aladdin is its enterprise resource management system which provides investment and risk management system.

Overall about 80% of total sales comes from investment advisory administration fees and lending securities about 10% in technology services and the remaining 10% comes from distribution fees and other revenues.

Geographic Reach

New York-based BlackRock has more than 70 offices in more than 30 countries. The company operates through three geographical segments that makes more than 65% of its revenue in the Americas. Europe accounts for around 30% and the Asia-Pacific region about 5%. BlackRock has clients and investments in more than 100 countries.

Sales and Marketing

BlackRock focuses on establishing and maintaining its investment management relationships by marketing its services through financial professionals pension consultants third-party distribution relationships or directly to investors themselves.

Clients include tax-exempt institutions (defined benefit pension plans charities and foundations); official institutions (central banks sovereign wealth funds supra nationals and other government entities); and taxable institutions (insurance companies financial institutions corporations and third-party fund sponsors and retail investors). More than 65% of BlackRock's assets are pension plan assets.

Financial Performance

Revenue increased $341 million to $14.5 billion in 2019 from 2018 primarily driven by higher base fees and 24% growth in technology services revenue.

In 2019 the company's net income increase by about $171 million to $4.5 billion from $4.3 billion in the prior year. The increase was primarily due to the increase on their revenue offsetting the increase on their expenses.

The company's cash at the end of 2019 decreased by $1.7 billion to $4.8 billion compared to $6.5 billion in 2018. Cash provided by operations was $2.9 billion while investing and financing activities used $2.0 billion and $2.6 billion respectively.

Strategy

BlackRock's highly diversified multi-product platform was created to meet client needs in all market environments. BlackRock is positioned to provide alpha-seeking active index and cash management investment strategies across asset classes and geographies. In addition BlackRock leverages its world-class risk management analytics and technology capabilities including the Aladdin platform on behalf of clients.

iShares ETFs' growth strategy is centered on increasing scale and pursuing global growth themes in client and product segments including Core Strategic which includes Fixed Income Factors Sustainable and Megatrends ETFs and Precision Exposures.

As the wealth management landscape shifts globally from individual product selection to a whole-portfolio approach BlackRock's retail strategy is focused on creating outcome-oriented client solutions. This includes having a diverse platform of alpha-seeking active index and alternative products as well as enhanced distribution and portfolio construction technology offerings. Digital wealth tools are an important component of BlackRock's retail strategy as BlackRock scales and customizes model portfolios extends Aladdin Wealth and digital wealth partnerships globally and helps advisors build better portfolios through portfolio construction and risk management powered by Aladdin.

Mergers and Acquisitions

In 2019 BlackRock has completed acquiring French alternative investment management software company eFront from Bridgepoint Advisers and eFront employees for about $1.3 billion. BlackRock will combine eFront with Aladdin its investment management platform to allow users to manage portfolios across public and private asset classes including alternative assets. The firm also agreed in 2019 to buy an approximately 80% stake in Distributed Solar Development from GE. GE's GE Renewable Energy unit will retain the remaining stake.

Company Background

BlackRock is led by CEO Laurence Fink who has overseen a string of major acquisitions in recent years expanding into private equity real estate energy and hedge funds as investors look to diversify beyond stock and bond funds.

Fink engineered a blockbuster merger with Barclays Global Investors (BGI) in 2009. In the deal which was several years in the making BlackRock bought Barclays Global Investors from UK banking giant Barclays for some $15 billion. The deal resulted in a new company operating under the BlackRock name. Barclays Bank retained a 20% stake in the combined firm but Fink remained in charge of the enterprise. The merger nearly tripled BlackRock's assets under management and propelled the company to the top of the international money management industry by enhancing its investment and risk management capabilities. The deal also gave BlackRock a much larger footprint outside the US and added more than 3500 new employees.

EXECUTIVES

President And Director, Robert S. (Rob) Kapito, age 63, $750,000 total compensation
Chairman And Ceo, Laurence D. (Larry) Fink, age 67, $900,000 total compensation
Senior Managing Director, Robert W. (Rob) Fairbairn, age 54, $350,000 total compensation
Senior Managing Director And Chief Risk Officer, Bennett W. Golub, age 62
Senior Managing Director And Global Head Of Multi-asset Strategies, J. Richard (Rich) Kushel, age 53, $500,000 total compensation
Senior Managing Director And Head Of Trading Liquidity And Investments Platform, Richard L. (Richie) Prager
Head Alladin Clien Business, Ryan D. Stork, age 48
Senior Managing Director Head Of Global Active Equities And Chairman Blackrock Alternative Investors, Mark Wiseman
Senior Managing Director And Global Head Of Ishares And Index Investments, Mark K. Wiedman
Senior Managing Director And Head Of Global Human Resources, Jeffrey A. Smith, age 49
Senior Managing Director Head Of The Americas Region And Global Head Of Blackrock Alternative Investors, Mark S. McCombe, age 54
Senior Managing Director And Head Of Europe Middle East And Africa (emea), David J. Blumer, age 51
Senior Managing Director And Cfo, Gary S. Shedlin, age 56, $500,000 total compensation
Senior Managing Director Coo And Global Head Blackrock Solutions, Rob L. Goldstein, age 46, $500,000 total compensation
Senior Managing Director And Global Head Business Operations And Technology, Derek K. Stein
Vice President, Ed Mallon
Vice President, Lawrence Garrity
Vice President, Katie Russell
Vice President Global Marketing, Laura Tyrholm
Vice President Portfolio Manager, Bernard Gordon
Vice President Brand And Advertising Ishares, Mona Lee
Vice President Finance, Jennifer Shoup
Vice President, Carlie Mcaninch
Vice President, John Kent
Vice President, Margaret Lassiter
Vice President Corporate Communications, Farrell Denby
Vice President, Vivek Hemdev
Vice President Product Tax Real Estate, Troy Wismer
Vice President Hr Business Partner, Anna Kim
Vice President Product Tax, Denise Xiong
Vice President Sourcing And Vendor Management Transaction Management Team, Dana Aurora
Vice President, Craig Dehner
Vice President, Uri Morris
Vice President Sourcing, Michael Schnalzer
Vice President, Amaurys Mercedes
Vice President, Colleen Wade
Vice President Fixed Income Portfolio Management Group, Sriram Reddy
Vice President User Experience And Design, Devjit Basu
Vice President, Santosh Yadav
Vice President, Kate Bruestle
Vice President Critical Infrastructure, Ed Cannon
Vice President, Ned Rosenman
Vice President Market Research, Katie Herzog
Vice President, David Edson
Vice President, Miranda Harrison

Vice President, Patricia Belcher
Vice President, Tyler Thomas
Vice President, Ryan Shriber
Vice President, Sukhbir Gill
Vice President, Charles Harrington
Vice President, Amy Goldfarb
Vice President, Stephanie Lupo
Vice President Access And Identity Management, Nikhil Mathur
Vice President Aladdin And Technology, Paul Dearman
Vice President, Diego Mora
Vice President Media Services, Lisa Sturdivant
Vice President, Rachel Barry
Vice President, Vincent Dellaglio
Vice President, Heinrich Schutze
Vice President, Davina Stickland
Vice President, Celia Chau
Vice President Internal Audit, Stella Yap
Vice President, Andrea Vigano
Vice President, Nancy Dambrosio
Vice President, Adam Hess
Vice President, Carol Wong
Vice President Financial Institutions Group, Felipe Arguello
Vice President Finance, Amit Soni
Vice President Senior Marketing Manager Marketing Germany And Austria, Karin Emmrich
Vice President Technology And Operations, Praveen Dasari
Vice President, Eric Neis
Vice President, Trevor Slaven
Vice President, David Benelli
Vice President, Gregory Rosta
Vice President, Lisa Kulan
Vice President, Tim Ott
Vice President, Henry Shen
Vice President Marketing, Elisabeth Nygren
Vice President Global Philanthropy, Greg Levin
Vice President, Anish Shah
Vice President Integrated Marketing, Molly Henning
Vice President Trader, Mark Mckenzie
Vice President Internal Audit, Jaspreet Dharia
Vice President Defined Contribution, Jeffrey Kern
Vice President, Don Hunt
Vice President, Meghan Sharin
Vice President, Jesse Weidenfeld
Vice President, Matthew Estes
Vice President, Megan Lynch
Vice President, Robert Pacicco
Vice President, Angela Pflug
Vice President, Uran Guma
Vice President, Nikhil Patel
Vice President, Sivan Gamliel
Vice President, Allie Selnick
Vice President, Nicholas Weiss
Vice President, Justine Duffin
Vice President, Karen Toll
Vice President Software Developer, Fouad Semaan
Vice President, Ye Liang
Vice President, Jeffrey Nauman
Vice President, Andrew Stack
Vice President Market Leader, Ian Uhar
Vice President, Benjamin Hopson
Vice President, Dennis Markey
Vice President, Kathy Carusio
Vice President, John Hrenko
Vice President Fixed Income Trading, Brian Smith
Vice President, Youxun Duan
Vice President, Suzanne Melcher
Vice President, Kellie Marquet
Vice President Institutional Client Business, Irina Donskaya
Vice President Portfolio Management Assistant Global Real Estate Securities, Charles Wright
Vice President Product Marketing Management (aladdin Business), Daniel Kallas
Vice President, Mark Yu
Vice President, Lakshmi Devarajan

Vice President, Katherine Monroe
Vice President, Summer Jolly
Vice President Legal And Compliance, Emily Cohen
Vice President, Sharon Loiseau
Vice President, Christopher Aiken
Vice President, Jamie Hill
Vice President, John Kavanaugh
Vice President, Kathleen Stremlo
Vice President Portfolio Manager, Kelly Lenahan
Vice President Strategic Initiatives Cash Management Marketing, Katlin Mongelluzzo
Vice President Head Of Data Analytics, Bryan Blick
Vice President Financial Institutions Group Marketing, Marci McAvoy
Vice President Defined Contribution, Joseph Maximos
Vice President, Patricia Currie
Vice President, Jacqueline Waraksy
Vice President, Joe Davis
Vice President, Lauren Shern
Vice President Performance And Yardi Operations, Lana Sokolov
Vice President, Tom Mantych
Vice President, Michael Garvey
Vice President, Drew Burton
Vice President Corporate Treasury Sales, Lauren Pralle
Vice President Global Head Of Index Construction, Nikita Surin
Vice President, Yang Kim
Vice President, Stephen Fagan
Vice President Ishares Us Strategy, Richard Fleischman
Vice President, Maria Lewis
Vice President Treasury, Brett Gottlieb
Vice President Digital Marketing, Mollie Warshaw
Vp Product Tax, Lou Steadman
Vice President Global Philanthropy, Jessica Baird
Vice President, Jeff Ingram
Vice President Implementation Manager At Blackrock Solutions, Samantha Gillette
Auditors: DELOITTE & TOUCHE LLP

LOCATIONS

HQ: BlackRock Inc
55 East 52nd Street, New York, NY 10055
Phone: 212 810-5300
Web: www.blackrock.com

2017 Sales

	$ mil.	% of total
Americas	8,406	67
Europe	3,432	28
Asia/Pacific	653	5
Total	**12,491**	**100**

PRODUCTS/OPERATIONS

2017 Sales

	$ mil.	% of total
Investment advisory administration fees & securities lending		
Equity	5,722	46
Fixed income	2,921	23
Multi-asset class	1,181	10
Alternative investments	1,105	9
Cash management	558	5
Black Rock Solutions & advisory	755	6
Distribution fees	24	-
Other revenue	225	2
Total	**12,491**	**100**

COMPETITORS

Allianz Global Investors	Federated Investors
Bank of New York Mellon	Legg Mason
Charles Schwab	Morgan Stanley
Dimensional Fund Advisors	Principal Global
	State Street
	UBS
	Waddell & Reed

HISTORICAL FINANCIALS

Company Type: Public

Income Statement

FYE: December 31

	REVENUE ($ mil.)	NET INCOME ($ mil.)	NET PROFIT MARGIN	EMPLOYEES
12/19	14,539	4,476	30.8%	16,200
12/18	14,198	4,305	30.3%	14,900
12/17	12,491	4,970	39.8%	13,900
12/16	11,155	3,172	28.4%	13,000
12/15	11,401	3,345	29.3%	13,000
Annual Growth	6.3%	7.6%	—	5.7%

2019 Year-End Financials

Debt ratio: 2.94%
Return on equity: 13.58%
Cash ($ mil.): 4,829
Current ratio: 2.48
Long-term debt ($ mil.): 4,955

No. of shares (mil.): 154
Dividends
Yield: 2.6%
Payout: 50.9%
Market value ($ mil.): 77,605

	STOCK PRICE ($) FY Close	P/E High/Low	PER SHARE ($) Earnings	Dividends	Book Value
12/19	502.70	18 13	28.43	13.20	217.31
12/18	392.82	22 13	26.58	12.02	205.48
12/17	513.71	17 12	30.23	10.00	198.93
12/16	380.54	21 15	19.04	9.16	180.13
12/15	340.52	19 15	19.79	8.72	174.37
Annual Growth	10.2%	— —	9.5%	10.9%	5.7%

Blackstone Group Inc (The)

Throw a rock and you're bound to hit a Blackstone investment. The Blackstone Group is one of the world's largest real estate private equity and alternative asset managers in the world with more than $570 billion in assets under management. Of approximately $570 billion private equity make up the firm's largest asset category with more than $180 billion under management and around 100 portfolio companies. Its real estate investment holdings constitute more than $160 billion making Blackstone one of the world's largest real estate investors. The firm manages investment vehicles including real estate private equity public debt and equity growth equity opportunistic non-investment grade credit real assets and secondary funds all on a global basis. Clients include public and corporate pensions financial institutions and individuals.

HISTORY

In 2013 the firm purchased the Hughes Center complex in Las Vegas for $347 million to eventually benefit from the region's rebound. Blackstone was also part of an investor group that bought Extended Stay Hotels owner HVM which was in bankruptcy. All of the hospitality investment activity helped bring in a dramatic rise in revenues in 2013.

In China following its strategy to invest in high-growth Chinese companies through its partnership with the Shanghai-Pudong district government a consortium led by Blackstone agreed in late 2013 to acquire China-based global consulting and technology services company Pactera Technology International Ltd. for about $600 million. The move marked Blackstone's foray into China's technology outsourcing industry a sector traditionally dominated by Indian firms.

In 2012 in capitalizing on the boom in energy markets Blackstone completed fundraising for its first energy-focused private equity fund Blackstone Energy Partners L.P. with total fund commitments of $2.4 billion. The firm also raised $13.3 billion for its seventh global real estate fund BREP VII making it the biggest real estate fund in the world. In 2013 Blackstone acquired secondary private fund of funds unit Strategic Partners Fund Solutions in a deal that added some $9.4 billion in assets under management.

Founded in 1985 by industry veterans Peter Peterson and CEO Stephen Schwarzman the once-reclusive Blackstone went public in June 2007. The public offering which was a first among major US private equity firms valued Blackstone at upwards of $4 billion.

EXECUTIVES

President And Coo, Hamilton E. (Tony) James, age 69, $350,000 total compensation

Chairman And Ceo, Stephen A. Schwarzman, age 73, $350,000 total compensation

Senior Managing Director And Head Of Private Equity Portfolio Operations, David L. (Dave) Calhoun, age 63

Senior Managing Director And Cfo, Michael S. Chae, age 51, $350,000 total compensation

Senior Managing Director Gso Capital Partners, Bennett J. Goodman, age 62

Senior Managing Director And Head Of Tactical Opportunities, David S. Blitzer, age 50

Senior Managing Director And Global Head Of Real Estate, Jonathan D. Gray, age 50

Senior Managing Director And Head Of Multi-asset Investing And External Relations, Joan Solotar, age 55, $350,000 total compensation

Vice Chairman And President And Ceo Blackstone Alternative Asset Management, J. Tomilson Hill, age 71, $350,000 total compensation

Global Head Of Private Equity, Joseph P. Baratta, age 49

Senior Managing Director And Chief Legal Officer, John G. Finley, age 63, $350,000 total compensation

Senior Managing Director And Cto, William Murphy

Chairman Asia-pacific, Christopher (Chris) Heady

Senior Managing Director And Head Of Energy Practice Gso Capital Partners, Dwight Scott, age 56

Senior Managing Director And Ceo Blackstone Insurance Solutions, Chris Blunt

Vice President Information Technology, Andrew Scott

Vice President Credit Business, Juliann O'Sullivan

Vice President, John Wander

Vice President, Donald Purdy

Vice President Of Information Technology, Daniel Moy

National Sales Manager For The Private Wealth Management Group, Joe Lohrer

Vice President, Brij Kalaria

Vice President, John Shields

Vice President, Raphael Kiam

Senior Vice President, Kaori Curran

Vice President, Stephen O'Connor

Vice President, Taylor Carvajal

Assistant Vice President, Shannon Farley

Vice President, Kuohsin Chen

Vice President, Brett Crandall

Vice President, Jack Pitts

Senior Vice President, Steve Long

Senior Vice President Credit Businesses, Thomas Iannarone

Vice President, Kevin Gee

Vice President, John Wrafter

Vice President, Michelle Harika

Vice President, Adam Hermida

Vice President, Daniel Chang

Vice President, Thomas Procida

Vice President, Cooper Wright

Vice President, Michael Pierog

Vice President, Milca Beltre

Vice President Real Estate Debt Strategies, Damiano Buffa

Vice President, Marni Blivice

Senior Vice President, Anna Guerin

Vice President, Jennifer Chang

Assistant Vice President, Matthew Moyer

Vice President, Bill Sheehan

Vice President, Ryan Chapman

Vice President, Christine Japlit

Vice President, Sarah Mccormick

Assistant Vice President, Renata Milaknyte

Assistant Vice President, Brice Blanton

Senior Vice President, Cindy Remin

Auditors: DELOITTE & TOUCHE LLP

LOCATIONS

HQ: Blackstone Group Inc (The)
345 Park Avenue, New York, NY 10154
Phone: 212 583-5000
Web: www.blackstone.com

PRODUCTS/OPERATIONS

2018 Sales

	% of total
Management and Advisory Fees net	44
Total Investment Income	43
Interest and Dividend Revenue and Other	12
Incentive Fees	1
Total	**100**

Selected Investments

Allcargo
Alliant Insurance Services
AlliedBarton Security Services
Antares Restaurant Group
Apria Healthcare
Axis Capital
BankUnited
Bayview Asset Management
Biomet
Caesars Entertainment (formerly Harrah's Entertainment)
Catalent Pharma Solutions
Celanese
Center Parcs
Charter Communications
China Animal Healthcare Ltd.
China National Bluestar Group
CMS Computers Ltd.
Crestwood Midstream Partners
CTI Holdings
Cumulus Media Partners
DJO
Dili Group
eAccess
Emcure
Equity Office Properties
Extended Stay America
Freescale Semiconductor Group
Gates Corporation
Gateway Rail Freight Ltd.
Gerresheimer Group
Gokaldas Exports Limited
Gold Toe-Moretz
Houghton Mifflin
Imperial Home Dé;cor
Independent Clinical Services
Intelenet Global Services
Intertrust
Klöckner Pentaplast
Leica Camera
Maldivian Air
Michaels Stores
Mivisa Envases S.A.U.
Monnet
Montecito

Moser Baer Energy
MTAR Technologies Private
Nuziveedu Seeds
Osum Oil Sands Corp.
PBF Energy
People's Choice TV
Performance Food Group
Pinnacle Foods Corporation
Polymer Group Inc.
RGIS Inventory Specialists
Sonalike International Tractors
SeaWorld Parks & Entertainment
Summit Materials
Stiefel Laboratories
SunGard
Team Health
Texas Genco
Tragus
TRW Automotive
UCAR
United Biscuits
Vivint Inc.
The Weather Channel
Western Integrated Networks

COMPETITORS

American Financial Group	Clayton Dubilier & Rice
Apollo Global Management	Goldman Sachs Investcorp
Bain Capital	KKR
Berkshire Hathaway	The Carlyle Group
BlackRock	

HISTORICAL FINANCIALS

Company Type: Public

Income Statement

FYE: December 31

	REVENUE ($ mil.)	NET INCOME ($ mil.)	NET PROFIT MARGIN	EMPLOYEES
12/19	7,338	2,049	27.9%	2,905
12/18	6,833	1,541	22.6%	2,615
12/17	7,119	1,470	20.7%	2,360
12/16	5,125	1,039	20.3%	2,120
12/15	4,646	709	15.3%	2,060
Annual Growth	12.1%	30.4%	—	9.0%

2019 Year-End Financials

Debt ratio: 34.01%
Return on equity: —
Cash ($ mil.): 2,523
Current ratio: 1.08
Long-term debt ($ mil.): 11,080

No. of shares (mil.): 671
Dividends
 Yield: 1.7%
 Payout: 42.1%
Market value ($ mil.): 37,545

	STOCK PRICE ($) FY Close	P/E High/Low	PER SHARE ($) Earnings	Dividends	Book Value
12/19	55.94	19 10	-3.03	0.97	10.44
12/18	29.81	17 12	2.26	2.42	9.62
12/17	32.02	16 13	2.21	2.32	10.06
12/16	27.03	19 14	1.56	1.66	10.04
12/15	29.24	39 25	1.04	2.90	10.04
Annual Growth	17.6%	— —	30.6%	(24.0%)	1.0%

BNSF RAILWAY COMPANY

BNSF Railway operates one of the largest railroad networks in North America. A wholly-owned subsidiary of Burlington Northern Santa Fe itself a unit of Berkshire Hathaway the company provides freight transportation over a network of about 32500 route miles of track across some 30 US states and three provinces in Canada. BNSF Railway owns or leases a fleet of about 8000 locomotives. It also has some 25 intermodal facilities that help to transport agricultural consumer and industrial products as well as coal. In addition to major cities and ports BNSF Railway serves smaller markets in alliance with short-line partners.

Operations

BNSF Railway transports a wide range of products and commodities through its four main product segments.

The Consumer Products segment generates about 35% of revenue and consists of the Domestic Intermodal International Intermodal and Automotive business units. The Industrial Products segment provides about 25% of revenue and comprises five business units: Construction Products Petroleum Products Building Products Chemicals and Plastics Products and Food and Beverages.

Agricultural Products represents 20% of revenue and includes the transportation of commodities like corn wheat ethanol soybeans fertilizer oil seeds flour and other grains. The Coal business (less than 20%) is primarily BNSF's operations that originate from the Powder River Basin of Wyoming and Montana.

The company also generates about 5% of revenue from its wholly-owned non-rail logistics subsidiary BSNF Logistics LLC through logistics and transportation services such as storage as well as demurrage (detention fees for delays in loading and unloading of freight).

Geographic Reach

Headquartered in Fort Worth TX BNSF Railway's network spreads across about 30 US states and three Canadian provinces.

Sales and Marketing

BNSF Railway serves smaller markets by working closely with 200 shortline partners. It also forms marketing agreements with other rail carriers expanding the marketing reach for each railroad and its customers.

Financial Performance

BNSF has seen steady growth in recent years with revenue reaching $23.9 billion in 2018 a 12% increase compared with $21.4 billion in 2017. The increase in 2018 was mainly due to increased volume and increased rates per car as well as tight truck capacity in the transportation sector which converted some business from highway to rail.

Net income however plummeted to $5.2 billion less than half that of the previous year. This was primarily due to an increased tax liability as a result of the Tax Cuts and Jobs Act.

Cash at the end of fiscal 2018 was $2.0 billion about the same as the prior year. Cash from operations contributed $7.9 billion to the coffers while investing activities used $3.2 billion mainly for capital expenditures related to equipment purchases. Financing activities used another $4.7 billion primarily for cash distributions to its parent company.

Strategy

BNSF plans capital spending of about $3.5 billion in 2019 for network maintenance and replacement of assets to ensure safe and reliable operations. These include expansion and efficiency projects focused on key growth areas along its Southern and Northern Trancon routes. The company faces challenges in its supply chain environment with competition from improving productivity in the trucking industry. Another hurdle is consumers' expectations for quicker and quicker delivery as online shopping continues to grow. In response BSNF is focusing on providing consistent reliable and efficient transportation services to its customers.

Company Background

BNSF's traces its roots to 1849 when the Aurora Branch Railroad was founded in Illinois with 12 miles of track. Over the years additional rail lines were built including Atchison Topeka & Santa Fe;Burlington Northern; Chicago Burlington & Quincy; Frisco; Great Northern; Northern Pacific; and Spokane Portland & Seattle.

BNSF was created in 1995 when Burlington Northern Inc. (the parent company of Burlington Northern Railroad) merged with Santa Fe Pacific Corporation (parent company of the Atchison Topeka & Santa Fe Railway). The company was acquired by Berkshire Hathaway in 2010 and BNSF now operates as a subsidiary of that company.

EXECUTIVES

President And Ceo, Carl R. Ice, age 63
Evp Law And Corporate Affairs, Roger Nober, age 55
Evp And Cfo, Julie A. Piggott
Evp And Chief Marketing Officer, Stevan B. Bobb
Evp Operations, Gregory C. Fox
Vice President Federal Government Affairs, Amy Hawkins
Executive Vice President Law And Government Affairs And Secretary, Jeffrey Moreland
Vice President Network Strategy, Dean Wise
Vice President Controller, Dannis Johnson
Executive Chairman, Matthew K. (Matt) Rose, age 61
Auditors: DELOITTE & TOUCHE LLP FORT WO

LOCATIONS

HQ: BNSF RAILWAY COMPANY
 2650 LOU MENK DR, FORT WORTH, TX 761312830
Phone: 800 795-2673
Web: WWW.BNSF.COM

PRODUCTS/OPERATIONS

2018 Sales

	$ mil.	% of total
Consumer Products	7,902	33
Industrial Products	5,967	25
Agricultural Products	4,697	20
Coal	4,012	17
Other revenues	1,277	5
Total	23,855	100

COMPETITORS

CSX	Kansas City Southern Railway
Canadian National Railway	Norfolk Southern
Canadian Pacific Railway	Union Pacific Railroad

HISTORICAL FINANCIALS

Company Type: Private

Income Statement

FYE: December 31

	REVENUE ($ mil.)	NET INCOME ($ mil.)	NET PROFIT MARGIN	EMPLOYEES
12/17	20,747	12,119	58.4%	41,000
12/16	19,278	4,260	22.1%	
12/14	22,714	4,397	19.4%	
12/13	21,552	4,271	19.8%	
Annual Growth	(0.9%)	29.8%	—	—

Boeing Co. (The)

Boeing is the world's largest aerospace company and one of only two major manufacturers (the other being Airbus) of 100-plus seat airplanes for the commercial airline industry. Its commercial jet aircraft models include the 737 narrow body; the 747 767 and 777 wide bodies; and the 787 Dreamliner as well as the beleaguered 737 MAX which has been grounded by the FAA since two early-2019 crashes. Serving the military science and space and sea exploration sectors the company also produces KC-46 aerial refueling aircraft the AH-64 Apache helicopter the 702 family of satellites CST-100 Starliner spacecraft and the Echo Voyager unmanned undersea vehicle. The company generates half of its revenue domestically.

Operations

Boeing's operations are divided into four reportable segments: Commercial Airplanes (BCA); Defense Space & Security (BDS); Boeing Global Services (BGS); and Boeing Capital (BCC) its global financing operations.

Boeing Commercial Airplanes represents more than 40% of sales and designs manufactures and services commercial jet aircraft for both passengers and cargo. More than 10000 Boeing-built commercial jetliners are in service worldwide which is almost half the world fleet. The company also offers the most complete family of freighters.

Defense Space & Security (about 35% of sales) provides design production modification service and support services for large-scale systems including missiles munitions aerial refuelers transporters and spacecraft.

Boeing Global Services generates about 25% of sales. The division caters to aerospace and defense needs including supply chain and logistics management maintenance upgrades and conversions spare parts training systems and data analytics and digital services.

Boeing Capital ensure that Boeing customers have the financing they need to buy and take delivery of their Boeing product and manages overall financing exposure.

Geographic Reach

The Chicago Illinois-based Boeing's principal operations are in the US Canada and Australia with some key suppliers and subcontractors located in Europe and Japan. About 95% of its manufacturing warehousing engineering and administration facilities are located in the US. Boeing brings in approximately 50% of its revenue from the US roughly 20% from Asia more than 10% from Europe more than 10% from the Middle East about 5% in Canada and the remaining 5% comes from Oceana Africa and Latin America.

Sales and Marketing

The main customer of Boeing's Defense Space & Security segment is the Department of Defense which generates about 85% of revenue (including foreign military sales through the US government). Other significant BDS revenue is derived from NASA and customers in international defense markets civil markets and the commercial satellite market.

More than 85% of Sales are generated from product sold and about 15% on Sales on services that provides maintenance training data analytics and information-based services to customers.

Financial Performance

Boeing's revenue has been fluctuating over the past five years with a total increase of 20% since 2015.

Revenues decreased by $24568 million in 2019 compared with 2018 primarily due to lower revenues at BCA partially offset by higher revenues

at BGS. Lower BCA revenues are primarily driven by lower 737 MAX deliveries and a revenue reduction of $8259 million recorded in 2019 for estimated potential concessions and other considerations to customers for disruptions and associated delivery delays related to the 737 MAX grounding net of insurance recoveries.

In 2019 the company reported losses of $636 million an $11.1 billion decline from its profits in 2018.

Cash at the end of fiscal 2019 was $9.5 billion an increase of $1.8 billion from the prior year. Cash from operations united $2.4 billion to the coffers investing activities used $1.5 billion mainly for additions to property plant and equipment and acquisitions. Financing activities generated $5.7 billion mainly from new borrowings.

Strategy

As part of Boeing's business strategy the company may merge with or acquire businesses and/or form joint ventures and strategic alliances. For example in 2018 the company completed the acquisition of KLX Inc. a provider of aviation parts and services.

The company also may make strategic divestitures from time to time. These transactions may result in continued financial involvement in the divested businesses such as through guarantees or other financial arrangements.

Mergers and Acquisitions

Boeing achieves growth by acquiring businesses that focus on specific technology products and target the needs of emerging markets such as services.

In early 2019 the company completed the acquisition of Houston Texas-based ForeFlight a leading provider of innovative mobile and web-based aviation applications for an undisclosed amount. The acquisition of ForeFlight aligns with Boeing's growth strategy of complementing organic investments with targeted strategic investments that position the company for long-term growth. "We are excited to build on ForeFlight's tremendous success in personal business and defense aviation so we can provide next-generation integrated tools to our aviation customers today" said Ken Sain Boeing Vice President of Digital Solutions and Analytics.

Company Background

The Boeing Company celebrated 100 years in business in 2016. Some of its first aircraft were used in World War I and the company began manufacturing commercial aircraft in 1919. The global aviation industry continued to grow even through The Great Depression and Boeing continued to deliver more commercial and military aircraft through the decades.

In 1947 Boeing set speed and distance records with its B-47 and its swept-back wings a design that would become standard on many commercial and military aircraft. Boeing also designed the first stage of the three-stage Saturn V rocket used for the Apollo space missions in the 1960s. The company went on to develop the Apache helicopter which is still in use today.

Most recently Boeing has been focused on future mobility products such as autonomous aircraft and next-generation space vehicles.

HISTORY

Bill Boeing who had already made his fortune in Washington real estate built his first airplane in 1916 with naval officer Conrad Westervelt. His Seattle company Pacific Aero Products changed its name to Boeing Airplane Company the next year. During WWI Boeing built training planes for the US Navy and began the first international airmail service (between Seattle and Victoria British Columbia). The company added a Chicago-San

Francisco route in 1927 and established an airline subsidiary Boeing Air Transport. The airline's success was aided by Boeing's Model 40A the first plane to use Frederick Rentschler's new air-cooled engine.

Rentschler and Boeing combined their companies as United Aircraft and Transport in 1929 and introduced the all-metal airliner in 1933. The next year new antitrust rules forced United Aircraft and Transportation to sell portions of its operations as United Air Lines and United Aircraft (later United Technologies). This left Boeing Airplane (as it was known until 1961) with the manufacturing concerns.

EXECUTIVES

Evp And Ceo Boeing Global Services, Stanley A. (Stan) Deal, age 56

Evp And General Counsel, J. Michael (Mike) Luttig, age 65, $903,673 total compensation

Svp Supply Chain And Operations, Patrick M. (Pat) Shanahan, age 58

Chairman President And Ceo, Dennis A. Muilenburg, age 56, $1,640,962 total compensation

President Phantom Works Boeing Defense Space And Security, Darryl W. Davis

Evp And President And Ceo Boeing Commercial Airplanes, Kevin G. McAllister, age 57, $92,308 total compensation

Svp Sales Asia Pacific And President Boeing India, Dinesh A. Keskar, age 66

Evp Business Development And Strategy And Cfo, Gregory D. (Greg) Smith, age 53, $911,442 total compensation

President Boeing Military Aircraft Boeing Defense Space And Security, Shelley K. Lavender, age 56

Svp And President Boeing International, Bertrand-Marc (Marc) Allen, age 46

Svp Information And Analytics And Cio, Theodore (Ted) Colbert, age 46

Svp Engineering And Cto, Gregory L. (Greg) Hyslop, age 61

President Boeing Capital Corporation, Timothy Myers

Evp And President And Ceo Defense Space And Security (bds), Leanne G. Caret, age 53

President Network And Space Systems, Jim Chilton

Vp Airplane Programs Engineering Commercial Airplanes, Patrick (Pat) Goggin

Senior Vice President Commercial Sales And Marketing, Ihssane Mounir

Vice President Strategy Global Services, Dennis Floyd

Vice President Attack Helicopters And Mesa Senior Site Executive, Kim Smith

Vice President Communications And Marketing, Mary Foster

Boeing Vice President Of Leasing Sales, Bill Collins

Vice President, Mark Jenks

Vice President, Bernard Hensey

Vice President, Karen Tang

Vice President, Mark Bertrand

Vice President, Steve Bachmann

Regional Vice President, David Cazer

Vice President Of Strategic Development, Bill Bonadio

Vice President Human Resources, Grace Miller

Vice President Customer Support, Donald Ruhmann

Deputy Vice President, Kevin Standerfer

Manager Government Relations, Mark Gaspers

Vice President Corporate Strategy, Rik Geiersbach

Vice President, Matt Wilks

Senior Vice President Gc, J M Luttig

National Account Manager, Jacqueline Stephenson

Vice President, Phyllis Ditocco

Vp And Gm Supply Chain Commercial Airplanes, Elizabeth Lund
Vice President Federal Legislative Affairs Government Operations, Art Cameron
Vice President Of Supply Chain Rate Capability For Commercial Airplanes Supplier Management, Beth Anderson
Vice President Of Sales For Digital Division, Keith P White
Vice President Integrated Defense System, Gregory Laxton
Vice President Business Systems And Administration, Renee L Stober
Vp Communications, Gordon Johndroe
Vice President Supply And Operations Chain, William Schnettgoecke
Vice President, Jay Byunn
Vice President And Managing Director, James Detwiler
Vice President Enterprise Strategy, Christopher Raymond
Vice President Intellectual Property Management, Peter Hoffman
Vice President, Lynn Johnson
Vice President, Brett Fischer
Vice President, Bruce Dennis
Vice President, Tobias Bright
Vice President Special Events, Lacey Jones
Vice President Digital Solutions, Per Noren
Vice President And General Manager For Supplier Management, Steve Schaffer
Vice President Communications Boeing Global Services, Conrad Chun
Vp And Chief Engineer Commercial Airplanes, John Hamilton
Vice President Of Sales And Marketing, Harry W Gray
Vice President, Ken Torok
Vice President Manufacturing Safety And Quality Commercial Airplanes, Walter Odisho
Vice President, Michael Sloup
Vice President Middle East Sales, Robert Johnstone
Vice President, Terry Kamm
Vice President Enterprise Strategy, Travis Sullivan
Vice President, Catherine J Pruss-Jones
Vice President Engineering, Russell E Shue
Vice President Supply Chain Boeing Global Services, Kenneth Shaw
Vice President, Shelly Huff
Vp And Program Manager Boeing Global Broadband System, Bruce Chesley
Vice President And Program Manager C 130 Avionics Modernization Program, Michael Harris
Office Of The Vice President Of Engineering, Patricia Sandoval
Vice President, Steve Wallace
Vice President Information Technology, Ralph Czeschin
Vp Human Resources, Wendy Livingston
Vice President Transaction Services, Edward Bayne
Vice President Edelman Employee Engagement Practice, Nicole Silva
Vice President Of Decision Support, Rebecca Fasano
Vice President Human Resources Commercial Airplanes, Joelle Denney
Vice President And Assistant General Counsel Boeing Commercial Airplanes, Matt Cooper
Svp Global Sales And Marketing Defense Space And Security, Thomas Bell
Vice President Cargo Helicopters, Stephen Parker
Vice President Director Of Marketing, Paul Mittmann
Senior Vice President Supplier Management, Jim Morris
Vice President Business And Supply Chain Systems, Lakshmi Eleswarpu
Vp Of Boeing International And President Of Israel, David Ivry
Vice President, Jeremy Griffin

Vice President, Michael Fleming
Vice President Communications, Linda Mills
Vice President, Stanley A Orr
Vice President Digital Transformation Commercial Airplanes, Michael Delaney
Vice President Global Trade Controls Office Of Internal Governance And Administration, Sue Gainor
Vice President Navy Systems, Mike Manazir
Vice President And General Manager, Charles Toups
Vice President, Jeff Rice
Vice President Space Intelligence And Missile Defense Systems, Roger Teague
Vice President Information Technology Business Partners Defense Space And Security, Denise Russell Fleming
Vice President Sales, Rachel Lohmar
Provost And Vice President For Academic Affairs, Michael Hannan
Vice Chairman, Raymond L. (Ray) Conner, age 64
Assistant Treasurer, Ruud Roggekamp
Secretary, Bruce J Cadiz
Assistant Treasurer, Verett Mims
Assistant Treasurer Risk Management And Insurance, Michael Tarling
Board Member, Thi Tran
Treasurer, Roger Pullman
Svp Finance And Treasurer, David Dohnalek
Secretary, Chris Tavares
Treasurer, Laura LU
Chapter Treasurer, Daniel Hill
Board Member, Guy Ferranti
Board Member, David Wang
Office Of The Treasurer, Kim Rainey
Usglc Treasurer, Jefferson Hofgard
Treasurer, Melinda Donaldson
Board Member, David Good
Secretary, Stanley Huang
Board Member, David Calhoun
Secretary Of The Corporation, Edward Higgins
Treasurer, Gordon Yip
Secretary, Joseph S Lyons
Secretary, Dan McNeil
Treasurer, Edward Puckett
Auditors: DELOITTE & TOUCHE LLP

LOCATIONS

HQ: Boeing Co. (The)
100 North Riverside Plaza, Chicago, IL 60606-1596
Phone: 312 544-2000
Web: www.boeing.com

2018 Sales

	$ mil.	% of total
US	44,676	44
Asia		
China	13,764	14
Other Asia	12,141	12
Europe	12,976	13
Middle East	9,745	10
Canada	2,583	3
Oceania	2,298	2
Africa	1,486	1
Latin American Caribbean & other	1,458	1
Total	**101,127**	**100**

PRODUCTS/OPERATIONS

2018 Sales

	$ mil.	% of total
Sales of products	90,229	89
Sales of services	10,898	11
Total	**101,127**	**100**

2018 Sales

	$ mil.	% of total
Commercial Airplanes	60,715	60
Defense Space & Security	23,195	23
Global Services	17,018	17
Boeing Capital	274	—
Adjustments	(75)	—
Total	**101,127**	**100**

Selected Products and Services

Commercial Airplanes
Products
737 Next Generation (short-to-medium-range two-engine jet)
747 (long-range four-engine jet)
767 (medium-to-long-range two-engine jet)
777 (long-range two-engine jet)
Boeing Business Jet
787 Dreamliner (in development; long-range super-efficient 200-250 passenger capacity)
747-8 (in development;
Services
Engineering modification and logistics
Maintenance repair and overhaul
Boeing Training & Flight Services
Defense Space & Security
Military Aircraft
AH-64 Apache
B-1B Lancer
B-2 Spirit
F/A-18 Hornet
F-15E Strike Eagle
F-22 Raptor
T-45 Flight Training System
A160 Hummingbird
Harpoon
Insitu
C-17 Globemaster III
CH-47D/F Chinook
V-22 Osprey
Global Services & Support
Integrated logistics
Maintenance modifications and upgrades
Training systems
Government services
Network & Space Systems
Electronic and mission
Cyber security
Infrastructure
Intelligence
Logistics command and control
Satellite and ground operations
Space exploration

COMPETITORS

AgustaWestland	Lockheed Martin
Airbus Group	Northrop Grumman
BAE SYSTEMS	Raytheon
Dassault Aviation	Rockwell Collins
Embraer	Space Exploration
General Dynamics	Technologies
Kaman	Thales
Leonardo	United Technologies

HISTORICAL FINANCIALS

Company Type: Public

Income Statement   FYE: December 31

	REVENUE ($ mil.)	NET INCOME ($ mil.)	NET PROFIT MARGIN	EMPLOYEES
12/20	58,158	(11,873)	—	141,000
12/19	76,559	(636)	—	161,100
12/18	101,127	10,460	10.3%	153,000
12/17	93,392	8,197	8.8%	140,800
12/16	94,571	4,895	5.2%	150,500
Annual Growth	**(11.4%)**	**—**	**—**	**(1.6%)**

2020 Year-End Financials

Debt ratio: 41.79%
Return on equity: —
Cash ($ mil.): 7,752
Current ratio: 1.39
Long-term debt ($ mil.): 61,890

No. of shares (mil.): 582
Dividends
Yield: 2.8%
Payout: —
Market value ($ mil.): 124,651

	STOCK PRICE ($)	P/E	PER SHARE ($)		
	FY Close	High/Low	Earnings	Dividends	Book Value
12/20	214.06	— —	(20.88)	6.17	(31.45)
12/19	325.76	— —	(1.12)	8.22	(15.31)
12/18	322.50	22 16	17.85	6.84	0.60
12/17	294.91	22 12	13.43	5.68	0.60
12/16	155.68	20 14	7.61	4.36	1.32
Annual Growth	8.3%	— —	—	9.0%	

BOK Financial Corp

With seven principal banking divisions in eight midwestern and southwestern states multi-bank holding company BOK offers a range of financial services to consumers and regional businesses. In addition to traditional deposit lending and trust services its banks provide investment management wealth advisory and mineral and real estate management services through a network of branches in Arizona Arkansas Colorado Kansas Missouri New Mexico Oklahoma and Texas. Brokerage subsidiary BOSC underwrites public private and municipal securities. BOK also owns electronic funds network TransFund and institutional asset manager Cavanal Hill.

Operations

BOK Financial operates through three primary segments: Commercial Banking Consumer Banking and Wealth Management. The Commercial Banking segment brings in more than 75% of BOK's total revenue with offerings including lending treasury and cash management and risk management products for small midsized and large companies. The Consumer Banking segment which brings in about 15% of total revenue is the retail arm providing lending and deposit services and all mortgage activities. The Wealth Management segment provides private bank and investment advisory services across all markets and it has more than $16 billion in assets under management. The segment is also engaged in trading and it underwrites state and municipal securities.

Geographic Reach

Most of Tulsa-based BOK Financial's locations are located in and around Tulsa; Oklahoma City; Dallas/Fort Worth; Houston; Albuquerque New Mexico; Denver; Phoenix; and Kansas City in Kansas and Missouri. The company's primary operations facilities lare in Tulsa; Oklahoma City; Dallas; and Albuquerque New Mexico.

Sales and Marketing

In 2017 BOK Financials spent $28.9 million on promotional costs versus $26.6 million in 2016 and $27.9 million in 2015.

Financial Performance

Thanks largely to the improving US economy BOK's revenues have been trending upward for the past five years. Net income has been somewhat more volatile but reached a peak in 2017.

Revenue increased 9% to $1.5 billion in 2017 as interest income increased 17%. Loan trading securities and interest-bearing cash and cash equivalents revenues saw significant growth that year. Asset management income also rose gaining some 20%. These increases were partially offset by a decline in mortgage banking revenue.

With the higher revenue plus certain lower operating expenses (including mortgage banking costs and insurance expenses) net income rose 44% to $331.1 million in 2017.

The company ended 2017 with $2.3 billion in net cash some $220 million less than it had at the end of 2016. Operating activities provided $214.9 million and investing activities provided $739.6 million. Financing activities used $1.2 billion.

Strategy

BOK emphasizes local decision-making at its flagship subsidiary Bank of Oklahoma and its operating divisions Bank of Albuquerque Bank of Arizona Bank of Arkansas Bank of Texas Colorado State Bank and Trust and Mobank. Commercial loans primarily to the energy services health care and wholesale and retail industries make up the majority of the company's loan portfolio. Commercial real estate residential mortgage car and consumer loans round out its lending activities.

The company is also focused on diversifying its revenue stream by growing its mortgage banking brokerage and wealth management operations.

With banking operations in several major oil- and natural gas-producing states more than 15% of the group's lending portfolio is in the energy sector. Because the energy industry has been challenged with low commodity prices BOK's energy-related charge-offs have grown significantly. In Q2 of 2018 net charge-offs reached $10.5 million — more than half of which was attributed to a single energy customer.

Mergers and Acquisitions

In October 2018 BOK Financial acquired financial services company CoBiz Financial which provides commercial banking and other financial services to businesses in Arizona and Colorado through its Colorado Business Bank and Bank of Arizona subsidiaries. The deal valued at $1 billion more than doubled BOK Financial's deposit market share in the two states.

EXECUTIVES

President And Ceo, Steven G. (Steve) Bradshaw, age 60, $484,275 total compensation
Evp And Cfo, Steven E. Nell, age 58, $439,354 total compensation
Svp And Corporate Controller, Stacy C. Kymes, age 49
Chief Credit Officer, Marc C. Maun, age 62
Chairman And Ceo Bank Of Texas, Norman P. Bagwell, age 57, $403,054 total compensation
Evp And Chief Human Resources Officer, Stephen D. Grossi
Evp And Cio, Donald T. Parker
Evp Consumer Banking, Patrick E. Piper
Evp Wealth Management And Ceo Bosc. Inc., Scott B. Grauer
Ceo Oklahoma City Market, John Higginbotham
Assistant Vice President Finance And Administration, Lanny L Randolph
Senior Vice President Perf. Reporting And Analysis, Kent Rugeley
Vice President Perf. Reporting And Analysis, Tamara Cobb
Senior Vice President And Chief Marketing Officer, Alan Nykiel
Senior Vice President, Guy Evangelista
Senior Vice President, Michael Bickel
Vice President, Alice Worthington
Vice President Middle Office Manager, John Williamson
Senior Vice President, Lee Allen
Vice President Business Performance Measurement, Richard Hubbard
Vice President, Debi Briscoe
Senior Vice President Director Of Contact Center Operations, John Holt
Vice President, Lisa Albers
Vice President Marketing, Margot McKoy
Vice President, Candice Williams
Senior Vice President, Jill Hall

Senior Vice President, Jeff Sanders
Vice President, Mary Campbell
Vice President And Trust Officer, Claudia Cepeda
Vice President And Portfolio Manager, Tim Hopkins
Senior Vice President Director Of Business Banking, John Anderson
Senior Vice President Manager Of Health Care Lending, Brad Vincent
Vice President Risk Management, Don Mallory
Vice President Accounting Control Reporting, Ed Disney
Assistant Vice President Information Technology Project Manager, Lisa Porter Lisa Porter
Vice President Trust Officer Iii, Mary Thomason
Chairman Bok Financial And Bank Of Oklahoma, George B. Kaiser, age 77
Board Member, Kimberley Henry
Auditors: Ernst & Young LLP

LOCATIONS

HQ: BOK Financial Corp
Bank of Oklahoma Tower, Boston Avenue at Second Street, Tulsa, OK 74192
Phone: 918 588-6000
Web: www.bokf.com

PRODUCTS/OPERATIONS

2017 Sales

	% of total
Commercial Banking	76
Consumer Banking	7
Wealth Management	17
Total	**100**

Selected Banking Subsidiaries

Bank of Albuquerque National Association
Bank of Arizona National Association
Bank of Arkansas National Association
Bank of Oklahoma National Association
Bank of Texas National Association
Colorado State Bank & Trust
Mobank

COMPETITORS

BBVA Compass Bancshares	JPMorgan Chase
Bank of America	Regions Financial
Bank of the West	UMB Financial
Comerica	Wells Fargo
Commerce Bancshares	Zions Bancorporation
First National of Nebraska	

HISTORICAL FINANCIALS

Company Type: Public

Income Statement

				FYE: December 31
	ASSETS ($ mil.)	NET INCOME ($ mil.)	INCOME AS % OF ASSETS	EMPLOYEES
12/19	42,172	500	1.2%	5,107
12/18	38,020	445	1.2%	5,313
12/17	32,272	334	1.0%	4,930
12/16	32,772	232	0.7%	4,884
12/15	31,476	288	0.9%	4,789
Annual Growth	**7.6%**	**14.8%**	**—**	**1.6%**

2019 Year-End Financials

Debt ratio: 0.72%	No. of shares (mil.): 70
Return on equity: 10.78%	Dividends
Cash ($ mil.): 1,258	Yield: 2.3%
Current ratio: —	Payout: 28.9%
Long-term debt ($ mil.): —	Market value ($ mil.): 6,169

	STOCK PRICE ($) FY Close	P/E High/Low	PER SHARE ($) Earnings	PER SHARE ($) Dividends	PER SHARE ($) Book Value
12/19	87.40	13 10	7.03	2.01	68.80
12/18	73.33	16 11	6.63	1.90	61.45
12/17	92.32	18 15	5.11	1.77	53.45
12/16	83.04	24 13	3.53	1.73	50.12
12/15	59.79	17 13	4.21	1.69	49.03
Annual Growth	10.0%	— —	13.7%	4.4%	8.8%

BON SECOURS MERCY HEALTH, INC.

Bon Secours Mercy Health (formerly Bon Secours Health System) is a Roman Catholic health care organization. Sponsored by the Bon Secours Ministries it is home to 43 hospitals with more than 2100 physicians. First founded in 1919 its facilities are in seven states in the eastern US from New York to Florida. In addition to its acute care hospitals the not-for-profit system operates a psychiatric hospital numerous nursing homes and assisted-living facilities as well as hospices and home health care agencies. Bon Secours merged with Cincinnati-based Mercy Health to create Bon Secours Mercy Health in 2018. The combined entity expanded into Ireland in 2019.

Geographic Reach

Bon Secours Mercy Health has hospitals in Florida Kentucky Maryland New York Ohio South Carolina and Virginia.

Sales and Marketing

Medicare and Medicaid payments account for around 35% of Bon Secours Mercy Health's total net patient revenue.

Strategy

Bon Secours Mercy Health plans to continue to grow its operations in existing and new communities targeting expansion in ambulatory care elderly services and home health and hospice. The health system has opened several new ambulatory care centers in existing service territories and it is conducting renovation and expansion efforts at some of its hospital facilities.

The system has also initiated information technology restructuring efforts; it has developed a new clinical information management system (electronic medical records) ConnectCare which is being implemented at its facilities in gradual stages.

The company branched out internationally through the purchase of Irish hospital operator Bon Secours Health System in 2019. Additionally its Global Ministry Initiative provides outreach for health care and social services in developing countries particularly Haiti Peru and South Africa.

Mergers and Acquisitions

Bon Secours MercyHealth in 2019 agreed to acquire three hospitals in southeastern Virginia expanding its operations in the region by some 500 beds. The hospitals are Southside Regional Medical Center in Petersburg Southampton Memorial Hospital in Franklin and Southern Virginia Regional Medical Center in Emporia. The hospitals are affiliates of Community Health Systems Inc. a hospital company selling facilities as it deal with financial difficulties.

In 2018 Bon Secours and Cincinnati-based Mercy Health joined forces to create a system with 43 hospitals in seven states. The combined entity has more than 2100 physicians and clinicians working in more than 1000 locations.

The following year Bon Secours Mercy Health acquired Ireland-based Bon Secours Health System which operates five hospitals and other health facilities.

EXECUTIVES

President Ceo And Director, Richard J. (Rich) Statuto
Svp And Cio, Skip Hubbard
Evp, Mark S. Nantz
Evp, Janice Burnett
Evp, Samuel L. Ross
Ceo Bon Secours St. Francis Health System, R. Craig McCoy
Ceo Bon Secours Charity, Mary Leahy
Senior Vice President Of Mission, Pam Phillips
Vice President Revenue Cycle Services, Vickie Kleski
Vice President Financial Planning And Analysis, James Siegel
Senior Vice President Human Resources, Fernando Fleites
Director Of Admissions, Carrie Newcomb
Vice President Ancillary Amb Services, Johnna S Reed
Vice President Revenue Cycle, Sheila Kuenzle
Vice President Treasury Services, Pamela Schmidt
Director Of Nursing Resources, Candace Porter
Senior Vice President Of Services, Robert Rosenthal
Medical Director And Residency Director, John Unkel
Medical Director And Physician, Mark Miranda
Pharmacy Manager, Ryan Cann
Director Of Pharmacy, Terri Spearman
Medical Director, Janet Eddy
Director Of Radiology, William Long
Medical Director Emergency Services, Adrienne Wasserman
Vice President Patient Care Cne, Sophie Crawford-Rosso
Vice President Service Line Strategy, Leigh Sewell
Vice President Corporate Communications, Terri Mcnorton
Senior Vice President Provider Networks, Wael Haidar
Vice President Patient Care Services, Leana Fox
Director Of Pharmacy, Kerri Musselman
Medical Director Clinical Ethics, Kelly Stuart
Vice President Bon Secours Hampton Roads Foundations, Judy Bilicki
Senior Vice President, Archuleta Bob
Vice President, Rose Marie Jasinski
Assistant Vice President Quality And Patient Safety, Kathleen Geisinger
Executive Vice President Chief Administrative Officer, Tim Davis
Radiology Director, Alan Bailey
Medical Records Director, Susan Griffith
Director Of Radiology, Hill Michael
Vice President Of Patient Services And Chief Nursing Executive, Brandi Fields
Vice President Of Clinical Operations, Jude Ade
Chairman, Charles H. Brown
Secretary, Maria Sorice
Unit Secretary, Corie Miller
Unit Secretary, Noel Townes
Secretary Admin, Huff Brenda
Senior Medical Secretary, Brian Raymond
Unit Secretary, Tamara Pearson
Unit Secretary, Eva White
Auditors: KPMG LLP BALTIMORE MD

LOCATIONS

HQ: BON SECOURS MERCY HEALTH, INC.
1701 MERCY HEALTH PL, CINCINNATI, OH 452376147
Phone: 410 442-5511
Web: WWW.BSMHEALTH.ORG

Selected Facilities

Florida
Bon Secours St. Petersburg Health System
Bon Secours - Maria Manor Nursing Care and Rehabilitation Center
Bon Secours Place at St. Petersburg
Bon Secours St. Petersburg Home Care Services
Kentucky
Bon Secours Kentucky Health System
Our Lady of Bellefonte Hospital (Ashland)
Maryland
Bon Secours Baltimore Health System
Bon Secours Hospital
Bon Secours Washington Village
Community Institute of Behavioral Sciences
Hollins Terrace/Benet House
New York
Bon Secours Charity Health System
Bon Secours Community Hospital (Port Jervis)
Good Samaritan Hospital (Suffern)
St. Anthony Community Hospital (Warwick)
Bon Secours New York Health System
Schervier Nursing Care Center (Riverdale)
Pennsylvania
Altoona Regional Health System (joint venture)
South Carolina
Bon Secours St. Francis Health System Inc.
St. Francis Hospital (Downtown and Eastside Campuses Greenville)
Roper St. Francis Healthcare (Charleston joint venture)
Virginia
Bon Secours Hampton Roads Health System
Bon Secours Maryview Nursing Care Center (Suffolk)
DePaul Medical Center (Norfolk)
Mary Immaculate Hospital (Newport News)
Maryview Medical Center (Portsmouth)
Province Place (Norfolk and Portsmouth)
St. Francis Nursing Care Center (Newport News)
Bon Secours Richmond Health System (joint venture)
Memorial Regional Medical Center (Mechanicsville)
Richmond Community Hospital
St. Francis Medical Center (Midlothian)
St. Mary's Hospital (Richmond)

Selected Affiliations
Cosponsoring Congregational Relationships
Bernardine Sisters of the Third Order of St. Francis (Newport News Virginia)
Sisters of Charity of Saint Elizabeth of Convent Station (New Jersey and New York)
Affiliated Organizations
Health Corporation of Virginia (Richmond)
Medical Society of South Carolina and Carolinas Health Care System (Charleston)
Life Care Services (Florida and Virginia)

PRODUCTS/OPERATIONS

2014 Sales

	$ mil.	% of total
Net Patient Service Revenue	3,328	96
Other revenue	133	4
Total	3,461	100

COMPETITORS

Adventist HealthCare	Highlands Health
Albany Medical Center	Inova
Albert Einstein Healthcare Network	Johns Hopkins Medicine
	MedStar Health
Appalachian Regional Healthcare	MediSys Health Network
Carilion Clinic	New York City Health and Hospitals
Catholic Health Initiatives	Novant Health
	Riverside Health
Centra Health Inc.	System (Virginia)
Christiana Care	Sentara Healthcare
Community Health	St. Agnes HealthCare

Systems	University of Maryland
Conemaugh Health	Medical System
System	University of Miami
Franklin Square	Hospital
Hospital Center	Upstate Affiliate
GBMC	Virginia Hospital
HCA	Center

HISTORICAL FINANCIALS

Company Type: Private

Income Statement FYE: December 31

	REVENUE ($ mil.)	NET INCOME ($ mil.)	NET PROFIT MARGIN	EMPLOYEES
12/19*	8,717	2,593	29.7%	19,000
08/10	3,084	(41)	—	—
08/09	2,895	(291)	—	—
08/08	187	51	27.6%	—
Annual Growth	41.8%	42.7%	—	—

*Fiscal year change

Booking Holdings Inc

Booking Holdings (formerly The Priceline Group) operates six of the world's leading online travel tools. Booking.com is its namesake and top brand and offers online reservation services for nearly 2.6 million properties — including hotels resorts apartments and homes — across over 230-plus countries. The holding company also owns Priceline which features discount bookings for hotels cars airline tickets and vacation packages; other brands include Agoda KAYAK RentalCars and OpenTable. Booking Holdings generates revenues from credit card processing rebates and customer processing fees advertising services restaurant reservations and management services and various other services such as travel-related insurance. It was founded in 1997 and generates some 90% of sales outside the US.

Operations

Booking Holdings (formerly The Priceline Group) operates an online global travel services network. It works to connect customers looking to make travel reservations with providers of travel services worldwide including nearly 2.6 million hotels and accommodations.

Internationally the company offers a retail price-disclosed hotel and accommodation reservation service through global brands Booking.com (the world's largest online hotel and accommodation website) and Agoda.com (an online hotel reservation service with operations primarily in Asia-Pacific Region). In the US it offers reservations via priceline.com brand for hotels rental cars airline tickets and vacations packages. KAYAK allows consumers to easily search and compare travel itineraries and prices including airline ticket accommodation reservation and rental car reservation information from hundreds of travel websites at once.

OpenTable allows consumers to set up restaurant reservations online and Rentalcars.com is a leading rental car reservation service.

More than 65% of Priceline Group's total revenue comes from agency revenue (commissions paid by travel service providers) while merchant revenue (service fees paid by travelers) and advertising revenue make up some 25% and nearly 10% of its total sales respectively.

Geographic Reach

Connecticut-based Booking Holdings (formerly The Priceline Group) serves more than 230 countries. Its ownership of Amsterdam-based Booking.com means the company generates about 80% of its total revenue from the Netherlands. The US and other international markets together generate over 20%.

Agoda.com is based in Singapore Priceline and KAYAK are both headquartered in Connecticut OpenTable is based in San Francisco and Rental-cars.com is located in Netherlands. Additional offices and data centers are located in the US UK Switzerland the Netherlands Germany Singapore and Hong Kong.

Sales and Marketing

Booking Holdings aggressively promotes its brands online relying on internet search engine (mostly Google) keyword purchases referrals from meta-search sites and travel research websites affiliate programs and other performance-based marketing and incentives.

The Company provides loyalty programs where participating consumers are awarded loyalty points on current transactions that can be redeemed in the future. The Company's largest loyalty program is at OpenTable where points can be redeemed for rewards such as qualifying reservations at participating restaurants third-party gift cards and accommodation reservations booked through some of the Company's other platforms.

It spent $4.4 billion on performance marketing in 2019 compared to $4.4 billion and $4.2 billion the prior two years. Brand marketing which is a specific focus for the company increased to $548 million in 2019 compared to $509 million and $435 million in 2018 and 2017 respectively.

Financial Performance

Revenue growth for Booking Holdings continued an upward trend since 2015. For that five-year span the revenue grew by 63% thanks to the rising popularity of the online travel booking business.

In fiscal 2019 the company saw its sales hit $15.1 billion up 4% from the prior year. Increase in revenue was due to increase in sales in accommodation reservation services.

Net income jumped 22% to $4.9 billion compared to 2018 due to increase in sales.

Cash at the end of 2019 was $6.3 billion an increase of $3.7 billion from the prior year. Cash from operations contributed $4.9 billion to the coffers while investing activities added another $7.1 billion from proceeds on the sale of investments. Financing activities used $8.2 billion primarily for stock repurchase program.

Strategy

Booking Holdings' strategy is to continue to participate broadly in this online growth by expanding its service offerings and markets. In particular the Company seeks to: Leverage technology to provide consumers with the best experience; Partner with travel service providers and restaurants to their mutual benefit; Operate multiple brands that collaborate with each other; and Invest in profitable and sustainable growth.

The company have also entered into commercial relationships with other online travel companies such as Didi (the leading ride hailing service in China) and Grab (the leading ride hailing company in Southeast Asia) whereby the customers of one company will have access to the services of the other. For example through the Booking.com app a Booking.com customer traveling in Southeast Asia can book a local ride arranged by Grab.

Mergers and Acquisitions

In 2019 Booking Holdings agreed to acquire Washington DC-based Venga which operates a guest management platform for restaurants and other businesses. The business will improve the offerings of OpenTable for its more than 51000 restaurant partners.

Company Background

Priceline founder Jay Walker launched a string of ventures before making the leap into e-commerce. In 1994 he founded Walker Digital an entrepreneurial think tank formed to develop business models that could germinate into new companies.

In 1996 Walker Digital found the impetus that would drive Priceline: Each day major airlines have more than 500000 empty seats. Walker's team reasoned that if the airlines were offered even a discounted price for these empty seats they'd jump at the chance to cut their losses. Based on that premise Walker Digital developed a "name your price" system and founded Priceline in 1997.

The company went public with a chart-busting IPO in 1999.

In April 2014 the company changed its name from Priceline.com to The Priceline Group to better reflect the growth of its business and all of its subsidiaries and brands including Booking.com priceline.com KAYAK OpenTable and others. Four years later it changed its name again — to Booking Holdings — reflecting its most important brand.

HISTORY

Priceline founder Jay Walker launched a string of ventures before making the leap into e-commerce. In 1994 he founded Walker Digital an entrepreneurial think tank formed to develop business models that could germinate into new companies.

In 1996 Walker Digital found the impetus that would drive Priceline: Each day major airlines have more than 500000 empty seats. Walker's team reasoned that if the airlines were offered even a discounted price for these empty seats they'd jump at the chance to cut their losses. Based on that premise Walker Digital developed a "name your price" system and founded Priceline in 1997.

The company launched its airfare service in 1998 and obtained financing from General Atlantic Partners and Paul Allen's Vulcan Ventures (now called Vulcan Northwest). That year it expanded into hotel reservations and added a car-buying service. Richard Braddock became chairman and CEO in 1998.

Priceline added home financing services to its offerings in 1999. The company went public with a chart-busting IPO later that year. Priceline also launched a rental car service. Branching into the retail arena it licensed its technology to WebHouse Club for use in selling grocery products. The company sued Microsoft in 1999 claiming that company's Expedia unit's name-your-own-price hotel reservation service violated Priceline's patent.

In 2000 the company licensed its business model to several international ventures including General Atlantic Partners' Priceline.com Europe (headed by Dennis Malamatinas former Burger King CEO) SOFTBANK's Priceline.com Japan (a deal that was later cancelled) MyPrice in Australia and New Zealand (also cancelled) and Asian conglomerate Hutchinson Whampoa. In collaboration with Alliance Capital (now AllianceBernstein) Priceline created subsidiary pricelinemortgage to act as mortgage broker.

Daniel Schulman became CEO later that year. Jay Walker resigned as vice chairman at the end of 2000 after taking on the role of CEO at Walker Digital. After deciding it would probably never be profitable WebHouse Club shut down ending Priceline's foray into grocery sales. Known for its splashy ads Priceline dumped pop icon William Shatner as its TV spokesperson in favor of Sex and the City star Sarah Jessica Parker. (Shatner returned in 2002.) Later that year the company fired Schulman and reappointed Braddock as CEO.

In 2002 the company joined with National Leisure Group to offer cruises from its website. Later that year Priceline purchased the assets of discount travel site Lowestfare.com. It also announced plans to sell cars under a marketing agreement with Autobytel. In late 2002 Braddock passed his CEO responsibilities to president Jeffery Boyd. (Braddock remained as chairman.)

A handful of new international destinations (Australia Japan Indonesia Malaysia South Korea Taiwan) was added in 2003 to Priceline's hotel reservation service. In April 2004 chairman Richard Braddock (former president of Citicorp and one of the last remaining high-profile board members) resigned from the company. Director Ralph Bahna was then named chairman. The following month Priceline acquired most of Travelweb.com. That September it bought Active Hotels of Britain for about $161 million in cash. In December 2004 Priceline acquired the remaining stake in Travelweb for about $4 million.

EXECUTIVES

Ceo Priceline.com, Brett Keller, age 52

Svp And General Counsel, Peter J. Millones, age 50, $330,000 total compensation

Svp International; Senior Manager Priceline.co.uk, Glenn D. Fogel, age 58, $315,000 total compensation

Svp Cfo And Chief Accounting Officer, Daniel J. Finnegan, age 57, $315,000 total compensation

Ceo Agoda.com, Robert Rosenstein, age 53

Ceo Kayak, Steve Hafner

President And Ceo Booking.com, Gillian Tans, age 49, $498,356 total compensation

Ceo Rentalcars.com, Ian Brown

Ceo Opentable Inc., Christa Quarles

Senior Vice President Of It Operations Of Priceline.com, Ken Jones

Vice President Associate General Counsel, Brian Macdonald

Senior Vice President Global Infrastructure, Glen Dalgleish

Chairman, Jeffery H. (Jeff) Boyd, age 63

Board Member, Craig Rydin

Board Member, Tim Armstrong

Board Member, Mirian Graddick-weir

Board Member, Nicholas J Read

Auditors: DELOITTE & TOUCHE LLP

LOCATIONS

HQ: Booking Holdings Inc
 800 Connecticut Avenue, Norwalk, CT 06854
Phone: 203 299-8000   **Fax:** 203 595-0160
Web: www.bookingholdings.com

2018 Sales

	$ mil.	% of total
The Netherlands	11,094	76
US	1,626	11
Other	1,807	13
Total	**14,527**	**100**

PRODUCTS/OPERATIONS

2018 Sales

	$ mil.	% of total
Agency	10,480	72
Merchant	2,987	21
Advertising and other	1,060	7
Total	**14,527**	**100**

Selected Products

Airline tickets
Cruises
Hotel rooms
Rental cars
Restaurant reservations
Vacation packages

Selected Brands

agoda.com
Booking.com
KAYAK
OpenTable
priceline.com
rentalcars.com

COMPETITORS

Airbnb	Facebook
Alibaba Group	Google
Amazon.com	Hotwire Inc.
American Express	Orbitz Worldwide
Apple Inc.	Travelocity
BCD Travel	TripAdvisor
Carlson Wagonlit	Yelp
Expedia	

HISTORICAL FINANCIALS

Company Type: Public

Income Statement				FYE: December 31
	REVENUE ($ mil.)	NET INCOME ($ mil.)	NET PROFIT MARGIN	EMPLOYEES
12/19	15,066	4,865	32.3%	26,400
12/18	14,527	3,998	27.5%	24,500
12/17	12,681	2,340	18.5%	22,900
12/16	10,743	2,134	19.9%	18,500
12/15	9,223	2,551	27.7%	15,500
Annual Growth	**13.0%**	**17.5%**	**—**	**14.2%**

2019 Year-End Financials

Debt ratio: 40.31%	No. of shares (mil.): 41
Return on equity: 66.11%	Dividends
Cash ($ mil.): 6,312	Yield: —
Current ratio: 1.83	Payout: —
Long-term debt ($ mil.): 7,640	Market value ($ mil.): 85,060

	STOCK PRICE ($) FY Close	P/E High/Low	PER SHARE ($) Earnings	Dividends	Book Value
12/19	2,053.73	18 15	111.82	0.00	143.25
12/18	1,722.42	26 19	83.26	0.00	192.52
12/17	1,737.74	43 31	46.86	0.00	232.31
12/16	1,466.06	37 23	42.65	0.00	199.64
12/15	1,274.95	29 20	49.45	0.00	177.29
Annual Growth	**12.7%**	**— —**	**22.6%**	**—**	**(5.2%)**

Booz Allen Hamilton Holding Corp.

Booz Allen Hamilton is a leading contractor for US Government defense and intelligence departments assisting in the fields of cyber security and intelligence operations. The firm which acts as prime contractor in nearly every instance generates billions in sales each year from the delivery of highly technical skills to the Department of Defense the National Security Agency the IRS and nearly every cabinet-level US Government department. It increasingly works with foreign governments and commercial clients as well. Investment firm The Carlyle Group owns a majority interest in the consulting firm which was founded in 1914.

Operations

Booz Allen Hamilton typically works under three contract types. Cost-Reimbursable Contracts which account for more than 55% of revenue provide for the payment of costs racked up during the completion of a contract (up to a pre-determined ceiling) plus a fee. Under Time-and-Materials Contracts which account for around 25% of Booz Allen's sales the company bills its clients for each labor hour and material costs and out-of-pocket expenses. Under Fixed-Price Contacts which also account for 20% of sales the company works to a pre-determined price.

More than 90% of the company's total sales were coming from prime contractors while subcontractors account for the rest.

Geographic Reach

Booz Allen's headquarters are located in McLean Virginia. The firm also has offices in Annapolis Junction Bethesda Maryland; Laurel Maryland; San Diego California; Herndon Virginia; Charleston South Carolina; Arlington Virginia; Alexandria Virginia; and Washington D.C.

Sales and Marketing

The majority (over 95%) of Booz Allen Hamilton's revenue comes from the US government. Defense clients including the US Army Navy/Marine Corps Air Force and Joint Combatant Commands account for nearly 50% of Booz Allen's revenue. Civil Clients including the Departments of Homeland Security Health and Human Services Veterans Affairs Treasury and Justice account for more than 25% of sales. Intelligence clients (more than 20% of sales) include the National Security Agency National Geospatial-Intelligence Agency and National Reconnaissance Office and military intelligence agencies such as the Defense Intelligence Agency Service Intelligence Centers and Intelligence Surveillance Reconnaissance units. Global commercial clients are comprised of US commercial and international clients which accounts for less than 5% of sales.

Financial Performance

For a five-year period starting in 2016 revenue registered steady growth and posted a 38% increase in that span.

Revenue for fiscal 2020 was $6.7 billion a 9% increase from prior year primarily driven by sustained client demand and increased client staff headcount to meet that demand. Revenue also benefited from higher billable expenses as compared to the prior year.

Net income rose 15% to $482.6 million in fiscal 2020 thanks to higher revenue and gains from Other income.

Booz Allen's cash on hand rose to $741.9 million during fiscal 2020. The company's operations generated $551.4 million while its investing activities used $128.1 million for purchases of property and equipment. Financing activities also generated $34.6 million.

Strategy

Vision 2020 is a comprehensive strategy to transform Booz Allen and create sustainable quality growth for the company. Fiscal 2020 was the seventh year of implementing the strategy but its design reaches back to before the government market began to contract in 2011 and 2012. The company anticipated the market downturn and set in place a strategy that would allow Booz Allen to emerge in a strong position vis- -vis its competitors. Under Vision 2020 the company is: Moving closer to the center of its clients' core missions; Increasing the technical content of its work; Attracting and retaining superior talent in diverse areas of expertise; Leveraging innovation to deliver complex differentiated end-to-end solutions; Creating a broad network of external partners and alliances;

and Expanding into the commercial and international markets.

The success of its strategy can be seen in: Backlog growth which achieved record levels during fiscal 2020 for the second consecutive year; Headcount growth and a corresponding shift in its talent portfolio to more technical expertise in disciplines such as systems development cyber and analytics; Accelerating industry-leading organic revenue growth; Enhanced profitability and margin expansion. To support its success against Vision 2020 long-term strategy the company is considering and have taken steps in preparation for the implementation of new financial management systems to among other things support business growth and facilitate the exploration of new lines of business in the future.

HISTORY

Edwin Booz graduated from Northwestern University in 1914 with degrees in economics and psychology and started a statistical analysis firm in Chicago. After serving in the army during WWI he returned to his firm renamed Edwin Booz Surveys. In 1925 Booz hired his first full-time assistant George Fry and in 1929 he hired a second James Allen. By then the company had a long list of clients including U.S. Gypsum the Chicago Tribune and Montgomery Ward which was losing a retail battle with Sears Roebuck and Co.

In 1935 Carl Hamilton joined the partnership and a year later it was renamed Booz Fry Allen & Hamilton. The firm prospered well into the next decade by providing advice based on "independence that enables us to say plainly from the outside what cannot always be said safely from within" according to a company brochure.

During WWII the firm worked increasingly on government and military contracts. Fry opposed the pursuit of such work for consultants and left in 1942. The firm was renamed Booz Allen & Hamilton. Hamilton died in 1946 and the following year Booz retired (he died in 1951) leaving Allen as chairman. He successfully steered the firm into lucrative postwar work for clients such as Johnson Wax RCA and the US Air Force.

A separate company Booz Allen Applied Research Inc. (BAARINC) was formed in 1955 for technical and government consulting including missile and weaponry work as well as consulting with NASA. By the end of the decade Time had dubbed Booz Allen "the world's largest most prestigious management consultant firm." The partnership was incorporated as a private company in 1962 and in 1967 commissioner Pete Rozelle requested its services for the merger of the National Football League and American Football League.

When Allen retired in 1970 Charlie Bowen became the new chairman and the company went public. However as the economy stalled during the energy crisis spending for consultants plunged. Jim Farley replaced Bowen in 1975 and the company was taken private again in 1976. A turnaround was engineered and the firm was soon helping Chrysler through its 1979 bailout and developing strategies for the breakup of AT&T in 1984.

Booz Allen again experienced trouble in the 1980s after Farley instituted a competition to select his successor. Michael McCullough was eventually chosen in 1984 but the 10-month election process turned into a dogfight that pitted partner against partner taking an enormous toll on morale. McCullough began restructuring the firm along industry lines creating a department store of services in an industry characterized by boutique houses. The turmoil was too much and by 1988 nearly a third of the partners had quit.

William Stasior became chairman in 1991 and reorganized Booz Allen yet again splitting it down public and private sector lines. Allen died in 1992 the same year the firm moved to McLean Virginia. The company began privatization work in the former Soviet Union and in Eastern Europe in 1992 and continued to emphasize government business including contracts with the IRS (1995) for technology modernization and with the General Services Administration (1996) to provide technical and management support for all federal telecommunications users.

In 1998 the company won a 10-year $200 million contract with the US Defense Department to establish a scientific and technical data warehouse. Ralph Shrader was appointed CEO in early 1999; Stasior retired as chairman later that year. Booz Allen acquired Scandinavian consulting firm Carta in 1999 and formed a venture capital firm for start-ups with Lehman Brothers in 2000. The company announced in late 2000 that it would spin off Aestix its e-commerce business but reconsidered amid a general economic slowdown and hostile IPO market. (The unit was integrated back into Booz Allen in 2002.)

Booz Allen saw an increase in work related to defense and national security after the terrorist attacks of September 11 2001. Engagements included work related to the reconstruction of Iraq (as a subcontractor on telecommunications projects managed by Lucent) and in 2003 Booz Allen was awarded a contract from the US Health Resources and Services Administration to help establish and operate a bioterrorism technical support center.

In 2008 Booz Allen spun off its commercial consulting business as an independent firm Booz & Company. The spinoff was part of a transaction in which investment firm The Carlyle Group acquired a controlling interest in the Booz Allen's government-related consulting business which retained the Booz Allen name.

Striving to alleviate debt Booz Allen launched an initial public offering on the New York Stock Exchange in November 2010.

EXECUTIVES

Executive Vice President And Chief People Officer, Betty Thompson
Evp Middle East And North Africa (mena), Nabih Maroun
Vp, Gary D. Labovich
President And Ceo, Horacio D. Rozanski, age 52, $1,437,500 total compensation
Evp Justice And Homeland Security Business, Thad W. Allen
Evp Directed Energy Innovation, Henry A. (Trey) Obering
Evp Cfo And Treasurer, Lloyd W. Howell, age 58, $1,000,000 total compensation
Evp Chief Administrative Officer (cao) And Chief Information Security Officer (ciso), Joseph W. (Joe) Mahaffee, age 62, $765,000 total compensation
Evp Strategic Transformation, Michael M. (Mike) Thomas
Evp Homeland Security And Transportation, Patrick F. Peck, age 62
Evp Client Service Officer (cso) Justice Homeland Security And Transportation (jht), Fred K. Blackburn
Vp, Gary C. Cubbage
Evp Civil Commercial Group (ccg), Karen M. Dahut, age 56, $1,000,000 total compensation
Evp, Maria Darby
Evp Joint Combatant Command, Judith H. (Judi) Dotson
Evp Infrastructure And Military Health, Laurene (Laurie) Gallo

Evp Engineering And Science And C4isr Crosscut, Patricia Goforth
Vp, Tom Greenspon
Evp Air Force Lead, Gregory Harrison
Evp Financial Services Group, David Kletter
Evp International Business, Christopher Ling
Vp, Joseph (Joe) Logue, age 55, $1,250,000 total compensation
Evp Innovation Service Officer (iso) And Cyber Functional Service Officer (fso), Angela M. (Angie) Messer
Evp And Deputy Lead Defense And Intelligence, Anthony (Tony) Mitchell
Vp, Susan L. Penfield
Evp Energy Business, Gary Rahl
Evp And Lead U.s. Defense And Military Intelligence And Operations, Joseph F. (Joe) Sifer
Evp Defense And Intelligence, Ted Sniffin
Evp Commercial Cyber Business, William (Bill) Stewart
Vp, Elizabeth M. (Betty) Thompson, age 65
Evp Strategic Innovation Group (sig), Gregory G. (Greg) Wenzel
Evp Cyber Business, Christopher Pierce
Vp, Joan A. Dempsey
Evp Civil Health Business, Kristine Martin Anderson
Evp Chief Legal Officer And Secretary, Nancy J. Laben, age 58
Vp And Cio, Kevin Winter
Evp Energy Chemicals And Utilities, Walid Fayad
Evp Middle East And North Africa, Ramez Shehadi
Evp Command Control Communications Computers Intelligence Surveillance And Reconnaissance (c4isr), Steve Soules
Evp Army Market, Brian M. McKeon
Evp Digital Practice Middle East And North Africa (mena), Raymond Khoury
Vice President And Group Administrative Officer Defense And Intelligence Market, Joan Wolfle
Vice President, Kevin Vigilante
Senior Vice President, Charles S Hamilton
Senior Vice President Citizen Services, Shannon Fitzgerald
Vice President Engineering And Science Business, Steve Harrell
Vice President, Theodore Kraemer
Senior Vice President And Digital Analytics And Strategy Lead, Julie Mcpherson
Vice President Security Sector, Patricia Hanback
Vice President Army Business, Jay Dodd
Vice President, Ralph Lawrence
Senior Vice President Commercial Health, Lucy Stribley
Senior Vice President Mena, Fady Kassatly
Svp Analytics, Josh Sullivan
Senior Vice President And Executive, Booz A Hamilton
Vice President Data Solutions And Machine Intelligence, Bryce Pippert
Vice President, Chris Pierce
Vice President Sales And Marketing, Scott Barr
Vice President Facility Infrastructure And Environment, Bob Miller
Vice President Technical Services, Felix Yao
Vice President Civil And Commercial Market, Marlene Aquino
Vice President Defense Market, Brian Pickerall
Vice President Of Information Technology, Joe Sifer
Vice President, John Druitt
Vice President, Scott Welles
Vice President, Rob Silverman
Vice President Defense Market, James Gibbons
Senior Vice President, Ken Mills
Executive Vice President Portfolio Strategic Projects, Matthew Calderone
Vice President And Lead Contracting Officer, Linda Asher
Senior Vice President Global Defense Group And Crosscut Market Strategy, Andrea Inserra

Vice President Enterprise Cloud Computing Business, Munjeet Singh

Vice President Consulting Services, Craig Todd

Senior Vice President U.s. Government Classified And National Geospatial Intelligence Agency, Kim Lynch

Vice President Digital Transformation Programs And Opportunities, Ralph Wade

Vice President Civil Health Business, John Peterson

Senior Vice President, Robert Smith

Vice President, Mark Hoffman

Senior Vice President And Cyber And Engineering Lead, Brad Medairy

Senior Vice President Nextgen Finance Modernization (ngfm) Program, Tim Lawrence

Vice President Civil Health Business, Travis Burd

Vice President Energy Environment And Infrastructure, Johnny Ayoub

Executive Vice President U.s. Commercial, Bill Phelps

Vice President Real Estate And Facilities Operations, Deane Edelman

Senior Vice President Technology Solutions, Natalie Givans

Vice President, Vincent Simpson

Vice President Law Enforcement, Bob Sogegian

Vice President Banking And Fintech Business Mena, Charles Habak

Senior Vice President Acquisition And Sustainment Efforts, Dick Johnson

Vice President Data Science And Advanced Analytics, Ezmeralda Khalil Sager

Vice President Air Force Military Intelligence And Cyber Business, Kim Bird

Senior Vice President Finance Energy And Economic Development, Mark Gamis

Senior Vice President Operations Practice Mena, Nadim Batri

Vice President Finance Energy And Economic Development, Paul Tartaglione

Senior Vice President Health Business, Richard Crowe

Senior Vice President U.s. Air Force Clients, Rick Holley

Vice President Navy And Marine Corps Headquarters And Operations, Steve Moore

Vice President Finance Energy And Economic Development, Terence Mandable

Executive Vice President U.s. Navy And Marine Corps, Thomas Crabtree

Senior Vice President Army Market, Bill Schuler

Senior Vice President Cf And Ao, Sam Strickland

Vice President, Chris Ellis

Senior Vice President And Director Of Center Cer, Wallave Angela

Chairman, Ralph W. Shrader, age 76

Secretary, Linda Ryan

Secretary, Jennifer Stingl

Treasurer, Phil Maes

Auditors: Ernst & Young LLP

LOCATIONS

HQ: Booz Allen Hamilton Holding Corp.
8283 Greensboro Drive, McLean, VA 22102
Phone: 703 902-5000
Web: www.boozallen.com

PRODUCTS/OPERATIONS

2018 sales

	$ mil.	% of total
US Government		
Defense Clients	3,114	47
Intelligence Clients	1,566	23
Civil Clients	1,761	26
Global Commercial Clients	261	4
Total	**6,704**	**100**

2018 sales

	$ mil.	% of total
Prime contractor		92
Sub-contractor		8
Total		**100**

Selected Markets Served

Civil government
  Benefits and entitlements
  Federal finance
  International development and diplomacy
Defense
  Air Force
  Army
  Joint staff and combatant commands
  Navy and Marine Corps
  Office of the Secretary of Defense and defense agencies
  Space
Energy
Environment
Health
  Health informatics
  Health not-for-profit/nongovernmental organizations
  International public health
  US public health
Homeland security
Intelligence
Law enforcement
Not-for-profit/nongovernmental organizations
Transportation
  Aviation infrastructure
  Highways and automotive technology
  Passenger rail and mass transit

Selected Practice Areas

Assurance and resilience
Economic and business analysis
Information technology
Modeling and simulation
Organization and strategy
Supply chain and logistics
Systems engineering and integration

COMPETITORS

A.T. Kearney	IBM
Accenture	L3 Technologies
BAE SYSTEMS	Leidos
Bain & Company	Lockheed Martin
Boeing	MAXIMUS
Boston Consulting	ManTech
CACI International	McKinsey & Company
CSRA	Northrop Grumman
Capgemini	PA Consulting
Computer Sciences Corp.	PRTM Management
Deloitte Consulting	Raytheon
General Dynamics	SAIC
HP Enterprise Services	Unisys

HISTORICAL FINANCIALS

Company Type: Public

Income Statement

FYE: March 31

	REVENUE ($ mil.)	NET INCOME ($ mil.)	NET PROFIT MARGIN	EMPLOYEES
03/20	7,463	482	6.5%	27,200
03/19	6,704	418	6.2%	26,100
03/18	6,171	305	4.9%	24,600
03/17	5,804	252	4.4%	23,300
03/16	5,405	294	5.4%	22,600
Annual Growth	**8.4%**	**13.2%**	—	**4.7%**

2020 Year-End Financials

Debt ratio: 45.60%
Return on equity: 62.84%
Cash ($ mil.): 741
Current ratio: 1.75
Long-term debt ($ mil.): 2,007
No. of shares (mil.): 138
Dividends
  Yield: 1.5%
  Payout: 30.5%
Market value ($ mil.): 9,522

	STOCK PRICE ($) FY Close	P/E High/Low	PER SHARE ($) Earnings	Dividends	Book Value
03/20	68.64	23 17	3.41	1.04	6.17
03/19	58.14	20 13	2.91	0.80	4.82
03/18	38.72	19 15	2.05	0.70	3.87
03/17	35.39	23 16	1.67	0.62	3.85
03/16	30.28	16 12	1.94	0.54	2.76
Annual Growth	**22.7%**	— —	**15.1%**	**17.8%**	**22.3%**

BorgWarner Inc

BorgWarner is a leading maker of engine and drivetrain products for the world's major automotive manufacturers. Products include turbochargers timing chain systems emissions and thermal systems four-wheel-drive and all-wheel-drive transfer cases (primarily for light trucks and SUVs) starters alternators hybrid electric motors and transmission components. Together automakers Ford and Volkswagen account for about 25% of sales. Other customers include BMW Daimler and General Motors. In addition to automotive customers BorgWarner also serves OEMs of commercial and off-highway vehicles. The company nets nearly 75% of its sales from outside the US.

Operations

BorgWarner's two operating segments are Engine Products (more than 60% of total sales) and drivetrain products (nearly 40% of sales). The Engine division manufactures products to optimize engines for fuel efficiency reduce emissions and enhance performance and includes turbochargers engine timing systems ignition systems air management and cooling and controls. The Drivetrain unit provides automotive transmission components all-wheel drive torque transfer systems and rotating electrical devices. Turbochargers for light vehicles is the company's largest product line representing around 30% of sales.

BorgWarner also operates seven joint ventures located in Japan China India and South Korea including NSK-Warner KK a leading producer of friction plates and one-way clutches in Japan and China.

Geographic Reach

BorgWarner operates nearly 70 manufacturing and technical facilities in some 20 countries (including nearly 20 in the US and about half a dozen each in Germany China and South Korea).

Europe is by far BorgWarner's largest market: Germany accounts for roughly 15% of total sales; Hungary and Poland account for around 10% and other Europe 10%. The US generates around 25% of its sales and South Korea and China together represent some 25%. Others generate the remaining total sales.

Sales and Marketing

BorgWarner markets its products to OEMs of light vehicles (passenger cars sport-utility vehicles vans and light trucks) and commercial and off-highway vehicles through separate sales teams for its Engine and Drivetrain business segments. Ford generates nearly 15% of the company's overall sales; Volkswagen accounts for more than 10%. Other key customers include Fiat Chrysler Automobiles and General Motors.

Financial Performance

Aside from a misfire in 2015 BorgWarner's Engine and Drivetrain revenue has been turbocharged in recent years with total sales rising about 27% between 2015 and 2019.

Sales in 2019 decreased 3% to $10.2 billion compared to $10.5 billion in 2018. The decrease was primarily driven by lower sales in Europe.

Net income decreased $185 million to $746 million in 2019 compared to $931 million in 2018 primarily driven by lower sales.

Cash at the end of 2019 was $832 million an increase of $93 million from the prior year. Cash from operations contributed $1.0 billion to the coffers while investing activities used $489 million mainly for capital expenditures. Financing activities used $420 million primarily used in repayment of long-term debt and dividend payments.

Strategy

BorgWarner is positioning itself to capitalize on growth in hybrid and electric vehicles while continuing to prosper in the gradually shrinking combustion market. To drive continued innovation in its Engine and Driveline products BorgWarner spends about 4% of annual revenue on R&D.

While global automotive demand has moderated especially in China the acquisitions of Sevcon (power electronics) and Remy (electric drive motor products) have given the company the capability to provide complete electric vehicle propulsion systems which should pay dividends down the road as more OEMs offer full-electric models.

To further enhance its hybrid and electric vehicle operations in early 2019 BorgWarner made two acquisitions Reinhart Motion Systems and AM Racing and combined them into a new subsidiary named Cascadia Motion. BorgWarner aims for Cascadia Motion to serve as an incubator for niche and emerging hybrid and electric propulsion applications including professional motorsports heavy duty vehicles buses and motorcycles.

Later in 2019 BorgWarner formed a joint venture with battery module and pack supplier Romeo Power Technology. The venture which is 60% owned by BorgWarner will extend the company's electric propulsion offerings to include battery modules and packs as well as intelligent battery management systems and proprietary thermal engineering for passive and active battery cooling.

To focus on propulsion-related products BorgWarner has shed some non-core operations. In 2019 the company sold its thermostat business to Arlington Industries Group. Later that year the company sold its BorgWarner Morse TEC division to Enstar Holdings (US) LLC a subsidiary of Enstar Group. BorgWarner Morse TEC has asbestos and other liabilities that BorgWarner wanted to eliminate.

Mergers and Acquisitions

In early 2020 the company entered into a definitive agreement to acquire Delphi Technologies PLC (Delphi Technologies) in an all-stock transaction valued at approximately $3.3 billion based on the closing price of BorgWarner stock in 2020.

Company Background

BorgWarner traces its roots to the 1928 merger of major Chicago auto parts companies Borg & Beck (clutches) Warner Gear (transmissions) Mechanics Universal Joint and Marvel Carburetor. The newly named Borg-Warner Corporation quickly began buying other companies including Ingersoll Steel & Disc (agricultural blades and discs) and Norge (refrigerators).

HISTORY

BorgWarner traces its roots to the 1928 merger of major Chicago auto parts companies Borg & Beck (clutches) Warner Gear (transmissions) Mechanics Universal Joint and Marvel Carburetor. The newly named Borg-Warner Corporation quickly began buying other companies including Ingersoll Steel & Disc (agricultural blades and discs) and Norge (refrigerators).

EXECUTIVES

Vp General Counsel And Secretary, John J. Gasparovic, age 62, $477,250 total compensation

Vp; President And General Manager Borgwarner Transmissions Systems, Robin Kendrick, age 55, $406,250 total compensation

Vp Marketing Public Relations Communications And Government Affairs, Scott D. Gallett, age 54

Evp And Cfo, Ronald T. (Ron) Hundzinski, age 61, $665,750 total compensation

Vp; President And General Manager Of Borgwarner Morse Tec, James R. Verrier, age 57, $1,245,000 total compensation

Vp And President And General Manager Borgwarner Emissions Systems, Brady D. Ericson, age 48, $415,000 total compensation

Vp And President And General Manager Borgwarner Morse Systems, Joseph F. Fadool, age 53, $416,250 total compensation

Vp; President And General Manager Borgwarner Turbo Systems, Frédéric B. Lissalde, age 52, $606,630 total compensation

Vp And President And General Manager Borgwarner Powerdrive Systems, Stefan Demmerle, age 55, $442,750 total compensation

Vice President And Treasurer, Jan Bertsch

Vice President Of Operations, Todd Bennington

Vp And Chief Compliance Officer, Laurene Horiszny

Vp Drivetrain It, Sandra Short

Vice President Global Supply Chain Management, Thomas Babineau

Vice President Global Supply Chain Management, Marco Caputo

Vice President Information Technology, Bernd Ruff

Vice President Human Resources, Shelley Bridarolli

Vice President And Treasurer, Tom Mcgill

Executive Vice President, Felecia Pryor

Director, Alexis P. Michas, age 62

Board Member, John McKernan

Secretary, Greg Dziegielewski

Board Member, Vicki Sato

Auditors: PricewaterhouseCoopers LLP

LOCATIONS

HQ: BorgWarner Inc
3850 Hamlin Road, Auburn Hills, MI 48326
Phone: 248 754-9200
Web: www.borgwarner.com

2017 Sales

	$ mil.	% of total
United States	2,280	23
Europe		
Germany	1,652	17
Hungary	655	7
Other Europe	1,427	15
China	1,560	16
South Korea	877	9
Mexico	920	9
Other regions	425	4
Total	**9,799**	**100**

PRODUCTS/OPERATIONS

2017 Sales

	$ mil.	% of total
Engine	6,061	62
Drivetrain	3,790	38
Elimination	(52.4)	-
Total	**9,799**	**100**

Selected Products

Engine Group
  Air-control valves
  Chain tensioners and snubbers
  Complete engine induction systems
  Complex solenoids and multi-function modules
  Crankshaft and camshaft sprockets
  Diesel cabin heaters
  Diesel cold starting systems (glow plugs and instant starting systems)

Electric air pumps
Engine hydraulic pumps
Exhaust gas-recirculation (EGR) coolers modules tubes and valves
Fan clutches
Fans and fan drives
Front-wheel and four-wheel-drive chain and timing-chain systems
High-temperature sensors (for exhaust gas aftertreatment systems)
Ignition coils
Intake manifolds
On-off fan drives
Single-function solenoids
Throttle bodies
Throttle position sensors
Tire pressure sensors
Transfer cases
Turbochargers
Drivetrain Group
  Four-wheel-drive and all-wheel-drive transfer cases
  Friction plates
  One-way clutches
  Torque converter lock-up clutches
  Transmission bands

Selected Joint Ventures

BERU Korea Co. Ltd. (51% South Korea ignition coils and pumps)
Borg-Warner Shenglong (Ningbo) Co. Ltd. (70% China fans and fan drives)
BorgWarner TorqTransfer Systems Beijing Co. Ltd. (80% China transfer cases)
BorgWarner Transmission Systems Korea Inc. (60% South Korea transmission components)
BorgWarner United Transmission Systems Co. Ltd. (66% China transmission components)
BorgWarner-Vikas Emissions Systems India Private Limited (60% India EGR coolers)
Divgi-Warner Limited (60% India transfer cases and automatic locking hubs)
SeohanWarner Turbo Systems Ltd. (71% South Korea turbochargers)

COMPETITORS

American Axle & Manufacturing	Magna Powertrain
DENSO	Meritor
Dana	Mitsubishi Heavy Industries
Delphi Automotive Systems	Modine Manufacturing
GKN	NGK SPARK PLUG
Honeywell International	Renold
IHI Corp.	Robert Bosch
JTEKT	Schaeffler
Kolbenschmidt Pierburg	Tsubaki Nakashima
	Valeo
	Visteon

HISTORICAL FINANCIALS

Company Type: Public

Income Statement

FYE: December 31

	REVENUE ($ mil.)	NET INCOME ($ mil.)	NET PROFIT MARGIN	EMPLOYEES
12/19	10,168	746	7.3%	29,000
12/18	10,529	930	8.8%	30,000
12/17	9,799	439	4.5%	29,000
12/16	9,071	118	1.3%	27,000
12/15	8,023	609	7.6%	30,000
Annual Growth	**6.1%**	**5.2%**	**—**	**(0.8%)**

2019 Year-End Financials

Debt ratio: 21.08%	No. of shares (mil.): 206
Return on equity: 16.70%	Dividends
Cash ($ mil.): 832	Yield: 1.5%
Current ratio: 1.65	Payout: 18.6%
Long-term debt ($ mil.): 1,741	Market value ($ mil.): 8,954

STOCK PRICE ($) FY Close	P/E High/Low	PER SHARE ($) Earnings	Dividends	Book Value
12/19	43.38	13 9	3.61	0.68	22.80
12/18	34.74	13 7	4.44	0.68	20.29
12/17	51.09	27 18	2.08	0.59	17.63
12/16	39.44	79 50	0.55	0.53	15.16
12/15	43.23	23 14	2.70	0.52	16.20
Annual Growth	0.1%	— —	7.5%	6.9%	8.9%

Boston Private Financial Holdings, Inc.

Boston Private Financial Holdings (BPFH) is a holding company for firms engaged in wealth management and private banking including Boston Private Bank & Trust which operates branches in New England New York Los Angeles and the San Francisco Bay Area. (The bank sold its branches in the Pacific Northwest in 2013.) BPFH also owns four other wealth advisory and investment management firms. The company offers private banking wealth advisory investment management deposits and lending and trust services to wealthy individuals corporations and institutional clients. All told BPFH and its affiliates have more than $30 billion in managed or advised assets.

Operations

In addition to Boston Private Bank & Trust Co. BPFH's other affiliates include: investment advisory firms Anchor Capital Advisors and Dalton Greiner Hartman Maher & Co.; wealth managers Bingham Osborn & Scarborough and KLS Professional Advisors Group; as well as newly-acquired Banyan Partners a registered investment advisor. BPFH sold its majority-owned affiliate Davidson Trust Co. (DTC) in 2012. DTC was part of the holding company's wealth advisory business.

Financial Performance

Boston Private Financial Holdings (BPFH) reported revenue of $339.5 million in 2013 an increase of less than 1% versus 2012. The modest uptick was due to increased recurring fees from its investment management wealth advisory and private banking wealth management and trust businesses as well as other income and a gain on the sale of loans. Assets under management and advisory (AUM) increased 19% during 2013 due to $3.7 billion of market appreciation and $0.2 billion of net flows. All three of the BPFH's segments experienced gains in AUM.

Net income grew 32% in 2013 compared with 2012 to $70.5 million on a decline in interest expense on deposits partially offset by a 2% increase in average balance. The lower interest rate environment in the US has allowed the company's banking arm to lower interest rates on money markets accounts and certificates of deposit.

Strategy

Since its founding in 1987 Boston Private has had a voracious appetite for acquiring smaller trust companies private banks and wealth managers. While the firm put the brakes on its expansion and shifted strategies amid the economic recession. Indeed it divested about a half-dozen money management subsidiaries as way to raise capital and reduce risk. Also in 2011 the company consolidated its four banking charters into Boston Private Bank & Trust to simplify its structure and cut costs.

However with the economy and financial markets on the mend the company has resumed making acquisitions most recently to build its wealth management business.

Mergers and Acquisitions

In October 2014 Boston Private Bank & Trust Co. acquired Banyan Partners LLC an independent registered investment advisory firm based in Palm Beach Florida. With more than $4.5 billion in client assets Banyan has offices in Boston Miami Naples Atlanta Wisconsin Texas and California. The purchase furthered the bank's aim of expanding the reach and accelerating the development of its wealth management business.

In May 2013 Boston Private Bank & Trust sold three offices in the Pacific Northwest to focus on its banking business in California and New England. The bank recorded a $10.6 million pretax gain on the sale.

EXECUTIVES

Evp General Counsel Secretary And Chief Legal Officer, Margaret W. (Megan) Chambers, age 61, $360,000 total compensation
Evp And Coo, Anne L. Randall
Ceo Private Banking Group; President Boston Private Bank & Trust Company, George G. Schwartz
Co-president Private Banking Group, James C. Brown
Evp Cfo And Chief Administrative Officer, David J. Kaye, age 56, $425,000 total compensation
Ceo; Ceo Boston Private Bank And Trust, Clayton G. (Clay) Deutsch, $675,000 total compensation
Evp And Chief Risk Officer, W. Timothy MacDonald, $350,000 total compensation
Ceo Boston Private Wealth Llc, Corey A. Griffin, $400,000 total compensation
Evp And Chief Human Resource Officer, Martha T. Higgins
President Boston Private Wealth Llc, Peter J. Raimondi
Co-president Private Banking Group, Torrance Childs
Evp Private Clients Group, Nicholas A.R. Hofer
Evp Commercial Banking Group, Robert J. Nentwig
Evp And Client Development Officer, Jacqueline S. Shoback
Svp And Chief Fiduciary Officer, Lynn Swenson
Assistant Vice President, Joe Lavigne
Senior Vice President Marketing, Allison Baird
Vice President Manager Of Cred, Susan Tackitt
Senior Vice President, Mary Rohan
Vice President Residential Lending, Richard Little
Vice President Office Manager, Mark Connor
Senior Vice President Residential Lending, Rob Kinasewich
Vice President Commercial Real Estate, Andrew Garfinkle
Assistant Vice President Back Bay Assistant Office Manager, Rudy Canelas
Senior Vice President Northern California Deposit Sales Manager, John Delaney
Vice President, William Massos
Vice President Certified Appraiser Residential Loan Officer, Rosa Amaya
Assistant Vice President Private Banking Relationship Officer, Ida Solari
Vice President Commercial Banking, Sean Burke
Senior Vice President And Trust Officer, Jeanne Barrett
Senior Vice President Commercial Loan Officer Commercial Lending New England, George Carroll
Executive Vice President General Counsel, Colleen Graham
Vice President Chicago Territory, Scott Mortensen
Vice President, Peter Karp
Executive Vice President Human Resources, Pat Butler

Vice President Sales, Jeffrey Forbes
Vice President Healthcare Life Sciences Solutions Sales, Jeff Forbes
Vice President Global Marketing, Lucian Lui
Vice President Government Affairs, Theresa Pattara
Vice President Senior Project Manager, Ted Finnerty
Director Of Loan And Mortgage Operations Senior Vice President, Elaine Fitzpatrick
Vice President Commercial Real Estate Lender, Melanie Prole
Vice President Office Manager, Kim Arcari
Enterprise Architect Vice President, Christopher Green
Chairman, Stephen M. Waters, age 73
Board Member, Gloria Larson
Board Member, Mark Furlong
Board Member, Joseph Guyaux
Board Member, Kimberly Stevenson
Auditors: KPMG LLP

LOCATIONS

HQ: Boston Private Financial Holdings, Inc.
Ten Post Office Square, Boston, MA 02109
Phone: 617 912-1900
Web: www.bostonprivate.com

PRODUCTS/OPERATIONS

2015 Sales

	$ mil.	% of total
Interest and dividend income		
Loans	192	51
Mortgage-backed securities	10	3
Investment securities	9	2
Federal funds sold and other	1	1
Fees and other income		
Investment management & trust fees	45	12
Wealth advisory fees	50	14
Wealth management and trust fees	51	14
Other	13	3
Total	374	100

Selected Subsidiaries & Affiliates

Anchor Capital Advisors LLC
Bingham Osborn & Scarborough LLC
Boston Private Bank & Trust Company
Dalton Greiner Hartman Maher & Co. LLC
KLS Professional Advisors Group LLC

COMPETITORS

Bank of America	FMR
Brown Brothers Harriman	JPMorgan Chase
Central Bancorp	Morgan Stanley
Century Bancorp (MA)	Sovereign Bank
Citigroup	TD Bank USA
Citizens Financial Group	TriState Capital
	Wells Fargo

HISTORICAL FINANCIALS

Company Type: Public

Income Statement

FYE: December 31

	ASSETS ($ mil.)	NET INCOME ($ mil.)	INCOME AS % OF ASSETS	EMPLOYEES
12/19	8,830	80	0.9%	779
12/18	8,494	80	0.9%	774
12/17	8,311	40	0.5%	925
12/16	7,970	71	0.9%	888
12/15	7,542	64	0.9%	890
Annual Growth	4.0%	5.4%		(3.3%)

2019 Year-End Financials

Debt ratio: 1.20%
Return on equity: 10.18%
Cash ($ mil.): 292
Current ratio: —
Long-term debt ($ mil.): —
No. of shares (mil.): 83
Dividends
  Yield: 3.9%
  Payout: 42.4%
Market value ($ mil.): 1,002

	STOCK PRICE ($)	P/E	PER SHARE ($)		
	FY Close	High/Low	Earnings	Dividends	Book Value
12/19	12.03	13 10	0.97	0.48	9.84
12/18	10.57	19 11	0.92	0.48	9.01
12/17	15.45	42 33	0.42	0.44	9.27
12/16	16.55	20 11	0.81	0.40	9.13
12/15	11.34	18 14	0.74	0.36	8.91
Annual Growth	1.5%	— —	7.0%	7.5%	2.5%

Boston Scientific Corp.

Boston Scientific makes medical supplies and devices used in interventional medical procedures. A leader in devices addressing heart conditions the firm focuses on manufacturing cardiovascular and cardiac rhythm management (CRM) products. It also makes devices used for electrophysiology endoscopy pain management (neuromodulation) urology and women's health. Its roughly 13000 diagnostic and treatment products – made in more than a dozen factories worldwide – include biopsy forceps catheters coronary and urethral stents defibrillators needles and pacemakers. Boston Scientific markets its products in about 120 countries but the US generates more than half of sales.

Operations

Boston Scientific operates in three primary segments: Cardiovascular MedSurg and Rhythm and Neuro.

Its largest segment Cardiovascular accounts for nearly 40% of annual revenues. That segment makes interventional cardiology products (coronary stents catheters guidewires) which account for more than 25% of the company's sales and peripheral intervention products (non-coronary vascular stents) which account for about 15%.

The MedSurg segment (30% of revenue) makes devices for endoscopy (nearly 20% of sales) and urology and pelvic health (about 15%). Endoscopy devices diagnose and treat pulmonary and gastrointestinal conditions through minimally invasive scopes and stent and needle systems.

The Rhythm and Neuro segment (some 30% of revenue) makes implantable devices (pacemakers and implanted coronary defibrillators or ICDs) for cardiac rhythm management (almost 20% of sales) as well as neuromodulation devices and electrophysiology devices (both account for about 10%).

Geographic Reach

Boston Scientific operates in around 40 countries and markets its products in some 120 nations around the world. Based in Marlborough Massachusetts it has seven manufacturing facilities in the US and nine manufacturing facilities abroad (in Ireland Costa Rica Malaysia Brazil Switzerland and Puerto Rico). The company provide localized training programs at about 15 Institutes for Advancing Science in the Americas Africa Asia and Europe and it has research operations in China Costa Rica UK India Ireland and Puerto Rico. It also has regional headquarters located in Singapore and France.

While the US is still Boston Scientific's largest single market international sales have grown to make up about 45% of total sales.

Sales and Marketing

Boston Scientific markets its products to some 37000 hospitals clinics outpatient facilities and medical offices around the world. In the US large group purchasing organizations (GPOs) hospital networks and other buying groups make up a significant portion of sales.

Boston Scientific markets products through direct forces in the US and European markets; it also uses dealers distributors and partners in certain countries.

Financial Performance

Boston Scientific's revenue has seen steady growth over the past five years increasing by 44% between 2015 and 2019. After a net income loss in 2015 it fought back to recover the last four years.

Revenue in 2019 climbed about 9% to some $10.7 billion due to strong growth in all its three operating segments.

Net income climbed to a massive $4.7 billion in 2019 an increase of $3 billion from 2018 due to higher revenue.

The company ended 2019 with $607 million in cash down by $222 million from 2018. Operating activities contributed $1.8 billion while investing activities used $5 billion (mostly on acquisition expenses) and financing activities contributed $3 billion via proceeds from long-term borrowings.

Strategy

Boston Scientific operates through five strategic imperatives: Strengthening category leadership: Expanding into high growth adjacencies; Drive global expansion; Fund the journey to fuel growth; and Develop key capabilities.

Execution of these strategic imperatives will drive innovation accelerate profitable revenue growth and increase stockholder value while strengthening its leadership position in the medical device industry.

The company will continue to invest on their core franchises and pursue opportunities to diversify and further expand their presence in strategic growth adjacencies and new global markets.

Mergers and Acquisitions

In 2019 Boston Scientific completed the purchase of UK-based BTG which makes minimally-invasive devices targeting cancer and vascular diseases and specialty pharmaceuticals for $4.2 billion.

In mid- 2019 the company acquired Veriflex a maker of a lumbar spinal stenosis device for $465 million. The deal expands Boston Scientific's pain management portfolio to include the only commercially-available minimally-invasive interspinous spacer.

Company Background

Boston Scientific traces its roots to the 1960s when co-founder John Abele bought a stake in surgical technology research firm Medi-tech. Abele teamed with Pete Nicholas in 1979 to form Boston Scientific for the purpose of acquiring Medi-tech.

The company expanded through product launches and acquisitions over the years. Purchases include Swiss company Symetis (transcatheter aortic valves 2017); Apama Medical (radiofrequency balloon catheter systems 2017); EndoChoice (infection control products 2016).

HISTORY

Many medical companies start near a hospital but Boston Scientific's roots sprouted at a children's soccer game where two dads found common ground. John Abele and Peter Nicholas had complementary interests: Wharton MBA Nichols wanted to run his own company; philosophy and physics graduate Abele wanted a job that would help people.

In 1979 the two men founded Boston Scientific to buy medical device maker Medi-Tech. (Abele had purchased a stake in Medi-tech in the 1960s.) Abele and Nicholas had to borrow half a million dollars from a bank and raise an additional $300000. Medi-Tech's primary product was a steerable catheter a soft-tipped device that could be maneuvered within the body. The catheter revolutionized gallstone operations in the early 1970s and Boston Scientific expanded on the success of the product. The company adapted it for a slew of new procedures for the heart lungs intestines and other organs.

Boston Scientific's sales were healthy in 1983 but the firm still lacked funds. It eagerly accepted $21 million from Abbott Laboratories in exchange for a 20% stake. New FDA regulations slowed product introduction and put a crimp in the company's growth.

Boston Scientific found a legal loophole in the late 1980s to avoid lengthy delays: The company described its products in the vaguest possible terms so upgraded devices were considered similar enough to predecessors to escape the in-depth scrutiny of the new approval process. Still Abele and Nicholas had to mortgage their personal properties to stay afloat before this linguistic legerdemain helped to clear government red tape.

Boston Scientific returned to profitability in 1991 and went public the next year buying back Abbott Laboratories' interest in the company as well.

Boston Scientific acquired a bevy of medical device companies throughout the late 1990s which expanded its range of cardiology products and doubled sales. Among them were SCIMED Life Systems Heart Technology Meadox Medicals EP Technologies and Symbiosis Target Therapeutics and Pfizer's catheter stent and angioplasty equipment business.

The company's Taxus drug-eluting stent was approved in the US in 2004 the second such device sold on the market. Major acquisitions in the 2000s included Guidant (with Abbott) and CryoCor.

EXECUTIVES

Chairman President And Ceo, Michael F. (Mike) Mahoney, age 55, $1,042,191 total compensation

President Electrophysiology, Joseph M. (Joe) Fitzgerald, age 56, $499,241 total compensation

Evp And Cfo, Daniel J. (Dan) Brennan, age 54, $544,421 total compensation

Svp And President Neuromodulation, Maulik Nanavaty, age 58

President Endoscopy, Michael P. (Mike) Phalen, age 61

Evp Chief Administrative Officer General Counseland Secretary, Timothy A. (Tim) Pratt, age 70, $640,017 total compensation

Evp And President Asia-pacific Middle East And Africa, Supratim Bose, age 67, $537,326 total compensation

Svp And President Endoscopy, David A. (Dave) Pierce, age 56

Svp And President Interventional Cardiology, Kevin J. Ballinger, age 47, $476,647 total compensation

Evp Operations, Edward F. Mackey, age 57, $410,548 total compensation

Svp Manufacturing And Supply Chain, John B. (Brad) Sorenson, age 52

Svp And President Europe, Eric Thépaut, age 58

Svp And President Endoscopy, Art Butcher

Evp And Global Chief Medical Officer, Ian Meredith

Svp And President Peripheral Interventions, Jeff Mirviss

Vice President Sales, Lee Sullivan

Vice President Government Affairs, Steve Lapierre

Vice President Marketing Science, Tom Robinson

Vice President Operations, Daniel Zaic

Vice President International Quality, Rosaleen Burke

Vice President Global Project Management, Eileen Rose

Vice President Of Operations, Matt Lavelle

Vice President Of Sales, Mike Jones
Area Vice President, Julie Reese
Vice President Corporate Tax, Douglas Cronin
Vice President Of Sales, Allen Meacham
Vice President Government Affairs, Paul Barry
Vice President Manager Director, Ru Zheng
Vice President Of Sales And Strategic Accounts,
  Samuel Conaway
Area Vice President Corporate Accounts, Ryan
  Farley
Vice President, Prabodh Mathur
Vice President Of Operations, Sean Aherne
Vice President Human Resources Business,
  Georgette Flowers
Vice President Global Marketing Endoscopy,
  Meghan Scanlon
Vp And Managing Director India, Prabal
  Chakraborty
Vice President Of Information Technology And
  General Superintendent, Neha Khera
National Sales Manager, Rahul Garg
Vice President Quality Neuromodulation, Patrick
  Crotteau
Vice President, Conor Dolan
Executive Vice President Operations, Edward
  Macky
Svp And President Emea, Eric Thepaut
Vice President Global Supply Chain, Tony Stallings
Svp And Cio, Jodi Eddy
Vice President Is Global Infrastructure Services,
  Tom Woehrle
Vice President Information Technology And Chief
  Digital Health Officer, David Feygin
Vice President Of Finance, David Inman
Vice President Business Development Venture
  Capi, Chris Kaster
Vice President Corporate Research, David Knapp
Vice President Firm Supervision, Sarah Simes
Global Vice President Medical Affairs, Sean
  Lilienfeld
Assistant Treasurer, Graeme Williamson
Auditors: Ernst & Young LLP

LOCATIONS

HQ: Boston Scientific Corp.
  300 Boston Scientific Way, Marlborough, MA 01752-
  1234
Phone: 508 683-4000
Web: www.bostonscientific.com

PRODUCTS/OPERATIONS

Selected Products

Cardiovascular
  Interventional Cardiology
  PolarCath peripheral dilation system
  PROMUS drug-eluting stents
  TAXUS drug-eluting stents
  VeriFLEX bare-metal stents
  WALLSTENT carotid artery stents
  Cardiac Rhythm Management (CRM)
  ACUITY steerable ventricular leads
  COGNIS cardiac resynchronization defibrillator
  LATITUDE remote patient monitoring system
  TELIGEN implantable cardiac defbrillator
  Other cardiovascular
  Cutting Balloon dilation device
  FilterWire EZ embolic protection system
  iLab ultrasound imaging catheter system
  Maverick balloon catheters
Endoscopy
  Radial Jaw 4 single-use biopsy forceps
  (gastrointestinal)
  RX Biliary System (bile duct surgeries)
  SpyGlass direct visualization system (pancreatic
  system)
Urology/Pelvic health
  Genesys Hydro ThermAblator (endometrial ablation
  system)
Neuromodulation
  Precision Spinal Cord Stimulation system (chronic
  pain)

Electrophysiology
  Blazer Prime temperature ablation catheters

Selected Acquisitions

COMPETITORS

Abbott Labs	Hologic
American Medical	Johnson & Johnson
Systems	LeMaitre Vascular
Bard	Medtronic
Cook Group	ZOLL
Edwards Lifesciences	

HISTORICAL FINANCIALS

Company Type: Public

Income Statement				FYE: December 31
	REVENUE ($ mil.)	NET INCOME ($ mil.)	NET PROFIT MARGIN	EMPLOYEES
12/19	10,735	4,700	43.8%	36,000
12/18	9,823	1,671	17.0%	32,000
12/17	9,048	104	1.1%	29,000
12/16	8,386	347	4.1%	27,000
12/15	7,477	(239)	—	25,000
Annual Growth	9.5%	—	—	9.5%

2019 Year-End Financials

Debt ratio: 32.74%
Return on equity: 41.59%
Cash ($ mil.): 563
Current ratio: 0.97
Long-term debt ($ mil.): 8,592

No. of shares (mil.): 1,394
Dividends
  Yield: —
  Payout: —
Market value ($ mil.): 63,078

	STOCK PRICE ($) FY Close	P/E High/Low	PER SHARE ($) Earnings	Dividends	Book Value
12/19	45.22	13 10	3.33	0.00	9.95
12/18	35.34	32 21	1.19	0.00	6.30
12/17	24.79	373274	0.08	0.00	5.11
12/16	21.63	94 62	0.25	0.00	4.94
12/15	18.44	— —	(0.18)	0.00	4.69
Annual Growth	25.1%	—	—	—	20.7%

Bridgewater Bancshares Inc

Auditors: CliftonLarsonAllen LLP

LOCATIONS

HQ: Bridgewater Bancshares Inc
  4450 Excelsior Boulevard, Suite 100, Bloomington,
  MN 55416
Phone: 952 893-6868
Web: www.bridgewaterbankmn.com

HISTORICAL FINANCIALS

Company Type: Public

Income Statement				FYE: December 31
	ASSETS ($ mil.)	NET INCOME ($ mil.)	INCOME AS % OF ASSETS	EMPLOYEES
12/19	2,268	31	1.4%	160
12/18	1,973	26	1.4%	140
12/17	1,616	16	1.0%	114
12/16	1,260	13	1.0%	—
Annual Growth	21.6%	33.4%		

2019 Year-End Financials

Debt ratio: 1.66%
Return on equity: 13.48%
Cash ($ mil.): 34
Current ratio: —
Long-term debt ($ mil.): —

No. of shares (mil.): 28
Dividends
  Yield: —
  Payout: —
Market value ($ mil.): 399

	STOCK PRICE ($) FY Close	P/E High/Low	PER SHARE ($) Earnings	Dividends	Book Value
12/19	13.78	13 9	1.05	0.00	8.45
12/18	10.55	14 11	0.91	0.00	7.34
12/17	0.00	— —	0.68	0.00	5.56
Annual Growth	—	—	15.6%	—	15.0%

Brighthouse Financial Inc

Auditors: DELOITTE & TOUCHE LLP

LOCATIONS

HQ: Brighthouse Financial Inc
  11225 North Community House Road, Charlotte, NC
  28277
Phone: 980 365-7100
Web: www.brighthousefinancial.com

HISTORICAL FINANCIALS

Company Type: Public

Income Statement				FYE: December 31
	ASSETS ($ mil.)	NET INCOME ($ mil.)	INCOME AS % OF ASSETS	EMPLOYEES
12/19	227,259	(740)	—	1,330
12/18	206,294	865	0.4%	1,260
12/17	224,192	(378)	—	1,260
12/16	221,930	(2,939)	—	1,100
12/15	226,725	1,119	0.5%	—
Annual Growth	0.1%	—	—	—

2019 Year-End Financials

Debt ratio: 1.92%
Return on equity: (-4.84%)
Cash ($ mil.): 2,877
Current ratio: —
Long-term debt ($ mil.): —

No. of shares (mil.): 106
Dividends
  Yield: —
  Payout: —
Market value ($ mil.): —

Brighthouse Life Insurance Co - Insurance Products

EXECUTIVES

Chb-Pres-Ceo, Eric T Steigerwalt
V Pres-Cfo, Anant Bhalla
V Pres-Cao, Lynn A Dumais
Manager, Deborah McKinney
Regional Sales Vice President, Erik Conroy
Market Research Consultant, Eve Varian
Account Management Vice Presid, Gretchen Bell
Senior Marketing Consultant, Jamie Marin
Regional Sales Vice President, Jason Shrock
Supervisor, Jessica Wellington
Senior Business Applications Q, Julie Richardt
Auditors: DELOITTE & TOUCHE LLP

LOCATIONS

HQ: Brighthouse Life Insurance Co - Insurance Products
11225 North Community House Road, Charlotte, NC 28277
Phone: 980 365-7100
Web: www.metlife.com

HISTORICAL FINANCIALS

Company Type: Public

Income Statement   FYE: December 31

	ASSETS ($ mil.)	NET INCOME ($ mil.)	INCOME AS % OF ASSETS	EMPLOYEES
12/19	216,153	(809)	—	—
12/18	195,830	967	0.5%	—
12/17	212,045	(883)	—	—
12/16	199,273	(2,937)	—	—
12/15	202,362	839	0.4%	—
Annual Growth	1.7%	—	—	—

2019 Year-End Financials

Debt ratio: 0.39%	No. of shares (mil.): 0
Return on equity: (-4.59%)	Dividends
Cash ($ mil.): 2,493	Yield: —
Current ratio: —	Payout: —
Long-term debt ($ mil.): —	Market value ($ mil.): —

Bristol Myers Squibb Co.

Pharmaceutical giant Bristol-Myers Squibb (BMS) treats an array of maladies through its vast lineup of therapies. The company's blockbuster drugs include Eliquis for stroke prevention cancer treatment Opdivo and rhemuatoid arthritis treatment Orencia. Most of the firm's sales come from products in the areas of hematology oncology cardiovascular fibrosis and immunology. BMS has global research facilities and manufacturing plants mainly in the US and Europe. The US accounts for about 60% of sales.

Operations

BMS operates in one segment: Biopharmaceuticals. The company has five blockbuster drugs experiencing growing sales. An oral Factor Xa inhibitor targeted at stroke prevention in adult patients with NVAF and the prevention and treatment of VTE disorders Eliquis brings in about $8 billion and anti-cancer indications including bladder blood colon head and neck kidney liver lung melanoma and stomach Opdivo brings in more than $7 billion in sales or about 30% of annual revenue each. Rheumatoid arthritis drug Orencia earns about $3 billion and leukemia medication Sprycel earns about $2 billion (about 10% of sales each) while melanoma drug Yervoy brings in about $1.5 billion (some 5%). The company added three more blockbuster drugs through its 2019 purchase of Celgene. Another promising drug experiencing rising sales is Empliciti for multiple myeloma.

Established brands include Baraclude Vidaza and other brands generate about 10%.

BMS' R&D efforts are focused on medicines that address serious unmet medical needs with a special emphasis on immuno-oncology and other cancer therapies. Other core therapeutic areas include immunoscience (especially lupus rheumatoid arthritis psoriasis and inflammatory bowel disease) cardiovascular care (heart disease) and fibrotic disease (lung and liver).

Geographic Reach

While New York City-based BMS serves a global customer base the US market accounts for about 60% of its annual revenue. Europe accounts for about 25% of sales rest of the world and other generate more than 15% of sales.

The company operates about 260 manufacturing R&D administration storage and distribution sites around the globe. BMS has four significant manufacturing sites in the US and three in Europe. It has around 10 major research and development facilities in the US and one in Europe.

Sales and Marketing

US wholesale drug distributors McKesson Cardinal Health and AmerisourceBergen together account for about 65% of BMS' annual sales. In addition to wholesalers the company also sells some products directly to customers including hospitals clinics government agencies retailers and pharmacies.

BMS employs a direct sales force to promote products to doctors pharmacists nurses physician assistants hospitals pharmacy benefit managers (PBMs) and managed-care organizations (MCOs). The company also uses television radio print and digital advertising and promotion activities to market its products to consumers.

Advertising and product promotion costs are included in marketing selling and administrative expenses and were $633 million in 2019 $672 million in 2018 and $740 million in 2017 respectively.

Financial Performance

BMS has seen steady revenue growth over the past five years with a growth of 58% between 2015 and 2019. On the other hand net income has been volatile for the last five years.

The company reported a 16% revenue increase in 2019 to some $26.1 billion as a result of higher demand for its prioritized brands including Eliquis and Opdivo and the Celgene acquisition which contributed $1.9 billion of revenues representing approximately one half of the growth.

Net income declined 30% from $4.9 billion in 2018 to $3.4 billion in 2019.

The company ended 2019 with $12.8 billion in cash up $5.9 billion from 2018. Operating activities contributed $8.1 billion while investing activities used $9.8 billion (mostly acquisition and other payments net of cash acquired) and financing activities provided $7.6 billion from issuance of long-term debt.

Strategy

BMS's strategy is to combine the resources scale and capability of a pharmaceutical company with the speed and focus on innovation of the biotech industry. Its focus as a biopharmaceutical company is on discovering developing and delivering transformational medicines for patients facing serious diseases in areas where it believes that the company has an opportunity to make a meaningful difference: oncology (both solid tumors and hematology) immunology cardiovascular and fibrosis. BMS's four strategic priorities as a combined company are to drive enterprise performance maximize the value of its commercial portfolio ensure the long-term sustainability of its pipeline through combined internal and external innovation and establish its new culture and embed its people strategy.

Mergers and Acquisitions

Acquisitions are a major piece of BMS' growth goals. In 2019 the company acquired New Jersey-based biopharma firm Celgene. Celgene became a wholly-owned subsidiary of Bristol-Myers Squibb Company. Under the terms of the transaction Celgene shareholders received one share of Bristol-Myers Squibb common stock and $50.00 in cash for each share of Celgene common stock. Celgene shareholders also received one contingent value right (the CVR) representing the right to receive $9.00 in cash which is subject to the achievement of future regulatory milestones for each share of Celgene common stock. Based on the closing share price of our common stock in late 2019 the aggregate purchase price was approximately $80.3 billion including approximately $35.7 billion in cash and approximately $40.4 billion in Bristol-Myers Squibb common stock. Celgene and BMS sold one of Celgene's major drug offerings Otezla to Amgen for $13.4 billion to meet FTC merger approval requirements.

Company Background

Squibb was founded by Dr. Edward Squibb in New York City in 1858. Bristol-Myers was founded as Clinton Pharmaceutical in Clinton New York in 1887 by William Bristol and John Myers to sell bulk pharmaceuticals. Bristol-Myers Squibb was formed through the merger of Bristol-Myers and Squibb in 1989. The firm was renamed after its founders in 1900. In 1929 the company was publicly held on the New York Exchange company.

EXECUTIVES

Evp And General Counsel, Sandra Leung, age 59, $919,945 total compensation
Chairman And Ceo, Giovanni Caforio, age 56, $1,513,077 total compensation
Evp Cfo And Global Business Operations, Charles A. Bancroft, age 61, $966,115 total compensation
Svp And Cio, Paul von Autenried, age 58
President Global Manufacturing And Supply, Louis S. (Lou) Schmukler, age 64
Svp And Head Of Worldwide Markets, Murdo Gordon, age 53, $737,225 total compensation
Evp And Chief Scientific Officer R&d, Thomas J. Lynch
Senior Vice President Strategy And Business Development, Paul Biondi
Vice President, John Pinter
Senior Vice President And Chief Procurement Officer, Farryn Melton
Senior Vice President Corporate Affairs And Investor Relations, John Elicker
Chief Sales Officer, Giselle Hughes
Vice President Head Of Commercial Law And Compliance European Markets Australia And Canada, Joshua Mclaughlin
Executive Medical Director, David Shepperly
Svp And Deputy General Counsel, Henry Hadad

Svp And Head Product Development, Christopher Sinko
Vice President Of Marketing, Jeff Conklin
Medical Director, William Petkun
Vice President, Anthony Waclawski
Associate Medical Director, Guoqiang Zhang
Vice President Medical Affairs And Pharmacovigilance, Hiroshi Tamada
Medical Director, Nina Kola
Vp And Assistant General Counsel Global Strategic Corporate Transactions, Luis Vilarin
Senior Vice President Chief Human Resources Officer, Ann Powell
Medical Director, Xuemei Li
Vice President, Alastair Binnie
Vp And Assistant General Counsel Hr And Chief Privacy Officer, James Beslity
Associate Medical Director, Poliana Patah
Senior Vice President Head Of Global Regulatory Sciences And Pharmacovigilance And Epidemiology, Mathias Hukkelhoven
Associate Medical Director, Yanfang Liu
Senior Vice President Pharmaceutical Man, Ricardo Zayas
Vice President Finance Us Pharmaceuticals, Phil Holzer
Vice President And Head R And D And Commercial Communications, Danielle Halstrom
Associate Medical Director Global Pharmacovigilance And Epidemiology, David Paar
Vice President Of Human Resources, Julie Taylor
Vp Regulatory Compliance And External Engagement, Lori Hirsch
Clinical Director, Von Potter
Vp Global Product Development And Supply Procurement, Catalina Vargas
Senior Vice President Controller, Karen Santiago
Vice President Of Marketing, Lisa Walker
Vice President Global Procurement, Sanjeev Majoo
Senior Vice President Corporate Strategy, Samuel Moed
Assistant Treasurer, Scott R Massengill
Assistant Treasurer Pension And Savings, Robert Chapman
Auditors: DELOITTE & TOUCHE LLP

LOCATIONS

HQ: Bristol Myers Squibb Co.
430 E. 29th Street, 14th Floor, New York, NY 10016
Phone: 212 546-4000   **Fax:** 212 546-4020
Web: www.bms.com

2017 Sales

	$ mil.	% of total
US	11,358	55
Europe	4,988	24
Other	3,877	18
Other revenues	553	3
Total	**20,776**	**100**

PRODUCTS/OPERATIONS

2017 Sales

	$ mil.	% of total
Prioritized brands		
Opdivo	4,948	24
Eliquis	4,872	23
Orencia	2,479	12
Sprycel	2,005	10
Yervoy	1,244	6
Empliciti	231	1
Established brands		
Baraclude	1,052	5
Sustiva franchise	729	4
Reyataz franchise	698	3
Hepatitis C franchise	406	2
Other	2,112	10
Total	**20,776**	**100**

Selected Pharmaceuticals

Cardiovascular
Eliquis (atrial fibrillation with Pfizer)

Immunology
Nulojix (kidney rejection)
Orencia (rheumatoid arthritis)
Metabolism
Bydureon (type 2 diabetes)
Byetta (type 2 diabetes)
Neuroscience
Emsam (major depressive disorder)
Oncology
Erbitux (colorectal head and neck cancer with Lilly)
Sprycel (chronic myeloid leukemia with Otsuka)
Yervoy (metastatic melanoma)
Virology
Baraclude (chronic hepatitis B)
Reyataz (HIV)
Sustiva Franchise (includes Atripla and Sustiva for HIV with Gilead)

COMPETITORS

AbbVie	Merck
Allergan plc	Mylan
Amgen	Novartis
Apotex	Pfizer
AstraZeneca	Regeneron
Biogen	Pharmaceuticals
Boehringer Ingelheim	Roche Holding
Eli Lilly	Sandoz International
Genentech	GmbH
GlaxoSmithKline	Sanofi
Johnson & Johnson	Teva

HISTORICAL FINANCIALS

Company Type: Public

Income Statement

FYE: December 31

	REVENUE ($ mil.)	NET INCOME ($ mil.)	NET PROFIT MARGIN	EMPLOYEES
12/19	26,145	3,439	13.2%	30,000
12/18	22,561	4,920	21.8%	23,300
12/17	20,776	1,007	4.8%	23,700
12/16	19,427	4,457	22.9%	25,000
12/15	16,560	1,565	9.5%	25,000
Annual Growth	**12.1%**	**21.8%**	**—**	**4.7%**

2019 Year-End Financials

Debt ratio: 35.96%—
Return on equity: 10.48%
Cash ($ mil.): 12,346
Current ratio: 1.60
Long-term debt ($ mil.): 43,387
Dividends
Yield: 2.5%
Payout: 81.5%
Market value ($ mil.): —

	STOCK PRICE ($) FY Close	P/E High/Low	Earnings	Dividends	Book Value
12/19	64.19	32 21	2.01	1.64	22.92
12/18	51.98	23 16	3.01	1.60	8.64
12/17	61.28	107 77	0.61	1.56	7.23
12/16	58.44	29 18	2.65	1.14	9.72
12/15	68.79	75 61	0.93	1.49	8.55
Annual Growth	**(1.7%)**	**— —**	**21.2%**	**2.4%**	**28.0%**

BRIXMOR LLC

EXECUTIVES

MBR, Michael Carroll
Chief Financial Officer*, Tiffanie Fisher
MBR*, Steven F Siegel
MBR*, Leonard Brumberg
MBR*, Steve Splain
Pres*, Michael Pappagallo
Exec V Pres*, Dean Bernstein
Exec V Pres*, Timothy Bruce
Exec V Pres*, Steven Siegel
Vice President, Diane Roberts
Administrative Assistant, Laurie Madsen
Auditors: ERNST & YOUNG LLP

LOCATIONS

HQ: BRIXMOR LLC
450 LEXINGTON AVE FL 13, NEW YORK, NY 100173956
Phone: 212 869-3000
Web: WWW.BRIXMOR.COM

HISTORICAL FINANCIALS

Company Type: Private

Income Statement

FYE: December 31

	ASSETS ($ mil.)	NET INCOME ($ mil.)	INCOME AS % OF ASSETS	EMPLOYEES
12/08	4,157	(550)	—	442
12/07	5,702	(486)	—	
Annual Growth	**(27.1%)**	**—**	**—**	**—**

Broadcom Inc (DE)

Broadcom Limited's products cover a broad range of semiconductors. The products include chips for wireless and wired communications as well as optoelectronics radio-frequency and microwave components power amplifiers and application-specific integrated circuits (custom chips). The company's thousands of products are used in a wide range of applications including mobile phones data networking and telecommunications equipment consumer appliances displays printers servers and storage networking gear and factory automation. Broadcom Limited was created with Avago Technologies acquired Broadcom Inc. The company took the Broadcom Limited name when the deal closed in early 2016.

Change in Company Type

Singapore-based Avago bought US-based Broadcom for $37 billion in 2015 with the transaction closing in February 2016. The deal has been one of the biggest in the wave of consolidation in the semiconductor business. Chip companies have sought strength in bulking up to offer a wider range of products. That was the logic of the Avago-Broadcom deal. It extends the market reach beyond what the individual companies had and it offers the opportunity to sell into each other's markets.

Operations

Broadcom designs makes and sell products for four basic market: wireless communications enterprise storage wired infrastructure and industrial.

Wireless communications generates 37% of Broadcom's revenue through the sale of radio frequency (RF) semiconductor devices and filters for the cell phone market.

The enterprise storage business supplies 32% of the company's revenue. Those products enable secure transfer of data to and from host machines such as servers personal computers and storage systems to the underlying storage devices such as hard disk drives (HDDs) and solid-state drives (SSDs).

Wired infrastructure such as transceivers that receive and transmit information along optical fibers makes up 22% of Broadcom's sales.

The industrial segment supplies devices for automotive military electronics displays and other uses.

Most of the company's product are made by third-party manufacturers such as ASE Korea Inc. Inari Technology SDN BHD Taiwan Semiconductor Manufacturing Company Ltd. and WIN Semiconductors Corp. Broadcom maintains manufacturing capability in Singapore and the US from some production and for developing new products.

Geographic Reach

China is the company's single largest market accounting for about 54% of sales. The US accounts for about 11% and Taiwan 3%. About a third of sales are to areas the company clusters under "other."

Sales and Marketing

Broadcom sells through its own sales staff and through distributors. It staff focus on sales to and support of Broadcom's large OEM customers. The company main are Avnet Inc. and Arrow Electronics Inc.

The company's biggest customer is Foxconn known formally as Hon Hai Precision Industry which accounts for 24% of revenue. Its top five customers account for 46% of the company's sales. Broadcom's sales to Apple directly and through Foxconn make up more than a fifth of revenue.

Financial Performance

Contributions from acquired companies helped boost Broadcom's 2015 (ended November) revenue a robust 60%. Sales reached $6.8 billion for the year compared to $4.27 billion in 2014. Sales rose in all segments and geography but were particularly strong in the enterprise business (150% higher) from the full year of results of products from LSI Corp. which was acquired in 2014.

Broadcom's net income also shot up in 2015 rising a whopping 419% to $1.36 billion compared to $0.26 billion in 2014. The increase came from the jump in revenue and higher operating expenses including research and development costs did little to take the edge off the profit rise.

Strategy

Avago and Broadcom made acquisitions a key part of their growth strategies but as they integrate their widespread operations they might not be in shopping mode.

Broadcom Limited invests in R&D to maintain a pipeline of new products. Its R&D spending has nearly doubled for each of the past three years. It reached $1 billion in 2015 and it expected to stay at that level or higher.

The company bolstered it manufacturing capacity by adding to its plant in Fort Collins Colorado and buying a facility in Eugene Oregon. The company will work on its proprietary products particularly in its wireless communications operation. The Fort Collins plant will get the capacity to make 8-inch wafers which contain more chips that the 6-inch wafers it has turned out.

Broadcom sells as well as buys. In October 2015 it sold Endace a network visibility operation which was acquired with the Emulex deal.

Mergers and Acquisitions

Broadcom in 2017 completed its $5.5 billion acquisition of Brocade Communications after a lengthy review by regulators. The deal gives Broadcom a bigger share of the market for chips designed for data centers and connected devices including cars. Brocade' makes fiber channel switches that increase the speed of data between servers and storage devices.

In 2017 Broadcom made an unsolicited offer of $103 billion to buy Qualcomm Inc. which rejected it. A combination of Broadcom and Qualcomm would be a dominant player in chips for communications from cell phones to data centers and devices. Such a deal would face regulatory scrutiny

even as Broadcom committed to moving its corporate headquarters to the US from Singapore.

In 2014 Avago acquired LSI Corp. in an all-cash deal valued at $6.6 billion. San Jose-based LSI designs semiconductors and software that accelerate storage and networking in data centers mobile networks and client computing. The purchase positions Avago as a leader in enterprise storage. The company anticipates $200 million of annual operating synergies by the end of fiscal year 2015.

In 2013 Avago acquired Javelin Semiconductor which will help in Avago's development of next-generation components for smartphones. Also that year the company agreed to purchase CyOptics which serves the data communications and telecommunications markets with Indium Phosphide (InP) optical chips and components. In 2010 it bought Wuxi expanding its presence in China as well as its motion control encoder product line. In 2008 the company supplemented its motion control product line with the acquisition of Nemi-con.

EXECUTIVES

President And Ceo, Hock E. Tan, age 68, $827,692 total compensation

Svp And General Manager Avago Wireless Semiconductor Division, Bryan T. Ingram, age 56, $508,654 total compensation

Vp And General Manager Isolation Products Division, Tze Siong Chong

Vp And General Manager Motion Control Products Division, Hassan Hussain

Svp And General Manager Asic Products Division, Frank Ostojic

Vp And General Manager Optoelectronic Products Division, Fatt Lun Ho

Svp And General Manager Fiber Optics Products Division, Philip Gadd

Svp Global Operations, Boon Chye Ooi, age 66, $568,467 total compensation

Svp And Cfo, Anthony E. Maslowski, age 59, $396,750 total compensation

Vp Cio And Global Information Technology, Andy Nallappan

Svp And General Manager Data Controller Division, Jim Bland

Vp And General Manager Preamp Components Division, Sally Doherty

Svp And General Manager Datacenter Storage Group, Tom Swinford

Vp And General Manager Industrial Fiber Products Division, Martin Weigert

Vp And General Manager Emulex Connectivity Division, Jeff Hoogenboom

Vp And General Manager Ip Licensing Division, Mark Terrano

Chairman, James V. Diller, age 84

Auditors: PricewaterhouseCoopers LLP

LOCATIONS

HQ: Broadcom Inc (DE)
1320 Ridder Park Drive, San Jose, CA 95131-2313
Phone: 408 433-8000
Web: www.broadcom.com

2015 Sales

	$ mil.	% of total
China	3,675	54
US	755	11
Singapore	208	3
Other countries	2,186	32
Total	**6,824**	**100**

PRODUCTS/OPERATIONS

2015 Sales

	$ mil.	% of total
Wireless communications	2,536	37
Enterprise storage	2,180	32
Wired infrastructure	1,479	22
Industrial & Other	629	9
Total	**6,824**	**100**

Selected Products

Ambient light sensors
Application-specific integrated circuits (ASICs)
Diodes
Fiber-optic transceivers
Light-emitting diodes (LEDs)
LED displays
Low noise amplifiers
mm-wave mixers
Motion control encoders and subsystems
Navigation interface devices
Optical Finger Navigation (OFN)
Optical mouse sensors
Optocouplers
Radio-frequency (RF) integrated circuits
RF amplifiers
RF filters
RF front-end modules
Serializer/deserializer (SerDes)

COMPETITORS

ANADIGICS	Oclaro
Analog Devices	OmniVision
Applied Micro Circuits	Technologies
Citizen Watch	Qorvo
Cree	Qualcomm CDMA
EPCOS	Renesas Electronics
Fairchild	STMicroelectronics
Semiconductor	Sensata
Finisar	Sharp Corp.
HEIDENHAIN Corp.	Skyworks
Hittite Microwave	Texas Instruments
IBM Microelectronics	Toshiba Semiconductor
Infineon Technologies	& Storage Products
Lite-On Technology	Viavi Solutions
Nichia	Vishay Intertechnology
OSRAM Licht	

HISTORICAL FINANCIALS

Company Type: Public

Income Statement				FYE: November 1
	REVENUE ($ mil.)	NET INCOME ($ mil.)	NET PROFIT MARGIN	EMPLOYEES
11/20	23,888	2,960	12.4%	21,000
11/19	22,597	2,724	12.1%	19,000
11/18*	20,848	12,259	58.8%	15,000
10/17	17,636	1,692	9.6%	14,000
10/16	13,240	(1,739)	—	—
Annual Growth	**15.9%**	—	—	—

*Fiscal year change

2020 Year-End Financials

Debt ratio: 54.08%	No. of shares (mil.): 407
Return on equity: 12.15%	Dividends
Cash ($ mil.): 7,618	Yield: 0.0%
Current ratio: 1.87	Payout: 205.3%
Long-term debt ($ mil.): 40,235	Market value ($ mil.): 142,299

	STOCK PRICE ($) FY Close	P/E High/Low		PER SHARE ($)		
			Earnings	Dividends	Book Value
11/20	349.63	58 25	6.33	13.00	58.72
11/19	296.59	47 33	6.43	10.60	62.74
11/18*	220.77	10 7	28.44	3.50	65.34
10/17	252.90	61 39	4.02	4.08	49.63
10/16	169.35	— —	(4.86)	1.94	47.43
Annual Growth	**19.9%**	— —	—	**60.9%**	**5.5%**

*Fiscal year change

Brookline Bancorp Inc (DE)

Boston-based Brookline Bancorp is the holding company for Brookline Bank Bank Rhode Island (BankRI) and First Ipswich Bank which together operate more than 50 full-service branches in eastern Massachusetts and Rhode Island. Commercial and multifamily mortgages backed by real estate such as apartments condominiums and office buildings account for the largest portion of the company's loan portfolio followed by indirect auto loans commercial loans and consumer loans. Established in 1997 as Brookline Savings Bank the bank went public five years later and changed its name to Brookline Bank in 2003.

Operations

Brookline Bancorp focuses its services and products to commercial enterprises. It offers commercial business and retail banking services such as cash management products on-line banking services consumer and residential loans and investment services. The holding company provides equipment financing through its Eastern Funding and Macrolease Corporation subsidiaries. Eastern Funding holds loans with higher-than-normal credit risk (and higher yields) due to the limited capital of its typical customers: coin-operated laundries dry cleaning businesses and convenience stores in the New York City metropolitan area.

Geographic Reach

Boston-based Brookline Bancorp operates primarily in Boston MA and Providence Rhode Island.

Financial Performance

Brookline Bancorp generated $263 million in interest & dividend income and another $32 million of non-interest income. Combined the $295 million of 2017 annual revenue exceeded the previous year's result by 12% aided heavily by the bank's one-time gain of $11 million on the sale of investment securities. Its loan portfolio grew 6% to $5.7 billion in 2017.

Despite the healthy improvement in revenue net income fell 4% to $50.5 million due in large part to an unusually high income tax bill triggered by the passing of the US Federal Tax Reform bill in late 2017.

Strategy

Brookline has grown from a sleepy suburban community savings bank to a publicly-traded commercial lender with loan volumes that put it among Massachusetts' top banks. Its operational approach of a holding company with local largely independent banks gives it certain advantages. The local banks are empowered to address local market needs whether in the form of products services or even interest rates on loans. This gives each bank the opportunity to build its own brand along with strong long-term relationships with commercial customers while leaving the corporate functions (IT risk management etc.) to the centralized holding company.

Mergers and Acquisitions

In 2018 the bank purchased for $264 million First Commons Bank N.A. to extend its reach into the western suburbs of Boston MA.

EXECUTIVES

President And Ceo, Paul A. Perrault, age 69, $715,000 total compensation
Coo, James M. Cosman, age 69, $265,000 total compensation

President And Ceo Bank Rhode Island, Mark J. Meiklejohn, age 56, $330,000 total compensation
Chief Risk Officer General Counsel And Secretary, Michael W. McCurdy, age 51
Chief Credit Officer, M. Robert Rose, age 68, $288,000 total compensation
President And Ceo The First National Bank Of Ipswich, Russell G. Cole, age 62
Cfo, Carl M. Carlson, age 56, $335,000 total compensation
Senior Vice President, Bill Mackenzie
Vice President Regional Manager, Cathy Pierce
Vice President, Tony Glazier
Vice President Of Commercial Lending, Tim Steiner
Vice President Underwriting And Operations, Gretchen Annese
Regional Vice President, Rob Callahan
Vice President, James Vallone
Vp Benefits And Payroll, Edgar Oteiza
Vice President, Michael Minicucci
Chairman, Joseph J. Slotnik, age 84
Treasurer, Reed H Whitman
Auditors: KPMG LLP

LOCATIONS

HQ: Brookline Bancorp Inc (DE)
131 Clarendon Street, Boston, MA 02116
Phone: 617 425-4600
Web: www.brooklinebancorp.com

PRODUCTS/OPERATIONS

2017 sales

	$ mil.	% of total
Interest and dividend income:		
Loans and leases	247	84
Debt securities	12	4
Marketable and restricted equity securities	3	1
Short-term investments	.4	-
Non-interest income:		
Deposit fees	10	3
Loan fees	1	-
Loan level derivative income net	2	1
Gain on sales of investment securities	11	4
Gain on sales of loans and leases held-for-sale	2	1
Other	4	2
Total	**295**	**100**

Selected Services

Personal
Checking
Savings
Borrowing
Investment Services
Business
Signature Business Banking
Business Checking Accounts
Business Savings
Business Lending
Business Online Banking
Cash Management
Service Center
Branch Locations
ATM Locations
Online Banking
Mobile Banking
Telephone Services
Mail Services
Order Checks
Order Foreign Currency
Overdraft Privilege Service

COMPETITORS

Bank of America
Berkshire Hills Bancorp
Boston Private
Central Bancorp
Century Bancorp (MA)
Citizens Financial Group
Eastern Bank
Sovereign Bank
TD Bank USA

HISTORICAL FINANCIALS

Company Type: Public

Income Statement

FYE: December 31

	ASSETS ($ mil.)	NET INCOME ($ mil.)	INCOME AS % OF ASSETS	EMPLOYEES
12/19	7,856	87	1.1%	811
12/18	7,392	83	1.1%	791
12/17	6,780	50	0.7%	765
12/16	6,438	52	0.8%	743
12/15	6,042	49	0.8%	718
Annual Growth	6.8%	15.2%	—	3.1%

2019 Year-End Financials

Debt ratio: 1.84%
Return on equity: 9.50%
Cash ($ mil.): 77
Current ratio: —
Long-term debt ($ mil.): —
No. of shares (mil.): 80
Dividends
Yield: 2.6%
Payout: 40.7%
Market value ($ mil.): 1,320

	STOCK PRICE ($) FY Close	P/E High/Low	PER SHARE ($) Earnings	Dividends	Book Value
12/19	16.46	15 12	1.10	0.44	11.79
12/18	13.82	19 12	1.04	0.40	11.23
12/17	15.70	25 20	0.68	0.36	10.42
12/16	16.40	22 14	0.74	0.36	9.82
12/15	11.50	17 13	0.71	0.36	9.45
Annual Growth	9.4%	— —	11.6%	5.5%	5.7%

Bryn Mawr Bank Corp

Bryn Mawr Bank Corporation stands atop a "big hill" in Pennsylvania. Bryn Mawr (which in Welsh translates as "big hill") is the bank holding company for Bryn Mawr Trust operates some 20 offices in Pennsylvania and Delaware. The bank offers traditional services as checking and savings accounts CDs mortgages and business and consumer loans in addition to insurance products equipment leasing investment management retirement planning tax planning and preparation and trust services. Founded in 1889 Bryn Mawr boasts more than $5 billion of assets under administration and management.

Operations

Bryn Mawr operates two business segments. Its Banking segment which makes up two-thirds of overall business provides commercial and retail banking services. The Wealth Management division which includes the Bryn Mawr Trust of Delaware and Lau Associates businesses makes up about one-third of the bank's overall revenue and provides a variety of custody investment management tax and brokerage services.

Broadly speaking the company generated 60% of its total revenue from interest and fees on loans and leases in 2014 while another 30% of its total revenue came from fees for wealth management services.

Bryn Mawr operated 19 full-service branches seven Life Care Community Offices five wealth offices and a full-service insurance agency in 2014.

Geographic Reach

The bank corporation has branches and offices across Montgomery Delaware Chester and Dauphin counties in Pennsylvania and New Castle county in Delaware.

Financial Performance

Bryn Mawr has enjoyed rising revenues and profits over the past several years reflecting strong growth in its loan business and wealth management business.

The bank's revenue rose by 4% to a record $131.23 million in 2014 mostly thanks to higher interest income from loans as it grew its loan assets by $153.9 million during the year. The company's Wealth Management services fees also grew by 5% thanks to new business acquisitions and solid market appreciation during the year which resulted in higher assets under management.

Higher revenue and a strong grip on costs in 2014 also boosted Bryn Mawr's net income by 14% to a record $27.84 million. Despite higher earnings the bank's operating cash declined by 6% to $37.68 million for the year as it made less in net proceeds from the sales of its loans held for resale.

Strategy

Bryn Mawr Bank Corporation continued to push its acquisition strategy in 2015 designed to broaden its service offerings boost its loan and deposit business and expand its branch network. The bank looks to strategically acquire smaller insurance businesses small to mid-sized banks and community banks wealth management companies and advisory and planning services firm that complement its existing businesses.

Besides acquisitions the company has been growing its wealth management business through marketing campaigns to raise brand awareness.

Mergers and Acquisitions

In April 2015 to grow its wealth management business the bank purchased Robert J. McAllister Agency which provides insurance and risk management solutions to individuals and businesses in the Philadelphia region.

In January 2015 Bryn Mawr acquired the Continental Bank Holdings and its Plymouth Meeting-based flagship Continental Bank adding some $433 million in loans and $480 million in deposits along with 10 full-service branches located in key markets in Montgomery Chester and Philadelphia counties.

In October 2014 Bryn Mawr bought the Rosemont Pennsylvania-based insurance agency Powers Craft Parker & Beard Inc. (PCPB) for $7 million to enhance its own insurance business among individuals and commercial clients.

In 2012 as part of a strategy to build its wealth management division the company acquired Davidson Trust adding some $1 billion in assets under management.

Company Background

In 2011 the company bought the private wealth management business of Hershey Trust Company for more than $14.5 million; that deal brought in approximately $1 billion of assets under management. In 2010 the company purchased First Keystone Financial adding about 10 bank branches in Pennsylvania and some $2.7 billion in trust and investment assets.

EXECUTIVES

Evp And Coo, Alison E. Gers, age 62, $250,000 total compensation

Evp And Chief Lending Officer Bryn Mawr Trust, Joseph G. (Joe) Keefer, age 61, $238,500 total compensation

President And Ceo, Francis J. Leto, age 60, $310,000 total compensation

Evp Secretary And Chief Risk Officer, Geoffrey L. Halberstadt

Cfo And Treasurer Bryn Mawr Bank Corporation; Evp Cfo And Treasurer Bryn Mawr Bank, Michael W. (Mike) Harrington, age 57

Evp Wealth Management Division, Harry R. Madeira

Senior Vice President, Richard Gentile

Senior Vice President Wealth Management, Barbara Pettit

Assistant Vice President, Leslie Herrick

Assistant Vice President And Trust Advisor, Nancy Fanucchi

Senior Vice President, Drew Camerota

Assistant Vice President And Trust Advisor, Yvonne Lalime

Vice President Operations Manager Retail Credit Center Division, Mandy Payne

Senior Vice President Commercial Lending, Mike Bunn

Senior Vice President Operations, Mame Skelly

Vice President Wealth Management Division, J Keefer-Hugill

Assistant Vice President Trust Tax Advisor, John Fotiou

Vice President; Executive Vice President And Chief Administrative Officer Of The Bank, Alison Eichert

Vice President, Cheryl Howard

Vice President, Sally Worrell

Vice President Relationship Manager, Shawn Williams

Vice President Director Of Investment Services, Bryan Andersen

Vice President Mortgage Division, Anne Stulpin

Vice President Comptrollers And Finance, Maral Kaloustian

Senior Vice President Managing Partner, Robert McLaughlin

Assistant Vice President And Senior Fiduciary Tax Acct, Amanda Decaria

Vice President, John Tucker

Svp And Relationship Manager, Joseph J Dimaio

Vice President Small Business Portfolio Manager, Kirsten Althoff

Assistant Vice President Service Manager Chadds Ford Branch, Leslie Paynter

Avp Recruitment Manager, Maria Delimitros

Svp And Chief Credit Officer, Liam Brickley

Senior Vice President Relationship Manager Bmt Wealth Management, Joanne Shallcross

Vice President Senior Mortgage Loan Officer, Patt Mcgowan

Senior Vice President And Director Of Facilities, Emanuel Ball

Senior Vice President Director Of Capital Markets, Mark Henderson

Senior Vice President Head Of Commercial And Industrial Banking, Jim Donovan

Senior Vice President Chief Investment Officer, Ernest E Cecilia

Senior Vice President Chief Operating Officer, Stephen M Wellman

Senior Vice President Commercial, Dennis B Levasseur

Senior Vice President, Ned Lee

Vice President Portfolio Manager, Brandon R Shuler

Chairman, Britton H. Murdoch

Board Member, Michael Clement

Auditors: KPMG LLP

LOCATIONS

HQ: Bryn Mawr Bank Corp
801 Lancaster Avenue, Bryn Mawr, PA 19010
Phone: 610 525-1700
Web: www.bmtc.com

PRODUCTS/OPERATIONS

2014 Sales

	$ mil.	% of total
Interest		
Interest & fees on loans & leases	78	60
Investment securities	4	3
Cash & cash equivalents	0	-
Noninterest		
Fees for wealth management services	36	30
Service charges on deposits	2	2
Net gain on sale of residential mortgages	1	1
Loan Servicing and other fees	1	1
Other	5	3
Total	**131**	**100**

Selected Subsidiaries

Bryn Mawr Advisors Inc.
Bryn Mawr Asset Management Inc.
Bryn Mawr Brokerage Co. Inc.
Bryn Mawr Financial Services Inc.
Bryn Mawr Trust Company of Delaware
Joseph W. Roskos Co. Inc.
Lau Associates LLC
The Bryn Mawr Trust Company
BMT Leasing Inc.
BMT Mortgage Services Inc.
BMT Settlement Services Inc.
Insurance Counsellors of Bryn Mawr Inc.

COMPETITORS

Alliance Bancorp of Pennsylvania	Royal Bancshares
Firstrust Savings Bank	Sovereign Bank
PNC Financial	Wells Fargo

HISTORICAL FINANCIALS

Company Type: Public

Income Statement				FYE: December 31
	ASSETS ($ mil.)	NET INCOME ($ mil.)	INCOME AS % OF ASSETS	EMPLOYEES
12/19	5,263	59	1.1%	684
12/18	4,652	63	1.4%	696
12/17	4,449	23	0.5%	680
12/16	3,421	36	1.1%	544
12/15	3,031	16	0.6%	530
Annual Growth	14.8%	37.1%	—	6.6%

2019 Year-End Financials

Debt ratio: 2.29%	No. of shares (mil.): 20
Return on equity: 10.05%	Dividends
Cash ($ mil.): 53	Yield: 2.4%
Current ratio: —	Payout: 34.3%
Long-term debt ($ mil.): —	Market value ($ mil.): 830

	STOCK PRICE ($) FY Close	P/E High/Low		PER SHARE ($) Earnings	Dividends	Book Value
12/19	41.24	14	11	2.93	1.02	30.45
12/18	34.40	16	11	3.13	0.94	28.04
12/17	44.20	34	28	1.32	0.86	26.23
12/16	42.15	20	11	2.12	0.82	22.50
12/15	28.72	33	29	0.94	0.78	21.42
Annual Growth	9.5%	—	—	32.9%	6.9%	9.2%

Builders FirstSource Inc.

Builders FirstSource supplier and manufacturer of building materials manufactured components and construction services to professional homebuilders sub-contractors remodelers and consumers. It also offers construction-related services. The company's products and services – which manufactured products include the factory-built roof and floor trusses wall panels and stairs vinyl windows custom millwork and trim as well as engineered wood that the company designs cuts and assembles?are offered through some 400 locations across roughly 40 US states. Homebuilders such as Pulte Homes and Lennar are among its largest customers. Builders is a supplier of structural building products and services for new residential construction repair and remodeling. Builders First-Source Inc. is a Delaware corporation formed in 1998 as BSL Holdings Inc. On October 13 1999 the name changed to Builders FirstSource Inc.

Operations

Builders FirstSource operates through four geographic reporting segments: West (which provides about 30% of net sales) South (25%) Southeast (more than 20%) and Northeast (20%).

By product category Builders' largest revenue generator is lumber and lumber sheet goods which account for nearly 30%. Manufactured products generate roughly 20% as well as windows doors and millwork (also provides more than 20% of sales).. Roughly 10% derives from siding metal and concrete products; another 10% comes from what the company classifies as other building and product services – including cabinets hardware turnkey framing shell construction and design. Gypsum roofing and insulation bring in the remainder.

Geographic Reach

Based in Dallas Texas Builders FirstSource is active in about 40 US states and the products and services offerings are distributed across approximately 400 locations across the US which have been organized into nine geographical regions. It serves about 75 of the country's top 100 metropolitan statistical areas.

Sales and Marketing

Builders FirstSource serves a range of customers from individual consumers to repair and remodel contractors to large homebuilders as well as multi-family builders. Its top 10 customers account for more than 15% of sales and include large homebuilders such as D.R. Horton Pulte Homes Lennar Hovnanian Enterprises Inc. and Taylor Morrison Home Corporation.

The company markets its products and services through a locally focused sales force of some 1900 and worked with approximately 1600 sales coordinators and product specialists.

According to ProSales magazine's 2019 the company was the largest building product supplier with manufacturing capabilities on this list.

Financial Performance

Huge gains by Builders FirstSource in the past five years peaking at $7.7 billion in 2018. The company's net income has been erratic: it fell to a loss in 2015 before rebounding in 2016?only to slide by about three-quarters the next year. 2019 saw net income was higher compared to 2018.

Builders' net sales declined by more than five percent in 2019 to end the year at $7.2 billion; commodity price deflation decreased net sales in 2019. Excluding the impact of commodity price deflation the company achieved more than five percent of the net sales growth in the single-family multi-family and repair and remodel/other end markets.

The company's net income jumped by almost 10% to $221.8 million in 2019 thanks mostly to net losses on debt extinguishment and other financing costs.

Builders gained $3 million of its cash stores in 2019 to end the year with $14.0 million. Its operations provided $504.0 million. It invested a net $199.2 million in property plant and equipment; financing activities used $300.9 million primarily for revolving credit facility payments.

Strategy

Builders Firstsource's long-term business plan provides for continued growth through strategic acquisitions and organic growth through the construction of new facilities or the expansion of existing facilities. Failure to identify and acquire suitable acquisition candidates on appropriate terms could have a material adverse effect on the company' growth strategy.

In terms of homebuilders the company seeks a more strategic relationship with suppliers that are able to offer a broad range of products and services and are allocating a greater share of wallet to a select number of larger full-service suppliers.

The company is working towards identifying measuring and mapping the environmental social and governance impacts of its business in an effort to be a good corporate citizen and proactively manage the impacts on the communities in which the company's caters. Helping home builders become more productive and efficient is fundamental to what Builders FirstSource does and is passionate about building this future together.

One core of the company's strategy is controlling costs and striving to be a low-cost building materials supplier in the markets it serves. It pays close attention to managing the working capital and operating expenses.

Mergers and Acquisitions

In early 2020 the company acquired certain assets and the operations of Bianchi & Company Inc. ("Bianchi") for $17.2 million in cash subject to certain adjustments. Bianchi is a supplier and installer of interior and exterior doors crown moldings open stair rail chair rail wainscoting commercial hollow metal frames and doors and other custom millwork.

In late 2019 The company acquired certain assets and the operations of Raney Components LLC and Raney Construction Inc. (collectively "Raney") for $59.0 million in cash subject to certain adjustments. Raney is a vertically-integrated manufacturer and installer of residential structures for production builder customers.

In mid-2019 the company acquired certain assets and the operations of Sun State Components ("Sun State") for $42.5 million in cash. Sun State is comprised of three truss locations which are located in Las Vegas Nevada; Surprise Arizona; and Kingman Arizona. Sun State manufactures roof trusses and floor trusses and distributes lumber and related products to residential homebuilders and commercial contractors.

Company Background

Builders FirstSource was founded in 1998 as BSL Holdings. It is the US' largest supplier of structural building products and services for new residential construction repair and remodeling.

EXECUTIVES

Svp And General Counsel, Donald F. McAleenan, age 65, $415,481 total compensation
President And Ceo, M. Chad Crow, age 52, $625,000 total compensation
Svp And Cfo, Peter Jackson

Vice President Treasury, Mark Cooper
Senior Vice President And Chief Operating Officer Of East, Dave Rush
Vice President, Gary Raven
Vice President Of Hr, Jan Smith
Vice President Sales And Marketing, Randy Craine
Vice President Sales, Matt Liska
Vice President, Greg Turnage
Vice President Sales, Chris Lemly
Vice President Credit, Bart Roberts
Svp Investor Relations, Jennifer Pasquino
Vice President Human Resources, John Foley
Vice President, Kelly Kimbrel
Vice President Of Purchasing, Jeff Rettig
Vice President Credit Southeast Region, Liz Hummell
Vice President Development Seattle, Steve Yoon
Vice President, Stephen Prochnow
Vice President Of Construction, Frank Navia
Vice President Of Financial Reporting, Kimberly Minna
Vp Of Marketing, Kellie Hughes
Vice President Investor Relations, Binit Sanghvi
Vp Logistics And Fleet Maintenance, Michael Birk
Chairman, Paul S. Levy, age 72
Board Member, Floyd F Sherman
Board Member, Kevin Kruse
Board Member, Daniel Agroskin
Auditors: PricewaterhouseCoopers LLP

LOCATIONS

HQ: Builders FirstSource Inc.
2001 Bryan Street, Suite 1600, Dallas, TX 75201
Phone: 214 880-3500   **Fax:** 214 880-3599
Web: www.bldr.com

2018 Sales

	$ mil.	% of total
West	2,461	32
South	2,051	27
Southeast	1,704	22
Northeast	1,340	17
Other	167	2
Total	**7,724**	**100**

PRODUCTS/OPERATIONS

2018 Sales

	$ mil.	% of total
Lumber and lumber sheet goods	2,902	37
Manufactured products	1,392	18
Windows doors and millwork	1,445	19
Siding metal and concrete products	697	9
Gypsum roofing and insulation	528	7
Other building products and services	758	10
Total	**7,724**	**100**

Selected Products

Building Materials
  Concrete
  Concrete block
  Decking
  Gypsum
  Paint
  Roofing
  Sheathing
Interior Items
  Builder hardware
  Cabinets
  Cabinet hardware
  Countertops
  Fireplaces
Lumber and Related Products
  Dimensional lumber
  Engineered wood
  Oriented strand board
  Plywood
  Pressure-treated lumber
Manufactured Components
  Floor trusses
  I-Joist floor systems
  Interior and exterior doors
  Open wall panels
  Roof trusses

Stairs
Millwork
  Columns
  Custom millwork
  Interior and exterior doors
  Moldings
  Special-order millwork
  Windows
Tools
  Pneumatic tools
  Power tools

COMPETITORS

84 Lumber	HD Supply
Ace Hardware	Lowe's
BMC Stock	McCoy Corp.
BlueLinx	Menard
Boise Cascade Company	True Value
Carter Lumber	Universal Forest
CertainTeed	Products

HISTORICAL FINANCIALS

Company Type: Public

Income Statement   FYE: December 31

	REVENUE ($ mil.)	NET INCOME ($ mil.)	NET PROFIT MARGIN	EMPLOYEES
12/19	7,280	221	3.0%	15,800
12/18	7,724	205	2.7%	15,000
12/17	7,034	38	0.6%	15,000
12/16	6,367	144	2.3%	14,000
12/15	3,564	(22)	—	14,000
Annual Growth	19.5%	—	—	3.1%

2019 Year-End Financials

Debt ratio: 39.74%	No. of shares (mil.): 116
Return on equity: 31.21%	Dividends
Cash ($ mil.): 14	Yield: —
Current ratio: 1.59	Payout: —
Long-term debt ($ mil.): 1,277	Market value ($ mil.): 2,949

	STOCK PRICE ($) FY Close	P/E High/Low		PER SHARE ($) Earnings	Dividends	Book Value
12/19	25.41	14	6	1.90	0.00	7.11
12/18	10.91	13	6	1.76	0.00	5.18
12/17	21.79	64	32	0.34	0.00	3.31
12/16	10.97	11	5	1.27	0.00	2.78
12/15	11.08	—	—	(0.22)	0.00	1.36
Annual Growth	23.1%			—	—	51.2%

Burlington Stores Inc

Burlington Stores (Burlington) takes the "Brrr!" out of your life. The clothing retailer which made its name selling coats operates nearly 700 no-frills retail stores offering off-price current brand-name clothing in about 45 states plus Puerto Rico. Although it is one of the nation's largest coat sellers the stores also sell a full wardrobe of products including children's apparel bath items furniture gifts jewelry linens and shoes. Sister chains include a pair of higher-priced Cohoes Fashions shops a pair of Super Baby Depot stores and about ten MJM Designer Shoe stores. Burlington was founded in 1972.

Operations

Almost all Burlington's sales are rung up at its Burlington Coat Factory Warehouse stores. Women's ready-to-wear apparel and accessories and footwear are its biggest earner at a quarter of sales which both account for more than 20% fol-

lowed by menswear (around 20%) youth and baby apparel (more than 15%) home (approximately15%) and coats (some 5%).

As its name suggests Super Baby Depot's two stores sell baby clothing accessories furniture and everything else a baby might need in the middle to higher price range. The company's MJM Designer Shoe sells brand names at significant discounts. Cohoes Fashions offers products similar to those offered by the mainline stores.

Geographic Reach

New Jersey-based Burlington has stores in about 45 states and Puerto Rico. Its almost five primary distribution centers which ship almost all its merchandise are located in Edgewater Park and Burlington New Jersey and San Bernardino and Redlands California. Nearly three warehouses support its distribution centers.

Sales and Marketing

Burlington Coat Factory takes less of a markup than its department store competition and has lower profit margins than other clothing retailers. It buys the coats early in the season (up to five months before department stores) to lock in lower prices.

The company's marketing channels include TV direct mail email digital and social marketing radio and out-of-home communications.

Burlington's advertising costs were $74.6 million $77.1 million and $82.3 million during the fiscal years 2019 2018 and 2017 respectively.

Financial Performance

Burlington Stores has recorded increasing revenue and profits over the last five years.

In fiscal 2020 (ended February 1) the company's sales grew 9% to $7.3 billion. Comparable store sales increased 3%.

Burlington earned net income of $465.1 million in fiscal 2020 compared with $414.7 million the year prior which is an increase of $50.4 million.

Burlington's cash on hand rose $275.5 million during fiscal 2020 ending the year at $409.7 million. The company's operations generated $891.7 million offset by the $324.6 million used in its investing activities and $291.6 million used in its financing. Burlington's main cash uses in 2020 were capital expenditures (such as store openings) and principal payments on long term debt.

Strategy

Burlington continues to explore expansion opportunities both within its current market areas and in other regions. The company believes that its ability to find satisfactory locations for its stores is essential for the continued growth of its business. The opening of stores generally is contingent upon a number of factors including the availability of desirable locations with suitable structures and the negotiation of acceptable lease terms.

Burlington's growth largely depends on its ability to successfully open and operate new stores as well as to expand its distribution capabilities in order to support that growth. The company intends to open 54 net new stores in 2020 while refreshing remodeling or relocating a portion of its existing store base annually.

HISTORY

Russian-Jewish immigrant Abe Milstein and a partner started coat wholesaler and manufacturer Milstein and Feigelson in 1924. Abe's son Monroe was a quick study. He graduated from New York University with a business degree in 1946 at age 19 and started his own coat and suit wholesaling business called Monroe G. Milstein Inc. His mother provided free labor at her son's company six days a week to keep the business alive. Abe ended his partnership in 1953 and joined his son's business.

Family relations were strained temporarily in 1972 when Monroe disregarded his father's advice

not to buy a faltering coat factory outlet store in Burlington New Jersey. (Abe believed that his son did not have enough retailing experience.) Monroe however thought owning a retail store would provide a guaranteed sales outlet for their merchandise and he bought Burlington Coat Factory for $675000 (using $60000 of his wife Henrietta's savings). His company also adopted the Burlington Coat Factory Warehouse moniker as its own.

To become less dependent on the season-specific coat business the company soon expanded its merchandise mix by adding a children's division (started by Henrietta deceased in 2001) and subleased departments. It opened a second store in Long Island New York in 1975.

Settling a trademark dispute with fabric maker Burlington Industries in 1981 Burlington Coat Factory agreed to say in advertising — as it does to this day — that the two companies are not affiliated. The 31-store company went public two years later using the money it raised to open almost 30 stores that year. As part of its expansion in the 1980s Burlington Coat Factory opened stores in warmer climates such as Texas and Florida.

The firm tried to grow through acquisitions that decade but failed in its attempts to buy a number of department store retailers. It made a successful bid in 1989 for New York discount retailer Cohoes.

Burlington Coat Factory's sales topped the $1 billion mark for the first time in fiscal 1993. Also that year the company bought Boston-based off-price family apparel chain Decelle. It then opened its first store outside the US (in Mexico) and tried new stand-alone store concepts based on successful in-store departments such as Luxury Linens and Baby Depot. A warm winter in 1994 hurt the company: Profits fell by two-thirds and it sold off inventory for two years afterward.

The company pulled a line of men's parkas in late 1998 after a Humane Society investigation revealed that the coats were trimmed with hair from dogs killed inhumanely in China. Burlington Coat Factory launched a baby gift registry in 2000 and later that year opened a silk floral division in selected stores. In 2001 the company acquired 16 stores formerly occupied by bankrupt Montgomery Ward. Burlington Coat Factory began operating MJM Designer Shoes in fiscal 2002 opening nine of the stand-alone specialty shoe stores. The company closed its Decelle stores in 2003 but converted most of them to the Burlington Coat Factory and Cohoes names while launching 25 new stores in 2004 (most under the Burlington Coat Factory moniker).

In 2005 the company opened two Super Baby Depot stores. Burlington Coat Factory was acquired by the Boston-based private equity firm Bain Capital Partners in April 2006 for about $2.1 billion.

In fiscal year 2006 the company opened three MJM Designer Shoes stores. The company's two stand-alone Luxury Linens stores were shut down and instead operate as departments within Burlington Coat Factory stores.

In December 2008 Thomas Kingsbury was named president and CEO of Burlington Coat Factory Warehouse succeeding Mark Nesci who retired after 37 years with the retailer. Prior to joining the company Kingsbury was a SEVP at Kohl's.

In February 2010 the company changed its fiscal year end from May to January to better comply with its peers in the retail industry. In October Burlington Coat Factory agreed to pay $10 million to settle a long-running legal fight with Italian luxury goods maker Fendi over the sale of counterfeit handbags and other leather goods.

Burlington went public in 2013.

EXECUTIVES

Chairman President And Ceo, Thomas A. (Tom) Kingsbury, age 67, $1,164,257 total compensation
Evp Human Resources, Joyce Manning Magrini, $386,539 total compensation
Cfo And Principal, Marc D. Katz, age 55, $654,400 total compensation
Evp General Counsel And Corporate Secretary, Janet L. Dhillon, age 57
Chief Merchandising Officer And Principal, Jennifer Vecchio, age 54, $677,195 total compensation
Chief Customer Officer And Principal, Fred Hand, age 56, $654,400 total compensation
Evp And Chief Marketing Officer, Hobart (Bart) Sichel, age 55, $326,923 total compensation
Evp Supply Chain Corporate Services And Asset Protection, Mike Metheny, age 53
Evp Merchandising, Rick Seeger, age 58, $629,826 total compensation
Evp Stores, Forrest David Coder
Evp Planning & Allocation And Merchandise Information Operations (mio), Eliot M. Rosenfield
Vice President E Commerce, Brian Questad
Vice President Supply Chain Support, Steven Bienstock
Regional Vice President, Marty Frent
Vice President Dmm, Heather Brown
Senior Vice President Real Estate Construction And Facilities, Gayle Aertker
Svp Profit Improvement, Pete Cupps
Vice President And Assistant Treasurer, Jeff Laub
Senior Vice President Visual Merchandise, Jean Marie Hill
Senior Vice President Planning And Allocation, Fran Jose
Executive Vice President Human Resources, Joyce Manning
Vice President Planning And Allocation, Michael Cane
Vice President Vice President, Nancy Pickus
Vp Facilities, Shirley Culman
Vice President Store Administration, Steve Riley
Svp Stores Territory 5 South East U.s. And Puerto Rico, Troy Steiner
Vice President Advertising, Warren Johnson
Executive Vice President Supply Chain, Charlie Guardiola
Vice President, Gerry Incollingo
Vice President, Melanie Grant
Vice President Marketing, Wendy Siskind
Vp Logistics, Lorenzo Figueroa
Vice President Legal, Stacy Haigney
Regional Vice President, Tracey Jwanier
Senior Vice President Asset Protection, James Connolly
Vice President Of Information Technology Transitional Services, Mike Prince
Senior Vice President And Chief Accounting Officer, John Crimmins
Svp Store Hr, Bruce Mager
Vp And Assistant Secretary, Christopher Schaub
Vice President Planning And Allocation Localization, Shireesh Annam
Regional Vice President, Richard Catapano
Evp Merchandising, Siiri Dougherty
Senior Vice President Gmm Ladies Apparel, Nancy Mair
Vice President Human Resources, Susan Katims
Svp Stores, Hank Wagner
Vice President Dmm, Lydia Veres
Vice President, Andrew Milstein
Vp Divisional Merchandise Manager Housewares And Tabletop, Michael Kasprowicz
Board Member, John Mahoney
Auditors: DELOITTE & TOUCHE LLP

LOCATIONS

HQ: Burlington Stores Inc
2006 Route 130 North, Burlington, NJ 08016
Phone: 609 387-7800
Web: www.burlingtonstores.com

2017 Stores

	No.
Texas	67
California	66
Florida	46
New York	41
Illinois	34
Pennsylvania	33
New Jersey	31
Ohio	24
Georgia	19
Michigan	18
Virginia	18
Maryland	16
North Carolina	15
Massachusetts	14
Arizona	12
Indiana	12
Washington	12
Connecticut	11
Puerto Rico	11
Wisconsin	10
Missouri	9
Minnesota	8
South Carolina	8
Tennessee	8
Colorado	7
Louisiana	7
Nevada	7
Alabama	6
Arizona	5
Kansas	5
Kentucky	5
Rhode Island	5
Utah	5
Oregon	4
Delaware	3
Iowa	3
Mississippi	3
Nebraska	3
New Hampshire	3
New Mexico	3
Oklahoma	3
Arkansas	2
Idaho	2
Maine	2
North Dakota	1
South Dakota	1
Online Store	1
Total	**629**

PRODUCTS/OPERATIONS

2019 Sales

	% of total
Women's ready-to-wear apparel	23
Accessories & Footwear	22
Menswear	20
Youth Apparel/Baby	16
Home	14
Coats	5
Total	**100**

2019 Stores

	No.
Burlington Stores	661
MJM Designer Shoes	9
Cohoes Fashions	2
Super Baby Depot	2
Online Store	1
Total	**629**

Selected Store Banners

Burlington Coat Factory Warehouse (value-priced apparel accessories linens bath items gifts)
Cohoes Fashions (higher-priced apparel and accessories)
MJM Designer Shoes (designer and fashion shoes)
Super Baby Depot (baby clothing accessories furniture)

COMPETITORS

Ascena Retail	Nordstrom
Babies "R" Us	Payless ShoeSource
Bed Bath & Beyond	Ross Stores
Belk	Saks
Bon-Ton Stores	Stein Mart
DSW	TJX Companies
Dillard's	Target Corporation
Kohl's	Wal-Mart
Macy's	

HISTORICAL FINANCIALS

Company Type: Public

Income Statement

				FYE: February 1
	REVENUE ($ mil.)	NET INCOME ($ mil.)	NET PROFIT MARGIN	EMPLOYEES
02/20	7,286	465	6.4%	47,000
02/19	6,668	414	6.2%	44,000
02/18*	6,110	384	6.3%	40,000
01/17	5,590	215	3.9%	40,000
01/16	5,129	150	2.9%	37,500
Annual Growth	**9.2%**	**32.6%**	**—**	**5.8%**

*Fiscal year change

2020 Year-End Financials

Debt ratio: 17.97%
Return on equity: 109.63%
Cash ($ mil.): 403
Current ratio: 0.97
Long-term debt ($ mil.): 1,001

No. of shares (mil.): 65
Dividends
  Yield: —
  Payout: —
Market value ($ mil.): 14,338

	STOCK PRICE ($) FY Close	P/E High/Low	PER SHARE ($) Earnings	Dividends	Book Value
02/20	217.47	33 20	6.91	0.00	8.01
02/19	171.87	28 18	6.04	0.00	4.81
02/18*	115.75	23 14	5.48	0.00	1.28
01/17	80.91	29 16	3.01	0.00	(0.71)
01/16	53.73	30 20	1.99	0.00	(1.37)
Annual Growth	**41.8%**	**— —**	**36.5%**	**—**	**—**

*Fiscal year change

Business First Bancshares Inc

Auditors: Hannis T. Bourgeois, LLP

LOCATIONS

HQ: Business First Bancshares Inc
500 Laurel Street, Suite 101, Baton Rouge, LA 70801
Phone: 225 248-7600
Web: www.b1bank.com

HISTORICAL FINANCIALS

Company Type: Public

Income Statement

				FYE: December 31
	ASSETS ($ mil.)	NET INCOME ($ mil.)	INCOME AS % OF ASSETS	EMPLOYEES
12/19	2,273	23	1.0%	355
12/18	2,094	14	0.7%	333
12/17	1,321	4	0.4%	219
12/16	1,105	5	0.5%	208
12/15	1,076	4	0.4%	184
Annual Growth	**20.6%**	**55.2%**	**—**	**17.9%**

2019 Year-End Financials

Debt ratio: 1.10%	No. of shares (mil.): 13
Return on equity: 8.72%	Dividends
Cash ($ mil.): 89	Yield: 1.5%
Current ratio: —	Payout: 24.0%
Long-term debt ($ mil.): —	Market value ($ mil.): 331

	STOCK PRICE ($) FY Close	P/E High/Low	PER SHARE ($) Earnings	Dividends	Book Value
12/19	24.93	14 13	1.74	0.38	21.47
12/18	24.23	23 17	1.22	0.24	19.68
Annual Growth	0.7%		9.3%	12.2%	2.2%

Byline Bancorp Inc

Auditors: Moss Adams LLP

LOCATIONS

HQ: Byline Bancorp Inc
180 North LaSalle Street, Suite 300, Chicago, IL
60601
Phone: 773 244-7000
Web: www.bylinebancorp.com

HISTORICAL FINANCIALS

Company Type: Public

Income Statement

FYE: December 31

	ASSETS ($ mil.)	NET INCOME ($ mil.)	INCOME AS % OF ASSETS	EMPLOYEES
12/19	5,521	57	1.0%	1,001
12/18	4,942	41	0.8%	943
12/17	3,366	21	0.6%	844
12/16	3,295	66	2.0%	791
12/15	2,479	(14)	—	—
Annual Growth	22.2%			

2019 Year-End Financials

Debt ratio: 0.68%	No. of shares (mil.): 38
Return on equity: 8.14%	Dividends
Cash ($ mil.): 80	Yield: 0.1%
Current ratio: —	Payout: 1.9%
Long-term debt ($ mil.): —	Market value ($ mil.): 749

	STOCK PRICE ($) FY Close	P/E High/Low	PER SHARE ($) Earnings	Dividends	Book Value
12/19	19.57	14 11	1.48	0.03	19.61
12/18	16.66	20 13	1.18	0.00	17.90
12/17	22.97	59 50	0.38	0.00	15.64
Annual Growth	(3.9%)		40.5%	—	5.8%

Cadence Bancorporation

EXECUTIVES

Chb-Ceo, Paul B Murphy Jr
V Chb*, Joseph W Evans
Pres, Samuel M Tortorici
Exec V Pres-Cfo, Valerie C Toalson
Exec V Pres-General Counsel-SE, Jerry W Powell
Exec V Pres, David F Black
Evp, R H Holmes IV
Chief Talent Officer, Sheila E Ray
Assistant Branch Manager, Samuel Garcia
Senior Manager, Sherry Lee
Appraisal Risk Management Depa, Rebecca Travis
Auditors: Ernst & Young LLP

LOCATIONS

HQ: Cadence Bancorporation
2800 Post Oak Boulevard, Suite 3800, Houston, TX
77056
Phone: 713 871-4000
Web: www.cadencebank.com

HISTORICAL FINANCIALS

Company Type: Public

Income Statement

FYE: December 31

	ASSETS ($ mil.)	NET INCOME ($ mil.)	INCOME AS % OF ASSETS	EMPLOYEES
12/19	17,800	201	1.1%	1,849
12/18	12,730	166	1.3%	1,811
12/17	10,948	102	0.9%	1,206
12/16	9,530	65	0.7%	1,193
12/15	8,811	39	0.4%	—
Annual Growth	19.2%	50.6%		

2019 Year-End Financials

Debt ratio: 1.53%	No. of shares (mil.): 127
Return on equity: 10.36%	Dividends
Cash ($ mil.): 977	Yield: 3.8%
Current ratio: —	Payout: 45.4%
Long-term debt ($ mil.): —	Market value ($ mil.): 2,313

	STOCK PRICE ($) FY Close	P/E High/Low	PER SHARE ($) Earnings	Dividends	Book Value
12/19	18.13	15 10	1.56	0.70	19.29
12/18	16.78	16 8	1.97	0.55	17.43
12/17	27.12	22 16	1.25	0.00	16.25
Annual Growth	(9.6%)		5.7%	—	4.4%

Cambridge Bancorp

Cambridge Bancorp is the nearly $2 billion-asset holding company for Cambridge Trust Company a community bank serving Cambridge and the Greater Boston area through about a dozen branch locations in Massachusetts. It offers standard retail products and services including checking and savings accounts CDs IRAs and credit cards. Residential mortgages including home equity loans account for about 50% of the company's loan portfolio while commercial real estate loans make up more than 40%. The company also offers commercial industrial and consumer loans. Estab-

lished in 1892 the bank also offers trust and investment management services.

Operations

The commercial bank operates a traditional retail banking line focused on lending as well as its Wealth Management Group which investment management and trust business. The bank had $1.8 billion in total assets and $2.4 billion in client assets under management at the end of 2015.

As with other retail banks Cambridge Bancorp makes the bulk of its revenue from interest income. About 58% of its total revenue came from loan interest during 2015 while another 10% came from interest on taxable and tax-exempt investment securities. The rest of its revenue came from wealth management income (24% of revenue) deposit account fees (3%) ATM/Debit card income (1%) and other non-interest income sources.

Geographic Reach

Cambridge Bancorp has 12 branches in Massachusetts in Cambridge Boston Belmont Concord Lexington Lincoln and Weston. It also has wealth management offices in Boston as well as in New Hampshire in Concord Manchester and Portsmouth.

Sales and Marketing

The company spent $2.38 million on marketing during 2015 up from $2.12 million in 2014.

Financial Performance

Cambridge's annual revenues and profits have been steadily rising over the past several years thanks to continued commercial real estate mortgage growth and as its Wealth Management business has nearly doubled its managed assets since 2011 spurring higher fee revenue.

The bank's revenue climbed 7% to $80.2 million during 2015 on 10% loan growth mostly driven by commercial real estate loans which spurred higher interest income. The company's wealth management business income grew 7% as its client assets continued to grow with new investor inflows.

Revenue growth in 2015 drove Cambridge Bancorp's net income up 5% to $15.7 million. The bank's operating cash levels rose 24% to $20 million for the year with an increase in cash-based earnings and favorable changes in working capital mostly related to a change in accrued interest receivable deferred taxes and other assets and liabilities.

Strategy

Cambridge Bancorp continued in 2016 to lean on the success of its commercial mortgage business though it plans to pivot more to commercial and industrial lending to diversify its commercial lending portfolio.

To better prepare for rising interest rates Cambridge Bancorp in 2015 and 2016 modified its commercial loan strategy from long-term fixed-rate loans (which are vulnerable to interest rate risk) to a new interest rate derivative product to offer an alternative long-term financing for its customers while helping the bank earn a variable rate of interest on its loans. For its consumer banking unit the bank in 2015 began a plan to sell the majority of its long-term residential mortgage production including secondary loans to the secondary market.

EXECUTIVES

Chairman President And Ceo, Denis K. Sheahan, age 54
Svp And Chief Investment Officer, James F. Spencer
Evp And Chief Lending Officer, Martin B. Millane
Evp And Cio Cambridge Trust, Lynne M. Burrow
Evp And Head Of Wealth Management Cambridge Trust, Michael A. Duca

Svp And Consumer Banking Director Cambridge Trust, Thomas A. Johnson
Cfo, Michael Carotenuto
Svp And President Cambridge Trust Company Of New Hampshire, Susan Martore-Baker
Svp And Marketing Director, Robert N. Siegrist
Assistant Vice President Business Banking, Kate Carlson
Vice President, Laura Mcgregor
Senior Vp Private Banker, Sara Sarkis
Svp Director Of Retail Banking, Michael Reed
Assistant Vice President And Tax Manager, Theresa Giglio
Avp Compliance Officer, Philip Pace
Assistant Vice President And Branch Manager, Fenton Martin
Vice President And Manager Of Community Business Development, Dina Scianna
Avp Hr Business Partner And Recruiter, Ashley Thomas
Auditors: Wolf & Company P.C

LOCATIONS

HQ: Cambridge Bancorp
  1336 Massachusetts Avenue, Cambridge, MA 02138
Phone: 617 876-5500
Web: www.cambridgetrust.com

PRODUCTS/OPERATIONS

2015 Sales

	% of total
Interest Income	
Interest on loans	58
Interest on taxable investment securities	7
Interest on tax exempt investment securities	3
Non-Interest Income	
Wealth Management Income	24
Deposits accounts fee	3
ATM/Debit card income	1
Bank Owned life insurance income	1
Gain on disposition on investment securities	1
Gain on loans held of sale	1
Other income	1
Loan related derivative income	-
Total	**100**

Products/Services

Personal Banking
Checking
Savings CDs & IRAs
Online Banking
Mobile Banking
Mortgages
Home Equity
Credit Cards
Personal Loans
More Services
Business Banking
Checking & Savings
Commercial Lending
Commercial Real Estate
Cash Management
Remote Deposit Capture
Online Banking
Mobile Banking
Professional Services Program
More Services
Wealth Management
Investment Process
Investment Management
Fiduciary & Planning Services
Estate Settlement
Wealth Management Personnel
Forums
Online Access

COMPETITORS

Bank of America	Eastern Bank
Cambridge Financial	Middlesex Savings
Central Bancorp	Peoples Federal
Century Bancorp (MA)	Bancshares Inc.
Citizens Financial Group	

HISTORICAL FINANCIALS

Company Type: Public

Income Statement   FYE: December 31

	ASSETS ($ mil.)	NET INCOME ($ mil.)	INCOME AS % OF ASSETS	EMPLOYEES
12/19	2,855	25	0.9%	321
12/18	2,101	23	1.1%	262
12/17	1,949	14	0.8%	247
12/16	1,849	16	0.9%	—
12/15	1,706	15	0.9%	—
Annual Growth	**13.7%**	**12.6%**	—	—

2019 Year-End Financials

Debt ratio: —	No. of shares (mil.): 5
Return on equity: 11.14%	Dividends
Cash ($ mil.): 61	Yield: 2.5%
Current ratio: —	Payout: 37.9%
Long-term debt ($ mil.): —	Market value ($ mil.): 433

	STOCK PRICE ($) FY Close	P/E High/Low	PER SHARE ($) Earnings	Dividends	Book Value
12/19	80.15	16 13	5.37	2.04	53.06
12/18	83.25	16 13	5.77	1.96	40.67
12/17	79.80	24 17	3.61	1.86	36.24
12/16	62.29	15 11	4.15	1.84	33.36
12/15	47.40	13 11	3.93	1.80	31.26
Annual Growth	**14.0%**	— —	**8.1%**	**3.2%**	**14.1%**

Camden National Corp. (ME)

Camden National Corporation is the holding company for Camden National Bank which boasts nearly 45 branches in about a dozen Maine counties and provides standard deposit products such as checking and savings accounts CDs and IRAs. Commercial mortgages and loans make up 50% of its loan portfolio while residential mortgages make up another 40% and consumer loans constitute the remainder. Subsidiary Acadia Trust provides trust fiduciary investment management and retirement plan administration services while Camden Financial Consultants offers brokerage and insurance services. The largest bank headquartered in Maine Camden National Bank was founded in 1875 and once issued its own US currency.

Operations

About 63% of Camden National's total revenue came from loan interest (including fees) in 2014 while another 15% came from interest on its US government and sponsored enterprise obligations (investment securities). The rest of its revenue came from deposit account service charges (5%) other service charges and fees (5%) income from fiduciary services (4%) brokerage and insurance commissions (2%) and other miscellaneous income sources. The bank had a staff of 471 employees at the end of 2014.

Geographic Reach

Camden National has around 45 branches in 12 counties throughout Maine with one commercial loan office in Manchester New Hampshire. Its primary markets are in the counties of Androscoggin Cumberland Hancock Kennebec Knox Lincoln Penobscot Piscataquis Somerset Waldo Washington and York.

Sales and Marketing

The company offers deposit and loan services to consumers institutions municipalities non-profits and commercial customers.

Financial Performance

The company has struggled to consistently grow its revenues and profits in recent years mostly due to shrinking interest margins on loans amidst the low-interest environment.

Camden National's revenue dipped by 3% to $112.8 million in 2014 mostly because the bank in 2013 had collected a non-recurring $2.7 million gain from the sale of its five Franklin County branches and because its mortgage banking income fell by $1.1 million as it decided to retain most of its 30-year fixed rate residential mortgage production in 2014.

Despite revenue declines in 2014 the bank's net income jumped by 8% to $24.6 million mostly because in 2013 it had recorded a non-recurring $2.8 million goodwill impairment charge related to its financial services reporting unit. Camden's operating cash levels rose by 1% to $29.9 million for the year on higher cash earnings.

Strategy

The bank competes with larger financial institutions by emphasizing customer service to build customer loyalty and long-term relationships. It also sometimes pursues acquisitions of banks and branches in its target markets in Maine to grow its loan and deposit business.

Camden may also be expanding its franchise beyond Maine in future years. In 2014 it opened a commercial loan office in Manchester New Hampshire enabling it to serve more customers across northern New England.

Mergers and Acquisitions

In March 2015 Camden National Corporation agreed to purchase SBM Financial along with its subsidiary The Bank of Maine subsidiary. The deal expected to be completed in late 2015 would add $813 million in assets and make Camden National Bank Maine's largest community bank.

In late 2012 the bank acquired 15 full-service branches from Bank of America for $12 million.

EXECUTIVES

Vice President Risk Management, Steve Matteo
Evp Coo And Cfo, Deborah A. Jordan, age 54, $223,327 total compensation
Vp And Human Resources Manager, June B. Parent, age 56, $189,248 total compensation
Evp Risk Management, Joanne T. Campbell, age 57, $124,585 total compensation
President And Ceo, Gregory A. (Greg) Dufour, age 59, $398,077 total compensation
Svp Information Technology, Scott Buckheit
Evp Commercial Lending, Timothy P. Nightingale, age 62, $213,846 total compensation
Vice President, Richard Nickerson
Vice President Compliance Manager, Jennifer Mazurek
Vice President Information Security Manager, Anthony Mazzeo
Vice President Credit Risk Officer, Susan Weber
Vice President Loan Servicing, Mark Richards
Vp Sr Mortgage Consultant, Phil Ingraham
Vice President Of Mortgage Operations, Paul Palmer
Senior Vice President Director Of Corporate Services, Susan Giffard
Vice President Commercial Portfolio Manager, Matthew Gilbert
Vice President Mortgage Equity Closings Qc Manager, Angela Arbour
Vice President Senior Trust Officer, Marsha Connors
Vice President, Patricia Harriman
Vp Technology Operations Manager, Tim Crawford

Vice President, Jane Merrill
Avp Financial Consultant, David Doane
**Chairman Camden National Corporation And
Camden National Bank,** Karen W. Stanley, age 74
Auditors: RSM US LLP

LOCATIONS

HQ: Camden National Corp. (ME)
2 Elm Street, Camden, ME 04843
Phone: 207 236-8821 **Fax:** 207 236-6256
Web: www.CamdenNational.com/healthprofunding

PRODUCTS/OPERATIONS

2014 Sales

	$ mil.	% of total
Interest		
Loans including fees	70	63
US government & agency securities	17	14
Other investments	0	1
Noninterest		
Service charges on deposit accounts & others	12	11
Income from fiduciary services	5	4
Brokerage and insurance commission	1	2
Other	5	5
Total	112	100

COMPETITORS

Bangor Savings Bank	People's United
Bar Harbor Bankshares	Financial
KeyCorp	TD Bank USA
Northeast Bancorp	The First Bancorp
Norway Bancorp	

HISTORICAL FINANCIALS

Company Type: Public

Income Statement

FYE: December 31

	ASSETS ($ mil.)	NET INCOME ($ mil.)	INCOME AS % OF ASSETS	EMPLOYEES
12/19	4,429	57	1.3%	639
12/18	4,297	53	1.2%	634
12/17	4,065	28	0.7%	636
12/16	3,864	40	1.0%	631
12/15	3,709	20	0.6%	652
Annual Growth	4.5%	28.5%	—	(0.5%)

2019 Year-End Financials

Debt ratio: 1.33%	No. of shares (mil.): 15
Return on equity: 12.58%	Dividends
Cash ($ mil.): 75	Yield: 2.6%
Current ratio: —	Payout: 33.4%
Long-term debt ($ mil.): —	Market value ($ mil.): 698

	STOCK PRICE ($) FY Close	P/E High/Low	PER SHARE ($) Earnings	Dividends	Book Value
12/19	46.06	13 10	3.69	1.20	31.26
12/18	35.97	14 10	3.39	1.10	27.95
12/17	42.13	26 20	1.82	0.92	25.99
12/16	44.45	19 11	2.57	0.80	25.30
12/15	44.09	26 21	1.73	0.80	23.69
Annual Growth	1.1%	— —	20.8%	10.7%	7.2%

CAMERON INTERNATIONAL CORPORATION

Cameron is a leading manufacturer provider and servicer of oil and gas industry equipment. The company makes products that control pressure at oil and gas wells including blowout preventers chokes controls wellheads measurement tools and valves. The company's products are used for offshore onshore and subsea applications. Cameron is a wholly owned subsidiary of oilfield product and services giant Schlumberger (a major provider of technology for reservoir characterization drilling production and processing services to the oil and gas industry).

Financial Performance

Cameron generates about 15% of Schlumberger's sales. The subsidiary's revenue declined 4% to $6.5 billion on lower sales for its OneSubsea and Valves & Measurements product segments. OneSubsea offers products and services for subsea oil and gas companies including wellheads subsea trees control systems and production system optimization. The company's Valves & Measurements products span valves and measurement systems for oil and gas flow for the upstream midstream and downstream sectors.

Strategy

To keep pace with rivals increasingly adopting automation technology Schlumbeger formed a joint venture in 2019 with Rockwell Automation to form Sensia. Sensia combines Cameron's sensor and measurement products with Rockwell's industrial automation technology and analytics capabilities. The new company's offerings will facilitate automated oilfield operations and connect equipment with software to gather data from sensors and devices. About two-fifths of the JV's revenue is expected to derive from North America.

EXECUTIVES

President Cameron Group, Olivier Le Peuch
Auditors: ERNST & YOUNG LLP HOUSTON TE

LOCATIONS

HQ: CAMERON INTERNATIONAL CORPORATION
4646 W SAM HOUSTON PKWY N, HOUSTON, TX
770418214
Phone: 713 939-2282
Web: WWW.SLB.COM

PRODUCTS/OPERATIONS

Selected Mergers and Acquisitions

COMPETITORS

ABB Inc.
Aker Solutions
Atlas Copco
CIRCOR International
Dresser-Rand
Dril-Quip
Ebara
FMC
Flotek
GE Oil
Ingersoll-Rand Industrial Technologies
McDermott
National Oilwell Varco
Weatherford International

HISTORICAL FINANCIALS

Company Type: Private

Income Statement

FYE: December 31

	REVENUE ($ mil.)	NET INCOME ($ mil.)	NET PROFIT MARGIN	EMPLOYEES
12/14	10,381	848	8.2%	23,000
12/13	9,838	724	7.4%	—
12/12	8,502	750	8.8%	—
Annual Growth	10.5%	6.3%	—	—

Campbell Soup Co

The one of the world's top soup maker Campbell Soup Company's range of products include Campbell's condensed and ready to-serve soups Swanson broth and stocks and Pacific Foods broth. Campbell also makes many other simple foods snacks and beverages including Pace Mexican sauce V8 juices and beverages and Pepperidge Farm baked goods (including those popular tiny Goldfish crackers). The company sold its U.S. refrigerated business Garden Fresh Gourmet business and Bolthouse Farms business in 2019. The company also sold its Kelsen business Arnott's business and European chips business also in 2019. Its biggest customer Wal-Mart accounts for around a fifth of all sales.

HISTORY

Campbell Soup Company began in Camden New Jersey in 1869 as a canning and preserving business founded by icebox maker Abram Anderson and fruit merchant Joseph Campbell. Anderson left in 1876 and Arthur Dorrance took his place. The Dorrance family assumed control after Campbell retired in 1894.

Arthur's nephew John Dorrance joined Campbell in 1897. The young chemist soon found a way to condense soup by eliminating most of its water. Without the heavy bulk of water-filled cans distribution was cheaper; Campbell products quickly spread.

In 1904 the firm introduced the Campbell Kids characters. Entering the California market in 1911 Campbell became one of the first US companies to achieve national distribution of a food brand. It bought Franco-American the first American soup maker in 1915.

The company's ubiquity in American kitchens made its soup can an American icon (consider Andy Warhol's celebrated 1960 print) and brought great wealth to the Dorrance family.

With a reputation for conservative management Campbell began to diversify acquiring V8 juice (1948) Swanson (1955) Pepperidge Farm (1961) Godiva Chocolatier (33% in 1966 full ownership in 1974) Vlasic pickles (1978) and Mrs. Paul's seafood (1982). It introduced Prego spaghetti sauce and LeMenu frozen dinners in the early 1980s.

Much of Campbell's sales growth in the 1990s came not from unit sales but from increasing its prices. In 1993 it took a $300 million restructuring charge and over the next two years it sold poor performers at home and abroad. John Sr.'s grandson Bennett Dorrance took up the role of vice chairman in 1993 becoming the first family member to take a senior executive position in 10 years.

Two years later Campbell paid $1.1 billion for Pace Foods (picante sauce) and acquired Fresh Start Bakeries (buns and muffins for McDonald's) and Homepride (popular cooking sauce in the UK).

As part of its international expansion in 1996 the firm acquired Erasco a top German soup maker and Cheong Chan a food manufacturer in Malaysia. However back at home it sold Mrs. Paul's. In 1997 Campbell sold its Marie's salad dressing operations and bought Groupe Danone's Liebig (France's leading wet-soup brand). Also that year Dale Morrison a relative newcomer to the firm succeeded David Johnson as president and CEO. To reduce costs and focus on other core segments in 1998 Campbell spun off Swanson frozen foods and Vlasic pickles into Vlasic Foods International. (Vlasic later filed bankruptcy and was snapped up in a leveraged buyout.) In 1999 Campbell redesigned its soup can labels altering an American icon.

Morrison resigned abruptly as president and CEO in 2000; Johnson returned to the helm during the search for a permanent chief. In early 2001 Douglas Conant previously of Nabisco Foods joined Campbell as president and CEO. A fresh plan was introduced to spend up to $600 million on marketing product development and quality upgrades (at the expense of shareholder dividends). In 2001 Campbell also bought the Batchelors Royco and Heisse Tasse brands of soup as well as the OXO brand of stock cubes from Unilever for about $900 million. The deal made Campbell the leading soup maker in Europe. In 2003 Campbell bought Snack Foods Limited a leading snack food maker in Australia and Irish dry soup maker Erin Foods from Greencore.

Campbell reorganized its North American business in 2004 into the following units: US Soup Sauces and Beverages; Campbell Away From Home and Canada Mexico and Latin America; Pepperidge Farm; and Godiva Worldwide. (In response to dietary trends the company announced that year that it was removing all trans-fatty acids from its Pepperidge Farm breads.) The company retired the Franco-American brand in 2004; products that carried the brand (most notably SpaghettiOs) now bear the Campbell brand. Also that year company chairman George M. Sherman retired and was replaced by Harvey Golub.

In 2006 Campbell sold its UK and Irish businesses to Premier Foods for about $870 million. Brands involved in the sale included Homepride sauces OXO stock cubes and Batchelors McDonnells and Erin soups.

In 2012 the company purchased Bolthouse Farms for about $1.55 billion from Madison Dearborn Partners. Bolthouse known for selling fresh carrots beverages and salad dressings was expected to further fuel Campbell's US beverage division which had benefited from the rising popularity of the V8 juice brand.

In fiscal 2013 Campbell expanded its access to manufacturing and distribution capabilities in Mexico for its beverages soups broths and sauces after it signed a deal with Grupo Jumex and Conservas La Costeñato. That year it also sold its European simple meals business closing facilities in Belgium France Germany and Sweden.

In August 2013 the soup giant acquired the Denmark-based baked snack maker Kelsen Group for $325 million.

In June 2013 it bought Plum Organics one of the top brands of organic baby food in the US. The company makes organic foods and snacks for babies toddlers and children a fast-growing premium food category. It hoped the purchase would bring a new generation of consumers to Campbell.

EXECUTIVES

President And Ceo, Denise M. Morrison, age 66, $1,100,000 total compensation
Vp And Controller, Anthony P. DiSilvestro, age 61, $642,500 total compensation
President Americas Simple Meals And Beverages, Mark R. Alexander, age 56, $696,667 total compensation
Svp And General Counsel, Adam G. Ciongoli, age 52, $700,000 total compensation
President Campbell Fresh, Edward L. (Ed) Carolan, age 51
President Global Biscuits And Snacks, Luca Mignini, age 57, $674,042 total compensation
Svp Global Research And Development And Quality, Carlos J. Barroso, age 61, $470,000 total compensation
President Campbell Soup Foundation, Kim Fremont Fortunato
Vp And Chief Technology And Information Officer, Francisco Fraga
Svp Integrated Global Services, Bethmara Kessler
Division Vice President Financial, Andrew Ridler
Vice President Business Development Grea, John Shannon
Senior Vice President Global Sales, Alyssa Bansky
Senior Vice President Corporate Strategy, Emily Waldorf
Vice President Sales Us Retail, James Sterbenz
Vice President Fin Cna, Stan Polomski
Government Relations, Luz Alena
Vice President External Development, Roger Wilson
Vice President Initiatives And Network Optimization, Dave Parcher
Vp Of Talent Management Of Culture Of And Organizational Development, Heidi Manna
Vice President Corporate Responsibility And Chief Sustainability Officer, Dave Stangis
Svp Us Sales, Jim Sterbenz
Vp Of Corporate Audit, Kevin Blatcher
Vice President Taxes, Richard Landers
Vice President Logistics, Skip Tappan
Vice President Global Talent And Change Management, David Walsh
Senior Vice President And Chief Legal And Public Affairs Officer, Ellen O Kaden
Vice President Global Procurement, Jose Turkienicz
Vice President Club Channel, Larry Daley
Vice President Global Procurement, Bob Frederick
Vice President Global Walmart, Ian Rowland
Vice President Global Packaging Procurement, Paul Capponi
Vice President Global Indirect Procurement, Chris Calabretta
Vp Human Resources, Xavier Boza
Vp Business Operations, Rick Pifer
Vice President Sales Strategy And Commercialization, Frank Andriuolo
Vp Research And Development Campbell Snacks, George Vindiola
Chairman, Les C. Vinney, age 71
Board Member, Randall Larrimore
Board Member, Bennett Dorrance
Board Member, Mary Malone
Board Member, Fabiola Arredondo
Auditors: PricewaterhouseCoopers LLP

LOCATIONS

HQ: Campbell Soup Co
1 Campbell Place, Camden, NJ 08103-1799
Phone: 856 342-4800   **Fax:** 856 342-3878
Web: www.campbellsoupcompany.com

2019 Sales

	$ mil.	% of total
US	7,492	91
Other	615	8
Total	**8,107**	**100**

PRODUCTS/OPERATIONS

2019 Sales

	$ mil.	% of total
Meals and Beverages	4,322	53
Snacks	3,784	47
Corporate	1	-
Total	**8,107**	**100**

2019 Sales

	$ mil.	% of total
Soup	2,368	29
Baked snacks	3,918	48
Other simple meals	1,082	14
Beverages	738	9
Total	**8,107**	**100**

Selected Brand Names

Domestic
  Away From Home
  Campbell
  Ecce Panis
  Pace
  Pepperidge Farm
  Plum Organics
  Prego
  Select Harvest
  StockPot
  Swanson
  V8 and V8 Splash
  Wolfgang Puck

Selected Subsidiaries

Ecce Panis Inc.
Pepperidge Farm Incorporated
Players Group Limited (Australia)
Sinalopasta S.A. de C.V. (Mexico)
Stockpot Inc.

COMPETITORS

Associated British Foods	Hanover Foods
B&G Foods	Harry's Fresh Foods
Barbara's Bakery	Heinz
Baxters	Hormel
Beech-Nut	Kellogg U.S. Snacks
Big Heart Pet Brands	Mondelez International
Bush Brothers	Morgan Foods
Canyon Creek Food	NORPAC
ConAgra	Nestlé
Dole Food	Odwalla
Frito-Lay	Pacific Coast Producers
General Mills	Peter Rabbit Farms
Gerber Products	Red Gold
Golden Enterprises	Reily Foods
Grimmway Enterprises	Renée's Gourmet Foods
H. J. Heinz Limited	Snyder's-Lance
Hain Celestial	Walkers Snack Foods

HISTORICAL FINANCIALS

Company Type: Public

Income Statement   FYE: August 2

	REVENUE ($ mil.)	NET INCOME ($ mil.)	NET PROFIT MARGIN	EMPLOYEES
08/20*	8,691	1,628	18.7%	14,500
07/19	8,107	211	2.6%	19,000
07/18	8,685	261	3.0%	23,000
07/17	7,890	887	11.2%	18,000
07/16	7,961	563	7.1%	16,500
Annual Growth	2.2%	30.4%	—	(3.2%)

*Fiscal year change

2020 Year-End Financials

Debt ratio: 50.08%	No. of shares (mil.): 302
Return on equity: 87.38%	Dividends
Cash ($ mil.): 859	Yield: 0.0%
Current ratio: 0.78	Payout: 26.1%
Long-term debt ($ mil.): 4,994	Market value ($ mil.): 14,970

	STOCK PRICE ($) FY Close	P/E High/Low	PER SHARE ($) Earnings	Dividends	Book Value
08/20*	49.57	10 8	5.36	1.40	8.49
07/19	40.96	62 46	0.70	1.40	3.66
07/18	40.94	62 38	0.86	1.40	4.53
07/17	52.85	22 18	2.89	1.40	5.44
07/16	62.27	37 25	1.81	1.25	4.95
Annual Growth	(5.5%)	— —	31.2%	2.9%	14.4%

*Fiscal year change

CANDID COLOR SYSTEMS, INC.

EXECUTIVES

Pres-Ceo, Jack E Counts Jr
SEC-Treas, Beverly Ellis
Designer, David J Wall
Chief Financial Officer, Clayton Sliger
Customer Support Manager, Cristina Oconnor
Customer Support Manager, Cristina O'Connor
Bankruptcy Automation Manager, Jack Smiley

LOCATIONS

HQ: CANDID COLOR SYSTEMS, INC.
1300 METROPOLITAN AVE, OKLAHOMA CITY, OK
731082042
Phone: 405 947-8747
Web: WWW.CANDID.COM

HISTORICAL FINANCIALS
Company Type: Private

Income Statement   FYE: July 31

	REVENUE ($ mil.)	NET INCOME ($ mil.)	NET PROFIT MARGIN	EMPLOYEES
07/07	21,742	2,534	11.7%	300
07/05	22	1	8.3%	—
07/04	21	2	10.9%	—
07/03	21	1	9.4%	—
Annual Growth	467.2%	498.3%	—	—

Capital City Bank Group, Inc.

Capital City Bank Group is the holding company for Capital City Bank (CCB) which serves individuals businesses and institutions from some 70 branches in Florida Georgia and Alabama. CCB offers checking savings and money market accounts; CDs; IRAs; Internet banking; and debit and credit cards. Commercial real estate mortgages account for about 40% of its loan portfolio; residential real estate loans also hover near 40%. The bank also originates business loans and consumer loans including credit cards. Capital City also performs data processing services for other financial institutions in its market area.

Operations

In addition to its CCB bank subsidiary which accounts for about 94% of Capital City Bank Group's total revenue the holding company operates three other subsidiaries: Capital City Trust a provider of trust and asset management services; Capital City Banc Investments which offers investments retirement plans and life and long-term care insurance through an agreement with third-party provider INVEST Financial Corporation a subsidiary of Jackson National Life Insurance Company; and data processor Capital City Services Co.

Geographic Reach

Florida is CCB's largest market accounting for about 78% of its revenue. Georgia and Alabama account for 21% and 1% respectively.

Financial Performance

Capital City Bank Group's revenue has slid since the onset of the recession and housing crisis which battered the Florida market and during the uneven recovery. Revenue fell 5% in 2011 vs. 2010 marking the fourth consecutive year of decline. Indeed revenue plunged 74% between 2007 and 2011. However in 2011 the group returned to profitability with net income of $4.9 million following losses in 2010 and 2009.

Interest income decreased by 10% while noninterest income increased 4% in 2011 vs. 2010. Lower interest and fees on loans contributed to the decline in interest income. Growth in bank card and retail brokerage fees contributed to the rise in non-interest income.

Strategy

Capital City Bank Group was founded in 1982 to acquire six banks and has never looked back. While its growth has slowed the company has continued its acquisition strategy buying 15 banks since 1984; it has also expanded by opening new offices. However its home state of Florida was one of the hardest hit during the recession. High unemployment levels contributed to an increase in nonperforming loans in the bank's portfolio which in turn translated to net losses in 2009 and 2010. (Nonperforming loans totaled $75 million or 4.6% of the company's total loan portfolio at the end of 2011.) Capital City is focusing on diversifying its portfolio and reducing problem assets.

EXECUTIVES

Evp And Cfo, J. Kimbrough (Kim) Davis, age 66, $260,000 total compensation
Chairman President And Ceo, William G. (Bill) Smith, age 66, $350,000 total compensation
Credit Administration, Dale A. Thompson
Chief People Officer And President Capital Services Company, Bethany H. (Beth) Corum
President Capital City Banc Investments; President Capital City Trust Company, Bill Moor
President Leon County, Ed West
Residential Mortgage, Tom Allen
Commercial Banking, Ed Canup
Community Banking, Mitch Englert
Vice President, Tolga Dincman
Assistant Vice President, Lisa Elam
Assistant Vice President And Market Leader, Susan Terry
Executive Vice President Co Founder, Katrina Williams
Senior Vice President, Cheryl Thompson
Vice President, Joel Ginaldi
Avp And Treasury Mgt Support Manager, Cindy Richardson
Vice President, Cristie Garrett
Assistant Vice President, Janette Wagner
Vice President And Community Banker, Valerie Hoffler
Senior Vice President, Craig Ellard
Assistant Vice President Mis Analysis, Canington Carol

Vice President Marketing, Walter Hoskins
Assistant Vice President, Sylvia White
Business Banking Assistant Vice President, Myles Bradley
Assistant Vice President, Edie Frasier
Vice President, Karen C Meadows
Assistant Vice President And Community Banker, Janie Stewart
Vice President Information Security, Leanne Staalenburg
Vice President And Trust Officer, Leitta Williamson
Assistant Vice President Business Banker, Terry Huiskens
Vice President, Alex Milton
Vice President, Courtney Armitage
Senior Vice President, Jim Scarboro
Vice President, Catherine Sherman
Vice President Auto Finance, Jim Philippou
Senior Vice President Human Resources Risk Manager, Pamela Gay
Assistant Vice President And Compliance Officer, Sheila D Reddick
Assistant Vice President, Francis M Rolfes
Senior Vice President, Lee Nichols
Vice President Of Human Resources, Linda Nwokeji
Senior Vice President, Brantley Henderson
Executive Vice President Community Banking Manager, Wellington Mary
Assistant Vice President, Yvonne Reed
Vice President Small Business Banker, Jill Tarbox
Senior Vp, Sherry Thompson
Vice President, Stewart Wasson
Auditors: Ernst & Young LLP

LOCATIONS

HQ: Capital City Bank Group, Inc.
217 North Monroe Street, Tallahassee, FL 32301
Phone: 850 402-7821
Web: www.ccbg.com

PRODUCTS/OPERATIONS

2015 Sales

	$ mil.	% of total
Interest		
Loans including fees	73	55
Investment securities	5	5
Funds sold	0	-
Noninterest income		
Deposit fee	22	17
Bank card fees	11	8
Wealth management fees	7	6
Mortgage Banking fees	4	3
Data processing fees	1	1
Other	6	5
Total	**133**	**100**

COMPETITORS

Ameris	Regions Financial
BBX Capital	SunTrust
Bank of America	Thomasville Bancshares
Delta Community Credit Union	

HISTORICAL FINANCIALS
Company Type: Public

Income Statement   FYE: December 31

	ASSETS ($ mil.)	NET INCOME ($ mil.)	INCOME AS % OF ASSETS	EMPLOYEES
12/19	3,088	30	1.0%	815
12/18	2,959	26	0.9%	819
12/17	2,898	10	0.4%	825
12/16	2,845	11	0.4%	853
12/15	2,797	9	0.3%	894
Annual Growth	2.5%	35.6%	—	(2.3%)

2019 Year-End Financials

Debt ratio: 1.92%
Return on equity: 9.79%
Cash ($ mil.): 378
Current ratio: —
Long-term debt ($ mil.): —

No. of shares (mil.): 16
Dividends
Yield: 1.5%
Payout: 26.3%
Market value ($ mil.): 512

	STOCK PRICE ($) FY Close	P/E High/Low	PER SHARE ($) Earnings	Dividends	Book Value
12/19	30.50	17 12	1.83	0.48	19.50
12/18	23.21	17 14	1.54	0.32	18.07
12/17	22.94	41 28	0.64	0.24	16.73
12/16	20.48	32 19	0.69	0.17	16.34
12/15	15.35	31 26	0.53	0.13	15.99
Annual Growth	**18.7%**	—	**36.3%**	**38.6%**	**5.1%**

Capital One Financial Corp

Thanks to its "What's in Your Wallet" branding campaign Capital One Financial is one of the most recognizable issuers of Visa and MasterCard credit cards in the US. It offers credit and debit card products auto loans and other consumer lending products in markets across the U.S. The company also offer products outside of the U.S. principally through Capital One (Europe) plc ("COEP") and through a branch of COBNA in Canada. Capital One holds some 45 million customer accounts in the US Canada and the UK and maintains a deposit portfolio worth roughly $250 billion. It boasts a banking network of hundreds of branches (mostly in about five US states) and maintains a strong online presence with its internet and mobile banking applications.

HISTORY

Capital One Financial is a descendant of the Bank of Virginia which was formed in 1945. The company began issuing products similar to credit cards in 1953 and was MasterCard issuer #001. Acquisitions and mergers brought some 30 banks and several finance and mortgage companies under the bank's umbrella between 1962 and 1986 when Bank of Virginia became Signet Banking.

Signet's credit card operations had reached a million customers in 1988 when the bank hired consultants Richard Fairbank and Nigel Morris (Fairbank is now chairman and CEO) to implement their "Information-Based Strategy." Under the duo's leadership the bank began using sophisticated data-collection methods to gather massive amounts of information on existing or prospective customers; it then used the information to design and mass-market customized products to the customer.

In 1991 — after creating an enormous database and developing sophisticated screening processes and direct-mail marketing tactics — Signet escalated the credit card wars luring customers from its rivals with its innovative balance-transfer credit card. The card let customers of other companies transfer what they owed on higher-interest cards to a Signet card with a lower introductory rate.

The new card immediately drew imitators (by 1997 balance-transfer cards accounted for 85% of credit card solicitations). After skimming off the least risky customers Fairbank and Morris began going after less desirable credit customers who could be charged higher rates. The result was what they call second-generation products — secured and unsecured cards with lower credit lines and higher annual percentage rates and fees for higher-risk customers.

The credit card business had grown to 5 million customers by 1994 but at a high cost to Signet which had devoted most of its resources to finding and servicing credit card holders. That year Signet spun off its credit card business as Capital One to focus on banking. (Signet was later acquired by First Union.)

The company moved into Florida and Texas in 1995 and into Canada and the UK in 1996; that year it established its savings bank mainly to offer products and services to its cardholders. In 1997 the company used this unit to move into deposit accounts buying a deposit portfolio from J. C. Penney. In 1998 the company began marketing its products to such clients as immigrants and high school students (whose parents must co-sign for the card). The company also expanded in terms of products and geography acquiring auto lender Summit Acceptance and opening a new office in Nottingham England.

In 1999 the firm's growth continued. The company stepped up its marketing efforts and was rewarded with significant boosts to its non-interest income and customer base. The next year the company launched The Capital One Place an Internet shopping site. In 2001 the company acquired AmeriFee which provides loans for elective medical and dental surgery; and PeopleFirst Inc. the nation's largest online provider of direct motor vehicle loans.

In response to industry-wide concern over subprime lending Capital One agreed in 2002 to beef up reserves on its subprime portfolio. Also in 2002 the company's UK operations proved profitable for the first time.

The company expanded into banking in 2005 and 2006 with the acquisitions of Hibernia and North Fork Bancorporation respectively. The deals gave it a boost in the banking sector expanding its presence both geographically in the Northeast and in the South and turning the company into one of the top bank holding companies in the US. The $13.2 billion stock-and-cash North Fork deal gave the company more than 300 bank branches in New York New Jersey and Connecticut.

The 2005 purchase of New Orleans-based Hibernia was a stock-and-cash transaction valued at some $5 billion nearly 10% less than the originally agreed-upon price. The transaction was delayed then renegotiated after Hurricane Katrina devastated Hibernia's home city. Hibernia which relocated to Houston adopted the Capital One moniker.

Capital One closed wholesale lender GreenPoint Mortgage Funding acquired as part of its acquisition of North Fork in 2007. The unit suffered from the credit woes that have plagued the subprime mortgage industry.

The company expanded its franchise into the Washington DC market in 2009 by buying Chevy Chase Bank for some $475 million in cash and stock.

In 2011 the company boosted its credit card business with the acquisition of GE Capital's $1.3 billion Hudson's Bay credit card portfolio tripling the number of Canadian customer accounts Capital One services. That year Capital One also acquired Kohl's existing $3.7 billion private-label credit card portfolio.

Capital One grew its US credit card business once again with the 2012 acquisition of HSBC's US card portfolio for some $2.6 billion.

In 2013 Capital One introduced its Capital One Quicksilver credit card offering cardholders a simple way to earn and redeem higher-than-average cash back rewards.

EXECUTIVES

General Counsel And Corporate Secretary, John G. Finneran, age 70, $1,016,538 total compensation

Chairman And Ceo, Richard D. (Rich) Fairbank, age 69

Head Of Finance And Corporate Development, Stephen S. (Steve) Crawford, age 55, $1,592,692 total compensation

Cfo, R. Scott Blackley, age 52, $617,769 total compensation

Cio, Robert M. Alexander, age 55

President Commercial Banking, Michael C. Slocum, age 63

Evp Europe, Sanjiv Yajnik, age 63, $962,654 total compensation

President Retail And Direct Banking, Jonathan W. Witter, age 50, $870,769 total compensation

Chief Enterprise Services Officer And Chief Of Staff To The Ceo, Frank G. LaPrade, age 53, $974,577 total compensation

Chief Risk Officer, Kevin S. Borgmann, age 48

President U.s. Card, Michael J. Wassmer, age 50

President International And Small Business Card, Christopher T. Newkirk, age 49

Vice President, Khary Scott

Vice President Human Resources, Sammy Duff

Senior Vice President, Lein B Tung

Vice President, Ashish Tandon

Vice President Senior Associate General Counsel, Kathryn Hu

Assistant Vice President Information S, Carl Pomplon

Senior Vice President, Richard Amador

Vice President, Sonu Mittal

Vice President, Anthony Fermo

Vice President, Brad Dolbec

Senior Vice President, Roy Aksdal

Vice President Human Resources, Guenet Beshah

Vice President Senior Director, John Walsh

Vice President, Hamilton Blanton

Vice President, Ehab Awadallah

Vice President Card Recoveries, Amanda Aghdami

Vice President Corporate Audit Services, Erika Ray

Vice President, Michael Lockery

Vice President Sales And Service Strategy, Shail Moorjani

Vice President, Stephanie Tyner

Managing Vice President Treasury Balance, Jeffrey Kuzbel

Managing Vice President, Johan Gericke

Vice President, Shahram Elghanayan

Senior Vice President, John Blackwelder

Vice President Private Banking, Bob Sferrazza

Vice President And Senior Business Relationship Banker, Franklin Carrero

Vice President, Theresa Bedeau

Senior Vice President, Gregory Horstman

Vice President Business Banking Group, Jamila Braithwaite

Vice President Business Banking, Nate Hoffman

Senior Vice President, Bryan N Pynchon

Assistant Vice President Commercial Real Estate, Alexander Thezan

Managing Vice President, John Walker

Vice President Business Banking, Maria Brosnahan

Vp Small Business Banking, Charles Middleton

Vice President, Kim Dean

Vice President, David P Blasini

Managing Vice President, Detelina Ivanova

Vice President Strategy, Sarah Strauss

Vice President Us Card, Emilia Lopez

Managing Vice President, Kara Lyons

Assistant Vice President Quality Assurance Manager, Gloria Stafford

Senior Vice President, Robbie Naquin

Vice President, Kader Ma

Senior Vice President, Ric Kearny
Vice President And Trust Officer, Jean Moncla
Vice President, Patrick Gemmell
Vice President Of Human Resources, Joel Martinez
Senior Vice President, Kristen Croxton
Assistant Vice President, Karen Eleser
Svp Commercial Real Estate, Jeff Wallace
Vice President Regional Executive North Tx North La, Laura Mathieu
Assistant Vice President, Hosai Akbarzadeh
Senior Vice President, Brian Hayes
Senior Vice President, Frank Arceri
Vice President Corporate Security, Timothy Rigg
Vice President Small Business Card, Jason Walker
Senior Vice President Origination, Brian Sykes
Assistant Vice President, Cristina Brum
Senior Vice President, Fran Nuchims
Vice President, Diana Macculley
Vice President, Henriette Henriette Harris
Assistant Vice President Loan Administrator, Terrie Harris
Vice President, Shelley Desilva
Vice President, Billy Mcardle
Vice President, Ken Shah
Assistant Vice President Branch Manager, Jessica Kitzmann
Vice President Private Underwriter, Curtis Vincent
Vice President, Enrico Panno
Senior Vice President, Tom Higgins
Assistant Vice President Manager, James Rocco
Senior Vice President, Richard Wolbach
Vice President Business Banking, Fabian Martin
Vice President, Sal Fratanduono
Assistant Vice President Merchant Services Sales Advisor, Diane Slatkin
Senior Vice President, Jennifer Driscoll
Front Line Manager Assistant Vice President, Patricia Milton
Senior Vice President, Andrew Mahtaney
Assistant Vice President, Cindy Lau
Senior Vice President, Jonathan Wood
Assistant Vice President, Stanley Liu
Vice President Business Banker, Joshua Prejean
Assistant Vice President Commercial Banking, Diane Lee
Senior Vice President Managing Underwriter, Marlene Schwartz
Assistant Vice President, Milos Milosevic
Vice President, Robert Plank
Senior Vice President, Diane Dolce
Assistant Vice President, Roland Annan
Vice President Senior Manager, Kathleen Cavanaugh
Assistant Vice President, Mitchell Hart
Vice President, Christine Pascarella
Vice President Regulatory Relations, Morris Thompson
Vice President Commercial Real Estate, Michael Monroe
Vice President Commercial Real Estate, Katie Kennedy
Vice President, Luis Otoya
Business Banker Vice President, Khadija Basir
Senior Vice President, Jon Oldham
Vice President Of Finance, Steve Braskamp
Vice President, Ilene O'Tero
Executive Vice President, Paul Widuch
Vice President, Ladan Karami
Assistant Vice President And Specialty Sales Process Manager, Darla Smith
Vice President Of Business Banking, Ryan Cash
Vice President Account Management, Kenneth Hund
Vice President Capital One, Brent Reynolds
Senior Vice President, Adam Ostrach
Vice President Finance, Darrell Alexander
Senior Vice President, Ali Zaidi
Vice President Finance, Rena Friske
Managing Vice President, Michelle Moss
Vice President Litigation, Nicholas Sladic

Vice President Human Resources Operations, Leslie Taylor
Senior Vice President Treasury Management Sales, Neil Becker
Mvp Portfolio Management, Jeffrey Juliane
Senior Vice President, Paul Darrigo
Vice President, Allen Rebstock
Vice President Institutional Equity Sales, James Brady
Senior Vice President, Alicia Cook
Senior Vice President, Kevin Michel
Senior Vice President, Jeff Lee
Senior Vice President, Shelby Davis
Vice President Deputy Chief Underwriter, Tina Quirin
Vice President Retail Bank Operations, John Dudas
Vice President Treasury Sales, Stacey Beckmann
Vice President, Jamie Lutton
Vice President Data Product Innovation, Philip Kim
Vice President Software Engineering, Tarik Essawi
Assistant Vice President, Andrew Kwok
Vice President, Karina Iturrios
Assistant Vice President, Melinda Rozsalyi
Vice President Underwriting, Joel Goodman
Vice President, Saideh Meeker
Vice President, Tressa Bauer
Assistant Vice President Branch Manager, Philip Allen
Senior Vice President Senior Director, Michael Prendergast
Vice President, Scott Miller
Vice President Relationship Manager, Chase Steinberg
Vice President New Product Development, Yumi Clark
Vice President Business Relationship Manager, Casey Collins
Auditors: Ernst & Young LLP

LOCATIONS

HQ: Capital One Financial Corp
1680 Capital One Drive, McLean, VA 22102
Phone: 703 720-1000
Web: www.capitalone.com

PRODUCTS/OPERATIONS

2018 Sales

	$ mil.	% of total
Interest		
Loans held for investment	24,728	76
Investment securities	2,211	7
Cash equivalents and other interest-earning assets	237	1
Interest Expense	4,301	-
Non-interest		
Interchange fees net	2,823	8
Service charges & other customer fees	1,585	5
Net securities gains (losses)	(209)	-
Others	1,002	3
Total	28	100

2018 Segment sales

	$ mil.	% of total
Credit card	17,687	63
Consumer banking	7,212	26
Commercial banking	2,896	10
Others	281	1
Total	28,076	100

2018 Loans

	% of total
Credit card	
Domestic credit card	43
International card business	4
Consumer banking	
Auto	23
Retail banking	1
Commercial banking	
Commercial and multifamily real estate	12
Commercial and industrial	17
Total	100

Selected Products

Auto Loans
Business Credit Cards
Commercial Banking
Investing
Personal Banking
Personal Credit Cards
Small Business Banking

COMPETITORS

Alliance Data Systems	GM Financial
American Express	HSBC USA
Bank of America	JPMorgan Chase
Citigroup	PNC Financial
Credit Acceptance	Regions Financial
Discover	Wells Fargo

HISTORICAL FINANCIALS

Company Type: Public

Income Statement

FYE: December 31

	ASSETS ($ mil.)	NET INCOME ($ mil.)	INCOME AS % OF ASSETS	EMPLOYEES
12/19	390,365	5,546	1.4%	51,900
12/18	372,538	6,015	1.6%	47,600
12/17	365,693	1,982	0.5%	49,300
12/16	357,033	3,751	1.1%	47,300
12/15	334,048	4,050	1.2%	45,400
Annual Growth	4.0%	8.2%	—	3.4%

2019 Year-End Financials

Debt ratio: 14.27%	No. of shares (mil.): 456
Return on equity: 10.11%	Dividends
Cash ($ mil.): 13,407	Yield: 1.5%
Current ratio: —	Payout: 14.4%
Long-term debt ($ mil.): —	Market value ($ mil.): 46,985

	STOCK PRICE ($) FY Close	P/E High/Low		PER SHARE ($) Earnings	Dividends	Book Value
12/19	102.91	9	7	11.05	1.60	127.06
12/18	75.59	9	6	11.82	1.60	110.47
12/17	99.58	29	22	3.49	1.60	100.37
12/16	87.24	13	8	6.89	1.60	98.94
12/15	72.18	13	10	7.07	1.50	89.68
Annual Growth	9.3%	—	—	11.8%	1.6%	9.1%

Capitol Federal Financial Inc

Dorothy and Toto may not be in Kansas anymore but Capitol Federal Financial is. The holding company owns Capitol Federal Savings Bank the largest bank headquarted there. The savings bankÂ serves metropolitan areasÂ of the Sunflower StateÂ as well asÂ Kansas City Missouri throughÂ aboutÂ 45 branches includingÂ nearly aÂ dozen inside retail stores such as Target Price Chopper and Dillons. Serving consumers and commercial customers theÂ thrift offers standard servicesÂ such as mortgages and loans depositsÂ and retail investments. Its Capitol Agency affiliate sells life liability homeowners renters and vehicle insurance.

EXECUTIVES

Chairman President And Ceo, John B. Dicus, age 59, $581,484 total compensation

Evp Cfo And Treasurer, Kent G. Townsend, age 58, $303,991 total compensation

Evp And Chief Lending Officer, Rick C. Jackson, $163,690 total compensation

Evp Corporate Services, Carlton A Ricketts

Evp General Counsel, Natalie Haag

Evp Retail Operations, Frank H. Wright, $202,362 total compensation

Vice President Information Technology Delivery Systems, Tamara Vande Velde

Executive Vice President Retail Operations, Daniel Lehman

Vice President Security Business, Kevin Moore

First Vice President, Rodney Martin

Vice President, David Richardson

Vice President Consumer Lending Man, Mike Cast

Vice President Security, Ed Cox

First Vice President Senior Loan Operations Manage, Jacque Taylor

Vice President, Wanda Espinosa

First Vice President: Mortgage Lending, Kevin Brittain

Vice President Information Technology Security And Risk, Steve Huff

First Vice President, Tara Van Houweling

First Vice President Director Of Marketing, Becky Moore

Assistant Vice President Network And Telecom Supervisor, Kevin Nelson

Vice President Deposit Services, Clint Devoe

Vice President Delivery Systems Manager, Travis Buchanan

First Vice President, Sarah Sanders

First Vice President, Sarah Shute

Vice President Accounting Manager, Angie Whalen

First Vice President, Joel Oliver

Vice President Chief Appraiser, Susan Sirridge

Vice President, Susan Fickler

Vice President, Debbie Wempe

Vice President Commercial Lending, Joseph Hoytal

Vice President, Christy Rudrow

Board Member, Reginald Robinson

Board Member, James Morris

Board Member, Michel Cole

Secretary Treasurer, Ashley Isbell

Auditors: DELOITTE & TOUCHE LLP

LOCATIONS

HQ: Capitol Federal Financial Inc
700 South Kansas Avenue, Topeka, KS 66603
Phone: 785 235-1341
Web: www.capfed.com

PRODUCTS/OPERATIONS

2016 Sales

	$ mil.	% of total
Interest Income		
Loans receivable	243	75
Mortgage backed securities	29	9
FHLB stock	12	4
Cash and cash equivalents	9	3
Investment securities	5	2
Non-Interest Income		
Retail fees and charges	14	4
Income from bank-owned life insurance	3	1
Other non-interest income	5	2
Total	**324**	**100**

COMPETITORS

Bank of America	Landmark Bancorp
Commerce Bancshares	U.S. Bancorp
First Federal of Olathe	UMB Financial

HISTORICAL FINANCIALS

Company Type: Public

Income Statement

FYE: September 30

	ASSETS ($ mil.)	NET INCOME ($ mil.)	INCOME AS % OF ASSETS	EMPLOYEES
09/20	9,487	64	0.7%	793
09/19	9,340	94	1.0%	773
09/18	9,449	98	1.0%	775
09/17	9,192	84	0.9%	708
09/16	9,267	83	0.9%	676
Annual Growth	0.6%	(6.2%)	—	4.1%

2020 Year-End Financials

Debt ratio: 18.86%	No. of shares (mil.): 138
Return on equity: 4.91%	Dividends
Cash ($ mil.): 185	Yield: 7.3%
Current ratio: —	Payout: 138.7%
Long-term debt ($ mil.): —	Market value ($ mil.): 1,287

	STOCK PRICE ($) FY Close	P/E High/Low	PER SHARE ($) Earnings	Dividends	Book Value
09/20	9.27	31 19	0.47	0.68	9.25
09/19	13.78	21 18	0.68	0.98	9.45
09/18	12.74	21 17	0.73	0.88	9.85
09/17	14.70	27 21	0.63	0.88	9.90
09/16	14.07	23 19	0.63	0.84	10.13
Annual Growth	(9.9%)	— —	(7.1%)	(5.1%)	(2.3%)

CapStar Financial Holdings Inc

Auditors: Elliott Davis, LLC

LOCATIONS

HQ: CapStar Financial Holdings Inc
1201 Demonbreun Street, Suite 700, Nashville, TN 37203
Phone: 615 732-6400
Web: www.capstarbank.com

HISTORICAL FINANCIALS

Company Type: Public

Income Statement

FYE: December 31

	ASSETS ($ mil.)	NET INCOME ($ mil.)	INCOME AS % OF ASSETS	EMPLOYEES
12/19	2,037	22	1.1%	289
12/18	1,963	9	0.5%	295
12/17	1,344	1	0.1%	175
12/16	1,333	9	0.7%	170
12/15	1,206	7	0.6%	166
Annual Growth	14.0%	31.2%	—	14.9%

2019 Year-End Financials

Debt ratio: —	No. of shares (mil.): 18
Return on equity: 8.50%	Dividends
Cash ($ mil.): 101	Yield: 1.1%
Current ratio: —	Payout: 24.0%
Long-term debt ($ mil.): —	Market value ($ mil.): 306

	STOCK PRICE ($) FY Close	P/E High/Low	PER SHARE ($) Earnings	Dividends	Book Value
12/19	16.65	14 11	1.20	0.19	14.87
12/18	14.73	30 19	0.67	0.08	14.35
12/17	20.77	169125	0.12	0.00	12.69
12/16	21.96	22 16	0.81	0.00	12.42
Annual Growth	(6.7%)	— —	10.3%	—	4.6%

Capstead Mortgage Corp.

Capstead Mortgage is a self-managed real estate investment trust (REIT) with holdings in mortgage-backed securities. It makes leveraged investments in single-family residential adjustable-rate mortgage securities issued and backed by government agencies such as Fannie Mae Freddie Mac and Ginnie Mae. It occasionally makes limited investments in credit-sensitive commercial mortgage assets as well. The REIT typically funds its investment activities through short-term borrowings or equity offerings. Founded in 1985 Capstead is one of the oldest publicly traded mortgage REITs in the US and manages an investment portfolio worth nearly $1.17 billion.

Operations

Capstead's nearly $1.17 billion investment portfolios are made up of almost exclusively short-duration adjustable-rate mortgage (ARM) Agency Securities.

Unlike fixed-term securities that pay a static rate of interest short-duration ARM securities correspond with interest rate changes and are able to change the interest payments in a relatively short amount of time (e.g. If interest rates rise ARM securities can raise the rate of interest paid to security holders within a year or a few years.). The securities also have limited or no credit risk because payments are guaranteed by government agencies.

Geographic Reach

Capstead's headquarters are located in Dallas Texas in office space leased by the company.

Financial Performance

Capstead Mortgage has struggled with declining revenues over the past few years largely due to depressed interest rates. Revenue fell below $100 million in 2016 and 2017. Net income also fell under the $100-million-mark in 2016 and stayed there the following year falling further year after year until it plunged into a loss in 2019.

Revenue rose 12% to $69.1 million in 2019 from $62 million in 2018. Capstead's interest income grew significantly that year despite higher recorded interest expenses.

Following Capstead's profit of $50.1 million in 2018 the company posted a loss of $35.3 million in 2019. Net income was negatively affected during 2019 primarily by losses on hedging-related derivatives of $91 million due largely to declining interest rates.

The company ended 2019 with $105.4 million in net cash a $45.1 million increase over what it had at the end of 2018. Operating activities provided $154.3 million and investing activities provided $738.9 million from residential mortgage investment collections. Financing activities used $848 million mostly for payments of repurchases arrangements payments on derivative settlements and dividends paid.

Strategy

Capstead's investment strategy involves managing a leveraged portfolio of residential mortgage pass-through securities consisting of relatively short-duration adjustable-rate mortgage (ARM) securities issued and guaranteed by government-sponsored enterprises either Fannie Mae or Freddie Mac or by an agency of the federal government Ginnie Mae.

This strategy differentiates Capstead from its peers because ARM loans underlying its investment portfolio can reset to more current interest rates within a relatively short period of time. This positions the company to benefit from a potential recovery in financing spreads that typically contract during periods of rising interest rates and can result in smaller fluctuations in portfolio values compared to portfolios containing a significant amount of longer-duration fixed-rate mortgage securities.

Company Background

After its founding in 1985 Capstead was initially a conduit for nonconforming loans but adopted its current strategy in 2000 and now invests only in securities with implied AAA ratings.

HISTORY

Former Chairman and CEO Ronn Lytle formed Capstead Mortgage (originally called Lomas Mortgage Corp.) and took it public in 1985 to structure and manage mortgage investments. Lytle had previously been an SVP at mortgage banking firm Lomas & Nettleman Co. (later Lomas Mortgage USA) which provided initial funding and some management services.

In 1989 the firm became Capstead Mortgage and acquired Strategic Mortgage Investment. Capstead Mortgage entered the mortgage servicing business in 1992 and acquired Tyler Cabot Mortgage Securities Fund. The company severed its ties to Lomas after 1992.

As market conditions changed the company adjusted its strategy. In 1994 Capstead Mortgage stopped issuing collateralized mortgage obligations and instead began acquiring interest-only mortgage securities. In 1996 the investor reduced its commitment to adjustable-rate mortgage securities and increased its investments in interest-only mortgage securities.

By early 1998 the firm had serviced more than 400000 mortgage loans and developed a mortgage investment portfolio worth more than $10 billion. Capstead Mortgage even ventured into originating mortgages. With its servicing income threatened by prepayments the firm sold its mortgage servicing and writing operations that year.

In 1999 the company began rebuilding its investment portfolio which had lost value due to mortgage investment market conditions; it accepted a $51 million cash infusion from privately held real estate investor Fortress Investment in return for a share of Capstead Mortgage's stock.

The following year Capstead Mortgage sold off $1.4 billion in medium-term and fixed-rate securities opting instead to invest in adjustable-rate securities.

Capstead made its first direct investment in real estate in 2002 investing in a portfolio of seven senior living properties in Georgia Florida Ohio Virginia and Texas. It sold one property about five months after the purchase and the rest at the end of 2005.

EXECUTIVES

Evp And Chief Investment Officer, Robert R. Spears, age 58, $525,000 total compensation

President Ceo And Cfo, Phillip A. Reinsch, age 59, $420,000 total compensation

Chairman, Jack Biegler, age 76

Auditors: Ernst & Young LLP

LOCATIONS

HQ: Capstead Mortgage Corp.
8401 North Central Expressway, Suite 800, Dallas, TX 75225-4404

Phone: 214 874-2323

Web: www.capstead.com

PRODUCTS/OPERATIONS

2017 Sales

	$ mil.	% of total
Interest	361	100
Investment premium amortization	(128.8)	-
Interest expense	145	-
Total	**87**	**100**

COMPETITORS

AG Mortgage Investment Trust

ARMOUR Residential REIT

Annaly Capital Management

Anworth Mortgage Asset

Dynex Capital

MFA Financial

Redwood Trust

HISTORICAL FINANCIALS

Company Type: Public

Income Statement

FYE: December 31

	ASSETS ($ mil.)	NET INCOME ($ mil.)	INCOME AS % OF ASSETS	EMPLOYEES
12/19	11,520	(35)	—	14
12/18	12,186	50	0.4%	15
12/17	13,733	79	0.6%	13
12/16	13,576	82	0.6%	14
12/15	14,446	108	0.7%	14
Annual Growth	(5.5%)	—	—	0.0%

2019 Year-End Financials

Debt ratio: 90.05%
Return on equity: (-3.31%)
Cash ($ mil.): 105
Current ratio: —
Long-term debt ($ mil.): —

No. of shares (mil.): 94
Dividends
Yield: 5.9%
Payout: —
Market value ($ mil.): 749

	STOCK PRICE ($) FY Close	P/E High/Low	PER SHARE ($) Earnings	Dividends	Book Value
12/19	7.92	— —	(0.62)	0.47	11.35
12/18	6.67	28 20	0.34	0.49	12.42
12/17	8.65	17 13	0.65	0.80	12.95
12/16	10.19	15 11	0.70	0.95	13.00
12/15	8.74	13 9	0.97	1.14	13.55
Annual Growth	(2.4%)	— —	—	(19.9%)	(4.3%)

Cardinal Health, Inc.

When your local pharmacy runs low on drugs or supplies it might just call Cardinal Health. The company is a top distributor of pharmaceuticals and other medical supplies and equipment in the US. Its pharmaceutical division provides supply chain services including branded generic and specialty pharmaceutical and OTC drug distribution. It also franchises Medicine Shoppe and Medicap Pharmacy retail pharmacies. Cardinal's medical division parcels out medical laboratory and surgical supplies. Customers include retail pharmacies hospitals health care systems surgery centers nursing homes doctor's offices clinical labs and other health care businesses. The US accounts for the majority of Cardinal's sales.

Operations

Cardinal Health operates through two primary segments — Pharmaceutical and Medical.

Pharmaceutical distribution primarily to pharmacy customers across the US accounts for more than 95%% of Cardinal Health's sales. Through its Specialty Solutions division it distributes specialty pharmaceutical products and provides consulting patient support logistics group purchasing and other services. Its Nuclear and Precision Health Solutions division prepare and deliver radiopharmaceuticals for use in nuclear imaging and other procedures. This division also contract manufactures a radiopharmaceutical treatment (Xofigo) and holds the North American rights to manufacture and distribute Lymphoseek a radiopharmaceutical diagnostic imaging agent.

Its Medical segment (accounts less than 5% of sales) manufactures and sources branded general and specialty medical surgical and laboratory products. These products include exam and surgical gloves; needle syringe and sharps disposal; compression; incontinence; nutritional delivery; wound care; cardiovascular and endovascular; single-use surgical drapes gowns and apparel; fluid suction and collection systems; urology; operating room supply; and electrode product lines. Also this segment also assembles and sells sterile and non-sterile procedure kits.

Geographic Reach

Based in Dublin Ohio Almost all of Cardinal Health's revenue generates in the US though it operates in about 45 countries worldwide.

Its Pharmaceutical segment operated one national logistics center; a number of primary pharmaceutical and specialty distribution facilities as well as nuclear pharmacy and radiopharmaceutical manufacturing facilities. The Medical segment operated medical-surgical distribution assembly manufacturing and other operating facilities in the US.

Outside the US and Puerto Rico its Medical segment operated manufacturing facilities in Canada Costa Rica the Dominican Republic Germany Ireland Japan Malaysia Malta Mexico and Thailand.

Sales and Marketing

Cardinal Health sells to thousands of pharmacies and provides support to hospitals throughout the US. Its largest customers are CVS Health (about 25% of total revenue) and OptumRx (nearly 15% of revenue); its five largest customers combined account for around half of its total revenues. Group purchasing organizations are also key to the company's business with Vizient and Premier together accounting for more than 20% of total revenues. Other customers include surgery centers clinics physician practices and clinical laboratories.

Though the bulk of the company's operations consist of direct promotion sales and distribution of drugs and medical supplies Cardinal Health does use some third-party distributors for the manufactured products from its Medical segment.

Financial Performance

Revenue for fiscal 2019 was $145.5 billion a 6% increase from the prior year primarily due to sales growth from pharmaceutical distribution and specialty pharmaceutical customers partially offset by the February 2018 divestiture of our China distribution business.

The company's net income increased by $1.1 billion to $1.4 billion compared to the prior year with $259 million.

Cash in the end of 2019 increased by $768 million to $2.5 billion compared to the prior year with $1.8 billion. Cash provided by operations and investing activities were $2.7 billion and $338 million respectively. Cash used for financing activities was $2.3 billion.

Strategy

The company has acquired a number of businesses over the years that have enhanced its core strategic areas of Cardinal Health Brand medical products generic pharmaceutical distribution and services specialty pharmaceutical products and services international and post-acute care. Cardinal Health expect to continue to pursue additional acquisitions in the future.

Mergers and Acquisitions

In early 2019 Cardinal Health acquired Mirixa which provides tools to help pharmacies manage medications from the National Community Pharmacists Association. Mirixa joined Cardinal's Outcomes MTM business.

Company Background

Cardinal Health harks back to Cardinal Foods a food wholesaler named for Ohio's state bird. In 1971 Robert Walter then 26 and with the ink still fresh on his Harvard MBA acquired Cardinal in a leveraged buyout.

In 1980 Cardinal moved into pharmaceuticals distribution with the acquisition of Zanesville. It went public in 1983 as Cardinal Distribution and Walter began looking for more acquisitions. Cardinal soon expanded nationwide by swallowing other distributors. In 1988 Cardinal sold its food group and narrowed its focus to pharmaceuticals.

HISTORY

Cardinal Health harks back to Cardinal Foods a food wholesaler named for Ohio's state bird. In 1971 Robert Walter then 26 and with the ink still fresh on his Harvard MBA acquired Cardinal in a leveraged buyout. He hoped to grow Cardinal by acquisitions but was frustrated when he found that the food distribution industry was already highly consolidated.

In 1980 Cardinal moved into pharmaceuticals distribution with the acquisition of Zanesville. It went public in 1983 as Cardinal Distribution and Walter began looking for more acquisitions. Cardinal soon expanded nationwide by swallowing other distributors. During the 1980s these purchases included two pharmaceuticals distributors headquartered in New York and a Massachusetts-based pharmaceuticals and food distributor.

In 1988 Cardinal sold its food group including Midland Grocery and Mr. Moneysworth to Roundy's and narrowed its focus to pharmaceuticals.

Drug distributors joined the rest of the pharmaceutical industry in its rush toward consolidation during the 1990s. Cardinal's acquisitions in those years included Ohio Valley-Clarksburg (1990 the Mid-Atlantic) Chapman Drug Co. (1991 Tennessee) PRN Services (1993 Michigan) Solomons Co. (1993 Georgia) Humiston-Keeling (1994 Illinois) and Behrens (1994 Texas).

One of Cardinal's most important acquisitions during this period was its cash purchase of Whitmire Distribution in 1994. Formerly Amfac Health Care Whitmire had been a subsidiary of Amfac one of Hawaii's "Big Five" landholders. When Amfac Health Care was spun off in 1988 its president Melburn Whitmire led a management group that acquired a majority interest. When Cardinal bought it Whitmire was the US's #6 drug wholesaler; the purchase bumped Cardinal up to #3. At that time the company changed its name to Cardinal Health and Melburn Whitmire became Cardinal's vice chairman.

In 1995 Cardinal made its biggest acquisition yet when it purchased St. Louis-based Medicine Shoppe International the US's largest franchisor of independent retail pharmacies. Founded by two St. Louis obstetricians in 1970 the Medicine Shoppe had 987 US outlets and 107 abroad at the time of its purchase by Cardinal (for $348 million in stock).

Over the next few years Cardinal continued to grow through acquisitions including automatic drug-dispensing system maker Pyxis pharmaceutical packaging company PCI Services and pharmacy management services company Owen Healthcare (which became Cardinal Health Pharmacy Management).

EXECUTIVES

Evp Customer Support Services And Cio, Patricia B. (Patty) Morrison, age 61

Chief Human Resources Officer, Pamela O. (Pam) Kimmet, age 61

President Nuclear Pharmacy Services, Tiffany P. Olson, age 61

Ceo And Director, Michael C. (Mike) Kaufmann, age 57, $721,311 total compensation

Ceo Medical Segment, Donald M. (Don) Casey, age 61, $671,311 total compensation

Chief Legal And Compliance Officer, Craig S. Morford, age 61, $531,311 total compensation

President Cardinal Health Specialty Solutions, Joseph I. DePinto, age 53

President U.s. Pharmaceutical Distribution, Jon Giacomin, age 55, $542,623 total compensation

Evp Global Sourcing, Craig Cowman

President Cordis, David J. Wilson

President Cardinal Health At Home, Steve Mason

President Global Commercial Solutions, Steve Blazejewski

Evp Strategy And Corporate Development, Michele Holcomb

Evp Deputy General Counsel And Corporate Secretary, Jessica L. Mayer

President Us Pharmaceutical Distribution, Debbie Weitzman

Svp And Cfo Cardinal Health Midecal Division, Jorge M. Gomez

Svp Eit Shared Services, Scot Lindsey

Vice President, Kraig Corwin

Senior Vice President Global Sourcing, Stefan Grunwald

Pharmacy Manager, John Miller

Vice President, Marc Delorenzo

Vice President Account Management, Jennifer Ferrang

Vice President Customer Service Management, Susan Dixon

Vice President, Eric Bolling

National Vice President Of Sales Laboratory Products, Angela Davis

Vice President And Associate General Counsel Finance, Rylan Rawlins

Vice President, Warren Hastings

Vice President, Sean Postol

Director Of Pharmacy, Norma Yeverino

Clinical Director, Steve Lundquist

Senior Vice President, Dennis Braun

Vice President And General Manager Cardinal Health Inventory Management Solutions, John Roy

Vice President Distribution Services, Paul Farnin

Vice President, John Sullivan

Pharmacy Manager, Jeremy Guthrie

Director Of Pharmacy, Laurie Sobas

Pharmacy Manager, Melissa Christopher

Vice President Strategic Marketing And Product Management, David Mitchell

Pharmacy Manager, Alan Alberto

Vice President, Steve Peale

Vice President Of Sales, Andy Grant

Vice President Compensation, Melanie Filas

Manager Government Relations, Laura Padgitt

Senior Vice President Marketing Managed Care And Customer Solutions Pharmaceutical Distribution, Christi Pedra

Director Of Pharmacy Practice, Kevin Walker

Vice President, Mike Good

Pharmacy Manager, Michael Wyant

Senior Vice President City Executive, Kevin Rourk

Pharmacy Manager, Tally Townsend

Senior Vice President Of Ecommerce Enterprise Architecture And Chief Information Security Officer, Talvis Love

Pharmacy Manager, Sam Ling

Director Of Pharmacy, Denise Payette

Vice President, Colleen McGuffin

Vice President, Jeff Brannon

Director Of Pharmacy Operations And Account Manager, Sue Raymoure

Pharmacy Manager, Gene Nickman

Vice President, Justin Hooper

Vice President Human Resources, Ola Snow

Group Vice President Health Systems, Therese Grossi

Executive Vice President Packaging Service Group, Renard Pawlak

Pharmacy Manager, Sherry Miller

Director Of Pharmacy, Jay Dyer

Pharmacy Manager, Todd Lamb

Vice President, Sean Mcnally

Vice President, Chris Lanctot

Director Of Pharmacy, Todd Worsham

Pharmacy Manager, Bevan Callicott

Pharmacy Manager, Ann Shea

Director Of Pharmacy, Lynn Staggs

Vice President, Justin Schomaker

Pharmacy Manager, Mary Johnson

Pharmacy Manager, John Miano

Pharmacy Manager, Arthur Bowman

Director Of Pharmacy, Sharon Greasheimer

Director Of Pharmacy, Mary Ndumele

Pharmacy Manager, Jeff Parrish

Vice President, Kendell Sherrer

Director Of Pharmacy, Rande Hempen

Pharmacy Manager, Jimmy Coker

Vice President Enterprise Information Technology, Cyndi Carter

Pharmacy Manager, Chad Walker

Vice President Of Marketing An, Erika Jurrens

Vice President, Katie Ballay

Vice President, Luke Whitworth

Senior Vice President Independent And Alternate Care Sales, Steve Lawrence

Vice President Enterprise Architecture And It Strategy, Jeff Greer

Pharmacy Manager, Abdul Kamara

Vice President Associate General Counsel, Cheryl Kahn

Vice President National Market Sales, Gregory Ewing

Pharmacy Manager, Matt Champ

Pharmacy Manager, Mark Wear

Vice President Strategic Account Management, Ken Rasbid

Vice President Information Technology, Pete Cornford

Vice President, Tina Lantz

Vice President Operations, Martha Huston

Executive Assistant To Ramon Gregroy Senior Vice President Customer Support Services, Molly Decker

Vice President Customer Service, Greg Stuart

Pharmacy Manager, Glenn Carmody

Vice President Human Resources, Maribel Delfaus

Pharmacy Manager, Kelli Love

Vice President, John Kilgour

Vice President Public Relations, Brett Ludwig

Vice President Sales, Ryan Schorr

Director Of Pharmacy, Anita Ward

Svp Government Relations, Sean Callinicos

Vice President Marketing, Michael Pintek

Pharmacy Manager, Gary Mantz

Senior Vice President General Counsel Medical
  Segment, Jennifer Spalding
Vice President Information Technology, Gregory
  Boggs
Vice President Investor Relations, Lisa Capodici
Vice President Corporate Development (mergers
  And Acquisitions), Jimmy Steinberg
Clinical Director Infectious Diseases, Katherine
  Shea
Pharmacy Manager, Kevin Marsh
Vice President Risk Management, Roxsann Wilson
Global Medical Director Cordis, Ali Almedhychy
Vice President Of Marketing Cardinal Health,
  Preety Sidhu
Svp Enterprise Corporate Accounts And
  Enterprise Marketing, Robert Rajalingam
Director Of Pharmacy, Carol Yuan
Senior Vice President General Manager Yong Yu,
  Elsie Lim
Vice President Engineering Fuse, Steve Langella
Vice President Community Relations, Jessie
  Cannon
Pharmacy Manager Radiation Safety Officer,
  Richard Medeiros
Evp Cio And Customer Support Services, Brian
  Rice
Vice President Enterprise Information
  Technology, Steven Callison
Vice President Of Tax, Hunter Scott
Pharmacy Manager, Erin Searles
Chairman, George S. Barrett, age 65
Board Member, Colleen Arnold
Assistant Secretary To The Board, Elaine Natsis
Treasurer, Diana Waltz
Board Member, Calvin Darden
Auditors: Ernst & Young LLP

LOCATIONS

HQ: Cardinal Health, Inc.
  7000 Cardinal Place, Dublin, OH 43017
Phone: 614 757-5000
Web: www.cardinalhealth.com

2018 Sales

	$ mil.	% of total
US	132,526	97
Other	4,283	3
Total	**136,809**	**100**

PRODUCTS/OPERATIONS

2018 Sales by Segment

	$ mil.	% of total
Pharmaceutical	121,241	89
Medical	15,581	11
Corporate	(13)	-
Total	**136,809**	**100**

COMPETITORS

AmerisourceBergen	Medline Industries
Becton Dickinson	Owens & Minor
CVS	PharMerica
Deroyal Industries	Rite Aid
Franz Haniel	Thermo Fisher
Henry Schein	Scientific
McKesson	Walgreen

HISTORICAL FINANCIALS

Company Type: Public

Income Statement

FYE: June 30

	REVENUE ($ mil.)	NET INCOME ($ mil.)	NET PROFIT MARGIN	EMPLOYEES
06/20	152,922	(3,696)	—	30,000
06/19	145,534	1,363	0.9%	49,500
06/18	136,809	256	0.2%	50,200
06/17	129,976	1,288	1.0%	40,400
06/16	121,546	1,427	1.2%	37,300
Annual Growth	**5.9%**	**—**	**—**	**(5.3%)**

2020 Year-End Financials

Debt ratio: 16.62%
Return on equity: (-90.82%)
Cash ($ mil.): 2,771
Current ratio: 1.10
Long-term debt ($ mil.): 6,765

No. of shares (mil.): 293
Dividends
  Yield: 3.7%
  Payout: —
Market value ($ mil.): 15,292

	STOCK PRICE ($) FY Close	P/E High/Low		PER SHARE ($) Earnings	Dividends	Book Value
06/20	52.19	—	—	(12.61)	1.93	6.11
06/19	47.10	13	9	4.53	1.91	21.16
06/18	48.83	96	60	0.81	1.86	19.61
06/17	77.92	21	16	4.03	1.81	21.54
06/16	78.01	21	17	4.32	1.61	20.35
Annual Growth	**(9.6%)**	**—**	**—**	**—**	**4.6%**	**(26.0%)**

Carmax Inc.

CarMax helps drivers find late-model used autos. The US's largest specialty used-car retailer buys reconditions and sells cars and light trucks through more than 215 superstores in 100-plus television markets (markets in which CarMax has a television advertising presence). Typically selling vehicles that are approximately ten years old with more than 100000 miles CarMax sells more than 832500 used cars per year. CarMax also operates two new-car franchises and sells older vehicles through more than 465000 in-store auctions each year at over 75 stores. Additionally it sells older cars and trucks with higher mileage and offers vehicle financing through its CarMax Auto Finance unit.

Operations

CarMax operates through two business segments: CarMax Sales Operations and CarMax Auto Finance (CAF).

CarMax Sales Operations which sells more than 832640 used cars per year represents the nation's largest used-car retailer. The company's finance arm CarMax Auto Financing (CAF) offers financing solely to CarMax customers and finances about 45% of the company's retail vehicle unit sales. CAF also services over 1 million customer accounts in its $13.5 billion portfolio of managed receivables.

The company's used vehicle sales generate about 85% of total revenue wholesale vehicle sales more than 10% and other products and services less than 5%.

Geographic Reach

While Richmond Virginia-based CarMax sells cars in more than 40 US states its largest markets are California Texas Florida North Carolina Georgia Tennessee and Virginia which together account for nearly half of store locations.

Its Auto Finance division operates out of Atlanta Georgia. The company have office buildings for their customer experience centers in Atlanta Georgia; Kansas City Missouri; and Phoenix Arizona.

Sales and Marketing

CarMax focuses on developing brand awareness and detailing the advantages of shopping at its stores. It reaches customers through TV and mobile phones carmax.com search engine optimization and in-person in their modern sales facilities.

CarMax's customers often take advantage of its transfer option which allows a customer to get a vehicle of their choice relocated to a more local CarMax store. About 35% of vehicles sold are transferred via customer request.

Financial Performance

In 2020 the company's revenue increased by 12% to $20.3 billion from $18.2 billion in the prior year. The increase was due to the 13% increase in used vehicle revenues in fiscal 2020 was primarily due to an 11% increase in unit sale; the 5% increase in wholesale vehicle revenues in fiscal 2020 was primarily due to a 4% increase in wholesale unit sales; Other sales and revenues increased 7% in fiscal 2020 driven by the 14% increase in EPP revenues.

Net income grew 5% to $888.4 million on the increased sales and a smaller provision for income taxes than in fiscal year 2019.

Cash at the end of fiscal 2020 was $656.4 million an increase of 9% from the prior year. Cash from operations used $236.6 million to the coffers and investing activities subtracted $389.4 million mainly for capital expenditures. Financing activities added $687 million.

Strategy

CarMax's marketing strategies are focused on developing awareness of the advantages of shopping at their stores and on carmax.com and on attracting customers who are already considering buying or selling a vehicle. These strategies are implemented through a broad range of media types including but not limited to traditional broadcast digital search video on demand and social.

The company's long-term strategy continues to be focused on completing the rollout of their retail concept including their omni-channel experience and to increase their share of used vehicle unit sales in each of the markets in which they operate. CarMax's omni-channel experience empowers customers to buy a car on their own terms whether completely from home in-store or through a seamlessly integrated combination of online and in-store experiences.

In order to execute their long-term strategy they have invested in various strategic initiatives to increase innovation specifically with regards to customer facing and customer-enabling technologies. The company continue to make improvements to their website and enhance customer experiences such as finance pre-approval home delivery online appraisal and express or curbside pick-up. They are also developing and implementing tools that help their associates be more efficient and effective. Additionally the company have centralized customer support in their customer experience centers ("CEC") which we believe provides a more seamless integration between the online and in-store experience for their customers.

Company Background

Looking for new retailing channels to conquer in 1993 Circuit City Stores began test-driving the used-car concept when it opened its first CarMax outlet in Richmond Virginia. Richard Sharp who also served as Circuit City's CEO became the chairman and CEO for CarMax Group.

A pioneer in the car industry CarMax offered computerized shopping play areas for children and no-haggle pricing. The company extended its geographical reach in 1995 and 1996. Circuit City spun off about 25% of CarMax to the public in 1997. Circuit City spun off CarMax as an independent company in 2002.

HISTORY

Looking for new retailing channels to conquer in 1993 Circuit City Stores began test-driving the used-car concept when it opened its first CarMax outlet in Richmond Virginia. Richard Sharp who was named Circuit City's CEO in 1986 became the chairman and CEO for CarMax Group as well.

A pioneer in the car industry CarMax offered computerized shopping play areas for children and no-haggle pricing. Competing car dealers criticized CarMax's TV ads which tarred rivals with a stereotype of sleaze and greed. Some dealers disputed CarMax's low-price claims.

The company extended its geographical reach into North Carolina Georgia and Florida in 1995 and 1996. In 1996 CarMax began selling new cars at an Atlanta store.

No longer riding it as a test-drive Circuit City spun off about 25% of CarMax to the public in 1997. The following year it moved into Illinois.

Also in 1998 CarMax bought a new-car Toyota dealership in Maryland and the multi-make Mauro Auto Mall of Wisconsin. It entered South Carolina that year and added a Georgia Mitsubishi dealership in early 1999. The company acquired two new-car franchises in the competitive Los Angeles market in mid-1999.

In mid-2001 Circuit City reduced its share in CarMax from 75% to about 65% having sold some stock to help remodel the company's electronics stores. Circuit City then spun off CarMax as an independent company in October 2002. President Austin Ligon took the CEO title at that time (Sharp remained chairman).

CarMax opened five superstores but sold four new-car dealerships in 2003.

EXECUTIVES

Vice President, Barbara Harvill
Vice President Marketing Carmax, Rob Sorenson
Vice President Regional Sales, Daniel Johnston
Region Vp Merchandising Atlanta Region, Jason K Day
Vice President Investor Relations, Katharine Kenny
Region Vice President And General Manager Los Angeles Region, Vaughn Sigmon
Evp Strategy And Business Transformation, Edwin J. (Ed) Hill, age 60, $597,209 total compensation
Evp General Counsel And Secretary, Eric M. Margolin, age 67, $572,801 total compensation
Evp And Cfo, Thomas W. (Tom) Reedy, age 56, $699,039 total compensation
President Ceo And Director, William D. (Bill) Nash, age 51, $902,308 total compensation
Evp And Coo, William C. (Cliff) Wood, age 53, $699,039 total compensation
Svp And Chief Marketing Officer, James (Jim) Lyski, age 57
Svp And Cio, Shamim Mohammad, age 51
Svp Carmax Auto Finance, Jon G. Daniels, age 48
Assistant Vice President Management Information Systems, Troy Downs
Assistant Vice President Associate Relations, Greg Stewart
Assistant Vice President Consumer Finance, Rusty Jordan
Vice President Business Operations And Customer Service, Lynn Mussatt
Regional Vice President Service Operations, Jason Lowery
Avp Construction Design And Grand Opening, Scott Sawyer
Vice President, Patricia Gangwer
Vice President Deputy General Counsel, Ross Longood
Assistant Vice President Assistant Controller, Veronica Hinckle

Vp Construction Design And Facilities, Dan Bickett
Assistant Vice President Risk And Servicing Analytics, Kevin Duck
Vice President Sales, Kevin Cox
Vice President Treasurer, Tom Reedy
Regional Vice President, Chris Bartee
Vice President Financial Services And Products, Robert Mitchell
Assistant Vice President Information Technology, Greg Shull
Vice President Information Technology, David Banks
Regional Vice President Purchasing, Bryan Windsor
Vice President Procurement And Strategic Sourcing, Julie Reed
Vice President And Deputy General Counsel, Greg Fitzharris
Vice President Marketing, Rob Sorensen
Regional Vice President General Manager Xf Nashville Region, Dave Cantu
Assistant Vice President Data Science, Nick Anderson
Chairman, Thomas J. (Tom) Folliard
Board Of Directors, Alan Colberg
Auditors: KPMG LLP

LOCATIONS

HQ: Carmax Inc.
12800 Tuckahoe Creek Parkway, Richmond, VA 23238
Phone: 804 747-0422
Web: www.carmax.com

2017 Stores

	No.
California	23
Florida	16
Texas	16
Virginia	10
Georgia	9
Illinois	9
North Carolina	9
Tennessee	8
Maryland	6
Colorado	5
Ohio	5
Alabama	4
Massachusetts	4
Wisconsin	4
Arizona	3
Missouri	3
Nevada	3
Pennsylvania	3
South Carolina	3
Connecticut	2
Indiana	2
Kansas	2
Kentucky	2
Minnesota	2
Mississippi	2
New Jersey	2
New York	2
Oklahoma	2
Oregon	2
Delaware	1
Idaho	1
Iowa	1
Louisiana	1
Michigan	1
Nebraska	1
New Mexico	1
Rhode Island	1
Utah	1
Washington	1
Total	**173**

PRODUCTS/OPERATIONS

2017 Sales

	$ mil.	% of total
Used vehicles	13,270	84
Wholesale vehicles	2,082	13
Other sales & revenue	522	3
Total	**15,875**	**100**

COMPETITORS

Asbury Automotive	Holman Enterprises
AutoNation	Internet Brands
AutoTrader	JM Family Enterprises
Brown Automotive	KAR Auction Services
Cox Automotive	McCombs Enterprises
Danner Company	Penske Automotive
DriveTime Automotive	Group
Ed Morse Auto	Serra Automotive
Group 1 Automotive	Sonic Automotive
Hendrick Automotive	

HISTORICAL FINANCIALS

Company Type: Public

Income Statement

FYE: February 29

	REVENUE ($ mil.)	NET INCOME ($ mil.)	NET PROFIT MARGIN	EMPLOYEES
02/20	20,319	888	4.4%	27,050
02/19	18,173	842	4.6%	25,946
02/18	17,120	664	3.9%	25,110
02/17	15,875	626	3.9%	24,344
02/16	15,149	623	4.1%	22,429
Annual Growth	**7.6%**	**9.3%**	—	**4.8%**

2020 Year-End Financials

Debt ratio: 72.94%
Return on equity: 24.87%
Cash ($ mil.): 58
Current ratio: 2.39
Long-term debt ($ mil.): 14,944

No. of shares (mil.): 163
Dividends
  Yield: —
  Payout: —
Market value ($ mil.): 14,239

	STOCK PRICE ($) FY Close	P/E High/Low	PER SHARE ($) Earnings	PER SHARE ($) Dividends	PER SHARE ($) Book Value
02/20	87.31	19 11	5.33	0.00	23.11
02/19	62.10	17 12	4.79	0.00	20.04
02/18	61.92	21 15	3.60	0.00	18.45
02/17	64.54	21 14	3.26	0.00	16.66
02/16	46.26	24 14	3.03	0.00	14.92
Annual Growth	**17.2%**	— —	**15.2%**	—	**11.6%**

Carrier Global Corp

EXECUTIVES

Pres-Ceo, David Gitlin
Exec Chb, John V Faraci
V Pres-Cfo, Timothy McLevish
V Pres-General Counsel, Kevin O'Connor
V Pres-Chief Hr Officer, Nadia Villeneuve
V Pres-Contrl, Kyle Crockett
Vp Strategy & Services, Ajay Agrawal
Pres Refrigeration, David Appel
Pres Hvac, Christopher Nelson
Pres Fire & Security, Jurgen Timperman

LOCATIONS

HQ: Carrier Global Corp
13995 Pasteur Boulevard, Palm Beach Gardens, FL 33418
Phone: 561 365-2000
Web: www.carrier.com

HISTORICAL FINANCIALS

Company Type: Public

Income Statement

	REVENUE ($ mil.)	NET INCOME ($ mil.)	NET PROFIT MARGIN	EMPLOYEES
12/19	18,608	2,116	11.4%	52,635
12/18	18,914	2,734	14.5%	54,384
12/17	17,814	1,227	6.9%	54,998
Annual Growth	2.2%	31.3%	—	(2.2%)

FYE: December 31

2019 Year-End Financials

Debt ratio: —
Return on equity: 15.10%
Cash ($ mil.): 952
Current ratio: 1.33
Long-term debt ($ mil.): —

Dividends
Yield: —
Payout: —
Market value ($ mil.): —

	STOCK PRICE ($) FY Close	P/E High/Low	PER SHARE ($) Earnings	Dividends	Book Value
12/19	0.00	— —	(0.00)	0.00	(0.00)
12/18	0.00	— —	(0.00)	0.00	(0.00)
Annual Growth	—	— —	—	—	—

Carter Bankshares Inc

Dominion Energy dominates the American energy market as one of its top distributors of electricity and natural gas. The company serves some 7 million retail energy customers across eight US states with a special concentration in Virginia the Carolinas and Ohio. The company boasts an impressive energy portfolio with about 30700 MW of generating capacity as well as one of the largest underground natural gas storage systems with 1 trillion cu. ft. of capacity. Operating subsidiaries include Virginia Power and Dominion Energy Gas.

Operations

In 2019 Dominion Energy strategically realigned its segments which resulted in the formation of five primary operating segments: Dominion Energy Virginia Gas Transmission & Storage Gas Distribution Dominion Energy South Carolina and Contracted Generation.

The Dominion Energy Virginia segment is composed of Virginia Power's regulated electric transmission distribution (including customer service) and generation (regulated electric utility and its related energy supply) operations which serve approximately 2.6 million residential commercial industrial and governmental customers in Virginia and North Carolina. The segment accounts for about 45% total sales.

Gas Transmission & Storage segment includes FERC regulated interstate natural gas transmission pipeline and underground storage systems in the eastern and Rocky Mountain regions of the U.S. (primarily through DETI DECG and Dominion Energy Questar Pipeline) LNG import/export and storage (through its 75% controlling interest in Cove Point) as well as a 50% noncontrolling partnership interest in Iroquois. It also includes nonregulated retail natural gas marketing development of renewable natural gas and LNG infrastructure and its investments in Atlantic Coast Pipeline Align RNG and Wrangler. The segment accounts for about 20% of total sales.

The Dominion Energy South Carolina segment is comprised of DESC's generation transmission and distribution of electricity to approximately 740000 customers in the central southern and southwestern portions of South Carolina and the distribution of natural gas to approximately 390000 residential commercial and industrial customers in South Carolina. The segment accounts for more than 15% of total sales.

The Gas Distribution segment includes Dominion Energy's regulated natural gas sales transportation gathering and distribution operations in Ohio West Virginia North Carolina Utah southwestern Wyoming and southeastern Idaho (through East Ohio Hope PSNC and Questar Gas) which collectively serve approximately 3.0 million residential commercial and industrial customers. The segment accounts for nearly 15% of total sales.

The Contracted Generation segment includes the operations of Millstone and associated energy marketing and price risk activities and Dominion Energy's long-term contracted renewable electric generation fleet as well as a 50% noncontrolling partnership interest in Fowler Ridge. The segment accounts for about 5% of total sales.

Geographic Reach

Headquartered in Richmond Virginia Dominion has operations in 18 states. Its Virginia Power subsidiary distributes power in North Carolina and Virginia.

Its East Ohio Gas Hope Gas and Questar subsidiaries distribute gas in Ohio West Virginia Utah Wyoming and Idaho..

Sales and Marketing

Dominion primarily sells electricity to retail customers consisting of residential homes and commercial businesses. Its subsidiary Virginia Power includes customers such as residential commercial and industrial customers as well as rural electric cooperatives and municipalities. The company serves more than 7 million utility and retail energy customers.

Financial Performance

Dominion has seen a steady rise in revenue in recent years with sales growing 42% between 2015 and 2019. Net income has fluctuated in recent years.

Revenue increased 23% in 2019 to some $16.6 billion due to a $1.5 billion increase from the SCANA Combination due to operations acquired ($2.5 billion) partially offset by a $1.0 billion charge for refunds of amounts previously collected from retail electric customers of DESC for the NND Project.

Net income declined 45% to about $1.4 billion in 2019 primarily due to charges for refunds of amounts previously collected from retail electric customers of DESC for the NND Project litigation acquired in the SCANA Combination a voluntary retirement program the planned early retirement of certain Virginia Power electric generation facilities and the absence of gains on the sales of certain equity method investments.

The company ended 2019 with $269 million in cash down $122 million from 2018. Operating activities contributed $5.2 billion while investing activities used $4.6 billion (mostly construction costs) and financing activities used $704 million mainly for debt and dividend payments.

Strategy

Dominion is focusing on its regulated power and gas infrastructure assets to reduce its exposure to volatile energy markets. It acquired western US gas utility Questar in 2016 and southeastern US utility SCANA in 2019. The firm exited certain retail energy marketing operations in 2018; it also sold three merchant power generation plants for $1.3 billion and its 50% stake in midstream gas services provider Blue Racer for $1.2 billion.

Dominion's five-year investment plan for the 2019-23 period includes a focus on upgrading the electric system in Virginia through investments in additional renewable generation facilities smart meters customer information platform intelligent grid devices and associated control systems physical and cyber security investments strategic undergrounding and energy conservation programs. Dominion Energy also plans to upgrade its gas and electric transmission and distribution networks and meet environmental requirements and standards set by various regulatory bodies.

Mergers and Acquisitions

In early 2019 Dominion acquired SCANA Corporation in a transaction valued at $13.4 billion adding some 1.6 million customers to Dominion's already massive base and expanding its power and gas utility operations in the Carolinas. SCANA and its subsidiaries including South Carolina Electric & Gas Company Public Service Company of North Carolina and SCANA Energy Marketing became part of Dominion's newly formed Southeast Energy segment. The deal included the assumption of financial obligations (including customer refunds) related to two SCANA nuclear reactors that will not be completed due to construction delays and cost overruns.

Also in 2019 Dominion acquired the remaining interest in majority owned subsidiary Dominion Energy Midstream Partners through a share exchange transaction valued at about $1.6 billion.

In addition the company acquired two solar projects in Virginia and one solar project in South Carolina in 2019. The previous year it purchased two solar projects in North Carolina and Virginia for $250 million.

Company Background

Dominion Energy traces its roots to the founding of the Upper Appomattox Company in Virginia in 1795. The company managed water rights and eventually ran power plants. The Virginia Railway and Power Company (VR&P) acquired Upper Appomattox in 1909 along with several other utilities in the following year. VR&P became Virginia Electric and Power Company (Virginia Power) after being acquired by engineering firm Stone & Webster in 1925. Virginia Power acquired Virginia Public Service Company and built numerous power plants in the following years. It expanded into gas exploration in the 1990s.

In 2000 Dominion bought Consolidated Natural Gas (CNG) for $9 billion making it one of the largest fully integrated gas and electric power companies in the US; it then sold CNG's Virginia Natural Gas to AGL Resources and the two firms' combined Latin American assets to Duke Energy. It sold its telecom business in 2004 the bulk of its oil and gas exploration operations in 2007 and utility Peoples Natural Gas in 2010. In 2016 Dominion bought gas utility Questar for $4.4 billion.

In 1983 Dominion Resources was incorporated as a parent company for Virginia Power. The holding company changed its name to Dominion Energy in 2017.

Auditors: Crowe LLP

LOCATIONS

HQ: Carter Bankshares Inc
1300 Kings Mountain Road, Martinsville, VA 24112
Phone: 276 656-1776
Web: www.cbtcares.com

HISTORICAL FINANCIALS

Company Type: Public

Income Statement

FYE: December 31

	ASSETS ($ mil.)	NET INCOME ($ mil.)	INCOME AS % OF ASSETS	EMPLOYEES
12/19	4,006	26	0.7%	977
12/18	4,039	11	0.3%	992
12/17	4,112	(0)	—	963
12/16	4,505	15	0.4%	—
12/15	4,893	39	0.8%	964
Annual Growth	(4.9%)	(9.2%)	—	0.3%

2019 Year-End Financials

Debt ratio: —
Return on equity: 5.85%
Cash ($ mil.): 125
Current ratio: —
Long-term debt ($ mil.): —

No. of shares (mil.): 26
Dividends
Yield: —
Payout: —
Market value ($ mil.): 625

	STOCK PRICE ($) FY Close	P/E High/Low	PER SHARE ($) Earnings	Dividends	Book Value
12/19	23.72	23 15	1.01	0.00	17.97
12/18	15.00	44 32	0.45	0.00	16.60
12/17	17.55	— —	(0.03)	0.00	16.46
12/16	13.29	23 20	0.61	0.30	16.55
12/15	13.50	9 8	1.49	0.40	16.24
Annual Growth	15.1%	— —	(9.3%)	—	2.5%

Casey's General Stores, Inc.

Casey's provides convenience for small-town customers. One of the largest convenience store chains in the country Casey's General Stores owns over 2200 stores across 15-plus states primarily in the Midwest. Its stores most of which operate in areas with fewer than 5000 people offer gasoline prepared foods such as pizza and donuts and other food and nonfood items traditionally found in convenience stores. In addition to Casey's and Casey's General Store locations the company operates two tobacco stores one liquor store and one grocery store. Prepared food items sales account for about 60% of Casey's revenue.

Operations

Casey's generates some 60% of its revenue from fuel over 25% from grocery and other merchandise and just more than 10% from prepared food and fountain drinks.

It has a broad selection of merchandise fuel and other products and services designed to appeal to the convenience needs of guests with stores typically stocking more than 3000 food and non-food items. The company sells nationally known brands as well as its own proprietary brands. Casey's has built up its selection of prepared foods over the years and now offers sandwiches and burgers pizza donuts chicken tenders and breakfast biscuits among other items.

Geographic Reach

Iowa-based Casey's operates stores in some 15 states including its largest markets — Iowa Illinois and Missouri—as well as Kansas Kentucky Minnesota Nebraska Wisconsin Indiana Michigan Ohio Oklahoma Arkansas Tennessee and the Dakotas.

It has distribution centers in Ankeny Iowa and Terre Haute Indiana.

Sales and Marketing

Casey's targets smaller communities by serving as both general and convenience stores including stocking a broader selection of products than typical of convenience stores.

Financial Performance

Casey's revenues in the last five years have steadily grown about 15% with a peak of $9.4 billion in 2019. Net income has been a little more sporadic however it has seen a 17% growth over the same period.

The company reported revenue of $9.2 billion in fiscal 2020 (ended April) down 2% from the prior year. The results were driven by a decrease in prices of fuel which affected the company's retail fuel sales as well as its fuel gallon sales.

Net income that year rose 29% to $263.8 million primarily due to increased fuel margin contribution and more operating stores than last year.

Cash at the end of fiscal 2020 was $78.3 million an increase of $15 million from the prior year. Cash from operations contributed $504.3 million to the coffers while investing activities used $466.6 million mainly for purchase of property and equipment. Financing activities used another $22.7 million primarily for dividends to shareholders and long-term debt repayments.

Strategy

Casey's updated long-term strategic plan is focused on four strategic objectives: reinvigorate hospitality and the guest experience be where the guest is best-in-class efficiencies and invest in its people and culture through new capabilities technology data and processes.

In line with this Casey's has acquired Fantasy's Convenience stores and Ride the Wave carwashes. Casey's plans to remodel these locations to enable the stores to offer pizza donuts made-to-order sub-sandwiches and many other freshly prepared food items. Additionally Casey's has partnered with DoorDash to provide delivery to nearly 600 locations which will provide delivery services for Casey's famous made-from-scratch pizza select appetizers and soda.

Lastly Casey's is looking to engage and interact with its customers through online and mobile channels as well as in stores. In 2019 it launched its new and improved website with a refreshed design and enhancements to its online ordering system all centered on making it easier than ever to order. It also launched its mobile app which allows customers to browse local menus customize pizzas and place their orders. The mobile app brings the same time-saving features from the newly-redesigned website.

Mergers and Acquisitions

During the year 2020 the Company acquired 18 stores through a variety of multi-store and single store transactions with several unrelated third parties. Of the 18 stores acquired 11 were reopened as a Casey's store during the 2020 fiscal year and seven will be opened during the 2021 fiscal year. In 2019 Casey's General Stores Inc. have acquired the Fantasy's Convenience stores and Ride the Wave carwashes located in the Omaha Nebraska metro area. Casey's plans to perform significant remodels at all nine of the locations that will enable the stores to offer pizza donuts made-to-order sub-sandwiches and many other freshly prepared food items. Terms were not disclosed.

Company Background

Donald Lamberti who had run his family's grocery store founded Casey's General Stores with Kurvin C. "K. C." Fish. The men converted a gas station into the first Casey's convenience store in 1968. To expand and build brand recognition the company began franchising outlets two years later. By focusing on small towns the company avoided competition and expensive building and property costs. A significant growth spurt in 1979 took Casey's from 119 stores to 226. Fish retired the following year and the company went public in 1983.

EXECUTIVES

Svp And Cfo, William J. (Bill) Walljasper, age 59, $550,000 total compensation
Vp Advertising, Michael R. (Mike) Richardson, $195,000 total compensation
President And Ceo, Terry W. Handley, age 61, $770,000 total compensation
Svp General Counsel And Secretary, Julia L. (Julie) Jackowski, age 55, $530,000 total compensation
Vp Information Technology, Rich Schappert
Svp Operations, John C. (Jay) Soupene, age 52
Board Director, David Lenhardt
Auditors: KPMG LLP

LOCATIONS

HQ: Casey's General Stores, Inc.
One SE Convenience Boulevard, Ankeny, IA 50021
Phone: 515 965-6100
Web: www.caseys.com

PRODUCTS/OPERATIONS

2019 Sales

	$ mil.	% of total
Fuel	5,848	63
Grocery & other merchandise	2,369	25
Prepared food & fountain	1,074	11
Other	60	1
Total	**9,352**	**100**

Selected Merchandise

Ammunition
Automotive products
Beverages
Food including fresh foods
Gasoline (self-service)
Health and beauty aids
Housewares
Pet products
Photo supplies
School supplies
Tobacco products

COMPETITORS

7-Eleven	Krause Gentle
Chevron	Kwik Trip
Couche-Tard	Martin & Bayley
Exxon Mobil	QuikTrip
Family Express	Royal Dutch Shell
Fareway Stores	Thorntons Inc.
Holiday Companies	Wallis Companies
Hy-Vee	

HISTORICAL FINANCIALS

Company Type: Public

Income Statement

FYE: April 30

	REVENUE ($ mil.)	NET INCOME ($ mil.)	NET PROFIT MARGIN	EMPLOYEES
04/20	9,175	263	2.9%	—
04/19	9,352	203	2.2%	36,841
04/18	8,391	317	3.8%	37,205
04/17	7,506	177	2.4%	35,014
04/16	7,122	225	3.2%	34,997
Annual Growth	6.5%	3.9%	—	—

2020 Year-End Financials

Debt ratio: 35.62%
Return on equity: 17.24%
Cash ($ mil.): 78
Current ratio: 0.36
Long-term debt ($ mil.): 714

No. of shares (mil.): 36
Dividends
Yield: 0.8%
Payout: 20.9%
Market value ($ mil.): 5,573

	STOCK PRICE ($)	P/E	PER SHARE ($)		
	FY Close	High/Low	Earnings	Dividends	Book Value
04/20	151.41	25 17	7.10	1.28	44.64
04/19	132.35	25 17	5.51	1.16	38.42
04/18	96.60	15 11	8.34	1.04	34.47
04/17	112.07	30 24	4.48	0.96	30.71
04/16	112.00	22 14	5.73	0.88	27.74
Annual Growth	7.8%	— —	5.5%	9.8%	12.6%

Caterpillar Inc.

The Caterpillar was company founder Benjamin Holt's nickname for his new farm tractor with crawler tracks used in place of iron wheels. Growing from that 1904 invention Caterpillar Inc. is the world's #1 manufacturer of construction and mining equipment which includes excavators loaders and tractors as well as forestry paving and tunneling machinery. It also manufactures diesel engines gas turbines and diesel-electric locomotives. Subsidiary Caterpillar Financial Services offers financing products and services for dealers and customers and its Progress Rail Services subsidiary provides remanufacturing and rail-related maintenance services. The US supplies about 40% of sales.

Operations

Caterpillar is organized into three main operating segments- Construction Industries Energy & Transportation and Resource Industries.

Construction Industries (about 40% of net sales) caters to customers using machinery in infrastructure forestry and building construction applications.

Energy and Transportation (almost 35%) makes and sells reciprocating engines turbines diesel-electric locomotives and related parts for power generation industrial oil and gas and transportation applications.

Resource Industries (nearly 20%) makes and sells machinery for mining quarry waste and material handling applications. It also develops and sells technology products for customers' fleet management systems and provides equipment management analytics and autonomous machine capabilities.

A fourth segment is Financial Products which accounts for less than 5% of revenue in providing financing for Caterpillar customers and dealers.

Geographic Reach

Caterpillar has construction mining and power equipment manufacturing operations scattered across the US and around the world. It also operates technical centers in Mossville IL. Wuxi China and Chennai India. Demonstration centers are located in Tinaja Hills Arizona; Edwards Illinois; Chichibu Japan and Malaga Spain. Additionally the company has marketing and operating locations parts distribution centers and remanufacturing facilities worldwide. The company is headquartered in Deerfield Illinois.

Caterpillar's strong international presence generates about 60% of revenue with around 20% of revenue from Europe Africa & Middle East (EAME) more than 20% from the Asia/Pacific region and about 10% from Latin America. The US supplies about 45% of Caterpillar's sales.

Sales and Marketing

Caterpillar machinery is distributed to customers in more than 190 countries through a worldwide network of about 120 dealers (45 are in the US) many of which provide sales rental service and aftermarket support. Most are independently owned and operated though Caterpillar owns and operates its own dealerships in Japan and covers up to 80% of the Japanese market.

Caterpillar serves the mining construction electric power generation industrial marine and oil and gas industries.

Financial Performance

For a five-year period starting in 2015 Caterpillar saw its sales and revenue fluctuates. Net income followed the same trend for that period.

Caterpillar's sales and revenues for 2019 were $53.8 billion a 2% decrease from 2018 sales and revenues of $54.7 billion. The decrease was primarily due to lower sales volume. The sales volume decline was mostly due to changes in dealer inventories partially offset by higher end-user demand.

The sales decreased translated to a $6.09 billion profit for Caterpillar in 2019 compared to a $6.14 billion profit the year before.

The company's coffers held about $8.3 billion in cash in 2019 compared to $7.9 billion in 2018. Operating activities generated $6.9 billion in 2019 while investing and financing activities used $1.9 billion and $4.5 billion respectively.

Strategy

Caterpillar is working to identify and prioritize business opportunities that offer the most potential for growth. Using a data-driven approach dubbed the "Operating & Executing (O&E) Model" the company is assessing its financial performance by product region and application and is investing in areas producing lower-than-acceptable returns. As a result Caterpillar is streamlining its operations and expanding its product offerings and services portfolio.

Services growth is a core focus of their strategy. The company have a bold goal to double their Machinery Energy and Transportation (ME&T) services sales to $28 billion by 2026 from their 2016 baseline.

At Caterpillar they define services as the value we provide to customers after the equipment purchase – everything from aftermarket parts to maintenance agreements to financing – with a goal of delivering a superior customer experience. The company invest time talent and resources in service offerings because they drive value for their customers. Services can reduce total owning and operating costs for customers and deliver revenue for Caterpillar and their dealers throughout the cycles.

Mergers and Acquisitions

In 2019 Caterpillar's Progress Rail Services subsidiary agreed to purchase Cleveland Track Material (CTM) for about ?35 million. CTM is part of Germany-based rail equipment provider Vossloh AG's North American operations. CTM is a leading manufacturer of special trackwork — including rail turnouts and crossings trackwork assemblies and switch points — for Class 1 and transit railroads. The deal should bolster Progress Rail's track services operations.

Company Background

In 1904 in Stockton California combine maker Benjamin Holt modified the farming tractor by substituting a gas engine for steam and replacing iron wheels with crawler tracks. This improved the tractor's mobility over dirt.

The British adapted the "caterpillar" (Holt's nickname for the tractor) design to the armored tank in 1915. Following WWI the US Army donated tanks to local governments for construction work. The caterpillar's efficiency spurred the development of earthmoving and construction equipment.

Holt merged with Best Tractor in 1925. The company renamed Caterpillar moved to Peoria Illinois in 1928 and went public in 1929. Cat expanded into foreign markets in the 1930s and phased out combine production to focus on construction and road-building equipment.

EXECUTIVES

Vp And Chief Procurement Officer, Frank J. Crespo
Svp And President And Ceo Progress Rail Services, William P. (Billy) Ainsworth
Vp Large Power Systems Division, Tana L. Utley
Vp Innovation & Technology Development Division (itdd) And Cto, Thomas J. (Tom) Bluth
Group President And Cfo, Bradley M. (Brad) Halverson, $786,312 total compensation
Group President Customer And Dealer Support, Robert B. (Rob) Charter, $729,768 total compensation
Vp Industrial Power Systems, Ramin Younessi
Group President Resources Industries, Denise C. Johnson
Ceo, D. James (Jim) Umpleby, $825,636 total compensation
Vp China Operations, Qihua Chen
Group President Energy And Transportation Group, Thomas (Tom) Pellette
Vp And President Solar Turbines, Pablo M. Koziner
Vp Global Information Services (gis) And Cio, Julie A. Lagacy
Vp Surface Mining & Technology Division (sm&t), Jean Savage
Interim Evp Law And Public Policy, Suzette M. Long
Group President Construction Industries, Bob De Lange
Vp Asia Pacific Cis Africa & Middle East Distribution Division (apds), Wai Man (Raymond) Chan
Vp Global Power Solutions, Thomas G. (Tom) Frake
Vp Building Construction Products (bcp), Kenneth J. (Ken) Hoefling
Vp Excavation, Zachary A. (Zach) Kauk
Vp Material Handling And Underground Division, Karl E. Weiss
Vp And President Caterpillar Financial Services Corporation, David T. (Dave) Walton
Vp Product Support & Logistics Division (psld), Chris Snodgrass
Vp Global Construction & Infrastructure (gci), Damien Giraud
Vp Earthmoving Division, Frederic Istas
Vice President, Steven Fisher
Vice President Cat Digital, Ogi Redzic
Vice President Of Marketing And Corporate And Strategic Development, Ricky Sweeney
Vice President Finance, Theresa Dickens
Vice President, Mark Bainbridge
Chairman, David L. (Dave) Calhoun
Assistant Secretary, Desmond Eppel
Assistant Secretary, Barbara Thomas
Treasurer, Patrick Mccartan
Auditors: PricewaterhouseCoopers LLP

LOCATIONS

HQ: Caterpillar Inc.
510 Lake Cook Road, Suite 100, Deerfield, IL 60015
Phone: 224 551-4000
Web: www.caterpillar.com

2018 Sales

	$ mil.	% of total
Outside United States	32,032	59
Inside United States	22,690	41
Total	**54,722**	**100**

2018 Sales

	$ mil.	% of total
North America	25,623	47
Asia/Pacific	12,475	23
EAME	11,929	22
Latin America	4,695	8
Total	**54,722**	**100**

PRODUCTS/OPERATIONS

2018 Sales

	$ mil.	% of total
Construction Industries	23,237	39
Energy & Transportation	22,785	38
Resources Industries	10,270	17
All other segments	482	1
Corporate Items & Eliminations	(4952)	-
Financial Products	3,279	5
Corporate Items & Eliminations	(379)	-
Total	**54,722**	**100**

Selected Brands

CAT
Caterpillar
CAT Financial
CAT Reman
CAT The Rental Store
Anchor
Asiatrak
Hindustan
Hypac
FG Wilson
MaK
MWM
Olympian
Perkins
Prentice
Progress Rail
SEM
Solar Turbines
Turner Powertrain Systems
Yellowmark
Kemper Valve & Fittings
M2M

COMPETITORS

ALSTOM	Hitachi Construction
Atlas Copco	Machinery
Bombardier	Hyundai Heavy
Charles Machine Works	Industries
Cummins	Komatsu
DEUTZ	Kubota
Deere	Navistar International
Detroit Diesel	Sandvik
Doosan Infracore	Sumitomo Heavy
GE	Industries
Generac Holdings	Volvo

HISTORICAL FINANCIALS

Company Type: Public

Income Statement

FYE: December 31

	REVENUE ($ mil.)	NET INCOME ($ mil.)	NET PROFIT MARGIN	EMPLOYEES
12/19	53,800	6,093	11.3%	102,300
12/18	54,722	6,147	11.2%	104,000
12/17	45,462	754	1.7%	98,400
12/16	38,537	(67)	—	98,400
12/15	47,011	2,102	4.5%	105,700
Annual Growth	3.4%	30.5%	—	(0.8%)

2019 Year-End Financials

Debt ratio: 48.00%
Return on equity: 42.57%
Cash ($ mil.): 8,284
Current ratio: 1.47
Long-term debt ($ mil.): 26,281

No. of shares (mil.): 550
Dividends
  Yield: 2.5%
  Payout: 35.8%
Market value ($ mil.): 81,236

	STOCK PRICE ($) FY Close	P/E High/Low		PER SHARE ($) Earnings	Dividends	Book Value
12/19	147.68	14	10	10.74	3.78	26.52
12/18	127.07	16	11	10.26	3.28	24.39
12/17	157.58	125	72	1.26	3.10	22.92
12/16	92.74	—	—	(0.11)	3.08	22.40
12/15	67.96	26	18	3.50	2.94	25.43
Annual Growth	21.4%	—		32.4%	6.5%	1.1%

Cathay General Bancorp

Cathay General Bancorp is the holding company for Cathay Bank which mainly serves Chinese and Vietnamese communities from some 30 branches in California and about 20 more in Illinois New Jersey New York Massachusetts Washington and Texas. It also has a branch in Hong Kong and offices in Shanghai and Taipei. Catering to small to medium-sized businesses and individual consumers the bank offers standard deposit services and loans. Commercial mortgage loans account for more than half of the bank's portfolio; business loans comprise nearly 25%. The bank's Cathay Wealth Management unit offers online stock trading mutual funds and other investment products and services through an agreement with PrimeVest.

Geographic Reach

California state-chartered Cathay Bank has branches in California Illinois Massachusetts New Jersey New York Texas and Washington. Overseas it has a branch in Hong Kong and offices in Shanghai and Taipei.

Financial Performance

The bank's revenue is on a downward trend. In 2012 revenue declined more than 5% vs. 2011 after posting a 3% decline in the previous annual comparison. Indeed between 2008 and 2012 revenue dipped by about 17% on lower interest income and dividend income. However the bank's profit picture is improving with net income up in 2012 for the third consecutive year.

Strategy

With 60% of its branches in California — a state hard hit by the downturn in the housing market — Cathay Bank's real estate secured loan portfolio has suffered as the value of the underlying collateral plummeted. In 2010 the company entered into a memorandum of understanding with the FDIC to reduce its concentration of commercial real estate loans improve its capital ratios reduce overall risk and strengthen asset quality. The moves have helped the company to cut its losses. The bank has also been successful growing deposits.

Mergers and Acquisitions

In 2016 Cathay Bank agreed to buy SinoPac Bancorp from Taiwan's Bank SinoPac for $340 million. SinoPac's Far East National Bank operates nine branches including five in Los Angeles. After the deal closes Cathay plans to close a number of branches. The transaction will help boost the company's balance sheet.

EXECUTIVES

Sevp And Coo, Irwin Wong, age 71, $339,777 total compensation
Evp And Chief Credit Officer Cathay Bank, Donald S. Chow, age 69, $312,615 total compensation
Evp Cfo And Treasurer, Heng W. Chen, age 68, $416,542 total compensation
Chairman President And Ceo Cathay General Bancorp And Chairman And Ceo Cathay Bank, Pin Tai, $424,900 total compensation
Evp And Chief Risk Officer Cathy Bank, Kim R. Bingham, age 63
Assistant Vice President Marketing, Chris Lu
Vice President And Portfolio Manager, Ronald Chen
Vice President Special Assets Department, Margaret Waye
Board Member, Felix Fernandez
Auditors: KPMG LLP

LOCATIONS

HQ: Cathay General Bancorp
777 North Broadway, Los Angeles, CA 90012
Phone: 213 625-4700
Web: www.cathaybank.com

2015 Branch offices

	No.
Southern California Branches	21
Northern California Branches	12
New York Branches	12
Illinois Branches	4
Washington Branches	3
Texas Branches	2
Massachusetts Branch	1
Nevada Branch	1
New Jersey Branch	1
Maryland Branch	1
Overseas Branch	1
Total	**59**

PRODUCTS/OPERATIONS

2015 sales

	$ mil.	% of total
Interest and Dividend income		
Loan receivable	427	88
Investment securities- taxable	21	4
Federal Home Loan Bank stock	3	1
Deposits with banks	1	-
Non-Interest income		
Securities losses net	(3.3)	-
Letters of credit commissions	5	1
Depository service fees	5	1
Other operating income	25	5
Total	**486**	**100**

Products/Services

Personal
Accounts
Checking Accounts
Savings Accounts
CDs
IRA CD
Debit Cards
Loans
Mortgage Loan
Home Equity Financing
Auto Loan
Credit Cards
Cathay Online Banking
Mobile Banking
Business/Commercial
Business Accounts
Business Checking Account
Business Savings Account
CDs
Cash Management Services
Merchant Deposit Capture
Zero Balance Account
Lockbox Service
Merchant Bankcard Services
Courier Deposit Service
Armored Transport Services
Cash Vault Services
Business Online Banking
Loans
Commercial Financing
Real Estate & Construction Financing
International Banking & Financing
Smart Capital Line
SBA Guaranteed Loan Program
Credit Cards

COMPETITORS

Bank of America	Grandpoint
Citibank	Hanmi Financial
East West Bancorp	Hope Bancorp
Far East National Bank	U.S. Bancorp

HISTORICAL FINANCIALS

Company Type: Public

Income Statement

FYE: December 31

	ASSETS ($ mil.)	NET INCOME ($ mil.)	INCOME AS % OF ASSETS	EMPLOYEES
12/19	18,094	279	1.5%	1,219
12/18	16,784	271	1.6%	1,277
12/17	15,640	176	1.1%	1,271
12/16	14,520	175	1.2%	1,129
12/15	13,254	161	1.2%	1,122
Annual Growth	8.1%	14.7%	—	2.1%

2019 Year-End Financials

Debt ratio: 0.82%
Return on equity: 12.64%
Cash ($ mil.): 593
Current ratio: —
Long-term debt ($ mil.): —

No. of shares (mil.): 79
Dividends
Yield: 3.2%
Payout: 36.0%
Market value ($ mil.): 3,034

	STOCK PRICE ($) FY Close	P/E High/Low		PER SHARE ($) Earnings	Dividends	Book Value
12/19	38.05	11	9	3.48	1.24	28.78
12/18	33.53	13	10	3.33	1.03	26.36
12/17	42.17	20	16	2.17	0.87	24.39
12/16	38.03	17	12	2.19	0.75	22.97
12/15	31.33	17	12	1.98	0.56	21.63
Annual Growth	5.0%	—	—	15.1%	22.0%	7.4%

CBRE Group Inc

As a commercial real estate services company CBRE Group provides leasing property sales occupier outsourcing and valuation businesses from about 530 offices worldwide. Subsidiary Trammell Crow provides property development services for corporate and institutional clients primarily in the US. CBRE Global Investors manages real estate investments for institutional clients. The company garners about 60% of its revenue from the Americas. CBRE was founded in San Francisco in 1906 and by the 1940s grew to be one of the largest commercial real estate services firms in the western US.c

HISTORY

Colbert Coldwell and Albert Tucker started real estate brokerage Tucker Lynch & Coldwell in 1906 in San Francisco. In 1922 the company expanded to Los Angeles where it began developing real estate in 1933 with a 60-acre subdivision in the burgeoning city.

Having profited from California's rapid growth in the 1950s and 1960s the firm expanded out of state. The partnership incorporated in 1962 as Coldwell Banker which went public in 1968. Sears Roebuck & Co. bought the company in 1981 for 80% above its market price. But by 1991 Sears had abandoned aims to become a financial services giant and sold Coldwell Banker's commercial operations to The Carlyle Group as CB Commercial Real Estate Services Group.

Free of Sears but $56 million in the red the company didn't return to profitability until 1993. Two years later it embarked on a shopping spree in real estate services buying tenant representatives Langon Rieder and Westmark Realty. In 1996 the company went public and bought mortgage banker L. J. Melody & Company (which was re-named CBRE | Melody); it purchased Koll Real Estate Services in 1997.

In 1998 the company widened its global scope with the acquisition of REI Limited the non-UK operations of Richard Ellis; it was renamed CB Richard Ellis Services. CB Richard Ellis also bought Hillier Parker May & Rowden (now operating in the UK as CB Hillier) a London-based provider of commercial property services.

CB Richard Ellis experienced a revenue crunch in 1999 and responded by restructuring its North American operations into three divisions (transaction financial and management services) and cutting management ranks by 30%. Growth continued in 1999 with the purchase of Pittsburgh-based Gold & Co. the addition of an office in Venezuela and a fat contract to manage more than 1100 locations for Prudential.

In 2000 the company committed significant resources to the Internet inking a deal to offer the lease management services of MyContracts.com and investing in Canadian real estate transaction tracker RealNet Canada.

A group of investors including then-CEO Ray Wirta chairman Richard Blum (and his BLUM Capital Partners) and Freeman Spogli took the company private in 2001. Blum Capital Partners bought the 60% of publicly traded CBRE that it did not already own forming CBRE Holding. Three years later the company went public once again.

In 2003 CBRE merged with top commercial real estate broker and property manager Insignia Financial. The next year the company changed its name to CB Richard Ellis Group and went public. It bought rival Trammell Crow in 2006 as well as a dozen or so other companies as it sought to fill in its holdings. The acquisitions deepened CBRE's outsourcing services especially project and facilities management for corporate and institutional clients in the US.

CBRE spun off former subsidiary Realty Finance Corporation in 2008 after the real estate investment trust continued to post losses in a troubled credit market.

Also in 2008 it opened its first offices in Bahrain and joined forces with Vanke to provide residential property management services in China. The following year CBRE expanded its existing UK-based investment banking business (advisory and restructuring services for real estate hospitality and gaming companies) to the Americas.

CBRE in 2011 made one of its largest deals in several years. The company bolstered its global real estate investment management business with the acquisition of ING Groep's real estate investment management operations for some $940 million. The Dutch firm's real estate investment management business in Asia and Europe was merged into CBRE Global Investors and more than doubled the size of the unit. The transaction also included US-based Clarion Real Estate Securities and interests in commercial real estate co-investments. (The ING deal helped boost CBRE's investment management revenue by more than 60% in 2012.)

In November 2012 CBRE acquired EA Shaw. a independent commercial and residential property partnership specializing in central London. The purchase significantly enhanced the firm's business in central London.

In 2013 CBRE acquired technical engineering services firm Norland Managed Services Ltd. which specialized in commercial buildings in the UK and Ireland and had a growing customer base in the US and Singapore.

The firm also in 2013 purchased The CAC Group a top commercial real estate services firm based in San Francisco. The move made CBRE the #1 provider of commercial property management and leasing in the market. CBRE also bought property and asset management specialist SOGES-MAINT-CBRE to build on its previous acquisitions in the Netherlands the Czech Republic Slovakia Poland Latvia and Lithuania. Additionally in 2013 CBRE acquired commercial real estate services business Resource Estate Partners and TPA Realty Services both based in Atlanta where it's working to boost its market share.

EXECUTIVES

President Ceo And Director, Robert E. (Bob) Sulentic, age 64, $990,000 total compensation

Ceo Global Workplace Solutions (gws), William F. (Bill) Concannon, age 64, $675,000 total compensation

Global President Capital Markets, Christopher R. Ludeman

Cfo And Global Director Of Corporate Development, James R. (Jim) Groch, age 58, $770,000 total compensation

Global Group President Geographies, Calvin W. (Cal) Frese, age 64, $680,000 total compensation

Global President Debt And Structured Finance, Brian F. Stoffers

Ceo Asia Pacific, Steven A. (Steve) Swerdlow

Global Group President Lines Of Business & Client Care, Michael J. (Mike) Lafitte, age 59, $700,000 total compensation

Global Chief Investment Officer And Ceo Cbre Global Investors And Cbre Clarion Securities, T. Ritson Ferguson, age 60, $800,000 total compensation

Chairman Asia Pacific, Robert (Rob) Blain, age 65, $560,000 total compensation

Evp And General Counsel, Laurence H. Midler, age 55, $325,000 total compensation

Global Director Client Care, Tony Long

Ceo Trammell Crow Company., Matt Khourie

President Cbre Global Investors, Daniel (Danny) Queenan

Evp Global Brokerage And Sales Management, Laura OBrien

Ceo Americas, Jack Durburg

Ceo Cbre Europe Middle East And Africa (emea), Martin Samworth

Global President Occupier Advisory And Transaction Services, Whitley Collins

Global President Asset Services And Valuation And Advisory Services (vas), Mary Jo Eaton

President Cbre Southern California - Hawaii, Lewis Horne

Vice Chairman Capital Markets And Institutional Properties, Michael Hines

Chief Digital And Technology Officer, Chandra Dhandapani

Vice Chairman Cbre Capital Markets Debt And Structured Finance, Rocco Mandala

Senior Vice President, Jeff Carr

Senior Vice President Debt And Structured Finance, Peter Gineris

First Vice President, Craig Lillibridge

Senior Vice President And Head Econic Incentive Solutions Group, Eric Stavriotis

Vice President, Sue Zickefoose

Senior Vice President, Gregg Haly

Executive Vice President Advisory And Transaction Chicago, Mark Pasquella

Senior Vice President Partner, Alden Anderson

Senior Vice President, Steven Brabant

Senior Vice President, Pat Viele

Vice President Of Corporate Marketing, Tracy Allen

Senior Vice President Los Angeles, Richard Ratner

Executive Vice President, Jeffrey C Babikian

First Vice President, Don Weis

Vice President, John Slivka

Executive Vice President Advisory And Transaction Chicago, Chris Reynolds

Senior Vice President, Michael Moran

First Vice President, Phillip Linton

Senior Vice President Global Head Of Total Rewards, Kelly Pool
Vice President, Andrew Ewald
Senior Vice President, Jim Koenig
Senior Vice President, Peter Kast
Vice President, Nancy Johnson
First Vice President, Taylor Hillenmeyer
Vice President, Julius Tabert
Senior Vice President, Trey Pennington
Vice President Information Technology, Mike Washington
Senior Vice President, Ned Burns
Senior Vice President, Dave Mcelroy
Vice President, Haydon Burns
Senior Vice President, Bradley Gingerich
Vice President Senior, Mary O'Connor
Vice President, Brian Beaty
Vice President, Mitchell Stravitz
Executive Vice President, Thomas Bohlinger
Senior Vice President, Greg Geraci
Senior Vice President, Jerome E Kranzel
Senior Vice President, Doug Jackson
Vice President, Andy Blunt
Senior Vice President, Phillip Sample
Senior Vice President, Michael Shustak
Senior Vice President, Eric Smith
Senior Vice President, Rod Apodaca
Senior Vice President Investment Properties, Alex Kozakov
Vice President, Justin Mohler
Senior Vice President, Cal Wessman
Senior Vice President Of Retail, Joe Belinske
First Vice President, John Boote
Senior Vice President Based, Daniel Woodward
First Vice President Brokerage Services, Andrew Stefanich
Senior Vice President, Chris Caras
Senior Vice President, Alan Krueger
Vice President, Ben Bastian
Vice President, Philip Weber
First Vice President, Michael Curran
Senior Vice President Of Industrial Properties, Mark Writt
Senior Vice President, Jed Stirnkorb
Vice President Human Resources, Mari Flynn
First Vice President, Daniel Brandel
Senior Vice President, Jon Schultz
Senior Vice President, Meredith Freese
Vice President, Leonard Santoro
Senior Vice President Partner, Rob Walles
Svp Retail Investments, Ian Schroeder
Vice President, Erik Parker
Senior Vice President, Michael Shover
Senior Vice President, Eric Comer
Vas Vice President, Clinton Bogart
First Vice President, Bob Pielsticker
Vice President, John Hamilton
Vice President, Matt Patyk
First Vice President, Dwayne Flynn
Vice President, Izzy Eichenstein
Vice President, Ryan Thornton
First Vice President, Steve Delaney
First Vice President, Patrick Wade
Vice President, Rabih Malaeb
Vice President Brokerage Services, Annah Moore
Senior Vice President, Brad Wilner
Senior Vice President, Carlos Vigon
Vice President, Joseph Orscheln
Senior Vice President, Nat Gambuzza
Vice President, Vincent Polce
Vice President, Jim Angelotti
Vice President Corporate Human Resources, Beverly Bradshaw
Vice President, Michael P Wall
Senior Vice President, Paul Chaput
Senior Vice President, Andy Wimsatt
Senior Vice President, Michael Wilson
Vice President, Nicholas Emerson
Sp Vice President, William Kuntz
Mai Vice President, Mark Mediavilla

Lp Senior Vice President, Van Wehr
Senior Vice President Institutional Properties Multifamily, Robert Dean
Vice President, Tommy Molin
Vice President Global Enterprise Systems, Will Wende
Senior Vice President, Jeremy Ballenger
First Vice President, Jared Ross
Vice President, Tom Zorn
Senior Vice President, Steve Preston
First Vice President, Will Lightfoot
Vice President, Daniel Boring
Vice President, John Makowski
Vice President, Angel Benschneider
Senior Vice President, Mike Fahey
Senior Vice President, Kevin Mclennan
Vice President, Bennett Johnson
First Vice President, Annie Prupas
Senior Vice President, Anthony Gaiti
Senior Vice President, Martin Rolh
Vice President, Johnsun Cha
Mai Vice President, Jonathan Barker
Executive Vice President, Bob Kraynak
Senior Vice President, Larry Dinner
First Vice President, Jessica Birmingham
Executive Vice President, Patrick Gallagher
Executive Vice President, Phil Voorhees
Senior Vice President, Jeff Kapcheck
Vice President, Brad Weiner
Vice President, Sonya Schmidt
Vice President, Whit Jordan
Senior Vice President, Darrell Hernandez
First Vice President, Peter Langhoff
Senior Vice President, Jason Lind
Senior Vice President, Ross Marshall
Senior Vice President, Rick Schuch
Senior Vice President, Robert Aycock
Senior Vice President Business Development, Letizia Rubino
Auditors: KPMG LLP

LOCATIONS

HQ: CBRE Group Inc
2100 McKinney Avenue, 12th Floor, Dallas, TX 75201
Phone: 214 979-6100
Web: www.cbre.com

2016 Sales

	$ mil.	% of total
Americas	7,226	55
Europe Middle East & Africa	3,917	30
Asia/Pacific	1,485	11
Global investment management	369	3
Development services	71	1
Total	**13,071**	**100**

2016 Sales

	$ mil.	% of total
US	6,917	55
UK	2,094	18
Other countries	4,059	27
Total	**13,071**	**100**

PRODUCTS/OPERATIONS

Selected Industries
CBRE Hotels
Data Centers
Energy & Sustainability
Golf & Resort Properties
Healthcare
Industrial & Logistics
Labor Analytics
Multifamily
Office
Public Institutions & Education
Residential
Retail
Alternative Investments Practice
Labor Analytics
Life Sciences

Selected Subsidiaries
CBRE Inc.
CBRE Capital Markets Inc.
CB/TCC LLC
CBRE Global Holdings SARL
CBRE Finance Europe LLP
CBRE Limited
CBRE Services Inc.
Norland Managed Services Ltd.
Trammell Crow Company LLC
CBRE Luxembourg Holdings SARL
CBRE Global Acquisition Company SARL
Relam Amsterdam Holdings
CBRE Limited Partnership

Selected service Investors
Financing
Investment Administration
Investment Banking
Leasing & Advisory
Loan Servicing
Property Management
Property Sales
Valuation & Advisory

Selected services for occupiers
Facilities Management
Leasing & Advisory
Management Consulting
Project Management
Valuation & Advisory
Workplace

Selected Business Lines
Advisory & Transaction Services
Asset Services
Capital Markets
Global Workplace Solutions
Valuation & Advisory Services
Investment Management (CBRE Global Investors)
Development Services (Trammell Crow Company)
CB/TCC LLC
CBRE Finance Europe LLPCBRE Luxembourg Holdings SARLCBRE Global Acquisition Company SARLRelam Amsterdam HoldingsCBRE Limited Partnership

COMPETITORS

BGC Partners	Inland Group
Cassidy Turley	Jones Lang LaSalle
Colliers International	Lincoln Property
Colliers International Group	Marcus & Millichap
Cushman & Wakefield	Mitsui Fudosan
Eastdil Secured	Realogy Holdings
	Savills Studley

HISTORICAL FINANCIALS
Company Type: Public

Income Statement   FYE: December 31

	REVENUE ($ mil.)	NET INCOME ($ mil.)	NET PROFIT MARGIN	EMPLOYEES
12/19	23,894	1,282	5.4%	100,000
12/18	21,340	1,063	5.0%	90,000
12/17	14,209	691	4.9%	80,000
12/16	13,071	571	4.4%	75,000
12/15	10,855	547	5.0%	70,000
Annual Growth	21.8%	23.7%	—	9.3%

2019 Year-End Financials

Debt ratio: 16.95%	No. of shares (mil.): 334
Return on equity: 22.96%	Dividends
Cash ($ mil.): 971	Yield: —
Current ratio: 1.17	Payout: —
Long-term debt ($ mil.): 1,761	Market value ($ mil.): 20,517

STOCK PRICE ($)		P/E		PER SHARE ($)		
	FY Close	High/Low		Earnings	Dividends	Book Value
12/19	61.29	16	10	3.77	0.00	18.62
12/18	40.04	16	12	3.10	0.00	14.66
12/17	43.31	22	15	2.03	0.00	11.84
12/16	31.49	20	14	1.69	0.00	8.94
12/15	34.58	24	19	1.63	0.00	8.12
Annual Growth	15.4%	—		23.3%	—	23.1%

CBTX Inc

Auditors: Grant Thornton LLP

LOCATIONS

HQ: CBTX Inc
9 Greenway Plaza, Suite 110, Houston, TX 77046
Phone: 713 210-7600
Web: www.communitybankoftx.com

HISTORICAL FINANCIALS

Company Type: Public

Income Statement   FYE: December 31

	ASSETS ($ mil.)	NET INCOME ($ mil.)	INCOME AS % OF ASSETS	EMPLOYEES
12/19	3,478	50	1.5%	500
12/18	3,279	47	1.4%	495
12/17	3,081	27	0.9%	462
12/16	2,951	27	0.9%	472
12/15	2,882	24	0.8%	
Annual Growth	4.8%	20.3%	—	—

2019 Year-End Financials

Debt ratio: —	No. of shares (mil.): 24
Return on equity: 9.87%	Dividends
Cash ($ mil.): 372	Yield: 1.2%
Current ratio: —	Payout: 19.3%
Long-term debt ($ mil.): —	Market value ($ mil.): 777

STOCK PRICE ($)		P/E		PER SHARE ($)		
	FY Close	High/Low		Earnings	Dividends	Book Value
12/19	31.12	17	13	2.02	0.40	21.45
12/18	29.40	20	15	1.89	0.20	19.58
12/17	29.66	24	23	1.22	0.05	17.97
Annual Growth	1.2%	—		13.4%	68.2%	4.5%

CDW Corp

Auditors: Ernst & Young LLP

LOCATIONS

HQ: CDW Corp
75 Tri-State International, Lincolnshire, IL 60069
Phone: 847 465-6000
Web: www.cdw.com

HISTORICAL FINANCIALS

Company Type: Public

Income Statement   FYE: December 31

	REVENUE ($ mil.)	NET INCOME ($ mil.)	NET PROFIT MARGIN	EMPLOYEES
12/19	18,032	736	4.1%	250
12/18	16,240	643	4.0%	250
12/17	15,191	523	3.4%	250
12/16	13,981	424	3.0%	8,516
12/15	12,988	403	3.1%	8,465
Annual Growth	8.5%	16.3%	—	(58.5%)

2019 Year-End Financials

Debt ratio: 41.47%	No. of shares (mil.): 143
Return on equity: 76.14%	Dividends
Cash ($ mil.): 154	Yield: 0.8%
Current ratio: 1.24	Payout: 26.5%
Long-term debt ($ mil.): 3,283	Market value ($ mil.): 20,426

STOCK PRICE ($)		P/E		PER SHARE ($)		
	FY Close	High/Low		Earnings	Dividends	Book Value
12/19	142.84	28	15	4.99	1.27	6.72
12/18	81.05	23	16	4.19	0.93	6.60
12/17	69.49	21	15	3.31	0.69	6.42
12/16	52.09	21	13	2.56	0.48	6.52
12/15	42.04	20	14	2.35	0.31	6.52
Annual Growth	35.8%	—		20.7%	42.1%	0.8%

Centene Corp

Centene provides health insurance to more than 15 million members in more than 45 US states and about 5 international markets. Centene is a leading Medicaid managed care provider serving low-income families and disabled people through state Medicaid plans the Children's Health Insurance Program (CHIP) Long-Term Services and Supports (LTSS) and other programs. Centene also offers Medicare military and commercial insurance plans. It provides specialty services in areas such as vision and dental benefits wellness home health and pharmacy benefits management. Centene has bought Medicaid insurer WellCare for nearly $20 billion.

Operations

Centene operates in two primary segments: Managed Care and Specialty Services.

The Managed Care segment accounting for more than 80% of total revenue provides Medicaid coverage under programs including CHIP LTSS behavioral health foster care and ABD (aged blind and disabled) programs. The state-based plans are operated under names such as Managed Health Services (Wisconsin and Indiana) Superior HealthPlan (Texas) and Buckeye Health Plan (Ohio). The segment also provides Medicare and military coverage and it operates commercial health plans for groups and individuals.

The Specialty Services segment (nearly 20% of total revenue) provides a range of health care services and products to the Managed Care segment and other customers. Its Envolve division provides health triage wellness and disease management services pharmacy solutions as well as vision and dental services. Other units offer case management (CaseNet) correctional healthcare services (Centurion) home-based primary care (US Medical Management) analytics (Interpreta) federal services

(Health Net Federal Services) and clinical healthcare (Community Medical Group).

Geographic Reach

Centene serves plan members in more than 45 states and about 5 international markets. California New York and Texas are its largest markets.

Headquartered in St. Louis Missouri the company also offers health administrations concession services in Spain and provider network management in the UK.

Sales and Marketing

Most of Centene's revenue comes under contract or subcontract with state Medicaid managed care programs. The State of California State of New York and the State of Texas are its largest customers. California brings 10% New York with 15% and another 10% of sales from Texas. Medicaid account for about 70% of sales while Medicare account for some 10%. Commercial health plans provided to employer groups and individuals account for more than 15% of revenue.

Its Specialty Services segment serves state programs health care organizations correctional facilities employer groups and other organizations.

Financial Performance

Centene's revenue has grown significantly over the past five years as the company acquires other firms adds and retains state contracts and enters new business areas with sales more than tripling between 2015 and 2019. Net income has also tripled over the past five years.

Revenues increased 24% to $74.6 billion in 2019 primarily due to the acquisition of Fidelis Care growth in the Health Insurance Marketplace business expansions and new programs in many states in 2018 and 2019 particularly Arkansas Illinois Iowa New Mexico and Pennsylvania. These increases were partially offset by the health insurer fee moratorium in 2019.

Net income rose 47% to $1.3 billion in 2019 due to the higher revenue figure offset by higher sales and service costs and increased income tax expenses.

The company ended 2019 with $12.1 billion in cash up $6.8 billion from 2018. Operating activities contributed $1.5 billion while investing activities used $1.5 billion primarily for purchases of investments and financing activities contributed $6.8 billion mostly for payments of long-term debt.

Strategy

Centene aims to increase its Medicaid Medicare and Health Insurance Marketplace membership through alliances with key providers outreach efforts development and implementation of community-specific products and acquisitions. In 2020 they have expanded their Health Insurance Marketplace footprints in several existing markets and they also completed the WellCare Acquisition further expanding their scale and presence.

Centene's primary growth strategies are to enter new markets and expand in existing markets via acquisitions. In 2020 the company began operating in Illinois under the first phase of an expanded contract for the Medicaid Managed Care Program. Its New Mexico subsidiary Western Sky Community Care also began operating under a new statewide contract in New Mexico for the Centennial Care 2.0 Program. The company also completed the acquisition of QCA Health Plan Inc. and QualChoice Life and Health Insurance Company Inc. which will expands their footprint in Arkansas by adding additional members primarily through commercial products.

Centene's growth strategy also includes expansion of health plans participating in government sponsored healthcare programs and specialty services businesses contract rights and related assets of other health plans both in their existing service areas and in new markets and start-up operations in new markets or new products in existing markets. They will continue to pursue opportunistic acquisitions to expand into new geographies and complementary business lines as well as to augment existing operations.

Mergers and Acquisitions

In 2020 Centene Corporation acquired all of the issued and outstanding shares of WellCare Health Plans Inc. The transaction is valued at nearly $20 billion. With the completion of the transaction the previously announced divestitures of Centene's Illinois Medicaid and Medicare Advantage plans WellCare's Missouri Medicaid and Medicare Advantage plans and WellCare's Nebraska Medicaid plan have closed.

In 2019 Centen purchased an additional 40% ownership in Ribera Salud for some $55 million bringing their total ownership to 90%. Ribera Salud manages health administration concessions in various regions in Spain.

Company Background

Centene traces its roots to the 1984 founding of a nonprofit Medicaid plan (Family Hospital Physician Associates) by former Wisconsin hospital bookkeeper Elizabeth "Betty" Brinn. The firm restructured as a Wisconsin holding company in 1993 and expanded into Indiana in 1996. It was renamed Centene and moved its headquarters to St. Louis in 1997.

Centene reincorporated in Delaware and became a publicly traded entity in 2001; it moved to the NYSE in 2003 and launched its Buckeye Health Plan in Ohio in 2004. It expanded into Georgia and Arizona in 2006 added Absolute Total Care in South Carolina in 2007 and moved into Florida and Massachusetts in 2009.

It expanded into more than 15 additional states between 2010 and 2018. Acquisitions included Cenpatico (2003) Opticare (2006) Celtic Group (2008) AcariaHealth (2013) and Health Net (2016).

EXECUTIVES

Svp Products, Kevin J. Counihan
President And Coo, Cynthia J. (Cindy) Brinkley, age 60, $650,000 total compensation
Chairman And Ceo, Michael F. Neidorff, age 77, $1,500,000 total compensation
Evp Mergers & Acquisitions And Chief Strategy Officer, Jesse N. Hunter, age 44, $650,000 total compensation
Evp Markets, Christopher D. Bowers, age 64
Evp General Counsel And Secretary, Keith H. Williamson, age 67, $600,000 total compensation
Evp Cfo And Treasurer, Jeffrey A Schwaneke, age 45, $632,671 total compensation
Evp And Cio, Mark J. Brooks, age 50
Vice President Sales Marketing And Business Development, Kristine Ziegler
Vice President Of Actuarial Services, Don Killian
Vice President Of Finance, Trip Peeples
Vice President Hospital Operations, Michael Bailey
Corporate Vice President Business Development, Wade Rakes
Senior Vice President Patient Services, Susan Ekvall
Vice President Assistant Controller, Katie Casso
Vice President Of Medical Affairs, David Harmon
Vice President Information Technology Security; Chief Information Security Officer, Dustin Wilcox
Vice President Medical Management, Kendra Case
Vice President Tax Services, Cynthia Lemons
Vice President, Arvan Chan
Senior Vice President Individual Business, Anand Shukla
Vice President Information Technology, Keith Hibbard
Director Of Pharmacy, Alicia Cyrus
Assistant Vice President Of Systems Information Technology, Cindy Adams

Medical Director, David Gilchrist
Vice President Human Resources, Barbara Basham
Vice President Actuarial Srvs And Risk Management, Steele Stewart
Vice President Of Business Development, Stacey Hull
Vice President Human Resources, Trevan Ross
Senior Vice President Business Development, Debra Cooper
Vice President Of Human Resour, Jalie Cohen
Vice President Of Human Resources, Mary-Katherine Kutac
Vice President Information Technology, Steele Sloane
Vice President Of User Experience, Amy Poole-yaeger
Vice President Of Operations, Kristine Cusimano
Vice President Of Human Resources, Stephanie Hall
Vice President Of Payment Innovation, Ananth Lalithakumar
Vice President, Donald Pifer
Vice President And Director, Carolyn Thomas
Corporate Medical Director, Julianne Mazurek
Senior Vice President Government Relations, Jonathan Dinesman
Vice President Operations, James Sefcik
Vice President Pharmacy Operations, Justin Weiss
Senior Vice President, Edmund Kroll
Vice President Facility Management And Construction, Andrea Cruce
Vice President Medical Management, Marion Sustakoski
Vice President Of Medical Affairs, Ronald Charles
Vice President Health Plan Operations, Kevin OToole
Executive Vice President, Mark Eggert
Vice President Compliance, Jeff Torres
Director Of Pharmacy, James Frank Reynolds
Vice President Product Solutions, Lisa McClellan
Vice President Customer Service, Rodney Long
Vice President Marketing, John Howell
Director Of Pharmacy Operations, Martha Exton
Vice President, William Scheffel
Vice President Pharmacy Operations Federal Programs, Jeff Borowiecki
Vice President Of Organizational Development, Tony Myers
Vice President Of Medical Management New Business, Judy Bauer
Vice President Procurement And Strategic Sourcing, Rob Cox
Senior Vice President Hoalth Services, Debra Smyers
Vice President Ethics And Compliance, Bob Miromonti
Vice President Finance, Steven Kerr
Senior Vice President Boston, Chris Dycus
Vice President Of Finance, Nitin Jain
Vice President Medical Management Clinical Systems, Alice Stewart
Evp Sales And Account Management Envolve Pharmacy Solutions, Carmen Fontanez
Vp Compliance, Kathleen Harkness
Vice President Strategy And Business Development, Brett Tindall
Clinical Director, Rachel Blaising
Vice President Information Technology Operations Strategy And Business Development, Brian Holman
Senior Vice President And Chief Security Risk Officer, Louis Desorbo
Senior Vice President Of Medical Affairs, Marcus Wallace
Vice President Product Development Hemophilia Acariahealth, Charles Signorino
Senior Vp Chief Security Risk Officer (csro), Lou Desorbo
Vice President Compliance And Government Affairs, Terrica Miller

Vice President Quality Buckeye Health Plan, Hagy Wegener
Vice President Medical Management Um Superior Health Plan, Janice Wierschke
Vice President Of Operations, Jackie Shearer-adams
Vp Finance, Sarah Baiocchi
Assistant Vice President Account Executive, Steven Merahn
Senior Vice President, Julie Bugala
Vice President Talent Acquisition, Dan Nielsen
Director Of Government Relations Coordinated Care Health Plan, Andrea Tull
Vice President Medicare, Franz Lorenz
Vice President Human Resources, Sheila Riordan
Vice President Ethics And Compliance, Donovan Ayers
Vice President Quality Improvment, Tal Zarom
Vice President Talent Management, Denise Grode
Vice President Of Product Performance, Abbie Lecoz
Vice President Legislative And Government Affairs Pennsylvania Health And Wellness, Norris Benns
Vice President, Ann Sciammacco
Vice President, Pam Perry
Vice President Human Resources Operations, Jaclyn Pettinari
Vice President Medicare Programs, Michael Franks
Senior Vice President Health Plans, Chris Bowers
Vice President Legislative And Government Affairs, Shawn Furey
Svp Social Responsibility, Patrick J Frawley
Vice President Compliance, Krug Iris
Vice President Assistant Treasurer, Louis Henderson
Vice President External Relations, Jennifer Guy
Medical Director, Dennis McCluskey
Senior Vice President Operations, Marcie Johnson
Vice President Implementation And Integration, Remedios Rodriguez
Secretary Treasurer, Patricia Atherton
Board Member, Tommy Thompson
Auditors: KPMG LLP

LOCATIONS

HQ: Centene Corp
7700 Forsyth Boulevard, St. Louis, MO 63105
Phone: 314 725-4477 **Fax:** 314 725-5180
Web: www.centene.com

PRODUCTS/OPERATIONS

2017 Sales

	$ mil.	% of total
Premiums	43,353	89
Premium tax & health insurer fee	2,762	6
Service	2,267	5
Total	**48,382**	**100**

2017 Sales by Segment

	$ mil.	% of total
Managed Care	45,842	79
Specialty Services	12,055	21
Adjustments	(9515)	-
Total	**48,382**	**100**

COMPETITORS

AMERIGROUP	Kaiser Foundation
Aetna	Health Plan
Anthem	Molina Healthcare
Blue Cross and Blue	Scott & White Health
Shield of Texas	Plan
CIGNA	UnitedHealth Group
Humana	WellCare Health Plans

HISTORICAL FINANCIALS

Company Type: Public

Income Statement   FYE: December 31

	REVENUE ($ mil.)	NET INCOME ($ mil.)	NET PROFIT MARGIN	EMPLOYEES
12/19	74,639	1,321	1.8%	56,600
12/18	60,116	900	1.5%	47,300
12/17	48,382	828	1.7%	33,700
12/16	40,607	562	1.4%	30,500
12/15	22,760	355	1.6%	18,200
Annual Growth	34.6%	38.9%	—	32.8%

2019 Year-End Financials

Debt ratio: 33.48%
Return on equity: 11.26%
Cash ($ mil.): 12,123
Current ratio: 1.57
Long-term debt ($ mil.): 13,638

No. of shares (mil.): 415
Dividends
Yield: —
Payout: —
Market value ($ mil.): 26,094

	STOCK PRICE ($) FY Close	P/E High/Low	PER SHARE ($) Earnings	Dividends	Book Value
12/19	62.87	41 13	3.14	0.00	30.24
12/18	115.30	64 43	2.26	0.00	26.47
12/17	100.88	43 24	2.35	0.00	19.75
12/16	56.51	43 29	1.72	0.00	17.14
12/15	65.81	81 35	1.44	0.00	8.96
Annual Growth	(1.1%)	— —	21.5%	—	35.5%

CenterPoint Energy, Inc

CenterPoint Energy Inc. one of the largest public utilities in the US distributes natural gas and electricity to more than 7 million customers. Through subsidiary CenterPoint Energy Resources Corp this holding company distributes natural gas to 4.6 million customers in six states. The company's other major subsidiary Houston Electric distributes electricity that reaches 2.5 million customers in the Texas Gulf Coast region including Houston. Beyond these regulated distributions (that requires rate approval from regional authorities) CenterPoint Energy also sells gas directly to some 31000 customers across 30 US states. These customers range from large industries and utilities to municipalities and educational institutions. In addition to its portfolio of about 55200 miles of power distribution lines and 76000 miles of gas distribution lines the holding company has about 55% equity investment in the master limited partnership Enable which maintains natural gas and crude oil infrastructure assets in five US states.

HISTORY

CenterPoint Energy's earliest predecessor Houston Electric Lighting and Power was formed in 1882 by a group including Emanuel Raphael cashier at Houston Savings Bank and Mayor William Baker. In 1901 General Electric's financial arm United Electric Securities Company took control of the utility which became Houston Lighting & Power (HL&P). United Electric sold HL&P five years later; by 1922 HL&P ended up in the arms of National Power & Light Company (NP&L) a subsidiary of Electric Bond & Share (a public utility holding company that had been spun off by General Electric).

In 1942 NP&L was forced to sell HL&P in order to comply with the 1935 Public Utility Holding Company Act. As the oil industry boomed in Houston after WWII so did HL&P.

HL&P became the managing partner in a venture to build a nuclear plant on the Texas Gulf Coast in 1973. Construction on the South Texas Project with partners Central Power and Light and the cities of Austin and San Antonio began in 1975. In 1976 Houston Industries (HI) was formed as the holding company for HL&P.

By 1980 the nuke was four years behind schedule and over budget. HL&P and its partners sued construction firm Brown & Root in 1982 and received a $700 million settlement in 1985. (The City of Austin also sued HL&P for damages but lost.) The nuke was finally brought online in 1988 with the final cost estimated at $5.8 billion.

Meanwhile HI diversified into cable TV in 1986 by creating Enrcom (later Paragon Communications) through a venture with Time Inc. Two years later it bought the US cable interests of Canada's Rogers Communications. HI left the cable business in 1995 selling out to Time Warner.

Developing Latin fever HI joined a consortium that bought 51% of Argentinean electric company EDELAP in 1992. (However in 1998 HI sold its stake to AES.) On a roll HI acquired 90% of Argentina's electric utility EDESE (1995); joined a consortium that won a controlling stake in Light a Brazilian electric utility (1996); bought a stake in Colombian electric utility EPSA (1997); and bought interests in three electric utilities in El Salvador (1998). It also won a permit to develop and operate a natural gas system in Mexico (1998).

Back in the US HI acquired gas dealer NorAm for $2.5 billion in 1997. The next year it bought five generating plants in California from Edison International and laid plans to build merchant plants in Arizona (near Phoenix) Illinois Nevada (near Las Vegas in partnership with Sempra Energy) and Rhode Island. Overseas HI finished a power plant in India in 1998. It also bought a 65% interest in Colombian electric utilities Electricaribe and Electrocosta; EPSA bought about 55% of CET in Colombia and Light bought about 75% of Metropolitana (S o Paulo Brazil).

In 1999 HI became Reliant Energy and HL&P became Reliant Energy HL&P. That year the company bought a 52% stake in Dutch power generation firm UNA; it bought the remaining 48% the next year. Also in 2000 Reliant Energy paid Sithe Energies (now a part of Dynegy) $2.1 billion for 21 power plants in the mid-Atlantic states. It sold its operations in Brazil Colombia and El Salvador that year and transferred all of its nonregulated operations to subsidiary Reliant Resources. Reliant Energy also announced plans to spin off Reliant Resources that year.

Reliant Energy netted about $1.7 billion in 2001 from the sale to the public of nearly 20% of Reliant Resources. Later that year Reliant Resources announced that it would acquire US independent power producer Orion Power Holdings in a $4.7 billion deal; the deal was completed in 2002. Deregulation took effect in Texas that year and Reliant Energy transferred its retail power supply business to Reliant Resources.

As the finances of wholesale energy companies came under scrutiny in 2002 the SEC issued a formal investigation into "round-trip" energy trades completed by Reliant Resources. These activities artificially inflated the company's trading volumes and led it to restate its 1999 2000 and 2001 financial results; it also reduced its energy marketing and trading workforce by about 35%.

Reliant Energy announced plans in 2001 to form a new holding company (CenterPoint Energy) for itself and Reliant Resources; it completed the name change in 2002.

CenterPoint Energy changed its name in 2002 in preparation for the spin-off of its 83% stake in Reliant Resources (now GenOn Energy) a global independent power producer and energy marketer; the spinoff was completed later that year. (Reliant Resources changed its name to Reliant Energy in 2004.) CenterPoint Energy transferred its nonregulated Texas retail power supply business to Reliant Resources before spinning off the unit.

EXECUTIVES

Evp And President Electric Division, Tracy B. Bridge, age 61, $481,250 total compensation
President Ceo And Director, Scott M. Prochazka, age 53, $996,525 total compensation
Svp Electric Utility Business, Kenneth M. Mercado
Svp Gas Operations, Richard A. (Rick) Zapalac
Evp And Cfo, William D. (Bill) Rogers, age 59, $485,000 total compensation
Svp Natural Gas Distribution, Scott E. Doyle
Svp Energy Services, Joseph J. (Joe) Vortherms
Svp Deputy General Counsel And Chief Ethics And Compliance Office, Carol Helliker
Vice President And Treasurer, Carla Kneipp
Svp And Chief Human Resources Officer, Susan Ortenstone
Division Vp Operations Support And Technology, John Slanina
Vice President Operations Support, Beverley Melchisedech
Vice President Marketing, Carol Burchfield
Post Oak Chapter Vice Presiden, Nicollette Hickman
Executive Vice President, Thomas Standish
Vp Minnesota Operations, Brad Tutunjian
Svp Strategic Planning And Business Development, James Dumler
Vp Texas State Relations, Jeff Bonham
Senior Vice President Supply Chain, Leslie Alexander
Vice President Cmp Services, Rob Ellis
Vice President Of Human Resources, Valencia Amenson
Vp Of Information Technology, Al Collins
Board Member, Susan Rheney
Chairman, Milton Carroll, age 69
Assistant Treasurer, Linda Geiger
Senior Secretary, Penny Hecox
Board Member, Peter Wareing
Secretary Iii, Jennifer Woodall
Vice Chairman, Jeremy Bloch
Senior Secretary, Nina LeBlanc
Board Member, Theodore Pound
Board Member, Scott Mclean
Board Member, Phillip Smith
Auditors: DELOITTE & TOUCHE LLP

LOCATIONS

HQ: CenterPoint Energy, Inc
1111 Louisiana, Houston, TX 77002
Phone: 713 207-1111
Web: www.centerpointenergy.com

PRODUCTS/OPERATIONS

2018 Sales

	$ mil.	% of total
Retail gas	4,161	39
Electric delivery	3,232	31
Wholesale gas	3,008	28
Energy products & services	156	2
Gas transportation & processing	32	-
Total	**10,589**	**100**

2018 Sales

	$ mil.	% of total
Energy Services	4,411	42
Electric Transmission & Distribution	3,232	30
Natural Gas Distribution	2,931	28
Other	15	-
Total	**10,589**	**100**

2018 Sales

	$ mil.	% of total
Utility	6,163	58
Non-utility	4,426	42
Total	**10,589**	**100**

COMPETITORS

AEP	Southern Company
AEP Texas Central	Southwestern Electric
AEP Texas North	Power
Ameren	Xcel Energy
OGE Energy	

HISTORICAL FINANCIALS

Company Type: Public

Income Statement
FYE: December 31

	REVENUE ($ mil.)	NET INCOME ($ mil.)	NET PROFIT MARGIN	EMPLOYEES
12/19	12,301	791	6.4%	14,262
12/18	10,589	368	3.5%	7,977
12/17	9,614	1,792	18.6%	7,977
12/16	7,528	432	5.7%	7,727
12/15	7,386	(692)	—	7,505
Annual Growth	**13.6%**	**—**	**—**	**17.4%**

2019 Year-End Financials

Debt ratio: 42.64%
Return on equity: 9.64%
Cash ($ mil.): 241
Current ratio: 0.99
Long-term debt ($ mil.): 14,244

No. of shares (mil.): 502
Dividends
Yield: 4.2%
Payout: 91.2%
Market value ($ mil.): 13,696

	STOCK PRICE ($) FY Close	P/E High/Low	PER SHARE ($) Earnings	Dividends	Book Value
12/19	27.27	23 18	1.33	1.15	16.64
12/18	28.23	40 34	0.74	1.11	16.08
12/17	28.36	7 6	4.13	1.07	10.88
12/16	24.64	25 17	1.00	1.03	8.03
12/15	18.36	— —	(1.61)	0.99	8.05
Annual Growth	**10.4%**	**— —**	**—**	**3.8%**	**19.9%**

Central Pacific Financial Corp

When in the Central Pacific do as the islanders do. This may include doing business with Central Pacific Financial the holding company for Central Pacific Bank which operates more than 35 branch locations and 110 ATMs across the Hawaiian Islands. Targeting individuals and local businesses the $5 billion bank provides such standard retail banking products as checking and savings accounts money market accounts and CDs. About 70% of the bank's loan portfolio is made up of commercial real estate loans residential mortgages and construction loans though it also provides business and consumer loans.

Operations

Central Pacific Financial operates through two core segments. The Banking Operations segment provides construction and real estate development loans commercial loans residential mortgage loans consumer loans trust services retail brokerage services and traditional banking products and services. The Treasury segment manages the company's investment securities portfolio and wholesale funding activities.

Boasting total assets of $5 billion Central Pacific Bank ranked as the fourth-largest bank by deposits in the state of Hawaii in 2014. The bank makes nearly 60% of its total revenue from interest and fees on loans and leases and nearly 20% from interest and dividends on its investment securities. It makes about 10% on service charges on deposit accounts and other charges and fees while the small remainder of its revenue comes from a mix of loan servicing fees gains on sales of residential loans and foreclosed assets income from fiduciary activities and income from bank-owned life insurance.

Central Pacific Financial's other wholly-owned subsidiaries include CPB Capital Trust II; CPB Statutory Trust III; CPB Capital Trust IV; and CPB Statutory Trust V. Central Pacific Bank holds 50% stakes in Pacific Access Mortgage Gentry Home-Loans and Island Pacific HomeLoans.

Geographic Reach

Honolulu-based Central Pacific boasts more than 35 branches and 110 ATMs across Hawaii. The island of Oahu holds 28 branches while the Maui Hawaii and Kauai islands host the remaining branches.

Sales and Marketing

Central Pacific Financial spent $2.34 million on advertising in 2014 compared to $2.67 million and $3.52 million in 2013 and 2012 respectively.

Financial Performance

Central Pacific Financial's revenue performance has been mixed in recent years. Its mortgage banking business has suffered from lower residential mortgage origination volumes while its loan business has been growing at a healthy clip thanks to higher loan balances from added assets.

Following two years of modest top-line growth driven by growing loan business Central Pacific's revenue dipped by 1% to $193.63 million in 2014 as it collected lower net gains on sales of foreclosed assets and lower net gains on sales of residential mortgage loans. The bank's interest income from loans continued to grow however as the bank added more than $403 million in new loan assets.

Central Pacific's net income declined by 76% to $40.45 million in 2014 mostly because in 2013 the bank received a $112.25 million income tax benefit as it reversed a significant portion of its valuation allowance for its doubtful accounts from 2009. Beyond this non-recurring event the bank managed to cut its salaries and employee benefit expenses by 22% saving about $8 million for the year.

The bank's operating cash also fell by 15% during the year to $71.43 million primarily due to lower cash earnings.

Strategy

Central Pacific reiterated in 2015 that its strategy is to continue growing its loan business particularly focusing on providing more commercial loans and mortgages as well as construction loans and leases to small and mid-sized companies business professionals and real estate developers. Though its residential mortgage and consumer loans made up just 25% of its loan portfolio that year the bank will also continue its focus on extended those loans to more local homebuyers and individuals.

The bank's key to drumming up its commercial loan business has traditionally come from its community-oriented commercial real estate team and banking officers which are able to develop deep relationships with local communities and industries that they serve.

EXECUTIVES

President And Ceo, A. Catherine Ngo, age 60, $345,833 total compensation
Chairman, John C. Dean, age 73, $265,625 total compensation
Svp And Chief Marketing Officer Central Pacific Financial Corp. And Central Pacific Bank, Wayne H. Kirihara
Interim Vice Chairman And Coo, Denis K. Isono, age 69, $244,792 total compensation
Evp And Cio Central Pacific Financial Corp. And Central Pacific Bank, Lee Y. Moriwaki, age 61, $205,625 total compensation
Evp Cfo And Treasurer, David S. Morimoto, age 52, $201,208 total compensation
Evp Chief Legal Officer And Risk Management Division Manager Central Pacific Financial Corp. And Central Pacific Bank, K.C. (Glenn) Ching, age 61
Evp Community Banking Division Manager Central Pacific Financial Corp. And Central Pacific Bank, David W. Hudson, age 61, $220,000 total compensation
Svp And Commercial Real Estate Lending Division Manager Central Pacific Financial Corp. And Central Pacific Bank, Arnold D. Martines, age 55
Assistant Vice President And Commercial Branch Manager, Jolene Kiyono
Assistant Vice President Commercial Real Estate Officer, Scott Nojiri
Vp Of Information Technology, Anna Hu
Vice President And Operations Support Manager, Susan Tachino
Vice President, Michael Waring
Vice President, Adrian Chee
Vice President And Manager Call Center, Norman Nakasone
Avp And Sr Mortgage Loan Officer, Juo Leung
Vice President And Manager Of The West Oahu Region, Susan Utsugi
Vice President And Commercial Branch Manager, Herman Chang
Vice President Mortgage Loan Manager, Trong Son
Assistant Vice President, Jaysen Kim
Vice President And Branch Manager, Linda Virtudes
Vice President, Francine Komine
Senior Vice President Controller, Neal Kanda
Vice President And Manager Business Continuity, Michael Shibata
Executive Vice President Director Of H, Karen Street
Vice President Of Qc, Sheryl Kurizaki
Vice President And Corporate Communications Manager, Dean Kawamura
Vice President Corporate Compliance Manager, Riley Angell
Vice President And Commercial Banking Officer, Roy Yonaoshi
Vice President And Kihei Branch Manager, Pat Matsumoto
Vice President, Gale Young
Board Member, Earl Fry
Board Member, Wayne Kamitaki
Board Member, Saedene Ota
Auditors: Crowe LLP

LOCATIONS

HQ: Central Pacific Financial Corp
220 South King Street, Honolulu, HI 96813
Phone: 808 544-0500 **Fax:** 808 531-2875
Web: www.centralpacificbank.com

PRODUCTS/OPERATIONS

2014 Sales

	$ mil.	% of total
Interest income		
Loans and leases	112	58
Securities	37	19
Non-interest income		
Other service charges and fees	11	6
Service Charges on deposit accounts	8	4
Loan Servicing fees	5	3
Others	18	10
Total	**193**	**100**

COMPETITORS

American Savings Bank	Mitsubishi UFJ
Bank of Hawaii	Financial Group
First Hawaiian	Territorial Bancorp

HISTORICAL FINANCIALS

Company Type: Public

Income Statement

FYE: December 31

	ASSETS ($ mil.)	NET INCOME ($ mil.)	INCOME AS % OF ASSETS	EMPLOYEES
12/19	6,012	58	1.0%	854
12/18	5,807	59	1.0%	844
12/17	5,623	41	0.7%	838
12/16	5,384	46	0.9%	837
12/15	5,131	45	0.9%	876
Annual Growth	4.0%	6.2%	—	(0.6%)

2019 Year-End Financials

Debt ratio: 0.86%
Return on equity: 11.43%
Cash ($ mil.): 102
Current ratio: —
Long-term debt ($ mil.): —

No. of shares (mil.): 28
Dividends
  Yield: 3.0%
  Payout: 44.3%
Market value ($ mil.): 837

	STOCK PRICE ($) FY Close	P/E High/Low	PER SHARE ($) Earnings	Dividends	Book Value
12/19	29.58	15 12	2.03	0.90	18.68
12/18	24.35	16 12	2.01	0.82	16.97
12/17	29.83	24 20	1.34	0.70	16.65
12/16	31.42	21 12	1.50	0.60	16.39
12/15	22.02	18 13	1.40	0.82	15.77
Annual Growth	7.7%	— —	9.7%	2.4%	4.3%

Century Bancorp, Inc.

Century Bancorp is the holding company for Century Bank and Trust which serves Boston and surrounding parts of northeastern Massachusetts from more than 25 branches. Boasting some $3.6 billion in total assets the bank offers standard deposit products including checking savings and money market accounts; CDs; and IRAs. Nearly two-thirds of its loan portfolio is comprised of commercial and commercial real estate loans. while residential mortgages and home equity loans make up around 30%. The bank also writes construction and land development loans business loans and personal loans. It offers brokerage services through an agreement with third-party provider LPL Financial.

Operations

Century Bank also provides cash management short-term financing and transaction processing services to municipalities in Massachusetts and Rhode Island. It offers automated lockbox collection services to its municipal customers as well as commercial clients. The bank also continues to open new branches in its traditional market area in metropolitan Boston.

The bank gets more than 80% of its revenue in the form of interest income (mostly from loans). It generated 32% of its total revenue from taxable loans in 2014 while another 18% came from non-taxable loans and 35% came from interest income on the bank's investment securities. On the non-interest side the bank made 8% of its overall revenue from service charges on deposit accounts 3% from lockbox fees and a negligible amount on brokerage commissions and gains on sales of securities or mortgage loans.

Geographic Reach

The bank operates more than 25 branches in 20 cities and towns across Massachusetts ranging from Braintree in the South to Andover in the northern part of the state.

Sales and Marketing

Most of Century Bank's business comes from small and medium-sized businesses needing commercial loans though the bank also serves retail customers as well as local governments and other institutions throughout Massachusetts.

The bank spent $1.79 million on advertising in 2014 compared to $1.75 million and $1.85 million in 2013 and 2012 respectively.

Financial Performance

Century Bancorp's revenues and profits have been steadily rising over the past few years thanks to increased loan business and declining loan loss provisions as its loan portfolio's credit quality has been improving in the strengthening economy.

The bank's revenue rose by more than 2% to a record $100.64 million in 2014 mostly as it collected more interest income from long-term securities and non-taxable loans during the year. The bank's earning securities assets grew by 8.5% during the year while the size of its loan business swelled by double-digits with increased tax-exempt lending and residential second mortgage lending; all of which boosted interest income during the year.

Higher revenue lower interest expenses on deposits and a continued dip in loan loss provisions in 2014 pushed Century's net income higher by 9% to a record $21.86 million. The bank's operating cash also grew by 7% to $22.39 million thanks to higher cash earnings.

Strategy

Century Bancorp has been growing organically through new branch openings and digital bank product launches in recent years. In 2014 for example the bank opened its new branch in Woburn Massachusetts and launched its all-new Century Bank Mobile App which boosted customer convenience and allowed the bank to better compete with larger banks with more expansive branch networks.

Showcasing its strong financial capitalization the bank received an "A" rating from the Standard and Poor's credit ratings agency in 2015 making Century Bank the only regional bank in the state to receive such a rating.

EXECUTIVES

Senior Vice President, Susan Delahunt
Evp Century Bank And Trust Company, Paul A. Evangelista, age 56, $337,614 total compensation
Evp Century Bank And Trust Company, David B. Woonton, age 64, $337,614 total compensation
President Ceo And Director, Barry R. Sloane, age 65, $569,207 total compensation
Cfo And Treasurer, William P. Hornby, age 53, $294,708 total compensation
Evp Century Bank And Trust Company, Linda Sloane Kay, age 58, $294,708 total compensation
Evp Century Bank And Trust, Brian J. Feeney, age 59, $294,708 total compensation
Vice President, Jim Smith
Vice President, Anna Gorska
Vice President, Nancy M Marsh
Senior Vice President, Brad Buckley
Senior Vice President Director Of Underwriting And Loan Review, Thomas Piemontese
Vice President, Bradford J Buckley
Senior Vice President, Deb Rush
Chairman, Marshall M. Sloane, age 93
Auditors: KPMG LLP

LOCATIONS

HQ: Century Bancorp, Inc.
  400 Mystic Avenue, Medford, MA 02155
Phone: 781 391-4000
Web: www.centurybank.com

PRODUCTS/OPERATIONS

2014 Sales

	$ mil.	% of total
Interest		
Loans	50	50
Securities	2	3
Other	32	32
Noninterest		
Service charges on deposit accounts	8	8
Lockbox fees	3	3
Gains on sales of Mortgage loans	2	3
Other	1	1
Total	**100**	**100**

COMPETITORS

Boston Private	Eastern Bank
Brookline Bancorp	Middlesex Savings
Cambridge Financial	Peoples Federal
Capital Crossing	Bancshares Inc.
Central Bancorp	Sovereign Bank
Citizens Financial Group	

HISTORICAL FINANCIALS

Company Type: Public

Income Statement

FYE: December 31

	ASSETS ($ mil.)	NET INCOME ($ mil.)	INCOME AS % OF ASSETS	EMPLOYEES
12/19	5,492	39	0.7%	460
12/18	5,163	36	0.7%	460
12/17	4,785	22	0.5%	447
12/16	4,462	24	0.5%	438
12/15	3,947	23	0.6%	438
Annual Growth	8.6%	14.6%	—	1.2%

2019 Year-End Financials

Debt ratio: 7.41%
Return on equity: 12.54%
Cash ($ mil.): 258
Current ratio: —
Long-term debt ($ mil.): —

No. of shares (mil.): 5
Dividends
  Yield: 0.5%
  Payout: 5.9%
Market value ($ mil.): 501

	STOCK PRICE ($) FY Close	P/E High/Low	PER SHARE ($) Earnings	Dividends	Book Value
12/19	89.96	11 8	7.13	0.48	59.73
12/18	67.73	11 8	6.50	0.48	53.96
12/17	78.25	18 12	4.01	0.48	46.75
12/16	60.00	12 7	4.41	0.48	43.11
12/15	43.46	9 8	4.13	0.48	38.53
Annual Growth	19.9%	— —	14.6%	(0.0%)	11.6%

CFJ PROPERTIES LLC

EXECUTIVES

Chb, Crystal Call Maggelet
Exec Committee MBR*, Andre Lortz
Exec Committee MBR*, Richard D Peterson
Executive Committee MBR, Richard Peterson
Senior Corporate Counsel, Tom Schofield
Auditors: KPMG LLP SALT LAKE CITY UTAH

LOCATIONS

HQ: CFJ PROPERTIES LLC
  5508 LONAS DR, KNOXVILLE, TN 379093221
Phone: 801 624-1000
Web: WWW.PILOTFLYINGJ.COM

HISTORICAL FINANCIALS

Company Type: Private

Income Statement

FYE: January 31

	REVENUE ($ mil.)	NET INCOME ($ mil.)	NET PROFIT MARGIN	EMPLOYEES
01/09	7,672	157	2.1%	6,250
01/07	6,769	50	0.7%	—
01/06	6,166	48	0.8%	—
Annual Growth	7.6%	47.7%	—	—

Charter Communications Inc (New)

Auditors: KPMG LLP

LOCATIONS

HQ: Charter Communications Inc (New)
  400 Atlantic Street, Stamford, CT 06901
Phone: 203 905-7801
Web: www.charter.com

COMPETITORS

AT&T	Mediacom
Apple Inc.	Communications
Bright House Networks	Netflix
Cablevision Systems	RCN Corporation
Clearwire	Skype
Comcast	Sprint Communications
Cox Communications	Suddenlink
DIRECTV	Communications
DISH Network	T-Mobile USA
EarthLink	Time Warner Cable
Frontier	United Online
Communications	Verizon
Hulu	Vonage
Insight Communications	YouTube
LodgeNet	

HISTORICAL FINANCIALS

Company Type: Public

Income Statement

FYE: December 31

	REVENUE ($ mil.)	NET INCOME ($ mil.)	NET PROFIT MARGIN	EMPLOYEES
12/20	48,097	3,222	6.7%	96,100
12/19	45,764	1,668	3.6%	95,100
12/18	43,634	1,230	2.8%	98,000
12/17	41,581	9,895	23.8%	94,800
12/16	29,003	3,522	12.1%	91,500
Annual Growth	13.5%	(2.2%)	—	1.2%

2020 Year-End Financials

Debt ratio: 57.38%	No. of shares (mil.): 193
Return on equity: 11.63%	Dividends
Cash ($ mil.): 998	Yield: —
Current ratio: 0.40	Payout: —
Long-term debt ($ mil.): 81,744	Market value ($ mil.): 128,163

	STOCK PRICE ($) FY Close	P/E High/Low	PER SHARE ($) Earnings	Dividends	Book Value
12/20	661.55	43 23	15.40	0.00	122.88
12/19	485.08	64 37	7.45	0.00	149.76
12/18	284.97	73 49	5.22	0.00	161.01
12/17	335.96	10 7	34.09	0.00	163.87
12/16	287.92	17 9	15.94	0.00	149.27
Annual Growth	23.1%	— —	(0.9%)	—	(4.7%)

Cheniere Energy Inc.

Cheniere Energy is a producer of liquefied natural gas (LNG) in the US exporting LNG to customers in over 30 nations around the world. The company purchases natural gas and processes it into LNG and offers customers the option to load the LNG onto their vessels at its terminals or it delivers the LNG to regasification facilities around the world. The company has two terminals on the US Gulf Coast in various stages of development: its Sabine Pass liquefaction project in southwest Louisiana and its Corpus Christi liquefaction facility in South Texas. Over 70% of revenue come from outside the US. Cheniere also has pipeline assets and operates an LNG and natural gas marketing business.

Operations

Cheniere's Sabine Pass project in southwest Louisiana has five liquefaction units or "Trains" as they are known in the LNG industry. When all Trains are completed (after its sixth Train is operational) its production capacity is expected to be approximately 30 million tonnes per annum (mtpa) of LNG. When its Corpus Christi liquefaction facility in South Texas is complete its aggregate production capacity is expected to be approximately 15 mtpa of LNG. The company has a contract with major engineering firm Bechtel for construction work.

Natural gas is transported to Cheniere's LNG facilities on third party pipelines as well as on pipelines Cheniere has constructed and owns and operates. Its pipelines include the Creole Trail nearly 95-mile pipeline interconnecting the Sabine Pass terminal with a number of large interstate pipelines; the Corpus Christi Pipeline about 25-mile pipeline that interconnect its Corpus Christi project with several inter- and intrastate natural gas pipelines; and the Midship Pipeline a new-build project that will connect new gas production from

the Anadarko Basin in Oklahoma to Gulf Coast and Southeast markets once it is complete.

Nearly all the company's revenue (some 95%) comes from LNG sold at its terminals and three percent of the revenue is from regasification.

Geographic Reach

The Houston Texas-based Cheniere Energy derives substantially all of its revenue from facilities in Louisiana and Texas. Sales to customers in the US account for about 30% of revenue; South Korea and India over 10% each; Ireland approximately 10%; Spain and the UK more than 5%; Singapore some 5%; and Japan two percent.

The company has offices in Houston Beijing London Singapore and Tokyo.

Sales and Marketing

Approximately 85% of Cheniere's expected LNG production capacity either completed or under construction is contracted through long-term agreements with customers. The remaining volumes of LNG are available to sell on the open market.

The company market and sell LNG produced by the Liquefaction Projects that is not required for other customers through their integrated marketing function.

Cheniere is highly dependent on revenue from four major customers: BG and its affiliates account for over 15% of revenue while Korea Gas Corporation (KOGAS) GAIL (India) and Naturgy generates some 10% of revenue each.

Financial Performance

Throughout the five-year period ending in 2019 Cheniere Energy reported year-over-year revenue growth as the company built more "Trains" (liquefaction units) and increased the volume of LNG it sold during the year. The company reported losses between 2015 and 2016 as it invested big in build-out. Net income eventually swung to a profit in 2018.

The company reported $9.7 billion in revenue in 2019 up from $8 billion in 2018. The increase in was primarily attributable to the increased volume of LNG sold following the achievement of substantial completion of these Trains.Net income was $648 million for the year an increase of $177 million from 2018. The increase was mostly attributable to increased gross margins increased tax benefit and increased LNG revenues.

Cash at the end of 2019 was $3 billion. Cash from operations was $1.8 billion while investing activities used $3.2 billion primarily to purchase property plant and equipment. Financing activities contributed another $1.2 billion.

Strategy

The company's primary business strategy is to be a full-service LNG provider to worldwide end-use customers. It will accomplish this objective by owning constructing and operating LNG and natural gas infrastructure facilities to meet its long-term customers' energy demands and safely efficiently and reliably operating and maintaining its assets; procuring natural gas and pipeline transport capacity to its facilities; commencing commercial delivery for its long-term SPA customers; safely on-time and on-budget completing its expansion construction projects including the development of Corpus Christi Stage 3; maximizing the production of LNG to serve its long-term customers and generating steady and stable revenues and operating cash flows; and maintaining a flexible capital structure to finance the acquisition development construction and operation of the energy assets needed to supply its customers.

Company Background

Cheniere Energy was founded in 1996. The company began developing its first LNG terminal in 1999 and was among the first companies to secure sites and commence development of new LNG terminals in North America. The company is particularly vulnerable to weather-related interruptions. While Hurricane Katrina in 2005 didn't directly hit its operations it significantly impacted workforce availability. Hurricanes Rita in 2005 Ike in 2008 and Harvey in 2017 all had a serious impact.

In February 2016 the Sabine Pass facility became the first to ship LNG from a commercial facility in the contiguous US. The company's Corpus Christi liquefaction facility in South Texas began operations in 2018.

EXECUTIVES

Svp International, Jean Abiteboul, age 68, $461,850 total compensation

Vp Human Resources, Ann Raden

President And Ceo, Jack A. Fusco, age 57

Evp Asset Group, R. Keith Teague, age 55, $565,385 total compensation

Director, Neal A. Shear, $38,462 total compensation

Svp And Cfo, Michael J. Wortley, age 43, $565,385 total compensation

Svp And General Counsel, Greg W. Rayford, $565,385 total compensation

Vice President Trading Cheniere International (uk Establishment), Nicolas Zanen

Senior Vice President Policy Government And Public Affairs, Chris Smith

Vice President State Government Affairs, Julie Nelson

Vice President And Chief Security Risk Officer, Mitch Price

Vice President Investor Relations, Katie L Pipkin

Chairman, G. Andrea Botta, age 66

Board Member, Nuno Brandolini

Auditors: KPMG LLP

LOCATIONS

HQ: Cheniere Energy Inc.
700 Milam Street, Suite 1900, Houston, TX 77002
Phone: 713 375-5000
Web: www.cheniere.com

PRODUCTS/OPERATIONS

2017 Sales

	$ mil.	% of total
LNG revenues	5,317	95
Regasification revenues	260	5
Other revenues	21	-
Other- related party	3	-
Total	**5,601**	**100**

Subsidiaries

Subsidiaries
Caldera LNG Holdings SpA Chile
Cheniere Cares Inc. Texas
Cheniere Chile SpA Chile
Cheniere CCH HoldCo I LLC Delaware
Cheniere CCH HoldCo II LLC Delaware
Cheniere Corpus Christi Holdings LLC Delaware
Cheniere Corpus Christi Pipeline L.P. Delaware
Cheniere Creole Trail Pipeline L.P. Delaware
Cheniere Energy Investments LLC Delaware
Cheniere Energy Operating Co. Inc. Delaware
Cheniere Energy Partners GP LLC Delaware
Cheniere Energy Partners LP Holdings LLC Delaware
Cheniere Energy Partners L.P. Delaware
Cheniere Energy Shared Services Inc. Delaware
Cheniere Field Services LLC Delaware
Cheniere GP Holding Company LLC Delaware
Cheniere Ingleside Marine Terminal LLC Delaware
Cheniere International Investments Holdings S.à.r.l Luxembourg
Cheniere International Investments S.à.r.l Luxembourg
Cheniere Land Holdings LLC Delaware
Cheniere Liquids LLC Delaware
Cheniere LNG Holdings GP LLC Delaware
Cheniere LNG O&M Services LLC Delaware
Cheniere LNG Terminals LLC Delaware
Cheniere Major Project Development LLC Delaware
Cheniere Marketing International HoldCo I L.P. Bermuda
Cheniere Marketing International HoldCo II Ltd. Bermuda
Cheniere Marketing International LLP United Kingdom
Cheniere Marketing LLC Delaware
Cheniere Marketing Ltd. United Kingdom
Cheniere Marketing PTE Ltd. Singapore
Cheniere Midship Holdings LLC Delaware
Cheniere Midstream Holdings Inc. Delaware
Cheniere Pipeline GP Interests LLC Delaware
Cheniere Pipeline Holdings LLC Delaware
Cheniere San Patricio Processing Hub LLC Delaware
Cheniere Southern Trail GP Inc. Delaware
Cheniere SPH Pipeline LLC Delaware
Cheniere Supply & Marketing Inc. Delaware
Concepción LNG Holding SpA Chile
Corpus Christi Liquefaction LLC Delaware
Corpus Christi Liquefaction Stage II LLC Delaware
Corpus Christi Liquefaction Stage III LLC Delaware
Corpus Christi LNG LLC Delaware
Corpus Christi Pipeline GP LLC Delaware
Corpus Christi Tug Services LLC Delaware
CQH Holdings Company LLC Delaware
CUI I LLC Delaware
Johnson Bayou Holdings LLC Delaware
Live Oak LNG Holdings LLC Delaware
Louisiana LNG Holdings LLC Delaware
Midship Holdings LLC Delaware
Midship Pipeline Company LLC Delaware
Nordheim Eagle Ford Gathering LLC Delaware
Sabine Pass Liquefaction LLC Delaware
Sabine Pass LNG-GP LLC Delaware
Sabine Pass LNG-LP LLC Delaware
Sabine Pass LNG L.P. Delaware
Sabine Pass Tug Services LLC Delaware

COMPETITORS

Ameren	PG&E Corporation
CMS Energy	Public Service
Calpine	Enterprise Group
DTE	Sempra Energy
Dominion Energy	TRII
Enbridge	TransCanada
ONEOK	

HISTORICAL FINANCIALS

Company Type: Public

Income Statement

FYE: December 31

	REVENUE ($ mil.)	NET INCOME ($ mil.)	NET PROFIT MARGIN	EMPLOYEES
12/19	9,730	648	6.7%	1,530
12/18	7,987	471	5.9%	1,372
12/17	5,601	(393)	—	1,230
12/16	1,283	(609)	—	911
12/15	270	(975)	—	888
Annual Growth	144.8%	—	—	14.6%

2019 Year-End Financials

Debt ratio: 86.87%	No. of shares (mil.): 253
Return on equity: —	Dividends
Cash ($ mil.): 2,474	Yield: —
Current ratio: 2.25	Payout: —
Long-term debt ($ mil.): 30,832	Market value ($ mil.): 15,487

	STOCK PRICE ($) FY Close	P/E High/Low	PER SHARE ($) Earnings	Dividends	Book Value
12/19	61.07	28 23	2.51	0.00	(0.06)
12/18	59.19	37 27	1.90	0.00	(2.05)
12/17	53.84	— —	(1.68)	0.00	(7.42)
12/16	41.43	— —	(2.67)	0.00	(5.87)
12/15	37.25	— —	(4.30)	0.00	(3.83)
Annual Growth	13.2%	— —	—	—	—

Chesapeake Energy Corp.

Chesapeake Energy is an independent exploration and production company with oil and gas assets across the US. The company has estimated 6.6 billion cubic feet of natural gas. Chesapeake has exploration and production assets in Marcellus Eagle Ford Brazos Valley Mid-Continent and Haynesville shale plays. Customers have included Valero Energy Corp. and Royal Dutch Shell.

Operations

Chesapeake's two sources of revenue are its production of oil natural gas and natural gas liquids (NGL) which accounts for about 55% of revenue and its marketing operations generate more than 45% of revenue.

The oil natural gas and NGL operations explore for acquire develop and produce energy throughout the company's production areas. Within the segment oil accounts approximately 50% of the company's revenue while natural gas generates about 45%. NGLs provide roughly 5% of sales.

Chesapeake's marketing operations provide commodity price structuring securing and negotiating of services for gathering hauling processing and transportation and contract administration and nomination services. Marketing also aggregates volumes sold to intermediary markets end markets and pipelines.

Geographic Reach

Chesapeake Energy which is based in Oklahoma City Oklahoma has operations in the Marcellus in Northern Appalachian Basin in Pennsylvania; Haynesville in Northwestern Louisiana Eagle Ford in South Texas Brazos Valley in Southeast Texas Powder River Basin in Wyoming and the Mid-Continent in Anadarko Basin in northwestern Oklahoma.

Sales and Marketing

Chesapeake sells through market-sensitive short-term or spot price contracts. Natural gas and NGL production is sold to purchasers under percentage-of-proceeds contracts percentage-of-index contracts or spot price contracts. Valero Energy accounted for more than 10% of revenue in 2019.

Financial Performance

Chesapeake's revenue has been slowly increasing in the past few years since its huge downfall in 2016. Between 2015 and 2019 the company's revenue decreased by 33% to $8.5 billion in 2019.

In 2019 revenue fell $8.5 billion about $1.7 billion from $10.2 billion in 2018 driven by a decrease in natural gas and NGL prices and production volumes resulted in a $650 million and $364 million decrease to revenues.

In 2019 the company had a net loss to $308 million.

Chesapeake's coffers held $6 million in cash at the end of 2019 compared to $4 million in 2018. Operating activities generated $1.6 billion in 2019 while investing activities provided $2.5 billion and financing activities used about $859 million. The company's main cash in 2019 was primarily used in drilling and completion costs business combination and issuance of term loans.

Strategy

Chesapeake Energy has been through the ups and downs of the oil-and-gas business over the years. Now the company is trying to adjust its operations and balance sheet to deliver sustained performance in a volatile industry.

The company's strategy is to create shareholder value through the development of its significant resource plays. Chesapeake Energy continues to focus on reducing debt increasing cash provided by operating activities improving margins through financial discipline and operating efficiencies and maintaining exceptional environmental and safety performance.

To accomplish these goals the company intends to allocate its capital expenditures to projects where the company believes that it could offer the highest return and value regardless of the commodity price environment to deploy leading drilling and completion technology throughout its portfolio and to take advantage of acquisition and divestiture opportunities to strengthen its cost structure and its portfolio. The company continues to seek opportunities to reduce cash costs per barrel of oil equivalent production (production gathering processing and transportation and general and administrative) through operational efficiencies including improving its production volumes from existing wells.

Mergers and Acquisitions

In 2019 Chesapeake bought WildHorse Resource Development Corporation for nearly $4 billion adding 20000 net acres in the Eagle Ford Shale and Austin Chalk formations in Texas.

HISTORY

Aubrey McClendon (who grew up near Maryland's Chesapeake Bay) and Tom Ward had been non-operating partners in about 600 wells in Oklahoma before forming their own company in 1989 to develop new fields in Texas and Oklahoma during the 1990s. The firm went public in 1993. In 1995 the company acquired oil and gas acreage in Louisiana as well as Princeton Natural Gas an Oklahoma City-based gas marketing firm.

Oil finds in Louisiana and strong production from its Texas and Oklahoma wells helped lift Chesapeake's sales in 1996. That year it acquired Amerada Hess' (later renamed Hess) half of their joint operations in two Oklahoma fields. In 1997 chairman McClendon and president Ward acquired control of Chesapeake.

The company's success was based on its "growth through the drillbit" strategy — developing new wells. But after a 1997 loss Chesapeake modified its strategy and sought to grow by acquiring other companies. That year it bought energy company AnSon Production. Chesapeake subsequently bought oil and gas explorer-producer Hugoton Energy and energy company DLB Oil & Gas.

In 1998 the company acquired a 40% stake in Canadian oil producer Ranger Oil and paid Occidental Petroleum $105 million for natural gas reserves in the Texas Panhandle. Chesapeake then began to transform itself from a hotshot driller to an acquirer of natural gas properties almost tripling its proved reserves. The company suffered a huge loss that year in part from the acquisitions and continuing lower gas prices.

With gas prices soaring again the company continued its buying spree into 2000 when it agreed to buy midcontinent natural gas producer Gothic Energy for $345 million in stock and assumed debt. The deal closed in 2001. The company also sold its Canadian assets that year in order to focus on its core US properties.

In 2002 Chesapeake acquired oil and gas producer Canaan Energy for about $118 million. Later that year the company announced plans to sell or trade its Permian Basin assets.

Chesapeake acquired in 2003 a 25% stake in Pioneer Drilling (which it subsequently sold). In 2004 the company acquired Barnett Shale assets from Hallwood Energy for $292 million. That year it also bought privately owned Concho Resources for $420 million. The next year the company acquired privately held BRG Petroleum which held assets of more than 450 wells with proved reserves of more than 275 billion cu. ft. of natural gas for $325 million.

In 2005 Chesapeake acquired 20% of Gastar Exploration (reduced to 15% by 2007). That year in a major move the company acquired Columbia Natural Resources for $2.2 billion.

To get better financial returns the company is selling assets to secure capital. Hurt by continuing low natural gas prices the company sold its midstream assets in 2012 and 2013 for $4.9 billion in three separate deals. As part of this move in 2012 the company sold its limited partner units and its general partner interests in Chesapeake Midstream Partners to Global Infrastructure Partners for $2 billion. That year the company also sold about $6.9 billion of its Permian basin properties in order to pay down debt.

To simplify its operations in 2012 Chesapeake spun off its oilfield service affiliate Chesapeake Oilfield Services.

In 2013 it also sold assets in the Northern Eagle Ford Shale and Haynesville Shale to an EXCO Resources subsidiary for $1 billion.

In 2013 the company sold its 50% undivided interest in 850000 acres in northern Oklahoma (its Mississippi Lime joint venture with Sinopec International Petroleum Exploration and Production) for $1.02 billion.

Other asset sales in 2013 included Granite Wash Midstream Gas Services (to a subsidiary of Mark-West Energy Partners for $252 million) and its interests in certain gathering system assets in Pennsylvania to Western Gas Partners for $134 million.

EXECUTIVES

Svp Information Technology And Cio, Cathlyn L. (Cathy) Tompkins, age 59

Evp And Cfo, Domenic J. (Nick) Dell'Osso, age 44, $725,001 total compensation

Evp Exploration And Production, Frank J. Patterson, age 61, $600,000 total compensation

Evp General Counsel And Corporate Secretary, James R. Webb, age 52, $625,000 total compensation

President And Ceo, Robert D. (Doug) Lawler, age 53, $1,300,000 total compensation

Evp Operations And Technical Services, M. Jason Pigott, age 46, $574,999 total compensation

Vice President Marketing And Corporate Business Development, Bryan Lemmerman

Vice President Drilling, Dave Bert

Vice President Marine Information Technology, Steve A Melton

Vice President Human Resources, James jay Hawkins

Vice President, Mandy Duane

Vice President Information Technology, Steve Evans

Vice President, Lacie Wilson

Vice President, Frank Gagliardi

Vice President Of Marketing, Mary Whitson

Senior Vice President Information Technology And Cio, Cathy Tompkins

Vice President Environment Health And Safety, Brittany Benko

Vice President Performance Solutions, Chris Mitchel

Vice President Marketing, Sarika Jewell

Evp And Cfo, Domenic Dell'osso Jr

Chairman, R. Brad Martin, age 68

Assistant Secretary, Anita Brodrick

Treasurer, Julian Carrillo

Auditors: PricewaterhouseCoopers LLC

LOCATIONS

HQ: Chesapeake Energy Corp.
6100 North Western Avenue, Oklahoma City, OK 73118
Phone: 405 848-8000
Web: www.chk.com

PRODUCTS/OPERATIONS

2018 Sales

	$ mil.	% of total
Oil natural gas and NGL	5,155	58
Marketing	5,076	42
Total	**10,231**	**100**

COMPETITORS

Adams Resources	Koch Industries Inc.
Anadarko Petroleum	Noble Energy
Apache	Occidental Petroleum
BP	Pioneer Natural
Chevron	Resources
ConocoPhillips	SandRidge Energy
Exxon Mobil	Southwestern Energy
Freeport-McMoRan Oil & Gas LLC	Unit Corporation

HISTORICAL FINANCIALS

Company Type: Public

Income Statement

FYE: December 31

	REVENUE ($ mil.)	NET INCOME ($ mil.)	NET PROFIT MARGIN	EMPLOYEES
12/19	8,595	(308)	—	2,300
12/18	10,231	873	8.5%	2,350
12/17	9,496	949	10.0%	3,200
12/16	7,872	(4,401)	—	3,300
12/15	12,764	(14,685)	—	4,400
Annual Growth	**(9.4%)**	—	—	**(15.0%)**

2019 Year-End Financials

Debt ratio: 58.41%	No. of shares (mil.): 9
Return on equity: (-13.08%)	Dividends
Cash ($ mil.): 6	Yield: —
Current ratio: 0.52	Payout: —
Long-term debt ($ mil.): 9,073	Market value ($ mil.): 8

	STOCK PRICE ($) FY Close	P/E High/Low		PER SHARE ($) Earnings	Dividends	Book Value
12/19	0.83	—	—	(50.00)	0.00	447.75
12/18	2.10	0	0	170.00	0.00	75.57
12/17	3.96	0	0	180.00	0.00	(109.43)
12/16	7.02	—	—	(1,290.00)	0.00	(326.24)
12/15	4.50	—	—	(4,486.00)	17.50	644.60
Annual Growth	**(34.6%)**	—	—	—	—	**(8.7%)**

Chevron Corporation

Chevron has earned its stripes as the #2 integrated oil company in the US behind Exxon Mobil. Its global operations explore for and produce oil and oil equivalents refines them into various fuels and other end products and sells them through gas stations airport fuel depots and industrial channels. Chevron boasts approximately11.4 billion barrels of proved reserves produces about 3.1 million barrels of oil per day and has refining capacity for nearly 1.7million barrels per day. The company sells refined products branded under the Chevron Texaco and Caltex names through approximately 7900 gas stations in the US and around 5100 outside the US.

HISTORY

Thirty years after the California gold rush a small firm began digging for a new product — oil. The crude came from wildcatter Frederick Taylor's well located north of Los Angeles. In 1879 Taylor and other oilmen formed Pacific Coast Oil attracting the attention of John D. Rockefeller's Standard Oil. The two competed fiercely until Standard took over Pacific Coast in 1900.

When Standard Oil was broken up in 1911 its West Coast operations became the stand-alone Standard Oil Company (California) which was nicknamed Socal and sold Chevron-brand products. After winning drilling concessions in Bahrain and Saudi Arabia in the 1930s Socal summoned Texaco to help and they formed Caltex (California-Texas Oil Company) as equal partners. In 1948 Socony (later Mobil) and Jersey Standard (later Exxon) bought 40% of Caltex's Saudi operations and the Saudi arm became Aramco (Arabian American Oil Company).

Socal exploration pushed into Louisiana and the Gulf of Mexico in the 1940s. In 1961 it bought Standard Oil Company of Kentucky (Kyso). The 1970s brought setbacks: Caltex holdings were nationalized during the OPEC-spawned upheaval and the Saudi Arabian government claimed Aramco in 1980.

In 1984 Socal was renamed Chevron and doubled its reserves with its $13 billion purchase of Gulf Corp. which had origins in the 1901 Spindletop gusher in Texas. Gulf became an oil power by developing Kuwaiti concessions but was hobbled when those assets were nationalized in 1975. After Gulf was rocked by disclosures that it had an illegal political slush fund Socal stepped in. The deal loaded the new company with debt and it cut 20000 jobs and sold billions in assets.

Chevron bought Tenneco's Gulf of Mexico properties in 1988 and in 1992 swapped fields valued at $1.1 billion for 15.7 million shares of Chevron stock owned by Pennzoil. It also moved into the North Sea in 1994.

In the 1990s Chevron gave its retailing units a tune-up. It allied with McDonald's (1995) to combine burger stands and gas stations in 12 western states. In addition the company sold 450 UK gas stations and a refinery to Shell (1997). Meanwhile Chevron sold its natural gas operation in 1996 for a stake in Houston-based NGC (later Dynegy ; sold in 2007) and it signed an onshore exploration contract in China the next year.

Poor economic conditions in Asia and slumping oil prices in 1998 forced Chevron to shed some US holdings including California properties. Looking for growth overseas in 1999 it bought Rutherford-Moran Oil increasing its interests in Thailand and Petrolera Argentina San Jorge Argentina's #3 oil company.

Chevron trimmed about 10% of its workforce in 1999 and 2000 in an effort to cut costs. As the rest of the industry consolidated Chevron discussed merging with Texaco but the talks collapsed in 1999. Later that year CEO Ken Derr retired and vice chairman Dave O'Reilly replaced him.

In 2000 Chevron formed a joint venture with Phillips Petroleum (later ConocoPhillips) that combined the companies' chemicals businesses as Chevron Phillips Chemical . That year talks with Texaco were revived and Chevron agreed to acquire its Caltex partner for about $35 billion in stock and about $8 billion in assumed debt. The deal completed in 2001 formed ChevronTexaco.

Part of the 2001 deal to acquire Texaco required Chevron to sell exclusive rights to the Texaco brand for a period of three years. A division of Royal Dutch Shell owned rights to the Texaco brand until 2004 and changed the name of the service stations to Shell. Once Chevron regained the rights to the Texaco name it revitalized the brand name by adding about 400 Texaco stations in the western US.

In 2002 ChevronTexaco divested its stakes in US downstream joint ventures Equilon (to Shell) and Motiva (to Shell and Saudi Aramco). It also sold part of a Gulf of Mexico pipeline and two natural gas plants in Louisiana to Duke Energy and its 12.5% stake in a natural gas liquids fractionator to Enterprise Products Partners. In 2004 ChevronTexaco sold 150 US natural gas and oil properties to XTO Energy for $912 million. The company changed its name to Chevron Corporation in 2005.

Chevron acquired Unocal in 2005 for more than $16 billion boosting its proved reserves by about 15%. Equally attractive to Chevron was the strategic position of Unocal's operations; at a time when industries are trying to get a foothold in China the reserves in Southeast Asia could easily be transported not only there but also to a surging India as well. Unocal's other operations easily supplied the US (from the Gulf of Mexico) and Europe (Caspian Sea) with gas and oil. Chevron bought a 5% stake in Indian refiner Reliance Petroleum for about $300 million in 2006. That year a company-led group of exploration firms announced a new successful oil strike in the Gulf of Mexico.

The company has also been growing its natural gas assets. In 2008 it announced plans to construct a $3.1 billion natural gas project in the Gulf of Thailand. The project will have the capacity to meet 14% of Thailand's natural gas needs.

Ultrapar acquired Chevron's Texaco-branded fuel distribution business in Brazil for $720 million in 2008 and the next year Chevron sold its Nigerian fuel marketing business.

A leading producer of viscous heavy oil in 2010 a Chevron-led consortium was awarded the rights to 40% of a heavy oil project in Venezuela's Orinoco Oil Belt.

In 2010 in the wake of the BP oil rig disaster in the Gulf of Mexico Chevron announced it was forming a $1 billion joint venture with Exxon Mobil Royal Dutch Shell and ConocoPhillips to create a rapid-response system capable of capturing and containing up to 100000 barrels of oil from an oil spill in water depths of 10000 feet.

Looking to develop a deepwater area unaffected by US regulations in 2010 the company acquired a 70% stake in three concessions in Liberia in West Africa. Other deepwater exploration asset acquisitions that year included purchases in China and the Turkish Black Sea.

In 2010 the company began to cut its US refining and marketing business staff by 20% and as part of this realignment it sold its 23% stake in Colonial Pipeline to a KKR affiliate.

In 2013 company acquired exploration interests in offshore Blocks EPP44 and EPP45 (more than 8 million acres in the Bight Basin off the South Australian coast).

Growing its LNG supply and export capacity in 2013 Chevron acquired a 50% operating interest in the Kitimat liquefied natural gas project and proposed Pacific Trail Pipeline and a 50% stake in 644000 acres of petroleum and natural gas rights in the Horn River and Liard Basins in British Columbia Canada. The company bought the assets from Apache for $405 million.

In a major move in 2011 Chevron acquired Atlas Energy in a $4.3 billion deal. The acquisition is part the company's strategy of finding new reserves to replace reserves lost from declining fields. It also marked Chevron's move to become a major

player in the prolific Marcellus Shale play in Pennsylvania where a number of majors are seeking to cash in on the improved drilling technology that has made the exploitation of unconventional gas finds more commercially viable. The purchase gave Chevron Atlas Energy's 850 billion cu. ft. of proved natural gas reserves and 80 million cu. ft. of daily natural gas production. It also complements Chevron's earlier acquisitions of shale gas assets in Canada Poland and Romania as well as its purchase of an additional 228000 acres in the Marcellus Shale from Chief Oil & Gas LLC and Tug Hill Inc. (The acquisitions added up to 5 trillion cubic feet of natural gas resources to Chevron's existing Marcellus Shale operations.)

An earlier chapter of Chevron's history reemerged in 2011 when the company was slapped with a bill for $18 billion in fines and charges by a court in Ecuador regarding environmental damages allegedly caused by Texaco (acquired in 2001) in the 1970s and 1980s. Chevron challenged the findings as illegitimate and unenforceable.

Restructuring its refinery and retail businesses to cut costs in 2011 Chevron sold its Chevron Ltd. UK unit which operated the Pembroke refinery to Valero for $730 million. In addition Valero agreed to pay more that $1 billion for other Chevron Ltd. assets including 1000 gas stations. That year Chevron also sold its fuels marketing and aviation businesses in 16 countries in the Caribbean and Latin America and some marketing businesses in five African countries.

In 2012 the company signed a 20-year deal with Tohoku Electric Power for the delivery of liquefied natural gas (LNG) from the Chevron-operated Wheatstone natural gas project in Australia.

Growing its shale assets in 2013 Chevron agreed to a $1.24 billion investment in YPF to help YPF develop the world's second-largest shale gas deposit and fourth-largest oil reservoir located in Argentina's Vaca Muerta region. In 2013 and 2012 the company also announced new exploration and production deals to expand its assets in China Kurdistan the Republic of Congo Surinam and the US.

In 2013 50%-owned affiliate GS Caltex opened a 53000-barrel-per-day gas oil fluid catalytic cracking unit at the Yeosu Refinery in South Korea.

The company consolidated the supply and trading functions in 2013 into a single supply and trading group within Chevron's Gas and Midstream organization.

EXECUTIVES

Vp And Cfo, Patricia E. (Pat) Yarrington, age 63, $1,073,242 total compensation

Chairman And Ceo, Michael K. (Mike) Wirth, age 60, $1,094,492 total compensation

Evp Downstream And Chemicals, Pierre R. Breber, age 55

Vp And General Counsel, R. Hewitt (Hew) Pate, age 58, $867,000 total compensation

Evp Technology Projects And Services, Joseph C. (Joe) Geagea, age 60, $906,367 total compensation

Evp Upstream, James W. (Jay) Johnson, age 61, $1,012,417 total compensation

Managing Director Chevron Nigeria Mid-africa, Clay Neff, age 58

National Sales Manager Consumer Products, Paul Dudley

Vice President Of Finance, Uriel Ose

Vice President, Elliott Ginger

Vice President, Petros Papazis

Vice President Marketing, Jeff Petro

Vice President, Marek Kacewicz

Vice President And General Cou, Wendy Daboval

Vice President Of Montgomery O, Julia Martin

Vice President Png Marketing, Stephen Green

National Account Manager, Steve Faggard
Assistant Vice President Information Technology
  Operations, Antonio Calombo
Vice President Of Membership, Yolanda Peria
Vice President Chevron Energy Solutions, Mark
  Emerson
Vice President, Martin Donohue
Executive Vice President, Sandy Cab
Vice President, Sergey Kuznetsov
Vice President Finance, Brenda Young
National Account Manager, Marcella Love
Vice President, Jay Byers
Executive Vice President, George Kirkland
Vice President, Francesca Fazzari
Vice President, Jay Close
Vice President Of Marketing, Viviane Tonon
Vice President And General Counsel, R Hewitt Pate
Vice President, Amir Hidayat
Vice President Jv Managing Director, Leon De
  Bruyn
Vice President, Andrew Kulpecz
Vice President, Nadine Barroca-Pursiano
Vice Chairman Of The Board, Glenn F Tilton
Secretary, H Xun
Treasurer Chevron Stations, Ravinder Bhumbla
Secretary, Lawrence Febo
Assistant Secretary And Managing Counsel, Chris
  Cavallo
Board Member, Gary P Luquette
Auditors: PricewaterhouseCoopers LLP

LOCATIONS

HQ: Chevron Corporation
  6001 Bollinger Canyon Road, San Ramon, CA 94583-
  2324
Phone: 925 842-1000   Fax: 925 894-6017
Web: www.chevron.com

2018 sales

	$ mil.	% of total
US	83,289	44
International	107,939	56
Adjustments	(32326)	
Total	158,902	100

PRODUCTS/OPERATIONS

2018 Sales

	$ mil.	% of total
Downstream	129,471	68
Upstream	60,713	32
Other	1,044	-
Adjustments	(32326)	-
Total	158,902	100

COMPETITORS

BP	Occidental Petroleum
ConocoPhillips	PEMEX
Devon Energy	PETROBRAS
Eni	PetrOleos de
Exxon Mobil	Venezuela
Hess Corporation	Repsol
Imperial Oil	Royal Dutch Shell
Koch Industries Inc.	Sinopec Corp.
Marathon Petroleum	TOTAL

HISTORICAL FINANCIALS

Company Type: Public

Income Statement				FYE: December 31
	REVENUE ($ mil.)	NET INCOME ($ mil.)	NET PROFIT MARGIN	EMPLOYEES
12/19	146,516	2,924	2.0%	48,200
12/18	166,339	14,824	8.9%	48,600
12/17	141,722	9,195	6.5%	51,900
12/16	114,472	(497)	—	55,200
12/15	138,477	4,587	3.3%	61,500
Annual Growth	1.4%	(10.6%)	—	(5.9%)

2019 Year-End Financials

Debt ratio: 11.36%
Return on equity: 1.96%
Cash ($ mil.): 5,686
Current ratio: 1.07
Long-term debt ($ mil.): 23,691

No. of shares (mil.): 1,882
Dividends
  Yield: 3.9%
  Payout: 309.0%
Market value ($ mil.): 226,820

	STOCK PRICE ($) FY Close	P/E High/Low	PER SHARE ($) Earnings	Dividends	Book Value
12/19	120.51	82 70	1.54	4.76	76.62
12/18	108.79	17 13	7.74	4.48	81.22
12/17	125.19	26 21	4.85	4.32	77.77
12/16	117.70	— —	(0.27)	4.29	76.95
12/15	89.96	46 28	2.45	4.28	81.11
Annual Growth	7.6%	— —	(11.0%)	2.7%	(1.4%)

CHEVRON PHILLIPS CHEMICAL COMPANY LLC

Among the world's largest petrochemical firms Chevron Phillips Chemical (CPChem) produces ethylene propylene polyethylene and polypropylene — sometimes used as building blocks for the company's other products such as pipes and food containers. CPChem also produces aromatics such as benzene and styrene specialty chemicals such as acetylene black (a form of carbon black) and mining chemicals. Chevron Phillips Chemical Company LP is CPChem's wholly-owned primary US operating subsidiary. CPChem is 50% owned by Chevron U.S.A. Inc. an indirect wholly-owned subsidiary of Chevron Corporation and 50% by wholly-owned subsidiaries of Phillips 66.

Operations
CPChem divides its operations into two segments: Olefins & Polyolefins and Specialties Aromatics and Styrenics.

The Olefins & Polyolefins segment produces ethylene polyethylene normal alpha olefins polyalphaolefins propylene and high-density polyethylene pipe and conduit and pipe fittings.

The Specialties Aromatics and Styrenics segments makes cyclohexane styrene polystyrene benzene mining chemicals Soltex drilling mud additive scentinel mercaptans specialty organosulfur compounds racing fuels and E-Series acetylene hydrogenation catalysts.

CPChem generates some 55% of sales from petrochemicals products one-third form polymers and more than 10% from specialty products.

The company's chemical products are used in more than 70000 consumer and industrial products. Its brands include Marlex Aromax Scentinel Soltex and K-Resin.

Geographic Reach
CPChem operates about 30 factories across Belgium Colombia Qatar Saudi Arabia Singapore and the US. It has two R&D and quality control centers in Bartlesville Oklahoma and Kingwood Texas. CPChem is active in Qatar Saudia Arabia and Singapore through joint venture

Sales and Marketing
CPChem serves a range of markets including Adhesives and Sealants Agricultural Appliances Automotive Building and Construction Chemical Manufacturing Drycleaning Textiles Pharmaceuticals Paint and Coatings Imaging and Photography Packaging and Electronics.

It holds the leading market position in the US for polyethelyne piping and is the world's largest marketer of cyclohexane. Subsidiary America Styrenics holds a nearly 30% market share in US polystyrene.

Financial Performance
CPChem has recorded growing sales over the past three years. In 2018 revenue climbed 25% to $11.3 billion. Profits dipped in 2017 but rebounded in 2018 growing 43% to $2.1 billion.

Strategy
External pressures on the petrochemicals industry including slowing growth the trade war between the US and China and a consumer backlash against plastic use have ushered in a period of consolidation. To diversify its output and geographic spread Chevron Phillips (CPChem) bid for Nova Chemicals in 2019 in a move that would make CPChem the third-largest producer of polyethylene in North America and the largest producer of high-density polyethylene.

Company Background
A coin toss determined whose name would go first when Chevron and Phillips Petroleum (now Phillips 66) formed 50-50 joint venture Chevron Phillips Chemical Company in 2000.

EXECUTIVES

Svp Petrochemicals, D. S. (Dave) Smith
President And Ceo, Mark E. Lashier
Vp And Cio, Peggy Colsman
Svp Cfo And Controller, Tim D. Leveille
Svp Projects And Supply Chain, R. E. (Ron) Corn
Svp Manufacturing, M. S. (Scott) Sharp
Svp Polymers, David Morgan
Vice President Of Business Development, John
  Lupe
Vice President, Linda Tolman
Vice President Controller, G Maxwell
National Account Manager, Steve Faggard
Vice President Manufacturing, Todd Monette
Senior Vice President Of Technology Research,
  Don Lycette
Auditors: ERNST & YOUNG LLP HOUSTON TX

LOCATIONS

HQ: CHEVRON PHILLIPS CHEMICAL COMPANY LLC
  10001 SIX PINES DR, THE WOODLANDS, TX
  773801498
Phone: 832 813-4100
Web: WWW.CPCHEM.COM

PRODUCTS/OPERATIONS

Selected Products
Olefins and polyolefins
  Ethylene
  Polyethylene
  Polyethylene pipe
  Polypropylene
  Propylene
Aromatics and styrenics

Benzene
Cumene
Cyclohexane
Paraxylene
Styrene
Specialty products
Acetylene black
Alpha olefins
Dimethyl sulfide
Drilling specialty chemicals
High-purity hydrocarbons and solvents
Mining chemicals
Neohexene
Performance and reference fuels
Polyalpha olefins
Polystyrene

Selected Joint Ventures

Americas Styrenics (50%)
Chevron Phillips Singapore Chemicals (Private) Limited
(50%)
KR Copolymer Co. Ltd. (60% South Korea)
Qatar Chemical Company Ltd. (Q-Chem 49%)
Saudi Chevron Phillips Company (50%)
Shanghai Golden Phillips Petrochemical Co. Ltd. (40%)

COMPETITORS

Dow Chemical	SABIC
ExxonMobil Chemical	Sasol
LyondellBasell	Total Petrochemicals
NOVA Chemicals	Westlake Chemical

HISTORICAL FINANCIALS

Company Type: Private

Income Statement   FYE: December 31

	REVENUE ($ mil.)	NET INCOME ($ mil.)	NET PROFIT MARGIN	EMPLOYEES
12/16	8,769	1,687	19.2%	6,472
12/15	9,859	2,651	26.9%	—
12/14	14,148	3,288	23.2%	—
Annual Growth	(21.3%)	(28.4%)	—	—

CHEVRON PHILLIPS CHEMICAL COMPANY LP

EXECUTIVES

Ceo, Peter Cella
Exec V Pres, Mark Lashier
Sr V Pres, Ron Corn
Sr V Pres, Tim Hill
V Pres, Mitch Eichelberger
Coordinator, Aprile Turner
Staff, Aaron Evitts
Coordinator, Tom Shomette
Safety Manager, Carolyn Rogers
Information Specialist, Marie Newhouse
Operations Manager, Art Orscheln
Auditors: ERNST & YOUNG LLP HOUSTON T

LOCATIONS

HQ: CHEVRON PHILLIPS CHEMICAL COMPANY LP
10001 SIX PINES DR, THE WOODLANDS, TX
773801498
Phone: 832 813-4100
Web: WWW.CPCHEM.COM

HISTORICAL FINANCIALS

Company Type: Private

Income Statement   FYE: December 31

	REVENUE ($ mil.)	NET INCOME ($ mil.)	NET PROFIT MARGIN	EMPLOYEES
12/16	7,106	1,301	18.3%	6,472
12/15	7,990	2,020	25.3%	—
12/14	11,758	2,444	20.8%	—
Annual Growth	(22.3%)	(27.0%)	—	—

Chimera Investment Corp

This Chimera has the body of a mortgage real estate investment trust (REIT) but its head is that of its external manager FIDAC (Fixed Income Discount Advisory Company) a fixed-income investment management firm wholly-ownedÂ by Annaly Capital Management. Formed in 2007 Chimera invests in residential mortgage loans; residential mortgage-backed securities (RMBS) such as those guaranteed by government agencies Fannie Mae and Freddie Mac; real estate-related securities; and other assets including collateralized debt obligations or CDOs. The REIT went public in 2007 shortly after it was formed.

EXECUTIVES

Board Member, Dennis Mahoney
Auditors: Ernst & Young LLP

LOCATIONS

HQ: Chimera Investment Corp
520 Madison Avenue, 32nd Floor, New York, NY 10022
Phone: 212 626-2300
Web: www.chimerareit.com

COMPETITORS

Annaly Capital Management	MFA Financial
Capstead Mortgage	Walter Investment Management
Impac Mortgage Holdings	

HISTORICAL FINANCIALS

Company Type: Public

Income Statement   FYE: December 31

	ASSETS ($ mil.)	NET INCOME ($ mil.)	INCOME AS % OF ASSETS	EMPLOYEES
12/19	27,118	413	1.5%	39
12/18	27,708	411	1.5%	38
12/17	21,222	524	2.5%	38
12/16	16,684	551	3.3%	38
12/15	15,344	250	1.6%	32
Annual Growth	15.3%	13.4%	—	5.1%

2019 Year-End Financials

Debt ratio: 30.65%	No. of shares (mil.): 187
Return on equity: 10.80%	Dividends
Cash ($ mil.): 109	Yield: 9.7%
Current ratio: —	Payout: 110.5%
Long-term debt ($ mil.): —	Market value ($ mil.): 3,849

	STOCK PRICE ($) FY Close	P/E High/Low	PER SHARE ($) Earnings	Dividends	Book Value
12/19	20.56	12 10	1.81	2.00	21.12
12/18	17.82	10 8	1.96	2.00	19.80
12/17	18.48	8 7	2.61	2.00	19.35
12/16	17.02	6 4	2.92	2.44	16.64
12/15	13.64	13 2	1.25	1.44	15.70
Annual Growth	10.8%	—	9.7%	8.6%	7.7%

CHINESE HOSPITAL ASSOCIATION

EXECUTIVES

Ceo, Brenda Yee
Cfo*, Thomas Bolger
Coo*, Linda Schumacher
Chief of Medicine, Joseph Woo
Director of Finance, Amy Wong
Lab Technician, Lisa Glaser
Training Manager, Josephine Lee
Executive Director, Angela Sun
Internal Medicine, Roderick Snow
Director, Scott Huang
Vice President, Chee Tong
Auditors: MOSS & ADAMS LLP SAN FRANCISC

LOCATIONS

HQ: CHINESE HOSPITAL ASSOCIATION
845 JACKSON ST, SAN FRANCISCO, CA 941334899
Phone: 415 982-2400
Web: WWW.CHINESEHOSPITAL-SF.ORG

HISTORICAL FINANCIALS

Company Type: Private

Income Statement   FYE: December 31

	REVENUE ($ mil.)	NET INCOME ($ mil.)	NET PROFIT MARGIN	EMPLOYEES
12/19	226,958	(10,648)	—	285
12/18	216	(28)	—	—
12/17	123	(11)	—	—
12/16	202	(13)	—	—
Annual Growth	938.3%	—	—	—

CHRISTIAN BROTHERS INVESTMENT SERVICES, INC.

EXECUTIVES

Ceo, Jeffrey McCroy
Chief Investment Officer, John W Geissinger
Cpo, Cece Novotny
Marketing Staff, Miranda McCoy
Accountant, Alex Chan

Director, Dean Armstrong
Caia Director Institutional De, Sean McCaffrey
Senior Compliance Officer, Diane Miller
Director, Julie Tanner
Managing Director Investor, Michael Nagy
Managing Director Relationship, Eric Bieniasz

LOCATIONS

HQ: CHRISTIAN BROTHERS INVESTMENT SERVICES, INC.
20 N WACKER DR STE 2000, CHICAGO, IL 606063002
Phone: 312 526-3343
Web: WWW.CBISONLINE.COM

HISTORICAL FINANCIALS
Company Type: Private

Income Statement				FYE: December 30
	ASSETS ($ mil.)	NET INCOME ($ mil.)	INCOME AS % OF ASSETS	EMPLOYEES
12/11	2,079	100	4.8%	45
12/10	2,167	68	3.1%	—
12/09	1,863	0	—	—
12/05	2,191	0	—	—
Annual Growth	(0.9%)	—	—	—

CHS Inc

CHS is a major cooperative marketer of grain oilseed and energy resources in the US. It represents farmers ranchers and co-ops from the Great Lakes to Texas trading grain and selling farm supplies through its stores to members. The group processes soybeans for use in food and animal feeds and grinds wheat into flour. In addition to grain marketing it operates through joint ventures and a variety of business segments for the sale of soybean oil and crop nutrient products. CHS also operates petroleum refineries that sell Cenex-brand fuels lubricants and other energy products. The company does about 90% of its business in North America.

HISTORY

To help farmers through the Great Depression the Farmers Union Terminal Association (a grain marketing association formed in 1926) created the Farmers Union Grain Terminal Association (GTA) in 1938. With loans from the Farmers Union Central Exchange (later known as CENEX) and the Farm Credit Association the organization operated a grain elevator in St. Paul Minnesota. By 1939 GTA had 250 grain-producing associations as members.

GTA leased terminals in Minneapolis and Washington and built others in Wisconsin and Montana in the early 1940s. It then took over a Minnesota flour mill and created Amber Milling. GTA also began managing farming insurance provider Terminal Agency. In 1958 the association bought 57 elevators and feed plants from the McCabe Company.

Adding to its operations in 1960 GTA bought the Honeymead soybean plant. The next year the co-op acquired Minnesota Linseed Oil. In 1977 it acquired Jewett & Sherman (later Holsum Foods) which helped transform the company into a provider of jams jellies salad dressings and syrups.

In 1983 GTA combined with North Pacific Grain Growers a Pacific Northwest co-op incorporated in 1929 to form Harvest States Cooperatives. Harvest States grew in the early and mid-1990s by acquiring salad dressing makers Albert's Foods Great American Foods and Saffola Quality Foods; soup stock producer Private Brands; and margarine and dressings manufacturer and distributor Gregg Foods.

The company started a joint venture to operate the Ag States Agency agricultural insurance company in 1995. The next year the co-op's Holsum Foods division and Mitsui & Co.'s edible oils unit Wilsey Foods merged to form Ventura Foods a distributor of margarines oils spreads and other food products.

Harvest States merged in 1998 with Minnesota-based CENEX a 16-state agricultural supply co-op that had been founded in 1931 as Farmers Union Central Exchange. (Among CENEX's major operations was a farm inputs services marketing and processing joint venture with dairy cooperative Land O'Lakes formed in 1987.) CENEX CEO Noel Estenson took the helm of the resulting co-op Cenex Harvest States Cooperatives which soon formed a petroleum joint venture called Country Energy with Farmland Industries.

CHS members rejected a proposed merger with Farmland Industries in 1999. Also that year Cenex/Land O'Lakes Agronomy (it became Agriliance in 2000 when Farmland Industries joined the joint venture) bought Terra Industries' $1.7 billion distribution business (400 farm supply stores seed and chemical distribution operations partial ownership of two chemical plants).

CHS bought the wholesale propane marketing operations of Williams Companies in 2000 and the co-op paid $14 million for tortilla and tortilla chip maker Sparta Foods. Additionally Estenson retired that year and company president John Johnson took over as CEO. CHS launched an agricultural e-commerce site (Rooster.com) in conjunction with Cargill and DuPont in 2000. The site was shut down the next year however because of a lack of funds. Also in 2001 the cooperative became the full owner of Country Energy by purchasing Farmland Industries' share.

In 2002 CHS acquired Agway's Grandin North Dakota-based sunflower business and formed a wheat-milling joint venture (Horizon Milling) with Cargill. In 2003 the company changed its name from Cenex Harvest States Cooperatives to CHS Inc. and began trading on the NASDAQ. It used the proceeds from the stock offering to repay its short-term debts.

In 2004 CHS purchased all of bankrupt Farmland Industries' ownership of Agriliance thus giving CHS a 50% ownership of Agriliance (with Land O'Lakes owning the other 50%). With an eye to this growing energy sector CHS acquired a 28% ownership of ethanol producer and marketer US BioEnergy Corporation in 2005. Also that year it sold off its Mexican foods business and sold 81% of its 20% ownership of crop-nutrient manufacturer CF Industries in an initial public offering.

CHS and Land O'Lakes realigned the businesses of their 50-50 joint venture Agriliance in 2007 with CHS acquiring its crop-nutrients wholesale-products business and Land O'Lakes acquiring the crop-protection products business. Canadian ag cooperative La Coop f d r e purchased Agriliance's retail agronomy operation the following year. Adding to its lubricants offerings in 2007 the company acquired two Minnesota companies: Nor-Lakes Services Midwest and The Farm-Oyl Company. In 2008 it sold off all its remaining shares of CF.

Recognizing the growing demand for soy-based food products and in turn to increase shareholder value the company in 2008 acquired Legacy Foods maker of Ultra Soy and TSP brands of textured soybean products for use by both human food and pet food manufacturers. Legacy's operations are overseen by CHS's oilseed processing division.

On the energy front CHS became the sole owner of Provista Renewable Fuels Marketing in 2008 by purchasing US BioEnergy's 50% interest in the biofuels maker. (VeraSun Energy bought out US BioEnergy later that year.

In 2009 CHS acquired Winona River & Rail including 90000 tons of dry-fertilizer storage capacity a dedicated river dock and a 65-car railroad track capacity. The acquisition of the Minnesota operations bolstered the company's storage capacity and rail access in the midwestern and upper Mississippi River regions. Later that year it formed a joint venture with Russia's farm operation Agrico Group (called ACG) in order to manage the export and worldwide marketing of its wheat and feed grains. In turn it gave CHS access to the Russian grain market and improved its ability to serve its global customers.

Also in 2009 CHS formed another of its joint ventures this time at home. It joined with Nebraska's Central Valley Ag Cooperative (CVA) to form Advanced Energy Fuels to provide customers with an industry-leading fuel delivery system.

Beyond the US the company was part of a grain marketing joint venture (Multigrain A.G.) with Brazilian commodities-company PMG Trading and Mitsui. In 2011 CHS sold a nearly 45% stake in Multigrain to the Japanese firm for Å 47 billion yen (roughly $510 million). Mitsui which already owned about a 45% stake also bought PMG's interest. The deal marked one of the largest overseas farming investments made by a Japanese trading house.

Building on the success of its joint ventures in 2013 CHS formed a flouring-milling partnership with agri-giants Cargill and ConAgra called Ardent Mills. The newly-formed partnership was North America's largest flour miller with annual sales of more than $4 billion. CHS held 12% of Ardent Mills while ConAgra and Cargill each owned 44%.

EXECUTIVES

President And Ceo, Jay D. Debertin, $667,242 total compensation
Evp Business Solutions, Lisa Zell, $438,600 total compensation
Evp And Coo Country Operations, Lynden E. Johnson
Evp And Coo Ag Business And Enterprise Strategy, Shirley Cunningham, $593,983 total compensation
Evp And Cfo, Timothy Skidmore, $487,135 total compensation
Evp And Chief Human Resources Officer, Adam Holton
Evp And General Counsel, James (Jim) Zappa, $423,667 total compensation
Vice President And General Manager, Roger Baker
Regional Vice President Operations, Christopher Cairo
Chairman, Daniel (Dan) Schurr
First Vice Chairman, Clinton J. (C.J.) Blew
Auditors: PricewaterhouseCoopers LLP

LOCATIONS

HQ: CHS Inc
5500 Cenex Drive, Inver Grove Heights, MN 55077
Phone: 651 355-6000
Web: www.chsinc.com

2018 Sales

	$ mil.	% of total
North America	29,475	90
EMEA	1,569	5
APAC	1,101	3
APAC	536	2
Total	**32,683**	**100**

PRODUCTS/OPERATIONS

2018 Sales

	$ mil.	% of total
Ag	25,052	81
Energy	8,068	19
Corporate and Other	64	-
Adjustments	(502.3)	-
Total	**32,683**	**100**

Selected Operations

Ag business
  Grain exporter
  Grain merchandising in Argentina
  Grain merchandising in Europe
  Grain merchandising in Spain
  Grain procurement and merchandising in Russia
  Grain procurement and merchandising in Ukraine
  Retail distribution of agronomy products
  Soybean procurement in Brazil
Corporate and Other
  Finance company
  Insurance agency
  Insurance brokerage
  Risk management products broker
Energy
  Crude oil transportation
  Finished product transportation
  Petroleum refining
Processing
  Food manufacturing and distribution
  Wheat milling in Canada
  Wheat milling in US

COMPETITORS

ADM	ConocoPhillips
Ag Processing Inc.	ExxonMobil Chemical
AmeriGas Partners	Flint Hills
CGC	GROWMARK
CITGO	JR Simplot
Cargill	Marathon Petroleum
Columbia Grain	Valero Energy
ConAgra	

HISTORICAL FINANCIALS

Company Type: Public

Income Statement

FYE: August 31

	REVENUE ($ mil.)	NET INCOME ($ mil.)	NET PROFIT MARGIN	EMPLOYEES
08/20	28,406	422	1.5%	10,493
08/19	31,900	829	2.6%	10,703
08/18	32,683	775	2.4%	10,495
08/17	31,934	127	0.4%	11,626
08/16	30,347	424	1.4%	12,157
Annual Growth	**(1.6%)**	**(0.1%)**	**—**	**(3.6%)**

2020 Year-End Financials

Debt ratio: 21.05%—
Return on equity: 4.84%
Cash ($ mil.): 140
Current ratio: 1.27
Long-term debt ($ mil.): 1,601

Dividends
  Yield: 6.6%
  Payout: —
Market value ($ mil.): —

	STOCK PRICE ($) FY Close	P/E High/Low	PER SHARE ($) Earnings	Dividends	Book Value
08/20	26.83	— —	(0.00)	1.88	(0.00)
08/19	27.03	— —	(0.00)	1.78	(0.00)
08/18	28.86	— —	(0.00)	1.88	(0.00)
08/17	29.35	— —	(0.00)	1.88	(0.00)
08/16	31.25	— —	(0.00)	1.88	(0.00)
Annual Growth	**(3.7%)**	**— —**	**—**	**(0.0%)**	

Cigna Corp (New)

EXECUTIVES

Pres-Ceo, David Cordani
Exec V Pres-Chief Marketing of*, Lisa Bacus
Exec V Pres-Chief Information*, Mark Boxer
Exec V Pres-General Counsel*, Nicole Jones
Chief Clinical Officer, Steve Miller
Exec V Pres-Chief Human Resour*, John Murabito
Exec V Pres-Cfo*, Eric Palmer
Hr Consultant, Margaret O'Callaghan
Information Protection Lead An, Matthew Collins
Customer Advocate, Megan Wetzel
Vice President Sales, Mike Evans
Auditors: PricewaterhouseCoopers LLP

LOCATIONS

HQ: Cigna Corp (New)
900 Cottage Grove Road, Bloomfield, CT 06002
Phone: 860 226-6000   **Fax:** 860 226-6741
Web: www.cigna.com

HISTORICAL FINANCIALS

Company Type: Public

Income Statement

FYE: December 31

	ASSETS ($ mil.)	NET INCOME ($ mil.)	INCOME AS % OF ASSETS	EMPLOYEES
12/19	155,774	5,104	3.3%	73,700
12/18	153,226	2,637	1.7%	73,800
12/17	61,753	2,237	3.6%	46,000
12/16	59,360	1,867	3.1%	41,000
12/15	57,088	2,094	3.7%	39,300
Annual Growth	**28.5%**	**24.9%**	**—**	**17.0%**

2019 Year-End Financials

Debt ratio: 23.39%
Return on equity: 11.82%
Cash ($ mil.): 4,619
Current ratio: —
Long-term debt ($ mil.): —

No. of shares (mil.): 372
Dividends
  Yield: 0.0%
  Payout: 0.3%
Market value ($ mil.): 76,179

	STOCK PRICE ($) FY Close	P/E High/Low	PER SHARE ($) Earnings	Dividends	Book Value
12/19	204.49	15 11	13.44	0.04	121.70
12/18	189.92	21 15	10.54	0.04	107.71
12/17	203.09	24 15	8.77	0.04	56.30
12/16	133.39	20 16	7.19	0.04	53.42
12/15	146.33	21 12	8.04	0.04	46.91
Annual Growth	**8.7%**	**— —**	**13.7%**	**(0.0%)**	**26.9%**

Cincinnati Financial Corp.

Cincinnati Financial Corporation (CFC) provides property casualty insurance marketed through independent insurance agencies in around 45 states primarily in the midwestern and southeastern US. Its flagship firm Cincinnati Insurance (operating through four subsidiaries) sells commercial property and casualty liability excess and surplus auto bond and fire insurance. Personal lines include homeowners auto and other personal line products. The Cincinnati Insurance companies also sell life coverage and annuities. Other CFC subsidiaries include CFC Investment (leasing and financing services) CSU Producers Resources (excess and surplus lines brokerage) and Cincinnati Global Underwriting (global specialty insurance).

Operations

CFC operates through five segments: Commercial Lines Insurance Investments Personal Lines Insurance Excess and Surplus Lines Insurance and Life Insurance.

The Commercial Lines Insurance segment which accounts for more than 40% of total revenue provides commercial property/casualty coverage including auto workers' compensation machinery and equipment and management liability.

The CFC Investment unit (almost 30% of sales) provides commercial financing leasing and real estate services to its independent insurance agents and their clients while the CSU Producers Resources business offers insurance brokerage services to independent agencies.

The Personal Lines Insurance segment accounting for nearly 20% of sales writes personal auto homeowners fire watercraft umbrella and other property/casualty policies.

The Life Insurance Excess and Surplus Lines and other income segments each account for about 5% of revenue.

Primary operating unit Cincinnati Insurance has two standard property/casualty subsidiaries: Cincinnati Casualty and Cincinnati Indemnity. Its Cincinnati Specialty Underwriters Insurance unit underwrites excess and surplus property/casualty policies while Cincinnati Life Insurance provide annuities and life insurance. The four subsidiaries are known as the Cincinnati Insurance Companies.

The company's Cincinnati Global Underwriting unit formerly MSP Underwriting is a London-based specialty insurance firm acquired in 2019.

CFC's earned premiums generates more than 70% of total revenue. Its net investment gains account for over 20%.

Geographic Reach

Headquartered in Ohio CFC markets its policies in around 45 states but does most of its business in the Midwest and Southeast US. The company writes about 15% of its business in Ohio and it is strong in Illinois Indiana Georgia North Carolina and Pennsylvania. Other states include Michigan Tennessee Virginia and Alabama. Cincinnati Life is licensed in almost 50 states and the District of Columbia.

Sales and Marketing

CFC maintains a force of more than 1800 field associates who provide local service and be accountable to its agencies for decisions we make at the local level.

The company's commercial lines segment targets primarily small to mid-sized businesses though it is working to expand its services for larger companies. CFC has tied its growth to increasing the number of new agencies with which it strikes new relationships.

Financial Performance

CFC revenue climbed steadily between 2014 and 2017 but declined in 2018. Overall sales increased 25% over the past five years. Net income fluctuated for the same period.

Revenue rose nearly 47% to $7.9 billion in 2019 due to contributed net earned premiums of $3.3 billion representing 41.9% of consolidated total revenues.

Net income jumped almost 600% to $2 billion in 2019 including a $1.6 billion increase for 2019 net investment gains after taxes. The improved 2019 net income also included an increase in property casualty underwriting income of $122 million after taxes and a $21 million increase in investment income after taxes.

The company ended 2019 with $767 million in cash down $17 million from 2018. Operating activities contributed $1.2 billion while investing activities used $679 million (mostly fixed maturity purchases) and financing activities used $546 million on shareholder dividends share repurchases and contract holder fund withdrawals.

Strategy

CFC's mission and strategy is to grow profitably and enhance the ability of local independent insurance agents to deliver quality financial protection to the people and businesses they serve by providing insurance market stability through financial strength producing competitive up-to-date products and services and developing associates committed to superior service.

The company's strategic priorities include meeting the wants and needs of its agent customers attracting and developing talented associates providing comprehensive product solutions achieving best-in-class field service and continually enhancing operational efficiency and effectiveness. CFC believes successful execution of its long-term strategy and related shorter-term initiatives will help achieve its long-term objectives despite potential unfavorable shorter-term effects of difficult economic market or pricing cycles.

Mergers and Acquisitions

In early 2019 the company expanded internationally through the purchase of MSP Underwriting a London-based specialty insurance firm from Munich Re for some Å 102 million. MSP Underwriting has since been renamed Cincinnati Global Underwriting. The purchase included management of Lloyd's Syndicate 318 through its Beaufort Underwriting Agency unit.

Company Background

Cincinnati Insurance was founded by the Schiff brothers in 1950 to offer property/casualty insurance to homeowners and small businesses. In 1968 Cincinnati Financial Corporation was formed as a holding company for the insurance operation; CFC went public in 1969.

The company expanded into real estate and life insurance services in the 1970s. It focused on personal lines in the 1960s and 1970s but grew its commercial offerings in the 1980s and 1990s.

HISTORY

Jack Schiff spent three years with the Travelers Company before he joined the Navy in WWII. He returned to Cincinnati to start his own independent insurance agency in 1946 and was joined by his younger brother Robert; both were Ohio State graduates whose affection for the Buckeyes led them in later years to close company banquets with the school fight song. The brothers incorporated Cincinnati Insurance with $200000 from investors in 1950.

Under Harry Turner the company's first president the company offered property/casualty insurance to small businesses and homeowners through its network of agents. By 1956 the company had spread into neighboring Kentucky and Indiana. During the next decade Cincinnati Insurance expanded its products and network adding auto burglary and commercial all-risk lines and enlisting agents throughout the Midwest.

In 1963 Turner took the chairman's seat and Jack Schiff became president introducing a more aggressive leadership style. In 1968 the company reorganized forming Cincinnati Financial Corporation as a holding company for the insurance operation and went public in 1969. CFC used the money to pay off debts and buy new businesses forming two subsidiaries: CFC Investment Company in 1970 to deal in commercial real estate and financing; and Queen City Indemnity (later

named The Cincinnati Casualty Company) in 1972 to offer direct-bill personal policies.

By 1973 operations included The Life Insurance Company of Cincinnati Queen City Indemnity and fellow Cincinnati giant Inter-Ocean Insurance Company. That year Jack Schiff added CEO to his title.

CFC continued to grow throughout the 1970s with a new emphasis on independent investments. In 1982 Cincinnati Financial veteran Robert Morgan became president and CEO. The company's conservative roots and investment base helped it shake off the early-1980s recession and a string of natural disasters that left many other insurers dangling in the wind.

Also during the 1980s the company started to shift its focus from personal to commercial lines. In 1988 it reorganized its life insurance subsidiaries under the Cincinnati Life banner and formed The Cincinnati Indemnity Company to offer workers' compensation and personal insurance.

EXECUTIVES

President Ceo And Director, Steven J. Johnston, age 60, $960,814 total compensation
Vice President Commercial, Anthony Henn
Svp Cfo And Treasurer, Michael J. (Mike) Sewell, age 56, $784,665 total compensation
Svp Chief Investment Officer Assistant Secretary And Assistant Treasurer, Martin F. Hollenbeck, age 60, $646,808 total compensation
Assistant Vice President Of Corporate Accounting, Jerry Litton
Vice President, David Sloan
Assistant Vice President, Ann Binzer
Vice President, Gary J Kline
Senior Vice President And Senior Marketing Officer, Glenn Nicholson
Assistant Vice President Information Technology, Michael Hingsbergen
Vice President Commercial Lines The Cincinnati Insurance Company, Bill Thomas
Vice President Marketing, Mark McBeath
Vice President, Mark Wietmarschen
Vice President, Rodney French
Vice President Information Technology, Rich Mathews
Assistant Vice President For Education, BradleyBrad Delaney
Vice President Sales And Marketing, Duane Swanson
Vice President Information Technology, Todd Taylor
Assistant Vice President Headquarters Claims, William Gregory
Vice President And Chief Information Security Officer, Mike Dockery
Executive Vice President Of Sales And Marketing, Jay Sherer
Vice President Financial Planning And Analysis, Tony Dunn
Vice President, David Mckinney
Vice President Of Commercial Lines, Chris Kendall
Vice President, Brian Mcnair
Vice President, Frederick Ferris
Vice President, Michael Abrams
Vice President And Corporate Compliance Officer, Helen Kyrios
Svp And Treasurer, Theresa Hoffer
Vice President Of Information Technology, Brad Delaney
Vice President Target Markets, Steve Spray
Assistant Vice President, Tony Henn
Senior Vice President, Kevin Guilfoyle
Vice President Commercial Lines Director Of Underwriting, Rick Ferris
Vice President Of Informaton Technology, Bill Geier

Vice President Reinsured Assumed, Claudio Ronzitti
Vice President, Gary Givler
Executive Vice President, Jf Scherer
Vice President Field Claims, Charles Robinson
Vice President Personal Lines, Joseph Kinsey
Vice President Corporate Comminications, Elizabeth Ertel
Vp And Director Product Management, Steve Ventre
Vice President Reinsured Assumed, John Davis
Vice President Reinsured Assumed, James Faust
Vice President Reinsured Assumed, Paul Lestourgeon
Assistant Vice President Headquarters Claims, John Crow
Vp And Director Risk Management, Vicki Hill
Assistant Vice President For Education, Bradley Delaney
Vice President Director Of Risk Management, Vicki Walno
Legal Secretary, Megan VanLeuven
Region Vice President, Pat Luchtel
Vice President Director Target Markets Product Development, Jody Wainscott
Avp Pricing Analytics, Daniel F Henke
Avp Commercial Lines, Matthew R Burrows
Vice President Pricing And Predictive Analytics, Robert Weishaar
Senior Vice President Of The Cincinnati Insurance Company, William Heuvel
Vice President, Michael Tiemeier
Vice President Premium Audit Manager, Tim Morris
Senior Vice President Worldwide Partner Organization, Bruce Klein
Senior Vice President Worldwide Strategy And Planning, Inder Sidhu
Senior Vice President Cisco Product Resiliency Research, Joel Bion
Vice President Biography Music Educator, Melissa Ray
Chairman, Kenneth W. (Ken) Stecher, age 73
Secretary Loss Control Field Manager, Mitchell Carson
Secretary, Susan Fitzgerald
Secretary, Pam Vehr
Assistant Treasurer, Kevin Smith
Secretary, Julie Sweeney
Secretary, Sean Givler
Board Member, BRENDA GAGNON
Board Member, William Bahl
Assistant Treasurer, William Loftis
Board Member, Kenneth Lichtendahl
Assistant Secretary Process Developmenteducation, David Pierce
Secretary Commercial Lines The Cincinnati Insurance Company, Pamela Cooper
Assistant Secretary It Support Services, Kevin Heslin
Assistant Secretary Headquarters Claims The Cincinnati Insurance Company, Dale Prisco
Board Member, David Osborn
Board Member, Douglas Skidmore
Secretary; Marketing Other; Sales Other, William M Clevidence
Assistant Treasurer, Christina Scherpenberg
Auditors: DELOITTE & TOUCHE LLP

LOCATIONS

HQ: Cincinnati Financial Corp.
6200 S. Gilmore Road, Fairfield, OH 45014-5141
Phone: 513 870-2000
Web: www.cinfin.com

PRODUCTS/OPERATIONS

2017 Sales

	$ mil.	% of total
Earned premiums	4,954	86
Net investment income	609	11
Realized investment gains	148	3
Fees	16	-
Other	5	-
Total	**5,732**	**100**

2017 Sales

	$ mil.	% of total
Commercial lines	3,170	55
Personal lines	1,246	22
Investment income	757	13
Life insurance	237	4
Excess & surplus	210	4
Other	112	2
Total	**5,732**	**100**

Selected Subsidiaries

CFC Investment Company
CSU Producer Resources Inc.
The Cincinnati Insurance Company
  The Cincinnati Casualty Company
  The Cincinnati Indemnity Company
  The Cincinnati Life Insurance Company
  The Cincinnati Specialty Underwriters Insurance
  Company

COMPETITORS

American Financial Group	Progressive Corporation
CNA Financial	Selective Insurance
Erie Indemnity	The Hartford
Farmers Group	Travelers Companies
Indiana Insurance	Westfield Insurance
Ohio Casualty	Zurich American
OneBeacon	

HISTORICAL FINANCIALS

Company Type: Public

Income Statement

FYE: December 31

	ASSETS ($ mil.)	NET INCOME ($ mil.)	INCOME AS % OF ASSETS	EMPLOYEES
12/19	25,408	1,997	7.9%	5,148
12/18	21,935	287	1.3%	4,999
12/17	21,843	1,045	4.8%	4,925
12/16	20,386	591	2.9%	4,754
12/15	18,888	634	3.4%	4,493
Annual Growth	7.7%	33.2%	—	3.5%

2019 Year-End Financials

Debt ratio: 3.48%
Return on equity: 22.57%
Cash ($ mil.): 767
Current ratio: —
Long-term debt ($ mil.): —

No. of shares (mil.): 162
Dividends
  Yield: 2.1%
  Payout: 40.2%
Market value ($ mil.): 17,129

	STOCK PRICE ($) FY Close	P/E High/Low		PER SHARE ($) Earnings	Dividends	Book Value
12/19	105.15	10	6	12.10	2.24	60.55
12/18	77.42	47	38	1.75	2.12	48.11
12/17	74.97	13	11	6.29	2.50	50.29
12/16	75.75	22	15	3.55	1.92	42.94
12/15	59.17	16	13	3.83	2.30	39.21
Annual Growth	15.5%	—	—	33.3%	(0.7%)	11.5%

Cintas Corporation

Cintas has a uniform approach to business. Supplying corporate identity uniform programs providing entrance and logo mats restroom supplies promotional products first aid safety fire protection products and services and industrial carpet and tile cleaning primarily in North America as well as Latin America Europe and Asia. Cintas provide their products and services to over one million businesses of all types from small service and manufacturing companies to major corporations that employ thousands of people. Cintas which sells leases and rents uniforms operates over 480 facilities in more than 330 cities; it leases over half of them. Besides offering rental and servicing of uniforms and other garments the company provides flame-resistant clothing mats mops and shop towels and other ancillary items. Other products offered by Cintas include uniforms floor care restroom supplies first-aid and safety products fire extinguishers and testing and safety and compliance training. Richard T. Farmer founded the company in 1929. Cintas is now run by Scott D. Farmer.

Operations

The company has two segments: Uniform Rental and Facility Services and First Aid and Safety Services.

Uniform Rental and Facility Services which accounts for around 80% of total consists of the rental and servicing of uniforms and other garments including flame resistant clothing mats mops and shop towels and other ancillary items. In addition to these rental items it provides restroom cleaning services and supplies and carpet and tile cleaning services.

First Aid and Safety Services which accounts for about 10% of sales consists of first aid and safety products and services.

The remainder of Cintas' businesses (10% of sales) consist primarily of Fire Protection Services and its Direct Sale business.

Geographic Reach

Cincinnati Ohio-based Cintas operates over 480 facilities including five manufacturing plants and about a dozen distribution centers in over 330 cities. It serves businesses in North America Asia Europe and Latin America. The company has approximately 11100 local delivery routes.

Sales and Marketing

The primary markets served by all Cintas businesses are local in nature and highly fragmented. Cintas competes with national regional and local providers and the level of competition varies at each of Cintas' local operations. Cintas provides its products and services to customers via local delivery routes originating from rental processing plants and branches and via its distribution network and local delivery routes or local representatives.

Cintas provides its products and services to more than 1 million businesses of all sizes. Cintas uses its corporate website www.cintas.com as a channel for routine distribution of important information including news releases analyst presentations and financial information.

Financial Performance

Cintas has seen robust revenue growth in the last five years. Its annual revenues have risen more than 48% since 2016. Net income was fluctuating for the same period.

Revenue increased to $7.1 billion in 2020 an increase of approximately 3% from the year prior. The increase was driven by organic growth as well as acquisitions.

Net income was $876 million in fiscal year 2020 a 1% decrease from $885 million in fiscal year 2019.

Cash at the end of fiscal 2020 was $145 million a $49 million increase from 2019. Cash provided by operating activities was $1.3 billion in fiscal 2020 while investing activities used $285.4 million. Financing activities used another $955 million.

Strategy

Cintas' principal strategy is to achieve revenue growth for all its products and services by increasing its penetration at existing customers and by broadening its customer base to include business segments to which the company have not historically served. Cintas will also continue to identify additional product and service opportunities for their current and future customers.

To pursue the strategy of increasing penetration the company have a highly talented and diverse team of service professionals visiting its customers on a regular basis. This frequent contact with customers enables them to develop close personal relationships. The combination of its distribution system and these strong customer relationships provides a platform from which it launches additional products and services.

The company pursues the strategy of broadening its customer base in several ways. Cintas has a national sales organization introducing all of its products and services to prospects in all its business segments. Its broad range of products and services allows its sales organization to consider any type of business a prospect. It also broadens its customer base through geographic expansion especially in its first aid and safety and fire protection businesses.

Company Background

In 1929 onetime animal trainer boxer and blacksmith Richard "Doc" Farmer started a business of salvaging old rags cleaning them and then selling them to factories. Farmer later began renting the rags to his customers. He would pick up the dirty rags clean them and return them to the factory. By 1936 the Acme Overall & Rag Laundry had established itself in Cincinnati with plans to convert an old bathhouse into a laundry. Farmer along with his adopted son Herschell suffered a setback from flood damage in 1937 but the family rebuilt and continued to grow the business.

HISTORY

In 1929 onetime animal trainer boxer and blacksmith Richard "Doc" Farmer started a business of salvaging old rags cleaning them and then selling them to factories. Farmer later began renting the rags to his customers. He would pick up the dirty rags clean them and return them to the factory. By 1936 the Acme Overall & Rag Laundry had established itself in Cincinnati with plans to convert an old bathhouse into a laundry. Farmer along with his adopted son Herschell suffered a setback from flood damage in 1937 but the family rebuilt and continued to grow the business.

Doc Farmer died in 1952 and Herschell assumed command of the company. Five years later Herschell turned the reins over to his 23-year-old son Richard who immediately moved Acme into the uniform rental market and the company blossomed. Throughout the 1960s the company grew enormously aided by Richard's innovative leadership. (Acme was the first to use a polyester-cotton blend that lasted twice as long as normal cotton work uniforms.) Through a holding company Richard established a string of uniform plants in the Midwest starting with a factory in Cleveland in 1968. Four years later the company changed its name to Cintas.

At this time the company began tapping into the new corporate identity market pushing the idea that uniforms convey a sense of professionalism and present a cleaner safer image. The company began to custom-design the uniforms adding logos and distinctive colors. This aspect of the business compelled Cintas to expand to help accommodate its national clients; by 1972 the company had offices throughout Ohio and in Chicago Detroit and Washington DC. By 1975 Cintas was operating in 13 states.

The company went public in 1983. For the rest of the 1980s Cintas rode the wave of consolidation in the uniform rental industry making a slew of acquisitions. The company also expanded from its blue-collar base into the service industry and began to supply uniforms to hotels restaurants and banks. By the early 1990s Cintas was a presence in most major US cities and its share of the US market had climbed to about 10%. Farmer turned over the title of CEO to president Robert Kohlhepp in 1995. That year the company acquired Cadet Uniform Services a Toronto uniform rental business for $41 million.

Scott Farmer Richard's 38-year-old son was named president and COO in 1997. That year Cintas made a number of acquisitions including Micron-Clean Uniform Service and Canadian firms Act One Uniform Rentals and DW King Services. The company also moved into the first aid supplies industry with its purchase of American First Aid and added clean-room garments to its expanding list of uniform rentals. In 1998 Cintas acquired uniform rental company Apparelmaster as well as Chicago-based Uniforms To You a $150 million design and manufacturing company. In an effort to expand its corporate uniform business the company acquired rival Unitog in 1999 for about $460 million.

As part of the integration of Unitog in 2000 Cintas closed several of Unitog's uniform rental operations distribution centers and manufacturing plants. The company also established first aid supplies and safety equipment unit Xpect. In 2002 Cintas purchased Omni Services marking its largest acquisition to date.

Cintas purchased more than 10 document management businesses and three first-aid and fire protection businesses in fiscal 2009.

In fiscal 2013 it launched its AR Red Suiting Collection (made with renewable-sourced fiber) as well as its Signature Series line of designer soap and toilet paper dispensers and related products.

EXECUTIVES

President And Coo, J. Phillip Holloman, age 65, $643,966 total compensation
Chairman And Ceo, Scott D. Farmer, age 61, $1,000,000 total compensation
Svp Secretary And General Counsel, Thomas E. Frooman, age 53, $499,550 total compensation
Vp Finance And Cfo, J. Michael (Mike) Hansen, age 52, $360,000 total compensation
Vp And Treasurer, Paul F. Adler, age 49, $250,000 total compensation
Vice President Communications, Michelle Goret
Senior Vice President Corporate Strategy And Development, Paul Jantsch
Senior Vice President, Dave Bingham
National Account Manager, John Shannon
Regional Vice President, Greg Eling
Senior Vice President Operations, Dave Pollack
Vice President Of Sales, Todd Schneider
Executive Vice President And Chief Administrative Officer, Mike Thompson
Vice President And Marriott Lodging Uniforms And Services, Donna L Williams
National Account Manager, Brooke Negus
National Account Manager, Ian Adams
National Account Manager Global Accounts And Strategic M, Jacqueline Nopka

National Account Manager, Kevin Truex
Board Of Directors, Melanie Barstad
Board Member, Joe Scaminace
Board Member, Jamie Johnson
Auditors: Ernst & Young LLP

LOCATIONS

HQ: Cintas Corporation
6800 Cintas Boulevard, P.O. Box 625737, Cincinnati, OH 45262-5737
Phone: 513 459-1200   **Fax:** 513 573-4030
Web: www.cintas.com

PRODUCTS/OPERATIONS

2016 sales

	$ mil.	% of total
Uniforms Rental & Facility Services	3,777	77
First aid and safety services	461	9
All others	665	14
Total	**4,905**	**100**

Selected Products and Services

Clean-room supplies
Entrance mats
Fender covers
Fire protection
First aid and safety products and services
Linen products
Mops
Restroom supplies
Towels
Uniform cleaning
Uniform rental and sales

COMPETITORS

ARAMARK	NCH
Alsco	Superior Uniform Group
Angelica Corporation	UniFirst
Iron Mountain Inc	

HISTORICAL FINANCIALS

Company Type: Public

Income Statement

	REVENUE ($ mil.)	NET INCOME ($ mil.)	NET PROFIT MARGIN	FYE: May 31 EMPLOYEES
05/20	7,085	876	12.4%	40,000
05/19	6,892	884	12.8%	45,000
05/18	6,476	842	13.0%	41,000
05/17	5,323	480	9.0%	42,000
05/16	4,905	693	14.1%	35,000
Annual Growth	**9.6%**	**6.0%**	—	**3.4%**

2020 Year-End Financials

Debt ratio: 33.11%	No. of shares (mil.): 103
Return on equity: 28.01%	Dividends
Cash ($ mil.): 145	Yield: —
Current ratio: 2.61	Payout: 31.4%
Long-term debt ($ mil.): 2,539	Market value ($ mil.): —

Cisco Systems Inc

Cisco Systems (Cisco) is a maker of the network gear — routers switches and servers as well as software — that moves information around the internet and corporate networks. The company which has dominated the market for internet protocol-based networking equipment also makes security devices internet conferencing systems and other networking equipment for businesses and government agencies. Software that controls networks has become an increasing focus for Cisco which also provides cloud connectivity. Most sales come from customers in the Americas. Cisco's primary customers are large enterprises and telecommunications service providers but it also sells products designed for small businesses and public sector.

Operations
Cisco offers products and services in four categories.

The company's infrastructure platforms which generate 55% of its revenue consist of switching routing wireless and data center products that provide networking capabilities and transport and store data.

Applications which account for more than 10% of revenue are primarily software-related offerings that run on the company's networking and data center platforms. The applications include collaboration offerings (unified communications Cisco TelePresence and conferencing) as well as AppDynamics and Internet of Things software.

The Security product category over 5% of revenue includes network security cloud and email security identity and access management advanced threat protection and unified threat management products.

The Other Products category consists of cloud and system management products and emerging technologies products. The Services segment beyond 25% of revenue provides service and support for customers including comprehensive advisory services.

Cisco contracts with independent third-party companies to make printed-circuit boards conduct in-circuit testing assemble products and make repairs.

Geographic Reach
Cisco does well in the US and the Americas which account for some 60% of its sales. Internationally Cisco runs up against competitors like Huawei and Nokia which have strongholds in Asia and Europe respectively. Cisco gets more than 25% of its revenue from customers in the Europe Middle East and Africa region and customers in the Asia/Pacific China and Japan region supply 15%.

Cisco's headquarters is in San Jose California and it has regional headquarters in Amsterdam and Singapore. The company has significant operations in Australia Belgium Canada China Germany India Japan Mexico Poland and the UK.

Sales and Marketing
Cisco customers primarily operate in the following markets: enterprise commercial service provider and public sector.

In enterprise market the company offers service and support packages financing and managed network services through service provider partners. Cisco sells these products through a network of third-party application and technology vendors and channel partners as well as selling directly to these customers. In commercial it also sells through a combination of its direct sales force and channel partners. Service providers offer data voice video and mobile/wireless services to businesses governments utilities and consumers worldwide. Public sector (include federal governments state and local and educational institution) sell through third-party application and technology vendors channel partners and direct sales.

Advertising costs were approximately $187 million $204 million and $166 million for fiscal 2020 2019 and 2018 respectively.

Financial Performance
Cisco's revenue has trended higher in the past five years with some fluctuations on the way. The company's net income has followed a similar pattern. Total revenue in fiscal 2020 decreased by 5% to $49.3 billion compared with fiscal 2019.

Product revenue decreased by 8% and service revenue increased by 3%.

The company's total revenue reflected declines across each of their geographic segments. Product revenue for the emerging countries of BRICM in the aggregate experienced a 25% product revenue decline with decreases in India China Mexico and Brazil.

The company's net income increased to $11.2 billion in 2019 compared to $11.6 billion in the prior year.

In 2020 Cisco had about $11.8 billion in cash compared to $11.77 billion in 2019. Its operations generated $15.4 billion in 2020 and investing activities provided $3.5 billion while financing activities used $18.9 billion (including $2.6 billion spent to repurchase stock).

Strategy

As the company's customers add billions of new connections to its enterprises and as more applications move to a multicloud environment the network becomes even more critical. Cisco's customers are navigating change at an unprecedented pace and the company's mission is to inspire new possibilities by helping transform its infrastructure expand applications and analytics address its security needs and empowers its teams. The company believe that its customers are looking for intent-based networks that provide meaningful business value through automation security and analytics across private hybrid and multicloud environments. Cisco's vision is to deliver highly secure software-defined automated and intelligent platforms for its customers.

The company are expanding its research and development (R&D) investments in certain product areas including cloud security cloud collaboration and application insights and analytics. Cisco are investing to optimize its product offerings for application to education healthcare and other specific industries. Cisco also make investments to enable increase automation and support the customer as the workplace changes. In addition it also continue to remain focused on investments around Software-Defined Wide Area Network (SD-WAN) multicloud environments 5G and WiFi-6 400G speeds optical networking next generation silicon and artificial intelligence (AI). Cisco are also accelerating its efforts to enable the delivery of network functionality as a service.

Mergers and Acquisitions

Cisco regularly acquires companies to expand technologies and fill gaps.

In mid-2020 Cisco completed the acquisition of ThousandEyes. ThousandEyes' internet and cloud intelligence platform expands visibility and insights into the digital delivery of applications and services over the internet and the cloud. ThousandEyes enables organizations to visualize any network as if it was their own quickly surface actionable insights and collaborate and solve problems with service providers. Financial terms were not disclosed.

Cisco agreed to buy Voicea which provides meeting transcription voice search and meeting highlights to add to its Webex portfolio of products. Voicea's technology blends artificial intelligence and automated speech recognition to provide digital notes from meetings.

In 2019 Cisco agreed to buy Acacia Communications which designs and manufactures high-speed optical interconnect technologies for about $2.6 billion. The deal allows Cisco to amplify its switching routing and optical networking products to address customer demanding for faster transmission of data. Acacia would join Cisco's Optical Systems and Optics business. The transaction was expected to close in second half of Cisco's 2020 fiscal year.

In 2019 Cisco acquired privately-held Luxtera which uses silicon photonics to make chips with optics capabilities for faster transmission for about $596 million. Cisco bought Luxtera's technology to increase the speed and capacity that its networking equipment can provide for webscale and enterprise data centers service provider market segments and other customers.

EXECUTIVES

Senior Vice President Cisco Research And Advanced Development, Joel Bion
Senior Vice President Operations Processes And Systems, Randy Pond
Senior Vice President, Bruce Klein
Senior Vice President Cloud And Managed Services Partner Organization, Edison Peres
Vice President, Ross Fowler
Senior Vice President Sports And Entertainment Solutions Group Sesg, David Holland
Evp And Chief Development Officer, Pankaj S. Patel, $749,135 total compensation
Evp Worldwide Sales And Field Operations, Chris Dedicoat, $691,490 total compensation
Svp Cloud Services And Platforms; Cto, Zorawar Biri Singh
Chairman And Ceo, Charles H. (Chuck) Robbins, age 54, $1,172,115 total compensation
Chairman And Ceo Cisco Greater China, Owen Chan
Svp And Chief Operations, Rebecca J. Jacoby
Svp And General Manager Collaboration Technology Group, Rowan M. Trollope
President Cisco Capital, Kristine A. (Kris) Snow, age 60
President Latin America Theater, Jordi Botifoll
President Smart+connected Communities And Deputy Chief Globalization Officer, Anil Menon
Svp And General Manager Cisco Security Solutions, Bryan Palma
Evp And Cfo, Kelly A. Kramer, $749,135 total compensation
Svp It, Guillermo Diaz
Svp And Chief Marketing Officer, Karen Walker
President Cisco India And Saarc, Sameer Garde
Vice President Director Of Technology, Jerry Tonies
Senior Vice President Marketing For The Insieme Business Unit, Soni Jiandani
Senior Vice President Us Public Sector Organization, Patrick Finn
Vice President Sales, Bejoy Antony
Vp Sales Strategy And Planning, Stephen Sinclair
Vice President Cisco Systems China, Hanh Tu
Segment Vice President, Chuck Look
Vice President Middle East And Turkey Operat, Mike Weston
Vice President Service Provider Operat, David Caspari
Vice President, Tony Bates
Senior Vice President Data Center, Luca Cafiero
Vice President Of Engineering Network Software And, Greg – Lavender
Regional Vice President Northeast, Mei Ling
Vice President Of Sales And Marketing, Joseph Bonney
Vice President, Andy Lockhart
It Vice President Of Switching Hardware, Scott Scheeler
Vice President Finance, Ken Mesuda
Svp, Brett Wingo
Vice President Corporate Marketing Cisco Canada, Willa Black
Vice President Emerging Markets, Milo Schacher
Executive Vice President General Sales Manager, Lily Zhou
Vice President, Tom Wilburn
Vice President Sales, Anant Deshpande
Vp Sales, Marylou Maco
Vice President Sales, Rajesh Shetty

Vice President Corporate Development, Rob Salvagno
Vp Gm, Steve Slattery
Vice President, Arcangelo Fanelli
Executive Vice President And Chief People Officer, Francine Katsoudas
Vice President, Bruce Laird
National Sales Manager, Femy Fonacier
Vice President Of Operations, Paris Arey
Vp.business Operations, Denise Peck
Vice President Data Center Cloud And Information Technology Transformation, Scott Clark
Vice President Product Management And Marketing, Tuqiang Cao
Vice President Canadian Services Operations, Derek Mak
Vp Customer Care Business Unit, Michael Mcnally
Vice President Law And Deputy General, Van Dang
Vice President Of Engineering, Jeffrey Allison
Senior Vice President Corporate Affairs, Tae Yoo
Vice President Market Development, Paul Bosco
Vice President Marketing Manager, Donna Cox
Vp Sales, Pankaj Lulla
Vice President And General Manager, Gene Quon
Senior Vice President Sales, Steve Ficklin
Vice President Corporate Development And Cisco Investments, Derek Idemoto
Vice President Marketing And Business Development, Aaron Stu
Vice President Of Product Management, Gennady Sirota
Vice President Global Iot Service Operations, Cliff Johnson
Vice President Plant, Don McClaughlin
Senior Vice President, David Chai
Vice President Marketing Cisco Systems, Ranajoy Punja
Vice President Global Video And Connected Life Solutions, Stephen Silva
Vice President Enterprise And Mid Market Solutions Marketing, Paul McNab
Vice President And Ct0, Bret Hartman
Vice President Of Innovation, Gordon Feller
Senior Vice President Software, John Brigden
Vice President Sales, Michael Hall
Regional Vice President Cisco Systems Administrator, Mark Guerrazzi
Vice President Communications Software, Todd Murray
Vice President U S Field Channels, Geoff Fancher
Senior Vice President And General Manager Networking And Security Business, Kip Compton
Vice President Sales, Bernadette Wightman
Vice President Marketing Cloud Services, Peder Ulander
Vp Marketing, Christoph Caspar
Vice President Federal Operations, Kelda – Morris
Vice President Informatics, Vilia Corvison
Vice President Advanced Services, Flint Brenton
Vice President Engineering Gigabit Switching Group, Andy Bechtolsheim
Senior Vice President, David Yen
Senior Vice President Manager Of Scott Scheeler, Ravikrishna Cherukuri
Vice President Sales Industry, Jan Schlosser
Vice President Finance At Cisco, Ted Hull Ted Hull
Area Vice President, John Moses
Vice President Engineering, Donald Williams
Vice Presidentproduct Management, Steve Chazin
Executive Vice President, Randall Pond
Area Vice President Us Sales, Georges Antoun
Vice President Of Talent, Annmarie Neal
Vpam Small Business Fl South North Carolina South Carolina, Richard Hinkley
Vpss Flexpod, Cesar Hurtado
Vp Global Services, Jerome Katz
Vice President, Kim Poineau
Vice President And Business Development, Mitch Null Zenger

Vice President, Jeanne Beliveau-dunn
Vice President Systems Engineering, Michael Koons
Area Vice President Enterprise Sales, Mark Houska
Vice President Customer Value Chain Management, David Ashley
Senior Vice President And Chief Strategy Officer, Anuj Kapur
Vice President Engg Routing Tech Grp, Bill Jennings
Vice President Sales, Clarence Jasin
Vice President Of Marketing, Thomas Hooker
Vice President Federal Operations, Ed McCrossen
Vice President Customer Value Chain Management, Jeff Devine
Vice President New Business Ventures, Sanjay Pol
Vice President Finance Operations, Debbie Normington
Area Vice President Us Sales, Roxann Swanson
Vice Presidentibsg, Richard Cantwell
Vice President Finance, Phil Roush
Vice President Of Corporate Portfolio Management A, Inder Singh
Vice President Information Technology Customer Strategy And Success, Lance Perry
Vice President Service Sales, Brian Jeffries
Senior Vice President Human Resources And Talent Acquisition, Jill Larsen
Vice President Engineering Network Software And Systems, Amit S Phadnis
Vice President Information Technology, Venbakm Gopalratnam
Vice President Of Marketing, Andy Blackburn
Vice President Of Software Engineering, Ramesh Bodapati
Vice President Sales, Timothy Hannon
Vice President Sales And Purchasing, Peter Buchmeier
Senior Vice President Advanced Services, Parvesh Sethi
Vice President Of Sales North America, Michael Trahtenhertz
Vice President, Marie Higa
Vice President Sales, Jeff Towson
Kfir Pravda Imtc Vice President Of Marketing, Cary Bryan
Vice President, Cathleen Ashley
Area Vice President Commercial Sales S, David Ruggiero
Vice President Subscriber Networks Sector, Robert Beebe
Vice President Engineering, John Wakerly
Vice President Consumer Marketing, Ken Wirt
Vice President World Wide Supply Chain Management, Steve Darendinger
Vice President And General Manager Sales And Busin, Ruma Balasubramanian
Vice President Marketing, Paul Buteaux
Vice President Systems Engineering, Maria Cannon
Vice President Corporate Development, Tom Mcdonough
Vice President, Joseph Puthussery
Auditors: PricewaterhouseCoopers LLP

LOCATIONS

HQ: Cisco Systems Inc
170 West Tasman Drive, San Jose, CA 95134
Phone: 408 526-4000
Web: www.cisco.com

2019 sales

	$ mil.	% of total
Americas	30,927	60
Europe the Middle East& Africa	13,100	25
Asia-Pacific regionJapan & China	7,877	15
Total	51,904	100

PRODUCTS/OPERATIONS

2019 sales

	$ mil.	% of total
Infrastructure Platforms	30,191	58
Applications	5,803	11
Security	2,730	5
Other Products	281	1
Services	4,352	9
Total	51,904	100

Selected Products

Access servers
Blade servers
Cable modems
Cables and cords
Content delivery devices
Customer contact software
Digital video recorders
Ethernet concentrators hubs and transceivers
Interfaces and adapters
Network management software
Networked applications software
Optical platforms
Power supplies
Routers
Security components
Switches
Telephony access systems
Television set-top boxes
Video networking
Virtual private network (VPN) systems
Voice integration applications
Wireless networking

COMPETITORS

AWS	Huawei Technologies
Arista Networks	Juniper Networks
Broadcom	Lenovo
Check Point Software	LogMeIn
Citrix Systems	Motorola Mobility
CommScope	NSN
Dell	Nutanix
Extreme Networks	Palo Alto Networks
F5 Networks	Symantec
Fireye	VMware
Fortinet	
Hewlett Packard Enterprise	

HISTORICAL FINANCIALS

Company Type: Public

Income Statement   FYE: July 25

	REVENUE ($ mil.)	NET INCOME ($ mil.)	NET PROFIT MARGIN	EMPLOYEES
07/20	49,301	11,214	22.7%	77,500
07/19	51,904	11,621	22.4%	75,900
07/18	49,330	110	0.2%	74,200
07/17	48,005	9,609	20.0%	72,900
07/16	49,247	10,739	21.8%	73,700
Annual Growth	0.0%	1.1%	—	1.3%

2020 Year-End Financials

Debt ratio: 15.37%—
Return on equity: 31.46%
Cash ($ mil.): 11,809
Current ratio: 1.72
Long-term debt ($ mil.): 11,578
Dividends
Yield: 0.0%
Payout: 53.7%
Market value ($ mil.): —

	STOCK PRICE ($) FY Close	P/E High/Low	PER SHARE ($) Earnings	Dividends	Book Value
07/20	46.40	21 13	2.64	1.42	8.95
07/19	56.53	22 15	2.61	1.36	7.90
07/18	42.57	23151519	0.02	1.24	9.36
07/17	31.52	18 15	1.90	1.10	13.27
07/16	30.53	14 11	2.11	0.94	12.64
Annual Growth	11.0%	— —	5.8%	10.9%	(8.3%)

CIT Group Inc (New)

A stalwart in the big-business landscape for over a century CIT Group is a financial holding company that offers lending leasing deposit products as well as ancillary products and services including cash management capital markets and advisory services to small- and mid-sized businesses in such industries as eerospace & defense aviation communication power and energy entertainment gaming health care industrial maritime restaurants services and technology. It operates a physical branch network in southern California and spans the US with its online banking platform. Founded in 1908 CIT expanded its consumer presence with the 2015 acquisition of OneWest. Majority of the company's revenue is generated from the US.

HISTORY

Henry Ittleson founded CIT Group as Commercial Credit and Investment Trust in St. Louis in 1908. Initially financing horse-drawn carriages it moved to New York in 1915 as Commercial Investment Trust (CIT) to participate in one of the milestones of modern consumer debt: Its auto financing program launched in collaboration with Studebaker was the first of its kind.

CIT diversified into industrial financing during the 1920s and went public in 1924 on the NYSE. Cars remained a strong focus though: When Ford Motor Co. ran into difficulties in 1933 it sold financing division Universal Credit Corp. to CIT. CIT continued to expand into industrial financing incorporating its industrial business as CIT Financial Corp. in 1942.

During the post-WWII boom CIT began financing manufactured home sales and offering small loans. In 1964 it consolidated factoring operations into Meinhard-Commercial Corp. By the end of the 1960s the firm started to retreat from auto financing focusing instead on industrial leasing factoring and equipment financing.

In 1980 RCA bought CIT seeking to buy financing to develop its other businesses. RCA found the debt from the purchase unwieldy however and sold CIT to Manufacturers Hanover Bank (Manny Hanny) in 1984. The bank bought CIT to expand outside its home state of New York: Though it could not open banks out of state Manny Hanny could still offer financial services through CIT which became The CIT Group in 1986.

Manny Hanny executives tried to bring aggressive management to staid top-heavy CIT. The company sold its Inventory Finance division in 1987 divested the consumer loan business in 1988 and consolidated the Meinhard-Commercial and Manufacturers Hanover factoring units in 1989. By then Manny Hanny was cash-strapped over losses incurred from foreign loans so it sold a 60% stake in CIT to The Dai-Ichi Kangyo Bank of Japan.

CIT gave Dai-Ichi entrée into US financial services and it began expanding CIT's range of services again including equity investment (1990) credit finance (from its purchase of Fidelcor Business Credit in 1991) and venture capital (1992). CIT also reentered the consumer loan market (including home equity lending) with a new Consumer Finance group (1992).

In 1995 Chemical Bank (Manny Hanny's successor; now part of JPMorgan Chase) sold an additional 20% share to Dai-Ichi bumping the Japanese bank's holdings to 80% and arranging to sell its remaining shares to Dai-Ichi. In 1997 instead of Dai-Ichi buying the rest of Chase's shares CIT bought them and spun them off to the public. In 1998 Dai-Ichi reduced its stake.

In 1999 CIT bought Newcourt Credit Group North America's #2 equipment finance and leasing firm; it also bought Heller Financial's commercial services unit. In 2000 the firm worked on integrating Newcourt and sold its Hong Kong consumer finance unit.

Tyco International bought CIT in 2001 renaming the new subsidiary Tyco Capital. Under Tyco's umbrella it sold its manufactured home loan portfolio to Lehman Brothers and recreational vehicle portfolio to Salomon Smith Barney in an effort to exit noncore businesses. Tyco however expanded too far too fast and the next year announced an about-face on its financial services subsidiary deciding to spin off the division and return it to its CIT identity.

Jeff Peek took the reins of the company from longtime chairman and CEO Al Gamper in 2004.

CIT Group's Student Loan Xpress unit was one of several companies in the student-lending industry that came under investigation for business practices in 2007. It discontinued its private student loans that year and in 2008 it stopped originating government-guaranteed student loans.

Amid losses the company also exited the consumer finance business to focus on commercial lending. In 2008 it sold its home loan unit to Lone Star Funds and its manufactured housing portfolio to Vanderbilt Mortgage and Finance. The previous year it sold its construction lending unit to Wells Fargo and its 30% stake in Dell Financial Services to Dell.

CIT was hit hard in the economic recession which nearly shut down the credit markets. The company struggled to stay afloat as liquidity levels sank (a situation exacerbated as nervous customers drew on their credit lines). It exited money-losing businesses sold units and secured $3 billion from company bondholders including PIMCO and Oaktree Capital. The company also converted to a bank holding company enabling it to access government bailout funds. Still struggling CIT filed for Chapter 11 in November 2009. The restructuring lasted six weeks and helped the company eliminate more than $10 billion in debt. None of CIT's operating subsidiaries were included in the bankruptcy.

Jeffrey Peek who oversaw CIT's untimely expansion activities stepped down as CEO in early 2010. He was succeeded by John Thain who has also led Merrill Lynch and New York Stock Exchange. No stranger to turning ailing companies around Thain is credited with bringing the NYSE into the modern era with electronic trading. He also merged NYSE with Euronext establishing the first trans-Atlantic exchange.

EXECUTIVES

President Cit Rail, George D. Cashman, age 66

Evp And Cfo, John J. Fawcett

Evp And Head Of Technology And Operations, Denise M. Menelly, age 58, $253,846 total compensation

Evp And Chief Marketing And Communications Officer, Gina M. Proia, age 48

President Cit Commercial Finance, James L. (Jim) Hudak, age 56, $503,526 total compensation

Evp And Chief Risk Officer, Robert C. Rowe, age 59

Evp General Counsel And Corporate Secretary, Stuart Alderoty, age 61

President Cit Real Estate Finance, Matthew E. (Matt) Galligan, age 66

Chairman And Ceo; President And Ceo Cit Bank, Ellen R. Alemany, age 64, $883,333 total compensation

Evp And Chief Strategy Officer, Kelley Morrell, age 40

President Consumer Banking Cit Business Capital And California, Steven (Steve) Solk, age 65

Evp And Chief Human Resources Officer, James J. (Jim) Duffy, age 65

President Aviation Lending, Jennifer Villa Tennity

Managing Director Aerospace Defense And Government Services, John Heskin

Svp, Monahan Mike

Senior Vice President, John Edel

Vice President, Julianne Allen

Vice President Strategic Marketing, Ann Crater

Vice President And Information Technology Manager Receibable Systems, Mike Noonan

Vice President Capital Equipment Finance, Bruce Fabian

Assistant Vice President Credit Scoring, Xiaoman Wang

Vice President Dealer Service, Rob Sureda

Vice President, Jeff Rushnak

Senior Vice President Bsa Aml And Ofac Sanctions Compliance Head, Michelle Goodsir

Vice President Human Resources, Kristen Doyle

Vice President Credit Risk Management, Ari Romanoff

Vice President, George Fikaris

Vice President Threat And Vulnerability Management Information, Roman Brozyna

Senior Vice President National Manager, Kenneth Wendler

Vice President National Accounts Manager, Mike Loconsolo

Senior Vice President Rail Finance, Jeffrey Lytle

Vice President, Ronald Gibney

Executive Vice President Chief Credit And Risk Officer Corporate Credit Risk Management, Nancy Foster

Vice President Aml Compliance, Rachel Benjamin

Assistant Vice President, Joshua Hare

Assistant Vice President, Rosalyn Jones

Vice President, Sohail Khan

Assistant Vice President, Soheir Krauss

Vice President, Debra Brown

Assistant Vice President Sales Support, Haley Werle

Vice President, Patricia Matos

Vice President, David Howson

Vice President, Kai Liang

Vice President, William Riggin

Vice President, Jim Condina

Senior Vice President, Eugene Schwartz

Sales Support Manager Assistant Vice President, James Bailey

Vice President Consumer Finance Operations, Krista Neal

Vice President Employment Human, Tammy Haynie

Vice President Sales, Thomas Gonnella

Vice President Finance, Frederick Rick

Operation Manager Vice President, Marvin Daniel

Vice President, Kristin Appelbaum

Assistant Vice President, Adam Schacter

Executive Vice President And Treasurer, Glenn Alan Votek

Vice President Applications Management, Martin Herman

Vice President Leveraged Finance, Nicole Rapport

Vice President Account Executive, Michael Rayner

Assistant Vice President Marketing, Evena Liao

Vice President, Diane Harris

Vice President Project And Service Management, Russell Hansen

Vice President Facility Operations, Vincent Sorrentino

Senior Vice President, Joseph Florio

Vice President, Daniel Bernstein

Assistant Vice President Content Marketing, Saryia Green

Vp Finance, Aashitha Ashokkumar

Senior Vice President, Michael Cleary

It Assistant Vice President Tech Operations, Gabby Lopez

Senior Vice President And Head Of Investor Relations, Barbara Callahan

Svp And Gm Locomotives, Ken Pierson

Evp, Kenneth Brause

Svp Financial Operations, Ed Sperling

Svp Internal Audit, Jacque Breslauer

Assistant Vice President, Robert Hensel

Assistant Vice President Hr Operations, Jennifer Hodsden

Vice President Digital And Social Media, Carolyn Menz

Vice President Account Executive, Vernon Wells

National Account Manager, Charlie Dillon

Vice President, Kevin Brown

Vice President Global Accounting Operations, Stacy Klein

Assistant Vice President Accounting Manager, Amey Kelley

Vice President Information Technology .net Enterprise Architecture, Harvey Orloff

Assistant Vice President Human Resources Project Management Office Project Manager, Janine Santangelo

Vp Corporate Treasury Services, Jay D'auria

Vice President Finance, David Camarneiro

Avp Technical, Ariel Rodriguez

Senior Vice President Head Of Consumer And Internet Banking Technology, Kedar Sathe

Vice President Of Factoring Operations For Ny Region, Sam Macrillo

Vice President Capital Markets, Elias Uribe

Avp, Rebecca Wong

Avp Sox, Liana Balseiro

Vp Regulatory Compliance And Controls, Nathan Lai

Avp Compliance Aml Edd, Cynthia Hernandez

Evp And Chief Strategy Officer, Kennth Mcphail

Vice President And Business Development Officer Commercial Services, Nicholas Nunnari

Vice President, Manesh Chandwani

Assistant Vice President, Oscar Menendez

Vice President Financial Analytics And Modeling, Cynthia Kim

Avp Treasury Controllers, Robert Bickerstaff

Assistant Vice President Accounts Payable, Warren Allen

Assistant Vice President Third Party Management, Jennifer Terribile

Vice President, William Sheridan

Assistant Vice President Accounting Manager, Irene Yang

Assistant Vice President Aml And Sanctions Program Strategy, Mark DiGaetani

Vp Of Business Development Of Technology Of Equipment Finance, Mike Hampton

Vice President Program Director, Mike Errico

Avp Audit Manager, Patricia Hennessy

Senior Vice President Of Information Technology, Fred Mistretta

Executive Vice President, Mark Links

Assistant Vice President, Eugene Oliva

Vice President Account Executive, Jeffrey Kremberg

Avp Tax Technology, Amanda Kateman

Vice President Sales Tax Audit And Compliance, Brenton Futch

Senior Vice President Corporate Strategy, Emmelene Lee

Vice President Sales And Business Development, Mark Hall

Senior Vice President Chief Information, Stephen Schwimmer

Vice President Marketing, Veru Narula

Vice President, Kenneth Nwele

Vice President Corporate Social Responsibility, Darrah Feldman

Avp Learning Strategy And Design, Will Constantine

Vice President Regulatory Reporting, Huan Jin

Avp Strategic Planning Marketing And Communications, Jon Mahoney

Executive Vice President, Donal Ratigan
Senior Vice President, Gene Schwartz
Vice President And Senior Counsel, Danny Park
Vice President, Bob Fogelson
Assistant Vice President, Rosie Nunez
Assistant Vice President Information Technology Business Analyst, Diane Ching
Senior Vice President Financial Investigations Unit, Bob Binnie
Senior Vice President, Ken Horner
Vp It And Epmo, James Irwin
Vice President, Jenn Matticks
Vice President, Jeanette Creque
Assistant Vice President Software Development, Ramit Bajpai
Board Member, William Freeman
Auditors: DELOITTE & TOUCHE LLP

LOCATIONS

HQ: CIT Group Inc (New)
11 West 42nd Street, New York, NY 10036
Phone: 212 461-5200
Web: www.cit.com

2016 Sales

	$ mil.	% of total
US	2,755	89
Europe	139	5
Rest of the world	198	6
Total	**3,093**	**100**

PRODUCTS/OPERATIONS

Products and Services

Account receivables collection
Acquisition and expansion financing
Asset management and servicing
Asset-based loans
Cash management and payment services
Credit protection
Debt restructuring
Debt underwriting and syndication
Deposits
Enterprise value and cash flow loans
Equipment leases
Factoring services
Financial risk management
Import and export financing
Insurance services
Letters of credit / trade acceptances
Merger and acquisition advisory services
Residential mortgage loans
Secured lines of credit
Small Business Administration loans

Sales 2016

	$ mil.	% of total
Commercial Banking	2,546	79
Consumer Banking	382	12
Non-Strategic Portfolios	26	1
Corporate & Other	252	8
Total	**3,207**	**100**

2017 Sales

	$ mil.	% of total
Interest income		
Interest & fees on loans	1,638	58
Other interest and dividends	197	4
Non-interest income		
Rental income on operating leases	1,007	33
Other income	364	5
Total	**3,207**	**100**

COMPETITORS

Ally Financial	ILFC
Citigroup	JPMorgan Chase
Comerica	ORIX
Deutsche Bank	Zions Bancorporation
First Republic (CA)	

HISTORICAL FINANCIALS

Company Type: Public

Income Statement

FYE: December 31

	ASSETS ($ mil.)	NET INCOME ($ mil.)	INCOME AS % OF ASSETS	EMPLOYEES
12/19	50,832	529	1.0%	3,609
12/18	48,537	447	0.9%	3,678
12/17	49,278	468	1.0%	4,167
12/16	64,170	(848)	—	4,410
12/15	67,498	1,056	1.6%	4,900
Annual Growth	**(6.8%)**	**(15.8%)**	**—**	**(7.4%)**

2019 Year-End Financials

Debt ratio: 9.49%	No. of shares (mil.): 94
Return on equity: 8.63%	Dividends
Cash ($ mil.): 2,685	Yield: 2.8%
Current ratio: —	Payout: 26.9%
Long-term debt ($ mil.): —	Market value ($ mil.): 4,323

	STOCK PRICE ($) FY Close	P/E High/Low		PER SHARE ($) Earnings	Dividends	Book Value
12/19	45.63	10	7	5.27	1.30	66.91
12/18	38.27	15	10	3.61	0.82	58.92
12/17	49.23	18	14	2.80	0.61	55.73
12/16	42.68	—	—	(4.20)	0.60	49.50
12/15	39.70	9	7	5.67	0.60	54.61
Annual Growth	**3.5%**	—	—	**(1.8%)**	**21.3%**	**5.2%**

Citigroup Inc

This is the Citi that never sleeps. One of the largest financial services firms known to man Citigroup (also known as Citi) has some 200 million customer accounts and serves clients around the globe. It offers deposits and loans (mainly through Citibank) investment banking brokerage wealth management and other financial services. Trading in more than 160 countries and with approximately 142 million Citi-branded credit cards in circulation worldwide few other banks can equal Citigroup's global reach. Hit hard by the 2008 financial crisis Citi has been refocusing on its original mission — traditional banking. Citi has some $1.9 trillion in assets and some $1.1 trillion in deposits. Citigroup generates some 45% of its sales from North America.

HISTORY

Empire builder Sanford "Sandy" Weill who helped build brokerage firm Shearson Loeb Rhoades sold the company to American Express (AmEx) in 1981. Forced out of AmEx in 1985 Weill bounced back in 1986 buying Control Data's Commercial Credit unit.

Primerica caught Weill's eye next. Its predecessor American Can was founded in 1901 as a New Jersey canning company; it eventually expanded into the paper and retail industries before turning to financial services in 1986. The firm was renamed Primerica in 1987 and bought brokerage Smith Barney Harris Upham & Co.

Weill's Commercial Credit bought Primerica in 1988. In 1993 Primerica bought Shearson from AmEx as well as Travelers taking its name and logo.

Weill set about trimming Travelers. He sold life subsidiaries and bought Aetna's property/casualty business in 1995. In 1996 he consolidated all property/casualty operations to form Travelers Prop-

erty Casualty and took it public. The next year Travelers bought investment bank Salomon Brothers and formed Salomon Smith Barney Holdings (now Citigroup Global Markets).

Weill sold Citicorp chairman and CEO John Reed on the idea of a merger in 1998 in advance of the Gramm-Leach-Bliley act which deregulated the financial services industry in the US. By the time the merger went through a slowed US economy and foreign-market turmoil brought significant losses to both sides. The renamed Citigroup consolidated in 1998 and 1999 laying off more than 10000 employees. So many executives (including co-chairmen and co-CEOs Weill and Reed) were paired through "co" titling that the company was dubbed "the ark."

In 1999 Citigroup moved deeper into subprime lending. Also that year former Treasury Secretary Robert Rubin joined Citigroup as a co-chairman.

In 2000 Reed retired and the company bought the investment banking business of British firm Schroders. Citigroup also bought subprime lender Associates First Capital (now part of CitiFinancial) for approximately $27 billion to expand its consumer product lines and its international presence. The deal however also brought Citigroup federal scrutiny regarding perceived predatory lending tactics. In 2001 the company bought New York-based European American Bank from ABN AMRO and purchased Grupo Financiero Banamex one of Mexico's biggest banks.

The company parlayed the $4 billion it netted from the 2002 spinoff of 20% of Travelers Property Casualty (it distributed most of the remaining stock to Citigroup shareholders) into a $5.8 billion purchase of California-based Golden State Bancorp the parent of the then-third-largest thrift in the US Cal Fed.

Also that year Citigroup paid some $215 million to settle federal allegations that Associates First Capital made customers unwittingly purchase credit insurance by automatically billing for the service. The agreement was one of the largest consumer-protection settlements ever.

The company also became embroiled in the Enron mess as regulators scrutinized short-term loans that Citigroup floated to the energy trader and were possibly used by Enron in transactions with offshore entities to mask debt and inflate cash flow figures. Citigroup neither confirmed nor denied allegations that it helped fudge Enron's books but in 2003 remitted more than $100 million earmarked to pay victims who lost money because of Enron's malfeasance.

A landmark ruling by the SEC in 2003 implied that Citigroup issued favorable stock ratings to companies in exchange for investment banking contracts (predictably the company neither confirmed nor denied the allegations). Also as part of the ruling erstwhile star analyst Jack Grubman agreed to pay some $15 million in fines for his overly rosy stock reports and accepted a lifetime ban from working in the securities industry. Citigroup forked over $400 million in fines the largest portion of a total of some $1.4 billion levied against 10 brokerage firms regarding conflicts of interest between analysts and investment bankers.

Amid the investigations Citigroup separated its stock-picking and corporate advisory businesses creating a retail brokerage and equity research unit called Smith Barney. In the SEC's 2003 ruling such a "Chinese Wall" between bankers and analysts was later made mandatory at all firms. Still Citigroup raked in net profits of nearly $18 billion (on revenues in excess of $94 billion) in 2003 one of the largest-ever yearly takes in US corporate history.

In 2004 the company — while admitting no wrongdoing — paid $2.65 billion to investors who were burned when WorldCom went bankrupt amid an accounting scandal. (Citigroup was one of the lead underwriters of WorldCom stocks and bonds.) The settlement was one of the largest ever for alleged securities fraud and compelled Citigroup to set aside an additional $5 billion to cover legal fees for this case and others involving Enron and spinning. The company eventually paid $2 billion in mid-2005 to investors who lost money on publicly traded Enron stocks and bonds again settling the matter while denying it broke any laws. Enron shareholders had argued that Citigroup helped Enron to set up offshore companies and shady partnerships to exaggerate the energy trader's cash flow.

In Japan where Citigroup is one of the leading foreign banks regulators pulled the plug on the company's private banking operations in 2004 after determining that Citigroup misled customers regarding the sale of certain structured bonds. The closures led to the forced resignation of three top executives in the company's asset management and private banking units about a month later.

Citigroup sold The Travelers Life and Annuity Company (now MetLife Life and Annuity Company of Connecticut) plus most of its international insurance business to MetLife in 2005. Later that year a convoluted deal with Legg Mason netted Citigroup that company's retail brokerage and capital markets business (and $1.5 billion of Legg Mason stock) in exchange for most of Citigroup's asset management and mutual fund division; Citigroup concurrently sold Legg Mason's capital markets operations to Stifel Financial.

Seeking growth internationally Citigroup was part of a consortium that acquired a controlling stake in Guangdong Development Bank in 2006. Also that year the company opened more than 800 bank branches and consumer finance offices outside the US.

Weill ended years of speculation in 2003 by anointing corporate and investment bank head Chuck Prince as his successor. Weill retired as chairman in 2006 and Prince assumed that title as well. Prince resigned in 2007 as Citigroup dealt with losses on mortgage-related securities and other investments.

Prince was succeeded by Vikram Pandit a Morgan Stanley veteran who came to Citigroup when it acquired hedge fund and private equity manager Old Lane Partners in 2007. Pandit was at Citigroup only a few months before he was named CEO but during that time he oversaw the company's alternative investments and led its institutional clients group. The following year Citigroup disbanded Old Lane and wound up its flagship fund.

Citigroup further expanded its fund services operations via its 2007 acquisition of BISYS. As part of the deal the company sold BISYS' insurance services division to investment firm J.C. Flowers & Co.

Also that year it picked up remnants of the subprime mortgage collapse when it acquired ACC Capital Holding's wholesale mortgage origination operations as well as the servicing rights to some $5 billion in home loans. It also bought ABN AMRO Mortgage Group and shelled out more than $1 billion to buy Egg one of the largest online-only banks in the world from Prudential plc. The deal boosted its UK consumer operations by adding some 3 million customers.

The company sold its trademark red umbrella logo back to insurance firm Travelers which began using the symbol nearly 150 years before. Citigroup acquired the iconic logo when it bought the insurance company in 1993 and held onto it after it spun off Travelers in 2002. But the company ultimately decided that customers associated the umbrella with insurance and sold it in 2007.

In order to shore up its balance sheet Citigroup sold some 5% of itself to the Abu Dhabi Investment Authority a Middle Eastern sovereign fund for $7.5 billion in 2007. It later raised more than $12 billion by selling preferred shares to investors including a Singapore government-owned investment fund former CEO Sandy Weill and Saudi investor Prince Al-Walid bin Talal who owns roughly 5% stake of Citigroup.

Citigroup bought a majority stake in one of Japan's largest brokerages Nikko Cordial in 2007. It acquired the remaining shares of Nikko Cordial in early 2008 and merged it with Citigroup Japan Holdings to form Nikko Citi Holdings.

In 2008 Citigroup sold several of its commercial finance lines to GE Capital. It sold its German consumer banking business to French bank Groupe Cr dit Mutuel.

As the global credit crisis mounted in 2008 the US government injected some $700 billion into the nation's banking industry including $45 billion investment in Citigroup. It further stepped in to aid the faltering bank by backing more than $300 in loans and securities to boost confidence in the bank and protect its investments. In exchange the government took a 34% stake in Citigroup. The company received approval to pay the funds back in 2009 and the government began reducing its ownership.

Citigroup shed numerous noncore operations (grouped into its new Citi Holdings division) to raise money to repay the government bailout funds. In 2009 it sold Japanese brokerage Nikko Cordial (nowSMBC Nikko) and other parts of Nikko Citi Holdings for $8.7 billion to Sumitomo Mitsui Financial Group. Also in 2009 Citigroup combined its Smith Barney and Quilter wealth management units with those of Morgan Stanley to create Morgan Stanley Smith Barney taking a 49% of the combined firm.

Sales in 2010 include its $1.93 billion Canadian MasterCard portfolio (to CIBC) a $3.5 billion real estate loan portfolio (to JPMorgan Chase) a $3.2 billion auto loan portfolio (to Santander) and a $1.6 billion portfolio of retail credit card assets (to GE). In 2011 it sold a $1.7 billion private equity portfolio to AXA. Also in 2010 the company spun off Primerica in an IPO selling remaining shares by 2011.

Furthermore Citigroup exited the student loan business in the wake of federal legislation eliminating subsidies for private lenders: It sold its 80% stake in Student Loan Corporation and much of its private student loans portfolio to Discover Financial Services and Sallie Mae. The company also sold three hedge fund businesses with a combined $4.2 billion in assets under management to New York-based SkyBridge Capital.

The firm began withdrawing from the consumer lending business in Europe by selling its Egg UK credit card business to Barclays in 2011 and its UK/Ireland Diners Club business to Affiniture Cards in 2012.

EXECUTIVES

Ceo Citibank N.a., Barbara J. Desoer, age 67
Ceo North America, William J. (Bill) Mills, age 64
President Citigroup Inc. And Ceo Institutional Clients Group, James A. (Jim) Forese, age 57, $500,000 total compensation
Ceo, Michael L. Corbat, age 59, $1,500,000 total compensation
Managing Director And Global Head Emerging Markets Sales And Trading Corporate And Investment Banking, Paco Ybarra
Cfo, John C. Gerspach, age 67, $500,000 total compensation
Ceo Global Consumer Banking, Stephen Bird, age 53, $499,623 total compensation
Ceo Citi Holdings, Francesco Vanni d'Archirafi

Head Operations And Technology, Don Callahan, age 63, $500,000 total compensation
Evp Global Public Affairs, Edward Skyler, age 46
Global Head Of Strategy And Mergers & Acquisitions, Jane Fraser, age 52, $500,000 total compensation
Ceo Europe Middle East And Africa, James C. Cowles, age 64
Ceo Citi Cards, Jud Linville
Ceo Asia Pacific, Francisco A. Aristeguieta Silva, age 54
Chief Risk Officer, Bradford Hu, age 56
Ceo Citi Mexico And Banco Nacional De México (banamex), Ernesto Torres Cantu
Assistant Vice President, George Gilbert
Assistant Vice President Systems Engineer, Jeffrey Serzon
Assistant Vice President And Business Information Security Officer, Veena Srinivasan
Senior Vice President Asset Management, Gustav Gollisz
Vice President Information Security, Bill Philhower
Vice President Account Managementdepositary Receipt Services, Maria Perez
Vice President, Charan Singh
Avp, Jennifer Chen
Senior Vice President, Ryan McCaughey
Senior Vice President Global Portfolio Management, Mary Imbriale-Holubec
Senior Vice President Network Architect, David Gubitosi
Vice President Rates Technology, Michael G Hole
Assistant Vice President, Melissa Alomar
Vice President Application Development Senior Manager Global Equities, Peter Micciche
Senior Vice President, Peter Sullivan
Consumer Liaison Manager Vice President, Deborah Smith
Vice President, Douglas Gourley
Svp Marketing Program Director, Chad Steinwolf
Senior Vice President, Linda Basher
Vice President, Dennis Lee
Senior Vice President Investment Finance, Greg Zann
Vice President Business Initiatives, Raj Mohan
Vp Control Administrator, Dawn Patak
Vice President Digital Channels, Michael Dellatte
Senior Vice President Storage Engineering, Eliot Wilson
Senior Vice President, Fabricio Calderon
Vice President, Joseph Pasciak
Vice President Information Technology Risk Management, Ram Kumar
Vice President, Christian Paz
Vice President Enhancement Services, Mike Maloney
Vice President, Anil Yitta
Vice President, Mayank Shah
Senior Vice President, Nareg Dermanuelian
Information Technology Management: Vice President, Jeffrey Bray
Sr Vice President, Bhupesh Kokate
Vice President, Rajeshwar Bhakey
Senior Vice President Relationship Manager, Betty Silfa
Relationship Manager Svp, Edia Cruz
Senior Vice President, Lesley Glazer
Senior Vice President, Dheepa Krishnamoorthy
Vice President, Paul Milora
Vice President Client Executive, Keri Reed
Vice President Finance, Ryan Hall
Assistant Vice President Equity Derivatives Trading, Peter Plevritis
Assistant Vice President, Sam Dyson
Assistant Vice President, Donna Chan
Svp Risk Management, Cheri Bockhorst
Senior Vice President Of Rel Technology Finance, Cheryl Gamache
Vice President, Brian Gelok
Vp Latam Gts Financial Analyst, Noelia Ozuna

Associate Vice President, Cesar Tobar
Assistant Vice President Cpb Technology, Elizabeth Reen
Senior Vice President, Chris Cralle
Assistant Vice President, Kenzel Fleming
Vice President Treasury, Austin Holbrook
Senior Vice President Compliance, Joseph Morgo
Vice President, Brad Randlett
Senior Vice President Manager Of Regulatory Reporting Department For Derivatives (otc And Et), Yanina Kulchitskaya
Assistant Vice President, Anthony Thomas
Senior Vice President, Frank Zhang
Vice President Crm Process Manager, Brian Lilly
Senior Vice President, Harim Shon
Assistant Vice President Recovery Senior Supervisor Litigation, John Linnenbrink
Senior Vice President, Tim Walter
Assistant Vice President At Citi Loan Syndications Group, Christopher Romanelli
Assistant Vice President, Timothy Seaton
Vice President, Kyle Moeller
Vice President, Donna McCafferty
Vice President, Kevin Vee
Vice President, Evan Elisseou
Executive Vice President Global Engineering And Security, Daniel Tigar
Senior Vice President, Vikram Mago
Vice President, Beth Mcabee
Vice President, Sibylle Baker
Vice President Customer Engagement Risk, Pankaj Agarwal
Senior Vice President, Diana Alfonso
Sr Project Analyst Vp, Ian Good
Vp Global Pmo, Eric Moon
Vice President Sales Development Counsultant Cit, Leta Bajraktari
Assistant Vice President, Sharon Eng
Senior Vice President, Ranjeet Jha
Assistant Vice President, Cherry Tam
Vice President And Senior Quality Assurance, Stella Zhang
Vice President, Elizabeth Clancey
Senior Vice President Remedial Management Senior Manager, Bernadette Walsh
Vice President And Compliance Officer, Yolette Mazile
Assistant Vice President, Darrell Drake
Senior Vice President, Patrick Defeciani
Executive Vice President, Mark Morgenlender
Vice President Client Development, Michael Vaughan
Vice President Technology, James Carney
Vice President, Jodi Rodgers
Assistant Vice President Transaction Services, Zirley Moyette
Senior Vice President Director, Anthony Mauro
Vice President, Dawn Cato
Assistant Vice President, Noreen Hanson
Assistant Vice President Change Management Shift Manager, Patrick Davis
Vp Model Risk Management, Michelle Stone
Vice President Infrastructure Senior Manager, Keith Skoog
Senior Vice President Global Strategic Operations, Jason Marchese
Vice President, Poonam Sharma
Vice President, Madhumita Sarkar
Vice President, Joseph Stanz
Vice President Of Market Research Glob, Tim Teran
Senior Vice President, Hao Hu
Assistant Vice President, Laurence Evans
Assistant Vice President, Anuja Raval
Vice President, Patrick Kosiek
Vice President, William Schwarz
Avp, Huseyin Tarkan
Vice President, Santhosh Babu
Senior Vice President, Rainer Butsch
Vice President Marketing, Reema Butala

Vice President Relationship Manager Commercial Banking, Madison Murphy
Vice President, Arkady Temchin
Avp, Errol Rathjen
Vice President, Imran Hirani
Senior Vice President Risk Management, Peter You
Vice President, Henry Palmer
Assistant Vice President, John Yiovanakos
Senior Vice President, Cathleen Bok
Vice President, Pei Wang
Avp Senior Client Service Officer, Frances Argento
Vice President, Krishna Prasad
Vice President, Marc Silva
Senior Vice President, Sasikiran Mylu
Vice President, Julian Stippig
Vice President, Andrea Vaswani
Vice President E Citi Director, Joan Haffenreffer
Vice President Of Marketing, Kathleen Desiderio
Senior Vice President Citi Cards, Ron Guggenheimer
Vice President, Linda Bauer
Vice President Risk Management, Alice Dymally
Senior Vice President, Kevin Louie
Vp Finance, David Wendel
Auditors: KPMG LLP

LOCATIONS

HQ: Citigroup Inc
388 Greenwich Street, New York, NY 10013
Phone: 212 559-1000
Web: www.citigroup.com

PRODUCTS/OPERATIONS

2017 Sales

	$ mil.	% of total
Net Interest	44,687	63
Non-interest		
Commissions & fees	12,939	18
Principal transactions	9,168	13
Administration & other fiduciary fees	3,079	4
Realized gains on sales of investments	778	1
Other	861	1
Adjustments	(63)	-
Total	**71,449**	**100**

2017 Sales

	% of total
Institutional Clients Group	50
Global Consumer Banking	46
Corporate/Other	4
Total	**100**

2017 Sales

	% of total
North America	47
Asia	20
Latin America	14
EMEA	15
Corporate/Other	4
Total	**100**

Selected Products

Banamex
Bill Consolidation
Checking
Citi Cards
Citi Private Bank
CitiMortgage
Commercial Real Estate Loans
Home Equity
Mortgages
Online Banking
Personal Loans
Savings
Student Loans

COMPETITORS

American Express	Goldman Sachs
Bank of America	HSBC
Bank of New York	JPMorgan Chase
Mellon	Mizuho Financial
Barclays	U.S. Bancorp
Capital One	UBS
Deutsche Bank	USAA
FMR	Wells Fargo
GE	

HISTORICAL FINANCIALS

Company Type: Public

Income Statement

FYE: December 31

	ASSETS ($ mil.)	NET INCOME ($ mil.)	INCOME AS % OF ASSETS	EMPLOYEES
12/19	1,951,158	19,401	1.0%	200,000
12/18	1,917,383	18,045	0.9%	204,000
12/17	1,842,465	(6,798)	—	209,000
12/16	1,792,077	14,912	0.8%	219,000
12/15	1,731,210	17,242	1.0%	231,000
Annual Growth	**3.0%**	**3.0%**	**—**	**(3.5%)**

2019 Year-End Financials

Debt ratio: 12.75%
Return on equity: 9.96%
Cash ($ mil.): 193,919
Current ratio: —
Long-term debt ($ mil.): —

No. of shares (mil.): 2,114
Dividends
  Yield: 2.4%
  Payout: 25.5%
Market value ($ mil.): 168,897

	STOCK PRICE ($) FY Close	P/E High/Low		PER SHARE ($) Earnings	Dividends	Book Value
12/19	79.89	10	7	8.04	1.92	91.41
12/18	52.06	12	7	6.68	1.54	82.85
12/17	74.41	—	—	(2.98)	0.96	78.11
12/16	59.43	13	7	4.72	0.42	81.20
12/15	51.75	11	9	5.40	0.16	75.12
Annual Growth	**11.5%**	**—**	**—**	**10.5%**	**86.1%**	**5.0%**

Citizens Financial Group Inc (New)

Citizens Financial Group offers a broad range of retail and commercial banking products and services to more than five million individuals small businesses middle-market companies large corporations and institutions. The company's main operating subsidiary is consumer bank Citizens Bank which spans some 1100 branches across eleven states as well as in New Zealand and boasts more than $165 billion in assets and $125 billion in deposits. The bank's branches offer standard retail and commercial services including loans leases trade financing deposits cash management commercial cards foreign exchange and others.

Operations

Citizens Financial offers customers mortgage lending auto loans education loans and commercial banking services. Altogether its portfolio includes 1100 branches 135 non-branch offices and 2700 ATMs.

The bank operates two segments: Consumer Banking offers deposit products mortgage and home equity lending credit cards business loans wealth management and investment services auto loans education loans unsecured loans and product financing in addition to select digital deposit products nationwide-which serves individuals and counts for more than 65% of the bank's total revenue.

On the other hand Commercial Banking offers lending and leasing deposit and treasury management services foreign exchange interest rate and commodity risk management solutions as well as loan syndications corporate finance merger and acquisition and debt and equity capital markets capabilities which serves businesses and accounts for about a third of revenue.

Interest income accounts for more than 65% of Citizens' revenue.

Geographic Reach

Rhode Island-based Citizens Financial operates branches in New England the Mid-Atlantic and the Midwest. Its largest markets are Boston Philadelphia Providence and Pittsburgh.

Sales and Marketing

Citizens Financial's serves to more than 5 million customers including individuals small businesses middle-market companies large corporations and institutions. Its business clients typicallyserve healthcare technology aerospace and defense and franchise finance.

The company serves customers through telephone service centers as well as through its online and mobile platforms.

Financial Performance

Citizens Financial has grown its revenue and profits since 2015. In fiscal 2019 the bank's net revenue (net interest income plus noninterest income) rose approximately 5% to $6.4 billion compared to 2018.

Total assets grew to $165.7 billion while deposits expanded $5.7 billion to $125.3 billion.

Net income grew slightly up 4% from $1.7 billion in 2018 to $1.8 billion in 2019.

The company's cash and due from banks at the end of the year was $1.4 billion. Operations generated $1.2 billion in cash while investing and financing activities used $51.0 million and $693.0 million respectively.

Strategy

The company's business strategies are designed to maximize the full potential of the businesses drive sustainable growth and enhance profitability such as; maintain a high-performing customer-centric organization develop differentiated value propositions to acquire deepen and retain core customer segments build excellent capabilities designed to help us stand out from competitors and embed risk management within our culture and operations.

In terms of its personnel the company focuses on hiring highly skilled and qualified personnel. The ability to implement the strategic plan and the future success depends on the ability to attract retain and motivate highly skilled and qualified personnel including the senior management and other key employees and directors.

Mergers and Acquisitions

In early 2020 Citizens Financial Group Inc. d that it has completed the acquisition of Trinity Capital an advisory firm in Los Angeles that offers a range of financial services to commercial clients. Trinity will become part of Citizens Capital Markets Inc. further accelerating the buildout of Citizens' financial advisory capabilities.

In 2019 the Company acquired certain assets and assumed certain liabilities of Bowstring Advisors LLC ("Bowstring") an Atlanta Georgia-based mergers and acquisitions advisory and capital raising firm for the consideration of $40 million. As part of this transaction the Company expanded its mergers and acquisitions advisory position with the addition of a referral network and experienced staff.

Also in 2019 the Company acquired Clarfeld Financial Advisors LLC ("Clarfeld") a Tarrytown New York-based boutique wealth management and financial advisory firm for total consideration of $110 million. As part of this transaction the

Company expanded its wealth management position with the addition of a robust client base.

Company Background

In September 2014 Royal Bank of Scotland (RBS) sold a 25% ownership interest or 140 million shares of the regional US bank for $21.50 each (below the company's expected range of $23 to $25 per share). The deal which valued Citizens Financial Group (CFG) at $3 billion was one of the largest bank IPOs on record. In October 2015 RBS sold its remaining stake (the last 20.9% of Citizens common stock) for $23.38 per share raising some $2.6 billion.

After being bought by RBS in 1988 Citizens Financial went on an acquisition spree making more than two dozen deals. In 2000 and through later years the company gobbled up Mellon's retail banking network Medford Bancorp and Port Financial in Massachusetts and Pennsylvania's Commonwealth Bancorp and Thistle Group Holdings among others. The company expanded into the Midwest by buying superregional bank Charter One in 2004. Following its acquisition of Charter One its largest deal yet Citizens Financial retained the Charter One Bank name in Midwestern markets but converted the bank's branches to Citizens Bank in New York and Pennsylvania. That was the company's last major acquisition however.

Like many banks the company was hamstrung by the mortgage crisis. It posted a nearly $1 billion loss in 2008 as its nonperforming loans roughly doubled. The developments compelled the company to re-evaluate its acquisition strategy and it has reversed its field: Citizens Financial sold 18 of its branches in northern New York to Community Bank System in 2008 and all 65 Charter One branches in Indiana to Old National Bancorp the following year. The company also pegged certain operations as noncore including its dealer finance program and portions of its auto lending business. In 2012 Citizens Financial unloaded more branches selling nearly 60 supermarket locations to People's United Financial. In 2013 it opted to unload its Chicago branches.

In 2015 RBS sold its remaining stake in Citizens Financial.

EXECUTIVES

Evp And Cfo, John F. Woods, age 55
Evp And Chief Risk Officer, Malcolm D. Griggs, age 59
Vice Chairman Commercial Banking, Donald H. (Don) McCree, age 58, $700,000 total compensation
Evp General Counsel And Chief Legal Officer, Stephen T. (Steve) Gannon, age 67, $600,000 total compensation
Vice Chairman Consumer Banking, Brad L. Conner, age 58, $700,000 total compensation
Chairman And Ceo, Bruce Van Saun, age 62, $1,487,000 total compensation
Chief Marketing Officer And Head Of Consumer Strategy, Beth Johnson
Head Of Technology Services, Brian OÅ'Connell
President Citizens Bank Rhode Island, Keith Kelly
Evp And Head Of Business Services, Mary Ellen Baker, age 61
Senior Vice President, Anthony Watson
Svp Hr, Joanna Robbins
Senior Vice President, Lawrence Bigelow
Vice President And Counsel, Lilach Cohen
Vice President Compliance Officer Rbs Cfg Compliance, Suzanne Brunner
Vice President Senior Risk Manager, Pat Coutu
Senior Vice President Cre Relationship Manager, Barbara Mackin
Chief Sales Officer, Chauncey Holden
Executive Vice President, Sean Rowles
Senior Vice President, Michael Stank
Senior Vice President, James McLaughlin

Senior Vice President, Sheryl Medeiros
Senior Vice President, Allen Lamboy
Senior Vice President, John Cooper
Senior Vice President, Jean-Marie Coletta
Senior Vice President, Kathryn Gallagher
Executive Vice President, Paul Howard
Senior Vice President, Catherine Brown
Svp And Head Consumer And Regional Operations, Jeff Leblanc
Assistant Vice President Portfolio Manager, Laurie Charest
Vice President Security Solution Architect, Pasquale Gallo
Executive Vice President, Kenneth Deveaux
Svp Head Operations Supply Chain Services, Alison Sorel
Senior Vice President, Claire Smith
Senior Vice President, Dave Howe
Vice President, Dave Mewkalo
Vice President, Andrew Nevins
Vice President Senior Recruiter, Scott Dorey
Evp Head Investor Relations, Ellen Taylor
Executive Vice President, Cindy Erickson
Senior Vice President, Steven Girard
Senior Vice President, Jeffrey LeBlanc
Senior Vice President, Kathleen Baker
Senior Vice President, Susan Baker Shipley
Senior Vice President, Donald Barry
Senior Vice President, F Gorham Brigham
Senior Vice President, Michael Brown
Senior Vice President, Gillian Cairns
Senior Vice President, Peter Camilleri
Executive Vice President, Craig Campbell
Senior Vice President, Dwayne Finney
Senior Vice President, Paul Flynn
Executive Vice President, Peter Galligan
Executive Vice President, Neil Grassie
Senior Vice President, Michael Hall
Executive Vice President, Paul Hanlon
Senior Vice President, William Harris
Senior Vice President, Thomas King
Senior Vice President, Daniel May
Senior Vice President, Paul McKinnon
Senior Vice President, James Morris
Senior Vice President, Michael Palinkos
Senior Vice President, Gregory Suchy
Senior Vice President, Carol Townsend
Senior Vice President, Michael Williams
Vice President Market Manager, Monica Burch
Vice President Senior Treasury Sales Specialist, William Cano
Vice President, Thomas Drew
Vice President, Ben Foltz
Vice President, Deven Dittrich
Vice President Solutions Architecture, Santosh Sinha
Senior Vice President Human Resources Analytics, Melissa Arronte
Senior Vice President Strategy And Architecture, Saumitra Pande
Senior Vice President, Louis Noppenberger
Senior Vice President Credit Products Manager, Mark Walker
Assistant Vice President Branch Manager, Anna Clune
Senior Vice President Business Development, John Lim
Senior Vice President, Edward Kloecker
Senior Vice President, Patrick Moody
Vice President, Biagio Maffettone
Assistant Vice President Sales Manager, Maria Esposito
Senior Vice President Commercial Real Estate, Alex Hofstetter
Vice President, Jeff Hoepf
Vice President Senior Strategy Consultant Private Wealth Management, Joe Savoca
Vice President Treasury Solutions, Debi Segars
Vp Contract Specialist, Paula Dunphy

Vice President Residential Lending Sales
  Manager, Jill Allen
Senior Vice President, Robert Lindberg
Vice President, Peter Yelle
Vice President Media Relations, Rory Sheehan
Assistant Vice President Senior User Experience
  Designer, Samuel Custer
Senior Vice President Professionals Banking, Jay
  Benegal
Vp Branch Digital Marketing, Sarah Cenedella
Vice President, Christopher Pelletier
Vice President Enterprise Risk Management,
  Staples Carmen
Business Banking Relationship Manager Vice
  President, Joseph Mcnamee
Vp Fraud Operations Sr Professional, Christina
  Brenner
Executive Vice President, Chapin Bates
Svp Risk Director, Chuck Doolittle
Vice President Business Banking Relationship
  Manager, Salman Anwer
Vp Middle Market Corporate Banking Portfolio
  Manager, Timothy Whalen
Vice President, Gillian Marcott
Vice President And Relationship Manager, Matthew
  Adams
Senior Vice President Community Developm,
  Eugene Clerkin
Vice President Flex Staffing Program, Cheryl
  Rebello
Senior Vice President, Christopher Hallee
Assistant Vice President International C, William
  Gamble
Senior Vice President Benefits, Sal Di Liberti
Senior Vp Chief Architect, James Mitcheson
Vp Network Service Delivery, Drew Yates
Head Talent Acquisition And Evp, Kristi Robinson
Vice President Senior Fx Trader, Paul Yong
Vp Senior Product Marketing Partner, Kaitlin
  Mccafferty
Vice President Relationship Manager Business
  Banking, Laura Gauger
Vice President Information Technology
  Governance, Brian Kaufman
Vice President Portfolio Manager Nonprofit And
  Healthcare Banking, Shaun Jafarzadeh
Senior Vp Head Of Asset Management, Frederick
  Mckibbin
Senior Vp And Senior Legal Counsel Corporate
  Transactions And Intellectual Property, Molly
  Frankel
Svp Head Of Digital Engagement, Robert Scott
Senior Vice President, Samual Bluso
Senior Vice President, Casey Brill
Avp Tbma Sr Business Analyst, Stephanie Geltrude
Vice President Recruitment (wealth), Terri
  Lawless-Munro
Evp And Head Of Commercial Underwriting And
  Portfolio Management And Strategy, David
  Harnisch
Vice President Private Wealth Advisor, Mickey
  Kittredge
Vice President, Jeffrey Szczypinski
Board Member, Wendy A Watson
Auditors: DELOITTE & TOUCHE LLP

LOCATIONS

HQ: Citizens Financial Group Inc (New)
  One Citizens Plaza, Providence, RI 02903
Phone: 401 456-7000   Fax: 401 455-5927
Web: www.citizensbank.com

2017 Branches

	No.
Pennsylvania	340
Massachusetts	246
New York	133
Ohio	103
Michigan	93
Rhode Island	78
New Hampshire	66
Connecticut	41
Delaware	23
Vermont	16
New Jersey	11
Total	**1,150**

PRODUCTS/OPERATIONS

2017 Sales

	$ mil.	% of total
Interest income		
Interest on loans & fees	4,249	66
Investment securities	625	10
Others	46	1
Non-interest income		
Service charges & fees	517	8
Card fees	233	3
Trust & investment services fees	158	2
Capital markets fees	194	3
Letter of credit & loan fees	121	2
Others	320	5
Net security impairment loss	(7)	-
Total	**6,454**	**100**

Sales 2017

	% of total
Consumer Banking	62
Commercial Banking	34
Others	4
Total	**100**

COMPETITORS

Bank of America	M&T Bank
Bank of New York	PNC Financial
Mellon	People's United
Citigroup	Financial
Fifth Third	Sovereign Bank
HSBC USA	TD Bank USA
Huntington Bancshares	U.S. Bancorp
JPMorgan Chase	Wintrust Financial
KeyCorp	

HISTORICAL FINANCIALS

Company Type: Public

Income Statement

FYE: December 31

	ASSETS ($ mil.)	NET INCOME ($ mil.)	INCOME AS % OF ASSETS	EMPLOYEES
12/19	165,733	1,791	1.1%	18,000
12/18	160,518	1,721	1.1%	18,100
12/17	152,336	1,652	1.1%	17,600
12/16	149,520	1,045	0.7%	18,000
12/15	138,208	840	0.6%	17,700
Annual Growth	**4.6%**	**20.8%**	**—**	**0.4%**

2019 Year-End Financials

Debt ratio: 5.45%	No. of shares (mil.): 433
Return on equity: 8.33%	Dividends
Cash ($ mil.): 3,683	Yield: 3.3%
Current ratio: —	Payout: 35.8%
Long-term debt ($ mil.): —	Market value ($ mil.): 17,589

	STOCK PRICE ($) FY Close	P/E High/Low		PER SHARE ($) Earnings	Dividends	Book Value
12/19	40.61	11	8	3.81	1.36	51.26
12/18	29.73	14	8	3.52	0.98	44.67
12/17	41.98	13	10	3.25	0.64	41.30
12/16	35.63	19	9	1.97	0.46	38.57
12/15	26.19	18	15	1.55	0.40	37.22
Annual Growth	**11.6%**	**—**	**—**	**25.2%**	**35.8%**	**8.3%**

CITY & COUNTY OF SAN FRANCISCO

The City of San Francisco is the 14th largest in the US and its dense population geographic detachment and cultural diversity have made San Francisco a favorite with both tourists and residents. San Francisco's government is a consolidated city-county bureaucracy with both entities led by an elected mayor. The government includes an executive branch led by the mayor and consisting of other elected officials and city departments and a legislative branch consisting of an 11-member Board of Supervisors. The city is also home to several federal institutions including the Federal Reserve Bank and the US Mint.

EXECUTIVES

Legal Secretary, Pamela Cheeseborough
Medical Director, Jan Gurley
Legal Secretary Labor Division, Sylvia Angelo
Legal Secretary, Catheryn Daly
Director Of Nursing, Lissette Waterman
Secretary, Vinnie Lew
Board Member, Niki Solis
Office Of The Treasurer And Tax Collector,
  Romualdo Castro
Board Member, Esther Lane
Auditors: MACIAS GINI & O'CONNELL LLP

LOCATIONS

HQ: CITY & COUNTY OF SAN FRANCISCO
  1 DR CARLTON B GOODLETT P, SAN FRANCISCO, CA
  941024604
Phone: 415 554-7500
Web: WWW.SFGOV.ORG

HISTORICAL FINANCIALS

Company Type: Private

Income Statement

FYE: June 30

	REVENUE ($ mil.)	NET INCOME ($ mil.)	NET PROFIT MARGIN	EMPLOYEES
06/19	7,561	563	7.4%	30,000
06/18	6,411	1,172	18.3%	—
06/17	5,971	569	9.5%	—
06/16	5,789	546	9.4%	—
Annual Growth	**9.3%**	**1.0%**	**—**	**—**

City Holding Co.

"Take Me Home Country Roads" may be the (unofficial) state song of West Virginia but City Holding hopes all roads lead to its City National Bank of West Virginia subsidiary which operates more than 80 branches in the Mountaineer State and in neighboring areas of southern Ohio eastern Kentucky and northern Virginia. Serving consumers and regional businesses the nearly $4 billion bank offers standard deposit products loans credit cards insurance trust and investment services. Residential mortgages and home equity loans constitute more than half of City Holding's $2.5 billion loan portfolio though the bank also writes commercial industrial commercial mortgage and installment consumer loans.

Operations

City National Bank (CNB) operates four main business divisions: Commercial banking Consumer Banking Mortgage Banking and Wealth Management and Trust Services.

Commercial Banking provides traditional banking products commercial and industrial loans and different kinds of real estate loans to corporations and other business customers. Consumer Banking provides deposit products installment loans and real estate loans and lines of credit. The bank's Mortgage Banking division offers fixed and adjustable-rate mortgages construction financing production of conventional and government-backed mortgages secondary marketing and mortgage servicing.

Wealth Management and Trust Services offers personal trust and estate administration investment management and investment and custodial services for commercial and individual customers. This includes management of investment accounts for individuals employee benefit plans and charitable foundations.

Altogether the company earned 62% of its total revenue from interest and fees on loans in 2014 plus another 7% from interest on its investment securities. About 14% of revenue came from service charges 8% came from bankcard revenue and 2% came from trust and investment management fee income.

Geographic Reach

City boasts around 80 branches in four US states including more than 55 branches in West Virginia nearly 15 in Virginia around 10 in Kentucky and less than a handful of branches in Ohio.

Sales and Marketing

The bank spent $3.27 million on advertising in 2014 compared to $2.67 million and $2.59 million in 2013 and 2012 respectively.

Financial Performance

City Holding's revenues and profits have mostly been on the uptrend in recent years as the bank has grown its loan business through acquisitions.

The bank's revenue dipped by 4% to $188.29 million in 2014 mostly because it generated less in loan interest due to an expected drop in accretion from fair value adjustments related to its recent Virginia Savings Bank and Community Bank acquisitions. Interest margins also shrank amidst the low interest environment which caused further headwinds to interest income. The bank did have some bright spots with 16% growth in trust and investment fee income and 11% growth in bankcard revenue as it continued to push those services.

Despite lower revenue in 2014 City Holdings net income jumped by 10% to $52.96 million – the highest its profit has been since 2007. The rise was mostly thanks to a combination of a non-income based tax rebate (non-recurring) decreased legal and professional fees from lower legal settlements a $2.7 million decline in loan loss provisions as the credit quality of the bank's loan portfolio improved and a $1.3 million reduction in interest expense on deposits.

City's operating cash fell to $53.35 million despite higher earnings during the year primarily because the bank used more of its cash toward purchasing assets and generated less net cash proceeds from its loans held for sale.

Strategy

City Holding's flagship subsidiary City National Bank has been growing its loan business and branch network in target markets through acquisitions in recent years. In mid-2015 for example the bank agreed to acquire three bank branches in Lexington Kentucky from American Founders Bank boosting CNB's presence in the state to 11

branches while adding $164.2 million in new deposits and $125 billion in performing loans to its books.

Beyond buying just select branches the bank has also been known to buy smaller community banks outright in its target markets.

To free up resources for more investment in its core business City National sold its insurance operations to The Hilb Group in early 2015 netting an after-tax gain of $5.80 million.

Mergers and Acquisitions

In January 2013 City Holding acquired Community Financial Corporation holding company of the 11-branch Community Bank in Virginia.

In 2012 the company entered a new market in Virginia through its acquisition of Virginia Savings Bank which had five branches in the northern part of the state.

EXECUTIVES

Evp Marketing Human Resources And Retail Banking, Craig G. Stilwell, age 64, $330,000 total compensation

President And Ceo, Charles R. (Skip) Hageboeck, age 57, $500,000 total compensation

Evp Commercial Banking, John A. DeRito, age 70, $250,000 total compensation

Cfo, David L. Bumgarner, age 55, $207,000 total compensation

Cio, Jeffrey D. (Jeff) Legge, $175,000 total compensation

Assistant Vice President And Trust Officer, John Chandler

Vice President, Kevin Thomas

Vice President, Madison Sayre

Vice President Of Customer Service, John Kelly

Assistant Vice President, Patricia Davis

Vice President Information Technology, Vince Workman

Vice President Business Development, Sharon Hughes

Vice President, Keith Unger

Vice President Human Resources, Lillian Komata

Senior Vice President Cco, Tim Whittaker

Senior Vice President Chief Administrative Officer And Chief Information Officer Of The Company And, Jeff Legge

Vice President, Clara Mullins

Avp, Pat Davis

Avp And Branch Manager, Massie Schemmel

Senior Vice President And Commercial Loan Officer, Lyle A Moffett

Assistant Vice President And Branch Manager, Ora Muth

Vice President Sec Treas, Virginia Stump

Vice President Sba Lending, Patrick Donnelly

Credit Officer Vice President, Julio Avila

Vice President Credit Team Lead, Thomas Trigg

Chairman, C. Dallas Kayser, age 68

Board Member, Tracy Hylton

Board Member, Sharon Rowe

Treasurer Secretary Vice President Systems Staff Finance Other Personnel, Jack Cipoletti

Auditors: Crowe LLP

LOCATIONS

HQ: City Holding Co.
25 Gatewater Road, Charleston, WV 25313
Phone: 304 769-1100
Web: www.bankatcity.com

PRODUCTS/OPERATIONS

2014 Sales

	$ mil.	% of total
Interest		
Loans including fees	116	62
Investment securities & other	13	7
Noninterest		
Service charges	265	14
Bankcard revenue	15	8
Other	171	9
Total	188	100

COMPETITORS

1st West Virginia Bancorp	Huntington Bancshares
BB&T	Ohio Valley Banc
Fifth Third	Premier Financial Bancorp
First Community Bancshares	United Bankshares
	WesBanco

HISTORICAL FINANCIALS

Company Type: Public

Income Statement

FYE: December 31

	ASSETS ($ mil.)	NET INCOME ($ mil.)	INCOME AS % OF ASSETS	EMPLOYEES
12/19	5,018	89	1.8%	918
12/18	4,899	70	1.4%	891
12/17	4,132	54	1.3%	839
12/16	3,984	52	1.3%	847
12/15	3,714	54	1.5%	853
Annual Growth	7.8%	13.4%	—	1.9%

2019 Year-End Financials

Debt ratio: 0.08%
Return on equity: 14.20%
Cash ($ mil.): 140
Current ratio: —
Long-term debt ($ mil.): —

No. of shares (mil.): 16
Dividends
Yield: 2.6%
Payout: 45.8%
Market value ($ mil.): 1,336

	STOCK PRICE ($) FY Close	P/E High/Low	PER SHARE ($) Earnings	Dividends	Book Value
12/19	81.95	15 12	5.42	2.16	40.36
12/18	67.59	18 14	4.49	1.91	36.29
12/17	67.47	21 17	3.48	1.75	32.17
12/16	67.60	20 12	3.45	1.71	29.25
12/15	45.64	15 12	3.53	1.66	27.62
Annual Growth	15.8%	— —	11.3%	6.8%	9.9%

CITY OF LOS ANGELES

Los Angeles may be a Mecca for the rich and famous but there is little glamour in running a city of more than 4 million people. Governing responsibilities are shared among the city's mayor and city council while various commissions departments and bureaus see to the daily operations that keep the wheels spinning. Elected every four years the mayor appoints most commission members (subject to approval by the city council) and serves as the city's executive officer. The City of Los Angeles is located in the County of Los Angeles.

EXECUTIVES

Medical Director Pathology And Lab Medicine Children's Hospital Los Angeles, Paul Pattengale

Vp Of Programming, Noah Silver

Managing Director. Candidate 2020, Kush Gaur

Head Secretary, Rosie Aldaz

LOCATIONS

HQ: CITY OF LOS ANGELES
200 N SPRING ST STE 303, LOS ANGELES, CA
900123239
Phone: 213 978-0600
Web: WWW.LACITY.ORG

HISTORICAL FINANCIALS

Company Type: Private

Income Statement

	REVENUE ($ mil.)	NET INCOME ($ mil.)	NET PROFIT MARGIN	EMPLOYEES
06/16	7,196	231	3.2%	41,000
06/09*	6,281	(285)	—	—
12/08	0	0	—	—
Annual Growth	274.6%			

FYE: June 30

*Fiscal year change

Civista Bancshares Inc

First Citizens Banc Corp. is the holding company for The Citizens Banking Company and its Citizens Bank and Champaign Bank divisions which together operate more than 30 branches in northern Ohio. The banks offer such deposit products as checking and savings accounts and CDs in addition to trust services. They concentrate on real estate lending with residential mortgages and commercial mortgages each comprising approximately 40% of the company's loan portfolio. The Citizens Banking Company's Citizens Wealth Management division provides financial planning brokerage insurance and investments through an agreement with third-party provider UVEST (part of LPL Financial).

EXECUTIVES

Vice President And Commercial Lender, John Desanto
Auditors: BKD, LLP

LOCATIONS

HQ: Civista Bancshares Inc
100 East Water Street, Sandusky, OH 44870
Phone: 419 625-4121

COMPETITORS

Fifth Third
Huntington Bancshares
KeyCorp
PNC Financial
U.S. Bancorp

HISTORICAL FINANCIALS

Company Type: Public

Income Statement

	ASSETS ($ mil.)	NET INCOME ($ mil.)	INCOME AS % OF ASSETS	EMPLOYEES
12/19	2,309	33	1.5%	457
12/18	2,138	14	0.7%	432
12/17	1,525	15	1.0%	350
12/16	1,377	17	1.3%	337
12/15	1,315	12	1.0%	326
Annual Growth	15.1%	27.7%	—	8.8%

FYE: December 31

2019 Year-End Financials

Debt ratio: 1.27%	No. of shares (mil.): 16
Return on equity: 10.77%	Dividends
Cash ($ mil.): 48	Yield: 1.7%
Current ratio: —	Payout: 20.4%
Long-term debt ($ mil.): —	Market value ($ mil.): 401

	STOCK PRICE ($) FY Close	P/E High/Low		PER SHARE ($) Earnings	Dividends	Book Value
12/19	24.00	11	8	2.01	0.42	19.78
12/18	17.42	23	15	1.02	0.32	19.16
12/17	22.00	16	13	1.28	0.25	18.09
12/16	19.43	10	5	1.57	0.22	16.49
12/15	12.83	8	7	1.17	0.20	15.96
Annual Growth	16.9%	—	—	14.5%	20.4%	5.5%

CNA Financial Corp

CNA Financial is an umbrella organization for a wide range of insurance providers including Continental Casualty and Continental Insurance. It primarily provides commercial policies such as workers' compensation and general liability. CNA also sells specialty insurance including professional liability (real estate agents lawyers architects) and vehicle warranty service contracts. The firm offers commercial surety bonds risk management claims administration and information services. Its products are sold by independent agents and brokers in the US and through partners abroad. Holding company Loews which is controlled and run by the Tisch family owns nearly 90% of CNA.

Operations

CNA Financial operates through three core property/casualty segments and two non-core segments. Its property/casualty segments are Specialty (more than 40% of revenue) Commercial (more than 35%) and International (about 10%) while non-core business segments are Life & Group (over 10%) and Corporate & Other.

The Specialty segment provides professional financial and specialty products and services through independent agents brokers and managing general underwriters. The Commercial segment includes products sold to small and mid-market organizations primarily through an independent agency distribution system; it also sells commercial insurance and risk management products to large corporations primarily through insurance brokers. The International segment offers management and professional liability products and services outside of the US; distribution is via a network of brokers independent agencies and managing general underwriters. The segment also sells on the Lloyd's marketplace.

About 70% of sales were generated from net earned premiums its net investment income account for some 20% amd the net insurance warranty revenue account for the rest.

Geographic Reach

CNA is headquartered in Chicago and has offices throughout the US (Arizona Florida New York South Dakota and Pennsylvania) and Canada; it also has locations in Europe.

Sales and Marketing

In the US independent agents and brokers market CNA products to customers including businesses of all sizes other insurers associations and professionals while partners handle the coverage abroad. The group primarily targets companies in the health care manufacturing life insurance financial services and construction industries.

Financial Performance

CNA's revenue since 2015 but has been steadily increasing. Net income is following the same path despite a slight dip in 2018.

In 2019 revenue increased 6% to $10.8 billion. An increase in earned premiums investment income and non-insurance warranty contributed to a rise in revenue for the year.

Net income increased by 23% to $1 billion in 2019. An increase in revenue and net investment gains contributed to the increase in net income.

The company ended 2019 with $242 million in net cash $68 million less than it had at the end of 2018. Operating activities provided $1.1 billion while investing activities used $225 million and investing activities used another $988 million. Main cash uses for the year were for dividends payment and purchases of matured securities.

Strategy

As part of its overall investment strategy the company invests in various assets which require future purchase sale or funding commitments. These investments are recorded once funded and the related commitments may include future capital calls from various third-party limited partnerships signed and accepted mortgage loan applications and obligations related to privately placed debt securities. As of December 31 2019 the company had commitments to purchase or fund approximately $945 million and sell approximately $85 million under the terms of these investments.

In June 2020 CNA launched The View From Home an innovative program offering eligible long-term care policyholders additional services to help age in place. The View From Home will launch its first phase of service offerings through a partnership with The Helper Bees an insurtech company dedicated to easing aging in place through digital technologies. Together CNA and The Helper Bees will offer select long-term care policyholders complimentary 12-month access to a Care Concierge program. While not an insurance benefit the Care Concierge program will provide personalized guidance in navigating the challenges a family or an individual faces when they require long-term care. A care concierge will work with the insured to understand their situation and educate them on resources including options not covered by insurance which may assist with aging in place.

Company Background

Merchant Henry Bowen along with a group of investors established Continental Insurance in the 1880s. In 1897 a group of Midwestern investors formed Continental Casualty. Both Continentals rose to the challenges presented by the World Wars and the Depression; they entered the 1950s ready for new growth.

In the 1960s Continental Insurance added interests in Diners Club and Capital Financial Services; in 1968 it formed holding company Continental Corp. Meanwhile Continental Assurance (which had formed its own holding company CNA Financial) went even farther afield adding mutual fund consumer finance nursing home and residential construction companies.

Both companies suffered losses arising from Hurricane Andrew in 1992 but CNA which had done some housecleaning in the 1970s was better able to deal with the blow than Continental which entered the 1990s in need of restructuring.

The two companies merged in 1995 to become one of the US's top 10 insurance companies.

EXECUTIVES

Evp General Counsel And Secretary, Jonathan D. (Jon) Kantor, age 64, $800,000 total compensation
President And Coo Cna Specialty, Mark I. Herman, age 61, $675,000 total compensation

Evp And Cfo, D. Craig Mense, age 68, $825,000 total compensation

President And Ceo Cna Canada, Nick Creatura

Chief Executive Hardy, David J. (Dave) Brosnan, age 57

Evp And Chief Underwriting Officer, Douglas M. (Doug) Worman

Evp Worldwide Property And Casualty Claim, Andrew J. Pinkes, age 57

Chairman And Ceo, Dino E. Robusto, age 61, $114,103 total compensation

Evp And Chief Actuary, Larry A. Haefner, age 63, $367,628 total compensation

President Worldwide Field Operations, Timothy J. (Tim) Szerlong, age 67, $700,000 total compensation

President Long Term Care, Albert J. (Al) Miralles, age 50

President And Coo Cna Commercial, Kevin Leidwinger, age 56

Evp Technology And Operations, Joseph (J.) Merten

Svp And Northeastern Zone Officer, Jim Romanelli

Senior Vice President And Western Zone Officer, Steve Marohn

Vice President Branch Services, Kelly Walsh

Vice President Boston Branch, Tom Allen

Svp Financial Institutions And Management Liability Cna Specialty, Paul Larson

Senior Vice President Construction, Song Kim

Senior Vice President And Chief Procurement Officer, Doug Kortfelt

Avp Professional Liability, Michelle Aliperti-urbielewicz

Svp And Chief Marketing Officer, Jennifer Livingstone

Svp Healthcare, Brice Dymtrow

Svp Of Underwriting Services, Katie Wilson

Board Member, Don Randel

Board Member, Michael Bless

Board Member, Andre Rice

Auditors: DELOITTE & TOUCHE LLP

LOCATIONS

HQ: CNA Financial Corp
  151 N. Franklin, Chicago, IL 60606
Phone: 312 822-5000   **Fax:** 312 822-6419
Web: www.cna.com

PRODUCTS/OPERATIONS

2018 Sales by Segment

	$ mil.	% of total
Specialty		
Management & professional	2,440	24
Warranty & alternative risks	1,169	11
Surety	571	6
Commercial		
Middle market	2,045	20
Small business insurance	472	5
Other commercial insurance	1,061	10
Life & Group	1,333	13
International		
Hardy	441	4
Europe	363	4
Canada	255	3
Corporate & Other	39	
Adjustments	(55)	
Total	**10,134**	**100**

Selected Solutions

Business interruption
Cargo (ocean marine)
CNA connect
CNA paramount
Commercial auto
Commercial general liability
Cyber liability
Directors & officers (d&o)
Employment practices liability (epl)
Epack extra
Equipment breakdown
Fidelity and crime insurance
Inland marine
International

Kidnap ransom and extortion
Professional liability (errors & omissions)
Property
Surety
Umbrella liability
Warranty
Workers' compensation

COMPETITORS

AIG	Old Republic
American Financial Group	The Hartford
Berkshire Hathaway	Travelers Companies
Everest Re	United Fire
Liberty Mutual	W. R. Berkley
Nationwide	Zurich Insurance Group

HISTORICAL FINANCIALS

Company Type: Public

Income Statement   FYE: December 31

	ASSETS ($ mil.)	NET INCOME ($ mil.)	INCOME AS % OF ASSETS	EMPLOYEES
12/19	60,612	1,000	1.6%	5,900
12/18	57,152	813	1.4%	6,100
12/17	56,567	899	1.6%	6,300
12/16	55,233	859	1.6%	6,700
12/15	55,047	479	0.9%	6,900
Annual Growth	**2.4%**	**20.2%**	**—**	**(3.8%)**

2019 Year-End Financials

Debt ratio: 4.42%		No. of shares (mil.): 271	
Return on equity: 8.54%		Dividends	
Cash ($ mil.): 242		Yield: 7.5%	
Current ratio: —		Payout: 106.5%	
Long-term debt ($ mil.): —		Market value ($ mil.): 12,162	

	STOCK PRICE ($) FY Close	P/E High/Low	Earnings	Dividends	Book Value
12/19	44.81	14 12	3.67	3.40	45.01
12/18	44.15	18 14	2.98	3.30	41.32
12/17	53.05	17 12	3.30	3.10	45.15
12/16	41.50	13 9	3.17	3.00	44.25
12/15	35.15	25 19	1.77	3.00	43.50
Annual Growth	**6.3%**	**— —**	**20.0%**	**3.2%**	**0.9%**

CNB Financial Corp. (Clearfield, PA)

CNB Financial is the holding company for CNB Bank ERIEBANK and FCBank. The banks and subsidiaries provide traditional deposit and loan services as well as wealth management merchant credit card processing and life insurance through nearly 30 CNB Bank- and ERIEBANK-branded branches in Pennsylvania and nine FCBank branches in central Ohio. Commercial industrial and agricultural loans make up more than one-third of the bank's loan portfolio while commercial mortgages make up another one-third. It also makes residential mortgages consumer and credit card loans. The company's non-bank subsidiaries include CNB Securities Corporation Holiday Financial Services Corporation and CNB Insurance Agency.

Operations

Commercial industrial and agricultural loans made up 36% of the bank's $16.74 billion loan portfolio at the end of 2015 while commercial mortgages made up another 33%. The rest of the portfolio was made up of residential mortgages (15% of loan assets) consumer (14%) overdrafts (less than 1%) and credit card loans (less than 1%).

The group makes more than 80% of its revenue from interest income. About 70% of its revenue came from loan interest during 2015 while another 15% came from interest income from taxable and tax-exempt securities. The remainder of its revenue came from deposit account service charges (4% of revenue) wealth and asset management fees (3%) and other miscellaneous income sources.

Geographic Reach

Clearfield Pennsylvania-based CNB Financial serves clients in its home state as well as in Ohio. CNB Financial serves a specific market area such as the Pennsylvania counties of Cambria Cameron Centre Clearfield Crawford Elk Erie Indiana Jefferson McKean and Warren.

Sales and Marketing

The group serves individuals businesses government and institutional customers.

CNB Financial has been increasing its advertising spend in recent years. It spent $1.6 million during 2015 up from $1.5 million and $1 million in 2014 and 2013 respectively.

Financial Performance

CNB Financial's revenues have risen more than 30% since 2011 as its loan assets have nearly doubled to $1.58 billion. The firm's profits have grown nearly 50% over the same period as low-interest rates and declining loan loss provisions have lowered operating costs.

The group's revenue climbed 1% to $102 million during 2015 thanks to a modest rise in interest income stemming mostly from 16% loan asset growth.

Despite revenue growth in 2015 CNB Financial's net income dipped 4% to $22.2 million mostly due to nearly 10% rise in salary and employee benefit costs from new hires and more expensive benefits. The group's operating cash levels jumped 16% to $34 million for the year thanks to favorable working capital changes related to accrued interest payables and other liabilities.

Strategy

CNB Financial has been acquiring other banks and opening branches in new geographic markets in recent years to boost its loan and deposit business. As a sign of success the bank noted that its assets have nearly doubled in size since 2009 from $1.16 billion to $2.29 billion at the end of 2015.

Toward its branch expansion plans the group's ERIEBANK brand entered Ohio by opening a loan production office there in 2014 with plans to open another by the end of 2016. After opening an FCBank branch in Dublin Ohio in 2014 the group in 2016 also continued to push its FCBank brand which has been enjoying double-digit loan and deposit business growth in the Columbus and Lancaster regions in Ohio. It plans to open a new FCBank branch in Worthington Ohio by the end of 2016.

Mergers and Acquisitions

In 2016 CNB looked expanded into Northeast Ohio after buying Mentor Ohio-based Lake National Bank — and its $152 million in assets — for nearly $25 million. Lake National Bank's operations were folded into ERIEBANK's operations when the transaction closed.

In 2013 extending its reach in Ohio CNB Financial acquired FC Banc Corp. for $41.6 million. The deal gave CNB Financial Farmers Citizens Bank which serves the northern Ohio communities of Bucyrus Cardington Fredericktown Mount Hope and Shiloh as well as the greater Columbus Ohio area.

Company Background

In 2012 CNB Financial acquired an Ebensburg Pennsylvania-based consumer discount company which brought with it a loan portfolio valued at about $1 million.

EXECUTIVES

Evp Human Resources, Mary Ann Conaway
Sevp And Chief Credit Officer Cnb Bank, Mark D. Breakey, age 61, $211,000 total compensation
President And Ceo, Joseph B. Bower, age 56, $458,000 total compensation
Sevp And Coo Cnb Bank, Richard L Greslick, age 44, $221,000 total compensation
Evp Cfo And Treasurer Cnb Bank And Treasurer Principal Financial Officer And Principal Accounting Officer Cnb Financial Corporation, Brian W. Wingard, age 46, $210,000 total compensation
Evp And Chief Commercial Banking Officer Cnb Bank, Joseph E. Dell, age 64, $211,000 total compensation
Evp Customer Experience, Leanne D. Kassab
Assistant Vice President Of Credit Administration, Gregory Dixon
Assistant Vice President Of Mortgage Lending, Eileen Ryan
Vice Presidents Commercial Banking, Joseph Yaros
Assistant Vice President Compliance, Kylie Ogden
Vice President, Andrew Roman
Senior Vice President Chief Lending Officer, Jeffrey Alabran
Senior Vice President, Martin T Griffith
Senior Vice President Of Operations, Vincent C Turiano
Vice President Information Technology, Bonnie Garito
Chairman, Peter F. Smith, age 65
Board Member, Jeffrey Powell
Board Member, Robert Montler
Board Member, Deborah Pontzer
Auditors: Crowe LLP

LOCATIONS

HQ: CNB Financial Corp. (Clearfield, PA)
1 South Second Street, P.O. Box 42, Clearfield, PA 16830
Phone: 814 765-9621
Web: www.cnbbank.bank

PRODUCTS/OPERATIONS

2015 Sales

	$ mil.	% of total
Interest and Dividend Income		
Loans including fees	71	70
Securities		
Taxable	11	10
Tax-exempt	3	4
Dividends	0	1
Non-Interest Income		
Wealth and asset management fees	3	3
Service charges on deposit accounts	4	4
Other service charges and fees	3	3
Other revenues	4	5
Total	102	100

Selected Services

Checking
Credit cards
Loans
Savings

COMPETITORS

AmeriServ Financial	M&T Bank
CBT Financial	Northwest Bancshares
Citizens Financial Group	PNC Financial
First Commonwealth Financial	S&T Bancorp

HISTORICAL FINANCIALS

Company Type: Public

Income Statement

FYE: December 31

	ASSETS ($ mil.)	NET INCOME ($ mil.)	INCOME AS % OF ASSETS	EMPLOYEES
12/19	3,763	40	1.1%	559
12/18	3,221	33	1.0%	556
12/17	2,768	23	0.9%	528
12/16	2,573	20	0.8%	507
12/15	2,285	22	1.0%	454
Annual Growth	13.3%	15.9%	—	5.3%

2019 Year-End Financials

Debt ratio: 7.93%
Return on equity: 14.12%
Cash ($ mil.): 192
Current ratio: —
Long-term debt ($ mil.): —

No. of shares (mil.): 15
Dividends
  Yield: 2.0%
  Payout: 25.8%
Market value ($ mil.): 498

	STOCK PRICE ($) FY Close	P/E High/Low		PER SHARE ($) Earnings	Dividends	Book Value
12/19	32.68	13	9	2.63	0.68	20.00
12/18	22.95	15	10	2.21	0.67	17.28
12/17	26.24	19	13	1.57	0.66	15.98
12/16	26.74	20	12	1.42	0.66	14.64
12/15	18.03	12	11	1.54	0.66	14.01
Annual Growth	16.0%			14.3%	0.7%	9.3%

CNO Financial Group Inc

Have a modest but stable income? Graying at the temples? CNO Financial Group finds that especially attractive and has life insurance and related products targeted at you and millions of others. With a focus on middle-income working families and seniors the holding company's primary units include Bankers Life and Casualty which provides Medicare supplement life annuities and long-term care insurance; Washington National which offers specified disease insurance accident insurance life insurance and annuities; and Colonial Penn which offers life insurance to consumers. The company also offers reinsurance. CNO Financial operates nationwide.

Operations

CNO operates through four segments: Bankers Life Washington National Colonial Penn and Long-term care in run-off. The Bankers Life segment accounts for about 70% of CNO's annual revenue and the Washington National segment accounts for more than 20%. Colonial Penn (nearly 10%) and Long-term care in run-off (1%) round out the group's sales.

CNO has some 3.5 million policies in force including third-party policies sold by its Bankers Life agents.

Geographic Reach

With operations throughout the US (including the District of Columbia and certain protectorates) CNO counts Florida Pennsylvania California and Texas among its largest markets. Together the four states account for more than a quarter of CNO's total premiums.

Sales and Marketing

CNO's largest segment Bankers Life sells products through its own team of around 4000 career agents; it also markets Medicare Advantage plans through distribution arrangements with Humana and United HealthCare. The Washington National segment uses a combination of brokers independent agents and worksite marketing programs. The smaller Colonial Penn segment sells policies through direct sales efforts including television advertising direct mail telemarketing and online sales campaigns.

The group's career agent distribution channel brings in the bulk of its business representing some three-fourths of premiums collected. Independent producers account for more than 15% of collected premiums and direct marketing accounts for some 10%.

CNO leases around 275 sales offices.

Financial Performance

CNO had steady single-digit growth until the 2014 sale of Conseco Life Insurance which brought revenue down for a couple of years. Revenue has been rising since but net income has been more turbulent.

In 2017 revenue increased 8% to $4.3 billion. This was largely due to increases in insurance policy and investment income but was partially offset by a decline in fees and other income. Subsidiary Bankers Life had higher collected premium and annuity account values that year. Washington National also had a strong year gaining a record in new annualized premium. Colonial Penn had a reduction in new annualized premium.

Despite the higher revenue in 2017 net income fell 51% to $175.6 million as operating expenses (primarily insurance policy benefits paid) and income tax expenses both rose.

The company ended 2017 with $578.4 million in net cash $100 million more than it had at the end of 2016. Operating activities provided $613.1 million in cash while financing activities used $274 million and investing activities used $239.6 million.

Strategy

CNO believes its target markets of seniors and middle-income families are often overlooked and underserved giving the company opportunity in the senior market which is expected to double over the next decade. One of its strategies is to market Medicare Supplement insurance which is popular among its target customers and cross-sell discretionary products such as life insurance and annuities.

A major priority is growth across a number of areas including broadening its product portfolio revamping its distribution channels to increase efficiency and reach and deepening its reach within certain of its target demographics. For example in 2016 the company launched its own broker-dealer (Bankers Life Securities) and registered investment advisor (Bankers Life Advisory Services) subsidiaries. Those financial services units are a direct response to Middle America 's increasing concern with financial security in retirement when health care costs typically increase.

The company is working to lower its relative exposure to the long-term care business which pose a higher level of tail risk. It stopped selling home health care long-term policies and comprehensive and nursing home long-term care policies with benefits exceeding three years. In 2018 CNO ceded the legacy (prior to 2003) comprehensive and nursing home long-term care policies of subsidiary Bankers Life and Casualty to Wilton Reassurance Company.

To increase profits CNO is working to reduce unnecessary costs across the entire organization while expanding its number of locations. It also works to attract and retain talented employees in part by offering professional development opportunities. For example it is dedicated to increasing the number of career agents holding a securities license which has already helped assets under administration and assets under management grow.

Company Background

In 2010 the company changed its name from Conseco to CNO Financial Group to reflect a broader identity. (The firm also sought to distance itself from historical financial instabilities associated with the Conseco brand.) The name change came after several years' worth of management efforts to conserve capital reduce complexity and debt and sequester or divest less profitable operations.

HISTORY

CNO Financial evolved from Security National an Indiana insurance company formed in 1979 by Stephen Hilbert. The former encyclopedia salesman and Aetna executive believed most insurance companies were bloated and the industry itself overcrowded as well as ripe for consolidation by a smart lean organization.

In 1982 the company began a growth-by-acquisition strategy with the purchase of Executive Income Life Insurance (renamed Security National Life Insurance). The next year it bought Consolidated National Life Insurance and renamed the expanded company Conseco.

The firm went public in 1985 using the proceeds to fund an acquisitions spree that included Lincoln American Life Insurance Lincoln Income Life (sold in 1990) Bankers National Life Insurance Western National Life Insurance (sold in 1994) and National Fidelity Life Insurance.

In 1990 the company formed Conseco Capital Partners (with General Electric and Bankers Trust) to finance acquisitions without seeming to burden the parent company with debt. This device financed the purchase of Great American Reserve and the 1991 acquisition of Beneficial Standard Life. The former Conseco bought Bankers Life Insurance in 1992 then sold 67% of the firm the next year. Also in 1993 the company formed the Private Capital Group to invest in non-insurance companies.

In 1994 the company tried to acquire the much larger Kemper Corp. but shied away from the debt load that the $2.6 billion deal would have entailed. The aborted deal cost $36 million in bank and accounting fees and spelled the end of the company's relationship with Merrill Lynch which had underwritten the company's IPO when a Merrill Lynch analyst downgraded its stock after the fiasco.

Meanwhile Private Capital's success led the company to form Conseco Global Investments. Other investments included stakes in racetrack and riverboat gambling operations in Indiana.

In 1996 and 1997 the firm absorbed eight life health property/casualty and specialty insurance companies and raised its interest in American Life Holdings to 100%.

Itching to move beyond insurance in 1998 the company bought Green Tree Financial the US's #1 mobile home financier. Charges of Green Tree's own fuzzy accounting practices helped torpedo the company's quest for a federal thrift charter. But the troubles had just begun. The mobile home finance industry took a dive as customers refinanced at lower rates and prepayments slammed Green Tree Financial reducing Conseco's earnings.

The company tried to recoup in 1999 by launching an ad campaign portraying the company as the "Wal-Mart of financial services." It also continued the acquisition spree. But Green Tree Financial (renamed Conseco Finance that year) couldn't stanch the flow of red ink: Buyers grew wary of the quality of the finance unit's loan securities and changes in accounting methods cost the parent company a $350 million charge against earnings for 1999.

In 2002 due to its financial woes the NYSE suspended trading in the company and its stock was moved to the OTC. The company also filed for Chapter 11 protection. As part of the reorganization agreement it agreed to sell Conseco Finance. The company's insurance operations were not subject to the Chapter 11 agreement.

In 2003 it finally unloaded the Conseco Finance unit to investor group CFN Investment Holdings and General Electric Co.'s consumer finance unit for $1 billion. The company emerged from bankruptcy in September 2003.

The company agreed to pay a fine of $6.3 million in 2008 after an investigation determined that its long-term care insurance business Conseco Senior Health had wrongly denied claims and mishandled complaints and that some sales and marketing practices at Banker's Life did not comply with industry standards. To put what it could in the past in late 2008 the firm spun off its closed block of long-term care insurance. The new entity was named Senior Health Insurance Company of Pennsylvania and consisted entirely of policies in run-off.

EXECUTIVES

Ceo And Director, Gary C. Bhojwani, age 52, $517,307 total compensation

Evp Coo And Cto, Bruce K. Baude, age 56, $559,487 total compensation

Chief Investment Officer And President 40|86 Advisors, Eric R. Johnson, age 60, $500,000 total compensation

Evp Human Resources, Susan L. (Sue) Menzel, age 54

President Bankers Life And Casualty Company, Scott L. Goldberg, age 49

Evp And Chief Actuary, Christopher J. (Chris) Nickele, age 64, $416,667 total compensation

Evp And General Counsel, Matthew J. (Matt) Zimpfer, age 53

Evp And Cfo, Erik M. Helding, age 47, $357,813 total compensation

President Washington National, Mike Heard

President Colonial Penn, Joel Schwartz

Avp Technical Services, Gevan Arnett

Senior Vice President Underwriting And New Business, David Vega

Vice President, Gregory Turner

Vice President Compensation And Benefits, Grace Brothers

Vice President Finance And Administration Bankers Life, Doug Williams

Vice President Product Marketing, Dana Allen

Vice President Corporate Finance And Treasurer, Jeff Kircher

Assistant Vice President Internet T Senior Director Customer Service, Ming Tong

Vice President Underwriting, Gail Mitchell

Vice President Corporate Development, Adam Auvil

Executive Vice President Government Relations, William Fritts

Vice President Valuation, Tim Bischof

Vice President Human Resources Services, Mark Rawas

Senior Vice President Enterprise Operations, Jean Linnenbringer

Vp And General Auditor, Tom Kleyle

Vice President Compensation Hris And Payroll, Mitch Schulz

Svp Of Sales And Distribution Of Bankers Life, Nathan Richardson

Chairman, Neal C. Schneider, age 76

Assistant Treasurer, Paul Podgorny

Board Member, Charles Jacklin

Auditors: PricewaterhouseCoopers LLP

LOCATIONS

HQ: CNO Financial Group Inc
11825 N. Pennsylvania Street, Carmel, IN 46032
Phone: 317 817-6100
Web: www.cnoinc.com

PRODUCTS/OPERATIONS

2017 Sales

	$ mil.	% of total
Insurance policy income	2,647	61
General account assets	1,285	30
Policyholder & reinsurer accounts & other special-purpose portfolios	265	6
Net realized investment gains excluding impairment losses	77	2
Fee revenue & other	48	1
Adjustments	(27.1)	-
Total	**4,297**	**100**

2017 Sales by Segment

	% of total
Bankers Life	67
Washington National	23
Colonial Penn	8
Long-term care in run-off	1
Corporate	1
Total	**100**

COMPETITORS

Aflac	MetLife
Allstate	Mutual of Omaha
Colonial Life &	New York Life
Accident	Northwestern Mutual
Gerber Life	Torchmark
MassMutual	

HISTORICAL FINANCIALS

Company Type: Public

Income Statement — FYE: December 31

	ASSETS ($ mil.)	NET INCOME ($ mil.)	INCOME AS % OF ASSETS	EMPLOYEES
12/19	33,630	409	1.2%	3,300
12/18	31,439	(315)	—	3,300
12/17	33,110	175	0.5%	3,300
12/16	31,975	358	1.1%	3,400
12/15	31,125	270	0.9%	3,500
Annual Growth	2.0%	10.9%	—	(1.5%)

2019 Year-End Financials

Debt ratio: 11.26%
Return on equity: 10.17%
Cash ($ mil.): 654
Current ratio: —
Long-term debt ($ mil.): —

No. of shares (mil.): 148
Dividends
  Yield: 2.3%
  Payout: 43.0%
Market value ($ mil.): 2,685

	STOCK PRICE ($) FY Close	P/E High/Low		PER SHARE ($) Earnings	Dividends	Book Value
12/19	18.13	7	5	2.61	0.43	31.58
12/18	14.88	—		(1.90)	0.39	20.78
12/17	24.69	25	18	1.02	0.35	29.05
12/16	19.15	10	7	2.01	0.31	25.82
12/15	19.09	15	11	1.39	0.27	22.49
Annual Growth	(1.3%)	—		17.1%	12.3%	8.9%

COASTAL FEDERAL CREDIT UNION

EXECUTIVES

Chb, Joan Nelson
Chb*, Richard S Bloom
SEC-Treas*, William F Smith
Exec V Pres*, Chuck Purvis
Exec V Pres-Coo*, Kris Kovacs
R Vpres,cfo*, Brad Miller
R Vp Chief ADM Offcr*, Brenda Hooks
Corporate Communications Staff, Michael Doi
Technology, Mike Day
Art Director, Paul Styron
Officer, Ashley Holland

LOCATIONS

HQ: COASTAL FEDERAL CREDIT UNION
1000 SAINT ALBANS DR, RALEIGH, NC 276097347
Phone: 919 420-8000
Web: WWW.COASTAL24.COM

HISTORICAL FINANCIALS
Company Type: Private

Income Statement				FYE: December 31
	ASSETS ($ mil.)	NET INCOME ($ mil.)	INCOME AS % OF ASSETS	EMPLOYEES
12/08	2,087	2	0.1%	400
12/07	1,881	13	0.7%	—
12/06	46	0	—	—
Annual Growth	566.5%	—	—	—

COBANK, ACB

You could say CoBank is dependent on its rural customers and vice versa. A member of the Farm Credit System (which is regulated by the FCA) the $110 billion cooperative bank provides seasonal and wholesale loans to agribusinesses as well as to rural power water and communications cooperatives across the US. The bank also leases vehicles farming equipment and agricultural facilities through various Farm Credit System affiliates. Its core agribusiness customers range from local and regional farmers' cooperatives to multinational food companies. It has counted Land O' Lakes Blue Diamond Almonds and National Beef as among its larger customers. Formed in 1989 CoBank merged with US AgBank in early 2012.

Operations

CoBank operates three main business segments: Strategic Relationships Agribusiness and Rural Infrastructure. Its Strategic Relationships loans made up 50% of its $80 billion loan portfolio at the end of 2014 while Agribusiness and Rural Infrastructure made up another 30% and 20% respectively.

About 76% of CoBank's total revenue came from loan interest in 2014 while another 16% came from interest income on investment securities. The rest of its revenue came from fee income (5% of revenue) prepayment income (1%) and other miscellaneous sources.

Geographic Reach

Based in Colorado the bank operates 15 regional offices throughout the US including locations in Iowa Georgia Texas Connecticut Kansas Missouri and Kentucky. It also has an international office in Singapore.

Sales and Marketing

CoBank mainly serves clients in rural America in the agribusiness water communications and power sectors.

Financial Performance

CoBank's annual revenues and profits have been rising over the past several years thanks to steady loan asset growth across all three of its target loan types (Strategic Relationships Agribusiness and Rural Infrastructure).

The bank's revenue jumped 5% to $2.2 million during 2014 mostly thanks to higher average loan volume and increased earnings from a strengthened balance sheet. CoBank's lending business grew with food and agribusiness customers Farm Credit Association customers and rural energy and communications customers which all in turn contributed to its top-line growth.

Revenue growth in 2014 drove CoBank's net income up 6% to $904.3 million for the year. The bank's operating cash levels dipped 2% to $883.1 million during the year due to unfavorable working capital changes related to accrued interest balance changes.

EXECUTIVES

Cfo, David P. Burlage
Chief Risk Officer, Lori L. O'Flaherty
Coo, Ann Trakimas
Evp Banking Services Group, Antony M. Bahr
Svp And Cio, James R. Bernsten
Evp Regional Agribusiness Banking Group, Amy H. Gales
Central Region President Regional Agribusiness Banking Group, Mike Hechtner
Chief Credit Officer, Daniel Key
Evp Corporate Agribusiness Banking Group, Jonathan B. Logan
Southern Region President Regional Agribusiness Banking Group, Lynn Scherler
Svp And Manager Communications Division, Robert F. (Rob) West
Eastern Region President Regional Agribusiness Banking Group, David Sparks
Western Region President Regional Agribusiness Banking Group, Leili Ghazi
Ceo, Robert B. Engel, $880,000 total compensation
President, Mary E. McBride
Chief Banking Officer; Member Management Executive Committee, Thomas Halverson
Vp And Managing Counsel Legal And Loan Processing Division, Chris Clayton
President Farm Credit Leasing, Mike Romanowski
Svp Power Energy And Utilities Banking Division, Todd E. Telesz
Svp Electric Distribution Water And Community Facilities, Nivin Elgohary
Vice President Lead Relationship Manager, David James
Vice President, Bert Johnson
Regional Vice President Southern Region Electric Distribution Division, Tamra Reynolds
Sector Vice President And Relationship Manager, Michael Tousignant
Vice President, Marshall Essig
Vice President Policy And Public Affairs, Sarah Tyree
Vice President And Executive D, Matthew Brill
Senior Vice President Communications Banking Division, Ted Koerner
Second Vice Chair, Kevin A. Still
First Vice Chair, Daniel T. (Dan) Kelley
Chairman, Everett M. Dobrinski
Auditors: PRICEWATERHOUSECOOPERS LLP DE

LOCATIONS

HQ: COBANK, ACB
6340 S FIDDLERS GREEN CIR, GREENWOOD VILLAGE, CO 801114951
Phone: 303 740-6527
Web: WWW.COBANK.COM

Selected Regional Offices
Ames IA
Atlanta GA
Austin TX
Enfield CT
Fargo ND
Louisville KY
Lubbock TX
Minneapolis MN
Omaha NE
Roseville CA
Spokane WA
St. Louis MO
Washington D.C.
Wichita KS

COMPETITORS

AgFirst	Northwest Farm Credit
AgStar	Rabo AgriFinance
AgriBank	Wells Fargo
Bank of America	
Farm Credit Services of Mid-America	

HISTORICAL FINANCIALS
Company Type: Private

Income Statement				FYE: December 31
	ASSETS ($ mil.)	NET INCOME ($ mil.)	INCOME AS % OF ASSETS	EMPLOYEES
12/18	139,015	1,190	0.9%	500
12/17	129,210	1,125	0.9%	—
12/16	126	945	749.8%	—
12/15	117,470	936	0.8%	—
Annual Growth	5.8%	8.3%	—	—

Coca-Cola Co (The)

The Coca-Cola Company is a nonalcoholic beverage company in the world and one of the world's most recognizable brands. It is home to more than 500 beverage brands some 20 of those billion-dollar-brands including four of the top five soft drinks: Coca-Cola Diet Coke Fanta and Sprite. In addition to soft drinks it markets waters enhanced water and sports drinks; juice drinks dairy and plant-based beverages ready-to-drink teas and coffees and energy drinks. Other top brands include Minute Maid Powerade Dasani Honest Tea and vitaminwater. With the world's largest beverage distribution system Coca-Cola reaches thirsty consumers in more than 200 countries. Nearly 70% of its sales comes from outside the US.

HISTORY

Atlanta pharmacist John Pemberton invented Coke in 1886. His bookkeeper Frank Robinson named the product after two ingredients coca leaves (later cleaned of narcotics) and kola nuts. By 1891 druggist Asa Candler had bought The Coca-Cola Company and within four years the soda-fountain drink was available in all states; it was in Canada and Mexico by 1898.

Candler sold most US bottling rights in 1899 to Benjamin Thomas and John Whitehead of Chattanooga Tennessee for $1. The two designed a regional franchise bottling system that created more than 1000 bottlers within 20 years. In 1916 Candler retired to become Atlanta's mayor; his family sold the company to Atlanta banker Ernest Woodruff for $25 million in 1919. Coca-Cola went public that year.

The firm expanded overseas and introduced the slogans "The Pause that Refreshes" (1929) and "It's the Real Thing" (1941). To keep WWII soldiers in Cokes at a nickel a pop the government built 64 overseas bottling plants. Coca-Cola bought Minute Maid in 1960 and began launching new drinks — Fanta (1960) Sprite (1960) TAB (1963) and Diet Coke (1982).

In 1981 Roberto Goizueta became chairman. Four years later with Coke slipping in market share the firm changed its formula and introduced New Coke which consumers soundly rejected (thus Coca-Cola Classic was born). In 1986 it consolidated the US bottling operations it owned into Coca-Cola Enterprises and sold 51% of the new company to the public. Goizueta also engineered the company's purchase of Columbia Pictures in 1982. (Columbia earned Coke a $1 billion profit when it sold the studio to Sony in 1989.)

In 1995 it bought Barq's root beer. Goizueta died of lung cancer in 1997; while he was at the helm the firm's value rose from $4 billion to $145 billion. Douglas Ivester the architect of Coca-Cola's restructured bottling operations succeeded him. An agreement to buy about 30 Cadbury Schweppes beverage brands — including Canada Dry Dr Pepper and Schweppes — outside the US and France was scaled down because of antitrust concerns. Completed in 1999 the deal also excluded Canada much of continental Europe and Mexico. (Cadbury in 2008 spun off its beverage division which became Dr Pepper Snapple Group.)

A battered Ivester resigned in 2000; president and COO Douglas Daft was named chairman and CEO. Coca-Cola began its largest cutbacks ever slashing nearly 5000 jobs and later agreed to pay nearly $193 million to settle a race-discrimination suit filed by African-American workers.

To fortify its portfolio in the fast-growing noncarbonated drinks segment Coca-Cola acquired Mad River Traders (teas juices sodas) and Odwalla (juices and smoothies) in 2001. The company also bought a 35% interest (San Miguel Corporation owned the rest) in bottler Coca-Cola Philippines from Coca-Cola Amatil. (In 2005 Coke bought the remaining percentage of the Philippine bottler.) The company announced the creation of a huge beverage and snack distribution joint venture with Procter & Gamble but the multibillion-dollar operation fell apart before it could begin. Coca-Cola also announced that it would invest $150 million to build bottling facilities in China.

In 2002 Coca-Cola introduced Vanilla Coke its biggest new product launch since the disastrous New Coke debacle. The company also secured distribution rights to Danone's Evian brand in North America and paid about $128 million when it formed a joint venture (CCDA Waters LLC) with Danone to produce market and distribute Danone's bottled water in the North America (including Dannon and Sparkletts brands under license). Also in 2002 Steven Heyer president and COO of Coca-Cola Ventures and Coca-Cola Latin America was named Coca-Cola's new president and COO. (The company's former president Jack Stahl had left after a reorganization in 2001.)

As part of the restructuring initiated by Daft in 2000 another 1000 employees (half in Atlanta) were laid off in 2003 after the company decided to combine several business units under the Coca-Cola North America umbrella. The company laid off 2800 employees worldwide in 2003.

Those layoffs led one former employee to sue claiming the soft drink maker improperly accounted for funds discriminated against minorities and in 2000 rigged test marketing of frozen Coca-Cola at a Virginia Burger King. Coca-Cola said it does not violate general accounting principles and does not discriminate. However the company said it had already disciplined employees involved in the Burger King tests and Coke executive Thomas Moore who led the fountain drinks division responsible for the questionable tests resigned. Coke also agreed to pay Burger King as much as $21 million to settle the matter. Coke said in 2003 it would reduce its revenue by $9 million to make up for accounting errors from the fountain drinks division that managed the troubled tests. Coke later settled its dispute with the former employee who first raised concerns about Coke's conduct agreeing to pay $500000 in severance and legal costs.

Later in 2003 trouble broke out for the company overseas. Claims surfaced in India that both Coke and Pepsi bottled in that country contain traces of DDT malathion and other pesticides that exceed government limits. Both Coke and Pepsi denied the reports in a joint press conference. Government labs cleared the colas saying the drinks were safe but not before both soft drink companies saw sales dip by as much as 50% in a two-week period.

Trying to boost the younger consumer's interest in its flagship cola Coca-Cola launched new marketing and ad campaigns in 2003. Efforts included changing graphics on Coke bottles and cans back to a more traditional look. However Coca-Cola took the opposite tactic to spur interest in Sprite unveiling Sprite Remix a tropical-flavored version of the soft drink. Minute Maid unveiled Minute Maid Premium Heart Wise which claims to lower cholesterol as long as people consistently drink two glasses a day.

Coca-Cola rolled out a lime version of its Diet Coke in 2004. (The non-diet version came out in 2005.) The flavor joined diet cherry lemon and vanilla. In making the announcement Coca-Cola said it also had reformulated its lemon flavor so that it tastes "lighter." Also in 2004 Coke opened an online music store in the UK called MyCoke-music.com. A month later Coke began selling its Dasani bottled water in the UK and 19 other countries. Later in 2004 the company recalled Dasani water in Europe because of elevated levels of bromate. In addition Daft retired as Coca-Cola's chairman and CEO in 2004 and former Coca-Cola HBC CEO E. Neville Isdell replaced him.

Responding to the growing awareness by consumers of health problems associated with obesity and inactive lifestyles in 2004 Coca-Cola created The Beverage Institute for Health & Wellness a beverage research and educational operation which the company hopes will lead to the creation of more healthful beverage products.

Having introduced Minute Maid products in Russia in 2004 Coke furthered its juice presence in the country with the 2005 purchase of Russian juice maker Multon. Coke bought the company in conjunction with Coca-Cola Hellenic Bottling Co. Later that year Coke began test marketing a Mountain Dew-like drink named Vault in Alabama North Carolina and Tennessee. (Surge a previous Mountain Dew competitor tried by Coke failed in testing.) In 2005 the company announced the phasing out of Vanilla Coke and introduction of Black Cherry Coke.

In 2005 Coke bought Danone's 49% stake in their North American bottled-water venture for about $100 million. The joint venture never turned a profit during its three-year run but Coke hopes full ownership of the Dannon and Sparkletts brands will prove profitable. Coke still shares North American import and marketing rights of Danone's premier water brand Evian which although the world's top-selling bottled water has seen declining in US sales.

The company's rivalry with PepsiCo goes beyond soda to juice products (Coca-Cola's Minute Maid vs. PepsiCo's Tropicana) bottled water (Dasani vs. Aquafina) and other noncarbonated products. Feeling pressure to stay competitive with these faster selling beverages Coca-Cola introduced an energy drink Full Throttle in 2005.

Also in 2005 Coke also announced a revamping of its global marketing team announcing the retirement of Sandy Allen president of its European division. In an effort to expand its international product offerings later that same year it acquired Brazilian juice maker Sucos Mais for some $48 million.

New drinks introduced in 2006 included Vault (a Mountain Dew knock-off). That year Blak a coffee-flavored Coke (with half the calories and twice the caffeine of a regular Coke that was in development for two years) was first test-marketed in France and subsequently introduced in the US. (The pricey soda — $1.99 for an 8-ounce bottle — was discontinued in the US in 2007 due to poor sales.)

Boosting its drinks in the reduced-calorie category in 2006 the company introduced a so-called "calorie-burning" drink called Enviga a green-tea-based drink. It is marketed through a joint venture with Nestl . (The joint venture called Beverage Partners Worldwide primarily focuses on black tea drinks.)

The company also launched a new line of premium coffee and tea beverages called Far Coast in 2006. The drinks were launched in Canada along with Far Coast concept stores where consumers can taste test the flavors. The company expanded its reach into coffee further with a deal with coffeehouse chain Caribou Coffee. Coca-Cola and Caribou created a new line of ready-to-drink iced coffee beverages.

In 2013 Coca-Cola opened a new bottling plant in Myanmar as part of a planned $200 million investment during the next five years there which also includes adding more than 22000 jobs during that time period.

In 2013 it bought ZICO Beverages a maker of ZICO Pure Premium Coconut Water.

Growing its distribution network in 2013 The Coca-Cola Company bought Sacramento Coca-Cola Bottling Company the sixth-largest independent Coca-Cola bottler in the nation that serves nine northern California counties.

EXECUTIVES

Evp And President Bottling Investments And Supply Chain, Irial Finan, age 63, $908,108 total compensation

Evp And President Coca-cola North America, J. Alexander M. (Sandy) Douglas, age 59, $698,091 total compensation

Evp And Chief Marketing Officer, Marcos de Quinto, age 61, $778,379 total compensation

President Europe Middle East And Africa (emea), Brian J. Smith, age 64

Svp And Cio, Barry N. Simpson, age 59

President And Ceo, James R. Quincey, age 56, $923,625 total compensation

Evp And Cfo, Kathy N. Waller, age 62, $749,365 total compensation

President Coca-cola Refreshments North America, Paul Mulligan

Vice President Of Operations National Di, Kraig Adams

Svp And Cto, Ed Hays, age 61

Svp And Chief Customer And Commercial Leadership Officer, Julie Hamilton, age 54
President Asia Pacific Group, John Murphy, age 58
President West Africa, Peter Njonjo
President South And East Africa, Kelvin Balogun
Svp And President The Mcdonalâ's Division, Craig Williams
President Latin America Group, Alfredo Rivera, age 58
President Coca-cola Ltd., Shane Grant
Regional Director-india Bangladesh Sri Lanka And Nepal Hindustan Coca-cola Beverages Pvt Ltd., Vamsi Mohan
Vice President Connections Planning, Katie Miller
Svp Special Projects, Brent Hastie
Vice President Retail Channel Strategy A, Kelly Marr
Vice President Contact Centers, Glenn Gemmill
Vice President Marketing, Allison Higbie
Vice President National Retail Sales West Region Sales, Katie Giesler
Vice President Sales National Accounts Cr, Dean McKillip
Vp Finance Us Region Sales, Greg Blumeyer
Vice President Strategic Partnership Marketing, Bruce Mcdonald
Vice President Flavor Supply, Bernard Mcguinness
Vice President System Of The Future Transactions, Roberto Moraes
Vice President National Sales, Scott Woodburn
Vice President Government Relations, Connell Stafford
Vice President Of Tamacc, Ish Arebalos
Vice President Sprite Flavors, Kim Venkatesh
Vice President Environment, Jefferson Seabright
Vice President Region Sales Strategic Initiatives, Greg Sample
Vice President Retail Marketi, Diane Wallace
Vice President, Matthew T Echols
Vice President Convenience Retail Channel Ccr, Jay J Ard
Vice President Finance, Mark Eppert
Vice President And Director Mergers And Acquisitions, Marie Quintero-johnson
Vp National Accounts, David Thompson
Global Vice President And General Manager (coca Cola Freestyle Division), Chris Hellmann
Vice President Customer Leadership Capab, Mike Harley
Vice President U S Sales Walmart Custome, Brian Sappington
Vice President Field Operations, Jonathan Leonard
Vp Global Design, James Sommerville
Vice President Field Service, Patrick Plunkett
Vp Commercial Leadership, Andrew Buckingham
Vice President Sales Bu, Doug C Herrington
Vice President Human Resources, Jose A Gomez
Chairman, Muhtar Kent, age 67
Board Member, Barry Diller
Board Member, Robert Kotick
Assistant Secretary, Fiona K Payne
Board Member, Maria Lagomasino
Board Member, Helene Gayle
Auditors: Ernst & Young LLP

LOCATIONS
HQ: Coca-Cola Co (The)
One Coca-Cola Plaza, Atlanta, GA 30313
Phone: 404 676-2121   **Fax:** 404 676-6792
Web: www.coca-colacompany.com

2018 Sales
	$ mil.	% of total
US	11,344	36
Other countries	20,512	64
Total	**31,856**	**100**

2018 Sales
	$ mil.	% of total
North America	11,768	36
Europe Middle East & Africa	7,702	24
Asia Pacific	5,197	16
Latin America	4,014	12
Bottling Investments	3,771	12
Corporate	105	-
Eliminations	(701)	-
Total	**31,856**	**100**

PRODUCTS/OPERATIONS

2018 Sales
	$ mil.	% of total
Concentrate operations	20,457	64
Finished product operations	11,399	36
Total	**31,856**	**100**

Selected Brands
Sparkling Beverages
  Core sparkling
  Barq's
  Coca-Cola
  Coca-Cola Zero/Coke Zero
  Diet Coke/Coca-Cola Light
  Fanta
  Fresca
  Inca Kola
  Lift
  Schweppes
  Sprite
  Thums Up
  Energy drinks
  Burn
  Nos
  Real Gold
Still Beverages
  Coffee & teas
  Ayataka teas
  Dogadan teas
  Georgia coffees
  Leão/Matte Leão teas
  Nestea teas
  Sokenbicha teas
  Juices and juice drinks
  Cappy
  Del Valle
  Dobriy
  Hi-C
  Minute Maid
  Minute Maid Pulpy
  Simply
  Other still beverages
  glaceau vitaminwater
  Fuze
  Sports drinks
  Aquarius
  Powerade
  Waters
  Bonaqua/Bonaqa
  Ciel
  Dasani
  Ice Dew
  Kinley
  ZICO Pure Premium Coconut Water

COMPETITORS
Danone	Monster Beverage
Dole Food	Naked Juice
Dr Pepper Snapple Group	Nestlé
	PepsiCo
IZZE	Red Bull
Kirin Holdings Company	Suntory Holdings
Kraft Heinz	Unilever PLC
Mondelez International	Wonderful Company

HISTORICAL FINANCIALS
Company Type: Public

Income Statement
FYE: December 31

	REVENUE ($ mil.)	NET INCOME ($ mil.)	NET PROFIT MARGIN	EMPLOYEES
12/19	37,266	8,920	23.9%	86,200
12/18	31,856	6,434	20.2%	62,600
12/17	35,410	1,248	3.5%	61,800
12/16	41,863	6,527	15.6%	100,300
12/15	44,294	7,351	16.6%	123,200
Annual Growth	(4.2%)	5.0%	—	(8.5%)

2019 Year-End Financials
Debt ratio: 49.51%—
Return on equity: 49.61%
Cash ($ mil.): 6,480
Current ratio: 0.76
Long-term debt ($ mil.): 27,516

Dividends
  Yield: 2.8%
  Payout: 88.4%
Market value ($ mil.): —

	STOCK PRICE ($) FY Close	P/E High/Low	Earnings	Dividends	Book Value
12/19	55.35	27 21	2.07	1.60	4.43
12/18	47.35	33 28	1.50	1.56	3.98
12/17	45.88	164 139	0.29	1.48	4.01
12/16	41.46	31 27	1.49	1.40	5.38
12/15	42.96	26 22	1.67	1.32	5.91
Annual Growth	6.5%	— —	5.5%	4.9%	(6.9%)

Cognizant Technology Solutions Corp.

Cognizant Technology Solutions is aware of the desire to shift business processes to digital technologies and it wants to help. To help customers make the switch the information technology outsourcing company provides intelligent systems automation cloud technologies and cyber security tools. Cognizant also offers digital services and solutions consulting application development systems integration application testing application maintenance infrastructure services and business process services. The company targets companies in financial services health care manufacturing retail and logistics as well as communications and media. Most of Cognizant's software development centers and employees are in India. Most of the company's revenue is generated in North America.

Operations
Cognizant's financial services business brings in around 35% of revenue followed by the healthcare segment about 30% the products and resources unit over 20% and its communications media and technology operation around 15%.

The company also offers digital services consulting application development systems integration application testing application maintenance infrastructure services and business process services.

Additionally it develops licenses implements and supports proprietary and third-party software products and platforms for the healthcare industry. Overall consulting and technology services generate almost 60% of the company's revenue while the remainder comes from outsourcing services.

Geographic Reach

Cognizant headquartered in Teaneck New Jersey has offices and operations in almost 80 cities including New York London Paris Melbourne Singapore and Sao Paulo in more than 35 countries.

Although it has operations worldwide Cognizant relies heavily on its North American customers (mostly those in the US) which generate more than 75% of its revenue. Combined Europe and the UK constitute the next biggest market accounting for almost 20% of sales.

Sales and Marketing

Cognizant markets and sells through its direct sales force which operates from offices in the US and around the world.

Cognizant's 10 biggest customers account for about 15% of its revenue.

Financial Performance

Cognizant's revenue marched steadily higher for the past five years rising at an annual rate of 8%. The company's net income has been fluctuating in the last five years peaking at 2018.

In 2019 revenue rose to $16.8 billion a 4% increase from $16.1 billion in 2018 with higher sales in each business segment and geographic market. Work to integrate digital technologies into customers' workflows and higher customer spending on discretionary projects helped drive sales higher. Net income was $1842 million in 2019 and $2101 million in 2018.

The decrease in net income is primarily due to a decrease in income from operations partially offset by lower foreign exchange losses as compared to 2018.

Cash and equivalents stood at $2.6 billion in 2019 compared to $1.2 billion in 2018. In 2019 operations generated $2.5 billion. Investing activities generated $1.6 billion. Financing activities used $2.6 billion.

Strategy

Cognizant has aligned its operations to pursue its digital strategy. The company's Digital Business area helps customers design and implement digital business models while the Digital Operations area provides digital tools for managing customers' business processes. The Cognizant Digital Systems and Technology area helps with their digital IT operations.

Cognizant works in a competitive business where margins are thin and companies try to keep costs low. The industry's practice of short-term contracts with customers makes it easy for customers to move to other service providers. Some of Cognizant's competitors are bigger companies with more resources which can make a difference in hiring employees and bidding for acquisitions.

Mergers and Acquisitions

With recent acquisitions Cognizant has expanded its reach in international markets while adding to its digital capabilities.

In mid-2020 Cognizant entered into an agreement to acquire Collaborative Solutions a privately-held global consultancy specializing in Workday enterprise cloud applications for finance and human resources. The transaction is expected to close in the second quarter of 2020 subject to the satisfaction of certain closing conditions including regulatory clearance.

In early 2020 Cognizant entered into an agreement to acquire Lev a privately-held digital marketing consultancy in the U.S. Lev helps businesses simplify and modernize their marketing campaigns using Salesforce Marketing Cloud to provide data-driven insight and personalization across the customer journey and ultimately drive revenue.

In the same year Cognizant entered into exclusive negotiations to acquire the French operations of EI-Technologies a Paris-based privately-held digital technology consulting firm and leading independent Salesforce specialist in France. The pro-posed acquisition would complement Cognizant's global Salesforce practice expanding client resources in Europe.

Cognizant also acquired Code Zero Consulting a privately-held provider of consulting and implementation services for cloud-based Configure-Price-Quote (CPQ) and billing solutions. The acquisition further strengthens Cognizant's cloud solutions portfolio and Salesforce CPQ and billing capabilities. Financial details were not disclosed.

In late 2019 Cognizant entered into an agreement to acquire Contino a privately-held technology consulting firm. Contino specializes in helping Global 2000 clients accelerate their digital transformation by leveraging enterprise DevOps methodologies a cloud-native development approach and advanced data platforms. Headquartered in London Contino has approximately 350 employees worldwide with operations in the United Kingdom the United States and Australia.

In 2019 Cognizant agreed to acquire Zenith Technologies a life sciences manufacturing technology services company headquartered in Cork Ireland. Zenith uses digital technologies to manage control and optimize drug and medical device production. The deal extends Cognizant's services offerings for connected biopharmaceutical and medical device manufacturers. The transaction was expected to close in the 2019 third quarter.

In early 2019 Cognizant acquired Meritsoft a privately-held financial software company based in Dublin Ireland. Meritsoft is best known for its FIN-BOS platform for post-trade processing an intelligent automation solution for managing taxes fees commissions and cash flow functions between financial institutions. Meritsoft's products are currently used by five of the world's eight leading investment banks. Financial details of the transaction were not disclosed.

Company Background

Cognizant Technology Solutions began as an in-house technology center for Dun & Bradstreet in 1994 and was spun off from D&B in 1996. Two years later Cognizant reorganized and spun off its market research operations into two public companies IMS Health and Nielsen Media Research in order to focus on IT services.

EXECUTIVES

President, Rajeev (Raj) Mehta, age 53, $574,100 total compensation

Svp Marketing And Strategy, Malcolm Frank, age 54, $417,000 total compensation

Executive Vice Chairman Cognizant India, Ramakrishnan Chandrasekaran, age 62, $152,925 total compensation

Cfo, Karen McLoughlin, age 55, $426,500 total compensation

Ceo And Director, Francisco D'Souza, age 51, $664,300 total compensation

Coo, Srinivasan Veeraghavachary

Evp And President Global Industries And Consulting, Ramakrishna Prasad Chintamaneni, age 50, $417,250 total compensation

Evp And President Global Client Services, Dharmendra Kumar Sinha, age 57, $356,504 total compensation

Vp And Head Global Corporate Strategy, Pascal Aguirre

Avp Analytics And Information Management, Jay Warren

Assistant Vice President Corporate Development, Sameer Desawale

Assistant Vice President Projects, Ronald Trella

Vice President Corp. Comm., Richard Lacroix

Senior Vice President Of Marketing, Robert Painter

Avp And Partner Cognizant Digital Business Interactive, Imran Masood

Vice President Corporate Communications, Rick Lacroix

Vice President And Corporate Controller, Robert Telesmanic

Vice President, Curtis Girod

Assistant Vice President Software Development, Bob Yengle

Associate Vice President Corporate Communications, Jodi Sorensen

Assistant Vice President Healthcare, Gopal Iyer

Avp And Partner Digital Strategy, John Mcvay

Vice President Corporate Development, Komal Misra

Assistant Vice President, Kshitij Nerurkar

Assistant Vice President Projects, Norma Hauer

Assistant Vice President Technology Services, Dave Bhattacharya

Vp And Partner Healthcare Consulting, Andrew Cohen

Vp Evolutionary Ai, Babak Hodjat

Vice President, Edward Abrams

Vice Chairman, Lakshmi Narayanan, age 67

Chairman, John E. Klein, age 78

Board Member, John N Fox

Auditors: PricewaterhouseCoopers LLP

LOCATIONS

HQ: Cognizant Technology Solutions Corp.
Glenpointe Centre West, 500 Frank W. Burr Blvd., Teaneck, NJ 07666
Phone: 201 801-0233   **Fax:** 201 801-0243
Web: www.cognizant.com

2018 Sales

	$ mil.	% of total
North America	12,293	76
Europe		
United Kingdom	1,274	10
Rest of Europe	1,563	6
Other	995	6
Total	**16,125**	**100**

PRODUCTS/OPERATIONS

Selected Services

Application design development integration and re-engineering
  Complex custom systems development
  Customer relationship management (CRM)
  Data warehousing/Business intelligence (BI)
  Enterprise resource planning (ERP)
  Software testing services
IT consulting and technology services
  Business and knowledge process consulting
  IT strategy consulting
  Program management consulting
  Technology consulting
Outsourcing services
  Application maintenance
  Business and knowledge process outsourcing
  Cloud
  CRM and ERP maintenance
  Custom application maintenance
  IT infrastructure outsourcing
  Mobility

2018 Sales

	$ mil.	% of total
Financial services	5,845	36
Health care	4,668	30
Products and Resources	3,415	21
Communications Media and Technology	2,197	13
Total	**16,125**	**100**

2018 Sales

	$ mil.	% of total
Consulting and Technology Services	9,309	59
Outsourcing Services	6,816	42
Total	**16,125**	**100**

Industries

Industries
Banking & Financial Services
Communications

Consumer Goods
Education
Energy & Utilities
Healthcare
Information Services
Insurance
Life Sciences
Manufacturing
Media & Entertainment
Retail
Technology
Transportation & Logistics
Travel & Hospitality

COMPETITORS

Accenture	Genpact
Atos	HCL Technologies
Capgemini	IBM Global Services
Computer Sciences	Infosys
Corp.	Tata Consultancy
EPAM	Wipro

HISTORICAL FINANCIALS

Company Type: Public

Income Statement
FYE: December 31

	REVENUE ($ mil.)	NET INCOME ($ mil.)	NET PROFIT MARGIN	EMPLOYEES
12/19	16,783	1,842	11.0%	292,500
12/18	16,125	2,101	13.0%	281,600
12/17	14,810	1,504	10.2%	260,000
12/16	13,487	1,553	11.5%	260,200
12/15	12,416	1,623	13.1%	221,700
Annual Growth	7.8%	3.2%	—	7.2%

2019 Year-End Financials

Debt ratio: 4.55%
Return on equity: 16.41%
Cash ($ mil.): 2,645
Current ratio: 2.55
Long-term debt ($ mil.): 700

No. of shares (mil.): 548
Dividends
Yield: 1.2%
Payout: 21.6%
Market value ($ mil.): 33,987

	STOCK PRICE ($) FY Close	P/E High/Low	PER SHARE ($) Earnings	Dividends	Book Value
12/19	62.02	23 17	3.29	0.80	20.11
12/18	63.48	23 17	3.60	0.80	19.80
12/17	71.02	30 20	2.53	0.45	18.14
12/16	56.03	25 19	2.55	0.00	17.64
12/15	60.02	26 19	2.65	0.00	15.23
Annual Growth	0.8%	— —	5.6%	—	7.2%

Colgate-Palmolive Co.

Colgate-Palmolive is a leader in toothpaste (it has more than 40% of the global market) and soap and cleaning products. The company also offers pet nutrition products through subsidiary Hill's Pet Nutrition which makes Science Diet and Prescription Diet pet foods. Many of its oral care products fall under the Colgate brand and include toothbrushes mouthwash and dental floss. Its Tom's of Maine unit covers the natural toothpaste niche. Personal and home care items include Ajax brand household cleaner Palmolive dishwashing liquid Softsoap shower gel and Sanex and Speed Stick deodorants. Colgate-Palmolive sells its products in more than 200 countries and generates most of its sales outside the US.

HISTORY

William Colgate founded The Colgate Company in Manhattan in 1806 to produce soap candles and starch. Colgate died in 1857 and the company was passed to his son Samuel who renamed it Colgate and Company. In 1873 the company introduced toothpaste in jars and in 1896 it began selling Colgate Dental Cream in tubes. By 1906 Colgate was making 160 kinds of soap 625 perfumes and 2000 other products. The company went public in 1908.

In 1898 Milwaukee's B. J. Johnson Soap Company (founded 1864) introduced Palmolive a soap made of palm and olive oils rather than smelly animal fats. It became so popular that the firm changed its name to The Palmolive Company in 1916. Ten years later Palmolive merged with Peet Brothers a Kansas City-based soap maker founded in 1872. Palmolive-Peet merged with Colgate in 1928 forming Colgate-Palmolive-Peet (shortened to Colgate-Palmolive in 1953). The stock market crash of 1929 prevented a planned merger of the company with Hershey and Kraft.

During the 1930s the firm purchased French and German soap makers and opened branches in Europe. Colgate-Palmolive-Peet introduced Fab detergent and Ajax cleanser in 1947 and the brands soon became top sellers in Europe. The company expanded to Asia in the 1950s and by 1961 foreign sales were 52% of the total.

Colgate-Palmolive introduced a host of products in the 1960s and 1970s including Palmolive dishwashing liquid (1966) Ultra Brite toothpaste (1968) and Irish Spring soap (1972). During the same time the company diversified by buying approximately 70 other businesses including Kendall hospital and industrial supplies (1972) Helena Rubinstein cosmetics (1973) Ram Golf (1974) and Riviana Foods and Hill's Pet Products (1976). The strategy had mixed results and most of these acquisitions were sold in the 1980s.

Reuben Mark became CEO of Colgate-Palmolive in 1984. The company bought 50% of Southeast Asia's leading toothpaste Darkie in 1985; it changed its name to Darlie in 1989 following protests of its minstrel-in-blackface trademark. Both Palmolive automatic dishwasher detergent and Colgate Tartar Control toothpaste were introduced in 1986. That year Colgate-Palmolive purchased the liquid soap lines of Minnetonka the most popular of which is Softsoap. In 1992 the company bought Mennen maker of Speed Stick (the leading US deodorant).

Increasing its share of the oral care market in Latin America to 79% in 1995 Colgate-Palmolive acquired Brazilian company Kolynos (from Wyeth for $1 billion) and 94% of Argentina's Odol Saic. The company also bought Ciba-Geigy's oral hygiene business in India increasing its share of that toothpaste market. At home however sales and earnings in key segments were dismal so in 1995 Colgate-Palmolive began a restructuring that included cutting more than 8% of its employees and closing or reconfiguring 24 factories in two years.

The company introduced a record 602 products in 1996 and continued to expand its operations in countries with emerging economies. In 1997 Colgate-Palmolive took the lead in the US toothpaste market for the first time in 35 years (displacing P&G).

In 1999 the company sold the rights to Baby Magic (shampoos lotions oils) in the US Canada and Puerto Rico to Playtex Products retaining the rights in all other countries. Two years later the company sold its heavy-duty laundry detergent business in Mexico (primarily the Viva brand) to Henkel one of Europe's leading detergent producers.

In 2002 Colgate-Palmolive introduced a teeth-whitening gel Simply White to compete with rival P&G's Crest Whitestrips. The company saw success that year when its Hill's Pet Nutrition subsidiary launched new specialty foods for cats and dogs; one of its dog foods reportedly slows brain aging in canines.

In late 2004 Colgate-Palmolive implemented a four-year restructuring plan. Its three primary objectives were to increase profit reallocate resources to promising growth areas and leverage global market efficiencies. It implemented the plan by reducing its global workforce by some 12% closing about 25 of its 78 factories and focusing on core units. Colgate-Palmolive also built new state-of-the-art plants to produce toothpaste in the US and Poland. The company believed that its savings estimated at $500 million altogether would allow it to fund investments in its key businesses as well as provide for new product development.

By selling its North American laundry detergent brands in 2005 Colgate-Palmolive began focusing on the high-margin pearly whites (with bite) of its portfolio — oral care and pet care. The company's purchase of natural oral-care products maker Tom's of Maine in 2006 marked its effort to target the natural niche. It bought some 84% of the firm for about $100 million.

Chairman and CEO Reuben Mark handed over the title of CEO to then-president and COO Ian Cook in July 2007 and the title of chairman to Cook in January 2009; Mark retired at the end of 2008.

Colgate-Palmolive in early 2010 sold its Code 10 brand which boasted about a 10% market share. Indian consumer goods maker Marico acquired the Malaysian hair-styling name; the move was intended to allow Colgate-Palmolive to focus on its oral personal and pet care businesses.

EXECUTIVES

Cfo, Dennis J. Hickey, age 71, $910,000 total compensation
Chairman President And Ceo, Ian M. Cook, age 68, $1,309,000 total compensation
Vice President Of Finance, Philip Shotts
President Global Oral Care, Suzan F. Harrison
Vp Colgate United Kingdom, Chris E. Pedersen
President Colgate Mexico, Ricardo (Ricky) Ramos
Chief Supply Chain Officer, Michael A. (Mike) Corbo
President Colgate Latin America, Panagiotis Tsourapas
Coo Global Innovation And Growth And Hill's Pet Nutrition, Noel R. Wallace
President And Ceo Hill's Pet Nutrition, Peter Brons-Poulsen
Coo North America Europe Africa/eurasia And Global Sustainability, P. Justin Skala, age 61, $734,333 total compensation
Vp And General Manager Colgate Canada, Derek A. Gordon
Vp And General Manager Colgate Caribbean, Bernal Saborio
Vp And Controller, Henning Jakobsen, age 60
President Colgate-africa/eurasia, Jean-Luc Fischer
Vp And General Manager Colgate Central Europe East, Wojciech Krol
Vp And General Manager Colgate Brazil, Andrea Lagioia
Vp And General Manager Colgate Venezuela, Francisco Munoz Ramirez
Cto, Patricia Verduin, age 60
President Colgate-north America, Juan Pablo Zamorano
Vp And General Manager Colgate Latin America, Massimo Poli
Vp; General Manager Colgate-venezuela, Ruben Young
Vp; General Manager Colgate-italy, Vinod Nambiar
Vp And General Manager Colgate-north Africa Middle East, Burc Cankat
Vp And General Manager Colgate Northern Europe, Philip Durocher
Cio, Mike Crowe

Vp And General Manager Colgate India And South Asia, Issam Bachaalani
President Colgate Europe, Prabha Parameswaran
Vp And General Manager Colgate-philippines, Arvind Sachdev
Vp Hill's Pet Nutrition-eurasia, David Scharf
Vp And General Manager Colgate Central Europe West, Dany Schmidt
Vp And General Manager Greater China, Stephen Lau
Vp And General Manager Colgate North America, Bill Van de Graaf
Vp And Gm Colgate Andina Region, Hector Pedraza
Chief Information And Business Services Officer, Thomas (Tom) Greene
Vp And General Manager Global Toothbrush Division, Christopher Rector
Vp And General Manager Colgate-north America, Anne-Marie Motte
Vp And General Manager Colgate-north America, Julie Dillon
Vp And General Manager Tom's Of Maine, Nancy Pak
Vp And General Manager Colgate Western Europe, Andrew Shepard
Vp And General Manager Colgate South Africa, Orlando Tenorio
Vp And General Manager Global Personal Care, John Hazlin
Vp And General Manager Colgate Southern Cone, Adriana Leite
Vp And General Manager Hawley & Hazel, Eddie Niem
Vice President Global Information Technology, Paul McGarry
Vice President Colgate Latin America, Pablo Mascolo
Vice President Sourcing, Katherine Freeley
Vice President Of Design, Robert Dietz
Vice President Deputy General Counsel Operations, Rosemary Nelson
Vp Safety Sustainability And Supply Chain Strategy, Ann Tracy
Vice President Global Supply Chain, Warren Pruitt
Vice President Global Legal, Peter Graylin
National Account Manager, Jenny Squier
Vice President Worldwide Shopper Marketing, Steve Fogarty
Vice President Global Information Technology, Marianne Delorenzo
Vice President Colgate Africa Middle East, Robert Tatera
Vice President, Tom Boyd
Vice President Global Advertising And Digital, Jack Haber
Vp And Corporate Treasurer, Elaine Paik
Vp And Gm Colgate Eurasia, Alan Wolpert
Vice President Ethics And Compliance, Bob Holland
Vice President Of Supply Chain, Manuel Arrese
Svp Chief Of Staff, John J Huston
Vice President Global Research And Development, Daniel Bagley
Senior Vice President Investor Relations, Jon Simon
National Account Manager, Susan Siao
Vice President Colgate Latin America, Jose Fernando Serrano
Vice President And General Manager Colgate Southern Europe, Riccardo Ricci
Senior Vice President Investor Relations, John Faucher
Vice President Global Legal, Lisa Mather
Vice President Hill 's Pet Nutrition, Donald Beatty
Vice President Corporate Audit, Gregory Malcolm
Vice President Colgate Asia Pacific, Iain Kielty
Vice President Colgate Africa Eurasia, Godfrey Nthunzi
Vice President Colgate Europe And Africa Eurasia, Robert Hofmann
Vice President Colgate Africa Eurasia, Debashish Roy
Vice President Hill 's Pet Nutrition, Michele Ross
Vice President Colgate Mexico, Diana Geofroy
Vice President And General Manager Colgate Central America, Francisco Munoz
Vice President Global Sustainability And Environmental Health And Safety, Lori Michelin
Vice President And Gm Colgate Cace, Shekar Bharatwaj
Senior Vice President General Counsel, Andrew Hendry
Vice President, Danielle Koffer
Vice President Colgate Latin America, Kim Faulker
Vp Chief Security Officer, Nancy Rolph
Executive Vice President Chief Growth And Strategy Officer, Justin Skala
Vice President Colgate Latin America, Jose Fernando Fernando Serrano
Vp And Gm Colgate Greater China, Winnie Wong
Executive Vice President Strategic Business Operations Customer And Partner Engagement Salesforce.com Inc., Lisa M Edwards
Executive Vice President Chief Growth And Strategy Officer, Peter Skala
Vice Chairman, Franck J. Moison, age 67
Board Member, Stephen Sadove
Board Member, Crystal Harris
Board Member, John Bilbrey
Board Member, Lorrie Norrington
Board Member, Michael Polk
Board Member, Charles Bancroft
Auditors: PricewaterhouseCoopers LLP

LOCATIONS

HQ: Colgate-Palmolive Co.
300 Park Avenue, New York, NY 10022
Phone: 212 310-2000 Fax: 212 310-3284
Web: www.colgatepalmolive.com

2018 Sales

	$ mil.	% of total
Oral personal & home care		
Latin America	3,605	23
North America	3,348	22
Asia Pacific	2,734	18
Europe	2,502	16
Africa/Eurasia	967	6
Pet nutrition	2,388	15
Total	**15,544**	**100**

PRODUCTS/OPERATIONS

2018 Sales

	$ mil.	% of total
Oral personal & home care	13,156	85
Pet nutrition	2,388	15
Total	**15,544**	**100**

Selected Brands

Home Care
  Ajax
  Brite
  Murphy Oil Soap
  Palmolive
  Suavitel
Oral Care
  Colgate
  Tom's of Maine
Personal Care
  Afta
  Irish Spring
  Sanex
  Softsoap
  Speed Stick
  Tender Care
Pet Nutrition
  Hill's Prescription Diet
  Hill's Science Diet

COMPETITORS

Church & Dwight	Nestlé
Clorox	Nu Skin
General Mills	Philips Oral
GlaxoSmithKline	Procter & Gamble
Hain Celestial	Reckitt Benckiser
Henkel	Sun Products
Johnson & Johnson	Unilever NV
Kimberly-Clark	

HISTORICAL FINANCIALS

Company Type: Public

Income Statement

FYE: December 31

	REVENUE ($ mil.)	NET INCOME ($ mil.)	NET PROFIT MARGIN	EMPLOYEES
12/19	15,693	2,367	15.1%	34,300
12/18	15,544	2,400	15.4%	34,500
12/17	15,454	2,024	13.1%	35,900
12/16	15,195	2,441	16.1%	36,700
12/15	16,034	1,384	8.6%	37,900
Annual Growth	(0.5%)	14.4%	—	(2.5%)

2019 Year-End Financials

Debt ratio: 52.20%	No. of shares (mil.): 854
Return on equity: 31,560.00%	Dividends
Cash ($ mil.): 883	Yield: 2.4%
Current ratio: 1.03	Payout: 62.1%
Long-term debt ($ mil.): 7,333	Market value ($ mil.): 58,838

	STOCK PRICE ($) FY Close	P/E High/Low	PER SHARE ($) Earnings	Dividends	Book Value
12/19	68.84	27 21	2.75	1.71	0.14
12/18	59.52	28 21	2.75	1.66	(0.12)
12/17	75.45	34 28	2.28	1.59	(0.07)
12/16	65.44	27 23	2.72	1.55	(0.28)
12/15	66.62	47 39	1.52	1.50	(0.33)
Annual Growth	0.8%	— —	16.0%	3.3%	—

COLORADO HOUSING AND FINANCE AUTHORITY

EXECUTIVES

Ceo, Cris A White
Chief Operating Officer*, Jaime Gomez
Cfo*, Patricia Hippe
Int Gen Coun*, Charles L Borgman
Senior Developer, Bill Spencer
Communications Specialist, Heather Johnson
Executive Officer, Julie Chelin
Executive Officer, Margaret Miller
Officer, Mike Pacheco
Business Specialis, Paige Omohundro
Compliance Staff, Shelia Anderson
Auditors: RSM US LLP DENVER COLORADO

LOCATIONS

HQ: COLORADO HOUSING AND FINANCE AUTHORITY
1981 BLAKE ST, DENVER, CO 802021229
Phone: 303 297-2432
Web: WWW.CHFAINFO.COM

HISTORICAL FINANCIALS

Company Type: Private

Income Statement   FYE: December 31

	ASSETS ($ mil.)	NET INCOME ($ mil.)	INCOME AS % OF ASSETS	EMPLOYEES
12/18	2,354	52	2.2%	150
12/17	2,192	52	2.4%	—
12/16	2,037	24	1.2%	—
Annual Growth	7.5%	46.9%	—	—

Columbia Banking System Inc

Columbia Banking System (CBS) is the roughly $13 billion-asset holding company for Columbia Bank. The regional community bank has about 150 branches in Washington from Puget Sound to the timber country in the southwestern part of the state as well as in northern Oregon and Idaho. Targeting retail and small to medium-sized business customers the bank offers standard retail services such as checking and savings accounts CDs IRAs credit cards loans and mortgages. Commercial and multifamily residential real estate loans make up about 45% of the company's loan portfolio while business loans make up another 40%.

Financial Performance

Bolstered by consistent growth in its loan and securities portfolio caused by acquisitions and organic growth Columbia Banking System (CBS) has seen rising revenue each of the last five years to yield an overall expansion of more than 50%; net income fared even better?more than doubling in that time as the bank consolidated physical branches.

The holding company increased its revenue 22% to $565.9 million in 2018 on a large increase in CBS's loan and securities portfolios following its 2017 acquisition of Pacific Continental the parent company of Pacific Continental Bank?which had $2.9 billion in assets.

CBS's net income rose 53% to $172.9 million on the strength of its revenue gains and a lower income tax provision caused by US tax reform.

The company used $64.9 million of its cash in 2018 to end the year with $277.6 million. Operations provided $237.2 million and financing activities?primarily Federal Home Loan Bank advances?generated $203.9 million. CBS used $506 million on investments which mainly comprised purchases of debt securities available for sale.

Strategy

Columbia Banking System (CBS) has grown its loan and securities base recently through a major acquisition while reducing its costs by consolidating physical branches and adopting digital banking technologies.

In 2017 CBS acquired Pacific Continental for $644.8 million. Pacific Continental is the holding company for Pacific Continental Bank which had 14 branches in Oregon and Washington. The purchase gave CBS $2.9 billion in assets (including $1.9 billion in loans) and $2.1 billion in deposits.

Amid the rising popularity of digital banking CBS consolidated one branch in 2017 and seven branches in 2018. It has plans to consolidate a further three branches in 3Q19. The company's 2018 digital banking initiatives include programs to enable digital commercial business and healthcare banking; use data to drive its workforce; upgrade its digital enterprise workflows; and expand its base of employees with expertise in the digital environment. CBS's Columbia Connect platform allows retail customers to deposit checks pay bills transfer funds or locate physical branches or ATMs via internet-connected devices.

Company Background

Columbia Banking System took advantage of the rash of bank failures in past years to increase its presence in the Pacific Northwest region. It added more than 30 branches in 2010 when it acquired most of the deposits and assets of failed banks Columbia River Bank and American Marine Bank a week apart. In similar transactions in 2011 it acquired most of the operations of the failed institutions Summit Bank First Heritage Bank and Bank of Whitman. Those deals added more than a dozen branches in Washington.

EXECUTIVES

Evp And Chief Credit Officer, Andrew L. (Andy) McDonald, age 61, $298,000 total compensation

Evp And Cfo, Clint E. Stein, age 49, $345,000 total compensation

Ceo, Hadley S. Robbins, age 63, $369,827 total compensation

Evp And General Counsel, Kumi Yamamoto Baruffi, age 50

Evp And Chief Human Resources Officer, David C. (Dave) Lawson, age 62, $247,500 total compensation

Vice President Senior Financial Advisor With Cb Financial, John Brunk

Vice President, Thomas Poole

Svp Chief Innovation Officer Banking Solutions And Innovation, Bruce Morehead

Vice President Commercial Banking Officer, Antoine White

Senior Vice President Relationship Manager, Gus Martin

Vice President, Harold Boucher

Vice President Private Banking Relationship Manager, Donna Himpler

Avp Wealth Advisor, Ron Polluconi

Vice President Account Credit Adm, Gary Crawford

Senior Vice President Director Loan Operations, Carol Friend

Vice President, Canen Madsen

Vice President Branch Manager Maple Valley Branch, Nick Duben

Senior Vice President Commercial Relationship Banking Officer Fox Tower, Lisa Banoff

Svp, Michael Evans

Vice President Branch Manager Iii, Alfredo Aguilar

Vice President, Chris Skandalis

Vice President Market Manager, Suzanne Vanamburgh

As Vice President Business Development Officer, Derek Rawnsley

Assistant Vice President Branch Manager, Marc Silva

Vice President Treasury Management Officer, Rhonda VanOrder

Chairman And Interim Ceo Columbia Banking System; Chairman Columbia Bank, William T. Weyerhaeuser, age 77

Auditors: DELOITTE & TOUCHE LLP

LOCATIONS

HQ: Columbia Banking System Inc
   1301 A Street, Tacoma, WA 98402-2156
Phone: 253 305-1900
Web: www.columbiabank.com

2018 Branches

	No.
Washington	74
Oregon	62
Idaho	14
Total	**150**

PRODUCTS/OPERATIONS

2018 Revenue

	% of total
Net Interest Income	
Loans	73
Taxable securities	10
Tax-exempt securities	2
Non-interest Income	15
Total	**100**

COMPETITORS

BECU	JPMorgan Chase
Bank of America	KeyCorp
Banner Corp	U.S. Bancorp
Heritage Financial	Washington Federal
HomeStreet	Wells Fargo

HISTORICAL FINANCIALS

Company Type: Public

Income Statement   FYE: December 31

	ASSETS ($ mil.)	NET INCOME ($ mil.)	INCOME AS % OF ASSETS	EMPLOYEES
12/19	14,079	194	1.4%	2,162
12/18	13,095	172	1.3%	2,137
12/17	12,716	112	0.9%	2,120
12/16	9,509	104	1.1%	1,819
12/15	8,951	98	1.1%	1,868
Annual Growth	12.0%	18.4%	—	3.7%

2019 Year-End Financials

Debt ratio: 0.25%	No. of shares (mil.): 72
Return on equity: 9.27%	Dividends
Cash ($ mil.): 247	Yield: 3.4%
Current ratio: —	Payout: 52.8%
Long-term debt ($ mil.): —	Market value ($ mil.): 2,934

	STOCK PRICE ($) FY Close	P/E High/Low		Earnings	PER SHARE ($) Dividends	Book Value
12/19	40.69	15	12	2.68	1.40	29.95
12/18	36.29	20	14	2.36	1.14	27.76
12/17	43.44	25	19	1.86	0.88	26.70
12/16	44.68	25	15	1.81	1.53	21.55
12/15	32.51	21	15	1.71	1.34	21.52
Annual Growth	5.8%	—	—	11.9%	1.1%	8.6%

Columbia Financial Inc

Auditors: KPMG LLP

LOCATIONS

HQ: Columbia Financial Inc
   19-01 Route 208 North, Fair Lawn, NJ 07410
Phone: 800 522-4167
Web: www.columbiabankonline.com

HISTORICAL FINANCIALS

Company Type: Public

Income Statement   FYE: December 31

	ASSETS ($ mil.)	NET INCOME ($ mil.)	INCOME AS % OF ASSETS	EMPLOYEES
12/19	8,188	54	0.7%	698
12/18	6,691	22	0.3%	663
12/17*	5,766	3	0.1%	—
09/17	5,429	31	0.6%	679
09/16	5,037	32	0.7%	—
Annual Growth	17.6%	18.4%	—	—

*Fiscal year change

2019 Year-End Financials

Debt ratio: 1.61%	No. of shares (mil.): 113
Return on equity: 5.60%	Dividends
Cash ($ mil.): 75	Yield: —
Current ratio: —	Payout: —
Long-term debt ($ mil.): —	Market value ($ mil.): 1,927

	STOCK PRICE ($) FY Close	P/E High/Low	PER SHARE ($) Earnings	Dividends	Book Value
12/19	16.94	35 30	0.49	0.00	8.64
12/18	15.29	88 74	0.20	0.00	8.39
Annual Growth	3.5%	— —	34.8%	—	1.0%

Comcast Corp

Comcast is one of the biggest pay-TV providers in the US with more than 30 million subscribers to its cable systems. Its broadband internet service has nearly 30 million subscribers video has about 21 million subscribers and its voice service has 10 more than million customers. On the content side the company owns NBCUniversal including the NBC TV network and movie studios Universal Pictures and DreamWorks Animation. Cable channels CNBC MSNBC and the USA Network are also under the Comcast tent. Other Comcast properties include the Universal Studios theme parks and Telemundo a leading Spanish-language TV network.

Operations

Comcast operates three primary businesses: Comcast Cable (Cable Communication) NBCUniversal (Cable Networks Broadcast Television Filmed Entertainment and Theme Parks) and Sky.

The cable business accounting for more than half of revenue offers internet video voice and security and automation services in the US under the Xfinity brand.

NBCUniversal operates four business segments: Cable Networks around 10% of revenue which provides entertainment news and information and sports content as well as regional sports and news networks; Broadcast Television nearly 10% of revenue consists primarily of the NBC and Telemundo broadcast networks; Filmed Entertainment about 5% of revenue owns Universal Pictures which makes and distributes movies; and NBCUniversal's Theme Parks also 5% of revenue consists primarily of Universal theme parks in Orlando Florida; Hollywood California; and Osaka Japan.

Sky (nearly 20% of revenue) consist of operation in Europe providing services including Sky News broadcast network and Sky Sports networks.

Comcast also provides wireless telephone service through its Xfinity Mobile brand. Through its majority-owned subsidiary Comcast Spectacor the company owns the Philadelphia Flyers of the NHL as well as the team's arena the Wells Fargo Center.

Geographic Reach

Comcast based in Philadelphia has operations of one kind or another in all 50 states. Its cable communications operations are along the East Coast in the South the Midwest the West Coast and Pacific Northwest. The company owns and operates about 10 NBC-affiliate TV stations in the some of the top markets in the country. In Europe Sky operates three of the four largest pay television markets in Western Europe: UK Italy and Germany.

Even with the international expansion through the Sky acquisition Comcast's revenue is concentrated in the US which supplies around 75% of sales.

Sales and Marketing

Comcast offers its services directly to residential and business customers through call centers door-to-door selling direct mail advertising television advertising internet advertising local media advertising telemarketing and retail outlets. The company spends about $7.6 billion a year on advertising marketing and promotion.

Financial Performance

Comcast's revenue had grown at a steady 9% average rate over the past five years as the company had added to its stable of telecom and content through acquisitions.

In 2019 revenue rose 15% to $108.9 billion up about $14.4 billion from 2018. Growth in their Cable Communications segment driven by increased revenue from residential high-speed internet business services and wireless partially offset by decreased revenue from advertising video and voice.

Net income increased to $13.1 billion in 2019 $1.3 billion more than in 2018. The increase was primarily due to the increase on their revenue but offset with also the increase of cost and expenses.

Comcast held $5.6 billion in cash and equivalents in 2019 compared to $3.9 billion in 2018. Operations generated $25.7 billion in 2019 while investing activities used $14.8 billion and financing activities used $9.2 billion.

Strategy

Comcast expects its capital expenditures for 2020 will be focused on the continued investment in scalable infrastructure to increase network capacity in its Cable Communications segment; increased investment in line extensions for the expansion of both business services and residential; and the continued deployment of wireless gateways the company's X1 platform cloud DVR technology Sky Q and international OTT platforms. In addition they expect to continue to invest in existing and new attractions at their Universal theme parks including the additional theme park being constructed in Orlando Florida. Capital expenditures for subsequent years will depend on numerous factors including acquisitions competition changes in technology regulatory changes the timing and rate of deployment of new services the capacity required for existing services and the timing of new attractions at their theme parks.

Mergers and Acquisitions

In 2019 Comcast acquired Deep Blue Communications which engineers installs and manages commercial WiFi networks. Comcast intends to combine its networks with Deep Blue's intelligent managed WiFi and create greater efficiency for businesses. Terms were not disclosed.

In 2019 Comcast bought BluVector which uses artificial intelligence and machine learning to provide cybersecurity protection to companies and government agencies. Verizon and BluVector planned to build on BluVector's existing business and to develop new cybersecurity technologies. Terms were not disclosed.

Company Background

In 1963 Ralph Roberts Daniel Aaron and Julian Brodsky bought American Cable Systems in Tupelo Mississippi. The company soon expanded throughout the state. In 1969 the company got a new name: Comcast combining "communications" and "broadcast." Two years later Comcast acquired franchises in western Pennsylvania and when it went public in 1972 it moved to Philadelphia.

Comcast bought up local operations nationwide through the early 1980s and gained its first foreign cable franchise in 1983 in London (it sold its affiliate there to NTL — now Virgin Media— in 1998). It took a 26% stake in the large Group W Cable in 1986. Roberts also lent financial support that year to a fledgling home-shopping channel called QVC— for "quality value and convenience."

A big step into telecommunications came in 1988 when Comcast bought American Cellular Network with Delaware and New Jersey franchises. Two years later Roberts' son Brian — who had trained as a cable installer during a summer away from college — became Comcast's president.

In 1992 Comcast bought Metromedia's Philadelphia-area cellular operations and began investing in fiber-optic and wireless phone companies. By then the company was a major QVC shareholder. With an eye toward Comcast's programming needs Brian persuaded FOX network head Barry Diller to become QVC's chairman. But when Diller tried to use QVC to take over CBS Comcast bought control of QVC in 1994 to quash the bid which went against cross-ownership bans. To pay for QVC Comcast had to sell its 20% stake in cable firm Heritage Communications in 1995. Diller left the company to oversee for a time InterActiveCorp parent of QVC's archrival HSN. Also in 1995 Comcast funded former Disney executive Richard Frank to launch the C3 (Comcast Content and Communication) programming company.

EXECUTIVES

Sevp And Ceo Nbcuniversal, Stephen B. (Steve) Burke, $2,797,499 total compensation

Chairman And Ceo, Brian L. Roberts, $3,013,510 total compensation

Chairman Nbc News And Msnbc, Andrew R. (Andy) Lack

Chairman And Ceo Universal Parks & Resorts (upr), Thomas L. (Tom) Williams

Chairman Nbc Broadcasting And Sports, Mark H. Lazarus

Sevp; President And Ceo Comcast Cable, David N. (Dave) Watson

Chairman Nbcuniversal Cable Entertainment Group, Bonnie Hammer

President Comcast Spotlight, Charlie Thurston

Sevp, David L. Cohen, $1,475,621 total compensation

Evp General Counsel And Secretary, Arthur R. Block, $900,000 total compensation

Svp And Managing Director And Head Of Funds Comcast Ventures, Amy L. Banse

Chairman Nbc Entertainment, Robert (Bob) Greenblatt

Evp And Chief Communications Officer, D'Arcy F. Rudnay

Head Of Comcast Mobile, Greg R. Butz

President And Ceo Comcast-spectator, David A. (Dave) Scott

Sevp And Cfo, Michael J. (Mike) Cavanagh, $1,843,408 total compensation

President And Ceo Cnbc, Mark Hoffman

President Comcast Business Services, William R. (Bill) Stemper

Chairman Nbcuniversal International, Kevin MacLellan

Chairman Nbcuniversal International Group And Nbcuniversal Telemundo Enterprises, Cesar Conde

Chairman Nbc Universal Content Distribution, Matt Bond

President Advertising, Marcien Jenckes

Chairman Universal Filmed Entertainment Group, Jeff Shell

Svp Global Chief Information Security Officer (gciso), Myrna Soto

Evp Global Corporate Development And Strategy, Bob Eatroff

President Comcast Foundation, Dalila Wilson-Scott

President Technology And Product Comcast Cable, Tony G. Werner

President Comcast Cable West Division, Steve White

President Comcast Cable Central Division, Bill Connors

Senior Vice President Financial Planning And Analysis, Greg Horn

Senior Vice President Investor Relations And Finance, Peter Armstrong

National Sales Manager, Paul Gilbert

Svp Greater Boston Region Comcast Cable, Tracy Pitcher

National Sales Manager, Gigi Dolan

Vice President Of Engineering, Richard Newcomb

Divisional Vice President For The Western Division Comcast Spotlight, Rick Stanley

Vice President Finance, Angela Masterson

Vice President, Randall Hounsell

Vice President Learning And Development Customer Service, Lisa Dicocco-newman

Vice President Intellectual Property, Mark Dellinger

Senior Vice President, Jan Hofmeyr

Vice President Human Resources, Greg Geshel

Senior Vice President Procurement, Jeur Abeln

National Account Manager, Joann Renner

Svp General Manager Digital, John Williamson

Division Vice President, Dave Kowolenko

Vice President Finance And Accounting, Chris Lawler

Senior Vice President Brand Marketing, Todd Arata

Vice President, Juan Otero

Vice President Comcast Assurance, Anthony Deshan

Svp Freedom Region Northeast Division Comcast Cable, Jim Samaha

Vice President Of Marketing, Michael Volosin

Senior Vice President Finance And Accounting, John Iadanza

Vice President, Jingyu Zhou

Svp Customer Experience Comcast Corp., Kyle Mcslarrow

Vice President, Scott Wood

Svp Customer Experience Comcast Cable, Piers Lingle

National Sales Manager, Jesse Woodnal

Vice President Affiliate Finance, Victor Viola

Vice President Corporate Development Comcast Corp., Mark Noble

Vice President Cdv Implementation, Mike Bradshaw

Vice President Of Government And Regulatory Affairs, Kevin Broadhurst

National Account Manager, Lisa Reese

National Sales Manager, Brad Carroll

Vice President Finance And Accounting, Barry Corcoran

Vice President Of Human Resources, Samantha Callahan

Senior Vice President Global Public Policy, Rebecca Arbogast

Vice President Strategic Development, Marc Siry

Senior Vice President Next Generation Access Networks, Elad Nafshi

Senior Vice President Communications Nbcuniversal News Group, Mark Kornblau

Vp Hr, Lori Boruch

Svp, Michael Cox

Vice President Enterprise Business Intelligence, Trace Hawkins

Vice President Business Services Comcast, Kalyn Hove

Vice President, Michael Ruger

Senior Vice President Of Finance, Susan Waarheid

Svp Greater Chicago Region Central Division Comcast Cable, John Crowley

Vice President Engineering, Michael Spaulding

Vp Customer Care Operations, Veronica Jellison

Vice President Financial Operations, Bruce Wilson

Svp Heartland Region Central Division Comcast Cable, Tim Collins

Vice President Design, Robb D'egidio

Senior Vice President Marketing Northeast Division Comcast Cable, Randy Waddell

Division Vice President, Leslie Buckley

Regional Vice President, Terry Taylor

Vice President And Deputy General Counsel, David Copas

Senior Vice President, Lisa Bonnell

Svp Applied Analytics, Marc Sirota

Vice President, Tom Donnelly

Svp External Affairs West Division Comcast Cable, Chris Mcdonald

Vice President Human Resources, Norene Miller

Senior Vice President Government, Sena Fitzmaurice

Senior Vice President Finance, Steven Croney

Svp Beltway Region Northeast Division Comcast Cable, Mary Mclaughlin

Svp And Gm Communications Data And Mibility Comcast Cable, Eric Schaefer

Evp Xfinity Services Comcast Cable, Matthew Strauss

Svp Engineering And Operations Central Division Comcast Cable, Dan Murphy

Vice President Human Resources, Michael Eagles

Vice President Marketing, Carolyne Hannan

Vice President, Rob Omberg

Vice President Sales And Marketing, Stephen Krom

National Sales Manager, Sara Doyle

Vice President Of Advertising Sales, Craig Coane

Evp Human Resources Comcast Cable, William Strahan

Vice President Sales And Marketing, Sameer Bhatti

Vice President Video Subscription Services, Michael Gatzke

Vp Product Design And Customer Experience, Rui Costa

Vice President Public Relations, Cindy Parsons

Senior Vice President Customer Care West Division Comcast Cable, Cathy Kilstrom

Svp Finance And Treasurer, William Dordelman

Vice President Outsourcing Strategy And Support Ecare, Joy Park

Vice President Of Operations, Tom Kearney

Vice President Technical Operations, Mike Burnett

Vice President Finance, Scott Knaub

Senior Vice President, Teresa Lucido

National Sales Manager, John Brocato

Vice President Marketing Communications, Barbara Hedges

National Sales Manager, Ella Parisi

Vice President Public Relations, Jeff Alexander

Senior Vice President Customer Care, Michael Mcardle

Vice President 2, Theressa Dulaney

Evp Global Corporate Development And Strategy, Robert Eatroff

Vice President Accounting And Finance, Greg Snyder

Division Vice President Customer Care, Chris Weeks

Senior Vice President Product Engineering And Operations, Cossette Cheryl

Vice President Government Affairs Central Division, Michael Mitchell

Vice President Public Relations, Alex Horwitz

Vice President Of Marketing, Dara Leslie

Vice President Government And Regulatory Affairs, Timothy Murnane

Vice President Xfinity.com, Philip Marcella

Vp Of Communications, Beth Bacha

National Sales Manager, James Ostrander

Senior Vice President Retail Sales And Service, Tom Devito

Regional Vice President, Jd Keller

Vice President, Thomas Fad

Vice President Product Marketing, Lisa Ahern

Vice President Human Resources, Carolyn Seckinger

Vice President Business Services Heartland Region, Michelle Pluskota

Vp Care Operations, Ken Fowler

National Sales Manager, Richard Miller

Assistant Vice President Operations, Stephen Trippe

Vice President Human Resources, Leon Barnes

Vice President Of Advertising Sales, Kim Woodworth

Vice President Sales, Kimberly A Barrett

Vice President, Tim Silvia

Vice President Benefit Innovation And Product, Jon Kipp

Vice President And General Manager High Speed Data Product Consumer Services, James Odom

Vice President Partner Solutions At Mlb Advanced Media, Mallory Delva

Vice President Of Field Operations, Jonathan Anglin

Vice President Public Policy, Jay Schwarz

Vice Chairman, Neil Smit

Auditors: DELOITTE & TOUCHE LLP

LOCATIONS

HQ: Comcast Corp
One Comcast Center, Philadelphia, PA 19103-2838
Phone: 215 286-1700
Web: www.comcastcorporation.com

2018 Sales

	$ mil.	% of total
US	82,233	87
International	12,274	13
Total	**94,507**	**100**

PRODUCTS/OPERATIONS

2018 Sales

	$ mil.	% of total
Cable Communications	55,143	57
NBC Universal		
Cable Networks	11,773	12
Broadcast Television	11,439	12
Filmed Entertainment	7,152	7
Theme parks	5,683	6
Headquarters & others	63	-
Eliminations	(349)	0
Sky	4,587	5
Corporate and others	1,403	1
Eliminations	(2387)	
Total	**94,507**	**100**

Cable Networks

Cable Networks
Bravo
CNBC
CNBC World
E!
Golf Channel
MSNBC
NBC Sports Network
Oxygen
Syfy
Universal HD
USA Network
Olympic Channel
USA Network

HISTORICAL FINANCIALS

Company Type: Public

Income Statement — FYE: December 31

	REVENUE ($ mil.)	NET INCOME ($ mil.)	NET PROFIT MARGIN	EMPLOYEES
12/20	103,564	10,534	10.2%	168,000
12/19	108,942	13,057	12.0%	190,000
12/18	94,507	11,731	12.4%	184,000
12/17	84,526	22,714	26.9%	164,000
12/16	80,403	8,695	10.8%	159,000
Annual Growth	6.5%	4.9%	—	1.4%

2020 Year-End Financials

Debt ratio: 37.89%—
Return on equity: 12.14%
Cash ($ mil.): 11,740
Current ratio: 0.93
Long-term debt ($ mil.): 100,614

Dividends
Yield: 1.7%
Payout: 40.3%
Market value ($ mil.): —

	STOCK PRICE ($) FY Close	P/E High/Low	PER SHARE ($) Earnings	Dividends	Book Value
12/20	52.40	23 14	2.28	0.90	19.72
12/19	44.97	16 12	2.83	0.82	18.17
12/18	34.05	17 12	2.53	0.76	15.82
12/17	40.05	16 7	4.75	0.47	14.77
12/16	69.05	39 30	1.79	0.68	11.35
Annual Growth	(6.7%)	— —	6.3%	7.5%	14.8%

COMENITY BANK

World Financial Network National Bank (WFNNB) will take credit for the credit it extends. The company is the private-label and co-branded credit card banking subsidiary of Alliance Data Systems. Along with affiliate World Financial Capital Bank the company underwrites cards on behalf of more than 85 businesses. The company's largest clients include apparel retailers L Brands and Redcats USA. WFNNB oversees about 120 million cardholder accounts and roughly $4 billion in receivables. Private equity giant Blackstone planned to acquire parent Alliance Data Systems for more than $6 billion but that deal was terminated in 2008.

EXECUTIVES

Pres, Timothy King
Computer Operations, Mike Schick
Project Manager, Connie Murphy
Information Technology, Paul Wroten
Client Sales Manager, Stacey Siak
Director Financial Planning, Don Borowy
Client Sales Manager, Jennifer Staten
Marketing Staff, Jeffrey Fasino
Administrative Assistant, Kurt Fraczkowski
Senior Vice President Chief Co, Michael F Swallow

LOCATIONS

HQ: COMENITY BANK
12921 S VISTA STATION BLV, DRAPER, UT 840202377
Phone: 614 729-4000
Web: WWW.COMENITY.COM

HISTORICAL FINANCIALS

Company Type: Private

Income Statement — FYE: December 31

	ASSETS ($ mil.)	NET INCOME ($ mil.)	INCOME AS % OF ASSETS	EMPLOYEES
12/14	9,149	389	4.3%	200
12/13	7,453	350	4.7%	—
12/05	332	10	3.2%	—
12/03	672	88	13.2%	—
Annual Growth	26.8%	14.4%	—	—

Comerica, Inc.

Comerica is the holding company for Comerica Bank which has about 435 branches primarily in five US states (Texas California Michigan Arizona & Florida) and in Canada and Mexico. The company is organized into three main segments. The Business Bank division is the largest offering commercial loans deposits and capital markets products to small- and middle-market businesses multinational corporations and government clients. The Retail Bank serves consumers while the Wealth Management arm provides fiduciary services investment management and advisory and retirement services. Comerica categorizes its securities portfolio and asset and liability management under an additional Finance segment. The company boasts total assets of nearly $75 billion and deposits of over $55 billion.

Operations

Comerica generates about 65% of its revenue from loan interest and fees. It derives between 5% and 10% of its revenue from each of investment securities interest card fees deposit account service charges and fiduciary income.

The bulk of Comerica's portfolio is made up of commercial loans which represent nearly 65% of the total. Commercial mortgages make up about 20%; real estate construction lending comprises more than 5%.

Comerica has strategically aligned its operations into three major business segments: the Business Bank the Retail Bank and Wealth Management. In addition to the three major business segments Finance is also reported as a segment. Comerica's net income is heavily weighted in its Business Bank segment—it provides more than 80% of the total. Wealth Management and the Retail Bank provide some 10% and more than 5% respectively. The Business Bank division offers commercial and lines of credit loans deposits cash management international trade finance letters of credit foreign exchange management services loan syndication services and capital markets products to small- and middle-market businesses multinational corporations and government clients. The Retail Bank serves consumers while the Wealth Management

arm provides fiduciary services investment management and advisory and retirement services. Comerica categorizes its securities portfolio and asset and liability management under an additional Finance segment.

Geographic Reach

Comerica operates around 550 locations including about 440 bank branches. Its other facilities offer trust services loan production and other financial services. California and Michigan each represent about 30% of the holding company's net income; Texas provides about 20%. Arizona Florida and Canada contribute the remainder. Comerica has roughly 190 branches in Michigan 120 in Texas 100 in California and 25 in its other markets.

Sales and Marketing

Beyond retail customers Comerica caters to small- and middle-market businesses multinational corporations and government entities and others operating in the energy automotive production and commercial and residential real estate industries. Middle-market clients represent some 55% of its loan portfolio.

The company's advertising expense were $34 million $30 million and $28 million for the years 2019 2018 and 2017 respectively.

Financial Performance

Comerica's revenue has grown by almost a quarter in the last five years thanks mainly to higher short-term rates most of those years. Despite reductions in 2015 and 2016 net income has more than doubled in that period due to increased net interest income the last two years particularly in 2018.

Progressing at a less than 1% the company's revenue totaled $3.3 billion in 2019; loan interest and fees drove most of the gains. Net income dipped by 3%.

Comerica's cash stores gained $1.2 billion in 2019 to end the year at $5.8 billion. Operations contributed $1.1 billion while investment activities used $494 million. Financing activities generated another $661 million.

Strategy

The Corporation has strategically aligned its operations into three major business segments: the Business Bank the Retail Bank and Wealth Management. These business segments are differentiated based on the type of customer and the related products and services provided. In addition to the three major business segments the Finance Division is also reported as a segment. The Other category includes items not directly associated with the business segments or the Finance segment. The performance of the business segments is not comparable with the Corporation's consolidated results and is not necessarily comparable with similar information for any other financial institution. Additionally because of the interrelationships of the various segments the information presented is not indicative of how the segments would perform if they operated as independent entities. Market segment results are also provided for the Corporation's three primary geographic markets: Michigan California and Texas. In addition to the three primary geographic markets Other Markets is also reported as a market segment.

Company Background

Elon Farnsworth founded Comerica precursor Detroit Savings Fund Institute in 1849 to serve Michigan clients. The company changed its name to Comerica in 1982. The holding company expanded into the Florida and Texas markets in 1982 and 1988 respectively.

HISTORY

Comerica traces its history to 1849 when Michigan governor Epaphroditus Ransom tapped Elon

Farnsworth to found the Detroit Savings Fund Institute. At that time Detroit was a major transit point for shipping between Lakes Huron and Erie as well as between the US and Canada. The bank grew with the town and in 1871 became Detroit Savings Bank.

By 1899 Detroit was one of the top 10 US manufacturing centers and thanks to a group of local tinkerers and mechanics that included Henry Ford was on the brink of even greater growth. Detroit Savings grew also fueled by the deposits of workers whom Ford paid up to $5 a day. Detroit Savings was not however the beneficiary of significant business with the auto makers; for corporate banking they turned first to eastern banks and then to large local banks in which they had an interest.

Detroit boomed during the 1920s as America went car-crazy but after the 1929 crash Detroiters defaulted on mortgages by the thousands. By 1933 Michigan's banks were in such disarray that the governor shut them down three weeks prior to the federal bank holiday. Detroit Savings was one of only four Detroit banks to reopen. None of the major banks associated with auto companies survived.

A few months later Manufacturers National Bank backed by a group of investors that included Edsel Ford (Henry's son) was founded. Although its start was rocky Manufacturers National was on firm footing by 1936; around the same time Detroit Savings Bank renamed itself the Detroit Bank to appeal to a more commercial clientele.

WWII and the postwar boom put Detroit back in gear. In the 1950s and 1960s both banks thrived. In the 1970s statewide branching was permitted and both banks formed holding companies (DETROITBANK Corp. and Manufacturers National Corp.) and expanded throughout Michigan. As they grew they added services; when Detroit's economy was hit by the oil shocks of the 1970s these diversifications helped them through the lean years.

DETROITBANK opened a trust operation in Florida in 1982 to maintain its relationship with retired customers and renamed itself Comerica to be less area-specific. Manufacturers National also began operating in Florida (1983) and made acquisitions in the Chicago area (1987). Comerica went farther afield buying banks in Texas (1988) and California (1991).

Following the national consolidation trend in 1992 Comerica and Manufacturers National merged (retaining the Comerica name) but did not fully integrate until 1994 when the new entity began making more acquisitions. To increase sales and develop its consumer business the company reorganized in 1996. It sold its Illinois bank and its Michigan customs brokerage business and acquired Fairlane Associates to expand its property/casualty insurance line.

As part of its strategy to have operations in all three NAFTA countries Comerica opened a bank in Mexico in 1997 and one in Canada in 1998. That year it dropped $66 million for the naming rights to the Detroit Tigers' baseball stadium which opened as Comerica Park in 2000. It also started a Web-based payment system for its international trade business.

To fortify its business lending operations in California Comerica bought Imperial Bancorp in 2001. At the beginning of 2002 chairman Eugene Miller handed the CEO reins to Ralph Babb who had been CFO. Later that year Babb became chairman as well.

EXECUTIVES

Chairman President And Ceo Comerica Incorporated And Comerica Bank, Ralph W. Babb, age 71, $1,265,000 total compensation
Evp And President Comerica Bank (california Market), Judith S. Love, age 63
Evp And Chief Risk Officer Comerica Incorporated And Comerica Bank, Michael H. Michalak, age 62
Evp And Cio Comerica Incorporated And Evp Comerica Bank, Paul R. Obermeyer, age 62
Evp Governance Regulatory Relations And Legal Affairs Comerica Incorporated And Comerica Bank, John D. Buchanan, age 56, $573,846 total compensation
President Comerica Incorporated And Comerica Bank, Curtis C. Farmer, age 57, $700,000 total compensation
Evp And Cfo, Muneera S. Carr, age 52
Evp And President Comerica Bank Michigan Market, Michael T. Ritchie, age 51
Evp And Chief Human Resources Officer Comerica Incorporated And Comerica Bank, Megan D. Burkhart, age 48
Evp And Chief Credit Officer, Peter W. Guilfoile, age 59
Evp And President Comerica Bank Texas Market, Peter L. Sefzik, age 44
Evp And General Auditor, Christine Moore
Assistant Vice President Senior Systems Engineer, David Walker
Vice President Texas Market, Greg Wilcox
Vice President, Cindy Morgan
Vice President Financial Systems Support, William Grace
Senior Vice President, Melanie Rice
Vice President And Senior Trust, Joan Dindoffer
Vice President Cbo, Angela Knight
Vice President Human Resources Staffing, Dan Dunn
Assistant Vice President Relationship Manager, Dave Sullivan
Vice President, Jon E Haffner
Vice President Marketing, Jason Logan
Vice President, Brian Miller
Assistance Vice President, Daphne Berry
First Vice President And Assistant Counselor, Keith Altenburg
Senior Vice President, Geoff Payne
Vice President Relationship Manager, Brad Bell
Vice President Western Market, Peter Wentworth
Vice President, Thomas Jones
Vice President, Padmanabhan Karatha
Assistant Vice President Texas Market, Marc Farmer
Vice President Credit Administration, Lori Yu
Banking Center Manager Vice President, Catherine Kelley
Senior Vice President Group Manager Stemmons, David A Milton
Vice President, Rhonda D Dantzler
Vice President Private Banking, Gary J Beyer
Assistant Vice President, Dave Samra
Treasury Management Vice President, Danette R Hames
Vice President Liquidity Risk Management, Brittany Butler
Vice President Middle Market Banking, Bryan L Johnston
Vice President Process Manager, Mary Hammond
Vice President, Marc P Abello
Vice President, Lynn M Ris
Vice President Business Consulting Manager, Kristin Class
Vice President, Lesley B Higginbotham
Vice President And Alternate Group Manager Commercial Real Estate, Cynthia V Porter
Vice President, Sheila Ausberry

Assistant Vice President Treasury Management, Pamela G Porter
Vice President, Nancy Blake
Vice President, Kristy Denby
Vice President Portfolio Risk Analytics, Nicholas Teson
Vice President, Linda Vance
Vice President Estate Administration, Angela W Aycock
Vice President Middle Market Banking, Heidi Spencer
Banking Center Manager Assistant Vice President, Teresa Nolasco
Vice President, John Mckee
Vice President U S. Banking Midwest, Mark Leveille
Vice President, Fred Hoops
Banking Center Manager Vice President, Gordon McKinley
Banking Center Manager Assistant Vice President, Lisa Thompson
Vice President, Judi Callis
Senior Vice President, Joshua D Rockwell
Senior Vice President, Paul Orsborn
Vice President Middle Market Banking, Rodney L Thompson
Vice President, Cynthia Walters
Vice President Agm, Matthew Breight
Vice President, Matt Maberry
Vice President, Raffi Khelghatian
Assistant Vice President, Christopher Hoffman
Vice President, Sharon Feigelson
Assistant Vice President, Cedric Jordan
Banking Center Manager Assistant Vice President, Henry Tran
Vice President Retail Prod Management, John MacMillan
Vice President, Amy Pillivant
Senior Vice President Texas Market North Texas Region Manager, Barry Brundage
Senior Vice President Midwest Region Commercial Real Estate Finance, James Preston
Vice President Business Banking, Karen Gladney
Vice President, Kathy Pitton
Vice President Product Development, William Anderson
Senior Vice President, Dan Evans
Vice President, Tom O'connell
Vice President, Peter Kennedy
Assistant Vice President, Bryndon Skelton
Vice President E Business Manager, Kellie Powell
Vice President, Michael Mccarty
Vice President U S Banking Midwest, Brandon Welling
Vice President Regional Banking Officer Financial Services Division, Laura Reyes
Vice President And Senior Counsel, Marinda Little
Senior Vice President Division Finance Officer Wim, Sajid Siddiqi
Vice President, Madhuri Bandla
Vice President, Evan Huckabay
Vice President, Teresa Bosco
Vice President, Maribeth Gomez
Vice President And Senior Counsel, Jennifer Perry
Vice President Private Banking, Todd Goodhue
Vice President, Barry Carroll
Vice President, Cheryl Degraff
Assistant Vice President, Ian Patterson
Senior Vice President, David Ohanian
Vice President And Human Resources Counsel, Von Hays
Vice President Project Manager, Grey Cole
Vice President Of Enterprise Project Management Office, Paul Gustafson
Vice President, Elizabeth Alvarado
Senior Vice President Middle Market Group, Alice Yang
Vice President Texas Market, Jim Young
Assistant Vice President Finance, Haiyan Li
Svptexas Marketing Gro, John Castellano

Vice President, Douglas Smith
Senior Vice President, Dennis Gilkerson
Banking Center Manager Assistant Vice President, Vanessa Ochoa
Vice President Ets Server Engineering, Alex Gonzalez
Vice President And Banking Center Manager Iv, Linda K Landers
Vice President, John Cavanaugh
Vice President, Charlie Heckenlaible
Assistant Vice President, Joe Fisher
Vice President Institutional Sales, Rick Clancy
Vice President, Brian Fitzgerald
First Vice President, Anne Coulter
Assistant Vice President, Megan Trapp
Vice President, Dennis Black
Assistant Vice President Branch Manager, Anna Quijano
Vice President Warehouse Lending, Rob W Marr
Vice President Relationship Manager, Erik McKay
Vice President Marketing, Deborah Srour
Vice President, Danny Sanchez
Assistant Vice President Learning, Scott Blackman
Vice President Regional Sales Manager, Stephanie Sealey
Svp Private Banking, Debbie Ludwig
Vice President Commercial Banking Officer, Adan Gonzalez
Vice President Business Banking, Derek Aten
Banking Center Manager Assistant Vice President, Jasko Korajkic
Vice President, Crystal Dennis
Vice President And Senior Commercial Portfolio Manager, Niranjan Duvvuru
Assistant Vice President Relationship Manager Business Banking, Nancy Correia
Vice President Ii, Garth Gorrall
Vice President Agm, Jim Kelley
Vice President, Abigail Soper
Vice President Relationship Manager, Rebecca Callahan
Vice President, Timothy Nomura
Vice President, Eric Brawner
Vice President, James Dox
Vice President, Pam Crooks
Banking Center Manager Assistant Vice President, Rachel Svoboda
Vice President Treasury Management, Stephanie Jamrog
Group Manager Senior Vice President, Sara Mann
Vice President Information Security Engineer, Dave Frank
Vice President, John Graham
Lead Sourcing Governance Analyst Vice President, Kathie Stevenson
Vice President Director Of Product Risk Control, Shelly Gannaway
Auditors: Ernst & Young LLP

LOCATIONS

HQ: Comerica, Inc.
Comerica Bank Tower, 1717 Main Street, MC 6404, Dallas, TX 75201
Phone: 214 462-6831
Web: www.comerica.com

2018 Banking Centers

	No.
Michigan	193
Texas	122
California	96
Other Markets	
Arizona	17
Florida	7
Canada	1
Total	436

Selected Markets

Arizona
California
Colorado
Florida
Illinois
Michigan
Nevada
Ohio
Texas
Washington

PRODUCTS/OPERATIONS

2018 Sales

	$ mil.	% of total
Net Interest Income		
Fees on Loans	2,262	61
Investment securities	265	7
Short-term investments	92	3
Interest expense	(267)	
Noninterest income		
Card fees	244	7
Service charges on deposit accounts	211	6
Fiduciary income	206	6
Other noninterest income	315	10
Total	3,328	100

2018 Sales

	% of total
Business Bank	85
Wealth Management	10
Retail Bank	5
Total	100

Selected Subsidiaries

Comerica Bank
Comerica Bank & Trust National Association
Comerica Capital Advisors Incorporated
Comerica Financial Incorporated
Comerica Holdings Incorporated
Comerica Insurance Group Inc.
Comerica Insurance Services Inc.
Comerica Investment Services Inc.
Comerica Investments LLC
Comerica Leasing Corporation
Comerica Merchant Services Inc.
Comerica Securities Inc.
Wilson Kemp & Associates Inc.
World Asset Management Inc.

COMPETITORS

Bank of America	Regions Financial
Citigroup	SVB Financial
Cullen/Frost Bankers	SunTrust
Fifth Third	TCF Financial
Huntington Bancshares	U.S. Bancorp
JPMorgan Chase	Wells Fargo
MUFG Americas Holdings	

HISTORICAL FINANCIALS

Company Type: Public

Income Statement   FYE: December 31

	ASSETS ($ mil.)	NET INCOME ($ mil.)	INCOME AS % OF ASSETS	EMPLOYEES
12/19	73,402	1,198	1.6%	7,948
12/18	70,818	1,235	1.7%	8,051
12/17	71,567	743	1.0%	8,190
12/16	72,978	477	0.7%	8,149
12/15	71,877	521	0.7%	9,103
Annual Growth	0.5%	23.1%	—	(3.3%)

2019 Year-End Financials

Debt ratio: 4.73%
Return on equity: 16.15%
Cash ($ mil.): 5,818
Current ratio: —
Long-term debt ($ mil.): —

No. of shares (mil.): 142
Dividends
Yield: 3.7%
Payout: 33.9%
Market value ($ mil.): 10,195

	STOCK PRICE ($) FY Close	P/E High/Low		PER SHARE ($) Earnings	Dividends	Book Value
12/19	71.75	11	7	7.87	2.68	51.56
12/18	68.69	14	9	7.20	1.84	46.89
12/17	86.81	21	15	4.14	1.09	46.07
12/16	68.11	26	11	2.68	0.89	44.47
12/15	41.83	18	14	2.84	0.83	43.03
Annual Growth	14.4%	—	—	29.0%	34.0%	4.6%

Commerce Bancshares Inc

Commerce Bancshares owns bank branch operator Commerce Bank. The financial institution boasts a network of more than 360 locations across several US states including Missouri Kansas Illinois Oklahoma and Colorado. The bank focuses on retail and commercial banking services such as deposit accounts mortgages loans and credit cards. Commerce Bank also runs a wealth management division that offers asset management trust private banking brokerage and estate planning services and also manages proprietary mutual funds. As part of its operations Commerce Bank has subsidiaries devoted to insurance leasing and private equity investments.

Operations

The company operates three main segments: Consumer Commercial and Wealth.

The Commercial segment which collects roughly 65% of the bank's total revenue provides corporate lending merchant and commercial bank card products leasing and international services as well as business and government deposit and cash management services. Fixed income investments are sold to individuals and institutional investors through the segment's Capital Markets Group.

Another 20% of bank revenue is generated through the Consumer segment which includes the retail branch network consumer installment lending personal mortgage banking and consumer debit and credit bank card activities. It provides services through a network of more than 200 full-service branches a 400-machine ATM network and alternative delivery channels such as extensive on-line banking and telephone banking services.

The remaining bank revenue (around 15%) comes from the Wealth segment which manages investments with a market value of $20.4 billion and administers an additional $14.8 billion in non-managed assets provides traditional trust and estate tax-planning services brokerage services and advisory and discretionary investment portfolio management services targeted to personal and institutional corporate customers. The Wealth segment also manages Commerce Bank's proprietary mutual funds.

Broadly speaking interest income from the bank's portfolio of loans make up more than 40% of total revenue. Roughly 60% of the portfolio is comprised of commercial loans (mostly business real estate loans but also construction and land loans and other business-related loans). Personal banking loans make up the remaining 40% of the portfolio and mostly include real estate loans and consumer lines of credit but also consumer credit cards revolving home equity loans and some over-draft lines of credit.

Geographic Reach

Commerce Bancshares through its Commerce Bank business operates more than 360 branch banks in five central US states with major focus in Peoria and Bloomington Illinois; St. Louis; Kansas City and Wichita Kansas; Denver; Tulsa Oklahoma; Nashville; Cincinnati; and Dallas. The bank also has commercial offices in Cincinnati Nashville and Dallas. The company's two largest markets include St. Louis and Kansas City. To this end the cities serve as the central hubs for its operation.

Sales and Marketing

The bank spent $14.2 million on marketing in fiscal 2013 down 6% from $15.1 million in 2012 and down 15% from the $16.8 million it spent on marketing in 2011.

Financial Performance

In the recent low interest environment Commerce Bancshares has seen its revenue slowly decline over the past few years from declining interest income from its loans and investment securities. In fiscal 2013 revenue fell by $8.9 million to $1.08 billion as the bank earned lower rates on investment securities and loans (from smaller interest margins) despite higher loan balances and lower rates paid on deposits. The bank was able to offset some of its revenue losses by earning $18.8 million more from bank card transaction trust and brokerage fees.

The bank's net income also dipped by $8.4 million (or 3%) to $261 million in 2013. This is mostly from the drop in revenue but also because the bank paid $6 million more toward employee salaries and benefits (from higher salaries) and $4.4 million more toward data processing and software expenses as bank card processing costs went up. Profits are still up significantly from the bank's recovery period in 2009 and 2010 when it earned $169.1 million and $221.7 million respectively.

The amount of cash provided from operations fell for the third straight year to $360.9 million in 2013 down 6% from the $383.1 million provided in 2012. This was primarily because of lower net income but also because it paid $11.7 million more toward its income tax obligations than in the prior year.

Unlike its revenue and earnings Commerce's assets have been growing. Total loans were $10.96 billion in 2013 representing an increase of $1.13 billion or 11% over balances in 2012. While loan assets have increased across the board business loan assets contributed the most growing by $580.5 million in 2013 to a total of $3.7 billion. Deposit assets also rose by 4% to $19.05 billion in 2013.

Strategy

Commerce Bancshares serves its local retail markets through relationship banking and high touch service. It works to grow its core revenue by expanding new and existing customer relationships leveraging improved technology and enhancing customer satisfaction. To respond to changes in consumer banking preferences the bank will work to improve its distribution strategy by de-emphasizing the central role of traditional branch banking and providing more customers access to its services through ATMs call centers mobile and house lines internet. It will also work to develop new products and focus on expense reductions wherever possible to improve the company's bottom line.

To grow its commercial business segment which already provides two-thirds of all bank revenue Commerce plans to invest in distinctive lower-risk/higher return businesses to increase its loan business. In addition it intends to deepen its relationships with existing commercial customers and provide more products to them to increase profitability while taking on little additional risk or cost.

Thanks to higher brokerage and trust fees Commerce Bancshares' Wealth division saw the largest segment revenue growth in 2013. The bank is optimistic that its new hires in the division will contribute to higher sales productivity over the next few years particularly in the institutional and St. Louis Family Office. In addition management believes that the improving US economy and booming stock market will improve investor confidence and M&A activity which should help grow the segment in the years ahead.

Mergers and Acquisitions

Commerce Bancshares in May 2013 inked a merger agreement with Summit Bancshares whereby Summit merged into a wholly-owned subsidiary of Commerce Bancshares. The transaction valued at approximately $40.6 million consisted entirely of Commerce Bancshares' stock and added more than $200 million in new loans to the bank's portfolio. The deal significantly boosted Commerce Bank's foothold in the Tulsa Oklahoma market and allowed it to enter the Oklahoma City market.

EXECUTIVES

Svp; Director Operations And Information Services, Robert J. Rauscher, age 62

Cfo, Charles G. (Chuck) Kim, age 60, $415,080 total compensation

Evp Commercial Line Of Business; President And Coo Commerce Bank Kansas City Region, Kevin G. Barth, age 60, $408,705 total compensation

Evp; Chief Human Resources Officer And Director Internal Support Services, Sara E. Foster, age 60

Chairman And Ceo, David W. Kemper, age 69, $896,073 total compensation

Evp Trust Line Of Business; President The Commerce Trust Company A Division Of Commerce Bank, V. Raymond (Ray) Stranghoener, age 69, $235,900 total compensation

Evp; Chief Credit Officer And Chief Risk Officer, Daniel D. Callahan

Svp; Director Commercial Card And Merchant Services, Jeff Burik

Svp; Director Community Bank Administration, Michael J. Petrie

President And Coo, John W. Kemper, $462,287 total compensation

Senior Vice President, Patricia R Kellerhals

Vice President Marketing Support, Christopher Schildz

Assistant Vice President Deposit Product Manager, Catherine Mills

Vice President, Paul Zietlow

Vice President Private Client Group, Joe Morris

Vice President Of Human Resources, Betty Maes

Vice President Commercial Marketing, Liz Lewis

Assistant Vice President Regional Marketing, Jenny Stanley

Vice President, Jeffrey Turner

Vice President, Joe Mccaddon

Vice President Regional Retail Sales Manager, Jen Bradley

Senior Vice President Retail And Small Business Group Manager, Robin Wandschneider

Assistant Vice President, Ron Nesemeyer

Vice President, Trishia Baker

Senior Vice President Portfolio Manager, WM Cody

Vice President Information Technology, Kaz Verwers

Assistant Vice President Information Tec, Andy Frank

Senior Vice President And Director Operations, Eric Rauscher

Vice President Business Banking Relationship Manager, Rob Gillespie

Vice President Of Investment Banking, Michael Hartmann

Vice President Branch Management, Robert Henson

Vice President Server Operations Manager Information Technology, Wanda Edgmond

Senior Vice President, Mark Tankesley

Senior Vice President, Debbie Housh

Assistant Vice President Information Technology Manager, Chad Boline

Vice President, Clive Veri

Vice President, Susan McGee

Vice President Of Information Technology, Allan Smith

Vice President Commercial Lending, Pam Hill

Executive Vice President, Raymond Stranghoener

Executive Vice President, Gaylyn McGregor

Svp Private Client Manager, Thomas Durfee

National Account Manager, Jennifer White

Vice President, Craig Duerksen

Assistant Vice President, Wilkerson Kurtis

Assistant Vice President Business Line Systems Manager, Kevin Belloma

Vice President, JO Hicks

Vice President, Barbara Mccaslin

Senior Vice President, Gordon Roewe

Senior Vice President, Nick Fafoglia

Vice President Commercial Banking, Benjamin Wanless

Vice President Finance, Lynn McLaughlin

Vice President, Judy Shilling

Svp Director Private Banking Credit, Kyle Rosborg

Vice President, Garth Kilburn

Vice President, Paul Manuel

Vice President, Brendan Carmichael

Senior Vice President, Bill White

Senior Vice President, Len Metzger

Vice President Commercial Card Services, Rob Perdue

Vice President Of Commercial Banking, Sam Jarvis

Vice President, Gerald Mckay

Vice President Business Banking, Janelle Schneider

Assistant Vice President Small Business Banking Specialist, Darin Crump

Vice President Mortgage Technology Manager, Sarah Vande

Vice President Senior Relationship Manager, Lee Tilghman

Vice President Information Technology, Williams Jonathan

Assistant Vice President, Andrew Fogt

Vice President Team Leader, Matt Dority

Vice President Business Banking Center Manager, Jamie Huch

Vice President Business Development, Brent Miller

Vice President, Bruce Talen

Assistant Vice President Branch Manager Iv, Hank Koehly

Senior Vice President, Joe Williams

Executive Vice President Chief Credit Officer Risk Manager, Robert Matthews

Assistant Vice President, Melissa Caputo

Vice President, Jim Watson

Vice President Investments, Rakesh Uthamchand

Vice President, Jack Stapleton

Vice President National Accounts, Venus Vega

Assistant Vice President, Cole Higginbotham

Vice President Retail Banking Manager, Kathy Wilkes

Assistant Vice President Small Business Banking, Sonya Tandy

Assistant Vice President, Angela Wright-Jones

Senior Vice President Commercial Banking, Matt Gomric

Senior Vice President Regional Credit Officer Oklahoma Market, Aaron Stone

Vice President, Ian Finch

Vice President Mortgage Sales And Production, Tim Rebori

Senior Vice President, Michael Boehn

Vice President National Account Executive, Heide Garza

Vp Business Transformation Program Manager, Stacy Regnier

Vice President Of Information Technology, Ken Isbell

Senior Vice President Commercial Payments Credit And Risk Officer, Rob Olsen

Vice President, Kristy Hess

Senior Vice President Commercial Loan Servicing, Jeremy Allen

Vice President Trust Administration, Brad Landsbaum

Senior Vice President Relationship Manager, Chris Hamm

Vice President Private Banking Officer, Ami Slader

Vice President, Niall Mooney

Vice President And Commercial Loan Officer, Jeffrey G Elliott

Senior Vice President Private Banking Team Leader, Shelly P Arnold

Executive Vice President, Doug Neff

Senior Vice President Corporate Banking, Aric Hassel

Assistant Vice President, Jerry Letoumeau

Vice President Senior Account Executive, Cindy Horan Horan

Senior Vice President, Debbie Laycock

Vice President Business Banking, Todd Norton

Vice President Of Information Technology, James G Smith

Assistant Vice President, Jason Ward

Vice President And Director Marketing (western Region), Terri Hurd

Vice President Senior Financial Planner, Kimberly Bridges

Vice President National Account Executive, Michael Venditto

Svp Private Client Wealth Advisor, Beth Kinzel

Svp Healthcare, Richard Heise

Vice Chairman, Seth M. Leadbeater, age 69

Vice Chairman, Jonathan M. Kemper, age 67

Board Member, Karen L Daniel

Auditors: KPMG LLP

LOCATIONS

HQ: Commerce Bancshares Inc
1000 Walnut, Kansas City, MO 64106
Phone: 816 234-2000   **Fax:** 816 234-2369
Web: www.commercebank.com

2016 Sales by Market

	% of total
Kansas City	32
St. Louis	28
Other regions	40
Total	**100**

PRODUCTS/OPERATIONS

2016 Sales

	$ mil.	% of total
Interest Income		
Interest and fees on loans	490	42
Interest on investment securities	207	18
Interest on long-term securities purchased under agreements to resell	13	1
Interest on loans held for sale	1	0
Interest on federal funds sold and short-term securities purchased under agreements to resell	0	0
Interest on deposits with banks	1	0
Non-Interest Income		
Bank card transaction fees	181	15
Trust fees	121	10
Deposit account charges and other fees	86	7
Consumer brokerage services	13	1
Loan fees and sales	11	1
Capital market fees	10	1
Other	48	4
Total	**1,187**	**100**

Selected Services

Commercial Banking
  Financing
  Treasury Services
  Commercial Card Products
  Merchant Services
  International Services
  Capital Markets
  Investment Management
  Corporate Trust
Personal Banking
  Checking Accounts
  Savings Accounts
  Money Market Accounts & CDs
  Borrowing Solutions & Loans
  Mortgages
  Credit Cards
  Check Cards & Prepaid Cards
  Online Banking Services & Mobile Banking
Small Business Banking
  Small Business Checking Accounts
  Small Business Online Services
  Small Business Loans
  Business Credit Cards & Check Cards
  Business Resource Center
  Merchant Services
Wealth Management
  The Commerce Trust Company
  Investment Management
  Private Banking Services
  Financial Advisory Services
  Trust Services
  Institutional Trust Services
  Corporate Trust
  Brokerage Services
  Insurance Services

Selected Subsidiaries

Capital for Business Inc.
CBI-Kansas Inc.
CFB Partners LLC
CFB Venture Fund L.P.
Clayton Financial Corp.
Clayton Holdings LLC
Clayton Realty Corp.
Commerce Bank National Association
Commerce Brokerage Services Inc.
Commerce Insurance Services Inc.
Commerce Investment Advisors Inc.
Commerce Mortgage Corp.
Illinois Financial LLC
Illinois Realty LLC
Tower Redevelopment Corporation

COMPETITORS

BOK Financial	First National of
Bank of America	Nebraska
Bank of the West	Great Western Bancorp
Capitol Federal	INTRUST
Financial	U.S. Bancorp
Dickinson Financial	UMB Financial
First Banks	Wells Fargo

HISTORICAL FINANCIALS

Company Type: Public

Income Statement   FYE: December 31

	ASSETS ($ mil.)	NET INCOME ($ mil.)	INCOME AS % OF ASSETS	EMPLOYEES
12/19	26,065	421	1.6%	4,835
12/18	25,463	433	1.7%	4,869
12/17	24,833	319	1.3%	4,857
12/16	25,641	275	1.1%	4,877
12/15	24,604	263	1.1%	4,859
Annual Growth	**1.5%**	**12.4%**	—	**(0.1%)**

2019 Year-End Financials

Debt ratio: 0.01%
Return on equity: 13.89%
Cash ($ mil.): 915
Current ratio: —
Long-term debt ($ mil.): —

No. of shares (mil.): 117
Dividends
  Yield: 1.5%
  Payout: 29.0%
Market value ($ mil.): 8,015

	STOCK PRICE ($) FY Close	P/E High/Low	PER SHARE ($) Earnings	Dividends	Book Value
12/19	67.94	20 16	3.41	0.99	26.57
12/18	56.37	21 16	3.43	0.85	23.88
12/17	55.84	24 21	2.50	0.78	23.07
12/16	57.81	27 18	2.15	0.74	22.27
12/15	42.54	24 20	2.01	0.71	19.01
Annual Growth	**12.4%**	— —	**14.2%**	**8.9%**	**8.7%**

COMMONSPIRIT HEALTH

Formed in 2019 through the merger of Catholic hospital systems Catholic Health Initiatives and Dignity Health CommonSpirit Health is a $29 billion not-for-profit organization with more than 140 hospitals in 21 states. Its hospitals range from large urban medical centers (many with educational and research programs) to small hospitals in rural areas. The company also operates clinics long-term care assisted-living and senior residential facilities (totaling more than 700 health care facilities) and provides home-based care services. The system is sponsored by nearly 20 different congregations of nuns. CommonSpirit is the largest not-for-profit health system in the US.

Operations

CHI's network includes acute-care hospitals including academic and teaching facilities rural facilities with critical-care access nursing colleges home-health agencies community health services organizations long-term care facilities assisted-care and residential senior homes research and development programs and labs. The company has about 25000 physicians and advanced practice clinicians.

Geographic Reach

CHI operates in Arkansas California Colorado Indiana Iowa Kansas Kentucky Minnesota Nebraska Nevada New Jersey New Mexico North Dakota Ohio Oregon Pennsylvania South Dakota Tennessee Texas Washington and Wisconsin — 21 states in all.

Strategy

The 2019 merger of California-based Dignity Health and Colorado-based Catholic Health Initiatives that resulted in the creation of CommonSpirit Health was just one of several health system transactions in a time of rising M&A activity. The systems joined forces to strengthen their operations enabling them to provide better care for more people. The combined system's operating goals include expanding its clinical capabilities shifting to providing care outside of the hospital investing in technology addressing social determinants of health and maintaining an experienced workforce.

Mergers and Acquisitions

After years of discussions CHI and Dignity Health merged in early 2019. The combined health system CommonSpirit Health is the largest not-for-profit hospital system in the US. The size of the system allows for it to provide expanded care to patients through such methods as virtual appointments a broader range of clinical programs and advanced technologies. The new organization with 142 hospitals in 21 states is headquartered in Chicago. Individual hospitals continue to operate under their existing names.

HISTORY

In 1860 the Sisters of St. Francis established a hospital in Philadelphia laying the foundation for a larger health care organization. In 1981 Franciscan Health System was formally established to be a national holding company for Catholic hospitals and related organizations. By the mid-1990s the system consisted of 12 member and two affiliate hospitals and 11 long-term-care facilities located in the mid-Atlantic states and the Pacific Northwest.

Sisters of Charity of Cincinnati and the Sisters of St. Francis Perpetual Adoration of Colorado Springs co-sponsored The Sisters of Charity Health Care Systems incorporated in 1979 as a multi-institutional health care network. By the mid-1990s the system included 20 hospitals in Colorado Kentucky Nebraska New Mexico and Ohio.

Three congregations collaborated to form Catholic Health Corporation in 1980 one of the first such health care partnerships between religious communities within the Roman Catholic Church in the US. By 1996 this coalition operated 100 health care facilities in 12 states.

The development of modern managed care health care systems put pressure on the smaller Catholic hospital operations so the three systems established Catholic Health Initiatives (CHI) in 1996 as a national entity serving five geographic regions. Patricia Cahill a lay health care veteran who previously served the Archdiocese of New York was appointed president and CEO of CHI. The following year CHI absorbed the 10-hospital Sisters of Charity of Nazareth Health Care System based in Bardstown Kentucky (founded in a log cabin in 1812).

That year CHI continued to seek new partnerships to improve efficiency. With Alegent Health it formed provider network Midwest Select with nearly 200 hospitals marketing discounted rates to businesses. CHI allied with the Daughters of Charity to form for-profit joint venture Catholic Healthcare Audit Network to provide operational financial compliance and information systems audits as well as due diligence reviews. CHI also joined insurance joint venture NewCap Insurance with the Daughters of Charity and Catholic Health East; the firm allowed CHI to operate independently of commercial insurers.

CHI made a secular tie-in with the University of Pennsylvania Health System in 1998 whereby the university's system would offer care through five Catholic hospitals (CHI made plans to transfer these hospitals to Catholic Health East in 2001). The next year CHI announced its first loss due to lackluster performance in the Midwest. During 2000 the company responded by streamlining operations and changing management resulting in a positive bottom line. In 2001 it sold three hospitals in Pennsylvania one in Delaware and one in New Jersey to Catholic Health East.

EXECUTIVES

President Ceo And Trustee, Kevin E. Lofton, age 65
President Enterprise Business Lines And Cfo, J. Dean Swindle
Svp Divisional Operations (texas), Michael H. Covert
Svp Marketing And Communications, Joyce M. Ross
Executive Vice President Mission, Thomas R. Kopfensteiner
Svp Divisional Operations And Ceo Chi Memorial (tennessee), Larry Schumacher, age 62
Svp Legal Services And General Counsel, Mitch H. Melfi
Evp Growth And Business Acquisitions, Paul W. Edgett

Svp Human Resources And Chief Human Resources Officer, Patricia G. (Pat) Webb
Svp Divisional Operations And Ceo Chi Health (nebraska And Southwest Iowa), Cliff A. Robertson
Senior Vice President And Division Executive Officer, Jeffrey S. Drop
Svp And Chief Nursing Officer, Kathleen D. Sanford
Svp Divisional Operations And Ceo Mercy Health Network (iowa), David H. Vellinga
Svp Divisional Operations And Ceo Chi Franciscan Health (tacoma), Ketul J. Patel
Svp And President And Ceo Kentuckyone Health, Ruth W. Brinkley
Ceo Chi St. Alexius Health, Matt Grimshaw, age 45
Interim Evp Operations, Anthony Jones
Svp And Chief Medical Officer, Robert J. Weil
Vice President Operational Finance Mercy Medical Center, Joseph Ruark
Vp Finance, Brent Schmidt
Auditors: ERNST & YOUNG LLP IRVINE CA

LOCATIONS

HQ: COMMONSPIRIT HEALTH
444 W LAKE ST STE 2500, CHICAGO, IL 606060097
Phone: 312 741-7000
Web: WWW.COMMONSPIRIT.ORG

COMPETITORS

Adventist Health System Sunbelt Healthcare
Allina Hospitals
Ascension Health
Baptist Health
Baptist Health (Arkansas)
BryanLGH Medical Center
Denver Health and Hospital Authority
Exempla Healthcare
HCA
Life Care Centers
Memorial Health System (Colorado)
Methodist Health System
OhioHealth
Tenet Healthcare
Universal Health Services

HISTORICAL FINANCIALS

Company Type: Private

Income Statement				FYE: June 30
	REVENUE ($ mil.)	NET INCOME ($ mil.)	NET PROFIT MARGIN	EMPLOYEES
06/19	7,170	9,008	125.6%	72,500
06/18	14,982	222	1.5%	—
06/17	15,547	128	0.8%	—
06/16	15,942	(703)	—	—
Annual Growth	(23.4%)	—	—	—

COMMONWEALTH OF KENTUCKY

EXECUTIVES

Governor, Matt Bevin
Lt Govenor, Jenean Hampton
Chief Information Security Off, Joe Manley
Staff, Donna Cordier
Coordinator, Joe Wolford
Coordinator, Laronda Davis
Project Coordinator, Teresa Bailey
First Supreme Court Judge, David C Buckingham

Government Affairs Manager, Amy Mefford
Aging Program Case Manager, Dorris Phillips
Lims Administrator, Gerry Morford

LOCATIONS

HQ: COMMONWEALTH OF KENTUCKY
700 CAPITAL AVE STE 100, FRANKFORT, KY 406013410
Phone: 502 564-2611
Web: WWW.KENTUCKY.GOV

HISTORICAL FINANCIALS

Company Type: Private

Income Statement				FYE: June 30
	REVENUE ($ mil.)	NET INCOME ($ mil.)	NET PROFIT MARGIN	EMPLOYEES
06/19	27,091	3	0.0%	34,000
06/18	25,692	338	1.3%	—
Annual Growth	5.4%	(99.0%)	—	—

COMMONWEALTH OF MASSACHUSETTS

EXECUTIVES

Governor, Charlie Baker
Lt Gov*, Karyn Polito
State Superior Court Judges, Kenneth V Desmond
State Superior Court Judges, James R Lemire
State Solicitor, Peter Sacks
Assistant Attorney General, Sookyoung Shin
MA Orange District Court Clerk, Joella E Fortier
Engagement Director, Deidre Travis-Brown
Deputy Director Office of Empl, John Langan
Superior Court Judge, Valerie A Yarashus
District Court Judge, Shelby M Smith
Auditors: KPMG LLP BOSTON MA

LOCATIONS

HQ: COMMONWEALTH OF MASSACHUSETTS
1 ASHBURTON PL FL 9, BOSTON, MA 021081518
Phone: 617 727-5000
Web: WWW.MASS.GOV

HISTORICAL FINANCIALS

Company Type: Private

Income Statement				FYE: June 30
	REVENUE ($ mil.)	NET INCOME ($ mil.)	NET PROFIT MARGIN	EMPLOYEES
06/17	53,391	323	0.6%	59,253
06/16	52,992	(31)	—	—
06/15	50,609	685	1.4%	—
06/14	47,709	(250)	—	—
Annual Growth	3.8%	—	—	—

COMMONWEALTH OF PENNSYLVANIA

EXECUTIVES

Governor, Tom Wolf
Lt Governor*, John Fetterman
General*, Linda Kelly
Chief of Staff*, Stephen Aichele
Acting Attorney General*, Bruce L Castor Jr
Portfolio Manager, James Del Gaudio
Compliance Staff, Megan Porta
Co-Chair PA Inter-Agency Elect, Robert Torres
Co-Chair PA Inter-Agency Elect, John Macmillan
Chair-PA Sch Safety SEC Commit, Charles H Ramsey
Forensic Laboratory Manager, Bruce Tackett
Auditors: CLIFTONLARSONALLEN LLP BALTIM

LOCATIONS

HQ: COMMONWEALTH OF PENNSYLVANIA
238 MAIN CAPITOL BUILDING, HARRISBURG, PA
171200022
Phone: 717 787-5962
Web: WWW.STATE.PA.US

HISTORICAL FINANCIALS

Company Type: Private

Income Statement FYE: June 30

	REVENUE ($ mil.)	NET INCOME ($ mil.)	NET PROFIT MARGIN	EMPLOYEES
06/19	78,418	(338)	—	89,207
06/18	73,689	2,198	3.0%	—
06/17	72,373	187	0.3%	—
06/16	67,822	(630)	—	—
Annual Growth	5.0%	—		

COMMONWEALTH OF VIRGINIA

EXECUTIVES

Gov, Ralph Northam
Lt Gov, Justin E Fairfax
Attorney Gen, Ronald F McDonnell
Press Secretary, Crystal Carson
SEC of Fin, Jody Wagner
Executive Director, Diana Cantor
Treasurer, Lee Andes
Treasurer, Manju Ganeriwala
Director, Tod Massa
Policy Director, Jennie O'Holleran
Special Asst For Constituent S, Rickee Jones
Auditors: MARTHA S MAVREDES CPA RICHMO

LOCATIONS

HQ: COMMONWEALTH OF VIRGINIA
101 N 14ST JAMES MONROE ST, RICHMOND, VA
23219
Phone: 804 225-3131
Web: WWW.VIRGINIA.GOV

HISTORICAL FINANCIALS

Company Type: Private

Income Statement FYE: June 30

	REVENUE ($ mil.)	NET INCOME ($ mil.)	NET PROFIT MARGIN	EMPLOYEES
06/19	40,939	1,480	3.6%	100,000
06/18	38,725	1,353	3.5%	—
06/17	36,395	18	0.1%	—
06/16	35,094	(744)	—	—
Annual Growth	5.3%	—		

CommScope Holding Co Inc

Auditors: Ernst & Young LLP

LOCATIONS

HQ: CommScope Holding Co Inc
1100 CommScope Place, SE, Hickory, NC 28602
Phone: 828 324-2200
Web: www.commscope.com

HISTORICAL FINANCIALS

Company Type: Public

Income Statement FYE: December 31

	REVENUE ($ mil.)	NET INCOME ($ mil.)	NET PROFIT MARGIN	EMPLOYEES
12/19	8,345	(929)	—	30,000
12/18	4,568	140	3.1%	20,000
12/17	4,560	193	4.2%	20,000
12/16	4,923	222	4.5%	25,000
12/15	3,807	(70)	—	23,000
Annual Growth	21.7%	—		6.9%

2019 Year-End Financials

Debt ratio: 68.13%
Return on equity: (-51.74%)
Cash ($ mil.): 598
Current ratio: 1.72
Long-term debt ($ mil.): 9,800
No. of shares (mil.): 194
Dividends
  Yield: —
  Payout: —
Market value ($ mil.): 2,761

	STOCK PRICE ($) FY Close	P/E High/Low		PER SHARE ($) Earnings	Dividends	Book Value
12/19	14.19	— —		(5.02)	0.00	9.44
12/18	16.39	56 21		0.72	0.00	9.13
12/17	37.83	42 31		0.98	0.00	8.63
12/16	37.20	32 17		1.13	0.00	7.19
12/15	25.89	— —		(0.37)	0.00	6.39
Annual Growth	(14.0%)	— —		—		10.2%

Community Bank System Inc

Community Bank System is right up front about what it is. The holding company owns Community Bank which operates about 195 branches across upstate New York and northeastern Pennsylvania where it operates as First Liberty Bank and Trust. Focusing on small underserved towns and non-urban markets the bank offers standard products and services such as checking and savings accounts certificates of deposit and loans and mortgages to consumer business and government clients. Boasting over $11.0 billion in assets the bank's loan portfolio consists of mostly business loans residential mortgages and consumer loans. Community Bank System's subsidiaries offer employee benefit services wealth management and insurance products and services.

Operations

Community Bank System operates three business segments. The Banking segment which made up 83% of the company's total revenue during 2015 provides lending and deposit services to individuals businesses and municipalities. Employee Benefit Services (12% of revenue) offers trust investment fund retirement plan actuarial healthcare consulting and other administrative services through Benefit Plan Administrative Services (BPAS). The All Other segment (5% of revenue) includes its Wealth Management (operating through Community Investment Services) and Insurance businesses (operating through CBNA Insurance Agency).

Nearly 70% of the company's revenue comes from interest income. About 49% of its revenue came from loan interest during 2015 while another 19% came from interest on taxable and nontaxable investments. The rest of its revenue came from deposit service fees (14% of revenue) employee benefit services (12%) wealth management and insurance services (5%) and other banking revenues (1%).

Geographic Reach

Community Bank System operated 194 branches and six back-office operating facilities in 36 counties in upstate New York and six counties in northeastern Pennsylvania at the end of 2015.

Sales and Marketing

The bank has been ramping up its advertising spend in recent years. It spent $3.6 million on advertising during 2015 up from $3.2 million and $3.0 million in 2014 and 2013 respectively.

Financial Performance

Community Bank System's annual revenues have been slowly trending higher since 2013 despite a decline in loan interest mostly as it's been building its non-interest related business lines. Meanwhile its net income has risen more than 15% as it's had to pay less in interest expenses on deposits amidst the low interest environment.

The bank's revenue grew 2% to $382.92 million during 2015 thanks to a combination of employee benefit services business growth from new customers and expanding business relationships with existing customers as well as from new service offerings; higher interest income from loans and taxable investments as such interest-earning asset balances grew modestly; and a 13% jump in wealth management and insurance services revenue stemming from the acquisition of OneGroup from the Oneida Financial Group acquisition.

Despite revenue growth in 2015 Community's net income dipped less than 1% to $91.23 million for the year due to costs related to the Oneida acquisition. The company's operating cash levels shrank 5% to $116.46 million mostly due to unfavorable working capital changes related to deferred income tax provisions and changes in other assets and liabilities.

Strategy
Community Bank System looks to continue building its loan and deposit business as well as its non-interest service lines organically and through strategic acquisitions of other banks and financial companies. The financial company in 2015 began exploring expansion opportunities into neighboring markets in eastern Ohio upper New England and New Jersey and in 2017 acquired Northeast Retirement Services (NRS) for around $146 million. NRS provides institutional transfer agency master recordkeeping services custom target date fund administration trust product administration and customized reporting services to institutional clients.

Mergers and Acquisitions
Community Bank System acquired Kinderhook Bank in 2019 for $93.4 million. Kinderhook has 11 offices in five New York counties (including in the Capital District of upstate New York) and holds nearly $640 million in assets and about $560 million in deposits. The deal extends Community Bank's reach into the Capital District markets.

In spring 2017 Community Bank acquired Vermont-based Merchants Bancshares. Merchants operates nearly 35 branches and has assets in excess of $1.8 billion; the acquisition will expand Community Bank's operations into Vermont and western Massachusetts.

Company Background
In mid-2012 the bank purchased about 20 branches in upstate New York from HSBC. The deal which was made to satisfy antitrust concerns regarding First Niagara's purchase of 195 branches in New York from HSBC strengthened Community Bank Systems' geographic footprint.

In 2011 the company bought bank holding company The Wilber Corporation adding about 20 locations in the Catskills Mountains region of central New York.

In 2011 expanding its trust and benefits administration business it bought retirement plan administrator CAI Benefits which has offices in New York and Northern New Jersey.

EXECUTIVES

Evp And Cfo, Scott A. Kingsley, age 55, $422,500 total compensation
President Ceo And Director, Mark E. Tryniski, age 59, $725,000 total compensation
Evp And Chief Banking Officer, Brian D. Donahue, age 64, $350,000 total compensation
Svp And Cto, J. Michael Wilson, age 49
Svp Retail Banking Sales And Marketing, Harold M. (Harry) Wentworth, age 55
Svp And Chief Investment Officer, Joseph J. Lemchak, age 58
President Pennsylvania Banking, Robert P. Matley, age 68
Svp Municipal Banking Director, Joseph E. Sutaris, age 52
Svp And Senior Commercial Lending Officer Northern New York, Nicholas S. (Nick) Russell, age 52
Svp And Chief Credit Administrator, Stephen G. Hardy, age 65
Evp And General Counsel, George J. Getman, age 63, $375,000 total compensation
Svp And Chief Risk Officer, Paul J. Ward
Svp And Chief Credit Officer, Joseph Serbun, $248,107 total compensation
Assistant Vice President Marketing An, Mary K Barnette
Executive Vice President Marketing, Aaron Kurtz

Executive Vice President Marketing, Deborah Fitch
Vice President Marketing, Art Gentry
Executive Vice President Marketing, Barbara Call
Vice President And Manager Financial Analysis, Robert Frost
Vice President Director Mortgage Lending, George J Burke
Vice President And Information Technology Manager, James Wilson
Senior Vice President, Marlene Walker
Finance Senior Vice President, Richard Heidrick
Vice President Of Human Resources, Denise Cooper
Vice President Information Technology, Brian Montalbano
Vice President And Marketing Director, Blake Boyer
Vice President Commercial Banker, Allison Mosher
Assistant Vice President Cash Management Sales Officer, Lindsay Horn
Vice President Commercial Banking, Craig Stevens
Senior Vice President And Regional Sales Manager, Theresa Kalil-Lennon
Vice President Commercial Relationship Officer, Michael Moore
Vp Commercial Banking Officer, Edward Michalek
Vp Commercial Loan Officer, Christopher Humphrey
Vp Br Manager, Diane Easton
Senior Vice President, Richard Kazmerick
Senior Vice President, Edward Nork
Executive Vice President Benefit Plan Administrator, Kathy Harvey
Vice President Advice Technology, James McElwain
Vice President Client Service, Kevin Wade
Svp Regional Executive, Jeffrey Levy
Vice President For Finance, Richard Halberg
Vice President Special Assets Commercial Loan Relationship Remediation, Barry Westington
Board Member, Brian Ace
Chair, Sally A. Steele, age 64
Board Member, Eric Stickels
Board Member, Raymond Pecor
Auditors: PricewaterhouseCoopers LLP

LOCATIONS

HQ: Community Bank System Inc
5790 Widewaters Parkway, DeWitt, NY 13214-1883
Phone: 315 445-2282
Web: www.communitybankna.com

PRODUCTS/OPERATIONS

2015 Sales

	$ mil.	% of total
Interest Income:		
Interest and fees on loans	187	49
Taxable investments	52	14
Nontaxable investments	19	5
Noninterest		
Deposit service fees	52	14
Employee benefit services	45	12
Wealth management	20	5
Other	5	1
Total	**382**	**100**

Selected Subsidiaries & Affiliates
Benefit Plans Administrative Services Inc.
Benefit Plans Administrative Services LLC
Brilie Corporation
CBNA Insurance Agency Inc.
CBNA Preferred Funding Corp.
CBNA Treasury Management Corporation
Community Bank N.A. (also dba First Liberty Bank & Trust)
Community Investment Services Inc.
First of Jermyn Realty Company
First Liberty Service Corporation
Flex Corporation
Hand Benefit & Trust Company
Hand Securities Inc.
Harbridge Consulting Group LLP
Nottingham Advisors Inc.

Town & Country Agency LLC
Western Catskill Realty Inc.

COMPETITORS

Arrow Financial	Financial Institutions
Bank of America	HSBC USA
Canandaigua National	JPMorgan Chase
Chemung Financial	KeyCorp
Citizens Financial Group	M&T Bank
	NBT Bancorp
Elmira Savings Bank	

HISTORICAL FINANCIALS
Company Type: Public

Income Statement
FYE: December 31

	ASSETS ($ mil.)	NET INCOME ($ mil.)	INCOME AS % OF ASSETS	EMPLOYEES
12/19	11,410	169	1.5%	3,038
12/18	10,607	168	1.6%	2,933
12/17	10,746	150	1.4%	2,874
12/16	8,666	103	1.2%	2,499
12/15	8,552	91	1.1%	2,490
Annual Growth	**7.5%**	**16.7%**		**5.1%**

2019 Year-End Financials

Debt ratio: 0.80%		No. of shares (mil.): 51	
Return on equity: 9.47%		Dividends	
Cash ($ mil.): 205		Yield: 2.2%	
Current ratio: —		Payout: 48.9%	
Long-term debt ($ mil.): —		Market value ($ mil.): 3,674	

	STOCK PRICE ($) FY Close	P/E High/Low	PER SHARE ($) Earnings	Dividends	Book Value
12/19	70.94	22 17	3.23	1.58	35.82
12/18	58.30	20 16	3.24	1.44	33.43
12/17	53.75	20 16	3.03	1.32	32.26
12/16	61.79	27 15	2.32	1.26	26.96
12/15	39.94	20 15	2.19	1.22	26.06
Annual Growth	**15.4%**	**— —**	**10.2%**	**6.7%**	**8.3%**

Community Health Systems, Inc.

Community Health Systems (CHS) owns or leases about 100 hospitals — mostly in rural areas or small cities — in about 20 states. Its hospitals (which house roughly 16240 beds) typically operate as part of larger regional networks or act as the sole or primary acute health care provider in a service area. Facilities offer a variety of medical surgical and emergency services; CHS also operates a couple of stand-alone rehabilitation or psychiatric facilities. The CHS network also includes physician practices urgent care clinics surgery centers cancer and imaging centers and occupational medicine clinics.

Operations
CHS operates through a single segment — hospital operations. The segment's holdings include inpatient centers and their related outpatient care facilities.

Altogether CHS employs some 2000 physicians and 1000 other licensed practitioners.

Geographic Reach
Headquartered in Franklin Tennessee CHS has hospitals in about 20 states with its largest market

concentrations in Florida Indiana Texas Alabama and Mississippi.

Sales and Marketing

CHS receives about 60% of its revenue from commercial insurance companies and managed care companies. Nearly 25% of sales come from Medicare and Medicaid reimbursements and a small portion of revenue comes from self-pay patients.

Financial Performance

For the last five years CHS's revenue has been declining. It has an overall decrease of 32% from 2015-2019. Its net loss after spiking in 2017 has gradually improved. Revenue in 2019 declined 7% to some $13.2 billion primarily due to lost revenues from hospital divestitures.

Net operating revenues on a same-store basis from hospitals that were operated throughout both periods increased $518 million or 4% during the year 2019 as compared to the year 2018.

Net loss of Community Health Systems Inc. was $675 million for the year ended 2019 compared to $788 million for the year ended 2018.

The company ended 2019 with $216 million in cash up by $20 million from 2018. Operating activities contributed $385 million while investing activities used $2 million (property and equipment purchases and other investments) and financing activities used $363 million on debt payments.

Strategy

The company have been implementing a portfolio rationalizing and deleveraging strategy by divesting hospitals and non-hospital businesses that are attractive to strategic and other buyers. Generally these businesses are not in one of their strategically beneficial service areas are less complementary to their business strategy and/or have lower operating margins. In connection with their divestiture initiative they have received offers from strategic buyers to buy certain of their assets. After considering these offers we have divested and expect to continue to divest hospitals and non-hospital businesses when they find such offers to be attractive and in line with their operating strategy.

CHS is committed to efficient cost effective and profitable operations that seek to ensure sustainable health systems and deliver long-term shareholder value. Their efforts are focused around the following key strategies which are designed to help them achieve their objectives: become a market leader and increase market share in the communities they serve; increase productivity and operating efficiencies to enhance profitability; continuously improve patient safety and quality of care; and optimize their portfolio through select divestitures of non-core assets while investing in markets with the best opportunities for growth.

Company Background

Community Health Systems (CHS) was founded in 1985 and went public in 1991. The company was reincorporated in Delaware in 1996 when it was acquired by investment firm Forstmann Little & Co. It also moved its headquarters from Houston to Nashville Tennessee that year.

In 2014 CHS added some 70 hospitals through the acquisition of Health Management Associates (HMA). CHS conducted an IPO in 2000.

In 2016 the company spun off nearly 40 of its hospitals along with its Quorum Health Resources unit (a provider of management services to non-affiliated hospitals) forming a new public company named Quorum Health Corporation. In 2017 it sold 30 hospitals for a total of some $1.7 billion. Also that year CHS sold an 80% stake in its home health and hospice operations to Almost Family for $128 million.

HISTORY

Community Health Systems (CHS) was founded in 1985.

In 1996 it was acquired by investment firm Forstmann Little & Co. in a leveraged buyout transaction worth some $1.1 billion. It also moved its headquarters from Houston to Nashville Tennessee that year.

CHS once again became a public entity through an IPO in 2000. It engaged is engaged in a flurry of acquisition activity of small regional hospitals each year following its IPO.

However CHS limited its purchases somewhat after plunking down $7 billion in 2007 to acquire Triad Hospitals (and its more than 50 hospitals). After conducting integration efforts at the former Triad hospitals CHS fully resumed its acquisition activity when it purchased five hospitals during 2010 including the Marion Regional Hospital in South Carolina the Forum Health (later Valley-Care) hospitals in Ohio and the Bluefield Hospital in West Virginia.

Buoyed by those purchases CHS launched a campaign to acquire fellow hospital operator and rival Tenet in late 2010 in a deal worth some $7.3 billion in cash stock and debt. However after much back and forth between the firms — including lawsuits and hostile tender offers — CHS halted its acquisition attempts the following year due to a lack of response from Tenet's shareholders and board members.

CHS instead completed several smaller purchases that year including the acquisition of the Mercy Health Partners Scranton operations in Pennsylvania from Catholic Health Partners. The company also purchased Tomball Regional Medical Center (TRMC) located near Houston.

As part of its periodic practice of divesting non-core centers in 2011 it sold two Oklahoma facilities SouthCrest Hospital and Claremore Regional Hospital to Ardent Health Services' Hillcrest Health-Care System unit for an undisclosed price. It also sold a Texas hospital Cleveland Regional Medical Center that year to New Directions Health Systems.

EXECUTIVES

Vice President Of Facilities Management, Gordon Carlisle

Evp And Cfo, W. Larry Cash, age 72, $850,000 total compensation

Chairman And Ceo, Wayne T. Smith, age 74, $1,600,000 total compensation

President Division Ii Operations, Michael T. Portacci, age 62, $663,341 total compensation

Evp Administration, Martin G. (Marty) Schweinhart, age 65

Svp Corporate Communications Marketing And Public Affairs, Tomi Galin

President And Coo, Tim L. Hingtgen, age 53, $655,007 total compensation

Vp And Chief Purchasing Officer, Tim G. Marlette

President Division Iii Operations, P. Paul Smith, age 57

Svp And Cio, Manish Shah

President Division Iv Operations, John W. McClellan

Chief Quality Officer; President Clinical Services, Lynn T. Simon, age 57

President Division I Operations, Martin J. Bonick, age 47

Svp And Chief Nursing Officer, Pamela T. Rudisill

Cfo, Thomas J. (Tom) Aaron

Vp Dir Finance, James Wright

Senior Vice President Of Managed Care, Richard T Willis

Senior Vice President Corporate Compliance And Privacy Officer, Andrea Bosshart

Vice President Of Finance, Nicole Slaughter

Vice President And Chief Strategy Officer, Wesley Littrell

Director Of Health, Lisa Naylor

Director Of Pharmacy, Marshall Robbins

Senior Vice President Internal Audit, Mark Buford

Vice President Of Operations, Matt Hayes

Senior Vice President Financial Services, Michael Lynd

Vice President, Terry Hendon

Vice President Division Operations, Christopher Costello

Medical Director, Scott Wagner

Clinic Manager, Amanda Anderton

Vice President, Laurence Bludau

Vice President Of Human Resource, Sam Pettit

Vice President Physician Business Services, Dan Adkins

Vice President Of Information Technology, Byung Kang

Vice President; Associate General Counsel Division Iv, Carol Hendry

Senior Vice President Human Resources, Ronald Shafer

Vice President Operations, David Fikse

Vice President Case Management And Appeals, Terri Yancey

Senior Vice President And Chief Human Resources Officer, James M Hayes

Radiology Director, Kay Byrd

Vice President, Minnie Head

Board Member, John Fry

Sec Treasbookkeeperestimator, Joan Hayden

Auditors: DELOITTE & TOUCHE LLP

LOCATIONS

HQ: Community Health Systems, Inc.
4000 Meridian Boulevard, Franklin, TN 37067
Phone: 615 465-7000
Web: www.chs.net

PRODUCTS/OPERATIONS

2017 Sales

	% of total
Managed care & other third-party payors	54
Medicare	23
Self-pay	13
Medicaid	10
Total	100

COMPETITORS

Adventist Health System Sunbelt Healthcare
Adventist Health System West
Ascension Health
Banner Health
CHRISTUS Health
Carolinas HealthCare System
Catholic Health Initiatives
Dignity Health
Encompass Health
HCA
LifePoint Health
Mercy Health
SSM Health Care
SunLink Health Systems
Sutter Health
Tenet Healthcare
Texas Health Resources
Trinity Health (Novi)
Universal Health Services
University Health Services
WellStar Health System

HISTORICAL FINANCIALS
Company Type: Public

Income Statement   FYE: December 31

	REVENUE ($ mil.)	NET INCOME ($ mil.)	NET PROFIT MARGIN	EMPLOYEES
12/19	13,210	(675)	—	80,000
12/18	14,155	(788)	—	87,000
12/17	15,353	(2,459)	—	95,000
12/16	18,438	(1,721)	—	120,000
12/15	19,437	158	0.8%	137,000
Annual Growth	(9.2%)	—	—	(12.6%)

2019 Year-End Financials
Debt ratio: 85.88%
Return on equity: —
Cash ($ mil.): 216
Current ratio: 1.50
Long-term debt ($ mil.): 13,385

No. of shares (mil.): 117
Dividends
  Yield: —
  Payout: —
Market value ($ mil.): 342

	STOCK PRICE ($) FY Close	P/E High	P/E Low	PER SHARE ($) Earnings	PER SHARE ($) Dividends	PER SHARE ($) Book Value
12/19	2.90	—	—	(5.93)	0.00	(18.82)
12/18	2.82	—	—	(6.99)	0.00	(13.20)
12/17	4.26	—	—	(22.00)	0.00	(6.69)
12/16	5.59	—	—	(15.54)	0.00	14.18
12/15	26.53	46	18	1.37	0.00	35.64
Annual Growth	(42.5%)	—	—	—	—	—

Community Trust Bancorp, Inc.

Community Trust Bancorp is the holding company for Community Trust Bank one of the largest Kentucky-based banks. It operates 70-plus branches throughout the state as well as in north-eastern Tennessee and southern West Virginia. The bank offers standard services to area businesses and individuals including checking and savings accounts credit cards and CDs. Loans secured by commercial properties and other real estate account for nearly 70% of the bank's portfolio which also includes business consumer and construction loans. Subsidiary Community Trust and Investment Company provides trust estate retirement brokerage and insurance services through a handful of offices in Kentucky and Tennessee.

Operations
Community Trust Bancorp's lending activities include making commercial construction mortgage and personal loans. It also offers lease-financing lines of credit revolving lines of credit term loans and other specialized loans including asset-backed financing.

Some 69% of Community Trust Bancorp's portfolio of loans is secured real estate (36% of which consists of commercial real estate).

Geographic Reach
Kentucky-based Community Trust Bancorp operates more than 70 banking locations across Kentucky West Virginia and Tennessee. Its trust offices are located in Kentucky and Tennessee.

Sales and Marketing
Community Trust Bancorp specializes in serving both small and medium-sized businesses.

Financial Performance
Despite weak loan demand Community Trust Bancorp has grown its revenue from 2009 to 2011

followed by a marginal decline in 2012. Thanks to a decline in both interest expenses and provisions for loan losses Community Trust Bancorp has seen its net income rise during the past five years.

While Community Trust Bancorp logged marginal decreases (1%) in revenue in fiscal 2012 vs. 2011 the financial institution posted net income increases of 16% to $45 million during the reporting period.

Mergers and Acquisitions
Community Trust Bancorp bought LaFollette First National Corporation the holding company for First National Bank of LaFollette for some $16 million. The 2010 acquisition gave the company its first four bank branches and first trust office in Tennessee.

Community Trust is considering additional acquisitions of smaller competitors. It also grows by opening new branches.

EXECUTIVES
Chairman President And Ceo And Chairman Community Trust Bank, Jean R. Hale, age 74, $548,077 total compensation
Evp And Cfo Community Trust Bancorp And Evp And Treasurer Community Trust Bank, Kevin J. Stumbo, age 60, $231,539 total compensation
Evp And Secretary Community Trust Bancorp President And Ceo Community Trust Bank And Vp Community Trust And Investment Company, Mark A. Gooch, age 62, $397,000 total compensation
Evp Community Trust Bancorp And Evp And Chief Credit Officer Community Trust Bank, James J. (Jim) Gartner, age 79
Evp Community Trust Bancorp And Evp Operations Community Trust Bank, James B. (Jim) Draughn, age 61, $241,231 total compensation
Evp Community Trust Bancorp And Evp And South Central Region President Community Trust Bank, Ricky D. Sparkman, age 57
Evp Community Trust Bancor And Evp And Eastern Region President Community Trust Bank, Richard W. (Rick) Newsom, age 65
Evp Community Trust Bancorp And Evp And President Central Kentucky Region Community Trust Bank Inc., Larry W. Jones, age 73, $249,231 total compensation
Evp Community Trust Bancorp And Evp And Chief Internal Audit And Risk Officer Community Trust Bank, Steven E. (Steve) Jameson, age 63
Evp Community Trust Bancorp And Evp And President North East Region Community Trust Bank Inc., D. Andrew Jones, age 57
Evp Community Trust Bancorp And President And Ceo Community Trust And Investment Co., Andy D. Waters, age 54
Evp Community Trust Bancorp Inc. And Evp And Senior Staff Attorney Community Trust Bank Inc., C. Wayne Hancock, age 45
Svp Facilities Manager, Brian Hatmaker
Executive Vice President, David Jones
Executive Vp, Rick Newsom
Assistant Vice President And Relationship Officer, Will Davis
Senior Vice President Operations Manager, Janice Evans
Vice President, Jeffery Stutes
Board Member, Lynn Parrish
Board Member, Anthony St Charles
Board Member, Nicholas Carter
Auditors: BKD, LLP

LOCATIONS
HQ: Community Trust Bancorp, Inc.
346 North Mayo Trail, P.O. Box 2947, Pikeville, KY 41502
Phone: 606 432-1414
Web: www.ctbi.com

PRODUCTS/OPERATIONS
2016 Sales

	$ mil.	% of total
Interest income		
Interest and fees on loans	133	69
Interest and dividends on securities	12	6
Noninterest income		
Service charges on deposit accounts	24	13
Gains on sales of loans	1	1
Trust and wealth management income	9	5
Loan related fees	4	2
Bank owned life insurance	2	1
Brokerage revenue	1	1
Securities gains (losses)	0	.
Other noninterest income	3	2
Total	**195**	**100**

Selected Products & Services
Business Banking
  Business CDs
  Business Checking
  Corporate Services
  Lending
  Merchant Services
  Online Services
  Savings & Money Market
Financial Services
Personal Banking
  Card Services
  CDs & IRAs
  Consumer Loans
  Home Equity
  Interest Checking
  Mobile Banking
  Mortgages
  Personal Checking
  Savings & Money Market
Wealth & Trust Management

COMPETITORS
BB&T	Republic Bancorp
Fifth Third	U.S. Bancorp
Home Federal	
Premier Financial	
Bancorp	

HISTORICAL FINANCIALS
Company Type: Public

Income Statement   FYE: December 31

	ASSETS ($ mil.)	NET INCOME ($ mil.)	INCOME AS % OF ASSETS	EMPLOYEES
12/19	4,366	64	1.5%	1,000
12/18	4,201	59	1.4%	978
12/17	4,136	51	1.2%	990
12/16	3,932	47	1.2%	996
12/15	3,903	46	1.2%	984
Annual Growth	2.8%	8.6%	—	0.4%

2019 Year-End Financials
Debt ratio: 1.36%
Return on equity: 10.95%
Cash ($ mil.): 264
Current ratio: —
Long-term debt ($ mil.): —

No. of shares (mil.): 17
Dividends
  Yield: 3.1%
  Payout: 40.8%
Market value ($ mil.): 830

	STOCK PRICE ($)	P/E	PER SHARE ($)		
	FY Close	High/Low	Earnings	Dividends	Book Value
12/19	46.64	13 10	3.64	1.48	34.56
12/18	39.61	16 11	3.35	1.38	31.81
12/17	47.10	18 14	2.92	1.30	30.00
12/16	49.60	18 12	2.70	1.26	28.40
12/15	34.96	14 12	2.66	1.22	27.12
Annual Growth	7.5%	—	8.2%	4.9%	6.2%

COMMUNITYBANK OF TEXAS, N.A.

EXECUTIVES

Prin, George Casseb
Fo*, Donna Dillon
Chief Financial Officer, Robert Pigott

LOCATIONS

HQ: COMMUNITYBANK OF TEXAS, N.A.
5999 DELAWARE ST, BEAUMONT, TX 777067607
Phone: 409 861-7200
Web: WWW.COMMUNITYBANKOFTX.COM

HISTORICAL FINANCIALS

Company Type: Private

Income Statement   FYE: December 31

	ASSETS ($ mil.)	NET INCOME ($ mil.)	INCOME AS % OF ASSETS	EMPLOYEES
12/18	3,280	48	1.5%	60
12/17	3,079	28	0.9%	—
12/16	2,950	28	1.0%	—
12/15	2,881	25	0.9%	—
Annual Growth	4.4%	25.0%	—	—

COMPUTER SCIENCES CORPORATION

Computer Sciences Corporation (CSC) has been one of the world's leading providers of systems integration and other information technology services. It offers application development data center management communications and networking development IT systems management and business consulting. It also provides business process outsourcing (BPO) services in such areas as billing and payment processing customer relationship management (CRM) and human resources. CSC boasts 2500 clients in more than 70 countries. In 2017 CSC merged with the Enterprise Services segment of Hewlett-Packard Enterprise to form DXC Technology Co. This report is based on CSC's last year as an independent company.

Change in Company Type

DXC is the result of mixing and matching of downsizing and upsizing corporate units. Computer Sciences Corp. spun out its government serv-ice unit several years ago which reduced CSC's revenue. Hewlett Packard Enterprise Services was part of Hewlett Packard Enterprise one of two companies created with Hewlett-Packard split up. The combination of HP Enterprise Services and CSC began in 2016 and concluded in April 2017 when DXC formally began operations. The new company is expected to have annual revenue of about $26 billion. This report reflects the final year of CSC as an independent company.

Operations

Prior to the creation of DXC CSC conducted business in through Global Business Services (GBS) and Global Infrastructure Services (GIS). GBS (55% of revenue) addresses key business challenges such as consulting applications services and software. GIS (45% of revenue) provides IT infrastructure services such as managed and virtual desktop solutions unified communications and collaboration services data center management cyber security and cloud-based offerings.

Geographic Reach

CSC has major operations throughout North America Europe Asia and Australia. The company has clients in more than 70 countries. About 40% of sales are made in the US and about 20% are in the UK the second biggest market.

Sales and Marketing

CSC's clients have included AboveNet Communications Deutsche Telekom DirecTV Vodafone and Ryman Hospitality Properties (formerly Gaylord Entertainment).

Financial Performance

After seven straight years of revenue declines CSC's sales rebounded in 2017 (ended March) to $7.6 billion a 7% increase from 2016. The increase was driven by the Global Business Services unit's business processing services offerings and contributions from recent acquisitions in the Digital Applications business. The Global Infrastructure Services unit posted a small revenue increase from new business and sales from acquisitions.

CSC lost about $123 million in 2017 down from a $251 million profit in 2016 mainly due to large restructuring charges.

Cash flow from operating activities rose to $978 million in 2017 from $802 million in 2016. The increase flowed from an increase in trade payables and a decrease in net account receivables.

Strategy

After going through corporate breakups DXC Technology bets that bigger will be better and stronger in competing in the worldwide market for IT services. The companies have a wide footprint and with some $26 billion in annual revenue and will have some weight to throw around. A question will be if the company can effectively compete with companies that provide similar services such as Cognizant WiPro Accenture IBM Global Service and Dell Technologies.

DXC has bulked up to ride the wave of digital transformation that its customers and potential customers are going through. The company's range of services could lead customers from legacy systems to private or public or hybrid cloud systems.

Mergers and Acquisitions

In 2016 CSC acquired Xchanging plc provider of technology-enabled business services for $633 million. Xchanging brings its Xuber software which is used by commercial insurance companies around the world.

Also in 2016 CSC acquired Aspediens a European provider in the service-management sector and a preferred partner of ServiceNow. The deal extended CSC's reach in software-as-a-service in Europe.

EXECUTIVES

Vice President, Debbie Granberry
Vice President Finance And Administration, Frank Sossi
Vice President Of Global Human Resources And Trans, Mike Darcy
Division Director Deputy Vice President General Manager, Richard Morrow
Senior Vice President And General Manager Security, Art Wong
Vice President, Brad Canel
Vp Corporate Communications, Caryn Kboudi
Svp Of Leasing, Michelle Waak
Auditors: DELOITTE & TOUCHE LLP MCLEAN

LOCATIONS

HQ: COMPUTER SCIENCES CORPORATION
1775 TYSONS BLVD STE 1000, TYSONS, VA 221024284
Phone: 703 245-9675
Web: WWW.CSC.COM

2017 Sales

	$ mil.	% of total
United States	2,986	40
United Kingdom	1,482	19
Australia	921	12
Other Europe	1,594	21
Other International	624	8
Total	**7,607**	**100**

PRODUCTS/OPERATIONS

2017 Sales

	$ mil.	% of total
Global Business Services	4,173	55
Global Infrastructure Services	3,434	45
Total	**7,607**	**100**

Selected Service Areas

Application outsourcing
Business process outsourcing
Customer relationship management
Data hosting
Enterprise application integration
Knowledge management
Management consulting
Risk management
Security
Supply chain management

Selected Solutions

Application Services
Big Data & Analytics
Business & Technology Consulting
Cloud Solutions & Services
Cybersecurity
Industry Software & Solutions
Infrastructure Services
Managed Services & Outsourcing
Mobility Solutions

COMPETITORS

ADP
Accenture
Atos
Booz Allen
CACI International
CIBER
Capgemini
Cognizant Tech Solutions
Computacenter
Convergys
Dell
Deloitte Consulting
Dimension Data
General Dynamics Information Technology
Getronics
HCL Technologies
Honeywell International
IBM Global Services
Infosys

Leidos
ManTech
NTT Data
Northrop Grumman
Siemens AG
Tata Consultancy
Tech Mahindra
Unisys
Wipro
Wipro Technologies

HISTORICAL FINANCIALS

Company Type: Private

Income Statement

FYE: March 31

	REVENUE ($ mil.)	NET INCOME ($ mil.)	NET PROFIT MARGIN	EMPLOYEES
03/17*	7,607	(100)	—	66,000
04/16	7,106	263	3.7%	—
04/15	12,173	7	0.1%	—
03/14	12,998	690	5.3%	—
Annual Growth	(16.4%)	—	—	—

*Fiscal year change

Conagra Brands Inc

ConAgra Foods fills the refrigerators freezers and pantries of most households. The company makes and markets name-brand packaged and frozen foods that are sold widely across the US including in Wal-Mart stores. ConAgra's cornucopia of America's best-known brands includes Banquet Birds Eye Slim Jim Reddi-wip Vlasic Angie's BOOMCHICKAPOP Duke's Earth Balance Gardein Frontera Healthy Choice and Marie Callender. More than 40 domestic manufacturing facilities located in Arkansas California Colorado Illinois Indiana Iowa Kentucky Maryland Michigan Minnesota Missouri Nebraska Nevada Ohio Pennsylvania Tennessee Washington and Wisconsin. ConAgra began as a flour-milling company in Nebraska in 1919 and over the decades transformed into a consumer goods company.

HISTORY

Alva Kinney founded Nebraska Consolidated Mills in 1919 by combining the operations of four Nebraska grain mills. It did not expand outside Nebraska until it opened a mill and feed processing plant in Alabama in 1942.

Consolidated Mills developed Duncan Hines cake mix in the 1950s. But Duncan Hines failed to raise a large enough market share and the company sold it to Procter & Gamble in 1956. Consolidated Mills used the proceeds to expand opening a flour and feed mill in Puerto Rico the next year. In the 1960s while competitors were moving into prepared foods the firm expanded into animal feeds and poultry processing. By 1970 it had poultry processing plants in Alabama Georgia and Louisiana. In 1971 the company changed its name to ConAgra (Latin for "in partnership with the land"). During the 1970s it expanded into the fertilizer catfish and pet accessory businesses.

Poorly performing subsidiaries and commodity speculation caused ConAgra severe financial problems until 1974 when Mike Harper a former Pillsbury executive took over. Harper trimmed properties to reduce debt and had the company back on its feet by 1976. ConAgra stayed focused on the commodities side of the business but was thus tied to volatile price cycles. In 1978 it bought United Agri Products (agricultural chemicals).

ConAgra moved into consumer food products in the 1980s. It bought Banquet (frozen food 1980) and within six years had introduced almost 90 new products under that label. Other purchases included Singleton Seafood (1981) Armour Food Company (meats dairy products frozen food; 1983) and RJR Nabisco's frozen food business (1986). ConAgra became a major player in the red meat market with the 1987 purchases of E.A. Miller (boxed beef) Monfort (beef and lamb) and Swift Independent Packing.

Confident it had found the right path ConAgra continued with acquisitions of consumer food makers including Beatrice Foods (Orville Redenbacher's popcorn Hunt's tomato products) in 1991. In 1997 the company agreed to pay $8.3 million to settle federal charges of wire fraud and watering down grain. That year ConAgra named vice chairman and president Bruce Rohde as CEO; he became chairman in 1998. Also in 1998 the company bought GoodMark Foods maker of Slim Jim and Nabisco's Egg Beaters and table spread unit(Parkay). ConAgra bought Holly Ridge Foods (pastries) in 1999 and announced a major restructuring.

ConAgra bought Emerge an agricultural and land-use information software provider from Litton Industries in 2000. It also acquired Seaboard's poultry division and refrigerated meat alternatives maker Lightlife (Tofu pups Smart Dogs) before buying major brand holder International Home Foods from HM Capital Partners (known as Hicks Muse Tate & Furst at the time) for about $2.9 billion. The company then became ConAgra Foods.

During 2001 the company drew SEC attention and was forced to restate earnings for the previous three years due to accounting no-no's in its United Agri Products division.

In 2002 the USDA forced ConAgra to recall 19 million pounds of ground beef because of possible E. coli contamination making it the second-largest food recall in US history. (The largest recall occurred in 1997 when Hudson Foods later purchased by Tyson Foods withdrew 35 million pounds of beef.) Later in 2002 ConAgra sold its fresh beef and pork processing business — one of the largest in the US — to Booth Creek Management and HM Capital Partners and it was renamed Swift & Company Swift & Company. (Swift was acquired by Brazilian beef giant JBS in 2007.)

In 2003 the company began supplying packaged meat products for grilling to George Foreman Foods which sells them via its Web site. That year it sold its Bumble Bee canned seafood business to members of Bumble Bee management and private investment firm Centre Partners Management and its blue cheese brands (Treasure Cave Nauvoo) to Canada's Saputo Inc. for undisclosed prices. It also sold its chicken processing business to Pilgrim's Pride for a stock and cash deal worth about $550 million in 2003.

Also in 2003 ConAgra agreed to pay $1.5 million in cash and job offers to settle an EEOC lawsuit charging bias against disabled workers at the company's California-based Gilroy Foods plant. The agreement involves the largest disability settlement in the agriculture industry. The dispute dated back to 1999 when Gilroy Foods then owned by Basic Vegetable Products (ConAgra bought the facility in 2000) after a strike failed to recall disabled workers who were on leaves of absence due to illness or pregnancy or who had a history of illness or injury.

In keeping with its strategy to focus on its branded and value-added food business in 2003 ConAgra sold United Agri Products to Apollo Management for stock and securities. The deal was worth about $600 million. In 2004 it sold its minority interest in the beef and pork processing operations of Swift Foods to HM Capital Partners. The deal was worth $194 million. ConAgra also sold Swift's feedlot operations to Smithfield Foods for an undisclosed amount.

ConAgra sold its turkey hatchery and breeding business to Ag Forte in 2004. It sold its Canadian and US crop inputs businesses and its Spanish feed and Portuguese poultry businesses that year as well. In addition it sold Casa de Oro Foods (the US's third-largest tortilla maker) to the Plaza Belmont Fund II. Also that year ConAgra introduced Golden Cuisine a line of frozen meals designed for seniors. The company began manufacturing and supplying Golden Cuisine to Meals On Wheels which distributes the meals which are formulated for seniors to the homebound elderly. That year ConAgra also introduced a high-fiber flour called Ultragrain that has the taste and texture of refined flour but the nutrition of whole grain.

In 2005 ConAgra sold its remaining 15 million shares of Pilgrim's Pride to that company for about $480 million. That year CEO Bruce Rhode retired. His replacement was former chairman and CEO of PepsiCo Beverages and Foods North America Gary Rodkin who began a company-wide restructuring. The company reorganized its business structure from three channels to two: Foodservice was merged with Food Ingredients and became ConAgra Foods Commercial ; the ConAgra Retail channel remained the same.

ConAgra agreed to pay a $14 million shareholder settlement in 2005 regarding a lawsuit claiming fictitious sales and mis-reported earnings at its former subsidiary United Agri Products.

In a move to demonstrate its commitment to the humane treatment of animals in 2006 ConAgra urged its poultry suppliers to consider slaughtering chickens in a more humane manner called controlled-atmosphere killing. The process which ConAgra has only suggested to its suppliers is approved by the People for the Ethical Treatment of Animals.

Rodkin continued the company redo focusing on portfolio trimming when in early 2006 he announced plans to sell a large part of ConAgra's refrigerated-meats business. The brands involved in the sale include some of the company's best-known: Armour Butterball and Eckrich. (The Brown 'N Serve Healthy Choice Hebrew National Pemmican and Slim Jim brands were not included in the portfolio reduction.) It sold its Cook's ham business to Smithfield Foods for $260 million that year.

Not long after that it agreed to sell of the rest of its refrigerated meats business that it had for sale to Smithfield as well. The deal which became final in October 2006 cost Smithfield $571 million in cash. That same month it sold its Butterball Turkey unit to Carolina Turkeys for $325 million. (Carolina subsequently changed its company name to Butterball LLC .)

Divesting almost faster than one can keep track of one day after the Butterball deal was completed ConAgra sold its MaMa Rosa's Pizza operations to investment firm the Plaza Belmont Management Group. (MaMa Rosa's is refrigerated — not frozen pizza — and competes in a different market than other pizzas albeit frozen powerhouses such as Di Giorno Tombstone or Tony's .)

In another move to improve long-term operating performance ConAgra announced its intention to sell off its seafood and domestic and imported cheese businesses. To that end the company sold its surimi business including the Louis Kemp brand to Trident Seafoods and its Singleton Seafood and Meridian Seafood to Singleton Fisheries. It sold its specialty and imported cheese operation Swissrose International to investment company Fairmount Food Group. Late in 2006 the company sold its oat-milling business to investment companies Sequel Holdings and Falcon Investment Advisors.

The company added to its Lamb Weston branded potato products with the 2008 acquisition of Watts Brothers. With operations in Washington and Oregon Watts is a vegetable-processing company that has annual sales of some $100 million. It has retail foodservice and industrial customers throughout the US as well as in Mexico Japan China and other Far East countries. The deal also included Watts' organic dairy fertilizer cold storage packaging and agricultural farming businesses.

In early 2007 salmonella was found in some of the company's Peter Pan and Great Value (a Wal-Mart product) brands of peanut butter forcing a nationwide recall of the peanut butter bearing the product code involved. Salmonella food poisoning was linked to some 600 people in 47 states. No deaths related to the peanut better were confirmed. The recall eventually included products made as far back as October 2004. ConAgra shut down the Sylvester Georgia plant that was involved in the outbreak and reopened it in Augusts 2007 having spent $15 million on renovation which included repairing the roof installing new equipment and creating a manufacturing process that better separated raw materials from the finished peanut butter.

Just two months later the company voluntarily stopped production at the Missouri plant that makes its Banquet and generic brands of frozen turkey and chicken pot pies after learning that the were linked to some 140 cases of salmonella in 30 states. ConAgra did not recall the pies but offered mail-in refunds and store returns. The USDA began an investigation and advised consumers not to eat the pies.

As part of its strategy to add to its brand-name offerings in 2007 ConAgra acquired Alexia Foods a maker of natural frozen potatoes appetizers and artisan breads for about $50 million in cash. Later that year the company paid a penalty of $45 million in the wake of SEC charges that alleged the company had misreported its profits for the fiscal years 1999 2000 and 2001.

The company acquired Lincoln Snacks Company in 2007. Lincoln's well-known brands such as Fiddle Faddle and Poppycock extended ConAgra's name-brand lineup which is in line with company strategy. That year it also announced the removal of the chemicals from its microwave popcorn products that are suspected of causing lung ailments in popcorn-plant workers.

ConAgra sold its trading and merchandising operations (ConAgra Trade Group) in 2008 to a group of investors that included the Ospraie Special Opportunities Fund for $2.8 billion. The sale was part of the company's long-term strategy to exit the commodities business and concentrate on its consumer food products. Saying it couldn't give the brand the attention it needs in 2008 the company sold its Knott's Berry Farm jam and jelly business to J. M. Smucker .

In a tragedy that made the evening news three ConAgra workers were killed and some 40 were injured in an explosion and fire at a company Slim Jim manufacturing plant in Garner North Carolina in June 2009. It was later determined that the blast was caused by a natural-gas leak. ConAgra partnered with the United Way forming the Garner Plant Fund that raised money to assist the victims and their families. The company also continued to pay workers salaries while the plant remained closed for investigation. ConAgra was fined $106000 by the government in 2010 and the plant was eventually closed.

During 2010 ConAgra unloaded its Gilroy Foods & Flavors business-to-business unit to Olam

International for $250 million. The sale excluded Gilroy's seasonings and flavors businesses.

In 2011 ConAgra Foods made an unsolicited takeover bid to buy Ralcorp Holdings a leading maker of private-label snack foods cereals and condiments. After proffering an initial bid of $82 per share ConAgra ultimately offered $94 (valuing Ralcorp at more than $5 billion). However Ralcorp spurned all bids saying they were not in the best interests of shareholders.

In May 2012 the company completed the acquisition of Odom's Tennessee Pride the #2 producer of frozen breakfast sandwiches in the US.

In January 2013 ConAgra completed its $6.8 billion purchase of Ralcorp Holdings.

In September 2013 it purchased the frozen dessert producer business of Harlan Bakeries which made frozen fruit pies cream pies pastry shells and loaf cakes.

In early 2013 ConAgra acquired Ralcorp the nation's #1 maker of private-label food in a deal valued at about $6.8 billion (including debt). The combined company was expected to generate $18 billion in sales and made ConAgra the largest private-brand packaged foods business in North America with annual private brand sales of about $4.5 billion a year. The private brands segment makes private-label ready-to-eat cereals cereal bars snack mixes cookies crackers and other products for retailers under their own brand names.

EXECUTIVES

Senior Vice President And Chief Litigation Counsel, Leo A Knowles

Evp General Counsel And Corporate Secretary, Colleen Batcheler, age 46, $521,635 total compensation

Evp And Cfo, John F. Gehring, age 59, $643,269 total compensation

Ceo, Sean M. Connolly, $1,100,000 total compensation

President Consumer Foods, Thomas M. (Tom) McGough, age 55, $636,538 total compensation

Evp And President Sales, Derek De La Mater

President Commercial Foods, Tom Werner, $438,654 total compensation

Evp And Chief Supply Chain Officer, Dave Biegger

Evp And Chief Human Resources Officer, Charisse Brock

Cio, Mindy Simon

Vp Talent Effectiveness, Tresia Nwamadi

Vice President Research And Development, Richard McArdle

Vp Research And Development Packaging, Eric Sinz

Senior Vice President Insights And Analytics, Bob Nolan

Vice President Product Readiness, Mark Evans

Vice President Customer Development, Michael Fitzpatrick

Vice President Information Technology, Scott Tylski

Vice President Business Development, Keith Chapman

Senior Vice President And General Manager Global Business Unit, Sharon Miller

Vice President Internal Audit, Brendy Sealock

Vice President Marketing, Mike Veal

Vice President Sustainable Development, Gail Tavill

Division Vp West, Wes Upchurch

Vice President Human Resources, Kelly Schaefer

Vice President General Manager, Taylor Strubell

Vice President Of Marketing, Andy Johnston

Vice President Assistant Treasurer, Scott Schneider

Vice President Research Quality And Innovation, Christian Rhynalds

Vice President General Manager Spicetec, Mark Duffy

Senior Vice President Marketing, Karen E Carey

Vice President Internal Audit, Allen Cooper

Senior Vice President Supply Chain, Mike Tracy

Senior Vice President Procurement, Dk Singh

Vice President Corporate Real Estate And Facilities, James Doyle

Vice President Finance, Teresa Wallfred

Vice President Program Management, Mark Grohe

Vice President Manufacturing, Charlie Gorman

Vice President Marketing, Karl Sears

Vice President Transportation And Warehousing, Ken Smith

Senior Vice President Sales, Bill Tragos

Vice President Supply Chain Integration, Craig Weiss

Senior Vice President Strategy And Business Development, Brian Davison

Vice President Finance Enterprise Procurement, Scott Luther

Vice President Program Implementation, Joe McSharry

Vp Enterprise Deployment, Jim Blakemore

Vice President Customer Facing Lead Ralcorp Integration, Dave Dobronski

Vice President Procurement, Bob Hellem

Vice President Precision Marketing, Delu Jackson

Vice President International Finance, Denise Hansen

Vice President Engineering, Jim Prunesti

Vice President Sales Kroger Team, Jeremy Attal

Senior Vice President Sales Grocery, Christopher Chromy

Chairman, Steven F. (Steve) Goldstone, age 75

Board Member, Jennifer Hudson

Auditors: KPMG LLP

LOCATIONS

HQ: Conagra Brands Inc
222 West Merchandise Mart Plaza, Suite 1300, Chicago, IL 60654
Phone: 312 549-5000
Web: www.conagrabrands.com

PRODUCTS/OPERATIONS

2018 sales

	$ mil.	% of total
Grocery & Snacks	3,279	34
Refrigerated & Frozen	2,804	30
International	793	8
Foodservice	934	10
Pinnacle Foods	1,727	18
Total	**9,538**	**100**

Selected Brands

Commercial foods
  ConAgra Mills
  Lamb Weston
  Spicetec Flavors & Seasonings
Consumer foods
  Act II
  Alexia
  Banquet
  Bertolli
  Blue Bonnet
  Chef Boyardee
  DAVID Seeds
  Egg Beaters
  Healthy Choice
  Hebrew National
  Hunt's
  Marie Callender's
  Odom's Tennessee Pride
  Orville Redenbacher's
  PAM
  Peter Pan
  P.F. Chang's
  Reddi-wip
  Slim Jim
  Snack Pack
  Swiss Miss
  Van Camp's
  Wesson

COMPETITORS

American Pop Corn	Jenny Craig
B&G Foods	Kellogg
Big Heart Pet Brands	Link Snacks
Boulder Brands	MOM Brands
Bush Brothers	Manischewitz Company
Campbell Soup	McCain Foods
Clorox	McIlhenny
Eden Foods	Monterey Gourmet Foods
Frito-Lay	Mott's
General Mills	Nestlé
Gilster-Mary Lee	Newman's Own
Goya	Nutrisystem
H. J. Heinz Limited	Pinnacle Foods
Hain Celestial	Schwan's
Hanover Foods	Seneca Foods
Heinz	Slim-Fast
Hormel	Smucker
Inventure foods	Snappy Popcorn
J-OIL MILLS	Weaver Popcorn Company
JR Simplot	

HISTORICAL FINANCIALS

Company Type: Public

Income Statement				FYE: May 31
	REVENUE ($ mil.)	NET INCOME ($ mil.)	NET PROFIT MARGIN	EMPLOYEES
05/20	11,054	840	7.6%	16,500
05/19	9,538	678	7.1%	18,000
05/18	7,938	808	10.2%	12,400
05/17	7,826	639	8.2%	12,600
05/16	11,642	(677)	—	20,900
Annual Growth	(1.3%)	—	—	(5.7%)

2020 Year-End Financials

Debt ratio: 43.70%
Return on equity: 10.83%
Cash ($ mil.): 553
Current ratio: 0.88
Long-term debt ($ mil.): 8,900

No. of shares (mil.): 487
Dividends
  Yield: 0.0%
  Payout: 49.4%
Market value ($ mil.): 16,948

	STOCK PRICE ($) FY Close	P/E High/Low		PER SHARE ($) Earnings	Dividends	Book Value
05/20	34.79	20	14	1.72	0.85	16.17
05/19	28.83	25	14	1.52	0.85	15.19
05/18	37.41	20	16	1.98	0.85	9.41
05/17	39.03	33	23	1.46	0.90	9.58
05/16	45.29	—	—	(1.56)	1.00	8.48
Annual Growth	(6.4%)		—	—	(4.0%)	17.5%

ConnectOne Bancorp Inc (New)

ConnectOne Bancorp (formerly Center Bancorp) is the holding company for ConnectOne Bank which operates some two dozen branches across New Jersey. Serving individuals and local businesses the bank offers such deposit products as checking savings and money market accounts; CDs; and IRAs. It also performs trust services. Commercial loans account for about 60% of the bank's loan portfolio; residential mortgages account for most of the remainder. It also has a subsidiary that sells annuities and property/casualty life and health coverage. The former Center Bancorp acquired rival community bank ConnectOne Bancorp in 2014 and took that name.

Geographic Reach

ConnectOne has 24 branches in Bergen Essex Hudson Manhattan Mercer Monmouth Morris and Union Counties in New Jersey.

Mergers and Acquisitions

In 2019 ConnectOne Bancorp agreed to acquire online business lending marketplace company BoeFly. BoeFly connects franchisors and small business owners with lenders and loan brokers in the US and has facilitated more than $5 billion in financing transactions. BoeFly's online platform and client network will enhance and expand ConnectOne's Small Business Adminstration (SBA) line of business.

EXECUTIVES

Vice President, Lisa Wagner
Senior Vice President, Leo Faresich
Vice President, Antonio Medici
Auditors: Crowe LLP

LOCATIONS

HQ: ConnectOne Bancorp Inc (New)
301 Sylvan Avenue, Englewood Cliffs, NJ 07632
Phone: 201 816-8900
Web: www.centerbancorp.com

COMPETITORS

BCB Bancorp	New York Community Bancorp
Bank of America	
Citizens Financial Corp.	Oritani Financial
	PNC Financial
Fulton Financial	Provident Financial Services
Hudson City Bancorp	
Investors Bancorp	Sovereign Bank
JPMorgan Chase	Valley National Bancorp
Kearny Financial	
Lakeland Bancorp	Westamerica

HISTORICAL FINANCIALS

Company Type: Public

Income Statement				FYE: December 31
	ASSETS ($ mil.)	NET INCOME ($ mil.)	INCOME AS % OF ASSETS	EMPLOYEES
12/19	6,174	73	1.2%	—
12/18	5,462	60	1.1%	—
12/17	5,108	43	0.8%	—
12/16	4,426	31	0.7%	—
12/15	4,016	41	1.0%	—
Annual Growth	11.3%	15.5%	—	—

2019 Year-End Financials

Debt ratio: 2.09%
Return on equity: 10.91%
Cash ($ mil.): 201
Current ratio: —
Long-term debt ($ mil.): —

No. of shares (mil.): 35
Dividends
  Yield: 1.3%
  Payout: 16.8%
Market value ($ mil.): 902

	STOCK PRICE ($) FY Close	P/E High/Low		PER SHARE ($) Earnings	Dividends	Book Value
12/19	25.72	13	9	2.07	0.35	20.85
12/18	18.47	17	9	1.86	0.30	18.99
12/17	25.75	21	16	1.34	0.30	17.63
12/16	25.95	26	15	1.01	0.30	16.62
12/15	18.69	16	13	1.36	0.30	15.87
Annual Growth	8.3%		—	11.1%	3.6%	7.1%

ConocoPhillips

EXECUTIVES

Ceo, Ryan M Lance
Chb-Ceo*, J J Mulva
Exec V Pres-Cfo-Treas*, John A Carrig
V Pres*, Matt Fox
Director, Eduardo Romero
Director, Jim Lowry
Director, Keith Garza
Senior Software Engineer, Yvonne Shonne Scott
Supervisor Sap Operations, Ron Hoofard
Manager, Sanjay Mehta
Executive Assistant, Carol Riddell
Auditors: Ernst & Young LLP

LOCATIONS

HQ: ConocoPhillips
925 N. Eldridge Parkway, Houston, TX 77079
Phone: 281 293-1000
Web: www.conocophillips.com

HISTORICAL FINANCIALS

Company Type: Public

Income Statement				FYE: December 31
	REVENUE ($ mil.)	NET INCOME ($ mil.)	NET PROFIT MARGIN	EMPLOYEES
12/19	36,670	7,189	19.6%	10,400
12/18	38,727	6,257	16.2%	10,800
12/17	32,584	(855)	—	11,400
12/16	24,360	(3,615)	—	13,300
12/15	30,935	(4,428)	—	15,900
Annual Growth	4.3%	—	—	(10.1%)

2019 Year-End Financials

Debt ratio: 21.12%
Return on equity: 21.49%
Cash ($ mil.): 5,088
Current ratio: 2.40
Long-term debt ($ mil.): 14,790

No. of shares (mil.): 1,084
Dividends
  Yield: 2.0%
  Payout: 20.8%
Market value ($ mil.): 70,549

	STOCK PRICE ($) FY Close	P/E High/Low		PER SHARE ($) Earnings	Dividends	Book Value
12/19	65.03	11	8	6.40	1.34	32.24
12/18	62.35	15	10	5.32	1.16	28.06
12/17	54.89	—	—	(0.70)	1.06	26.00
12/16	50.14	—	—	(2.91)	1.00	28.27
12/15	46.69	—	—	(3.58)	2.94	32.17
Annual Growth	8.6%		—	—	(17.9%)	0.1%

Consolidated Edison Co. of New York, Inc.

Consolidated Edison Company of New York (Con Edison of New York) keeps the nightlife pulsing in The Big Apple. The utility a subsidiary of Consolidated Edison distributes electricity throughout most of New York City and Westchester County. The company distributes electricity to 3.4 million residential and business customers in New York City; it also delivers natural gas to about 1.1 million customers. The utility also provides steam services to 1703 customers in portions of the New York metropolitan area. Con Edison of New York owns and operates more than 133900 miles of overhead and underground power distribution lines.

Operations

The company has three segments: electric gas and steam — which contributed 79% 15% and 6% of total revenues in 2015.

Its assets include more than 4300 miles of gas distribution mains a gas liquefaction and storage facility and electric and steam generating stations. It also owns a range of power transmission assets which are operated by the New York Independent System Operator. Con Edison of New York's electric generating facilities consist of plants located in New York City with an aggregate capacity of 724 MW.

The company's distribution system had a transformer capacity of 29762 MVA with 36929 miles of overhead distribution lines and 97286 miles of underground distribution lines. The underground distribution lines represent the single longest underground electric delivery system in the United States.

Geographic Reach

Con Edison of New York has distribution facilities throughout New York City and Westchester County and operates manufactured gas plants at 51 sites.

Sales and Marketing

Con Edison of New York delivers electricity to state and municipal customers of NYPA and economic development customers of municipal electric agencies. Its customers include residential commercial industrial public authorities retail choice customers.

Financial Performance

In fiscal 2015 its net revenues decreased by 4% due to the lower gas steam and electric sales.

Revenues from electric decreased due to lower purchased power expenses and lower fuel expenses offset in part by higher revenues from the electric rate plan.

Con Edison of New York's gas revenues declined due to a decrease in gas purchased for resale expenses offset in part by higher revenues from the gas rate plan (reflecting higher delivery volumes attributable to oil-to-gas conversions). However revenues from steam increased due primarily to higher fuel expenses and higher revenues from the steam rate plan offset by the weather impact on revenues and lower purchased power costs.

In fiscal 2015 net income increased by 2% due to lower gas purchased for resale and purchased power.

Cash from operating activities increased by 16% due to lower income taxes paid net of refunds received offset in part by increased pension contributions.

Strategy

In 2016 Con Edison of New York filed a request with the New York State Public Service Commission for an electric rate increase of $482 million. It also entered into an agreement to sell certain electric transmission projects to NY Transco.

The company (in 2015) partnered with Drive Electric Vehicle Research Forward to help promote electric vehicles.

In 2014 Con Edison of New York was in the middle of a four-year $1 billion storm hardening program in the wake of 2012's Superstorm Sandy. Investments include the installation of 3000 devices that isolate and clear temporary faults on overhead electric systems and more than 150 smart switches that minimize outages caused by fallen trees. More than a mile of flood walls and 260 pieces of submersible equipment also have been installed. For its efforts the utility was named as the winner of the 2014 Outstanding System Reliability Award by the PA Consulting Group. The award recognizes the PA Consulting Group

ReliabilityOne regional award recipient that demonstrated superior annual system-wide reliability performance for its customers. Con Edison of New York was also named best in the Northeast Region.

Company Background

Citing a 20% growth rate during the 2000s Con Edison of New York in 2011 spent almost $1.8 billion ($2 billion in 2010) to upgrade the company's aging electrical delivery systems (new high-voltage transmission cables) in New York City and surrounding areas. In 2010 Con Edison of New York and sister company Orange and Rockland also received $200 million in federal grants to install smart grid technology (automated more efficient meters and other systems) across their service area. By mid-2011 the company had also supported the installation of 8.5 MW of solar power units across its service region.

EXECUTIVES

Chairman And Ceo, Kevin Burke, age 70, $1,107,200 total compensation
Svp And Cro, Robert N. Hoglund, age 59, $584,200 total compensation
President Of Consolidated Edison Company Of New York; Inc., Craig S. Ivey, age 57
President And Ceo Orange And Rockland Utilities Inc., John T. McAvoy, age 59
Owner, Linda Goldberg
Auditors: PricewaterhouseCoopers LLP

LOCATIONS

HQ: Consolidated Edison Co. of New York, Inc.
4 Irving Place, New York, NY 10003
Phone: 212 460-4600

COMPETITORS

Commerce Energy Group	New York Power
Delmarva Power	Authority
Green Mountain Energy	Public Service
Integrys Energy	Enterprise Group
Services	Rochester Gas and
NYSEG	Electric
National Grid USA	

HISTORICAL FINANCIALS

Company Type: Public

Income Statement   FYE: December 31

	REVENUE ($ mil.)	NET INCOME ($ mil.)	NET PROFIT MARGIN	EMPLOYEES
12/19	10,821	1,250	11.6%	14,890
12/18	10,680	1,196	11.2%	13,685
12/17	10,468	1,104	10.5%	14,010
12/16	10,165	1,056	10.4%	13,531
12/15	10,328	1,084	10.5%	13,393
Annual Growth	1.2%	3.6%	—	2.7%

2019 Year-End Financials

Debt ratio: 32.14%	No. of shares (mil.): 235
Return on equity: 9.24%	Dividends
Cash ($ mil.): 933	Yield: —
Current ratio: 0.86	Payout: 72.9%
Long-term debt ($ mil.): 14,614	Market value ($ mil.): —

Consolidated Edison Inc

Utility holding company Consolidated Edison (Con Edison) is the night light for the city that never sleeps. Con Edison's main subsidiary Consolidated Edison Company of New York distributes electricity to 3.5 million residential and business customers in a 660-mile service territory centered on New York City. It delivers natural gas to about 1.1 million customers and operates the country's largest steam distribution service to deliver energy to parts of Manhattan. Subsidiary Orange and Rockland Utilities serves more than 300000 electric and gas customers in New York and New Jersey. Con Edison also owns or operates renewable energy facilities and advises large clients on energy efficiency programs.

Operations

Con Edison owns and operates the following business units: Consolidated Edison Company of New York (CECONY) Clean Energy Businesses Orange and Rockland Utilities (O&R) and Con Edison Transmission (CET).

CECONY produces more than 80% of Con Edison's total revenue by distributing electricity natural gas and steam in New York City. The unit purchases the majority of its electricity from third parties and delivers it through its extensive distribution network of 39 transmission substations 62 area substations and nearly 135000 miles of distribution lines. Its gas operations liquefy store and distribute gas via 4400 miles of mains and 376000 service lines. CECONY operates the largest steam distribution system in the US.

The Clean Energy Businesses unit generates more than 5% of revenue. The unit develops owns and operates renewable and energy infrastructure projects to wholesale and retail customers. It has generating capacity of more than 2600 MW through its solar (85%) and wind (15%) facilities. The business also sells services to manage the energy dispatch fuel requirements and risk management for various non-affiliated generating plants in addition to energy-efficiency consultancy.

O&R (more than 5% of sales) delivers electricity and gas to customers in southeastern New York and New Jersey. The unit purchases its electricity from outside sources and delivers it through its own distribution network of transmission substations area substations and nearly 6000 miles of distribution lines. Gas requirements and purchase contracts are shared with its affiliate subsidiary CECONY which manages the procurement process. O&R gas is delivered through its own mains and service lines.

The Con Edison Transmission segment invests in electric transmission facilities and gas pipeline and storage facilities through its wholly owned subsidiaries Consolidated Edison Transmission (CET Electric) and Con Edison Gas Pipeline and Storage (CET Gas).

Geographic Reach

Con Edison's utility operations serve customers primarily in New York City greater New York state and New Jersey. Affiliates provide services to Pennsylvania West Virginia and Virginia.

Most of its assets are in the New York City vicinity. Its non-CECONY business segments have assets throughout the US including New Jersey Massachusetts Nebraska California Texas Minnesota Nevada and Arizona.

Sales and Marketing

Con Edison's businesses sell electricity purchased in wholesale markets to retail customers provide energy-related products and services to wholesale and retail customers and develop own and operate renewable and energy infrastructure projects. The CECONY unit counts some 3.5 million customers while Con Edison's O&R unit boasts 300000 electric customers in southeastern New York and northern New Jersey and 100000 gas customers in southeastern New York. The Clean Energy Businesses division serves both wholesale and retail customers and offers consultancy to government and commercial entities.

Financial Performance

Con Edison's revenue remained in $12 to $12.5 billion. Meanwhile net income has followed the opposite trajectory growing during that period before falling in 2019.

In 2019 the company's sales grew 2% to $12.6 billion amid uplift in electric gas and steam revenue. Net income dipped 3% to $1.3 billion as increases in operating expenses across the board weighed on margins.

Con Edison's cash balance increased by $211 million ending the year $1.2 billion. The company's operating activities generated $3.1 billion and its financing activities bore cash of $859 million while its investing activities absorbed $3.8 billion. Con Edison's primary cash used in higher investments in electric and gas transmission projects and increased utility construction costs.

Strategy

One of the companies under Consolidated Edison is CECONY. CECONY's mission comprises four goals: to provide energy services to customers safely reliably efficiently and in an environmentally sound manner; to provide a workplace that allows employees to realize their full potential; to improve the quality of life in the communities that the company serves; and to provide a fair return to investors. The company achieves these goals through three strategic priorities: improving public and employee safety achieving operational excellence and enhancing the customer experience.

HISTORY

Several professionals led by Timothy Dewey formed The New York Gas Light Company in 1823 to illuminate part of Manhattan. In 1884 five other gas companies joined New York Gas Light to form the Consolidated Gas Company of New York.

Thomas Edison's incandescent lamp came on the scene in 1879 and The Edison Electric Illuminating Company of New York was formed in 1880 to build the world's first commercial electric power station (Pearl Street) financed by a group led by J.P. Morgan. Edison supervised the project and in 1882 New York became the first major city with electric lighting.

Realizing electricity would replace gas Consolidated Gas acquired electric companies including Anthony Brady's New York Gas and Electric Light Heat and Power Company (1900) which joined Edison's Illuminating Company in 1901 to form the New York Edison Company. More than 170 purchases followed including that of the New York Steam Company (1930) a cheap source of steam for electric turbines.

The Public Utility Holding Company Act of 1935 ushered in the era of regulated regional monopolies. The next year New York Edison combined its holdings to form the Consolidated Edison Company of New York (Con Ed).

Con Ed opened its first nuclear station in 1962. By then Con Ed had a reputation for inefficiency and poor service and shareholders were angry about its slow growth and low earnings. Environmentalists joined the grousers in 1963 when Con Ed began constructing a pumped-storage plant in Cornwall near the Hudson River. Charles Luce a former undersecretary with the Department of Interior was recruited to rescue Con Ed in 1967. He added power plants and beefed up customer service.

In the 1970s inflation and the energy crisis drove up oil prices (Con Ed's main fuel source) and in 1974 Luce withheld dividends for the first time since 1885. He persuaded the New York State Power Authority to buy two unfinished power plants saving Con Ed $200 million. In 1980 Luce ended the Cornwall controversy and donated the land for park use. He retired in 1982.

The utility started buying power from various suppliers and in 1984 began a two-year price freeze a boon to rate-hike-weary New Yorkers. The New York State Public Service Commission didn't approve another rate increase until 1992.

In 1997 Con Ed government officials consumer groups and other energy firms outlined the company's deregulation plan which included the formation of the Consolidated Edison Inc. holding company (known as Con Edison) and a power marketing unit in 1998. The next year Con Edison sold New York City generating facilities to KeySpan Northern States Power and Orion Power for a total of $1.65 billion.

Also in 1999 Con Edison bought Orange and Rockland Utilities for $790 million to increase its New York base and expand into New Jersey and Pennsylvania. In an effort to push into New England the company that year agreed to buy Northeast Utilities (NU since renamed Eversource Energy) for $3.3 billion in cash and stock and $3.9 billion in assumed debt. But the deal broke down in 2001. NU accused Con Edison of improperly trying to renegotiate terms while Con Edison accused NU of concealing information about unfavorable power supply contracts.

Con Edison's Indian Point Unit 2 nuclear plant was shut down temporarily in 2000 after a radioactive steam leak; later that year it agreed to sell Indian Point Units 1 and 2 to Entergy for $502 million. The sale was completed in 2001. That year Con Edison also incurred an estimated $400 million in costs related to emergency response and asset damage from the September 11 terrorist attacks on New York City.

In 2013 Con Edison announced plans to make it easier and less expensive for customers to convert from heating oil to lower cost natural gas in Manhattan and the Bronx. Its gas infrastructure expansion program includes investing a $100 million on new mains regulators and other upgrades in several neighborhoods.

It also plans to develop 25 MW of solar energy resources in New York City by the end of 2015. The solar power generated in the New York project would annually offset about 16000 tons of carbon dioxide.

EXECUTIVES

Senior Vice President Public Affairs, Frances Resheske

Vice President Human Resources, Claude Trahan, age 69

President And Ceo Con Edison Transmission Inc., Joseph P. Oates, age 59

Svp And Cfo Con Edison And Cecony, Robert N. Hoglund, age 59, $721,242 total compensation

Chairman And Ceo Coned And Cecony, John T. McAvoy, age 59, $1,220,767 total compensation

President Consolidated Edison Company Of New York Inc. (cecony), Timothy P. Cawley, age 55, $409,033 total compensation

Svp And General Counsel Consolidated Edison And Cecony, Elizabeth D. Moore, age 65, $608,017 total compensation

President And Ceo Con Edison Clean Energy Businesses Inc., Mark Noyes, age 55

Office Of The Vice President Central Engineering, Laurens Irizarry

Auditors: PricewaterhouseCoopers LLP

LOCATIONS

HQ: Consolidated Edison Inc
4 Irving Place, New York, NY 10003
Phone: 212 460-4600
Web: www.conedison.com

PRODUCTS/OPERATIONS

2018 Sales

	$ mil.	% of total
Electric	8,612	70
Gas	2,327	19
Non-utility	767	6
Steam	631	5
Total	**12,337**	**100**

2018 sales

	$ mil.	% of total
CECONY	10,680	87
Clean Energy Business	891	7
O&R (Orange and Rockland)	763	6
Con Edison Transmissino	4	-
Other	-1	-
Total	**12,337**	**100**

Selected Subsidiaries

Consolidated Edison Inc. (Con Edison)
Consolidated Edison Company of New York Inc. (CECONY)
Con Edison Clean Energy Businesses Inc.
  Consolidated Edison Development Inc.
  Consolidated Edison Energy Inc.
Consolidated Edison Solutions Inc.
Con Edison Transmission Inc.
  Consolidated Edison Transmission LLC (CET Electric)
  Consolidated Edison Gas Pipeline and Storage LLC (CET Gas)
Orange and Rockland Utilities Inc. (O&R)
Pike County Light & Power Company
Rockland Electric Company (RECO)

COMPETITORS

AEP	PPL Corporation
Avangrid	Public Service
CH Energy	Enterprise Group
Green Mountain Energy	South Jersey
NSTAR	Industries
National Fuel Gas	USPowerGen
National Grid USA	

HISTORICAL FINANCIALS

Company Type: Public

Income Statement — FYE: December 31

	REVENUE ($ mil.)	NET INCOME ($ mil.)	NET PROFIT MARGIN	EMPLOYEES
12/19	12,574	1,343	10.7%	14,890
12/18	12,337	1,382	11.2%	15,307
12/17	12,033	1,525	12.7%	15,591
12/16	12,075	1,245	10.3%	14,960
12/15	12,554	1,193	9.5%	14,806
Annual Growth	0.0%	3.0%	—	0.1%

2019 Year-End Financials

Debt ratio: 34.39%	No. of shares (mil.): 333
Return on equity: 7.73%	Dividends
Cash ($ mil.): 981	Yield: 3.2%
Current ratio: 0.68	Payout: 72.5%
Long-term debt ($ mil.): 18,527	Market value ($ mil.): 30,127

	STOCK PRICE ($)	P/E	PER SHARE ($)		
	FY Close	High/Low	Earnings	Dividends	Book Value
12/19	90.47	23 18	4.08	2.96	54.12
12/18	76.46	19 16	4.42	2.86	52.11
12/17	84.95	18 15	4.94	2.76	49.74
12/16	73.68	20 15	4.12	2.68	46.88
12/15	64.27	18 14	4.05	2.60	44.55
Annual Growth	8.9%	— —	0.2%	3.3%	5.0%

Constellation Brands Inc

Constellation Brands is a leading wine beer and spirits company in North America. The company is the world's largest premium wine producer offering more than 100 brands sourced from the world's premier wine-growing regions; brands include Robert Mondavi Clos du Bois and Meiomi. On the beer front Constellation holds the exclusive license to produce import and sell Mexican beer giant Grupo Modelo's Corona and Modelo brand in the US; it also owns a number of small-scale craft beer brands. Spirits the company's smallest business includes the premium spirits Casa Noble and SVEDKA vodka. Brothers Richard and Robert Sands control the company which was founded by the late Marvin Sands.

Operations

Constellation Brands reports its business in four segments: Beer Wine and Spirits Corporate Operations and Other and Canopy but its two main segments are Beer and Wine & Spirits. The beer segment accounting for about 65% of group revenue has an exclusive license to import and sell Grupo Modelo's Corona Modelo and other brands. Wine & Spirits accounting for more than 30% covers a wide range of wine and spirits over a spectrum of price points. Wine brands include Charles Smith Wines Meiomi and Ruffino while spirits brands include SVEDKA a Swedish import and the largest imported vodka brand in the US. The remaining revenue came from canopy segment.

Geographic Reach

New York-based Constellation Brands has operations in the US Mexico New Zealand Italy and Canada and sells its products in about 150 countries. That being said the company gets virtually all its revenue from two countries: it generates over 95% of its sales in the US and most of the rest comes from Canada. The company is also a leading wine company in New Zealand.

Sales and Marketing

Constellation Brands staffs in-house marketing sales and customer service teams to increase its sales. These teams deploy a variety of marketing strategies conducting market research consumer and trade advertising price promotions point-of-sale materials event sponsorship on-premise promotions and public relations activities.

The company owns about 15 of the top 100 wine brands in the US. Products are primarily distributed by wholesale distributors with generally separate distribution networks utilized for beer and wine and spirits as well as state alcohol beverage control agencies.

The company advertising expenses was approximately $769.5 million $700.8 million and $615.7 million for the years 2020 2019 and 2018 respectively.

Financial Performance

Constellation Brands' has recorded strong revenue and profit growth over the last five years and it boasts enviable margins.

In fiscal 2020 (ended February 28) the company's sales grew 3% to $8.3 billion as the Beer category grew 8%.

Net loss attributable to CBI was $11.8 million for Fiscal 2020 from $3.4 billion for fiscal 2019.

Constellation Brands' cash on hand declined $12.2 million during fiscal 2020 ending the year at $81.4 million. The company's operations generated $2.6 billion while financing used $2 billion and investing activities used $531 million. Its main cash uses were capital expenditures dividends and share repurchases. It also issued debt worth $3.7 billion to support its investment program.

Strategy

Constellation Brands' overall strategy is to drive industry-leading growth build unrivaled shareholder value and shape the future of its industry by building brands that people love. The company positions its portfolio to benefit from the consumer-led trend toward premiumization which it believes will continue to result in faster growth rates in the higher-end of the beer wine and spirits categories.

To capitalize on premiumization trends become more competitive and grow its business Constellation Brands has employed a strategy dedicated to a combination of organic growth and acquisitions with a focus on the higher-margin higher-growth categories of the beverage alcohol industry. Key elements of this strategy include:

Leveraging its leading position in total beverage alcohol and its scale with wholesalers and retailers to expand distribution of its product portfolio; Strengthening relationships with wholesalers and retailers by providing consumer and beverage alcohol insights; Investing in brand building and innovation activities; Positioning itself for success with consumer-led products that identify meet and stay ahead of evolving consumer trends and market dynamics; Realizing operating efficiencies through expanding and enhancing production capabilities and maximizing asset utilization; and developing employees to enhance performance in the marketplace.

In its wine and spirits business as part of its efforts to focus on higher-end brands improve margins and create operating efficiencies Constellation Brands has acquired higher-margin higher-growth wine brands and portfolios of brands including Meiomi and Prisoner. It has strategically optimized the value of this business through the divestiture of the Canadian wine business and the anticipated completion of the transactions to divest a portion of its wine and spirits business which include lower-margin lower-growth products. In addition the company added higher-end brands to its spirits portfolio through the acquisitions of Casa Noble tequila and High West craft whiskeys.

Mergers and Acquisitions

Constellation has been through a heavy-acquisition period as it reshapes its portfolio towards premium brands. In 2020 Constellation announced its purchase of Empathy Wines a high-performing digitally-native wine brand and direct-to-consumer (DTC) platform co-founded by entrepreneur and media personality Gary Vaynerchuk with business partners Jon Troutman and Nate Scherotter. Empathy Wines focuses on producing high quality sustainably made wines sold direct-to-consumer through its eCommerce platform powered by consumer insights and content-driven digital marketing. This move aligns with Constellation's wine and spirits vision to be a bold and innovative high-end portfolio of distinctive brands and products that deliver exceptional consumer experiences. As part of the agreement Constellation will work with the Empathy Wines team to further scale the brand's growth while leveraging their rich consumer insights and analytics proven brand building expertise and high-performing digital technology to build DTC and digital capabilities that Constellation intends to scale across its wine and spirits brands to help deliver strong and sustainable growth for its portfolio.

Company Background

The company was established in 1945 by Marvin Sands in the Finger Lakes region of New York as Canandaigua Industries Company. Since that time the company has grown through internal expansion and by acquisitions across all segments of the beverage alcohol industry.

HISTORY

Marvin Sands the son of winemaker Mordecai (Mack) Sands exited the Navy in 1945 and entered distilling by purchasing an old sauerkraut factory in Canandaigua New York. His business Canandaigua Industries struggled while making fruit wines in bulk for local bottlers in the East. Aiming at regional markets the company began producing its own brands two years later. Marvin opened the Richards Wine Cellar in Petersburg Virginia in 1951 and put his father in charge of the unit. In 1954 Marvin developed his own brand of "fortified" wine — boosted by 190-proof brandy — and named it Richards Wild Irish Rose after his son Richard.

The company slowly expanded buying a number of small wineries in the 1960s and 1970s. It went public in 1973 changing its name to Canandaigua Wine. A year later the company expanded to the West Coast thus gaining access to the growing varietal market.

Canandaigua continued to grow through acquisitions and new product introductions in the early 1980s. In 1984 when wine coolers became popular the company introduced Sun Country Coolers doubling sales to $173 million by 1986.

The short-lived wine cooler fad made Canandaigua realize that its distribution network could handle more volume so it began looking for additional brands. After a flurry of acquisitions in the late 80s and 90s the company changed its name in 1997 to Canandaigua Brands.

Founder Marvin Sands died in 1999. His son Richard who had been CEO since 1993 succeeded his father as chairman. In 2000 the firm changed its name to Constellation Brands.

In June 2013 Constellation Brands completed its acquisition of Grupo Modelo's US beer business from Anheuser-Busch InBev for approximately $5.23 billion. The transaction included full ownership of Crown Imports LLC which provided Constellation with complete independent control of all aspects of the US commercial business; a state-of-the-art brewery in Nava (Piedras Negras) Mexico; and an exclusive perpetual brand license in the US to import market and sell Corona and the Modelo brands. The deal gave Constellation ownership of six of the top 20 imported beer brands in the US.

EXECUTIVES

President And Ceo, Robert S. (Rob) Sands, age 61, $1,310,383 total compensation

Evp And Coo, William A. (Bill) Newlands, age 61

Evp And General Counsel, Thomas J. (Tom) Mullin, age 69, $497,663 total compensation

Evp And President Beer, F. Paul Hetterich, age 57, $600,000 total compensation

Evp And President Wine And Spirits Division, Christopher (Chris) Stenzel, age 52

Evp And Chairman Beer, William F. (Bill) Hackett, age 68, $607,046 total compensation
Svp And Cio, Joseph D. (Joe) Bruhin
Evp And Chief Human Resources Officer, Thomas M. (Tom) Kane, age 59
Evp And Cfo, David Klein, age 56, $600,000 total compensation
Vp Americas Region, Erwin Petznek
Vice President Strategic Accounts, Mark Elder
Vice President, Jennifer Murray
Senior Vice President Human Resources Wine + Spirits Division, Melina Param
Vice President Deputy General Counsel Mexico, Abdon Hernandez
National Account Manager, ED Corbett
Vice President Security, Peter Moore
National Account Manager, Jorey Newcomb
Vice President Corporate Indirect Procurement, Charlie Shikany
Vice President And Controller, Deb Price
Senior Vice President Public Affairs, Ginny Clark
Vice President Strategic Accounts, Phil Parker
National Account Manager, Stephen Civello
Vice President Assistant Treasurer, Sandy Dominach
Vice President Human Resources Operations, Dan Towner
Vice President Events Sponsorship Field Marketing, Rene Ramos
Vp And Deputy General Counsel, Barb Laverdi
Svp Finance Wine + Spirits Division, Lisa Schnorr
Vice President Chief Winemaker, Chris Millard
Senior Vice President Operations, Martin Van Der Merwe
Vice President, John Alvarado
National Account Manager, Chris Beletti
National Account Manager, Eric Ramey
National Account Manager, Paul Hays
Vice President Associate General Counsel, Brian Bennett
Vice President On Premise, Scott Waters
Vice President National Accounts, Shawn Keller
National Account Manager, Fred Ashenbrenner
Senior Vice President Corporate Communications, Michael McGrew
Senior Vice President Human Resources, Julie Bassett
Chief Sales Officer Beer Division, William Renspie
Senior Vice President Operations Beer Division, Michael Othites
Vice President And Associate General Counsel, K Kristann Carey
National Account Manager, Matt Pinchera
Senior Vice President General Counsel Beer Division, Jeffrey LaBarge
National Sales Manager, Frank Labar
Vice President Associate General Counsel, Lonette Merriman
Svp Controller, Tom Mccorry
Svp Production Wine + Spirits Division, Sam Glaetzer
Svp Chief Growth Officer And Chief Of Staff, Mallika Monteiro
Executive Vice President And President Beer Division, Paul Hetterich
Svp Public Affairs, Matt Stanton
Vice President General Manager Texas, David Lancaster
Chairman, Richard Sands, age 69
Board Member, Annie Johnson
Auditors: KPMG LLP

LOCATIONS

HQ: Constellation Brands Inc
207 High Point Drive, Building 100, Victor, NY 14564
Phone: 585 678-7100
Web: www.cbrands.com

2019 Sales

	$ mil.	% of total
US	7,894	97
International	221	3
Total	**8,116**	**100**

PRODUCTS/OPERATIONS

2019 Sales

	$ mil.	% of total
Beer	5,202	64
Wine	2,532	31
Spirit	381	5
Total	**8,116**	**100**

Selected Subsidiaries and Operations

Constellation Spirits Inc.
Constellation Wines U.S.
Crown Imports LLC (beer)
Vincor International Inc. (wine Canada)

Selected Brands

Wine
  Black Box
  Clos du Bois
  Estancia
  Franciscan Estate
  Inniskillin
  Kim Crawford
  Mark West
  Mount Veeder
  Nobil
  Robert Mondavi
  Ruffino
  SIMI
  Wild Horse
Beer
  Corona Extra
  Corona Light
  Modelo Especial
  Negra Modelo
  Pacifico
Spirits
  SVEDKA Vodka

COMPETITORS

Andrew Peller	Lion
Anheuser-Busch InBev	MillerCoors
Bacardi	PatrOn Spirits
Beam Suntory	Pernod Ricard
Boston Beer	SABMiller
Bronco Wine Co.	Scheid Vineyards
Brown-Forman	Sebastiani Vineyards
Carlsberg	Taittinger
Diageo	Terlato Wine
E. & J. Gallo	Treasury Wine Estates
GIV	Trinchero Family
Halewood	Estates
Heineken	W.J. Deutsch
Jackson Family Wines	Willamette Valley
Korbel	Vineyards
LVMH	Wine Group

HISTORICAL FINANCIALS

Company Type: Public

Income Statement — FYE: February 29

	REVENUE ($ mil.)	NET INCOME ($ mil.)	NET PROFIT MARGIN	EMPLOYEES
02/20	8,343	(11)	—	9,000
02/19	8,116	3,435	42.3%	9,800
02/18	7,585	2,318	30.6%	9,600
02/17	7,331	1,535	20.9%	8,700
02/16	6,548	1,054	16.1%	9,000
Annual Growth	**6.2%**	**—**	**—**	**0.0%**

2020 Year-End Financials

Debt ratio: 44.59%
Return on equity: (-0.10%)
Cash ($ mil.): 81
Current ratio: 1.51
Long-term debt ($ mil.): 11,210
No. of shares (mil.): 192
Dividends
  Yield: 0.0%
  Payout: —
Market value ($ mil.): 33,238

	STOCK PRICE ($) FY Close	P/E High/Low		PER SHARE ($) Earnings	Dividends	Book Value
02/20	172.38	—	—	(0.07)	3.00	62.92
02/19	169.16	13	8	17.57	2.96	65.62
02/18	215.48	19	13	11.55	2.08	42.06
02/17	158.81	22	18	7.52	1.60	35.41
02/16	141.43	28	20	5.18	1.24	32.89
Annual Growth	**5.1%**			**—**	**24.7%**	**17.6%**

Core Mark Holding Co Inc

A convenience store wholesale distributors Core-Mark Holding supplies packaged consumables (including cigarettes alternative nicotine products candy snacks and food) to over 40000 customer locations. Traditional convenience stores are the company's primary customer as well as alternative outlets selling consumer packaged goods grocery stores mass merchandisers drug stores liquor stores cigarette and tobacco shops hotel gift shops military exchanges college and corporate campuses casinos hardware stores airport concessions and other specialty and small format stores. Cigarettes and other tobacco products are Core-Mark's top sellers generating more than three-fourths of net sales. The company operates primarily in the US serving customers in all 50 US states; it also has customers in five Canadian provinces.

Operations
Core-Mark offers more than 60000 stock keeping units from suppliers and manufacturers. Cigarettes account for about two-thirds of its revenue with other tobacco products bringing in about 10%. Food — including fast food candy snacks groceries beverages and fresh products generates more than 20% of revenue and non-food products such as health and beauty aids and general merchandise contributes the rest.

The company purchases brand name and private label products from approximately 3300 active suppliers and manufacturers in the US and Canada. Two suppliers — Altria Group (parent of Philip Morris USA) and R.J. Reynolds Tobacco Company — together account for about 55% of total purchases.

Geographic Reach
Texas-based Core-Mark operates in the US where it generates more than 90% of its revenue. The company's remaining revenue comes from Canada.

Core-Mark operates a network of over 30 distribution centers in the US and Canada (excluding two distribution facilities it operates as a third-party logistics provider). More than two dozen of its distribution centers are located in the US and the rest are in Canada.

The company has information technology offices in Plano Texas and Richmond British Columbia.

Sales and Marketing
Core-Mark's primary customer base consists of traditional convenience stores including major national and super-regional convenience store operators as well as independently owned convenience stores. Other customers include grocery stores cigarette and tobacco shops drug and liquor stores hotel gift shops military exchanges college and corporate campuses casinos hardware stores airport concessions and other specialty and small for-

mat stores that carry convenience products. The company service both convenience store chain customers and independent operators with ten or fewer stores which comprise approximately 65% of the convenience retail store market.

Canadian convenience store operator Murphy U.S.A is Core-Mark's largest customer representing about 13% of sales.

Financial Performance

Acquisitions and organic growth have pushed Core-Mark's revenue up 51% since 2015. Net income has been a little more sporadic but is still up 12% during that time.

In 2019 the company reported revenue of $16.7 billion up 2% from the prior year. Sales of food and non-food products rose 7% due to a strong growth in alternative nicotine products and increases in the fresh food beverages and candy categories.

Net income was also up that year jumping 24% to $57.7 million on the rise in revenue.

Cash at the end of 2019 was $14.1 million a decrease of $13.2 million from the prior year. Cash from operations contributed $89.7 million to the coffers while investing activities used $31 million mainly for capital expenditures. Financing activities used another $71.2 million for line of credit repayments.

Strategy

Core-Mark's strategy includes the following initiatives designed to further enhance the value it provides to its retail customers: fresh products and food services vendor consolidation initiative focused marketing initiative center of excellence and acquisitions and expansion.

As consumer tastes change the company is focused on expanding its fresh food and meal replacement capabilities. It is investing in chill docks and tri-temp trailers which enables the delivery of a broad range of chilled items. In addition it is partnering with strategically-located dairies kitchens bakeries and other entities to offer a greater selection of premium items such as fried chicken fresh pizza sandwiches and wraps cut fruit doughnuts and bread.

Continued investment in and growth of Core-Mark's Vendor Consolidation Initiative (VCI) and Focused Marketing Initiative (FMI) are also key elements of its strategy. VCI capitalizes on the fragmented convenience store supply chain by consolidating deliveries from disparate product segments. For the company's independent customers FMI offers pricing strategy category insights and marketing services to increase sales and profitability.

Since 2010 Core-Mark has expanded its distribution network product selection and customer base via six acquisitions. It has also added three primary distribution centers.

Company Background

The company's roots reach back to 1888 when it was known as Glaser Bros. a family-run candy and tobacco distribution business in San Francisco.

EXECUTIVES

Svp And Cfo, Christopher M. (Chris) Miller, age 59, $312,885 total compensation

President And Coo, Scott E. McPherson, age 50, $296,640 total compensation

Ceo And Director, Thomas B. Perkins, age 61, $515,412 total compensation

President Core-mark Canada, Eric J. Rolheiser, age 49

Svp Us Distribution-west, Christopher K. (Chris) Hobson, age 51, $270,375 total compensation

Svp Us Distribution East, William G. Stein, age 50, $263,718 total compensation

Chairman, Randolph I. Thornton, age 74
Auditors: DELOITTE & TOUCHE LLP

LOCATIONS

HQ: Core Mark Holding Co Inc
1500 Solana Boulevard, Suite 3400, Westlake, TX 76262
Phone: 940 293-8600
Web: www.core-mark.com

2018 Sales

	$ mil.	% of total
US	14,844	91
Canada	1,494	9
Corporate	56	—
Total	**16,395**	**100**

PRODUCTS/OPERATIONS

2018 Sales

	$ mil.	% of total
Cigarettes	10,974	67
Food	1,659	10
Candy	992	6
Fresh	474	3
Other tobacco products	1,387	9
Health beauty & general	711	4
Beverages	191	1
Equipment/other	5	-
Total	**16,395**	**100**

COMPETITORS

AMCON Distributing	H. T. Hackney
Associated Food	McLane
C&S Wholesale	Performance Food Group
Coca-Cola	SUPERVALU
Eby-Brown	Sobeys
Frito-Lay	Southco Distributing
GSC Enterprises	SpartanNash

HISTORICAL FINANCIALS

Company Type: Public

Income Statement   FYE: December 31

	REVENUE ($ mil.)	NET INCOME ($ mil.)	NET PROFIT MARGIN	EMPLOYEES
12/19	16,670	57	0.3%	8,555
12/18	16,395	45	0.3%	8,087
12/17	15,687	33	0.2%	8,413
12/16	14,529	54	0.4%	7,688
12/15	11,069	51	0.5%	6,655
Annual Growth	**10.8%**	**2.9%**	**—**	**6.5%**

2019 Year-End Financials

Debt ratio: 20.13%
Return on equity: 9.96%
Cash ($ mil.): 14
Current ratio: 1.89
Long-term debt ($ mil.): 382
No. of shares (mil.): 45
Dividends
Yield: 1.6%
Payout: 36.0%
Market value ($ mil.): 1,227

	STOCK PRICE ($) FY Close	P/E High/Low	Earnings	Dividends	Book Value
12/19	27.19	32 19	1.25	0.45	13.12
12/18	23.25	40 18	0.99	0.41	12.41
12/17	31.58	60 37	0.72	0.37	12.03
12/16	43.07	79 28	1.17	0.33	11.48
12/15	81.94	81 47	1.11	0.28	10.71
Annual Growth	**(24.1%)**	**— —**	**3.1%**	**13.1%**	**5.2%**

Corning Inc

Once known for kitchenware and lab products Corning Incorporated makes a diverse range of glass and ceramic products for optical communications mobile consumer electronics display technology automotive and life sciences markets. Its products include damage-resistant cover glass for mobile devices precision glass for advanced displays optical fiber and automotive emissions control products to name a few. Corning's signature Gorilla Glass cover glass for mobile devices is known for surviving high and repeated drops. The company operates more than 115 manufacturing and processing facilities in around 15 countries but generates more than half of its sales in the Asia Pacific region.

Operations

Corning operates in five segments: Optical Communications; Display Technologies; Specialty Materials; Environmental Technologies; and Life Sciences.

Its largest segment Optical Communications accounts for about 35% sales and is classified into two main product groups?carrier network and enterprise network. The carrier network group consists primarily of products and solutions for optical-based communications infrastructure for services such as video data and voice communications. The enterprise network group consists of optical-based communication networks.

Display Technologies which manufactures glass substrates primarily for flat panel liquid crystal displays brings in nearly 30% of sales.

The Specialty Materials business about 15% of sales manufactures products that provide more than 150 material formulations for glass glass ceramics and fluoride crystals for various customer needs. It is powered by superstar product Gorilla Glass which is used in consumer electronics devices such as notebook computers mobile phones and TVs.

Environmental Technologies manufactures ceramic substrates and filters for automotive and diesel products. It accounts for nearly 15% of total sales.

Life Sciences makes glass and plastic equipment for labs and other scientific applications account for around 10% of sales.

Geographic Reach

Corning's US-based customers generate more than 30% of its revenue. The Asia-Pacific region accounts for more than half of sales with China representing more than 25% and Korea about 10%.

The company operates more than 100 manufacturing and processing facilities in 15 countries. Its display glass manufacturing operations are in South Korea Japan Taiwan and China.

Its optical fiber manufacturing facilities are in North Carolina China and India. Cabling operations are mainly in North Carolina and Poland. Its hardware and equipment products are produced in Texas and Arizona in the US and in other facilities worldwide. Corning's Specialty Materials segment includes Gorilla Glass which is manufactured in Kentucky South Korea Japan and Taiwan.

Corning manufactures ceramic substrates and filter products for its Environmental Technologies segment in New York Virginia China Germany and South Africa. Products for its Life Sciences segment are made in eight US states as well as in Mexico France Poland and China.

Sales and Marketing

Corning's display glass products within the Display Technologies segment are sold to customers directly using the company's manufacturing facilities throughout Asia. Products such as optical-based communication networks within its Optical Communications segment are sold to businesses governments and individuals for their own use.

The Environmental Technologies segment sells its products worldwide to catalyzers and manufacturers of emission control systems who then sell to automotive and diesel vehicle or engine manufacturers. Products in the Life Sciences segment are marketed globally primarily through distributors to pharmaceutical and biotechnology companies contract manufacturing organizations academic institutions hospitals and government entities.

Financial Performance

Corning's revenue has seen a general upward trend in revenue with 25% increase from 2015 to 2019.

The company posted net sales of $115 billion in 2019 a 2% increase compared with $11.3 billion in 2018. Growth in 2019 was driven by sales increases in all its three divisions: Environmental Technologies was up $210 million the Life Sciences segment $69 million and Specialty Materials up $70 million.

Net income decrease to $960 million in 2019 compared with $1.1 billion the previous year. The decrease was due primarily to Higher costs of $238 million primarily driven by accelerated depreciation and asset write-offs for our Display Technologies and Optical Communications segments; and lower segment net income of $83 million primarily driven by lower sales in our Display Technologies and Optical Communications segments.

Cash at the end of fiscal 2019 was $2.4 billion an increase of $79 million from the prior year. Cash from operations contributed $2.0 billion to the coffers while investing activities used $1.9 billion including capital expenditures. Financing activities used another $47 million for dividends to stockholders and the company's stock repurchase program.

Strategy

Corning introduced its 2020-2023 Strategy & Growth Framework. From 2020 to 2023 the company plans to invest $10 billion to $12 billion for growth and to return $8 billion to $10 billion to shareholders.

In October 2015 Corning announced a strategy and capital allocation framework (the "Framework") that reflects the Company's financial and operational strengths as well as its ongoing commitment to increasing shareholder value. The Framework outlined its leadership priorities and articulated the opportunities it saw across its businesses. Corning designed the Framework to create significant value for shareholders by focusing to its portfolio and leveraging its financial strength

Corning's Frameworks outline the company's leadership priorities. With the completed Strategy and Capital Allocation Framework and new Strategy & Growth Framework Corning plans to focus its portfolio and utilize its financial strength. The probability of success increases as it invest in its world-class capabilities. Corning is concentrating approximately 80% of its research development and engineering investment along with capital spending on a cohesive set of three core technologies four manufacturing and engineering platforms and five market-access platforms. This strategy allows Corning to quickly apply its talents and repurpose its assets across the company as needed to capture high-return opportunities.

Company Background

Amory Houghton started Houghton Glass in Massachusetts in 1851 and moved it to Corning New York in 1868. By 1876 the company renamed Corning Glass Works was making several types of technical and pharmaceutical glass. In 1880 it supplied the glass for Thomas Edison's first light bulb. Other early developments included the red-yellow-green traffic light system and borosilicate glass (which can withstand sudden temperature changes) for Pyrex oven and laboratory ware.

By 1945 the company's had introduced the first mass-produced television tubes freezer-to-oven ceramic cookware (Pyroceram Corning Ware) and car headlights. After WWII Corning emphasized consumer product sales and expanded globally. In the 1970s the company pioneered the development of optical fiber and auto emission technology (now two of its principal products).

EXECUTIVES

Chairman And Ceo, Wendell P. Weeks, age 61, $1,337,740 total compensation
Vice Chairman And Corporate Development Officer, Lawrence D. (Larry) McRae, age 62, $731,971 total compensation
Svp And Cfo, R. Tony Tripeny, age 61, $504,808 total compensation
Evp And Corning Innovation Officer, Martin J. (Marty) Curran, age 61
Evp Corning Optical Telecommunications, Clark S. Kinlin, age 60
President Corning Glass Technologies (cgt), James P. Clappin, age 63, $686,538 total compensation
Evp Corning Technologies And International, Eric S. Musser, age 61
Svp Corporate Research, David L. Morse, age 68, $631,010 total compensation
Vice President Sales And Marketing, Aparna Krishnamurthy
Vice President Treasurer, Melinda Lee
Vice President Of Sales, Duncan Rogers
Vice President Flat Glass Photovoltaics Program, Marc Giroux
Vice President New Opportunity Development New Business Development, Robert Ritchie
Vice President Of Information Management, Nader Balti
Vice President Technology, Claudio Mazzali
Vice President, Susan Ford
Vice President Of Sales, Eric Marinakis
Vice President Of Product Management, Jeff Kunst
Division Vice President, John Sharkey
Vice President Of Chemical Engineering, Thomas Capek
Senior Vice President, Alan Eusden
Vice President, Adriane Brown
Vice President Sales, Dave Johnson
Vice President, Robert France
Senior Vice President Global Benefits And Compensation, John P MacMahon
Vice President Carrier Market Development, Robert Whitman
Senior Vice President Science And Technology, Jean-pierre Mazeau
Vice President Network Technology, Shingo Ihara
Vice President Corporate Controller, Ed Schlesinger
Vice President Tax, Jude Lemke
Vice President Commercial Technology, Bill Cune
Vice President Marketing And Technical Support, Dave Purwin
Vice President Global Commercial Operations, J David Johnson
Vice President And Gm Corning Life Sciences, Richard Eglen
Senior Vice President And General Manager, Mike Bell
Vice President Strategy Corning Optical Communications And Corporate Development, Steve Miller
Division Vice President And Commercial Director, Thomas Lynch
Vice President Of Finance, Rob Hutton
National Sales Manager, Ryan Ehrhart
Vice President Financial Services And Assistant Treasurer, Jill Baker
Vice President And Treasurer, Greg Mills
Vice President Communications And Technology, Hank Blackwood
Board Member, Darlene Salvagin
Treasurer, Lee Starnes
Board Member, Lisa Emel
Assistant Treasurer, Rob Vanni
Us Treasurer, Ida Meadows
Secretary, Kathy McClure
Board Member, Kevin Martin
Assistant Treasurer, Chris Tubbs
Auditors: PricewaterhouseCoppers LLP

LOCATIONS

HQ: Corning Inc
One Riverfront Plaza, Corning, NY 14831
Phone: 607 974-9000
Web: www.corning.com

2018 Sales

	$ mil.	% of total
North America		
United States	3,569	31
Canada	296	3
Mexico	53	-
Asia Pacific		
China	2,716	24
Korea	1,259	11
Taiwan	921	8
Japan	415	4
Other	436	4
Europe		
Germany	451	4
Other	905	8
All other	377	3
Total	11,398	100

PRODUCTS/OPERATIONS

2018 Sales

	$ mil.	% of total
Optical Communications	4,192	37
Display Technologies	3,276	29
Specialty Materials	1,479	13
Environmental Technologies	1,289	11
Life Sciences	946	8
All Other	216	2
Total	11,398	100

Selected Products

Display technologies
   Liquid crystal displays (LCD)
   Organic light-emitting diode (OLED) displays
Telecommunications
   Optical fiber and cable
   Optical networking components
Environmental technologies
   Industrial and stationary emissions products
   Mobile emissions and automotive catalytic converter products
Life sciences
   Genomics and laboratory equipment
Specialty Materials
   Gorilla Glass
Other
   Polarized glass
   Semiconductor materials

COMPETITORS

Asahi Glass	Nippon Electric Glass
CommScope	Nippon Sheet Glass
Dai Nippon Printing	Prysmian
Eppendorf	SCHOTT
Heraeus Holding	Thermo Fisher
IBIDEN	Scientific
NGK INSULATORS	

HISTORICAL FINANCIALS

Company Type: Public

Income Statement

FYE: December 31

	REVENUE ($ mil.)	NET INCOME ($ mil.)	NET PROFIT MARGIN	EMPLOYEES
12/19	11,503	960	8.3%	49,500
12/18	11,290	1,066	9.4%	51,500
12/17	10,116	(497)	—	46,200
12/16	9,390	3,695	39.4%	40,700
12/15	9,111	1,339	14.7%	35,700
Annual Growth	6.0%	(8.0%)	—	8.5%

2019 Year-End Financials

Debt ratio: 28.56%
Return on equity: 7.19%
Cash ($ mil.): 2,434
Current ratio: 2.12
Long-term debt ($ mil.): 8,179

No. of shares (mil.): 762
Dividends
Yield: 2.7%
Payout: 60.1%
Market value ($ mil.): 22,182

	STOCK PRICE ($) FY Close	P/E High/Low	PER SHARE ($) Earnings	Dividends	Book Value
12/19	29.11	32 24	1.07	0.80	16.94
12/18	30.21	30 22	1.13	0.72	17.50
12/17	31.99	— —	(0.66)	0.62	18.30
12/16	24.27	7 5	3.23	0.54	19.32
12/15	18.28	25 16	1.00	0.48	16.63
Annual Growth	12.3%	— —	1.7%	13.6%	0.5%

Costco Wholesale Corp

Operating more than 780 membership warehouse stores Costco is the nation's largest wholesale club operator (ahead of Wal-Mart's SAM'S CLUB). Primarily under the Costco Wholesale banner it serves nearly 99 million cardholders in some 45 US states Washington DC and Puerto Rico and about 10 other countries. The company carries an average of approximately 3700 active stock keeping units (SKUs) per warehouse in its core warehouse business significantly less than other broadline retailers. (many in bulk packaging) ranging from alcoholic beverages and appliances to fresh food pharmaceuticals and tires. Certain club memberships also offer products and services such as car and home insurance real estate services and travel packages. Costco generates most of its sales in the US.

HISTORY

From 1954 to 1974 retailer Sol Price built his Fed-Mart discount chain into a $300 million behemoth selling general merchandise to government employees. Price sold the company to Hugo Mann in 1975 and the next year with son Robert Rick Libenson and Giles Bateman opened the first Price Club warehouse in San Diego to sell in volume to small businesses at steep discounts.

Posting a large loss its first year prompted Price Club's decision to expand membership to include government utility and hospital employees as well as credit union members. In 1978 it opened a second store in Phoenix. With the help of his father Sol's other son Laurence began a chain of tire-mounting stores (located adjacent to Price Club outlets on land leased from the company and using tires sold by the Price Clubs).

The company went public in 1980 with four stores in California and Arizona. Price Club moved into the eastern US with its 1984 opening of a store in Virginia and continued to expand including a joint venture with Canadian retailer Steinberg in 1986 to operate stores in Canada; the first Canadian warehouse opened that year in Montreal.

Two years later Price Club acquired A. M. Lewis (grocery distributor Southern California and Arizona) and the next year it opened two Price Club Furnishings offering discounted home and office furniture.

Price Club bought out Steinberg's interest in the Canadian locations in 1990 and added stores on the East Coast and in California Colorado and British Columbia. However competition in the East from ensconced rivals such as SAM'S CLUB and PACE forced the closure of two stores two years later. A 50-50 joint venture with retailer Controladora Comercial Mexicana led to the opening of two Price Clubs in Mexico City one each in 1992 and 1993.

Price Club merged with Costco Wholesale in 1993. Founded in 1983 by Jeffrey Brotman and James Sinegal (a former EVP of Price Company) Costco Wholesale went public in 1985 and expanded into Canada.

In 1993 Price/Costco opened its first warehouse outside the Americas in a London suburb. Merger costs led to a loss the following year and Price/Costco spun off its commercial real estate operations as well as certain international operations as Price Enterprises (now Price Legacy). In 1995 the company launched its Kirkland Signature brand of private-label merchandise. Two years later the company changed its corporate name to Costco Companies.

Costco began online sales and struck a deal to buy two stores in South Korea in 1998 and opened its first store in Japan in 1999. Under industrywide pressure over the way members-only chains record fees Costco took a $118 million charge for fiscal 1999 to change accounting practices. That year the company made yet another name change to Costco Wholesale (emphasizing its core warehouse operations).

In 2000 the company purchased private retailer Littlewoods' 20% stake in Costco UK increasing Costco's ownership to 80%. Costco began expanding into the Midwest in 2001 as part of plans to open 40 new clubs a year including ones in China.

During fiscal 2002 Costco opened 29 new warehouse clubs. In December 2002 the retailer opened its first home store — called Costco Home — in Kirkland Washington stocked with mostly high-end furniture. A second Costco Home store opened in Tempe Arizona in December 2004.

Costco increased its equity interest in Costco Wholesale UK in October 2003 to 100% when it purchased Carrefour Nederland's 20% stake.

In 2006 Costco began offering more than 200 generic prescription medicines (100 count) for $10 or less. The following year Costco.com logged sales in excess of $1 billion.

In July 2009 Costco shuttered its two Costco Home stores which were located in Washington and Arizona. The retailer cited the weak economy and market for home furnishings and the fact that the concept didn't fit with its expansion plans for their closure. In August the company opened its first warehouse club in Australia.

CEO Jim Sinegal stepped down in 2012 after more than 20 years at the helm. Sinegal who together with chairman Jeffrey Brotman founded Costco in 1983 handed the reins to Craig Jelinek a 28-year veteran and former president and COO of the company.

In 2012 Costco bought the remaining 50% stake in Costco Mexico for $789 million from its joint venture partner Controladora Comercial Mexicana.

EXECUTIVES

Svp Operations, Roger A. Campbell
Evp Costco Wholesale Industries, Timothy L. Rose, age 67
Evp Information Systems, Paul G. Moulton, age 69, $602,519 total compensation
Evp Administration And Human Resources, Franz E. Lazarus, age 73
Evp And Coo Eastern And Canadian Divisions, Joseph P. (Joe) Portera, age 68, $645,297 total compensation
President And Ceo, W. Craig Jelinek, age 68, $699,810 total compensation
Evp And Coo Southwest And Mexico Divisions, Dennis R. Zook, age 71, $642,618 total compensation
Evp And Cfo, Richard A. Galanti, age 64, $712,888 total compensation
Evp International, James P. (Jim) Murphy, age 67
Evp And Coo Northern Division And Midwest Region, John D. McKay, age 63
Svp And General Manager Northeast Region, Jeffrey R. Long
Svp And General Manager Midwest Region, John B. Gaherty
Svp And General Manager Mexico, Jaime Gonzalez
Evp And Coo Merchandising, Douglas W. (Doug) Schutt, age 61
Svp And General Manager Bay Area Region, Jeffrey Abadir
Svp And General Manager Northwest Region, Mario Omoss
Svp And General Manager San Diego Region, Yoram Rubanenko
Svp And General Manager Eastern Canada Region, Pierre Riel
Svp And General Manager Los Angeles Region, Caton Frates
Svp And General Manager Western Canada Region, Russ Miller
Pharmacy Manager, Hassan Awada
Vice President Of Operations, Julie Cruz
Senior Vice President E Commerce And Publishing, Don Burdick
Avp General Merchandise Manager Kirkland Signature, Tess Wilkins
Assistant Vice President Finance And Investor Relations, Jeff Elliott
Vice President Regional Operations Manager, Darby Greek
Pharmacy Manager, Jeff Mrowczynski
Pharmacy Manager, Jai Abraham
Vice President, Todd Thull
Senior Vice President General Manager Europe, Stephen Pappas
Assistant Vice President Information Systems, Tim Bowersock
Assistant Vice President Risk Management, Dellanie Fragnoli
Senior Vice President Merchandising Fresh Foods, Jeffrey Lyons
Pharmacy Manager, Bill Jones
Senior Vice President General Manager Bay Area Region, Jeff Abadir
Vice President Merchandise Accounting Controller, Joseph Grachek
Vice President Member Services, Mona Silva
Vice President Member Services, Colleen Johnson
Pharmacy Manager, Jeremy Skarda
Pharmacy Manager, Christina Song
Board Member, Susan Decker
Board Member, John Meisenbach
Board Member, Jeffrey Raikes
Member Board Of Directors, Jeff Raikes
Board Member, Ken Denman
Board Member, Sue Decker
Auditors: KPMG LLP

LOCATIONS

HQ: Costco Wholesale Corp
999 Lake Drive, Issaquah, WA 98027
Phone: 425 313-8100
Web: www.costco.com

2018 Sales

	$ mil.	% of total
US	102,286	72
Canada	20,689	15
Other	18,601	13
Total	**141,576**	**100**

PRODUCTS/OPERATIONS

2018 Sales

	$ mil.	% of total
Sales	138 434	98
Membership fees	3,142	2
Total	**141,576**	**100**

2018 Sales

	% of total
Food & Sundries (dry & institutionally packaged candy snacks beverages cleaning products)	41
Hardlines (major appliances electronics health & beauty hardware garden & patio)	16
Fresh food (meat bakery deli & produce)	14
Softlines (apparel small appliances)	11
Ancillary (pharmacy fuel)	18
Total	**100**

COMPETITORS

Amazon.com	Office Depot
BJ's Wholesale Club	Safeway
Best Buy	Sam's Club
Big Lots	Staples
Dollar General	Target Corporation
Dollar Tree	Wal-Mart
Home Depot	Walgreens Boots
Kroger	

HISTORICAL FINANCIALS

Company Type: Public

Income Statement

FYE: August 30

	REVENUE ($ mil.)	NET INCOME ($ mil.)	NET PROFIT MARGIN	EMPLOYEES
08/20*	166,761	4,002	2.4%	273,000
09/19	152,703	3,659	2.4%	254,000
09/18	141,576	3,134	2.2%	245,000
09/17	129,025	2,679	2.1%	231,000
08/16	118,719	2,350	2.0%	218,000
Annual Growth	**8.9%**	**14.2%**	**—**	**5.8%**

*Fiscal year change

2020 Year-End Financials

Debt ratio: 13.70%
Return on equity: 23.94%
Cash ($ mil.): 12,277
Current ratio: 1.13
Long-term debt ($ mil.): 7,514

No. of shares (mil.): 441
Dividends
Yield: 0.0%
Payout: 29.9%
Market value ($ mil.): 153,720

	STOCK PRICE ($) FY Close	P/E High/Low	PER SHARE ($) Earnings	Dividends	Book Value
08/20*	348.37	38 31	9.02	2.70	41.44
09/19	294.76	36 23	8.26	2.44	34.67
09/18	233.13	33 22	7.09	2.14	29.21
09/17	158.24	30 23	6.08	8.90	24.65
08/16	163.93	32 26	5.33	1.70	27.61
Annual Growth	**20.7%**	**—**	**14.1%**	**12.3%**	**10.7%**

*Fiscal year change

COUNTY OF LOS ANGELES

The County of Los Angeles could easily be its own country; all it really needs is just an "r." It encompasses more than 4000 square miles 88 cities two islands and has a population of more than 10 million. The regional level of state government provides such services as law enforcement property assessment tax collection public health protection and other social services within its boundaries (sometimes sharing and often providing municipal services for unincorporated cities). The county's elected Board of Supervisors provide political direction filling executive legislative and judicial roles while the various departments manage daily operations. LA County has an annual budget of nearly $30 billion.

EXECUTIVES

Secretary Ii, Diana Maldonado
Treasurer And Tax Collector, Nune Yaghjyan
Auditors: MACIAS GINI & O'CONNELL LLP L

LOCATIONS

HQ: COUNTY OF LOS ANGELES
500 W TEMPLE ST STE 437, LOS ANGELES, CA 900122724
Phone: 213 974-1101
Web: WWW.LACOUNTY.GOV

HISTORICAL FINANCIALS

Company Type: Private

Income Statement

FYE: June 30

	REVENUE ($ mil.)	NET INCOME ($ mil.)	NET PROFIT MARGIN	EMPLOYEES
06/18	21,191	403	1.9%	100,000
06/17	20,064	393	2.0%	—
06/16	18,922	307	1.6%	—
06/15	18,435	482	2.6%	—
Annual Growth	**4.8%**	**(5.8%)**	**—**	**—**

CrossFirst Bankshares Inc

Auditors: BKD, LLP

LOCATIONS

HQ: CrossFirst Bankshares Inc
11440 Tomahawk Creek Parkway, Leawood, KS 66211
Phone: 913 312-6822
Web: www.crossfirstbankshares.com

HISTORICAL FINANCIALS

Company Type: Public

Income Statement

FYE: December 31

	ASSETS ($ mil.)	NET INCOME ($ mil.)	INCOME AS % OF ASSETS	EMPLOYEES
12/19	4,931	28	0.6%	357
12/18	4,107	19	0.5%	360
12/17	2,961	5	0.2%	—
Annual Growth	**29.0%**	**120.6%**	**—**	**—**

2019 Year-End Financials

Debt ratio: 0.02%
Return on equity: 5.21%
Cash ($ mil.): 187
Current ratio: —
Long-term debt ($ mil.): —

No. of shares (mil.): 51
Dividends
Yield: —
Payout: —
Market value ($ mil.): 749

	STOCK PRICE ($) FY Close	P/E High/Low	PER SHARE ($) Earnings	Dividends	Book Value
12/19	14.42	25 21	0.58	0.00	11.58
12/18	0.00	— —	0.47	0.00	10.88
12/17	0.00	— —	0.12	0.00	9.36
Annual Growth	**—**		**—119.8%**	**—**	**11.2%**

Crown Holdings Inc

Crown Holdings is a leading global manufacturer of consumer packaging products including steel and aluminum food and beverage cans. Its portfolio includes beverage food and aerosol cans and ends glass bottles specialty packaging metal vacuum closures steel crowns and aluminum caps under brands Liftoff SuperEnd and Easylift. Crown also supplies can-making equipment and parts. Its roster of customers has included Anheuser-Busch InBev Coca-Cola SC Johnson Unilever Friesland Campina and Procter & Gamble. Crown traces its historical roots all the way back to 1892. Most of its net sales is generated outside the US.

Operations

The Company's business is generally organized by product line and geography within four divisions: Americas (almost 30% of revenue) Europe (almost 30% of revenue) Asia Pacific (over 10% revenue) and Transit Packaging (about 20% revenue).

The Americas Division manufactures beverage food and aerosol cans and ends glass bottles specialty packaging metal vacuum closures steel crowns and aluminum caps.

The European Division manufactures beverage food and aerosol cans and ends promotional packaging and metal vacuum closures and caps.

The Asia Pacific Division is a reportable segment primarily consisting of beverage can operations. It also includes non-beverage can operations primarily food cans and specialty packaging.

Transit Packaging Division is a reportable segment which includes the Company's industrial and protective solutions and equipment and tools businesses. Industrial solutions include steel strap plastic strap industrial film and other related products that are used in a wide range of industries. Protective solutions include transit protection products such as airbags edge protectors and honeycomb products.

Non-reportable segments (over 10% of revenue) include the Company's aerosol can businesses in North America and Europe the Company's food can business in North America the Company's promotional packaging business in Europe and the Company's tooling and equipment operations in the U.S. and United Kingdom.

By product Crown's metal beverage cans business accounts for about half of total revenue while metal food cans and transit packaging represent about 20% each. Metal packaging and other products account for the remaining revenue.

Geographic Reach

Crown operates almost 240 plants in more than 45 countries some in Brazil Spain Canada Mexico Belgium Germany India Sweden and Switzerland among others. Over 70% of sales come from outside the US. The Americas division has nearly 50 operating facilities. The European division 60 and the Asia Pacific division almost 30. Transit Packaging operates approximately 100 facilities. The company also has three can-making equipment and spare part operations in the US and the UK.

Crown's US headquarters is stationed in Yardley Pennsylvania while its European headquarters is in Baar Switzerland. In addition its Asia Pacific headquarters resides in Singapore and its Transit Packaging headquarters is in Glenview Illinois. It has additional research facilities in Alsip Illinois and Wantage England.

Sales and Marketing

Crown markets and sells products to customers through its own sales and marketing staffs. In some instances contracts with customers are centrally negotiated but products are ordered through and distributed directly by its local facilities. Its top 10 global customers collectively represent about 30% of its overall revenue.

Customers include Anheuser-Busch InBev Coca-Cola Keurig Dr Pepper Heineken Molson Coors Pepsi-Cola and Refresco among others.

Financial Performance

Excluding its dip in 2016 Crown's revenue has been increasing in the last five years. It has an overall growth of 33%. The company's net income follows a similar pattern except that its decline occurred in 2017.

Net sales increased from $11.2 billion in 2018 to $11.7 billion in 2019 primarily due to $569 from an additional three months of Signode's operations and 3% higher global beverage sales unit volumes partially offset by the impact of foreign currency translation.

The company posted net income of $510 million in 2019 up 16% from $439 million in 2018.

Cash at the end of fiscal 2019 was $663 million an increase of $4 million from the prior year. Cash from operations contributed $1.2 million to the coffers while investing activities used $374 million mainly for capital expenditures. Financing activities used $786 million for payments of long-term debt.

Strategy

Crown grows its businesses in specific international growth markets while improving its operations and results in more mature markets through disciplined pricing cost control and careful capital allocation.. However with international expansion Crown like its rivals risks exposure to unfavorable foreign-currency exchange rates of the euro pound sterling and Canadian dollar as well as cyclical consumer spending on food and beverages. Its net sales are also impacted by the rise or decrease in the cost of aluminum and steel which is passed on to customers.

However the company believes that technological innovation will help mitigate for usual risks and cycles. Not content with making containers the same old way Crown Holdings operates research development and engineering centers in the US and the UK. Its mission is to promote development of value-added metal packaging systems design cost-efficient manufacturing processes provide continuous quality and/or production ef-

ficiency improvements and provide value-added engineering services and technical support. One of the company's key strategies is to drive sales by offering a number of different can sizes.

Crown is specifically targeting Southeast Asia and Mexico as regions ripe with growth opportunities. In 2018 the company opened new manufacturing facilities in Myanmar and expanded existing capacity at its plant in Cambodia. In Mexico it began operations at a new glass factory to serve the expanding beer market in the region. In addition markets such as Brazil Europe and Southeast Asia have also experienced higher volumes and market expansion.. Crown has also been building new plants and expanding its European operations in Spain and Italy.

HISTORY

Formed as Crown Cork & Seal Co. (CC&S) of Baltimore in 1892 the company was consolidated into its present form in 1927 when it merged with New Process Cork and New York Patents. The next year CC&S expanded overseas and formed Crown Cork International. In 1936 CC&S acquired Acme Can and benefited from the movement at the time from home canning to processed canning. A decade later the company launched its new product in 1946 — the first aerosol can.

EXECUTIVES

President Ceo And Director, Timothy J. Donahue, age 58, $915,000 total compensation

Svp And Cfo, Thomas A. Kelly, age 61, $575,000 total compensation

President Crown Technology, Daniel A. Abramowicz

Evp And Coo, Gerard H (Jerry) Gifford, age 65, $600,000 total compensation

President Crown Aerosol Packaging North America, C. Anderson (Andy) Bolton

President Crown Food Packaging North America Crown Closures And Specialty Packaging, James D. (Jim) Wilson

President Americas Division, Djalma Novaes, age 59, $510,000 total compensation

President Crown Beverage Packaging South America, Wilmar Arinelli

President Crown Beverage Packaging Mexico, Abel Coello Quintanilla

President Crown Beverage Packaging North America, Timothy J. (Tim) Lorge

Svp Crown Beverage Packaging China And Hong Kong, Robert H. Bourque, age 50, $302,413 total compensation

President Crown Europe, Didier Sourisseau, age 54

Vice President Health And Safety European Division, Eddy Geelen

Division Vice President, George Fernandez

Vice President Planning And Development, Torsten Kreider

Vice President Operations North America Beverage Division, Doug Pyer

Vice President, Randall Chaffins

Vice President Steel Sourcing, Daniel Shackell

Regional Vice President Sales, Michelle Hinton

Vice President, Joseph Pierce

V.p. Of Operations, Ken Tutin

Vice President Sales, Ralph Menichini

Executive Vice President, Ronald Thoma

Svp Sourcing Americas Division, Edward Vesey

Vice President Sales And Marketing, David Rayzis

Vice President Commercial Food Europe, Olivier Aubry

Vice President Labor And Employee Relations, Vince Pepenelli

Vp And Controller Europe, Inigo D'ornellas

Divisional Vice President Of Sales, Greg Wise

Chairman, John W. Conway, age 74

Board Member, Josef Muller

Board Member, Arnold Donald
Board Member, Aaron Miller
Board Member, Jim Turner
Auditors: PricewaterhouseCoopers LLP

LOCATIONS

HQ: Crown Holdings Inc
770 Township Line Road, Yardley, PA 19067
Phone: 215 698-5100
Web: www.crowncork.com

2018 Sales

	$ mil.	% of total
US	3,018	27
Mexico	763	7
Brazil	732	7
UK	685	6
Spain	666	6
Other regions	5,287	47
Total	**11,151**	**100**

PRODUCTS/OPERATIONS

2018 Sales

	$ mil.	% of total
Metal beverage cans & ends	5,551	50
Metal food cans & ends	2,452	22
Transit packaging	1,800	16
Other metal packaging	884	8
Other products	464	4
Total	**11,151**	**100**

2017 Sales

	$ mil.	% of total
Americas beverage	3,282	29
European food	1,982	18
European beverage	1,489	13
Asia Pacific	1,316	12
Transit Packaging	1,800	16
Non-reportable segments	1,282	12
Total	**11,151**	**100**

Selected Products

Metal packaging
   Aerosol cans
   Beverage cans
   Closures and caps
   Crowns
   Ends
   Food cans
Plastics packaging
Other products
   Can making equipment and spares

Selected Markets

Food and beverage
Health and beauty
Household / Industrial
Luxury Goods
Promotional
Construction
Agriculture

COMPETITORS

Amcor	Berry Global
AptarGroup	Metal Container
Arconic	Corporation
Ardagh Group	Owens-Illinois
BWAY	Silgan
Ball Corp.	Sonoco Products

HISTORICAL FINANCIALS

Company Type: Public

Income Statement				FYE: December 31
	REVENUE ($ mil.)	NET INCOME ($ mil.)	NET PROFIT MARGIN	EMPLOYEES
12/19	11,665	510	4.4%	33,000
12/18	11,151	439	3.9%	33,000
12/17	8,698	323	3.7%	24,000
12/16	8,284	496	6.0%	24,000
12/15	8,762	393	4.5%	24,000
Annual Growth	7.4%	6.7%	—	8.3%

2019 Year-End Financials

Debt ratio: 51.31%
Return on equity: 38.49%
Cash ($ mil.): 607
Current ratio: 1.03
Long-term debt ($ mil.): 7,818

No. of shares (mil.): 135
Dividends
  Yield: —
  Payout: —
Market value ($ mil.): 9,835

	STOCK PRICE ($) FY Close	P/E High/Low		PER SHARE ($) Earnings	Dividends	Book Value
12/19	72.54	20	11	3.78	0.00	12.63
12/18	41.57	18	12	3.28	0.00	6.93
12/17	56.25	26	22	2.38	0.00	4.48
12/16	52.57	16	12	3.56	0.00	2.62
12/15	50.70	20	16	2.82	0.00	1.03
Annual Growth	9.4%	—	—	7.6%	—	87.0%

CSX Corp

Through its main subsidiary CSX Transportation (CSXT) CSX Corporation operates a major rail system of some 20000 route miles in the eastern US. The freight carrier links some 25 states 70 ports 230 short-line railroads the District of Columbia and two Canadian provinces (Ontario and Quebec). Freight hauled by the company includes a wide variety of merchandise (food chemicals and consumer goods) coal and automotive products. CSX also transports via intermodal containers and trailers.

Operations

CSX's principal operating subsidiary is CSX Transportation which operates through three lines of businesses: merchandise (its largest segment by revenue) coal and intermodal.

It has a fleet of more than 3500 locomotives and approximately 69400 railcars (gondolas hoppers and box/flat cars). CSXT handles the company's real estate sales leasing acquisition and management and development activities.

Other subsidiaries include CSX Intermodal Terminals which provides intermodal terminal and trucking services across the eastern US; Total Distribution Services a storage and distribution company for the automotive industry; Transflo Terminal Services a logistics company for transferring shipments from rail to truck; and CSX Technology which provides IT services to its parent company.

Geographic Reach

Based in Jacksonville FL CSX operates in about two dozen states primarily in the Eastern US and along the Eastern Seaboard. It also operates in Washington DC and the two Canadian provinces of Ontario and Quebec.

The company's largest terminals are based on numbers of railcars or intermodal containers processed and are located in Illinois Georgia New York Indiana Ohio Tennessee and Kentucky.

Sales and Marketing

CSX serves customers in a wide range of industries including chemicals automotive agricultural and food products mineral fertilizers forest products and metal and equipment.

Financial Performance

CSX's financial performance is highly dependent on fluctuations in fuel prices. Revenue increased for the second consecutive year in 2018 after two years of decline in 2016 and 2015 due to the ongoing steep decline in oil prices.

CSX revenue decreased 3% to $11.9 billion in 2019 due to volume declines lower other revenue and decreases in fuel recovery.

Net income jumped less than 1% to $3.3 billion in 2019due to an almost $1 billion tax expense.

Cash at the end of 2019 was $958 million an increase of $100 million from the prior year. Cash from operations contributed $4.9 billion to the coffers while investing activities used $2.1 billion mainly for investment purchases and property additions (infrastructure freight cars and locomotives). Financing activities used another $2.6 billion for loan payments dividends to stockholders and the company's stock repurchase program.

Strategy

CSX reduced its management workforce by approximately 950 employees during 2017. The Company was focused on driving efficiencies through process improvement and responding to business mix shifts. These management reductions were designed to further streamline general and administrative and operating support functions to speed decision making and further control costs.

The Company is focused on developing and strictly maintaining a scheduled service plan with an emphasis on optimizing assets. When this operating model is executed effectively customer service is improved enabling the Company to better compete for an increased share of the U.S. freight market. Further this model leads to reduced costs and strong free cash flow generation.

Company Background

CSX traces its history back to 1827 when the Baltimore and Ohio Railroad Company (B&O) started operations. Since then numerous railroads have combined with then B&O to create what has now become CSX. Each merger added new geographic reach to valuable markets cities and ports along the way. CSX was incorporated in 1978 in Virginia and in 1980 acquired Chessie Systems and Seaboard Coast Line Industries allowing the company to connect northern population centers and Appalachian coal fields with growing southeastern markets. It later it acquired Conrail Inc. which connected New England and the New York metropolitan area with Chicago and midwestern markets. The resulting CSX conglomerate serves every major market in the eastern US with freight transportation and intermodal services.

EXECUTIVES

President Ceo And Director, James M. Foote
Evp And Cfo, Frank A. Lonegro, $500,000 total compensation
President Csx Technology, Kathleen Brandt
Vp And Chief Transportation Officer, Mike Pendergrass
President Csx Real Property Inc., Shantel Davis
Evp Chief Legal Officer And Corporate Secretary, Nathan D. Goldman
Evp Corporate Affairs And Chief Of Staff, Mark K. Wallace
Assistant Vice President, Sean Craig
Assistant Vice President Operations Process Excellence, John Murphy
Assistant Vice President Risk Management, Geoffrey Aughenbaugh

Vice President Legal Affairs, Peter Shudtz
Assistant Vice President Finance, Erik Palm
Assistant Vice President Commercial Fina, Amy Rice
Assistant Vice President Advanced Engineering, Timothy Male
Vice President Strategic Infrastructure Initiatives, Louis Renjel
Vice President Network Operations, Cary Helton
Vice President Human Resources, Alison Brown
Assistant Vice President Operations Finance, John Hart
Vice President Of Industrial Products, Dean Piacente
Senior Vice President Human Resources And Labor Relations, Bob Haulter
Assistant Vice President Pensions And Investments, Richard G Patsy
Regional Vp State Government Affairs Philadelphia Nj And Ny City, Rodney Oglesby
Assistant Vice President Information Technology Operations, Caroline Crawford
Resident Vice President, David Hall
Assistant Vice President, Salvatore Macedonio
Senior Vice President Of Operations West, Brian Barr
Associate Vice President Of Information Technology Operations, Tim Mciver
Senior Vice President Of Network Operations, Jamie Boychuk
Vice President Of Intermodal And Automotive, Marclare Kenney
Svp Operations East, Robert Frulla
Chairman, Edward J. (Ned) Kelly
Board Of Directors, Steve Halverson
Vp Treasurer And Investor Relations Officer, David Baggs
Board Member, David Moffett
Board Member, John Breaux
Board Member, John McPherson
Board Member, Linda Riefler
Board Member, Dennis Reilley
Vice Chair, Joseph Przybylowicz
Auditors: Ernst & Young LLP

LOCATIONS

HQ: CSX Corp
  500 Water Street, 15th Floor, Jacksonville, FL 32202
Phone: 904 359-3200
Web: www.csx.com

PRODUCTS/OPERATIONS

2018 Sales

	$ mil.	% of total
Merchandise	7,491	61
Coal	2,246	18
Intermodal	1,931	16
Other	582	5
Total	**12,250**	**100**

Selected Subsidiaries

CSX Transportation
CSX Intermodal Terminals
Total Distribution Services Inc.
Transflo Terminal Services Inc.
CSX Technology

COMPETITORS

APL Logistics
Burlington Northern Santa Fe
Canadian National Railway
Canadian Pacific Railway

Hub Group
J.B. Hunt
Norfolk Southern
Schneider National
Union Pacific
Washington Companies

HISTORICAL FINANCIALS

Company Type: Public

Income Statement   FYE: December 31

	REVENUE ($ mil.)	NET INCOME ($ mil.)	NET PROFIT MARGIN	EMPLOYEES
12/19	11,937	3,331	27.9%	21,000
12/18	12,250	3,309	27.0%	22,500
12/17	11,408	5,471	48.0%	24,000
12/16	11,069	1,714	15.5%	27,000
12/15	11,811	1,968	16.7%	29,000
Annual Growth	0.3%	14.1%	—	(7.8%)

2019 Year-End Financials

Debt ratio: 42.44%
Return on equity: 27.29%
Cash ($ mil.): 958
Current ratio: 1.52
Long-term debt ($ mil.): 15,993

No. of shares (mil.): 773
Dividends
  Yield: 1.3%
  Payout: 22.9%
Market value ($ mil.): 55,968

	STOCK PRICE ($) FY Close	P/E High/Low		PER SHARE ($) Earnings	Dividends	Book Value
12/19	72.36	19	15	4.17	0.96	15.32
12/18	62.13	20	13	3.84	0.88	15.35
12/17	55.01	10	6	5.99	0.78	16.53
12/16	35.93	21	12	1.81	0.72	12.58
12/15	26.13	19	12	2.00	0.70	12.07
Annual Growth	29.0%	—	—	20.2%	8.2%	6.1%

Cullen/Frost Bankers, Inc.

One of the largest independent bank holding companies in Texas Cullen/Frost Bankers owns Frost Bank and other financial subsidiaries through a second-tier holding company The New Galveston Company. The community-oriented bank serves individuals and local businesses as well as clients in neighboring parts of Mexico through 120-plus branches in Texas metropolitan areas. It offers commercial and consumer deposit products and loans trust and investment management services mutual funds insurance brokerage and leasing. Subsidiaries include Frost Insurance Agency Frost Brokerage Services Frost Investment Advisors and investment banking arm Frost Securities. Cullen/Frost has total assets of $26.5 billion.

Geographic Reach

San Antonio-based Cullen/Frost Bankers has branches throughout Texas including the Austin Corpus Christi Dallas Fort Worth Houston Permian Basin the Rio Grande Valley and San Antonio regions.

Financial Performance

Cullen/Frost reported revenue of $945.3 million in 2013 an increase of 3% versus 2012 on increased interest income on loans and deposits and an increase in trust and investment management fees. Net income was $237.9 a flat comparison with the prior year. 2013 marked the third consecutive year of rising revenue following a dip in 2010. The bank's fortunes are rising along with the thriving energy and technology sectors in Texas.

Strategy

Cullen/Frost has built its insurance business through acquisitions in recent years; since 2009 it has bought agencies in Dallas Houston San Antonio and San Marcos that provide group employee benefit plans. The company continues to seek out acquisition opportunities while it also looks for ways to expand and diversify within its existing markets. To reduce its reliance on interest rate spreads Cullen/Frost wants to grow its income from fees such as insurance commissions trust investment fees and service charges on deposit accounts.

Mergers and Acquisitions

In June 2014 Frost Bank acquired Odessa Texas-based Western National Bank (WNB) increasing its presence in the oil-rich Permian Basin Midland and Odessa markets in West Texas. Seven of WNB's eight branches were converted to the Frost name (an office in San Antonio was closed) increasing the number of Frost branches statewide to more than 120. The acquisition of WNB added $1.8 billion in assets $1.6 billion in deposits and $668 million in total loans to Cullen/Frost. The purchase of WNB was the first time in nearly seven years that Frost acquired another bank.

EXECUTIVES

Chairman And Ceo, Phillip D. Green, age 65, $565,000 total compensation

President Frost Bank; Evp Frost Wealth Advisors, Patrick B. (Pat) Frost, age 60, $485,000 total compensation

President, Paul H. Bracher, age 63, $500,000 total compensation

Evp And Cfo, Jerry Salinas, $400,000 total compensation

Vice President, Stephanie Conti

Vice President Of Marketing, Bobby Jacob

Vice President Of Marketing, Linda Hopkins

Senior Vice President, John Wilson

Vice President Of Marketing, Howard Kasanoff

Senior Vice President It, Harvey Gutierrez

Senior Executive Vice Presiden, William Sirakos

Senior Vice President Director Of Investor Relatio, Greg Parker

Vice President Of Finance, Vicki Ball

Vice President Community Development, Betty Davis

Senior Vice President, David Hamilton

Senior Vice President Treasury Management, Darlene Selsor

Vice President, Hilary Stull

Senior Vice President, Andrew A Merryman

Executive Vice President, David Perdue

Senior Vice President, John Hind

Vice President Of Operation, Cliff McCauley

Vice President Of Finance, Gregory Dreier

Vice President, Oscar Molina

Vice President East Dallas Market Leader, Michael Alcantar

Senior Vice President, Cliff Perez

Senior Vice President, Cathy Garison

Senior Vice President, Vennesa Starr

Vice President, Jonathan Pursch

Senior Vice President, Clay Cary

Senior Vice President, Casey Maxfield

Assistant Vice President Accounting, Mike Benson

Executive Vice President, Matt Bryant

Vice President Executive Benni, Darleen Schauer

Senior Vice President, Jill Stacy

Vice President Sales, Talal Tay

Vice President, Julius Eccell

Vice President Of Marketing, Wendy Erickson

Vice President Of Finance, Wayne Baker

Vice President Marketing, Ericka Pullin

Senior Executive Vice President, Michael S Cain

Senior Vice President, Mark Seeberger

Senior Vice President, Edward Porras

Senior Vice President, James Watson

Senior Vice President, Scott Tellkamp

Senior Vice President, David Seitze

Vice President Of Operation, Erica Noriega

Senior Vice President Capital Markets, Mark Brell

Senior Vice President, Roger Lind

Vice President, Teresa Woods

Vice President, Clay Jones

Vice President Private Banking Officer, Beverly Hankinson

Vice President Of Information Technology, Diane Madalin

Vice President Public Finance Division, Jeff Nuckols

Senior Vice President, Terrie Ramirez

Senior Vice President, Leigh Olejer

Vice President, Floyd Wilson

Vice President Research And Strategy Marketing Department Rb7, Tammy Herrera

Senior Vice President, Michael Nutter

Senior Vice President, Mike Davis

Vice President Of Employee Benefits, Tony Zavala

Senior Vice President, Donna Normandin

Vice President Of Finance, Andrea Knight

Vice President, Susan Carruthers

Vice President Internal Audit, Natalie McCabe

Regional Vice President, Lorraine Neff

Vice President, Olga Harrison

Senior Executive Vice President Operations And Processing, Gary Mcknight

Assistant Vice President, Hope S Molina

Vice President, Matt Badders

Senior Vice President Institutional Trust Administration, Steven A Klein

Senior Vice President, Terry Frank

Senior Vice President, Letty Dominguez

Vice President Of Finance, Mark Cranmer

Senior Vice President Community Leader, Jeff Fuller

Vice President Technology Infrastructure, Robert Jacobs

Senior Vice President Wealth Advisor Private Trust, John Sands

Assistant Vice President Capital Markets, Kyle Woodland

Senior Vice President Compliance, Jan Robertson

Senior Vice President Corporate Banki, Susie Howell

Senior Vice President Capital Markets, Victor Quiroga

Executive Vice President, Charlie Schuchardt

Vice President Of Marketing, Daryl Hoffmann

Senior Vice President Workout Officer, Jennifer Crabtree

Vice President Sales, Dorothy Wood

Senior Vice President Of Investment Division, Jeanne Glorioso

Senior Vice President North Texas Sales Manager Public Finance, Shirley Cox

Assistant Vice President Of Network Engineering, Danny Leal

Vice President Trust Real Estate, Hampton Pratka

Senior Vice President Application Support, Jeff Sanders

Senior Vice President, Shannon Watt

Assistant Vice President, Elsie Boone

Senior Vice President Investments, Linnie Phebus

Executive Vice President Marketing, Debbie Danmeter

Senior Vice President, Carol Lampier

Assistant Vice President, Beth Pence

Assistant Vice President Employee Benefits, Brenda Smith

Senior Vice President, Gina Prill

Assistant Vice President, Rene Ramirez

Svp It Change Management, Brenda Gonzales

Vice President, Duncan Morrow

Senior Vice President Special Assets, Betsy Gleiser

Assistant Vice President Corporate Banking, Jim Dixon

Vice President, Zada Cisneros

Executive Vice President, Roderick Washington

Vice President Of Marketing, John Greenwood

Senior Vice President Compliance, Verna Fletcher
Senior Executive Vice President, James Allen
Executive Vice President, Louis Barton
Senior Vice President, Stacy L Flores
Senior Vice President Of Private Trust Services,
Debbie Eippert
Senior Vice President, Mark Ritter
Assistant Vice President, J Rosow Jaroszewski
Vice President, Ken Orsburn
Vice President Business Development, Taylor
Benson
Assistant Vice President, Patricio Perez
Assistant Vice President, Lauren Urban
Assistant Vice President, Yolanda Gonzales
Vice President, Michael Aubuchon
Vice President, Van C Carter
Vice President, Gloria Andrus
Vice President And Corporate C, Jon K Daubert
Vice President, Anna Sanchez
Senior Vice President, Brent Bike
Vice President, Anabell Rodriguez
Vice President, Sallie Newman
Vice President, Gwen Dominic
Assistant Vice President, Justin Steinbach
Assistant Vice President, Samuel Lopez
Vice President, Laura Pinto
Senior Vice President, Carole Kilpatrick
Assistant Vice President, Karla Riley
Vice President Intl Private Banking, Elvia Daley
Assistant Vice President, Trey McCord
Vice President Sales, Linda Wileman
Vice President Sba Loan Coordinator, Kathy Raia
Senior Vice President Trust Internal Audit,
Deanna Rankin
Vice President, Allison Byers
Senior Vice President, Lou Kissling
Sr. Vice Pres., Barbara Kelly
Vice President In Human Resources Department,
Janet Lane
Vice President, Albert Shannon
Executive Vice President And General Counsel,
Stanley McCormick
Executive Vice President, Chas Mella
Vice President, James Winton
Executive Vice President Marketing, Brandi Doster
Vice President, Sherry Mcgillicuddy
Senior Vice President, Kaye Carpenter
Vice President, Ileana Payne
Vice President Business Services, Gloria Kopycinski
Principal Vice President, Christy Bachmeyer
Vice President, Susan Essex
Auditors: Ernst & Young LLP

LOCATIONS

HQ: Cullen/Frost Bankers, Inc.
  111 W. Houston Street, San Antonio, TX 78205
Phone: 210 220-4011   Fax: 210 220-5578
Web: www.frostbank.com

PRODUCTS/OPERATIONS

2016 Sales

	$ mil.	% of total
Interest		
Loans including fees	458	40
Securities	313	28
Interest-bearing deposits	16	1
Federal funds sold and resell agreements	0	-
Non-interest		
Trust and investment management fees	104	9
Service charges on deposit accounts	81	7
Insurance commissions & fees	47	4
Interchange and debit card transaction fees	21	2
Other charges commissions and fees	39	4
Net gain (loss) on securities transactions	15	1
Other	41	4
Total	**1,138**	**100**

2016 Sales

	% of total
Banking	88

Frost Wealth Advisors	12
Total	**100**

Selected Subsidiaries

Carton Service Corporation
Cullen BLP Inc.
Cullen/Frost Capital Trust II
Frost Bank
Frost Brokerage Services Inc.
Frost Insurance Agency Inc.
Frost Investment Advisors Inc.
Main Plaza Corporation
Tri-Frost Corporation

COMPETITORS

BBVA Compass	JPMorgan Chase
Bancshares	Lone Star Bank
Bank of America	PlainsCapital
Broadway Bancshares	Prosperity Bancshares
Capital One	Texas Capital
Comerica	Bancshares
Extraco	Wells Fargo
First Financial	Woodforest Financial
Banksharses	
International	
Bancshares	

HISTORICAL FINANCIALS

Company Type: Public

Income Statement   FYE: December 31

	ASSETS ($ mil.)	NET INCOME ($ mil.)	INCOME AS % OF ASSETS	EMPLOYEES
12/19	34,027	443	1.3%	4,659
12/18	32,292	454	1.4%	4,370
12/17	31,747	364	1.1%	4,270
12/16	30,196	304	1.0%	4,217
12/15	28,567	279	1.0%	4,211
Annual Growth	**4.5%**	**12.3%**	**—**	**2.6%**

2019 Year-End Financials

Debt ratio: 0.69%	No. of shares (mil.): 62
Return on equity: 12.19%	Dividends
Cash ($ mil.): 3,431	Yield: 2.8%
Current ratio: —	Payout: 39.6%
Long-term debt ($ mil.): —	Market value ($ mil.): 6,128

	STOCK PRICE ($) FY Close	P/E High/Low	PER SHARE ($) Earnings	Dividends	Book Value
12/19	97.78	15 12	6.84	2.80	62.42
12/18	87.94	17 12	6.90	2.58	53.49
12/17	94.65	18 15	5.51	2.25	51.95
12/16	88.23	19 9	4.70	2.15	47.30
12/15	60.00	19 14	4.28	2.10	46.63
Annual Growth	**13.0%**	**— —**	**12.4%**	**7.5%**	**7.6%**

Cummins, Inc.

Cummins makes diesel- and natural gas-powered engines for the heavy- and mid-duty truck RV automotive and industrial markets as well as for the marine rail mining and construction industries. In addition to its flagship Engine segment other business segments include Components (filtration products and fuel systems) Power Systems (vehicle and residential generators) New Power (electric and hybrid powertrain systems) and Distribution (product distributors and servicing). Cummins' major customers include OEMs Chrysler Daimler Ford Komatsu PACCAR Navistar and Volvo. More than 55% of the company's total sales

come from the US. The company traces its historical roots back to 1919 when it was founded by Clessie Cummins.

Operations

Cummins' Engine segment is its largest accounting for more than one-third of total sales. It makes a broad range of diesel- and natural gas-powered engines under the Cummins brand as well as other brand names for the heavy- and medium-duty truck bus recreational vehicle and light-duty automotive markets.

The Distribution and Components segments each contribute about a quarter of total sales. Distribution comprises a network of approximately 600 company-owned and independent distributors that serve 190 countries worldwide. The Components segment manufactures products that are complementary to commercial diesel applications including more than 8300 filtration products some branded as Fleetguard. Other products within this segment include turbo technologies for air handling in engines and exhaust after-treatment technologies. It also offers new used and remanufactured fuel systems.

Power Systems represents about 15% of revenue and sells power products such as alternators transfer switches and controls. It serves the commercial and consumer markets as well as military organizations. Brands include AVK and Stamford (alternators).

The New Power segment designs manufactures sells and supports electrified power systems ranging from fully electric to hybrid along with innovative components and subsystems including battery fuel cell and hydrogen production technologies.

Geographic Reach

Cummins' main domestic operating facilities are located in Columbus IN (headquarters); Memphis TN; Walton KY; and Lakewood NY. Key international locations reside in Belgium Brazil China India Mexico Russia South Africa the UK and the UAE. The US generates more than 55% of its total sales.

Sales and Marketing

Cummins has a large geographic reach and serves customers through a network of 600 wholly-owned and independent distributor locations and more than 7600 dealer locations spanning about 190 countries and territories. Major customer PACCAR accounts for more than 15% of the company's net sales.

Financial Performance

Sales decreased 1% holding the $20 million-mark with $23.6 billion in 2019 (2018 revenue was $23.8 billion). The decrease was due to the decrease of their Engine segment with about $510 million and $166 million decrease in power systems segment.

Profits increased in 2019 to $2.3 billion driven primarily by increased gross margin lower variable compensation expenses and gains on corporate owned life insurance partially offset by restructurings higher research development and engineering expenses and lower equity royalty and interest income from investees.

Cash at the end of fiscal 2018 was $1.3 billion down slightly ($66 million) from the prior year. Cash from operations contributed $3.2 billion to the coffers while investing activities used $1.2 billion mainly for capital expenditures. Financing activities used another $3.1 billion for dividends to stockholders and the company's stock repurchase program.

Strategy

Cummins design and/or manufacture their strategic components used in or with their engines and power generation units including cylinder blocks and heads turbochargers connecting rods camshafts crankshafts filters alternators electronic and emission controls automated transmissions and fuel systems. Other important elements include working with suppliers to measure and improve their environmental footprint; selecting and managing suppliers to comply with their supplier code of conduct; and assuring their comply with Cummins' prohibited and restricted materials policy.

Mergers and Acquisitions

Cummins acquired Hydrogenics a provider of fuel cell technologies in 2019. The addition of Hydrogenics boosts Cummins' clean fuel operations with both fuel cell and hydrogen generation capabilities and allows it to offer integrated fuel cell solutions to customers.

Company Background

Chauffeur Clessie Cummins believed that Rudolph Diesel's cumbersome and smoky engine could be improved for use in transportation. Borrowing money and work space from his employer Columbus Indiana banker W.G. Irwin Cummins founded Cummins Engine in 1919. Irwin invested more than $2.5 million in the company and in the mid-1920s Cummins produced a mobile diesel engine. Truck manufacturers were reluctant to switch from gas to diesel so Cummins used publicity stunts such as racing in the Indianapolis 500 to advertise his engine.

The company was profitable by 1937 the year Irwin's grandnephew Irwin Miller took over. During WWII the Cummins engine was used in cargo trucks. Sales jumped from $20 million in 1946 to more than $100 million by 1956. That year Cummins started its first overseas plant in Scotland. It bought crankshaft camshaft and piston and valve supplier Atlas Crankshafts in 1958. By 1967 it had 50% of the diesel engine market.

EXECUTIVES

Vice President, Tony Satterthwaite

Chairman And Ceo, N. Thomas (Tom) Linebarger, $1,375,000 total compensation

Vp And Chief Administrative Officer, Marya M. Rose, $634,000 total compensation

President And Coo, Richard J. (Rich) Freeland, $848,000 total compensation

Vp And President Distribution Business, Livingston L. (Tony) Satterthwaite, $570,000 total compensation

Group Vp China And Russia, Steven M. (Steve) Chapman

Vp And Cio, Sherry A. Aaholm

Chairman And Managing Director Cummins India Ltd., Anant Talaulicar, $537,500 total compensation

Vp And President Engine Business, Srikanth Padmanabhan

Vp And Cfo, Patrick J. (Pat) Ward, $726,000 total compensation

President Cummins Turbo Technologies (ctt), Tracy A. Embree

Vp And President Power Systems, Norbert Nusterer

Vp Engineering Cummins Engine Business, Jennifer Rumsey

Vice President Chief Manufacturing And Procurement Officer, Ignacio Garcia

Vice President, Donald Trapp

Vice President, Luis Pasquotto

Hhp Vice President Rebuild, Terry Wham

Vice President Corporate Controller, Christopher Clulow

Lead Vpi Sqie, Larry Frasier

Vice President Research And Technology, Wayne Eckerle

Vice President Finance And Newsletter Coordinator, Tamara Henthorne

Senior Vice President Information Technology, Karthikeyan Gopal

Vice President Cummins Business Services, Diana Rey-Marrero

Second Vice President Corporate Development, Jeff Lawrence

Vpi Manufacturing Program Manager, Hamilton Harper

Vice President Engine Business Quality, Robert Weimer

Vice President, Cindy Moore

Vice President, David Taylor

Vice President Government Relations, Stephen May

Vice President Of Operations, Rick Miller

National Account Manager, Jeff Poferl

Vice President Managing Director Holset, David Moorehouse

Vice President, Kris Urban

Vice President Power Generation, Ken Peterson

Vice President Cummins Filtration, Amy Davis

Vice President, Tim Millwood

Vice President Corporate Strategy And Business Development, Thad Ewald

Vp And Controller Engine Business, Michael Miller

Vice President Corporate Strategy And Business Development, Thaddeaus Ewald

Vice President Automotive Business, Arun Ramachandran

Vpi Materials Readiness Leader, Anoop Mampetta

Executive Vice President, J T White

Vice President Of Finance, Michael Doherty

Vice President Of Aftermarket Support, Joe Dunn

Vpi Sourcing Manager, Adam Kasch

Vice President Financial Operations, Marc Smith

Vpi Sourcing Manager, Larry Detwiler

Vpi Financial Analyst, Roger Clark

Vpi Sourcing Manager, Wray Hendrickson

Vice President Of Operations Cummins Inc South Region, Craig Sanford

Vice President Chief Manufacturing Officer, Jim Lyons

Vpi Manager, Allison Gu

Vice President Turbo Technologies, Tracey Embree

Vice President Sales, Phil Bush

Vice President, Gary L Rickle

Vice President, Ivan Sheffield

Vice President Business Development, Curtis Hallowell

Secretary, Maria Ward

Board Member, Bill Miller

Board Member, William Miller

Board Member, Franklin Chang-diaz

Auditors: PricewaterhouseCoopers LLP

LOCATIONS

HQ: Cummins, Inc.
500 Jackson Street, P.O. Box 3005, Columbus, IN 47202-3005
Phone: 812 377-5000   **Fax:** 812 377-4937
Web: www.cummins.com

2018 Sales

	$ mil.	% of total
United States	13,218	56
China	2,324	10
India	965	4
Other International	7,264	30
Total	**23,771**	**100**

PRODUCTS/OPERATIONS

2018 Sales

	$ mil.	% of total
Engine	10,566	35
Distribution	7,828	26
Components	7,166	24
Power Generation	4,626	15
Electrified Power	7	-
Intersegment eliminations	(6422)	-
Total	**23,771**	**100**

Selected Products

Components business
  Emission solutions
  Filtration (heavy-duty air fuel hydraulic and lube filtration and chemicals)
  Fuel systems (new fuel systems remanufactured electronic control modules)
  Turbo technologies (turbochargers)
Emissions solutions
Engine business
  Bus engines
  Heavy- and medium-duty truck engines
  Industrial engines for construction mining
  agricultural rail and marine equipment
  Light commercial vehicle engines
  Marine diesels (recreational and commercial)
Filtration business
  Air system
  Cooling system (crankcase ventilation)
  Diesel emission additives
  Fuel system (hydraulic)
  Lube system (transmission)
Fuel systems
  Common rail pump
  Extreme pressure injection system
  High Pressure Injection (HPI) system
  Remanufactured products
Power generation business
  Diesel and alternative-fuel electrical generator sets
Turbo technologies

COMPETITORS

Aisin Seiki	Mitsubishi Heavy
Allison Transmission	Industries
BAE Systems Inc.	Parker-Hannifin
BorgWarner	Regal Beloit
Caterpillar	Robert Bosch
China Yuchai	Rolls-Royce Power
DENSO	Systems
DEUTZ	Tenneco
Donaldson Company	

HISTORICAL FINANCIALS

Company Type: Public

Income Statement

FYE: December 31

	REVENUE ($ mil.)	NET INCOME ($ mil.)	NET PROFIT MARGIN	EMPLOYEES
12/19	23,571	2,260	9.6%	61,615
12/18	23,771	2,141	9.0%	62,610
12/17	20,428	999	4.9%	58,600
12/16	17,509	1,394	8.0%	55,400
12/15	19,110	1,399	7.3%	55,200
Annual Growth	**5.4%**	**12.7%**	**—**	**2.8%**

2019 Year-End Financials

Debt ratio: 11.99%	No. of shares (mil.): 150
Return on equity: 30.43%	Dividends
Cash ($ mil.): 1,129	Yield: 2.7%
Current ratio: 1.50	Payout: 30.5%
Long-term debt ($ mil.): 1,576	Market value ($ mil.): 26,969

	STOCK PRICE ($) FY Close	P/E High/Low		PER SHARE ($) Earnings	Dividends	Book Value
12/19	178.96	13	9	14.48	4.90	49.81
12/18	133.64	15	10	13.15	4.44	46.51
12/17	176.64	30	23	5.97	4.21	43.81
12/16	136.67	18	10	8.23	4.00	40.87
12/15	88.01	19	11	7.84	3.51	42.27
Annual Growth	**19.4%**	**—**	**—**	**16.6%**	**8.7%**	**4.2%**

Customers Bancorp Inc

Customers Bancorp makes it pretty clear who they want to serve. Boasting some $8.5 billion in assets the bank holding company operates about 15 branches mostly in southeastern Pennsylvania but also in New York and New Jersey. It offers personal and business checking savings and money market accounts as well as loans certificates of deposit credit cards and concierge or appointment banking (they come to you seven days a week). Around 95% of the bank's loan portfolio is made up of commercial loans while the rest consists of consumer loans. It was formed in 2010 as a holding company for Customers Bank which was created in 1994 as New Century Bank.

Operations

Customers Bancorp operates two main business lines: Commercial Lending and Consumer Lending. Its Commercial Lending business provides commercial and industrial loans small and middle-market business banking and small business administration (SBA) loans multi-family and commercial real estate loans and commercial loans to mortgage originators. Its Consumer Lending division mostly makes local market mortgage loans and home equity loans. More than 95% of the bank's loan portfolio was made up of commercial loans at the end of 2015 while the rest consisted of consumer loans.

Broadly speaking the bank makes roughly 90% of its revenue from interest income. About 66% of its revenue came from loan interest during 2015 while another 19% came from interest loans held for sale and 4% came from interest on investment securities. The remainder of its revenue came from mortgage warehouse transactional fees (4%) and other miscellaneous and non-recurring sources.

Geographic Reach

The bank had 14 branches at the end of 2015 including nine in Philadelphia and Southeastern Pennsylvania; four in Berks County Pennsylvania; one in Westchester County New York; and one in Mercer County New Jersey. It also had a handful of additional offices in Boston; New York City; Portsmouth New Hampshire; Providence Rhode Island; and Suffolk County New York.

Sales and Marketing

Customers Bancorp's customers include private businesses business customers non-profits and consumers. Its commercial lending division typically makes loans to companies with revenues between $1 million to $50 million needing between $0.5 million to $10 million in credit.

The bank has been ramping up its advertising spend in recent years. It spent $1.48 million on advertising in 2015 up from $1.33 million and $1.27 million in 2014 and 2013 respectively.

Financial Performance

The bank's annual revenues have nearly quadrupled since 2011 as its loan assets have more than tripled (its loan assets reached $5.45 billion by of the end of 2015). Meanwhile growing revenues strong cost controls and low interest rates have pushed the bank's annual profits up almost 15-fold over the same period.

Customers Bancorp's revenue jumped 29% to $277.5 million during 2015 mostly as its average balance of interest-earning loan and securities assets rose by 31% to $6.7 billion for the year.

Revenue growth in 2015 drove the bank's net income up 36% to $58.5 million. Customer Bancorp's operating cash levels declined sharply to $356.6 million for the year as the bank originated more loans held for sale than it actually sold.

Strategy

With its eye on becoming the leading regional bank holding company Customers Bancorp continued in 2016 to focus on expanding its market share with its high-touch personalized Concierge Banking services and its "high-tech" BankMobile offerings which include remote account opening remote deposit capture and mobile banking. The BankMobile and online banking channels allow Customers Bancorp to slow expensive branch-expansion plans and cut operating costs significantly while giving customers faster access to banking services.

But even with digital banking the bank occasionally opens new branches (and selectively acquire others) to grow its loan and deposit business. In January 2016 it opened and replaced an existing branch in Hamilton New Jersey onto Route 33 in the same city. In June 2015 Customers opened a new Long Island location in Mellville New York to expand its private and commercial banking services to local clients there.

Mergers and Acquisitions

In December 2015 Customers Bank expanded its deposit business and added 2 million new student customers after buying the One Account Student Checking and Refund Management Disbursement Services business from higher education refund disbursement provider Higher One Inc for $42 million.

Company Background

In late 2011 Customers purchased Berkshire Bancorp and picked up five branches in Berks County Pennsylvania for about $11.3 million.

EXECUTIVES

Chairman And Ceo, Jay S. Sidhu, age 68, $300,000 total compensation
President And Coo, Richard A. Ehst, age 74, $225,000 total compensation
Executive Vice President President Of Community Banking, Warren Taylor, age 62, $190,000 total compensation
Evp And Chief Credit Officer, Thomas Jastrem
Evp And Chief Administrative Officer, Jim Collins
Evp And Chief Lending Officer, Timothy D. Romig
Evp And President Special Assets Group, Robert A. White
Evp And Cfo, James D. Hogan
Evp And Director Multi-family And Investment Cre Lending, Kenneth A. Keiser
Senior Vice President, Randy Hanks
Vice President, John Gerhart
Assistant Vice President And Appraisal Review Officer, Richard Nagy
Senior Vice President, Mary Moffitt
Vice President Commercial Lending, Andrew Herbein
Vp Assistant Bsa Officer, Melissa Krueger
Vice President, Margaret Donovan
Senior Vice President Credit O, Barbara Bergman
Senior Vice President, William Hirst
Assistant Vice President Capital Markets, Dana Galvin
Vice President, Scott Gates
Assistant Vice President And Assistant Branch Manager, Lisa Gearheart
Senior Vice President, Travis L Gray
Vice President Commercial Credit Manager, Jason Rauenzahn
Assistant Vice President Sox Internal Control Manager, Frank Bommentre
Senior Vice President, Kevin Cornwall
Assistant Vice President, Terry Meehan
Assistant Vice President And Credit Analyst, Angela Edwards
Vice President Senior Underwriter In Small Business Lending, Gino Cavaliere
Senior Vice President Facilities And Security, James Zardecki
Vice President Commercial Lending, John Camero
Senior Vice President Ne Director Of Pla, Paula Pais
Vice President And Government Guaranteed Lender, Jennifer Mason
Vice President Sales And Industrial Group, Kurt Kolesha

Vice President Government Guaranteed Lending Sba And Usda, Mario Campbell
Vice President And Government Guaranteed Lender, Jennifer Mckay
Vice President, Joanne Jolin
Vice President Sba Loan Specialist, Stacey Kuzniasz
Senior Vice President Commercial Real Estate Lending, Stephen King
Senior Vice President Regional Chief Lending Officer, Robert Fischer
Assistant Vice President Collateral Manager, Donna Abel
Executive Vice President And Manager Market, Brett Long
Senior Vice President Information Technology Strategy, Alex Balagour
Vice President, Kimberly Miller
Senior Vice President, Veder Reddick
Vice President Commercial Lending, Brett V Long
Vice President, Brent Black
Vice President Insurance Risk Management, Antonette Tumminello
Senior Vice President Senior Credit Officer, Clifford Gaysunas
Senior Vice President Relationship Manager, Richard Donnelly
Senior Vice President, Samuel H Smith
Vice President Of Sales Strategy And Operations Cb Private And Commercial Banking, Robert Fraioli
Vice President And Fraud Prevention And Investigation Manager, Georgia Felty
Senior Vice President Audit Director, Brion Watson
Vice President Lead Corporate Counsel, Michael Detommaso
Senior Vice President Director Of Operations Deposit Administration, Robert J Diegel
Vice President Special Assets Financial Reporting, Doan Dang
Assistant Vice President And Lead Information Technology Auditor, Patrick Direnzo
Vice President Special Assets Group, Kathy Hansen
Vice President, Kimberly Stack
Senior Vice President Director Of Mortgage Servicing, Debra Hutchinson
Assistant Vice President, John Chung
Vice President, Diane Billman
Vice President, Keith Munley
Vice President Consumer Lending Compliance, Matt Kachurka
Vice President Manager Of Network Administration, Joseph Thren
Vice President And Senior Analyst, Joann Zerbo
Senior Vice President, Robert Fine
Vice President Financial Crime Compliance Officer, Marsha Thomas
Senior Vice President And Loan Operations, Joseph M Swarr
Avp Portfolio Manager, Chris Lacroix
Vice President, Lucia Deangelo
Vice President And Client Manager, Kinwa Auyeung
Senior Vice President Commercial Deposit Officer, Todd Goldstein
Assistant Vice President Private And Commercial Banking, Mary Haley
Senior Vice President Commercial Deposit Services Manager, Lary Snow
Vice President And Sba Processor, Theresa Busa
Senior Vice President And Senior Relationship Manager, Jay Farland
Senior Vice President And Credit Officer, John Powers
Assistant Vice President And Portfolio Manager, Charles Macchione
Senior Vice President And Credit Analysis Manager, Carol Macelree
Senior Vice President And Regional Credit Officer, Charles Margiotti

Assistant Vice President And Policy And Procedures Manager, Elizabeth Podguski
Auditors: DELOITTE & TOUCHE LLP

LOCATIONS

HQ: Customers Bancorp Inc
  701 Reading Avenue, West Reading, PA 19611
Phone: 610 933-2000
Web: www.customersbank.com

PRODUCTS/OPERATIONS

2015

	$ mil.	% of total
Interest income		
Loans receivable including fees	182	66
Loans held for sale	51	19
Investment securities	10	4
Other	5	2
Non interest income		
Mortgage warehouse transnational fees	10	4
Bank-owned life insurance	7	3
Gains on sales of loans	4	1
Deposit fees	0	0
Mortgage loan and banking income	0	0
Gain (loss) on sale of investment securities)	(0.09)	0
Other	4	1
Total	**277**	**100**

Products include
Equipment Loans
Mortgage Warehouse Loans
Multi-Family And Commercial Real Estate Loans
Residential Mortgage Loans
Small Business Loans

COMPETITORS

Bank of America	Huntington Bancshares
Capital One	JPMorgan Chase
Citigroup	KeyCorp
Comerica	PNC Financial
Fifth Third	U.S. Bancorp
HSBC	Wells Fargo

HISTORICAL FINANCIALS

Company Type: Public

Income Statement   FYE: December 31

	ASSETS ($ mil.)	NET INCOME ($ mil.)	INCOME AS % OF ASSETS	EMPLOYEES
12/19	11,520	79	0.7%	867
12/18	9,833	71	0.7%	827
12/17	9,839	78	0.8%	765
12/16	9,382	78	0.8%	739
12/15	8,401	58	0.7%	517
Annual Growth	**8.2%**	**7.9%**	**—**	**13.8%**

2019 Year-End Financials

Debt ratio: 2.65%	No. of shares (mil.): 31
Return on equity: 7.89%	Dividends
Cash ($ mil.): 212	Yield: —
Current ratio: —	Payout: —
Long-term debt ($ mil.): —	Market value ($ mil.): 746

	STOCK PRICE ($) FY Close	P/E High/Low		Earnings	PER SHARE ($) Dividends	Book Value
12/19	23.81	12	8	2.05	0.00	33.60
12/18	18.20	18	9	1.78	0.00	30.86
12/17	25.99	17	12	1.97	0.00	29.35
12/16	35.82	15	9	2.31	0.00	28.26
12/15	27.22	15	9	1.96	0.00	20.59
Annual Growth	**(3.3%)**	**—**	**—**	**1.1%**	**—**	**13.0%**

CVB Financial Corp

CVB Financial is into the California Vibe Baby. The holding company's Citizens Business Bank offers community banking services to primarily small and midsized businesses but also to consumers through nearly 50 branch and office locations across central and southern California. Boasting more than $7 billion in assets the bank offers checking money market CDs and savings accounts trust and investment services and a variety of loans. Commercial real estate loans account for about two-thirds of the bank's loan portfolio which is rounded out by business consumer and construction loans; residential mortgages; dairy and livestock loans; and municipal lease financing.

Operations

In addition to its 40 business financial centers CVB operates seven Commercial Banking Centers (CBCs). The CBCs operate primarily as sales offices and focus on business clients professionals and high-net-worth individuals. The bank also has three trust offices.

Citizens Business Bank provides auto and equipment leasing and brokers mortgage loans through its Citizens Financial Services Division; CitizensTrust offers trust and investment services.

Overall the bank made 63% of its total revenue from interest income on loans and leases in 2014 with another 24% of total revenue coming from interest income on the bank's investment securities. About 5% of total revenue came from service charges on deposit accounts and 3% came from trust and investment services income.

Geographic Reach

CVB Financial has 40 Business Financial Centers located in the Inland Empire Los Angeles County Orange County San Diego County and the Central Valley regions in California.

Sales and Marketing

CVB Financial provides services to companies from a variety of industries including: industrial and manufacturing dairy and livestock agriculture education nonprofit entertainment medical professional services title and escrow government and property management.

Financial Performance

CVB's revenue has been in decline in recent years due to shrinking interest margins on loans amidst the low-interest environment. The firm's profits however have been rising thanks to declining loan loss provisions as its loan portfolio's credit quality has been improving in the strengthening economy.

CVB enjoyed a breakout year in 2014 with revenue rebounding by 12% to $289.32 million mostly thanks to higher interest income as the bank grew its loan and lease assets by 7% during the year and grew its investment security assets by 18%. Most of its loan growth came from commercial real estate loans while SFR mortgage loans consumer loans and construction loans also helped boost the company's top line. The bank's non-interest income also jumped by 44% during the year thanks to a $6 million gain on loans held-for-sale and a net $3.6 million decrease in its FDIC loss sharing asset.

Higher revenue and a $16.1 million loan loss provision recapture in 2014 also drove the bank's net income higher by 9% to $104.02 million.

Despite higher earnings for the year CVB's operating cash levels shrank by 22% to $87.70 million as the bank used more cash toward employee payments and income taxes.

Strategy

CVB Financial continues to seek out acquisitions of smaller banking trust and investment companies

to grow its loan and deposit business as well as its geographic reach in key markets in (mostly Southern) California. With its 2014 acquisition of American Security Bank for example CVB boosted its assets by 6% to over $7 billion while adding branches in more than a handful of key markets in Southern California.

Remaining profitable throughout the economic downturn CVB Financial credits its success in part to its strict loan underwriting standards. The bank targets family-owned or other privately held businesses with annual revenues of up to $200 million with the goal of maintaining its client relationships for decades.

Mergers and Acquisitions

In March 2014 CVB Financial through its Citizens Business Bank (CBB) subsidiary purchased Southern California-based American Security Bank (the flagship subsidiary of American Bancshares) for a total of $57 million. The deal would add American Security Bank's $431 million in assets and boost CBB's branch presence across key markets in Newport Beach Corona Laguna Niguel Lancastar Victorville and Apple Valley.

In 2016 CVB Financial agreed to buy the $416 million-asset Valley Commerce Bancorp the holding company for Valley Business Bank. Valley Business has four banking locations in California's Visalia Tulare Fresno and Woodlake.

Company Background

In 2009 CVB Financial healthier than most California banks acquired the failed San Joaquin Bank after the FDIC took it over. The deal added five branches banking centers in the Bakersfield area.

EXECUTIVES

Evp And General Counsel Cvb Financial Corporation And Citizens Business Bank, Richard H. Wohl, age 61

President And Ceo Cvb Financial And Citizens Business Bank, Christopher D. (Chris) Myers, age 57, $800,000 total compensation

Evp And Cfo, E. Allen Nicholson, age 53

Evp And Cio, Elsa I. Zavala

Evp And Dairy And Livestock Industries Group Manager Citizens Business Bank, G. Larry Zivelonghi

Evp And Senior Lender, Ted J. Dondanville

Svp And Regional Manager Citizens Business Bank, David A. Brager, $300,000 total compensation

Evp And Coo Citizens Business Bank, David C. Harvey, $300,000 total compensation

Evp; Head Citizenstrust, R. Daniel Banis

Evp And Chief Risk Officer Citizens Business Bank, Yamynn De Angelis

Evp Ventura/santa Barbara, Donald R. Toussaint

Executive Vice President, Daniel Banis

Vice President Relationship Manager, Nadine Ortega

Senior Vice President Chief Risk Officer, Yamynn Deangelis

Senior Vice President, Michael D Stain

Vice President Relationship Manager, Jason Gould

Vice President Senior Product Manager, John Outwater

Senior Vice President, John Stenz

Vice President And Relationship Manager, Maria Padilla

Evp Of Cfo, Allen Nicholson

Vice President Specialty Service Officer Commercial Banking Group, Martha Ponce

Vice President Special Assets Portfolio Manager, Bruce Adams

Vp And Special Assets Portfolio Manager, Verona Chion

Vice President Center Manager, Pamela Gaspar

Vice President Credit Officer, Frank Yu

Avp Senior Regional Loan Consultant For Citizens Home Lending, Rosita Rapelian

Vice Chairman, George A. Borba, age 87
Chairman, Raymond V. O'Brien
Auditors: KPMG LLP

LOCATIONS

HQ: CVB Financial Corp
  701 North Haven Ave., Suite 350, Ontario, CA 91764
Phone: 909 980-4030
Web: www.cbbank.com

Selected Branch Locations
Fresno County
Kern County
Los Angeles County
Madera County
Orange County
Riverside County
San Bernardino County
Tulare County

PRODUCTS/OPERATIONS

2014 Sales

	$ mil.	% of total
Interest		
Loans including fees	181	62
Investment securities	68	24
Other	2	1
Noninterest		
Service charges on deposit accounts	15	5
Trust & investment services	8	3
Bankcard services	3	1
BOLI income	2	1
Other	10	3
Adjustments	(3.6)	-
Total	**289**	**100**

COMPETITORS

Bank of America	Popular Inc.
Bank of the West	Provident Financial
City National	Holdings
Comerica	U.S. Bancorp
JPMorgan Chase	Wells Fargo
MUFG Americas Holdings	

HISTORICAL FINANCIALS

Company Type: Public

Income Statement — FYE: December 31

	ASSETS ($ mil.)	NET INCOME ($ mil.)	INCOME AS % OF ASSETS	EMPLOYEES
12/19	11,282	207	1.8%	—
12/18	11,529	152	1.3%	—
12/17	8,270	104	1.3%	—
12/16	8,073	101	1.3%	—
12/15	7,671	99	1.3%	—
Annual Growth	10.1%	20.3%	—	—

2019 Year-End Financials

Debt ratio: 0.23%	No. of shares (mil.): 140
Return on equity: 10.81%	Dividends
Cash ($ mil.): 188	Yield: 3.1%
Current ratio: —	Payout: 47.8%
Long-term debt ($ mil.): —	Market value ($ mil.): 3,023

	STOCK PRICE ($) FY Close	P/E High/Low	PER SHARE ($) Earnings	Dividends	Book Value
12/19	21.58	16 14	1.48	0.68	14.23
12/18	20.23	20 15	1.24	0.56	13.22
12/17	23.56	26 21	0.95	0.52	9.70
12/16	22.93	25 15	0.94	0.36	9.15
12/15	16.92	20 16	0.93	0.48	8.68
Annual Growth	6.3%	— —	12.3%	9.1%	13.2%

CVS Health Corporation

CVS Health Corp. is a leading pharmacy benefits manager with approximately 105 million plan members as well as the nation's largest drugstore chain (topping Walgreens). It runs approximately 9900 retail and specialty drugstores. In addition to its standalone pharmacy operations the company operates CVS locations inside Target stores and runs a prescription management company Caremark Pharmacy Services. The company also offers walk-in health services through its retail network of MinuteClinics that are located in around 1100 CVS stores. CVS also serves an estimated 37 million people through traditional voluntary and consumer-directed health insurance products and related services.

HISTORY

Brothers Stanley and Sid Goldstein who ran health and beauty products distributor Mark Steven branched out into retail in 1963 when they opened up their first Consumer Value Store in Lowell Massachusetts with partner Ralph Hoagland.

The chain grew rapidly amassing 17 stores by the end of 1964 (the year the CVS name was first used) and 40 by 1969. That year the Goldsteins sold the chain to Melville Shoe to finance further expansion.

Melville had been founded in 1892 by shoe supplier Frank Melville. Melville's son Ward grew the company creating the Thom McAn shoe store chain and later buying its supplier. By 1969 Melville had opened shoe shops in Kmart stores (through its Meldisco unit) launched one apparel chain (Chess King sold in 1993) and purchased another (Foxwood Stores renamed Foxmoor and sold in 1985).

In 1972 CVS bought the 84-store Clinton Drug and Discount a Rochester New York-based chain. Two years later when sales hit $100 million CVS had 232 stores — only 45 of which had pharmacies. The company bought New Jersey-based Mack Drug (36 stores) in 1977. By 1981 CVS had more than 400 stores.

CVS's sales hit $1 billion in 1985 as it continued to add pharmacies to many of its older stores. In 1987 Stanley's success was recognized company-wide when he was named chairman and CEO of CVS's parent company which by then had been renamed Melville.

CVS bought the 490-store Peoples Drug Stores chain from Imasco in 1990 giving it locations in Maryland Pennsylvania Virginia West Virginia and Washington DC. CVS created PharmaCare Management Services in 1994 to take advantage of the growing market for pharmacy services and managed-care drug programs. Pharmacist Tom Ryan was named CEO that year.

With CVS outperforming Melville's other operations in 1995 Melville decided to concentrate on the drugstore chain. By that time Melville's holdings had grown to include discount department store chain Marshalls and furniture chain This End Up both sold in 1995; footwear chain Footaction spun off as part of Footstar in 1996 along with Meldisco; the Linens 'n Things chain spun off in 1996; the Kay-Bee Toys chain sold in 1996; and Bob's Stores (apparel and footwear) sold in 1997.

Melville was renamed in late 1996. Amid major consolidation in the drugstore industry in 1997 CVS — then with about 1425 stores — paid $3.7 billion for Revco D.S. which had nearly 2600 stores in 17 states mainly in the Midwest and Southeast. The next year the company bought

Arbor Drugs (200 stores in Michigan later converted to the CVS banner) for nearly $1.5 billion.

CVS opened about 180 new stores and relocated nearly 200 in 1998 as it shifted from strip malls to freestanding stores. (It also closed nearly 160 stores.) Stanley retired as chairman in 1999 and was succeeded by Ryan.

In 1999 the company bought online drugstore pioneer Soma.com renamed CVS.com. It also launched the CVS ProCare pharmacy to serve customers in need of complex drug therapies. A year later CVS bought Stadtlander Pharmacy of Pittsburgh from Bergen Brunswig (now Amerisource-Bergen) for $124 million.

In early 2001 Wolverine Equities paid $288 million for 96 stores which CVS said it would continue to operate. In 2001 CVS opened 43 stores in new markets including Miami and Fort Lauderdale Florida; Las Vegas; and Dallas Houston and Fort Worth Texas. As part of a strategic restructuring begun in 2001 CVS closed more than 200 stores and moved others from strip malls to freestanding locations.

In July 2002 CVS was among the winning bidders for the remaining assets of bankrupt rival Phar-Mor. CVS acquired the majority of Phar-Mor's prescription lists. In October CVS named KB Toys as the exclusive toy supplier to its drugstores. CVS opened 266 new stores in 2002 and another 150 new stores in 2003.

In April 2003 specialty pharmacy division CVS ProCare changed its name to PharmaCare Specialty Pharmacy.

With those store closings behind it the drugstore chain began opening stores in Minneapolis the 10th-largest drugstore market in the US in 2004. CVS opened about 10 stores in the Los Angeles area in 2004 marking the drugstore chain's return to Southern California after a 12-year absence. CVS is also targeting other high-traffic markets including Chicago Florida Las Vegas Phoenix and Texas for expansion.

In July 2004 CVS completed the acquisition of 1260 Eckerd stores Eckerd Health Services (which included Eckerd's $1 billion mail order and pharmacy benefits management businesses) and three distribution centers from J. C. Penney Company for $2.15 billion. The acquisition of the Eckerd stores (622 in Florida) gave CVS more stores than archrival Walgreen. CVS completed the conversion of Eckerd stores in Alabama Arizona Colorado Florida Kansas Louisiana Mississippi Missouri New Mexico Oklahoma and Texas to its own banner within about a year.

In June 2005 CVS agreed to pay $110 million to settle a shareholders' lawsuit filed in 2001 that alleged the company had made misleading statements to artificially raise its stock price and violated accounting practices. CVS denied the charges and said the settlement was "purely a business decision."

In June 2006 CVS completed the acquisition of some 700 stand-alone Sav-On and Osco drugstores from Albertson's. CVS was part of a consortium that bought the nation's #2 supermarket chain and split it up amongst themselves. The transaction gave CVS access to Southern California and key Midwest markets. In September the company purchased the retail-based health clinic operator MinuteClinic for an undisclosed amount. The acquisition allowed CVS to provide in-store care to its customers for minor ailments.

In March 2007 CVS changed its name to CVS Caremark Corporation following its acquisition of the pharmacy benefits manager Caremark RX after months of bidding between CVS and Express Scripts. Ultimately CVS paid about $26.5 billion for Caremark. In November CEO Ryan added the chairman's title to his job description following the retirement of Mac Crawford.

In October 2008 CVS Caremark acquired Longs Drug Stores for about $2.9 billion. Longs Drug operates 521 pharmacies in California Hawaii Nevada and Arizona. The purchase included Long's Rx America subsidiary a pharmacy benefits management service to more than 8 million members. Also in 2008 the company opened about 190 new retail pharmacies.

In 2008 CVS settled a lawsuit regarding drug-switching allegations for $36.7 million. The company had been accused of switching Medicaid customers to a more expensive capsule form of Zantac from a tablet form; CVS denied the allegations.

In June 2009 CVS agreed to pay almost $1 million to settle allegations stemming from the sale of expired OTC medications infant formula and dairy products.

CVS Caremark in early 2011 won a contract to administer Aetna's retail pharmacy network. CVS Caremark is managing both purchasing and prescription filling for Aetna's mail-order and specialty pharmacy operations. Prior to his retirement in May 2011 Ryan assumed the title of non-executive chairman in March when Larry Merlo took over as president and CEO of CVS.

In 2012 CVS opened drugstores in four new states: Arkansas Colorado Oregon and Washington.

In September 2014 the company changed its name to CVS Health Corporation to reflect its broader commitment to health care. The corporate name change coincided with the cessation of tobacco sales at its retail stores in September.

EXECUTIVES

Evp Health Plans, Tracy L. Bahl, age 57
President And Ceo, Larry J. Merlo, age 64, $1,630,000 total compensation
Evp; President Cvs/pharmacy, Helena B. Foulkes, age 55, $950,000 total compensation
Evp And Cio, Stephen J. Gold, age 61
Evp And Chief Human Resources Officer, Lisa Bisaccia, age 64
Svp And Chief Marketing Officer, Norman de Greve
Evp Specialty Pharmacy Cvs/caremark, Alan M. Lotvin, age 58
Evp And Chief Medical Officer, Troyen A. Brennan, age 66, $637,500 total compensation
Evp And Head Of Retail Operations, Scott Baker
Evp And Coo, Jonathan C. Roberts, age 64, $950,000 total compensation
Evp And Cfo, David M. (Dave) Denton, age 55, $850,000 total compensation
Evp And Associate Chief Medical Officer; President Cvs/minuteclinic, Andrew J. (Andy) Sussman, age 54
Evp Sales And Marketing Cvs/caremark, J. David Joyner, age 55
Evp Chief Health Strategy Officer And General Counsel, Thomas M. Moriarty, age 57, $750,000 total compensation
Evp Enterprise Strategy And Corporate Development, Joshua (Josh) Flum
Evp And President Omnicare, Robert O. (Rocky) Kraft, age 50
Svp And Chief Compliance Officer, David Falkowski
Vice President Sales, Edward Devaney
Senior Vice President Sales And Account Services, James Margiotta
Vice President Corporate Communications, Karen Brown
Senior Vice President Pharmacy And Clinical Programs, Stephen Hobson
Vice President Strategic Procurement, Anna M Umberto
Senior Vice President Investor Relations, Michael McGuire
Senior Vice President Chief Compliance Officer, John Buckley

Pharmacy Manager, Vijay Patel
Senior Vice President Chief Accounting Officer Controller, James Clark
Senior Vice President Tax, John Kennedy
Pharmacy Manager, Kim Nguyen
Senior Vice President Trade Relations, Gary Loeber
Pharmacy Manager, Brian Jackson
Pharmacy Manager, Michael Brito
Pharmacy Manager, Komal Patel
Pharmacy Manager, JoAnne Tran
Pharmacy Manager, Deanne Medouris
Pharmacy Manager, James Przybylowicz
Pharmacy Manager, Harsh Patel
Vice President And Ciso, Frank Price
Vice President Coalition Business Unit, Bruce Macrae
Senior Vice President Logistics And Supply Chain, Ron Link
Vice President Information Technology, Dawn Pagano
Svp Government And Public Affairs, Melissa Schulman
Vice President Rx Merchandising, Brian Whalen
Pharmacy Manager, Benjamin King
Senior Vice President Payer Relations And Managed Care Cvs Pharmacy, Tom Gibbons
Vice President Retail Pharmacy Systems, Dennis MacQuarrie
Vice President Of Sales, Atin Bhadouria
Vice President Clinical Services Operations, Julie Sheer
Pharmacy Manager, Joseph Morasutti
Vice President, Shannon Penberthy
Senior Vice President Assistant General Counsel, Elizabeth Ferguson
Vice President, Joan O'Rourke
Vp Retail Omni Channel Digit, Catherine Lewenberg
Vice President, Stephen Holodak
Pharmacy Manager, Mariam Al-Khudhair
Pharmacy Manager, Tricia Miller
Pharmacy Manager, Ashlie Miller
Vice President Health Plan Sales At Cvs Caremark, Michelle Manolovic
Svp Investor Relations, Nancya R Christal
Vice President Account Management; Health Plan Client Services, Sabrina Williams
Evp Cvs Health And President Omnicare, C Daniel Haron
Executive Vice President Sales And Account Services, John Joyner
Chairman, David W. (Dave) Dorman, age 66
Board Member, Jean-pierre Millon
Board Member, Nancy-ann Deparle
Board Member, William Weldon
Board Member, Tony White
Auditors: Ernst & Young LLP

LOCATIONS

HQ: CVS Health Corporation
One CVS Drive, Woonsocket, RI 02895
Phone: 401 765-1500   **Fax:** 401 762-2137
Web: www.cvshealth.com

PRODUCTS/OPERATIONS

2018 Sales

	$ mil.	% of total
Products	183,910	95
Premiums	8,184	4
Services	1,825	1
Net investment income	660	-

Total	194,579	100

2018 Sales

		$ mil.	% of total
Pharmacy services		134,128	60
Retail/LTC Segment		83,989	37
Health care benefits		5,549	3
Corporate and other	606		
Adjustments		(29693)	-
Total		194,579	100

COMPETITORS

Anthem	OptumRx
Blue Cross	PharMerica
CIGNA	Prime Therapeutics
Express Scripts	Rite Aid
Humana	Wal-Mart
MedImpact	Walgreen
Medicare & Medicaid Services	

HISTORICAL FINANCIALS

Company Type: Public

Income Statement

FYE: December 31

	REVENUE ($ mil.)	NET INCOME ($ mil.)	NET PROFIT MARGIN	EMPLOYEES
12/19	256,776	6,634	2.6%	290,000
12/18	194,579	(594)	—	295,000
12/17	184,765	6,622	3.6%	246,000
12/16	177,526	5,317	3.0%	250,000
12/15	153,290	5,237	3.4%	243,000
Annual Growth	13.8%	6.1%	—	4.5%

2019 Year-End Financials

Debt ratio: 30.78%
Return on equity: 10.87%
Cash ($ mil.): 5,683
Current ratio: 0.94
Long-term debt ($ mil.): 64,699

No. of shares (mil.): 1,302
Dividends
Yield: 2.6%
Payout: 39.3%
Market value ($ mil.): 96,726

	STOCK PRICE ($) FY Close	P/E High/Low		PER SHARE ($) Earnings	Dividends	Book Value
12/19	74.29	15	10	5.08	2.00	49.05
12/18	65.52	—	—	(0.57)	2.00	44.96
12/17	72.50	13	10	6.44	2.00	37.17
12/16	78.91	22	15	4.90	1.70	34.71
12/15	97.77	24	20	4.63	1.40	33.78
Annual Growth	(6.6%)	—	—	2.3%	9.3%	9.8%

Dacotah Banks Inc.

EXECUTIVES

Ceo, Richard Westra
Pres, Robert Fouberg
SEC, Kenneth L Gosch
Cfo, Chad Bergan
Sr V Pres, Joe Senger
Dir, Tom Heisler
Sr V Pres, Bob Compton
V Pres, Steven Schaefer
V Pres, Kent Edson
Pres Market Faulkton, SD, Dwight Hossle
Senior Account Representative, David Boehnke
Auditors: Eide Bailly LLP

LOCATIONS

HQ: Dacotah Banks Inc.
401 South Main Street, Suite 212, P.O. Box 1496,
Aberdeen, SD 57402-1496
Phone: 605 225-4850 **Fax:** 605 225-4929
Web: www.dacotahbank.com

HISTORICAL FINANCIALS

Company Type: Public

Income Statement   FYE: December 31

	ASSETS ($ mil.)	NET INCOME ($ mil.)	INCOME AS % OF ASSETS	EMPLOYEES
12/19	2,701	30	1.1%	—
12/18	2,577	28	1.1%	—
12/17	2,406	17	0.7%	—
12/16	2,297	22	1.0%	—
12/15	2,234	21	1.0%	—
Annual Growth	4.9%	9.6%		

2019 Year-End Financials

Debt ratio: 0.81%   No. of shares (mil.): 11
Return on equity: 9.87%   Dividends
Cash ($ mil.): 201   Yield: 0.0%
Current ratio: —   Payout: 19.3%
Long-term debt ($ mil.): —   Market value ($ mil.): 382

	STOCK PRICE ($) FY Close	P/E High/Low	PER SHARE ($) Earnings	Dividends	Book Value
12/19	34.00	20 12	2.74	0.53	29.04
12/18	51.01	22 12	2.51	0.47	20.70
12/17	33.00	25 18	1.57	0.43	19.17
12/16	28.25	135 12	2.07	0.40	18.20
12/15	245.00	133 111	1.92	0.36	21.76
Annual Growth	(39.0%)	— —	9.3%	10.2%	7.5%

DAIRY FARMERS OF AMERICA, INC.

Dairy Farmers of America (DFA) is one of the world's largest dairy cooperatives with more than 13000 member farmers across the US. Along with fresh and shelf-stable fluid milk the co-op produces cheese butter powders and sweetened condensed milk for industrial wholesale and retail customers. It also offers contract manufacturing services. The company's brands include Borden and Cache Valley for consumer cheese; Keller's Creamery Plugra Breakstone's Falfurrias and Oakhurst Dairy; and other dairy products under Sport Shake (sports beverage) La Vaquita (queso) Kemps Guida's Dairy and Cass Clay. The company owns more than 85 production plants nationwide.

Geographic Reach

DFA is based in Kansas City Missouri and divides the US into seven areas: Central (which shares the main headquarters) Mideast (Medina OH) Mountain (Salt Lake City UT) Northeast (East Syracuse NY) Southeast (Knoxville TN) Southwest (Grapevine TX) and Western (Corona CA).

Sales and Marketing

DFA's customers include food manufacturers school cafeterias large restaurant and retailers among others.

Mergers and Acquisitions

In mid-2020 DFA acquired Dean Foods a dairy processor in the country based in Texas for $433 million. Dean Foods is a leading food and beverage company and the largest processor and direct-to-store distributor of fresh fluid milk and other dairy and dairy case products in the United States. The acquisition helps DFA in expanding its milk market.

Company Background

DFA was established in 1998 by leaders of four of the nation's leading milk cooperatives: Associated Milk Producers Mid-America Dairymen Milk Marketing and Western Dairymen Cooperative.

HISTORY

Mid-America Dairymen (Mid-Am) the largest of the cooperatives that merged to form Dairy Farmers of America (DFA) was born in 1968. At that time several Midwestern dairy co-ops banded together to attack common economic problems such as reduced government subsidies price drops resulting from a rising milk surplus dealer consolidation and improvements in production processing and packaging. The merging organizations — representing 15000 dairy farmers — were Producers Creamery Company (Springfield Missouri) Sanitary Milk Producers (St. Louis) Square Deal Milk Producers (Highland Illinois) Mid-Am (Kansas City Missouri) and Producers Creamery Company of Chillicothe (north central Missouri).

During the early 1970s Mid-Am struggled with internal restructuring. Most dairy farmers and co-ops were hit hard by the energy crisis and the government's decision to allow increased dairy imports in 1973 the same year the US Justice Department filed an antitrust suit against Mid-Am. (A judge cleared the co-op 12 years later.)

In 1974 Mid-Am lost almost $8 million on revenues of $625 million chalked up to record-high feed prices a weakened economy a milk surplus and a massive inventory loss. Co-op veteran Gary Hanman was named CEO that year. Over the next two years Mid-Am cut costs sold corporate frills downsized management and began marketing more of its own products under the Mid-America Farms label thus reducing dependency on commodity sales.

Mid-Am expanded its research and development efforts throughout the 1980s. The co-op opened its services to farmers in California and New Mexico in 1993 and a series of mergers in 1994 and 1995 nearly doubled its size. In 1997 it purchased some of Borden's dairy operations including rights to the valuable Elsie the Cow and Borden's trademarks.

Wary of falling milk prices Mid-Am merged with Western Dairymen Cooperative Milk Marketing and the Southern Region of Associated Milk Producers at the end of 1997 to form DFA. Hanman moved into the seat of CEO at the new co-op. DFA began a series of joint ventures with the #1 US dairy processor Suiza Foods (now Dean Foods).

DFA added California Gold (more than 330 farmers 1998) and Independent Cooperative Milk Producers Association (730 dairy farmer members in Michigan and parts of Ohio and Indiana 1999). In another joint venture with Suiza in early 2000 DFA sold its 50% stake in the US's #3 fluid milk processor Southern Foods in exchange for 34% of a new company named Suiza Dairy Group.

After mollifying the government's antitrust fears DFA acquired the butter operations of Sodiaal North America in 2000. It then molded all its butter businesses into a new entity Keller's Creamery. However another acquisition did not fare as well. The same year DFA acquired controlling interest in Southern Belle Dairy only to have the merger challenged three years later by the Department of Justice. Arguing that the merger formed a monopoly in school milk sales in several states the Department of Justice filed suit which a federal judge later dismissed.

During 2001 the cooperative went in with Land O'Lakes 50/50 to purchase a cheese plant from Kraft. Later in the year as Suiza Foods acquired Dean Foods (and took on its name) DFA sold back its stake in Suiza Dairy Group to the new Dean Foods. DFA then teamed up with a group of dairy investors to form a new 50/50 joint venture National Dairy Holdings which received 11 processing plants from Dean Foods as part of the exchange for Suiza Dairy.

EXECUTIVES

Senior Adviser; President Affiliate Division, Alan J. Bernon, age 65
President Farm Services, Gregory I. (Greg) Wickham
Coo And Ceo Dairylea, Richard P. (Rick) Smith
Evp; President Global Dairy Products Group, Mark Korsmeyer
Svp Finance, David Meyer
Executive Vice President Of Commercial Operations, Doug Glade
Vice President Sales And Marketing Global Ingredients, Lavonne Dietrich
Vice President Operations Fluid, Ray Mccoy
Assistant Vice President Legal, Heather Grossman
Vice President Milk Logistics, Ernest Yates
Vice Chairman, Bill Siebenborn
Chairman, Randy Mooney
Vice Chairman, Wayne Palla
Vice Chairman, George Mertens
Treasurer, Danelle Bender
Auditors: KPMG LLP KANSAS CITY MO

LOCATIONS

HQ: DAIRY FARMERS OF AMERICA, INC.
1405 N 98TH ST, KANSAS CITY, KS 661111865
Phone: 816 801-6455
Web: WWW.DFAMILK.COM

PRODUCTS/OPERATIONS

Selected Products and Brands
Consumer brands
  Borden cheese
  Breakstone's butter
  Cache Valley cheese
  Keller's Creamery butter
  Plugrá; butter
  Sport Shake energy milk shake
Contract manufacturing
  Cheese dips
  Cheese powders & flavors
  Coffee-based flavored drinks
  Instant formula
  Sour cream
  Sports drinks
Dairy ingredients
  Cheeses (American & Italian)
  Nonfat dry milk powder
  Skim milk powder
  Sweetened condensed milk

COMPETITORS

Arla Foods	Glanbia plc
Associated Milk Producers	Great Lakes Cheese
	HP Hood
Berkeley Farms	Humboldt Creamery
California Dairies Inc.	Lactalis
	Land O'Lakes
ConAgra	Marathon Cheese
Darigold Inc.	Mayfield Dairy Farms
Dean Foods	Northwest Dairy
Farmland Dairies	Prairie Farms Dairy
Foremost Farms	Quality Chekd
Friendship Dairies	Sargento
Garelick Farms	

Company Type: Private

Income Statement				FYE: December 31
	REVENUE ($ mil.)	NET INCOME ($ mil.)	NET PROFIT MARGIN	EMPLOYEES
12/16	13,528	136	1.0%	21,000
12/15	13,803	98	0.7%	—
12/14	17,856	48	0.3%	—
Annual Growth	(13.0%)	67.6%	—	—

Dana Inc

Dana is a global leader in providing power-conveyance and energy-management solutions for vehicles and machinery. In addition to its core offerings which include driveline products (rear and front axles driveshafts transmissions) it provides power technologies (sealing and thermal-management products) and service parts. It makes products for vehicles in the light medium/heavy (commercial) and off-highway markets that carry brand names such as Spicer Victor Reinz and Long. Dana operates in about 150 facilities across the globe. It traces its historical roots back to 1904 when it introduced the automotive universal joint. More than 50% of its sales comes from North America.

Operations

Dana divides its operations across four business segments: Light Vehicle (roughly 40% of total sales) Commercial Vehicle (about 20%) Off-Highway (more than 25%) and Power Technologies (approximately 10%).

Dana's Light Vehicle and Power Technologies segments primarily support light vehicle OEMs with products for light trucks SUVs crossover SUVs (CUVs) vans and passenger cars while the Commercial Vehicle segment sells to makers of on-highway commercial vehicles – primarily trucks and buses. The Off-Highway segment serves manufacturers of wheeled vehicles used in construction mining and agricultural applications.

Geographic Reach

Headquartered in Maumee Ohio Dana manufactures its products in about 150 facilities in nearly 35 countries in North and South America Europe and the Asia Pacific region. The company also has engineering centers located throughout the world. Dana operates other facilities in Maumee and Detroit that house administrative operations such as finance and accounting human resources procurement and supply chain management and information technology.

North America accounts for more than 50% of Dana's revenue while Europe contributes approximately 30%. The Asia Pacific region generates about 10% and South America accounts for the remaining sales.

Sales and Marketing

Ford Motor accounts for approximately 20% of Dana's total revenue and Fiat Chrysler Automobile represents about 10%. Other large customers are OEMs such as PACCAR Inc Toyota Motor Company and Volkswagen A. Dana's 10 largest customers account for about 60% of total sales.

Financial Performance

Dana's revenue has recovered over the last three years after decline in 2016. Profits have fluctuated wildly since 2015 ending on a high note achieving record sales in 2019 to $8.6 billion or an increase of 42%.

The company posted sales of $8.6 billion in 2019 a $477 higher than in 2018. Weaker global construction/mining and agricultural equipment markets and a softening in the Chinese economy offset the organic sales increase in North America driven by stronger medium/heavy truck production and the conversion of sale backlog.

Net income in 2019 was $226 million a decrease of $201 million compared to $427 million in 2018. This was primarily due to the noncontrolling interests net income.

Cash at the end of fiscal 2019 was $518 million a decrease of $20 million from the prior year. Cash from operations contributed $637 million to the coffers while investing activities used $1123 million mainly for purchases of property plant and equipment and acquisitions. Financing activities provided $479 million mainly due to repayment of long-term debt and dividends paid to common stockholders.

Strategy

Wanting to reduce its dependence on any one geographic market Dana is expanding into growth regions several growth initiatives that are targeting emerging markets like China and India. The company is also capitalizing on new technologies around hybrid and electric vehicle components.

The company has recently opened two new engineering facilities in Asia and gear manufacturing facilities in Thailand and India. The company added five facilities in China since the start of the year. The increase is the result of Dana's recent acquisition of the SME Group as well as the Drive Systems segment of Oerlikon Group including the Graziano and Fairfield brands. Its acquisition of the power-transmission and fluid power businesses of Brevini Group in 2017 added eight new countries to Dana's manufacturing footprint and allowed the company to leverage one of Brevini's facilities in China to consolidate its Power Technologies business there.

On the technology front Dana has developed a new and more efficient electronically disconnecting all-wheel drive technology that is now being used on a Ford Motor vehicle platform. Its investment in TM4 in 2018 adds electric motors power inverters and control systems used in hybrid and electric vehicles.

Dana Incorporated launched a new series of eight Spicer Torque-Hub drives expanding the company's offering of drive and motion technologies for crawler cranes and other large tracked vehicles. The company introduced the complete range of Fairfield jack-up gearboxes for offshore applications as well as the availability of eight new Brevini heavy-duty winch drives for the marine market. It also introduced a line of aftermarket Dana axles and Spicer drivetrain components for the new Jeep Gladiator (JT). The line of axle upgrades includes Ultimate Dana 60 front- and rear-axles as well as Ultimate Dana 44 AdvanTEK front axles. The company also offers Spicer nickel chromoly axle shafts extended service ball joints ultimate performance driveshafts nodular iron differential covers blue-coated corrosion-resistant u-joints and Spicer ring and pinion gear sets.

In collaboration with Lonestar Specialty Vehicles the company launched of a fully electrified terminal tractor at the North American Commercial Vehicle show. The new Spicer Electrified e-Powertrain system is designed and manufactured by Dana as a complete electric powertrain solution for use on vehicles built by Lonestar SV.

Mergers and Acquisitions

In 2019 Dana purchased Nordresa for $12 million a maker of battery-management systems and electric powertrain controls for electric commercial vehicle powertrains. Nordresa's expertise – combined with Dana's motors inverters chargers gear-boxes and thermal management products – allow Dana to provide complete electric powertrains.

Also in 2019 Dana acquired Italy-based SME Group a maker of low-voltage AC induction and synchronous reluctance motors inverters and controls for off-highway electric vehicle applications for industries such as construction and agriculture. SME's low-voltage products significantly expand Dana's electrified product portfolio.

Dana's 2019 $626 million acquisition of Oerlikon Group's Drive Systems segment is putting Dana closer to its customers in key growth areas such as China and India. Oerlikon makes high-precision gears planetary hub drives for wheeled and tracked vehicles and products and software that support electric vehicle manufacturing.

Company Background

The company was founded as C.W. Spicer in 1904 in Plainfield NJ by Clarence Spicer with his patented encased universal joints or "U-joints." In 1909 Spicer renamed his business Spicer Manufacturing Company. Attorney Charles Dana purchased a controlling interest in Spicer Manufacturing in 1914 and two years later became president and treasurer. Spicer went public in 1922 and in 1946 became Dana Corporation. It acquired Reinz Company in 1993 and formed the new Victor Reinz for its gaskets sealing products and heat shields. In 1997 Dana made the largest acquisition in the company's history by purchasing Clark-Hurth Components from Ingresoll-Rand to create its Off-Highway Components Group. In 2016 Dana Holding Corporation changed its name to Dana Incorporated.

EXECUTIVES

President Light Vehicle Driveline Technologies, Robert (Bob) Pyle, $477,000 total compensation

Evp And Group President Commercial Vehicle Driveline Technologies, Mark E. Wallace, $580,000 total compensation

President And Ceo, James K. (Jim) Kamsickas, $1,100,000 total compensation

President Off-highway Drive And Motion Technologies, Aziz S. Aghili, $515,000 total compensation

President Power Technologies, Dwayne E. Matthews

Evp And Cfo, Jonathan M. Collins, $381,944 total compensation

Svp Dana China, Antonio Valencia

Svp And Cto, Christophe Dominiak

Vice President Human Resources Light Vehicle Driveline Technologies, Dave Currie

Vice President Global Sales Commercial Vehicles, Tim Farney

Chairman, Keith E. Wandell

Auditors: PricewaterhouseCoopers LLP

LOCATIONS

HQ: Dana Inc
3939 Technology Drive, Maumee, OH 43537
Phone: 419 887-3000　　**Fax:** 419 887-5200
Web: www.dana.com

2018 Sales

	$ mil.	% of total
North America	4,106	50
Europe	2,484	31
Asia/Pacific	1,007	12
South America	546	7
Total	**8,143**	**100**

PRODUCTS/OPERATIONS

2018 Sales

	$ mil.	% of total
Light Vehicle Driveline Technologies	3,575	44
Off-Highway Drive and Motion Technologies	1,844	22
Commercial Vehicle Driveline Technologies	1,612	20
Power Technologies	1,112	14
Total	**8,143**	**100**

Selected Products

Automotive (light vehicle driveline)
  Axles (front and rear)
  Differentials
  Driveshafts
  Modular assemblies
  Side rails
  Torque couplings
Commercial vehicle (medium-heavy)
  Axles
  Driveshafts
  Steering shafts
  Suspension and tire management systems
Off-highway
  Axles
  Driveshafts
  Electronic controls
  Torque converters
  Transaxles
  Transmissions
Power technologies
  Cooling and heat transfer
  Cover modules
  Engine sealing systems
  Heat shields
  Gaskets
Structures (for light and medium/heavy)
  Cradles
  Frames
  Side rails

COMPETITORS

American Axle & Manufacturing	Magna International
Boler	Mahle International
Carraro	Meritor
DENSO	Modine Manufacturing
ElringKlinger	Valeo
Freudenberg-NOK	Wanxiang
GKN	ZF Friedrichshafen

HISTORICAL FINANCIALS

Company Type: Public

Income Statement   FYE: December 31

	REVENUE ($ mil.)	NET INCOME ($ mil.)	NET PROFIT MARGIN	EMPLOYEES
12/19	8,620	226	2.6%	36,300
12/18	8,143	427	5.2%	20,900
12/17	7,209	111	1.5%	30,100
12/16	5,826	640	11.0%	24,900
12/15	6,060	159	2.6%	23,100
Annual Growth	**9.2%**	**9.2%**	**—**	**12.0%**

2019 Year-End Financials

Debt ratio: 32.83%
Return on equity: 14.05%
Cash ($ mil.): 508
Current ratio: 1.71
Long-term debt ($ mil.): 2,336

No. of shares (mil.): 143
Dividends
Yield: 2.2%
Payout: 25.6%
Market value ($ mil.): 2,620

	STOCK PRICE ($) FY Close	P/E High/Low		PER SHARE ($) Earnings	Dividends	Book Value
12/19	18.20	13	7	1.56	0.40	13.01
12/18	13.63	12	4	2.91	0.40	9.30
12/17	32.01	46	24	0.71	0.24	6.99
12/16	18.98	5	2	4.36	0.24	8.04
12/15	13.80	23	13	0.99	0.23	4.85
Annual Growth	**7.2%**	**—**	**—**	**12.0%**	**14.8%**	**28.0%**

Danaher Corp

Danaher is a diversified industrial and medical conglomerate whose products test analyze and diagnose. Its subsidiaries design manufacture and market products and offer services geared to worldwide professional medical and dental industrial and commercial markets. Danaher operates through three segments: Life Sciences Diagnostics (research and clinical tools) Environmental & Applied Solutions (turbine pumps and air/water analysis and treatment equipment). It has facilities in more than 60 countries and generates more than 35% of sales from customers in the US.

Operations

Built largely through acquisitions Danaher's three business segments reflect a well-balanced portfolio. Top segments Life Sciences and Diagnostics account from 35-40% revenue each. The Life Sciences segment's products include mass spectrometry; cellular analysis and lab automation; filtration; and microscopy. The Diagnostics segment offers clinical lab critical care and anatomical pathology.

Key Danaher subsidiaries include Beckman Coulter X-Rite Esko BV Linx Printing Technologies and Trojan Technologies.

Geographic Reach

Danaher has more than 210 manufacturing and distribution facilities worldwide. More than 90 are in the US spread over more than 20 states; another 120 locations are in 30 countries throughout Asia Europe North America South America and Australia. The company generates about 40% of its revenue from North America primarily the US (more than 35% of sales). Western Europe represents almost a quarter of sales while the countries Danaher terms its "high-growth markets" including countries in Eastern Europe the Middle East Africa Latin America and the Asia/Pacific region together bring in 30% of sales.

Financial Performance

Danaher Corp.'s sales have risen strongly over the past five years as it has expanded its portfolio through acquisitions offset by a few spinoffs.

In 2019 the company's revenue grew 5% to $17.9 billion thanks to contributions from acquired businesses in the Life Sciences and Environmental & Applied Solutions segments in addition to strong organic growth in both high-growth and development markets and currency tailwinds.

Net income growth was also positive at around 13% with Danaher posting a net profit of $3 billion. Higher sales were partially offset by higher income taxes.

Danaher's cash on hand grew $19.9 billion during 2019 ending the year at $19.9 billion. The company's operations generated $4.0 billion partially offset by the $1.2 billion used in investing activities and the $16.4 billion was provided by their financing activities. Danaher's main cash uses in 2019 were acquisitions ($331 million) and dividends ($526.7 million).

Strategy

Danaher strives to create shareholder value primarily through three strategic priorities: enhancing its portfolio in attractive science and technology markets through strategic capital allocation; strengthening its competitive advantage through consistent application of the DANAHER BUSINESS SYSTEM ("DBS") tools; and consistently attracting and retaining exceptional talent.

Danaher measures its progress against these strategic priorities over the long-term based primarily on financial metrics relating to revenue growth profitability cash flow and capital returns.

Mergers and Acquisitions

In 2020 Danaher has acquired General Electric's BioPharma unit for about $21.4 billion. The biopharma business makes instruments and software that support the research and development of pharmaceuticals and is part of GE's healthcare segment. Danaher plans to slot the acquisition and its $3 billion annual sales as a stand-alone operating company within its $6.5 billion Life Sciences segment.

In 2019 the company acquired five businesses for total consideration of $331 million in cash. The businesses acquired complement existing units of each of the Company's three segment. The aggregate annual sales of these five businesses at the time of their respective acquisitions in each case based on the company's revenues for its last completed fiscal year prior to acquisition were $72 million.

Company Background

Danaher (from the Celtic word dana meaning "swift flowing") is named for a fishing stream off the Flathead River in Montana. The term is also an appropriate description of the spotlight-averse Rales brothers. The two have proven to be fishers not only of trout but also of companies buying underperforming companies with strong market shares and recognizable brand names.

Once dubbed "raiders in short pants" by Forbes Steven and Mitchell Rales began making acquisitions in their 20s. In 1981 they bought their father's 50% stake in Master Shield a maker of vinyl building products. The brothers bought tire manufacturer Mohawk Rubber the following year. In 1983 they acquired control of publicly traded DMG a distressed Florida real-estate firm; the next year they sold DMG's real estate holdings and folded Mohawk and Master Shield into the company which they renamed Danaher.

HISTORY

Danaher (from the Celtic word dana meaning "swift flowing") is named for a fishing stream off the Flathead River in Montana. The term is also an appropriate description of the spotlight-averse Rales brothers. The two have proven to be fishers not only of trout but also of companies buying underperforming companies with strong market shares and recognizable brand names.

Once dubbed "raiders in short pants" by Forbes Steven and Mitchell Rales began making acquisitions in their 20s. In 1981 they bought their father's 50% stake in Master Shield a maker of vinyl building products. The brothers bought tire manufacturer Mohawk Rubber the following year. In 1983 they acquired control of publicly traded DMG a distressed Florida real-estate firm; the next year they sold DMG's real estate holdings and folded Mohawk and Master Shield into the company which they renamed Danaher.

EXECUTIVES

Evp And Cfo, Daniel L. Comas, age 56, $862,357 total compensation

President And Ceo, Thomas P. Joyce, age 59, $1,100,000 total compensation

Vp And Group Executive Danaher Motion, William K. (Dan) Daniel, age 55, $730,144 total compensation

Svp Human Resources, Angela S. Lalor, age 54, $603,986 total compensation

Evp Life Sciences, Rainer M. Blair, age 55

Vp Global Talent Acquisition, Mark Hamberlin

Vice President Of Business Development For Product Iden, Pasha Fedorenko

Vice President, Craig Overhage

Vice President Human Resources, Dennis Mabes

Global Vice President Human Resources Water Qua, Larry Byrnes

Vice President And Treasurer, Frank Mcfaden
Vice President Regulatory Affairs And Quality
  Assurance, Frances Zee
Corporate Vice President And Chief Financial
  Officer Asia, Samuel Liao
Vice President Compensation, Joe Cavallaro
Vice President, James Lico
Vice President Internal Audit, Christopher Sandberg
Vp Operations, Mike Rok
Vice President And Bu Manager, Raj Karanam
Vice President And Chief Counsel Mergers And
  Acquisitions, Attila Bodi
National Sales Manager, Jim White
Vice President Business Development And
  Strategy Dental, Mischa Reis
Vice President Sales (tektronix Division), Eben
  Jenkins
Vice President Human Resources High Growth
  Markets, Richard D Wachter
Vice President Strategic Development, Bill King
Vice President, Daniel Rakas
Executive Vice President, Dan Comas
Vice President Dbso, Michael Weatherred
V.p. Finance, Christopher Bouda
Vice President Organizational Development,
  Suzanne Wolfe
Senior Vp, Jim Ditkoff
Regional Vice President, Howard Hagan
Vice President Of Americas, Ernie Lauber
Chairman, Steven M. Rales, age 68
Board Member, Donald Ehrlich
Board Member, Alan Spoon
Board Member, Teri List-stoll
Board Member, Elias A Zerhouni
Auditors: Ernst & Young LLP

LOCATIONS

HQ: Danaher Corp
2200 Pennsylvania Avenue, N.W., Suite 800W,
Washington, DC 20037-1701
Phone: 202 828-0850   Fax: 202 828-0860
Web: www.danaher.com

2018 Sales

	$ mil.	% of total
United States	7,374	37
China	2,357	12
Germany	1,247	6
Japan	918	5
All other	7,995	40
Total	**19,893**	**100**

2018 sales

	%
North America	39
Nigh-growth markets	31
Western Europe	24
Other developed markets	6
Total	**100**

PRODUCTS/OPERATIONS

2018 Sales

	$ mil.	% of total
Diagnostics	6,257	31
Life Sciences	6,471	33
Environmental & Applied Solutions	4,319	22
Dental	2,844	14
Total	**18,329**	**100**

2018 Sales

	$ mil.	% of total
Research and medical products	12,686	64
Dental products	2,844	14
Analytical and physical instrumentation	2,437	12
Product identification	1,925	10
Total	**19,839**	**100**

COMPETITORS

ABB	National Instruments
Advantest	Parker-Hannifin
Bosch Rexroth Corp.	PerkinElmer
Datamax-O'Neil	Rockwell Automation
Emerson Electric	SPX
GE	Schneider Electric
Greenlee Textron	Siemens Water
Hitachi	Technologies
Johnson & Johnson	Snap-on
Medical	Stanley Black and
Keysight	Decker
Labfacility	Thermo Fisher
Makita	Scientific
Mettler-Toledo	Wayne

HISTORICAL FINANCIALS

Company Type: Public

Income Statement

FYE: December 31

	REVENUE ($ mil.)	NET INCOME ($ mil.)	NET PROFIT MARGIN	EMPLOYEES
12/19	17,911	3,008	16.8%	60,000
12/18	19,893	2,650	13.3%	71,000
12/17	18,329	2,492	13.6%	67,000
12/16	16,882	2,553	15.1%	62,000
12/15	20,563	3,357	16.3%	81,000
Annual Growth	(3.4%)	(2.7%)	—	(7.2%)

2019 Year-End Financials

Debt ratio: 35.00%
Return on equity: 10.29%
Cash ($ mil.): 19,912
Current ratio: 5.19
Long-term debt ($ mil.): 21,516

No. of shares (mil.): 695
Dividends
Yield: 0.4%
Payout: 20.1%
Market value ($ mil.): 106,745

	STOCK PRICE ($) FY Close	P/E High/Low	PER SHARE ($) Earnings	Dividends	Book Value
12/19	153.48	37 24	4.05	0.68	43.52
12/18	103.12	29 24	3.74	0.64	40.22
12/17	92.82	26 22	3.53	0.56	37.84
12/16	77.84	28 21	3.65	0.57	33.23
12/15	92.88	20 17	4.74	0.54	34.49
Annual Growth	13.4%	— —	(3.9%)	5.9%	6.0%

Darden Restaurants, Inc.

You could call this company Olive Darden. After all Darden Restaurants' spot as the No. 1 casual-dining company has been fueled by its Olive Garden chain of more than 900 Italian-themed restaurants. But Darden is more than garden operating approximately 1865 restaurants in the US and Canada (fully-owned and franchises). Other concepts include LongHorn Steakhouse The Capital Grille (upscale steakhouse) Bahama Breeze (Caribbean food and drinks) Eddie V's (seafood) Yard House (American food) Seasons 52 (casual grill and wine bar) and Cheddar's (meals from "scratch"). . Overall Darden restaurants serve over 355 million diners in fiscal 2020.

Operations

Darden organizes its operations into four business segments that are based on a combination of the size and economic characteristics of each of its restaurant brands. These include Olive Garden LongHorn Steakhouse Fine Dining and Other Business.

Olive Garden's nearly 870 owned restaurants dish up more than 50% the company's revenue while LongHorn Steakhouse includes over 520 owned restaurants and provides over 20% of revenue. Fine Dining runs over 60 Capital Grilles and nearly 25 Eddie V's restaurants that serve higher-priced menus such as steak and seafood entrees in the $30-$100 range. The segment provides more than 5% of revenue.

Another some 20% of revenue comes from the company's Other segment composed of the Yard House (about 80 locations) Bahama Breeze (around 40) Cheddar's (some 165) and Seasons 52 (about 45) restaurants. It also includes results from franchise operations which number more than 60 across the US Latin America and the Middle East.

Geographic Reach

Orlando Florida-based Darden owns and operates over 1800 restaurants in the US and Canada and franchises some 30 restaurants in the US including Puerto Rico and Guam. About 30 franchises are located in Latin America and less than 5 are in the Middle East.

Sales and Marketing

Olive Garden uses national network TV advertising supplemented with cable local TV and digital advertising. LongHorn Steakhouse uses local TV and digital advertising to build engagement and loyalty by market. The company's other brands rely on local and digital marketing. Darden also uses on outdoor billboard direct mail and email advertising as well as radio newspapers digital coupons search engine marketing and social media. It engages in research to monitor guest satisfaction and evolving food service trends and expectations.

The company continues to make improvements to its online and mobile ordering system for Olive Garden and LongHorn Steakhouse and uses customer relationship management programs data analytics and data-driven marketing approaches to target existing and potential diners across its portfolio of brands.Darden's marketing expenses were $238 million $255 million and $252 million in 2020 2019 and 2018 respectively.

Financial Performance

Sales in 2020 fell about 8% to $7.8 billion from $8.5 billion in 2019 primarily due to the fall on their Olive Garden and LongHorn Steakhouse revenue because of the pandemic.

Net loss from continuing operations for fiscal 2020 was $49.2 million compared with net earnings from continuing operations for fiscal 2019 of $718.6 million.

Darden finished 2020 with $763.3 million in cash compared to $457.3 million in 2019. Cash from operations and financing activities were $717.4 million and $138.7 million respectively. Investing activities used $462.6 million.

Strategy

The company believes that capable operators of strong multi-unit brands have the opportunity to increase their share of the restaurant industry's full-service segment. Generally the restaurant industry is considered to be comprised of three segments: quick service fast casual and full-service. All of their restaurants fall within the full-service segment which is highly fragmented and includes many independent operators and small chains. Darden believes that they have strong brands and that the breadth and depth of their experience and expertise sets them apart in the full-service restaurant industry. This collective capability is the product of investments over many years in areas that are critical to success in their business including restaurant operations excellence brand management excellence supply chain talent management and information technology among other things.

Although the fourth quarter of fiscal 2020 required the company to focus on adapting their business to account for the impacts of the COVID-19 pandemic their operating philosophy remains focused on strengthening the core operational fundamentals of the business by providing an outstanding guest experience rooted in culinary innovation attentive service engaging atmosphere and integrated marketing. Darden enables each brand to reach its full potential by leveraging its scale insights and experience in a way that protects uniqueness and competitive advantages. Additionally their brands can capitalize on data insights to deliver customized one-to-one customer relationship marketing. The company holds themselves accountable for operating their restaurants with a sense of urgency to achieve their commitments to all of their stakeholders.

Company Background

Bill Darden opened his first restaurant — a luncheonette in Waycross GA called The Green Frog promising "Service with a Hop" — in 1938 when he was just 19-years-old.

EXECUTIVES

Ceo And Director, Eugene I. (Gene) Lee, age 59, $953,750 total compensation
Svp And Chief Human Resources Officer, Danielle Kirgan, $378,462 total compensation
Evp And President Olive Garden, David C. (Dave) George, age 64, $576,539 total compensation
Svp And Cfo, Ricardo (Rick) Cardenas, age 52, $474,539 total compensation
President Yard House, Michael (Mike) Kneidinger
Vp Operations The Capital Grille, Brian Foye
President Longhorn Steakhouse, Todd Burrowes, $442,211 total compensation
Svp And Cio, Chris Chang
President The Capital Grille And Eddie V's, John Martin
Senior Vice President Division, Sam Pereira
Svp Corporate Controller, John Madonna
Vice President Of Finance, Mark Cooper
Senior Vice President Human Resource Olive Garden, Paula Manchester
Senior Vp, Mone Isaia
Vice President, Kathy Janiga
Senior Vice President Division, Paula Britton
Vice President Quality Assurance, Ana Hooper
Svp And Treasurer, Bill White
Vice President Associate General Counsel (erisa And Tax), Tonya Moore
Senior Vice President Corp Marketing, Angela Simmons
Senior Vice President Strategy And Insights, Ali Charri
Vice President Communications, Justin Sikora
Senior Vice President Operations, Thomas Hall
Senior Vice President Franchising And President International Operations, Michael Beacham
Svp And Chief Development Officer, Rich Renninger
Svp And Cio, Christopher Chang
Vice President Culinary Operations Olive Garden, Timothy Blaise
Executive Vice President Of Ma, Jose Duenas
Vice President, Carlito Jocson
Vice President Enterprise Beverage Strategy And Innovation, Helen Mackey
Executive Vice President Of Marketing, Debby Shimick
Vice President Of Division, Anthony Morrow
Svp Development, Joe Mutti
Vice President Of Division, Summara Jones
Vice President Design, Ryan Hatfield
Chairman, Charles M. (Chuck) Sonsteby
Secretary, Stephanie Talamas

Board Member, Margaret Atkins
Treasurer, Pommels Craig
Auditors: KPMG LLP

LOCATIONS

HQ: Darden Restaurants, Inc.
  1000 Darden Center Drive, Orlando, FL 32837
Phone: 407 245-4000
Web: www.darden.com

PRODUCTS/OPERATIONS

Restaurant Brands

Bahama Breeze
Eddie V's
LongHorn Steakhouse
Olive Garden
The Capital Grille
Yard House
Seasons 52
Cheddar's Scratch Kitchen

2018 Sales

	$ mil.	% of total
Olive Garden	4,082	51
LongHorn Steakhouse	1,703	21
Fine Dining	575	7
Other Business	1,720	21
Total	**8,080**	**100**

COMPETITORS

Bob Evans	DineEquity
Brinker	Hooters
Carlson Restaurants	OSI Restaurant
Cheesecake Factory	Partners
Cracker Barrel	Perkins & Marie
Denny's	Callender's

HISTORICAL FINANCIALS

Company Type: Public

Income Statement   FYE: May 31

	REVENUE ($ mil.)	NET INCOME ($ mil.)	NET PROFIT MARGIN	EMPLOYEES
05/20	7,806	(52)	—	177,895
05/19	8,510	713	8.4%	184,514
05/18	8,080	596	7.4%	180,656
05/17	7,170	479	6.7%	178,729
05/16	6,933	375	5.4%	150,000
Annual Growth	3.0%	—		4.4%

2020 Year-End Financials

Debt ratio: 12.05%	No. of shares (mil.): 129
Return on equity: (-2.18%)	Dividends
Cash ($ mil.): 763	Yield: 0.0%
Current ratio: 0.61	Payout: —
Long-term debt ($ mil.): 928	Market value ($ mil.): 9,984

	STOCK PRICE ($) FY Close	P/E High/Low		PER SHARE ($) Earnings	Dividends	Book Value
05/20	76.86	—	—	(0.43)	2.64	17.95
05/19	120.13	22	15	5.69	3.00	19.44
05/18	87.88	21	16	4.73	2.52	17.77
05/17	87.95	23	16	3.80	2.24	16.76
05/16	67.48	25	18	2.90	2.10	15.47
Annual Growth	3.3%	—	—	—	5.9%	3.8%

DaVita Inc

DaVita performs dialysis treatments for patients suffering from end-stage renal disease (ESRD or chronic kidney failure). The firm is one of the US' largest providers of dialysis — its administrative services reach more than 206900 patients through about 2755 outpatient centers across the US. The company also offers home-based dialysis services as well as inpatient dialysis in some 900 hospitals. It operates one separately licensed and highly automated clinical laboratory that specialize in routine testing of dialysis patients and serve the company's network of clinics.

Operations

DaVita's separate operating segments include its U.S. dialysis and related lab services business each of its ancillary services and strategic initiatives its kidney care operations in each foreign sovereign jurisdiction its other health operations in each foreign sovereign jurisdiction and its equity method investment in the Asia Pacific joint venture.

The US dialysis and related lab services business qualifies as a separately reportable segment and all other ancillary services and strategic initiatives operating segments including the international operating segments have been combined and disclosed in the other segments category. The US dialysis segment generates more than 90% of company's total sales while the remaining sales is from Other - Ancillary services.

The company sold its DaVita Medical Group (DMG) unit (formerly known as HealthCare Partners or HCP) to UnitedHealth Group's Optum unit for $4.3 billion in 2019; DMG's Nevada operations were sold to Intermountain Healthcare as part of the transaction. DMG provides integrated health care services and manages medical care offices in California Colorado Florida Nevada New Mexico and Washington.

Of its primary payer medicare and medicare advantage accounts for nearly 55% of sales. Around 95% of sales were generated from dialysis patient services.

Geographic Reach

The company provided dialysis and administrative services and related laboratory services throughout the US via a network of about 2755 outpatient dialysis centers in more than 45 US states and the District of Columbia serving a total of approximately 206900 patients and provided acute inpatient dialysis services in approximately 900 hospitals. The company divested its DaVita Medical Group (DMG) unit in 2019 which operated and managed medical groups and physician practice networks in California Colorado Florida Nevada New Mexico and Washington.

DaVita operated or provided administrative services to about 260 outpatient dialysis centers which includes consolidated and nonconsolidated centers located in ten countries outside of the US serving approximately 28700 patients. Its international dialysis operations have continued to grow steadily and expand as a result of acquiring and developing outpatient dialysis centers in various strategic markets. International outpatient dialysis centers are located in Germany Poland Malaysia Brazil Saudi Arabia Colombia Portugal Taiwan China and Singapore.

The company's corporate headquarters are located in Denver Colorado. The company has also six business offices located in California Pennsylvania Tennessee and Washington for its US dialysis business. Its laboratory is based in Florida where it operate its lab services. DaVita also have other administrative offices in the US and worldwide.

Sales and Marketing

Almost 90% of DaVita's dialysis patients are covered under some form of government-based program with about 75% of its dialysis patients covered under Medicare and Medicare-assigned plans.

Financial Performance

DaVita's revenue has risen steadily since 2015. Increased sales volume and payment rates at its existing and acquired dialysis centers have driven an overall expansion of more than 14%. Net income has shifted erratically in the last five years dropping 76% in 2018 but bouncing back 409% the following year.

The company's revenue slightly fell by $16.4 million to $11.4 billion in 2019 because revenues from Medicare Medicaid and Commercial collected significantly decreased.

DaVita's net income jumped 409% to $811 million that year income from continuing and discontinued operations both increased.

The company has $1.2 billion in cash at the end of 2019 $793.3 million more from prior year. Operating and investing activities generated $2.1 billion and $3 billion respectively. The company used $4.7 billion on financing activities mainly for payments of long-term debt.

Strategy

DaVita have made and continue to make investments in building its integrated care capabilities including the operation of certain strategic business initiatives that are intended to integrate care amongst healthcare participants across the renal care continuum from chronic kidney disease (CKD) to ESRD to kidney transplant. Through improved technology and data sharing as well as an increasing focus on value based contracting and care these initiatives seek to bring together physicians nurses dieticians pharmacists hospitals dialysis clinics transplant centers and payors with a view towards improving clinical outcomes for our patients and reducing the overall cost of comprehensive kidney care.

The other strategic business initiatives of DaVita are clinical research programs and vascular access service. For clinical research programs DaVita Clinical Research uses its extensive applied database and real-world healthcare experience to assist in the design recruitment and completion of retrospective and prospective pragmatic and clinical trials. Revenues are based upon an established fee per study as determined by contract with drug companies and other sponsors and are recognized as earned according to the contract terms. Vascular access services Management fees generated from providing management and administrative services are recognized as earned typically based on a percentage of revenues or cash collections generated by the clinics. Revenues associated with the vascular access clinics that are majority-owned are recognized in the period when the services are provided.

From time to time DaVita decide to dispose of certain assets or businesses. DaVita sold its DaVita Medical Group (DMG) segment to UnitedHealth in 2019 for $4.3 billion. The sale of DMG results in a less diversified portfolio of businesses and the company have a greater dependency on the performance of its kidney care business for its financial results.

Mergers and Acquisitions

In 2017 DaVita bought Colorado-based Renal Ventures for $415 million. Renal Ventures operates 36 dialysis clinics in six states; it also has units that operate infusion and vascular centers. That year it also purchased Pacific Northwest independent physician association Northwest Physicians Network (NPN). That buy gave DaVita 1000 primary and specialty care physicians.

HISTORY

Hospital chain National Medical Enterprises (NME now Tenet) formed Medical Ambulatory Care in 1979 to run its in-hospital dialysis centers. The unit bought other centers in NME's markets. In 1994 the subsidiary's management backed by a Donaldson Lufkin & Jenrette — now Credit Suisse First Boston (USA) — investment fund bought the dialysis business and renamed it Total Renal Care (TRC).

To become a leader in its consolidating field TRC began buying other centers and soon added clinical laboratory and dialysis-related pharmacy services and home dialysis programs. It went public in 1995.

The next year the firm added 66 facilities 32 from its acquisition of Caremark International's dialysis business. In 1997 TRC expanded abroad buying UK-based Open Access Sonography (vein care) and partnering with UK-based Priory Hospitals Group.

In 1998 TRC bought Renal Treatment Centers nearly doubling its size. But the acquisition costs caused a loss that year and sparked shareholder lawsuits (settled in 2000) over alleged misleading statements. The firm also became embroiled in a reimbursement dispute with Florida's Medicare program. Problems continued into 1999 as the company struggled to meld operations. The company took a charge to cover a billing shortfall and chairman and CEO Victor Chaltiel and COO/CFO John King resigned. New management began improving billing procedures and took other cost-cutting measures.

The company changed its name in 2000 to DaVita an Italian phrase loosely translated as "he/she gives life." It also sold its international operations to competitor Fresenius.

In 2005 the company acquired Gambro's US dialysis operations for about $3 billion adding some 565 dialysis clinics to its operations. To meet FTC requirements for the deal DaVita sold about 70 clinics to RenalAmerica a company founded by former Gambro Healthcare executive Michael Klein.

In 2007 DaVita expanded its health care offerings by acquiring a majority stake in HomeChoice Partners a provider of home infusion services. The company added about 80 new centers through acquisitions in 2009.

DaVita significantly widened its domestic network of dialysis centers when it acquired regional dialysis chain DSI Renal for $690 million in 2011. To secure approval for the deal from the FTC DaVita agreed to divest 30 clinics but overall the acquisition added more than 100 dialysis centers to its holdings.

Elsewhere around the world DaVita entered Germany with the 2011 purchase of DV Care. It also expanded into the Middle East through the acquisition of a majority stake in Lehbi Care a leading Riyadh-based kidney care company with three clinics.

The company has also been looking to branch out into new areas of health care including medical practice management a mission it accomplished through the 2012 purchase of private medical group management firm HealthCare Partners through a merger transaction worth some $4.4 billion.

Following the deal the company changed its legal name from DaVita to DaVita HealthCare Partners to reflect its broadened operations; the dialysis division continues to operate under the DaVita name while HealthCare Partners operates as an independent subsidiary of DaVita HealthCare Partners. The two companies both count California and Florida as key markets and DaVita HealthCare Partners has used HealthCare Partners' integrated care model to help it offer a wider range of health care services.

Internationally the company entered China in 2012 through a joint venture to provide dialysis services with Chinese biotech company 3SBio.

EXECUTIVES

Senior Vice President Agricultural Marketing North America Australia, Douglas Devries
Executive Chair Davita Medical Group, Charles G. (Chuck) Berg, age 63
Chairman And Ceo, Kent J. Thiry, age 64, $1,273,077 total compensation
Cfo, Joel Ackerman, age 55
Group Vp Purchasing And Public Affairs, LeAnne M. Zumwalt, age 61, $400,000 total compensation
Chief Compliance Officer, Jeanine M. Jiganti, age 61
Chief Accounting Officer, James K. (Jim) Hilger, age 58, $375,000 total compensation
Ceo Davita Kidney Care, Javier J. Rodriguez, age 49, $865,385 total compensation
Chief Medical Officer Davita Kidney Care, Allen R. Nissenson, age 73
President Colorado Springs Health Partners, Oraida Roman
Ceo Davita International, Robert Lang
Director Of Pharmacy Operations, Randy Ferreter
Medical Director, John Burns
Vice President, Rebecca Griggs
Vice President Revenue Management, David Corlett
Senior Vice President Strategy, James Rechtin
Vice President Integration, Douglas Allen
Division Vice President, Brandon King
Director Of Clinical Services, Cicely Gibson
Vice President Corporate Development, Scott Lloyd
Vice President Finance, Chitra Goswami
Vice President Revenue Operations, Chad Hull
Vice President, Stuart Bachelder
Director Of Clinical Services, Karla Close
Vice President, Maxwell Larson
Vice President Federal Government Affairs, Joelle Thornhill
Vice President Application Development, James Richardson
Division Vice President Dvp, Rick Duckworth
Group Medical Director, Mihran Naljayan
Division Vice President, Christopher Marchese
Vice President Associate General Counsel, Samantha Caldwell
Board Member, Phyllis Yale
Board Member, Paul Diaz
Auditors: KPMG LLP

LOCATIONS

HQ: DaVita Inc
2000 16th Street, Denver, CO 80202
Phone: 720 631-2100
Web: www.davita.com

PRODUCTS/OPERATIONS

2018 Revenues by Payer

	% of total
Government-based programs	
Medicare and Medicare-assigned plans	59
Medicaid and Managed Medicaid	6
Other government-based programs	4
Commercial	31
Total	**100**

2018 Dialysis Revenues

	% of total
Outpatient hemodialysis centers	79
Peritoneal dialysis and home-based hemodialysis	16
Hospital inpatient hemodialysis	5
Total	**100**

2016 Sales

	$ mil.	% of total
US dialysis and related lab services	10,335	90
Other - Ancillary services and strategic initiatives	1,196	10
Adjustments	(127.2)	-
Total	**11,404**	**100**

Selected Operations

Astro Hobby West Mt. Renal Care Limited Partnership
Austin Dialysis Centers L.P.
Beverly Hills Dialysis Partnership
Brighton Dialysis Center LLC
Capital Dialysis Partnership
Carroll County Dialysis Facility L.P.
Central Carolina Dialysis Centers LLC
Chicago Heights Dialysis LLC
Continental Dialysis Center Inc.
Dallas-Fort Worth Nephrology L.P.
Dialysis of Des Moines LLC
Dialysis Specialists of Dallas Inc.
Downriver Centers Inc.
Downtown Houston Dialysis Center L.P.
Durango Dialysis Center LLC
DVA Healthcare of Maryland Inc.
East End Dialysis Center Inc.
Elberton Dialysis Facility Inc.
Empire State DC Inc.
Greenwood Dialysis LLC
Hawaiian Gardens Dialysis LLC
HealthCare Partners LLC
HuntingtonPark Dialysis LLC
Indian River Dialysis Center LLC
Jedburg Dialysis LLC
Kidney Centers of Michigan L.L.C.
Lincoln Park Dialysis Services Inc.
Mason-Dixon Dialysis Facilities Inc.
Middlesex Dialysis Center LLC
Natomas Dialysis
Nephrolife Care (India) Pte. Ltd.
North Colorado Springs Dialysis LLC
Open Access Lifeline LLC
Palomar Dialysis LLC
Physicians Choice Dialysis of Alabama LLC
Physicians Dialysis of Houstin LLP
Renal Life Link Inc.
Renal Treatment Centers Inc.
RMS Lifeline Inc.
Rocky Mountain Dialysis Services LLC
Shining Star Dialysis Inc.
Soledad Dialysis Center LLC
Summit Dialysis Center L.P.
Tortugas Dialysis LLC
Total Renal Care Inc.
Total Renal Laboratories Inc.
Total Renal Research Inc.
TRC West Inc.
Tulsa Dialysis Center LLC
Upper Valley Dialysis L.P.

COMPETITORS

Apria Healthcare	Lincare Holdings
Critical Care Systems	Molina Healthcare
International	Permanente Medical
Dialysis Clinic Inc	Groups
FMCNA	Quest Diagnostics
Gentiva	U.S. Renal Care
LabCorp	UnitedHealth Group

HISTORICAL FINANCIALS

Company Type: Public

Income Statement

FYE: December 31

	REVENUE ($ mil.)	NET INCOME ($ mil.)	NET PROFIT MARGIN	EMPLOYEES
12/19	11,388	810	7.1%	65,000
12/18	11,404	159	1.4%	77,700
12/17	10,876	663	6.1%	74,500
12/16	14,745	879	6.0%	70,300
12/15	13,781	269	2.0%	60,400
Annual Growth	**(4.7%)**	**31.7%**	**—**	**1.9%**

2019 Year-End Financials

Debt ratio: 46.84%
Return on equity: 27.79%
Cash ($ mil.): 1,102
Current ratio: 1.56
Long-term debt ($ mil.): 7,977

No. of shares (mil.): 125
Dividends
  Yield: —
  Payout: —
Market value ($ mil.): 9,442

	STOCK PRICE ($) FY Close	P/E High/Low		PER SHARE ($) Earnings	Dividends	Book Value
12/19	75.03	14	8	5.27	0.00	16.95
12/18	51.46	86	52	0.92	0.00	22.26
12/17	72.25	21	15	3.47	0.00	25.70
12/16	64.20	18	13	4.29	0.00	23.89
12/15	69.71	66	53	1.25	0.00	23.22
Annual Growth	**1.9%**			**43.3%**	**—**	**(7.6%)**

DCP Midstream LP

DCP Midstream is one of the natural gas gatherers in North America and also a producer and a marketer of natural gas liquids (NGLs). It also engages in natural gas compressing treating processing transporting and selling. DCP Midstream also transports and sells NGLs and distributes propane wholesale. The company operates natural gas gathering and transmission systems (62000 miles of pipe) in more than 15 states (including Alabama Arkansas Colorado Kansas Louisiana Maine Massachusetts Michigan New Mexico New York Oklahoma Pennsylvania Texas Vermont Virginia and Wyoming) more than 10 fractioning facilities four NGL pipelines and seven propane natural gas liquids terminals. DCP Midstream Partners LP merged with DCP Midstream LLC in 2017 to become DCP Midstream LP.

Operations

DCP Midstream has two reportable segments: Logistics and Marketing (L&M) and Gathering and Processing (G&P).

L&M transports trades markets and stores natural gas and NGLs and brings in more than 60% of total sales.G&P comprises the gathering compressing treating and procession of natural gas; the production and fractionation of NGLs; and recovering condensate. It generated about 40% of sales.

Overall the sales of natural gas alone accounts for some 30% of sale. The combined sales of natural gas NGLs and condensate accounts for about 80%.

Geographic Reach

Denver Colorado based - DCP Midstream operates assets in more than 15 states in the continental US: Alabama Arkansas Colorado Kansas Louisiana Maine Massachusetts Michigan New Mexico New York Oklahoma Pennsylvania Texas Vermont Virginia and Wyoming.

The company's logistics and marketing activities take place in Colorado Kansas Louisiana Michigan Oklahoma New Mexico and Texas while its gathering and processing operations are conducted through around 50 facilities spread across the North Permian Midcontinent and South of the US.

An NGL storage facility which holds ethane propane and butane is located in Marysville Michigan and has access to Marcellus Utica and Canadian NGLs

The natural gas supply for its gathering pipelines and processing plants is derived primarily from natural gas wells located in Colorado Louisiana Michigan Oklahoma Texas Wyoming and New Mexico.

Sales and Marketing

DCP Midstream's customers include multi-national petrochemical and refining companies to small regional retail propane distributors. Substantially all of the company's NGL sales are made at market-based prices.

The company typically sells propane to propane distributors under annual sales agreements.

DCP Midstream markets its NGLs residue gas and condensate and provide logistics and marketing services to third-party NGL producers and sales customers in significant NGL production and market centers in the United States.

Financial Performance

The company's revenue has been fluctuating in the last five years with an overall growth of 3% between 2015 and 2019. Net income resurfaced in 2016 and rose until 2018 then dropped in 2019.

Total operating revenues decreased $2.2 billion in 2019 compared to 2018 primarily as a result of the $2.2 billion decrease from its Logistics and Marketing segment due to lower commodity prices and a $1.5 billion decrease from its Gathering and Processing segment also due to lower commodity prices and decreased volumes in the Midcontinent region.

Net income dropped 94% from $298 million in 2018 to $17 million in 2019. The lower costs and expenses in 2019 were offset by lower operating revenues.

The company's cash at the end of 2019 remained flat at $1 million from the previous year. Operating activities generated $859 million while investing activities used $760 million (mainly for capital expenditures and investments in unconsolidated affiliates). Financing activities used another $99 million mainly for payments of debt.

Strategy

DCP Midstream's primary business objectives are to achieve sustained company profitability a strong balance sheet and profitable growth thereby sustaining and ultimately growing its cash distribution per unit. The company intends to accomplish these objectives by prudently executing the following business strategies:

Operational Performance. The company believes its operating efficiency and reliability enhance its ability to attract new natural gas supplies by enabling it to offer more competitive terms services and service flexibility to producers.

Organic Growth. DCP Midstream intends to use its strategic asset base in the United States and its position as one of the largest processors of natural gas and as one of the largest producers and marketers of NGLs in the United States as a platform for future growth. The company plans to grow its business by constructing new NGL and natural gas pipeline infrastructure expanding existing infrastructure and constructing new gathering lines and processing facilities.

Strategic Partnerships and Acquisitions. The company intends to pursue economically attractive and strategic partnership and acquisition opportunities within the midstream energy industry both in new and existing lines of business and areas of operation.

Company Background

In 2013 DCP Midstream bought a 47% stake in an Eagle Ford joint venture from the owner of its general partner for $626 million bringing its ownership interest in the joint venture to 80%.

In 2012 DCP Midstream acquired the Texas-based Crossroads processing plant and gathering system from Penn Virginia Resource Partners for $63 million. The bolt-on acquisition allows the company to expand its market position in East Texas and provide services to drillers in the Haynesville shale and Cotton Valley regions.

In 2011 DCP Midstream acquired the Seaway Products Pipeline Co. from ConocoPhillips. The pipeline now called Southern Hills Pipeline and being converted to NGL service is expected to be operational by mid-2013. It will provide NGL access from the Midcontinent to the Texas Gulf Coast.

Expanding in Michigan in 2009 the company acquired gas gathering and treating assets for $45.1 million. In 2010 it acquired a 350-mile interstate natural gas liquids pipeline system in Colorado's Denver-Julesburg Basin from Buckeye Partners for $22 million.

In 2010 DCP Midstream moved to extend its Northeast wholesale propane business into the MidAtlantic region acquiring UGI's Atlantic Energy for $49 million. That year it also purchased of NGL storage company Marysville Hydrocarbon Holdings (in Michigan) for about $95 million.

In terms of the company's origins the D in DCP Midstream Partners (formerly Duke Energy Field Services) is for Duke Energy; the CP ConocoPhillips. These two energy majors formed DCP Midstream Partners in 2005. Following the spinoff of Spectra Energy from Duke Energy in 2007 Spectra Energy assumed Duke Energy's 50% holding in DCP.

EXECUTIVES

Group Vp And Chief Environmental Health And Safety Officer, Jerry Barnhill, age 58
Group Vp And Chief Transformation Officer, Bill Johnson
President Commercial, Don Baldridge, age 50, $182,077 total compensation
Chairman President And Ceo, Wouter T. van Kempen, age 50
Group Vp And Cfo, Sean P. OÁ'Brien, age 50
President Asset Operations, Brian Frederick
Group Vp And Cfo, Sean O'brien
Vice President, Paul Kennedy
Vice President Of Quality Information Technology And Regulatory Affairs, Rusty Bondeson
Group Vice President, Richard Cargile
Group Vice President Trading Marketing, William Waldheim
Vice President And General Auditor, Irene G Lofland
Executive Vice President, Mark Borer
Vice President Procurement, Bill Prentice
Vice President Of Business Development, Greg Smith
Vice President Of Information Technology, Quay Chan
Vice President Of Information Technology, Susie Sjulin
Vice President Of Information Technology, William Johnson
Vice President Of Information Systems, Lori Martinez
Vice President, Mark Krabbe
Vp Engineering, Chris Root
Vice President Global Technology Operations, Jordan Pittman
Senior Vice President Information Technology Infrastructure, Craig McCarty
Vice President, Russell Bishop
Vice President Of It, Peter Wright
Vice President Corporate Planning And Strategic Initiatives, Timothy Osullivan
Senior Paralegal And Assistant Secretary, Stacey Metcalfe
Board Member, Rick Nelson
Board Member, Billy Waycaster
Treasurer, Evelyn Kastner
Board Member, William Kimble
Auditors: DELOITTE & TOUCHE LLP

LOCATIONS

HQ: DCP Midstream LP
370 17th Street, Suite 2500, Denver, CO 80202
Phone: 303 595-3331
Web: www.dcpmidstream.com

PRODUCTS/OPERATIONS

2018 Sales

	$ mil.	% of total
Logistics & Marketing	9,014	61
Gathering & Processing	5,843	39
Intersegment eliminations	(5035)	-
Total	**9,822**	**100**

2018 Sales

	$ mil.	% of total
Sales of natural gas propane NGLs and condensate	9,374	95
Transportation processing and other	489	5
Trading and marketing (losses) gains net	(41)	-
Total	**9,822**	**100**

COMPETITORS

BP NGL
Crestwood Midstream Partners LP
Enterprise Products
Kinder Morgan
Magellan Midstream
Martin Midstream Partners
SandRidge Energy
Williams Companies
XTO Energy

HISTORICAL FINANCIALS

Company Type: Public

Income Statement   FYE: December 31

	REVENUE ($ mil.)	NET INCOME ($ mil.)	NET PROFIT MARGIN	EMPLOYEES
12/19	7,625	17	0.2%	—
12/18	9,822	298	3.0%	—
12/17	8,462	229	2.7%	—
12/16	1,497	312	20.8%	—
12/15	1,898	228	12.0%	—
Annual Growth	**41.6%**	**(47.7%)**	**—**	**—**

2019 Year-End Financials

Debt ratio: 41.93%	No. of shares (mil.): 208
Return on equity: —	Dividends
Cash ($ mil.): 1	Yield: 12.7%
Current ratio: 0.60	Payout: —
Long-term debt ($ mil.): 5,321	Market value ($ mil.): 5,102

	STOCK PRICE ($) FY Close	P/E High/Low	PER SHARE ($) Earnings	Dividends	Book Value
12/19	24.49	— —	(1.05)	3.12	31.70
12/18	26.49	75 42	0.61	3.12	50.71
12/17	36.33	97 69	0.43	3.12	51.69
12/16	38.38	24 10	1.64	3.12	22.67
12/15	24.67	52 23	0.91	3.12	24.16
Annual Growth	**(0.2%)**	**— —**	**—**	**(0.0%)**	**7.0%**

Dean Foods Co.

Dean Foods is one of the nation's largest milk bottler and purveyor of dairy products. The company markets fluid milk ice cream and cultured dairy products as well as beverages (juices teas and bottled water). It operates under more than 50 local regional and private label brands including DairyPure Mayfield Pet Country Fresh Meadow Gold and TruMoo a leading national flavored milk brand. Dean Foods owns and operates a number

of smaller regional dairy companies including Friendly's Berkeley Farms and Garelick Farms. The company distributes dairy products across the US from regional manufacturing facilities. In late 2019 Dean Foods filed for Chapter 11 bankruptcy with the intention of selling itself.

Bankruptcy
In late 2019 the "U.S. Bankruptcy Court for the Southern District of Texas has entered a final order granting the Company authority to access the full amount of its $850 million in debtor-in-possession ("DIP") financing. The Company had previously received interim approval from the Court to access up to $475 million of the DIP financing. The Court also granted all other relief sought including providing final approvals for certain other of the Company's "First Day Motions" intended to support the business." Deans Foods and substantially all of the company's subsidiaries initiated Chapter 11 reorganization proceedings in the Southern District of Texas.

Operations
About 65% of Dean Foods' revenue comes from its fluid milk while ice cream products account for nearly 15%. The rest of the company's sales come from fresh cream extended shelf-life and other dairy products cultured products and other beverages each accounting for around 5% or less of sales; excess raw materials and other bulk commodities account for nearly 10% of sales). The company's heavy reliance on fluid milk puts it at the mercy of milk prices consumer demand and competition. Changes in any of those forces could affect the company's operations.

Company' branded and private label brands each account for about half of product sales. Excess raw materials and other bulk commodities both account for around 5% of sales. Due to the perishable nature of the company's products the company delivers the majority of its products directly to its customers' locations in refrigerated trucks or trailers that the company owns or leases.

Geographic Reach
Dean Foods based in Dallas Texas has a wide reach around the US operating more than 55 production facilities throughout nearly 30 states with distribution capabilities across all 50 states.

Sales and Marketing
Dean Foods markets its products through advertising and other promotions including media agency coupons trade shows and other promotional activities.

Dean Foods' customers include food retailers distributors foodservice outlets educational institutions and governmental entities throughout the US. Walmart and its subsidiaries including Sam's Club is the company's largest customer accounting for around 15% of revenue.

The company's products are sold primarily on a local or regional basis through local and regional sales forces although some national customer relationships are coordinated by a centralized corporate sales department.

Dean Foods' advertising expense totaled $19.3 million in 2019 $41.6 million in 2018 and $39.1 million in 2017.

Financial Performance
Dean Foods' revenue growth performance have been inconsistent the past five years. Net income for the Company incurred losses for three years for that period.

In 2019 sales slipped by 5% to $7.3 billion primarily due to fluid milk volume declines from year-ago levels partly offset by increased pricing as a result of increases in dairy commodity costs from year-ago levels and pricing actions taken during the year ended December 31 2019 to offset inflation.

Dean Foods lost $499.9 million in 2019 higher compared to losses incurred in 2018 the result of lower revenue and higher costs (including non-cash charges on impaired assets).

The company's coffers held $80 million in cash at the end of 2019 compared to $24.2 million the year before. In 2019 operations used $47.3 million investing activities also used $83.4 million and financing activities generated $186.6 million.

Strategy

Dean Foods has evolved over the past 20 years through periods of rapid acquisition consolidation integration and the separation of our operations including the spin-off of The WhiteWave Foods Company ("WhiteWave") and sale of Morningstar Foods ("Morningstar") in 2013. Today it is a leading food and beverage company and the largest processor and direct-to-store distributor of fresh fluid milk and other dairy and dairy case products in the United States.

The Company vision is to be the most admired and trusted provider of wholesome great-tasting dairy products at every occasion. Its strategy is to invest and grow its portfolio of brands while strengthening its operations and capabilities to achieve a more profitable core business. its strategy is anchored by its commitments to safety quality and service and delivering sustainable profit growth and total shareholder return.

Within its business strategies corporate responsibility remains an integral part of its efforts. As it work to strengthen its business the Company is committed to do it in a way that is right for its employees shareholders consumers customers suppliers and the environment. It intends to realize savings by reducing waste and duplication while continuing to support programs that improve its local communities. Dean Foods believe that its customers consumers and suppliers value its efforts to operate in an ethical environmentally sustainable and socially responsible manner.

HISTORY

Investment banker Gregg Engles formed a holding company in 1988 with other investors including dairy industry veteran Cletes Beshears to buy the Reddy Ice unit of Dallas-based Southland (operator of the 7-Eleven chain). The company also bought Circle K's Sparkle Ice and combined it with Reddy Ice. By 1990 it had acquired about 15 ice plants.

The company changed its name to Suiza Foods when it bought Suiza Dairy in 1993 for $99 million. The Puerto Rican dairy was formed in 1942 by Hector Nevares Sr. and named for the Spanish word for "Switzerland." By 1993 it was Puerto Rico's largest dairy controlling about 60% of the island's milk market.

Suiza Foods bought Florida's Velda Farms manufacturer and distributor of milk and dairy products in 1994. The company went public in 1996 the same year it bought Swiss Dairy (dairy products California and Nevada) and Garrido y Compañía (coffee products Puerto Rico).

The company became one of the largest players in the North American dairy industry through its acquisitions in 1997. It paid $960 million for Morningstar (Lactaid brand lactose-free milk Second Nature brand egg substitute) which — like Suiza Foods itself — was a Dallas-based company formed in 1988 through a Southland divestiture. The company entered the Midwest with its $98 million purchase of Country Fresh and the Northeast with the Bernon family's Massachusetts-based group of dairy and packaging companies including Garelick Farms and Franklin Plastics (packaging).

Suiza Foods strengthened its presence in the southeastern US in 1998 with its $287 million acquisition of Land-O-Sun Dairies operator of 13 fluid-dairy and ice-cream processing facilities. Also that year Suiza Foods purchased Continental Can

(plastic packaging) for about $345 million and sold Reddy Ice to Packaged Ice for $172 million.

After settling an antitrust lawsuit brought by the US Department of Justice in 1999 Suiza Foods bought dairy processors in Colorado Ohio and Virginia. That year Suiza Foods combined its US packaging operations with Reid Plastics to form Consolidated Containers retaining about 40% of the new company.

In 2001 Suiza Foods announced it had agreed to purchase rival Dean Foods for $1.5 billion and the assumption of $1 billion worth of debt. Dean Foods had begun as Dean Evaporated Milk founded in 1925 by Sam Dean a Chicago evaporated-milk broker. By the mid-1930s it had moved into the fresh milk industry. The company went public in 1961 and was renamed Dean Foods in 1963.

Suiza Foods completed the acquisition and took on the Dean Foods name later in 2001. The new Dean Foods bought out Dairy Farmers of America's interest in Suiza Dairy and merged it with the "old" Dean's fluid-dairy operations to create its internal division Dean Dairy Group.

Along with the purchase of "old" Dean came a 36% ownership of soy milk maker WhiteWave and in 2002 Dean Foods purchased the remaining 64% for approximately $189 million. By the end of the year Dean had sold off some smaller businesses (boiled peanuts and contract hauling) and its Puerto Rico operations for $119 million in cash.

EXECUTIVES

Ceo, Ralph P. Scozzafava, age 61, $850,000 total compensation

Evp General Counsel Corporate Secretary And Government Affairs, Russell F. Coleman

Evp And Chief Human Resources Officer, Kimberly (Kim) Warmbier, age 58, $432,000 total compensation

Svp Logistics, S. Craig McCutcheon, age 59

Evp Supply Chain, Brad Cashaw, age 56, $343,674 total compensation

Interim Cfo, Scott K. Vopni, age 52

Vice President National Accounts, Tom Arcand

Svp Human Resources, Jose Motta

Vice President Director Manager, Joan Salyers

Vice President Business Development Group, Christopher Anderson

Group Vice President Sales, Ed Hinson

Vice President Legal Departmet, Karen Hess

Vice President Sales, Terry Dana

Vice President Finance, Kim Lechner

Vp Of It Infrastructure, Thomas Ehrman

Group Vice President Sales, Bill Riley

Vice President Research And Development Fresh Dairy Direct, Kathleen Dacunha

Vice President, Scott Toth

Vice President Director Manager, Abi Rasti

Senior Vice President And Credit Manager, Ed Gorden

Vice President Sales South Region, Marvin Monroe

Vice President Prc, Gary Tritt

Vice President Corporate Development, Steve Schultz

Vice President Tax Planning, Shan Luton

Vice President Legal, Mark Niermann

Vice President Of Finance, Tim Jones

Vice President, David Hurst

National Account Manager, Hunter Jarvis

Vice President Of Sales National Accounts, Tim Heil

Vice President Ehs, Mark Longmier

Vice President Government Relations, Anne Divjak

Chairman, Jim L. Turner, age 74

Assistant Treasurer, Edgar Deguia

Auditors: DELOITTE & TOUCHE LLP

LOCATIONS

HQ: Dean Foods Co.
2711 North Haskell Avenue, Suite 3400, Dallas, TX 75204
Phone: 214 303-3400
Web: www.deanfoods.com

2018 Sales

	% of total
Domestic	99
Foreign	1
Total	**100**

PRODUCTS/OPERATIONS

2018 Sales

	$ mil.	% of total
Fluid milk	4,756	61
Ice cream	1,077	14
Excess bulk materials	515	7
Fresh cream	397	5
Other beverages	278	3
Cultured	260	5
Extended shelf life and other dairy products	189	2
Other bulk commodities	157	2
Other	123	2
Total	**7,795**	**100**

2018 Fresh Dairy Direct Sales

	% of total
Private-label brands	50
Company brands	50
Total	**100**

Selected Brands

Alpro (Europe)
Alta Dena
Berkeley Farms
Borden (licensed)
Brown Cow
Brown's Dairy
Dean's
Friendly's
Garelick Farms
Gandy's
Hershey's (licensed)
Horizon Organic
Knudsen (licensed)
LAND O'LAKES (licensed)
Mayfield Creamery
Oak Farms
Over the Moon
Pet (licensed)
Provamel (Europe)
Robinson Dairy
Silk
Swiss Premium
Tru Moo
Tuscan
WhiteWave

Selected Products

Bottled waters
Eggnog
Eggs
Cottage cheese
Half-and-half
Ice cream
Juice
Milk
Pudding
Sour cream
Soymilk
Whipping cream

COMPETITORS

Associated Milk Producers	H-E-B
Aurora Organic Dairy	Hain Celestial
Ben & Jerry's	Lifeway Foods
Blue Bell	Maryland & Virginia Milk Producers
California Dairies Inc.	Mondelez International
ConAgra	National Dairy
Dairy Farmers of America	Nestlé USA
	Organic Valley
	Prairie Farms Dairy

Danone
Darigold Inc.
Dreyer's
Foster Dairy Farms
Galaxy Nutritional
 Foods
Grupo LALA

Rockview Dairies
Stonyfield Farm
Tillamook County
 Creamery Association
Vitasoy International
Wal-Mart

HISTORICAL FINANCIALS
Company Type: Public

Income Statement				FYE: December 31
	REVENUE ($ mil.)	NET INCOME ($ mil.)	NET PROFIT MARGIN	EMPLOYEES
12/19	7,328	(499)	—	14,500
12/18	7,755	(326)	—	15,000
12/17	7,795	61	0.8%	16,000
12/16	7,710	119	1.6%	17,000
12/15	8,121	(8)	—	16,960
Annual Growth	(2.5%)	—	—	(3.8%)

2019 Year-End Financials

Debt ratio: 19.97%
Return on equity: (-820.67%)
Cash ($ mil.): 80
Current ratio: 0.88
Long-term debt ($ mil.): 4

No. of shares (mil.): 91
Dividends
 Yield: 350.0%
 Payout: —
Market value ($ mil.): 6

	STOCK PRICE ($) FY Close	P/E High/Low	PER SHARE ($) Earnings	Dividends	Book Value
12/19	0.06	— —	(5.45)	0.21	(1.97)
12/18	3.81	— —	(3.58)	0.30	3.31
12/17	11.56	32 13	0.67	0.36	7.20
12/16	21.78	17 12	1.31	0.36	6.74
12/15	17.15	— —	(0.09)	0.28	5.97
Annual Growth	(75.7%)	— —	—	(6.9%)	—

Deere & Co.

Deere & Co. is one of the world's largest makers of farm equipment and a major producer of construction forestry and commercial and residential lawn care equipment. Deere operates through three business segments. Its agriculture and turf and construction and forestry segments make up its equipment operations; the financial services segment provides financing and leasing for John Deere dealers. Deere famous for its "Nothing Runs Like a Deere" slogan sells John Deere and other brands through dealer networks and also sells lawn and garden products through home improvement retailers like The Home Depot and Lowes. Most of the company's revenue is generated in North America.

Operations

Deere's largest operating segment is agriculture and turf which accounts for about 60% of revenue. Consolidated into five product platforms?crop harvesting turf and utility hay and forage crop care and tractors?this segment makes such products as loaders combines pickers and golf course equipment and outdoor power products. Besides John Deere brands include Frontier Kemper Green Systems Hagie Mazzotti and Monosem as well as SABO in Europe.

The company's construction and forestry segment generates nearly a third of sales. This segment manufactures 90% of the types of construction equipment used in North America. Besides John Deere brands include Wirtgen V ¶gele Hamm Kleeman Benninghoven Waratah and Ciber. Forestry equipment (attachments) are distributed under the John Deere and Waratah brand names.

In addition the company licenses certain John Deere-designed and -manufactured construction equipment to Bell Equipment for sale in Africa. Its joint venture with Hitachi Construction Machinery allows for specific products to be manufactured and sold in North Central and South America. Deere also owns Nortrax Inc. a John Deere dealer for construction and forestry equipment with locations in the US and Canada.

Besides equipment the company's financial services segment (less than 10% of revenue) provides financing and leasing for new and used equipment purchased from John Deere dealers as well as wholesale financing to the dealers themselves. Financial services also provides revolving charge accounts and extended equipment warranties.

Geographic Reach

Deere is based in Moline IL in the middle of the US corn belt. Accordingly North America (the US and Canada) accounts for about 60% of the company's revenue.

The company doesn't break out revenue from other specific regions but it operates around two dozen manufacturing facilities in North America. To get equipment and parts where they need to go Deere has two centralized parts distribution centers and nine regional parts depots and distribution centers throughout North America. It also has manufacturing and distribution operations in Europe South America Africa and Asia and Australia. It has sales and administrative offices worldwide.

Sales and Marketing

Through US and Canadian facilities Deere markets products to about 2000 dealer locations most of which are independently owned and operated. Of these about 1540 sell agricultural equipment while some 435 sell construction earthmoving material handling and forestry equipment. Some dealer locations are owned by Deere's Nortrax subsidiary. Outside the US and Canada Deere agriculture and turf equipment is also sold to distributors and dealers for resale in over 100 countries.

Deere advertising expense was 215 million in 2019 $188 million in 2018 and $169 million in 2017.

Financial Performance

Revenue for Deere & Company has picked up significantly in 2017 and 2018 after a downward trend in previous years. Net sales in 2019 climbed 5% to a record high of $39.3 billion compared with $37.4 billion in 2018. The increase was due to higher sales new worldwide customers and added sales from the acquisition of the Wirtgen Group. Growth is attributed to higher demand in the North American housing market and economic growth worldwide. Of note were higher sales in the oil and gas sector.

Net income also saw a healthy 37% increase to $3.3 billion in 2019 partially offset by increases to the provision for income taxes including those related to the US tax reform legislation.

Cash at the end of fiscal 2019 was around $4 billion. Cash from operations contributed $3.4 billion to the coffers while investing activities used $3.9 million. Financing activities provided $509 million primarily due to borrowings of $6.4billion.

Strategy

Going forward Deere aims to build on its current leadership position in agricultural equipment and strengthen its position in the construction equipment market. The company is focused on incorporating more technology into its products and expanding globally.

Deere is working to develop technology such as vehicle automation and autonomy digitalization and life-cycle management for its products. It made almost $2.9 billion in research and development investments and capital expenditures in 2019. With the machine learning capabilities gained from its Blue River Technologies acquisition Deere is well positioned to develop artificial intelligence features for many of its products. For example Blue River's see-and-spray technology which helps growers reduce the use of herbicides is being tested for new crops such as cotton.

The company's Combine Advisor product uses a combination of artificial intelligence and cameras to help farmers improve yield and grain quality. It is also working on new technology to reduce emissions from diesel engines and is continuing its use of new battery technology in small equipment such as lawn mowers and Gators (its branded utility vehicles). Larger equipment still uses hybrid electric-diesel power but Deere is investing in research for an all-electric tractor.

Mergers and Acquisitions

Deere & Company acquired Brazil-based Unimil a company specializing in aftermarket service parts for sugarcane harvesters in 2019. Deere is committed to the Brazilian sugarcane business and is making investments that could reduce customers' production costs in this sector.

Also in 2019 the company acquired OnLink a maker of golf course performance optimization software. The company is incorporating OnLink's technology that includes a cloud-based golf course management platform that collects data on golf equipment labor water chemicals and nutrients and playing conditions.

Company Background

Vermont-born John Deere moved to Grand Detour Illinois in 1836 and set up a blacksmith shop. Deere and other pioneers had trouble with the rich black soil of the Midwest getting stuck to iron plows designed for sandy eastern soils so in 1837 Deere used a circular steel saw blade to create a self-scouring plow that moved so quickly it was nicknamed the "whistling plow." He sold only three in 1838 but by 1842 he was making 25 a week.

Deere moved his enterprise to Moline in 1847. His son Charles joined the company in 1853 beginning a long tradition of family management. (All five Deere presidents before 1982 were related by blood or marriage.) Charles eventually set up an independent dealership distribution system and added wagons buggies and corn planters to the product line.

Deere & Company was incorporated in 1868 and the John Deere Credit Company began operation in 1958.

EXECUTIVES

Executive Vice President Worldwide Parts Services Global Supply M, H Markley
Vp Of Forestry And Business Development Candf Division, Martin Wilkinson
Vice President Information Technology, Ganesh Jayaram
Vice President Worldwide Supply Management Logistics, Thomas Knoll
Chairman President And Ceo, Samuel R. (Sam) Allen, $1,500,000 total compensation
Senior Vice President, Markwart Pentz
President Agriculture And Turf Americas Australia And Global Harvesting And Turf Platforms, James M. Field, $686,266 total compensation
President Worldwide Construction And Forestry Global Labor Relations And Security, Max A. Guinn
President Agriculture And Turf Division Europe Asia Africa And Global Tractor Platform, Mark von Pentz
Svp And Cfo, Rajesh (Raj) Kalathur, $615,312 total compensation

President Agricultural Solutions And Cio, John C. May, $599,840 total compensation
Vp Global Supply Management And Logistics, Pierre Guyot
Svp John Deere Power Systems Worldwide Parts Services Advanced Technology And Engineering And Global Supply Management And Logistics, Jean H. Gilles, $614,823 total compensation
Svp And Chief Administrative Officer, Marc A. Howze
President John Deere Financial, Cory J. Reed
Vice President Of Marketing, Hans Becherer
Vice President Global Human Resources, Mary Jones
Senior Vice President Engineering Manufacturing And Supply Management Worldwide Construction Andamp; Forestry Division, Brian Rauch
Senior Vice President Manufacturing And Engineering Global Tractor A, Adel Zkri
Vice President And Chief Compliance Officer, Laurie Simpson
Svp Global Tractor Platform Ag And Turf Division, Bernard Haas
Vice President Strategic Partnerships Worldwide Construction And Forestry Division, Douglas Gage
Vp Of Information Technology, Richard Courtade
Vice President Of Sales, Vanessa Stifferclaus
Vp Of Information Technology, Scott Mcdaniel
Vice President, Weylon Heiser
Vice President And Comptroller, Ryan Campbell
Vp And Treasurer, Thomas Spitzfaden
Vice President Of Finance, Jesus Rasgado
Vice President Information Service, Curt Hoppasted
Senior Vice President, John Stone
Vice President Agribusiness, Lynn White
Vice President Information Systems, Ray Lybarger
Vice President, Arthur Woodcock
Vice President H R, Heather Rogers
Vice President And Deputy Financial Offi, Marie Ziegler
Senior Vice President Of Finance, Michael Matera
Senior Vice President Global Tractor Platform, Bernhard Haas
Vice President Of Planning And Corporate Development, Dan Reilly
Vice President, Holly Dierks
Vice President Of Information Technology, Dave Gerse
Vice President Of Human Resources, Beverly Curtis
Vice President, Ken Taylor
Senior Vice President Of Commercial Se, Dave Werning
Senior Vice President Marketing, Pentz Von
Vice President Corporate Communications And Global Brand Management, Frances B Emerson
Vice President Assistant Sec, Danny Langston
Vice President Of Management Informati, Richard Townsend
Vp Of Information Technology, Scott Hemesath
Vp Of Information Technology, Adam Winders
Vice President Marketing, Bev Mickelson
Vice President, Patricia Dyar
Executive Vice President, Adel Zakaria
Senior Vice President, Robert Porter
Vp Of Information Technology, Bailey Ogle
Vice President Of Human Resources, Cara Pifer
Vp Of Information Technology, Robert Drumm
Vice President Marketing Us And Canada, Sandquist Jayma
Vp Of Information Technology, Nathan Livingston
Vice President Insurance Strategic Planning And Business Development, Patrick Mack
Vice President Taxes, Margaret Curry
Vice President And Deputy General Counsel Deere And Company And Senior Vice President And Chief Couns, Matthew Haney

Vice President Taxes, James McCabe
Vp Of Information Technology, Gregory Zuber
Vp Of Information Technology, Andrea Larsen
Vice President Finance, Charles Dahl
Vice President, Bill Norton
Vice President Information Technology, James Wagner
Vice President Senior Loan Officer, Trisha Kalscheur
Senior Vice President And Finance Director John Deere Financial, Steven Owenson
Director Of Nursing Services, Kimberly Campbell
Vice President Pension Fund And Investments, Jeffrey Trahan
Vp Marketing, Ron Jump
Senior Vice President Information Technology, Dave Rodger
Vice President Of Sales, Jerry Hoeksema
Finance Vice President, Mary Blixt
Board Member, Crandall Bowles
Board Member, Shukla Abhishek
Secretary, Paul Nagel
Secretary, Michael Driscoll
Board Member, Robert Dunbar
Treasurer, Terry Card
Board Member, Dmitri Stockton
Board Member, Michael Johanns
Board Member, Sheila Talton
Board Member, Alan Heuberger
Board Member, Gregory Page
Board Member, Jed Stockton
Treasurer, Kay Meadows
Treasurer, Philipp Wilson
Treasurer, Thomas Hoeksema
Board Member, Jeri Isbell
Board Member, Michael Grebe
Treas, Robert Null Dentler
Auditors: DELOITTE & TOUCHE LLP

LOCATIONS

HQ: Deere & Co.
One John Deere Place, Moline, IL 61265
Phone: 309 765-8000   **Fax:** 309 765-9929
Web: www.johndeere.com

2018 Sales

	$ mil.	% of total
US & Canada	21,632	58
Outside U.S. and Canada	14,971	40
Other	755	2
Total	**37,358**	**100**

PRODUCTS/OPERATIONS

2018 Sales

	$ mil.	% of total
Agriculture & turf	23,191	62
Construction & forestry	10,160	27
Financial services	3,252	9
Other	755	2
Total	**37,358**	**100**

Selected Products and Services

Agricultural and turf equipment
  Balers
  Combines
  Cotton harvesting equipment
  Golf course equipment
  Harvesters
  Hay and forage equipment
  Irrigation
  Landscape and nursery
  Loaders
  Mowers (commercial riding lawn equipment and walk-behind mowers)
  Planting and seeding equipment
  Power products (outdoor)
  Sprayers
  Tillage
  Tractors (large medium and utility)
  Utility vehicles
Construction and forestry equipment

  Articulated dump trucks
  Backhoe loaders
  Crawler dozers
  Crawler loaders
  Excavators
  Landscape loaders
  Log skidders and loaders
  Material handling equipment
  Motor graders
  Skid-steer loaders
Credit
  Leasing
  Retail and wholesale financing
Power systems
  Diesel and natural gas engines (marine industrial mining)
  Powertrain components
  Transmissions

COMPETITORS

AGCO	Kubota
Caterpillar	Mahindra
Claas KG auf Aktien mbH	Navistar International
Doosan Heavy Industries	PACCAR
Komatsu	Terex
	Toro Company
	Volvo

HISTORICAL FINANCIALS

Company Type: Public

Income Statement

FYE: November 1

	REVENUE ($ mil.)	NET INCOME ($ mil.)	NET PROFIT MARGIN	EMPLOYEES
11/20	35,540	2,751	7.7%	69,634
11/19*	39,258	3,253	8.3%	73,489
10/18	37,357	2,368	6.3%	74,413
10/17	29,737	2,159	7.3%	60,476
10/16	26,644	1,523	5.7%	56,800
Annual Growth	7.5%	15.9%	—	5.2%

*Fiscal year change

2020 Year-End Financials

Debt ratio: 61.26%	No. of shares (mil.): 313
Return on equity: 22.66%	Dividends
Cash ($ mil.): 7,066	Yield: 0.0%
Current ratio: 0.77	Payout: 34.9%
Long-term debt ($ mil.): 32,734	Market value ($ mil.): 70,858

	STOCK PRICE ($) FY Close	P/E High/Low	PER SHARE ($) Earnings	Dividends	Book Value
11/20	225.91	27 13	8.69	3.04	41.25
11/19*	176.11	17 13	10.15	3.04	36.45
10/18	133.00	23 13	7.24	2.58	35.45
10/17	133.25	20 13	6.68	2.40	29.70
10/16	88.30	18 15	4.81	2.40	20.71
Annual Growth	26.5%	— —	15.9%	6.1%	18.8%

*Fiscal year change

Delek US Holdings Inc (New)

EXECUTIVES

Chb-Pres-Ceo, Ezra Uzi Yemin
Exec V Pres-Cfo*, Kevin L Kremke
Exec V Pres-Coo*, Frederec Green
Exec V Pres-Cco*, Avigal Soreq
Exec V Pres Hr*, Donald N Holmes
Unknown, Blake Waterson

Project Coordinator, Alexandra Dalton
Help Desk Manager, Gary McCullough
Database Manager, Russell Guier
Laboratory Supervisor, Demica Smith
Director of Accounting, Ashley Dubler
Auditors: Ernst & Young LLP

LOCATIONS

HQ: Delek US Holdings Inc (New)
  7102 Commerce Way, Brentwood, TN 37027
Phone: 615 771-6701
Web: www.Delekus.com

COMPETITORS

7-Eleven	Motiva Enterprises
CITGO	Murphy Oil
Chevron	Publix
ConocoPhillips	Racetrac Petroleum
Costco Wholesale	The Pantry
Cumberland Farms	Wal-Mart
Exxon Mobil	Winn-Dixie
Gate Petroleum	

HISTORICAL FINANCIALS
Company Type: Public

Income Statement				FYE: December 31
	REVENUE ($ mil.)	NET INCOME ($ mil.)	NET PROFIT MARGIN	EMPLOYEES
12/19	9,298	310	3.3%	3,814
12/18	10,233	340	3.3%	3,717
12/17	7,267	288	4.0%	3,941
12/16	4,197	(153)	—	1,326
12/15	5,762	19	0.3%	4,584
Annual Growth	12.7%	100.0%	—	(4.5%)

2019 Year-End Financials

Debt ratio: 29.46%
Return on equity: 18.83%
Cash ($ mil.): 955
Current ratio: 1.26
Long-term debt ($ mil.): 2,030
No. of shares (mil.): 73
Dividends
  Yield: 3.4%
  Payout: 22.9%
Market value ($ mil.): 2,463

	STOCK PRICE ($) FY Close	P/E High/Low		PER SHARE ($) Earnings	Dividends	Book Value
12/19	33.53	11	7	4.06	1.14	22.68
12/18	32.51	15	7	3.95	0.96	20.93
12/17	34.94	9	5	4.00	0.30	20.44
12/16	24.07	—	—	(2.49)	0.60	16.01
12/15	24.60	128	70	0.32	0.60	18.56
Annual Growth	8.1%	—	—	88.7%	17.4%	5.1%

Dell Technologies Inc

Auditors: PricewaterhouseCoopers LLP

LOCATIONS

HQ: Dell Technologies Inc
  One Dell Way, Round Rock, TX 78682
Phone: 800 289-3355
Web: www.delltechnologies.com

HISTORICAL FINANCIALS
Company Type: Public

Income Statement				FYE: January 31
	REVENUE ($ mil.)	NET INCOME ($ mil.)	NET PROFIT MARGIN	EMPLOYEES
01/20*	92,154	4,616	5.0%	165,000
02/19	90,621	(2,310)	—	157,000
02/18	78,660	(3,728)	—	145,000
02/17	61,642	(1,672)	—	138,000
01/16	50,911	(1,104)	—	
Annual Growth	16.0%	—	—	—

*Fiscal year change

2020 Year-End Financials

Debt ratio: 43.80%
Return on equity: —
Cash ($ mil.): 9,302
Current ratio: 0.70
Long-term debt ($ mil.): 44,319
No. of shares (mil.): 743
Dividends
  Yield: —
  Payout: —
Market value ($ mil.): 36,236

	STOCK PRICE ($) FY Close	P/E High/Low		PER SHARE ($) Earnings	Dividends	Book Value
01/20*	48.77	11	7	6.03	0.00	(1.27)
02/19	49.65	—	—	(6.04)	0.00	(6.35)
Annual Growth	(0.4%)	—	—	—	—	—

*Fiscal year change

Delta Air Lines Inc (DE)

Delta Air Lines is one of the world's largest airlines by traffic. Through its regional carriers the company serves about 300 destinations in about 50 countries and it operates a mainline fleet of 1000-plus aircraft as well as maintenance repair and overhaul (MRO) and cargo operations. The airline serves more than 200 million customers each year and offers more than 15000 daily flights. Delta is a founding member of the SkyTeam marketing and code-sharing alliance (airlines extend their networks by selling tickets on flights) which includes carriers Air France KLM and Virgin Atlantic. Customers from the US account for approximately 70% of sales.

Operations

Delta divides its operations into two chief segments: airline and refinery. The airline segment which accounts for 90% of Delta's sales provides scheduled air transportation for passengers and cargo throughout the US and around the world and other ancillary airline services including maintenance and repair services for third parties.

The refinery segment (some 10% of total sales) provides jet fuel to the airline segment from its own production and through jet fuel obtained via agreements with third parties. The costs included in the refinery segment are primarily for the benefit of the airline segment.

By product type economy/coach tickets accounts for more than 45% of total revenue while business cabin and premium tickets generate about 30%. Loyalty travel awards travel-related services cargo and other services accounts the remainder.

Geographic Reach

Atlanta Georgia-based Delta operates from hubs in Amsterdam Atlanta Boston Detroit London-Heathrow Los Angeles Mexico City Minneapolis-St. Paul New York-LaGuardia New York-JFK Paris-Charles de Gaulle Salt Lake City SOo Paulo Seattle Seoul-Incheon and Tokyo-Haneda. The US market is its largest representing about 70% of net sales.

Delta directly owns an oil refinery in Pennsylvania operated by subsidiary Monroe Energy. Monroe which supplies a large chunk of Delta's jet fuel is loss-making and Delta execs are having a hard time finding a willing buyer.

Sales and Marketing

Delta's tickets are sold through various distribution channels including telephone reservations Delta.com and traditional brick and mortar and online travel agencies.

Delta annual advertising expense was $288 million $267 million and $273 million for the years ended 2019 2018 and 2017 respectively.

Financial Performance

The revenue growth of Delta for a five-year period starting in 2015 showed an upward trend except in 2016 when it dipped 3%. Net income followed the same trend with a 7% dip in 2016.

In 2019 revenue grew by 6% to $47 billion compared to $44 billion in 2018. Growth was driven by increase in ticket revenues for both main cabin and business cabin and premium products.

Delta's net income grew 21% to $4.8 billion from $3.9 billion in 2018. The increase in 2019 resulted from a $2.6 billion increase in revenue and lower fuel expense on an 8% decrease in the market price per gallon of fuel and improved fuel efficiency.

Delta's cash position strengthened in 2019 ending the year $982 million higher at $3.7 billion. It generated $8.4 billion from its operations while investing activities used $4.6 billion and financing activities used $2.9 billion. Delta's primary cash uses during the year were investments in flight equipment and ground property long-term debt repayments stock repurchases and dividend payouts.

Strategy

An important part of the Company strategy to expand its global network has been to make significant investments in airlines in other parts of the world and expand its commercial relationships with these carriers including through joint ventures. It expects to continue exploring ways to expand its relationships with other carriers as part of its global business strategy. Delta's alliance with SkyTeam extends the airline's reach to more than 900 destinations in over 140 countries around the globe. The company gets a boost in global coverage with airlines around the world coming aboard the SkyTeam alliance. Delta has five joint ventures with foreign carriers.

To boost its position in the important region of China Delta acquired a 3% stake in China Eastern one of the leading airlines in China. The move allows Delta and China Eastern to compete more effectively on routes between the US and China and provided more travel options for customers in both countries.

Looking to Europe Delta has joint ventures with Air France and KLM and plans to build its presence in its strategically advantaged hubs in Paris and Amsterdam while de-emphasizing higher Europe point-of-sale markets. It also holds a 49% equity investment in Virgin Atlantic which improved its presence in London one of Delta's largest revenue markets from the US.

Targeting the Asia/Pacific region for growth in 2018 Delta and Korean Air formed a joint venture increasing air traffic between the United States and certain countries in Asia.

Delta also has joint venture with Virgin Australia serving traffic between U.S. and Australia/New Zealand; and Mexican airline Aeroméxico which includes a joint MRO operation in Queretaro (in addition to trans-border flights between the US and Mexico).

HISTORY

Delta Air Lines was founded in Macon Georgia in 1924 as the world's first crop-dusting service Huff-Daland Dusters to combat boll weevil infestation of cotton fields. It moved to Monroe Louisiana in 1925. In 1928 field manager C. E. Woolman and two partners bought the service and renamed it Delta Air Service after the Mississippi Delta region it served. About 80 years later Delta became one of the world's largest airlines by traffic after its $2.8 billion acquisition of Northwest Airlines in 2008.

EXECUTIVES

Executive Vice President Human Resources And Labor Relations, Michael Campbell
Senior Vice President New York, Gail Grimmett
Vice President In Flight Service Business Operations, David Watson
Ceo, Edward H. (Ed) Bastian, age 62, $741,669 total compensation
President, Glen W. Hauenstein, age 59, $604,997 total compensation
Evp And Cfo, Paul A. Jacobson, age 48, $525,000 total compensation
Sevp And Coo, Wayne G. (Gil) West, $617,977 total compensation
Evp And Chief Human Resources Officer, Joanne Smith
Svp And Cio, Rahul Samant
Evp Global Sales; President International, Steve Sear
Evp And Chief Legal Officer, Peter W. Carter, $500,000 total compensation
Vice President Corporate Real Estate, Shane Jones
Vice President Of Communications, Bridget Carey
Svp Network Planning, Joe Esposito
Svp Global Sales, Bob Somers
Executive Vice President And Chro, Anne Smith
Vice President Marketing, Lidia Chiang
Senior Vice President Operations And Customer Center, Dave Holtz
Vice President And Chief Accounting Officer, Craig Meynard
Vice President Of Application, Richard Stone
Vice President, Cherylope Taylor
Vice President Global Human Resources Services, Chris Collins
Vice President And Treasurer, Kenneth Morge
Assistant Vice President Corporate Communications, Jonathan Kennedy
Vice President, Patrick Redahan
Vice President Technical Services, Mark Benson
Assistant Vice President Retail Information Technology, Timothy W Harms
Sevp And Coo, Gil West
Svp Hr, Rob Kight
Vice President Information Systems, Robert Olson
Senior Vice President Delta Connection, Don Bornhurst
Senior Vice President Delta Connection, Donald Bornhorst
National Account Manager, Laura Cascino
Vice President, Shreve Lee
Department Head, Mandell Pressley
Senior Vice President Flight Operations, Steve Dickson
Vice President Of Global Diversity And Community Affai, Jerome Miller
Vice President Global Distribution And Digital Strategy, Rhonda Crawford
Svp Supply Chain Management And Fleet Strategy, Greg May
Aa To Vice President, Keila Workley
Vice President Of Business Operations, Thomas E Schull
Regional Vice President, Wynetta Mccrary
Svp Global Alliances, Nat Pieper
Regional Vice President, Richard R Marr
Vp Customer Engagement And Loyalty And Ceo Delta Vacations, Sandeep Dube
Aa To Executive Vice President, Mary Mitchell
Senior Vice President And Deputy General Counsel, Matthew Knopf
Vice President Channel Technology, Matthew Matt Cincera
Aa To Senior Vice President, Maylin Fischer
Vice President Mergers And Acquisitions, Terrance Schwartz
Senior Vice President Finance And Controller, Bryan Treadway
Vice President Sales, Chuck Imhof
Svp Worldport Operations, Greg Kennedy
Vp Of It Infrastructure And Reliability, Dan Blanchard
Svp Legal Regulatory And International, Christine Wilson
Svp Delta Technical Operations, Don Mitacek
Vp Transatlantic, Roberto Ioriatti
Vice President Information Technology Revenue Technology And Data Analytics, Matt Schrag
Senior Vice President Europe Middle East Africa And India, Corneel Koster
Executive Vice President, Jim O'brien
Vice President Of Sales Mro Services, Sonny Stern
Senior Vice President Safety Engineering And Compliance, Kimberly Hill
Vice President Of Operations, Lora Sarah
Vice President Sales Latin America, Paul R Jones
Senior Vice President Central Region, Trevor O Pickle
Atg Vice President Fld Stns Xy, Kristin K Rice
Atg Vice President Human Resources Xy, Jannie Richardson
Vpcorp Audit, Brandi Thomas
Atg Vice President Fld Stns Xy, Kristin Rice
Vice President Sales Latin America, Paul Jones
Senior Business Intelligence Developer, Maria Brigiotta
Svp Of Network Planning, Bob Cortelyou
Senior Vice President Supply Chain Manag, Gregory May
Vice President Of Business Operations, Helen Zhang
Senior Vice President, William Carroll
Chairman, Francis S. (Frank) Blake, age 70
Managing Director Finance And Assistant Treasurer, Andy Nelson
Spec Acs Safetysecretarycompl, Clifton Jackson
Spec Acs Safetysecretarycompl, Abhishek Chauhan
Board Member, Allan Carter
Board Member, Tom Seip
Auditors: Ernst & Young LLP

LOCATIONS

HQ: Delta Air Lines Inc (DE)
  Post Office Box 20706, Atlanta, GA 30320-6001
Phone: 404 715-2600
Web: www.delta.com

2018 Sales

	$ mil.	% of total
Domestic	31,233	70
Atlantic	7,042	16
Latin America	3,181	7
Pacific	2,982	7
Total	44,438	100

PRODUCTS/OPERATIONS

2018 sales

	$ mil.	% of total
Tickets - Main Cabin	21,196	48
Ticket - business cabin and premium products	13,754	31
Loyalty travel awards	2,651	6
Travel-related services	2,154	5
Cargo	865	2
Other	3,818	8
Total	**44,438**	**100**

2018 Sales

	$ mil.	% of total
Airline	43,890	89
Refinery	5,458	11
Intersegment Sales/Other	(4910)	
Total	**44,438**	**100**

Selected Aircraft

Type
B-717-200
B-737-700
B-737-800
B-737-900ER
B-747-400
B-757-200
B-767-300
B-777-200ER
E190-100
MD-88

COMPETITORS

Air Canada
AirTran Airways
American Airlines Group
British Airways
Cathay Pacific
Japan Airlines
JetBlue
Lufthansa
Qantas
SAS
Singapore Airlines
Southwest Airlines
United Continental
Virgin Atlantic Airways

HISTORICAL FINANCIALS

Company Type: Public

Income Statement

	REVENUE ($ mil.)	NET INCOME ($ mil.)	NET PROFIT MARGIN	EMPLOYEES
12/19	47,007	4,767	10.1%	91,224
12/18	44,438	3,935	8.9%	89,000
12/17	41,244	3,577	8.7%	87,000
12/16	39,639	4,373	11.0%	84,000
12/15	40,704	4,526	11.1%	83,000
Annual Growth	3.7%	1.3%	—	2.4%

FYE: December 31

2019 Year-End Financials

Debt ratio: 18.53%
Return on equity: 32.82%
Cash ($ mil.): 2,882
Current ratio: 0.41
Long-term debt ($ mil.): 8,873
No. of shares (mil.): 642
Dividends
  Yield: 2.5%
  Payout: 21.0%
Market value ($ mil.): 37,589

	STOCK PRICE ($) FY Close	P/E High/Low		Earnings	Dividends	Book Value
12/19	58.48	9	6	7.30	1.51	23.89
12/18	49.90	11	8	5.67	1.31	20.13
12/17	56.00	11	9	4.95	1.02	19.67
12/16	49.19	9	6	5.79	0.68	16.81
12/15	50.69	9	7	5.63	0.45	13.93
Annual Growth	3.6%			6.7%	35.2%	14.4%

DHPC TECHNOLOGIES, INC.

EXECUTIVES

Ceo-Pres, John M Curtis
Director, Robert Lake
Engineer, Tom Tokash
Senior Consultant, Dan Glasel
Engineer, Kevin Sullivan
Associate, David Gandarillas
Chief Scientist, Frank Barone
Contracts Manager, Natalya Gnyp
Training Manager, Susan Missenheim
Electrical Engineer, Jenny Maung
Software Engineer, John Morgan

LOCATIONS

HQ: DHPC TECHNOLOGIES, INC.
10 WODBRDGE CTR DR STE 65, WOODBRIDGE, NJ
07095
Phone: 732 791-5400
Web: WWW.DHPCTECH.COM

HISTORICAL FINANCIALS

Company Type: Private

Income Statement				FYE: May 11
	REVENUE ($ mil.)	NET INCOME ($ mil.)	NET PROFIT MARGIN	EMPLOYEES
05/17*	38,584	1,320	3.4%	150
12/09	11	1	9.0%	—
12/07	6	1	29.2%	—
06/06	1,726	0	0.0%	—
Annual Growth	32.6%	179.9%	—	—

*Fiscal year change

Dick's Sporting Goods, Inc

Dick's Sporting Goods sells a full range of sports and outdoor merchandise from A (adidas cleats) to Y (Yeti coolers). The company's some 850 namesake stores across the US offers sporting goods apparel and footwear and accessories through its in-store services and specialty shop-in-shops for leisure pursuits ranging from football golf and cycling to hunting and climbing. In addition to well-known brand names Dick's carries exclusive brands such as Walter Hagen Second Skin and Top-Flite. The company also operates about 95 Golf Galaxy and more than 25 Field & Stream stores as well as associated e-commerce sites.

Operations

Dick's reports through three primary merchandise categories: hardlines apparel and footwear. Hardlines which includes equipment and gear is the largest segment and accounts for about 45% of sales. Apparel and footwear brings in some 35% and over 20% respectively.

The company purchases merchandise from approximately 1200 vendors including Nike (its largest) which represents more than 20% of the total. Beyond Nike and other well-known national and international brands it sells products under its private-label brands such as Field & Stream Fit-

ness Gear Lady Hagen and Quest. Dick's own brands contribute about 15% of sales.

Geographic Reach

Headquartered in Coraopolis Pennsylvania Dick also has a total of about 860 stores in 45-plus US states; its largest markets are California Florida New York North Carolina Ohio Pennsylvania and Texas which together account for more than 40% of total stores.

It also has distribution centers in Goodyear Arizona; Atlanta Georgia; Plainfield Indiana; Conklin New York; and Smithton Pennsylvania and a customer support center in Coraopolis Pennsylvania.

Sales and Marketing

Dick offers their products to athletes through their network of retail stores and e-commerce sites.

The company is focused on developing its omnichannel offering designed to serve customers however they prefer to shop — in stores online or through a combination of both.

It markets its products through traditional channels such as newspaper direct mail and seasonal use of local and national television and radio but is increasingly moving toward digital and personalized appeals enabled by its customer marketing database and ScoreCard loyalty program. In 2019 the company launched ScoreCard Gold an enhancement to their loyalty program targeting top-tier athletes.

Dick's advertising expenses were $339 million $322 million and $330 million for 2019 2018 and 2017 respectively.

Financial Performance

Net sales increased 4% in fiscal 2019 to $8.8 billion from $8.4 billion in fiscal 2018 due primarily to a $305.2 million or 4% increase in consolidated same store sales.

The company's net income decreased by $3.6 million to $297.5 million in 2019 compared to $319.9 million in 2018. The fall was due to the increase on both costs of goods sold and pre-opening expenses.

Cash held by the company at the end of fiscal 2019 decreased by $44.3 million to $69.3 million compared to $113.7 million in fiscal 2018. Cash provided by operations was $404.6 million while cash used for investing and financing activities were $129.3 million and $319.7 million respectively.

Strategy

The key elements of their business strategy are: Focus on their Athletes; Authentic Sporting Goods Retailer; Drive Omni-channel Growth; Differentiating DICK'S Sporting Goods; and Investing in Youth Sports.

DICK's key partners invest in their stores to showcase their brands. The company carry a wide variety of well-known brands including adidas Asics Brooks Callaway Golf Columbia Easton Nike Patagonia TaylorMade The North Face Titleist Under Armour and Yeti. DICK seek to leverage their partnerships to offer authenticity and credibility to their customers while differentiating ourselves from their competitors. The company's brand partnerships also provide them with access to exclusive products and allow them to differentiate their athletes' shopping experience through initiatives such as their brand shops which provide the company's athletes with a wider and deeper selection of products from key brands.

Company Background

Dick's was founded in 1948 when Dick Stack father of company chairman and CEO Edward Stack opened a bait and tackle shop. Edward joined the business full-time in 1977 and became CEO in 1984 when the company only had two locations.

In 1999 the company changed its name from Dick's Clothing and Sporting Goods to Dick's Sporting Goods. It went public in 2002.

EXECUTIVES

V Pres-controller, Oliver Joseph
Chairman And Ceo, Edward W. (Ed) Stack, age 65, $1,000,000 total compensation
Cto, Paul J. Gaffney, age 49
Vp Treasurer And Controller, Lee J. Belitsky, age 59, $541,983 total compensation
President, Lauren R. Hobart, age 51, $520,000 total compensation
Evp And Chief Merchant, Keri Jones
Svp Information Technology And Cio, Kurt J. Schnieders
Evp And Chief Strategy Officer, Michele B. Willoughby, age 54, $538,024 total compensation
Svp Operations, Don Germano
Executive Vice President Global Merchandising, John Duken
Regional Vice President, Tom Mcalorum
Vice President Business Systems And Procurement, Miles Mewhertre
Regional Vice President, Dave Shappee
Vice President Controller And Treasurer, Joe Oliver
Vice President Retail Technology, David Lammers
Senior Vice President Retail Operations, George Hill
Senior Vice President Operations, Donald Germano
Senior Vice President Supply Chain, George Giacobbe
Vice President Total Rewards, Todd Lombardi
Vice President Of Store Planning Construction And Purchasing, Scott Blyze
Senior Vice President Chief Accounting Officer, Joseph Oliver
Vp Of Technology Services, Greg White
Vice President Of Logistics And Vendor Relations, Terri Seagroatt
Vp Strategy And Innovation, Ryan Eckel
Vice President Retail Technology, Dave Lammers
Vp Tax, Todd Hipwell
Regional Vice President, John Dell'angelo
Vice President Of Marketing, Tom Hassett
Svp General Counsel And Secretary, John Hayes
Vice President Customer Innovation Technology, Rafeh Massod
Vice President Of Product Development Softlines, Meredith Laginess
Vice President Of Marketing, Thomas Hassett
Svp Product Development And Design, Nina Barjesteh
Vp Data Science Analytics And Crm, Vimal Kohli
Vice President Application Development, Bob Griffith
Vice Chairman, William J. (Bill) Colombo, age 64
Treasurer, Moussa Coulibaly
Auditors: DELOITTE & TOUCHE LLP

LOCATIONS

HQ: Dick's Sporting Goods, Inc
345 Court Street, Coraopolis, PA 15108
Phone: 724 273-3400
Web: www.DICKS.com

2018 Locations

	No.
California	67
Pennsylvania	52
Texas	53
Florida	54
Ohio	50
New York	49
North Carolina	42
Virginia	34
Illinois	34
Michigan	28
Georgia	24
Indiana	21
Massachusetts	21
New Jersey	22
Tennessee	20
Other states	288
Total	**858**

PRODUCTS/OPERATIONS

2018 Sales

	% of total
Hardlines	43
Apparel	35
Footwear	20
Other	2
Total	**100**

Selected Categories

Archery
Backpacking
Baseball
Basketball
Boating
Bowling
Camping
Cycling
Exercise
Fishing
Football
Golf
Hockey (ice and roller)
Hunting
In-line skating
Lacrosse
Optics/telescopes
Paintball
Racquetball/squash
Running
Skateboarding
Snow sports
Soccer
Tennis
Volleyball
Water sports

COMPETITORS

Academy Sports	Hibbett Sports
Amazon.com	L.L. Bean
Big 5	REI
Cabela's	Sportsman's Warehouse
Costco Wholesale	Target Corporation
Finish Line	Wal-Mart
Foot Locker	Zumiez

HISTORICAL FINANCIALS

Company Type: Public

Income Statement

FYE: February 1

	REVENUE ($ mil.)	NET INCOME ($ mil.)	NET PROFIT MARGIN	EMPLOYEES
02/20	8,750	297	3.4%	41,600
02/19	8,436	319	3.8%	40,700
02/18*	8,590	323	3.8%	45,200
01/17	7,921	287	3.6%	40,500
01/16	7,270	330	4.5%	37,200
Annual Growth	**4.7%**	**(2.6%)**	—	**2.8%**

*Fiscal year change

2020 Year-End Financials

Debt ratio: 3.38%	No. of shares (mil.): 83
Return on equity: 16.41%	Dividends
Cash ($ mil.): 69	Yield: 0.0%
Current ratio: 1.16	Payout: 32.9%
Long-term debt ($ mil.): 224	Market value ($ mil.): 3,695

	STOCK PRICE ($) FY Close	P/E High/Low		PER SHARE ($) Earnings	Dividends	Book Value
02/20	44.23	15	9	3.34	1.10	20.73
02/19	35.25	12	9	3.24	0.90	20.29
02/18*	31.49	18	8	3.01	0.68	18.84
01/17	51.31	24	14	2.56	0.61	17.49
01/16	39.08	21	12	2.83	0.55	16.01
Annual Growth	**3.1%**	—	—	**4.2%**	**18.9%**	**6.7%**

*Fiscal year change

DIGNITY HEALTH

Dignity Health has steadily grown to become the hospital provider in the state of California and the fifth-largest health system in the US. The not-for-profit health care provider operates a network of more than 40 cute care hospitals and 400-plus care-centers including neighborhood hospitals urgent care surgery and imaging centers home health and primary care clinics located in California Arizona and Nevada. Dignity Health is the official health care provider of the San Francisco Giants. It has more than 10000 active physicians. In 2019 Dignity Health merged with Denver-based hospital group Catholic Health Initiatives to create CommonSpirit Health the largest not-for-profit health system in the US.

Operations

Dignity Health offers inpatient outpatient sub-acute and home health care services as well as physician services through affiliates including Dignity Health Medical Foundation. Through another affiliate U.S. HealthWorks Dignity Health provides occupational health and urgent care services in about 20 additional states.

Geographic Reach

Dignity Health operates some 40 hospitals urgent care centers clinics emergency rooms and specialty care centers in California Nevada and Arizona. It has more than 65 facilities in California approximately 15 in Arizona and less than 5 in Nevada. Its headquarters is located in San Francisco California.

Sales and Marketing

Dignity Health serves all communities with physical mental and spiritual needs.

Strategy

Although Dignity Health combined with Catholic Health Initiatives in 2019 to become part of the larger CommonSpirit Health system it continues to pursue its own strategic goals. Those include improving quality of care in a just work environment implementing clinical and administrative changes to cut costs and expanding operations in existing markets and new markets.

Mergers and Acquisitions

After years of discussions Dignity Health and Catholic Health Initiatives merged in early 2019. The combined health system named CommonSpirit Health and with more than 140 hospitals in nearly 20 states is the largest not-for-profit hospital system in the US. The size of the new system allows it to provide expanded care to patients through such methods as virtual appointments a broader range of clinical programs and advanced technologies. The new organization is headquartered in Chicago. The group's hospitals continue to operate under their existing names.

Company Background

Dignity Health traces its roots to 1857. The Sisters of Mercy Catholic order was established in Dublin in 1831. In the 1850s eight Sisters arrived in San Francisco and began caring for residents with cholera typhoid and influenza. They established St. Mary's Hospital now that city's oldest continuously operating hospital. The order merged operations with another community of Sisters of Mercy in 1986 to create Catholic Healthcare West. The combined system had one retirement home and 10 hospitals throughout California.

The system changed its name to Dignity Health in early 2012 as part of a governance restructuring program. While the firm remained a not-for-profit organization with Catholic roots and its Catholic hospitals continued to be sponsored by their founding congregations (and governed by the Catholic health care directives) the parent organi-

zation itself was no longer an official ministry of the Catholic church. In 2019 Dignity Health joined forces with Catholic Health Initiatives to create CommonSpirit Health the nation's largest not-for-profit health system.

HISTORY

Dignity Health formerly Catholic Healthcare West (CHW) traces its roots to 1857 when the Sisters of Mercy founded St. Mary's Hospital in San Francisco. The order expanded in that area and in 1986 two different communities of the Sisters of Mercy merged their hospitals into an organization with one retirement home and 10 hospitals from the Bay Area to San Diego. Declining membership in Roman Catholic religious orders combined with consolidation in the field led the orders to see merger as their only route to survival.

CHW continued to add facilities including AMI Community Hospital in Santa Cruz California in 1990. Since CHW already owned the area's only other acute care hospital Dominican Santa Cruz Hospital CHW in 1993 was ordered not to acquire any more acute care hospitals in Santa Cruz County without FTC approval.

As the trend to managed care became a stampede in the 1990s CHW moved more into preventive care and began reigning in costs through productivity improvement plans. It continued to add hospitals including tax-supported institutions trying to compete with national for-profit systems.

The network increased its medical clout in 1994 by allying with San Diego-based Scripps one of the state's largest HMO systems. In 1995 the Daughters of Charity Province of the West realigned its six-hospital operation with CHW. The next year the Dominican Sisters (California) the Dominican Sisters of St. Catherine of Siena (Wisconsin) and the Sisters of Charity of the Incarnate Word allied their California hospitals with CHW. New community hospitals included Bakersfield Memorial Sierra Nevada Memorial (Grass Valley) Sequoia Hospital (Redwood City) and Woodland Healthcare.

Charity and cost-consciousness clashed in 1996 when union members staged a walkout to protest nonunion outsourcing of vocational nursing housekeeping and kitchen jobs. This dispute was settled but CHW continued to be a target for union organizers with a bitter battle against the Service Employees International Union (SEIU) starting in 1998.

The year 2000 brought CHW more problems with labor relations: SEIU argued that the organization was resistant to unionization. Continued losses led the organization to implement major restructuring the following year as its 10 regional divisions were consolidated into four.

The company parted ways with one of its sponsoring organizations the Franciscan Sisters of the Sacred Heart of Frankfort Illinois in 2003. The sponsorship ended when CHW closed St. Francis Medical Center of Santa Barbara. However the hospital operator that fiscal year posted its first operating profit in seven years.

The company changed its name from Catholic Healthcare West (CHW) to Dignity Health in early 2012 as part of a governance restructuring program. While the firm remained a not-for-profit organization with Catholic roots and its Catholic hospitals continued to be sponsored by their founding congregations (and governed by the Catholic health care directives) the parent organization itself was no longer an official ministry of the Catholic church.

The company's rebranding and restructuring aimed to give it more flexibility to pursue its growth strategy of widening its presence into additional regions of the US while lowering the overall cost of care (a desire of most large hospital operators as the US government works to reform its ailing health system). At the time of the governance shift Dignity Health operated 25 Catholic hospitals and 15 non-Catholic hospitals.

EXECUTIVES

Evp Sponsorship Mission Integration And Philanthropy, Bernita McTernan
President And Ceo, Lloyd H. Dean
Evp And Chief Human Resources Officer, Darryl L. Robinson
Evp And Chief Administrative Officer, Elizabeth Shih
Sevp And Coo, Marvin O'Quinn
Sevp And Cfo, Daniel J. Morissette
Sevp And Chief Strategy Officer, Charles P. Francis
Evp And Cio, Deanna L. Wise
Evp And Chief Medical Officer, Robert L. Wiebe
Evp And General Counsel, Rick Grossman
Evp Sponsorship And Mission Integration, Elizabeth Keith
Medical Director Health Informatics, David Camitta
Director Of Him, Swaran Dwarka
Senior Vice President And Chief Strategy Officer, Charlie Francis
Vice President Human Resources Southern California West Service Area, Ed Gonzales
Vice President Ambulatory Services, Margie Roper
Senior Vice President Of Philanthropy, Fred Najjar
Director Of Radiology, Richard Siegel
Senior Vice President Of Operations For Greater Sacramento Area, Laurie Harting
Vice President Strategy And Business Development, Susan Macmillan
Director Of Pharmacy, Jason Glick
Vice President Employee And Labor Relations, Scott Fuller
Medical Director, Christina Kwasnica
Senior Vice President Of Operations For Bay Area Service Area, Todd Strumwasser
Medical Director, Javier Cardenas
Vice President Of Philanthropy, Jessa Brooks
Chairman, Caretha Coleman
Vice Chair, Judy Carle
Auditors: DELOITTE & TOUCHE LLP SAN FRA

LOCATIONS

HQ: DIGNITY HEALTH
185 BERRY ST STE 300, SAN FRANCISCO, CA 941071773
Phone: 415 438-5500
Web: WWW.DIGNITYHEALTH.ORG

Selected Facilities
Arizona
Barrow Neurological Institute (Phoenix)
Chandler Regional Medical Center
Mercy Gilbert Medical Center
St. Joseph's Hospital and Medical Center (Phoenix)
California
Arroyo Grande Community Hospital
Bakersfield Memorial Hospital
California Hospital Medical Center (Los Angeles)
Community Hospital of San Bernardino
Dominican Hospital (Santa Cruz)
French Hospital Medical Center (San Luis Obispo)
Glendale Memorial Hospital and Health Center
Marian Medical Center (Santa Maria)
Mark Twain St. Joseph's Hospital (San Andreas)
Mercy General Hospital (Sacramento)
Mercy Hospital of Bakersfield
Mercy Hospital of Folsom
Mercy Medical Center Merced Community Campus
Mercy Medical Center Merced Dominican Campus
Mercy Medical Center Mt. Shasta
Mercy Medical Center Redding
Mercy San Juan Medical Center (Carmichael)
Mercy Southwest Hospital (Bakersfield)
Methodist Hospital of Sacramento
Northridge Hospital Medical Center

Oak Valley Hospital (Oakdale)
Saint Francis Memorial Hospital (San Francisco)
Sequoia Hospital (Redwood City)
Sierra Nevada Memorial Hospital (Grass Valley)
St. Bernardine Medical Center (San Bernardino)
St. Elizabeth Community Hospital (Red Bluff)
St. John's Pleasant Valley Hospital (Camarillo)
St. John's Regional Medical Center (Oxnard)
St. Joseph's Behavioral Health Center (Stockton)
St. Joseph's Medical Center (Stockton)
St. Mary Medical Center (Long Beach)
St. Mary's Medical Center (San Francisco)
Woodland Healthcare
Nevada
St. Rose Dominican Hospital Rose de Lima Campus (Henderson)
St. Rose Dominican Hospital San Martí;n Campus (Las Vegas)
St. Rose Dominican Hospital Siena Campus (Henderson)

PRODUCTS/OPERATIONS

Sponsoring Organizations
Congregation of the Dominican Sisters of St. Catherine of Siena of Kenosha (Kenosha Wisconsin)
Congregation of the Sisters of Charity of the Incarnate Word (Houston Texas)
Sisters of Mercy of the Americas West Midwest Community (Omaha Nebraska; formerly Auburn Regional Community of the Sisters of Mercy and Burlingame Regional Community of the Sisters of Mercy in California)
Sisters of St. Dominic Congregation of the Most Holy Rosary (Adrian Michigan)
Sisters of St. Francis of Penance and Christian Charity St. Francis Province (Redwood City California)
Sisters of the Third Order of St. Dominic Congregation of the Most Holy Name (San Rafael California)

COMPETITORS

Adventist Health System West
Banner Health
Community Health Systems
Community Hospital of the Monterey Peninsula
Ensign Group
HCA
John C. Lincoln Health Network
John Muir Health
Loma Linda University Medical Center
Memorial Health Services
Prospect Medical
Providence St. Joseph Health
Salinas Valley Memorial
Shasta Regional Medical Center
Stanford Health Care
Sutter Health
Tenet Healthcare
UCSF Medical
Universal Health Services
VITAS Healthcare

HISTORICAL FINANCIALS

Company Type: Private

Income Statement   FYE: June 30

	REVENUE ($ mil.)	NET INCOME ($ mil.)	NET PROFIT MARGIN	EMPLOYEES
06/09	8,957	(799)	—	55,494
06/08	8,401	169	2.0%	—
Annual Growth	6.6%	—	—	—

Dime Community Bancshares Inc (New)

The Bridgehampton National Bank which operates 40 branches on primary market areas of Suffolk and Nassau Counties on Long Island and the New York City boroughs. Founded in 1910 the bank offers traditional deposit services to area individuals small businesses and municipalities including savings money market accounts and CDs. Deposits are invested primarily in mortgages which account for some 80% of the bank's loan portfolio. Title insurance services are available through bank subsidiary Bridge Abstract. In addition it offers merchant credit and debit card ATMs cash management services and individual retirement accounts through Bridge Financial Services LLC. Bridge Bancorp bought Hamptons State Bank in 2011 to fortify its presence on Long Island.

Operations
The company offers a full service of commercial and consumer banking business including accepting time savings and demand deposits. These deposits together with funds generated from operations and borrowings are invested primarily in: commercial real estate loans; multi-family mortgage loans; residential mortgage loans; secured and unsecured commercial and consumer loans and home equity loans just to name a few.

It also provides the Certificate of Deposit Account Registry Service (CDARS) and Insured Cash Sweep (ICS) programs. In addition it offers merchant credit and debit card processing automated teller machines cash management services lockbox processing online banking services remote deposit capture safe deposit boxes and individual retirement accounts as well as investment services through Bridge Financial Services LLC which offers a full range of investment products and services through a third-party broker dealer. Furthermore bank operations also include Bridge Abstract LLC (Bridge Abstract) a wholly-owned subsidiary of BNB Bank which is a broker of title insurance services.

Geographic Reach
New York-based Bridge Bancorp's market area is Suffolk County in eastern Long Island. It operates 40 branch locations in the primary market areas of Suffolk and Nassau Counties on Long Island and the New York City boroughs including about 35 in Suffolk and Nassau Counties two in Queens and two in Manhattan. It has six branches located in Montauk Southold Westhampton Beach Southampton Village East Hampton Village and Mattituck; and one drive-up facility located in Sag Harbor.

Sales and Marketing
The company engages in a full service commercial and consumer banking business including accepting time savings and demand deposits from the consumers businesses and local municipalities in its market area. The customer base is comprised principally of small businesses municipal relationships and consumer relationships.

Marketing and advertising increased to $4.7 million in 2019 compared to $4.6 million in 2018. In 2017 marketing and advertising got $4.7 million.

Financial Performance
The company had a net interest income of $136.5 million a 1% increase from the previous year.

Net income for 2019 was $51.7 million a 32% increase from the previous year. The increase is primarily attributable to the higher sales volume for the year.

The company's cash at the end of 2019 was $117.2 million. Operating activities generated $70.0 million while investing activities used $352.6 million mainly for net increase in loans. Financing activities generated $104.5 million.

Strategy

The company established five strategic objectives: Acquiring new customers in growth markets; Building new sales and marketing disciplines; Deepening customer relationships; Expanding use of automation; and improving talent management.

Company Background

The Bank was established in 1910 and is headquartered in Bridgehampton New York. In May 2011 it acquired HSB which increased its presence in an existing market with a branch located in the Village of Southampton. In 2014 it acquired FNBNY Bancorp and its wholly-owned subsidiary the First National Bank of New York.

EXECUTIVES

President And Ceo, Kevin M. O'Connor, age 57, $300,000 total compensation

Svp And Chief Lending Officer Bridgehampton National Bank, Kevin L. Santacroce, $180,000 total compensation

Svp And Cio Bridgehampton National Bank, Thomas H. Simson, $175,000 total compensation

President Ceo And Director, Kevin OConnor

Chief Financial Officer, Adam Hall

Evp And Chief Retail Banking Officer, James J. Manseau, $235,000 total compensation

Senior Vice President And Regional Manager, Ralph Meyer

Vice Chairman, Dennis A. Suskind, age 77

Chairman, Marcia Z. Hefter, age 76

Chief Financial Officer Executive Vice President Treasurer, John Mccaffery

Board Member, Christian Yegen

Board Member, Daniel Rubin

Auditors: Crowe LLP

LOCATIONS

HQ: Dime Community Bancshares Inc (New)
2200 Montauk Highway, Bridgehampton, NY 11932
Phone: 631 537-1000
Web: www.bridgenb.com

COMPETITORS

Bank of America	JPMorgan Chase
Bank of New York Mellon	Suffolk Bancorp

HISTORICAL FINANCIALS

Company Type: Public

Income Statement				FYE: December 31
	ASSETS ($ mil.)	NET INCOME ($ mil.)	INCOME AS % OF ASSETS	EMPLOYEES
12/19	4,921	51	1.1%	496
12/18	4,700	39	0.8%	473
12/17	4,430	20	0.5%	480
12/16	4,054	35	0.9%	477
12/15	3,781	21	0.6%	433
Annual Growth	6.8%	25.1%	—	3.5%

2019 Year-End Financials

Debt ratio: 1.60%	No. of shares (mil.): 19
Return on equity: 10.87%	Dividends
Cash ($ mil.): 117	Yield: 2.7%
Current ratio: —	Payout: 35.5%
Long-term debt ($ mil.): —	Market value ($ mil.): 665

	STOCK PRICE ($) FY Close	P/E High/Low	PER SHARE ($) Earnings	Dividends	Book Value
12/19	33.53	13 10	2.59	0.92	25.06
12/18	25.49	19 12	1.97	0.92	22.93
12/17	35.00	37 29	1.04	0.92	21.78
12/16	37.90	19 13	2.00	0.92	21.36
12/15	30.43	22 17	1.43	0.92	19.62
Annual Growth	2.5%	— —	16.0%	(0.0%)	6.3%

Discover Financial Services

Discover Financial Services is best known for issuing Discover-brand credit cards. The company provides direct banking products and services and payment services through their subsidiaries. They offer credit card loans private student loans personal loans home equity loans and deposit products. Discover also licenses Diners Club which processes transactions for Discover-branded credit and debit cards provides payment transaction processing and settlement services. But there's more to this business than just plastic. The company also offers direct banking services makes student and personal loans and runs the PULSE Network ATM system. Discover spun off from Morgan Stanley in 2007.

Operations

Discover Financial Services has two operating segments: Direct Banking and Payment Services.

Direct Banking is the largest accounting for almost all of its revenue. It includes Discover-branded credit cards issued to individuals and small businesses as well as other consumer products and services such as private student loans personal loans home loans prepaid cards and other consumer lending and deposit products.

The company's smaller Payment Services segment includes the PULSE network Diners Club and Network Partners businesses. The PULSE network of ATMs and point-of-sale (POS) terminals is accessible by cardholders served by around 4100 financial institutions in the US; it also provides access to cash from about 2.1 million ATMs in about 135 countries. The Diners Club business generates revenues from royalties that licensees (generally financial institutions) pay to issue Diners Club branded cards to its customers. Discover's Network Partners are financial institutions networks and commercial service providers that pay the company to process payments on the Discover network.

Discover makes more than 80% of its money from net interest income particularly from credit card loans (which account for nearly 70% of interest income). Other loans make up some 15% of interest income. The rest of its total revenue comes from net discounts and interchanges (about 10%) investment securities and other interest income protection products loan fees transaction processing and other non-recurring income sources.

Geographic Reach

More than 30% of Riverwoods Illinois-based Discover Financial Services' credit card loans are tied to customers across California Texas New York and Florida. Furthermore more than 30% of the company's personal student and purchase credit-impaired (PCI) loans are originated in New York California Pennsylvania and Illinois.

Sales and Marketing

Discover markets its credit cards and other loan products through digital channels such as direct mail internet media advertising and merchant or partner relationships.

Discover also offer rewards such as Cashback Bonus which allows their cardmembers to redeem any amount based on their spending.

The company's advertising spend totaled $264 million in 2019 $258 million in 2018 and $219 million in 2017.

Financial Performance

Like many in its industry Discover Financial Services has enjoyed several years of growth thanks to increased spending on credit and debit cards and higher credit card balances. Since 2015 the company has expanded its revenue by about a quarter. Net income had a massive gain in 2019 resulted in five-year growth of 30 %.

Discover's revenue increased 7% to $11.5 billion in 2019 compared with the previous year. Revenue from its Direct Banking segment increased 9% due to loan growth higher yields on credit card loans. Growth of 12% in the Payment Services segment was attributed to higher transaction volume across several of its service channels.

The company posted a net income of $3 billion in 2019 a 7% increase from the prior year. The increase was driven by the 10% increase in its interest income.

Discover's cash cash equivalents and restricted cash for 2019 was $7 billion. Operations contributed $6.2 billion while investing activities used $15.3 billion mainly for net principal disbursed on loans originated for investment as well as for purchases of available-for-sale investment securities. Financing activities provided $897 million primarily from a net increase in deposits and proceeds from issuance of securitized debt.

Strategy

In order to attract and retain customers and merchants Discover continues to develop new programs features and benefits and market them through a variety of channels. Marketing efforts may promote no annual fee Cashback Bonus FICO Credit Score for free Freeze it Social Security Number Alerts New Account Alerts balance transfer offers and other rewards programs. Through the development of a large prospect database use of credit bureau data and use of a customer contact strategy and management system they continuously develop their modeling and customer engagement capabilities which helps optimize product pricing and channel selection. The company also leverage strategic partnerships and sponsorship properties such as the NHL and the Big Ten Conference to help drive loan growth.

To remain organizationally effective Discover aims to effectively empower integrate and deploy their management and operational resources and incorporate global and local business regulatory and consumer perspectives into their decisions and processes. In order to execute on their objective to be the leading consumer bank and payments partner they will seek to develop and implement innovative and efficient technology solutions and marketing initiatives while effectively managing legal regulatory compliance security operational and other risks as well as expenses. Examples include the implementation of a broader rollout of their checking product and a structure for a more competitive global network business.

Company Background

Discover Financial Services spun off from Morgan Stanley in 2007.

To gain access to federal funds made available through the Troubled Asset Relief Program (TARP) Discover Financial converted to a bank holding company in 2009. It received $1.2 billion from the program which it repaid the following year.

Discover boosted its lending operations in 2010 with its $600 million purchase of Citibank's 80% stake in Student Loan Corporation. It also acquired a $4.2 billion portfolio of private student loans from Citibank. The company later divested its portfolio of federal student loans after the government overhauled its lending program and became the sole provider of government-backed student loans in 2010. The following year Discover bought another $2.5 billion in student loans from Citibank.

In 2012 Discover issued its first cards outside the US (in Ecuador) and entered into an alliance with National Payments Corporation to increase network acceptance in India.

EXECUTIVES

Chairman And Ceo, David W. Nelms, $1,000,000 total compensation
President And Coo, Roger C. Hochschild, $800,000 total compensation
Evp And Cfo, R. Mark Graf, $650,000 total compensation
Evp And President Payment Services, Diane E. Offereins, $650,000 total compensation
Evp And President Consumer Banking, Carlos M. Minetti, $650,000 total compensation
Evp General Counsel And Secretary, Kelly McNamara Corley
Evp And President Credit And Card Operations, James V. Panzarino
Evp And Cio, Glenn P. Schneider
Evp And Chief Risk Officer, Brian D. Hughes
Svp And Chief Marketing Officer, Julie A. Loeger
Vice President Infrastructure Services, Larry Holstein
Vice President Business Development, Reese Bogle
Vice President Technology Products, Joseph Bonefas
Vice President Enterprise Computing Services, Lut Calcote
Vice President Of Information Technology Audit, Vesela Zlateva
Vice President Deposit Products, Dan Matysik
Vice President Marketing And Core Processes, Jack Garland
Vice President Information Technology, Lisa Koehler
Vice President Enterprise Compliance Programs, Katherine Licup
Vice President Discover Network Strategic Development, Joe Hurley
Vice President External Reporting And Accounting Policy, Shifra Kolsky
Vice President Cardmember Assistance, Tracy Hedrick
Vice President Application Development Shared Services, Amy Hernandez
Executive Assistant Executive Vice President, Kim Schneider
Vice President Of Marketing, Mark Scarborough
Vice President, Charles Barsky
Vice President Corporate Planning, Steve Trussell
Senior Vice President Credit And Decision Management, Dan Capozzi
Vice President Compliance, Layne Bussell
Vice President Discover Network Strategic Development, Allison Parker
Vice President And Assistant General Counsel Litigation, Sherri Nagel
Vice President Network Services, Rob Tourt
Vice President, Dave Sutter
Vice President Of Purchasing, Gerry Fitzmaurice
Vice President Digital Marketing, Szabolcs Paldy
Vice President, Shilpa Wadhera
Vice President, Philip Law
Vp And Chief Credit Officer Student Loans, Robert Zelikson

Vp Of Operations Center, Keith Carroll
Vice President, Alisa Ellis
Vice President And Head Us Government Relations, Richard Santoro
Vice President Global Acceptance, Curtis Chia
Vice President Investor Relations, Timothy Schmidt
Vice President Customer Relations, Dale Southerland
Assistant Treasurer, Bill Franklin
Board Member, Jeffrey Aronin
Board Member, Mary Bush
Board Member, Candace Duncan
Board Member, Cynthia Glassman
Board Member, Joseph Eazor
Board Member, Mark Thierer
Auditors: Deloitte & Touche LLP

LOCATIONS

HQ: Discover Financial Services
2500 Lake Cook Road, Riverwoods, IL 60015
Phone: 224 405-0900
Web: www.discover.com

PRODUCTS/OPERATIONS

2018 Sales

	$ mil.	% of total
Direct banking	12,537	98
Payment services	311	2
Total	**12,848**	**100**

2018 Sales

	$ mil.	% of total
Interest		
Credit card loans	8,835	69
Other loans	1,726	14
Investment securities	40	0
Other	292	2
Non-interest		
Net discount & interchange revenue	1,074	8
Loan fees	402	3
Protection products	204	2
Transaction processing	178	1
Other	97	1
Total	**12,848**	**100**

COMPETITORS

Ally Financial	JPMorgan Chase
American Express	MasterCard
Bank of America	PNC Financial
Barclays Bank Delaware	Sallie Mae
Capital One	USAA
Citigroup	Visa Inc
First Data	Wells Fargo

HISTORICAL FINANCIALS

Company Type: Public

Income Statement

FYE: December 31

	ASSETS ($ mil.)	NET INCOME ($ mil.)	INCOME AS % OF ASSETS	EMPLOYEES
12/19	113,996	2,957	2.6%	17,200
12/18	109,553	2,742	2.5%	16,600
12/17	100,087	2,099	2.1%	16,500
12/16	92,308	2,393	2.6%	15,549
12/15	86,936	2,297	2.6%	15,036
Annual Growth	**7.0%**	**6.5%**	**—**	**3.4%**

2019 Year-End Financials

Debt ratio: 22.55%	No. of shares (mil.): 310
Return on equity: 25.73%	Dividends
Cash ($ mil.): 6,924	Yield: 1.9%
Current ratio: —	Payout: 18.9%
Long-term debt ($ mil.): —	Market value ($ mil.): 26,308

	STOCK PRICE ($) FY Close	P/E High/Low		PER SHARE ($) Earnings	Dividends	Book Value
12/19	84.82	10	6	9.08	1.68	38.24
12/18	58.98	10	7	7.79	1.50	33.58
12/17	76.92	14	11	5.42	1.30	30.43
12/16	72.09	13	7	5.77	1.16	29.13
12/15	53.62	13	10	5.13	1.08	26.74
Annual Growth	**12.1%**	**—**	**—**	**15.3%**	**11.7%**	**9.4%**

Discovery Inc

The company is a provider of non-fiction TV programming and it tends to be culturally neutral and maintains its relevance for an extended period of time. with about 20 cable TV networks that together reach approximately 4 billion subscribers in more than 220 countries and territories in 50 languages. Properties include the Discovery Channel HGTV Food Network TLC Animal Planet Investigation Discovery Travel Channel Science Channel and MotorTrend (previously known as Velocity domestically and currently known as Turbo in most international countries). Discovery also operates stream mobile devices video on demand ("VOD") and broadband channels. The US accounts for more than 60% of revenue.

HISTORY

John Hendricks a history graduate who wanted to expand the presence of educational programming on TV founded Cable Educational Network in 1982. Three years later he introduced the Discovery Channel. Devoted entirely to documentaries and nature shows the channel premiered in 156000 US homes. After dodging bankruptcy (it had $5000 cash and $1 million in debt to the BBC) within a year the Discovery Channel had 7 million subscribers and a host of new investors including Cox Communications and TCI (later AT&T Broadband). It expanded its programming from 12 hours to 18 hours a day in 1987.

Discovery continued to attract subscribers reaching more than 32 million by 1988. The next year it launched Discovery Channel Europe to more than 200000 homes in the UK and Scandinavia. The company began selling home videos in 1990 and entered the Israeli market. The following year Discovery Communications Inc. (DCI) was formed to house the company's operations and it bought The Learning Channel (TLC founded 1980). The company revamped TLC's programming and in 1992 introduced a daily six-hour commercial-free block of children's programs. The next year it introduced its first CD-ROM title In the Company of Whales based on the Discovery Channel documentary.

DCI increased its focus on international expansion in 1994 moving into Asia Latin America the Middle East North Africa Portugal and Spain. The next year the company introduced its website and began selling company merchandise such as CD-ROMs and videos. DCI solidified its move into the retail sector in 1996 with the acquisition of The Nature Company and Scientific Revolution chains (renamed Discovery Channel Store). Also that year it launched its third major cable channel Animal Planet.

The company continued expanding internationally throughout the mid-1990s establishing operations in Australia Canada India New Zealand and

South Korea (1995); Africa Brazil Germany and Italy (1996); and Japan and Turkey (1997). DCI also added to its stable of cable channels with the purchase of 70% of the Travel Channel from Paxson Communications (later ION Media Networks) in 1997. (It acquired the remaining 30% interest in 1999.) The company's 1997 original production "Titanic: Anatomy of a Disaster" attracted 3.2 million US households setting a network ratings record.

The following year DCI and the BBC launched Animal Planet in Asia through a joint venture and agreed to market and distribute new cable channel BBC America. It also bought CBS 's Eye on People renaming the channel Discovery People (DCI shut the channel down in 2000). DCI spent $330 million launching its new health and fitness channel Discovery Health in 1999 and formed partnerships with high-speed online service Road Runner (to provide interactive information and services to Road Runner customers) and Rosenbluth Travel (to provide vacation packages based on DCI programming).

DCI reorganized its Internet activities into one unit called Discovery.com in 2000 with plans to eventually take it public. Later that year the Discovery Channel set back-to-back records with the two highest-rated documentaries ever on cable "Raising the Mammoth" (10.1 million people) and "Walking With Dinosaurs" (10.7 million people). In 2001 the company cut about 50 jobs as part of a restructuring. Later that year Discovery Communications struck a three-year deal to lease time from NBC on Saturday mornings (paying $6 million per season) to show its Discovery Kids programs.

In 2002 the company launched a 24-hour high-definition television network called Discovery HD Theater. Two years later founder John Hendricks relinquished his CEO duties (he remained chairman). President Judy McHale replaced him.

DCI started off 2005 by rebranding its aviation-themed Discovery Wings channel as the Military Channel. Later that year former majority owner Liberty Media placed its stake in DCI into a new company called Discovery Holding which it then spun off to Liberty shareholders.

Early in 2007 former NBC Universal Cable executive David Zaslav was named CEO replacing McHale. DCI later bought out 25%-partner Cox Communications in exchange for $1.3 billion in cash along with such assets as the Travel Channel and Antenna Audio. It also began shuttering its chain of Discovery Channel Stores as part of a cost-cutting effort.

Joint venture partners Discovery Holding and Advance/Newhouse (an affiliate of Advance Publications) combined their stakes in Discovery Communications in 2008 spinning off DCI as a public company.

Over the next few years DCI worked diligently to launch new networks targeting a diverse selection of audience segments. In 2010 it rolled out The Hub a channel targeting kids ages 2-11. Another 50/50 joint venture with toy maker Hasbro The Hub offers programming based on many of Hasbro's popular brands including G.I. Joe Scrabble Tonka and Transformers.

In early 2011 the company helped launch OWN talk show host Oprah Winfrey's new network and 3net one of the first networks dedicated to providing 3D programming 24 hours a day.

EXECUTIVES

President Ceo And Director, David M. Zaslav, age 61, $3,000,000 total compensation

Group President Discovery Channel Animal Planet And Science Channel, Rich Ross, age 59

President Own: Oprah Winfrey Network And Harpo Studios, Erik Logan

Chief Commercial Officer, Paul (Guyardo) Guagliardo, age 56, $1,400,000 total compensation

Group President Investigation Discovery American Heroes Channel And Destination America, Henry S. Schleiff, age 71

Cto, John Honeycutt

President Discovery Networks International, Jean-Briac (JB) Perrette, $1,381,557 total compensation

President And Managing Director Discovery Networks Asia-pacific, Arthur Bastings

President And Ceo Discovery Education, Bill Goodwyn

President International Development Digital And Discovery Nordics, Michael (Mike) Lang, age 55

Chief Corporate Operations And Communications Officer, David C. Leavy

Chief Development Distribution And Legal Officer, Bruce L. Campbell, age 53, $1,544,423 total compensation

President And General Manager Tlc, Nancy Daniels

President And Managing Director Discovery Networks Latin America/u.s. Hispanic And Canada, Enrique R. (Henry) Mart nez

Chief Human Resources And Global Diversity Officer, Adria Alpert-Romm, age 65, $801,058 total compensation

President And Managing Director Discovery Networks Central & Eastern Europe Middle East And Africa, Kasia Kieli

Cfo, Gunnar Wiedenfels

Ceo Eurosport, Peter Hutton

President Domestic Distribution, Eric Phillips

President And Managing Director Discovery Networks Southern Europe, Marinella Soldi

President International Content Group, Susanna Dinnage

Vice President Operations And Prod Development Partnerships, Kevin Malone

Vice President Operations, Toni Herbert

Vice President Financial Planning And Analysis, Matthew Deprey

Executive Vice President Advertising Sales Mtv Networks Kids And Family Group, Jim Perry

Vice President Technology, Jim Boyle

Carrie D Storer Senior Vice President Human Resources And Compliance Legal, Carrie Storer

Senior Vice President Of Operations, Veronica Cajigas

Vice President, John Saag

Vice President, Michela Giorelli

Senior Vice President Investor Relations, Craig Felenstein

Senior Vice President Distribution, Meg Lowe

Senior Vice President Us Media Operations, Don Johnson

Vice President Strategy And Account Management, Todd Richards

Chairman, Robert J. (Bob) Miron, age 83

Auditors: PricewaterhouseCoopers LLP

LOCATIONS

HQ: Discovery Inc
  8403 Colesville Road, Silver Spring, MD 20910
Phone: 240 662-2000
Web: www.discoverycommunications.com

PRODUCTS/OPERATIONS

2017 Sales

	$ mil.	% of total
Distribution	3,474	51
Advertising	3,073	45
Other	326	4
Total	**6,873**	**100**

2017 Sales

	$ mil.	% of total
US networks	3,434	50
International networks	3,281	48
Education & other	158	2
Corporate & adjustments	(2)	-
Total	**6,873**	**100**

Selected Mergers and Acquisitions

FY2012
Revision3 ($30 million; San Francisco CA; digital video provider)

Selected Operations

Cable channels
  Animal Planet
  Discovery Channel
  Discovery Kids
  Investigation Discovery
  Planet Green
  Science Channel
  TLC (The Learning Channel)
Commerce and education
  Discovery Education
  DiscoveryStore.com
Business and Brands
U.S. Networks
Discovery Networks International
Discovery Education
Discovery Commerce
Discovery Digital Media
Revision3
Discovery Enterprises International
Discovery Studios

COMPETITORS

A&E Networks	NBCUniversal
AMC Networks	PBS
CBS Corp	Turner Broadcasting
Disney	Viacom
E! Entertainment Television	

HISTORICAL FINANCIALS

Company Type: Public

Income Statement

FYE: December 31

	REVENUE ($ mil.)	NET INCOME ($ mil.)	NET PROFIT MARGIN	EMPLOYEES
12/19	11,144	2,069	18.6%	9,200
12/18	10,553	594	5.6%	9,000
12/17	6,873	(337)	—	7,000
12/16	6,497	1,194	18.4%	7,000
12/15	6,394	1,034	16.2%	7,000
Annual Growth	**14.9%**	**18.9%**	**—**	**7.1%**

2019 Year-End Financials

Debt ratio: 45.71%   No. of shares (mil.): 525
Return on equity: 22.64%   Dividends
Cash ($ mil.): 1,552   Yield: —
Current ratio: 1.61   Payout: —
Long-term debt ($ mil.): 14,810   Market value ($ mil.): 17,189

	STOCK PRICE ($) FY Close	P/E High/Low		PER SHARE ($) Earnings	Dividends	Book Value
12/19	32.74	12	9	2.88	0.00	18.84
12/18	24.74	39	24	0.86	0.00	16.00
12/17	22.38	—	—	(0.59)	0.00	12.07
12/16	27.41	15	12	1.96	0.00	13.29
12/15	26.68	22	16	1.58	0.00	13.30
Annual Growth	**5.3%**	—	—	**16.2%**	**—**	**9.1%**

DISH Network Corp

DISH Network believes entertainment (and news and sports) is a dish best served from the sky and over the internet. The company is one of the biggest pay-TV providers in the US serving about 12 million household subscribers as well as hotels motels and other commercial accounts. Programming includes premium movies on-demand video service regional and specialty sports local and international channels and pay-per-view in addition to basic video programming. Its relatively Sling TV offering provides streaming video over the internet. DISH generates almost all sales in the US.

Operations

DISH Network's revenue comes from its satellite and streaming pay-TV subscriptions. The satellite service relies on satellite dishes that are set up on customers' structures (homes and commercial buildings) to receive signals. Signals reach those dishes from the 13 satellites that DISH owns or leases orbiting some 22300 miles above the equator. (DISH Network added another nine satellites in a deal with EchoStar.) The company also leases set-top boxes and video recorders to subscribers.

The Sling streaming service is transmitted over the internet and is geared to consumers who don't subscribe to cable or satellite services. Sling-branded pay-TV services consist of live streaming programming for US and international markets.

Among DISH Network's assets is a range of radio spectrum for wireless service.

Geographic Reach

While virtually all of DISH Network's revenue is from US customers the company gets a fraction of sales from Canada and Mexico. The company based in the Denver suburb of Englewood operates 10 call centers in about ten states. Its major digital broadcast operations facilities are in Cheyenne Wyoming and Gilbert Arizona.

Sales and Marketing

DISH Network gains new subscribers through third parties including national retailers and telecommunications firms local and regional electronics stores and small satellite retailers among other channels. Of its 12 million subscribers nearly 10 million are DISH customers and two million are Sling subscribers.

Financial Performance

The company's revenue dropped 6% to $12.8 billion in 2019 from 2018 primarily due to the fall on its subscriber-related revenue.

Net income fell to $1.4 billion in 2019 from $1.6 billion in 2018 primarily due to the fall on its revenue and also due to the presence of income tax provisions.

The holdings of cash and equivalents in DISH Network's coffers climbed to $2.5 billion in 2019 from $887.9 million in 2018. Operations provided $2.7 billion in 2019 while investing activities used $717.8 million and financing activities used $328.2 million.

Strategy

The company's Pay-TV business strategy is to be the best provider of video services in the United States by providing products with the best technology outstanding customer service and great value. DISH Network promotes its Pay-TV services as providing their subscribers with a better "price-to-value" relationship than those available from other subscription television service providers.

On July 26 2019 Dish Network entered into an Asset Purchase Agreement (the "APA") with T-Mobile US Inc. ("TMUS") and Sprint Corporation. Pursuant to the APA after the consummation of the Sprint-TMUS merger and at the closing of the transaction NTM will sell to the company and they will acquire from NTM certain assets and liabilities associated with the Prepaid Business for an aggregate purchase price of $1.4 billion.

As the pay-TV industry is mature the company's strategy has included an emphasis on acquiring and retaining higher quality subscribers even if it means that they will acquire and retain fewer overall subscribers.

Mergers and Acquisitions

In 2020 DISH announced that it has completed its $1.4 billion acquisition of Boost Mobile. With this purchase DISH officially enters the retail wireless market serving more than nine million customers. "Today we are proud to welcome hundreds of employees thousands of independent retailers and millions of customers to the DISH family" said Erik Carlson president and CEO DISH. "This marks an important milestone in DISH's evolution as a connectivity company. It positions us well as we continue to build out the first virtualized stand-alone 5G network in America."

In 2019 DISH Network Corporation and EchoStar Corporation announced that they have executed an agreement that will transfer certain EchoStar operations and other assets that comprise the company's Broadcast Satellite Service (BSS) Business including nine direct broadcast satellites and the certain key employees responsible for satellite operations licensing for the 61.5-degree orbital slot and select real estate properties to DISH in exchange for approximately 22.9 million shares of DISH Network Corporation stock that will be distributed to EchoStar shareholders.

Company Background

Charlie Ergen a former financial analyst for Frito-Lay founded a Denver company called Echosphere a retailer of large-dish C-band satellite TV equipment with his wife Cantey and James DeFranco in 1980. Echosphere which preceded DISH Network evolved into a national manufacturer and distributor which in 1987 began its move toward the new direct broadcast satellite (DBS) delivery system. It filed for a DBS license and set up subsidiary EchoStar Communications Corporation to build launch and operate DBS satellites. In 1992 the FCC granted the company an orbital slot.

By 1994 Echosphere was the US's largest distributor of conventional home satellite equipment but the future clearly rested with DBS and EchoStar. A 1995 reorganization renamed the firm EchoStar Communications; the Echosphere distributor business became a subsidiary. EchoStar also created the DISH (Digital Sky Highway) Network brand aiming for an easier-to-remember name than its rivals' "DSS" and "USSB."

EXECUTIVES

Evp Strategic Planning, Bernard L. (Bernie) Han, age 55, $500,000 total compensation

Evp, James (Jim) DeFranco, age 68, $374,640 total compensation

Chairman And Ceo, Charles W. (Charlie) Ergen, age 66, $1,000,000 total compensation

Evp Corporate Development, Thomas A. (Tom) Cullen, age 60, $450,000 total compensation

President And Coo, W. Erik Carlson, age 50, $515,000 total compensation

Evp General Counsel And Secretary, R. Stanton Dodge, age 52, $296,155 total compensation

Evp And Cto, Vivek Khemka, age 47

Evp Operations, John W. Swieringa, age 42

Evp Customer Acquisition And Retention, Brian V. Neylon, age 54

Svp And Cfo, Steven E. (Steve) Swain, age 52, $357,539 total compensation

Evp Marketing Programming And Media Sales, Warren W. Schlichting, age 58, $372,885 total compensation

Svp And Cio, Rob Dravenstott

Svp And Chief Marketing Officer, Jay Roth

Vice President Corporate Development, Theodore Henderson

Vice President Wireless Development, David Zufall

Vice President Sales, Christopher Samuelson

Vice President, Melissa Gonzalez

Vice President Dns Operations, Dennis Newman

National Sales Manager, Jessica Palframan

Vice President Of Finance, Kevin Gelston

National Account Manager, Brett Temple

Vice President Human Resources, Aaron Lapoint

National Account Manager, Brian Cox

National Accounts Manager, Christopher Guthery

Vice President Of Operation, Douglas Mohr

Vice President Of Commercial Sales, Robert Grosz

Marketing Vice President, Alfredo Rodriguez

Senior Vice President And Deputy General Counsel, Jeffrey Blum

National Sales Manager Latino Sales, Juan Colmenares

National Accounts Manager, Stephen Butters

Vp Partner Marketing, Bassil Khatib

Vice President Corporate Communications, Bob Toevs

Vice President Of Marketing, Melanie Polvoriza

Vice President Of Corporate Initiatives, Rex Povenmire

Vice President Programming, Carolyn Crawford

Vice President New Products And Operations, Nathan Knight

National Account Manager, Levi Boscardin

National Accounts Manager, Stephen Rudberg

National Account Manager, Laura Haessler

Vice President Human Resources, Rob Fuchs

Vice President Engineering, Russell Bangert

Senior Vice President Sec, David K Moskowitz

Svp Manufacturing, Jim Larocque

Senior Vice President Software Engineering, Dan Minnick

Vice President, Shannon Picchione

Vice President, Jim Defranco

Senior Vice President Of Sales, Carlos Barberi

Vice President Of Sales And Marketing, Michael Kinner

Vp Of Marketing, Bassil Elkhatib

Vice President Of Marketing, Shathabi Ravindra

Vice President, Jeff Anderson

Vice President Hardwareengineering, Mark Gomez

Vp Engineering, Terry Pattison

Vice President And Associate General Counsel, Katzin Lawrence R

National Sales Manager Strategic Channels, Josh Rogers

V.p. Brand Marketing, Kurt Simon

Senior Vice President Product Developmen, Rao Paddy

Vice President And Ciso, Artie Wilkowsky

National Sales Manager Of Specialized Distribution, Seth Van Sickel

Vice President Sales, Chris Samuelson

Senior Vice President Human Resources, Robert Fuchs

Senior Vice President, Schneider Kathy

Auditors: KPMG LLP

LOCATIONS

HQ: DISH Network Corp
9601 South Meridian Boulevard, Englewood, CO 80112
Phone: 303 723-1000   **Fax:** 303 723-1499
Web: www.dishnetwork.com

2018 Sales

	$ mil.	% of total
United States	13,578	100
Canada and Mexico	43	-
Total	**13,621**	**100**

PRODUCTS/OPERATIONS

2018 Sales

	$ mil.	% of total
Subscriber-related revenue	13,456	99
Equipment sales and other revenue	165	1
Total	**13,621**	**100**

COMPETITORS

AT&T	Grande Communications
Altice USA	Hulu
Amazon.com	Netflix
Charter Communications	Roku
Comcast	Time Warner Cable
Cox Communications	Verizon
DIRECTV	YouTube

HISTORICAL FINANCIALS

Company Type: Public

Income Statement				FYE: December 31
	REVENUE ($ mil.)	NET INCOME ($ mil.)	NET PROFIT MARGIN	EMPLOYEES
12/19	12,807	1,399	10.9%	16,000
12/18	13,621	1,575	11.6%	16,000
12/17	14,391	2,098	14.6%	17,000
12/16	15,094	1,449	9.6%	16,000
12/15	15,068	747	5.0%	18,000
Annual Growth	**(4.0%)**	**17.0%**		**(2.9%)**

2019 Year-End Financials

Debt ratio: 42.55%
Return on equity: 13.88%
Cash ($ mil.): 2,443
Current ratio: 0.89
Long-term debt ($ mil.): 12,968

No. of shares (mil.): 523
Dividends
Yield: —
Payout: —
Market value ($ mil.): 18,552

	STOCK PRICE ($) FY Close	P/E High/Low		PER SHARE ($) Earnings	Dividends	Book Value
12/19	35.47	15	9	2.60	0.00	22.11
12/18	24.97	15	7	3.00	0.00	18.37
12/17	47.75	15	10	4.07	0.00	14.87
12/16	57.93	19	13	3.05	0.00	9.97
12/15	57.18	49	35	1.61	0.00	5.92
Annual Growth	**(11.3%)**			**12.7%**	**—**	**39.0%**

Disney (Walt) Co. (The)

EXECUTIVES

Sr Exec V, Christine M McCarthy
Sr Exec V Pres-Gen Counsel-Sec, Alan N Braverman
Sr Exec V Pres-Cso, Kevin A Mayer
Sr Exec V Pres-Chief Hr Office, M Jayne Parker
Senior Vice President, Dorothy Attwood
Director, Jeff Good
Sr Manager, John Hezlep
Manager, Jon Edwards
Director, Kara Hansen
Manager Software Infrastructur, Laurence Spolidoro
Manager, Lesley Adams
Auditors: PricewaterhouseCoopers LLP

LOCATIONS

HQ: Disney (Walt) Co. (The)
500 South Buena Vista Street, Burbank, CA 91521
Phone: 818 560-1000
Web: www.disney.com

COMPETITORS

21st Century Fox	NBCUniversal
AOL	SeaWorld
CBS Corp	Six Flags
Discovery Communications	Sony Pictures Entertainment
DreamWorks Animation	Time Warner
Liberty Interactive	Viacom
Lucasfilm	Yahoo!
MGM	

HISTORICAL FINANCIALS

Company Type: Public

Income Statement				FYE: October 3
	REVENUE ($ mil.)	NET INCOME ($ mil.)	NET PROFIT MARGIN	EMPLOYEES
10/20*	65,388	(2,864)	—	203,000
09/19	69,570	11,054	15.9%	223,000
09/18	59,434	12,598	21.2%	201,000
09/17	55,137	8,980	16.3%	199,000
10/16	55,632	9,391	16.9%	195,000
Annual Growth	**4.1%**	**—**	**—**	**1.0%**

*Fiscal year change

2020 Year-End Financials

Debt ratio: 29.09%
Return on equity: (-3.27%)
Cash ($ mil.): 17,914
Current ratio: 1.32
Long-term debt ($ mil.): 52,917

No. of shares (mil.): 1,781
Dividends
Yield: 0.0%
Payout: —
Market value ($ mil.): 218,262

	STOCK PRICE ($) FY Close	P/E High/Low		PER SHARE ($) Earnings	Dividends	Book Value
10/20*	122.55	—	—	(1.58)	0.88	46.93
09/19	129.96	22	15	6.64	1.76	49.85
09/18	116.94	14	12	8.36	1.68	32.78
09/17	98.57	20	16	5.69	1.56	27.23
10/16	92.86	21	15	5.73	1.42	27.09
Annual Growth	**7.2%**			**—**	**(11.3%)**	**14.7%**

*Fiscal year change

Dollar General Corp

Dollar General commands the field of discount general merchandise. The fast-growing retailer boasts more than 16360 discount stores in some 45 US states mostly in the South the Midwest and the Southwest. It generates most of its sales from consumables (including paper and cleaning products; health and beauty aids; and refrigerated shelf-stable and perishable foods). The stores also offer seasonal items cookware and small appliances and apparel. Dollar General targets low- and fixed-income shoppers pricing items at about $10 or less. The no-frills stores typically measure around 7400 sq. ft. and are in small towns that are off the radar of giant discounters.

Operations

Dollar General generates nearly 80% of its sales from consumables which includes paper and cleaning products packaged food and snacks perishables health and beauty merchandise and pet supplies. Seasonal products including decorations toys

and small electronics greeting cards gardening supplies and other items — bring in more than 10% of sales with home products and apparel accounting for the rest.

Its stores offer private-label products as well as merchandise from such well-known national and international manufacturers as Clorox Procter & Gamble Hanes Nestle and PepsiCo.

A substantial portion of Dollar General's goods come from China putting the company at risk in the ongoing tariff battle between the US and China. Tariffs could lead to higher prices for goods and force the company to raise prices to its price-sensitive customers.

Geographic ReachDollar General operates more than 16360 stores in about 45 US states. About 10% of its stores are in Texas with Florida Georgia and North Carolina its next largest markets. Overall its stores are concentrated in the southern southwestern midwestern and eastern US. The Tennessee-based company has distribution centers in more than 15 states; its largest (each bigger than 1 million sq. ft.) are in Georgia Oklahoma Ohio Missouri Indiana South Carolina Virginia Pennsylvania Texas and Wisconsin.

Sales and MarketingDollar General's core customers include low- and fixed-income households often underserved by other retails. Because those customers generally live in small towns (fewer than 20000 people) the company doesn't allocate large amounts of money for advertising. Advertising costs were $91.0 million in 2019 $70.5 million in 2018 and $68.8 million in 2017.

Financial Performance

Dollar General's sales and profits have been rising the past several years thanks to aggressive store expansion and increased same-store sales. Revenue is up 36% since fiscal 2016 and net income is up 47%.

In fiscal 2019 (ended January) sales increased 8% to about $27.8 billion from the prior year driven by increase in same-stores sales by 4% reflecting an increase in average transaction amount and customer traffic compared to 2018. The increase in net sales was positively affected by new stores modestly offset by sales from closed stores.

Benefiting from the growth in revenue net income rose to $1.7 billion that year from $1.6 billion in 2018 despite a corresponding increase in selling general and administrative expenses.

Cash at the end of fiscal 2019 was $240.3 million an increase of $4.8 million from the prior year. Cash from operations contributed $2.2 billion to the coffers while investing activities used $782.5 million mainly for capital expenditures. Financing activities used another $1.5 billion primarily for dividends to stockholders and stock repurchase program.

StrategyWith its small-box stores typically measuring some 7400 sq. ft Dollar General targets cost-conscious consumers who seek value and convenience for either fill-in shopping periodic trips to stock up or more frequent trips to meet essential needs. Competition is tight on all sides however with encroachment from smaller nimbler companies as well as those big names with more resources. Competitors include Family Dollar and Dollar Tree Big Lots and 99 Cents Only in addition to retail giants like Walmart and Target. It also counts low-cost grocers such as Aldi and Lidl as competitors. To stay ahead of the competition Dollar General continues to aggressively open new stores in existing and new states. In fiscal 2019 the company opened some 975 stores and relocated or remodeled about 1025 stores. For 2020 Dollar General plans to open approximately 1000 new stores remodel approximately 1500 stores and relocate approximately 80 stores for a total of 2580 real estate projects. Other strategic initiatives include DG Fresh a pilot to shift to self-distribution for perishable goods and Fast Track a program designed to improve both labor productivity and customer convenience. Dollar General is also focused on expanding its non-consumables categories and continues to invest in technology and digital tools improve the in-store experience. In mid-2020 it announced its plans to expand its distribution center presence by adding one traditional distribution center in Kentucky and three DG Fresh cold storage facilities in Kentucky Oklahoma and California. In total the addition of these new facilities is expected to create 600 new career opportunities.

Company Background

J.L. Turner founded Dollar General in 1939 as J.L. Turner and Son Wholesale. The first Dollar General store was opened in 1955.

The company went public in 1968 as Dollar General Corporation and remained public for nearly 40 years. In 2007 it was purchased by investment firm Kohlberg Kravis Roberts (KKR). It went public again in 2009 and KKR sold its remaining shares in late 2013.

HISTORY

J. L. Turner was 11 when his father was killed during the 1890s in a Saturday night wrestling match. This forced J. L. to drop out of school and work on the family farm which was weighted by a mortgage. By his 20s J. L. who never learned to read well was running an area general store. Experiencing some success he branched out and purchased two stores of his own. They failed but J. L. rebounded going to work for a wholesaler. With the onset of the Depression J. L. found he could buy out the inventories of failing merchants for next to nothing using short-term bank loans that were quickly repaid.

In 1939 J. L. was joined by his son Cal. The two each put up $5000 to start a new Scottsville Kentucky-based dry goods wholesaling operation called not surprisingly J.L. Turner & Son. It was not until 1945 when the company experienced a glut of women's underwear that it expanded into retail. J.L. Turner & Son sold off the dainties in their first store located in Albany Kentucky. Within a decade the company was operating 35 stores. In 1956 J.L. Turner & Son introduced its first experimental Dollar General Store — all items priced less than a dollar — in Springfield Kentucky. Like the company's first stores the dollar store concept would grow: Dollar General Stores numbered 255 a decade later.

Cal Jr. J. L.'s 25-year-old grandson joined the family business in 1965 and became a director in 1966. The company changed its name to Dollar General and went public two years later. In 1977 Cal Jr. was named president and CEO. That year Dollar General acquired Arkansas-based United Dollar Stores.

The early 1980s saw Dollar General continue its acquisition-powered growth. The company bought INTERCO's 280-store P.N. Hirsch chain and the 203-store Eagle Family Discount chain in 1983 and 1985 respectively. To cope with expanded distribution demands Dollar General opened an additional distribution center in Homerville Georgia in 1986 to help out the original Scottsville facility. The acquisitions led by Cal Jr.'s brother Steve ended up costing the company dearly; Dollar General's 1987 stock price dropped nearly 85%. The next year they also cost Steve his job: He was forced out by the company's new chairman Cal Jr. In addition to ousting Steve Cal Jr. replaced more than half of Dollar General's executives in 1988. The retailer began moving toward everyday low pricing (la Wal-Mart) in the late 1980s.

Growth from then on was powered by internal expansion. In 1990 the company operated nearly 1400 stores; by 1995 it had more than 2000. To accommodate the growth Dollar General built a third distribution center in Ardmore Oklahoma in 1995 and another in South Boston Virginia in 1997.

While continuing to focus on small towns and neighborhoods Dollar General has expanded beyond the Southeast and Midwest opening its first stores in New York and New Jersey in 2001. In 2004 the company opened more than 700 locations and expanded into Arizona New Mexico and Wisconsin.

In April 2005 the company settled a Securities and Exchange Commission investigation into the circumstances that resulted in a $100 million earnings restatement for the years 1998 through 2000 with payment of a $10 million civil penalty.

To support its growth Dollar General opened a new distribution center in South Boston (its ninth) in 2006 and one in Union County South Carolina in mid-2005. Also in 2006 the retailer expanded its warehouse in Ardmore Oklahoma.

In July 2007 Dollar General was taken private by Kohlberg Kravis & Roberts GS Capital Partners (an affiliate of Goldman Sachs) and Citi Private Equity an investment arm of Citigroup in a deal valued at $7.3 billion.

In November 2009 the company went public with an offering valued at $716 million. The fast-growing chain opened its 9000th store in late July 2010.

Dollar General in August 2014 bid $78.50 per share for its smaller rival Family Dollar Stores. The all-cash offer which valued Family Dollar at about $9.7 billion topped a standing offer for Family Dollar from Dollar Tree of $74.50 in cash and stock. The addition of Family Dollar's 8200 stores would solidify Dollar General's standing as the largest in its industry. By July 2015 however Dollar Tree had prevailed in the bid and completed its acquisition that month. Before Dollar Tree's triumph Dollar General revealed that it may have had to sell between 1500 and 4000 stores prior to the deal closing in order to comply with regulators.

EXECUTIVES

Senior Vice President And Chief Information Officer, Bruce Ash
Ceo, Todd J. Vasos, $1,083,375 total compensation
Evp And Chief People Officer, Robert D. (Bob) Ravener, $521,999 total compensation
Evp And General Counsel, Rhonda M. Taylor, $539,371 total compensation
Evp And Chief Merchandising Officer, Jason S. Reiser
Evp And Cfo, John W. Garratt, $511,603 total compensation
Evp Store Operations, Jeffrey C. (Jeff) Owen, $613,924 total compensation
Evp And Cio, Carman Wenkoff
Vice President Assistant Controller, Lee Carlisle
Vice President Dmm, Brian Hartshorn
Svp Global Sourcing Operations, Steve Jacobson
Vice President, Mary Kirby
Vice President And Credit Administrator, John Flanigan
Division Vice President Store Operations, Tracey Herrmann
Vice President Operations, Bill Bass
Evp Global Supply Chain, Mike Kindy
Vice President Investor Relations, Mary Pilkington
Vice President Of Human Resources, Chris Snow
Vice President Transportation, Jeff Harpole
Senior Vice President Chief Accounting Officer, Anita Elliott
Svp Non Consumables, Emily Taylor
Vice President Dmm, Jerry Reinhardt

Vice President, Valarie Edmondson
Vice President Fpa And Zbb, Peter Hinrichs
Vice President Real Estate, Stephen Krumholz
Senior Vice President General Merchandise Manager Non Consumables, Lawrence Gatta
Vice President Marketing, Dave Stewart
Vice President Distribution, Adam Janatsch
Vice President Of Risk Management, Tina Schaell
Division Vice President, John Culbreth
Vice President Tax, Neal E Miller
Vice President External Marketing And Communications, Curtis Corl
Vp And Cto, Julie Elmore
Vice President, Johanna Blankush
Vice President Government Affairs, Steve Brophy
Chairman, Michael M. Calbert
Board Member, Sandra Cochran
Treasurer, Francis Hicks
Auditors: Ernst & Young LLP

LOCATIONS

HQ: Dollar General Corp
100 Mission Ridge, Goodlettsville, TN 37072
Phone: 615 855-4000 **Fax:** 615 855-5527
Web: www.dollargeneral.com

2018 Stores

	No.
Texas	1,485
Georgia	872
Florida	856
North Carolina	817
Ohio	798
Tennessee	780
Alabama	760
Other states	9,104
Total	**15,472**

PRODUCTS/OPERATIONS

2018 Sales

	$ mil.	% of total
Consumables	19,865	77
Seasonal	3,050	12
Home Products	1,506	6
Apparel	1,204	5
Total	**25,625**	**100**

Selected Merchandise

Basic apparel
Cleaning supplies
Dairy products
Frozen foods
Health and beauty aids
Housewares
Packaged foods
Seasonal goods
Stationery

COMPETITORS

99 Cents Only	Fred's
ALDI	Kroger
Big Lots	Lidl
CVS	Rite Aid
Costco Wholesale	Target Corporation
Dollar Tree	Wal-Mart
Family Dollar Stores	Walgreen

HISTORICAL FINANCIALS

Company Type: Public

Income Statement

	REVENUE ($ mil.)	NET INCOME ($ mil.)	NET PROFIT MARGIN	EMPLOYEES
				FYE: January 31
01/20*	27,753	1,712	6.2%	143,000
02/19	25,625	1,589	6.2%	135,000
02/18	23,470	1,538	6.6%	129,000
02/17	21,986	1,251	5.7%	121,000
01/16	20,368	1,165	5.7%	113,400
Annual Growth	8.0%	10.1%	—	6.0%

*Fiscal year change

2020 Year-End Financials

Debt ratio: 12.76%
Return on equity: 26.18%
Cash ($ mil.): 240
Current ratio: 1.14
Long-term debt ($ mil.): 2,911

No. of shares (mil.): 251
Dividends
Yield: 0.8%
Payout: 20.0%
Market value ($ mil.): 38,650

	STOCK PRICE ($) FY Close	P/E High/Low	PER SHARE ($) Earnings	Dividends	Book Value
01/20*	153.41	25 17	6.64	1.28	26.60
02/19	115.04	20 14	5.97	1.16	24.73
02/18	99.44	19 12	5.63	1.04	22.80
02/17	73.14	22 15	4.43	1.00	19.64
01/16	75.06	21 15	3.95	0.88	18.76
Annual Growth	19.6%	— —	13.9%	9.8%	9.1%

*Fiscal year change

Dollar Tree Inc

Dollars may not grow on trees but Dollar Tree brings in the green. The fast-growing company operates more than 15000 Dollar Tree and Family Dollar discount stores across the US and in about five provinces in Canada. The stores carry a mix of housewares toys seasonal items food health and beauty aids. At Dollar Tree shops most goods are priced at $1 or less while Family Dollar merchandise is usually less than $10. The stores are generally located in high-traffic strip centers and malls often in midsized cities and small towns.

Operations

Dollar Tree reports its operations through the Dollar Tree and Family Dollar brands. Dollar Tree brand generates about 50% of the company's revenue while more than 45% comes from Family Dollar.

The Dollar Tree division built around merchandise at the $1 price point has about 7500 stores with an average of some 8000-10000 sq. ft. of sales space. Family Dollar operates through nearly 7785 stores which are a bit smaller at 6000-8000 sq. ft. of sales space; it offers competitively priced merchandise often less than $10.

From a product standpoint Dollar Tree segment's consumables category (candy food health and beauty products household paper products) accounts for more than 25% of the company's revenue; variety merchandise (toys housewares gifts) electronics and seasonal offerings bring in the rest. Family Dollar's consumables products account for over 35% of total revenue. Home products apparel and accessories and seasonal electronics produce more than 10% combined.

Geographic Reach

Virginia- based Dollar Tree operates stores across the US. Its largest markets are Texas Florida Ohio North Carolina and California which together account for about a third of locations. It has some 225 stores in Canada with about half in Ontario.

The Dollar Tree segment has more than 10 distribution centers in the US two distribution centers in Canada and a store support center in Chesapeake Virginia. The Family Dollar segment has more than 10 distribution centers across the US and a store support center in Matthews North Carolina (which is being moved to Virginia in late 2019).

Sales and Marketing

The Dollar Tree brand primarily serves middle income customers in suburban locations with Family Dollar serving lower income customers in urban and rural locations.

The company's advertising costs totaled $102.9 million in fiscal 2019 compared to $99.9 million in 2018 and $106.3 million in 2017.

Financial Performance

Net sales increased 4% or $787.5 million in 2019 compared to 2018 resulting from increases in comparable store net sales in the Dollar Tree and Family Dollar segments and sales of $796.3 million at new stores partially offset by lost sales resulting from store closures primarily on the Family Dollar segment.

Net income increased from a loss $1.6 billion to an income of $827 million in 2020. The increase was due to lower selling general and administrative expenses from $7.9 billion in 2019 to $5.8 billion in 2020.

Cash at the end of fiscal 2020 was $586 million an increase of $139.3 million from the prior year. Cash from operations contributed $1.9 billion to the coffers while investing activities used $1.0 billion mainly for capital expenditures. Financing activities used another $709.8 million for payments on long-term debt primarily.

Strategy

Continue to execute its proven and best?in?class retail business strategy. Dollar Tree will continue to execute its proven strategies that have generated a history of success and continued growth for the company. Key elements of its strategy include: aiming continuously to "Wow" the customer with a compelling fun and fresh merchandise assortment comprising a variety of the things you want and things you need all at incredible values in bright clean and friendly stores; maintaining a flexible sourcing merchandise model that allows a variety of products to be sold as long as desired merchandise margin thresholds are met; growing and improving both the Dollar Tree and Family Dollar brands; pursuing a "more better faster" approach to the roll-out of new Dollar Tree and Family Dollar stores to broaden their geographic footprint; maintaining customer relevance by ensuring that it reinvent themselves constantly through new merchandise categories and initiatives; leveraging the complementary merchandise expertise of each segment including Dollar Tree's sourcing and product development expertise and Family Dollar's consumer package goods and national brands sourcing expertise; and maintaining a prudent approach with its use of capital for the benefit of its shareholders.

Operates a diversified and complementary business model across both fixed?price and multi?price point strategies. The company plans to operate and grow both the Dollar Tree and Family Dollar brands. It will utilize the reach and scale of its combined company to serve a broader range of customers in more ways offering better prices and more value for the customer.

Company Background

In 1953 K. R. Perry opened a variety store in Norfolk Virginia called Ben Franklin; it was later renamed K&K 5&10. By 1970 Perry and two other men established a mall concept store called K&K Toys also in Virginia although it eventually grew to some 130 locations along the East Coast.

A third chain Only $1.00 was started in 1986 with stores located alongside K&K Toys stores.

K&K Toys was sold in the early 1990s to KB Toys and proceeds from the sale were used to expand the dollar store chain. By 1995 that chain Only $1.00 had become Dollar Tree and gone public.

Dollar Tree expanded through new store openings and acquisitions culminating in the 2015 purchase of North Carolina-based Family Dollar for about $9 billion.

EXECUTIVES

Chief Supply Chain Officer, Gary A. Maxwell, age 58
Cfo, Kevin S. Wampler, age 57, $690,385 total compensation
President Ceo And Director, Gary M. Philbin, age 63, $1,121,154 total compensation
Cio, Joshua R. (Josh) Jewett, age 50
President And Coo Family Dollar Stores, Duncan C. Mac Naughton, age 58, $61,538 total compensation
Chief Administrative Officer, Michael (Mike) Matacunas, age 53, $537,500 total compensation
Chief Merchandising Officer, Robert H. (Bob) Rudman, age 69, $740,385 total compensation
President And Coo Dollar Tree, Michael Witynski, age 57
Vice President, Frank Torrell
Vice President Human Resources Services, Bruce Paolini
Vice President Treasurer, Roger Dean
Vice President, Deborah Miller
Svp Store Operations, Tom Mcaloon
President And Coo, Bob Sasser, age 68
Board Member, Stephanie Stahl
Auditors: KPMG LLP

LOCATIONS

HQ: Dollar Tree Inc
500 Volvo Parkway, Chesapeake, VA 23320
Phone: 757 321-5000
Web: www.dollartree.com

2018 Canadian Stores

	No.
Ontario	110
British Columbia	49
Alberta	37
Saskatchewan	16
Manitoba	13
Total	**225**

2018 US Stores

	No.
Texas	1,622
Florida	1,107
Ohio	757
North Carolina	721
California	725
Georgia	665
New York	641
Michigan	628
Pennsylvania	622
Other states	7,524
Total	**15,012**

PRODUCTS/OPERATIONS

2018 Sales

	% of total
Consumables	62
Other	38
Total	**100**

2018 Sales

	$ mil.	% of total
Dollar Tree	11,712	51
Family Dollar	11,111	49
Total	**22,823**	**100**

Selected Products

Books
Candy
Cards
Food
Gifts
Health and beauty care products
Housewares
Party goods
Personal accessories
Seasonal goods
Stationery
Toys

COMPETITORS

99 Cents Only	OllieÂ's Bargain
ALDI	Outlet
Big Lots	Rite Aid
CVS	SUPERVALU
Dollar General	Savers Inc.
Five Below	Target Corporation
Fred's	Wal-Mart
Kmart	Walgreen

HISTORICAL FINANCIALS

Company Type: Public

Income Statement

FYE: February 1

	REVENUE ($ mil.)	NET INCOME ($ mil.)	NET PROFIT MARGIN	EMPLOYEES
02/20	23,610	827	3.5%	193,100
02/19	22,823	(1,590)	—	182,100
02/18*	22,245	1,714	7.7%	176,100
01/17	20,719	896	4.3%	176,800
01/16	15,498	282	1.8%	167,800
Annual Growth	11.1%	30.8%	—	3.6%

*Fiscal year change

2020 Year-End Financials

Debt ratio: 19.27%
Return on equity: 13.94%
Cash ($ mil.): 539
Current ratio: 1.20
Long-term debt ($ mil.): 3,522

No. of shares (mil.): 236
Dividends
Yield: —
Payout: —
Market value ($ mil.): 20,612

	STOCK PRICE ($) FY Close	P/E High/Low		PER SHARE ($) Earnings	Dividends	Book Value
02/20	87.07	34	25	3.47	0.00	26.42
02/19	96.69	—	—	(6.66)	0.00	23.70
02/18*	108.83	16	9	7.21	0.00	30.26
01/17	74.05	26	19	3.78	0.00	22.82
01/16	81.32	66	48	1.26	0.00	18.76
Annual Growth	1.7%	—	—	28.8%		8.9%

*Fiscal year change

Dominion Energy Inc (New)

Dominion Energy dominates the American energy market as one of its top distributors of electricity and natural gas. The company serves some 7 million retail energy customers across eight US states with a special concentration in Virginia the Carolinas and Ohio. The company boasts an impressive energy portfolio with about 30700 MW of generating capacity as well as one of the largest underground natural gas storage systems with 1 trillion cu. ft. of capacity. Operating subsidiaries include Virginia Power and Dominion Energy Gas.

HISTORY

In 1781 the Virginia General Assembly established a group of trustees including George Washington and James Madison to promote navigation on the Appomattox River. The group (named the Appomattox Trustees) formed the Upper Appomattox Company in 1795 to secure its water rights. The company eventually began operating hydroelectric plants on the river and by 1888 it had added a steam-powered plant to its portfolio.

The Virginia Railway and Power Company (VR&P) led by Frank Jay Gould purchased the Upper Appomattox Company (which had changed its name) in 1909. The next year the firm acquired several electric and gas utilities as well as some electric streetcar lines.

In 1925 New York engineering company Stone & Webster acquired VR&P. The company became known as Virginia Electric and Power Company (Virginia Power) and was placed under Engineers Public Service (EPS) a new holding company. Virginia Power purchased several North Carolina utilities following its acquisition.

During the 1930s the Depression (and the popularity of the automobile) led the company to exit the trolley business. The Public Utility Holding Company Act of 1935 (repealed 2005) which ushered in an era of regulated utility monopolies forced EPS to divest all of its operations except Virginia Power. However the utility soon merged with the Virginia Public Service Company thus doubling its service territory.

The company added new power plants to keep up with growing customer demand in the 1950s. Always an innovator it also built an extra-high-voltage transmission system the first in the world.

In the 1970s Virginia Power's first nuclear plants became operational. By 1980 however the firm was near bankruptcy. That year William Berry who had completed a 23-year rise through the ranks to become president canceled two other nuclear units. He also became an early supporter of competition in the electric utility industry. In 1983 he formed Dominion Resources as a parent company for Virginia Power and halted nearly all plant construction. Two additional subsidiaries were soon formed: Dominion Capital in 1985 and Dominion Energy in 1987.

In 1990 the year Thomas Capps took over as CEO Dominion sold its natural gas distribution business and in 1995 Dominion Energy began developing natural gas reserves through joint ventures and by purchasing three natural gas exploration and production companies.

The company acquired UK utility East Midlands Electricity in 1997. However after it was hit by a hefty windfall tax by the newly elected Labour Party and its hopes for mergers with other UK utilities were dashed it sold East Midlands to PowerGen just 18 months after acquiring it.

In 1999 Dominion prepared for energy deregulation through reorganization. It separated its electricity generation activities from its transmission and distribution operations. In 2000 Dominion bought Consolidated Natural Gas (CNG) for $9 billion making it one of the largest fully integrated gas and electric power companies in the US; it then sold CNG's Virginia Natural Gas to AGL Resources and the two firms' combined Latin American assets to Duke Energy.

Virginia Power moved to head off state and federal lawsuits in 2000 by agreeing to spend $1.2 billion over 12 years to reduce pollution from coal-fired plants. The company also agreed to pay $1.3 billion for Eversource Energy's Millstone nuclear power complex that year (the deal closed in 2001). Also in 2000 Dominion changed its brand name from Dominion Resources to just Dominion and rebranded several of its subsidiaries as well.

In 2001 Dominion bought exploration and production company Louis Dreyfus Natural Gas for about $1.8 billion in cash and stock and $500 million in assumed debt; the acquisition added 1.8 trillion cu. ft. of natural gas equivalent to Dominion's proved reserves. The company also sold the assets of its financial services unit Dominion Capital that year.

The following year Dominion purchased a 500-MW Chicago power plant from US power producer Mirant (now GenOn Energy) for $182 million and it purchased the Cove Point LNG (liquefied natural gas) import facility from The Williams Companies for $217 million.

Dominion began to prepare for power deregulation implemented in most of its service territories by expanding its nonregulated electric operations. The company also divested its non-US operations to focus on its businesses in the Northeast Mid-Atlantic and Midwest. In 2004 it sold its telecom business to private firm Elantic Networks. The firm completed the acquisition of three fossil-fueled plants (2800 MW) from USGen New England a subsidiary of National Energy & Gas Transmission for $656 million in 2005. That was the same year Dominion purchased the 550-MW Kewaunee nuclear plant from WPS Resources subsidiary Wisconsin Public Service and Alliant Energy subsidiary Wisconsin Power & Light for $220 million.

At the end of 2006 Dominion Exploration & Production had proved reserves of 6.5 trillion cu. ft. of natural gas equivalent. The next year Dominion began to dismantle the unit selling its offshore operations in the Gulf of Mexico to Eni; its assets in Alabama Michigan and Texas to Loews Corp.; its Mid-Continent operations to Linn Energy; and operations in the Rocky Mountain and Gulf Coast regions to XTO Energy. Dominion Resources pocketed almost $14 billion from the sales.

To free up cash and hone its business focus the company has sold most of its exploration and production operations in recent years. In 2010 the company sold its remaining Appalachian exploration and production assets to CONSOL Energy for about $3.5 billion. The acquisition doubled CONSOL's natural gas reserves to 3 million cu. ft. (In 2007 Dominion sold the bulk of its oil and gas exploration and production assets — excluding its Appalachian operations because at the time they offered less risk — for nearly $14 billion.)

In a related move Dominion agreed to sell its Appalachian gas distribution companies The Peoples Natural Gas Company and Hope Gas located in Pennsylvania and West Virginia to investment firm SteelRiver Infrastructure Partners for $910 million. After receiving approval from Pennsylvania the deal was rejected in late 2009 by West Virginia saying the terms of the agreement were not in the public interest. The company then sold just Peoples Natural Gas to SteelRiver in 2010 for $780 million.

Dominion's divestments allow it to concentrate its efforts on its core power generation and gas and electricity distribution businesses along with its trading and marketing activities.

In 2012 Dominion announced plans to sell three fossil fuel-fired merchant power stations (one in Massachusetts and two in Illinois) as part of its transition to cleaner burning and renewable power plants.

On the gas side of the business in 2012 Dominion and Caiman Energy II LLC formed a $1.5 billion joint venture (Blue Racer Midstream LLC) to provide midstream services to natural gas producers operating in the Utica shale in Ohio and portions of Pennsylvania.

In 2013 Dominion Virginia Power put the Altavista Power Station into commercial operation with renewable biomass as its fuel the first of three such stations to be converted from coal to biomass.

After no acquisitions during the 2008-13 period Dominion then pursued several costly acquisitions.

Betting on stable revenues from natural gas distribution in 2016 Dominion bought Questar Corp. for $4.4 billion.

In 2017 Dominion Energy acquired several wholly-owned merchant solar projects in California North Carolina and Virginia for $356 million and Virginia Power acquired two solar developments in North Carolina.

EXECUTIVES

Ceo Dominion Generation Group, Paul D. Koonce, age 60, $680,138 total compensation

Chairman President And Ceo, Thomas F. Farrell, age 65, $1,502,372 total compensation

Svp And Chief Administrative Officer, Mark F. McGettrick, age 62, $850,055 total compensation

Evp; Ceo Dominion Generation Group, David A. Christian, age 65, $680,138 total compensation

President And Chief Nuclear Officer Dominion Nuclear, David A. Heacock, age 62, $528,098 total compensation

President And Ceo Dominion Virginia Power, Robert M. (Bob) Blue, age 52

Svp And Cio, P. Rodney Blevins

Svp Dominion Transmission, Diane G. Leopold, age 53

President Dominion Questar, Craig C. Wagstaff

Vp Transmission, Scot C. Hathaway

Svp Corporate Affairs And Chief Legal Officer, Mark O. Webb, age 55

President Dominion Midstream Operations, Paul F. Ruppert

Vice President State And Electric Public Policy, William Murray

Vice President Of Information Technology, Kris Morelli

Vice President Nuclear Operations, Daniel G Stoddard

Senior Vice President, Barbara Roland

Senior Vice President Pipeline Customer Service And Business Development, Donald Raikes

Vice President Government Affairs, Daniel Weekley

Vice President Customer Service Dominion Virginia Power, Charlene Whitfield

Senior Vice President Distribution, Edward Ed Baine

Vice President Nuclear Engineering, Mark Sartain

Vp Financial Management, Dennis Millet

Board Member, William Barr

Auditors: DELOITTE & TOUCHE LLP

LOCATIONS

HQ: Dominion Energy Inc (New)
120 Tredegar Street, Richmond, VA 23219
Phone: 804 819-2000   **Fax:** 804 775-5819
Web: www.dom.com

PRODUCTS/OPERATIONS

2016 Sales

	$ mil.	% of total
Dominion Generation	6,757	55
Dominion Energy	2,766	22
DVP	2,233	18
Corporate and Other	602	5
Adjustments & Eliminations	(621)	-
Total	**11,737**	**100**

2016 Sales

	$ mil.	% of total
Electric Sales	8,867	76
Gas transportation and Storage	1,636	14
Gas Sales	854	7
Other	380	3
Total	**11,737**	**100**

Selected Subsidiaries and Business Units

Dominion Generation Corporation (power plant management)
Dominion Energy (energy marketing gas and power transmission)
  Dominion Transmission Inc. (natural gas pipelines)
Dominion Virginia Power
  Consolidated Natural Gas
  Dominion East Ohio (or The East Ohio Gas Company gas distribution)
  Dominion Hope (or Hope Gas Inc. West Virginia gas distribution)
  Dominion North Carolina Power (or Virginia Electric and Power Company electricity distribution)
  Dominion Retail Inc. (retail energy marketing)
  Virginia Electric and Power Company (electricity distribution)

COMPETITORS

AEP	Exelon
CenterPoint Energy	Koch Industries Inc.
Duke Energy	NiSource
Entergy	Piedmont Natural Gas

HISTORICAL FINANCIALS

Company Type: Public

Income Statement

FYE: December 31

	REVENUE ($ mil.)	NET INCOME ($ mil.)	NET PROFIT MARGIN	EMPLOYEES
12/19	16,572	1,358	8.2%	19,100
12/18	13,366	2,447	18.3%	21,300
12/17	12,586	2,999	23.8%	16,200
12/16	11,737	2,123	18.1%	16,200
12/15	11,683	1,899	16.3%	14,700
Annual Growth	**9.1%**	**(8.0%)**	**—**	**6.8%**

2019 Year-End Financials

Debt ratio: 33.46%
Return on equity: 5.21%
Cash ($ mil.): 166
Current ratio: 0.61
Long-term debt ($ mil.): 33,824
No. of shares (mil.): 838
Dividends
  Yield: 4.4%
  Payout: 275.9%
Market value ($ mil.): 69,403

	STOCK PRICE ($) FY Close	P/E High/Low	PER SHARE ($) Earnings	Dividends	Book Value
12/19	82.82	50 41	1.62	3.67	38.18
12/18	71.46	21 17	3.74	3.34	29.53
12/17	81.06	18 15	4.72	3.04	26.58
12/16	76.59	23 20	3.44	2.80	23.26
12/15	67.64	25 20	3.20	2.59	21.25
Annual Growth	**5.2%**	**— —**	**(15.6%)**	**9.1%**	**15.8%**

Dover Corp

Dover a diversified global manufacturer and solutions provider delivering innovative equipment and components consumable supplies aftermarket parts software and digital solutions and support services through five operating segments: engineered systems (products for printing and identification transportation waste handling and industrial markets); fluids (fluid handling products for retail fueling oil and gas chemical and hygienic markets); fueling solutions refrigeration and food equipment (systems and products serving the commercial refrigeration and food service industries); pumps & process solutions (specialty pumps fluid handling and plastics and polymer processing equipment); and imaging & identification (coding product traceability and digital textile printing

equipment). It generates more than 45% of revenue outside the US. Dover traces its historical roots back to 1947.

Operations

Dover operates through five segments: Engineered Systems Fueling Solutions Refrigeration and Food Equipment Pumps & Process Solutions and Imaging & Identification.

The Engineered Systems segment accounts for around 25% of total revenue provides a wide range of products software and services that have a broad customer applications across a number of markets including aftermarket vehicle services solid waste handling industrial automation aerospace and defense industrial winch and hoist and fluid dispensing.

Fueling Solutions segment (about 25% of revenue) focused on providing components equipment and software and service solutions enabling safe transport of fuels and other hazardous fluids along the supply chain as well as the safe and efficient operation of retail fueling and vehicle wash establishment.

Refrigeration & Food Equipment generates about 20% of sales and makes refrigeration systems refrigeration display cases commercial glass refrigerator and freezer doors and brazed plate heat exchangers used for industrial heating and cooling and residential climate control.

Pumps & Process Solutions segment (about 20% of revenue) manufactures specialty pumps fluid handling components plastics and polymer processing equipment and highly engineered components for rotating and reciprocating machines.

Imaging & Identification segment accounts for about 15% of revenue supplies precision marking and coding product traceability and digital textile printing equipment as well as related consumables software and services.

Geographic Reach

Based in Illinois Dover has a significant worldwide presence and operates in Australia Brazil Canada China France Germany Italy India Mexico the Netherlands Switzerland Sweden and the UK.

The US generates nearly 55% of Dover's revenue while Europe accounts for more than 20%. Other countries in the Americas generate around 10% as does the Asia/Pacific region.

Sales and Marketing

Dover sells directly to customers as well as through a network of distributors. It caters to the supermarket industry including big-box retail and convenience stores the commercial/industrial refrigeration industry institutional and commercial food service and food production markets and beverage can-making industries.

Dover advertising costs were $24609 in 2019 $26831 in 2018 and $33369 in 2017.

Financial Performance

Dover's revenue has seen steady growth the last five years rising 21% between 2019 and 2015. The company's Engineered Products segment has been the chief growth driver.

Sales in 2019 increased about 2% to $7.1 billion compared to $7 billion in 2019. Growth in 2019 was led by organic growth in Dover's Fueling Solutions and Engineered Systems segments partially offset by its Refrigeration & Food Equipment segment. A favorable pricing environment also boosted revenue.

Net income increase about 20% to $677.9 million in 2019 compared to 2018 primarily due to higher earnings from continued operations.

Cash at the end of 2019 was $397.3 million an increase of $1.0 billion from the prior year. Cash from operations contributed $945.3 million to the coffers while investing activities used $384.3 million mainly for acquisition and purchase of property plant and equipment. Financing activities used

$558.0 million primarily for repurchases of common stock.

Strategy

Dover aim to grow by making organic investments in research and development developing new products and technologies improving digital capabilities expanding our geographic coverage and by pursuing disciplined strategic acquisitions that will enhance its portfolio and position Dover for long-term growth. It continually evaluate how its assets and capabilities can position Dover to grow in markets adjacent to its core businesses (for example new applications geographies product segments or adjacent technologies) where Dover can be advantaged.

n addition to product innovation Dover plan to grow by developing digital technologies. In 2018 it opened its new Digital Labs center in the greater Boston area and have continued to invest in this facility and its team of software developers data scientists and product managers to enhance ooutdigital capability. The Digital Labs team is driving digital transformation across its businesses along the following three areas: (i) e-commerce – more efficient and streamlined digital customer interfaces that make it easy to do business with Dover companies; (ii) connected products – development of value-add connected sensorized and softwareaugmented solutions built on top of Dover's core equipment and component offerings in its endmarkets; and (iii) digital manufacturing – driving increased efficiency safety and quality in its manufacturing operations by employing cutting-edge automation and "digital factory" solutions. Dover believe that the Digital Labs center will enhance the effectiveness of its products and fuel and commercial growth strategy. By leveraging a central resource for Industrial Internet of Things ("IIoT") and connected product initiatives Dover are able to reduce redundancy of support infrastructure while managing the proliferation of common parts such as sensors to keep its projects cost-competitive.

Between 2017 and 2019 Dover spent $319.3 billion to purchase seven businesses. On the other hand in the same period it sold several businesses for $400.8 million. In mid-2018 Dover also spun off its former energy segment — equipment used in the extraction and handling of oil and gas – as Apergy Corporation.

Mergers and Acquisitions

Dover's acquisition activity is significant.

In 2020 Dover agreed to acquire Germanybased EM-tec GmBh a leading designer and manufacturer of flow measurement devices that serve a wide array of medical and biopharmaceutical applications. Following the close of the transaction Em-tec will become part of the PSGÂ® business unit within Dover's Pumps & Process. The addition of Em-tec further expands Dover's reach into biopharma and other hygienic applications and enhances its portfolio of flow control technologies with flow rate sensors. Terms of the transaction were not disclosed.

In the same year Dover agreed to acquire USbased Soft-Pak a leading independent provider of integrated back office route management and customer relationship management software solutions to the waste and recycling fleet industry. Following the close of the transaction Soft-Pak will become part of the Environmental Solutions Group ("ESG") business unit. The acquisition enhances ESG's industry-leading digital offerings centered around connected refuse vehicle and productivityenhancing solutions.

Also in 2020 the company agreed to acquired US- based Systech a leading provider of software and solutions for product traceability regulatory compliance and brand protection. Following the close of the transaction Systech will become part of the Imaging and Identification segment. The acquisition will enhance Imaging and Identification segment portfolio of product identification and traceability solutions with complementary and highly-demanded software and service offerings catering to a large and growing global brand protection market.

In mid-2019 Dover acquired Ohio-based All-Flo Pump Company which was rolled into the Pump Solutions Group (PSG) unit within Dover's Fluids segment. All-Flo is a manufacturer of specialty airoperated double-diaphragm (AODD) pumps used in a wide range of industrial applications. The addition of All-Flo enhances PSG's lineup of AODD pumps and expands its geographic and channel reach.

Earlier in 2019 Dover bought Michigan-based Belanger Inc. a leading manufacturer of vehicle wash equipment and systems. Belanger adds to the vehicle wash systems operations of Dover's Fluids segment.

Company Background

George Ohrstrom a New York stockbroker formed Dover in 1955 and took it public that year. Originally headquartered in Washington DC Dover consisted of four companies: C. Lee Cook (compressor seals and piston rings) Peerless (spaceventing heaters) Rotary Lift (automotive lifts) and W.C. Norris (components for oil wells). In 1958 Dover made the first of many acquisitions and entered the elevator industry by buying Shepard Warner Elevator.

HISTORY

George Ohrstrom a New York stockbroker formed Dover in 1955 and took it public that year. Originally headquartered in Washington DC Dover consisted of four companies: C. Lee Cook (compressor seals and piston rings) Peerless (spaceventing heaters) Rotary Lift (automotive lifts) and W.C. Norris (components for oil wells). In 1958 Dover made the first of many acquisitions and entered the elevator industry by buying Shepard Warner Elevator.

EXECUTIVES

Vp; President And Ceo Dover Fluids, William W. (Bill) Spurgeon, age 62, $650,000 total compensation
President And Ceo, Robert A. (Bob) Livingston, age 66, $1,030,000 total compensation
President And Ceo Dover Energy, Sivasankaran (Soma) Somasundaram, age 55, $502,000 total compensation
Svp And Cfo, Brad M. Cerepak, age 61, $670,000 total compensation
President And Ceo Dover Engineered Systems, C. Anderson Fincher, age 49, $530,000 total compensation
President And Ceo Refrigeration And Food Equipment, William T. Bosway
President Dover Business Services, S. Gary Kennon
Vice President Communications, Adrian Sakowicz
Vice President Global Human Resources, Cynthia Wells
Vice President Of Human Resources, Gerry Vinci
Executive Vice President, James Moyle
Vice President Internal Audit, Cynthia Boumann
Vice President And Treasurer, Jim Moran
Vice President And Deputy General Counsel, Alison Rhoten
Vice President Human Resources, David Schmit
Vice President Marketing, Noelle Britton
Vice President Sales (institutional Accounts), Beth Hammer
Vice President Human Resources, Mike Russell
Vice President Software Engineering, Sreedhar Patnala

Vice President Corporate Development, Andrey Galiuk
Vp And Associate Counsel Mergers And Acquisitions, Matthew Gaudette
Chairman, Michael F. (Mike) Johnston, age 72
Board Member, Stephen Wagner
Board Member, Stephen Todd
Vice President Treasurer, James Moran
Board Member, Keith Wandell
Auditors: PricewaterhouseCoopers LLP

LOCATIONS

HQ: Dover Corp
3005 Highland Parkway, Downers Grove, IL 60515
Phone: 630 541-1540
Web: www.dovercorporation.com

2017 Sales

	$ mil.	% of total
Americas		
United States	4	57
Other Americas	735	9
Europe	1,504	19
Asia	774	10
Other	391	5
Total	**6,830**	**100**

PRODUCTS/OPERATIONS

2017 Sales

	$ mil.	% of total
Engineered Systems	2,576	33
Fluids	2,250	29
Refrigeration & Food Equipment	1,599	20
Energy	1,406	18
Intra-segment eliminations	(1.3)	-
Total	**6,794**	**100**

Selected Brands

Engineered Systems
Caldera
Destaco
JK Group
Fluids
CPC
Dover Fueling Solutions
HydroEnergy
Accelerated
Cook Compression
Dover Artifical Lift
Refrigeration & Food Equipment
Anthony
Belvac
Hillphoenix

COMPETITORS

Alfa Laval	Middleby
Brother Industries	Navistar
Carlisle Companies	Oshkosh Truck
Crane Co.	PACCAR
Danaher	Paul Mueller
Danfoss	RAKON LIMITED
Dayco Products	SPX
Domino Printing	Schlumberger
Fortive	Sequa
Franklin Electric	Siemens AG
Gardner Denver	Smith Bits
Hussmann International	Snap-on
IDEX	Swagelok
Illinois Tool Works	Tatung
Ingersoll-Rand	Thermador Groupe
KEMET	Vesuvius
KSB AG	Wastequip
Kaydon	Weatherford
Lufkin Industries	International
Manitowoc	Zebra Technologies

HISTORICAL FINANCIALS

Company Type: Public

Income Statement
FYE: December 31

	REVENUE ($ mil.)	NET INCOME ($ mil.)	NET PROFIT MARGIN	EMPLOYEES
12/19	7,136	677	9.5%	24,000
12/18	6,992	570	8.2%	24,000
12/17	7,830	811	10.4%	29,000
12/16	6,794	508	7.5%	29,000
12/15	6,956	869	12.5%	26,000
Annual Growth	0.6%	(6.0%)	—	(2.0%)

2019 Year-End Financials

Debt ratio: 35.42%
Return on equity: 23.37%
Cash ($ mil.): 397
Current ratio: 1.46
Long-term debt ($ mil.): 2,985

No. of shares (mil.): 144
Dividends
Yield: 1.6%
Payout: 42.0%
Market value ($ mil.): 16,632

	STOCK PRICE ($) FY Close	P/E High/Low		PER SHARE ($) Earnings	Dividends	Book Value
12/19	115.26	25	15	4.61	1.94	21.02
12/18	70.95	28	18	3.75	1.90	19.11
12/17	100.99	19	15	5.15	1.82	28.31
12/16	74.93	24	16	3.25	1.72	24.45
12/15	61.31	14	10	5.46	1.64	23.51
Annual Growth	17.1%	—	—	(4.1%)	4.3%	(2.8%)

Dow Inc

Auditors: DELOITTE & TOUCHE LLP

LOCATIONS

HQ: Dow Inc
2211 H.H. Dow Way, Midland, MI 48674
Phone: 989 636-1000
Web: www.dow.com

HISTORICAL FINANCIALS

Company Type: Public

Income Statement
FYE: December 31

	REVENUE ($ mil.)	NET INCOME ($ mil.)	NET PROFIT MARGIN	EMPLOYEES
12/20	38,542	1,225	3.2%	35,700
12/19	42,951	(1,359)	—	36,500
12/18	60,278	4,499	7.5%	37,000
12/17	55,508	466	0.8%	—
12/16	48,158	4,318	9.0%	—
Annual Growth	(5.4%)	(27.0%)	—	—

2020 Year-End Financials

Debt ratio: 27.83%
Return on equity: 9.41%
Cash ($ mil.): 5,104
Current ratio: 1.72
Long-term debt ($ mil.): 16,491

No. of shares (mil.): 743
Dividends
Yield: 5.0%
Payout: 170.7%
Market value ($ mil.): 41,247

	STOCK PRICE ($) FY Close	P/E High/Low		PER SHARE ($) Earnings	Dividends	Book Value
12/20	55.50	35	13	1.64	2.80	16.73
12/19	54.73	—	—	(1.84)	2.10	18.26
Annual Growth	0.3%	—	—	—	7.5%	(2.2%)

DTE Energy Co

DTE Energy provides Detroit with a reliable spark. The holding company's utility operations consist primarily of DTE Electric and DTE Gas. DTE Electric distributes electricity to some 2.2 million customers in southeastern Michigan. The utility's power plants have a generating capacity of more than 11700 MW. The company's DTE Gas unit distributes natural gas to 1.3 million customers throughout Michigan. DTE Energy runs non-regulated businesses in gas storage & pipelines power & industrial operations and energy trading.

HISTORY

DTE Energy's predecessor threw its first switch in 1886 when George Peck and local investors incorporated the Edison Illuminating Company of Detroit. Neighboring utility Peninsular Electric Light was formed in 1891 and both companies bought smaller utilities until they merged in 1903 to form Detroit Edison. A subsidiary of holding company North American Co. Detroit Edison was incorporated in New York to secure financing for power plants.

Detroit's growth in the 1920s and 1930s led the utility to build plants and buy others in outlying areas. Detroit Edison acquired Michigan Electric Power which had been divested from its holding company under the Public Utility Holding Company Act of 1935 and was itself divested from North American in 1940.

The post-WWII boom prompted Detroit Edison to build more plants most of them coal-fired. In 1953 it joined a consortium of 34 companies to build Fermi 1 a nuclear plant brought on line in 1963. Still strapped for power Detroit Edison built the coal-fired Monroe plant which began service in 1970. In 1972 Fermi 1 had a partial core meltdown and was taken off line.

Detroit Edison began shipping low-sulfur Montana coal through its Wisconsin terminal in 1974 which reduced the cost of obtaining the fuel. The next year it began building another nuke Fermi 2. The nuke had cost more than $4.8 billion by the time it went on line in 1988. That year the utility began its landfill gas recovery operation (now DTE Biomass Energy).

A recession pounded automakers in the early 1990s leading to cutbacks in electricity purchases. In 1992 Congress passed the Energy Policy Act allowing wholesale power competition. In 1993 a fire shut down Fermi 2 for almost two years. Michigan's public service commission (PSC) approved retail customer-choice pilot programs for its utilities in 1994. Detroit Edison and rival Consumers Energy (now CMS Energy) took the PSC to court.

DTE Energy became Detroit Edison's holding company in 1996. The next year it formed DTE Energy Trading (to broker power) and DTE-Co-Energy (to provide energy-management services and sell power to large customers). It also formed Plug Power with Mechanical Technology to develop fuel cells that convert natural gas to power without combustion.

In 1997 and 1998 the PSC bolstered by state court decisions issued orders to restructure Michigan's utilities. The transition to retail competition began in 1998. That year DTE Energy and natural gas provider Michigan Consolidated Gas (MichCon) began collaborating on some operations including billing and meter reading. DTE and GE formed a venture to sell and install Plug Power fuel cell systems.

A higher court shot down the PSC's restructuring orders in 1999 but DTE Energy and CMS Energy decided to implement customer choice using PSC guidelines. That year the US Department of Energy selected DTE Energy to install the world's first super power-cable which could carry three times as much electricity as conventional copper. Also in 1999 DTE Energy agreed to acquire MCN Energy MichCon's parent.

In 2000 DTE Energy formed subsidiary International Transmission (ITC) to hold Detroit Edison's transmission assets; the next year ITC joined the Midwest Independent System Operator which began to manage ITC's network. It also completed its $4.3 billion purchase of MCN Energy in 2001. Full deregulation of Michigan's electricity market was completed in 2002. International Transmission was sold in 2003 to affiliates of Kohlberg Kravis Roberts and Trimaran Capital Partners for $610 million.

In 2007 it sold its Michigan Antrim Shale gas exploration and production assets to Atlas Energy Resources (which later was acquired by Chevron) for about $1.3 billion. That year due to the expiration of synthetic fuel production tax credits DTE Energy exited the synfuels business. In 2010 it sold its rail service unit (DTE Rail Services) to FreightCar America for $23 million.

In 2012 DTE Energy signed a deal with Spectra Energy and Enbridge to jointly develop the NEXUS Gas Transmission system a 250-mile long pipeline project to transport the growing supplies of Ohio Utica shale gas to markets in Michigan Ohio and Ontario.

To raise cash to pay down debt and to focus on its core businesses in 2012 the company sold its Unconventional Gas Production business (88000 acres of gas and oil production assets in the western Barnett and Marble Falls shale areas of Texas) for $255 million.

In 2013 the company opened the northern portion of the Bluestone Project. The 44.5 mile pipeline (which interconnects with Millennium Pipeline in New York) transports up to 600000 million cu. ft. per day to both the Millennium Pipeline in Broome County New York and the Tennessee Gas Pipeline in Susquehanna County Pennsylvania. (The southern portion of Bluestone interconnects with Tennessee Pipeline).

In 2013 DTE Energy has reached an agreement to sell its historic Marysville Power Plant (an idled coal-fired plant on the St. Clair River) to Commercial Development Company.

EXECUTIVES

Svp And General Counsel, Bruce Peterson
Chairman And Ceo, Gerard M. Anderson, $1,293,519 total compensation
President Dte Gathering And Processing, Richard L. Redmond, age 63
Chairman And President Dte Energy Foundation, Faye A. Nelson, age 67
President And Coo Dte Electric, Trevor F. Lauer, age 56
President And Coo, Gerardo (Jerry) Norcia, $650,926 total compensation
President And Coo Dte Gas, Mark W. Stiers, age 58
President Dte Energy Services, David Ruud, age 53
President Dte Biomass Energy, Mark Cousino
Svp And Cfo, Peter B. Oleksiak, age 54, $553,519 total compensation
President Dte Energy Trading, Steven Mabry
Vp And Cio, Steve Ambrose
President Dte Gas Stprage And Pipelines, David Slater
President Dte Energy Foundation, Lynette Dowler
Executive Vice President Major Enterprise Projects, Ron May
Vp And Cio, Steven Ambrose
Vice President Dte Methane Resources, Jan Stewart

Vice President Regulatory Affairs, Daniel Brudzynski
Senior Vice President Distribution Operations, Heather Rivard
Vice President Distribution Operations, Marco Bruzzano
Vice President Corporate Strategy, Camilo Serna
Senior Vice President Commercial Develop, Gregg Russell
Vice Chairman And Chief Administrative Officer, David E. (Dave) Meador, age 63
Secretary, Francesca Racz
Auditors: PricewaterhouseCoopers LLP

LOCATIONS

HQ: DTE Energy Co
   One Energy Plaza, Detroit, MI 48226-1279
Phone: 313 235-4000
Web: www.dteenergy.com

PRODUCTS/OPERATIONS

2018 Sales

	$ mil.	% of total
Utility		
Electric	5,298	37
Gas	1,436	10
Eliminations	(64)	-
Non-Utility		
Energy Trading	5,557	36
Power and Industrial Products	2,204	14
Gas Storage and Pipelines	485	3
Corporate and Other	3	-
Eliminations	(707)	-
Total	**14,212**	**100**

COMPETITORS

AEP	Indiana Michigan Power
CMS Energy	Nicor Gas
CMS Enterprises	PG&E Corporation
Consumers Energy	SEMCO ENERGY
DPL	WEC Energy
Dairyland Power	Xcel Energy
Exelon Energy	

HISTORICAL FINANCIALS

Company Type: Public

Income Statement FYE: December 31

	REVENUE ($ mil.)	NET INCOME ($ mil.)	NET PROFIT MARGIN	EMPLOYEES
12/19	12,669	1,169	9.2%	10,700
12/18	14,212	1,120	7.9%	10,600
12/17	12,607	1,134	9.0%	10,200
12/16	10,630	868	8.2%	10,000
12/15	10,337	727	7.0%	10,000
Annual Growth	**5.2%**	**12.6%**	**—**	**1.7%**

2019 Year-End Financials

Debt ratio: 41.66%	No. of shares (mil.): 192
Return on equity: 10.67%	Dividends
Cash ($ mil.): 93	Yield: 2.9%
Current ratio: 0.77	Payout: 64.6%
Long-term debt ($ mil.): 15,935	Market value ($ mil.): 24,962

	STOCK PRICE ($) FY Close	P/E High/Low		PER SHARE ($) Earnings	Dividends	Book Value
12/19	129.87	21	17	6.31	3.85	60.73
12/18	110.30	19	15	6.17	3.59	56.27
12/17	109.46	18	15	6.32	3.36	53.03
12/16	98.51	21	16	4.83	3.06	50.22
12/15	80.19	23	18	4.05	2.84	48.88
Annual Growth	**12.8%**	—	—	**11.7%**	**7.9%**	**5.6%**

Duke Energy Carolinas LLC

LOCATIONS

HQ: Duke Energy Carolinas LLC
   526 South Church Street, Charlotte, NC 28202-1803
Phone: 704 382-3853

HISTORICAL FINANCIALS

Company Type: Public

Income Statement FYE: December 31

	REVENUE ($ mil.)	NET INCOME ($ mil.)	NET PROFIT MARGIN	EMPLOYEES
12/19	7,395	1,403	19.0%	—
12/18	7,300	1,071	14.7%	—
12/17	7,302	1,214	16.6%	—
12/16	7,322	1,166	15.9%	—
12/15	7,229	1,081	15.0%	—
Annual Growth	**0.6%**	**6.7%**	**—**	**—**

2019 Year-End Financials

Debt ratio: 27.01%—	
Return on equity: 11.46%	Dividends
Cash ($ mil.): 18	Yield: —
Current ratio: 0.92	Payout: —
Long-term debt ($ mil.): 11,442	Market value ($ mil.): —

Duke Energy Corp

Duke Energy is one of the top electric power holding companies in the US serving about 7.8 million retail customers in six US states covering more than 90000square miles of service area in the Southeast and Midwest. Its substantial coal nuclear and natural gas assets generate more than 50000 MW of electricity. The company also serves about 1.6 million natural gas customers through more than 65000 miles of pipelines. Duke Energy's rate-regulated utilities serve customers in the Carolinas Florida Ohio Indiana and Kentucky. The company also owns some renewable energy assets like wind and solar farms.

HISTORY

Surgeon Gill Wylie founded Catawba Power Company in 1899; its first hydroelectric plant in South Carolina was on line by 1904. The next year Wylie and James "Buck" Duke (founder of the American Tobacco Company and Duke University's namesake) formed Southern Power Company with Wylie as president.

In 1910 Buck Duke became president of Southern Power and organized Mill-Power Supply to sell electric equipment and appliances. He also began investing in electricity-powered textile mills which prospered as a result of the electric power and continued to bring in customers. He formed the Southern Public Utility Company in 1913 to buy other Piedmont-region utilities. Wylie died in 1924 the same year the company was renamed Duke Power; Buck Duke died the next year.

Growing after WWII the company went public in 1950 and moved to the NYSE in 1961. It also formed its real estate arm Crescent Resources in

the 1960s. Insulating itself from the 1970s energy crises Duke invested in coal mining and three nuclear plants the first completed in 1974.

In 1988 Duke began to develop power projects outside its home region and it also bought neighboring utility Nantahala Power and Light. The next year it formed a joint venture with Fluor's Fluor Daniel unit to provide engineering and construction services to power generators. Mill-Power Supply was sold in 1990.

By the 1990s Duke had moved into overseas markets acquiring an Argentine power station in 1992. It also tried its hand at telecommunications creating DukeNet Communications in 1994 to build fiber-optic systems and in 1996 it joined oil giant Mobil to create a power trading and marketing business. As the US power industry traveled toward deregulation Duke also sought natural gas operations. It targeted PanEnergy which owned a major pipeline system in the eastern half of the US. Duke Power bought PanEnergy in 1997 to form Duke Energy Corporation.

Seeing an opportunity in 1998 Duke formed Duke Communication Services to provide antenna sites to the fast-growing wireless communications industry. It also acquired a 52% stake in Electroquil an electric power generating company in Guayaquil Ecuador. That year it purchased a pipeline company in Australia from PG&E; it also bought three PG&E power plants to compete in California's deregulated electric utility marketplace.

Duke merged its pipeline business Duke Energy Trading and Transport with TEPPCO Partners and acquired gas processing operations from Union Pacific Resources. It sold Panhandle Eastern Pipe Line and gas-related assets in the Midwest to CMS Energy in 1999 to reduce operations in the region and made plans to build a pipeline extending from Alabama to Florida (completed in 2002).

To further enhance natural gas operations in other regions Duke bought El Paso's East Tennessee Natural Gas pipeline unit in 2000 and a 20% stake in Canadian 88 Energy; it also purchased $1.4 billion in South American generation assets including assets from Dominion Resources and the gas trading operations of Mobil (now Exxon Mobil) in the Netherlands. Also in 2000 Duke and Phillips Petroleum (now ConocoPhillips) merged their gas gathering and processing and NGL operations into Duke Energy Field Services.

In 2001 Duke announced the $8 billion acquisition of Westcoast Energy; the purchase which was completed in 2002 added more than a million natural gas customers and 6900 miles of gas pipeline in Canada. That year Duke sold its Duke Engineering & Services unit to Framatome ANP and its DukeSolutions unit to Ameresco. Duke Energy Field Services purchased Chevron's 33% stake in Discovery Producer Services which operates a Gulf of Mexico gas pipeline and nearby processing facilities.

Duke set out to sell $1.5 billion in assets in 2003 to focus on core operations. The company sold its Empire State Pipeline subsidiary to National Fuel Gas for $240 million and sold its stakes in the Alliance Pipeline Alliance Canada Marketing and the Aux Sable refinery to Enbridge and Fort Chicago Energy Partners for $245 million. Also that year Duke sold its stake in Foothills Pipe Lines to TransCanada for $181 million and it sold $300 million in renewable energy facilities to privately owned Highstar Renewable Fuels.

In 2004 the company sold an Indonesian power plant to Freeport-McMoRan in a $300 million deal and it sold its 30% interest in the Vector Pipeline to Enbridge and DTE Energy for $145 million. It also sold the assets of its merchant finance business (Duke Capital Partners) and its stake in Canadian 88 Energy (now Esprit Exploration). Following this trend in 2005 Duke Energy sold its

620-MW Grays Harbor facility (Washington) to an affiliate of Invenergy for $21 million.

In 2006 Duke sold a 50% stake in its real estate subsidiary Crescent Resources to Morgan Stanley Real Estate. That year the company bought an 825-MW power plant in Rockingham County North Carolina from Dynegy for $195 million.

In a major industry power move in 2006 the company bought energy provider Cinergy in a $9 billion stock swap. Reorganizing its business lines to focus on its US power businesses that year Duke Energy sold its commercial marketing and trading businesses to Fortis and in 2007 it spun off its natural gas transmission business as Spectra Energy. The company also exited the European energy marketing business; it also left the proprietary (third-party) energy trading business in North America (primarily made up of Duke Energy North America or DENA sold to LS Power Equity Partners for a reported $1.5 billion). Duke also wound down its energy-trading joint venture with Exxon Mobil.

In 2008 Duke moved to strengthen its alternative energy assets by buying wind energy producer Catamount Energy for about $240 million plus assumed debt. Catamount had about 500MW of renewable energy in operation.

That year as part of its refocusing on its energy businesses the company stopped reporting on its Crescent Resources unit (a joint venture with Morgan Stanley Real Estate Fund which manages land holdings and develops real estate projects).

It acquired its first solar project Blue Wing Solar now a 14-MW solar farm in San Antonio from juwi solar in January 2010.

That year it formed a partnership with Integrys Energy Services and Smart Energy Capital to build solar projects across the US. In 2010 Duke Energy also teamed up with Areva to build a $250 million biomass-fueled power plant in Shelton in Washington state.

To raise cash that year Duke Energy sold its 50% stake in DukeNet communications to investment firm Alinda Capital Partners for $137 million.

Boosting its role in the transmission sector in 2011 Duke Energy formed a transmission utility joint venture with American Transmission. Duke-American Transmission Co. builds owns and operates new power transmission infrastructure across North America.

Through its Duke Energy Renewables unit in 2011 the company acquired the Shirley Wind Power Project a 20-MW wind farm in Wisconsin from Central Hudson Energy Group. The project has a 20-year contract to sell its output to Wisconsin Public Service Corp.

In late 2011 the Renewables unit acquired three commercial solar projects in southwestern North Carolina. It bought the photovoltaic projects from ESA Renewables and the power from each solar farm is sold through Blue Ridge Mountain EMC to the Tennessee Valley Authority. The unit has four other commercial solar farms in North Carolina all located outside of Duke Energy's regulated service territories in the state. That year it also snapped up two solar farms in Arizona (in Ajo and Bagdad) from Recurrent Energy doubling its portfolio of commercial solar projects in operation and expanding its footprint further into the western US.

Not neglecting its international growth markets in 2012 Duke Energy International acquired CGE Group's Iberoamericana de Energ a Ibener S.A. subsidiary in Chile including hydroelectric generating assets with 140 MW capacity for $415 million. Chile is Duke's the fourth largest non-US country in terms of generating capacity.

In a major US expansion in 2012 Duke acquired Progress Energy in a $32 billion deal. The acquisition created a more than $100 billion enterprise with the US' largest regulated customer base and was aimed at securing major costs savings in fuel purchasing power generating plant operations and other economies of scale benefits.

In 2012 Duke had almost 1300 MW of wind and solar powered plants in operation.

Growing its solar footprint in California in 2013 Duke Energy Renewables acquired a 4.5 MW solar project the largest solar generation facility in San Francisco from solar project developer Recurrent Energy. That year it also bought the 21-megawatt Highlander solar power projects in Twentynine Palms California. All told Duke Energy Renewables has more than 100 MW of solar generating capacity (16 solar farms in the US).

EXECUTIVES

Evp And Cfo, Steven K. Young, age 60, $625,000 total compensation

Svp Global Risk Management And Insurance And Chief Risk Officer, Keith G. Butler, age 60

Evp Chief Legal Officer And Corporate Secretary, Julie S. Janson, age 55, $520,833 total compensation

Evp; President Natural Gas Business, Franklin H. Yoho, age 61

Svp And Chief Distriution Officer, Michael A. Lewis, age 58

Evp Market Solutions And President Carolinas Region, Lloyd M. Yates, age 59, $661,458 total compensation

Chairman President And Ceo, Lynn J. Good, age 60, $1,291,667 total compensation

Evp And President Midwest And Florida, Douglas F. (Doug) Esamann, age 62

Svp Nuclear Support, Dhiaa M. Jamil, age 63, $737,500 total compensation

President Duke Energy Indiana, Melody Birmingham-Byrd

State President North Carolina, David B. Fountain

State President Ohio And Kentucky, James P. (Jim) Henning

Svp And Chief Nuclear Officer, John W. (Bill) Pitesa

Vp And Cio, Christopher B. (Chris) Heck

Evp Administration And Chief Human Resources Officer, Melissa H. Anderson, age 55

State President South Carolina, Kodwo Ghartey-Tagoe

State President Florida, Harry K. Sideris

Vice President Call Center Operations, Larry Eiser

Svp Financial Planning And Analysis, Bill Currens

Vice President Of Marketing, Jack Farley

Vice President Human Resources Business Partners, Jim O'Connor

Vice President, David Litchfield

Vice President Commercial Strategy, Chip Wood

Executive Vice President, John McArthur

Vice President, Steve Immel

Executive Vice President, Kevin Howell

Vice President, Michael Engelman

Vice President Finance, Bill Dickey

Vice President, Angeline Clinton

Vice President Business Development, John Upchurch

Vice President Corporate Finance And Investor Relations, Kenneth Lockwood

Site Vice President, Dave Baxter

Vice President, John Stowell

Senior Vice President Government Relations, David Dave Marventano

Vice President Internal Audit And Chief Ethics And Compliance Officer, Jeffrey Stone

Vice President, Rudi Zipter

Vice President Asset Management, Ron Snead

Vice President, Arthur Raymond

Vice President And Chief Diversity Officer, Joni Davis

Vice President Talent Management, Lisa Marcuz

Vice President Litigation, Vijay Bondada

Vice President And Chief Ethics And Compliance Officer, Sandra Wyckoff

Svp Corporate Development, Karl Newlin

Executive Vice President And Chief Human Resources Officer, Jennifer L Weber

Executive Vice President, Mario Alonso

Vice President, Eric Bruce

Executive Vice President, Nick Caruso

Executive Vice President, Robert Doty

Executive Vice President, Alec Dreyer

Vice President, Gene Foster

Executive Vice President, Catherine James

Vice President, Griff Jones

Executive Vice President, Henry Jones

Vice President, Jane Jones

Vice President, Norelle Lundy

Vice President, Donna McGinnis

Senior Vice President, Jeffrey McParland

Executive Vice President, Holli Nichols

Vice President, Margaret Nollen

Vice President, Mike Sanders

Vice President, April Farris

Board Member, Bob Davis

Pac Treasurer, William Mayhew

Board Member, Robert Davis

Board Member, Charles Moorman

Board Member, Carlos Saladrigas

Board Member, Tom Skains

Board Of Directors, Dan Dimicco

Board Member, Theodore Craver

Board Of Directors, Marie Mckee

Board Member, Austin Mckee

Treasurer, Brad Robinson

Auditors: Deloitte & Touche LLP

LOCATIONS

HQ: Duke Energy Corp
550 South Tryon Street, Charlotte, NC 28202-1803
Phone: 704 382-3853
Web: www.duke-energy.com

PRODUCTS/OPERATIONS

2018 Sales

	$ mil.	% of total
Electric Utilities and Infrastructure	22,273	90
Gas Utilities and Infrastructure	1,881	8
Commercial Renewables	477	2
Other	89	
Eliminations	(199)	-
Total	**24,521**	**100**

2018 Sales

	$ mil.	% of total
Regulated electric	22,097	90
Regulated natural gas	1,773	7
Nonregulated electric and other	651	3
Total	**24,521**	**100**

COMPETITORS

AEP	PG&E Corporation
AES	Piedmont Natural Gas
Avista	SCANA
CenterPoint Energy	Southern Company
Entergy	TVA
Exelon	Williams Companies

HISTORICAL FINANCIALS

Company Type: Public

Income Statement

	REVENUE ($ mil.)	NET INCOME ($ mil.)	NET PROFIT MARGIN	EMPLOYEES
12/19	25,079	3,748	14.9%	28,793
12/18	24,521	2,666	10.9%	30,083
12/17	23,565	3,059	13.0%	29,060
12/16	22,743	2,152	9.5%	28,798
12/15	23,459	2,816	12.0%	29,188
Annual Growth	1.7%	7.4%	—	(0.3%)

2019 Year-End Financials

Debt ratio: 38.57%
Return on equity: 8.27%
Cash ($ mil.): 311
Current ratio: 0.62
Long-term debt ($ mil.): 54,985

No. of shares (mil.): 733
Dividends
 Yield: 4.1%
 Payout: 77.5%
Market value ($ mil.): 66,857

	STOCK PRICE ($) FY Close	P/E High/Low	PER SHARE ($) Earnings	Dividends	Book Value
12/19	91.21	19 17	5.06	3.75	63.88
12/18	86.30	24 19	3.76	3.64	60.27
12/17	84.11	21 18	4.36	3.49	59.63
12/16	77.62	28 23	3.11	3.36	58.62
12/15	71.39	22 16	4.05	3.24	57.74
Annual Growth	6.3%	— —	5.7%	3.7%	2.6%

DuPont de Nemours Inc

DuPont (formerly DowDuPont Inc) is back on its own after its brief merger with Dow. In 2019 the company completed the separation of its materials science business through the spun-off of Dow and its agriculture business through the spun-off of Corteva. DuPont is now organized into five business segments: Electronics & Imaging (products used in the semiconductor display and printing industries); Transportation & Industrial (resins adhesives and lubricants used in industries including aerospace automotive electronics industrial healthcare and consumer markets); Nutrition & Biosciences (products used in the food beverage and pharmaceutical industries); Safety & Construction (fibers and foams non-wovens water purification and protective garments); and Non-Core (metallization pastes backsheet materials silicone encapsulants and adhesives). About 40% of the company's revenue comes from Asia Pacific.

Operations

DuPont operates through five reportable segments: Nutrition & Biosciences; Safety & Construction; Transportation & Industrial; Electronics & Imaging; and Non-Core.

Nutrition & Biosciences is an innovation-driven and customer-focused segment that provides solutions for the global food and beverage dietary supplements pharma home and personal care energy and animal nutrition markets. This segment generates about 30% of company's total revenue.

Safety & Construction is the global leader in providing innovative engineered products and integrated systems for a number of industries including worker safety water purification and separation aerospace energy medical packaging and building materials. Nearly a quarter of the company's sales comes from this segment.

Transportation & Industrial provides high-performance engineering resins adhesives silicones lubricants and parts to engineers and designers in the transportation electronics healthcare industrial and consumer end-markets to enable systems solutions for demanding applications and environments. It accounts for about a quarter of the DuPont's revenue.

Electronics & Imaging is a leading global supplier of differentiated materials and systems for a broad range of consumer electronics including mobile devices television monitors personal computers and electronics used in a variety of industries. This segment accounts for more than 15% of the total revenue.

The Non-Core segment is a global supplier of key materials for the manufacturing of photovoltaic cells and panels including innovative SOLAMET metallization pastes TEDLAR backsheet materials and FORTASUN silicone encapsulants and adhesives. Approximately 10% of the revenue comes from this segment.

Geographic Reach

Delaware-based DuPont has manufacturing processing marketing and research and development facilities regional purchasing offices and distribution centers located throughout the world. The US is the largest market in terms of revenue accounting for about a-third. Outside US Asia Pacific also generates 40% of company's total revenue followed by EMEA presented some 25% more than 5% comes Latin America and the remaining revenue is from Canada.

Sales and Marketing

Most products are marketed primarily through the company's sales organization and through distributors in some regions. The company has a diverse worldwide network which markets and distributes its brands to customers globally. This network consists of the DuPont's sales and marketing organization partnering with distributors independent retailers cooperatives and agents throughout the world.

Financial Performance

DuPont's revenue dipped 5% from $22.6 billion in 2018 to $21.5 billion in 2019. The decline was due to lower sales in all of the company's segments.

In 2019 net income available for DuPont common stockholders totaled $498 million an 87% decrease from the previous year.

The company's cash at the end of 2019 was $1.6 billion. Operating activities provided $1.4 billion while investing activities used $2.3 billion mainly for capital expenditures. Financing activities used another $11.6 billion primarily for cash held by Dow and Corteva.

Strategy

In the past couple of years DuPont has been strengthening its portfolio of water purification and separation technologies. The company has done this by acquiring multiple companies of the same nature. Some of these acquisitions contribute to innovation and cost reduction of the company's operations.

Mergers and Acquisitions

In early 2020 DuPont completed the 2019 acquisitions of Desalitech inge GmbH Memcor and OxyMem Limited; adding to its leading portfolio of water purification and separation technologies including ultrafiltration reverse osmosis and ion exchange resins. These four recent acquisitions support DuPont's goal to increase access to the products and technologies needed to meet global customers' current and future challenges including the increased need to recycle water while reducing the energy requirements to generate clean water. The recent acquisitions further broaden DuPont's portfolio and enhance the company's ability to accelerate innovation and offer customers better levels of service while reducing the life cycle costs of clean water.

In late 2019 DuPont Safety & Construction (DuPont) has signed an agreement to acquire the Ultrafiltration Membrane business from BASF including inge GmbH. The transaction including the business' international workforce its headquarters and production site in Greifenberg Germany and associated intellectual property currently owned by BASF SE is expected to close by the end of 2019 subject to customary closing conditions and regulatory approvals. Financial terms of the agreement were not disclosed.

Around the same time the company also acquired the Memcor business including ultrafiltration and membrane biofiltration technologies from Evoqua Water Technologies Corp. The Evoqua ultrafiltration and membrane biofiltration (MBR) technologies add to DuPont's leading portfolio of water purification and separation capabilities including ultrafiltration reverse osmosis and ion exchange resins. Together with the intended acquisition of BASF's ultrafiltration business which is also expected to close by the end of 2019 subject to customary closing conditions and regulatory approvals DuPont will be even better positioned to provide the products technology and geographic diversification needed to meet current and future customer demand.

Company Background

DuPont is a Delaware corporation formed in 2015 (formerly DowDuPont Inc) for the purpose of effecting an all-stock merger of equals transactions between The Dow Chemical Company (Historical Dow) and E. I. du Pont de Nemours and Company (Historical EID).

EXECUTIVES

Ceo And Director, Edward D. (Ed) Breen
General Counsel And Secretary, Stacy L. Fox
Coo Agriculture Division, James C. Collins
Coo Materials Science Division, James R. (Jim) Fitterling
Cfo, Howard I. Ungerleider
Coo Specialty Products Division, C. Marc Doyle
Co-controller Dowdupont And Vp Controllers And Tax Dow, Ron Edmonds
Co-controller, Jeanmarie F. Desmond
Evp Corteva Agriscience Business Platform, Rajan Gajaria
Chairman, Andrew N. Liveris

LOCATIONS

HQ: DuPont de Nemours Inc
974 Centre Road, Building 730, Wilmington, DE 19805
Phone: 302 774-3034
Web: www.investors.dupont.com

COMPETITORS

3M	L'Air Liquide
Ahlstrom	LANXESS
Air Products	Lucite
Akzo Nobel	Mitsubishi Chemical
Asahi Kasei	Holdings
BASF SE	Mitsui Chemicals
Bayer AG	Occidental Chemical
Cargill	Olin
Chevron Phillips Chemical	PPG Industries
	Reliance Industries
ConAgra	SABIC
DIC Corporation	Scotts Miracle-Gro
Eastman Chemical	Shell Chemicals
Evonik Degussa	Sherwin-Williams
ExxonMobil Chemical	Shin-Etsu Chemical
FMC	Sumitomo

Formosa Plastics   Syngenta
Henkel   Taminco
Koch Industries Inc.   The Linde Group

HISTORICAL FINANCIALS
Company Type: Public

Income Statement
FYE: December 31

	REVENUE ($ mil.)	NET INCOME ($ mil.)	NET PROFIT MARGIN	EMPLOYEES
12/19	21,512	498	2.3%	35,000
12/18	22,594	3,845	17.0%	—
12/17	11,672	1,159	9.9%	—
Annual Growth	35.8%	(34.5%)	—	—

2019 Year-End Financials

Debt ratio: 25.14%
Return on equity: 0.74%
Cash ($ mil.): 1,540
Current ratio: 1.20
Long-term debt ($ mil.): 13,617

No. of shares (mil.): 738
Dividends
  Yield: 0.9%
  Payout: 29.9%
Market value ($ mil.): 47,416

	STOCK PRICE ($) FY Close	P/E High/Low	PER SHARE ($) Earnings	Dividends	Book Value
12/19	64.20	114 45	0.67	0.60	55.50
12/18	53.48	15 10	4.96	4.56	124.67
12/17	71.22	34 30	2.15	5.28	(0.00)
/0.00	—	— (0.00)	0.00	(0.00)	
/0.00	—	— (0.00)	0.00	(0.00)	
Annual Growth	—	— —	—	—	—

DXC Technology Co

Auditors: DELOITTE & TOUCHE LLP

LOCATIONS

HQ: DXC Technology Co
1775 Tysons Boulevard, Tysons, VA 22102
Phone: 703 245-9675
Web: www.dxc.technology

HISTORICAL FINANCIALS
Company Type: Public

Income Statement
FYE: March 31

	REVENUE ($ mil.)	NET INCOME ($ mil.)	NET PROFIT MARGIN	EMPLOYEES
03/20	19,577	(5,369)	—	138,000
03/19	20,753	1,257	6.1%	130,000
03/18	24,556	1,751	7.1%	150,000
03/17	7,607	(123)	—	—
Annual Growth	37.0%	—	—	—

2020 Year-End Financials

Debt ratio: 38.25%
Return on equity: (-66.16%)
Cash ($ mil.): 3,679
Current ratio: 1.14
Long-term debt ($ mil.): 8,672

No. of shares (mil.): 253
Dividends
  Yield: 6.4%
  Payout:
Market value ($ mil.): 3,309

	STOCK PRICE ($) FY Close	P/E High/Low	PER SHARE ($) Earnings	Dividends	Book Value
03/20	13.05	— —	(20.76)	0.84	18.87
03/19	64.31	23 11	4.47	0.76	42.48
03/18	100.53	17 11	6.04	0.72	47.26
03/17	0.00	— —	(0.88)	0.00	(0.00)
Annual Growth	—	— —	—	—	—

Eagle Bancorp Inc (MD)

For those nest eggs that need a little help hatching holding company Eagle Bancorp would recommend its community-oriented EagleBank subsidiary. The bank serves businesses and individuals through more than 20 branches in Maryland Virginia and Washington DC and its suburbs. Deposit products include checking savings and money market accounts; certificates of deposit; and IRAs. Commercial real estate loans represent more than 70% of its loan portfolio while construction loans make up another more than 20%. The bank which has significant expertise as a Small Business Administration lender also writes business consumer and home equity loans. EagleBank offers insurance products through an agreement with The Meltzer Group.

Operations

Like other retail banks Eagle Bancorp makes the bulk of its money from loan interest. About 86% of its total revenue came from loan interest (including fees) during 2015 while another 4% came from interest on investment securities. The rest of its revenue came from deposit account service charges (2% of revenue) and non-recurring income sources.

The bank has two direct subsidiaries: Bethesda Leasing LLC which holds the bank's foreclosed real estate (owned and acquired); and Eagle Insurance Services LLC which provides commercial and retail insurance products through a referral arrangement with insurance broker The Meltzer Group.

Geographic Reach

The Bethesda Maryland-based bank operates 21 branches in Maryland Virginia and Washington DC (as of mid-2016) including nine in Northern Virginia seven in Montgomery County and five in the District of Columbia.

Sales and Marketing

Eagle Bancorp serves local businesses professional clients individuals sole proprietors small and medium-sized businesses non-profits and investors. Other clients are from the healthcare accountant and attorney markets.

The bank spent $2.7 million on marketing and advertising during 2015 up 38% from the $2 million it spent in 2014 mostly due to higher digital and print advertising and sponsorship costs.

Financial Performance

Eagle Bancorp's annual revenue has more than doubled since 2011 mostly thanks to strong loan growth with the addition of new branches. Meanwhile its net income has more than tripled as the bank has kept a lid on credit loss provisions and overhead costs.

The bank's revenue jumped 33% to $279.8 million during 2015 largely thanks to a rise in interest income as its loan assets grew 16%.

Strong revenue growth in 2015 coupled with an absence of merger expenses drove Eagle Bancorp's net income up 55% to $84.1 million. The bank's operating cash levels spiked 66% to $98.5 million for the year thanks to a strong rise in cash-based earnings.

Strategy

The company has been focused on growing within its existing markets. Its strategy for further growth includes continuing to seek opportunities to open or acquire new banking locations while waiting out record low interest rates. Eagle's strict loan underwriting standards — it didn't write subprime residential mortgages and didn't buy securities backed by subprime mortgages — has helped it have fewer problem loans the downfall for many banks.

Beyond its core lending and deposit businesses Eagle Bancorp continues to expand its other product offerings as well. In 2015 it introduced a Full Service Equipment Leasing program which provided alternative and convenient financing for all types of business equipment for customers.

Mergers and Acquisitions

In November 2014 Eagle Bancorp significantly expanded its presence in Northern Virginia after it purchased Fairfax County-based Virginia Heritage. The deal added six Virginia Heritage Bank branches (renamed as EagleBank) in northern Virginia along with $917.4 million in assets — including $715 million in loans and $737 million in deposits.

EXECUTIVES

Evp; Sevp And Coo Eaglebank, Susan G. Riel, age 71, $478,806 total compensation
Chairman President And Ceo; Chairman And Ceo Eaglebank; President Ronald D. Paul Cos., Ronald D. Paul, age 65, $863,565 total compensation
Evp; Evp And Chief Credit Officer Eaglebank, Janice L. Williams, age 63, $391,758 total compensation
Evp And General Counsel Eagle Bancorp And Eaglebank, Laurence E. Bensignor, age 64
Evp; Evp And Chief Lending Officer Commercial Real Estate Eaglebank, Antonio F. Marquez, age 62, $368,256 total compensation
Evp; Evp And Chief Lending Officer Commercial And Industrial Eaglebank, Lindsey S. Rheaume, age 60
Evp And Cfo, Charles D. Levingston, age 40
Vice President, Joan Grant
Senior Vice President Commercial Banking Team Leader, Derek Whitwer
Vice President, Linda Dawkins
Vice President Facilities Operations Manager, Shawn Cox
Assistant Vice President Branch Relationship Manager, Aida Tannous
Vice Chairman Of The Board Of Company And Bank, Norman Pozez
Vice President Treasurer, Scott Clark
Auditors: Crowe LLP

LOCATIONS

HQ: Eagle Bancorp Inc (MD)
7830 Old Georgetown Road, Third Floor, Bethesda, MD 20814
Phone: 301 986-1800
Web: www.eaglebankcorp.com

PRODUCTS/OPERATIONS

Selected Subsidiaries

EagleBank
  Bethesda Leasing LLC
  Eagle Insurance Services LLC
  Fidelity Mortgage Inc.
Eagle Commercial Ventures LLC

COMPETITORS

BB&T	OBA Financial Services
Bank of America	PNC Financial
Capital One	Sandy Spring Bancorp
M&T Bank	SunTrust

HISTORICAL FINANCIALS

Company Type: Public

Income Statement · FYE: December 31

	ASSETS ($ mil.)	NET INCOME ($ mil.)	INCOME AS % OF ASSETS	EMPLOYEES
12/19	8,988	142	1.6%	492
12/18	8,389	152	1.8%	470
12/17	7,479	100	1.3%	466
12/16	6,890	97	1.4%	469
12/15	6,076	84	1.4%	434
Annual Growth	10.3%	14.2%	—	3.2%

2019 Year-End Financials

Debt ratio: 2.42%	No. of shares (mil.): 33
Return on equity: 12.43%	Dividends
Cash ($ mil.): 202	Yield: 0.9%
Current ratio: —	Payout: 10.5%
Long-term debt ($ mil.): —	Market value ($ mil.): 1,617

	STOCK PRICE ($) FY Close	P/E High/Low		PER SHARE ($) Earnings	Dividends	Book Value
12/19	48.63	14	9	4.18	0.44	35.82
12/18	48.71	15	10	4.42	0.00	32.25
12/17	57.90	23	17	2.92	0.00	27.80
12/16	60.95	22	15	2.86	0.00	24.77
12/15	50.47	22	13	2.50	0.00	22.07
Annual Growth	(0.9%)	—	—	13.7%	—	12.9%

East West Bancorp, Inc

East West Bancorp banks in both hemispheres of the world. It's the holding company for East West Bank which provides standard banking services and loans through more than 130 branches in major US metropolitan areas and about 10 offices across in China Hong Kong and Taiwan. Boasting $29 billion in assets East West Bank focuses on making commercial and industrial real estate loans which account for the majority of the company's loan portfolio. Catering to the Asian-American community it also provides international banking and trade financing to importers/exporters doing business in the Asia/Pacific region. East West Bank offers multilingual service in English Cantonese Mandarin Vietnamese and Spanish.

Operations

East West Bancorp operates two business segments. The commercial banking segment (which generated 62% of its total revenue in 2014) includes commercial industrial and commercial real estate primarily generates commercial and industrial real estate loans and offers a wide variety of international finance and trade services and products. The retail banking segment (33% of total revenue) focuses primarily on retail operations through the East West Bank's branch network. The bank also offers insurance products through East West Insurance.

Broadly speaking the bank made 93% of its revenue from loan interest (including fees) in 2014 and another 7% from interest on investment securities investment in Federal Home Loan Bank and Federal Reserve Bank Stock and short-term investments. It had a staff of roughly 2700 employees at the end of 2014.

Geographic Reach

East West's bank network in the US is mainly in California (in and around Los Angeles the San Francisco Bay area Orange County and Silicon Valley) and in the Atlanta Boston Houston New York and Seattle metropolitan areas. Internationally the bank has five branches in Hong Kong and Greater China (Shanghai Shantou and Shenzhen) and five representative offices in Beijing Chongqing Guangzhou Xiamen and Taiwan.

Sales and Marketing

East West Bancorp caters its banking and loan business to companies in the manufacturing wholesale trade and service sectors.

Financial Performance

The bank has struggled to consistently grow its revenues in recent years due to shrinking interest margins on loans amidst the low-interest environment. Its profits however have been rising thanks to declining loan loss provisions as its loan portfolio's credit quality has improved with higher property valuations in the strengthened economy.

East West had a breakout year in 2014 as its revenue climbed by 17% to $1.14 billion mostly thanks to an increase in non-covered loan volumes. Higher revenue in 2014 drove East West Bancorp's net income higher by 16% to $342.5 million. Lower income tax provisions resulting from additional purchases of affordable housing partnerships and tax-credited investments also help pad the bank's bottom line.

The bank's operating cash levels dipped by 8% to $392.9 million mostly due to unfavorable working capital changes related to accrued interest receivables and other asset balances.

Strategy

East West Bancorp's long-term vision reiterated in 2015 is to "serve as the financial bridge between the United States and Greater China" by reaching more customers with its cross-border products and capabilities. Its full-service branches in Greater China offer traditional letters of credit and trade finance between businesses while also providing the bank a way to serve existing clients and establish new business relationships.

Toward its international expansion plans the company opened two new branches in Greater China's Shenzhen and Shanghai Pilot Free Trade Zone during 2014 which would better position it to help its customers and facilitate their financial needs between Greater China and the US.

The bank may also occasionally pursue acquisitions of other banks to broaden its market reach and grow its loan and deposit business.

Mergers and Acquisitions

In 2014 East West Bancorp expanded its presence in Texas and California after it purchased Metrocorp along with its 19 MetroBank and Metro United Bank branches in the Houston Dallas and San Diego markets. The deal also added $1.7 billion in assets and $1.4 billion in new loan assets.

Company Background

East West Bancorp was founded in 1998.

In 2009 the company acquired more than 60 branches and most of the banking operations of larger rival United Commercial Bank which had been seized by regulators. The deal gave East West Bank about 40 more California branches plus some 20 additional US locations beyond the state.

EXECUTIVES

Evp Chief Risk Officer General Counsel And Secretary East West Bancorp And East West Bank, Douglas P. Krause, age 64, $403,090 total compensation

Chairman And Ceo East West Bancorp And East West Bank, Dominic Ng, age 61, $1,000,000 total compensation

Vice Chairman East West Bancorp And East West Bank, John M. Lee, age 88

Evp And Head Of International And Commercial Banking, Andy Yen, age 62, $370,977 total compensation

Evp And Cfo East West Bancorp And East West Bank, Irene H. Oh, age 42, $403,090 total compensation

Evp And Chief Credit Officer East West Bank, Albert Sun, age 65

President And Coo East West Bancorp And East West Bank, Gregory L. Guyett, age 56

Evp Head Of U.s. Eastern And Texas Regions And Head Of Consumer And Business Banking, Wendy Cai-Lee

First Vice President And Customer Communications Manager, Manni Liu

Senior Vice President, Frances Ng

Vice President, Samsonz Lam

First Vice President Relationship Manager, Steve Reichmuth

Vice President Assistant Branch Manager El Monte, Fiona Yao

Vice President Bm, Betty Liaw

Vice President Business Development Officer, Ellen Chiang

Senior Vice President, Mary Wei

Assistant Vice President Credit Analyst, Joseph Au

Senior Vice President, Timothy Monter

Senior Vice President Head Of Special Assets, Stuart Bonomo

Vice President Portfolio Manager Commercial Real Estate Eastern Region, Akmar Wallace

Vice President Tms Sales Consultant Ii, Stacy So

Vp Gts Merchant Sales Manager, Dustin Sullivan

Vice President, Taurat Hossain

First Vice President, Johnny Cheng

First Vice President Head Of Information Technology Operations, Bill Likes

First Vice President Loan Support Manager, Peggy Donovan

First Vice President Interest Rates And Foreign Exchange, Supat Tipayamongkol

Senior Vice President, Andrew Stein

Senior Vice President, Al Cheng

Assistant Vice President, Elvira Valenzuela

Vice President, Joe Solano

Auditors: KPMG LLP

LOCATIONS

HQ: East West Bancorp, Inc
135 North Los Robles Ave., 7th Floor, Pasadena, CA 91101
Phone: 626 768-6000
Web: www.eastwestbank.com

PRODUCTS/OPERATIONS

2011 Sales

	$ mil.	% of total
Commercial lending	619	57
Retail banking	358	33
Other& adjustments	112	10
Total	**1,091**	**100**

COMPETITORS

Bank of America	Hanmi Financial
Bank of East Asia	Hope Bancorp
Cathay General Bancorp	JPMorgan Chase
Citibank	U.S. Bancorp
City National	Wells Fargo
Comerica	

HISTORICAL FINANCIALS

Company Type: Public

Income Statement

FYE: December 31

	ASSETS ($ mil.)	NET INCOME ($ mil.)	INCOME AS % OF ASSETS	EMPLOYEES
12/19	44,196	674	1.5%	3,300
12/18	41,042	703	1.7%	3,200
12/17	37,150	505	1.4%	3,000
12/16	34,788	431	1.2%	2,873
12/15	32,350	384	1.2%	2,833
Annual Growth	8.1%	15.1%	—	3.9%

2019 Year-End Financials

Debt ratio: 0.34%
Return on equity: 14.28%
Cash ($ mil.): 3,457
Current ratio: —
Long-term debt ($ mil.): —

No. of shares (mil.): 145
Dividends
  Yield: 2.1%
  Payout: 23.4%
Market value ($ mil.): 7,092

	STOCK PRICE ($) FY Close	P/E High/Low		PER SHARE ($) Earnings	Dividends	Book Value
12/19	48.70	12	8	4.61	1.06	34.46
12/18	43.53	15	8	4.81	0.86	30.52
12/17	60.83	18	14	3.47	0.80	26.58
12/16	50.83	17	9	2.97	0.80	23.78
12/15	41.56	17	13	2.66	0.80	21.70
Annual Growth	4.0%	—	—	14.7%	7.2%	12.3%

Eastman Chemical Co

Eastman Chemical Company is a chemical manufacturer with a focus on additives chemical intermediates advanced materials and fibers. From manufacturing sites in the US and about five European countries it turns out chemicals fibers plastics rubber materials polymers and solvents. Eastman's products wind up in scores of consumer and industrial products including building materials automotive paints tires personal and home care products packaging animal nutrition and crop protection products water treatment and health and wellness products. The company was once part of film giant Eastman Kodak. US and Canada generate the largest sales at about 40%.

HISTORY

Eastman Chemical went public in 1994 but the company traces its roots to the 19th century. George Eastman after developing a method for dry-plate photography established the Eastman Dry Plate and Film Company in 1884 in Rochester New York (the name was changed to Eastman Kodak in 1892).

In 1886 Eastman hired scientist Henry Reichenbach to help create and manufacture new photographic chemicals. As time passed Reichenbach and the company's other scientists came up with chemicals that were either not directly related to photography or had uses in addition to photography.

Eastman bought a wood-distillation plant in Kingsport Tennessee in 1920 and formed the Tennessee Eastman Corporation to make methanol and acetone for the manufacture of photographic chemicals. The company by this time called Kodak introduced acetate yarn and Tenite a cellulose ester plastic in the early 1930s. During WWII the company formed Holston Defense to make explosives for the US armed forces.

Kodak began to vertically integrate Tennessee Eastman's operations during the 1950s acquiring A. M. Tenney Associates Tennessee Eastman's selling agent for its acetate yarn products in 1950. It also established Texas Eastman opening a plant in Longview to produce ethyl alcohol and aldehydes raw materials used in fiber and film production. At the end of 1952 Kodak created Eastman Chemical Products to sell alcohols plastics and fibers made by Tennessee Eastman and Texas Eastman. Also that year Tennessee Eastman developed cellulose acetate filter tow for use in cigarette filters. In the late 1950s the company introduced Kodel polyester fiber.

Kodak created Carolina Eastman Company in 1968 opening a plant in Columbia South Carolina to produce Kodel and other polyester products. It also created Eastman Chemicals Division to handle its chemical operations.

In the late 1970s Eastman Chemicals Division introduced polyethylene terephthalate (PET) resin used to make containers. It acquired biological and molecular instrumentation manufacturer International Biotechnologies in 1987.

Eastman Chemicals Division became Eastman Chemical Company in 1990. In 1993 it exited the polyester fiber business. When Kodak spun off Eastman Chemical in early 1994 the new company was saddled with $1.8 billion in debt.

Eastman's 1996 earnings were reduced when oversupply lowered prices for PET. Eastman opened plants in Argentina Malaysia and the Netherlands in 1998.

Eastman added to its international locations in 1999 by opening a plant in Singapore and an office in Bangkok. It also bought Lawter International (specialty chemicals for ink and coatings) with locations in Belgium China and Ireland. In 2000 the company began restructuring into two business segments (chemicals and polymers) and acquired resin and colorant maker McWhorter Technologies.

In 2001 Eastman acquired most of Hercules' resins business. In November the company announced that it had postponed plans to split into two companies (one focusing on specialty chemicals and plastics the other concentrating on polyethylene plastics and acetate fibers) until mid-2002 due to the weak economy. In early 2002 the company announced that it had cancelled those plans altogether and would operate the two as separate divisions.

The following year Eastman announced it would split off part of its coatings adhesives specialty polymers and inks (CASPI) segment. The division had been underperforming and had been hit particularly hard by the high costs of raw materials and a general overcapacity in the marketplace. Eastman sold a portion of CASPI to investment firm Apollo Management for $215 million. Businesses included in the sale were composites inks and graphic arts raw materials liquid and powder resins and textile chemicals. (Apollo called the acquired businesses Resolution Specialty Materials and then joined RSM with Resolution Performance Products and another of its chemical companies Borden Chemical to form the new Hexion Specialty Chemicals in 2005.)

It restructured its divisional alignment in 2006 in an attempt to group together related product groups and technologies. In the process Eastman disbanded its former Voridian Division.

At the end of 2007 the company decided to divest its PET facilities in the UK and the Netherlands as well as its Dutch PTA plants. Eastman sold the facilities to Indorama for about $330 million.

Chairman and CEO Brian Ferguson retired in 2009 after nearly seven years as CEO. James Rogers who had been president of the company and head of the chemicals and fibers group became

his successor and Ferguson became executive chairman.

In 2009 the company joined with SK Chemicals in a joint venture to construct a cellulose acetate tow facility in Ulsan South Korea. Eastman owns 80% of the JV and operates the plant. It also bought a facility in China in 2010 in a joint venture with Mazzucchelli 1849 SPA. The previous year Eastman had expanded an acetate tow facility it owns in the UK.

Eastman Chemical acquired Genovique Specialties Corporation a global provider of benzoate plasticizers from Arsenal Capital Partners in 2010. Genovique produces benzoic acid sodium benzoate and specialty plasticizers with operations in North America Europe and Asia.

Eastman bought Houston-based Sterling Chemicals for $100 million in 2011. The company plans to use Sterling's plasticizers manufacturing plant to produce its own line of non-phthalate plasticizers Eastman 168 for its PCI segment. The non-phthalate plasticizers used to soften vinyl are an alternative to phthalates which have seen restrictions because of safety concerns.

To raise cash for core businesses in 2011 Eastman sold its Texas-based TX Energy unit to Zero Emission Energy Plants. The TX Energy facility will convert petroleum coke an oil refining waste product into hydrogen and pipeline-quality carbon dioxide.

Eastman Chemicals completed its exit of its Performance Polymers segment in 2011 by selling its polyethylene terephthalate (PET) business to DAK Americas LLC for about $600 million. Eastman Chemicals had been a top producer of PET a plastic used to make packaging for soft drinks food and water.

In a major move in 2012 Eastman acquired US-based chemicals firm Solutia in a $4.7 billion cash-and-stock deal. With the addition of Solutia Eastman became a top-tier specialty chemicals company. Its products include rubber materials specialty polymers (synthetic plastics) solvents adhesives plasticizers (additives to soften plastics such as PVC) and specialty fluids.

The Solutia purchase not only broadened Eastman Chemicals' portfolio but also its geographic reach. The addition was a significant step in the company's growth strategy particularly in the Asia/Pacific region and other emerging markets and the company expected the transaction to accelerate the expansion of its businesses worldwide.

That year Eastman also bought Dynaloy a specialty chemical company in Indianapolis. Dynaloy sells cleaning products used in the manufacture of semiconductors and the acquisition supports Eastman's efforts to expand its CASPI segment.

In 2012 Eastman's joint venture with Sinopec Yangzi Petrochemical announced plans to build a major hydrogenated hydrocarbon resin plant in Nanjing China capable of producing 50000 metric tons of Eastman's Adhesives and Plasticizers segment's Regalite hydrocarbon resins.

To meet customer growth in 2013 the company's Fibers segment joint venture with China National Tobacco completed a new 30000 metric ton acetate tow manufacturing facility in Hefei China.

EXECUTIVES

Evp And Cfo, Curtis E. (Curt) Espeland, age 55, $736,887 total compensation
Evp Additives And Functional Products And Advanced Materials; Chief Marketing Officer Eastman Chemical Company, Mark J. Costa, age 53, $1,102,895 total compensation
Svp And Chief International Ventures Officer, Michael H. K. Chung, age 66

Svp And Cto, Stephen G. (Steve) Crawford, age 55, $484,892 total compensation
Evp And Chief Commercial Officer, Brad A. Lich, age 52, $611,007 total compensation
Svp Chief Manufacturing And Engineering Officer, Mark K. Cox, age 54
Vp And Cio, Keith Sturgill
Evp Additives Functional Products And Chemical Intermediates, Lucian Boldea
Senior Vice President Fibers And Global Supply Chain, Richard Johnson
Vice President Global Public Affairs And Policy, Etta Clark
National Sales Manager, Vince Volk
Corporate Medical Director, Ibrahim Heiba
Vice President Director Of Information Technology Risk Management, Rick Noller
Vice President Information Technology, Michael Stoltz
Board Member, Julie Holder
Secretary Treasurer, Greg Allen
Auditors: PricewaterhouseCoopers LLP

LOCATIONS

HQ: Eastman Chemical Co
200 South Wilcox Drive, Kingsport, TN 37662
Phone: 423 229-2000
Web: www.eastman.com

2016 Sales

	$ mil.	% of total
US & Canada	4,025	45
Europe Middle East & Africa	2,305	24
Asia/Pacific	2,163	25
Latin America	515	6
Total	**9,008**	**100**

PRODUCTS/OPERATIONS

2016 Sales

	$ mil.	% of total
Additives & Functional Products	2,979	33
Chemical Intermediates	2,534	28
Advanced Materials	2,457	27
Fibers	992	11
Other	46	1
Total	**9,008**	**100**

Selected Brands and Products

ABALYN rosin resins
ABITOL hydroabietyl alcohols
ADMEX plasticizers
ASPIRA family of resins
BENZOFLEX plasticizers
BIOEXTEND high performance additives
CADENCE resins for calendered films
CELLOLYN synthetic resins
CHROMSPUN acetate yarn
CRYSTEX insoluble sulfur
CYPHREX microfibers
DRESINATE rosin soaps
DURASTAR polymer
DYMEREX rosins
EASTAPURE electronic chemicals
EASTAR copolyesters
EASTEK polymer dispersion
EASTMAN AQ polymers
EASTMAN cellulose esters
EASTMAN coalescents
EASTMAN G polymers
EASTMAN low volatile pure monomer resins
EASTMAN NPG glycol
EASTMAN plasticizers
EASTMAN solvents
EASTMAN TXIB formulation additive
EASTOFLEX amorphous polyolefins
EASTOTAC resins
ECDEL elastomers
EMBRACE family of resins
ENDEX hydrocarbon resins
ENERLOGIC low-e window film
ESTRON acetate yarn
FLEXVUE film
FORAL hydrogenated rosins
FORALYN hydrogenated rosin esters

FORMULAONE high performance auto tint
GILA DIY window film
HUPER OPTIK & DESIGN film
IQUE film
KRISTALEX hydrocarbon resins
LLUMAR window film
METALYN rosin esters
NANOLUX film
NEOSTAR elastomer
OPTIFILM family of products
PAMOLYN fatty acids
PENTALYN synthetic resins
PERENNIAL WOOD
PERMALYN resins
PICCO hydrocarbon resins
PICCOLASTIC hydrocarbon resins
PICCOTAC hydrocarbon resins
PICCOTEX hydrocarbon resins
PLASTOLYN hydrocarbon resins
POLY-PALE rosin resins
PROBENZ sodium benzoate
PROVISTA copolymer
REGALITE hydrocarbon resins
REGALREZ hydrocarbon resins
SAFLEX PVB polymers
SANTOFLEX antidegradants
SKYDROL aviation hydraulic fluids
SKYKLEEN solvents
SOLUS performance additive
SPECTAR copolyester
STAYBELITE-E hydrogenated rosins
SUN-X film
SUSTANE SAIB
TACOLYN resin dispersions
TENITE cellulosics
TENOX antioxidants
TEXANOL ester alcohol
THE GLASS POLYMER
THERMINOL heat transfer fluids
TiGLAZE copolyester
TMPD glycol
TRITAN copolyester
VANCEVA PVB polymers
VELATE coalescents
VISTA window film
V-KOOL film
XIR coated PET

Selected Mergers and Acquisitions

COMPETITORS

Akzo Nobel	DSM
BASF SE	Dow Chemical
Celanese	ExxonMobil Chemical
Clariant	Huntsman Corp
DIC Corporation	Solvay

HISTORICAL FINANCIALS

Company Type: Public

Income Statement

FYE: December 31

	REVENUE ($ mil.)	NET INCOME ($ mil.)	NET PROFIT MARGIN	EMPLOYEES
12/19	9,273	759	8.2%	14,500
12/18	10,151	1,080	10.6%	14,500
12/17	9,549	1,384	14.5%	14,000
12/16	9,008	854	9.5%	14,000
12/15	9,648	848	8.8%	15,000
Annual Growth	**(1.0%)**	**(2.7%)**	**—**	**(0.8%)**

2019 Year-End Financials

Debt ratio: 36.12%
Return on equity: 12.91%
Cash ($ mil.): 204
Current ratio: 1.86
Long-term debt ($ mil.): 5,611
No. of shares (mil.): 135
Dividends
Yield: 3.1%
Payout: 45.4%
Market value ($ mil.): 10,775

	STOCK PRICE ($) FY Close	P/E High/Low	PER SHARE ($) Earnings	Dividends	Book Value
12/19	79.26	15 11	5.48	2.52	43.83
12/18	73.11	14 9	7.56	2.30	41.53
12/17	92.64	10 8	9.47	2.09	37.81
12/16	75.21	13 10	5.75	1.89	30.95
12/15	67.51	15 11	5.66	1.66	26.67
Annual Growth	**4.1%**	**— —**	**(0.8%)**	**11.0%**	**13.2%**

eBay Inc.

eBay is a well-known e-commerce platform for online auctions and boasts more than 180 million users and over 1 billion listings globally. Trading goods every second of every day eBay offers an online forum for buying and selling merchandise worldwide from fine antiques to the latest video games. It generates revenue through listing and selling fees and through advertising. The company also sells tickets to concerts sporting events and other entertainment via its StubHub platform and provides online classified listings via its Classifieds platform. eBay is available across digital platforms including mobile. Some 60% of its sales are outside the US. In 2019 eBay sell StubHub to viagogo for a purchase price $4.1 billion in cash.

HISTORY

Pierre Omidyar created a flea market in cyber-space when he launched online auction service Auction Web on Labor Day weekend in 1995. Making a name for itself largely through word of mouth the company incorporated in 1996 the same year it began to charge a fee to auction items online. That year it enhanced its service with Feedback Forum (buyer and seller ratings).

The company changed the name to eBay in 1997 and began promoting itself through advertising. By the middle of that year eBay was boasting nearly 800000 auctions each day and Benchmark Capital came on board as a significant financial backer.

Margaret ("Meg") Whitman a former Hasbro executive replaced Omidyar as CEO in early 1998. EBay made a blockbuster debut as a public company later that year. The company moved closer to household name status the same year by launching a national ad campaign and inking alliance deals with AOL and WebTV.

eBay showed its acquisitive streak in 1999 with purchases of Alando (online auctions in Germany) and Billpoint (person-to-person credit card technology). It also made one of its first investments in an outside company with the purchase of 6% of TradeOut.com an online seller of corporate surplus materials. The company set the jewel in its 1999 acquisition crown when it acquired upscale auction house Butterfield & Butterfield (now just Butterfields). eBay also expanded down under through a joint venture with Australia-based ecorp (formerly PBL Online). A bit of the bloom came off the rose in 1999 when online service interruptions (one "brownout" in June persisted for 22 hours) revealed a chink in eBay's armor. The company called its top 10000 users to convey its apologies and pledged to improve its website's performance.

In 2000 eBay agreed to develop person-to-person and merchant-to-person auction sites for Disney's GO Network began distributing information through wireless products and joined with banking giant Wells Fargo to offer eBay sellers the option of accepting online checks. Also that year the US Department of Justice began an investigation to determine if eBay had violated antitrust laws in its dealings with competitors. In other legal news a class-action lawsuit was filed against the company claiming that eBay was an auctioneer and therefore must authenticate the items on its site. (A trial court dismissed the case in early 2001.)

Also in 2000 the company expanded into Japan through eBay Japan with computer firm NEC acquiring 30% of the Japanese subsidiary and eBay owning the rest; it also launched Canadian and Austrian sites. In addition eBay took an equity stake in online used-car dealer AutoTrader.com and launched a co-branded used-car auction website and it acquired online trading community Half.com.

eBay strengthened its European position in 2001 through the purchase of French Internet auction firm iBazar. It also launched sites in Ireland New Zealand and Switzerland. eBay made a deal that year to provide its e-commerce capabilities to Microsoft developers and to add business-to-business auctions to its consumer operations. In addition the company began offering virtual storefronts for retailers to sell fixed-price items and purchased auctioneer of foreclosed property HomesDirect. In late 2001 eBay sold its iBazar's Brazilian subsidiary to MercadoLibre Latin America's leading auction site in exchange for a 19.5% stake (now 18%) in MercadoLibre.

Disappointed with the performance of eBay Premiere (fine art and other high-end merchandise) in 2002 the company partnered with Sotheby's in a deal that moved Sotheby's entire online business into the eBay website replacing eBay Premiere (Sotheby's later pulled out of the deal citing lagging sales). eBay also sold its traditional auction house Butterfields and shuttered its eBay Japan operations after its dismal performance in that market. In 2003 the company continued to grow through acquisitions with its purchases of EachNet (after acquiring a minority stake in the Chinese e-commerce company in 2002) FairMarket and Internet Auction.

In 2004 eBay took several steps toward diversifying its business. It expanded its international presence through acquisitions in China and India and spent heavily to establish operations there. Three years later eBay shifted its China strategy entering into a joint venture with Chinese Internet gaming firm TOM Online.

The company purchased about a 25% stake in online classifieds provider craigslist and announced plans to offer a music downloading service. Overall in 2004 more than 60% of eBay's new registered users were in the international business.

2005 was a particularly acquisitive year for eBay. That year it picked up Internet listing site Rent.com for about $415 million. Then eBay's international classifieds group Kijiji (Swahili for "village") acquired London-based Gumtree.com and Spain's LoQUo.com a community-based listings website that operates sites for several Spanish cities alongside ones for France Germany Norway Portugal and the UK. Kijiji next acquired opusforum a local classifieds website based in Germany for an undisclosed sum.

Later in 2005 eBay closed on three major deals. It acquired Shopping.com — a provider of online comparison shopping and consumer reviews with sites in France the UK and the US — for about $635 million. It also purchased PayPal VeriSign's payment gateway business for about $370 million. Also in 2005 eBay acquired start-up online telecom service provider Skype of Luxembourg for nearly $3 billion. Skype's Web-based software allowed its 220 million registered users to make phone calls over the Internet. The acquisition proved costly

however. eBay took about $1.5 billion in Skype-related charges in the third quarter of 2007.

Keeping the acquisitions rolling in 2006 eBay snatched up the leading Swedish online auctioneer Tradera.com for $48 million; eBay made the purchase to strengthen its Swedish trading opportunities in the future. Later in 2006 Internet power-house Yahoo! and eBay entered an agreement to join forces on advertising Web searches online payments (through eBay's PayPal platform) and a co-branded toolbar. Key elements of the arrangement's design included Yahoo! providing advertisements throughout eBay's site and the integration of PayPal into Yahoo!'s e-commerce infrastructure.

eBay bought German auction management software company Via-Online in 2007. Via-Online operated sales tool Afterbuy.com and eBay made the deal to ramp up support for its Germany sellers. Looking to diversify its online marketplace operations also that year eBay acquired ticket seller StubHub for about $310 million. The company followed that up with the significant $900 million purchase of Bill Me Later in 2008.

In 2008 eBay settled its long-running patent dispute with MercExchange agreeing to buy the three MercExchange patents it had been accused of violating. MercExchange had sued eBay in 2001 claiming that eBay's "Buy It Now" option infringed on its patent technology. A federal judge ruled that eBay should pay MercExchange $30 million in damages in the case. Terms of the settlement were not disclosed.

Later in 2008 eBay announced it would end its arrangement with LiveAuctioneers.com that allowed customers to participate in live auctions hosted by other companies. eBay said ending the deal allowed it to better concentrate on growing listings in its core product.

To encourage further growth in its auctions the company reduced fees and rolled out an improved matching feature in 2008. The feature implemented a ranking system that took into account time remaining feedback scores quality of listing pictures and other criteria.

Whitman who led eBay for a decade stepped down as president and CEO of the company in 2008. She was succeeded by John Donahoe who previously led the company's highest revenue-producing unit eBay Marketplaces. Also that year eBay acquired the California-based visual media company VUVOX Network to further develop rich media capabilities in the eBay marketplace.

In a program that ran through the bulk of 2009 eBay partnered with resurrected automaker General Motors to sell new cars online. Prospective buyers could place bids for vehicles from more than 225 GM dealers in California at gm.ebay.com. The program did not move as many cars as anticipated however prompting the automaker to halt sales and shift its attention to marketing. eBay in 2009 paid about $1 billion for a majority stake (99.2%) in Gmarket a leading online marketplace in South Korea.

eBay also sold a majority of Skype in 2009. Four years after investing in the service eBay acknowledged that Skype did not complement the rest of its operations. It sold off a 70% stake in Skype to investors led by the private-equity firm Silver Lake in a deal involving $1.9 billion in cash and a $125 million note. As part of the agreement eBay retained a 30% interest in the Skype. (eBay had purchased Skype for nearly $3 billion but in 2007 it took a write-down for about half that amount.) eBay sold its share in Skype to Microsoft in 2011.

In 2010 eBay acquired popular German shopping site Brands4Friends for about $200 million. It made the deal to become a leading online fashion destination in Europe. The company continued its shopping spree in Germany the following year

when it bolstered PayPal assets by acquiring the German company BillSAFE adding over 15 million accounts. The deal gave eBay purchase-on-invoice capabilities that are popular to merchants and consumers in Austria German the Netherlands and Switzerland.

eBay bought mobile software application developer Critical Path in 2010. Critical Path had worked with eBay to develop several of its applications for Apple's iPhone. The acquisition doubled the size of eBay's mobile team which is working to capitalize on the growing numbers of consumers who are shopping on their smart phones.

In its largest acquisition since purchasing Skype in 2011 eBay bought GSI Commerce a provider of such services as website development and maintenance order fulfillment and digital advertising for $2.4 billion.

In 2012 eBay sold Rent.com to PRIMEDIA. eBay spun off PayPal in 2015.

EXECUTIVES

President And Ceo, Devin N. Wenig, age 53, $1,000,000 total compensation
President Stubhub, Scott Cutler
Svp And General Counsel, Marie Oh Huber, age 59, $389,462 total compensation
Svp Ebay North America, Harry A. (Hal) Lawton, age 46, $650,000 total compensation
Svp And Cto, Stephen (Steve) Fisher, age 55, $625,000 total compensation
Svp And Cfo, Scott F. Schenkel, age 52, $650,000 total compensation
Svp Global Operations, Wendy Jones
Svp Ebay Europe, Paul Todd
Svp Ebay Asia Pacific, Jay Lee
Svp And Chief Product Officer, Raymond J. (R.J.) Pittman, age 50, $580,000 total compensation
Svp And Chief People Officer, Kristin Yetto
Vice President Intellectual Property, Jay Monahan
Vp Of Applied Research, Tom Pinckney
Vice President Ebay Customer Service Solutions And Technology, Scott Murray
Vice President Core Product Experience, Mohan Patt
Vice President Of Data, Zoher Karu
Vice President Deputy General Counsel Head Of Legal Americas And Global Product And Technology, Karin Schwab
Vice President Talent Acquisition Management And Development, Lou Sanchez
Senior Vice President Information Technology, Andre Tozzi
Vice President Mobile Products, Kevin Hurst
Vice President Sales, Todd Pearson
National Account Manager, Jessica Schrenker
Vice President Product Development, Jay Hanson
Senior Vice President Finance Chief Financial Officer, Bob Swan
Vice President, Don Albert
Vice President Global Customer Experience Ebay Europe, Jean-marc Codsi
Vice President Investor Relations, Thomas Hudson
Vice President Legal, John Muller
Vice President Of Engineering, Daniel Fain
Vice President Of Compensation Benefits And Human Resources, Robin Colman
Vice President Information Technology, Omar Jabbar
Vice President Engineering, Japjit Tulsi
Senior Vice President Chief Product Officer Sharing, Rj Pittman
Vp It, Rami Mazid
Vice President And General Manager Selling Experience, Sunil Rajasekar
Vice President, Bob Kupbens
Vice President Finance And Chief Audit Executive, Meeta Sunderwala
Vice President Fulfillment, Gearold Feury

LOCATIONS

HQ: eBay Inc.
  2025 Hamilton Avenue, San Jose, CA 95125
Phone: 408 376-7008
Web: www.ebay.com

2018 Sales

	$ mil.	% of total
US	4,373	41
Germany	1,591	15
UK	1,481	14
South Korea	1,195	11
Rest of world	2,106	19
Total	**10,746**	**100**

PRODUCTS/OPERATIONS

2018 Sales

	$ mil.	% of total
Net transaction revenues:		
Marketplace	7,416	69
StubHub	1,068	10
Marketing services and other revenues:		
Marketplace	1,225	11
Classifieds	1,022	10
StubHub Corporate and other	15	-
Total	**10,746**	**100**

COMPETITORS

Alibaba.com	HSN
Amazon.com	Naspers
Buy.com	Overstock.com
Costco Wholesale	Spectrum Group
Digital River	Tickets.com
Etsy	Wal-Mart
Facebook	Wayfair
Google	

HISTORICAL FINANCIALS

Company Type: Public

Income Statement

FYE: December 31

	REVENUE ($ mil.)	NET INCOME ($ mil.)	NET PROFIT MARGIN	EMPLOYEES
12/20	10,271	5,667	55.2%	12,700
12/19	10,800	1,786	16.5%	13,300
12/18	10,746	2,530	23.5%	14,000
12/17	9,567	(1,016)	—	14,100
12/16	8,979	7,266	80.9%	12,600
Annual Growth	3.4%	(6.0%)	—	0.2%

2020 Year-End Financials

Debt ratio: 40.20%	No. of shares (mil.): 684
Return on equity: 175.76%	Dividends
Cash ($ mil.): 1,428	Yield: 1.2%
Current ratio: 1.80	Payout: 8.9%
Long-term debt ($ mil.): 7,745	Market value ($ mil.): 34,371

	STOCK PRICE ($) FY Close	P/E High/Low		PER SHARE ($) Earnings	Dividends	Book Value
12/20	50.25	7	3	7.89	0.64	5.21
12/19	36.11	20	13	2.09	0.56	3.61
12/18	28.07	18	10	2.55	0.00	6.86
12/17	37.74	—	—	(0.95)	0.00	7.84
12/16	29.69	5	3	6.35	0.00	9.70
Annual Growth	14.1%	—	—	5.6%	—	(14.4%)

Ecolab Inc

Ecolab cleans up by cleaning up. The company offers cleaning sanitation pest-elimination and maintenance products and services to the energy healthcare hospitality and industrial sectors among others. Its cleaning and sanitizing operations serve hotels schools commercial and institutional laundries and quick-service restaurants. Other units focus on products for textile care water care healthcare food and beverage processing and pest control. It also makes chemicals used in water treatment for industrial processes including in the paper and energy industries. The US is Ecolab's largest market accounting for about 55% of revenue.

Operations

Ecolab provides cleaning and sanitizing programs and products equipment repair and pest elimination for markets such as food service food and beverage processing chemical processing oil and gas production healthcare government and education and textile care.

Ecolab has three operating segments: Global Industrial (consisting of the Global Water Global Food & Beverage Global Paper Global Life Sciences and Global Textile Care operating units); Global Institutional (Global Institutional Global Specialty and Global Healthcare operating units); and Global Energy (operating under the ChampionX name).

The Global Industrial segment (accounting for more than 35% of sales) provides water treatment and cleaning and sanitizing services to large industrial clients in the chemical commercial laundry food manufacturing and paper industries. Global Institutional also generates around 35% of sales and Global Energy accounts for more than 20% of sales.

Geographic Reach

St. Paul Minnesota-based Ecolab has broad reach across the world operating in more than 170 countries. The US accounts for about 55% of the company's total revenue. Europe accounts for about 20% the Asia/Pacific region around 10%; Latin America around 5% the Middle East and Africa 5% and Canada 5%.

Sales and Marketing

Ecolab serves customers in a range of segments including buildings and facilities chemical processing education facility care food and beverage processing food retail foodservice government healthcare lodging and oil and gas.

Some of Ecolab's products are sold to distributors agents or licensees. Deliveries to customers are made from manufacturing plants and a network of distribution centers and third-party logistics service providers using common carriers Ecolab's own delivery vehicles and distributors' vehicles.

Financial Performance

After hitting a peak of $14.9 billion in revenue in 2019 Ecolab's sales continuously increases from the past four years. But Ecolab's revenue grew in 2017 and again in 2018 when it posted record revenue through organic growth and contributions from acquisitions.

In 2019 revenue rose 2% to about $14.9 billion up about $238 million from 2018 driven by higher sales in each segment and geographic region. Overall Ecolab sold more products and services at higher prices in 2019 compared to 2018. Acquisitions also contributed to the company's sales increase.

Net income rose to $1.6 billion in 2019 from $1.4 billion in 2018 due to charges for restructuring acquisition-related activities and the company's commitment to the Ecolab Foundation.

Ecolab had about $186 million in cash in 2019 compared to $294 million the year before. In 2019 operations generated $2.4 billion while investing activities used about $1.2 billion and financing activities used about $1.3 billion.

Strategy

Acquisition has been a growth engine for Ecolab spreading its reach and expanding line of products and services to provide water processing management to food and beverage hospitality and laundry customers worldwide. In 2018 and 2019 the company extended its offerings and enlarged its footprint in Europe with the acquisitions of Holchem in Germany and Bioquell in the UK.

Ecolab's 2020 growth strategy rests on integrating digital into its back end and products and positioning the company as a desirable destination for talent. To reach those goals Ecolab is restructuring to simplify and automate processes and tasks reduce complexity and management layers consolidate facilities and focus on long-term growth areas. The company expects savings to total $325 million by 2021.

The company plans to spin off its Upstream Energy business composed of the WellChem and Oil Field Chemicals businesses into an independent publicly traded company by mid-2020. The upstream business has an increasingly different business model than the rest of Ecolab and the company believes that two more focused companies would better serve their customers. The upstream business had sales of about $2.4 billion in 2018.

With trade tensions in global markets Ecolab may suffer from higher raw material costs needed for its products that include an array of organic and inorganic chemicals.

Mergers and Acquisitions

In 2020 Ecolab Inc. has reached an agreement to acquire CID Lines a leading provider of livestock biosecurity and hygiene solutions. CID Lines' strong product portfolio range of applications and regulatory expertise for farming environments give Ecolab a foothold in the growing livestock and poultry biosecurity segment as well as opportunities to leverage their global presence to drive expansion particularly in Asia where this segment is rapidly developing.

In 2019 Ecolab Inc. has acquired the business of privately held Chemstar Corporation a U.S.-based supplier of food safety and cleaning and sanitizing solutions focused on the grocery and food retail markets. Chemstar's food safety solutions align well with their existing offerings and will enhance and broaden their ability to meet the needs of our food retail customers.

In 2019 Ecolab Inc has acquired Lobster Ink a leading provider of end-to-end online customer training solutions. Addressing customers' growing need for effective training this acquisition combines Lobster Ink's innovative customer training capabilities and digital platform with Ecolab's expertise in food safety hygiene water management and public and planet health.

In 2019 Ecolab closed on its acquisition of Bioquell a provider of hydrogen peroxide vapor biodecontamination systems and services for the life sciences and healthcare industries. Based in the UK Bioquell's 2017 sales were approximately Å 29 million.

HISTORY

Salesman Merritt Osborn founded Economics Laboratory in 1924 as a specialty chemical maker; its first product was a rug cleaner for hotels. It added industrial and institutional cleaners and consumer detergents in the 1950s. The company went public in 1957. By 1973 it had been organized into five divisions: industrial (cleaners and specialty chemical formulas) institutional (dishwasher products sanitation formulas) consumer (dishwasher detergent and laundry aids coffee filters floor cleaners) food-processing (detergents) and international (run by future CEO Fred Lanners).

EXECUTIVES

Chairman And Ceo, Douglas M. (Doug) Baker, age 62, $1,187,500 total compensation

Cfo, Daniel J. (Dan) Schmechel, age 60, $581,250 total compensation

Evp And Cio, Stewart H. McCutcheon

President And Coo, Thomas W. (Tom) Handley, age 65, $581,250 total compensation

Evp General Counsel And Assistant Secretary, Michael C. McCormick

Evp; President Global Institutional, Michael A. (Mike) Hickey, age 58, $543,125 total compensation

Evp And Cto, Larry L. Berger, age 59

Evp; President International Regions, Christophe Beck, age 52, $548,125 total compensation

Svp And General Manager Global Healthcare, Paul B. Chaffin

Evp; President Global Water And Process Services, Timothy P. Mulhere, age 57

Evp Human Resources, Laurie M. Marsh, age 56

Evp; President Global Energy, Stephen M. (Steve) Taylor, age 58, $518,818 total compensation

Evp; President Global Services And Specialty, Roberto D. (Bobby) Mendez

Evp General Counsel And Secretary, James J. (Jim) Seifert, age 63

Evp And President Europe, Darrell Brown

Evp Global Textile Care, Andreas Weilinghoff

Evp; President Global Food And Beverage, Jill S. Wyant, age 48

Evp And Chief Supply Chain Officer, Alex Blanco, age 59, $450,000 total compensation

Svp Global Marketing And Communications, Elizabeth A. (Beth) Simermeyer

Vp Middle East And Africa, Vishal Sharma

Evp Asia Pacific, Sean Toohey

Evp And General Manager Global Food And Beverage, Nicholas (Nick) Alfano

Svp And President Latin America, John Guttery

Senior Vice President Catalyst Program, Marc Adams

Evp And Gm Global Food And Beverage, Nick Alfano

Assistant Vice President Corporate Accounts, Cargile Kelly

Executive Vice President And Chief Information Officer, Anil Arcalgud

Vice President And Assistant Controller, Colleen Crawford

Vice President Human Resources Talent, Sue Metcalf

Avp Global Foodservice, Rob Sloan

Vp Corporate Sustainability, Emilio Tenuta

Senior Vice President External Relations, Michael Monahan

Vice President Institutional Global Corporate Accounts Finance, William Fiedler

Senior Vice President And Corporate Controller, Bryan Hughes

Vice President Food Safety And Public Health, Ruth Petran

Senior Vice President Worldwide Customer Experience Sikorsky, Michael Weber

Executive Vice President And Chief Digital Officer, Charles Koontz

Vice President Business Development, Jeremiah Keehn

Senior Vice President And President Middle East And Africa, Arjan Boogaards

Senior Vice President And General Manager Global Healthcare, Gergely Sved

Executive Vice President And President Greater China, Connell Zhang

Vice President Supply Chain, Jose Luis Josan

Assistant Vice President Area Sales, George Panas
Board Member, Stephen Chazen
Auditors: PricewaterhouseCoopers LLP

LOCATIONS

HQ: Ecolab Inc
1 Ecolab Place, St. Paul, MN 55102
Phone: 800 232-6522
Web: www.ecolab.com

2018 Sales

	$ mil.	% of total
United States	7,748	53
Europe	2,858	19
Asia Pacific excluding Greater China	1,239	8
Latin America	906	6
MEA	519	4
Canada	687	5
Greater China	709	4
Total	**14,668**	**100**

PRODUCTS/OPERATIONS

2018 Sales

	$ mil.	% of total
Global Industrial	5,462	37
Global Institutional	5,204	35
Global Energy	3,501	23
Other	877	5
Effect of foreign currency translation	(378.1)	2
Total	**14,668**	**100**

Selected Services

Equipment Care
Facility Cleaning
Food Retail Solutions
Food Safety Specialties
Foodservice Water Management
Front and Back of House
Housekeeping ; Guest Rooms
HVAC Performance Services
Laundry
Pest Elimination
Pool and Spa
Restaurants
Water Safety
Water Treatment

COMPETITORS

3M Purification	ISS A/S
Ashland	Medline Industries
Chemed	Rollins Inc.
Diversey	STERIS
GE Water and Process	ServiceMaster
Technologies	Zep Inc.
Healthcare Services	

HISTORICAL FINANCIALS
Company Type: Public

Income Statement   FYE: December 31

	REVENUE ($ mil.)	NET INCOME ($ mil.)	NET PROFIT MARGIN	EMPLOYEES
12/19	14,906	1,558	10.5%	50,200
12/18	14,668	1,429	9.7%	49,000
12/17	13,838	1,508	10.9%	48,400
12/16	13,152	1,229	9.3%	47,565
12/15	13,545	1,002	7.4%	47,000
Annual Growth	**2.4%**	**11.7%**	—	**1.7%**

2019 Year-End Financials

Debt ratio: 30.45%
Return on equity: 18.68%
Cash ($ mil.): 186
Current ratio: 1.33
Long-term debt ($ mil.): 5,973

No. of shares (mil.): 288
Dividends
Yield: 0.9%
Payout: 35.5%
Market value ($ mil.): 55,660

	STOCK PRICE ($) FY Close	P/E High/Low	PER SHARE ($) Earnings	Dividends	Book Value
12/19	192.99	39 26	5.33	1.85	30.11
12/18	147.35	32 26	4.88	1.69	27.82
12/17	134.18	26 23	5.13	1.52	26.33
12/16	117.22	30 24	4.14	1.42	23.65
12/15	114.38	36 29	3.32	1.34	23.35
Annual Growth	**14.0%**	— —	**12.6%**	**8.4%**	**6.6%**

Edison International

Edison International is a major power provider in California through its Southern California Edison (SCE) subsidiary which distributes electricity to 15 million people in a 50000 square-mile area of central coastal and southern California. The distribution system which takes power from substations to customers includes over 53000 line-miles of overhead lines 38000 line-miles of underground lines and approximately 800 substations all of which are located in California. SCE also has about 7000 MW of generating capacity and energy storage facilities primarily located in California. Through its Edison Energy subsidiary Edison International owns and operates additional solar and wind power projects.

HISTORY

In 1896 a group including Elmer Peck and George Baker organized West Side Lighting to provide electricity in Los Angeles. The next year the company merged with Los Angeles Edison Electric which owned the rights to the Edison name and patents in the region and Baker became president. Edison Electric installed the first DC-power underground conduits in the Southwest.

John Barnes Miller took over the top spot in 1901. During his 31-year reign the firm bought many neighboring utilities and built several power plants. In 1909 it took the name Southern California Edison (SCE).

SCE doubled its assets by buying Southern California electric interests from rival Pacific Light & Power in 1917. However in 1912 the City of Los Angeles had decided to develop its own power distribution system and by 1922 SCE's authority in the city had ended. A 1925 earthquake and the 1928 collapse of the St. Francis Dam severely damaged SCE's facilities.

SCE built 11 fossil-fueled power stations (1948-1973) and moved into nuclear power in 1963 when it broke ground on the San Onofre plant with San Diego Gas & Electric (brought online in 1968). It finished consolidating its service territory with the 1964 purchase of California Electric Power. In the late 1970s SCE began to build solar geothermal and wind power facilities.

Edison Mission Energy (EME) was founded in 1986 to develop buy and operate power plants around the world. The next year investment arm Edison Capital was formed as well as a holding company for the entire group SCEcorp. EME began to build its portfolio in 1992 when it snagged a 51% stake in an Australian plant and bought hydroelectric facilities in Spain. In 1995 it bought UK hydroelectric company First Hydro; it also began building plants in Italy Turkey and Indonesia.

The 1994 Northridge earthquake that cut power to a million SCE customers was nothing compared to the industry's seismic shifts. In 1996 SCEcorp became the more worldly Edison International. California's electricity market opened to competition in 1998 and the utility began divesting SCE's generation assets; it sold 12 gas-fired plants. Overseas EME picked up 25% of a power plant being built in Thailand and a 50% stake in a cogeneration facility in Puerto Rico.

SCE got regulatory approval to offer telecom services in its utility territory in 1999. That year EME snapped up several plants in the Midwest from Unicom for $5 billion. Overseas it purchased two UK coal-fired plants from PowerGen (which it sold to American Electric Power in 2001 for $960 million). The next year EME CEO Edward Muller (who had held the post since 1994) abruptly resigned and Edison bought Citizens Power from the Peabody Group.

In 2000 SCE got caught in a price squeeze brought on in part by deregulation. Prices on the wholesale power market soared but the utility was unable to pass along the increase to customers because of a rate freeze. The company gained some prospect of relief in 2001 when California's governor signed legislation to allow a state agency to buy power from wholesalers under long-term contracts. In addition the California Public Utilities Commission (CPUC) approved a substantial increase in retail electricity rates and the Federal Energy Regulatory Commission approved a plan to limit wholesale energy prices during periods of severe shortage in 11 western states.

To reduce debt Edison International agreed to sell its transmission grid to the state for $2.8 billion. While the California legislature debated the agreement however the CPUC announced a settlement in which SCE would be allowed to keep its current high rates in place until its debts are paid off. The settlement which was approved in 2002 eliminated the need for the sale of the company's transmission grid.

Also in 2001 the company sold most of its Edison Enterprises businesses including home security services unit Edison Select which was sold to ADT Security Services.

In 2004 Edison International committed to taking a lead position in developing comprehensive national programs to reduce greenhouse gas emissions primarily carbon dioxide.

In 2006 SCE signed the largest wind energy deal ever completed by a US utility providing for 1500 MW of wind power from plants in the Tehachapi area of California.

EME marketed energy in the US and Turkey and had interests in more than 40 power plants in the US and one in Turkey that gave it a net physical generating capacity of about 10780 MW. EME filed for bankruptcy protection in 2012 citing high operating losses due to low realized energy and capacity prices high fuel costs and low generation at its Midwest Generation plants.

In 2013 SCE decided to permanently retire Units 2 and 3 of its San Onofre Nuclear Generating Station. Unit 2 was taken out of service January 2012 for a planned routine outage. Unit 3 was also taken offline a few weeks later after station operators found a small leak in a tube inside a steam generator.

In 2013 Edison Energy acquired SoCore Energy a Chicago-based solar portfolio development and commercial rooftop installation company focusing on the solar energy needs of multisite retailers REITs and industrial clients and bought a minority stake in Clean Power Finance a financial services and software provider for the solar industry.

In 2016 Edison International subsidiary SoCore Energy acquired equity interests in about 20 community solar garden development projects in Minnesota as part of the SunEdison bankruptcy proceedings. The price was $80 million.

EXECUTIVES

President Edison Energy, Ronald L. Litzinger, age 61, $600,000 total compensation
President Ceo And Director, Pedro J. Pizarro, age 55, $836,782 total compensation
Vp And Cio Southern California Edison, Todd L. Inlander
Ceo Southern California Edison Company (sce), Kevin M. Payne, age 59, $421,171 total compensation
Svp Commercial Operations Edison Energy And President Edison Transmission Llc, Steven D. Eisenberg
Evp And Cfo, Maria Rigatti, age 56, $392,891 total compensation
Evp And General Counsel, Adam S. Umanoff, age 60, $548,391 total compensation
President Socore Energy, Rob Scheuermann
President Southern California Edison (sce), Ronald O. Nichols, age 66
Vp Operational Finance Sce, Chris Dominski
Vice President, Cindy Creed
Vice President, Weston Williams
Vice President Regulatory Operations, Akbar Jazayeri
Senior Vice President Human Resources, John Kelly
Senior Vice President Government Affairs, Gaddi Vasquez
Vp And Corporate Controller, Aaron Moss
Senior Vice President, Drew Murphy
Vice President Local Public Affairs Sce, Christopher Thompson
Vice President Tax Edison International And Sce, Andrea Wood
Vice President Of Distribution, Gregory Ferree
Vice President Of Investor Relations, Sam Ramraj
Chairman, William P. (Bill) Sullivan, age 70
Board Of Directors, Troy Nguyen
Board Member, Linda Stuntz
Board Member, James Morris
Board Member, Michael Camunez
Auditors: PricewaterhouseCoopers LLP

LOCATIONS

HQ: Edison International
2244 Walnut Grove Avenue, P.O. Box 976, Rosemead, CA 91770
Phone: 626 302-2222
Web: www.edisoninvestor.com

PRODUCTS/OPERATIONS

Selected Subsidiaries

Edison Energy (solar power activities)
Southern California Edison Company (SCE electric utility)

COMPETITORS

AES	NV Energy
Avista	NextEra Energy
Berkshire Hathaway	PG&E Corporation
Energy	PacifiCorp
CMS Energy	Portland General
Calpine	Electric
Constellation Energy	Sacramento Municipal
Group	Utility
Electricité de France	Sempra Energy
Los Angeles Water and	
Power	

HISTORICAL FINANCIALS

Company Type: Public

Income Statement

FYE: December 31

	REVENUE ($ mil.)	NET INCOME ($ mil.)	NET PROFIT MARGIN	EMPLOYEES
12/19	12,347	1,284	10.4%	12,937
12/18	12,657	(423)	—	12,574
12/17	12,320	565	4.6%	12,521
12/16	11,869	1,311	11.0%	12,390
12/15	11,524	1,020	8.9%	12,768
Annual Growth	1.7%	5.9%	—	0.3%

2019 Year-End Financials

Debt ratio: 29.35%
Return on equity: 10.81%
Cash ($ mil.): 68
Current ratio: 0.64
Long-term debt ($ mil.): 17,864

No. of shares (mil.): 361
Dividends
  Yield: 3.2%
  Payout: 65.6%
Market value ($ mil.): 27,297

	STOCK PRICE ($) FY Close	P/E High/Low		PER SHARE ($) Earnings	Dividends	Book Value
12/19	75.41	20	14	3.77	2.48	36.75
12/18	56.77	—	—	(1.30)	2.43	32.10
12/17	63.24	48	37	1.72	2.23	35.82
12/16	71.99	20	14	3.97	1.98	36.82
12/15	59.21	22	18	3.10	1.73	34.89
Annual Growth	6.2%	—	—	5.0%	9.3%	1.3%

EDUCATIONAL FUNDING OF THE SOUTH, INC.

Reading is fundamental but funding is crucial to higher education. That's where Educational Funding of the South comes in. Known as Edsouth the not-for-profit public benefit corporation provides student loan funding by purchasing loans from originators. Nearly 500 lending institutions participate in one or more of Edsouth's educational loan programs. Edsouth is one of the nation's largest holders of student loans. The organization was founded in 1988. Formerly known as Volunteer State Student Funding Corporation it changed its name to Educational Funding of the South in 1996.

EXECUTIVES

Ceo, Ron Gambill
Executive Assistant, Sonna Biraghi
Auditors: KRAFT CPAS NASHVILLE TENNESS

LOCATIONS

HQ: EDUCATIONAL FUNDING OF THE SOUTH, INC.
12700 KINGSTON PIKE, FARRAGUT, TN 379340917
Phone: 865 342-0684
Web: WWW.EDSOUTH.ORG

COMPETITORS

Bank of America
Brazos Higher Education Service Corp.
College Loan Corporation
Discover
JPMorgan Chase
Nelnet
Sallie Mae

HISTORICAL FINANCIALS

Company Type: Private

Income Statement   FYE: September 30

	ASSETS ($ mil.)	NET INCOME ($ mil.)	INCOME AS % OF ASSETS	EMPLOYEES
09/12*	2,924	(20)	—	3
12/06	4,223	252	6.0%	—
12/05	4,484	26	0.6%	—
12/04	3,881	30	0.8%	—
Annual Growth	(3.5%)	—	—	—

*Fiscal year change

EMCOR Group, Inc.

EMCOR Group is an electrical and mechanical construction specialist and facilities services firms. It plans installs operates maintains and protects complex mechanical and electrical systems. These include systems for power generation and distribution lighting water and wastewater treatment voice and data communications fire protection plumbing and heating ventilation and air-conditioning (HVAC). EMCOR also provides facilities services including management and maintenance support. Through some 80 subsidiaries and joint ventures the company serves a range of commercial industrial institutional and utility customers. EMCOR's domestic operations account for most of its revenue.

Operations

EMCOR Group operates five main business segments based on service: United States mechanical construction and facilities services more than 35% of revenue; United States electrical construction and facilities services about 25% of revenue; United States building services nearly 25% of revenue; United States industrial services over 10% of revenue; and United Kingdom building services 5% of revenue.

EMCOR specialize principally in providing construction services relating to electrical and mechanical systems in all types of facilities and in providing various services relating to the operation maintenance and management of facilities including refineries and petrochemical plants.

Geographic Reach

More than 95% of Norwalk Connecticut-based EMCOR's revenue comes from work performed in the US. The remainder is derived from the UK.

Sales and Marketing

The company services are provided to a broad range of commercial industrial utility and institutional customers through approximately 80 operating subsidiaries and joint venture entities.

EMCOR have a broad customer base with many long-standing relationships. They perform construction services pursuant to contracts with owners (such as corporations municipalities and other governmental entities) general contractors systems suppliers construction managers developers other subcontractors and tenants of commercial properties. Institutional and public works projects are frequently long-term complex projects that require significant technical and management skills and the financial strength to obtain bid and performance bonds which are often a condition to bidding for and winning these projects.

Their United Kingdom subsidiary primarily focuses on building services and currently provides a broad range of services under multi-year agreements to public and private sector customers including utilities airlines airports real estate property managers manufacturers governmental agencies and the finance sector.

Financial Performance

EMCOR's revenue and profits have grown steadily in recent years.

In 2019 EMCOR's sales rose about 15% to $9.2 billion from $8.1 billion in 2018 driven by across-the-board increases in its segments and contributions made by acquisitions. The company saw increased activity in commercial and institutional projects while it experienced slowdowns in some transportation and manufacturing projects that neared completion.

The company's net income jumped to $325.1 million in 2019 up of 15% to $283.5 million from 2018 due to the rise in sales.

EMCOR held $359.9 million in cash and equivalents in 2019 compared to $366.2 million the year before. In 2019 operations generated $355.7 million while investing activities used $345.3 million and financing activities used $19.2 million.

Strategy

As part of the company's growth strategy it acquires companies that expand complement and/or diversify its businesses.

The acquisition of Batchelor & Kimball Inc. strengthens Emcor's position and broadens its capabilities in the Southern and Southeastern regions of the United States and the results of its operations have been included within the United States mechanical construction and facilities services segment.

Mergers and Acquisitions

In 2019 EMCOR acquired Batchelor & Kimball a leading provider of mechanical construction and maintenance services. The acquisition strengthens EMCOR's position in mechanical construction and maintenance services and broadens its capabilities across the South and Southeast regions.

Company Background

EMCOR's history goes back to the late 1880s when a forerunner Jamaica Water Supply Co. was incorporated in 1887 to supply water to some residents of Queens and Nassau Counties in New York. The company's size grew and contracted over the years before declaring bankruptcy in the mid-1990s. The current EMCOR grew out of the reorganized company.

HISTORY

EMCOR's forerunner Jamaica Water Supply Co. was incorporated in 1887 to supply water to some residents of Queens and Nassau Counties in New York. In 1902 it bought Jamaica Township Water Co. and by 1906 it was generating revenue — reaching $1.6 million by 1932. Over the next 35 years the company kept pace with the population of its service area.

In 1966 the enterprise was acquired by Jamaica Water and Utilities which then bought Sea Cliff Water Co. In 1969 and 1970 it acquired Welsbach (electrical contractors) and A to Z Equipment (construction trailer suppliers); it briefly changed its name in 1974 to Welsbach Corp. before becoming Jamaica Water Properties in 1976.

Diversification proved unprofitable however and in 1977 Martin Dwyer and his son Andrew took over the management of the struggling firm. Despite posting million-dollar losses in 1979 it was profitable by 1980.

The Dwyers acquired companies in the electrical and mechanical contracting security telecommunications computer energy and environmental businesses. In 1985 Andrew Dwyer became president and the firm changed its name the next year to JWP.

Between 1986 and 1990 JWP acquired more than a dozen companies including Extel (1986) Gibson Electric (1987) Dynalectric (1988) Drake & Scull (1989) NEECO and Compumat (1990) and Comstock Canada (1990).

In 1991 JWP capped its strategy of buying up US computer systems resellers by acquiring Businessland. It then bought French microelectronics distributor SIVEA. Later that year JWP bought a 34% stake in Resource Recycling Technologies (a solid-waste recycler).

JWP's shopping spree extended the firm's reach but the company began to struggle when several sectors turned sour. A price war in the information services business and a weak construction market led to a loss of more than $600 million in 1992. That year president David Sokol resigned after questioning JWP's accounting practices. He turned over to the SEC a report that claimed inflated profits.

Cutting itself to about half its former size the company sold JWP Information Services in 1993. (JWP Information Services later became ENTEX Information Services which was acquired by Siemens in 2000.) However JWP continued to struggle and in early 1994 it filed for bankruptcy. Emerging from Chapter 11 protection in December 1994 the reorganized company took the name EMCOR. That year Frank MacInnis former CEO of electrical contractor Comstock Group stepped in to lead EMCOR.

In 1995 the SEC using Sokol's information charged several former JWP executives with accounting fraud claiming they had overstated profits to boost the value of their company stock and their bonuses. EMCOR later reached a non-monetary settlement with the SEC. The company sold Jamaica Water Supply and Sea Cliff in 1996; it also achieved profitability that year.

Focusing on external growth EMCOR acquired a number of firms in 1998 and 1999 including Marelich Mechanical Co. and Mesa Energy Systems BALCO Inc. and the Poole & Kent group of mechanical contracting companies based in Baltimore and Miami. To meet increased demands for facilities services in 2000 EMCOR consolidated the operations of three of its mechanical contractors (BALCO J.C. Higgins and Tucker Mechanical) into one company EMCOR Services which operates in New England.

That year about six years after emerging from bankruptcy EMCOR began trading on the New York Stock Exchange. In 2002 EMCOR bought 19 subsidiaries from its financially troubled rival Comfort Systems USA including its largest unit Shambaugh & Son. Later that year it expanded its facilities services operations with the acquisition of Consolidated Engineering Services (CES) an Archstone-Smith subsidiary that operated in 20 states.

EMCOR broadened its facilities services operations by acquiring the US facility management services unit of Siemens Building Technologies in 2003; in 2005 it added Fluidics Inc. a mechanical services company based in Philadelphia.

In 2007 EMCOR acquired FR X Ohmstede Acquisitions Co. a leading provider of aftermarket maintenance and repair services and replacement parts for oil refinery equipment.

The company added to its industrial services operations by acquiring South Carolina-based facilities maintenance provider MOR PPM in 2008.

In 2009 EMCOR bought LT Mechanical of North Carolina a leading plumbing and mechanical contractor. The following year it bought Pennsylvania-based engineering and facilities services firm Scalise Industries broadening its mechanical services business.

EXECUTIVES

Evp And Cfo, Mark A. Pompa, age 56, $670,000 total compensation
Evp Shared Services, R. Kevin Matz, age 62, $530,000 total compensation
Ceo Emcor Uk, Keith Chanter, age 61
President Ceo And Director, Anthony J. (Tony) Guzzi, age 55, $1,071,000 total compensation
Vp Marketing And Communications, Mava K. Heffler
President And Ceo Emcor Construction Services, Michael J. (Mike) Parry, age 71
President And Ceo Emcor Building Services, Michael P. (Mike) Bordes
President And Ceo Emcor Industrial Services And Ohmstede, Bill Reid
Vice President Of Sales And Marketing Emcor Group Inc, Jeff Budzinski
Vice President Information Systems And Technology, Peter Baker
Vice President Massachusetts Operations, Gary Picco
Senior Vice President Information Systems And Technology Building Services, Timothy Reed
Vice President, Charlie Hadsell
Vice President And Controller, William Feher
Vice President Facility Services, Anthony Scalise
Vice President Midwest Region, John Schmitz
Vice President Estimating, Jerry Gallagher
Chairman, Stephen W. Bershad, age 78
Auditors: Ernst & Young LLP

LOCATIONS

HQ: EMCOR Group, Inc.
301 Merritt Seven, Norwalk, CT 06851-1092
Phone: 203 849-7800
Web: www.emcorgroup.com

PRODUCTS/OPERATIONS

2018 Sales

	$ mil.	% of total
United States mechanical construction and facilities services	3,202	37
United States electrical construction and facilities services	1,954	24
United States building services	1,875	23
United States industrial services	865	11
United Kingdom building services	414	5
Total	**8,130**	**100**

Selected Operations

Mechanical and Electrical Construction
  Building plant and lighting systems
  Data communications systems
  Electrical power distribution systems
  Energy recovery
  Heating ventilation and air-conditioning (HVAC) systems
  Lighting systems
  Low-voltage systems (alarm security communications)
  Piping and plumbing systems
  Refrigeration systems
  Voice communications systems
Facilities Services
  Facilities management
  Installation and support for building systems
  Mobile maintenance and service
  Program development and management for energy systems
  Remote monitoring
  Site-based operations and maintenance
  Small modification and retrofit projects
  Technical consulting and diagnostic services

Selected Subsidiaries

Dyn Specialty Contracting Inc.
EMCOR Construction Services Inc.
EMCOR-CSI Holding Co.
EMCOR Facilities Services Inc.
EMCOR Group (UK) plc
EMCOR International Inc.
EMCOR (UK) Limited
EMCOR Mechanical/Electrical Services (East) Inc.
  EMCOR (UK) Limited

FR X Ohmstede Acquisitions Co.
MES Holdings Corporation
RepconStrickland Inc.

COMPETITORS

AECOM
Comfort Systems USA
Fluor
Honeywell
  International

IES Holdings
ISS GROUP LIMITED
Johnson Controls Power
  Solutions
Matrix Service

HISTORICAL FINANCIALS

Company Type: Public

Income Statement
FYE: December 31

	REVENUE ($ mil.)	NET INCOME ($ mil.)	NET PROFIT MARGIN	EMPLOYEES
12/19	9,174	325	3.5%	36,000
12/18	8,130	283	3.5%	33,000
12/17	7,687	227	3.0%	32,000
12/16	7,551	181	2.4%	31,000
12/15	6,718	172	2.6%	29,000
Annual Growth	**8.1%**	**17.2%**	**—**	**5.6%**

2019 Year-End Financials

Debt ratio: 6.46%
Return on equity: 17.12%
Cash ($ mil.): 358
Current ratio: 1.37
Long-term debt ($ mil.): 294

No. of shares (mil.): 56
Dividends
  Yield: 0.3%
  Payout: 5.7%
Market value ($ mil.): 4,852

	STOCK PRICE ($) FY Close	P/E High/Low		Earnings	PER SHARE ($) Dividends	Book Value
12/19	86.30	16	10	5.75	0.32	36.59
12/18	59.69	17	12	4.85	0.32	31.09
12/17	81.75	22	16	3.82	0.32	28.46
12/16	70.76	24	14	2.97	0.32	25.64
12/15	48.04	19	15	2.72	0.32	24.18
Annual Growth	**15.8%**	**—**	**—**	**20.6%**	**(0.0%)**	**10.9%**

Emerson Electric Co.

Emerson Electric is a global leader that designs and manufactures products and delivers services that bring technology and engineering together to provide innovative solutions for customers in a wide range of industrial commercial and consumer markets around the world. Emerson also makes measurement and analytical instruments that provide data about the physical properties of gases and liquids. Want another example of an Emerson product? Look in your kitchen sink. Its Tools & Home Products segment includes brands such as Emerson Emerson Professional Tools Badger Greenlee Grind2Energy InSinkErator Klauke Pro-Team and RIDGID. Emerson operates approximately 200 manufacturing locations with some 130 outside of the US. About 55% of total sales were from Americas region.

Operations

Emerson Electric operates within three segments: Automation Solutions; and Climate Technologies and Tools & Home Products which together comprise the Commercial & Residential Solutions.

Automation Solutions (about two-thirds of sales) enables process hybrid and discrete manufacturers to maximize production protect personnel and the environment and optimize their energy efficiency and operating costs through a broad offering of products and integrated solutions including measurement and analytical instrumentation industrial valves and equipment and process control software and systems.

The Commercial & Residential Solutions business generates about a third of revenue and consists of the Climate Technologies and Tools & Home Products segments. This business provides products that promote energy efficiency enhance household and commercial comfort and protect food quality and sustainability through heating air conditioning and refrigeration technologies.

Across both segments the company's brand names have included ASCO Aventics Bettis DeltaV Fisher Fusite Dixell Copeland Sensi InSinkErator Keystone Klauke KTM RIDGID and Pro Team.

Geographic Reach

The Americas form Emerson Electric's largest market representing about 55% its sales. Asia Middle East and Africa region accounts for nearly 30% while Europe represent about 20%. The company has approximately 200 manufacturing locations worldwide of which approximately 70 were located in the US and some 130 were located outside the US primarily in Europe and Asia and to a lesser extent in Canada and Latin America.

Emerson Electric headquarter is in St. Louis Missouri.

Sales and Marketing

Emerson Electric sells its products through a variety of distribution channels including its direct sales force a network of independent sales representatives and distributors purchasing products for resale. Emerson serves industries such as oil and gas pulp and paper chemicals power food and beverage and life sciences.

Financial Performance

Net sales for 2020 were $16.8 billion a decrease of $1.6 billion or 9% compared with 2019. Sales decreased $1.0 billion in Automation Solutions and $526 million in Commercial & Residential Solutions.

Net earnings attributable to common stockholders in 2020 were $2.0 billion down 15% compared with 2019. The decline in sales volume largely attributable to the negative effects of COVID-19 resulted in a decline in operating results of $0.27 per share while restructuring costs and special advisory fees reduced earnings by $0.42 per share in the current year ($0.12 per share in the prior year).

Cash held by the company at the end of 2020 decreased to $1.1 billion. Cash provided by operations was $2.9 billion while cash used for investing and financing activities were $2.7 billion and $2.1 billion respectively. Main uses of cash were purchases of businesses and dividends paid.

Mergers and Acquisitions

In late 2020 Emerson has completed the purchase of Massachusetts-based 7AC Technologies Inc. 7AC is a technology start-up offering an emerging approach to air conditioning technology that enables energy savings and sustainable air management. Emerson a longtime leader in advanced heating and cooling technologies has been collaborating with 7AC to commercialize a new technology that enables customers such as commercial building owners and retailers to achieve desired relative humidity and temperature in a single step. The membrane-based liquid desiccant technology is flexible fully modular and can be incorporated into various applications. Terms were not disclosed.

In 2020 Emerson has completed the acquisition of the Progea Group an industry-leading provider based in Italy of industrial internet of things (IIoT) plant analytics human machine interface (HMI) and supervisory control and data acquisition (SCADA) technologies for an undisclosed amount. The addition of Progea's capabilities in analytics industrial visualization and IIoT will build upon

Emerson's embedded software and control portfolio for manufacturing infrastructure and building automation applications and enable customers to streamline comprehensive machine and plant control systems to a single partner.

Also in 2020 Emerson completed the purchase of Open Systems International Inc. (OSI Inc.) for $1.6 billion in an all cash transaction. OSI Inc. is a leading operations technology software provider helping customers in the global power industry as well as other end markets transform and digitize operations to more seamlessly incorporate renewable energy sources and improve energy efficiency and reliability. Emerson's domain expertise in power generation combined with OSI Inc.'s complementary software and reach within the power transmission and distribution sectors enables the end-to-end ability to monitor control and optimize operations in real-time across the power enterprise.

Company Background

Emerson Electric was founded in 1890 in St. Louis by brothers Alexander and Charles Meston inventors who developed uses for the alternating-current electric motor which was new at the time. The company was named after former Missouri judge and US marshal John Emerson who financed the enterprise and became its first president. Emerson's best-known product was an electric fan introduced in 1892. Between 1910 and 1920 the company helped develop the first forced-air circulating systems.

EXECUTIVES

Svp And Cto, Randall D. Ledford
Chairman And Ceo, David N. Farr, $1,300,000 total compensation
Vice President Architecture And Research, Chris Stephen
Evp And Coo, Edgar Purvis
Evp; Business Leader Commercial And Industrial Solutions, James J. (Jim) Lindemann
Evp Emerson Storage Solutions & Professional Tools, Patrick J. (Pat) Sly
Evp And Cfo, Frank J. Dellaquila, $620,000 total compensation
President, Edward L. Monser, $720,000 total compensation
Vp Planning, Mark J. Bulanda
Chairman Automated Solutions, Steven A. (Steve) Sonnenberg
Evp Organizational Planning And Development, Steve J. Pelch
Evp; Business Leader Emerson Climate Technologies, Robert T. (Bob) Sharp
Evp; Group Business Leader Automated Solutions, Michael H. Train
Vice President Marketing Key Accounts And Distribution Customer, Jim Bolit
Vice President Global Security, Tony Vermillion
Vice President And Treasurer, David Rabe
Vice President Sales North America, Tim Erman
Vice President Managing Director China, Choonhwee Tan
Vice President Product Safety, Steve Bryant
Vice President Human Resources Americas, Tom Sheehan
Vice President Asia Pacific Daniel Measurement And Cont, Keven Dunphy
Vice President Business Development, Matthew Fox
Vice President Latin America, Fernando Llopart
Vice President Global Supply Chain, Eric Carlson
Vice President Information Technology Risk Management, Jim Loge
Vice President, Steve Nahrup
Senior Vice President Finance And Controller, Ada Aguirre
Vice President Sales, Scott Whitley

Se Area Vice President, Steve Moore
Group Vice President Storage Solutions, Russ Kerstetter
Vice President Marketing And Sales Americas, Bob M Brown
National Account Manager, Justin Conley
Vice President Pension Investments, David Meade
Vice President Human Resources, Jill Lutes
Vice President Lifecycle Services Process Systems And Sol, Sean Sims
Vice President Global Human Resources, Timothy M Volk
Vice President Operations, Kent Schultz
Vice President Of Global Quality Safety And Approvals Rosemount, Kelly Klein
National Account Manager, Traci Olmstead
Senior Vice President Materials And Logistics, Larry Lawrence
Vice President Global Supply Chain, Ken Poczekaj
Vice President Shared Services, Fred Burdell
Senior Vice President Information Technology Servicing Operations, Ana Victoria
Vice President Engineering, Robert Jantz
Vp And Cio, Jake Fritz
Vice President Global Logistics, Greg Fromknecht
Vice President Human Resources Information Systems (hris), Jim Rhodes
Vice President Global Projects, Denis Lawlor
Vice President Emerson Professional Tools Sales, Mark Downie
Vice President It Emerson Process Management, Lisa Nelson
Vp Pressure Engineering, Dave Wehrs
Vice President Global Sales, Gregg Berres
Vice President Flow, Austin Childs
Vp Supply Chain, Tom King
Vice President Development, Catherine Merkel
Vice President Global Operations, Theodor Cojocaru
National Accounts Manager, Al Schuler
Vice President, Michael Keating
Vice President Application Engineering Emerson Climate Technologies, Al Maier
Vice President Of Operations, Scott Latona
Vp Human Resources Emerson Automation Solutions, Demetrios Georgacopoulos
Vice President Engineering, Jason Hill
Vice President Technology Development, Chuck Ketterer
Vice President Engineering, Don Haugh
Vice President Employment Law, Charlie Morgan
Vice President, Charles Woodard
Vice President Finance, Gerry Lawrence
Vice President And General Management In Brazil, Rafael Jaramillo
Vice President Controller And Chief Accounting Officer, Rick Schlueter
Vice President Global Operations, Dan Ackermann
Vice President Global Sales And Business Development, Joerg Brahm
Vice President Group Leader Mergers And Acquisitions, Vanessa Mckenzie
Vice President Technology, Bill Butler
Vice President Engineering Services And, Carlos Obella
Vice President Human Resources Latin America, Dario Kanevsky
Vice President And Managing Director, John Ruese
Vice President Operations, Anuar Barake
Vice President And Corporate Controller, Michael Baughman
Vice President Procurement Process Systems And Solutions, Vincent Grindlay
Vice President, Rick Gehrin
Vice President And General Manager, Eric Claggett
Vice President Human Resources Europe, Ralf Buttkus
Vice President And General Counsel Emerson Asia Pacific, Mei Yin Lim

Vice President Advanced Manufacturing Engineering, Gary Diller
Vice President Global Supply Chain, Douglas Johnson
Vice President And General Manager, Lara Kauchak
Vice President, Scott-h Olson
Vp Sales Cargo Solutions, Doug Thurston
Evp And Coo Emerson Commercial And Residential Solutions, Jim Lindemann
Vice President Communications And Channel Marketing, Bob Labbett
Vice President, Dennis Belanger
Regional Treasurer, Martin Benedict Fernandez
Secretary Iii Emerson Process Management, Susan Amberson
Treasurer, Alan Mielcuszny
Board Member, Joshua Bolten
Board Member, Gloria Flach
Auditors: KPMG LLP

LOCATIONS

HQ: Emerson Electric Co.
8000 W. Florissant Avenue, P.O. Box 4100, St. Louis, MO 63136
Phone: 314 553-2000
Web: www.emerson.com

2018 Sales

	$ mil.	% of total
United States and Canada	8,620	49
Asia	3,936	23
Europe	2,898	17
Middle East/Africa	1,105	6
Latin America	849	5
Total	**17,408**	**100**

PRODUCTS/OPERATIONS

2018 Sales

	$ mil.	% of total
Automation Solutions		
Valves actuators and regulators	3769	
Measurement and analytical instrumentation	3604	
Process control systems and solutions	2121	
Industrial solutions	1947	
Total Automation Solutions	11,441	66
Commercial & Residential Solutions		
Climate technologies	4454	
Tools and home products	1528	
Total Commercial & Residential Solutions	5,982	34
Eliminations	(15)	
Total	**17,408**	**100**

PRODUCTS

Automation Solutions
Density & Viscosity Measurement
Flame & Gas Detection
Flow Measurement
Gas Analysis
Level Measurement
Liquid Analysis
Marine Measurement & Analytical
Pipeline Integrity
Pressure
Tank Gauging System
Temperature Measurement
Wireless Acoustic & Discrete
Wireless Infrastructure
Commercial & Residential Solutions
Ceiling Fans & Lighting
Construction & Plumbing Tools
Food Waste Disposers
Grind2Energy
Heating & Air Conditioning
Home Repair & Maintenance
Indoor Outdoor Heating Cables
Instant Hot Water Dispensers
Monitoring Systems & Facility Control
Refrigeration
Sensing & Protection Devices
Thermostats
Vacuum Equipment
Industries
AUTOMATION SOLUTIONS INDUSTRIES
Automotive

Chemical
Downstream Hydrocarbons
Food & Beverage
Industrial Energy & Onsite Utilities
Life Sciences & Medical
Marine
Mining Minerals & Metals
Oil & Gas
Packaging
Power Generation
Pulp & Paper
Water & Wastewater
COMMERCIAL & RESIDENTIAL SOLUTIONS
Commercial Buildings & Construction
Energy & Utilities
Facility Management & Maintenance
Food Retail
Food Service & Hospitality
Residential Construction & Home Improvement
Transportation

Selected Brands
AMS Suite
Baumann
Bettis
Bristol
CSI
Emerson Process Management

COMPETITORS

ABB	Rockwell Automation
Danaher	Rolls-Royce
Honeywell	Siemens AG
International	TE Connectivity
Mitsubishi Electric	United Technologies
OMRON	Yokogawa Electric

HISTORICAL FINANCIALS

Company Type: Public

Income Statement   FYE: September 30

	REVENUE ($ mil.)	NET INCOME ($ mil.)	NET PROFIT MARGIN	EMPLOYEES
09/20	16,785	1,965	11.7%	83,500
09/19	18,372	2,306	12.6%	88,000
09/18	17,408	2,203	12.7%	87,500
09/17	15,264	1,518	9.9%	76,500
09/16	14,522	1,635	11.3%	103,500
Annual Growth	3.7%	4.7%	—	(5.2%)

2020 Year-End Financials

Debt ratio: 32.72%
Return on equity: 23.56%
Cash ($ mil.): 3,315
Current ratio: 1.52
Long-term debt ($ mil.): 6,326

No. of shares (mil.): 598
Dividends
 Yield: 3.0%
 Payout: 62.5%
Market value ($ mil.): 39,211

	STOCK PRICE ($) FY Close	P/E High/Low	PER SHARE ($) Earnings	Dividends	Book Value
09/20	65.57	24 12	3.24	2.00	14.06
09/19	66.86	21 15	3.71	1.96	13.47
09/18	76.58	23 17	3.46	1.94	14.22
09/17	62.84	27 21	2.35	1.92	13.59
09/16	54.51	22 17	2.52	1.90	11.77
Annual Growth	4.7%	— —	6.5%	1.3%	4.5%

Employers Holdings Inc

Because workers' compensation is nothing to gamble with small business owners can turn to Employers Holdings. The Reno-based holding company provides workers' compensation services including claims management and services focused on select small businesses in low and medium hazard industries. The company provides workers' compensation through its Employer Insurance Company of Nevada (EICN) and Employers Compensation Insurance Company. Employers Holdings also operates Employers Assurance and Employers Preferred Insurance Company both of which also offer workers' compensation.

Operations

The company has two reportable segments: Employers and Cerity. Almost all of its revenues came from employers' segment.

The Employers segment is defined as traditional business offered under our EMPLOYERS brand name (Employers) through our agents including business originated from our strategic partnerships and alliances.

The Cerity segment is defined as business offered under our Cerity brand name which includes our direct-to-customer business.

Corporate and Other activities consist of those holding company expenses that are not considered to be underwriting in nature the financial impact of the LPT agreement and legacy business assumed and ceded by Cerity Insurance Company.

Nearly 85% of sales were generated from its net premiums earned while the rest came from net investment income and realized gains on investment.

Geographic Reach

While Employers Holdings distributes its products in more than 45 states and the District of Columbia approximately half of its premiums come from California.

Its corporate headquarters is located in Reno Nevada and also has offices in more than 5 states.

Sales and Marketing

Employers Holdings uses a network of approximately 4100 independent agencies to brings its wares to the public; these agencies bring in about three-fourths of the company's in-force premiums. The company also markets its products through brokers and local trade groups and associations. Furthermore it markets its products along with ADP's payroll services in several states. Employers Holdings is forging additional distribution partners in other markets.

Financial Performance

Employers Holdings' revenue has been relatively stable for the past five years.

In fiscal 2019 revenue rose 4% to $835.9 million. That change was primarily driven by gains on investments as premiums earned were lower compared to the previous year.

The net income of the company for 2019 increased by $15.8 million to $157.1 million. Increased income from investments lower losses and LAE and lower commission expense contributed to the rise in net income.

Cash at the end of fiscal 2019 was $155.2 million. Net cash provided by operating activities was $123.1 million and another $49.2 was provided by investing activities. Financing activities used $119.1 million for acquisition of stocks dividends payment and redemption of payable notes.

Strategy

The company's business strategy is to pursue profitable growth opportunities across market cycles and maximize total investment returns within the constraints of prudent portfolio management. It pursues profitable growth opportunities by focusing on disciplined underwriting and claims management utilizing medical provider networks designed to produce superior medical and indemnity outcomes establishing and maintaining strong long-term relationships with independent insurance agencies developing and implementing new technologies designed to transform the way small businesses and insurance agents utilize digital capabilities and developing important alternative distribution channels. It continues to execute a number of ongoing business initiatives including: achieving internal and customer-facing business process excellence; diversifying its risk exposure across geographic markets; and utilizing a multi-company pricing platform and territory-specific pricing. Additionally it continues to execute its plan of aggressive development and implementation of new technologies and capabilities that it believe will fundamentally transform and enhance the digital experience of its customers including continued investments in new technology data analytics and process improvement capabilities focused on improving the agent experience and enhancing agent efficiency; and the launch and further development of digital insurance solutions including direct-to-customer workers' compensation coverage.

The capital strategy is focused on supporting its business operations by maintaining capital levels commensurate with its desired ratings from independent rating agencies satisfying regulatory constraints and legal requirements and sustaining a level of financial flexibility to prudently manage its business through insurance and economic cycles while allowing it to take advantage of investment opportunities including acquisitions of insurance and insurance-related entities as and when they arise.

EXECUTIVES

President And Ceo, Douglas D. Dirks, $927,569 total compensation

Evp Chief Legal Officer And General Counsel, Lenard T. Ormsby, $485,708 total compensation

Evp Corporate And Public Affairs, Ann W. Nelson, $354,501 total compensation

Evp And Chief Administrative Officer, John P. Nelson, $334,391 total compensation

Evp And Coo, Stephen V. Festa, $488,299 total compensation

Evp And Cio, Tracey L. Berg

Svp And Chief Underwriting Officer, Lawrence S. (Larry) Rogers

Evp And Cfo, Michael S. Paquette, age 57

Vice President, Christina Ozuna

Vice President Deputy General Counsel, Mary Lynn

Vice President, Jim Werbeckes

Vice President Human Resources, Chris Mclauchlin

Vice President Of Treasury And Investments, Matthew Hendricksen

Vice President Customer Support, Dennis Dix

Vice President, Sam King

Vice President Ciso, Bertrum Carroll

Vice President Claims, David Macy

Chairman, Michael D. (Mike) Rumbolz, age 67

Auditors: Ernst & Young LLP

LOCATIONS

HQ: Employers Holdings Inc
 10375 Professional Circle, Reno, NV 89521
Phone: 888 682-6671
Web: www.employers.com

2015 Premiums In-force

	% of total
California	57
others	43
Total	**100**

PRODUCTS/OPERATIONS

2015 Sales

	$ mil.	% of total
Net premiums earned	690	91
Net investment income	72	9
Realized losses on investments	(10.7)	-
Other income	0	-
Total	**752**	**100**

Selected Products & Services

Claims Management

Fraud Prevention
Loss Control
Loss Run Report
Managed Care Services
PrecisePay (Pay-As-You-Go)
Premium Audit
Return to Work Program
Safety Promotion Programs
Workers' Compensation Insurance

Selected Subsidiaries

AmSERV Inc.
EIG Services Inc.
Elite Insurance Services Inc.
Employers Assurance Company
Employers Compensation Insurance Company
Employers Group Inc.
Employers Insurance Company of Nevada
Employers Occupational Health Inc.
Employers Preferred Insurance Company
Pinnacle Benefits Inc.

COMPETITORS

AMERISAFE	Republic Indemnity
AmTrust Financial	Safety Insurance
Baldwin & Lyons	SeaBright Insurance
Berkshire Hathaway	Selective Insurance
CNA Financial	State Auto Financial
Donegal	State Compensation
EMC Insurance	Insurance Fund
Liberty Mutual	The Hartford
Meadowbrook Insurance	TowerGroup
Navigators	Travelers Companies
ProAssurance	United Fire
RLI	Zurich Insurance Group

HISTORICAL FINANCIALS

Company Type: Public

Income Statement				FYE: December 31
	ASSETS ($ mil.)	NET INCOME ($ mil.)	INCOME AS % OF ASSETS	EMPLOYEES
12/19	4,004	157	3.9%	704
12/18	3,919	141	3.6%	704
12/17	3,840	101	2.6%	672
12/16	3,773	106	2.8%	693
12/15	3,755	94	2.5%	716
Annual Growth	1.6%	13.6%	—	(0.4%)

2019 Year-End Financials

Debt ratio: —	No. of shares (mil.): 31
Return on equity: 14.39%	Dividends
Cash ($ mil.): 154	Yield: 2.1%
Current ratio: —	Payout: 19.1%
Long-term debt ($ mil.): —	Market value ($ mil.): 1,309

	STOCK PRICE ($) FY Close	P/E High/Low	PER SHARE ($) Earnings	Dividends	Book Value
12/19	41.75	9 8	4.83	0.88	37.18
12/18	41.97	11 9	4.24	0.80	31.08
12/17	44.40	16 12	3.06	0.60	29.07
12/16	39.60	12 7	3.24	0.36	26.16
12/15	27.30	10 7	2.90	0.24	23.62
Annual Growth	11.2%	— —	13.6%	38.4%	12.0%

Energy Transfer LP

Energy Transfer LP (ET) transfers natural gas and other energy resources through its massive network of US-based pipelines. The company's operations occur primarily through primary subsidiary Energy Transfer Operating LP (ETO) and Sunoco LP although it has interests in a number of LPs and other subsidiaries. The company operates pipelines that transport natural gas natural gas liquids refined products crude oil and Liquefied Natural Gas(LNG) across the US. It also owns and operates associated terminalling storage and fractionation facilities. Energy Transfer LP generates about 30% of revenue through a controlling stake in Sunoco LP. In 2019 the company agreed to acquire SemGroup Corporation for $5 billion.

Operations

Energy Transfer's revenue streams are its crude oil transportation and services; investment in Sunoco LP; the transportation of NGL and refined products; midstream services; interstate transportation and storage; intrastate transportation and storage; and its investment in USAC.

Energy Transfer's crude oil transportation and services provides transportation terminaling and acquisition and marketing services to crude oil markets throughout the southwest Midwest and northeastern US. The company owns and operates more than 10000miles of trunk and gathering pipelines in the southwest and Midwest in the US. The segment accounts for more than 30% of sales.

Energy Transfer's investment in Sunoco LP brings in nearly 30% of revenue. Sunoco LP is a fuel distributor to third-party dealers and distributors fuel traders and other commercial customers. It also supplies some 5400 Sunoco-branded or third-party-branded gas stations all operated by third parties. Sunoco also operates 75 retail stores in Hawaii and New Jersey.

The NGL (natural gas liquids) and Refined Products Transportation and Services segment represents around a fifth of sales. It owns some 4500 miles of NGL pipelines fractionation facilities; a NGL storage facility in Mont Belvieu; and other NGL storage assets.

Energy Transfer's Midstream Segment generates 10% of annual sales. It owns natural gas gathering compression treating processing storage and transportation assets.

The Interstate Transportation and Storage segment connects natural gas suppliers with industrial end users and other pipelines via storage facilities and gathering systems. It owns and operates approximately 12500 miles of interstate natural gas pipelines and another approximately 6770 miles through joint venture interests. The segment accounts for almost 20% of sales.

The Intrastate Transportation and Storage segment has similar operations to the above contained within Texas. It owns and operates 9400 miles of pipeline and three natural gas storage facilities. The segment accounts for about 10% of sales.

USAC provides compression services. This segment generates the remainder of the company's revenue.

Geographic Reach

Based in Dallas TX Energy Transfer operates entirely within the US. It has significant operations in Texas Louisiana Oklahoma West Virginia Pennsylvania and New York. Its pipelines reach as far as North Dakota Arizona and Idaho.

The Sunoco LP subsidiary is headquartered in Philadelphia PA.

Sales and Marketing

Energy Transfer's customers include petrochemical companies commercial and industrial end-users oil and gas producers municipalities gas and electric utilities midstream companies and independent power generators.

Sunoco supplies approximately 5474 gas stations some Sunoco-brands and some under third-party brands such as Chevron Exon and Valero. Sunoco is Chevron's largest fuel supplier.

Financial Performance

Except in 2016 Energy Transfer's sales have been rising.

In 2019 Energy Transfer's revenue grew less than 1% to $54.2 billion due mainly to higher prices.

Net income attributable to partners grew 112% to $3.6 billion.

Energy Transfer's cash on hand decreased $128 million during 2019 ending the year at $291 million. The company's operating activities generated $8 billion partially offset by $6.9 billion used in investing activities and $1.2 billion used in its financing.

Strategy

Energy Transfer has engaged and will continue to engage in a well-balanced plan for growth through strategic acquisitions internally generated expansion measures aimed at increasing the profitability of existing assets and executing cost control measures where appropriate to manage operations.

The company intends to continue to operate as a diversified growth-oriented limited partnership. The company believes that by pursuing independent operating and growth strategies Energy Transfer will be best positioned to achieve its objectives. The company balance its desire for growth with goal of preserving a strong balance sheet ample liquidity and investment grade credit metrics.

Following is a summary of the business strategies of its core businesses:

Growth through acquisitions. Energy Transfer intends to continue to make strategic acquisitions that offer the opportunity for operational efficiencies and the potential for increased utilization and expansion of existing assets while supporting investment grade credit ratings.

Engage in construction and expansion opportunities. The company intends to leverage existing infrastructure and customer relationships by constructing and expanding systems to meet new or increased demand for midstream and transportation services.

Increase cash flow from fee-based businesses. Energy Transfer intends to increase the percentage of business conducted with third parties under fee-based arrangements in order to provide for stable consistent cash flows over long contract periods while reducing exposure to changes in commodity prices.

Enhance profitability of existing assets. The company intends to increase the profitability of existing asset base by adding new volumes under long-term producer commitments undertaking additional initiatives to enhance utilization and reducing costs by improving operations.

Mergers and Acquisitions

In late 2019 Energy Transfer acquired fellow pipeline and energy infrastructure firm SemGroup Corporation in a transaction valued at about $5 billion. Its headquarters is located in Oklahoma US. The deal enhances Energy Transfer's midstream infrastructure connectivity increases the company's crude oil and natural gas liquids (NGL) infrastructure and adds direct pipelines to the Houston Ship Channel and the Nederland Terminal. SemGroup Corporation provides gathering transportation storage distribution marketing and other midstream services primarily to producers refiners of petroleum products and other market participants located in the Gulf Coast Midwest and Rocky Mountain regions of the United States of America and Canada.

Company Background

In 2012 Energy Transfer Equity bought diversified gas player Southern Union for $9.4 billion (including $3.7 billion in debt). The acquisition made Energy Transfer Equity one of the largest natural gas infrastructure companies in the US.

That year the company also completed a $2 billion merger of a wholly owned Energy Transfer Partners subsidiary with and into Southern Union subsidiary CrossCountry Energy LLC which owns an indirect 50% interest in Citrus Corp. the owner of the Florida Gas Transmission pipeline system. After the merger CrossCountry Energy remained as the surviving entity a wholly owned subsidiary of Energy Transfer Partners.

In 2010 Energy Transfer Equity acquired the general partner stake of Regency Energy Partners and sold a 49.9% stake in its Midcontinent Express Pipeline to that company. The move was seen as a way for the company to diversify its general partner operations with the aim of getting a better return for shareholders. Regency Energy Partners focuses on the gathering processing marketing and transportation of natural gas and natural gas liquids in Arkansas Kansas Louisiana and Texas.

Energy Transfer Equity was formed in 2002 as La Grange Energy a Texas limited partnership. In early 2005 it changed its name to Energy Transfer Company. In August 2005 it converted from a Texas limited partnership to a Delaware limited partnership and became Energy Transfer Equity.

EXECUTIVES

President, John W. McReynolds, age 68, $577,280 total compensation
Cfo, Thomas E. (Tom) Long, age 64, $454,154 total compensation
Evp And General Counsel, Thomas P. Mason, age 63, $571,729 total compensation
President And Coo Etp, Marshall S. (Mackie) McCrea, $1,009,231 total compensation
Evp And Head Tax, Bradford D. (Brad) Whitehurst, $503,354 total compensation
Vice President Commercial, Steven Breckon
Senior Vice President Commercial Operations Allegheny Region, Alan Vaina
Vp Engineering, Rodney Rogers
Vice President Human Resources And Administration, Robert M Kerrigan
Vice President Human Resources, Gene Weldon
Vice President Market Services, Bradley Holmes
Vice President Executive Operations, Laura Whitfield
Vice President Engineering, Charles Frey
Senior Vice President Commercial Operations, Mario Rivera
Senior Vice President Commercial Operations, Brian Beebe
Vice President Lng Operations, Jeff Brightwell
Vice President Business Development, Martin Anthony
Vice President Commercial Operations, Glenn Emery
V.p. Operations, Jim Kerns
Senior Vice President, Stephen Looney
Senior Vice President, Heejung Ryoo
Vice President Procurement Fleet Budget, Kelly Henry
Vp Engineering, Chuck Frey
Vice President Of Marketing, Gregg Russell
Senior Vice President Fleet Management Engineering Production And Supply Chain, Trey Shaddox
Assistant Treasurer, Debbie Gomez
Board Member, Steve Anderson
Secretary Ii, Debbie Perry
Auditors: Grant Thornton LLP

LOCATIONS

HQ: Energy Transfer LP
8111 Westchester Drive, Suite 600, Dallas, TX 75225
Phone: 214 981-0700
Web: www.energytransfer.com

PRODUCTS/OPERATIONS

2016 Sales

	$ mil.	% of total
Investment in ETP	21,827	58
Investment in Sunoco LP	15,698	41
Investment in lake Charles LNG	197	1
Adjustments	(218)	-
Total	**37,504**	**100**

2016 Sales

	$ mil.	% of total
Refined product sales	14,020	37
Crude sales	6,766	18
NGL sales	4,841	13
Gathering transportation and other fees	4,172	11
Natural gas sales	3,619	10
Other	4,086	11
Total	**37,504**	**100**

Selected Subsidiaries and Operating Units

EASTERN GULF CRUDE ACCESS LLC
ETP- Energy Transfer Partners L.P.
ETP GP- Energy Transfer Partners GP L.P. the general partner of ETP
ETP LLC- Energy Transfer Partners L.L.C. the general partner of ETP GP
Holdco- ETP Holdco Corporation
Regency GP- Regency Energy Partners GP LP the general partner of Regency
Regency LLC- Regency Energy Partners GP LLC the general partner of Regency GP
Regency- Regency Energy Partners LP
Southern Union- Southern Union Company
Sunoco Logistics- Sunoco Logistics Partners L.P.
Sunoco- Sunoco Inc.

COMPETITORS

AmeriGas Partners	Exxon Mobil
Atmos Energy	Ferrellgas Partners
Chevron	Kinder Morgan
Crestwood Midstream Partners LP	Magellan Midstream
	ONEOK
DCP Midstream Partners	Star Gas Partners
Enbridge	Suburban Propane

HISTORICAL FINANCIALS

Company Type: Public

Income Statement

FYE: December 31

	REVENUE ($ mil.)	NET INCOME ($ mil.)	NET PROFIT MARGIN	EMPLOYEES
12/19	54,213	3,592	6.6%	12,812
12/18	54,087	1,694	3.1%	11,768
12/17	40,523	954	2.4%	29,486
12/16	37,504	995	2.7%	30,992
12/15	42,126	1,189	2.8%	30,078
Annual Growth	**6.5%**	**31.8%**	**—**	**(19.2%)**

2019 Year-End Financials

Debt ratio: 51.63%—
Return on equity: —
Cash ($ mil.): 291
Current ratio: 1.02
Long-term debt ($ mil.): 51,028

Dividends
Yield: 9.5%
Payout: 101.6%
Market value ($ mil.): —

	STOCK PRICE ($) FY Close	P/E High/Low		PER SHARE ($) Earnings	Dividends	Book Value
12/19	12.83	11	8	1.36	1.22	8.12
12/18	13.21	17	10	1.15	1.22	7.85
12/17	17.26	23	18	0.83	1.15	(1.11)
12/16	19.31	21	4	0.92	1.14	(1.62)
12/15	13.74	63	10	1.11	1.02	(0.89)
Annual Growth	**(1.7%)**	**—**		**5.2%**	**4.6%**	**—**

Energy Transfer Operating LP

Energy Transfer Operating (ETO) is the main operating subsidiary of diversified energy asset firm Energy Transfer LP. ETO's crude oil segment (about 30% of sales) operates more than 9500 miles of pipelines that provide crude transportation services to oil markets in the Southwest Midwest and Northeast US. The NGL and Refined Products segment (20% of sales) operates about 4700 miles of natural gas liquids (NGL) pipelines and fractionation facilities. The company's midstream activities (nearly 15% of sales) include the gathering compression and treating of natural gas. Other operations include more than 28000 miles of interstate and intrastate natural gas pipelines and an LNG import terminal and regasification facility in Louisiana. The company derives about 30% of revenue through a 35% stake in Sunoco LP.

EXECUTIVES

Ceo, Kelcy L Warren
Pres-Coo, Matthew S Ramsey
L.P., Gen Ptnr, Energy T GP
Superintendent, Chuck Massey
Materials Manager, Floyd Gaines
Office Assistant, Liz Morgan
Auditors: Grant Thornton LLP

LOCATIONS

HQ: Energy Transfer Operating LP
8111 Westchester Drive, Suite 600, Dallas, TX 75225
Phone: 214 981-0700
Web: www.energytransfer.com

PRODUCTS/OPERATIONS

2011 Sales

	% of total
Crude oil acquisition & marketing	92
Terminal facilities	4
Crude oil pipelines	3
Refined product pipelines	1
Total	**100**

COMPETITORS

Buckeye Partners	Magellan Midstream
CITGO	Marathon Petroleum
Enbridge Energy	Plains All American
Enterprise Products	Pipeline
Kinder Morgan Energy Partners	RKA Petroleum
	TransMontaigne
Kinder Morgan Management	TransMontaigne Partners

HISTORICAL FINANCIALS

Company Type: Public

Income Statement

FYE: December 31

	REVENUE ($ mil.)	NET INCOME ($ mil.)	NET PROFIT MARGIN	EMPLOYEES
12/19	54,032	4,084	7.6%	12,517
12/18	54,087	3,020	5.6%	11,768
12/17	29,054	2,081	7.2%	506,829
12/16	9,151	705	7.7%	2,575
12/15	10,486	393	3.7%	2,500
Annual Growth	**50.7%**	**79.5%**	**—**	**49.6%**

Debt ratio: 51.10%—
Return on equity: —
Cash ($ mil.): 253
Current ratio: 1.01
Long-term debt ($ mil.): 50,334

Dividends
Yield: 4.1%
Payout: —
Market value ($ mil.): —

	STOCK PRICE ($) FY Close	P/E High/Low	PER SHARE ($) Earnings	Dividends	Book Value
12/19	24.22	— —	(0.00)	1.06	(0.00)
12/18	22.01	— —	(0.00)	0.46	(0.00)
Annual Growth	2.4%		—	23.0%	

Entergy Corp

Entergy is into energy. The integrated utility holding company's subsidiaries distribute electricity to some 2.9 million customers in four southern states (Arkansas Louisiana Mississippi and Texas) and provide natural gas to about 200000 customers in Louisiana. Entergy owns power plants that have a combined generating capacity of about 30000 MW including approximately 9000 MW of nuclear power. Entergy also provides ownership operation and decommissioning of nuclear power plants in the northern US. The company's regulated utilities have little retail competition as they are deemed by state regulators as the sole providers of electricity in their service areas.

Operations

The company operates two business segments: Utility and Entergy Wholesale Commodities.

The Utility segment produces 85% of revenue by generating transmitting distributing and selling electric power to customers in its regulated service areas in the US Gulf States region. It also provides natural gas utility services to customers in and around Baton Rouge Louisiana and New Orleans. The segment is composed of several regulated utility companies including: Entergy Arkansas Inc. Entergy Louisiana LLC Entergy Mississippi Inc. Entergy New Orleans Inc. and Entergy Texas. Four nuclear power plant sites with capacity of more than 5300 MW are owned and operated by corporations that roll up into this segment. Of its generation capacity about 40% is from natural gas more than 25% is from nuclear and the rest comes from coal-fired plants. Hydroelectric power provided less than 1% of Entergy Arkansas's generation in 2019.

Entergy Wholesale Commodities segment produces about 15% of total revenue through its ownership operation and decommissioning of nuclear power plants (about 2900 MW of capacity) and fossil fuel plants (some 400 MW of capacity) and the sale of its electricity on the wholesale market. It also provides management services to Nebraska's Cooper Nuclear Station (800 MW of capacity).

Geographic Reach

Entergy's Utility segments operates power plants in Arkansas Mississippi and its headquarters in Louisiana. It provides power to customers in those states and in Texas. Entergy New Orleans distributes and transports natural gas within New Orleans and Louisiana through approximately 2600 miles of gas pipeline.

The Wholesale Commodities segment has power plants and customers in New York Michigan Nebraska Arkansas and Louisiana.

Sales and Marketing

Entergy delivers electricity to more than 710000 customers in Arkansas about 1.1 million in Louisiana more than 450000 in Mississippi and some 460000 in Texas. It provides natural gas to approximately 100000 customers in New Orleans and nearly another 100000 throughout the rest of Louisiana. Entergy's retail business (mostly through the regulated utility companies) generates some 40% of sales volume from industrial businesses nearly 25% from commercial enterprises more than 25% from residential and the rest from government agencies wholesale and other customers.

Entergy Wholesale Commodities segment sells both energy and capacity from its nuclear plants to retail power providers utilities electric power cooperatives power trading organizations and other power generation companies such Consumers Energy companies from which Entergy purchased plants with the promise to continue providing energy to them. It also sells to transmission-sharing entities such as NYISO and MISO.

The company's regulated utilities have little retail competition as they are deemed by state regulators as the sole providers of electricity in their service areas.

Financial Performance

Entergy's revenue has not been consistently increasing over the past five years moving up and down from year to year. It had its peak on 2015 with $11.5 billion revenue. Net income on the other hand after its sharp decreases in 2015 and 2016 had an increase in 2017 and has been continuously increasing since then.

In 2019 revenue fell by 1% to $10.9 billion. The decrease was driven by the $174 million loss in the Entergy Wholesale Commodities segment.

Net income rose to $1.3 billion in 2019 46% increase from 2018 primarily due to higher retail electric price and lower nuclear refueling outage expenses partially offset by lower volume/weather higher interest expense and higher depreciation and amortization expenses.

Cash holdings at the end of 2019 is $426 million a decrease from $481 million the year prior. Operations generated a net inflow of $2.8 billion in cash which was more than offset by $4.5 billion used in investing activities. Financial activities brought in a net cash inflow of $1.6 billion primarily for retirement of long-term debt.

Strategy

Entergy plans to spend on routine capital projects that are necessary to support reliability of its service equipment or systems and to support normal customer growth. These capital investments includes investments in Lake Charles Power Station Washington Parish Energy Center Sunflower Solar Facility New Orleans Power Station Montgomery County Power Station and Searcy Solar Facility and investments in Entergy's Utility nuclear fleet. They also plan to invest in transmission spending to enhance reliability reduce congestion and enable economic growth distribution spending to enhance reliability and improve service to customers. Entergy Wholesale Commodities invests in component replacements software and security and dry cask storage.

Entergy's strategy is to operate and grow a world-class utility business that creates sustainable value for its customers employees communities and owners. Their current scope includes electricity generation transmission and distribution and natural gas distribution. Entergy also continually seeks opportunities to grow its utility business to benefit all stakeholders and to optimize its portfolio of assets in an ever-dynamic market. The Utility business segment will continue to modernize its operations maintain reliability and better serve its customers while growing the business. The Entergy Wholesale Commodities business segment will continue to manage the risk of its operating portfolio as Entergy completes its exit from the merchant power business.

Mergers and Acquisitions

In October 2019 Entergy Mississippi acquired the Choctaw Generating Station an 810 MW natural gas fired combined-cycle turbine plant located near French Camp Mississippi from a subsidiary of GenOn Energy Inc. The purchase price for the Choctaw Generating Station was approximately $305 million.

Company Background

Entergy has had a colorful and varied start in the beginning of the 20th Century. Its roots can be traced back to Arkansas Power & Light (1913) New Orleans Public Service Inc (1922) Louisiana Power & Light and Mississippi Power & Light (both formed in 1927). In 1949 these four companies along with other utilities were combined into a Maine holding company Electric Power and Light. In 1949 after a small phase when the unified company was dissolved a new holding company Middle South Utilities emerged that year to take over the four utilities' assets. In 1989 following a badly botched construction plan of two nuclear facilities (behind schedule and over budget)- whereby Middle South tried to pass on the costs to customers but eventually settled the disputes— the company changed its name to Entergy to distance itself from the controversy.

HISTORY

Arkansas Power & Light (AP&L founded in 1913) consolidated operations with three other Arkansas utilities in 1926. Also that year New Orleans Public Service Inc. (NOPSI founded in 1922) merged with two other Big Easy electric companies. Louisiana Power & Light (LP&L) and Mississippi Power & Light (MP&L) were both formed in 1927 also through consolidation of regional utilities.

AP&L LP&L MP&L NOPSI and other utilities were combined into a Maine holding company Electric Power and Light which was dissolved in 1949. A new holding company Middle South Utilities emerged that year to take over the four utilities' assets.

In 1971 the company bought Arkansas-Missouri Power. In 1974 it brought its first nuclear plant on line and formed Middle South Energy (now System Energy Resources) to develop two more nuclear facilities Grand Gulf 1 and 2. Unfortunately Grand Gulf 1 was completed behind schedule and about 400% over budget. When Middle South tried to pass on the costs to customers controversy ensued. Construction of Grand Gulf 2 was halted and the CFO Edwin Lupberger took charge in 1985. Two years later nuke-related losses took the company to the brink of bankruptcy.

The company moved to settle the disputes by absorbing a $900 million loss on Grand Gulf 2 in 1989. To distance itself from the controversy Middle South changed its name to Entergy. In 1991 NOPSI settled with the City of New Orleans over Grand Gulf 1 costs.

That year Entergy anticipating deregulation branched out into nonregulated industries and looked abroad for growth opportunities. In 1993 a consortium including Entergy acquired a 51% interest in Edesur a Buenos Aires electric utility. In 1995 Entergy agreed to buy a 20% stake in a power plant under construction in India but the state government soon halted the project accusing the participating US companies of exploiting India.

Entergy completed its acquisition of CitiPower an Australian electric distributor in 1996 and the next year it bought the UK's London Electricity.

But diversification had drained funds. Lupberger resigned in 1998 and a new management team began selling noncore businesses such as CitiPower and London Electricity. NYMEX began trading electricity futures in 1998 using Entergy and Cinergy as contract-delivery points.

EXECUTIVES

Group President Utility Operations, Theodore H. (Theo) Bunting, age 62, $607,806 total compensation

Chairman And Ceo, Leo P. Denault, age 61, $1,191,462 total compensation

Svp And Coo, Paul D. Hinnenkamp

Evp, Roderick K. (Rod) West, age 52, $654,514 total compensation

President And Ceo Entergy Mississippi Inc, Haley R. Fisackerly, $248,346 total compensation

Evp Nuclear Operations And Chief Nuclear Officer, A. Christopher (Chris) Bakken, $426,990 total compensation

Evp And Cfo, Andrew S. (Drew) Marsh, age 47, $553,284 total compensation

President And Ceo Entergy New Orleans Inc, Charles Rice

President And Ceo Entergy Arkansas Inc., Rick Riley

Evp And General Counsel, Marcus V. Brown, age 58, $563,208 total compensation

President And Ceo Entergy Texas Inc, Sallie Rainer

President And Ceo Entergy Louisiana Llc And Entergy Gulf States Louisiana L.l.c., Phillip R. May

Evp Shared Services And Human Resources; Chief Diversity Officer, Don Vinci

Vice President Information Technology Entergy Corp., Robyn Murhammer

Senior Vice President Of Nuclear Business Development, Randy Hutchinson

Vice President, Charles Fink

Vice President, Bill Abler

Vice President Of Marketing, Liz Gaiennie

Vice President Transmission, Jim Schott

Vice President Asset Management, Rose Albarado

Vice President, William Maguire

Vice President, David Fishel

Site Vice President Vermont Yankee, Chris Wamser

Vice President Engineering, Mike Knight

Svp Nuclear Strategy And Operations Entergy Nuclear, Donna Jacobs

Evp And Cao, Donald Vinci

Svp And Chief Accounting Officer, Alyson Mount

Vice President, Michael Twornay

Vice President Federal Governmental Affairs, Daniel Turton

Vice President Finance, Bob Cushman

Site Vice President, Bob Smith

Vice President Of Governmental Affairs, Kenneth Theobalds

Vice President Critical Infrastructur, Chris Peters

Vice President And Associate Broker, Mike Wilson

Senior Vice President Human Resources Chro And Chief Diversity Officer, Andrea Rowley

Executive Vice President Nuclear Operations; Chief Nuclear Officer Entergy Nuclear, Chris Bakken

Svp Federal Policy Regulatory And Governmental Affairs, Mike Twomey

Vice President Customer Service Entergy Mississippi, Lea Turnipseed

Site Vice President Waterford 3 Steam Electric Station, Sergio Vazquez

Vice President Energy Technology And Analytics, Raiford Smith

Executive Vice President And General Counsel Of Entergy Corporation And Subsidiares, Marc Brown

Vice President Information Technology, Paul Hull

Vice President, Paul Rousseau

Executive Vice President, G Traub

Secretary, Kim Leddy

Secretary, Nicole Grille

Secretary, Gwen Hymel

Secretary, Julie Mullet

Secretary, Cheryl Morse

Board Member, Perry Rodrigue

Board Member, Charles E Watkins

Secretary Iii, Sandra Bailey

Senior Secretary, Cynthia Washington

Board Of Directors, Dave McElwee

Senior Secretary, Linda Lay

Treasurer, Edward Green

Board Member, Kirkland Donald

Board Member, Philip Frederickson

Senior Secretary, Marie Montanarello

Secretary, Karla Jones

Senior Secretary, Shirley Halliburton

Board Member, Blanche L Lincoln

Board Member, Stuart Levenick

Board Member, Karen Puckett

Treasurer, Susan Morris

Board Member, Michael Putziger

Auditors: DELOITTE & TOUCHE LLP

LOCATIONS

HQ: Entergy Corp
639 Loyola Avenue, New Orleans, LA 70113
Phone: 504 576-4000
Web: www.entergy.com

PRODUCTS/OPERATIONS

2017 Sales

	$ mil.	% of total
Utility	9,417	85
Entergy Wholesale Commodities	1,656	15
Eliminations	(0.1)	—
Total	**11,074**	**100**

2017 Sales

	$ mil.	% of total
Electric	9,278	84
Competitive businesses	1,656	15
Natural gas	1,389	1
Total	**11,074**	**100**

Selected Subsidiaries

Entergy Arkansas Inc. (electric utility)
Entergy Louisiana LLC. (electric utility)
Entergy Mississippi Inc. (electric utility)
Entergy New Orleans Inc. (electric and gas utility)
Entergy Nuclear Inc. (nuclear plant operation)
Entergy Operations Inc. (plant management and maintenance for Entergy utilities)
Entergy Services Inc. (management services for Entergy utilities)
System Energy Resources Inc. (plant management and supply to Entergy utilities)
System Fuels Inc. (fuel storage and delivery to Entergy utilities)

COMPETITORS

AEP
Atmos Energy
CenterPoint Energy
OGE Energy
Oncor Electric Delivery
Southern Company

HISTORICAL FINANCIALS

Company Type: Public

Income Statement   FYE: December 31

	REVENUE ($ mil.)	NET INCOME ($ mil.)	NET PROFIT MARGIN	EMPLOYEES
12/19	10,878	1,258	11.6%	13,635
12/18	11,009	862	7.8%	13,688
12/17	11,074	425	3.8%	13,504
12/16	10,845	(564)	—	13,513
12/15	11,513	(156)	—	13,579
Annual Growth	**(1.4%)**	**—**		**0.1%**

2019 Year-End Financials

Debt ratio: 38.32%
Return on equity: 12.88%
Cash ($ mil.): 425
Current ratio: 0.54
Long-term debt ($ mil.): 17,078

No. of shares (mil.): 199
Dividends
  Yield: 3,0%
  Payout: 91.9%
Market value ($ mil.): 23,858

	STOCK PRICE ($) FY Close	P/E High/Low		PER SHARE ($) Earnings	Dividends	Book Value
12/19	119.80	19	13	6.30	3.66	52.61
12/18	86.07	19	15	4.63	3.58	47.94
12/17	81.39	38	31	2.28	3.50	45.37
12/16	73.47	—	—	(3.26)	3.42	46.25
12/15	68.36	—	—	(0.99)	3.34	53.67
Annual Growth	**15.1%**	**—**	**—**	**—**	**2.3%**	**(0.5%)**

Enterprise Bancorp, Inc. (MA)

Enterprise Bancorp caters to more customers than just entrepreneurs. The holding company owns Enterprise Bank and Trust which operates more than 20 branches in north-central Massachusetts and southern New Hampshire. The $2 billion-asset bank offers traditional deposit and loan products specializing in lending to businesses professionals high-net-worth individuals and not-for-profits. About half of its loan portfolio is tied to commercial real estate while another one-third is tied to commercial and industrial and commercial construction loans. Subsidiaries Enterprise Investment Services and Enterprise Insurance Services provide investments and insurance geared to the bank's target business customers.

Operations
More than 50% of Enterprise Bancorp's $1.86 billion loan portfolio was tied to commercial real estate loans at the end of 2015 while commercial and industrial and commercial construction loans made up another 25% and 11% of the bank's loan assets. The rest of the bank's portfolio was tied to residential mortgages (9% of loan assets) home equity loans and lines of credit (4%) and consumer loans (less than 1%).

Nearly 80% of the bank's total revenue comes from loan interest while investment advisory fees and deposit and interchange fees each make up another 5%.

Geographic Reach
The Lowell Massachusetts-based bank operated 23 branches mostly located in the greater Merrimack Valley and North Central regions of Massachusetts and Southern New Hampshire at the end of 2015.

Sales and Marketing
Enterprise spent $2.7 million on advertising and public relations during 2015 down from $2.9 million in 2014.

Financial Performance
The bank's annual revenues have risen more than 40% since 2011 as its loan assets have swelled by 50% to $1.86 billion. Meanwhile its net income has grown more than 50% as it's kept a lid on loan loss provisions and operating costs.

Enterprise Bancorp's revenue climbed 8% to $98.4 million during 2015 thanks to 11% loan asset growth driven by a "seasoned" lending team a sales and service culture and geographic market expansion. Commercial construction loans grew the fastest rate during the year though all loans grew albeit at a slightly slower rate.

Revenue growth in 2015 drove the bank's net income up 10% to $16.1 million despite higher salary and employee benefit expenses. Enterprise Bancorp's operating cash levels nearly doubled to $25.7 million for the year largely thanks to positive changes in working capital mainly related to pre-paid expenses and other assets.

Strategy

Enterprise Bancorp has traditionally expanded its loan and deposit business by opening new branches rather than by acquiring other banks. Enterprise hopes to take advantage of the trend to switch from larger banks to smaller community-oriented institutions. The company has also invested in upgrading its branches and operations systems.

EXECUTIVES

Evp And Cfo Enterprise Bancorp And Enterprise Bank And Trust, James A. (Jim) Marcotte, age 62, $194,806 total compensation

Ceo Enterprise Bancorp And Enterprise Bank And Trust, John P. (Jack) Clancy, age 62, $400,000 total compensation

President Enterprise Bancorp And Enterprise Bank And Trust, Richard W. (Dick) Main, age 72, $258,918 total compensation

Evp And Coo Enterprise Bank And Trust, Stephen J. Irish, age 65, $194,804 total compensation

Evp And Chief Commercial Lending Officer Enterprise Bank And Trust, Brian H. Bullock, age 62

Evp And Chief Banking Officer Enterprise Bank And Trust, Steven R. Larochelle, age 56

Svp And Sales Manager, Chester J. (Chet) Szablak, age 62

Executive Vice President Chief Human Resources Officer, Jamie Gabriel

Senior Vice President Regional Commercial Lending Manager, Ryan Dunn

Vice Chairman Enterprise Bancorp And Enterprise Bank And Trust, Arnold S. Lerner, age 90

Chairman Enterprise Bancorp And Enterprise Bank And Trust, George L. Duncan, age 79

Auditors: RSM US LLP

LOCATIONS

HQ: Enterprise Bancorp, Inc. (MA)
222 Merrimack Street, Lowell, MA 01852
Phone: 978 459-9000
Web: www.enterprisebanking.com

PRODUCTS/OPERATIONS

2015 Sales

	$ mil.	% of total
Interest and dividend income:		
Loans and loans held for sale	77	79
Investment securities	5	5
Other interest-earning assets	0	-
Non-interest income:		
Investment advisory fees	4	5
Deposit and interchange fees	4	5
Net gains on sales of investment securities	1	2
Income on bank-owned life insurance net	0	1
Gains on sales of loans	0	1
Other income	2	3
Total	**98**	**100**

Products and Services

Lending Products:
Residential Loans
Home Equity Loans and Lines of Credit
Consumer Loans
Credit Risk and Allowance for Loan Losses
Deposit Products:
Cash Management Services

Product Delivery Channels
Investment Services
Insurance Services

COMPETITORS

Bank of America	Peoples Federal
Citizens Financial	Bancshares Inc.
Group	Sovereign Bank
Eastern Bank	TD Bank USA

HISTORICAL FINANCIALS

Company Type: Public

Income Statement

FYE: December 31

	ASSETS ($ mil.)	NET INCOME ($ mil.)	INCOME AS % OF ASSETS	EMPLOYEES
12/19	3,235	34	1.1%	538
12/18	2,964	28	1.0%	508
12/17	2,817	19	0.7%	482
12/16	2,526	18	0.7%	468
12/15	2,285	16	0.7%	426
Annual Growth	**9.1%**	**20.6%**	—	**6.0%**

2019 Year-End Financials

Debt ratio: 0.46%
Return on equity: 12.39%
Cash ($ mil.): 63
Current ratio: —
Long-term debt ($ mil.): —

No. of shares (mil.): 11
Dividends
  Yield: 1.8%
  Payout: 23.6%
Market value ($ mil.): 401

	STOCK PRICE ($) FY Close	P/E High/Low		Earnings	PER SHARE ($) Dividends	Book Value
12/19	33.87	12	9	2.89	0.64	25.09
12/18	32.16	17	12	2.46	0.58	21.80
12/17	34.05	23	18	1.66	0.54	19.97
12/16	37.56	22	12	1.70	0.52	18.72
12/15	22.85	16	13	1.55	0.50	17.38
Annual Growth	**10.3%**	—	—	**16.9%**	**6.4%**	**9.6%**

Enterprise Financial Services Corp

Enterprise Financial Services wants you to boldly bank where many have banked before. It's the holding company for Enterprise Bank & Trust which mostly targets closely-held businesses and their owners but also serves individuals in the St. Louis Kansas City and Phoenix metropolitan areas. Boasting $3.8 billion in assets and 16 branches Enterprise offers standard products such as checking savings and money market accounts and CDs. Commercial and industrial loans make up over half of the company's lending activities while real estate loans make up another 45%. The bank also writes consumer and residential mortgage loans. Bank subsidiary Enterprise Trust offers wealth management services.

Operations

Enterprise Trust the company's wealth management unit targets business owners wealthy individuals and institutional investors providing financial planning business succession planning and related services. The unit also invests in Missouri state tax credits from funds for affordable housing development which it then sells to clients and others.

About 82% of Enterprise Financial's total revenue came from loan interest (including fees) in 2014 while another 7% came from interest on its taxable and tax-exempt investment securities. The rest of its revenue came from wealth management income (4%) service fees (3%) gains on state tax credits (1%) and other miscellaneous income sources. The bank had a staff of 452 full-time employees at the end of 2014.

Geographic Reach

Enterprise Bank & Trust operates eight banking locations in or around Kansas City six banking locations and a support center in the St. Louis area and two banking locations in the Phoenix metro area.

Financial Performance

The company has struggled to consistently grow its revenues in recent years mostly due to shrinking interest margins on its loans amidst the low-interest environment. Its profits however have mostly trended higher thanks to declining loan loss provisions as its loan portfolio's credit quality has improved with higher property valuations in the strengthened economy.

Enterprise Financials' revenue fell by 9% to $148.4 million in 2014 mostly due to double-digit declines in interest income as its purchased credit-impaired (PCI) loan balances and accelerated payments declined and as interest margins on its loans continued to shrink. The bank's portfolio loan balances increased however helping to offset some of its interest income decline.

Lower revenue and higher loan loss provisions (it received a loan loss benefit of $642 thousand in 2013) in 2014 caused the bank's net income to dive 18% to $27.2 million. Enterprise Financial's operating cash levels rose by 7% to $31.5 million despite lower earnings for the year mostly thanks to favorable changes in its working capital related to a $12-million change in other asset balances.

Strategy

Enterprise Financial Services planned in 2015 to continue its long-term strategy of keeping a "relationship-oriented distribution and sales approach"; growing its fee income and niche businesses; practicing "prudent" credit and interest rate risk management; and using advanced technology and controlled-expense growth. The company added that it planned on "operating branches with larger average deposits and employing experienced staff who are compensated on the basis of performance and customer service."

Though it just had two branches in Phoenix in 2015 the bank believes the fast-growing Phoenix market offers long-term growth opportunities for the company with its underlying demographic and geographic factors. Indeed at the end of 2014 the market had over 90000 privately-held businesses and 80000-plus households each with investable assets of more than $1 million.

Mergers and Acquisitions

In 2017 Enterprise Financial Services completed the acquisition of Jefferson County Bancshares the holding company of Eagle Bank and Trust Company in Missouri. The deal added 13 branches in metropolitan St. Louis and Perry County Missouri. The acquisition expanded EFS's assets to nearly $5 billion.

Company Background

In a restructuring move Enterprise Financial Services sold life insurance arm Millennium Brokerage in 2010 five years after investing in the company.

EXECUTIVES

President Enterprise Bank And Trust, Scott R. Goodman, age 56, $318,150 total compensation

Evp And Cfo, Keene S. Turner, age 40, $333,125 total compensation

Ceo, James B. Lally, age 52, $331,342 total compensation
Chief Credit Officer Enterprise Bank & Trust, Douglas N. Bauche, age 51, $253,270 total compensation
Senior Vice President Trust Officer, Steven Ray
Senior Vice President Treasury Management, Rhonda Harrelson
Vice President Operations, Colleen Shea
Senior Vice President Commercial Banking, James Tighe
Senior Vice President Treasury Management, Mark Lawson
Vice President Treasury Management, Shirley Jacobs
Senior Vice President, Debbie Barstow
Vice President Relationship Manager, Brian Bonfanti
Executive Vice President Wholesale, Greg Willert
Vice President Finance, Matt Eusterbrock
Chairman, John S. Eulich, age 69
Auditors: Deloitte & Touche LLP

LOCATIONS

HQ: Enterprise Financial Services Corp
 150 North Meramec Avenue, Clayton, MO 63105
Phone: 314 725-5500
Web: www.enterprisebank.com

PRODUCTS/OPERATIONS

2011 Sales

	$ mil.	% of total
Interest		
Loans including fees	130	79
Securities	11	7
Other	0	1
Noninterest		
Wealth management	6	4
Service charges on deposit accounts	5	3
Gain on state tax credits net	3	2
Other service charges and fee income	1	1
Other	4	3
Adjustments	(3.5)	—
Total	**161**	**100**

Selected Acquisitions

COMPETITORS

BOK Financial	Midwest BankCentre
Bank of America	Pulaski Financial
Commerce Bancshares	U.S. Bancorp
First Clover Leaf Financial	Wells Fargo

HISTORICAL FINANCIALS

Company Type: Public

Income Statement

FYE: December 31

	ASSETS ($ mil.)	NET INCOME ($ mil.)	INCOME AS % OF ASSETS	EMPLOYEES
12/19	7,333	92	1.3%	805
12/18	5,645	89	1.6%	650
12/17	5,289	48	0.9%	635
12/16	4,081	48	1.2%	479
12/15	3,608	38	1.1%	459
Annual Growth	**19.4%**	**24.6%**	**—**	**15.1%**

2019 Year-End Financials

Debt ratio: 2.39%	No. of shares (mil.): 26
Return on equity: 12.61%	Dividends
Cash ($ mil.): 164	Yield: 1.2%
Current ratio: —	Payout: 17.4%
Long-term debt ($ mil.): —	Market value ($ mil.): 1,280

	STOCK PRICE ($) FY Close	P/E High/Low	PER SHARE ($) Earnings	Dividends	Book Value
12/19	48.21	14 11	3.55	0.62	32.67
12/18	37.63	15 10	3.83	0.47	26.47
12/17	45.15	22 18	2.07	0.44	23.76
12/16	43.00	18 10	2.41	0.41	19.31
12/15	28.35	16 10	1.89	0.26	17.53
Annual Growth	**14.2%**	**— —**	**17.1%**	**24.0%**	**16.8%**

Enterprise Products Partners L.P.

Doing business through wholly owned subsidiary Enterprise Products Operating LLC (EPO) Enterprise Products Partners is one of the leading players in the North American midstream market. EPO connects producers of natural gas natural gas liquids (NGL) crude oil in major North American supply basins with domestic and international consumers. Operations include natural gas processing NGL fractionation petrochemical services and crude oil transportation. It owns some 50000 miles of pipelines about 14 billion cu. ft. of natural gas storage and approximately 260 million barrels of storage for NGLs refined products and crude oil. It owns more than 20 natural gas processing plants almost 25 NGL and propylene fractionators and nearly 20 deep water docks. The company derives nearly all its sales from the US.

Operations

Enterprise Products operates through four business segments: NGL (natural gas liquids) Pipelines and Services Crude Oil Pipelines and Services Petrochemical and Refined Products Services and Natural Gas Pipelines and Services.

The NGL Pipelines and Services segment generates more than 40% of sales and comprises the activities of more than 20 natural gas processing plants nearly 20000 miles of pipelines and more than 15 NGL fractionators. The plants collect and purify natural gas for end-use. It also includes EPO's NGL import and LPG export terminal operations in addition to marketing activities comprising a fleet of about 850 railcars that serve customers throughout the US and Canada.

The Crude Oil Pipelines & Services segment brings in over 30% of revenue. It includes about 5300 miles of crude oil pipelines and related operations crude oil storage and marine terminals and crude oil marketing activities. Perhaps its most important pipeline is the Seaway pipeline that connects the Cushing Oklahoma crude oil hub with markets in Southeast Texas.

The Petrochemical and Refined Products Services segment engages in petrochemical and refined products transportation and services. It fractionates propylene to create the building blocks of carpet fibers molded plastic parts for appliances cars and medical products and packaging film. It accounts for almost 20% of revenue.

Natural Gas Pipelines and Services segment includes almost 20000 miles of pipeline used to gather and transport natural gas from shale plays Eagle Ford Haynesville Permian and others. It leases underground salt dome natural gas storage facilities and conducts to natural gas marketing activities. It accounts for approximately 10% of revenue.

Overall Enterprise Products generates almost all of its sales from third parties.

Geographic Reach

Houston TX-based Enterprise Products operates the vast majority of its facilities in Texas along the Gulf Coast with particular emphasis in the Mont Belvieu refinery and transport complex. Key locations from which it gathers natural gas and crude oil include Colorado Louisiana New Mexico Texas and Wyoming. It has a presence in shale plays: Eagle Ford Haynesville Barnett Permian Piceance San Juan and Greater Green River supply basins. Its NGL pipelines extend throughout the US Midwest Rocky Mountains Southeastern and Gulf Coast including states such as Georgia New York Oklahoma and Minnesota.

Sales and Marketing

Enterprise Products sells product and services to refineries industrial companies commercial customers and regional natural gas processing plants. It generates much of its revenue from fees calculated by the volume of product it transports. The company's customer base is diversified with largest customer Vitol accounting for more than 10% of annual revenue.

Financial PerformanceEnterprise Products' sales are at the mercy of global commodity prices. As such over the last five years the company's sales have fluctuated. It has an overall growth of 21%. In 2019 the company's sales dipped 10% to $32.8 billion primarily due to a $3.87 billion decrease in marketing revenues. Revenues from the marketing of NGLs petrochemicals and refined products decreased a combined net $2.54 billion year-to-year primarily due to lower sales prices which accounted for a $4.7 billion decrease partially offset by higher sales volumes which resulted in a $2.16 billion increase. Net income grew 10% to $4.6 billion. The increase was due to lower in costs and expenses. Enterprise Products' cash and equivalents at the end of 2019 was $410 million. Operations generated $6.5 billion partially offset by the $4.6 billion used in investing activities and the $1.9 billion used in financing. Enterprise Products' main cash uses were capital expenditures and repayments of debts.

Strategy

Enterprise Products' integrated midstream energy asset network links producers of natural gas NGLs and crude oil from some of the largest supply basins in the US Canada and Gulf of Mexico with domestic consumers and international markets.

Its business strategy seeks to leverage this network to: capitalize on expected demand growth including exports for natural gas NGLs crude oil and petrochemical and refined products; maintain a diversified portfolio of midstream energy assets and expand this asset base through growth capital projects and accretive acquisitions of complementary midstream energy assets; enhance the stability of cash flows by investing in pipelines and other fee-based businesses; and share capital costs and risks through business ventures or alliances with strategic partners including those that provide processing throughput or feedstock volumes for growth capital projects or the purchase of such projects' end products.

Company Background

Enterprise Products was founded in April 1998 and conducted its IPO in July 1998. The company is investing heavily in serving shale plays especially the Eagle Ford in South Texas and is building midstream facilities to serve the surge in natural gas production.

In a major expansion move in 2009 the company acquired rival TEPPCO Partners L.P. in a $26 billion all-stock deal which boosted its pipelines and oil refined products and NGL storage capacity. The TEPPCO Partners purchase made the company the largest publicly traded energy partnership in the US. The expanded company's assets include 60 liquid storage terminals 25 natural gas storage facilities 17 fractionation facilities and six offshore hub platforms.

That year the company acquired Enterprise GP Holdings which controlled the general partner of Enterprise. The $8 billion deal was aimed at reducing long-term capital costs and simplifying the business structure of Enterprise Products Partners.

In 2010 in a move to increase its footprint in the lucrative Haynesville/Bossier Shale play Enterprise acquired two natural gas gathering and treating systems in northwest Louisiana and East Texas from M2 Midstream LLC for $1.2 billion.

In 2012 it opened a fifth NGL fractionator at its Mont Belvieu facility to process Eagle Ford hydrocarbons and a fifth in 2012.

That year Enterprise joined Enbridge Energy Partners and Anadarko Petroleum in advancing development of the Texas Express Pipeline by the companies' joint venture. The 20-inch diameter pipeline will extend about 580 miles from Skellytown Texas to the Mont Belvieu NGL fractionation complex. The pipeline also provides access to other producers in several regions: West Texas the Rocky Mountains southern Oklahoma and the Mid-continent area.

The family of Chairman Dan Duncan controls more than 30% stake in Enterprise.

EXECUTIVES

President, W. Randall (Randy) Fowler, age 64, $521,178 total compensation
Ceo, A. James (Jim) Teague, age 74, $800,000 total compensation
Evp Commercial, William (Bill) Ordemann, age 61, $451,150 total compensation
Svp And Cfo, Bryan F. Bulawa, age 51
Svp And Cio, Paul G. Flynn
Evp Operations And Engineering, Graham W. Bacon, age 56, $375,000 total compensation
Svp Commercial, Brent Secrest
Vice President Gulf Coast Gathering Processing And Transportation, Rockey Storie
Vice President, Tony Chovanec
Senior Vice President, Daniel Boss
Vice President Crude Oil Pipelines And Terminals, Greg Mills
Vice President Planning And Analysis, Randy Scheirman
Vice President Domestic, Angela Deloach
Svp Regulatory Affairs, Craig Murray
Senior Vice President, Charles Brabson
Executive Vice President And Chief Commercial Officer, Jim Teague
Vice President Deputy General Counsel Assistant Secretary, Stephanie Hildebrandt
Senior Vice President, Anthony C Chovanec
Svp General Counsel And Secretary, Harry Weitzel
Svp Of Government Affairs And Public Relations, James A Cisarik
Executive Vice President Operations, Christopher Cragg
Vice President Commercial Activity And Business Development, Terrance Mcgill
Vice President Engineering, Matt Isom
Executive Vice President, Stefan Koellmann
Vice President Strategy Supply And Risk Management, Robert Stibolt
Chairman, Randa D. Williams, age 58
Secretary, Ruth Darling
Auditors: Deloitte & Touche LLP

LOCATIONS

HQ: Enterprise Products Partners L.P.
  1100 Louisiana Street, 10th Floor, Houston, TX 77002
Phone: 713 381-6500
Web: www.enterpriseproducts.com

PRODUCTS/OPERATIONS

2018 Sales

	$ mil.	% of total
NGL Pipelines & Services	42,102	41
Crude Oil Pipelines & Services	46,533	46
Petrochemical & Refined Products Services	9,305	9
Natural Gas Pipelines & Services	4,176	4
Adjustments and Eliminations	(65583.4)	-
Total	**36,534**	**100**

COMPETITORS

Anadarko Petroleum	Kinder Morgan
CenterPoint Energy	Magellan Midstream
Crestwood Midstream Partners LP	ONEOK
Dominion Energy	Occidental Petroleum
Duke Energy	Plains All American Pipeline
Enbridge	Spectra Energy
Energy Transfer Equity	TRII
Exxon Mobil	Williams Companies

HISTORICAL FINANCIALS

Company Type: Public

Income Statement — FYE: December 31

	REVENUE ($ mil.)	NET INCOME ($ mil.)	NET PROFIT MARGIN	EMPLOYEES
12/19	32,789	4,591	14.0%	—
12/18	36,534	4,172	11.4%	—
12/17	29,241	2,799	9.6%	—
12/16	23,022	2,513	10.9%	—
12/15	27,027	2,521	9.3%	—
Annual Growth	4.9%	16.2%	—	—

2019 Year-End Financials

Debt ratio: 44.75%—
Return on equity: —
Cash ($ mil.): 334
Current ratio: 0.86
Long-term debt ($ mil.): 25,643

Dividends
  Yield: 6.2%
  Payout: 80.8%
Market value ($ mil.): —

	STOCK PRICE ($) FY Close	P/E High/Low	Earnings	Dividends	Book Value
12/19	28.16	15 12	2.09	1.76	11.31
12/18	24.59	16 12	1.91	1.72	10.92
12/17	26.51	23 18	1.30	1.67	10.43
12/16	27.04	25 16	1.20	1.59	10.41
12/15	25.58	29 17	1.26	1.51	10.08
Annual Growth	2.4%	— —	13.5%	3.8%	2.9%

EOG Resources, Inc.

Large-scale shale is the Holy Grail for oil prospector EOG Resources. It engages in exploration development production and marketing of natural gas and crude oil originating in the Eagle Ford Shale and Barnett Shale in Texas and the Bakken formation in North Dakota. Of its approximately 3.3 million BOE reserves EOG holds nearly 1.7 million barrels in crude oil and condensates with an approximately 5.3 billion cubic feet of natural gas. The US is the company's largest market.

Operations

EOG is the biggest operator (by volume produced) in the lucrative Eagle Ford Shale play in South Texas. The company also has a presence in the Delaware Basin owning about 160000 net acres in the Leonard Shale and over 345000 net acres in the Wolfcamp Shale. Additionally EOG has acreage in the Wolfcamp Shale within the Midland Basin.

Sales of crude oil and crude condensates account for around 55% of total sales natural gas sales account for roughly 10% and NGLs (natural gas liquids) nearly 5%.

EOG also conducts gas gathering processing and marketing which together bring in more than 30% of the company's sales. It sells oil and natural gas in local downstream markets transported either by pipeline.

EOG operates its own sand mine and sand processing plants in Wisconsin and Texas to support EOG exploration and development operations.

Geographic Reach

Based in Texas EOG has a presence in three major shale plays of the US? the Eagle Ford Shale and Barnett Shale in Texas and the Bakken Formation in North Dakota. Though most of its assets are in the US EOG also has operations in Canada offshore Trinidad and the Sichuan Basin in China.

The US accounts for over 95% of the company's proved reserves.

Sales and Marketing

EOG sells two major products?wellhead crude oil & condensates and natural gas. To sell beyond its local market EOG markets these products to downstream customers via extensive pipelines. Crude is also distributed by rail and truck. Its major sales points include Midwest the Permian Basin Cushing Oklahoma Corpus Christi Louisiana and other U.S Gulf Coast locations.

The company's Trinidad natural gas operations were sold to the National Gas Company of Trinidad and Tobago while its Chinese natural gas operations were sold to PetroChina.

Financial Performance

EOG has seen revenue climb from $8.7 billion in 2015 to a peak of $17.4 billion by 2019 only to fall drastically to $7.7 billion by 2016.

In 2019 revenue slightly increased by less than 1% to $17.4 billion mostly coming from a 30% decrease in NGLs revenue due to a lower composite average wellhead NGLs price ($518 million). Natural gas revenue decline by 9% to $1.2 billion due to a lower composite wellhead natural gas price ($280 million).

Net income fell to $2.7 billion in 2019 to $3.4 billion in 2018. This was primarily due higher expenses mostly to marketing costs.

Cash holdings grew $472 million to $2.0 billion at the end of 2019. Operations generated $8.1 billion which was offset by $6.2 billion used for investments (mostly in additions of new oil & gas properties) plus $1.5 billion of outflows to financing activities (primarily in debt repayments).

Strategy

EOG's business strategy is to maximize the rate of return on investment of capital by controlling operating and capital costs and maximizing reserve recoveries. Pursuant to this strategy each prospective drilling location is evaluated by its estimated rate of return. This strategy is intended to enhance the generation of cash flow and earnings from each unit of production on a cost-effective basis allowing EOG to deliver long-term production growth while maintaining a strong balance sheet. EOG is focused on cost-effective utilization of advanced technology associated with three-dimensional seismic and microseismic data the development of reservoir simulation models the use of improved drilling equipment completion technologies for horizontal drilling and formation evaluation. These advanced technologies are used as appropriate throughout EOG to reduce the risks and costs associated with all aspects of oil and gas exploration development and exploitation. EOG implements its strategy primarily by emphasizing the drilling of internally generated prospects in order to find and develop low-cost reserves. Maintaining the lowest possible operating cost structure that is consistent with efficient safe and environmentally responsible operations is also an important goal in the implementation of EOG's strategy.

HISTORY

In 1987 Enron formed Enron Oil & Gas from its existing InterNorth and Houston Natural Gas operations to concentrate on exploration for oil and natural gas and their production. Enron maintained full ownership until 1989 when it spun off 16% of Enron Oil & Gas to the public raising about $200 million. Later offerings reduced its holdings to just over 50%.

Enron Oil & Gas in 1992 was awarded a 95% working interest in three fields off Trinidad that previously had been held by government-owned companies. Two years later the company assumed the operations of three drilling blocks off Bombay (including the Tapti field) as well as a 30% interest in them. Natural gas prices fell in the winter of 1994 causing Enron Oil & Gas to focus its 1995 drilling on crude oil exploitation and the enhancement of its natural gas reserves. Natural gas prices rebounded in 1996. That year Enron Oil & Gas was awarded a 90% interest in an offshore area of Venezuela. In 1997 the company inked a 30-year production contract with China. The company made a major discovery of natural gas in offshore Trinidad in 1998. That year Mark Papa succeeded Forrest Hoglund as CEO (Papa became chairman in 1999).

In 1999 Enron traded most of its remaining stake in Enron Oil & Gas to the company in exchange for Enron Oil & Gas' operations and assets in India and China. Consequently the company changed its name from Enron Oil & Gas to EOG Resources.

The next year EOG won contracts to develop properties in Canada's Northwest Territories. It also moved into the Appalachian Basin in 2000 through the acquisition of Somerset Oil & Gas. Buoyed by a strong performance that year the company increased its capital spending on North American exploration by more than 30% and in 2001 it bought Energy Search a small natural gas exploration and production company that operated in the Appalachian Basin.

EXECUTIVES

Chairman And Ceo, William R. Thomas, age 68, $925,000 total compensation
President And Coo, Gary L. Thomas, age 71, $835,000 total compensation
Svp And Chief Information And Technology Officer, Sandeep Bhakhri
Vp Human Resources Administration, Patricia L. Edwards
Evp And Cfo, Timothy K. Driggers, age 59, $480,000 total compensation
Vp And General Manager Fort Worth, Kenneth E. Dunn
Vp And General Manager Canada Shale Project, Lloyd W. (Bill) Helms, age 62, $470,000 total compensation
Vp Drilling, Robert C. Smith
Vp And General Manager San Antonio, Sammy G. Pickering
Evp Exploration And Production, David W. Trice, age 49

Vp And General Manager Forth Worth, J. Pat Woods
Vp And General Manager Midland, Ezra Y. Yacob
Svp Operations, John J. Boyd
Vp Land, Steven D. Wentworth
Evp General Counsel And Corporate Secretary, Michael P. Donaldson, $475,000 total compensation
Vp And General Manager Oklahoma City, Nathan J. Andrews
Vp And General Manager Corpus Christi, Kenneth D. Marbach
Vp And General Manager Denver, Kenneth W. Boedeker
Vp And General Manager Artesia, Reese T. Lantrip
Vp And Treasurer, Robert West
Vice President Of Information Technology, Jim Coleman
Vice President Investor And Public Relations, David Streit
Vice President Engineering, Cory Helms
Senior Vice President And Chief Accounting Officer, Ann Janssen
Vice President, Steve Wentworth
Vice President, Sara Miller
Vice President Global Network Services, Liz Panfely
Vice President Executive Exploration, Charles Sheppard
Vice President Exploration, Charlie Sheppard
Vp And Gm International, J Pat Woods
Vice President, Rosemary Bussell
Auditors: DELOITTE & TOUCHE LLP

LOCATIONS

HQ: EOG Resources, Inc.
1111 Bagby, Sky Lobby 2, Houston, TX 77002
Phone: 713 651-7000
Web: www.eogresources.com

2017 sales

	$ mil.	% of total
United States	10,872	97
Trinidad	284	3
Other International	51	-
Total	**11,208**	**100**

PRODUCTS/OPERATIONS

2017 sales

	$ mil.	% of total
Crude oil & condensate	6,256	55
Natural Gas Liquids	729	7
Natural Gas	921	8
Gains on Mark-to-Market Commodity Derivative Contracts	19	-
GatheringProcessing and Marketing	3,298	29
Gains on Asset DispositionsNet	(99.1)	-
OtherNet	81	1
Total	**11,208**	**100**

COMPETITORS

Anadarko Petroleum
Chevron
ConocoPhillips
Enerplus
Newfield Exploration
Oasis Petroleum

Occidental Petroleum
Parsley Energy LLC
Pioneer Natural Resources
Royal Dutch Shell

HISTORICAL FINANCIALS

Company Type: Public

Income Statement

	REVENUE ($ mil.)	NET INCOME ($ mil.)	NET PROFIT MARGIN	EMPLOYEES
12/19	17,379	2,734	15.7%	2,900
12/18	17,275	3,419	19.8%	2,800
12/17	11,208	2,582	23.0%	2,664
12/16	7,650	(1,096)	—	2,650
12/15	8,757	(4,524)	—	2,760
Annual Growth	**18.7%**	**—**	**—**	**1.2%**

FYE: December 31

2019 Year-End Financials

Debt ratio: 13.94% No. of shares (mil.): 581
Return on equity: 13.34% Dividends
Cash ($ mil.): 2,027 Yield: 0.0%
Current ratio: 1.18 Payout: 21.5%
Long-term debt ($ mil.): 4,160 Market value ($ mil.): 48,741

	STOCK PRICE ($) FY Close	P/E High/Low		PER SHARE ($) Earnings	Dividends	Book Value
12/19	83.76	23	14	4.71	1.02	37.19
12/18	87.21	22	14	5.89	0.76	33.39
12/17	107.91	24	19	4.46	0.67	28.15
12/16	101.10	—	—	(1.98)	0.67	24.24
12/15	70.79	—	—	(8.29)	0.67	23.54
Annual Growth	**4.3%**			**—**	**10.9%**	**12.1%**

EQUINOR MARKETING & TRADING (US) INC.

Check the stats. Oil. Hundreds of thousands of barrels of oil gasoline and more. Statoil Marketing & Trading is a wholesaler of oil and petroleum products. The company is the US trading arm of StatoilÂ the leading Scandinavian oil and gas enterprise. Statoil Marketing & Trading delivers about 600000 barrels a day in the form of crude oil gasoline liquefied petroleum gas (LPG) propane and butane to the North American market. In addition to supplying Norwegian crude the company trades crude oil from Africa South America and North America.Â Statoil Marketing & Trading sells itÂ oil products primarilyÂ to customers in Northeastern Canada the US East Coast and Gulf Coast.

EXECUTIVES

Vice President Of Administration, Geir Bjornstad
Executive Vice President Development And Production International, Torgrim Reitan
Executive Vice President Development And Production Brazil, Margareth Ovrum
Vice President Human Resources Services, Siv Oftedal
Vice President Operations Subsea, Rune Aase
Vice President Legal, Paul Owen
Vice President Project Management, Erik Westad
Vice President Project Management, Johnny Wollberg
Vice President Quality, Magne Ottera
Vice President, Sverre Serck-hanssen
Vice President Of Supply Chain, Mauro Andrade
Vp Tax, Tom Geczik
Executive Vice President Technology Projects And Drilling, Anders Opedal

Vice President Communications, Nathaniel Teti
Auditors: KPMG LLP STAMFORD CONNECTICU

LOCATIONS

HQ: EQUINOR MARKETING & TRADING (US) INC.
120 LONG RIDGE RD 3EO1, STAMFORD, CT
069021839
Phone: 203 978-6900
Web: WWW.STATOIL.COM

COMPETITORS

Global Partners	Irving Oil Limited
Gulf Oil	Shell Oil
Hess Corporation	Tauber Oil

HISTORICAL FINANCIALS

Company Type: Private

Income Statement   FYE: December 31

	REVENUE ($ mil.)	NET INCOME ($ mil.)	NET PROFIT MARGIN	EMPLOYEES
12/17	9,874	(28)	—	5
12/16	5,984	(259)	—	—
12/15	6,947	(132)	—	—
12/14	12,075	(140)	—	—
Annual Growth	(6.5%)	—	—	—

Equitable Holdings Inc

Auditors: PricewaterhouseCoopers LLP

LOCATIONS

HQ: Equitable Holdings Inc
1290 Avenue of the Americas, New York, NY 10104
Phone: 212 554-1234
Web: www.axa.com

HISTORICAL FINANCIALS

Company Type: Public

Income Statement   FYE: December 31

	ASSETS ($ mil.)	NET INCOME ($ mil.)	INCOME AS % OF ASSETS	EMPLOYEES
12/19	249,870	(1,733)	—	7,900
12/18	220,797	1,820	0.8%	7,800
12/17	235,648	850	0.4%	7,500
12/16	216,614	1,272	0.6%	—
12/15	0	333	—	—
Annual Growth	—	—	—	—

2019 Year-End Financials

Debt ratio: 1.65%	No. of shares (mil.): 463
Return on equity: (-12.65%)	Dividends
Cash ($ mil.): 5,500	Yield: 2.3%
Current ratio: —	Payout: 29.9%
Long-term debt ($ mil.): —	Market value ($ mil.): 11,491

	STOCK PRICE ($) FY Close	P/E High/Low		PER SHARE ($) Earnings	Dividends	Book Value
12/19	24.78	—	—	(3.51)	0.58	29.19
12/18	16.63	7	5	3.27	0.26	26.22
Annual Growth	10.5%			—	22.2%	2.7%

Equity Bancshares Inc

LOCATIONS

HQ: Equity Bancshares Inc
7701 East Kellogg Drive, Suite 300, Wichita, KS 67207
Phone: 316 612-6000
Web: www.equitybank.com

HISTORICAL FINANCIALS

Company Type: Public

Income Statement   FYE: December 31

	ASSETS ($ mil.)	NET INCOME ($ mil.)	INCOME AS % OF ASSETS	EMPLOYEES
12/19	3,949	25	0.6%	607
12/18	4,061	35	0.9%	627
12/17	3,170	20	0.7%	526
12/16	2,192	9	0.4%	415
12/15	1,585	10	0.6%	297
Annual Growth	25.6%	25.5%	—	19.6%

2019 Year-End Financials

Debt ratio: 0.52%	No. of shares (mil.): 15
Return on equity: 5.48%	Dividends
Cash ($ mil.): 91	Yield: —
Current ratio: —	Payout: —
Long-term debt ($ mil.): —	Market value ($ mil.): 477

	STOCK PRICE ($) FY Close	P/E High/Low		PER SHARE ($) Earnings	Dividends	Book Value
12/19	30.87	22	15	1.61	0.00	30.95
12/18	35.25	19	14	2.28	0.00	28.87
12/17	35.41	22	18	1.62	0.00	25.62
12/16	33.64	34	19	1.07	0.00	22.09
12/15	23.39	16	15	1.54	0.00	20.37
Annual Growth	7.2%			1.1%	—	11.0%

EQUITY ONE, INC.

LOCATIONS

HQ: EQUITY ONE, INC.
1 INDEPENDENT DR STE 114, JACKSONVILLE, FL
322025005
Phone: 212 796-1760

COMPETITORS

Agree Realty	Kimco Realty
AmREIT	Kite Realty
CBL & Associates Properties	Realty Income
DDR	Regency Centers
EDENS	Vornado Realty
	Weingarten Realty

HISTORICAL FINANCIALS

Company Type: Private

Income Statement   FYE: December 31

	ASSETS ($ mil.)	NET INCOME ($ mil.)	INCOME AS % OF ASSETS	EMPLOYEES
12/16	3,494	72	2.1%	155
12/14	3,262	61	1.9%	—
12/13	3,354	88	2.6%	—
12/12	3,502	7	0.2%	—
Annual Growth	(0.1%)	78.2%	—	—

Erie Indemnity Co.

Erie Indemnity may be near a lake but it prefers pools. Founded in 1925 as an auto insurer it now provides management services that relate to the sales underwriting and issuance of policies of one customer: Erie Insurance Exchange. The Exchange is a reciprocal insurance exchange that pools the underwriting of several property/casualty insurance firms. The principal personal lines products are private passenger automobile and homeowners. The principal commercial lines products are commercial multi-peril commercial automobile and workers compensation. Historically due to policy renewal and sales patterns the Exchange's direct and affiliated assumed written premiums are greater in the second and third quarters than in the first and fourth quarters of the calendar year. Erie Indemnity charges a management fee of 25% of all premiums written or assumed by the Exchange.

Operations

Management fees account for more than 75% of Erie Indemnity's revenue; service agreements and investment income account for the remainder.

The Exchange and its subsidiaries (Erie Insurance Erie Insurance Company of New York Erie Insurance Property and Casualty and Flagship City Insurance) together operate as a property/casualty insurer and are collectively referred to as the Property and Casualty Group. The group also owns Erie Family Life Insurance.

Personal lines — primarily private passenger automobile and homeowners products — comprise some 70% of the direct and assumed premiums written; commercial lines — primarily multi-peril workers' compensation and commercial automobile — make up the rest.

Geographic Reach

Erie Indemnity operates in a dozen mid-western mid-Atlantic and southeastern states (Illinois Indiana Kentucky Maryland New York North Carolina Ohio Pennsylvania Tennessee Virginia West Virginia and Wisconsin) as well as in the District of Columbia.

Indemnity and the Exchange also operate 25 field offices in 12 states to perform primarily claims-related activities. The Exchange owns seven field offices and the remaining field offices are leased from third parties. Commitments for properties leased from other parties expire periodically through 2027. They expect that most leases will be renewed or replaced upon expiration. Rental costs of shared facilities are allocated based upon usage or square footage occupied.

Sales and Marketing

The Exchange is represented by independent agencies that serve as its sole distribution channel. In addition to their principal role as salespersons the independent agents play a significant role as underwriting and service providers and are an integral part of the Exchange's success. Erie Indemnity's distribution network includes about 12000 independent agents.

Sales and advertising costs decreased $3.2 million to $53.4 million due to decreased personnel costs.

Financial Performance

Erie Indemnity's revenue which has been rising for the past five years increased nearly 5% to $1.5 billion in 2019. This was driven by an increase in net management fee income and administrative service income but offset by a slight decline in service agreement income.

Net income rose 10% to $316.8 million in 2019 partially due to increase in operating income and total investment income.

Cash flow at the end of the year rise to $336.7 million. Cash from operations increase to almost 40% to $364.5 million while cash used in investing activities increase to $124.6 million and $169.6 million used in financing activities.

Strategy

Through careful risk selection and pricing practices as well as by maintaining a diverse product mix Erie Indemnity seeks to maintain long-term underwriting profit growth for the Exchange. It also seeks to provide consistent support services to policyholders and agents. Towards that end the company is upgrading its technology platforms (such as its claims management system). Additionally it was an early adopter of drone technology which it uses to deploy drones to hard-to-reach claims sites. In order to support their business processes and strategic initiatives in a cost and resource efficient manner they must maintain the effectiveness of existing technology systems and continue to both develop new and enhance existing technology systems.

Chief among Erie Indemnity's strategies for growth are efforts to increase its property/casualty group premiums. Furthermore it is working to improve its competitive position by expanding the size of its agency force and increasing market penetration in existing territories. It also intends to expand geographically and broaden the types of products it offers. For example in 2016 it began providing small to midsized companies with protection against cloud computing risks.

In the normal course of business they collect use store and where appropriate disclose data concerning individuals and businesses. They also conduct business using third-party vendors who may provide software data storage cloud-based computing and other technology services. They have on occasion experienced and will continue to experience cyber threats to their data and systems. They employ a company-wide cybersecurity program of technical administrative physical and disclosure controls intended to reduce the risk of cyber threats and protect our information as well as to communicate potential material threats and incidents.

Because of its reliance on sole customer Erie Insurance Exchange Erie Indemnity's performance is ultimately tied to that of the Exchange. That makes the company somewhat vulnerable to that firm's ability to withstand catastrophic losses or the possibility that the Exchange will lower its management fee rates.

In early 2019 the Credit Facility converted to a fully-amortized term loan with monthly payments of principal and interest at a fixed rate of about 5% over a period of 28 years. They capitalize applicable interest charges incurred during the construction period of long-term building projects as part of the historical cost of the asset.

Limited partnership investments primarily include U.S. and foreign private equity investments and are recorded using the equity method of accounting. The partnerships record assets on their balance sheet at fair value. While they perform various procedures in review of the general partners' valuations they rely on the general partners' financial statements as the best available information to record their share of the partnership unrealized gains and losses resulting from valuation changes. Due to the availability of financial statements provided by the general partner their share of limited partnership results is generally recorded on a quarter lag within equity in earnings (losses) of limited partnerships. Cash contributions made to and distributions received from the partnerships are recorded in the period in which the transaction

occurs. We have made no new limited partnership commitments since 2006 and the balance of limited partnership investments is expected to continue to decrease over time as additional distributions are received.

Company Background

Erie Indemnity's structure and relationship to other parts of the larger Erie Insurance Group are complex to say the least. The company operated as a property/casualty insurer through its wholly-owned subsidiaries Erie Insurance Co. Erie New York and Erie Insurance Property and Casualty throughout 2010. At year-end however Erie Indemnity sold all of its outstanding capital stock and voting shares of these subsidiaries to the Exchange. As a result now all of its former property/casualty insurance operations are owned by the Exchange and Erie Indemnity serves as the management company. The sale of the subsidiaries did not affect its pooling agreement. The company also sold its approximate 22% ownership in Erie Family Life to the Exchange which became Erie's' full parent.

EXECUTIVES

President And Ceo, Timothy G. NeCastro, $492,085 total compensation

Evp And Cio, Robert C. (Bob) Ingram, age 61, $456,923 total compensation

Evp Claims And Customer Service, Lorianne Feltz

Svp And Chief Investment Officer, Bradley G. Postema, $418,558 total compensation

Evp And General Counsel, Sean J. McLaughlin, age 65, $426,923 total compensation

Svp And Controller, Gregory J. (Greg) Gutting, age 56, $406,885 total compensation

Evp Sales And Products, Doug Smith

Senior Vice President Law Division, Sheryl Rucker

Vice President Special Investigations, David Rioux

Executive Vice President Sales And Marketing, John Kearns

Vice President Information Technology Operations And Service Management, Andrew Abramczyk

Vice President, Rebecca Dudenhoeffer

Vice Chairman, Jonathan Hirt Hagen, age 57

Chairman, Thomas B. Hagen, age 84

Auditors: Ernst & Young LLP

LOCATIONS

HQ: Erie Indemnity Co.
100 Erie Insurance Place, Erie, PA 16530
Phone: 814 870-2000
Web: www.erieinsurance.com

PRODUCTS/OPERATIONS

2017 Sales

	$ mil.	% of total
Operating revenue		
Net management fees	1,662	97
Service agreements	29	2
Investment income	28	1
Total	**1,720**	**100**

COMPETITORS

ACE USA	Navigators
Alleghany Corporation	Old Republic
Gallagher	Transatlantic Holdings
Marsh & McLennan	Travelers Companies

HISTORICAL FINANCIALS

Company Type: Public

Income Statement

FYE: December 31

	ASSETS ($ mil.)	NET INCOME ($ mil.)	INCOME AS % OF ASSETS	EMPLOYEES
12/19	2,016	316	15.7%	5,700
12/18	1,778	288	16.2%	5,500
12/17	1,665	197	11.8%	5,300
12/16	1,548	210	13.6%	5,000
12/15	1,407	174	12.4%	4,800
Annual Growth	9.4%	16.0%	—	4.4%

2019 Year-End Financials

Debt ratio: 4.85%	No. of shares (mil.): 46
Return on equity: 30.07%	Dividends
Cash ($ mil.): 336	Yield: 2.1%
Current ratio: —	Payout: 58.9%
Long-term debt ($ mil.): —	Market value ($ mil.): 7,668

	STOCK PRICE ($) FY Close	P/E High/Low	PER SHARE ($) Earnings	Dividends	Book Value
12/19	166.00	40 19	6.06	3.60	24.53
12/18	133.31	22 18	5.51	3.36	21.08
12/17	121.84	30 26	3.76	3.13	18.56
12/16	112.45	25 20	4.01	2.19	17.69
12/15	95.64	27 21	3.33	2.77	16.66
Annual Growth	14.8%	— —	16.1%	6.7%	10.2%

Eversource Energy

The largest energy delivery company in New England Eversource Energy serves roughly four million electric and gas customers via its six distinct utility companies in Connecticut Massachusetts and New Hampshire. Eversource delivers its energy through about 628000 overhead and underground lines and covers over 3200 square miles of natural gas distribution. Its electricity-focused utility companies include Public Service Company of New Hampshire (PSNH) The Connecticut Light and Power Company and NSTAR Electric Company. Eversource's gas utilities are NSTAR Gas and Yankee Gas which supply natural gas to about 300000 customers in central and eastern Massachusetts and about 241000 customers in Connecticut respectively. The company also operates a water utilities subsidiary Eversource Aquarion Holdings in Connecticut Massachusetts and New Hampshire.

HISTORY

In 1966 three old intertwined New England utilities merged. One was The Hartford Electric Light Company (HELCO) founded in 1883 by Austin Dunham in Hartford Connecticut. In 1915 the company signed the first power exchange agreement in the US with Connecticut Power (CP) which HELCO acquired in 1920.

The second founded in 1886 was Western Massachusetts Electric (WMECO) which merged with Western Counties in the 1930s to become WMECO. The third was Connecticut Light and Power (CL&P). Founded as Rocky River Power in 1905 it took the CL&P name in 1917. In 1929 it built the US's first large-scale pumped-storage hydroelectric plant.

In the 1950s HELCO formed Yankee Atomic Electric with CL&P WMECO and others to build an experimental nuclear reactor. In 1965 members of the group began jointly building the Connecticut Yankee nuke (on line in 1968). After years of co-operation CL&P HELCO and WMECO merged in 1966 and Northeast Utilities (NU) was born. It was the first multistate utility holding company created since the Public Utility Holding Company Act of 1935 had broken up the old utility giants. Holyoke Water Power joined NU the following year.

The 1970s energy crisis spurred NU to continue building nukes including Maine Yankee Vermont Yankee and two Millstone units. But by the 1980s construction delays had raised the cost of the final unit Millstone 3.

Regulators forced CL&P to spin off its gas utility Yankee Energy System in 1989. The next year NU acquired bankrupt utility Public Service Company of New Hampshire (PSNH) and its new Seabrook nuke. (PSNH emerged from bankruptcy in 1991.)

The 1995 shutdown of Millstone 1 began NU's nuclear troubles. In 1996 regulators closed all of its nukes except Seabrook because of safety concerns and NU mothballed Connecticut Yankee. The next year Michael Morris replaced CEO Bernard Fox who left after federal regulators ordered NU to comply with regulations and fix management problems — NU managers had routinely retaliated against whistleblowers — the first time a utility had been given such an order. New managers came in including a former whistleblower but NU couldn't avoid a record-setting $2.1 million fine. NU received permission to restart the Millstone units in 1998-99. But it had to absorb the $1 billion in power replacement associated with the shutdown.

Meanwhile as deregulation loomed NU created a retail marketer (now Select Energy) and a telecommunications arm (Mode 1 Communications) in 1996. Two years later retail competition began in Massachusetts and deregulation legislation was passed in Connecticut (deregulation went into effect there in 2000).

In 1999 NU sold its Massachusetts plants to New York's Consolidated Edison and auctioned off its non-nuclear plants in Connecticut to its subsidiary Northeast Generation and Northern States Power (now Xcel Energy). NU agreed to plead guilty to 25 federal felony counts and pay $10 million in penalties for polluting water near Millstone and lying to regulators.

That year Consolidated Edison agreed to buy NU for $3.3 billion in cash and stock and $3.9 billion in assumed debt. The deal broke down in 2001 however; Con Edison charged NU with misrepresenting information about power-supply contracts and NU charged Con Edison with improperly attempting to renegotiate the terms of the acquisition.

Bringing an old family member home NU bought Yankee Energy System for $679 million in 2000. Later that year Dominion Resources which had helped NU restart Millstone 2 and Millstone 3 (Millstone 1 had been taken out of service) agreed to buy the Millstone complex for $1.3 billion. The sale closed in 2001.

Also in 2001 NU subsidiary Select Energy bought Niagara Mohawk's energy marketing unit NU sold the distribution business of its Holyoke Water Power utility to the City of Holyoke for $18 million and retail electric competition began in New Hampshire. The company agreed to sell CL&P's 10% stake in the Vermont Yankee nuclear facility to Entergy in 2001; the deal was completed the following year.

NU sold its 40% interest in the Seabrook Nuclear Generating facility in 2002 to FPL Group.

In 2006 NU sold nonregulated subsidiary Select Energy which marketed and traded energy to wholesale and retail customers to Hess Corporation. That year the company also sold its competitive generation assets in Connecticut and Massa-

chusetts to Energy Capital Partners for $1.34 billion.

In 2007 Connecticut Light and Power Company completed the installation of electric service to Yankee Gas Services Company's new liquefied natural gas facility in Waterbury.

To give better access and service to its customers in 2009 NU relocated its headquarters from Berlin Connecticut to a larger building in downtown Hartford.

The 2012 acquisition of NSTAR (with 1.1 million power and 300000 gas customers) for $4.2 billion boosted the financial resources of Eversource to pay for planned transmission projects aimed at bringing cleaner power from northern New England and Canada to population centers in southern New England. The "merger of equals" (NSTAR and Eversource) created a major energy player in the US Northeast which serves more than half the total utility customers in New England. NSTAR shareholders hold about 44% of the expanded company.

EXECUTIVES

Evp And Coo, Werner J. Schweiger, age 60, $592,108 total compensation
Evp And General Counsel, Gregory B. Butler, age 62, $514,494 total compensation
President And Ceo, James J. (Jim) Judge, age 64, $959,690 total compensation
Evp Enterprise Energy Strategy And Business Development Eversource Energy And Eversource Service, Leon J. (Lee) Olivier, age 72, $1,232,250 total compensation
Evp Customer And Corporate Relations Eversource Energy And Eversource Service, Joseph R. (Joe) Nolan, age 56, $419,364 total compensation
Evp Human Resources And Information Technology Eversource Energy And Eversource Service, Christine M. (Chris) Carmody, age 57
Svp And Cfo, Philip J. (Phil) Lembo, age 64, $439,208 total compensation
Vp Internal Audit And Security, Ron Smith
Vice President Energy Supply, James Daly
Vice President Operations Executive, Robert Coates
Vice President Controller And Chief Accounting Officer, Jay Buth
Evp And Cfo, Phillip Lembo
Vp Engineering New Hampshire, Paul Ramsey
Svp Regulatory Affairs And Chief Communications Officer, Jim Hunt
Vice President New Hampshire Electric Operations, Joseph Purington
Vice President Employee And Labor Relations, Chris Hall
Vice President Communications, Beth Foley
Vice President Electric System Operations, Michael Hayhurst
Chairman, Thomas J. (Tom) May, age 73
Board Member, Dennis Harrington
Secretary, Richard Morrison
Auditors: DELOITTE & TOUCHE LLP

LOCATIONS

HQ: Eversource Energy
300 Cadwell Drive, Springfield, MA 01104
Phone: 800 286-5000
Web: www.eversource.com

PRODUCTS/OPERATIONS

2018 Sales

	$ mil.	% of total
Retail Tariff Sales		
Residential	4,439	52
Commercial	3,028	36

Industrial	442	5
Wholesale Transmission Revenue	264	3
Wholesale Market Sales Revenue	241	3
Other Revenue from Contracts with Customers	81	1
Reserve for Revenue Subject to Refunds	(24.3)	-
Alternative Revenue Programs	(46.1)	-
Other Revenue	21	-
Total	**8,448**	**100**

2018 Sales

	$ mil.	% of total
Electric distribution	6,957	67
Electric transmission	1,286	12
Natural gas distribution	1,022	10
Water distribution	212	2
Other	936	9
Eliminations	(1965.8)	-
Total	**8,488**	**100**

Selected Subsidiaries & Affiliates

The Connecticut Light and Power Company (CL&P eletric utility)
NSTAR Electric Company (electric utility)
NSTAR Gas Company (natural gas utility)
Public Service Company of New Hampsire (PSNH electric utility)
Western Massachusetts Electric Company (WMECO electric utility)
Yankee Gas Services Company (natural gas utility)

COMPETITORS

Avangrid	NiSource
Con Edison	Public Service
Green Mountain Power	Enterprise Group
National Grid	Unitil
New Hampshire Electric	

HISTORICAL FINANCIALS

Company Type: Public

Income Statement

FYE: December 31

	REVENUE ($ mil.)	NET INCOME ($ mil.)	NET PROFIT MARGIN	EMPLOYEES
12/19	8,526	909	10.7%	8,234
12/18	8,448	1,033	12.2%	7,998
12/17	7,751	988	12.7%	8,084
12/16	7,639	942	12.3%	7,762
12/15	7,954	878	11.0%	7,943
Annual Growth	1.8%	0.9%	—	0.9%

2019 Year-End Financials

Debt ratio: 37.86%	No. of shares (mil.): 329
Return on equity: 7.54%	Dividends
Cash ($ mil.): 15	Yield: 2.5%
Current ratio: 0.67	Payout: 76.9%
Long-term debt ($ mil.): 14,310	Market value ($ mil.): 28,063

	STOCK PRICE ($) FY Close	P/E High/Low	PER SHARE ($) Earnings	Dividends	Book Value
12/19	85.07	30 22	2.81	2.14	38.29
12/18	65.04	22 16	3.25	2.02	36.25
12/17	63.18	21 17	3.11	1.90	(2.18)
12/16	55.23	20 17	2.96	1.78	5.94
12/15	51.07	20 16	2.76	1.67	4.88
Annual Growth	13.6%	— —	0.4%	6.4%	67.4%

Exchange Bank (Santa Rosa, CA)

Exchange Bank serves personal and business customers from some 20 branch offices throughout Sonoma County California. It also has a branch in nearby Placer County. The bank provides standard products including checking and savings accounts Visa credit cards online banking and a variety of real estate business and consumer loans. It also offers investment services such as wealth management personal trust administration employee benefits plans and individual retirement accounts. Effective early 2014 Exchange Bank is on its eighth president since its inception in 1890. The Doyle Trust which was established by co-founder Frank Doyle owns a majority of the bank.

Operations

Exchange Bank's lending activity is concentrated in Sonoma County. Commercial real estate loans represent more than half of its loan portfolio. Exchange Bank believes it will continue to benefit from growth in the local technology and biomedical industries and lower unemployment increased tourism and a decline in commercial real estate vacancies in Sonoma County.

Geographic Reach

Based in Santa Rosa California Exchange Bank operates primarily in Sonoma County but also in Placer and Contra counties.

Sales and Marketing

Exchange Bank counts some 25000 customers among its clients serving them through about 20 branch offices. It caters to customers online as well through its website which in fiscal 2013 earned 1.5 million customer visits.

Financial Performance

Revenue dropped 4% in fiscal 2013 to $85.9 million as compared to $89.1 million in 2012. Exchange Bank attributes the decrease to lower interest income resulting from a decline in interest received on term loans offset in part by increased interest on securities. From $12.26 million in 2012 the firm's net income grew some 28% to $15.73 million. Exchange Bank points to noteworthy drops in the provision for loan and lease losses and a decrease in interest and non-interest income for the net income gains.

EXECUTIVES

Vice President Commercial, Connie Mcmannus
Vice President And General Manager Dumac Leasing, Kenneth Taylor
Avp And Re Closing And Disbursement Specialist, Donna Smith
Vice President, Beth Huang
Vice President Sba Loan Department, Scott Dykstra
Vp Residential Underwriting Manager, Colleen Oller
Vice President Commercial Banking, Tina Sheldon
Assistant Vice President And Bank Operations Analy, Jane Daniel
Vice President And Real Estate Loan Officer, Wynn Spain
Vice President, Lori Decosta
Senior Vice President Corporate And Business Development Manager, Howard Daulton
Senior Vice President, Sam Brown
Avp Of Learning And Development Manager, Erin Williams
Assistant Vice President, Patty Brookins
Vice President And General Manager, Ken Taylor
Vice President Retail Banking, Becky Morgan
Vice President, Rich Carlson

Senior Vice President Human Resources, Lori Zaret
Special Assets Officer And Assistant Vice President, Christy Somers
Vice President, Jason Hinde
Senior Vice President Real Estate Loan, Louise Mason
Senior Vice President, Gary Searby
Vice President Business Banking Officer And Commercial Loan Officer, Bill Espindola
Vp Of Business Development, Richard Carlson
Business Development Officer Vice President, Brian Kilkenny
Vice President, Wade Connelly
Assistant Vice President, Maryanne Harris
Vice President, Terry Fassold
Executive Vice President, Troy Sanderson
Vice President Commercial Underwriter, Antonio Uribe
Executive Vice President And Chief Credit Officer, Michael Sullivan
Auditors: Crowe LLP

LOCATIONS

HQ: Exchange Bank (Santa Rosa, CA)
545 Fourth Street, Santa Rosa, CA 95401
Phone: 707 524-3000
Web: www.exchangebank.com

COMPETITORS

Bank of America	U.S. Bancorp
First Northern	Wells Fargo
JPMorgan Chase	Westamerica
MUFG Americas Holdings	

HISTORICAL FINANCIALS

Company Type: Public

Income Statement

FYE: December 31

	ASSETS ($ mil.)	NET INCOME ($ mil.)	INCOME AS % OF ASSETS	EMPLOYEES
12/19	2,673	36	1.4%	—
12/18	2,653	38	1.5%	—
12/17	2,584	19	0.8%	—
12/16	2,179	21	1.0%	—
12/15	2,062	21	1.0%	—
Annual Growth	6.7%	14.8%	—	—

2019 Year-End Financials

Debt ratio: —	No. of shares (mil.): 1
Return on equity: 14.53%	Dividends
Cash ($ mil.): 264	Yield: 2.4%
Current ratio: —	Payout: 20.6%
Long-term debt ($ mil.): —	Market value ($ mil.): 307

	STOCK PRICE ($) FY Close	P/E High/Low		PER SHARE ($) Earnings	Dividends	Book Value
12/19	179.00	9	7	21.29	4.40	157.97
12/18	165.00	9	7	22.46	3.85	135.08
12/17	152.00	14	11	11.38	3.40	118.53
12/16	125.00	11	6	12.54	2.80	110.35
12/15	89.00	7	6	12.27	2.20	100.98
Annual Growth	19.1%			14.8%	18.9%	11.8%

Exelon Corp

Exelon is lighting up the utility industry with high-powered energy generation and extensive electricity delivery. The utility holding company does enough of both to be designated one of the largest in the US. Its Exelon Generation subsidiary holds power-generating assets of almost 31000 MW (some 20000 MW is produced at about 25 nuclear plants). Exelon distributes electricity and gas to 10 million customers in Illinois Maryland the District of Columbia Delaware New Jersey and Pennsylvania through its regulated utility companies. Its Constellation subsidiary provides energy products and services to about 2 million residential public sector and business customers.

HISTORY

Thomas Dolan and local investors formed the Brush Electric Light Company of Philadelphia in 1881 to provide street and commercial lighting. Competitors sprang up and in 1885 Brush merged with the United States Electric Lighting Company of Pennsylvania to form a secret "electric trust" or holding company. Dolan became president in 1886 and bought four other utilities.

In 1895 Martin Maloney formed Pennsylvania Heat Light and Power to consolidate the city's electric companies. By the next year it had acquired among other businesses Columbia Electric Light Philadelphia Edison and the electric trust. In 1899 a new firm National Electric challenged Maloney by acquiring neighboring rival Southern Electric Light. Before retiring Maloney negotiated the merger of the two firms forming Philadelphia Electric in 1902.

Demand rose rapidly into the 1920s fueled in part by the company's promotion of electric appliances. In 1928 the year after it completed the Conowingo Hydroelectric Station Philadelphia Electric was absorbed by the much larger United Gas Improvement. United Gas avoided large layoffs during the Depression but passage of the Public Utility Holding Company Act (PUHCA) in 1935 sounded its death knell. (PUHCA was repealed in 2005.) In 1943 the SEC forced United Gas to divest Philadelphia Electric.

Philadelphia Electric built several plants in the 1950s and 1960s in response to a postwar electricity boom. A small experimental nuclear reactor was completed at Peach Bottom Pennsylvania in 1967 and in 1974 the company placed two nuclear units in service at the plant. The Salem (New Jersey) nuke (Unit 1) followed in 1977. The company relied on these plants during the OPEC oil crisis. Another one Limerick Unit 1 began operations in 1986 and Unit 2 went on line in 1990 but the Peach Bottom plant was shut down from 1989 to 1991 because of management problems (later resolved).

The company began reorganizing in 1993 and changed its name the next year to PECO Energy Company. It also sold Maryland retail subsidiary Conowingo Power retaining the hydroelectric plant. In 1995 rival PP&L rejected PECO's acquisition bid citing PECO's nuclear liabilities.

A year later PECO teamed with AT&T Wireless to offer PCS in Philadelphia (service was launched in 1997). EnergyOne a national venture formed in 1997 by PECO UtiliCorp United (now Aquila) and AT&T offered consumers a package of power phone and Internet services on one bill. However the slow deregulation process caused the venture to fail.

PECO also joined with British Energy in 1997 to form AmerGen hoping to buy nukes at rock-bottom prices from utilities eager to unload them. AmerGen purchased three nuclear facilities in 1999 and 2000: Unit 1 of the Three Mile Island (Pennsylvania) facility; a plant in Clinton Illinois; and an Oyster Creek (New Jersey) location.

In 1999 PECO announced plans to acquire Chicago's Unicom the parent company of Commonwealth Edison (ComEd). After the deal was completed in 2000 the combined company took the name Exelon and established its headquarters in Chicago.

Pennsylvania's utility markets were fully deregulated in 2000. To expand its power generation business Exelon that year bought 49.9% of Sithe Energies for $682 million. In 2001 Exelon agreed to buy two gas-fired power plants (2300 MW) in Texas from TXU for $443 million; the deal was completed in 2002.

Also in 2002 Exelon purchased Sithe Energies' stakes in six New England power plants with 2000 MW of capacity (plus 2400 MW under construction) for $543 million plus the assumption of $1.15 billion in debt. The company also sold its Philadelphia PCS venture interest to former partner AT&T Wireless Services (now part of AT&T Mobility). Sithe Energies was sold to Dynegy in 2005 for $135 million.

To focus on core utility operations the company sold its infrastructure construction business InfraSource and its facility and infrastructure management business Exelon Solutions. Exelon then completed the sale of its interest in telecommunications joint venture PECO TelCove which provides voice and data services to its partner TelCove and sold its district heating and cooling division (Thermal Chicago).

In 2008 in a move to expand its geographic reach Exelon made a $6.2 billion bid to buy NRG Energy. Though the offer to buy NRG met with resistance Exelon had kept up its pursuit of the company. Toward the end of 2008 it announced an exchange offer for NRG's shares. By the expiration date of the offer early the next year it had acquired just more than 50% of those shares. In addition to announcing another extension of the offer Exelon said it hoped NRG's Board would allow it to do due diligence and begin negotiations for an acquisition. But an NRG proxy vote rejection in 2009 led Exelon to terminate its offer.

In 2010 in a bid to grow its renewable energy segment and lower its carbon emissions the company acquired wind power developer John Deere Renewables for about $860 million. The deal added 735 MW of operating wind power capacity (and 230 MW under development) to Exelon's generation assets.

To meet stricter environmental regulations the company has been bulking up its non-fossil fuel generating assets. Growing its cleaner-burning plant fleet in Texas in 2011 the company bought Wolf Hollow a 720 MW combined-cycle natural gas-fired power plant in north Texas from Sequent Wolf Hollow for $305 million.

Expanding its green energy assets that year the company also acquired Antelope Valley Solar Ranch One from First Solar. The 230-MW solar power project is under development in northern Los Angeles County. The $1.4 billion investment complements Constellation Energy's solar power holdings and marks Exelon's first move into the California merchant power market.

In 2012 the company bought Constellation Energy in a $7.9 billion stock deal. The acquisition part of an industry-wide consolidation trend gives Exelon access to Constellation's major retail operations in Maryland enabling it to grow its retail profile.

The US Department of Justice required Exelon and Constellation to divest three electricity generating plants in Maryland to proceed with the merger. It contended that combining the companies' assets would potentially enable the merged firm to raise wholesale electricity prices and reduce output.

As part of the integration of Constellation Energy's assets in 2013 Exelon announced that three commercial nuclear power plants operated by the Constellation Energy Nuclear Group in New York and Maryland will be integrated into the Exelon Generation nuclear fleet.

EXECUTIVES

President And Ceo, Christopher M. (Chris) Crane, age 61, $1,255,515 total compensation

Svp And Chief Information And Digital Officer, Mike Koehler, age 53

President Exelon Power, Ronald J. (Ron) DeGregorio, age 57

Evp; Coo Excelon Generation, Michael J. Pacilio, age 59

Sevp And Cfo, Jonathan W. (Jack) Thayer, age 48, $784,802 total compensation

Evp Customer Operations Regulatory And External Affairs Comed, Anne R. Pramaggiore, age 61

Sevp And Chief Commercial Officer And President And Ceo Exelon Generation, Kenneth W. (Ken) Cornew, age 54, $857,477 total compensation

Evp And Ceo Constellation, Joseph (Joe) Nigro, age 55

Sevp And Chief Strategy Officer, William A. (Bill) Von Hoene, age 66, $831,350 total compensation

President And Ceo Pepco Holdings, David M. (Dave) Velazquez, age 61

President And Chief Nuclear Officer Exelon Nuclear, Bryan C. Hanson, age 54

Evp; President And Ceo Peco, Craig L. Adams, age 67

Ceo Baltimore Gas And Electric, Calvin G. Butler, age 50

Evp And Chief Enterprise Risk Officer, Paymon Aliabadi, age 57

Evp Governmental And Regulatory Affairs And Public Policy, Joseph Dominguez, age 56

Sevp And Ceo Exelon Utilities, Denis P. O'Brien, age 59, $800,378 total compensation

Svp And Chief Supply Officer, M. Bridget Reidy

Senior Vice President State Governmental And Regulatory Affairs, David Fein

Senior Vice President Operations Support, Christopher Mudrick

Vice President Corporate Affairs, Melissa Sherrod

Vpres Clinton Power Station, Mark Newcomer

Vice President And Deputy General Counsel Employment And Benefits, Susan Rider

Vice President, Nadim Kazi

Vice President, Dean Hengst

Vice President Nuclear Oversight, Edward Callan

Senior Vice President And Chro, Amy Best

Vice President And Deputy General Counsel, Nina Jezic

Vp Corp Communications, Jean Medina

Senior Vice President Corporate Finance, Daniel Eggers

Vp Tech Services And Smart Grid And Smart Meter Peco Energy, John Mcdonald

Senior Vice President Corporate Affairs Philanthropy And Customer Engagement, Maggie Fitzpatrick

Senior Vice President And Chief Financial Officer Of Peco, Phillip Barnett

Vice President Regulatory Policy And S, Michael Guerra

Site Vice President, Garey Stathes

Vice President, Formica Vivian

Senior Vice President, Ramic Edita

Vice President Of Distribution Operations, William Mcbride

Vice President Finance Exelon Nuclear, Jeanne Jones

Vice President Corporate And Information Security Services, Kevin Perkins

Senior Vice President Corporate Controller, Fabian Souza

Vice President, Marlow Colvin

Vice President, William Scott

Senior Vice President Operations, Daniel Enright

Senior Vice President Exelon Generation And President Exelon Power, John Barnes

Vice President Bsc Human Resources, Matthew English

Vice President Finance Phi, Marissa Humphrey

Vice President Marketing, Richard Gwebster

Vice President West Power Origination, Thompson Brent

Executive Assistant To M Bridget Reidy Executive Vice President Corporate Operations, Griffith Evan

Site Vice President, Tracey Gorham

Vice President Market Risk And Analytics, Daniel Scobell

Vice President Supply Chain, Ed Jandacek

Vice President And Controller, Robert Aiken

Vice President Marketing, Mark Page

Chairman, Mayo A. Shattuck, age 65

Board Member, Brian Boggetto

Secretary Iv, Maria Boweolsen

Treasurer, Robert Miller

Auditors: PricewaterhouseCoopers LLP

LOCATIONS

HQ: Exelon Corp
10 South Dearborn Street, P.O. Box 805379, Chicago, IL 60680-5379
Phone: 800 483-3220
Web: www.exeloncorp.com

PRODUCTS/OPERATIONS

2016 Sales

	$ mil.	% of total
Generation	17,751	54
ComEd	5,254	16
PECO	2,994	9
BGE	3,233	10
PHI	3,643	11
Other	(1515)	-
Total	**31,360**	**100**

2016 Sales

	$ mil.	% of total
Competitive businesses revenues	16,324	52
Rate-regulated utility revenues	15,036	48
Total	**31,360**	**100**

Selected Operating Units Subsidiaries and Affiliates

Exelon Energy Delivery
Baltimore Gas and Electric (BGE electric and gas utility)
Commonwealth Edison Company (ComEd electric utility)
PECO Energy Company (PECO electric and gas utility)
Pepco Holdings LLC (PHI)
Potomac Electric Power Company (Pepco electric utility)
Delmarva Power & Light Company (DPL electric and gas utility)
Atlantic City Electric Company (ACE electric utility)
Exelon Generation Company LLC
  Constellation
  Exelon Power
  Exelon Hydro
  Exelon Solar
  Exelon Wind
  Exelon Power Team
  Exelon Energy (nonregulated retail power sales)
  Exelon Nuclear (nuclear power generation)
Exelon Transmission Company

COMPETITORS

AES	FirstEnergy
Alliant Energy	Green Mountain Energy
Ambit Energy	Jersey Central Power &
Ameren	Light
American Transmission	NextEra Energy
Dominion Energy	PPL Corporation
Duke Energy	Public Service
Duquesne Light	Electric and Gas
Holdings	UGI

HISTORICAL FINANCIALS

Company Type: Public

Income Statement   FYE: December 31

	REVENUE ($ mil.)	NET INCOME ($ mil.)	NET PROFIT MARGIN	EMPLOYEES
12/19	34,438	2,936	8.5%	32,713
12/18	35,985	2,010	5.6%	33,383
12/17	33,531	3,770	11.2%	34,621
12/16	31,360	1,134	3.6%	34,396
12/15	29,447	2,269	7.7%	29,762
Annual Growth	4.0%	6.7%	—	2.4%

2019 Year-End Financials

Debt ratio: 30.24%
Return on equity: 9.32%
Cash ($ mil.): 587
Current ratio: 0.85
Long-term debt ($ mil.): 31,719

No. of shares (mil.): 973
Dividends
Yield: 3.1%
Payout: 61.1%
Market value ($ mil.): 44,359

	STOCK PRICE ($) FY Close	P/E High/Low		PER SHARE ($)	
			Earnings	Dividends	Book Value
12/19	45.59	17 15	3.01	1.45	33.12
12/18	45.10	23 17	2.07	1.38	31.77
12/17	39.41	11 8	3.97	1.31	30.99
12/16	35.49	30 22	1.22	1.26	27.96
12/15	27.77	15 10	2.54	1.24	28.25
Annual Growth	13.2%	— —	4.3%	4.0%	4.1%

Exelon Generation Co LLC

Exelon Generation Company has built an excellent reputation by generating electricity. The company a subsidiary of Exelon Corporation is one of the largest electric wholesale and retail power generation companies in the US. In 2013 Exelon Generation had a generation capacity of more than 44560 MW (primarily nuclear but also fossil-fired and hydroelectric and other renewable energy-based plants). Subsidiary Exelon Nuclear operates the largest fleet of nuclear power plants in the US. Exelon Generation's Exelon Power unit oversees a fleet of more than 100 fossil- and renewable-fueled plants (more than 15875 MW of capacity) in Illinois Maryland Massachusetts Pennsylvania and Texas.

Operations

The company operates as an integrated business leveraging its owned and contracted electric generation capacity to market and sell power to wholesale and retail customers. It has ownership interests in eleven nuclear generating stations currently in service consisting of 19 units with an aggregate of 17263 MW of capacity. It also owns a 50% interest in CENG a joint venture with EDF. CENG is governed by a board of ten directors five of which are appointed by Generation and five by EDF.

Geographic Reach

The Mid-Atlantic represents operations in the eastern half of PJM and accounted for 37% of Exelon Generation's generating capacity in 2013; Midwest (western half of PJM the entire US footprint of MISO 34%); New England (the operations within the ISO-NE 8%); New York (ISO-NY 3%); ERCOT (Texas) 12%; and Other areas 6%).

The Mid-Atlantic region includes Pennsylvania New Jersey Maryland Virginia West Virginia Delaware the District of Columbia and parts of North Carolina. Midwest includes portions of Illinois Indiana Ohio Michigan Kentucky and Tennessee; and the United States footprint of MISO excluding MISO's Southern Region which covers all or most of North Dakota South Dakota Nebraska Minnesota Iowa Wisconsin and the remaining parts of Illinois Indiana Michigan and Ohio not covered by PJM; and parts of Montana Missouri and Kentucky.New England represents the operations within ISO-NE covering the states of Connecticut Maine Massachusetts New Hampshire Rhode Island and Vermont. New York represents the operations within ISO-NY which covers the state of New York in its entirety. ERCOT represents operations within Electric Reliability Council of Texas covering most of the state of Texas. "Other Regions" is an aggregate of other geographic regions not considered individually significant.

Sales and Marketing

Exelon Generation's customers include distribution utilities municipalities cooperatives financial institutions and commercial industrial governmental and residential customers in competitive markets. The company also sells natural gas and renewable energy and other energy-related products and services and engages in natural gas exploration and production activities.

Financial Performance

The company's revenues increased by 8% in 2013 primarily due to increased capacity prices and higher nuclear volume partially offset by lower realized energy prices higher nuclear fuel costs and lower mark-to-market gains.

Net income increased by 90% in 2013 primarily due to higher revenues net of purchased power and fuel expense lower operating and maintenance expense and higher earnings from Exelon Generation's interest in CENG; partially offset by impairment of certain generating assets and higher depreciation costs property taxes and interest expenses.

Strategy

Exelon Generation leverages owned and contracted electric generation capacity to market and sell power wholesale. The company's integrated business operations include the physical delivery and marketing of power obtained through its generation capacity and through long-term intermediate-term and short-term contracts. Exelon Generation maintains an effective supply strategy through ownership of generation assets and power purchase and lease agreements. The company has also contracted for access to additional generation through bilateral long-term power agreements.

Exelon Generation's electricity generation strategy is to pursue opportunities that provide generation to load matching and that diversify the generation fleet by expanding Generation's regional and technological footprint. The company leverages its energy generation portfolio to ensure delivery of energy to both wholesale and retail customers under long-term and short-term contracts and in wholesale power markets.

In 2012 a subsidiary of Exelon Generation sold three coal-fired plants (Brandon Shores and H.A. Wagner generating station in Anne Arundel County Maryland and the C.P. Crane plant in Baltimore County Maryland) to Raven Power Holdings LLC a subsidiary of Riverstone Holdings LLC to comply with certain of the regulatory approvals required by the company's merger with Constellation Energy for net proceeds of $371 million which resulted in a pre-tax loss of $272 million.

Exelon Nuclear operates the largest nuclear fleet in the US (10 stations with 17 nuclear units) and has about 20% of the industry's total capacity. Exelon Generation has submitted an application to the Nuclear Regulatory Commission to build a new nuclear generating facility in Texas. The company hasn't made the decision to build the facility but wanted to get a start on the potentially onerous process. The last license to result in the construction of a new nuclear facility in the US was granted in 1973. However the Fukushima nuclear plant disaster in early 2011 placed nuclear power expansion plans under serious scrutiny from regulators.

Mergers and Acquisitions

In a major move to grow its retail operations in 2012 parent Exelon Corporation bought Constellation Energy in a $7.9 billion stock deal. The purchase of Constellation Energy (which gets 17% of its power from nuclear plants) helped the company boost its nuclear-generated power plant assets.

Company Background

Growing its cleaner-burning plant fleet in Texas in 2011 Exelon Corporation bought the 720 MW capacity Wolf Hollow plant in north Texas from Sequent Wolf Hollow for $305 million.

In 2010 to grow its renewable energy unit the company acquired wind power developer John Deere Renewables for about $860 million. The purchase adds 735 MW of operating wind power capacity to its generation capacity.

EXECUTIVES

MBR, John W Rowe
MBR, John Young
MBR-Ceo, Christopher M Crane
Chm, Mayo A Shattuck III
Svp, Bryan Hanson
Paralegal, Jenifer Newman
Svp, Generation Development, Thomas S O'Neill
Svp, Doyle N Beneby
Svp and President and Chief Nu, Bryan C Hanson
Senior Supervisor, Leah Dawes
Technician, Brian Higgins
Auditors: PricewaterhouseCoopers LLP

LOCATIONS

HQ: Exelon Generation Co LLC
300 Exelon Way, Kennett Square, PA 19348-2473
Phone: 610 765-5959
Web: www.exeloncorp.com

PRODUCTS/OPERATIONS

2013 Sales

	$ mil.	% of total
Mid-Atlantic	5	33
Midwest	4	27
New England	1	8
ERCOT	1	8
Other Regions	1	6
New York	0	5
Others	2	13
Total	**15**	**100**

COMPETITORS

AES	Duke Energy
AMP	NextEra Energy
Buckeye Power	Wolverine Power Supply
CMS Energy	

HISTORICAL FINANCIALS

Company Type: Public

Income Statement				FYE: December 31
	REVENUE ($ mil.)	NET INCOME ($ mil.)	NET PROFIT MARGIN	EMPLOYEES
12/19	18,924	1,125	5.9%	13,082
12/18	20,437	370	1.8%	14,110
12/17	18,466	2,694	14.6%	15,011
12/16	17,751	496	2.8%	14,717
12/15	19,135	1,372	7.2%	14,512
Annual Growth	(0.3%)	(4.8%)	—	(2.6%)

2019 Year-End Financials

Debt ratio: 16.69%—
Return on equity: 8.43%
Cash ($ mil.): 303
Current ratio: 0.97
Long-term debt ($ mil.): 4,792

Dividends
Yield: —
Payout: —
Market value ($ mil.): —

Expedia Group Inc

Expedia a market leader in online travel services (with rival Booking Holdings) is often the go-to online trip-planner. It offers tools that allow users to book nearly 1.6 million properties including over 765000 of Vrbo's over 2.1 million online bookable alternative accommodations listings in 200 countries and territories over 500 airlines packages rental cars cruises insurance as well as activities and experiences. They include flagship Expedia.com online travel bookers Travelocity and Orbitz accommodations manager Hotels.com vacation rental site HomeAway travel discounter Hotwire hotel meta-searcher Trivago luxury package provider Classic Vacations and several sites focused on international destinations. More than 55% of sales come from customers in the US.

Operations

Expedia operates through four segments: Core OTA (online travel agency) Trivago Vrbo and Egencia.

Core OTA accounts for roughly 80% of Expedia's total revenue and includes the brands Hotwire and Hotels.com. Trivago which generates 10% of total revenue is a hotel price-comparison platform that scans prices across 400 booking websites. Vrbo offers vacation rental website Vrbo which operates localized websites around the world and HomeAway and also brings in around 5% of revenue. Egencia segment at 5% of sales is a full-service travel management company that offers travel products and services to businesses and their corporate travelers.

Expedia has three principal revenue sources: Lodging (70% of sales) Air fares (about 10% of sales) and Advertising and Media (more than 5%). The remaining approximately 15% of sales arise from car rental insurance destination services and fees from corporate customers.

Geographic Reach

Based in Seattle Washington Expedia has offices throughout the Americas Europe and Asia/Pacific region and operates in about 200 countries.

The US accounts for more than 55% of revenue.

Sales and Marketing

Selling and marketing expense primarily relates to direct costs including traffic generation costs from search engines and internet portals television radio and print spending private label and affiliate program commissions public relations and other costs.

For the years ended December 31 2019 2018 and 2017 Expedia's advertising expense were $3.5 billion $3.4 billion and $3.3 billion.

Financial Performance

Expedia's revenue has been consistently increasing in the last five years. It has an overall growth of 81%. Except in 2016 where the company's net income declined by 63% Expedia's net income improved. However its net income has an overall decline of 26% in the last five years.

Sales grew 8% to $12.1 billion in 2019 thanks to strong growth in its core Online Travel Agency businesses and Vrbo. Trivago saw sales fall 10% while the smaller Egencia unit grew 3%. By type lodging air and other assorted revenue sources all strengthened but advertising revenue growth fell from 2% in 2018 to 1% in 2019.

Expedia's net income which grew 39% to $565 million in 2019 lags far behind rival Booking Holdings which reported net income of $4.0 billion in 2018. The growth came from higher revenue operating performance being equal.

Expedia's cash position increased by $1.4 billion during 2019 ending the year at $4.1 billion. Its operations generated $2.8 billion while investing activities used $1.6 billion and financing activities provided $175 million. The company's main cash uses in 2019 were capital expenditures investments debt repayments and stock repurchases.

Strategy

Brand Expedia Hotels.com Expedia Partner Solution and Egencia brands operate both domestically and through international points of sale including in Europe Asia Pacific Canada and Latin America. In addition ebookers offers multi-product online travel reservations in Europe and the Wotif portfolio of brands are focused principally on the Australia and New Zealand markets. The Vrbo portfolio offers alternative accommodations websites all around the world. The company own a majority share of trivago a leading metasearch company. In December 2016 trivago successfully completed its initial public offering and trades on the Nasdaq Global Select Market under the symbol "TRVG." In addition they have commercial agreements in place with Trip.com and eLong in China Traveloka in Southeast Asia as well as Despegar in Latin America among many others. In conjunction with the commercial arrangements with Traveloka and Despegar we have also made strategic investments in both companies. In 2019 approximately 37% of their worldwide gross bookings and 43% of worldwide revenue were through international points of sale. Their strategy includes focus on expanding their global reach and their goal is to continue to increase their mix of international revenue as they execute on their global expansion plans.

The company also intend to continue leveraging these technology investments when launching additional points of sale in new countries introducing new website features adding supplier products and services including new business model offerings as well as proprietary and user-generated content for travelers.

Mergers and Acquisitions

Expedia isn't shy about acquiring parts of the travel planning experience that it doesn't already have. The approach has brought some well-recognized travel sites under its corporate umbrella.

In 2019 Expedia agreed to acquire Liberty Expedia a holding company whose main interest is a 16% stake in Expedia itself. Liberty Expedia also owned Bodybuilding.com via subsidiary Vitalize. The acquisition improves Expedia's corporate governance and meaningfully reduces its share count.

Company Background

Originally a division of Microsoft Expedia was sold to IAC/InterActiveCorp which acquired the computer maker's majority stake in 2002 and the minority interest it did not already own in 2003. Two years later IAC spun off Expedia into a separate publicly traded firm.

EXECUTIVES

President Ecommerce Platform, J. Tucker Moodey
President Hotwire Group, Henrik V. Kjellberg, age 50
President Hotels.com And Ean, Johan Svanstrom, age 49
President Expedia Lodging Partner Services, Cyril Ranque
President Egencia, Rob Greyber
President Ceo And Director, Mark D. Okerstrom, $750,000 total compensation
Evp General Counsel And Secretary, Robert Dzielak, $575,000 total compensation
President Brand Expedia Group, Aman Bhutani, age 44
Chief People Officer, Nikki Krishnamurthy
President Homeaway, John Kim
Svp And General Manager Expedia Affiliate Network, Ariane Gorin
Vice President Of Employee Engagement, Kristin Graham
Senior Vice President Marketing Packages And Canada, Sean C Shannon
Vice President Technology Brand Expedia Group, Michael Nixon
Vice President Global Supply Operations, Sean Huberty
Vice President Floor Operations, Hal Grant
Global Vice President Expedia Media Solutions, Noah Tratt
Vice President Technology, Bhala Dalvi
Vice President Marketing And Demand Information Technology, Alex Hopwood
Vice President Associate General Counsel, Ronen Elad
Vice President Transport Americas, Julie Kyse
Senior Vice President Sales, Bruce Freeman
Vice President Of Finance, Bank Rec
Senior Vice President Marketing And Innovation, Helen Maher
Vice President Finance, Dominique Bourgault
Vice President Marketing, Matthew Wells
Senior Vice President Global Product And Design, Arthur Chapin
Vice President Enterprise Risk And Security, David Montague
Senior Vice President Global Marketing, Aaron Price
Senior Vice President Commercial Strategy And Services, Gregory Schulze
Vice President Marketing Egencia, Wendy White
Vice President And Associate General Counsel, Robert Zech
Vice Chairman, Victor A. Kaufman, age 76
Chairman, Barry Diller, age 78
Auditors: Ernst & Young LLP

LOCATIONS

HQ: Expedia Group Inc
1111 Expedia Group Way W, Seattle, WA 98119
Phone: 206 481-7200
Web: www.expediainc.com

2018 Sales

	$ mil.	% of total
United States	6,202	55
All other countries	5,021	45
Total	**11,223**	**100**

PRODUCTS/OPERATIONS

2018 Sales

	$ mil.	% of total
Core OTA (online travel agency)	8,760	78
trivago	691	6
HomeAway	1,171	11
Egencia	601	5
Total	**11,223**	**100**

2018 Sales

	$ mil.	% of total
Merchant	5,950	53
Agency	3,010	27
Advertising and media	1,092	11
HomeAway	1,171	9
Total	**11,223**	**100**

BRANDS

BRANDS
CarRentals.com
Classic Vacations
Egencia
Expedia
Expedia Affiliate Network (EAN)
Expedia CruiseShipCenters
Expedia Local Expert
Expedia Media Solutions
HomeAway
Hotels.com
Hotwire
Orbitz
SilverRail
Traveldoo
Travelocity
trivago
Wotif Group

SELECTED SUBSIDIARIES

Classic Vacations LLC
Cruise LLC
EAN.com LP
Egencia France SAS
Egencia LLC
EXP Holdings Luxembourg S.A.
Expedia Asia Holdings Mauritius
Expedia do Brasil Agencia de Viagens e Turismo Ltda.

COMPETITORS

Airbnb	Prestige Travel
American Express	Priceline
BCD Travel	Sabre
Carlson Wagonlit	Travelport
Concur Technologies	TripAdvisor
GetThere	Uniglobe Travel
Google	WorldRes
Pegasus Solutions	ebookers.com

HISTORICAL FINANCIALS

Company Type: Public

Income Statement   FYE: December 31

	REVENUE ($ mil.)	NET INCOME ($ mil.)	NET PROFIT MARGIN	EMPLOYEES
12/19	12,067	565	4.7%	25,400
12/18	11,223	406	3.6%	24,500
12/17	10,059	377	3.8%	22,615
12/16	8,773	281	3.2%	20,075
12/15	6,672	764	11.5%	18,730
Annual Growth	**16.0%**	**(7.3%)**	**—**	**7.9%**

2019 Year-End Financials

Debt ratio: 23.06%
Return on equity: 14.00%
Cash ($ mil.): 3,315
Current ratio: 0.72
Long-term debt ($ mil.): 4,189

No. of shares (mil.): 142
Dividends
 Yield: 1.2%
 Payout: 39.5%
Market value ($ mil.): 15,421

	STOCK PRICE ($) FY Close	P/E High/Low	PER SHARE ($) Earnings	Dividends	Book Value
12/19	108.14	36 25	3.77	1.32	27.82
12/18	112.65	51 37	2.65	1.24	27.89
12/17	119.77	64 45	2.42	1.16	29.80
12/16	113.28	70 49	1.82	1.00	27.54
12/15	124.30	23 13	5.70	0.84	32.37
Annual Growth	**(3.4%)**	**— —**	**(9.8%)**	**12.0%**	**(3.7%)**

Expeditors International of Washington, Inc.

As a freight forwarder Expeditors International of Washington keeps cargo moving. The company purchases air and ocean cargo space on a volume basis and resells that space to its customers at lower rates than they could obtain directly. The company also acts as a customs broker for air and ocean freight shipped by its customers and offers supply chain management services. Customers include global businesses engaged in retailing and wholesaling electronics high technology industrial and manufacturing. The company's estimated average airfreight consolidation weighs approximately 3000 pounds and that a typical consolidation includes merchandise from several shippers.

Operations

Expeditors operates in three segments: airfreight ocean freight and ocean and customs brokerage and other.

Customs brokerage and other services about 35% of revenue aids in the movement of shipments across borders by providing such services as adding up duties and taxes and arranging inspections. Beyond the border entry the segment provides additional services including warehousing product distribution and time-definite transportation.

Expeditors provides these services not only for its own shipping customers but also for businesses that have not hired the company as a forwarder a class of client that accounts for a significant portion of the segment's revenue. Expeditors' airfreight services segment roughly 35% of revenue represents airlines as an agent in addition to providing freight consolidation for shippers. Besides shipping on scheduled flights the company sometimes charters aircraft for the delivery of backlogs. By not purchasing its own aircraft the company avoids the costs of large capital expenditures and operating costs.

Ocean freight and ocean services nearly 25% of revenue operates as a non-vessel operating common carrier which is a contractor with ocean shipping lines for a set number of containers. Expeditors also obtains less-than container load freight to fill containers. The segment additionally provides such order management services as document management and SKU visibility.

Geographic Reach

Expeditors is headquartered in Seattle Washington and has regional headquarters in London Dubai Singapore and Shanghai. It operates from approximately 450 facilities in more than 100 countries.

North America is its largest market generating about 35% of revenue followed by North Asia with about 30% Europe with about 15% and others generate the remaining.

Sales and Marketing

Expeditors caters to its customers' supply chains. Therefore its marketing efforts target people in logistics and supply chain management roles. The company determines the routing consolidates shipments bound for a particular airport distribution point and then selects the airline for transportation to the distribution point.. The company primarily targets the aviation and aerospace health care oil and energy automotive technology and retail sectors.

Financial Performance

Except for a dip in 2016 Expeditors' revenue has seen steady growth the last two years rising about 24% between 2015 and 2019. In recent years the strongest growth has come from the company's airfreight services segments.

Sales in 2019 increased about $37.1 million to $8.2 billion compared to $8.1 billion in 2018.

Net income decreased about 5% to $590.4 million in 2019 compared to $618.2 million 2018.

Cash at the end of 2019 was $1.2 billion an increase of $306.8 million from the prior year. Cash from operations contributed $771.9 million to the coffers while investing activities used $46.0 million mainly for property and equipment purchases. Financing activities used $418 million primarily for stock repurchases and dividends.

Strategy

Expeditors continues to focus on executing key strategic initiatives that are designed to achieve long-term earnings growth. The strategic plan is to grow the company's business by focusing on the right markets and within each market on the right customers that lead to profitable business growth.

Expeditors' teams are aligned on the specific markets of its focused priorities; on the targeted accounts within those markets; and on ways that the company can continue to differentiate the company from its competitors. While the company continues to emphasize expanding its business in North America the company simultaneously remains focused on growth based on three key strategic initiatives: first ensure that every operating unit's base-line growth strategies for air ocean and customs services grow at the relevant market growth rate of each unit; lign and integrate its European?Asian Pacific and European?North Americas interests to the same degree that the company's Asian Pacific and Americas interests have historically been aligned. This alignment is expected to result in additional growth in these markets beyond our base-line growth expectations; leverage its long and deeply entrenched presence in China – as well as the reputation that the company have with the strategic carriers servicing China – to build a stronger import presence.

Mergers and Acquisitions

In mid-2020 Expeditors acquired Portland-based Fleet Logistics' Digital Platform. The purchase will support Expeditors' online less-than-truckload (LTL) shipping platform Koho and aligns with Expeditors' strategy and focus on Digital Solutions.

Company Background

Expeditors International of Washington was founded in 1979 in Seattle Washington.

EXECUTIVES

Evp Europe, Timothy C. Barber, age 60, $100,000 total compensation
President Global Services, Eugene K. Alger, age 59, $100,000 total compensation

Svp And Cfo, Bradley S. (Brad) Powell, age 60, $100,000 total compensation
President Global Products, Daniel R. Wall, age 51, $100,000 total compensation
President And Ceo, Jeffrey S. Musser, age 54, $100,000 total compensation
President Global Geographies And Operations, Richard H. Rostan
Svp And Cio, Christopher J. McClincy, age 45
Svp Global Sales And Marketing, J. Jonathan Song
Svp Global Sales And Marketing, Jonathan Song
Vice President Accounting And Reporting, Dominic Kistner
Svp General Counsel And Corporate Secretary, Benjamin Clark
Senior Vice President Global Order Management, Michelle Weaver
Svp Account Management, Steven Grimmer
Director, Robert R. Wright, age 60
Auditors: KPMG LLP

LOCATIONS

HQ: Expeditors International of Washington, Inc.
1015 Third Avenue, Seattle, WA 98104
Phone: 206 674-3400   **Fax:** 206 674-3459
Web: www.expeditors.com

2016 Sales

	$ mil.	% of total
Asia		
North Asia	2,598	36
South Asia	684	9
North America		
US	1,962	27
Other North America	268	4
Europe	1,115	16
Middle East Africa and India	426	6
Latin America	111	2
Eliminations	(2463)	-
Total	**6,920**	**100**

PRODUCTS/OPERATIONS

2017 Sales

	$ mil.	% of total
Airfreight services	2,877	42
Ocean freight & ocean services	2,107	30
Customs brokerage & other services	1,936	28
Total	**6,920**	**100**

Selected Products and Services

Air freight-consolidation
Air freight forwarding
Customs brokerage services
Warehousing and Distribution Services
Direct Ocean Forwarding
Order Management
Transcom

COMPETITORS

APL Logistics
C.H. Robinson
  Worldwide
CEVA Logistics
DHL
FedEx Trade Networks
Kintetsu World Express
Kuehne + Nagel
  International
Mitsui-Soko

NYK Line
Nippon Express
Panalpina
Schenker
Sino-Global
Sinotrans
UPS Supply Chain
  Solutions
Yamato Holdings

HISTORICAL FINANCIALS

Company Type: Public

Income Statement

FYE: December 31

	REVENUE ($ mil.)	NET INCOME ($ mil.)	NET PROFIT MARGIN	EMPLOYEES
12/19	8,175	590	7.2%	18,000
12/18	8,138	618	7.6%	17,400
12/17	6,920	489	7.1%	16,500
12/16	6,098	430	7.1%	16,000
12/15	6,616	457	6.9%	15,397
Annual Growth	5.4%	6.6%	—	4.0%

2019 Year-End Financials

Debt ratio: —
Return on equity: 28.24%
Cash ($ mil.): 1,230
Current ratio: 2.37
Long-term debt ($ mil.): —

No. of shares (mil.): 169
Dividends
  Yield: 1.2%
  Payout: 27.6%
Market value ($ mil.): 13,234

	STOCK PRICE ($) FY Close	P/E High/Low		PER SHARE ($) Earnings	Dividends	Book Value
12/19	78.02	23	19	3.39	1.00	12.94
12/18	68.09	22	17	3.48	0.90	11.58
12/17	64.69	24	19	2.69	0.84	11.29
12/16	52.96	24	18	2.36	0.80	10.26
12/15	45.10	21	18	2.40	0.72	9.29
Annual Growth	14.7%	—	—	9.0%	8.6%	8.6%

Exxon Mobil Corp

Exxon Mobil Corporation is the world's #1 publicly traded oil company rivaled only by giants like Shell BP and Total. Its vast portfolio holds more than 22 billion barrels of oil equivalent of proved reserves spread across some 15 countries on six continents. The company has a huge daily average output: about 1.7 million barrels of crude oil 269000 barrels of NGLs and 9.4 billion cubic feet of natural gas. Its biggest business is selling refined products through approximately 19000 gas stations around the world. Exxon Mobil is also a provider in the chemicals industry manufacturing olefins polyolefins and aromatics that form the base for many plastic products. The company's brands?ExxonMobil Exxon Esso Mobil and XTO? enjoy global recognition.

HISTORY

Exxon's 1999 acquisition of Mobil reunited two descendants of John D. Rockefeller's Standard Oil Company. Rockefeller a commodity trader started his first oil refinery in 1863 in Cleveland. Realizing that the price of oil at the well would shrink with each new strike Rockefeller chose to monopolize oil refining and transportation. In 1870 he formed Standard Oil and in 1882 he created the Standard Oil Trust which allowed him to set up new ostensibly independent companies including the Standard Oil Company of New Jersey (Jersey Standard); Rochester New York-based Vacuum Oil; and Standard Oil of New York (nicknamed Socony).

Initially capitalized at $70 million the Standard Oil Trust controlled 90% of the petroleum industry. In 1911 after two decades of political and legal wrangling the Supreme Court broke up the trust into 34 companies the largest of which was Jersey Standard.

Walter Teagle who became president of Jersey Standard in 1917 secretly bought half of Humble

Oil of Texas (1919) and expanded operations into South America. In 1928 Jersey Standard joined in the Red Line Agreement which reserved most Middle East oil for a few companies. Teagle resigned in 1942 after the company was criticized for a prewar research pact with German chemical giant I.G. Farben.

The 1948 purchase of a 40% stake in Arabian American Oil Company combined with a 7% share of Iranian production bought in 1954 made Jersey Standard the world's #1 oil company at that time.

Meanwhile Vacuum Oil and Socony reunited in 1931 as Socony-Vacuum and the company adopted the Flying Red Horse (Pegasus — representing speed and power) as a trademark. The fast-growing diversifying company changed its name to Socony Mobil Oil in 1955 and became Mobil in 1976.

Other US companies still using the Standard Oil name objected to Jersey Standard's marketing in their territories as Esso (derived from the initials for Standard Oil). To end the confusion in 1972 Jersey Standard became Exxon a name change that cost $100 million.

Nationalization of oil assets by producing countries reduced Exxon's access to oil during the 1970s. Though it increased exploration that decade and the next Exxon's reserves shrank.

Oil tanker Exxon Valdez spilled some 11 million gallons of oil into Alaska's Prince William Sound in 1989. Exxon spent billions on the cleanup and in 1994 a federal jury in Alaska ordered the company to pay $5.3 billion in punitive damages to fishermen and others affected by the spill. (Exxon appealed and in 2001 the jury award was reduced to $2.5 billion and in 2008 to $507.5 million).

With the oil industry consolidating Exxon merged its worldwide oil and fuel additives business with that of Royal Dutch/Shell in 1996. The next year under FTC pressure Exxon agreed to run ads refuting claims that its premium gas enabled car engines to run more efficiently. Another PR disaster followed in 1998 when CEO Lee Raymond upset environmentalists by publicly questioning the global warming theory.

Still Exxon was unstoppable. It acquired Mobil for $81 billion in 1999; the new company had Raymond at the helm and Mobil's Lucio Noto as vice chairman. (Noto retired in 2001.) To get the deal done Exxon Mobil had to divest $4 billion in assets. It agreed to end its European gasoline and lubricants joint venture with BP and to sell more than 2400 gas stations in the US.

In 2000 Exxon Mobil sold 1740 East Coast gas stations to Tosco for $860 million. It sold a California refinery and 340 gas stations to Valero Energy for about $1 billion.

More than a decade after the Exxon Valdez wreaked environmental havoc off the shores of Alaska Exxon Mobil attempted to atone in 2001 by joining the California Fuel Cell Partnership a group studying possible alternatives to and supplements for gasoline in fuel-burning engines. That year Exxon Mobil also announced that it was proceeding with a $12 billion project (with Japanese Indian and Russian partners) to develop oil fields in the Russian Far East.

In 2002 Exxon Mobil sold its 50% stake in a Colombian coal mine as part of its strategy to divest coal assets in order to focus on its core businesses. That year the company sold its Chilean copper mining subsidiary (Disputada de Las Condes) to mineral giant Anglo American for $1.3 billion. Exxon Mobil sold its 3.7% stake in China Petroleum & Chemical Corp. (Sinopec) in early 2005. Later that year the company was ordered to pay $1.3 billion to about 10000 gas station owners for overcharges dating back to 1983; the average amount for each station owner was about $130000.

Shortages caused by Hurricane Katrina prompted Exxon Mobil to receive a 6 million barrel of crude oil loan primarily from the US Strategic Petroleum Reserve and increase gasoline production at its Baton Rouge facility.

Exiting the low-margin retail gasoline business in order to focus on its other operations in 2008 the company began to sell to distributors its remaining 820 company-owned US gas stations and another 1400 outlets operated by dealers.

In 2009 the company signed up to partner with TransCanada to jointly develop the $26 billion Alaska Pipeline Project. A long-term project if and when built the pipeline will deliver natural gas from Alaska's North Slope to US markets.

Also in 2009 it made its first major investment in developing biofuels agreeing to spend $600 million in an algae-to-fuel project with biotech firm Synthetic Genomics.

In a move to replace the decline of oil reserves from its mature fields in 2010 Exxon Mobil acquired XTO Energy. The $41 billion all-stock deal sharply boosted Exxon shale properties in the continental US including the Haynesville shale. Exxon followed up by acquiring Ellora Energy that same year for $695 million which further solidified Exxon's Haynesville position in Texas and Louisiana.

In 2010 in response to the BP oil rig disaster in the Gulf of Mexico Exxon Mobil joined forces with other US oil companies to create a $1 billion rapid-response joint venture capable of capturing and containing some 100000 barrels of oil in water depths of 10000 feet.

In 2011 the company reported a major oil find in the Gulf with potentially 700 million barrels of recoverable oil equivalent.

That year Exxon Mobil acquired two Pittsburgh-area natural gas producers (Phillips Resources and TWP) for $1.7 billion giving the company access to hundreds of thousands of leased acres of the Marcellus Shale in southwestern Pennsylvania.

In 2012 Saudi Basic Industries Corporation and Exxon Mobil agreed to build a world-scale specialty elastomers facility (to be completed in 2015) at the Al-Jubail Petrochemical Company manufacturing joint venture in Saudi Arabia.

To raise cash to pay down debt in 2012 the company sold its North Sea assets to Apache for $1.25 billion.

In 2013 Rosneft and Exxon Mobil agreed to expand their cooperation under their 2011 Strategic Cooperation Agreement to include an additional 150 million acres of exploration acreage in the Russian Arctic and potential participation by Rosneft in the Point Thomson project in Alaska. They also agreed to conduct a joint study on a potential LNG project in the Russian Far East. (In 2011 Exxon Mobil agreed to spend $1 billion in a joint venture with Rosneft to jointly explore oil and gas fields in the Black Sea.). However US economic sanctions on Russia in 2014 forced the company to suspend its operations in the Arctic with Rosneft.

In 2013 Exxon Mobil acquired Canada's Celtic Exploration for about about $2.5 billion Exxon Mobil's largest transaction since it bought Texas' XTO Energy for a whopping $41 billion in 2010. The Celtic deal gives Exxon 545000 net acres in the liquids-rich Montney shale 104000 net acres in the Duvernay shale and other acreage in Alberta.

EXECUTIVES

Svp And Principal Financial Officer, Andrew P. (Andy) Swiger, age 64, $1,287,500 total compensation

President Exxonmobil Chemical Company, John R. Verity
Chairman And Ceo, Darren W. Woods, age 55, $1,000,000 total compensation
Vp And President Exxonmobil Upstream Ventures, B. W. Corson
Vp And General Counsel, R. M. Ebner
Vp Human Resources, M. A. Farrant
President Exxonmobil Production Company, N. W. Duffin
President Exxonmobil Fuels Lubricants And Specialties Marketing Company, B. W. Milton
President Exxonmobil Refining And Supply Company, D. G. Wascom
President Exxonmobil Research And Engineering Company, T. J. Wojnar
President Exxonmobil Global Services Company, L. D. DuCharme
Vice President, Hugh Comer
Vice President Information Technology, Nigel Searle
Vice President Procurement, Jean Baderschneider
National Accounts Manager, Juan Rodriguez
Vice President, Ashok Sapaliga
Vice President Engineering Exxonmobil Upstream Research Company, Jayme K Meier
Senior Vice President Finance And Administration And Controller, Daniel Lyons
Vice President, Pat Doolan
Vice President, Elijah White
Vice President, Atinuke Abanishe
National Account Manager, Richard Bowen
Department Head, Michael Hotaling
Vice President, Rupert Dalwood
Vice President, Pam Darwin
Vice President Upstream Engineering, Gerry Gabriel
Senior Vice President, John Williams
Vice President Engineering, Erika Anzaldua
Government Relations Advisor, Robert Nolan
Vice President, Jim Parsons
Vice President, M Jay Wood
Vice President Engineering, Kenneth Warren
Vice President, Evelyn Miller
Vice President, Tina Fitts
Vice President Strategy And Planning, Ian Carr
Vice President Research And Development Exxonmobil Research And Engineering, Vijay Swarup
Government Relations, Alfredo Balena
Vice President Americas, John Dashwood
Vice President Of Engineering, Roman Perez
Vice President, Henrique Fagundes
Vice President, Christopher Vandewater
Vp And General Tax Counsel, James Spellings Jr
Dvp, Stephen Casmer
Vice President Technical, Carl Ding
Treasurers Benefits Finance And Investments, Cindy Kessel
Secretary, Cathy Coleman
Secretary, Suzanne Manahan-smith
L And S Downstream Treasurers Credit Analyst, Patricia Beckwith
Financial Advisor Upstream Treasurers, Todd Norman
Assistant Treasurer, Kate Shae
Assistant Treasurer, Namisa Taylor
Auditors: PricewaterhouseCoopers LLP

LOCATIONS

HQ: Exxon Mobil Corp
5959 Las Colinas Boulevard, Irving, TX 75039-2298
Phone: 972 940-6000   **Fax:** 972 444-1505
Web: www.exxonmobil.com

2018 Sales

	% of total
US	35
International	65
Total	**100**

PRODUCTS/OPERATIONS

2018 Sales

	$ mil.	% of total
Downstream	221,331	79
Chemical	32,443	12
Upstream	25,517	9
Corporate and Financing	38	-
Total	**279,332**	**100**

COMPETITORS

BP	Royal Dutch Shell
Chevron	Saudi Aramco
Gazprom	Sinopec Corp.
PetroChina	Statoil
Reliance Industries	TOTAL
Rosneft	

HISTORICAL FINANCIALS

Company Type: Public

Income Statement   FYE: December 31

	REVENUE ($ mil.)	NET INCOME ($ mil.)	NET PROFIT MARGIN	EMPLOYEES
12/19	264,938	14,340	5.4%	74,900
12/18	290,212	20,840	7.2%	71,000
12/17	244,363	19,710	8.1%	69,600
12/16	226,094	7,840	3.5%	71,100
12/15	268,882	16,150	6.0%	73,500
Annual Growth	(0.4%)	(2.9%)	—	0.5%

2019 Year-End Financials

Debt ratio: 12.94%—
Return on equity: 7.48%
Cash ($ mil.): 3,089
Current ratio: 0.78
Long-term debt ($ mil.): 26,342

Dividends
Yield: 4.9%
Payout: 102.0%
Market value ($ mil.): —

	STOCK PRICE ($) FY Close	P/E High/Low	PER SHARE ($) Earnings	Dividends	Book Value
12/19	69.78	25 20	3.36	3.43	45.26
12/18	68.19	18 13	4.88	3.23	45.27
12/17	83.64	20 16	4.63	3.06	44.28
12/16	90.26	51 39	1.88	2.98	40.34
12/15	77.95	24 18	3.85	2.88	41.10
Annual Growth	(2.7%)	— —	(3.3%)	4.5%	2.4%

Facebook Inc

Facebook is the face of social media for good and bad. The social networking juggernaut which continues to grow even as it struggles with public relations issues related to privacy security and fake news lets users share information post photos and videos play games and otherwise connect with one another online. The site which allows outside developers to build apps that integrate with Facebook boasts 2.5 billion monthly active users. In addition to its namesake platform Facebook owns photo and video sharing site Instagram messaging applications Messenger and WhatsApp and virtual reality platform Oculus. The company generates revenue through advertising; approximately 55% of total sales accounts outside the US.

Operations

Facebook boasts more than 2.5 billion monthly Facebook users and serves a total of 7 million advertisers.

In a move that emphasizes the growing importance of the products and services it offers beyond its core platform the company has said it will stop sharing user numbers for each individual service (Facebook Instagram WhatsApp and Facebook Messenger) and instead provide one combined figure for all of its apps.

Beyond its core offerings the company has investments in longer-term technology initiatives such as artificial intelligence augmented and virtual reality and connectivity efforts.

Geographic Reach

Global in its reach the Menlo Park California-based Facebook generates about 55% of its revenue from outside of the US. The majority of its international business comes from customers located in Western Europe Australia Brazil Canada and China.

The company has approximately 70 offices and 15 data center facilities located all over the world.

Sales and Marketing

Advertising accounts for nearly all of Facebook's revenue. The company uses a global sales force to attract and retain advertisers. It also serves advertising customers through a self-service ad platform.

Users have generally found the site through word-of-mouth as well as internal marketing efforts. Facebook spent $1.57 billion $1.10 billion and $324 million in FY 2019 2018 and 2017 respectively.

Financial Performance

Facebook has experienced exponential growth over the past few years enabling it to dominate the social networking world as the most trafficked site of its kind in the US. Its revenue grew from nearly $17.9 billion in 2015 to more than $70.7 billion in 2019 while its net income grew from $2.9 billion to $22.1 billion. Despite record-breaking business the company cannot rest on its laurels.

While still in growth mode Facebook's annual growth rate slowed some in 2019 when revenue increased 27% from the prior year (versus 37% in 2018). Monthly active users grew 8% and the average price per ad decreased by 5% (versus the increase of 13% in 2018).

Net income decreased by 16% from $22.1 billion in 2018 to $18.5 billion in 2019 on the jump in cost and expense. (The prior year profits rose 39%.) Operating expenses consists primarily of expenses associated with the delivery and distribution of their products.

Cash at the end of 2019 was $19.3 billion. Cash from operations contributed $36.3 billion to the coffers while investing activities used $19.9 billion. Financing activities used another $7.3 billion.

Strategy

As part of its business strategy the company has made and intends to continue to make acquisitions to add specialized employees and complementary companies products or technologies. Facebook may not be able to find suitable acquisition candidates and may not be able to complete acquisitions on favorable terms if at all. In some cases the costs of such acquisitions may be substantial and there is no assurance that they will receive a favorable return on investment for their acquisitions.

In 2019 the company continued to focus on its main revenue growth priorities: helping marketers use its products to connect with consumers where the company is and (ii) making marketers' ads more relevant and effective.

Company Background

Facebook was launched in 2004 by Harvard student Mark Zuckerberg as an online version of the Harvard Facebook. The name comes from books of freshmen's faces majors and hometowns that are distributed to students.

In 2012 Facebook began publicly trading after filing one of the largest IPOs in US history.

EXECUTIVES

Coo, Sheryl K. Sandberg, age 51, $738,077 total compensation
Chairman And Ceo, Mark Zuckerberg, age 36, $1 total compensation
Cto, Michael (Mike) Schroepfer, age 45, $658,846 total compensation
Cio, Atish Banerjea, age 54
Cfo, David M. (Dave) Wehner, age 51, $662,692 total compensation
Chief Product Officer, Christopher K. (Chris) Cox, age 37, $658,846 total compensation
Vice President Global Public Policy, Joel Kaplan
Vice President Partnerships, Dan Rose
Vice President Global Marketing Solutions, Carolyn Everson
Vice President Growth And Analytics, Javier Olivan
Vice President Product Marketing, Ty Ahmad-Taylor
Vp And Virtual Reality Chief, Hugo Barra
Vice President Data Center Design Engineering, Jay Park
Senior Vice President Business Development Sales And Marketing, Cree Crawford
Vice President Small Business, Dan Levy
Vp. Mobile And Global Access Policy, Kevin Martin
Vice President Social Good, Naomi Gleit
Vice President Ads And Business Platform, Mark Rabkin
Vice President Global Operations, Justin Osofsky
Vp And Deputy General Counsel, Paul Grewal
Vp Of Hr, Janelle Gale
Board Member, Susan Desmond-hellmann
Auditors: Ernst & Young LLP

LOCATIONS

HQ: Facebook Inc
1601 Willow Road, Menlo Park, CA 94025
Phone: 650 543-4800
Web: www.facebook.com

2017 Sales

	$ mil.	% of total
US	17,734	44
International	22,919	56
Total	**40,653**	**100**

PRODUCTS/OPERATIONS

2017 Sales

	$ mil.	% of total
Advertising	39,942	98
Payments & other fees	711	2
Total	**40,653**	**100**

Selected Products and Features

Products for Users
  Timeline
  News feed
  Photos & videos
  Messages
  Groups
  Lists
  Events
  Places
  Notifications
  Facebook Pages
Products for Developers
  Open Graph
  Social plugins
  Like button
  Recommendations
  Comments
  Facebook Payments
  Apps on Facebook
Products for Advertisers & Marketers
  Facebook Ads
  Sponsored Stories
  Ad analytics

COMPETITORS

Bebo	Pinterest
Friendster	Snapchat
Google	Tencent Holdings
IAC	Tumblr
LiveJournal	Twitter
Meetup	Yelp
Memory Lane	craigslist
Microsoft	

HISTORICAL FINANCIALS

Company Type: Public

Income Statement

FYE: December 31

	REVENUE ($ mil.)	NET INCOME ($ mil.)	NET PROFIT MARGIN	EMPLOYEES
12/20	85,965	29,146	33.9%	58,601
12/19	70,697	18,485	26.1%	49,942
12/18	55,838	22,112	39.6%	35,587
12/17	40,653	15,934	39.2%	25,105
12/16	27,638	10,217	37.0%	17,048
Annual Growth	32.8%	30.0%	—	36.2%

2020 Year-End Financials

Debt ratio: —
Return on equity: 25.35%
Cash ($ mil.): 17,576
Current ratio: 5.05
Long-term debt ($ mil.): —
Dividends
Yield: —
Payout: —
Market value ($ mil.): —

	STOCK PRICE ($) FY Close	P/E High/Low	PER SHARE ($) Earnings	Dividends	Book Value
12/20	273.16	30 14	10.09	0.00	45.03
12/19	205.25	32 20	6.43	0.00	35.43
12/18	131.09	28 16	7.57	0.00	29.48
12/17	176.46	33 21	5.39	0.00	25.58
12/16	115.05	37 26	3.49	0.00	20.47
Annual Growth	24.1%	— —	30.4%	—	21.8%

Fannie Mae

The Federal National Mortgage Association better known as Fannie Mae is a government-sponsored enterprise (GSE) that provides liquidity in the US mortgage market. Like its brother Freddie Mac the company buys mortgages from lenders and packages them for resale transferring risk from lenders and allowing them to offer mortgages to those who may not otherwise qualify. Through its single-family and multifamily business segments Fannie Mae provided over $650 billion in liquidity to the mortgage market in 2019 which enabled the financing of approximately 3 million home purchases refinancing or rental units.

HISTORY

In 1938 President Franklin Roosevelt created Fannie Mae as part of the government-owned Reconstruction Finance Corporation; its mandate was to buy FHA (Federal Housing Administration) loans. Fannie Mae began buying VA (Veterans Administration) mortgages in 1948. It was rechartered as a public-private mixed-ownership corporation in 1954.

The Housing Act of 1968 divided the corporation into the Government National Mortgage Association (Ginnie Mae which retained explicit government backing) and Fannie Mae which went public (with only an implicit US guarantee). Fannie

Mae retained its treasury backstop authority whereby the secretary of the treasury can purchase up to $2.24 billion of the company's obligations.

The company introduced uniform conventional loan mortgage documents in 1970 began to buy conventional mortgages in 1972 and started buying condo and planned-unit development mortgages in 1974. By 1976 it was buying more conventional loans than FHA and VA loans.

As interest rates rose in the 1970s Fannie Mae's profits declined and by 1981 it was losing more than $1 million a day. Then it began offering mortgage-backed securities (MBSs) — popular as an investment product because of their implicit guarantee from the government. By 1982 the company funded 14% of US home mortgages.

Fannie Mae began borrowing money overseas and buying conventional multifamily and co-op housing loans in 1984. The next year it tightened credit rules and began issuing securities aimed at foreign investors such as yen-denominated securities. Fannie Mae issued its first real estate mortgage investment conduit (REMIC) securities (shares in mortgage pools of specific maturities and risk classes) and introduced a program to allow small lenders to pool loans with other lenders to create MBSs in 1987.

After CEO David Maxwell's 1991 retirement with a reported $29 million pension package Fannie Mae's powerful Washington lobby squelched calls to limit executive salaries. Other attempts to make the company more competitive with private concerns were more successful. In 1992 Fannie Mae's capital requirements were raised; a new mandate also required the organization to lend greater support to inner-city buyers. A new client/server computer system helped the company handle the deluge of new and refinanced loans that came in 1993 (Fannie Mae had struggled to improve its information systems in the 1980s pouring more than $100 million into a mainframe system that was obsolete before it went online).

In 1997 Fannie Mae officially adopted its longtime nickname. The next year Fannie Mae named White House budget chief Franklin Raines to succeed CEO James Johnson.

Fannie Mae is no stranger to bad news or bad press. In 1999 the Department of Housing and Urban Development began investigating charges that the company's automated underwriting systems were racially biased. The next year the agency released a study that found it to be negligent in promoting homeownership in low-income neighborhoods. In response Fannie Mae eased credit requirements in an effort to boost minority homeownership (1999) and announced plans to loan some $2 trillion to minority and low-income homebuyers (2000). This move however invoked criticism that the company was exposing itself to increased risk from buyers more likely to default.

Following the lead of rival Freddie Mac in 2000 Fannie Mae offered securities for sale over the Internet. In 2002 it tightened standards for mortgage refinance cash-out loans it would buy as mortgage defaults rose (even as home sales and mortgage refinancings were helping prop up the sagging US economy).

In response to those who thought it was in bed with the federal government Fannie Mae kicked off the covers and put one foot on the floor. In 2003 it fulfilled a voluntary commitment to register its common stock with the SEC and came permanently under that organization's disclosure and oversight requirements.

But the move did not stop controversy from swirling around the lender. Chairman and CEO Franklin Raines CFO Timothy Howard and auditor KPMG were ousted in December 2004 after the SEC determined Fannie Mae had violated accounting rules. The inquiry was prompted by accusations Fannie Mae had manipulated earnings; earnings from 2001 through 2003 were restated and those from 2004 and 2005 were each released more than a year late.

In 2006 federal regulators hit the firm with a whopping $400 million fine. Investigators claimed that its former executives willfully overstated earnings by more than $10 billion — and then tried to impede an investigation into the discrepancies — in order to reap performance bonuses. Chairman Stephen Ashley and CEO Daniel Mudd who'd been brought in to replace Franklin Raines in late 2004 were brought to task by the Senate Banking Committee in regard to accounting misdeeds.

Though the Justice Department eventually dropped criminal charges against the firm Fannie Mae agreed to major changes in its accounting internal controls and management practices. It additionally agreed to appoint an independent chief risk officer as well as an organizational review overseen by a compliance committee. Meanwhile the lender suspended its home construction loan program — worth about $10 billion — while it got its financial house in order.

Fannie suffered huge losses in 2007 and 2008 as a result of the subprime mortgage crisis which saw a tremendouse increase in loan defaults. The government stepped in loans and in 2008 seized both Fannie and Freddie. It also shuffled their management teams: Fannie CEO Mudd was replaced by Herbert Allison former TIAA-CREF. Allison was later tapped by the Obama administration to run the Treasury Department's financial recovery program. Former COO Michael Williams was named CEO in 2009.

The Federal Housing Finance Agency (FHFA) was created in 2008 to oversee both Fannie and Freddie as well as the 12 Federal Home Loan Banks. The FHFA was granted more authority than its predecessor agencies the Federal Housing Finance Board and the Office of Federal Housing Enterprise Oversight.

In an historic move the government in 2008 placed the two GSEs in conservatorship which is a legal status similar to bankruptcy rather than risk the possibility that the companies might fail. The government assumed a nearly 80% stake in the troubled companies in a $111 billion bailout (with a commitment of up to $400 billion). In 2011 the Obama administration proposed to restructure the housing market in a plan that will reduce the government's role and eventually eliminate the GSEs.

In 2009 the Making Home Affordable Program was introduced to provide assistance to borrowers in default through refinancings and other loan modifications.

EXECUTIVES

President Ceo And Director, Timothy J. (Tim) Mayopoulos, age 61, $600,000 total compensation
Evp And Head Multifamily, Jeffery R. Hayward, age 64, $475,000 total compensation
Evp And Cfo, David C. Benson, age 61, $600,000 total compensation
Evp Single-family Underwriting Pricing And Capital Markets, Andrew Bon Salle, $500,000 total compensation
Evp General Counsel And Corporate Secretary, Brian P. Brooks, $500,000 total compensation
Evp And Chief Risk Officer, Kimberly H. Johnson
Svp Operations And Technology, Bruce Lee
Vice President, Stephanie Bahr
Vice President, Karen Jez
Vice President Information Technology, Beth Applegate
Vice President Of Internal Audit Technology, Don Farineau
Vice President, Mike Hernandez
Vice President Internal Audit, John Lengel
Vice President Investigations, Leslie Arrington
Vice President Single Family Mortgage Business, Katrina Jones
Vice President Single Family Business, Greg Awad
Senior Vice President And Chief Human Resources Officer, Elcio Barcelos
Chairman, Egbert L. J. Perry, age 64
Board Member, Kenneth Duberstein
Board Member, Ryan Zanin
Auditors: DELOITTE & TOUCHE LLP

LOCATIONS

HQ: Fannie Mae
1100 15th Street, NW, Washington, DC 20005
Phone: 800 232-6643
Web: www.fanniemae.com

Selected Locations
Atlanta
Chicago
Dallas
Pasadena
Philadelphia
Washington DC

PRODUCTS/OPERATIONS

2018 Sales

	$ mil.	% of total
Interest income		
Mortgage loans	114,605	95
Trading securities	1,336	1
Federal funds	742	1
Available-for-sale securities	230	-
Others	136	-
Interest expense	(96098)	-
Non-interest income		
Fair value gains (losses) net	1,121	1
Fee and other income	979	1
Investment gains net	952	1
Total	**24,003**	**100**

2018 Sales

	% of total
Single-Family	85
Multifamily	15
Total	**100**

Selected Business Segments
Single-Family Credit Guaranty
Multifamily

COMPETITORS

Freddie Mac	VBA
Ginnie Mae	Wells Fargo

HISTORICAL FINANCIALS

Company Type: Public

Income Statement				FYE: December 31
	ASSETS ($ mil.)	NET INCOME ($ mil.)	INCOME AS % OF ASSETS	EMPLOYEES
12/19	3,503,319	14,160	0.4%	7,500
12/18	3,418,318	15,959	0.5%	7,400
12/17	3,345,529	2,463	0.1%	7,200
12/16	3,287,968	12,313	0.4%	7,000
12/15	3,221,917	10,954	0.3%	7,300
Annual Growth	2.1%	6.6%		0.7%

2019 Year-End Financials

Debt ratio: 98.97%	No. of shares (mil.): 1,158
Return on equity: 135.84%	Dividends
Cash ($ mil.): 21,184	Yield: —
Current ratio: —	Payout: —
Long-term debt ($ mil.): —	Market value ($ mil.): 3,613

STOCK PRICE ($)		P/E		PER SHARE ($)		
	FY Close	High/Low		Earnings	Dividends	Book Value
12/19	3.12	134	37	0.03	0.00	12.61
12/18	1.06	4	2	0.57	0.00	5.39
12/17	2.65	—	—	(1.12)	0.00	(3.18)
12/16	3.90	449	110	0.01	0.00	5.24
12/15	1.64	—	—	(0.05)	0.00	3.48
Annual Growth	17.4%	—	—	—	—	38.0%

HISTORICAL FINANCIALS
Company Type: Private

Income Statement   FYE: December 31

	ASSETS ($ mil.)	NET INCOME ($ mil.)	INCOME AS % OF ASSETS	EMPLOYEES
12/16	21,222	192	0.9%	200
12/13	16,212	179	1.1%	—
/	0	0	—	—
Annual Growth				

LOCATIONS
HQ: FARM CREDIT WEST
  3755 ATHERTON RD, ROCKLIN, CA 957653701
Phone: 916 724-4800
Web: WWW.FARMCREDITWEST.COM

HISTORICAL FINANCIALS
Company Type: Private

Income Statement   FYE: December 31

	ASSETS ($ mil.)	NET INCOME ($ mil.)	INCOME AS % OF ASSETS	EMPLOYEES
12/12	6,668	151	2.3%	165
12/11	6,282	176	2.8%	—
12/10	6,129	0	—	—
Annual Growth	4.3%	—	—	—

FARM CREDIT BANK OF TEXAS

The largest member of the federal Farm Credit System the Farm Credit Bank of Texas provides loans and financial services to about 20 lending cooperatives and financial institutions in Alabama Louisiana Mississippi New Mexico and Texas. These include agricultural credit associations which provide agricultural production loans agribusiness financing and rural mortgage financing; and federal land credit associations which offer real estate loans on farms ranches and other rural property. Farm Credit Bank of Texas is owned by the lending cooperatives it serves.

EXECUTIVES

Senior Vice President Policy Compliance, Matthew Byerly
Senior Vice President, Rusty Lampman
Vice President, Steve Donnell
Vice President And Controller, Vicki Rodriguez
Vice President Business Development, Jeremy Lightfoot
Vice President, Paul Rudd
Vice President Product Development, Paul Barton
Vice President Business Systems Unit Manager, Ed Benson
Vice President, Darren Cannon
Senior Vice President And Cco, John Logsdon
Vice President Regional Manager, Chris Amend
Vice President Lending, Boyd J Chambers
Vice President, Heath Davis
Vice President Collateral Risk Management, Brad Swinney
Vice President, Amy Pala
Vice President Branch Manager, Angela Shannon
Assistant Vice President Operations, William Foley
Vice President, Ronnie Sellers
Assistant Vice President At The Clarksdale Branch Office, Bobby Spinks
Vp Of Compliance, Thomas Ringler
Vice President, Jason Gandy
Vp Of It Compliance, Igor Stojanovski
Vice President, Mike Tippit
Senior Vice President, Doug Reinart
Senior Vice President Relationship Manager, Brett Valentine
Board Of Directors, Buddy Cortese
Auditors: PRICEWATERHOUSECOOPERS LLP AU

LOCATIONS
HQ: FARM CREDIT BANK OF TEXAS
  4801 PLAZA ON THE LK # 1200, AUSTIN, TX 787461081
Phone: 512 465-0400
Web: WWW.FARMCREDITBANK.COM

FARM CREDIT SERVICES OF AMERICA

EXECUTIVES

Pres-Ceo, Doug Stark
Exec V Pres*, Neil Olsen
Sr V Pres-Cfo*, Eugene College
Sr V Pres*, Michelle Mapes
Sr V Pres*, David Martin
Turner Youth Initiative Direct, Twila Phillips
Engineer, Dave Cook
Senior Vice President Agribusi, Marshall Hansen
Auditors: PRICEWATERHOUSECOOPERS LLP M

LOCATIONS
HQ: FARM CREDIT SERVICES OF AMERICA
  5015 S 118TH ST, OMAHA, NE 681372210
Phone: 800 884-3276
Web: WWW.FCSAMERICA.COM

HISTORICAL FINANCIALS
Company Type: Private

Income Statement   FYE: December 31

	ASSETS ($ mil.)	NET INCOME ($ mil.)	INCOME AS % OF ASSETS	EMPLOYEES
12/15	24,772	514	2.1%	10,000
12/04	8,475	294	3.5%	—
12/03	7,633	114	1.5%	—
12/02	0	132	—	—
Annual Growth	—	11.0%	—	—

FARM CREDIT WEST

EXECUTIVES

Ceo-Pres, Mark D Littlefield
Sr V Pres, Chris N Brumfield
Exec V Pres, John C Boyes
Exe V Pres, William M Noland
Cfo, Chris Doherty
Exec V Pres-Fiscal ADM, Ernest M Hodges
Prin, K E Graff
Loan Officer, Danielle Vietti
Senior Vice President Chief, Denise Warkomski
Human Resources Generalist, Tanya Berry
Executive Vice President Chief, Dan Clawson
Auditors: PRICEWATERHOUSECOOPERS LLP SA

Farmers & Merchants Bancorp (Lodi, CA)

EXECUTIVES

Chb-pres-ceo, Kent A Steinwert
Vice President Of Software, Bill Russell
Assistant Vice President, Benea Schmidt
Vice President Banking Services, Carol Mcmurran
Vice President And Chief Appraiser, Jon Schrader
Vice President, Pam Mcglynn
Vice President Retail Credit Sales Manager, Gary Spears
Assistant Vice President Retail Administration, Jackie Phillips
Vice President Commercial Loan Officer, Claire Forsythe
Vice President Relationship Manager, Corinne Santos
Vice President Treasury Relationship Manager, Mike Caselli
Vice President Director Of Treasury Operations, Patty Ducato
Vice President Treasury Management Specialist LI, Patricia Preston
Senior Vice President, Carol Murray
Assistant Vice President Operations Supervisor, Carrie Henshaw
Vice President Commercial Account Officer, Jesse Pataria
Avp Branch Manager, Michael Pierce
Auditors: Moss Adams LLP

LOCATIONS
HQ: Farmers & Merchants Bancorp (Lodi, CA)
  111 W. Pine Street, Lodi, CA 95240
Phone: 209 367-2300
Web: www.fmbonline.com

HISTORICAL FINANCIALS
Company Type: Public

Income Statement   FYE: December 31

	ASSETS ($ mil.)	NET INCOME ($ mil.)	INCOME AS % OF ASSETS	EMPLOYEES
12/19	3,721	56	1.5%	365
12/18	3,434	45	1.3%	376
12/17	3,075	28	0.9%	330
12/16	2,922	29	1.0%	339
12/15	2,615	27	1.0%	316
Annual Growth	9.2%	19.6%	—	3.7%

Debt ratio: 0.28%	No. of shares (mil.): 0
Return on equity: 16.47%	Dividends
Cash ($ mil.): 294	Yield: 1.8%
Current ratio: —	Payout: 20.5%
Long-term debt ($ mil.): —	Market value ($ mil.): 609

	STOCK PRICE ($) FY Close	P/E High/Low	PER SHARE ($) Earnings	Dividends	Book Value
12/19	768.10	13 10	71.18	14.20	465.68
12/18	700.00	13 11	56.82	13.90	397.10
12/17	676.00	20 17	35.03	13.55	368.90
12/16	640.00	17 13	37.44	13.10	346.80
12/15	540.00	17 13	34.82	12.90	318.46
Annual Growth	9.2%	— —	19.6%	2.4%	10.0%

Farmers & Merchants Bank of Long Beach (CA)

Auditors: KPMG LLP

LOCATIONS

HQ: Farmers & Merchants Bank of Long Beach (CA)
302 Pine Avenue, Long Beach, CA 90802
Phone: 562 437-0011
Web: www.fmb.com

HISTORICAL FINANCIALS

Company Type: Public

Income Statement   FYE: December 31

	ASSETS ($ mil.)	NET INCOME ($ mil.)	INCOME AS % OF ASSETS	EMPLOYEES
12/19	7,605	85	1.1%	—
12/18	7,308	85	1.2%	—
12/17	6,991	64	0.9%	747
12/16	6,729	71	1.1%	—
12/15	6,153	64	1.1%	—
Annual Growth	5.4%	7.1%		

2019 Year-End Financials

Debt ratio: —	No. of shares (mil.): 0
Return on equity: 8.11%	Dividends
Cash ($ mil.): 118	Yield: 1.5%
Current ratio: —	Payout: 18.6%
Long-term debt ($ mil.): —	Market value ($ mil.): 1,009

	STOCK PRICE ($) FY Close	P/E High/Low	PER SHARE ($) Earnings	Dividends	Book Value
12/19	7,849.00	13 12	661.23	123.00	8,425.
12/18	7,700.00	14 12	654.07	121.00	7,850
12/17	7,860.00	16 14	494.65	119.00	7,325
12/16	6,800.00	13 11	546.16	119.00	6,952
12/15	6,240.00	13 12	496.06	119.00	6,532
Annual Growth	5.9%	— —	7.4%	0.8%	6.6%

Farmers National Banc Corp. (Canfield,OH)

Farmers National Banc is willing to help even nonfarmers grow their seed income into thriving bounties of wealth. The bank provides commercial and personal banking from nearly 20 branches in Ohio. Founded in 1887 Farmers National Banc offers checking and savings accounts credit cards and loans and mortgages. Farmers' lending portfolio is composed of real estate mortgages consumer loans and commercial loans. The company also includes Farmers National Insurance and Farmers Trust Company a non-depository trust bank that offers wealth management and trust services.

Geographic Reach

Farmers National Banc operates 19 branches located throughout Mahoning Trumbull Columbiana Stark and Cuyahoga Counties. Farmers Trust Company operates two offices located in Boardman and Howland Ohio.

Financial Performance

The company's revenues have ranged from $40 million to $60 million in the past decade. In 2013 overall sales fell 1% to $54 million; the slight dip was due to lessened interest income on loans and taxable securities. (Financial institutions make their money on interest income from loans and non-interest income from fees.) Its non-interest income experienced growth from service charges insurance agency commissions and consulting fees for retirement planning.

Profits decreased by 22% to $8 million in 2013 due to increase in a provision for loan losses and non-interest expenses such as salary and employee benefits.

Mergers and Acquisitions

In 2013 the bank added retirement planning services to their portfolio with the acquisition of Cleveland-based National Associates Inc. for $4.4 million. The acquisition was part of its plan to boost noninterest income and complement its existing retirement services.

EXECUTIVES

Vice President Retail Operations Manager, Jim Swift
Vice President Commercial Lending Relationship Manager, Darrell Smucker
Senior Vice President Commercial Lending Team Leader, Thomas Stocksdale
Vp Commercial Lending Relationship Manager, David Benavides
Senior Vice President, Michael Oberhaus
Board Member, Anne Crawford
Board Member, David Paull
Board Member, Gregory Bestic
Vice Chairman Of The Board, James Smail
Board Member, Terry Moore
Board Member, Edward Muransky
Auditors: CliftonLarsonAllen LLP

LOCATIONS

HQ: Farmers National Banc Corp. (Canfield,OH)
20 South Broad Street, Canfield, OH 44406
Phone: 330 533-3341
Web: www.farmersbankgroup.com

PRODUCTS/OPERATIONS

Selected Products

Personal
Certificate of Deposit
Checking Accounts
Children's Accounts
Consumer Loans
Home Equity Loans & Lines
Mortgage Loans
Online Banking
Personal Credit Card
Personal Debit Card
Phone Banking
Retirement
Savings Accounts
Business
Business Credit Card
Business Debit Card
Business Deposits
Business Loans
Cash Management
Remote Deposit Capture
Wealth Management and Insurance
Farmers Trust Company
Farmers National Investments
Farmers National Insurance
On-line banking

COMPETITORS

CSB Bancorp	JPMorgan Chase
Central Federal	Killbuck Bancshares
Consumers Bancorp	National Bancshares
Cortland Bancorp	Ohio Legacy
FFD Financial	Tri-State 1st Banc
Fifth Third	United Community
First Financial	Financial
Bancorp	Wayne Savings
First Niles Financial	Bancshares
Home Loan Financial	

HISTORICAL FINANCIALS

Company Type: Public

Income Statement   FYE: December 31

	ASSETS ($ mil.)	NET INCOME ($ mil.)	INCOME AS % OF ASSETS	EMPLOYEES
12/19	2,449	35	1.5%	450
12/18	2,328	32	1.4%	453
12/17	2,159	22	1.1%	445
12/16	1,966	20	1.0%	441
12/15	1,869	8	0.4%	432
Annual Growth	7.0%	45.2%	—	1.0%

2019 Year-End Financials

Debt ratio: 1.84%	No. of shares (mil.): 27
Return on equity: 12.73%	Dividends
Cash ($ mil.): 70	Yield: 2.3%
Current ratio: —	Payout: 30.4%
Long-term debt ($ mil.): —	Market value ($ mil.): 452

	STOCK PRICE ($) FY Close	P/E High/Low	PER SHARE ($) Earnings	Dividends	Book Value
12/19	16.32	13 10	1.28	0.38	10.82
12/18	12.74	14 10	1.16	0.30	9.44
12/17	14.75	19 15	0.82	0.22	8.79
12/16	14.20	20 11	0.76	0.16	7.88
12/15	8.60	24 20	0.36	0.12	7.35
Annual Growth	17.4%	— —	37.3%	33.4%	10.1%

FB Financial Corp

Dominion Energy dominates the American energy market as one of its top distributors of electricity and natural gas. The company serves some 7 million retail energy customers across eight US states with a special concentration in Virginia the Carolinas and Ohio. The company boasts an impressive energy portfolio with about 30700 MW of generating capacity as well as one of the largest underground natural gas storage systems with 1 trillion cu. ft. of capacity. Operating subsidiaries include Virginia Power and Dominion Energy Gas.

Operations

In 2019 Dominion Energy strategically realigned its segments which resulted in the formation of five primary operating segments: Dominion Energy Virginia Gas Transmission & Storage Gas Distribution Dominion Energy South Carolina and Contracted Generation.

The Dominion Energy Virginia segment is composed of Virginia Power's regulated electric transmission distribution (including customer service) and generation (regulated electric utility and its related energy supply) operations which serve approximately 2.6 million residential commercial industrial and governmental customers in Virginia and North Carolina. The segment accounts for about 45% total sales.

Gas Transmission & Storage segment includes FERC regulated interstate natural gas transmission pipeline and underground storage systems in the eastern and Rocky Mountain regions of the U.S. (primarily through DETI DECG and Dominion Energy Questar Pipeline) LNG import/export and storage (through its 75% controlling interest in Cove Point) as well as a 50% noncontrolling partnership interest in Iroquois. It also includes nonregulated retail natural gas marketing development of renewable natural gas and LNG infrastructure and its investments in Atlantic Coast Pipeline Align RNG and Wrangler. The segment accounts for about 20% of total sales.

The Dominion Energy South Carolina segment is comprised of DESC's generation transmission and distribution of electricity to approximately 740000 customers in the central southern and southwestern portions of South Carolina and the distribution of natural gas to approximately 390000 residential commercial and industrial customers in South Carolina. The segment accounts for more than 15% of total sales.

The Gas Distribution segment includes Dominion Energy's regulated natural gas sales transportation gathering and distribution operations in Ohio West Virginia North Carolina Utah southwestern Wyoming and southeastern Idaho (through East Ohio Hope PSNC and Questar Gas) which collectively serve approximately 3.0 million residential commercial and industrial customers. The segment accounts for nearly 15% of total sales.

The Contracted Generation segment includes the operations of Millstone and associated energy marketing and price risk activities and Dominion Energy's long-term contracted renewable electric generation fleet as well as a 50% noncontrolling partnership interest in Fowler Ridge. The segment accounts for about 5% of total sales.

Geographic Reach

Headquartered in Richmond Virginia Dominion has operations in 18 states. Its Virginia Power subsidiary distributes power in North Carolina and Virginia.

Its East Ohio Gas Hope Gas and Questar subsidiaries distribute gas in Ohio West Virginia Utah Wyoming and Idaho..

Sales and Marketing

Dominion primarily sells electricity to retail customers consisting of residential homes and commercial businesses. Its subsidiary Virginia Power includes customers such as residential commercial and industrial customers as well as rural electric cooperatives and municipalities. The company serves more than 7 million utility and retail energy customers.

Financial Performance

Dominion has seen a steady rise in revenue in recent years with sales growing 42% between 2015 and 2019. Net income has fluctuated in recent years.

Revenue increased 23% in 2019 to some $16.6 billion due to a $1.5 billion increase from the SCANA Combination due to operations acquired ($2.5 billion) partially offset by a $1.0 billion charge for refunds of amounts previously collected from retail electric customers of DESC for the NND Project.

Net income declined 45% to about $1.4 billion in 2019 primarily due to charges for refunds of amounts previously collected from retail electric customers of DESC for the NND Project litigation acquired in the SCANA Combination a voluntary retirement program the planned early retirement of certain Virginia Power electric generation facilities and the absence of gains on the sales of certain equity method investments.

The company ended 2019 with $269 million in cash down $122 million from 2018. Operating activities contributed $5.2 billion while investing activities used $4.6 billion (mostly construction costs) and financing activities used $704 million mainly for debt and dividend payments.

Strategy

Dominion is focusing on its regulated power and gas infrastructure assets to reduce its exposure to volatile energy markets. It acquired western US gas utility Questar in 2016 and southeastern US utility SCANA in 2019. The firm exited certain retail energy marketing operations in 2018; it also sold three merchant power generation plants for $1.3 billion and its 50% stake in midstream gas services provider Blue Racer for $1.2 billion.

Dominion's five-year investment plan for the 2019-23 period includes a focus on upgrading the electric system in Virginia through investments in additional renewable generation facilities smart meters customer information platform intelligent grid devices and associated control systems physical and cyber security investments strategic undergrounding and energy conservation programs. Dominion Energy also plans to upgrade its gas and electric transmission and distribution networks and meet environmental requirements and standards set by various regulatory bodies.

Mergers and Acquisitions

In early 2019 Dominion acquired SCANA Corporation in a transaction valued at $13.4 billion adding some 1.6 million customers to Dominion's already massive base and expanding its power and gas utility operations in the Carolinas. SCANA and its subsidiaries including South Carolina Electric & Gas Company Public Service Company of North Carolina and SCANA Energy Marketing became part of Dominion's newly formed Southeast Energy segment. The deal included the assumption of financial obligations (including customer refunds) related to two SCANA nuclear reactors that will not be completed due to construction delays and cost overruns.

Also in 2019 Dominion acquired the remaining interest in majority owned subsidiary Dominion Energy Midstream Partners through a share exchange transaction valued at about $1.6 billion.

In addition the company acquired two solar projects in Virginia and one solar project in South Carolina in 2019. The previous year it purchased two solar projects in North Carolina and Virginia for $250 million.

Company Background

Dominion Energy traces its roots to the founding of the Upper Appomattox Company in Virginia in 1795. The company managed water rights and eventually ran power plants. The Virginia Railway and Power Company (VR&P) acquired Upper Appomattox in 1909 along with several other utilities in the following year. VR&P became Virginia Electric and Power Company (Virginia Power) after being acquired by engineering firm Stone & Webster in 1925. Virginia Power acquired Virginia Public Service Company and built numerous power plants in the following years. It expanded into gas exploration in the 1990s.

In 2000 Dominion bought Consolidated Natural Gas (CNG) for $9 billion making it one of the largest fully integrated gas and electric power companies in the US; it then sold CNG's Virginia Natural Gas to AGL Resources and the two firms' combined Latin American assets to Duke Energy. It sold its telecom business in 2004 the bulk of its oil and gas exploration operations in 2007 and utility Peoples Natural Gas in 2010. In 2016 Dominion bought gas utility Questar for $4.4 billion.

In 1983 Dominion Resources was incorporated as a parent company for Virginia Power. The holding company changed its name to Dominion Energy in 2017.

Auditors: Crowe LLP

LOCATIONS

HQ: FB Financial Corp
211 Commerce Street, Suite 300, Nashville, TN 37201
Phone: 615 564-1212
Web: www.firstbankonline.com

HISTORICAL FINANCIALS

Company Type: Public

Income Statement				FYE: December 31
	ASSETS ($ mil.)	NET INCOME ($ mil.)	INCOME AS % OF ASSETS	EMPLOYEES
12/19	6,124	83	1.4%	1,399
12/18	5,136	80	1.6%	1,356
12/17	4,727	52	1.1%	1,386
12/16	3,276	40	1.2%	1,108
12/15	2,899	47	1.7%	1,038
Annual Growth	20.6%	15.0%	—	7.7%

2019 Year-End Financials

Debt ratio: 4.97%	No. of shares (mil.): 31
Return on equity: 11.69%	Dividends
Cash ($ mil.): 101	Yield: 0.8%
Current ratio: —	Payout: 12.0%
Long-term debt ($ mil.): —	Market value ($ mil.): 1,229

	STOCK PRICE ($) FY Close	P/E High/Low		PER SHARE ($)		
				Earnings	Dividends	Book Value
12/19	39.59	15	11	2.65	0.32	24.56
12/18	35.02	17	13	2.55	0.20	21.87
12/17	41.99	23	13	1.86	0.00	19.54
12/16	25.95	12	9	2.10	4.03	13.71
Annual Growth	11.1%	—	—	6.0%	(46.9%)	15.7%

FBL Financial Group Inc

Insurance holding company FBL Financial Group (FBL) is the parent of Farm Bureau Life Insurance Company. Through its subsidiary the firm sells life insurance annuities and investment products to farmers ranchers and agricultural businesses. Farm Bureau Life sells insurance and annuities through an exclusive network of about 1860 agents across some 15 states in the Midwest and West. (In Colorado it operates as Greenfields Life Insurance.) The company markets its products through an affiliation with the American Farm Bureau Federation. FBL also manages for a fee two Farm Bureau-affiliated property/casualty insurance companies. The Iowa Farm Bureau Federation owns majority of the company.

Operations

FBL divides its business into two segments annuity and life insurance. Traditional and universal life insurance products sold primarily in Iowa Kansas and Oklahoma account for about 55% of sales. Annuities including fixed rate and index are also big in Iowa and Kansas and account for about 25% of revenue.

The two Farm Bureau-affiliated property/casualty insurers that FBL manages are Farm Bureau Property & Casualty and Western Agricultural Insurance. The two affiliates underwrite auto crop and other property/casualty policies for individuals and groups under FBL's corporate and other segment which accounts for more than 10% of revenue.

Geographic Reach

FBL offers its services in about 15 western and midwestern states. Iowa Kansas Oklahoma and Wyoming are key markets. Its corporate headquarters is located in West Des Moines Iowa.

Sales and Marketing

Sales through distribution channels are currently conducted in about 15 states which characterized as follows: multi-line states and life partner state. The company's agency force is one of our most important competitive advantages as the agents are able to develop long term personal relationships through a deep understanding of their customers' needs. It has over 1195 agents and managers in multi-line states that were supported by some 1150 sales associates who assist them and provide a variety of support in the sales process.

Financial Performance

FBL's total revenue in 2019 totaled $774.7 million an 8% growth from the previous year. The growth was due to higher sales in all of the company's segments.

Net income for 2019 was $126.3 million a 35% growth from the previous year. Higher expenses were offset by higher total revenues.

Cash and cash equivalents at the end of the year were $17.3 million. Operating activities generated $213.1 million while investing activities used $154.6 million mainly for fixed maturities. Financing activities used $60.2 million primarily for contract holder account withdrawals.

Strategy

FBL's core business strategies leverage areas where it has competitive advantages. The company's exclusive agent distribution channel enables deep customer engagement and long-term customer relationships. It benefits from close ties to the unique needs of the agricultural market and affinity with the Farm Bureau brand and its cross-sell culture results in industry leading cross-sell rates.

Mergers and Acquisitions

In the 3rd quarter of 2020 FBL Financial Group Inc. has received a non-binding proposal from Farm Bureau Property & Casualty Insurance Company to acquire all of the outstanding shares of Class A common stock and Class B common stock of the Company that are not currently owned by FBPCIC or the Iowa Farm Bureau Federation at a purchase price of $47.00 per share in cash. The Iowa Farm Bureau Federation owns approximately 60% of the Company's Class A common stock and approximately 67% of the Company's Class B common stock. The Proposal is subject to certain conditions.

EXECUTIVES

Ceo, James P. (Jim) Brannen, age 58, $700,000 total compensation
Cfo And Treasurer, Donald J. (Don) Seibel, age 56, $360,706 total compensation
Chief Investment Officer, Charles T. Happel, age 58, $353,496 total compensation
Coo Life Companies, Raymond W. Wasilewski, age 61
Cio, Casey Decker
Coo Property Casualty Companies, Daniel D. Pitcher, age 58, $383,778 total compensation
Vice President Human Resources, Lori K Strottman
Vice President Audit Services, Tricia Erb
Vice President Sales, Christopher Shryack
P And C Member Services Operations Vice President, Jerry Kristan
Vice President Commercial Lines, Steve Wittmuss
Regional Vice President, Jay Seiboldt
Vice Chairman, Jerry L. Chicoine, age 77
Chairman, Craig D. Hill, age 64
Auditors: Ernst & Young LLP

LOCATIONS

HQ: FBL Financial Group Inc
5400 University Avenue, West Des Moines, IA 50266-5997
Phone: 515 225-5400
Web: www.fblfinancial.com

Selected Areas of Operation

Farm Bureau Life Insurance Company
Multi-line (life and property/casualty)
Arizona
Iowa
Kansas
Minnesota
Nebraska
New Mexico
South Dakota
Utah
Life only
Idaho
Montana
North Dakota
Oklahoma
Wisconsin
Wyoming
Farm Bureau Property & Casualty Insurance Company and Western Agricultural Insurance Company
Arizona
Iowa
Kansas
Minnesota
Nebraska
New Mexico
South Dakota
Utah

PRODUCTS/OPERATIONS

2015 Sales

	$ mil.	% of total
Life Insurance	409	57
Annuity	212	29
Gains on derivatives	10	1
Losses on investments	(2.7)	-
Corporate & other	93	13
Total	**722**	**100**

Selected Subsidiaries

Insurance
Farm Bureau Life Insurance Company
Noninsurance
5400 Holdings L.L.C.
FBL Assigned Benefit Company
FBL Financial Group Capital Trust
FBL Financial Group Capital Trust II
FBL Financial Services Inc.
FBL Investment Management Services Inc.
FBL Leasing Services Inc.
FBL Marketing Services L.L.C.

COMPETITORS

AIG
Allstate
American Equity Investment Life Holding Company
American Farmers & Ranchers Mutual Insurance Co.
COUNTRY Financial
Farm Family Holdings
Farmers & Merchants Investment
Great American Financial Resources
MetLife
Midland National Life
Nationwide
Prudential
State Farm
Thrivent Investment Management

HISTORICAL FINANCIALS

Company Type: Public

Income Statement

FYE: December 31

	ASSETS ($ mil.)	NET INCOME ($ mil.)	INCOME AS % OF ASSETS	EMPLOYEES
12/19	10,480	126	1.2%	1,751
12/18	9,833	93	1.0%	1,647
12/17	10,066	194	1.9%	1,692
12/16	9,566	107	1.1%	1,644
12/15	9,132	113	1.2%	1,637
Annual Growth	3.5%	2.7%	—	1.7%

2019 Year-End Financials

Debt ratio: 0.93%
Return on equity: 9.45%
Cash ($ mil.): 17
Current ratio: —
Long-term debt ($ mil.): —
No. of shares (mil.): 24
Dividends
Yield: 5.8%
Payout: 87.0%
Market value ($ mil.): 1,453

	STOCK PRICE ($) FY Close	P/E High/Low		PER SHARE ($) Earnings	Dividends	Book Value
12/19	58.93	14	10	5.09	3.42	60.24
12/18	65.65	23	17	3.75	3.34	47.90
12/17	69.65	10	8	7.75	3.26	55.71
12/16	78.15	19	13	4.28	3.68	47.73
12/15	63.64	15	11	4.53	3.60	45.73
Annual Growth	(1.9%)	—	—	3.0%	(1.3%)	7.1%

Federal Agricultural Mortgage Corp

Farmer Mac (Federal Agricultural Mortgage Corporation) is Fannie Mae and Freddie Mac's country cousin. Like its city-slicker kin it provides liquidity in its markets (agricultural real estate and rural housing mortgages) by buying loans from lenders and then securitizing the loans into Farmer Mac Guaranteed Securities. Farmer Mac buys both conventional loans and those guaranteed by the

US Department of Agriculture. Farmer Mac was created by Congress in 1987 to establish a secondary market for agricultural mortgage and rural utilities loans. It is a stockholder-owned publicly-traded corporation based in Washington DC with an underwriting office in Iowa.

Operations

Farmer Mac operates four segments: Farm & Ranch which accounted for 39% of revenue during 2015 purchases mortgage loans secured by first liens on agricultural real estate including part-time farms and rural housing; Institutional Credit (28% of revenue) which buys or guarantees general lender obligations secured by eligible pools of loans; the USDA Guarantees segment (18%) which buys USDA-backed agricultural rural development business and industry and community facilities loans; and Rural Utilities (10%) which buys mortgages tied to eligible rural utilities loans.The organization generates more than 90% of its revenue from interest income stemming from a roughly even mix of loans and backed loan securities. About 47% of its revenue came from interest on Farmer Mac Guaranteed or USDA securities during 2015 while another 41% came from interest on loans. The rest came from interest on other investments (5% of revenue) guarantee and commitment fees (5%) and gains on financial derivatives and hedging activities (1%).

Geographic Reach

The Washington DC-based group serves the US from satellite operations in Ames Iowa; Boise Idaho; Canton Michigan; Fresno California; Johnston Iowa; and Scottsdale Arizona.

Sales and Marketing

Farmer Mac markets its services personally and directly to agricultural lenders by participating regularly in events such as state and national banking conferences. It also has alliances with the American Bankers Association and the Independent Community Bankers of Alliances and has a business relationship with the members of the Farm Credit System.

Financial Performance

Farmer Mac's annual revenues have risen more than 25% since 2011 thanks to a stronger agricultural economy as well as product developments which have driven customer and overall loan asset growth over the years. Its annual profits have also trended higher but have fluctuated more due to the volatility of the gains it's made from financial derivatives hedging activities and other trading securities.

The group's revenue climbed 4% to $284 million during 2015 mostly thanks to double-digit interest income growth as its loan assets grew 12% to $3.96 billion and as its Farm & Ranch loans USDA Securities and AgVantage securities balances grew as well. Farmer Mac's non-interest income shrank 39% as it collected $37.4 million less in trading securities gains as it did in 2014.

Revenue growth and a decline in interest expenses in 2015 drove Farmer Mac's net income up 43% to $68.7 million. The lender's operating cash levels jumped 19% to $184 million as its cash-based earnings rose and as working capital increased with changes in other assets.

Strategy

Farmer Mac seeks to improve the availability of long-term credit at stable interest rates to rural communities. To this end its primary strategy for managing interest rate risk is to fund asset purchases with liabilities that have similar duration and cash flow characteristics so that they will perform similarly as interest rates change.

EXECUTIVES

President And Ceo, Timothy L. (Tim) Buzby, age 51, $643,750 total compensation
Evp Cfo And Treasurer, R. Dale Lynch, age 53, $375,950 total compensation
Svp Agricultural Finance, J. Curtis Covington, age 64
Svp General Counsel And Secretary, Stephen P. Mullery, age 53, $340,930 total compensation
Vice President Corporate Affairs, Chris Bohanon
Executive Vice President Chief Financial Officer, Dale Lynch
Senior Vice President Business Strategy And Financial Research, Brian Brinch
Chairman, Lowell L. Junkins, age 76
Vice Chairman, Myles J. Watts, age 69
Auditors: PricewaterhouseCoopers LLP

LOCATIONS

HQ: Federal Agricultural Mortgage Corp
1999 K Street, N.W., 4th Floor, Washington, DC 20006
Phone: 202 872-7700

PRODUCTS/OPERATIONS

2015 Sales

	$ mil.	% of total
Interest income		
Farmer Mac Guaranteed Securities and USDA Securities	134	47
Loans	117	41
Investments and cash equivalents	13	5
Noninterest income		
Guarantee and commitment fees	14	5
Gains on financial derivatives and hedging activities	2	1
Other	3	1
Total	**285**	**100**

2015 Sales

	% of total
Farm & Ranch	39
USDA Guarantees	28
Rural Utilities	18
Institutional Credit	10
Corporate	4
Reconciling Adjustments	1
Total	**100**

Selected Operations

Farm & Ranch (Farmer Mac I)
USDA Guarantees (Farmer Mac II)
Rural Utilities

COMPETITORS

AgFirst	Fannie Mae
AgStar	Farm Credit Services
AgriBank	of Mid-America
Bank of America	Freddie Mac
Citigroup	

HISTORICAL FINANCIALS

Company Type: Public

Income Statement

FYE: December 31

	ASSETS ($ mil.)	NET INCOME ($ mil.)	INCOME AS % OF ASSETS	EMPLOYEES
12/19	21,709	109	0.5%	103
12/18	18,694	108	0.6%	103
12/17	17,792	84	0.5%	88
12/16	15,606	77	0.5%	81
12/15	15,540	68	0.4%	71
Annual Growth	**8.7%**	**12.4%**	**—**	**9.7%**

2019 Year-End Financials

Debt ratio: 87.97%	No. of shares (mil.): 10
Return on equity: 14.12%	Dividends
Cash ($ mil.): 604	Yield: 3.3%
Current ratio: —	Payout: 32.2%
Long-term debt ($ mil.): —	Market value ($ mil.): 894

	STOCK PRICE ($) FY Close	P/E High/Low		PER SHARE ($) Earnings	Dividends	Book Value
12/19	83.50	10	7	8.69	2.80	74.62
12/18	60.44	11	6	8.83	2.32	70.54
12/17	78.24	12	8	6.60	1.44	66.69
12/16	57.27	10	4	5.97	1.04	61.05
12/15	31.57	8	5	4.19	0.64	51.79
Annual Growth	**27.5%**	**—**	**—**	**20.0%**	**44.6%**	**9.6%**

Federal Home Loan Bank New York

Federal Home Loan Bank of New York (FHLBNY) provides funds for residential mortgages and community development to more than 330 member banks savings and loans credit unions and life insurance companies in New York New Jersey Puerto Rico and the US Virgin Islands. One of a dozen Federal Home Loan Banks in the US it is cooperatively owned by its member institutions and supervised by the Federal Housing Finance Agency. FHLBNY like others in the system is privately capitalized; it receives no taxpayer funding. The bank instead raises funds mainly by issuing debt instruments in the capital markets.

Operations

FHLBNY is a secured lender that requires collateral for its advances which are typically used by members to underwrite residential mortgages or to invest in US Treasury and agency securities mortgage-backed securities and other real estate-related assets.

A large part of FHLBNY's business is in making collateralized loans or advances to members. It serves the public through its mortgage programs. Three members — Citibank (25%) Met Life (14%) and New York Community Bank (11%) — accounted for half of total advances.

Geographic Reach

Based in New York FHLBNY serves not only New York but New Jersey Puerto Rico and the US Virgin Islands.

Sales and Marketing

FHLBNY caters to more than 330 member banks credit unions life insurance companies and savings and loans.

Financial Performance

Revenue dropped by 14% to $801 million in fiscal 2013 from 2012's $934.9 million. FHLBNY attributes the decline to a decrease in interest income and other income. Net income also dropped some 16% in 2013 to $304.6 million vs. $360.7 million in 2012. It attributes net income decreases to declining revenue and rising other expenses. Operating cash flow decreased in fiscal 2013 to $525.6 million compared to 2012's $678.9 million.

Strategy

Credit unions are a possible area of growth for FHLBNY. The bank has identified more than 50 credit unions and banks that are not members but are eligible. To be under consideration an institution must have more than $50 million in assets ($100 million for banks) be an established wholesale lender maintain a high deposit-to-loan ratio and have management that has done business with an FHLB in the past.

Beginning in 2014 it's also funding — with the help of $35.5 million in subsidies — 48 affordable housing initiatives throughout New Jersey New

York Puerto Rico the US Virgin Islands Florida Maryland and Pennsylvania. The effort involves the creation or rehabilitation of more than 3000 affordable housing units.

EXECUTIVES

Vice President Director Of Human Resources, Mildred Tse-Gonzalez
Senior Vice President Acting Chief Risk Officer, Melody Feinberg
Assistant Vice President, Claudia Kim
Vice President, Edward Samson
Vice President Calling Office, Alfred O'connell
Vice President Director Of Sales, Tom Settino
Senior Vice President, Phil Scott
Vice President, Eugene Khesin
Assistant Vice President Financial Risk Management, Kimberly Whitenack
Senior Vice President, Jonathan West
Vp Director Of, Muriel Brunken
Auditors: PricewaterhouseCoopers LLP

LOCATIONS

HQ: Federal Home Loan Bank New York
101 Park Avenue, New York, NY 10178
Phone: 212 681-6000
Web: www.fhlbny.com

PRODUCTS/OPERATIONS

2013 Sales

	$ mil.	% of total
Interest		
Advances	444	55
Long-term securities	244	30
Mortgage loans held for portfolio	68	9
Available-for-sale securities	16	2
Other	14	2
Non-interest	13	2
Total	**801**	**100**

HISTORICAL FINANCIALS

Company Type: Public

Income Statement				FYE: December 31
	ASSETS ($ mil.)	NET INCOME ($ mil.)	INCOME AS % OF ASSETS	EMPLOYEES
12/19	162,062	472	0.3%	342
12/18	144,381	560	0.4%	314
12/17	158,918	479	0.3%	308
12/16	143,606	401	0.3%	280
12/15	123,248	414	0.3%	273
Annual Growth	7.1%	3.3%	—	5.8%

2019 Year-End Financials

Debt ratio: 48.60%
Return on equity: 6.19%
Cash ($ mil.): 603
Current ratio: —
Long-term debt ($ mil.): —
No. of shares (mil.): 57
Dividends
  Yield: —
  Payout: 76.1%
Market value ($ mil.): —

Federal Home Loan Bank Of Cincinnati

Auditors: PricewaterhouseCoopers LLP

LOCATIONS

HQ: Federal Home Loan Bank Of Cincinnati
600 Atrium Two, P.O Box 598, Cincinnati, OH 45201-0598
Phone: 513 852-7500
Web: www.fhlbcin.com

HISTORICAL FINANCIALS

Company Type: Public

Income Statement				FYE: December 31
	ASSETS ($ mil.)	NET INCOME ($ mil.)	INCOME AS % OF ASSETS	EMPLOYEES
12/19	93,491	276	0.3%	234
12/18	99,202	339	0.3%	229
12/17	106,895	313	0.3%	226
12/16	104,635	268	0.3%	211
12/15	118,796	248	0.2%	203
Annual Growth	(5.8%)	2.6%	—	3.6%

2019 Year-End Financials

Debt ratio: 93.62%
Return on equity: 5.65%
Cash ($ mil.): 570
Current ratio: —
Long-term debt ($ mil.): —
No. of shares (mil.): 33
Dividends
  Yield: —
  Payout: 74.0%
Market value ($ mil.): —

Federal Home Loan Bank Of Dallas

Auditors: PricewaterhouseCoopers LLP

LOCATIONS

HQ: Federal Home Loan Bank Of Dallas
8500 Freeport Parkway South, Suite 600, Irving, TX 75063-2547
Phone: 214 441-8500
Web: www.fhlb.com

HISTORICAL FINANCIALS

Company Type: Public

Income Statement				FYE: December 31
	ASSETS ($ mil.)	NET INCOME ($ mil.)	INCOME AS % OF ASSETS	EMPLOYEES
12/19	75,381	227	0.3%	203
12/18	72,773	198	0.3%	197
12/17	68,524	150	0.2%	205
12/16	58,212	79	0.1%	218
12/15	42,083	67	0.2%	207
Annual Growth	15.7%	35.6%	—	(0.5%)

2019 Year-End Financials

Debt ratio: 47.42%
Return on equity: 6.01%
Cash ($ mil.): 1,690
Current ratio: —
Long-term debt ($ mil.): —
No. of shares (mil.): 24
Dividends
  Yield: —
  Payout: 33.4%
Market value ($ mil.): —

Federal Home Loan Bank Of Des Moines

Auditors: PricewaterhouseCoopers, LLP

LOCATIONS

HQ: Federal Home Loan Bank Of Des Moines
909 Locust Street, Des Moines, IA 50309
Phone: 515 412-2100
Web: www.fhlbdm.com

HISTORICAL FINANCIALS

Company Type: Public

Income Statement				FYE: December 31
	ASSETS ($ mil.)	NET INCOME ($ mil.)	INCOME AS % OF ASSETS	EMPLOYEES
12/19	129,603	384	0.3%	379
12/18	146,515	460	0.3%	372
12/17	145,099	518	0.4%	351
12/16	180,605	649	0.4%	307
12/15	137,381	131	0.1%	279
Annual Growth	(1.4%)	30.8%	—	8.0%

2019 Year-End Financials

Debt ratio: 93.43%
Return on equity: 5.38%
Cash ($ mil.): 1,030
Current ratio: —
Long-term debt ($ mil.): —
No. of shares (mil.): 45
Dividends
  Yield: —
  Payout: 70.0%
Market value ($ mil.): —

Federal Home Loan Bank Of San Francisco

The city by the bay is the home to the Federal Home Loan Bank of San Francisco one ofÂ a dozenÂ regional banks in the Federal Home Loan Bank System chartered by Congress inÂ 1932 to provide credit to residential mortgage lenders. TheÂ government-sponsored enterpriseÂ is privately owned by its members which include some 400 commercial banks credit unions industrial loan companies savings and loans insurance companies and housing associatesÂ headquartered in Arizona California and Nevada. The bank links members to worldwide capital markets which provide them with low-cost funding. Members then pass these advances along to their customers in the form of affordable home mortgage and economic development loans.

EXECUTIVES

Senior Vice President Chief Banking Officer, Stephen P Traynor
Vice President Secured And Unsecured Credit Risk Management, Reimund Sauer
Vice President Model Validation, Michael Roginsky
Assistant Vice President Strategic Solutions And Architecture, Gary Wells
Assistant Vice President Portfolio And Derivatives Operations, Gwen Hill
Assistant Vice President Compliance, Jamie Leong
Vice President Solution Delivery, Michael Rich
Avp Model Validation, Wen Zheng
Vice President Secondary Marketing, Michael Roth
Assistant Vice President Collateral Risk Management, Douglas Aguilar
Vice President Business Continuity Management And Corporate Services, Sarah Salk
Assistant Vice President, Aashish Khatri
Vice President Senior Human Resources Business Partner, Barbara Waite
Assistant Vice President Hris Payroll, Joe Troiano
Vice President Head Of Total Rewards, Eric Grove
Vice President And Treasurer, Tony Ruscitti
Auditors: PricewaterhouseCoopers LLP

LOCATIONS

HQ: Federal Home Loan Bank Of San Francisco
333 Bush Street, Suite 2700, San Francisco, CA 94104
Phone: 415 616-1000
Web: www.fhlbsf.com

PRODUCTS/OPERATIONS

2013

	$ mil.	% of total
Interest income	1,086	97
Other income	5	3
Total	**1,091**	**100**

HISTORICAL FINANCIALS

Company Type: Public

Income Statement			FYE: December 31	
	ASSETS ($ mil.)	NET INCOME ($ mil.)	INCOME AS % OF ASSETS	EMPLOYEES
12/19	106,842	327	0.3%	282
12/18	109,326	360	0.3%	282
12/17	123,385	376	0.3%	287
12/16	91,941	712	0.8%	274
12/15	85,707	638	0.7%	263
Annual Growth	**5.7%**	**(15.4%)**	**—**	**1.8%**

2019 Year-End Financials

Debt ratio: 92.42%
Return on equity: 4.93%
Cash ($ mil.): 2,387
Current ratio: —
Long-term debt ($ mil.): —
No. of shares (mil.): 30
Dividends
  Yield: —
  Payout: 63.0%
Market value ($ mil.): —

Federal Reserve Bank of Atlanta, Dist. No. 6

One of 12 regional banks in the Federal Reserve System the Federal Reserve Bank of Atlanta oversees Fed member banks and thrifts and their holding companies throughout the Southeast including Alabama Florida Georgia and parts of Louisiana Mississippi and Tennessee. It conducts examinations and investigations of member institutions distributes cash issues savings bonds and Treasury securities and assists the Fed in setting monetary policy such as interest rates. The bank also processes checks and acts as a clearinghouse for payments between banks. Fed Reserve Banks are independent arms within the government and return earnings (gleaned mostly from investments in government bonds) to the US Treasury.

Operations

Of the 12 regional banks in the Federal Reserve System only the Atlanta bank processes both paper and electronic checks for the system.

Financial Performance

In 2012 FRB Atlanta reported about $5.5 billion in total current income about 7% of the $81.6 billion in total income for the Federal Reserve System.

Company Background

The Federal Reserve Bank of Atlanta was established in 1914.

EXECUTIVES

Senior Vice President Supervision And Regulation, William Estes
First Vp And Coo, Marie C. Gooding
Evp, Cheryl L. Venable
Evp, David E. Altig
President And Ceo, Raphael W. Bostic
Evp, Michael Johnson
Vice President Marketing, Anita Brown
Vice President, Michael Chriszt
Assistant Vice President Systems, Brad Joiner
Assistant Vp Macropolicy And Research Economist And Policy Adviser, Tao Zha
Vice President And General Auditor, Brian Bowling
Vice President Marketing, Rob Lilly
Vice President, Christina Wilson
Assistant Vice President, Gregory Fuller
Vice President Marketing, Ken Willis
Assistant Vice President, Robert Hawkins
Vp Finance, Elizabeth Bibby
Assistant Vp Check Function Office, Charles Weems
Vice President Marketing, Lane Smith
Senior Vice President Retail Payments Office, Blake Lyons
Vice President In Charge, Daron Peschel
Assistant Vice President Of Business Development, Evette Jones
Vice President, Nell Campbell
Vice President Of Regional Research, John Robertson
Vice President, Suzanna Costello
Assistant Vice President, Allen Stanley
Assistant Vice President, Stephen Levy
Vice President Marketing, Christopher Oakley
Assistant Vice President, Annella Campbell-drake
Assistant Vice President, Jeffrey Schiele
Vice President, Mine Yucel
Vice President Human Resources, Tammy Cummings
Vice President Sales And Marketing, Janice Angus-foster
Assistant Vice President, Kathryn Hinton
V.p, John Branigin
Vice President, Cindy Rasche
Svp Cio Ciso, Russell Eubanks
Vice President, Kevin Jansen
Assistant Vice President, Michael Williams
Vice President, Sheryl Britsch
Vice President Operations, Ken Wilc
Vice President Information Technology, Gregory Johnston
Assistant Vice President, Shilpa Dutt
Assistant Vice President, William Wheeler
Senior Vice President, Keith Melton
Senior Vice President And Chief Audit Executive, Azher Abbasi
Assistant Vice President, Paula Armstrong
Assistant Vice President, Jim Fuchs
Vice President Of Service Management Operations, Lina Gladstein
Vice President And Regional Economist, Rae Rosen
Assistant Vice President, Christine Johnson
Senior Vice President, Chris Haley
Assistant Vice President, Michael Coldwell
Assistant Vice President, Maria Massei-rosato
Assistant Vice President, Ken Townsend
Assistant Vice President, Jonathan Atkinson
Assistant Vice President, Lisa Gravely
Vice President, Ann Worthy
Deputy Chairman, Michael J. (Mike) Jackson
Deputy Chairman, Thomas A. (Tom) Fanning
Board Member, Lee Thomas
Auditors: KPMG LLP

LOCATIONS

HQ: Federal Reserve Bank of Atlanta, Dist. No. 6
1000 Peachtree Street, N.E., Atlanta, GA 30309-4470
Phone: 404 498-8500
Web: www.frbatlanta.org

HISTORICAL FINANCIALS

Company Type: Public

Income Statement				FYE: December 31
	REVENUE ($ mil.)	NET INCOME ($ mil.)	NET PROFIT MARGIN	EMPLOYEES
12/19	7,042	(26)	—	—
12/18	6,948	(138)	—	—
12/17	6,971	48	0.7%	—
12/16	6,502	66	1.0%	—
12/15	6,562	(992)	—	—
Annual Growth	**1.8%**	**—**	**—**	**—**

2019 Year-End Financials

Debt ratio: 76.61%
Return on equity: (-1.24%)
Cash ($ mil.): 312,947
Current ratio: 4.41
Long-term debt ($ mil.): 243,959
No. of shares (mil.): 31
Dividends
  Yield: —
  Payout: —
Market value ($ mil.): —

Federal Reserve Bank of New York, Dist. No. 2

The Federal Reserve Bank of New York is the largest in the Federal Reserve System to oversee US bank activities. It issues currency clears check drawn and lends to banks in its district. In addition to the duties it shares with twelve other regional Federal Reserve Banks the New York Fed trades US government securities to regulate the money supply intervenes on foreign exchange markets and stores monetary gold for foreign central banks and governments. The New York Fed's district is relatively small (made up of New York Puerto Rico the US Virgin Islands northern New Jersey and Fairfield County Connecticut) but the bank is the largest in the Federal Reserve System in assets and volume of transactions.

Operations

Secured in a vault 80 feet below street level in the New York Fed's Manhattan headquarters is billions of dollars worth of gold of the world's official monetary gold reserves. The vault rests on Manhattan Island's bedrock considered to be one of the few foundations adequate enough to support the weight of the vault and its contents.

Federal Reserve Bank of New York provides variety of services and operations include participating in formulating and conducting monetary; transfers of funds automated clearinghouse and check collection distributing coin and currency; performing fiscal agency functions for the U.S. Department of the Treasury certain federal agencies and other entities; serving as the federal government's bank; providing short-term loans to depository institutions; serving consumers and communities by providing educational materials and information regarding financial consumer protection rights and laws; and supervising bank holding companies state member banks savings and loan holding companies U.S. offices of foreign banking organizations corporations and certain financial market utilities.

Geographic Reach

Federal Reserve Bank of New York headquarters are located in Liberty Street New York United States.

Company Background

The U.S. Congress founded Federal Reserve Bank of New York in 1913. In additions the Act of 1913 provided the establishment of the Federal Reserve Banks.

EXECUTIVES

Evp And Head Emerging Markets And International Affairs Group, Terrence J. Checki
Executive Vice President, Dino Kos
First Vice President, Christine M. Cumming
Executive Vice President, Roseann Stichnoth
Executive Vice President Risk Group, Sandra C. (Sandy) Krieger
Evp And Head Research And Statistics Group, James J. McAndrews
Evp Markets Group, Brian P. Sack
Evp And General Auditor, Edward C. Smith
Evp Corporate, Edward F. Murphy
President And Ceo, William C. Dudley
Executive Vice President, William T. Christie
Executive Vice President, Susan W. Mink
Evp And Head Communications, Krishna Guha
Executive Vice President Markets Group, Simon M. Potter
Chief Of Staff And Vice President, James P. Bergin
Executive Vice President And Chief Risk Officer, Joshua Rosenberg
Senior Vp, Stephanie Heller
Assistant Vice President, Eileen Goodman
Senior Vice President Financial Institution Supervision Group, Caroline Frawley
Assistant Vice President Of Financial Services Gro, Christopher Armstrong
Senior Vice President Information Security, James Mahon
Assistant Vice President Financial Management And Discount Window, Maria Grac Ambrosio
Senior Vp, Michael Recupero
Assistant Vice President, Rona Stein
Assistant Vice President Of Legal Group, Sean Omalley
Assistant Vice President, Sarah Adelson
Assistant Vice President Of Financial Institution Supervision Group, Brian Hefferle
Assistant Vice President Of Financial Institution Supervision Group, Louis Braunstein
Vice President Director Environmental Affairs, Tom Buhse
Assistant Vice President, Keith Pulsifer
Senior Executive Specialist Executive Vice President, Marlene Williams
Vice President And Counsel In The Legal Group, Michele Kalstein

Assistant Vice President, Thomas Reilly
Assistant Vice President Of Financial Institution Supervision Group, Glen Reppy
Senior Vice President, Nancy Bercovici
Assistant Vice President, Patrick Coyne
Vice President, Haeran Kim
Vice President Information Technology, Jeffrey C Blye
Vice President, Jack Gutt
Assistant Vice President Of Legal Group, Brett Phillips
First Vice President, Jamie B Stewart
Assistant Vice President, GERALD MCCRINK
Assistant Vice President, Suzanne Elio
Senior Vice President And Chief Information Security Officer, Joeseph Leonard
Executive Vice President And Chief Technology And Strategy Officer, James Lammers
Avp Technology Group Richmond, Nicholas Baronian
Assistant Vice President Director Of Community Development Analysis, Claire Kramer Mills
Chairman, Lee C. Bollinger
Chairman, Emily K. Rafferty
Secretary, Kyla Whitt
Auditors: KPMG LLP

LOCATIONS

HQ: Federal Reserve Bank of New York, Dist. No. 2
33 Liberty Street, New York, NY 10045-0001
Phone: 212 720-5000
Web: www.newyorkfed.org

Selected Offices
Buffalo New York
East Rutherford New Jersey
New York City
Utica New York

HISTORICAL FINANCIALS
Company Type: Public

Income Statement				FYE: December 31
	REVENUE ($ mil.)	NET INCOME ($ mil.)	NET PROFIT MARGIN	EMPLOYEES
12/19	56,535	226	0.4%	—
12/18	62,509	(652)	—	—
12/17	65,090	(503)	—	—
12/16	64,509	328	0.5%	—
12/15	68,534	(5,604)	—	—
Annual Growth	(4.7%)	—	—	—

2019 Year-End Financials

Debt ratio: 25.92%	No. of shares (mil.): 213
Return on equity: 1.78%	Dividends
Cash ($ mil.): 2,240,588	Yield: —
Current ratio: 1.72	Payout: —
Long-term debt ($ mil.): 587,443	Market value ($ mil.): —

Federal Reserve Bank of San Francisco, Dist. No. 12

One of 12 regional banks in the Federal Reserve System the Federal Reserve Bank of San Francisco through five branch offices oversees hundreds of banks and thrifts in nine western states and American Samoa Guam and the Northern Mariana Islands - the largest of the twelve districts. It provides short-term loans to depository institutions distributes money issues savings bonds and Treasury securities and assists the Federal Reserve in setting monetary policy. The bank also processes checks and acts as a clearinghouse for payments between banks. Federal Reserve Banks are not-for-profit and return earnings (mostly from investments in government bonds) to the US Treasury.

Operations

The Federal Reserve Bank performs five general functions to promote the effective operation of the US economy and more generally the public interest. The Federal Reserve conducts the nation's monetary policy to promote maximum employment stable prices and moderate long-term interest rates in the US economy; promotes the stability of the financial system and seeks to minimize and contain systemic risks through active monitoring and engagement in the US and abroad; promotes the safety and soundness of individual financial institutions and monitors their impact on the financial system as a whole; fosters payment and settlement system safety and efficiency through services to the banking industry and the US government that facilitate US-dollar transactions and payments; and promotes consumer protection and community development through consumer-focused supervision and examination research and analysis of emerging consumer issues and trends community economic development activities and the administration of consumer laws and regulations.

Over 55% of sales were generated from net treasury securities while about 45% comes from net federal agency and government-sponsored enterprise mortgage-backed securities.

Geographic Reach

The bank headquartered in San Francisco California oversees the Twelfth Federal Reserve District which includes the nine western states of Alaska Arizona California Hawaii Idaho Nevada Oregon Utah and Washington and also the American Samoa Guam and the Commonwealth of the Northern Mariana Islands.

Branch offices reside in Los Angeles; Portland Oregon; Salt Lake City; and Seattle. It also has a cash processing center in Phoenix.

EXECUTIVES

Vice President, John Fernald
Svp And Cio Seattle Branch, Mark A. Gould
President And Ceo, John C. Williams
Svp, Teresa M. Curran
Svp Information And Technology And Cio, Gopa Kumar
Vice President Microeconomic And Macroeconomic Research, Sylvain Leduc
Group Vice President, Stanley Crisp
Group Vice President, Fred Furlong
Group Vice President, Reuven Glick
Group Vice President, Clifford Croxall
Senior Vice Presiden, Stephen Hoffman
Group Vice President, Patrick Loncar
Vice President, Summer Cole
Vice President, Thomas Cunningham
Group Vice President, Mongkha Pavlick
Group Vice President, Frederick T Furlong
Vice President Microeconomic And Macroeconomic Research, Scar Jord
Vice President Research, Robert Valletta
Vice President, Dan Wilson
Executive Vice President, Elaine S Couture
Group Vice President, David Bohm
Chairman, Roy A. Vallee
Deputy Chairman, Alexander R. (Alex) Mehran
Auditors: KPMG LLP

HQ: Federal Reserve Bank of San Francisco, Dist. No. 12
101 Market Street, San Francisco, CA 94105
Phone: 415 974-2000
Web: www.frbsf.org

HISTORICAL FINANCIALS

Company Type: Public

Income Statement				FYE: December 31
	REVENUE ($ mil.)	NET INCOME ($ mil.)	NET PROFIT MARGIN	EMPLOYEES
12/19	12,188	133	1.1%	—
12/18	13,978	(330)	—	—
12/17	14,660	116	0.8%	—
12/16	13,437	51	0.4%	—
12/15	12,696	(2,426)	—	—
Annual Growth	(1.0%)	—	—	—

2019 Year-End Financials

Debt ratio: 45.77%
Return on equity: 2.32%
Cash ($ mil.): 479,981
Current ratio: 1.88
Long-term debt ($ mil.): 226,783

No. of shares (mil.): 94
Dividends
 Yield: —
 Payout: —
Market value ($ mil.): —

Federal Reserve System

Where do banks go when they need a loan? To the Federal Reserve System which sets the discount interest rate the base rate at which its member banks may borrow. Known as the Fed the system oversees a network of 12 Federal Reserve Banks located in major US cities; these in turn regulate banks in their districts and ensure they maintain adequate reserves. The Fed also clears money transfers issues currency and buys or sells government securities to regulate the money supply. Through its powerful New York bank the Fed conducts foreign currency transactions trades on the world market to support the US dollar's value and stores gold for foreign governments and international agencies.

Operations

By setting the discount rate and the federal funds rate (the rate at which banks borrow from each other) the Board influences the pace of lending and many believe the pace of the economy itself. In response to the economic downturn in 2008 the Fed aggressively cut the discount interest rate in an effort to jump-start the US economy.

Fed board members are appointed by the US president and confirmed by the Senate for one-time 14-year terms staggered at two-year intervals to prevent political stacking. Seven governors comprise the majority of the 12-person Federal Open Market Committee which determines monetary policy. The five remaining members are reserve bank presidents who rotate in one-year terms with New York always holding a place. National member banks must own stock in their Federal Reserve Bank though it is optional for state-chartered banks.

A seven-member Board of Governors oversees the Fed's activities. The board was chaired by Alan Greenspan from the Reagan administration until 2006. As chairman under four different presidents Greenspan wielded more power than perhaps any Fed chief in history and securities markets rose and fell on his every word. Greenspan was replaced by former chairman of President George W. Bush's Council of Economic Advisers and Fed board member Ben Bernanke who himself was replaced by former Vice Chair of the Board of Governors Jenet L. Yellen on February 3 2014.

Geographic Reach

The company's banks are located in Boston New York Philadelphia Cleveland Richmond Atlanta Chicago St. Louis Minneapolis Kansas City Dallas and San Francisco.

Financial Performance

The Reserve Banks' income in 2015 was $114 billion. The total expenses for the entire Federal Reserve System for 2015 were $13 billion.

HISTORY

When New York's Knickerbocker Trust Company failed in 1907 it brought on a panic that was stemmed by J. P. Morgan who strong-armed his fellow bankers into supporting shaky New York banks. The incident showed the need for a central bank.

Morgan's actions sparked fears of his economic power and spurred congressional efforts to establish a central bank. After a six-year struggle between Eastern money interests and populist monetary reformers the 1913 Federal Reserve Act was passed. Twelve Federal Reserve districts were created but New York's economic might ensured it would be the most powerful.

New York bank head Benjamin Strong dominated the Fed in the 1920s countering the glut of European gold flooding the US in 1923 by selling securities from the Fed's portfolio. After he died in 1928 the Fed couldn't stabilize prices. Such difficulty along with low rates encouraging members to use Fed loans for stock speculation helped set the stage for 1929's crash.

During the Depression and WWII the Fed yielded to the demands of the Treasury to buy bonds. But after WWII it sought independence using Congress to help free it from Treasury demands. This effort was led by chairman William McChesney Martin with the assistance of New York bank president Alan Sproul (also a rival for the chairmanship). Martin diluted Sproul's influence by governing by consensus with the other bank leaders.

The Fed managed the economy successfully in the postwar boom but it was stymied by inflation in the late 1960s. In the early 1970s the New York bank also faced the collapse of the fixed currency exchange-rate system and the growth of currency trading. Its role as foreign currency trader became even more crucial as the dollar's value eroded amid rising oil prices and a slowing economy.

The US suffered from double-digit inflation in 1979 as President Jimmy Carter appointed New York Fed president Paul Volcker as chairman. Volcker believing that raising interest rates a few points would not suffice allowed the banks to raise their discount rates and increased bank reserve requirements to reduce the money supply. By the time inflation eased Ronald Reagan was president.

During the 1980s and 1990s US budget fights limited options for controlling the economy through spending decisions so the Fed's actions became more important. Its higher profile brought calls for more access to its decision-making processes. Alan Greenspan took over as chairman in 1987 after being designated by Reagan (and reappointed by presidents George H. W. Bush Bill Clinton and George W. Bush). He stepped down during the second Bush administration and was replaced by Ben Bernanke.

While the US economy seemed immune to the Asian currency crisis of 1997 and 1998 the Federal Reserve remained relatively quiescent. But when Russia defaulted on some of its bonds in 1998 leading to the near-collapse of hedge fund Long-Term Capital Management the New York Federal Reserve Bank brokered a bailout by the fund's lenders and investors.

This led in 1999 to new guidelines for banks' risk management. The next year the Fed faced up to the Internet age taking a look at e-banking supervision. After raising interest rates to stave off inflation during the go-go late 1990s the Fed cut rates an unprecedented 11 times in 2001 (to a 40-year low of 1.75%) to help spur the flagging post-boom economy.

Rate changes and subsequent economic changes continued with a low of 1% in 2003. In all rates were adjusted a total of 18 times between 2002 and 2006.

In 2008 the US faced an economic crisis as severe as any seen since the Great Depression that claimed numerous victims including Bear Stearns (the Fed brokered and assisted its purchase by JP-Morgan Chase) and Lehman Brothers. Together with former Secretary of the Treasury Henry Paulson chairman Ben Bernanke pushed for the passage of a $700 billion rescue plan — the largest in history. Through the plan the government purchased toxic assets including troubled mortgages and distressed properties. As his predecessor did during the economic downturn earlier this decade Bernanke also aggressively cut the discount interest rate in an effort to jump-start the economy.

EXECUTIVES

President Federal Reserve Bank Of Dallas, Robert S. (Rob) Kaplan
President Federal Reserve Bank Of Atlanta, Dennis P. Lockhart
President Federal Reserve Bank Of Chicago, Charles L. (Charlie) Evans
President Federal Reserve Bank Of Richmond, Jeffrey M. (Jeff) Lacker
President Federal Reserve Bank Of San Francisco, Janet L. Yellen
President Federal Reserve Bank Of Boston, Eric S. Rosengren
President And Ceo Federal Reserve Bank Of St. Louis, James B. Bullard
President Federal Reserve Bank Of New York, William C. Dudley
President Federal Reserve Bank Of Minneapolis, Neel T. Kashkari
President Federal Reserve Bank Of Philadelphia, Patrick T. Harker
President Federal Reserve Bank Of Kansas City, Ester L. George
President Federal Reserve Bank Of San Francisco, John C. Williams
President Federal Reserve Bank Of Cleveland, Loretta J. Mester
Vice President, Paul Rimmereid
Vice President Treasury Services, Harvey Mitchell
Vice President, Patrick Defontnouvelle
Vice President And Discount Officer, Vish P Viswanathan
Assistant Vice President, Thomas Weber
Vice Chairman, Stanley Fischer
Secretary, Ann Misback
Board Of Governors, Kelvin Chen
Auditors: KPMG LLP

LOCATIONS

HQ: Federal Reserve System
20th Street and Constitution Avenue N.W.,
Washington, DC 20551
Phone: 202 452-3245　　　**Fax:** 202 728-5886
Web: www.federalreserve.gov

HISTORICAL FINANCIALS

Company Type: Public

Income Statement   FYE: December 31

	REVENUE ($ mil.)	NET INCOME ($ mil.)	NET PROFIT MARGIN	EMPLOYEES
12/19	103,846	565	0.5%	—
12/18	113,120	(2,218)	—	—
12/17	116,764	133	0.1%	—
12/16	112,207	894	0.8%	—
12/15	113,468	(17,195)	—	—
Annual Growth	(2.2%)	—	—	—

2019 Year-End Financials

Debt ratio: 42.16%
Return on equity: 1.45%
Cash ($ mil.): 4,106,951
Current ratio: 2.04
Long-term debt ($ mil.): 1,759,427
No. of shares (mil.): 633
Dividends
Yield: —
Payout: —
Market value ($ mil.): —

FEDERAL-MOGUL HOLDINGS LLC

Auditors: GRANT THORNTON LLP SOUTHFIELD

LOCATIONS

HQ: FEDERAL-MOGUL HOLDINGS LLC
27300 W 11 MILE RD # 101, SOUTHFIELD, MI 480346193
Phone: 248 354-7700
Web: WWW.FEDERALMOGUL.COM

HISTORICAL FINANCIALS

Company Type: Private

Income Statement   FYE: December 31

	REVENUE ($ mil.)	NET INCOME ($ mil.)	NET PROFIT MARGIN	EMPLOYEES
12/16	7,434	90	1.2%	53,700
12/15	7,419	(104)	—	—
12/14	7,317	(161)	—	—
Annual Growth	0.8%	—	—	—

FedEx Corp

Holding company FedEx Corporation operates through subsidiaries FedEx Express FedEx Ground and FedEx Freight among others. Its FedEx Express unit is the world's largest express transportation provider to more than 220 countries and territories from about 2200 FedEx Office shops. It maintains a fleet of about 680 aircraft and over 183000 r vehicles. To complement the express delivery business FedEx Ground provides small-package ground delivery in North America and less-than-truckload (LTL) carrier FedEx Freight hauls larger shipments. FedEx Office stores offer a variety of document-related and other business services and serve as retail hubs for other FedEx units. In addition its TNT Express subsidiary is an international express transportation and small-package ground delivery company. About 70% of revenue is generated in the US.

Operations

FedEx offers a broad portfolio of transportation e-commerce and business services through its subsidiaries which operate independently and are managed collaboratively under the FedEx brand.

FedEx Express generating about 50% of revenue is the world's largest express transportation company. Its business operations provide fast time-definite delivery of packages and freight to more than 220 countries and territories through an integrated global network.

FedEx Ground generates nearly 35% of revenue and provides small-package ground delivery services primarily in North America. This segment includes FedEx SmartPost a business-to-consumer package delivery business that uses the US Postal Service for final mile delivery.

FedEx Freight (around 10%) offers LTL freight services throughout North America as well as Puerto Rico and the US Virgin Islands. (LTL carriers consolidate freight from multiple shippers into a single truckload.) This unit's offerings include FedEx Freight Priority and FedEx Freight Economy.

FedEx Services provides sales and marketing technology support and other back-office functions such as billing and collection and customer service for other FedEx divisions. This unit includes FedEx Office and Print Services (document and business services for FedEx Express and FedEx Ground shipping services). The remainder of sales comprises other operations including logistics and supply chain services brokerage and freight forwarding.

Geographic Reach

FedEx operates in or delivers goods to more than 220 countries and territories. Its primary sorting facility is located in Memphis TN and it has a second national hub in Indianapolis IN. FedEx Express operates additional US hubs in Texas New Jersey California North Carolina Illinois and Alaska. It also has major hubs in France Germany China and Japan. The US accounts for roughly 70% of net sales annually.

FedEx's headquarter is located in Memphis Tennessee.

Sales and Marketing

FedEx promotes its brands through television print digital advertising sponsorships and special events. It also serves customers in airports worldwide. The company's advertising and promotional expenses were $427 million in 2020 $468 million in 2019 and $442 million in 2018.

Financial Performance

FedEx has achieved several consecutive years of unprecedented growth with revenue increasing 37% since fiscal 2016 (ended May 31).

Revenue decreased 1% to $69.2 billion in 2020 primarily due to the elimination of business from a large customer and the impact from macroeconomic weakness including the impact of the COVID-19 pandemic.

The company's net income increased $746 million to $1.3 billion in 2019 compared to $540 million in the prior year. The increase was primarily due to lower other expenses with $748 million in 2019 from $3.8 billion in the prior year.

Cash at the end of 2020 was $4.9 billion an increase of $2.6 billion from the prior year. Cash from operations contributed $5.1 billion to the coffers while investing activities used $5.8 billion mainly for capital expenditures. Financing activities provided $3.4 billion from proceeds from debt issuances.

Strategy

FedEx has developed a unique business strategy whereby their companies compete collectively operate independently and manage collaboratively which allows them to provide a broad portfolio of transportation e-commerce and business services to their customers. FedEx's companies compete collectively by standing as one brand worldwide and speaking with one voice; they operate independently by focusing on their independent networks to meet distinct customer needs; and they manage collaboratively by working together to sustain loyal relationships with their workforce customers and investors.

The company's "compete collectively operate independently manage collaboratively" strategy allows them to manage their business as a portfolio in the long-term best interest of the enterprise not a particular operating company.

Mergers and Acquisitions

In mid-2019 FedEx Express acquired Israel's FC Express the international express division of Flying Cargo Group. FC Express (previously a FedEx licensee) provides logistics warehousing fulfillment and distribution service in Israel. FedEx plans to incorporate FC Express into its international operations along with TNT.

HISTORY

From his undergraduate classes at Yale and his experience as a charter airplane pilot Fred Smith got the idea that increased automation of business processes would create the need for a reliable overnight delivery service and he presented his case in a term paper in 1965. After serving in the Marine Corps in Vietnam Smith began raising money to develop the overnight delivery idea. He founded Federal Express in 1971 with $4 million inherited from his father and $80 million from investors. Overnight and second-day delivery to two dozen US cities began in 1973.

Several factors contributed to FedEx's early success: Airlines turned their focus from parcels to passengers; United Parcel Service (UPS) union workers went on strike in 1974; and competitor REA Express went bankrupt. FedEx went public in 1978.

EXECUTIVES

Evp Market Development And Corporate Communications, T. Michael Glenn, age 64, $850,028 total compensation

Evp And Cfo, Alan B. Graf, age 64, $920,840 total compensation

Chairman And Ceo, Frederick W. (Fred) Smith, age 76, $1,279,632 total compensation

President And Coo, David J. Bronczek, age 66, $960,936 total compensation

Vp Human Resources, Beth Casteel

Senior Vice President Strategic Marketing Planning And Analysis, James Webb
Evp Information Services And Cio, Robert B. (Rob) Carter, age 60, $778,216 total compensation
Coo Fedex Express; President International, Michael L. Ducker, age 67
Evp General Counsel And Secretary, Christine P. Richards, age 65, $617,640 total compensation
President And Ceo Fedex Express, David L. Cunningham
President And Ceo Fedex Ground, Henry J. Maier
Vice President Customer Services, Casey Zettler
Svp Chief Hr And Diversity Officer Fedex Express, Shannon Brown
Vice President Wro, Betty Hale
Vice President Products Services And Network Planning, Jeff Euler
Svp Operations Fedex Ground, Scott Ray
Svp Sales Fedex Office, Aimee Dicicco
Vice President Global Sales Operations, Chris Suhoza
Vice President Internal Audit, Karl Stingily
Senior Vice President Senior Executive Assistant Ii, Paula Baker
Vice President Strategic Planning And Support, Dale Chrystie
Vice President Admin, Carolyn Dupuy
Vice President Senior Assistant Ii, Melissa Drum
Vice President Senior Assistant Ii, Peggy Carlisle
Vp Admin, Alicia Malone
Vice President Admin, Caroline Clarkson
Vice President, Rita Cowans
Vice President And Ww Controller, Jerry Bateman
Evp Global Sales And Solutions, Don Colleran
Vice President Assistant, Nancy Tarr
Vice President Operations Americas For Fedex Trade Networks, John Gazitua
Vice President Finance, Jane Amaba
Vice President Corporate Sales, Michael Moriarty
Svp And General Counsel Fedex Supply Chain, Bradley R Peacock
Vice President Executive Creative Direct, Kelly Liu
Vice President Digital Access Marketing, Tom Wicinski
Vice President Litigation, Joseph Milcoff
Vice President Marketing, Lawrence Lanier
Vice President, Dottie Berry
Vice President Strategic Planning, Stephanie Cohen
Vice President Sourcing, Susan Spence
Vice President, Don Gibson
Vice President Field Sales, Dave Russell
Svp Sales, Dan Mullally
Vice President Customer Engagement Marketing, Rebecca Huling
Senior Marketing Vice President, Kim Winstead
Executive Vice President Market Dev Corp Comm Presi Fedex Service, Michael Glenn
Vice President Brand Experience And Marketing, Monica Skipper
Vp Assistant, Deanna Davidson
Vice President Marketing, Randy Scarborough
Vice President Finance, Tom Holland
Senior Vice President Central Support, Leonard Feiler
Vice President Quality Assurance And F, Margaret Pelech
Senior Vice President Executive Assistant, Debbie Cain
Vice President Senior Assistant Ii, Patti Hofer
Vice President Investor Relations, A Mickey Foster
Vice President Operations Planning And Engineering Fedex Freight, Gary Bouch
Senior Vice President Agfs, Michael K Pigors
Vice President Admin, Debby Davis
Evp And Coo Fedex Ground, Ward Strang
Vice President Of Environmental Affairs And Sustainabiltiy, Mitchell Jackson
Vice President Global Operations Planning Fedex Office, Jerod Littlefield
Senior Vice President Systems, James Rubino

Vice President It Security Federal Express, Gene Sun
Vice President Of Fedex Cross Border, Charles F Hull
Vice President, Tim Leonard
Vice President, Susan Sweat
Vp Human Resources, Judy Edge
Vice President Information Technology Fedex Services, Jeff Roemer
Vice President Of Human Resources, Sean McNamee
Vice President, Jill Brannon
Vice President, Cheryl O'brien
Senior Vice President Global Product Marketing, Jill Brown
Vice President Assistant, Francine Coleman
Senior Vice President Admin, Mary Macon
Vice President Legal, Sean S Mcnamee
Vice President Healthcare, Kevin J Mcpherson
Senior Vice President Sales, Aimee L Dicicco
Vice President Regulatory Affairs And Compliance, Cynthia D Allen
Vice President Senior Assistant, Demetra Walton
Executive Vice President Global Sales And Solutions, Donald F Colleran
Vice President Of Marketing, Donald J Miller
Vice President Human Resources, Tom Tannehill
Legal Secretary V, Tina Blackwell
Vice President Air Network Operations Planning And Engin, Patrick Donlon
Vice President Senior Assistant, Vallerie M Bledsoe
Vice President, Robert Pratka
Vp Assistant, Lillian Ventura
Svp Integrated Marketing And Communications, Patrick Fitzgerald
Senior Vice President Finance International Fedex Express, Helena Jansson
Vp Int'l Sales Administrative Assistant, Rhonda Edmondson
Corporate Vice President Customer And Business Transactions Legal, Jim Ferguson
Application Application Development Advisor, Rebecca Holden-williams
Vice President, Paul Melander
Corporate Vp Operations And Service Support, Gloria Boyland
Vice President, Frank Lerose
Svp Global Portfolio Marketing, Brie Carere
Vice President Healthcare, Kevin Mcpherson
Vice President At Fedex Trade Networks, Cristiano Koga
Vice President Information Technology Tower Group International, Carol Smith
Vice President Retail Operations, Jeff Hyman
Vice President Finance, Mark Cox
Vice President, Thomas Mangrum
Vice President, Vernon Thomas
Board Member, David Steiner
Board Member, Amber Inglis
Board Member, Bob Griffith
Board Member, Kim Jabal
Auditors: Ernst & Young LLP

LOCATIONS

HQ: FedEx Corp
942 South Shady Grove Road, Memphis, TN 38120
Phone: 901 818-7500
Web: www.fedex.com

2018 Sales

	$ mil.	% of total
US	47,584	69
Other countries	22,109	31
Total	69,693	100

PRODUCTS/OPERATIONS

2018 Sales

	$ mil.	% of total
FedEx Express	37,331	54
FedEx Ground	20,522	29
FedEx Freight	7,582	11
FedEx Services	1,691	2
Corporate eliminations and other	2,567	4
Total	69,693	100

Services

FedEx Trade Networks
FedEx Supply Chain Systems
FedEx SmartPost
GENCO

COMPETITORS

ABF Freight System	Royal Mail
Amazon.com	Ryder System
Canada Post	The UPS Store
DHL	UPS
Japan Post	US Postal Service
La Poste	Xerox
Nippon Express	YRC Worldwide
Old Dominion Freight	

HISTORICAL FINANCIALS

Company Type: Public

Income Statement

FYE: May 31

	REVENUE ($ mil.)	NET INCOME ($ mil.)	NET PROFIT MARGIN	EMPLOYEES
05/20	69,217	1,286	1.9%	245,000
05/19	69,693	540	0.8%	239,000
05/18	65,450	4,572	7.0%	227,000
05/17	60,319	2,997	5.0%	169,000
05/16	50,365	1,820	3.6%	168,000
Annual Growth	8.3%	(8.3%)	—	9.9%

2020 Year-End Financials

Debt ratio: 29.92%
Return on equity: 7.11%
Cash ($ mil.): 4,881
Current ratio: 1.58
Long-term debt ($ mil.): 21,952
No. of shares (mil.): 261
Dividends
  Yield: 0.0%
  Payout: 53.0%
Market value ($ mil.): 34,201

	STOCK PRICE ($) FY Close	P/E High/Low	PER SHARE ($) Earnings	Dividends	Book Value
05/20	130.56	36 18	4.90	2.60	69.84
05/19	154.28	129 74	2.03	2.60	68.08
05/18	249.12	16 12	16.79	2.00	73.01
05/17	193.84	18 13	11.07	1.60	59.92
05/16	164.97	28 19	6.51	1.00	51.91
Annual Growth	(5.7%)	— —	(6.9%)	27.0%	7.7%

Fidelity National Financial Inc

To make sure that buying a dream home does not become a nightmare Fidelity National Financial (also known as FNF) provides title insurance escrow home warranties and other services related to real estate transactions. It is now the top dog in the residential and commercial title insurance sectors (the second-largest is First American) and issues more title insurance policies than any other title company in the US. The company operates through underwriters including Fidelity National

Title Insurance Commonwealth Land Title Alamo Title and National Title of New York. It sells its products both directly and through independent agents.

Operations
FNF is organized into two segments: Title and Corporate and Other.

The Title segment brings in most of the group's revenues (nearly 100% of the company's total sales); it includes title insurance and related closing services. Through subsidiary ServiceLink FNF provides mortgage transaction services such as facilitating the production and management of mortgage loans.

Corporate and Other segment includes the operations of the parent holding company real estate technology subsidiaries other smaller non-title businesses and unallocated corporate overhead expenses and eliminations.

Geographic Reach
FNF's insurance businesses operate exclusively within the US. Naturally the biggest markets are in states with the greatest populations: California Texas Florida New York and Illinois combined account for nearly 50% of its title insurance premiums.

The company leases offices in around 45 states and Washington DC as well as in Canada and India. FNF is headquartered in Florida US.

Sales and Marketing
FNF uses direct sales representatives and independent agents to market its title and escrow products to residential and commercial real estate customers. The company maintains over 1300 retail offices to provide residential title insurance. It markets its commercial title insurance through a network of approximately 5300 agents in major urban real estate markets.

Financial Performance
FNF's revenues have been steadily rising over the last five years. It has seen growth of 27% between 2015 and 2019. With the exception of 2018 its net income has also been on the rise.

Total revenue in 2019 increased $875 million to $8.5 billion compared to 2018 primarily attributable to increases in both its direct and agency premiums increases in interest and investment income and non-cash valuation gains on its equity and preferred investment holdings partially offset by a decrease in escrow title-related and other fees.

Net income in 2019 rose 69% to $1.1 billion from $628 million the prior year due to higher revenues that year despite a corresponding increase in expenses.

FNF ended 2019 with $1.4 billion in cash and cash equivalents $119 million more than it had at the beginning of the year. Operating activities provided $1.1 billion. Investing activities used $520 million mainly for purchases of short-term investments and for Cannae Holdings Inc. Financing activities used another $482 million primarily for subsidiary dividends and treasury stock purchases.

Strategy
FNF's strategy is to maximize operating profits by increasing its market share and managing operating expenses throughout the real estate business cycle. In order to accomplish this FNF has implemented multiple strategies.

FNF will continue to operate multiple title brands independently. FNF believes that in order to maintain and strengthen its title insurance customer base it must operate its strongest brands in a given marketplace independently of each other.

The company will also consistently deliver superior customer service. FNF believes customer service and consistent product delivery are the most important factors in attracting and retaining customers. Its goal is to continue to improve the experience of its customers in all aspects of the business.

As FNF operates in a cyclical industry and its ability to diversify its revenue base within its title insurance business and manage the duration of its investments allow it to better operate in this cyclical business. It continues to monitor evaluate and execute upon the consolidation of administrative functions legal entity structure and office consolidation as necessary to respond to the continually changing marketplace.

FNF also continues to improve its products and technology to maintain values that support its strategy and to effectively manage costs based on economic factors. Adapting to evolving industry standards and continuing to evaluate and manage its cost structure aids FNF's performance.

Mergers and Acquisitions
In mid-2020 FNF acquired FGL Holdings (F&G). FNF issued approximately 27 million shares of FNF common stock and paid approximately $1.8 billion in cash to former holders of FGL ordinary and preferred shares. Iowa-based F&G is one of the leading providers of annuity and life insurance products. FNF Chairman William Folley II stated "The acquisition of F&G offers FNF entry to an industry that is counter-cyclical to FNF's title insurance business."

Company Background
The current company arose in 2006 when a previous company also named Fidelity National Financial split apart its title insurance operations from its information services business. What had been Fidelity National Title Group took on its former parent's name while Fidelity National Information Services took on the former parent's remaining operations. The two companies share a history and some stray holdings but are otherwise separate.

Like all title insurers Fidelity National Financial shivered when the big chill hit the real estate market in 2008. But while the company slowed it remained quick enough to take advantage of opportunities. When its ailing rival LandAmerica Financial Group filed Chapter 11 in 2008 the company bought up the choice bits for $235 million. This purchase helped make it into the largest title insurer in the US and caught the attention of the FTC prompting the company to divest a few holdings to soothe the agency's nerves. The 2009 sale of Fidelity National Capital only brought in $50 million but took $214 million of debt off company ledgers. The 2010 sale of its 32% stake in Sedgwick Claims Management brought in some $225 million.

EXECUTIVES

Evp And Chief Legal Officer, Peter T. Sadowski, age 66, $431,671 total compensation

Ceo, Raymond R. (Randy) Quirk, age 74, $831,692 total compensation

Evp General Counsel And Corporate Secretary, Michael L. (Mike) Gravelle, age 59, $550,500 total compensation

Evp Corporate Strategy, Brent B. Bickett, age 56, $550,500 total compensation

Coo, Roger S. Jewkes, age 62, $630,000 total compensation

President Fidelity National Title Group National Agency Operations, Erika Meinhardt, age 62

Evp And Cfo, Anthony J. (Tony) Park, age 54, $483,000 total compensation

President, Michael J. (Mike) Nolan, age 61, $557,308 total compensation

Senior Vice President, Colleen Haley

Vice President, James Sindoni

Vice President Regional Controller, Sylvia Freyling

Assistant Vice President Legal Administrator, Madeline Lovejoy

Assistant Vice President And Administrative Assistant, Jennifer Edwards

Assistant Vice President And Underwriting Counsel, Shira Burns

Assistant Vice President And Branch Manager, Tiffanie Hobgood

Assistant Vice President And Senior Counsel, Michael Behrens

Assistant Vice President Business Development, Scott Nordell

Vice President, Holly Stapley

Assistant Vice President, Jodi Reimer

Vice President Of Account, Kimberly Abkin

Assistant Vice President Special Projects Wireless Team Lead, Andrea Mcmahon

Vice President Inbound Sales, Terri Adamo

Vice President And Associate Counsel, Ian Rothenberg

Assistant Vice President, Cathy Kennedy

Vice President Managing Counsel, Rob Shepard

Vice President Agency Support Services, Lisa Beville

Vice President And Counsel, Nathaniel Yingling

Asistant Vice President, Jose Flores

Vice President, Matt Semple

Vice President And Area Counsel, Kevin Campbell

Vice President, Ann Wilbanks

Vice President, Jason Allen

Assistant Vice President And Agency Account Manager, Melodye Marvin

Vice President Digital Strategy, Bill Risser

Vice President Sales Executive, April Palmer

Assistant Vice President Claims Counsel, Michelle Statz

Vice President Commercial Underwriting Counsel, Walter Wilson

Assistant Vice President, Sandy Dow

Assistant Vice President Agency Auditor, Mary Rooney

Vice President, Tamara Strickland

Assistant Vice President, Erik Deppe

Assistant Vice President, Mercy Palmer

Assistant Vice President Asset Accounting Manager, Melissa Mannion

Vice President State Pa Agency Manager Commonwealth Land And Chicago Title, Adrienne Verdone

Vice President Kitsap Operations, Mary Schofield

Vice President, Chris Martin

Vice President Information Technology, Dan Leisle

Vice President, George Tellez

Assistant Vice President, Judith Lanahan

Senior Vice President, Kenji Kikuchi

Vice President And Sales Manager Fidelity National Title Santa Barbara, Jennifer Lemert

Assistant Vice President, Kelli Moquin

Vice President, Jason Somers

Assistant Vice President And Nw Indiana Escrow Manager, Susan Miedema

Vice President, John Maddie

Vice President And Area Manager And Stat, Mark Schittina

Assistant Vice President And Sales Executive, Len Hyde

Senior Claims Counsel Vice President, Cheri Taylor

Avp It Strategy Manager, Janine Dapaah

Vice President Agency Counsel, Thomas Bartlett

Assistant Vice President And Director 401k Plan, Eva Chavis

Vice President, Amy Tueckes

Assistant Vice President, David Scott

Senior Claims Counsel And Vice President, Scott Aronowitz

Vice President, Melissa Mccarty

Assistant Vice President, Todd Niemczyk

Vice President, Debby Boyd

Vice President, Beth Rennie

Vice President, Chris Jaramillo

Assistant Vice President, Holly Odonnell

Senior Vice President, Rick Ransom

Vice President Of Business Development, Ryan Pulliam
Vice President, Tabitha Campbell
Assistant Vice President Sales Representative, Christine Rifkin
Assistant Vice President, Kristin Wyckoff
Vice President Human Resources, David Faliszek
Assistant Vice President, Susan Sever
Executive Vice President, Phil Shea
Senior Vice President, Kevin Gallagher
Assistant Vice President Reo Manager, Pati Walter
Vice President, Keith Weller
Vice President Sales, Ron Nyeholt
Assistant Vice President, Deborah Bayha
Senior Vice President And Manager New York National Commercial Services, Joanna Patilis
Assistant Vice President, Ginger Heintz
Vice President Sales, John Ravita
Assistant Vice President Associate Branch Counsel, Francis Hoffman
Assistant Vice President, Brandie Cho
Vice President Business Development, Janis Okerlund
Vice President, Brett Larocque
Vice President Business Development, Eileen Saul
Escrow Officer And Assistant Vice President, Kristin Bailey
Assistant Vice President Analyst Corporate Compliance, Gina Stanley
Legal Assistant Assistant Vice President, Patricia Jandrue
Vice President, Dorry Bragg
Vice President, Gerry Grady
Assistant Vice President, Lois Watson
Assistant Vice President And Agency Account Manager, John Stilla
Vice President Business Development, Paul Jackson
Vice President, Sam Kitamura
Senior Vice President, Morris Evans
Vice President System Admin, Tommy Bach
Managing Counsel Vice President, Elizabeth Skinner
Vice President And Georgia Underwriting Counsel, David Swan
Senior Vice President And Sales Manager, Tine Dickey
Vice President, Mary Garcia
Senior Vice President, Kelly Feese
Vice President Of Information Technology, Jon Parks
Assistant Vice President And Agency Representative, Tiffany Mcdonough
Vice President, John Hlivka
Vice President National Business Development, Mark Gronke
Vice President Manager, Traci Watson
Executive Vice President, Ray Marine
Vice President Managing Director, Scott Morgano
Vice President, Jill Evans
Executive Vice President National Agency Operations, John Obzud
Vice President And Senior Escrow Officer, Lisa Wikert
Vice President Underwriter, Shanna Cole
Vice President And Litigation Counsel, Scott Lascari
Vice President Sales, Toni Mccarty
Vice President, Emi Tsuji
Vice President And Executive Director, Grant Miller
Senior Vice President Field Operations Manager, Ruth Stolhanske
Assistant Vice President Agency Representative, Theresa Bartow
Agency Representative Assistant Vice President, Kristen Costello
Assistant Vice President Associate Counsel, Paul Mcgeough
Managing Counsel Vice President, Todd Moody
Vice President Escrow Officer, Darla Wagner

Assistant Vice President And Chief Title Officer, Dan Cowgill
Vice President, Sam Smith
Vice President And Area Manager, Rob Cohen
Vice President Counsel, Douglas Whitaker
Vice President And Senior Claims Counsel, Andrea Baird
Assistant Vice President And Associate Trial Counsel, Austin James
Claims Counsel And Assistant Vice President, Kelly Pritchard
Claims Counsel And Assistant Vice President, Stacy Young
Vice President Maryland Agency Manager, Joe Shepherd
Senior Managing Major Claims Counsel Senior Vice President, John Klein
Senior Recoupment Counsel Assistant Vice President, Anthony Medina
Senior Vice President, Rich Cannan
Assistant Vice President And Senior Escrow Officer, Linda Tyrrell
Vice President Business Development, Thomas Kane
Senior Vice President, Andy Giddings
Assistant Vice President And Escrow Officer, Nancy Wilcoxon
Vice President Commercial Escrow Officer, Samantha Maestas
Vice President, Mark Rizzo
Senior Vice President Credit Card Services, Barbara Hunter
Claims Counsel Assistant Vice President, Derek Eilander
Vice President And Major Transactions Counsel, Sarah Webb
Claims Counsel Assistant Vice President, Jodi Hansen
Vice President Agency Counsel, Tom Bartlett
Auditors: Ernst & Young LLP

LOCATIONS

HQ: Fidelity National Financial Inc
601 Riverside Avenue, Jacksonville, FL 32204
Phone: 904 854-8100
Web: www.fnf.com

PRODUCTS/OPERATIONS

2017 Sales

	$ mil.	% of total
Agency title insurance premiums	2,723	36
Escrow title-related & other fees	2,637	34
Direct title insurance premiums	2,170	28
Interest & investment income	131	2
Net realized gains	2	-
Total	**7,663**	**100**

COMPETITORS

American Coast Title	Stewart Information
Equity Title Company	Services
First American	Title Resource Group
Investors Title	United General Title
North American Title	Insurance
Old Republic	
Old Republic National Title	

HISTORICAL FINANCIALS

Company Type: Public

Income Statement — FYE: December 31

	ASSETS ($ mil.)	NET INCOME ($ mil.)	INCOME AS % OF ASSETS	EMPLOYEES
12/19	10,677	1,062	9.9%	25,063
12/18	9,301	628	6.8%	23,436
12/17	9,151	771	8.4%	24,367
12/16	14,463	650	4.5%	55,219
12/15	13,931	527	3.8%	54,091
Annual Growth	(6.4%)	19.1%	—	(17.5%)

2019 Year-End Financials

Debt ratio: 7.85%	No. of shares (mil.): 275
Return on equity: 21.21%	Dividends
Cash ($ mil.): 1,376	Yield: 2.7%
Current ratio: —	Payout: 45.4%
Long-term debt ($ mil.): —	Market value ($ mil.): 12,497

	STOCK PRICE ($) FY Close	P/E High/Low		PER SHARE ($) Earnings	Dividends	Book Value
12/19	45.35	12	8	3.83	1.26	19.53
12/18	31.44	18	13	2.26	1.20	16.81
12/17	39.24	20	14	2.38	1.02	16.20
12/16	33.96	16	12	2.34	0.88	17.71
12/15	34.67	21	17	1.89	0.80	16.53
Annual Growth	6.9%	—	—	19.3%	12.0%	4.3%

Fidelity National Information Services Inc

At Fidelity National Information Services (FIS) the check will never get lost in the mail. The company helps financial institutions merchants companies and governmental entities conduct transactions through its range of software and services. It also offers outsourcing and consulting for the financial services industry. For banks and other financing entities the company's offerings address financial functions such as core processing decision and risk management and retail payment solutions. FIS also provides payment services such as electronic funds transfer check and ticket processing and credit card production and activation. In 2019 FIS acquired Worldpay a payment processor to expand its capabilities. North America accounts for about three-quarters of company's total revenue.

Operations

As a result of the Company's acquisition of Worldpay the Company reorganized its reportable segments and recast all prior-period segment information presented to align with the new reportable segments. The new segments are Merchant Solutions ("Merchant") Banking Solutions ("Banking") and Capital Market Solutions ("Capital Markets") which are organized based on the markets and clients served aligned with the solutions they provide as well as the Corporate and Other segment.

Merchant Solutions generates almost 20% of revenue and focuses on serving merchants of all sizes globally enabling them to accept electronic payments including credit debit and prepaid payments originated at a physical point of sale as well as in card-not-present environments such as eCommerce and mobile.

Banking Solutions generates over 55% of revenue and focuses on serving all sizes of financial institutions for core processing and ancillary applications solutions; digital solutions; fraud risk management and compliance solutions; electronic funds transfer and network services solutions; payment solutions; wealth and retirement solutions; item processing and output services solutions; and services capitalizing on the continuing trend to outsource these solutions.

Capital Markets Solutions generates almost 25% of revenue and focuses on serving global financial services clients with a broad array of buy- and sell-side solutions.

The Corporate and Other segment consists of corporate overhead expense certain leveraged functions and miscellaneous expenses that are not included in the operating segments as well as certain non-strategic businesses.

Overall Fidelity's transaction processing and services generate over 70% of its revenue.

Geographic Reach

FIS based in Jacksonville Florida operates through some 200 owned or leased locations in Brazil India Africa Southeast Asia and the Middle East.

FIS relies on its North American operations for 75% of its revenue. The company does business in more than 140 countries but most of its international revenue comes from customers in Brazil Canada the UK Australia India and Germany.

Sales and Marketing

FIS markets its products and services through direct and indirect field sales as well as inbound and outbound lead generation and telesales. It claims about 20000 clients around the world.

Financial Performance

In 2019 after reporting lower revenue two years in a row in 2017 and 2018 FIS' revenue shot up to over $10.3 billion. In terms of revenue the company has an overall growth of 57% in the last five years.

In 2019 revenue rose 23% to $10.3 billion from $8.4 billion in 2018.

Net income fell to $298 million in 2019 from $846 million in 2018.

FIS's coffers held $3.2 billion in cash and equivalents in 2019 compared to $703 million in 2018. Operations produced $2.4 billion in 2019 while investing activities used $7.5 billion and financing activities provided $7.6 billion.

Strategy

Fidelity's strategy is built on the following pillars:

Building Buying or Partnering to Add Solutions to Cross-Sell Existing Clients and Win New Clients – The company continues to invest in growth through internal software development as well as through acquisitions and equity investments that complement and extend its existing solutions and capabilities providing the company with additional solutions to cross-sell existing clients and capture the interest of new clients.

Supporting Clients Through Innovation - Changing market dynamics particularly in the areas of information security regulation and innovation are transforming the way Fidelity's clients operate which is driving incremental demand for its integrated solutions and services around its intellectual property.

Continually Improving to Drive Margin Expansion - Fidelity strives to optimize its performance through investments in infrastructure enhancements workforce and other measures that are designed to drive margin expansion.

Expanding Client Relationships – Fidelity's leveraged solutions and processing expertise can produce meaningful value and cost savings for its clients through more efficient operating processes improved service quality and convenience for clients' customers.

Building Global Diversification - Fidelity continues to deploy resources in strategic global markets where it expects to achieve meaningful scale.

Mergers and Acquisitions

In 2019 FIS bolstered the services it provides with the $35 billion acquisition of Worldpay a payment processor. The deal brought significant payment resources to FIS as other companies in the industry have consolidated.

EXECUTIVES

Corporate Evp And Coo Institutional And Wholesale, Marianne C. Brown, age 61, $700,000 total compensation
Cio, Ido Gileadi
President Integrated Financial Solutions, Gary A. Norcross, age 55, $1,000,000 total compensation
Evp North American Financial Solutions, Anthony M. Jabbour, age 52, $700,000 total compensation
Corporate Evp Chief Administrative Officer And Corporate Secretary, Michael P. Oates, age 61, $475,000 total compensation
Evp And Cfo, James W. (Woody) Woodall, age 50, $605,000 total compensation
Corporate Evp And Chief Risk Officer, Gregory G. (Greg) Montana, age 51, $365,000 total compensation
Evp International Markets, Raja Gopalakrishnan
Ceo Capco, Lance Levy
Evp And Chief Legal Officer, Marc Mayo
Coo Integrated Financial Solutions, Bruce Lowthers
Senior Vice President Global Commercial Services Supply Chain And Real Estate, Kevin Gouin
Vice President Implementation Services, Chris Wichman
Senior Vice President Eft Services, Serena Smith
Svp Fis Output Solutions, Keith Shaffer
Vice President, Brian Paulson
Senior Vice President And Legal Executive, Duncan Mitchell
Vice President, John Kopriva
Vice President Marketing And Strategy, Linda Netherton
Senior Vice President Financial Services Products, Trevor Mast
Assistant Vice President Chargeback Services, Christine Sterling
Vice President, Pete Foy
Assistant Vice President, Marie Storey
Senior Vice President Marketing, Stephen Kane
Vice President, Gina Gitter
Vice President, Sean Oliver
Vice President, Robert Brennen
Vp Product Development, Floyd Berus
Vice President Sales And Marketing, Robert Boitano
Senior Vice President Loyalty Services, Robert Legters
Vice President Operations, John Oleon
Assistant Vice President Finance, Dawn Frye
Assistant Vice President Treasury, Alex Alley
Assistant Vice President, Kimberly Sadler
Vice President Advanced Technology Solutions, Hank Godwin
Vice President Business Recovery Services Advanced Technology Solutions, Ovid Babb
Assistant Vice President Global Midrange Applications, Alex Pisieczko
Senior Vice President Channel Architecture And Strategy, Bernie Schramm
Vice President New Solutions Architecture, Will Starnes
Vice President Acbs Global Sales, Gregg Cerniglia
Senior Vice President Operations, Mike Amble

Svp Fis Global Marketing And Communications, Kim Snider
Vice President Channels Delivery, Sethu Thottikamath
Vice President Enterprise Architecture, Roy Jutze
Senior Vice President And General Manager, Michelle Bowen
Vice President And Managing Director, Jim Gorski
Sales Senior Vice President, Michael Whitacre
Vice President Customer Service, Christopher Hermann
Vice President Fidelity Information Services Testing, Laura Belliot
Vice President Infrastructure Services, David Plante
Assistant Vice President Fraud Product Mangement, Eric Kraus
Svp And Deputy Ciso, Ivana Cojbasic
Vice President Strategic Account Sales, Lucy Mills
Vice President Application Services India, Vishad Gupta
Vice President Technology Operations, Joseph Dedovesh
Vice President International Treasury, Andres Shuyama
Vice President Sales, Ryan Fetzer
Vice President Sales And Product Management, Matt Phillips
Vice President Human Resources, Kristen Cimock
Senior Vice President And Deputy General Counsel Corporate, Charles Curley
Vice President Product Management, Somesh Chablani
Vice President Product Management, Paul Zur Nieden
Chief People Officer, Denise Williams
Senior Vice President Development, Aaron Gerdeman
Vice President Brokerage Solutions And Strategy, David Hoffman
Senior Vice President Business Development, Chad Davis
Vice President Payment Solutions Sales, Amy Hammon
Vice President And General Manager Merchant Services, Dawn Murray
Vice President, John Francis
Vice President Program Management Ps, Mary Spyridakis
National Account Manager, Steven Romeo
Vice President Product Strategy, Dan Peacock
Vice President Sales And Relationship Management, Darryl Wims
Vice President Corporate And Executive Communications, Jen Becker
Senior Vice President Information Securi, Hamish Craig
Vice President; Director Of Client Services Technology, Craig Hennerberg
Application Architect Vice President, Virginija Paulius
Vp Of Prepaid Product Development, Tracy Kirkland
Senior Vice President, Peter Lennon
Chief People Officer, Dee Williams
Senior Vice President, Erik Hoag
Vice President Client Services And Application Delivery, Jon Hamilton
Vice President Global Operations Financi, Jose Fajardo
Vice President, Patrick Hogan
Vice President Corporate Controller, Thomas Warren
Vice President Information Technology, Leslie Harlow
Vice President Product Strategy, Ernie Buday
Svp Group Executive, Tom Mcbride
Assistant Vice President And Division Counsel, Stephen Teplin
Senior Vice President, Mark Metzendorf

Vice President Information Technology Operations, Eric Van Riper
Vice President Account Management, Carla Pipes
Vice President Product Manager, Lee Detlaff
Vice President Sales, Dan Buttolph
Senior Vice President Risk Management, Rick Floress
Vice President, Mandy Poole
Senior Vice President Client Services And Kiodex Global Market Data Capital Markets, Brian Lane
Vice President And Trust Relationship Manager, Kerry Larkins
Senior Vice President Account Management, Kim Klett
Vice President Account Management, Ellen Burnham
Chairman, Frank R. Martire, age 72
Auditors: KPMG LLP

LOCATIONS

HQ: Fidelity National Information Services Inc
601 Riverside Avenue, Jacksonville, FL 32204
Phone: 904 438-6000
Web: www.fisglobal.com

2018 Sales

	$ mil.	% of total
North America	6,283	75
All others	2,140	25
Total	**8,423**	**100**

PRODUCTS/OPERATIONS

2018 Sales

	$ mil.	% of total
IFS	4,401	52
GFS	3,718	44
Corporate & Other	304	4
Total	**8,423**	**100**

SOLUTIONS

SOLUTIONS
Banking and Wealth
Institutional and Wholesale
Management Consulting
Payments

COMPETITORS

ACI Worldwide	IBM
Accenture	Infosys
Alliance Data Systems	Jack Henry
First Data	MasterCard
Fiserv	Oracle Financial
Global Payments	Services Software
HP Enterprise Services	SEI Investments
Heartland Payment	Total System Services
Systems	Visa Inc

HISTORICAL FINANCIALS

Company Type: Public

Income Statement

FYE: December 31

	REVENUE ($ mil.)	NET INCOME ($ mil.)	NET PROFIT MARGIN	EMPLOYEES
12/19	10,333	298	2.9%	55,000
12/18	8,423	846	10.0%	47,000
12/17	9,123	1,319	14.5%	53,000
12/16	9,241	568	6.1%	55,000
12/15	6,595	631	9.6%	55,000
Annual Growth	**11.9%**	**(17.1%)**	**—**	**0.0%**

2019 Year-End Financials

Debt ratio: 24.09%
Return on equity: 1.00%
Cash ($ mil.): 1,152
Current ratio: 0.84
Long-term debt ($ mil.): 17,229

No. of shares (mil.): 614
Dividends
Yield: 1.0%
Payout: 212.1%
Market value ($ mil.): 85,401

	STOCK PRICE ($) FY Close	P/E High/Low	PER SHARE ($) Earnings	Dividends	Book Value
12/19	139.09	209 147	0.66	1.40	80.52
12/18	102.55	43 36	2.55	1.28	31.24
12/17	94.09	24 19	3.93	1.16	32.54
12/16	75.64	46 32	1.72	1.04	29.70
12/15	60.60	33 26	2.19	1.04	28.72
Annual Growth	**23.1%**	**— —**	**(25.9%)**	**7.7%**	**29.4%**

Fifth Third Bancorp (Cincinnati, OH)

Fifth Third Bancorp is the holding company of Fifth Third Bank which boasts assets of more than $140 billion and about 1150 branches in about 10 states in the Midwest and Southeast. Fifth Third offers branch banking (deposit accounts and loans for consumers and small businesses) commercial banking (lending leasing and syndicated and trade finance for corporations) consumer lending (residential mortgages home equity loans and credit cards) and wealth and asset management (private banking brokerage and asset management). In 2019 it acquired MB Financial making the combined company the fourth largest bank in Chicago by deposits.

Operations

Fifth Third Bancorp operates four business segments: Commercial Banking Branch Banking Wealth and Asset Management and Consumer Lending. Commercial Banking generate roughly 40% of total revenue. Branch Banking accounts for more than 35% while Wealth and Asset Management contributes about 10%; and Consumer Lending provides around 5%.

Commercial Banking provides financial services?like credit intermediation and cash management?to middle-market businesses and government and professional clients. Its additional services include international trade finance and derivatives and asset-based lending. Net interest income generates more than 65% of the segment's revenue.

Branch Banking offers a standard range of deposit loan and lease products to individuals and businesses. It offers depository and loan products such as checking and saving accounts home equity loans and lined of credit credit cards and loans for automobile and other personal financing needs. Some 75% of its revenue comes from net interest income.

Wealth and Asset Management is divided into four primary businesses: retail broker FTS risk management company Fifth Third Insurance Agency high-net worth client wealth management firm Fifth Third Private Bank and institutional advisory services provider Fifth Third Institutional Services. Fifth Third's Consumer Lending division includes the Bancorp's residential mortgages automobile and other indirect lending activities. Net interest income and mortgage banking account for about 50% and 45% of the segment's revenue respectively.

Geographic Reach

Cincinnati Ohio-based Fifth Third Bancorp has around 1150 full-service branches and nearly 2500 ATMs in Ohio Kentucky Indiana Michigan Illinois Florida Tennessee West Virginia Georgia and North Carolina.

Sales and Marketing

In addition to retail customers and affluent individuals Fifth Third Bancorp targets agribusinesses dealers government agencies healthcare-related companies US financial institutions and businesses seeking energy financing.

Commercial Banking offers services to large and middle-market businesses and government and professional customers. Wealth & Asset Management targets individuals companies and not-for-profit organizations. Branch Banking and Consumer Lending largely tend to the needs of retail consumers and small businesses.

Financial Performance

Fifth Third Bancorp's revenue has floundered somewhat in recent years alternately showing modest gains of about 10% or ticking down slightly for five-year growth of 27%. Its net income has fared better over that period showing an expansion of about 50% between 2015 and 2019 thanks mostly to an increase of about 40% in 2017 when the company sold of some of its shares in former subsidiary Vantiv.

The company's net income grew by some 15% to $2.5 billion thanks to those revenue gains and a lower income tax expense caused by a retrospective accounting policy change for its investments in affordable housing projects that qualified low-income housing tax credits.

Fifth Third added $597 million to its cash in 2019 to end the year with $3.3 billion. Operations contributed $1.8 billion and financing activities?mostly net changes in deposits?used $430 million. Investing activities used $797 million mainly for available for sale debt and other investment.

Strategy

In a move to strengthen its position in the Chicago deposit market Fifth Third Bancorp acquired MB Financial in 2019. MB Financial had about $20 billion in assets. The combination created the fourth largest Chicago bank by deposits second in estimated retail deposits and second in middle market relationships (with a 20% share).

Fifth Third is also investing in digital banking channels to move in front of the fast forming FinTech (Financial Technology) changes that are enveloping the industry. As a result Fifth Third has cut back its branch network and is seeing reduced operating costs all while giving customers faster access to banking services. To ensure it is keeping pace with the change the bank is partnering with and investing in several FinTech companies such as Current and CommonBond.

Fifth Third kicked off a 3-year growth plan in late 2016 termed NorthStar with the intention of strengthening its brand value growing tighter long-term relationships with its customers and leveraging data analytics to drive better operational efficiencies. To those ends it upgraded its mortgage and teller systems expanded its suite of credit card and treasury management products and invested in its commercial verticals (such as Healthcare with the Coker Capital acquisition).

Mergers and Acquisitions

In early 2019 Fifth Third Bancorp acquired Chicago-based bank holding company MB Financial for $3.6 billion. With about $20 billion the integration of MB's MB Financial Bank into Fifth Third created the fourth largest Chicago bank by deposits second in estimated retail deposits and second in middle market relationships (with a 20% share).

Company Background

William W. Scarborough and 11 other entrepreneurs opened Fifth Third Bancorp's precursor The Bank of the Ohio Valley in Cincinnati Ohio in 1858. In 1927 Fifth-Third National and The Union Trust Company merged to form The Fifth Third Union Trust Company.

HISTORY

In 1863 a group of Cincinnati businessmen opened the Third National Bank inside a Masonic temple to serve the Ohio River trade. Acquiring the Bank of the Ohio Valley (founded 1858) in 1871 the firm progressed until the panic of 1907. Third National survived and in 1908 consolidated with Fifth National forming the Fifth Third National Bank of Cincinnati. The newly organized bank acquired two local banks in 1910.

A second bank consolidation in 1919 resulted in Fifth Third's affiliation with Union Savings Bank and Trust Company permitting the bank to establish branches theretofore forbidden by regulators. The company acquired the assets and offices of five more banks and thrifts that year operating them as branches.

In 1927 the bank merged its operations with the Union Trust Company forming the Fifth Third Union Trust. With its combined strength it weathered the Great Depression and acquired three more banks between 1930 and 1933. However the Depression also brought massive banking regulations to the industry limiting Fifth Third's acquisitions.

In the postwar years and during the 1950s and 1960s the bank expanded its consumer banking services offering traveler's checks. Under CEO Bill Rowe son of former CEO John Rowe the firm emphasized the convenience of its locations and increased hours of operations.

In the 1970s Fifth Third shifted its lending program's emphasis from commercial loans to consumer credit and launched its ATM and telephone banking services. Aware that the bank was technologically unprepared for the onslaught of electronic information Fifth Third expanded its data processing and information services resources forming the basis for its Midwest Payment Systems division.

The company formed Fifth Third Bancorp a holding company and began to branch within Ohio (branching had previously been limited to the home county) in 1975. Ten years later more deregulation allowed the bank to move into contiguous states. Focused on consumer banking and with cautious underwriting policies Fifth Third weathered the real estate bust and leveraged-buyout problems of the 1980s and acquired new outlets cheaply by buying several small banks as well as branches from larger banks. It acquired the American National Bank in Kentucky and moved further afield with its purchase of the Sovereign Savings Bank in Palm Harbor Florida in 1991.

The company continued to expand buying several banks and thrifts in Ohio in 1997 and 1998. In 1999 Fifth Third moved into Indiana in a big way with its purchase of CNB Bancshares then solidified its position in the state with the acquisition of Peoples Bank of Indianapolis. Fifth Third also moved into new business areas buying mortgage banker W. Lyman Case broker-dealer The Ohio Company (1998) and Cincinnati-based commercial mortgage banker Vanguard Financial (1999). The company began to offer online foreign exchange via its FX Internet Trading Web in 2000.

In 2001 Fifth Third bought money manager Maxus Investments and added some 300 bank branches with its purchase of Capital Holdings (Ohio and Michigan) and Old Kent Financial (Michigan Indiana and Illinois) its largest-ever acquisition.

Fifth Third exited the property/casualty insurance brokerage business in 2002 selling its operations to Hub International. Also that year Fifth Third arranged to enter Tennessee via its planned purchase of Franklin Financial. But the deal was stalled as industry regulators investigated Fifth Third's risk management procedures and internal controls. A moratorium on acquisitions was placed on the bank during the investigation. It was lifted in 2004 and the purchase of Franklin was completed not long afterwards. That opened the door for Fifth Third's acquisition of First National Bankshares of Florida in 2005. Two years later it continued growing with its purchase of R-G Crown Bank from R&G Financial which added some 30 branches in Florida in addition to locations in Georgia.

EXECUTIVES

President Ceo And Director, Greg D. Carmichael, age 58, $994,287 total compensation

Evp And Coo, Lars C. Anderson, age 59, $675,002 total compensation

Evp And Chief Risk Officer, Frank R. Forrest, age 65, $519,713 total compensation

Evp, Philip R. McHugh, age 55

Evp And Chief Corporate Responsibility And Reputation Officer, Brian Lamb

Evp And Chief Administrative Officer, Teresa J. Tanner, age 51

Evp And Cfo, Tayfun Tuzun, age 55, $519,342 total compensation

Evp, Chad M. Borton, age 49, $491,260 total compensation

Evp And Treasurer, James C. Leonard, age 50

Evp And Chief Strategy Officer, Timothy N. Spence, age 41, $450,008 total compensation

Evp And Chief Operations And Technology Officer, Aravind Immaneni

Evp Chief Legal Officer And Corporate Secretary, Jelena McWilliams

Evp, Richard Stein

Vice President Finance, Dan Flanigan

Vice President Information Technology, Ken Valentine

Assistant Vice President Principal Application Developer, Aaron Stockmeister

Vice President Edm Database Administration, Tracey Tebelman

Vice President Recruiting, Nancy Pinckney

Vice President Middle Market Relationship Manager, Adam Herr

Avp And Senior Manager Applications, Terry Grooms

Vice President Director Of Wealth And Asset Management Marketing, Tricia Eltonhead

Senior Vice President, Jeffrey Leithauser

Vice President Of Facilities, Al Druckenmiller

Vice President, Sara Clark

Vice President, Kevin Zgonc

Vice President Mortgage, Alisa Hunter

Assistant Vice President, Michelle Knight

Vice President Investment Executive, Charles Huff

Vice President Legal Counsel, Shannon Barrow

Vice President Food And Agribusiness Group, Marc Crady

Vice President Senior Relationship Man, Brian Knutson

Senior Vice President And C10 Commercial Bank, Sidney Deloatch

Vice President Commercial Lending, Jerry Hartley

Assistant Vice President Manager Information Security Operations, Christopher Fant

Vice President Chief Operational Risk Officer, John Wallace

Assistant Vice President Senior Compliance Officer, Janis Scharenberg

Assistant Vice President And Relationship Manager, Natan Milgrom

Vice President And Trust Officer, David Garber

Vice President Manager Project Manager, Colleen Foster

Vice President Of Enterprise Architecture, Gary Schnettler

Vice President, Greg Vollmer

Vice President And Director Commercial Analytics, Stephen Boras

Vice President Portfolio Manager, Keith McFarland

Vice President Credit Officer, David Eaton

Vice President And Chief Financial Officer Of Eastern Michigan, John Worthington

Vice President Manager Financial Services, Terrence Lyons

Vice President Information Technology Compliance, Jeffrey A Jones

Vice President, Douglas Schuchter

Senior Vice President And Managing Director, David Williams

Vice President Corporate Banking, William Whitley

Vice President Treasury Management Officer, Alicia Mattice

Senior Vice President And Director Operations, Paul Moore

Vice President, Brian Gardner

Vice President, Tim Tierney

Vice President Financial Audit Senior Manager, Chris Bezold

Vice President, William Hummel

Vice President Institutional Real Estate, Brad Boersma

Assistant Vice President, Brad Pinson

Vice President, Keith Goodpaster

Assistant Vice President, Maher Kaddoura

Vice President, Libby Chapin

Vice President Area Investment Manager, Crystal Kolcz

Vice President, Mark Telles

Vice President, Karen Mundy

Assistant Vice President, Anoopa McKim

Vice President Commercial Lending Middle Market, Kathleen Mekesa

Senior Vice President And Director Business Controls Chief Administrative Office, Peg Jula

Assistant Vice President Information Technology Projects, Michele Mcdonel

Vice President Indirect Originations, Edward Mcelveen

Vice President, Dean Haberkamp

Vice President, Valena Allen

Assistant Vice President Financial Center Manager, Lakita Tucker

Vice President Global Payments, Jason Dement

Assistant Vice President Senior Market Intelligence Analyst, Ashley Wyant

Vice President Legal Counsel, Peter Jurs

Vice President, Jennifer Dunigan-wernke

Vice President Business Banking, Tracey Siarkowski

Vice President Commercial Banking, Tim Egloff

Senior Vice President Senior Credit Officer, Kristof Schneider

Vice President Commercial Banking, Mary Weldon

Vice President Commercial Portfolio Manager, Jonathan Roe

Vice President Product And Risk Manager, April Cothran

Equipment Management Vice President, Donald Mcgill

Vice President, Mark Ransom

Vice President, Joe Acito

Vice President Professional Services, John Huber

Vice President Commercial Loan Operations, Margie Johnson

Vice President Private Bank, David W Herrenbruck

Vice President, Joanne Hindel

Structured Finance Group Assistant Vice President, Paul Bahra

Vice President, Sonia Sonecha

Vice President Treasury Management, Kate Nagy

Vice President Of Marketing, Richard Steimer

Senior Vice President, Jeanne Reynolds

Assistant Vice President Institutional Investments Client Services Specialist, Rachel Trent

Vice President, Patrick Farnan

Financial Center Manager Assistant Vice President, Archard Mathis

Vice President Enterprise Qa, William Nearhood
Vice President, Michael Olinsky
Senior Vice President, Tom Plodzeen
Vice President Officer, George Hunter
Vice President, Michael Hossack
Vice President Portfolio Manager, Neil Vajda
Vice President Treasury Management Officer, Douglas Henderson
Vice President, Tammy Schaefer
Vice President Sba Alternative Lending, Chris Intemann
Vice President, Terry Feucht
Vice President, Jason Fronheiser
Fcm Vice President, Rubia Marins
Vice President And Director Of Accounting, Glen Napolitano
Financial Center Manager Avp, Rick Bugaj
Vice President Of Capital Markets Accounting Group, Bryan Preston
Vice President, Mark Gregory
Vice President Portfolio Manager, Christopher Staples
Vice President Consumer Risk Management, Warren Butterworth
Vice President, Thomas Begam
Vice President Employee Relations, Kathie Davis
Vice President Recovery Manager, Jeremy Hejl
Vice President Business Controls Manager, Tina Doyle
Vice President Senior Wealth Management Advisor, Craig Vaness
Vice President, Jon Powell
Vice President Healthcare Treasury Management, Lynne Pearson
Vice President Legal Counsel, Melissa Stegman
Assistant Vice President Special Assets Group, Monique Suranye
Financial Center Manager And Vice President, Adrian Mendieta
Senior Vice President Audit Director, Ryan Dirks
Vice President Of Business Banking, Lisa Sammons
Vice President Sag Core, Chris C Cagle
Investment Executive Vice President, Jason Tosh
Vice President Business Loan Center Manager, Philip Ottinger
Assistant Vice President And Counsel, Gregory Sova
Senior Vice President Charitable Management Services, Deborah Moses
Vice President, John Burlowski
Vice President Commercial Equipment Finance, Charles Bonano
Vice President Area Sales Manager, Greg Elmore
Vice President Global Payments, Jim McNamara
Senior Vice President Commercial Banking, John Fittro
Vice President Team Lead, David Fuller
Vice President Product Management, Wade Edwards
Vice President Investor Reporting Loan Servicing Manager, Mark Fairchild
Vice President Senior Manager Of Treasury Analytics, Todd Okeson
Vice President Team Lead Documentation, Barbara Yerdon
Vice President Data Warehouse And Business Intelligence, Mark Jenkins
Senior Vice President, Frank Conway
Auditors: DELOITTE & TOUCHE LLP

LOCATIONS

HQ: Fifth Third Bancorp (Cincinnati, OH)
38 Fountain Square Plaza, Cincinnati, OH 45263
Phone: 800 972-3030
Web: www.53.com

Selected Markets
Florida
Georgia
Indiana
Illinois
Kentucky
Michigan
North Carolina
Ohio
Tennessee
West Virginia

PRODUCTS/OPERATIONS

2018 Sales

	$ mil.	% of total
Interest		
Loans & leases including fees	4,078	51
Securities & other	1,080	13
Interest on other short-term investments	25	-
Interest Expense	(1043.0)	
Non-Interest		
Service charges on deposits	549	7
Wealth and asset management revenue	444	6
Corporate banking revenue	438	5
Mortgage banking net revenue	212	3
Card & processing revenue	329	4
Securities gains net	(54.0)	-
Other	887	11
Total	**6,945**	**100**

2018 Sales

	% of total
Commercial Banking	37
Branch Banking	40
Consumer Lending	6
Wealth and Asset Management	9
Corporate and Other	8
Total	**100**

Selected Subsidiaries
Fifth Third Financial Corporation
Fifth Third Bank
GNB Management LLC
GNB Realty LLC
ClearArc Capital Inc.
Fifth Third Holdings LLC
Fifth Third Insurance Agency Inc.
Fifth Third International Company
The Fifth Third Auto Leasing Trust
Fifth Third Mortgage Company — Michigan LLC
Old Kent Mortgage Services Inc.
Fifth Third Community Development Corporation
Fifth Third New Markets Development Co. LLC
Fifth Third Investment Company
Fountain Square Life Reinsurance Company Ltd. (Turks and Caicos Islands)
Vista Settlement Services LLC

COMPETITORS

Bank of America	KeyCorp
Citigroup	Northern Trust
Comerica	PNC Financial
Harris	U.S. Bancorp
Huntington Bancshares	Wells Fargo
JPMorgan Chase	

HISTORICAL FINANCIALS
Company Type: Public

Income Statement
FYE: December 31

	ASSETS ($ mil.)	NET INCOME ($ mil.)	INCOME AS % OF ASSETS	EMPLOYEES
12/19	169,369	2,512	1.5%	19,869
12/18	146,069	2,193	1.5%	17,437
12/17	142,193	2,194	1.5%	18,125
12/16	142,177	1,564	1.1%	17,844
12/15	141,082	1,712	1.2%	18,261
Annual Growth	**4.7%**	**10.1%**	**—**	**2.1%**

2019 Year-End Financials
Debt ratio: 8.78%
Return on equity: 13.41%
Cash ($ mil.): 3,575
Current ratio: —
Long-term debt ($ mil.): —
No. of shares (mil.): 708
Dividends
 Yield: 3.0%
 Payout: 30.5%
Market value ($ mil.): 21,792

	STOCK PRICE ($) FY Close	P/E High/Low		PER SHARE ($) Earnings	Dividends	Book Value
12/19	30.74	9	7	3.33	0.94	29.91
12/18	23.53	11	7	3.06	0.74	25.13
12/17	30.34	11	8	2.83	0.60	23.59
12/16	26.97	14	7	1.93	0.53	21.59
12/15	20.10	11	8	2.01	0.52	20.18
Annual Growth	**11.2%**	**—**	**—**	**13.5%**	**16.0%**	**10.3%**

Financial Institutions Inc.

Financial Institutions may not have a luxurious name but they specialize in five star service. The holding company owns Five Star Bank which provides standard deposit products such as checking and savings accounts CDs and IRAs to retail and business customers through some 50 branches across western and central New York. Indirect consumer loans originated through agreements with area franchised car dealers account for the largest percentage of the company's loan portfolio (35%) followed by commercial mortgages. The company also sells insurance while its Five Star Investment Services subsidiary offers brokerage and financial planning services.

Operations

Financial Institutions operates through two business segments: banking which includes the bank's retail and commercial banking operations; and insurance which sells insurance to both personal and business clients through its Scott Danahy Naylon Co (SDN) subsidiary.

About 65% of the company's total revenue came from loan interest (including fees) in 2014 while another 15% came from interest on its investment securities. The rest of its revenue came from deposit account service charges (7%) ATM and debit card fees (4%) insurance income (2%) investment advisory (2%) and other miscellaneous income sources.

Geographic Reach

Five Star Bank boasts 50 branches and an ATM network across Western and Central New York in the counties of Allegany Cattaraugus Cayuga Chautauqua Chemung Erie Genesee Livingston Monroe Ontario Orleans Schuyler Seneca Steuben Wyoming and Yates.

Sales and Marketing

The company offers financial and banking services to individuals municipalities and businesses in Western and Central New York.

Financial Performance

Financial Institution's revenues and profits have been rising over the past few years thanks to growing loan business (organically and from 2012 acquisitions) lower interest expenses and rising fee-based revenue.

The company's revenue rose by 2% to $126.4 million in 2014 mostly thanks to the addition of insurance income from stemming from the bank's acquisition of SDN. Financial's loan interest grew by 1% on organic loan business growth while interest on investment securities grew by 7% as it purchased more interest-earning assets.

Higher revenue and a decline in loan loss provisions from a more credit-worthy loan portfolio in 2014 drove Financial Institution's net income higher by 15% to a record $29.4 million. The company's operating cash levels dipped by 5% to $35.2 million during the year due to unfavorable changes in working capital related to its contributions to its defined benefit pension plan.

Strategy

Financial Institutions' long-term strategy reiterated in 2015 has been to "maintain a community bank philosophy which consists of focusing on and understanding the individualized banking needs of individuals municipalities and businesses of the local communities surrounding their primary service area." The firm believes this focus will enable it to better respond to customer needs and provide a higher level of personalized services giving it a competitive advantage over larger competitors.

The company has also pursued acquisitions to bolster its service lines to grow its non-interest business. Its 2014 acquisition of a New-York based full-service insurance agency for example launched it beyond banking into the insurance business.

Mergers and Acquisitions

In January 2015 Financial Institutions bolstered its investment service business after acquiring Courier Capital which offers customized investment management investment consulting and retirement plan services to some 1100 individuals businesses and institutions.

In 2014 Financial Institutions expanded its services into the insurance business after acquiring Buffalo-based Scott Danahy Naylon Co. (SDN) a full-service insurance agency for a total of $16.9 million plus a promise of $3.4 million in future payments contingent on SDN meeting revenue performance goal targets through 2017.

Company Background

In 2012 Five Star Bank acquired four retail branches owned by HSBC Bank and four owned by First Niagara Bank in upstate New York.

Five Star Bank was formed in 2005 when the company consolidated its four banking subsidiaries (First Tier Bank & Trust National Bank of Geneva Wyoming County Bank and Bath National Bank) into a single entity. First Tier Bank & Trust absorbed the other three banks and changed its name to Five Star Bank.

EXECUTIVES

Vice President Customer Service, David Macintyre
Evp Cfo And Treasurer, Kevin B. Klotzbach, age 67, $230,000 total compensation
President And Ceo, Martin K. Birmingham, $420,000 total compensation
Evp Commercial Executive And Regional President, Jeffrey P. Kenefick, $209,100 total compensation
Svp And Director Of Human Resources And Enterprise Planning, Paula D. Dolan, $140,000 total compensation
Evp And Chief Risk Officer, Kenneth V. Winn
Vice President Marketing, John Bennett
Executive Vice President, Basar Ordukaya
Vice President Of Commercial Lending, Robert McFadden
Second Vice President, William Andrews
Senior Vice President And Treasurer, Marc Swanson
Vice President, Karen Urban
Senior Vice President And Manager Work, Steven Ambrose
Vice President Information Technology Operations, Chip Shepard
Senior Vice President, Darren Haugen
Vice Presidenti Information Technology, R McLaughlin
Senior Vice President Chief Commercial Credit Officer Of The Bank, David Case

Senior Vice President Candi Lending Executive And Buffalo Regional President Of The Bank, Edward Oexle
Senior Vice President Consumer Lending Manager, Jonathan Chase
Executive Vice President Chief Community Commercial And Strategic Development Officer Of The Compa, Jeff Kenefick
Senior Vice President Business Banking Executive, Vito Caraccio
Senior Vice President Commercial Real Estate Executive Of The Bank, Craig Burton
Board Member, Samuel M Gullo
Chairman, Robert N. Latella, age 77
Treasurer, Kevin Kotzbach
Board Member, Susan Holliday
Auditors: RSM US LLP

LOCATIONS

HQ: Financial Institutions Inc.
220 Liberty Street, Warsaw, NY 14569
Phone: 585 786-1100
Web: www.fiiwarsaw.com

PRODUCTS/OPERATIONS

2013 Sales

	$ mil.	% of total
Interest income		
Loans including fees	81	66
Investment securities	17	14
Noninterest income		
Service charges on deposits	9	9
ATM & debit card	5	4
Investment advisory	2	2
Other	7	5
Total	**123**	**100**

COMPETITORS

Astoria Financial	HSBC USA
Citibank	KeyCorp
Community Bank System	M&T Bank
ESL Federal Credit Union	

HISTORICAL FINANCIALS

Company Type: Public

Income Statement

FYE: December 31

	ASSETS ($ mil.)	NET INCOME ($ mil.)	INCOME AS % OF ASSETS	EMPLOYEES
12/19	4,384	48	1.1%	722
12/18	4,311	39	0.9%	725
12/17	4,105	33	0.8%	656
12/16	3,710	31	0.9%	654
12/15	3,381	28	0.8%	691
Annual Growth	**6.7%**	**14.6%**	**—**	**1.1%**

2019 Year-End Financials

Debt ratio: 0.90%	No. of shares (mil.): 16
Return on equity: 11.70%	Dividends
Cash ($ mil.): 112	Yield: 3.1%
Current ratio: —	Payout: 33.7%
Long-term debt ($ mil.): —	Market value ($ mil.): 514

	STOCK PRICE ($) FY Close	P/E High/Low	PER SHARE ($) Earnings	Dividends	Book Value
12/19	32.10	11 9	2.96	1.00	27.43
12/18	25.70	14 10	2.39	0.96	24.88
12/17	31.10	17 12	2.13	0.85	23.94
12/16	34.20	16 12	2.10	0.81	22.02
12/15	28.00	15 12	1.90	0.80	20.71
Annual Growth	**3.5%**	**— —**	**11.7%**	**5.7%**	**7.3%**

First American Financial Corp

First American Financial knows that when you're buying real estate you'll probably want some insurance to go along with it. In addition to title insurance closing and escrow services from its First American Title Insurance subsidiary the company's specialty insurance arm provides residential property and casualty insurance and home warranties. Its First American Trust unit offers banking and trust services to the escrow and real estate industries. Other offerings include settlement valuation and real estate data. Vast majority of First American Financial's revenue comes from the US.

Operations

First American Financial is one of the largest title insurers in the US. Its title insurance and services segment accounts for more than 90% of revenue. The unit is focused on issuing title insurance for commercial and residential real estate transactions in the US and abroad; it also provides escrow closing exchange documentation banking and other title insurance-related services. The company also provides real property-related data services to mitigate risk and facilitate transactions.

The remainder of revenue comes from the specialty insurance segment which offers property and casualty policies including homeowners renters and property hazard coverage. It also markets home warranties.

Direct premiums and escrow fees account for about 45% of total revenue while agent premiums represent about 40%. Information and other provides some 15% of revenue.

Geographic Reach

With headquarters in Santa Ana California First American Financial issues policies in 49 states and Washington DC. The US market accounts approximately 95% of title insurance and services revenue. The company has international title insurance and closing services operations in Canada the UK South Korea and Australia.

First American Financial's specialty insurance division is licensed to issue policies in all 50 states and actively issues them in more than 45 states. Its policy liability is concentrated in the western US; California accounts for the majority. The company's home warranty business reaches over 35 states and the District of Columbia.

Sales and Marketing

First American Financial distributes its title insurance and related products through independent issuing agents and a direct sales force. For residential products it markets to real estate agents brokers and attorneys; mortgage brokers and originators; homebuilders; and escrow service providers. For its refinance and default-related services the company targets mortgage originators servicers and government-backed entities. Commercial lines are primarily marketed to real estate investors (e.g. real estate investment trusts (REITs) insurance brokers insurance companies and asset managers). Other clients include law firms commercial and investment banks mortgage brokers and commercial real estate owners.

First American Financial's casualty insurance is marketed through direct distribution channels (including cross-selling to existing customers) and through a network of independent brokers. The company promotes its home warranty business through real estate brokers and agents and direct consumer outreach.

Financial Performance

Except for a slight dip in revenue in 2018 the overall growth trend for the last five years was encouraging. Revenue grew 20% for that period. Net income also enjoyed growth for the same period.

The firm's revenue increased by 8% to $6.2 billion in 2019 driven by increases in direct premiums and escrow fees agent premiums and investment income.

Net income increased by 49% to $707.4 million in 2019 largely in part to higher revenue.

First American increased its cash by $18.8 million in 2019 ending the year with $1.5 billion. Operations provided $913.1 million and financing activities used $445.1 million (due to repayments of secured financings payable). The company used $452.2 billion for investments mostly on advances under secured financing agreements.

Strategy

In addition to the company's debt and equity securities portfolio it maintains certain money-market and other short-term investments. It also holds strategic equity investments in companies engaged in its businesses or similar or related businesses. The company's investment policies are designed to comply with regulatory requirements and to align the investment portfolio asset allocation with strategic objectives.

The company utilizes lower cost labor in countries such as India and the Philippines among others.

Mergers and Acquisitions

In early 2020 First American Financial acquired Idaho-based Docutech a leading provider of document eClose and fulfillment technology for the mortgage industry for $350 million. "The acquisition of Docutech reflects our steadfast commitment to invest in and grow our core business. Moreover it demonstrates our dedication to improving the home-buying experience for consumers and driving the digital transformation of the real estate settlement process." said Dennis J. Gilmore Chief Executive Officer at First American Financial Corporation.

In addition to early 2020 acquisition First American Financial acquired Arizona-based Title Security Agency LLC which specializes in title and escrow services for residential and commercial transactions and has 17 offices in Arizona for an undisclosed amount. "The addition of Title Security Agency LLC expands our abilities to serve customers in Arizona and enhances our expertise in the Arizona market." said Chris Leavell Chief Operating Officer at First American Title Insurance a subsidiary of First American Financial.

Company Background

First American Financial was birthed out of the 1889 split of Orange County California from Los Angeles when two companies formed to perform title services in the new county. The two companies merged in 1994 to form First American's predecessor Orange County Title Company.

HISTORY

In 1889 when Los Angeles was on its way to becoming a real city the more countrified residents to the south (including The Irvine Company's founding family) formed Orange County a peaceful realm of citrus groves where land transactions were assisted by title companies Orange County Abstract and Santa Ana Abstract. In 1894 the firms merged under the leadership of local businessman C. E. Parker. For three decades the resulting Orange County Title limited its business to title searches.

In 1924 as real estate transactions became more complex (in part because of mineral-rights issues related to Southern California's oil boom) Orange County Title began offering title insurance and es-

crow services. The company remained under Parker family management until 1930 when H. A. Gardner took over and guided it through the Depression. In 1943 the company returned to Parker family control.

In 1957 the company began a major expansion beyond Orange County. The new First American Title Insurance and Trust name acknowledged the firm's expansion into trust and custody operations. Donald Kennedy (C. E. Parker's grandson) took over in 1963 and took the company public the next year.

In 1968 First American Corporation was formed as a holding company for subsidiaries First American Title Insurance and First American Trust. This structure facilitated growth as the firm began opening new offices and buying all or parts of other title companies including Title Guaranty Co. of Wyoming Security Title & Trust (San Antonio) and Ticore Inc. (Portland Oregon) all purchased in 1968.

The 1970s were a quiet time for the company but it began growing again in the 1980s as savings and loan deregulation jump-started the commercial real estate market in Southern California. First American diversified into home warranty and real estate tax services. In 1988 on the brink of the California meltdown the company bought an industrial loan corporation to make commercial real estate loans.

EXECUTIVES

Evp, Kenneth D. DeGiorgio, age 48, $749,615 total compensation

Ceo And Director, Dennis J. Gilmore, age 61, $949,231 total compensation

Coo First American Title Insurance Company, Christopher M. Leavell, age 57, $699,615 total compensation

Evp And Cfo, Mark E. Seaton, age 44, $574,231 total compensation

Vice President Of Operations, Shawna Mixon

Vp And Chief Accounting Officer, Matthew F. Wajner, age 44, $274,769 total compensation

Vice President Southern California Area Operations Director, Chris Clemens

Svp And Business Development Officer First American Trust, Kenneth Petersen

Svp And Legal Counsel First American Trust, Stephen Minana

Vice President Corporate Information Technology, Desai Priti

Svp And Managing Director Northeast Region National Commercial Services, Michael Hillman

Vice President, Michael Kennedy

Vice President, Amanda Pomerantz

Vice President National Accounts, Valerie Kolytiris

Senior Vice President Sales, Caitlin Stearns

Vice President, Trish Brown

Vice President Business Development Manager, Lisa Jackson

Assistant Vice President Trust Services, Kathy Vian

Vice President, Jack Hanrahan

Executive Vice President, Scott Callender

Vice President And Wealth Management Advisor First American Trust, Nicholas Henry

Vice President And Relationship Manager First American Trust, Jamie Kim

Vp And Senior Relationship Manager First American Trust, Jody Hudson

Vp And Senior Relationship Manager First American Trust, Denise Mehus

Assistant Vice President Information Security And Continuity Officer, David Nasta

Vp And State Manager West Virginia First American Title Insurance Company, Laura Wareheim

Vp And Portfolio Manager First American Trust, Michael Serrano

Svp And Senior Portfolio Manager First American Trust, Kevin Wilcox

Svp And Relationship Manager First American Trust, Neil Schoenblum

Vice President And Wealth Management Advisor First American Trust, Kris Lanzer

Vice President Of Sales, Tori Robinson

Vice President Of Marketing, Sandeep Narayan

Vice President Sales, Omar Kubba

Assistant Vice President Client Solutions Manager, Carolee Richards

Division Vice President Operations, Kristen Estrella

Vice President And Manager, Amanda Harris

Vice President Sales, Michele Klein

Chairman, Parker S. Kennedy

Board Member, Mark Oman

Auditors: PricewaterhouseCoopers LLP

LOCATIONS

HQ: First American Financial Corp
1 First American Way, Santa Ana, CA 92707-5913
Phone: 714 250-3000   **Fax:** 714 250-3151
Web: www.firstam.com

2016 Sales

	% of total
US	94
International	6
Total	**100**

PRODUCTS/OPERATIONS

2018 Sales

	$ mil.	% of total
Direct premiums and escrow fees	2,507	43
Agent premiums	2,284	39
Information and other	781	14
Net investment income	230	4
Net realized investment losses	(56.5)	-
Total	**5,747**	**100**

2018 Sales

	$ mil.	% of total
Title Insurance and Services	5,282	92
Specialty Insurance	469	8
Corporate	(3.1)	-
Eliminations	(1.2)	-
Total	**5,747**	**100**

2018 Sales (title insurance and services segment

	% of total
US	94
International	6
Total	**100**

Selected Products and Services

Title and Settlement Services
  Title Insurance - Residential
  Title Insurance - Commercial
  Title Insurance - Homebuilders
  Escrow Settlement Services
  Escrow Settlement Services - Commercial
Asset Disposition Services
  Auction Services
  Asset Closing Services
  REO Title Services
  REO Direct Production Services
Equity Services
  Title Insurance Services
  Settlement Services
  Signature Services-Origination
  National Recording Services
Due Diligence
  ALTA Land Title Survey and Coordination Services
  ExpressMap
  Flood Elevation Certificates and Determination
  Zoning Reports
Disclosure Reports
  Natural Hazard Disclosure Report
1031 Exchange Services
  Delayed Exchanges
  Improvement - Build-to-Suit Exchanges

Personal Property Exchanges
Reverse Exchanges
UCC Services
EAGLE 9 UCC Insurance Policy for Buyers
EAGLE 9 UCC Lenders Insurance Policy
EAGLE 9 UCC Foreclosure Notice Policy
EAGLE 9 UCC Vacation Interest Policy
Trustee Services
Direct Source Entry and Review
Foreclosure Processing
Senior Lien Monitoring
Loss Mitigation - Borrower Assistance
Loss Mitigation Title Services
Property Reports - Residential
Document Retrieval Services
Property Reports - Commercial
Lien Priority Insurance
Foreclosure Title Services
National Foreclosure Title Services
Mortgage Priority Reporting
Trustee Sale Guarantee
Trustee Servicing Solutions
Non-National Foreclosure Title Services
Commercial Foreclosure Services — Southwest
Software Solutions
Custom Software Solutions

COMPETITORS

American Coast Title	Old Republic National
American Home Shield	Title
Equity Title Company	Stewart Information
Fidelity National	Services
Financial	Ticor Title Co.
Home Buyers Warranty	Title Resource Group
Investors Title	United General Title
North American Title	Insurance
Old Republic	

HISTORICAL FINANCIALS

Company Type: Public

Income Statement — FYE: December 31

	ASSETS ($ mil.)	NET INCOME ($ mil.)	INCOME AS % OF ASSETS	EMPLOYEES
12/19	11,519	707	6.1%	18,412
12/18	10,630	474	4.5%	18,251
12/17	9,573	423	4.4%	18,705
12/16	8,831	342	3.9%	19,531
12/15	8,254	288	3.5%	17,955
Annual Growth	8.7%	25.2%	—	0.6%

2019 Year-End Financials

Debt ratio: 8.74%	No. of shares (mil.): 112
Return on equity: 17.33%	Dividends
Cash ($ mil.): 1,485	Yield: 2.8%
Current ratio: —	Payout: 33.1%
Long-term debt ($ mil.): —	Market value ($ mil.): 6,560

	STOCK PRICE ($) FY Close	P/E High/Low		PER SHARE ($) Earnings	Dividends	Book Value
12/19	58.32	10	7	6.22	1.68	39.30
12/18	44.64	15	10	4.19	1.60	33.56
12/17	56.04	15	10	3.76	1.44	31.37
12/16	36.63	14	10	3.09	1.20	27.36
12/15	35.90	16	12	2.62	1.00	25.28
Annual Growth	12.9%			24.1%	13.8%	11.7%

First Bancorp (NC)

Don't confuse this First Bancorp with Virginia's First Bancorp or First BanCorp in Puerto Rico. This one is the holding company for First Bank which operates about 100 branch locations in east-central North Carolina east South Carolina and western Virginia (where it operates under the name First Bank of Virginia). In addition to offering standard commercial banking services such as deposit accounts and lending the bank offers investment products and discount brokerage services. Another subsidiary First Bank Insurance Services offers property/casualty products. First Bank focuses its lending on mortgages which account for more than half of its loan portfolio.

EXECUTIVES

Evp And Cfo First Bancorp And First Bank, Eric P. Credle, age 51, $325,000 total compensation
President And Director First Bancorp And President And Ceo First Bank, Michael G. Mayer, age 60, $425,000 total compensation
President Ceo And Director, Richard H. Moore, age 59, $525,000 total compensation
Senior Vice President Retail Market Manager, Carol Clagett
Senior Vice President Legal Division, Kirsten Foyles
Vice President, Jason Williams
Assistant Vice President, Laurie Byrd
Mortgage Loan Originator Assistant Vice President, Patrick Blackburn
Chairman First Bancorp And First Bank, James C. Crawford, age 63
Board Member, Dennis Wicker
Board Member, John Gould
Auditors: BDO USA, LLP

LOCATIONS

HQ: First Bancorp (NC)
300 S.W. Broad St., Southern Pines, NC 28387
Phone: 910 246-2500
Web: www.localFirstbank.com

PRODUCTS/OPERATIONS

2016 Sales

	$ mil.	% of total
Interest Income	130	84
Non-interest Income	25	16
Total	156	100

COMPETITORS

BB&T	NewBridge Bancorp
BNC Bancorp	PNC Financial
Bank of America	South Street Financial
CommunityOne Bancorp	SunTrust
First Citizens BancShares	Wells Fargo

HISTORICAL FINANCIALS

Company Type: Public

Income Statement — FYE: December 31

	ASSETS ($ mil.)	NET INCOME ($ mil.)	INCOME AS % OF ASSETS	EMPLOYEES
12/19	6,143	92	1.5%	1,111
12/18	5,864	89	1.5%	1,098
12/17	5,547	45	0.8%	1,166
12/16	3,614	27	0.8%	861
12/15	3,362	27	0.8%	840
Annual Growth	16.3%	35.8%	—	7.2%

2019 Year-End Financials

Debt ratio: 0.88%	No. of shares (mil.): 29
Return on equity: 11.39%	Dividends
Cash ($ mil.): 231	Yield: 1.3%
Current ratio: —	Payout: 16.9%
Long-term debt ($ mil.): —	Market value ($ mil.): 1,181

	STOCK PRICE ($) FY Close	P/E High/Low	Earnings	PER SHARE ($) Dividends	Book Value
12/19	39.91	13 10	3.10	0.54	28.80
12/18	32.66	14 10	3.01	0.40	25.71
12/17	35.31	21 15	1.82	0.32	23.38
12/16	27.14	21 13	1.33	0.32	17.66
12/15	18.74	15 12	1.30	0.32	17.33
Annual Growth	20.8%	— —	24.3%	14.0%	13.5%

First Bancorp Inc (ME)

It may not actually be the first bank but The First Bancorp (formerly First National Lincoln) was founded over 150 years ago. It is the holding company for The First a regional bank serving coastal Maine from more than 15 branches. The bank offers traditional retail products and services including checking and savings accounts CDs IRAs and loans. Residential mortgages make up about 40% of the company's loan portfolio; business loans account for another 40%; and home equity and consumer loans comprise the rest. Bank subsidiary First Advisors offers private banking and investment management services. Founded in 1864 the bank now boasts more than $1.4 billion in assets.

Operations
Subsidiary First Advisors acts as the bank's Trust and Investment services division which managed some $740 million in investor assets as of late 2014.

The First Bancorp generated 57% of its total revenue from interest income on loans (including fees) while another 25% came from interest and dividends on its investments. Service charges on deposit accounts (4%) Fiduciary and investment management income (3%) mortgage origination (2%) and net securities gains (2%) made up most of the rest of its total revenue.

Geographic Reach
The Damariscotta-based bank boasts more than 15 branches in Mid-Coast Eastern and Down East regions of Maine in Lincoln Knox Hancock Washington and Penobscot counties.

Sales and Marketing
The community-oriented bank concentrates on marketing to small businesses and individuals within its local markets.

Financial Performance
The First Bancorp's revenues have slowly declined over the past few years mostly with as its loan business has stagnated and as its interest margins on loans and investments have been shrinking in the low-interest rate environment. Its profits however have been steadily rising thanks to declining loan loss provisions as its loan portfolio's credit quality has improved with the strengthened economy.

The company's revenue inched up by less than one-tenth of a percent to $62.07 million in 2014 mostly as the bank carried more interest-earning investment assets during the year. The bank's non-interest income however declined by 9% as it collected less from the origination and sale of refinanced mortgage loans into the secondary market.

The First Bancorp's net income jumped by 13% to $14.7 million in 2014 thanks primarily to a continued decline in loan loss provisions as its portfolio's credit quality improved. Slightly higher revenue and lower interest expenses on deposits also helped pad the company's bottom line. The bank's operating cash levels fell by 18% to $20.5 million after adjusting its earnings for non-cash items related to its loan loss provisions and its net proceeds from the sale of its mortgage loans held for sale.

Strategy

As management reiterated in early 2015 remaining well capitalized "remains a top priority for The First Bancorp" and has been key to its profit growth over the past several years. Indeed its de-risking initiatives for its loan portfolio assets have taken the bank's risk-based capital ratio from 11.13% in 2008 to 16.27% at the end of 2014 well above the FDIC's suggested threshold of 10%. As a result the bank's loan loss provisions have declined over the period and its profits have blossomed despite a lack of revenue growth.

Company Background

First National Lincoln acquired competitor FNB Bankshares and its First National Bank of Bar Harbor subsidiary in 2005. It merged that bank into its own subsidiary The First National Bank of Damariscotta which was renamed The First.

EXECUTIVES

Treasurer The First Bancorp Inc. And Evp And Cfo First National Bank, F. Stephen Ward, age 67, $254,400 total compensation

Evp And Clerk The First Bancorp Inc. And Evp Banking Services And Senior Loan Officer The First National Bank, Charles A. Wootton, age 63, $241,100 total compensation

Evp And Chief Administrative Officer First National Bank, Susan A. Norton, age 60, $210,000 total compensation

Evp And Treasurer First National Bank, Richard M. Elder, age 54, $179,400 total compensation

Evp And Cio The First, Tammy L. Plummer, age 54

President And Ceo The First Bancorp And The First N.a., Tony C. McKim, age 53, $430,000 total compensation

Board Member, Robert B Gregory

Chairman, David B. Soule, age 75

Vice Chairman, Mark N. Rosborough, age 72

Board Member, Stuart Smith

Board Member, Renee Kelly

Board Member, Cornelius Russell

Auditors: Berry Dunn McNeil & Parker, LLC

LOCATIONS

HQ: First Bancorp Inc (ME)
Main Street, Damariscotta, ME 04543
Phone: 207 563-3195
Web: www.thefirstbancorp.com

PRODUCTS/OPERATIONS

2007 Sales

	$ mil.	% of total
Interest		
Loans including fees	60	74
Investments & other	11	14
Noninterest		
Service charges on deposit accounts	2	3
Fiduciary & investment management income	1	1
Other	6	8
Total	81	100

COMPETITORS

Bangor Savings Bank	KeyCorp
Bar Harbor Bankshares	Northeast Bancorp
Camden National	TD Bank USA

HISTORICAL FINANCIALS

Company Type: Public

Income Statement

FYE: December 31

	ASSETS ($ mil.)	NET INCOME ($ mil.)	INCOME AS % OF ASSETS	EMPLOYEES
12/19	2,068	25	1.2%	245
12/18	1,944	23	1.2%	239
12/17	1,842	19	1.1%	235
12/16	1,712	18	1.1%	235
12/15	1,564	16	1.0%	223
Annual Growth	7.2%	12.0%	—	2.4%

2019 Year-End Financials

Debt ratio: 0.49%	No. of shares (mil.): 10
Return on equity: 12.63%	Dividends
Cash ($ mil.): 25	Yield: 3.9%
Current ratio: —	Payout: 50.6%
Long-term debt ($ mil.): —	Market value ($ mil.): 329

	STOCK PRICE ($) FY Close	P/E High/Low	PER SHARE ($) Earnings	Dividends	Book Value
12/19	30.23	13 10	2.34	1.18	19.50
12/18	26.30	14 11	2.17	1.06	17.63
12/17	27.23	18 14	1.81	1.06	16.74
12/16	33.10	20 11	1.66	0.90	15.98
12/15	20.47	15 11	1.51	0.86	15.58
Annual Growth	10.2%	— —	11.6%	8.2%	5.8%

First Bancshares Inc (MS)

Hoping to be first in the hearts of its customers The First Bancshares is the holding company for The First a community bank with some two dozen branch locations in southern Mississippi's Hattiesburg Alabama and Louisiana. The company provides such standard deposit products as checking and savings accounts NOW and money market accounts and IRAs. Real estate loans account for about 80% of the bank's lending portfolio including about equal portions of residential mortgages commercial mortgages and construction loans. The bank also writes business loans and consumer loans. The bank which has expanded beyond Mississippi through several acquisitions has approximately $970 million in assets.

EXECUTIVES

Assistant Vice President Branch Manager, Whitney Boyd

Vp Appraisal Analyst, Lindsey Smith

Board Member, David Bomboy

Board Member, Fred Mcmurry

Board Member, Ted Parker

Auditors: Crowe LLP

LOCATIONS

HQ: First Bancshares Inc (MS)
6480 U.S. Highway 98 West, Suite A, Hattiesburg, MS 39402
Phone: 601 268-8998
Web: www.thefirstbank.com

COMPETITORS

BancorpSouth	Peoples Financial
Community Bancshares of Mississippi	Renasant
Hancock Holding	Trustmark

HISTORICAL FINANCIALS

Company Type: Public

Income Statement

FYE: December 31

	ASSETS ($ mil.)	NET INCOME ($ mil.)	INCOME AS % OF ASSETS	EMPLOYEES
12/19	3,941	43	1.1%	697
12/18	3,003	21	0.7%	641
12/17	1,813	10	0.6%	487
12/16	1,277	10	0.8%	315
12/15	1,145	8	0.8%	305
Annual Growth	36.2%	49.3%	—	23.0%

2019 Year-End Financials

Debt ratio: 2.18%	No. of shares (mil.): 18
Return on equity: 9.65%	Dividends
Cash ($ mil.): 168	Yield: 0.8%
Current ratio: —	Payout: 12.1%
Long-term debt ($ mil.): —	Market value ($ mil.): 668

	STOCK PRICE ($) FY Close	P/E High/Low	PER SHARE ($) Earnings	Dividends	Book Value
12/19	35.52	14 11	2.55	0.31	28.91
12/18	30.25	25 17	1.62	0.20	24.49
12/17	34.20	31 24	1.11	0.15	19.92
12/16	27.50	15 8	1.64	0.15	17.19
12/15	18.34	11 8	1.62	0.15	19.24
Annual Growth	18.0%	— —	12.0%	19.9%	10.7%

First Bank (Williamstown, NJ)

EXECUTIVES

Coo, Ryan K Manville

Senior Vice President Market Executive, Marianne Desimone

Svp Controller, Donald Theobald

Vp Business Development Officer, Frank Puleio

Vp Internal Auditor, Maria Mayshura

Evp Chief Financial Officer, Stephen Carman

Evp Chief Deposits Officer, Emilio Cooper

Vp Credit Officer, Thao Nguyen

Vice President Commercial Lending Relationship Manager, Brett Lawrence

Assistant Treasurer And Loan Accounting Assistant And Manager, Samantha Dayton

Auditors: RSM US LLP

LOCATIONS

HQ: First Bank (Williamstown, NJ)
2465 Kuser Road, Hamilton, NJ 08690
Phone: 877 821-2265
Web: www.firstbanknj.com

Company Type: Public

Income Statement   FYE: December 31

	ASSETS ($ mil.)	NET INCOME ($ mil.)	INCOME AS % OF ASSETS	EMPLOYEES
12/19	2,011	13	0.7%	221
12/18	1,711	17	1.0%	188
12/17	1,452	6	0.5%	153
12/16	1,073	6	0.6%	110
12/15	855	3	0.5%	101
Annual Growth	23.8%	36.4%	—	21.6%

2019 Year-End Financials

Debt ratio: 1.09%
Return on equity: 6.38%
Cash ($ mil.): 47
Current ratio: —
Long-term debt ($ mil.): —

No. of shares (mil.): 20
Dividends
　Yield: 1.0%
　Payout: 13.4%
Market value ($ mil.): 226

	STOCK PRICE ($) FY Close	P/E High/Low	PER SHARE ($) Earnings	Dividends	Book Value
12/19	11.05	17 15	0.69	0.12	11.07
12/18	12.12	15 12	0.95	0.12	10.43
12/17	13.85	30 23	0.48	0.08	9.36
12/16	11.60	20 10	0.61	0.00	7.78
12/15	6.61	17 14	0.41	0.00	7.26
Annual Growth	13.7%	—	13.9%	—	11.1%

First Busey Corp

First Busey Corporation keeps itself busy taking care of deposits and making loans. It's the holding company for Busey Bank which boasts $4 billion in assets and 40 branches across Illinois Florida and Indiana. The bank offers standard deposit products and services using funds from deposits to originate primarily real estate loans and mortgages. Subsidiary Busey Wealth Management which manages $5 billion in assets provides asset management trust brokerage and related services to individuals businesses and foundations while FirsTech provides retail payment processing services. Most of Busey Bank's branches are located in downstate Illinois.

Operations

First Busey Corporation operates three business segments Busey Bank which generated more than 99% of its total revenue in 2014 and serves retail and corporate customers; FirsTech which provides remittance processing for online bill payments lock box and walk-in payments; and Busey Wealth Management which provides asset management tax preparation philanthropic advisory services and investment and fiduciary services to individuals businesses and foundations.

Real estate loans including commercial and residential mortgages accounted for 70% of the bank's loan portfolio in 2014 while commercial loans (25%) construction loans (4%) and consumer installments and other loans (0.5%) comprised the rest.

About 55% of First Busey's total revenue came from loan interest (including fees) while another 10% came from interest income on taxable and non-taxable investment securities. The rest of its revenue came from trust fees (11%) deposit account service charges (7%) remittance processing fees (6%) commissions and brokers' fees (2%) and various types of gains on securities and loan sales.

Geographic Reach

Busey Bank has nearly 30 branches in Illinois seven locations in southwest Florida and another office in Indianapolis. Its FirsTech subsidiary accepts payments from its 3000 agent locations across 36 US states.

Sales and Marketing

The bank which staffed 801 employees at the end of 2014 serves individuals businesses and foundations.

Financial Performance

First Busey's revenues have declined in recent years due to shrinking interest margins on loans amidst the low-interest environment. Its profits however have been rising thanks to lower interest expenses on deposits and declining loan loss provisions as its loan portfolio's credit quality has improved with higher property valuations in the strengthened economy.

The bank's revenue dipped by 2% to $167 million mostly as it collected smaller gains from loan sales due to lower refinancing volumes as interest rates began to rise. The bank's loan interest income also continued to decline with lower yields on loan and security assets in the low-interest environment.

Despite generating less revenue in 2014 First Busey's net income jumped by 14% to $32.8 million thanks to continued declines in interest expenses on deposits and lower loan loss provisions. The company's operating cash levels fell by 31% to $68.1 million after adjusting its earnings for non-cash items related to its net proceeds from its loans held-for-sale.

Strategy

First Busey sometimes strategically acquires smaller banks in its target markets to boost its market share broaden its service offerings and boost its loan and deposit business.

Mergers and Acquisitions

In 2019 First Busey agreed to acquire Fort Myers Florida-based wealth advisory firm Investors' Security Trust which will be integrated into the wealth management division of Busey Bank. The combined entity will have assets under management of more than $9.2 billion.

EXECUTIVES

Evp And Chief Risk Officer, Barbara J. Harrington, age 60

President Ceo And Director, Van A. Dukeman, age 61, $537,308 total compensation

Chief Credit Officer, Robert F. (Bob) Plecki, age 59, $268,654 total compensation

President And Ceo Firstech, Howard F. Mooney, age 55, $240,216 total compensation

Evp And President And Ceo Busey Bank, Christopher M. (Chris) Shroyer, age 54, $268,654 total compensation

Evp And General Counsel, John J. Powers

Coo And Cfo, Robin N. Elliott, $256,731 total compensation

Vice President Senior Retirement Plan Services Advisor, Charlee Seaton

Senior Vice President Commercial Real Estate, Kent Poli

Senior Vice President Loan Operations, Michael Stevenson

Vice President, Kelly Dennemann

Assistant Vice President Special Assets, Shana Reed-harper

Executive Vice President, Robert Ballsrud

Assistant Vice President, Emerson Schoonover

Vice President Retail Market Manager, Tami Crouch

Vice President, Brenda Carlson

Senior Vice President, Janice Wolters

Assistant Vice President Risk Management Analyst, Annie Feleccia

Vice President Senior Loan Officer, Brian Church

Assistant Vice President Wealth Advisor Assistant, Monya Russell

Vice President Retail Market Manager, Linda Smith

Vice President Commercial Credit Manager, Thomas Richlak

Senior Vice President Relationship Manager Middle Market, Karen Johnson

Assistant Vice President Wire Services Manager, Karen Aulph

Vice President, Tom Carter

Senior Vice President, Ed Paine

Vice President, Sally Brumfield

Chairman, Gregory B. (Greg) Lykins, age 72

Vice Chairman, Ed Scharlau

Auditors: RSM US LLP

LOCATIONS

HQ: First Busey Corp
100 W. University Avenue, Champaign, IL 61820
Phone: 217 365-4544

PRODUCTS/OPERATIONS

2014 Sales

	$ mil.	% of total
Interest		
Loans including fees	92	55
Interest & dividends on securities	15	10
Noninterest		
Trust fees	19	11
Service charges on deposit accounts	12	7
Remittance processing	9	6
Gain on sales of loans	4	3
Commissions and broker's fees net	2	2
Other	10	6
Total	**167**	**100**

COMPETITORS

Bank of America
CIB Marine Bancshares
Fifth Third
First Mid-Illinois Bancshares
First Midwest Bancorp
JPMorgan Chase
Mercantile Bancorp
PNC Financial
Wintrust Financial

HISTORICAL FINANCIALS

Company Type: Public

Income Statement   FYE: December 31

	ASSETS ($ mil.)	NET INCOME ($ mil.)	INCOME AS % OF ASSETS	EMPLOYEES
12/19	9,695	102	1.1%	1,531
12/18	7,702	98	1.3%	1,270
12/17	7,860	62	0.8%	1,347
12/16	5,425	49	0.9%	1,295
12/15	3,998	39	1.0%	795
Annual Growth	24.8%	27.5%	—	17.8%

2019 Year-End Financials

Debt ratio: 2.25%
Return on equity: 9.29%
Cash ($ mil.): 529
Current ratio: —
Long-term debt ($ mil.): —

No. of shares (mil.): 54
Dividends
　Yield: 3.0%
　Payout: 44.9%
Market value ($ mil.): 1,507

	STOCK PRICE ($) FY Close	P/E High/Low	PER SHARE ($) Earnings	Dividends	Book Value
12/19	27.50	15 13	1.87	0.84	22.28
12/18	24.54	16 12	2.01	0.80	20.36
12/17	29.94	22 19	1.45	0.72	19.21
12/16	30.78	22 13	1.40	0.68	15.54
12/15	20.63	17 5	1.32	0.17	13.01
Annual Growth	7.5%	—	9.1%	49.1%	14.4%

First Business Financial Services, Inc.

Business comes first at First Business Financial Services which serves small and midsized companies entrepreneurs professionals and high-net-worth individuals through First Business Bank and First Business Bank - Milwaukee. The banks offer deposits loans cash management and trust services from a handful of offices in Wisconsin and Kansas. Over 60% of the company's loan portfolio is made up of commercial real estate loans. Subsidiary First Business Capital specializes in asset-based lending while First Business Equipment Finance provides commercial equipment financing. First Business Trust & Investments offers investment management and retirement services.

Operations

First Business Financial Services backs its subsidiaries with low-cost corporate services such as human resources finance IT and marketing. First Business Credit Cards provides revolving lines of credit and term loans for financial and strategic acquisitions capital expenditures working capital used to support rapid growth bank debt refinancing debt restructuring and other corporate financing needs.

The company generated 80% of its total revenue from interest on loans and leases in 2014 and another 5% from interest on its securities. About 7% of revenue came from trust and investment services fee income while service charges on deposits and loan fees made up 4% and 2% of revenue respectively.

Geographic Reach

The company's primary market areas are in Wisconsin Kansas and Missouri. First Business's loan production offices are in Wisconsin in Oshkosh Green Bay Appleton and Kenosha while its two Kansas offices are in Leawood and Overland Park. In Wisconsin it targets Madison Milwaukee Appleton Green Bay Oshkosh and their surrounding communities.

Sales and Marketing

Beyond individual customers the bank generally targets businesses with annual sales between $2 million and $75 million.

Financial Performance

The company has struggled to consistently grow its revenues in recent years due to shrinking interest margins on loans amidst the low-interest environment. Its profits however have been rising thanks to declining loan loss provisions as its loan portfolio's credit quality has improved with higher property valuations in a strengthened economy.

First Business had a breakout year in 2014 however as its revenue rose 9% to $67.8 million on higher loan interest as its commercial and industrial loans comercial real estate and other mortgage loans and direct financing leases businesses all enjoyed "favorable volume variances." The bank's non-interest income also jumped by 20% which was mostly driven by growth in trust and investment services fee income on higher assets under management.

Higher revenue and lower interest expenses on deposits in 2014 pushed the company's net income up by 3% to $14.1 million. First Business' operating cash levels fell by 25% to $11.9 million due to unfavorable changes in working capital related to an increase in accrued interest payable and other liabilities.

Strategy

First Business Financial Services continued in 2015 to focus on maintaining its loan asset quality while organically growing its loan and lease portfolio in addition to growing its customer account based to increase its fee-based revenues on its variety of treasury management trust and investment services and SBA loans. It also planned to boost its investment in utilizing technology to support these initiatives while staying efficient as the business grows.

The company occasionally opens new offices or strategically acquires other banks and financial companies to extend its reach into its target markets and to grow its loan and deposit business. In 2014 its FBB-Milwaukee bank subsidiary expanded more into the southeastern area of Wisconsin after opening a loan production office in Kenosha; while its acquisition of Aslin Group and Alterra Bank furthered its exposure to new markets and loan and deposit business in Kansas.

Mergers and Acquisitions

In November 2014 First Business Financial Services expanded its Midwest market and extended its reach into Kansas after its acquisition of Leawood-based Aslin Group including its Alterra Bank subsidiary. The deal added $223 million in total assets including $182 million in new loan assets and $192 million in new deposits.

EXECUTIVES

President And Ceo, Corey A. Chambas, age 57, $416,000 total compensation
Svp And Chief Credit Officer, Michael J. Losenegger, age 62, $221,950 total compensation
President And Ceo First Business Capital, Charles H. (Chuck) Batson, age 66, $242,927 total compensation
President And Ceo First Business Bank - Madison, Mark J. Meloy, age 58, $201,800 total compensation
President First Business Trust & Investments, Joan A. Burke, age 68
President And Ceo First Business Bank - Milwaukee, David J. (Dave) Vetta, age 65
Cfo, Edward G. (Ed) Sloane, age 59
President Kenosha Region, Wesley Ricchio
Svp And Coo First Business Capital Corp., Peter Lowney
Coo And Interim President And Ceo Alterra Bank, David R. Seiler
Cio, Daniel S. Ovokaitys, age 46
Senior Vice President Compliance And Risk Management, Theresa Wiese
Vice President, Josh Hoesch
Senior Vice President First Business Bank Madison, Beth Korth
Assistant Vice President Business Development Officer, Jerimiah Janssen
Senior Vice President Commercial Banking, Kelly Foster
Vice President Of Treasury Management, Wade Hanna
Vice President Consumer Loans, Penny Byrne
Vice President Business Development, Greg Lherault
Assistant Vice President Private Banking, Peggy Stoop
Vice President Private Wealth Management, Monica Schlicht
Vice President Commercial Real Estate, Ryan Hughes
Vice President Business Development Officer, Chris Mckernan
Vice President Internal Loan Review, Gretchen Griffin
Vice President Talent Development Manager, Bonnie Van
Vice President Commercial Banking, Jessica Meier
Vice President, Cymbre Vanfossen
Vice President Business Development Officer, Anne Roslin
Vice President Commercial Banking, Austin Thompson
Chairman, Jerome R. (Jerry) Smith, age 69
Auditors: Crowe LLP

LOCATIONS

HQ: First Business Financial Services, Inc.
401 Charmany Drive, Madison, WI 53719
Phone: 608 238-8008
Web: www.firstbusiness.com

COMPETITORS

Associated Banc-Corp	TCF Financial
Bank Mutual	U.S. Bancorp
Harris	

HISTORICAL FINANCIALS

Company Type: Public

Income Statement
FYE: December 31

	ASSETS ($ mil.)	NET INCOME ($ mil.)	INCOME AS % OF ASSETS	EMPLOYEES
12/19	2,096	23	1.1%	301
12/18	1,966	16	0.8%	289
12/17	1,794	11	0.7%	264
12/16	1,780	14	0.8%	272
12/15	1,782	16	0.9%	258
Annual Growth	4.1%	9.0%	—	3.9%

2019 Year-End Financials

Debt ratio: 15.71%	No. of shares (mil.): 8
Return on equity: 12.44%	Dividends
Cash ($ mil.): 67	Yield: 2.2%
Current ratio: —	Payout: 24.2%
Long-term debt ($ mil.): —	Market value ($ mil.): 226

	STOCK PRICE ($) FY Close	P/E High/Low		PER SHARE ($) Earnings	Dividends	Book Value
12/19	26.33	10	7	2.68	0.60	22.67
12/18	19.51	14	10	1.86	0.56	20.57
12/17	22.12	21	15	1.36	0.52	19.32
12/16	23.72	15	11	1.71	0.48	18.55
12/15	25.01	25	12	1.90	0.44	17.34
Annual Growth	1.3%	—	—	9.0%	8.1%	6.9%

First Citizens BancShares Inc (DE)

First Citizens BancShares owns First-Citizens Bank which operates more than 550 branches in 20 states mainly in the southeastern and western US and urban areas scattered nationwide. The $32 billion-asset bank provides standard services such as deposits loans mortgages and trust services in addition to processing and operational support to other banks. Real estate loans including commercial residential and revolving mortgages and construction and land development loans comprise most of its loan portfolio. Subsidiaries First Citizens Investor Services First Citizens Securities Corporation and First Citizens Asset Management offers investment and discount brokerage services to bank clients.

Operations

The company provides consumer business and commercial banking wealth investments and insurance through a network of branch offices internet banking mobile banking telephone banking and ATMs.

More than 60% of the bank's total revenue came from loan and lease interest during 2015 while another 6% came from interest income on investment securities. The rest of its revenue came from merchant services (6% of revenue) service charges on deposit accounts (6%) wealth management services (6%) cardholder services (4%) mortgage income (1%) insurance commissions (1%) and other miscellaneous income sources.

Geographic Reach

First Citizens BancShares has nearly 560 branches in almost 20 states (Arizona California Colorado Florida Georgia Kansas Maryland Missouri New Mexico North Carolina Oklahoma Oregon South Carolina Tennessee Texas Virginia Washington and West Virginia) and Washington DC.

Sales and Marketing

First Citizens BancShares serves both individuals and commercial entities operating in the healthcare dental practices legal services property management agribusiness nonprofit and trade association markets.

The bank has been ramping up its advertising spend in recent years. It spent $12.4 million in 2015 up from $11.4 million and $8.2 million in 2014 and 2013 respectively.

Financial Performance

First Citizens BancShares' annual revenues have risen more than 35% since 2013 thanks to growth in its variety of non-banking business. Its profits have also been trending higher thanks to declining loan loss provisions as its loan portfolio's credit quality has improved with higher property valuations in the strengthened economy.

The bank's revenue jumped 30% to $1.44 billion during 2015 mostly thanks to higher loan and lease interest income stemming from added loan business from the acquisition of First Citizens Bancorporation. Its non-interest income sources grew 36% during the year as well.

Strong revenue growth in 2015 drove First Citizen's net income up 52% to $210.3 million. The bank's operating cash levels rose 28% to $233 million with the rise in cash-based earnings.

Strategy

FCB has expanded its branch network into new markets while bolstering its loan and deposit business by acquiring small community banks in new territory.

Mergers and Acquisitions

In 2019 First Citizens Bancshares acquired Spartanburg South Carolina-based First South Bancorp the holding company for First South Bank. First South had $236 million in assets $206 million in deposits and $183 million in gross loans. The deal expanded First Citizens' geographic reach in South Carolina.

Company Background

First Citizens BancShares has been fortifying its presence along the West Coast by snapping up failed financial institutions. Since 2009 it has acquired most of the banking operations of Temecula Valley Bank Washington-based Venture Bank and First Regional Bank in Southern California. It also acquired the failed Florida-based bank Sun American and entered Colorado through the acquisitions of United Western Bank and Colorado Capital Bank. All were FDIC-assisted transactions and each acquired institution became branches of First-Citizens Bank. The deals added about 50 branches to the bank's network. First Citizens BancShares continues to seek out acquisitions of other seized institutions.

Though the company has been able to grow geographically thanks to the economic downturn its IronStone Bank division which focused on business customers suffered from weakened markets

in Florida and Georgia. (First Citizens Bancshares merged IronStone into First-Citizens Bank in 2011 to increase efficiency and unify the company's brand.) It has remained profitable thanks in part to its acquisitions which include loss-sharing agreements with the FDIC but has had to increase its provisions for loan losses each of the last five years.

The Holding family which occupies several positions in the company's board room and executive suite controls First Citizens BancShares.

EXECUTIVES

Coo Bancshares And First-citizens Bank & Trust Company, Edward L. (Ed) Willingham, age 65, $585,125 total compensation

President And Corporate Sales Executive Of Bancshares And First-citizens Bank & Trust Company, Peter M. Bristow, age 54

Chairman And Ceo First Citizens Bancshares First-citizens Bank & Trust And Ironstone Bank, Frank B. Holding, age 59, $902,875 total compensation

Evp Finance And Cfo, Craig L. Nix, age 48

Evp Business Banking Segment Manager And Director First-citizens Bank & Trust; President Ironstone Bank, Hope Holding Connell, age 57, $563,750 total compensation

Evp And Chief Human Resources Officer First-citizens Bank & Trust, Lou J. Davis, age 67

Evp And Chief Credit Officer First-citizens Bank & Trust; Group Vp And Chief Credit Officer Ironstone, Ricky T. Holland, age 66

Executive Vice President And General Auditor Of Fcb, Donald Preskenis

Senior Vice President, Morris Turner

Senior Vice President Commercial Relationship Manager, Ivy Dill

Senior Vice President Commercial Banking, Stephanie Logan

Vice President, Rhonda Chapman

Vice President Marketing, Christine Thompson

Vice President, Scott German

Vice President Business Banking, Jessica Chisholm

Vice President Sba Loan Officer, Alan Black

Assistant Vice President Commercial Underwriter, Dickson Mbora

Avp Mortgage Banker Product Specialist, Tommy Harris

Vice President, Amy Maughon

Commercial Banker Senior Vice President, Davis Robinson

Financial Sales Manager Assistant Vice President, Chris Rivera

Vice President Business Development Officer, Debra Stewart

Vice President Business Banking, Kevin Scott

Vice President Commercial Banking, Drew Schiavone

Vice President Business Banker, Joanne Fockler

Avp Business Banking Specialist, Alexi Strish

Senior Vice President, Virginia Lee

Business Banker Vice President, Ryan Cannon

Vice President Financial Sales Manager, Kim Adams

Senior Vice President Financial Sales Manager, Rebecca Hardwick

Vice President Business Banking, Chris Crary

Vice President Premier Relationship Banker, Kelli Peele

Vice President Senior Business Analyst Loan Officer, Joanna Warrick

Vice President Business Banker, Isaac Chavira

Vice President And Associate Counsel, Carrie Mcmillan

Senior Vice President, Allen Sprinkle

Vp Of Sba Lending Central Region, Brett Stacey

Senior Vice President Enterprise Risk Management, Brian Paull

Vice President Business Banker, Laura Mccombs

Vice President, Luis Clavijo

Vice President Sales Manager, Bonita Davis

Senior Vice President Regional Mortgage Sales Manager, John Adams

Senior Vice President, Rick Adyniec

Vice President Commercial Banking, Shawn Mcbride

Vice President Commercial Lending, Branden Conrad

Vice President Business Banking, Bill Mcgowan

Senior Vice President Commercial Banking, Scott Russell

Senior Vice President Commercial Banking, Stephanie Gan

Vice President Private Banker, Shawn Gaffin

Vice President Of Information Technology, Therese Zumbahlen

Assistant Vice President Brand Marketing Specialist, Linda Kline

Auditors: Dixon Hughes Goodman LLP

LOCATIONS

HQ: First Citizens BancShares Inc (DE)
4300 Six Forks Road, Raleigh, NC 27609
Phone: 919 716-7000
Web: www.firstcitizens.com

2013 Branches

	No.
North Carolina	253
Virginia	48
California	21
Florida	18
Georgia	14
Washington	7
Texas	7
Colorado	6
Tennessee	6
West Virginia	5
Arizona	2
New Mexico	2
Oklahoma	2
Oregon	2
District of Columbia	1
Kanas	1
Maryland	1
Missouri	1
Total	**397**

PRODUCTS/OPERATIONS

2013 Sales

	$ mil.	% of total
Interest		
Loans & leases	757	72
Investment securities including dividends	36	3
Overnight investments	2	-
Noninterest		
Service charges on deposit accounts	60	5
Wealth management services	59	5
Merchant services	56	4
Cardholder services	48	4
Fees from processing services	22	1
Other service charges and fees	15	1
Adjustments	(72.3)	-
Other	72	5
Total	**1,060**	**100**

COMPETITORS

BB&T	JPMorgan Chase
BBVA Compass	PNC Financial
Bancshares	Regions Financial
Bank of America	SunTrust
Capital One	Synovus
Citibank	Wachovia Corp
First Horizon	Wells Fargo

HISTORICAL FINANCIALS

Company Type: Public

Income Statement

FYE: December 31

	ASSETS ($ mil.)	NET INCOME ($ mil.)	INCOME AS % OF ASSETS	EMPLOYEES
12/19	39,824	457	1.1%	7,176
12/18	35,408	400	1.1%	6,683
12/17	34,527	323	0.9%	6,799
12/16	32,990	225	0.7%	6,296
12/15	31,475	210	0.7%	6,232
Annual Growth	6.1%	21.4%	—	3.6%

2019 Year-End Financials

Debt ratio: 0.78%
Return on equity: 12.93%
Cash ($ mil.): 1,484
Current ratio: —
Long-term debt ($ mil.): —

No. of shares (mil.): 10
Dividends
Yield: 0.3%
Payout: 4.0%
Market value ($ mil.): 5,657

	STOCK PRICE ($) FY Close	P/E High/Low		PER SHARE ($) Earnings	Dividends	Book Value
12/19	532.21	13	9	41.05	1.60	337.38
12/18	377.05	14	11	33.53	1.45	300.04
12/17	403.00	16	12	26.96	1.25	277.60
12/16	355.00	19	12	18.77	1.20	250.82
12/15	258.17	15	12	17.52	1.20	239.14
Annual Growth	19.8%	—	—	23.7%	7.5%	9.0%

First Commonwealth Financial Corp (Indiana, PA)

First Commonwealth Financial is the holding company for First Commonwealth Bank which provides consumer and commercial banking services from nearly 115 branches across 15 central and western Pennsylvania counties as well as in Columbus Ohio. The bank's loan portfolio mostly consists of commercial and industrial loans including real estate operating agricultural and construction loans. It also issues consumer loans such as education automobile and home equity loans and offers wealth management insurance financial planning retail brokerage and trust services. The company has total assets of some $6.7 billion with deposits of roughly $4.5 billion.

Operations

The bank made 65% of its total revenue from interest and fees on loans in 2014 while another 12% came from interest and dividends on its investments. Another 6% of First Commonwealth's revenue came from service charges on deposit accounts while trust income and insurance and retail brokerage commissions each made up 2% of the bank's total revenue.

Geographic Reach

The bank boasts nearly 115 branch offices in western and central Pennsylvania and Columbus Ohio. It also has loan production offices in downtown Pittsburgh Pennsylvania and Cleveland Ohio.

Sales and Marketing

First Commonwealth Financial spent $2.95 million on advertising in 2014 compared to $3.13 million and $4.16 million in 2013 and 2012 respectively.

Financial Performance

First Commonwealth's revenues have been slowly decline over the past few years due to shrinking interest margins on loans amidst the low-interest environment. The firm's profits however have been rising thanks to declining loan loss provisions as its loan portfolio's credit quality has been improving in the strengthening economy.

The bank's revenue dipped by more than 1% to $263.04 million in 2014 mostly as interest margins on loans continued to decline as it issued new loans with lower rates in the low-interest environment.

Despite lower revenue in 2014 the bank's net income jumped by 7% to $44.45 million for the year mostly thanks to further decreases in loan loss provisions with a strengthening credit portfolio and lower interest expenses on deposits. First Commonwealth's operating cash fell by 4% to $82.14 million despite higher earnings mostly as the bank collected less in cash proceeds from the sales of its mortgage loans held for sale.

Strategy

First Commonwealth Financial has historically expanded its branch reach through the acquisition smaller banks and thrifts in its market area. However in recent years the company has also been adding non-banking businesses such as insurance firms to bolster its existing non-banking service lines.

Mergers and Acquisitions

First Commonwealth Bank acquired 13 branches in Canton and Ashtabula Ohio from FirstMerit Bank in 2016. The acquisition related to FirstMerit's acquisition by Huntington Bancshares added some $735 million in deposits and some 34000 customers. It is also buying Ohio's DCB Financial parent company of Delaware County Bank & Trust for some $106 million. That deal will add nine full-service branches in central Ohio.

In 2014 First Commonwealth Bank entered the Columbus Ohio market for the first time with its purchase of the Ohio-based First Community Bank for $14.75 million cash.

Also in 2014 the bank bolstered its insurance business through its acquisition of Thompson/McLay Insurance Associates which boasted long-term client relationships in the home auto commercial and specialty insurance lines. The deal added the insurance firm's experienced sales and account management personnel as well as the popular Thompson/McLay Insurance Associates brand which it would keep as a division of its own insurance agency.

EXECUTIVES

Evp And Chief Revenue Officer, Jane Grebenc, $355,833 total compensation
Evp And Chief Credit Officer, I. Robert (Bob) Emmerich, $274,500 total compensation
President And Ceo, Thomas Michael (Mike) Price, age 57, $435,567 total compensation
Evp Cfo And Treasurer, James R. Reske, $237,372 total compensation
Evp And Chief Audit Executive, Leonard V. Lombardi, age 60
Evp Business Integration, Norman J. Montgomery, $261,792 total compensation
Evp Chief Risk Officer General Counsel And Secretary, Matthew C. (Matt) Tomb
Evp Human Resources, Carrie Riggle
Senior Vice President Controller, Teresa Ciambotti
Vice President Administration, Wendy Reynolds
Vice President Of Networking Security, Sheila Hoover
Vice President, Terry Lingenfelter
Vice President, Kevin Cribbs

Assistant Vice President And Hris Manager, Karen Livermore
Vice President And Office Manager Of Murrysville And Export Offices, John Mango
Vice President And Commercial Real Estate, Brian Pukylo
Vice President Treasury Managment Officer, Valarry Wolfe
Assistant Vice President Operations, Mona Straw
Vice President And Staffing Manager, Vicki Fox
Vice President Office Manager Ii, David Louis
Vice President Bank Secrecy Act Officer First Commonwealth Bank, David Mcgreevy
Executive Vice President First Commonwealth Advisors, David Buckiso
Senior Vice President Relationship Manager, David McGowan
Assistant Vice President Benefits Administration, Natalie Felix
Senior Vice President Relationship Manager, Douglas Sako
Vice President Business Banker, Dan Poirier
Vice President Commercial Portfolio Manager, Misty Cleary
Assistant Vice President Corporate Loan Officer, Ronald DiBiase
Vice President Corporate Banking, Mark Woleslagle
Senior Vice President Internal Audit, Steven Melletz
Business Banker Vice President, Susan Henigin
Vice President Sec And Regulatory Reporting, Morgan Cypher
Vice President Secured Credit, Joe Innocenti
Senior Vice President Financial Solutions Market Leader, Scott Vidovich
Executive Vice President And Chief Credit Officer Of First Commonwealth Bank, Brian Karrip
Assistant Vice President, Bradley Wojnar
Assistant Vice President Middle Market Banker I, Sharon Nies
Vice President Special Assets Administration, Brenda Wainwright
Vice President Senior Corporate Banker First Commonwealth Bank, Matthew Zuro
Svp Senior Treasury Managment Officer, Valarry Frymoyer
Vice President Senior Treasury Officer, Tricia Baker
Senior Vice President Commercial Banking, Mary Patton
Assistant Vice President And Foreclosure Oreo Officer, Mark Oresick
Vp Budget And Profitability Manager, Melissa M Burba
Senior Vice President, Regis Scanlon
Assistant Vice President Financial Solutions Center Manager, Mikey Boyer
Vice President Finance, Kristin Robertucci
Assistant Vice President Community Engagement Manager, Elizabeth Saraceno
Vice President Of Treasury Management, Amy Holbrook
Senior Vice President Private Banking, Walters Barbara
Vice President, Charles Bennett
Senior Vice President Corporate Banking, Huey Bartolini
Vice President Commercial Banking, John Simkonis
Senior Vice President Managing Director, Antonio Benton
Evp Chief Audit Executive, Len Lombardi
Executive Vice President, Joe Culos
Senior Vice President Chief Administrative Officer, Ronald J Nardis
Chairman, David S. (Dave) Dahlmann, age 70
Auditors: KPMG LLP

LOCATIONS

PRODUCTS/OPERATIONS

2014 Sales

	$ mil.	% of total
Interest		
Loans including fees	171	65
Taxable investments	31	12
Noninterest		
Service charges on deposit accounts	15	7
Insurance & retail brokerage commissions	6	2
Trust income	6	2
Others	32	12
Total	**263**	**100**

Selected Subsidiaries

First Commonwealth Bank
  First Commonwealth Insurance Agency
  First Commonwealth Home Mortgage LLC (49.9%)
First Commonwealth Financial Advisors Incorporated

COMPETITORS

Allegheny Valley Bancorp	F.N.B. (PA)
AmeriServ Financial	Fidelity Bancorp (PA)
Citizens Financial Group	Northwest Bancshares
Dollar Bank	PNC Financial
	S&T Bancorp

HISTORICAL FINANCIALS

Company Type: Public

Income Statement

FYE: December 31

	ASSETS ($ mil.)	NET INCOME ($ mil.)	INCOME AS % OF ASSETS	EMPLOYEES
12/19	8,308	105	1.3%	1,571
12/18	7,828	107	1.4%	1,512
12/17	7,308	55	0.8%	1,476
12/16	6,684	59	0.9%	1,376
12/15	6,566	50	0.8%	1,311
Annual Growth	**6.1%**	**20.4%**	**—**	**4.6%**

2019 Year-End Financials

Debt ratio: 2.82%	No. of shares (mil.): 98
Return on equity: 10.37%	Dividends
Cash ($ mil.): 121	Yield: 2.7%
Current ratio: —	Payout: 37.3%
Long-term debt ($ mil.): —	Market value ($ mil.): 1,427

	STOCK PRICE ($) FY Close	P/E High/Low	PER SHARE ($) Earnings	Dividends	Book Value
12/19	14.51	14 11	1.07	0.40	10.74
12/18	12.08	16 10	1.08	0.35	9.90
12/17	14.32	26 21	0.58	0.32	9.11
12/16	14.18	21 12	0.67	0.28	8.43
12/15	9.07	18 14	0.56	0.28	8.09
Annual Growth	**12.5%**	**— —**	**17.6%**	**9.3%**	**7.3%**

First Community Bankshares Inc (VA)

First Community Bancshares doesn't play second fiddle to other area banks. The firm is the holding company for First Community Bank which provides traditional services like checking and savings accounts CDs and credit cards and serves communities through some 55 branches across Virginia West Virginia North Carolina and Tennessee. Commercial real estate loans make up 45% of its loan portfolio while commercial business loans make up another 5%. First Community Bancshares offers insurance through subsidiary Greenpoint Insurance and wealth management and investment advisory services through Trust Services and First Community Wealth Management.

Operations

First Community Bancshares operates through four main business activities: commercial and consumer banking lending activities wealth management and insurance services. Its Trust Services and First Community Wealth Management subsidiary had managed assets with a market value of nearly $700 million in 2014.

The bank which had a staff of 678 employees at the end of 2014 generated 70% of its total revenue from loan interest (including fees and loans held for investment) in 2014 and another 8% from interest on taxable and non-taxable securities. The rest of its revenue came from deposit account service charges (9%) insurance commissions (4%) wealth management (1%) and other miscellaneous sources of income.

Sales and Marketing

The bank serves individuals and businesses across several industries including: manufacturing mining services construction retail healthcare military and transportation.

Financial Performance

The company has struggled to grow its revenues in recent years due to shrinking interest margins on loans amidst the low-interest environment. Its profits however have been rising thanks to falling interest expenses and declining loan loss provisions as its loan portfolio's credit quality has improved with higher property valuations in the strengthened economy.

First Community Bancshares's revenue dipped by 2% to $136.1 million in 2014 as its interest income on loans and securities declined with fewer assets and because it took on a $1.39 million loss from the sale of its investment securities during the year.

Despite revenue declines in 2014 the bank's net income jumped 9% to $25.5 million thanks to continued declines in interest expenses on deposits and loan loss provisions. First Community's operating cash levels fell by 6% to $41.7 million for the year after adjusting its earnings for non-cash items related to its loan loss provisions and the proceeds of its mortgage loan sales.

Strategy

Faced with shrinking revenues in recent years First Community has been strategically changing its geographic positioning selling off some of its branches in certain areas and acquiring new branches in others. In late 2014 it acquired seven branches from Bank of America in Southwestern Virginia and Central North Carolina and sold 13 of its branches to Charleston-based CresCom Bank including 10 of its branches in Southeastern North Carolina and three in South Carolina.

Mergers and Acquisitions

In 2014 First Community purchased seven branches from Bank of America including six branches in Southwestern Virginia and one in Central North Carolina. The deal also added $318.9 million in new deposits as well as real estate and assumed leases associated with the branches.

Company Background

After slowing its acquisition activity during the economic downturn First Community resumed in 2012 buying Peoples Bank of Virginia which added four branches in the Richmond area. The company also acquired the failed Waccamaw Bank in a FDIC-facilitated transaction. That deal brought in 16 branches in North Carolina.

EXECUTIVES

Evp And Coo, E. Stephen (Steve) Lilly, age 61, $252,000 total compensation
Chairman And Ceo, William P. Stafford, age 56, $200,013 total compensation
Cfo, David D. Brown, age 45, $225,000 total compensation
President; Ceo First Community Bank, Gary R. Mills, $300,000 total compensation
President First Community Bank, Martyn A. Pell, $255,000 total compensation
Vice President Director Of Operations, Garry Stutts
Assistant Vice President Credit Administration, Jeff Noble
Senior Vice President Market President, Mark Evans
Senior Vice President On The Corporate Staff, John Spracher
Vice President And Sales And Service Leader, Brad Ferguson
Vice President Financial Center Manager, Kevin Ford
Vice President, Adam Jante
Vice President. Regulatory Compliance Officer, Jean Prazecky Crcm
Assistant Vice President Eb Officer, Shirley Smith
Board Member, Samuel Elmore
Board Member, C William Davis
Board Member, M Adam Sarver
Auditors: Dixon Hughes Goodman LLP

LOCATIONS

PRODUCTS/OPERATIONS

2011 Sales

	$ mil.	% of total
Interest		
Loans including fees	80	61
Securities	13	10
Deposits in banks	0	-
Noninterest		
Service charges on deposit accounts	13	10
Insurance commissions	6	5
Net gains on sales of securities	5	4
Wealth management	3	3
Other service charges commissions & fees	5	4
Other	3	3
Adjustments	(2.3)	-
Total	**129**	**100**

COMPETITORS

BB&T	Huntington Bancshares
Bank of America	SunTrust
City Holding	United Bankshares
First Citizens BancShares	WesBanco
Highlands Bankshares Inc.	

HISTORICAL FINANCIALS

Company Type: Public

Income Statement

	ASSETS ($ mil.)	NET INCOME ($ mil.)	INCOME AS % OF ASSETS	EMPLOYEES
12/19	2,798	38	1.4%	527
12/18	2,244	36	1.6%	519
12/17	2,388	21	0.9%	562
12/16	2,386	25	1.1%	580
12/15	2,462	24	1.0%	673
Annual Growth	3.3%	12.1%	—	(5.9%)

FYE: December 31

2019 Year-End Financials

Debt ratio: —
Return on equity: 10.19%
Cash ($ mil.): 69
Current ratio: —
Long-term debt ($ mil.): —

No. of shares (mil.): 18
Dividends
Yield: 3.0%
Payout: 39.8%
Market value ($ mil.): 570

	STOCK PRICE ($) FY Close	P/E High/Low	PER SHARE ($) Earnings	Dividends	Book Value
12/19	31.02	15 12	2.46	0.96	23.33
12/18	31.48	16 12	2.18	0.21	20.79
12/17	28.73	24 19	1.26	0.68	20.63
12/16	30.14	22 12	1.45	0.60	19.95
12/15	18.63	16 11	1.31	0.54	18.95
Annual Growth	13.6%	— —	17.1%	15.5%	5.3%

First Financial Bancorp (OH)

First Financial Bancorp spreads itself thick. The holding company's flagship subsidiary First Financial Bank operates nearly 110 branches in Ohio Indiana and Kentucky. Founded in 1863 the bank offers checking and savings accounts money market accounts CDs credit cards private banking and wealth management services through its First Financial Wealth Management subsidiary. Commercial loans including real estate and construction loans make up more than 50% of First Financial's total loan portfolio; the bank also offers residential mortgage and consumer loans. First Financial Bancorp boasts more than $7 billion in assets including nearly $5 billion in loans.

Operations

The company's private banking business First Financial Wealth Management had $2.4 billion in assets under management in early 2015.

Sales and Marketing

First Financial spent $3.60 million on marketing in 2014 compared to $4.27 million and $5.55 million in 2013 and 2012 respectively.

Financial Performance

First Financial's revenue has been in decline in recent years due to shrinking interest margins on loans amidst the low-interest environment. The company has also struggled to grow its profits much past the $65 million-mark though profit levels are more than twice as high as they were prior to 2009.

The company's revenue dipped by 2% to $311.82 million in 2014 mostly as its loan interest income declined by nearly 4% as interest margins continued to shrink in the low-interest environment. First Financial's non-interest income fell by double-digits mostly due to lower FDIC loss shar-

ing income lower income from the accelerated discount on prepaid covered loans and smaller gains on investment securities sales.

Despite lower revenue in 2014 First Financial's net income rebounded by 34% to $65 million for the year mostly thanks to an 80% reduction in loan and lease loss provisions as the bank's loan portfolio's credit quality improved with the strengthening economy. The company's non-interest expenses also declined by double-digits mostly because the bank in 2013 incurred a non-recurring $22.4 million FDIC indemnification valuation adjustment.

First Financial's operating cash declined by 66% to $56.65 million after adjusting its earnings for non-cash items related to the indemnification asset decrease and net sales proceeds on its loans held for sale.

Strategy

First Financial has been focusing on branch expansion (on its own or through acquisitions) in three core metropolitan markets: Cincinnati Dayton and Indianapolis. In 2014 for example First Financial acquired three Ohio-based banks and their branches in 2014 expanding its branch network in Central Ohio while adding new loan and deposit business at the same time.

Mergers and Acquisitions

In 2017 First Financial agreed to acquire Main-Source Financial Group with an expected deal completion in 2Q 2018. The purchase extends its reach in Indiana (80 branches) Ohio Illinois and Kentucky.

In 2014 to expand further into key markets in Columbus and Central Ohio First Financial purchased The First Bexley Bank which served commercial and consumer bank clients from its one branch location in Bexley Ohio. Similarly that year it purchased Insight Bank operated a branch in Worthington Ohio and a mortgage origination office in Newark Ohio; and bought Worthington-based Guernsey Bancorp and its three branches in Central Ohio.

Company Background

In the past the bank acquired 16 branches in western Ohio from Liberty Savings Bank and bought 22 Indianapolis-area branches from Flagstar Bank in 2011. Together the two acquisitions furthered the bank's growth strategy for the key markets of Dayton and Indianapolis.

EXECUTIVES

President Western Markets Commercial Banking And Wealth Management, C. Douglas (Doug) Lefferson
President And Ceo, Claude E. Davis
President And Coo, Anthony M. (Tony) Stollings
Chief Credit Officer, Richard S. Barbercheck
Svp And Cfo, John Gavigan
President Mortgage Banking, Jill A. Stanton
Evp And Chief Compliance Officer, Holly M. Foster
President Corporate Banking, Brad Ringwald
Vice President Commercial Underwriter, Brian Englert
Assistant Vice President Sales Center Manager Iii, Cooley Andrew
Vice President Of Mortgage Lending, Wade Spain
Vice President Information Technology Support Services, Roland Lima
Vice President, Stephen Vegh
First Vice President Director Of Corporate Facilities, Jeffrey Weingartner
Vice President Deposit Operations, Ronald Kloska
First Financial Center Banking Center Manager Assistant Vice President, Julie Estep
Vice President Digital Sales Channel Manager, Brano Tomic
Vice President Credit Reporting And Analytics, Angie Henderson

Assistant Vice President Business Banking Branch Manager, Kimberly Stitt
Vice President Mortgage Operations, Debbie Kassinos
Assistant Vice President, Mark Gregg
Vice President And Fiduciary Manager, Paul Schwarz
Vice President, Josh Riley
Assistant Vice President Mortgage Sales Manager, Mark Spangler
Vice President Commercial Banking First Financial Bank, Jason King
Vice President And Senior Trust Officer, Linda Glass
Assistant Vice President, Teresa Peyton
Vice President Business Development Officer, Kevin Stewart
Vice President Credit Risk Review, Mike Hurley
Vice President, Barbara Engelhart
Vice President, Jimmy Chandler
Svp Director Of Mortgage Sales, Andy Applewhite
Vice President, Jim Nichols
Vice President, Bradley Cummings
Vice President, Thom Frantz
First Vice President Commercial Credit Officer, Jean M Messenger
Vice President Corporate Information Technology, Desai Priti
Vice President Of Human Resources, Jennifer Harper
Executive Vice President Marketing, Dan Clark
Vice President, Landon Hammond
Senior Vice President And Branch Manager, Tim Laws
Vice President And Trust Officer, Seth Keele
Chairman, Murph Knapke
Vice Chairman, J. Wickliffe Ach
Board Member, J Ach
Board Member, Vince Berta
Board Member, Tim Lancaster
Board Member, David Copeland
Board Member, Murray Edwards
Board Member, Tucker Bridwell
Auditors: Crowe LLP

LOCATIONS

HQ: First Financial Bancorp (OH)
255 East Fifth Street, Suite 800, Cincinnati, OH 45202
Phone: 877 322-9530
Web: www.bankatfirst.com

PRODUCTS/OPERATIONS

2014 Sales

	$ mil.	% of total
Interest		
Loans including fees	208	66
Investment securities	44	14
(Adjustment)	(5.5)	-
Noninterest		
Service charges on deposit accounts	20	7
Trust and wealth management fees	13	5
Bankcard income	10	3
Net gains from sales on loans	4	1
Accelerated discount on covered/formerly covered loans	4	1
Others	10	3
Total	311	100

COMPETITORS

AMB Financial	Logansport Financial
Commercial Bancshares	MutualFirst Financial
Farmers National	PNC Financial
Fifth Third	Peoples Community
First Defiance Financial	Bancorp
	Peoples-Sidney
First Franklin	SB Financial Group
LCNB	U.S. Bancorp
Liberty Capital	

HISTORICAL FINANCIALS

Company Type: Public

Income Statement   FYE: December 31

	ASSETS ($ mil.)	NET INCOME ($ mil.)	INCOME AS % OF ASSETS	EMPLOYEES
12/19	14,511	198	1.4%	2,123
12/18	13,986	172	1.2%	2,131
12/17	8,896	96	1.1%	1,366
12/16	8,437	88	1.0%	1,521
12/15	8,147	75	0.9%	1,471
Annual Growth	15.5%	27.5%	—	9.6%

2019 Year-End Financials

Debt ratio: 1.18%
Return on equity: 9.16%
Cash ($ mil.): 257
Current ratio: —
Long-term debt ($ mil.): —

No. of shares (mil.): 98
Dividends
  Yield: 3.5%
  Payout: 43.2%
Market value ($ mil.): 2,506

	STOCK PRICE ($) FY Close	P/E High/Low	PER SHARE ($) Earnings	Dividends	Book Value
12/19	25.44	14 11	2.00	0.90	22.82
12/18	23.72	17 11	1.93	0.78	21.23
12/17	26.35	19 15	1.56	0.68	14.99
12/16	28.45	20 10	1.43	0.64	13.96
12/15	18.07	17 13	1.21	0.64	13.13
Annual Growth	8.9%	— —	13.4%	8.9%	14.8%

First Financial Bankshares, Inc.

Texas hold 'em? Well sort of. First Financial Bankshares is the holding company for eleven banks consolidated under the First Financial brand all of which are located in small and midsized markets in Texas. Together they have about 50 locations. The company maintains a decentralized management structure with each of the subsidiary banks having their own local leadership and decision-making authority. Its First Financial Trust & Asset Management subsidiary administers retirement and employee benefit plans in addition to providing trust services. First Financial Bankshares also owns an insurance agency.

EXECUTIVES

Chairman President And Ceo; Chairman First Financial Bank N.a., F. Scott Dueser, age 67, $754,167 total compensation
Evp And Cfo, J. Bruce Hildebrand, age 65, $445,000 total compensation
Evp And Chief Administrative Officer, Ronald D. (Ron) Butler, age 59, $405,000 total compensation
Evp Lending, Marna Yerigan
Evp Lending, T. Luke Longhofer
Evp And Cio, Thomas S. (Stan) Limerick
Evp And Lending Officer, Gary S.Gragg, age 60, $325,000 total compensation
Evp Retail And Training, Monica Houston
Evp Chief Risk Officer, Randy Roewe
Executive Vice President, Rodney Foster
Senior Vice President, Kay Berry
Vice President, Jay Evans
Vice President, Wade Spain
Vice President Branch Manager N.a, Shay Minor
Vice President, Isabel Montoya
Senior Vice President Mortgage Lending, Janet O'Dell

Vice President Of Human Resources, Jennifer Harper
Executive Vice President, Joe Love
Vice President Mortgage Lending, Jayden Slentz
Vice President Commercial And Real Estate Lender, Alicia Bland
Senior Vice President Advertising And Marketing, Will Christoferson
Vice President Information Technology, Reid Sharp
Vice President, Robert Charles
Board Member, Ron Giddiens
Auditors: Ernst & Young, LLP.

LOCATIONS

HQ: First Financial Bankshares, Inc.
  400 Pine Street, Abilene, TX 79601
Phone: 325 627-7155
Web: www.ffin.com

PRODUCTS/OPERATIONS

2015 sales

	$ mil.	% of total
Interest Income		
Interest and fees on loans	151	51
Interest on investment securities	69	24
Interest on federal funds sold and interest-bearing deposits in banks	0	0
Non-Interest Income		
ATM interchange and credit card fees	21	7
Trust fees	19	6
Service charges on deposit accounts	17	6
Real estate mortgage operations	10	4
Net gain on sale of available-for-sale securities	0	-
Net gain on sale of foreclosed assets	0	-
Net loss on sale of assets	(0.8)	-
Other	4	2
Total	295	100

Products/ServicesPersonal

Learn
Online Banking
Mobile Banking
Consumer Education
FAQS
Privacy & Security Information
Resources
Testimonials
Tools
Bank
Checking
Savings
Invest
CDS & IRAS
Broker Services
Borrow
Mortgage Loans
Mortgage Lenders
Auto Loans
Recreational Loans
Home Equity Loans
Personal Line of Credit
CD Secured Loans
Banking with First Financial
Mobile Banking
Online Banking
Pay Bills
Get Cash
Make Deposit
Move Money
Keep Track
Business
Learn
Online Banking
Mobile Banking
Business Education
Starting your Business
Growing your Business
Tools
Business Banking Services
Manage Cash
Send Payments
Receive Payments
Manage Fraud and Risk
Other Services
Trust & Wealth Management
Investment Management
Trust Management

Estate Management
Oil & Gas Management
Real Estate and Property Management
Company Retirement Plans

Selected Subsidiaries

First Financial Bank National Association Abilene Texas.
First Technology Services Inc. Abilene Texas (wholly owned subsidiary of First Financial Bank National Association Abilene Texas).
First Financial Trust & Asset Management Company National Association Abilene Texas.
First Financial Insurance Agency Inc. Abilene Texas.
First Financial Investments Inc. Abilene Texas.

COMPETITORS

BBVA Compass Bancshares
Bank of America
Cullen/Frost Bankers
JPMorgan Chase
Wells Fargo
Woodforest Financial

HISTORICAL FINANCIALS

Company Type: Public

Income Statement   FYE: December 31

	ASSETS ($ mil.)	NET INCOME ($ mil.)	INCOME AS % OF ASSETS	EMPLOYEES
12/19	8,262	164	2.0%	1,345
12/18	7,731	150	1.9%	1,350
12/17	7,254	120	1.7%	1,300
12/16	6,809	104	1.5%	1,300
12/15	6,665	100	1.5%	1,270
Annual Growth	5.5%	13.2%	—	1.4%

2019 Year-End Financials

Debt ratio: —
Return on equity: 14.45%
Cash ($ mil.): 279
Current ratio: —
Long-term debt ($ mil.): —

No. of shares (mil.): 134
Dividends
  Yield: 1.3%
  Payout: 38.9%
Market value ($ mil.): 4,737

	STOCK PRICE ($) FY Close	P/E High/Low	PER SHARE ($) Earnings	Dividends	Book Value
12/19	35.10	53 24	1.21	0.47	9.09
12/18	57.69	60 40	1.11	0.82	7.83
12/17	45.05	53 41	0.91	0.38	7.02
12/16	45.20	58 31	0.80	0.35	6.39
12/15	30.17	47 32	0.77	0.62	6.15
Annual Growth	3.9%	— —	12.0%	(6.9%)	10.3%

First Financial Corp. (IN)

Which came first the First Financial in Indiana Ohio South Carolina or Texas? Regardless this particular First Financial Corporation is the holding company for First Financial Bank which offers traditional banking deposit accounts and loans as well as trust private banking wealth management and investment services through more than 70 branches in west-central Indiana and east-central Illinois. About 60% of its loan portfolio is tied to commercial loans while the rest is split between residential and consumer loans. Subsidiary Forrest Sherer sells personal and commercial insurance while subsidiary Morris Plan originates indirect auto loans through dealerships in the bank's market area.

Operations

About 59% of the bank's $1.76 billion loan portfolio was tied to commercial business loans to finance business asset purchases and expansion at the end of 2015 while the remainder of the portfolio was tied to 1-4 family residential real estate mortgages (25% of loan assets) and consumer loans (16%).

Nearly 75% of First Financial's revenue comes from interest income. About 57% of its total revenue came from loan interest (including fees) during 2015 while another 16% came from interest income on taxable and tax-exempt investment securities. The rest of its revenue came from deposit account service charges (7% of revenue) insurance commissions (5%) trust and financial services (4%) gains on mortgage loan sales (2%) and other miscellaneous income sources.

Geographic Reach

The Terre Haute Indiana-based bank operated 71 branches in west-central Indiana and east-central Illinois at the end of 2015.

Financial Performance

First Financial Corporation's annual revenues and profits have been trending lower over the past several years due to shrinking margins in the low-interest environment and as its loan assets have declined more than 5% since 2011.

The bank's revenue fell 4% to $147.86 million during 2015 mostly as its interest-earning loan and investment assets and the interest margins they command continued to decline. Its non-interest income tumbled at a similar rate due to reduced investment service and insurance agency income.

Revenue declines in 2015 caused First Financial's net income to dive nearly 11% to $30.2 million. The bank's operating cash levels plunged almost 30% to $41.26 million for the year as cash earnings shrank.

Strategy

First Financial Corporation continued in 2016 to expand its branch network in hopes to build its loan and deposit business. Indeed its branch network has steadily grown from 65 branches at the end of 2011 to 71 branches at the end of 2015.

Mergers and Acquisitions

In January 2019 First Financial agreed to purchase HopFed Bancorp in a deal valued at nearly $130 million. The Hopkinsville Kentucky-based company has 18 branches and three loan production offices in Kentucky and Tennessee new markets for First Financial.

Company Background

In 2011 First Financial bought Freestar Bank adding more than a dozen branches in central Illinois. It was the largest acquisition in the company's history.

With roots dating back to 1834 First Financial Bank is not only one of the oldest banks in Indiana but also the entire country. It is also one of the oldest continually operating businesses in its hometown of Terre Haute. Another local business Princeton Mining Company owns nearly 10% of First Financial Corporation.

EXECUTIVES

Vice Chairman And Ceo, Norman D. Lowery, age 52, $630,297 total compensation
Personal Trust Department Assistant Vice Presiden, Carol Myers
Vice President, Brad Williams
Assistant Vice President Of Marketing And First Gold Club Coordinator, Sally Whitehurst
Vice President Collections, Jeff Nickels
Vice President, Thom Frantz
Vice President Human Resources, Racheal Carter
Vice President Director Of Consumer Lending, Carl Britton

Assistant Vice President Cra Officer, Chris Shaw
Vice President, Eric Feathers
Board Member, Gregory L Gibson
Chairman, B. Guille Cox
Board Member, Ronald Rich
Board Member, William Krieble
Auditors: Crowe LLP

LOCATIONS

HQ: First Financial Corp. (IN)
One First Financial Plaza, Terre Haute, IN 47807
Phone: 812 238-6000
Web: www.first-online.com

PRODUCTS/OPERATIONS

2011 Sales

	$ mil.	% of total
Interest		
Loans including related fees	91	61
Securities	22	15
Other	2	1
Noninterest		
Service charges & fees on deposit accounts	9	6
Other service charges & fees	8	6
Insurance commissions	7	5
Trust & financial services	4	3
Other	4	3
Total	**149**	**100**

COMPETITORS

FFW	Huntington Bancshares
Fifth Third	JPMorgan Chase
First Midwest Bancorp	Old National Bancorp
First Robinson Financial	PNC Financial

HISTORICAL FINANCIALS

Company Type: Public

Income Statement				FYE: December 31
	ASSETS ($ mil.)	NET INCOME ($ mil.)	INCOME AS % OF ASSETS	EMPLOYEES
12/19	4,023	48	1.2%	957
12/18	3,008	46	1.5%	816
12/17	3,000	29	1.0%	847
12/16	2,988	38	1.3%	846
12/15	2,979	30	1.0%	896
Annual Growth	7.8%	12.8%	—	1.7%

2019 Year-End Financials

Debt ratio: 0.25%
Return on equity: 9.77%
Cash ($ mil.): 127
Current ratio: —
Long-term debt ($ mil.): —
No. of shares (mil.): 13
Dividends
  Yield: 2.2%
  Payout: 28.3%
Market value ($ mil.): 628

	STOCK PRICE ($) FY Close	P/E High/Low	Earnings	PER SHARE ($) Dividends	Book Value
12/19	45.72	12 10	3.80	1.03	40.58
12/18	40.15	14 10	3.80	2.52	36.06
12/17	45.35	22 18	2.38	2.50	33.77
12/16	52.80	17 10	3.12	0.99	33.92
12/15	33.97	16 14	2.35	0.98	32.21
Annual Growth	7.7%	— —	12.8%	1.3%	5.9%

First Foundation Inc

Auditors: Eide Bailly LLP

LOCATIONS

HQ: First Foundation Inc
18101 Von Karman Avenue, Suite 700, Irvine, CA 92612
Phone: 949 202-4160
Web: www.ff-inc.com

HISTORICAL FINANCIALS

Company Type: Public

Income Statement				FYE: December 31
	ASSETS ($ mil.)	NET INCOME ($ mil.)	INCOME AS % OF ASSETS	EMPLOYEES
12/19	6,314	56	0.9%	485
12/18	5,840	42	0.7%	482
12/17	4,541	27	0.6%	394
12/16	3,975	23	0.6%	335
12/15	2,592	13	0.5%	295
Annual Growth	24.9%	43.2%	—	13.2%

2019 Year-End Financials

Debt ratio: 11.77%
Return on equity: 9.59%
Cash ($ mil.): 65
Current ratio: —
Long-term debt ($ mil.): —
No. of shares (mil.): 44
Dividends
  Yield: 1.1%
  Payout: 16.1%
Market value ($ mil.): 777

	STOCK PRICE ($) FY Close	P/E High/Low	Earnings	PER SHARE ($) Dividends	Book Value
12/19	17.40	14 10	1.25	0.20	13.74
12/18	12.86	20 12	1.01	0.00	12.57
12/17	18.54	36 17	0.78	0.00	10.34
12/16	28.50	41 28	0.70	0.00	8.69
12/15	23.59	41 29	0.58	0.00	8.13
Annual Growth	(7.3%)	— —	21.2%	—	14.0%

First Guaranty Bancshares, Inc.

EXECUTIVES

V Chb-Pres-Ceo, Alton B Lewis Jr
Chb*, Marshall T Reynolds
Cfo, Eric J Dosch
Member FDIC, Evan Baranosky
Commercial Lender, Irvin Williams
Manager, Luke Hammonds
Senior Credit Analyst, Michael Wiggins
Training Specialist, Miranda Derveloy
Information Technology Procure, Donnamarie Turnage
Auditors: Castaing, Hussey & Lolan, LLC

LOCATIONS

HQ: First Guaranty Bancshares, Inc.
400 East Thomas Street, Hammond, LA 70401
Phone: 985 345-7685
Web: www.eguaranty.com

HISTORICAL FINANCIALS

Company Type: Public

Income Statement

FYE: December 31

	ASSETS ($ mil.)	NET INCOME ($ mil.)	INCOME AS % OF ASSETS	EMPLOYEES
12/19	2,117	14	0.7%	457
12/18	1,817	14	0.8%	373
12/17	1,750	11	0.7%	349
12/16	1,500	14	0.9%	304
12/15	1,459	14	1.0%	289
Annual Growth	9.7%	(0.5%)	—	12.1%

2019 Year-End Financials

Debt ratio: 2.99%
Return on equity: 9.09%
Cash ($ mil.): 66
Current ratio: —
Long-term debt ($ mil.): —
No. of shares (mil.): 9
Dividends
  Yield: 2.9%
  Payout: 48.5%
Market value ($ mil.): 212

	STOCK PRICE ($) FY Close	P/E High/Low		PER SHARE ($) Earnings	Dividends	Book Value
12/19	21.77	16	12	1.47	0.64	17.04
12/18	23.21	19	13	1.46	0.64	15.20
12/17	25.00	24	18	1.25	0.54	14.86
12/16	23.93	16	10	1.53	0.53	13.51
12/15	18.75	13	10	1.66	0.54	12.84
Annual Growth	3.8%	—	—	(3.0%)	4.2%	7.3%

First Hawaiian Inc

Auditors: DELOITTE & TOUCHE LLP

LOCATIONS

HQ: First Hawaiian Inc
999 Bishop Street, 29th Floor, Honolulu, HI 96813
Phone: 808 525-7000
Web: www.fhb.com

HISTORICAL FINANCIALS

Company Type: Public

Income Statement

FYE: December 31

	ASSETS ($ mil.)	NET INCOME ($ mil.)	INCOME AS % OF ASSETS	EMPLOYEES
12/19	20,166	284	1.4%	2,100
12/18	20,695	264	1.3%	2,200
12/17	20,549	183	0.9%	2,300
12/16	19,661	230	1.2%	2,200
12/15	19,352	213	1.1%	2,250
Annual Growth	1.0%	7.4%	—	(1.7%)

2019 Year-End Financials

Debt ratio: 0.00%
Return on equity: 11.01%
Cash ($ mil.): 694
Current ratio: —
Long-term debt ($ mil.): —
No. of shares (mil.): 129
Dividends
  Yield: 3.6%
  Payout: 48.8%
Market value ($ mil.): 3,748

	STOCK PRICE ($) FY Close	P/E High/Low		PER SHARE ($) Earnings	Dividends	Book Value
12/19	28.85	14	11	2.13	1.04	20.32
12/18	22.51	17	11	1.93	0.96	18.72
12/17	29.18	26	20	1.32	0.88	18.14
12/16	34.82	21	15	1.62	0.20	17.75
Annual Growth	(4.6%)	—	—	7.1%	51.0%	3.4%

First Horizon Corp

First Horizon National would like to be on banking consumers' horizons in the Volunteer State and beyond. The bank holding company operates about 300 First Tennessee Bank branches in its home state and neighboring markets. Boasting roughly $41 billion in total assets it offers traditional banking services like loans deposit accounts and credit cards as well as trust asset management financial advisory and investment services. Subsidiary FTN Financial performs securities sales and trading fixed-income underwriting and other investment banking services.

Change in Company Type

In 2019 First Horizon National Corp. and IBERIABANK Corporation announced that they have entered into a definitive agreement under which the companies will combine in an all-stock merger of equals. Under the terms of the agreement which was unanimously approved by the Boards of Directors of both companies the combined holding company and bank will operate under the name First Horizon name and will be headquartered on Memphis Tenn. Once the transaction is completed the combined company will be one of the largest financial services headquartered in the South and one of the top 25 banks in the U.S. in deposits.

Operations

First Horizon operates three core business segments: Regional Banking Fixed Income and Corporate.

Regional Banking is the company's largest division and provides traditional banking products and services to retail and commercial customers mostly in Tennessee but also in neighboring markets. The division also provides investments financial planning trust services and asset management as well as correspondent banking services such as credit depository and other banking related services for financial institutions. Fixed Income operates through FHN Financial and offers fixed income sales trading and strategies for institutional customers in the United States and abroad. The company also provides investment services and balance sheet management solutions.

Geographic Reach

First Horizon National operates approximately 300 First Tennessee Bank and Capital Bank Branches in eight states. More than 55% of the branches are in Tennessee while the remaining are in the states of Georgia (northwestern area) Mississippi (northwestern area) North Carolina Virginia South Carolina Texas and Florida. FTN Financial has more than 25 financial offices in more than 15 states across the US.

Financial Performance

First Horizon's revenue rose to $1.9 billion in 2018 an approximately 45% increase from the year prior. The increase was driven by growth in both net interest income and non-interest income. Net income was $538.8 million in 2018 an increase from $159.3 million in fiscal year 2017. The growth was due to increases in net interest income and noninterest income somewhat offset by higher non-interest expense. Reported earnings were also improved by the inclusion of Capital Bank and other strategic transactions expected to boost growth returns and profitability.

Strategy

First Horizon National has its eye on growth. In 2019 First Horizon National Corp. and IBERIABANK Corporation announced that they have entered into a definitive agreement under which the companies will combine in an all-stock merger of equals. The combined holding company and bank will operate under the name First Horizon name and will be headquartered on Memphis Tenn. Once the transaction is completed the combined company will be one of the largest financial services headquartered in the South and one of the top 25 banks in the U.S. in deposits.

The company began the process of rolling out unified brands and a new logo with its existing brands in 2019. As part of that plan Capital Bank First Tennessee Bank FTB Advisors and FTN Financial will become First Horizon Bank First Horizon Advisors and FHN Financial respectively.

First Horizon announced in 2019 an agreement to buy 30 branches from SunTrust Banks to expand its presence in key growth markets in North Carolina Virginia and Georgia. The acquired bank branches will operate under the First Horizon Bank brand.

Mergers and Acquisitions

First Horizon announced in 2019 an agreement to buy 30 branches from SunTrust bank to enhance its presence in key growth markets in North Carolina Virginia and Georgia. The acquired bank branches will operate under the First Horizon Bank brand.

Company Background

Frank S. Davis submitted a national charter to establish First National Bank of Memphis in 1864. The bank continued to grow over the years and in 1977 First National changed its name to First Tennessee to reflect the bank's expansion beyond Memphis. At the start of the recession First Horizon began selling non-core assets and refocused growth closer to home. First Horizon exited the Baltimore-Washington DC and Atlanta markets. The company also sold some 230 First Horizon Home Loan offices as well as the unit's loan origination and servicing operations outside of Tennessee to MetLife. After the sale First Horizon Financial outsourced some its mortgage origination processing and servicing operations within Tennessee to PHH Mortgage. In 2004 the company changed its name to First Horizon National Corporation. In 2008 the bank discontinued its specialty construction and consumer lending activities beyond Tennessee. It exited the institutional equity research business in 2010 and sold its First Horizon Insurance unit to Brown & Brown the following year. Also in 2011 First Horizon sold a subsidiary that provided administrative services for health savings accounts.

EXECUTIVES

Evp And Chief Human Resources Officer, John M. Daniel, age 65

Evp Regional Banking; Coo First Tennessee Bank, David T. Popwell, age 59, $450,000 total compensation

Chairman President And Ceo, D. Bryan Jordan, age 58, $815,000 total compensation

Evp And General Counsel, Charles T. Tuggle, age 71, $475,000 total compensation

Evp Corporate Communications, Kimberley C. (Kim) Cherry

Evp Technology And Operations And Cio, Bruce A. Livesay
Evp And Cfo, William C. (BJ) Losch, age 49, $425,000 total compensation
Evp And Chief Risk Officer, Yousef A. Valine, age 60, $362,692 total compensation
President Ftn Financial, Michael E. Kisber, age 60, $600,000 total compensation
Evp And Chief Credit Officer, Susan L. Springfield, age 55
Evp And Chief Operating And Financial Officer Ftn Financial, Michael K. Waddell
Evp Consumer Banking First Tennessee Bank, David W. Miller
Evp Corporate Banking, Steve J. Hawkins
President First Tennessee Bank Mid-atlantic Region, Billy Frank, age 49
President First Tennessee Bank Mid-atlantic Region, John Fox, age 67
Regional President First Tennessee Bank Tennessee Banking Group, Richard Shaffer, age 55
Evp And Chief Audit Executive, Vernon H. Stafford
Senior Vice President Facilities Management, Stephen Bieber
Vice President Risk Management, Kathleen Mooney
Vice President Business Process Services, Nancy Bradley
Senior Vice President And Chief Investment.., Karen Kruse
Senior Vice President, Christine Bland
Vice President, David Ward
Vice President Senior Financialadvisor, Michael Null Hardin
Svp And Credit Risk Manager, Darin Johnson
Vice President, Jack Yokley
Board Member, Luke Yancy
Board Member, Scott Niswonger
Board Member, Colin Reed
Board Member, Cecelia Stewart
Board Member, Rajesh Subramaniam
Auditors: KPMG LLP

LOCATIONS

HQ: First Horizon Corp
165 Madison Avenue, Memphis, TN 38103
Phone: 901 523-4444
Web: www.firsthorizon.com

PRODUCTS/OPERATIONS

2014 Sales

	$ mil.	% of total
Interest		
Loans including fees	571	45
Investment securities	93	7
Trading securities	32	3
Loans held for sale	11	1
Other	1	-
Noninterest		
Capital markets	200	16
Deposit transactions & cash management	112	9
Mortgage banking	71	6
Brokerage management fees & commissions	49	4
Trust services and investment management	27	2
Bankcard income	23	2
Bank owned life insurance	16	1
Other	49	4
Total	**1,259**	**100**

COMPETITORS

Athens Federal Community Bank	JPMorgan Chase
BB&T	Regions Financial
Bank of America	SunTrust
Citigroup	Trustmark
	Wells Fargo

HISTORICAL FINANCIALS

Company Type: Public

Income Statement

FYE: December 31

	ASSETS ($ mil.)	NET INCOME ($ mil.)	INCOME AS % OF ASSETS	EMPLOYEES
12/19	43,310	440	1.0%	5,017
12/18	40,832	545	1.3%	5,577
12/17	41,423	165	0.4%	5,984
12/16	28,555	227	0.8%	4,288
12/15	26,195	85	0.3%	4,293
Annual Growth	13.4%	50.5%	—	4.0%

2019 Year-End Financials

Debt ratio: 1.83%
Return on equity: 9.51%
Cash ($ mil.): 1,116
Current ratio: —
Long-term debt ($ mil.): —

No. of shares (mil.): 311
Dividends
  Yield: 3.3%
  Payout: 40.5%
Market value ($ mil.): 5,158

	STOCK PRICE ($) FY Close	P/E High/Low		Earnings	PER SHARE ($) Dividends	Book Value
12/19	16.56	12	10	1.38	0.56	15.35
12/18	13.16	12	7	1.65	0.48	14.09
12/17	19.99	31	24	0.65	0.36	13.11
12/16	20.01	22	12	0.94	0.28	10.31
12/15	14.52	48	36	0.34	0.24	9.83
Annual Growth	3.3%			41.9%	23.6%	11.8%

First Internet Bancorp

First Internet Bancorp was formed in 2006 to be the holding company for First Internet Bank of Indiana (First IB). Launched in 1999Â the bankÂ was the first state-chartered FDIC-insured institution to operate solely via the Internet.Â It now operates two locationsÂ in Indianapolis after adding one via its 2007 purchase of Landmark Financial (the parent of Landmark Savings Bank) a deal that also brought aboard residential mortgage brokerage Landmark Mortgage.Â First IB offers traditional checking and savings accounts in addition to CDs IRAs credit and check cards consumer installment and residential mortgage loans and lines of credit. It serves customers in all 50 states.

EXECUTIVES

Vice President Asset Quality, Gregg Feigh
Vice President Commercial Banking, Maria Bryce
Vice President Loan Servicing, David Sewell
Vice President Commercial Lender, Carl Osberg
Vice President Commercial Lending, Jim Laine
Vice President Commercial Lending, Kevin Lynch
Vice President Of Commercial Banking Group, Christy Smith
Vice President Commercial Relationship Manager, Charles Fippen
Vice President Commercial Banking, Suzy Sottong
Vp Human Resources, Angie Redmon
Vice President, Denise Clevenger
Vice President, Bill Kennedy
Vp Secondary Marketing Manager, Bill Steadman
Vice President Commercial Banking Relationship Manager, Meghan Marrello
Vice President Public Finance Closing Administrator, Tina Montgomery
Auditors: BKD, LLP

LOCATIONS

HQ: First Internet Bancorp
11201 USA Parkway, Fishers, IN 46037
Phone: 317 532-7900
Web: www.firstinternetbancorp.com

COMPETITORS

Bank of America	Citibank
BofI	E*TRADE Bank

HISTORICAL FINANCIALS

Company Type: Public

Income Statement

FYE: December 31

	ASSETS ($ mil.)	NET INCOME ($ mil.)	INCOME AS % OF ASSETS	EMPLOYEES
12/19	4,100	25	0.6%	231
12/18	3,541	21	0.6%	201
12/17	2,767	15	0.6%	206
12/16	1,854	12	0.7%	192
12/15	1,269	8	0.7%	152
Annual Growth	34.0%	29.7%	—	11.0%

2019 Year-End Financials

Debt ratio: 1.70%
Return on equity: 8.50%
Cash ($ mil.): 327
Current ratio: —
Long-term debt ($ mil.): —

No. of shares (mil.): 9
Dividends
  Yield: 1.0%
  Payout: 11.3%
Market value ($ mil.): 231

	STOCK PRICE ($) FY Close	P/E High/Low		Earnings	PER SHARE ($) Dividends	Book Value
12/19	23.71	10	7	2.51	0.24	31.30
12/18	20.44	18	8	2.30	0.24	28.39
12/17	38.15	19	12	2.13	0.24	26.65
12/16	32.00	14	10	2.30	0.24	23.76
12/15	28.69	18	7	1.96	0.24	23.28
Annual Growth	(4.7%)			6.4%	(0.0%)	7.7%

First Interstate BancSystem Inc

This Treasure State bank wants to be your treasury. First Interstate BancSystem is the holding company for First Interstate Bank which has about 80 branches in Montana western South Dakota and Wyoming. Serving area consumers businesses and municipalities the bank provides traditional services including deposit accounts wealth management and loans. Commercial loans including mortgages make up more than half of the bank's loan portfolio; residential real estate agricultural and construction loans round out its lending activities. On the wealth management side the bank has more than $8 billion in trust assets held in a fiduciary or agent capacity.

Financial Performance

The company's revenue decreased in fiscal 2013 compared to the previous period. It reported $369.3 million in revenue for fiscal 2013 down from $388.8 million in fiscal 2012. However despite the decreased annual revenue the company's net income increased in fiscal 2013 to $86 million up from a net income of $58 million the prior fiscal year. Cash flow increased by about $15 million in fiscal 2013 compared to 2012 levels.

Strategy

The company is always looking for opportunities for expansion including organic growth as well as growth through acquisitions. It expanded into the northwest growth market with the acquisition of Cascade Bancorp for around $589 million.

EXECUTIVES

Svp And Cio, Kevin J. Guenthner, age 56, $205,385 total compensation

President And Ceo, Kevin P. Riley, age 60, $307,270 total compensation

Evp And Chief Banking Officer, Bill Gottwals

Evp And Cfo, Marcy D. Mutch, age 60

Executive Vice President And Chief Banking Officer, Michael Huston

Assistant Vice President And Personal Banking Officer, Julie Mazza

Vice Chairman, James R. Scott, age 70

Secretary, Jana Garza

Auditors: RSM US LLP

LOCATIONS

HQ: First Interstate BancSystem Inc
401 North 31st Street, Billings, MT 59116-0918
Phone: 406 255-5390
Web: www.fibk.com

PRODUCTS/OPERATIONS

Selected ServicesBanking
Checking Accounts
Credit Cards
Debit Cards
Escrow Services
Foreign Currency
Overdraft Protection
Personal Resources
Prepaid Cards
Savings Accounts
Borrowing
AdvanceLine
Auto & Recreation
Debt Consolidation
Home Equity
Home Mortgage
Personal Loans
Create & Build Wealth
Long-Term Planning
Planning for the Unexpected
Saving for College
Saving for Retirement
Wealth Resources
Protect & Preserve Wealth
Asset Management
Employee Exit Strategies
Health Concerns
Investment Services
Retirement Plan Services

Sales 2015

	$ mil.	% of total
Interest income	282	70
Non-interest income	121	30
Total	**403**	**100**

COMPETITORS

Bank of the West	Great Western Bancorp
Crazy Woman Creek	U.S. Bancorp
Eagle Bancorp	Wells Fargo
Glacier Bancorp	

HISTORICAL FINANCIALS

Company Type: Public

Income Statement — FYE: December 31

	ASSETS ($ mil.)	NET INCOME ($ mil.)	INCOME AS % OF ASSETS	EMPLOYEES
12/19	14,644	181	1.2%	2,473
12/18	13,300	160	1.2%	2,330
12/17	12,213	106	0.9%	2,207
12/16	9,063	95	1.1%	1,721
12/15	8,728	86	1.0%	1,742
Annual Growth	**13.8%**	**20.2%**	—	**9.2%**

2019 Year-End Financials

Debt ratio: 0.69%	No. of shares (mil.): 65
Return on equity: 9.76%	Dividends
Cash ($ mil.): 241	Yield: 2.9%
Current ratio: —	Payout: 45.9%
Long-term debt ($ mil.): —	Market value ($ mil.): 2,735

	STOCK PRICE ($) FY Close	P/E High/Low	PER SHARE ($) Earnings	Dividends	Book Value
12/19	41.92	15 13	2.83	1.24	30.87
12/18	36.56	17 13	2.75	1.12	27.94
12/17	40.05	22 16	2.05	0.96	25.28
12/16	42.55	20 12	2.13	0.88	21.87
12/15	29.07	16 12	1.90	0.80	20.92
Annual Growth	**9.6%**	—	**10.5%**	**11.6%**	**10.2%**

First Merchants Corp

First Merchants is the holding company that owns First Merchants Bank which operates some 120 branches in Indiana Illinois and western Ohio. Through its Lafayette Bank & Trust and First Merchants Private Wealth Advisors divisions the bank provides standard consumer and commercial banking services including checking and savings accounts CDs check cards and consumer commercial agricultural and real estate mortgage loans. First Merchants also provides trust and asset management services. Founded in 1982 First Merchants has nearly $9.4 billion worth of consolidated assets.

Operations

Real estate loans made up about 70% of First Merchants's loan portfolio while commercial and industrial agricultural and consumer loans account for the remainder of the bank's lending activity.

Geographic Reach

Muncie Indiana-based First Merchants's 120-plus bank branches are located across Indiana and in two counties each in Illinois and Ohio.

Sales and Marketing

First Merchants's marketing expense was $3.73 million in 2017 $3 million (2016) and $3.5 million (2015).

Financial Performance

Revenue jumped by 19% to $348.2 million in 2017 driven by higher interest income from more organic and inorganic loan business and more investment security income following the bank's recent acquisitions. The bank also collected significantly more non-interest income from deposit account service charges electronic card fees and insurance-related gains as it grew its customer base through acquisitions. Higher revenue drove the bank's net income up 18% to $96 million.

Total cash on hand at the end of fiscal 2017 stood at $154.9 million which was $27 million higher than cash at the start of the year. Cash from operations contributed $126 million and cash generated through financing activities added $535.8 while investments in securities and other uses used $635.3 million.

Strategy

A key part of the First Merchants's growth strategy is to expand geographically through acquisitions of small community banks operating in its key Indiana Illinois and western Ohio markets.

In 2017 and 2018 First Merchants added more nearly 3 dozen branches to its banking network after acquiring Michigan-based Monroe Bank & Trust Ohio-based Arlington Bank and Independent Alliance Banks located in Indiana. The bank has in recent years acquired 1-2 community banks operating in these states each year often adding a handful of branches as well as loans and other assets through each transaction.

Mergers and Acquisitions

In 2018 First Merchants acquired MBT Financial Corporation the holding company for Monroe Bank & Trust and its 20 branches serving Monroe Michigan and the southeastern Michigan area.

In 2017 First Merchants bought Columbus Ohio-based Arlington Bank. for $82.6 million. The same year it spent $238.8 million to acquire a majority stake in Independent Alliance Banks and IAB's 16 banking centers located in and around Fort Wayne Indiana.

EXECUTIVES

First Vice President Corporate Controller, Jeff Lorentson

Evp And Cfo, Mark K. Hardwick, age 49, $317,347 total compensation

Svp And Cio, Stephan H. Fluhler, $205,268 total compensation

President And Ceo, Michael C. (Mike) Rechin, age 61, $502,181 total compensation

Evp And Chief Banking Officer, Michael J. (Mike) Stewart, age 54, $310,077 total compensation

Evp And Chief Credit Officer, John J. Martin, age 53, $249,193 total compensation

Svp And Chief Risk Officer, Jeffery B. Lorentson

Vice President, Darlisa E Davis

Assistant Vice President, Kris Lacy

Vice President Assistant Director Operations, Jon Graves

Vice President, Tom Dunson

Vice President Of Loans, Christopher Allen

Vice President Marketing Manager, Dana Talaga

Vice President Cash Management, Jennifer Wehrly

Vice President Commercial Lending, Greg Lanter

Vice President, Lentz Gregory

Executive Vice President Mortgage Operations, Debra Rynearson

Senior Vice President Human Re, Leslie Holland

Vice President And Purchasing Director, Lisa Brothers

Vice President Secretary And Shareholder Relations Officer, Cynthia Holaday

Vice President, Joseph Keyler

Vice President, Alex Jones

Assistant Vice President Relationship Manager, Michael Kahne

Vice President, Margaret Hoke

Senior Vice President, John Ditmars

Senior Vice President And Director Of Human Resources, Kim A Ellington

Vice President Structured Finance, Dave Decraene

Vice President Retail Lending Leader, Jill Engerer

Vice President, Candy Shumard

Vice President, James F Zimmerman

Assistant Vice President, Tammy Hall

First Vice President, Mark Stevenson

Vice President, Jeffrey Lorentson

Vice President, Dan House

Vice President, Josh McKenney

Vice President, Adam Treibic
Assistant Vice President Merchant Services, Brad Garrison
Senior Vice President, Mark Engle
Vice President Manager Mortgage Sales, Elizabeth Chenore
Vice President Senior Product Manager, LuAnne Whewell
Vice President Relationship Manager Iii, Kevin Wagner
Assistant Vice President Business Banking Officer, Duane Kamminga
Senior Vice President And Director Of Finance, Michele Kawiecki
Vice President Information Systems Director, Kevin Scharnowske
Assistant Vice President Banking Center Manager, Sally Conyers
Vice President, William Robertson
Vice President And Client Advisor, Rita K Smith
Vice President, Benjamin J Hartings
Assistant Vice President Manager Facilities Projects And Planning, Lindsay S Sweet
Vice President Relationship Manager Iii, Kevin M Orourke
Vice President Retirement Plan Advisor, Kristopher Feldmeyer
Vice President Manager Commercial Lending, Scott Casbon
Senior Vice President, Brian Emmons
Assistant Vice President Banking Center Manager, Robert Holland
Assistant Vice President Executive Assistant To The Chief Operating Officer Chief Financial Officer, Nicole Weaver
Vice President, Paul Orner
Vice President Manager Commercial Banking, John Novosel
Vice President Relationship Manager Iii, Kevin Orourke
Vice President Commercial Lending, Clark Scott
Vice President Account Executive, Lehman Gary
Vice President, Hohl Matt
Senior Vice President Director Of Human Resources, Steven Harris
Vice President, Ctfa King
Assistant Vice President Manager Recordkeeping, Brenda Hiser
Board Member, Terry Walker
Chairman, Charles E. Schalliol, age 73
Board Member, Gary Lehman
Board Member, Jean Wojtowicz
Board Member, William Hoy
Board Member, Patrick Sherman
Board Member, Robert R Halderman
Auditors: BKD, LLP

LOCATIONS

HQ: First Merchants Corp
200 East Jackson Street, Muncie, IN 47305-2814
Phone: 765 747-1500
Web: www.firstmerchants.com

PRODUCTS/OPERATIONS

2017 Sales

	$ mil.	% of total
Interest		
Loans	274	71
Investment Securities	38	10
Federal Reserve and Federal Home Loan Bank stock	.9	-
Interest Expense/Other	(36.9)	-
Non-interest		
Service charges on deposits	18	5
Fiduciary activities	11	3
Other customer fees	20	5
Earnings on cash surrender value of life insurance	3	1
Net gains and fees on sales of loans	7	2
Net realized gains on sales of available for sale securities	2	1
Others	5	2
Total	**348**	**100**

COMPETITORS

Ameriana Bancorp	NorthWest Indiana
Bank of America	Bancorp
Citigroup	Old National Bancorp
Harris	STAR Financial Group
JPMorgan Chase	U.S. Bancorp
MutualFirst Financial	

HISTORICAL FINANCIALS

Company Type: Public

Income Statement
FYE: December 31

	ASSETS ($ mil.)	NET INCOME ($ mil.)	INCOME AS % OF ASSETS	EMPLOYEES
12/19	12,457	164	1.3%	1,891
12/18	9,884	159	1.6%	1,702
12/17	9,367	96	1.0%	1,684
12/16	7,211	81	1.1%	1,449
12/15	6,761	65	1.0%	1,529
Annual Growth	**16.5%**	**25.9%**	**—**	**5.5%**

2019 Year-End Financials

Debt ratio: 1.11%
Return on equity: 10.30%
Cash ($ mil.): 295
Current ratio: —
Long-term debt ($ mil.): —
No. of shares (mil.): 55
Dividends
Yield: 2.4%
Payout: 31.5%
Market value ($ mil.): 2,303

	STOCK PRICE ($) FY Close	P/E High/Low	PER SHARE ($) Earnings	Dividends	Book Value
12/19	41.59	13 10	3.19	1.00	32.26
12/18	34.27	15 10	3.22	0.84	28.54
12/17	42.06	21 17	2.12	0.69	26.52
12/16	37.65	19 11	1.98	0.54	22.04
12/15	25.42	16 13	1.72	0.41	20.92
Annual Growth	**13.1%**		**16.7%**	**25.0%**	**11.4%**

First Mid Bancshares Inc

Money doesn't grow on trees so when farmers inÂ Illinois need a little cash they turn to First Mid-Illinois Bank & Trust. The primary subsidiary of First Mid-Illinois Bancshares isÂ a major supplier of farm credit (including real estate machinery and production loans; inventory financing; and lines of credit) in its market area. In addition to agricultural loans the bank offers commercial consumer and real estate lending. ItÂ also provides deposit products such as savings and checking accounts plus trust and investment services through a partnership with Raymond James.Â First Mid-Illinois Bank & Trust has about 40 branches.Other subsidiaries provideÂ data processing servicesÂ and insurance products and services.

EXECUTIVES

Vp Conversions And Special Projects Implementation Manager, Rhonda Rawlings
Vice President Director Of Retirement Services, Kelly Jackson
Vice President Marketing, Rodney Morris
Executive Vice President, Clay Dean
Assistant Vice President, Jaci Manzella
Vice President, Darlene Johnson
Assistant Vice President, Dena Clifton
Senior Management (senior Vice President General Manager Director), Jason Tucker
Assistant Vice President Mortgage Lending, Mary White
Senior Vice President, Robert Weber
Senior Vice President Risk Management, Christopher Slabach
Senior Vice President, Andrew Zavarella
Assistant Vice President Mortgage Loan Administration, Sue Radloff
Sr Vp Director Of Loan Operations, Nancy Zike
Vice President Regional Lending Manager, Dave Garrett
Vice President Director Of Marketing, Laura Zuhone
Sr V Pres, Rhonda Gatons
Executive Vice President Market President, Matthew Carr
Vice President, Jack Franklin
Assistant Vice President Mortgage Loan O, Kim Weaver
Vice President, Gregory Kuhn
Board Member, Holly Bailey
Board Member, Gary Melvin
Board Member, Mary Westerhold
Board Member, Robert Cook
Board Member, James Zimmer
Auditors: BKD, LLP

LOCATIONS

HQ: First Mid Bancshares Inc
1421 Charleston Avenue, Mattoon, IL 61938
Phone: 217 234-7454   **Fax:** 217 258-0485
Web: www.firstmid.com

PRODUCTS/OPERATIONS

Selected Subsidiaries
The Checkley Agency Inc. (dba First Mid Insurance Group)
First Mid-Illinois Bank & Trust N.A.
First Mid-Illinois Statutory Trust I II
Mid-Illinois Data Services Inc.

COMPETITORS

Bank of America	Northern Trust
Fifth Third	PNC Financial
First BancTrust	U.S. Bancorp
First Busey	

HISTORICAL FINANCIALS

Company Type: Public

Income Statement
FYE: December 31

	ASSETS ($ mil.)	NET INCOME ($ mil.)	INCOME AS % OF ASSETS	EMPLOYEES
12/19	3,839	47	1.2%	827
12/18	3,839	36	1.0%	818
12/17	2,841	26	0.9%	592
12/16	2,884	21	0.8%	598
12/15	2,114	16	0.8%	513
Annual Growth	**16.1%**	**30.5%**	**—**	**12.7%**

2019 Year-End Financials

Debt ratio: 0.62%
Return on equity: 9.56%
Cash ($ mil.): 84
Current ratio: —
Long-term debt ($ mil.): —
No. of shares (mil.): 16
Dividends
Yield: 2.1%
Payout: 27.3%
Market value ($ mil.): 588

	STOCK PRICE ($) FY Close	P/E High/Low	PER SHARE ($) Earnings	Dividends	Book Value
12/19	35.25	13 11	2.87	0.76	31.58
12/18	31.92	17 12	2.52	1.04	28.59
12/17	38.54	20 14	2.13	0.66	24.32
12/16	34.00	17 11	2.05	0.62	22.51
12/15	26.00	14 10	1.81	0.59	24.25
Annual Growth	7.9%	— —	12.2%	6.5%	6.8%

First Midwest Bancorp, Inc. (Naperville, IL)

There's a lot of cabbage in corn country. Just ask First Midwest Bancorp the holding company for First Midwest Bank. Through nearly 110 branches the bank mainly serves suburban Chicago though its market extends into central and western Illinois and neighboring portions of Iowa and Indiana. Focusing on area small to mid-sized businesses it offers deposit products loans trust services wealth management insurance and retirement plan services; it has $7.2 billion of client trust and investment assets under management. Commercial real estate loans account for more than half of the company's portfolio.

Operations

More than 85% of the company's loan portfolio consists of corporate loans (the majority of which are secured by commercial real estate) while the remainder of the portfolio consists of consumer loans (which include home equity loans lines of credit and 1-4 family mortgages). Illustrative of its commitment to business lending First Midwest does not originate sub-prime lending or investment banking activities.

The bank's subsidiaries include: equipment leasing and commercial financier First Midwest Equipment Finance Co.; investment security managers First Midwest Securities Management LLC and First Midwest Holdings Inc.; Section 8 housing venture investor LIH Holdings; and Synergy Property Holdings LLC which manages the bank's OREO properties.

Geographic Reach

The company operates 109 banking offices largely located in various communities throughout the suburban metropolitan Chicago market as well as central and western Illinois and eastern Iowa. It owns 145 automated teller machines most of which are housed at banking locations. First Midwest and Allpoint together provide access to more than 50000 free ATMs worldwide.

Sales and Marketing

The company serves different industry segments including manufacturing health care pharmaceutical higher education wholesale and retail trade service and agricultural. First Midwest spent about $8.2 million on advertising and promotions in 2014 up from $7.8 million in 2013 and $5.1 million in 2012.

Financial Performance

Following a modest rebound in 2013 First Midwest's revenue in 2014 dipped by less than 1% to $426.48 million mostly because of a 76% drop in net securities gains as the bank in 2013 was able to collect a non-recurring equity investment sale gain of $34 million. Lower mortgage banking income resulting from lower market pricing also contributed to the modest dip in revenue. The bank did however report higher interest income as its loan business grew higher wealth management fees with growth in assets under management and higher service charge fees as deposit accounts grew.

After healthy profit growth in 2013 net income fell by nearly 13% to $69.31 million in 2014 mostly as the bank incurred higher costs associated with the acquisition and integration of Popular and Great Lakes and because the bank had higher loan loss provision expenses. In 2013 First Midwest had posted a large jump in net income thanks to higher revenue a decrease in the provision for loan and covered loan losses and lower interest and non-interest expenses.

Continuing its annual cash declines the bank's operations provided $122.93 million (or 10% less cash than in 2013) mostly due to lower earnings.

Mergers and Acquisitions

First Midwest Bancorp acquired Bridgeview Bank in 2019. Bridgeview has about $1.1 billion in assets $755 million in loans and $1 billion in deposits.

In early 2017 the company completed the acquisition of another Chicago-area bank Standard Bancshares. The deal will add 35 branches $2.3 billion in assets $2.1 billion in deposits and $1.9 million in loans.

Company Background

First Midwest capitalized on the rash of bank failures that have occurred in the Chicago area amid the recessionary economy. Its relative financial soundness put it in a position to acquire three failed Illinois banks through separate FDIC-facilitated transactions in 2009 and 2010: First DuPage Bank Peotone Bank and Trust and Palos Bank and Trust. The deals which included loss-sharing agreements with the regulator added a total of nearly 10 branches. In 2012 the company acquired the deposits and loans of Waukegan Savings Bank in another FDIC-assisted deal that added two more branches to its network. First Midwest will continue to consider acquisitions of failed banks in the Chicago area.

EXECUTIVES

President Ceo And Director; Chairman And Ceo First Midwest Bank, Michael L. Scudder, age 59, $750,000 total compensation

Evp Cio And Coo First Midwest Bank, Kent S. Belasco, age 69, $224,000 total compensation

Evp And Cfo First Midwest Bancorp Inc. & First Midwest Bank, Paul F. Clemens, age 68, $376,000 total compensation

Sevp And Coo; Vice Chairman And President First Midwest Bank, Mark G. Sander, age 61, $545,000 total compensation

Evp And Treasurer First Midwest Bancorp Inc. & First Midwest Bank, James P. Hotchkiss, age 63

Evp And Chief Risk Officer First Midwest Bancorp Inc. & First Midwest Bank, Kevin L. Moffitt

Evp Corporate Secretary And General Counsel, Nicholas J. Chulos

Senior Vice President, Heidi Smithson

Vice President Field, Phillip Tan

Vice President, Juan Cortez

Vice President, Scott Nelson

Executive Vice President And Director Commercial Banking First Midwest Bank, Victor Carapella

Senior Vice President, Jim Schramm

Vice President Compliance Review Manager, Beth Uhlir

First Vice President, Ed Garner

Vice President, Marianne Coneset

Vice President Administration, Connie Steinke

Executive Vice President Chief Administrative Officer, Dean Glassberg

Vice President, Mike Trunck

Vice President, Martha Sandoval

Vice President Employee Relations, Pam Porter

Vice President, Sue Barreto

Senior Vice President, Steve Rankins

Vice President, Jodie Speers

Senior Vice President Director Applic, John Hudak

Senior Vice President Financial Planning, Rich Padula

Senior Vice President, Matthew Burns

Vice President Public Funds, Susan Wade

Vice President And Assistant General Counsel, Steve Babinski

Senior Vice President Businessbanking Group Manager, Chris Esposito

Assistant Vice President, Donald Knapp

Vice President Commercial Banking, Steven Olson

Senior Vice President Wealth Management, Chris Ksoll

Senior Vice President, John Gaughan

Assistant Vice President, Megan Miller

Business Banking Relationship Manager Iii And Assistant Vice President, Michelle Payla

Vice President, Nick Yerkes

Vice President, Michele Morgan

Vice President Business Banking, Dave Kurow

Vice President, Chad Lyons

Vice President, Gia Ormond

Vice President Commercial Banking, Abdullah Tadros

Vice President Community Banking Officer Community Real Estate Group, Richard Rischall

Vice President, Todd Troeger

Vice President Administration, Dorothy Karr

Vice President, Angela Hart

Senior Vice President Total Rewards, Steven Kull

Svp Head Structured Finance, Joseph Angel

Executive Vice President And Chief Risk Officer, Jeff Newcom

Vice President Business Banking, Tony Martino

Senior Vice President, Steve Clingen

Vice President Sales Regional Sales Manager, Joe Creamons

Vice President Middle Market Banking, Chris Hannon

Vice President Commercial Banking Officer, Tim Meyer

Vice President Abl Relationship Manager Business Credit, Thomas Brennan

Vice President Trust Relationship Manager, Michael Lambert

Vice President Senior Talent Acquisition Manager, Jeff Boulos

Senior Vice President Structured Finance, Aaron Markos

Vice President, Keith Massey

Vice President Cra Manager, Mary Morstadt

Vice President Franchise Banking Group, Kara Symeonides

Vice President, Robert Rodie

Senior Vice President Manager Business Banking, Brian Burke

Senior Vice President, Matthew Brennan

Vice President, Rick Lang

Vice President Group Sales Manager, Joseph Palazzolo

Senior Vice President, Jim Ringer

Vice President Senior Human Resources Consultant, Anita Dwyer

Vice President, Dana Pike

Vice President Centralized Credit Underwriting, Jesse Newkirk

Assistant Vice President Credit Analyst Manager, Matthew Rudny

Senior Vice President Audit Services Director, Ted Roknich

Vice President Mainframe Relationship Manager, Mary Mesch

Vice President First Midwest Bank, Nancy Henningfield

Vice President Regional Recruitment Manager, Linda Cleveland

Senior Vice President, Phil Ostroski

Senior Vice President, Neil Prendergast

Vice President Mortgage Underwriting Manager, Erin Wehman

Assistant Vice President Branch Manager, Evelyn Nieves

Avp Hr Consultant (business Partner), Amy Crabbe

Senior Vice President Healthcare Banking Coverage Group, James Goody

Vice President, Terrence Duffy

Executive Vice President And Senior Counsel, James Carroll

Senior Vice President Structured Finance, Jeffrey Skinner

Svp And Director Corporate Communications, Maurissa Kanter

Executive Vice President And Chief Human Resources Officer, Doug Rose

Executive Vice President And Chief Credit Officer, Kevin Geoghegan

Senior Vice President, Karen Kuppler

Vice President, Constance Simms

Vice President, David Rutledge

Senior Vice President Healthcare Finance, Michael Mason

Vice President Treasury Management Business Development, Joe Koscal

Assistant Vp Hr Technology, Daniel Wilman

Vice President, Donna Becker

Vice President Credit Administration, Salena Fuoss

Chairman, Robert P. (Bob) O'Meara, age 82

Board Member, Barbara Boigegrain

Auditors: Ernst & Young LLP

LOCATIONS

HQ: First Midwest Bancorp, Inc. (Naperville, IL)
8750 West Bryn Mawr Avenue, Suite 1300, Chicago, IL 60631-3655
Phone: 708 831-7483
Web: www.firstmidwest.com

PRODUCTS/OPERATIONS

2016

	$ mil.	% of total
Interest Income		
Loans	338	63
Investment securities - taxable	28	5
Investment securities - tax-exempt	8	2
Other short-term investments	2	0
Noninterest Income		
Service charges on deposit accounts	40	8
Wealth management fees	33	6
Card-based fees	29	5
Merchant servicing fees	12	2
Mortgage banking income	10	2
Capital market products income	10	2
Other service charges commissions and fees	9	2
Net gain on sale-leaseback transaction	5	1
BOLI income	3	1
Net securities gains	1	0
Other income	3	1
Total	537	100

COMPETITORS

Bank of America	Meta Financial Group
BankFinancial	Northern Trust
Cummins-Allison	PrivateBank
Fifth Third	QCR Holdings
First Busey	West Suburban Bancorp
Harris	Wintrust Financial
JPMorgan Chase	

HISTORICAL FINANCIALS

Company Type: Public

Income Statement   FYE: December 31

	ASSETS ($ mil.)	NET INCOME ($ mil.)	INCOME AS % OF ASSETS	EMPLOYEES
12/19	17,850	199	1.1%	2,122
12/18	15,505	157	1.0%	2,046
12/17	14,077	98	0.7%	2,152
12/16	11,422	92	0.8%	1,882
12/15	9,732	82	0.8%	1,790
Annual Growth	16.4%	24.9%	—	4.3%

2019 Year-End Financials

Debt ratio: 1.31%
Return on equity: 9.03%
Cash ($ mil.): 299
Current ratio: —
Long-term debt ($ mil.): —

No. of shares (mil.): 109
Dividends
  Yield: 2.3%
  Payout: 31.0%
Market value ($ mil.): 2,536

	STOCK PRICE ($) FY Close	P/E High/Low	Earnings	Dividends	Book Value
12/19	23.06	13 10	1.82	0.54	21.56
12/18	19.81	18 12	1.52	0.45	19.32
12/17	24.01	27 22	0.96	0.39	18.16
12/16	25.23	22 14	1.14	0.36	15.46
12/15	18.43	19 15	1.05	0.36	14.70
Annual Growth	5.8%	—	14.7%	10.7%	10.0%

First National Bank Alaska

First National Bank Alaska is a financial anchor in Anchorage. Founded in 1922 the bank is one of the state's oldest and largest financial institutions. With about 30 branches throughout The Last Frontier (and about 20 ATMs in rural communities) the bank offers traditional deposit products such as checking and savings accounts CDs and IRAs as well as loans and mortgages credit and debit cards and trust and investment management services. The family of longtime president Daniel Cuddy owns a majority of First National Bank Alaska; he took the helm of the bank in 1951.

Geographic Reach

In order to help serve clients in remote locales First National Bank Alaska opened its first branch with a full-service customer kiosk at a joint air force/army base outside of Anchorage where customers can make routine banking transactions without teller assistance. The bank may add such kiosks at other branches.

Financial Performance

The company's total annul revenue has slowly declining across recent fiscal years. However it has managed to stay profitable.

EXECUTIVES

Senior Vice President Commercial Lending, Bill Inscho

Senior Vice President, Brent Kimball

Executive Vice President And Chief Financial Officer, Michele Schuh

Assistant Vice President, Darcy Steger

Vice President, Lita Beck

Vice President, Alan Dablemont

Vice President, Jennifer Mahlen

Vice President Dimond Lending Division, Melissa Reiser

Assistant Vice President, Allen Jackson

Assistant Vice President, Sheila Lomboy

Senior Vice President And Specialty Lending Director, Stacy Tomuro

Assistant Vice President Escrow Manager, Michelle Frain

Senior Vice President, Rick Flake

Senior Vice President, Pamela Keeler

Senior Vice President, Elaine Kroll

Executive Vice President, Bill Renfrew

Senior Vice President, Karl Heinz

Board Secretary, Cheri Gillian

Auditors: Crowe LLP

LOCATIONS

HQ: First National Bank Alaska
101 West 36th Avenue, P.O. Box 100720, Anchorage, AK 99510-0720
Phone: 907 777-4362   Fax: 907 265-3528
Web: www.FNBAlaska.com

COMPETITORS

Alaska Pacific Bancshares	KeyCorp
Alaska USA	Northrim BanCorp
	Wells Fargo

HISTORICAL FINANCIALS

Company Type: Public

Income Statement   FYE: December 31

	ASSETS ($ mil.)	NET INCOME ($ mil.)	INCOME AS % OF ASSETS	EMPLOYEES
12/19	3,808	55	1.5%	—
12/18	3,753	54	1.4%	—
12/17	3,653	36	1.0%	—
12/16	3,609	41	1.1%	—
12/15	3,569	36	1.0%	—
Annual Growth	1.6%	11.4%	—	—

2019 Year-End Financials

Debt ratio: —
Return on equity: 10.55%
Cash ($ mil.): 127
Current ratio: —
Long-term debt ($ mil.): —

No. of shares (mil.): 3
Dividends
  Yield: 5.9%
  Payout: 82.0%
Market value ($ mil.): 770

	STOCK PRICE ($) FY Close	P/E High/Low	Earnings	Dividends	Book Value
12/19	243.00	16 13	17.56	14.40	172.91
12/18	252.00	162 15	17.07	11.40	159.96
12/17	2,065.00	210 144	11.49	10.00	156.70
12/16	1,750.00	134 97	13.04	8.50	155.37
12/15	1,403.00	142 124	11.30	50.00	153.43
Annual Growth	(35.5%)	—	11.6%	(26.7%)	3.0%

First of Long Island Corp

When it comes to banking The First of Long Island wants to be the first thing on Long Islanders' minds. The company owns The First National Bank of Long Island which offers a variety of lending investment and deposit services through around 45 commercial and retail branches on New

York's Long Island and the boroughs of Manhattan and Queens. Residential and Commercial Mortgages (particularly tied to multifamily properties) make up more than 90% of the bank's loan portfolio though the bank also writes revolving home equity business and consumer loans. Its two bank subsidiaries include insurance agency The First of Long Island Agency and investment firm FNY Service.

Operations

The First National Bank of Long Island also operates an investment management division that offers trust and investment management estate and custody services.

The bank makes more than 90% of its revenue from interest income. About 70% of its total revenue came from loan interest during 2015 while another 21% came from interest income on taxable and non-taxable investment securities. The rest of its revenue came from deposit account service charges (3% of revenue) investment management division income (2%) gains on securities sales (1%) and other income sources.

Geographic Reach

The New York City-based bank operated 45 branches at the end of 2015 including 41 in Long Island and two each in Manhattan and Queens.

Sales and Marketing

First serves individuals professionals corporations institutions and governmental clients through its branches.

The bank markets its services through customer service personnel tele-sales lending relationships referral sources and advertisements. It spent $877000 on marketing during 2015 compared to $927000 and $670000 in 2014 and 2013 respectively.

Financial Performance

The First of Long Island's annual revenues have risen more than 20% since 2011 as its loan assets have more than doubled to $2.25 billion. Meanwhile the bank's profits have swelled more than 30% thanks to revenue growth and low interest expenses.

First's revenue jumped 13% to $101 million during 2015 mostly thanks to higher interest income as its average loan balances grew 26% and as its non-taxable security assets rose by 6%. The bulk of the loan asset growth was tied to residential mortgages while most of the rest came from multifamily commercial mortgage growth.

Double-digit revenue growth drove the bank's net income up 12% to $25.9 million. First's operating cash levels dipped 1% to $35 million despite the rise in earnings due to unfavorable working capital changes mostly related to a decrease in accrued expenses and other liabilities.

Strategy

The bank has been opening new branches utilizing "effective relationship management" using targeted solicitation efforts and expanding its product and service offerings to boost its loan and deposit business in recent years.

In early 2016 the company planned to open between eight and 12 more The First National Bank of Long Island branches in Queens after opening two branches there in Howard Beach and Whitestone in 2015. It also planned to open branches in Brooklyn. Expanding its branch network on Long Island the bank in 2015 launched new branches in Patchogue and Melville.

EXECUTIVES

Svp And Evp And Senior Lending Officer Commercial Lending The First National Bank Long Island, Donald L. Manfredonia, age 68, $222,500 total compensation

Svp, Richard Kick, age 62, $230,100 total compensation

Svp And Treasurer; Evp Cfo And Cashier The First National Bank Of Long Island, Mark D. Curtis, age 65, $242,700 total compensation

President And Ceo The First Of Long Island Corporation And The First National Bank Of Long Island, Michael N. Vittorio, age 67, $468,000 total compensation

Svp And Secretary; Sevp The First National Bank Of Long Island, Sallyanne K. Ballweg, age 64, $264,000 total compensation

Evp And Chief Risk Officer First National Bank Of Long Island, Christopher Becker

Vice President, Jane Reed

Assistant Vice President, Giuseppe Sparacino

Vice President, Robert Eisen

Vice President And Trust Officer, Sharon Pazienza

Vice President Director Of Human Resources, Sue Hempton

Vice President Director Of Marketing, Laura Ierulli

Avp Branch Administration, Kalpa Ved

Senior Vice President And Chief Investment Officer, Jay Mcconie

Vice President, Nicholas Ulrich

Executive Vice President, Christopher Hilton

Assistant Vice President And Senior Credit Analyst, Michael Moscati

Chairman The First Of Long Island Corporation And The First National Bank Of Long Island, Walter C. Teagle, age 70

Auditors: Crowe LLP

LOCATIONS

HQ: First of Long Island Corp
10 Glen Head Road, Glen Head, NY 11545
Phone: 516 671-4900
Web: www.fnbli.com

PRODUCTS/OPERATIONS

2015 Sales

	$ mil.	% of total
Interest and dividend income:		
Loans	70	70
Investment securities		
Taxable	8	8
Nontaxable	13	13
Noninterest income		
Investment Management Division income	2	2
Service charges on deposit accounts	2	3
Net gains on sales of securities	1	1
Other	2	3
Total	**100**	**100**

Selected Services:

Checking
Savings
Saving for Retirement & Education
Online Banking & Bill Pay
FirstLink Online Banking
Quicken/Quickbooks
FirstPay Bill Pay
PopMoney
Account to Account Transfers

COMPETITORS

Astoria Financial
Bank of America
Citibank
Dime Community Bancshares
Flushing Financial
JPMorgan Chase
New York Community Bancorp
Ridgewood Savings Bank
Suffolk Bancorp

HISTORICAL FINANCIALS

Company Type: Public

Income Statement

FYE: December 31

	ASSETS ($ mil.)	NET INCOME ($ mil.)	INCOME AS % OF ASSETS	EMPLOYEES
12/19	4,097	41	1.0%	341
12/18	4,241	41	1.0%	344
12/17	3,894	35	0.9%	333
12/16	3,510	30	0.9%	314
12/15	3,130	25	0.8%	302
Annual Growth	**7.0%**	**12.6%**	**—**	**3.1%**

2019 Year-End Financials

Debt ratio: —
Return on equity: 10.69%
Cash ($ mil.): 38
Current ratio: —
Long-term debt ($ mil.): —

No. of shares (mil.): 23
Dividends
  Yield: 2.7%
  Payout: 40.8%
Market value ($ mil.): 600

	STOCK PRICE ($) FY Close	P/E High/Low	PER SHARE ($)		
			Earnings	Dividends	Book Value
12/19	25.08	15 12	1.67	0.69	16.26
12/18	19.95	18 12	1.63	0.62	15.27
12/17	28.50	22 18	1.43	0.58	14.37
12/16	28.55	30 19	1.34	0.55	12.90
12/15	30.00	26 19	1.22	0.52	11.85
Annual Growth	**(4.4%)**	**— —**	**8.2%**	**7.3%**	**8.2%**

First Republic Bank (San Francisco, CA)

Founded in 1985 First Republic Bank offers private banking real estate lending wealth management trust and custody services for businesses and high-net-worth clients through about 90 offices. Its main geographic focus is on urban markets such as San Francisco Los Angeles New York Portland and San Diego. The company generates most of its revenue from commercial banking operations. It also offers investment advice and brokerage and trust services through its wealth management division. First Republic Bank has around $115 billion of assets under management.

Operations

Commercial banking accounts for more than 80% of First Republic Bank's total revenue. It claims about $90 billion in deposits (mostly checking) and about $90 billion in loans (around half single-family real estate loans).

First Republic Bank's wealth management services generate nearly 20% of revenue and are conducted via subsidiaries: First Republic Investment Management (investment advice) First Republic Securities Company (brokerage services) and First Republic Trust Company (trust services).

The interest income accounts for nearly 85% of the company's total sales.

Geographic Reach

First Republic Bank operates about 90 offices nearly 80 of which are licensed deposit-taking offices primarily located in San Francisco (headquarters) Palo Alto Los Angeles Santa Barbara Newport Beach and San Diego California; Portland Oregon; Boston Massachusetts; Palm Beach Florida; Greenwich Connecticut; New York New York; and Jackson Wyoming.

California accounts for over 60% of First Republic Bank's outstanding loans and some 55% of total deposits giving the region significant control over the company's success.

Sales and Marketing

First Republic Bank advertises via digital media newspaper television and radio ads; its primary marketing goal is to attract deposits in its Preferred Banking offices wealth management sweep deposits and others. The vast majority of new clients are referred by word of mouth from existing clients.

Business customers represent about 55% of total deposits with consumer clients accounting for the rest. Its advertising and marketing expenses were $66.0 million in 2019 $60.5 million in 2018 and $48.4 million in 2017.

Financial Performance

The company's revenue increased by $250.5 million to $2.8 billion in 2019 compared to $2.5 billion in prior year. Net interest income for Commercial Banking was $2.7 billion in 2019 compared to $2.4 billion in 2018 and $2.1 billion in 2017. The increase in 2019 was primarily due to an increase in interest-earning assets partially offset by a decrease in net interest margin.

Net income was $930.3 million in 2019 compared to $853.8 million in 2018 and $757.7 million in 2017 an increase of 9% in 2019 and an increase of 13% in 2018.

Cash at the end of 2019 was $1.7 billion a decrease of $1.1 billion from the prior year. Cash from operations contributed $938.5 million to the coffers while investing activities used $17.0 billion mainly for loan originations. Financing activities added another $15.0 billion as a result of a net increase in deposits.

Strategy

First Republic's core business principles and service-based culture have successfully guided its efforts over the past 34 years. The company believes focusing on these principles will enable to expand its capabilities for providing value added services to its urban coastal client base and generate steady long-term growth. The company focuses on delivering superior client service originating high quality loans growing core deposits growing its wealth management business and attracting and retaining high quality service professionals.

First Republic have traditionally attracted new clients through its mortgage lending activities providing an opportunity for its relationship managers to introduce other services to these clients. The company remain committed to underwriting and originating high quality loans for existing and new clients. This enables the company to expand its business in a disciplined manner while maintaining superior credit quality.

Company Background

First Republic was founded in 1985 by CEO Jim Herbert.

EXECUTIVES

Evp Secretary And General Counsel, Edward J. Dobranski, age 69

Chairman And Ceo, James H. Herbert

Evp And Chief Credit Officer, David B. Lichtman

President First Republic Securities, David Tateosian

Sevp And Chief Banking Officer, Michael D. (Mike) Selfridge, age 52

Chairman First Republic Trust Company, Michael J. Harrington

Evp And President Private Wealth Management, Bob Thornton

Evp And Chief Marketing Officer, Dianne Snedaker

Svp Chief Deposit Officer And Chief Investment Officer, Hafize Gaye (Gaye) Erkan

Evp And Cfo, Michael J. (Mike) Roffler

Evp; Chief Bsa And Aml And Security Officer, Bill Ward

Evp And Cio, Dale A. Smith

Evp And Coo, Jason C. Bender

President First Republic Trust Company, Kelly Johnston

Senior Vice President Foreign Exchange, Kate Kent-Sheehan

Associate Vice President, Brent Chapman

Vice President Investment Consultant, Maureen Mcnally

Vice President Portfolio Manager, Stephen Marotto

Vice President Business Analysis, Greg Boudreaux

Vice President Compliance Risk Manager, Steven Sears

Vice President Residential Lending, Lionel Antunes

Vice President, Michael Curley

Senior Vice President Chief Auditor Internal Audit, Justin Gibson

Vice President, Todd Brantley

Vice President First Republic Investment Management, Reynolds Ospina

Vice President Strategic Planning And Special Projects, Tim Maguire

Vice President Of Retail Marketing, Gwenn Murphy

Vice President Credit Risk Officer, Sean Callum

Vice President Director Single Family Lending, Paula Lazar

Vice President Lending Services, Pj Pamulo

Senior Vice President Chief Accounting Officer, Olga Tsokova

Vice President, David Weitgenant

Senior Vice President, Michael Scrivens

Vice President Finance, Erwin Hom

Vice President Wealth Manager, Jeff Greene

Vice President, Andrew Gibson

Vice President Director Deposit Technology, Dave McLelland

Vice President Digital Technologies, Yvonne Yang

Vice President, Justin Launer

Senior Vice President, Helene Jepson

Vice President Compensation, Mea Kwon

Vice President Head Of Operations Analysis And Process Improvement, Kushal Gandhi

Vice President, Tim Ross

Vice President Governance And Compliance, Teresa Joyce

Vp Trading, Lynn Rueb

Senior Vice President, Christian Nelson

Vice President Head Analytics, Subrmanian Iyer

Cfa Vice President, Garret Giglia

Vice President Credit Risk Manager, Earl Crawford

Vice President, Roger Duke

Vice President And Associate General Counsel, Hilary Gevondyan

Vice President And Investment Consultant, Aaron Nichols

Vice President Corporate Security And Investigations Bsa Aml, Eric Breshears

Vice President Compliance Officer, Lalesh Muni

Vice President And Head Of Digital Channels (business Operations), Jonathan Kropf

Vice President And Assistant General Counsel Private Wealth Management, Debra Achkire

Senior Vice President, Jeff Cougoule

Vice President Core Business Integration Enterprise Data And Client Insights, Amy Farnstrom

Senior Vice President, David Breslin

Vice President Info Security Programs Information Security, David Estabrook

Vice President Facilities And Admin. Services, Shannon Flynn

Vice President, Adam Rose

Vice President Marketing, Kymberlie Boston-keplinger

Vice President Head Of Talent Acquisition, Lisa Hess

Vice President Lending Services, Leslie Gibin

Vp Pmo Operations, Jean Burns

Vice President Senior Attorney, Benjamin Spohn

Vice President Core Transformation, Mercedes Broening

Vice President, Gilmar Valencia

Vice President Deputy Chief Auditor, Robert Pearce

Vice President And Wealth Manager First Republic Private Wealth Management, Rick Will

Vice President And Wealth Manager New York, Gregory Carafello

Vice President And Wealth Manager New York, Chad Cohen

Vice President Vendor Management, Helen Lee

Senior Vice President Financial Planning, Justin Mesko

Vice President Wealth Management And Derivative Strategy, Annie Northrop

Vice President Of Solutions Architecture, Laban Eilers

Vice Chair, Katherine August-deWilde, age 69

Assistant Treasurer, Aaron Frank

Auditors: KPMG LLP

LOCATIONS

HQ: First Republic Bank (San Francisco, CA)
111 Pine Street, 2nd Floor, San Francisco, CA 94111
Phone: 415 392-1400
Web: www.firstrepublic.com

PRODUCTS/OPERATIONS

2018 Sales

	% of total
Commercial Banking	82
Wealth Management	18
Total	**100**

COMPETITORS

Bank of Marin	JPMorgan Chase
Bank of New York Mellon	MUFG Americas Holdings
Boston Private	Merrill Lynch
Citigroup	Morgan Stanley
City National	TriState Capital
Goldman Sachs	UBS
	Wells Fargo

HISTORICAL FINANCIALS

Company Type: Public

Income Statement

	ASSETS ($ mil.)	NET INCOME ($ mil.)	INCOME AS % OF ASSETS	EMPLOYEES
12/19	116,263	930	0.8%	4,812
12/18	99,205	853	0.9%	4,480
12/17	87,780	757	0.9%	4,025
12/16	73,277	673	0.9%	3,566
12/15	58,981	522	0.9%	—
Annual Growth	18.5%	15.5%	—	—

FYE: December 31

2019 Year-End Financials

Debt ratio: 1.10%	No. of shares (mil.): 168
Return on equity: 10.04%	Dividends
Cash ($ mil.): 1,699	Yield: 0.6%
Current ratio: —	Payout: 14.7%
Long-term debt ($ mil.): —	Market value ($ mil.): 19,805

STOCK PRICE ($)		P/E		PER SHARE ($)		
	FY Close	High/Low		Earnings	Dividends	Book Value
12/19	117.45	22	16	5.20	0.75	58.42
12/18	86.90	22	16	4.81	0.71	52.62
12/17	86.64	24	20	4.31	0.67	48.35
12/16	92.14	23	14	3.93	0.63	44.78
12/15	66.06	21	15	3.18	0.59	39.05
Annual Growth	15.5%	—	—	13.1%	6.2%	10.6%

FirstEnergy Corp

FirstEnergy's first goal is to generate and deliver power but its second goal is to stay profitable in a market undergoing deregulation. Its ten utilities provide electricity to 6 million customers in the Midwest and the Mid-Atlantic. FirstEnergy controls approximately 3780 megawatts from regulated scrubbed coal and hydro facilities in West Virginia New Jersey and Virginia. Stretching from the Ohio-Indiana border to the New Jersey shore the companies operate a vast infrastructure of more than 269000 miles of distribution lines and are dedicated to providing customers with safe reliable and responsive service.

Operations

FirstEnergy has two primary operating segments: Regulated Distribution and Regulated Transmission. More than 85% of total revenue comes from Regulated Distribution and about 15% from Regulated Transmission.

The Regulated Distribution segment distributes electricity through FirstEnergy's ten utilities which serve 6 million customers in a service area. It has a controlling interest in about 3800 MWs of generation capacity in West Virginia Virginia and New Jersey. It fulfills the additional electricity needs of its customers through power purchase agreements.

The Regulated Transmission segment transmits electricity through transmission facilities owned and operated by Transmission Company and a number of FirstEnergy's utilities. Transmission operations include approximately 24500 miles of lines and two regional transmission operation centers.

Geographic Reach

FirstEnergy operates and serves customers in a service area of 65000 square miles in Maryland New Jersey New York Ohio Pennsylvania and West Virginia.

Its controls approximately 3780 megawatts from regulated scrubbed coal and hydro facilities in West Virginia New Jersey and Virginia.

Sales and Marketing

The Regulated Distribution segment sells roughly equal amounts of electricity to its residential and commercial customers and slightly less to its industrial customers. Generally there is no competition for electric distribution service in its service territories in Ohio Pennsylvania West Virginia Maryland New Jersey and New York.

Financial Performance

Until 2018 the company's financial performance was steady through trending slightly upward until it slightly fell in 2019. Net income also slightly fell down in 2019 but improved a lot in 2018 despite the loss in the later year.

In 2019 revenue fell 2% to $11.0 billion this was due from Regulated Distribution primarily from retail generation and wholesale sales.

The company decrease its net income of $912 million for 2019 primarily due to low income from continuing operation and Regulated Distribution segment. Regulated Distribution's net income decreased $166 million in 2019 as compared to 2018 primarily resulting from the SCOH ruling that ceased collection of Rider DMR a higher pension and OPEB mark-to-market adjustment the absence of the reversal of a reserve on recoverability of certain REC purchases in Ohio and lower revenues associated with decreased weather-related usage.

It has $679 million in cash holdings. Operations generated $2.5 billion and financing activities provided $656 million offset by $2.9 billion in investing cash outflow.

Strategy

FirstEnergy's strategy is to invest in its Regulated Transmission and Regulated Distribution segments as a fully regulated company FirstEnergy is also focused on improving the balance sheet over time consistent with its business profile and maintaining investment grade ratings at its regulated businesses and FE.

FirstEnergy's 2019 Strategic Plan "Energized by Possibility" articulates their vision for the next five years. It includes the company's approach to the rapid changes in the electric utility industry fueled by evolving customer expectations emerging technologies and a lower-carbon economy. The plan outlines key initiatives related to our core values including: Providing customer with reliable electricity and innovative programs products and services; Fostering a culture of innovation and embracing forward-thinking perspectives and emerging technologies; Helping customers and communities thrive while making the environment better; Creating a diverse and inclusive workplace; Leveraging teamwork to create thoughtful innovative solutions that bring value to customers; Keeping safety first every day to protect our communities employees and assets; and Achieving operational excellence and strong financial performance to meet our commitments to stakeholders.

HISTORY

FirstEnergy came to light in 1893 as the Akron Electric Light and Power Company. After several mergers the business went bankrupt and was sold in 1899 to Akron Traction and Electric Company which became Northern Ohio Power and Light (NOP&L).

In 1930 Commonwealth and Southern (C&S) bought NOP&L and merged it with four other Ohio utility holding companies to form Ohio Edison. The new firm increased sales during the Depression by selling electric appliances.

The Public Utility Holding Company Act of 1935 (passed to rein in uncontrolled utilities) caught up with C&S in 1949 forcing it to divest Ohio Edison. Rival Ohio Public Service was also divested from its holding company and in 1950 Ohio Edison bought it.

In 1967 after two decades of expansion Ohio Edison and three other Ohio and Pennsylvania utilities formed the Central Area Power Coordination Group (CAPCO) to share new power-plant costs including the construction of the Beaver Valley nuclear plant (1970-76). Although the CAPCO partners agreed in 1980 to cancel four planned nukes in 1985 Ohio Edison took part in building the Perry Unit 1 and Beaver Valley Unit 2 nuclear plants.

The federal Energy Policy Act of 1992 allowed wholesale power competition and to satisfy new federal requirements Ohio Edison formed a six-state transmission alliance in 1996 with fellow utilities Centerior Energy Allegheny Power System and Dominion Resources' Virginia Power to coordinate their grids.

Ohio Edison paid about $1.5 billion in 1997 for Centerior Energy formed in 1986 as a holding company for Toledo Edison and Cleveland Electric. Ohio Edison and Centerior both burdened by high-cost generating plants merged to cut costs and the expanded energy concern was renamed FirstEnergy Corp.

Looking toward deregulation FirstEnergy began buying mechanical construction contracting and energy management companies in 1997 including Roth Bros. and RPC Mechanical. In 1998 it added nine more. FirstEnergy then ventured into natural gas operations by purchasing MARBEL Energy. The company also created separate subsidiaries for its nuclear and transmission assets.

In 2000 FirstEnergy agreed to acquire New Jersey-based electric utility GPU in an $11.9 billion deal; it became one of the largest US utilities in 2001 when it completed the acquisition which added three utilities (Jersey Central Power & Light Metropolitan Edison and Pennsylvania Electric) serving 2.1 million electricity customers.

Beefing up its generation assets in 2011 the company acquired Allegheny Energy in a $8.5 billion deal. The acquisition increased FirstEnergy's power generation capacity by 70% and its customer base by 35% dramatically boosting its position as a leading regional energy provider focused on both regulated utility operations and a competitive generation business.

EXECUTIVES

President Maryland Operations, James A. Sears

Evp Corporate Strategy Regulatory Affairs And Chief Legal Officer, Leila L. Vespoli, age 61, $758,606 total compensation

Plant Manager, Donald R. (Donny) Schneider, age 59, $552,404 total compensation

Svp Corporate Services And Cio, Bennett L. Gaines, age 66

Svp Marketing And Branding, Dennis M. Chack, age 69

Svp And President Utilities Business, Steven E. (Steve) Strah, age 56, $553,286 total compensation

President Ceo And Director, Charles E. (Chuck) Jones, age 65, $1,133,840 total compensation

Evp And Cfo, James F. (Jim) Pearson, age 66, $659,884 total compensation

Evp And President Firstenergy Generation, James H. (Jim) Lash, age 69, $583,187 total compensation

Regional President The Cleveland Electric Illuminating Company, John E. Skory

Regional President Metropolitan Edison Company, Edward L. Shuttleworth

Regional President Ohio Edison Company, Randall A. Frame

Regional President West Penn Power Company, David W. McDonald

President Jersey Central Power And Light, James V. Fakult

Regional President Pennsylvania Electric Company, Scott R Wyman

President West Virginia Operations, Holly C Kauffman

President Pennsylvania Operations, Linda L. Moss, age 55

Svp And Coo Firstenergy Nuclear Operating Company, Samuel L. Belcher

Regional President Toledo Edison Company, Richard S. Sweeney

Executive Vice President, Charles Lasky

Senior Vice President Strategic Planning And Opera, Mark Clark

Vice President Controller And Chief Accounting Officer, Jason Lisowski

Vp And Treasurer, Steve Staub

Vice President, Ernie Maley

Vice President Transmission, Carl Bridenbaugh

Vice President And General Counsel, Robert
 Reffner
Chairman, George M. Smart, age 74
Assistant Treasurer, Bill Wang
Board Member, Michael Anderson
Board Member, Tom Mitchell
Board Member, James O'neil
Auditors: PricewaterhouseCoopers LLP

LOCATIONS

HQ: FirstEnergy Corp
 76 South Main Street, Akron, OH 44308
Phone: 800 736-3402
Web: www.firstenergycorp.com

PRODUCTS/OPERATIONS

2016 Sales

	$ mil.	% of total
Regulated Distribution	9,629	63
Competitive Energy Services	4,549	30
Regulated Transmission	1,151	7
Corporate/Other and Reconciling Adjustments	(767)	
Total	**14,562**	**100**

COMPETITORS

AEP	Exelon
Avista	National Fuel Gas
CMS Energy	NiSource
Constellation Energy	PPL Corporation
Group	PSEG Energy Holdings
DPL	Peoples Natural Gas
Delmarva Power	Pepco Holdings
Dominion Energy	Public Service
Duquesne Light	Enterprise Group
Duquesne Light	TVA
Holdings	Vectren
EnergySolve	WGL Holdings

HISTORICAL FINANCIALS

Company Type: Public

Income Statement

FYE: December 31

	REVENUE ($ mil.)	NET INCOME ($ mil.)	NET PROFIT MARGIN	EMPLOYEES
12/19	11,035	912	8.3%	12,316
12/18	11,261	1,348	12.0%	12,494
12/17	14,017	(1,724)	—	15,617
12/16	14,562	(6,177)	—	15,707
12/15	15,026	578	3.8%	15,781
Annual Growth	**(7.4%)**	**12.1%**	**—**	**(6.0%)**

2019 Year-End Financials

Debt ratio: 49.64%	No. of shares (mil.): 540
Return on equity: 13.23%	Dividends
Cash ($ mil.): 627	Yield: 3.1%
Current ratio: 0.50	Payout: 71.3%
Long-term debt ($ mil.): 19,618	Market value ($ mil.): 26,276

	STOCK PRICE ($) FY Close	P/E High/Low	PER SHARE ($) Earnings	Dividends	Book Value
12/19	48.60	29 22	1.68	1.52	12.90
12/18	37.55	20 15	1.99	1.44	13.31
12/17	30.62	— —	(3.88)	1.44	8.81
12/16	30.97	— —	(14.49)	1.44	14.11
12/15	31.73	30 21	1.37	1.44	29.33
Annual Growth	**11.2%**	**— —**	**5.2%**	**1.4%**	**(18.6%)**

Fiserv Inc

Fiserv Inc. is a leading global provider of financial services technology. The company provides account processing systems electronic billing and payment systems and presentment services account-to-account transfers person-to-person payments debit network solutions debit card processing and services general purpose credit retail private label and commercial credit card processing and services and payments infrastructure services; internet and mobile banking systems; and related services including card and print personalization services item processing and source capture services loan origination and servicing products stored value network solutions and fraud and risk management products and services. It also provides consulting services business operations services and related software products that promote change in deposit behavior to transition check capture from branch and teller channels to digital self-service deposit channels including mobile merchant and ATM. Fiserv serves customers of all sizes including banks credit unions other financial institutions and merchants. Most of Firserv's revenue is generated in the US. Fiserv bought First Data a payments processor for $22 billion.

HISTORY

When First Bank System of Minneapolis bought Milwaukee-based Midland Bank in 1984 the head of Midland's data processing operation George Dalton bought the unit and then merged that operation with Sunshine State Systems a newly independent Florida processing company headed by Leslie Muma. Christened Fiserv the company went public in 1986. It grew by providing outsourcing services to small banks and thrifts.

In the 1990s Fiserv began targeting larger clients. But industry consolidation sometimes hurt the company as when the 12-year term of a 1995 contract with Chase Manhattan was reduced to three after Chase and Chemical Bank merged in 1996.

As banks moved into new areas Fiserv went along. In the late 1990s it acquired BHC Financial and Hanifen Imhoff Holdings (securities transaction processing). Other purchases that broadened its service list included Automated Financial Technology (credit union software) and Network Data Processing (administrative software for insurance companies). The push into software continued with 1999 purchases in the field of workers' compensation systems.

Also in 1999 Fiserv bolstered its client list by buying QuestPoint's check servicing business. It moved into retirement plan administration with the purchase of a unit from what is now SunAmerica Financial Group. In 2000 a deal to provide back-office services for American Express' online Membership Banking unit fell apart but Fiserv recovered its momentum with enhanced mortgage servicing offerings and an agreement to provide technology services to cahoot the online banking unit of the UK's Abbey National (which was acquired by Spanish group Banco Santander in 2004).

Fiserv continued its acquisitive activities in 2001 buying Benefit Planners (a leading employee benefit program administrator with operations in Europe the Middle East South America and the US) Facilities and Services Corporation (a California-based insurance software maker) NCSI (information and services targeting the flood insurance industry) and the bank processing operations of NCR Corporation. The company that year also sold its

Human Resources Information Services unit to buyout firm Gores Group.

Fiserv boosted its ATM and electronic funds transfer (ETF) business with the 2002 purchase of the Consumer Network Services unit of Electronic Data Systems (now HP Enterprise Services).

The company embarked on a series of sales in the next few years. It sold its securities clearing operations to a unit of FMR in 2005. Three years later it sold most of its health business to United-Health for some $480 million. The sale included Fiserv Health Plan Administration Fiserv Health Plan Management Innoviant Pharmacy Avidyn Health and other units but not WorkingRx (workers' compensation) and CareGain (technology) which remained with Fiserv.

The company also sold the bulk of its Fiserv Trust Company (also known as Fiserv Investment Support Services or Fiserv ISS) business including advisor services and institutional retirement services to TD AMERITRADE. In a separate transaction the newly formed Trust Institution Bank (headed by former Fiserv ISS management) acquired most of the company's investment administration services business.

Fiserv acquired one of the largest electronic payments firms CheckFree in 2007 boosting its capabilities in the payments landscape. In a smaller deal Fibought payment processor i_Tech from First Interstate BancSystem in 2008.

All of the acquisition activity led the company to higher debt levels which it began paying down through a combination of cost-cutting measures and divesting noncore operations. In 2008 it sold most of its health business to UnitedHealth and the bulk of Fiserv Trust Company to TD AMERITRADE. The following year it sold 51% of Fiserv Insurance Services (now StoneRiver) to investment firm Stone Point Capital for some $540 million. It also sold Loan Fulfillment Solutions a provider of mortgage-related services including settlement and title certification. As it added new operations and jettisoned others the company introduced a new marketing strategy in 2009 to unify its brands under the Fiserv banner.

In 2010 Fiserv acquired AdviceAmerica which provides desktop technology for financial advisers. It also introduced ZashPay a peer-to-peer platform available to consumers.

EXECUTIVES

Evp And Coo, Mark A. Ernst, $600,000 total compensation
Chief Sales Officer; Group President International, Steven (Steve) Tait
President Ceo And Director, Jeffery W. Yabuki, $840,000 total compensation
Evp Human Resources, Kevin P. Pennington
Group President Depository Institution Services, Byron C. Vielehr, $470,000 total compensation
Evp Corporate Development, James W. Cox, $450,000 total compensation
Group President Digital Banking, Kevin J. Schultz
Cfo, Robert W. (Bob) Hau, $499,599 total compensation
Evp General Counsel And Secretary, Lynn S. McCreary
Group President Financial Institutions, Kevin P. Gregoire, $450,000 total compensation
President Billing And Payments Group, Devin B. McGranahan, $86,961 total compensation
Cio, Jim Grech
Vice President Planning And Communications India, Vikram Talwar
Vice President Institutional Retirement Plan Services, John Newman
Vice President, Rebekkah Wilson
Senior Vice President, Jed Delker

Senior Vice President Of Technology And Business Development, Oscar Mireles
Vice President Information Technology Operations, Ed Jolly
Vice President Global Sales, Vicki O'Connor
Vice President Information Technology Infrastructure, John Albor
Vice President Market Development, Kathy Herziger-Snider
Vice President And Assistant General Counsel Regulatory Compliance, Lisa Liban
Vice President Platform, Steve Hodgins
Vice President Human Resources Wisconsin, Heidi Swartz
Senior Vice President Enterprise Operations, Mark Prout
Senior Vice President, Allan MacKinnon
Senior Vice President, Craig Ponsonby
Senior Vice President, Alan Eugley
Vice President And Head Of Internal Systems, Phil Demuth
Vice President Sales And Business Development Latin America, Rodrigo Silva
Senior Vice President Sales And Account Management, Dan Galway
Svp Sales North America, Andres Pasantes
Senior Vice President Product Management Card Services, David Keenan
Svp Finkit Digital Banking, Lee Cameron
Svp Market Strategy Bank Solutions, John Macaluso
Chairman, Daniel P. Kearney
Board Member, Glenn Renwick
Board Member, Doyle Simons
Board Member, Matthew Sherman
Auditors: DELOITTE & TOUCHE LLP

LOCATIONS

HQ: Fiserv Inc
255 Fiserv Drive, Brookfield, WI 53045
Phone: 262 879-5000   Fax: 262 879-5013
Web: www.fiserv.com

PRODUCTS/OPERATIONS

2017 Sales

	$ mil.	% of total
Payments		
Digital Money Movement	1,460	25
Card and Related Services	1,682	29
Other	325	5
Financial		
Account and Item Processing	2,094	36
Lending Solutions	54	1
Other	247	4
Corporate and Other	(39)	-
Total	**5,823**	**100**

Selected Subsidiaries

BillMatrix Corporation
CheckFree Corporation
CheckFreePay Corporation
Corillian Corporation
Fiserv Global Services Inc.
Fiserv (Europe) Limited (UK)
Information Technology Inc.
ITI of Nebraska Inc.
XP Systems Corp.

COMPETITORS

ACI Worldwide	Jack Henry
Accenture	MasterCard
Apple Inc.	PayPal
Banc of America	TEMENOS Group AG
Merchant Services	Total System Services
Black Knight	Vantiv
Fidelity National	Visa Inc
Information Services	Western Union
Intuit	

HISTORICAL FINANCIALS

Company Type: Public

Income Statement

FYE: December 31

	REVENUE ($ mil.)	NET INCOME ($ mil.)	NET PROFIT MARGIN	EMPLOYEES
12/19	10,187	893	8.8%	44,000
12/18	5,823	1,187	20.4%	24,000
12/17	5,696	1,246	21.9%	24,000
12/16	5,505	930	16.9%	23,000
12/15	5,254	712	13.6%	22,000
Annual Growth	18.0%	5.8%	—	18.9%

2019 Year-End Financials

Debt ratio: 28.24%
Return on equity: 5.06%
Cash ($ mil.): 893
Current ratio: 1.08
Long-term debt ($ mil.): 21,612

No. of shares (mil.): 679
Dividends
Yield: —
Payout: —
Market value ($ mil.): 78,617

	STOCK PRICE ($) FY Close	P/E High/Low	PER SHARE ($) Earnings	Dividends	Book Value
12/19	115.63	67 40	1.71	0.00	48.51
12/18	73.49	51 24	2.87	0.00	5.84
12/17	131.13	45 36	2.89	0.00	6.58
12/16	106.28	53 41	2.08	0.00	5.90
12/15	91.46	64 46	1.50	0.00	5.90
Annual Growth	6.0%	—	3.4%	—	69.3%

Flagstar Bancorp, Inc.

Flagstar Bancorp is the holding company for Flagstar Bank which operates around 110 branches (including 10 in retail stores) mostly in Michigan. Beyond offering traditional deposit and loan products Michigan's largest bank specializes in originating purchasing and servicing one-to-four family residential mortgage loans across all 50 states through a network of brokers and correspondents. Around 70% of the Flagstar's revenue is linked to mortgage origination and servicing while another 25% comes from its community banking business. Boasting $14 billion in assets Flagstar is one of the nation's 10 largest savings banks.

Operations

Flagstar Bancorp operates four business segments: Mortgage Originations which made up 58% of its total revenue during 2015 and acquires and sells one-to-four family residential mortgage loans; Mortgage Servicing (12% of revenue) which charges a fee to service and sub-service mortgage loans for its own community bank and other parties; and Community Banking (24%) which provides deposit and loan products (including warehouse lending) to businesses individuals government entities and held-for-investment portfolio groups.

Unlike traditional banks which focus on interest income Flagstar makes most of its revenue from its mortgage banking business. Only about 43% of its revenue came from interest during 2015 (mostly from loans) while most of the rest came from gains on mortgage loan sales (36% of revenue) loan fees and charges (8%) and other mortgage-banking related fees (10%).

Geographic Reach

The Troy Michigan-based company had 99 branches in Michigan and another 10 locations in retail locations in nine highly-populous states. Its mortgage banking business does business in all 50 states.

Sales and Marketing

Flagstar spent $9 million on advertising in 2015 compared to $10 million and $9 million in 2014 and 2013 respectively.

Financial Performance

As with other mortgage bankers Flagstar has struggled to grow its revenues over the past few years as many borrowers have already refinanced their loans to take advantage of low interest rates. The lender has also been in and out of the red in recent years suffering losses in 2014 and 2011.

Flagstar Bancorp's revenue rebounded 28% to $825 million during 2015 however thanks to a combination of higher interest income and mortgage sales. On the mortgage side a 40% jump in loan sale gains were driven by higher fallout-adjusted lock volumes improved margins and lower representation and warranty provisions. The company's interest income grew 24% as it continued to build its average loans held-for-sale loans held-for-investment and investment security assets.

Strong revenue growth in 2015 and a sharp decline in loan loss provisions on an improving quality credit portfolio drove the company's net income up 28% to $158 million (compared to a $70 million loss in 2014). Despite earnings growth Flagstar's operations used $9.55 billion in cash or about 17% more than in 2014 mostly as it used more cash to originate mortgage loans.

Strategy

While home mortgage lending remains key to Flagstar the company hopes to diversify its revenue streams so the business eventually accounts for about a third of sales. Over the past few years the company has been transforming its branches into full-service community banks and moving toward cross-selling an expanded suite of retail commercial and government banking services.

In February 2016 the company expanded and diversified more into commercial lending after launching its national homebuilder lending platform designed to offer financing to residential developers and homebuilders across the US. In past years it introduced a line of consumer loans such as credit cards and home equity lines of credit and added services for small and midsized businesses like treasury management and specialty lending.

Company Background

In 2011 to raise capital after suffering the effects of the housing bust the company sold 27 bank branches in the suburbs north of Atlanta along with their deposits to PNC. The company also sold its 22 Indiana branches to First Financial Bancorp later that year. In addition to bringing in some cash the divestitures help Flagstar focus on its Michigan operations.

MP Thrift an affiliate of private equity firm MatlinPatterson Global Advisors assumed a controlling stake of Flagstar in 2009. Today it owns 64% of the company.

EXECUTIVES

Evp And Director Performing Servicing, Mark Landschulz, age 55
President Mortgage Banking, Leonard (Len) Israel
President Ceo And Director, Alessandro P. DiNello, age 65
Evp And Senior Deputy General Counsel, Paul D. Borja, age 59, $749,982 total compensation
Evp And Treasurer, Brian D.J. Boike, age 43
Evp And Coo, Lee M. Smith
Evp And Cfo, James K. Ciroli
Evp And Chief Risk Officer, Steve Figliuolo
Evp And Director Mis And Analytics, William D. Belekewicz
Evp And Cio, Tony Buttrick
Evp Secondary Marketing, Palmer T. Heenan
Evp And Director Mortgage Fulfillment, Donna M. Krall

Evp And Chief Lending Officer Commercial Banking, Thomas R. Kuslits
Evp And Chief Human Resources Officer, Cynthia M. Myers
Evp And Chief Credit Officer, Joseph M. Redoutey
Evp And Chief Compliance Officer, Karen A. Sabatowski
Chairman, John D. Lewis
Auditors: PricewaterhouseCoopers LLP

LOCATIONS

HQ: Flagstar Bancorp, Inc.
5151 Corporate Drive, Troy, MI 48098-2639
Phone: 248 312-2000
Web: www.flagstar.com

PRODUCTS/OPERATIONS

2015 Sales

	$ mil.	% of total
Interest income		
Loans	295	36
Investment securities	59	7
Interest-earning deposits and other	1	-
Non interest income		
Net gain on loan sales	288	36
Loan fees & charges	67	8
Deposit fees and charges	25	3
Loan administration income	26	3
Net return on mortgage serving assets	28	3
Net (loss) gain on sale of assets	(1)	-
Representation and warranty benefit (provision)	19	2
Other non-interest income	18	2
Total	**825**	**100**

2015 Sales

	% of total
Mortgage origination	58
Community Banking	24
Mortgage Servicing	12
Others	6
Total	**100**

Selected Products/Services

Personal Banking
Banking
Checking Accounts
Checking
Savings Accounts
Savings Accounts: Personal
Banking Goals
View All Rates
Online Banking Login: Personal Accounts
Mobile Banking
Detroit Red Wings Partnership
Foreign Currency
Loans
Home Loans
Refinance
Home Equity Solutions
Credit Cards
Money Market
Investment Accounts: Personal

COMPETITORS

Bank of America	JPMorgan Chase
Comerica	KeyCorp
Fifth Third	Northern Trust
Harris	PNC Financial
Huntington Bancshares	

HISTORICAL FINANCIALS

Company Type: Public

Income Statement

FYE: December 31

	ASSETS ($ mil.)	NET INCOME ($ mil.)	INCOME AS % OF ASSETS	EMPLOYEES
12/19	23,266	218	0.9%	4,453
12/18	18,531	187	1.0%	3,938
12/17	16,912	63	0.4%	3,525
12/16	14,053	171	1.2%	2,886
12/15	13,715	158	1.2%	2,713
Annual Growth	14.1%	8.4%	—	13.2%

2019 Year-End Financials

Debt ratio: 2.13%	No. of shares (mil.): 56
Return on equity: 12.98%	Dividends
Cash ($ mil.): 426	Yield: 0.4%
Current ratio: —	Payout: 4.2%
Long-term debt ($ mil.): —	Market value ($ mil.): 2,166

	STOCK PRICE ($) FY Close	P/E High/Low		PER SHARE ($) Earnings	Dividends	Book Value
12/19	38.25	10	7	3.80	0.16	31.57
12/18	26.40	12	8	3.21	0.00	27.19
12/17	37.42	35	23	1.09	0.00	24.41
12/16	26.94	11	6	2.66	0.00	23.51
12/15	23.11	11	6	2.24	0.00	27.07
Annual Growth	13.4%	—	—	14.1%	—	3.9%

FLORIDA DEPARTMENT OF LOTTERY

The State of Florida Department of the Lottery runs instant-play scratch tickets and lotto games including Florida Lotto Mega Money Fantasy 5 and Cash 3. In addition to its own games Florida is part of the Multi-State Lottery Association which operates the popular Powerball drawing. Proceeds from the games are contributed to Florida's Educational Enhancement Trust Fund which provides funding for a variety of education programs from pre-kindergarten up to the state university level. The lottery has returned more than $19 billion to the state since starting in 1988.

EXECUTIVES

Secretary, Jim Poppell

LOCATIONS

HQ: FLORIDA DEPARTMENT OF LOTTERY
250 MARRIOTT DR, TALLAHASSEE, FL 323012983
Phone: 850 487-7777
Web: WWW.FLALOTTERY.COM

COMPETITORS

Georgia Lottery
Seminole Tribe of Florida

HISTORICAL FINANCIALS

Company Type: Private

Income Statement

FYE: June 30

	REVENUE ($ mil.)	NET INCOME ($ mil.)	NET PROFIT MARGIN	EMPLOYEES
06/19	7,157	36	0.5%	400
06/03	2,872	117	4.1%	—
06/02	2	0	2.0%	—
06/01	2,284	981	43.0%	—
Annual Growth	6.6%	(16.7%)	—	—

FLORIDA HOUSING FINANCE CORP

Owning a home in Florida is just a bit easier thanks to Florida Housing Finance Corporation. Established in 1997 by the Florida Legislature as a public corporation Florida Housing's mission is to help Floridians obtain safe decent housing that might otherwise be unavailable to them. Florida Housing pursues its mission through a number of programs that provide financial assistance for first time homebuyers and for developers of multifamily dwellings that serve elderly and low income Floridians. Florida Housing partners with various local state and federal agencies as well as developers and not-for-profit organizations to achieve its goals.

EXECUTIVES

Exec Dir, Stephen Auger
Exec Dir*, Harold Price
Executive Officer, Vicki Robinson
Director of Asset Management, Laura J Cox
Controller, Angie Sellers
Senior Financial Administrator, Melanie Weathers
Homeownership Programs Adminis, Charles White
CIO, David Hearn
Director of Homeownerhip Progr, David Westcott
Human Resources Administrator, Jessica Cherry
Program Administrator, Robert Dearduff
Auditors: ERNST & YOUNG LLP ORLANDO F

LOCATIONS

HQ: FLORIDA HOUSING FINANCE CORP
227 N BRONOUGH ST # 5000, TALLAHASSEE, FL 323011367
Phone: 850 488-4197
Web: WWW.FLORIDAHOUSING.ORG

PRODUCTS/OPERATIONS

Selected Programs

First Time Homebuyer Program
Down Payment Assistance
Homeownership Loan Program
Mortgage Credit Certificate
Multifamily Development Programs
Multifamily Mortgage Revenue Bonds
Florida Affordable Housing Guarantee Program
HOME Investment Partnerships
Elderly Housing Community Loan Program
Low Income Housing Tax Credits
State Apartment Incentive Loan
Predevelopment Loan Program
State Housing Initiative Partnerships
Demonstration Loans
Affordable Housing Catalyst Program

HISTORICAL FINANCIALS

Company Type: Private

Income Statement

FYE: December 31

	ASSETS ($ mil.)	NET INCOME ($ mil.)	INCOME AS % OF ASSETS	EMPLOYEES
12/19	5,373	224	4.2%	130
12/18	4,974	125	2.5%	—
12/17	4,764	206	4.3%	—
12/16	4,567	141	3.1%	—
Annual Growth	5.6%	16.6%	—	—

Florida Power & Light Co.

Florida Power & Light (FPL) sheds extra light onto the Sunshine State. The company a subsidiary of utility holding company NextEra Energy serves more than 5 million electricity customers in eastern and southern Florida. FPL's typical 1000-kWh residential customer bill is approximately 30% lower than the latest national average and among the lowest in the U.S. FPL's service reliability is better than 99.98%. .. FPL's has one of the cleanest power plant fleets across the US.

Operations

The company operates nuclear power plants which include St. Lucie Power Plant and Turkey Point Power Plant.

St. Lucie plant generates enough power to supply the annual needs of more than 1.1 million homes.

Turkey Point plant generates enough power to supply the annual needs of more than 900000 homes.

Geographic Reach

Juno Beach FL-headquartered FPL serves retail customers along Florida's Atlantic and southern Gulf Coasts.

Sales and Marketing

FPL serves more than 5 million customer accounts or an estimated 10 million-plus people across the state of Florida. FPL's typical 1000-kWh residential customer bill is approximately 30% lower than the latest national average and among the lowest in the U.S.

Strategy

In late 2020 Florida Power & Light Company (FPL) announced it currently has 14 new solar energy centers under construction across the state. It exceeds its previous peak of simultaneously constructing 10 solar energy centers in 2019. The new sites will add approximately 4.1 million solar panels to the state and support FPL SolarTogether – the company's popular community solar program which launched earlier this year and is the largest of its kind in the United States. This also brings FPL closer to fulfilling its 30-by-30 plan.

In mid-2020 the company constructed a wave of solar energy centers. This is on the heels of Florida leading the largest first quarter in solar installations for the utility-scale solar industry in the US. The six new solar energy centers which are on track to go into operation by the end of this year will support FPL SolarTogether – the company's highly popular community solar program and the largest of its kind in the US.

Company Background

In 2013 FPL began installing solar panels at about 100 schools in 23 counties. It also agreed to a plan whereby more than 400 homes being built or refurbished by Habitat for Humanity and other non-profits would be fitted with solar-powered water heaters.

Between 2011 to 2013 FPL invested $9 billion to strengthen and improve its electric generation and delivery system. The company has revived a $2 billion plan to convert a plant in Port St. John and a plant in Riviera Beach from heavy fuel to natural gas. It also got a further 510 MW of capacity from its Turkey Point and St. Lucie nuclear power plants in 2012 and 2013.

In 2010 the Florida Public Service Commission turned down the company's proposed 30% retail rate hike or $1.3 billion. FPL adjusted its expansion programs accordingly.

Moving further to meet federal requirements for green energy production in 2010 the company commissioned the Space Coast Next Generation Solar Energy Center at the Kennedy Space Center three solar farms built in tandem with NASA to produce 10 MW of clean energy enough to serve 1100 homes. It also brought into service the 75-MW Martin Next Generation Solar Energy Center designed to power about 11000 homes. The hybrid facility connects more than 190000 solar thermal mirrors to an existing combined-cycle natural gas power plant.

EXECUTIVES

Evp Engineering Construction And Corporate Services, Robert L. (Bob) McGrath, age 67
Evp Finance And Cfo, Moray P. Dewhurst, age 65
Evp, Charles E. Sieving, age 47
President And Ceo, Eric E. Silagy
Evp Human Resources, Shaun J. Francis
Vice President And Agc, Robert Sendler
Vice President Smart Grid Solutions And Meter Operations, Bryan Olnick
Senior Vice President Power Delivery Florida Power And Light Company, Manny Miranda
Vice President And Chief Communications Officer Nextera Energy Inc., Rob Gould
Executive Vice President, Wanda Cantres
Vice President Corporate Real Estate, Timothy Oliver
National Account Manager, Ellis Adger
Chairman, Lewis (Lew) Hay, age 64
Ward Secretary, Bonnie Foreman
Auditors: DELOITTE & TOUCHE LLP

LOCATIONS

HQ: Florida Power & Light Co.
  700 Universe Boulevard, Juno Beach, FL 33408
Phone: 561 694-4000
Web: www.nexteraenergy.com

PRODUCTS/OPERATIONS

2016 Operating Revenues

	% of total
Residential	89
Commercial	11
Total	**100**

2016 Sales

	$ mil.	% of total
Retail base	5,807	53
Fuel cost recovery	3,120	29
Other	1,962	18
Total	**10,114**	**100**

COMPETITORS

Clay Electric
Florida Public
  Utilities
Gulf Power
JEA
Orlando Utilities
  Commission

Progress Energy
  Florida
Seminole Electric
Southern Company Gas
Sumter Electric
Tampa Electric

HISTORICAL FINANCIALS

Company Type: Public

Income Statement

FYE: December 31

	REVENUE ($ mil.)	NET INCOME ($ mil.)	NET PROFIT MARGIN	EMPLOYEES
12/19	12,192	2,334	19.1%	8,900
12/18	11,862	2,171	18.3%	9,100
12/17	11,972	1,880	15.7%	8,700
12/16	10,895	1,727	15.9%	8,900
12/15	11,651	1,648	14.1%	8,800
Annual Growth	1.1%	9.1%	—	0.3%

2019 Year-End Financials

Debt ratio: 27.35%	No. of shares (mil.): 0
Return on equity: 11.01%	Dividends
Cash ($ mil.): 77	Yield: —
Current ratio: 0.60	Payout: —
Long-term debt ($ mil.): 14,131	Market value ($ mil.): —

Fluor Corp.

Fluor is one of the world's largest international design engineering and contracting firms. Through subsidiaries it provides engineering procurement construction (EPC) and maintenance as well as project management services for a variety of industrial sectors around the world. Its construction portfolio includes manufacturing plants refineries pharmaceutical facilities health care buildings power plants and telecommunications and transportation infrastructure. The group also provides operations and maintenance services for its projects as well as administrative and support services to the US government. The company generates most of its revenue internationally.

HISTORY

Fluor's history began in 1890 when three Fluor brothers immigrants from Switzerland opened a Wisconsin lumber mill under the name Rudolph Fluor & Brothers. In 1912 John Simon Fluor formed a construction firm in Santa Ana California. Fluor's company soon began a relationship with Southern California Gas which led it to specialize in oil and gas construction. The company incorporated as Fluor Construction in 1924 later began making engine mufflers. In 1930 it expanded outside of California with a contract to build Texas pipelines.

After WWII Middle East oil reserves were aggressively developed by Western companies. Fluor cashed in on the stampede winning major contracts in Saudi Arabia. During the early 1960s it continued to emphasize oil and gas work establishing a contract drilling unit and in the 1970s it began work on giant energy projects.

In 1977 Fluor made its biggest purchase: Daniel International a South Carolina engineering and construction firm with more than $1 billion in annual revenues. The contracting firm founded by Charles Daniel in 1934 initially did construction work for the textile industry then later worked for the chemical pharmaceutical metal and power industries.

Flush with cash Fluor bought St. Joe Minerals in 1981. A drop in oil prices in the 1980s killed demand for the big projects that were its bread and butter. As metal prices fell St. Joe didn't help the bottom line either. John Robert Fluor the last of the founding family to head the firm died in 1984.

When David Tappan stepped in as CEO he faced a $573 million loss the first year. The white-haired son of missionaries to China Tappan — known as the Ice Man — dumped subsidiaries and halved the payroll. In 1986 he merged Daniel into Fluor's engineering unit forming Fluor Daniel.

Leslie McCraw succeeded Tappan as CEO in 1991. McCraw saw Fluor as overly conservative and three years later he began setting up offices around the world while decentralizing Fluor's structure and adding new business such as temporary staffing and equipment leasing. Fluor also shed some of its commodity companies including its lead business in 1994. In 1996 Fluor's environmental services unit merged with Groundwater Technology and was spun off as a public company Fluor Daniel GTI.

Fluor saw mixed results from its expansion. Amid fierce competition and pricing pressure Fluor Daniel began cutting its overhead in early 1997 by reorganizing and selling noncore businesses.

Ill with cancer McCraw stepped down in 1998 and Philip Carroll who had overhauled Shell Oil took over as CEO. Carroll reorganized Fluor into four business units and tagged $90 million to rebuild its internal information management systems. Fluor also unloaded its 52% stake in Fluor Daniel GTI to The IT Group for $36 million.

Fluor in 1999 cut 5000 jobs further streamlined operations and focused on growth industries such as biotechnology and telecommunications. The next year the company split its construction and coal mining operations into two separate publicly traded companies one to concentrate on engineering and construction and one on coal mining. Former Fluor subsidiary A. T. Massey Coal was spun off as Massey Energy.

Carroll his restructuring job complete announced in December 2001 that he would retire the following February. That year the company also made plans to dispose of noncore operations of the company's construction equipment and temporary staffing businesses. Alan Boeckmann who had been president and COO succeeded Carroll in 2002.

The next year Fluor acquired Del-Jen a provider of outsourced services to US military bases and to the US Department of Labor. It also picked up five specialty operations and maintenance business groups from Philip Services. And in 2003 the company decided to dissolve its Duke/Fluor Daniel joint venture.

Fluor moved its headquarters from California to Dallas in 2006. The move resulted in the elimination of about 100 jobs. That year the company also entered the health care construction market.

In 2007 the company saw growth in all of its business segments with the exception of its government contracts in part because of the conclusion of projects for FEMA and in Iraq. The following year Fluor formed Fluor Offshore Solutions which is dedicated to global oil and gas clients in the offshore market. The company's construction segment acquired two private engineering companies in Europe — Belgium's UNEC Engineering N.V. and Spain's Europea de Ingenieria y Asesoramiento — increasing Fluor's ability to support its clients from a local level.

In early 2011 Alan Boeckmann retired as CEO after nearly a decade at the helm. He was succeeded by longtime company executive David Seaton who previously led Fluor's energy and chemicals global sales and China operations among others.

EXECUTIVES

Vice President Dod Business Development, Kenneth Ken J Oscar

Evp Chief Legal Officer And Secretary, Carlos M. Hernandez, $630,032 total compensation

President Power, Chris Tye

Evp And Cfo, Biggs C. Porter, $841,318 total compensation

President Government, Bruce A. Stanski, $600,018 total compensation

Evp Systems And Supply Chain, Ray F. Barnard, $564,689 total compensation

President Ameco, Tracey Cook

Evp Project Support Services, Garry W. Flowers

Chairman And Ceo, David T. Seaton, $1,295,029 total compensation

President Energy And Chemicals Americas, Jim Brittain

President Energy And Chemicals Asia/pacific, Ken R. Choudhary

President Energy And Chemicals Europe Africa And Middle East, Taco de Haan

President Life Sciences And Advanced Manufacturing, Juan G. Hern ̇ndez

President Mining And Metals, Rick Koumouris

Svp Information Technology And Cio, Robert C. Taylor

Evp Business Development And Strategy, Jose L. M. Bustamante

President Infrastructure, Hans Dekker

President Construction And Fabrication, Jack Penley

Vice President Health Safety And Environmen, Jeffrey Ruebesam

Senior Vice President Government Relations, David Marventano

Sr Vp Global Projects, Joe Mcaneny

Vice President, Stewart Cameron

Vice President, Jose Herrero

Vice President Sales And Marketing, Larry Bolander Larry Bolander

Senior Vice President Supply Chain And C, Wheeler Mike

Senior Vice President Procurement And Chief Procurement Officer, Mike Wheeler

Vice President And General Manager Fluor Philippines Malaysia And Singapore, Dan Spinks

Vice President Law And Chief Compliance Officer, Dawn Stout

Senior Vice President Chief Human Resources Officer, Mark Landry

Construction Vice President, David Gates

Vice President Sales, David Eppinger

Vice President And Project Director, Dennis Carr

Upper Mgt. Vp, Linda Fleming

Senior Vice President, Lou Del Tufo

Vice President Process Engineering And Technology, Claus-Peter Haelsig

Vice President Sales, G Hemann

Vice President Business Services, Dave Fraley

Vice President Construction, Ian Swanbeck

Vice President Nuclear Power Projects, Michael Lackey

Vice President, Richard C Meserole

Vice President And Vc Summer Consortium Project Director, Frederick P Hughes

Senior Vice President Energy, Larry Burns

Executive Vice President Business Development And Strategy, Jose Luis Bustamante

Vice President, Jamie Hernandez

Board Member, Nader Sultan

Board Member, Armando Olivera

Member Board Of Directors, Deborah McWhinney

Board Member, Mike Criss

Board Member, Lynn Swann

Board Member, Samuel Locklear

Auditors: Ernst & Young LLP

LOCATIONS

HQ: Fluor Corp.
6700 Las Colinas Boulevard, Irving, TX 75039
Phone: 469 398-7000
Web: www.fluor.com

2018 Sales

	$ mil.	% of total
United States	8,306	43
Canada	361	2
Europe	4,883	26
Middle East and Africa	2,091	11
Central and South America	1,988	10
Asia/Pacific (includes Australia)	1,536	8
Total	**19,166**	**100**

PRODUCTS/OPERATIONS

2018 Sales

	$ mil.	% of total
Energy & Chemicals	7,698	40
Mining Industrial Infrastructure & Power	5,186	27
Government	3,772	20
Diversified Services	2,510	13
Total	**19,166**	**100**

Selected Services
Construction management
Design
Engineering procurement and construction (EPC)
Operations and maintenance
Program management
Project development and finance
Project management
Staffing

Selected Industries Served
Chemicals and petrochemicals
Government
Life Sciences
Manufacturing
Metals
Mining
Oil and gas production
Petroleum refining
Power generation
Transportation

Selected Subsidiaries
American Equipment Company Inc.
  American Construction Equipment Company Inc.
Fluor Constructors International Inc.
Fluor Enterprises Inc.
  Daniel International Corporation
  Fluor Daniel Mexico S.A.
  ICA-Fluor Daniel S. de R.L. de C.V. (49% Mexico)
Fluor Holding Company LLC
TRS Staffing Solutions Inc.

COMPETITORS

ACS	Jacobs Engineering
AECOM	KBR
Bechtel	Kiewit Power
Chicago Bridge & Iron	Constructors
Chiyoda Corp.	Petrofac
EMCOR	Quanta Services
Granite Construction	SNC-Lavalin
Hyundai Engineering	
and Construction	

HISTORICAL FINANCIALS
Company Type: Public

Income Statement
FYE: December 31

	REVENUE ($ mil.)	NET INCOME ($ mil.)	NET PROFIT MARGIN	EMPLOYEES
12/19	14,348	(1,522)	—	50,182
12/18	19,166	224	1.2%	53,349
12/17	19,520	191	1.0%	56,706
12/16	19,036	281	1.5%	61,551
12/15	18,114	412	2.3%	38,758
Annual Growth	**(5.7%)**	**—**	**—**	**6.7%**

2019 Year-End Financials

Debt ratio: 21.22%
Return on equity: (-68.40%)
Cash ($ mil.): 1,997
Current ratio: 1.40
Long-term debt ($ mil.): 1,651

No. of shares (mil.): 140
Dividends
Yield: 3.8%
Payout: —
Market value ($ mil.): 2,646

	STOCK PRICE ($) FY Close	P/E High/Low	PER SHARE ($) Earnings	Dividends	Book Value
12/19	18.88	— —	(10.87)	0.73	10.61
12/18	32.20	39 19	1.59	0.84	21.22
12/17	51.65	42 27	1.36	0.84	23.89
12/16	52.52	28 20	2.00	0.84	22.44
12/15	47.22	21 14	2.81	0.84	21.56
Annual Growth (20.5%) (16.2%)		— —	—	(3.4%)	

Flushing Financial Corp.

Flushing Financial Corp. (FFC) is the holding company for Flushing Bank which operates more than 15 branches in the New York City metropolitan area. The bank offers services catering to the sizable populations of Asians and other ethnic groups in Queens where it has the most full-service offices. Deposit products include CDs and checking savings money market and negotiable order of withdrawal (NOW) accounts. Mortgages secured by multifamily residential commercial and mixed-use real estate account for most of the company's $5.2 billion loan portfolio.

Operations

Flushing Financial generates some 85% of revenue from fees and interest on loans. About 85% of the company's lending is for mortgages including more than 40% for multifamily residences followed by commercial real estate (around 25%) and one-to-four family mixed-use properties (around 10%). Business loans account for the remainder of its lending activity.

Its deposits are equally dominated by negotiable order of withdrawal (NOW) accounts and CDs which comprise about 60% of its $4.4 billion total.

Geographic Reach

Flushing Bank operates solely in the New York City metropolitan area including Nassau County. The company's NYC branches are in Brooklyn Manhattan and Queens. Around half of its banking offices are in Queens where the company is focused on fostering its links to Asian communities.

Sales and Marketing

Flushing's marketing activities revolve primarily around promoting its online banking services which attracted nearly 10% of deposits in 2017 and outreach to Asian communities at its branches in the Queens borough of New York City.

The company has two online banking brands: iGObanking.com (offering savings and checking accounts among other traditional products) and BankPurely (positioned as an environmental sustainable philanthropic banking solution).

Flushing also has an advisory board to promote awareness of the bank's role in the Asian communities of Queens which account for more than $500 million in deposits and $450 million in loans and lines of credit outstanding. The company's employees also speak Cantonese and Mandarin in its locations that serve primarily Chinese customers.

Financial Performance

Although Flushing's revenue and net income fell by double-digits in 2017 both metrics have trended positively over the last five years as the economic environment strengthened in the New York City region and the bank expanded its asset base.

In 2017 the company reported revenue of $183.5 million down 18% from the previous year despite an increase in interest from assets. Net income was also down falling 37% to $41.1 million. Both declines resulted from an uncharacteristic $48 million bump earned in 2016 from the sale of three branch buildings.

The company's cash increased by $15.7 in 2017 to $51.5 million. Cash from operations added $83.5 million to the coffers while investing activities used $254.1 million for purchases of securities available for sale loan purchases and net originations of loans. Financing activities provided $186.3 million as a result of a net increase in interest-bearing deposits and proceeds from borrowings.

Strategy

Flushing's business strategy is centered on improving net interest income and automating bank services. The company is also working to further its presence in New York City-area Asian communities which make up a large portion of its customer base.

In its efforts increase net interest income the company is continuing a strategy which seeks higher loan prices instead of greater volume. The company is focused on growing multifamily residence mortgage loans non-owner occupied commercial mortgages and commercial business loans while pulling back on loans for one-to-four family mixed-use properties and construction. Results in 2017 showed evidence of this strategy with two of Flushing's three focus areas ticking up a point or two and both of the deemphasized areas declining.

As part of its automation push Flushing expects a 20% expense savings following the rollout of its Universal Banker model which is designed to improve efficiency at its physical branches. The technology — which Flushing has deployed at about 60% of its locations — utilizes automated bank telling from assisted service kiosks that include an option to video chat with a banker for assistance.

The bank also continues to invest in services for NYC's Asian populations. In 2018 Flushing announced plans to open a Universal Banker branch in the city's Chinatown area.

Company Background

Flushing Bank was founded as a mutual savings bank in 1929 and converted to a holding company structure in 1994.

EXECUTIVES

Sevp And Chief Of Real Estate Lending Flushing Financial And Flushing Savings Bank, Francis W. (Frank) Korzekwinski, age 57, $418,111 total compensation

President Ceo And Director Flushing Financial And Flushing Savings Bank, John R. Buran, age 70, $899,176 total compensation

Sevp Coo And Corporate Secretary Flushing Financial And Flushing Savings Bank, Maria A. Grasso, age 55, $481,222 total compensation

Evp Residential Mixed-use And Small Multifamily Real Estate Lending, Jeoung (A. J.) Jin, age 53

Evp And Cio, Allen M. Brewer, age 67

Evp And Chief Audit Officer, Robert G. (Bob) Kiraly, age 64

Evp And Director Of Government Banking, Patricia Mezeul, age 60

Evp Commercial Real Estate Lending, Ronald Hartmann, age 64

Evp Business Banking Flushing Financial And Flushing Savings Bank, Theresa Kelly, age 58, $285,704 total compensation

Evp And Chief Risk Officer, Gary P. Liotta, age 60

Evp Cfo And Treasurer, Susan Cullen

Evp And Director Of Distribution And Client Development, Michael Bingold, age 57

Evp And Chief Of Staff, John F. Stewart

Svp And Chief Investment Officer, Frank J. Akalski, age 65

Vice President Cash Management Team Leader, Anthony Campisi

Assistant Vice President Commercial Real Estate Loan Officer, Albert Bozzolo

Senior Vice President Director Strategic Development And Delivery, Caterina dePasquale

Vice President Business Development, Steven Glass

Assistant Vice President, Patrick Dolan

Vice President Business Develo, Nick Symanski

Vice President Information Security, Joe Rinaldi

Senior Vice President And Director Of Operations, Barbara Beckmann

Vice President, Rhonda Delorenzo

Assistant Vice President Loan Servicing, Marcia Witter

Vice President Business Banking, Louis Matti

Senior Vice President, Michael Nedder

Vice President Business Banking, Denis Healy

Vice President Business Banking, Jonathan Stern

Assistant Vice President Bsa Department, Karen Williams

Senior Vice President Team Leader Business Banking, Gus Buitrago

Senior Vice President, Joseph Baldasare

Assistant Vice President Instructor Led Training Manager, Quwana Hamilton

Vice President And Loan Review Officer, James Kumpas

Vice President Of Vendor Management, Alana Domill-maltese

Vice President, Jin Kim

Vice President And Budget And Financial Foreca, Edward Zekraus

Vice President And Credit Relationship Manager, Elizabeth Carroll

Assistant Vice President And Training Specialist Ii, Marva Webb

Executive Vice President And Chief Audit Officer, Rosina Manzi

Vice President And Senior Sharepoint Administrator, Thomas Cunnane

Chairman Flushing Financial And Flushing Savings Bank, John E. Roe, age 86

Board Member, Michael Russo

Board Member, Sang Han

Auditors: BDO USA, LLP

LOCATIONS

HQ: Flushing Financial Corp.
220 RXR Plaza, Uniondale, NY 11556
Phone: 718 961-5400
Web: www.flushingbank.com

PRODUCTS/OPERATIONS

2017 Sales

	$ mil.	% of total
Interest and dividend income		
Interest and fees on loans	209	84
Interest and dividends on securities		
Interest	24	10
Dividends	0	-
Other interest income	0	-
Total interest expense	(61.5)	-
Non-interest income		
Banking services fee income	4	2
Net gain on sale of loans	0	-
Net loss on sale of securities	(0.2)	-
Net loss from fair value adjustments	(3.5)	-
Federal Home Loan Bank of New York stock dividends	3	1
Gains from life insurance proceeds	1	1
Bank owned life insurance	3	1
Other income	1	1
Total	**183**	**100**

Apple Bank for Savings
Astoria Financial
Bank of America
Bank of New York
Mellon
Citigroup
Dime Community
Bancshares

First of Long Island
HSBC USA
JPMorgan Chase
Korea Exchange Bank
New York Community
Bancorp

HISTORICAL FINANCIALS

Company Type: Public

Income Statement

FYE: December 31

	ASSETS ($ mil.)	NET INCOME ($ mil.)	INCOME AS % OF ASSETS	EMPLOYEES
12/19	7,017	41	0.6%	474
12/18	6,834	55	0.8%	480
12/17	6,299	41	0.7%	467
12/16	6,058	64	1.1%	470
12/15	5,704	46	0.8%	442
Annual Growth	5.3%	(2.8%)	—	1.8%

2019 Year-End Financials

Debt ratio: 1.69%
Return on equity: 7.31%
Cash ($ mil.): 49
Current ratio: —
Long-term debt ($ mil.): —

No. of shares (mil.): 28
Dividends
Yield: 3.8%
Payout: 58.7%
Market value ($ mil.): 608

	STOCK PRICE ($) FY Close	P/E High/Low		PER SHARE ($) Earnings	Dividends	Book Value
12/19	21.61	16	13	1.44	0.84	20.59
12/18	21.53	15	11	1.92	0.80	19.64
12/17	27.50	22	18	1.41	0.72	18.63
12/16	29.39	13	8	2.24	0.68	17.95
12/15	21.64	14	11	1.59	0.64	16.41
Annual Growth	(0.0%)	—	—	(2.4%)	7.0%	5.8%

FNB Corp

F.N.B. Corporation is the holding company for First National Bank of Pennsylvania which serves consumers and small to midsized businesses though almost 290 bank branches in Pennsylvania northeastern Ohio and Maryland. The company also has more than 70 consumer finance offices operating as Regency Finance in those states as well as Tennessee and Kentucky. In addition to community banking and consumer finance F.N.B. also has segments devoted to insurance and wealth management. It also offers leasing and merchant banking services. F.N.B. has extended its reach in its target states through acquisitions of banks including Metro Bancorp Annapolis Bancorp and PVF Capital Corp.

Operations

F.N.B operates four segments. The Community Banking segment which made up almost 90% of the company's total revenue during 2015 provides commercial and consumer banking services including corporate banking small business banking investment real estate financing asset-based lending capital markets services and lease financing as well as traditional consumer banking products.

The company's Wealth Management segment (5% of revenue) offers trust and other fiduciary services while the Insurance segment (2% of revenue) offers commercial and personal insurance through major carriers. F.N.B.'s Consumer Finance segment (6% of revenue) which operates through subsidiary Regency Finance Company provides installment loans to individuals and buys installment loans from retail merchants.

Like other retail banks F.N.B. makes the bulk of its money from interest income. Nearly 70% of the bank's total revenue came from loan and lease interest (including fees) during 2015 while 9% came from interest on taxable and non-taxable securities. The rest of money came from service charges (10% of revenue) trust income (3%) insurance commissions and fees (2%) securities commissions and fees (2%) mortgage banking (1%) and other non-interest income sources.

Geographic Reach

Most of the Pittsburgh-based company's branches are concentrated in Pennsylvania with the next largest markets being in Ohio Maryland and West Virginia. Its consumer finance offices are mostly in Pennsylvania and Tennessee with others in Kentucky and Ohio.

Sales and Marketing

F.N.B. boosted its advertising and promotional spend by 7% to $8.4 million during 2015 mostly because of higher expenses associated with the bank's recent acquisitions as it worked to get the name out in new territories such as in Cleveland Ohio and Baltimore.

Financial Performance

F.N.B. Corporation's annual revenues have risen nearly 40% since 2011 as its loan assets have nearly doubled with new branch openings and acquisitions. Its profits have doubled as well over the period as the company has kept a lid on growing costs.

The bank's revenue climbed 6% to $709.21 million during 2015 thanks to continued loan business growth stemming from recent bank acquisitions.

Revenue growth in 2015 drove F.N.B.'s net income up 11% to $159.65 million. The company's operating cash levels plunged 50% to $223.48 million for the year due to unfavorable changes in working capital related to securities classified as trading in business combination and sold.

Strategy

F.N.B. Corporation grows its loan and deposit business while expanding into new markets by acquiring smaller banks and select bank branches. In 2016 it agreed to buy North Carolina-based Yadkin Financial for $1.4 billion. That deal will add around 100 banking locations in the Carolinas and some $7.5 billion in assets. The combined bank will have some 400 branches across the Mid-Atlantic and Southeast US.

Mergers and Acquisitions

In April 2016 the company bought 17 branch locations in the Pittsburgh area from Fifth Third Bank as well as $100000 in loans and over $300000 in deposits.

In February 2016 F.N.B. Corporation purchased Metro Bancorp along with its $3 billion in assets and more than 30 Metro Bank branches in south-central Pennsylvania. The deal effectively merged Metro Bank into F.N.B.'s First National Bank of Pennsylvania subsidiary.

In September 2015 the bank purchased five branches in southeastern Pennsylvania from Bank of America along with almost $155000 in associated deposits.

In October 2013 F.N.B. moved to expand its presence in the greater Cleveland area by purchasing PVF Capital Corp. which owned Park View Federal Savings Bank with some 20 offices in Cleveland and northeastern Ohio.

In April 2013 F.N.B. purchased Annapolis Bancorp the parent company of BankAnnapolis in an all-stock transaction valued at about $51 million. The deal expanded F.N.B.'s reach into Maryland.

Company Background

F.N.B. which moved its headquarters from Pennsylvania to Florida in 2001 spun off First National Bankshares of Florida at the start of 2004 and returned to the Pittsburgh area. F.N.B. still operates two loan offices in Florida but these primarily manage the company's legacy loan portfolio there.

The bank is again rooted firmly in the Keystone State and bordering markets. After returning it expanded via several acquisitions prior to the Parkvale deal including bank holding companies NSD Bancorp Slippery Rock Financial North East Bancshares Omega Financial and Iron and Glass Bancorp. In 2011 F.N.B. expanded in northeastern Pennsylvania through the acquisition of Comm Bancorp. The deal valued at some $70 million brought in 15 branches.

EXECUTIVES

Svp And Corporate Controller, Timothy G. Rubritz, age 67, $215,016 total compensation
Chief Legal Officer, James G. Orie, age 61, $165,000 total compensation
Cfo, Vincent J. Calabrese, age 57, $385,008 total compensation
Chief Credit Officer, Gary Guerrieri, age 59, $350,016 total compensation
President And Ceo; Ceo First National Bank, Vincent J. (Vince) Delie, age 55, $770,016 total compensation
President First National Bank, John C. Williams, $385,008 total compensation
President Charlotte Region, Gregory L. (Greg) Heaton
Vice President Of It Network Services, Brian Diegan
Vp Mortgage Sales Manager, Steve Dipangrazio
Vice President Business Development Officer, Leslie Harrison
Senior Vice President, Paul Puleo
Vice President, Mark Renzini
Assistant Vice President Business Development Officer, Donnie Rhodes
Credit Support Senior Vice President Credit Officer First National Bank, Ron Scarton
Senior Vice President, Craig Muthler
Vice President, Michael Griffo
Vice President, Chris Grobelny
Vice President, Colleen Ensinger
Vice President Commercial Loan Officer, Shane Moser
Vice President Financial Advisor, Daniel Richardson
Assistant Vice President Germantown Branch Merchant Services First National Bank, Jean Carpinone
Vice President Wealth Advisor Maryland Region, Nick Ey
Public Square Assistant Vice President Relationship Manager Investment Real Estate, Dean Razek
Vice President Business Development Officer, Sean Laurin
Senior Vice President Managing Director, Nick Bellino
Svp Regional Manager Of Commercial Banking, Douglas Brown
Svp Market Executive, Craig Caplan
Vice President And Relationship Advisor, Keith Nazak
Senior Vice President, Stewart Rea
Vice President Branch Manager, Deanna Belk
Vp Commercial Lending, Maria Continenza
Vp Business Banking, Philip Persons
Senior Vice President, Mike Hendricks
Evp Capital Markets And Specialty Finance Businesses, D Bryant Mitchell
Senior Vice President Regional Credit Officer, Susan Carson

Vice President Regional Underwriting Manager,
Amar Grover
Assistant Vice President Branch Manager, Amanda
Escobar
Vice President, Cindy Davidson
Vice President, John Wiggins
Vice President Market Manager, Tammy Welker
Senior Vice President, Anthony Leone
Vice President, Margaret Howe
Assistant Vice President, Curtis Beggs
Vice President, Charles Evans
Vice President, Deric Mims
Vice President, Dan Stout
Assistant Vice President Business Banker, Justin
Holladay
**Assistant Vice President Retail Lending Loan
Underwriter,** Kimberly Bowers
Vice President Wealth Advisor, Kevin Day
Vice President, Dan Veneziale
Vice President Enterprise Data Management,
Cannabilla Prashanth
Vice President Bdo, Michael Byers
Vice President, Brett Atkins
Vice President Bdo, Jon Fabyonic
Chairman, Stephen J. (Steve) Gurgovits, age 76
Board Member, Stephen Martz
Board Member, Sheila Stewart
Treasurer, Ken Wu
Auditors: Ernst & Young LLP

LOCATIONS

HQ: FNB Corp
One North Shore Center, 12 Federal Street,
Pittsburgh, PA 15212
Phone: 800 555-5455
Web: www.fnb-online.com

PRODUCTS/OPERATIONS

2015 Sales by Segment

	$ mil.	% of total
Community banking	616	87
Consumer finance	42	6
Wealth management	35	5
Insurance	13	2
parent & other	1	-
Total	**709**	**100**

2015 Sales

	$ mil.	% of total
Interest		
Loans including fees	482	68
Securities including dividends	64	9
Other	0	-
Non-interest		
Service charges	70	10
Trust Services	20	3
Insurance commissions & fees	16	2
Securities commissions & fees	13	2
Other	40	6
Total	**709**	**100**

Selected Subsidiaries

F.N.B. Capital Corporation (merchant banking)
First National Bank of Pennsylvania
 Bank Capital Services LLC (also dba F.N.B.
 Commercial Leasing)
 First National Trust Company
 F.N.B. Investment Advisors
 First National Investment Services Company
First National Insurance Agency LLC
Regency Finance Company
 Citizens Financial Services Inc.
 F.N.B. Consumer Discount Company
 Finance and Mortgage Acceptance Corporation

COMPETITORS

Bank of America	Huntington Bancshares
Citizens Financial	M&T Bank
Group	Northwest Bancshares
Dollar Bank	PNC Financial
Fifth Third	S&T Bancorp

First Commonwealth	Sandy Spring Bancorp
Financial	Sovereign Bank
Fulton Financial	United Community
Glen Burnie Bancorp	Financial

HISTORICAL FINANCIALS

Company Type: Public

Income Statement

FYE: December 31

	ASSETS ($ mil.)	NET INCOME ($ mil.)	INCOME AS % OF ASSETS	EMPLOYEES
12/19	34,615	387	1.1%	4,223
12/18	33,102	373	1.1%	4,420
12/17	31,417	199	0.6%	4,748
12/16	21,844	170	0.8%	3,821
12/15	17,557	159	0.9%	3,205
Annual Growth	**18.5%**	**24.8%**	**—**	**7.1%**

2019 Year-End Financials

Debt ratio: 1.17%
Return on equity: 8.16%
Cash ($ mil.): 599
Current ratio: —
Long-term debt ($ mil.): —

No. of shares (mil.): 325
Dividends
 Yield: 3.7%
 Payout: 40.6%
Market value ($ mil.): 4,128

	STOCK PRICE ($) FY Close	P/E High/Low		PER SHARE ($) Earnings	Dividends	Book Value
12/19	12.70	11	8	1.16	0.48	15.02
12/18	9.84	13	8	1.12	0.48	14.21
12/17	13.82	26	19	0.63	0.48	13.63
12/16	16.03	21	14	0.78	0.48	12.18
12/15	13.34	17	14	0.86	0.48	11.95
Annual Growth	**(1.2%)**	**—**	**—**	**7.8%**	**(0.0%)**	**5.9%**

Foot Locker, Inc.

Foot Locker is a leading retailer of athletic footwear with chains in the US and more than 25 other countries. It has about 2190 Foot Locker Kids Foot Locker and Lady Foot Locker stores in the US as well as in Canada Europe and the Asia-Pacific region. The company's other chains — totaling nearly 940 stores — include Champs Sports Footaction (mostly located in the US) and Runners Point and Sidestep (mostly located in Europe). The primarily mall-based stores offer footwear apparel and accessories from leading global brands such as NIKE and Adidas as well as emerging brands. Foot Locker also sells via ecommerce sites mobile devices and catalogs. The US market accounts for some 70% of total revenue.

HISTORY

With the idea of selling merchandise priced at no more than five cents Frank Woolworth opened the Great Five Cent Store in Utica New York in 1879; it failed. That year he moved to Lancaster Pennsylvania and created the first five-and-dime. Woolworth moved his headquarters to New York City (1886) and spent the rest of the century acquiring other dime-store chains. He later expanded to Canada (1897) England (1909) France (1922) and Germany (1927).

The 120-store chain with $10 million in sales incorporated as F.W. Woolworth & Company in 1905 with Woolworth as president. In 1912 the company merged with five rival chains and went public with 596 stores making $52 million in sales the first year. The next year paying $13.5 million in cash Woolworth finished construction of the Woolworth Building then the world's tallest build-

ing (792 feet). When he died in 1919 the chain had 1081 stores with sales of $119 million.

Woolworth became more competitive after WWII by advertising establishing revolving credit and self-service moving stores to suburbs and expanding merchandise selections. In 1962 it opened Woolco a US and Canadian discount chain.

From the 1960s through the 1980s the company grew by acquiring and expanding in the US and abroad. It picked up Kinney (shoes 1963) Richman Brothers (men's clothing 1969) Holtzman's Little Folk Shop (children's clothing 1983) Champs Sports (sporting goods 1987) and Mathers (shoes Australia 1988).

The company introduced Foot Locker the athletic shoe chain in 1974 later developing Lady Foot Locker (1982) and Kids Foot Locker (1987). In 1993 Woolworth launched an ambitious restructuring plan focusing on specialty stores (mostly apparel and shoes). It also closed 400 US stores and sold 122 Canadian Woolco stores to Wal-Mart that year. Former Macy's president Roger Farah became CEO in 1994. Farah eliminated 16 divisions and dozens of executives.

A year later the firm sold its Kids Mart/Little Folks children's wear chain. In 1996 Woolworth began a major remodeling program that included removing its venerable lunch counters. (Another alleged renovation at the Woolworth chain — the firing of older workers who were replaced by teenagers — led to an Equal Employment Opportunity Commission lawsuit against the company in 1999.) The changes failed and the next year the company closed its US Woolworth stores and bought athletic-products catalog company Eastbay.

In 1998 Woolworth changed its name to Venator Group and sold the Woolworth Building a national landmark (headquarters remained in the building). The company then shed itself of more than 1400 stores including Kinney shoes and Footquarters (both closed).

Internet site eVenator was launched in 1999 to sell Eastbay Champs and Foot Locker merchandise. Venator came out the champ in a proxy fight against investment group Greenway Partners in July 1999. Shortly thereafter Farah was replaced as CEO (he remained chairman) by president Dale Hilpert.

In 2000 Venator slashed 7% of its workforce in the US and Canada (a small part of the planned 30% cut) and closed 465 stores. COO Matt Serra became president and Hilpert became chairman when Farah resigned later that year.

In March 2001 Hilpert resigned replaced by Carter Bacot as chairman and Serra added CEO to his title. Venator later sold its Canadian Northern Group unit to investment firm York Management Services and closed its Northern Reflections stores in the US. Venator changed its name to Foot Locker in November. It also sold gift retailer San Francisco Music Box Co. and its hospitality division's fast-food franchises before the end of the year.

In early 2004 chairman Bacot become lead director and president and CEO Serra added chairman to his title.

In 2004 Foot Locker capitalizing on the Chapter 11 filing of Footstar Inc. purchased from the company 350 of its Footaction stores. The company also acquired 11 stores in Ireland from Champion Sports Group later in the same year.

The company's short-lived family footwear retail concept — called Footquarters — launched in early 2007 but was quickly discontinued due to poor performance. The locations were converted to Foot Lockers and Champs Sports outlet stores. Also in early 2007 Foot Locker made an unsolicited $1.2 billion bid for rival Genesco that was rejected by

Genesco's board. Foot Locker closed about 275 mostly underperforming stores in 2007.

In 2008 the company reduced its store count by about 145 locations across its five chains in a bid to boost profitability by focusing on its most profitable locations and improving operations. In November Foot Locker acquired the CCS brand from dELia*s for about $103 million. The CCS brand includes skateboarding and snowboarding equipment apparel and footwear targeting primarily teenage boys.

J.C. Penney executive Kenneth Hicks was recruited to succeed Serra as president and CEO in August 2009. Serra who had held the CEO title since 2001 retained the chairman's title until his retirement in January 2010. At that time Hicks became chairman.

In July 2013 Foot Locker acquired Germany's Runners Point Group a specialty athletic store and online retailer based in Recklinghausen in a deal valued at ?72 million Euros ($94 million). The move gave Foot Locker shops in Germany that operated under the Runners Point and Sidestep banners as well as stores in the Netherlands Austria and Switzerland.

EXECUTIVES

Evp And Cfo, Lauren B. Peters, age 58, $657,500 total compensation
Chairman President And Ceo, Richard A. (Dick) Johnson, age 62, $1,087,500 total compensation
President And Ceo Foot Locker Europe, Lewis P. Kimble, age 61, $642,460 total compensation
Evp And Ceo North America, Stephen D. (Jake) Jacobs, age 57, $844,445 total compensation
Svp And Chief Human Resources Officer, Paulette R. Alviti, age 49, $486,250 total compensation
Svp And Cio, Pawan Verma, age 43, $216,071 total compensation
Vp Human Resources Corporate, Juan Mejia
Vice President, Dennis Sheehan
Vice President Brand Marketing Lady Foot Locker Six:02, Kirta Carroll
Vice President Leasing East Region, Cooper Daniel
Auditors: KPMG LLP

LOCATIONS

HQ: Foot Locker, Inc.
330 West 34th Street, New York, NY 10001
Phone: 212 720-3700
Web: www.footlocker-inc.com

2018 Sales

	$ mil.	% of total
US	5,647	71
International	2,292	29
Total	**7,939**	**100**

PRODUCTS/OPERATIONS

2018 Stores

Type	No.
Foot Locker US	886
Foot Locker Europe	642
Champs Sports	535
Kids Foot Locker	428
Footaction	250
Lady Foot Locker	57
Runners Point	107
Foot Locker Canada	107
Foot Locker Asia Pacific	99
Sidestep	80
SIX:02	30
Total	**0** **3,221**

2018 Sales

	$ mil.	% of total
Athletic Stores	6,714	85
Direct-to-Customers	1,225	15
Total	**7,939**	**100**

COMPETITORS

Academy Sports	L.L. Bean
Amazon.com	Modell's
Caleres	Shoe Carnival
DSW	Sports Authority
Dick's Sporting Goods	Target Corporation
Finish Line	Wal-Mart
Genesco	Zappos.com
Hibbett Sports	

HISTORICAL FINANCIALS

Company Type: Public

Income Statement — FYE: February 1

	REVENUE ($ mil.)	NET INCOME ($ mil.)	NET PROFIT MARGIN	EMPLOYEES
02/20	8,005	491	6.1%	50,999
02/19	7,939	541	6.8%	49,331
02/18*	7,782	284	3.6%	49,209
01/17	7,766	664	8.6%	50,168
01/16	7,412	541	7.3%	47,025
Annual Growth	**1.9%**	**(2.4%)**	**—**	**2.0%**

*Fiscal year change

2020 Year-End Financials

Debt ratio: 1.85%
Return on equity: 19.78%
Cash ($ mil.): 907
Current ratio: 2.00
Long-term debt ($ mil.): 122
No. of shares (mil.): 104
Dividends
Yield: 0.0%
Payout: 33.7%
Market value ($ mil.): 3,956

	STOCK PRICE ($) FY Close	P/E High/Low	PER SHARE ($) Earnings	Dividends	Book Value
02/20	37.97	14 8	4.50	1.52	23.74
02/19	55.06	13 9	4.66	1.38	22.19
02/18*	48.38	35 13	2.22	1.24	21.02
01/17	68.01	16 10	4.91	1.10	20.61
01/16	67.56	19 13	3.84	1.00	18.64
Annual Growth	**(13.4%)**	**— —**	**4.0%**	**11.0%**	**6.2%**

*Fiscal year change

Ford Motor Co. (DE)

Ford Motor is striving to build smart vehicles for a smart world. One of the "Big Three" automakers in the US (with GM and Fiat Chrysler) the company manufactures cars trucks and SUVs under the Ford and Lincoln brands ?- and finances sales through Ford Motor Credit. Ford which does business worldwide is making significant investments in a strategic shift to move it from solely an automaker to a leader in vehicle technology and mobility services. Nearly 65% of total sales comes from US.

Operations

Ford operates through Automotive Ford Credit and Mobility.

Ford's Automotive segment represents more than 90% of revenue and includes the sale of Ford and Lincoln brand vehicles. The Ford Credit segment contributes less than 10% of revenue and includes vehicle-related financing and leasing through Ford Motor Credit Company. Outside the US Europe is Ford Credit's largest operation are the UK and Germany.

Ford's Mobility segment includes Ford Smart Mobility which designs and builds mobility services and makes investments in start-ups and technology companies. Mobility is also Ford's locus for the development of autonomous vehicle technologies

Geographic Reach

Ford's business units span the five regions of North America South America Europe the Middle East and Africa and Asia-Pacific.

The US accounts for nearly 65% of Ford's revenue. Other major markets include the UK Canada and Germany each accounting for about 5% of sales.

Sales and Marketing

Ford's vehicles parts and accessories are sold through more than 11500 dealerships worldwide most independently-owned. In addition to retail sales these dealerships sell vehicles to commercial fleet customers rental car companies and governments.

Ford's advertising expenses were $3.6 billion $4.0 billion and $4.1 billion for the years 2019 2018 and 2017 respectively.

Financial Performance

For full year 2019 revenue was down 3% to $155.9 billion. The decrease was primarily due to the fall on their automotive segments.

The company's net income fell by about 98% to $84 million in 2019. The fall was due to the loss from their operations from an income of $4.3 billion in 2018 to a loss of $640 million in 2019.

Cash held by the company by the end of 2019 increased by $2.6 billion to $18.6 billion compared to $16.9 million in the prior year. Cash provided by operations and financing activities were $18.1 billion and $3.4 billion respectively. Cash used for investing activities was $19.4 billion.

Strategy

Speaking of Europe 2019 also brought tighter focus for Ford's operations on the Continent. Ford aims to refresh the company's European lineup streamline operations and return the business to profitability. Moving forward Ford's Europe division will be organized across three customer-focused areas: Commercial Vehicles Passenger Vehicles and Imports (US-made products like the Mustang). Ford will introduce at least three models over five years and offer more electrified products across its lineup. Ford also plans to beef up its already-strong presence in Europe's commercial vehicle market.

In late 2019 Ford and India-based Mahindra & Mahindra formed a joint venture that will build vehicles under the Ford brand for the Indian market and Ford and Mahindra branded vehicles for other high-growth emerging markets. Mahindra will hold a 51% controlling stake in the new venture and Ford will hold 49%.

Company Background

Henry Ford started the Ford Motor Company in 1903 in Dearborn Michigan. In 1908 Ford introduced the Model T produced on a moving assembly line that revolutionized both carmaking and manufacturing. By 1920 some 60% of all vehicles on the road were Fords.

After Ford omitted its usual dividend in 1916 stockholders sued. Ford responded by buying back all its outstanding shares in 1919 and didn't allow outside ownership again until 1956.

Despite the debut of the Mercury (1938) market share slipped behind General Motors and Chrysler. Henry Ford II decentralized Ford following the GM model. Henry Ford died in 1947 at the age of 83. In 1950 the carmaker recaptured second place. Ford rolled out the infamous Edsel line in 1958 and launched the Mustang in 1964.

Ford acquired Hertz in 1994. To focus on its struggling automotive operations Ford sold its Hertz car rental business in 2005.

With the automotive industry reeling from the Great Recession companies made decisions to streamline their operations for survival. In mid-2010 Ford sold all of Volvo Car Corporation to

Geely Automotive a subsidiary of China-based Zhejiang Geely Holding Group. At the onset of 2011 Ford's Mercury model production was discontinued.

Ford's $65 million acquisition of app-based crowd-sourced shuttle service Chariot (completed in 2017) is allowing it to use data algorithms to schedule trips in real time. Chariot uses 100 Ford Transit 15-seat vans; its 28 routes have been based on demand from riders. Ford is expanding the service from two cities (San Francisco and Austin) to eight with at least one route outside the US.

Amid shifting consumer tastes in 2018 Ford announced it would phase out virtually all its car offerings in North America except for the Mustang to focus on more profitable trucks SUVs and crossovers.

HISTORY

Henry Ford started the Ford Motor Company in 1903 in Dearborn Michigan. In 1908 Ford introduced the Model T produced on a moving assembly line that revolutionized both carmaking and manufacturing. By 1920 some 60% of all vehicles on the road were Fords.

After Ford omitted its usual dividend in 1916 stockholders sued. Ford responded by buying back all of its outstanding shares in 1919 and didn't allow outside ownership again until 1956.

Ford bought Lincoln Motor Company in 1922 and discontinued the Model T in 1927. Its replacement the Model A came in 1932. With Henry Ford's health failing his son Edsel became president that year. Despite the debut of the Mercury (1938) market share slipped behind General Motors and Chrysler. After Edsel's death in 1943 his son Henry II took over and decentralized Ford following the GM model. Henry Ford died in 1947 at the age of 83. In 1950 the carmaker recaptured second place. Ford rolled out the infamous Edsel line in 1958 and launched the Mustang in 1964.

Ford acquired Hertz in 1994 and two years later bought #3 rental agency Budget Rent a Car (sold 1997). Also in 1996 it sold a 19% stake in finance unit Associates First Capital in an IPO and increased its stake in Mazda to one-third. The next year Ford sold its heavy-duty truck unit to Daimler's Freightliner subsidiary (since renamed Daimler Trucks North America) for about $200 million and spun off 19% of Hertz in an IPO. Also in 1997 it launched automotive systems supplier Visteon (formerly Ford Automotive Products Operations) at the Frankfurt Motor Show.

Decades later in order to focus on its struggling automotive operations Ford sold its Hertz car rental business in 2005 to a private equity group made up of Clayton Dubilier & Rice The Carlyle Group and Merrill Lynch Global Private Equity for $5.6 billion and the assumption of nearly $10 billion of Hertz debt.

In mid-2009 the US Department of Energy approved $5.9 billion in low-interest loans to Ford for converting its US plants to making cleaner more efficient engines transmissions and vehicles. As a result Ford reported it would spend $550 million to convert its Michigan Assembly Plant where Ford Expedition and Lincoln Navigator SUVs were produced into a modern facility for making its next-generation Focus small car. The new Focus rolled off the assembly line in 2010 with an all-electric version of the Focus to follow in 2011. Ford consolidated operations from its Wayne Assembly Plant as part of the project and worked with the UAW on more flexible work rules for the Michigan Assembly Plant. In addition Ford converted its Cuautitlan Assembly Plant in Mexico from SUV production to assembly of small cars commencing in 2011. The Mexican plant began building the new Fiesta subcompact in 2010.

With the automotive industry reeling from the Great Recession companies made decisions to streamline their operations for survival. In mid-2010 Ford sold all of Volvo Car Corporation to Geely Automotive a subsidiary of China-based Zhejiang Geely Holding Group. Volvo's headquarters and manufacturing operations remain in Sweden and Belgium with Stefan Jacoby (former CEO of Volkswagen Group of America) serving as president and CEO of Volvo Cars. At the onset of 2011 Ford's Mercury model production was discontinued.

EXECUTIVES

Vp Operations Support Finance And Strategy Ford Of Europe And Premier Automotive Group, Robert L. (Bob) Shanks, age 67, $858,000 total compensation
President Ford Motor Company Fund & Community Services, James G. (Jim) Vella
Chairman And Ceo Ford China, Jason Luo, age 54
Evp And President Global Markets, James D. (Jim) Farley, age 57, $918,750 total compensation
Evp And President Global Operations, Joseph R. (Joe) Hinrichs, age 54, $1,053,500 total compensation
Vp Strategic Planning And Cfo Ford Of Europe, Dave L. (Dave) Schoch, age 68
Vp And Coo Ford Europe, Steven Armstrong
Chief Marketing Officer And President Lincoln, A. Kumar Galhotra
Vp And President Global Ford Customer Service Division, Frederiek Toney, age 64
Group Vp And President Asia Pacific, Peter Fleet
Vp; President Changan Ford Automotive, Nigel Harris, age 59
Evp Product Development And Cto, Raj Nair, age 55
Evp And President Mobility, Marcy Klevorn, age 60
President Ford Middle East And Africa, Jacques Brent
President Ford South America, Lyle Watters
President And Ceo Ford Motor Company Of Canada Limited, Mark Buzzell
Group Vp; Chairman And Ceo Ford Motor Credit Company, Joy Falotico
Ceo, Jim Hackett, age 65
President And Ceo Ford Motor Company Southern Africa (fmcsa), Jeffery Nemeth
President Asean, Yukontorn (Vickie) Wisadkosin
Vp Quality And New Model Launch, Linda Cash
Interim Head Human Resources, Kiersten Robinson
Vice President Design, Moray Callum
Ric Pte Navp Portfolio Manager Vehicle Solutions, Mark Anders
Vice President Quality Ford Europe, Gunnar Herrmann
Senior Vice President And Director Of Fm, Michael Patterson
Vice President Communications For Asia Pacific And Africa, Karen Hampton
National Account Manager, Vic Kachel
National Accounts Manager, Chris Trewin
Senior Vice President, Jason Rau
National Account Manager, Bob Miller
Executive Vice President, John Frankiline
Group Vice President Communications, Ray Day
Vice President, Michael Null Parente
Vice President Marketing Sales And Service, Roelant Dewaard
Group Vp Sustainability Environment And Safety Engineering, Kimberly Pittel
Vp And Cio, Jeff Lemmer
Vice President, Curt Magleby
National Account Manager, Mark Lowrey
Manager Government Relations, Sam Scales
National Account Manager, Joel Nielsen
National Vice President, Vera Newton
Vice President Of Admissions, Allison Kozulla

Executive Vice President Marketing And Sales
Executive Vice President Asia Pacific, David McClelland
Government Relations, Marilee Chlebicki
Vice President Finance Ford Of Canada, Bob Eaton
National Account Manager, Bridget Butterfield
Vice President Ford X, Sundeep Madra
Vice President, Matt A Gelso
Vice President, Erin Jasso
Regional Vice President, Kelly Olsen
Executive Chairman, William C. (Bill) Ford, age 62
Secretary Treasurer, Ed Hogan
Financial Strategy Treasurers Office, Mark Turner
Board Member, Christopher Thornton
Auditors: PricewaterhouseCoopers LLP

LOCATIONS

HQ: Ford Motor Co. (DE)
  One American Road, Dearborn, MI 48126
Phone: 313 322-3000
Web: www.corporate.ford.com

2017 Sales

	$ mil.	% of total
US	93,844	60
United Kingdom	9,619	6
Canada	10,580	7
Germany	7,265	5
All Others	35,468	22
Total	**156,776**	**100**

PRODUCTS/OPERATIONS

Selected Products
Automotive Products
  Automotive relays
  Camera modules
  Car navigation systems
  Car speakers
  Charging systems
  Cockpit systems
  EV relays
  Head up displays
  Instrument panel switches
  Lithium-ion batteries
  Telematics control units
Cars
  C-Max
  Fiesta
  Focus
  Fusion
  Mustang
  Taurus
Crossovers and SUVs
  EcoSport
  Escape
  Edge
  Flex
  Explorer
  Expedition
Commercial Vehicles
  Chassis Cab
  E-Series Cutaway
  F-650
  F-750
  Stripped Chassis
  Super Duty Pickup
  Transit Chassis Cab and Cutaway
  Transit Connect
Hybrids and Electric Vehicles
  C-Max Hybrid
  C-Max Energi
  Focus Electric
  Fusion Hybrid
  Fusion Energi
Performance Vehicles
  F-150 Raptor
  Fiesta ST
  Focus RS
  Focus SST
  GT
  Mustang Shelby GT350
Trucks and Vans
  F-150
  Super Duty
  Transit Connect
  Transit Passenger Wagon

2017 Sales

	$ mil.	% of total
Automotive	145,653	93
Financial services	11,113	7
Other	10	-
Total	**156,776**	**100**

COMPETITORS

BMW	Mitsubishi Motors
Daimler	Nissan
Fiat Chrysler	Peugeot
General Motors	Renault
Honda	Suzuki Motor
Hyundai Motor	Tata Motors
Isuzu	Toyota
Kia Motors	Volkswagen
Mazda	Volvo

HISTORICAL FINANCIALS
Company Type: Public

Income Statement — FYE: December 31

	REVENUE ($ mil.)	NET INCOME ($ mil.)	NET PROFIT MARGIN	EMPLOYEES
12/20	127,144	(1,279)		186,000
12/19	155,900	47	0.0%	190,000
12/18	160,338	3,677	2.3%	199,000
12/17	156,776	7,602	4.8%	202,000
12/16	151,800	4,596	3.0%	201,000
Annual Growth	**(4.3%)**	**—**	**—**	**(1.9%)**

2020 Year-End Financials

Debt ratio: 60.50%—
Return on equity: (-3.99%)
Cash ($ mil.): 25,243
Current ratio: 1.20
Long-term debt ($ mil.): 110,341

Dividends
  Yield: 5.1%
  Payout: —
Market value ($ mil.): —

	STOCK PRICE ($) FY Close	P/E High/Low	Earnings	Dividends	Book Value
12/20	8.79	— —	(0.32)	0.45	7.71
12/19	9.30	1051778	0.01	0.60	8.37
12/18	7.65	14 8	0.92	0.73	9.03
12/17	12.49	7 6	1.90	0.65	8.78
12/16	12.13	12 10	1.15	0.85	7.34
Annual Growth	**(7.7%)**	**— —**	**—**	**(14.7%)**	**1.3%**

Fortive Corp

Auditors: Ernst & Young LLP

LOCATIONS

HQ: Fortive Corp
  6920 Seaway Blvd., Everett, WA 98203
Phone: 425 446-5000
Web: www.fortive.com

HISTORICAL FINANCIALS
Company Type: Public

Income Statement — FYE: December 31

	REVENUE ($ mil.)	NET INCOME ($ mil.)	NET PROFIT MARGIN	EMPLOYEES
12/19	7,320	738	10.1%	25,000
12/18	6,452	2,913	45.2%	24,000
12/17	6,656	1,044	15.7%	26,000
12/16	6,224	872	14.0%	24,000
12/15	6,178	863	14.0%	22,000
Annual Growth	**4.3%**	**(3.8%)**	**—**	**3.2%**

2019 Year-End Financials

Debt ratio: 36.29%
Return on equity: 10.57%
Cash ($ mil.): 1,205
Current ratio: 1.06
Long-term debt ($ mil.): 4,828

No. of shares (mil.): 336
Dividends
  Yield: 0.3%
  Payout: 3.7%
Market value ($ mil.): 25,667

	STOCK PRICE ($) FY Close	P/E High/Low	Earnings	Dividends	Book Value
12/19	76.39	45 32	1.97	0.28	21.99
12/18	67.66	10 8	8.21	0.28	19.72
12/17	72.35	25 18	2.96	0.28	10.90
12/16	53.63	22 19	2.51	0.14	7.77
Annual Growth	**9.2%**	**— —**	**(5.9%)**	**18.9%**	**29.7%**

Fox Corp

Auditors: Ernst & Young LLP

LOCATIONS

HQ: Fox Corp
  1211 Avenue of the Americas, New York, NY 10036
Phone: 212 852-7000
Web: www.FOXCorporation.com

HISTORICAL FINANCIALS
Company Type: Public

Income Statement — FYE: June 30

	REVENUE ($ mil.)	NET INCOME ($ mil.)	NET PROFIT MARGIN	EMPLOYEES
06/20	12,303	999	8.1%	9,000
06/19	11,389	1,595	14.0%	7,700
06/18	10,153	2,187	21.5%	7,600
06/17	9,921	1,372	13.8%	—
06/16	8,894	1,072	12.1%	—
Annual Growth	**8.4%**	**(1.7%)**	**—**	**—**

2020 Year-End Financials

Debt ratio: 36.53%
Return on equity: 9.94%
Cash ($ mil.): 4,645
Current ratio: 3.93
Long-term debt ($ mil.): 7,946

No. of shares (mil.): 604
Dividends
  Yield: 2.5%
  Payout: 42.5%
Market value ($ mil.): 16,218

	STOCK PRICE ($) FY Close	P/E High/Low	Earnings	Dividends	Book Value
06/20	26.82	24 12	1.62	0.69	16.69
06/19	36.64	16 13	2.57	0.23	16.03
Annual Growth	**(7.5%)**	**— —**	**(10.9%)**	**31.6%**	**1.0%**

Freddie Mac

These siblings know there's no place like home. Government-sponsored enterprises (GSEs) Freddie Mac (officially Federal Home Loan Mortgage Corporation) and Fannie Mae were established to provide liquidity stability and affordability to the US housing market. They do so by purchasing mortgages from lenders and packaging them for resale thereby mitigating risk and allowing lenders to provide mortgages to those who may not otherwise qualify. The agency also provides assistance for rental housing. Freddie Mac generates the vast majority of its revenue from mortgage loans. Due to losses related to the subprime mortgage crisis the government seized Fannie and Freddie in 2008. Government plans to divest the firms into private ownership have proven difficult; they remain GSEs. As Donald H. Layton retired as Chief Executive Officer of the company in earl 2019 the board appointed David M. Brickman to succeed him effective mid-2019.

HISTORY

Ah the '60s — free love great tunes and a war nobody wanted to pay for with taxes. By the '70s inflation was rising and real income was starting to fall. To divert a construction industry recession Congress created a new entity to buy home mortgages and boost the flow of money into the housing market.

Fannie Mae had been buying mortgages since 1938 but focused on Federal Housing Administration (FHA) and Veterans Administration loans. In 1970 Congress created Freddie Mac and enlarged Fannie Mae's field of action to include conventional mortgages. Still rising interest rates in the 1970s were brutal to the US real estate market.

In the early 1980s dealers devised a way to securitize the company's loans — seen as somewhat frumpy investments — by packaging them into more alluring bond-like investments made even sexier by the implicit government guarantee. When three major government securities dealers collapsed in 1985 ownership of some Freddie Mac securities was in doubt and the Federal Reserve Bank of New York quickly automated registration of government securities.

In 1984 Freddie Mac issued shares to members of the Federal Home Loan Bank (the overseer of US savings and loans). By 1989 the shares had been converted to common stock and were traded on the NYSE. Freddie Mac's board expanded from three political appointees to 18 members.

Nationwide real estate defaults (rampant in the wake of the late 1980s crash) kindled concern about Freddie Mac's reserve levels and whether it might need to tap its US Treasury line of credit. In response Congress in 1992 created the Office of Federal Housing Enterprise Oversight to regulate Freddie Mac and Fannie Mae. Initial examinations sounded no alarms. A 1996 Congressional Budget Office report questioned whether the government should continue its implicit guarantees of the pair's debt securities.

In 1997 Freddie Mac officially adopted its longtime nickname. The next year it launched a system to cut loan approval time from weeks to minutes (it agreed to develop a similar version for the FHA). The streamlining was crucial to pacts in which mortgage lenders (including one of the US's largest Wells Fargo) promised to sell Freddie Mac their loan originations. In 1999 Freddie Mac hired former House Speaker Newt Gingrich as a consultant.

Freddie Mac made a major Internet push in 2000 with its first online taxable bond offering. A wired venture involving Freddie Mac Microsoft and such big lenders as Chase Manhattan (now part of JPMorgan Chase & Co.) Bank of America and Wells Fargo drew fire from small banks that said it would push them out of the online lending business.

In 2001 Freddie Mac bought Tuttle Decision Systems a loan-pricing software system provider. Critics responded that Freddie Mac overstepped its government charter with such a move.

In a move initiated by its auditor Freddie Mac re-audited its earnings from 2000 to 2003 uncovering accounting irregularities and employee misconduct. Further investigations executive oustings restructuring and numerous lawsuits followed. In late 2003 Freddie Mac announced the findings of its re-audit. The company admitted to understating earnings by $4.4 billion between 2000 and 2002 and overstating profits by $989 million in 2001 all in an attempt to smooth out results and show steady profit growth.

In 2006 the company paid a record $3.8 million fine to settle allegations by the Federal Election Commission that the company made illegal campaign contributions to members of the US House-Financial Services Committee. It also agreed to pay $4.65 million to settle a lawsuit related to its employee 401(k) plan. Freddie Mac did receive good news that year though when the Department of Justice dropped criminal charges against the company for misstating earnings from 2000 to 2002.

As the subprime mortgage crisis began heating up in 2007 and 2008 Freddie Mac announced plans to stop purchasing risky subprime mortgages. However the company tried to help restore stability to the teetering mortgage market by investing in billions of dollars in new jumbo mortgages raising its loan limits to more than $700000.

Although the government stepped in with loans to help Freddie the company still struggled with subprime mortgage losses. The government seized Fannie Mae and Freddie Mac in 2008 and placed them in conservatorship. Freddie Mac's leadership was also shaken up. David Moffat resigned as CEO in 2009 and chairman John Koskinen stepped in to serve as his interim replacement. Later that year Charles Haldeman Jr. the former head of Putnam Investments was selected to lead the company.

The Federal Housing Finance Administration (FHFA) was created in 2008 to oversee Fannie and Freddie as well as the 12 Federal Home Loan Banks. The FHFA was granted more authority than its predecessor agencies the Federal Housing Finance Board and the Office of Federal Housing Enterprise Oversight.

EXECUTIVES

Evp General Counsel And Corporate Secretary, William H. (Bill) McDavid, age 72, $500,000 total compensation

Ceo, Donald H. (Don) Layton, age 69, $600,000 total compensation

Vice President, James Bowden

Evp And Chief Administrative Officer, Jerry Weiss, age 59, $450,000 total compensation

Evp Multifamily Business, David M. Brickman

Chairman, Christopher S. Lynch, age 62

Evp And Cio, Stacey Goodman, age 57

Evp Single-family Business, David B. (Dave) Lowman, age 59, $500,000 total compensation

Evp And Cfo, James G. Mackey, age 53, $500,000 total compensation

Evp Investments And Capital Markets, Michael Hutchins

Evp And Chief Enterprise Risk Officer, Anil Hinduja, $500,000 total compensation

Vice President Prepayment And Portfolio Modeling, Jonathan Veum

Vice President Executive Compensation, Daniel Scheinkman

Vice President Human Resources Talent Management, Dru Fearing

Vice President And Deputy General Counsel, Melinda Reingold

Vice President Underwriting, Stephen Lansbury

Senior Vice President Division Chief Risk Officer Single Family, Donna Corley

Executive Vice President General Counsel Corporate Secretary, Robert Bostrom

Vice President Multifamily Capital Markets, Robert Koontz

Senior Vice President, Michael Lipson

Vice President Risk Process And Governance, Ken Moskowitz

Vice President Quality Control, James J Johnson

Vice President Single Family Underwriting And Quality Control, Pamela Padgett

Senior Vice President Corporate Controller And Principal Accounting Officer, Donald Kish

Vice President Servicing Operations, Ken Burke

Senior Vice President And Principal Deputy General Counsel, Alicia Myara

Vice President Multiclass Issuance, Mike Dawson

Svp Enterprise Capital Liquidity And Market Risk, Jorge Reis

Vice President Loan Servicing, Carl Mclaughlin

Vice President And Chief Economist, Sean Becketti

Vice President Of Planning And Analysis, Peter Zou

Senior Vice President Sales And Relationship Mgt, Chris Boyle

Vice President Change Management, Bill Cary

Vice President Government Affairs, Barbara Fox

Vice President Sales And Relationship Mgmt, Randy Jones

Vice President Multifamily Asset Management, Pamela Dent

Vice President Single Family Data Delivery Services, Susan Burke

Vice President, Buckner Bill

Assistant Vice President, Rush Brandon

Vice President Mha Complinace Program Disbursements, Thomas Lee

Vice President Chief Credit Officer Single Family, Behera Pradyot

Associate Vice President Ii Account Manager, Ates James

Vice President It Delivery, Ike Snyder

Vice President Affordable Lending And Access To Credit, Danny Gardner

Senior Vice President Human Resources Diversity And Inclusion And Chief Diversity Officer, Jacqueline Welch

Vp And Chief Economist, Sam Khater

Vice President, Beth Ryan

Vice President Sourcing, Sally W Baker

Vp Customer Technology Integration, Richard Lang

Vice President, Cheryl Wyatt

Vice Chair, Mark Friend

Auditors: PricewaterhouseCoppers LLP

LOCATIONS

HQ: Freddie Mac
8200 Jones Branch Drive, McLean, VA 22102-3110
Phone: 703 903-2000
Web: www.freddiemac.com

PRODUCTS/OPERATIONS

2017 Sales

	$ mil.	% of total
Interest		
Mortgage loans	63,735	85
Securities	3,415	5
Other	657	1
Non-interest	6,869	9
Adjustments	(53643)	
Total	**20,692**	**100**

COMPETITORS

FHLB Atlanta

Company Type: Public

Income Statement
FYE: December 31

	ASSETS ($ mil.)	NET INCOME ($ mil.)	INCOME AS % OF ASSETS	EMPLOYEES
12/19	2,203,623	7,214	0.3%	6,912
12/18	2,063,060	9,235	0.4%	6,642
12/17	2,049,776	5,625	0.3%	6,185
12/16	2,023,376	7,815	0.4%	6,004
12/15	1,986,050	6,376	0.3%	5,462
Annual Growth	2.6%	3.1%	—	6.1%

2019 Year-End Financials

Debt ratio: 95.71%
Return on equity: 106.10%
Cash ($ mil.): 5,189
Current ratio: —
Long-term debt ($ mil.): —

No. of shares (mil.): 650
Dividends
  Yield: —
  Payout: —
Market value ($ mil.): 1,953

	STOCK PRICE ($) FY Close	P/E High/Low		PER SHARE ($) Earnings	Dividends	Book Value
12/19	3.00	—	—	(0.18)	0.00	14.03
12/18	1.06	2	1	1.12	0.00	6.89
12/17	2.52	—	—	(1.00)	0.00	(0.48)
12/16	3.74	147	36	0.03	0.00	7.81
12/15	1.62	—	—	(0.01)	0.00	4.52
Annual Growth	16.7%	—		—		32.7%

Freeport-McMoRan Inc

Freeport McMoran (FCX) is one of the world's major mining companies with holdings in copper molybdenum and gold. It is a leading copper producer with proven or probable reserves of more than 115 billion pounds; the company also has about 29.6 million ounces of gold reserves and about 3.6 billion pounds of molybdenum reserves. FCX's mines are in the Americas and Indonesia. The company consumes much of its raw output itself manufacturing copper rods and other intermediate goods. With customers across the Americas Europe and Asia the US is FCX's biggest market at around 35% of company revenue.

HISTORY

The Freeport Sulfur Company was formed in Texas in 1912 by Francis Pemberton banker Eric Swenson and several investors to develop a sulfur field. The next year Freeport Texas was formed as a holding company for Freeport Sulfur and other enterprises.

During the 1930s the company diversified. In 1936 Freeport pioneered a process to remove hydrocarbons from sulfur. The company joined Consolidated Coal in 1955 to establish the National Potash Company. In 1956 Freeport formed an oil and gas subsidiary Freeport Oil.

Internationally Freeport formed an Australian minerals subsidiary in 1964 and a copper-mining subsidiary in Indonesia in 1967. The company changed its name to Freeport Minerals in 1971 and merged with Utah-based McMoRan Oil & Gas (formerly McMoRan Explorations) in 1982.

McMoRan Explorations had been formed in 1969 by William McWilliams Jim Bob Moffett and Byron Rankin. In 1973 McMoRan formed an exploration and drilling alliance with Dow Chemical and signed a deal with Indonesia to mine in the remote Irian Jaya region. McMoRan went public in 1978.

Moffett became chairman and CEO of Freeport-McMoRan in 1984. The company formed Freeport-McMoRan Copper in 1987 to manage its Indonesian operations. The unit assumed the Freeport-McMoRan Copper & Gold name in 1991. Two years later Freeport-McMoRan acquired Rio Tinto Minera a copper-smelting business with operations in Spain.

To support expansion in Indonesia Freeport-McMoRan spun off its copper and gold division in 1994. In 1995 Freeport-McMoRan Copper & Gold (FCX) formed an alliance with the UK's RTZ Corporation to develop its Indonesian mineral reserves. Local riots that year closed the Grasberg Mine and FCX's political risk insurance was canceled. Despite these setbacks higher metal prices and growing sales in 1995 helped the company double its operating income.

An Indonesian tribal leader filed a $6 billion lawsuit in 1996 charging FCX with environmental human rights and social and cultural violations. The company called the suit baseless but offered to set aside 1% of its annual revenues or about $15 million to help local tribes. Tribal leaders rejected the offer and in 1997 a judge dismissed the lawsuit.

In 1997 FCX pulled out of Bre-X Minerals' Busang gold mine project which independent tests later proved to be a fraud of historic proportions. Amid widespread rioting Indonesia's embattled president Suharto was forced out of office in 1998. The new government investigated charges of cronyism involving FCX.

FCX received permission from the Indonesian government in 1999 to expand the Grasberg Mine and increase ore output up to 300000 metric tons per day. However the next year an overflow accident killed four workers in Grasberg and as a result of the accident the Indonesian government ordered FCX to reduce its production at the mine by up to 30%. Normal production at the mine resumed in early 2001.

FM Services (administrative legal and financial services) was added as a subsidiary in 2002. In 2003 FCX bought an 86% stake in PT Puncakjaya Power a supplier of power to PT-FI.

The $26 billion acquisition of Phelps Dodge in 2007 brought that company's global copper gold and molybdenum business into the fold. The deal placed FCX in a position to thrive as a global competitor in the rank just below metals and mining giants such as BHP Billiton Rio Tinto and Vale. A year later FCX sold the wire and cable business it acquired in the Phelps Dodge deal to General Cable Corporation for $735 million.

Following the acquisition — and benefiting from high copper prices and a good business climate — the company began to invest in its development projects. It was also able to retire a sizable portion of its debt much of it accumulated from the Phelps Dodge acquisition.

Political and environmental controversy in Indonesia has been a problem for FCX since its major protector former President Suharto was forced to resign in 1998 after more than 30 years in power. Sectarian violence in Indonesia where FCX is one of the largest employers also makes the company vulnerable to work stoppages. Anglo-Australian mining giant Rio Tinto is jointly involved with FCX in developing mineral properties in Indonesia's politically and environmentally sensitive Papua region. The company's Tenke Fungume copper and gold mine named Too is located in the Democratic Republic of Congo which also can be an unstable environment in which to do business. Tenke Fungume is jointly owned with Lundin Mining and the Congolese government. It began production in 2009.

Beginning in 2013 FCX has also moved into the oil and gas market to broaden its portfolio as a natural resource player though acquisitions.

In 2013 the company bought Plains Exploration & Production for $16.3 billion (including $9.7 billion of debt). Assets acquired included oil production facilities in California a production base in the Eagle Ford trend in Texas and deepwater Gulf of Mexico and onshore Haynesville assets.

That year to enhance FCX's cobalt marketing position it acquired 56% of a large scale cobalt chemical refinery in Kokkola Finland. The joint venture will operate under the name Freeport Cobalt FCX will be the operator. Other JV partners include Lundin Mining (24%) and La G n rale des Carri res et des Mines (20%).

EXECUTIVES

Evp And Chief Administrative Officer, Michael J. Arnold, age 68, $550,000 total compensation
Vice Chairman President And Ceo, Richard C. Adkerson, age 73, $1,250,000 total compensation
Vice President Taxes, Hugh O Donahue
Evp Cfo And Treasurer, Kathleen L. Quirk, age 56, $650,000 total compensation
President Americas And Africa Mining, Harry M. (Red) Conger, age 88, $500,000 total compensation
Vp And Cio, Bertrand (Bert) Odinet
Vice President Sales, Dennis Wright
Svp International Relations And Federal Government Affairs, W Russell King
Chairman, Gerald J. Ford, age 76
Auditors: Ernst & Young LLP

LOCATIONS

HQ: Freeport-McMoRan Inc
  333 North Central Avenue, Phoenix, AZ 85004-2189
Phone: 602 366-8100
Web: www.fcx.com

2018 Sales

	$ mil.	% of total
Indonesia Mining	5,559	25
Rod & Refining	5,134	24
North America Copper Mines	4,694	22
South America	3,655	17
Atlantic Copper Smelting & Refining	2,302	10
Molybdenum mines	410	2
Corporate other & eliminations	(3126)	-
Total	**18,628**	**100**

2018 sales

	% of total
US	31
Switzerland	16
Indonesia	12
Japan	10
Other	31
Total	**100**

PRODUCTS/OPERATIONS

2018 Sales

	$ mil.	% of total
Copper		
Concentrate	6,180	31
Cathode	4,366	22
Rod and other refined copper products	2,396	12
Purchased Copper	1,053	5
Gold	3,231	16
Molybdenum	1,190	6
Other	1,490	8
Adjustments to revenue	-961	-
Embedded derivatives	-317	-
Total	**18,628**	**100**

Selected subsidiaries

Atlantic Copper Holding SA (smelting and refining Spain)
Chino Mines Company
Climax Molybdenum Company

FM Service Company (administrative and financial services)
Plains Exploration & Production (oil and gas US)
PT Freeport Indonesia Co. (91% mining)
  PT Smelting (Gresik) Co. (25% smelting Indonesia)

COMPETITORS

Anglo American	Glencore
Antofagasta	KGHM Polska Miedz
BHP Billiton	Rio Tinto Limited
Codelco	Southern Copper
First Quantum Minerals	Vale Limited

HISTORICAL FINANCIALS

Company Type: Public

Income Statement

FYE: December 31

	REVENUE ($ mil.)	NET INCOME ($ mil.)	NET PROFIT MARGIN	EMPLOYEES
12/19	14,402	(239)	—	68,100
12/18	18,628	2,602	14.0%	50,200
12/17	16,403	1,817	11.1%	53,200
12/16	14,830	(4,315)	—	59,100
12/15	15,877	(12,195)	—	72,000
Annual Growth	(2.4%)	—	—	(1.4%)

2019 Year-End Financials

Debt ratio: 24.08%	No. of shares (mil.): 1,451
Return on equity: (-2.50%)	Dividends
Cash ($ mil.): 2,020	Yield: 1.5%
Current ratio: 2.47	Payout: 133.3%
Long-term debt ($ mil.): 9,821	Market value ($ mil.): 19,037

	STOCK PRICE ($) FY Close	P/E High/Low		PER SHARE ($) Earnings	Dividends	Book Value
12/19	13.12	—	—	(0.17)	0.20	6.41
12/18	10.31	11	5	1.78	0.15	6.76
12/17	18.96	15	9	1.25	0.00	5.51
12/16	13.19	—	—	(3.16)	0.00	4.19
12/15	6.77	—	—	(11.31)	0.57	6.28
Annual Growth	18.0%			—	(23.1%)	0.5%

Frontier Communications Corp

Frontier Communications provides phone data and internet video and satellite TV (through a partnership with DISH Network) services to urban and rural customers in about 30 US states. The company has about 4.1 million customer 3.5 million broadband subscribers. Frontier is active mostly in rural and small to mid-sized markets where it is the incumbent local-exchange carrier (ILEC). In 2020 the sale of Frontier Communications' Northwest operations completed with Ziply Fiber taking over nearly 500000 residential and business internet phone and TV subscribers. The $1.35 billion deal covers customers across Washington Oregon Idaho and Montana. The new owner also committed $500 million in improvements to the network.

Operations

Frontier Communications' data and internet services contribute about 45% of revenue while local and long distance services account for about a third of the company's revenue followed by video services more than 10% and other services and subsidy revenue account the remainder.

The company offers a range of services including broadband video voice and other services and products to residential customers over a combination of fiber and copper-based networks. For business customers Frontier offers broadband Ethernet traditional circuit-based services service (UCaaS) and voice over Internet Protocol (VoIP). The company also sells customer premise equipment and related maintenance services.

Geographic Reach

Norwalk Connecticut-based Frontier has operations spread throughout the US in about 30 states in the South Southwest West and Midwest. Some location includes Connecticut North Carolina South Carolina Minnesota Illinois New York and Ohio.

Sales and Marketing

Frontier Communication dials in new customers through its broadband offerings and tries to sell other services such as voice and video to them. The company conduct business with both consumer (which accounts about 50% of the revenue) and commercial customers (about 45% of revenue). The remainder comes from subsidy revenue. The company offers services to multi-location companies government educational institutions and non-profits. Its wholesale customers are often referred to as carriers or service providers and include national operators such as AT&T and Verizon.

Financial Performance

Frontier's revenue has been gradually declining since 2017.

The company's revenue dropped 6% to $8.1 billion in 2019 down about $504 million from 2018. This was primarily due to the $221 million decrease in Voice Services revenue.

Frontier plunged its net loss to $5.9 billion in 2019 compared to loss of $643 million in 2018. The increase in net loss was primarily driven by the $5725 million goodwill impairment charge a decrease in revenues of $504 million and a loss on disposal of $446 million partially offset by decreased Network related Selling general and administrative and other operating expenses.

The company's coffers held $810 million in cash and equivalents in 2019 compared to $404 million in 2018. In 2019 Frontier's operations generated $1.5 billion while investing activities used $1.1 billion. Financing activities generated $32 million.

Strategy

In customer care and technical support the company is trying to reduce the need to send technicians on house calls. Part of the changes are designed to improve call center interactions with customers. So far the company had reached 20% of the targeted reductions in dispatches.

Frontier has new products on the way to keep current customers and attract new ones. In 2019 the company announced Simply Wi-Fi Secure a product aimed at small business customers. Also in 2019 Frontier plans to deploy the capability for 10GB fiber service across our FiOS footprint for commercial customers as well as for 5G backhaul capability.

In 2019 Frontier entered into a definitive agreement to sell its operations and associated assets in Washington Oregon Idaho and Montana (Northwest Operations) for $1352 million subject to certain closing adjustments including adjustments for working capital and certain pension and retiree medical liabilities. The sale is expected to close during the first half of 2020 subject to customary closing conditions. In connection with the sale Frontier has entered into a transition services agreement with the purchaser to provide various network and support services for a minimum of six months following the transaction closing.

Company Background

Frontier Communications was formed in 1935 as Citizens Utilities Company to acquire Public Utilities Consolidated Corporation a Minneapolis-based company with interests in electric gas water and telephone utilities throughout the US. From 1950 to 1970 the company bought utilities in rural and suburban areas of Arizona California Hawaii Illinois Indiana Ohio and Pennsylvania. The company continued to expand by buying smaller rural phone companies.

EXECUTIVES

Evp Field Operations, John J. Lass, age 63, $436,156 total compensation
Evp Consumer Sales Marketing And Product, John Maduri
President And Ceo, Daniel J. McCarthy, age 55, $981,251 total compensation
Evp And Chief People Officer, Kathleen Weslock, age 64
Evp General Counsel And Corporate Secretary, Mark D. Nielsen, age 55, $387,500 total compensation
Evp And Cto, Steve Gable, age 46, $458,750 total compensation
Evp And Cfo, R. Perley McBride, $199,432 total compensation
Evp Commercial Sales Operations, Kenneth A. Arndt
Evp Operational Transformation, Tim Travaille
Svp And Gm Connecticut Operations, Paul Quick
Svp-gen Mgr Pennsylvania, Elena Kilpatrick
Vice President, David Schwartz
Assistant Vice President New Technology, David Puente
Assistant Vice President Carrier Services, Kim Czak
Vp Network Planning And Inside Plant Engineering, Ron Poteete
Avp Broadband Video Services, Nathan Amburn
National Sales Manager Retail, Zabrina Mitchell
Vice President Engineering, John Hansen
Vice President National Osp Engineering, David Woods
Vice President Talent Acquisition, Mark Westphal
Vp Of Commercial New Products, Marcelo Oliveira
Svp Commercial Products And Marketing, Daniel Peiretti
Senior Vp Commercial Sales, Joe Pellitteri
Assistant Vice President Advanced Video Advertising, James Frogameni
Assistant Vice President Contact Center Support, Davy Roach
Chairman, Pamela D. A. Reeve, age 71
Auditors: KPMG LLP

LOCATIONS

HQ: Frontier Communications Corp
401 Merritt 7, Norwalk, CT 06851
Phone: 203 614-5600
Web: www.frontier.com

PRODUCTS/OPERATIONS

2018 Sales

	$ mil.	% of total
Consumer	4,380	51
Commercial	3,848	45
Subsidy and other regulatory revenue	383	4
Total	**8,611**	**100**

2018 Sales

	$ mil.	% of total
Customer Revenue		
Data and internet services	3,878	45
Voice Services	2,721	32
Video services	1,085	13
Others	544	6
Subsidy and other regulatory revenue	383	4
Total	**8,611**	**100**

COMPETITORS

AT&T	Hulu
Altice USA	Netflix
Amazon.com	Time Warner Cable
CenturyLink	U.S. TelePacific
Charter Communications	Verizon
Comcast	Vonage
Cox Communications	XO Holdings
FairPoint Communications Inc.	

HISTORICAL FINANCIALS

Company Type: Public

Income Statement

FYE: December 31

	REVENUE ($ mil.)	NET INCOME ($ mil.)	NET PROFIT MARGIN	EMPLOYEES
12/19	8,107	(5,911)	—	18,300
12/18	8,611	(643)	—	21,200
12/17	9,128	(1,804)	—	22,700
12/16	8,896	(373)	—	28,300
12/15	5,576	(196)	—	19,200
Annual Growth	9.8%	—		(1.2%)

2019 Year-End Financials

Debt ratio: 98.94%	No. of shares (mil.): 105
Return on equity: —	Dividends
Cash ($ mil.): 760	Yield: —
Current ratio: 1.08	Payout: —
Long-term debt ($ mil.): 16,308	Market value ($ mil.): 94

	STOCK PRICE ($) FY Close	P/E High/Low		PER SHARE ($) Earnings	Dividends	Book Value
12/19	0.89	—	—	(56.80)	0.00	(41.80)
12/18	2.38	—	—	(8.37)	1.20	15.16
12/17	6.76	—	—	(25.99)	1.20	28.99
12/16	3.38	—	—	(7.65)	6.30	57.81
12/15	4.67	—	—	(4.35)	6.30	72.09
Annual Growth	(33.9%)			—	—	—

Fulton Financial Corp. (PA)

Fulton Financial is a financial holding company with $20 billion in assets that owns four community banks in semi-rural and suburban areas of Pennsylvania Maryland Delaware New Jersey and Virginia. Through some 240 branches the banks offer standard products such as checking savings and credit accounts CDs retirement accounts mortgages and loans. Commercial loans — including for real estate and industrial financial and agricultural loans — account for most of the company's loan portfolio.? The company owns several non-banking units including Fulton Insurance an agency selling life insurance and related products.

Operations

More than 70% of Fulton Financial's revenue comes from net interest income particularly from loans including fees. The remainder is derived from non-interest income mostly from service charges on deposit accounts investment management and trust services and other service charges and fees. Commercial real estate loans account for about 40% of the company's nearly $16 billion loan portfolio; industrial financial and agricultural commercial loans contribute more than 25% to that lineup.

Residential mortgages and home equity each account for around 10% of the portfolio.

Fulton Financial's four subsidiary banks include Fulton Bank Fulton Bank of New Jersey The Columbia Bank and Lafayette Ambassador Bank. Fulton Bank (120-plus branches) accounts for about 60% of the holding company's total assets with Fulton Bank of New Jersey (some 65 branches) contributing about 20% and the other two banks accounting for some 10% each. In October 2018 Fulton merged subsidiary banks FNB Bank and Swineford National Bank (which each held less than 2% of its total assets) into lead bank Fulton Bank.

Geographic Reach

Fulton Financial and its subsidiary banks operate about 240 branches in suburban and semi-rural markets in the northeastern US. Lead bank Fulton Bank serves customers in Pennsylvania Delaware and Virginia. Fulton Bank of New Jersey Lafayette Ambassador Bank and The Columbia Bank serve New Jersey Pennsylvania and Maryland respectively.

Headquartered in Lancaster Pennsylvania the holding company has operations centers in East Petersburg Pennsylvania and Mantua New Jersey.

Sales and Marketing

Fulton Financial increased its marketing spend by 14% in 2017 compared with 2016 primarily for promotions to increase deposits. Commercial customers are the holding company's leading customer segment.

Financial Performance

Amid its expansion into new markets Fulton Financial saw its revenue tick up about 10% to more than $780 million between 2013 and 2017 thanks mostly to increased net interest income particularly loans including fees. Net income trended up more than 5% to about $170 million. However its cash stores were halved to less than $110 million (owing to increased use for financings and decreased proceeds from sales of mortgage loans held for sale); its debt also went up almost 20% to about $1 billion in that time.

The company's revenue gained 10% in 2017 to $783.3 million driven primarily by increased income from loans including fees in Fulton's commercial and residential mortgage commercial loan construction and leasing portfolios. Increased loan revenues also drove the company's 2017 net income up 6% to $172 million.

Fulton had cash of $108.3 million at the end of 2017 down $10.5 million from the prior year. Operations contributed $258.8 million and investments used $1.2 billion related mostly to a net increase in loans. Financings added $897.1 million due to a net increase in demand and savings deposits.

Strategy

Fulton Financial is shifting its strategy away from allowing its subsidiary banks autonomy in their regions to instead focus on consolidation of its banks expansion without geographic restriction and alignment with its customer segments. The company believes such a strategy will enable it to more efficiently manage risk through centralized risk management and compliance operations. In October 2018 Fulton merged subsidiary banks FNB Bank and Swineford National Bank into lead bank Fulton Bank. The company plans to absorb its remaining subsidiary banks into Fulton Bank by the end of 2019.

Fulton's near-term strategy is to invest in Philadelphia Pennsylvania a quickly growing urban market. The company hired a regional president and a commercial team for the area in 2016 and opened a mortgage loan production office in May 2018. The company also has regulatory approval to open two full service branches in the area which are targeted to open in early 2019. The company also plans to grow its presence in Baltimore Maryland.

Mergers and Acquisitions

In early 2019 Fulton Financial agreed to buy the wealth management business of Altoona Pennsylvania-based Forney Financial Solutions. The deal broadens Fulton's services for clients in the central part of the state.

Company Background

Fulton Financial traces its history back to the creation of Fulton National Bank in Lancaster Pennsylvania in 1882. It began acquiring other banks in the late 1940s and launched a holding company structure in 1982.

EXECUTIVES

Svp Community Banking; Chairman And Ceo Fulton Bank, Craig A. Roda, $398,805 total compensation

Sevp Coo And Interim Cfo, Philmer H. (Phil) Rohrbaugh, age 68, $478,543 total compensation

Sevp; President And Coo Fulton Bank, Curtis J. Myers, $371,347 total compensation

Sevp And Chief Credit Officer, Meg R. Mueller

Sevp And Cio, Angela M. Sargent

Chairman President And Ceo, E. Philip (Phil) Wenger, $944,103 total compensation

Sevp And Chief Risk Officer, Beth Ann L. Chivinski

President Small Business Administration Lending, Lynn Ozer

President And Coo Fulton Mortgage Company, Jeffrey J. Scheuren

Vice President Marketing, Theresa Bachman

Executive Vice President Marketing Corporate Communications, David Hostetter

Vice President Workforce Readiness And Advancement, Tonya Aument

Vice President, Gregory Palmer

Senior Vice President Loan Operations, Georgina Condran

Vice President Sales Learning And Enablement Manager, Matthew Bills

Vice President Ancillary Services Manager, Doug Tshudy

Svp Marketing Communications Director, Jennifer Brown

Vice President And Corporate Training Director, William Glover

Vice President, Constance Beck

Vice President Chief Appraiser, Jeffrey Gorman

Vice President, Walter Zalis

Vice President, Stephanie Lavenberg

Vice President Senior Cash Management Sales Officer, Steve Schreiber Steve Schreiber

Sr Vice President, Forest Crigler

Vice President Senior Human Resources Business Partner, Lisa Whitacre

Senior Vice President Director Of Retail, Randy Metz

Vice President, Marc Ryan

Vice President Corporate Workout Manager, Chris Demko

Senior Vice President Bank Controller, Linda Schroeder

Senior Vice President Funds Management, Keith Paich

Vice President, Joe Warner

Vice President, Christopher Bigos

Vice President, Tammy Snyder

Senior Vice President, Jim Wagner

Senior Vice President, Chris Sugra

Senior Vice President, James Bush

Vice President Special Assets, Virginia Akin

Vice President Commercial Sales Performance Program Manager, Coleen Toy

Vice President, Michael Thompson

Vice President Consumer Loan Review, Domenick Vitale

Senior Vice President Underwriting Manager, Bruce Spicer

Senior Vice President, Sal Marone

Vice President, Federico Manno

Vice President, Nancy Sellers

Avp Merchant Sales Officer, Diane Smith

Senior Vice President And Corporate Tax Director, Brian Demild

Vice President Relationship Manager Private Banking, Jessica Malone

Vice President Retirement Services, Amy White

Senior Vice President Chief Learning And Development Officer, Debra Hamilton

Vice President Loan Servicing Group Manager, Amy Snyder

Senior Vice President And Senior Portfolio Manager, Walter J Banta

Senior Vice President, Willie A Maddox

Vice President And Portfolio Manager, Laurie Bodisch

Vice President Trust Support Services And Technology Manager, Loretta Gockley

Senior Relationship Manager And Vice President, Max Tabak

Senior Vice President, Richard J Mason

Vice President Manager Of Charities And Endowments, Sheri Leo

Vice President And Senior Leasing Sales Officer, Sharon Wingenroth

Vice President, Todd Dietrich

Senior Vice President, John D Harding

Vice President And Senior Leasing Officer, Jason D Ibach

Executive Vice President And Chief Investment Officer, Keith P Aleardi

Vice President Product Implementation And Process Manager, Angela Schadt

Vice President Manager, Colleen A Lukacs

Vice President, Debbie Truckermiller

Vice President Senior Regional Loan Review Manager, John Sawn

Vice President Deputy Bsa Director, Jamie Thomas

Vice President, Jim Pesavento

Senior Vice President Sba Portfolio Manager, Alan Wilson

Senior Vice President, Richard Mason

Senior Vice President, John Harding

Vice President And Senior Leasing Officer, Jason Ibach

Vice President Manager, Colleen Lukacs

Senior Vice President And Senior Portfolio Manager, Walter Banta

Senior Vice President, Willie Maddox

Vice President, Keith Silfee

Vice President Relationship Manager, Kenneth Norman

Senior Vice President And Managing Director Bsa And Aml And Ofac, Matthew Mandrell

Vice President, Celeste Rau

Vice President And Relationship Manager, Jayne Kredatus

Vp Senior Commerial Relationship Manager, Mark Ritter

Vice President Private Banking, Connie Beck

Vice President, Mike Weber

Senior Management (senior Vice President General Manager Director), Sharon Hake

Vice President Of Cash Management, Frances Haldeman

Vice President, Todd Shaw

Senior Vice President Corporate Banking Division, Tim Peachey

Senior Executive Vice President And Head Of Consumer Banking, Angela Snyder

Vice President Senior Counsel, Amy Macinanti

Member Board Of Directors, Lisa Crutchfield

Board Member, Joe Ballard

Board Member, Scott Snyder

Auditors: KPMG LLP

LOCATIONS

HQ: Fulton Financial Corp. (PA)
One Penn Square, P.O. Box 4887, Lancaster, PA 17604
Phone: 717 291-2411
Web: www.fult.com

PRODUCTS/OPERATIONS

2017 Sales

	$ mil.	% of total
Interest		
Loans including fees	604	69
Investment securities	59	7
Other	5	1
Expense	(93.5)	-
Non interest		
Service charges on deposit accounts	51	6
Other service charges & fees	52	6
Investment management & trust services	49	5
Mortgage banking income	19	2
Investment securities gains	9	1
Other	25	3
Total	**783**	**100**

COMPETITORS

First Commonwealth Financial	Mid Penn Bancorp
	PNC Financial
Investors Bancorp	Sovereign Bank
M&T Bank	TD Bank USA

HISTORICAL FINANCIALS

Company Type: Public

Income Statement

FYE: December 31

	ASSETS ($ mil.)	NET INCOME ($ mil.)	INCOME AS % OF ASSETS	EMPLOYEES
12/19	21,886	226	1.0%	3,500
12/18	20,682	208	1.0%	3,500
12/17	20,036	171	0.9%	3,700
12/16	18,944	161	0.9%	3,500
12/15	17,914	149	0.8%	3,460
Annual Growth	5.1%	10.9%	—	0.3%

2019 Year-End Financials

Debt ratio: 3.28%	No. of shares (mil.): 164
Return on equity: 9.86%	Dividends
Cash ($ mil.): 517	Yield: 3.2%
Current ratio: —	Payout: 40.5%
Long-term debt ($ mil.): —	Market value ($ mil.): 2,862

	STOCK PRICE ($) FY Close	P/E High/Low	PER SHARE ($) Earnings	Dividends	Book Value
12/19	17.43	13 11	1.35	0.56	14.26
12/18	15.48	16 12	1.18	0.52	13.21
12/17	17.90	20 17	0.98	0.47	12.73
12/16	18.80	21 13	0.93	0.41	12.18
12/15	13.01	17 13	0.85	0.38	11.72
Annual Growth	7.6%	— —	12.3%	10.2%	5.0%

Gallagher (Arthur J.) & Co.

One of the world's largest insurance brokers Arthur J. Gallagher (Gallagher) provides commercial insurance brokerage consulting and third-party property/casualty claims settlement and administration services to businesses and organizations around the world through a network of subsidiaries and agencies. It places (arranges directly with underwriters) traditional and niche/practice groups in addition to offering retirement solutions and managing employee benefits programs. Risk management services include claims management insurance property appraisal services and loss control consulting. The global company operates more than 580 sales and service offices located throughout the U.S. and more than 300 sales and service locations in about 50 nations and does business in more than 150 countries. It also have investments in companies that own clean coal production facilities in the US. Most of Gallagher's revenue comes from the US.

Operations

Gallagher has grown to become one of the world's top five insurance brokers based on revenue. The company operates through three reportable segments: Brokerage Corporate and Risk Management.

The Brokerage segment accounting for nearly 70% of annual revenue distributes property/casualty life health disability and reinsurance coverage. It also provides employee benefits consulting and administration. A majority of Gallagher's brokerage income comes from commissions paid by insurance companies (upon placement of their policies). Retail insurance brokerage accounts for more than 80% of the segment's revenue. Wholesale brokerage operates through approximately 300 offices primarily located across the U.S. and Bermuda which places insurance with the Lloyd's of London exchange.

Gallagher's Corporate segment which makes up nearly 20% of sales primarily generates income from its ownership of about 35 refined coal production facilities which utilize pollution reduction technologies from clean energy firm Chem-Mod. The division has a 46.5% stake in Chem-Mod and a 12% stake in dormant emissions-reduction firm C-Quest.

The smaller Risk Management segment (nearly 15% of sales) provides contract claim settlement and administration services for enterprises and public entities that choose to self-insure some or all of their property/casualty coverages and for underwriting enterprises that choose to outsource some or all of their property/casualty claims departments. These operations also provide claims management loss control consulting and insurance property appraisal services.

Geographic Reach

Headquartered in Rolling Meadows Illinois Gallagher gets some 75% of its revenue from the US and almost 15% in UK. The company operates in about 50 nations and through a brokerage and consultant network serves more than 150 nations. Its largest overseas markets include Australia Bermuda Canada the Caribbean New Zealand and the UK.

Sales and Marketing

Most of Gallagher's brokerage business comes from retail customers which include commercial public entity industrial not-for-profit and religious organizations as well as some individuals. Gallagher's brokerage segment provide insurance services through unrelated agents brokers consultants and management advisors. The company manages its brokerage operations through a network of more than 580 sales and service offices in the US and another over 300 overseas offices. Risk management services are provided to commercial not-for-profit organizations and captive and public entities.

Financial Performance

Gallagher's growth efforts in both the brokerage segment and the risk management segment have helped the company to increase new customer volumes and retention rates driving substantial annual revenue and net income increases in recent years. Sales increased about 41% between 2015 and 2019 while profits rose by about 80% over the same period.

In 2019 revenue rose 4% to $7.2 billion as Brokerage earnings increased 15% and Risk Management earnings increased 4% despite a 25% decrease in Corporate earnings. Sales increased across geographies as well.

Net income rose 6% to $668.8 million in 2019 largely driven by the corresponding increase in revenues despite a slight increase in expenses.

The company ended 2019 with $2.6 billion in cash up $387.1 million from 2018. Operating activities contributed $1.1 billion while investing activities used $1.4 billion (mostly acquisitions and capital expenditures) and financing activities contributed $638.4 million via an expanded credit line.

Strategy

A key component of Gallagher's growth strategy is the ongoing acquisition of small regional insurance agencies and benefits consulting firms. The company targets strong sales organizations with a focus on middle-market clients or expertise in niche property/casualty lines (such as aviation energy hospitality and health care).

In addition to growth through acquisitions Gallagher has influenced the growth of its business by expanding and strengthening its relationships with independent brokerage partners in countries where we do not have a local office presence. Through this global network of correspondent insurance brokers and consultants Gallagher is able to serve its clients' coverage and service needs in more than 150 countries around the world.

The firm also invests in clean energy owning some 35 commercial clean coal production facilities that aim to reduce power plant emissions of mercury sulfur dioxide and other chemicals. Gallagher also owns a 46.5% controlling interest in Chem-Mod which has been marketing The Chem-Mod Solution proprietary technologies principally to refined fuel plants that sell refined fuel to coal-fired power plants owned by utility companies including plants in which the company holds interests.

Mergers and Acquisitions

In early 2020 Gallagher has purchased a minority stake in Malaysian broker SP&G Insurance Brokers Sdn Bhd a multi-discipline commercial insurance broker specializing in coverages for the aviation market as well as offering clients additional expertise and insurance solutions for property & casualty marine engineering and other risks. The transaction expands Gallagher's commercial insurance footprint in Asia and further extends its client reach in the global aviation sector.

In mid-2019 Gallagher acquired the aerospace retail and wholesale insurance division of Jardine Lloyd Thompson. The deal will help Gallagher offer new products and services to its clients in the aerospace industry including airlines and manufacturers. Other 2019 purchases include EHE Group (BonusDrive auto voluntary benefits) UK broker Stackhouse Poland and US broker LSG Insurance Partners.

In early 2019 Gallagher acquired of Baton Rouge Louisiana-based The Chapman Group Inc. Urbandale Iowa-based Partners Advantage Insurance Services LLC and AMZ Financial Insurance Services LLC wholly owned subsidiaries of Inversion Holding Company LLC and Louisiana-based Interstate Insurance Underwriters LLC. The acquisitions give Gallagher's Risk Placement Services (RPS) a presence in Northern Louisiana.

Company Background

Gallagher is led by J. Patrick Gallagher grandson of founder Arthur Gallagher who formed the company back in 1927. Gallagher went public in 1984 and was listed on the New York Stock Exchange in 1987.

EXECUTIVES

Corporate Vice President And President U.s. Wholesale Brokerage, David McGurn

Chairman Employee Benefits Consulting And Brokerage, James W. (Jim) Durkin, age 70, $725,000 total compensation

Chairman President And Ceo, J. Patrick (Pat) Gallagher, age 67, $1,000,000 total compensation

Cfo, Douglas K. (Doug) Howell, age 58, $850,000 total compensation

President U.s. Wholesale Brokerage, Joel D. Cavaness, age 58

Chairman Brokerage Services, James S. (Jim) Gault, age 68, $800,000 total compensation

President And Ceo Risk Management Services, Scott R. Hudson, age 58

Ceo Brokerage Services, Thomas J. (Tom) Gallagher, age 62, $750,000 total compensation

Global Chief Service Officer, Vishal Jain

Ceo Employee Benefits Consulting And Brokerage, William F. Ziebell, age 57

Ceo Arthur J. Gallagher Australia, Sarah Lyons

Executive Vice President, Mike Temple

Vice President, John Segredo

Senior Vice President, Diana Bertoni

Area Vice President, Jerry Guy

Area Senior Vice President, Barb Galuppi

Vice President Loss Control, Jim Stover

Vice President Merger And Acquisitions, Kevin Doyle

Area Vice President, Rob Erzen

Area Senior Vice President, Maureen O'Connell

Vice President, Bruce Beardsley

Vice President Corporate Ethics And Sustainability, Tom Tropp

Area Executive Vice President, Tim Gonsior

Assistant Vice President Real Estate And Hospitality, Sandy Gilder

Area Vice President Marine, Marc Dunn

Area Vice President, Jack Zogg

Aavp And Director Of Operations Tampa Bay Branch, Randi Watson

Senior Vice President, Susan Ruvolo

Division President, Teresa Koster

Area Executive Vice President, Daniel Johnson

Area Executive Vice President, Eric Olson

Area Vice President, Kelly Bonanno

Area Vice President, Cindy Caslin

Area Vice President, Frank Szemko

Vice President Sourcing And Services, Cara Richardson

Area Vice President Of Business Insurance Sales And Risk Management Consulting, John Sence

Area Assistant Vice President Property Loss Control, Scott Quackenbush

Area Vice President And Consultant, Janet Brendis

Area Vice President Human Capital And Employee Benefits, Bobby Desai

Area Assistant Vice President, Patricia Husker

Vp Global Cash Management, Patricia Hinton

Area Vice President, Paul Nelson

Area Vice President, Judy Worrall

Senior Vice President, Daniel R'bibo

Area Vp Insurance And Risk Management, Bob Perlman

Area Vice President, Al Lasarre

Senior Vice President Property And Casualty Insurance, Frank Cook

Area Senior Vice President, Glen H Evelyn

Senior Vice President Digital Marketing Strategy, Jen Wachtel

Vice President Marketing And Customer Insights, Felicia Stanczak

Area Senior Vice President, Melissa Ginter

Area Senior Vice President Atlanta Transportation, Eden Hancock

Assistant Vice President Property, Jason Tegan

Auditors: Ernst & Young LLP

LOCATIONS

HQ: Gallagher (Arthur J.) & Co.
2850 Golf Road, Rolling Meadows, IL 60008-4050
Phone: 630 773-3800
Web: www.ajg.com

2017 Sales

	$ mil.	% of total
U.S.	4,737	77
U.K.	717	12
Australia	270	4
Canada	155	3
New Zealand	150	2
Other foreign	127	2
Total	**6,159**	**100**

PRODUCTS/OPERATIONS

2017 Sales

	$ mil.	% of total
Brokerage		
Commissions	2,627	43
Fees	868	14
Supplemental commissions	163	3
Contingent commissions	111	2
Investment income	59	1
Risk management		
Fees	768	12
Investment income	0	-
Corporate		
Clean energy & other investment income	1,560	25
Total	**6,159**	**100**

Selected Subsidiaries

AJG Financial Services Inc.
AJG Coal Inc.
Arthur J. Gallagher & Co. (Bermuda) Limited (insurance & reinsurance placement captive risk services)
Artex Risk Solutions (Bermuda) Ltd.
Arthur J. Gallagher & Co. (Canada) Ltd.
Arthur J. Gallagher Australasia Holdings Pty Ltd (Australia)
Arthur J. Gallagher Brokerage & Risk Management Services LLC
Arthur J. Gallagher Risk Management Services Inc.
Arthur J. Gallagher Service Company
Arthur J. Gallagher (UK) Limited (Lloyd's of London brokerage)
Risk Management Partners Ltd. (customized insurance & risk management)
Gallagher Bassett Services Inc. (risk analysis)
Gallagher Bassett International Ltd. (UK)
Gallagher Bassett Services Pty Ltd. (Australia)
Gallagher Benefit Services Inc. (employee benefit program management)
Heath Lambert Limited (Gallagher Heath UK)
Protected Insurance Company
Risk Placement Services Inc.

COMPETITORS

ACE USA
Aon
BroadSpire
Brown & Brown
Chubb Limited
Hub International
Jardine Lloyd

Liberty Mutual
Marsh & McLennan
Sedgwick Claims Management Services
Travelers Companies
Willis Towers Watson

HISTORICAL FINANCIALS

Company Type: Public

Income Statement
FYE: December 31

	REVENUE ($ mil.)	NET INCOME ($ mil.)	NET PROFIT MARGIN	EMPLOYEES
12/19	7,195	668	9.3%	33,300
12/18	6,934	633	9.1%	30,362
12/17	6,159	463	7.5%	26,800
12/16	5,594	414	7.4%	24,800
12/15	5,392	356	6.6%	21,500
Annual Growth	**7.5%**	**17.0%**	**—**	**11.6%**

2019 Year-End Financials

Debt ratio: 23.46%
Return on equity: 13.85%
Cash ($ mil.): 604
Current ratio: 1.02
Long-term debt ($ mil.): 3,816
No. of shares (mil.): 188
Dividends
Yield: 1.8%
Payout: 48.8%
Market value ($ mil.): 17,913

	STOCK PRICE ($) FY Close	P/E High/Low		PER SHARE ($) Earnings	Dividends	Book Value
12/19	95.23	27	20	3.52	1.72	27.41
12/18	73.70	23	18	3.40	1.64	24.45
12/17	63.28	26	20	2.54	1.56	22.68
12/16	51.96	22	16	2.32	1.52	20.17
12/15	40.94	24	19	2.06	1.48	20.57
Annual Growth	**23.5%**	**—**	**—**	**14.3%**	**3.8%**	**7.4%**

GEISINGER HEALTH

Geisinger Health System provides health care to a large portion of the Keystone State. The health care system serves more than 3 million residents of nearly 50 counties spanning central and northeastern Pennsylvania. Founded in 1915 the organization's flagship facility is Geisinger Medical Center a 400-bed medical-surgical hospital located in Danville. It includes the Janet Weis Children's Hospital. With joint venture partner HealthSouth Geisinger also runs a rehabilitation hospital in Danville. As part of its operations the health system runs the 240-bed Geisinger Wyoming Valley Medical Center as well as numerous outpatient facilities and doctors' offices located throughout the region.

Geographic Reach

Geisinger Health System extends the reach of its health care system to millions of central and northeastern Pennsylvania residents across about 50 counties.

Financial Performance

In fiscal 2014 the hospital reported net revenue of $9.8 billion a $1 billion increase over the prior year.

Strategy

Geisinger Health System has been working to standardize its procedural operations to improve the quality of care at its facilities and cut costs. Initiatives include assigning care coordinators and providing home visits for high-risk patients to avoid repeat hospitalizations. The health network also implemented an electronic medical records system and began using networking technology to reach into rural markets. Known as "telemedicine" the system's networking technologies are used among other things to facilitate remote two-way consultations between system physicians and rural patients. Additionally Geisinger runs the Geisinger Health Plan a not-for-profit HMO with some 230000 members.

In addition to its clinical operations Geisinger Health System also pursues industry partnerships and licensing opportunities through Geisinger Ventures its business development unit. The unit works to commercialize (and sometimes spin off) medical and technology-related innovations.

Mergers and Acquisitions

Geisinger has grown through several strategic acquisitions as of late. The health care system purchased central Pennsylvania's Cancer Care Centers in late 2014 adding four facilities to its network.

EXECUTIVES

Evp And Coo, Frank Trembulak
Evp Finance And Cfo, Kevin F. Brennan
Evp And Chief Medical Officer, Albert Bothe

Evp And Managing Partner Geisinger Consulting Services, Bruce H. Hamory
Evp And System Chief Nursing Officer, Susan M. Robel
Evp Clinical Operations, Lynn Miller
Evp And Chief Scientific Officer, David H. Ledbetter
President And Ceo, David T. Feinberg
President And Ceo Geisinger Health Plans, Steven R. Youso
Chief Medical Executive Geisinger Northeast Region, Robert J. Weil
Vice President Supply Chain Services, Deborah Templeton
Senior Vice President Finance, Thomas Sokola
Assistant To Greg Snow Vice President Of Revenue Cycle, Denise Baylor
Vice President Human Resources, Rick Flynn
Vice President Clinical Informatics, Joan Topper
Director Of Pharmacy, David Klinger
Senior Vice President And Chief Inform, Thomas Barna
Vice President Of Sales, Chris Fanning
Medical Director Government Programs, Perry Meadows
Associate Medical Director, David Withers
Pharmacy Manager, Nannette Leganza
Assistant Vice President, Kristy Hine
Medical Director, Carrie L Delone
Associate Vice President Compensation, Kelly Moore
Auditors: KPMG LLP PHILADELPHIA PA

LOCATIONS

HQ: GEISINGER HEALTH
100 N ACADEMY AVE, DANVILLE, PA 178229800
Phone: 800 275-6401
Web: WWW.GEISINGER.ORG

PRODUCTS/OPERATIONS

Selected Services
Adolescent & Young Adult Medicine
Allergy
Anesthesia
Audiology
Bariatric Surgery
Cancer Institute
Cardiology
Colorectal Surgery
Cosmetics Program
Critical Care
Dental Medicine
Dermatology
Ear Nose & Throat
Emergency Medicine
Endocrinology & Metabolism
Fertility Center
Gastroenterology
Gynecology
Gynecologic Oncology
Heart Services
Hip & Knee Center
Imaging Services
Infectious Disease
Internal Medicine
Joint Replacement
Laboratory Medicine
LASIK Surgery
Mammography
Maternal Fetal Medicine
Mental Health
Minimally Invasive Surgery
Mohs Surgery
Neonatology
Nephrology
Neurodevelopmental Pediatrics
Neuroscience Institute
Neurology
Neurosurgery
Obstetrics
Ophthalmology
Orthopaedics
Osteoporosis

Pain Management
Palliative Medicine
Pediatrics (General)
Pediatric Allergy & Immunology
Pediatric Anesthesia & Sedation
Pediatric Cardiology
Pediatric Dental Surgery
Pediatric Dentistry
Pediatric Dermatology
Pediatric Endocrinology
Pediatric Gastroenterology
Pediatric General Surgery
Pediatric Genetics
Pediatric Hematology/Oncology
Pediatric Hospitalists
Pediatric Infectious Disease
Pediatric Intensive Care
Pediatric Interventional Radiology
Pediatric Nephrology
Pediatric Neurology
Pediatric Neuropsychology
Pediatric Neurosurgery
Pediatric Ophthalmology
Pediatric Orthopaedics
Pediatric Otolaryngology
Pediatric Plastic Surgery
Pediatric Psychology & Psychiatry
Pediatric Pulmonology
Pediatric Rehabilitation
Pediatric Rheumatology
Pediatric Transplant Surgery
Pediatric Trauma
Pediatric Urology
Pediatric Weight Management & Nutrition
Plastic & Reconstructive Surgery
Podiatry
Psychiatry
Pulmonary Medicine
Radiology
Rehabilitation
Rheumatology
Sleep Services
Spine Medicine
Sports Medicine
Surgery
Thoracic Surgery
Transplant Surgery
Trauma Center
Urogynecology
Urology
Vascular Surgery
Weight Management Clinic
Women's Health

Selected Facilities
Geisinger HealthSouth Rehabilitation Hospital (Danville)
Geisinger Medical Center (Danville)
  The Janet Weis Children's Hospital
Geisinger Wyoming Valley Medical Center (Wilkes-Barre)
  Pearsall Heart Hospital
Geisinger South Wilkes-Barre Outpatient Center
Shamokin Area Community Hospital

COMPETITORS

Ascension Health
Blue Cross of Northeastern Pennsylvania
Capital BlueCross
Community Health Systems
HealthAmerica
Highmark
PinnacleHealth System
UPMC
Universal Health Services
Wyoming Valley Health Care System

HISTORICAL FINANCIALS
Company Type: Private

Income Statement   FYE: June 30

	REVENUE ($ mil.)	NET INCOME ($ mil.)	NET PROFIT MARGIN	EMPLOYEES
06/20	7,121	(190)	—	13,030
06/19	7,145	174	2.4%	
06/18	6,536	359	5.5%	—
06/17	6,337	552	8.7%	—
Annual Growth	4.0%	—	—	—

General Dynamics Corp

General Dynamics is a prime military contractor to the Pentagon (the US government accounts for over 65% of sales). The company's Marine Systems unit builds surface combatants auxiliary and combat-logistics ships and nuclear submarines. The Aerospace division - composed of Gulfstream Aerospace and Jet Aviation - makes and refurbishes business jets primarily for civilian customers. The company's Information Technology segment provides IT services and IT infrastructure to the US government. The Combat Services unit makes battle tanks wheeled combat/tactical vehicles munitions weapons systems and armament. Mission Systems handles C4ISR (command control communications computers intelligence surveillance and reconnaissance) solutions for naval air ground space and cyber systems. About 85% of the company's total sales comes from North America.

Operations

General Dynamics has five operating segments: Aerospace Marine Systems Information Technology Combat Systems and Mission Systems.

On the civilian side of the business the company's Aerospace segment (about a quarter of revenue) produces mid- and large-cabin business jet aircraft for which the company provides maintenance refurbishment and outfitting.

General Dynamic's Marine Systems group (nearly 25% of revenue) is a major shipbuilder for the US Navy and it provides MRO (maintenance/repair/overhaul) services. Through Electric Boat Marine Systems manufactures the Virginia-class nuclear-powered submarine and Columbia-class ballistic-missile submarine while Bath Iron Works builds the Arleigh Burke-class guided-missile destroyer (DDG-51). NASSCO builds auxiliary and support ships for the US Navy as well as oil tankers and container ships for commercial customers.

The Information Technology segment (some 20% of revenue) offers IT services (consulting design integration operations and maintenance cloud applications development and cyber defense). Other operations include IT infrastructure modernization (system development and engineering data center and cloud strategy migration and operations); and professional services (logistics training and life sciences).

The Combat Systems division (roughly 20% of revenue) is composed of European Land Systems; Land Systems; and Ordnance and Tactical Systems. It offers combat vehicles weapons systems and munitions for the U.S. government and its non-U.S. partners.

Mission Systems division (nearly 15% of revenue) is a provider of C4ISR (command control communications computers intelligence surveillance and reconnaissance) products and systems. Its core offerings are space intelligence and cyber systems; ground systems and products; and naval air and electronic systems.

Overall the company generates almost 60% of total sales from products and more than 40% from services.

Geographic Reach

Headquartered in Reston Virginia General Dynamics operates around the world serving government and commercial customers on five continents spanning more than 45 countries. The North America represents its largest market generating around 85% of sales.

Sales and Marketing

General Dynamics' main customer is the US Department of Defense. About 65% of its revenues stem from the US government and some 15% come from US commercial customers. The company offers services through different types of contracts. Its fixed-price contracts generate around 70% of the total revenue followed by the cost-reimbursement contract for about 25%.

Financial Performance

General Dynamics' revenues – apart from a slight dip in 2016 – have seen steady growth over the last five years rising 24% between 2015 and 2019. As the U.S. government is its biggest customer the company's financial performance is heavily reliant on it. The signing of the Bipartisan Budget Act of 2019 raised discretionary spending limits and thus represented an increase of approximately 3% over the total FY 2019 spending level.

Revenue increased 9% to $39.4 billion in 2019 with growth in all of its segments. The increase was driven by deliveries of the new G500 and G600 aircraft in General Dynamics' Aerospace segment and new contracts from the U.S. government for military vehicles in the Combat Systems segment and submarines in the Marine Systems segment.

General Dynamics' net income rose 4% to $3.5 billion in 2019 mainly due to a decrease in effective tax rate from increased R&D tax credits and favorable 2019 regulatory developments associated with implementing the Tax Cuts and Jobs Act.

The company's cash and cash equivalents stood at $902 million at the end of 2019 compared with $963 million in the prior year. Cash from operations contributed $2.9 billion while investing activities used $994 million mainly for capital expenditures. Financing activities used another $1.9 billion mostly for dividends and commercial paper repayments.

Strategy

General Dynamics employs a unique business model that keeps it focused on its priorities which are exceeding customer expectations executing on backlog managing costs implementing continuous improvement and maximizing earnings cash and return on invested capital.

The company's continued investment in research and development leads to new aircraft that consistently broaden customer offerings while raising the bar for safety and performance. As part of its sustainability strategy Gulfstream in 2019 made its first customer sales of sustainable aviation fuel. In 2019 the all-new G600 was introduced to customers joining the G500 which was launched in 2018.

Additionally General Dynamics acquired Deep Learning Analytics in 2019 with extensive expertise in AI that specializes in deploying deep learning algorithms on small power-efficient appliances and mobile devices. The new investment brings a wealth of artificial intelligence and machine learning knowledge experience and capabilities to its customers across all domains.

The company is also the lead contractor for the US Navy's next-generation ballistic missile submarine the Columbia-class. The Navy considers the Columbia-class sub a top priority offering strategic nuclear deterrent capabilities for decades. The Columbia-class submarines are scheduled to replace the Ohio-class fleet when it reaches the end of its service life in 2027.

Mergers and Acquisitions

In 2019 Jet Aviation a wholly owned subsidiary of General Dynamics acquired full ownership of the San Juan fixed-base operator (FBO) at Luis Muñoz Marin International Airport in Puerto Rico a provider of premium business aviation services at one of the most convenient U.S. points of entry for international flights. A new larger hangar will open in the first quarter of 2019 to replace the one destroyed by Hurricane Maria in 2017. The hangar – 20000 square feet of hangar space and 2500 square feet of office space – will offer customers parking facilities refueling third party aircraft maintenance meeting space an executive passenger lounge flight-planning workstations and a pilots' suit.

HISTORY

In 1899 John Holland founded Electric Boat Company a New Jersey ship and submarine builder. The company built ships PT boats and submarines during WWII but when faced with waning postwar orders CEO John Jay Hopkins diversified with the 1947 purchase of aircraft builder Canadair. Hopkins formed General Dynamics in 1952 merging Electric Boat and Canadair and buying Consolidated Vultee Aircraft (Convair) a major producer of military and civilian aircraft in 1954.

EXECUTIVES

Evp Marine Systems, John P. Casey, age 65, $747,500 total compensation

Vp Strategic Planning, Phebe N. Novakovic, age 62, $1,585,000 total compensation

Vp And President General Dynamics Mission Systems, Christopher (Chris) Marzilli, age 60

Vp And President Electric Boat, Jeffrey S. Geiger, age 58

Vp; President Bath Iron Works, Dirk Lesko

Vp And President Gulfstream Aerospace Corp., Mark L. Burns, age 60

Vp And President Jet Aviation, Robert E. (Rob) Smith

Evp Combat Systems, Mark C. Roualet, age 62, $747,500 total compensation

Vp; President Nassco, Kevin M. Graney

Evp General Dynamics Information Systems And Technology Group; President General Dynamics Information Technology, S. Daniel (Dan) Johnson, age 73, $713,750 total compensation

Vp And President European Land Systems, Alfonso J. Ramonet

Svp And Cfo, Jason W. Aiken, age 47, $701,250 total compensation

Vp And President Land Systems, Gary L. Whited, age 59

President General Dynamics Information Technology, M. Amy Gilliland

Executive Vice President, Gerard Demuro

Vice President Air Force It Business Development Gd Defense Systems, Paul Besson

Vice President Human Resources, Sharon Matsumura-crowe

Director Government Relations, Jen Navarro

Director Of Government Relations, Gerry Lamb

Vice President Finance, Dale Kaminski

Vice President Sales, Murray Rapp

Vp Manufacturing, Howard Bruce

Vice President Information Technology, Tommy Augustsson

Manager Of Public And Government Relations, Dennis DuBard

Vice President And Gm General Dynamics Ordnance And Tactical Systems, Steve Elgin

Director Of Surgery, Todd Tarby

Vice President, Jack Picker

Svp Finance And Operations, William Wylie

Vice President Tax, Ken Hayduk

Vice President And General Counsel Electric Boat, Matthew S Luxton

Vice President President Ordnance And Tactical Systems, Michael S Wilson

Vp It Mis, Jason Sye

Vice President Quality And Radiological Controls, William P Lennon

Vice President Human Resources, Sharon Dunbar

Vice President Planning And Development, Bob Helm

Vice President New Marketing, Chris Trella

Vice President Investor Relations, Howard A Rubel

Vice President, Vincent Shugrue

Vice President Marketing, Dean Bartles

Executive Vice President Information Systems And Technoloy, S Daniel Johnson

Vice President Of Supply Chain Materials And Strategic Sourcing Electric Boat, T Blair Decker

Senior Vice President Hardware Engineering, Dan Riccio

Vice President Machine Products, Frank Pellegrino

Board Member, Lester Lyles

Board Member, Rudy deLeon

Board Member, Laura Schumacher

Board Member, Mark Malcolm

Board Member, Catherine Reynolds

Secretary, John Glenn

Auditors: KPMG LLP

LOCATIONS

HQ: General Dynamics Corp
11011 Sunset Hills Road, Reston, VA 20190
Phone: 703 876-3000
Web: www.gd.com

2016 Sales

	$ mil.	% of total
North America	24,122	77
Europe	2,355	8
Africa/Middle East	2,668	8
Asia/Pacific	1,914	6
South America	294	1
Total	**31,353**	**100**

PRODUCTS/OPERATIONS

2016 Sales

	$ mil.	% of total
Information Systems and Technology	9,187	29
Aerospace	8,362	27
Marine Systems	8,202	26
Combat Systems	5,602	18
Total	**31,353**	**100**

2016 Sales

	$ mil.	% of total
Products	19,885	63
Services	11,468	37
Total	**31,353**	**100**

COMPETITORS

BAE SYSTEMS	Leidos
Boeing	Lockheed Martin
Bombardier	Motorola Solutions
Cisco Systems	Navistar International
DRS Technologies	Nokia
Dassault Aviation	Northrop Grumman
Day & Zimmermann	Peugeot
FLIR Systems	Raytheon
HP Enterprise Services	Renco
Harris Corp.	Rockwell Collins
ITT Corp.	Textron
L3 Technologies	United Technologies

Company Type: Public

Income Statement				FYE: December 31
	REVENUE ($ mil.)	NET INCOME ($ mil.)	NET PROFIT MARGIN	EMPLOYEES
12/19	39,350	3,484	8.9%	102,900
12/18	36,193	3,345	9.2%	105,600
12/17	30,973	2,912	9.4%	98,600
12/16	31,353	2,955	9.4%	98,800
12/15	31,469	2,965	9.4%	99,900
Annual Growth	5.7%	4.1%	—	0.7%

2019 Year-End Financials

Debt ratio: 24.43%
Return on equity: 27.53%
Cash ($ mil.): 902
Current ratio: 1.18
Long-term debt ($ mil.): 9,010

No. of shares (mil.): 289
Dividends
Yield: 2.2%
Payout: 34.6%
Market value ($ mil.): 51,073

	STOCK PRICE ($)	P/E		PER SHARE ($)		
	FY Close	High/Low	Earnings	Dividends	Book Value
12/19	176.35	16 13	11.98	3.99	46.88
12/18	157.21	20 13	11.18	3.63	40.64
12/17	203.45	22 18	9.56	3.28	38.52
12/16	172.66	18 13	9.52	2.97	36.29
12/15	137.36	17 14	9.08	2.69	34.31
Annual Growth	6.4%	— —	7.2%	10.4%	8.1%

General Electric Co

From turbines and oilfield equipment to aircraft engines and power plants General Electric is plugged in to industrial equipment businesses that shape the modern world. The company produces aircraft engines locomotives and other transportation equipment generators and turbines lighting and oil and gas exploration and production equipment. GE also has a healthcare products business which it plans to separate into a standalone company and a financial services division the size of which it is reducing (especially its energy and industrial finance business). More than 40% of GE's sales comes from its US operations.

HISTORY

General Electric was established in 1892 in New York the result of a merger between Thomson-Houston and Edison General Electric. Charles Coffin was GE's first president and Thomas Edison who left the company in 1894 was one of the directors.

GE's financial strength (backed by the Morgan banking house) and its research focus contributed to its initial success. Early products included such Edison legacies as light bulbs elevators motors toasters and other appliances under the GE and Hotpoint labels. In the 1920s GE joined AT&T and Westinghouse in a radio broadcasting venture Radio Corporation of America (RCA) but GE sold off its RCA holdings in 1930 because of an antitrust ruling.

By 1980 GE had reached $25 billion in revenues from plastics consumer electronics nuclear reactors and jet engines. But it had become rigid and bureaucratic. Jack Welch became president in 1981 and shook up the company. He decentralized operations and adopted a strategy of pursuing only high-achieving ventures and dumping those that didn't perform. GE shed air-conditioning (1982)

housewares (1984) and semiconductors (1988) and with the proceeds acquired Employers Reinsurance (1984); RCA including NBC (1986 but sold RCA in 1987); CGR medical equipment (1987); and investment banker Kidder Peabody (1990).

In the early 1990s GE grew its lighting business. It bought mutual fund wholesaler GNA in 1993 and GE Investment Management (now GE Financial Network) began selling mutual funds to the public.

GE sold scandal-plagued Kidder Peabody to Paine Webber in 1994. General Electric Capital Services (GECS) expanded its lines buying Amex Life Insurance (Aon's Union Fidelity unit) and Life Insurance Co. of Virginia in 1995 and First Colony the next year. The company sold its struggling GEnie online service in 1996 and formed an NBC and Microsoft venture the MSNBC cable news channel. In 1997 GE Engine Services bought aircraft engine maintenance firms Greenwich Air Services and UNC.

GE acquired Lockheed Martin's medical imaging unit in 1997 and added to the medical systems business with the 1998 purchase of Marquette Medical Systems. In 1998 GECS became the first foreign company to enter Japan's life insurance market when it bought assets from Toho Mutual Life Insurance and set up GE Edison Life.

In 1999 GECS bought the 53% of Montgomery Ward it didn't already own along with the retailer's direct-marketing arm as Montgomery Ward emerged from bankruptcy. (Ward declared bankruptcy again in 2000.) In 2000 it reorganized GE Information Systems to form an e-commerce unit Global eXchange Services (GXS). (GE sold 90% of GXS to buyout firm Francisco Partners in 2002.)

Later in 2000 the company announced its biggest acquisition of the Welch era. Moving in at the last minute GE trumped a rival bid from United Technologies and agreed to pay $45 billion in stock for manufacturing giant Honeywell International and to assume $3.4 billion in Honeywell debt.

Welch by then viewed as one of the best corporate leaders in the US had agreed to postpone his retirement from April 2001 until the end of that year in order to oversee the completion of the Honeywell acquisition. But European regulators concerned about the potential strength of the combined GE-Honeywell aircraft-related businesses blocked the Honeywell deal that summer. Welch then stepped down and Jeff Immelt formerly president and CEO of GE Medical Systems succeeded him in September 2001.

Immelt initially set about reshaping GE by spinning off its life and mortgage insurance businesses into a new entity Genworth Financial which went public in 2004 (completely divested in 2006). GE acquired UK-based Amersham a medical diagnostics and life sciences company since renamed GE Healthcare Medical Diagnostics.

In 2006 GE sold off most of its remaining insurance businesses including GE Insurance Solutions and Employers Reinsurance in a sale to Swiss Re. The company kept its US life reinsurance business.

Citing rising commodities costs GE sold its advanced materials unit which produced silicone quartz and ceramics products to Apollo Management and sold its GE Plastics unit (now SABIC Innovative Plastics) to SABIC for more than $11 billion in 2007. Also that year GE shut down the operations of wholesale subprime lender WMC Mortgage.

At the same time GE built some of its traditional businesses through acquisitions. In early 2007 the company's aviation division acquired aircraft systems manufacturer Smiths Aerospace from Smiths Group. GE Energy bought oil and gas production

equipment supplier Vetco Gray and the US retail natural gas distribution network of Knight (then named Kinder Morgan).

In 2011 GE sold a controlling stake in NBCUniversal to Comcast. GE retained a 49% stake in the media venture.

In 2013 GE sold its 49% stake in NBCUniversal for nearly $17 billion to Comcast as part of its strategy to focus on its industrial operations. There was already a structure in place for Comcast to eventually take full ownership of NBCUniversal but stronger than expected growth from the joint venture accelerated those plans.

GE in 2013 acquired Texas-based Lufkin Industries which specializes in providing artificial lift technologies for the oil and gas industry as well as making industrial gears. The $3.3 billion deal broadened the GE Oil & Gas unit and supports the company's plans to tighten its focus on industrial customers by providing services and equipment. In 2014 GE launched Predictivity a portfolio of web-based products to help oil and gas customers in the Asia/Pacific region improve operational and fiscal productivity.

To further boost its industrial operations the partnered with XD Electric Group in 2013 to combine GE's grid automation capabilities with XD's high-voltage power equipment. GE Energy Financial Services has also recently invested in Japan's largest solar power project to be built in Okayama Prefecture; it holds a 60% stake in the project.

In 2013 to boost its global reach GE's financial arm bought a $2.3 billion portfolio of commercial real estate loans from Deutsche Postbank that comprised 90% British as well as German and French properties. GE Capital also acquired MetLife's banking unit in 2013 adding some $6.4 billion in deposits and an established online banking platform.

That year the company also bought Italy-based industrial manufacturer Avio's aviation business which it renamed Avio Aero for $4.3 billion. The move expanded GE's activities in the appealing jet propulsion segment and strengthens its global supply chain.

In 2014 GE sold GE Money Bank AB business in Sweden Denmark and Norway to Santander for $2.3 billion. That year the company also announced plans to exit its North American Retail Finance operations.

EXECUTIVES

Svp Business Transformation, Daniel Janki
Chairman And Ceo, John L. Flannery, age 58
Svp; Chairman And Ceo Ge Capital, Richard A. (Rich) Laxer
President And Ceo Ge Fanuc Intelligent Platforms Technology Infrastructure, Maryrose T. Sylvester
Svp And President And Ceo Ge Aviation, David L. Joyce, age 63, $1,333,333 total compensation
Svp And Cto, Victor (Vic) Abate, age 51
Svp And President And Ceo Ge Power, Steve Bolze, age 57
Cfo, Jamie S. Miller, age 51
President And Ceo Ge Africa, Jay W. Ireland
President And Ceo Ge Europe And Alstom Integration Leader, Mark Hutchinson, age 60
Svp And Chairman President And Ceo Ge Asset Management, Dmitri L. Stockton, age 56
President And Ceo Ge Korea, Chris Khang
Svp And President And Ceo Power Services, Paul A. McElhinney
President And Ceo Baker Hughes A Ge Company, Lorenzo Simonelli, age 47
Svp And President And Ceo Ge Power, Russell Stokes, age 49
Svp And Chief Digital Officer Ge And Ceo Ge Digital, William (Bill) Ruh, age 59

President And Ceo Ge Renewable Energy, Jérme Pécresse

Vp Global Services Organization (gso), Pete McCabe

Ceo Ge Malaysia, Datuk Mark Rozario

Ceo Ge Australia, Max York

Ceo Ge New Zealand And Ge Papua New Guinea, Kevin Hart

President And Ceo Ge Apac, Wouter Van Wersch

Government Affairs And Policy Director Ge Japan, Eriko Asai

Vice President, Kevin Czarnecki

Assistant Vice President, Valerie Bouchereau

Vice President Of Sales, Michael Sylstra

Regional Vice President Sales, Bjorn Gidner

Vice President Strategic Initiatives, Allison Garrigan

Senior Vice President Vice Public Relations, Rene Buhay

Senior Vice President, Kathleen Chomienne

Legal Secretary, Marlene Gerardi

Senior Vice President, Matthew Pauley

Vice President Risk Analyst, Debra Bresnan

Senior Vice President, Thomas Costello

Vice President Engineering, Luciano Cerone

Vice President, John Laws

Vice President National Direct Sales, David Robinson

Vice President Risk, Dennis Duffany

Vice President Speciality Solutions Sales Southeast, Randy Goins

Assistant Vice President: Franchiefinance, Vince Malizia

Vice President Retail Finance, Stephen Motta

National Account Manager Sears, Gary Howard

Assistant Vice President, Dennis Leonard

Senior Vice President, Bob Vail

Senior Vice President, David Richman

National Account Manager, Jack Hodes

Vice President Labor And Employment, Amber Kagan

Vice President Middle East Ge Energy, Joseph Anis

Vice President Business Operations Ge Power And Water China, Yang Dan

Vice President Global Services Ge Transportation, Pascal Schweitzer

Vice President Global Services Turbomachinery Solutions Ge Oil And Gas, Maria Sferruzza

Chief Accounting Officer Vice President Controller, Thomas Timko

Government Relations, Pamela Farrell

Vice President Senior Account Executive, Eric Busch

Vice President Engineering, Louis Gasper

Vice President General Manager Civil Programs, Stefanie Darlington

Senior Vice President Engineering, Milan Shah

Board Member, Shannon Winlove-smith

Board Member, Heather Bunyard

Advisory Board Member, Jill Johnson

Board Member, Elisa Morales

Board Member, Jody Engel

Board Member, Michael Tengelin

Vice Chairman, Jesse Rock

Board Member, Eric Denoyel

Treasurer Ge Aviation, David Martin

Treasurer, Craig Stevens

Board Member, Richard J Hawkins

Auditors: Deloitte & Touche LLP

LOCATIONS

HQ: General Electric Co
5 Necco Street, Boston, MA 02210
Phone: 617 443-3000
Web: www.ge.com

Sales 2016

	% of total
US	43
Europe	17
Asia	17
Americas	9
Middle East & Africa	14
Total	**100**

PRODUCTS/OPERATIONS

2018 Sales

	$ mil.	% of total
Power	27,300	22
Aviation	30,566	24
Healthcare	19,784	16
Oil & Gas	22,859	18
Lighting	1,723	1
Capital	9,551	8
Renewable Energy	9,533	8
Transportation	3,898	3
Corporate items & eliminations	(3600.0)	-
Total	**121,615**	**100**

2018 Sales

	$ mil.	% of total
US	46,754	38
Outside US	74,861	62
Total	**121,615**	**100**

COMPETITORS

ABB	Rockwell Automation
ALSTOM	Rolls-Royce
Agilent Technologies	Schneider Electric
Atlas Copco	Siemens AG
Caterpillar	Textron
Emerson Electric	ThyssenKrupp
FANUC	Toshiba
ITT Corp.	United Technologies
Raytheon	

HISTORICAL FINANCIALS

Company Type: Public

Income Statement   FYE: December 31

	REVENUE ($ mil.)	NET INCOME ($ mil.)	NET PROFIT MARGIN	EMPLOYEES
12/19	95,214	(4,979)	—	205,000
12/18	121,615	(22,355)	—	283,000
12/17	122,092	(5,786)	—	313,000
12/16	123,693	8,831	7.1%	295,000
12/15	117,386	(6,126)	—	333,000
Annual Growth	**(5.1%)**	**—**	**—**	**(11.4%)**

2019 Year-End Financials

Debt ratio: 33.54%—
Return on equity: (-16.79%)
Cash ($ mil.): 36,394
Current ratio: 1.53
Long-term debt ($ mil.): 67,155

Dividends
Yield: 0.3%
Payout: —
Market value ($ mil.): —

	STOCK PRICE ($) FY Close	P/E High/Low	Earnings	PER SHARE ($) Dividends	Book Value
12/19	11.16	— —	(0.62)	0.04	3.24
12/18	7.57	— —	(2.62)	0.37	3.56
12/17	17.45	— —	(0.72)	0.84	7.40
12/16	31.60	37 31	0.89	0.93	8.67
12/15	31.15	— —	(0.61)	0.92	10.48
Annual Growth	**(22.6%) (25.4%)**	**— —**	**—**	**(54.3%)**	

GENERAL ELECTRIC INTERNATIONAL, INC.

EXECUTIVES

Pres, Giuseppe Recchi
V Pres*, Candace F Carson
V Pres*, Daniel Janki
SEC*, Pierrot Christophe
SEC*, Kristen Urso-Rio
Treas*, Michael J Geary
Senior Specialist, A Carbone
Power Performance Mana, Jerry King
Fbw Integrator, Joseph Desormeaux
Leader, Tyler Zimmer
Fleet Manager, Carrie McConnell
Auditors: KPMG LLP CINCINNATI OHIO

LOCATIONS

HQ: GENERAL ELECTRIC INTERNATIONAL, INC.
191 ROSA PARKS ST, CINCINNATI, OH 452022573
Phone: 617 443-3000
Web: WWW.GE.COM

HISTORICAL FINANCIALS

Company Type: Private

Income Statement   FYE: December 31

	REVENUE ($ mil.)	NET INCOME ($ mil.)	NET PROFIT MARGIN	EMPLOYEES
12/17	14,100	685	4.9%	125
12/16	13,364	1,339	10.0%	—
12/15	13,288	82	0.6%	—
12/14	12,884	(304)	—	—
Annual Growth	**3.1%**	**—**	**—**	**—**

General Mills Inc

General Mills is high in the ranks of consumer-packaged goods companies. Some of its #1 and #2 market-leading brands include Betty Crocker dessert mixes Gold Medal flour Pillsbury cookie dough and Yoplait yogurt. It competes with Kellogg to be the top cereal maker with a brand arsenal that includes Kix Chex Cheerios Lucky Charms and Wheaties. While most of the firm's sales come from the US General Mills is working to extend the reach and position of its brands globally and has facilities across five major continents. General Mills also owns the Haagen-Dazs ice cream brand in the US.

HISTORY

Cadwallader Washburn built his first flour mill in 1866 in Minneapolis which eventually became the Washburn Crosby Company. After winning a gold medal for flour at an 1880 exposition the company changed the name of its best flour to Gold Medal Flour.

In 1921 advertising manager Sam Gale created fictional spokeswoman Betty Crocker so that correspondence to housewives could go out with her signature. The firm introduced Wheaties cereal in 1924. James Bell named president in 1925 consolidated the company with other US mills in 1928 to form General Mills the world's largest miller. The companies operated independently of one another with corporate headquarters coordinating advertising and merchandising.

General Mills began introducing convenience foods such as Bisquick (1931) and Cheerios (1941). During WWII it produced war goods such as ordnance equipment and developed chemical and electronics divisions.

When Edwin Rawlings became CEO in 1961 he closed half of the flour mills and divested such unprofitable lines as electronics. This cost $200 million in annual sales but freed resources for such acquisitions as Kenner Products (toys 1967) and Parker Brothers (board games 1968) which made General Mills the world's largest toy company.

During the next 20 years the company made many acquisitions including Gorton's (frozen seafood 1968) Monet (jewelry 1968) Eddie Bauer (outerwear 1971) and The Talbots (women's clothing 1973). It bought Red Lobster in 1970 and acquired the US rights to Yoplait yogurt in 1977. When the toy and fashion divisions' profits fell in 1984 they were spun off as Kenner Parker Toys and Crystal Brands (1985). Reemphasizing food in 1989 the firm sold many businesses including Eddie Bauer and Talbots.

To expand into Europe General Mills struck two important joint ventures: Cereal Partners Worldwide (with Nestlé in 1989) and Snack Ventures Europe (with PepsiCo in 1992).

As part of a cereal price war in 1994 the company cut coupon promotion costs by $175 million and lowered prices on many cereals. But some retailers did not pass on the price cuts to consumers due to shortages that developed after the FDA found an unauthorized pesticide in some cereals. General Mills destroyed 55 million boxes of cereal at a cost of $140 million. Stephen Sanger became CEO in 1995. That year the company sold Gortons to Unilever and spun off its restaurant businesses as Darden Restaurants.

Focused on a food-only future in the late 1990s General Mills picked up several smaller businesses including Ralcorp Holdings' Chex snack and cereal lines and Gardetto's Bakery snack mixes as well as the North American rights to Olibra an appetite suppressant food additive made by Scotia Holdings. Entering the natural foods market in 2000 General Mills launched Sunrise organic cereal and bought organic foods producer Small Planet Foods.

Big changes came in 2001 when General Mills became the #1 cereal maker in the US overtaking Kellogg for the first time since 1906. The company then completed its $10.5 billion purchase of Pillsbury from Diageo in October 2001. A month later General Mills sold competing product lines to International Multifoods. Also that year the company launched a 50-50 joint venture with DuPont to develop soy beverages marketed under the 8th Continent brand name. While busily integrating Pillsbury in 2002 General Mills saw its income fall and watched as Kellogg regained the lead in the cereal market. In 2003 the SEC began an investigation into the company's sales and accounting practices (which it terminated in 2005 taking no action against General Mills).

In 2004 General Mills filed a universal shelf registration with the SEC the result of which is that Diageo had to register the common shares of General Mills that it owns before it could sell those shares in a public offering. Also as a result of the shelf registration two Diageo-designated members of General Mills' board (including Diageo CEO Paul Walsh) resigned as a result of a change in the two companies' stockholders agreement that terminated Diageo's right to designate two General Mills' board members. Diageo sold part of its approxi-mate 20% stake in General Mills. General Mills in turn sold an $835 million stake to an affiliate of Lehman Brothers Holding and used $750 million to buy back the Diageo shares and $85 million to pay down debt.

Also in 2004 the company sold its US H ¤agen-Dazs ice cream shop franchise business to Dreyer's Grand Ice Cream. In 2005 it sold its stake in Snack Ventures Europe joint venture to PepsiCo for $750 million. That year the company introduced Yoplait Healthy Heart which contains cholesterol-lowering plant sterols.

Diageo sold two-thirds of its 20% stake in General Mills in 2005. Later that year General Mills announced the sale of Lloyd's barbecue business to Hormel Foods. In 2006 Cereal Partners Worldwide (its joint venture with Nestlé) acquired the Australian breakfast cereal operations of Uncle Tobys from Burns Philp.

After more than 10 years of being ignored the Jolly Green Giant came out of retirement in 2005 as part of a multi-million dollar marketing campaign by General Mills to up its veggie sales. The next year General Mills declined to renew its licensing agreement with Archer Daniels Midland regarding the sale and marketing of Pillsbury Bakery Flour to the industrial and foodservice sectors. General Mills integrated the brand which consists of mixes and frozen bakery products into its bakery ingredients segment.

In order to develop healthier products in 2006 the company entered a supply agreement for DHA (an omega-3 fatty acid said to play a role in mental and cardiovascular health) with Martek Biosciences maker of DHA (which is already widely used in infant formula).

General Mills pulled its reduced-sugar children's cereal from the market in 2007 due to poor sales. Sweetened with SPLENDA the cereals never took off with consumers perhaps due to resistance to the sugar replacement. (Kellogg and Kraft use sugar in their reduced-sugar cereal offerings.) That year the company acquired UK chilled pastry company Saxby Bros.

Also in 2007 CEO Sanger stepped down. President and COO Ken Powell replaced him. The following year General Mills and DuPont sold their soy-milk joint venture 8th Continent to Stremicks Heritage Foods.

To better focus on its core brands and foodservice offerings the company in mid-2010 sold its Delicity chain of bakeries in Argentina to Tentissimo Group which also operates restaurants under the Tentissimo banner in the country. The deal included the Delicity brand five company-owned bakeries and franchiser rights which apply to the roughly 55 bakery locations operated by franchisees. General Mills also agreed to continue supplying dough products to the chain. It had owned Delicity since acquiring Pillsbury in 2001.

In 2008 the company sold its PopÂ·Secret operations to Diamond Foods for some $190 million in cash. PopÂ·Secret is the second-largest-selling branded popcorn in the US after Orville Redenbacher which is made by ConAgra. (ConAgra also makes Act II microwaveable popcorn.) While General Mills said it is concentrating its efforts on increasing the sales of its more lucrative core brands the high price of corn most probably also figured into the decision to jettison PopÂ·Secret.

General Mills made no divestures in 2009 but in 2010 the company ceased making Perfect Portions refrigerated biscuits and exited the kids' refrigerated yogurt beverage and microwave soup segments in its US retail operations; internationally it also stopped the manufacture of foodservice breadcrumbs with the sale of its Brazilian bread and pasta plant for $6 million. These product cessations were made in response to its declining financial results particularly in its international segment.

To better focus on its retail sales channels in late 2010 General Mills sold its Croissant King (acquired in 2005) and van den Bergh's (acquired in 1999) frozen bakery business in Australia to Ireland's Kerry Group. The sale includes frozen dough and pastry products sold to professional bakers.

Following that divestiture General Mills in 2011 acquired Australia's Pasta Master a maker of chilled Italian meals pasta and sauces. The purchase valued at nearly $40 million broadened General Mills' ready-to-cook pasta offerings.

To help offset weakness in its core cereal business General Mills is beefing up its yogurt empire through acquisitions such as its $1.2 billion purchase of a controlling stake in Yoplait in 2011 a brand that it had licensed for several decades. The company acquired the 50% stake in Yoplait owned by French investment firm PAI Partners plus 1% from dairy cooperative Social. Additionally General Mills acquired a 50% share of a related firm that owns Yoplait's global branding rights. General Mills aims to expand Yoplait's operations in France Europe and the rest of the world. Also in 2011 General Mills acquired Dean Foods' Mountain High all-natural yogurt business for about $85 million. The brand became part of General Mills' Yoplait USA division.

In line with its strategy to grow its business in global markets General Mills acquired Parampara's ready-to-cook spice and sauce mixes made and marketed in India and also exported to the US Canada and Japan. In 2012 it bought Brazilian food maker Yoki Alimentos which makes and markets more than 600 items under nine brands including Yoki and Kitano. The deal doubles General Mills' annual sales in Latin America.

EXECUTIVES

Executive Vice President And Chief Finan, James Lawrence

Svp; Ceo Cereal Partners Worldwide, David P. (Dave) Homer

Evp And Coo International, Christopher D. (Chris) O'Leary, age 61, $730,133 total compensation

Vp; President Annieâ's Foods, John M. Foraker, age 57

Svp External Relations; President General Mills Foundation, Kimberly A. (Kim) Nelson, age 57

Svp; President Greater China, Gary Chu

Evp And Cfo, Donal L. (Don) Mulligan, age 60, $736,050 total compensation

Svp; President Big G Cereals, James H. (Jim) Murphy

Evp Supply Chain, John R. Church, age 54, $577,767 total compensation

Svp; President Meals, Michele S. Meyer

Svp; President Sales And Channel Development, Shawn P. O'Grady, age 56

Ceo, Jeffrey L. Harmening, age 53, $775,000 total compensation

Evp Innovation Technology And Quality, Peter C. Erickson, age 59

Svp; President Latin America, Sean N. Walker

Svp; President Europe Australia And New Zealand, Jonathon J. (Jon) Nudi

Vp; President Snacks, Anton Vincent

Vp; President Yoplait International, Olivier Faujour

Vp; President Asia Middle East And Africa, Christina Law

Vp; President Yoplait Usa, David Clark

Vp; President Convenience And Foodservice, Bethany C. Quam

Vp; President Baking, Elizabeth M. Nordlie

Vice President Finance North American Retail, Brett White

Vice President Executive Director, Vijay K Sood

Vice President Corporate Services, Mike Nordstrom

Vice President Marketing Big G, John Haugen

Vice President Information Technology, Samuel Gale
Vice President It, Jodi Benson
Vice President, Kymm Pollack
Vice President Consumer Insight, Gayle Fuguitt
Vice President And Chief Tax Officer, Gerald Morris
Vice President Corporate Strategy, Peter McDonald
Senior Vice President, Tom Eggemeier
Vice President And Deputy General Counsel, Eric Wedepohl
Vice President Marketing Yoplait Division, Steve Young
Vice President Benefits, Ann Carlson
Vp Of Human Resources International General Mills, Mike Switzer
National Account Manager, Kurt Schuitema
Vice President Comp Ben, Michael Davis
Senior Vice President; President Bakeries And Foodservice, David E Dudick
Executive Vice President, Roderick Palmore
Vice President, James Cooper
Vice President Worldwide Sourcing, John Wiebold
Vice President Sales Walmart, David Wurm
Vice President Controller, Richard Lund
Vp Sales, David Nagel
Vice President Of Human Resources, Victor Huang
Vice President, Sheila Gallagher
Vice President Engineering, Gregg Stedronsky
Vice President, Gene Kahn
Vice President Sales Admin, Ruth Welter
Senior Vice President Marketing, Jeff Rotsch
Vice President Information Technology, Zachariah Watne
National Account Manager, Dudley Whiteley
Senior Business Intelligence Developer, Steve Schober
Vice President Marketing Partnerships And Commercialization, Dave Wagner
Vice President Innovation Technology And Quality Global Cereal Platform, Mayank Patel
Vice President Media, Rick Hosfield
Vice President Of Human Resources, Joseph Mucha
Vp Marketing, Steve Rogers
Vp Research And Development, John Mendesh
Vice President Trade And Marketing, Steve Mayle
Vice President And Chief Tax Officer, Jerry Morris
National Sales Manager, Breanne Tindale
National Sales Manager Foodservice, Esme Plessis
Vice President Legal And External Affairs, Alice Lee
Vice President Human Resources, Sandy Ohlsson
Senior Vice President; President Consumer Foods Sales, Shawn P Ogrady
Vice President Qro, Liz Westring
Vice President Global Ecommerce, Gregory Pulsifer
Vice President, Doug Mcclure
National Sales Manager Vend Nfr, Richard Anastasio
Vice President President Foodservice, Maria Morgan
Vice President, Clifton Hyder
Vice President Product Marketing, Eric Tamblyn
Chairman, Kendall J. (Ken) Powell, age 67
Corporate And Security Counsel Assistant Secretary, Chris Rauschl
Board Member, Heidi Miller
Secretary, Christopher Rauschl
Board Member, Juliana Chugg
Assistant Treasurer, Craig Shafer
Board Member, David Cordani
Treasurer, Daniel Shaheen
Auditors: KPMG LLP

LOCATIONS

HQ: General Mills Inc
Number One General Mills Boulevard, Minneapolis, MN 55426
Phone: 763 764-7600   **Fax:** 763 764-8330
Web: www.generalmills.com

2019 sales

	% of total
US	74
Non-US	26
Total	**100**

PRODUCTS/OPERATIONS

2019 sales

	$ mil.	% of total
Snacks	3,359	20
Cereal	2,672	16
Convenient meals	2,241	15
Yogurt	2,193	13
Baking mixes & integrates	1,704	10
Dough	1,692	10
Pet	1,430	8
Super-premium ice cream	813	5
Other	452	3
Total	**16,865**	**100**

2019 sales

	$ mil.	% of total
North America Retail	9,925	59
Convenience Stores & Foodservice	1,969	12
Europe & Australia	1,886	11
Asia & Latin America	1,653	10
Pet	1,430	8
Total	**16,563**	**100**

Selected Brands

Dessert and baking mixes
  Betty Crocker
  Bisquick
  Gold Medal
  SuperMoist
  Warm Delights
Dry dinners and shelf stable and frozen vegetable products
  Annie's
  Bac*O's
  Betty Crocker
  Chicken Helper
  Diablitos
  Green Giant
  Hamburger Helper
  Old El Paso
  Potato Buds
  Simply Steam
  Suddenly Salad
  Valley Selections
  Tuna Helper
  Wanchai Ferry
Frozen pizza and pizza snacks
  Jeno's
  Party Pizza
  Pillsbury Pizza Minis
  Pillsbury Pizza Pops
  Pizza Rolls
  Totino's
Grain fruit and savory snacks
  Annie's
  Bugles
  Chex Mix
  Fiber One
  Fruit By The Foot
  Fruit Roll-Ups
  Gardetto's
  Gushers
  Lärabar
  Nature Valley
  Stickerz
Ice cream and frozen desserts
  Häagen-Dazs
Organic products
  Annie's
  Cascadian Farm
  Muir Glen
Ready-to-eat cereals
  Basic 4
  Cheerios
  Chex
  Cinnamon Toast Crunch
  Clusters
  Cocoa Puffs
  Cookie Crisp
  Fiber One
  Golden Grahams

  Kix
  Lucky Charms
  Oatmeal Crisp
  Reese's Puffs
  Total
  Trix
  Wheaties
Ready-to-serve soup
  Progresso
Refrigerated and frozen dough products
  Big Deluxe
  Golden Layers
  Grands!
  Jus-Rol
  La Salte Â Â a
  Latina
  Pasta Master
  Pillsbury
  Savorings
  Toaster Scrambles
  Toaster Strudel
  V.Pearl
  Wanchai Ferry
Refrigerated yogurt
  Go-GURT
  Fiber One
  Mountain High
  Trix
  Yoplait
  Yoplait Kids
  Yoplait Whips!
  YoPlus

COMPETITORS

B&G Foods	Hain Celestial
Barbara's Bakery	Hanover Foods
Bay State Milling	Heinz
Ben & Jerry's	Kellogg
Big Heart Pet Brands	King Arthur Flour
Birds Eye	Lakeside Foods
Blue Bell	MOM Brands
Bob's Red Mill Natural	Manischewitz Company
Foods	McKee Foods
Campbell Soup	Mondelez International
Carvel	Mrs. Fields
Chelsea Milling	Nature's Path
Cold Stone Creamery	Nestlé
ConAgra	Pinnacle Foods
Dairy Queen	Pro-Fac
Danone	Procter & Gamble
Dole Food	Ralston Food
Dreyer's	Seneca Foods
Fresh «ns	Stonyfield Farm
Friendly's Ice Cream	Victoria Packing
Frito-Lay	YoCream
Gilster-Mary Lee	

HISTORICAL FINANCIALS

Company Type: Public

Income Statement   FYE: May 31

	REVENUE ($ mil.)	NET INCOME ($ mil.)	NET PROFIT MARGIN	EMPLOYEES
05/20	17,626	2,181	12.4%	35,000
05/19	16,865	1,752	10.4%	40,000
05/18	15,740	2,131	13.5%	40,000
05/17	15,619	1,657	10.6%	38,000
05/16	16,563	1,697	10.2%	39,000
Annual Growth	1.6%	6.5%	—	(2.7%)

2020 Year-End Financials

Debt ratio: 43.95%	No. of shares (mil.): 609
Return on equity: 28.40%	Dividends
Cash ($ mil.): 1,677	Yield: 0.0%
Current ratio: 0.68	Payout: 55.0%
Long-term debt ($ mil.): 10,929	Market value ($ mil.): 38,442

	STOCK PRICE ($)	P/E	PER SHARE ($)		
	FY Close	High/Low	Earnings	Dividends	Book Value
05/20	63.04	18 13	3.56	1.96	13.21
05/19	52.81	18 13	2.90	1.96	11.72
05/18	42.64	16 11	3.64	1.96	10.35
05/17	57.32	26 20	2.77	1.92	7.50
05/16	62.87	23 19	2.77	1.78	8.26
Annual Growth	0.1%	— —	6.5%	2.4%	12.5%

General Motors Co

General Motors (GM) one of the world's largest auto manufacturers makes and sells cars and trucks worldwide under well-known brands such as Buick Cadillac Chevrolet and GMC. Business divisions GM North America and GM International handle the automotive end of the business while General Motors Financial Co. provides financing services. Looking toward the future of transportation the company is investing in developing electric vehicles and autonomous vehicles and it has established a ride-sharing service dubbed Maven. GM's biggest single market is the US which accounts for about 80% of sales.

Operations

General Motors operates through four segments: GM North America (GMNA) GM International (GMI) GM Financial and Cruise.

GMNA generates more than 75% of revenue and manufactures vehicles marketed under the Buick Cadillac Chevrolet and GMC brands. GMI (almost 15% of sales) sells these same brands to customers outside North America with the addition of the Holden lineup of vehicles. The company also has ownership stakes in companies in China where vehicles are also made and sold under the local Baojun Buick Cadillac Chevrolet and Wuling brands.

GM Financial contributes about 10% of the company's total revenue. It provides automotive financing and retail loan and lease lending products and services. It also offers commercial products to dealers such as new and used vehicle inventory financing inventory insurance working capital capital improvement loans and storage center financing.

The company's GM Cruise unit includes the business operations of its autonomous vehicle technology development.

Geographic Reach

Headquartered in Detroit GM has more than 100 locations in the US engaged in manufacturing assembly distribution warehousing engineering and testing. It has locations with similar functions in more than 30 other countries. Its major facilities outside the US are in Argentina Brazil Canada China Colombia Ecuador South Korea and Mexico.

GM Financial operates at nearly 45 locations globally. Around 30 are in the US. The US generates about 80% of GM's overall revenue.

Sales and Marketing

GM's cars and trucks are marketed and sold through a network of approximately 12600 independent distributors dealers and authorized sales service and parts outlets all over the world. Vehicles are also sold directly to fleet customers including rental car companies commercial fleet customers leasing companies and governments.

GM is a constant presence on television and other media spending $3.7 billion $4.0 billion and $4.3 billion in the years ended December 31 2019 2018 and 2017 respectively.

Financial Performance

For the last five years GM's revenue struggled to maintain its growth and net income also fluctuated.

In 2019 the company revenue decreased by 7% to $137 billion compared with $147 billion in 2019. It was primarily due to decrease in net wholesale volumes due to lost production resulting from the UAW strike and to unfavorable Other primarily due to the foreign currency effect resulting from the weakening of the Canadian Dollar against the U.S. Dollar.

Net income also fell 16% to $6.7 billion from $8 billion in 2018. Cash at the end of fiscal 2019 was $22.9 billion a decrease of $553 million from the prior year.

Cash from operations contributed $15 billion to the coffers while investing activities used $10.9 billion mainly for purchases of property and leased vehicles and investments in securities. Financing activities used another $4.7 billion for dividends to stockholders and payments of debt.

Strategy

One of GM's long-term strategy is to reduce petroleum consumption and GHG emissions by investing in the development of its hydrogen fuel cell technology. This initiative will help the company identify consumer and infrastructure needs to understand the business case for potential production of vehicles with this technology.

The Company is also focusing on the production and manufacture of electric vehicles that they envision to be increasingly important to their business. GM is committed to an all-electric future. Its next-generation vehicle technology will be launched in the new Cadillac EV scheduled to debut in 2022. It's also exploring lightweighting its new transmission systems and engines.

GM views Chinese market as important to their global growth strategy and are employing a multi-brand strategy led by its Buick Chevrolet and Cadillac brands. In the coming years the Company plans to leverage its global architectures to increase the number of product offerings under the Buick Chevrolet and Cadillac brands in China and continue to grow its business under the local Baojun and Wuling brands with Baojun focusing its expansion in less developed cities and markets. The Company operates in the Chinese market through a number of joint ventures and maintaining strong relationships with its joint venture partners is an important part of its China growth strategy.

Company Background

In the early years of the auto industry hundreds of carmakers each produced a few models. William Durant who bought a failing Buick Motors in 1904 reasoned that manufacturers could benefit from banding together and formed the General Motors Company in Flint MI in 1908. In 1909 GM purchases Cadillac AC Spark Plug and Rapid Motor Vehicle Company. It later developed the General Motors Truck Company (which later became GMC) Chevrolet Motor Company of Michigan General Motors Export Company and general Motors of Canada.

After the stock market crash of 1929 GM bought out the Fokker Aircraft Company and the General Motors Aviation Company was launched. During WWII the company began making military vehicles including trucks guns airplane engines airplanes and parts tanks and shells among other products. It also provided the mobility system for the Lunar Roving Vehicle during the 1971 Apollo 15 space mission to the moon.

General Motors has manufactured some of the most popular vehicles ever made including the Cadillac Corvette El Camino Malibu and Camaro. The auto giant went through a six-week period of bankruptcy protection in 2009. GM was split into two companies when it emerged from Chapter 11 – General Motors and Motors Liquidation (the name for leftover assets). In 2011 Motors Liquidation sold the majority of its assets which encompassed almost 90 industrial sites in 14 states which cleared the way for GM bondholders to receive stock in the new company.

EXECUTIVES

Svp; President And Ceo Gm Financial, Daniel E. (Dan) Berce, age 67

Evp Legal And Public Policy And General Counsel, Craig B. Glidden, age 62, $583,333 total compensation

Evp; President Europe; Chairman Management Board Opel Group, Karl-Thomas Neumann, age 59, $822,133 total compensation

Evp; President Cadillac, Carel Johannes de Nysschen, age 59

Evp Global Product Development Purchasing And Supply Chain, Mark L. Reuss, age 56, $1,100,000 total compensation

Chairman And Ceo, Mary T. Barra, age 59, $1,750,000 total compensation

Executive Director Global Technology Engineering, Matthew (Matt) Tsien, age 59

Evp And President Gm International, Barry Engle, age 57

Evp Global Manufacturing, Alicia Boler Davis

Evp; President North America, Alan S. Batey, age 56

President, Daniel (Dan) Ammann, age 48, $1,200,000 total compensation

Svp Global Information Technology And Cio, Randall D. (Randy) Mott

Evp And Cfo, Charles K. (Chuck) Stevens, age 60, $1,000,000 total compensation

President And Managing Director General Motors India, Sanjiv Gupta

Vp Global Purchasing And Supply Chain, Robert E Socia, age 68

U.s. Vice President Sales And Service, Kurt Mcneil

Vice President Autonomous And Ev Programs, Ken Morris

Vice President Gm Public Policy, Catherine Clegg

Senior Medical Director, Patrick Stover

Vice President Engineering Technical Center India, Lavern Sula

Vice President, Paras Dholakia

Vice President, Carlos Diaz

Medical Director, Donna Smith

Vice President And Treasurer, Rick Westenberg

Vice President Legal Affairs S, Elizabeth Shaffer

Vice President Of Industry Dealer Affairs, Bill Powell

Senior Vice President Gm International Operations, Julian Blissett

Senior Vice President Global Human Resources, Kim Brycz

Vice President, Jina Hwang

Vice President, Troy Hill

Senior Business Intelligence Developer, Rob Persons

Svp Global Human Resources, Kimberly kim Brycz

Senior Vice President Global Communications, Antonio Cervone

Vice President, Julian Bernal

Treasurer And Vice President Of Investor Relations, Rocky Gupta

Uaw Vice President, Tim Stannard

Senior Vice President Global Public Policy General Motors Company, Everett Eissenstat

Vice President Of The Business Unit, Lynch Richard

Vice President, Greg Ross

Svp; President Cadillac, Stephen steve Carlisle

Treasurer's Office, Nick Coupe

Treasurer, Niyant Shah

LOCATIONS

HQ: General Motors Co
   300 Renaissance Center, Detroit, MI 48265-3000
Phone: 313 667-1500
Web: www.gm.com

PRODUCTS/OPERATIONS

2018 Sales

	$ mil.	% of total
GM North America	113,792	77
GM International	19,148	13
GM Financial	14,016	10
Corporate	203	.
Eliminations	(110)	-
Total	**147,049**	**100**

2018 Sales

	$ mil.	% of total
Automotive		
U.S.	104,413	71
Non-U.S.	28,632	20
GM Financial		
U.S.	12,169	8
Non-U.S.	1,835	1
Total	**147,049**	**100**

Selected Brands

Buick
Cadillac
Chevrolet
GMC
Holden
Isuzu
Baojun
Jiefang
Wuiling

COMPETITORS

BMW	Mitsubishi Motors
Chery Automobile	Nissan
Daimler	Peugeot
FCA US	Renault
Fiat Chrysler	Subaru
Ford Motor	Toyota
Honda	Volkswagen

HISTORICAL FINANCIALS

Company Type: Public

Income Statement   FYE: December 31

	REVENUE ($ mil.)	NET INCOME ($ mil.)	NET PROFIT MARGIN	EMPLOYEES
12/19	137,237	6,732	4.9%	164,000
12/18	147,049	8,014	5.4%	173,000
12/17	145,588	(3,864)	—	180,000
12/16	166,380	9,427	5.7%	225,000
12/15	152,356	9,687	6.4%	215,000
Annual Growth	(2.6%)	(8.7%)	—	(6.5%)

2019 Year-End Financials

Debt ratio: 45.31%
Return on equity: 16.69%
Cash ($ mil.): 23,243
Current ratio: 0.88
Long-term debt ($ mil.): 65,924

No. of shares (mil.): 1,429
Dividends
   Yield: 4.1%
   Payout: 33.2%
Market value ($ mil.): 52,301

	STOCK PRICE ($) FY Close	P/E High/Low		PER SHARE ($) Earnings	Dividends	Book Value
12/19	36.60	9	7	4.57	1.52	29.25
12/18	33.45	8	5	5.53	1.52	27.57
12/17	40.99	—	—	(2.60)	1.52	24.95
12/16	34.84	6	4	6.00	1.52	29.26
12/15	34.01	6	4	5.91	1.38	25.81
Annual Growth	1.9%	—	—	(6.2%)	2.4%	3.2%

Genuine Parts Co.

What do spark plugs hydraulic hoses paper clips and magnet wire have in common? They're all Genuine Parts. The diversified company is the sole member and majority owner of National Automotive Parts Association (NAPA) a voluntary trade association that distributes auto parts nationwide. Genuine Parts Company (GPC) operates about 6000 NAPA Auto Parts stores in more than 55 US states. It also distributes parts through chains in Canada Mexico Australasia and across Europe. Other subsidiaries include auto parts distributor Balkamp industrial parts supplier Motion Industries and Business products distributor S.P. Richards.

HISTORY

Genuine Parts Company (GPC) got its start in Atlanta in 1928 when Carlyle Fraser bought a small auto parts store. That year GPC had the only loss in its history. Three years earlier a group that included Fraser had founded the National Automotive Parts Association (NAPA) an organization of automotive manufacturers remanufacturers distributors and retailers.

The Depression was a boon for GPC because fewer new-car sales meant more sales of replacement parts. During the 1930s GPC's sales rose from less than $350000 to more than $3 million. One tool it developed to spur sales during the Depression was its monthly magazine Parts Pups which featured pretty girls and corny jokes (discontinued in the 1990s). GPC acquired auto parts rebuilder Rayloc in 1931 and established parts distributor Balkamp in 1936.

WWII boosted sales at GPC because carmakers were producing for the war effort but scarce resources limited auto parts companies to producing functional parts. GPC went public in 1948.

The postwar boom in car sales boosted GPC's sales in the 1950s and 1960s. It expanded during this period with new distribution centers across the country. GPC bought Colyear Motor Sales (NAPA's West Coast distributor) in 1965 and introduced a line of filters and batteries in 1966 that were the first parts to carry the NAPA name.

GPC moved into Canada in 1972 when it bought Corbetts a Calgary-based parts distributor. That acquisition included Oliver Industrial Supply. During the mid-1970s GPC began to broaden its distribution businesses adding S.P. Richards (office products 1975) and Motion Industries (industrial replacement parts 1976). In the late 1970s GPC acquired Bearing Specialty and Michigan Bearing as part of Motion Industries.

In 1982 the company introduced its now familiar blue-and-yellow NAPA logo. Canadian parts distributor UAP (formerly United Auto Parts) and GPC formed a joint venture UAP/NAPA in 1988 with GPC acquiring a 20% stake in UAP.

During the 1990s GPC diversified its product lines and its geographic reach. Its 1993 acquisition of Berry Bearing made the company a leading distributor of industrial parts. The next year GPC formed a joint venture with Grupo Auto Todo of Mexico.

NAPA formed an agreement in 1995 with Penske Corporation to be the exclusive supplier of auto parts to nearly 900 Penske Auto Centers. GPC purchased Horizon USA Data Supplies that year adding computer supplies to S.P. Richards' product mix.

A string of acquisitions in the late 1990s increased GPC's industrial distribution business (including Midcap Bearing Power Drives & Bearings and Amarillo Bearing).

GPC paid $200 million in 1998 for EIS a leading wholesale distributor of materials and supplies to the electrical and electronics industries. Late in 1998 after a 10-year joint venture it bought the remaining 80% of UAP it didn't already own. GPC continued to expand its auto parts distribution network in 1999 acquiring Johnson Industries an independent distributor of auto supplies for large fleets and car dealers. GPC also acquired Oklahoma City-based Brittain Brothers a NAPA distributor that serves about 190 auto supply stores in Arkansas Missouri Oklahoma and Texas.

In 2000 the company bought a 15% interest in Mitchell Repair Information (MRIC) a subsidiary of Snap-on Incorporated that provides diagnostic and repair information services. The next year Johnson Industries acquired Coach and Motors a distribution center in Detroit.

GPC acquired NAPA Hawaii which serves more than 30 independently owned NAPA stores and four company-owned ones in Hawaii and Samoa in 2003. Also that year the company sold its interest in the partnership that distributes industrial parts in Mexico Refacciones Industriales de México.

President Thomas Gallagher became the company's fourth CEO in more than 75 years when he was named to the position in August 2004. Former CEO Larry Prince remained as chairman until early in 2005 when Gallagher was elected chairman; Prince remains on the board. Also during 2005 the company acquired a 25% interest in Altrom Canada Corp.

GPC subsidiary Motion Industries in mid-2006 acquired Lewis Supply Co. a provider of casters cutting tools machinery accessories and other general mill supplies. In October the company merged HorizonUSA Data Supplies previously a wholly owned subsidiary of S.P. Richards into S.P. Richards.

In early 2008 the company sold its Johnson Industries subsidiary which provided automotive supplies to fleets and new car dealers. In October GPC's S.P. Richards unit acquired ActionEmco's business assets in the midwestern US including its Grand Rapids Michigan distribution center. Also that year Motion Industries acquired Texas-based Drago Supply Company Mill Supply Corp. and Monroe Rubber and Plastic Supply.

In 2009 GPC added eight companies to its industrial and automotive operations for about $70 million and snapped up the remaining 11% interest in Balkamp that it did not already control for some $60 million making it a wholly owned subsidiary. These deals compare to a broader acquisition strategy in 2008 which added a dozen companies to all four of GPC's business segments (automotive industrial office products and electrical and electronic) for nearly $135 million.

Also in 2010 it acquired Canada's BC Bearing a distributor of bearing and power transmission components.

In late 2013 Motion acquired AST Bearings an industrial distributor specializing in high-precision miniature and specialty bearing with locations in New Jersey and California as well as Paragon Service & Supply (PS&S) of Lima Ohio. PS&S distributes industrial cutting tools abrasives and metalworking equipment.

In 2013 GPC acquired the remaining 70% of Melbourne-based Exego Group for approximately $800 million. (In January 2012 it purchased a 30% share in the company for around $150 million in cash). Exego an aftermarket distributor of automotive replacement parts and accessories has about 430 stores across Australia and New Zealand. The Exego stake allows GPC an entry point into Asia.

In 2012 GPC bought rival auto parts distributor Quaker City Motor Parts Co. for $343 million and thus became the only member of NAPA. Delaware-based Quaker was a long-standing NAPA distributor with annual sales of about $300 million and some 270 auto parts stores.

EXECUTIVES

Svp Finance And Corporate Secretary, Carol B. Yancey, age 57, $507,500 total compensation

Svp Human Resources, James R. (Jim) Neill, age 58, $319,000 total compensation

President And Ceo, Paul D. Donahue, age 64, $840,000 total compensation

President And Coo U.s. Automotive Parts Group, Lee A. Maher, $489,670 total compensation

President And Ceo Motion Industries, Timothy P. (Tim) Breen, age 59, $456,000 total compensation

Vice President And Corporate Controller, David Haskett

Executive Vice President Global Procurement S.p. Richards Company, Steven Lynn

Vice President Southeast Division S.p. Richards Company, Lester Christian

Svp Hr U.s. Automotive Parts Group, Todd Helms

Vice President Sales S.p. Richards Company, John Burgess

Vice President Organizational Development U.s. Automotive Parts Group, J Michael Phillips

Vice President Real Estate And Construction, Karl Koenig

Group Svp, Kevin Herron

Senior Vice President Of Human Resources, Jim R Neill

Vp Sales And Marketing Rayloc, Scott Rolf

Vice President Retail, Cameron Richardson

Vice President Integrated Business Solutions U.s. Automotive Parts Group, Jett Kuntz

Vice President Employee Relations, Vickie Smith

Vice President Western Division, Thomas Skov

Vice President Customer Relations And Sales, Stephen Yancey

Senior Vice President Human Resources S.p. Richards Company, G Henry Martin

Senior Vice President Logistics And Operations Eis, William Knight

Senior Vice President Finance And Supply Chain Rayloc, Michael Gaffney

Evp And Coo Eis, Matthew C Tyser

Senior Vice President Planning And Acquisition, Treg Brown

Executive Vice President Auto Parts Division Napa Canada Uap Inc., John Buckley

Vice President Product Development Napa Canada Uac Inc., Thomas Hunt

Vice President Distribution And Logistics Napa Canada Uap Inc., Mark Miron

Senior Vice President Marketing Distribution And Purchasing Motion Industries, Randall Breaux

Senior Vice President Hose And Rubber Shops And Service Centers Motion Industries, Anthony Cefalu

Vice President Of Safety And Industrial Of Motion Industries, Frederick Cowie

Vice President Business Systems Motion Industries, M Keith Knight

Vice President Operations Motion Industries, N Joe Limbaugh

Vice President Government Sales And Export Motion Industries, C Jeff Rouse

Vice President Of Supply Chain Of S.p. Richards Company, Dennis Flynn

Senior Vice President Of Merchandising Of S.p. Richards Company, John Reagan

Vice President Sales Emerging Markets S.p. Richards Company, Jason Smith

Vice President Sales S.p. Richards Company, Thomas Testa

Vice President Cleaning And Breakroom Supply S.p. Richards Company, Chris Whiting

Senior Vice President Sales And Marketing S.p. Richards Company, Bryan Wight

Vice President Western Division S.p. Richards Company, Gregory Nissen

Vice President Northeast Division S.p. Richards Company, Ray Sreca

Vice President Midwest Division U.s. Automotive Parts Group, Dennis Gibbs

Executive Vice President Finance And Administration Napa Canada Uap, Frank Pipito

Vice President Sales And Marketing Napa Canada Uap, Simon Weller

Senior Vice President Marketing Eis, David Brower

Senior Vice President And Group Executive Central Motion Industries, James Randazzo

Vice President Ecommerce And Marketing Services S.p. Richards Company, Paul Gatens

Vice President Sales S.p. Richards Company, A Gaius Gough

Vice President Emerging Products And Services S.p. Richards Company, Manning Lomax

Vice President Human Resources U.s. Automotive Parts Group, Thu-Quyen Clifton

Vice President Marketing And Category Management, Matthew LeTexier

Vice President Traction Heavy Vehicle Parts, Charles Stille

Executive Vice President Heavy Vehicle Parts Division Napa Canada Uap, Pierre Rachiele

Vice President Heavy Vehicle Operations, Simon Bourque

Vice President Accounting Napa Canada Uap Inc, Martin Brisebois

Vice President Corporate Planning And Strategic Development Napa Canada Uap, Francois Cadoret

Vice President Paint Body And Equipment, Eric Levielle

Vice President Napa Store Operations Napa Canada Uap, Michel Pomerleau

Senior Vice President Marketing And Distribution Eis, Ronald Harris

Vice President Human Resources S.p. Richards Company, James Starr

Vice President Operational Excellence S.p. Richards Company, Richard Weeks

Assistant Vice President Financial Analysis, Christine Powell

Vice President Supply Chain And Logistics U.s. Automotive Parts Group, J Richard Borman

Vice President Major Accounts U.s. Automotive Parts Group, Dennis Tolivar

Executive Vice President Global Procurement, Scott LeProhon

Group Senior Vice President U.s. Automotive Parts Group, M Todd McMurtrie

Vice President Benefits And Communication, Lisa Hamilton

Vice President Wholesale Product Management U.s. Automotive Parts Group, Byron Frantz

Assistant Vice President And Mortgage Production Branch Operations Manager, Dave Lloyd

Vice President Supply Chain, J Scott Mosteller

Vice President Finance Motion Industries, J Marvin Marvin Walker

Senior Vice President Of Finance And Chief Financial Officer Of S.p. Richards Company, J Phillip Welch

Senior Vice President Human Resources Napa Canada Uap Inc, Marie Claire Dupuis

Vice President Product Management Heavy Vehicle Parts Division, Marc Phillipe Beaudoin

Vice President Franchise Administration, Goscinskit Henry

Senior Vice President Digital, Rob Milstead

Vice President Southern Division U.s. Automotive Parts Group, Patrick Wolfe

Senior Vice President Operations And Logistics S.p. Richards Company, E Chadwick Lee

Vice President Compensation, Phillip Johnson

Senior Vice President Sales U.s. Automotive Parts Group, Daniel Askey

Vice President Information Services Rayloc, Joseph Lashley

Vice President Finance And Treasurer Balkamp Inc., Mary Knudsen

Vice President Napa Tools And Equipment Sales U.s. Automotive Parts Group, David Nicki

Vice President Retail Product Management And Merchandising U.s. Automotive Parts Group, Michael Briggs

Senior Vice President Human Resources And Communications Uap Inc., Caroline Tremblay

Vice President Supply Chain Management, Rick Spong

Chairman, Thomas C. (Tom) Gallagher, age 73

Board Member, Elizabeth Camp

Board Member, Gary Fayard

Board Member, John Johns

Board Member, Robert Loudermilk

Board Member, Wendy Needham

Board Member, John Holder

Board Member, Donna Hyland

Board Member, P Russell Hardin

Auditors: Ernst & Young LLP

LOCATIONS

HQ: Genuine Parts Co.
2999 Wildwood Parkway, Atlanta, GA 30339
Phone: 678 934-5000
Web: www.genpt.com

2018 Sales

	$ mil.	% of total
US	13,927	74
Europe	1,624	10
Canada	1,624	9
Australasia	1,193	6
Mexico	129	1
Total	**18,735**	**100**

PRODUCTS/OPERATIONS

2018 Sales

	$ mil.	% of total
Automotive	10,526	56
Industrial	6,298	34
Office products	1,910	10
Total	**18,735**	**100**

Selected Operations

Automotive Parts Group
  Altrom Canada Corp. (distribution of import automotive parts Canada)
  Balkamp (majority-owned subsidiary; distribution of replacement parts and accessories for cars heavy-duty vehicles motorcycles and farm equipment)
  Grupo Auto Todo S.A. de C.V. (Mexico)
  UAP Inc. (auto parts distribution Canada)
Electrical/Electronic Materials Group
  EIS Inc. (products for electrical and electronic equipment including adhesives copper foil and thermal management materials)
Industrial Parts Group
  Motion Industries (Canada) Inc.
  Motion Industries Inc.
Office Products Group
  S.P. Richards Company

COMPETITORS

Advance Auto Parts	General Parts
Applied Industrial Technologies	Gould Paper
Arrow Electronics	Graybar Electric
AutoZone	Hahn Automotive
Avnet	Ingersoll-Rand
CARQUEST	Kaman Industrial Technologies
Coast Distribution	MSC Industrial Direct
Cole Office Products	O'Reilly Automotive

Complete Office	Office Depot
D & H Distributing	Pep Boys
Essendant	Staples
Ford Motor	W.W. Grainger
General Motors	

HISTORICAL FINANCIALS

Company Type: Public

Income Statement
FYE: December 31

	REVENUE ($ mil.)	NET INCOME ($ mil.)	NET PROFIT MARGIN	EMPLOYEES
12/19	19,392	621	3.2%	55,000
12/18	18,735	810	4.3%	50,000
12/17	16,308	616	3.8%	48,000
12/16	15,339	687	4.5%	40,000
12/15	15,280	705	4.6%	39,600
Annual Growth	6.1%	(3.1%)	—	8.6%

2019 Year-End Financials

Debt ratio: 23.39%	No. of shares (mil.): 145
Return on equity: 17.43%	Dividends
Cash ($ mil.): 276	Yield: 2.8%
Current ratio: 1.24	Payout: 55.9%
Long-term debt ($ mil.): 2,802	Market value ($ mil.): 15,444

	STOCK PRICE ($) FY Close	P/E High/Low	PER SHARE ($) Earnings	Dividends	Book Value
12/19	106.23	27 21	4.24	3.05	25.28
12/18	96.02	19 16	5.50	2.88	23.64
12/17	95.01	24 19	4.18	2.70	23.27
12/16	95.54	23 17	4.59	2.63	21.52
12/15	85.89	23 17	4.63	2.46	20.97
Annual Growth	5.5%	— —	(2.2%)	5.5%	4.8%

Genworth Financial, Inc. (Holding Co)

Insurance and investment specialist Genworth Financial specializes in life insurance long-term care and retirement investments in the US market. Internationally Genworth offers mortgage insurance and other payment protection products. The firm also provides private residential mortgage insurance in the US. Traditionally Genworth has focused its retirement investment products including fixed annuities However facing declines in its core lines of business the company has suspended most sales of its long-term care life insurance and fixed annuity products. Chinese conglomerate China Oceanwide Holdings is buying Genworth for $2.7 billion.

Change in Company Type

In 2020 Genworth Financial Inc. moving forward and with plans to address its near-term liabilities and financial obligations and maximize shareholder value while China Oceanwide Holdings Group Co. Ltd. (Oceanwide) finalizes its funding plan for the acquisition of Genworth. Genworth and Oceanwide also announced that they have agreed to a 15th waiver and agreement of each party's right to terminate the previously announced merger agreement. The 15th waiver extends the previous deadline of June 30 2020 to no later than September 30 2020.

The extension gives Oceanwide additional time to finalize the financing for the transaction purchase price of $5.43 per share which may include

debt funding of up to $1.8 billion through Hony Capital and/or other third parties. Oceanwide has indicated that the financing has been delayed due to the COVID-19 pandemic and uncertain macroeconomic conditions.

Operations

Genworth operates in four segments: US Life Insurance US Mortgage Insurance Australia Mortgage Insurance and Runoff.

The US Life Insurance segment is Genworth's largest unit bringing in some 75% of total revenue. It provides long-term coverage products and services traditional life insurance policies and fixed annuity products in the US. However the company has suspended sales of all three types of products.

The two mortgage insurance segments primarily offer prime mortgage insurance coverage for individually underwritten loans; they also offer selective bulk mortgage insurance. The runoff segment managed products that are no longer actively marketed including variable annuity variable life and corporate-owned life policies.

Geographic Reach

While US operations account for around 90% of revenues Genworth's international operations include significant mortgage insurance businesses in Australia and Mexico. The firm is looking to expand its mortgage insurance operations into emerging markets. For example it has a minority stake in a joint venture in India.

Genworth financial headquarter is located in Richmond Virginia.

Sales and Marketing

Genworth's products are sold through direct sales brokerage general agencies and independent marketing organizations as well as by banks and financial advisors.

The company markets its mortgage products to financial groups and mortgage lenders that require mortgage insurance for customer financing. It has a field sales force throughout the US and a telephone sales force that primarily works with smaller lenders. Genworth also has a call center to support all customer segments.

Financial Performance

Genworth's revenue was on a downward trend until 2018 when the company had a slight recovery. And after three years in the black the company became profitable again in 2017.

In 2019 revenue increased 2% to $8.1 billion. Premium income rose 13% that year and net investment also rose 3% that same year.

Net income jumped 188% to $343 million in 2019 due to a decline in operating expenses and helped by modest growth in revenue.

The company ended 2019 with $3.3 billion in net cash about $1.2 billion more than it had at the end of 2018. Operating activities provided $2.1 billion in cash while investing activities provided another $1.3 billion. Investing activities used $2.2 billion that year.

Strategy

Genworth is focused on improving business performance addressing financial leverage and increasing financial and strategic flexibility across the organization. Its strategy includes maximizing its opportunities in its mortgage insurance businesses and stabilizing U.S. life insurance businesses.

The company's primary investment objective is to meet its obligations to policyholders and contract holders while increasing value to its stockholders by investing in a diversified high quality portfolio comprised primarily of income producing securities and other assets. Genworth's investment strategy focuses on: Managing interest rate risk as appropriate through monitoring asset durations relative to policyholder and contract holder obligations; Selecting assets based on fundamental research-driven strategies; Emphasizing fixed-in-

come low-volatility assets while pursuing active strategies to enhance yield; Maintaining sufficient liquidity to meet unexpected financial obligations; Regularly evaluating our asset class mix and pursuing additional investment classes when prudent; and Continuously monitoring asset quality and market conditions that could affect our assets.

Company Background

Genworth Financial traces its roots back to 1871 when it was founded as The Life Insurance Company of Virginia. The company was acquired by General Electric in 1996. GE combined a number of insurance businesses under the Genworth name and spun the unit off in a 2004 IPO.

HISTORY

The company was formed in 2004 to acquire certain insurance and financial services business from General Electric (GE). GE retained a controlling stake in Genworth Financial after its stock offering but sold its remaining stake in 2006.

During the downturn in the US housing market (starting in 2008) the company faced losses in its US mortgage insurance segment. After considering divestitures Genworth instead simply yanked hard on those operations making its underwriting criteria more stringent and restricting new business. The company also conducted extensive restructuring programs including a 15% workforce reduction in 2009 and a de-risking of its investment portfolio to recover from the economic downturn. Nonetheless the company saw income and cash flow losses during those years as a result of poor returns on investments.

In 2009 the company launched an IPO of its Canadian mortgage insurance business.

In late 2010 Genworth expanded its asset management operations with the purchase of hedge fund and managed futures producer Altegris Capital. The purchase brought in alternative investments and $2.2 billion in assets under management.

Despite steady growth in the sales of its Medicare supplemental products in 2011 the company sold the block of products (held by the former Continental Life Insurance Company unit) to Aetna for $290 million. In addition in 2011 the company stopped offering mortgage insurance policies in New Zealand.

EXECUTIVES

Svp And Cfo Genworth Mi Canada, Philip Mayers
President And Ceo, Thomas J. (Tom) McInerney, age 64, $996,804 total compensation
President And Ceo Us Mortgage Insurance, Rohit Gupta
Evp Human Resources, Michael S. Laming, age 69, $491,692 total compensation
Evp And Chief Strategy Officer, Scott J. McKay, age 59
Evp And Coo, Kevin D. Schneider, age 58, $722,683 total compensation
President And Ceo Genworth Mortgage Insurance Canada, Stuart Levings
President And Ceo U.s. Life Insurance, David OÂ'Leary
Evp And Chief Investment Officer, Daniel J. (Dan) Sheehan, age 54, $598,083 total compensation
Evp And Chief Risk Officer, Lori M. Evangel, age 57, $455,271 total compensation
Evp And General Counsel, Ward E. Bobitz, age 55, $423,642 total compensation
Evp And Cfo, Kelly L. Groh, age 51, $538,657 total compensation
President And Ceo Genworth Mortgage Insurance Australia, Georgette C. Nicholas
Senior Vice President, Roger Levy

Svp Hr Global Mortage Insurance And U.s. Life Insurance, Simon Bartle
National Account Manager, Lea Fosz
Senior Vice President Audit, Derek Venable
Vice President Talent Acquisition And Global Staffing Services, Chris Jordan
Senior Vice President Corporate Development, Charles Taben
Vice President And Associate General Cnsl, Arthur O'Connor
Assistant Vice President Finance, Beth Adcock
Regional Vice President, Erin Kirkeeng
Vice President International Government Relations, Scott Quesenberry
Vice President Accounting Policy, Mitch Rosen
Regional Vice President, Maureen Doherty
Senior Vice President Of Sales, Matthew Young
Regional Vice President, Bridget Collins
Senior Vice President, Peter Hurst
Vice President National Account Manager, Carmen Richardson
Associate Vice President And Actuary, Vanesa Barbera
Regional Sales Vice President, Chuck Breen
Vice President And Associate General Counsel, David Dodd
Vice President Of Asset And Liability Management, Robert Causey
Svp And Chief Risk Officer Investments, Benjamin Perlman
Svp And Chief Commercial Officer U.s. Life Insurance, Larry Nisenson
Vice President Marketing And Communications, Susan Carter
Divisional Vice President, Stan J Mensing
Vice President Products And Services Marketing, Miller Tammy
Assistant Vice President And Actuary Life Insurance Experience Studies, Mike Krugel
Vice President, Angela Daniel
Vice President Corporate Accounts, David Stagnitti
Medical Director, James Wright
Vice President Reinsurance Operations, Mark Holbrook
Vp Of Operations, Duncan Hall
Svp Chief Risk Officer For Us Mortgage Insurance, Mike Derstine
Vice President International Financial Planning And Analysis, Tim Knieriem
Vice President, Saul Goodman
Vice President U S Benefits, Matthew Turner
Pharmacy Manager, Eto Joshua
Evp Human Resources, Pam Harrison
Vice President Long Term Care Claims, Leo Savino
Senior Vice President Product Management, Vincent Bodnar
Vice President Corporate Systems, Jp Raffenot
Vice President Government Relations, Kris Barnier
Chairman, James S. (Jim) Riepe, age 77
Assistant Secretary And Senior Paralegal, Theresa Myers
Board Member, Susan Conrad
Board Member, Greg Moloney
Board Member, Robert Restrepo
Auditors: KPMG LLP

LOCATIONS

HQ: Genworth Financial, Inc. (Holding Co)
6620 West Broad Street, Richmond, VA 23230
Phone: 804 281-6000
Web: www.genworth.com

2018 Sales

	$ mil.	% of total
US	7,466	89
Canada	526	6
Australia	526	5
Other countries	9	5
Total	8,430	100

PRODUCTS/OPERATIONS

2018 Sales by Segment

	$ mil.	% of total
US Life	6,318	75
US Mortgage Insurance	841	10
Canada Mortgage Insurance	526	8
Australia Mortgage Insurance	440	5
Run-off	294	4
Corporate & other	24	
Total	8,430	100

2018 Sales

	$ mil.	% of total
Premiums	4,519	53
Net investment income	3,262	38
Net investment losses	(146)	-
Policy fees & and other income	795	9
Total	8,430	100

Selected Products and Services

Fixed annuities
Life insurance
Long-term care insurance
Mortgage
Retirement solutions
Wealth management solutions

COMPETITORS

AEGON USA
AIG
MGIC Investment
MassMutual
New York Life
PMI Group
Radian Group
US Department of Veterans Affairs

HISTORICAL FINANCIALS

Company Type: Public

Income Statement
FYE: December 31

	ASSETS ($ mil.)	NET INCOME ($ mil.)	INCOME AS % OF ASSETS	EMPLOYEES
12/19	101,342	343	0.3%	3,100
12/18	100,923	119	0.1%	3,500
12/17	105,297	817	0.8%	3,500
12/16	104,658	(277)	—	3,400
12/15	106,431	(615)	—	4,100
Annual Growth	(1.2%)	—	—	(6.8%)

2019 Year-End Financials

Debt ratio: 3.54%
Return on equity: 2.58%
Cash ($ mil.): 3,341
Current ratio: —
Long-term debt ($ mil.): —

No. of shares (mil.): 504
Dividends
Yield: —
Payout: —
Market value ($ mil.): 2,218

	STOCK PRICE ($) FY Close	P/E High/Low		Earnings	Dividends	Book Value
12/19	4.40	7	4	0.67	0.00	28.14
12/18	4.66	20	11	0.24	0.00	24.85
12/17	3.11	3	2	1.63	0.00	26.89
12/16	3.81	—	—	(0.56)	0.00	25.39
12/15	3.73	—	—	(1.24)	0.00	25.75
Annual Growth	4.2%	—	—	—	—	2.2%

GEORGIA HOUSING FINANCE AUTHORITY

EXECUTIVES

Exec Dir, Carmen Chubb
Principal*, Marcia Paul
Attrny, Julie Livingston
Manager, Sally Adams
Deputy Director, Kirby Davis
Operations Executive, Robert Rego
Information Technology Team ME, Michael Landrum
Auditors: REZNICK GROUP PC ATLANTA

LOCATIONS

HQ: GEORGIA HOUSING FINANCE AUTHORITY
60 EXECUTIVE PK S NE FL 2, ATLANTA, GA 303292257
Phone: 404 679-4840

HISTORICAL FINANCIALS

Company Type: Private

Income Statement
FYE: June 30

	ASSETS ($ mil.)	NET INCOME ($ mil.)	INCOME AS % OF ASSETS	EMPLOYEES
06/19	2,589	26	1.0%	196
06/09	1,318	17	1.3%	—
06/08	1,289	7	0.6%	—
06/07	1,201	9	0.8%	—
Annual Growth	6.6%	8.4%	—	—

Georgia Power Co

Georgia Power is the largest subsidiary of US utility holding company Southern Company. The regulated utility provides electricity to about 2.6 million residential commercial and industrial customers throughout most of Georgia. It has interests in about 10 gas/oil nearly 15 solar one nuclear and over 15 hydroelectric power plants that give it about 14400 MW of generating capacity. Georgia Power sells wholesale electricity to several cooperatives and municipalities in the region. The utility also offers energy efficiency.

Operations

Georgia Power generates purchases transmits distributes and sells electricity in Georgia. It generates power from coal and natural gas as well as from renewable sources such as solar hydroelectric and wind.

In 2019 the company purchased some 390 kilowatt hours of power from other providers.

On the financing front the company invests in domestic equity international equity fixed income trust-owned life insurance special situations real estate investments and private equity.

Geographic Reach

The company serves retail customers in Georgia (headquarters). It also sells power to wholesale customers across the US Southeast. Georgia Power provides electric service to customers in some 155 of the state's almost 160 counties.

Sales and Marketing

The company serves a total of about 2.6 million customers of which 2.3 million are residential about 315330 are commercial over 10620 are industrial and about 9820 are others.

About 40% of sales came from residential customers around 35% accounts from commercial customers industrial with some 15% and less than 5% from wholesale.

Financial Performance

Georgia Power has maintained its revenues in the $8.3 billion to $8.4 billion range for the past five years. Meanwhile net income has been inconsistent for the past five years recording its highest in 2019 and its lowest in 2018.

Revenue in 2019 remained in the similar level with 2018 as retail and wholesale revenues decreased offset by an increase in other revenues.

Net income increased from $793 million in 2018 to $1.7 billion in 2019.

Cash and cash equivalents at the end of the year were $52 million a 53% decrease from $112 million in 2018. Cash provided by operations was $2.9 billion. Investing activities used $3.9 billion primarily for property additions while financing activities provided $918 million primarily from senior notes and FFB Loan.

Strategy

Georgia Power has agreements with Southern Nuclear under which Southern Nuclear renders the following nuclear-related services at cost: general executive and advisory services; general operations management and technical services; administrative services including procurement accounting employee relations systems and procedures services; strategic planning and budgeting services; other services with respect to business and operations; and for Georgia Power construction management. These costs are primarily included in other operations and maintenance expenses or capitalized to property plant and equipment. Costs for these services in 2019 2018 and 2017 amounted to $760 million $780 million and $675 million respectively.

Company Background

The company was founded in 1927.

EXECUTIVES

Evp Cfo Treasurer And Comptroller, W. Ron Hinson, age 63

Evp And Chief Production Officer Southern Company Generation, Theodore J. (Ted) McCullough, age 57

Chairman President And Ceo, Paul Bowers

Svp Marketing, Kenny Coleman

Evp External Affairs, Chris Cummiskey

Evp Customer Service And Operations, Pedro Cherry

Vice President And Senior Production Officer Gulf Power, Michael Burroughs

Region Vice President, Cathy Hill

Vice President Of Corporate Communi, Jason Cuevas

Executive Vice President, Larry Westbrook

Senior Vice President Human Resources, Leonard Owens

Executive Vice President External Affairs, Craig Barrs

Vice President Administrative Services, Brian Ivey

Sr. Vice President External Affairs, William Barrs

Executive Vice President; President External Affairs, Chris Womack

Executive Vice President Nuclear Development, Joe Miller

Vice President Comptroller, David Poroch

Vice President Customer Services, Kevin Kastner

Vice Chairman, Dan Burer

Secretary, Rick Perry

Auditors: DELOITTE & TOUCHE LLP

LOCATIONS

HQ: Georgia Power Co
241 Ralph McGill Boulevard, N.E., Atlanta, GA 30308
Phone: 404 506-6526
Web: www.georgiapower.com

PRODUCTS/OPERATIONS

Selected Services

Residential Customers
My Account
Pay My Bill
Turn On/Off Power
Payment Arrangements
Paperless Billing
Budget Billing
Prices/Rate
Save Money and Energy
Energy Audits
Money-Saving Tips
Rebates & Incentives
Electric Vehicles
Products & Programs
Water Heaters
Heat Pumps
Lighting
Power Credit
Green Energy
Smart Meter
Multifamily
Business Customers
My Account
Pay My Bill
Turn On/Off Power
Budget Billing
Prices/Rates
Save Money and Energy
Energy Audits
Money-Saving Tips
Rebates & Incentives
Electric Vehicles
Programs & Services
Water Heaters
Heat Pumps
Outdoor Lighting
Electric Cooking
Forklifts
Green Energy
Smart Meter
Energydirect

2016 Sales

	$ mil.	% of total
Retail		
Residential	3,318	40
Commercial	3,077	37
Industrial	1,291	15
Other retail	86	1
Wholesale	217	2
Other	394	5
Total	**8,383**	**100**

COMPETITORS

Atmos Energy	Progress Energy
Duke Energy Progress Inc.	SCANA
	Sawnee EMC
Energen	South Carolina
Entergy	Electric & Gas
Flint Energies	Southern Company Gas
MEAG Power	TECO Energy
Oglethorpe Power	Walton EMC

HISTORICAL FINANCIALS

Company Type: Public

Income Statement

FYE: December 31

	REVENUE ($ mil.)	NET INCOME ($ mil.)	NET PROFIT MARGIN	EMPLOYEES
12/19	8,408	1,720	20.5%	6,938
12/18	8,420	793	9.4%	6,967
12/17	8,310	1,428	17.2%	6,986
12/16	8,383	1,347	16.1%	7,527
12/15	8,326	1,277	15.3%	7,989
Annual Growth	0.2%	7.7%	—	(3.5%)

2019 Year-End Financials

Debt ratio: 27.35%	No. of shares (mil.): 9
Return on equity: 11.71%	Dividends
Cash ($ mil.): 52	Yield: —
Current ratio: 0.60	Payout: 91.6%
Long-term debt ($ mil.): 10,791	Market value ($ mil.): —

German American Bancorp Inc

German American Bancorp is the holding company for German American Bank which operates some 65 branches in southern Indiana and Kentucky. Founded in 1910 the bank offers such standard retail products as checking and savings accounts certificates of deposit and IRAs. It also provides trust services while sister company German American Investment Services provides trust investment advisory and brokerage services. German American Bancorp also owns German American Insurance which offers corporate and personal insurance products. The group's core banking operations provide more than 90% of its total sales.

Geographic Reach

German American is headquartered in Jasper Indiana. Its subsidiaries operate from more than 60 locations in southern Indiana and Kentucky.

Sales and Marketing

German American Bancorp spent $3.5 million on advertising in 2017. Advertising expenses totaled $2.7 million in 2016 and $3.7 million in 2015.

Financial Performance

German American's revenue has been climbing steadily for the past five years thanks to the company's acquisitions of other area banks. Similarly net income has also been on the rise. In 2017 the company marked its eighth consecutive year of record earnings.

In 2017 revenue increased 4% to $131.8 million. That increase was partially due to the addition of River Valley Financial Bank which German American acquired in 2016. Growth in the company's loan portfolio also boosted net interest income. This was slightly offset by a 1% decline in non-interest income. Although trust and insurance operations rose other operating income declined $1.1 million (29%).

Net income rose 16% to $35.2 million in 2017; in addition to having higher revenue the company recognized a benefit related to the reduced corporate tax rate that year.

German American ended 2017 with $70.4 million in net cash $5.5 million more than it had at the end of 2016. Operating activities provided $54.9 million in cash and financing activities provided $139.9 million. Investing activities used $189.3 million.

Strategy

German American Bancorp has grown recently through a number of acquisitions including bank branches an insurance office and other bank holding companies. These acquisitions have also helped the company grow into new geographic markets including locations in Kentucky.

Growth by acquisition can be somewhat risky though. The company could unknowingly acquire problem assets or have difficulties integrating other banks it purchases. These issues could bring down its financial performance.

German American operates in a relatively small region which leaves it vulnerable to economic downturns in that area. If economic conditions in its market decline German American faces the risk of increased delinquencies and charge-offs. The company's larger more widespread competitors would be less impacted in such a case.

Mergers and Acquisitions

German American Bancorp agreed to acquire Citizens First in early 2019 in a cash-and-stock transaction valued at about $70 million. German American will gain Citizens' branch offices in the Barren Hart Simpson and Warren counties of Kentucky. Citizens has about $475 million in assets loans of some $375 million and deposits of around $390 million.

In October 2018 German American Bancorp acquired Kentucky's First Security Bank for $101 million. With that deal the company expanded into Kentucky's Owensboro Bowling Green and Lexington markets.

EXECUTIVES

Vice President, Lisa Matheis

General Technical; Senior Vice President, Floyd Alsman

Chairman And Ceo, Mark A. Schroeder, age 67, $342,500 total compensation

President, Clay W. Ewing, age 65, $250,000 total compensation

Evp Cfo And Senior Administrative Officer, Bradley M. Rust, age 54, $210,000 total compensation

Svp And Chief Credit Officer, Keith A. Leinenbach, age 61, $180,000 total compensation

Svp And Head Of Retail Banking, Randall L. Braun, age 60, $180,000 total compensation

Vice President Deposit Services Secruity, Dale Altstadt

Senior Vice President Of Technology And Operations, Clay Barrett

Senior Vice President Commercial Banking, Joe Hauersperger

Vice President, Christina Lebeau

Vice President Private Banking, Sherri Alley

Vice President Region Commercial Banker, Rodney Russell

Vice President, Ashley McCreary

Vice President Commercial Banking, Rob Bingham

Vice President Commercial Banking, John Newcomer

Vice President, Eric Kehl

Senior Vice President Retail Banking, Brock Goggins

Senior Vice President Senior Wealth Advisor, Alan VanCleef

Regional Senior Vice President, Steve Walker

Auditors: Crowe LLP

LOCATIONS

HQ: German American Bancorp Inc
711 Main Street, Jasper, IN 47546
Phone: 812 482-1314
Web: www.germanamerican.com

PRODUCTS/OPERATIONS

2017 Sales

	$ mil.	% of total
Interest		
Loans including fees	91	64
Securities including dividends	19	13
Short-term investments	0	-
Non-interest		
Insurance	8	6
Service charges on deposit accounts	6	4
Trust & investment product fees	5	4
Other	12	9
Adjustments	(11.1)	-
Total	131	100

COMPETITORS

Fidelity Federal	Home Financial Bancorp
Fifth Third	Old National Bancorp
First Bancorp of Indiana	Porter Bancorp
First Capital	SVB&T

HISTORICAL FINANCIALS

Company Type: Public

Income Statement

FYE: December 31

	ASSETS ($ mil.)	NET INCOME ($ mil.)	INCOME AS % OF ASSETS	EMPLOYEES
12/19	4,397	59	1.3%	817
12/18	3,929	46	1.2%	738
12/17	3,144	40	1.3%	614
12/16	2,955	35	1.2%	597
12/15	2,373	30	1.3%	596
Annual Growth	16.7%	18.5%	—	8.2%

2019 Year-End Financials

Debt ratio: 1.33%	No. of shares (mil.): 26
Return on equity: 11.47%	Dividends
Cash ($ mil.): 105	Yield: 1.9%
Current ratio: —	Payout: 31.7%
Long-term debt ($ mil.): —	Market value ($ mil.): 950

	STOCK PRICE ($) FY Close	P/E High/Low	PER SHARE ($) Earnings	Dividends	Book Value
12/19	35.62	16 12	2.29	0.68	21.51
12/18	27.77	19 13	1.99	0.60	18.37
12/17	35.33	30 17	1.77	0.52	15.90
12/16	52.61	34 19	1.57	0.48	14.43
12/15	33.32	23 18	1.51	0.45	12.67
Annual Growth	1.7%	— —	10.9%	10.7%	14.2%

GGP, INC.

Auditors: DELOITTE & TOUCHE LLP CHICAGO

LOCATIONS

HQ: GGP, INC.
350 N ORLEANS ST STE 300, CHICAGO, IL 606541607
Phone: 312 960-5000
Web: WWW.GGP.COM

COMPETITORS

CBL & Associates Properties	Prime Retail
DDR	Simon Property Group
Glimcher Realty	Tanger Factory Outlet
	Taubman Centers

JMB Realty	Trade Street
Kimco Realty	Residential
Lincoln Property	Vornado Realty
Macerich	Weingarten Realty

HISTORICAL FINANCIALS

Company Type: Private

Income Statement

FYE: December 31

	ASSETS ($ mil.)	NET INCOME ($ mil.)	INCOME AS % OF ASSETS	EMPLOYEES
12/12	27,282	(471)	—	1,500
12/11	29,518	(306)	—	—
12/10	32,367	(256)	—	—
12/09	28,149	(1,304)	—	—
Annual Growth	(1.0%)	—	—	—

Gilead Sciences Inc

Gilead Sciences has biotech balms for infectious diseases including hepatitis HIV and infections related to AIDS. The company's drug franchise includes Truvada an oral formulation indicated in combination with other antiretroviral agents for the treatment of HIV-1 infection in certain patients. The company co-promotes another HIV treatment called Atripla in the US and Europe with Bristol-Myers Squibb (BMS). Other products on the market include AmBisome used to treat systemic fungal infections such as those that accompany AIDS or kidney disease. Beyond HIV/AIDS Gilead also markets Hematology and Oncology medicines and the Yescarta CAR-T cell therapy for cancer. About three-quarters of its sales are in the US.

Operations

Gilead primarily focuses on discovering developing and commercializing innovative medicines in areas of unmet medical need producing treatments for HIV liver diseases including hepatitis B and hepatitis C and cancer. Its main source of revenue continues to be its antiviral franchise which accounts for about 75% of product sales and primarily consists of HIV medications. Biktarvy is Gilead's top-selling drug accounting for about 20% of sales.

Aside from the Atripla partnership with BMS Gilead has collaborations with other companies including Japan Tobacco which promotes HIV drugs.

Gilead continues to advance its R&D pipeline; the company had about 105 active clinical studies in 2019. It had more than 25 clinical trials in Phase III.

The company's portfolio of nearly 25 marketed products contains a number of firsts such as the first complete treatment regimens for HIV and chronic hepatitis.

Geographic Reach

Gilead relies on the US market for a significant portion of its revenue about 75%. Europe accounts for more than 15% of revenue while other international markets provide about 10%.

Gilead is based in Foster City California and it has R&D facilities in Emeryville Oceanside and Santa Monica California; Gaithersburg Maryland; Edmonton Canada Seattle Washington and Amsterdam Netherlands. It has manufacturing sites in California Canada and Ireland. The company's commercial operations are in approximately 35 countries around US and international.

Sales and Marketing

Gilead products are marketed through commercial teams and/or in conjunction with third-party distributors and corporate partners. The commercial teams promote products through direct field contact with physicians hospitals clinics and other healthcare providers. The company generally grant third-party distributors the exclusive right to promote the product in a territory for a specified period of time. Gilead sell and distribute its products in Europe and countries outside the United States where the product is approved either through commercial teams third-party distributors or corporate partners.

Three wholesale distributors — McKesson Cardinal Health and AmerisourceBergen — account for over 85% of Gilead's US sales.

Financial Performance

After peaking at $32.6 billion in 2015 Gilead's revenue dropped about a third to $21.1 billion in 2018 and recovered by about 1% in 2019.

Total revenues increased to $22.4 billion and total product sales increased to $22.1 billion in 2019 compared to $22.1 billion and $21.7 billion in 2018 respectively primarily due to higher sales of its HIV products partially offset by lower sales of Ranexa and Letairis and HCV products.

Net income of Gilead changed to $5.4 billion in 2019 compared to $5.5 billion in 2018 primarily due to pre-tax up-front collaboration and licensing expenses of $3.9 billion related to its collaboration with Galapagos partially offset by the net favorable fluctuation in tax effects of intra-entity intangible asset transfers to different tax jurisdictions and an increase in net unrealized gains from equity securities.

The company had $11.6 billion in cash and equivalents in 2019 compared to $17.9 billion in 2018. Operations generated $9.1 billion in 2019 while investing activities provided $7.8 billion and financing activities used $7.6 billion.

Strategy

Gilead's focus is to create possibilities for patients through scientific breakthroughs and innovation by leveraging pillars of a durable core business existing pipeline opportunities and strategy to drive additional growth. The company's strategy includes ambitions and priorities which enables the company to achieve those ambitions. The strategic ambitions define what success looks like over the next decade and are summarized as (i) bring 10+ transformative therapies to patients by 2030; (ii) be the biotech employer and partner of choice; and (iii) deliver shareholder value in a sustainable and responsible manner. Gileads's strategic priorities reflect how the company will deliver those ambitions: (i) expand internal and external innovation; (ii) strengthen portfolio strategy and decision making; (iii) increase patient benefit and access; and (iv) continue to evolve our culture.

In 2020 the company expects underlying growth in its base business which is expected to offset the full-year impact of cardiopulmonary products loss of exclusivity which occurred in 2019 and the initial generic version of Truvada in the United States in late 2020. The company will also continue to invest to support the growth of Biktarvy Descovy for PrEP launch preparation for competitive launches of filgotinib in RA in the United States Japan and Europe and continued investments in pipeline cell therapy and external partnerships. Gilead's overall plan is now guided by the newly established corporate strategy that provides focus and guides resource and capital allocation priorities. The company expect data read-outs in 2020 including filgotinib for ulcerative colitis KTE-X19 for acute lymphoblastic leukemia (ALL) axicabtagene ciloleucel CD19 for indolent B-cell non-Hodgkin lymphoma (iNHL) and second line diffuse large B-cell lymphoma and GLPG-1972 for os-

teoarthritis. To further augment the product pipeline the company continue to pursue opportunities for collaborations partnerships and strategic investments that fit into its long-term strategic plan.

Mergers and Acquisitions

In 2020 Gilead Sciences Inc. completed the previously announced transaction for Toro Merger Sub Inc. a wholly owned subsidiary of Gilead to acquire US-based Forty Seven Inc. for $95.50 per share net to the seller in cash without interest or approximately $4.9 billion in the aggregate. As a result of the completion of the merger Forty Seven has become a wholly owned subsidiary of Gilead and the common stock of Forty Seven will no longer be listed for trading on the Nasdaq Global Select Market.

Company Background

Dr. Michael Riordan started Gilead Sciences in 1987 backed by venture capital firm Menlo Ventures. The name was derived from the Biblical phrase "Is there no balm in Gilead?" In 1990 Glaxo Wellcome (now GlaxoSmithKline) agreed to fund Gilead's research into code-blocking treatments for cancer. Gilead went public in 1992.

HISTORY

Dr. Michael Riordan started Gilead Sciences in 1987 backed by venture capital firm Menlo Ventures. The name was derived from the Biblical phrase "Is there no balm in Gilead?" In 1990 Glaxo Wellcome (now GlaxoSmithKline) agreed to fund Gilead's research into code-blocking treatments for cancer. Gilead went public in 1992.

In 1994 the company formed an alliance with American Home Products' Storz Instruments (now part of Bausch & Lomb) to develop and market a topical treatment for an ophthalmic virus. Two years later Gilead joined forces with Roche to develop treatments for influenza.

Vistide was approved in the US in 1996 and in Europe in 1997. But more-effective HIV therapies brought declining demand for Vistide.

The company bounced back with Tamiflu (the fruit of its Roche partnership) which was approved in 1999. Sales were brisk during that flu season. Also that year Gilead expanded its pipeline and geographic reach with the $550 million all-stock acquisition of NeXstar Pharmaceuticals which focused on antifungals antibiotics and cancer treatments.

In 2000 Gilead sought approval for Tamiflu in Japan and Europe (it withdrew the European application after regulators there asked for more information) and also sought approval for pediatric uses for the drug which was granted. The following year it resubmitted Tamiflu for approval in Europe.

Chairman Donald Rumsfeld resigned in 2001 to become US secretary of defense and was replaced by retired Sears Roebuck executive James Denny. Perhaps the Defense connection helped: Vistide became one of the many drugs that researchers began studying as possible alternatives to vaccines should a smallpox bio-attack occur in the US.

EXECUTIVES

Evp Pharmaceutical Development And Manufacturing, Taiyin Yang, age 66
Evp Research, William A. Lee, age 64, $363,333 total compensation
Evp Research And Development And Chief Scientific Officer, Norbert W. Bischofberger, age 64, $1,044,231 total compensation
President And Ceo, John F. Milligan, age 59, $1,465,385 total compensation
Coo, Kevin Young, $787,645 total compensation

Evp And Cfo, Robin L. Washington, age 57, $900,385 total compensation
Evp Commercial And Access Operations (asia Latin America And Africa) And Corporate And Medical Affairs, Gregg H. Alton, age 54, $925,385 total compensation
Evp Clinical Research And Development Operations, Andrew Cheng
Evp Clinical Research, John G. McHutchison
Evp Strategy, Martin B. Silverstein, age 65
Evp And General Counsel, Brett Pletcher
Evp Human Resources, Katie L. Watson
Senior Medical Director, Belinda Jump
Vice President Commercial Operations, Clifford Samuel
Vice President Of U S Marketing And Sales, Jean Kress
V P Risk Management, Marti Dodson
Vice President Information Technology, Mark Hill
Senior Vice President Public Affairs, Amy Flood
Vice President Information Systems, Michael Louie
Vice President Project And Portfolio Managment, Laura Lehman
Vice President Public Affairs, Sonia Choi
Vp Corp Legal, Jason Okazaki
National Sales Manager Oncology, Boyd Marianna
Vice President Director Of Information Technology Risk Management, Ramulu Badam
Executive Vice President Corporate Development And Strategy, Andrew Dickinson
Medical Director, Beatrix Bartok
Vice President Human Resources, Matt Hostetler
Evp Of Worldwide Commercial Operations, Laura Hamill
Vice President Corporate Development, Jeremy Bender
Vp Oncology Therapeutics, Pankaj Bhargava
Vice President Of Regional Sales, Ashwin Mathur
Vice President Human Resources, Jyoti Mehra
Vice President Tax, Terilea Wielenga
Vice President Government Affairs And Policy, Michael Boyd
Vice President Clinical Development, Roger Sidhu
Chairman, John C. Martin, age 68
Board Member, Nicholas G Moore
Treasurer, Brad Vollmer
Auditors: Ernst & Young LLP

LOCATIONS

HQ: Gilead Sciences Inc
  333 Lakeside Drive, Foster City, CA 94404
Phone: 650 574-3000
Web: www.gilead.com

2018 Sales

	$ mil.	% of total
US	16,269	74
Europe	4,006	18
Other International	1,852	8
Total	**30,390**	**100**

PRODUCTS/OPERATIONS

2018 Sales

	$ mil.	% of total
Genvoya	4,624	21
Truvada	2,997	14
Epclusa	1,966	9
Odefsey	1,598	7
Descovy	1,581	7
Harvoni	1,222	6
Atripla	1,206	5
Biktarvy	1,457	5
Other	5,299	24
Royalty contract and other revenue	450	2
Total	**22,127**	**100**

Selected Products

Antiviral
  Atripla (HIV with Bristol-Myers Squibb)
  Complera/Eviplera (HIV)

Emtriva (HIV)
Harvoni (HCV infection)
Hepsera (hepatitis B)
Sovaldi (HCV infection)
Stribild (HIV)
Tamiflu (flu treatment royalties from Roche)
Truvada (fixed-dose combination of Viread and Emtriva for HIV)
Viread (HIV chronic hepatitis B with liver disease)
Vistide (AIDS-related cytomegalovirus retinitis)
Other products
AmBisome (antifungal with Astellas)
Cayston (cystic fibrosis)
Flolan (pulmonary hypertension)
Letairis (pulmonary arterial hypertension)
Lexiscan/Rapiscan (cardiovascular with Astellas)
Macugen (age-related macular degeneration royalties from Eyetech)
Ranexa (chronic angina)
Products in development
Aztreonam (cystic fibrosis)
Cobicistat (HIV/AIDS)
Elvitegravir (HIV/AIDS)
GS-1101 (leukemia and lymphoma)
GS-7977 (hepatitis C)
Intesgrase (HIV)
Ranolazine (cardiovascular diabetes)

COMPETITORS

AbbVie	Merck
Abbott Labs	Novartis
Actelion	Pfizer
Bristol-Myers Squibb	Shire
GlaxoSmithKline	United Therapeutics

HISTORICAL FINANCIALS

Company Type: Public

Income Statement — FYE: December 31

	REVENUE ($ mil.)	NET INCOME ($ mil.)	NET PROFIT MARGIN	EMPLOYEES
12/19	22,449	5,386	24.0%	11,800
12/18	22,127	5,455	24.7%	11,000
12/17	26,107	4,628	17.7%	10,000
12/16	30,390	13,501	44.4%	9,000
12/15	32,639	18,108	55.5%	8,000
Annual Growth	(8.9%)	(26.2%)	—	10.2%

2019 Year-End Financials

Debt ratio: 39.91%	No. of shares (mil.): 1,266
Return on equity: 24.53%	Dividends
Cash ($ mil.): 11,631	Yield: 3.8%
Current ratio: 3.10	Payout: 59.7%
Long-term debt ($ mil.): 22,094	Market value ($ mil.): 82,265

	STOCK PRICE ($) FY Close	P/E High/Low	PER SHARE ($) Earnings	Dividends	Book Value
12/19	64.98	17 15	4.22	2.52	17.79
12/18	62.55	21 14	4.17	2.28	16.68
12/17	71.64	24 18	3.51	2.08	15.63
12/16	71.61	10 7	9.94	1.84	14.42
12/15	101.19	10 8	11.91	1.29	13.03
Annual Growth	(10.5%)	— —	(22.8%)	18.2%	8.1%

Glacier Bancorp, Inc.

Glacier Bancorp is on a Rocky Mountain high. The holding company owns about a dozen community bank divisions with about 100 locations in Montana Idaho Utah Washington Arizona Colorado and Wyoming. Serving individuals small to midsized businesses not-for-profits and public entities the banks offer traditional deposit products and credit cards in addition to retail brokerage and investment services through agreements with third-party providers. Its lending activities consist of commercial real estate loans (about half of the company's loan portfolio) as well as residential mortgages business loans and consumer loans.

Financial Performance

Glacier's financial results are on a steady upward swing since 2012 with yearly increases in interest income and near-annual improvement in non-interest income and net income.

In 2017 the company generated $375 million in interest income and $112 million in non-interest income for total revenue of $487 million. Its loan portfolio grew by $601 million or 11% in the year bringing the size of its loan portfolio to just less than $6.5 billion.

Net income for the year was $116 million 4% more than 2016 due to the higher revenue partially offset by an increase in loan loss provisions employee compensation and income tax expense.

Glacier Bancorp ended 2017 with $200 million in cash an increase of nearly $50 million over the previous year. Financing activities used $230 million for loan repayments stock dividends and a decrease in deposits. Investing activities added $24 million to the coffers and operating activities contributed $255 million mostly from net income a deferred tax expense and proceeds from selling some of its loan portfolio.

Strategy

Glacier Bancorp hopes to capitalize on additional acquisition opportunities that it expects to arise as small banks deal with new industry regulations. To this end it has been on a buying spree in recent years. In early 2018 it acquired Inter-Mountain Bancorp (Montana) Columbine Capital Corporation (Colorado); in 2017 it purchased TFB Bancorp (Arizona); in 2016 it bought Treasure State Bank (Montana) and in 2015 Glacier acquired Canon Bank Corporation (Colorado) and Montana Community Banks (Montana). In total these purchases cost $377 million.

The company is also banking on organic growth with the populations of the states in its market area growing faster than the national average thanks to an influx of retiring Baby Boomers and an increase in energy- and natural resource-related jobs.

EXECUTIVES

Evp And Cfo, Ron J. Copher, $352,651 total compensation
Evp And Chief Administrative Officer, Don J. Cherry, $299,950 total compensation
President And Ceo, Randall M. (Randy) Chesler, age 62, $153,846 total compensation
Vice President And Cra And Compliance Officer, Lanette Marcum
Senior Vice President, Robert Taylor
Vice President Internal Auditor, Judy Overcast
Vice President Compliance, April Kelso
Vice President, Ryan T Screnar
Senior Vice President Business Developme, Steve Lloyd
Senior Vice President Consumer Lending, Greg Wilcox
Vice President Finance, Mike Romm
Senior Vice President Business Development, Don Lloyd
Vice President Internal Auditor, Jessica Rice
Vice President Of Human Resources, Roger Bamford
Vice President Of Human Resources, Christopher Murphy
Vice President Internal Auditor, Leslie Thompson
Vice President, Melody Pieri
Vice President Corporate Bsa Officer, Mary Strozzi
Assistant Vice President Internal Audit, Leslie Hall
Senior Vice President Enterprise Wide Risk Manager, T Frickle
Assistant Vice President Benefits Administrator, Jill Klocke
Vice President, Don McCarthy
Vice President Risk Management, T J Frickle
Senior Vice President, Lynn Riley
Chairman, Dallas I. Herron, age 75
Board Member, Sherry Cladouhos
Board Member, Mark Semmens
Auditors: BKD, LLP

LOCATIONS

HQ: Glacier Bancorp, Inc.
49 Commons Loop, Kalispell, MT 59901
Phone: 406 756-4200
Web: www.glacierbank.com

PRODUCTS/OPERATIONS

2016 Sales

	$ mil.	% of total
Interest income		
Commercial loans	227	47
Investment securities	81	17
Residential real estate loans	33	7
Consumer and other loans	32	7
Non-interest income		
Service charges and other fees	67	14
Gain on sale of loans	30	6
Miscellaneous loan fees and charges	4	1
(Loss) gain on sale of investments	(0.6)	-
Other income	10	2
Total	487	100

Selected Services

Commercial loan
Consumer loan
Deposits
Mortgage origination services
Real estate loan
Retail brokerage services
Transaction and savings

Selected Bank Divisions

1st Bank (Wyoming)
Bank of the San Juans (Colorado)
Big Sky Western Bank (Montana)
Citizens Community Bank (Idaho)
Collegiate Peaks Bank
First Bank of Montana
First Bank of Wyoming
First Security Bank (Montana)
First State Bank (Wyoming)
Foothills Bank
Glacier Bank (Montana)
Mountain West Bank (Idaho)
North Cascades Bank (Washington)
Valley Bank of Helena (Montana)
Western Security Bank (Montana)

COMPETITORS

Eagle Bancorp	U.S. Bancorp
First Citizens Banc Corp	Wells Fargo
First Interstate	Zions Bancorporation

HISTORICAL FINANCIALS

Company Type: Public

Income Statement — FYE: December 31

	ASSETS ($ mil.)	NET INCOME ($ mil.)	INCOME AS % OF ASSETS	EMPLOYEES
12/19	13,684	210	1.5%	3,046
12/18	12,115	181	1.5%	2,723
12/17	9,706	116	1.2%	2,354
12/16	9,450	121	1.3%	2,291
12/15	9,089	116	1.3%	2,245
Annual Growth	10.8%	16.0%	—	7.9%

Debt ratio: 1.23% No. of shares (mil.): 92
Return on equity: 12.11% Dividends
Cash ($ mil.): 330 Yield: 3.0%
Current ratio: — Payout: 59.2%
Long-term debt ($ mil.): — Market value ($ mil.): 4,244

	STOCK PRICE ($) FY Close	P/E High/Low	PER SHARE ($) Earnings	Dividends	Book Value
12/19	45.99	19 16	2.38	1.41	21.25
12/18	39.62	22 17	2.17	1.01	17.93
12/17	39.39	27 21	1.50	1.44	15.37
12/16	36.23	24 14	1.59	1.10	14.59
12/15	26.53	20 14	1.54	1.05	14.15
Annual Growth	14.7%	— —	11.5%	7.6%	10.7%

Global Partners LP

Global Partners imports petroleum products from global sources but its marketing is largely regional. The company wholesales heating oil residual fuel oil diesel oil kerosene distillates and gasoline to commercial retail and wholesale customers in New England and New York. A major player in the regional home heating oil market Global Partners operates storage facilities at 25 bulk terminals each with a storage capacity of more than 50000 barrels and with a collective storage capacity of 10.8 million barrels. It also owns and supplies a network of gasoline stations. Wholesale revenues accounts for the bulk of the company's sales.

Operations

Global Partners consists of three operating segments: Wholesale Gasoline Distribution and Station Operations (GDSO) and Commercial.

Wholesale accounts for more than 55% of total sales and sells unbranded gasoline and diesel to unbranded gasoline customers and other resellers of transportation fuels. It also sells home heating oil diesel kerosene and residual oil to home heating oil retailers and wholesale distributors; as well as crude oil to refiners.

GDSO generates more than third of total sales and sells branded and unbranded gasoline to gasoline stations and other sub-jobbers such as gasoline convenience store car wash and other ancillary services at company operated stores and leased gas stations.

Commercial brings in the remaining nearly 10% of sales and sells unbranded gasoline custom blended fuels home heating oil diesel kerosene residual oil renewable fuels and natural gas. Its customers are public sector and large commercial and industrial end users. The segment also includes the sale of custom blended distillates and residual oil delivered by barge or from a terminal dock to ships through its bunkering activity.

Geographic Reach

Waltham Massachusetts-based Global Partners has a network of refined petroleum products and renewable fuels terminals throughout the Northeast region (Connecticut Maine Massachusetts New Hampshire New Jersey New York Pennsylvania Rhode Island and Vermont). The company also operates around mid-continent region of the United States and Canada.

It has some 1550 owned leased and/or supplied gas stations including about 290 convenience stores in the Northeast. The company have two rail facilities in New York and Oregon capable of handling ethanol and another two rail facilities in North Dakota capable of handling crude oil.

Sales and Marketing

Global Partners gets its revenue primarily from convenience store sales at its directly operated stores and rental income from dealer leased or commission agent leased gasoline stations. Global Partners also is one of the largest distributors of gasoline distillates residual oil and renewable fuels to wholesalers retailers and commercial customers in New England and New York.

In the Commercial segment it serves customers in the public sector and large commercial and industrial end users of unbranded gasoline home heating oil diesel kerosene residual oil bunker fuel and natural gas.

Financial Performance

The company's total sales were $13.1 billion and $12.7 billion for 2019 and 2018 respectively an increase of $0.4 billion or 3% due to an increase in volume sold. Their aggregate volume of product sold was 6.5 billion gallons and 5.8 billion gallons for 2019 and 2018 respectively an increase of 0.7 billion gallons. The increase in volume sold includes increases of 533 million gallons in their Wholesale segment primarily in gasoline and gasoline blendstocks 98 million gallons in their Commercial segment and 26 million gallons in their GDSO segment.

In 2019 the company's net income was $68 million less than from its prior year. Even though the company gained more revenue the company lost their gain on trustee taxes worth $52.6 million in 2018.

The company's cash in 2019 was $3.9 million more than its cash in 2018 to $12.0 million. In 2019 the company's cash provided by operating activities was $94 million while investing activities used $67.2 million and also financing activities used $23.3 million.

Strategy

Global Partners has undertaken initiatives to strategically position itself by strengthening its balance sheet and enhancing its liquidity in order to be in a position to invest in opportunities fundamental to its growth strategy.

The initiatives include: Amendment of the company's credit agreement to among other things extend the maturity date for its working capital revolving credit facility and revolving credit facility from April 30 2020 to April 29 2022 and reduce the applicable rate under its revolving credit facility by 0.25% for borrowings of base rate loans Eurocurrency rate loans and cost of funds rate loans and for issuances of letters of credit; Completion of the private placement of an aggregate principal amount of $400.0 million of our 7.00% senior notes due 2027 the proceeds of which were used to pay the full redemption of the company's 6.25% senior notes due 2022 which redemption occurred on August 30 2019 and repay a portion of the borrowings outstanding under the company's credit agreement; Ongoing divestiture of non-strategic assets.

Company Background

Through AE Holdings the Slifka family controls about 21% of Global Partners; Kayne Anderson Capital Advisors L.P 12%.

Global Partners was founded in 1933 as a one-truck heating oil retailer by current CEO Eric Slifka's grandfather Abraham Slifka.

In 2010 in order to expand its wholesale supply business the company acquired about 190 retail gas stations in three states in the Northeast from Exxon Mobil and some of its dealers for $202.3 million. Pursuing a strategy of growing its storage capacity in 2010 Global Partners also acquired three terminals in Newburgh New York from Warex Terminals for $47.5 million.

In 2012 the company signed a long-term lease agreement with Getty Realty to supply gasoline to and operate about 90 of Getty's gas station in Queens Manhattan and the Bronx as well as in Long Island and Westchester County.

Boosting its gas station network in 2012 Global Partners acquired Alliance Energy a gasoline distributor and gas stations/convenience store operator controlled by the Slifka family for $180 million.

Growing its portfolio in 2013 Global Partners acquired Cascade Kelly Holdings LLC (a crude oil and ethanol facility near Portland Oregon) for $95 million. That year it also acquired 60% of Basin Transload LLC (which operates two crude oil transloading facilities in Columbus and Beulah North Dakota with a combined rail loading capacity of 160000 barrels per day) for $85 million. The transaction complements its purchase of West Coast crude oil transload and ethanol facility near Portland.

EXECUTIVES

Svp Light Oil Supply And Distribution, Mark A. Romaine, age 51, $500,000 total compensation
Evp Chief Accounting Officer And Co-director Mergers And Acquisitions, Charles A. (Chuck) Rudinsky, age 72, $273,000 total compensation
Vp Marketing Manager Distillates And Gasoline Wholesale, Joseph (Joe) DeStefano
President Ceo And Director, Eric Slifka, age 54, $800,000 total compensation
Evp General Counsel And Secretary, Edward J. Faneuil, age 67, $450,000 total compensation
Cfo, Daphne H. Foster, age 62, $400,000 total compensation
Evp Director And President Alliance Gasoline, Andrew Slifka, age 51, $425,000 total compensation
Svp Information Technology, Bill Gifford
Vice President Of Marketing Information Technology, Mary McCarty
Vice President, Bruce Atkins
Vice President Of Rail Products Division, Matt Snyder
Vice President Information Security And Compliance, Carl Stolfi
Executive Vice President Of Information Technology, Gregory Rudoy
Vp National Business Group, Ken Whalley
Vice President Heavy Oil Marketing, Dennis Bowersox
Vice President Credit, Robert J Fraczkiewicz
Vice President Health And Safety Operations, Tom Keefe
Senior Vice President, Mark Cosenza
Vice President, Steve Lundgren
Vice President Credit, Bob Fraczkiewicz
Vice President, Jane Michalek
Vice President, Eileen Sweeney
Vice President Gdso North, Kevin Jackson
Senior Vice President Of Retail Development, Dino Dethomas
Vice President Wholesale New England, Joe Moceri
Assistant Vice President Of Terminal Operations, Steven Mccool
Board Member, Robert McCool
Chairman, Richard Slifka, age 79
Board Member, David Mckown
Treasurer, Greg Hanson
Board Member, Kenneth Watchmaker
Senior Executive Assistant To Edward J. Faneuil Vice President Group Chief Officer And Secretary, Lillian Santangelo
Auditors: Ernst & Young LLP

LOCATIONS

HQ: Global Partners LP
P.O. Box 9161, 800 South Street, Waltham, MA 02454-9161
Phone: 781 894-8800
Web: www.globalp.com

PRODUCTS/OPERATIONS

2016 Sales

	$ mil.	% of total
Wholesale	4,107	50
Gasoline distribution & station operations	3,443	42
Commercial	689	8
Total	**8,239**	**100**

Selected Products

Biofuels
Bunker oil
Diesel oil
Distillates
Gasoline
Home heating oil
Kerosene
Residual fuel oil

COMPETITORS

Bayside Fuel	Koch Industries Inc.
Exxon Mobil	Sprague Resources
George Warren	Tauber Oil
Gulf Oil	Warren Equities
Highlands Fuel	
Delivery	

HISTORICAL FINANCIALS

Company Type: Public

Income Statement

FYE: December 31

	REVENUE ($ mil.)	NET INCOME ($ mil.)	NET PROFIT MARGIN	EMPLOYEES
12/19	13,081	35	0.3%	3,860
12/18	12,672	103	0.8%	2,500
12/17	8,920	58	0.7%	2,000
12/16	8,239	(199)	—	1,770
12/15	10,314	43	0.4%	1,890
Annual Growth	**6.1%**	**(4.7%)**	**—**	**19.5%**

2019 Year-End Financials

Debt ratio: 42.98%
Return on equity: —
Cash ($ mil.): 46
Current ratio: 1.33
Long-term debt ($ mil.): 1,058

No. of shares (mil.): 34
Dividends
Yield: 10.1%
Payout: 86.2%
Market value ($ mil.): 687

	STOCK PRICE ($) FY Close	P/E High/Low	PER SHARE ($) Earnings	Dividends	Book Value
12/19	20.16	26 20	0.81	2.05	13.43
12/18	16.30	7 5	2.95	1.88	14.64
12/17	16.70	12 9	1.74	1.85	11.54
12/16	19.45	— —	(5.91)	1.85	11.63
12/15	17.57	37 14	1.11	2.74	19.20
Annual Growth	**3.5%**	**— —**	**(7.6%)**	**(7.0%)**	**(8.5%)**

Globe Life Inc

Globe Life (formerly Torchmark) specializes in providing individual life insurance and supplemental health insurance to middle-income families. Globe Life's subsidiaries including American Income Life and Globe Life and Accident offer whole and term life insurance policies and supplemental health insurance coverage including illness accident and Medicare Supplement policies. Globe Life has some 4.2 million policyholders and sells its products through direct marketing efforts and a network of exclusive and independent agents. Substantially all of Globe Life's business is conducted in the US.

Operations

Globe Life operates in four segments: life insurance supplemental health insurance annuities and investments.

The life insurance segment (more than 55% of revenue) offers individual life products including whole life coverage (traditional and interest-sensitive) and term life insurance.

The supplemental health segment (about 25% of sales) offers critical illness accident Medicare Supplement and limited-benefit surgical and hospital policies.

The investments segment (approximately 20% of sales) manages the group's capital resources including investments and the management of corporate debt and liquidity.

The annuity segment (less than 1%) manages runoff fixed-benefit contracts that are no longer actively marketed by the company.

The company's underwriting subsidiaries include Globe Life and Accident which reaches middle-income customers with life and health insurance products including Medicare Supplement coverage and juvenile and senior life policies. The American Income Life subsidiary sells life and health insurance to working families while Liberty National Life provides life and health policies to middle-income families. The Family Heritage Life unit provides limited-benefit health products in non-urban markets while United American primarily sells Medicare Supplement insurance.

As part of a brand recognition strategy the company changed its name from Torchmark to Globe Life in 2019. Globe Life's subsidiaries will gradually transition to the Globe Life brand.

Geographic Reach

Globe Life conducts substantially all of its business in the US. The company is headquartered in McKinney Texas along with its Globe Life and Accident Liberty National and United American subsidiaries. American Income Life is based in Waco Texas and Family Heritage Life is based in Cleveland Ohio.

United American also has offices in Omaha Nebraska and Syracuse New York. Globe Life and Accident has offices in Oklahoma City Oklahoma and Allen Texas. American Income has a network of marketing offices across the US with minor agent distribution in Canada and New Zealand.

Sales and Marketing

Globe Life's subsidiaries market and distribute products through more than 10000 producing and independent agents. The Globe Life and Accident unit also utilizes direct mail electronic media insert media and an inbound call center.

Financial Performance

The company's revenue in 2019 increased by 6% to $3.6 billion from $3.4 billion in 2018. The increase was primarily due to the increase on their Life insurance segment.

Net income increased 8% to $761 million in 2019 compared with $701 million in 2018. This increase was primarily related to favorable underwriting income.

The company ended 2019 with $75.9 million in cash down by $45.1 million from 2018. Operating activities contributed $1.4 billion while investing activities used $809.3 million (mostly fixed maturity acquisitions) and financing activities used $590.5 million via treasury stock acquisitions and dividend and deposit payments.

Strategy

The company changed its name from Torchmark to Globe Life in 2019 to increase its ability to build brand recognition with potential customers and agent recruits. Globe Life's subsidiaries will continue to operate as separate legal entities but will gradually transition to the new brand. The Globe Life name was chosen to leverage branding

initiatives conducted by the Globe Life and Accident subsidiary in recent years.

Globe Life's insurance strategy is centered on selling life and health products to middle-income households which it sees as an underserved market. In recent years the company has especially been focused on young families with children. It has also been focused on expanding its distribution channels. For example American Income Life has expanded its reach beyond unions (which have declined in membership) to include other infinity groups third-party vendor leads and referrals. In addition the Liberty National unit is expanding its producing agent network to widen its focus beyond small towns into more densely populated areas.

Company Background

The company was founded as Heralds of Liberty in 1900 as a fraternal organization. After running into some trouble over its business practices the company recapitalized as a stock company named Liberty National in 1929. It expanded through acquisitions of several other insurance companies over the following decades.

Liberty National reorganized itself as a holding company in 1980 to accommodate the purchase of Globe Life and Accident; it also purchased United American in 1981. The company's name was changed to Torchmark in 1982 and then to Globe Life in 2019.

HISTORY

It began as a scam plain and simple. In 1900 the Heralds of Liberty was founded as a fraternal organization — but its real reason for existence was to funnel money to its founders according to Frank Samford CEO of Torchmark (now Globe Life) from 1967 to 1985; Samford was also the great-grandson of the governor who signed the group's charter and the son of the state insurance commissioner who oversaw the Heralds of Liberty's rehabilitation into a real insurance company.

The Heralds offered a joint life distribution plan under which policyholders were divided by age; when a person died his or her beneficiary was paid along with the holder of the lowest-numbered insurance certificate in the class (if they were paid at all; the Heralds were not scrupulous about that). Postal authorities called this plan a lottery and it was illegal in many states. But the Heralds' fraternal order status allowed it to circumvent Alabama insurance laws until 1921 when its infractions could no longer be ignored.

The organization operated under state supervision until 1929 when it was recapitalized as stock company Liberty National. By 1934 despite the Depression the company was financially sound.

In 1944 Liberty National merged with funeral insurance company Brown-Service whose large sales force began selling Liberty National's policies. The added sales helped the company grow and make acquisitions from the 1950s through the 1970s. Even after it discontinued funeral insurance the company still paid out benefits. (As late as 1985 half of all Alabamans who died had the policies.)

Liberty National reorganized itself as a holding company in 1980 to accommodate the purchase of Globe Life And Accident. In 1981 it acquired Continental Investment Corp. which owned United Investors Life Insurance Waddell & Reed (financial services) and United American Insurance. In 1982 the holding company became Torchmark. Throughout its growth spurt it refrained from offering high-yield financial products and thus escaped the worst effects of the economic disruptions of the late 1980s. Its 1990 acquisition of Family Service Life Insurance put it back in the funeral insurance business (it exited again in 1995 and sold the unit in 1998).

Sales in the 1990s were affected by a decline in cash-value life insurance and Medicare supplements. Slack sales forced the company to stop having agents collect premiums personally and by 1996 all accounts were handled by mail.

In 1998 the company sought to sell its 28% stake in property insurer Vesta Insurance Group after that company became the target of numerous lawsuits. Torchmark was only able to reduce its stake to 24% on the open market but in 2000 Vesta bought out Torchmark's holdings.

Torchmark was haunted in 2000 by its own version of the undead — burial policies. An investigation by Alabama regulators was sparked by a Florida court order forcing the company to stop collecting premiums on old burial policies for which African-Americans had been charged higher premiums. In 2001 and 2002 Torchmark was hit by another dozen lawsuits including allegations of overcharging.

Torchmark changed its name to Globe Life in 2019.

EXECUTIVES

Co-chairman And Co-ceo, Larry M. Hutchison, age 66, $870,865 total compensation
Co-chairman And Co-ceo, Gary L. Coleman, age 67, $870,865 total compensation
Ceo American Income Life And Liberty National Life, Roger C. Smith, age 67, $594,846 total compensation
Evp And Chief Administrative Officer, Vern D. Herbel, age 62, $519,846 total compensation
Evp And Cfo, Frank M. Svoboda, age 58, $499,692 total compensation
Evp And Chief Investment Officer, W. Michael Pressley, age 68, $499,692 total compensation
Evp And Chief Actuary, Ben W. Lutek, age 61
President Lnl Agency Division, Steven J. (Steve) DiChiaro, age 53
Evp And General Counsel, R. Brian Mitchell, age 56
President And Ceo Globe Life Direct Response, Bill E. Leavell, age 57
President Family Heritage Life Insurance, Kenneth J. (Ken) Matson, age 53
President United American Insurance And First United American Insurance, Michael C. Majors, age 58
Evp And Cio, James E. (Bo) McPartland, age 53
Evp And Chief Strategy Officer, J. Matthew Darden, age 49
President Ail Agency Division American Income, Steven K. Greer, age 47
Senior Vice President Facilities, Douglas Gockel
Avp Agent Recruiting And Leads, Kimberley Smith
Executive Vice President And Chief Strategy Officer, James Darden
Executive Vice President Chief Strategy Officer, Gregory Smith
Assistant Secretary, Christopher Moore
Board Member, Steven Johnson
Board Member, Charles Adair
Board Member, Robert Ingram
Board Member, Linda Addison
Auditors: DELOITTE & TOUCHE LLP

LOCATIONS

HQ: Globe Life Inc
3700 South Stonebridge Drive, McKinney, TX 75070
Phone: 972 569-4000
Web: www.torchmarkcorp.com

PRODUCTS/OPERATIONS

2017 Revenues

	$ mil.	% of total
Insurance		
Life	2,306,547	56
Health	976,373	23
Annuity	15	-
Investment income	847,885	20
Realized investment gain	23,611	1
Other income	1,142	-
Total	**4,155,573**	**100**

Selected Subsidiaries

American Income Life Insurance Company
Family Heritage Life Insurance Company of America
Globe Life and Accident Insurance Company
Liberty National Life Insurance Company
United American Insurance Company

COMPETITORS

Aflac	Monumental Life
Allstate	Northwestern Mutual
Amalgamated Life	Penn Treaty
Gerber Life	Prudential
Guardian Life	State Farm
Lincoln Financial	Texas Life
Group	USAA
MassMutual	Unum Group
MetLife	

HISTORICAL FINANCIALS

Company Type: Public

Income Statement				FYE: December 31
	ASSETS ($ mil.)	NET INCOME ($ mil.)	INCOME AS % OF ASSETS	EMPLOYEES
12/19	25,977	760	2.9%	3,196
12/18	23,095	701	3.0%	3,102
12/17	23,474	1,454	6.2%	3,102
12/16	21,436	549	2.6%	3,128
12/15	19,853	527	2.7%	3,115
Annual Growth	**7.0%**	**9.6%**	**—**	**0.6%**

2019 Year-End Financials

Debt ratio: 5.23%
Return on equity: 11.97%
Cash ($ mil.): 75
Current ratio: —
Long-term debt ($ mil.): —

No. of shares (mil.): 107
Dividends
Yield: 0.6%
Payout: 10.2%
Market value ($ mil.): 11,338

	STOCK PRICE ($) FY Close	P/E High/Low		PER SHARE ($)		
				Earnings	Dividends	Book Value
12/19	105.25	15	11	6.83	0.68	67.72
12/18	74.53	15	11	6.09	0.63	48.92
12/17	90.71	7	6	12.22	0.59	54.38
12/16	73.76	16	11	4.49	0.56	38.69
12/15	57.16	15	12	4.16	0.53	33.14
Annual Growth	**16.5%**			**13.2%**	**6.2%**	**19.6%**

Goldman Sachs Group Inc

Goldman Sachs has long possessed the Midas touch in the investment banking world. One of the world's most powerful investment banks Goldman Sachs offers a gamut of investment banking and asset management services to corporate and government clients worldwide as well as institutional and wealth individual investors. It is a world leader in merger and acquisitions advice and equities and debt underwriting. Through its Global Markets division Goldman Sachs is a major market maker offering fixed income equities currency and commodity products. The bank boasts nearly $2 trillion in assets under supervision covering all major asset classes. Goldman Sachs was founded in 1869. Vast majority of its revenue comes from its domestic operation.

HISTORY

German immigrant-cum-Philadelphia retailer Marcus Goldman moved to New York in 1869 and began buying customers' promissory notes from jewelers to resell to banks. Goldman's son-in-law came aboard in 1882 and the firm became Goldman Sachs & Co. in 1885.

Two years later Goldman Sachs began offering US-UK foreign exchange and currency services. To serve such clients as Sears Roebuck it expanded to Chicago and St. Louis. In 1896 it joined the NYSE.

While the firm increased its European contracts Goldman's son Henry made it a major source of financing for US industry. In 1906 it co-managed its first public offering United Cigar Manufacturers (later General Cigar). By 1920 it had underwritten IPOs for Sears B.F. Goodrich and Merck.

Sidney Weinberg made partner in 1927 and stayed until his death in 1969. In the 1930s Goldman Sachs entered securities dealing and sales. After WWII it became a leader in investment banking co-managing Ford's 1956 IPO. In the 1970s it pioneered buying blocks of stock for resale.

Under Weinberg's son John Goldman Sachs became a leader in mergers and acquisitions. The 1981 purchase of J. Aron gave the firm a significant commodities presence and helped it grow in South America.

Seeking capital after 1987's market crash Goldman Sachs raised more than $500 million from Sumitomo for a 12% nonvoting interest in the firm (since reduced to 3%). The Kamehameha Schools/Bishop Estate of Hawaii an educational trust also invested.

The 1994 bond crash and a decline in new debt issues led Goldman Sachs to cut staffing for the first time since the 1980s. But problems went deeper. Partners began leaving and taking their equity. Cost cuts a stronger bond market and the long bull market helped the firm rebound; firm members sought protection through limited liability partnership status. The firm also extended the period during which partners can cash out (slowing the cash drain) and limited the number of people entitled to a share of profits. Overseas growth in 1996 and 1997 focused on the UK and Asia.

After three decades of resistance the partners in 1998 voted to sell the public a minority stake in the firm but market volatility led to postponement. Goldman Sachs also suffered from involvement with Long-Term Capital Management ultimately contributing $300 million to its bailout.

In 1999 Jon Corzine then co-chairman and co-CEO announced that he would leave the group after seeing it through its IPO and Goldman Sachs finally went public that year in an offering valued at close to $4 billion. In 2000 Corzine was elected to a US Senate seat. The New Jersey Democrat spent more than $64 million on his campaign (a record) nearly $61 million of it from his own personal wealth (also a record). Corzine went on to win New Jersey's gubernatorial race in 2005.

In early 2004 Goldman president and COO John Thain left the firm to assume the helm of the New York Stock Exchange. Lloyd Blankfein was named his successor and became chairman and CEO in

2006 when his predecessor Henry "Hank" Paulson was named secretary of the US Treasury.

At the height of the economic crisis Goldman Sachs converted to a bank holding company. It formed subsidiary Goldman Sachs Bank USA (GS Bank USA) to manage bank loan trading mortgage originations and other activities. The Federal Reserve mandated the change for Goldman Sachs and fellow investment bank Morgan Stanley. The shift marked a monumental change on Wall Street as it put an end to the independent brokerage firm model that had been a mainstay in the US since reform measures were implemented during the Great Depression. Rivals Merrill Lynch Lehman Brothers and Bear Stearns had already merged with larger banks or filed for bankruptcy. The bank holding company structure brought increased regulation but allowed Goldman Sachs to acquire commercial banks — all in an effort to shore up the company's balance sheet.

In the days following the Federal Reserve announcement Warren Buffett's Berkshire Hathaway invested $5 billion in Goldman Sachs and acquired an option to assume $5 billion more of the company's common shares. Goldman Sachs made an additional $5 billion worth of stock available in a public offering. Additionally the US government stepped in with funding for Goldman Sachs in late 2008 when it announced an economic stimulus plan to buy some $250 billion worth of preferred shares of the nation's top banks; approximately $10 billion went to Goldman Sachs.

The capital infusions helped but didn't completely shield Goldman Sachs from the financial crisis the effects of which were felt worldwide. To cut costs the company trimmed some 10% of its workforce. It eventually returned to profitability in 2009 and paid back the money it received from the government but still drew ire from politicians over what have been perceived to be extravagant pay packages for its top employees. (The firm's extravagant year-end bonuses had become the stuff of legend.)

Goldman Sachs opened a new $1.8-billion headquarters building in New York City's lower Manhattan in 2009.

In 2012 Goldman spent some $5.65 billion to buy back preferred shares that Warren Buffet's Berkshire Hathaway acquired in 2008. The repurchase would save the firm money as it had been paying some 10% interest on the shares (or some $500 million annually).

Also in 2012 Goldman acquired the Bermuda-based insurance and reinsurance operations of Ariel Reinsurance; an addition that should bring in a steady stream of fees. Additionally that year the company arranged to sell hedge fund administrator Goldman Sachs Administration Services to State Street for some $550 million.

In 2013 Goldman Sachs Asset Management acquired the Global Treasury Funds assets which consists of a variety of money market funds from RBS Asset Management to strengthen its strong fixed income and liquidity management businesses in Europe and around the world.

Goldman bought the remaining 20% stake it didn't already own in Endesa Gas T&D in 2013. It purchased the natural gas transport firm from Spanish power utility Endesa for about $174 million.

In January 2013 Goldman sold approximately 45% of its ordinary shares of ICBC.

EXECUTIVES

Head Merchant Banking Division, Richard A. Friedman, age 62

Evp General Counsel And Secretary, Gregory K. Palm, age 71

Chairman Goldman Sachs Bank Usa And Goldman Sachs International Bank, Esta E. Stecher, age 63

Evp And Cfo, R. Martin Chavez, age 56

Chairman And Ceo, Lloyd C. Blankfein, age 65, $2,000,000 total compensation

Evp And Head Of Global Compliance, Sarah E. Smith

Vice Chairman Ceo Goldman Sachs International And Co-head Investment Banking Division, Richard J. Gnodde, age 60

President And Co-coo, David M. Solomon, age 58

President Goldman Sachs Japan, Masanori Mochida

President Asia/pacific Outside Japan, Kenneth W. Hitchner

Evp Chief Of Staff And Secretary, John F.W. Rogers, age 63

Global Co-head Investment Management Division, Timothy J. O'Neill

Evp And Global Head Human Capital Management, Edith W. Cooper, age 58

Global Co-coo Equities Franchise, Michael D. Daffey

Head Conflicts Resolution Group, Gwen R. Libstag

President And Co-coo, Harvey M. Schwartz, age 55, $1,850,000 total compensation

Global Co-head Securities Division, Isabelle Ealet

Vice Chairman And Global Co-head Securities Division, Pablo J. Salame, age 54

Head Global Investment Research, Steven H. Strongin

Global Co-head Investment Management Division, Eric S. Lane

Chief Strategy Officer And Head Latin America, Stephen M. Scherr

Global Co-head Securities Division, Ashok Varadhan

Chief Risk Officer, Craig W. Broderick

Co-head Investment Banking Division, John Waldron

Global Head Credit Trading, Justin G. Gmelich

Co-head Of Global Mergers And Acquisitions, Gregg R. Lemkau

Head Of The Global Financing Group And Head Of Latin America, Marc Nachmann

Chairman Global Financial Institutions Group (fig), Mike Esposito

Coo Goldman Investment Banking Division, Luke Sarsfield

Co-head Global Financial Institutions Group, Todd Leland

Global Co-coo Equities Franchise, Paul M. Russo

Head Of The Global Special Situations Group (gssg), Julian Salisbury

Ceo Goldman Sachs Singapore Pte., Jason Moo

Vice President Technology, Ted Najjar

Vice President Equities Technology, Chris Carignan

West Coast Technology Vice President, Brandon Johnson

Vice President Investment Management Division, Ganesh Jois

Vice President, Seth Lonsk

Vice President, Lorraine Sperling

Vice President Gsam Insurance Asset Management Relationship Manager, Brian Rapino

Vice President, Jill Toporek

Vice President, Jeff Boyd

Vice President, Bryan Doyle

Vice President, Cameron Birdwell

Vice President, Tom Healy

Vice President Corporate Insurance, Jenny Chin

Vice President Global Securities Services, Megan Chastain

Vice President, Anuraag Verma

Vp And Executive Director Network Architect, James Morris

Vice President, Diana Tuminez

Vice President, Charu Govil

Vice President Technology, Krishnamurthy Vaidyanathan

Vice President, Curtis L Ambrose

Vice President, Thomas Croft

Vice President, Ovadiah Jacob

Vice President Global Securities Services, Caitlin Walsh

Vice President, Scott Maxfield

Vice President Investment Banking, Siddharth Shrivastava

Vice President Fx Ecommerce Product Management, Soomin Hu

Vice President Private Wealth Management Investment Management Division, Cristin Dalecki

Vice President Leveraged Finance Investment Banking, Jamie Tam

Vice President, Laura Mcdonald

Vice President, Karen Ho

Vice President, Nancy Benchoff

Vice President, Doreen Fattore

Vice President, Christina Tedeschi

Vice President, Subhek Garg

Vice President, Gitika Gumbar

Vice President, Taylor Yi

Vice President Information Technology Manager, Greg Killeen

Vice President, Krishnan Narayanan

Vice President Asset Management, Jordan Kaufman

Vice President, Gary Godshaw

Vice President, Christopher Higgins

Vice Present, John Sobral

Vice President, Kevin Carmody

Vice President Private Wealth Management Compliance, Diana Ryan

Vice President, Gabriel Haddad

Vice President, David Menachery

Technology Fellow And Vice President, Michael Ahern

Vice President, Bradley Goetschius

Vice President, Linda Avery

Vice President, Emma Taylor

Vice President, Hugh Chisholm

Vice President, Nikhil Reddy

Vice President Global Data Centre Operations, George Jurrjens

Vice President, Eric Altier

Vice President, Eric Riley

Vice President, Peter Linehan

Vice President, Arpita Mazumdar

Vice President, Douglas Wu

Vice President Technology, Eugene Gauthier

Vice President Private Wealth Management Investment Management Division, Neil Stone

Vice President, Matthew Korenberg

Vice President, Richard Lerner

Vice President Assistant General Counsel, Michael Huber

Vice President Technology, Stephen Chan

Vice President, Allison Marsh

Vice President And Associate General Counsel, Margaret Vaden

Vice President, Sean Butkus

Vice President Systems Management, Jeff Levine

Vice President, Christopher Wright

Vice President Investment Banking Division, Thomas Lynch

Vice President Tax Department, Nicolle Lewis

Vice President, Frank Drury

Vice President, Naomi Leslie

Vice President, Jeffrey Gido

Vice President, Robert Leggett

Vice President, Andre Benjamin

Vice President, Michael Darling

Vice President, Melissa Teng

Vice President, Lakshmanan Ramakrishnan

Vice President, Vanessa Schmidt

Vice President, Jane Kearsey

Vice President, Richard Jiang

Vice President, Jia Shan

Vice President Prime Brokerage, John Chiesa

Vice President, Nikhil Khanna

Vice President Of Information Technology, Prasert Chirachanakul
Vice President, Farley Friedman
Vice President, Joseph Pozzi
Vice President, WILLIAM CARINCI
Vice President, Sagar Solat
Vice President Information Security, Anita Nandakumar
Vice President, Erica Olsen
Vice President, Virender Bedi
Vice President, David Kirschner
Vice President Infrastructure Technology Audit, Manfred Elezovski
Vice President Investment Banking Division, Dave Park
Vice President, David Bao
Vice President And Tax Counsel, James Nolan
Vice President, Farzana Morbi
Vice President, Philip Pallone
Vice President Technology Finance, David Beneventano
Vice President, Giovanni Sansalone
Vice President, Ruben Salinas
Vice President Technology, Mayank Sharma
Vice President Technology Engineering Campus Recruiting, Mallory Leib
Vice President, Caitlin DeSantis
Technology Fellow And Vice President, Haodong Ma
Vice President Software Engineer, Javier Vazquez
Vice President Legal Department Technology Intellectual Property And Contracts Group, Marie Willemsen
Vice President, Nita Birla
Vice President, Ivan Kriakov
Vice President Information Systems, Reto Frei
Vice President, Greg Larson
Vice President, Michael Watts
Vice President, Stephen Blumenfeld
Auditors: PricewaterhouseCoopers LLP

LOCATIONS

HQ: Goldman Sachs Group Inc
  200 West Street, New York, NY 10282
Phone: 212 902-1000   Fax: 212 902-3000
Web: www.gs.com

2018 Sales

	% of total
Americas	61
Europe the Middle East & Africa	25
Asia	14
Total	100

PRODUCTS/OPERATIONS

2018 Sales

	$ mil.	% of total
Net interest income	3,767	38
Non Interest income		
Market making	9,451	18
Investment banking	7,862	18
Investment management	6,514	14
Commissions & fees	3,199	7
Other	5,823	12
Total	36,616	100

2018 Sales

	% of total
Institutional Client Services	37
Investment Banking	21
Investment Management	19
Investing & Lending	23
Total	100

Selected Subsidiaries

Goldman Sachs & Co.
Goldman Sachs Bank USA
Goldman Sachs Credit Partners L.P. (Bermuda)
Goldman Sachs Financial Markets L.P.
Goldman Sachs International (UK)
Goldman Sachs Japan Co. Ltd.

Goldman Sachs Mortgage Company
GSTM LLC
  Goldman Sachs Execution & Clearing L.P.
J. Aron & Company

COMPETITORS

BMO Capital Markets	FMR
Barclays	JPMorgan Chase
CIBC World Markets	Lazard
Citigroup Global Markets	Merrill Lynch
Credit Suisse	Morgan Stanley
Credit Suisse (USA)	Nomura Securities
Deutsche Bank	RBC Capital Markets
	UBS

HISTORICAL FINANCIALS

Company Type: Public

Income Statement   FYE: December 31

	ASSETS ($ mil.)	NET INCOME ($ mil.)	INCOME AS % OF ASSETS	EMPLOYEES
12/19	992,968	8,466	0.9%	38,300
12/18	931,796	10,459	1.1%	36,600
12/17	916,776	4,286	0.5%	36,600
12/16	860,165	7,398	0.9%	34,400
12/15	861,395	6,083	0.7%	36,800
Annual Growth	3.6%	8.6%	—	1.0%

2019 Year-End Financials

Debt ratio: 25.88%
Return on equity: 9.38%
Cash ($ mil.): 133,546
Current ratio: —
Long-term debt ($ mil.): —

No. of shares (mil.): 347
Dividends
  Yield: 1.8%
  Payout: 19.7%
Market value ($ mil.): 79,865

	STOCK PRICE ($) FY Close	P/E High/Low		PER SHARE ($) Earnings	Dividends	Book Value
12/19	229.93	11	8	21.03	4.15	259.87
12/18	167.05	11	6	25.27	3.15	245.24
12/17	254.76	29	23	9.01	2.90	219.43
12/16	239.45	15	8	16.29	2.60	221.31
12/15	180.23	18	14	12.14	2.55	206.75
Annual Growth	6.3%		—	14.7%	12.9%	5.9%

Goodyear Tire & Rubber Co.

Goodyear Tire & Rubber sells tires under the Goodyear Dunlop Kelly Fulda Debica and Sava brand names. The company manufactures and sells its tires across the Americas Europe Middle East & Africa (EMEA) and the Asia Pacific region including Australia and New Zealand. Goodyear also makes and markets rubber-related chemicals for various applications. It operates approximately 1000 tire and auto service centers where it offers its products for retail sale and provides automotive repair and other services. Goodyear has marketing operations in almost every country in the world although the US generates about 45% of its revenue.

HISTORY

In 1898 Frank and Charles Seiberling founded a tire and rubber company in Akron Ohio and named it after Charles Goodyear (inventor of the vulcanization process 1839). The debut of the Quick Detachable tire and the Universal Rim (1903) made Goodyear the world's largest tire maker by 1916.

Goodyear began manufacturing in Canada in 1910 and over the next two decades it expanded into Argentina Australia and the Dutch East Indies. The company established its own rubber plantations in Sumatra (now part of Indonesia) in 1916.

Financial woes led to reorganization in 1921 and investment bankers forced the Seiberlings out. Succeeding caretaker management Paul Litchfield began three decades as CEO in 1926 a time in which Goodyear emerged to become the world's largest rubber company.

Goodyear blimps served as floating billboards nationwide by the 1930s. During that decade Goodyear opened company stores acquired tire maker Kelly-Springfield (1935) and began producing tires made from synthetic rubber (1937). After WWII Goodyear was an innovative leader in technologies such as polyester tire cord (1962) and the bias-belted tire (1967).

By 1980 Goodyear had introduced radial tire brands such as the all-weather Tiempo the Eagle and the Arriva as it led the US market.

Thwarting British financier Sir James Goldsmith's takeover attempt in 1986 CEO Robert Mercer raised $1.7 billion by selling the company's non-tire businesses (Motor Wheel Goodyear Aerospace) and by borrowing heavily.

Recession overcapacity and price-cutting in 1990 led to hard times for tire makers. After suffering through 1990 its first money-losing year since the Depression Goodyear lured Stanley Gault out of retirement. He ceased marketing tires exclusively through Goodyear's dealer network by selling tires through Wal-Mart Kmart and Sears. Gault also cut costs through layoffs plant closures and spending reductions and returned Goodyear to profitability in 1991.

The company increased its presence in the US retail market in 1995 when it began selling tires through 860 Penske Auto Centers and 300 Montgomery Ward auto centers. President Samir Gibara succeeded chairman Gault as CEO in 1996. That year Goodyear bought Poland's leading tire maker T C Debica and a 60% stake in South African tire maker Contred (acquiring the rest in 1998).

In 1997 Goodyear formed an alliance with Sumitomo Rubber Industries under which the companies agreed to make and market tires for one another in Asia and North America. The next year Goodyear sold its Celeron Oil subsidiary which operated the All American Pipeline and acquired the remaining 26% stake in tire distributor Brad Ragan (commercial and retail outlets in the US) for $20.7 million.

The company acquired Sumitomo Rubber Industries' North American and European Dunlop tire businesses in 1999. The acquisition returned Goodyear to its #1 position in the tire-making industry. However the company recorded drastically low profits that year because it had cut tire production and was unable to meet supplier demands.

To improve profitability Goodyear increased tire prices in 2000 and began consolidating its manufacturing operations. Goodyear also announced plans to combine its commercial tire service centers with those of Treadco through a joint venture named Wingfoot Commercial Tire Systems. Despite record sales in 2000 the company's profits hit some hard road prompting Goodyear to lay off 10% of its workforce and implement other cost-cutting efforts.

Early in 2001 the company announced that it would close its Mexican tire plant. The same year the company agreed to replace Firestone Wilderness AT tires with Goodyear tires for Ford owners as part of Ford's big Firestone tire recall.

Early in 2002 Goodyear announced that its recent job cuts and manufacturing consolidation resulted in an $85 million decrease in annual operating costs. Later in the year the tire maker became embroiled in an age discrimination lawsuit claiming unfair job evaluations for the company's older employees. Blaming a slow US economy Goodyear announced plans to cut 450 jobs at its Union City Tennessee manufacturing plant. The job cuts were just the beginning of what would be a series of operational adjustments made as part of a Capital Structure Improvement Plan formally launched in 2003.

Although Goodyear once owned about 10% of its Sumitomo Rubber Industries it sold more than 20 million shares of its Japanese counterpart stock back to the tire maker in 2003. Later in the year as the company was embroiled in a lengthy debate with the United Steelworkers union it was announced that the Huntsville Alabama tire manufacturing plant would be closed. Goodyear also announced that it would cut 500 non-union salaried employees in North America. Later that same year it was announced that Goodyear was chosen by Volvo to be the truck manufacturer's primary tire supplier in North America; Goodyear had a similar contract with Mack Trucks.

Qantas Airways announced in early 2004 that it chose Goodyear to provide tires for the Australia-based company's Jetstar Airways. Later in the year Goodyear acquired the shares of Slovenia-based Sava Tires it did not already own and the company's Goodyear Dunlop Tires Europe unit purchased the Sweden-based Dackia retail tire stores. The company announced more job cuts in the non-tire sector in 2004 affecting Goodyear's engineered products and chemical units.

In 2005 Goodyear sold its stake in Goodyear Sumatra Plantations (rubber plantations in Indonesia) to rival Bridgestone for $62 million. Later that year the company sold its Wingtack adhesive resin business to Sartomer Company Inc. (a subsidiary of France's TOTAL S.A.) for about $65 million. As 2005 wound to a close the company sold its farm tire business to Titan International for $100 million.

Goodyear called off plans to sell its Chemical Products division. Instead the company integrated its chemical operations with those of its North American Tire division to take greater advantage of operational synergies. The company did however move forward with plans to jettison its Engineered Products division. In 2005 Goodyear secured the services of J.P. Morgan Securities and Goldman Sachs to help it explore opportunities for the sale of Engineered Products. The company struck a deal for The Carlyle Group in 2007 to buy its Engineered Products division for about $1.5 billion.

In 2011 Goodyear sold its tire reinforcement wire business (located in Luxembourg and North Carolina) to South Korea-based Hyosung for $50 million. The same year it sold its farm tire business in Latin America to a Titan International unit for $99 million. In 2010 Goodyear had agreed to sell its farm tire business in Europe as well as Latin America to Titan but the European part of the deal fell through and Goodyear does not have a time frame for making that sale. (In 2005 Titan had purchased Goodyear's North American farm tire business.) Also in 2011 Goodyear closed a facility in Union City Tennessee.

Intent on making more tires at lower-cost facilities Goodyear relocated its tire-making operations from Dalian China to Pulandian China in 2012. Additionally Goodyear is expanding or modernizing plants in Brazil Chile Germany and the US.

EXECUTIVES

Chairman President And Ceo, Richard J. (Rich) Kramer, age 56, $1,233,333 total compensation
Svp General Counsel And Secretary, David L. (Dave) Bialosky, age 63, $565,000 total compensation
Evp And Cfo, Laura K. Thompson, age 55, $621,667 total compensation
President Americas, Stephen R. (Steve) McClellan, age 54, $610,000 total compensation
Svp Global Operations And Technology, Joseph (Joe) Zekoski, age 68
President North America Consumer, R. Scott Rogers, age 51
President Europe Middle East And Africa (emea), Chris Delaney, age 59
Svp Global Human Resources And Chief Human Resources Officer, John T. Lucas, age 60, $547,333 total compensation
Svp Global Sales And Marketing, Richard Kellam, age 59
Vp And Cto, Christopher Helsel, age 55
President Asia Pacific, Ryan Patterson, age 46
Senior Vice President Global Communications, Paul Fitzhenry
Vice President Human Resources North American Tire, Gary Vanderlind
Vice President Global Labor Relations, Jim Allen
Vp Of Consumer Experience Of Americas, Andy Traicoff
Vice President Total Rewards At The Goodyear Tire And Rubber Company, Annie Granchi
Vice President Global Manufacturing, Marcelo Toscani
Vice President Global Engineer, Dallas Olson
Vice President Of It, John Flounders
Vice President Human Resources, Patrick Murphy
Vice President Product Quality And Plant Technology, Donald Stanley
Vice President Public Relations Americas, Laura Duda
Vice President And General Auditor, Kristian Hoeh
Vp Of Operations Emea, Paul Connolly
Senior Secretary, Monica Hill
Board Member, James Firestone
Secretary Marketing Department, Marilyn Chapanar
Senior Secretary, Melissa Gould
Assistant Treasurer, Ken Barfuss
Emea Treasurer, Christopher Collins
Senior Secretary Gtr A Research, Wanda Albino
Senior Secretary, Sarah Mcmillen-gore
Auditors: PricewaterhouseCoopers LLP

LOCATIONS

HQ: Goodyear Tire & Rubber Co.
200 Innovation Way, Akron, OH 44316-0001
Phone: 330 796-2121   **Fax:** 330 796-4099
Web: www.goodyear.com

2018 Sales

	$ mil.	% of total
Americas	8,168	53
Europe Middle East and Africa	5,090	33
Asia Pacific	2,217	14
Total	**15,475**	**100**

2018 Sales

	$ mil.	% of total
United States	6,692	43
Germany	1,883	12
Other international	6,900	45
Total	**15,475**	**100**

PRODUCTS/OPERATIONS

Selected Products

Automotive repair services
Chemical products
Natural rubber
Tires
Automotive
Aviation
Buses
Construction
Farm
Mining
Motorcycles
Trucks
Tread rubber
Wholesale tires

Selected Subsidiaries

Celeron Corporation
Dunlop Grund und Service Verwaltungs GmbH (Germany)
Dunlop Tyres Limited (UK)
Goodyear Canada Inc.
Goodyear Dalian Tire Company Ltd. (China)
Goodyear de Chile S.A.I.C.
Goodyear de Colombia S.A.
Goodyear do Brasil Produtos de Borracha Ltda (Brazil)
Goodyear Dunlop Tires Austria GmbH
Goodyear Dunlop Tires Belgium N.V.
Goodyear Dunlop Tires Czech s.r.o.
Goodyear Dunlop Tires Danmark A/S
Goodyear Dunlop Tires Espana S.A. (Spain)
Goodyear Dunlop Tires Finland OY
Goodyear Dunlop Tires Hellas S.A.I.C. (Greece)
Goodyear Dunlop Tires Hungary Ltd.
Goodyear Dunlop Tires Ireland Ltd
Goodyear Dunlop Tires Italia SpA (Italy)
Goodyear Dunlop Tires Polska Sp z.o.o. (Poland)
Goodyear Dunlop Tires Portugal Unipessoal Lda
Goodyear Dunlop Tires Slovakia s.r.o.
Goodyear Dunlop Tires Suisse S.A. (Switzerland)
The Kelly-Springfield Tyre Company Ltd (UK)
Wingfoot Corporation

COMPETITORS

Bridgestone	Pep Boys
Continental AG	Pirelli
Cooper Tire & Rubber	Sime Darby
Hankook Tire	Titan International
Kumho Tire	Toyo Tire & Rubber
Marangoni	Yokohama Rubber
Michelin	Zeon
Midas	

HISTORICAL FINANCIALS

Company Type: Public

Income Statement

FYE: December 31

	REVENUE ($ mil.)	NET INCOME ($ mil.)	NET PROFIT MARGIN	EMPLOYEES
12/19	14,745	(311)	—	63,000
12/18	15,475	693	4.5%	64,000
12/17	15,377	346	2.3%	64,000
12/16	15,158	1,264	8.3%	66,000
12/15	16,443	307	1.9%	66,000
Annual Growth	(2.7%)	—	—	(1.2%)

2019 Year-End Financials

Debt ratio: 32.95%
Return on equity: (-6.75%)
Cash ($ mil.): 908
Current ratio: 1.12
Long-term debt ($ mil.): 4,753
No. of shares (mil.): 232
Dividends
Yield: 4.1%
Payout: 78.0%
Market value ($ mil.): 3,619

	STOCK PRICE ($) FY Close	P/E High/Low	PER SHARE ($) Earnings	Dividends	Book Value
12/19	15.56	— —	(1.33)	0.64	18.70
12/18	20.41	12 7	2.89	0.58	20.95
12/17	32.31	27 21	1.37	0.44	19.17
12/16	30.87	7 5	4.74	0.31	17.91
12/15	32.67	31 21	1.12	0.25	14.68
Annual Growth	(16.9%)	— —	—	26.5%	6.2%

GOVERNMENT OF DISTRICT OF COLUMBIA

Our nation's capital is its own jurisdiction — and the Government of the District of Columbia manages it. The government body manages ticket and tax payments housing and property issues children and youth services and motor vehicles registration among other duties for Washington DC. More than 658000 people live in Washington DC and many more commute to the city every day to work for the federal government. Washington DC is overseen by a mayor and a 13-member city council. It acquires contracts with more than 30 local government agencies. The Government of the District of Columbia was created in 1790 with donated land from Maryland and Virginia as part of the Residence Act.

EXECUTIVES

Cfo, Jeffrey S. DeWitt
City Administrator, Rashad M. Young
Mayor, Muriel Bowser
Cto, Archana Vemulapalli
Secretary, Mary Pelzer
Auditors: SB & COMPANY LLC WASHINGTON

LOCATIONS

HQ: GOVERNMENT OF DISTRICT OF COLUMBIA
441 4TH ST NW, WASHINGTON, DC 200012714
Phone: 202 727-0252
Web: WWW.DC.GOV

PRODUCTS/OPERATIONS

Selected Services
311 Service Request Online
Children and Youth Services
District Neighborhoods
Emergency Preparedness
Health and Human Services
Housing and Property
Pay a Ticket
Public Safety
Public Works Sanitation and Utilities
Taxpayer Service Center
Transportation and Motor Vehicles

HISTORICAL FINANCIALS

Company Type: Private

Income Statement   FYE: September 30

	REVENUE ($ mil.)	NET INCOME ($ mil.)	NET PROFIT MARGIN	EMPLOYEES
09/16	12,095	(78)	—	34,600
09/15	11,637	583	5.0%	—
09/11	9,822	102	1.0%	—
09/05	0	0	—	—
Annual Growth	—	—	—	—

Grainger (W.W.) Inc.

W.W. Grainger distributes about 1.6 million industrial products from supplies to equipment and tools. The company offers material-handling equipment safety and security supplies lighting and electrical products power and hand tools pumps and plumbing supplies cleaning and maintenance supplies and metalworking tools. Its more than 3.5 million customers are government manufacturing transportation commercial and contractors. Grainger sells through a network of branches distribution centers catalogs sales and service representatives and websites. More than three quarters of its revenue are generated from customers in the US.

Operations

Grainger's US business is its largest operating segment representing more than 70% of net sales. The segment's product lines include lighting and electrical equipment power and hand tools pumps and plumbing and cleaning and maintenance supplies. The US business purchases products from approximately 5000 key suppliers most of which are manufacturers.

The majority of products sold by the US business are nationally branded products. In addition about 20% of its sales were private label MRO (maintenance repair and operations) items bearing Grainger's trademarks including DAYTON SPEEDAIRE AIR HANDLER TOUGH GUY WESTWARD CONDOR and LUMAPRO.

Acklands-Grainger the company's core Canadian business focuses on distributing industrial and safety products via about 60 domestic branches and distribution centers. The business represents about 5% of the company's sales.

Besides a wide range of products Grainger also provides services that include inventory management and energy efficiency assistance for lower maintenance costs. The company's KeepStock program offers vendor-managed inventory customer-managed inventory and onsite vending machines. Other offerings include its endless assortment businesses US-based Zoro (online MRO distributor) and MonotaRO which operates in Japan and other Asian countries primarily through websites and catalogs.

Geographic Reach

More than 75% of Grainger's sales stem from the US about 5% in Canada and the rest in Europe Asia and Latin America. With locations in all 50 states the US business has about 280 branches and more than 15 distribution centers. The company also has over 50 branches and five distribution centers in Canada.

Grainger headquarter is located in Lake Forest Illinois.

Sales and Marketing

Grainger offers its services to a range of industries such as government manufacturing transportation commercial and contractors. It markets its products through sales and service representatives distribution centers e-commerce platforms branches and contact centers.

Grainger's advertising expense was $316 million $241 million and $187 million for 2019 2018 and 2017 respectively.

Financial Performance

Grainger has seen solid revenue growth in recent years. Its annual revenues have risen 15% since 2015 driven in part by an uptick in the economy and mid-sized customer growth.

Grainger's net sales of $11.5 billion for the year ended 2019 increased $265 million or 3% compared to the same period in 2018. The increase in net sales was primarily driven by volume increases in the U.S. business from market share gain and continued double-digit growth in the endless assortments businesses partially offset by lower sales in the Canada business and other businesses.

Net earnings attributable to W.W. Grainger Inc. for the year ended 2019 increased $67 million or 8% to $849 million from $782 million in the same period in 2018. The increase in net earnings primarily resulted from lower SG&A and other expense net.

Cash held by the company at the end of 2019 decreased by $178 million to $360 million compared to $538 million in the prior year. Cash provided by operating activities was $1 billion in fiscal 2019 while investing activities used $202 million. Financing activities used another $1.0 billion.

Strategy

In the large and fragmented MRO industry Grainger's strategy is to relentlessly expand its leadership position (i.e. supply chain infrastructure broad in-stock product offering and deep customer relationships) by being the go-to partner for customers who build and run safe sustainable and productive operations. To execute this strategy the Company competes with two business models: high-touch solutions and endless assortment. Grainger's high-touch solutions businesses serve customers with complex needs primarily in North America and Europe. The endless assortment businesses are focused on customers with less-complex needs and includes Zoro Tools Inc. (Zoro) in the United States (U.S.) and MonotaRO Co. Ltd. (MonotaRO) in Japan. Competing with these two models allows Grainger to leverage its scale and advantaged supply chain to meet the changing needs of its customers. The company has been reducing its footprint in Canada amid a challenging market in recent years. Grainger has reduced the number of Canadian branches from 181 in 2014 to approximately 50 branches in 2018.

HISTORY

In 1919 William W. Grainger a motor designer and salesman saw the opportunity to develop a wholesale electric-motor sales and distribution company. He set up an office in Chicago in 1927 and incorporated the business a year later. With sales generated primarily through postcard mailers and an eight-page catalog called MotorBook Grainger started shipping motors to mail-order customers.

Utilities and factories began to shift from direct-current to alternating-current power systems in the late 1920s. Uniform DC-powered assembly lines gave way to individual workstations each powered by a separate AC motor. This burgeoning market opened the way for distributors such as W.W. Grainger to tap into segments that high-volume manufacturers found difficult to reach. In the early 1930s W.W. Grainger opened offices in Atlanta Dallas Philadelphia and San Francisco; by 1936 it had 15 sales branches.

W.W. Grainger entered a boom period after WWII and by 1949 it had branches in 30 states. The company continued to expand in the 1950s and 1960s then went public in 1967.

William Grainger retired in 1968 and his son David succeeded him as CEO. The company expanded into electric motor manufacturing with the purchase of the Doerr Companies in 1969. Ten years later it opened its 150th branch.

Grainger's distribution became decentralized with the 1983 opening of its 1.4-million-sq.-ft. automated regional distribution center in Kansas City. The next year Grainger surpassed $1 billion in sales. The company sold its Doerr Electric subsidiary to Emerson Electric in 1986. It added 91 branches in 1987 and 1988.

After a 17-year hiatus the company started making acquisitions again buying Vonnegut Industrial Products in 1989; Bossert Industrial Supply and Allied Safety in 1990; Ball Industries a distributor of sanitary and janitorial supplies in 1991; and Lab Safety Supply in 1992. Grainger began integrating its sanitary supply business with its core activities in 1993.

For the first time in company history no Grainger held the CEO position when president Richard Keyser was appointed in 1995 replacing David Grainger. That year the company moved its headquarters to Lake Forest Illinois.

EXECUTIVES

Svp And General Counsel, John L. Howard, age 63, $673,828 total compensation

Svp And Chief People Officer, Joseph C. High, age 67, $495,250 total compensation

Svp And Cfo, Ronald L. Jadin, age 60, $721,885 total compensation

Chairman And Ceo, Donald G. (D.G.) Macpherson, age 53, $875,000 total compensation

Svp Global Supply Chain Branch Network Contact Centers And Corporate Strategy, Paige K. Robbins, age 51, $441,769 total compensation

Vice President Digital Engineering And Information Management, Scot Gillespie

Vice President Customer Information And Business Insights, Shailesh Sood

Vice President Of Human Resources Global Enterprise, Tom Culhane

Regional Sales Vice President, Daniel Moscaritolo

Vice President Marketing, Jim Penvillo

Regional Sales Vice President, Lloyd Peterson

Vice President Of Information Technology, Kathleen Tullis

Regional Sales Vice President, Brian Norris

Vice President International Market Development, Bonnie McIntyre

National Accounts Manager, Michael Taylor

Vice President Of Information Technology, Linda Mclaughlin

Vice President Corporate Strategy And Continuous Improvement, Elizabeth Ubell

Senior Vice President Communications And Investor Relations, Laura Brown

Vice President User Services. Mergers And Acquisitions And Specialty Brands, Bill Koenig

Vp; President Grainger International, Fred Costello

Vice President Eps Support Services, Mike Smuda

Vice President Controller, Eric Tapia

Senior Vice President Human Resources, Lawrence Pilon

Vp Operations And Infrastructure, Linda Worley-ray

Vp And Cio, Gregory Harman

Vp And President Acklands Grainger Inc., John Kaul

Vp Finance Us Business, Toni Sullivan

Svp And Cfo, Thomas B Okray

Vice President Of Information Technology, Garrett Goluszka

Board Member, Michael Roberts

Board Member, Mike Roberts

Board Member, Neil Novich

Board Member, Arlyn Perez

Board Member, Stuart Levenick

Board Member, Amber Watson

Auditors: Ernst & Young LLP

LOCATIONS

HQ: Grainger (W.W.) Inc.
100 Grainger Parkway, Lake Forest, IL 60045-5201
Phone: 847 535-1000   **Fax:** 847 535-0878
Web: www.grainger.com

2016 Sales

	$ mil.	% of total
US	7,834	77
Canada	739	7
Other countries	1,563	16
Total	**10,137**	**100**

PRODUCTS/OPERATIONS

2016 Sales

	$ mil.	% of total
US-based businesses	7,522	74
Canada-based businesses	733	7
Other businesses	1,880	19
Total	**10,137**	**100**

Selected Products

Adhesives
Air compressors
Air-filtration equipment
Electric motors
Electrical products
Fasteners
Fleet and vehicle maintenance products
Hand tools
Heating and ventilation equipment
Janitorial and plumbing supplies
Lab supplies
Library equipment
Lighting equipment
Material handling
Pneumatics and hydraulics
Power tools
Pumps
Safety products
Security products
Spray paints
Test Instruments

COMPETITORS

Ace Hardware
Applied Industrial Technologies
Fastenal
Genuine Parts
Gexpro
Graybar Electric
Industrial Distribution Group
International Library Furniture
Kaman Industrial Technologies
Lowe's
MSC Industrial Direct
McMaster-Carr
WESCO International
Wilson

HISTORICAL FINANCIALS

Company Type: Public

Income Statement				FYE: December 31
	REVENUE ($ mil.)	NET INCOME ($ mil.)	NET PROFIT MARGIN	EMPLOYEES
12/19	11,486	849	7.4%	25,300
12/18	11,221	782	7.0%	24,600
12/17	10,424	585	5.6%	25,700
12/16	10,137	605	6.0%	25,600
12/15	9,973	769	7.7%	25,800
Annual Growth	**3.6%**	**2.5%**	**—**	**(0.5%)**

2019 Year-End Financials

Debt ratio: 36.89%
Return on equity: 44.97%
Cash ($ mil.): 360
Current ratio: 2.12
Long-term debt ($ mil.): 1,914

No. of shares (mil.): 53
Dividends
  Yield: 1.6%
  Payout: 33.2%
Market value ($ mil.): 18,174

	STOCK PRICE ($) FY Close	P/E High/Low		PER SHARE ($) Earnings	Dividends	Book Value
12/19	338.52	22	17	15.32	5.68	34.55
12/18	282.36	27	16	13.73	5.36	34.39
12/17	236.25	26	16	10.02	5.06	30.00
12/16	232.25	24	18	9.87	4.83	30.57
12/15	202.59	22	16	11.58	4.59	36.54
Annual Growth	**13.7%**	**—**	**—**	**7.2%**	**5.5%**	**(1.4%)**

Granite Point Mortgage Trust Inc

Auditors: Ernst & Young LLP

LOCATIONS

HQ: Granite Point Mortgage Trust Inc
3 Bryant Park, Suite 2400A, New York, NY 10036
Phone: 212 364-5000
Web: www.gpmtreit.com

HISTORICAL FINANCIALS

Company Type: Public

Income Statement				FYE: December 31
	ASSETS ($ mil.)	NET INCOME ($ mil.)	INCOME AS % OF ASSETS	EMPLOYEES
12/19	4,460	70	1.6%	—
12/18	3,361	63	1.9%	—
12/17	2,499	53	2.1%	—
12/16	1,495	35	2.4%	—
12/15	722	0	0.0%	—
Annual Growth	**57.6%**	**374.9%**	**—**	**—**

2019 Year-End Financials

Debt ratio: 30.32%
Return on equity: 7.60%
Cash ($ mil.): 80
Current ratio: —
Long-term debt ($ mil.): —

No. of shares (mil.): 54
Dividends
  Yield: 9.1%
  Payout: 122.6%
Market value ($ mil.): 1,008

	STOCK PRICE ($) FY Close	P/E High/Low		PER SHARE ($) Earnings	Dividends	Book Value
12/19	18.38	15	14	1.32	1.68	18.60
12/18	18.03	13	11	1.42	1.62	18.99
12/17	17.74	32	29	0.60	0.70	19.19
Annual Growth	**0.9%**	**—**	**—**	**21.8%**	**24.5%**	**(0.8%)**

Graybar Electric Co., Inc.

Graybar Electric is one of the largest distributors of electrical and communications and data networking products and is a provider of related supply chain management and logistics services in the US. The employee-owned company distributes more than 1 million electrical communications and data networking products through a network of around 290 distribution facilities.. It also offers supply chain management and logistics services. . Graybar Electric serve customers in the construction industrial & utility vertical markets and commercial institutional and government (CIG) primarily in the US.

Operations

The company purchase all of the products it sell from others and it neither manufacture nor contract to manufacture any products it sell. In addition to its extensive product offering the company provides a wide range of supply chain management services that when combined with its network of locations are designed to deliver convenience cost savings and improved efficiency for its customers.

Graybar is a distributor of electrical and communications and data networking products to the construction CIG and industrial & utility verticals in North America.

Geographic Reach

Graybar's business is primarily based in the US as its headquarters are located in St. Louis Missouri. Other operations include distribution facilities in Canada and Puerto Rico. The company serves its customers through a network of nearly 290 locations across the US and Canada.

It also operates in about 15 geographical districts in the US each of which maintains multiple distribution facilities that consist primarily of warehouse space. Most of the districts have around 20 sales and distribution facilities.

Sales and Marketing

Among the company's strengths is a diverse and large customer base with approximately 146000 clients. Graybar gets some 60% of its sales from the construction sector. Other customers come from the institutional commercial and government (more than 20%) and industrial and utility (20%) sectors.

Graybar distributes one million products purchased from more than 4500 manufacturers and suppliers. The company sells approximately 50% of the products from its top 25 suppliers.

Financial Performance

The company's 2019 net sales totaled $7.5 billion an increase of $321.4 million or 5% compared to net sales of $7.2 billion for the year ended December 31 2018. In 2019 net sales in their construction CIG and industrial & utility verticals increased 5% 3% and 3% respectively.

Net income attributable to Graybar Electric Company Inc. for the year ended December 31 2019 was $144.5 million which was $1.2 million or 1% higher than net income attributable to Graybar Electric Company Inc. of $143.3 million for the year ended December 31 2018.

Graybar's cash on hand grew $1.9 million during 2019 ending the year at $60.8 million. The company's operations generated $249.4 million offset by $39.4 million used in its investing activities. Financing activities used another $208.1 million payment of dividends.

Strategy

The company manage their liquidity and capital levels so that they have the capability to invest in the growth of their business meet debt service obligations finance anticipated capital expenditures pay dividends make benefit payments finance information technology needs fund acquisitions and finance other miscellaneous cash outlays. Graybar believe that maintaining a strong company financial condition enables us to competitively access multiple financing channels maintain an optimal cost of capital and enable their company to invest in strategic long-term growth plans.

Graybar achieved positive results in 2019 by investing in the people services and technology to grow their business and improve their productivity. The company believe these investments contributed to their strong performance last year and will also serve as foundational building blocks for success in the years to come. As they work to transform their company for the future Graybar remain focused on providing an exceptional customer experience boosting efficiency in the supply chain and inspiring a culture of innovation agility and growth throughout the company.

HISTORY

After serving as a telegrapher during the Civil War Enos Barton borrowed $400 from his widowed mother in 1869 and started an electrical equipment shop in Cleveland with George Shawk. Later that year Elisha Gray a professor of physics at Oberlin College who had several inventions (including a printing telegraph) to his credit bought Shawk's interest in the shop and the firm of Gray & Barton moved to Chicago where a third partner joined.

The company incorporated as the Western Electric Manufacturing Co. in 1872 with two-thirds of the company's stock held by two Western Union executives. As the telegraph industry took off the enterprise grew rapidly providing equipment to towns and railroads in the western US.

Western Electric then formed a new distribution business in 1926 Graybar Electric Co. (from "Gray" and "Barton") the world's largest electrical supply merchandiser. In 1929 employees bought the company from Western Electric for $3 million in cash and $6 million in preferred stock. During the 1930s it marketed a line of appliances and sewing machines under the Graybar name.

EXECUTIVES

Regional Vp Western Region, Dennis E. DeSousa, age 62, $276,571 total compensation

Svp North American Business, Robert C. Lyons, age 64, $268,435 total compensation

Svp Marketing, William P. Mansfield, age 58, $256,288 total compensation

Svp And Cfo, Randall R. Harwood, age 64, $280,000 total compensation

Svp Sales And Director, David G. Maxwell

Chairman President And Ceo, Kathleen M. Mazzarella, age 59, $854,921 total compensation

Svp Secretary And General Counsel, Matthew W. Geekie, age 58, $313,119 total compensation

Svp Human Resources And Director, Beverly L. Propst, age 50, $284,632 total compensation

Vp And Cio, David Meyer

Svp Supply Chain Management, Scott S. Clifford, age 49

Vice President Education Graybar Electric, Chris Althauser

Vice President Of Marketing, Rob Bezjak

District Vice President, Joseph Lamotte

Auditors: Ernst & Young LLP

LOCATIONS

HQ: Graybar Electric Co., Inc.
34 North Meramec Avenue, St. Louis, MO 63105
Phone: 314 573-9200
Web: www.graybar.com

2018 Sales

	% of total
US	95
Other countries	5
Total	**100**

PRODUCTS/OPERATIONS

2018 Sales

	% of total
Construction	60
Commercial Institutional and Government	19
Utility & Industrial	21
Total	**100**

Selected Products

Ballasts
Batteries
Cable
Conduit
Connectors
Emergency lighting
Enclosures
Fiber-optic cable
Fittings
Fluorescent lighting
Fuses
Hand tools
Hangers/fasteners
Heating and ventilating equipment
Industrial fans
Lighting
Lubricants
Paints
Patch cords
Smoke detectors
Testing and measuring instruments
Timers
Transfer switches
Transformers
Utility products
Wire

Selected Subsidiaries

Commonwealth Controls Corporation
Distribution Associates Inc.
Graybar Business Services Inc.
Graybar Canada Limited
Graybar Commerce Corporation
Graybar Electric Canada Limited
Graybar Financial Services Inc.
Graybar International Inc.
Graybar Services Inc.

COMPETITORS

Anixter International	Rexel Canada
Border States Electric	Rexel Inc.
Communications Supply	Richardson Electronics
Consolidated	SUMMIT Electric Supply
Electrical	Sonepar USA
Gexpro	United Electric Supply
HD Supply	W.W. Grainger
HWC	WESCO International
Premier Farnell	

HISTORICAL FINANCIALS

Company Type: Public

Income Statement

FYE: December 31

	REVENUE ($ mil.)	NET INCOME ($ mil.)	NET PROFIT MARGIN	EMPLOYEES
12/19	7,523	144	1.9%	9,100
12/18	7,202	143	2.0%	8,700
12/17	6,631	71	1.1%	8,500
12/16	6,385	93	1.5%	8,500
12/15	6,110	91	1.5%	8,300
Annual Growth	5.3%	12.2%	—	2.3%

2019 Year-End Financials

Debt ratio: 5.94%	No. of shares (mil.): 22
Return on equity: 16.43%	Dividends
Cash ($ mil.): 60	Yield: —
Current ratio: 1.46	Payout: 78.0%
Long-term debt ($ mil.): 7	Market value ($ mil.): —

Great Southern Bancorp, Inc.

Despite its name Great Southern Bancorp is firmly entrenched in the heartland. It is the holding company for nearly 200-year-old Great Southern Bank which offers loans deposit accounts CDs IRAs and credit cards through more than 75 branches in Missouri plus more than two dozen locations in Iowa Kansas Nebraska Minnesota and Arkansas. The firm's Great Southern Travel division is one of the largest travel agencies in Missouri. It serves both leisure and corporate travelers through about a dozen offices. Great Southern Insurance offers property/casualty and life insurance while Great Southern Financial provides investment products and services through an agreement with Ameriprise.

Operations

Great Southern loan portfolio is mostly made up of real estate loans. Commercial real estate mortgages and construction and land development loans accounted for around half of its loan portfolio at the end of 2015 while single-family residential mortgages made up another roughly 15%. The bank also writes consumer (including home equity) construction and business loans.

The bank made 82% of its total revenue from loan interest during 2015 while the rest of its revenue came from service charges and fees (9% of revenue) and other non-interest income sources.

Sales and Marketing

The bank served more than 169000 households mostly in Missouri but also in Arkansas Iowa Kansas Minnesota and Nebraska. It spent $2.3 million on advertising during 2015 compared to $2.4 million and $2.17 million in 2014 and 2013 respectively.

Financial Performance

Great Southern has struggled to consistently grow its revenues in recent years despite a 30% rise in loan assets since 2011 mostly as it's been selling off more of its interest-earning mortgage-backed securities assets. Its profits have been rising thanks to declining loan loss provisions as its loan portfolio's credit quality has improved with higher property valuations in the strengthened economy.

The bank's revenue dipped less than 1% to $197.93 million during 2015 as the bank continued to sell more of its mortgage-backed securities which led to lower interest income. It also earned $2.14 million less in gains from security sales than it did in 2014.

Despite modest revenue declines in 2015 Great Southern's net income climbed 7% to $46.5 million mostly as in 2014 it incurred prepayment penalties when it repaid $130 million of its FHLB advances. The bank's operating cash levels rose 6% to $71.42 million thanks to the increase in cash-denominated earnings.

Strategy

Great Southern Bancorp continues to expand its bank network to grow its loan and deposit business either through new branch openings or by acquiring branches in new geographic markets. Its branch network has grown from 104 branches in 2011 to 110 at the end of 2015.

Mergers and Acquisitions

In 2015 the bank purchased 12 branches and related deposit and loan business in the St. Louis area from Cincinnati-based Fifth Third Bank more than doubling its branch presence in the St. Louis area.

EXECUTIVES

Vp Operations And Secretary Great Southern Bank, Douglas W. (Doug) Marrs, age 62, $122,602 total compensation
Vice President Human Resources, Matt Snyder
Vice President, Bob Ogden
Svp And Chief Lending Officer Of The Bank, Steven G. Mitchem, age 68, $227,429 total compensation
President Ceo And Director Great Southern Bancorp And Great Southern Bank, Joseph W. (Joe) Turner, age 55, $299,237 total compensation
Svp And Cfo Great Southern Bank, Rex A. Copeland, age 55, $235,201 total compensation
Vp Information Systems, Linton J. (Lin) Thomason, age 63
Vice President, Jennifer Cook
Vice President Information Services, Lynn Thomason

Assistant Vice President, Denit Patrick
Vice President Commercial Lending, Kent Lammers
Vice President Operations, Tonia Tillman
Chairman Great Southern Bancorp And Great Southern Bank, William V. Turner, age 87
Board Member, Douglas Pitt
Auditors: BKD, LLP

LOCATIONS

HQ: Great Southern Bancorp, Inc.
1451 E. Battlefield, Springfield, MO 65804
Phone: 417 887-4400
Web: www.greatsouthernbank.com

COMPETITORS

Arvest Bank	Hawthorn Bancshares
BancorpSouth	NASB Financial
Bank of America	Scottrade
Commerce Bancshares	U.S. Bancorp
First Bancshares (MO)	UMB Financial
Guaranty Federal	Wells Fargo

HISTORICAL FINANCIALS

Company Type: Public

Income Statement

FYE: December 31

	ASSETS ($ mil.)	NET INCOME ($ mil.)	INCOME AS % OF ASSETS	EMPLOYEES
12/19	5,015	73	1.5%	1,191
12/18	4,676	67	1.4%	1,182
12/17	4,414	51	1.2%	1,225
12/16	4,550	45	1.0%	1,263
12/15	4,104	46	1.1%	1,270
Annual Growth	5.1%	12.2%	—	(1.6%)

2019 Year-End Financials

Debt ratio: 1.99%
Return on equity: 12.97%
Cash ($ mil.): 220
Current ratio: —
Long-term debt ($ mil.): —

No. of shares (mil.): 14
Dividends
 Yield: 3.2%
 Payout: 40.5%
Market value ($ mil.): 903

	STOCK PRICE ($) FY Close	P/E High/Low		PER SHARE ($) Earnings	Dividends	Book Value
12/19	63.32	12	9	5.14	2.07	42.29
12/18	46.03	13	9	4.71	1.20	37.59
12/17	51.65	16	9	3.64	1.82	33.48
12/16	54.65	17	11	3.21	0.88	30.77
12/15	45.26	16	11	3.28	0.86	28.67
Annual Growth	8.8%	—	—	11.9%	24.6%	10.2%

Great Western Bancorp Inc

LOCATIONS

HQ: Great Western Bancorp Inc
225 South Main Avenue, Sioux Falls, SD 57104
Phone: 605 334-2548
Web: www.greatwesternbank.com

HISTORICAL FINANCIALS

Company Type: Public

Income Statement

FYE: September 30

	ASSETS ($ mil.)	NET INCOME ($ mil.)	INCOME AS % OF ASSETS	EMPLOYEES
09/20	12,604	(680)	—	1,714
09/19	12,788	167	1.3%	1,666
09/18	12,116	157	1.3%	1,664
09/17	11,690	144	1.2%	1,689
09/16	11,531	121	1.1%	1,649
Annual Growth	2.2%	—	—	1.0%

2020 Year-End Financials

Debt ratio: 2.41%
Return on equity: (-44.33%)
Cash ($ mil.): 432
Current ratio: —
Long-term debt ($ mil.): —

No. of shares (mil.): 55
Dividends
 Yield: 6.1%
 Payout: —
Market value ($ mil.): 685

	STOCK PRICE ($) FY Close	P/E High/Low		PER SHARE ($) Earnings	Dividends	Book Value
09/20	12.45	—	—	(12.24)	0.76	21.14
09/19	33.00	15	10	2.92	1.10	33.76
09/18	42.19	17	14	2.67	0.90	31.24
09/17	41.28	18	13	2.45	0.74	29.83
09/16	33.32	16	11	2.14	0.56	28.34
Annual Growth	(21.8%)	—	—	—	7.9%	(7.1%)

GREENSTONE FARM CREDIT SERVICES ACA

One of the largest associations in the Farm Credit System GreenStone offers FARM CREDIT SERVICES (FCS) providesÂ short intermediate and long-term loans; equipment and building leases; appraisal services; and life and crop insurance to farmers in Michigan and Wisconsin. ItÂ serves about 15000 members and has nearlyÂ 40 locations. Through an alliance with AgriSolutions a farm software and consulting company Greenstone provides income tax planning and preparation services farm business consulting and educational seminars. FCS Mortgage provides residential loans for rural properties as well as loans for home improvement construction and refinancing.

EXECUTIVES

Executive Vice President, Melissa Stolicker
Senior Vice President Chief Legal Counsel, Peter Lemmer
Senior Vice President Chief Information Officer, Steve Junglas
Vice President Human Resources, Bethany Barker
Regional Vice President, Cindy Birchmeier
Assistant Vice President Credit, Sarah J Morack
Vice President Credit, Kevin Emison
Vice President Commercial Lending, Daniel Gitter
Vice President Of Marketing And Public Relations, Melissa Rogers
Senior Vice President Chief Financial Officer, Travis Jones
Vice President Credit, Steve Kluemper
Vice President Commercial Lending, Troy Click
Vice President Credit, Thomas Urban

Regional Vice President Sales And Customer
 Relations, Ben Mahlich
Regional Vice President Sales And Customer
 Relations, Melissa Humphrey
Second Vice President, Shane Kenner
Vice President Commercial Lending, Kyle Hurley
Avp Credit And Syndicated Lending, Bonnie
 Coponen
Vice President Capital Markets, Brad Hibbert
Secretary Treasurer, Tracy Koch
Auditors: PRICEWATERHOUSECOOPERS LLP MI

LOCATIONS

HQ: GREENSTONE FARM CREDIT SERVICES ACA
 3515 WEST RD, EAST LANSING, MI 488237312
Phone: 517 324-0213
Web: WWW.GREENSTONEFCS.COM

COMPETITORS

COUNTRY Financial   Rabobank Group
FB BanCorp

HISTORICAL FINANCIALS

Company Type: Private

Income Statement				FYE: December 31
	ASSETS ($ mil.)	NET INCOME ($ mil.)	INCOME AS % OF ASSETS	EMPLOYEES
12/07	4,317	69	1.6%	380
12/06	3,691	63	1.7%	—
Annual Growth	17.0%	8.9%	—	—

Group 1 Automotive, Inc.

Group 1 Automotive is a new and used car re-tailer with more than 185 dealerships some 240 franchises and about 50 collision service centers. It operates in the US UK and Brazil. The US is the biggest market and the company is present in 15 US states. Group 1's largest concentration of dealerships is in its home state of Texas. Of the some 30 car and light truck brands Group 1 offers Toyota/Lexus vehicles are its biggest sellers followed by BMW/MINI and Volkswagen/Audi/Porsche/SEAT/SKODA. The company also offers financing provides maintenance and repair services and sells replacement parts. It went public in 1997.

Operations

Group 1 Automotive's had three reportable segments: U.S. (more than 75%) U.K. (20%) and Brazil (about 5%).

The U.S. and Brazil segments are led by the President U.S. and Brazilian Operations and the U.K segment is led by a Managing Director each reporting directly to the Company's Chief Executive Officer who is the Chief Operating Decision Maker. Each of the segments is comprised of retail automotive franchises that sell new and used cars and light trucks; arrange related vehicle financing; sell service insurance contracts; provide automotive maintenance and repair services; and sell vehicle parts. The vast majority of the Company's corporate activities are associated with the operations of the U.S. segment and therefore the corpo-rate financial results are included within the U.S. segment.

The company's brand offerings include: Toyota BMW Porsche SEAT SKODA Ford Lincoln Audi Buick Cadillac Mercedes-Benz Smart Sprinter Chrysler Honda Nissan Lexus Chevrolet Volkswagen Dodge Jaguar Land Rover Mini Jeep Acura GMC RAM Hyundai Kia Genesis and Other.

Geographic Reach

The company lease their corporate headquarters located at Houston Texas as well as their regional headquarters in Brazil. They own their regional headquarters in the U.K. At fiscal year 2019 they had more than 185 dealerships about 245 franchises and nearly 50 collision centers in the United States United Kingdom and Brazil.

The company operations are located in geographically diverse markets that extend domestically across 15 states aggregated into one U.S. region and internationally in the U.K. and Brazil representing their three reportable segments: U.S. U.K. and Brazil.

Sales and Marketing

The Company expenses the costs of advertising as incurred. Advertising expense is included in Selling general and administrative expenses in the Consolidated Statements of Operations and totaled $75.2 million for both fiscal year 2019 and 2018. The Company receives advertising assistance from certain automobile manufacturers which the Company is required to spend on qualified advertising and which is subject to audit and chargeback by the manufacturer. The assistance is accounted for as a reduction to SG&A expenses as earned and amounted to $15.4 million in 2019 respectively.

Financial Performance

Group 1's revenue has steadily increased the past five years.

In 2019 revenue rose about to $12.0 billion compared to $11.6 billion in 2019 despite a drop in used vehicle wholesale sales in the US and the UK. The increase in U.S. same store revenue was driven by growth in all of our revenue streams with the exception of used vehicle wholesale sales.

The company's profit raised to $174.0 million in 2019 from $157.8 million in 2018.

Group 1 had $28.1 million in cash in 2019 compared to $18.7 million the year before. Operations produced $370.9 million in 2019 while investing activities used $291.6 million and financing activities used $67.0 million.

The company carries about $1.5 billion in debt which could hamper its ability to raise new debt and limit its flexibility in responding to industry and economic changes.

Strategy

The company's business strategy primarily focuses on the performance of their existing dealerships to achieve growth capture market share and maximize the investment return to their stockholders and also focuses on enhancing their dealership portfolio through strategic acquisitions and dispositions. They constantly evaluate opportunities to improve the overall profitability of their dealerships. For 2020 their priorities are: Used Vehicle Retail Growth; Parts and Service Growth; Digital Initiatives to Enhance the Customer Experience; and Cost Management as They Continue to Grow Gross Profit.

Group 1 acquisition strategy they seek to acquire large profitable well-established dealerships and franchises that are leaders in their markets to: enhance brand and geographic diversity with a primary focus on import and luxury brands; expand their brand product and service offerings in their existing markets; expand into geographic areas they currently do not serve; and/or capitalize on economies of scale and cost savings opportunities in their existing markets in areas such as used vehicle sourcing advertising purchasing data pro-cessing personnel utilization and the cost of floor-plan financing thereby increasing operating efficiency.

Their divestiture strategy is they continually review the investments in their dealership portfolio for disposition opportunities based upon a number of criteria including: the rate of return on their capital investment over a period of time; location of the dealership in relation to existing markets and their ability to leverage our cost structure; potential future capital investment requirements; the brand; and existing real estate obligations coupled with their ability to exit those obligations or identify an alternate use for real estate.

Mergers and Acquisitions

In 2019 the Company acquired four dealerships representing six franchises in the U.S. and four dealerships representing five franchises in the U.K. Aggregate consideration paid for these dealerships which were accounted for as business combinations totaled $143.2 million. They also opened one dealership representing one franchise in the U.S. and two dealerships representing three franchises in the U.K.

In mid-2019 Group 1 expanded its presence in the New Mexico market with the acquisition of two BMW/MINI dealerships in Albuquerque and Santa Fe. The deal also includes BMW Motorrad franchises in Albuquerque and Santa Fe making Group 1 the exclusive seller of BMW Motorcycles in New Mexico.

In late-2019 the Company acquires two Lexus Dealerships in New Mexico. The dealerships are located in Albuquerque and Santa Fe. These stores are the only Lexus franchises in the state of New Mexico and are expected to generate approximately $90 million in annualized revenues.

EXECUTIVES

President Ceo And Director, Earl J. Hesterberg, age 67, $1,100,000 total compensation
Vp Manufacturer Relations, Peter C. DeLongchamps, age 59, $456,300 total compensation
Svp Human Resources Training And Operations Support, Frank Grese, age 68, $540,000 total compensation
Svp And Cfo, John C. Rickel, age 59, $583,500 total compensation
Vp And General Counsel, Darryl M. Burman, age 62, $440,300 total compensation
Vp Information Systems, James R. Druzbik
Vice President Human Resources, Brooks O'hara
Vice President Human Resources, Brooks OHara
Vice President Corporate Development, Larry Caudill
Svp Hr Training And Operations Support, Frank Grese Jr
Chairman, Stephen D. Quinn, age 65
Corporate Treasurer, Kim Craig
Auditors: DELOITTE & TOUCHE LLP

LOCATIONS

HQ: Group 1 Automotive, Inc.
 800 Gessner, Suite 500, Houston, TX 77024
Phone: 713 647-5700   Fax: 713 647-5858
Web: www.group1auto.com

2018 Sales

	$ mil.	% of total
U.S.	8,723	75
U.K.	2,437	21
Brazil	440	4
Total	11,601	100

Dealership presence

Dealership presence
United States
 Alabama
 California

Florida
Georgia
Kansas
Louisiana
Maryland
Massachusetts
Mississippi
New Hampshire
New Jersey
New Mexico
Oklahoma
South Carolina
Texas
United Kingdom
Brighton
Chelmsford
Chingford
Farnborough
Hailsham
Harold Wood
Hindhead
Southend
Stansted
Worthington
Brazil
Sao Paolo
Parana
Mato Grosso do Sul

2018 Sales

	% of total
Grocery trade	52
Building and technical trade	39
Car trade	9
Total	**100**

Selected Kesko Divisions

Anttila (department stores home and specialty goods)
Kesko Agro Ltd. (agriculture and machinery)
Kesko Food Ltd. (groceries)
Rautakesko Ltd. (building supplies interior decoration
  and hardware)
VV-Auto (auto dealerships)

PRODUCTS/OPERATIONS

2018 Sales

	$ mil.	% of total
New vehicle retail	6,181	52
Used vehicle retail	3,166	28
Used vehicle wholesale	369	3
Parts & service	1,416	12
Finance insurance & other	467	4
Total	**11,601**	**100**

Selected Brands

Domestic
  Ford
  Chevrolet
  Dodge
  Jeep
  GMC
  Chrysler
  Buick
  RAM
Import
  Toyota
  Nissan
  Honda
  Volkswagen
  Hyundai
  Mazda
  Subaru
  Scion
  Kia
  Peugeot
  Renault
Luxury
  BMW
  Acura
  MINI
  Land Rover
  Lexus
  Mercedes
  Audi
  Volvo
  Cadillac
  Lincoln
  Porsche

Sprinter
smart
Jaguar

COMPETITORS

Ancira	Lookers
Asbury Automotive	Pendragon
AutoNation	Penske Automotive
CarMax	Group
David McDavid Auto	Phil Long Dealerships
Group	Sonic Automotive
Herb Chambers	Sytner
Lithia Motors	

HISTORICAL FINANCIALS

Company Type: Public

Income Statement   FYE: December 31

	REVENUE ($ mil.)	NET INCOME ($ mil.)	NET PROFIT MARGIN	EMPLOYEES
12/19	12,043	174	1.4%	15,296
12/18	11,601	157	1.4%	14,570
12/17	11,123	213	1.9%	14,108
12/16	10,887	147	1.4%	13,500
12/15	10,632	94	0.9%	12,886
Annual Growth	**3.2%**	**16.6%**	**—**	**4.4%**

2019 Year-End Financials

Debt ratio: 55.57%
Return on equity: 14.80%
Cash ($ mil.): 23
Current ratio: 1.04
Long-term debt ($ mil.): 1,432

No. of shares (mil.): 18
Dividends
Yield: 1.0%
Payout: 12.9%
Market value ($ mil.): 1,863

	STOCK PRICE ($) FY Close	P/E High/Low		PER SHARE ($) Earnings	Dividends	Book Value
12/19	100.00	12	6	9.34	1.09	67.41
12/18	52.72	11	6	7.83	1.04	59.80
12/17	70.97	8	5	10.08	0.97	53.80
12/16	77.94	12	7	6.67	0.91	43.46
12/15	75.70	25	19	3.90	0.83	39.22
Annual Growth	**7.2%**	**—**	**—**	**24.4%**	**7.1%**	**14.5%**

GROWMARK, INC.

Agricultural and energy cooperative GROW-MARK serves farm commercial and residential customers across the US and in parts of Canada. Under the Growmark FS name it offers a host of plant food and crop protection products as well as biotechnology services and training and agricultural marketing and consulting. The company also operates a full-line seed company Seedway and provides grain facility planning and grain marketing services. Lastly GROWMARK's energy offers a complete line of refined and renewable fuels lubricants and propane to member cooperatives and retail energy distributors including winterized fuels diesel exhaust fluid (DEF) biodiesel and bioblends.

Operations

GROWMARK delivers high quality agronomy and energy products as well as premium services from expert advisors. Its long-term relationships with manufacturers and refiners coupled with the company's extensive terminal network means GROWMARK has access to a broad and reliable supply of fertilizers fuel and propane. The company also offers private label crop protection products and proprietary brands of corn and soybean seeds.

In addition GROWMARK also provides grain marketing services through its subsidiary MID-CO COMMODITIES and has partnership with COFCO International. Its commercial construction provides equipment facilities and services that improve the operating efficiency of the company's customers. It is equipped to provide system consultations through complete turnkey construction services such as consultation development planning construction and operation. GROWMARK logistics includes brokerage services specializing in transporting and storing liquid fuel propane anhydrous ammonia bulk and packaged motor oils and crop inputs including seed liquid and dry fertilizer and bulk and packaged crop protection products while its Electronic Payments Network currently processes and settles more than 9.7 million transactions and approximately $500 million annually. The company keeps pace with regulatory and market demands for bank cards fleet cards DEBIT cards gift cards ACH/electronic check conversion and PC/web-based payments. Lastly GROWMARK Agronomy Equipment has national account relationships with John Deere Case IH AGCO and Caterpillar to provide its customers with competitive pricing and service from local dealer on application equipment tractors loaders construction equipment and small equipment.

GROWMARK's high performing product lines include proprietary brands FS InVISION FS HiSOY FS Wheat FS Alfalfa as well as distribution agreements with DEKALB Asgrow and NK.

Geographic Reach

GROWMARK is headquartered in Bloomington Illinois and serves customers in more than 40 US states and Ontario Canada. Its Electronic Payments Network serves network merchants across more than 15 states.

Its Seedway business has about 25 office and warehouse locations in Vermont North and South Carolina Mexico New York Pennsylvania and Florida among others.

Sales and Marketing

GROWMARK is serving cooperatives retailers grain companies and other business customers of all industries including freight brokerage and credit card processing.

Strategy

GROWMARK Inc. and Southern States Cooperative announced in September 2020 plans to close on a transaction that aligns the organizations operationally to yield increased innovation growth and returns for the farmer-owners of both cooperative systems.

GROWMARK will assume the wholesale agronomy and energy (fuels and propane) assets of Southern States along with several retail locations serving farmers in Delaware and Maryland. GROWMARK will provide crop inputs fuels propane and a variety of customer support and marketing services to Southern States and its member cooperatives. They in turn will continue to deliver custom solutions with access to GROWMARK's product mix distribution expertise and drive for innovation.

GROWMARK's vision is to be the best agricultural cooperative system in North America and this partnership enables both organizations to further that goal together. It is committed to delivering an unsurpassed customer experience to the patrons it serves across North America. The cooperative model is uniquely positioned to deliver that so this combination of efforts is great news for farmers invested in the cooperative organizations.

Company Background

GROWMARK traces its history back to 1920 and the establishment of local cooperatives by Farm Bureau members. One of those cooperatives Farm Bureau Service Company of Iowa in the early 1960s merged with Illinois Farm Supply Company (founded in 1927) to form the foundation of what is today GROWMARK. The GROWMARK name started being used in 1980.

EXECUTIVES

Vice President Agronomy, Jim Spradlin
Vice Chairman, John Reifsteck
Ceo, Jeff Solberg
Vp And General Counsel, Brent Bostrom
Vp Eastern Retail Operations, Steve Buckalew
Vp And Cfo, Marshall Bohbrink
Vp Energy, Kevin Carroll
Vp Midwest Retail And Acquisitions, Shelly Kruse
Vp Grain, Brent Ericson
Vice President Human Resources & Compliance, Gary Swango
Vp Agronomy, Mark Orr
Vp Financial And Risk Management, Mike Woods
Vp Member Services, Denny Worth
Region Vice President, Barry Schmidt
Senior Vice President, Jeffrey M Solberg
Vice President Corporate Services, Stan Nielsen
Vice President Information Technology, Carla Makowski
Vice Chairman, Rick Nelson
Vice Chairman, Chet Esther
Assistant Treasurer, Karmy Kays
Treasurer, Jeffrey Lynch
Auditors: ERNST & YOUNG LLP CHICAGO IL

LOCATIONS

HQ: GROWMARK, INC.
1701 TOWANDA AVE, BLOOMINGTON, IL 617012057
Phone: 309 557-6000
Web: WWW.GROWMARK.COM

COMPETITORS

ADM	Marathon Oil
AGRI Industries	NC Hybrids
Ag Processing Inc.	Orscheln Farm and Home
BP	Pfister Hybrid Corn
Barkley Seed	Pioneer Hi-Bred
Bayer CropScience	Rabo AgriFinance
CHS	Sakata Seed
Cargill	Seed Enterprises
Chevron	Southern States
Costco Wholesale	Terra Nitrogen
DeBruce Grain	Wal-Mart
Exxon Mobil	Wilbur-Ellis

HISTORICAL FINANCIALS

Company Type: Private

Income Statement				FYE: August 31
	REVENUE ($ mil.)	NET INCOME ($ mil.)	NET PROFIT MARGIN	EMPLOYEES
08/19	8,745	75	0.9%	7,000
08/18	8,522	65	0.8%	—
08/17	7,291	115	1.6%	—
08/16	7,031	101	1.4%	—
Annual Growth	7.5%	(9.4%)	—	—

Guaranty Bancshares Inc

Guaranty Bancshares is the holding company for Guaranty Bond Bank which operates about a dozen branches in northeast Texas and another in West Texas. Guaranty Bond Bank's deposit products and services include CDs and savings checking NOW and money market accounts.Â Its lending activities include one- to four-family residential mortgages (more than a third of the company's loan portfolio) in addition to commercial mortgage construction business agriculture and personal loans. The company's GB Financial division provides wealth management retirement planning and trust services.

EXECUTIVES

Senior Vice President, Terry Todd
Senior Vice President, Steve Bledsoe
Executive Vice President General Counsel, Randall Kucera
Auditors: Whitley Penn LLP

LOCATIONS

HQ: Guaranty Bancshares Inc
16475 Dallas Parkway, Suite 600, Addison, TX 75001
Phone: 888 572-9881
Web: www.gnty.com

PRODUCTS/OPERATIONS

2008 Sales		
	$ mil.	% of total
Interest		
Loans including fees	31	70
Securities	6	13
Other	1	2
Noninterest		
Service charges	4	8
Other	3	7
Total	**46**	**100**

COMPETITORS

BancorpSouth	Southside Bancshares
Bank of America	Wells Fargo
Capital One	Woodforest Financial
Cullen/Frost Bankers	

HISTORICAL FINANCIALS

Company Type: Public

Income Statement				FYE: December 31
	ASSETS ($ mil.)	NET INCOME ($ mil.)	INCOME AS % OF ASSETS	EMPLOYEES
12/19	2,318	26	1.1%	467
12/18	2,266	20	0.9%	454
12/17	1,962	14	0.7%	407
12/16	1,828	12	0.7%	397
12/15	1,682	10	0.6%	—
Annual Growth	8.3%	27.0%	—	—

2019 Year-End Financials

Debt ratio: 0.47%	No. of shares (mil.): 11
Return on equity: 10.38%	Dividends
Cash ($ mil.): 45	Yield: 2.1%
Current ratio: —	Payout: 31.1%
Long-term debt ($ mil.): —	Market value ($ mil.): 380

	STOCK PRICE ($) FY Close	P/E High/Low		PER SHARE ($) Earnings	Dividends	Book Value
12/19	32.88	15	12	2.25	0.64	22.65
12/18	29.82	20	16	1.77	0.55	20.68
12/17	30.65	25	20	1.40	0.40	18.75
12/16	26.50	—	—	1.35	0.52	16.22
12/15	26.50	—	—	1.15	0.50	15.47
Annual Growth	5.5%		—	18.3%	6.2%	10.0%

GWG Holdings Inc

Auditors: Grant Thornton LLP

LOCATIONS

HQ: GWG Holdings Inc
325 North St. Paul Street, Suite 2650, Dallas, TX 75201
Phone: 612 746-1944
Web: www.gwgh.com

HISTORICAL FINANCIALS

Company Type: Public

Income Statement				FYE: December 31
	ASSETS ($ mil.)	NET INCOME ($ mil.)	INCOME AS % OF ASSETS	EMPLOYEES
12/19	3,635	108	3.0%	130
12/18	1,480	(119)	—	75
12/17	818	(20)	—	65
12/16	643	0	0.1%	70
12/15	398	(7)	—	50
Annual Growth	73.8%	—		27.0%

2019 Year-End Financials

Debt ratio: 44.59%	No. of shares (mil.): 30
Return on equity: 35.16%	Dividends
Cash ($ mil.): 79	Yield: —
Current ratio: —	Payout: —
Long-term debt ($ mil.): —	Market value ($ mil.): 300

	STOCK PRICE ($) FY Close	P/E High/Low		PER SHARE ($) Earnings	Dividends	Book Value
12/19	9.82	6	2	2.65	0.00	10.94
12/18	8.83	—	—	(22.32)	4.30	8.51
12/17	8.32	—	—	(5.72)	0.00	22.99
12/16	7.94	—	—	(0.53)	0.00	11.25
12/15	6.44	—	—	(1.02)	0.00	2.72
Annual Growth	11.1%	—	—	—	—	41.6%

Halliburton Company

Founded in 1919 Halliburton is one of the world's largest providers of products and services to the energy industry. It manufactures drill bits and other downhole and completion tools provides pressure pumping services locates hydrocarbons and manages geological data drills new wells and optimizes production once the well is operational. The company serves major national and independent oil and natural gas companies throughout the world. North America accounts for about 55% of company sales.

Operations

Halliburton operates two business segments: Completion & Production and Drilling & Evaluation.

The Completion and Production segment the core business of the company accounting for some 65% of annual sales provides cementing stimulation intervention pressure control specialty chemicals artificial lift and completion services. This segment comprises several product service lines such as Production Enhancement Pipeline & Process Services Production Solutions Artificial Life and Multi-chem.

The Drilling and Evaluation segment (more than 35% of revenue) offers field and reservoir modeling drilling evaluation and precise and wellbore placement services and technology that enable clients to model measure drill and optimize their well construction activities. Product service lines in this segment include Drill Bits and Services Wireline and Perforating Testing and Subsea Baroid (drilling fluid solutions) Sperry Drilling (well bore services) Landmark Software and Services and Halliburton Project Management.

Geographic Reach

Houston TX-headquartered Halliburton has operations stretching from the North Sea to Southeast Asia spanning some 80 countries. Its Completion and Production segment has operations in Arbroath UK; Johor Bahru Malaysia; and Louisiana US. Drilling and Evaluation segment has offices in Alvarado and The Woodlands Texas; and Nisku Canada.

North America (mostly US) accounts for nearly 55% of Halliburton's revenues. Middle East and Asia bring in an additional 20% of revenue.

Sales and Marketing

Halliburton serves national international and independent upstream energy companies engaged in the exploration and production of oil & gas commodities. Most of its services and products are marketed through its own servicing and sales organizations.

Financial Performance

Like most companies in the oil and gas industry Halliburton's revenue fell in the aftermath of the oil price downturn of 2014. From a high of $23.6 billion in 2015 revenue halved to under $16 billion in 2016 before recovering in the following three years.

In 2019 the company generated $22.4 billion in revenue a 7% decrease from the $23.9 billion generated in 2018 with its Completion and Production segment declining by 12% and its Drilling and Evaluation segment improving by 4%.

Net income to 168% as Halliburton posted $1.1 billion loss in profits in 2019 compared to $1.6 billion for 2018.

The company's cash and cash equivalents jumped by $260 million ending 2019 with $2.3 billion on hand. Cash from operations generated $2.4 billion while cash from investing used $1.49 billion primarily for capital expenditures. Financing activities used a further $695 million primarily for dividends to shareholders.

Strategy

The company continue to strengthen its product service lines through a combination of organic growth investment and selective acquisitions. It plan to continue executing strategies in 2020. Prudently allocating capital into strategic markets around the world; collaborating with and engineering solutions to maximize asset value for its customers; leveraging its broad technology offerings to provide value to its customers and enable them to more efficiently drill and complete their wells; investing in technology that will help its customers reduce reservoir uncertainty increase op-

erational efficiency and improve well productivity - as well as help to reduce its costs and deliver acceptable returns; improving working capital and managing its balance sheet to maximize financial flexibility; seeking additional ways to be one of the most cost-efficient service providers in the industry by optimizing costs maintaining capital discipline and leveraging our scale and breadth of operations; and striving to achieve superior returns and cash flow generation for its shareholders.

Internationally the company expect a third consecutive year of customer spending growth. They believe they have the right footprint and an enhanced technology portfolio to compete successfully across the international markets. Its pipeline of projects is strong and we expect continued growth in its Drilling and Evaluation division as its iCruise rotary steerable drilling platform roll-out continues new offshore drilling activity begins around the world and operate a full year of its Norway integrated contracts. Pricing in certain international regions is improving and expect this momentum to continue in 2020.

Company Background

Halliburton got its start in 1919 as the Better Method Oil Well Cementing Company. The company's first assignment was to use cement to hold a steel pipe in a well which kept oil out of the water table strengthen well walls and reduce the risk of explosions. This method was patented in 1924 as the company incorporated in Oklahoma as the Halliburton Oil Well Cementing Company.

The company grew through acquisitions since the 1940s. After the 1973 Arab oil embargo Halliburton benefited from the surge in global oil exploration and later as drilling costs surged it became a leader in well stimulation.

Halliburton served the US military in Iraq and Afghanistan.

HISTORY

Halliburton got its start in 1919 as the Better Method Oil Well Cementing Company. The company's first assignment was to use cement to hold a steel pipe in a well which kept oil out of the water table strengthen well walls and reduce the risk of explosions. This method was patented in 1924 as the company incorporated in Oklahoma as the Halliburton Oil Well Cementing Company.

The company grew through acquisitions between the 1950s and the 1970s. In 1962 it bought Houston construction giant Brown & Root an expert in offshore platforms. After the 1973 Arab oil embargo Halliburton benefited from the surge in global oil exploration and later as drilling costs surged it became a leader in well stimulation.

In the 1990s Halliburton expanded abroad entering Russia in 1991 China in 1993 and Germany in 1995. The company is known to have won many US military contracts through the former US Vice President Dick Cheney especially in Iraq and Afghanistan.

The company realigned its work into Eastern and Western Hemisphere operations in 2006 and in 2007 divided its service offerings into two divisions: Completion and Production and Drilling and Evaluation.

EXECUTIVES

Evp Administration And Chief Human Resources Officer, Lawrence J. Pope, age 51, $535,000 total compensation

Evp And General Counsel, Robb L. Voyles, age 62

President Eastern Hemisphere, Joseph D. (Joe) Rainey, age 63, $809,950 total compensation

President Western Hemisphere, James S. (Jim) Brown, age 65, $873,000 total compensation

President And Ceo, Jeffrey A. (Jeff) Miller, age 56, $970,000 total compensation

Evp And Cfo, Christopher T. (Chris) Weber, age 47

Evp Global Business Lines, Eric Carre

Svp And Cio, Ken Braud

Vice President Audit Services, Lyn Beaty

Regional Vice President Apac, Rao Abdullah

Vice President Mergers And Acquisitions, Michael Cheeseman

Global Account Vice President, Edmond Durre

Vp And Treasurer, Timothy Mckeon

Account Vice President, Carl Shaw

Vice President Of Artificial Lift, Chuck Ervin

Vice President Of Manufacturing, James Shevchek

Vice President Australasia, Michael Segura

Vice President Director Of Information Technology Risk Management, Ronald Higginbotham

Vice President And Chief Ethics And Compliance Officer, Jeffrey Spalding

Chairman, David J. (Dave) Lesar, age 67

Auditors: KPMG LLP

LOCATIONS

HQ: Halliburton Company
3000 North Sam Houston Parkway East, Houston, TX 77032
Phone: 281 871-2699
Web: www.halliburton.com

2018 Sales

	$ mil.	% of total
North America	14,431	60
Middle East/Asia	4,554	19
Europe/Africa/CIS	2,945	12
Latin America	2,065	9
Total	**23,995**	**100**

PRODUCTS/OPERATIONS

2018 Sales

	$ mil.	% of total
Completion and Production	15,973	67
Drilling and Evaluation	8,022	33
Total	**23,995**	**100**

2018 Sales

	$ mil.	% of total
Services	18,444	77
Product sales	5,551	23
Total	**23,995**	**100**

Areas of Expertise

Areas of Expertise
Clean Energy
Deepwater
Heavy Oil
High Pressure/Temperature
Mature Fields
Unconventional Resources

Selected Products and Services

Artificial Lift
Cementing
Consulting
Coring
Drill Bits
Drilling
Fluid Services
Formation Evaluation
Hole Enlargement
Pipeline & Process Services
Project Management
Real Time Services
Reservoir Testing / Analysis
Sand Control
Wellbore Service Tools
Software and Services
Stimulation
Subsea
Well Completions
Well Intervention
Wireline and Perforating

Selected Brands

Baroid
Landmark
Multi-Chem
Pinnacle
Sperry Drilling

COMPETITORS

Baker Hughes	RPC
McDermott	Schlumberger
National Oilwell Varco	TechnipFMC

HISTORICAL FINANCIALS

Company Type: Public

Income Statement				FYE: December 31
	REVENUE ($ mil.)	NET INCOME ($ mil.)	NET PROFIT MARGIN	EMPLOYEES
12/20	14,445	(2,945)	—	40,000
12/19	22,408	(1,131)	—	55,000
12/18	23,995	1,656	6.9%	60,000
12/17	20,620	(463)	—	55,000
12/16	15,887	(5,763)	—	50,000
Annual Growth	(2.4%)	—		(5.4%)

2020 Year-End Financials

Debt ratio: 47.52%
Return on equity: (-45.23%)
Cash ($ mil.): 2,563
Current ratio: 2.14
Long-term debt ($ mil.): 9,132

No. of shares (mil.): 885
Dividends
Yield: 1.6%
Payout: —
Market value ($ mil.): 16,727

	STOCK PRICE ($) FY Close	P/E High/Low	PER SHARE ($) Earnings	Dividends	Book Value
12/20	18.90	— —	(3.34)	0.32	5.62
12/19	24.47	— —	(1.29)	0.72	9.13
12/18	26.58	30 13	1.89	0.72	10.93
12/17	48.87	— —	(0.53)	0.72	9.53
12/16	54.09	— —	(6.69)	0.72	10.86
Annual Growth	(23.1%) (15.2%)	— —			—(18.7%)

Hancock Whitney Corp

Hancock Whitney is the holding company of Hancock Whitney Bank which has nearly 200 branches and more than 260 ATMs throughout the Gulf South from Florida to Texas. The community-oriented bank offers traditional and online products and services such as deposit accounts treasury management and investment brokerage services and loans to commercial small business and retail customers. The company also provides trust and investment management services to retirement plans corporations and individuals as well as discount investment brokerage services annuity and life insurance products and consumer financing services. Formerly Hancock Holding Company Hancock Whitney consolidated its two brands (Whitney Bank and Hancock Bank) in 2018 and changed its name.

EXECUTIVES

President Ceo And Director, John M. Hairston, age 57, $707,000 total compensation
Coo, D. Shane Loper, age 54, $400,000 total compensation
Cfo, Michael M. Achary, age 59, $400,000 total compensation

President Whitney Bank, Joseph S. Exnicios, age 64, $375,000 total compensation
Chief Credit Officer Whitney Bank, Suzanne C. Thomas, age 65
Chief Credit Risk Officer, Samuel B. Kendricks, age 60
Chief Investment Officer, David J. Lundgren
Executive Vice President General Counsel Corporate Secretary, Joy Phillips
Vice President And Private Banker, Larry Cuervo
Senior Vice President Financial And Estate Planner, Emile Koury
Assistant Vice President, Kim Gibson
Assistant Vice President, Jimmy Campbell
Assistant Vice President Technology, Roland Pittman
Vice President Senior Business Banker, Kai Sonnenschein
Assistant Vice President Merchant Services Sales Specialist, Lisa Parks
Assistant Vice President And Trust Officer, Kevin Peyton
Vice President, Rachel Nunez
Vice President Retirement Plan Services, Amy Grace
Vice President Social Media And Public Relations, Janel Evans
Vice President, Brandon Perry
Vice President Specialty Asset Management, Steve Rapier
Chairman, James B. Estabrook, age 76
Auditors: PricewaterhouseCoopers LLP

LOCATIONS

HQ: Hancock Whitney Corp
Hancock Whitney Plaza,, 2510 14th Street, Gulfport, MS 39501
Phone: 228 868-4000
Web: www.hancockbank.com

PRODUCTS/OPERATIONS

2017 Sales

	$ mil.	% of total
Interest income		
Loans including fees	772	66
Securities	124	11
Other	4	-
Interest expense	(108.3)	-
Non interest income		
Service charges on deposit accounts	83	7
Bank card and ATM fees	53	5
Trust fees	44	4
Investment and annuity fees	20	2
Secondary mortgage market operations	15	1
Insurance commissions and fees	3	-
Other	49	4
Total	**1,062**	**100**

Selected Services

Banking
Checking
Credit Cards
Currency Exchange
Home Equity Loans and Lines
Investment Services
Investments
Loans & Credit
Mobile Banking
Mortgage
Online & Mobile Banking
Online Banking
Personal Loans and Lines
Savings

COMPETITORS

BancorpSouth	MidSouth Bancorp
Capital One	Regions Financial
First Horizon	Renasant
IBERIABANK	Trustmark
Investar	

HISTORICAL FINANCIALS

Company Type: Public

Income Statement				FYE: December 31
	ASSETS ($ mil.)	NET INCOME ($ mil.)	INCOME AS % OF ASSETS	EMPLOYEES
12/19	30,600	327	1.1%	4,136
12/18	28,235	323	1.1%	3,933
12/17	27,336	215	0.8%	3,887
12/16	23,975	149	0.6%	3,724
12/15	22,839	131	0.6%	3,921
Annual Growth	7.6%	25.6%	—	1.3%

2019 Year-End Financials

Debt ratio: 0.76%
Return on equity: 10.00%
Cash ($ mil.): 542
Current ratio: —
Long-term debt ($ mil.): —

No. of shares (mil.): 87
Dividends
Yield: 2.4%
Payout: 28.4%
Market value ($ mil.): 3,840

	STOCK PRICE ($) FY Close	P/E High/Low	PER SHARE ($) Earnings	Dividends	Book Value
12/19	43.88	12 9	3.72	1.08	39.62
12/18	34.65	15 9	3.72	1.02	35.98
12/17	49.50	21 17	2.48	0.96	33.86
12/16	43.10	24 11	1.87	0.96	32.29
12/15	25.17	20 15	1.64	0.96	31.14
Annual Growth	14.9%	— —	22.7%	3.0%	6.2%

Hanmi Financial Corp.

Hanmi Financial owns Hanmi Bank which serves Korean-American and other ethnic communities in California Colorado Georgia Illinois New Jersey New York Texas Virginia and Washington. The company which holds $5.5 billion in assets offers traditional banking services to small and midsized businesses from about 40 branches and eight loan offices. Real estate loans — including for retail hospitality mixed-use apartment office industrial gas station faith-based facility and warehouse properties — account for about 80% of its loan portfolio; commercial and industrial loans and leases receivable make up most of the rest.

Operations

Hanmi Financial originates real estate loans (including commercial construction and residential property) commercial and industrial loans (including commercial term commercial lines of credit and international) equipment lease financing consumer loans and Small Business Administration (SBA) loans. The bank also offers traditional deposit products including checking savings negotiable order of withdrawal (NOW) and money market accounts and CDs.

Hanmi's $4.6 billion loan portfolio is made up mostly of real estate loans — particularly commercial property loans including retail (about 20% of total portfolio) hospitality (20%) and other loans (30%). Other loans include loans for mixed-use apartment office industrial gas station faith-based facility and warehouse properties. Residential property loans comprise around 10%.

Commercial and industrial loans and leases receivable together make up about 15% of the bank's portfolio.

Geographic Reach

Headquartered in a penthouse suite on Los Angeles' Wilshire Boulevard Hanmi Financial has one bank branch in each of New Jersey New York and

Virginia; some five branches in Illinois; about 10 branches in Texas; and around 25 branches in California. The majority of its loan and deposit concentration is in Southern California.

Sales and Marketing

Hanmi Financial's lending is concentrated in real estate loans commercial loans and leases and Small Business Administration (SBA) loans for small and middle market businesses in California Texas Illinois and New York — primarily among Korean-American and other multi-ethnic communities.

Financial Performance

Since 2013 Hanmi Financial has grown its revenue and net income by about 60% and 40% respectively thanks to increasing net interest income. But the company also depleted its cash stores by about 15% and more than doubled its long-term debt in that time mostly due to Federal Home Loan Bank advances in 2016.

The bank's revenue increased 9% in 2017 compared with 2016 reaching $210.2 million. Higher interest and fees on loans and leases drove the improvement which was partially offset by higher expense for interest on deposits. Average loans and leases and the percentage of loans and leases in Hanmi's mix of interest-earning assets both increased in 2017.

Net income slipped 3% to $54.7 million owing mostly to an increase in the bank's income tax provision which included a $3.9 million charge for a one-time revaluation adjustment connected with the Tax Cuts and Jobs Act (TCJA).

Hanmi added $6.6 million to its cash stores in 2017 for a total of $153.8 million. Operations and financings provided $79.9 million and $445.1 million respectively. Investment activity used $518.4 million.

Strategy

Hanmi Financial is working to diversify its loan portfolio to reduce its reliance on commercial real estate and increase its composition of leases and commercial industrial and residential real estate loans. Since 2014 the company has increased the proportion of its portfolio made up of leases and residential real estate while maintaining the proportion of commercial and industrial loans.

After a review of its cost structure and operating efficiency in 2018 the company is moderating its growth expectations lowering its non-interest expenses and consolidating about 10% of its branches.

Hanmi also hired a Chief Technology officer in 2018 to implement a strategy to improve the company's use of technology including using it to increase efficiency of regulatory compliance activities (for which the company heavily relies on human capital).

Mergers and Acquisitions

In its first foray outside of California in late 2013 Hanmi agreed to acquire Central Bancorp Inc. the parent of Texas-based United Central Bank. United Central Bank serves multi-ethnic communities in Texas Illinois Virginia California New York and New Jersey through some two dozen branches. Once the acquisition is complete Hanmi will have about 50 branches and two loan production offices serving a broad range of ethnic communities in California Texas Illinois New York New Jersey Virginia and Georgia.

Company Background

Hanmi Financial was founded in 1982.

EXECUTIVES

Sevp And Coo, Bonita I. (Bonnie) Lee, age 57
Chief Compliance And Bsa Officer, Jean Lim
Evp And Cfo, Michael W. McCall

President Ceo And Director, Chong Guk (C. G.) Kum
Evp And Chief Credit Officer, Randall G. Ewig
Evp And Chief Administrative Officer, Greg D. Kim
Evp And Chief Banking Officer, Peter Yang
Evp And Chief Lending Officer, Anthony Kim
Assistant Vice President, Sue Kim
Assistant Vice President Compliance Officer, Michael Santiago
First Vice President And Branch Manager, Annie Chung
Vice President Human Resources Officer, Ashley Sowa
Senior Vice President And Operations Administrator, Nancy Lee
Senior Vice President Regional Retail Banking Manager, Shellie Merritt
Vice President And Business Development Officer, Yusin Lee
Chairman, Joseph K. Rho, age 79
Auditors: Crowe LLP

LOCATIONS

HQ: Hanmi Financial Corp.
3660 Wilshire Boulevard, Penthouse Suite A, Los Angeles, CA 90010
Phone: 213 382-2200
Web: www.hanmi.com

PRODUCTS/OPERATIONS

2017 Sales

	$ mil.	% of total
Net interest income	176	84
Non-interest income	33	16
Total	**210**	**100**

COMPETITORS

Bank of America	Far East National Bank
Broadway Financial	Hope Bancorp
Cathay General Bancorp	JPMorgan Chase
East West Bancorp	Woori

HISTORICAL FINANCIALS

Company Type: Public

Income Statement   FYE: December 31

	ASSETS ($ mil.)	NET INCOME ($ mil.)	INCOME AS % OF ASSETS	EMPLOYEES
12/19	5,538	32	0.6%	633
12/18	5,502	57	1.1%	635
12/17	5,210	54	1.0%	642
12/16	4,701	56	1.2%	638
12/15	4,234	53	1.3%	622
Annual Growth	6.9%	(11.7%)	—	0.4%

2019 Year-End Financials

Debt ratio: 3.76%	No. of shares (mil.): 30
Return on equity: 5.88%	Dividends
Cash ($ mil.): 121	Yield: 4.8%
Current ratio: —	Payout: 72.1%
Long-term debt ($ mil.): —	Market value ($ mil.): 616

	STOCK PRICE ($) FY Close	P/E High/Low		PER SHARE ($) Earnings	Dividends	Book Value
12/19	20.00	23	16	1.06	0.96	18.29
12/18	19.70	18	10	1.79	0.96	17.87
12/17	30.35	21	15	1.69	0.80	17.34
12/16	34.90	20	11	1.75	0.66	16.42
12/15	23.72	16	12	1.68	0.47	15.45
Annual Growth	(4.2%)	—	—	(10.9%)	19.5%	4.3%

Hanover Insurance Group Inc

Founded in 1852 The Hanover Insurance Group is one of the oldest property/casualty insurance holding companies around. Through Hanover Insurance Company the group provides personal and commercial automobile homeowners and workers' compensation coverage as well as commercial multi-peril insurance and professional liability coverage. The group sells its products through a network of independent agents throughout the US; Michigan Massachusetts and New York account for about 40% of its business. In Michigan it operates as Citizens Insurance Company. Hanover's Opus Investment Management subsidiary provides institutional investment management services.

Operations

Hanover's primary domestic segments are Commercial Lines Personal Lines and Other.

Primarily through the Hanover Insurance Company unit Hanover writes more than $5 billion in gross premiums each year. Commercial Lines account for nearly 60% of annual revenues while Personal lines account for about 40%.

Hanover's Other segment comprises Opus Investment Management which provides investment advisory services to affiliates; it also manages assets for unaffiliated clients including insurance companies retirement plans and foundations.

Geographic Reach

Hanover is licensed to sell property and casualty insurance in all 50 US states and the District of Columbia. It actively markets Commercial Lines policies in more than 35 states and Personal Lines policies in nearly 20 states. The group is highly dependent on three states: Michigan is the company's largest market accounting for some 20% of all commercial and personal lines. Massachusetts and New York account for nearly 10% each.

In addition to its headquarters in Worcester Massachusetts the company has about 40 regional offices in cities across the US.

Sales and Marketing

Hanover sells through a network of agents and brokers including about 2100 agent partners. The company's customers include individuals families and businesses.

Financial Performance

The company's revenue increased by 9% to $4.9 billion in 2019 from $4.5 billion in the prior year. Commercial Lines net premiums written were $2.7 billion for the year ended December 31 2019 compared to $2.6 billion for the year ended December 31 2018. This $96.5 million increase was primarily driven by pricing increases and strong retention.

Net income was $425.1 million in 2019 compared to $391.0 million in 2018 an increase of $34.1 million primarily due to an increase in the net change in fair value of equity securities and from an increase in operating income in 2019.

Cash held by the company at the end of 2019 decreased by $808.3 million to $215.7 million from $1.0 billion in 2018. Cash provided by operations was $602.9 million while cash provided was used for investing activities and financing activities were $311.9 million and $1.1 billion respectively.

Strategy

Hanover's business strategy focuses on providing their agents and customers with competitive insurance products delivered with clear and consistent underwriting and pricing expectations while prudently growing and diversifying their product and geographical business mix. The company conduct their business with an emphasis on disciplined underwriting pricing quality claim handling and customer service. In 2019 Hanover wrote approximately $4.6 billion in net premiums. Agency relationships and active agency management are core to their strategy.

Hanover's strategy in Commercial Lines focuses on building deep relationships with partner independent agents through differentiated product offerings industry segmentation and franchise value through limited distribution. The company continue to make enhancements to their products and technology platforms that are intended to drive more total account placements in their small commercial and middle market business while delivering enhanced margins in their specialty businesses. This aligns with the company's focus of delivering the capabilities that will help expand the depth and breadth of their partnerships with a limited number of agents.

HISTORY

In 1842 a group of Worcester Massachusetts businessmen tried to form a mutual life insurance company. After a failed first attempt they succeeded with the help of lobbyist Benjamin Balch. In 1844 the State Mutual Life Assurance Co. of Worcester set up business in the back room of secretary Clarendon Harris' bookstore. The first president was John Davis a US senator. The company issued its first policy in 1845.

In the early years State Mutual reduced risk by issuing policies only for residents of such "civilized" areas as New England New Jersey New York Pennsylvania and Ohio. It also restricted movement requiring policyholders to get permission for travel outside those areas. By the 1850s the company had begun issuing policies in the Midwest (with a 25% premium surcharge) the South (for 30% extra) and California (for a pricey extra $25 per $1000) with a maximum coverage of $5000.

The Civil War was a problem for many insurers who had to decide what to do about Southern policyholders and payment on war-related claims. State Mutual chose to pay out its Northern policyholders' benefits despite the extra cost. In 1896 the firm began offering installment pay-out plans for policyholders concerned that their beneficiaries would fritter away the whole payment.

The first 30 years of the 20th century were for the company a time of growth that was stopped short by the Depression. But despite a great increase in the number of policy loans and surrenders for cash value State Mutual's financial footing remained solid.

After WWII the company entered group insurance and began offering individual sickness and accident coverage. In 1957 it was renamed State Mutual Life Assurance Co. of America. The firm added property/casualty insurance in the late 1950s through alliances with such firms as Worcester Mutual Fire Insurance. During the 1960s State Mutual continued to develop property/casualty buying interests in Hanover Insurance and Citizens Corp.

The firm followed the industrywide shift into financial services in the 1970s adding mutual funds a real estate investment trust and an investment management firm. This trend accelerated in the 1980s and State Mutual began offering financial planning services as well as administrative and other services for the insurance and mutual fund industries (the mutual fund administration operations were sold in 1995). Managing this growth was another story: Its acquisitions left it bloated and disorganized. Technical systems were in disarray by the early 1990s and the agency force had grown to more than 1400. In response the com-

pany began a five-year effort to upgrade systems cut fat and reduce sales positions.

In view of its shifting focus State Mutual became Allmerica Financial in 1992. Three years later it demutualized. In 1997 it bought the 40% of Allmerica Property & Casualty it didn't already own.

EXECUTIVES

Evp General Counsel And Assistant Secretary, J. Kendall Huber, age 65, $498,077 total compensation
Evp And Cfo, Jeffrey M. (Jeff) Farber, age 55, $150,000 total compensation
Svp And Chief Claims Officer, Mark Welzenbach, age 60
President And Ceo, John C. (Jack) Roche, age 56, $470,385 total compensation
Chief Growth Innovation Officer, Richard W. (Dick) Lavey
Chief Investment Officer; President Opus Investment Management, Ann K. Tripp, age 61
Ceo And Chief Underwriting Officer Chaucer, John Fowle, age 50
Chief Technology Innovation Officer, Mark L. Berthiaume, age 63
Evp And Chief Human Resources Officer, Christine Bilotti-Peterson, age 49
Evp Corporate Development And Strategy, Mark L. Keim, age 54
Evp; President Specialty, Bryan J. Salvatore
Vice President Management Liability Of Commercial Lines Business, Helen Savaiano
Vice President And General Auditor, Don Gilbert
Vice President, Charles Kingsbury
Vice President Investor Relations, Oksana Lukasheva
Assistant Vice President Program Director, Dennis Warren
Vice President Claims, James McSheffrey
Rvp, George Agyen
Vice President, Roger Pare
Assistant Vice President And Senior Counsel, Donald Grzybowski
Vice President Corporate Real Estate, James Johnson
Regional Vice President, Scott Betlesky
Assistant Vice President Investment Operations, Michael Pastore
Vice President And Corporate Counsel, Harris Berenson
Vice President And Chief Product Officer Personal Lines, Gavin Blair
Vice President Distribution, Michael Lewis
Regional Vice President, Paul Alan Anderson
Assistant Vice President Business Integration, Kevin Pray
Avp Network Telecommunications Pc Services Collabo, Steve White
Assistant Vice President Marine Uw Development, Mary Corcoran
Assistant Vice President Allied Healthcare, Eric Paynter
Assistant Vice President Technology, James Marengo
Assistant Vice President Sales Effectiveness Sales Training Field Operations, Larry Kaczmarek
Director Media Relations, Emily Trevallion
Assistant Vice President Product Management, Joseph Brophy
Vice President Marketing And Comm., Jennifer F Luisa
Assistant Vice President Property Large Loss, Joe Green
Vice President Of Information Technology, Patty Kularski
Branch Vice President, Mark Mcgregor
Regional Vice President, Gregory L Parr
Regional Vice President, Steve Schaeberle

Assistant Vice President And Financial Officer, Randy Dinjian
Assistant Vice President, Lisa Binnie
Assistant Vice President Industry Solutions, Diana Obrian
Assistant Vice President Cl Operations, Julee Gianoulis
Vice President, William Cahill
Assistant Vice President Human Resources, Liz Berry
Assistant Vice President Learning And Development, Jim Gulinello
Vice President And Chief Security, Brian Haugli
Vice President Fidelity And Crime, Steven Vardilos
Regional Vice President, Scott Couger
Assistant Vice President, Richard Drake
Assistant Regional Vice President For Nys, Steve Cibelli
Zonal Vice President Pl, Kendra Schenkel
Avp Risk Solutions Field Operations, Wayne Grudzien
Assistant Vice President Human Resources Strategic Business Partner, Kelly Villanueva
Assistant Vice President Workers' Compensation Claims, Michael Berezin
Branch Vice President, Michael Sharr
Vice President Claims, Doug Kratzer
Vice President Product Management, Jeff Berridge
Regional Vice President Nh Vt, Mike Lee
Assistant Vice President Commercial Umbrella, John Lyons
Regional Vice President Cl, Angela Roman-Grimaldi
Vice President Casualty Underwriting Commercial Lines, Coleman Johnson
Vice President Quality And Learning Middle Market, Kim Callanan
Vice President Excess And Surplus Lines, Daniel Kearney
Avp Financial Officer Of Middle Market, Benjamin Selchan
Avp Industry Solutions Construction, Bill Meyer
Assistant Vice President Head Of Medical Strategy, Helen Weber
Vice President Risk Solutions, Christina Villena
Vice President Small Commercial Renewal Organization, Matt Hudnall
Regional Assistant Vice President Claims, Kevin Pendergast
Vp Corporate Development, Kevin Coyle
Vice President Personal Lines Strategic Initiatives, Brad Mccreedy
Vice President State Management, Matt Hardin
Vice President Distribution Management Professional Lines, Jon Martin
Rvp, Dina Amato
Vice President Tax, Anna Feinhaus
Assistant Vice President Data Science, Derek Winkler
Vice President Human Resources And Shared Services, William Bailey
Vice President, Sarah Medina
Avp State Manager, Nathan Santamaria
Chairman, Michael P. Angelini, age 77
Auditors: PricewaterhouseCoopers LLP

LOCATIONS

HQ: Hanover Insurance Group Inc
440 Lincoln Street, Worcester, MA 01653
Phone: 508 855-1000   **Fax:** 508 855-6332
Web: www.hanover.com

PRODUCTS/OPERATIONS

2017 Sales

	$ mil.	% of total
Net premiums earned		
Commercial lines	2,399	46
Personal lines	1,580	31
Chaucer	853	16
Net investment income	298	6
Net realized investment gains	23	
Fees & other	29	1
Total	**5,184**	**100**

Selected Products

Personal Lines
 Auto Insurance
 Companion Products
 Dwelling Fire
 Home Care Services
 Homeowners Insurance
 Identity Integrity
 Umbrella
 Valuable Items
 Watercraft
Small Commercial and Middle Market Core Products
 Business Owner's Policy
 Commercial Automobile
 Commercial Package
 General Liability
 Property
 Umbrella
 Workers' Compensation
Specialized Products
 AIX Specialty Programs
 Commercial Umbrella and Excess
 Healthcare
 Industrial Property Risk
 Management Liability
 Marine (inland and ocean)
 Professional Liability
 Surety (commercial and contract)

COMPETITORS

Alleghany Corporation	Liberty Mutual
Allstate	Markel Insurance
American Automobile	Nationwide
Association (AAA)	Progressive
American Financial	Corporation
Group	State Farm
Auto-Owners Insurance	Travelers Companies
GEICO	USAA

HISTORICAL FINANCIALS

Company Type: Public

Income Statement

FYE: December 31

	ASSETS ($ mil.)	NET INCOME ($ mil.)	INCOME AS % OF ASSETS	EMPLOYEES
12/19	12,490	425	3.4%	4,300
12/18	12,399	391	3.2%	4,200
12/17	15,469	186	1.2%	4,600
12/16	14,220	155	1.1%	4,900
12/15	13,790	331	2.4%	4,800
Annual Growth	**(2.4%)**	**6.4%**	**—**	**(2.7%)**

2019 Year-End Financials

Debt ratio: 5.23%
Return on equity: 14.48%
Cash ($ mil.): 215
Current ratio: —
Long-term debt ($ mil.): —

No. of shares (mil.): 38
Dividends
 Yield: 7.1%
 Payout: 91.5%
Market value ($ mil.): 5,248

	STOCK PRICE ($) FY Close	P/E High/Low	PER SHARE ($) Earnings	Dividends	Book Value
12/19	136.67	13 10	10.46	9.70	75.94
12/18	116.77	14 11	9.09	2.22	69.85
12/17	108.08	25 18	4.33	2.04	70.53
12/16	91.01	25 20	3.59	1.88	67.39
12/15	81.34	11 9	7.40	1.69	66.15
Annual Growth	**13.9%**	**— —**	**9.0% 54.8%**		**3.5%**

HarborOne Bancorp Inc (New)

Auditors: Crowe LLP

LOCATIONS

HQ: HarborOne Bancorp Inc (New)
 770 Oak Street, Brockton, MA 02301
Phone: 508 895-1000
Web: www.harborone.com

HISTORICAL FINANCIALS

Company Type: Public

Income Statement

FYE: December 31

	ASSETS ($ mil.)	NET INCOME ($ mil.)	INCOME AS % OF ASSETS	EMPLOYEES
12/19	4,058	18	0.5%	675
12/18	3,653	11	0.3%	658
12/17	2,684	10	0.4%	581
12/16	2,448	5	0.2%	614
12/15	2,163	5	0.3%	387
Annual Growth	**17.0%**	**33.4%**	**—**	**14.9%**

2019 Year-End Financials

Debt ratio: 5.05%
Return on equity: 3.57%
Cash ($ mil.): 211
Current ratio: —
Long-term debt ($ mil.): —

No. of shares (mil.): 58
Dividends
 Yield: —
 Payout: —
Market value ($ mil.): 642

	STOCK PRICE ($) FY Close	P/E High/Low	PER SHARE ($) Earnings	Dividends	Book Value
12/19	10.99	60 30	0.33	0.00	11.40
12/18	15.89	56 42	0.36	0.00	10.98
12/17	19.16	67 49	0.33	0.00	10.52
12/16	19.34	— —	(0.00)	0.00	10.25
Annual Growth	**(13.2%)**	**— —**	**—**	**—**	**2.7%**

Hartford Financial Services Group Inc.

The Hartford Financial Services Group is a major US provider of commercial and personal property/casualty insurance. Its commercial operations include workers' compensation auto and liability coverage as well as specialty insurance policies. The Hartford also offers consumer homeowners and auto coverage. The group has been the direct auto and home insurance writer for AARP's members for about 35 years. In addition the company provides group life accident and disability benefits. Through its mutual fund division the firm offers wealth management products and services. The Hartford has been in business since 1810.

HISTORY

In 1810 a group of Hartford Connecticut businessmen led by Walter Mitchell and Henry Terry founded the Hartford Fire Insurance Co. Frequent fires in America's wooden cities and executive ignorance of risk assessment and premium-setting often left the firm on the edge of insolvency. (In 1835 stockholders staged a coup and threw management out.) Still each urban conflagration — including the Great Chicago Fire of 1871 — gave The Hartford an opportunity to seek out and pay all its policyholders thus teaching the company to underwrite under fire as it were and to use such disasters to refine its rates.

The company's stag logo was initially a little deer as shown on a policy sold to Abraham Lincoln in 1861. A few years later however Hartford began using the majestic creature (from a Landseer painting) now familiar to customers. By the 1880s Hartford operated nationwide as well as in Canada and Hawaii. In 1913 it formed an accident and indemnity subsidiary to protect automobiles and property from risks beyond fire.

The company survived both world wars and the Depression but emerged in the 1950s in need of organization. It set up new regional offices and added life insurance buying Columbian National Life (founded 1902) in 1959 which became Hartford Life Insurance Co.

In 1969 Hartford was bought by ITT (formerly International Telephone and Telegraph) whose CEO Harold Geneen was an avid conglomerateur. Consumer advocate Ralph Nader strongly opposed the acquisition — he fought the merger in court for years and felt vindicated when ITT spun off Hartford in 1995. Others opposed it too because ITT had engineered the merger based on an IRS ruling (later revoked) that Hartford stockholders wouldn't have to pay capital gains taxes on the purchase price of their stock.

Insurance operations consolidated under the Hartford Life Insurance banner in 1978. Through the 1980s Hartford Life remained one of ITT's strongest operations. A conservative investment policy kept Hartford safe from the junk bond and real estate manias of the 1980s.

Hartford reorganized its property/casualty operations along three lines in 1986 and in 1992 it organized its reinsurance business into one unit. The company faced some liability in relation to Dow Corning's breast-implant litigation but underwriting standards after 1985 reduced long-term risk. In 1994 the company began selling insurance products to AARP members under an exclusive agreement. In 1996 the company finished its spin-off from ITT which was acquired by Starwood Hotels & Resorts two years later.

To grow its reinsurance operation Hartford acquired the reinsurance business of Orion Capital (later known as Royal & SunAlliance USA) in 1996. It posted a loss of $99 million due in large part to asbestos and pollution liabilities. Late that year the firm changed its name to The Hartford Financial Services Group.

To shore up reserves and fund growth in 1997 the company spun off 19% of Hartford Life. The Hartford expanded into nonstandard auto insurance in 1998 by buying Omni Insurance Group (since sold in 2006). The company also sold its London & Edinburgh Insurance Group in 1998 to Norwich Union (now part of Aviva formerly CGNU). In 1999 The Hartford acquired the reinsurance business of Vesta Fire Insurance a subsidiary of Vesta Insurance Group.

In 2000 Hartford bought back the part of Hartford Life it had spun off. The Hartford also bought the financial products and excess and surplus specialty insurance lines of Reliance Group Holdings. Assurances G n rales de France bought the company's Dutch subsidiary Zwolsche Algemeene. In 2001 the company bought Fortis Financial a US subsidiary of Belgian insurer Fortis and sold Hartford Seguros its Spanish subsidiary to Liberty Mutual.

Before the financial crisis hit Hartford Life invested in its data management with the acquisition of a defined contribution recordkeeping business (Princeton Retirement Group 2007) and a web-based technology company (TopNoggin 2008). Following the same strategy The Hartford acquired Sun Life's US 401K plan administration business.

Like so many others in the insurance and financial services industry The Hartford had its share of losses during the 2008 financial crisis due to its investment holdings in Fannie Mae Freddie Mac and Lehman Brothers. In mid-2009 the US Treasury stepped in and offered The Hartford and other major life insurers access to its Troubled Asset Relief Program (TARP). The Hartford borrowed $3.4 billion to shore up its capital reserves. As the company and the economy stabilized the loan was repaid by early 2010 including an additional $21.7 million dividend payment.

Prior to the creation of TARP funds the Treasury first made money available to banks through its Capital Purchase Program (CPP). To make itself more eligible The Hartford worked quickly to transform itself into a bank — at least on paper. In 2009 The Hartford acquired Federal Trust Corporation a regional bank holding company for $10 million. However shortly thereafter TARP funds became available and The Hartford readily accepted them and the strings attached. Two years later the company recognized that banking was not among its core competencies or passions and made arrangements to sell Federal Trust Corporation to CenterState Banks.

Chairman and CEO Ramani Ayer had planned on retiring at the end of 2008 but agreed to stay at the helm through 2009. His final year was marked by efforts to stem the company's losses stemming from the global economic and financial crisis that began in 2008. Former head of consumer banking at Bank of America Liam McGee was appointed as the company's new CEO in late 2009.

The Hartford then conducted restructuring measures including exiting international markets and disposing of non-core assets. It ended sales of variable annuities in Japan and the UK in 2009 and sold its Canadian mutual funds business and its Brazilian joint venture in 2010. In early 2011 The Hartford also sold off its third-party claims administration business Specialty Risk Services (SRS) unit to Sedgwick Claims Management Services for $278 million. In addition in late 2011 the company formed an agreement with Wellington Management which took over management of several of Hartford's mutual funds.

During 2010 the company reshaped its reporting segments into the commercial markets consumer markets and wealth management categories. In 2011 it also placed a number of operations into a separate runoff segment including its exited international operations and its discontinued institutional annuities and private placement life insurance operations.

Despite all of its efforts to recover from the financial crisis of 2008-2009 (which caused heavy investment losses for The Hartford) via cost-cutting and restructuring measures in early 2012 the company began facing investor pressure to separate its life and property/casualty operations through spinoff or asset sale transactions. After reviewing its options The Hartford soon gave in to the demands. While it retained its mutual funds business the firm exited its annuity business and sold the bulk of its life insurance operations (including individual life retirement plans and Woodbury Financial Services units) in 2012 and 2013. It also sold Hartford Life Insurance KK in 2014.

In 2016 The Hartford bought Maxum Specialty Insurance Group for $168 million. Maxum Indemnity is an authorized excess and surplus lines provider in 49 states plus the District of Columbia Puerto Rico and the US Virgin Islands with operations throughout the US.

The Hartford struck another major deal in 2017 when it bought Aetna's domestic group life and disability business for $1.45 billion. That transaction made The Hartford the nation's second-largest group life and disability insurer after market leader MetLife. The purchase also included digital assets that enhanced The Hartford's distribution capabilities.

Perhaps in order to limit its exposure in Europe (and especially in the UK which has been increasingly volatile in anticipation of the nation's pending withdrawal from the European Union) The Hartford sold its UK property/casualty run-off units Hartford Financial Products International and Downlands Liability Management to Catalina Holdings (Bermuda). The $259 million deal closed in mid-2017.

EXECUTIVES

Senior Vice President National Client Practices, Brian Griffith

President, Douglas G. (Doug) Elliot, age 60, $918,750 total compensation

Evp Group Benefits, Michael (Mike) Concannon, age 58

Chairman And Ceo, Christopher J. Swift, age 59, $1,075,000 total compensation

Chief Investment Officer; President Hartford Investment Management And Talcott Resolution, Brion Johnson, age 60, $525,000 total compensation

Cfo And Head Strategy Property And Casualty And Group Benefits, Jonathan R. Bennett, age 56

Evp And Property And Casual Chief Underwriting Officer, A. Morris (Mo) Tooker

Cfo, Beth A. Bombara, age 52, $687,500 total compensation

Evp Human Resources, Martha (Marty) Gervasi, age 58

Svp U.s. Wealth Management Group, James E. (Jim) Davey, age 55

Evp And Chief Risk Officer, Robert R. Rupp, age 67, $600,000 total compensation

Evp Operations Technology And Data, William A. (Bill) Bloom, age 56

Svp And Secretary, David C. Robinson, age 55

Evp Personal Lines, Raymond J. (Ray) Sprague, age 61

Evp Small Commercial, Stephanie Bush

Chief Claims Officer, John Kinney

Vice President Marketing Communications And Sponsorships, Laura Marzi

Senior Vice President Treasure, John Giamalis

Assistant Vice President Service Strategy, Sue Sweeney

Assistant Vp Enterprise Talent Solutions, Courtney Sterling

Assistant Vice President, Theresa Milone

Assistant Vice President Human Resources, Daniel O'Shea

Assistant Vice President Server And Storage Engineering, Ryan Wilhelm

Senior Vice President Product And Strategy, Mike Fish

Vice President Strategy And Corporate Development, Devi Mohanty

Vice President And Actuary Middle Market, Eric Besman

Assistant Vice President Operations, Mike Renfrew

Assistant Vice President Security, Daniel Lewis

Assistant Vice President And Actuary, Luis Marques

Assistant Vice President Media And Public Relations, Thomas Hambrick

Vp Chief Underwriting Officer, Larry Christianson

Vice President Human Resources, Suzanne Tamburro

Vice President Large Loss, Stephen Deane

Regional Vice President, Meg Carter

Assistant Vice President, Carolyn L Kopper

Assistant Vice President Claim Account Management, Sean Faherty

Assistant Vice President And Assistant General Counsel, Donna Gesualdi

Assistant Vp National Account Underwriting, Charles Gill

Assistant Vice President, Matt Wright

Vice President Marketing Analytics And Media Execution, Gary Coleman

Regional Vice President, Brian Carey

Vice President Associate General Counsel And Director Employment Law, David Kulle

Vice President Market Risk Officer, Christopher Abreu

Vice President Strategy, Kari Ratajczak

Vice President And Head Of Construction And, Thomas Boudreau

Assistant Vice President And Chief Marketing Officer Middle Market, Kelly Trella

Vp Division Sales Executive, Landon Reid

Assistant Vice President Sales Excellence, Noelle Crawford

Assistant Vice President Underwriting Officer Cons, Debby Mcgee

Avp Claim Compliance, Stephanie Raymond

Regional Vice President, Anthony Phifer

National Account Manager, Shelly Birkholz

Assistant Vice President Industry Practices, Melissa Zaparanick

Vice President Of Communications, Donna Gendreau

National Account Manager Group Benefits, Sarah Berard

Vice President Enterprise Process Improvement, Troy Nagel

Assistant Vice President Underwriting Officer, Matthew Giuffre

Vice President Loss Control Commercial Markets, Carl Carano

Senior Vice President And General Auditor, Michael Hession

Assistant Vp And Senior Counsel, Leslie Soler

Vice President Human Resources, Gary West

Vp Programs And Partnerships, Kenneth Zygiel

Assistant Vice President, Jeanne Fenster

Assistant Vice President And Actuary, Ken Kasner

Mbr 1st Vice President, Mayer Goldberger

Evp-chief Underwriting Officer, A Morris Tooker

Vpres Strategy & Business Deve, Ray Sprague

Legal Secretary, Sandra Branz

Assistant Vice President Assistant General Counsel, Liz Steigman

Assistant Vice President Enterprise Risk Management, Dan OConnell

Senior Vice President, Michael Hotaling

Assistant Vice President Commercial Markets Technology, Ann Nemphos

Vice President Group Benefits Specialty Products, Matthew Montminy

Assistant Vice President Project Management Office, Bill Lombardi

Senior Tax Counsel Assistant Vice President, William Elwell

Vice President And General Cou, Danielle Woolsey

Assistant Vice President Senior Counsel, Cedric Delacruz

Assistant Vice President Property Line Lead, Eric Cannon

Vice President And Actuary, Elizabeth Horvath

Regional Vice President, Cindy Roth

Assistant Vice President And Assistant Treasurer, Mike Fixer

Assistant Vice President Program Management, Jennifer Paul

Assistant Vice President Counsel, Catherine Gregory

Senior Vice President Investor Relations, Richard Costello

Assistant Vice President Information Security, Timothy Carling

Assistant Vice President Information Technology, Gurunatham Pellakuru

Assistant Vice President Product Management, Chad Mirock

Vice President Government Affairs, Cliff Leach

Regional Vice President, Tracy Charbonneau

Assistant Vice President And Counsel, Andrew Daly

Vice President Small Commercial Operations, Colleen Batman

Regional Vice President, Jim Reeves

Assistant Vice President Programs Business Development, Tim Brady

Assistant Vice President, James Plante

Assistant Vice President Claims, Barbara Agulnek

Assistant Vice President, Perry Roschelle

Avp Application Development And Corporate It And Enterprise Risk Management It, Tom Mika

Vice President, Scott Elliott

Vice President, Lampton Enochs

Vice President Project Management Office, Ellen Below

Vice President Strategy And Business Performance Management, Robert Wentling

Assistant Vice President Project Management And Planning, Bob Leyden

Vice President, Neal Wolin

Assistant Vice President And Counsel, Michael Petropoulos

Senior Vice President And Controller, Scott Lewis

Avp And Actuary, Ethan Triplett

Vice President Large Loss, Charlene Ridgeway

Avp Claims Data Science, Kari Palmer

Vp Digital Customer Experience, Ryan Denning

Assistant Vice President, Steve Thompson

Senior Vice President Controller And Chief Accoun, Elizabeth Bombara

Assistant Vice President Operational Risk Management, Lori Gattinella

Medical Director, Edward Berman

Assistant Vice President Information Technology Commercial Markets And Sales, Michael Garbiel

Senior Vice President Small Commercial Sales, Lisa Morgan

Vice President Finance, Thomas Peloquin

Vice President Planning Information Technology, Lynda Godkin

Vice President Liquidity And Market Risk Management, Nancy O'Connor

Avp Underwriting, Aishwarya Kothakota

Assistant Vice President, Tracey Kamenash

Assistant Vice President, Deb Szaraburak

Assistant Vice President, John Montone

Avp Marine Field Sales, Harold Fowlkes

Assistant Vice President Information Technology, Carolyn Small

Assistant Vice President Prod Development, Bryan R Smith

Assistant Vice President Small Commercial Information Technology, Brian Pierz

Assistant Vice President, Thomas Mika

Vice President Product Management, Brent Radeloff

Vp Of Director Of Hr Of Hartford Life, Peg Lesiak

Senior Vice President, Mary Boyd

Assistant Vice President Strategic Marketing Small Business, Daniel Campany

Senior Vice President Specialty Commercial, M Ross Fisher

Assistant Vice President Distribution Technology Strategy, Jim Rogers

Senior Vice President Corporate Asset, Robert Paiano

Assistant Vice President Agency Compensation, Keith Lawler

Vice President Claims Operations, Matthew Scott

Vice President E Business Delivery, Thomas Nogles

Vice President Of Information Delivery Services, Rich Filthaut

Vice President Digital Strategy, Kevin Keller

Vice President Internal Communications And Corporate Sustainability, Paula Angelo

Assistant Vice President Security, Daniel J Lewis

Vice President Liability Field Claims, Richard Bowman

Rvp Claims Group Benefits Minn, Christopher Lancaster

Assistant Vice President Controller, John Vachon

Avp Enterprise Strategy And Business Development, Ariadna Khafizova

Avp Underwriting Officer Construction Group, Michael Mcgann

Assistant Vice President, Maria Manuele

Regional Vice President, James Walz

Assistant Vice President Product Manager, David Case

Avp And Director It And Customer Service For Europe, Joanne Stjames

Senior Vice President Operations, Michelle Buswell

Auditors: Deloitte & Touche LLP

LOCATIONS

HQ: Hartford Financial Services Group Inc.
One Hartford Plaza, Hartford, CT 06155
Phone: 860 547-5000
Web: www.thehartford.com

PRODUCTS/OPERATIONS

2017 Sales by Segment

	$ mil.	% of total
Commercial Lines	7,954	47
Group Benefits	4,092	24
Personal Lines	3,975	23
Mutual Funds	807	5
Property & Casualty Other Operations	120	1
Corporate	26	-
Total	**16,974**	**100**

COMPETITORS

AIG	Nationwide
Allstate	State Farm
Berkshire Hathaway	Travelers Companies
CNA Financial	Unum Group
Liberty Mutual	Zurich Insurance Group
MetLife	

HISTORICAL FINANCIALS
Company Type: Public

Income Statement   FYE: December 31

	ASSETS ($ mil.)	NET INCOME ($ mil.)	INCOME AS % OF ASSETS	EMPLOYEES
12/19	70,817	2,085	2.9%	19,500
12/18	62,307	1,807	2.9%	18,500
12/17	225,260	(3,131)	—	16,400
12/16	223,432	896	0.4%	16,900
12/15	228,348	1,682	0.7%	17,400
Annual Growth	**(25.4%)**	**5.5%**	**—**	**2.9%**

2019 Year-End Financials

Debt ratio: 6.14%
Return on equity: 14.20%
Cash ($ mil.): 185
Current ratio: —
Long-term debt ($ mil.): —
No. of shares (mil.): 359
Dividends
  Yield: 1.9%
  Payout: 25.5%
Market value ($ mil.): 21,851

	STOCK PRICE ($) FY Close	P/E High/Low		Earnings	PER SHARE ($) Dividends	Book Value
12/19	60.77	11	7	5.66	1.20	45.25
12/18	44.45	12	8	4.95	1.10	36.48
12/17	56.28	—		(8.61)	0.94	37.82
12/16	47.65	21	16	2.27	0.86	45.20
12/15	43.46	12	10	3.96	0.78	43.91
Annual Growth	**8.7%**	**—**	**—**	**9.3%**	**11.4%**	**0.8%**

HBT Financial Inc

Auditors: RSM US LLP

LOCATIONS

HQ: HBT Financial Inc
401 North Hershey Road, Bloomington, IL 61704
Phone: 888 897-2276
Web: www.hbtbank.com

HISTORICAL FINANCIALS
Company Type: Public

Income Statement   FYE: December 31

	ASSETS ($ mil.)	NET INCOME ($ mil.)	INCOME AS % OF ASSETS	EMPLOYEES
12/19	3,245	66	2.1%	747
12/18	3,249	63	2.0%	742
12/17	3,312	56	1.7%	—
12/16	0	58	—	—
Annual Growth	**—**	**4.5%**		

2019 Year-End Financials

Debt ratio: 1.16%
Return on equity: 19.86%
Cash ($ mil.): 284
Current ratio: —
Long-term debt ($ mil.): —
No. of shares (mil.): 27
Dividends
  Yield: 0.7%
  Payout: 374.7%
Market value ($ mil.): 521

	STOCK PRICE ($) FY Close	P/E High/Low		Earnings	PER SHARE ($) Dividends	Book Value
12/19	18.99	6	5	3.33	12.48	12.12
12/18	0.00			3.54	2.36	18.88
Annual Growth	**—**	**—**	**—**	**(2.0%)**	**74.2%**	**(13.7%)**

HCA Healthcare Inc

HCA dispenses TLC for a profit. HCA Healthcare (formerly HCA Holdings) through its HCA Inc. (Hospital Corporation of America) unit operates about 185 hospitals — mostly acute care centers as well as three psychiatric facilities and two rehabilitation hospital — located in the US and UK. It also runs about 125 ambulatory surgery centers — as well as urgent care rehab and other outpatient centers — that form health care networks in many of the communities it serves. In total its hospitals are home to some 49000 beds. HCA's facilities are located in about 20 states; roughly half of its hospitals are in Florida and Texas. The HCA International unit operates the company's hospitals and clinics in the UK.

HISTORY

In 1987 Dallas lawyer Rick Scott and Fort Worth Texas financier Richard Rainwater founded Columbia Hospital Corp. to buy two hospitals in El Paso Texas. The partners eventually sold 40% of the hospitals to local doctors hoping that ownership would motivate physicians to increase productivity and efficiency.

The company entered the Miami market the next year and by 1990 had four hospitals. After merging with Smith Laboratories that year Columbia went public and then acquired Sutter Laboratories (orthopedic products). By the end of 1990 it had 11 hospitals.

Columbia moved into Florida in 1992 with the purchase of several hospitals and facilities. The next year it acquired Galen Health Care which operated 73 hospitals and had been spun off from health plan operator Humana earlier in the year. The merger thrust the hospital chain into about 15 new markets.

Columbia bought Hospital Corporation of America (HCA) in 1994. Thomas Frist his son Thomas Frist Jr. and Jack Massey (former owner of Kentucky Fried Chicken now part of TRICON) founded HCA in Nashville Tennessee in 1968. By 1973 the company had grown to 50 hospitals.

Meanwhile the medical industry was changing — insurers Medicare and Medicaid began scrutinizing payment procedures while the growth of HMOs (which aimed to restrict hospital admissions) cut hospital occupancy rates. HCA began paring operations in the late 1980s selling more than 100 hospitals. In 1989 the younger Frist led a $5.1 billion leveraged buyout of the company. He sold more assets and in 1992 took HCA public again but losses and a tumbling stock price made it a takeover target.

Later in 1994 the newly christened Columbia/HCA acquired the US's largest operator of outpatient surgery centers Dallas-based Medical Care America. A year later it bought 117-hospital HealthTrust a 1987 offshoot of HCA. Columbia/HCA was unstoppable in 1996 with some 150 acquisitions.

In 1997 the government began investigating the company's business practices. After executive indictments the company fired Scott and several other top officers. Frist Jr. became chairman and CEO pledging to shrink the company and tone down its aggressive approach. Columbia/HCA sold its home care business more than 100 of its less-desirable hospitals and almost all the operations of Value Health a pharmacy benefits and behavioral health care management firm it had recently bought.

The trimming continued in 1998: The company sold nearly three dozen outpatient surgery centers and more than a dozen hospitals. That year Columbia/HCA sued former financial executive Samuel Greco and several vendors accusing them of defrauding the company of several million dollars. In 1999 it spun off regional operators LifePoint Health (23 facilities) and Triad Hospitals (34) to trim its holdings. The next year it sold some 120 medical buildings to MedCap Properties a joint venture formed with First Union Capital Partners.

During 2000 the company bought out partner Sun Life and Provincial Holdings' (now AXA UK) interest in several London hospitals and bought three hospitals there from St. Martins Healthcare. It also renamed itself HCA - The Healthcare Company. While continuing a strategy of consolidating and streamlining operations (and resolving remaining legal matters) in 2001 the company streamlined its name even further to simply HCA Inc.

By 2002 HCA began shaking off its shaky past. Profits stabilized allowing it to reinvest millions into modernizing facilities and equipment at its hospitals and surgery centers. It entered the Kansas City market in 2003 by acquiring a local hospital chain.

The company finally closed the books during 2003 on the numerous government investigations launched in 1997 into its business practices. In the five years leading up to 2003 HCA paid out some $2 billion in settlements for Medicare fraud and other claims. These settlements took their toll on the firm's bottom line.

To expand its outpatient services HCA beginning in 2004 began purchasing imaging centers. In early 2005 the firm acquired Tampa Florida's Total I Imaging and its five centers that offer diagnostic services. In 2005 HCA's iMage1 Network part of HCA's outpatient services group bought more than a handful of imaging centers located in the Tampa Florida area from Ultra Open MRI Corp.

The devastating hurricane season of 2005 hit HCA's operations hard as they are concentrated in the southern US. When Hurricane Katrina hit HCA evacuated its Tulane University Hospital and Clinic (it reopened in early 2006). Hurricane Rita spurred HCA to evacuate three Houston-area hospitals (Mainland Medical Center in Texas City East Houston Regional Medical Center in Houston and Clear Lake Regional Medical Center in Webster) and partially evacuate two others.

In 2006 a group of investors — including Thomas Frist Jr. as well as Bain Capital Kohlberg Kravis Roberts and the private equity arm of Merrill Lynch — took HCA private in a $30 billion leveraged buyout. In 2009 Richard Bracken became CEO of the company.

The hospital operator maintained its private status for several years until it once again went public in 2011 as a way to pay off some debt.

EXECUTIVES

Chairman And Ceo, R. Milton Johnson, age 63, $1,391,667 total compensation
President And Coo, Samuel N. (Sam) Hazen, age 60, $995,834 total compensation
President Service Line And Operations Integration, A. Bruce Moore, age 60, $574,989 total compensation
Evp And Cfo, William B. (Bill) Rutherford, age 56, $793,750 total compensation
President American Group, Jon M. Foster, age 58, $762,781 total compensation
President Clinical Services And Chief Medical Officer, Jonathan B. (Jon) Perlin, age 59, $795,833 total compensation
President National Group, Charles J. (Chuck) Hall, age 67, $797,088 total compensation
Svp Marketing And Corporate Affairs, Jana J. Davis, age 61
Svp And Cio, P. Martin (Marty) Paslick, age 60
President Physician Services Group, Michael S. Cuffe, age 54
Svp And Chief Nursing Officer, Jane D. Englebright, age 61
Physical Therapy Director, Mary B Peterson
Assistant Vice President Risk, Joseph Haase
Vice President, Michael Marotta
Director Of Radiology Services, Phyllis Barker
Vice President Field Operations, Jay Levy
Assistant Vice President Strategic Resource Group, Brian Marger
Assistant Vice President Technical Services, Bill Fitzgerald
Assistant Vice President Development, Bobby Stokes
Assistant Vice President Owned Hospitals, Ron Redding
Vice President Managed Care, James Koss

Vice President Physician Services, Patrick Kueny
Director Of Pharmacy, Ron Nagata
Assistant Vice President Information Technology Strategy And Planning, David Catino
Vice President Human Resources Operations Support, Yonnie Chesley
Vice President Human Resources Midwest Division, Rich Lowe
Vice President Information Technology, Cyndi Talley
Regional Vice President Of Operations, John Lowe
Medical Director Behavioral Health Unit West Valley Medical Center Hca Mountain Division, Lawrence Banta
Medical Director Of Trauma Services, Darwin Ang
Vice President Quality Risk Management, Cheryl Roberts
Director Of Nursing, Kristina Wallace
Nursing Director, CHERYL THOMPSON
Vice President, Lyn Garrett
Respiratory Therapy Director, Victor Ortega
Auditors: Ernst & Young LLP

LOCATIONS

HQ: HCA Healthcare Inc
One Park Plaza, Nashville, TN 37203
Phone: 615 344-9551
Web: www.hcahealthcare.com

2018 Locations

	No.
US	
Texas	47
Florida	45
Tennessee	13
Virginia	11
Georgia	9
Utah	8
Colorado	7
Missouri	5
California	5
Kansas	4
Louisiana	4
Nevada	3
South Carolina	3
Idaho	2
Kentucky	2
New Hampshire	2
Oklahoma	2
Alaska	1
Indiana	1
Mississippi	1
UK	6
Total	**179**

Selected Segments

American Group
  Colorado
  Southern Georgia
  Kansas
  Southern Kentucky
  Louisiana
  Mississippi
  Missouri
  Oklahoma
  Tennessee
  Texas
National Group
  Alaska
  California
  Florida
  Southern Georgia
  Idaho
  Indiana
  Northern Kentucky
  Nevada
  New Hampshire
  North Carolina
  South Carolina
  Utah
  Virginia

Selected US Facilities

Alaska
Alaska Regional Hospital (Anchorage)
California
Good Samaritan Hospital (San Jose)
Los Robles Medical Center (Thousand Oaks)
Regional Medical Center of San Jose
Riverside Community Hospital
West Hills Hospital & Medical Center
Colorado
Centrum Surgical Center (Greenwood Village)
Medical Center of Aurora
North Suburban Medical Center (Thornton)
Presbyterian/St. Luke's Medical Center (Denver)
Rose Medical Center (Denver)
Sky Ridge Medical Center (Lone Tree)
Spalding Rehabilitation Hospital (Aurora)
Swedish Medical Center (Englewood)
Florida
Aventura Hospital and Medical Center
Blake Medical Center (Bradenton)
Brandon Regional Hospital
Capital Regional Medical Center (Tallahassee)
Central Florida Regional Hospital (Sanford)
Columbia Hospital (West Palm Beach)
Doctors Hospital of Sarasota
Edward White Hospital (St. Petersburg)
Fawcett Memorial Hospital (Port Charlotte)
Gulf Coast Medical Center (Panama City)
JFK Medical Center (Atlantis)
Kendall Regional Medical Center (Miami)
Lake City Medical Center
Largo Medical Center
Memorial Hospital Jacksonville
Memorial Hospital of Tampa
North Florida Regional Medical Center (Gainesville)
Northwest Medical Center (Margate)
Ocala Regional Medical Center
Osceola Regional Medical Center (Kissimmee)
Palms of Pasadena Hospital (St. Petersburg)
Palms West Hospital (Loxahatchee)
South Bay Hospital (Sun City Center)
St. Lucie Medical Center (Port St. Lucie)
Town and Country Hospital (Tampa)
Twin Cities Hospital (Niceville)
University Hospital and Medical Center (Tamarac)
West Florida Hospital (Pensacola)
Westside Regional Medical Center (Plantation)
Georgia
Atlanta Outpatient Surgery Center (Atlanta)
Cartersville Medical Center
Coliseum Medical Centers (Macon)
Doctors Hospital (Augusta)
Eastside Medical Center (Snellville)
Fairview Park Hospital (Dublin)
Northlake Surgical Center (Tucker)
Polk Medical Center (Cedartown)
Redmond Regional Medical Center (Rome)
Idaho
Eastern Idaho Regional Medical Center (Idaho Falls)
West Valley Medical Center (Caldwell)
Indiana
Terre Haute Regional Hospital
Kansas
Allen County Hospital (Iola)
Galichia Heart Hospital (Wichita)
Menorah Medical Center (Overland Park)
Overland Park Regional Medical Center
Wesley Medical Center (Wichita)
Kentucky
Frankfort Regional Medical Center
Greenview Regional Hospital (Bowling Green)
Louisiana
Dauterive Hospital (New Iberia)
Lafeyette Surgicare
Lakeview Regional Medical Center (Covington)
Rapides Regional Medical Center (Alexandria)
Tulane Medical Center (Metarie)
Tulane University Hospital & Clinic (New Orleans)
Women's & Children's Hospital (Lafayette)
Mississippi
Garden Park Medical Center (Gulfport)
Missouri
Centerpoint Medical Center (Independence)
Lafayette Regional Health Center (Lexington)
Lee's Summit Hospital
Research Medical Center (Kansas City)
Research Psychiatric Center (Kansas City)
Nevada
Flamingo Surgery Center (Las Vegas)

MountainView Hospital (Las Vegas)
Southern Hills Hospital and Medical Center (Las Vegas)
Sunrise Hospital and Medical Center (Las Vegas)
New Hampshire
Parkland Medical Center (Derry)
Portsmouth Regional Hospital
Salem Surgery Center
Oklahoma
Edmond Medical Center
Oklahoma Surgicare (Oklahoma City)
Oklahoma University Medical Center (Oklahoma City)
South Carolina
Colleton Medical Cemter (Walterboro)
Grand Dunes Surgery Center (Myrtle Beach)
Grand Strand Regional Medical Center (Myrtle Beach)
Summerville Medical Center
Trident Regional Medical Center (Charleston)
Tennessee
Centennial Medical Center (Nashville)
Hendersonville Medical Center
Horizon Medical Center (Dickson)
Parkridge East Hospital (Chattanooga)
Parkridge Valley Hospital (Chattanooga)
Skyline Medical Center (Nashville)
StoneCrest Medical Center (Smyrna)
Summit Medical Center (Hermitage)
Texas
Bailey Square Surgery Center (Austin)
Bayshore Medical Center (Pasadena)
Clear Lake Regional Medical Center (Webster)
Conroe Regional Medical Center
Corpus Christi Medical Center
Del Sol Medical Center (El Paso)
Denton Regional Medical Center
Green Oaks Hospital (Dallas)
Kingwood Medical Center
Las Colinas Medical Center (Irving)
Mainland Medical Center (Texas City)
Medical Center of Arlington
Medical Center of Lewisville
Medical Center of McKinney
Medical Center of Plano
Medical City Dallas Hospital
Methodist Hospital (San Antonio)
Metropolitan Methodist Hospital (San Antonio)
North Austin Medical Center
North Hills Hospital (North Richland Hills)
Plaza Medical Center of Fort Worth
Rio Grande Regional Hospital (McAllen)
Round Rock Medical Center
St. David's Medical Center (Austin)
Valley Regional Medical Center (Brownsville)
West Houston Medical Center
Woman's Hospital of Texas (Houston)
Utah
Brigham City Community Hospital
Lakeview Hospital (Bountiful)
Ogden Regional Medical Center
St. Mark's Hospital (Salt Lake City)
Timpanogos Regional Hospital (Orem)
Virginia
CJW Medical Center (Richmond)
Dominion Hospital (Falls Church)
Henrico Doctors' Hospital (Richmond)
John Randolph Medical Center
LewisGale Medical Center (Salem)
Pulaski Community Hospital
Reston Hospital Center
Spotsylvania Regional Medical Center (Fredricksburg)

Selected International Facilities

UK
Harley Street Clinic (London)
Lister Hospital (London)
London Bridge Hospital (London)
The Portland Hospital for Women and Children (London)
Princess Grace Hospital (London)
The Wellington Hospital (London)

PRODUCTS/OPERATIONS

2018 Sales

	$ mil.	% of total
Payer sources		
Managed care & other insurers	24,467	52
Medicare	9,831	21
Managed Medicare	5,497	12
Managed Medicaid	2,403	5
Medicaid	1,358	3
International	1,156	3
Other	1,965	4
Total	**46,677**	**100**

COMPETITORS

Ascension Health
CHRISTUS Health
Catholic Health
  Initiatives
Community Health
  Systems
Encompass Health

Tenet Healthcare
Texas Health Resources
Trinity Health (Novi)
United Surgical
  Partners
Universal Health
  Services

HISTORICAL FINANCIALS

Company Type: Public

Income Statement   FYE: December 31

	REVENUE ($ mil.)	NET INCOME ($ mil.)	NET PROFIT MARGIN	EMPLOYEES
12/19	51,336	3,505	6.8%	280,000
12/18	46,677	3,787	8.1%	262,000
12/17	43,614	2,216	5.1%	253,000
12/16	41,490	2,890	7.0%	241,000
12/15	39,678	2,129	5.4%	233,000
Annual Growth	**6.7%**	**13.3%**	—	**4.7%**

2019 Year-End Financials

Debt ratio: 74.84%
Return on equity: —
Cash ($ mil.): 621
Current ratio: 1.44
Long-term debt ($ mil.): 33,577

No. of shares (mil.): 338
Dividends
  Yield: 1.0%
  Payout: 16.0%
Market value ($ mil.): 50,026

	STOCK PRICE ($) FY Close	P/E High/Low	PER SHARE ($) Earnings	Dividends	Book Value
12/19	147.81	15 11	10.07	1.60	(8.30)
12/18	124.45	13 8	10.66	1.40	(14.44)
12/17	87.84	15 12	5.95	0.00	(19.44)
12/16	74.02	11 8	7.30	0.00	(19.71)
12/15	67.63	18 13	4.99	0.00	(19.06)
Annual Growth	**21.6%**	— —	**19.2%**	—	—

HEALTHPARTNERS, INC.

EXECUTIVES

Pres-Ceo, Mary Brainerd
Exec V Pres-Chief Mktg Offcr*, Andrea Walsh
Cfo*, David A Dziuk
Coordinator, Renee Hannan
Team Leader Appl, Chao Nguyen
Admin Asst, Kristi Brandt
Senior Director, Frank Muller
Business Analyst, Laurie Lorence
Project Coordinator, Lesley Pereira
Information Specialist, Milagros Ogania
Information Specialist, Pierre Gingerichboberg
Auditors: KPMG LLP MINNEAPOLIS MINNES

HQ: HEALTHPARTNERS, INC.
8170 33RD AVE S, BLOOMINGTON, MN 554254516
Phone: 952 883-6000
Web: WWW.HEALTHPARTNERS.COM

HISTORICAL FINANCIALS

Company Type: Private

Income Statement				FYE: December 31
	REVENUE ($ mil.)	NET INCOME ($ mil.)	NET PROFIT MARGIN	EMPLOYEES
12/19	7,251	278	3.8%	22,000
12/18	7,061	143	2.0%	—
12/97	1,247	(2)	—	—
12/96	1,178	9	0.8%	—
Annual Growth	8.2%	16.0%	—	—

Heartland Financial USA, Inc. (Dubuque, IA)

Heartland Financial USA is an $11.3 billion multi-bank holding company that owns flagship subsidiary Dubuque Bank and Trust (Iowa) and ten other banks that together operate more than 120 branches in about a dozen states primarily in the West and Midwest. In addition to standard deposit loan and mortgage services the banks also offer retirement wealth management trust insurance and investment services. Heartland also owns consumer lender Citizens Finance which has about a dozen offices in Illinois Iowa and Wisconsin.

Operations

Heartland Financial USA operates two main segments: community and other banking and retail mortgage banking services which account for about 90% and 10% of revenue respectively. The community banking business generates revenue from interest earned on loans and investment securities and fees from deposit services. Its retail mortgage banking services division collects revenue from interest from mortgage loans held for sale gains on sales of loans on the secondary market the servicing of mortgage loans for investors and loan origination fee income.

About three-quarters of Heartland's loan portfolio comes from commercial and commercial real estate loans but — in keeping with the bank's Midwestern identity — it also makes agricultural residential mortgage and consumer loans.

Heartland's subsidiaries include: Citywide Banks (approximately $1.9 billion total deposits) New Mexico Bank & Trust ($1.2 billion) Dubuque Bank and Trust Company ($1.1 billion) Wisconsin Bank & Trust ($890 million) First Bank & Trust ($820 million) Premier Valley Bank ($710 million) Illinois Bank & Trust ($690 million) Morrill & Janes Bank and Trust ($560 million) Arizona Bank & Trust ($520 million) Rocky Mountain Bank ($420 million) and Minnesota Bank & Trust ($180 million).

Geographic Reach

Dubuque Iowa-based Heartland Financial USA operates through about 145 locations (including branches and loan production offices) in local communities in Iowa Illinois Wisconsin New Mexico Arizona Montana Colorado Minnesota Kansas Missouri Texas and California. The company's three largest bank subsidiaries by number of locations are Colorado's Citywide Banks with about 25 and Wisconsin Bank & Trust and New Mexico Bank & Trust with about 20 each.

Sales and Marketing

Heartland Financial USA offers its banking services to businesses public sector and non-profit entities and individuals.

The company's Commercial Card team works with its commercial clients to help cut manual processes and costs from employee travel entertainment spending and vendor payments.

Financial Performance

As it grows its assets and loan portfolio via acquisitions Heartland Financial USA had positive overall performance in the last five years increasing revenue by some 70% and net income by more than 100% — all while expanding its cash by about 55% and reducing long-term debt by nearly 20%.

Revenue ticked up 6% to $432.3 million in 2017 on increased interest income mostly from interest and fees on a larger loan portfolio following the company's acquisitions of Citywide Banks and Founders Bancorp.

Net income trended down 6% to $75.3 million owing to higher income taxes salaries employee benefits and professional fees.

Heartland added $37.3 million to its cash stores in 2017 to end the year with $196 million. Operations and investments brought in $155.9 million and $27.3 million respectively. Financing activities used up $145.9 million due to a net decrease from savings accounts and repayments of short term Federal Home Loan Bank advances.

Strategy

Heartland Financial USA's strategy for the past two decades is centered on expanding through acquisitions in its existing and adjacent markets while balancing growth in newer western markets with the stability of its established midwestern markets. The company's goal is to have at least $1 billion in assets in each state where it operates.

Mergers and Acquisitions

In 2019 Heartland Financial USA acquired Overland Park Kansas-based Blue Valley Ban the holding company for Bank of Blue Valley. Blue Valley has $712 million in assets $564 million in gross loans outstanding and $587 million in deposits. The acquisition expands Heartland's presence in the Kansas City and Johnson County markets.

Heartland added its eleventh subsidiary in May 2018 through its acquisition of Lubbock Texas-based First Bank Lubbock Bancshares for $189.9 million. Operating under the name First Bank & Trust (which Heartland retained) the bank held $681.1 million in gross loans held to maturity and deposits of $893.8 million. First Bank & Trust has eight branches in West Texas and eight mortgage lending services offices throughout Texas.

In February 2018 the company acquired Minnetonka Minnesota-based Signature Bancshares for $61.4 million and incorporated it into its Minnesota Bank & Trust subsidiary. Signature had two branches in the Twin Cities metropolitan area with $324.5 million in gross loans held to maturity and deposits of $357.3 million.

Heartland acquired Citywide Banks (headquartered in Aurora Colorado) in July 2017 for $211.2 million. At the time of purchase Citywide had $985.4 million in net loans outstanding and $1.2 billion in deposits. Following incorporation of Citywide into its Centennial Bank and Trust subsidiary (which then adopted Citywide's name) Heartland had more than 25 branches in Colorado.

In February 2017 Heartland Financial USA acquired San Luis Obispo California-based Founders Bancorp which it incorporated into its Premier Valley Bank subsidiary for $31 million. The company's Founders Community Bank held loans totaling $96.4 million and the purchase increased Heartland's total number of branches in California from five to nine.

Company Background

Heartland Financial USA was founded in 1981 although it traces its roots back to the 1935 establishment of Dubuque Bank and Trust. It made its first bank acquisition in in 1989 - Key City Bank - and has continued acquiring community banks since.

EXECUTIVES

Vice President Marketing, Dawn Oelke

President And Ceo Minnesota Bank & Trust, Catherine T. (Kate) Kelly

Chairman President And Ceo Heartland Financial Usa Inc.; Vice Chairman Dubuque Bank & Trust Wisconsin Bank & Trust New Mexico Bank & Trust Arizona Bank & Trust Rocky Mountain Bank Centennial Bank And Trust(1) Minnesota Bank & Trust And Premier Valley Bank, Lynn B. Fuller, age 70, $486,388 total compensation

Evp Lending, Douglas J. Horstmann, age 66, $275,156 total compensation

President And Ceo New Mexico Bank & Trust, R. Greg Leyendecker

President And Ceo Wisconsin Bank & Trust, Kevin S. Tenpas

President Of Heartland Director Rocky Mountain Bank And President Heartland Financial Usa Inc. Insurance Services, Bruce K. Lee, age 59, $383,519 total compensation

Evp Human Resources And Organizational Development, Mark G. Murtha, age 58

Evp Deputy Chief Financial Officer And Principal Accounting Officer, Janet M. Quick

President Centennial Bank And Trust, Steven E. Ward

Svp And Coo Wealth Management Group, Bruce C. Rehmke

Evp Commercial Sales, Frank E. Walter, age 73

Evp Senior General Counsel And Corporate Secretary, Michael J. Coyle, age 74

Evp Operations, Brian J. Fox, age 71, $190,000 total compensation

Evp And Chief Risk Officer, Rodney L. Sloan, age 60

Evp And Cfo Heartland Financial Usa Treasurer Citizens Finance Parent Co.. And Director Heartland Financial Usa Inc. Insurance Services, Bryan R. McKeag, age 59, $305,625 total compensation

Evp Finance And Corporate Strategy, David L. Horstmann, age 70

President And Ceo Arizona Bank & Trust, Jerry L. Schwallier

President And Ceo Rocky Mountain Bank, Curtis Chrystal

President And Ceo Morrill & Janes Bank And Trust Co., Kurt M. Saylor

Evp Private Client Services, Kelly J. Johnson, age 58

President And Ceo Illinois Bank And Trust, Jeff Hultman

Chief Investment Officer, Nancy Tengler

Evp And Chief Credit Officer, Drew Townsend

Evp And Private Wealth Management Director, Rick O. Terry

President And Ceo Heartland Mortgage, Paul Johnstun

Ceo Centennial Bank And Trust, Jim Basey

President Heartland Mortgage, Jack Lloyd

Vice President Finance, Sandra Wild

Vice President Administrative Services And Facilities, Joseph Berretta

Vice President, Kate Barth

Vice President, Jean Harkey

Vice President Of Retirement Plan Services, Lisan Adams

Vice President Electronic Banking And Fraud, Linda Maas

Retail Credit Officer Avp, Gina Carlson

Vice President Corporate Training Director, Bonnie Bollin

Assistant Vice President Commercial Services, Lynn Stoffregen

Vice President, Rachel Steiner

Vice President Information Technology, Les Oelke

Svp Bsa Director, Julie Shanahan

Senior Vice President Special Assets Reo, John Hawkins

Vice President, Shelley Phillips

Vice President, Troy Steger

Vice President, Craig Sciara

Vice President Business Development And Manager, Eric Foy

Vice President Credit Administration, Tom Steinhaus

Senior Vice President And Corporate Compliance Director, Chris Spellman

Senior Vice President Credit Administration Officer, Joe Davis

Assistant Vice President, Michelle Schoen

Deputy General Counsel And Corporate Secretary Svp, Angela Kelley

Assistant Vice President Information Services, Brent Wilke

Vice President Personal Loans Mortgage Loans, Michelle Skinder

Tm Wire Transfer Manager Avp, Cori Freihoefer

Vp Engineering, Mary Burns

Vice President Director Financial Planning And Performance Management, Michael G Flood

Credit Admin Officer Iv Senior Vice President, Ralph Atkinson

Credit Admin Officer Iv Senior Vice President, Jeffery Viviano

Vice President Compliance Officer, Kaci Brownell

Executive Vice President And Chief Human Resources Officer, Deborah Deters

Vice President Director Financial Planning And Performance Management, Michael Flood

Senior Vice President Director Investments, Tom Thornton

Vice President Sales, Brian Jackson

Vice President, Linda A Bessey

Vice President Commercial Banker, Bradley Kemp

Vice Chairman Of The Board Of Heartland Financial Usa Inc.; Chairman And Director Of Dubuque Bank And Trust, Mark C. Falb, age 72

Vice Chairman Of The Board Of Heartland Financial Usa Inc.; Director And Vice Chairman Of The Board Of Dubuque Bank And Trust, Thomas L. Flynn, age 64

Board Member, Duane White

Auditors: KPMG LLP

LOCATIONS

HQ: Heartland Financial USA, Inc. (Dubuque, IA)
1398 Central Avenue, Dubuque, IA 52001
Phone: 563 589-2100 **Fax:** 563 589-2011
Web: www.htlf.com

PRODUCTS/OPERATIONS

2017 Sales

	$ mil.	% of total
Interest		
Loans & leases including fees	304	65
Securities	58	13
Other	1	.
Interest expense	(33.3)	.
Noninterest		
Gains on sales of loans	22	5
Service charges and fees	39	8
Trust fees	15	3
Loan serving income	5	1
Brokerage & insurance commissions	4	1
Security gains	7	2
Other	8	2
Total	**432**	**100**

Selected Subsidiaries

Arizona Bank & Trust
Citywide Banks (Colorado)
Dubuque Bank and Trust Company (Iowa)
 DB&T Community Development Corp.
 DB&T Insurance
Illinois Bank & Trust
Minnesota Bank & Trust
Morrill & Janes Bank and Trust Company (Kansas)
New Mexico Bank & Trust
Premier Valley Bank (California)
Rocky Mountain Bank (Montana)
Wisconsin Bank & Trust

COMPETITORS

Associated Banc-Corp	First Banks
BBVA Compass Bancshares	U.S. Bancorp
Bank of America	Wells Fargo
Bank of the West	Zions Bancorporation

HISTORICAL FINANCIALS

Company Type: Public

Income Statement

FYE: December 31

	ASSETS ($ mil.)	NET INCOME ($ mil.)	INCOME AS % OF ASSETS	EMPLOYEES
12/19	13,209	149	1.1%	1,908
12/18	11,408	117	1.0%	2,045
12/17	9,810	75	0.8%	2,008
12/16	8,247	80	1.0%	1,864
12/15	7,694	60	0.8%	1,799
Annual Growth	**14.5%**	**25.5%**	**—**	**1.5%**

2019 Year-End Financials

Debt ratio: 2.07%
Return on equity: 10.27%
Cash ($ mil.): 382
Current ratio: —
Long-term debt ($ mil.): —

No. of shares (mil.): 36
Dividends
 Yield: 1.4%
 Payout: 18.0%
Market value ($ mil.): 1,826

	STOCK PRICE ($) FY Close	P/E High/Low	PER SHARE ($) Earnings	Dividends	Book Value
12/19	49.74	12 10	4.14	0.73	43.00
12/18	43.95	17 12	3.52	0.59	38.44
12/17	53.65	20 16	2.65	0.51	33.10
12/16	48.00	15 8	3.22	0.50	28.37
12/15	31.36	14 9	2.83	0.45	29.56
Annual Growth	**12.2%**	**— —**	**10.0%**	**12.9%**	**9.8%**

Heritage Commerce Corp

Heritage Commerce is the holding company for Heritage Bank of Commerce which operates about 15 branches in the southern and eastern regions of the San Francisco Bay area. Serving consumers and small to midsized businesses and their owners and managers the bank offers savings and checking accounts money market accounts and CDs as well as cash management services and loans. Commercial and commercial real estate loans make up most of the company's loan portfolio which is rounded out by land construction and home equity loans.

EXECUTIVES

Evp And Cfo, Lawrence D. McGovern, age 65, $260,753 total compensation

President And Ceo, Walter T. (Walt) Kaczmarek, age 68, $368,509 total compensation

Evp And Director Business Development, Robert P. (Bob) Gionfriddo, age 74

Evp Banking Division, Michael E. Benito, $244,826 total compensation

Coo, Keith A. Wilton, $243,025 total compensation

Evp And Chief Credit Officer, David E. Porter, $260,738 total compensation

Evp And Corporate Secretary, Deborah K. (Debbie) Reuter

Evp Hoa And Deposit Services, Teresa Powell

Vice President, Nancy Landy

Vice President Business Development Officer, David Beronio

Senior Vice President, Mike Hansen

Vice President And Financial Planning And Analysis, Minny Sue

Vice President Account Manager, Greg Ketell

Vice President Audit, Michael Egbujor

Vice President, John Rosendahl

Assistant Vice President And Credit Risk Officer, Joann Nguyen

Director, Jack W. Conner, age 80

Auditors: Crowe LLP

LOCATIONS

HQ: Heritage Commerce Corp
224 Airport Parkway, San Jose, CA 95110
Phone: 408 947-6900
Web: www.heritagecommercecorp.com

PRODUCTS/OPERATIONS

2017 Sales

	$ mil.	% of total
Interest		
Loans including fees	86	74
Taxable securities	13	12
Other	6	6
Interest expense	(5.4)	-
Noninterest		
Service charges & fees on deposit accounts	3	3
Increase in cash surrender value of life insurance	1	1
Gain on sales of SBA loans	1	1
Servicing income	1	1
Other	2	2
Total	**111**	**100**

COMPETITORS

Bank of America	JPMorgan Chase
Bank of the West	MUFG Americas Holdings
Citibank	SVB Financial
Comerica	U.S. Bancorp
First Republic (CA)	Wells Fargo

HISTORICAL FINANCIALS

Company Type: Public

Income Statement

FYE: December 31

	ASSETS ($ mil.)	NET INCOME ($ mil.)	INCOME AS % OF ASSETS	EMPLOYEES
12/19	4,109	40	1.0%	357
12/18	3,096	35	1.1%	302
12/17	2,843	23	0.8%	278
12/16	2,570	27	1.1%	263
12/15	2,361	16	0.7%	260
Annual Growth	**14.9%**	**25.1%**	**—**	**8.2%**

2019 Year-End Financials

Debt ratio: 0.96%
Return on equity: 8.57%
Cash ($ mil.): 457
Current ratio: —
Long-term debt ($ mil.): —

No. of shares (mil.): 59
Dividends
 Yield: 3.7%
 Payout: 43.2%
Market value ($ mil.): 762

	STOCK PRICE ($) FY Close	P/E High/Low	PER SHARE ($) Earnings	Dividends	Book Value
12/19	12.83	17 13	0.84	0.48	9.71
12/18	11.34	21 13	0.84	0.44	8.49
12/17	15.32	26 21	0.62	0.40	7.10
12/16	14.43	20 13	0.72	0.36	6.85
12/15	11.96	26 17	0.48	0.32	7.64
Annual Growth	1.8%	— —	15.0%	10.7%	6.2%

Heritage Financial Corp (WA)

Heritage Financial is ready to answer the call of Pacific Northwesterners seeking to preserve their heritage. Heritage Financial is the holding company for Heritage Bank which operates more than 65 branches throughout Washington and Oregon. Boasting nearly $4 billion in assets the bank offers a range of deposit products to consumers and businesses such as CDs IRAs and checking savings NOW and money market accounts. Commercial and industrial loans account for over 50% of Heritage Financial's loan portfolio while mortgages secured by multi-family real estate comprise about 5%. The bank also originates single-family mortgages land development construction loans and consumer loans.

Operations
The bank also does business under the Central Valley Bank name in the Yakima and Kittitas counties of Washington and under the Whidbey Island Bank name on Whidbey Island.

About 79% of Heritage Financial's total revenue came from loan interest (including fees) in 2014 while another 7% came from interest on its investment securities. The rest of its revenue came from service charges and other fees (8%) Merchant Visa income (1%) and other miscellaneous fees. The company had a staff of 748 employees at the end of that year.

Geographic Reach
The Olympia-based bank operates more than 65 branches across Washington and the greater Portland area. It has additional offices in eastern Washington mostly in Yakima county.

Sales and Marketing
Heritage targets small and medium-sized businesses along with their owners as well as individuals.

Financial Performance
Fueled by loan and deposit growth from a series of bank acquisitions Heritage Financial's revenues and profits have been on the rise in recent years.

The company's revenue jumped 70% to a record $137.6 million in 2014 mostly thanks to new loan business stemming from its acquisition of Washington Banking Company. Deposit service charge income also increased thanks to new deposit business from the acquisition.

Higher revenue in 2014 allowed Heritage Financial's net income to more than double to a record $21 million while its operating cash levels rose 66% to $51.3 million on higher cash earnings and net proceeds from the sale of its loans.

Strategy
The bank reiterated in 2015 that it would continue to pursue strategic acquisitions of community banks to grow market share across the Pacific Northwest (its region of expertise) expand its business lines and grow its loan and deposit business.

With its focus on business and commercial lending the bank also in 2015 emphasized the importance of seeking high asset quality loans lending to familiar markets that have a historical record of success. Recruiting and retaining "highly competent personnel" to execute its strategies was also key to its long-term agenda.

Mergers and Acquisitions
In May 2014 Heritage acquired Washington Banking Company and its Whidbey Island Bank subsidiary for $265 million which "significantly expanded and enhanced" its product offerings across its core geographic market.

In July 2013 the bank acquired Puyallup Washington-based Valley Community Bancshares and its eight Valley Bank branches for $44 million.

In January 2013 the company purchased Lakewood Washington-based Northwest Commercial Bank along with its two branch locations in Washington state for $5 million.

EXECUTIVES

President Ceo And Director Heritage Financial And Ceo Heritage Bank, Brian L. Vance, age 65, $494,316 total compensation
Evp And Cfo Heritage Financial And Heritage Bank, Donald J. Hinson, age 59, $255,084 total compensation
Evp And Chief Credit Officer Heritage Bank, David A. Spurling, age 67, $237,342 total compensation
Evp Heritage Financial And President And Coo Heritage Bank, Jeffrey J. (Jeff) Deuel, $291,516 total compensation
Evp And Chief Lending Officer Heritage Bank, Bryan D. McDonald, age 48, $261,374 total compensation
Vice President And Financial Reporting Manager, Patrice Hernandez
Avp, Debbie Libbing
Senior Vice President Commercial Banking Team Leader, Katherine Thompson
Avp Mortgage Loan Officer, Teresa Munn
Chairman, Brian S. Charneski, age 58
Board Member, Stephen Dennis
Auditors: Crowe LLP

LOCATIONS

HQ: Heritage Financial Corp (WA)
201 Fifth Avenue S.W., Olympia, WA 98501
Phone: 360 943-1500
Web: www.HF-WA.com

PRODUCTS/OPERATIONS

2014 Sales

	$ mil.	% of total
Interest income		
Interest and fees on loans	110	79
Investment securities	10	7
Others	0	-
Non-interest income		
Service charges and others	11	8
Merchant Visa income	1	1
Others	4	5
Total	**137**	**100**

COMPETITORS

Bank of America	U.S. Bancorp
Columbia Banking	Washington Federal
FS Bancorp	Wells Fargo
KeyCorp	

HISTORICAL FINANCIALS

Company Type: Public

Income Statement
FYE: December 31

	ASSETS ($ mil.)	NET INCOME ($ mil.)	INCOME AS % OF ASSETS	EMPLOYEES
12/19	5,552	67	1.2%	884
12/18	5,316	53	1.0%	859
12/17	4,113	41	1.0%	735
12/16	3,878	38	1.0%	760
12/15	3,650	37	1.0%	717
Annual Growth	11.1%	15.9%	—	5.4%

2019 Year-End Financials

Debt ratio: 0.37%	No. of shares (mil.): 36
Return on equity: 8.61%	Dividends
Cash ($ mil.): 228	Yield: 2.9%
Current ratio: —	Payout: 46.4%
Long-term debt ($ mil.): —	Market value ($ mil.): 1,036

	STOCK PRICE ($) FY Close	P/E High/Low	PER SHARE ($) Earnings	Dividends	Book Value
12/19	28.30	18 14	1.83	0.84	22.10
12/18	29.72	25 19	1.49	0.72	20.63
12/17	30.80	23 16	1.39	0.61	16.98
12/16	25.75	20 13	1.30	0.72	16.08
12/15	18.84	16 12	1.25	0.69	15.68
Annual Growth	10.7%	— —	10.0%	5.0%	9.0%

Hershey Company (The)

Hershey Company works to spread Almond Joy and lots of Kisses. With a portfolio of more than 80 global brands the #1 chocolate producer in North America has built a big business making such well-known chocolate and candy brands as Hershey's Kisses Reese's peanut butter cups Twizzlers Mounds and Almond Joy candy bars York peppermint patties and Kit Kat wafer bars. Hershey also makes grocery goods – including baking products toppings sundae syrup cocoa mix cookies snack nuts breath mints and bubble gum – and has expanded into popcorn and other savory snacks. Products are sold to wholesale distributors and retailers throughout North America and exported overseas; the US accounts for most of sales.

Operations
Hershey's operations consist of two business segments North America which accounts for some 90% of revenue and International and Other about 10%.

The company makes and sells more than 80 brands led by Hershey's and Reese's as well as Krackle Kit Kat Kisses and York. Other popular brand franchises are Twizzlers Mounds York Ice Breakers Jolly Rancher and Bubble Yum which fall within the company's sweets and refreshment business unit. Through acquisitions Hershey has added snack brands such as Skinny Pop popcorn and other "better-for-you" snacks and Krave jerky.

In international markets the company adds regional brands such as Pelon Pelo Rico confectionery products (Mexico) IO-IO snack products (Brazil) and Maha Lacto confectionery products and Jumpin and Sofit beverage products (India).

Confectionery and confectionery-based products account for about 95% of total sales with the up-and-coming snacks portfolio generating the rest.

Geographic Reach

Hershey's North America segment accounts for some 90% of revenue (mostly from the US) and it caters to the traditional chocolate and non-chocolate confectionery market as well as grocery and growing snacks markets in the US and Canada.

International and Other (about 10% of revenue) include operations in China Mexico Brazil India and Malaysia primarily for consumers in these regions. The segment also distributes and sells confectionery products in export markets within Asia Latin America Middle East Europe Africa and other regions and includes Hershey's Chocolate World stores in Hershey Pennsylvania; New York; Las Vegas; Niagara Falls (Ontario); and Singapore. The US accounts for about 85% of revenue and other countries accounts for about 15% of revenue.

Its headquarters is located in Pennsylvania.

Sales and Marketing

Hershey leverages a staff of full-time sales representatives and food brokers to peddle its products to customers. In general the confectionery company counts wholesale distributors chain grocery stores mass merchandisers chain drug stores vending companies wholesale clubs convenience stores and concessionaires among its vast customer set. Its distribution network ships products from its manufacturing plants to strategically located distribution centers using common carriers to deliver products to customers.

Hershey is heavily reliant on its largest customer McLane Co. the primary distributor of Hershey products to Walmart which accounts for nearly 30% of total sales.

The company's advertising expenses totaled $513.3 million in 2019 $479.9 million in 2018 and $541.3 million in 2017 respectively

Financial Performance

Net sales increased 3% in 2019 to almost $8 billion compared with 2018 reflecting a favorable price realization of 2% due to higher prices on certain products a 1% benefit from net acquisitions and divestitures (predominantly driven by the 2019 acquisition of ONE Brands and the 2018 acquisition of Pirate Brands partially offset by 2018 divestitures) and a volume increase of less than 1% partially offset by an unfavorable impact from foreign currency exchange rates of less than 1%. Excluding foreign currency our 2019 net sales increased 3%. Consolidated volumes increased due to solid marketplace growth in select international markets.

Net income decreased $27.9 million to $1.1 billion or 2% in 2019 compared with 2018. The decrease in both net income and EPS-diluted was driven primarily by higher impairment charges and SM&A in 2019 partially offset by higher gross profit lower business realignment costs and lower income taxes.

Cash at the end of 2019 was $493.3 million a decrease of $94.7 million from the prior year. Cash from operations contributed to the coffers was $1.8 billion while investing activities used $780.5 million mainly for acquisitions. Financing activities used another $1.1 billion mainly for payments of short-term debt.

Strategy

The foundation of their marketing strategy is their strong brand equities product innovation and the consistently superior quality of their products. Hershey devote considerable resources to the identification development testing manufacturing and marketing of new products. The company utilize a variety of promotional programs directed towards their customers as well as advertising and promotional programs for consumers of their products to stimulate sales of certain products at various times throughout the year.

The company's strategy focuses on: maintaining undisputed lead in US confection and capturing incremental snacking occasions; driving profitable growth allocating capital resources and optimizing cost structure; and expanding competitive advantage through differentiated capabilities.

Mergers and Acquisitions

In late 2019 in a move that bolsters its line of healthier snacks the company completed the acquisition of nutrition bar maker One Brands for approximately $397 million. The purchase complements Hershey's existing Oatmega business acquired as part of the 2018 acquisition of Amplify Snack Brands and its investment in European protein-bar maker FULFIL Holdings.

Company Background

The Hershey Company is the legacy of Milton Hershey of Pennsylvania Dutch origin. Apprenticed in 1872 at age 15 to a candy maker Hershey started Lancaster Caramel Company at age 30. In 1893 at the Chicago Exposition he saw a new chocolate-making machine and in 1900 he sold the caramel operations for $1 million to start a chocolate factory. Chocolate proved to be a wise decision as the company made the name Hershey synonymous with American chocolate over the century.

HISTORY

The Hershey Company is the legacy of Milton Hershey of Pennsylvania Dutch origin. Apprenticed in 1872 at age 15 to a candy maker Hershey started Lancaster Caramel Company at age 30. In 1893 at the Chicago Exposition he saw a new chocolate-making machine and in 1900 he sold the caramel operations for $1 million to start a chocolate factory.

The factory was completed in 1905 in Derry Church Pennsylvania and renamed Hershey Foods the next year. Chocolate Kisses individually hand-wrapped in silver foil were introduced in 1907. Two years later the candy man founded the Milton Hershey School an orphanage; the company was donated to a trust in 1918 and for years existed solely to fund the school. Hershey went public in 1927.

EXECUTIVES

Senior Vice President, Thomas Hernquist
President And Ceo, Michele G. Buck, age 59
Svp And Chief Product Supply And Technology Officer, Terence L. O'Day, age 70, $590,061 total compensation
Svp And Cfo, Patricia A. Little, age 60, $629,412 total compensation
President International, Steven C. Schiller
President U.s., Todd W. Tillemans
Vice President Us Finance, Todd Cunfer
Vice President, Joe Beck
National Account Manager, Mike Jauch
Vice President Finance, Gayla Molinelli
Vice President Technology And, Simon Viltz
Vice President Corporate Communications And Corporate Social Responsibility, Leigh E Horner
Senior Vice President General Counsel Secretary, Damien Atkins
Chairman, John P. (J.P.) Bilbrey, age 63
Vp Treasurer, Rosa Stroh
Vice Chairman For Finance And Informatics, Doug Eggli
Assistant Secretary, Kathleen Purcell
Auditors: Ernst & Young LLP

LOCATIONS

HQ: Hershey Company (The)
  19 East Chocolate Avenue, Hershey, PA 17033
Phone: 717 534 4200   **Fax:** 717 531-6161
Web: www.hersheys.com

2018 Sales

	$ mil.	% of total
North America	6,901	89
International and Other	889	11
Total	**7,791**	**100**

2018 Sales

	$ mil.	% of total
US	6,535	84
Other	1,255	16
Total	**7,791**	**100**

PRODUCTS/OPERATIONS

2018 Sales

	$ mil.	% of total
Confectionery	7,453	96
Snacks	337	4
Total	**7,791**	**100**

COMPETITORS

Ferrero	Mars Incorporated
Flowers Foods	Mondelez International
Ghirardelli Chocolate	Nestlé
Godiva Chocolatier	Otis Spunkmeyer
Guittard	Russell Stover
Kellogg	Smucker
Lindt & Spr ngli	Tootsie Roll

HISTORICAL FINANCIALS

Company Type: Public

Income Statement				FYE: December 31
	REVENUE ($ mil.)	NET INCOME ($ mil.)	NET PROFIT MARGIN	EMPLOYEES
12/19	7,986	1,149	14.4%	16,140
12/18	7,791	1,177	15.1%	16,420
12/17	7,515	782	10.4%	16,910
12/16	7,440	720	9.7%	17,980
12/15	7,386	512	6.9%	20,710
Annual Growth	**2.0%**	**22.4%**	**—**	**(6.0%)**

2019 Year-End Financials

Debt ratio: 52.41%	No. of shares (mil.): 208
Return on equity: 73.28%	Dividends
Cash ($ mil.): 493	Yield: 2.0%
Current ratio: 1.05	Payout: 49.6%
Long-term debt ($ mil.): 3,530	Market value ($ mil.): 30,694

	STOCK PRICE ($) FY Close	P/E High/Low		PER SHARE ($) Earnings	Dividends	Book Value
12/19	146.98	29	18	5.46	2.99	8.33
12/18	107.18	20	16	5.58	2.76	6.67
12/17	113.51	31	27	3.66	2.55	4.34
12/16	103.43	33	24	3.34	2.40	3.70
12/15	89.27	46	35	2.32	2.24	4.60
Annual Growth	**13.3%**	**—**	**—**	**23.9%**	**7.5%**	**16.0%**

Hertz Global Holdings Inc (New)

Hertz Global Holdings is a world leader in car rental. On its own and through agents and licensees Hertz operates about 12400 rental locations in about 160 countries under the Hertz Dollar and Thrifty brands. About 65% of its US revenue comes from airport locations. Its fleet includes approximately 180700 cars from General Motors Nissan Toyota and other manufacturers. In addition to its signature car rental services its Donlen subsidiary offers fleet leasing and management services. The newest iteration of Hertz was formed in 2016 when it was spun off from Herc Holdings.

Operations

Hertz's three core operating segments include: US Car Rental which consists of company-owned and franchisee car rental locations in the US; International Car Rental; and All Other Operations which includes Donlen the firm's fleet leasing and management subsidiary. The US Car Rental business accounts for more than 70% of sales followed by International car rental accounts for more than 20% and last other operations accounts for about less than 10%.

Geographic Reach

Florida-based Hertz operates throughout North America Europe Latin America Asia Australia the Caribbean New Zealand Africa and the Middle East. It has a reservation and financial center near Dublin Ireland and European headquarters outside London.

Hertz operates about 1600 US and about 2000 non-US airport rental locations. It has about 2000 US and about 6200 off-airport locations which primarily serve courtesy car customers and travelers going to or from airports.

US countries operations accounts for about 80% and international countries operations accounts for more than 20%.

Sales and Marketing

Hertz advertises its car rental services through television newspapers direct mail and the internet. Its other forms of marketing and promotion include travel industry business partnerships and press and public relations activities. About 60% of US vehicles rental revenues is from business purposes and the remaining about 40% from leisure purposes.

Hertz Global had an advertising expense amounted to $318 million $238 million and $191 million in years 2019 2018 and 2017 respectively.

Financial Performance

Total revenues increased $275 million in 2019 to $9.8 billion compared to 2018 due to an increase of $459 million in their U.S. RAC segment partially offset by a decrease of $107 million and $76 million in their International RAC and All Other Operations segments respectively. U.S. RAC revenues increased due to a 4% increase in volume and a 2% increase in Total RPD.

Hertz reported a net loss of $58 million recovering about $167 million compared to the prior year. The recovery was due to the increase on their revenue while maintaining almost the same expenses.

Cash held by the company at the end of 2019 decreased by $50 million to $1.36 billion compared to $1.41 billion in 2018. Cash provided by operations and financing activities were $2.9 billion and $1.5 billion respectively. Cash used for investing activities was $4.4 billion.

Strategy

The company's strategy includes optimization of their vehicle rental operations disciplined performance management and evaluation of all locations and the pursuit of same-store sales growth.

Hertz develop and maintain a talent management strategy that defines current and future talent requirements (e.g. experience skills location requirements timing etc.) based on their strategic direction outlines coordinated recruiting and development plans across businesses and regions and considers employee mobility centers of excellence and shared service concepts to optimize resource plans and leverage labor arbitrage.

Company Background

In 1918 22-year-old John Jacobs opened a Chicago car rental business with 12 Model T Fords that he had repaired. By 1923 when Yellow Cab entrepreneur John Hertz bought Jacobs' business it had revenues of about $1 million. Jacobs continued as top executive of the company renamed Hertz Drive-Ur-Self System. Three years later General Motors acquired the company when it bought Yellow Truck from John Hertz. Hertz introduced the first car rental charge card in 1926 opened its first airport location at Chicago's Midway Airport in 1932 and initiated the first one-way (rent-it-here/leave-it-there) plan in 1933. The company expanded into Canada in 1938 and Europe in 1950.

EXECUTIVES

President And Chief Executive Officer Director, Kathryn V. (Kathy) Marinello
Executive Vice President Of Pricing Revenue Management And Fleet Operations, Frederic (Fred) Deschamps
President Donlen Corporation, Tom Callahan
Executive Vice President Global Sales, Robert J. (Bob) Stuart
Executive Vice President And Chief Retail Operations Officer North America, Paul Stone
Executive Vice President And Chief Financial Officer, Jamere Jackson
Executive Vice President And Chief Human Resources Officer, Murali Kuppuswamy
Executive Vice President And Chief Marketing Officer, Jodi Allen
Executive Vice President General Counsel And Secretary, Richard Frecker
Executive Vice President And Chief Information Officer, Opal G. Perry
Vice President Infrastructure Services, Craig Bonza
Vice President Marketing International, Vincent Gillet
Svp And Cto, Robert Moore
Svp And Treasurer, Scott Massengill
Vice President Business Applications, Barry Lewis
Executive Vice President Global Sales, Bob Stuart
Vice President It Transformation And Customer Systems, Brent Lessing
Vice President Talent Acquisition, Stephanie Worley
Senior Vice President Operations Services, Rob Solomon
Vice President Global Bus Systems Management, Susan Palazzese
Vp Corporate And Ip Law And Associate General Counsel, Brian Waldbaum
Senior Vice President And Chief Accounting Officer, Eric Esper
Vice President Information Technology, William Ruppel
Division Vice President, Jeff Pitz
Senior Vp Human Resources Operations (north America), A Guthrie
Vice President Sales And Marketing Hertz Canada, Tom Froggatt
Chairman, Henry R. Keizer
Auditors: Ernst & Young LLP

LOCATIONS

HQ: Hertz Global Holdings Inc (New)
8501 Williams Road, Estero, FL 33928
Phone: 239 301-7000
Web: www.hertz.com

2018 sales

	$ mil.	% of total
US	7,211	76
International	2,293	24
Total	**9,504**	**100**

PRODUCTS/OPERATIONS

2018 sales

	$ mil.	% of total
Worldwide Vehicle Rental		
US Rental Car	6,480	68
International Rental Car	2,276	24
All other operations	748	8
Total	**9,504**	**100**

COMPETITORS

Avis Budget	Ryder System
Enterprise Rent-A-Car	Uber
Europcar	

HISTORICAL FINANCIALS

Company Type: Public

Income Statement

FYE: December 31

	REVENUE ($ mil.)	NET INCOME ($ mil.)	NET PROFIT MARGIN	EMPLOYEES
12/19	9,779	(58)	—	38,000
12/18	9,504	(225)	—	38,000
12/17	8,803	327	3.7%	37,000
12/16	8,803	(491)	—	36,000
12/15	9,017	273	3.0%	—
Annual Growth	2.0%	—	—	—

2019 Year-End Financials

Debt ratio: 69.39%	No. of shares (mil.): 142
Return on equity: (-4.10%)	Dividends
Cash ($ mil.): 865	Yield: —
Current ratio: 1.40	Payout: —
Long-term debt ($ mil.): 17,089	Market value ($ mil.): 2,237

	STOCK PRICE ($) FY Close	P/E High/Low		Earnings	PER SHARE ($) Dividends	Book Value
12/19	15.75	—	—	(0.49)	0.00	12.46
12/18	13.65	—	—	(2.68)	0.00	12.63
12/17	22.10	7	2	3.94	0.00	18.10
12/16	21.56	—	—	(5.85)	0.00	12.95
Annual Growth	(7.5%)	—	—	—	—	(1.0%)

Hewlett Packard Enterprise Co

Hewlett Packard Enterprise (HPE) once part of the storied Hewlett-Packard Corp. designs and sells servers storage and networking equipment and provides technology services to help its large enterprise customers put together and deploy IT systems. HPE has software-defined IT offerings for private public and hybrid cloud environments as well as technologies for industrial Internet of Things (IoT) applications. HPE is a global company and around two-thirds of its revenue comes from outside the US. It has a rich technology history and maintains a cache of around 15000 worldwide patents.

Operations

HPE has four operating segments: Hybrid IT Intelligent Edge Financial Services and corporate investments.

The Hybrid IT segment over 85% of revenue provides software-defined servers storage data center networking and HPE Pointnext services. The traditional server and storage systems within the Hybrid IT segment face pricing and unit volume challenges as customers migrate to cloud-based systems.

The Intelligent Edge business almost 10% of revenue is composed of a portfolio of secure edge-to-cloud solutions operating under the Aruba brand (HPE Aruba Product HPE Aruba Services) that include wireless LAN campus and data center switching software-defined wide-area-networking security and associated services to enable secure connectivity for businesses of any size. The primary business drivers for Intelligent Edge solutions are mobility and IoT.

The Financial Services segment over 10% of revenue provides leasing financing IT consumption and utility programs and asset management services.

Corporate Investments includes CMS Hewlett Packard Labs and certain business incubation projects.

In some circumstances HPE uses third party contractors to make its hardware.

Geographic Reach

San jose California-based HPE has operations and customers around the world. It has around 15 locations in the US and Puerto Rico and over five outside the US including sites in the UK India China Singapore and Taiwan.

The company's international customers provide about two-thirds of revenue and overseas sales have outpaced domestic sales in recent years.

Sales and Marketing

HPE customers are mostly large companies and government agencies organizations that usually are willing to spend on IT. The company reaches them through its own sales staff resellers distribution partners OEMs independent software vendors system integrators and consulting services companies. HPE account managers maintain relationships between the company's businesses and large enterprise customers.

Financial Performance

HPE's revenue has gradually decreased since 2015. Although it grew in 2018 by 6.9% it has once again took a 5.6% decrease in 2019 due to the decrease of the company's products sales.

HPE's net income for 2019 ($1 billion) is 45% less than 2018's net income ($1.9 billion). These amounts primarily included $488 million of net income tax charges related to changes in U.S. federal and state valuation allowances.

At 2019 and 2018 HPE's cash and cash equivalents were $3.8 billion and $4.9 billion. Cash provided by investing activities were $3 billion and $4 billion in 2019 and 2018 cash used in investing activities from $1.9 billion to $3.5 billion. Cash used in financing activities from 2018 to 2019 were $5.6 billion and $1.6 billion. The company's cash from operating activities increased by over 25% from $3 billion in 2018 to $4 billion in 2019.

Strategy

HPE delivers unique open and intelligent technology solutions with a consistent experience across all clouds and edges to help customers develop new business models engage in new ways and increase operational performance.

As part of HPE's business strategy they may acquire companies or businesses divest businesses or assets enter into strategic alliances and joint ventures and make investments to further their business (collectively "business combination and investment transactions"). For example in September 2019 we acquired Cray Inc. a global supercomputer leader.

Mergers and Acquisitions

In late 2019 HPE acquired Cray Inc. a maker of high-performance computers for $1.4 billion net of cash. "Bringing together Cray and HPE establishes the most comprehensive end-to-end portfolio across compute storage software and services in the fast-growing high performance computing and artificial intelligence market segments" said Phil Davis president Hybrid IT Hewlett Packard Enterprise.

EXECUTIVES

President And Ceo, Margaret C. (Meg) Whitman, age 64, $1,500,058 total compensation
Evp And Chief Marketing And Communications Officer, Henry Gomez, age 57
Evp General Counsel And Secretary, John F. Schultz, age 56
Evp And Coo, Christopher P. (Chris) Hsu, age 49, $675,026 total compensation
Evp Human Resources, Alan May, age 62
Evp And General Manager Enterprise Group, Antonio Neri, age 53, $725,028 total compensation
Evp And Cfo, Timothy C. (Tim) Stonesifer, age 53, $675,026 total compensation
Vice President, Sunil Pandita
Vice President Global Healthcare Services, Mary Mirabelli
Vice President Global Accounts, Gerri Gold
Vice President Finance, Andrew Alhagi
Vp Enterprise Group Quality And Customer Experience, Rhonda Rubinstein
Senior Vice President Experience Marketing, Susan Popper
Vice President Executive Assistant, Jeff Dolce
National Sales Manager, Mark McBroom
Vp Software Sales Americas West, Mark Fazio
Global Vp Hpe Pointnext, Erik Vogel
Vp And Gm Public Sector Sales, Doug Harvey
Vice President Global Procurement, Cory Locke
Vice President Finance, Maksim Razumkin
Vice President Product Management, Stephen Spellicy
Vice President Communications And Media Solutions Research And Development, Paul Mitalas
Ww Vice President Sales Big Data, Bruce Jones
Vice President And General Manager Enterprise Services Asia, John Johasky
Vp And Managing Director Central Eastern Emea, Johannes Koch
Vice President And Gm Applications Development And Management Global Practice, Rick Sullivan
Svp And Global Head Of Corporate Development, Vishal Bhagwati
Global Plm Campus Networking Vice President, Michael Dickman
Vice President And Managing Director, Thomas Adams
Vice President And Deputy Labs Director, Andrew Wheeler
Vice President, Jim O'grady
Vp Ww Strategic Alliances, Gary O'neal
Vice President Global And Enterprise Risk Management, Erin Scott
Vice President Marketing And Digital Demand Generation, Paul Greenland
Vp Business Operations And Planning Ww Technology Services, Deb Lawson
Vice President Product Management, Mat Mathews
Vice President Operations Separation Management Office, Travis Henley
Vice President Aruba (americas), Louis Serlenga
Senior Vice President And General Manager Big Data, Colin Mahony
Project Manager Vps, George Young
Vice President, Louis Kim
Vice President, Janet Morris
Vice President Alliance Sales And Channels, Samuel Chun
Senior Vice President, Bill Philbin
Corporate Vp And Industry Group Head, Jai Venkat
Vice President Engineering And Quality, John Grosso
Vice President Channel And Marketing Consumer Pcs, Bruce Greenwood
Vice President, Jim Kuo
Chairman, Patricia F. (Pat) Russo, age 67
Senior Vice President Finance Treasurer, Kirt Karros
Board Member, Michael Angelakis
Board Member, Ray Ozzie
Auditors: Ernst & Young LLP

LOCATIONS

HQ: Hewlett Packard Enterprise Co
11445 Compaq Center West Drive, Houston, TX 77070
Phone: 650 687-5817
Web: www.hpe.com

2018 Sales

	$ mil.	% of total
US	10,192	33
Other Countries	20,660	67
Total	**30,852**	**100**

PRODUCTS/OPERATIONS

2018 Sales

	$ mil.	% of total
Products	19,504	63
Services	10,901	35
Financing Income	447	2
Total	**30,852**	**100**

2018 Sales

	$ mil.	% of total
Hybrid IT		
Compute	13,823	43
Storage	3,706	12
DC Networking	225	1
HPE Pointnext	7,279	23
Intelligent Edge		
HPE Aruba Product	2,619	8
HPE Aruba Services	310	1
Financial Services	3,671	12
Eliminations	(781)	-
Total	**30,852**	**100**

COMPETITORS

Amazon.com	Juniper Networks
Arista Networks	Lenovo
Cisco Systems	Microsoft
Dell	NetApp
Fujitsu	Oracle
Hitachi	salesforce.com
IBM	

HISTORICAL FINANCIALS
Company Type: Public

Income Statement   FYE: October 31

	REVENUE ($ mil.)	NET INCOME ($ mil.)	NET PROFIT MARGIN	EMPLOYEES
10/20	26,982	(322)	—	59,400
10/19	29,135	1,049	3.6%	61,600
10/18	30,852	1,908	6.2%	60,000
10/17	28,871	344	1.2%	66,000
10/16	50,123	3,161	6.3%	195,000
Annual Growth	(14.3%)	—	—	(25.7%)

2020 Year-End Financials

Debt ratio: 29.51%
Return on equity: (-1.94%)
Cash ($ mil.): 4,233
Current ratio: 0.88
Long-term debt ($ mil.): 12,186

No. of shares (mil.): 1,287
Dividends
Yield: 0.0%
Payout: —
Market value ($ mil.): 11,120

	STOCK PRICE ($) FY Close	P/E High/Low	Earnings	PER SHARE ($) Dividends	Book Value
10/20	8.64	— —	(0.25)	0.48	12.47
10/19	16.41	22 16	0.77	0.45	13.21
10/18	15.25	16 10	1.23	0.38	14.92
10/17	13.92	118 62	0.21	0.32	14.71
10/16	22.47	13 7	1.82	0.22	18.87
Annual Growth	(21.3%)	— —	—	21.5%	(9.8%)

Hills Bancorporation

There's gold in them thar hills! Hills Bancorporation is the holding company for Hills Bank and Trust which has about a dozen branches located in the eastern Iowa counties of Johnson Linn and Washington. The bank provides standard commercial services to area individuals businesses government entities and institutional customers. Offerings include deposit accounts loans and debit and credit cards. Hills Bank and Trust also administers estates personal trusts and pension plans and provides farm management and investment advisory and custodial services. The bank traces its roots to 1904.

EXECUTIVES

Senior Vice President Director Of Retail, Tracy Stotler
Vice President Of Investments Trust And Wealth Management, Aaron Schaefer
Auditors: BKD, LLP

LOCATIONS

HQ: Hills Bancorporation
131 Main Street, Hills, IA 52235
Phone: 319 679-2291
Web: www.hillsbank.com

COMPETITORS

Ames National	MidWestOne
Bank of America	Regions Financial
Citigroup	U.S. Bancorp
Iowa First	Wells Fargo
Meta Financial Group	West Bancorporation

HISTORICAL FINANCIALS
Company Type: Public

Income Statement   FYE: December 31

	ASSETS ($ mil.)	NET INCOME ($ mil.)	INCOME AS % OF ASSETS	EMPLOYEES
12/19	3,300	45	1.4%	484
12/18	3,042	36	1.2%	481
12/17	2,963	28	0.9%	499
12/16	2,655	31	1.2%	503
12/15	2,493	28	1.1%	464
Annual Growth	7.3%	12.4%		1.1%

2019 Year-End Financials

Debt ratio: —
Return on equity: 11.18%
Cash ($ mil.): 241
Current ratio: —
Long-term debt ($ mil.): —

No. of shares (mil.): 9
Dividends
Yield: 0.0%
Payout: 18.3%
Market value ($ mil.): 613

	STOCK PRICE ($) FY Close	P/E High/Low	Earnings	PER SHARE ($) Dividends	Book Value
12/19	65.50	15 12	4.85	0.89	45.66
12/18	60.75	16 14	3.92	0.75	41.10
12/17	54.00	18 16	3.01	0.70	38.03
12/16	48.11	17 13	3.40	0.65	35.63
12/15	45.00	27 14	3.04	0.63	33.23
Annual Growth	9.8%	— —	12.4%	9.2%	8.3%

Hilltop Holdings, Inc.

With about $16.9 billion in assets diversified financial holding company Hilltop Holdings provides banking mortgage origination insurance and financial advisory services through its PlainsCapital Bank PrimeLending Hilltop Securities subsidiaries and National Lloyds. PlainsCapital offers community commercial and private banking through about 60 branches throughout Texas and holds more than $11.1 billion in deposits. PrimeLending generates mortgages in all 50 states and District of Columbia through approximately 1200 loan offices. Hilltop Securities is an investment bank and is among the US' top financial advisors to municipalities based on transaction volume. Niche property and casualty insurance underwriter National Lloyds targets low-value dwellings in Texas.

Operations

Hilltop operates in four business segments: origination broker-dealer banking and insurance.

The mortgage origination segment (nearly 40% of sales) includes the operations of PrimeLending which offers a variety of loan products. The broker-dealer segment (roughly 30%) includes the operations of Hilltop Securities and HTS Independent Network. The banking segment (about 25%) includes the operations of the bank and provides business and consumer banking services from offices located throughout Texas. The insurance segment (less than 10%) includes the operations of NLC which operates through its wholly owned subsidiaries NLIC and ASIC in Texas and other areas of the southern US.

More broadly Hilltop generated around one-third of its total revenue interest income while noninterest income made up the remainder of revenue.

Geographic Reach

Based in Dallas Texas Hilltop's banking segment conducted business at some 70 locations throughout Texas including five support facilities. Hilltop securities conducts business from more than 50 locations in about 20 states and PrimeLending conducts business from over 300 locations in some 45 states.

Sales and Marketing

Hilltop's business banking customers primarily consist of agribusiness energy healthcare institutions of higher education real estate (including construction and land development) and wholesale/retail trade companies. The company provides these customers with extensive banking services such as online banking business check cards and other add-on services as determined on a customer-by-customer basis.

Hilltop's advertising expense totaled $3.6 million $4.6 million and $4.7 million during 2019 2018 and 2017 respectively.

Financial Performance

Hilltop Holdings generates revenue from net interest income and noninterest income. The company generated $441.3 million in net interest income during 2019 compared to $436.3 million in 2018. Changes in net interest income during 2019 compared with 2018 primarily included an increase within the company's banking segment and corporate segment partially offset by a decrease in its mortgage origination segment. The company generated $1.2 billion in noninterest income during 2019 a minimal increase from $1 billion the year prior. The increase in noninterest income was predominantly attributable to increases of $102.3 million in gains from derivative and trading portfolio activities within its broker-dealer segment and $86.3 million in net gains from sale of loans other mortgage production income and mortgage loan origination fees within its mortgage origination segment.

Net income in 2019 was $225.3 million an 86% increase compared with the $121.4 million net income in 2018. The 2019 period included costs associated with the Leadership Changes and efficiency initiative-related charges which in the aggregate totaled $11 million before income taxes.

Hilltop's cash holdings decreased $135.7 million ending 2019 with $642.8 million in cash. Operating activities used $433.0 million while investing activities used another $604.3 million mainly for loans held for investment and purchases of securities. Financing activities generated $901.6 million from notes payable proceeds and deposits.

Strategy

Hilltop Holdings has a synergistic durable and differentiated business model and its optimized capital funding and liquidity provides unique advantages and stability to each of its businesses. The company's strong capital and diversified model provides additional benefits to its customers as it is positioned for growth across geographies products and industries.

In 2020 the company launched its newly redesigned corporate website featuring a streamlined design improved functionality and easy access to essential information for investors customers and others seeking to learn more about the Dallas-based financial holding company. This new website allows visitors to easily find what they need to better understand the scope of Hilltop's organization and the diverse services it provides.

Hilltop also completed the sale of its wholly owned subsidiary National Lloyds Corporation to Align in mid-2020. Gross proceeds to Hilltop from this transaction were approximately $154.1 million subject to post-closing adjustments. Hilltop believes Align will help take National Lloyds to the next level.

In 2019 the company also hired nine new financial advisors to its Private Client Group. The hires brought about $760 million in assets under management to Hilltop.

Company Background

The company began life as Affordable Residential Communities (ARC) and spent its early days as a real estate investment trust (REIT). It went public in 2004 dropped its REIT status in 2006 and built up its collection of manufactured housing communities through acquisitions.

After several years of losses in the housing business the company chose to transition into another industry. It acquired NLASCO a niche provider of fire and homeowners insurance for manufactured homes and other low-value properties at the start of 2007. The company then renamed itself Hilltop Holdings.

EXECUTIVES

President And Co-ceo, Jeremy B. Ford, age 45, $700,000 total compensation

Vice Chairman And Co-ceo; Chairman Plainscapital Bank, Alan B. White, age 71, $1,350,000 total compensation

Coo Subsidiaries, James R. Huffines, age 69, $690,000 total compensation

Chief Administrative Officer, Darren E. Parmenter, age 57, $335,000 total compensation

Chairman And Ceo Hilltop Securities, Hill A. Feinberg, age 73, $500,000 total compensation

President And Ceo Plainscapital Bank, Jerry L. Schaffner, age 62

Cfo, William B. Furr, age 42, $143,438 total compensation

Ceo Primelending, Todd L. Salmans, age 71, $750,000 total compensation

Cio, Toby Pennycuff

Senior Vice President Corporate Controller, Keith Bornemann

Assistant Vice President, Scott Wade

Senior Vice President Corporate Development, Erik Yohe

Vice President, Christopher Torley

Vice President It Audit Manager, Bo Yan

Assistant Vice President Internal Audit, Jessica Moore

Vice President, Taylor Pool

Vice President Information Technology Sox Compliance, Brian Wilk

Vice President, Matthew Weaver

Assistant Vice President Corporate Communications Manager, Michelle Parish

Assistant Vice President Internal Auditor Ii, Meshack Mulupi

Vice President Employee Benefits Manager, Lonna Shepherd

Vice President Capital Planning Manager, Sean Ridenour

Vice President Attorney, Emily Stevenson

Vice President, Haki Redda

Svp Director Of Accounting Policy, Rick Martin

Senior Vice President Director Enterprise Data, Dan Gardner

Senior Vice President Operations, Donald Karas

Senior Vice President, Perry Tipton

Senior Vice President, Nick Bulaich

Assistant Vice President, John Barganski

Assistant Vice President, Ashley Allen

Senior Vice President, Ed Stull

Vice President, Alan Goldfarb

Vice President, William Skelton

Vice President, Erick Macha

Senior Vice President, David Quintanilla

Vice President Credit Analyst Supervisor, Joey Couch

First Vice President, Mark Katz

Senior Vice President Financial Advisor, Wayne Daugherty

Vice President Portfolio Manager, Dan Grant

Vice President Financial Advisor, Stephen Crossman

Chairman, Gerald J. Ford, age 76

Board Member, Joris W Brinkerhoff

Board Of Directors, Markham Green

Board Member, Andrew Littlefair

Board Member, Charlotte Anderson

Board Member, Tracy Bolt

Board Member, Taylor Crandall

Board Member, Arthur Sherman

Auditors: PricewaterhouseCoopers LLP

LOCATIONS

HQ: Hilltop Holdings, Inc.
6565 Hillcrest Avenue, Dallas, TX 75205
Phone: 214 855-2177
Web: www.hilltop-holdings.com

PRODUCTS/OPERATIONS

2018 Revenue

	$ mil.	% of total
Interest income		
Loans including fees	436	27
Securities borrowed	66	4
Taxable Securities	51	3
Tax-exempt securities	6	1
Other	18	1
Non-interest income		
Net gains from sale of loans and other mortgage production income	445	28
Net insurance premiums earned	136	9
Securities commissions and fees	151	9
Investment and securities advisory fees and commissions	90	6
Mortgage loan origination fees	103	6
Other	96	6
Total	**1,602**	**100**

Selected Services

Financial Advisory
Clearing
Retail Brokerage
Investment Banking Services
Internet Banking
Business Check Cards

Selected Subsidiaries

PlainsCapital Bank
PrimeLending
HilltopSecurities
National Lloyds Corporation

COMPETITORS

American Modern Insurance	International Bancshares
BBVA Compass Bancshares	JPMorgan Chase
Bank of America	Morgan Keegan
Comerica	Raymond James Financial
Costco Wholesale	Republic Group
Cullen/Frost Bankers	Texas Capital Bancshares
Fannie Mae	Travelers Companies
Foremost Insurance	Wells Fargo
Freddie Mac	
ING	

HISTORICAL FINANCIALS

Company Type: Public

Income Statement

FYE: December 31

	ASSETS ($ mil.)	NET INCOME ($ mil.)	INCOME AS % OF ASSETS	EMPLOYEES
12/19	15,172	225	1.5%	4,950
12/18	13,683	121	0.9%	5,200
12/17	13,365	132	1.0%	5,500
12/16	12,738	145	1.1%	5,400
12/15	11,867	210	1.8%	5,300
Annual Growth	6.3%	1.7%	—	(1.7%)

2019 Year-End Financials

Debt ratio: 2.31%
Return on equity: 11.12%
Cash ($ mil.): 484
Current ratio: —
Long-term debt ($ mil.): —

No. of shares (mil.): 90
Dividends
  Yield: 1.2%
  Payout: 14.6%
Market value ($ mil.): 2,260

	STOCK PRICE ($) FY Close	P/E High/Low		PER SHARE ($) Earnings	Dividends	Book Value
12/19	24.93	11	7	2.44	0.32	23.20
12/18	17.83	21	13	1.28	0.28	20.83
12/17	25.33	22	16	1.36	0.24	19.92
12/16	29.80	20	10	1.48	0.06	18.98
12/15	19.22	12	8	2.09	0.00	17.56
Annual Growth	6.7%	—	—	3.9%	—	7.2%

Hilton Worldwide Holdings Inc

If you need a bed for the night Hilton has a few hundred thousand of them. Hilton Worldwide is one of the world's largest hoteliers with a lodging empire that includes about 6100 properties comprising about 972000 in about 120 countries operating under such names as Doubletree Embassy Suites and Hampton Inn as well as its flagship Hilton brand. Many of its hotels serve the mid-market segment though its Hilton and Conrad hotels offer full-service upscale lodging. In addition its Homewood Suites and Home2 Suites chains offers extended-stay services. Hilton became a public company again in 2013.

Operations

Hilton's management and franchise segment which accounts for nearly 80% of revenue includes more than 700 managed hotels about 5290 franchised hotels and the licensing of Hilton's brands. The segment derives revenue from a host of franchising management and licensing fees.

The ownership segment (more than 20% of sales) consists of about 65 properties comprising nearly 60 hotels and derives revenue from providing hotel room rentals food and beverage and other services at the company's owned and leased hotels.

Hilton controls an extensive portfolio of brands. The company's largest chains Hampton Inn and Hampton Inn & Suites include about 2550 locations and target mid-market travelers with moderately priced rooms and limited amenities. At the other end of the scale the company's Conrad chain offers luxury services and distinctive locations while its Waldorf-Astoria Collection is a prestigious collection of hotels inspired by the New York landmark.

Hilton's "focused service" (i.e. cheaper) hotel brands include Hilton Garden Inn Hampton by Hilton Tru by Hilton Homewood Suites by Hilton Motto by Hilton Hilton Grand Vacations and Home2 Suites by Hilton. The company's Hilton Grand Vacations subsidiary operates about 55 time-share vacation resorts.

Geographic Reach

Headquartered in Mclean Virginia the company has regional corporate offices in Watford UK; Dubai UAE; Singapore; Tokyo Japan; and Shanghai China. Additional Hilton support offices include its Hilton Honors and other commercial services office in Addison Texas; centralized operations centers in Memphis Tennessee and Glasgow Scotland; and our Hilton Reservations and Customer Care office in Carrollton Texas.

Hilton's holdings comprise about 972000 rooms in nearly 120 countries. The company divides its business into three geographic regions Americas; Europe Middle East and Africa ("EMEA"); and Asia Pacific. The Americas region includes North America South America and Central America including all Caribbean nations.

Properties in the US represent almost 80% of the company's system-wide hotel rooms and generate a similar portion of revenue.

Sales and Marketing

Hilton relies on traditional advertising and promotions along with a variety of direct marketing techniques such as email social media marketing and postal mailings to drum up business. When the company's hotel rooms are booked through internet travel intermediaries Hilton pays commissions and transaction fees for sales of rooms through such services.

The company also has a robust customer loyalty program Hilton Honors it uses to try to generate return business. As part of the company's hotel management business hotel owners pay for participation in the Hilton Honors guest loyalty program.

The owners also pay Hilton usage fees which cover the costs of advertising and marketing programs internet technology and reservation systems and quality assurance program expenses.

Financial Performance

Aside from a blip in 2016 when it sold off operations and hotels Hilton has enjoyed strong and steady revenue in recent years.

In 2019 the company's sales grew 6% to $9.4 billion thanks to growth in system-wide revenue per available room (RevPAR) particularly in Turkey which is recovering from political turmoil and China where its new hotels are entering a new phase of maturity.

Net income grew 15% to $886 million due to an increase in revenue.

Hilton's cash position increased in 2019 ending the year $630 million. The company generated $1.4 billion from its operations while investing activities used $123 million and financing activities used $1.1 billion. The company's main cash uses were debt repayments stock repurchases dividend payouts and capital expenditures.

Strategy

Hilton's strategic objectives include the continued expansion of its global footprint and fee-based business. However staffing shortages in various parts of the world could slow Hilton's ability to grow and expand its businesses. Payroll costs are always a major component of the company's operating expenses at its hotels and franchised hotels.

In addition to current hotel portfolio focusing on the growth of the business by expanding the share in the global hospitality industry through development pipeline. At the end of 2019 nearly 470 hotels opened consisting of more than 65000 rooms contributing to over 58000 net rooms growth in the system during the year. Additionally more than 116000 new rooms were approved for development and added to the development pipeline.

HISTORY

Conrad Hilton got his start in hotel management by renting out rooms in his family's New Mexico home. He served as a state legislator and started a bank before leaving for Texas in 1919 hoping to make his fortune in banking. Hilton was unable to shoulder the cost of purchasing a bank however but recognized a high demand for hotel rooms and made a quick change in strategy buying his first hotel in Cisco Texas. Over the next decade he bought seven more Texas hotels.

Hilton lost several properties during the Depression but began rebuilding his empire soon thereafter through the purchase of hotels in California (1938) New Mexico (1939) and Mexico (1942). He even married starlet Zsa Zsa Gabor in 1942 (they later divorced of course). Hilton Hotels Corporation was formed in 1946 and went public. The company bought New York's Waldorf-Astoria in 1949 (a hotel Hilton called "the greatest of them all") and opened its first European hotel in Madrid in 1953. Hilton paid $111 million for the 10-hotel Statler chain the following year.

Hilton took his company out of the overseas hotel business in 1964 by spinning off Hilton International and began franchising the following year to capitalize on the well-known Hilton name. Barron Hilton Conrad's son was appointed president in 1966 (he became chairman upon Conrad Hilton's death in 1979). Hilton bought two Las Vegas hotels (the Las Vegas Hilton and the Flamingo Hilton) in 1970 and launched its gaming division. The company returned to the international hotel business with Conrad International Hotels in 1982 and opened its first suite-only Hilton Suites hotel in 1989.

In the 1990s Hilton expanded its gaming operations buying Bally's Casino Resort in Reno in 1992 and launching its first riverboat casino the Hilton Queen of New Orleans in 1994. Two years later it acquired all of Bally Entertainment making it the largest gaming company in the world. Also that year Stephen Bollenbach the former Walt Disney CFO who had negotiated the $19 billion acquisition of Capital Cities/ABC was named CEO — becoming the first nonfamily-member to run the company.

Hilton formed an alliance with Ladbroke Group in 1997 (later Hilton Group owner of Hilton International and the rights to the Hilton name outside the US) to promote the Hilton brand worldwide. Hilton also put in a bid that year to acquire ITT owner of Sheraton hotels and Caesars World but was thwarted when ITT accepted a higher offer from Starwood Hotels & Resorts. Hilton was foiled once again in 1998 when a deal with casino operator Circus Circus (now part of MGM Resorts International) that would have separated Hilton's hotel and casino operations fell through. With a downturn in the gambling industry translating into sluggish results in Hilton's gaming segment the company spun off its gaming interests as Park Place Entertainment later that year.

In 1999 Hilton made a massive acquisition with the $3.7 billion purchase of Promus Hotel Corp. The following year Hilton sold its Flamingo Casino-Kansas City a remaining casino property left over from the Park Place spinoff to Isle of Capri Casinos for $33.5 million. In 2001 it sold 56 of its leases and management contracts to RFS Hotel Investors for about $60 million.

Hilton continued selling properties in 2002 with the sales of two Doubletree hotels and all 41 Red Lion locations to WestCoast Hospitality (now Red Lion Hotels) for about $51 million. It also sold its Harrison Conference Center portfolio (14 conference centers and university hotels) to ARAMARK for $55 million. At the end of that same year the company formed a $400 million venture with CNL Hospitality (now CNL Hotels & Resorts) to buy and refurbish hotel properties.

Following an extended downturn in the hospitality business brought on by recession and post-9/11 fears about terrorism Hilton began to invest in refurbishments for many of its properties and added about 150 locations in 2004.

Hilton Hotels acquired Hilton International from Hilton Group (now Ladbrokes) for about $5.7 billion in 2006. The deal re-unified the Hilton brand globally and added about 400 new locations to the company's portfolio. The year after the acquisition Hilton Hotels sold its Scandic Hotels business to private equity firm EQT for $1.1 billion and later sold LivingWell Health Clubs to Bannatyne Fitness; both brands had been included in the Hilton International transaction.

Also in 2007 the company was taken private by The Blackstone Group through a $26 billion buyout. The acquisition included about $6 billion in debt. Christopher Nassetta later replaced Bollenbach as CEO. Hilton Hotels was renamed Hilton Worldwide in 2009. Through a financial restructuring in 2010 Hilton was able to cut about $4 billion of its $20 billion debt. In early 2011 its newest brand Home2 Suites by Hilton opened its first property.

Hilton sold its Waldorf Astoria New York hotel for $1.95 billion in 2015.

EXECUTIVES

Evp And President Development Architecture And Construction, Ian R. Carter, age 58, $739,302 total compensation

President Ceo And Director, Christopher J. (Chris) Nassetta, age 58, $1,200,000 total compensation

Evp And Chief Human Resources Officer, Matthew W. (Matt) Schuyler, age 54

Evp And General Counsel, Kristin A. Campbell, age 58, $638,308 total compensation

Evp Global Brands, James E. (Jim) Holthouser, age 61, $600,000 total compensation

Evp And Cfo, Kevin J. Jacobs, age 47, $743,404 total compensation

Evp And President Americas, Joe Berger

President Europe Middle East & Africa, Simon Vincent

Evp And Chief Commercial Officer, Chris Silcock

Head Architecture Design And Construction, Matt Richardson

Evp And President Asia Pacific (apac), Alan Watts

Svp Team Member And Executive Communications, Katrina Jones

Svp Hr Systems And Services, Doug Krey

Executive Vice President Chief Commercial Officer, Christopher Silcock

Vp System Engineering, Hector Dominguez

Senior Vice President Strategy And Research, Nathalie Corredor

Senior Vice President Luxury Lifestyle Resort And Corporate Development, Greg Hartmann

Svp Architecture And Construction Americas, Phil Keipper

Senior Vice President Customer Journeyman Delivery, Virginia Suliman

Svp And Global Head Doubletree By Hilton And Curio Brand, Dianna Vaughan

Executive Vice President Corporate Affairs, Katie Fallon

Vp Corporate Communications, Nigel Glennie

Vp Operations Australia, Heidi Kunkel

Senior Vice President Hotel Operations, Keith Harrison

Vice President Customer Engagement Loyalty And Partnerships Emea, Heather Laverne
Chairman, Jonathan D. Gray, age 50
Board Member, Elizabeth Smith
Board Member, John Schreiber
Board Member, Melanie Healey
Auditors: Ernst & Young LLP

LOCATIONS

HQ: Hilton Worldwide Holdings Inc
7930 Jones Branch Drive, Suite 1100, McLean, VA 22102
Phone: 703 883-1000
Web: www.hiltonworldwide.com

2018 sales

	$ mil.	% of total
U.S.	6,848	77
UK	545	6
All other	1,513	17
Total	**8**	**100**

PRODUCTS/OPERATIONS

2018 sales

	$ mil.	% of total
Other revenues from managed and franchised properties	5,238	59
Franchise and licensing fees	1,530	17
Owned and leased hotels	1,484	17
Base and other management fees	235	3
Other fees and revenues	98	1
Total	**8,906**	**100**

Selected Brands

Conrad Hotels & Resorts
Doubletree
Embassy Suites Hotels
Hampton Inn
Hampton Inn & Suites
Hilton
Hilton Garden Inn
Hilton Grand Vacations Club
Homewood Suites by Hilton
Waldorf Astoria Hotels & Resorts

Selected Hotels

Chicago's Palmer House Hilton
Hilton Barcelona
Hilton Bora Bora Nui Resort & Spa
The Hilton Hawaiian Village on Waikiki Beach
Hilton Manchester Deansgate
Hilton Orlando
Hilton San Francisco on Union Square
Hilton Sedona
The New York Hilton

COMPETITORS

Accor	Interstate Hotels
Best Western	Loews
Carlson Hotels	Marriott
Choice Hotels	Omni Hotels
FRHI Hotels and	Red Lion Hotels
Resorts	Ritz-Carlton
Four Seasons Hotels	Starwood Hotels &
Hyatt	Resorts
InterContinental	Wyndham Destinations
Hotels	

HISTORICAL FINANCIALS
Company Type: Public

Income Statement

	REVENUE ($ mil.)	NET INCOME ($ mil.)	NET PROFIT MARGIN	EMPLOYEES
12/19	9,452	881	9.3%	173,000
12/18	8,906	764	8.6%	169,000
12/17	9,140	1,259	13.8%	163,000
12/16	11,663	348	3.0%	169,000
12/15	11,272	1,404	12.5%	164,000
Annual Growth	**(4.3%)**	**(11.0%)**	**—**	**1.3%**

2019 Year-End Financials

Debt ratio: 53.44%
Return on equity: 2,553.62%
Cash ($ mil.): 538
Current ratio: 0.73
Long-term debt ($ mil.): 7,956

No. of shares (mil.): 278
Dividends
Yield: 0.5%
Payout: 18.9%
Market value ($ mil.): 30,942

	STOCK PRICE ($) FY Close	P/E High/Low	PER SHARE ($) Earnings	Dividends	Book Value
12/19	110.91	37 22	3.04	0.60	(1.73)
12/18	71.80	35 25	2.50	0.60	1.87
12/17	79.86	21 7	3.85	0.60	6.53
12/16	27.20	26 16	1.05	0.84	17.91
12/15	21.40	7 5	4.26	0.42	18.18
Annual Growth	**50.9%**	**— —**	**(8.1%)**	**9.3%**	**—**

Hingham Institution for Savings

The Hingham Institution for Savings serves businesses and retail customers in Boston's south shore communities operating more than 10 branches in Massachusetts in Boston Cohasset Hingham Hull Norwell Scituate South Hingham and South Weymouth. Founded in 1834 the bank offers traditional deposit products such as checking and savings accounts IRAs and certificates of deposit. More than 90% of its loan portfolio is split between commercial mortgages and residential mortgages (including home equity loans) though the bank also originates construction business and consumer loans. More than 95% of the company's revenue comes from loan interest.

Operations

The Hingham Institution for Savings made 96% of its total revenue from loan interest during 2015 while about 2% came from interest in equities CODs and other investments. The rest of its revenue mostly came from service fees on deposit accounts.

Of its $1.4 billion loan portfolio (at the end of 2015) about 48% was made up of commercial real estate mortgages (including multi-family housing) while 45% was tied to residential mortgages (including home equity). The remainder of the portfolio was made up of residential and commercial construction loans (7% of loan assets) and commercial business loans and consumer loans (1%).

Subsidiary Hingham Unpledged Securities Corporation holds title to certain securities available for sale.

Geographic Reach

The company mostly serves clients in Boston the South Shore and the island of Nantucket. Its branches are in Boston Cohasset Hingham Hull Nantucket Norwell Scituate South Hingham and South Weymouth Massachusetts.

Sales and Marketing

The Hingham Institution for Savings serves both individuals and small businesses in its three target markets in Massachusetts. Some of its clients (as of mid-2016) include Lyons Associates The Hub TCR Development SYA+FH Steven Young Architect + Fine Home Builder and Park Drive Inc.

The bank spent $489000 on marketing expenses during 2015 down from $557000 in each of 2014 and 2013.

Financial Performance

The bank's annual revenues have slowly trended higher over the past several years as the promising Boston real estate market has fueled its commercial real estate and residential loan business growth.

Hingham's revenue dipped 1% to $64.34 million during 2015 despite 13% mortgage loan growth mostly because in 2014 it earned a gains on life insurance distributions. The bank also continued to lose fee income as it has eliminated many fees on its deposit products to simplify offerings and attract customer deposits.

Revenue declines and higher income tax provisions in 2015 (in 2014 it earned non-taxed death benefit proceeds) caused the bank's net income to fall 13% to $19.34 million. Hingham's operating cash levels rose 11% to $20.2 million for the year thanks to a jump in cash-based earnings.

Strategy

The Hingham Institution for Savings continued in 2016 to focus on originating commercial multi-family and single-family mortgage loans in its target markets of Boston the South Shore and the island of Nantucket in Massachusetts especially as the healthy real estate market in and around Boston has provided a tailwind for its lending business.

EXECUTIVES

Chief Executive Officer; President; Director, Robert H. Gaughen, $319,615 total compensation
Vice President Of Retail Banking, Andrew Vebber
Assistant Vice President Retail Lending, Patricia Talbot
Auditors: Wolf & Company, P.C.

LOCATIONS

HQ: Hingham Institution for Savings
55 Main Street, Hingham, MA 02043
Phone: 781 749-2200 **Fax:** 781 740-4889
Web: www.hinghamsavings.com

COMPETITORS

Bank of America	Independent Bank (MA)
Citizens Financial	Peoples Federal
Group	Bancshares Inc.
Eastern Bank	Sovereign Bank

HISTORICAL FINANCIALS
Company Type: Public

Income Statement
FYE: December 31

	ASSETS ($ mil.)	NET INCOME ($ mil.)	INCOME AS % OF ASSETS	EMPLOYEES
12/19	2,590	38	1.5%	90
12/18	2,408	30	1.3%	96
12/17	2,284	25	1.1%	101
12/16	2,014	23	1.2%	103
12/15	1,768	19	1.1%	111
Annual Growth	**10.0%**	**19.1%**	**—**	**(5.1%)**

2019 Year-End Financials

Debt ratio: 0.03%
Return on equity: 16.93%
Cash ($ mil.): 9
Current ratio: —
Long-term debt ($ mil.): —

No. of shares (mil.): 2
Dividends
Yield: 0.9%
Payout: 13.9%
Market value ($ mil.): 449

	STOCK PRICE ($) FY Close	P/E High/Low	PER SHARE ($) Earnings	Dividends	Book Value
12/19	210.20	12 9	17.83	2.04	115.75
12/18	197.74	16 14	13.90	1.73	99.67
12/17	207.00	19 14	11.81	1.62	87.29
12/16	196.78	18 11	10.89	1.52	75.50
12/15	119.80	15 9	9.02	2.14	64.83
Annual Growth	**15.1%**	**— —**	**18.6%**	**(1.2%)**	**15.6%**

HollyFrontier Corp

HollyFrontier refines crude oil to produce gasoline diesel and jet fuel as well as lubricants and asphalt selling its products to customers in the Southwest US the Rocky Mountains (extending into the Pacific Northwest) and Plains states. The company operates refineries and other production facilities in Kansas Oklahoma New Mexico Utah and Wyoming as well as Texas Arizona and Ontario Canada. HollyFrontier has more than 55% stake in Holly Energy Partners (HEP) which operates crude oil and petroleum product pipelines. The company sells lubricants and other specialty products through its Petro-Canada Lubricants and Red Giant Oil subsidiaries. US customers generate some 95% of the company's revenue.

Operations

HollyFrontier's refining segment about 85% of revenue produces gasoline diesel fuel jet fuel fuel oil commodity and modified asphalt base oils and liquid petroleum gas (LPG). It turns out around 455000 barrels per day of products from its El Dorado Tulsa Navajo Cheyenne and Woods Cross refineries. It also produces asphalt via the HFC Asphalt business that has plants in Arizona New Mexico and Oklahoma.

By product gasoline accounts for more than 50% HollyFrontier's refined products sales; diesel fuel accounts for around 35%; and jet fuel and asphalt less than 5% each.

Lubricants and Specialty Products more than 10 of revenue consists of the company's Petro-Canada Lubricant Red Giant Oil Sonneborn and the Tulsa subsidiaries. Petro-Canada produces automotive industrial and food grade lubricants and greases base and process oils and specialty fluids and Red Giant provides lubricants to the railroad industry. Sonneborn provides specialty hydrocarbon chemicals such as white oils petrolatums and waxes for the personal care cosmetic pharmaceutical and food processing industries. Tulsa refinery produces high quality base oils process oils waxes horticultural oils and asphalt performance products.

The HEP segment charges tariffs for transporting petroleum products and crude oil through its pipelines.

Geographic Reach

Dallas-based HollyFrontier's refinery operations (Cheyenne Wyoming; El Dorado Kansas; Navajo in Artesia New Mexico; Tulsa Oklahoma; and Woods Cross Utah) serve customers in the US Mid-Continent Rocky Mountain and Southwest regions of the US.

Sales and Marketing

HollyFrontier's principal customers for gasoline include other refiners convenience store chains independent marketers and retailers. Diesel fuel is sold to other refiners truck stop chains wholesalers and railroads. Jet fuel is sold for commercial airline use. LPG's are sold to LPG wholesalers and LPG retailers. They produce and purchase asphalt products that are sold to governmental entities paving contractors or manufacturers. Asphalt is also blended into fuel oil and is either sold locally or is shipped to the Gulf Coast.

The primary markets for the El Dorado Refinery's refined products are Colorado and the Plains States. The Woods Cross Refinery's primary market is Utah. The Cheyenne Refinery primarily markets its products in eastern Colorado including metropolitan Denver eastern Wyoming and western Nebraska. It also sells a significant portion of its diesel directly from the truck rack at the refinery eliminating transportation costs.

Asphalt products are marketed in Arizona New Mexico Oklahoma Kansas Missouri Texas and northern Mexico. Products are shipped via third-party trucking companies to commercial customers that provide asphalt-based materials for commercial and government projects.

Financial Performance

HollyFrontier's revenue over the past five years reflects the boom-and-bust nature of the oil business. Sales reached $13.2 billion in 2015 but collapsed to $10.5 billion in 2016. Since then revenue has increased two straight years until 2019. In 2019 revenue increased by 32% to $17.5 billion compared to $13.2 billion in 2015.

Sales decreased by 1% to $17.5 billion in 2019 from $17.7 billion in 2018 driven by a decrease in sales prices and lower refined product volumes.

Net income dropped by $325.6 million to $772.4 million in 2019 from $1.098 million in 2018 primarily due to a goodwill impairment charge and lower gross refining margins.

HollyFrontier's coffers fell by 23% to $ 885.2 million in 2019 compared to $1.1 billion the year before. Operations generated $ 1548.6 million in 2019 while investing activities used $ 972.9 million mainly from acquisition additions to properties plants and equipment and financing activities used $ 848.3 million primarily because of treasury stock purchase credit agreements repayments and dividends.

Strategy

One of the ways the company may grow its business is through the construction of new refinery processing units (or the purchase and refurbishment of used units from another refinery) and the expansion of existing ones. Projects are generally initiated to increase the yields of higher-value products increase the amount of lower cost crude oils that can be processed increase refinery production capacity meet new governmental requirements or maintain the operations of our existing assets. Additionally HollyFrontier's growth strategy includes projects that permit access to new and/or more profitable markets.

An additional component of the company's growth strategy is to selectively acquire complementary assets or businesses for the company's refining operations in order to increase earnings and cash flow.

The latest deal for Sonneborn in 2019 turned HollyFrontier into a leading provider of lubricants and specialty products.

Although the regulatory front has been quiet HollyFrontier could face changes in environmental regulations that could require pricey changes at its refineries to reduce pollution. The company took steps to mitigate some of those issues by building a biodiesel facility at its Artesia New Mexico refinery. The company is to process soybean oil and other feedstocks into biodiesel with production capacity of about 125 million gallons a year. By increasing its biodiesel production HollyFrontier would avoid having to buy production credits.

Mergers and Acquisitions

In 2019 HollyFrontier acquired Sonneborn a provider of white oils petrolatums and waxes for $655 million.

Company Background

HollyFrontier was formed in 2011 when Holly Corp. and Frontier Oil merged.

HISTORY

HollyFrontier was founded in 1947 as General Appliance Corp. to process other companies' crude oil; the current name was adopted in 1952. As Holly the company grew with the number of gas-guzzling cars in the 1950s and 1960s and in the 1970s it developed its Navajo refinery in New Mex-

ico. In 1981 Holly began producing higher-grade gasoline and started an asphalt company at Navajo.

In 1984 Holly became a partner in Montana Refining and later bought the entire business. It upgraded the Navajo refinery in the early 1990s to meet the demand for unleaded gasoline. In 1995 Amoco Mapco and Holly formed a joint venture the 265-mile Río Grande Pipeline (completed in 1997) to transport natural gas liquids to Mexico.

Also in 1997 FINA and Holly allied to expand and use Holly's pipelines in the southwestern US. A proposed merger with another southwestern refiner Giant Industries died in 1998 because of federal antitrust concerns and a billion-dollar lawsuit filed against Holly by Longhorn Partners Pipeline. Court papers revealed in 2000 that Holly had paid $4 million to fight Longhorn's request for a permit to transport gasoline in its Houston-to-El Paso pipeline. The permit if approved would compete with Holly's own interests in western Texas.

Later in 2000 Holly cut its workforce by about 10% mostly at Navajo Refining. The next year Navajo Refining secured a $122 million contract to provide JP-8 jet fuel to the Defense Department.

In a move to expand its production capacity in 2003 Holly acquired ConocoPhillips' Woods Cross refinery and related assets for $25 million. Holly agreed to be acquired by Frontier Oil for about $450 million that year but the companies terminated the agreement and litigation between the parties resulted.

In 2004 the company spun off its Navajo refinery-related refined petroleum pipeline and other distribution assets as Holly Energy Partners L.P.; it retains a 45% interest in the company.

In 2005 the Delaware Chancery Court ruled that Frontier Oil had not proved that Holly had repudiated the merger agreement and awarded Frontier Oil only $1 in damages. Also that year Holly acquired the remaining 51% of NK Asphalt Producers that it did not already own. The company sold its intermediate feedstock pipelines connecting two refining facilities in Lovington and Artesia New Mexico to Holly Energy Partners for $81.5 million.

To free up cash in 2008 it sold 136 miles of crude oil trunk lines and some tankage assets to Holly Energy Partners for $180 million.

To expand market share in 2011 the company acquired regional rival Frontier Oil and Holly changed its corporate name to HollyFrontier.

The all-stock deal created an enterprise valued at $7 billion and added Frontier's Kansas and Wyoming refineries to the company's portfolio. The acquisition which boosted HollyFrontier's refining capacity to 443000 barrels a day is expected to create cost savings of at least $30 million per year.

The purchase was part of a multi-year strategy of expanding refinery capacity through selective acquisitions of complementary assets. (Earlier the company bought Sunoco's 85000-barrels-per-day Tulsa refinery. Building the largest refinery complex in the Midcontinent the company also acquired Sinclair Oil's 75000-barrels-per-day Tulsa refinery for $128.5 million).

Responding to increased demand in 2012 HollyFrontier announced planned to expand the capacity of its Woods Cross Utah refinery from 31000 barrel per day to 45000 barrel per day.

Building up its infrastructure to create greater efficiencies in 2013 HollyFrontier and Holly Energy Partners agreed to build a rail facility to enable crude oil loading and unloading near HollyFrontier's Artesia and/or Lovington New Mexico refining facilities. The rail project which will be connected to Holly Energy's crude oil pipeline transportation system in southeastern New Mexico will have a capacity of up to 70000 barrels per day and will enable access to a variety of crude oil types.

EXECUTIVES

Vice President Of Sales, Gregory White
Senior Vice President, David G Blair
Senior Vice President Refinery Operations, Gary Fuller
Vice President Corporate Ehands Holly Corporation, David Jelmini
Svp Refining Operations, James M. Stump, age 53, $510,000 total compensation
President And Ceo, George J. Damiris, age 60, $1,100,000 total compensation
Svp Commercial And President Hollyfrontier Refining & Marketing Llc, Thomas G. Creery, age 61
Svp General Counsel And Secretary, Denise C. McWatters, age 60, $470,000 total compensation
Vp Information Technology, Nellson D. Burns
Evp And Cfo, Richard L. Voliva, age 42
Vice President And Refinery Manager, Lynn Keddington
Vice President Investor Relations, Julia Heidenreich
Assistant Vice President, Margaret Schieffer
Vp Supply, Tom Creery
Senior Vice President General Counsel Chief Compliance Officer And Secretary, Vaishali Bhatia
Assistant Vice President Senior Economist, Jeffery Gunther
Vice President Engineering And Process Development Holly Refining And Marketing, Janusz Siwek
Vice President Accounting, Kathryn Walker
Vice President, Scott Surplus
Vice President Investor Relations, Marcus Hickerson
Vice President And Controller, John W Gann
Vice President Internal Audit, Joseph Fronzaglio
Vice President Information Technology, Nelson Nelso
Vice President Refining, Dana Leach
Vp And Controller, Jw Gann
Vice President And Refinery Manager, Tony Conetta
Vice President, Ajay Seth
Vice President And Chro, Dale Kunneman
Vice President, Andrew Ashby
Vice President Information Technology Infrastructure And Operations, Jon Rabiega
Vice President Information Technology Business Partner, David Lair
Vice President, Patrick Gray
Vice President Of Operations, Robert Weber
Chairman, Michael C. Jennings, age 55
Board Member, Michael Rose
Board Member, Jerry Pinkerton
Treasurer, Steve Wise
Board Member, Douglas Bech
Board Member, Anna Catalano
Auditors: Ernst & Young LLP

LOCATIONS

HQ: HollyFrontier Corp
2828 N. Harwood, Suite 1300, Dallas, TX 75201
Phone: 214 871-3555
Web: www.hollyfrontier.com

2018 Sales

	% of total
North America	
Mid-Continent	53
Southwest	24
Rocky Mountains	15
Northeast	2
Canada	5
Europe and Asia	1
Total	

PRODUCTS/OPERATIONS

2018 Sales

	$ mil.	% of total
Refining	16,176	87
Lubricants and Specialty Products	1,812	10
HEP	506	3
Corporate Other Eliminations	(780.8)	
Total	**17,714**	**100**

COMPETITORS

BP	Sunoco
Crown Central	Tesoro
Exxon Mobil	Valero Energy
George Warren	Williams Companies
Marathon Petroleum	

HISTORICAL FINANCIALS

Company Type: Public

Income Statement				FYE: December 31
	REVENUE ($ mil.)	NET INCOME ($ mil.)	NET PROFIT MARGIN	EMPLOYEES
12/19	17,486	772	4.4%	4,074
12/18	17,714	1,097	6.2%	3,622
12/17	14,251	805	5.7%	3,522
12/16	10,535	(260)	—	2,676
12/15	13,237	740	5.6%	2,704
Annual Growth	**7.2%**	**1.1%**	**—**	**10.8%**

2019 Year-End Financials

Debt ratio: 20.19%
Return on equity: 12.98%
Cash ($ mil.): 885
Current ratio: 1.96
Long-term debt ($ mil.): 2,455

No. of shares (mil.): 161
Dividends
Yield: 2.6%
Payout: 26.6%
Market value ($ mil.): 8,207

	STOCK PRICE ($)	P/E		PER SHARE ($)		
	FY Close	High/Low		Earnings	Dividends	Book Value
12/19	50.71	13	8	4.61	1.34	36.94
12/18	51.12	13	7	6.19	1.32	34.39
12/17	51.22	11	5	4.52	1.32	30.27
12/16	32.76	—	—	(1.48)	1.32	26.40
12/15	39.89	14	8	3.90	1.31	29.15
Annual Growth	**6.2%**		**—**	**4.3%**	**0.6%**	**6.1%**

Home Bancorp Inc

Making its home in Cajun Country Home Bancorp is the holding company for Home Bank a community bank which offers deposit and loan services to consumers and small to midsized businesses in southern Louisiana. Through about two dozen branches the bank offers standard savings and checking accounts as well as lending services such as mortgages consumer loans and credit cards. Its loan portfolio includes commercial real estate commercial and industrial loans as well as construction and land loans. Home Bancorp also operates about half a dozen bank branches in west Mississippi which were formerly part of Britton & Koontz Bank.

Geographic Reach

Home Bancorp serves the Louisiana areas of Greater Lafayette Baton Rouge Greater New Orleans and Northshore (of Lake Pontchartrain). Its markets in Mississippi include Vicksburg and Natchez.

Financial Performance

Although the company saw assets and loans grow in 2013 net income fell 20% that year to $7.3 million on lower operating income.

Mergers and Acquisitions

In early 2014 Home Bancorp spent about $35 million on Britton & Koontz Capital Corporation the holding company of Britton & Koontz Bank; the deal added five branches in west Mississippi to Home Bancorp's operations.

EXECUTIVES

Chb-Pres-Ceo, John W Bordelon
Exec V Pres-Coo, Jason P Freyou
Exec V Pres-Cfo, Joseph B Zanco
Cfo, David T Kirkley
Auditors: Wipfli LLP

LOCATIONS

HQ: Home Bancorp Inc
503 Kaliste Saloom Road, Lafayette, LA 70508
Phone: 337 237-1960   **Fax:** 337 264-9280
Web: www.home24bank.com

COMPETITORS

Capital One	MidSouth Bancorp
IBERIABANK	Regions Financial
JPMorgan Chase	Teche Holding
Louisiana Bancorp	

HISTORICAL FINANCIALS

Company Type: Public

Income Statement				FYE: December 31
	ASSETS ($ mil.)	NET INCOME ($ mil.)	INCOME AS % OF ASSETS	EMPLOYEES
12/19	2,200	27	1.3%	—
12/18	2,153	31	1.5%	—
12/17	2,228	16	0.8%	—
12/16	1,556	16	1.0%	—
12/15	1,551	12	0.8%	—
Annual Growth	**9.1%**	**22.1%**		**—**

2019 Year-End Financials

Debt ratio: 0.25%
Return on equity: 9.00%
Cash ($ mil.): 40
Current ratio: —
Long-term debt ($ mil.): —

No. of shares (mil.): 9
Dividends
Yield: 2.1%
Payout: 26.4%
Market value ($ mil.): 363

	STOCK PRICE ($)	P/E		PER SHARE ($)		
	FY Close	High/Low		Earnings	Dividends	Book Value
12/19	39.19	13	11	3.05	0.84	34.19
12/18	35.40	14	10	3.40	0.71	32.14
12/17	43.22	19	14	2.28	0.55	29.57
12/16	38.61	17	10	2.25	0.41	24.47
12/15	25.98	14	11	1.79	0.37	22.80
Annual Growth	**10.8%**		**—**	**14.3%**	**22.7%**	**10.7%**

Home BancShares Inc

Home BancShares is the holding company for Centennial Bank which operates some 160 branches in Arkansas Florida and Alabama with an additional branch in each of New York City and Los Angeles (through which the company is building out a national lending platform). With $14.9 billion in assets the bank offers traditional services such as checking savings and money market accounts and CDs. About 60% of its lending portfolio is focused on commercial real estate loans — including non-farm and non-residential and construction and land development. The bank also writes residential mortgages and business and consumer loans. Through a subsidiary Home BancShares offers insurance services.

Operations

About 80% of Home Bancshares' $10.8 billion loan portfolio comprises real estate loans including non-farm and non-residential commercial loans which make up more than 40% of the total. Residential one-to-four-family loans and commercial construction and land development loans contribute about 20% and 15% respectively. Commercial and industrial loans make up around 10%.

The holding company has built a $6.3 billion portfolio of non-farm and non-residential commercial real estate loans primarily secured by commercial real estate. Around 50% 30% and 15% of the company's commercial real estate loan portfolio is in Florida Arkansas and with its Centennial Finance Group (CFG). Home Bancshares established the group in 2015 to manage loans acquired in the company's acquisition of the Florida Panhandle business of Banco Popular and to originate new loans (with a focus on commercial real estate and commercial and industrial loans) via a national lending platform.

About 30% and 60% of the company's $2.6 billion residential real estate loan portfolio are for one-to-four-family properties and non-owner occupied one-to-four family properties respectively.

The company's commercial and industrial loans account for about $1.3 billion of the portfolio; Arkansas Florida and Centennial CFG house about 40% 35% and 25% of that segment respectively.

Geographic Reach

Conway Arkansas-based Home Bancshares' holding company's Centennial Bank operates about 90 branches in Florida more than 75 in Arkansas around five in Southern Alabama and one in each of New York City and Los Angeles.

Sales and Marketing

Home Bancshares' non-farm and non-residential lending (comprising about 40% of the total) is made up of loans for shopping and retail centers hotels and motels offices industrial warehouses churches marinas and nursing homes.

Residential one-to-four-family residential mortgages for individuals make up some 20% of the company's portfolio. About 30% and 60% of its residential mortgage loans are for one-to-four-family owner-occupied and non-owner-occupied properties respectively.

The holding company also lends heavily to residential and commercial developers to construct commercial properties and develop land. Construction and land development loans make up about 15% of its portfolio.

Around 10% of the value of Home Bancshares' loans go to commercial and industrial clients.

Financial Performance

Home Bancshares reported revenue of $555.5 million in 2017 up 174% from 2013 and net income of $135.1 million up 103% over the same period. The company's cash stores and long-term debt both about tripled during that time to $635.9 million and $1.7 billion respectively.

The holding company's revenue increased 13% in 2017 compared with 2016 owing to increased interest income from loans.

Home Bancshares' net income fell 24% due mostly to an increase in income tax expense related to the passage of the Tax Cuts and Jobs Act.

The company's $419.3 million to its cash in 2017. Operating activities provided $176.9 million down from the previous year based on decreased net income and increased charges from indemni-

fication and other assets and accrued interest payable on other liabilities. Investments used $355.5 million while financings added $597.8 million driven mostly by proceeds from issuance of subordinated debentures.

Strategy

Home Bancshares' strategy is focused on expanding in its core Florida market through the purchase of local managed community banks including four in 2017 and 2018.

In addition to growing its geographic footprint Home Bancshares is also diversifying its product offerings through acquisitions. In 2018 the company bought the Shore Premier Finance division of Union Bankshares. Shore originated direct consumer loans for high-end sail and power boats in southeast Florida.

Mergers and Acquisitions

Home Bancshares acquired Giant Holdings The Bank of Commerce and Stonegate Bank in 2017 as well as former Union Bankshares subsidiary Shore Premier Finance in 2018.

The holding company purchased Giant Holdings for $96 million. Giant operated six branches in the Ft. Lauderdale Florida area and had $398.1 million in total assets $327.8 million in loans and $304 million in deposits.

Home Bancshares acquired The Bank of Commerce from Bank of Commerce Holdings as part of that company's bankruptcy for $4.2 million. Bank of Commerce - which had $182.5 million in assets $127.5 million in loans and $141.7 million in deposits - operated three branches in the Sarasota Florida area.

Home Bancshares bought Stonegate Bank for $820 million adding the company's $3.1 billion in total assets $2.4 billion in loans and $2.6 billion in deposits to its books. Stonegate had 24 offices in Florida markets including Broward and Sarasota counties.

In 2018 the company acquired the Shore Premier Finance division of Union Bankshares for $374.5 million in cash and 1.3 million shares. Shore originates direct consumer loans for high-end sail and power boats at 16 locations in southeast Florida. At the deal's close Shore had $384.2 million in assets including $383.4 million in total loans.

Company Background

Home Bancshares formed in 1998 as First State Bank.

EXECUTIVES

Cfo And Treasurer And Director, Randy E. Mayor, age 55, $300,000 total compensation
President And Ceo, C. Randall (Randy) Sims, age 65, $390,000 total compensation
Regional President Centennial Bank, Robert F. Birch, age 70, $290,000 total compensation
President And Ceo Centennial Bank, Tracy M. French, age 58, $290,000 total compensation
Chief Lending Officer, Kevin D. Hester, age 56
Coo Home Bancshares Inc. And Centennial Bank, John (Stephen) Tipton
Vice President Security, Jenni Holbrook
Vice President, Brian Jackson
Vp Association Services, Kathy Naughton
Vp Sr Business Development Officer, Tami Licato
Chairman, John W. Allison, age 73
Vice Chairman, Robert H. Adcock, age 71
Board Member, Thomas Longe
Board Member, Mike Beebe
Auditors: BKD, LLP

LOCATIONS

HQ: Home BancShares Inc
719 Harkrider, Suite 100, Conway, AR 72032
Phone: 501 339-2929
Web: www.homebancshares.com

COMPETITORS

Arvest Bank	Bear State Financial
BB&T	Regions Financial
BBX Capital	Simmons First
Bank of America	Woodforest Financial
Bank of the Ozarks	

HISTORICAL FINANCIALS

Company Type: Public

Income Statement				FYE: December 31
	ASSETS ($ mil.)	NET INCOME ($ mil.)	INCOME AS % OF ASSETS	EMPLOYEES
12/19	15,032	289	1.9%	1,920
12/18	15,302	300	2.0%	1,815
12/17	14,449	135	0.9%	1,744
12/16	9,808	177	1.8%	1,503
12/15	9,289	138	1.5%	1,424
Annual Growth	12.8%	20.3%	—	7.8%

2019 Year-End Financials

Debt ratio: 6.59%	No. of shares (mil.): 166
Return on equity: 11.91%	Dividends
Cash ($ mil.): 490	Yield: 2.5%
Current ratio: —	Payout: 30.0%
Long-term debt ($ mil.): —	Market value ($ mil.): 3,271

	STOCK PRICE ($) FY Close	P/E High/Low	PER SHARE ($) Earnings	Dividends	Book Value
12/19	19.66	12 10	1.73	0.51	15.10
12/18	16.34	15 9	1.73	0.46	13.76
12/17	23.25	33 24	0.89	0.40	12.70
12/16	27.77	35 15	1.26	0.34	9.45
12/15	40.52	46 28	1.01	0.28	8.55
Annual Growth	(16.5%)	—	14.4%	16.7%	15.3%

Home Depot Inc

When embarking on household projects many start their journey at The Home Depot. As the world's largest home improvement chain and one of the largest retailers in the US the company operates nearly 2300 stores in North America. It targets the do-it-yourself (DIY) and professional markets with its selection of up to 40000 items including lumber flooring plumbing supplies garden products tools paint and appliances. Home Depot also offers installation services for carpeting cabinetry and other products for its do-it-for-me (DIFM) customers. It conducts e-commerce operations through its websites (including thecompanystore.com) and mobile apps. More than 90% of its total revenue generates within the US.

HISTORY

Bernard Marcus and Arthur Blank founded The Home Depot in 1978 after they were fired (under disputed circumstances) from Handy Dan Home Improvement Centers. They joined Handy Dan coworker Ronald Brill to launch a "new and improved" home center for the do-it-yourselfer (DIY). In 1979 they opened three stores in the fast-growing Atlanta area and expanded to four stores in 1980.

Home Depot went public opened four stores in South Florida and posted sales of $50 million in 1981. The chain entered Louisiana and Arizona next. By 1983 sales were more than $250 million.

In 1984 Home Depot's stock was listed on the NYSE and the company acquired nine Bowater Home Centers in the South. Through subsequent stock and debenture offerings Home Depot continued to grow entering California (Handy Dan's home turf) with six new stores in 1985.

Back on track in 1986 sales exceeded $1 billion in the firm's 60 stores. Home Depot began the current policy of "low day-in day-out pricing" the following year achieving Marcus' dream of eliminating sales events. The company entered the competitive northeastern market with stores in Long Island New York in 1988 and opened its first EXPO Design Center in San Diego.

Home Depot's sales continued to rise during the 1990-92 recession and the retailer kept opening stores. It entered Canada in 1994 when it acquired a 75% interest in Aikenhead's a DIY chain that it converted to the Home Depot name (it bought the remaining 25% in 1998).

A series of gender-bias lawsuits plagued the company in 1994 as female workers claimed they were not treated on an equal basis with male employees. Home Depot reached a $65 million out-of-court settlement in 1997 but not before the company was ordered to pay another female employee $1.7 million in a case in California.

Troubles aside Home Depot roared past the 500-store mark in 1997. That year Blank succeeded Marcus as the company's CEO; Marcus remained chairman. Home Depot bought National Blind & Wallpaper Factory (a mail-order firm) and Maintenance Warehouse (a direct-mail marketer) that year.

The company introduced its 40000-sq.-ft. Villager's Hardware stores designed to compete with smaller hardware shops in 1999 in New Jersey. It also bought Georgia Lighting an Atlanta lighting designer distributor and retailer. Home Depot later began adding large appliances to some stores following competitor Lowe's (most stores had them by 2000).

In 2000 Home Depot bought Apex Supply (a 20-plus-location plumbing distributor in Georgia South Carolina and Tennessee) and opened a flooring-only test store in Texas. Later that year the company named General Electric executive Robert Nardelli as its president and CEO. Marcus and Blank were named co-chairmen.

The company opened 200 new stores in 2001 and bought Total HOME a home improvement chain with four stores in Mexico. Additionally Marcus was named chairman after Blank stepped down. Later in the year Marcus retired and Nardelli became chairman. Also that year the company said it was scrapping its Villager's Hardware experiment to test a small-store concept in urban areas.

In 2002 Home Depot opened its first small store a 61000-sq.-ft. outlet in New York City. Further increasing its presence in Mexico the company acquired the four-store Del Norte chain in Ciudad Ju rez that year.

Also in 2002 Home Depot created a new subsidiary HD Builder Solutions through the acquisition of Floors Inc. Arvada Hardwood Floor Company and FloorWorks Inc. The next year the company acquired roofing installer IPUSA and replacement windows and siding installer RMA Home Services.

Home Depot expanded its business in the home-builder market in January 2004 by purchasing Creative Touch Interiors a floor and counter installer in California and Nevada. Additionally early that year Home Depot opened its largest store ever

— 205000 sq. ft. — in wealthy Anaheim Hills California. It also announced in February 2004 that it had partnered with AARP to hire people older than 50.

In addition that month Home Depot became the exclusive retailer of Maytag's SkyBox a home beverage dispenser. It acquired Home Mart a 20-unit Mexican chain in that June giving it a total of more than 40 stores in Mexico. Also in 2004 the company acquired White Cap Construction Supply; agreed to settle discrimination claims of some Colorado employees for $5.5 million; opened two trend-setting urban-oriented stores in Manhattan; and bought 18 stores from Kmart.

In mid-2005 Home Depot acquired National Waterworks Holdings (now National Waterworks Inc.) and Williams Bros. Lumber of Georgia and folded them both into its The Home Depot Supply business (called HD Supply until it was sold). In September Home Depot Direct launched 10 Crescent Lane a high-end home decorating catalog and Web site offering furniture lighting and decorative accessories housewares and more. While some Home Depot locations in Louisiana and Texas were temporarily shut down by hurricanes Katrina and Rita its stores (and those of rival Lowe's and other building suppliers) are among the first places people visited in the wake of the disaster. In the immediate aftermath of the storms Home Depot stocked nontraditional items such as food and diapers in affected areas. Also in 2005 the company shuttered 15 EXPO Design Center stores which cater to affluent homeowners and converted five others to The Home Depot format. In all in 2005 Home Depot spent about $2.5 billion to acquire 21 companies.

The company's direct-to-consumer division launched a pair of high-end catalogs in 2005: 10 Crescent Lane and Paces Trading Company. However the catalogs which featured home furnishings and lighting products were discontinued in 2006 and selected products were folded back into the main Home Depot store catalog and website.

In January 2006 Home Depot acquired carpet and upholstery cleaning franchisor Chem-Dry and folded it into its At-Home Services division. (Chem-Dry has some 4000 franchises worldwide including 2500 in the US). In March the company completed its largest acquisition to date: the construction repair and maintenance products distributor Hughes Supply Inc. for $3.2 billion. That purchase was followed in May by the acquisition of Cox Lumber Co. a Tampa-based provider of trusses doors and lumber-related products. Also Home Depot acquired Home Decorators Collection a company specializing in catalog and online sales of home decor merchandise in 2006. Lured by the growth potential of the vast Chinese market the retailer purchased a majority stake in Taiwan-based Home-Way for about $100 million in late 2006. Home-Way operates DIY warehouse stores in northern China.

Joining the trend of big-box retailers adding gasoline and convenience store services to fuel sales Home Depot opened its first Home Depot Fuel locations in Tennessee and Georgia in 2006.

In early 2007 Nardelli left the company and vice chairman and EVP Frank Blake took the top spot. Home Depot decided to close its handful of flooring-only stores that year. The apparent nail in Nardelli's coffin was his autocratic management style and hefty compensation package (strategically based on options rather than shareholder returns and estimated at $245 million over five years). Nardelli left Home Depot with a $210 million severance package.

The company sold its HD Supply business in 2007 to Bain Capital Carlyle Group and Clayton Dubilier & Rice. The retailer used the proceeds to

help it make a $10 billion stock repurchase of more than 15% of its market capitalization.

The Home Depot closed two stores in China in fiscal 2011. In fiscal 2013 it closed the last of its big-box stores there.

EXECUTIVES

President Southern Division, Tim Hourigan
Evp Corporate Services And Cfo, Carol B. Tomé, age 63, $1,079,231 total compensation
President The Home Depot Mexico, Ricardo E. Saldivar, age 67
Chairman President And Ceo, Craig A. Menear, age 62, $1,300,000 total compensation
Evp Supply Chain And Product Development, Mark Q. Holifield, age 63, $775,385 total compensation
Evp And Cio, Matthew A. (Matt) Carey, age 55, $730,385 total compensation
Svp Talent Organization And Performance Systems, Timothy M. (Tim) Crow, age 64, $586,308 total compensation
Evp U.s. Stores, Ann-Marie Campbell, age 54, $665,385 total compensation
President The Home Depot Canada, Jeff Kinnaird
Evp Outside Sales And Service, William G. (Bill) Lennie, age 64
Evp General Counsel And Corporate Secretary, Teresa W. Roseborough, age 61
President Western Division, Aaron Flowe
Svp And President Online, Kevin Hofmann
Evp Merchandising, Edward P. (Ted) Decker, age 57
President Northern Division, Crystal Hanlon
Regional Vice President, Heidi Thompson
Svpa, April Haubenschild
Vice President Of Finance, Scott Bohrer
Vice President Human Resources, Michael Hagan
Vice President Employment Practices And Associate Relations, Derek W Bottoms
Vice President Finance, Jordan Broggi
Vice President Information Technology, Daniel Grider
Vice President, Renee Murray
Vice President Internal Communications, Dennis Depot
Vice President Of Marketing, Lisa Destefano Orebaugh
Regional Vice President, Quonta Vance
Vice President Of Tax, Karen Dewalt
Vice President, Katie Brubaker
Vice President Merchandising Operations, Mark Healy
Vice President Finance Canada, Peter Muench
Vice President Service Operations And Home Renovation Services, Chuyu Xi
Vice President Merchandising Execution, Tim Wilkerson
Merchandising Vice President, Mike Hogenmiller
Senior Vice President Supply Chain, Thomas Shortt
Vice President Real Estate, Michael Laferle
Senior Vice President Store Operations, Hector Padilla
Vice President Of Pro Business, Jt Rieves
Svp Merchandising Building Materials, Giles Bowman
Vice President And Deputy General Counsel, Peter Muniz
Senior Vice President Of Operations, Tim Applebee
National Sales Manager, Jeff Capone
Vice President Marketing, Lisa DeStefano
Vice President Online, Prat Vemana
Executive Vice President Cio, Matt Carey
Vice President Learning And Development, Tom Spahr
Senior Vice President Business Development, David Cochran
Merchandising Vice President, Mark G Healy
Vice President Supply Chain, Serge Carestia

Department Head, William Morgan
Vice President Customer Service, Sherri Allen
Vice President Asset Protection, Scott Glenn
National Account Manager, Tyler Trzaska
Board Member, Albert Carey
Auditors: KPMG LLP

LOCATIONS

HQ: Home Depot Inc
2455 Paces Ferry Road, Atlanta, GA 30339
Phone: 770 433-8211   **Fax:** 770 431-2707
Web: www.homedepot.com

2018 Sales

	$ mil.	% of total
US	99,386	92
Other	8,817	8
Total	**108,203**	**100**

2018 Stores

	No.
US	1,981
Canada	182
Mexico	124
Total	**2,287**

PRODUCTS/OPERATIONS

2018 Sales

	$ mil.	% of total
Indoor garden	10,438	10
Appliances	9,001	8
Paint	8,461	8
Lumber	8,388	8
Tools	8,109	8
Plumbing	8,052	7
Building materials	7,772	7
Kitchen and bath	7,721	7
Flooring	7,475	7
Outdoor garden	7,257	7
Hardware	6,194	6
Millwork	5,743	5
Electrical	5,576	5
Other	8,016	7
Total	**108,203**	**100**

Selected Private Labels and Proprietary Brands

EcoSmart (lighting)
Everbilt (plumbing parts and pumps)
Glacier Bay (fixtures)
Hampton Bay (lighting)
Husky (hand tools)
LifeProof (flooring)
RIDGID (power tools)
Stanley (hand tools)
Vigoro (lawn care products)

COMPETITORS

84 Lumber	Menard
Ace Hardware	Sears Holdings
Amazon.com	Sherwin-Williams
BMC Stock	Target Corporation
Best Buy	Tractor Supply
Do it Best	True Value
Lowe's	Wal-Mart
Lumber Liquidators	

HISTORICAL FINANCIALS

Company Type: Public

Income Statement

FYE: February 2

	REVENUE ($ mil.)	NET INCOME ($ mil.)	NET PROFIT MARGIN	EMPLOYEES
02/20	110,225	11,242	10.2%	415,700
02/19*	108,203	11,121	10.3%	413,000
01/18	100,904	8,630	8.6%	413,000
01/17	94,595	7,957	8.4%	406,000
01/16	88,519	7,009	7.9%	385,000
Annual Growth	**5.6%**	**12.5%**	**—**	**1.9%**

*Fiscal year change

2020 Year-End Financials

Debt ratio: 61.45%	No. of shares (mil.): 1,077
Return on equity: —	Dividends
Cash ($ mil.): 2,133	Yield: 0.0%
Current ratio: 1.08	Payout: 53.0%
Long-term debt ($ mil.): 28,670	Market value ($ mil.): 245,664

	STOCK PRICE ($) FY Close	P/E High/Low	PER SHARE ($) Earnings	PER SHARE ($) Dividends	PER SHARE ($) Book Value
02/20	228.10	23 18	10.25	5.44	(2.89)
02/19*	184.37	22 16	9.73	4.12	(1.70)
01/18	207.23	28 19	7.29	3.56	1.26
01/17	138.33	21 17	6.45	2.76	3.60
01/16	125.76	25 19	5.46	2.36	5.04
Annual Growth	**16.1%**	**— —**	**17.1%**	**23.2%**	

*Fiscal year change

HOME PROPERTIES, LIMITED PARTNERSHIP

LOCATIONS

HQ: HOME PROPERTIES, LIMITED PARTNERSHIP
850 CLINTON SQ, ROCHESTER, NY 146041730
Phone: 585 546-4900
Web: WWW.HOMEPROPERTIES.COM

HISTORICAL FINANCIALS

Company Type: Private

Income Statement

FYE: December 31

	ASSETS ($ mil.)	NET INCOME ($ mil.)	INCOME AS % OF ASSETS	EMPLOYEES
12/07	3,216	61	1.9%	1,000
12/06	3,240	110	3.4%	—
12/05	2,977	26	0.9%	—
12/01	1,346	2	0.2%	—
Annual Growth	**15.6%**	**75.1%**	**—**	**—**

HomeStreet Inc

HomeStreet aims to offer home and business mortgages to all in the West Coast and Hawaii. HomeStreet principally engaged in commercial banking consumer banking and real estate lending including commercial real estate and single family mortgage lending. In addition to the banking and lending operations of its wholly owned subsidiaries HomeStreet also sells insurance products and services for consumer clients under the name Home-Street Insurance. Founded in 1921 HomeStreet has about $6.8 billion assets.

Operations

HomeStreet primary subsidiaries are Home-Street Bank and HomeStreet Capital Corp. (HCC).

HomeStreet Bank provides commercial and consumer loans including mortgage loans deposit products private banking and cash management services. Its loan products include commercial business and agriculture loans consumer loans single family residential mortgages loans secured by commercial real estate and construction loans for res-

idential and commercial real estate projects. HCC sells and services multifamily mortgage loans in conjunction with HomeStreet Bank.

HomeStreet gets most of its revenue from interest income.

Geographic Reach

Seattle-based HomeStreet operates bank branches in California Hawaii Idaho Oregon Utah and Washington. HomeStreet also operates four primary commercial lending centers about 60 retail deposit branches and one insurance office. In addition it also operates three facilities for the purpose of administrative and other functions in addition to the principal offices: a call center and operations support facility located in Federal Way Washington; a loan fulfillment center in Lynnwood Washington and an operations support center in Spokane Washington.

Sales and Marketing

HomeStreet provides financial services for small- and middle-market businesses as well as consumers through bank branches ATMs online mobile and telephone banking channels.

HomeStreet spend $5.9 million $6.9 million and $6.8 million in advertising expense during 2019 2018 and 2017 respectively.

Financial Performance

Company's revenue increased to $263.3 million 2019 compared from the prior year with $229.5 million.

Net income which included both continuing and discontinued operations was $17.5 million in the year ended December 31 2019 a decrease of $22.5 million or 56% from $40.0 million for the year ended December 31 2018. The decrease in net income in 2019 was primarily due to the $20.6 million loss on disposal and restructuring-related expenses net of tax taken in the year ended December 31 2019 compared to the $5.0 million in restructuring related expenses net of tax taken in the year ended December 31 2018 a $4.9 million non-cash tax benefit from the revaluation of its deferred tax liability related to the Tax Reform Act taken in 2018 a decline in single-family mortgage servicing income related to the first quarter 2019 sales of single family mortgage servicing rights and a decline in single family net gain on mortgage loan sale and origination activities primarily from the HLC Business Sale.

Cash held by the company at the end of 2019 decreased to $57.9 million compared from the prior year with $58.6 million. Cash provided by operations and investing activities were $258.8 million and $83.9 million respectively. Cash used for financing activities was $343.5 million mainly for repayment of federal funds purchased and securities sold under agreements to repurchase.

Strategy

As a part of Home Street's growth strategy it opened several de novo retail deposit branches between 2012 and 2019 to expand its branch network and increase its core deposit base while also expanding its offerings of community banking products and services. The company focused its de novo branch openings branches in markets that it believes are underserved by community banks. In 2019 Home Street added two de novo branches in Northern California. Overall from its IPO through December 31 2019 the company added 24 de novo branches and acquired nine branches. At the same time it grew and diversified the Bank through acquisitions of whole banks and retail deposit branches in attractive growth markets on the West Coast to increase its scale in existing markets enter new markets and add to or acquire additional professionals for its commercial and consumer lending teams. Between 2013 and 2019 the company acquired four banks expanding its network in Eastern Washington and Southern California and nine individual branches to complement its existing networks in Washington Oregon and California.

Company Background

HomeStreet went public in February 2012 with an offering worth $55 million. The company sold 1.6 million shares priced at $44 each. HomeStreet had postponed two previous attempts to go public in 2011 that had planned to sell many more shares. Proceeds from the 2012 IPO were used to meet capital-ratio requirements required by regulators in the wake of allegations that the bank engaged in unsafe practices.

HomeStreet was hit hard by the economic downturn and slowdown in the housing market. Trouble in its core mortgage lending business led to losses in 2009 and 2010 and the bank entered into agreements with regulators to improve its capital position earnings and management. It brought in a new management team and launched a turnaround plan to stabilize the business which included tightening its lending standards restructuring troubled loans when necessary and the sale of real estate backed by nonperforming loans. The measures helped HomeStreet return to profitability in 2011 and remain in the black for several years thereafter.

EXECUTIVES

Chairman President And Ceo Homestreet Inc. And Homestreet Bank, Mark K. Mason, age 60, $537,500 total compensation

Evp Chief Administrative Officer General Counsel And Corporate Secretary Homestreet Inc. And Homestreet Bank, Godfrey B. Evans, age 66, $247,200 total compensation

Sevp Commercial Banking Homestreet Bank, David H. Straus, age 73

Evp Homestreet Inc. And Evp Residential Construction And Affiliated Businesses Homestreet Bank, Richard W. H. (Rich) Bennion, age 70, $203,000 total compensation

Evp And Retail Banking Director Homestreet Bank, Paulette Lemon, age 63

Evp And Human Resources Director Homestreet Bank, Pamela J. (Pam) Taylor, age 68

Evp Chief Risk Officer And Chief Credit Officer Homestreet Inc. And Homestreet Bank, Jay C. Iseman, age 60, $200,000 total compensation

Sevp Mortgage Lending Director, Rose Marie David, age 56, $200,000 total compensation

Evp Commercial Real Estate And Commercial Capital President Homestreet Bank, William D. Endresen, age 65

Evp And Residential Construction Lending Director Homestreet Bank, Jeff Todhunter

Evp Chief Investment Officer And Treasurer Homestreet Inc. And Homestreet Bank, Darrell S. van Amen, age 54

Vice President Commercial Lending Manager, George Brace

Vice President Loan Officer, Carmen Esteban

Auditors: DELOITTE & TOUCHE LLP

LOCATIONS

HQ: HomeStreet Inc
601 Union Street, Suite 2000, Seattle, WA 98101
Phone: 206 623-3050
Web: www.homestreet.com

PRODUCTS/OPERATIONS

2015 Sales

	$ mil.	% of total
Interest		
Loans	152	34
Investment securities available for sale	11	3
Other	0	-
Non-interest		
Net gains on mortgage origination & sales activities	236	53
Mortgage servicing	24	6
Depositor & other retail banking fees	5	1
Gain on sale of investment securities available for sale	2	1
Bargain purchase gain	7	2
Insurance agency commission income from WMS Series LLC and other	4	-
Total	**446**	**100**

Selected Services

Personal Banking
Home LoansInvestmentInsurancePrivate Bank
Commercial Banking
Builder Financing/Residential ConstructionCommercial LendingCommercial Real EstatePartnership Programs

COMPETITORS

American Savings Bank	KeyCorp
Bank of America	Sound Financial
Bank of Hawaii	U.S. Bancorp
Banner Corp	Umpqua Holdings
First Hawaiian	Washington Federal
JPMorgan Chase	Wells Fargo

HISTORICAL FINANCIALS

Company Type: Public

Income Statement

FYE: December 31

	ASSETS ($ mil.)	NET INCOME ($ mil.)	INCOME AS % OF ASSETS	EMPLOYEES
12/19	6,812	17	0.3%	1,071
12/18	7,042	40	0.6%	2,036
12/17	6,742	68	1.0%	2,419
12/16	6,243	58	0.9%	2,552
12/15	4,894	41	0.8%	2,139
Annual Growth	8.6%	(19.3%)	—	(15.9%)

2019 Year-End Financials

Debt ratio: 1.84%	No. of shares (mil.): 23
Return on equity: 2.47%	Dividends
Cash ($ mil.): 57	Yield: —
Current ratio: —	Payout: —
Long-term debt ($ mil.): —	Market value ($ mil.): 812

	STOCK PRICE ($) FY Close	P/E High/Low		PER SHARE ($) Earnings	Dividends	Book Value
12/19	34.00	52	32	0.65	0.00	28.45
12/18	21.23	22	14	1.47	0.00	27.39
12/17	28.95	13	9	2.54	0.00	26.20
12/16	31.60	14	8	2.34	0.00	23.48
12/15	21.71	12	9	1.96	0.00	21.08
Annual Growth	11.9%	—	—	(24.1%)	—	7.8%

HOMETOWN AMERICA MANAGEMENT CORP.

EXECUTIVES

Ceo, Richard Cline
Cao*, Tom Curatolo
Coo*, Greg Oberry
Community Manager, John McGrath

LOCATIONS

HQ: HOMETOWN AMERICA MANAGEMENT CORP.
150 N WACKER DR STE 2800, CHICAGO, IL 606061610
Phone: 312 604-7500
Web: WWW.HOMETOWNAMERICA.COM

HISTORICAL FINANCIALS

Company Type: Private

Income Statement

FYE: December 31

	ASSETS ($ mil.)	NET INCOME ($ mil.)	INCOME AS % OF ASSETS	EMPLOYEES
12/07	3,059	56	1.9%	1,000
12/06	2,815	55	2.0%	—
12/05	2,454	55	2.3%	—
12/04	2,288	18	0.8%	—
Annual Growth	10.2%	44.8%	—	—

HomeTrust Bancshares Inc.

EXECUTIVES

Ceo-Pres, Dana L Stonestreet
Exec V Pres-Cfo-Treas, Tony J Vuncannon
Exec V Pres-CIO, Howard L Sellinger
Pres-Coo, C Hunter Westbrook
Exec V Pres-Chief ADM Officer-, Teresa White
Exec V Pres-Cro, R Parrish Little
Evp-Commercial Banking Group E, Mark Demarcus
Chro, Paula C Labian
Independent Director, Robert Dinsmore
Independent Director, Robert James
Customer Care Specialist, Robert Meadows
Auditors: Dixon Hughes Goodman LLP

LOCATIONS

HQ: HomeTrust Bancshares Inc.
10 Woodfin Street, Asheville, NC 28801
Phone: 828 259-3939
Web: www.htb.com

HISTORICAL FINANCIALS

Company Type: Public

Income Statement
FYE: June 30

	ASSETS ($ mil.)	NET INCOME ($ mil.)	INCOME AS % OF ASSETS	EMPLOYEES
06/20	3,722	22	0.6%	590
06/19	3,476	27	0.8%	582
06/18	3,304	8	0.2%	520
06/17	3,206	11	0.4%	486
06/16	2,717	11	0.4%	465
Annual Growth	8.2%	18.8%	—	6.1%

2020 Year-End Financials

Debt ratio: —
Return on equity: 5.56%
Cash ($ mil.): 482
Current ratio: —
Long-term debt ($ mil.): —

No. of shares (mil.): 17
Dividends
Yield: 1.6%
Payout: 17.7%
Market value ($ mil.): 272

	STOCK PRICE ($) FY Close	P/E High/Low		PER SHARE ($) Earnings	Dividends	Book Value
06/20	16.00	20	9	1.30	0.27	23.99
06/19	25.14	20	16	1.46	0.18	22.74
06/18	28.15	65	50	0.44	0.00	21.49
06/17	24.40	41	27	0.65	0.00	20.96
06/16	18.50	32	26	0.65	0.00	20.00
Annual Growth	(3.6%)	—	—	18.9%	—	4.6%

Honeywell International Inc

Jet engines and Muck Boots seem worlds apart but they coexist at Honeywell International. More than a century old the company is a diverse industrial conglomerate its four segments making and selling products from aircraft engines flight safety and landing systems to smart controls for commercial buildings to personal safety products such as gas masks and footwear. The company does business worldwide and generates more than half its sales in the US.

Operations

Honeywell is organized across four segments: Aerospace; Performance Materials and Technologies; Honeywell Building Technologies; and Safety and Productivity Solutions.

The Aerospace segment accounts for about 40% of the company's revenue. It provides products and services for aircraft and vehicles sold to OEMs and other customers in a variety of end markets?air transport; regional business and general aviation aircraft; airlines and aircraft operators; defense and space contractors.

Performance Materials and Technologies (almost 30% of revenue) operates in three divisions. Honeywell UOP provides process technology for fuel production for the petroleum refining gas processing and petrochemical industries; Process Solutions sells automation controls and software for the oil and gas pulp and paper industrial power and several other industries; and Advanced Materials manufactures high-performance products such as fluorocarbons specialty films waxes additives and advanced fibers to name a few.

The company's former Home and Building Technologies segment?now just Honeywell Building Technologies?(over 15%) sells building automation controls for commercial customers.

The Safety and Productivity Solutions segment (over 15%) offers products that improve productivity workplace safety and asset performance. Safety products include personal protection equipment and footwear. Productivity solutions include gas detection technology mobile devices and software for computing and data collection supply chain and warehouse automation equipment and sensors switches and controls.

Geographic Reach

Headquartered in Charlotte North Carolina Honeywell has approximately 930 locations of which over 240 are manufacturing sites. The US accounts for around 60% of total revenue.

Sales and Marketing

Honeywell's Aerospace business sells its products and services to original equipment manufacturers (OEMs) and other end markets like air transport regional business and general aviation aircraft; airlines and aircraft operators; defense and space contractors. The Building Technologies segment sells to commercial building owners. Performance Materials and Technologies targets several industries including oil and gas refining pulp and paper industrial power generation petrochemicals biofuels life sciences metals minerals and mining. The Safety and Productivity Solutions business sells its products globally to a variety of industries.

Financial Performance

After an ascending trend for the past few years Honeywell's revenues decreased by 12% in 2019 due to the spin-offs.

Honeywell's net income dipped to $6.1 billion in 2019 a $620 million decrease from 2018. Cash at the end of fiscal 2019 was $9.1 billion a decrease of $220 million from the prior year.

Cash from operations contributed $6.9 billion to the coffers while investing activities used $533 million primarily used for expenditures for property plant and equipment. Financing activities used another $6.6 billion primarily for commercial paper and other short-term borrowings.

Strategy

FFor all its segments Honeywell is focused on several initiatives to spur growth including R&D activities to develop new technologies. The company aims to become an industrial software company offering products for the connected plane home building and factory. Other initiatives that target lower costs are process improvements in its manufacturing and administrative operations and cost control efforts for asbestos and environmental remediation and pension and retirement benefits.

Honeywell's strategy for growth includes both acquisitions and the divestiture of under-performing units. In order to streamline its operations Honeywell in late 2018 completed the spin-off of its turbo charger unit and home heating and security businesses to create two new publicly traded companies. The new business featuring its turbo charger technology (formerly the Transportation Systems business) is now Garrett Motion Inc. Its former Homes and ADI Global Distribution business is now Resideo a company providing home comfort and security systems. After the spin-offs Honeywell believes its remaining portfolio will consist of high-growth businesses each aligned to the global megatrends of energy efficiency infrastructure investment urbanization and safety.

Mergers and Acquisitions

In late 2019 Honeywell acquired Rebellion Photonics a Houston-based provider of innovative intelligent visual gas monitoring solutions that maximize safety operational performance emissions mitigation and compliance in the oil and gas petrochemical and power industries. The acquisition will become part of Honeywell's Safety and Productivity Solutions business which provides a wide range of gas detection technologies safety gear mobility solutions and software to help workers stay safe and productive.

In the same year Honeywell acquired privately held TruTrak Flight Systems a leader in autopilots for experimental light-sport and certified aircraft. The acquisition will become part of Honeywell's BendixKing business helping to deliver affordable technologies to the experimental and general aviation markets. This market has grown by double digits over the past five years.

HISTORY

During WWI Germany controlled much of the world's chemical industry causing dye and drug shortages. In response Washington Post publisher Eugene Meyer and scientist William Nichols organized the Allied Chemical & Dye Corporation in 1920.

Allied opened a synthetic ammonia plant in 1928 near Hopewell Virginia and became the world's leading producer of ammonia. After WWII Allied began making nylon refrigerants and other products. The company became Allied Chemical Corporation in 1958.

Seeking a supplier of raw materials for its chemical products Allied bought Union Texas Natural Gas in 1962. In the early 1970s CEO John Connor sold many of the firm's unprofitable businesses and invested in oil and gas exploration. By 1979 when Edward Hennessy became CEO Union Texas produced 80% of Allied's income.

Hennessy led the company into the electronics and technical markets. Under a new name Allied Corporation (1981) it bought the Bendix Corporation an aerospace and automotive company in 1983. In 1985 Allied merged with Signal Companies (founded by Sam Mosher in 1922) to form AlliedSignal. The company spun off more than 40 unprofitable chemical and engineering businesses over the next two years.

Larry Bossidy hired from General Electric in 1991 as the new CEO began to cut waste and buy growth businesses. In 1998 alone the company made 13 acquisitions. Late in 1999 the company acquired Honeywell (which dated back to 1906) in a deal valued at $15 billion and changed its name to Honeywell International. Honeywell after trying to make a go of it in the computer and telecommunications industries had refocused on its core products lines — thermostats security systems and other automation equipment.

In 2016 Honeywell was engaged in talks to merge with industry powerhouse United Technologies Corp. in a merger valued at around $90 billion. The talks ended however after United Technologies refused to explore the deal further fearing that the massive transaction could not clear steep regulatory hurdles.

EXECUTIVES

President And Ceo Aerospace, Timothy O. (Tim) Mahoney, age 63, $917,019 total compensation
President And Ceo Global High Growth Regions, Shane Tedjarati
President And Ceo Home And Building Technologies (hbt), Terrence S. Hahn, age 54
President Technology Solutions, Krishna Mikkilineni, age 60, $717,678 total compensation
President And Ceo Performance Materials And Technologies, Rajeev Gautam, age 67
President And Ceo Safety And Productivity Solutions (sps), John Waldron, age 44
Svp And Cfo, Thomas A. (Tom) Szlosek, age 56, $840,000 total compensation
President And Ceo, Darius Adamczyk, age 54, $1,120,383 total compensation

President And Ceo Honeywell Transportation
Systems, Olivier Rabiller
President Honeywell Intelligrated, Pieter Krynauw
President Honeywell Thailand, Mai Trang Thanh
Svp Of Finance, Greg Lewis
Vice President General Manager Resins And
Chemicals, Qamar S Bhatia
Vice President Marketing, Brian Holliday
Vice President Electrical Sourcing, Lawrence
Polizzotto
Vice President Marketing, Athanasios Karras
Vice President Americas Htt, Anthony Schultz
Vice President Human Resources (performance
Materials And Technologies), Shaun Zitting
Chairman President And Ceo, David M. (Dave) Cote,
age 67
Auditors: DELOITTE & TOUCHE LLP

LOCATIONS

HQ: Honeywell International Inc
300 South Tryon Street, Charlotte, NC 28202
Phone: 704 627-6200   **Fax:** 973 455-4807
Web: www.honeywell.com

2017 Sales

	$ mil.	% of total
US	22,722	56
Europe	10,400	26
Other International	7,412	18
Total	**40,534**	**100**

PRODUCTS/OPERATIONS

2017 Sales

	$ mil.	% of total
Aerospace	14,779	36
Performance Materials and Technologies	10,339	26
Home and Building Technologies	9,777	24
Safety and Productivity Solutions	5,639	14
Total	**40,534**	**100**

2017 Sales

	$ mil.	% of total
Product sales	32,317	80
Service sales	8,217	20
Total	**40,534**	**100**

Selected Products and Services

Aerospace
Aircraft engines
Auxiliary turbine power unites
Cockpit systems and displays
Cabin management and entertainment
Air and thermal management
Biofuel for aviation
BendixKing avionics
Buildings
Building automation systems
Software and controls
Construction and maintenance
Security and fire services
Combustion controls
Footwear
Oliver safety footwear
Muck boots
Xtratuf boots
Healthcare
Workflow automation for hospitals
Patient monitoring systems
Pharmaceutical laboratory products
Pharmaceutical packaging films
Industrial
Facility security and maintenance
Energy solutions
Honeywell Smart Energy for utilities
Instrumentation for measurement and control
Fuels and chemicals for clean power
Manufacturing
Sensors and switches
Advanced fibers and composites
Renewable energy from biomass
Honeywell MXProLine Quality Control System
Honeywell HydroBlock anti-graffiti barrier film
Oil and Gas
Refining technology

Petrochemicals
Gas processing equipment
Adsorbents for contaminant removal
Honeywell Green Diesel fuel
Industrial water treatment
Gas tank terminal operations controls
Personal protective equipment
Rope and performance fibers
Performance Materials
Catalysts
Refrigerants
Honeywell Electronic Materials
Research chemicals
Honeywell Aclar barrier film for pharmaceutical
packaging
Honeywell Spectra fiber for braided fishing line
Honeywell Specialty Additives
Productivity
Barcode scanners
Mobile computer devices
Printers and media for RFID labels tags etc.
Wearable devices
OEM scan engines and modules
Workflow solutions
Vocollect voice technology for data collection
Global tracking and messaging
Search and rescue technology and services
Safety
Protective equipment
Honeywell Instant Alert cloud-based notification and
emergency messaging

COMPETITORS

3M	Kion Group
Albemarle	MSA Safety
BASF SE	Rockwell Automation
BorgWarner	Rockwell Collins
Dow Chemical	Schneider Electric
Emerson Electric	Siemens AG
GE	TE Connectivity
Garmin	Thales
Itron	United Technologies
Johnson Controls Power	Zebra Technologies
Solutions	

HISTORICAL FINANCIALS

Company Type: Public

Income Statement   FYE: December 31

	REVENUE ($ mil.)	NET INCOME ($ mil.)	NET PROFIT MARGIN	EMPLOYEES
12/19	36,709	6,143	16.7%	113,000
12/18	41,802	6,765	16.2%	114,000
12/17	40,534	1,655	4.1%	131,000
12/16	39,302	4,809	12.2%	131,000
12/15	38,581	4,768	12.4%	129,000
Annual Growth	(1.2%)	6.5%	—	(3.3%)

2019 Year-End Financials

Debt ratio: 27.27%
Return on equity: 33.49%
Cash ($ mil.): 9,067
Current ratio: 1.34
Long-term debt ($ mil.): 11,110

No. of shares (mil.): 711
Dividends
Yield: 1.9%
Payout: 39.2%
Market value ($ mil.): 125,865

	STOCK PRICE ($) FY Close	P/E High/Low	PER SHARE ($) Earnings	Dividends	Book Value
12/19	177.00	21 15	8.41	3.36	26.02
12/18	132.12	18 14	8.98	3.06	24.94
12/17	153.36	72 54	2.14	2.74	23.01
12/16	115.85	19 15	6.20	2.45	25.46
12/15	103.57	18 15	6.04	2.15	24.11
Annual Growth	14.3%	—	8.6%	11.8%	1.9%

Hope Bancorp Inc

EXECUTIVES

**Senior Executive Vice President Regional
President Eastern Region,** Kyu Kim
Vice President And Systems Support Manager,
Joshua Chu
Senior Vice President And Chief Credit Officer,
Peter Koh
**Senior Vice President And Manager Loan Center
Iii We Are Now Bank Of Hope,** Christie Yoo
**Vice President Information Technology
Procurement Manager,** Karina Moran
**Vice President And Business Development Officer
Commercial Lending Center I,** Brian Chung
**Assistant Vice President And Loan Servicing
Officer Northern California Commercial Lending
Center Bank Of Hope,** Aekyung Park
Assistant Vice President And Loan Officer, Hyelim
Choe
**Executive Vice President Managing Director Of
The Corporate Banking Group Of Bank Of Hope,**
Steven Canup
**First Vice President And Portfolio Manager
Commercial Lending Center I Bank Of Hope,** Kay
Kim
Svp Institutional Banking, Scott Schaidle
Senior Vice President 8c Branch Manager, Cindy
Chi
Senior Vice President Vendor Risk Management,
Bradley Martin
**Aap Senior Vice President Tms Operations
Manager,** Rachel Lim
**Vice President And Operational Risk Management
Assistant,** Katelyn Kang
**First Vice President And Senior Financial
Analyst,** Joonhyok Shin
Vice President International Operations, Lisa Lee
Avp And Loan Officer Bank Of Hope, James Chong
Avp Loan Officer, Gina Choi
Senior Vice President And Sba Manager, Sylvester
Kim
Senior Vice President Branch Manager, Eric Lee
**Senior Vice President International Operations
Manager,** Linda Kim
First Vice President, Alex Cho
**Senior Vice President And Marketing Manager
Senior Business Analyst Loan Department,** Gene
Pak
Assistant Vice President Treasury Management,
Joseph Han
Assistant Vice President And Service Officer Ii,
Gloria Wang
Svp And Area Manager Business Centers, Christina
So
Vice President And Sba Loan Officer, Ellie Park
Managing Director Middle Market Lending, Mark
Smith
Vice President Project Manager, David Son
**Senior Vice President Chief Corporate Banking
Officer,** Alex Kim
Senior Vice President Tms Department Manager,
Anthony Bourg
Vice President Business Systems Analyst, Jonas
Dimas
Auditors: Crowe LLP

LOCATIONS

HQ: Hope Bancorp Inc
3200 Wilshire Boulevard, Suite 1400, Los Angeles, CA
90010
Phone: 213 639-1700   **Fax:** 213 235-3033
Web: www.bankofhope.com

2015 Sales

	$ mil.	% of total
Interest income	313	88
Non-interest income	43	12
Total	**357**	**100**

COMPETITORS

Bank of America	Grandpoint
Broadway Financial	Hanmi Financial
Cathay General Bancorp	U.S. Bancorp
East West Bancorp	Wells Fargo
Far East National Bank	Woori

HISTORICAL FINANCIALS

Company Type: Public

Income Statement

FYE: December 31

	ASSETS ($ mil.)	NET INCOME ($ mil.)	INCOME AS % OF ASSETS	EMPLOYEES
12/19	15,667	171	1.1%	1,441
12/18	15,305	189	1.2%	1,494
12/17	14,206	139	1.0%	1,470
12/16	13,441	113	0.8%	1,372
12/15	7,912	92	1.2%	938
Annual Growth	**18.6%**	**16.7%**	**—**	**11.3%**

2019 Year-End Financials

Debt ratio: 1.93%	No. of shares (mil.): 125
Return on equity: 8.68%	Dividends
Cash ($ mil.): 698	Yield: 3.7%
Current ratio: —	Payout: 40.8%
Long-term debt ($ mil.): —	Market value ($ mil.): 1,869

	STOCK PRICE ($) FY Close	P/E High/Low		PER SHARE ($) Earnings	Dividends	Book Value
12/19	14.86	11	9	1.35	0.56	16.19
12/18	11.86	13	8	1.44	0.54	15.03
12/17	18.25	22	15	1.03	0.50	14.23
12/16	21.89	20	13	1.10	0.45	13.72
12/15	17.22	17	11	1.16	0.42	11.79
Annual Growth	**(3.6%)**	**—**	**—**	**3.9%**	**7.5%**	**8.3%**

Horace Mann Educators Corp.

Naming itself in honor of Horace Mann considered the father of public education Horace Mann Educators is an insurance holding company that primarily serves K-12 school teachers and other public-school employees throughout the US. Through its operating subsidiaries the company offers homeowners auto (majority of revenue) and individual and group life insurance as well as retirement annuities. Horace Mann employs some 800 agents many of whom are former teachers themselves. Writing business in all 50 states and the U.S. Virgin Islands and the District of Columbia the company derives about 35% of its direct premiums and contract deposits from five states — California Texas North Carolina Minnesota and Pennsylvania.

Operations

Horace Mann maintains a long-standing relationship with the country's biggest education association the National Education Association.

The company divides it business into Property/Casualty insurance Supplemental Retirement and Life insurance. Property/casualty is the largest contributor to revenue with auto being the largest component of that group. The property/casualty retirement life and supplemental segments account for some 50% 35% about 10% and some 5% respectively of the company's insurance premiums and contract deposits.

Nearly 65% of sales were generated from insurance premiums & contract charges earned around 25% came from net investment income and net realized investment gains and other account for the rest.

Geographic Reach

The company is based in Springfield Illinois. It leases office space in suburban Chicago Illinois suburban Dallas Texas (approximately 114000 of rentable square feet) suburban Raleigh North Carolina and Cherry Hill New Jersey.

The top five states and their portion of total direct insurance premiums and contract deposits were California about 10%; Texas nearly 10%; North Carolina more than 5%; Minnesota about 5%; and Pennsylvania some 5%.

Sales and Marketing

The company serves approximately 470000 educator households in roughly half of the of the K-12 public school buildings in its market footprint in the US with significant opportunity to grow in this niche market.

The company aims to provide multiple complementary distribution channels to meet individual educator preferences with more than 800 local agents.

Financial Performance

For the last five years the company revenue is on the upswing and registered 32% overall growth since 2015.

In 2019 the company posted a 20% increase in revenue ending the year with $1.4 billion. Insurance premiums investment gains and Other income all increased offset by a decrease in net investment income.

For 2019 the company's net income increased from $166.1 million to $184.4 million compared to 2018. The increase in net income was primarily due to recognition of a $106.9 million after tax realized investment gain in the second quarter of 2019 associated with an annuity reinsurance transaction.

Cash at the end of the year was $25.5 million. Net cash provided by operating activities was $127.6 million and another $55.9 million was generated by investing activities. Financing activities used $169.9 million for principal repayment on FHLB funding agreements.

Strategy

The company's vision is to be the company of choice to provide financial solutions for educators and others who serve their communities. Management believes the unique value of the company is providing solutions tailored for educators at each stage of their lives empowering them to achieve lifelong financial success.

Over the past several years the company has established its solutions orientation for the education market through a focus on products distribution and infrastructure (PDI): Products designed to meet educators' needs and protect their unique risks; Knowledgeable trusted distribution tailored to educator preferences; and Modern scalable infrastructure that is easy to do business with.

In addition the company completed three transactions in 2019 that supported its PDI strategy: acquiring NTA and Benefit Consultants Group Inc. (BCG) as well as reinsuring a $2.9 billion block of legacy annuity business. The annuity reinsurance transaction reduced the company's interest rate risk while releasing capital that was redeployed

into higher-margin products through the acquisition of NTA.

As a result the company has become a larger more diverse company that expects to continue its transformation by leveraging its market leadership to increase its share of the education market.

Mergers and Acquisitions

In mid-2019 Horace Mann Educators Corporation it has closed the acquisition of supplemental insurance provider National Teachers Associates Life Insurance Company (NTA). NTA is subsidiary of Reinsurance Group of America Incorporated a leading global life reinsurer and it has reinsured a $2.9 billion block of Horace Mann's annuity business. Combined with acquisition of National Teachers Associates Life Insurance Company (NTA) the reinsurance transaction sets the stage for strong earnings growth and accelerated shareholder value creation while also reducing earnings volatility.

In early 2019 Horace Mann acquired retirement plan coordinator Benefits Consultants Group further expanding its operations in the retirement market. . Terms were not disclosed.

EXECUTIVES

Executive Vice President Senior Vice President Vice President, Jeff Jaynes

Evp And Cfo, Dwayne D. Hallman, age 57, $444,000 total compensation

President And Ceo, Marita Zuraitis, age 59, $742,333 total compensation

Evp Annuity And Life, Matthew P. Sharpe, $394,000 total compensation

Evp Property And Casualty, William J. Caldwell, $325,000 total compensation

Vice President Human Resources, Kathi Karr

Vice President Chief Actuary, Robert Rich

Assistant Vice President Product Manager, Angel Plaza

Assistant Vice President Claims Training, Jill Kilroy

Assistant Vice President Finance, Troy Gayle

Vice President Of Human Resources Finance, Rob Billingsley

Vice President Corporate Accounting And Reporting, Ladd Turner

Vice President Of Information Technology Operation, Robert E Rich

Board Member, Stephen Hasenmiller

Chairman, Gabriel L. Shaheen, age 67

Board Member, Ronald Helow

Auditors: KPMG LLP

LOCATIONS

HQ: Horace Mann Educators Corp.
1 Horace Mann Plaza, Springfield, IL 62715-0001
Phone: 217 789-2500
Web: www.horacemann.com

PRODUCTS/OPERATIONS

2016 Sales

	$ mil.	% of total
Insurance premiums & contract charges earned	759	67
Net investment income	361	32
Net realized investment gains	4	-
Other income	4	1
Total	**1,128**	**100**

HISTORICAL FINANCIALS

Company Type: Public

Income Statement

FYE: December 31

	ASSETS ($ mil.)	NET INCOME ($ mil.)	INCOME AS % OF ASSETS	EMPLOYEES
12/19	12,478	184	1.5%	1,538
12/18	11,031	18	0.2%	1,495
12/17	11,198	169	1.5%	1,496
12/16	10,576	83	0.8%	2,061
12/15	10,059	93	0.9%	2,034
Annual Growth	5.5%	18.5%	—	(6.7%)

2019 Year-End Financials

Debt ratio: 2.39%
Return on equity: 12.91%
Cash ($ mil.): 25
Current ratio: —
Long-term debt ($ mil.): —

No. of shares (mil.): 41
Dividends
Yield: 2.6%
Payout: 36.8%
Market value ($ mil.): 1,800

	STOCK PRICE ($) FY Close	P/E High/Low		PER SHARE ($) Earnings	Dividends	Book Value
12/19	43.66	11	8	4.40	1.15	38.01
12/18	37.45	107	81	0.44	1.14	31.50
12/17	44.10	12	8	4.08	1.10	36.88
12/16	42.80	21	14	2.02	1.06	32.15
12/15	33.18	17	14	2.20	1.00	31.18
Annual Growth	7.1%	—	—	18.9%	3.6%	5.1%

Horizon Bancorp Inc

For those in Indiana and Michigan Horizon Bancorp stretches as far as the eye can see. The company is the holding company for Horizon Bank (and its Heartland Community Bank division) which provides checking and savings accounts IRAs CDs and credit cards to customers through more than 50 branches in north and central Indiana and southwest and central Michigan. Commercial financial and agricultural loans make up the largest segment of its loan portfolio which also includes mortgage warehouse loans (loans earmarked for sale into the secondary market) consumer loans and residential mortgages. Through subsidiaries the bank offers trust and investment management services; life health and property/casualty insurance; and annuities.

Operations

Horizon boasted more than $2.08 billion in total assets and $1.48 billion in deposits in 2014. Commercial loans made up 49% of the bank's total loan portfolio. The bank employed nearly 450 full and part time employees that year.

Horizon's subsidiaries include: Horizon Investments which manages the bank's investment portfolio; Horizon Properties which manages the real estate investment trust; Horizon Insurance Services which sells through the company's Wealth Management; and Horizon Grantor Trust which

holds title to certain company-owned life insurance policies.

The bank generated 61% of its revenue from interest income on loans in 2014 while another 13% came from interest on its taxable and tax-exempt investments. About 8% of revenues came from gains on its mortgage sales while the remainder of revenues were mostly generated by a mix of service charges on deposit accounts interchange fees and fiduciary activities fees.

Geographic Reach

The bank's more than 30 branches serve customers in north and central Indiana and southwest and central Michigan. Its mortgage-banking services are offered across the Midwest.

Financial Performance

Horizon Bancorp's revenues and profits have been trending higher over the past few years mostly as it's continued to grow its loan business and deposit customer base through acquisitions.

The bank's revenue rose by 2% to $102.5 million in 2014 mostly as the bank increased its interest-earning assets during the year. Its non-interest income also increased thanks to higher service charges on deposits and interchange fee income resulting from the growth in transactional deposit accounts and volume.

Despite higher revenue in 2014 the company's net income fell by 9% to $18.1 million for the year on higher provisions for loan losses due to loan growth and a write off of a commercial account coupled with an increase in transaction costs related to its Summit acquisition and an increase in salaries and employee benefits due to growth. Horizon's operating cash levels fell by 62% to $17.7 million after adjusting its earnings for non-cash items related to its net proceeds on the sale of its held-for-sale loans.

Strategy

Horizon Bancorp continues to expand its geographic reach and loan business through acquisitions and new branches. It acquired several banks and opened new branches throughout 2016 and 2017.

Mergers and Acquisitions

In 2017 Horizon Bancorp agreed to buy Wolverine Bancorp for $92 million and Lafayette Community Bancorp for $32 million

In 2016 Horizon Bancorp bought LaPorte Bancorp for $98.9 million boosting its total assets by 20% to more than $3.24 billion while expanding its branch reach into the LaPorte area of Indiana. It also agreed to buy CNB Bancorp which operates Central National Bank & Trust in Attica Indiana.

In 2015 Horizon Bancorp agreed to buy Peoples Bancorp and subsidiary Peoples Federal Savings Bank of DeKalb County.

In April 2014 the company purchased SCP Bancorp including subsidiary Summit Community Bank and its two branches.

EXECUTIVES

President Ceo Chief Administrative Officer And Director; Chairman And Ceo Horizon Bank, Craig M. Dwight, age 63, $300,000 total compensation

Evp; President And Coo Horizon Bank, Thomas H. Edwards, age 67, $187,000 total compensation

Cfo, Mark E. Secor, age 54, $131,921 total compensation

President Laporte County Indiana Horizon Bank, Steven C. Kring

President Southwest Michigan Horizon Bank, Donald E. (Don) Radde, age 67, $166,000 total compensation

President Porter County Indiana Horizon Bank, David G. Rose

Executive Vice President And Senior Bank Operations Officer, Kathie A Deruiter

Chairman, Robert C. Dabagia, age 81

Board Member, Larry Middleton
Board Member, Peter Pairitz
Board Member, Spero Valavanis
Board Member, Susan Aaron
Board Member, Lawrence Burnell
Board Member, James Dworkin
Board Member, Daniel Hopp
Board Member, Michele Magnuson
Board Member, Steven Reed
Board Member, Eric Blackhurst
Auditors: BKD, LLP

LOCATIONS

HQ: Horizon Bancorp Inc
515 Franklin Street, Michigan City, IN 46360
Phone: 219 879-0211
Web: www.horizonbank.com

PRODUCTS/OPERATIONS

Selected Subsidiaries

Horizon Bank National Association
Horizon Insurance Services Inc.
Horizon Investments Inc.
Horizon Trust & Investment Management N.A.

COMPETITORS

1st Source Corporation	Farmers Mutual of NE
American United Mutual	Fifth Third
Bank of America	First Merchants
Brotherhood Mutual	Indiana Farmers Mutual

HISTORICAL FINANCIALS

Company Type: Public

Income Statement

FYE: December 31

	ASSETS ($ mil.)	NET INCOME ($ mil.)	INCOME AS % OF ASSETS	EMPLOYEES
12/19	5,246	66	1.3%	839
12/18	4,246	53	1.3%	716
12/17	3,964	33	0.8%	701
12/16	3,141	23	0.8%	665
12/15	2,652	20	0.8%	558
Annual Growth	18.6%	34.1%	—	10.7%

2019 Year-End Financials

Debt ratio: 1.07%
Return on equity: 11.59%
Cash ($ mil.): 107
Current ratio: —
Long-term debt ($ mil.): —

No. of shares (mil.): 44
Dividends
Yield: 2.3%
Payout: 30.3%
Market value ($ mil.): 855

	STOCK PRICE ($) FY Close	P/E High/Low		PER SHARE ($) Earnings	Dividends	Book Value
12/19	19.00	13	10	1.53	0.44	14.59
12/18	15.78	24	11	1.38	0.39	12.82
12/17	27.80	30	26	0.95	0.32	11.94
12/16	28.00	40	26	0.79	0.27	10.25
12/15	27.96	33	26	0.84	0.25	9.93
Annual Growth	(9.2%)	—	—	16.2%	14.8%	10.1%

Hormel Foods Corp.

The maker of such thrifty pantry staples as SPAM lunch meat and Dinty Moore stew Hormel Foods produces a slew of refrigerated processed meats and deli items ethnic entrees and frozen foods sold under the flagship Hormel brand as well as Don Miguel and MegaMex (Mexican) and Lloyd's (barbeque). Food service offerings include Hormel Natural Choice meats Café H Austin Blues and Bread Ready pre-sliced meats. Hormel is also a major US turkey and pork processor churning out Jennie-O turkey Cure 81 hams and Always Tender pork. More than 40 Hormel brands are ranked #1 or #2 in their respective markets. Vast majority of its total sales were from domestic operations.

HISTORY

George Hormel opened his Austin Minnesota slaughterhouse in an abandoned creamery in 1891. By 1900 Hormel had modernized his facilities to compete with larger meat processors. In 1903 the enterprise introduced its first brand name (Dairy Brand) and a year later began opening distribution centers nationwide. The scandal that ensued after the discovery in 1921 that an assistant controller had embezzled over $1 million almost broke the company causing Hormel to initiate tighter controls. By 1924 it was processing more than a million hogs annually. Hormel introduced canned ham two years later.

Jay Hormel George's son became president in 1929; under his guidance Hormel introduced Dinty Moore beef stew (1936) and SPAM (1937). A Hormel executive won a contest and $100 by submitting the name a contraction of "spiced ham." During WWII the US government bought over half of Hormel's output; it supplied SPAM to GIs and Allied forces.

In 1959 Hormel introduced its Little Sizzlers pork sausage and sold its billionth can of SPAM. New products rolled out in the 1960s included Hormel's Cure 81 ham (1963). By the mid-1970s the firm had more than 750 products.

The company survived a violent nationally publicized strike triggered by a pay cut in 1985. In the end only 500 of the original 1500 strikers returned to accept lower pay scales.

Sensing the consumer shift toward poultry Hormel purchased Jennie-O Foods in 1986. Later acquisitions included the House of Tsang and Oriental Deli (1992) Dubuque (processed pork 1993) and Herb-Ox (bouillon and dry soup mix 1993). After more than a century as Geo. A. Hormel & Co. the company began calling itself Hormel Foods in 1993 to reflect its expansion into non-pork foods. Former General Foods executive Joel Johnson was named president and CEO that year (and chairman two years later).

Hormel proved it could take a joke with the 1994 debut of its tongue-in-cheek SPAM catalog featuring dozens of SPAM-related products. But when a 1996 Muppets movie featured a porcine character named Spa'am Hormel sued Jim Henson Productions; a federal court gave Spa'am the go-ahead.

Also in 1996 Hormel teamed up with Mexican food processor Grupo Herdez to sell Herdez sauces and other Mexican food products in the US. It then formed a joint venture with Indian food producer Patak Spices (UK) to market its products in the US. Late that year Hormel paid $64 million for a 21% interest in Spanish food maker Campofrio Alimentacion.

Earnings fell in 1996 due in part to soaring hog prices. The company was hit hard again in 1998 when production contracts with hog growers meant it wound up paying premium rates despite a market glut. In 1998 the Smithsonian Institution accepted two cans of SPAM (one from 1937 the other an updated 1997 version) for its History of Technology collection.

SPAM sales soared in 1999 as nervous consumers stockpiled provisions for the millennium. To build its growing HealthLabs division Hormel acquired Cliffdale Farms (2000) and Diamond Crystal Brands nutritional products (a division of Imperial Sugar) in 2001 — boosting its share of the market for easy-to-swallow foods sold to hospitals and nursing homes.

In early 2001 Hormel acquired family-owned The Turkey Store for approximately $334 million and folded it into its Jennie-O division.

Hormel produced its 6 billionth can of SPAM in 2002 and traded $115 million in stock to acquire the rest of Imperial Sugar's Diamond Crystal Brands unit which packages single-serve packets of sugar sweeteners seasonings and plastic cutlery for the foodservice industry.

To further diversify in 2003 Hormel acquired food manufacturer Century Foods International (whey-based protein powders beverages and nutrition bars) and added it to its burgeoning specialty foods group. In 2004 Hormel sold off its stake in Campofrio to Smithfield Foods.

Its last act of business in 2004 was to purchase Southern California's Clougherty Packing for about $186 million. The pork processor's facilities help extend Hormel's capacity for further-processed foods in the southwestern US.

In 2005 the company purchased Mexican food manufacturer Arriba Foods for $47 million in cash. Later that year it bought Lloyd's Barbecue Company from General Mills.

Responding to the growing trend of the US population to dine out Hormel expanded its foodservice segment (which it refers to as its specialty foods business) with the 2005 purchase of foodservice food manufacturer and distributor Mark-Lynn Foods. Mark-Lynn's products include salt and pepper packets ketchup mustard sauces and salad dressings creamers and sugar packets as well as jellies desserts and drink mixes.

Adding to its grocery product offerings in 2006 the company acquired canned ready-to-eat chicken producer Valley Fresh Foods for $78 million. It also bought pepperoni and pasta maker Provena Foods and sausage and sliced meat maker Saag's Products. It added another to its list of countries in which it has joint ventures in 2006 when it formed a JV with San Miguel to raise and market hogs and animal feed in Vietnam. The JV is 49%-owned by Hormel.

Hormel acquired Burke Corporation a maker of pizza toppings and other fully cooked meat items in 2007 for $115 million in cash. The acquisition allowed Hormel to extend its pizza-topping operations into the foodservice sector. The following year it acquired Boca Grande Foods for $23.5 in cash. Boca Grande makes Poco Pac branded jams jellies and pancake syrup portion-control products for foodservice operators.

EXECUTIVES

Vice President For Specialty Foods, Michael Tolbert
Vice President Legislative Affairs, Joe Swedberg
Vice President Marketing For Foodservice Group, David F Weber
Evp And President Hormel Business Units, Steven G. Binder, age 63, $500,965 total compensation
Group Vp And President Hormel Foods International, Larry L. Vorpahl, age 57

Vp And Chief Accounting Officer, James N. Sheehan, age 65
Group Vp Refrigerated Foods, Thomas R. Day, age 62, $337,900 total compensation
Svp Supply Chain, Bryan D. Farnsworth, age 63
Group Vp And President Consumer Products Sales, Deanna T. Brady, age 55
Vp Wal-mart Sales, Donald H. (Don) Kremin, age 60
Director Purchasing, James P. Snee, age 52, $509,595 total compensation
Group Vp And President Jennie-o Turkey Store, Glenn R. Leitch, age 59, $380,500 total compensation
Group Vp Foodservice, Jeffrey R. Baker, age 55
Group Vp Grocery Products, Luis G. Marconi, age 53
Vp Information Technology Services, Mark D. Vaupel
Vice President Business Planning, Mike Gyarmaty
Vice President, Alan Rasell
Vice President, Brett Asleson
National Sales Manager, Jeff Schultz
National Sales Manager, Mark Engelhardt
National Sales Manager, Michael Dougherty
Vice President Of Sales In The Consumer Products Sales Division, Kurt Mueller
Vice President Consumer Insights And Corporate Innovation, Scott Aakre
Vp And Controller, Jana Haynes
Vp Operations Production Mfg, Jeffrey A Nuytten
Vp And Svp Sales Consumer Product Sales, Patrick Schwab
Vice President And Senior Vice President Sales And Consumer Product Sales, Erinn Mueller
Vp Treasurer, Rollie Gentzler
Vice President Supply Chain, Bill Snyder
Svp. Human Resources, Janet Hogan
Senior Vice President Marketing Cytosport Inc., Karen Wiernik
Vp Operations Grocery Products, Timothy Fritz
Senior Vice President Retail Business Unit Jennie O Turkey Store Llc, Barry Lynch
Svp Corporate Staff Retiring As Svp Corporate Staf, James Jorgenson
Vice President, Joel Johnson
National Account Manager, Mose Munro
Board Member, Dakota Pippins
Vice President Finance And Treasurer, Gary Jamison
Board Member, Terrell Crews
Auditors: Ernst & Young LLP

LOCATIONS

HQ: Hormel Foods Corp.
1 Hormel Place, Austin, MN 55912-3680
Phone: 507 437-5611   **Fax:** 507 437-5489
Web: www.hormel.com

2018 sales

	$ mil.	% of total
US	8	94
Foreign	588	6
Total	**9,545**	**100**

PRODUCTS/OPERATIONS

2018 sales

	$ mil.	% of total
Refrigerated Foods	4,771	50
Grocery Products	2,522	26
Jennie-O Turkey Store	1,627	17
International & Other	624	7
Total	**9,545**	**100**

Selected Products and Brands

Refrigerated
  Country Crock Side Dishes
  Hormel
  Hormel Always Tender flavored pork and beef products
  Hormel Black Label and Microwave Ready bacon
  Hormel Cure 81 ham
  Hormel Fresh Pantry meats

Hormel Little Sizzlers pork sausage
Hormel Natural Choice meats
Hormel pepperoni minis and stix
Hormel refrigerated entrees
Hormel Wranglers franks
Hormel Snac Cups
Lloyd's Barbeque products
Saag's sausages
Jennie-O Turkey Store
  Bratwursts and breakfast/dinner sausages
  Breast meat products
  Deli
  Di Lusso deli meats
  Farmer John deli meats
  Hormel 100 percent natural deli meats
  Hormel Deli beef dry sausage ham and turkey
  Hormel party trays
  Ground turkey
  Marinated turkey tenderloins
  So-Easy Entrees
  Turkey burger patties and franks
  Whole turkeys
Grocery products
  Dinty Moore stew Hearty Meals varieties microwave-ready products
  Herb-Ox bouillon
  Herdez Salsa
  Hormel
  Hormel bacon toppings
  Hormel Chili Master
  Hormel chunk meats
  Hormel Compleats microwave meals
  Hormel corned beef and roast beef with gravy
  Hormel dried beef
  Hormel Kid's Kitchen microwave cups
  Hormel Mary Kitchen hash
  Hormel microwave cups
  Not-So-Sloppy-Joe sloppy joe sauce
  Skippy peanut butter
  SPAM products (classic hickory smoke flavored hot and spicy lite low-sodium spread singles and oven-roasted turkey)
  Stagg chili
  Valley Fresh chunk meats and broths
Specialty Foods
  Century Foods International (dairy and vegetable proteins nutraceuticals)
  Diamond Crystal Brands (salts sugar substitutes)
  Hormel Foods Ingredients (sauces powders broths oils Omega-3 additives)
  Private Label products (canned meats prepared foods and desserts bouillon sweeteners salts seasonings)
Other
  MegaMex Mexican brands
  Bufalo hot sauces
  CHI-CHI'S Mexican hot sauces taco tubs dips seasoning mixes and tortillas
  Do Â Â a Marí;a Authentic Mexican products
  Don Miguel burritos appetizers empanadas taquitos tacos flautas chimichangas enchiladas
  El Torito sauces dressings and corn cakes
  Embasa Mexican peppers salsas
  Herdez imported salsas
  La Victoria Mexican salsas taco sauces enchilada sauces green chile peppers
  Wholly Guacamole
  World Food ethnic brands
  House of Tsang entrees sauces and oils
  Marrakesh Express Mediterranean products (couscous risotto)
  Peloponnese Greek foods olives

Selected Foodservice Brands

Always Tender Pork
Austin Blues barbeque meats
Authentic Barbeque
Bread Ready pre-sliced meats
Café; H ethnic meats
Cure 81 Ham
Dry Sausage
Fast 'N Easy Fully Cooked Meats
Hormel Chili
Masterpieces Toppings
Natural Choice meats
Old Smokehouse bacon
Old Tyme breakfast sausage
Old Tyme ham
Special Recipe Sausage
Stagg Chili

COMPETITORS

B&G Foods	H. J. Heinz Limited
Boar's Head	JBS USA
Bob Evans	Perdue Incorporated
Bridgford Foods	Pilgrim's Pride
Bush Brothers	Pinnacle Foods
Butterball	Plainville Farms
Campbell Soup	Sanderson Farms
Cargill	Seaboard
ConAgra	Smithfield Foods
Cooper Farms	The Dial Corporation
Foster Farms	Tyson Foods
General Mills	

HISTORICAL FINANCIALS

Company Type: Public

Income Statement

FYE: October 25

	REVENUE ($ mil.)	NET INCOME ($ mil.)	NET PROFIT MARGIN	EMPLOYEES
10/20	9,608	908	9.5%	19,100
10/19	9,497	978	10.3%	18,800
10/18	9,545	1,012	10.6%	20,100
10/17	9,167	846	9.2%	20,200
10/16	9,523	890	9.3%	21,100
Annual Growth	0.2%	0.5%	—	(2.5%)

2020 Year-End Financials

Debt ratio: 13.16%
Return on equity: 14.75%
Cash ($ mil.): 1,714
Current ratio: 2.38
Long-term debt ($ mil.): 1,044

No. of shares (mil.): 539
Dividends
  Yield: 0.0%
  Payout: 56.0%
Market value ($ mil.): 26,784

	STOCK PRICE ($) FY Close	P/E High/Low		PER SHARE ($) Earnings	Dividends	Book Value
10/20	49.61	31	24	1.66	0.93	11.90
10/19	40.57	25	21	1.80	0.84	11.08
10/18	41.17	22	16	1.86	0.75	10.49
10/17	30.38	24	19	1.57	0.68	9.34
10/16	38.22	49	20	1.64	0.58	8.42
Annual Growth	6.7%	—		0.3%	12.5%	9.0%

Horton (DR) Inc

The largest US homebuilder by volume D.R. Horton constructs single-family homes that range in size from 1000 sq. ft. to more than 4000 sq. ft. and sell for an average price of about $300000 under the D.R. Horton Emerald Homes Express Homes and Freedom Homes brand names. Texas-based D.R. Horton is active in about 90 markets in nearly 30 states and generates about 75% of its revenue from the Southeast South Central and Western regions of the US. Beyond single-family detached homes which account for nearly 90% of sales D.R. Horton builds duplexes townhomes and condominiums. It also provides mortgage title and closing services through its DHI Mortgage subsidiary

Operations

The primary activity of D.R. Horton is acquiring land developing infrastructure on the land (utilities roads) and building residential homes. Its homes range in size from 1000 square feet to more than 4000 square feet and in price from $100000 to more than $1 million. The builder sells approximately 57000 homes in a year.

The company's homebuilding operations are its core business generating around 95% of consoli-

dated revenue. Those operations generate nearly all of their revenue from the sale of completed homes; land and lots provides less than 1% of the division's sales. Around 90% of home revenue is generated from the sale of single-family detached homes with the remainder from the sale of attached homes — including townhomes duplexes and triplexes.

Through its DHI Mortgage subsidiary D.R. Horton provides mortgages which it generally sells to third parties. Financial services provide less than 5% of the company's revenue. The company also conducts insurance-related operations constructs and owns income-producing rental properties owns non-residential real estate including ranch land and improvements and owns and operates oil and gas-related assets.

Geographic Reach

Arlington TX-based D.R. Horton is active in approximately 30 states. The company generates about 30% of its sales in the Southeast (Alabama Florida Georgia Mississippi and Tennessee) about 25% in the South Central US (Louisiana Oklahoma and Texas) and roughly 20% in the West (California Hawaii Nevada Oregon Utah and Washington). Eastern states (Delaware Georgia Maryland New Jersey North Carolina Pennsylvania South Carolina and Virginia) provide more than 10% of sales and the Midwest (Colorado Illinois Indiana and Minnesota) and Southwest (Arizona and New Mexico) regions together produce about 10%.

Sales and Marketing

The builder markets and sells its homes under the D. R. Horton Emerald Homes Express Homes and Freedom Homes brand names. Homes marketed under the D.R. Horton brand represent around 60% of closings and home sales revenue. About 35% of the company's closings are conducted under its Express Homes brand (which also provides about 30% of home sales revenue).

D.R. Horton-branded communities are focused mostly on first-time and first-time move-up buyers. The Express Homes brand primarily courts entry-level buyers concerned with affordability. The Emerald Homes brand focuses on higher-end move-up and luxury homes. The company's Freedom Homes brand offers homes at affordable prices to active adult buyers seeking a low-maintenance lifestyle.

D.R. Horton markets and sells homes mostly through commissioned employees and independent real estate brokers. It also markets through digital and print media billboards radio television magazine and newspapers.

D.R. Horton advertising expenses was $47.0 million $44.1 million and $45.4 million in fiscal 2019 2018 and 2017 respectively.

Financial Performance

D.R. Horton has enjoyed growing revenue and higher profits over the past several years thanks to a strengthening housing market. The company has seen its revenue increased by 63% since fiscal 2015 while net income grew by about 116 % and its cash stores added some 8%. It also skimmed 2% off its long-term debt in that time.

In 2019 revenue rose to $17.6 billion 9% higher than 2018 on increased home sales. Its financial services albeit a small portion of overall revenue posted an 18% increase in sales generating about $441.7 million.

The rise in sales along with decrease in income tax expense boosted net income 11% to $1.6 billion.

Cash on hand at the end of 2019 was $1.5 billion up $8 million from the prior year. Operating activities contributed $892.1 million and investments used $394 million. The company spent $490.1 million on financings.

Strategy

D.R. Horton's ability to weather the Great Recession (2008-2009) — which hit homebuilders especially — allowed it to make long-term investments that are now paying off. As the US economy continues its multi-year growth trend the housing market continues to climb upward creating a welcome tailwind for D.R. Horton.

In recent years it has focused on expanding its product offerings to more consistently include a broad range of homes for entry-level move-up and luxury buyers across most of its geographic markets. Its entry-level homes have experienced strong demand from homebuyers as the entry-level segment of the new home market remains underserved with low inventory levels relative to demand.

The company's operating strategy focuses on enhancing long-term value to their shareholders by leveraging their financial and competitive position in their core homebuilding business to increase the returns on their inventory investments and generate strong profitability and cash flows while managing risk and maintaining financial flexibility to make opportunistic strategic investments

Company Background

Donald R. Horton was selling homes in Fort Worth Texas when he hit upon a strategy for increasing sales — add options to a basic floor plan. In 1978 he borrowed $33000 to build his first home added a bay window for an additional charge and sold the home for $44000. Donald soon added floor plans and options that appealed to regional preferences.

By 1991 Horton and his family owned more than 25 companies that were combined as D.R. Horton which went public in 1992.

HISTORY

Donald R. Horton was selling homes in Fort Worth Texas when he hit upon a strategy for increasing sales — add options to a basic floor plan. In 1978 he borrowed $33000 to build his first home added a bay window for an additional charge and sold the home for $44000. Donald soon added floor plans and options that appealed to regional preferences.

The depressed Texas market drove the company to expand beyond the Dallas/Fort Worth area in 1987 when it entered the then-hot Phoenix market. It continued to expand into the Southeast Mid-Atlantic Midwest and West in the late 1980s and early 1990s. By 1991 Horton and his family owned more than 25 companies that were combined as D.R. Horton which went public in 1992.

D.R. Horton acquired six geographically diverse construction firms in 1994 and 1995. In 1996 the company started a mortgage services joint venture expanded its title operations and added three more firms.

In 1998 the company bought four builders including Scottsdale Arizona-based Continental Homes. Continental had been expanding beyond its Arizona and Southern California base and had entered the lucrative retirement community market. After the Continental purchase Donald Horton stepped down as president remaining chairman. Richard Beckwitt took over as president and Donald Tomnitz became CEO. In 1999 the company acquired Century Title and Midwest builder Cambridge Properties.

D.R. Horton sold its St. Louis assets to McBride & Son Enterprises in 2000 after spending five years trying to break into the St. Louis homebuilding market. Tomnitz also took over the duties of president in 2000 when Beckwitt retired.

D.R. Horton gained homebuilding operations in Houston and Phoenix when it bought Emerald Builders in 2001. In February 2002 the company acquired Schuler Homes for $1.2 billion including debt.

Sales continued to climb in fiscal 2003 and 2004. D.R. Horton experienced its 27th consecutive year of earnings and revenue growth in 2004 and broke records by being the first residential homebuilder to sell more than 45000 homes in the US in a fiscal year; in fiscal 2005 the company closed 51172 homes. By 2007 however it was evident that the heady days were over with a rise in cancellations and a larger value of backlog orders.

CEO Donald Tomnitz summed up the housing market crash when he said "I don't want to be too sophisticated here but '07 is going to suck all 12 months of the calendar year." Indeed the company suffered a loss that year and the next when sales orders declined and cancellation rates rose due to tightened mortgage markets and severe liquidity shortages. Adding to homebuilders' difficulties an influx of foreclosed homes on the market brought down the demand for new homes.

D.R. Horton responded to the downturn in 2008 by reducing land and housing inventory controlling construction and inventory costs and using its cash to reduce debt. Despite drops in many markets D.R. Horton saw improvements in its eastern market where home affordability and employment led to a higher demand for new homes.

EXECUTIVES

President West Region, J. Matt Farris
Evp And Cfo, William W. (Bill) Wheat, age 54, $500,000 total compensation
President Financial Services, Randall C. (Randy) Present
Vp And Cio, Rick Rawlings
President Central Region, Rick Horton
President Southeast Region, David V. Auld, age 63, $700,000 total compensation
Svp Busienss Development, Michael Murray, $500,000 total compensation
President East Region, Tom Hill
President North Region, Doug Brown
President Florida Region, Paul Romanowski
Vice President And Division Counsel, Carolyn Mitchell
Assistant Vice President And Environmental Manager, Edward Perez
Vice President Human Resources, Paula Hunter-perkins
Vice President Of Construction, David Gude
Chairman, Donald R. Horton, age 70
Auditors: Ernst & Young LLP

LOCATIONS

HQ: Horton (DR) Inc
   1341 Horton Circle, Arlington, TX 76011
Phone: 817 390-8200
Web: www.drhorton.com

2018 Homebuilding Sales by Region

	% of total
West	24
South central	24
Southeast	33
East	12
Midwest	5
Southwest	4
Total	**100**

PRODUCTS/OPERATIONS

2018 Homebuilding Sales by Region

	% of total
West	24
South Central	24
Southeast	29
East	12
Midwest	6
Southwest	5
Total	**100**

2018 Sales by Service

	$ mil.	% of total
Home building		
Home sales	15502.0	96
Land/lot sales	121	1
Financial services	375	2
Forestar	109	1
Eliminations	(39.1)	-
Other adjustments	(1.2)	-
Total	**16,068**	**100**

COMPETITORS

Beazer Homes	Meritage Homes
David Weekley Homes	NVR
Hovnanian Enterprises	PulteGroup
KB Home	TRI Pointe
Lennar	Taylor Morrison
M.D.C.	Toll Brothers
M/I Homes	William Lyon Homes

HISTORICAL FINANCIALS

Company Type: Public

Income Statement

FYE: September 30

	REVENUE ($ mil.)	NET INCOME ($ mil.)	NET PROFIT MARGIN	EMPLOYEES
09/20	20,311	2,373	11.7%	9,716
09/19	17,592	1,618	9.2%	8,916
09/18	16,068	1,460	9.1%	8,437
09/17	14,091	1,038	7.4%	7,735
09/16	12,157	886	7.3%	6,976
Annual Growth	13.7%	27.9%	—	8.6%

2020 Year-End Financials

Debt ratio: 22.65%
Return on equity: 21.66%
Cash ($ mil.): 3,018
Current ratio: 8.35
Long-term debt ($ mil.): 4,283

No. of shares (mil.): 364
Dividends
   Yield: 0.9%
   Payout: 12.6%
Market value ($ mil.): 27,529

	STOCK PRICE ($) FY Close	P/E High/Low		PER SHARE ($) Earnings	Dividends	Book Value
09/20	75.63	12	4	6.41	0.70	32.53
09/19	52.71	12	8	4.29	0.60	27.20
09/18	42.18	14	10	3.81	0.50	23.88
09/17	39.93	14	10	2.74	0.40	20.66
09/16	30.20	14	10	2.36	0.32	18.21
Annual Growth	25.8%		—	28.4%	21.6%	15.6%

Howard Bancorp Inc

EXECUTIVES

Chb-Ceo, Mary Ann Scully
Exec V Pres-Cfo-Treas, George C Coffman
Exec V Pres-SEC, Charles E Schwabe
Evp-Cfo, Robert L Carpenter Jr
Coo, Robert D Kunisch Jr
Loan Assistant, Ariel Helm
Underwriter, Brandi Abel

Underwriter, Kathy Diperna
Vice President, Marc Czosnowski
Relationship Administrator, Toni Carlson
Svp, Erica Starr
Auditors: Dixon Hughes Goodman LLP

LOCATIONS

HQ: Howard Bancorp Inc
3301 Boston Street, Baltimore, MD 21224
Phone: 410 750-0020
Web: www.howardbank.com

HISTORICAL FINANCIALS

Company Type: Public

Income Statement

FYE: December 31

	ASSETS ($ mil.)	NET INCOME ($ mil.)	INCOME AS % OF ASSETS	EMPLOYEES
12/19	2,374	16	0.7%	307
12/18	2,266	(3)	—	337
12/17	1,149	7	0.6%	306
12/16	1,026	5	0.5%	300
12/15	946	1	0.1%	257
Annual Growth	25.8%	96.1%	—	4.5%

2019 Year-End Financials

Debt ratio: 3.51%
Return on equity: 5.55%
Cash ($ mil.): 109
Current ratio: —
Long-term debt ($ mil.): —
No. of shares (mil.): 19
Dividends
Yield: —
Payout: —
Market value ($ mil.): 322

	STOCK PRICE ($) FY Close	P/E High/Low	PER SHARE ($) Earnings	Dividends	Book Value
12/19	16.88	20 14	0.89	0.00	16.48
12/18	14.30	— —	(0.22)	0.00	15.48
12/17	22.00	31 20	0.75	0.00	13.47
12/16	15.10	20 16	0.73	0.00	12.27
12/15	13.24	94 69	0.16	0.00	13.34
Annual Growth	6.3%	— —	53.6%	—	5.4%

Howmet Aerospace Inc

Formerly known as Arconic Inc the company is now renamed as Howmet Aerospace Inc. a global leader in lightweight metals engineering and manufacturing – primarily made multi-material products which include aluminum titanium and nickel – can help you fly drive build and generate power. Created in 2016 when it was spun off from the aluminum giant Alcoa Howmet has retained the parts businesses of its predecessor?engineered products like fastening systems or castings; and global rolled products like aluminum sheets and plates. With operations in some 20 countries Howmet is a top provider of specialty materials to the aerospace commercial transportation automotive defense building and construction oil & gas and packaging industries. It generates about two-third of its revenue in the US.

HISTORY

In 1886 two chemists one in France and one in the US simultaneously discovered an inexpensive process for aluminum production. The American Charles Hall pursued commercial applications. Two years later with an investor group led by Captain Alfred Hunt Hall formed the Pittsburgh Re-

duction Company. Its first salesman Arthur Davis secured an initial order for 2000 cooking pots.

In 1889 the Mellon Bank loaned the company $4000. In 1891 the firm recapitalized with the Mellon family holding 12% of the stock.

Davis led the business after Hunt died in 1899 and stayed on until 1957 (he died in 1962 at age 95). The company introduced aluminum foil (1910) and found applications for aluminum in new products such as airplanes and cars. It became the Aluminum Company of America in 1907.

By the end of WWI Alcoa had integrated backward into bauxite mining and forward into end-use production. By the 1920s the Mellons had raised their stake to 33%.

The government and Alcoa had debated antitrust issues in court for years since the smelting patent expired in 1912. Finally a 1946 federal ruling forced the company to sell many operations built during WWII as well as its Canadian subsidiary (Alcan).

In the competitive aluminum industry of the 1960s Alcoa's lower-cost production helped it seize market share especially in beverage cans. In the 1970s Alcoa began offering engineered products such as aerospace components and in the 1980s it invested in research acquisitions and plant modernization.

Paul O'Neill (former president of International Paper) arrived as CEO in 1987 and shifted the company's focus back to aluminum. Sales and earnings set records the next two years but plunged afterward reflecting a weak global economy and record-low aluminum prices. Then the fall of the Soviet Union in the early 1990s led to a worldwide glut as Russian exports soared.

In 1994 Alcoa cut its production as part of a two-year accord with Western and Russian producers. That year the company agreed to pool its alumina and chemical operations with Australia's Western Mining Corp.

Alcoa formed a joint venture with Shanghai Aluminum Fabrication Plant in China. The company expanded in Europe in 1996 acquiring Italy's state-run aluminum business followed by the purchase of Inespal Spain's state-run aluminum operations in 1998. Alcoa also bought #3 US aluminum producer Alumax for $3.8 billion in 1998 but only after divesting its cast-plate operations.

Known by the nickname "Alcoa" since the late 1920s the company adopted that as its official name in 1999. O'Neill retired as CEO in 1999; COO Alain Belda succeeded him. Later that year Alcoa bought the 50% of aluminum auto parts maker A-CMI that it did not already own from Hayes Lemmerz International.

In 2000 Alcoa bought aluminum extrusion maker Excel Extrusions from Noranda (now called Falconbridge) and paid $4.5 billion for Reynolds Metals after agreeing to divest some assets — including all of Reynolds' alumina refineries — to satisfy regulators. The same month Alcoa acquired Cordant Technologies. Alcoa also assumed Cordant's 85% ownership of Howmet International (castings) as a result of the transaction — and later acquired the remainder of Howmet. Late in 2000 President-elect George W. Bush named Alcoa's chairman Paul O'Neill to be treasury secretary. (O'Neill subsequently resigned the post in December 2002.)

Alcoa sold its majority stake in the Worsley alumina refinery (Australia) to BHP Billiton in 2001 for about $1.5 billion as part of its refinery divestments. Treasury Secretary O'Neill completed the sale of his more than $90 million worth of Alcoa stock and options in June. In late November Alcoa and BHP Billiton combined their North American metals distribution businesses to create Integris Metals — a joint venture with revenues of about

$1.5 billion. (The two subsequently sold the JV to Ryerson in 2005.)

In 2013 Alcoa and Russia's VSMPO-AVISMA the world?s largest manufacturer of titanium ingots and forged products agreed to join forces to meet growing demand for high-end titanium and aluminum products for aircraft manufacturers worldwide. The joint venture combines Alcoa's expertise in manufacturing value-add products with VSMPO-AVISMA's leadership in titanium production to manufacture high-end aerospace goods such as landing gear and forged wing components at Alcoa's plant in Samara.

In 2013 Alcoa completed the expansion of aluminum lithium capacity at its Kitts Green facility in the UK to serve the growing demand for the company's 3rd-generation aluminum lithium alloys. Alcoa projects its aluminum lithium revenues will quadruple by 2020 to nearly $200 million.

In 2013 the company also announced a second major North American expansion to meet the growing demand for light durable and recyclable aluminum sheet for automotive production.

EXECUTIVES

Evp Corporate Development Strategy And New Ventures, Christoph Kollatz, age 59, $531,250 total compensation
Ceo And Director, Charles P. (Chip) Blankenship, age 54
President International Project Development And Asset Management, Kenneth (Ken) Wisnoski, age 65
Evp; Group President Alcoa Engineered Products And Solutions, Karl Tragl, age 58, $453,125 total compensation
Evp And Group President Alcoa Transportation And Construction Solutions, Tim D. Myers, age 54
President Arconic Global Rolled Products And Arconic Defense, Eric V. Roegner, age 51
Evp And Cto, Raymond J. (Ray) Kilmer
Evp And Cfo, Ken Giacobbe, $386,250 total compensation
Evp Human Resources And Environment Health Safety And Sustainability, Vas Nair, age 54
Evp Legal, Kate Ramundo
Vice President Finance, Jim Herring
Vice President Controller, Paul Myron
Vice President Compensation And Benefits, Brian Redmond
Vice President Strategy And Marketing, Raj Reddy
Executive Vice President Human Resources, Neil Marchuk
Vp Operations, Torben Kaese
Vice President Human Resources, Melissa Miller
Vice President Finance And Group Controller, Shelley Wheat
Chair, John C. Plant, age 67
Vice President Treasurer, Peter Hong
Chief Securities And Governance Counsel And Assistant Secretary, Margaret Lam
Auditors: PricewaterhouseCoopers LLP

LOCATIONS

HQ: Howmet Aerospace Inc
201 Isabella Street, Suite 200, Pittsburgh, PA 15212-5872
Phone: 412 553-1940
Web: www.howmet.com

2018 Sales

Country	$ mil.	% of total
United States	9,137	65
France	936	7
Hungary	823	6
United Kingdom	737	5
China	632	4
Russia	553	4
Germany	302	2
Brazil	214	2
Canada	285	2
Japan	170	1
Other	225	2
Total	**12,960**	**100**

PRODUCTS/OPERATIONS

2018 Sales by Segment

	$ mil.	% of total
Engineered Products and Solutions	6,316	44
Global Rolled Products	5,764	41
Transportation and construction Solutions	2,126	15
Eliminations of intersegment sales	(160)	-
Corporate	(32)	15
Total	**14,014**	**100**

2018 Sales by product

	$ mil.	% of total
Innovative products	5,588	40
Engines	2,940	21
Engineered structures	1,839	13
Fastening systems	1,531	11
Architectural aluminum systems	1,140	8
Aluminum wheels	969	7
Other	7	-
Total	**14**	**100**

Selected Products

Engineered Products and Solutions
  Arconic Engines
  Arconic Engineered Structures
  Arconic Fastening Systems
Global Rolled Products
  Aerospace and Automotive Products
  Brazing Commercial Transportation and Industrial Solutions
Transportation and Construction Solutions
  Building and Construction Systems
  Arconic Wheel and Transportation Products
Certified Reference Material
  Spectrochemical Reference Materials

COMPETITORS

Accuride
Aleris Corp.
Apogee Enterprises
Berkshire Hathaway
Constellium
Doncasters
Eramet
Kaiser Aluminum
Kobe Steel
Nippon Steel & Sumitomo Metal Corporation
Novelis

HISTORICAL FINANCIALS

Company Type: Public

Income Statement   FYE: December 31

	REVENUE ($ mil.)	NET INCOME ($ mil.)	NET PROFIT MARGIN	EMPLOYEES
12/19	14,192	470	3.3%	41,700
12/18	14,014	642	4.6%	43,000
12/17	12,960	(74)	—	41,500
12/16	12,394	(941)	—	41,500
12/15	22,534	(322)	—	60,000
Annual Growth	**(10.9%)**	**—**	**—**	**(8.7%)**

2019 Year-End Financials

Debt ratio: 33.79%
Return on equity: 9.23%
Cash ($ mil.): 1,648
Current ratio: 1.42
Long-term debt ($ mil.): 4,906

No. of shares (mil.): 432
Dividends
Yield: 0.3%
Payout: 11.6%
Market value ($ mil.): 13,319

	STOCK PRICE ($) FY Close	P/E High/Low	PER SHARE ($) Earnings	Dividends	Book Value
12/19	30.77	30 16	1.03	0.12	10.64
12/18	16.86	23 12	1.30	0.24	11.53
12/17	27.25	— —	(0.28)	0.24	10.20
12/16	18.54	— —	(2.31)	0.09	11.66
12/15	9.87	— —	(0.93)	0.00	27.58
Annual Growth	**32.9%**		**—**	**—**	**(21.2%)**

HP Inc

Just about every office — from home to big business — has two basic items: personal systems and printers. That's pretty much the business of HP Inc. one of two companies created from the breakup of Hewlett-Packard Co. in 2015. HP makes a full line of computing devices from desktops and laptops for commercial and consumer use to tablets and point-of-sale systems. Its printers include large format commercial printers and inkjet and laser printers as well as 3D printers. And don't forget printer supplies such as ink cartridges. HP is a leading PC maker. The company generates over a third of its revenue in the US.

Operations

HP reports its operations through three business segments: Personal Systems Printing and Corporate Investments.

Personal Systems makes and sells commercial PCs consumer PCs desktop notebook workstations thin clients commercial tablets and mobility devices retail point-of-sale systems displays and accessories software and support. The segment generates over two thirds of HP's revenue.

Printing produces consumer and commercial printers supplies media services as well as scanning devices. Over a third of the company's revenue rolls out of the unit.

Corporate Investments includes HP Labs and business incubation projects. As a research-oriented unit it contributes a negligible amount of revenue.

HP buys some components from other companies. That includes the laser printer engines and laser toner cartridges it obtains from Canon. Processors for the company's computers come from Intel and AMD and the machines runs on Microsoft software.

While the company operates some of its own manufacturing it outsources a significant portion of the work to third party companies

Geographic Reach

HP based in Palo Alto California gets about two-thirds of revenue from customers outside the US. The company has operations throughout the world with significant facilities in the Singapore Malaysia China India Sounth Korea Taiwan Spain and Israel as well its US operations. It has regional headquarters in Geneva Switzerland and Singapore.

Sales and Marketing

HP markets its products directly as well as through a wide range of third-party channels including retailers resellers and distributors and original equipment manufacturers and systems integrators.

The company's advertising expenses totaled approximately $652 million $568 million and $544 million in fiscal years 2019 2018 and 2017 respectively.

Financial Performance

The HP's revenue took a dip in 2016 compared to its revenue in 2015 but its increase in the last three years has made up for it. The company's revenue in 2016 decreased by a little over 6% compared to its revenue in 2015 however 2019 has almost 18% increase compared to its revenue in 2016.

HP has posted three years of higher revenue on rising sales of PCs and printers after the company's split with Hewlett Packard Enterprise in 2015.

The company's sales rose less than 1% to $58.8 billion in 2019 (ended November) compared from the previous year the increase was primarily driven by the growth in Notebooks Desktops and Workstation in Personal Systems partially offset by unfavorable foreign currency impacts and a decline in Printing Supplies. Personal Systems revenue increased 3% on higher sales of notebook and desktops computers which benefited from higher volume and prices. Printing revenue decreased to 4% driven by decline Supplies Consumer Hardware and unfavorable foreign currency impacts partially offset by an increase in Commercial Hardware revenue.

Despite the jump in sales HP's gross margin increase to 19% in 2019 compared to 18.2% in 2018 due to an increase in Personal Systems driven by lower supply chain costs.

HP's coffers held $4.5billion in cash and equivalents in 2019 compared to $5.2 billion in 2018. In 2019 operations generated $4.6 billion investing activities used $438 million and financing activities used $4.8 billion which used for the company's stock repurchase program.

Strategy

HP's strategy is focused on leveraging its existing portfolio of products and services to meet the demands of a continually changing technological landscape and to offset certain areas of industry decline.

HP found life as a PC-and-printer company refreshing in 2018. PC sales rose for the year and brought printer and printer supply sales with them spurred by strong cyclical demand for PCs a wave of upgrades to the Windows 10 operating system and the acquisition of the Samsung printer business.

The company has increased production of computers that convert back and forth to notebooks and tablets and released the Spectre Folio convertible in 2019. For the home market the company started selling the HP Tango which features combined voice-activated and app-based printing. In 3D printing HP introduced the Metal Jet platform which enables 3D mass production to metals manufacturing.

HP's Device-as-a-Service program in which is helps companies manage their PC and printing needs grew 50% year-to-year. The program uses data and analytics to help lower costs and improve efficiency for users.

While the company roosts at the top rungs of PC and printer sales HP faces stiff price and product competition from established competitors like Lenovo Acer and Dell Technologies as well as newcomers offering new technologies.

Mergers and Acquisitions

In late 2019 announced the acquisition of Bromium an end point security start-up. Bromium protects enterprises by using virtualization-based security to isolate browser-based attacks malicious downloads email attachments and other applications in unique hardware-enforced micro-virtual machines. Bromium technology complements and enhances HP's existing security platform with hardware enforced application isolation and containment to protect against advanced attacks while providing real-time threat intelligence.

In 2018 HP bought Apogee Corp. a UK-based printing company for about Â 380 million. The deal should help HP expand in managed print services leveraging Apogee's long-term contracts for providing printing and publishing services.

Company Background

HP is a successor to what could be considered the first Silicon Valley company.

Encouraged by Stanford professor Frederick Terman in 1938 engineers Bill Hewlett and David Packard started Hewlett-Packard (HP) in a garage in Palo Alto California with $538. Hewlett was the idea man while Packard served as manager; the two were so low-key that the company's first official meeting ended with no decision on exactly what to manufacture. Finding good people took priority over finding something to sell. The first product ended up being an audio oscillator. Walt Disney Studios one of HP's first customers bought eight to use in the making of Fantasia.

Hewlett-Packard grew into one of the top technology companies producing personal computers workstations printers and software that led their markets. The company's fortunes were tempered with the onslaught of the dot-com boom and competition from companies like Dell. In the early 2000s Hewlett-Packard bought Compaq a major PC competitor to strengthen it across the computer markets. But by 2015 Hewlett-Packard split into HP Inc. which concentrates on PCs and printers and Hewlett Packard Enterprise which focuses on hardware software and services for bigger companies.

EXECUTIVES

Chief Supply Chain Officer, Stuart C. Pann, age 61
Coo, Jon E. Flaxman, age 63, $700,027 total compensation
Svp; General Manager Graphics And Imaging Hp Imaging And Printing Group, Stephen (Steve) Nigro
Cto, Shane D. Wall, age 55
President Personal Systems Business, Ron Coughlin
Evp And Cfo, Catherine A. (Cathie) Lesjak, age 61, $850,033 total compensation
President Imaging And Printing Business, Enrique Lores, age 55
President Americas, Christoph Schell
President Asia Pacific And Japan (apj), Richard Bailey
President And Ceo, Dion J. Weisler, $1,200,046 total compensation
President Europe Middle East And Africa (emea), Nick Lazaridis
Chief Human Resources Officer, Tracy S. Keogh, $600,023 total compensation
Managing Director And General Manager Hp India, Sumeer Chandra
Vice President Big Data, Pankaj Dugar
Vice President Americas Channels And Alliances, Archie Miller
Vice President Human Resources, Kelly Parrish
Vice President And Associate General Counsel, Todd Sulger
National Account Manager, Jay Khaira
Senior Vice President Global Sales Best, Kelly Ducourty
Vice President Ecommerce, Suresh Subramanian
National Sales Manager, Spencer Wilson
Vice President Head Of Current Business Management Inkjet Printing Systems, Mark Quiroz
Vice President, Todd Gustafson
Vice President Of Mobility Pro, Keith Hartsfield
Vice President Education Printing And Personal Systems, Gus Schmedlen
Assistant Vice President Operations, Sushanto Das
Vp Inkjet Printing Americas, Emre Ozguc

Vice President, Santiago Morera
Assistant Vice President Loan Administration Associate, Thomas Persons
Vice President And General Manager Commercial Pc, Alex Cho
Vice President And General Manager Americas Solutions Business, David N Prezzano
Vp And Managing Director Hp Inc Africa, Elisabeth Moreno
Vice President Global Head Of Commercial Notebook Product Management, Bill Gorden
Vice President Marketing, Joseph Pacula
Senior Vice President Tax, Barbara Barton Weiszhaar
Senior Vice President, Schell Christoph
Chairman, Charles V. (Chip) Bergh, age 62
Board Member, Bethany Madrid
Board Member, Stacey Mobley
Board Member, Robert Bennett
Board Member, Stacy Brown-philpot
Auditors: Ernst & Young LLP

LOCATIONS

HQ: HP Inc
  1501 Page Mill Road, Palo Alto, CA 94304
Phone: 650 857-1501
Web: www.hp.com

2018 Sales

	$ mil.	% of total
US	20,602	35
Other countries	37,870	65
Total	**58,472**	**100**

PRODUCTS/OPERATIONS

2018 Sales

	$ mil.	% of total
Notebooks	22,547	39
Desktops	11,567	20
Workstations	2,246	4
Other	1,301	2
Supplies	13,575	23
Commercial Hardware	4,674	8
Consumer Hardware	2,556	4
Corporate Investments	5	
Other	1	
Total	**58,472**	**100**

2018 Sales

	$ mil.	% of total
Personal Systems	37,661	64
Printing	20,805	36
Corporate Investment	5	
Other	1	
Total	**58,472**	**100**

Selected Products and Services

Personal Systems
  Calculators
  Desktop PCs
  Digital entertainment centers
  DVD writers
  Handheld computers
  Notebook computers
  Televisions (LCD plasma)
  Workstations
Imaging and Printing
  Commercial printing
  Digital presses
  Printers
  Digital imaging
  Projectors
  Scanners
  Personal printing
  All-in-ones (copier fax printer scanner)
  Ink jet printers
  Laser printers
  Shared printing
  Networked inkjet laser and multifunction printers
  Office all-in-ones
  Services
  Supplies

COMPETITORS

ADP	Lexmark
ASUSTeK	NEC
Acer	Océ
Apple Inc.	Oki Electric
Brother Industries	Panasonic Corp
Canon	Ricoh Company
Dell	Samsung Electronics
Epson	Sharp Corp.
Fuji Xerox	Sony
Fujitsu	Toshiba
Hitachi	Unisys
Konica Minolta	Xerox
Lenovo	

HISTORICAL FINANCIALS

Company Type: Public

Income Statement   FYE: October 31

	REVENUE ($ mil.)	NET INCOME ($ mil.)	NET PROFIT MARGIN	EMPLOYEES
10/20	56,639	2,844	5.0%	53,000
10/19	58,756	3,152	5.4%	56,000
10/18	58,472	5,327	9.1%	55,000
10/17	52,056	2,526	4.9%	49,000
10/16	48,238	2,496	5.2%	49,000
Annual Growth	**4.1%**	**3.3%**	**—**	**2.0%**

2020 Year-End Financials

Debt ratio: 17.93%
Return on equity: —
Cash ($ mil.): 4,864
Current ratio: 0.79
Long-term debt ($ mil.): 5,543

No. of shares (mil.): 1,304
Dividends
  Yield: 0.0%
  Payout: 35.2%
Market value ($ mil.): 23,420

	STOCK PRICE ($) FY Close	P/E High/Low		PER SHARE ($) Earnings	Dividends	Book Value
10/20	17.96	12	7	2.00	0.70	(1.71)
10/19	17.37	12	8	2.07	0.64	(0.82)
10/18	24.14	8	6	3.26	0.56	(0.41)
10/17	21.55	15	10	1.48	0.53	(2.07)
10/16	14.49	11	6	1.43	0.50	(2.27)
Annual Growth	**5.5%**	**—**	**—**	**8.7%**	**9.2%**	**—**

HSBC USA, Inc.

HSBC USA a subsidiary of British banking behemoth HSBC Holdings operates HSBC Bank USA one of the largest foreign-owned banks in the country. Boasting $200 billion in assets and 230-plus branches across 10 US states (including 145 in New York making it one of the state's largest banks by branches) the bank offers personal commercial and mortgage banking services as well as wealth management investment banking private banking brokerage and trust services. Its largest markets are in New York California New Jersey and Florida. Roughly 75% of HSBC USA's loan portfolio is made up of commercial loans and around 70% of its total revenue comes from interest income.

Operations

The company operates four business segments: Retail Banking and Wealth Management (RBWM); Commercial Banking which serves small and multinational businesses in five hubs where 50% of US corporate imports and exports happen (California Florida Illinois New York and Texas); Global Banking and Markets which offers advisory services and trading services for major government corporate and institutional clients; and Private Bank which serves high net worth and ultra-high net worth individuals and their families particularly focusing on multi-generational families business owners and entrepreneurs.

About 75% of HSBC USA's $82.92 billion-loan portfolio was made up of commercial loans (including global banking business and corporate banking and construction and other real estate loans) at the end of 2015. The rest of its portfolio was made up of consumer loans especially residential mortgages with some home equity credit card and other loans.

The bank makes around 70% of its revenue from interest income. About 41% of its total revenue came from loan interest during 2015 while another 27% came from interest on securities trading securities and short-term investments. The rest of its revenue came from trust and investment management fees (3% of revenue) credit card fees (1%) trading revenue (1%) residential mortgage banking revenue (1%) other fees and commissions (15%) gains on securities at fair value (5%) and other miscellaneous sources.

Geographic Reach

HSBC USA serves customers nationwide with the highest concentration of its bank branches located in New York City Los Angeles San Francisco Chicago Atlanta Houston Seattle Miami and Washington DC. The company operates foreign branches and representative offices in the Caribbean Canada Latin America Europe and Asia.

Sales and Marketing

HSBC USA serves a variety of customers such as individuals (including high net worth individuals) small businesses corporations institutions and governments. It boasted 2.4 million customers at the end of 2015 30% of which live in New York and 29% in California.

The bank has been ramping up its advertising spend in recent years. It spent $60 million on advertising in 2015 up from $53 million and $43 million in 2014 and 2013 respectively.

Financial Performance

The US division of HSBC has been struggling to grow its revenue over the past several years as low interest rates have continued to eat away at its interest margins and as its non-interest revenues have been in decline. The bank has been recovering from losses in 2013 and 2012 caused by goodwill impairments and regulatory expenses.

HSBC USA's revenue turned a corner in 2015 jumping 11% to $5.17 billion during the year mostly thanks to higher interest income on 8% commercial loan asset growth and double-digit security asset growth.

Despite strong revenue growth in 2015 the company's net income fell 7% to $330 million mainly because its credit loss provisions increased by $173 million mostly as it made more commercial loans with exposure to the oil and gas industry. HSBC USA's operating cash levels dropped 22% to $4.65 billion for the year due to unfavorable working capital changes primarily related to changes in trading assets and liabilities.

Strategy

HSBC USA as part of the broader HSBC group aims to become the world's leading international bank and seeks to connected emerging economies with developed markets. The US division like parent HSBC also continued in 2016 to look for ways to cut operating costs to boost efficiency and overall profits.

In 2014 HSBC USA became one of the nation's first major banks to roll out a new fraud protection device which employs two-factor authentication for its personal Internet customers.

Company Background

HSBC and HSBC USA restructured their operations in 2011 which included divesting operations and cutting staff. As part of the restructuring HSBC sold 195 retail branches in New York and Connecticut to First Niagara for $1 billion. Through HSBC USA and its HSBC Finance affiliate HSBC also sold its card and retail services business to Capital One Financial. In 2010 HSBC USA exited its noncore wholesale banknotes business. The company also closed and consolidated about a dozen branches in Connecticut and New Jersey. The moves are part of the company's strategy to focus more on commercial and corporate banking in New York and other key urban markets itself part of HSBC's restructuring to create a leaner group.

EXECUTIVES

Chairman President And Ceo Hsbc North America Holdings Inc. And Hsbc Bank Usa, Patrick J. (Pat) Burke, age 58
Sevp And Cfo, Mark A. Zaeske
Sevp And Coo Usa, Vittorio M. Severino
Sevp And Head Of Global Banking And Markets Americas, Thierry Roland
Sevp And Head Of Strategy And Planning, Loren C. Klug, age 59
Evp And Head Of Private Banking Americas, Marlon Young, age 64, $389,423 total compensation
Sevp And Chief Risk Officer, Rhydian H. Cox
Sevp And Head Of Commercial Banking, Wyatt E Crowell
Evp And Head Of Human Resources Usa, Maureen A. Gillan-Myer
Evp And Head Of Regulatory Remediation, Stephen R. Nesbitt
Sevp And Chief Auditor, Richard E. O'Brien
Evp And Corporate Secretary, Karen Pisarczyk
Sevp And Head Of Retail Banking And Wealth Management, Pablo Sanchez
Sevp And General Counsel, Mark Steffensen
Evp And Chief Accounting Officer, William Tabaka
Auditors: PricewaterhouseCoopers LLP

LOCATIONS

HQ: HSBC USA, Inc.
452 Fifth Avenue, New York, NY 10018
Phone: 212 525-5000
Web: www.us.hsbc.com

PRODUCTS/OPERATIONS

2013 Sales

	$ mil.	% of total
Interest		
Loans	1,876	39
Securities	876	19
Other	227	4
Non-interest		
Other fees & commissions	706	14
Trading revenue	474	9
Servicing and other fees from HSBC affiliates	202	4
Other securities gains	202	4
Trust income	123	3
Other	150	4
Total	**4,836**	**100**

COMPETITORS

Astoria Financial	KeyCorp
Bank of America	M&T Bank
Capital One	New York Community
Citibank	Bancorp
Citizens Financial	PNC Financial
Group	TD Bank USA
JPMorgan Chase	Wells Fargo

HISTORICAL FINANCIALS

Company Type: Public

Income Statement

FYE: December 31

	ASSETS ($ mil.)	NET INCOME ($ mil.)	INCOME AS % OF ASSETS	EMPLOYEES
12/19	175,375	113	0.1%	4,828
12/18	172,448	320	0.2%	4,933
12/17	187,235	(179)	—	5,107
12/16	201,301	129	0.1%	6,114
12/15	188,278	330	0.2%	6,173
Annual Growth	(1.8%)	(23.5%)	—	(6.0%)

2019 Year-End Financials

Debt ratio: 14.65%	No. of shares (mil.): 0
Return on equity: 0.58%	Dividends
Cash ($ mil.): 32,234	Yield: —
Current ratio: —	Payout: —
Long-term debt ($ mil.): —	Market value ($ mil.): —

	STOCK PRICE ($) FY Close	P/E High/Low	PER SHARE ($) Earnings	Dividends	Book Value
12/19 25,568,627.00	0.00	— —	(0.00)	0.00	
Annual Growth					

Humana Inc.

Medicare has made Humana a big-time player in the insurance game. Humana is a Medicare Advantage HMO PPO and PFFS organization providing Medicare Advantage plans and prescription drug coverage to approximately 5 million members throughout the US. It also administers managed care plans for other government programs including Medicaid plans in Florida and Texas and TRICARE (for military personnel) in the South. Additionally Humana offers commercial health plans and specialty (life dental and vision) coverage; it also provides its members with access through their networks of health care providers such outpatient surgery centers primary care providers specialist physicians dentists and providers of ancillary health care services. All told it covers more than 20 million members in the US.

HISTORY

In 1961 Louisville Kentucky lawyers David Jones and Wendell Cherry bought a nursing home as a real estate investment. Within six years their company Extendicare was the largest nursing home chain in the US (with only eight homes).

Faced with a glutted nursing home market the partners noticed that hospitals received more money per patient per day than nursing homes so they took their company public in 1968 to finance hospital purchases (one per month from 1968 to 1971). The company then sold its 40 nursing homes. Sales rose 13 times over in the next five years and in 1973 the firm changed its name to Humana.

By 1975 Humana had built 27 hospitals in the South and Southwest. It targeted young privately insured patients and kept its charity caseload and bad-debt expenses low. Three years later #3 forprofit hospital operator Humana moved up a notch when it bought #2 American Medicorp.

In 1983 the government began reimbursing Medicare payments based on fixed rates. Counting on its high hospital occupancy in 1984 the company launched Humana Health Care Plans rewarding doctors and patients who used Humana hospitals. However hospital occupancy dropped and the company closed several clinics. When its net income fell 75% in 1986 the firm responded by lowering premiums to attract employers.

In 1991 co-founder Cherry died. With hospital profits down in 1993 Jones spun off Humana's 76 hospitals as Galen Healthcare which formed the nucleus of what is now HCA - The Healthcare Company. Humana used the cash to expand its HMO membership buying Group Health Association (an HMO serving metropolitan Washington DC) and CareNetwork (a Milwaukee HMO). The next year Humana added 1.3 million members when it bought EMPHESYS and the company's income which had stagnated since the salad days of the late 1980s and early 1990s seemed headed in the right direction.

In the mid-1990s cutthroat premiums failed to cover rising health care costs as members' hospital use soared out of control particularly in the company's new Washington DC market. Profits dropped 94% and Humana's already tense relationship with doctors and members worsened. President and COO Wayne Smith and CFO Roger Drury resigned as part of a management shake-up and newly appointed president Gregory Wolf offered to drop the company's gag clause after the Florida Physicians Association threatened to sue.

A reorganized Humana rebounded in 1997. The company pulled out of 13 unprofitable markets including Alabama (though it did not drop TRICARE its military health coverage program in that state) and Washington DC. Refocusing on core markets in the Midwest and Southeast Humana bought Physician Corp. of America (PCA) and ChoiceCare a Cincinnati HMO. Wolf replaced Jones as CEO in 1997.

To cut costs Humana agreed in 1998 to be bought by United HealthCare (now UnitedHealth Group). The deal was abandoned however when United HealthCare took a $900 million charge in advance of the purchase. Humana found savings by pruning its Medicare HMO business.

Humana did everything but party in 1999. The company faced RICO charges for allegedly overcharging members for co-insurance; it agreed to repay $15 million in Medicare overpayments to the government; and it became the first health insurance firm to be slapped with a class-action suit over its physician incentives and other coverage policies.

Humana sold PCA in 2000 saying that it had paid too much for the company; subsidiary PCA Property & Casualty was also sold marking the company's exit from the workers' compensation business. That year Humana also sold its underperforming Florida Medicaid HMO to Well Care HMO and agreed to pay more than $14 million to the government for submitting false Medicare payment information.

In 2001 Humana bought a unit of Anthem that provides health benefits to the military. Expanding its holdings in the southeast Humana acquired Louisiana's Ochsner Health Plan in 2004.

It further grew its product line with the 2007 acquisition of Atlanta-based CompBenefits a provider of dental and vision benefits to nearly 5 million members. The acquisition gave Humana a full-service vision offering and expanded its dental benefits operations. Later that year the company bought KMG America a life and health insurer and third-party administrator for more than 1 million members. Humana combined CompBenefits KMG America and its previous dental benefits operations into a new unit in 2008 called Humana Specialty Benefits.

In 2008 Humana acquired about 25000 Medicare Advantage members in Nevada from UnitedHealth which was divesting the operations as part of its merger deal with Sierra Health Services for $225 million. And later that year it acquired smaller Florida-based Medicare Advantage provider Metcare Health Plans from Metropolitan Health Networks.

Additional acquisitions include the 2008 acquisition of OSF HealthPlans an Illinois-based managed care company belonging to OSF Healthcare. The deal worth about $90 million gave Humana another 60000 commercial members as well as some new Medicare customers in Illinois. The company had already wrapped up its acquisition of Tennessee-based PHP Companies (which does business as Cariten Healthcare) from Covenant Health. Humana spent $250 million in late 2008 to gain Cariten's managed care operations in East Tennessee adding 70000 commercial customers and 45000 Medicare members.

One of Humana's competitive TRICARE contracts was awarded to another party in 2009; however after Humana objected and bids were re-evaluated the decision was reversed in 2011 (with no negative impact on the company's operations).

In 2010 Humana moved into an all new specialty business area with its acquisition of Concentra a provider of occupational medicine urgent care and wellness programs from Welsh Carson Anderson & Stowe for some $790 million. Humana made the purchase to bolster its consumer-focused initiatives and provide a platform for future service-offering expansion efforts.

To widen its cost-control services and advance its IT offerings Humana partnered with software firm Anvita Health in 2010. The analytics firm provided analytics capabilities to identify at-risk members and also served other insurers benefit managers health care professionals and electronic health record providers. (Humana wound up acquiring Anvita in late 2011.)

Early in 2012 Humana purchased MD Care a Medicare Advantage provider serving some 15000 members in four Southern California counties. It also acquired Arcadian Management Services a Medicare Advantage HMO with some 64000 members in 15 states including California. To complete its acquisition of Arcadian Humana was required to sell select Medicare Advantage plans serving some 12000 former Arcadian members to CIGNA (in Texas and Arkansas) and WellCare Health Plans (in Arizona).

EXECUTIVES

President And Ceo, Bruce D. Broussard, age 57, $1,235,446 total compensation

Svp And Chief Consumer Officer, Jody L. Bilney, age 58, $573,452 total compensation

Svp And Chief Medical Officer, Roy A. Beveridge, age 62

Svp And Cio, Brian P. LeClaire, age 59

Svp And Chief Human Resources Officer, Timothy S. (Tim) Huval, age 53, $573,453 total compensation

Svp And Cfo, Brian A. Kane, age 47, $636,254 total compensation

Svp And Chief Strategy Officer, Christopher H. (Chris) Hunter, age 51, $465,865 total compensation

President And Intermountain Region Market Leader Senior Products, Catherine Field

Market Vice President, Jordan Swanson

Vice President Information Technology, Michael Richmond

Medical Director, Arthur Tomases

Vice President Public Sector, Tim Snyder

Health Services Director, Yvonne Shell

Segment Vice President, John Delorimier

Medical Director, Earl Jackman

Medical Director, Teresita Hernandez

National Account Manager, Melissa Staton

Vice President Information Technology Transformation And Shared Services, Faheem Zuberi

Vice President, Gary Williams

Vice President National Contracting, Jason Lyvers

National Sales Manager Strategic Alliances, Lynn Pereira

Vice President Direct Marketing Services, Khursheed Zafar

Medical Director, Bryan Carr

Vice President Primary Care Operations, Kate Blackmon

Srvpnr Lan Operating Systems, Wes Johnson

Medical Director, Donn Perisee

Market Vice President Dfw And Houston Senior Products, Lesli C Young

Vice President Of Clinical Compliance, Meliss A Koellner

Medical Director, Rebecc Colon

Director Of Nursing Services, Jennifer Grottkau

Segment Vice President, Thoma P Klammer

Vice President, Kristin Martin

Medical Director, Cind M Dunn

National Sales Manager, Mallor Strange

Senior Vice President And Chief Consumer Officer, Jod Bilney

Medical Director, Cind Dunn

Vice President And Chief Medical Officer Integrated Care Delivery Metcare, Yogi Hernandez

Medical Director, Ann Vaughters

Medical Director, Allan Kogan

Regional Vice President, Peggy Taylor

Medical Director, Cristi Trecroce

Region Vice President Finance, Debbie Findlay

Vice President, Greg Mclaurim

Vp Sales, Corey Murphy

Enterprise Vice President Consumer Experience, Jon Kerekes

Chairman, Kurt J. Hilzinger, age 59

Board Member, Christopher Mitchell

Board Member, Jerry Valentine

Board Member, Marissa Peterson

Board Member, Adrienne F Jones

Secretary Treasurer, Jeff Fernandez

Board Member, David Jones

Board Member, Garry O'Brien

Board Member, Bobbi Mcdonald

Board Member, Alexis Nash

Vice Chairman Sales, John Wiesler

Auditors: PricewaterhouseCoopers LLP

LOCATIONS

HQ: Humana Inc.
500 West Main Street, Louisville, KY 40202
Phone: 502 580-1000
Web: www.humana.com

PRODUCTS/OPERATIONS

2018 Sales

	$ mil.	% of total
Premiums		
Individual Medicare Advantage	35,656	63
Group Medicare Advantage	6,103	11
Fully insured	5,962	10
Medicare stand-alone PDP	3,584	6
Specialty	1,359	2
Medicaid & other	2,277	4
Services	1,457	3
Investment income	514	1
Total	**56,912**	**100**

	$ mil.	% of total
Retail	48,255	60
Healthcare Services	23,811	30
Group and Specialty	7,679	10
Individual Commercial	8	—
Other Businesses	136	—
Adjustments	(22977)	—
Total	**56,912**	**100**

Selected Products and Services

Government
Medicaid managed care plans
Medicare Advantage plans
Medicare prescription drug plans
TRICARE (military personnel)

Commercial
Administrative services only (ASO)
HMO plans
HumanaOne (individual insurance)
POS (point-of-service) plans
PPO plans
Specialty products
Dental insurance
Life insurance
Short-term disability insurance

COMPETITORS

Aetna	Kaiser Foundation
Anthem	Health Plan
CIGNA	Molina Healthcare
HCSC	UnitedHealth Group
HealthSpring	WellCare Health Plans

HISTORICAL FINANCIALS

Company Type: Public

Income Statement

FYE: December 31

	ASSETS ($ mil.)	NET INCOME ($ mil.)	INCOME AS % OF ASSETS	EMPLOYEES
12/19	29,074	2,707	9.3%	47,200
12/18	25,413	1,683	6.6%	43,600
12/17	27,178	2,448	9.0%	47,900
12/16	25,396	614	2.4%	54,200
12/15	24,705	1,276	5.2%	51,700
Annual Growth	4.2%	20.7%	—	(2.3%)

2019 Year-End Financials

Debt ratio: 19.23%	No. of shares (mil.): 132
Return on equity: 24.39%	Dividends
Cash ($ mil.): 4,054	Yield: 0.6%
Current ratio: —	Payout: 11.6%
Long-term debt ($ mil.): —	Market value ($ mil.): 48,419

	STOCK PRICE ($) FY Close	P/E High/Low	PER SHARE ($) Earnings	Dividends	Book Value
12/19	366.52	18 12	20.10	2.20	91.12
12/18	286.48	29 21	12.16	2.00	74.95
12/17	248.07	15 12	16.81	1.89	71.49
12/16	204.03	53 37	4.07	0.87	71.56
12/15	178.51	25 16	8.44	1.15	69.77
Annual Growth	19.7%	— —	24.2%	17.6%	6.9%

Hunt (J.B.) Transport Services, Inc.

J.B. Hunt Transport Services is one of the largest transportation delivery and logistics companies in North America. Through its divisions the company transports freight including general merchandise automotive parts building materials chemicals electronics food and beverages and forest and paper products. Its Intermodal unit the company's largest maintains about 5000 tractors more than 6375 drivers and about 96745 pieces of trailing equipment and moves customers' cargo by combinations of truck and train. The company also offers dedicated contract services truckload freight transportation and transportation management and logistics services. The company traces its roots back to 1961 when it was founded by Johnnie Bryan Hunt and Johnnie D. Hunt.

Operations

The company divides its operations across four segments: Intermodal (JBI) Dedicated Contract Services (DCS) Integrated Capacity Solutions (ICS) and Truckload (JBT).

J.B. Hunt's Intermodal segment is the company's largest and generates more than 50% of the company's net sales. JBI offers intermodal freight services (a combination of truck and rail) to customers in Canada Mexico and the US relying on its partnerships with major North American rail carriers. Pickups and deliveries (drayage services) are handled by company-owned tractors on either end of the rail component.

The Dedicated Contract Services unit (roughly 30% of total sales) provides dedicated truck fleets drivers and supply chain services for freight transport including final mile delivery. DCS uses its network of just about 120 cross-dock and delivery network locations primarily in the US. Integrated Capacity Solutions (approximately 15% of sales) which provides traditional freight brokerage and transportation logistics solutions using third-party carriers integrated with company-owned equipment and Truckload (about 5%) which offers full-load dry-van freight services using its own tractors and employee drivers or independent contractors who agree to transport freight in our trailers.

Geographic Reach

J.B. Hunt is headquartered in Lowell AK and owns or leases more than 45 other facilities in the US for maintenance and fueling. It also operates more than 115 cross-dock and other delivery system networks for its Dedicated Contract Services segment the remaining three locations outsourced and 37 leased or owned remote sales offices or branches in its ICS segment. In addition it owns or leases small facilities offices and parking yards throughout the US.

J.B. Hunt does business in North America (primarily in the US) with very minor operations in foreign countries.

Sales and Marketing

J.B. Hunt markets its services through a nationwide sales and marketing network. It uses a specific sales force within its Dedicated Contract Services segment due to the length and complexity of the sales cycle. In addition the Integrated Capacity Solutions segment utilizes its own local groups of salespeople.

Financial Performance

J.B. Hunt has enjoyed significant growth over the last several years with revenue increasing 48% since 2015.

Sales in 2019 jumped 6% to $9.2 billion from $8.6 billion in 2018. The increase was primarily due to an increased revenue in DCS related to an increase in revenue producing trucks higher truck productivity defined as revenue per truck per week and an acquisition in the first quarter 2019.

Net earnings in 2019 increased by 5% to $516.3 million compared to $489.6 million from the previous year.

Cash at the end of fiscal 2018 was $35.0 billion an increase of $27 billion from the prior year. Cash from operations contributed $1.10 in 2019 billion to the coffers while investing activities used $804 million mainly from a decrease in equipment purchases net of proceeds from the sale of equipment partially offset by the purchases of Cory and RDI Last Mile Co. (RDI). Financing activities used another $267 million primarily from an increase in treasury stock purchased partially offset by higher proceeds from long-term debt issuances net of long-term debt repayments.

Strategy

J.B. Hunt is well-positioned to leverage opportunities in the fast-growing e-commerce market with its range of services from full load highway and intermodal and final-mile delivery. Companies are increasingly outsourcing their transportation fleet needs another benefit to the J.B. Hunt. To ensure growth the company has made recent strategic acquisitions is improving its digital services and revamping its technology infrastructure and is expanding its geographic footprint.

The company continues to build out its Final Mile Services business with the 2019 acquisition of Cory 1st Choice Home Delivery – specialize in furniture delivery aligned with the growing trend in big and bulky item delivery.

The company launched its Marketplace for J.B. Hunt 360Â° a digital platform for matching carriers and shippers and continues to make enhancements to the application. To support its digital initiatives J.B. Hunt is in the midst of an enterprise-wide information technology overhaul that includes moving all its systems from a legacy mainframe to a cloud-based infrastructure.

The company also aims to expand geographically targeting the intermodal and brokerage businesses in Canada and Mexico and developing and expanding its operations in Puerto Rico and its inbounds programs from China.

Mergers and Acquisitions

In 2019 J.B. Hunt acquired Cory 1st Choice Home Delivery a trucking firm specializing in furniture delivery. 1st Choice will be integrated with J.B. Hunt's Final Mile Services division part of its Dedicated contract Services business unit. The acquisition increases the Final Mile business to include 100 locations and more than 3 million square feet of warehouse and facilities space.

In late 2019 its subsidiary J.B. Hunt Transport Inc. acquired the assets of RDI Last Mile Co. The transaction was funded using J.B. Hunt's existing revolving credit facility.

Company Background

J.B. Hunt was founded by Johnnie Bryan Hunt in 1961. Hunt had been in business since the late 1950s in Arkansas selling rice hulls as poultry litter. In 1961 he began the J.B. Hunt Company with help from future Arkansas governor Winthrop Rockefeller who owned Winrock grass company where Hunt bought sod for one of his side businesses. Hunt developed a machine to compress the rice hulls which made their transportation profitable and within a few years the company was the world's largest producer of rice hulls for poultry litter.

Still looking for new opportunities Hunt bought some used trucks and refrigerated trailers in 1969 though the company continued to focus on its original business. In the 1980s J.B. Hunt's trucking division grew dramatically and became lucrative as the trucking industry was being deregulated. In

1981-82 the Hunt trucking business had higher margins than most trucking firms. In 1983 when J.B. Hunt Transport Services went public Hunt sold the rice hull business to concentrate on trucking.

HISTORY

Johnnie Bryan (J.B.) Hunt's life was a classic tale of rolling from rags to riches — with a little help from a Rockefeller. Hunt grew up in a family of sharecroppers during the Depression and he left school at age 12 to work for his uncle's Arkansas sawmill. In the late 1950s after driving trucks for more than nine years Hunt noticed that the rice mills along his eastern Arkansas route were burning rice hulls. Believing the hulls could be used as poultry litter Hunt got a contract to haul away the hulls and began selling them to chicken farmers.

In 1961 he began the J.B. Hunt Company with help from future Arkansas governor Winthrop Rockefeller who owned Winrock grass company where Hunt bought sod for one of his side businesses. Hunt developed a machine to compress the rice hulls which made their transportation profitable and within a few years the company was the world's largest producer of rice hulls for poultry litter.

Still looking for new opportunities Hunt bought some used trucks and refrigerated trailers in 1969 though the company continued to focus on its original business. In the 1980s J.B. Hunt's trucking division grew dramatically and became lucrative as the trucking industry was being deregulated. In 1981-82 the Hunt trucking business had higher margins than most trucking firms. In 1983 when J.B. Hunt Transport Services went public Hunt sold the rice hull business to concentrate on trucking.

EXECUTIVES

Evp Operations And Coo, Craig Harper, age 63, $375,000 total compensation

President Dedicated Contract Services; Evp Enterprise Solutions, John N. Roberts, age 55, $807,747 total compensation

Evp And Cio, Stuart L. Scott, age 54

Evp Sales And Marketing Truck And Intermodal, Terrence D. (Terry) Matthews, age 62, $478,819 total compensation

Svp Tax And Risk Management And Corporate Secretary, David G. Mee, age 60, $480,660 total compensation

Evp; President Integrated Capacity Solutions, Shelley Simpson, age 48, $476,923 total compensation

Evp; President Dedicated Contract Services, Nicholas (Nick) Hobbs, age 57, $454,808 total compensation

Vice President Sales, Kevin Kapales

Vice President Sales National Accounts, Mark Calcagni

Vice President Pricing And Revenue Management, Ed Harwell

Vice President Of Transportation, Nick Gowen

Vice President Of Operations, Andrew Deblock

Senior Vice President, Brian Webb

Vice President Intermodal Pricing, Darren Field

Vice President Pricing, Stacey Griffin

Vice President Finance, Erin Taylor

Vice President Of Operations, Jon Payne

Vice President Of Sales, Chris Sandor

Vice President Personnel, Sherry Moncrief

Vice President Of Trans, Greg Price

Vice President Memphis, John Flynt

National Account Manager, Chris Putnam

Vice President Pricing, Sarthak Verma

National Sales Manager, Ed Page

Vice President Of Is, Jay Davidson

National Sales Manager, Keith Brown

Vice President Strategic Accounts, Clay Cox

National Account Manager, Kevin Boortz

Senior Vice President Sales, Paul Bingham

Vice President Of Maintenance, Derek Kennemer

Svp And Treasurer Finance, Kevin Bracy

Vice President Intermodal Operations, Michael Brothers

Vice President Of Sales And Marketing, Jessica Brooks

National Account Manager, Linda Peak

Vice President Business Development, Raul Cavazos

Svp Operations, John Vargo

Vp Intermodal Operations, John Mckuin

Vice President Sales, Jason Bohannon

National Account Manager, Kim Armstrong

National Account Manager, Christopher Trout

Vice President National Accounts, Bill Copelin

Vice President Of Maintenance, Michael Ralston

Vice President Maintenance Maintenance Manager, Charles Radcliffe

National Account Manager, Todd Witt

International Vice President Marketing, John Hammond

Senior Vice President Sales, Spencer Frazier

National Sales Manager, Bill Gasaway

Vice President Of Sales, David Will

Svp And Controller Finance, John Kuhlow

National Sales Manager, John Perrine

Vice President Sales Southern Region, Shannon Foley

National Account Manager, Jack Willis

Vice President Of Operations, Brian Dieringer

Vice President Sales Eastern Region, Bill Fedorchak

National Account Manager, Rick Thurow

Vp Human Resources, Mark Greenway

Vice President Strategic Accounts, David Keefauver

Senior Vice President Sales And Marketing, Gregory Breeden

National Account Manager, Tina Sanders

Vice President Of Strategic Accounts, Gabe Waldrop

Vice President Of Operations, Steve Rogers

National Sales Manager, Ben Mallard

Vice President Of Sales, Bill Carver

Vice President, Steve Guthrie

Vice President, Keith Stevens

National Sales Manager, Jack Page

National Sales Manager, Randall Markis

Vice President Tax, Juli Dorrough

Senior Vice President Infrastructure And Operations, Vana Matte

Chairman, Kirk Thompson, age 67

Board Member, Alex Hunt

Auditors: Ernst & Young LLP

LOCATIONS

HQ: Hunt (J.B.) Transport Services, Inc.
615 J.B. Hunt Corporate Drive, Lowell, AR 72745
Phone: 479 820-0000
Web: www.jbhunt.com

PRODUCTS/OPERATIONS

2018 Sales

	$ mil.	% of total
Intermodal (JBI)	4,717	55
Dedicated contract services (DCS)	2,163	25
Integrated capacity solutions (ICS)	1,335	15
Trucking (JBT)	417	5
Intersegment adjustments	(17)	
Total	**8,615**	**100**

Selected Trucking Services

Dedicated
Expedited
Final Mile
Flatbed
Intermodal
Less Than Truckload
Refrigerated
Truckload

COMPETITORS

C.H. Robinson Worldwide	Republic Services
CSX	Ryder System
Expeditors	Schneider National
Hub Group	Swift Transportation
Kansas City Southern	Waste Management
Norfolk Southern	XPO logistics
Old Dominion Freight	YRC Worldwide

HISTORICAL FINANCIALS

Company Type: Public

Income Statement   FYE: December 31

	REVENUE ($ mil.)	NET INCOME ($ mil.)	NET PROFIT MARGIN	EMPLOYEES
12/19	9,165	516	5.6%	29,056
12/18	8,614	489	5.7%	27,621
12/17	7,189	686	9.5%	24,681
12/16	6,555	432	6.6%	22,190
12/15	6,187	427	6.9%	21,562
Annual Growth	10.3%	4.8%	—	7.7%

2019 Year-End Financials

Debt ratio: 23.68%
Return on equity: 23.64%
Cash ($ mil.): 35
Current ratio: 1.43
Long-term debt ($ mil.): 1,295
No. of shares (mil.): 106
Dividends
Yield: 0.8%
Payout: 24.6%
Market value ($ mil.): 12,404

	STOCK PRICE ($) FY Close	P/E High/Low	PER SHARE ($) Earnings	Dividends	Book Value
12/19	116.78	25 18	4.77	1.04	21.34
12/18	93.04	29 20	4.43	0.96	19.33
12/17	114.98	19 13	6.18	0.92	16.76
12/16	97.07	26 17	3.81	0.88	12.70
12/15	73.36	25 19	3.66	0.84	11.41
Annual Growth	12.3%	— —	6.8%	5.5%	16.9%

Huntington Bancshares Inc

Huntington Bancshares is the holding company for The Huntington National Bank which operates more than 855 branches mostly in Ohio and Michigan. In addition to traditional retail and commercial banking services the bank offers mortgage banking capital market services equipment leasing brokerage services investment management recreational vehicle and marine financing and trust and estate services. The company's automobile finance business provides car loans to consumers and real estate and inventory finance to car dealerships throughout the Midwest. Founded in 1866 the company boasts total assets of approximately $114 billion.

Operations

Huntington Bancshares operates through four main business segments: Consumer and Business Banking Commercial Banking Vehicle Finance and the Regional Banking and The Huntington Private Client Group (RBHPCG). The company also records a Treasury/Other function.

Huntington's Consumer and Business Banking division which contributes about 55% to total revenue provides traditional banking products and services to consumer and small business customers as well as investment insurance foreign exchange hedging and treasury management services.

Its Commercial Banking division (almost 30% of revenue) is made up of six business units: Middle Market (addressing companies with annual sales of $20 million-500 million) Specialty Banking (for select industries in the Midwest) Asset Finance (a combination of its Huntington Equipment Finance Huntington Public Capital Technology and Healthcare Equipment Leasing and Lender Finance divisions) Capital Markets/Institutional Corporate Banking (offering corporate risk management services; institutional sales trading and underwriting; and institutional corporate banking) Commercial Real Estate (serving real estate developers REITs and commercial customers) and Treasury Management (which helps businesses manage working capital and reduce expenses).

Vehicle Finance (about 10% of revenue) lends to customers purchasing automobiles light-duty trucks recreational vehicles and marine craft. The company also finances new and used inventory acquisition by franchised dealerships through the segment.

Huntington's Regional Banking and The Huntington Private Client Group (RBHPCG) accounts for under 10% of sales. Through The Huntington Private Bank Huntington offers high net-worth clients deposit lending wealth management legacy planning investment and portfolio management fiduciary administration and trust services.

Treasury/Other covers technology and operations other unallocated assets liabilities revenue and expense.

The company's loan portfolio is composed of a managed mix of consumer and commercial credits. The consumer accounts for more than 50% of sales and this includes sales from automobile home equity residential mortgage RV and marine and other consumer. It's commercial (under commercial: commercial and industrial around 40% and commercial real estate: construction and commercial nearly 10%) generates nearly 50% of sales.

Geographic Reach

Huntington Bancshares is headquartered in Columbus Ohio. The holding company operates more than 10 private client offices and more than 855 branches in Ohio Michigan Pennsylvania Indiana Illinois Wisconsin West Virginia and Kentucky. Ohio is home to about 425 branches; Michigan has more than 275.

Sales and Marketing

In addition to traditional bank branches Huntington Bancshares distributes its products and services through convenience branches (in grocery stores and retirement centers for example) and an ATM network as well as via internet and mobile services.

Financial Performance

Amid a positive market environment Huntington Bancshares' revenue has increased modestly or moderately each year since 2015 for overall five-year growth of around 22%. Net income more than doubled in that time mostly due to gains made in 2017.

The holding company's revenue added 4% to $4.6 billion in 2019 on growth in its Consumer & Business Banking Commercial Banking and Regional Banking and The Huntington Private Client Group (RBHPCG) segments.

Huntington's net income climbed 1% in 2019 compared with 2018 ending the year at $1.4 billion. Strong sales combined with lower expenses drove the improvement.

The company's cash stores $1.2 billion a decreased of $1.5 billion from the year before. Operations provided $1.5 billion and financings used $1.2 billion (mostly from an increase in deposits). Huntington used $1.9 billion on investments primarily for net loan and lease activity (excluding sales and purchases) and purchase of available-for-sale securities.

Strategy

Overall Huntington strategy involves an active corporate development program that seeks to identify partnership and possible investment opportunities in technology-driven companies that can augment Huntington's distribution and product capabilities.

In its automobile RV and marine finance portfolios Huntington is targeting borrowers with high FICO and internal custom scores. This strategy and operational capabilities allow to appropriately manage the origination quality across the entire portfolio including the newer markets. Although increased origination volume and entering new markets can be associated with increased risk levels the company believes that disciplined strategy and operational processes significantly mitigate these risks.

Furthermore Huntington is investing in its digital technology to personalize clients' banking experience. In February 2019 the company launched its Huntington Heads Up platform an AI-based tool to help customers manage their finances by making spending and saving suggestions.

Company Background

With the economy in the Midwest wracked by the recession Huntington posted losses in 2008 and 2009 — more than $3 billion in the latter year alone — mainly attributable to credit losses due to nonperforming assets and the write down of goodwill related to past acquisitions. It returned to profitability in 2010 thanks in part to higher interest margins as a result of the company's focus on lower-cost customer checking accounts.

HISTORY

Pelatiah Webster (P. W.) Huntington descendant of both a Revolutionary War leader and a Declaration of Independence signer went to work at sea in 1850 at age 14. He returned to go into banking and in 1866 founded what would become Huntington National Bank of Columbus. As the business grew he conscripted four of his five sons. The bank took a national charter in 1905 and became The Huntington National Bank of Columbus. It survived the hard times of 1907 and 1912 through the Huntington philosophy of sitting on piles of cash.

P. W. died in 1918 and his son Francis became president. Francis expanded the company into trust services. Unlike many bankers in the 1920s he refused to make speculative loans based on the stock market. Francis died in 1928 and was succeeded by brother Theodore. By 1930 Huntington's trust assets accounted for more than half of the total. The family's conservative philosophy helped the bank sail through the 1933 bank holiday although when it reopened the amount of cash it could pay out was restricted to 10% of deposits.

P. W.'s son Gwynne chaired the bank during its post-WWII expansion. His death in 1958 ended the Huntington family reign. The bank began opening branches and adding new services such as mortgage and consumer loans. In 1966 in order to expand statewide the bank formed a holding company Huntington Bancshares. In the 1960s and 1970s the corporation added new operations including mortgage and leasing companies and an international division to help clients with foreign exchange.

In 1979 the company consolidated its 15 affiliates into The Huntington National Bank. Three years later the company bit off more than it could chew with the acquisitions of Reeves Banking and Trust Company of Dover and Union Commerce Corporation of Cleveland. The latter purchase loaded the company with debt. Nevertheless it continued to expand particularly after 1985 when banking regulations allowed interstate branch banking and it soon had operations in Florida Indiana Kentucky Michigan and West Virginia.

Huntington Bancshares was largely insulated from the real estate problems of the late 1980s and early 1990s thanks to its continuing conservative lending policies. But the company was at risk from the nationwide consolidation of the banking industry which made it a potential takeover target. It increased its service offerings and bolstered its place in the market through acquisitions. In 1996 Huntington Bancshares bought life insurance agency Tice & Associates and began cross-selling bank and insurance products. Important banking acquisitions in 1997 included First Michigan Bank and several Florida companies.

Also in 1997 the company took advantage of deregulation to consolidate its interstate operations (except for The Huntington State Bank) into a single operating company. In 1998 Huntington Bancshares continued to build its Huntington insurance services unit with the acquisition of Pollock & Pollock. In 1999 the bank launched a mortgage program aimed at wealthy clients and sold its credit card receivables portfolio to Chase Manhattan (now JPMorgan Chase & Co.). In 2000 the company bought Michigan's Empire Banc Corporation.

Former BANK ONE executive Thomas Hoaglin was named president and CEO in 2001. Later that year he became chairman when Frank Wobst retired after leading the company for 20 years.

In 2002 the company consolidated some branches in the Midwest to cut costs and exited the retail banking market in Florida selling some 140 retail branches there to SunTrust. After the mid-2007 acquisition of Sky Financial Sky's CEO Marty Adams became president and COO of Huntington Bancshares. He retired at the end of 2007 and Hoaglin resumed the president's role until his own retirement in 2009; Stephen Steinour then took the helm.

EXECUTIVES

Executive Vice President And Director Corporate Tax, Edward Kane

President Northwest Ohio Region, Sharon S. Speyer

Evp General Counsel And Secretary, Richard A. Cheap, age 68, $279,833 total compensation

Chairman President And Ceo, Stephen D. (Steve) Steinour, age 62, $1,061,538 total compensation

Sevp And Managing Director Auto Finance Commercial Real Estate And Community Development Lending And Investment, Nicholas G. (Nick) Stanutz, age 65, $465,000 total compensation

Sevp Retail And Business Banking, Mary W. Navarro, age 64, $541,154 total compensation

Sevp And Chief Risk Officer, Helga S. Houston, age 59, $542,308 total compensation

Sevp And Director Regional Banking And The Huntington Private Client Group, James E. (Jim) Dunlap, age 67, $518,333 total compensation

President Central Ohio And Columbus Region, James E. Kunk

Sevp And Director Corporate Operations And Corporate Services, Mark E. Thompson, age 61, $315,340 total compensation

President Central Ohio Region, Sue E. Zazon

President West Virginia Region, Andrew J. Paterno

President Western Pennsylvania And Ohio Valley Region, Susan (Susie) Baker Shipley

Sevp And Cfo, Howell D. (Mac) McCullough, age 62, $596,538 total compensation

President Greater Cleveland Region, Sean P. Richardson

President Chicago Region, Peter K. Gillespie

Vp Commercial Banking Greater Akron/canton Region, William C. Shivers

Sevp And Chief Credit Officer, Daniel J. Neumeyer, age 60

Sevp And Chief Technology And Operations Officer, Paul G. Heller, age 56, $590,385 total compensation

President West Michigan Region, John Irwin

President Southern Ohio And Northern Kentucky Region, Kevin Jones

Sevp And Director Commercial Banking, Richard (Rich) Remiker, age 62

Sevp And Chief Human Resources Officer, Rajeev (Raj) Syal, age 54

President Akron Region, Nicholas Browning

President Indiana Region, John Corbin

President Wisconsin Region, Kevin Leissring

President East Michigan, David Lochner

Sevp Private Bank; Regional Banking Director And Chair Michigan, Sandra E. Pierce, $222,789 total compensation

Evp And Chief Communications And Marketing Director, Julie C. Tutkovics

Assistant Vice President, Stacy Oberman

Senior Vice President Treasury Management Sales Manager, Robin Triplett

Vice President, Denise Stone

Business Banking Relationship Manager Sr. Vice Preside, Connie Condo

Assistant Vice President, Jill Pazerski

Vice President, Bruce Sautter

Vice President, Couturier Jan

Assistant Vice President And Senior Product Manage, Amy Beck

Vice President International Services, Robert Storbeck

Vice President, Geoffrey Mowery

Vice President Sec Reporting Manager, Jeff Endres

Vice President Executive Recruiter, Mary Smith

Vice President, James Matousek

Vice President, Philip Francis

Assistant Vice President Section Manager, Gayla Strickler

Vice President Community Development, Eric Stachler

Vice President Credit Specialist Senior, Robert Hiss

Vice President National Sales Manager And Key Accounts, Patrick Prato

Vice President Senior Sba Lender, Paul Collinsworth

Vice President Senior Sales Executive, Bret Haggy

Vice President I Treasury Management Industry Solutions, Brett Bailey

Assistant Vice President, Brock McFann

Vice President Risk Manager Retail And Business Banking, Heidi Sims

Senior Vice President, Peter Arendt

Senior Vice President Marketing Operations Director, Janice Tedesco

Vice President Enterprise Technology Systems, Carolyn Jones

Senior Vice President Information Technology Risk, Christine Holland

Assistant Vice President Treasury Management Sales Executive, Faith Hansen

Vice President Custody Services, Kevin Speert

Vice President, Nadine Liggett

Assistant Vice President, John Breitling

Vice President Segment Risk Manager Senior, Pamela Birnbrich

Assistant Vice President, Jenny Nickles

Vice President, Brad Udy

Assistant Vice President 1 Portfolio Manager, Nick Markovich

Senior Vice President Regional Banking Process Solutions, Steven Clemens

Senior Vice President, Neil S Clark, age 69

Senior Vice President Total Rewards, Craig Wilkins

Assistant Vice President Treasury Group Finance Manager, Erik Kyre

Vp And Senior Product Manager, Shannon Gardner

Senior Vice President, Mary Cline

Senior Vice President Sales, Jon Greenwood

Senior Vice President Credit Risk Management, Tim Barber

Vice President Tm Liquidity And Fraud Group Product Manager, Ashley Sanders

Vice President Private Banker, Erin Kallmerten

Vice President Business Unit Controller, Scott Dupler

Vice President Director Of Investor Relations, Mark Muth

Vice President Treasury Management Sales, John Tremoulis

Assistant Vice President Senior Human Resources Generalist, Susan Lelonek

Vice President, Joseph Ahee

Executive Vice President Senior Commercial Credit Approval Officer, Josh Eichenhorn

Senior Vice President Treasury Management, Steve Veach

Vice President, Daniel Erlandson

Vice President, Terry Kuney

Vice President, Diana Ferrara

Assistant Vice President Home Lending Compliance Senior Manager, Omar Ramsay

Vice President Loan Syndications, Chad Lowe

Vice President Credit Review, Lucia West

Senior Vice President Deposit Product Pricing And Fees Director, David Schamer

Vice President, Dan Hewitt

Vice President Information Technology Operations And Service Desk, John Mingus

Vice President, Roy Dsa

Vice President Human Resources Senior Staffing Specialist, Karis Spence

Vice President Senior Sourcing Manager, Jay Gomer

Senior Vice President Retail Marketing, Karen Maruna

Assistant Vice President, Tony Ruberg

Senior Vice President, Michael Price

Vice President Front End Collections, Dave Mortenson

Senior Vice President Auto Finance, Brad Norman

Assistant Vice President Regional Property Manager, Cheryl Pitzer

Vice President Of The Mortgage Group, Linda Zack

Vice President, Renee Ross

Vice President Business Banking, Brian Burrell

Vice President, Dan Lowrie

Assistant Vice President, Schlosser James

Vice President, Terri Whitman

Executive Vice President Marketing, Chandra Kimble

Vice President Commercial Loans, John Leuhmann

Senior Vice President, Bruce Shearer

Vice President Senior Commercial Relationship Manager, Kevin Contat

Vice President Commercial Banking, Grant Friend

Vice President Legal, Kelly Semer

Assistant Vice President And Branch Manager, Amber Babik

Assistant Vice President Third Party, Michael Adams

Vice President, Michael Williams

Vice President R Receivables Specialist, Rick Dison

Vice President And Manager Customer Information And Market Research, Joyce Smith

Vice President, Bill Crum

Senior Vice President Senior Regional Credit Officer, Jeff Blendick

Vice President Senior Relationship Manager, Jason Ratkovich

Assistant Vice President Deposit Pricing And Product Lead Analyst, Dominic Monley

Vice President, Gary Bogan

Vice President, Christina Brown

Vice President Business Banking Relationship Manager, Robert Haslinger

Vice President Senior Product Manager, Lash Chapel

Vice President, Bob Mohr

Vice President Sales, Tom Obrian

Assistant Vice President, Mel Jenkins

Vice President District Manager, Eric Kelemen

Assistant Vice President, Kathryn Kasinec

Assistant Vice President Scrum Master, Laura Elliott

Vice President, Laura Greetham

Senior Vice President, Allen Card

Assistant Vice President Commercial Loan Closer, Marianne Kartson

Assistant Vice President Senior Risk Specialist, Selvan Kumar

Assistant Vice President Branch Manager Ii, Scott Johnson

Assistant Vice President Auto Finance Credit Rep Senior, Jeremy Menning

Vice President Relationship Manager, David Stiller

Senior Vice President Market Manager, Brad Balmert

Senior Vice President Change Management Director, Lin Hillis

Vice President Commercial Real Estate Portfolio Manager, Thomas Buck

Vice President, Dee Giles

Senior Vice President, Chuck Ramseur

Vice President Lease Administration Manager, Lynn Putterbaugh

Vice President Business Banking, Julie Roth

Assistant Vice President Asset Recovery And Remarketing Manager, Wendy Westwick

Vice President, Thomas Hannaford

Assistant Vice President Network Infrastructure Manager, Kevin Kohlheim

Cml Strategy Implementation Manager Senior Vice President, Michelle Friend

Vice President And Team Leader Special Assets Division, Alfred Casino

Assistant Vice President Senior Risk Man, Na Jin

Senior Vice President Segment Risk Officer, Mindy Ball

Auditors: PricewaterhouseCoopers LLP

LOCATIONS

HQ: Huntington Bancshares Inc
41 South High Street, Columbus, OH 43287
Phone: 614 480-2265
Web: www.huntington.com

2016 Bank Branches

	No.
Ohio	523
Michigan	353
Pennsylvania	53
Indiana	46
Illinois	39
Wisconsin	37
West Virginia	30
Kentucky	10
Total	**1,091**

2016 sales

	No.
Consumer and Business Banking	43
Commercial Banking	23
Commercial Real Estate and Vehicle Finance	24
Regional Banking and The Huntington Private Client Group	8
Home Lending	2
Total	**100**

PRODUCTS/OPERATIONS

2018 Bank Branches

	No.
Ohio	451
Michigan	300
Pennsylvania	49
Indiana	41
Illinois	37
Wisconsin	31
West Virginia	25
Kentucky	10
Total	**944**

2018 Sales

	$ mil.	% of total
Interest		
Loans & leases	3,305	63
Available-for-sale and other securities	376	7
Held-to-maturity securities	211	4
Other	57	1
Interest Expense	(760.0)	
Noninterest		
Service charges on deposit accounts	364	7
Cards and payment processing income	224	4
Mortgage banking income	108	2
Trust services	171	3
Insurance income	82	2
Capital markets fees	91	2
Bank-owned life insurance income	67	1
Gain on sales of loans	55	1
Net gains on sales of securities	(21.0)	-
Other	180	3
Impairment losses recognized in earnings on available-for-sale securities		
Total	**4,510**	**100**

COMPETITORS

Citizens Financial Group	PNC Financial
Comerica	Park National
Fifth Third	Regions Financial
JPMorgan Chase	TFS Financial
KeyCorp	U.S. Bancorp
	Wells Fargo

HISTORICAL FINANCIALS

Company Type: Public

Income Statement

FYE: December 31

	ASSETS ($ mil.)	NET INCOME ($ mil.)	INCOME AS % OF ASSETS	EMPLOYEES
12/19	109,002	1,411	1.3%	15,664
12/18	108,781	1,393	1.3%	15,693
12/17	104,185	1,186	1.1%	15,770
12/16	99,714	711	0.7%	15,993
12/15	71,044	692	1.0%	12,243
Annual Growth	**11.3%**	**19.5%**	**—**	**6.4%**

2019 Year-End Financials

Debt ratio: 9.03%	No. of shares (mil.): 1,020
Return on equity: 12.32%	Dividends
Cash ($ mil.): 1,713	Yield: 3.8%
Current ratio: —	Payout: 44.9%
Long-term debt ($ mil.): —	Market value ($ mil.): 15,382

	STOCK PRICE ($) FY Close	P/E High/Low		PER SHARE ($) Earnings	Dividends	Book Value
12/19	15.08	12	9	1.27	0.58	11.56
12/18	11.92	14	9	1.20	0.50	10.61
12/17	14.56	15	12	1.00	0.35	10.09
12/16	13.22	19	11	0.70	0.29	9.49
12/15	11.06	14	12	0.81	0.25	8.30
Annual Growth	**8.1%**			**11.9%**	**23.4%**	**8.7%**

Huntington Ingalls Industries, Inc.

Huntington Ingalls Industries (HII) is the sole designer builder and refueler of the US Navy's nuclear aircraft carriers. Rivaling nuclear submarine builder General Dynamics HII is the largest naval shipbuilder in America; it also maintains and repairs nuclear submarines and aircraft carriers. In addition HII builds expeditionary warfare ships surface combatants submarines and Coast Guard surface ships and provides aftermarket fleet support. Almost all its offerings are sold to the US government.

Operations

The shipbuilder has three reportable segments: Newport News Ingalls and Technical Solutions.

Newport News includes the manufacture of nuclear-powered aircraft carriers and submarines and services such as overhaul repair maintenance and fleet support. It accounts for more than 55% of Huntington Ingalls Industries' net sales.

The Ingalls segment accounts for roughly 30% of net sales. It designs and constructs non-nuclear ships for the US Navy and US Coast Guard including amphibious assault ships expeditionary warfare ships surface combatants and national security cutters.

Technical Solutions (about 15%) includes information technology fleet maintenance and modernization nuclear management and operations and oil and gas engineering and support.

Geographic Reach

Headquartered in Newport News VA HII operates in about 45 US states and some 15 countries. It has offices in Huntsville AL; San Diego CA; Broomfield CO; Pascagoula MS; Houston TX; Fairfax Hampton Newport News Suffolk and Virginia Beach VA; and Washington DC.

Sales and Marketing

In addition to the US government HII provides services for commercial customers in the private sector specifically in the energy and oil and gas industries. The US government is its largest customer with the US Navy accounting for almost 90% of its net sales. The US Coast Guard generates about 5%.

Financial Performance

Huntington Ingalls' revenue has been increasing steadily over the past five years.

Sales in 2019 were up 9% reaching $89 billion compared with $8.2 billion the previous year. Higher volumes specifically in aircraft carriers and submarines were cited as primary factors for growth.

Net earnings amounted to $549 million a 34% decrease from $836 million in 2018. The decrease was primarily due to higher cost of products sales and services revenues.

Cash at the end of fiscal 2019 was $75 million a decrease of $240 million from the prior year. Cash from operations contributed $896 million to the coffers while investing activities used $627 million mainly for capital expenditures and acquisitions. Financing activities used another $434 million for dividends to stockholders and the company's stock repurchase program.

Strategy

Huntington Ingalls Industries continues to benefit from strong Navy and Coast Guard expenditures for ships. To prepare for current and future programs the company has been deploying capital to reactivate its East Bank facilities for Ingalls Shipbuilding in Pascagoula MS and continues to outfit the Joint Manufacturing Assembly Facility (JMAF) at Newport News Shipbuilding in Virginia.

In 2018 the US Navy awarded a multiyear contract for seven destroyers valued at $9.8 billion to Ingalls Shipbuilding and in 2019 it awarded Newport News Shipbuilding a contract for two aircraft carriers?the CVN 80 and 81?worth almost $15 billion.

Diversification in the growing non-shipbuilding sector is providing revenue growth for HII. Recent bolt-on acquisitions within its Technology Solutions division are adding threat analytics and cybersecurity capabilities to its professional services portfolio allowing the company to reach key new customers in the intelligence and special operations communities as well as additional defense and federal agencies.

Mergers and Acquisitions

In early 2019 HII acquired Virginia- based Fulcrum IT Services an information technology and government consulting company for $195 million. Fulcrum joins HII's Technical Solutions division and expands its capabilities in enhanced situational awareness and predictive threat analytics through Fulcrum's advanced engineering cyber security software development big data engineering and intelligence and special operations experience.

EXECUTIVES

President And Ceo, C. Michael (Mike) Petters, age 60, $328,847 total compensation

Evp Communications, Jerri Fuller Dicskeski

Evp; President Newport News Shipbuilding, Matthew J. (Matt) Mulherin, age 60, $515,000 total compensation

Evp And General Counsel, Kellye L. Walker, age 53, $505,096 total compensation

Evp And Chief Human Resources Officer, William R. (Bill) Ermatinger

Evp And President Technical Solutions, Andy Green

Evp; President Ingalls Shipbuilding, Brian Cuccias, $514,906 total compensation

Evp Business Management And Cfo, Christopher D. Kastner, age 56, $463,462 total compensation

Evp Government And Customer Relations, Mitchell B. (Mitch) Waldman

Evp Strategy And Development, Michael S. Smith

Vice President Of Operations, Scott Stabler

Corporate Vice President, Bruce Hawthorne

Corp Vice President Benefits And Compensatio, Jim Taylor

Vice President Legislative Affairs, Carrie Apostolou

Vp And Controller Newport News Shipbuilding, Carolyn Pittman

Vice President Of Energy, Pete Diakun

Vice President, Matt Mulherin

Corporate Vice President Associate General Counsel And Secretary, Charles Chuck Monroe

Vice President Program Management Ingalls Shipbuilding, Kari Wilkinson

Vice President Construction John F. Kennedy (cvn79) Newport News Shipbuilding, Lucas Hicks

Vice President Of Nuclear, Barry Fletcher

Chairman, Thomas B. Fargo, age 72

Board Member, Anastasia Kelly

Board Member, Victoria Harker

Board Member, Thomas Schievelbein

Board Member, John Welch

Auditors: DELOITTE & TOUCHE LLP

LOCATIONS

HQ: Huntington Ingalls Industries, Inc.
4101 Washington Avenue, Newport News, VA 23607
Phone: 757 380-2000
Web: www.huntingtoningalls.com

PRODUCTS/OPERATIONS

2018 Sales

	$ mil.	% of total
Newport News	4,722	57
Ingalls	2,607	31
Technical Solutions	988	12
Intersegment eliminations	(141)	-
Total	**8,176**	**100**

2018 Sales

	$ mil.	% of total
Product sales	6,023	74
Service revenues	2,153	26
Total	**8,176**	**100**

Selected Products

Aircraft carriers (nuclear-powered)
Amphibious assault ships
National Security Cutters (US Coast Guard ships)
Expeditionary warfare ships
Fleet services
Submarines (nuclear-powered)
Surface combatants

COMPETITORS

BAE SYSTEMS
Direction des Constructions Navales
Electric Boat
General Dynamics
Northrop Grumman
Todd Shipyards

HISTORICAL FINANCIALS

Company Type: Public

Income Statement

FYE: December 31

	REVENUE ($ mil.)	NET INCOME ($ mil.)	NET PROFIT MARGIN	EMPLOYEES
12/19	8,899	549	6.2%	42,000
12/18	8,176	836	10.2%	40,000
12/17	7,441	479	6.4%	38,000
12/16	7,068	573	8.1%	37,000
12/15	7,020	404	5.8%	36,000
Annual Growth	6.1%	8.0%	—	3.9%

2019 Year-End Financials

Debt ratio: 18.29%
Return on equity: 35.37%
Cash ($ mil.): 75
Current ratio: 0.94
Long-term debt ($ mil.): 1,286
No. of shares (mil.): 40
Dividends
Yield: 1.4%
Payout: 24.7%
Market value ($ mil.): 10,236

	STOCK PRICE ($) FY Close	P/E High/Low	PER SHARE ($) Earnings	Dividends	Book Value
12/19	250.88	19 14	13.26	3.61	38.92
12/18	190.31	14 9	19.09	3.02	36.18
12/17	235.70	24 18	10.46	2.52	38.98
12/16	184.19	15 10	12.14	2.10	35.78
12/15	126.85	17 12	8.36	1.70	31.77
Annual Growth	18.6%	— —	12.2%	20.7%	5.2%

HY-VEE, INC.

Give Hy-Vee a high five for being one of the largest privately owned US supermarket chains despite serving some modestly sized towns in the Midwest. The company runs more than 240 stores in eight Midwestern states. It distributes products to its stores through several subsidiaries including Amber Pharmacy D&D Foods Inc. Hy-Vee Construction and Midwest Heritage. Charles Hyde and David Vredenburg founded the employee-owned firm in 1930. It takes its name from a combination of its founders' names.

Operations

Hy-Vee Inc. offers groceries ready to go meals pastries and cakes. Through its subsidiaries Hy-Vee established a distribution system that secures the highest quality merchandise and transports its products quickly and efficiently to its customers.

Geographic Reach

Iowa-based Hy-Vee Inc. operates 240 retail stores in Illinois Iowa Kansas Minnesota Missouri Nebraska South Dakota and Wisconsin.

Sales and Marketing

Hy-Vee Inc. sell its products through online and its own groceries located in eight Midwestern states in the US.

Financial Performance

Hy-Vee Inc. is an employee-owned corporation operating retail stores across eight Midwestern states with sales of $11 billion annually.

Strategy

Hy-Vee Inc. announced recently the launch of its newest subsidiary Vivid Clear Rx. The new subsidiary will offer affordable pharmacy benefit management services to Hy-Vee's more than 88000 employees as well as other employers looking to maximize their employee benefits spending. With the launch of Vivid Clear Rx it is leveraging its experience in the pharmacy industry and the expertise it gained from serving millions of pharmacy patients to help other employers make the most of every health care dollar they're investing in their employees.

Vivid Clear Rx will offer a full range of flexible pharmacy benefit management services powered by RxSense's RxAgile enterprise technology which will provide clarity to those utilizing the company's services. RxSense is providing Vivid Clear Rx with a full-service suite of modules for pharmacy benefit management that will supplement assets that Hy-Vee already owns and operates. RxSense's analytics product RxIQ will provide Vivid Clear Rx with real-time health plan performance insights through customizable data dashboards; financial operational and clinical action alerts; and the ability to quickly evaluate data by claim type pharmacy or geography.

EXECUTIVES

Vp General Merchandise, Jon S. Wendel
Chairman President And Ceo, Randy Edeker
Evp And Chief Customer Officer, Sheila Laing
Evp Cfo And Treasurer, Mike Skokan
Vice Chairman Evp And Chief Administrative Officer, Andy McCann
Evp Western Region, Brett Bremser
Evp And Coo, Jay Marshall
Evp Eastern Region, Darren Baty
Vice President Retail Information Technology, Julie Proffitt
Assistant Vice President Operations, Jim Watters
Senior Vice President And Chief Health Officer, Kristin Williams
Assistant Vice President Employee Benefits, Kristine Hennings
Pharmacy Manager, Marrianne Ryno
Assistant Vice President Sec, Angie Rosenberger
Assistant Vice President Operations, Rob Eslick
Group Vice President, Jason Pride
Assistant Vice President Bakery Operations, Tony Byington
Group Vice President Equipment Purchasing, Mark Brauer
Assistant Vice President Meat Operations, Kenan Judge
Assistant Vice President Engineering, Adam Bishop
Assistant Vice President For Marketing Projects, Erin Bailey
Assistant Vice President Logistics, Jody Sandy
Vice President Sales, Katie Graham
Assistant Vice President, Tony Kaska
Assistant Vice President Auditing Services, Juli Egeland
Assistant Vice President Western Region, Pat Hensley
Vice President Special Projects, Gary Goodhall
Vice President Government Relations, Noreen Otto
Assistant Vice President Store Setup, Mark Millsap
Vice President Distribution, Tod Hockenson
Vice President Information Technology Operation, Cevin Anderson
Assisant Vice President, Chuck Seaman
Vice President Customer Care, Denise Broderick
Vice President, Karl Kruse
Assistant Vice President Information Technology Operations, Travis Hoover
Assistant Vice President Risk Management, Janet Crocker
Group Vice President Information Technology, Tom Settle
Assistant Vice President Of Produce Operations, Jason Sheridan
Assistant Vice President, Marshall Sanders
Avp Produce Operations, Mike Orf
Vice President Store Development, Jeff Markey
Assistant Vice President Risk Management, John Brummit
Assistant Vice President Information Technology Projects, Angie Dachenbach
Pharmacy Manager, Rick Awbrey
Pharmacy Manager, Jeff Jorgensen
Pharmacy Manager, Brad Moriarty
Pharmacy Manager, Heather Yennie
Vice President Business Development, Kevin Sherlock
Vice President Of Real Estate, Pete Hosch
Gvp Ecommerce, Brandon Williams
Vice President Of Human Resources, Karen Boriskey
Assisant Treasurer, Jeff Pierce
Secretary To Greg Frampton, Stacey Groff
Assistant Secretary, Michael Jurgens
Senior Vice President Secretary And General Counsel, Steve Meyer

LOCATIONS

HQ: HY-VEE, INC.
5820 WESTOWN PKWY, WEST DES MOINES, IA 502668223
Phone: 515 267-2800
Web: WWW.HY-VEE.COM

PRODUCTS/OPERATIONS

Selected Subsidiaries

D & D Foods Inc. (salads dips and meats)
Florist Distributing Inc. (flowers plants and florist supplies)
Hy-Vee Construction L.C. (construction)
Hy-Vee Pharmacy Solutions (specialty pharmacy services)
Hy-Vee Weitz Construction L.C. (construction)
Lomar Distributing Inc. (specialty foods)
Midwest Heritage Bank FSB (banking)
Perishable Distributors of Iowa Ltd. (meat fish seafood and ice cream)

COMPETITORS

ALDI	Niemann Foods
Associated Wholesale Grocers	Rite Aid
Ball's Food	Roundy's
CVS	SUPERVALU
Casey's General Stores	Save-A-Lot Food Stores
Fareway Stores	Target Corporation
Kmart	Wal-Mart
Kroger	Walgreen

HISTORICAL FINANCIALS

Company Type: Private

Income Statement   FYE: September 30

	REVENUE ($ mil.)	NET INCOME ($ mil.)	NET PROFIT MARGIN	EMPLOYEES
09/19	10,672	0	—	83,000
09/18*	10,290	0	—	
12/16	9,842	0	—	
09/13	8,014	0	—	
Annual Growth	4.9%	—	—	—

*Fiscal year change

Icahn Enterprises LP

Icahn Enterprises has a can-do attitude when it comes to making money. The holding company has investments in companies active across seven industry segments: investment energy automotive food packaging metals real estate and home fashion. Subsidiaries include CVR Energy Pep Boys Viskase and WestPoint Home among others. Icahn has investments in major brands such as Herbalife Caesars Entertainment HP Inc. Xerox and Hertz. The firm targets companies it deems to be undervalued and takes an activist investment approach to its holdings. Most of Icahn's business is in the US which accounts for some 95% of revenue. Billionaire corporate raider Carl Icahn and his affiliates control his namesake firm.

Operations

Icahn Enterprises holds and operates companies across several industries each of which is called out as a distinct business segment in the company's financial statements. Automotive and Energy segments together comprise more than 85% of annual company revenue. The remaining segments each generate less than 5% of revenue.

Icahn's Energy segment (some 60% of revenue) operates through CVR Energy which is engaged in petroleum refining and nitrogen fertilizer manufacturing. Its Automotive segment generates nearly 30% of revenue and includes IEH Auto Parts Pep Boys the franchise businesses of Precision Tune Auto Care and American Driveline Systems the franchisor of AAMCO and the licensor of Cottman Transmission service centers.

Food Packaging subsidiary Viskase is a producer of cellulosic fibrous and plastic casings used to prepare and package processed meat products and Home Fashion subsidiary WestPoint Home (WPH) sells bedding bath and home decor products. The company's Metal segment does business through PSC Metals which collects processes and sells ferrous and non-ferrous metals and processes steel pipe and plate products in the Midwest and Southern US. PSC also collects industrial and obsolete scrap metal processes it into reusable forms and supplies the recycled metals to its customers.

Real Estate assets include a portfolio of commercial rental properties development properties golf and club operations and a resort property. Its Railcar segment is being conducted through a wholly owned subsidiary American Railcar Leasing LLC.

Through Icahn's Investment segment the company holds significant positions in Herbalife Caesars Entertainment HP Cheniere Energy Occidental Petroleum Xerox Newell Brands Hertz and Cloudera.

Geographic Reach

Icahn Enterprises' corporate operations are headquartered in New York City though a move to Miami is scheduled for 2020.

The company's Energy segment is headquartered in Sugar Land Texas and has offices refineries plants and storage facilities mainly in Kansas and Oklahoma.

Icahn Automotive is headquartered in Kennesaw Georgia. The segment has company-operated stores franchise locations and distributions centers throughout the US.

Food Packaging subsidiary Viskase is headquartered in Lombard Illinois. Operations include manufacturing facilities distribution centers and service centers throughout North America Europe South America and Asia.

PSC Metals is headquartered in Mayfield Heights Ohio. The business has recycling yards warehouses and storage and distribution centers throughout the Midwestern and Southeastern US.

Real Estate assets include commercial rental properties throughout the US as well as development properties and golf and club operations in Cape Cod Massachusetts and Vero Beach Florida and a resort property in Aruba.

WestPoint Home (WPH) is headquartered in New York City and has retail space manufacturing and distribution facility in Florida and a manufacturing facility in Bahrain.

Sales and Marketing

Customers for CVR Refining's products primarily include retailers railroads and farm cooperatives and other refiners/marketers. The company focuses its marketing efforts in the central mid-continent area because of its relative proximity to its refineries and pipeline access. Icahn's CRV engages in rack marketing which is the supply of product through tanker trucks and railcars directly to customers located in close geographic proximity to its refineries and to customers at throughput terminals on third-party refined products distribution systems. CVR Refining also makes bulk sales (sales into third-party pipelines) into mid-continent markets and other destinations utilizing third-party product pipeline networks.

Financial Performance

Icahn Enterprises has seen fluctuating revenue in the last five years rising for about four years before slightly falling in 2019. Despite this revenue grew 44% between 2015 and 2019. Its net income has also struggled in the same period posting profits only in 2017 in-between two consecutive years of net losses.

Revenue was $9 billion in 2019 down from $11.8 billion in 2019. During 2019 net loss from holding company investment activities contributed to the drop as did declines in Food Packaging Real Estate Energy Metals and Railcar. Such decreases offset growth from Automotive and Mining.

Net loss attributable to Icahn Enterprises from continuing operations for 2019 was $1.1 billion a further decline from the prior year's net loss of $238 million. This was largely due to a loss of $775 million in Investment compared to a profit of $319 million in 2018. Its Holding Company Automotive Food Packaging and Home Fashion segments reported further losses together with a loss from its Metals segment of $22 million against a $5 million profit the year prior.

Cash at the 2019 year-end was $4.9 billion. Operating activities used $1.5 billion largely affected by the year's loss and further spending on security purchases. Investing activities provided $586 million from proceeds from sale of investments. Financing activities provided another $566 million from Holding Company senior notes proceeds.

Strategy

Icahn Enterprises' strategy known as The Icahn Formula is to seek undervalued or bankrupt assets

improve their operations enhance their valuation and sell them for a profit. The firm typically purchases substantial stakes in companies with an eye toward gaining control of them often by waging proxy battles for seats on their boards of directors.

As it is a diversified holding company owning subsidiaries engaged in seven diversified reporting segments it has significant positions in various investments as of 2019 which include Herbalife Ltd. Caesars Entertainment Corporation HP Inc. Cheniere Energy Inc. Occidental Petroleum Corporation Xerox Corporation Newell Brands Inc. Hertz Global Holdings Inc. and Cloudera Inc. Icahn also sold Ferrous Resources in 2019 which owns mining rights in Brazil for $550 million.

Furthermore the company's business strategy includes these key elements: capitalizing on growth opportunities in its existing business driving accountability and financial discipline in the management of its business seeking to acquire undervalued assets and using activism to unlock value.

Company Background

Carl Icahn developed a reputation on Wall Street as a corporate raider in the 1980s when he clashed with management at TWA and Texaco. Icahn has a personal fortune worth nearly $18 billion according to Forbes magazine.

EXECUTIVES

Cfo And Director, SungHwan Cho, age 45, $822,616 total compensation

Chief Accounting Officer, Peter Reck, age 53, $300,000 total compensation

President Ceo And Director, Keith Cozza, age 41, $1,557,736 total compensation

Senior Vice President Commercial Strategy Americas Federal Mogul Motoparts, Phil Halberg

Vice President South America Viskase, Newton Martins

Senior Vice President Global Sales And Corporate Strategy Powertrain Federal Mogul, Richard Llope

Senior Vice President And General Manager Rings And Liners Valve Seats And Guides Powertrain Federal Mogul, Michael Hedderich

Senior Vice President Finance Federal Mogul Powertrain, Shaun Merry

Senior Vice President And General Manager Global Valvetrain Powertrain Federal Mogul, Jean-Philippe Keller-Comte

Senior Vice President And Chief People Officer Icahn Automotive, Athony Tony Papa

Senior Vice President Global Braking Federal Mogul Motorparts, Neville Rudd

Senior Vice President Globla Oe Sales And Commercial Strategy Emea Federal Mogul Motorparts, Detlev Baudach

Senior Vice President And General Manager Sealing And Gaskets Federal Mogel Powertrain, Andrea Pappagallo

Senior Vice President And General Manager Bearings Federal Mogel Powertrain, Olaf Weidlich

Vice President Engineering And Technolgoy Asia Pacific Federal Mogul, Weibo Weng

Senior Vice President And General Manager Global Pistons Powertrain Federal Mogul, Bernhard Motel

Senior Vice President Corporate Development And Strategy Icahn Automotive, James Healy

Vice President Corporate Technology And Cybersecurity, Dustin Goodwin

Vice President Treasury Management, Courtney Mather

Chairman, Carl C. Icahn, age 84

Board Member, Jack Wasserman

Treasurer, John Saldarelli

Board Member, William Leidesdorf

Auditors: Grant Thornton LLP

LOCATIONS

HQ: Icahn Enterprises LP
16690 Collins Avenue, Penthouse Suite, Sunny Isles Beach, FL 33160
Phone: 305 422-4000
Web: www.ielp.com

2017 Sales

	% of total
United States	69
Germany	9
Other countries	22
Total	**100**

PRODUCTS/OPERATIONS

2017 Sales

	$ mil.	% of total
Automotive	10,528	48
Energy	5,918	27
Railcar	2,306	11
Gaming	960	4
Real Estate	590	2
Metal	408	2
Home Fashion	183	1
Mining	93	-
Holding company	68	-
Investment	297	1
Total	**21,744**	**100**

Selected Subsidiaries

Ace Nevada Corp.
American Entertainment Properties Corp.
American Railcar Industries
AREP Oil & Gas Holdings LLC
AREP Real Estate Holdings LLC
Atlantic Coast Entertainment Holdings Inc.
Bayswater Development LLC
Federal-Mogul Corporation
Icahn Capital LP
Icahn Capital Management LP
Icahn Enterprises Holdings L.P.
Icahn Offshore LP
Icahn Onshore LP
New Seabury Properties L.L.C.
PEP Boys: Manny Moe and jack
PSC Metals Inc.
Tropicana Entertainment Inc.
Trump Taj Mahal
Viskase Companies Inc.
WestPoint Home LLC

COMPETITORS

Apollo Global Management	Leucadia National
	MSD Capital
Berkshire Hathaway	Soros Fund Management
Blackstone Group	The Trump Organization
Clark Enterprises	Vulcan
D. E. Shaw	Wesco Financial
KKR	

HISTORICAL FINANCIALS

Company Type: Public

Income Statement   FYE: December 31

	REVENUE ($ mil.)	NET INCOME ($ mil.)	NET PROFIT MARGIN	EMPLOYEES
12/19	8,992	(1,098)	—	28,033
12/18	11,777	1,507	12.8%	29,034
12/17	21,744	2,430	11.2%	89,034
12/16	16,348	(1,128)	—	90,960
12/15	15,272	(1,194)	—	73,786
Annual Growth	(12.4%)	—	—	(21.5%)

2019 Year-End Financials

Debt ratio: 33.25%	No. of shares (mil.): 214
Return on equity: —	Dividends
Cash ($ mil.): 4,945	Yield: 13.0%
Current ratio: 3.28	Payout: —
Long-term debt ($ mil.): 8,192	Market value ($ mil.): 13,166

	STOCK PRICE ($) FY Close	P/E High/Low	PER SHARE ($) Earnings	Dividends	Book Value
12/19	61.50	— —	(5.38)	8.00	25.49
12/18	57.08	7 4	11.46	7.00	34.12
12/17	53.00	4 3	14.80	6.00	29.42
12/16	59.92	— —	(8.07)	6.00	14.88
12/15	61.30	— —	(9.29)	6.00	30.32
Annual Growth	0.1%	— —	—	7.5%	(4.3%)

ICE DATA SERVICES, INC.

EXECUTIVES

Pres, Scott A Hill
Treasurer, Martin Hunter
Secretary, Octavia Spencer
Vice President, Chuck Adkins
Vice President Information TEC, Scott Caudell
Director Evaluated Op, Steve Miano
Oracle Database Administrator, Sudhir Patel
Senior Relationship Manager, Kevin Mulvey
Global Data Administration Man, Nick Benkovich
Director, Joseph Greiner
Manager, Lisa Dizenzo

LOCATIONS

HQ: ICE DATA SERVICES, INC.
32 CROSBY DR STE 100, BEDFORD, MA 017301448
Phone: 781 687-8500

HISTORICAL FINANCIALS

Company Type: Private

Income Statement   FYE: December 31

	ASSETS ($ mil.)	NET INCOME ($ mil.)	INCOME AS % OF ASSETS	EMPLOYEES
12/13	3,968	33	0.8%	2,600
12/12	3,962	1	0.0%	—
12/11	4,093	(29)	—	—
Annual Growth	(1.5%)	—	—	—

Illinois Tool Works, Inc.

Illinois Tool Works (ITW) manufactures and services equipment for the automotive construction electronics food beverage decorative surfaces and medical components industries. The company makes metal and plastic fasteners components and assemblies used in light vehicles automobiles and industrial applications. It also manufactures cooking equipment such as ovens ranges and broilers equipment and software for testing and measuring materials structures gases and fluids. The company's brands include Shakeproof Instron and Rain-X. ITW has operations in about 55 countries but the customers in the US supply about 45% of the company's revenue. It was founded in 1912.

Operations

ITW operates through seven segments: Automotive OEM more than 20% of revenue; Test & Measurement and Electronics Specialty Products and Food Equipment all about 15%; and Polymers & Fluids and Construction Products and Welding about 10% each.

The company's segments operate brands that are well-known to customers. Among them are Deltar and Shakeproof in Automotive; Hobart in Food Equipment; Instron in Test & Measurement and Electronics; Miller in Welding; Rain-X and Permatex in Polymers & Fluids; Paslode in Construction Products; and Hi-Cone in Specialty Products.

Geographic Reach

ITW operates about 280 plants and offices in about 55 countries (excluding the United States) notably China France Germany and the UK. The Illinois-based company depends on the US for about 45% of its sales. Other major markets include Europe the Middle East and Africa (EMEA) about 30% of revenue; and the Asia/Pacific region more than 15% of revenue.

Sales and Marketing

ITW distributes its products directly to industrial manufacturers and through independent distributors. It serves customers in a range of industries including automotive manufacturers automotive aftermarket general industrial commercial food equipment and construction.

Advertising costs were $48 million $50 million and $53 million for the years ended 2019 2018 and 2017 respectively.

Financial Performance

ITW has enjoyed 4-year revenue gain starting in 2015 but hit a snag and decrease in revenue in 2019. Income for the same period registered a fluctuation.

In 2019 revenue dipped to $14.1 billion a decrease of $659 million from 2018 due to unfavorable effect of foreign currency translation lower organic revenue and divestitures.

Net income slipped to $2.5 billion in 2019 from $2.6 billion in 2018 for the same reasons why revenue have gone down.

ITW's coffers held $2 billion in cash in 2019 compared to $1.5 billion the year before. Operations generated cash totaling $3 billion in 2019 while investing and financing activities used $183 million and $2.3 billion respectively.

Strategy

ITW focuses on a five-year enterprise strategy with key initiatives that include portfolio management business structure simplification and strategic sourcing. This entails making internal investments that support organic growth to sustain its core businesses.

ITW's portfolio management initiative includes divesting businesses that are no longer aligned with the company's long-term objectives. This strategy has cut expenses and increased operating income.

Business Structure Simplification was implemented to simplify and scale up ITW's operating structure to support increased engineering marketing and sales resources and improve global reach and competitiveness.

The Strategic Sourcing initiative established sourcing as a core strategic and operational capability at ITW.

Company Background

In the early years of the 20th century Byron Smith founder of Chicago's Northern Trust Company recognized that rapid industrialization was outgrowing the capacity of small shops to supply machine tools. Smith encouraged two of his four sons to launch Illinois Tool Works (ITW) in 1912. Harold C. Smith became president of ITW in 1915 and expanded its product line into automotive parts.

ITW developed the Shakeproof fastener the first twisted-tooth lock washer in 1923. When Harold C. died in 1936 his son Harold B. took up the torch and he decentralized the company and exhorted salesmen to learn customers' businesses so they could develop products before customers recognized they needed them. Smith plowed profits back into research as WWII spurred demand.

EXECUTIVES

Evp Test And Measurement And Electronics, Steven L. (Steve) Martindale, age 63
Chairman And Ceo, E. Scott Santi, age 58, $1,205,313 total compensation
Evp Specialty Products, Roland M. Martel, age 66, $534,434 total compensation
Evp Polymers And Fluids, Juan Valls, age 59
Svp And Cfo, Michael M. Larsen, age 51, $702,152 total compensation
Evp Automotive Oem, Sundaram (Naga) Nagarajan, age 57, $520,456 total compensation
Evp Welding, John R. Hartnett, age 60
Vp And Cio, Mike Parisi
Evp Construction Products, Michael R. Zimmerman, age 59
Evp Food Equipment, Lei Zhang Schlitz, age 53
Executive Vice President, Jane Warner
Vice President Strategic Marketing, Hannelore Rittinger
National Account Manager, Bob Beal
Vice President And General Manager, Cary Moreth
Vice Chairman, Christopher (Chris) O'Herlihy, age 56
Auditors: Deloitte & Touche LLP

LOCATIONS

HQ: Illinois Tool Works, Inc.
155 Harlem Avenue, Glenview, IL 60025
Phone: 847 724-7500
Web: www.itw.com

2017 Sales

	$ mil.	% of total
North America		
United States	6,243	43
Canada/Mexico	996	7
Europe Middle East and Africa	4,102	29
Asia Pacific	2,577	18
South America	396	3
Total	**14,314**	**100**

PRODUCTS/OPERATIONS

2017 Sales

	$ mil.	% of total
Automotive OEM	3,271	23
Food Equipment	2,123	15
Test & Measurement and Electronics	2,069	14
Specialty Products	1,938	14
Polymers & Fluids	1,724	12
Construction Products	1,672	12
Welding	1,538	10
Intersegment revenue	(21)	-
Total	**14,314**	**100**

Selected Products

Construction products
　Anchors for concrete applications
　Anchors for retail
　Fasteners concrete applications
　Fasteners for retail
　Fasteners for wood and metal applications
　Metal plate truss components
　Packaged hardware for retail
Decorative surfaces
　Decorative high-pressure laminate for furniture office and retail space and countertops
　High-pressure laminate worktops
Food equipment
　Cooking equipment
　Ovens
　Ranges
　Broilers
　Food processing equipment
　Slicers
　Mixers
　Scales
　Kitchen exhaust systems
　Pollution-control systems
　Refrigeration equipment
　Refrigerators
　Freezers
　Prep tables
　Ventilation Systems
　Warewashing equipment
Industrial packaging
　Metal jacketing
　Paper products that protect goods in transit
　Plastic products that protect goods in transit
　Plastic strapping
　Plastic stretch film
　Steel strapping
Polymers and fluids
　Adhesives
　Industrial
　Construction
　Consumer
　Chemical fluids that clean or add lubrication to machines
　Epoxy and resin-based coating products for industrial applications
　Hand wipes and cleaners for industrial applications
　Pressure-sensitive adhesives and components
　Telecommunications
　Electronics
　Medical
　Transportation
　Resin-based coating products for industrial applications
Power systems and electronics
　Airport ground support equipment
　Arc welding equipment
　Component packaging
　Electronic components
　Equipment for microelectronics assembly
　Metal arc welding consumables
　Metal solder materials for PC board fabrication
Transportation
　Fillers for auto body repair
　Fluids for auto aftermarket maintenance and appearance
　Metal components for automobiles and light trucks
　Patch products for the marine industry
　Plastic components for automobiles and light trucks
　Polyester coatings for the marine industry
　Polymers for auto aftermarket maintenance and appearance
　Putties for auto body repair
Other
　Equipment and related software for testing and measuring of materials and structures
　Film used to decorate consumer products
　Foil used to decorate consumer products
　Plastic reclosable packaging for consumer food storage
　Plastic consumables that multi-pack cans and bottles and related equipment
　Plastic for appliances and industrial applications
　Metal fasteners for appliances and industrial applications

COMPETITORS

3M	Marmon Group
BASF SE	NCH
Cummins	Nordson
ESAB	Park-Ohio Holdings
Emerson Electric	PennEngineering
Federal Screw Works	Snap-on
GE	Stanley Black and
Graco	Decker
IBIDEN	Textron
Koch Enterprises	TriMas
Lincoln Electric	Victor Technologies
Manitowoc	W. R. Grace

HISTORICAL FINANCIALS

Company Type: Public

Income Statement
FYE: December 31

	REVENUE ($ mil.)	NET INCOME ($ mil.)	NET PROFIT MARGIN	EMPLOYEES
12/19	14,109	2,521	17.9%	45,000
12/18	14,768	2,563	17.4%	48,000
12/17	14,314	1,687	11.8%	50,000
12/16	13,599	2,035	15.0%	50,000
12/15	13,405	1,899	14.2%	48,000
Annual Growth	1.3%	7.3%	—	(1.6%)

2019 Year-End Financials

Debt ratio: 51.49%
Return on equity: 80.29%
Cash ($ mil.): 1,981
Current ratio: 2.90
Long-term debt ($ mil.): 7,754

No. of shares (mil.): 319
Dividends
　Yield: 2.3%
　Payout: 54.5%
Market value ($ mil.): 57,446

	STOCK PRICE ($) FY Close	P/E High/Low	PER SHARE ($) Earnings	Dividends	Book Value
12/19	179.63	23 16	7.74	4.14	9.46
12/18	126.69	23 16	7.60	3.56	9.92
12/17	166.85	35 25	4.86	2.86	13.43
12/16	122.46	22 14	5.70	2.40	12.26
12/15	92.68	19 16	5.13	2.07	14.36
Annual Growth	18.0%	— —	10.8%	18.9%	(9.9%)

Independent Bank Corp (MA)

Independent Bank wants to rock the northeast. Its banking subsidiary Rockland Trust operates almost 75 retail branches as well as investment and lending offices in Eastern Massachusetts and Rhode Island. Serving area individuals and small to midsized businesses the bank offers standard services such as checking and savings accounts CDs and credit cards in addition to insurance products financial planning trust services. Commercial loans including industrial construction and small business loans make up more than 70% of Rockland Trust's loan portfolio. Incorporated in 1985 the bank boasts total assets of some $7.5 billion.

Operations

About 28% of Independent Bank's loan portfolio is made up of consumer real estate loans which include residential mortgages and home equity loans and lines; while personal loans and auto loans make up around 1% of the portfolio. Through an agreement with LPL Investment Holdings Rockland Trust offers investment products such as securities and insurance.

Independent Bank generated 70% of its total revenue from interest and fee income on loans in 2014 and another 6% from interest and dividends on investment securities. Investment management fees made up 6% of total revenue for the year while deposit account fees and interchange and ATM fees combined made up 11%.

Geographic Reach

Rockland Trust boasts nearly 75 retail branches and three limited-services branches located in Eastern Massachusetts in the counties of Barnstable Bristol Middlesex Norfolk Plymouth and Worcester.

Sales and Marketing

The company's borrowers include consumers and small-to-medium sized businesses with credit needs up to $250000 and revenues of less than $2.5 million. Independent Bank spent $3.86 million on advertising in 2014 compared to $4.28 million and $3.95 million in 2013 and 2012 respectively.

Financial Performance

Independent Bank Corp's revenues and profits have trended higher in recent years thanks to continued loan business growth from both acquisitions and through organic expansion higher deposit account and ATM fee income from customer base growth and thanks to a decline in loan loss provisions as the credit quality of its loan portfolio has improved with the strengthened economy.

The bank's revenue rose by 5% to $286.40 million in 2014 mostly thanks to higher interest income as its loan business growth continued to outpace the margin-eating impacts of low interest rates. Independent's non-interest income also rose by 3% thanks to a combination of higher interchange and ATM fees and investment management fees.

Higher revenue and lower interest expenses on deposits in 2014 drove Independent Bank Corp's net income up by 19% to $59.85 million. Despite higher earnings the company's operating cash dove sharply primarily because of working capital changes related to its loans held for sale and changes in other assets.

Strategy

Independent Bank planned in 2015 to grow its loans organically between 4-6% for the year while growing its deposits between 3% and 4%. The company has also been expanding its fee-based revenue business especially in its investment management segment with expectations of growing the business by another 3% to 4% in 2015.

In addition to organic growth in other financial services areas Independent Bank has expanded via acquisitions.

Mergers and Acquisitions

In 2019 Independent Bank acquired Hyde Park Massachusetts-based Blue Hills Bancorp—the holding company for The Blue Hills Bank—for about $170 million. The acquisition furthers Independent's strategy of acquiring banks in overlapping and adjacent markets.

Company Background

In past years Independent Bank launched institutional asset managers Bright Rock Capital Management (2010) and Compass Exchange Advisors (2006) and formed a handful of mutual funds.

EXECUTIVES

Executive Vice President Director Of Retail Delivery Business Banking & Home Equity Lending, Jane L. Lundquist, age 63, $262,981 total compensation

President Ceo And Director Independent Bank Corp. And Rockland Trust, Christopher (Chris) Oddleifson, age 61, $589,616 total compensation

Cfo, Robert D. Cozzone

Executive Vice President Commercial Banking, Gerard F. Nadeau, age 62, $322,308 total compensation

Chief Information Officer, Barry Jensen

Chairman, Donna L. Abelli

Auditors: Ernst & Young LLP

LOCATIONS

HQ: Independent Bank Corp (MA)
2036 Washington Street, Hanover, MA 02339
Phone: 781 878-6100
Web: www.RocklandTrust.com

PRODUCTS/OPERATIONS

2012 Sales

	$ mil.	% of total
Interest		
Loans	178	69
Taxable securities including dividends	16	6
Other	1	-
Noninterest		
Service charges on deposit accounts	16	6
Wealth management	14	6
Interchange & ATM fees	9	4
Other	21	9
Adjustments	(0.1)	-
Total	**258**	**100**

COMPETITORS

Bank of America	Hingham Institution
Citizens Financial	for Savings
Group	Sovereign Bank
Eastern Bank	TD Bank USA

HISTORICAL FINANCIALS

Company Type: Public

Income Statement
FYE: December 31

	ASSETS ($ mil.)	NET INCOME ($ mil.)	INCOME AS % OF ASSETS	EMPLOYEES
12/19	11,395	165	1.4%	1,348
12/18	8,851	121	1.4%	1,188
12/17	8,082	87	1.1%	1,108
12/16	7,709	76	1.0%	1,103
12/15	7,210	64	0.9%	1,051
Annual Growth	**12.1%**	**26.3%**	**—**	**6.4%**

2019 Year-End Financials

Debt ratio: 1.64%
Return on equity: 11.88%
Cash ($ mil.): 150
Current ratio: —
Long-term debt ($ mil.): —

No. of shares (mil.): 34
Dividends
Yield: 2.1%
Payout: 37.2%
Market value ($ mil.): 2,862

	STOCK PRICE ($) FY Close	P/E High/Low		PER SHARE ($) Earnings	Dividends	Book Value
12/19	83.25	17	13	5.03	1.76	49.69
12/18	70.31	21	15	4.40	1.52	38.23
12/17	69.85	24	19	3.19	1.28	34.38
12/16	70.45	24	19	2.90	1.16	32.02
12/15	46.52	21	15	2.50	1.04	29.40
Annual Growth	**15.7%**	**—**		**19.1%**	**14.1%**	**14.0%**

Independent Bank Corporation (Ionia, MI)

Independent Bank Corporation is the holding company for Independent Bank which serves rural and suburban communities of Michigan's Lower Peninsula from more than 100 branches. The bank offers traditional deposit products including checking and savings accounts and CDs. Loans to businesses account for about 40% of the bank's portfolio; real estate mortgages are more than a third. Independent Bank also offers additional products and services like title insurance through subsidiary Independent Title Services and investments through agreement with third-party provider PrimeVest.

Operations

The company also owns Mepco Finance which acquires and services payment plans for extended automobile warranties.

Financial Performance

The company's revenue has been trending down year-over-year. However its net income and cash on hand have both been spiking up across recent fiscal years.

Strategy

As Michigan's economy has exhibited signs of stabilizing and the company's results have relatively improved as well. Independent Bank has reduced its number of high-risk loans non-performing loans and delinquency rates.

EXECUTIVES

Assistant Vice President Senior Business Analyst, Phil Hamlin

Vice President Team Leader Commercial Loans, Stephen Hale

Executive Vice President, Stefanie Kimball

Vice President Sales Manager, Sue Fulk

Assistant Vice President Bank Manager, Chelsee Warman

Senior Vice President Mortgage Operations Manager, Susan Johnson

Executive Vice President And General Cou, Mark Collins

Auditors: Crowe LLP

LOCATIONS

HQ: Independent Bank Corporation (Ionia, MI)
4200 East Beltline, Grand Rapids, MI 49525
Phone: 616 527-5820
Web: www.independentbank.com

COMPETITORS

Bank of America	Flagstar Bancorp
Chemical Financial	Huntington Bancshares
Fifth Third	JPMorgan Chase
Firstbank	Mercantile Bank

HISTORICAL FINANCIALS

Company Type: Public

Income Statement
FYE: December 31

	ASSETS ($ mil.)	NET INCOME ($ mil.)	INCOME AS % OF ASSETS	EMPLOYEES
12/19	3,564	46	1.3%	994
12/18	3,353	39	1.2%	976
12/17	2,789	20	0.7%	911
12/16	2,548	22	0.9%	885
12/15	2,409	20	0.8%	831
Annual Growth	**10.3%**	**23.4%**	**—**	**4.6%**

2019 Year-End Financials

Debt ratio: 1.11%
Return on equity: 13.48%
Cash ($ mil.): 65
Current ratio: —
Long-term debt ($ mil.): —

No. of shares (mil.): 22
Dividends
Yield: 3.1%
Payout: 39.7%
Market value ($ mil.): 509

	STOCK PRICE ($) FY Close	P/E High/Low		PER SHARE ($) Earnings	Dividends	Book Value
12/19	22.65	12	9	2.00	0.72	15.58
12/18	21.02	16	12	1.68	0.60	14.38
12/17	22.35	24	20	0.95	0.42	12.42
12/16	21.70	21	13	1.05	0.34	11.71
12/15	15.23	18	14	0.86	0.26	11.28
Annual Growth	**10.4%**	**—**		**23.5%**	**29.0%**	**8.4%**

Independent Bank Group Inc.

It makes sense that a company that calls itself Independent Bank Group (IBG) would do business in a state that was once its own country. The bank holding company does business through subsidiary Independent Bank which operates about 40 banking offices and 70 branches in North and Central Texas Houston and Colorado. The banks offer standard personal and business accounts and services including some focused on small business owners. IBG has total assets of nearly $8.9 billion and loans of about $6.4 billion. The company traces its roots back 100 years but took its current shape in 2002.

Operations

In addition to its banking activities Independent Bank Group (IBG)also owns IBG Adriatica a mixed use development in the Dallas-Fort Worth area. The company does not intend to move into real estate but purchased the development where one of its branches is located to help maintain business in the area. It had also made commercial loans to several tenants of the development and saw the purchase as a way to protect its investments rather than have the entire property go into foreclosure.

Financial Performance

Independent Bank Group has shown increasing net income for several years and in fiscal 2016 grew revenue a further 20% to $210.0 million. Net income has likewise been consistently growing reaching $53.5 million up 39%. Cash from operations increased 85% to $80.3 million.

Strategy

Independent Bank Group's strategy is all about growth. It seeks organic growth in loans and deposits in existing locations by developing customer relationships while maintaining the quality of its loan portfolio. It also makes acquisitions: since 2010 it has made nine acquisitions most recently of Carlile Bancshares and its subsidiary Northstar Bank and Grand Bank in Dallas.

Mergers and Acquisitions

Independent Bank Group acquired Carlile Bancshares and its subsidiary Northstar Bank for around $434 million in 2017.

EXECUTIVES

Chairman President And Ceo, David R. Brooks, age 62, $650,000 total compensation
Evp And Coo, James C. (Jim) White, age 55
Vice Chairman And Chief Lending Officer And President Independent Bank Central Texas, Brian E. Hobart, age 55, $350,000 total compensation
Executive Vice President And Chief Financial Officer, Michelle S. Hickox, age 53, $265,000 total compensation
Evp And Secretary And Evp And Senior Operations Officer Independent Bank, Jan C. Webb, age 62
Senior Vice President, Amy Feagin
Vice President Commercial Lending, Kyle Morse
Assistant Vice President, Mallory Smith
Senior Vice President Credit Administration Manager, Stephanie Carrington
Vice President Market Manager, Tisha Reyes
Assistant Vice President, Brent Garrett
Senior Vice President Director Of Financial Reporting, Leslie Beseda
Senior Vice President Program Management, Chris Phelps
Svp Hr Director Texas, Pam Murray
Vice President, Montgomery Brenda

Senior Vice President Director Of Human Resources, Murray Pam
Executive Vice President, Duane Reaves
Senior Vice President, Julie Crump
Senior Vice President, Noorani Feroz
Senior Vice President Commercial Relationship Manager, Charlie Cartwright
Executive Vice President, Ralph Ramsey
Senior Vice President Commercial Lending, Landon Gann
Vice President Commercial Lending, Joe Booth
Avp; Talent Aquisition Senior Partner, Shayla Maxey
Assistant Vice President Senior Financial Analyst, Lesli Gilbert
Vice President, Richard Cervenka
Vice President, Paul Langdale
Senior Vice President Mortgage Operations, Scott Stone
Vice President Commercial Lending, Robin Thomas
Executive Vice President And Chief Credit Officer, Russ Lessmann
Vice President, Stefani Dayton
Senior Vice President, David Stanley
Vice President And Manager Compensation And Benefits, Laura Kurowski
Vice Chairman And Chief Risk Officer, Daniel W. Brooks, age 60
Auditors: RSM US LLP

LOCATIONS

HQ: Independent Bank Group Inc.
7777 Henneman Way, McKinney, TX 75070-1711
Phone: 972 562-9004
Web: www.ibtx.com

PRODUCTS/OPERATIONS

2012 Loan Portfolio

	% of total
Real estate	
Commercial	47
Residential	23
Construction land & land development	7
Single-family interim construction	5
Commercial	12
Agricultural	3
Consumer	3
Total	**100**

Selected Acquisition

Town Center Bank (2010 North Texas)
Farmersville Bancshares Inc. (2010 North Texas)
I Bank Holding Company Inc. (2012 Austin/Central Texas)
The Community Group Inc. (2012 Dallas/North Texas)

COMPETITORS

BBVA Compass Bancshares	HSBC International Bancshares
Bank of America	JPMorgan Chase
Broadway Bancshares	Lone Star Bank
Capital One	PlainsCapital
Citigroup	Prosperity Bancshares
Comerica	Texas Capital Bancshares
Cullen/Frost Bankers	
Extraco	Wells Fargo
First Financial Bankshares	Woodforest Financial

HISTORICAL FINANCIALS

Company Type: Public

Income Statement   FYE: December 31

	ASSETS ($ mil.)	NET INCOME ($ mil.)	INCOME AS % OF ASSETS	EMPLOYEES
12/19	14,958	192	1.3%	1,469
12/18	9,849	128	1.3%	1,087
12/17	8,684	76	0.9%	924
12/16	5,852	53	0.9%	577
12/15	5,055	38	0.8%	587
Annual Growth	**31.2%**	**49.3%**	**—**	**25.8%**

2019 Year-End Financials

Debt ratio: 1.71%	No. of shares (mil.): 42
Return on equity: 9.77%	Dividends
Cash ($ mil.): 565	Yield: 1.8%
Current ratio: —	Payout: 22.6%
Long-term debt ($ mil.): —	Market value ($ mil.): 2,381

	STOCK PRICE ($) FY Close	P/E High/Low	PER SHARE ($) Earnings	Dividends	Book Value
12/19	55.44	14 11	4.46	1.00	54.48
12/18	45.77	18 10	4.33	0.54	52.50
12/17	67.60	24 18	2.97	0.40	47.28
12/16	62.40	22 9	2.88	0.34	35.63
12/15	32.00	21 13	2.21	0.32	34.09
Annual Growth	**14.7%**	**— —**	**19.2%**	**33.0%**	**12.4%**

Insight Enterprises Inc.

Insight Enterprises distributes computer hardware and software and provides IT services for businesses schools and government agencies and departments. The company offers thousands of products from hundreds of manufacturers (including Microsoft HP Inc. IBM and Cisco) as well as cloud services. Insight also provides integration services to knit hardware and software together for its customers. The company uses field sales agents and an e-commerce site to reach its clients. Geographically Insight gets about 75% of sales from customers in the US and in terms of customers its large business clients provide about 75% of sales.

Operations

Insight sells technology in three areas: Hardware software and services.

In hardware about 60% of sales the company offer products from Cisco Systems Dell Technologies HP Inc. Lenovo Hewlett Packard Enterprise Co. NetApp Apple Microsoft IBM and hundreds of others.

The software segment over 25% of sales carries products from Microsoft VMware Adobe IBM Software Symantec Citrix and more.

Insight's services business about 15%of sales combines the hardware and software aspects for its customers. Among the needs it addresses are supply chain outfitting the workforce with appropriate equipment helping companies move operations to cloud environments and implementing digital technologies.

Geographic Reach

Insight's sales are concentrated in the US which provides about 75% of revenue with Canada contributing another few percentage points. Europe Middle East and Africa region contributes about 20% and Asia-Pacific with less than 5%. The

Tempe Arizona-based company has operations in about 20 counties.

Sales and Marketing

Although the company sells software and hardware from hundreds of companies Insight relies on five major vendors Microsoft Dell Cisco System HP Inc. and Lenovo for over 50% of its sales. Microsoft alone accounts for over 15% of Insight's sales.

Insight makes almost 75% of its sales to large corporate customers while government and small and medium business customers about split the other remainder.

Insight's advertising expense were $62.9 million $57.4 million and $47.1 million for the years 2019 2018 and 2017 respectively.

Financial Performance

Insight has posted rising sales for the past five years (since 2015). Boosted by a 22% jump in 2017 from 2016 due to increased integration work and acquisitions the company's total sales have an overall growth of 44%.

In 2019 revenue rose about 9% to $7.7 billion up about $2.4 billion from 2018 on stronger hardware and services sales. Hardware revenue increased 10% driven by sales of client devices storage and networking products to large customers. Service sales jumped 25% from cloud maintenance and enterprise agreement fees as well as contributions from the Cardinal acquisition. Software sales also grew 14%.

Insight's net income declined 3% to $159.4 million in 2019 from 2018 due to increase in costs of goods sold and expenses.

The company's cash and equivalents dipped to $116.3 million in 2019 decrease of about $28 million from 2018. Operations generated $127.9 million in 2019 while investing activities activities used $733.3 million and financing activities generated $159 million.

Strategy

Insight's business strategy consists of the following:

Digital Innovation – The company leverages emerging technologies to build innovative applications to improve clients' business performance engage customers and uncover new revenue streams;

Cloud and Data Center Transformation – Insight helps businesses modernize and secure critical platforms to transform IT;

Connected Workforce – The company helps clients deliver a secure modern experience to their workforce driving productivity in the workplace and helping to attract and retain talent in this competitive marketplace;

Supply Chain Optimization – Through Insight's core business it helps clients effectively and efficiently acquire all of their information technology needs leveraging the company's scale and supply chain expertise.

Mergers and Acquisitions

In 2020 Insight Enterprises announced the acquisition of consulting and services firm vNext. vNext is a market leader in digital consulting services and managed services and specializes in Microsoft Cloud solutions. "Acquiring vNext was an obvious move for us. The quality of our workforce our common values and our view of the market have enabled us to quickly forge a shared vision: to be the partner of choice for enterprise digital transformation initiatives in the French market" said Richard Ramos general manager of Insight France.

In mid-2019 Insight Enterprises completed the acquisition of PCM Inca provider of IT products and services. The addition of PCM expands Insight's footprint in the United States Canada and the United Kingdom allowing the company to further capitalize on driving digital transformation modernizing and securing their data platforms empowering their employees with tools that fuel productivity and simplifying IT procurement and asset management.

Company Background

Eric Crown worked for a small computer retail chain in the mid-1980s before leaving to market PCs. In 1986 he and his brother Tim pooled $2000 from credit cards and $1300 in savings and anticipating a drop in hard drive prices placed an ad for low-cost hard drives in a computer magazine. The ad pulled in $20000 worth of sales and since costs did indeed drop the profit was enough to start a new company Hard Drives International. In 1988 they changed the name to Insight Enterprises; by 1991 the Crowns also sold Insight-branded PCs software and peripherals (discontinued in 1995). The company passed the $100 million revenue mark in 1992.

Over the years through organic growth and acquisitions Insight expanded into new markets and exited others and growing to compete with top distributors and integrators such as CDW and Accenture.

HISTORY

Eric Crown worked for a small computer retail chain in the mid-1980s before leaving to market PCs. In 1986 he and his brother Tim pooled $2000 from credit cards and $1300 in savings and anticipating a drop in hard drive prices placed an ad for low-cost hard drives in a computer magazine. The ad pulled in $20000 worth of sales and since costs did indeed drop the profit was enough to start a new company Hard Drives International. In 1988 they changed the name to Insight Enterprises; by 1991 the Crowns also sold Insight-branded PCs software and peripherals (discontinued in 1995). The company passed the $100 million revenue mark in 1992.

Insight shifted its marketing focus to catalogs in 1993 and had a circulation of more than 7 million by 1995. The company went public that year and entered an alliance with Computer City (acquired by CompUSA in 1998) to handle its mail-order fulfillment. It also launched its website. The next year subsidiary Insight Direct began to offer on-site service warranties and in 1997 retailing subsidiary Direct Alliance was chosen to provide product fulfillment for Internet software firm Geo Publishing. That year the company began sponsoring the Copper Bowl a college football game played in Arizona which was renamed the Insight.com Bowl (and later the Insight Bowl).

Looking beyond the US in 1998 Insight established operations in Canada and acquired direct marketers Choice Peripherals (UK) and Computerprofis Computersysteme (Germany). At home it added direct marketer Treasure Chest Computers. Sales passed the billion-dollar mark that year.

The company formed an alliance with Daisytek International in 1999 that expanded its product line by more than 10000. Soon thereafter Insight walked away from a merger with UK-based computer wholesaler Action Computer Supplies when Action's profits slumped.

Insight withdrew its planned IPO and spinoff of Direct Alliance in 2001 due to poor market conditions. Also that month Eric became chairman and Tim became CEO (they had previously shared the title of co-CEO). Insight ended up buying Action Computer Supplies in 2001. It also shut down its German operations and acquired computer direct marketers in both the UK and Canada in late 2001.

In April 2002 Insight acquired Comark a leading private reseller of computers peripherals and computer supplies in the US and began integrating its operations into Insight North America's existing operational structure.

Tim stepped down as president and CEO and became chairman in late 2004 while Eric assumed the title of chairman emeritus. The company appointed IBM veteran Richard Fennessy to the position of president and CEO. That year Insight spun off its UK-based Internet service provider PlusNet.

In 2006 Insight Enterprises bought software and mobile solutions firm Software Spectrum.

EXECUTIVES

President And Ceo, Kenneth T. (Ken) Lamneck, age 65, $800,000 total compensation
Cio, Michael Guggemos, age 55, $398,989 total compensation
Cfo, Glynis A. Bryan, age 61, $466,140 total compensation
President Insight Us, Steven W. Dodenhoff, age 57, $488,625 total compensation
President Insight Emea, Wolfgang Ebermann, age 55, $578,726 total compensation
Vice President Marketing, David Locker
Vice President Sales, Rob McConnell
Svp Finance And Operations Emea, Russell Leighton
Vice President Sales, Luke Purdon
Vice President Sales, Collin Ryan
Vice President Sales, Christy Arnold
Vp And Gm Digital Innovation, Stan Lequin
Vice President Sales, Jason Sullivan
Senior Vice President Na And Apac Software, Andrea Mattea
Senior Vice President Human Resources, Jennifer Fernandez
Vice President Sales, Mark Zawacki
Vice President Inside Sales, Brenda Hudson
Vice President Of Information Technology, Joseph Flynn
Vice President Support Services, Michael Parsons
Vp Services Emea, Rolf Adam
Vice President Services, Matt Jackson
Vice President Human Resources, Jen Vasin
Vice President, Mickey Bland
Chairman, Timothy A. (Tim) Crown, age 56
Auditors: KPMG LLP

LOCATIONS

HQ: Insight Enterprises Inc.
6820 South Harl Avenue, Tempe, AZ 85283
Phone: 480 333-3000
Web: www.insight.com

2018 Sales

	$ mil.	% of total
North America	5,363	75
Europe Middle East & Africa	1,530	22
Asia/Pacific	186	3
Total	**7,080**	**100**

2018 Sales

	$ mil.	% of total
United States	5,100	72
United Kingdom	843	12
Others Foreign	1,136	16
Total	**7,080**	**100**

PRODUCTS/OPERATIONS

2018 Sales

	$ mil.	% of total
Hardware	4,293	60
Software	1,956	28
Services	830	12
Total	**7,080**	**100**

Selected Products

Computer memory and processors
Desktop computers
Monitors
Networking equipment
Notebook computers
Printers and printing consumables
Servers
Software
Storage devices
Tablet computers

Selected Services

Business optimization software
  Business productivity
  Core infrastructure
  Software asset management
Collaboration
  Call/contact center
  Unified communications/messaging
  Video collaboration/conferencing
Cloud services
  Collaboration
  Infrastructure
  Messaging
  Security
Data center
  Infrastructure solutions
  Server solutions
  Storage solutions
Infrastructure and security
  Network infrastructure
  Security infrastructure
Managed services
  Business process outsourcing
  Connected real estate and sports
  Financing and leasing
  IT asset disposal
  Maintenance
  Product provisioning
  Remote network operations
  Telecom expense management
  Warehouse/integration
  Mobility
  Big Data
  Creativity
  Data protection

COMPETITORS

Accenture	HP
Amazon.com	IBM
Best Buy	Lenovo
Buy.com	Microsoft
CDW	Newegg
CompuCom	PC Mall
Convergys	PFSweb
Dell	SHI International
Digital River	Zones

HISTORICAL FINANCIALS

Company Type: Public

Income Statement				FYE: December 31
	REVENUE ($ mil.)	NET INCOME ($ mil.)	NET PROFIT MARGIN	EMPLOYEES
12/19	7,731	159	2.1%	11,261
12/18	7,080	163	2.3%	7,420
12/17	6,703	90	1.4%	6,697
12/16	5,485	84	1.5%	5,930
12/15	5,373	75	1.4%	5,761
Annual Growth	9.5%	20.4%	—	18.2%

2019 Year-End Financials

Debt ratio: 20.57%
Return on equity: 14.85%
Cash ($ mil.): 114
Current ratio: 1.62
Long-term debt ($ mil.): 857

No. of shares (mil.): 35
Dividends
  Yield: —
  Payout: —
Market value ($ mil.): 2,479

	STOCK PRICE ($) FY Close	P/E High/Low		PER SHARE ($) Earnings	Dividends	Book Value
12/19	70.29	16	9	4.43	0.00	32.90
12/18	40.75	12	7	4.55	0.00	27.82
12/17	38.29	19	14	2.50	0.00	23.54
12/16	40.44	18	9	2.32	0.00	20.11
12/15	25.12	16	12	1.98	0.00	18.48
Annual Growth	29.3%	—	—	22.3%	—	15.5%

Intel Corp

Intel Corp. is one of the computer chip companies Intel offers platform products that incorporate various components and technologies including a microprocessor and chipset a stand-alone SoC or a multichip package. It has dominated the PC chip market processors such as Intel Core processor family and the Intel Quark Intel Atom Celeron Pentium Intel Xeon and Itanium trademarks make up its CPU brands. Intel also includes autonomous cars and small low-power devices as well as a broad range of solutions targeting the data center wireless networking military medical and industrial market segments. The company's latest data center solutions target a wide range of use cases within cloud computing network infrastructure and intelligent edge applications and support high-growth workloads including AI and 5G. In addition Intel Corp. exited 5G smartphone modem business to increase the focus of its 5G efforts on the broader opportunity to modernize network and edge infrastructure. Intel was founded in 1968. The China including Hong Kong is the company's largest market accounting to nearly 30% of the company's total sales.

Operations

The company manages its business through these operating segments: Client Computing Group (more than 50%) Data Center Group (nearly 35%) Internet of Things Group (around 5%) Non-Volatile Memory Solutions Group (more than five percent) Programmable Solutions Group (less than five percent) and All other (nearly one percent).

DCG and CCG are the reportable operating segments. IOTG Mobileye NSG and PSG do not meet the quantitative thresholds to qualify as reportable operating segments; however it was elected to disclose the results of these non-reportable operating segments. The Internet of Things portfolio presented as Internet of Things is comprised of the IOTG and Mobileye operating segments.

Intel Corp.'s Client Computing Group is the company's workhorse. The business includes platforms designed for end-user form factors focusing on higher growth segments of 2-in-1 thin-and-light commercial and gaming and growing adjacencies such as connectivity graphics and memory.

The Data Center Group develops workload-optimized platforms for compute storage and network functions. It also makes chips for server-platforms and related products designed for the enterprise cloud government and communication infrastructure markets.

The Internet of Things Group develops high-performance compute for targeted verticals and embedded markets. The customers include retailers manufacturers healthcare providers energy companies automakers and governments. In addition Mobileye is the global leader in the development of computer vision and machine learning-based sensing data analysis localization mapping and driving policy technology.

The Programmable Solutions offers programmable semiconductors primarily FPGAs structured ASICs and related products for a broad range of market segments including communications data center industrial and military.

Non-Volatile Memory Solutions offers memory and storage products.

Intel makes most of its products in its own manufacturing facilities which allows the company to control the process for quality speed and flexibility. For some communications connectivity networking field programmable and memory components the company outsources manufacturing to third parties. Intel handles test and assembly in-house and through contractors.

Geographic Reach

Intel Corp. is based in California and has more than 100 locations around the globe with three assembly and test facilities in China Malaysia and Vietnam and six water fabrication in Arizona Oregon New Mexico Ireland Israel and other countries. Sales are well-distributed geographically with customers in China (including Hong Kong) generating about 30% of Intel's sales followed by Singapore and US customers over 20% each and customers in Taiwan who kick in nearly 15% of revenue.

Sales and Marketing

Intel sells its products primarily to original equipment manufacturers (OEMs) cloud service providers and original design manufacturers (ODMs). In addition Intel products are sold to makers of industrial and communications equipment.

Its customers also include those who buy PC components and other products through distributor reseller retail and OEM channels. Intel's worldwide reseller sales channel consists of thousands of indirect customers who are systems builders that purchase microprocessors and other products from distributors. The microprocessors and other products are also available in direct retail outlets.

Intel's three largest customers account for more than 40% of revenue. They are Dell Technologies more than 15% of sales and Lenovo Group (nearly 15%) and HP Inc. with around 10%.

Advertising costs including direct marketing recorded within MG&A expenses were $832 million in 2019 $1.2 billion in 2018 and $1.4 billion in 2017.

Financial Performance

Intel has posted company-record revenue in each of the past four years as it has maintained revenue from computer-related products and sales of its lineup of newer products for data centers and cloud computing have grown.

In 2019 the company's revenue totaled $72 billion a 2% increase from 2018.

Intel's profit declined less than a percentage. It totaled around $21 billion in 2019.

Intel's coffers held $4.2 billion in cash and equivalents in 2019 about $1.2 billion more than in 2018. Operations generated $33.1 billion in 2019 while investing and financing activities used $14.4 billion and $17.6 billion respectively.

Strategy

Intel deploys various forms of capital to execute its strategy in a way that seeks to reflect its corporate values help customers succeed and create value for stakeholders.

Leveraging cash flow to invest in itself and grow its capabilities supplement and strengthen its capabilities through acquisitions and strategic investments and provide returns to stockholders.

Investing significantly in R&D and IP to ensure that the company's process and product technologies are competitive in its strategic pursuit of making the world's best semiconductors and realizing data-centric opportunities.

Investing timely and at a level sufficient to meet customer demand for current technologies and prepare for future technologies.

Developing the talent needed to remain at the forefront of innovation and create a diverse inclusive and safe workplace.

Building trusted relationships for both Intel and its stakeholders including employees suppliers customers local communities and governments.

Continually striving to reduce its environmental footprint through efficient and responsible use of natural resources and materials used to create products.

Mergers and Acquisitions

In 2020 Intel acquires Camberwell London-based Rivet Networks and joins the Wireless Solutions Group within the Client Computing Group. Rivet Networks' key products including its Killer brand will integrate into Intel's broader PC Wi-Fi portfolio. This partnership will Boost Intel's Wi-Fi offerings for PC platforms Terms were not disclosed.

Intel acquires Moovit for approximately &900 million to enhance the daily mobility habits and needs of millions of Moovit users with the state-of-the-art safe affordable and eco-friendly transportation enabled by self-driving vehicles. Moovit is headquartered in Israel and is known for its urban mobility application that offers travelers around the world the best multimodal trip planning by combining public transportation bicycle and scooter services ride-hailing and car-sharing.

In 2019 Intel bought the Smart Edge software business from Toronto-based Pivot Technology Solutions for $27 million to aid in Intel's development of chips for the 5G mobile network market. Smart Edge software helps split up information and store it closer to users to make computing devices respond faster. The software is designed to run on Intel's chips.

Intel agreed to acquire California-based Barefoot Networks in 2019 to beef up its offerings for cloud computing applications. Barefoot designs and make chips that manage communication via Ethernet which is used to connect networked computers and servers. Barefoot's products fill a gap in Intel's portfolio and could help it compete more effectively against Broadcom the foremost product of such devices.

In 2019 Intel acquired UK's Omnitek a provider of video and vision for programmable processors that enable customized vision and artificial intelligence. Terms of the deal were not disclosed.

Intel acquired Ineda Systems a fabless chip company in 2019. Ineda's chips are used in autonomous driving artificial intelligence and the Internet of Things. The company is based in Hyderbad India where Intel plans to put a technology development center.

Company Background

The founding of Intel is one of the legendary stories of Silicon Valley. In 1968 three engineers from Fairchild Semiconductor created Intel in Mountain View California to develop technology for silicon-based chips. ("Intel" is a contraction of "integrated electronics.") The trio consisted of Robert Noyce (who co-invented the integrated circuit or IC in 1958) Gordon Moore and Andy Grove.

Intel initially provided computer memory chips such as DRAMs (1970) and EPROMs (1971). These successes funded the microprocessor designs that revolutionized the electronics industry. In 1971 Intel introduced the 4004 microprocessor promoted as "a micro-programmable computer on a chip."

EXECUTIVES

Corporate Vp And Gm Global Supply Management, Jacklyn A Sturm

Evp Corporate Strategy, Thomas M Kilroy, age 64

Interim Ceo, Robert H. (Bob) Swan, age 60, $194,800 total compensation

Evp And General Manager Product Assurance And Security, Leslie S. Culbertson

Vp Sales And Marketing Group; President Intel Americas, Gregory R. (Greg) Pearson, age 60, $545,000 total compensation

Vp Finance And Enterprise Services; Assistant Cfo, Stacy J. Smith, age 58, $800,000 total compensation

Svp And General Manager Automated Driving Group (adg), Douglas L. (Doug) Davis, age 59

Svp And General Manager Technology And Manufacturing Group, Sohail U. Ahmed

Svp And General Manager Non-volatile Memory (nvm) Solutions Group, Robert B. Crooke

Svp And General Manager Client Computing Group, Diane M. Bryant, age 59, $618,700 total compensation

Svp And Managing Director Intel Labs And Cto, Michael C. (Mike) Mayberry, age 63

Svp And General Manager Intel Product Assurance And Security Engineering Group, Joshua M. (Josh) Walden, age 58

Svp And General Manager Platform Engineering Group, Amir Faintuch

Svp And General Manager Software And Services Group (ssg), Douglas W. (Doug) Fisher

Evp And General Counsel, Steven R. (Steve) Rodgers

Evp And General Manager Data Center Group, Navin Shenoy

Svp And Chief Marketing Officer, Steven L. Fund

Svp And Chief Strategy Officer, Aicha S. Evans

Svp And General Manager Internet Of Things (iot) Group, Thomas P. (Tom) Lantzsch

Svp And President Intel Capital, Wendell M. Brooks

Corporate Vp And Cio, Paula C. Tolliver

Group President Technology Systems Architecture And Client Group And Chief Engineering Officer, Venkata M. (Murthy) Renduchintala, age 55, $900,000 total compensation

Corporate Vp And General Manager Technology And Manufacturing Group, Ann B. Kelleher

Corporate Vp And General Manager Programmable Solutions Group (psg), Daniel R. (Dan) McNamara

Corporate Vp And General Manager Artificial Intelligence Products Group, Naveen G. Rao

Vice President Tmg And General Manager Intel Ireland, Eamonn Sinnott

Intel Information Technology Vpro Amt Product Manager, Omer Livne

Vice President Platform Engineering Group And Gm Quality Advancement, John Pierron

Vice President Sales And Marketing Group Gm Global Communications Group, Paul Bergevin

Vice President Platform Engineering Capability, Mandy Mock

Senior Vice President, Arun Chandrasekhar

Northeast Regional Vice President, Praveen Kundurthy

Vice President Data Center Group And Gm Cloud Service Provider Group, Raejeanne Skillern

Corporate Vp Non Volatile Memory Solutions Group Worldwide Manufacturing, Keyvan Esfarjani

Vice President Platform Engineering Group And Director Manufacturing Validation Engineering Pre S, Jagannath Keshava

National Sales Manager Intel Malaysia, Simon Chan

Technical Assistant To Kim Stevenson Corporate Vice President And Cio Intel, Debbie Doran

Vice President Sales Andamp; Marketing Group Andamp; Director Management Andamp; Operations, Kit Chee

Vice President, Lei Shao

Vice President Of Systems, Patricia A Mcdonald

Vice President Data Center Group And Director Platform Hardware Engineering Division, Viktor Tymchenko

Vice President Technology And Manufacturing Group And Director Lead Technology Vehicle Development, Ying Zhang

Vice President Intel Labs And Director Integrated Platform Research Lab, Vida Ilderem

Vice President Associate General Counsel, Mark Friedman

Executive Vice President And Chief Development Officer, Gadi Oren

Corporate Vp And Cfo Data Center Group, Christina Min

Technical Advisor To Intel Vp (sales Marketing Group), Iris Wu

Vice President, Paul Stacey

Vice President Director Manager, Ulf Hofemeier

Vice President Applications And Support, John Kreatsoulas

Vice President Tmg Plant Manager Nm Site Fab 11x, Kirby Jefferson

Corporate Vice President And Gm Data Center Engineering And Architecture Group, Zane Ball

Vice President Government And Policy Group, Peter Cleveland

Corporate Vice President Deputy General Counsel Corporate Secretary, Suzan Miller

Vp And Germany Country Manager, Christin Eisenschmid

Vice President And General Manager, Gadi Singer

Vice President Software And Services Group And Director Open Source Technology Center Core Operati, Hillarie Prestopine

Corporate Vp And Gm Datacenter Solutions Group, Jason Waxman

Vice President Non Volatile Memory Solutions Group And Director Manufacturing And Automation Syste, Kumud Srinivasan

Vice President Core And Visual Computing Group And Gm Visual Technologies Team, Ari Rauch

Vice President Communication And Devices Group And Gm Modem And Platform Software Group, Abhay Joshi

Vice President Intel Capital Global Business Development Intel Sports, Howard Wright

Vice President Of Finance And Director Of Investor R, Shelley Floyd

Vice President, Armin Sarstedt

Vice President, Shahaf Kieselstein

Vice President Consumer Product Management, Alan LeFort

Vice President Executive Assistant, Valerie Montoya

Vice President Global Marketing And Communications, Alyson Griffin

Corporate Vice President And Gm Global Accounts Sales And Marketing Group, Christopher J Bruno

Corporate Vice President And Gm Assembly Test Manufacturing, Robin Martin

Vp Of New Technology Group And Gm Of New Business Group, Jerry Bautista

Vice President Information Technology And Chief Data Officer Enterprise Data And Platforms Informa, Aziz Safa

Vp Of Automated Driving Group And Gm Of Automated Driving Solutions, Katherine Winter

Senior Vice President And General Manager Network Platforms Group, Sandra Rivera

Vice President Information Technology Group And General Manager Information Technology Client And Collaboration Solutions, Dave Aires

Vice President Platform Engineering Group, Anwar Awad

Vice President Architecture Data Center Group, Anil Rao

Vice President Engineering, Raheel Khan

Vice President Of Visual Technology Architecture Group, Martin Ashton

Vice President Sales And Marketing Group And General Manager Sales Non Volatile Memory Solutions Group, John Vossoughi

Vice President, Amir Khosrowshahi

Senior Vice President Intel President And Chief Executive Officer Of Mobileye An Intel Company, Amnon Shashua

Vice President Network Platforms Group And Gm Network Custom Solutions Division, Cristina Rodriguez

Corporate Vice President And Corporate Secretary, Susie Giordano

Vice President Intel Capital And Director Mergers And Acquisition, Raheel A Shah

Vice President, Doug Davis

Vice President Software And Services Group And Director Platform Application Engineering, Peter Baker

Vice President Client Computing Group And Gm Business Client Platforms Division, Thomas Garrison

Vice President Global Marketing And Communications And Gm Global Client Marketing, Robert DeLine

Vice President Technology And Manufacturing Group And Director Assembly And Test Technology Develo, Jeffrey Pettinato

Vice President Client Computing Group And Gm Client Planning And Architecture, Adam King

Vice President Technology And Manufacturing Group And 22nm Plant Manager Arizona Fab Sort Manufa, Joseph McDonnell

Vice President Client Computing Group And Gm Mobility Client Platform, Christopher Walker

Vice President Data Center Group; President And Gm Intel Federal Llc, O'Neil Green

Corporate Vp And Gm Internet Of Things Group Sales, Rosemary M Schooler

Vp Software And Services Group And Gm Client Systems And Software, Michael C Uhl

Corporate Vp Platform Engineering Group And Gm Product Development Solutions, Kalyan Thumaty

Corporate Vp And Gm Integrated Ip And Technology Group, Daaman Hejmadi

Corporate Vp And Gm Global Data Center Group Sales, Rupal Shah Hollenbeck

Vice President Human Resources; Chief Diversity And Inclusion Officer, Barbara Whye

Vice President Law And Policy Group And Associate General Counsel Data Center Group, C Matt Swafford

Vice President, Steve Eckert

Vp General Finance, Nevin Chen

Vice President Technology And Manufacturing Group And Director Specialized Technologies, Bernhard Sell

Vice President Customer Experience Group, Rina Raman

Vice President Core And Visual Computing Group General Manager Developer Products Division, Lisa Lizarrago

Vp Hardware Engineering And Chief Architect Throughput Computing Socs, Balaji Kanigicherla

Information Technology Operations Vice President, Busch Doug

Chairman, Andy D. Bryant, age 69

Club Treasurer, Varun Setlur

Treasurer, Mahendra Malliwal

Vice Chair Of The Board Of Directors, Bernie Keany

Board Member, Kai Wang

Board Member, Edison F Rodrigues

Board Member, Aneel Bhusri

Board Member, Allen Wilson

Vp Finance And Assistant Treasurer Cash Investments And Capital Markets, Gary Kershaw

Auditors: Ernst & Young LLP

LOCATIONS

HQ: Intel Corp
2200 Mission College Boulevard, Santa Clara, CA 95054-1549
Phone: 408 765-8080   **Fax:** 408 765-2633
Web: www.intc.com

2018 Sales

	$ mil.	% of total
China (including Hong Kong)	18,824	27
Singapore	15,409	22
US	14,303	20
Taiwan	10,646	15
Other	11,666	16
Total	**70,848**	**100**

PRODUCTS/OPERATIONS

2018 Sales

	$ mil.	% of total
Client computing Group	37,004	52
Data Center Group	22,991	33
Internet of Things Group	4,307	6
Non-Volatile Memory Solutions Group	3,455	5
Programmable Solutions Group	2,123	3
All others	968	1
Total	**70,848**	**100**

Selected Products

Systems and Devices
  Laptops
  Desktops
  Tablets
  Smartphones
  Drones
Processors
  Intel Core
  Intel Xeon
  Intel Atom
  Pentium
  Celeron
  Intel Quark
Boards and Kits
  Intel NUC Boards and Kits
  Intel IoT RFP Ready Kits
  Server Motherboards
  Intel Quark D2000 Development Kit
Chipsets
  Mobile
  Desktop
  Server
  Embedded
FPGAs and Programmable Devices
  Intel FPGAs
  Intel Agilex
  Intel Stratix
  Intel Cyclone
Memory and Storage
  Solid State Drives
  Intel Optane Memory

COMPETITORS

AMD	SK Hynix
ARM Holdings	STMicroelectronics
Apple Inc.	Samsung Electronics
Fujitsu Semiconductor	Silicon Integrated
GLOBALFOUNDRIES	Systems
Maxim Integrated	Sony
Products	TSMC
Microchip Technology	Texas Instruments
Micron Technology	Toshiba Semiconductor
NVIDIA	& Storage Products
QUALCOMM	

HISTORICAL FINANCIALS

Company Type: Public

Income Statement

	REVENUE ($ mil.)	NET INCOME ($ mil.)	NET PROFIT MARGIN	EMPLOYEES
12/20	77,867	20,899	26.8%	110,600
12/19	71,965	21,048	29.2%	110,800
12/18	70,848	21,053	29.7%	107,400
12/17	62,761	9,601	15.3%	102,700
12/16	59,387	10,316	17.4%	106,000
Annual Growth	7.0%	19.3%	—	1.1%

FYE: December 26

2020 Year-End Financials

Debt ratio: 23.78%—
Return on equity: 26.41%
Cash ($ mil.): 5,865
Current ratio: 1.91
Long-term debt ($ mil.): 33,897

Dividends
  Yield: 0.0%
  Payout: 26.7%
Market value ($ mil.): —

	STOCK PRICE ($) FY Close	P/E High/Low		PER SHARE ($) Earnings	Dividends	Book Value
12/20	47.07	14	9	4.94	1.32	19.95
12/19	60.08	13	9	4.71	1.26	18.10
12/18	46.75	12	9	4.48	1.20	16.60
12/17	46.16	23	16	1.99	1.08	14.91
12/16	36.27	17	13	2.12	1.04	14.19
Annual Growth	6.7%	—	—	23.6%	6.1%	8.9%

Intercontinental Exchange Inc

Intercontinental Exchange (ICE) is a leading provider of regulated marketplaces and clearing services for global commodity trading primarily of electricity and agricultural commodities metals interest rates equities exchange traded funds or ETFs credit derivatives digital assets bonds and currencies and also offer mortgage and technology services. It manages a handful of global over-the-counter (OTC) markets and regulated futures exchanges. The firm also owns ICE Futures Europe a leading European energy futures and options platform as well as NYSE Holdings (including the New York Stock Exchange). ICE Data provides real-time daily historical and derived pricing data order book and transaction information related to our trading venues which span global commodity and financial markets. The company serves clients in approximately 155 countries. ICE's largest geographical market is the US with nearly 65% of the company's revenue.

Operations

Intercontinental Exchange (ICE) began operating two distinct business segments: Trading and Clearing and Data and Listings with total revenue split between the two both about 50%.

The Trading and Clearing segment performs trade execution clearing and benchmark administration. It provide execution and risk management services to businesses investors and traders across major asset classes such as commodities interest rates credit default swaps or CDS bonds foreign exchange equities and mortgage-related products. Its exchanges host approximately two-thirds of the world's traded crude and refined oil futures contract volume. It holds global benchmarks in energy agricultural commodities metals interest rates credit derivatives digital assets bonds and currency exchange rates equity indexes and also offer mortgage and technology services.

The Data and Listings segment provide a range of data and listing services for global financial and commodity including pricing and reference data exchange data analytics feeds index services desktops and connectivity solutions as well as corporate and ETF listing services on their cash equity exchanges.

Geographic Reach
Intercontinental Exchange (ICE) is based in Atlanta GA and also has principal executive offices in New York New York. It also has offices buildings in Asia Canada the EU Israel the UK and the US. The company operates six clearing houses positioned in major market centers around the globe including in Canada the EU Singapore the UK and the US.

The company makes nearly 65% of revenue from its US activities.

Sales and Marketing
Intercontinental Exchange (ICE) serves industries such as energy financial services and agricultural markets.

Financial Performance
Revenues less transaction-based expenses increased $223 million in 2019 from 2018. The increase in revenues includes $34 million in unfavorable foreign exchange effects arising from the stronger U.S. dollar in 2019 from 2018.

Net income was $1.9 billion in 2019 a drop from $2.0 billion in fiscal year 2018. The decrease can be attributed in part to favorable foreign exchange effects.

Cash provided by operating activities was $2.7 billion in 2019 while investing activities used $594 million. Financing activities used another $1.8 billion. The company ended the year with $2.2 billion in cash and cash equivalents.

Strategy
The company seeks to advance the company's leadership position in their markets by focusing its efforts on the following key strategies for growth: expand ICE's data offerings and the markets they serve to address the rising demand for information; enhance their extensive trading clearing and risk management capabilities; maintain leadership in the company's listings businesses; further develop their technology infrastructure and increase distribution; and strengthen competitive position through select acquisitions and strategic relationships.

ICE maintains a Cybersecurity Strategy or CSS which emphasizes consideration of the nature of the company's business ongoing intelligence collection regarding cybersecurity threats and initiatives to specifically address prominent areas of cybersecurity risk. The CSS outlines the key priorities for the company's cybersecurity program and the methods by which theInformation Security department seeks to accomplish those goals. The CSS is ratified by the Risk Committee of the company's Board of Directors and when applicable also by the corporate governance committees of our regulated subsidiaries.

Mergers and Acquisitions
In early 2020 Intercontinental Exchange Inc. it has agreed to acquire US-based Bridge2 Solutions a leading provider of loyalty solutions for merchants and consumers. Following the completion of the transaction Bakkt a majority-owned subsidiary of ICE intends to acquire Bridge2 Solutions from ICE using proceeds from Bakkt's Series B round of funding. Terms not disclosed.

In 2019 Intercontinental Exchange Inc. (ICE) acquired a family of fixed income vitality indices including the Merrill Lynch Volatility Estimate (MOVE) family of indices from Bank of America Merrill Lynch. The MOVE Index is a well-recog-

nized measure of U.S. interest rate volatility that tracks the movement in US MOVE. The accompanying fixed income volatility indices will become part of ICE Data Indices' comprehensive family of more than 5000 global fixed income equity commodity and currency indices that leverage ICE Data Services' pricing reference data and analytics solutions.Also in 2019 Intercontinental Exchange (ICE) agreed to acquire mortgage e-recording company Simplifile for $335 million. Simplifile's network connects lenders settlement agents and county recording offices to streamline residential mortgage transaction recording. Simplifile will become part of ICE Mortgage Services.

Company Background
Intercontinental Exchange (ICE) has grown rapidly through a series of acquisitions and portfolio diversification. In 2010 it acquired Climate Exchange a leader in the development of traded emissions markets. Expanding its options market portfolio in 2011 the company acquired broker/dealer Ballista which offers an electronic options platform for the execution of large and complex multi-leg options transactions. Also that year it bought 12% of Brazilian clearing-house operator Cetip SA for $514 million. In 2012 ICE bought WhenTech a provider of options technology including valuation analytics and risk management.

The company has also added to its OTC contracts offerings through the recently formed ICE Clear Europe. In 2011 alone it launched more than 250 new contracts for oil natural gas power emissions and refined petroleum products. ICE that year also launched new futures contracts including currency futures contracts and coal and natural gas option contracts. In Canada in early 2012 the company began trading new futures contracts on wheat and barley.

In 2017 ICE purchased 100% of TMX Atrium a company that provides low-latency access to markets and market data across 12 countries and 30 trading venues including in Toronto New Jersey and Chicago. That year the company also acquired Virtu BondPoint for $400 million which provides electronic fixed income trading solutions for more than 500 financial services firms.

EXECUTIVES

Senior Vice President Associate General Counsel, Andrew Surdykowski
Chairman And Ceo, Jeffrey C. (Jeff) Sprecher, $1,050,000 total compensation
Svp And Chief Strategic Officer, David S. (Dave) Goone, $664,583 total compensation
Svp And Coo, Charles A. (Chuck) Vice, $764,583 total compensation
President And Coo Ice Futures Canada, E. Bradley (Brad) Vannan
President Ice Futures Europe, David J. Peniket
Cto, Mayur V. Kapani
President And Coo Ice Clear U.s., Hester Serafini
President Nyse Group, Thomas W. (Tom) Farley, $664,583 total compensation
Cfo, Scott A. Hill, $714,583 total compensation
Chief Commercial Officer, Benjamin R. (Ben) Jackson
President Ice Clear Credit, Stanislav (Stan) Ivanov
President Ice Benchmark Administration Limited, Finbarr Hutcheson
President And Coo Ice Data Services, Lynn Martin
President Ice Futures U.s., Trabue Bland
Vice President Clearing Techno, Joseph Albert
Vice President Government Relations, Peter Roberson
Executive Vice President, Michael Walsh
Assistant Vice President Information Technology Security, David Jonas
Vice President, Brian Norris

Vice President Product Development, RJ Cummings
Senior Vice President Operations, Mark Wassersug
Vice President Content Management, Kyu Kang
Svp And Cio, Timothy April
Vice President Talent Management, Kelly Fritz
Senior Vice President Chief People Officer, Steve Erdman
Vice President Data Center Operations And Trading Floor Support, Anthony Monteleone
Vice President Nyse Post Trade Development, David Savage
Vice President, Charles Dennis
Assistant Vice President Business Analyst Commercial Real Estate, Bland Trabue
Board Member, Judith Sprieser
Treasurer Ice Clear U.s., Martin Hunter
Board Member, Vincent Tese
Board Member, Fredrick W Hatfield
Auditors: Ernst & Young LLP

LOCATIONS

HQ: Intercontinental Exchange Inc
5660 New Northside Drive, Atlanta, GA 30328
Phone: 770 857-4700   **Fax:** 770 937-0020
Web: www.theice.com

2016 Sales

	$ mil.	% of total
Transaction & clearing fees net	3,384	57
Data services fees	1,978	33
Listing fees	419	7
Other revenues	177	3
Total	**5,958**	**100**

2016 Sales

	% of total
US	61
Other countries	39
Total	**100**

2016 Sales

	% of total
Trading and clearing segment	47
Data and Listing segment	53
Total	**100**

PRODUCTS/OPERATIONS

Founding Partners
BP p.l.c.
Deutsche Bank AG
The Goldman Sachs Group Inc.
Morgan Stanley Dean Witter & Co.
Royal Dutch Shell plc
Socié;té; Gé;né;rale
TOTAL S.A.

COMPETITORS

APX	GFI Group
BGC Partners	NEX
Bloomberg L.P.	NYMEX Holdings
CBOE	Nasdaq
CHOICE! Energy	Reuters
CME	Unitil
Enporion	

HISTORICAL FINANCIALS
Company Type: Public

Income Statement
FYE: December 31

	REVENUE ($ mil.)	NET INCOME ($ mil.)	NET PROFIT MARGIN	EMPLOYEES
12/20	8,244	2,089	25.3%	8,890
12/19	6,547	1,933	29.5%	5,989
12/18	6,276	1,988	31.7%	5,161
12/17	5,834	2,514	43.1%	4,952
12/16	5,958	1,422	23.9%	5,631
Annual Growth	8.5%	10.1%	—	12.1%

2020 Year-End Financials

Debt ratio: 13.10%
Return on equity: 11.34%
Cash ($ mil.): 583
Current ratio: 0.99
Long-term debt ($ mil.): 14,126

No. of shares (mil.): 561
Dividends
Yield: 1.0%
Payout: 31.8%
Market value ($ mil.): 64,678

	STOCK PRICE ($) FY Close	P/E High/Low		PER SHARE ($) Earnings	Dividends	Book Value
12/20	115.29	30	18	3.77	1.20	34.76
12/19	92.55	28	21	3.42	1.10	31.15
12/18	75.33	24	19	3.43	0.96	30.23
12/17	70.56	17	13	4.23	0.80	29.03
12/16	56.42	119	22	2.37	0.68	26.42
Annual Growth	19.6%	—	—	12.3%	15.3%	7.1%

INTERMOUNTAIN HEALTH CARE INC

If you whoosh down the side of one of Idaho's majestic mountains and take a nasty spill Intermountain Health Care (dba Intermountain Healthcare) can pick you up and put you back together. From air ambulance services to urgent care clinics and general hospitals Intermountain has all the tools to mend skiers (and non-skiers alike) in Utah and southern Idaho. With about 1600 physicians the not-for-profit health system operates 22 hospitals and some 180 clinics as well as urgent care centers and rehabilitation centers. Intermountain also has an insurance arm named SelectHealth.

Operations

Intermountain Healthcare's hospitals range from general surgical to specialty care including orthopedic and pediatric facilities. Along with the full spectrum of physical health care services Intermountain also offers comprehensive mental health and substance abuse programs for patients of all ages. The organization's spectrum of care includes acute inpatient residential treatment day treatment chemical dependency inpatient/detoxification and intensive outpatient programs.

The system conducts cancer research through its partnership with Huntsman Cancer Institute at the University of Utah. The two share data best practices funding and co-conduct clinical trials. They also operate a number of cancer-specific treatment centers including multi-disciplinary tumor-specific clinics designed to provide one-stop service for cancer patients to meet with different cancer specialists on the same day for a more comprehensive treatment plan. Other areas of research include cardiovascular intensive medicine surgical care and behavioral health.

On the physician side the Intermountain Medical Group administers multi-specialty health care services in clinics located throughout the region. The group also operates urgent care clinics under the InstaCare and KidsCare banners.

Entering itself into the "what doesn't Intermountain do?" category the health system also provides health and dental insurance plans through its SelectHealth division.

Geographic Reach

Intermountain Healthcare serves the health care needs of Utah and Idaho residents.

Financial Performance

In 2016 Intermountain Healthcare's revenue grew 14% to $7.6 billion in fiscal 2016. This was due to increases in net patient services income and investment income. Net patient services accounted for 63% of the system's total revenue that year.

The company used $7 billion of that revenue towards operating expenses including salaries and benefits medical supplies and facilities maintenance and other business services as well as towards funds dedicated to future needs.

Strategy

Intermountain Healthcare uses its dedicated supply chain organization to continuously improve system efficiency. In addition to delivering medical supplies the unit also oversees hospital vehicles.

The system partners with several leading IT companies (including Xi3 Intel Dell and NetApp) to operate its Healthcare Transformation Lab on the campus of its flagship hospital Intermountain Medical Center in Murray Utah. The lab researches develops and measures new ideas to improve patient care.

In 2016 the system launched Navican Genomics its genomics research and testing arm. Also that year it partnered with the Stanford Genome Technology Center to establish a collaborative research program.

Intermountain has a number of projects underway to add expand or replace existing facilities.

Company Background

Intermountain was formed in 1975 when the Church of Jesus Christ of Latter Day Saints donated 15 hospitals to local communities.

EXECUTIVES

Senior Vice President Community Health, Mikelle Moore
Senior Vice President, Greg Poulsen
Ceo Intermountain Medical Group And Vp Physician Division, Linda C. Leckman
President And Ceo Selecthealth, Patricia R. Richards
Evp And Cfo, Bert R. Zimmerli
Evp And Coo, Laura S. Kaiser
Regional Vp Central Region, Moody L. Chisholm
Vp And Cio, Marc Probst
President And Ceo, A. Marc Harrison, age 56
Regional Vp Soutwest Region, Terri Kane
Svp And Coo, Robert Allen
Vp Clinical Operations And Chief Nursing Officer, Kim Henrichsen
Ceo Urban North Region And Mckay-dee Hospital Center, Timothy T. Pehrson
Chief Medical Officer, Brent E. Wallace
Ceo Primary Childrenâ's Medical Center, Katherine A. (Katy) Welkie
Regional Vp South Region, Steve Smoot
Vp Supply Chain And Support Services, Joe Walsh
Assistant Vice President Of Risk Management Services, Harlan Hammond
Assistant Vice President Investments, Stacy Jennings
Assistant Vice President Communications, Tom Vitelli
Assistant Vice President Compensation And Benefits, David Adams
Vice President Marketing And Communication, Todd Frehse
Assistant Vice President, Katherina Holzhauser
Vice President Healthcare Transformation, Joe Mott
Vice President, George Null Hamilton
Director Of Pharmacy, Scott Yardley
Medical Director, Scott Whittle
Vice President Of Pharmacy Affairs, Eric Cannon
Vice President Human Resources, Dan Zuhlke
Vice President And General Counsel, Doug Hammer
Medical Director, Tamara Lewis
Avp Pharmacy Services, Nannette Berensen

Assistant Vice President Clinical Is Operations, Tammy Madsen
Medical Director Community Health And Prevention, Tamara Sheffield
Vice President Rural Region, Rob Allen
Medical Director Imaging Services, Keith White
Pharmacy Manager, Robb Dengg
Pharmacy Manager, Bevan Jensen
Director Of Him, Mary Staub
Pharmacy Manager, Heather Hansen
Assistant Vice President Telehealth Services, Brian Wayling
Medical Director Clinical Genetics Institute, Steven Bleyl
Clinical Director Primary Children's Pediatric Behavioral Health Clinic, Nancy Cantor
Nursing Director, David Hurst
Vice President Of Operational Finance, Mark Runyon
Medical Director Informatics, Farukh Usmani
Director Of Pharmacy, Tom Dockendorf
Pharmacy Director Vice President Of Pharmacy Services, Matt Mitchell
Vice President Marketing, Caralee Lyon
Operating Room Dir, Travis Fullmer
Director Of Radiology, Coby Knudsen
Operating Room Dir, Dorothy Evans
Medical Director, Masood Safaee
Vice Chairman, Bruce T. Reese
Chairman, A. Scott Anderson
Secretary, Nicole Houghton
Secretary, Jeri Lay
Secretary, Sheri Jones
Medical Secretary, Janet Staker
Medical Secretary, Renee Harston
Scheduling Secretary, Jeanine Price
Secretary, JoAnn Fountain
Medical Secretary, Sherri Longhurst
Secretary, Stephanie Stromberg
Secretary, Jodi Simmons
Secretary, Heidi Null Leon
Auditors: KPMG LLP SALT LAKE CITY UTA

LOCATIONS

HQ: INTERMOUNTAIN HEALTH CARE INC
36 S STATE ST STE 1600, SALT LAKE CITY, UT 841111633
Phone: 801 442-2000
Web: WWW.INTERMOUNTAINHEALTHCARE.ORG

PRODUCTS/OPERATIONS

2016 Sales

	$ mil.	% of total
Net patient services	4,368	57
Non-patient activities	3,010	40
Non-operating income	237	3
Total	**7,617**	**100**

Selected Hospitals

Alta View Hospital (Sandy UT)
American Fork Hospital (Utah)
Bear River Valley Hospital (Tremonton UT)
Cassia Regional Medical Center (Burley ID)
Delta Community Medical Center (Utah)
Dixie Regional Medical Center (St. George UT)
Fillmore Community Medical Center (Utah)
Garfield Memorial Hospital (Panguitch UT)
Heber Valley Medical Center (Heber City UT)
Intermountain Medical Center (Murray UT)
LDS Hospital (Salt Lake City)
Logan Regional Hospital (Orem UT)
McKay-Dee Hospital Center (Ogden UT)
   McKay-Dee Behavioral Health Institute
Orem Community Hospital (Utah)
Park City Medical Center (Park City UT)
Primary Children's Medical Center (Salt Lake City)
Riverton Hospital (Riverton UT)
Sanpete Valley Hospital (Mt. Pleasant UT)
Sevier Valley Hospital (Richfield UT)
TOSH - The Orthopedic Specialty Hospital (Murray UT)
Utah Valley Regional Medical Center (Provo UT)
Valley View Medical Center (Cedar City UT)

COMPETITORS

CHRISTUS Health	Regence BlueCross
Encompass Health	BlueShield of Utah
HCA	St. Mark's
LifePoint Health	University of Utah
Ogden Regional Medical	Hospitals & Clinics
Center	

HISTORICAL FINANCIALS

Company Type: Private

Income Statement   FYE: December 31

	REVENUE ($ mil.)	NET INCOME ($ mil.)	NET PROFIT MARGIN	EMPLOYEES
12/19	8,812	1,212	13.8%	35,000
12/18	7,724	420	5.4%	—
12/17	6,940	1,061	15.3%	—
12/16	6,716	606	9.0%	—
Annual Growth	**9.5%**	**26.0%**	—	—

International Bancshares Corp.

International Bancshares is leading post-NAFTA banking in South Texas. One of the state's largest bank holding companies it does business through nearly 200 locations of International Bank of Commerce (IBC) IBC-Oklahoma Commerce Bank IBC Zapata and IBC Brownsville. The company facilitates trade between the US and Mexico and serves Texas' growing Hispanic population; about 30% of its deposits come from south of the border. In addition to commercial and international banking services for small and midsized businesses International Bancshares provides retail deposit services insurance and investment products mortgages and consumer loans. The bulk of the company's portfolio is made up of commercial financial and agricultural loans and real estate loans for construction.

Operations

Operating under a single segment International Bancshares garners around 70% of its revenue from interest income particularly loans including fees. Non-interest income - mostly from service charges on deposit accounts and other banking service charges commissions and fees - accounts for the rest.

Commercial financial and agricultural loans represent half of International Bancshares' $6.5 billion portfolio. Mortgages and construction real estate loans comprise roughly 20% and 30% of that total respectively.

Geographic Reach

Based in the border city of Laredo Texas International Bancshares has many customers living in Mexico especially northern Mexico. The holding company has nearly 200 branches in South Central and Southeast Texas and Oklahoma. Its primary market area in Texas is bordered on the east by the Galveston area the northwest by Dallas the southwest by Del Rio and to the southeast by Brownsville.

The branches are in the regions of Laredo San Antonio Austin Dallas Houston Zapata Eagle Pass the Rio Grande Valley of Texas the Coastal Bend area of Texas and throughout the State of Oklahoma.

Sales and Marketing

A large proportion of International Bancshares' business is with customers in Mexico; deposits from such clients comprise around 30% of its deposit base.

Financial Performance

International Bancshares has seen modest sputtering growth since 2013 adding approximately 5% to its revenue and 25% to its net income. Cash and long-term debt have fallen less than 5% and about 15% respectively in that time.

International Bancshares' revenue ticked up 4% to $526.6 million in 2017 owing to increased interest income caused by higher loan volume and overall yield. The company's interest expense also decreased following early termination of long-term repurchase agreements by its lead subsidiary bank.

The holding company's net income increased 18% to $157.4 million based on the same interest income improvement and a reduction in its provision for probable loan losses and a tax refund.

Cash stores fell $3.8 million to $265.4 million. Operations provided $196.8 million down slightly from 2016; financing provided $203.1 million mostly due to a net increase in other borrowed funds (which include Federal Home Loan Bank borrowings). Investments used $403.8 million owing primarily a large net decrease in loans.

Strategy

International Bancshares is attempting to shift its focus from commercial banking for small and midsized businesses to consumer and retail banking including mortgage lending and opening branches in retail properties and shopping malls. About 52% of the company's portfolio comprised commercial financial and agricultural loans compared with 56% in 2013. The share accounted for by mortgages increased from 16% in 2013 to 18% in 2017.

Company Background

International Bancshares was founded in 1966.

EXECUTIVES

Senior Vice President, Anselmo Castro
Executive Vice President And Senior Auditor, William Cuellar
Vp And Director; President And Ceo International Bank Of Commerce Mcallen, R. David Guerra, age 67, $245,668 total compensation
Chairman And Ceo; Ceo International Bank Of Commerce Laredo, Dennis E. Nixon, age 77, $659,632 total compensation
President Coo And Cfo International Bank Of Commerce Laredo, Imelda Navarro, age 62, $235,960 total compensation
President And Ceo Commerce Bank Laredo Texas, Ignacio Urrabazo
President And Ceo International Bank Of Commerce Eagle Pass Texas, Hector J. Cerna
Chairman And Ceo International Bank Of Commerce Houston Texas, Jay Rogers
President And Ceo International Bank Of Commerce Zapata Texas, Renato Ramirez
President And Ceo International Bank Of Commerce Austin Texas, Robert B. (Bob) Barnes
Svp, Eliza Gonzalez
President International Bank Of Commerce Houston Texas, Jeff Samples
President And Ceo International Bank Of Commerce San Antonio, Mike K. Sohn
President And Ceo International Bank Of Commerce Port Lavaca, Derek Schmidt
President And Ceo Corpus Christi, Harold Shockley
President And Ceo International Bank Of Commerce Brownsville, Al Villareal
Ceo San Antonio Service Center, Julie Tarvin
President Southwest Region International Bank Of Commerce, Brian Henry

President International Bank Of Commerce Tulsa, Andrew Levinson
President International Bank Of Commerce Zapata, Ricardo Ramirez
Evp Corporate International, Gerardo (Gerald) Schwebel
President And Ceo International Bank Of Commerce Oklahoma, Bill Schonacher
Evp And International Loan Officer, Natividad Lozano
Senior Vice President Of Marketing And International Banking, Dora Brown
Assistant Vice President, W S Bauer
Senior Vice President, Wilfredo Martinez
Assistant Vice President, Monique Jackson
Vice President Area Sales Manager, Rene Arriaga
First Vice President Auditor, Ramiro Herrera
First Vice President, Angelica Padron
Vice President, Jennifer Alvarado
Senior Vice President Of It, Hector Vasquez
Vice President Of Accounting, Alvaro Martinez
Vice President Human Resources, Rosie Ramirez
Vice President Accounting And Operations, David Shinn
Senior Vice President, Eddie Aldrete
Assistant Vice President Support Services, Fernando Santos
Executive Vice President Ibc Service Center, Rene Avila
Executive Vice President, Carlos Martinez
Vice President, Mirta Salcedo
Executive Vice President, Lee Reed
Vice President Life Sales, Markham Benn
Assistant Vice President Commercial Lending, Jose Palafox
Vice President, Anna Mercado
Assistant Vice President Commercial Lender, Bernardo De La Garza
Assistant Vice President, Trena Grob
Senior Vice President, Allen Wise
Senior Vice President Crm Practice Manager Senior Data Analyst, Shannon Galloway
Assistant Vice President, Debra Lozano
Senior Vice President Mortgage Division Manager, Dustin Wells
Assistant Vice President And Training, Shayla White
Auditors: RSM US LLP

LOCATIONS

HQ: International Bancshares Corp.
1200 San Bernardo Avenue, Laredo, TX 78042-1359
Phone: 956 722-7611
Web: www.ibc.com

PRODUCTS/OPERATIONS

2017 Sales

	% of total
Interest income	
Loans including fees	57
Investment securities	16
Other	-
Interest expense	-
Non interest income	
Service charges on deposit accounts	13
Other service charges commissions & fees	9
Other investments net	3
Other	2
Net investment securities transactions	-
Total	**100**

Selected Services

Business Investors
Business Online Banking Services
Checking Options
Commercial Insurance
Home and Personal Loans
IBC First Equity
IBC Investment Services
Individual Investors
Life And Health

Manage Your Account
Mobile Banking
Online Banking Center
Online Banking Services
Other Personal Services
Overdraft Courtesy
Personal
Personal Insurance

COMPETITORS

BancFirst	JPMorgan Chase
Bank of America	Lone Star National
Broadway Bancshares	Bancshares
Citigroup	Midland Financial
Cullen/Frost Bankers	Wells-Fargo
Falcon Bancshares	
First Victoria	
National Bank	

HISTORICAL FINANCIALS

Company Type: Public

Income Statement				FYE: December 31
	ASSETS ($ mil.)	NET INCOME ($ mil.)	INCOME AS % OF ASSETS	EMPLOYEES
12/19	12,112	205	1.7%	3,314
12/18	11,871	215	1.8%	3,390
12/17	12,184	157	1.3%	3,273
12/16	11,804	133	1.1%	3,216
12/15	11,772	136	1.2%	3,218
Annual Growth	0.7%	10.7%	—	0.7%

2019 Year-End Financials

Debt ratio: 6.28%	No. of shares (mil.): 65
Return on equity: 10.11%	Dividends
Cash ($ mil.): 256	Yield: 2.4%
Current ratio: —	Payout: 32.7%
Long-term debt ($ mil.): —	Market value ($ mil.): 2,808

	STOCK PRICE ($) FY Close	P/E High/Low	PER SHARE ($) Earnings	Dividends	Book Value
12/19	43.07	14 10	3.12	1.05	32.49
12/18	34.40	15 10	3.24	0.75	29.56
12/17	39.70	18 14	2.36	0.66	27.83
12/16	40.80	21 11	2.02	0.60	26.14
12/15	25.70	15 11	2.05	0.58	25.13
Annual Growth	13.8%	— —	11.1%	16.0%	6.6%

International Business Machines Corp

International Business Machines (IBM) bets that cognition is the ignition for growth. The company is investing in it what is calls cognitive computing systems led by the Watson artificial intelligence platform that help customers analyze massive amounts of data to make better decisions. Among other areas the company is betting on for growth are artificial intelligence security cloud systems quantum computing and more. IBM's information technology business services and software units are among the largest in the world. While IBM has placed less emphasis on hardware the company maintains enterprise server and data storage product lines that are among industry leaders.

Operations

IBM manages its sprawling operations in five segments.

Global Technology Services which generates more than a third of revenue provides comprehensive IT infrastructure and platform services that create business value for clients. Offerings include maintenance for IBM products and other technology platforms as well as support.

Cloud & Cognitive Software which provides about a third of revenue brings together IBM's software platforms and solutions enabling the company to deliver integrated and secure cloud data and AI solutions to our clients. It includes all software except operating system software reported in the Systems segment. Cloud & Cognitive Software Capabilities includes cognitive applications cloud & data platforms; and transaction processing platforms.

Global Business Services more than 20% of revenue provides consulting application management services and global process services to help customers move their businesses to digital platforms.

Systems about 10% of revenue is IBM's hardware business providing technologies for hybrid cloud and cognitive workloads. The unit sells servers storage systems and operating systems software. The segment also designs semiconductor and systems technology in collaboration with IBM Research.

Global Financing provides credit for customers to buy IBM products. It also handles used equipment returned from leases as well as other used and surplus equipment. The unit accounts for about 2% of revenue.

Geographic Reach

IBM has clients in about 175 countries with sales outside the US accounting for approximately 65% of revenue. Customers in Europe the Middle East and Africa (EMEA) generate about a third of sales and those in Asia/Pacific supply about 20% of sales.

Sales and Marketing

IBM operates country-based units where consultants product specialists and other workers facilitate the adoption and fulfillment of its products and services. It serves clients across most industries; leading industry groups include financial services industrial and communications.

Financial Performance

After a small recovery from 2018 by about $452 million IBM's revenue continues to fall down with an almost 5% difference from 2015.

Total revenue of $77.1 billion in 2019 decreased 3% from the prior year as reported. Global Financing total revenue decreased 18% compared to the prior year. This was due to a decrease in internal revenue of 24% driven by decreases in internal used equipment sales and internal financing. Systems revenue of $7.6 billion decreased 5.3 percent year to year as reported. Systems Hardware revenue of $5.9 billion declined 7% as reported driven primarily by declines in Power Systems and Storage Systems. Operating Systems Software revenue of $1.7 billion grew 1% as reported. GTS revenue of $27.4 billion decreased 6% as reported in 2019 compared to the prior year. Cloud & Cognitive Software revenue of $23.2 billion increased 5% as reported in 2019 compared to the prior year. There was strong growth in Cloud & Data Platforms as reported and at constant currency driven primarily by the acquisition of Red Hat in the third quarter of 2019.

Net income increased by 8% to $9.4 billion in 2019 from $8.7 billion in 2018 due to a low operating cost with $40.7 billion in 2019 compare to the $42.7 billion in 2018.

IBM had cash and equivalents of $8.3 billion in 2019 down by about $3.3m billion from the year before. In 2019 the company's operations generated $14.8 billion in cash while investing activities used $26.9 billion and financing activities provided more than $9 billion.

Strategy

IBM's strategy begins with their clients. IBM is distinguished as being first and foremost an Enterprise company serving the world's leaders in their industries.

Serving enterprises requires a distinct set of skills as their clients entrust them with building integrating and running the world's mission-critical systems. These are systems that cannot fail systems that require the highest levels of privacy and security. They are built with the company's software and systems designed and managed by IBM services. For example IBM manages approximately ninety percent of the credit card transactions and half of the world's wireless connections. They do this with an unparalleled commitment to their clients' data security.

IBM is unique in bringing innovative technology and industry expertise on a foundation of trust and security as an integrated proposition to their clients. This integrated proposition allows the company to deliver business impact that matters to their clients impact that requires bringing together technologies such as hybrid cloud data and AI insight with workflow and advanced industry skills. This integrated proposition helps their clients transform themselves from traditional businesses to what they call Cognitive Enterprises.

Mergers and Acquisitions

IBM in 2019 acquired Red Hat for $34 billion one of the biggest software acquisitions in history. The deal brings Red Hat's open source software to IBM's cloud efforts. Red Hat became a unit in IBM and reports as part of the Cloud and Cognitive Software segment. The deal was proposed in 2018 and closed in 2019.

Company Background

In 1914 National Cash Register's star salesman Thomas Watson left to rescue the flagging Computing-Tabulating-Recording (C-T-R) Company the pioneer in US punch card processing that had been incorporated in 1911. Watson aggressively marketed C-T-R's tabulators supplying them to the US government during WWI and tripling company revenue to almost $15 million by 1920. The company became International Business Machines (IBM) in 1924 and soon dominated the global market for tabulators time clocks and electric typewriters. It was the US's largest office machine maker by 1940.

IBM perfected electromechanical calculation (the Harvard Mark I 1944) but initially dismissed the potential of computers. When Remington Rand's UNIVAC computer (1951) began replacing IBM machines IBM quickly responded. The company unveiled its first computer in 1952. With its superior research and development and marketing IBM built a market share near 80% in the 1960s and 1970s.

In 1993 CEO John Akers was replaced by Louis Gerstner the first outsider to run IBM. He began to turn the ailing antiquated company around by slashing costs and nonstrategic divisions cutting the workforce shaking up entrenched management and pushing services. In 1994 Big Blue reported its first profit in four years. It also began making computer chips that year.

Since then IBM has tried to keep ahead of its aging product lineup. It introduced the Watson artificial intelligence platform (named after Thomas Watson) in 2011 as part of its renewal program that took it into cloud computing cybersecurity blockchain and it hopes someday into quantum computing.

EXECUTIVES

Svp Ibm Watson And Cloud Platform, David W. Kenny, age 58

Vice President Of Legal, Martha Rendeiro
Svp Solutions Portfolio And Research, John E. Kelly, age 67, $754,000 total compensation
Chairman President And Ceo, Virginia M. (Ginni) Rometty, age 62, $1,600,000 total compensation
Svp Ibm Cloud, Robert J. LeBlanc, age 61
Svp Global Business Services, Mark Foster, age 61
Svp Global Markets And Chairman Ibm Europe, Erich Clementi, age 61, $703,500 total compensation
Svp Global Markets, Martin J. Schroeter, age 55, $754,000 total compensation
Svp Ibm Watson Group, Michael D. (Mike) Rhodin, age 59, $630,000 total compensation
Svp Ibm Systems, Thomas W. (Tom) Rosamilia, age 59
Svp Global Markets, Bruno V. Di Leo, age 62
Svp Ibm Analytics, Robert J. (Bob) Picciano, age 61
Svp And Cfo, James J. Kavanaugh, age 53
Svp Ibm Industry Platforms, Bridget A. van Kralingen, age 56, $665,000 total compensation
Svp Ibm Global Technology Services, Martin Jetter, age 60, $650,000 total compensation
Cio, Fletcher Previn
Vice President, Mike Wing
Vice President Information Technology, Bryan Adair
Vice President Import Compliance And Supply Chain Security, Theo Fletcher
Vice President, John Kirkwood
Vice President Office Of The Cto Watson And Cloud Unit, Kendall Lock
Vice President Software Ibm Research, David Mcqueeney
Vice President Of Human Resources, Gary Kildare
Vice President Finance And Operations Ibm Channels, David Colistra
Vice President Finance And Director, James W Boyken
Senior Vice President, David Kalis
Vice President Of Marketing, Annie Cheung
Vice President Software Sales, Barry Gibbons
Vice President Financial Risk Assessment, Natalia Ruderman
Vice President Of Sales Operat Vice President Of Operations, Bill Lintner
Vice President Marketing And Communications, Brad Timothy
Vice President And Partner, Srinivas Attili
Executive Vice President World Wide Sales Tivoli S, Baba Gold
Vp Industry Sales, Mark Easton
Vice President Strategic Services, Randall Dalia
Vice President Telecommunications Industry Americas, Dave Mancl
Vice President Z Operating Systems, Maria Boonie
Vice President Worldwide Sales, Robert Wong
Vice President And Partner Digital Service Line Leader, Susan Wedge
Vice President Software Business Partners And Midmarket, Mark Register
Vice President Of Human Resources Technology, Steve Rolando
Vice President And Fellow, Brad Mccredie
Vice President Human Resources Business, Tania Mcveety
Vice President Of Marketing, Kristen Lauria
Vice President Partner Energy And Utility Industry Leader, Jim Bales
Vice President North America Microelectronics Sales, David Faircloth
Vice President Sales, Arlene Garcia
Vice President Ibm Cloud, Gilbert Molinar
Vice President Human Resources Sales Incentive Compensation, Richard Rabjohn
Vice President Human Resources Ibm Canada Ltd, Anne Berend
Vice President Global Sales, Rick Fuchs
Vice President Business Development, Mark Bytner
Vice President, Don Jue
Vice President, Daniel Delena

Vice President Of Marketing And Strategy, Roland Hagan
Vice President Of Human Resources, Jonathan Schoonmaker
Vice President For Information Technology, Radha Ratnaparkhi
Vice President Semiconductor Research And Development Center, Gary Patton
Vice President Ar Bcs, Christine Kinser
Vice President Of Marketing, Ann Rubin
Vice President, Vince Masi
Vice President Technology, Jay Cook
Vice President Marketing, Deon Newman
Vice President, David Simms
Vice President, Juhi Jotwani
Vice President Human Resources Software Group, Thomas Fleming
Vice President Marketing Nonesuch, Patrick Clarke
Svp Director Research, Paul Horn
Vice President Marketing And Communications, Maria Reeves Hayes
Senior Vice President Marketing Storage Technologies, Jim Kely
Vice President, James Wallis
Vice President Partner Enablement, William Bill Liebler
Senior Vice President, Bob Moffat
Vice President Iseries Marketing, Peter Bingaman
Vice President Watson Research Center, Vladimir Zolotov
Vice President Information Security Strategy, John Hsieh
International Leader Vice President Worldwide Sales, David Valovcin
Vice President Ibm Enterprise Storage Ds8870 And Tape, Calline Sanchez
Vice President East Coast Sales, Craig Singler
Vice President, Ben Edwards
Vice President Ibm Storage Systems, Michael Kuhn
Vice President Sales, Michele Stern
Vice President Ibm Gbs Global Leader Chemicals And Petroleum Industrial Products; Industrial Sector Leader Ap, Manish Chawla
Vice President Cognitive Computing Watson, Guruduth Banavar
Vice President Us Insurance Industry, Jane Schneider
Vice President Of Global Community Initiatives, Paula Baker
Vice President Of Marketing, Chris Maclaughlin
Vice President Global Cloud Infrastructure, Sonny Fulkerson
Vice President Information Technology, Dennis Jay
Assistant Vice President Services Overall, Jen Noble
Vice President Of Business Development, Janine Grasso
Worlwide Vice President Of Sales Systems And Tech, Bob Hoey
Vice President Business Operations, John White
Worldwide Vice President Business Partners Sales Ibm Software Group, Vincent Zandvliet
Vice President Sales, Peter Andino
Vice President Marketing, Kevin Taylor
Vice President Tax And Treasurer, Simon Beaumont
Vice President Security Growth Initiatives Security Services, Shelley Westman
Vice President General Business North America, Scott Ferber
Vice President Technical Sales Support, Walt Ling
Vice President, Luis Fernandez
Vice President Finance, Neal Marx
Vice President Storage Systems, Brian Hamel
Vice President Human Resources, Horst Gallo
Vice President For Software Standards And Cloud Co, Angel Thompson
Vice President Of Marketing Communication, Lisa Baird
Vice President Global Sales Operations, William Meikle

Vice President Diversity Employee Experience, Patricia Lewis
Vice President Of Marketing, Katharyn White
Vice President Of Sales: East Smb, John Schultz
Vice President Marketing, Jennifer Bucher
Vp It Service, Sam Lee
Vice President Technical Support Services, John Porter
Vice President And Chief Techn, Jason Wilkinson
Vice President Of Strategy Global Business Services, Ian Watson
Vice President Of Supply Chain Management, Tom Edwards
Vice President, Allen Downs
Vice President And Partner Sap Leader, Mark Towell
Senior Vice President And Trust Officer, George Araujo
Senior Vice President Ibm Systems And Technology Group, Andrew Mason
Vp Hpc And Cognitive Systems, David Turek
Vice President, Bob Curran
Vice President Business Development Its, Anil Philip
Honda North America Client Vice President, Jeff Schlageter
Vice President, Michael Karasick
Vice President Marketing Ibm Security, Lindsey Lurie
Vice President Development Websphere, Buff Jones
Vice President Global Business Development, Dan Friedman
Vice President Strategic Business Growth Markets Unit, Eduardo Joia
Vice President And Partner, Romas Pencyla
Vice President Global Technology Services Strategic Outsourcing North America, Steve Loehr
Vice President Resiliency Services Portfolio, Daniel Witteveen
Vice President Human Resources Global Mobility, Monica Lombardo
Vice President Z Systems Software, Michael Perera
Vice President Finance And Planning, Rob Delbene
Vice President And General Manager Strategic Sourcing, Joseph Msays
Vice President Zseries Software Sales Swg, Raymond Jones
Vice President Marketing Programs At Ibm, Bevin Maguire
Vice President And Partner Ibm Watson Health Consulting Group, Matt Porta
Vice President Ww Client Support Information Management Swg, Rosanne DeVries
Vice President Software Sales Strategy And Transformation, Robert Guidotti
Vice President Integrated Marketing For The Ibm Software Group, Mark Rosen
Vice President Global Business Operations, Anthony Lostaglio
Assistant To John Manasso General Manager Kathy Bennett Vice President, Alexandria Kornegay
Vice President Of Finance, Bill Chrystie
Vice President Of Worldwide Support For Ibm Security Systems, Will Raabe
Vice President Global Logistics, Gregory Smith
Vice President Client Excellence And Base Growth North America Gts Infrastructure Services, Jim Batterton
Vice President Corporate Events, Heidi Terens
Vice President Business Analytics Transformation, Douglas Dow
Vice President C And N Global Development, Janice McGinty-polito
Auditors: PricewaterhouseCoopers LLP

LOCATIONS

HQ: International Business Machines Corp
One New Orchard Road, Armonk, NY 10504
Phone: 914 499-1900   **Fax:** 914 765-4190
Web: www.ibm.com

2018 Sales

	$ mil.	% of total
Americas	36,994	46
Europe/Middle East/Africa	25,491	32
Asia Pacific	17,106	22
Total	**79,591**	**100**

PRODUCTS/OPERATIONS

2018 Sales

	$ mil.	% of total
Technology Services & Cloud Platforms	34,462	44
Cognitive Solutions	18,481	23
Global Business Services	16,817	21
Systems	8,034	10
Global Financing	1,590	2
Other	2,017	-
Total	**79,591**	**100**

Selected Services

Global Technology Services
  Cloud Services
  Mobility Services
  Networking Services
  Outsourcing and Managed Services
  Resiliency Services
  Security Services
  Site and Data Center Services
  Systems Services
  Technical Support Services
Financing
Technology services
  Application Management
  Global Process Services
  IT Infrastructure Services
  IT Outsourcing
Training
  Offerings
  Certification
  Conferences & Events
Additional Services
  System Lab Services
  Consulting Alliances
  Mobile Enterprise Services
  Project Financing
  Working Capital
Technology Services
  Business Process Outsourcing
  Infrastructure
  System Integration
  Systems Management
  Web Hosting

Selected Products

Systems
  Power Systems
  Z Systems
  LinuxOne
  Middleware
  Application Platform
  Smarter Process
Servers
Software
  Application development
  Business Analytics (Cognos SPSS)
  Cloud & Smarter Infrastructure
  Enterprise Content Management
  IBM Platform Computing
  Information Management (DB2 Informix InfoSphere)
  Rational (Software and Systems Delivery)
  IBM Security
  WebSphere (Integration a nd Optimization)
  Z Systems Software
Storage
  Software Defined Storage
  Flash Storage
  Optical Libraries
  Storage Area Networking
  Tape/Virtual Tape Storage
  Storage networking

COMPETITORS

AWS	Hewlett Packard
Accenture	Enterprise
Apple Inc.	Hitachi
Capgemini	Infosys
Cisco Systems	Microsoft
Cognizant Tech	NEC
Solutions	NTT DATA
DXC Technology	Oracle
Dell	SAP
Deloitte Consulting	Tata Consultancy
Fujitsu	Wipro Technologies
Google	

HISTORICAL FINANCIALS

Company Type: Public

Income Statement

FYE: December 31

	REVENUE ($ mil.)	NET INCOME ($ mil.)	NET PROFIT MARGIN	EMPLOYEES
12/19	77,147	9,431	12.2%	383,800
12/18	79,591	8,728	11.0%	350,600
12/17	79,139	5,753	7.3%	366,600
12/16	79,919	11,872	14.9%	380,300
12/15	81,741	13,190	16.1%	377,757
Annual Growth	**(1.4%)**	**(8.0%)**	—	**0.4%**

2019 Year-End Financials

Debt ratio: 41.33%
Return on equity: 50.12%
Cash ($ mil.): 8,313
Current ratio: 1.02
Long-term debt ($ mil.): 54,102

No. of shares (mil.): 887
Dividends
  Yield: 4.8%
  Payout: 74.6%
Market value ($ mil.): 118,908

	STOCK PRICE ($) FY Close	P/E High/Low	PER SHARE ($) Earnings	Dividends	Book Value
12/19	134.04	14 11	10.56	6.43	23.49
12/18	113.67	18 11	9.52	6.21	18.82
12/17	153.42	29 23	6.14	5.90	19.08
12/16	165.99	14 9	12.38	5.50	19.29
12/15	137.62	13 10	13.42	5.00	14.77
Annual Growth	**(0.7%)**	— —	**(5.8%)**	**6.5%**	**12.3%**

International Paper Co

International Paper (IP) is one of the world's largest manufacturers of printing papers. Products include uncoated paper used in printers and market pulp for tissue and paper products. In the US IP is #1 in containerboard production where 80% of materials are converted to industrial corrugated boxes. Most of its around 270 mills converting and packaging plants and recycling facilities are in the US. It also runs a pulp and paper business in Russia via a 50/50 joint venture with Ilim Holding. About 75% of IP's revenue is generated in the US.

Operations

IP operates in three segments: Industrial Packaging (almost 70% of net sales) Printing Papers (about 20%) and Global Cellulose Fibers (more than 10%).

Industrial Packaging is the largest manufacturer of containerboard in the US with a production capacity of more than 13 million tons annually. Products include linerboard and recycled linerboard medium and recycled medium whitetop and saturating kraft. About 80% of Industrial Packaging production is converted into corrugated boxes and other packaging by its 176-plus North American container plants.

The Printing Papers segment produces printing and writing papers mainly uncoated papers. These are sold under private label and International Paper brands such as Hammermill Springhill Williamsburg Postmark and several others. The Global Cellulose Fibers product portfolio includes fluff (filler in diapers and incontinence products) market pulp (used for tissue and paper products) and specialty pulps used for such things as textiles filtration and paints and coatings.

Geographic Reach

Headquartered in Memphis TN IP has manufacturing operations in Europe North and South America North Africa and Asia (India and Russia). In the US it operates more than 25 pulp paper and packaging mills about 165 converting and packaging plants around 15 recycling plants and three bag facilities. Outside the US the Company operates some 15 mills roughly 45 converting and packaging plants and two recycling plants.

The Company operates its primary research and development center in Loveland Ohio as well as several other product development facilities including the Global Cellulose Fibers technology center in Federal Way WA.

The US is IP's largest market representing about 75% of sales each year. EMEA is its second-largest market generating around 15% followed by the Asia Pacific region?less than 5%.

Sales and Marketing

IP's products are used in copiers desktop and laser printers digital imaging filtration construction materials and paints and coatings. End-use applications include advertising and promotional materials such as brochures pamphlets greeting cards books annual reports and direct mail.

The company sells products directly to end users and converters as well as through agents resellers and paper distributors.

Financial Performance

The Company's revenue decreased to $22.4 billion in 2019 compared to $23.3 billion in the prior year. The decrease was due to lower revenues on industrial packaging segment and global cellulose segment.

Net income in 2019 decreased to $1.2 billion mainly due to lower revenues and loss of income in discontinued operations.

Cash held by the Company at the end of 2019 decreased to $511 million compared to $589 million in the prior year. Cash provided by operations was $3.6 billion while cash used for investing and financing activities were $1.3 billion and $2.4 billion respectively. Main uses for cash were invested in capital projects and reduction of debt.

Strategy

IP direct research and development activities to short-term long-term and technical assistance needs of customers and operating divisions and to process equipment and product innovations. Activities include product development within the operating divisions; studies on innovation and improvement of pulping bleaching chemical recovery paper making converting and coating processes; packaging design and materials development; mechanical packaging systems environmentally sensitive printing inks and reduction of environmental discharges; re-use of raw materials in manufacturing processes; recycling of consumer and packaging paper products; energy conservation; applications of computer controls to manufacturing operations; innovations and improvement of products; and development of various new products.

IP continued to invest strategically to strengthen its Industrial Packaging business. In its North American corrugated packaging business it made targeted investments to enhance its capabilities and reinforce its strong position in the fastest growing segments. In its EMEA Packaging business IP completed selective acquisitions to expand its converting network around the Madrid Spain mill. Lastly in January 2020 IP monetized approximately 19% of its investment in Graphic Packaging in exchange for $250 million.

HISTORY

In 1898 nearly 20 northeastern pulp and paper firms consolidated to lower costs. The resulting International Paper had 20 mills in Maine Massachusetts New Hampshire New York and Vermont. The mills relied on forests in New England and Canada for wood pulp. When Canada enacted legislation to stop the export of pulpwood in 1919 International Paper formed Canadian International Paper.

During the 1940s and 1950s the company bought Agar Manufacturing (shipping containers 1940) Single Service Containers (Pure-Pak milk containers 1946) and Lord Baltimore Press (folding cartons 1958). It diversified in the 1960s and 1970s buying Davol (hospital products 1968; sold to C. R. Bard 1980) American Central (land development 1968; sold to developers 1974) and General Crude Oil (gas and oil 1975; sold to Mobil Oil 1979).

Decades later International Paper picked up Shorewood Packaging for $850 million in 2000. That year it made an unsolicited $6.2 billion bid for Champion International— which had previously agreed to be acquired by UPM-Kymmene— igniting a bidding war. UPM withdrew its offer however and International Paper acquired Champion for about $9.6 billion.

After surviving the Great Recession IP made one of its most significant acquisitions to date in 2012 when it acquired Temple-Inland one of North America's top producers of corrugated packaging in a transaction valued at $4.5 billion.

EXECUTIVES

National Account Manager, Todd J Taylor
Svp Human Resources Government Relations And Global Citizenship, Thomas G. (Tom) Kadien, age 64, $629,167 total compensation
Svp Consumer Packaging, Catherine I. Slater, age 56
Svp Industrial Packaging The Americas, Timothy S. (Tim) Nicholls, age 59, $710,000 total compensation
Chairman And Ceo, Mark S. Sutton, age 59, $1,200,000 total compensation
Svp Manufacturing Technology Ehs And Global Sourcing, Tommy S. Joseph, age 60, $600,000 total compensation
Svp Pulp, Jean-Michel Ribieras, age 57, $420,000 total compensation
Svp And President Ip Latin America, Glenn R. Landau, age 51
Svp Paper The Americas, W. Michael Amick, age 56, $500,000 total compensation
Svp And President Europe The Middle East Africa And Russia, John V. Sims, age 57
Svp North American Container, Gregory T. Wanta, age 54
Svp Global Cellulose Fibers, Jean-Michel Ribiéras, age 57
Senior Vice President Online Marketing, Chris Werner
National Account Manager, Jennifer Mugavero
Vice President Investments, Robert Hunkeler
Vice President Supply Chain North American Papers Pulp And Coated Paperboard, Fred Towler
Svp Corporate Development, Carleton Ealy
Vice President, Jim Johnson
National Account Manager, Doug Arters
Vice President And General Manager Xpedx Illinois Division, Thomas Plath
National Account Manager, Thomas Hendricks

National Account Manager, Axel Iglesias
Vice President Pulp, John Fisher
Carolinas Vice President Operations, John Hash
Vp And General Manager Containerboard And Recycling, Thomas Cleves
Sales Executive Vice President, Matthew Lewis
Vice President, Pamela Hollingsworth
National Account Manager, Jenae Lewis
Vice President, Pat Leggett
Vice President Corporate Audit, Marc Van Lieshout
National Accounts Manager, Michael T Murphy
Senior Vice President Consumer Pkg, Catherine I Slater
Senior Vice President, Debbie Ellington
National Sales Manager, Dennis Smith
National Accounts Manager, Mark Mang
National Account Manager, Mike Nelson
National Accounts Manager, Michael Murphy
National Accounts Manager, Dan Hensley
Svp Paper The Americas, W Michael Amick Jr
Vice President Deputy General Counsel Chief Ethics And Compliance Officer, Deon Vaughan
National Account Manager, Lauren Sickinger
Vp Human Resources, Elizabeth Patrick
Vice President, Dave Bohlman
Vice President Of Operations, Red Jentz
Vp Communications, Leslie Jorgensen
Board Member, J Steven Whisler
Board Member, Jay Johnson
Board Member, A Johnson
Board Member, Steven Whisler
Secretary, Vallie Williford
Auditors: DELOITTE & TOUCHE LLP

LOCATIONS

HQ: International Paper Co
6400 Poplar Avenue, Memphis, TN 38197
Phone: 901 419-7000
Web: www.internationalpaper.com

2016 Sales

	$ mil.	% of total
Americas		
US	15,918	76
Other countries	1,581	7
EMEA	2,862	14
Pacific Rim & Asia	718	3
Total	**21,079**	**100**

PRODUCTS/OPERATIONS

2016 Sales

	$ mil.	% of total
Industrial packaging	14,191	67
Printing papers	4,058	19
Consumer packaging	1,954	9
Global Cellulose Fibers	1,092	5
Adjustments	(216)	-
Total	**21,079**	**100**

Selected Operations and Products

Consumer Packaging
  Cold cups and lids
  Consumer-ready packaging (Shorewood Packaging folding carton set-up box)
  Folding carton board
  Food buckets and lids
  Hot cups and lids
  Milk container and lids
  Starcote tobacco board
Distribution North America (xpedx)
  Building services and away-from-home markets with facility supplies
  Commercial printers with printing papers and graphic pre-press printing presses post press equipment
  Manufacturers with packaging supplies and equipment
  Warehousing and delivery services
Industrial Packaging
  Automotive packaging
  Corrugated pallet
  Die-cut package
  Flapless
  Kraft linerboard

Laminated bulk bin
Liquid bulk
Litho lamination
Medium paper
Retail displays
Saturating kraft
Slotted container
White top liner
Papers
  HP (Hewlett-Packard) home and commercial papers
  Office papers
Pulp
  Fluff pulp
  Paper and tissue pulp
Recycling products
  Old corrugated containers and kraft corrugated cuttings
  Old newspaper

COMPETITORS

Amcor	Nippon Paper
Cascades Inc.	Packaging Corp. of
ENCE Energia y	America
Celulosa SA	Smurfit Kappa
Georgia-Pacific	Stora Enso
Louisiana-Pacific	UPM-Kymmene
M-real	Weyerhaeuser
Mondi	

HISTORICAL FINANCIALS

Company Type: Public

Income Statement

FYE: December 31

	REVENUE ($ mil.)	NET INCOME ($ mil.)	NET PROFIT MARGIN	EMPLOYEES
12/19	22,376	1,225	5.5%	51,000
12/18	23,306	2,012	8.6%	53,000
12/17	21,743	2,144	9.9%	56,000
12/16	21,079	904	4.3%	55,000
12/15	22,365	938	4.2%	56,000
Annual Growth	**0.0%**	**6.9%**	**—**	**(2.3%)**

2019 Year-End Financials

Debt ratio: 29.17%	No. of shares (mil.): 392
Return on equity: 16.25%	Dividends
Cash ($ mil.): 511	Yield: 4.3%
Current ratio: 0.77	Payout: 65.5%
Long-term debt ($ mil.): 9,597	Market value ($ mil.): 18,056

	STOCK PRICE ($) FY Close	P/E High/Low		PER SHARE ($) Earnings	Dividends	Book Value
12/19	46.05	15	12	3.07	2.01	19.67
12/18	40.36	13	8	4.85	1.93	18.38
12/17	57.94	11	10	5.13	1.86	15.79
12/16	53.06	25	15	2.18	1.78	10.56
12/15	37.70	26	16	2.23	1.64	9.42
Annual Growth	**5.1%**	**—**	**—**	**8.3%**	**5.3%**	**20.2%**

Interpublic Group of Companies Inc.

The Interpublic Group of Companies (IPG) is one of the world's largest advertising and marketing services conglomerates. The company has offices in more than 100 countries from which it operates three global networks that provide integrated large-scale advertising and marketing services: McCann Worldgroup; Foote Cone & Belding (FCB); and MullenLowe Group. IPG Mediabrands is the global media and data arm of IPG and includes the UM and Initiative agencies. The firm also has agencies that specialize in certain practice areas such as Octagon (sports entertainment and lifestyle marketing) and MRM//McCann (digital services). The US is IPG's largest market.

HISTORY

Standard Oil advertising executive Harrison McCann opened the H. K. McCann Company in 1911 and signed Standard Oil of New Jersey (later Exxon) as his first client. McCann's ad business boomed as the automobile became an integral part of American life. His firm merged with Alfred Erickson's agency (created 1902) in 1930 forming the McCann-Erickson Company. At the end of the decade the firm hired Marion Harper a top Yale graduate as a mailroom clerk. Harper became president in 1948.

Harper began acquiring other ad agencies and by 1961 controlled more than 20 companies. That year he unveiled a plan to create a holding company that would let the ad firms operate separately allowing them to work on accounts for competing products but giving them the parent firm's financial and information resources. He named the company Interpublic Inc. after a German research company owned by the former H. K. McCann Co. The conglomerate continued expanding and was renamed The Interpublic Group of Companies in 1964. Harper's management capabilities weren't up to the task however and the company soon faced bankruptcy. In 1967 the board replaced him with Robert Healy who saved Interpublic and returned it to profitability. The company went public in 1971.

The 1970s were fruitful years for Interpublic; its ad teams created memorable campaigns for Coke ("It's the Real Thing" and "Have a Coke and a Smile") and Miller Beer ("Miller Time" and Miller Lite ads). After Philip Geier became chairman in 1980 the company gained a stake in Lowe Howard-Spink (1983; it later became The Lowe Group) and bought Lintas International (1987). Interpublic bought the rest of The Lowe Group in 1990.

Interpublic bought Western International Media (now known as Initiative) and Ammirati & Puris (which was merged with Lintas to form Ammirati Puris Lintas) in 1994. As industry consolidation picked up in 1996 Interpublic kept pace with acquisitions of PR company Weber Group and Draft-Worldwide. Interpublic bought a majority stake in artist management and film production company Addis-Wechsler & Associates (now Industry Entertainment) in 1997 and later formed sports marketing and management group Octagon.

Interpublic acquired US agencies Carmichael Lynch and Hill Holliday Connors Cosmopulos in 1998. It also boosted its PR presence with its purchase of International Public Relations (UK) the parent company of public relations networks Shandwick and Golin/Harris. Interpublic strengthened its position in the online world in 1999 when it bought 20% of Stockholm-based Internet services company Icon Medialab International. That year the company merged agencies Ammirati and Lowe & Partners Worldwide to form Lowe Lintas & Partners Worldwide (in 2002 they changed the name to just Lowe & Partners Worldwide).

Interpublic bought market research firm NFO Worldwide for $580 million in 2000 and merged Weber Public Relations with Shandwick International to form Weber Shandwick Worldwide one of the world's largest PR firms. Later that year the company bought ad agency Deutsch for about $250 million. John Dooner took the position of chairman and CEO at the end of the year after Geier resigned. His first move proved a big one:

Interpublic acquired True North Communications for $2.1 billion in stock in 2001.

The honeymoon was short lived; facing a recession the mounting debt from its buying spree and with the revelation of accounting discrepancies at McCann-Erickson WorldGroup (renamed McCann Worldgroup in 2004) Dooner stepped aside as chairman and CEO in 2003. Interpublic chose vice chairman David Bell (former CEO of True North) as Dooner's replacement. After almost two years of work to improve Interpublic's balance sheet Bell was replaced by former MONY Group chief Michael Roth.

In 2005 Roth was tasked with straightening out Interpublic's financial controls and improving its balance sheet. Later that year the company revealed extensive bookkeeping problems primarily in its overseas operations leading to a financial restatement going back to 2000.

In order to simplify its operating structure in 2006 Interpublic integrated direct marketer Draft Inc. with advertising agency Foote Cone & Belding (forming DraftFCB). A year later it restructured its vast network of media brands to report under a single management structure (Mediabrands).

Looking to India in mid-2007 Interpublic bought all the shares of FCB Ulka a top-five ad agency in the country that operated from six offices. Interpublic integrated the Indian agency with its Draft-FCB operations. At the same time it acquired the remaining 51% stake it didn't hold in Lintas India Private Limited at a cost of $50 million in cash and integrated it into its Lowe Worldwide network.

In 2010 Interpublic acquired Brazilian creative advertising strategy firm CUBOCC and London-based marketing agency Delaney Lund Knox Warren & Partners (DLKW). During 2011 the company acquired several marketing agencies. In early 2012 Interpublic obtained German consumer lifestyle agency Nicole Weber Communications (NWC) and UK-based digital and interactive agency FUSE.

EXECUTIVES

Svp And Managing Director, Terry D. Peigh
Chairman And Ceo, Michael I. Roth, age 74, $1,500,000 total compensation
Evp And Cfo, Frank Mergenthaler, age 59, $1,000,000 total compensation
Evp And Chief Strategy And Talent Officer, Philippe Krakowsky, age 58, $1,000,000 total compensation
Svp And Managing Director, Peter Leinroth
Svp General Counsel And Secretary, Andrew Bonzani, age 56, $800,000 total compensation
Svp Controller And Chief Accounting Officer, Christopher F. Carroll, age 53, $587,714 total compensation
Svp And Cio, John Halper
Vice President Associate General Counsel And Assistant Secretary, Robert Dobson
Vice President Business Strategy, Helene Yan
Vice President Associate General Counsel Managing Attorney Chief Of Staff And Latam Regional Coordinator, William Crosby
Svp And Chief Growth Officer, Simon Bond
Vice President Financial Planning And Analysis, Michael Delvecchio
Senior Vice President And Account Group Director Accentmarketing, Alice Rivera
Executive Vice President Creative Director And Managing Partner Accentmarketing, Diana Ocasio-Fant
Vice President Global Client Finance Director Mediabrands, Nicole Aronzon
Vice President Global Sourcing And Chief Procurement Officer, Eliseo Rojas
Svp, Renu Hooda

Vice President Real Estate And Insurance, Richard Haray
Senior Vice President External Affairs, Nancy Nichols
Senior Vice President And Deputy Managing Director T, Michelle Maggs
Executive Vice President Chief Growth Officer, Barry Wacksman
Vice President Crrd Pm, Lori Woodcock
Executive Vice President Worldwide Director Of Employee Learning Hfd, Stewart Alter
Senior Vice President Group Mng. Director, Kevin Scher
Executive Vice President Account Director, Craig Bagno
Vice President Global Training Manager, Adeline Mahoney
Senior Vice President Art Director, Kris Kiger
Vice President Executive Creative Director Mobile And Emerging Platforms Group, Richard Ting
Senior Vice President Creative Director, Marcia J Goddard
Vice President Finance, Andy Queen
Vice President Director Of Payroll Admin, Francelia Febus
Senior Vice President Broadcast Operations, Eileen Feeney
Vice President, Patrick Reyes
Vice President Account Director Brand Century Regal 365 Golf, Michael Crone
Vice President Creative Director, Kathleen Vanhoff
Vice President Worldgroup Technology, Ed Recinto
Senior Vice President, Michael Presson
Vice President Strategic Planning, BRIAN SCRANTON
Experiential Marketing Vice President, John Sattler
Vice President Strategy Director, Barbara Hirsch
Executive Vice President Executive Creative Director, Auge Reichenberg
Senior Vice President Group Strategy Director, Julieta Smith
Vice President Account Director, Tanya Kennedy
Vice President Senior Producer, Chance Bassett
Vice President Ad Operations Analytics And Product Management, Liam Ross
Senior Vice President Talent Acquisition, Aimee Collin
Senior Vice President Head Of Technical Operations, James Brennan
Senior Vice President Group Managing Director, Nick Allen
Vice President Client Partner, Ethan Chamberlin
Board Member, Mary Guilfoile
Board Member, Jocelyn Carter-miller
Board Member, William Kerr
Board Member, Patrick Moore
Auditors: PricewaterhouseCoopers LLP

LOCATIONS

HQ: Interpublic Group of Companies Inc.
909 Third Avenue, New York, NY 10022
Phone: 212 704-1200
Web: www.interpublic.com

COMPETITORS

Dentsu	Omnicom
Dentsu Aegis	Publicis Groupe
Hakuhodo	WPP
Havas	

HISTORICAL FINANCIALS

Company Type: Public

Income Statement   FYE: December 31

	REVENUE ($ mil.)	NET INCOME ($ mil.)	NET PROFIT MARGIN	EMPLOYEES
12/19	10,221	656	6.4%	54,300
12/18	9,714	618	6.4%	54,000
12/17	7,882	579	7.3%	50,200
12/16	7,846	608	7.8%	49,800
12/15	7,613	454	6.0%	49,200
Annual Growth	7.6%	9.6%	—	2.5%

2019 Year-End Financials

Debt ratio: 18.74%
Return on equity: 25.38%
Cash ($ mil.): 1,192
Current ratio: 0.93
Long-term debt ($ mil.): 2,771

No. of shares (mil.): 387
Dividends
  Yield: 4.0%
  Payout: 55.9%
Market value ($ mil.): 8,940

	STOCK PRICE ($) FY Close	P/E High/Low	PER SHARE ($) Earnings	Dividends	Book Value
12/19	23.10	14 12	1.68	0.94	7.17
12/18	20.63	16 12	1.59	0.84	6.24
12/17	20.16	17 12	1.46	0.72	5.74
12/16	23.41	16 13	1.49	0.60	5.15
12/15	23.28	21 16	1.09	0.48	4.87
Annual Growth	(0.2%)	— —	11.4%	18.3%	10.1%

Intuit Inc

Intuit's fact is: It handles other people's taxes – and their bookkeeping and other financial management tasks. The company is a leading developer of software used for small business accounting (QuickBooks) and consumer tax preparation (TurboTax). Mint the online service helps manage personal finances and budgeting. Professional accountants boot up Intuit's Lacerte ProSeries and ProConnect Tax Online products. Nearly 80% of revenue comes from products hosted on Intuit's servers what the company calls connected services. Intuit claims more than 50 million users for its products and services. The company perform its operation on its offices in the US Canada and the UK.

Operations

Intuit operates in three segments Small Business & Self-Employed Consumer and Strategic Partner.

The Small Business & Self-Employed segment nearly 55% of sales offers QuickBooks financial and business management online services and desktop software payroll and payment processing products and financing for small businesses.

The Consumer segment about 40% of sales offers the TurboTax income tax preparation products and services as well as the Mint financial planning service.

The Strategic Partner segment more than 5% of sales sells Intuit's professional tax products like Lacerte ProSeries ProFile and ProConnect Tax Online.

Overall its services and others account nearly 80% of total sales while about 20% for its products.

Geographic Reach

California-based Intuit has operations in some 20 locations in nine countries including US Canada India the UK Israel and Australia. International sales consistently account for less than 5% of Intuit's sales.

Sales and Marketing

Intuit relies on web marketing and targeted advertising such as search engine optimization and purchasing key words from major search engine companies; placing its mobile application in proprietary online stores (including Google's Play Store and Apple's App Store) direct-response mail and email campaigns telephone solicitations TV radio and print advertisements social media and coordinated promotional offers with major retailers.

The company spent approximately $778 million $800 million and $615 million on advertising for FY 2020 2019 and 2018 respectively.

Financial Performance

Intuit has reported five consecutive years of higher revenue and the company enjoyed strong net income for the same period.

In 2020 (ended July) revenue rose 13% to about $7.7 billion up $895 million from 2019. Small Business & Self-Employed segment revenue increased 15% primarily due to growth in the Online Ecosystem. The Consumer segment revenue increased 13% primarily due to a shift in mix to its higher priced offerings including TurboTax Live and growth in TurboTax federal unit.

Net income increased $269 million or 17% in fiscal 2020 (ended July) compared with fiscal 2019 due to the increase in operating income.

Intuit's coffers held $6.7 billion in cash in 2020 (ended July) compared to $2.4 billion the year before. Operations generated $2.4 billion while financing activities added another $2 billion to the coffers. Investing activities used $97 million for purchases of corporate and fund investments.

Strategy

Intuit's strategy starts with customer obsession. It listens to and observe its customers and then use advanced technology including AI to develop innovative solutions designed to solve its problems and help the company grow and prosper. Its strategy for delivering on its bold goals is to become an AI-driven expert platform where the company and others can solve its customers' most important problems. It plans to accelerate the development of the platform by applying AI in three key areas: Machine learning; Knowledge engineering; and natural language processing.

As it builds its AI-driven expert platform Intuit is prioritizing its resources on five strategic priorities across the company. These priorities focus on solving the problems that matter most to customers and include: Revolutionizing speed to benefit; Connecting people to experts; Unlocking smart money decisions; Being the center of small business growth; and Disrupting the small business mid-market. As the external environment evolves the company continues to innovate and adapt these strategy and anticipate its customers' needs.

Mergers and Acquisitions

In 2019 Intuit acquired Origami Logic developer of a data integration ingestion and analytics platform for analyzing multiple data sets for estimated $64.5 million in venture funding. Intuit intends to use the technology to help customers get more information out of their data.

HISTORY

After earning his MBA from Harvard founder Scott Cook spent three years in marketing at Procter & Gamble and four years with consultancy Bain & Company before establishing Intuit in 1983. Research showed that consumers wanted an easy-to-use personal finance software package. Quicken was introduced in 1984.

Intuit was near collapse in 1986 when it received its first big order from software retailer Egghead.com. Intuit released QuickBooks in 1992 and went public in 1993. The next year it acquired a number of firms including tax preparation software developer ChipSoft which brought TurboTax onboard.

In 1995 Microsoft's $2 billion bid to buy Intuit was halted by a Justice Department antitrust lawsuit. Also that year Intuit launched an online banking service and forged its first ties with the Web by bundling a browser and free Internet access with Quicken. It sold its online banking and bill presentation business to CheckFree in 1997. In 1998 the company bought Lacerte Software a provider of software and services to tax professionals.

EXECUTIVES

Evp And Chief People Officer, Sherry Whiteley
Chairman And Ceo, Brad D. Smith, age 56, $1,000,000 total compensation
Evp General Counsel And Secretary, Laura A. Fennell, age 59, $575,000 total compensation
Evp And General Manager Small Business Group, Sasan K. Goodarzi, age 52, $625,000 total compensation
Evp And General Manager Proconnect Group, CeCe Morken
Svp And Cto, H. Tayloe Stansbury, age 59, $625,000 total compensation
Evp And General Manager Consumer Tax Group, Daniel A. (Dan) Wernikoff, age 48, $725,000 total compensation
Svp And General Manager Consumer Ecosystem Group, Al Ko
Evp And Chief Marketing And Sales Officer, Lucas Watson
Evp And Cfo, Michelle Clatterbuck, age 52
Vice President Global Communications Small Business Division, Heather McLellan
Vice President Corporate Finance And Treasurer, Jerry Natoli
Senior Vice President And Chief Communications Officer, Rob Lanesey
Vice President Communications, Sandra Corradetti
Vice President Of Design, Kurt Walecki
Vice President Of Product Management, Barry Saik
Svp Technology Accounting Professionals Division, Mamie Jones
Vice President Corporate Development, Erika Swanson
Senior Vice President Investment Services, Rajneesh Gupta
Vice President Marketing, Patti Newcomer
Vice President Engineering Financial Data Platform, Bhushan Heda
Vice President Tax Regulatory Affairs, David Sullivan
Vice President Of Design, Leslie Witt
Vp And Fellow Marketing Technologies, Aditi Dhagat
Vice President Mid Market Segment Leader Sbseg, Kelly Vincent
Board Of Directors, Stephen Bennett
Board Member, Jeff Weiner
Auditors: Ernst & Young LLP

LOCATIONS

HQ: Intuit Inc
  2700 Coast Avenue, Mountain View, CA 94043
Phone: 650 944-6000
Web: www.intuit.com

PRODUCTS/OPERATIONS

2019 Sales

	$ mil.	% of total
Small Business	3,533	52
Consumer Tax	2,775	41
ProConnect	476	7
Total	6,784	100

2019 Sales

	$ mil.	% of total
Product	1,623	24
Service and other	5,161	76
Total	**6,784**	**100**

Products and services

Individuals
Manage budgeting and taxes with confidence
Mint Budgeting
Quicken Personal Finance
QuickBooks Self-Employed
TurboTax Tax Preparation
Small Businesses
The tools you need to run your company
Checks & Supplies
Demandforce Marketing
Intuit Payroll Services
QuickBooks Business Finance
QuickBooks Payments
Accountants
Pro software for the range of client needs
Intuit Tax Online
Lacerte Pro Tax Software
ProSeries Pro Tax Software
QuickBooks for Accountants

COMPETITORS

ADP	H&R Block
Bank of America	JPMorgan Chase
CCH Incorporated	Jackson Hewitt
Elavon	PayPal
Fidelity National	Paychex
Information Services	Square
First Data	Thomson Reuters
Fiserv	Universal Tax
Global Payments	Wells Fargo

HISTORICAL FINANCIALS

Company Type: Public

Income Statement				FYE: July 31
	REVENUE ($ mil.)	NET INCOME ($ mil.)	NET PROFIT MARGIN	EMPLOYEES
07/20	7,679	1,826	23.8%	10,600
07/19	6,784	1,557	23.0%	9,400
07/18	5,964	1,211	20.3%	8,900
07/17	5,177	971	18.8%	8,200
07/16	4,694	979	20.9%	7,900
Annual Growth	**13.1%**	**16.9%**		**7.6%**

2020 Year-End Financials

Debt ratio: 30.82%
Return on equity: 41.13%
Cash ($ mil.): 6,442
Current ratio: 2.26
Long-term debt ($ mil.): 2,031
No. of shares (mil.): 261
Dividends
Yield: 0.6%
Payout: 41.8%
Market value ($ mil.): 80,189

	STOCK PRICE ($) FY Close	P/E High/Low	Earnings	PER SHARE ($) Dividends	Book Value
07/20	306.37	44 28	6.92	2.12	19.51
07/19	277.31	47 31	5.89	1.88	14.41
07/18	204.24	46 28	4.64	1.56	9.10
07/17	137.21	38 28	3.72	1.36	5.30
07/16	110.99	31 21	3.69	1.20	4.50
Annual Growth	**28.9%**		**17.0%**	**15.3%**	**44.3%**

Invesco Mortgage Capital Inc

Invesco Mortgage Capital is ready to roll now that the mortgage industry has finally reversed its course. Invesco Mortgage is a real estate investment trust (REIT) that finances and manages residential and commercial mortgage-backed securities and mortgage loans. It purchases agency-backed mortgages secured by the likes of Fannie Mae and Freddie Mac and is managed and advised by sibling Invesco Institutional a subsidiary of Invesco Ltd. The firm's mortgage-backed securities portfolio is concentrated within the four populous states of California Florida Texas and New York.

Operations

Invesco Mortgage conducts its business through IAS Operating Partnership L.P. The company primarily invests in residential mortgage-backed securities (RMBS) and commercial mortgage-backed securities (CMBS) that are guaranteed by a US government agency such as the Government National Mortgage Association (Ginnie Mae). It generates about 90% of total revenue from mortgage-backed and credit risk transfer securities.

Geographic Reach

Atlanta Georgia-based Invesco Mortgage's residential mortgage-backed securities (RMBS) portfolio is centered around California (about 45% of total) New York (almost 10%) and Florida (more than 5%). Its commercial mortgage-backed securities (CMBS) portfolio is concentrated in California (about 15%) New York (some 15%) Texas (nearly 10%) and Florida (more than 5%).

Financial Performance

Invesco Mortgage's net income has been fluctuating for the past five years but it has recorded its worst in 2018 when the company had a $70.8 million loss. Net income in 2019 was $364.1 million.

Cash and cash equivalents at the end of the year were $289.5 million 113% more than the previous year. Cash provided by operating activities was $343.4 million. Investing activities used $4.3 billion primarily for purchase of mortgage-backed and credit risk transfer securities while financing activities provided $4.1 billion primarily from proceeds from repurchase agreements.

Strategy

A part of Invesco Mortgage's strategy is to invest in a diversified pool of mortgage assets that generate attractive risk-adjusted returns. Its target assets generally include Agency RMBS Agency CMBS non-Agency RMBS non-Agency CMBS GSE CRT residential and commercial mortgage loans and other real estate-related financing arrangements. In addition to direct purchases of its target assets the company also invests in ventures managed by an affiliate of its manager which in turn invests in its target assets.

The company generally finances its investments through short- and long-term borrowings structured as repurchase agreements and secured loans. It has also financed investments through the issuances of debt and equity and may utilize other forms of financing in the future.

EXECUTIVES

Chief Investment Officer, John M. Anzalone, age 55
Chief Investment Officer, Jason Marshall, age 45
President, Robson J. (Rob) Kuster, age 47
Cfo, Richard L. Phegley
Evp Residential Credit, David Lyle
Evp Commercial Credit, Kevin Collins
Chairman, James S. Balloun, age 82
Auditors: PricewaterhouseCoopers LLP

LOCATIONS

HQ: Invesco Mortgage Capital Inc
1555 Peachtree Street N.E., Suite 1800, Atlanta, GA 30309
Phone: 404 892-0896
Web: www.invescomortgagecapital.com

PRODUCTS/OPERATIONS

2014 Sales

	$ mil.	% of total
Interest income		
Mortgage-backed and credit risk transfer securities	579	86
Residential loans	88	13
Commercial loans	9	1
Total interest income	676	100
Other income	-572.8 -	
Total	**103**	**100**

COMPETITORS

Annaly Capital Management	Redwood Trust
Anworth Mortgage Asset	Walter Investment Management
Capstead Mortgage	iStar Financial Inc
Impac Mortgage Holdings	

HISTORICAL FINANCIALS

Company Type: Public

Income Statement				FYE: December 31
	ASSETS ($ mil.)	NET INCOME ($ mil.)	INCOME AS % OF ASSETS	EMPLOYEES
12/19	22,346	364	1.6%	—
12/18	17,813	(70)		—
12/17	18,657	348	1.9%	—
12/16	15,706	254	1.6%	—
12/15	16,772	103	0.6%	—
Annual Growth	**7.4%**	**36.8%**		—

2019 Year-End Financials

Debt ratio: 7.38%
Return on equity: 13.95%
Cash ($ mil.): 172
Current ratio: —
Long-term debt ($ mil.): —
No. of shares (mil.): 144
Dividends
Yield: 11.1%
Payout: 1,321.4%
Market value ($ mil.): 2,402

	STOCK PRICE ($) FY Close	P/E High/Low	Earnings	PER SHARE ($) Dividends	Book Value
12/19	16.65	7 6	2.42	1.85	20.32
12/18	14.48		(1.03)	1.68	20.49
12/17	17.83	6 5	2.75	1.63	23.57
12/16	14.60	8 5	1.98	1.60	20.09
12/15	12.39	24 18	0.67	1.70	19.72
Annual Growth	**7.7%**	— —	**37.9%**	**2.1%**	**0.8%**

Investar Holding Corp

Auditors: HORNE LLP

LOCATIONS

HQ: Investar Holding Corp
10500 Coursey Boulevard, Baton Rouge, LA 70816
Phone: 225 227-2222

HISTORICAL FINANCIALS

Company Type: Public

Income Statement
FYE: December 31

	ASSETS ($ mil.)	NET INCOME ($ mil.)	INCOME AS % OF ASSETS	EMPLOYEES
12/19	2,148	16	0.8%	324
12/18	1,786	13	0.8%	255
12/17	1,622	8	0.5%	258
12/16	1,158	7	0.7%	152
12/15	1,031	7	0.7%	951
Annual Growth	20.1%	24.2%	—	(23.6%)

2019 Year-End Financials

Debt ratio: 2.27%
Return on equity: 7.94%
Cash ($ mil.): 44
Current ratio: —
Long-term debt ($ mil.): —

No. of shares (mil.): 11
Dividends
  Yield: 0.9%
  Payout: 13.5%
Market value ($ mil.): 269

	STOCK PRICE ($) FY Close	P/E High/Low	PER SHARE ($) Earnings	Dividends	Book Value
12/19	24.00	15 13	1.66	0.23	21.55
12/18	24.80	21 15	1.39	0.17	19.22
12/17	24.10	26 20	0.96	0.07	18.15
12/16	18.65	18 12	1.10	0.04	15.88
12/15	17.60	18 14	0.97	0.03	15.05
Annual Growth	8.1%	— —	14.4%	63.3%	9.4%

Investors Bancorp Inc (New)

EXECUTIVES

Sevp And Coo, Domenick A. Cama, age 64, $621,000 total compensation
President And Ceo, Kevin Cummings, age 65, $935,000 total compensation
Evp And Chief Lending Officer, Richard S. Spengler, age 58, $400,000 total compensation
Evp And Chief Retail Banking Officer, Paul Kalamaras, $375,000 total compensation
Svp And Cfo, Sean Burke
Chairman, Robert M. Cashill, age 77
Auditors: KPMG LLP

LOCATIONS

HQ: Investors Bancorp Inc (New)
  101 JFK Parkway, Short Hills, NJ 07078
Phone: 973 924-5100
Web: www.investorsbank.com

PRODUCTS/OPERATIONS

2014 Sales

	$ mil.	% of total
Interest		
Loans receivable and held-for-sale	603	86
Mortgage-backed securities	44	6
Federal Home Loan Bank stock	6	1
Municipal bonds & other debt	5	1
Other	0	.
Non-interest		
Fees & service charges	19	3
Gain on loan transaction	5	2
Others	17	1
Total	702	100

COMPETITORS

Bank of America
Bank of New York Mellon
Citigroup
ConnectOne Bancorp
Fulton Financial
M&T Bank
New York Community Bancorp
OceanFirst Financial
PNC Financial

HISTORICAL FINANCIALS

Company Type: Public

Income Statement
FYE: December 31

	ASSETS ($ mil.)	NET INCOME ($ mil.)	INCOME AS % OF ASSETS	EMPLOYEES
12/19	26,698	195	0.7%	1,793
12/18	26,229	202	0.8%	1,962
12/17	25,129	126	0.5%	1,959
12/16	23,174	192	0.8%	1,829
12/15	20,888	181	0.9%	1,768
Annual Growth	6.3%	1.9%	—	0.4%

2019 Year-End Financials

Debt ratio: 3.18%
Return on equity: 6.95%
Cash ($ mil.): 174
Current ratio: —
Long-term debt ($ mil.): —

No. of shares (mil.): 247
Dividends
  Yield: 3.6%
  Payout: 63.7%
Market value ($ mil.): 2,948

	STOCK PRICE ($) FY Close	P/E High/Low	PER SHARE ($) Earnings	Dividends	Book Value
12/19	11.92	17 14	0.74	0.44	10.60
12/18	10.40	20 14	0.72	0.38	10.50
12/17	13.88	34 29	0.43	0.33	10.21
12/16	13.95	22 16	0.64	0.26	10.09
12/15	12.44	24 19	0.55	0.25	9.89
Annual Growth	(1.1%)	— —	7.7%	15.2%	1.7%

IQVIA Holdings Inc

IQVIA Holdings has plenty to CRO about. One of the world's largest contract research organizations (CROs) it helps pharmaceutical biotechnology and medical device companies develop and sell their products. The firm provides a comprehensive range of clinical trials management services including patient recruitment data analysis laboratory testing and regulatory filing assistance. Its consulting offerings include strategic advice at each stage of drug discovery and development. The company also provides data analytics technology and expertise to medical researchers government agencies and health care payers. IQVIA gets about 45% of its revenue in the US.

Operations

IQVIA operates through three segments: Research & Development Solutions Technology & Analytics Solutions and Contract Sales & Medical Solutions.

The Research & Development segment which accounts for more than half of revenue offers project management virtual trials Q2 Solutions (clinical trial laboratory and research services) clinical trial support and strategic planning and design services.

The Technology & Analytics Solutions segment about 40% of revenue provides technology insight workflow analytics and consulting national and sub-national information and reference information; it has access to data on the treatments and outcomes of more than 800 million unidentified patients.

The Contract Sales & Medical Solutions segment more than 5% of revenue provides health care provider and patient engagement services as well as medical affairs services.

The company has a 60% stake in a joint venture with Quest Diagnostics. Named Q2 Solutions the venture provides clinical trials lab services.

Geographic Reach

IQVIA splits its headquarters between Durham North Carolina and Danbury Connecticut and it has more than 300 offices in about 85 countries in the Americas Europe Africa and the Asia/Pacific region.

The US supplies more than 40% of IQVIA's revenue while the UK provides about 10%. Regionally the Americas account for about half of the company's revenue Europe and Africa provide about a third and the Asia/Pacific region supplies about 20%.

Sales and Marketing

IQVIA has a broad base of customers which include most of the top 100 global pharmaceutical and biotechnology companies (in terms of revenue). Customers in pharmaceutical biotechnology device and diagnostic and consumer health businesses account for most of IQVIA's revenue. Other clients include payers government and regulatory agencies providers pharmaceutical distributors and pharmacies.

Financial Performance

The company's revenue grows for the past five years reaching the peak by $11.1 billion a 93% increase from 2015 to 2019.

In 2019 their revenues increased $676 million or 7% as compared to 2018. This increase was comprised of constant currency revenue growth of approximately $835 million or 8% and a negative impact of approximately $159 million from the effects of foreign currency fluctuations. The constant currency revenue growth was comprised of a $444 million increase in Technology & Analytics Solutions a $378 million increase in Research & Development Solutions and a $13 million increase in Contract Sales & Medical Solutions.

Net income fell to $191 million in 2019 from $259 million in 2019 due to $57 million increase on their income tax expense to $116 million in 2019.

IQVIA had $837 million in cash and equivalents in 2019 compared to $891 million the year before. In 2019 operations generated $1.4 billion while investing and financing activities used $1.2 billion and $276 million respectively.

Strategy

IQVIA's strategy for achieving growth includes: continue to innovate by leveraging their information advanced analytics transformative technology and significant domain expertise; build upon their extensive client relationships; expand portfolio through strategic acquisitions; and expand the penetration of their offerings to the broader healthcare marketplace.

As a leader in the development and commercialization of new pharmaceutical therapies the company can empower their therapeutic scientific and domain experts with expansive levels of information including product level tracking in 90 markets and information about treatments and outcomes on more than 800 million non-identified patients. By integrating these capabilities in the IQVIA CORE they have the ability to optimize the clinical trial process and enable their clients to reduce costs and get their products to market more quickly through more informed site selection faster patient recruitment practices and virtual trials. They transform Real World Evidence by linking prospective and retrospective approaches and introduce innovation such as secondary control arms which eliminate the need for a placebo group. The bring best in class SaaS platforms purpose built for life sciences to their clients to help them run the client's clinical and commercial operations more efficiently.

Mergers and Acquisitions

In 2019 IQVIA acquired Linguamatics a bioinformatics company that employs natural language processing. The deal boosts IQVIA's ability to find additional information in patient data.

Company Background

The company was founded as Quntiles by Dennis Gillings a British biostatistician who had worked with Hoechst (later part of Sanofi) on data analysis in the 1970s. Gillings set up Quintiles (Quantitative Information Technology In The Life and Economic Sciences) in 1982 at the University of North Carolina where he was then teaching. The company grew as drug companies began outsourcing some of the more irksome tasks of drug development. Quintiles went public in 1994.

The company used the proceeds of the IPO to expand its health economics segment with the purchases of Benefit International (1995) and Lewin Group (1996). These purchases introduced it to such new clients as governments and HMOs. Quintiles' 1996 purchase of Innovex (unrelated to the computer hardware maker of the same name) made it the world's largest CRO.

The company changed its name to IQVIA in 2017 following the merger with IMS Health.

HISTORY

Quintiles was founded by Dennis Gillings a British biostatistician who had worked with Hoechst (later part of Sanofi) on data analysis in the 1970s. Gillings set up Quintiles (Quantitative Information Technology In The Life and Economic Sciences) in 1982 at the University of North Carolina where he was then teaching. The company grew as drug companies began outsourcing some of the more irksome tasks of drug development. Quintiles went public in 1994.

The company used the proceeds of the IPO to expand its health economics segment with the purchases of Benefit International (1995) and Lewin Group (1996). These purchases introduced it to such new clients as governments and HMOs. Quintiles' 1996 purchase of Innovex (unrelated to the computer hardware maker of the same name) made it the world's largest CRO. The buying spree continued in 1997 and 1998. Among the purchases were some intended to strengthen Quintiles' marketing services (Data Analysis Systems Inc. Q.E.D. International and France-based Serval). The firm also formed new collaborations with such academic research organizations as Johns Hopkins Medicine.

In 1999 Quintiles expanded its marketing arm with the purchase of Pharmaceutical Marketing Services (parent of the leading pharmaceuticals industry research company Scott-Levin) and jumped headlong into data mining with its purchase of ENVOY — which processed insurance claims. Quintiles found the core business uninspiring and sold it to Healtheon (now Emdeon formerly WebMD) the next year. But it kept rights to ENVOY's stream of treatment outcome and insurance data gleaned from health care providers hospitals payers and pharmacies — a treasure house of information useful to salespeople and health providers.

The company continued in 2000 to add offices in Europe Asia and Latin America. It also opened additional offices in the US and Europe to help Japanese pharmaceutical companies market their products in those regions. Late in the year Quintiles bought the clinical development unit of Pharmacia.

In 2001 Quintiles became embroiled in a legal dispute with WebMD involving the availability of data associated with ENVOY; the company challenged WebMD's efforts to withhold such data. The two companies settled the squabble later that year and agreed to sever all ties. Also in 2001 Quintiles streamlined operations and cut about 5% of its workforce.

The future structure of the CRO came into question at the end of 2002. Gillings presented the company with a buyout offer; he planned to take the company private so he could pursue a new growth strategy Wall Street would surely find risky. The board rejected that offer in October 2002 but it opened up an auction. Some leading equity firms reportedly made offers but Gillings — with backing from Blackstone Group and BANK ONE's One Equity Partners (later part of JPMorgan Chase) — placed another offer for Quintiles and won the prize in April 2003. Some five months later Quintiles went private.

EXECUTIVES

Chairman And Ceo, Ari Bousbib, age 58, $390,137 total compensation

Cfo, Michael R. (Mike) McDonnell, age 56, $650,000 total compensation

Svp And Executive Director Quintilesims Institute, Murray L. Aitken

President Novella Clinical, W. Richard Staub, age 57, $485,923 total compensation

President Clinical Operations Research And Development Solutions, Cynthia L. Verst

President Customer Solutions Management Group, Paul Spreen

President Information And Technology Solutions, Kevin C. Knightly, age 58, $119,399 total compensation

President Asia/pacific, Anand Tharmaratnam

President Central East And South Europe, Elisabeth Beck

President North Europe Middle East And Africa, Alistair Grenfell

President Japan, Norihiko Minato

President Latin America, Nilton Paletta

Evp And General Counsel, James H. (Jim) Erlinger, age 61, $468,333 total compensation

President Real-world Insights (rwi), Jon Resnick

President Integrated Engagement Services, W. Scott Evangelista

Svp And Cio, Karl Guenault

President United States And Canada, Hossam Sadek

President Data Sciences Safety And Regulatory Research And Development Solutions, Margaret Keegan

Ceo Qâ Solutions, Costa Panagos

Vp Administration And Chief Of Staff To The Ceo Ims Health, Trudy Stein

Svp Strategy Marketing And Communications, Marla Kessler

President Global Services, José Luis Fern ndez

Vice President And Global Head Of Risk Management, Stella Blackburn

Vice President Commercial Sales, Jay Schwartz

Vice President Executive Strategist, David Hauser

Auditors: PricewaterhouseCoopers LLP

LOCATIONS

HQ: IQVIA Holdings Inc
4820 Emperor Blvd., Durham, NC 27703
Phone: 919 998-2000
Web: www.quintiles.com

2018 Sales

	$ mil.	% of total
Americas	4,998	48
Europe & Africa	3,448	33
Asia/Pacific	1,966	19
Total	**10,412**	**100**

PRODUCTS/OPERATIONS

2018 Sales by Segment

	$ mil.	% of total
Research & Development Solutions	5,465	52
Technology & Analytics Solutions	4,137	40
Contract Sales & Medical Solutions	810	8
Total	**10,412**	**100**

Selected Therapeutic Specialties

Cardiovascular
Central nervous system
Gastrointestinal/NASH
Infectious diseases
Internal medicine
Oncology
Pediatrics
Rheumatology
Women's health

COMPETITORS

Accenture	PRA Health Sciences
CMIC HOLDINGS CO. LTD.	Pharmaceutical Product
Covance	Development
ICON	Publicis Groupe
Kantar Group	Veeva Systems
PAREXEL	Verisk Health

HISTORICAL FINANCIALS

Company Type: Public

Income Statement

FYE: December 31

	REVENUE ($ mil.)	NET INCOME ($ mil.)	NET PROFIT MARGIN	EMPLOYEES
12/19	11,088	191	1.7%	67,000
12/18	10,412	259	2.5%	58,000
12/17	9,739	1,309	13.4%	55,000
12/16	6,878	115	1.7%	50,000
12/15	5,737	387	6.7%	36,100
Annual Growth	17.9%	(16.2%)	—	16.7%

2019 Year-End Financials

Debt ratio: 50.08%	No. of shares (mil.): 192
Return on equity: 3.00%	Dividends
Cash ($ mil.): 837	Yield: —
Current ratio: 1.05	Payout: —
Long-term debt ($ mil.): 11,545	Market value ($ mil.): 29,712

	STOCK PRICE ($) FY Close	P/E High/Low		PER SHARE ($) Earnings	Dividends	Book Value
12/19	154.51	165	112	0.96	0.00	31.22
12/18	116.17	103	75	1.24	0.00	33.99
12/17	97.90	18	13	5.88	0.00	38.97
12/16	76.05	105	73	0.76	0.00	36.67
12/15	68.66	25	18	3.08	0.00	(4.73)
Annual Growth	22.5%	—	—	(25.3%)	—	—

Jabil Inc

Jabil Inc. makes a jabillion different kinds of electronics. The company is one of the providers of outsourced Electronics Manufacturing Services (EMS) in the world. It makes electronics components and parts on a contract basis for computers smartphones printers and other consumer electronics as well as more complex specialized products for the defense and aerospace capital equipment cloud computing and storage automotive industrial and energy networking and telecommunications print and retail and smart home and appliances industries. Jabil also provides Diversified Manufacturing Services (DMS) that focuses in the edge devices and accessories healthcare mobility and packaging industries. The company's manufacturing and supply chain management services and solutions range from product innovation design planning fabrication and assembly delivery and managing the flow of resources and products. US-based Jabil operates in more than 100 sites in about 30 countries with international customers accounting for about 90% of sales.

Operations

Jabil conducts business in two segments: Electronics Manufacturing Services (EMS) and Diversified Manufacturing Services (DMS).

The EMS segment (more than 60% of revenue) focuses on IT supply chain design and engineering technologies largely centered on core electronic. The products Jabil makes for its customers are used in the automotive and transportation capital equipment cloud computing and storage defense and aerospace industrial and energy networking and telecommunications print and retail and smart home and appliances industries.

The DMS segment (about 40% of revenue) focuses on manufacturing services for material sciences technologies and healthcare. It works with customers to develop and manufacture products in the edge devices and accessories healthcare mobility and packaging industries.

Geographic Reach

Headquartered in St. Petersburg Florida Jabil has manufacturing plants in the US Canada and Mexico as well as Europe Asia South Africa Asia and South America. The company conducts operations in facilities that are located worldwide including but not limited to China Hungary Malaysia Mexico Singapore and the US.

Singapore and China are its largest markets accounting for more than 25% and 20% of sales respectively. Mexico accounts for about 20% of revenue.

Sales and Marketing

Jabil depends on a small number of customers for a significant percentage of revenue. Its top customer is Apple accounting for more than 20% of sales. In fiscal year 2019 the company's five largest customers accounted for more than 40% of the company's net revenue and approximately 85 customers accounted for approximately 90% of the company's net revenue.

The company also markets its services and solutions through its website and its Blue Sky Innovation Centers.

Financial Performance

Jabil's string of annual revenue increases continued for a fifth year in 2019 (ended August) with a 14% jump from 2018.

The company reported sales of $25.3 billion in 2019 up $3.2 billion from 2018. This was primarily due to the 26% increase in the EMS segment.

In 2019 net income attributable to Jabil totaled $287.1 million a 233% growth from $86.3 million in 2018.

Jabil had about $1.2 billion in cash and equivalents in 2019 compared to $1.3 billion in 2018. Operations generated about $1.2 billion in cash in 2019 while investing and financing activities used $872.5 million and $415.8 million respectively.

Strategy

Jabil's vision for the future is to become the world's most technologically advanced manufacturing services and solutions provider. As it works to achieve its vision it continues to pursue the following strategies:

Establishing and Maintaining Long-Term Customer Relationships. An important element of Jabil's strategy is to establish and maintain long-term relationships with leading companies in expanding industries with size and growth characteristics that can benefit from highly automated continuous flow manufacturing on a global scale.

Product Diversification. The company focuses on balancing its portfolio of products and product families to those that align with higher return areas of its business including manufacturing supply chain management services comprehensive electronics design production and product management services. The company has made concentrated efforts to diversify its industry sectors and customer base.

Utilizing Customer-Centric Business Units. Most of the company's business units are dedicated to serve one customer each and operate by primarily utilizing dedicated production equipment production workers supervisors buyers planners and engineers to provide comprehensive manufacturing solutions that are customized to each customer's needs.

Leveraging Global Production. The company believes that global production is a key strategy to reduce obsolescence risk and secure the lowest possible landed costs while simultaneously supplying products of equivalent or comparable quality throughout the world.

Offering Systems Assembly Direct-Order Fulfillment and Configure-to-Order Services. Jabil's systems assembly direct-order fulfillment and configure-to-order services allow customers to reduce product cost and risk of product obsolescence by reducing total work-in-process and finished goods inventory.

Offering Design Services. The company offers a wide spectrum of value-add design services to achieve improvements in performance cost time-to-market and manufacturability.

Pursue Acquisition Opportunities Selectively. Traditionally electronics manufacturing service companies have acquired manufacturing capacity from their customers to drive growth expand their footprint and gain new customers.

Mergers and Acquisitions

In late-2019 Jabil completed the third closing of their acquisition of certain assets of JJMD for a cash payment of $117.1 million primarily for inventory and the assumption of certain employee liabilities. The purchase price for the third closing is subject to certain post-closing adjustments based on conditions within the Framework Agreement.

Company Background

Jabil Circuit was named for founders James Golden and Bill Morean. The duo who originally ran an excavation business started Jabil in suburban Detroit in 1966 to provide assembly and reworking services to electronics manufacturers. Jabil incorporated in 1969 and began making printed circuit boards for Control Data Corporation (later renamed Control Data Systems) that year.

William D. Morean the founder's son who had worked summers at Jabil while in high school joined the company in 1977. The next year the younger Morean took over Jabil's day-to-day operations. The company had entered the automotive electronics business in 1976 through a $12 million contract with General Motors.

During the 1980s Jabil began building computer components adding such customers as Dell NEC Sun Microsystems and Toshiba. Jabil moved its headquarters to St. Petersburg Florida in 1983. William Morean became Jabil's chairman and CEO in 1988.

EXECUTIVES

Ceo And Director, Mark T. Mondello, age 56, $1,100,000 total compensation

Evp And Coo, William D. (Bill) Muir, age 52, $700,000 total compensation

Evp Corporate Development And Chief Of Staff, Courtney J. Ryan, age 50

Cfo, Forbes I. J. Alexander, age 60, $700,000 total compensation

Evp And Ceo Healthcare, Steven D. (Steve) Borges, age 51

Evp General Counsel And Corporate Secretary, Robert L. (Bobby) Katz, age 58

Evp And Ceo Green Point, Hwai Hai (HH) Chiang, $445,000 total compensation

Evp And Ceo Jabil Packaging Solutions, Erich Hoch, age 50

Evp And Ceo Engineered Solutions Group, Michael J. Loparco, age 49

Evp And Ceo Enterprise And Infrastructure, Alessandro Parimbelli, age 52, $444,392 total compensation

President, William E. (Bill) Peters, age 57, $700,000 total compensation

Svp And Cio, Gary L. Cantrell

Evp Human Resources And Human Development, Scott D Slipy, age 54

Executive Vice President National Operations, Mark Butler

Vice President Of Finance After Market Services Division, Brian Greff

Vice President Real Estate And Construction, Jacky Lau

Vice President After Market Services, Hartmut Liebel

Assistant Vice President Sales National Accounts, Dennis Maddock

Vp And Cio Jabil Digital Solutions, Bhaskar Ramachandran

Vp Global Security, David Benner

Chairman, Timothy L. (Tim) Main, age 63

Vice Chairman, Thomas A. Sansone, age 71

Board Member, Steven Raymund

Auditors: Ernst & Young LLP

LOCATIONS

HQ: Jabil Inc
10560 Dr. Martin Luther King, Jr. Street North, St. Petersburg, FL 33716
Phone: 727 577-9749
Web: www.jabil.com

2018 Sales

	$ mil.	% of total
Singapore	7	33
China	4,585	21
Mexico	3,533	16
U.S.	1,844	8
Malaysia	1,389	6
Hungary	897	4
Other	2,651	12
Total	**22,095**	**100**

PRODUCTS/OPERATIONS

2018 Sales

	$ mil.	% of total
Electronics Manufacturing Services	12,268	56
Diversified Manufacturing Services	9,826	44
Total	**22,095**	**100**

Services

Component selection sourcing and procurement
Design and prototyping
Engineering
Order fulfillment
Printed circuit board and backplane assembly
Product testing
Repair and warranty
Systems assembly
Test development
Tooling design (molds and dies)

COMPETITORS

ASUSTeK	Flextronics
AptarGroup	Hon Hai
BenQ	Inventec
Benchmark Electronics	Key Tronic
CATCHER TECHNOLOGY CO.	Plexus
LTD.	Sanmina
Celestica	Venture Corp.
Compal Electronics	Wistron

HISTORICAL FINANCIALS

Company Type: Public

Income Statement

FYE: August 31

	REVENUE ($ mil.)	NET INCOME ($ mil.)	NET PROFIT MARGIN	EMPLOYEES
08/20	27,266	53	0.2%	240,000
08/19	25,282	287	1.1%	200,000
08/18	22,095	86	0.4%	199,000
08/17	19,063	129	0.7%	170,000
08/16	18,353	254	1.4%	138,000
Annual Growth	10.4%	(32.1%)	—	14.8%

2020 Year-End Financials

Debt ratio: 18.95%
Return on equity: 2.91%
Cash ($ mil.): 1,393
Current ratio: 1.01
Long-term debt ($ mil.): 2,678

No. of shares (mil.): 150
Dividends
  Yield: 0.9%
  Payout: 133.3%
Market value ($ mil.): 5,134

	STOCK PRICE ($) FY Close	P/E High/Low	PER SHARE ($) Earnings	Dividends	Book Value
08/20	34.15	121 51	0.35	0.32	12.05
08/19	28.81	17 12	1.81	0.32	12.29
08/18	29.56	63 49	0.49	0.32	11.85
08/17	31.35	44 29	0.69	0.32	13.24
08/16	21.19	19 13	1.32	0.32	13.04
Annual Growth	12.7%	— —	(28.2%)	(0.0%)	(2.0%)

Jacobs Engineering Group, Inc.

Jacobs Engineering Group provides a full spectrum of professional services including consulting technical scientific and project delivery for government and private sector throughout the world. Jacobs handles project design architectural and engineering construction and construction management services operations and maintenance services and process scientific and systems consulting services. Around 75% of revenue comes from the US while the rest originates in other countries primarily in Europe. In 2020 Jacobs acquired a 65% stake of PA Consulting for about $2.4 billion.

Operations

Jacobs operates in two global lines of business: People & Places Solutions (PPS) and Critical Mission Solutions (CMS).

People & Places Solutions provides end-to-end solutions for its clients' most complex projects – whether connected mobility water smart cities advanced manufacturing or the environment. In doing so the company employs predictive analytics artificial intelligence and automation digital twin technology IoT smart sensors geospatial visualization and advanced delivery processes and tools for consulting planning architecture design engineering and implementation as well as long-term operation of facilities and infrastructure. PPS accounts for around 65% of the total revenue.

Critical Mission Solutions provides a full spectrum of cybersecurity data analytics software application development enterprise and mission IT systems integration and other highly technical consulting solutions to government agencies as well as commercial customers. CMS accounts for more than 35% of the company's revenue.

Geographic Reach

Dallas TX-based Jacobs' largest market is the US where it garners around 75% of its revenue. Europe accounts for about 15%; Australia and New Zealand together provides some 5% and Canada with less than 5%.

The company provides its services through office and subsidiaries located primarily in North America Europe the Middle East India Australia New Zealand and Asia.

Sales and Marketing

About one-third of Jacobs' revenue is earned directly or indirectly from U.S. federal agencies.

Critical Mission Solutions serves broad sectors including U.S. government services cyber nuclear commercial and international sectors.

People & Places Solutions clients include national state and local government in the US. Europe U.K. Middle East Australia New Zealand and Asia as well as multinational private sector clients throughout the world.

Financial Performance

Jacobs has significantly grown in the last five years with revenues consistently rising every year. Between 2016 and 2020 the company's revenues more than doubled from $6.3 billion to a record $13.6 billion.

Jacobs ended 2020 with revenue of $13.6 billion up 7% from the previous year. The increase in revenues was due to primarily to the full year of revenues in fiscal 2020 from the KeyW acquisition completed in June 2019 impacts from the March 2020 John Wood Group nuclear business acquisition and growth in its legacy People & Places Solutions businesses offset in part by impacts from the COVID-19 pandemic.

The company's net income increased by 42% to $491.8 million due mostly to slight increase in cost of contracts and other expenses.

Jacobs' cash stores increased by $231.4 million in 2020 ending at $862.4 million. Operations provided $806.8 million an improvement from the previous year. Investments used $429.1 million mainly for acquisitions of businesses. Financing activities used $208.3 million mainly for long-term borrowings repayments and common stock repurchases.

Strategy

Jacobs launched a three-year accelerated profitable growth strategy after spending three years transforming its portfolio. The company's new strategy is focused on innovation and the continued transformation to build upon its position as the leading solutions provider for its clients.

This transformation included the $3.2 billion acquisition of CH2M Hill Companies Ltd and the $3.4 billion divestiture of the company's energy chemicals and resources business. The alignment of revenue synergies was key to the successful integration of CH2M and created a model for successful integration of CH2M and created a model for successful follow-on integrations like The KeyW Holding Corporation and John Wood Group's nuclear business.

These acquisitions positioned the company as a leader in high-value government services and technology-enabled solutions enhancing its portfolio by adding intellectual property-driven technology with unique proprietary C5ISR (command control communications computer combat systems intelligence surveillance and reconnaissance) rapid solutions and amplifying Jacobs' position as a Tier-1 global nuclear services provider.

Jacobs' three-pillar strategy based on the foundation of company values drives it to become the employer of choice deliver connected and sustainable solutions and leverage technology-enabled execution.

Mergers and Acquisitions

In 2020 Jacobs acquired a 65% stake in PA Consulting for Å 1.825 billion ($2.4 billion). The remaining 35% stake will be held by PA employees following the exit of existing majority stakeholder The Carlyle Group. Its partnership with PA forms a unique offering in the market that combines strategic front-end consulting and deep domain knowledge across key sectors with next generation science and technology expertise.

Also in 2020 Jacobs acquired Reston Virginia The Buffalo Group a leader in advanced cyber and intelligence solutions further strengthening Jacobs' leading portfolio of national priority mission-focused government solutions in the cyber domain and the Intelligence Community (IC). The terms of the acquisition were not disclosed.

In early 2020 Jacobs completed its acquisition of Wood Nuclear part of John Wood Group for an enterprise value of approximately Å 250 million ($325 million). The transaction enhances Jacobs' credentials as a global leader of total lifecycle nuclear services and technology-enabled solutions providing strategic support to clients' mission-critical defense and clean energy priorities nuclear clean-up and decommissioning environmental restoration and operational support.

Company Background

Jacobs Engineering Group was founded in 1947 by Joseph J. Jacobs as a one-man engineering consultancy in Pasadena California. The company has acquired more than 70 businesses since its founding.

In 1967 it opened its first regional office but kept management decentralized to replicate the small size and hard-hitting qualities of its home office. Three years later Jacobs Engineering went public.

HISTORY

Joseph Jacobs graduated from the Polytechnic Institute of Brooklyn in 1942 with a doctorate in engineering. He went to work for Merck designing processes for pharmaceutical production. Later he moved to Chemurgic Corp. near San Francisco where he worked until 1947 when he founded Jacobs Engineering as a consulting firm. Jacobs also sold industrial equipment avoiding any apparent conflict of interest by simply telling his consulting clients.

When equipment sales outstripped consulting work by 1954 Jacobs hired four salesmen and engineer Stan Krugman who became his right-hand man. Two years later the company got its first big chemical design job for Kaiser Aluminum. Jacobs incorporated his sole proprietorship in 1957.

In 1960 the firm won its first construction contract to design and build a potash flotation plant and Jacobs Engineering became an integrated design and construction firm. In 1967 it opened its first regional office but kept management decentralized to replicate the small size and hard-hitting qualities of its home office. Three years later Jacobs Engineering went public.

The firm merged with Houston-based Pace Companies which specialized in petrochemical engineering design in 1974. Also that year the firm became Jacobs Engineering Group and began building its first major overseas chemical plant in Ireland.

By 1977 sales had reached $250 million. A decade of lobbying paid off that year when the firm won a contract for the Arab Potash complex in Jordan. Jacobs began to withdraw from his firm's operations in the early 1980s but the 1982-83 recession and poor management decisions pounded earnings. Jacobs returned from retirement in 1985 fired 14 VPs cut staff in half and pushed the firm to pursue smaller process-plant jobs and specialty construction.

After abandoning a 1986 attempt to take the company private Jacobs began making acquisitions to improve the firm's construction expertise. In 1992 he relinquished his role as CEO to president Noel Watson. The next year the company expanded its international holdings by acquiring the UK's H&G Process Contracting and H&G Contractors.

The firm's $38 million purchase of CRS Sirrine Engineers and CRSS Constructors in 1994 was the company's largest buy at that point and added new markets in the paper and semiconductor industries. By 1995 Jacobs Engineering was working on a record backlog.

Continuing its acquisition drive the company bought a 49% interest in European engineering specialist Serete Group in 1996; it bought the rest the next year. Also in 1997 it gained control of Indian engineering affiliate Humphreys & Glasgow (now Jacobs H&G) increasing its 40% stake to 70% and bought CPR Engineering a pulp and paper processing specialist. It also formed a joint venture with Krupp UHDE to provide design engineering and construction management services in Mexico.

In 1999 the company paid $198 million for St. Louis construction and design firm Sverdrup which had completed projects in some 65 countries. The next year Jacobs Engineering purchased half of Dutch firm Stork Engineering's business (it acquired the rest in 2001). But the company's bid to buy the assets of bankrupt power plant construction company Stone & Webster in 2000 was topped by Shaw Group.

After being accused of overcharging the US government Jacobs Engineering settled a whistleblower lawsuit (for $35 million) in 2000 while continuing to deny the allegations. However the next year Jacobs continued to receive federal contracts including contracts for boosting security at the US Capitol complex and providing logistics to the US Special Operations Command. Jacobs completed its acquisition of the UK-based GIBB unit of engineering consulting firm LawGibb Group in 2001 as well as the purchase of McDermott Engineers and Constructors (Canada).

EXECUTIVES

Group Vice President, Walter Barber
Svp Information Technology, Cora L. Carmody, age 63
Chairman President And Ceo, Steven J. Demetriou, age 61, $125,000 total compensation
Evp And Cfo, Kevin C. Berryman, age 61, $544,832 total compensation

President Industrial, Robert V. (Bob) Pragada, age 52
Evp Operations, Joseph G. Mandel, age 60, $699,996 total compensation
Evp Operations, Phillip J. Stassi, age 65, $639,423 total compensation
President Aerospace And Technology, Terence D. Hagen, age 55
Gvp Consulting Operations, Robert McWhinney
Vice President Information Technology, Pete Young
Division Vice President Director Construction Services, Joseph Franco
Vice President, Albert Pozotrigo
Gvp Federal Operations, James Thiesing
Vice President, David Lewia
Vice President Global Information Technology Security, George Hull
Vice President, Jonathan Doros
Svp And Gm Global Environmental Solutions Aerospace Technology Environmental And Nuclear, Jan Walstrom
Vice President For Professional Affairs, Kimberly Cornett Pe
Auditors: Ernst & Young LLP

LOCATIONS

HQ: Jacobs Engineering Group, Inc.
  1999 Bryan Street, Suite 1200, Dallas, TX 75201
Phone: 214 583-8500
Web: www.jacobs.com

2018 Sales

	$ mil.	% of total
US	9,519	64
Europe	2,768	18
Canada	863	6
Asia	316	2
India	212	1
Australia and New Zealand	719	5
South America and Mexico	159	1
Middle East and Africa	425	3
Total	**14,984**	**100**

PRODUCTS/OPERATIONS

2018 Sales by Segment

	$ mil.	% of total
Aerospace Technology Environmental and Nuclear	4,372	29
Buildings Infrastructure and Advanced Facilities	6,184	41
Energy Chemicals and Resources	4,427	30
Total	**14,984**	**100**

COMPETITORS

AECOM	HOK
Aker Solutions	KBR
Amec Foster Wheeler	Leidos
BWX Technologies	Lockheed Martin
Bechtel	Tetra Tech
Fluor	Turner Construction
HDR	WS Atkins
HNTB Companies	

HISTORICAL FINANCIALS

Company Type: Public

Income Statement

FYE: October 2

	REVENUE ($ mil.)	NET INCOME ($ mil.)	NET PROFIT MARGIN	EMPLOYEES
10/20*	13,566	491	3.6%	55,000
09/19	12,737	847	6.7%	52,000
09/18	14,984	163	1.1%	80,800
09/17	10,022	293	2.9%	54,700
09/16	10,964	210	1.9%	54,900
Annual Growth	**5.5%**	**23.6%**	**—**	**0.0%**

*Fiscal year change

2020 Year-End Financials

Debt ratio: 13.57%	No. of shares (mil.): 129
Return on equity: 8.39%	Dividends
Cash ($ mil.): 862	Yield: 0.8%
Current ratio: 1.54	Payout: 18.3%
Long-term debt ($ mil.): 1,676	Market value ($ mil.): 12,227

	STOCK PRICE ($) FY Close	P/E High/Low		PER SHARE ($) Earnings	Dividends	Book Value
10/20*	94.24	28	17	3.71	0.76	44.82
09/19	90.69	15	9	6.08	0.66	43.01
09/18	76.50	66	47	1.17	0.60	41.16
09/17	58.27	26	20	2.42	0.45	36.78
09/16	51.72	32	20	1.73	0.00	35.26
Annual Growth	**16.2%**	**—**	**—**	**21.0%**	**—**	**6.2%**

*Fiscal year change

JARDEN LLC

EXECUTIVES

Chair, Patrick D Campbell
Ceo, Debra A Crew
Pres, Ravi Saligram
Vp Human Resources, Brian Stull
Bi Architecture Lead, Calvin Francart
Director Marketing, Fernando Pacheco
Senior Channel Marketing Manag, Sarah Chirillo
Data Analyst, Aileen Wall
It Procurement Specialist, Alicia Miastkowski
Amazon Sales Manager Technical, Allison Kennedy
Marketing Operations Manager, Amanda Gillis
Auditors: PRICEWATERHOUSECOOPERS LLP NE

LOCATIONS

HQ: JARDEN LLC
  221 RIVER ST, HOBOKEN, NJ 070305989
Phone: 201 610-6600
Web: WWW.NEWELLBRANDS.COM

COMPETITORS

AZZ	Johnson Outdoors
Academy Sports	Kaz
Amazon.com	Kellwood
Amer Sports	Lasko Products
Andis	Lifetime Brands
BWAY	Lowe's
Bass Pro Shops	MEGA Brands
Bauer Hockey	Mattel
Bed Bath & Beyond	Mayborn Group
Burton	Mizuno
Cabela's	NACCO Industries
CalCedar	NIKE
Canadian Tire	New Balance
Carrefour	Newell Rubbermaid
Church & Dwight	Owens-Illinois
Conair Consumer	Patch Products
Products	Philips Avent
Costco Wholesale	Procter & Gamble
Crayola	Quiksilver
Daiwa	REI
De'Longhi	Richco
Deswell	Rollerblade
Dick's Sporting Goods	Rossignol
EBSCO	Russell Hobbs
Easton-Bell Sports	SEB
Elmer's Products	Sealy
Energizer Holdings	Simmons
Evenflo	Spectrum Brands
Female Health	Suncast
Gaming Partners	Target Corporation
International	Tecnica
Gerber Products	Tegrant

Habasit America
Hamilton Beach
Hanesbrands
Head N.V.
Hillerich &
  Bradsby
HoMedics
Home Depot
Honeywell ACS
Igloo Products
Intex DIY
Invensys
Johnson & Johnson

UTC Climate Controls
  & Security
Universal Security
  Instruments
VF Corporation
W.C. Bradley Co.
Wahl Clipper
West Pharmaceutical
  Services
Whirlpool
Worthington Industries
adidas

HISTORICAL FINANCIALS

Company Type: Private

Income Statement

	REVENUE ($ mil.)	NET INCOME ($ mil.)	NET PROFIT MARGIN	EMPLOYEES
12/15	8,603	146	1.7%	17,000
12/14	8,287	242	2.9%	—
12/13	7,355	203	2.8%	—
12/12	6,696	243	3.6%	—
Annual Growth	**8.7%**	**(15.6%)**	**—**	**—**

FYE: December 31

JetBlue Airways Corp

Airline JetBlue Airways offers one-class service?with leather seats satellite radio and TV and movies?to over 42 million passengers a year and takes them to about 100 Domestic cities. It has 1000 daily flights in approximately 30 US states Washington DC Puerto Rico and 21 countries in the Caribbean and Latin America. Domestic flights represent its largest market accounting for about three-quarters of total company sales. Most of its flights arrive or depart from Boston New York Orlando Fort Lauderdale Los Angeles and San Juan Puerto Rico. JetBlue's fleet of more than 250 aircraft consists mainly of Airbus A320s and A321s but also includes Embraer E190s. Dubbed "New York's Hometown Airline" about half of JetBlue's flights are to and from the New York metropolitan area.

HISTORY

JetBlue took to the skies in 2000 as the third airline start-up for founder and CEO David Neeleman. The first airline Neeleman helped create Morris Air was formed in 1984. Named after his business partner June Morris the discount airline was operating 22 planes out of Salt Lake City by 1993. While with Morris Air Neeleman pioneered ticketless travel which a decade later would become an industry standard.

Impressed with Morris Air's efficient and strategic network its e-ticket system and Neeleman Southwest Airlines acquired its smaller rival in 1993. Neeleman left Southwest after just six months but not without signing a non-compete clause that prevented him from attempting to repeat his Morris Air success in the US for five years.

Not willing to sit still for long (a characteristic he attributes to attention deficit disorder) Neeleman partnered with David Evans to create Open Skies an integrated e-ticket Internet booking and sales management tool that they began to market to smaller airlines.

Meanwhile Neeleman had skirted the terms of his non-compete agreement to help the founders of Canadian low-fare carrier WestJet get their project off of the ground serving as a consultant and a board member.

In 1999 a year after his non-compete agreement expired Neeleman sold Open Skies to Hewlett-Packard and set to work creating a new airline. In a matter of weeks he had managed to gather $130 million the most ever raised for a start-up airline from investors that included Chase Capital and financier George Soros. Neeleman immediately began acquiring new Airbus A320 jets and fitting them with satellite TV.

JetBlue's first flight was from New York to Fort Lauderdale in 2000. During the year the airline added nine more destinations in California Florida New York Utah and Vermont. By 2001 the airline was operating 20 new A320s with an ambitious 131 on order.

On September 11 of that year terrorists commandeered four passenger aircrafts and turned them into instruments of destruction killing some 3000 people. The events shocked the world and crippled the airline industry. Despite the climate however JetBlue continued to expand its network and it went public in 2002.

The industry star took some heat in 2003 for violating its own privacy policy when it gave the personal information of 1.1 million customers to the Department of Defense as part of anti-terrorism project.

JetBlue added nine new destinations in 2004 including Boston — a major market not dominated by a single carrier and lacking what the company deemed to be sufficient low-fare domestic service.

Consecutive losses in the fourth quarter of 2005 and the first quarter of 2006 — caused in part by rising fuel costs— led the carrier to raise fares on some routes redouble its efforts to keep expenses down and slow some of its expansion plans.

As part of the effort to improve the company's operations JetBlue's board in May 2007 asked David Neeleman to step down as CEO in favor of former president Dave Barger. Neeleman remained with the company as nonexecutive chairman until May 2008.

To grow JetBlue increased capacity at its base at New York's JFK airport with the opening of a new terminal in October 2008. The 630000 sq. ft. Terminal 5 has 26 gates solely used by JetBlue and can accommodate 250 daily departures. The $875 million renovation took three years; it has the largest single security checkpoint in the US and an adjacent 1500-space parking lot.

JetBlue expanded service in 2009 to Bogota Colombia and the Caribbean islands of St. Maarten and Jamaica.

In 2010 JetBlue ink a limited partnership with AMR Corp.'s legacy airline American; the two are sharing activities in New York and Boston including customer "interline" service one-stop booking and check-in and bag transfers for connecting flights. The partnership gives the younger low-cost carrier eight pairs of the Texas-based carrier's take-off and landing slots at Ronald Reagan Washington National Airport and swells American Airlines' New York market with 12 pairs of JetBlue's slots at John F. Kennedy International Airport.

In early 2011 the airline signed an interline agreement with Virgin Atlantic that allows passengers to make connecting flights on transatlantic routes using a single itinerary and baggage check.

EXECUTIVES

Evp Corporate Affairs General Counsel And Secretary, James G. (Jim) Hnat, age 49, $425,000 total compensation
President And Ceo, Robin Hayes, age 53, $550,000 total compensation
Evp Customer Experience, Joanna Geraghty
Evp Operations, Jeff Martin
Cio, Eash Sundaram
Evp People, Mike Elliott
Evp Commercial And Planning, Martin (Marty) St. George, $400,000 total compensation
Evp And Cfo, Stephen J. (Steve) Priest, age 50
Vice President Government And Airport Affairs, Jeffrey Goodell
Vice President Flight Operations, Bart Roberts
Senior Vice President Airline Planning, Scott Laurence
Vice President Security, Ken Maxwell
Vice President Network Planning, John Checketts
Vice President Customer Support, Frankie Littleford
Vice President Marketing, Elizabeth Windram
Vice President Information Technology Technology And Integration, Ramki Ramaswamy
Vice President Airports Focus Cities, Mike Parkinson
Vice President Operational Planning And Analysis, David Jehn
Vice Chairman, Frank V. Sica, age 69
Chairman, Joel C. Peterson, age 73
Auditors: Ernst & Young LLP

LOCATIONS

HQ: JetBlue Airways Corp
  27-01 Queens Plaza North, Long Island City, NY 11101
Phone: 718 286-7900
Web: www.jetblue.com

2018 Sales

	$ mil.	% of total
Domestic	5,386	70
Caribbean & Latin America	2,272	30
Total	**7,658**	**100**

PRODUCTS/OPERATIONS

2018 Sales

	$ mil.	% of total
Passenger	7,381	96
Other	277	4
Total	**7,658**	**100**

COMPETITORS

AirTran Airways
Alaska Air
American Airlines
  Group
Delta Air Lines

Frontier Airlines
Southwest Airlines
United Continental
Virgin America
WestJet

HISTORICAL FINANCIALS

Company Type: Public

Income Statement

	REVENUE ($ mil.)	NET INCOME ($ mil.)	NET PROFIT MARGIN	EMPLOYEES
12/19	8,094	569	7.0%	21,569
12/18	7,658	188	2.5%	20,892
12/17	7,015	1,147	16.4%	19,978
12/16	6,632	759	11.4%	18,406
12/15	6,416	677	10.6%	16,862
Annual Growth	**6.0%**	**(4.3%)**	**—**	**6.3%**

FYE: December 31

2019 Year-End Financials

Debt ratio: 19.58%
Return on equity: 12.09%
Cash ($ mil.): 959
Current ratio: 0.67
Long-term debt ($ mil.): 1,990

No. of shares (mil.): 282
Dividends
  Yield: —
  Payout: —
Market value ($ mil.): 5,279

	STOCK PRICE ($)	P/E		PER SHARE ($)		
	FY Close	High/Low	Earnings	Dividends	Book Value
12/19	18.72	10 8	1.91	0.00	17.02
12/18	16.06	38 25	0.60	0.00	15.07
12/17	22.34	7 5	3.47	0.00	15.06
12/16	22.42	10 7	2.22	0.00	11.91
12/15	22.65	13 7	1.98	0.00	9.97
Annual Growth	(4.7%)	— —	(0.9%)	—	14.3%

Johnson & Johnson

Johnson & Johnson (J&J) is a diversified health care giant operating through more than 260 companies located in more than 60 countries. Its Pharmaceuticals division is focused on manufacturing medicines for infectious diseases neurological cardiovascular pulmonary hypertension autoimmune and oncology ailments. Top sellers are psoriasis drugs Remicade and Stelara and cancer drug Zytiga. J&J's Medical Devices division offers surgical equipment orthopedic products and contact lenses among other items. Finally J&J's Consumer business makes over-the-counter (OTC) drugs and products for baby skin oral women's and first-aid care. The company operates worldwide but makes about half of revenue in the US.

HISTORY

Brothers James and Edward Mead Johnson founded their medical products company in 1885 in New Brunswick New Jersey. In 1886 Robert joined his brothers to make the antiseptic surgical dressings he developed. The company bought gauze maker Chicopee Manufacturing in 1916. In 1921 it introduced two of its classic products the Band-Aid and Johnson's Baby Cream.

Robert Jr. became chairman in 1932 and served until 1963. A WWII Army general he believed in decentralization; managers were given substantial freedom a principle still used today. Subsidiary Ortho Pharmaceutical (birth control products) was formed in 1931 and the Ethicon (sutures) unit was acquired in 1947. In 1959 Johnson & Johnson bought McNeil Labs which launched Tylenol (acetaminophen) as an OTC drug the next year. Foreign acquisitions included Switzerland's Cilag-Chemie (1959) and Belgium's Janssen (1961). The company focused on consumer products in the 1970s gaining half the feminine protection market and making Tylenol the top-selling painkiller.

Trouble struck in 1982 when someone laced Tylenol capsules with cyanide killing eight people. The company's response is now a damage-control classic: It immediately recalled 31 million bottles and totally redesigned its packaging to prevent future tampering. The move cost $240 million but saved the Tylenol brand. The next year prescription painkiller Zomax was linked to five deaths and was pulled.

New products in the 1980s included ACUVUE disposable contact lenses and Retin-A. The company bought LifeScan (blood-monitoring products for diabetics) in 1986. In 1989 it began a joint venture with Merck to sell Mylanta and other drugs bought from ICI Americas.

The firm continued its acquisition and diversification strategy in the 1990s. After introducing the first daily-wear disposable contact lenses in 1993 it bought skin-care product maker Neutrogena (1994) to enhance its consumer lines. To diversify its medical products and better compete for hospital business it bought Mitek Surgical Products (1995) and heart disease product maker Cordis (1996). The FDA cleared J&J's Renova wrinkle and fade cream in 1996. The company also began selling at-home HIV test Confide but pulled it the next year after low sales and other problems.

Later acquisitions included Neutrogena (1994) DePuy (1998) Centocor Biotech (1999) Micrus Endovascular (2010) Crucell (2010) and Synthes (2012).

In early 2017 the company acquired Swiss biotech Actelion which focuses on rare diseases for $30 billion. It also purchased Abbott Medical Optics (now J&J Surgical Vision) from Abbott Laboratories for $4.3 billion.

EXECUTIVES

Vp Group Finance, Dominic J. Caruso, age 63, $909,500 total compensation

Evp And Worldwide Chairman Consumer Group, Jorge S. Mesquita, age 58

Evp And Group Worldwide Chairman, Sandra E. Peterson, age 62, $963,462 total compensation

Chairman And Ceo, Alex Gorsky, age 59, $1,600,000 total compensation

Company Group Chairman Consumer Medical Devices, Ashley A. McEvoy

Evp And Chief Scientist Officer, Paulus (Paul) Stoffels, age 58, $1,144,000 total compensation

Evp And Worldwide Chairman Pharmaceuticals, Joaquin Duato, age 57, $875,000 total compensation

Evp And Chief Human Resources Officer, Peter M. Fasolo, age 57

Evp And General Counsel, Michael H. Ullmann, age 61, $645,385 total compensation

Evp And World Chairman Medical Devices, Gary Pruden, age 58

Company Group Chairman Pharmaceuticals The Americas, Jennifer Taubert

Vice President Franchise Medical Leader, Christopher Nessel

Vice President Clinical Trials, Mark Travers

Vp Hr, Martha Liano

Vice President Global Consumer Care, Sandi Hassett

Vice President Global Pharmaceutical Supply Chain, Courtney Billington

Vice President International Total Rewards And Global Benefits, Lisa Davis

Vp Engineering, Gary Warren

Vp Finance Medical Device Innovation, Greg Herlan

Vice President Procurement, David Radeke

Vice President Law, James Bergin

Vice President Of Human Resources, Teresa Vaughn

Vice President Business Development Pharmaceuticals Group, Patrick Verheyen

Vice President Head Discovery Immunology, Murray Mckinnon

Vice President R And D Global Otc Technology, Gerry McNally

Vice President Human Resources, Danielle Devine

Corporate Vice President Worldwide Government Affairs And Policy, Clifford Holland

Vice President Global Consumer Insights, Jim Norgren

Vp Worldwide Compensaiton, Donna Ng

Vice President North America For Global Marketing Group, Darryl Nicholson

Vice President Human Resources, Marc Schorpion

National Sales Manager, Christos Chantzis

Vp Drug Channel Us Sales, Sarah Arthur

Vice President World Wide Consumer Supply Chain, Robert Wuesthoff

Vice President Oncology Sci Innovation, Pamela Carroll

Vice President Research And Development Healthcare Compliance, Frank Konings

Vice President Business Development, Michael Grissinger

Vice President Human Resources, Brenda Bass

Vice President Compensation And Benefits Tax Counsel, Michele Lee

Vice President, Brenda Squaire

Vice President Of Medical Affairs, Diego Miralles

Vice President, Shashi Mandapaty

Vice President Global Medical Affairs, Craig Tendler

Vice President Of Risk Management, Wayne Klokis

Vice President Comm And Public Affairs Med Dev, Tom Sanford

Vice President New Business Development, Alan Rae

Vice President Global Regional Affairs, Robin Keen

Vice President Global Engineering, Michael Maggio

Vice President Business Transformation, Angie Caswell

Area Vice President Northeast, Travis Williams

Vice President Of Global Health, Scott Ratzan

Vice President Prod Stewardship, Susan Nettesheim

Worldwide Vice President Human Resources, Elizabeth Adefioye

Vice President Quality Assurance J And J Consumer Group Of Companies, Teresa Gorecki

Vice President Global Account Management, Jack Gelman

Vice President Global Pharmaceutical Communications, Craig Rothenberg

Vice President Sterile Process Technolog, Rainer Newman

Vice President Global Strategic Marketing, Aldo Denti

Vice President Of Business Development, David Keller

Vice President Commercial Analytics Operations, Jim Gabriele

Vice President Business Development, Robert Havard

Vice President, Pauline McNulty

Vice President Marketing Mcneil Consumer Healthcare, Catherine Devine

Vice President, Ravi Pande

Vice President Human Resources, Tim Raher

National Account Manager, Stephen Drees

Vice President Of Operations, Jos Gonzales

Vice President Product Communications, Kellie McLaughlin

Vice President, Efrem Dlugacz

Vice President Global Pharma R And D Sourcing, Vasco Grilo

Vice President Human Resources At Jandj, Hilde Claes

Vice President Business Development, Denise McGinn

Vice President Marketing, Joe Marrone

Vp Marketing, David Sampson

National Sales Manager, John Mattiola

National Accounts Manager, Cheryl Coleman

Vp Marketing, George Maxwell

Vice President, Catherine Lau

Vice President Planning Global Surgery Supply Chain, Matt Perry

Vice President Global Talent Management, Luani Alvarado

Vice President Marketing Policy And Advocacy, John Hoffman

Vice President Quality And Compliance, Jacqueline Berretta

Vice President Research And Development, Steve Aridgides

Vice President, Jay Kosminsky

World Wide Vice President Human Resources, Paul Anthony

Vice President, Vincent Burton

Senior Vice President, Brenda Whittaker

Vice President Global Tox And Path, Peggy Guzzie-peck

Vice President Us Medical Affairs Virology, Richard Nettles

Vp Preclinical, Alfred Tonelli

Vice President, Robert Berger

Vice President Human Resources North America, Jon Williamson

Vice President State Govt Affairs, Don Bohn

Vice President Business Development Neuroscience, Cindy Warren

Vice President Of Human Resources, Nancy Shapiro

Vice President Research Analytics, Elizabeth Blackwood

Vice President Immunology Research And Development, Dan Baker

Regional Vice President, Mark Sienkiewicz

Vice President Business Development, Susan Morano

Vice President Health And Wellness Enterprise Solutions, Susan Denman

Vice President Information Technology Babycenter, Tom Alessi

Vpcx Infrastructure Services, Nick Fisher

Vice President, Li Mao

Vp Cfo Global Consumer Supply Chain, Jill Freedman

Senior Vice President, Instructor Sunywcc

Vice President Quality Systems, Cherian George

Vice President Supply Chain North America Otc, Gaspar Zuniga

Vp Health System Innovation, Brad Moore

Vice President Quality Systems And Services, Jackie Maestri

Worldwide Vice President Global Sales Strategy And Revenue Growthmanagement, Lynne Owen

Vice President Cardiovascular And Metabolism Scientific Innovation, James Tobin

Vice President Global Brand Protection, Richard Kaeser

Vice President Global Consumer Care, Sandra Hassett

Vice President U.s. Sales And Marketing, David Hummell

Vice President R And D, Erin Johnson

Vice President Esp Technology Programs, Salvatore Trovato

Marketing Vp Global Orthopedics Business Model Innovation, Patrice Betts

Ww Vp And Head Of Supply Chain, Craig Russell

Worldwide Vice President Global Ecommerce And Digital, Manuel Suro

Vice President Law, Conde Kathryn

Vice President Idar Gcdo, Weston Darren

Vice President Consumer Medical Device Communications, Donna Lorenson

Vice President Compensation And Benefits Tax Counsel, Liza Leandre

Vice President Global Commercial Leader Gu Oncology Franchise Janssen Oncology, Reshema Kemps-polanco

Vice President, Sally Macaluso

Vice President Of Immunology Scientific Innovation, Jackie Papkoff

Vice President Strategy And External Innovation Janssen Research And Development, Catherine Oyler

Senior Vice President Global Oncology Therapeutic Area Head, Peter Lebowitz

Vice President North America Marketing Operations, Ajay Dhaul

Vice President Cvm Scientific Innovation, Thomas Gustafson

Vice President Law Consumer North America, Parisa Mazaheri

Vice President Assistant To, Licette Devarie

Vice President Strategic Account Management, Liz Weiss

Vice President, Matthaus Dengler

Board Member, Charles Prince

Vice Chairman Of The Executive Committee And Chief Scientific Officer, Paul Stoffels

Board Member, Dirk Collier

Treasurer, Michelle Ryan

Board Member, Mary Beckerle

Board Member, Adam Williams

Board Member, Alan Davis

Auditors: PricewaterhouseCoopers LLP

LOCATIONS

HQ: Johnson & Johnson
One Johnson & Johnson Plaza, New Brunswick, NJ 08933
Phone: 732 524-0400   Fax: 732 214-0332
Web: www.jnj.com

2017 Sales

	$ mil.	% of total
US	39,863	52
Europe	17,126	22
Asia/Pacific & Africa	13,420	18
Western hemisphere excluding US	6,041	8
Total	76,450	100

PRODUCTS/OPERATIONS

2017 Sales by Segment

	$ mil.	% of total
Pharmaceutical	36,356	47
Medical Devices	26,592	35
Consumer	13,602	18
Total	76,450	100

COMPETITORS

3M Health Care	Genzyme
Abbott Labs	GlaxoSmithKline
Alcon	Kimberly-Clark Health
Allergan plc	L'Oréal USA
Amgen	Medtronic
ArthroCare	Mentholatum Company
AstraZeneca	Merck
B. Braun Melsungen	Mylan
Bard	Novartis
Bausch & Lomb	NutraSweet
Baxter International	Perrigo
Bayer AG	Pfizer
Beckman Coulter	Procter & Gamble
Becton Dickinson	Roche Holding
Biogen	Sanofi
Boehringer Ingelheim	Shire
Boston Scientific	Smith & Nephew
Bristol-Myers Squibb	St. Jude Medical
Chattem	Stryker
Colgate-Palmolive	Terumo
Cook Incorporated	Teva
Dr. Reddy's	The Dial Corporation
Edwards Lifesciences	UCB
Eli Lilly	Zimmer Biomet

HISTORICAL FINANCIALS

Company Type: Public

Income Statement

				FYE: December 29
	REVENUE ($ mil.)	NET INCOME ($ mil.)	NET PROFIT MARGIN	EMPLOYEES
12/19	82,059	15,119	18.4%	132,200
12/18	81,581	15,297	18.8%	135,100
12/17*	76,450	1,300	1.7%	134,000
01/17	71,890	16,540	23.0%	126,400
01/16	70,074	15,409	22.0%	127,100
Annual Growth	4.0%	(0.5%)	—	1.0%

*Fiscal year change

2019 Year-End Financials

Debt ratio: 17.56%—
Return on equity: 25.43%
Cash ($ mil.): 17,305
Current ratio: 1.26
Long-term debt ($ mil.): 26,494

Dividends
Yield: 0.0%
Payout: 66.6%
Market value ($ mil.): —

	STOCK PRICE ($) FY Close	P/E High/Low	PER SHARE ($) Earnings	Dividends	Book Value
12/19	145.75	26 22	5.63	3.75	22.59
12/18	127.27	26 21	5.61	3.54	22.44
12/17*	139.72	299233	0.47	3.32	22.43
01/17	115.21	21 16	5.93	3.15	26.02
01/16	102.72	19 16	5.48	2.95	25.82
Annual Growth	9.1%	— —	—	0.7%	6.2% (3.3%)

*Fiscal year change

JOHNSON CONTROLS, INC.

EXECUTIVES

Ceo, Alberto Ventura

Chb-Ceo, George R Oliver

Exec V Pres-Cfo*, Brian Stief

V Pres-Gen Counsel-Sec*, Brian J Cadwallader

V Pres-Corp Contrl*, Suzanne M Vincent

Cpo-V Pres of Controls Operati*, Michael Bartschat

Central Region Sales, Joe Tieman

Project Manager, John Brumm

Project Manager, John Snell

Marketing Grant Research, Judith Mouton

Account Executive, Kevin Vercher

Auditors: PRICEWATERHOUSECOOPERS LLP MI

LOCATIONS

HQ: JOHNSON CONTROLS, INC.
5757 N GREEN BAY AVE, MILWAUKEE, WI 532094408
Phone: 800 382-2804
Web: WWW.JOHNSONCONTROLS.COM

COMPETITORS

3M	Honeywell
A123 Systems	International
Addison	Illinois Tool Works
Alcoa	Inci Aku
Building Technologies	International Paper
Caterpillar	Invensys
Comfort Systems USA	Lear Corp
DENSO	Lennox
Deere	Lockheed Martin
Delphi Automotive Systems	Magna International
Dow Chemical	Northrop Grumman
DuPont	Paloma Group
Eagle-Picher	Raytheon
East Penn Manufacturing	Rieter Automotive North America
Eaton	Robert Bosch
Emerson Electric	SPX
Exide	Trane Inc.
Faurecia	United Technologies
GS Yuasa	Valeo
General Dynamics	Visteon
General Motors	Whirlpool
Goodman Global	Yazaki North America
Goodyear Tire & Rubber	

HISTORICAL FINANCIALS

Company Type: Private

Income Statement   FYE: September 30

	REVENUE ($ mil.)	NET INCOME ($ mil.)	NET PROFIT MARGIN	EMPLOYEES
09/15	37,179	1,679	4.5%	105,000
09/14	42,828	1,335	3.1%	—
09/13	42,730	1,297	3.0%	—
Annual Growth	(6.7%)	13.8%	—	—

Jones Financial Companies LLLP

Auditors: PricewaterhouseCoopers, LLP

LOCATIONS

HQ: Jones Financial Companies LLLP
12555 Manchester Road, Des Peres, MO 63131
Phone: 314 515-2000
Web: www.edwardjones.com

HISTORICAL FINANCIALS

Company Type: Public

Income Statement   FYE: December 31

	REVENUE ($ mil.)	NET INCOME ($ mil.)	NET PROFIT MARGIN	EMPLOYEES
12/19	9,369	1,092	11.7%	49,000
12/18	8,469	990	11.7%	47,000
12/17	7,506	872	11.6%	45,000
12/16	6,557	746	11.4%	43,000
12/15	6,619	838	12.7%	41,000
Annual Growth	9.1%	6.8%	—	4.6%

2019 Year-End Financials

Debt ratio: —	No. of shares (mil.): 1
Return on equity: —	Dividends
Cash ($ mil.): 2,707	Yield: —
Current ratio: 1.15	Payout: —
Long-term debt ($ mil.): —	Market value ($ mil.): —

Jones Lang LaSalle Inc

Jones Lang LaSalle (JLL) provides real estate without borders. Its services include commercial leasing real estate brokerage management advisory and financing through about 340 corporate offices in about 50 countries around the world. The company's LaSalle Investment Management arm is a diversified real estate management firm with more than $65 billion in assets under management. JLL has commercial real estate expertise across office retail health care industrial and multifamily residential properties. It manages approximately 5.1 billion sq. ft. worldwide. JLL was formed through the 1999 merger of Jones Lang Wootton (founded in England in 1783) and LaSalle Partners (founded in the US in 1968).

HISTORY

Jones Lang Wootton had roots in London's Paternoster Row auction houses in 1783. LaSalle Partners originally known as IDC Real Estate was founded in El Paso Texas in 1968. The two companies could not have started out in a more disparate fashion yet their combined force is now one of the largest real estate services firms in the world.

Richard Winstanley opened an auction house in 1783 and his son James joined him in that business in 1806. In 1840 the Joneses entered the picture — the Winstanleys created a partnership with one James Jones. The business moved to King Street (in the Guildhall section of London) in 1860 and remained in that location for some 100 years in various incarnations — James' son Frederick took over the business renaming it Frederick Jones and Co. When James retired in 1872 the firm was again renamed to Jones Lang and Co. and was controlled by C. A. Lang. Jones Lang merged with Wootton and Son in 1939 becoming Jones Lang Wootton and Sons.

Jones Lang Wootton was active in redrawing the property lines in London after the Blitz. In 1945 the firm began contacting small landowners and by combining small parcels of land secured development leasing and/or purchase contracts. When the rebuilding of London began in 1954 Jones Lang Wootton was in a secure place to be right at the forefront of that new development. The firm began engaging in speculative development in the West End and in the City of London.

The year 1958 saw the expansion of Jones Lang Wootton into Australia; the firm had offices throughout the Asia/Pacific region by 1968. Further expansion took place closer to home in Scotland (1962) and Ireland (1965) and the first continental European office in Brussels (also 1965). The firm moved into the Manhattan market in 1975.

On the other side of the story IDC Real Estate (the name change to LaSalle Partners came in 1977) was a group of partnerships initially focused on investment banking investment management and land. The firm began offering development management services in 1975; it moved into property management leasing and tenant representation in 1978 and facility management operations in 1980.

It built market share by buying other firms including Kleinwort Benson Realty Advisors Corp. (1994) and UK-based investment adviser CIN Property Management (1996).

The firm leveraged its experience and long-term client base to pursue an acquisition strategy taking advantage of trends shaping commercial real estate — globalization consolidation and merchant banking. LaSalle went public in 1997 amalgamating the Galbreath Company (a property and development management firm with which it merged that year) with its other partnerships and becoming a corporation.

In 1998 it acquired the project management business of Satulah Group and two retail management business units from Lend Lease and took real estate investment trust LaSalle Hotel Properties public. In 1999 the firm strengthened its world position by merging with Jones Lang Wootton; the company was renamed Jones Lang LaSalle.

The merger with Jones Lang Wootton combined Wootton's strength in Asia and Europe with LaSalle Partners' large presence in North America to create a worldwide real estate services firm. In 2006 the company acquired Spaulding & Slye strengthening operations in the Mid-Atlantic and New England. Also that year it opened an office in Dubai and acquired RSP Group which operates in North Africa and the Middle East. In 2007 Jones Lang LaSalle bought German property advisory firm Kemper's Holding and took a stake in the former Trammell Crow Meghraj one of the largest private real estate companies in India.

The company broadened its presence in key North American markets when it acquired The Staubach Company in 2008. Jones Lang LaSalle paid $613 million for the rival real estate services firm which was founded by football legend and former Dallas Cowboys quarterback Roger Staubach.

Jones Lang LaSalle slowed its acquisition pace during the economic recession. But managed to cut a few deals. In 2009 Jones Lang LaSalle teamed up with Real Estate Disposition to begin offering online auction sales a product to help customers quickly sell commercial property and other distressed assets.

In another deal Jones Lang LaSalle acquired the third-party leasing and management duties of General Growth Properties in 2010 as part of the mall owner's restructuring efforts. The deal added about 20 shopping centers to Jones Lang LaSalle's management portfolio.

EXECUTIVES

Ceo Americas, Gregory P. (Greg) O'Brien, age 57, $400,000 total compensation
Ceo Lasalle Investment Management, Jeff A. Jacobson, age 58, $400,000 total compensation
President Ceo And Director, Christian Ulbrich, age 54, $481,619 total compensation
Ceo Europe Middle East And Africa, Guy Grainger
Managing Director Shanghai And East China, Anthony Couse, $420,902 total compensation
Global Ceo Corporate Solutions, John Forrest
Chief Administrative Officer, Patricia (Trish) Maxson, age 61
Global Chief Executive Officer Capital Markets, Richard Bloxam
Ceo Jll Netherlands, Pieter Hendrikse
Global Chief Financial Officer, Stephanie Plaines
Vice President Finance, Bill Grice
Senior Vice President, David Roberts
Vice President, Mia Eglinton
Vice President, Bob Gross
Senior Vice President Information Technology, David Laduke
Vice President Corporate Solutions Energy And Sustainability Clean Tech, Michael Bosco
Vice President Facility Management, Quentin Graves
Senior Vice President, Kevin Brant
Senior Vice President Of Engineering, Miles Anderson
Vice President, Michael Billing
Executive Vice President Strategic Advisory, Clay Dickinson
Vice President, Truitt Alday
Vice President Of Sponsorship Marketing, Sally Hertz
Vice President, Laurie Christian
Senior Vice President, Louis Molinini
Vice President, William Schuch
Assistant Vice President, Clayton Kline
Assistant Vice President, Jim Woodard
Senior Vice President, Peter Richardson
Vice President, Jeremiah Riordan
Executive Vice President, Wade Clark
Senior Vice President International Desk, Julie Steffen
Executive Vice President, Jim Plummer
Senior Vice President, Brad Shokes
Vp Human Resources, Darline Scelzo
Senior Vice President Hotels And Hospitality, Nick Baer
Vice President Public Relation, Paige Steers

Senior Vice President, Peter Ladas
Senior Vice President Strategic Consulting, James Rice
Executive Vice President, Darcy Miramontes
Executive Vice President, Jay Schliesman
Vice President Prosite Director Operations, George O'donnell
Vice President, Barry Josowitz
Senior Vice President Finance Client Manager And Compliance, Greg Sheehan
Vice President, Ryan Matthews
Vice President Strategic Sourcing West Region, Tim Hamill
Vice President Corp. Property Services, Kevin Griffin
Vice President Project And Development Services, Pam Heckman
Vice President, Alex Holton
Vice President, Cliff West
Vice President, Ben Casper
Vice President Retail, Mike Horner
Senior Vice President Hotels, John L Strauss
Vice President, Michele Barkinge
Executive Vice President, Jorg Mast
Vice President, Tony Haning
Senior Vice President, Darren Eades
Senior Vice President, Tom Fox
Svp, Bruce Gordon
Vice President, Bret Felberg
Senior Vice President, Zach Anderson
Vice President, Steve Borup
Vp And Director Geographic Information Systems, Michael Startin
Vice President, Teri Bell
Senior Vice President Regional Finance Director, Cliff Marnick
Vice President, Tom Doupe
Senior Vice President, Chuck Straw
Executive Vice President Supply Chain Management, Gerald Donovan
Senior Vice President Of Development And Asset Strategy, Jeffrey Adkison
Senior Vice President, Cameron Driscoll
Associate Vice President, Matthew Felice
Senior Vice President Tenant R, Patrick Bolick
Executive Vice President, Michael Diaz
Vice President, Michael Streit
Senior Vice President, Jim Rice
Executive Vice President Of Human Resources, Renee Cassella
Senior Vice President, Kyle Harding
Senior Vice President, Stephen Steinberg
Vice President, Dan Reynolds
Executive Vice President Tenant Reperesentation, Rob Nielsen
Senior Vice President, Andrea Sylvester
Senior Vice President, Jim Cahlin
Svp Global Technology Programs, Kimberly Griffiths
Executive Vice President, Gregg Raus
Senior Vice President Business Consulting, Shannon Curley
Vice President Corporate Properties Group, Allen Merrill
Vice President, Scott Harrison
Senior Vice President, Steve Ostrowski
Vice President Strategic Consulting Workplace And Occupancy Planning, Laura Delafuente
Assistant Vice President, Yorke Allen
Vice President, Koley X MacKay
Vice President, Michelle Monhaut
Senior Vice President, Bradley McGill
Vice President, Heather Filkins
Senior Vice President, Tim Glenn
Senior Vice President, Evamarie Smith
Senior Vice President National Director, Gary Gersten
Senior Vice President, Steve Trapp
Senior Vice President, Leo O'loughlin
Vice President, Matthew Ruffing
Senior Vice President, Jeff Groh

Senior Vice President Retail, Mike Longmore
Senior Vice President, Arthur Frye
Senior Vice President, William M Korchak
Senior Vice President, David Oh
Senior Vice President Transition Manager, Cathy Frampton
Vice President, Stephen Chastain
Vice President Engineering And Operati, Bruce Sirota
Senior Vice President Group Property Management, Steve Mace
Vp Retail Development Strategy Services, Cynthia Pearl
Senior Vice President, Robert Tomsovic
Senior Vice President, Seth Heikkila
Vice President, Michael Koerner
Vice President Pmp, Chris Ferreira
Senior Vice President, Arthur Turowski
Vice President Associate Director, Julie Bane
Vice President, Dana English
Senior Vice President Lease Administration, Michael Mavilla
Senior Vice President, Luanne Atkinson
Senior Vice President, Chris Hile
Vice President, Judy Caruthers
Executive Vice President, George Nicholas
Senior Vice President Project, Don Bucci
Vice President, Alex Witt
Vice President, Paul Kelsey
Senior Vice President, Joshua Sloan
Vice President, Lori Horvath
Senior Vice President, Brian Walsh
Senior Vice President, Brendan Mcarthur
Executive Vice President, Pat Harlan
Senior Vice President, Sam Durkin
Vice President, Coleen Cecil
Senior Vice President, Brian Ackerman
Executive Vice President, Glenn Aspinwall
Vice President, Jon Packee
Senior Vice President, Sherri Lusk
Senior Vice President, Andrew Whipple
Vice President Procurement Lead, Stacey Bonenberger
Senior Vice President, Griffin Guthneck
Vice President, Chris Chornohos
Executive Vice President, Nate Demetsky
Vice President, Jamie Vari
Vice President, Ryan Lawrence
Senior Vice President, Joe Greco
Vice President, Lesa French
Executive Vice President, Bruno Fiorvento
Vice President, Matthew Amato
Vice President Associate Director, Jesse Mangum
Senior Vice President, David Chapin
Vice President, Michael Paul
Senior Vice President, Mark Newman
Auditors: KPMG LLP

LOCATIONS

HQ: Jones Lang LaSalle Inc
200 East Randolph Drive, Chicago, IL 60601
Phone: 312 782-5800   Fax: 312 782-4339
Web: www.jll.com

2017 Sales by Business Segment

	$ mil.	% of total
Americas	3,354	42
Europe Middle East Africa	2,586	33
Asia Pacific	1,636	21
Investment management	355	4
Total	**7,932**	**100**

PRODUCTS/OPERATIONS

2017 Sales

	$ mil.	% of total
Real Estate Services		
Property and facility management	2,381	30
Leasing	2,023	26
Project and development services	1,348	17

Capital Markets & Hotels	1,138	14
Advisory Consulting and Other	684	9
LaSalle Investment Management	355	4
Total	**7**	**100**

Selected Services

Investor services
  Agency leasing
  Property management
  Valuations and consulting
Occupier services
  Facilities management
  Project and development services
  Tenant representation
Construction management
Capital markets
Hotel advisory
Strategic consulting

COMPETITORS

BGC Partners	Hines
CBRE Group	Lend Lease
Colliers International	Newmark Knight Frank
Colliers International Group	Prologis
	Savills
Cushman & Wakefield	

HISTORICAL FINANCIALS

Company Type: Public

Income Statement   FYE: December 31

	REVENUE ($ mil.)	NET INCOME ($ mil.)	NET PROFIT MARGIN	EMPLOYEES
12/19	17,983	535	3.0%	93,400
12/18	16,318	484	3.0%	90,000
12/17	7,932	254	3.2%	81,900
12/16	6,803	318	4.7%	77,300
12/15	5,965	438	7.4%	61,500
Annual Growth	31.8%	5.1%	—	11.0%

2019 Year-End Financials

Debt ratio: 13.26%	No. of shares (mil.): 51
Return on equity: 12.15%	Dividends
Cash ($ mil.): 451	Yield: 0.4%
Current ratio: 1.07	Payout: 8.8%
Long-term debt ($ mil.): 1,177	Market value ($ mil.): 8,974

	STOCK PRICE ($) FY Close	P/E High/Low	PER SHARE ($) Earnings	Dividends	Book Value
12/19	174.09	16 11	10.87	0.86	99.28
12/18	126.60	17 12	10.54	0.82	80.95
12/17	148.93	27 18	5.55	0.72	71.48
12/16	101.04	23 13	6.98	0.64	61.70
12/15	159.86	18 15	9.65	0.56	59.68
Annual Growth	2.2%	— —	—	3.0% 11.3%	13.6%

JPMorgan Chase & Co

Boasting some $2.7 trillion in assets JPMorgan Chase is the largest bank holding company in the US and among the largest half-dozen in the world. With nearly 5000 branches in about 25 states it is among the nation's top mortgage lenders and credit card issuers (it holds some $170 billion in credit card loans). The bank also boasts formidable investment banking and asset management operations through its subsidiaries JPMorgan Chase Bank and institutional investment manager JPMorgan Asset Management. Active in more than 100 markets the company generates about 75% of its sales comes from North America. JPMorgan Chase can trace its history back to the Bank of Manhattan Company founded in 1799.

HISTORY

JPMorgan Chase & Co.'s roots are in The Manhattan Company created in 1799 to bring water to New York City. A provision buried in its incorporation documents let the company provide banking services; investor and future US Vice President Aaron Burr brought the company (eventually the Bank of Manhattan) into competition with The Bank of New York founded by Burr's political rival Alexander Hamilton. JPMorgan Chase still owns the pistols from the notorious 1804 duel in which Burr mortally wounded Hamilton.

In 1877 John Thompson formed Chase National naming it for Salmon Chase Abraham Lincoln's secretary of the treasury and the architect of the national bank system. Chase National merged with John D. Rockefeller's Equitable Trust in 1930 becoming the world's largest bank and beginning a long relationship with the Rockefellers. Chase National continued growing after WWII and in 1955 it merged with the Bank of Manhattan. Christened Chase Manhattan the bank remained the US's largest into the 1960s.

When soaring 1970s oil prices made energy loans attractive Chase invested in Penn Square an obscure oil-patch bank in Oklahoma and the first notable bank failure of the 1980s. (The legal aftereffects of Penn Square's 1982 failure dragged on until 1993.) Losses following the 1987 foreign loan crisis hit Chase hard as did the real estate crash. In 1995 the bank went looking for a partner. After talks with Bank of America it settled on Chemical Bank.

Chemical Bank opened in 1824 and was one of the US's largest banks by 1900. As with Chase Chemical Bank began as an unrelated business (New York Chemical Manufacturing) in 1823 largely in order to open a bank (it dropped its chemical operations in 1844). Chemical would merge with Manufacturers Hanover in 1991.

After its 1996 merger with Chase Chemical Bank was the surviving entity but assumed Chase's more prestigious name. Initial cost savings from the merger were substantial as jobs and branch offices were eliminated. In 1997 Chase acquired the credit business of The Bank of New York and the corporate trustee business of Mellon Financial but underwent another round of belt-tightening the next year when it took a $320 million charge and cut 4500 jobs. The bank also suffered losses related to its involvement with the ill-starred Long-Term Capital Management hedge fund.

In 1999 Chase focused on lending buying two mortgage originators and forming a marketing alliance with subprime auto lender AmeriCredit (now General Motors Financial Company). Chase also bought Mellon Financial's residential mortgage unit and Huntington Bancshares' credit card portfolio. It bought UK investment bank Robert Fleming Holdings in 2000.

In 2001 it closed its $30 billion buy of J.P. Morgan and renamed itself JPMorgan Chase & Co. The new firm eliminated some 10% of its combined workforce as a result of the merger. Chairman Sandy Warner (who ran J.P. Morgan) retired at year-end and was replaced by former Chase Manhattan leader CEO William Harrison.

JPMorgan Chase had more than $1 billion in exposure to Enron but in 2003 recovered some $600 million after a court battle with the failed energy trader's insurers which claimed the losses stemmed from loans by JPMorgan Chase disguised as oil and gas transactions. Nonetheless JPMorgan Chase ended up paying some $135 million to settle actions relating to the questionable loans.

In 2004 JPMorgan Chase joined forces with venerable investment bank Cazenove; the joint venture called JPMorgan Cazenove handles corporate finance and capital markets activities in the UK.

The next year JPMorgan Chase and its investment banking arm J.P. Morgan Securities avoided a trial by paying some $2 billion to settle claims from investors who lost money on bonds that the firm underwrote in 2000 and 2001 for scandal-ridden WorldCom which eventually declared bankruptcy (WorldCom became MCI and later was acquired by Verizon Communications).

On the heels of the its massive BANK ONE buy in 2004 JPMorgan Chase made several smaller purchases including global trade management and logistics software maker Vastera (renamed JPMorgan Chase Vastera) trading technology firm Neovest and the credit card business of Sears Canada. JPMorgan Chase also sold online brokerage subsidiary J.P. Morgan Invest and its BrownCo unit to E*TRADE. The following year the company acquired student lender Collegiate Funding Services which JPMorgan Chase combined with its existing Chase Education Finance division. The company also got the go-ahead from the FTC and bought Kohl's $1.6 billion credit card portfolio.

Enron continued to haunt the company: in 2005 it forked over $2.2 billion to settle part of an investor class-action suit over fraud charges related to the Enron debacle and paid another $350 million to the infamous energy trading firm which asserted that JPMorgan Chase and about 10 other banks aided and abetted the company's collapse. However the next year the company got some good news regarding its alleged involvement with the collapse of Enron when the class action suit against it was dismissed.

Also in 2006 the company cut ties with private equity investment arm J.P. Morgan Partners which divided into two companies CCMP Capital and Panorama Capital. JPMorgan Chase retained the former private equity operations of BANK ONE One Equity Partners.

In keeping with the lesson learned regarding its $2 billion fine to settle claims in the WorldCom debacle in 2006 the bank was quick to settle its part of another class-action lawsuit this time brought by investors claiming they were cheated in the dot-com IPO boom. JPMorgan Chase paid $425 million to settle that case. It paid a much smaller settlement of $3.8 million for its part in the demise of the ill-fated telecom Global Crossing.

All was not lawsuits and settlements in 2006 however: that year it swapped its corporate trust business for Bank of New York's nearly 340-branch network in the New York metropolitan area. Both units were valued at about $2 billion with JPMorgan Chase paying Bank of New York around $150 million more to make up the difference.

William Harrison retired as chairman at the end of 2006; he was succeeded by president and CEO (and the CEO of BANK ONE when it was acquired) Jamie Dimon.

As one of the largest mortgage and home equity providers in the country JPMorgan Chase was hurt by the subprime mortgage crisis and subsequent fall in home values in 2007. About a third of its loans were home equity loans and it had to write off more than $500 million in home equity loans that year.

In 2008 the bank assumed full ownership of payments processor Chase Paymentech Solutions which had been a joint venture with First Data. First Data assumed 49% of Chase Paymentech's assets and clients in the deal.

Also that year as part of a plan to stimulate the economy the US government invested in JPMorgan Chase and other banks. The bank got $25 billion of the $700 billion taxpayer-funded bailout package that was approved in late 2008 with the stipulation that the banks use the money and not hoard it. The investment came with restrictions on executive pay and other rules and JPMorgan returned the money the following year saying it was doing just fine without it.

Led by CEO Jamie Dimon JPMorgan Chase closed a couple of very high profile deals as the economic crisis claimed numerous victims. It acquired Bear Stearns one of Wall Street's top investment banks and the operations of Washington Mutual (WaMu) the largest bank to fail in US history. Both deals closed in 2008.

Initially JPMorgan Chase made a bargain-basement offer of $270 million (around $2 a share) for the struggling Bear Stearns which was drowning in subprime mortgage investment debt. It ultimately raised its offer to around $10 a share or some $1.2 billion. The deal came after the Fed extended a $30 billion lifeline to Bear Stearns to keep the firm afloat; JPMorgan Chase was one of the lenders.

The company also stepped in to buy WaMu when that bank failed and was seized by regulators. It paid $1.9 billion for the bank's operations and assumed some $31 billion in losses. JPMorgan began integrating WaMu's branches with its own retail network phasing out the WaMu brand and closing about 10% of the combined branches (especially in markets where there was overlap). Shortly after the acquisition JPMorgan cut 9200 WaMu jobs — about 20% of its workforce.

In 2009 JPMorgan Chase sold specialist firm Bear Wagner acquired in the Bear Stearns deal to Barclays Capital.

JPMorgan Chase agreed to pay more than $153 million to the Securities and Exchange Commission in order to settle a claim that it misled investors during the 2007 housing market crash. The company was among others that were investigated for improper sales practices.

In 2010 JPMorgan acquired the European and Asian segments of RBS Sempra Commodities the energy trading joint venture between Royal Bank of Scotland and Sempra Energy. The $1.6 billion deal did not include RBS Sempra's more valuable North American segment. JPMorgan integrated the business into the bank's existing global commodities business doubling its corporate client numbers.

Also in 2010 the company bought the private equity administration services of Schroders. That deal added more than $6 billion in committed capital. J.P. Morgan Worldwide Securities Services already had some $15.3 trillion in assets under custody. In 2011 the company sold its 41% stake in mutual fund company American Century to CIBC for some $848 million.

EXECUTIVES

Ceo Jpmorgan Emea And Jp Morgan Securities Plc, Vis Raghavan
Vice President, Josephine Norris
First Vice President District Manager, Sean Cummings
Vice President, Jeanne Garcia
1st Vice President, Patti Shultz
Vice President Technology Program Director, Mark Koban
Vice President Information Technology, Jay Barret
Vice President Human Resources, Jim Odonnell
Vice President, Madhu Tumma
Vice President Information Technology, Dennis Ramawy
Vice President, Michael Green
Desktop Support Vice President, Jeff Morgan
Vice President Of Technology, Tracey Ball
Vice President Market Risk Technology, Kevin Ford
Vice President Trading Technologies, Ann Billak
Vice President Talent And Development Operations, Ning Ham
Senior Vice President Middle Market Banking, Jim Nicholas
Senior Vice President Client Care, Terry Hansen
Vice President Of It, Jose Sousa
Vice President Strategic Event Marketing, Lisl Stanton
Vice President Controller, Michael Bourke
Svp Shared Services Consumer Bank, John Samenuk
Vice President, Richard Hixson
Vice President Technology Director, Ed White
Assistannt Vice President, Jason Silbaugh
Vice President Finance, Matthew Gallino
Vice President, Jose Poblete
Vice President Client Service J.p. Morgan Securities Llc, Barbara Fuqua
Vice President Global Investment Banking, Michael Shaw
Vice President, Chet Zhang
Vice President Risk Modeling Manager Mortgage Banking Modeling And Analytics, Tracy Wu
Global Vice President Information Technology Investment Banking Division, Brian Zitterkopf
Senior Vice President, Carol Mark
Vice President Corporate And Investment Bank Strategy And New Business Development, John Curry
Senior Vice President, Dan Howat
Vice President, Anatoly Morosov
Vice President, Jeff Wright
Vice President Balance Data Mart Ib Si, Robert Depowski
Vice President Information Technology Operations Support, Sekou H Kaalund
Vice President Of Information Technology, Lonnie Goldman
Vice President, Gene Huang
Vice President, Harvey Klyce
Vice President, Kenneth Coons
Vice President Investment Bank Technology, Farhan Jaffery
Senior Vice President, Nancy McDonnell
Vice President, Ryan P Griswold
Vice President Global Strategic Relationships, Brooks Reynolds
Vice President Architecture, Prasad Chaubal
Vice President, Laura Cussen
Vice President Executive Recruiter Ii, Tom Suhm
Vice President Global Market Tech, Robert Stepanski
Vice President Accounting Manager, Jeanne Higgins
Vice President Business Relationship Manager, Jaime Garcia
First Vice President, Michael V McCann
Vice President Human Resources And Employee Development And Training, Sophia Chu
Vice President, Curt Barrentine
Vice President Client Advisor, Dan Brown

Vice President Information Risk And Business Continuity Management, Dennis McFadden
Assistant Vice President Banker, Javier Varela
Vice President, Sue Kay
Vice President Of Architecture, Adam Goldin
Vice President Marketing Analysis Manager, Matthew Reynolds
Vice President Of Application Infrastructure Arc, Alan Higgins
Vice President, Vinay Somashekar
Vice President, Bruce Goldberg
Vice President, Donna Kopelman
Vice President, Christopher Preuster
Vice President Equity Prime Brokerage, Andrew Hannigan
Vice President, Claudia Castillo
Vice President Senior P And A Manager, Charles Chiappone
Vice President Finance, Laurie Goodman
Vice President, Ryan Mccauley
Senior Vice President, Gerry Murphy
Vice President Receivables Product Management, Ron Victor
Vice President Customer Experience, Kelly Ballas
Executive Vice President, Emmett Vollenweider
Vice President, Michelle Erny
Assistant Vice President And Fixed Income Trading Operations, Joy Hayes
Vice President Of Desktop Computing And Application Integration, Leonard Friedman
Vice President, Jason Hand
Vice President, Nazli Beirne
First Vice President, David Shaw
Vice President Of Central Technology Operations Retail Financial Services, Kevin Kirkpatrick
Vice President, John Mathai
Vice President, Bob Cummings
Vice President Marketing And Communicati, Monica Mack
Vice President, Robert Grigg
Vice President, Laura Bosma
Vice President Of Infrastructure, Michael Knight
Vice President Regulatory And Compliance Project Management, Himani Ranjan
Vice President Crm Retention Management, Gail Timmerman
Vice President, Kelly Devlin
Vice President, Luc Droal
Vice President Of Business Development, Kyle Smith
Vice President Senior Lead Architect, Mark Cates
Vice President Business Development, Dionisia Coffman
Senior Banker Senior Vice President, David Sagers
Vice President, Molly Morgan
Vice President Application Development Manager, Kiran Mudichintala
Assistant Vice President Credit Risk Officer, Kelly Shrader
Vice President, John Tabback
Vice President Client Satisfaction, Giovanna Pape
Vice President, Muhammad Hasan
Senior Vice President Chase Business Credit, Rachel Surdick
Senior Vice President Special Credits Group, Phil Martin
Vice President, David Salaverry
Vice President Commercial Banking, Bill Cook
Vice President, Chris Collins
Vice President, Keith Jia
Vice President Customer Analytics, Stella Ng
Vice President Of Technology, Miguel Choto
Vice President Digital And Interactive Marketing Manager, Tanya Morris
Global Technology Vice President, Tom Pryor
Vice President, Denise Connors
Senior Vice President, Mary Reilly
Vice President, Kevin Connor
Vice President Enterprise Technology Services, Josiah Lam

Vice President Area Manager, Sherry Minda
Assistant Vice President, Daniel Miller
Senior Vice President, Bill W Handley
Vice President Treasury Services Manager, Jenny Chan
Vice President Asset Management, Rawle Sealy
Senior Vice President, John Ireton
Vice President Senior Marketing Manager Digital, Kerrie Alutto
Senior Vice President, Randolph Lopez
Vice President, Jennifer Theriault
Vice President, James Carillo
Vice President, Roger Willcut
Vice President, Gina Shera
Vice President, Alessandro Bagnara
Assistant Vice President, Desiree Brown
Vice President, Deya Booker
Vice President, Angelines Jover
Auditors: PricewaterhouseCoopers LLP

LOCATIONS

HQ: JPMorgan Chase & Co
383 Madison Avenue, New York, NY 10179
Phone: 212 270-6000
Web: www.jpmorganchase.com

PRODUCTS/OPERATIONS

2016 Sales

	$ mil.	% of total
Interest		
Loans	36,634	35
securities	7,304	7
Trading assets	7,292	7
Federal funds sold & securities purchased under resale agreements	2,265	2
Deposits with banks	1,863	2
Securities borrowed	(332)	-
Other	875	1
Non-interest		
Asset management administration & commissions	14,591	14
Principal transactions	11,566	11
Investment banking fees	6,448	6
Lending- and deposit-related fees	5,774	5
Credit card income	4,779	4
Mortgage fees and related income	2,491	2
Securities gains	141	-
Other	3,795	4
Total	**101,006**	**100**

COMPETITORS

American Express	Goldman Sachs
Bank of America	HSBC
Bank of New York Mellon	Morgan Stanley
	PNC Financial
Barclays	RBC Financial Group
CIBC	State Bank Financial
Capital One	Corporation
Citigroup	SunTrust
Citigroup Global Markets	TD Bank USA
	UBS
Credit Suisse (USA)	Wells Fargo
Deutsche Bank	

HISTORICAL FINANCIALS

Company Type: Public

Income Statement				FYE: December 31
	ASSETS ($ mil.)	NET INCOME ($ mil.)	INCOME AS % OF ASSETS	EMPLOYEES
12/19	2,687,379	36,431	1.4%	256,981
12/18	2,622,532	32,474	1.2%	256,105
12/17	2,533,600	24,441	1.0%	252,539
12/16	2,490,972	24,733	1.0%	243,355
12/15	2,351,698	24,442	1.0%	234,598
Annual Growth	3.4%	10.5%	—	2.3%

2019 Year-End Financials

Debt ratio: 10.45%—
Return on equity: 14.07%
Cash ($ mil.): 263,631
Current ratio: —
Long-term debt ($ mil.): —

Dividends
Yield: 2.3%
Payout: 30.7%
Market value ($ mil.): —

	STOCK PRICE ($) FY Close	P/E High/Low		PER SHARE ($) Earnings	Dividends	Book Value
12/19	139.40	13	9	10.72	3.30	84.74
12/18	97.62	13	10	9.00	2.48	78.31
12/17	106.94	17	13	6.31	2.04	74.65
12/16	86.29	14	9	6.19	1.84	71.38
12/15	66.03	12	9	6.00	1.68	67.58
Annual Growth	20.5%	—	—	15.6%	18.4%	5.8%

KAISER FOUNDATION HOSPITALS INC

Kaiser Foundation Hospitals is on a roll. The hospital group operates nearly 40 acute care hospitals and 680 medical offices in eight states (California Colorado Georgia Hawaii Maryland Oregon Virginia and Washington) and Washington D.C. The company's largest presence is in California where the majority of its hospitals are located. Kaiser Foundation Hospitals employs more than 21000 physicians representing all medical specialties. Kaiser Foundation Hospital's doctors group is controlled by Permanente Medical Groups and its HMO is offered through Kaiser Foundation Health Plan. Altogether the group provides care for about 11.7 million members.

Operations
Kaiser Foundation Hospitals works with other organizations to tackle such issues as obesity access to care and violence. It also works to promote health in the communities it serves through wellness programs.

In 2016 Kaiser Foundation Hospitals logged 44 million office visits. It facilitated 106000 births performed 129000 surgeries and filled 90 million prescriptions.

Company Background
Kaiser Foundation Hospitals was founded in 1945.

EXECUTIVES

Evp Kaiser Foundation Hospitals And Health Plan; Group President Kaiser Permanente Northern California And Mid-atlantic States; President Kaiser Permanente Northern California, Gregory A. Adams
Evp Kaiser Foundation Hospitals And Health Plan; Group President Kaiser Permanente Southern California And Hawaii; President Kaiser Permanente Southern California, Benjamin K. Chu
Chairman Southern California Permanente Medical Group And Executive Medical Director, Edward Ellison
Senior Management Senior Vice President General Manager Director, Anne Mcnealis
Secretary, Sandra Walker

LOCATIONS

HQ: KAISER FOUNDATION HOSPITALS INC
1 KAISER PLZ, OAKLAND, CA 946123610
Phone: 510 271-6611
Web: WWW.HEALTHY.KAISERPERMANENTE.ORG

PRODUCTS/OPERATIONS

Selected Hospitals
Antioch Medical Center
Fremont Medical Center
Fresno Medical Center
Hayward Medical Center
Manteca Medical Center
Modesto Medical Center
Oakland Medical Center
Redwood City Medical Center
Richmond Medical Center
Roseville Women and Children's Center
San Jose Medical Center
Santa Clara Medical Center
Sacramento Medical Center
South San Francisco Medical Center
South Sacramento Trauma Center
Santa Rosa Medical Center
San Francisco Medical Center
San Rafael Medical Center
Vacaville Medical Center
Vallejo Medical Center
Walnut Creek Medical Center
Baldwin Park Medical Center
Downey Medical Center
Fontana Medical Center
Los Angeles Medical Center
Moreno Valley Community Hospital
Orange County - Anaheim Medical Center
Orange County - Irvine Medical Center
Panorama City Medical Center
Riverside Medical Center
San Diego Medical Center
Harbor City (South Bay Medical Center)
Woodlands Hills Medical Center
West Los Angeles Medical Center
Sunnyside Medical Center (Portland Oregon area)
Moanalua Medical Center (Hawaii)

COMPETITORS

Adventist Health System West	Dignity Health
Ascension Health	HCA
Banner Health	LifePoint Health
CHRISTUS Health	Sutter Health
Catholic Health Initiatives	Tenet Healthcare
Community Health Systems	The Cleveland Clinic
	Universal Health Services

HISTORICAL FINANCIALS
Company Type: Private

Income Statement   FYE: December 31

	REVENUE ($ mil.)	NET INCOME ($ mil.)	NET PROFIT MARGIN	EMPLOYEES
12/09	14,795	429	2.9%	175,668
12/08	0	0	99.0%	—
12/05	9,852	774	7.9%	—
Annual Growth	10.7%	(13.7%)	—	—

Kansas City Life Insurance Co (Kansas City, MO)

Kansas City Life Insurance and its subsidiaries provide insurance products throughout the US to individuals (life and disability coverage and annuities) and to groups (life dental vision and disability insurance). Subsidiary Grange Life sells traditional life insurance universal life products and fixed annuities. The insurance companies sell through independent agents and agencies. Kansas City Life Insurance was established in 1895 and is based in Kansas City Missouri. Chairman and CEO R. Philip Bixby and his family control the company.

Operations
Kansas City Life operates in three business segments: Individual Insurance Old American and Group Insurance.

The Individual Insurance segment (which brings in about 35% of the company's revenue) consists of individual insurance products for both Kansas City Life Sunset Life and Grange Life and the assumed reinsurance transactions.

Old American (around 20% of revenue) consists of individual insurance products designed largely as final expense products.

The Group Insurance segment (more than 10% of the company's revenue) consists of group life dental vision disability products accident and critical illness products.

Geographic Reach
Kansas City Life sells insurance products to some 50 states and the District of Columbia.

Some of its largest state markets by mortgage loans include California Texas Minnesota Ohio New Jersey and Georgia.

Sales and Marketing
Kansas City Life markets its products through independent agents and agencies.

Financial Performance
Revenue for 2019 increased to $512.7 million compared from the prior year with $461.0 million mainly due to higher insurance revenues.

The company earned net income of $24.4 million in 2019 compared to $15.7 million in 2018.

Cash held by the company decreased by $17.5 million to $14.2 million. Cash provided by operations and financing activities were $0.1 million and $6.1 million respectively. Cash used for investing activities was $23.7 million mainly for purchases of fixed maturity securities.

Strategy
Plan fiduciaries set investment policies and strategies and oversee its investment allocation which includes selecting investment managers commissioning periodic asset-liability studies and setting long-term strategic targets. Long-term strategic investment objectives include preserving the funded status of the pension plan and balancing risk and return.

Company Background
The Bixby family owns about 60% of Kansas City Life through trusts and investment partnerships.

Founded in 1895 the company built up its operations through a number of historical acquisitions including GuideOne Life (2003) Old American (1991) and Sunset Life (1974). The company exited its banking operations (Generations Bank) in 2007.

EXECUTIVES

Svp And Actuary Kansas City Life And Vp And Actuary Sunset Life Insurance Company Of America, Mark A. Milton, age 61, $325,812 total compensation

Chairman President And Ceo, R. Philip Bixby, age 66, $779,160 total compensation

Vice Chairman And Evp And President Old American Insurance Company, Walter E. (Web) Bixby, age 61, $347,088 total compensation

Svp Finance Cfo And Director, Tracy W. Knapp, age 57, $322,344 total compensation

Svp Sales And Marketing Kansas City Life; Vp Sales And Marketing Sunset Life, Donald E. (Don) Krebs, age 62, $300,060 total compensation

Svp Operations, Stephen E (Steve) Ropp, age 60

Assistant Vice President Systems And Computer Operations, Rick Komer

Vice President Taxes, John Nogalski

Regional Vice President West, Chris Bor

Medical Director, Charlotte Lee

Regional Vice President, Bill Browning

Assistant Vice President, Dawn Roy

Vice President, Timothy Knott

Senior Vice President General Counsel, Craig Mason

Regional Vice President Special Markets, Robert Petzold

Assistant Vice President, Stephen Mack

Assistant Vice President Corporate Communications, Holly Ropp

Assistant Vice President Marketing Services, Jim Wilcox

Assistant Vice President Underwriting, James Bixby

Senior Vice President Finance, Philip A Williams

Assistant Vice President And Chief Underwriter, Michael Augustine

Senior Vice President Sales And Marketing, Don Krebs

Assistant Vice President Group Underwriting, Keith Fortmann

Auditors: BKD LLP

LOCATIONS

HQ: Kansas City Life Insurance Co (Kansas City, MO)
3520 Broadway, Kansas City, MO 64111-2565
Phone: 816 753-7000   **Fax:** 816 753-4902
Web: www.kclife.com

PRODUCTS/OPERATIONS

2017 Sales

	$ mil.	% of total
Insurance		
Individual insurance	145	32
Group insurance	59	13
Old American	88	20
Net investment income	145	33
Net realized investment gains	4	1
Other	6	1
Total	**450**	**100**

Selected Subsidiaries

Old American Insurance Company
Sunset Financial Services
Sunset Life Insurance Company of America

COMPETITORS

AEGON USA	MassMutual
Advance Insurance of Kansas	MetLife
	National Western
American Equity Life	Nationwide
American Heritage Life Insurance	New York Life
	Northwestern Mutual
American National Insurance	Phoenix Companies
	Primerica
Americo	Protective Life
Citizens Inc.	Prudential

Delphi Financial Group	Security Benefit Group
FBL Financial	The Hartford
Homesteaders Life	Torchmark
Kemper Corp	Universal American

HISTORICAL FINANCIALS

Company Type: Public

Income Statement

FYE: December 31

	ASSETS ($ mil.)	NET INCOME ($ mil.)	INCOME AS % OF ASSETS	EMPLOYEES
12/19	5,219	24	0.5%	—
12/18	4,971	15	0.3%	—
12/17	4,530	51	1.1%	—
12/16	4,449	22	0.5%	—
12/15	4,421	29	0.7%	441
Annual Growth	**4.2%**	**(4.4%)**	**—**	**—**

2019 Year-End Financials

Debt ratio: —
Return on equity: 3.25%
Cash ($ mil.): 14
Current ratio: —
Long-term debt ($ mil.): —

No. of shares (mil.): 9
Dividends
   Yield: 3.2%
   Payout: 54.0%
Market value ($ mil.): 325

	STOCK PRICE ($) FY Close	P/E High/Low	Earnings	PER SHARE ($) Dividends	Book Value
12/19	33.55	15 13	2.52	1.08	83.72
12/18	37.00	28 21	1.62	1.08	71.43
12/17	45.25	9 8	5.32	1.08	76.13
12/16	47.50	21 15	2.30	1.08	70.80
12/15	38.29	18 15	2.75	1.08	68.55
Annual Growth	**(3.2%)**	**— —**	**(2.2%)**	**(0.0%)**	**5.1%**

Kearny Financial Corp (MD)

Auditors: Crowe LLP

LOCATIONS

HQ: Kearny Financial Corp (MD)
120 Passaic Avenue, Fairfield, NJ 07004
Phone: 973 244-4500
Web: www.kearnybank.com

HISTORICAL FINANCIALS

Company Type: Public

Income Statement

FYE: June 30

	ASSETS ($ mil.)	NET INCOME ($ mil.)	INCOME AS % OF ASSETS	EMPLOYEES
06/20	6,758	44	0.7%	552
06/19	6,634	42	0.6%	565
06/18	6,579	19	0.3%	565
06/17	4,818	18	0.4%	466
06/16	4,500	15	0.4%	459
Annual Growth	**10.7%**	**29.8%**	**—**	**4.7%**

2020 Year-End Financials

Debt ratio: 17.36%
Return on equity: 4.06%
Cash ($ mil.): 180
Current ratio: —
Long-term debt ($ mil.): —

No. of shares (mil.): 83
Dividends
   Yield: 3.5%
   Payout: 61.7%
Market value ($ mil.): 684

	STOCK PRICE ($) FY Close	P/E High/Low	Earnings	PER SHARE ($) Dividends	Book Value
06/20	8.18	26 14	0.55	0.29	12.96
06/19	13.29	31 26	0.46	0.37	12.65
06/18	13.45	65 54	0.24	0.25	12.74
06/17	14.85	73 57	0.22	0.10	12.53
06/16	12.58	74 62	0.18	0.08	12.50
Annual Growth	**(10.2%)**	**— —**	**32.2%**	**38.0%**	**0.9%**

Kellogg Co

From the company's home base in Battle Creek Michigan Kellogg Company battles with rival General Mills for the #1 spot in the US cereal market. Kellogg founded in 1906 boasts many familiar cereal brands including Kellogg's Corn Flakes Frosted Flakes Froot Loops Special K and Rice Krispies. While the company works to fill the world's cereal bowls it actually makes more money these days from its snacks and convenience brands such as Kashi Pringles and Cheez-It Eggo waffles and Nutri-Grain and Bear Naked cereal bars. The company divested some of its cookie brands in 2019 including Famous Amos and Keebler Though its products are sold worldwide the company generates around 60% of its revenue domestically.

Operations

Kellogg operates through four segments based geographic location – North America (US and Canada businesses about 60% of total revenue); AMEA which consist of Africa Middle East Australia and other Asian and Pacific Markets (more than 15%); Europe (around 15%); and Latin America which consist of Central and South America and includes Mexico (over 5% of total sales).

Overall Snacks generate nearly half of sales while cereal accounts for more than 35%. Frozen and noodles represent about 10% and 5% respectively.

Geographic Reach

Headquartered in Battle Creek Michigan Kellogg manufactures its products in more than 20 countries and markets them in more than 180. It generates nearly 60% of its revenue in the US.

The company's manufacturing facilities in the US include four cereal plants and warehouses in Battle Creek Michigan; Lancaster Pennsylvania; Memphis Tennessee; and Omaha Nebraska and other facilities in California Georgia Kansas Kentucky Michigan New Jersey North Carolina Ohio Pennsylvania and Tennessee.

Outside the US Kellogg has additional manufacturing locations (some with warehousing facilities) in about 20 countries in Europe Asia Africa and South America. The company has joint ventures in China Nigeria and Ghana.

Sales and Marketing

Kellogg's top five customers including Wal-Mart generate a third of Kellogg's total sales and almost half of US sales.

Products are sold to retailers through direct sales forces broker and distributor arrangements. Broker and distributor arrangements are leveraged to market its products in less-developed areas or in markets outside its focus. The company spent $676 million $752 million and $732 million for advertising expenses in 2019 2018 and 2017.

Financial Performance

After declining in 2016 and 2017 Kellogg's revenue skyrocketed in 2018 followed by another increase in 2019. Its net revenue after peaking in 2018 declined in 2019. Despite the decline it has an overall growth of 56%.

Revenue grew to $13.5 billion in 2019 an approximately $31 billion increase from the year prior. The increase was driven by AMEA operations partially offset by the three other segments.

Net income was $960 million in 2019 a decrease of 25% from $1.3 billion in fiscal year 2018. Selling general and administrative expenses fell 1% in fiscal 2019 to $3 million as a result of the ongoing "Project K" efficiency and effectiveness program.

The company ended fiscal 2019 with $397 million in cash and cash equivalents. Cash provided by operating activities was $1.2 billion in 2019 while investing activities provided another $774 million. Financing activities used another $1.9 billion.

Strategy

Kellogg is working at cutting costs and expanding revenue as consumers are turning away from its old reliable cereal lines as awareness of the health risks of sugar increases.

Its ongoing "Project K" efficiency and effectiveness program began in 2013 and its initiatives continue through 2019. This On the flip side Kellogg in 2019 sold its cookie fruit snack pie crust and ice cream cone businesses to Luxembourg-based Ferrero Group for about $1.3 billion as it reshapes its portfolio. The list of brands includes Keebler Famous Amos Mother's Murray and Stretch Island as well as Little Brownie Bakers which supplies cookies to the Girl Scouts.

Company Background

Will Keith (W. K.) Kellogg first made wheat flakes in 1894 while working for his brother Dr. John Kellogg at Battle Creek Michigan's famed homeopathic sanitarium. John sold the flakes via mail order (1899) in a partnership that W. K. managed. In 1906 W. K. started his own firm to produce corn flakes.

After finding success in the US with its innovative cereal varieties the company expanded internationally beginning in Canada (1914) and followed in Australia (1924) and England (1938).

HISTORY

Will Keith (W. K.) Kellogg first made wheat flakes in 1894 while working for his brother Dr. John Kellogg at Battle Creek Michigan's famed homeopathic sanitarium. While doing an experiment with grains (for patients' diets) the two men were interrupted; by the time they returned to the dough it had absorbed water. They rolled it anyway toasted the result and accidentally created the first flaked cereal. John sold the flakes via mail order (1899) in a partnership that W. K. managed. In 1906 W. K. started his own firm to produce corn flakes.

As head of the Battle Creek Toasted Corn Flake Company W. K. competed against 42 cereal companies in Battle Creek (one run by former patient C. W. Post) and roared to the head of the pack with his innovative marketing ideas. A 1906 Ladies' Home Journal ad helped increase demand from 33 cases a day earlier that year to 2900 a day by year-end. W. K. soon introduced Bran Flakes (1915) All-Bran (1916) and Rice Krispies (1928). International expansion began in Canada (1914) and followed in Australia (1924) and England (1938).

EXECUTIVES

Ceo And Director, Steven A. (Steve) Cahillane, age 55
Vice Chairman Corporate Development And Chief Legal Officer, Gary H. Pilnick, age 56, $719,092 total compensation

Svp; President Kellogg North America, Paul T. Norman, age 56, $783,319 total compensation
Chief Growth Officer, Clive Sirkin
President U.s. Specialty Channels, Wendy Davidson, age 49
Svp And Cfo, Fareed A. Khan, age 55
President U.s. Morning Foods, Craig Bahner, age 55
Svp Global Snacks Category, Jim Cali, age 59
President Asia/pacific, Amit Banati, age 51
Svp And Cio, Brian S. Rice, age 57
President Us Snacks Division, Deanie Elsner
President Kellogg Canada, Carol Stewart
Ceo Kashi Company, David J. Denholm
Svp Global Supply Chain, Alistair D. Hirst, age 60, $552,770 total compensation
Svp; President Kellogg Latin America, Maria F. Mejia
President Kellogg Europe, Chris Hood, $540,896 total compensation
President U.s. Frozen Foods, Andrew Loucks
Svp Global Breakfast Category, Doug VanDeVelde
Vp Shared Services, David Pelyhes
Vp Manufacturing, Peter Moait
Vice President Of Global Insights And Planning, Mike Mickunas
Vice President Global Procurement Cpo, Michele Tyler
Vice President Nutrition, Guy Johnson
Vice President And Treasurer, Joel Vanderkooi
Vice President Treasury And Investor Relations, Joel R Wittenberg
Senior Vice President Morning Foods Supply Chain, George Chumakov
Vice President Frozen Foods Supply Chain, Sharron Moss-Higham
Vice President Sales, Kristina Geier
Vp Of Strategy Corporate Development In Transition, Steve Hyde
Vice President Industry Initiatives, Dave Jones
Vice President Human Resources, Shawn Zimmerman
Svp Global Hr, Melissa Howell
Vice President Human Resources Emea, Samantha Thomas Berry
National Account Manager, Laura Scherer
Vice President Human Resources Global Supply Chain And Global Functions, Jim Stockman
Vp Supply Chain, Jeffrey Arnold
It Vice President Engineering Global Technical Services, Pablo Lewin
Vice President Dsd Distribution And Logistics, Michael Wohlgemuth
Vice President Global Nutrition Scientific Affairs And Technology Scouting, Nelson Almeida
Vice President Corporate Controller, Kurt Forche
Vp Sales Us Frozen Foods, Sheila Gamble
Vice President. Supply Chain, Mike Gallaway
Vice President, Richard Olsen
Chairman, John A. Bryant, age 55
Assistant Treasurer, James Damico
Board Member, Cynthia Milligan
Board Member, Carolyn Tastad
Abm, Eric Hines
Board Member, Mary Laschinger
Board Member, Stephanie Burns
Board Member, Richard Dreiling
Board Member, Carter Cast
Auditors: PricewaterhouseCoopers LLP

LOCATIONS

HQ: Kellogg Co
One Kellogg Square, P.O. Box 3599, Battle Creek, MI 49016-3599
Phone: 269 961-2000
Web: www.kelloggcompany.com

2016 Sales

	$ mil.	% of total
United States	8,560	63
International	4,965	37
Total	**13,525**	**100**

2016 Sales

	$ mil.	% of total
United States	8,438	65
International	4,576	35
Total	**13,014**	**100**

PRODUCTS/OPERATIONS

2016 Sales

	$ mil.	% of total
U.S. Snacks	3,198	25
U.S. Morning Foods	2,931	23
Europe	2,377	18
North America Other	1,598	12
U.S. Specialty	1,214	9
Asia Pacific	916	7
Latin America	780	6
Total	**13,014**	**100**

2016 Sales

	$ mil.	% of total
Cereal	5,440	42
Snacks	6,660	51
Frozen	914	7
Total	**13,014**	**100**

Selected Cereal Brands

Asia and Australia
  BeBig
  Cerola
  Chex
  Frosties
  Goldies
  Kellogg's Iron Man Food
  Nutri-Grain
  Rice Bubbles
  Sultana Bran
Canada
  Vector
  Vive
Europe
  Choco Pops
  Chocos
  Country Store
  Frosties
  Fruit 'n' Fibre
  Honey Loops
  Kellogg's Crunchy Nut Corn Flakes
  Kellogg's Crunchy Nut Red Corn Flakes
  Kellogg's Extra
  Muslix
  Optima
  Pops
  Ricicles
  Smacks
  Start
  Sustain
Latin America
  Choco Krispis
  Choco Zucaritas
  Crusli Sucrilhos
  Musli
  NutriDia
  Sucrilhos Chocolate
  Vector
  Zucaritas
US
  All-Bran
  Apple Jacks
  Bran Buds
  Cinnamon Crunch
  Cocoa Krispies
  Complete Bran Flakes
  Complete Wheat Flakes
  Corn Pops
  Cracklin' Oat Bran
  Crispix
  Crunch
  Cruncheroos
  Froot Loops
  Frosted Krispies
  Frosted Mini-Wheats

Just Right
Kellogg's Corn Flakes
Kellogg's Frosted Flakes
Kellogg's Low-Fat Granola
Kellogg's Raisin Bran
Mueslix
Pops
Product 19
Raisin Bran
Rice Krispies
Smacks/Honey Smacks
Smart Start
Special K
Special K Red Berries

Selected Other Brands
Cereal Bars and Granola
  All-Bran
  Bear Naked
  Choco Krispies
  Froot Loops
  GoLean
  Kashi
Convenience Foods
  Austin
  Cheez-It
  Chips Deluxe
  Club
  Croutettes Croutons
  E. L. Fudge
  Famous Amos
  Fudge Shoppe
  Hi-Ho
  Keebler
  Kellogg's Corn Flake Crumbs
  Krispy Munch'Ems
  Murray
  Pop-Tarts
  Pop-Tarts Pastry Swirls
  Pop-Tarts Snak-Stix
  Pringles
  Ready Crust
  Rice Krispies Squares
  Rice Krispies Treats
  Right Bites
  Sandies
  Soft Batch
  Stretch Island
  Sunshine
  Toasteds
  Town House
Frozen Waffles and Pancakes
  Eggo
  Froot Loops
  Nutri-Grain
  Special K
Water and Water Mixes
  Special K
  Special K2O
Meat and Egg Alternatives
  Gardenburger
  Loma Linda
  Morningstar Farms
  Natural Touch
  Worthington

COMPETITORS
Amy's Kitchen	McKee Foods
Barbara's Bakery	Mondelez International
Bob's Red Mill Natural	Nestlé
Foods	Patty King
Boca Foods	PepsiCo
Campbell Soup	Pinnacle Foods
ConAgra	PowerBar
Frito-Lay	Ralston Food
General Mills	Schulze and Burch
Gilster-Mary Lee	Snyder's-Lance
Goodman Fielder	Weetabix
Hain Celestial	Wellness Foods
J & J Snack Foods	Wessanen
Jordans & Ryvita	granoVita
MOM Brands	

HISTORICAL FINANCIALS
Company Type: Public

Income Statement   FYE: December 28

	REVENUE ($ mil.)	NET INCOME ($ mil.)	NET PROFIT MARGIN	EMPLOYEES
12/19	13,578	960	7.1%	31,000
12/18	13,547	1,336	9.9%	34,000
12/17	12,923	1,269	9.8%	33,000
12/16*	13,014	694	5.3%	37,369
01/16	13,525	614	4.5%	33,577
Annual Growth	0.1%	11.8%	—	(2.0%)

*Fiscal year change

2019 Year-End Financials
Debt ratio: 45.10%
Return on equity: 36.00%
Cash ($ mil.): 397
Current ratio: 0.72
Long-term debt ($ mil.): 7,195

No. of shares (mil.): 341
Dividends
  Yield: 0.0%
  Payout: 80.7%
Market value ($ mil.): 23,621

	STOCK PRICE ($) FY Close	P/E High/Low	PER SHARE ($) Earnings	Dividends	Book Value
12/19	69.16	25 19	2.80	2.26	8.04
12/18	57.25	19 14	3.83	2.20	7.56
12/17	67.98	21 16	3.62	2.12	6.40
12/16*	73.71	44 35	1.96	2.04	5.44
01/16	72.27	42 35	1.72	1.98	6.08
Annual Growth	(1.1%)	—	13.0%	3.4%	7.2%

*Fiscal year change

Kemper Corp (DE)

Kemper is among the largest nonstandard auto insurers in the US and holds a strong position in the overall personal vehicle coverage market. The Kemper family of companies specializes in property/casualty insurance and life and health insurance products for individuals families and businesses. Policies include auto homeowners property life accident and health coverage. Kemper serves more than 6.4 million policyholders and has nearly $13 billion in assets. The company's policies are sold through independent and direct agents across the US.

Operations
The company operates through three operating segments: Specialty Property and Casualty Insurance Preferred Property and Casualty Insurance and Life and Health Insurance.

The Specialty Property and Casualty Insurance segment (roughly 65% of total revenue) provides personal and commercial automobile insurance to low-income customers or those with poor driving or payment records.

The Preferred Property and Casualty Insurance segment (about 15% of total revenue) offers preferred automobile (both standard and nonstandard risk) homeowners fire renters umbrella and other personal insurance.

The Life and Health Insurance segment (more than 15%) provides individual life accident and health insurance. It primarily does business through the Kemper Home Service Companies group of businesses (including United Insurance Reliable Life and Union National Life) which provide individual life and supplemental accident and health insurance products to customers with limited incomes. The smaller Reserve National unit sells specialty individual accident life and health

insurance policies including illness and hospitalization plans.

The company is reorganizing its operating divisions under four sub-brands: Kemper Auto Kemper Personal Insurance Kemper Life and Kemper Health.

Geographic Reach
Headquartered in Chicago Illinois Kemper sells its policies in 50 US states and Washington DC.

The Specialty Property and Casualty unit earns most of its revenue in California Texas and Florida while the Preferred Property and Casualty Insurance segment gets two-thirds of sales from California New York Texas North Carolina and Pennsylvania.

The Life and Health Insurance segment earns nearly half of sales in Texas Louisiana Alabama Mississippi and Georgia.

Sales and Marketing
Kemper offers its services through independent and direct agents and brokers. The Specialty Property and Casualty segment's products are offered by 21000 independent insurance agents and brokers while the Preferred Property and Casualty Insurance segment sells via 4800 independent agents. Kemper Home Services uses a network of some 2000 career agents while Reserve National uses about 3500 independent agents.

The company's Specialty Property and Casualty Insurance segment targets value-seeking consumers who may have difficulty obtaining preferred or standard auto insurance policies due to driving or payment histories. Meanwhile the Preferred Property and Casualty Insurance segment targets individuals who have favorable loss histories and risk characteristics.

Financial Performance
Kemper's revenue has climbed steadily over the past five years including a sizable bump from acquisition activities in 2018 for total growth of 50% between 2015 and 2019. Net income fluctuated rising in 2018 and 2017 but declining in 2015 and 2016. Overall earnings grew 562% over the five-year period.

The company reported a 35% sales increase in 2019 to some $5 billion largely due to higher earned premiums related to its acquisition of Infinity Property and Casualty. Kemper also reported growth in sales of its legacy personal specialty auto products and higher investment income that year.

Net income increased 179% in 2019 to $531.1 million due to higher Adjusted Consolidated Net Operating Income higher investment results and lower acquisition related transaction integration and other costs.

The company ended 2019 with $136.8 million in cash up $61.7 million from 2018. Operating activities contributed $534.3 million while investing activities used $633.4 million and financing activities provided $160.8 million via dividend payments.

Strategy
Kemper is making some changes to rejuvenate the company and focus strongly on niche and underserved markets. Its 2018 acquisition of Infinity Property and Casualty served to increase the scale of its specialty auto offerings grow its distribution network and expand its share in key geographic markets. The company hopes the purchase will accelerate growth and enhance product offerings for policyholders.

Following the acquisition Kemper announced a rebranding effort through which it is regrouping its operating divisions under four sub-brands over time to better reflect its core offerings: Kemper Auto Kemper Personal Insurance Kemper Life and Kemper Health. The brand refresh includes a new slogan: Affordable protection in an ever-changing world. In 2019 the company announced plans to move its collector vehicle book of business to fellow insurer Hagerty to increase its focus on core specialty and preferred auto lines.

Like other property/casualty insurers the company is struggling with an increase in catastrophe losses in recent years from wildfires hurricanes and other weather or man-made events. The company is working to reduce catastrophe exposure through reinsurance (risk-sharing) agreements and selective underwriting practices.

Company Background

James Kemper founded National Underwriters insurance exchange in 1913 to provide supplementary fire insurance for lumbermen.

The insurance holding company was formed in 1990. It changed its name from Unitrin to Kemper in August 2011; it also rebranded several of its business units under the Kemper name.

The name change followed a downsizing where the company shed or shuttered several operations. Its Fireside Bank subsidiary which purchased sub-prime loan contracts from used automobile dealers halted lending activities in 2009 and ceased banking operations in 2012. Kemper also narrowed its Reserve National subsidiary's focus on specialized life and health policies.

Kemper's disposal-heavy strategy followed a period of expansion in its consumer insurance options via acquisitions of smaller companies. It returned to growth through the 2015 purchase of nonstandard auto insurer Alliance United Group for $70 million.

EXECUTIVES

Executive Vice President Chief Financial Officer A, Eric Draut

Vp And Chief Accounting Officer, Richard Roeske, age 60, $371,000 total compensation

Evp Kemper Preferred, Naimish Patel

Svp And Chief Investment Officer, John M. Boschelli, age 52, $400,000 total compensation

President And Ceo, Joseph P. (Joe) Lacher, age 51, $750,000 total compensation

President Property And Casualty, George D. (Chip) Dufala, age 48, $214,519 total compensation

Evp; General Manager Kemper Specialty California, Timothy D. Bruns

President Kemper Home Service, Thomas D. Myers

Chief Risk Officer, Shekar G. Jannah

Svp Operations And Systems, Charles T. Brooks, age 54

Svp; President Life And Health, Mark A. Green, age 53, $240,692 total compensation

Svp And Cfo, James J. McKinney, age 41

Vice President Human Resources, Lisa M King

Vice President, Brad Andrekus

Vice President Human Resources Kemper Division, Scott Tomlinson

Vice President Senior Human Resources Manager, Rick Hammett

Assistant Vice President, Calvin Nash

Vp It, Greg Olds

Vp And Treasurer, Christopher Moses

Vice President Predictive Analytics, Ioan Seceleanu

Vice President Information Services, Harry Yee

Vice President Of Actuarial Services, Bradley Andrekus

Assistant Vice President Planning And Analysis, Justin Westcott

Vice President, Jack Broughton

Vice President National Product Management Strategy, David Pearlmutter

Senior Vice President Product Underwriting And Pricing, Eric Neely

Associate Vice President Financial Analysis And Planning, Edward Aguirre

Svp Secretary And General Counsel, C Thomas Evans Jr

Vice President Human Resources, Robin Buendia

Vice President Sales, Steve Bell

Vice President Is, Bhaskar Bulusu

Avp, Tom Crisanti

Assistant Vice President, Polly Mccann

Chairman, Robert J. (Bob) Joyce

Board Member, George Cochran

Board Member, Lacy Johnson

Auditors: DELOITTE & TOUCHE LLP

LOCATIONS

HQ: Kemper Corp (DE)
200 E. Randolph Street, Suite 3300, Chicago, IL 60601
Phone: 312 661-4600
Web: www.kemper.com

PRODUCTS/OPERATIONS

2016 sales

	$ mil.	% of total
Property/casualty insurance	1,688	66
Life & health insurance	821	32
Net realized gains on the sales of investments	33	1
Net impairment losses recognized in earning	(33)	-
Other	13	1
Total	**2,522**	**100**

Selected Insurance Options

Auto
Boat
Collectibles
Commercial Auto
Condo
Home
Identity Fraud
Life and Health
Package
Personal Catastrophe Liability
Personal Valuables
Renters

COMPETITORS

Allstate	Penn-America
Citizens Financial	Security National
Citizens Inc.	Financial
GEICO	State Farm
Liberty Mutual Agency	USAA
Nationwide	

HISTORICAL FINANCIALS

Company Type: Public

Income Statement

FYE: December 31

	ASSETS ($ mil.)	NET INCOME ($ mil.)	INCOME AS % OF ASSETS	EMPLOYEES
12/19	12,989	531	4.1%	8,900
12/18	11,544	190	1.6%	8,100
12/17	8,376	120	1.4%	5,550
12/16	8,210	16	0.2%	5,750
12/15	8,036	85	1.1%	5,600
Annual Growth	12.8%	57.8%	—	12.3%

2019 Year-End Financials

Debt ratio: 5.99%
Return on equity: 15.13%
Cash ($ mil.): 136
Current ratio: —
Long-term debt ($ mil.): —

No. of shares (mil.): 66
Dividends
Yield: 1.3%
Payout: 16.9%
Market value ($ mil.): 5,167

	STOCK PRICE ($) FY Close	P/E High/Low		PER SHARE ($) Earnings	Dividends	Book Value
12/19	77.50	11	8	7.96	1.03	59.59
12/18	66.38	26	16	3.22	0.96	47.10
12/17	68.90	30	16	2.33	0.96	41.11
12/16	44.30	138	72	0.33	0.96	38.52
12/15	37.25	25	21	1.65	0.96	38.82
Annual Growth	20.1%	—	—	48.2%	1.8%	11.3%

Keurig Dr Pepper Inc

Whether you like your caffeine hot or cold Keurig Dr Pepper (KDP) has you covered. The company formerly Dr Pepper Snapple Group is one of North America's largest beverage companies with more than 125 owned licensed and partner brands. It owns the top single-serve coffee system in the US (Keurig) and one of the US's leading soft drinks (Dr Pepper) as well as Green Mountain coffee Canada Dry ginger ale A&W root beer Snapple tea and juice and Mott's fruit juice among many other products. KDP operates facilities across North America. The company serves major retailers in the U.S. Canada and Mexico. Their largest retailer was Walmart representing approximately 13% of sales in 2019. Dr Pepper Snapple Group was acquired by Keurig Green Mountain in 2018 and renamed Keurig Dr Pepper.

Operations

KDP operates its business into four reporting segments: Coffee Systems Packaged Beverages Beverage Concentrates and Latin America Beverages.

Coffee Systems segment generates about 40% of sales and sells a variety of Keurig brewers brewer accessories and other coffee-related equipment. This segment also produce other specialty beverages in K-Cup pods (including hot and iced teas hot cocoa and other beverages) and traditional whole bean and ground coffee in other package types including bags fractional packages and cans.

Packaged Beverages segment manufactures and distribute packaged beverages of the company's brands such as Snapple Mott's Bai Clamato Hawaiian Punch Core Yoo-Hoo ReaLemon Vita Coco coconut water evian Mr and Mrs T mixers Forto Coffee Shoc Dr Pepper Canada Dry 7UP A&W Sunkist soda Squirt Big Red RC Cola and Vernors. This segment accounts for nearly 45% of sales.

Other segment includes Beverage Concentrates (about 15% of sales) and Latin America Beverages (5% of sales).

Geographic Reach

KDP operates across North America but generates most of its sales in the US. It has dual headquarters in Burlington Massachusetts and Plano Texas and more than 125 other facilities across the US Canada and Mexico.

Sales and Marketing

The company primarily serves retailers such as supermarkets mass merchandisers club stores e-commerce retailers office superstores and convenience stores. In 2019 their largest retailer was Walmart representing approximately 13% of net sales.

Some of their NCB brands such as Snapple Bai Core Yoo-Hoo Mistic and Nantucket Nectars are licensed for distribution in various territories to bottlers and a number of smaller distributors such as beer wholesalers wine and spirit distributors independent distributors and retail brokers.

KDP distribute brewers accessories and K-Cup pods (owned licensed and partner brands) to away from home channel participants which include restaurants hotel chains office coffee distributors as well as an e-commerce platform at www.keurig.com where end-use consumers can purchase their products.

As of 2019 their partner brands includes Starbucks Kirkland Signature Dunkin' Donuts Great Value Peet's Coffee Caribou Coffee Eight O'Clock Folgers Newman's Own Organics McCafé Maxwell House Kroger Krispy Kreme Celestial Seasonings Lipton Tazo Panera and Tim Hortons.

KDP's advertising expenses mostly for radio television and print ads were $670 million and $411 for 2019 and 2018.

Financial Performance

Net sales for the year ended December 31 2019 increased $3.7 billion to $11.1 billion compared with net sales of $7.4 billion for the year ended December 31 2018 primarily driven by the incremental impact in the current year of the DPS Merger completed in 2018.

Net income attributable to KDP increased $668 million to $1.3 billion for the year ended December 31 2019 compared to $586 million for the year ended December 31 2018 primarily driven by the incremental impact in the current year of the DPS Merger completed in 2018 including the favorable comparison to the $158 million of transaction costs and the $131 million impact of the inventory step-up associated with the DPS Merger recorded in the year ended December 31 2018.

Cash held by the company at the end of 2019 decreased by $28 million to $111 million compared to $139 million in the prior year. Cash provided by operations was $2.5 billion while cash used for investing and financing activities were $150 million and $2.4 billion respectively.

Strategy

KDP have strategically-located distribution capabilities which enables them to better align their operations with their customers and their channels to ensure the company's products are available to meet consumer demand to reduce transportation costs and to have greater control over the timing and coordination of new product launches. The company actively manage transportation of their products using their fleet (owned and leased) of approximately 6000 vehicles in the U.S. and 1700 in Mexico as well as third party logistics providers.

KDP have entered into strategic relationships for the manufacturing distribution and sale of K-Cup pods with well-regarded beverage companies such as Starbucks Corporation Dunkin' Brands Group Inc. The J.M. Smucker Company Kraft Heinz Newman's Own Organics McDonald's Peet's Coffee & Tea and Tim Hortons as well as with retailers such as Costco The Kroger Co. and Walmart for their private label brands. As independent companies the company's strategic partners make their own business decisions which may not align with KDP's interests.

Company Background

Touted as the oldest soft drink in the US Dr Pepper was invented in 1885 by Charles Alderton a pharmacist in Waco Texas. It was originally called a "Waco" by customers of the pharmacy where Alderton worked and later named Dr Pepper according to legend after Dr. Charles Pepper a friend of the drugstore owner.

The company was eventually purchased by Cadbury Schweppes which had assembled a large group of beverage companies including (by the year 2000) Snapple Beverage Group. Cadbury Schweppes Americas Beverages as it was known was spun off from Cadbury Schweppes in 2008 and renamed Dr Pepper Snapple Group.

In 2018 Keurig Green Mountain acquired Dr Pepper Snapple Group and Keurig Dr Pepper (KDP) was born.

EXECUTIVES

President And Ceo, Larry D. Young, $1,132,692 total compensation

Cfo, Martin M. (Marty) Ellen, $604,808 total compensation

Evp And Chief Commercial Officer, James R. (Jim) Trebilcock

President Packaged Beverages, Rodger L. Collins, $604,462 total compensation

Evp And General Counsel, James L. (Jim) Baldwin, $478,769 total compensation

Evp Supply Chain, Derry L. Hobson, $499,769 total compensation

President Beverage Concentrates And Latin American Beverages, James J. (Jim) Johnston, $604,462 total compensation

Evp Research And Development, David J. Thomas

Ceo Bai Brands, Iain Hancock

Vice President Sales, Ben McElroy

Vice President Sales Operations, Mark Beaton

Vice President, Roy Wright

Vice President Drug And Dollar Channels, Eddie Hicks

Senior Vice President, Joe Rowland

National Accounts Manager, Sherry Batts

Vp Purchasing, David Lainchbury

Chairman, Wayne R. Sanders

Treasurer, Lisa Papageorge

Auditors: DELOITTE & TOUCHE LLP

LOCATIONS

HQ: Keurig Dr Pepper Inc
53 South Avenue, Burlington, MA 01803
Phone: 781 418-7000
Web: www.keurig.com

2016 Sales

	$ mil.	% of total
U.S.	5,768	90
International	672	10
Total	**6,440**	**100**

PRODUCTS/OPERATIONS

2016 Sales

	$ mil.	% of total
Packaged Beverages	4,696	73
Beverage Concentrates	1,284	20
Latin America Beverages	460	7
Total	**6,440**	**100**

Selected Brands

7UP
A&W
Aguafiel (Mexico only)
Cadbury
Canada Dry
Clamato
Crush
Diet Rite
Dr Pepper
Hawaiian Punch
IBC
Margaritaville (licensed)
Mott's
Mr & Mrs T
Nantucket Nectars
Orangina
Pe Â Â afiel (Mexico only)
RC Cola
Rose's (licensed)
Schweppes
Snapple
Squirt
Stewart's (licensed)
Sunkist (licensed)
Vernors
Yoo-Hoo

COMPETITORS

American Beverage
Austin Coca-Cola
Big Heart Pet Brands
Campbell Soup
Citrus World
Coca-Cola
Coca-Cola Bottling Consolidated
Coca-Cola Bottling company of southern california
Coca-Cola Bottling of Northern New England
Coca-Cola FEMSA
Coca-Cola North America
Coca-Cola Refreshments
Coca-Cola Tennessee
Coke United
Cott
Country Pure Foods
Dole Food
Faygo
G & J Pepsi-Cola Bottlers
Gatorade
Great Plains Coca-Cola
Great Western Juice
Hornell Brewing
IZZE
Jones Soda
Jugos del Valle
Lane Affiliated
Mondelez International
Monster Beverage
National Beverage
Nestlé
Ocean Spray
Odwalla
Old Orchard
Pepsi Bottling Ventures
Pepsi-Cola Bottling Company of NY
Pepsi-Cola Bottling of Central Virginia
Pepsi-Cola of Ft. Lauderdale
PepsiCo
Philadelphia Coca-Cola
Red Bull
Reed's
South Beach Beverage
Sunny Delight
Swire Coca-Cola
Tree Top
Tropicana
Wet Planet Beverages
Wonderful Company

HISTORICAL FINANCIALS

Company Type: Public

Income Statement

FYE: December 31

	REVENUE ($ mil.)	NET INCOME ($ mil.)	NET PROFIT MARGIN	EMPLOYEES
12/19	11,120	1,254	11.3%	25,500
12/18	7,442	586	7.9%	25,500
12/17	6,690	1,076	16.1%	21,000
12/16	6,440	847	13.2%	20,000
12/15	6,282	764	12.2%	19,000
Annual Growth	15.3%	13.2%	—	7.6%

2019 Year-End Financials

Debt ratio: 29.75%	No. of shares (mil.): 1,406
Return on equity: 5.48%	Dividends
Cash ($ mil.): 101	Yield: 2.0%
Current ratio: 0.35	Payout: 68.1%
Long-term debt ($ mil.): 13,096	Market value ($ mil.): 40,728

	STOCK PRICE ($) FY Close	P/E High/Low	Earnings	PER SHARE ($) Dividends	Book Value
12/19	28.95	35 28	0.88	0.60	16.53
12/18	25.64	229 41	0.53	105.06	16.03
12/17	97.06	17 14	5.89	2.32	13.64
12/16	90.67	22 18	4.54	2.12	11.65
12/15	93.20	24 18	3.97	1.92	11.62
Annual Growth	(25.3%)	— —	(31.4%)	(25.2%)	9.2%

KeyCorp

With a focus on retail operations KeyBank a subsidiary of KeyCorp operates about 1100 branches and more than 1400 ATMs in some 15 states across the US. Its operations are divided into two groups: Consumer Bank offers traditional services such as deposits loans credit cards securities lending personal financial and planning services access to mutual funds treasury services and international banking services. Commercial Bank community development financing securities underwriting investment banking and capital markets products and brokerage. KeyCorp is also one of the largest servicers of commercial and multifamily loans in the US.

HISTORY

KeyCorp predecessor Commercial Bank of Albany was chartered in 1825. In 1865 it joined the new national banking system and became National Commercial Bank of Albany. After WWI National Commercial consolidated with Union National Bank & Trust as National Commercial Bank and Trust which then merged with First Trust and Deposit in 1971.

In 1973 Victor Riley became president and CEO. Under Riley National Commercial grew during the 1970s and 1980s through acquisitions. Riley sought to make the company a regional powerhouse but was thwarted when several New England states passed legislation barring New York banks from buying banks in the region.

As a result the company renamed Key Bank in 1979 turned west targeting small towns with less competition. Thus situated it prospered despite entering Alaska just in time for the 1986 oil price collapse. Its folksy image and small-town success earned it a reputation as the "Wal-Mart of banking."

Meanwhile in Cleveland Society for Savings followed a different path. Founded as a mutual savings bank in 1849 the institution succeeded from the start. It survived the Civil War and postwar economic turmoil and built Cleveland's first skyscraper in 1890. It continued to grow even during the Depression and became the largest savings bank outside the Northeast in 1949.

In 1955 the bank formed a holding company Society National. Society grew through the acquisitions of smaller banks in Ohio until 1979 when Ohio allowed branch banking in contiguous counties. Thereafter Society National opened branches as well. In the mid-1980s and the early 1990s the renamed Society Corporation began consolidating its operations and continued growing.

A 1994 merger of National Commercial with Society more than doubled assets for the surviving KeyCorp; compatibility of the two companies' systems and software simplified consolidation. KeyCorp sold its mortgage-servicing unit to NationsBank (now Bank of America) in 1995 and over the next year bought investment management finance and investment banking firms.

In 1997 KeyCorp began trimming its branch network divesting 200 offices including its 28-branch KeyBank Wyoming subsidiary. It expanded its consumer lending business that year by buying Champion Mortgage. In cooperation with USF&G (now part of The St. Paul Travelers Companies) and three HMOs KeyCorp began offering health insurance to the underserved small-business market.

In 1998 the company bought Leasetec which leases computer storage systems globally through its StorageTek subsidiary; it also bought McDonald & Company Investments (now McDonald Investments; sold in 2007) with an eye toward reaching its goal of earning half of its revenues from fees. Also in 1998 KeyCorp began offering business lines of credit to customers of Costco Wholesale the nation's largest wholesale club.

As part of a restructuring effort KeyCorp sold 28 Long Island New York branches to Dime Bancorp in 1999. The next year the company sold its credit card portfolio to Associates First Capital (now part of Citigroup) and bought National Realty Funding a securitizer of commercial mortgages. In 2001 it acquired Denver-based investment bank The Wallach Company.

The company expanded further in the Denver area with its 2002 purchase of Union Bankshares. Two years later KeyCorp bought Seattle-area bank EverTrust Financial Group.

In 2007 the company bought Tuition Management Systems which provides outsourced tuition billing accounting and counseling services for schools and colleges; the unit was later merged into its Key Education Resources operations. Also that year KeyCorp sold investment bank and brokerage McDonald Investments to UBS Financial Services.

The company bought New York-based U.S.B. Holding Co. and its Union State Bank subsidiary for some $550 million in early 2008. The deal added more than 30 branches nearly doubling KeyCorp's presence in the Hudson River Valley region.

EXECUTIVES

Vice Chairman And President Banking, Christopher M. (Chris) Gorman, age 59, $638,462 total compensation

Evp General Counsel; Secretary Keybank National Association, Paul N. Harris, age 61

Vice Chairman And Cfo, Donald R. Kimble, age 60, $638,462 total compensation

Co-president Key Community Bank, Edward J. (E.J.) Burke, $550,000 total compensation

Sevp And Chief Risk Officer, William L. (Bill) Hartmann, $500,000 total compensation

Chairman And Ceo, Beth E. Mooney, age 64, $1,000,000 total compensation

Co-president Key Community Bank, Dennis A. Devine, $571,154 total compensation

Cio, Amy G. Brady

Evp And Director Corporate Center, Katrina M. (Trina) Evans

Chief Human Resources Officer, Craig A. Buffie

Evp; Head Real Estate Capital, Angela G. Mago

Evp; President Keybank Capital Markets, Andrew J. (Randy) Paine, $500,000 total compensation

Executive Vice President Marketing, Bonnie Squadere

Vice President Database Marketing, Jonathan Boyer

Vice President, Alison Sammon

Assistant Vice President, Paul Pace

Assistant Vice President Senior Financial Analyst Planning And Forecasting, Danny Pho

Vice President Global Trade Services, Robert Kurek

Senior Vice President, Mark Kleinhaut

Vice President, Colleen Daly

Senior Vice President, Kim Monson

Executive Vice President Marketing, Darlene Kohring

Vice President Financial Risk Governance Manager, Anna Norcross

Vice President Information Technology Project Management, Lari Greenleaf

Vice President National Ach Edi Operat, Eric Foust

Vice President Of Information Technology, Roy Woodbury

Vice President And Manager Regional Reporting, Melissa Werner

Vice President Information Technology Delivery Manager Wealth And Commercial Segments, Mark Melaragno

Senior Vice President Central Ohio District, Thomas Spilman

Senior Vice President Payment Deposit, Dominic Cugini

Vice President Credit Risk Management, Bob Fisco

Senior Vice President, Elizabeth Mccaffery

Senior Vice President Capital Planning, Jay Luzar

Vice President And Compliance Officer, Tamara Darnow

Senior Treasury Services Sales Officer Vice President, Anwar Smiley

Vice President Commercial Banker, Yong Lee

Vice President, Nicholas T Stuart

Vice President Meeting Marketing Manager, Laurie Masters

Vice President, Aaron Gray

Executive Vice President, George Emmons

Co Chief Operating Officer, Douglas Preiser

Vice President, Lynda Fennern

Senior Vice President, Patrick Fish

Vice President Consumer Finance, Dan Sukys

Vice President Corporate Communications, Alison Altre-Kerber

Vice President And Trust Team Lead Real Estate, Emily Mogen

Vice President Of Marketing Strategist, Jill Dalton

Vice President Senior Business Banker, John Marriott

Vice President Credit Officer, Kellie Whelan

Assistant Vice President Retail Banking, Michael Emerson

Senior Vice President And Finance Director, William Shaw

Vice President Credit Risk Reviewer, Greg Newhouse

Senior Vice President Commercial Banking, Stephen Markley

Vice President Private Banking, Andrew Bowen

Vice President Team Leader, Pete Dunbar

Senior Vice President, James Harnett

Vice President Product Manager, Natalie Treibatch

Vice President Credit Officer, Jay Coleman

Vice President Senior Portfolio Manager, Jeff Stegeman

Senior Vice President Enterprise Architecture, Mike Onders

Vice President Business Development, Alice Karn

Vice President Senior Treasury Advisor Institutional Banking, Michael Thomas

Vice President Client Services Consumer Segment, Cheryl Towns

Vice President District Operations Manager, Monica Cichon

Senior Cash Management Advisor And Assistant Vice President Treasury Services, Kristina Simpson

Vice President And Senior Trust Officer, Daryl Hembry

Senior Vice President Real Estate Finance, Craig Younggren

Vice President And District Operations Manager, Laurie Dickinson

Vice President Community Bank Sales Systems, Robert Brzezinski

Senior Vice President Corporate Bank Technology And Sales Tool Team Manager, Brian Utrup

Senior Vice President District Retail Leader, Curtis Hollis

Senior Vice President And Manager Instit, Flavio Giust

E C Manager Assistant Vice President System Administrator, Margaret Mason

Vice President Network Solutions Engineering, Daniel Godlewski

Assistant Vice President Portfolio Manager, Sara Smith

Assistant Vice President Team Lead, Lashawn Dalton

Executive Vice President And Director Call Center Sales And Service, Dean Kontul

Senior Vice President Senior Relationship Manager, David Brown

Senior Vice President Asset Management, Amy Paine

Vice President Consumer Credit Risk Management, Kevin Takac

Executive Vice President Human Resources, Beth Yates

Executive Vice President Marketing, David Odell
Vice President And Senior Lit Counsel, Michelle Deshon
Vice President, Eric Klenz
Executive Vice President Marketing, Carla Mansur
Senior Vice President, Jeff Link
Vice President, Aaron Klein
Vice President Sba Sales Manager, Julie Sweet
Relationship Manager Vice President Commercial Banking, Hanna Piechocka
Senior Vice President, Alyce Juby
Vice President, Jennie Bacon
Assistant Vice President, Erik Vohs
Vice President Senior Relationship Manager, Brian Flewelling
Vice President Commercial Banking Relationship Manager, Adam Clinton
Vice President, Dan Schock
Vice President, Gordon Ostler
Assistant Vice President Business Banking Relationship Manager, Jennifer Regelski
Assistant Vice President And Relationship Manager, Brian Herrick
Senior Vice President Senior Portfolio Manager, Chris Sim
Executive Vice President, Brian Fishel
Vice President, Eric Hafertepen
Vice President Business Banking, John Fidler
Assistant Vice President, Max Rebello
Vice President, Seth Reimer
Vice President And Senior Portfolio Manager, Lynn Wilson
Vice President Credit Officer Business Banking, Peg Misencik
Vice President Senior Bus. Relationship Manager, Rachel Galusha
Assistant Vice President Business Banking Relationship Manager, Nicholas Emmett
Senior Commercial Relationship Manager Vice President, Sabrina Webster
Senior Vice President, Sanya Valeva
Assistant Vice President, Teena Heasley
Vice President, Sally Barton
Vice President, Selina Moriarty
Senior Vice President, Jerold Myler
Vice President, Michael Keach
Vice President, Suzan Jones
Senior Vice President, Sharon Lochocki
Senior Vice President, Denise Povolny
Senior Vice President And Senior Relationship Manager, Jun Chea
Vice President Relationship Manager, Todd Remy
Vice President Commercial Relationship Manager, Thomas Gunter
Vice President, Paul Taubeneck
Assistant Vice President Key Center Manager, Nicole Bier
Senior Vice President, Lawrence Mack
Vice President, Charles Arenas
Vice President Rocky Mountain And Agri Business Service Team Manager, Chantel West
Senior Vice President Senior Investment Portfolio Manager, Cheryl Ennis
Vice President Senior Business Banking Relationship Manager, Ed Korsok
Credit Executive Senior Vice Presidfent, Gary Knapp
Senior Vice President Director Of National Facilities, Brian Lawhead
Vice President Corporate Treasury Service Manager Enterprise Commercial Payments, Tami Riley
Senior Vice President Eastern Regional Manager, John Manginelli
Assistant Vice President; Senior Treasury Client Manager, Lynn Barclay
Vice President, William Schlag
Vice President Of Technology, Dani Madi
Vice President Global Information Technology Asset Management, Warren Edris

Vice President Federal Sales, Gina Ringgenberg
Assistant Vice President Asset Based Lending, Andrew Ashley
Vice President, Dale Williams
Assistant Vice President Lead Project Manager, Volney Schafer
Vice President And Senior Relationship Manager, Bart Gebers
Vice President Institutional Equity Sale, Christopher Brady
Assistant Vice President Branch Manager, David Butler
Vice President, George Mohan
Senior Vp, John Murphy
Senior Vice President, Kenneth Lynch
Senior Vice President, Nick Edwards
Senior Vice President, Peter Rand
Associate Vice President, Jill M Mcauley
Assistant Vice President Ap Accounting And Audit Manager, Dore Wawrzyniak
Vice President Regional Facilities Manager, Chris Headrick
Auditors: Ernst & Young LLP

LOCATIONS

HQ: KeyCorp
127 Public Square, Cleveland, OH 44114-1306
Phone: 216 689-3000
Web: www.key.com

PRODUCTS/OPERATIONS

2018 Sales

	$ mil.	% of total
Interest		
Loans	4,023	54
Securities available for sale	409	6
Held-to-maturity securities	284	4
Loans held for sale	66	1
Trading account assets	46	-
Short-term investments	29	-
Other investments	21	-
Interest Expense	969	-
Less: TE adjustment	31	-
Noninterest		
Trust & investment services	499	7
Investment banking and debt placement fees	650	9
Service charges on deposits	349	5
Corporate Service income	233	3
Cards and payments income	270	4
Corporate owned life insurance income	137	2
Operating lease income and other leasing gains	89	1
Mortgage servicing fees	82	1
Consumer mortgage income	30	-
Other income	176	2
Total	**6,455**	**100**

2018 Sales

	$ mil.	% of total
Key Community Bank	3,971	62
Key Corporate Bank	2,255	35
Other Segment	151	2
Reconciling Items	78	1
Total		100

2018 Loan Portfolio

	% of total
Commercial Loans	
Commercial and Industrial	51
Commercial Real Estate	
Commercial Mortgage	16
Construction	2
Commercial Lease Financing	5
Consumer Loans	
Real estate-residential mortgage	6
Home equity loans	13
Consumer direct loans	2
Credit cards	1
Consumer indirect loans	4
Total	**100**

COMPETITORS

Bank of America	Huntington Bancshares
Citigroup	JPMorgan Chase
Citizens Financial Group	M&T Bank
	Northern Trust
Comerica	PNC Financial
Fifth Third	Sovereign Bank
Flagstar Bancorp	U.S. Bancorp
HSBC USA	Wells Fargo

HISTORICAL FINANCIALS

Company Type: Public

Income Statement

FYE: December 31

	ASSETS ($ mil.)	NET INCOME ($ mil.)	INCOME AS % OF ASSETS	EMPLOYEES
12/19	144,988	1,717	1.2%	17,045
12/18	139,613	1,866	1.3%	18,180
12/17	137,698	1,296	0.9%	18,415
12/16	136,453	791	0.6%	15,700
12/15	95,133	916	1.0%	13,359
Annual Growth	11.1%	17.0%	—	6.3%

2019 Year-End Financials

Debt ratio: 8.50%	No. of shares (mil.): 977
Return on equity: 10.52%	Dividends
Cash ($ mil.): 1,772	Yield: 3.5%
Current ratio: —	Payout: 43.8%
Long-term debt ($ mil.): —	Market value ($ mil.): 19,778

	STOCK PRICE ($) FY Close	P/E High/Low		PER SHARE ($) Earnings	Dividends	Book Value
12/19	20.24	13	9	1.62	0.71	17.44
12/18	14.78	13	8	1.71	0.57	15.30
12/17	20.17	18	14	1.13	0.38	14.05
12/16	18.27	23	12	0.80	0.33	14.12
12/15	13.19	15	11	1.05	0.29	12.86
Annual Growth	11.3%	—	—	11.5%	25.1%	7.9%

KIEWIT CORPORATION

EXECUTIVES

Ceo, Bruce E Grewcock
Exec V Pres, Richard W Colf
Exec V Pres, Douglas E Patterson
Exec V Pres, Scott L Cassels
Sr V Pres, Steven Hansen
Treas, Stephen S Thomas
SEC, Michael F Norton
Major Project Mana, Joe Wingerter
Career, Heather Semple
Law Specialist, Simson Chan
Superintendent, Gary Dyer
Auditors: KPMG LLP OMAHA NE

LOCATIONS

HQ: KIEWIT CORPORATION
3555 FARNAM ST STE 1000, OMAHA, NE 681313302
Phone: 402 342-2052
Web: WWW.KIEWIT.COM

HISTORICAL FINANCIALS

Company Type: Private

Income Statement
FYE: December 28

	REVENUE ($ mil.)	NET INCOME ($ mil.)	NET PROFIT MARGIN	EMPLOYEES
12/13	11,826	796	6.7%	10,441
12/12	11,220	512	4.6%	—
12/11	10,381	796	7.7%	—
Annual Growth	6.7%	(0.0%)	—	—

Kimberly-Clark Corp.

One of the world's largest makers of personal paper products Kimberly-Clark operates through three business segments: Personal Care Consumer Tissue and K-C Professional. Kimberly-Clark's largest unit Personal Care makes products such as diapers (Huggies Pull-Ups) feminine care items (Kotex) and incontinence care products (Poise Depend). Through its Consumer Tissue segment the manufacturer offers facial and bathroom tissues paper towels and other household items under the names Cottonelle Kleenex Viva and Scott (plus the Scott Naturals line). Kimberly-Clark's K-C Professional unit makes WypAll commercial wipes among other items. The US accounts for around half of Kimberly-Clark's sales.

Operations

Kimberly-Clark has three reportable segments: Personal Care (about 50%) Consumer Tissue (roughly 35%) and K-C Professional (nearly 20%).

Personal Care offers products such as disposable diapers training and youth pants swimpants baby wipes feminine and incontinence care products and other related products. Its products are sold under the Huggies Pull-Ups Little Swimmers GoodNites DryNites Kotex U by Kotex Intimus Depend Plenitud Poise and other brands.

Consumer Tissue's products include facial and bathroom tissue paper towels napkins and related products and are sold under the Kleenex Scott Cottonelle Viva Andrex Scottex Neve and other brand names.

K-C Professional (KCP) partners with businesses and provides supporting products such as wipers tissue towels apparel soaps and sanitizers sold under the Kleenex Scott WypAll Kimtech and KleenGuard brands.

Geographic Reach

Dallas Texas-based Kimberly-Clark maintains a broad global presence as part of its growth strategy. It boasts some 85 manufacturing facilities in about 35 countries across the US Canada Europe Asia and Latin America and records sales in more than 175 countries. Consumer tissue and KCP products are produced in more than 50 facilities and personal care products are produced in over 45 facilities.

Kimberly-Clark generates more than 50% of sales in US.

Sales and Marketing

Kimberly-Clark sells its household items directly to supermarkets mass merchandisers drugstores warehouse clubs variety and department stores and other retail outlets as well as through distributors and e-commerce. For the away-from-home market it serves the company sells through distributors and directly to high-volume public facilities and to manufacturing lodging office building food service and health care establishments.

Its largest customer worldwide retailer Wal-Mart represents about 15% of net sales.

Kimberly-Clark's advertising expense were $757 million $655 million and $648 million for the years 2019 2018 and 2017 respectively.

Financial Performance

Kimberly-Clark has struggled to attain meaningful revenue growth in recent years while profits have fluctuated. In fiscal 2019 the company's sales decline less than 1% to $18.4 was due to the 3% decrease of its sales outside US. By segment Personal Care and K-C Professional are the strongest performers and Consumer Tissue the weakest.

Kimberly-Clark's net income jumped 52% to $2.2 billion due to restructuring program undertaken in 2018. The company incurred layoff expenses asset write-offs and impairments and depreciation. It hopes the restructuring will generate $500 million in pre-tax savings by 2021.

Kimberly-Clark's cash on hand fell slightly during 2018 ending the year $77 million lower at $539 million. The company's operations generated $2.7 billion while its investing activities used $1.0 billion and its financing used $1.8 billion. Kimberly-Clark's main cash uses in 2019 were capital expenditures share repurchases debt repayments and dividends.

Strategy

With business performance lower than desired Kimberly-Clark undertook a global restructuring program in 2018 that will see 10 factories close and certain low-margin businesses divested (mainly in the consumer tissue segment) as well as potentially saving some $500-550 million in annual costs. The restructuring which resulted in 5000-5500 job cuts should leave Kimberly-Clark on surer footing to invest in its brands and growth initiatives. The company has earmarked $1.1-1.3 billion in capex for 2019 an increase on the $0.9 and $0.8 billion in the two preceding years.

The company's strategy includes operations growth outside the U.S. especially in developing markets such as China Eastern Europe ASEAN and Latin America.

HISTORY

John Kimberly Charles Clark Havilah Babcock and Frank Shattuck founded Kimberly Clark & Company in Neenah Wisconsin in 1872 to manufacture newsprint from rags. The company incorporated as Kimberly & Clark Company in 1880 and built a pulp and paper plant on the Fox River in 1889.

In 1914 the company developed cellu-cotton a cotton substitute used by the US Army as surgical cotton during WWI. Army nurses used cellu-cotton pads as disposable sanitary napkins and six years later the company introduced Kotex the first disposable feminine hygiene product. Kleenex the first throwaway handkerchief followed in 1924. Kimberly & Clark joined with The New York Times Company in 1926 to build a newsprint mill (Spruce Falls Power and Paper) in Ontario Canada. Two years later the company went public as Kimberly-Clark.

EXECUTIVES

Chairman And Ceo, Thomas J. (Tom) Falk, age 62, $1,318,750 total compensation
Svp And Cfo, Maria G. Henry, age 53, $772,500 total compensation
President Latin America, Sergio Cruz
President Global Brands And Innovation, Anthony J. (Tony) Palmer, age 60, $655,000 total compensation
President Coo And Director, Michael D. Hsu, age 56, $833,750 total compensation

Svp And Chief Supply Chain Officer, Sandra J. MacQuillan, age 53, $392,424 total compensation
President Asia-pacific Region, Achal Agarwal
President Europe Middle East And Africa, Gustavo Calvo Paz
President Kimberly-clark Professional, Kim Underhill
Vice President Investor Relations, Paul Alexander
Vice President Kimberly Clark Professional Asia Pacific, Richard Thorne
Vice President Of Operations, Deanna Thornton
Vice President Its Infrastructure, Ryan Ramirez
Vp Government Relations, Susan Phillips
Vice President Internal Audit, Stephen Frimpong
Vice President Walmart International Development, John Scholes
Vice President Transportation, Scott Degroot
Vice President Human Resources, Rick Purdy
Vice President Global Communications, Christopher Wyse
Vice President Of Human Resources, Tina Busch
Vp Industry And Customer Development, Dennis Delcastro
National Account Manager, Patricia Lopez
Global Vp Logistics, Shane Azzi
Vice President And General Manager Walmart Family Care Business, Jason Epps
Treasurer, Kim Kap
Auditors: DELOITTE & TOUCHE LLP

LOCATIONS

HQ: Kimberly-Clark Corp.
P.O. Box 619100, Dallas, TX 75261-9100
Phone: 972 281-1200
Web: www.kimberly-clark.com

2018 Sales

	$ mil.	% of total
North America	9,532	51
Outside North America	9,256	49
Total	**18,486**	**100**

PRODUCTS/OPERATIONS

2018 Sales

	$ mil.	% of total
Personal Care	9,037	49
Consumer Tissue	6,015	33
K-C Professional	3,382	18
Corporate & other	52	-
Total	**18,486**	**100**

Selected Products and Brands

Baby & Child Care
  Huggies
  Pull-Ups
  GoodNites
  DryNites
  Little Swimmers
  Kleen Bebe
  Green Finger
Family Care
  Kleenex
  Andrex
  Hakle
  Cottonelle
  Scottes
  Page
  Neve
  Petalo
  Wondersoft
  Tela
  Scott
  Viva
Feminine Care
  U by Kotex
  Kotex
  Intimus
  CAmelia
K-C Professional
  KleenGuard
  Kimtech
  WypAll
  Scott
  Kleenex

HISTORICAL FINANCIALS

Company Type: Public

Income Statement

FYE: December 31

	REVENUE ($ mil.)	NET INCOME ($ mil.)	NET PROFIT MARGIN	EMPLOYEES
12/19	18,450	2,157	11.7%	40,000
12/18	18,486	1,410	7.6%	41,000
12/17	18,259	2,278	12.5%	42,000
12/16	18,202	2,166	11.9%	42,000
12/15	18,591	1,013	5.4%	43,000
Annual Growth	(0.2%)	20.8%	—	(1.8%)

2019 Year-End Financials

Debt ratio: 50.69%	No. of shares (mil.): 341
Return on equity: —	Dividends
Cash ($ mil.): 442	Yield: 3.0%
Current ratio: 0.73	Payout: 70.6%
Long-term debt ($ mil.): 6,213	Market value ($ mil.): 46,966

	STOCK PRICE ($) FY Close	P/E High/Low	PER SHARE ($) Earnings	Dividends	Book Value
12/19	137.55	23 17	6.24	4.12	(0.01)
12/18	113.94	30 24	4.03	4.00	(0.65)
12/17	120.66	21 17	6.40	3.88	1.97
12/16	114.12	23 19	5.99	3.68	(0.12)
12/15	127.30	47 37	2.77	3.52	(0.30)
Annual Growth	2.0%	— —	22.5%	4.0%	—

Kinder Morgan Inc.

Kinder Morgan Inc. (KMI) is one of the largest energy infrastructure companies in North America. It operates approximately 83000 miles of pipelines and more than 145 terminals that transport natural gas refined petroleum products crude oil condensate CO_2 and other products to its customers across America. It generates most of its sales in the US. In late 2019 KMI sold its 70% stake in Kinder Morgan Canada Limited to Pembina Pipeline Corporation.

Operations

KMI reports via four segments: Natural Gas Pipelines Terminals Products Pipelines and CO_2.

Natural Gas Pipelines is KMI's most significant business segment accounting for more than 60% of total revenue. This line of business operates approximately 71000 miles of pipelines and storage facilities which supply roughly 40% of all consumed natural gas in the US.

Terminals is the transportation arm of KMI and brings in roughly 15% of annual sales. With approximately 50 liquid terminals more than 30 bulk terminals and over 15 Jones Act approved tankers KMI is the largest independent terminal operator in North America. (Jones Act restricts US point-to-point maritime shipping to vessels that are 75% US-owned.) The terminals transload store or blend refined petroleum products crude oil chemicals ethanol and bulk products to US and parts of Canada.

The Products Pipelines segment includes approximately 9000 miles of pipelines roughly 60 terminals making this sector the largest independent transporter of petroleum products (more than 2 million barrels per day). Moving gasoline jet fuel diesel crude and NGL products and this sector brings about 15% of annual sales.

Although KMI is the largest CO_2 transporter in North America. Transporting approximately 1.2 billion cubic feet/day this segment only accounts for about 10% of the company's total sales.

Overall services generate around 55% of the company's revenue. Over 35% comes from commodities while the rest is generated from others.

Geographic Reach

Delaware-based KMI has operations in the US Canada and Mexico. KMI buys and sells significant volumes of natural gas in Texas. US customers account for more than 95% of the company's revenue and the remaining are generated from customers in Canada Mexico and other foreign countries.

Sales and Marketing

KMI customers include major oil companies energy producers and shippers as well as local distributors. The company does business under extended transport and sales contracts. KMI conducts its Midstream assets on a fee-based arrangement and its CO_2 business has third-party contracts with minimum volume requirements.

Financial Performance

Revenue at KMI fluctuated in the last five years. During that period the revenue has an overall decline of 8%. On the other hand its net income has a promising growth in the same period.

In 2019 annual sales decreased 7% to $13.2 billion primarily due to the decrease in natural gas and product sales.

Net income rose from $1.6 billion in 2018 to $2.2 billion in 2019.

Cash holdings declined to $209 million at the end of 2019. Operations provided $4.7 billion offset by $31.7 billion used in investments and a further $6.2 billion used by financing activities.

Strategy

Kinder Morgan's strategy is to: focus on stable fee-based energy transportation and storage assets that are central to the energy infrastructure of growing markets within North America; increase utilization of existing assets while controlling costs operating safely and employing environmentally sound operating practices; exercise discipline in capital allocation and in evaluating expansion projects and acquisition opportunities; leverage economies of scale from expansions of assets and acquisitions that fit within its strategy; and maintain a strong financial profile and enhance and return value to stockholders.

Company Background

Kinder Morgan Energy Partners (KMP) was founded in February 1997 when a group of investors led by Executive Chairman Richard D. Kinder and Vice Chairman William V. Morgan decided to build an energy company by utilizing the master limited partnership (MLP) financial structure as a growth vehicle—something that had never been done before.

Their innovative approach proved so successful that in two decades KMP has becomes the largest publicly traded pipeline limited partnership in America based on enterprise value. Initially the company grew mostly through acquisitions of existing operations but eventually took on the construction of projects.

Separately in 1999 Mr. Kinder took over the reins of KN Energy from Lakewood Colorado a natural gas pipeline company serving small communities and rural areas in Kansas and Nebraska and turned it to Kinder Morgan Inc. Kinder Morgan's second publicly traded company.

EXECUTIVES

President And Ceo, Steven J. (Steve) Kean, age 59, $1 total compensation
Vp And Cfo, Kimberly A. (Kim) Dang, age 51, $375,000 total compensation
President Kinder Morgan Canada, Ian D. Anderson, age 63
Vp; President Natural Gas Pipelines, Thomas A. (Tom) Martin, $375,000 total compensation
Vp Corporate Development, Dax Sanders, $375,000 total compensation
President Products Pipelines, Ronald G. (Ron) McClain
President Terminals, John W. Schlosser
Vp And Cio, Mark Huse
President Co2, Jesse Arenivas, $325,000 total compensation
Vice President Information Technology, Dan Henningsen
Senior Vice President, Harlan Bergen
Vice President, Alan Cooke
Executive Vice President And Chief Operating Officer, Scott Stoness
Vice President, Douglas Lawing
Vice President Employee Benefits, Mark Smith
Vice President, Bruce Boyd
Vice President Marketing, Jim Kehlet
Vice President Project Management, Scott Bare
Vice President Commercial, Greg Lang
Vice President, Dirk Cockrum
Vice President, David Michels
Vice President Of Engineering, Lanny Shoeling
Vice President Of Business Development, David Grisko
Vice President Technology, Dan Rizzo
Vice President Business Development, Michael Varagona
Vice President Pacific Business Development And Marketing, Mary Morgan
Vice President Operations (central Region), Michael Catt
Vice President Operations, Steven Romano
Vice President, Louis Zimmerman
Assistant Vice President, Guadalupe L Rivera
Vice President, Terri Kinder
Sr Executive Vice President, Brian Moore
Vice President, Doug Story
Executive Chairman, Richard D. (Rich) Kinder, age 76
Board Member, Michael Morgan
Board Member, Robert Vagt
Secretary Treasurer, Melinda Giles
Vice President And Treasurer, Anthony Ashley
Board Member, Arthur Reichstetter
Board Member, William Smith
Auditors: PricewaterhouseCoopers LLP

LOCATIONS

HQ: Kinder Morgan Inc.
  1001 Louisiana Street, Suite 1000, Houston, TX 77002
Phone: 713 369-9000
Web: www.kindermorgan.com

2017 Sales

	$ mil.	% of total
US	13,073	95
Canada	503	4
Mexico	129	1
Total	**13,705**	**100**

PRODUCTS/OPERATIONS

2017 Sales

	$ mil.	% of total
Natural Gas Pipelines	8,618	63
Terminals	1,966	14
Products Pipelines	1,661	12
CO2	1,196	9
Kinder Morgan Canada	256	2
Corporate and intersegment eliminations	8	
Total	**13,705**	**100**

2017 Sales

	$ mil.	% of total
Services	7,901	58
Natural gas sales	3,053	22
Product sales and other	2,751	20
Total	**13,705**	**100**

COMPETITORS

Denbury Resources	Energy Transfer Equity
Devon Energy	Enterprise Products
EnLink Midstream Partners	ONEOK
Enbridge	TRII
	Williams Companies

HISTORICAL FINANCIALS

Company Type: Public

Income Statement   FYE: December 31

	REVENUE ($ mil.)	NET INCOME ($ mil.)	NET PROFIT MARGIN	EMPLOYEES
12/20	11,700	119	1.0%	10,524
12/19	13,209	2,190	16.6%	954
12/18	14,144	1,609	11.4%	11,012
12/17	13,705	183	1.3%	10,897
12/16	13,058	708	5.4%	11,121
Annual Growth	**(2.7%)**	**(36.0%)**	**—**	**(1.4%)**

2020 Year-End Financials

Debt ratio: 48.20%—
Return on equity: 0.36%
Cash ($ mil.): 1,184
Current ratio: 0.63
Long-term debt ($ mil.): 32,131

Dividends
Yield: 7.5%
Payout: 2,075.0%
Market value ($ mil.): —

	STOCK PRICE ($) FY Close	P/E High/Low	PER SHARE ($) Earnings	Dividends	Book Value
12/20	13.67	445200	0.05	1.04	13.88
12/19	21.17	22 16	0.96	0.95	14.90
12/18	15.38	30 22	0.66	0.73	14.89
12/17	18.07	22941676	0.01	0.50	15.17
12/16	20.71	93 48	0.25	0.50	15.44
Annual Growth	**(9.9%)**	**—**	**(33.1%)**	**20.0%**	**(2.6%)**

KNIGHTS OF COLUMBUS

Good Knight! The Knights of Columbus is a formidable volunteer group boasting about 15900 councils made up of 1.9 million Roman Catholic male members in the US Canada Mexico Cuba the Philippines Poland and several other countries. The fraternal organization is also a force to be reckoned with in the insurance world providing life insurance annuities and long-term care insurance to its members and their families. More than 1500 full-time insurance agents work across the United States and Canada. In addition the group manages the Knights of Columbus Museum in New Haven Connecticut featuring exhibits of reli-

gious art and history. The group was founded in 1882 by Father Michael J. McGivney.

Operations

The Knights of Columbus (KoC) was formed to render financial aid to members and their families. Mutual aid and assistance are offered to sick disabled and needy members and their families. Social and intellectual fellowship is promoted among members and their families through educational charitable religious social welfare war relief and public relief works. KoC is also engaged in religious education the support of public policy issues and charitable activities such as disaster relief.

The entity is a Catholic family fraternal service organization. This theme permeates the entire Service Program: all Church community council family culture of life and youth activities. The Service Program is designed to establish each council as an influential and important force within the community elevate the status of the programming personnel provide more meaningful and relevant programs of action establish direct areas of responsibility build leadership and ensure the success of council programs.

The group's supreme council has more than 75 state council organizations.

Geographic Reach

The Knights of Columbus is made up of local councils throughout the US Canada Mexico Puerto Rico Guam Saipan and the US Virgin Islands. It also has councils in the Bahamas Cuba the Dominican Republic Guatemala Lithuania Panama the Philippines Poland South Korea and Ukraine. The United States Canada and the Philippines have the largest membership numbers.

Financial Performance

In 2019 Knights of Columbus Insurance reported nearly $9 billion in annual sales and more than $26 billion in assets under its management.

Strategy

Known for its charitable giving the Knights of Columbus is also an insurance company providing insurance to its membership.

The organization has 1500 agents who are also members of the Knights. Knights of Columbus launched its new life insurance product in early 2020. This new product provides affordable guaranteed lifetime coverage flexible premium payment options and a low-cost guaranteed death benefit that will ensure future obligations are met.

To expand its reach Knights have led major charitable initiatives including Coats for Kids the Ultrasound Initiative and Christians at Risk and have also sponsored events and programs with organizations such as Special Olympics and the Global Wheelchair Mission.

Knights of Columbus also has various charity programs such as its Christian refugee fund disaster relief and its Leave No Neighbor Behind which supports communities affected by the COVID-19 pandemic.

Company Background

The Knights of Columbus was founded in New Haven by Father Michael J. McGivney in 1882 and has been selling insurance since its founding.

EXECUTIVES

Supreme Knight, Carl A. Anderson
Supreme Secretary, Michael J. (Mike) O'Connor
Supreme Chaplain, William E. Lori
Deputy Supreme Knight, Patrick E. Kelly
Supreme Treasurer, Ronald F. Schwarz
Assistant Vice President Of Application Development, Niki Kratzert
Vice President, Gary Nolan
Vice President Actuary, Marc Andre-Brunet
Senior Vice President Chief Communications Officer, Kevin Shinkle

Vice President Portfolio Manager, Gil Marchand
Treasurer, Logan Ludwig
Treasurer, Keith Ryan
Treasurer, Ron Schwarz

LOCATIONS

HQ: KNIGHTS OF COLUMBUS
1 COLUMBUS PLZ STE 1700, NEW HAVEN, CT 065103326
Phone: 203 752-4000
Web: WWW.KOFC.ORG

HISTORICAL FINANCIALS

Company Type: Private

Income Statement   FYE: December 31

	ASSETS ($ mil.)	NET INCOME ($ mil.)	INCOME AS % OF ASSETS	EMPLOYEES
12/13	20,534	113	0.6%	2,300
12/12	19,401	127	0.7%	—
12/11	18,026	81	0.4%	—
12/10	16,861	86	0.5%	—
Annual Growth	**6.8%**	**9.5%**	**—**	**—**

Kohl's Corp.

Clothing retailer Kohl's operates about 1160 namesake department stores across the US as well as more than 10 FILA outlets. Competing with discount and mid-level department stores the company sells moderately priced name-brand and private-label apparel shoes accessories and housewares. Its private-label brands include Apt. 9 Croft & Barrow and Jumping Beans; Kohl's also sells exclusive brands through agreements with Lauren Conrad Vera Wang and the Food Network among others. Approximately 95% of the company's stores are freestanding or in strip centers with the rest located in malls.

Operations

By product Kohl's generates more than 25% of sales from women's clothing and some 20% from men's clothing. Most of the remainder of sales come from home products (nearly 20%) children's clothing (more than 10%) and accessories and footwear (about 10% each).

The company generates about 5% of revenue from credit card operations third-party advertising on the Kohl's website and unused gift cards among other non-merchandise items.

Kohl's boasts a strong portfolio of national exclusive and private-label brands with nearly 65% of its sales tied to national brands and the rest coming from private and exclusive brands.

Geographic Reach

Kohl's network of some 1160 stores covers the entire US. Its largest markets are the Midwest (with more than a quarter of stores and led by Illinois with about 65) and West (with about 20% of stores and led by California with more than 115); other leading states include Texas Ohio Florida New York and Pennsylvania.

Facilities that serve Wisconsin-based Kohl's e-commerce brick-and-mortar businesses are in Ohio Virginia Missouri New York Georgia Illinois California Maryland Indiana and Texas.

Sales and Marketing

Kohl's sells its products through its stores online and through in-store kiosks that offer customers free shipping to their homes. As an omni-channel retailer the company doesn't make a clear distinction between store and digital sales and thus doesn't report them separately.

Financial Performance

Kohl's has seen slow growth over the past five years with few new store openings and sluggish movement in comparable store sales. Revenue hasn't moved around $19-20 billion since fiscal 2015. Its profit has been sporadic amid rising merchandise costs and investments in IT and marketing to accelerate growth.

The retailer's revenue fell slightly in fiscal 2019 to $19.97 billion down 1% from the prior year. Net sales decreased to $282 million or 1.5% to $18.9 billion for 2019. The decrease was primarily due to a 1.3% decrease in comparable sales driven by a decrease in average transaction value.

Net income in 2019 was $691 million down by 14% from the prior year. The decrease was due to lower revenue higher impairments and higher selling general and administrative expenses.

Cash at the end of 2019 was $723 million a decrease of $211 million from the prior year. Cash from operations contributed $1.7 billion to the coffers while investing and financing activities used $837 million and $1.0 billion respectively. Main cash uses were for acquisition of property and equipment stock purchases and dividends payment.

Strategy

In October 2020 Kohl's shared the company's new strategic framework with the investment community including new initiatives to position the company for long-term success. As part of its strategy Kohl's has set a new vision: to be the most trusted retailer of choice for the active and casual lifestyle. The strategy informed by customer insights is designed to drive top-line growth and expand operating margin supported by disciplined capital management and agile organizational culture to create long-term shareholder value.

The new strategy will build on Kohl's strong foundation of 65 million customers industry-leading loyalty and charge card programs more than 1160 stores and large and growing digital business. To accomplish the vision to be the most trusted retailer of choice for the active and casual lifestyle Kohl's will focus on three key areas that will drive top-line growth: Be the destination for active casual and beauty for the entire family from the most trusted brands always delivering quality and discovery; Lead with loyalty and value through a best-in-class rewards program; and Offer a differentiated omnichannel experience that is easy and inviting no matter how customers want to shop..

Kohl's has a track record of disciplined financial management and this will continue to be an important focus. The company is committed to prudent balance sheet management with a long-term objective of sustaining its investment grade rating a status it has held for more than two decades. The company is also committed to a long-term capital return program and this follows a long history of returning significant capital to shareholders.

The company's strategic efforts are supported by its strong organizational focus. Kohl's will continue to foster a workplace culture of agility accountability and experimentation while also further amplifying its efforts on diversity and inclusion and environmental social and corporate governance (ESG) stewardship.

Company Background

Max Kohl (father of Sen. Herbert Kohl of Wisconsin) opened his first grocery store in Milwaukee in the late 1920s. Over the years he and his three sons developed it into a chain and in 1938 Kohl's incorporated.

Kohl opened a department store (half apparel half hard goods) in 1962 next door to a Kohl's grocery. In the mid-1960s he hired William Kellogg (no association with the cereal Kelloggs) a twentysomething buyer in the basement discount department at Milwaukee's Boston Store for his expertise in budget retailing. Kohl and Kellogg began developing the pattern for the store carving out a niche between upscale department stores and discounters (offering department store quality at discount store prices).

Kohl's went public in 1992

EXECUTIVES

Executive Vice President General Merch, Jack Boyle
Svp Marketing, Julie Gardner
Chairman President And Ceo, Kevin B. Mansell, $1,400,441 total compensation
Sevp And Chief Administrative Officer, Richard D. (Rick) Schepp, $911,250 total compensation
Cfo, Bruce H. Besanko
Ceo-elect, Michelle Gass, $1,113,750 total compensation
President, Sona Chawla, $1,113,750 total compensation
Vice President Of Application Management Development, Dennis Kester
Vice President Of Human Resources Stores, Kate Beck
Vice President Of Procurement, Chris Montgomery
Innovation Vice President, Ratnakar Lavu
Vp Of Corporate Communications, Jen Johnson
Vice President Information Systems, Shelley Mathwick
Assistant Vice President Credit Market, Brent Cook
Vice President, Andy Jaskaniec
Territory Vice President Of Loss Prevention, David Ruffing
Vice President Finance, Gary Stoltmann
Vice President Portfolio Management, Laura Berg
Executive Vice President Marketing, William Setliff
Vice President Compensation And Analytics, Matt Carpenter
Vice President District Manager, Randy Blackburn
Senior Vice President Dmm Merchandising, Larry Azar
Vice President Internal Audit, Steve Zamansky
Senior Vice President Fraud Operations, Troy Carrothers
Vice President Human Resources, Merle Mack
Vp Information Technology, Sunil Bhardwaj
Svp Technology, Ritch Houdek
Vice President Of Application Development, Scott Vifquain
Vice President Of Strategic Sourcing And Procurement, David Maley
Vice President Of Application Development, Dan Mueller
Executive Vice President, Will Setliff
Vice President Finance, Tom Taugher
Vice President District Manager, Shane Knoy
Executive Vice President General Merch, Steve Thomas
Vice President Production, Ron Katanick
Vice President Of Property Development, Mark D Griepentrog
Vice President Of Trend, Sofia Wacksman
Svp Human Resource, Dallas Moon
Vice President Administration, Gregg Bartel
Svp Loss Prevention, Randy Meadows
Executive Vice President General Merchandise Manager Men 's And Kids, Jeff Manby
Senior Vice President, Pat Peery
Vice President District Manager, Dave Schmit
Vice President District Manager, Stan Kirchgessner
Vice President, Charles Mangini
Senior Vice President Logistics, Gregg Barta
Vice President Sales, Brenda Thompson
Executive Vice President Of Store Administration, Janelle Havner

Senior Vice President E Commerce And Strategy, Michael Molitor
Vice President Finance, Gary Stoltman
Svp Merchandise Planning And Allocation, Kelli Harpel
Vice President Of Data Processing, Lynn Allison
Vice President And Director Distribution Operations, Reginald Davis
Territory Vice President Loss Prevention, Jeff Schmit
Vice President Consumer Public Relations And Social Media, Lisa Hellman
Executive Vice President Operations And Business S, David Brearton
Executive Vice President Research Development And, Jean Spence
Vice President Digital Technology, Klarissa Marenitch
Vp Of Pricing And Promotions, Lee Mackedanz
Vice President, Richard Kohl
Board Member, Nina Vaca
Board Member, Frank Sica
Board Member, John Schlifske
Board Member, Adrianne Shapira
Board Member, Jonas Prising
Secretary, Arlene Montalvo
Secretary, Tandra Wright
Auditors: Ernst & Young LLP

LOCATIONS

HQ: Kohl's Corp.
N56 W17000 Ridgewood Drive, Menomonee Falls, WI 53051
Phone: 262 703-7000   **Fax:** 262 703-6373
Web: www.kohls.com

2018 Stores

	No.
Midwest	312
West	237
Southeast	186
Northeast	158
South Central	150
Mid-Atlantic	116
Total	**1,159**

PRODUCTS/OPERATIONS

2018 Sales

	$ mil.	% of total
Women's	5,366	27
Men's	4,025	20
Home	3,642	18
Children's	2,492	12
Footwear	1,917	9
Accessories	1,725	9
Other	1,062	5
Total	**20,229**	**100**

2018 Store Locations

	No.
Strip centers	780
Freestanding	297
Community & regional malls	82
Total	**1,159**

Selected National Brands

adidas
Arrow
Calphalon
Candies
Carter's
Chaps
Columbia
Cuisinart
Daisy Fuentes
Dickies
Dockers
everGirl
George Foreman
Gloria Vanderbilt Home
Gold Toe
Haggar
Hanes

Healthtex
Henckels
HoMedics
Jockey
KitchenAid
Krups
Laura Ashley Lifestyles
Lee
l.e.i.
Levi's
Mudd
NIKE
Nine & Company
Oneida
OshKosh B'Gosh
Pfaltzgraff
Pyrex
Reebok
Skechers
Speedo
Unionbay
Urban Pipeline
Villager

Selected Private-label and Exclusive Brands
Apt. 9
Croft & Barrow
Elle
Food Network
Jumping Beans
LC Lauren Conrad
Simply Vera
SO
Sonoma Goods for Life

COMPETITORS

Amazon.com	Old Navy
Ascena Retail	Ross Stores
Bed Bath & Beyond	Saks
Belk	Stein Mart
Burlington Coat	TJX Companies
Factory	Target Corporation
Dillard's	Wal-Mart
Macy's	

HISTORICAL FINANCIALS
Company Type: Public

Income Statement — FYE: February 1

	REVENUE ($ mil.)	NET INCOME ($ mil.)	NET PROFIT MARGIN	EMPLOYEES
02/20	19,974	691	3.5%	122,000
02/19	20,229	801	4.0%	129,000
02/18*	19,095	859	4.5%	137,000
01/17	18,686	556	3.0%	138,000
01/16	19,204	673	3.5%	140,000
Annual Growth	1.0%	0.7%	—	(3.4%)

*Fiscal year change

2020 Year-End Financials

Debt ratio: 23.00%
Return on equity: 12.62%
Cash ($ mil.): 723
Current ratio: 1.68
Long-term debt ($ mil.): 3,223

No. of shares (mil.): 156
Dividends
Yield: 0.0%
Payout: 61.3%
Market value ($ mil.): 6,669

	STOCK PRICE ($) FY Close	P/E High/Low		PER SHARE ($) Earnings	Dividends	Book Value
02/20	42.75	17	10	4.37	2.68	34.94
02/19	66.69	17	12	4.84	2.44	33.91
02/18*	63.47	13	7	5.12	2.20	32.30
01/17	39.00	19	11	3.11	2.00	29.75
01/16	49.75	23	12	3.46	1.80	29.52
Annual Growth	(3.7%)	—	—	6.0%	10.5%	4.3%

*Fiscal year change

Kraft Heinz Co (The)

Bringing together packaged food giants Kraft Foods and H.J. Heinz The Kraft Heinz Company is one of the largest food and beverage companies in the world. In addition to its two namesakes the company's portfolio of iconic brands (eight of them billion-dollar brands) include such names as Oscar Meyer Capri Sun Ore-Ida Kool-Aid Jell-O Planters Philadelphia Lunchables Maxwell House and Velveeta. Kraft Heinz which generates nearly half its sales from condiments and sauces and cheese and dairy products offers its goods through retailers and foodservice distributors in more than 200 countries across the globe.

Operations
Kraft Heinz's operations are organized across some half a dozen specific product categories. Its largest categories are condiments and sauces (about a quarter of sales) and cheese and dairy (about 20%). Others include frozen and chilled foods; meats and seafood; and ambient or shelf-stable meals (at about 10% each); as well as refreshment beverages coffee infant and nutrition nuts and salted snacks and desserts toppings and baking.

The company's leading brands include Kraft and Heinz of course as well as Oscar Mayer Planters Maxwell House and Velveeta. It also licenses brands from third parties such as Capri-Sun TGI Fridays and McCafe.

Geographic Reach
Unlike many of its major competitors Kraft Heinz counts the US as its largest market by far accounting for about 70% of total revenue. Canada and the EMEA (Europe Middle East and Africa) region together contribute nearly 20% with the remaining revenue coming from Latin America and the Asia-Pacific region.

The company has co-headquarters in Pittsburgh Pennsylvania and Chicago Illinois. It also owns other facilities across the world including about 85 manufacturing and processing plants.

Sales and Marketing
Kraft Heinz's products are sold through its sales organizations and through independent brokers agents and distributors. This network sells to chain wholesale cooperative and independent grocery accounts as well as drug stores and pharmacies value and club stores and foodservice distributors. It also caters to hotels restaurants hospitals health care facilities and certain government agencies. Products are also sold online through various e-commerce platforms and retailers.

Kraft Heinz is heavily reliant on its largest customer Wal-Mart Stores which represents more than 20% of sales.

Financial Performance
Kraft Heinz's total revenue for the last five years has been fluctuating. It has an overall growth of 36% between 2015 and 2019. Its net revenue has also been fluctuating with a notable loss in 2018.

Net sales decreased 45% to $25 billion in 2019 compared to $26.3 billion in 2018 primarily due to the unfavorable impacts of foreign currency and acquisitions and divestitures.

Operating income increased 130% to income of $3.1 billion in 2019 compared to a loss of $10.2 billion in 2018. This increase was primarily driven by lower impairment losses in the current year.

Cash at the end of 2019 was $2.3 billion an increase of $1.1 billion from the prior year. Cash from operations contributed $3.6 billion to the coffers while investing activities added $1.5 billion mainly from sale of business. Financing activities used $3.9 billion primarily for payments of long term debt.

Strategy
With a new CEO taking the reins in mid-2019 the company is seeking to move past its problems with a renewed focus on brand building and organic growth powered by a better understanding of customers. Kraft Heinz sees initial opportunities in the Philadelphia Heinz and Planter's brands.

Kraft Heinz is currently actively reviewing the enterprise strategy for the company. As part of this strategic review the company expects to develop updates to the five-year operating plan in 2020 which could impact the allocation of investments among reporting units and brands and impact growth expectations and fair value estimates. Additionally as a result of this strategic review process Kraft Heinz could decide to divest certain non-strategic assets. As a result the ongoing development of the enterprise strategy and underlying detailed business plans could lead to the impairment of one or more of its reporting units or brands in the future.

Mergers and Acquisitions
In early 2019 Kraft Heinz completed the acquisition of Primal Nutrition LLC makers of Primal Kitchen branded products. California-based company its purchase price for this acquisition is $200M. "Primal Kitchen is an authentic premium and growing brand that complements our core Condiments & Sauces categories. We are excited to partner with the Company's strong team to drive growth across multiple categories and reach more consumers looking for these amazing products." said Paulo Basilio U.S. Zone President for Kraft Heinz.

Company Background
Kraft Heinz was formed from the 2015 merger of Kraft Foods and H.J. Heinz. Ultimately however it traces its history back some 150 years

EXECUTIVES

Head U.s. Meat And Dairy Business, Howard Friedman
Ceo And Director, Bernardo V. Hees, age 51, $1,000,000 total compensation
Evp Global Operations, Eduardo Pelleissone, age 46, $600,000 total compensation
Evp Global Foodservice, Emin Mammadov, age 43
Head U.s. Meals And Sauces Business, Eduardo Luz, age 47
Zone President United States, Paulo Basilio, age 45, $600,000 total compensation
Zone President Amea, Marcos Romaneiro, age 37, $395,437 total compensation
Zone President Latin America, Francisco Sa, age 54
Head U.s. Beverages And Snack Nuts Business, Tom Lopez
President U.s. Foodservice, David Toy
Svp Marketing Innovation Research And Development, Nina Barton
President Kraft Heinz Canada, Carlos Piani, $169,481 total compensation
Svp Global People Performance And Information Technology, Melissa Werneck
Zone President Europe, Rafael Oliveira
Head U.s. Commercial Finance, Andre Maciel
Vp And Category Head Planters, David Knopf, age 32
Vice President, Bill Durbin
National Account Manager, Angie Carpenter
Global Performance Vice President, Simone Hirakuri
Senior Vice President Of Sales, Michael Crouse
National Account Manager, Travis Ulrich
Sr V Pres Global General Couns, James Savina
Vice President Sales And Foodservice Canada, Dan Lafrance
Vice President Investor Relations, Chris Jakubik
Customer Vice President Sales, Betsy Wollney
Vp Of It, Gustavo De Souza

LOCATIONS

HQ: Kraft Heinz Co (The)
  One PPG Place, Pittsburgh, PA 15222
Phone: 412 456-5700
Web: www.kraftheinzcompany.com

2018 Sales

	$ mil.	% of total
US	18,122	69
Canada	2,173	8
EMEA	2,718	10
Rest of world	3,255	13
Total	26,268	100

PRODUCTS/OPERATIONS

2018 Sales

	$ mil.	% of total
Condiments and sauces	6,752	26
Cheese and dairy	5,287	20
Meats and seafood	2,505	9
Ambient meals	2,576	10
Frozen and chilled meals	2,548	10
Refreshment beverages	1,507	6
Coffee	1,438	5
Desserts toppings and baking	1,038	4
Nuts and salted snacks	967	4
Infant and nutrition	756	3
Other	894	3
Total	26,268	100

COMPETITORS

B&G Foods	Hormel
Campbell Soup	Kellogg
ConAgra	McCormick & Company
Frito-Lay	Mondelez International
General Mills	Nestlé USA
Hershey	Unilever PLC
Hillshire Brands	

HISTORICAL FINANCIALS

Company Type: Public

Income Statement

FYE: December 28

	REVENUE ($ mil.)	NET INCOME ($ mil.)	NET PROFIT MARGIN	EMPLOYEES
12/19	24,977	1,935	7.7%	37,000
12/18	26,268	(10,192)	—	38,000
12/17	26,232	10,999	41.9%	39,000
12/16*	26,487	3,632	13.7%	41,000
01/16	18,338	634	3.5%	42,000
Annual Growth	8.0%	32.2%	—	(3.1%)

*Fiscal year change

2019 Year-End Financials

Debt ratio: 28.83%	No. of shares (mil.): 1,221
Return on equity: 3.76%	Dividends
Cash ($ mil.): 2,279	Yield: 0.0%
Current ratio: 1.03	Payout: 101.2%
Long-term debt ($ mil.): 28,216	Market value ($ mil.): 38,608

	STOCK PRICE ($) FY Close	P/E High/Low	PER SHARE ($) Earnings	Dividends	Book Value
12/19	31.62	30 16	1.58	1.60	42.28
12/18	43.57	— —	(8.36)	2.50	42.34
12/17	77.76	11 8	8.95	2.45	54.17
12/16*	87.32	32 24	2.81	2.35	47.15
01/16	72.76	— —	(0.34)	1.70	54.37
Annual Growth	(18.8%)	— —	—	(1.5%)	(6.1%)

*Fiscal year change

Kroger Co (The)

Kroger is the world's largest traditional grocer despite Wal-Mart overtaking the chain as the world's largest seller of groceries years ago. It operates more than 2755 supermarkets in 35 states under variety of local banners; 2270 locations have pharmacies and more than 1565 have fuel centers. The company offers Pickup and Harris Teeter ExpressLane – personalized order online pick up at the store services – at about 1990 of its supermarkets and provide home delivery service to over 95% of Kroger households. It also has 35 food processing plants in the US mostly bakeries and dairies.

Operations

Kroger's supermarkets are generally operated under one of the following formats: combination food and drug stores multi-department stores marketplace stores or price impact warehouses.

Its supermarkets on average stock over 16000 private label items. Private label products are primarily produced and sold in three "tiers": Private Selection one of its premium quality brands; Kroger which represents the majority of its private label items; and Big K Check This Out and Heritage Farm which are some of its value brands. In addition the company continues to grow its natural and organic brand offerings with Simple Truth and Simple Truth Organic.

Approximately 30% of its brands and more than 40% of its grocery brands sold in its supermarkets are produced in production plants while the remaining brand items are produced by outside manufacturers. The company operates 35 food production plants consisting of primarily dairies (16) and deli or bakery (9) plants. Other plants include grocery product plants (5) beverage plants (2) cheese plants (2) and meat plants (1).

Kroger's retail operations represent almost all of its consolidated sales and is its only reportable segment. Additionally non-perishables accounted for about half of its total revenue while fresh merchandise accounts for about a quarter. Other product categories include supermarket fuel (over 10%) and Pharmacy (about 10%).

Geographic Reach

Cincinnati-based Kroger operates supermarkets in about 35 US states from coast to coast. Key markets include California (more than 300 locations) Texas (210) Ohio (205) and Georgia (170).

Sales and Marketing

Kroger offers a robust loyalty card program which offer discounts and other benefits to customers. The loyalty card program reaches 60 million households and is used in more than 95% of Kroger transactions. The company can leverage the shopping and personal data collected through the loyalty card program to develop targeted marketing strategies. Kroger also offers its customer shopping insights to product manufacturers through its Kroger Precision Marketing unit.

The Company's advertising costs totaled $854 million in 2019 $752 million in 2018 and $707 million in 2017.

Financial Performance

Kroger's revenue performance showed a steady growth (except for a slight decline in fiscal 2018) but profits has shown fluctuating trend for the past five years.

Revenue increased slightly to $122.3 billion in fiscal 2019 a 434 million increase from the year prior. The increase was due to an increase in total sales to retail customers without fuel partially offset by decreased supermarket fuel sales a reduction in convenience store sales due to the sale of our convenience store business unit in the first quarter of 2018 and decreased sales due to the disposal of Turkey Hill Dairy and You Technology in the first quarter of 2019.

Net income was $1.7 billion in fiscal year 2019 a 47% decrease from $3.1 billion in 2018.

Cash at the end of fiscal 2019 was $399 million a $30 million decrease from 2018. Cash provided by operating activities was $4.7 billion while investing activities used $2.6 billion. Financing activities used another $2.1 billion.

Strategy

Kroger's long-term growth strategy hinges on its successful execution of their Restock Kroger initiative. The four main areas of this initiative are: Redefine customer experience; Partner to create value: Develop talent; and Live its purpose. By executing the Restock Kroger framework it is repositioning its business by widening and deepening its competitive moats.

The Company's financial strategy is to continue to use its strong free cash flow to invest in the business to drive long-term sustainable growth through the identification of high-return projects. The Company will allocate capital toward driving profitable sales growth in stores and digital improving productivity and building a seamless digital ecosystem and supply chain.

Company Background

In 1883 Barney Kroger invested his life savings of $372 to open a grocery store at 66 Pearl Street in downtown Cincinnati. In 1972 Kroger became the first grocery retailer in America to test an electronic scanner. Mergers have played a key role in Kroger's growth over the years. In 1983 100 years after the company's founding Kroger merged with Dillon Companies Inc. in Kansas to become a coast-to-coast operator of food drug and convenience stores. The biggest merger in Kroger's history came in 1999 when the company teamed up with Fred Meyer Inc. in a $13 billion deal that created a supermarket chain with the broadest geographic coverage and widest variety of formats in the food retailing industry. In 2014 Kroger finalized its merger with Harris Teeter a regional chain of more than 200 stores. This merger brought to Kroger a well-known brand and complementary base of stores in high-growth markets primarily in the Mid-Atlantic region and the District of Columbia. Later that year Kroger merged with Vitacost.com an e-commerce company in the nutrition and healthy living market. In 2015 Kroger merged with Roundy's in Wisconsin adding Pick 'N Save Metro Market and Mariano's stores in Wisconsin and Illinois to the Kroger family.

HISTORY

Bernard Kroger was 22 when he started the Great Western Tea Company in 1883 in Cincinnati. Kroger lowered prices by cutting out middlemen sometimes by making products such as bread. Growing to 40 stores in Cincinnati and northern Kentucky the company became Kroger Grocery and Baking Company in 1902. It expanded into St. Louis in 1912 and grew rapidly during the 1910s and 1920s by purchasing smaller cash-strapped companies. Kroger sold his holdings in the company for $28 million in 1928 the year before the stock market crash and retired.

The company acquired Piggly Wiggly stores in the late 1920s and bought most of Piggly Wiggly's corporate stock which it held until the early 1940s. The chain reached its largest number of stores — a whopping 5575 — in 1929. (The Depression later trimmed that total.) A year later Kroger manager Michael Cullen suggested opening self-service low-price supermarkets but company executives demurred. Cullen left Kroger and began King Kullen the first supermarket. If he was ahead of his time at Kroger it wasn't by much; within five years the company had 50 supermarkets.

During the 1950s Kroger acquired companies with stores in Texas Georgia and Washington DC. It added New Jersey-based Sav-on drugstores in 1960 and it opened its first SupeRx drugstore in 1961. The company began opening larger supermarkets in 1971; between 1970 and 1980 Kroger's store count grew just 5% but its selling space nearly doubled.

In 1983 the grocer bought Kansas-based Dillons Food Stores (supermarkets and convenience stores) and Kwik Shop convenience stores. Kroger sold most of its interests in the Hook and SupeRx drug chains (which became Hook-SupeRx) in 1987 and focused on its food-and-drugstores. (It sold its remaining stake to Revco in 1994.) The next year it faced two separate takeover bids from the Herbert Haft family and from Kohlberg Kravis Roberts. The company warded off the raiders by borrowing $4.1 billion to pay a special dividend to shareholders and to buy shares for an employee stock plan.

To reduce debt Kroger sold most of its equity in Price Saver Membership Wholesale Clubs and its Fry's California stores. In 1990 the company made its first big acquisition since the 1988 restructuring by buying 29 Great Scott! supermarkets. Joseph Pichler became CEO that year.

Kroger sold its Time Saver Stores unit in 1995. In 1999 Kroger acquired Fred Meyer operator of about 800 stores mainly in the West in a $13 billion deal. Late in 1999 it announced it was buying nearly 75 stores (mostly in Texas) from Winn-Dixie Stores; the deal was called off in 2000 shortly after the FTC withheld its approval. But the company kept buying — acquisitions included 20 former Hannaford stores in Virginia in 2000 as well as 16 Nebraska food stores bought from food distributor Fleming and seven New Mexico stores bought from Furrs Supermarkets in 2001.

Kroger acquired 17 supermarkets (16 in the Houston area) from Albertson's (now Albertsons LLC) and another seven stores from Winn-Dixie in the Dallas/Fort Worth area in 2002.

In April 2003 Kroger introduced Naturally Preferred its own brand of some 140 natural and organic items including baby food pastas cereal snacks milk and soy products.

In 2012 with pharmacies in many of its stores nationwide Kroger purchased specialty pharmacy company Axium Pharmacy Holdings based in Florida. The move satisfied Kroger's long-term growth plans and allowed the grocery chain to serve customers that require complex drug therapies.

EXECUTIVES

Chairman And Ceo, W. Rodney McMullen, age 59, $1,251,781 total compensation
Evp And Cfo, J. Michael Schlotman, age 62, $850,360 total compensation
President Harris Teeter Supermarkets, Frederick J. (Fred) Morganthall, age 68, $691,487 total compensation
Sr V Pres, James Thorne
Evp And Cio, Christopher T. (Chris) Hjelm, age 58, $703,367 total compensation
Svp Drug/general Merchandising And Procurement, Michael J. (Mike) Donnelly, age 61, $757,036 total compensation
President Central Division, Katie Wolfram, age 65
President Mid-atlantic Division, Jerry L. Clontz
President Houston Division, Marlene Stewart, age 64
Vp Merchandising Fred Meyer Stores, Dan De La Rosa
Vp Manufacturing, Erin S. Sharp, age 62
President Dillons Division, Joe Grieshaber
President Nashville Division, Zane Day
Vp People Operations, Michael Marx
President Mariano's, Don Rosanova
President Smith's, Kenny Kimball
President Dillons Division, Colleen Juergensen
Group Vp And Chief Digital Officer, Yael Cosset, age 46
Senior Vice President, R Williams
Vice President, Jeremy Stover
Pharmacy Manager, Eric Manchester
Vice President Of Finance, Mary Adcock
Vp Digital Business, Matt Thompson
Director Of Surgery, Frank Zagar
Vice President, Bruce Gack
Vice President Finance Controller Quik Stop Division, Jim Bradshaw
Senior Vice President, Mark Tuffin
Svp Retail Divisions, Steve Mckinney
Vice President Of Marketing, Barbara White
Vice President Human Resource, Steve Jones
Pharmacy Manager, Peggy Gilligan
Pharmacy Manager, Diane Chance
Vice President Information Systems And Services, Nick Kaufman
Merchandising Vice President, Chris Albi
Senior Vice President New Business Development, Alessandro Tosolini
Vice President Of Brand Management, James Jenson
Pharmacy Manager, Gayle Townsend
Pharmacy Manager, Avi Bhatia
Vp Technical Strategy And Architecture, Ryan Kean
Vice President Sales And Marketing, Norm Carhill
Pharmacy Manager, Cc Hepburn
Department Head, Jeffrey Everling
Pharmacist (manager), Lauren Luken
Pharmd, Carrie Mott
Vice President Of Merchandising, Michael Cristal
Pharmacy Manager, Benjamin Thrailkill
Assistant Treasurer, Kathy Hanna
Auditors: PricewaterhouseCoopers LLP

LOCATIONS

HQ: Kroger Co (The)
1014 Vine Street, Cincinnati, OH 45202
Phone: 513 762-4000   **Fax:** 513 762-1400
Web: www.thekrogerco.com

PRODUCTS/OPERATIONS

2017 Sales

	$ mil.	% of total
Supermarket	96,900	84
Supermarket fuel sales	13,979	12
Other stores & manufacturing	4,458	4
Total	**115,337**	**100**

2017 Stores

	No.
Supermarkets & multidepartment stores	2,796
Convenience stores	784
Jewelry	319
Total	**3,899**

2017 Sales

	$ mil.	% of total
Non-perishable	60,220	52
Perishable	27,666	24
Fuel	13,979	12
Pharmacy	10,432	9
Other	3,040	3
Total	**115,337**	**100**

Selected Kroger Stores

Multidepartment stores
  Fred Meyer
Supermarkets
  Baker's
  City Market Food & Pharmacy
  Dillon Food Stores
  Fry's Food & Drug Stores
  Gerbes Supermarkets
  Harris Teeter Supermarkets
  Jay C Food Stores
  King Soopers
  Kroger
  Kroger Fresh Fare
  Owen's
  Pay Less Super Markets
  Quality Food Centers (QFC)
  Ralphs
  Scott's Food & Pharmacy
  Smith's Food & Drug Centers
Warehouse stores
  Food 4 Less
  FoodsCo
Jewelry stores
  Barclay Jewelers
  Fox's Jewelers
  Fred Meyer Jewelers
  Littman Jewelers
Food Production
  Bread and other baked goods
  Cheese
  Coffee
  Crackers
  Cultured products (cottage cheese yogurt)
  Deli products
  Fruit juices and fruit drinks
  Ice cream
  Juice
  Meat
  Milk
  Nuts
  Oatmeal
  Peanut butter
  Snacks
  Soft drinks
  Spaghetti sauce
  Water

Selected Private-Label Brands

Bath & Body Therapies (body and bath)
Banner brands (Kroger Ralphs King Soopers)
Everyday Living (kitchen gadgets)
FMV (For Maximum Value)
HD Design (upscale kitchen gadgets)
Moto Tech (automotive)
Naturally Preferred (premium quality natural and organic brand)
Office Works (office and school supplies)
Private Selection (premium quality brand)
Splash Spa (body and bath)
Splash Sport (body and bath)

COMPETITORS

99 Cents Only	Raley's
A&P	Randall's
Albertsons	Rite Aid
CVS	SUPERVALU
Costco Wholesale	Safeway
Dollar General	Save Mart
Family Dollar Stores	Stater Bros.
GNC	Sterling Jewelers
Giant Eagle	Target Corporation

H-E-B
Hy-Vee
IGA
Kmart
Marsh Supermarkets
Meijer
NBTY
Publix
Tesco
Vitamin Shoppe
Wal-Mart
Walgreen
Wegmans
Whole Foods
Winn-Dixie
Zale

HISTORICAL FINANCIALS

Company Type: Public

Income Statement

	REVENUE ($ mil.)	NET INCOME ($ mil.)	NET PROFIT MARGIN	EMPLOYEES
				FYE: February 1
02/20	122,286	1,659	1.4%	435,000
02/19	121,162	3,110	2.6%	453,000
02/18*	122,662	1,907	1.6%	449,000
01/17	115,337	1,975	1.7%	443,000
01/16	109,830	2,039	1.9%	431,000
Annual Growth	2.7%	(5.0%)	—	0.2%

*Fiscal year change

2020 Year-End Financials

Debt ratio: 31.10%
Return on equity: 20.18%
Cash ($ mil.): 399
Current ratio: 0.76
Long-term debt ($ mil.): 12,111

No. of shares (mil.): 788
Dividends
Yield: 0.0%
Payout: 29.4%
Market value ($ mil.): 21,166

	STOCK PRICE ($) FY Close	P/E High/Low		PER SHARE ($) Earnings	Dividends	Book Value
02/20	26.86	15	10	2.04	0.60	10.92
02/19	28.07	9	6	3.76	0.53	9.88
02/18*	29.34	16	9	2.09	0.49	7.97
01/17	33.36	20	14	2.05	0.45	7.25
01/16	38.81	37	16	2.06	0.40	7.05
Annual Growth	(8.8%)			—	(0.2%) 11.0%	11.5%

*Fiscal year change

L Brands, Inc

L Brands (formerly Limited Brands) is as much of a shopping-mall mainstay as food courts and teenagers. The company operates over 2900 specialty stores in North America the UK and China primarily under the Victoria's Secret PINK and Bath & Body Works (BBW) banners as well as corresponding websites and catalogs. Originally focused on apparel the company turned into a segment leader focused on women's intimate and other apparel personal care and beauty and home fragrance products. L Brands also owns apothecary C.O. Bigelow and The White Barn Candle Co. Most of the company's revenue are generated in the US. L Brands completed the sale of its La Senza business and the closing of all its Henri Bendel stores and websites in 2019.

Operations

L Brands has realigned its reportable segments into Victoria's Secret Bath & Body Works (BBW) and Victoria's Secret and Bath and Body Works International. Nearly 55% of sales come from domestic Victoria's Secret stores and direct channel operations. The Victoria's Secret segment sells women's intimate and other apparel personal care and beauty products under the Victoria's Secret and PINK brand names.

About 40% of sales come from the BBW segment. The Bath & Body Works segment sells personal care soaps sanitizers and home fragrance

products under the Bath & Body Works White Barn Candle Company C.O. Bigelow and other brand names.

The remaining revenue comes from Victoria's Secret and BBW International and other revenues which include the revenues from the company's sourcing function as well as sales from its previous Henri Bendel and La Senza operations. Victoria's Secret and Bath & Body Works International segments include the Victoria's Secret and Bath & Body Works company-owned and partner-operated stores.

Mast Global is a merchandise sourcing and production function serving the Company and its international partners and Corporate functions including non-core real estate equity investments and other governance functions such as treasury and tax.

Geographic Reach

In addition to its nearly 2700 US stores L Brands has about 230 company-owned retail stores in Canada the UK and China.

In addition to its company-owned stores L Brands' products are available at approximately 720 Victoria's Secret Victoria's Secret Beauty and Accessories and Bath & Body Works partner locations in more than 70 countries.

Based in Ohio the company also has several distribution and product development facilities located in New York and Ohio as well as Canada Hong Kong mainland China and various other international locations.

Sales and Marketing

L Brands utilizes merchandise presentation in-store marketing music and its sales associates to reinforce the image represented by its brands. It also uses marketing advertising and promotional programs to attract customers through various media including social media websites mobile applications email print and television.

The company spent $428 million on advertising and marketing expenses in 2019 down from $476 million and $383 million in 2018 and 2017 respectively.

Financial Performance

L Brands has seen limited revenue growth in recent years as it has struggled amid intense competition. Its annual revenues have risen 6% since 2016. The company's net income has fluctuated in the last five years with its peak at $1.3 billion in 2016.

Revenue decreased to $12.9 billion in 2019 an approximately 5% decrease from the year prior. The decrease was driven by a comparable sales decrease of 1% as opposed to a 3% increase of last year's.

The company experienced a net loss of $366 million in 2019 a drastic fall from last year's net income of $644 million. Decrease in operating income as well as a goodwill impairment charge of $720 million due to the company's Greater China and Victoria's Secret reporting units.

Cash on hand at the end of 2019 was $1.5 billion. Cash provided by operating activities was $1.2 billion in 2019 while investing activities used $480 million mostly for capital expenditures. Financing activities used another $666 million mainly for payments of long-term debts repayments of foreign facilities and for dividends.

Strategy

Continuing to battle underperformance at its top brands L Brands has made significant changes to its business to refocus its resources on core categories and accelerate growth. It is focused on growing its business in North America extending its brand internationally and further focus on the fundamentals of their business.

As part of its strategic plan the company announced the sale of 55% of the Victoria's Secret business to Sycamore for approximately $525 mil-

lion. The company believes this transaction will highlight the value and performance of the stand-alone Bath & Body Works business enhance management focus and reduce structural complexity.

The company will continue to invest in its White Barn concept which continues to yield strong results. By 2020 the company plans on increasing the square footage of its Bath & Body Works North America through the opening of new Bath & Body Works stores. Aside from opening new stores in North America it has also opened more than 40 new stores internationally bringing the total stores in the Middle East Latin America Southeast Asia and Europe to approximately 300 stores.

HISTORY

After a disagreement with his father in 1963 over the operation of the family store (Leslie's) Leslie Wexner then 26 opened the first Limited store in Columbus Ohio with $5000 borrowed from his aunt. The company was named from Wexner's desire to do one product line well — moderately priced fashionable attire for teenagers and young women.

When The Limited went public in 1969 it had only five stores but the rapid development of large covered malls spurred growth to 100 stores by 1976. Two years later The Limited acquired MAST Industries an international apparel purchasing and importing company. The company opened Express in 1980 to serve the teen market.

The Limited grew with acquisitions including the 1982 purchases of Lane Bryant (large sizes) and Victoria's Secret (lingerie). That year it formed the Brylane fashion catalog division and acquired Roaman's a bricks-and-mortar and catalog merchandiser of plus sizes.

Wexner bought The Lerner Stores (budget women's apparel) and Henri Bendel (high fashion) in 1985 sportswear retailer Abercrombie & Fitch (A&F) in 1988 and London-based perfumer Penhaligon's in 1990 (sold in 1997). The Limited introduced several in-store shops including Cacique (French lingerie) in 1988 and Limited Too (girls' fashions) which were later expanded into stand-alone stores. It also launched Structure (men's sportswear) in 1989 and Bath & Body Works shops in 1990. All of these stores were in malls often strategically clustered together.

The company closed many The Limited and Lerner stores in 1993 and sold 60% of its Brylane catalog unit to Freeman Spogli (Brylane went public in 1997). It opened four Bath & Body Works stores in the UK (its first non-US stores) to compete with British rival The Body Shop.

In 1994 The Limited bought Galyan's Trading Company a chain of sporting goods superstores. The company began spinning off its businesses while keeping controlling stakes; it spun off Intimate Brands (Victoria's Secret Cacique and Bath & Body Works) in 1995 and A&F in 1996. (The Limited sold its remaining 84% in A&F in 1998.)

The Limited closed more than 100 of its women's apparel stores in 1997 and Intimate Brands shuttered the Cacique chain; the next year The Limited closed nearly 300 more stores companywide (excluding the Intimate Brands chains) and the majority of its Henri Bendel stores.

In 1998 The Limited launched White Barn Candle Co. (candle and home fragrance stores). The following year the company spun off Limited Too its most successful chain as Too Inc. and reduced its interest in Galyan's to 40%. (Galyan's management and buyout firm Freeman Spogli bought the remaining 60% of the sporting goods chain.) The Limited (as well as Intimate Brands) declared a two-for-one stock split in 2000.

To boost profits in 2001 The Limited folded the Structure brand into the Express unit and spun off its Galyan's and Alliance Data Systems subsidiaries retaining 22% and 20% respectively. The Limited sold its Lane Bryant unit to Charming Shoppes for $335 million that year.

The Limited bought back the remaining shares of Intimate Brands it did not already own in March 2002 and over the course of the year phased it into a business segment. In May 2002 the company changed its name to Limited Brands from The Limited. Later that year Limited Brands sold off its remaining stake in Lerner New York and in late 2003 sold its Structure label (which it had rebranded as Express Men's) to Sears Roebuck and Co.

In 2007 Limited Brands completed its acquisition of lingerie maker and retailer La Senza based in Montreal for about $600 million. It also sold a 75% stake in its 251-store Limited Stores business to Sun Capital Partners taking a loss on the sale. In mid-2010 it sold the rest. Three years later in 2013 it finally changed the company name from The Limited to L Brands. In 2018 the company agreed to sell its La Senza business and shuttered its Henri Bendel business as it refocused on its biggest brands.

EXECUTIVES

Evp And Cfo, Stuart B. Burgdoerfer, age 56, $890,923 total compensation

Chairman And Ceo, Leslie H. Wexner, age 82, $2,000,000 total compensation

Evp And Cio, Steven M. Stone, age 59

Coo, Charles C. (Charlie) McGuigan, age 63, $1,290,385 total compensation

President And Ceo Bath & Body Works, Nicholas P.M. (Nick) Coe, age 57, $1,080,769 total compensation

Assistant Vice President Stores Staffing, Susan Moorer

Senior Vice President And Chief Techno, Kurt Schnieders

Vice President, Kyle Kuhn

Vice President Human Resources, Cheryl Stevens

Executive Vice President Retail Operations, Mark Giresi

Vice President Project Management, Beth Knuckles

Senior Vice President, Claudia Lucas

Assistant Vice President Compensation, Gina Johnson

Senior Vice President, Paul Jones

Senior Vice President Human Resources Limited Brands Victorias Secret Direct, Sheena Null Foley

Vice President Application Services, Nada Aried

Vice President Retail Selling Technologies, Anne Ritchey

Vice President, Bryan Eccard

Vice President Integration Global Sourcing And Logistics, Laura Warren

Avp Ecommerce, Ryan Davis

Vice President Brand Human Resources, Andre Joyner

Evp And Chief Human Resources Officer, Shelley Milano

Vice President, Polly Sinesi

Associate Vice President Production Operations, Lisa Szekely

Vice President Production And Operations, Marlene Manser

Vice President Legal, Heidi Yurkiw

Svp Enterprise Technology Operations, Brian Belcher

Vice President Production And Sourcing, Chris Kennedy

Executive Vice President Licensing, Alessandro Fabrini

Assistant Vice President Product Quality And Manufacturing Engineering, Steve Smith

Ass Vice President Consumer Insights, Cliona Miller

Vice President Human Resources Shared Services, Joyce Stearn

Senior Vice President Marketing, Edward Wolf

Vice President Marketing, Shannon Glass

Assistant Vice President Beauty Finance, Shannon Damen

Vice President, Thomas Mc Fadden

Avp Financial Reporting, Kevin Wynk

Senior Vice President International, Mary Mitchell

Vice President Store Design And Construction, Rebecca Cheng

Treasurer, Timothy Faber

Board Member, David Kollat

Board Member, Donna James

Board Member, Abigail S Wexner

Auditors: Ernst & Young LLP

LOCATIONS

HQ: L Brands, Inc
Three Limited Parkway, Columbus, OH 43230
Phone: 614 415-7000
Web: www.lb.com

PRODUCTS/OPERATIONS

2017 Stores

	No.
Bath & Body Works U.S.	1,591
Victoria's Secret U.S.	1,131
La Senza Canada	122
Bath & Body Works Canada	102
Victoria's Secret Canada	46
Victoria's Secret Beauty and Accessories	31
Henri Bendel	29
Victoria's Secret U.K.	18
La Senza U.S.	4
Total	**3,074**

2017 Sales

	$ mil.	% of total
Victoria's Secret	7,781	62
Bath & Body Works	3,852	31
Victoria's Secret and Bath & Body Works International	423	3
Other	518	4
Total	**12,574**	**100**

Selected Retail Brands

Bath & Body Works
C.O. Bigelow
Henri Bendel
La Senza
Pink
The White Barn Candle Company
Victoria's Secret

COMPETITORS

Abercrombie & Fitch	Macy's
American Eagle Outfitters	Mary Kay
Avon	Natori
Body Shop	Nordstrom
CVS	Revlon
Dillard's	Saks
Estée Lauder	Sephora USA
Frederick's of Hollywood	Shiseido Americas
Fruit of the Loom	Target Corporation
Hanesbrands	The Gap
Jockey International	Ulta
Kiehl's	VF Corporation
	Wal-Mart
	Warnaco Group

HISTORICAL FINANCIALS

Company Type: Public

Income Statement

FYE: February 1

	REVENUE ($ mil.)	NET INCOME ($ mil.)	NET PROFIT MARGIN	EMPLOYEES
02/20	12,914	(366)	—	94,400
02/19	13,237	644	4.9%	88,900
02/18*	12,632	983	7.8%	93,200
01/17	12,574	1,158	9.2%	93,600
01/16	12,154	1,253	10.3%	87,900
Annual Growth	1.5%	—	—	1.8%

*Fiscal year change

2020 Year-End Financials

Debt ratio: 54.80%	No. of shares (mil.): 277
Return on equity: —	Dividends
Cash ($ mil.): 1,499	Yield: 0.0%
Current ratio: 1.37	Payout: —
Long-term debt ($ mil.): 5,487	Market value ($ mil.): 6,415

	STOCK PRICE ($) FY Close	P/E High/Low		PER SHARE ($) Earnings	Dividends	Book Value
02/20	23.16	—	—	(1.33)	1.20	(5.41)
02/19	27.15	21	11	2.31	2.40	(3.16)
02/18*	47.51	18	10	3.42	2.40	(2.69)
01/17	59.01	24	15	3.98	4.40	(2.55)
01/16	96.15	23	18	4.22	4.00	(0.89)
Annual Growth	(29.9%)	—	—	—	(26.0%)	—

*Fiscal year change

L3Harris Technologies Inc

L3Harris Technologies (formerly Harris Corp. and L3 Technologies) is an agile global aerospace and defense technology innovator delivering end-to-end solutions that meet customers' mission-critical needs that provide advance defense and commercial technologies across air land sea space and cyber domains for government and commercial customers in approximately 130 countries. It makes tactical communications and other integrated vision solutions; air traffic management; and intelligence surveillance and reconnaissance systems. Although about three-quarters of L3Harris' revenue comes from US government agencies particularly the Department of Defense it also has customers in the commercial sector. In 2019 the former Harris Corp. and L3 Technologies combined to form L3Harris Technologies the sixth largest defense contractor in the US.

Change in Company Type

Harris Corp. in 2019 merged with L3 Technologies to form L3Harris Technologies a company with around $10 billion in revenue. The all-stock deal resulted in Harris shareholders owning about 55% of the company and L3 shareholders owning the rest. The company falls in line behind Lockheed Martin Boeing General Dynamics and Northrop Grumman as one of the biggest defense contractors in the US and in the top 10 internationally.

Operations

L3Harris operated in four business segments.

The Integrated Mission segment approximately 30% of revenue provides multi-mission ISR including fleet management support services sensor development modifications and periodic depot maintenance; command control communications computers and cyber intelligence surveillance and reconnaissance equipment for maritime platforms. It also makes advanced EO/IR sensors and surveillance and targeting systems and provide modernization and life extension maintenance upgrade and support services for military aircraft.

The Space and Airborne Systems segment roughly 25% of revenue provides intelligence space protection geospatial complete Earth observation universe exploration positioning navigation and timing and environmental equipment for national security defense civil and commercial customers. Among its products are advanced sensors antennas and payloads as well as ground processing and information analytics.

Its Communication Systems segment nearly 25% of revenue develops and makes tactical radio communications SATCOM terminals and night vision systems and equipment for public safety networks.

The Aviation Systems segment over 20% of revenue provides precision engagement sensors and systems small UAVs antennas and arrays RF amplifiers and microwave electronic devices. This segment also provides airport security and detection solutions commercial and military pilot training and flight and maintenance simulation solutions to commercial airlines aircraft manufacturers DoD and foreign military agencies and mission-critical infrastructure communications and networking solutions for ATM for the U.S. Federal Aviation Administration ("FAA") and international airspace national service providers.

The product sales accounts for approximately 75% of the company's total revenue.

Geographic Reach

Headquartered in Melbourne Florida L3Harris operates approximately 400 locations in Canada Europe Australia the Middle East South America Africa Asia and the US. Customers in the US account for around 70% of revenue.

Sales and Marketing

L3Harris largest customers being various departments of the US government agencies such as Department of Defense and their prime contractors the U.S. Intelligence Community the U.S. Department of Homeland Security foreign governments and domestic and foreign commercial customers. . US government-related revenue including prime contractors and supported foreign defense organizations accounts for nearly 75% of sales.

Financial Performance

Revenue rose 36% to $2.4 billion in 2020 (ended June) from 2019.

Net income dipped about $127 million to $822 million in 2020 from 2019.

The company's coffers held $824 million in cash in 2020 compared to $530 million the year before. In 2020 operations generated $939 million while investing activities used $1.3 billion and financing activities used $2 billion.

Strategy

In recent years L3Harris have successfully integrated Exelis reshaped The Company's portfolio of businesses to focus on high-growth high-margin technology-differentiated businesses combined with L3 in a transformative merger of equals and have made investments in technology and innovation that have led to several new product launches and strategic program awards. Execution of this multi-year strategy set the stage for financial results during the Fiscal Transition Period that have exceeded the targets we set at the beginning of the period.

The company has divested services businesses to narrow its focus on technology and it has reorganized to take advantage of similar functions among its businesses. The new segments are In-

tegrated Mission Systems Space and Airborne Systems Communication Systems and Aviation Systems.

L3Harris plans to reduce costs by about $500 million eliminating duplication combining processes and other methods.

While its plans to partner with other defense contractors to get parts of contracts its scope should enable the company to move into a prime contracting role in some of its areas of expertise such as communications networking and electronics.

Mergers and Acquisitions

Harris Corporation and L3 Technologies announced that they have received the necessary regulatory approvals for their all-stock merger in 2019. Upon closing Harris will be renamed L3Harris Technologies Inc. and shares of L3Harris common stock will trade on the NYSE under ticker symbol "LHX". L3 shares will cease trading upon market and convert into 1.3 L3Harris shares for each L3 share.

EXECUTIVES

Chairman President And Ceo, William M. (Bill) Brown, age 57, $1,172,913 total compensation

Svp And Chief Global Business Development Officer, Dana A. Mehnert, age 58, $527,770 total compensation

Svp Integration And Engineering, Sheldon J. Fox, age 62, $521,346 total compensation

Vp Environmental-energy Solutions Business Government Communications Systems Division, Carl D'Alessandro, age 56

Svp Human Resources And Administration, Robert L. Duffy, age 52, $459,885 total compensation

Cio, Henry Debnam

President Electronic Systems, Edward J. (Ed) Zoiss, age 54

President Space And Intelligence Systems, William H. (Bill) Gattle, age 58

President Communication Systems, Christopher D. (Chris) Young, age 59, $411,749 total compensation

Svp And Cfo, Rahul Ghai, age 48, $376,238 total compensation

Senior Vice President Of Business Development, Alex Heidt

Vice President Corporate Technology, Kent Buchanon

Vice President Controller, Daniel Heneghan

Vice President Operations, Paul North

Vice President Sales, John Koening

Broker And Vice President, George Hurst

Vice President Products And Systems, Shawn Baerlocher

Senior Vice President, Neal Serven

Vice President Information Technology, Michele St Mary

Vice President, Brett Kleefisch

Vice President, Daniel Flugstad

Vice President General Counsel, Eugene Cavallucci

Vice President Information Technology, Mark Gawron

Vice President, Paul Eisner

Vice President Human Resources, Ken Laprade

Vice President Lean Six Sigma, Phil Burroughs

Vice President Finance Public Safety And Professional Communications, William Cullen

Vice President, Erick Sanz

Vp And Managing Director Middle East Operations, Chris Tucker

Vice President Business Development, Jeff Smith

Board Member, Thomas Dattilo

Engineering Team Manager Treasurer, David Bruder

Treasurer, Steve Thompson

Treasurer, Harmon David

Auditors: Ernst & Young LLP

LOCATIONS

HQ: L3Harris Technologies Inc
1025 West NASA Boulevard, Melbourne, FL 32919
Phone: 321 727-9100
Web: www.l3harris.com

2019 sales

	$ mil.	% of total
US	6,530	96
Other countries	271	4
Total	**6,817**	**100**

PRODUCTS/OPERATIONS

2019 sales

	$ mil.	% of total
Communication Systems	2,177	32
Space and Intelligence Systems	2,057	30
Electronic Systems	2,583	38
Adjustments	(16)	38
Total	**6,801**	**100**

Selected Product Groups

Government Communications Systems
  Civil programs
  Aviation
  Weather
  IT services
  Mission command-and-control
  National intelligence programs
Radio-frequency (RF) Communications
  Antennas and accessories
  Information assurance
  Internet protocol voice and data networks
  Public safety
  Tactical radio communications

COMPETITORS

BAE Systems Inc.	Motorola Solutions
Boeing	Northrop Grumman
General Dynamics	Raytheon
IBM	United Technologies
Lockheed Martin	

HISTORICAL FINANCIALS

Company Type: Public

Income Statement
FYE: January 3

	REVENUE ($ mil.)	NET INCOME ($ mil.)	NET PROFIT MARGIN	EMPLOYEES
01/20*	9,263	822	8.9%	50,000
06/19	6,801	949	14.0%	18,200
06/18	6,182	718	11.6%	17,500
06/17	5,900	553	9.4%	17,000
07/16	7,467	324	4.3%	21,000
Annual Growth	5.5%	26.2%	—	24.2%

*Fiscal year change

2020 Year-End Financials

Debt ratio: 18.14%
Return on equity: 12.25%
Cash ($ mil.): 824
Current ratio: 1.57
Long-term debt ($ mil.): 6,694

No. of shares (mil.): 218
Dividends
  Yield: 1.3%
  Payout: 35.8%
Market value ($ mil.): 45,930

	STOCK PRICE ($) FY Close	P/E High/Low		PER SHARE ($) Earnings	Dividends	Book Value
01/20*	210.47	58	48	3.67	2.87	103.50
06/19	189.13	25	16	7.86	2.74	28.37
06/18	144.54	28	18	5.92	2.28	28.09
06/17	109.08	25	18	4.44	2.12	24.48
07/16	82.59	34	27	2.59	2.00	24.52
Annual Growth	26.3%	—	—	9.1%	9.4%	43.3%

*Fiscal year change

Laboratory Corporation of America Holdings

Laboratory Corporation of America (LabCorp) is a top provider of clinical laboratory services performing blood and other tests on more than 3 million specimens a day. Its customers include managed care organizations contract research organizations (CROs) hospitals doctors government agencies drug companies independent clinical labs food and nutritional companies and employers. Services range from routine urinalyses HIV tests and Pap smears to specialty testing for diagnostic genetics disease monitoring forensics identity clinical drug trials and allergies. Through LabCorp Diagnostics and Covance it provides end-to-end drug development support. LabCorp operates about 60 primary labs where tests are performed.

Operations

LabCorp operates through two primary segments: LabCorp Diagnostics (LCD) and Covance Drug Development (CCD).

The LCD segment which accounts for around 60% of LabCorp's annual revenue offers nearly 5000 different tests. Many of the tests it performs each year are routine tests (including blood chemistry analyses urinalyses blood cell counts and HIV tests) and nutritional chemistry and safety tests. It also offers specialty testing services for women's health allergies infectious disease oncology pain management and other areas. Covance (around 40% of revenue) provides end-to-end drug development medical device and companion diagnostic development solutions from early-stage research to clinical development and commercial market access.

Geographic Reach

Most of LabCorp's operations are conducted through its extensive network of facilities throughout the US (which accounts for about 80% of revenue). The company also has joint ventures in Canada.

Covance operates a network of facilities in the US Switzerland Belgium Singapore and China. Covance has pre-clinical laboratories in Wisconsin Virginia Michigan and Indiana.

It also operates labs in the UK Germany and China. Altogether LabCorp based in Burlington North Carolina operates in about 100 countries.

Sales and Marketing

LCD offers its diagnostic services through a sales force focused on serving the specific needs of customers in different market segments. These market segments generally include primary care women's health specialty medicine (e.g. infectious disease endocrinology gastroenterology and rheumatology) oncology ACOs and hospitals and health systems. LabCorp's LCD segment receives about 15% of its net revenue from Medicare and Medicaid programs.

CDD's global sales activities are conducted by sales personnel in North America Europe and the Asia-Pacific region. The sales force provides customer coverage across the biopharmaceutical industry for services including lead optimization pre-clinical safety assessment analytical services clinical trials central laboratories biomarkers and companion diagnostics market access and technology solutions.

Financial Performance

LabCorp's revenue has grown by 36% over the past five years.

In 2019 revenue rose about 2% to about $11.6 billion about a $221 million more than 2018. The 2019 revenue was primarily driven by an increase in the CDD segment.

LabCorp's net income fell to $823.8 million in 2019 from $883.7 million in 2018.

The company had $337.5 million in cash in 2019 compared to $426.8 million the year before. In 2019 operations produced $1.4 billion and investing activities used $1.3 billion while financing activities used $253 million.

Strategy

One of LabCorp's key selling points is the end-to-end nature of the data it collects throughout the company from drug development to testing to trials. The company's customers see the data generated in early phase development as a foundation to the ensuing trial and maintain their relationship with the company.

Part of the Company's strategy involves deploying capital in investments that enhance the Company's business which includes pursuing strategic acquisitions to strengthen the Company's scientific capabilities and enhance therapeutic expertise enhance esoteric testing and global drug development capabilities and increase presence in key geographic areas. Since 2015 LabCorp has invested net cash of some $7.2 billion and equity of $1.8 billion in strategic acquisitions. The company is focused on expanding its advanced testing capabilities especially in the areas of genetic and cancer testing.

Key acquisition in 2019 was of Georgióbased MNG.

Closer to consumers LabCorp has partnered with Walgreens to offer diagnostic tests in stores over the next few years. The in-store centers are branded LabCorp at Walgreens and provide specimen collection services for LabCorp testing.

Mergers and Acquisitions

In 2019 LabCorp acquired Georgióbased MNG which specializes in complex biochemical testing for neurology. MNG expands LabCorp's capabilities in neurology and neurogenetics.

EXECUTIVES

Evp Cfo And Treasurer, Glenn A. Eisenberg, age 58, $653,438 total compensation
Ceo Covance Drug Development, John D. Ratliff, age 60
Svp Chief Legal Officer Secretary And Chief Compliance Officer, F. Samuel Eberts, age 60, $486,875 total compensation
Chairman President And Ceo, David P. (Dave) King, age 62, $1,133,333 total compensation
Svp And Cio, Lance V. Berberian, age 57, $396,112 total compensation
Director Of Nursing, Scott Fleming
Vice President Information Technology Business Relations, George Meister
Senior Vice President, Dale Phipps
Vice President Of Human Resources Atlantic Division, Mickey McGinn
Vp Of It, Devin Lorsson
Senior Vice President Chief Medical Officer, Mark Brecher
Vice President Information Technology Enterprise Solutions, Mahesh Nair
Senior Vice President And Chief Supply Chain Officer, Mark Schroeder
Vice President Information Technology, Mark Ysteboe
Vice President, Traci Butler
Associate Vp And Technical Director Dna Identification Testing Division, Uwe Heine
Medical Director Mid America Division, Kyle Eskue
Medical Director West Division, Praveena Yetur
Medical Director Northeast Division, Araceli Reyes
Vice President And Director Medical Drug Monitoring; Discipline Director Forensic Toxicology, Glynn Chaney
Assistant Vice President And Information Technology Director Atlantic Division, Ronald K Tirpak
Senior Vice President, Chris Bosler
Vice President Translational Research, Margery Connelly
Executive Vice President, Ben Miller
Vice President, James Whelan
Executive Vice President And Upstate Market Leader, Melissa Fuller
Assistant Vice President Information Technology (viromed Laboratories), Vickie Grawey
Vice President, Carl Epple
Assistant Vice President Pre Analytical, Edwin Johnson
Vice President Human Resources, Ford Patrick
Senior Vice President Information Technology Project Management, Glenn Mogolowitz
Senior Vice President, Tom Kaminski
Auditors: DELOITTE & TOUCHE LLP

LOCATIONS

HQ: Laboratory Corporation of America Holdings
358 South Main Street, Burlington, NC 27215
Phone: 336 229-1127
Web: www.labcorp.com

2018 Sales

	% of total
US	78
Switzerland	5
Canada	3
United Kingdom	4
Other	10
Total	**100**

PRODUCTS/OPERATIONS

2018 Sales

	$ mil.	% of total
LCD	7,030	62
CDD	4,313	38
Intercompany eliminations	(10.5)	-
Total	**11,333**	**100**

Selected Subsidiaries

DIANON Systems Inc. (pathology Connecticut)
Dynacare Laboratories Inc. (clinical labs; Tennessee Washington Wisconsin Canada)
Esoterix Inc. (esoteric testing Colorado)
Integrated Genetics (formerly Genzyme Genetics fertility testing labs across the US)
Integrated Oncology (formerly US Labs esoteric oncology tests US)
Litholink Corporation (kidney patient testing Illinois)
Monogram Biosciences Inc. (HIV resistance testing and personalized medicine California)
National Genetics Institute (NGI infection testing and blood screening California)
Viro-Med Laboratories Inc. (molecular microbial testing Minnesota)

Selected Services

General and specialty laboratory testing
Ambulatory monitoring services
Bone marrow/HLA services
Clinical trials services
Drug testing services
DNA identification services
Forensic identity services
Health care provider services
Hospital services
Insurance/health plan services
Paternity testing
Patient services

HISTORICAL FINANCIALS

Company Type: Public

Income Statement
FYE: December 31

	REVENUE ($ mil.)	NET INCOME ($ mil.)	NET PROFIT MARGIN	EMPLOYEES
12/19	11,554	823	7.1%	65,000
12/18	11,333	883	7.8%	61,000
12/17	10,441	1,268	12.1%	60,000
12/16	9,641	732	7.6%	52,000
12/15	8,680	436	5.0%	50,000
Annual Growth	7.4%	17.2%		6.8%

2019 Year-End Financials

Debt ratio: 34.93%
Return on equity: 11.33%
Cash ($ mil.): 337
Current ratio: 1.12
Long-term debt ($ mil.): 5,880

No. of shares (mil.): 97
Dividends
 Yield: —
 Payout: —
Market value ($ mil.): 16,443

	STOCK PRICE ($) FY Close	P/E High/Low	PER SHARE ($) Earnings	Dividends	Book Value
12/19	169.17	21 15	8.35	0.00	77.85
12/18	126.36	22 14	8.61	0.00	70.49
12/17	159.51	13 10	12.21	0.00	67.03
12/16	128.38	20 14	7.02	0.00	53.61
12/15	123.64	29 24	4.34	0.00	48.81
Annual Growth	8.2%	— —	17.8%	—	12.4%

Ladder Capital Corp

This specialty finance firm is looking to climb to the top of the commercial real-estate lending business. Ladder Capital Corp. is a non-bank operating company engaged in three major lines of business: commercial mortgage lending mortgage backed securities and real-estate assets. Its loans typically range from $5 million to $100 million. More than 50% of its loans originate in the Northeast. Hotel retail and office properties account for about three-quarters of Ladder's loan portfolio. Since its founding in 2008 the commercial real estate finance firm has originated $5.4 billion in conduit loans. Ladder Capital went public in 2014 with an offering valued at $225 million.

IPO

The company's February 2014 IPO raised $225 million by offering 13.3 million shares at $17 the midpoint of the $16 to $18 range. Ladder Capital intends to use the IPO proceeds to grow its loan origination and related commercial real estate business lines and for general corporate purposes.

Geographic Reach

Ladder Capital is headquartered in New York City and has branches in Los Angeles and Boca Raton Florida.

EXECUTIVES

Cfo, Marc A. Fox, age 60
Ceo, Brian R. Harris, age 59, $1,000,000 total compensation
Head Asset Management, Robert M. Perelman, age 57
Head Merchant Banking And Capital Markets, Thomas Harney, age 58, $400,000 total compensation
President, Pamela McCormack, age 49, $600,000 total compensation
Chairman, Alan H. Fishman, age 74
Board Member, Michael Mazzei
Auditors: PricewaterhouseCoopers LLP

LOCATIONS

HQ: Ladder Capital Corp
 345 Park Avenue, New York, NY 10154
Phone: 212 715-3170
Web: www.laddercapital.com

2013 Loans by Region

	% of total
Northeast	56
South	20
Southwest	10
Midwest	5
West	1
Other	8
Total	100

PRODUCTS/OPERATIONS

2013 Loans by Type

	% of total
Hotel	34
Retail	22
Office	20
Multifamily	15
Condo	7
Mixed use	2
Total	100

COMPETITORS

CIT Group   Citigroup

HISTORICAL FINANCIALS

Company Type: Public

Income Statement
FYE: December 31

	ASSETS ($ mil.)	NET INCOME ($ mil.)	INCOME AS % OF ASSETS	EMPLOYEES
12/19	6,669	122	1.8%	76
12/18	6,272	180	2.9%	74
12/17	6,025	95	1.6%	72
12/16	5,578	66	1.2%	69
12/15	5,895	73	1.3%	73
Annual Growth	3.1%	13.5%	—	1.0%

2019 Year-End Financials

Debt ratio: 29.55%
Return on equity: 8.45%
Cash ($ mil.): 58
Current ratio: —
Long-term debt ($ mil.): —

No. of shares (mil.): 119
Dividends
 Yield: 7.5%
 Payout: 136.0%
Market value ($ mil.): 2,159

	STOCK PRICE ($) FY Close	P/E High/Low	PER SHARE ($) Earnings	Dividends	Book Value
12/19	18.04	16 13	1.15	1.36	12.19
12/18	15.47	10 7	1.84	1.54	12.35
12/17	13.63	13 11	1.13	1.22	11.10
12/16	13.72	14 9	1.06	1.29	8.86
12/15	12.42	14 8	1.42	2.23	8.34
Annual Growth	9.8%	— —	(5.1%)	(11.6%)	9.9%

Lakeland Bancorp, Inc.

Lakeland Bancorp is the holding company for Lakeland Bank which serves northern and central New Jersey from around 50 branch offices. Targeting individuals and small to midsized businesses the bank offers standard retail products such as checking and savings accounts money market and NOW accounts and CDs. It also offers financial planning and advisory services for consumers. The bank's lending activities primarily consist of commercial loans and mortgages (around three-quarters of the company's loan portfolio) and residential mortgages. Lakeland also offers commercial lease financing for commercial equipment.

Operations

Lakeland Bancorp operates through a single business segment. Around 70% of its $4.3 billion loan portfolio is made up of commercial mortgages. Industrial commercial loans residential mortgages real estate construction loans and home equity and consumer loans each represent between 5%-10% of the company's lending activity. The company holds $5.5 billion in assets and $4.4 billion in deposits.

Geographic Reach

Headquartered in Oak Ridge New Jersey Lakeland Bancorp boasts about 50 banking offices across the New Jersey counties of Bergen Essex Morris Ocean Passaic Somerset Sussex Union and Warren. The company also has a branch in Highland Mills New York; six New Jersey regional commercial lending centers in Bernardsville Jackson Montville Newton Teaneck and Waldwick; and two commercial loan production offices serving Middlesex and Monmouth counties in New Jersey and the Hudson Valley region of New York.

Sales and Marketing

Lakeland Bancorp serves a variety of customers from individuals to businesses to municipalities.

One-fifth of Lakeland's commercial loan segment - the largest in its portfolio - is made up of owner-occupied real estate loans. Multifamily and retail loans make up about 15% each and industrial and office loans each comprise around 10%.

Financial Performance

Lakeland Bancorp has seen major five-year growth expanding revenue by 53% to $190.7 million net income by 111% to $52.6 million and cash by 39% to $142.9 million between 2013 and 2017. However the company's debt has risen 85% to $296.9 million in that time.

The holding company's revenue increased 14% in 2017 owing primarily to increased net interest income from growing average earning assets. Net income added 27% on the strength of those gains.

Lakeland's cash dipped $32.9 million in 2017. Operations and financings contributed $67.5 million and investments used $355.1 million. Financings provided $254.8 million down nearly $200 million from the previous year following an increase in net deposits federal funds purchased and securities sold under repurchase agreements.

Strategy

Lakeland Bancorp is focused on growth through acquisitions. The company has acquired at least eight community banks since its inception including Highlands Bancorp. which operates in northern New Jersey. The company also offers internet banking mobile banking and cash management services.

Mergers and Acquisitions

In January 2019 Lakeland Bancorp acquired Vernon New Jersey-based Highlands Bancorp in a deal valued at $56.7 million. The holding company - which operated branches in the New Jersey municipalities of Sparta Totowa and Denville - had consolidated total assets of $5.53 billion.

Company Background

Lakeland Bancorp was founded in 1969. It organized into a bank holding company in 1989.

EXECUTIVES

President And Ceo Lakeland Bancorp And Lakeland Bank, Thomas J. Shara, age 62, $650,000 total compensation

Sevp And Coo, Ronald E. (Ron) Schwarz, age 63, $266,769 total compensation

Sevp And Regional President, Robert A. Vandenbergh, age 68, $360,212 total compensation

Evp And Senior Government Banking And Financial Services Officer, Jeffrey J. Buonforte, age 68, $205,075 total compensation

Evp And Chief Credit Officer, James R. Noonan, age 68

Evp And Chief Risk Officer, James M. Nigro

First Svp And Chief Accounting Officer, Thomas F. Splaine, age 55

First Svp And Chief Technology And Information Security Officer, Mary Kaye Nardone

Evp And Chief Retail Officer, Ellen Lalwani

Evp And Chief Lending Officer, David S. Yanagisawa, $220,000 total compensation

Evp Chief Administrative Officer General Counsel And Corporate Secretary, Timothy J. Matteson, age 50

Evp And Regional President, Michael A. Schutzer

Vice President Asset Based Lending, Steven Breeman

Vice President Commercial Lending, Bruce Bready

Vice President, Scott Heiman

Vice President Area Manager, Hafeza Mohammed

Executive Vice President And Chief Lending Officer Of The Company And The Bank, John Rath

Vice President Relationship Management, Patricia Tostanoski

Chairman Lakeland Bancorp And Lakeland Bank, Mary Ann Deacon, age 68

Board Member, Brian M Flynn

Board Member, Lawrence Inserra

Auditors: KPMG LLP

LOCATIONS

HQ: Lakeland Bancorp, Inc.
250 Oak Ridge Road, Oak Ridge, NJ 07438
Phone: 973 697-2000
Web: www.lakelandbank.com

PRODUCTS/OPERATIONS

2017 Sales

	$ mil.	% of total
Interest		
Loans & fees	172	80
Investment securities and other	17	8
Interest expense	(25.0)	-
Non-interest		
Service charges on deposit accounts	10	5
Commissions & fees	4	2
Income on bank owned life insurance	2	1
Other	7	4
Total	190	100

Selected Services

401K and IRA Rollovers
Certificates of deposit & individual retirement accounts
Checking accounts
Consumer loans
Home loans
Insurance
Investment management
Online services
Retirement income planning
Savings and money market accounts

COMPETITORS

Bank of America	PNC Financial
Bank of New York Mellon	Sovereign Bank
Capital One	Sussex Bancorp
Clifton Bancorp	TD Bank USA
Hudson City Bancorp	Valley National Bancorp
Investors Bancorp	Wells Fargo
JPMorgan Chase	
New York Community Bancorp	

HISTORICAL FINANCIALS

Company Type: Public

Income Statement

FYE: December 31

	ASSETS ($ mil.)	NET INCOME ($ mil.)	INCOME AS % OF ASSETS	EMPLOYEES
12/19	6,711	70	1.1%	692
12/18	5,806	63	1.1%	652
12/17	5,405	52	1.0%	621
12/16	5,093	41	0.8%	592
12/15	3,869	32	0.8%	551
Annual Growth	14.8%	21.5%	—	5.9%

2019 Year-End Financials

Debt ratio: 4.23%
Return on equity: 10.48%
Cash ($ mil.): 282
Current ratio: —
Long-term debt ($ mil.): —
No. of shares (mil.): 50
Dividends
Yield: 2.8%
Payout: 36.3%
Market value ($ mil.): 878

	STOCK PRICE ($) FY Close	P/E High/Low	PER SHARE ($) Earnings	Dividends	Book Value
12/19	17.38	13 10	1.38	0.49	14.36
12/18	14.81	16 11	1.32	0.45	13.14
12/17	19.25	20 16	1.09	0.40	12.31
12/16	19.50	21 10	0.95	0.37	11.65
12/15	11.79	15 12	0.85	0.33	10.57
Annual Growth	10.2%	—	12.9%	10.4%	8.0%

Lakeland Financial Corp

Lakeland Financial is the holding company for Lake City Bank which serves area business customers and individuals through around 50 branches scattered across about 15 northern and central Indiana counties. With $4.8 billion in assets the community bank offers such standard retail services as checking and savings accounts money market accounts and CDs. Commercial loans including agricultural loans and mortgages make up about 90% of the bank's loan portfolio. Lake City Bank also offers investment products and services such as corporate and personal trust brokerage and estate planning.

EXECUTIVES

Evp And Retail Banking Manager, Kevin L. Deardorff, age 59, $217,963 total compensation

President And Ceo Lakeland Financial And Lake City Bank, David M. Findlay, age 58, $493,360 total compensation

Evp And Chief Credit Officer, Michael E. Gavin

Evp And Cfo, Lisa M. O'Neill, age 52, $206,286 total compensation

Svp And General Counsel, Kristin L. Pruitt, age 48

Evp And Commercial Banking Manager, Eric H. Ottinger, $218,263 total compensation

Vice President And Trust Officer, Patricia Culp

Senior Vice President And Chief Fiduciary Officer, James Westerfield

Vice President, Mark Rensner

Vice President, Michael E Gavin

Vice President Commercial Banking Officer, Mike Ryan

Chairman Lakeland Financial And Lake City Bank, Michael L. Kubacki, age 68

Auditors: Crowe LLP

LOCATIONS

HQ: Lakeland Financial Corp
202 East Center Street, Warsaw, IN 46580
Phone: 574 267-6144
Web: www.lakecitybank.com

PRODUCTS/OPERATIONS

2017 Sales

	$ mil.	% of total
Interest		
Loans	151	75
Securities	14	7
Other	0	-
Interest expense	(29.8)	-
Noninteresst		
Service charges on deposit accounts	13	7
Loan and service fees	7	4
Wealth advisory fees	5	3
Investment brokerage fees	1	-
Other	7	4
Total	171	100

COMPETITORS

1st Source Corporation	PNC Financial
KeyCorp	Peoples Bancorp (IN)
Northeast Indiana Bancorp	

HISTORICAL FINANCIALS

Company Type: Public

Income Statement

FYE: December 31

	ASSETS ($ mil.)	NET INCOME ($ mil.)	INCOME AS % OF ASSETS	EMPLOYEES
12/19	4,946	87	1.8%	568
12/18	4,875	80	1.6%	553
12/17	4,682	57	1.2%	539
12/16	4,290	52	1.2%	524
12/15	3,766	46	1.2%	518
Annual Growth	7.1%	17.1%	—	2.3%

2019 Year-End Financials

Debt ratio: —
Return on equity: 15.55%
Cash ($ mil.): 99
Current ratio: —
Long-term debt ($ mil.): —
No. of shares (mil.): 25
Dividends
Yield: 2.3%
Payout: 34.6%
Market value ($ mil.): 1,245

	STOCK PRICE ($) FY Close	P/E High/Low	PER SHARE ($) Earnings	Dividends	Book Value
12/19	48.93	15 12	3.38	1.16	23.50
12/18	40.16	16 12	3.13	1.00	20.76
12/17	48.49	23 18	2.23	0.63	18.72
12/16	47.36	26 16	2.05	0.73	17.12
12/15	46.62	26 20	1.83	0.63	15.83
Annual Growth	1.2%	—	16.5%	16.5%	10.4%

Lam Research Corp

Lam Research is a leading manufacturer of the equipment used to make semiconductors. Its plasma etch machines are used to create tiny circuitry patterns on silicon wafers. The company also makes cleaning equipment that keeps unwanted particles from contaminating processed wafers. Lam also provides products and services to maximize equipment performance. Lam's customers include some of the world's largest chip makers such as Micron Technology and Samsung Electronics. Customers in four Asian countries account for nearly 85% of Lam's revenue. The company traces its historical roots back to 1980.

Operations

Lam makes equipment for processes used to make semiconductors.

Its products for deposition processes include the ALTUS VECTOR SABRE SOLA SPEED and Striker lines. For etch processes Lam makes the Flex Kiyo Versys and Syndion lines as well as others. The clean processes product lines include Coronus DV-Prime Da Vinci EOS and the SP Series. The Metryx line is Lam's offering for mass metrology processes.

The company handles most of its own manufacturing but outsources some aspects to contractors.

Geographic Reach

Lam's sales are concentrated in South Korea (about 25% of revenue) China (about 30%) Taiwan (nearly 20%) and Japan (about 10%). The US accounts for less than 10% of sales.

The Fremont California-based company has facilities in the US China Europe Japan South Korea Southeast Asia and Taiwan.

Sales and Marketing

Lam relies on four customers — Micron Technology Samsung Electronics Company SK Hynix and Taiwan Semiconductor Manufacturing Company.

Makers of memory chips account for nearly 60% of revenue foundries account for about 30% and logic and integrated device makers account for some 10%.

Financial Performance

Lam's revenue climbed steadily from 2016 through 2018 but retreated in 2019. Revenue has rebounded in 2020 however not as much as the previous years. Net income has also shown some inconsistency but remained at a steady $2 billion average in the recent years.

In fiscal 2020 (ended June) revenue increased 4% to $10 billion compared to fiscal 2019. The increase reflected stronger customer demand for semiconductor equipment.

The company's net income rose to $2.3 billion in 2019 an increase of about $60.3 million from the prior year. Selling general and administrative expenses decreased by about 3% primarily due decreases in spending for customer-related sales costs spending for supplies restructuring charges and spending for travel and entertainment partially offset by an increase in spending for rent repair and utilities.

Lam had $5.2 billion in cash and cash equivalents in its coffers in 2020 compared to $3.9 billion in 2019. Its operating activities generated $2.1 billion in 2020 while investing and financing activities used $244.1 million and $623.9 million respectively. Lam's primary cash uses in 2020 were security purchases capital expenditures and repayments on revolving credit facilities.

Strategy

The semiconductor business is notoriously cyclical rising and falling according to the strength of the overall economy and the capital equipment needs of Lam's customers. The volatility struck Lam in 2019 when revenue slumped to $9.6 billion from $11 billion the year before.

The high expense of semiconductor manufacturing equipment has resulted in consolidation of manufacturers. Samsung and Intel are among the few companies left that make their own products. So far Lam has maintained a mix of sales to manufacturers such as Samsung and to contract chip makers such as Taiwan Semiconductor.

A heavy investor in innovation the company's R&D expenses increased about 5% in 2020. The company unveiled a technological breakthrough for extreme ultraviolet (EUV) lithography?a dry resist technology that will help extend EUV lithography's resolution productivity and yield. Lam also launched a new plasma etch technology and system solution designed to provide chipmakers with advanced functionality and extendibility required for future innovation.

EXECUTIVES

Evp Global Products Group, Richard A. (Rick) Gottscho, age 69, $545,296 total compensation
Svp And Cto Corporate Technology Development, David J. (Dave) Hemker
President And Ceo, Martin B. Anstice, age 53, $937,789 total compensation
Evp And Cfo, Douglas R. (Doug) Bettinger, age 53, $548,827 total compensation
Evp And Coo, Timothy M. (Tim) Archer, age 53, $624,061 total compensation
Svp Chief Legal Officer And Secretary, Sarah A. O'Dowd, age 70, $434,488 total compensation
Svp Strategic Development Corporate Marketing And Communications, Gary Bultman
Vp Pl, Thorsten Lill
Vice President And General Manager Surface Integrity Group (sig), Mark Merrill
Vice President Organization Development, Amir Yasseri
Corporate Vice President, Harmeet Singh
Vice President, Mohsen Salek
Vice President Sales Operations, Neil Fernandes
Vice President And General Manager Ibm And Global, Wendell Isom
Vice President Regional Operations, Vince Brigman
Senior Vice President, Audrey Charles
Vice President Of Information Technology, Susan Wilkerson
Group Vice President Global Sales And Corporate Marketing, Steven Lindsay
Vice President Global Operations Lam Research Corporation, Abdi Hariri
Vice President Marketing, Dinesh Kalakkad
Vice President Corporate Marketing, Gary Blutman
Corporate Vice President Global Quality, Jerry Sowers
Vice President Engineering Pilot Operations, Karsten Theess
Vice President, Joon Park
Vice President, Joseph Han
Group Vice President Asia Pacific, Daniel Liao
Group Vp Customer Support Business Group Gm, Pat Lord
Senior Vice President, Sesha Varadarajan
Vice President, Natan Solomon
Svp Global Customer Operations, Scott Meikke
Vice President Computational Products, David Fried
Senior Vice President Global Customer Operations, Scott Meikle
Chairman, Stephen G. (Steve) Newberry, age 66
Board Member, Helen Tsai
Board Member, Catherine Lego
Auditors: Ernst & Young LLP

LOCATIONS

HQ: Lam Research Corp
4650 Cushing Parkway, Fremont, CA 94538
Phone: 510 572-0200 **Fax:** 510 572-6454
Web: www.lamresearch.com

2019 Sales

	$ mil.	% of total
Korea	2,205	23
China	2,161	22
Japan	1,161	20
Taiwan	1,596	17
Southeast Asia	615	6
United States	748	8
Europe	356	4
Total	**9,653**	**100**

PRODUCTS/OPERATIONS

Selected Products

Plasma ("dry") wafer-etching equipment
Plasma-based bevel clean system
Single-wafer spin and linear clean products
Three-dimensional integrated circuit etch equipment
Transformer Coupled Plasma (TCP) silicon etch equipment

COMPETITORS

ASM International	SCREEN Holdings
Applied Materials	Tokyo Electron
Hitachi	Wonik IPS Co. Ltd.
High-Technologies	

HISTORICAL FINANCIALS

Company Type: Public

Income Statement

FYE: June 28

	REVENUE ($ mil.)	NET INCOME ($ mil.)	NET PROFIT MARGIN	EMPLOYEES
06/20	10,044	2,251	22.4%	11,300
06/19	9,653	2,191	22.7%	10,700
06/18	11,077	2,380	21.5%	10,900
06/17	8,013	1,697	21.2%	9,400
06/16	5,885	914	15.5%	7,500
Annual Growth	14.3%	25.3%	—	10.8%

2020 Year-End Financials

Debt ratio: 39.91%	No. of shares (mil.): 145
Return on equity: 45.58%	Dividends
Cash ($ mil.): 4,915	Yield: 0.0%
Current ratio: 3.43	Payout: 30.4%
Long-term debt ($ mil.): 4,970	Market value ($ mil.): 43,966

	STOCK PRICE ($) FY Close	P/E High/Low		PER SHARE ($) Earnings	Dividends	Book Value
06/20	302.52	22	12	15.10	4.60	35.67
06/19	187.84	14	9	13.70	4.40	32.70
06/18	174.70	16	9	13.17	2.55	41.94
06/17	151.78	16	8	9.24	1.65	43.21
06/16	82.28	15	11	5.22	1.20	38.09
Annual Growth	38.5%	—	—	30.4%	39.9%	(1.6%)

Lauder (Estee) Cos., Inc. (The)

Auditors: KPMG LLP

LOCATIONS

HQ: Lauder (Estee) Cos., Inc. (The)
767 Fifth Avenue, New York, NY 10153
Phone: 212 572-4200
Web: www.elcompanies.com

HISTORICAL FINANCIALS

Company Type: Public

Income Statement

FYE: June 30

	REVENUE ($ mil.)	NET INCOME ($ mil.)	NET PROFIT MARGIN	EMPLOYEES
06/20	14,294	684	4.8%	48,000
06/19	14,863	1,785	12.0%	48,000
06/18	13,683	1,108	8.1%	46,000
06/17	11,824	1,249	10.6%	46,000
06/16	11,262	1,114	9.9%	46,000
Annual Growth	6.1%	(11.5%)	—	1.1%

2020 Year-End Financials

Debt ratio: 34.51%
Return on equity: 16.40%
Cash ($ mil.): 5,022
Current ratio: 1.72
Long-term debt ($ mil.): 4,914

No. of shares (mil.): 360
Dividends
Yield: 0.7%
Payout: 39.2%
Market value ($ mil.): 68,024

	STOCK PRICE ($) FY Close	P/E High/Low	PER SHARE ($) Earnings	Dividends	Book Value
06/20	188.68	116 76	1.86	1.39	10.91
06/19	183.11	37 25	4.82	1.67	12.15
06/18	142.69	53 31	2.95	1.48	12.77
06/17	95.98	29 22	3.35	1.32	11.91
06/16	91.02	32 25	2.96	1.14	9.71
Annual Growth	20.0%	—	(11.0%)	5.1%	3.0%

Lear Corp.

Lear Corporation is a leading manufacturer of seating and related components for automobiles. In addition to seating the company's E-Systems business produces automotive electronics and manufactures wire harnesses junction boxes terminals and connectors and body control modules. The company operates from some 260 facilities in about 40 countries. It generates more than 80% of revenue outside the US. Its largest customers are General Motors Ford Daimler and Volkwagen. Lear traces its history back to 1917 when it was founded in Detroit as American Metal Products.

Operations

Lear's operations are split between Seating (around 75% of sales) and E-Systems (about 25%).

The Seating segment consists of the manufacture and delivery of complete seat systems and seat components including seat covers and surface materials such as leather and fabric seat structure and mechanisms. Products and brands include Eagle Ottawa leather Guilford textiles and its new sustainable SoyFoam product.

E-Systems makes complete electrical distribution systems as well as sophisticated electronic control modules electrification products connectivity products and software solutions for the cloud vehicles and mobile devices. Some products include control modules smart junction boxes gateway modules lighting control modules audio domain controllers amplifiers and communication modules that are applicable to all vehicle types.

Geographic Reach

Based in Southfield MI Lear operates from about 260 facilities in some 40 countries. The company's operations include around 85 just-in-time manufacturing facilities 125 dedicated component manufacturing facilities about 35 administrative and technical support facilities and approximately 10 advanced technology canters and a small number of advanced technology centers

Lear's home market the US generates approximately 20% of sales annually. Other important markets are Mexico (about 15% of revenue) China (almost 15%) and Germany (roughly 10%).

Sales and Marketing

Lear serves the worldwide automotive and light truck market. More than 50% of Lear's sales are generated from four customers. General Motors accounts for close to 20% of revenue followed by Ford with around 15% and Daimler and Volkswagen each accounts for 11%.

The Seating segment's top five customers are General Motors Daimler Ford Fiat Chrysler and Volkswagen. The E-system segment's top customers are Ford General Motors Renault-Nissan Jaguar Land Rover and Volkswagen.

Financial Performance

Increasing global auto sales particularly in the advantageous crossover and sport utility vehicle segment have helped Lear enjoy unprecedented growth over the years. Sales have decreased approximately 9% since 2015.

Revenue decreased by 6% to $19.8 billion in 2019 over a $21.1 billion in 2018 mainly due to the decrease from external customers' revenue.

Net income decreased 1234% to $754 million mainly due to a higher provision for income taxes in 2019.

Cash at the end of fiscal 2019 was $1.5 billion a decreased of $20.6 million from the prior year. Cash from operations contributed $1.3 billion to the coffers while investing activities used $922.4 million mainly for additions to property plant and equipment. Financing activities used another $361.9 million for dividends to stockholders and the company's stock repurchase program.

Strategy

Lear Corporation is well-positioned to capitalize on several current trends in the automotive industry. The company focuses on the major imperatives for success as an automotive supplier: quality service cost and efficiency and innovation and technology. The shift to SUVs and increasing demands for luxury and performance features and autonomy and connectivity capabilities is driving growth as Lear has the goods to supply vehicles with the latest features and technology.

The consumer shift to crossover vehicles and SUVs increases the percentage of vehicle content supplied by the company. In China utility vehicle production has increased from 20% to 41% in the past five years. Lear continually realigns its manufacturing footprint to leverage operations in low-cost countries but is focused on China which it believes is the world's largest major automotive market with above-average growth potential.

Lear has expanded component and software capabilities both through internal development efforts and through acquisitions. In 2018 the company acquired an Israeli firm specializing in GPS for cars. Its expertise in V2X communication technology allows the company to provide high-speed communication between vehicles and road infrastructure even in extreme weather conditions. It has also developed standardized seat structures and mechanisms that can be adapted across multiple segments of its manufacturing operations.

Mergers and Acquisitions

One way Lear has achieved milestone revenue growth recently is through acquisitions.

In 2019 Lear completed its previously announced acquisition of Xevo Inc. (Xevo) a Seattle-based leading automotive software supplier that develops solutions for cloud car and mobile devices by acquiring all of its outstanding shares for $322 million. The acquisition of Xevo will enhance Lear's capabilities in software services and data analytics and strengthen its market position in connectivity. Also in 2019 the company through its Lear Innovation Ventures (LIV) subsidiary made an investment in Israel-based Maniv Mobility a company focused on advancing mobility technology.

Company Background

Lear dates back to 1917 when American Metal Products began supplying seats to Detroit's fledgling car industry. The seat maker incorporated in 1928 and grew during the 1950s and 1960s by buying other auto parts makers. In 1966 American Metal Products was acquired by Lear Siegler a manufacturer of aerospace auto parts and climate-control equipment. The company's aerospace unit sputtered in the 1970s but the seat business did well. By 1985 metal seat frames had become Lear Siegler's major auto parts revenue producer. Spurred by growing competition with Japanese carmakers the company built a plant near a General Motors factory in Michigan to allow for swift delivery of its car seats. In 1989 the company became Lear Seating.

Lear Seating bought a slice of Ford's North American automotive and trim operation and manufacturing factory in Ciudad Ju rez Mexico in 1993. As a result of the purchase the company entered into a long-term supply agreement with Ford. The following year Lear Seating went public. In 1995 it bought Automotive Industries and inked a contract to provide seats for Brazil's top-selling car the Volkswagen Gol. To reflect the broader scope of its business the company dropped "Seating" from its name and became Lear Corporation in 1996.

The company narrowed its product focus and sold its interior product lines (instrument panels door panels flooring acoustic systems and other interior products) in 2006. In the midst of the Great Recession Lear filed for Chapter 11 bankruptcy emerging in late 2009.

EXECUTIVES

President Ceo And Director, Raymond E. (Ray) Scott, age 54, $855,098 total compensation
Svp; President Asia/pacific Operations, Jay K. Kunkel, age 60
Evp Business Development And General Counsel, Terrence B. (Terry) Larkin, age 65, $855,098 total compensation
Svp And Cfo, Jeffrey H. Vanneste, age 60, $787,437 total compensation
Svp; President E-systems, Frank C. Orsini, age 47, $736,375 total compensation
Vp Global Engineering E Systems, Mike Fawaz
Vice President Korea, Dean M Ackerman
Vp Global Facilities And Real Estate, Doug Daugherty
Global Vice President Leadership Development, Noelle Gill
Vice President Human Resources North America, Pete Camarata
Multi Cultural Vice President, Jolito Bustamante
Vice President Talent Acquisition, Dave McNulty
Vice President Of Sales And Marketing, Siva Vinta
Vice President, Joe Duran
Svp Human Resources, Thomas Didonato
Vp Hse, Jack Nunes
Global Vice President Trim Cover Sales And Prgm Management, Dreta Roggenbuck
Vice President Connectivity, Doug Moeller
Vice President Of It Infrastructure, Jon Damm
Vp Finance And Investor Relations, John Trythall

Vice President Software And Systems Engineering, Michael Badalament
Vice President Global Engineering Structures And Mechanisms, Chris Florea
Chairman, Henry D. G. Wallace, age 74
Assistant Treasurer, Ed Lowenfeld
Auditors: Ernst & Young LLP

LOCATIONS

HQ: Lear Corp.
  21557 Telegraph Road, Southfield, MI 48033
Phone: 248 447-1500   **Fax:** 248 447-5250
Web: www.lear.com

2018 Sales

	$ mil.	% of total
US	3,717	18
Mexico	3,236	15
China	2,781	13
Germany	2,187	10
Other countries	9,225	44
Total	**21,148**	**100**

PRODUCTS/OPERATIONS

2018 Sales

	$ mil.	% of total
Seating	16,021	76
E-Systems	5,126	24
Total	**21,148**	**100**

2018 Sales by Customer

	% of total
GM	18
Ford	16
BMW	7
Others	59
Total	**100**

Selected Products

Seating
  Adjusters
  Automotive seats
  Fabrics
  Head restraints
  Mechanisms
  Seat foam
  Structure systems
  Trim covers
Electrical power management
  Electrical distribution and power management systems
  Fuse boxes
  Junction boxes
  Terminals and connectors
  Wire harness assemblies
  High-power electrical systems
  Hybrid electrical systems
  Specialty electronics
  Audio sound systems
  In-vehicle television tuner module
  LED electronics (interior/exterior)
  Lighting control module
  Media console
  Radio amplifiers
  Wireless systems
  Keyless entry systems
  Passive entry systems
  Tire pressure monitoring systems

COMPETITORS

Continental AG	Robert Bosch
DENSO	Sumitomo
Faurecia	TE Connectivity
Honda	TS TECH CO
LEONI	Toyota Boshoku
Magna International	Valeo
Molex	Visteon
Peugeot	Yazaki

HISTORICAL FINANCIALS

Company Type: Public

Income Statement

FYE: December 31

	REVENUE ($ mil.)	NET INCOME ($ mil.)	NET PROFIT MARGIN	EMPLOYEES
12/19	19,810	753	3.8%	164,100
12/18	21,148	1,149	5.4%	169,000
12/17	20,467	1,313	6.4%	165,000
12/16	18,557	975	5.3%	148,400
12/15	18,211	745	4.1%	136,200
Annual Growth	**2.1%**	**0.3%**	**—**	**4.8%**

2019 Year-End Financials

Debt ratio: 18.35%
Return on equity: 17.63%
Cash ($ mil.): 1,487
Current ratio: 1.37
Long-term debt ($ mil.): 2,293

No. of shares (mil.): 60
Dividends
  Yield: 2.1%
  Payout: 23.5%
Market value ($ mil.): 8,292

	STOCK PRICE ($) FY Close	P/E High/Low	PER SHARE ($) Earnings	PER SHARE ($) Dividends	PER SHARE ($) Book Value
12/19	137.20	12 8	12.75	3.00	71.97
12/18	122.86	12 7	17.22	2.80	66.74
12/17	176.66	10 7	18.59	2.00	62.06
12/16	132.37	10 7	13.33	1.20	44.03
12/15	122.83	13 10	9.59	1.00	39.31
Annual Growth	**2.8%**	**— —**	**7.4%**	**31.6%**	**16.3%**

Leidos Holdings Inc

Leidos Holdings provides cybersecurity information technology and analytics services to government agencies and companies in the defense intelligence homeland security civil and health markets. The company's areas of expertise include operations and logistics; sensors; software development; and systems engineering. It also operates one of the country's largest health system integrators. Most of the company's revenue (over 85%) comes from the US government.

Operations

Leidos Holdings operates through three segments: Defense Solutions Civil and Health.

Defense Solutions which accounts for about 50% of total sales offers technology development and integration capabilities in surveillance and reconnaissance integrated systems and global services for the US intelligence community the military and other government and commercial customers.

The Civil segment which accounts for nearly 35% of revenue provides aviation services security products digital transformation services federal environment and infrastructure management and logistics services.

The Health segment about 20% of revenue provides complex systems integration managed health services digital transformation and life sciences research and development.

Geographic Reach

Leidos has some about 335 offices in about 40 states across the US the District of Columbia and various foreign countries. Leidos owned buildings in Maryland Florida and Tennessee.

Over 90% of sales were generated in the US alone. The Leidos' corporate headquarters is located in Reston Virginia.

Sales and Marketing

The US government accounts for over 85% of Leidos Holdings' revenue with the US Department of Defense accounting for nearly 50%. Other major federal customers are the Navy Air Force the Defense Advanced Research Projects Agency the Department of Homeland Security and NASA. International customers account for about 10% of revenue.

Financial Performance

Leidos' revenue has been rising for the last five years with an overall growth of 135% between 2019 and 2015. Its net income follows a similar pattern.

The 9% increase ($900 million) of the company's revenue from $10.2 billion in 2018 to $11.1 billion in 2019 was due to the increase in revenue of all segments primarily Defense Solutions.

Net income rose 15% ($86 million) from $581 million in 2018 to $667 million in 2019.

Cash generated by operations increased $224 million to $992 million in 2019 from 2018. Investing activities generated $65 million while financing activities used $709 million mainly for repurchases of stock. Overall cash cash equivalents and restricted cash at end of year was $717 million.

Strategy

Leidos acquires businesses as part of its growth strategy to provide new or enhance existing capabilities and offerings to customers. The Company also selectively pursues strategic investments and joint ventures.

Mergers and Acquisitions

In 2020 Leidos announced that it has completed the acquisition of Florida-based L3Harris Technologies' ("L3Harris") Security Detection and Automation businesses for approximately $1 billion in cash. The acquired businesses provide airport and critical infrastructure screening products automated tray return systems and other industrial automation products. The transaction was announced in early 2020.

In early 2020 Leidos Holdings Inc. announced that it has completed the acquisition of Dynetics Inc. an industry-leading applied research and national security solutions company headquartered in Alabama US for approximately $1.65 billion in cash. Dynetics will operate as a wholly-owned subsidiary of Leidos and Dynetics' Chief Executive Officer David King will continue to lead the business reporting directly to Leidos' Chairman and Chief Executive Officer Roger Krone.

During 2019 Leidos announced it has entered into a definitive agreement to acquire Pennsylvania-based IMX Medical Management Services (IMX) a URAC accredited commercial independent review organization and its affiliated businesses including First Rehabilitation Resources a URAC accredited commercial case management organization primarily serving the mid-Atlantic and northeastern United States. Terms were not disclosed.

EXECUTIVES

Chairman And Ceo, Roger A. Krone, age 64, $988,462 total compensation
Evp And Cfo, James C. (Jim) Reagan, age 61, $561,538 total compensation
Evp And Chief Human Resources Officer, Ann M. Addison, age 58
President Technology Group And Cto, John J. Fratamico, age 62
Evp And Chief Of Business Development And Strategy, Gerard A. (Gerry) Fasano, age 54
President Health Group, Jonathan W. Scholl, age 58
Evp And General Counsel, Vincent A. (Vince) Maffeo, age 69, $575,000 total compensation
President Civil Group, Angela L. Heise, age 45
President Defense And Intelligence Group, Timothy J. Reardon, age 55, $162,240 total compensation

President Advanced Solutions Group, Michael L. Chagnon
Vp Strategic Accounts And Government Relations, Rob Thomas
Vice President, John Russell
Vice President, Jack Gumbert
Vice President, Steve Ventsam
Vice President Business Development, Karen Walton
Senior Vice President Corporate Controller And Chief Accounting Officer, Ken Sharp
Vice President And Senior Pricing Director, Mark Achenbach
Assistant Vice President Senior Program Manager Fo, Richard Deason
Vice President Security Solutions, Jeffrey Murter
Vice President For Cybersecurity, Robert Pate
Vice President Production, Paul Dickinson
Vice President Information Technology, Chris Russeau
Vice President Chief Engineer, Derek Lewis
Vice President And Director Human Resources Shared Services, Gayle Connatser
Svp, Paul Greiner
Vice President, Paul Bollinger
Senior Vice President, Doug Charles
Executive Vice President, W Roper
Executive Vice President, J Warner
Vice President Information Technology Quality User Experience, Gisele Moro
Vice President Director Of Operations Contracts, Graeme Ritchie
Vice President Business Development, Robert Foster
Vice President, Nevin Carr
Vice President And Division Manager, Brian Follmer
Senior Vice President Enterprise Shared Service Director, Chris Buffoni
Vice President Government Compliance, Matthew Popham
Vice President Program Risk Assessment And Execution, Daniel Wollenhaupt
Vice President Contracts And Procurement Director, Florin Pueblos
Svp Investor Relations, John Sweeney
Svp Transportation Solutions, Fran Hill
Svp Leidos Civil Health, Doreen Cohen
Senior Vice President Of Government Affairs, Valerie Baldwin
Senior Vice President And Chief Information Security Officer, Jr Williamson
Board Member, Gary May
Board Member, Lawrence Nussdorf
Board Member, Surya Mohapatra
Board Member, Gregory Dahlberg
Board Member, Frank Kendall
Auditors: DELOITTE & TOUCHE LLP

LOCATIONS

HQ: Leidos Holdings Inc
1750 Presidents Street, Reston, VA 20190
Phone: 571 526-6000
Web: www.leidos.com

PRODUCTS/OPERATIONS

2016 Sales

	$ mil.	% of total
National Security solutions	3,610	51
Information Systems & Global Solutions	1,971	28
Health and engineering	1,463	21
Adjustments	(-1)	-
Total	**7,043**	**100**

Selected Capabilities:

Civil:
Aviation
Cyber Solutions
Energy
Environment & Infrastructure
Exploration & Mission Support
Financial Solutions
Homeland & Transportation Security
Defense & Intelligence:
Airborne
Command & Control
Data Analytics
Enterprise IT
Federal Cybersecurity
Intelligence Services
Operations & Logistics
Sensors
Training
Health:
Federal Health IT
Hospitals & Health Systems
Life Sciences
Advanced Solutions:
Airborne Systems Integration
Maritime

COMPETITORS

Accenture
American Science and Engineering
BAE Systems Technology Solutions
Battelle Memorial
Boeing
Booz Allen
CACI International
Computer Sciences Corp.
Engility
Exelis
General Dynamics
HP Enterprise Services
Honeywell Technology Solutions
IBM Global Services
KBR
KEYW
Kratos Defense & Security Solutions
L3 Technologies
ManTech
OSI Systems
Raytheon Intelligence Information and Services
Serco
Unisys

HISTORICAL FINANCIALS

Company Type: Public

Income Statement — FYE: January 3

	REVENUE ($ mil.)	NET INCOME ($ mil.)	NET PROFIT MARGIN	EMPLOYEES
01/20*	11,094	667	6.0%	34,000
12/18	10,194	581	5.7%	32,000
12/17	10,170	366	3.6%	31,000
12/16	7,043	244	3.5%	32,000
01/16	4,712	242	5.1%	18,000
Annual Growth	**23.9%**	**28.8%**	**—**	**17.2%**

*Fiscal year change

2020 Year-End Financials

Debt ratio: 31.88%	No. of shares (mil.): 141
Return on equity: 19.53%	Dividends
Cash ($ mil.): 668	Yield: 1.3%
Current ratio: 1.21	Payout: 28.8%
Long-term debt ($ mil.): 2,925	Market value ($ mil.): 14,027

	STOCK PRICE ($) FY Close	P/E High/Low	PER SHARE ($) Earnings	Dividends	Book Value
01/20*	99.48	21 11	4.60	1.32	24.21
12/18	52.40	19 13	3.80	1.28	22.66
12/17	64.57	27 20	2.38	1.28	22.32
12/16	51.14	24 16	2.35	14.92	20.90
01/16	56.26	18 11	3.27	1.28	14.83
Annual Growth	**15.3%**	**— —**	**8.9%**	**0.8%**	**13.0%**

*Fiscal year change

LELAND STANFORD JUNIOR UNIVERSITY

The Leland Stanford Junior University better known as simply Stanford University is one of the top universities in the US. It boasts respected programs across seven schools and 18 interdisciplinary institutes such as business engineering law and medicine among others. Stanford serves more than 16500 students (taught by 2240 faculty members) from all 50 US states and more than 90 other countries. Its student-teacher ratio sit at about 5:1. A private institution Stanford is supported through an endowment of some $27.7 billion one of the largest in the US. The university was established in 1885 by Leland Stanford Sr. who made his fortune selling provisions to California gold miners; it was named after his son Leland Stanford Jr.

Operations

Stanford University is widely recognized as one of the top US research universities and sports a host of laboratories and research centers including the Stanford Institute for Economic Policy Research and the Stanford Linear Accelerator Center. Its faculty members include around 17 Nobel Prize winners a handful of Pulitzer Prize winners and more than 30 MacArthur fellows.

The university also offers 35 varsity sports and 20 club sports; it boasts more than 110 NCAA team championships.

Geographic Reach

Stanford is located in the heart of California's Silicon Valley known worldwide as an epicenter for technology and research ventures. Google (headquartered in Silicon Valley) got its start at Stanford when Sergey Brin and Larry Page developed the page-rank algorithm while they were still computer science graduate students.

The university is located on 8180 contiguous acres and has almost 700 major buildings.

Financial Performance

Stanford University reported total operating revenue of $12.3 billion in fiscal 2019 (ended August 31) an increase of 8%. The rise mainly came from higher patient services revenue from the Stanford Hospitals and Clinics organization. Student income sponsored support and investment income were broadly comparable with the prior year.

Net income rose 32% to $623 million due to comparatively lower expenses.

Stanford's cash balance grew $432.2 million to $1.6 billion during 2019. Operating activities generated $299.3 million and financing generated $628.9 million while investing activities used $496.0 million.

The university's sizable endowment grew 5% to $27.7 billion in fiscal 2019.

HISTORY

In 1885 Leland Stanford Sr. and his wife Jane established Leland Stanford Junior University in memory of their son Leland Jr. who had died of typhoid at age 15. Stanford made his fortune selling provisions to California gold miners and as a major investor in the Central Pacific Railroad one of the two companies that built the first transcontinental railway. It was Stanford who connected the tracks laid eastward by Central Pacific and westward by Union Pacific with a gold railway spike in 1869. He also served as California's governor and as a US senator.

The Stanfords donated more than 8000 acres of land from their own estate to establish an unconventional university one that was coeducational and nondenominational with a focus on preparing students for a profession. Stanford opened its doors in 1891 to a freshman class of 559 students. It awarded its first degrees four years later and among the graduates was future US president Herbert Hoover.

Leland Stanford Sr. died in 1893 and in 1903 Jane Stanford turned the university over to the board of trustees. After weathering significant damage in 1906 from the Great San Francisco Earthquake the university established a law school in 1908 and its medical school five years later.

During WWI the university mobilized half of its students into the Students' Army Training Corps. The School of Education was established in 1917 followed by the School of Engineering and Graduate School of Business eight years later. In 1933 a rule limiting the number of women admitted to Stanford was abolished.

Wallace Sterling who became president of the university after WWII initiated the transformation of Stanford into a world-class institution with a reputation for teaching and research. Under Sterling the university initiated development on the Stanford Research Park.

In 1958 Stanford opened its first overseas campus (near Stuttgart Germany) and the Stanford Medical Center was completed the following year. The university created a computer science department in 1965 and two years later opened the Stanford Linear Accelerator Center dedicated to physics research.

Donald Kennedy became president in 1980. The next year students voted to abandon the university's official mascot the "Indians" in response to concerns raised by Native American students. The nickname "Cardinal" was adopted in its place. The term refers to the school's color cardinal red.

Also during Kennedy's tenure it was revealed that Stanford had overcharged the Office of Naval Research for indirect costs associated with research. The scandal led to Kennedy's resignation in 1992 and in 1994 the Office of Naval Research and the university settled a related lawsuit for $1.2 million and a stipulation that Stanford had not committed any wrongdoing. Gerhard Casper succeeded Kennedy as president.

In 1997 Stanford and the University of California at San Francisco combined their teaching hospitals in a public/private merger. Two years later after the controversial experiment had harmed both hospitals' financial pictures the merger was terminated and the two hospitals agreed to go their separate ways.

In 1999 Casper announced his intention to resign as president. The school tapped provost John Hennessy as his replacement. Soon after his appointment in 2000 Hennessey launched a campaign to raise $1 billion. Former Stanford professor and Netscape co-founder Jim Clark donated $150 million later that year to support Stanford's biomedical engineering and sciences program. The school also launched a new company SKOLAR which developed an online search engine for the medical industry.

EXECUTIVES

President, John L. Hennessy
Provost, John W. Etchemendy
Dean School Of Humanities And Science, Richard P. Saller
Vp Business Affairs And Cfo, Randall S. (Randy) Livingston
Dean School Of Earth Energy And Environmental Sciences, Pamela Matson
Associate Vp It Services, Bill Clebsch

President And Ceo Stanford Health Care, Amir Dan Rubin
Vice Provost And Dean Of Research, Ann Margaret Arvin
Dean Graduate School Of Business, Garth Saloner
Dean Graduate School Of Education, Deborah Stipek
Dean School Of Engineering, Persis S. Drell
Dean Law School, M. Elizabeth Magill
Dean School Of Medicine, Lloyd Minor
President And Ceo Stanford Children's Health, Christopher Dawes
Vice President Human Resources, David Jones
Vice President, Britt Hedman
Vice President Slac National Accelerator Laboratory, William Madia
Associate Vice President Of Sponsored Research, Russell Brewer
Medical Director Performance Improvement, Terry Platchek
Medical Director, Kirsti Weng
Associate Vice President For University Affairs, Phil Taubman
Assoc. Vice President Of Human Resources Benefits, Leslie Schlaegel
Vice President, Carolyn Manning
Vp Finance, Wakuna Galega
Vice President Human Resources, Elizabeth Zacharias
Associate Vice President For The Arts, Matthew Tiews
Medical Director Emergency Medicine, Sam Shen
Medical Director, James Lau
Vpge, Rebecca Jantzen
Clinical Director Ibd, Sarah Streett
Medical Director Clinical Assistant Professor Of Medicine Division Of Primary Care And Population Health, Kurt Hafer
Associate Vice President Human Resources Communications, Melissa Mcvicker
Executive Vice President Technology, Ruth Ohara
Vice President, Anupam Singhal
Vpue Facilities Service Manager, Omar Ochoa
Assistant Vice President Of Development, Donna Lawrence
Director Of Pharmacy, Michael Brown
Senior Advisor To The Vice President F, Carol Dressler
Vice President Finance, David Connor
Vice President And Corporate Controller, James Martin
Vice President, Bill Madia
Vice President Ambulatory Care Services, Tim Engberg
Vice President Engineering, Douglas Gray
Co Vice President, Giselle Tran
Vice President And General Manager, Brian Freed
Vp Operations, Will Pfalzgraff
Vp Records, Andrew Doyle
Vice Chair, Mary Goldstein
Board Member, Udai Baisiwala
Auditors: PRICEWATERHOUSECOOPERS LLP SA

LOCATIONS

HQ: LELAND STANFORD JUNIOR UNIVERSITY
450 JANE STANFORD WAY, STANFORD, CA 943052004
Phone: 650 723-2300
Web: WWW.STANFORD.EDU

PRODUCTS/OPERATIONS

2014 Sales

	$ mil.	% of total
Healthcare services	3,942	50
Sponsored reseach support	1,266	16
Investment income	1,181	15
Student income	533	7
Special program fee and other income	641	7
Gifts	212	3
Net assets released from restrictions	146	2
Total	**7,924**	**100**

Selected Schools

Undergraduate
  School of Earth Sciences
  School of Engineering
  School of Humanities and Sciences
Graduate
  School of Business
  School of Earth Sciences
  School of Education
  School of Engineering
  School of Humanities and Sciences
  School of Law
  School of Medicine

Selected Interdisciplinary Research Centers

Alliance for Innovative Manufacturing at Stanford
Center for Computer Research in Music and Acoustics
Center for Integrated Facility Engineering
Center for Integrated Systems

Selected Laboratories Centers and Institutes

Center for Research on Information Storage Materials
Center for the Study of Language and Information
Edward L. Ginzton Laboratory
Institute for International Studies
Institute for Research on Women and Gender
John and Terry Levin Center for Public Service and Public Interest Law
Stanford Center for Buddhist Studies
Stanford Humanities Center
Stanford Institute for Economic Policy Research
W.W. Hansen Experimental Physics Laboratory

Selected Medical Research Facilities

Center for Biomedical Ethics
Center for Research in Disease Prevention
Human Genome Center
Richard M. Lucas Center for Magnetic Resonance Spectroscopy & Imaging
Sleep Disorders Center
Other Selected Research Facilities
Hoover Institution on War Revolution and Peace
Hopkins Marine Station
Martin Luther King Jr. Papers Project
Stanford Linear Accelerator Center

HISTORICAL FINANCIALS

Company Type: Private

Income Statement — FYE: August 31

	REVENUE ($ mil.)	NET INCOME ($ mil.)	NET PROFIT MARGIN	EMPLOYEES
08/19	12,262	1,961	16.0%	15,000
08/18	11,311	2,653	23.5%	—
08/17	5,604	2,972	53.0%	—
08/06	4,511	3,007	66.7%	—
Annual Growth	8.0%	(3.2%)	—	—

LendingClub Corp

LOCATIONS

HQ: LendingClub Corp
595 Market Street, Suite 200, San Francisco, CA 94105
Phone: 415 632-5600
Web: www.lendingclub.com

HISTORICAL FINANCIALS

Company Type: Public

Income Statement				FYE: December 31
	ASSETS ($ mil.)	NET INCOME ($ mil.)	INCOME AS % OF ASSETS	EMPLOYEES
12/19	2,982	(30)	—	1,538
12/18	3,819	(128)	—	1,768
12/17	4,640	(153)	—	1,837
12/16	5,562	(145)	—	1,530
12/15	5,793	(5)	—	1,382
Annual Growth	(15.3%)	—	—	2.7%

2019 Year-End Financials

Debt ratio: 57.32%
Return on equity: (-3.48%)
Cash ($ mil.): 243
Current ratio: —
Long-term debt ($ mil.): —

No. of shares (mil.): 88
Dividends
  Yield: —
  Payout: —
Market value ($ mil.): 1,120

	STOCK PRICE ($) FY Close	P/E High/Low	PER SHARE ($) Earnings	Dividends	Book Value
12/19	12.62	— —	(0.35)	0.00	10.14
12/18	2.63	— —	(1.50)	0.00	10.12
12/17	4.13	— —	(1.90)	0.00	11.05
12/16	5.25	— —	(1.90)	0.00	12.26
12/15	11.05	— —	(0.05)	0.00	13.72
Annual Growth	3.4%		—	—	(7.3%)

Lennar Corp

Lennar is one of the largest homebuilding land-owning loan-making leviathans in the US. The company builds single-family attached and detached homes and multi-family rental properties in more than 20 states under brand names including Lennar and CalAtlantic Group. Lennar targets first-time move-up active adult and luxury homebuyers and markets its homes as "everything included." The company delivered more than 51000 homes in 2019 at an average price of around $400000. Lennar traces its roots back to 1954 as a local Miami homebuilder.

HISTORY

Lennar is the creation of Leonard Miller and Arnold Rosen and the name of the company is a combination of their given names. Rosen a Miami homebuilder formed F&R Builders in 1954. A year later Miller graduated from Harvard with no firm career plans. Having worked summers in Florida Miller decided it would be a good place to make his fortune and the 23-year-old began selling real estate there.

With $10000 earned from commissions Miller bought 42 lots and in 1956 entered a joint venture with Rosen to build homes on the lots. They worked well together and Miller soon joined F&R. The operation grew emphasizing marketing and concentrating on low- and medium-priced single-family homes for first-time buyers and retirees.

After expanding into commercial real estate in the late 1960s the duo folded F&R into a new company — Lennar Corporation — in 1971 and went public. During the 1970s and 1980s the company hawked Jacuzzi tubs and designer homes (such as the Calvin and the Liz) and promised customers "$10000 worth of extras" free at Midnight Madness shopping mall sales. Lennar also began expanding acquiring land and builders in the Phoenix area in 1973. Rosen retired in 1977.

Spurred by a recession Lennar began offering mortgage services nationwide in 1981 keeping the potentially lucrative servicing for itself and selling its mortgages to Fannie Mae Ginnie Mae and Freddie Mac among others. In 1984 it dissolved its construction operations and began subbing out its work (a practice that it continues today). Lennar was relatively unscathed by the recession of the late 1980s in part because Miller had foreseen a slump and had cut corporate debt and overhead. When other builders were overextending themselves by buying land in good times Miller had used profit to pay down debt so he would have the resources to buy land cheap when bad times arrived.

During the 1990s Lennar targeted other Sun Belt markets and began buying portfolios of distressed property in partnership with heavy hitters like Morgan Stanley. Although Miller had looked at Texas as a development site since 1987 it was not until 1991 that Lennar entered the state beginning in Dallas.

The company bought up the secured debt of Bramalea Homes in Southern California in 1995 and entered Northern California with its acquisition of Renaissance Homes. Lennar's acquisition of Village Homes and Exxon's Friendswood Development in 1996 made it Houston's top home builder and Lennar surpassed $1 billion in sales.

In 1997 Stuart Miller became president and CEO (Leonard his father remained chairman). That year Lennar also spun off its commercial real estate operations as LNR Property a separately traded public company and acquired Pacific Greystone a Los Angeles builder.

The following year the company strengthened its position in the western US acquiring three California homebuilders: Winncrest Homes (Sacramento) ColRich Communities (San Diego) and Polygon Communities (Southern California and Sacramento). Lennar also purchased North American Title an escrow and title services company operating in Arizona California and Colorado.

In 2000 Lennar bought fellow builder U.S. Home for about $1.1 billion in a deal that expanded its operations into 13 states. The company acquired the North and South Carolina operations of The Fortress Group in late 2001 giving Lennar the Don Galloway Homes and Sunstar Homes brands. Through its FG Acquisition Corporation subsidiary Lennar acquired 93% of The Fortress Group in 2002; it also added Maryland-based Patriot Homes and assets of California homebuilders Pacific Century Homes and Cambridge Homes to bring its homebuilding operations to 16 states.

In July 2002 Leonard Miller died of liver cancer. Stuart Miller continues to lead the company as its president and CEO. The company acquired nine homebuilders that year which expanded its operations into markets in Chicago (Concord Homes and Summit Homes) Baltimore the Carolinas and California's Central Valley; some of the acquisitions strengthened Lennar's position in its existing markets. Lennar subsidiary North American Title Group acquired The Sentinel Title Corporation

with nine branches in Maryland Virginia and Washington DC.

Lennar continued to acquire in 2003 adding Seppala Homes and Coleman Homes (with a backlog of about 300 homes and 3000 owned or controlled homesites) expanding its positions respectively in South Carolina and the Central Valley of California. The company's North American Title Group Inc. subsidiary acquired Mid America Title Company (Waukegan Illinois) which strengthened Lennar's homebuilding operations in the Chicago market.

In mid-2003 an entity jointly owned by Lennar and LNR Property Corporation (real estate investment finance and management) agreed to acquire The Newhall Land and Farming Company (master-planned communities) for about $1 billion. The deal closed in January 2004 enabling LNR to buy existing income-producing commercial assets from the venture and Lennar to option certain current homesites. Also that year Lennar's Texas operations grew with its cash purchase of San Antonio-based Connell-Barron Homes and the company expanded into Jacksonville by acquiring Classic American Homes for an undisclosed cash price. Lennar closed out the year with increased revenues and earnings of 18% and 26% respectively over the previous year and a strong backlog of about 15550 homes valued at about $5 billion.

As the real estate market continued to thrive Lennar acquired regional builders mortgage operations and title and closing businesses. During 2005 Lennar entered the Boston New York City and Reno markets; it also expanded its Jacksonville operations by acquiring Admiral Homes. The condo and apartment buildings in New York and Boston were valued at more than $2 billion.

Along with the rest of the homebuilding industry Lennar started to see trouble in 2006 as interest rates rose and years of overbuilding began taking their toll. Fallout from the subprime mortgage crisis and global credit crunch further unraveled the market. Lennar's average price per home fell by $40000 and the number of homes delivered fell by approximately 40000 (in 2009 as compared with fiscal 2005).

In early 2007 Lennar and its spun-off investment unit LNR Properties reduced their stakes in LandSource a joint venture that invests in raw land (among the riskiest of real estate investments particularly vulnerable to market downturns). MW Housing Partners an investment vehicle of the California Public Employees' Retirement System bought 68% of LandSource for $900 million in cash and property; Lennar lowered its stake from 50% to 16%. The sale proved to be fortuitous for Lennar: Not only did it bring the company much-needed cash but it also reduced Lennar's exposure to the debt-laden LandSource which filed for Chapter 11 bankruptcy protection a year later. LandSource emerged from bankruptcy as the debt-free Newhall Land Development. In 2009 Lennar bought back a 15% stake in the reorganized company for $140.

Lennar survived the economic downturn by shifting its focus and tightening its belt. As one of the larger builders it weathered the downturn by exiting slower markets lowering prices and reducing staff. The company also bought fewer home sites and tightened its lending standards to reduce its exposure to loan defaults. Lennar also increased its focus on the first-time buyer and limited the number of home plans offered.

EXECUTIVES

Vp And Coo, Jonathan M. (Jon) Jaffe, age 60, $800,000 total compensation

Vp And Cfo, Bruce E. Gross, age 61, $650,000 total compensation

Ceo, Stuart A. Miller, age 62, $1,000,000 total compensation

President, Richard (Rick) Beckwitt, age 60, $800,000 total compensation

Ceo Rialto Capital Management, Jeffrey P. (Jeff) Krasnoff

Regional President Lennar Land And Homebuilding, Jeff Roos

Regional President Lennar Land And Homebuilding, Rob Hutton

President Strategic Holdings Inc., David J. Kaiserman

President North American Title Group, Thomas J. (Tom) Fischer

President Rialto Capital Management, Jay Mantz

Secretary And General Counsel, Mark Sustana, age 59, $450,000 total compensation

President Universal American Mortgage And Eagle Home Mortgage, James T. (Jimmy) Timmons

Regional President Lennar Land And Homebuilding, Fred Rothman

President Lennar Multifamily Communities, Todd Farrell

Regional President Lennar Multifamily Communities, Ed Easley

Cio, Laura Lete

Regional President Lennar Homebuilding And Land, Greg McGuff

President Lennar International, Chris Marlin

Vice President Of Marketing And Sales, Susan Wilke

Vice President Sales And Marketing, Carlos Gonzalez

Vice President Sales And Marketing, Courtney Jaskiewicz

Vice President Sales, Dan Koontz

Svp National Finance Group, Joy Condon

Vice President Of Sales, Joe Catanzariti

Vice President Compensation Payroll And Hrms, Manny Murias

Executive Vice President, Al Lee

Division President, Mark Torres

Division President Carolinas, Jeff Harris

Vice President Sales And Marketing, Will Grimes

Vice President Operations Atlanta South, Chris Recker

Regional Vice President Land, Matthew Wineman

Vice President Sales And Marketing, Gerry Riley

Vice President Marketing, Janice Hinshaw

Vice President Controller, Ryan Smith

Vice President Land Division, Anthony Mignone

Vice President Purchasing, Scott Handt

Vice President Forward Planning, Geoffrey Smith

Vice President Of Land Acquisition, Jeff Minich

Vice President Of Finance, Lance Ellis

Vice President Controller, Ryan Gatchalian

Vice President Acquisition, Christina Hart

Division President, JJ Abraham

Vice President Of Construction, Al Kaufman

Vice President Of Land And Acquisitions, Greg Urech

Vp Of Construction Orlando, Mark Revell

Regional Vice President Land, Jim Bavouset

Senior Vice President Of Operations And Technology, Alex Burris

Vice President Land Acquisitions, David Stearn

Vice President Land Acquisition, John Cheney

Regional Vice President, Darin Mcmurray

Vice President Property Operations East, Simon Andrew

Vice President Land Acquisition, Richard Maier

Division President, WORTH JENKINS

Vice President Of Construction, John Bishop

Vice President Quality Assurance, Norm Greuel

Vice President Of Construction, Kevin Stream

Vice President Corporate Development, Christian Falk

Vice President Supply Chain Management And Strategic Initiatives, Paul Dodge

Vice President Of Sales And Marketing, Karen Morgan

Vice President Of Marketing, Stacy Sanders

Vice President Loan Servicing, Brian Westerbeke

Chief Sales Officer, Juan Gomez-sanchez

Division President, John Merlino

Vice President Sales And Marketing, Jeff Morin

Vice President Sales And Marketing, Garrett Chan

Vice President Development, Michelle Coletti

Vice President Quality Assurance, Norman Greuel

Vice President Of International Sales, Paulo Neto

Vice President Regional Operations Center, Brian McElwain

Senior Vice President Sales And Marketing, Dale Human

Senior Vice President, Jeff Mccall

Vp Sales, Tammy Hathaway

Vp Operations, Mike Gillett

Vp Land Acquisition, Mike Freeman

Vp Sales And Marketing, Julie Hollyday

Vice President Of Operations, Robert Smart

Vice President Of Land Development, Kurt Bruskotter

Vice President Of National Purchasing, Kemp Gillis

Vice President Of Finance And Operations, Jeffrey Mitchem

Vice President Purchasing, Jeremy Ickovic

Vice President Marketing, Christina Traver

Vice President Of Land Development, Joseph Fortino

Vice President Of Acquisitions, Michael Mashioff

Senior Vice President, Matt Sonntag

Designated Broker Vice President Sales Marketing Calatlantic Homes, Katy Spencer

Executive Vice President, Valerie Capone

Vice President Land Acquisition And Development, Keith Lash

Vice President Land Development, Al Eriksson

Board Member, Theron I Gilliam

Vice Chairman Rialto Capital Management, Eric Feder

Assistant Treasurer, Gerry Rodriguez

Board Member, Janice Stucker

Assistant Treasurer, Jacqui DeSouza

Treasurer And Vice President Fivepoint Communities, Mike White

Assistant Secretary, Indira Jimenez

Auditors: DELOITTE & TOUCHE LLP

LOCATIONS

HQ: Lennar Corp
700 Northwest 107th Avenue, Miami, FL 33172
Phone: 305 559-4000
Web: www.lennar.com

Selected Markets

East

Florida
New Jersey
North Carolina
South Carolina
Central
Georgia
Illinois
Indiana
Maryland
Minnesota
Tennessee
Virginia
Texas
West
Arizona
California
Colorado
Nevada
Oregon

Utah
Washington
Other: Urban divisions and other homebuilding related investments including FivePoint.

PRODUCTS/OPERATIONS

2018 Sales

	$ mil.	% of total
Homebuilding West	8,060	40
Homebuilding East	6,250	30
Homebuilding Texas	2,421	12
Homebuilding Central	2,291	11
Homebuilding Other	55	-
Lennar Financial Services	867	4
Lennar Multifamily	421	2
Rialto	205	1
Total	**20,572**	**100**

Selected Subsidiaries

360 Developers LLC
Eagle Bend Commercial LLC
Eagle Home Mortgage LLC
Heritage of Auburn Hills LLC
Lennar Associates Management LLC
Lennar Homes of California Inc.
Lennar Homes of Texas Sales and Marketing Ltd.
Lennar Ventures LLC
LH-EH Layton Lakes Estate LLC
Majestic Woods LLC
North American Title Company (MD)
Raintree Village L.L.C.
Savell Gulley Development LLC
Universal American Mortgage Company LLC
U.S. Home of Arizona Construction Co.

COMPETITORS

Beazer Homes
D.R. Horton
Hovnanian Enterprises
KB Home
M.D.C.
Meritage Homes
NVR
PulteGroup
TRI Pointe
Taylor Morrison
Toll Brothers

HISTORICAL FINANCIALS

Company Type: Public

Income Statement

FYE: November 30

	REVENUE ($ mil.)	NET INCOME ($ mil.)	NET PROFIT MARGIN	EMPLOYEES
11/20	22,488	2,465	11.0%	9,495
11/19	22,259	1,849	8.3%	10,106
11/18	20,571	1,695	8.2%	11,626
11/17	12,646	810	6.4%	9,111
11/16	10,950	911	8.3%	8,335
Annual Growth	**19.7%**	**28.2%**	**—**	**3.3%**

2020 Year-End Financials

Debt ratio: 19.90%
Return on equity: 14.48%
Cash ($ mil.): 2,859
Current ratio: 19.75
Long-term debt ($ mil.): 5,955

No. of shares (mil.): 312
Dividends
　Yield: 0.0%
　Payout: 7.9%
Market value ($ mil.): 23,721

	STOCK PRICE ($) FY Close	P/E High/Low		PER SHARE ($) Earnings	Dividends	Book Value
11/20	75.86	11	4	7.85	0.63	57.55
11/19	59.65	11	7	5.74	0.16	50.49
11/18	42.73	13	7	5.44	0.16	44.97
11/17	62.78	18	12	3.38	0.16	32.81
11/16	42.54	13	9	3.85	0.16	29.96
Annual Growth	**15.6%**	**—**	**—**	**19.5%**	**40.6%**	**17.7%**

LETTIE PATE EVANS FOUNDATION

EXECUTIVES

President, Charles H McTier
V Pres, P Russell Harding
Treasurer, J Lee Tribble
Secretary, Erik S Johnson
Officer, Elizabeth A Smith
Vice-Chairman, James M Sibley
Executive Director, Antone Callaway
Manager, Amy Todd
Vice President, Susan Shows
Vice President Marketing, John Cooper

LOCATIONS

HQ: LETTIE PATE EVANS FOUNDATION
191 PEACHTREE ST NE # 3540, ATLANTA, GA
303031740
Phone: 404 522-6755
Web: WWW.LPEVANS.ORG

HISTORICAL FINANCIALS
Company Type: Private

Income Statement				FYE: December 31
	ASSETS ($ mil.)	NET INCOME ($ mil.)	INCOME AS % OF ASSETS	EMPLOYEES
12/16	2,694	90	3.3%	12
12/15	44	11	25.0%	—
12/14	33	0		—
12/12	33	0	0.3%	—
Annual Growth	198.4%	444.0%	—	—

Liberty Media Corp (DE)

Dominion Energy dominates the American energy market as one of its top distributors of electricity and natural gas. The company serves some 7 million retail energy customers across eight US states with a special concentration in Virginia the Carolinas and Ohio. The company boasts an impressive energy portfolio with about 30700 MW of generating capacity as well as one of the largest underground natural gas storage systems with 1 trillion cu. ft. of capacity. Operating subsidiaries include Virginia Power and Dominion Energy Gas.

Operations

In 2019 Dominion Energy strategically realigned its segments which resulted in the formation of five primary operating segments: Dominion Energy Virginia Gas Transmission & Storage Gas Distribution Dominion Energy South Carolina and Contracted Generation.

The Dominion Energy Virginia segment is composed of Virginia Power's regulated electric transmission distribution (including customer service) and generation (regulated electric utility and its related energy supply) operations which serve approximately 2.6 million residential commercial industrial and governmental customers in Virginia and North Carolina. The segment accounts for about 45% total sales.

Gas Transmission & Storage segment includes FERC regulated interstate natural gas transmission

pipeline and underground storage systems in the eastern and Rocky Mountain regions of the U.S. (primarily through DETI DECG and Dominion Energy Questar Pipeline) LNG import/export and storage (through its 75% controlling interest in Cove Point) as well as a 50% noncontrolling partnership interest in Iroquois. It also includes nonregulated retail natural gas marketing development of renewable natural gas and LNG infrastructure and its investments in Atlantic Coast Pipeline Align RNG and Wrangler. The segment accounts for about 20% of total sales.

The Dominion Energy South Carolina segment is comprised of DESC's generation transmission and distribution of electricity to approximately 740000 customers in the central southern and southwestern portions of South Carolina and the distribution of natural gas to approximately 390000 residential commercial and industrial customers in South Carolina. The segment accounts for more than 15% of total sales.

The Gas Distribution segment includes Dominion Energy's regulated natural gas sales transportation gathering and distribution operations in Ohio West Virginia North Carolina Utah southwestern Wyoming and southeastern Idaho (through East Ohio Hope PSNC and Questar Gas) which collectively serve approximately 3.0 million residential commercial and industrial customers. The segment accounts for nearly 15% of total sales.

The Contracted Generation segment includes the operations of Millstone and associated energy marketing and price risk activities and Dominion Energy's long-term contracted renewable electric generation fleet as well as a 50% noncontrolling partnership interest in Fowler Ridge. The segment accounts for about 5% of total sales.

Geographic Reach

Headquartered in Richmond Virginia Dominion has operations in 18 states. Its Virginia Power subsidiary distributes power in North Carolina and Virginia.

Its East Ohio Gas Hope Gas and Questar subsidiaries distribute gas in Ohio West Virginia Utah Wyoming and Idaho..

Sales and Marketing

Dominion primarily sells electricity to retail customers consisting of residential homes and commercial businesses. Its subsidiary Virginia Power includes customers such as residential commercial and industrial customers as well as rural electric cooperatives and municipalities. The company serves more than 7 million utility and retail energy customers.

Financial Performance

Dominion has seen a steady rise in revenue in recent years with sales growing 42% between 2015 and 2019. Net income has fluctuated in recent years.

Revenue increased 23% in 2019 to some $16.6 billion due to a $1.5 billion increase from the SCANA Combination due to operations acquired ($2.5 billion) partially offset by a $1.0 billion charge for refunds of amounts previously collected from retail electric customers of DESC for the NND Project.

Net income declined 45% to about $1.4 billion in 2019 primarily due to charges for refunds of amounts previously collected from retail electric customers of DESC for the NND Project litigation acquired in the SCANA Combination a voluntary retirement program the planned early retirement of certain Virginia Power electric generation facilities and the absence of gains on the sales of certain equity method investments.

The company ended 2019 with $269 million in cash down $122 million from 2018. Operating activities contributed $5.2 billion while investing activities used $4.6 billion (mostly construction costs)

and financing activities used $704 million mainly for debt and dividend payments.

Strategy

Dominion is focusing on its regulated power and gas infrastructure assets to reduce its exposure to volatile energy markets. It acquired western US gas utility Questar in 2016 and southeastern US utility SCANA in 2019. The firm exited certain retail energy marketing operations in 2018; it also sold three merchant power generation plants for $1.3 billion and its 50% stake in midstream gas services provider Blue Racer for $1.2 billion.

Dominion's five-year investment plan for the 2019-23 period includes a focus on upgrading the electric system in Virginia through investments in additional renewable generation facilities smart meters customer information platform intelligent grid devices and associated control systems physical and cyber security investments strategic undergrounding and energy conservation programs. Dominion Energy also plans to upgrade its gas and electric transmission and distribution networks and meet environmental requirements and standards set by various regulatory bodies.

Mergers and Acquisitions

In early 2019 Dominion acquired SCANA Corporation in a transaction valued at $13.4 billion adding some 1.6 million customers to Dominion's already massive base and expanding its power and gas utility operations in the Carolinas. SCANA and its subsidiaries including South Carolina Electric & Gas Company Public Service Company of North Carolina and SCANA Energy Marketing became part of Dominion's newly formed Southeast Energy segment. The deal included the assumption of financial obligations (including customer refunds) related to two SCANA nuclear reactors that will not be completed due to construction delays and cost overruns.

Also in 2019 Dominion acquired the remaining interest in majority owned subsidiary Dominion Energy Midstream Partners through a share exchange transaction valued at about $1.6 billion.

In addition the company acquired two solar projects in Virginia and one solar project in South Carolina in 2019. The previous year it purchased two solar projects in North Carolina and Virginia for $250 million.

Company Background

Dominion Energy traces its roots to the founding of the Upper Appomattox Company in Virginia in 1795. The company managed water rights and eventually ran power plants. The Virginia Railway and Power Company (VR&P) acquired Upper Appomattox in 1909 along with several other utilities in the following year. VR&P became Virginia Electric and Power Company (Virginia Power) after being acquired by engineering firm Stone & Webster in 1925. Virginia Power acquired Virginia Public Service Company and built numerous power plants in the following years. It expanded into gas exploration in the 1990s.

In 2000 Dominion bought Consolidated Natural Gas (CNG) for $9 billion making it one of the largest fully integrated gas and electric power companies in the US; it then sold CNG's Virginia Natural Gas to AGL Resources and the two firms' combined Latin American assets to Duke Energy. It sold its telecom business in 2004 the bulk of its oil and gas exploration operations in 2007 and utility Peoples Natural Gas in 2010. In 2016 Dominion bought gas utility Questar for $4.4 billion.

In 1983 Dominion Resources was incorporated as a parent company for Virginia Power. The holding company changed its name to Dominion Energy in 2017.

Auditors: KPMG LLP

LOCATIONS

HQ: Liberty Media Corp (DE)
  12300 Liberty Boulevard, Englewood, CO 80112
Phone: 720 875-5400
Web: www.libertymedia.com

HISTORICAL FINANCIALS
Company Type: Public

Income Statement   FYE: December 31

	REVENUE ($ mil.)	NET INCOME ($ mil.)	NET PROFIT MARGIN	EMPLOYEES
12/19	10,292	106	1.0%	6,753
12/18	8,040	531	6.6%	4,641
12/17	7,594	1,354	17.8%	4,393
12/16	5,276	680	12.9%	3,626
12/15	4,795	64	1.3%	3,503
Annual Growth	21.0%	13.4%	—	17.8%

2019 Year-End Financials

Debt ratio: 35.02%
Return on equity: 0.64%
Cash ($ mil.): 1,222
Current ratio: 0.62
Long-term debt ($ mil.): 15,416
No. of shares (mil.): 599
Dividends
  Yield: —
  Payout: —
Market value ($ mil.): 27,547

	STOCK PRICE ($) FY Close	P/E High/Low	PER SHARE ($) Earnings	Dividends	Book Value
12/19	45.97	— —	(1.33)	0.00	27.19
12/18	30.70	— —	(0.00)	0.00	27.31
12/17	34.16	— —	(0.00)	0.00	27.42
12/16	31.33	34 16	1.12	0.00	25.10
12/15	38.08	212175	0.19	0.00	32.68
Annual Growth	4.8%	—	—	—	(4.5%)

Liberty Media Corp (DE)

Auditors: KPMG LLP

LOCATIONS

HQ: Liberty Media Corp (DE)
  12300 Liberty Boulevard, Englewood, CO 80112
Phone: 720 875-5400
Web: www.libertymedia.com

HISTORICAL FINANCIALS
Company Type: Public

Income Statement   FYE: December 31

	REVENUE ($ mil.)	NET INCOME ($ mil.)	NET PROFIT MARGIN	EMPLOYEES
12/19	7,794	494	6.3%	6,667
12/18	5,771	676	11.7%	4,555
12/17	5,425	1,124	20.7%	4,393
12/16	5,014	413	8.2%	3,626
12/15	4,552	259	5.7%	
Annual Growth	14.4%	17.5%		

2019 Year-End Financials

Debt ratio: 29.42%
Return on equity: 4.64%
Cash ($ mil.): 493
Current ratio: 0.42
Long-term debt ($ mil.): 9,244
No. of shares (mil.): 316
Dividends
  Yield: —
  Payout: —
Market value ($ mil.): 15,298

	STOCK PRICE ($) FY Close	P/E High/Low	PER SHARE ($) Earnings	Dividends	Book Value
12/19	48.34	31 23	1.53	0.00	33.74
12/18	36.80	24 17	2.01	0.00	32.54
12/17	39.66	14 10	3.31	0.00	32.31
12/16	34.52	44 33	0.88	0.00	30.09
12/15	39.25	— —	(0.00)	0.00	(0.00)
Annual Growth	5.3%	—	—	—	—

Lilly (Eli) & Co

Eli Lilly is a leading pharmaceutical company that develops depression endocrinology oncology and cardiovascular care medicines. Its top-selling drugs include Cymbalta for depression and pain Alimta for lung cancer Humalog and Humulin insulin for diabetes and Cialis for erectile dysfunction. Lilly also makes medications to treat schizophrenia and bipolar disorder (Zyprexa) osteoporosis (Forteo) ADHD (Strattera) gastric and lung cancer (Cyramza) and diabetes (Jardiance and Trulicity). The company which has around 10 production and distribution facilities in about 10 countries generates most of its revenue in the US.

HISTORY

Colonel Eli Lilly pharmacist and Union officer in the Civil War started Eli Lilly and Company in 1876 with $1300. His process of gelatin-coating pills led to sales of nearly $82000 in 1881. Later the company made gelatin capsules which it still sells. Lilly died in 1898 and his son and two grandsons ran the business until 1953.

Eli Lilly began extracting insulin from the pancreases of hogs and cattle in 1923; 6000 cattle glands or 24000 hog glands made one ounce of the substance. Other products created in the 1920s and 1930s included antiseptic Merthiolate sedative Seconal and treatments for pernicious anemia and heart disease. In 1947 the company began selling diethylstilbestrol (DES) a drug to prevent miscarriages. Eli Lilly researchers isolated the antibiotic erythromycin from a species of mold found in the Philippines in 1952. Lilly was also the major supplier of Salk polio vaccine.

The company enjoyed a 70% share of the DES market by 1971 when researchers noticed that a rare form of cervical cancer afflicted many of the daughters of women who had taken the drug. The FDA restricted the drug's use and Lilly found itself on the receiving (and frequently losing) end of a number of trailblazing product-liability suits that stretched into the 1990s.

The firm diversified in the 1970s buying Elizabeth Arden (cosmetics 1971; sold 1987) and IVAC (medical instruments 1977). It launched such products as analgesic Darvon and antibiotic Ceclor.

Lilly's 1982 launch of Humulin a synthetic insulin developed by Genentech made it the first company to market a genetically engineered product. In 1986 the company introduced Prozac; that year it also bought biotech firm Hybritech for $300 million (sold in 1995 for less than $10 million). In 1988 Lilly introduced anti-ulcerative Axid. It founded pesticides and herbicides maker DowElanco with Dow Chemical in 1989.

Trying to find a new product outlet the firm bought pharmacy benefit management company PCS Health Systems from what is now McKesson in 1994. But an FTC mandate to offer rival drugs and a lack of mail-order sales contributed to poor results which ultimately led Lilly to sell PCS to Rite Aid and exit this arena completely in 1998.

Eli Lilly in 1995 bought medical communications network developer Integrated Medical Systems. That year the firm and developer Centocor introduced ReoPro a blood-clot inhibitor used in angioplasties. The next year it launched antipsychotic Zyprexa Humalog and Gemzar and Prozac was approved to treat bulimia nervosa.

In 1997 the firm sold its DowElanco stake to Dow. In 1998 the Lilly Endowment passed the Ford Foundation as the US's largest charity largely due to Prozac (it has since been passed by the Bill & Melinda Gates Foundation). That year Lilly began trying to stop Chinese drugmakers from infringing on its patents for Prozac's active ingredient.

In 1999 a US federal judge found the firm illegally promoted osteoporosis drug Evista as a breast cancer preventative similar to AstraZeneca's Nolvadex. Lilly halted tests on its variation of heart drug Moxonidine after 53 patients died. Also that year Zyprexa was approved to treat bipolar disorder.

In 2000 the firm began marketing Prozac under the Sarafem name for severe premenstrual syndrome. A federal appeals court knocked more than two years off Prozac's patent reducing the expected 2003 expiration date to 2001 creating a negative impact on Lilly's annual sales (Prozac had accounted for 30% of revenues). Lilly suffered another blow when a potential successor to Prozac failed in clinical trials and became embroiled in legal maneuverings with generics maker Barr Pharmaceuticals.

While the firm fretted over Prozac and its patents it continued work to find its next blockbuster. In 2000 Lilly and partner ICOS announced favorable results from a study of erectile dysfunction treatment Cialis which was approved in Europe in 2002 and in the US in 2004. (Several years later Lilly acquired ICOS and with it full ownership of the Cialis franchise.)

In 2001 Lilly bought a minority stake in Isis Pharmaceuticals a developer of antisense drugs and licensed from it an antisense lung cancer drug. Also that year the firm launched Lilly BioVentures a venture fund aimed at private biotech startup companies. In 2002 the company settled with eight states in an infringement-of-privacy case involving the company's accidental disclosure of e-mail addresses for more than 600 Prozac patients.

In late 2004 the druggernaut was one of several pharmas hit by bad news about drug side effects. Lilly announced its attention-deficit disorder drug Strattera had been linked to rare liver problems. The company agreed to add warning labels about the potential side effects to the drug's packaging and advertisements. The company also began facing trouble over Zyprexa as consumer lawsuits claiming diabetes and high blood pressure began pouring in. The majority of suits were settled in 2005 and 2007 for some $1.2 billion.

Generalized anxiety disorder drug Cymbalta was approved by the FDA and released in 2006 and osteoporosis drug Evista was approved for an expanded indication as a breast cancer preventative for postmenopausal women in 2007.

Also in 2007 the company acquired and absorbed development partner ICOS for $2.1 billion; the deal gave Lilly full ownership of Viagra-competitor Cialis. Lilly dropped a joint-development effort with another partner Alkermes for an inhaled insulin device in 2008.

The company gradually reduced its workforce by more than 10% between 2003 and 2008 to fight off the effects of generic competition and other challenges. Other restructuring measures included an employee attrition plan announced in 2007 a management restructuring in 2008 and a manufacturing consolidation program launched in 2008.

After a lengthy lawsuit regarding its patents for its top seller Zyprexa a federal judge ruled in Lilly's favor in 2008 against generic manufacturers IVAX Dr. Reddy's Laboratories and Teva Pharmaceutical Industries. Federal courts ruled that the drug's patents would remain valid until October 2011.

To fuel growth in the biopharmaceuticals market the firm completed a $1 billion biotech research facility in Indianapolis in 2008. It further expanded through the 2008 acquisition of biotech firm ImClone for about $6.5 billion; ImClone began operating as a research subsidiary of Lilly following the transaction. ImClone already had one approved blockbuster therapy Erbitux for colorectal and head/neck cancers and was developing numerous other cancer therapy candidates. Lilly also expanded its biotech oncology program earlier that year by purchasing development partner SGX Pharmaceuticals for $64 million. SGX was absorbed into Lilly's research operations.

EXECUTIVES

Svp And President Elanco Animal Health, Jeffrey N. (Jeff) Simmons, age 53
Svp And President Diabetes Business Unit And Lilly Usa, Enrique A. Conterno, age 53, $727,960 total compensation
President Manufacturing Operations, Maria Crowe, age 60
Svp And President Lilly International, Alfonso G. (Chito) Zulueta, age 57
Svp And President Lilly Oncology, Susan (Sue) Mahony, age 55
President And Ceo, David A. Ricks, age 52
Svp And President Lilly Bio-medicines, Christi Shaw
Svp And President Manufacturing Operations, Myles O'Neill
Svp Enterprise Risk Management And Chief Ethics And Compliance Officer, Melissa Stapleton Barnes, age 51
Svp And General Counsel, Michael J. Harrington, age 57, $827,400 total compensation
Svp And Cio, Aarti Shah
Svp And Cfo, Josh Smiley
Svp Science And Technology And President Lilly Research Labs, Daniel (Dan) Skovronsky
Svp Development Center Of Excellence And Chief Medical Officer, Timothy Garnett
Vice President Gra International, Susan Forda
Department Head Space Planning, Brent Blanchard
National Account Manager Managed Healthcare Services, Ruthanna Curry
Vice President Medical Affiars, Robert Heine
Vice President Medicine Development Unit Diabetes And Clinical Transformation, Rob Metcalf
Senior Vice President Finance And Treasurer, Philip Johnson
Senior Medical Director, Thomas Hardy
Medical Director, Anurita Majumdar
Vice President And Medical Director China, Li Wang
Vice President Global Product Team Leader, Benjamin Anderson
Government Relations, Joel Worthington
National Sales Manager, Paul Huibers
Vice President Parenteral Manufacturing Operations, Ken Whitehead
Medical Director, Jana Farr
Medical Director, Susan Kindig
Medical Director, Bo Chao
Assistant Vice President Communications, Tracy Henrikson
Associate Vp It, Geri Kern

Senior Vice President Global Quality, Johna Norton
Vice President Human Resources, Giorgio Davidoni
Medical Director Diabetes, Elisa Razzoli
Vice President, Marie Schiller
Medical Director Lilly Oncology, Heather Wasserstrom
National Account Manager Channel Accounts, Kristen Tinglum
Associate Vice President Organizational Learning And Development, Kristin Zemanek
Pharmd Surveillance Assoc, Russell Nichols
Senior Medical Director, Paulo Reis
National Account Manager, Nguyen Trang
Vice President, Gregory Plowman
National Sales Manager, Hostettler Danica
Medical Director Onc Platform Team, Merchant Fonny
Vice President Global Regulatory Affairs, Daniel Binette
Vice President For Information Technology, Alex Vorobeychik
Chairman, John C. Lechleiter
Board Of Visitors, Sonia Arnold
Board Member, Jessi Pitrelli
Secretary, Jose P Fernandes
Board Member, Brenda Pfister
Auditors: Ernst & Young LLP

LOCATIONS

HQ: Lilly (Eli) & Co
Lilly Corporate Center, Indianapolis, IN 46285
Phone: 317 276-2000
Web: www.lilly.com

2018 Sales

	$ mil.	% of total
US	13,875	57
Europe	4,231	17
Japan	2,493	10
Other	3,955	16
Total	**24,555**	**100**

PRODUCTS/OPERATIONS

2018 Sales

	$ mil.	% of total
Trulicity	3,199	13
Humalog	2,996	12
Alimta	2,132	9
Cialis	1,851	8
Forteo	1,575	6
Humulin	1,331	5
Other Products	8,325	34
Animal Health	3,142	13
Total	**24,555**	**100**

Selected Products and Indications

Neuroscience
Amyvid (florbetapir F 18 injection)
Cymbalta (duloxetine hydrocholoride; depression anxiety pain; also for managing fibromyalgia and chronic musculoskeletal pain in the US)
Prozac (fluoxetine hydrochloride; depression panic disorder obsessive-compulsive disorder and bulimia nervosa)
Strattera (atomoxetine hydrochloride ADHD)
Symbyax (olanzapine and fluoxetine hydrochloride bipolar and treatment-resistant depression)
Zyprexa (olanzapine schizophrenia and bipolar)
Zyprexa Relprevv (Zypadhera in the EU long-acting injectable Zyprexa)
Endocrinology (including diabetes)
Actos (pioglitazone hydrochloride type 2 diabetes)
Alimta (non-small cell lung cancer)
Axiron (testosterone topical for testosterone deficiency)
Erbitux (colorectal cancers head and neck cancers)
Evista (raloxifene hydrochloride osteoporosis and breast cancer prevention in postmenopausal women)
Forteo (osteoporosis)
Gemzar (pancreatic cancer metastatic breast cancer non-small cell lung cancer; bladder cancer in the EU)
Glucagon (injection rDNA origin)

Humalog (insulin lispro injection rDNA origin; diabetes)
Humalog Mix 75/25 (75% Insulin lispro protamine suspension 25% insulin lispro injection rDNA origin; diabetes)
Humalog Mix 50/50 (50% Insulin lispro protamine suspension 50% insulin lispro injection rDNA origin; diabetes)
Humalog Pen (insulin lispro rDNA origin; diabetes)
Humatrope (somatropin for injection rDNA origin; growth disorders)
Humulin (human insulin rDNA origin; diabetes)
Humulin Pen (human insulin rDNA origin; diabetes)
Tradjenta (type 2 diabetes)
Oncology (cancer)
Alimta (pemetrexed non-small cell lung cancer and malignant pleural mesothelioma)
Erbitux (colorectal head and neck cancers; from ImClone)
Gemzar (gemcitabine hydrochloride; pancreatic breast lung bladder and ovarian cancers)
Cardiovascular
Adcirca (pulmonary arterial hypertension)
Cialis (tadalafil erectile dysfunction; benign prostatic hyperplasia in US)
Efient/Effient (atherothrombotic events)
Livalo (statin high cholesterol)
ReoPro (percutaneous coronary intervention)
Animal Health (Elanco)
Apralan (antibiotic to control enteric infections in calves and swine)
Coban Monteban and Maxiban (anticoccidal for poultry)
Comfortis (flea infestation prevention tablets for dogs)
Micotil Pulmotil and Pulmotil AC (antibiotics for respiratory disease in cattle swine and poultry respectively)
Paylean Optaflexx (leanness and performance enhancers for swine and cattle respectively)
Posilac (protein supplement for enhanced milk productivity in cows)
Reconcile (separation anxiety for dogs)
Rumensin (feed additive)
Surmax/Maxus (performance enhancer for swine and poultry)
Trifexis (chewable tablet for dogs to prevent flea infestations and heartworm disease and control intestinal parasite infections)
Tylan (antibiotic)
Other pharmaceuticals (including anti-infectives)
Ceclor (bacterial infections)
Vancocin (staphylococcal infections)

COMPETITORS

Abbott Labs	Merck
Amgen	Novartis
AstraZeneca	Novo Nordisk
Bayer AG	Pfizer
Bristol-Myers Squibb	Roche Holding
Dr. Reddy's	Sanofi
GlaxoSmithKline	Takeda Pharmaceutical
Johnson & Johnson	

HISTORICAL FINANCIALS

Company Type: Public

Income Statement   FYE: December 31

	REVENUE ($ mil.)	NET INCOME ($ mil.)	NET PROFIT MARGIN	EMPLOYEES
12/19	22,319	8,318	37.3%	33,625
12/18	24,555	3,232	13.2%	38,680
12/17	22,871	(204)	—	40,655
12/16	21,222	2,737	12.9%	41,975
12/15	19,958	2,408	12.1%	41,275
Annual Growth	2.8%	36.3%	—	(5.0%)

2019 Year-End Financials

Debt ratio: 38.99%	No. of shares (mil.): 957
Return on equity: 133.78%	Dividends
Cash ($ mil.): 2,438	Yield: 1.9%
Current ratio: 1.16	Payout: 29.0%
Long-term debt ($ mil.): 13,817	Market value ($ mil.): 125,848

	STOCK PRICE ($) FY Close	P/E High/Low	Earnings	Dividends	Book Value
12/19	131.43	15 12	8.89	2.58	2.72
12/18	115.72	38 24	3.13	2.25	9.30
12/17	84.46	— —	(0.19)	2.08	10.54
12/16	73.55	33 25	2.58	2.04	12.72
12/15	84.26	40 30	2.26	2.00	13.18
Annual Growth	11.8%	— —	40.8%	6.6%	(32.6%)

HISTORICAL FINANCIALS
Company Type: Private

Income Statement   FYE: December 31

	REVENUE ($ mil.)	NET INCOME ($ mil.)	NET PROFIT MARGIN	EMPLOYEES
12/09	10,048	(451)	—	1,300
12/08	17,479	94	0.5%	—
Annual Growth	(42.5%)	—	—	—

LIMETREE BAY TERMINALS LLC

HOVENSA brings together US and Latin American know-how and operations to handle oil products in the US Virgin Islands. HOVENSA is a joint venture of Hess and Venezuelan oil giant PDVSA (its major crude oil supplier). Once the largest private employer in the US Virgin Islands the company operated a 500000-barrels-per-day crude oil refinery on St. Croix along with two specialized oil processing complexes a 150000-barrels-per-day fluid catalytic cracking unit and a 58000-barrels-per-day delayed coker unit. However the St. Croix refinery had run up losses for years; it was shut down in 2012 and was put up for sale in 2013.

Strategy
Citing high operating and maintenance costs (the refinery was fueled by oil not the cheaper natural gas) and the growth of lower-cost refineries in emerging markets HOVENSA has posted $1.3 billion in losses since 2009. As a result the company decided to cut its losses by converting the refinery into an oil storage terminal which can take advantage of St. Croix's strategic location. Its 55-ft. deep harbor enables it to receive crude oil tanker deliveries from Venezuela and around the world. The storage terminal employs about 100 workers. The shutdown of the refinery resulted in more than 2000 employes being laid off.

Company Background
In 2009 the global economic downturn depressed demand for oil caused a dip in production and prompted the company to lay off 270 employees (about 21% of its total contract workers).

Crude thoughput has declined steadily at HOVENSA due to weaker refining margins and planned and unplanned maintenance from 402000 barrels per day (bpd) in 2009 to 390000 bpd in 2010 to 284000 bpd in 2011.

Auditors: ERNST & YOUNG LLP NEW YORK N

LOCATIONS
HQ: LIMETREE BAY TERMINALS LLC
1 ESTATE HOPE, CHRISTIANSTED, VI 00820
Phone: 340 692-3000

COMPETITORS

Chevron	Royal Dutch Shell
ConocoPhillips	Sunoco
Exxon Mobil	Valero Energy
Marathon Oil	

Lincoln National Corp.

Lincoln National which operates as Lincoln Financial Group provides retirement planning and life insurance to individuals and employers through annuities 401k and savings plans and a variety of life dental and disability insurance products. The company does business through such subsidiaries as Lincoln National Life Insurance Lincoln Life & Annuity Company of New York and First Penn-Pacific Life Insurance Company. Lincoln Financial is also active in the investment management business offering individual and institutional clients such financial services as pension plans trusts and mutual funds through its subsidiaries.

Operations
Lincoln Financial operates through four segments: Life Insurance Annuities Group Protection and Retirement Plan Services.

The company's largest segment Life Insurance (more than 40% of total sales) offers term universal and variable policies; a linked benefit product; and a critical illness rider.

The Annuities segment (more than 25% of sales) offers fixed and variable annuities.

Group Protection (some 25% of sales) offers non-medical policies — primarily term life dental critical illness accident vision and disability products — to the employer market.

Retirement Plan Services (more than 5% of sales) provides employers with plans and services primarily in the defined contribution retirement plan marketplace.

Geographic Reach
Headquartered in Radnor Pennsylvania Lincoln Financial also has offices in Atlanta (Group Protection); Dover New Hampshire; Fort Wayne Indiana (Annuities and Retirement Plan Services); Greensboro North Carolina (Life Insurance); Omaha Nebraska; and Philadelphia.

Sales and Marketing
Lincoln Financial Network distributes Lincoln Financial products through a network of some 1000 planners and agents. Lincoln Financial Distributors is the company's wholesale distributor serving brokers consultants planners agents third party administrators financial advisors and other intermediaries. Lincoln Financial Distributors has more than 600 internal and external wholesalers and approximately 8600 active producers.

Group Protection distributes its products through employee benefits brokers third-party administrators and other employee benefit firms.

Financial Performance
Lincoln Financial has seen overall revenue growth over the past few years especially in 2017 and 201. Net income growth has been sporadic though.

In 2018 revenue increased 15% to $16.4 billion as insurance premiums fee income and net investment income all rose. Contributing to the rise in earned premiums was the addition of Liberty Life Assurance Company of Boston acquired midway through the year.

However net income fell 21% to $1.6 billion in 2018. This drop was largely due to a one-time federal income tax benefit received in 2017 which boosted net income that year by 74%. Acquisition-related expenses and the company's digitization initiative also cut into the bottom line.

The company ended 2018 with $2.3 billion in net cash some $7 million more than it had at the end of 2017. Operating activities provided $1.9 billion in cash and financing activities provided another $4.6 billion while investing activities used $5.8 billion.

Strategy
Like any company with heavy exposure to global macroeconomic conditions Lincoln Financial is vulnerable to capital market downturns which could lead to corporate losses. Additionally a number of the company's competitors have greater access to funds offer a broader range of products and enjoy a greater market share than Lincoln does. To meet the challenges of difficult economic times in the market the company has adopted strategies to strengthen its business that include investing in high-quality corporate securities to reduce asset risk escalating share repurchases and debt repayment and repricing life and annuity products to guarantee new business that is profitable. It is investing in product innovations and distribution channels to drive up revenues. And the company targets the fastest-growing industry segments while steering away from long-term guarantee products.

Lincoln Financial is also investing in technology to increase margins. Its current enterprise-wide digitization initiative is designed to improve customer experiences and provide for ease in meeting changing marketplace shifts. It expects to see annual benefits of between $90 million and $150 million beyond 2020 through the initiative.

Lincoln Financial is exploring additional financial strategies to address the statutory reserve strain that comes with its term and universal life products that contain secondary guarantees. It will shift its business to focus on products with shorter-duration liabilities and more limited liabilities.

Mergers and Acquisitions
In 2018 Lincoln Financial acquired Liberty Life Assurance Company of Boston from Liberty Mutual Insurance for $1.5 billion. The deal included Liberty's group benefits operations. Through the purchase Lincoln expanded its distribution reach.

Company Background
Lincoln National traces its roots to the founding of the Fraternal Assurance Society of America in 1902. After a founding member absconded with funds the remaining members obtained permission from Abraham Lincoln's son Robert to use his father's name and image to clean up the organization's reputation.

The company bought up other firms in the 1950s and 1960s and in 1968 it formed holding company Lincoln National. Soon it began diversifying buying Chicago Title and Trust (1969; sold 1985) as well as more life and reinsurance companies. Lincoln National also went into the health benefits business setting up its own HMO and investing in EMPHESYS (which it took public in 1994 divesting the remainder of its stock in 1995).

With the growth of retirement savings from baby boomers hitting their 50's the company shifted gears into wealth management. Lincoln National bought CIGNA's annuity and individual life insurance business and Aetna's US individual life insurance operations in 1998.

In 1999 after nearly a century in the heartland Lincoln National moved its headquarters to Philadelphia.

EXECUTIVES

President And Ceo; President Lincoln Financial Group, Dennis R. Glass, age 70, $1,200,000 total compensation

Evp Chief Human Resources Officer And Head Brand And Enterprise Communications, Lisa M. Buckingham, age 54, $578,448 total compensation

President Annuity Solutions Lincoln Financial Distributors And Lincoln Financial Network, Wilford H. (Will) Fuller, age 49, $650,000 total compensation

Evp And Cfo, Randal J. Freitag, age 57, $669,708 total compensation

Evp And Chief Investment Officer, Ellen Cooper, age 55

Evp And General Counsel, Kirkland L. Hicks, age 49, $575,000 total compensation

Evp Cio And Head Of Administrative Services, Kenneth S. Solon, age 59

Senior Vice President, Beth O'Brien

Assistant Vice President, Gina Boulton

Vice President And Chief Underwriter, Jordan J Carreira

Assistant Vice President, Richard Clay

Vice President, Joe Mitchell

Sales Vice President, Eric Patterson

Senior Vice President And Head Insurance Solutions Distribution, Andrew Bucklee

Assistant Vice President, Jennifer Flanagan

Senior Vice President Human Resources, George Murphy

Assistant Vice President Actuary, Henry Cheng

Senior Vice President, Andrew Yorks

Assistant Vice President And Senior Counsel, Jennifer Petruccelli

Assistant Vice President, Andy Scanlon

National Account Manager, Beth Griffith

Senior Counsel And Assistant Vice President, Michael Arnold

National Account Manager, Matt Jasa

Assistant Vice President Desktop Support Manager, Gina Hill

Assistant Vice President Financial Reporting And Expense Controls, Kathy Tibke

Vice President Human Resources, Rebecca Silva

Vice President, Brian Jenkins

Assistant Vice President Human Resources Business Partner, Carol Dowling

Second Vice President Corporate Actuary, Mike Antrobus

Vice President Customer Service, Wanda Pritchett

Vice President Talent Management, Nancy Rogers

Vp And Head Consultant Relations Retirement Plan Services, Jason Key

Senior Counsel And Assistant Vice President, Wayne Mcclain

Senior Vice President And Chief Human Resources Officer, Lisa Bettinger-buckingham

Vice President Institutional Retirement Distribution Retirement Plan Services, Jayson West

Vice President Of Human Resources Administration, Stephen Dovey

Senior Vice President Strategic Relationship Management, Rachel Jacobs

Assistant Vice President Underwriting, Frank Asplund

Assistant Vice President, Marc Tomlinson

Assistant Vice President Information Technology Shared Services, Michele Fedgechin

Assistant Vice President Total Rewards, Amber Chandler

Assistant Vice President Internal Audit, Claude Campbell

Sales Vice President, David Duckworth

Assistant Vice President And Senior Counsel, Sam Goldstein

Sales Vice President, Valerie Staublin

Assistant Vice President, David Furman

Assistant Vice President Field Development, Angela Whitcher

Avp Business Analysis Digital Technology, Casey Mathews

Vice President, Madhu Divyakola

Vice President Internal Communications, Claudia Wieber

Vice President Stable Value, William McLaren

Svp Human Resources, Patricia Insley

Assistant Vice President Procurement Strategy And Performance Excellence, John Hendrick

Tax Assistant Vice President, Jan Webb

Assistant Vice President Retirement Benefits, John Arko

Assistant Vice President And Counsel, Jeff Davis

Assistant Vice President Strategic Planning, Jeff Ryan

Assistant Vice President, Laurel Ciechon

Assistant Vice President Finance, Chris Reed

Vice President Commercial Real Estate Investments, Nick Heinzelmann

Vice President Talent Acquisition, Michael Kellar

Assistant Vice President And Associate Actuary, Jeffrey Curley

Senior Vice President Head Of Fixed Income, John Morriss

Senior Vice President Product And Solutions Management Rps, Ralph Ferraro

Senior Vice President And Head Annuity Life Retirement Group Protection And Distribution Informa, Robert Klaczak

Senior Vice President Finance Group Protection, Roger Martin

Senior Vice President Funds Management And Investments Law, Ronald Holinsky

Vice President And Associate General Counsel, Andrea Fox

Svp And Chief Ethics And Compliance Officer, Steve Harris

Avp Internet Architecture, Jae Park

Vice President, Matthew Condos

Senior Vice President And Head Enterprise Litigation And Legal Operations, Richard Spenner

National Account Manager, Tracey Lemelin

National Account Manager, Juanita Morris-gettings

Vice President Human Resources, Michael Semo

Assistant Vice President Enterprise Business Systems, Ken Weaver

Senior Vice President Life Product Management Individual Life Insurance, Stafford Thompson

Vice President Sales, Kevin Swantek

National Sales Manager, Tad Fifer

Vice President, Donald Keller

Medical Director, Mark Bell

Avp And Senior Counsel, Matt Creech

Vice President And Chief Counsel Group Protection, Tom Waldman

Assistant Vice President, Matt Pons

Vice President And Associate General Counsel, Mary Potter

National Account Manager, Tammy Mcginn

Vice President Chief Architect, Matthew Daniels

Vice President Data Center Network And Storage Services, Joseph Brannan

Vice President Individual Annuity New Business, Scott Bodenhafer

Vice President Account Management, Kerry Brooks

Avp National Accounts, Eli Oake-libow

Vice President Actuarial Valuation, William Obert

Regional Vice President Claims, Jeanette Zenner

Vice President Broker Dealer Operations, Jeff Sheftic

Assistant Vice President Sales Training Group Protection, Karen Rice

Assistant Vice President, Jerry Danielson

Vice President Distribution, Charles Callery

Vp Customer Service, Wendy Chase

Vice President National Account Sales, John Lemire

Assistant Vice President Product Risk Management, Tim Stickney

Assistant Vice President Shared Services, Rich Fargnoli

Assistant Vice President Application Development, Robert Mealey

Assistant Vice President Information Technology, Teresa Hopkins

Vice President; Senior Equity Trader, Gary Abrams

National Sales Manager, Watson Christi

Assistant Vice President, Tracy L Dyer

Vice President Of Investment And Planning Services, John Zurovitch

Assistant Vice President Consumer Marketing Analytics Corporate Marketing Communications And Strategy, Urvashi Singh

Vice President Regulatory And Litigation Counsel, Paul Chryssikos

Assistant Vice President Producer Solutions Operations, Kimberley Donahue

Svp Head Of Investment Products And Platforms, Edward Walters

Board Member, Eric Johnson

Chairman, William H. Cunningham, age 76

Board Member, Isaiah Tidwell

Board Member, Marilyn Ondecker

Board Member, David McDunn

Board Member, Deirdre Connelly

Corporate Treasurer, Christopher Giovanni

Vice President And Assistant Treasurer, Shantanu Mishra

Board Director, Pat Pittard

Auditors: Ernst & Young LLP

LOCATIONS

HQ: Lincoln National Corp.
150 N. Radnor Chester Road, Suite A305, Radnor, PA 19087
Phone: 484 583-1400
Web: www.lfg.com

PRODUCTS/OPERATIONS

2018 Sales

	$ mil.	% of total
Fee income	5,986	36
Net investment income	5,085	31
Insurance premiums	4,601	28
Realized gain excluding other-than-temporary impairment losses on securities	148	1
Amortization of deferred gain on business sold through reinsurance	9	-
Other	602	4
Adjustments	(7)	-
Total	**16,424**	**100**

2018 Sales by Segment

	$ mil.	% of total
Life Insurance	6,922	42
Annuities	4,383	27
Group Protections	3,757	23
Retirement Plan Services	1,178	7
Other	235	1
Adjustments	(51)	-
Total	**16,424**	**100**

Selected Subsidiaries

First Penn-Pacific Life Insurance Company
Lincoln Financial Advisors
Lincoln Financial Distributors
Lincoln Financial Foundation
Lincoln Financial Securities Corporation
Lincoln Investment Management Company
The Lincoln National Life Insurance Company
Lincoln National Management Corporation

COMPETITORS

AEGON
AIG
AXA Financial
American Equity Investment Life Holding Company
Guardian Life

John Hancock Financial Services
MassMutual
Nationwide Financial
New York Life
Northwestern Mutual
Principal Financial
Prudential
TIAA
Torchmark
Unum Group

HISTORICAL FINANCIALS

Company Type: Public

Income Statement   FYE: December 31

	ASSETS ($ mil.)	NET INCOME ($ mil.)	INCOME AS % OF ASSETS	EMPLOYEES
12/19	334,761	886	0.3%	11,357
12/18	298,147	1,641	0.6%	11,034
12/17	281,763	2,079	0.7%	10,194
12/16	261,627	1,192	0.5%	10,282
12/15	251,937	1,154	0.5%	10,535
Annual Growth	7.4%	(6.4%)	—	1.9%

2019 Year-End Financials

Debt ratio: 1.81%	No. of shares (mil.): 196
Return on equity: 5.21%	Dividends
Cash ($ mil.): 2,563	Yield: 2.5%
Current ratio: —	Payout: 37.0%
Long-term debt ($ mil.): —	Market value ($ mil.): 11,605

	STOCK PRICE ($) FY Close	P/E High/Low	PER SHARE ($) Earnings	Dividends	Book Value
12/19	59.01	15 12	4.38	1.48	100.11
12/18	51.31	11 6	7.40	1.32	69.71
12/17	76.87	8 7	9.22	1.16	79.43
12/16	66.27	13 6	5.03	1.00	63.97
12/15	50.26	13 10	4.51	0.80	55.84
Annual Growth	4.1%	— —	(0.7%)	16.6%	15.7%

Lithia Motors Inc

Lithia Motors has its foot on the growth pedal. The auto dealer specializes in famed US auto brands such as Chrysler General Motors and Ford through about 190 stores in select markets in 20 states. The firm sells some 30 brands of new domestic and imported vehicles and all brands of used vehicles and trucks through its stores and online. It also offers financing and replacement parts. The company generates almost a quarter of its revenue in California. Chairman Sidney DeBoer controls Lithia Motors through Lithia Holding Co.

Operations

Lithia has three segments: Import (more than 40% of sales) Domestic (around 35%) and Luxury (almost 25%).

The Domestic segment comprises retail automotive franchises that sell new vehicles manufactured by Chrysler General Motors and Ford. The Import segment covers retail automotive franchises that sell new vehicles made by Honda Toyota Subaru Nissan and Volkswagen. The Luxury segment sells new vehicles manufactured made by BMW Mercedes-Benz and Lexus.

The franchises in each segment also sell used vehicles parts and automotive services and automotive finance and insurance products.

Geographic Reach

Medford Oregon-based Lithia sells vehicles across 20 US states. California is Lithia's biggest market accounting for about a quarter of the company's total sales (and over 20% of total stores) followed by Oregon and Texas.

Sales and Marketing

Lithia sells through its stores and online website. It also maintains mobile versions of its websites and a mobile application in anticipation of greater adoption of mobile technology.

It also employs search engine optimization search engine marketing online display advertising (including re-targeting) social advertising and traditional media to reach more online prospects.

Advertising expenses were $111.9 million $108.7 million and $93.3 million in 2019 2018 and 2017 respectively.

Financial Performance

Lithia Motors has seen solid revenue growth in recent years as a growing economy has strengthened vehicle sales. It has a 61% overall growth from 2015.

Revenue increased to $12.7 billion in 2019 an approximately 7% increase from the year prior. The increase was driven by all segments except used vehicle wholesale.

During 2019 Lithia had a net income of $271.5 million compared to net income of $265.7 million during 2018.

Cash provided by operating activities was $500 million in fiscal 2019 while investing activities used $438 million. Financing activities used 9.1 million. Cash and cash equivalents at the end of 2019 totaled $84 million.

Strategy

Lithia builds long-term value for its customers employees and shareholders through the following strategies:

Driving operational excellence innovation and diversification. The company utilizes performance-based action plans to increase market share drive operational performance develop high-performing teams and foster manufacturer relationships.

Growth through acquisition and network optimization. Lithia increases its physical network of stores through acquisitions to strategically grow its presence and create density in its network providing convenience for customers.

Thoughtful capital allocation. The company constantly evaluates how to allocate capital including returning cash to its investors and investing in its stores. During 2019 Lithia paid $27.6 million in dividends. It also invested in its facilities utilizing $124.9 million for capital expenditures.

Mergers and Acquisitions

Lithia Motors has made a number of acquisitions in 2019. In August 2019 the company acquired Hazelton Honda in Pennsylvania which expands Lithia's store network into Eastern Pennsylvania. In mid-2019 Lithia acquired a Jaguar-Land Rover dealership in Mission Viejo California from Pendragon. It also added dealerships in New Jersey and West Virginia.

Company Background

Lithia Motors was founded in 1946 by Walt De-Boer as a Chrysler-Plymouth-Dodge dealership in Ashland Oregon. Walt's son Sidney is its chairman and grandson Bryan is president and CEO of the growing auto dealer.

EXECUTIVES

Svp Mergers And Acquisitions/operations, Bryan B. DeBoer, age 53, $950,000 total compensation
Vp Financial Planning, Christopher (Chris) Holzshu, age 46, $485,100 total compensation
Svp Operations, Scott A. Hillier, age 57, $485,100 total compensation
Svp And Cfo, John F. North, age 43, $302,500 total compensation
Vp Information Technology And Cio, Mark Smith

Svp Operations Dch Operations, George C. Liang, age 64, $378,000 total compensation
Regional Manager Vice President, Ken Wright
Vice President, TIM FREEBORN
Chairman, Sidney B. (Sid) DeBoer, age 76
Auditors: KPMG LLP

LOCATIONS

HQ: Lithia Motors Inc
150 N. Bartlett Street, Medford, OR 97501
Phone: 541 776-6401
Web: www.lithia.com

2016 Stores

	No.
California	35
Oregon	25
Texas	16
Montana	11
New Jersey	11
New York	10
Alaska	9
Washington	8
Iowa	7
Hawaii	5
Nevada	4
Idaho	4
North Dakota	3
New Mexico	2
Vermont	2
Massachusetts	1
Wyoming	1
Total	**154**

PRODUCTS/OPERATIONS

2016 Sales

	$ mil.	% of total
Import	3,764	43
Domestic	3,381	39
Luxury	1,528	18
Corporate and other	3	-
Total	**8,678**	**100**

2016 Sales

	$ mil.	% of total
New vehicles	4,938	57
Used vehicle retail	2,227	25
Service body & parts	844	10
Finance & insurance	330	4
Used vehicle wholesale	276	3
Fleet & other	60	1
Total	**8,678**	**100**

COMPETITORS

Ancira	Group 1 Automotive
AutoNation	Internet Brands
Autobytel	McCombs Enterprises
CarMax	Penske Automotive
David McDavid Auto Group	Group
Gillman Auto	Sonic Automotive

HISTORICAL FINANCIALS

Company Type: Public

Income Statement   FYE: December 31

	REVENUE ($ mil.)	NET INCOME ($ mil.)	NET PROFIT MARGIN	EMPLOYEES
12/19	12,672	271	2.1%	14,320
12/18	11,821	265	2.2%	13,643
12/17	10,086	245	2.4%	12,899
12/16	8,678	197	2.3%	11,170
12/15	7,864	183	2.3%	9,574
Annual Growth	12.7%	10.4%	—	10.6%

2019 Year-End Financials

Debt ratio: 58.15% No. of shares (mil.): 23
Return on equity: 20.38% Dividends
Cash ($ mil.): 84 Yield: 0.8%
Current ratio: 1.20 Payout: 10.5%
Long-term debt ($ mil.): 1,430 Market value ($ mil.): 3,410

	STOCK PRICE ($) FY Close	P/E High/Low		PER SHARE ($) Earnings	Dividends	Book Value
12/19	147.00	14	7	11.60	1.19	63.26
12/18	76.33	12	6	10.86	1.14	52.05
12/17	113.59	13	8	9.75	1.06	43.38
12/16	96.83	14	9	7.72	0.95	36.22
12/15	106.67	18	12	6.91	0.76	31.59
Annual Growth	8.3%	—	—	13.8%	11.9%	19.0%

Live Nation Entertainment Inc

Live Nation Entertainment holds center stage as the world's largest ticket seller and promoter of live entertainment. All total the company connects over 580 million fans across all of our concerts and ticketing platforms in 46 countries. Through Ticketmaster it sells more than 485 million tickets annually for events at arenas stadiums theaters festival sites clubs and other venues across the world. Live Nation owns operates has exclusive booking rights for or has an interest in some 275 venues including the House of Blues clubs. Also a leading artist management firm the company has nearly 110 managers providing services to more than 500 artists. Live Nation has offices in 40 countries and generates two-thirds of its revenue in the US.

Operations

Live Nation's reportable segments are Concerts Ticketing and Sponsorship & Advertising.

Its Concerts segment accounts for more than 80% of revenue. Operations involve global promotion of live music events in Live Nation-owned and operated venues and in rented third-party venues. The segment also operates and manages music venues and produces music festivals across the world.

Live Nation's Ticketing segment accounts for nearly 15% of revenues. It sells tickets for events on behalf of clients and retains a fee or service charge for these services. It sells tickets through websites mobile apps ticket outlets and telephone call centers.

Sponsorship & Advertising generates about 5% of revenues. The segment sells space across its venues tickets websites and other properties to help brands reach fans.

Geographic Reach

Beverly Hills California-based Live Nation owns operates leases or has booking rights in some 145 North American venues and about 80 international ones. The company generates over a third of its revenue from international operations.

Sales and Marketing

Live Nation promotes its events and sells tickets through websites (www.livenation.com and www.ticketmaster.com) and apps. It also sells tickets in numerous retail outlets and call centers.

The company spent $452.7 million $443.2 million and $378.1 million on advertising and promotional expenses for the years 2019 2018 and 2017 respectively.

Financial Performance

Live Nation's revenue increased consistently year-over-year over the last five years as supply and demand for live entertainment continues to grow along with festival attendance and large strategic sponsors. Profits during this time however were all over the map. The company recorded losses in 2015 and 2017 before reporting strong earnings in 2018 and 2019.

Live Nation continued to see strong demand for live events in 2019 driving 7% revenue growth to $11.5 billion up from $10.8 billion in 2018. Its Concerts segment was the largest contributor to revenue growth Overall Concerts sales grew by 1.5 million an increase of 19% over the prior year.

Net income grew in to $69.9 million 2019 from $60.2 million in 2018.

Cash at the end of 2019 was $2.5 billion including the face value of tickets sold for clients. The firm generally does not use client cash for financing or investing as the amounts are payable to clients on a regular basis. Cash from operations was $469.8 million while investing activities used $691 million. Financing activities provided $328.9 million.

Strategy

Live Nation's strategy is to grow and innovate through the initiatives listed below.

Expanding its Concert Platform. Live Nation will deliver more shows grow its fan base and increase its ticket sales by continuing to build portfolio of concerts globally expanding business into additional top global music markets and further building presence in existing markets.

Growing its Revenue per Show. Live Nation will grow revenue per show across its venues through more effective ticket pricing broader ticketing distribution and more targeted promotional marketing.

Selling More Tickets and Investing in Product Improvements. Live Nation is focused on selling tickets through a wide set of sales channels including mobile and online and leveraging its fan database.

Growing Sponsorship and Advertising Partnerships. Live Nation will continue to drive growth in its sponsorship relationships and capture a larger share of the global music sponsorship market.

Company Background

Robert Sillerman began his career teaching advertisers how to reach young consumers. He started investing in radio and TV stations and founded SFX Broadcasting (named for a scrambling of his initials) in 1992. In early 1997 the firm entered the live entertainment field with the formation of SFX Concerts. In 1998 it acquired national concert producer PACE Entertainment.

Radio station owner Clear Channel Communications bought the firm for about $4 billion in 2000. SFX became Clear Channel Entertainment and was spun off as a publicly traded company in 2005. The company gained House of Blues-branded music venues the following year when it acquired rival HOB Entertainment for $354 million. In 2010 the company acquired Ticketmaster Entertainment and became Live Nation Entertainment.

HISTORY

Robert Sillerman began his career teaching advertisers how to reach young consumers. He started investing in radio and TV stations and founded SFX Broadcasting (named for a scrambling of his initials) in 1992. In early 1997 the firm entered the live entertainment field with the formation of SFX Concerts and the purchase of concert promoter Delsener/Slater.

When SFX Broadcasting agreed to be bought in 1997 by Capstar Broadcasting 87% controlled by investment firm Hicks Muse Tate & Furst (now HM Capital) SFX Entertainment was formed to house the live entertainment operations (it was spun off in 1998). In 1998 the company continued its rapid acquisition rate with the purchases of sports marketing and management team FAME New England concert promoter Don Law and national concert producer PACE Entertainment.

In 1999 the company bought concert promoter The Cellar Door Companies (which almost doubled SFX's size) sports marketing firm Integrated Sports International sporting event management company The Marquee Group sports talent agency Hendricks Management 50% of urban-music producer A.H. Enterprises and troubled theatrical producer Livent. SFX also made its first foray abroad through its purchase of Apollo Leisure a UK-based live entertainment firm. The company rolled all of its sports talent and marketing businesses into a new division SFX Sports Group that year.

In 2000 SFX jumped on the other side of the acquisition train when it was bought by radio station owner Clear Channel Communications for about $4 billion. Sillerman stepped down as chairman and CEO and was replaced by Clear Channel EVP Brian Becker. Later that year SFX acquired Philadelphia-based concert promoter and venue operator Electric Factory Concerts; Core Audience Entertainment Canada's second-largest concert promoter and events marketer; and the Cotter Group a North Carolina-based motorsports marketing agency.

In 2001 SFX acquired a majority interest in the International Hot Rod Association. It also bought professional golf talent agency Signature Sports Group. Later that year the company changed its name to Clear Channel Entertainment. It also continued expansion into Europe with the acquisition of Trident Agency and Milano Concerti music promotion businesses in Italy.

While operating as Clear Channel Entertainment Live Nation spent nearly $2 billion on acquisitions (Pace Entertainment Livent) almost single-handedly consolidating the live entertainment industry.

Before being spun off in December 2005 the company changed its name to CCE Spinco then Live Nation. Also that year Randall Mays became chairman and Michael Rapino replaced Becker as CEO. As part of the Clear Channel spinoff the company relocated from Houston to headquarters in tony Beverly Hills. It trimmed the fat by shutting down operating divisions such as museum exhibitions and music publishing (and laying off about 400 employees in the process) in order to focus on its core businesses of live music concerts venue management and website brand development.

In 2006 the company acquired rival HOB Entertainment for $354 million. Live Nation used the acquisition to expand its presence in the midsized venue business and fill in geographic gaps in its existing amphitheater network. As part of the deal Live Nation gained high-profile House of Blues-branded music venues such as San Francisco's Fillmore Auditorium Jones Beach in New York and London's Apollo Theatre and Wembley Arena. The company subsequently began re-branding many of its midsize clubs "Fillmore" after the San Francisco venue.

The company had in 2005 formed Delirium Concert LP a joint venture with Cirque du Soleil. The Delirium tour began in 2006. The following year Live Nation signed a $120 million deal with pop icon Madonna. Through its North American Music segment in 2007 Live Nation promoted or produced some 10000 live music events including tours for Van Halen Dave Matthews Band and Kenny Chesney. International Music operations for the year included Cirque De Soleil's Delirium as well as UK's Reading Festival. Also in 2007 the company produced global tours for legends such as The Police The Rolling Stones Genesis and The Who and presented some 5000 theatrical performances such as the UK touring production of Chicago through its Global Theater operations.

In 2008 the company divested itself of its North American theatrical assets. Later that year the company signed pacts with U2 and Jay-Z. Michael Cohl chairman and Live Nation Artists chief who spearheaded the deals later resigned over conflicts with CEO Rapino. Also in 2008 the company sold its motor sports operations. In early 2010 the company acquired Ticketmaster Entertainment and Live Nation changed its name to Live Nation Entertainment.

EXECUTIVES

President House Of Blues Entertainment, Ronald (Ron) Bension, age 65

Evp General Counsel And Secretary, Michael G. Rowles, age 55, $750,000 total compensation

Co-president North America Concerts, Mark Campana, age 62

Ceo And Director, Michael (Mike) Rapino, age 55, $2,300,000 total compensation

Chairman Global Music And President Global Touring, Arthur Fogel, age 67

President And Coo, Joe Berchtold, age 55, $1,100,000 total compensation

President European Music Clear Channel Music Group, Alan Ridgeway, age 53, $730,025 total compensation

Cfo, Kathy Willard, age 54, $850,000 total compensation

President Media And Sponsorship, Russell Wallach, age 54

President Live Nation Europe - Concerts, John Reid, age 58

Evp Mergers And Acquisitions And Strategic Finance, John Hopmans, age 61

President Ticketmaster North America, Jared Smith, age 42

Co-president North America Concerts, Bob Roux, age 62

President Ticketmaster International, Mark Yovich, age 45

Cio, David Huckabay

President Production Film And Television, Heather Parry

Vice President National Sales, Craig Hoover

Senior Vice President Of Global Information Technology Financial Systems, Tim Moran

Vice President Legal Business Affairs, Chris Laffoon

Senior Vice President Relationship And Loyalty Marketing, Phil Seward

Senior Vice President Marketing And Business Development, David Fortin

Senior Vice President, Gary Mckenzie

Senior Vice President, Stacie George

Vice President Information Technology Ap, Alysia Piccioni

Vice President Finance House Of Blues Clubs, Nathan Scott

Vice President Of Sales, Kate Walsh

Vp Of Marketing, Jim Sutcliffe

Vice President Planning, George Duran

Vice President Human Resources, Shawn Imitatesdog

Regional Vice President, Danny Eaton

Vice President Controller, Bill Janney

Regional Vice President Of Finance, Frank Brayer

Senior Vice President Marketing, Joey Scoleri

Svp Marketing Solutions, Jeff Condon

Vice President Legal Affairs, Leslie Holland

Senior Vice President Of Legal Affairs, Sheila Small

Senior Vice President Human Resources, Laura Morton-rowe

Vice President Marketing, Brad Locker

Svp Government Relations, Becky Relic

Svp And Treasurer, Bill Lowe

Executive Vice President Operations, Robert Simeone

Evp Client Revenue North America, Cole Gahagan

Vice President Information Technology, Dave Gerardi

Senior Vice President Aoministration, Linda Gross

Vp Marketing, Kim Shiver

Senior Vice President, Django Bayless

Vice President Marketing And Publicity, Annasivia Britt

Regional Vice President, Rob Scolaro

Vice President Midwest Music, Dan Kemer

Svp Mergers And Acquisitions, Michael Wichser

Vice President Programmatic And Product Innovation, Mike Finnegan

Vice President, Michael McGaw

Vice President Account Management, Joe Ventura

Vice President Of Business Development And Strategy, Christopher Sumner

Regional Vice President, Louis Giangola

Vice President Technology Optimization, Brent Eubanks

Vice President Strategy And Insights Media And Sponsorship, Amanda Fraga

Vp Media And Publisher Partnerships, Dan Gerber

Vice President Business Development, Patti Kim

Svp Marketing And Sales, Barry Gabel

Senior Vice President Software Development, Alex Hazboun

Svp Technology And General Manager Privacy Ticketmaster, Elizabeth Gotto

Svp Live Nation Network, Gabriel Sassoon

Senior Vice President Premium Seat Sales, Bryan Dockett

Vice President Brand Strategist, Denise Quattrochi

Vice President Of Foundation Room House Of Blues, Victor Sutter

Vice President Diversity And Inclusion, Elizabeth Morrison

Vice President Analytics And Optimization, Christine Chu

Vice President Engineering And Data Science, Wojciech Jawor

Vice President, Julie Jin

Chief Security Officer And Vp Security Operations, Carol Haave

Senior Vice President Media And Sponsorship, Jon Landa

Vp Field Management And Communications, Pepper Meek

Vice President Touring, Omar Al-joulani

Vice President, Amit Kapoor

Vice President Touring, Omar Al

Senior Vp Creative Services, Alyssa Tobias

Vice President Talent, David Lefkowitz

Chairman, Gregory B. (Greg) Maffei, age 59

Auditors: Ernst & Young LLP

LOCATIONS

HQ: Live Nation Entertainment Inc
9348 Civic Center Drive, Beverly Hills, CA 90210
Phone: 310 867-7000
Web: www.livenationentertainment.com

2017 Sales

	$ mil.	% of total
Domestic operations	6,772	65
Foreign operation:		
UK operations	785	8
Other operations	2,779	27
Total	**10,337**	**100**

PRODUCTS/OPERATIONS

2017 Sales

	$ mil.	% of total
Concerts	7,892	76
Ticketing	2,143	21
Sponsorship & advertising	445	4
Other revenue	21	-
Eliminations	(164.6)	-
Total	**10,337**	**100**

COMPETITORS

Brillstein
CAA
Dodger Properties
Feld Entertainment
IMG
International Creative Management
Jujamcyn Theaters
MSG Networks
Nederlander Producing Company
Octagon
On Stage Entertainment
Palace Sports & Entertainment
Ryman
SMG Management
Shubert Organization
TBA Global
United Talent
Universal Music Group
Warner Music
WestwoodOne
William Morris Endeavor Entertainment

HISTORICAL FINANCIALS

Company Type: Public

Income Statement

	REVENUE ($ mil.)	NET INCOME ($ mil.)	NET PROFIT MARGIN	EMPLOYEES
12/19	11,547	69	0.6%	10,500
12/18	10,787	60	0.6%	9,500
12/17	10,337	(6)	—	8,800
12/16	8,354	2	0.0%	8,300
12/15	7,245	(32)	—	7,700
Annual Growth	**12.4%**			**8.1%**

FYE: December 31

2019 Year-End Financials

Debt ratio: 30.15%
Return on equity: 6.23%
Cash ($ mil.): 2,470
Current ratio: 1.02
Long-term debt ($ mil.): 3,271

No. of shares (mil.): 213
Dividends
  Yield: —
  Payout: —
Market value ($ mil.): 15,274

	STOCK PRICE ($) FY Close	P/E High/Low	PER SHARE ($) Earnings	Dividends	Book Value
12/19	71.47	— —	(0.02)	0.00	5.36
12/18	49.25	— —	(0.09)	0.00	5.23
12/17	42.57	— —	(0.48)	0.00	5.68
12/16	26.60	— —	(0.23)	0.00	5.52
12/15	24.57	— —	(0.33)	0.00	6.11
Annual Growth	**30.6%**	— —	—	—	(3.2%)

Live Oak Bancshares Inc

Auditors: Dixon Hughes Goodman LLP

LOCATIONS

HQ: Live Oak Bancshares Inc
1741 Tiburon Drive, Wilmington, NC 28403
Phone: 910 790-5867
Web: www.liveoakbank.com

HISTORICAL FINANCIALS

Company Type: Public

Income Statement   FYE: December 31

	ASSETS ($ mil.)	NET INCOME ($ mil.)	INCOME AS % OF ASSETS	EMPLOYEES
12/19	4,814	18	0.4%	635
12/18	3,670	51	1.4%	506
12/17	2,758	100	3.6%	528
12/16	1,755	13	0.8%	425
12/15	1,052	20	2.0%	366
Annual Growth	46.2%	(3.3%)	—	14.8%

2019 Year-End Financials

Debt ratio: 0.00%	No. of shares (mil.): 40
Return on equity: 3.52%	Dividends
Cash ($ mil.): 134	Yield: 0.6%
Current ratio: —	Payout: 27.2%
Long-term debt ($ mil.): —	Market value ($ mil.): 766

	STOCK PRICE ($) FY Close	P/E High/Low	PER SHARE ($) Earnings	Dividends	Book Value
12/19	19.01	45 29	0.44	0.12	13.21
12/18	14.81	25 11	1.24	0.12	12.29
12/17	23.85	9 7	2.65	0.10	10.95
12/16	18.50	50 30	0.39	0.07	6.51
12/15	14.20	31 20	0.65	0.02	5.84
Annual Growth	7.6%	— —	(9.3%)	56.5%	22.6%

LIVE OAK BANKING COMPANY

EXECUTIVES

Ceo, Chip Mahan
Chb, James Mahan III
Prin, David Lucht
Coo, Neil Underwood
Cfo, Brett Caines
Pres, Scott Custer
Financial Controller, Amy Rogers
Loan Officer, Anna Taylor
Loan Officer, Bert Smith
Treasurer, Betty Norris
Senior Loan Officer, Brian Faulk

LOCATIONS

HQ: LIVE OAK BANKING COMPANY
1741 TIBURON DR, WILMINGTON, NC 284036244
Phone: 910 790-5867

HISTORICAL FINANCIALS

Company Type: Private

Income Statement   FYE: December 31

	ASSETS ($ mil.)	NET INCOME ($ mil.)	INCOME AS % OF ASSETS	EMPLOYEES
12/17	2,666	114	4.3%	30
12/16	1,700	21	1.3%	—
12/15	1,008	22	2.2%	—
12/14	634	21	3.5%	—
Annual Growth	61.4%	73.3%	—	—

LKQ Corp

LKQ distributes replacement parts and components needed to repair passenger cars and trucks. It's one of the leading aftermarket parts suppliers in the US through subsidiary Keystone Automotive. LKQ also offers reconditioned remanufactured and refurbished parts including wheels bumpers mirrors and engines as well as recycled parts that are reclaimed from salvage vehicles. Customers include collision repair and mechanical repair shops. Additionally LKQ operates self-service retail yards that allow customers to come in search through and buy recycled auto parts. LKQ which generates just some half its sales in the US was formed in 1998.

Operations

LKQ operates through three reportable segments: Europe (about 45%) North America (more than 35%) and Specialty (more than 10%). Other segment generates the remaining sales.

The Europe and North America segments consist of wholesale operations (aftermarket refurbished recycled and OEM parts) and self-service retail operations (which allows consumers to come directly to the yard to pick parts off of salvage vehicles) in their respective markets. Leading products include brake pads clutches electrical products such as spark plugs and batteries filters and oil and automotive fluids.

The Specialty segment serves major markets in the US and Canada focusing on six product segments: truck and off-road; speed and performance; RV; towing; wheels tires and performance handling; and miscellaneous accessories. RV appliances & air conditioners towing hitches truck bed covers vehicle protection products and wheels tires & suspension products are among the segment's leading offerings.

Geographic Reach

Headquartered in Chicago Illinois LKQ operates about 550 facilities in the US and some 1150 facilities in over two dozen other countries. It has regional headquarters in Nashville Tennessee as well as Tamworth England; Schiedam and Amsterdam the Netherlands; Milan Italy; Prague Czech Republic; and Poing Germany. Certain back-office support functions are performed in Bangalore India.

The US is its largest market accounting approximately 50% of total revenue. Its European operations are led by the UK (nearly 15% of revenue) and Germany (more than 10%); other markets generate the remaining sales. Europe include the Benelux region (Belgium Netherlands and Luxembourg) Italy Czech Republic Poland Slovakia Austria Sweden and Norway.

Sales and Marketing

LKQ sells its products to wholesale customers such as collision and mechanical repair shops and new and used car dealerships as well as to retail customers. Customers of self-service yards are frequently do-it-yourself mechanics small independent repair shops auto rebuilders and resellers.

The company markets its products directly to customers through sales personnel e-commerce partners and distributors. It has an extensive and growing network of some 1700 facilities. LKQ's marketing activities include catalogs advertising sponsorships and promotional activities product-level marketing and online initiatives.

Financial Performance

Powered by its acquisition strategy LKQ has achieved substantial growth over the past five years. Revenue has jumped 74% since 2015 with net income up 28% during that time.

In 2019 the company reported sales of $12.5 billion up 5% from the prior year. The growth in parts and services revenue represented increases in segment revenue of 11.8% in Europe and 0.9% in North America and a decrease of 0.9% in Specialty. The decrease in other revenue was primarily driven by a $21 million organic decrease largely attributable to the North America segment.

Net income increased 13% that year to $541.3 million. The rise was due to increase in income from continuing operations before provision for income taxes and gain in income from discontinued operations.

Cash at the end of 2019 was $528.4 million an increase of $191.1 million from the prior year. Cash from operations contributed to the coffers was $1.1 billion while investing activities used $264.9 million mainly for acquisitions. Financing activities used another $600.7 million for purchases of treasury stocks and repayments of credits and receivables.

Strategy

LKQ's mission is to be the leading global value-added distributor of vehicle parts and accessories by offering its customers the most comprehensive available and cost-effective selection of part solutions while building strong partnerships with its employees and the communities in which it operates.

The company have four primary strategic pillars to build economic value: growth through diversified product offerings; growth through geographic expansion; adaptation to evolving technology; and rationalization of its asset base to enhance margins and return on capital. LKQ believes its supply network with a broad inventory of quality alternative collision and mechanical repair products and specialty vehicle aftermarket products high fulfillment rates and superior customer service provides the company with a competitive advantage.

To execute this strategy LKQ is focused on a number of key areas including: Extensive distribution network; Broad product offering; High fulfillment rates; Strong business relationships; Acquisitions; Technology driven business processes; Adaptation to evolving technology in the automotive industry; and Rationalized asset base.

Mergers and Acquisitions

In late 2019 the company acquired Auto Data Labels Inc. a leading manufacturer and distributor of replacement vehicle information labels in North America. Auto Data Labels produces various types of replacement vehicle information labels for all years vehicle makes and models including labels for Vehicle Identification Federal Safety certification tire pressure under hood and vehicle warning. Terms were not disclosed.

In early 2019 the company acquired all assets of Texas-based Elite Electronics which provides services in about 15 states specializes in various automotive diagnostic and repair services. The company's services include airbag replacements theft and vandalism repair frame replacements and full mechanical services. The acquisition has allowed LKQ to enter the vehicle services market by combining its auto parts and distribution network with Elite's services. Terms were not disclosed.

Company Background

LKQ was created in 1998 through the combination of a number of wholesale recycled products businesses located in Florida Michigan Ohio and Wisconsin. It has grown through internal development and 270-plus acquisitions.

EXECUTIVES

Ceo And Managing Director European Operations, John S. Quinn, age 61, $565,000 total compensation

Svp Development, Walter P. Hanley, age 54, $400,000 total compensation

President And Ceo, Dominick P. (Nick) Zarcone, age 61, $1,000,000 total compensation

Svp And Cio, Ashley T. Brooks

Svp Operations Wholesale Parts Division, Justin L. Jude, age 43

Evp And Cfo, Varun Laroyia

Svp General Counsel And Corporate Secretary, Victor Casini

Vice President Investor Relations, Joseph Boutross

National Accounts Manager North America, Steven Crutchfield

Senior Vice President, Bruce Morgan

Vice President, Dudley Smith

Vice President, Adam Gifford

Senior Vp Strategy And Innovation, Robert Reppa

Vp Global Infrastructure And Architecture, Todd Baxter

Chairman, Joseph M. Holsten, age 67

Board Member, Amanda Allen

Board Member, Guhan Subramanian

Auditors: DELOITTE & TOUCHE LLP

LOCATIONS

HQ: LKQ Corp
500 West Madison Street, Suite 2800, Chicago, IL 60661
Phone: 312 621-1950
Web: www.lkqcorp.com

2018 Sales

	$ mil.	% of total
US	6,193	52
UK	1,665	14
Germany	975	8
Other countries	3,044	26
Total	**11,877**	**100**

PRODUCTS/OPERATIONS

2018 Sales

	$ mil.	% of total
North America	5,182	44
Europe	5,222	44
Specialty	1,473	12
Total	**11,877**	**100**

Products & Services
Accessories
Fleet Service
Refinishing
Vehicle & Salvage Disposal
Warranty
Wheels

COMPETITORS

Cardone Industries	Halfords
Copart	Jasper Engines
Delphi Automotive	Kirk's Automotive

Systems	O'Reilly Automotive
Federal-Mogul	Titan International
Fred Jones Enterprises	U.S. Auto Parts
Genuine Parts	Valeo
Hahn Automotive	

HISTORICAL FINANCIALS

Company Type: Public

Income Statement

FYE: December 31

	REVENUE ($ mil.)	NET INCOME ($ mil.)	NET PROFIT MARGIN	EMPLOYEES
12/19	12,506	541	4.3%	51,000
12/18	11,876	480	4.0%	51,000
12/17	9,736	533	5.5%	43,000
12/16	8,584	463	5.4%	42,500
12/15	7,192	423	5.9%	31,100
Annual Growth	**14.8%**	**6.3%**	**—**	**13.2%**

2019 Year-End Financials

Debt ratio: 31.63%
Return on equity: 11.06%
Cash ($ mil.): 523
Current ratio: 2.15
Long-term debt ($ mil.): 3,715

No. of shares (mil.): 306
Dividends
  Yield: —
  Payout: —
Market value ($ mil.): 10,950

	STOCK PRICE ($) FY Close	P/E High/Low		PER SHARE ($) Earnings	Dividends	Book Value
12/19	35.70	21	13	1.75	0.00	16.33
12/18	23.73	28	15	1.53	0.00	15.13
12/17	40.67	24	16	1.71	0.00	13.58
12/16	30.65	24	16	1.50	0.00	11.19
12/15	29.63	23	17	1.38	0.00	10.19
Annual Growth	**4.8%**	—	—	**6.1%**	**—**	**12.5%**

Lockheed Martin Corp

EXECUTIVES

Chm, Patrick Dewar
Pres*, Richard Kirkland
V Pres*, Christopher Gregoire
V Pres*, John Ward
V Pres*, Kevin Darrenkamp
Prin*, Edward Whalen
General, Kreg Purcell
Administrator, Chad Vaughn
Information Technology Manager, Rod Traff
Senior Manager Information TEC, Chitra Raghu
Director of Mis Is, Charles Brookman
Auditors: Ernst & Young LLP

LOCATIONS

HQ: Lockheed Martin Corp
6801 Rockledge Drive, Bethesda, MD 20817
Phone: 301 897-6000
Web: www.lockheedmartin.com

HISTORICAL FINANCIALS

Company Type: Public

Income Statement

FYE: December 31

	REVENUE ($ mil.)	NET INCOME ($ mil.)	NET PROFIT MARGIN	EMPLOYEES
12/20	65,398	6,833	10.4%	114,000
12/19	59,812	6,230	10.4%	110,000
12/18	53,762	5,046	9.4%	105,000
12/17	51,048	2,002	3.9%	100,000
12/16	47,248	5,302	11.2%	97,000
Annual Growth	**8.5%**	**6.5%**	**—**	**4.1%**

2020 Year-End Financials

Debt ratio: 24.00%
Return on equity: 149.08%
Cash ($ mil.): 3,160
Current ratio: 1.39
Long-term debt ($ mil.): 11,669

No. of shares (mil.): 279
Dividends
  Yield: 2.7%
  Payout: 42.2%
Market value ($ mil.): 99,039

	STOCK PRICE ($) FY Close	P/E High/Low		PER SHARE ($) Earnings	Dividends	Book Value
12/20	354.98	18	11	24.30	9.80	21.56
12/19	389.38	18	12	21.95	9.00	11.17
12/18	261.84	20	14	17.59	8.20	4.96
12/17	321.05	46	36	6.89	7.46	(2.40)
12/16	249.94	15	12	17.49	6.77	5.23
Annual Growth	**9.2%**	—	—	**8.6%**	**9.7%**	**42.5%**

Loews Corp.

When it comes to diversification Loews definitely has the low-down. The holding company's main interest is insurance through publicly traded subsidiary CNA Financial which offers commercial property casualty coverage. It also owns hotels in the US and Canada through its Loews Hotels subsidiary. The group's energy holdings include contract oil-drilling operator Diamond Offshore Drilling (which operates roughly 20 offshore oil rigs) and interstate natural gas transmission pipeline systems operator Boardwalk Pipeline. Loews is controlled and run by the Tisch family including co-chairmen and cousins Andrew and Jonathan.

Operations

Loews is organized into five segments: CNA Financial Corporation Boardwalk Pipeline Partners LP Diamond Offshore Drilling Inc. Loews Hotels Holding Corporation and Corporate.

Flagship unit CNA Financial Corporation is the company's cash cow accounting for more than 70% of its annual revenue. Its specialty offerings include professional financial and property and casualty products; the company also offers commercial property and casualty coverage. CNA's other operations primarily include its run-off long-term care business. Affiliates include The Continental Insurance Company and CNA Surety.

Boardwalk Pipeline Partners LP (accounts nearly 10% of sales) consists of interstate natural gas pipeline systems originating in the Gulf Coast region Oklahoma and Arkansas and extending north and east; natural gas storage facilities in four states; and natural gas liquids pipelines and storage facilities in Louisiana and Texas.

Diamond Offshore Drilling Inc. (accounts roughly 5% of sales) owns and operates rigs located offshore of more than five countries including the US.

Loews Hotels Holding Corporation (around 5% of sales) operates about 25 hotels and resorts – nearly 20 in the US and one in Canada.

The newly established Altium Packaging LLC arm which is part of the Corporate segment manufactures plastic packaging for the beverage food and household chemical industries.

Loews' insurance premiums generate around 50% of total revenue. The company's net investment income accounts for more than 15% of revenue.

Geographic Reach

Through its subsidiaries diversified Loews headquartered in New York has operations in the US Canada and beyond. Its CNA Financial unit operates primarily in the US. Loews Hotels has around 25 properties in the US and one property in Canada. Diamond Offshore has drilling rigs located off the coasts of the US Mexico Brazil Scotland and Singapore and it markets its products worldwide. Boardwalk Pipeline operates approximately 14000 miles of pipelines in nearly 15 US states and serves customers in the northeastern and southeastern US. Altium Packaging LLC has offices in Nebraska and Georgia; it operates about 60 manufacturing plants in the US and another in Canada.

Sales and Marketing

Loews' largest division CNA Financial markets its products through independent brokers agents and managing general underwriters. CNA Financial targets professionals and small to large businesses as well as insurers associations and other groups.

Diamond Offshore's main customers include oil and gas companies ranging from large corporations to independent businesses as well as government-owned entities. Major customers include Hess Occidental and PetrOleo Brasileiro SA. Boardwalk Pipeline serves gas producers distributors transporters and marketers as well as electric and industrial plants.

Altium Packaging's largest customer is Dean Foods Company which brings in some 10% of its revenue. The unit sells its products to approximately 9400 customers.

Financial Performance

Except for a 2% dip in 2016 the company experienced remarkable revenue growth for the last five years. Net income also enjoyed steady growth peaking in at 2017.

Revenue in 2019 rose by 6% to $14.9 billion due to increases in insurance premiums and net investment income.

Net income attributable to Loews Corporation for 2019 was $932 million compared to $636 million in 2018. The increase was due to higher earnings at CNA and Boardwalk Pipelines as well as higher parent company net investment income. These increases were partially offset by lower results at Diamond Offshore and Loews Hotels & Co.

Cash at the end of fiscal 2019 was $336 million a $69 million decrease from prior year. Cash provided by operating activities was $1.7 billion. Cash used for investing activities was $671 million and cash used for financing activities was $1.1 billion mostly for debt payments and stock purchases.

Strategy

As part of its overall investment strategy Loews invests in various assets which require future purchase sale or funding of commitments. These investments are recorded once funded and the related commitments include future capital calls from various third-party limited partnerships signed and accepted mortgage loan applications and obligations related to privately placed debt securities. As of December 31 2019 the company had commitments to purchase or fund approximately $945 million and sell approximately $85 million under the terms of these investments.

The company also employs hedge fund strategy. Hedge fund strategies include both long and short positions in fixed income equity and derivative instruments. These hedge fund strategies may seek to generate gains from mispriced or undervalued securities price differentials between securities distressed investments sector rotation or various arbitrage disciplines. Within hedge fund strategies approximately 44.0% were equity related 32.3% pursued a multi-strategy approach 18.8% were focused on distressed investments and 4.9% were fixed income related as of December 31 2019.

HISTORY

In 1946 Larry Tisch who earned a business degree from New York University at age 18 dropped out of Harvard Law to run his parents' New Jersey resort. Younger brother Bob joined him in creating a new entity Tisch Hotels. The company bought two Atlantic City hotels in 1952 quickly making them profitable. Later Tisch purchased such illustrious hotels as the Mark Hopkins The Drake the Belmont Plaza and the Regency.Moving beyond hotels the brothers bought money-losing companies with poor management. Discarding the management along with underperforming divisions they tightened operational control and eliminated such frills as fancy offices company planes and even memos.

In 1960 Tisch Hotels gained control of MGM's ailing Loew's Theaters to take advantage of their desirable city locations. The company then began demolishing more than 50 stately movie palaces and selling the land to developers. In 1968 the company bought Lorillard the oldest US tobacco company; it shed Lorillard's unprofitable pet food and candy operations and reversed its slipping tobacco market share.

Taking the Loews name in 1971 the company bought CNA Financial in 1974. The Tisch method turned losses of more than $200 million to profits of more than $100 million the very next year. It bought Bulova Watch in 1979 and guided by Larry's son Andrew it gradually returned to profitability.

In the early 1980s Loews entered the energy business by investing in oil supertankers. The company sold its last movie theaters in 1985. Then in 1987 Loews helped CBS fend off a takeover attempt by Ted Turner and ended up with about 25% of the company. Larry became president of the broadcaster.

In 1989 Loews acquired Diamond M Offshore a Texas drilling company and with the acquisition of Odeco Drilling in 1992 the company amassed the world's largest fleet of offshore rigs. The next year Loews grouped its drilling interests as Diamond Offshore Drilling.

In 1994 CNA expanded its insurance empire buying The Continental Corp. The next year Loews sold its interest in CBS and the following year Diamond Offshore Drilling merged with Arethusa (Off-Shore) Limited.

As deft as the Tisch brothers had been in accumulating their riches Larry's bearish investment strategy (short-selling stocks) cost Loews in the late 1990s (more than $900 million alone during 1997's bull market). Larry and Bob retired as co-CEOs at the end of 1998; Larry's son James already president and COO became CEO.

That year Lorillard signed on to the 46-state tobacco lawsuit settlement; the first payment cost the company $325 million (payments continue until 2025). Facing a softened insurance market CNA sold unprofitable lines to focus on commercial insurance; in 1999 it transferred its auto and homeowners lines to Allstate (it continues writing and renewing these policies) and put its life and life reinsurance units up for sale in 2000. Also that year Lorillard was hit with $16 billion of a record-breaking $144 billion punitive damage award in a smokers' class-action suit in Florida. CNA Financial paid out over $450 million in 2001-02 for claims related to the attacks on the World Trade Center.

In 2004 the company continued to expand its natural resource offerings when its subsidiary Boardwalk Pipelines (formerly known as TGT Pipeline) acquired Gulf South Pipeline which operates natural gas pipeline and gathering systems in Texas Louisiana Mississippi Alabama and Florida including several major supply hubs. Loews had acquired gas pipeline operator Texas Gas

Transmission in 2003. Texas Gas operates natural gas pipeline systems reaching from the Louisiana Gulf Coast and East Texas north through Louisiana Arkansas Mississippi Tennessee Kentucky Indiana and into Ohio and Illinois.

Tobacco had long been a staple in Loews' portfolio until the company kicked the habit. Prior to quitting the company kept its 62% ownership of Lorillard rolled up as Carolina Group and traded it as a tracking subsidiary. Lorillard which included the Kent Newport and True cigarette brands in the US accounted for more than 20% of Loews' revenues. However after a steady stream of tobacco-related litigation the company spun Lorillard off into an independent public company in 2008 eliminating the Carolina Group and exiting the industry. Additionally while accessories make the outfit in 2008 Loews slipped its Bulova subsidiary off of its wrist and handed it to competitor Citizen Watch for $250 million.

Larry Tisch died at the age of 80 in 2003. Chairman Bob Tisch died of cancer in late 2005. Tisch also was co-owner of the New York Giants of the National Football League.

In keeping with the Loews strategy of acquiring what can be turned around letting go of what can't and the wisdom to know the difference the company spent $4 billion to acquire oil and gas exploration operator HighMount Exploration & Production and disposed of its tobacco interests and Bulova subsidiary in 2008.

EXECUTIVES

Co-chairman Loews Corporation And Chairman And Ceo Loews Hotels, Jonathan M. Tisch, age 66, $975,000 total compensation

President And Ceo, James S. Tisch, age 68, $975,000 total compensation

Svp And Cfo, David B. Edelson, age 60, $975,000 total compensation

Svp And Chief Investment Officer, Richard W. Scott, age 66

Svp, Kenneth I. Siegel, age 63, $975,000 total compensation

Vp Information Technology, Herb E. Hofmann

Senior Vice President And Chief Business Officer Loews Hotels And Resorts, Constantine Dimas

Regional Vice President, Felicia Marockie

Vice President Loews Cna Holdings Investments, Winifred Harrison

Senior Vice President Of Sales, David Wiener

Senior Vice President, Marc Shapiro

Vice President, Ramu Venkatachalam

Vp Of Engineering, Joe Thomas

Svp General Counsel And Corporate Secretary, Marc Alpert

Evp And Chro, Liz Aguinaga

Vice President Human Resources Diamond Offshore, R Lynn Charles

Vice President Operations Diamond Offshore, Steven Nelson

Svp Investments And Treasury Cna Financial, Amy Adams

Svp Sales And Distribution, John Hennessy

Senior Vice President Cna, Steve Wachtel

Vp Of Hr And Chro Of Diamond Offshore, Aaron Sobel

Vp. Product And Process Systems, Lindsay Lovvorn

Svp Chief Diversity Officer And Head Operations, Joyce Trimuel

Vice President Operations Diamond Offshore, Jimmy Moore

Evp Technology And Operations Cna Financial Corporation, Joseph Merten

Svp Of International Of Cna Commercial, Kathleen Ellis

Svp Underwriting Services Cna Commercial, Barb Sandelands

Svp Business Strategy Technology And Operations, Caroline King

Svp Special Projects And Strategic Initiatives Diamond Offshore, Lyndol Dew

Senior Vice President Administration Diamond Offshore, Mark Baudoin

Senior Vice President Tax Diamond Offshore, Stephen Elwood

Svp Technical Services Diamond Offshore, Karl Sellers

Vice President Health Safety And Environment Diamond Offshore, Neil Hall

Vice President Contracts And Marketing Diamond Offshore, Kane Liddelow

National Sales Manager, Jay Smith

Vice President Corporate Development, Ben Tisch

National Sales Manager, Michael Westfield

National Sales Manager, Rania Hammad

Vice President Of Sales And Marketing, Christopher Cawley

Vice President Operations Loews Hotels Universal Orlando, David Bartek

Vice President Accounting And Assistant Corporate Controller, Tracy Bress

National Sales Manager Southeast, Dan Sadler

National Sales Manager, Cristina Godwin

National Sales Manager, Mike Westfield

National Sales Manager, Melanie Lee

National Sales Manager, Jey Dutertre

National Sales Manager, Emily Friel

Vice President Of Operations, David Weidlich

Evp And Cfo Of Cna Financial Corporation, D Craig Mense

Svp And Cto, Bahr Omidfar

Svp Of Underwriting Of Workers' Compensation Of Cna, Chris Thurman

Evp And General Counsel Of Cna Financial Corporation, Scott Weber

Assistant Vp Of It Services Of Cna, Tony Katrib

National Sales Manager, Jeremy Keippela

Vice President Editorial, Erin Mcknight

Executive Vp, Alexander Tisch

National Sales Manager, Renee Pineda

National Sales Manager, Jennifer Kukulski

Co-chairman, Andrew H. Tisch, age 71

Board Member, Charles Diker

Board Member, Philip Laskawy

Treasurer, Andrew Stegen

Vice Chairman Loews Hotels And Resorts, Paul Whetsell

Board Member, Anthony Welters

Board Member, Jacob Frenkel

Board Member, Joseph Bower

Auditors: DELOITTE & TOUCHE LLP

LOCATIONS

HQ: Loews Corp.
667 Madison Avenue, New York, NY 10065-8087
Phone: 212 521-2000
Web: www.loews.com

PRODUCTS/OPERATIONS

2017 Sales

	$ mil.	% of total
Insurance premiums	6,988	51
Net investment income	2,182	16
Contract drilling revenues	1,451	11
Investment gains	122	-
Other	2,992	22
Total	**13,735**	**100**

2017 Sales by Segment

	$ mil.	% of total
CNA Financial	9,583	70
Diamond Offshore	1,500	11
Boardwalk Pipeline	1,325	10
Loews Hotels	682	5
Corporate & Other	645	4
Total	**13,735**	**100**

Selected Subsidiaries

Boardwalk Pipeline Partners LP (51%)
CNA Financial Corporation (89%)
Diamond Offshore Drilling Inc. (53%)
Loews Hotels Holding Corporation (100%)

COMPETITORS

AIG	Noble
American Financial Group	Shaner Hotel Group
Berkshire Hathaway	Statoil
Cincinnati Financial	The Hartford
Menasha	Travelers Companies
	W. R. Berkley

HISTORICAL FINANCIALS

Company Type: Public

Income Statement

FYE: December 31

	ASSETS ($ mil.)	NET INCOME ($ mil.)	INCOME AS % OF ASSETS	EMPLOYEES
12/19	82,243	932	1.1%	18,605
12/18	78,316	636	0.8%	17,900
12/17	79,586	1,164	1.5%	18,100
12/16	76,594	654	0.9%	15,800
12/15	76,029	260	0.3%	16,700
Annual Growth	**2.0%**	**37.6%**	**—**	**2.7%**

2019 Year-End Financials

Debt ratio: 13.93%
Return on equity: 4.95%
Cash ($ mil.): 336
Current ratio: —
Long-term debt ($ mil.): —

No. of shares (mil.): 290
Dividends
  Yield: 0.4%
  Payout: 13.6%
Market value ($ mil.): 15,273

	STOCK PRICE ($) FY Close	P/E High/Low	PER SHARE ($) Earnings	Dividends	Book Value
12/19	52.49	18 14	3.07	0.25	65.71
12/18	45.52	27 21	1.99	0.25	59.34
12/17	50.03	15 13	3.45	0.25	57.83
12/16	46.83	25 18	1.93	0.25	53.96
12/15	38.40	59 49	0.72	0.25	51.67
Annual Growth	**8.1%**	**— —**	**43.7%**	**(0.0%)**	**6.2%**

Lowe's Companies Inc

Lowe's Companies has built a strong business out of lumber cement power tools and other merchandise. The company is the nation's #3 home improvement chain (after True Value) with about 1730 stores mostly US-based locations. Its stores offer approximately 3500 products for repair and improvement projects (such as lumber paint plumbing and electrical supplies and tools) gardening and outdoor living and home furnishing and decorating. Lowe's is also one of the country's leading retailers of home appliances. It targets both the professional and consumer markets with national brand-name merchandise as well as its own private labels (Kobalt Harbor Breeze Sta-Green). The company only operates in North America with the vast majority of sales generated in the US.

Operations

No single product line dominates Lowe's sales profile. Its biggest earner at around 15% of revenue is the lumber and building materials and appliances category. Another three categories (seasonal & outdoor lawn & garden and rough plumbing & electrical) each bring in about 10%. The remaining revenues came from Kitchen & Bath tools millwork paint flooring hardware light-ning décor and others. Associated installation services are included in the sales for select categories; services overall represent just less than 5% of revenue.

The company sales in terms of merchandise division its Home décor accounts for about 35% of revenue Building products accounts for more than 30% Hardlines accounts for about 30% and others division for less than 5%.

The company offers a broad range of national brands including Whirlpool GE Sherwin-Williams Dewalt Valspar Husqvarna and John Deere. It also sells its own branded products such as Kobalt tools allen+roth home decor Holiday Living seasonal products Harbor Breeze ceiling fans and Reliabilt doors and windows.

Lowe's portfolio of stores includes about 185 RONA locations in Canada.

Geographic Reach

Lowe's has nearly 1730 stores across approximately 50 US states. It also has some 250 stores in Canada. Its operations in Mexico was totally closed in 2019.. The US accounts for just more than 90% of total revenue.

The company headquartered in Mooresville NC operates three contact centers in Wilkesboro NC; Albuquerque NM; and Indianapolis IN. It also has some 15 regional and flatbed distribution centers across the US as well as about half a dozen in Canada.

Sales and Marketing

Lowe's is focused on developing its omnichannel offering designed to serve customers however they prefer to shop — in stores online or through a combination of both. In addition to stores shopping options include e-commerce sites mobile apps contact centers and direct phone sales. Product sales account for about 95% of total revenue while service and other sales account for the remaining revenue.

The company's customer base falls into two main groups — individual homeowners/renters (including the do-it-yourself and do-it-for-me crowds) and professional customers primarily in the construction maintenance and repair trades.

Lowe's has been ramping up its advertising spend in recent years. Advertising costs were $871 million in 2019 compared to $963 million in 2018 and $968 million 2017.

Financial Performance

Lowe's has witnessed solid sales growth over the last five years with revenue up 22% since 2015 even as the number of physical stores has declined. Net income however has been a little more sporadic.

Net sales for fiscal 2019 increased 1.2% over fiscal year 2018 to $72.1 billion. The increase in total sales was driven by an increase in comparable sales offset by a decrease in sales due to closed stores and the exit of the Mexico and Orchard Supply Hardware (Orchard) businesses.

Net earnings for fiscal 2019 increased 85.0% to $4.3 billion.

Cash at the end of fiscal 2019 was $716 million an increase of $205 million from the prior year. Cash from operations contributed $4.3 billion to the coffers while investing activities used $1.4 billion mainly for capital expenditures. Financing activities used another $2.7 billion for dividends to stockholders and Lowe's stock repurchase program.

Strategy

During 2018 and 2019 the Company initiated a strategic reassessment of its business which has resulted in the exit of Orchard Supply Hardware and its operations in Mexico as well as the closure of under-performing stores across the U.S. and Canada.

The company's strategy focuses on responsible sourcing offering safe and eco-friendly products maintaining a diverse healthy engaged and skilled workforce supporting local communities through safe and affordable housing and operating ethically and responsibly.

Lowe's regularly considers and enters strategic transactions including mergers acquisitions joint ventures investments and other growth market and geographic expansion strategies with the expectation that these transactions will result in increases in sales cost savings synergies and other various benefits.

Additionally the company forms strategic relationships with selected suppliers to market and develop products under a variety of recognized and respected national and international brand names.

Company Background

Lowe's Companies was founded in 1921 as Mr. L. S. Lowe's North Wilkesboro Hardware in North Wilkesboro North Carolina. A family operation by 1945 Mr. Lowe's store (which also sold groceries snuff and harnesses) was run by his son Jim and his son-in-law H. Carl Buchan. Buchan bought Lowe's share of the company in 1956 and incorporated as Lowe's North Wilkesboro Hardware; he wanted Lowe's as part of the company name because he liked the slogan "Lowe's Low Prices."

Lowe's has been publicly held since 1961.

HISTORY

Lowe's Companies was founded in 1921 as Mr. L. S. Lowe's North Wilkesboro Hardware in North Wilkesboro North Carolina. A family operation by 1945 Mr. Lowe's store (which also sold groceries snuff and harnesses) was run by his son Jim and his son-in-law H. Carl Buchan. Buchan bought Lowe's share of the company in 1956 and incorporated as Lowe's North Wilkesboro Hardware; he wanted Lowe's as part of the company name because he liked the slogan "Lowe's Low Prices." The chain expanded from North Carolina into Tennessee Virginia and West Virginia. By 1960 Buchan had 15 stores and sales of $31 million — up $4 million from a decade before.

Buchan planned to create a profit-sharing plan for Lowe's employees but in 1960 he died of a heart attack at age 44. In 1961 Lowe's management and the executors of Buchan's estate established the Lowe's Employees Profit Sharing and Trust which bought Buchan's 89% of the company (later renamed Lowe's Companies). That year they financed the transaction through a public offering which diluted the employees' stock. Lowe's was listed on the NYSE in 1979.

Robert Strickland who had joined the company in 1957 became chairman in 1978. Revenues increased from $170 million in 1971 to more than $900 million with a net income of $25 million in 1979. Traditionally the majority of Lowe's business was in sales to professional homebuilders but in 1980 housing starts fell and company profits dropped. Concurrently The Home Depot introduced its low-price warehouse concept. Instead of building warehouse stores of its own Strickland changed the stores' layouts and by 1982 had redesigned half of the 229 stores to be more oriented toward do-it-yourself (DIY) consumers. The new designs featured softer lighting and displays of entire room layouts to appeal to women who made up over half of all DIY customers. In 1982 Lowe's made more than half of its sales to consumers for the first time in its history.

Although Lowe's had more than 300 stores by 1988 its outlets were only about 20000 sq. ft. (one-fifth the size of Home Depot's warehouse stores). By 1989 Lowe's which had continued to target contractors as well as DIYers was overtaken by Home Depot as the US's #1 home retail chain.

Since 1989 the company has focused on building larger stores taking a charge of $71 million in 1991 to phase out smaller stores and build warehouse outlets. In 1993 Lowe's opened 57 large stores (half were replacements for existing stores) almost doubling its total floor space.

The retailer opened 29 new stores in 1995. During 1996 Lowe's added a net of 37 stores and in 1997 it opened 42 stores in new markets. Also that year president and CEO Leonard Herring retired and was replaced by former COO Robert Tillman who also took the post of chairman when Strickland stepped down in 1998.

Also in 1998 the company entered a joint venture to sell an exclusive line of Kobalt-brand professional mechanics' tools produced by Snap-on and to better serve commercial customers began allowing them to special order items not stocked in stores. In addition Lowe's announced it would spend $1.5 billion over the next several years on a 100-store push into the western US. Lowe's westward expansion was fueled when it purchased Washington-based 38-store Eagle Hardware & Garden in 1999 in a stock swap deal worth $1.3 billion. The company gradually converted the Eagle stores into Lowe's.

In 2001 the company earmarked $2.4 billion of its $2.7 billion capital budget for store expansions and new distribution centers.

Robert Niblock was promoted from CFO to president in March 2003. Lowe's sold its some 30 outlets operating as The Contractor Yard to The Strober Organization in February 2004. In April 2004 the company opened its first predominantly urban-oriented store suited to the needs of city dwellers and building superintendents in Brooklyn.

Chairman and CEO Robert Tillman retired in January 2005. He was succeeded by president Robert Niblock.

Lowe's entered the Canadian market in 2007.

The home improvement chain expanded its distribution footprint in 2008 opening a regional distribution center in Pittston Pennsylvania and a flatbed distribution center in Purvis Mississippi.

During 2010 Lowe's opened its first location in Mexico (in Monterrey). In 2011 the company made a rare acquisition: online home-improvement retailer ATG Stores based in Kirkland Washington.

In 2013 the company acquired a majority stake of California-based Orchard Supply Hardware (OSH) adding 70 stores to the 110 stores that Lowe's already operated in California.

EXECUTIVES

Chairman President And Ceo, Robert A. Niblock, age 57, $1,300,000 total compensation
Cfo, Marshall A. Croom, age 59
President Orchard Supply Hardware, Lara L. Lee
Chief Supply Chain Officer, Brent G. Kirby
Chief Development Officer And President International, Richard D. Maltsbarger, age 44
Chief Customer Officer, Michael P. McDermott
Cio, Paul D. Ramsay, age 55
Managing Director Loweâ's India, James A. Brandt
President And Managing Director Loweâ's Mexico, Juan L. Pier Castello
President Atgstores.com, Michelle M. Newbery
President And Ceo Loweâ's Canada, Sylvain PrudÂ'homme
Svp Corporate Finance And Treasurer, Tiffany Mason
Svp Services, Kevin Measel
Regional Vice President For Eastern North Carolina, Jeff Blocker
Vice President Installed And Special Order Sales, Gary Gross
Svp Store Operations, William Edwards
Vice President Of Client Services, Marian Craig

Vice President Of Merchandisin, Daryl Tilley
Vice President Information Technology Business Management, Kathy Higgins
Vice President, Kimberly Wells
Regional Vice President Of Stores, Jeffrey Sain
Vice President Global Sourcing And Quality Assurance, Zach Miller
Senior Vice President, Belinda Rumple
Regional Vice President Distribution, Calvin Adams
Vice President Of Asia Sourcing, Scott Jenkins
Vice President Vendor Service Management, Ron Lutz
Vice President Real Estate Construction And Store Design Canada, Jeff Boyd
Vice President Corporate Communication, Tracey Ahearn
Senior Vice President Chief Accounting Officer, Matthew Hollifield
Vice President Merchandising Fashion Fixtures, Ann Haines
Vice President Transportation, Rick Gabrielson
Senior Vice President, Susan Burtt
Vice President Contact Center Operations, Donna Neale
Svp Strategy And Development, James Han
Vice President, Beth Macdonald
Vice President Merchandising Canada, Alan Blundell
Svp Chief Compliance Officer And Associate General Counsel, Jeff Vining
Svp And Chief Digital Officer, Vikram Singh
Vice President Of Merchandising, Dennis Lenahan
Merchandising Vice President, Revis Felts
Vice President Store Operations, Clay Clement
Evp, William P Boltz
Vp Hr Business Partner Shared Services, Angela Kirkby
Planning Vice President Supply Chain, Melissa Handy
Vice President Store Operations, Kissel Goldman
Vice President Information Technology Supply Chain, Timothy Stall
Vice President Operations Engineering, Ram Krishnamurthy
Vice President Of Store Operations, Laura Gump
Executive Vice President, Joe Mcfarland
Vice President In Home And Specialty Sales, Angela Huggins
Vice President Store Operations, Steve Mckalvey
Svp Gmm Decor, Jeff Epstein
Senior Vice President Of Learning, Jenny Lucas
Board Member, Bob Scott
Board Member, James Morgan
Secretary Treasurer, Arlene Holland
Board Member, Marshall Larsen
Board Member, Robert Johnson
Board Member, Lauren Douglas
Auditors: DELOITTE & TOUCHE LLP

LOCATIONS

HQ: Lowe's Companies Inc
1000 Lowes Blvd., Mooresville, NC 28117
Phone: 704 758-1000
Web: www.lowes.com

2018 Stores

	No.
US	1,723
Canada	279
Mexico	13
Total	**2,015**

2018 Sales

	% of total
US	92
Other	8
Total	**100**

PRODUCTS/OPERATIONS

2018 Sales

	$ mil.	% of total
Building & Maintenance	28,581	40
Appliances	27,987	39
Seasonal	12,786	18
Other	1,955	3
Total	**71,309**	**100**

Selected Product Categories

Appliances
Fashion Fixtures
Flooring
Home Fashions
Kitchens
Lawn & Garden
Lumber & Building Materials
Millwork
Outdoor Power Equipment
Paint
Rough Plumbing & Electrical
Seasonal Living
Tools & Hardware

Selected Proprietary Brands

allen+roth
Aquasource
Garden Treasures
Harbor Breeze
Kobalt
Portfolio
Reliabilt
Top Choice
Utilitech

COMPETITORS

84 Lumber	Lumber Liquidators
Ace Hardware	Menard
Amazon.com	Sears Holdings
Beacon Roofing	SiteOne
Best Buy	Tractor Supply
Builders FirstSource	True Value
Do it Best	Wal-Mart
Home Depot	

HISTORICAL FINANCIALS

Company Type: Public

Income Statement

FYE: January 31

	REVENUE ($ mil.)	NET INCOME ($ mil.)	NET PROFIT MARGIN	EMPLOYEES
01/20*	72,148	4,281	5.9%	320,000
02/19	71,309	2,314	3.2%	300,000
02/18	68,619	3,447	5.0%	310,000
02/17	65,017	3,093	4.8%	290,000
01/16	59,074	2,546	4.3%	270,000
Annual Growth	**5.1%**	**13.9%**	**—**	**4.3%**

*Fiscal year change

2020 Year-End Financials

Debt ratio: 48.91%	No. of shares (mil.): 763
Return on equity: 152.88%	Dividends
Cash ($ mil.): 716	Yield: 1.8%
Current ratio: 1.01	Payout: 55.7%
Long-term debt ($ mil.): 16,768	Market value ($ mil.): 88,691

	STOCK PRICE ($) FY Close	P/E High/Low		PER SHARE ($) Earnings	Dividends	Book Value
01/20*	116.24	22	17	5.49	2.13	2.58
02/19	97.11	41	29	2.84	1.85	4.55
02/18	101.50	26	18	4.09	1.58	7.08
02/17	73.29	24	18	3.47	1.33	7.43
01/16	71.66	28	24	2.73	1.07	8.41
Annual Growth	**12.9%**			**19.1%**	**18.8%**	**(25.5%)**

*Fiscal year change

Lumen Technologies Inc

CenturyLink provides cyber links throughout the country on one of the longest fiber networks in the US. Historically a regional wireline local and long-distance telephone provider it's connecting with the times by transforming into a broadband and network services provider for business residential and government clients. The company is the one of the largest US wireline telecom companies with about 450000 route miles of fiber optic cable globally and it's the incumbent local carrier in about 37 states. It spends approximately $3.6 billion a year on capital projects to build out its network.

Operations

The company has five reportable segments that provides products and services to its customers and channel partners. This include enterprise segment (accounts nearly 30% of revenue) consumer segment (accounts about one-fourth) wholesale segment (accounts nearly 20%) international and global accounts management (accounts about 15%) and small and medium business which accounts the remaining revenue.

While most of its customized customer interactions involve multiple integrated technologies and services CenturyLink organizes its products and services according to the core technologies that drive them.

This includes following categories: IP and data services transport and infrastructure services voice and collaboration services and IT and managed services.

IP and Data Services (accounts 30% of revenue) provides VPN Data Network. Ethernet Internet Protocol (IP) and content delivery services provide to its customers with the ability to meet their streaming video and far-reaching digital content distribution needs through Content Delivery Network (CDN) services and Vyvx Broadcast Solutions. Transport and Infrastructure (nearly 30%) offers wavelength that deliver high bandwidth optical networks dark fiber private line colocation and data center services and professional services. Voice and Collaboration (nearly 20%) offers voice that includes primary rate interface service local inbound service switched one-plus toll free long distance and international services and voice over IP (VoIP) and its IT and Managed Services (not more than 5%). The remaining revenue comes from broadband voice regulatory revenue and other services.

It conducts most of its operations under the brand "CenturyLink". The satellite television service is offered on a co-branded basis under the "DIRECTV".

Geographic Reach

CenturyLink operates a terrestrial and subsea fiber optic long-haul network throughout North America Europe Latin America and Asia Pacific which connects to its metropolitan fiber network operations. The company based in Monroe Louisiana also provide services in over 60 countries with most of the revenue being derived in the US.

Sales and Marketing

CenturyLink reaches business customers through offices in major and secondary markets in the US and bigger markets in some countries. Marketing to residential customers includes direct sales representatives inbound call centers telemarketing and third parties including retailers satellite television providers door to door sales agents and digital marketing firms. It supports distribution with digital marketing direct mail bill inserts newspaper and television advertising website promotions public relations activities and sponsorship of community events and sports venues.

The company's advertising expense was $62 million $98 million and $218 million for the FY 2019 2018 and 2017 respectively.

Financial Performance

The company's consolidated revenue decreased by $1.0 billion or 4% for the year ended December 31 2019 as compared to the year ended December 31 2018 largely due to continued declines in voice revenue as customers transition to other voice and non-voice services their de-emphasis of low margin equipment sales within Transport and Infrastructure churn in legacy contracts within IT and Managed Services and the de-recognition of their prior failed-sale leaseback partially offset by growth in their IP and Data services and Broadband revenue.

The company lost $5.3 billion in 2019 falling further from $1.7 billion loss in 2018. It had higher expenses in 2018 including a $503 million tax payment.

CenturyLink had $1.7 billion in cash and equivalents in 2019 compared to $518 million in 2018. Operations generated $6.9 billion in 2018 while investing activities used $3.6 billion and financial activities used $1.9 billion.

Strategy

CenturyLink incur capital expenditures on an ongoing basis to expand and improve its service offerings enhance and modernize the company's networks and compete effectively in their markets. The company evaluates capital expenditure projects based on a variety of factors including expected strategic impacts (such as forecasted impact on revenue growth productivity expenses service levels and customer retention) and expected return on investment. The amount of capital investment is influenced by among other things demand for the company's services and products cash flow generated by operating activities cash required for other purposes and regulatory considerations (such as CAF Phase II infrastructure buildout requirements).

CentryLink's capital expenditures continue to be focused on enhancing network operating efficiencies and supporting new service developments.

EXECUTIVES

Evp Controller And Assistant Secretary, David D. Cole, age 62, $482,687 total compensation
President And Ceo, Glen F. Post, age 67, $1,250,000 total compensation
Senior Vice President Business Service Delivery And Operations, Todd Schafer
President Small And Mid-size Business (smb) And Ges/sled, Vernon L. Irvin, age 58
Evp And Cfo, Sunit S. Patel, age 58
Evp Chief Administrative Officer General Counsel And Secretary, Stacey W. Goff, age 54, $540,758 total compensation
Evp And Cto, Aamir Hussain, $496,049 total compensation
President Consumer Markets, Maxine L. Moreau, age 58
Evp Human Resources, Scott A. Trezise, age 51
President Global Accounts Management And International, Laurinda Y. Pang, age 50
Svp Cyber Engineering And Technology Services, William E. (Bill) Bradley
President Advanced Solutions Group And Chief Enterprise Relationship Officer, Gary Gauba
President And Coo, Jeffrey K. (Jeff) Storey
President Wholesale Indirect Channels And Alliances, Lisa Miller
President Strategic Enterprise Federal Government And Ges/sled, Ed Morche

Vice President Of Sales, Harman Steve
Senior Vice President Information Technology,
  Alfonso Rivera
Vice President And General Counsel, Laurie
  Korneffel
Vice President Human Resources And Chief
  Diversity Officer, Richard Guidi
Regional Vice President Project Management,
  Monte Johnson
Vice President Product Management, David
  Shacochis
National Account Manager, Frank Palazzo
Area Vice President Strategic Initiatives, Dana
  Albright
Vice President Regional Reg And Legislative
  Affairs, William Hanchey
Vice President Of Corporate Development And
  Strategy, Kenneth Dunn
Vice President Compensation And Analytics, Jill
  Turner
Senior Vice President, Clay Bailey
Vice President Network Service Operations, Jeff
  Mitchell
Marketing Vice President, Mike Conaghan
Vice President Corporate Development, Bryan
  Taylor
Area Vice President, Beth Mitchell
Area Vice President, Jackie Slate
Vice President Of Technology Systems, Judy Betts
Vice President Corporate Tax, Jon Robinson
Vice President Product Strategy, Pasha Mohammed
Senior Vice President Product Development,
  Phillip Bronsdon
Vice President Consumer Markets, Christi Uhrig
Nw Region Vice President, Mark Reynolds
Vice President Global Infrastructure Operations,
  Todd Miller
Vice President Of Information Systems, Adam
  Youmans
Area Vice President Global Markets, Mike Raney
Assistant Vice President, John Benedict
National Sales Manager, Jane Jensen
Svp Strategic Government, David Young
Senior Vice President Digital Platform
  Development, Paritosh Bajpay
Executive Vice President, Thomas Mathews
Vice President Sales (sap Services And Global
  Its), Rahul Sethi
Executive Vice President, Tina Laird
Regional Vice President Service Delivery, David
  Capote
Regional Vice President Of Sales, Sonia Ramsey
Vp Network Implementation, Jeff O'hara
Vice President Sap Global Delivery And Solutions,
  Shyam Avvari
Vice President General Manager, Warren Greenberg
Channel Vice President, Tom Marx
Vice President Corporate Finance, David Panzer
Chairman, Harvey P. Perry, age 75
Vice Chairman, W. Bruce Hanks, age 65
Treasurer, Steve Nolen
Auditors: KPMG LLP

LOCATIONS

HQ: Lumen Technologies Inc
  100 CenturyLink Drive, Monroe, LA 71203
Phone: 318 388-9000   Fax: 318 789-8656
Web: www.centurylink.com

PRODUCTS/OPERATIONS

2018 Sales by Category

	$ mil.	% of total
Transport and Infrastructure	8,248	35
IP and Data Services	7,279	31
Voice and Collaboration	6,572	28
Regulatory	723	3
IT and Managed Services	621	3
Total	23,443	100

2018 Sales

	% of total
Business segment	74
Consumer segment	23
Other	3
Total	100

Selected Products & Services

Local and long-distance voice
High-speed Internet
MPLS
Private line (including special access)Data integration
Ethernet
Colocation
Managed hosting (including cloud hosting)
Network
Public access
Video
Wireless
Other ancillary services

COMPETITORS

AT&T
Cavalier Telephone
Comcast
Cox Communications
DISH Network
Equinix
FairPoint
  Communications Inc.
Farmers
  Telecommunications

Frontier
  Communications
Nsight
Sprint Communications
Telephone & Data
  Systems
Time Warner Cable
Verizon
XO Holdings

HISTORICAL FINANCIALS

Company Type: Public

Income Statement

FYE: December 31

	REVENUE ($ mil.)	NET INCOME ($ mil.)	NET PROFIT MARGIN	EMPLOYEES
12/19	22,401	(5,269)	—	42,500
12/18	23,443	(1,733)	—	45,000
12/17	17,656	1,389	7.9%	51,000
12/16	17,470	626	3.6%	40,000
12/15	17,900	878	4.9%	43,000
Annual Growth	5.8%	—	—	(0.3%)

2019 Year-End Financials

Debt ratio: 53.59%
Return on equity: (-31.65%)
Cash ($ mil.): 1,693
Current ratio: 0.66
Long-term debt ($ mil.): 32,394

No. of shares (mil.): 1,090
Dividends
  Yield: 0.0%
  Payout: —
Market value ($ mil.): 14,400

	STOCK PRICE ($) FY Close	P/E High/Low		PER SHARE ($) Earnings	Dividends	Book Value
12/19	13.21	—	—	(4.92)	1.00	12.36
12/18	15.15	—	—	(1.63)	2.16	18.36
12/17	16.68	12	6	2.21	2.16	21.97
12/16	23.78	28	19	1.16	2.16	24.52
12/15	25.16	26	15	1.58	2.16	25.86
Annual Growth	(14.9%) (16.9%)	—	—	—	(17.5%)	3.0%

Luther Burbank Corp

Auditors: Crowe LLP

LOCATIONS

HQ: Luther Burbank Corp
  520 Third Street, Fourth Floor, Santa Rosa, CA 95401
Phone: 844 446-8201
Web: www.lutherburbanksavings.com

HISTORICAL FINANCIALS

Company Type: Public

Income Statement

FYE: December 31

	ASSETS ($ mil.)	NET INCOME ($ mil.)	INCOME AS % OF ASSETS	EMPLOYEES
12/19	7,045	48	0.7%	277
12/18	6,937	45	0.6%	278
12/17	5,704	69	1.2%	266
12/16	5,064	52	1.0%	274
12/15	4,362	35	0.8%	—
Annual Growth	12.7%	8.4%	—	—

2019 Year-End Financials

Debt ratio: 2.22%
Return on equity: 8.17%
Cash ($ mil.): 88
Current ratio: —
Long-term debt ($ mil.): —

No. of shares (mil.): 56
Dividends
  Yield: 1.9%
  Payout: 27.7%
Market value ($ mil.): 646

	STOCK PRICE ($) FY Close	P/E High/Low		PER SHARE ($) Earnings	Dividends	Book Value
12/19	11.53	14	11	0.87	0.23	10.97
12/18	9.02	17	10	0.79	0.19	10.31
12/17	12.04	8	7	1.62	1.58	9.74
Annual Growth	(1.1%)	—	—	(14.4%)	(38.2%)	3.0%

M & T Bank Corp

Bank holding company M&T Bank offers deposit loan trust investment brokerage mortgage and insurance services to individuals and small- and mid-sized businesses. With about $120 billion in total assets and almost $95 billion in deposits the bank operates more than 750 branches and over 1800 ATMs in some part of US and District of Columbia. Its lending is largely focused in those states but it originates from its loans via offices in other states and Canada. The firm also manages a proprietary line of mutual funds through Wilmington Funds Management. M&T was founded in 1856 as Manufacturers and Traders Trust in Buffalo New York.

Operations

M&T Bank comprises two wholly-owned bank subsidiaries: M&T Bank and Wilmington Trust. The reportable segments are Business Banking Commercial Banking Commercial Real Estate Discretionary Portfolio Residential Mortgage Banking and Retail Banking.

The Retail Banking segment offers standard banking services and a variety of services to consumers through several delivery channels which include branch offices automated teller machines telephone banking and Internet banking. The consumer credit deposit products and generates nearly 30% of the company's total revenue. About 20% comes from its other activities not classified under its reporting segments. Those include trust income and allocation methodologies for internal transfers for funding charges and credits tied to earning assets and interest-bearing liabilities.

Commercial Banking brings in almost 20% of revenue and markets credit and banking services to middle-market and large corporate clients. Commercial Real Estate generates about 15% of revenue and offers credit and deposit products to clients seeking loans on apartments multifamily buildings offices and retail and industrial locations. Business Banking contributes around 10% of revenue and targets small businesses and professionals. It provides loans (including Small Business Administration loans) leases credit and deposit products cash management direct deposit merchant credit card and letters of credit and payroll services.

Residential Mortgage Banking originates and services consumer mortgages which it sells to investors or its Discretionary Portfolio division. It accounts for about 5% of the holding company's revenue. The company's Discretionary Portfolio segment produces less than 5% of its revenue. It includes investment and trading account securities residential real estate loans and other assets short-term and long-term borrowed funds brokered deposits and Cayman Islands office deposits. This segment also provides foreign exchange services to customers.

Overall net interest income accounts for about 70% of total sales and non-interest income generates the remaining 30%.

Geographic Reach

Buffalo New York-based M&T Bank has operations in New York Maryland New Jersey Pennsylvania Delaware Connecticut Virginia West Virginia and the District of Columbia. It has commercial banking offices Ontario Canada and Cayman Islands.

Sales and Marketing

M&T Bank caters to customers through multiple channels including physical branches and business banking centers telebanking the internet and ATMs. M&T markets its commercial and lending services and products to consumers small businesses middle-market and large corporations professionals governmental clients and financial institutions.

Advertising and marketing expenses for 2019 2018 and 2017 were $93.4 million $85.7 million and $69.2 million respectively.

Financial Performance

Despite stagnancy in 2015 M&T's Retail Banking segment posted revenue gains from 2016 to 2019 that led to an overall increase of some 33%. Overall the company has expanded its revenue by about a third and its net income by about 80% since 2015.

M&T's revenue increased 5% to some $6.1 billion in 2019. Net income slightly rose by less than one percent. It was boosted by increases in all segments.

The bank had $169.1 million to its cash in 2019 to end the year with stores of $1.4 billion. Operations provided $2.4 billion?an increase from 2018 caused by a gain in sales of assets and decrease in asset write down. Net cash provided by investing activities gained $727.0 million and financing activities depleted $3.3 million due to a net decrease in deposits dividend payments and long-term debt payments.

Strategy

Growth in the company's business including through acquisitions may increase its need for additional qualified personnel. The Company is increasingly competing for personnel with financial technology providers and other less regulated entities who may not have the same limitations on compensation as the Company does. If the Company is not able to hire or retain highly skilled and qualified individuals it may be unable to execute its business strategies and may suffer adverse consequences to its business financial condition and results of operations.

M&T has expanded its business through past acquisitions and may do so in the future.

Company Background

M&T Bank traces its roots to the 1856 founding of Manufacturers and Traders Trust in Buffalo New York. M&T Bank reorganized as a bank holding company in 1969 called First Empire State. It changed its name in 1998 to M&T Bank.

EXECUTIVES

Group Vice President Commercial Equipment Finance, Mohannad Jishi

Evp Wealth And Institutional Services Division M&t Bank Corp And M&t Bank, William J. (Bill) Farrell, age 62

Vice President Business And Professional Banking, Carl Speicher

Evp M&t Bank Corporation And Evp And Co-head Commercial Banking M&t Bank, Brian E. Hickey, age 68, $299,231 total compensation

Evp M&t Bank Corporation And Vice Chairman And Evp M&t Bank, Kevin J. Pearson, age 59, $725,000 total compensation

Evp And Chief Credit Officer M&t Bank Corporation And M&t Bank, Robert J. Bojdak, age 65

Evp And Cio M&t Bank Corporation And M&t Bank, Michele D. Trolli, age 59

Chairman And Ceo M&t Bank Corporation And M&t Bank, René F. Jones, age 56, $725,000 total compensation

President Coo And Director M&t Bank Corporation And M&t Bank, Richard S. Gold, age 60, $725,000 total compensation

Evp And Treasurer M&t Bank Corporation And M&t Bank, D. Scott N. Warman, age 54

Evp And Cfo M&t Bank Corporation And M&t Bank, Darren J. King, age 50, $600,000 total compensation

Evp And Area Executive M&t Bank Corporation And M&t Bank, Gino A. Martocci, age 54

Evp Human Resources M&t Bank Corp And M&t Bank, Janet M. Coletti, age 56

Evp M&t Bank Corporation And Evp Wilmington Trust Wealth Management M&t Bank, Doris P. Meister, age 64

Evp Retail And Business Banking M&t Bank, Neil J. Hosty

Evp M&t Bank Corporation And Evp Mortgage And Customer Asset Management M&t Bank, Michael J. Todaro, age 58

Regional President Western New York And President M&t Charitable Foundation, Shelley Drake

Vice President Systems Manger, Sheila Brown

Assistant Vice President Platform Management Group, Erik Steensen

Assistant Vice President And Performance Test Team Leader, Paula Henderson

Vice President Information Technology, Krista Swann

Assistant Vice President Technology Infrastructure Operations, Zana Vernon

Vice President, Kim Phelan

Vice President Marketing Director West Mortgage Division, Randy Daniels

Assistant Vice President Operations, Katie Schultz

Vice President Healthcare Finance, Mark Cartwright

Assistant Vice President Information Systems, Bob Roeder

Vice President, Maureen Stevens

Vice President Global Sourcing, Patti Haan

Senior Vice President, Ayan Das Gupta

Vice President Private Banking, Julie Enders

Vice President Of Corporate Applications, Diane Blanchard

Vice President Pa Special Assets, Sarah Pugh

Vice President, Ron Rozanski

Group Vice President, Jim Kaiser

Assistant Vice President Senior Software Engineering, Ashish Vikram

Vice President Compliance Officer, Lori Kunzelman

Vice President Senior Real Estate Counsel, Donna Suchan

Vice President Human Resources Business Partner, Amy Walker

Vice President Trust Risk Manager, Dawn Snelling

Vice President Human Resources Business Partner Mortgage And Consumer Lending, Donna Harlacher

Assistant Vice President Talent Acquisition Senior Recruiter, Roni Thomas

Assistant Vice President Team Lead, Bemina Rohde

Vice President, Patrick Wood

Vice President, David Dick

Assistant Vice President And Compliance Officer, Barbara Moynihan

Assistant Vice President Relationship Manager, Sam Higgins

Assistant Vice President Regulatory Affairs Capital Adequacy, David Zolnowski

Vice President, Brendan Mahoney

Vice President, Beth Beshaw

Vice President, Karen Boyle

Assistant Vice President Accounting Policy, Nick Ambrose

Vice President Accounting Policy, Timothy Cahlstadt

Vice President Commercial Banking, William Johnston

Vice President, Michael Gast

Vice President Senior Commercial Real Estate Relationship Mananger, Mike McCarthy

Assistant Vice President Internal Audit, David Keenan

Assistant Vice President Branch Manager, Lauren Perrone

Group Vice President, Kelley A Attig

Group Vice President For Residential Lending, Nick Buscaglia

Vice President, James Beardi

Vice President, Juliet Alexander

Vice President Senior Product Manager, David Reif

Vice President, Benjamin Levy

Group Vp, Clifford Johnson

Group Vp And Corporate Secretary, Marie King

Vice President, Stephanie Kercher

Vice President And Assistant Corporate Secretary, Karl Braun-Kolbe

Vice President, Gerald Brautlacht

Vice President Solutions Delivery, Boris Roginsky

Senior Vice President Quantative Risk, Carol Bartosz

Vice President Human Resources And Senior Employee Relations Specialist, Jon C Helmin

Svp And Assistant Treasurer, Douglas Sheline

Vice President End User Computing Manager, Mike Ferger

Avp Technology Infrastructure, Laurie Popielarski

Vice President Senior Project Manager, David Lee

Vice President Cybersecurity, Lynne Erickson

Senior Vice President Human Resources, Dan Boscarino

Group Vp, Arthur Bronson

Group Vp And Assistant Secretary, Randall Krolewicz

Avp; Project Manager Technology Infrastructure, Deb Gaydek

Vice President Corporate Training Support Services, Lynne Kreiner

Group Vice President Technology Infrastructure Operations, Mark Kumro

Svp Alternative Banking, Michael Shryne

Vice President Admin, Detra Miller

Administrative Vice President Information Technology Operations, Gary Fusco

Vice President Consumer Risk Management, Scott Warman

Vice President, Brooke Baker

Administrative Vice President Retail Banking, Matt Calhoun

Vice President Of Data Center Baltimore Md, John Lewis

Vice President Security Engineering, Rob Nichols

Group Vice President, John Federici
Vice President, Randy Taylor
Vice President Information Security And Access Management, Joan Sherwood-Wetherwax
Assistant Vice President Team Lead End User Experience, David Cuviello
Group Vice President, Denise Cramer
Vice President Business And Retail Web Banking Central Technology, Muhammad Akhtar
Vice President Of Healthcare Division, Sharon Obrien
Vice President Indirect Relationship Manager, Jim Eriksen
Vice President Product Management (digital Workspace), Amy LePenske
Group Vice President Enterprise Data Services, Seetharaman Kishor
Vice President Information Technology, Kalimuthu Chithambaram
Vice President Data Services, Shashi Shankar
Senior Vice President Digital And Telephone Banking, Paris Roselli
Vice President And Legal Counsel, Demario Carswell
Assistant Vice President Branch Manager, Jerry Laspisa
Vice President, Steven Wendelboe
Vice President Human Resources Business Partner, Vivek Siddhu
Vice President Commercial Credit Modeling, Vito Flitt
Vice President And Business And Professional Banking, Sue Simpson
Vice President, Vickie Quezada
Vice President Commercial Real Estate, Paul Ciancimino
Group Vice President, Trevor Foote
Vp Mortgage Originations, Julie Deglopper
Vice President Group Sales Manager, John Vilardo
Assistant Vice President, Marianne Tyree
Vice President, Gloria Diodato
Vice President Business Relationship Manager, Ana Saraiva
Vice President, Kimberly Austing
Assistant Vice President, Russ Whitley
Vice President And Manager Of Cyber And Network Security, Eric Ayotte
Vice President, Paul Bradley
Vice President Human Resources And Finance Business Systems, Terica Phillips-Gadley
Vice President Residential Mortgage Accounting Manager, Diane Kinton
Vice President, Lyn Rex
Vice President Debt Capital Markets, Ajibola Fadahunsi
Vice President, Amy Devine
Risk Analyst Avp, Robin Grzechowiak
Vp Sr User Experience Lead, Ivan Ereiz
Vice President Commercial Real Estate, Corey Rosenfield
Vice President, Bradley Myers
Group Vice President, Jill Rank
Vice President, Ivy Gafner
Vice President Special Assets, Kenneth Paulin
Vice President, Douglas Simon
Vice President Marketing And Communications Manager Institutional Retirement Services And Mandt Insurance, Craig Vollmer
Vice President, Monty Sayler
Vice President, Hugh Tran
Group Vice President, Randy Chestnut
Vice President, David Tellerday
Vice President, Carole Stafford
Vice President, Michele Kubik
Vice President, Keller Hoak
Vice President Financial Institutions Div., David Gordon
Vice President, Jeffrey Millard
Assistant Vice President Indirect Lending, Alan Helfgott

Vice President, Aaron Nodar
Vice President, Gaye Boyette
Vice President Consumer Lending, John Enny
Vice President, Suzanne Rosaschi
Assistant Vice President, Sheila Johnson
Auditors: PricewaterhouseCoopers LLP

LOCATIONS

HQ: M & T Bank Corp
One M & T Plaza, Buffalo, NY 14203
Phone: 716 635-4000
Web: www.mtb.com

PRODUCTS/OPERATIONS

Selected Subsidiaries
M&T Life Insurance Company
M&T Insurance Agency Inc
M&T Mortgage Reinsurance Company Inc.
M&T Real Estate Trust
M&T Realty Capital Corporation
M&T Securities Inc.
Wilmington Trust Company
Wilmington Trust Investment Advisors Inc.
Wilmington Funds Management Corporation
Wilmington Trust Investment Management LLC

2018 Sales

	$ mil.	% of total
Interest income		
Loans and leasesincluding fees	4,164	62
Investment securities	324	5
Deposits at banks	108	2
Others	1	0
Interest expense	(526.4)	-
Non-interest income		
Trust income	537	9
Service charges on deposit accounts	429	7
Mortgage banking revenue	360	6
Brokerage services income	51	1
Others	477	8
Total	**5,928**	**100**

2018 Sales

	$ mil.	% of total
Retail Banking	1,675	28
Commercial Banking	1,110	19
Commercial Real Estate	849	14
Business Banking	546	9
Residential Mortgage	319	5
Discretionary Portfolio	218	4
All Others	1,209	21
Total		100

COMPETITORS

Citigroup	KeyCorp
Citizens Financial Group	Northwest Bancshares
Fulton Financial	PNC Financial
HSBC USA	Sovereign Bank
JPMorgan Chase	SunTrust
	TriState Capital

HISTORICAL FINANCIALS

Company Type: Public

Income Statement   FYE: December 31

	ASSETS ($ mil.)	NET INCOME ($ mil.)	INCOME AS % OF ASSETS	EMPLOYEES
12/19	119,872	1,929	1.6%	17,773
12/18	120,097	1,918	1.6%	17,267
12/17	118,593	1,408	1.2%	16,794
12/16	123,449	1,315	1.1%	16,973
12/15	122,787	1,079	0.9%	17,476
Annual Growth	(0.6%)	15.6%		0.4%

2019 Year-End Financials

Debt ratio: 5.83%
Return on equity: 12.38%
Cash ($ mil.): 9,093
Current ratio: —
Long-term debt ($ mil.): —
No. of shares (mil.): 130
Dividends
 Yield: 2.4%
 Payout: 29.5%
Market value ($ mil.): 22,164

	STOCK PRICE ($) FY Close	P/E High/Low	Earnings	Dividends	Book Value
12/19	169.75	13 10	13.75	4.10	120.37
12/18	143.13	15 11	12.74	3.55	111.62
12/17	170.99	20 16	8.70	3.00	108.28
12/16	156.43	20 13	7.78	2.80	105.56
12/15	121.18	18 16	7.18	3.50	101.36
Annual Growth	**8.8%**	**— —**	**17.6%**	**4.0%**	**4.4%**

Macatawa Bank Corp.

Macatawa Bank Corporation is the holding company for Macatawa Bank. Since its 1997 founding the company has grown into a network of more than 25 branches serving western Michigan's Allegan Kent and Ottawa counties. The bank provides standard services including checking and savings accounts CDs safe deposit boxes and ATM cards. It also offers investment services and products through an agreement with a third-party provider. With deposit funds the bank primarily originates commercial and industrial loans and mortgages which account for nearly 75% of its loan book. Macatawa Bank also originates residential mortgages and consumer loans.

Operations
The bank carries total assets of $1.58 billion total loans of $1.12 billion and total deposits of $1.31 billion.

Through its Infinex affiliate the bank provides various brokerage services (including discount brokerage) personal financial planning and consultation regarding mutual funds.

The firm's Trust Department manages assets of approximately $648 million and offers retirement plan and personal trust services. Its personal trust services include financial planning investment management services trust and estate administration and custodial services.

Geographic Reach
Macatawa Bank operates more than 25 branches along with a lending and operation service facility in its primary market in western Michigan which includes the counties of Ottawa Kent and northern Allegan.

Sales and Marketing
Macatawa Bank targets small businesses mission-driven (non-profit) organizations builders manufacturers and service industry companies. Some of its clients include associations businesses churches financial institutions government authorities individuals and non-profit organizations.

Financial Performance
Macatawa's revenue has been declining ever since its peak in 2007. Revenue in fiscal 2014 fell by 2% to $63 million as the bank collected lower interest margins on its commercial residential and consumer loan portfolios amidst customer refinancing in the low interest-rate environment. The bank also generated less income from its short-term investments which hindered top line growth further.

Despite falling revenue the bank enjoyed its highest profit since 2007 as net income jumped by 10% to $10.47 million in 2014. This was thanks to a combination of lower interest expense on deposits and an improving real estate market which led to fewer losses from non-performing assets and fewer provisions for credit losses as real estate values improved.

Operations provided $16.62 million or 2% more cash than in 2013 thanks to higher earnings and because the bank wrote off more in non-cash accrued expenses and other liabilities.

EXECUTIVES

Assistant Vice President, Ron Buit
Vice President Commercial Lending, Frederick Lake
Vice President, Jason Coney
Vice President, Jason ME Coney
Vice President Mortgage Loan Officer, Bob Martin
Vice President Senior Audit Manager, Rick Wesolek
Vice President Treasury Management Sales, Kristin Timmer
Vice President Macatawa Bank, Linda Clatch
Vice President Commercial Banking, Andrew Schmidt
Vice President Retail Banking, Krista Geyer
Vice President Wealth Advisor, John Simonds
Vice President Team Lead Retail Banking Grand Rapids, Sandy Siedlecki
Commercial Banker Vice President, Mike Vanommen
Vice President Branch Manager Senior, Ben Overway
Vice President Private Banking Manager, Kirsen Doolittle
Branch Manager Senior Vice President, Eric Swensson
Board Of Directors, Chuck Geenen
Auditors: BDO USA, LLP

LOCATIONS

HQ: Macatawa Bank Corp.
10753 Macatawa Drive, Holland, MI 49424
Phone: 616 820-1444
Web: www.macatawabank.com

PRODUCTS/OPERATIONS

2014 Sales

	$ mil.	% of total
Interest		
Loans including fees	42	67
Securities	3	5
Other	0	2
Noninterest		
ATM and debit card fees	4	8
Service charges & fees	4	7
Trust fees	2	4
Gain on sales of loans	2	3
Other	2	4
Total	**63**	**100**

COMPETITORS

Comerica	Huntington Bancshares
Fifth Third	PNC Financial
Flagstar Bancorp	

HISTORICAL FINANCIALS

Company Type: Public

Income Statement				FYE: December 31
	ASSETS ($ mil.)	NET INCOME ($ mil.)	INCOME AS % OF ASSETS	EMPLOYEES
12/19	2,068	31	1.5%	364
12/18	1,975	26	1.3%	371
12/17	1,890	16	0.9%	368
12/16	1,741	15	0.9%	374
12/15	1,729	12	0.7%	385
Annual Growth	4.6%	25.7%	—	(1.4%)

2019 Year-End Financials

Debt ratio: 1.00%
Return on equity: 15.66%
Cash ($ mil.): 272
Current ratio: —
Long-term debt ($ mil.): —

No. of shares (mil.): 34
Dividends
  Yield: 2.5%
  Payout: 30.7%
Market value ($ mil.): 380

	STOCK PRICE ($) FY Close	P/E High/Low		PER SHARE ($) Earnings	Dividends	Book Value
12/19	11.13	12	10	0.94	0.28	6.38
12/18	9.62	16	12	0.78	0.25	5.61
12/17	10.00	22	19	0.48	0.18	5.09
12/16	10.41	22	12	0.47	0.12	4.78
12/15	6.05	16	13	0.38	0.11	4.48
Annual Growth	16.5%	—	—	25.4%	26.3%	9.2%

Macy's Inc

Auditors: KPMG LLP

LOCATIONS

HQ: Macy's Inc
151 West 34th Street, New York, NY 10001
Phone: 513 579-7780
Web: www.macysinc.com

HISTORICAL FINANCIALS

Company Type: Public

Income Statement				FYE: February 1
	REVENUE ($ mil.)	NET INCOME ($ mil.)	NET PROFIT MARGIN	EMPLOYEES
02/20	25,331	564	2.2%	123,000
02/19	25,739	1,108	4.3%	130,000
02/18*	24,837	1,547	6.2%	130,000
01/17	25,778	619	2.4%	148,300
01/16	27,079	1,072	4.0%	157,900
Annual Growth	(1.7%)	(14.8%)	—	(6.1%)

*Fiscal year change

2020 Year-End Financials

Debt ratio: 19.65%
Return on equity: 8.83%
Cash ($ mil.): 685
Current ratio: 1.18
Long-term debt ($ mil.): 3,621

No. of shares (mil.): 309
Dividends
  Yield: 0.0%
  Payout: 83.4%
Market value ($ mil.): 4,929

	STOCK PRICE ($) FY Close	P/E High/Low		PER SHARE ($) Earnings	Dividends	Book Value
02/20	15.95	14	8	1.81	1.51	20.64
02/19	25.73	12	7	3.56	1.51	20.93
02/18*	24.89	7	3	5.04	1.51	18.61
01/17	29.11	22	14	1.99	1.49	14.22
01/16	40.41	22	11	3.22	1.39	13.70
Annual Growth	(20.7%)	—	—	(13.4%)	2.0%	10.8%

*Fiscal year change

Magellan Health Inc.

Magellan Health is one of the largest managed behavioral health care companies in the US. The company manages mental health plan employee assistance and work/life programs through its nationwide third-party provider network. Magellan also provides radiology benefits management specialty pharmaceutical management and Medicaid management. Overall it serves about 55 million members through contracts with federal and local government agencies insurance companies and employers. Magellan's Pharmacy Management segment's services include benefit management dispensing administration clinical programs medical pharmacy management and care coordination.

Operations

Magellan operates through two primary business segments: Healthcare (which brings in over 65% of revenue) and Pharmacy Management (some 35% of revenue).

The Healthcare segment provides managed behavioral health care services and employee assistance program (EAP) services as well as managing other specialty areas including diagnostic imaging and musculoskeletal health. It also provides the integrated management of physical behavioral and pharmaceutical health care for special populations through Magellan Complete Care (MCC).

Magellan's Pharmacy Management segment offers products and services to help its clients manage pharmacy benefit programs. It provides pharmacy benefit management (PBM) services pharmacy benefit administration (PBA) for Medicaid and other government-sponsored programs medical pharmacy management and programs to integrate management of specialty drugs across medical and pharmacy benefits in complex cases.

Corporate segment of the Company is comprised primarily of amounts not allocated to the Healthcare and Pharmacy Management segments that are largely associated with costs related to being a publicly traded company.

Geographic Reach

Magellan Health operates about 55 offices in 24 states and Washington DC. The Company's headquarters is located in Phoenix Arizona. All of the company's revenue are generated from US and named to the Fortune 500 List of America's Largest Companies.

Sales and Marketing

Magellan's customers include health plans employer groups government and military agencies labor unions third-party administrators and pharmaceutical manufacturers The government accounts for about 75% of total revenue though.

The company has a network of health care providers as well as a third-party network of facilities including psychiatric and substance abuse hospitals partial hospitalization facilities rehab centers and community health centers.

Financial Performance

Except in 2019 Magellan's revenues have been climbing upward over the past five years but net income has been volatile from year to year.

In 2019 the company's revenue decreased 2% to $7.2 billion. This was primarily due to the $379 million decrease in PBM segment. This decrease is primarily due to terminated contracts of $325.8 million and decreased membership and utilization of $154.6 million mainly due to a reduction in the Part D footprint.

Net income rose 131% to $56 million that year.

The company ended 2019 with $325.2 million in net cash $52.9 million more than it had at the end of 2018. Operating activities provided $115.8 million while investing activities used $19.5 million and financing activities used another $43.4 million.

Strategy

Magellan is focused on measured growth while executing against a multi-year margin improvement plan for the current portfolio of customers to bring earnings in line with industry competitive levels. The Company's strategy is organized around four main focus areas:

Retaining customers and driving new sales: To drive revenue and profit growth long term the Company has targeted plans to retain existing customers and add new customers across both segments. In Pharmacy Management and Healthcare the Company is targeting growth through new business wins increased retention and upselling existing and newly developed services to existing customers.

Improving margins by reducing cost of care lowering Pharmacy costs of goods sold and driving operational improvements across the organization: Within Pharmacy Management the Company will continue to grow PBM while retaining specialty carve-out contracts and lowering our cost of goods sold. Within Healthcare the Company will execute against targeted medical action plans and will have market competitive loss ratios for each customer.

Maximizing and expanding Magellan's key value drivers (Pharmacy Management and Healthcare).

Engaging the Company's workforce: The Company will focus on talent acquisition development and retention as well as streamlining the Company's organizational structure.

Company Background

William Fickling once a star basketball player at Auburn University started his career in his father's real estate office in Georgia. In 1969 Fickling founded Charter Medical as a holding company for the family's six nursing homes and one hospital. The company went public in 1971 as an owner/manager of general acute care hospitals. By the mid-1980s it had focused on psychiatric facilities and was adding addiction treatment centers to its portfolio.

The company went into Chapter 11 in 1991 emerging in 1992 with a plan to focus on behavioral health care; it also went public again. As part of its reorganization Charter in 1995 bought Magellan Health Services and took that name. It also bought 51% of Green Spring Health Services a managed care company specializing in mental health and substance abuse. (It bought the rest in 1998.)

EXECUTIVES

Chairman And Ceo, Barry M. Smith, age 66, $1,000,000 total compensation
Cfo, Jonathan N. (Jon) Rubin, age 56, $535,600 total compensation
General Counsel And Secretary, Daniel N. (Dan) Gregoire, age 65, $470,350 total compensation
Ceo Magellan Healthcare, Sam K. Srivastava, age 52, $609,000 total compensation
Cto, Srinivas (Srini) Koushik
Chief Medical Officer, Karen Amstutz
Ceo Magellan Rx Management, Mostafa M. Kamal, age 39, $412,000 total compensation
Vice President, Tom Lenhart
Vice President Human Resources, Alli Lagrow
Senior Vice President And Chief Compliance Officer At Magellan Health Services, John DiBernardi
Vice President Human Resources Enterprise, Erin Kirchhardt
Vice President Benefits, Christine Barnard
Senior Vice President Specialty Sales, Terah Cochrane
Vice President Client Analytics, Peter Lee
Clinical Director, Rebecca Mutchler
Vice President Government Affairs, Lindsey Napier
Vice President Information Technology, Marco Smalls
Vice President Strategy And Corporate Development, Sprague Mark
Vice President Federal Affairs, Brian Coyne
Vice President Human Resources, Stacy Conti
Bernie Levine Vice President Designated Broker, Jennifer Rock
Senior Vice President Business Development, Thomas O'Connor
Associate Medical Director, Lashondra Washington
Vice President Business Development, Corrado Panno
Auditors: Ernst & Young LLP

LOCATIONS

HQ: Magellan Health Inc.
4801 E. Washington Street, Phoenix, AZ 85034
Phone: 602 572-6050
Web: www.magellanhealth.com

PRODUCTS/OPERATIONS

2018 Sales by Segment

	$ mil.	% of total
Healthcare	4,638	62
Pharmacy Management	2,865	38
Adjustments	(190.3)	-
Total	**7,314**	**100**

2018 Sales

	$ mil.	% of total
Managed care & other	4,878	67
Pharmacy benefit management	2,435	33
Total	**7,314**	**100**

COMPETITORS

APS Healthcare	Horizon Health
CIGNA Behavioral Health	Mental Health Network
ComPsych	OptumRx
Comprehensive Care	PharMerica
First Health Group	Schaller Anderson Inc
Health Net	UBH

HISTORICAL FINANCIALS

Company Type: Public

Income Statement

FYE: December 31

	REVENUE ($ mil.)	NET INCOME ($ mil.)	NET PROFIT MARGIN	EMPLOYEES
12/19	7,159	55	0.8%	10,100
12/18	7,314	24	0.3%	10,500
12/17	5,838	110	1.9%	10,700
12/16	4,836	77	1.6%	9,700
12/15	4,597	31	0.7%	6,900
Annual Growth	**11.7%**	**15.5%**		**10.0%**

2019 Year-End Financials

Debt ratio: 22.08%	No. of shares (mil.): 24
Return on equity: 4.17%	Dividends
Cash ($ mil.): 325	Yield: —
Current ratio: 1.84	Payout: —
Long-term debt ($ mil.): 679	Market value ($ mil.): 1,927

	STOCK PRICE ($) FY Close	P/E High/Low	PER SHARE ($) Earnings	Dividends	Book Value
12/19	78.25	35 24	2.28	0.00	56.77
12/18	56.89	112 54	0.97	0.00	53.70
12/17	96.55	21 14	4.51	0.00	52.74
12/16	75.25	23 15	3.22	0.00	46.76
12/15	61.66	57 37	1.21	0.00	43.18
Annual Growth	**6.1%**	**— —**	**17.2%**	**—**	**7.1%**

MAINE MUNICIPAL BOND BANK

EXECUTIVES

President, Robert Lenna

LOCATIONS

HQ: MAINE MUNICIPAL BOND BANK
127 COMMUNITY DR 101, AUGUSTA, ME 043308010
Phone: 207 622-9386
Web: WWW.MMBB.COM

HISTORICAL FINANCIALS

Company Type: Private

Income Statement

FYE: June 30

	ASSETS ($ mil.)	NET INCOME ($ mil.)	INCOME AS % OF ASSETS	EMPLOYEES
06/19	2,707	54	2.0%	18
06/18	2,443	14	0.6%	—
06/17	2,410	12	0.5%	—
Annual Growth	**6.0%**	**106.5%**	**—**	**—**

ManpowerGroup Inc

Millions of women and men have helped power this firm to the upper echelon of the staffing industry. ManpowerGroup's portfolio of services includes recruitment for permanent temporary and contract professionals as well as administrative and industrial positions. In addition to recruitment and assessment the company also offers training and development career management outsourcing and workforce consulting services. Its Experis brand specializes in IT engineering and finance jobs while its Right Management brand offers career development and coaching. ManpowerGroup operates a global network of over 2500 owned or franchised offices in about 75 countries and territories.

Operations

The company operates through five operating segments: Americas Southern Europe Northern Europe APME and Right Management.

The company provide services as Manpower Experis ManpowerGroup Solutions through both branch and franchise offices. The Americas segment had more than 560 branch and more than 170 franchise offices. Manpower and Experis operations provide a variety of workforce solutions and services including permanent temporary and contract recruitment assessment and selection and training. The segment accounts for a fifth of the company's revenue.

In Southern Europe the company provides permanent temporary and contract recruitment assessment and selection training and outsourcing services throughout Europe. It provides a comprehensive suite of workforce solutions and services offered through Manpower Experis or ManpowerGroup Solutions including permanent temporary and contract recruitment assessment and selection training and outsourcing. The segment accounts for about 45% of revenue.

Northern Europe segment operates in United Kingdom Germany the Nordics and the Netherlands providing a comprehensive suite of workforce solutions and services through Manpower Experis and ManpowerGroup Solutions. Collectively the company operate through about 400 branch offices in this region. The segment accounts for more than 20% of revenue.

In APME segment the company operates through more than 135 branch offices. The company operates provide a variety of workforce solutions and services offered through Manpower and ManpowerGroup Solutions including permanent temporary and contract recruitment assessment and selection training and outsourcing. The segment accounts more than 10% of revenue.

Right Management is a global expert in talent and career management workforce solutions. They design and deliver solutions to align talent strategy with business strategy.

Geographic Reach

ManpowerGroup is based in Milwaukee Wisconsin and operates a global network of some 2500 owned or franchised offices in about 75 countries and territories.

Southern Europe (including France and Italy) is the company's largest market accounting for more than 45% of the company's revenue followed by Northern Europe with about 25%. The Americas supply about 20% of revenue with Asia/Pacific and the Middle East together contributing nearly 15%.

Sales and Marketing

ManpowerGroup's client mix consists of small and medium-sized businesses and large national multinational clients which comprised approximately 60% of our revenues in 2019.

Advertising expenses were $25.7 $27.9 and $26.6 in 2019 2018 and 2017 respectively.

Financial Performance

Since 2015 ManpowerGroup's revenue has had an upward trend except in 2019. The company has had an overall 8% growth in the last five years Its net income for the last five years also follow the same trend.

The company reported $20.9 billion in revenue for 2019 down about 5% from $22.0 billion in 2018. The decrease was due to the overall decrease of the company's service types.

ManpowerGroup's net income decreased by about 16% to $465.7 million in 2019 from $556.7 million in 2018. The decrease was due to the decrease of the company's revenue and increase on their income taxes.

Cash at the end of 2019 was $1.0 billion. The company's cash provided by operating activities was $814.4 million. Investing activities used $16.2 million. Financing activities used $337.4 million.

Strategy

An important element of ManpowerGroup's strategy is to diversify revenue beyond its core staffing and employment services to increase business in areas such as workforce management outsourcing and consulting. It believes the rise of machine learning and artificial intelligence gives it an important opportunity and role to play as the job market evolves by focusing on learning development and training efforts so workers can gain hard-to-find skills and remain employable.

The company is also focused on improved productivity and cutting costs in countries experiencing a softening environment. At the same time ManpowerGroup continues to add resources in growth markets and is investing in technology initiatives in various countries to provide better data insights and innovative delivery models including analytics and cloud-based and mobile applications.

Mergers and Acquisitions

In 2019 ManpowerGroup acquired the remaining 51% controlled interest in their Swiss franchise to obtain full ownership in the entity. Additionally as the part of the purchase agreement they acquired the remaining 20% interest in Experis AG. Both Manpower Switzerland and Experis AG are reported in their Southern Europe segment. The aggregated cash consideration paid was $219.5 million.

Company Background

Milwaukee lawyers Elmer Winter and Aaron Scheinfeld founded Manpower in 1948. It originally concentrated on supplying temporary help to industry during the first few years of the postwar boom. In the next few years the company ex-

panded and in 1956 it began franchising. During the 1960s Manpower opened franchises in Europe Asia and South America. Unlike many of its competitors however it continued to emphasize blue-collar placements.

HISTORY

Milwaukee lawyers Elmer Winter and Aaron Scheinfeld founded Manpower in 1948. It originally concentrated on supplying temporary help to industry during the first few years of the postwar boom. In the next few years the company expanded and in 1956 it began franchising. During the 1960s Manpower opened franchises in Europe Asia and South America. Unlike many of its competitors however it continued to emphasize blue-collar placements.

EXECUTIVES

Evp Global Strategy And Talent, Mara E. Swan, $560,000 total compensation
President And Coo, Darryl E. Green, $800,000 total compensation
Chairman And Ceo, Jonas Prising, $1,200,000 total compensation
President Manpowergroup North America, Becky Frankiewicz
Svp Operational Excellence And It; President Asia/pacific And Middle East, Sriram (Ram) Chandrashekar, $568,035 total compensation
Evp And Cfo, John T. (Jack) McGinnis, $519,231 total compensation
Svp Experis North America, Sean Costello
Vice President Human Resources And Communications, Nadia Ciani
Vice President Global And North America Sales Operations, Rajesh Namboothiry
Vice President And General Manager Global Sales, Patrick Davis
Svp Gm Manpower Japan, Makoto Matsunaga
Vice President Client Solutions, Liz Duensing
Board Member, John Ferraro
Board Of Directors, Patricia Hemingway Hall
Auditors: Deloitte & Touche LLP

LOCATIONS

HQ: ManpowerGroup Inc
100 Manpower Place, Milwaukee, WI 53212
Phone: 414 961-1000   **Fax:** 414 332-0796
Web: www.manpower.com

2017 Sales

	$ mil.	% of total
Southern Europe	8,657	41
Northern Europe	5,306	25
Americas	4,216	20
Asia Pacific & Middle East	2,636	13
Right Management	218	1
Total	**21,034**	**100**

PRODUCTS/OPERATIONS

Selected Services

Staffing
Industrial trades
Manpower Professional
  Engineering
  Finance
  Information technology
  Telecommunications
Office and clerical

COMPETITORS

Adecco	Randstad Holding
Kelly Services	Robert Half
Kforce	TrueBlue
Korn/Ferry	Volt Information

PageGroup

HISTORICAL FINANCIALS

Company Type: Public

Income Statement

FYE: December 31

	REVENUE ($ mil.)	NET INCOME ($ mil.)	NET PROFIT MARGIN	EMPLOYEES
12/19	20,863	465	2.2%	28,000
12/18	21,991	556	2.5%	30,000
12/17	21,034	545	2.6%	29,000
12/16	19,654	443	2.3%	28,000
12/15	19,329	419	2.2%	27,000
Annual Growth	1.9%	2.7%	—	0.9%

2019 Year-End Financials

Debt ratio: 11.64%	No. of shares (mil.): 58
Return on equity: 17.35%	Dividends
Cash ($ mil.): 1,025	Yield: 2.2%
Current ratio: 1.46	Payout: 27.4%
Long-term debt ($ mil.): 1,012	Market value ($ mil.): 5,697

	STOCK PRICE ($) FY Close	P/E High/Low		PER SHARE ($) Earnings	Dividends	Book Value
12/19	97.10	13	8	7.72	2.18	46.75
12/18	64.80	16	7	8.56	2.02	43.21
12/17	126.11	16	11	8.04	1.86	41.99
12/16	88.87	15	9	6.27	1.72	35.27
12/15	84.29	18	12	5.40	1.60	35.94
Annual Growth	3.6%	—	—	9.3%	8.0%	6.8%

Marathon Petroleum Corp.

Marathon Petroleum is the largest oil refiner in the US. Once part of Marathon Oil Corporation Marathon Petroleum processed more than 3 million barrels of crude oil a day at more than 15 refineries in the US. It also holds stakes in pipelines and is one of the largest asphalt and light oil product terminal operators in the US. The company distributes petroleum products wholesale to private-brand marketers and to large commercial and industrial consumers as well as to the spot market. It completed the $23 billion milestone acquisition of Andeavor in 2019.

Operations

Marathon's operations consist of three business segments.

Its Refining & Marketing segment which makes up around 70% of the company's total revenue refines crude oil and other feedstocks at more than 15 refineries in the US Gulf Coast and Midwest regions purchases ethanol and refined products for resale and distributes refined products. It sells refined products to wholesale marketing customers buyers on the spot market its Speedway business segment and to independent entrepreneurs who operate Marathon retail outlets.

The Retail segment (more than 25% of sales) sells transportation fuels and convenience products in the retail market in the Midwest primarily through Speedway convenience stores. It has long-term supply contracts with gas stations operating under the ARCO brand.

The Midstream segment (nearly 5% of revenue) transports crude oil and other feedstocks to Marathon Petroleum's refineries and other locations delivers refined products to wholesale and retail markets and affiliated pipeline assets and investments.

Marathon holds stakes in about 17200 miles of pipeline (MPLX LP) and is one of the largest asphalt and light oil product terminal operators in the US (about 20terminals). In addition the company has a large US private inland product fleet that includes roughly two dozen inland towboats and more than 285 barges.

Geographic Reach

Ohio-based Marathon Petroleum sells refined products at some 6900 Marathon-branded gas stations in some 35 US states DC and Mexico. It is also one of the largest wholesale suppliers of gasoline and distillates to resellers and consumers within its 40-state market area. Nearly 30% of the gas stations are in Ohio Michigan and Indiana.

Sales and Marketing

Marathon Petroleum sells to wholesale suppliers of gasoline and distillates to resellers and consumers. Customers include independent retailers wholesale customers their Marathon brand jobbers and Speedway brand convenience stores airlines transportation companies and utilities. It also sells gasoline distillates and asphalt for export primarily out of their Garyville and Galveston Bay refineries.

Financial Performance

Marathon's revenue was on an upward trend in the last five years despite a blip in 2016.

In 2019 the company's operating revenue grew 28% to $123.9 billion thanks to increased sales and other operating revenues.

Despite rising sales net income fell 10% to $3.3 billion in 2019. The decrease in income was due to a $27.7 billion raise in cost and expenses and increase in net interest and other financial costs.

Cash and cash equivalents at the end of the period were $1.5 billion. The company's operations generated $9.4 billion financing used $3.4 billion and investing activities used another $6.3 billion. Marathon's main cash uses were for additions to property plant and equipment and repayment of long-term debts.

Strategy

The company's business strategy is based on five strategic pillars designed to define how it creates value through competitive advantages: superior execution integrated value chain growth through innovation strong financial discipline and sustainability. These strategic pillars are supported by its commitment to maintaining a high-performing culture and workforce. It continuously strives to enhance its workforce through active recruitment of the best candidates including those from diverse backgrounds. It develops its high quality workforce through coaching mentoring and the delivery of robust training programs focused on leadership commercial skills safety environmental stewardship diversity and inclusion and other professional and technical skills.

In October 2019 it announced its intention to separate its retail transportation fuel and convenience store business which is operated primarily under the Speedway brand into an independent publicly traded company through a tax-free distribution to MPC shareholders of publicly traded stock in the new independent retail transportation fuel and convenience store company.

Company Background

Marathon Petroleum Corporation founded in 1887

EXECUTIVES

Evp Supply Transportation And Marketing, Gary R. Heminger, age 66, $1,600,000 total compensation
Evp Human Resources Health And Administrative Services, Rodney P. Nichols, age 67
President Speedway, Anthony R. (Tony) Kenney, age 67, $687,500 total compensation
Svp Marketing, Thomas M. (Tom) Kelley, age 60

Svp Cfo And Treasurer, Timothy T. Griffith, age 50, $600,000 total compensation
Svp Supply Distribution And Planning, C. Michael Palmer, age 66, $637,500 total compensation
President, Donald C. (Don) Templin, age 56, $800,000 total compensation
Svp Transportation And Logistics, John S. Swearingen, age 60
Vp And Cio, Donald W. Wehrly, age 60
Svp Refining, Raymond L. Brooks, age 59
President Mplx Lp, Mike Hennigan
Senior Vice President Marketing, Tom Kelley
Vice President And Controller, C Kristopher Hagedorn
Evp, C Michael Palmer
Executive Vice President Markwest Operations, Gregory S Floerke
Vice President Tax, D Rick Linhardt
Board Member, Audrey Davis
Vp Finance And Treasurer, Thomas Kaczynski
Board Member, Charles Bunch
Board Member, Michael Beatty
Board Member, Christopher Helms
Auditors: PricewaterhouseCoopers LLP

LOCATIONS

HQ: Marathon Petroleum Corp.
539 South Main Street, Findlay, OH 45840-3229
Phone: 419 422-2121
Web: www.marathonpetroleum.com

PRODUCTS/OPERATIONS

2018 Sales

	% of total
Refining & marketing	73
Speedway	21
Midstream	6
Total	**100**

2018 Sales

	% of total
Refined products	88
Merchandise	6
Crude oil & refinery feedstocks	4
Transportation & other	2
Total	**100**

Selected Products

Asphalt
Branded Distillates
Branded Gasoline
Branded Lubricants
Heavy Oil
Petroleum Coke
Specialty Products
Wholesale Light Products

COMPETITORS

BP	Koch Industries Inc.
CITGO	Motiva Enterprises
Chevron	Murphy Oil
ConocoPhillips	Shell Oil Products
Exxon Mobil	Sunoco
Hess Corporation	Tesoro
HollyFrontier	Valero Energy

HISTORICAL FINANCIALS

Company Type: Public

Income Statement

FYE: December 31

	REVENUE ($ mil.)	NET INCOME ($ mil.)	NET PROFIT MARGIN	EMPLOYEES
12/19	124,813	2,637	2.1%	60,910
12/18	97,102	2,780	2.9%	60,350
12/17	75,369	3,432	4.6%	43,800
12/16	63,364	1,174	1.9%	44,460
12/15	72,258	2,852	3.9%	45,440
Annual Growth	14.6%	(1.9%)	—	7.6%

2019 Year-End Financials

Debt ratio: 29.26%
Return on equity: 7.66%
Cash ($ mil.): 1,527
Current ratio: 1.25
Long-term debt ($ mil.): 28,127

No. of shares (mil.): 649
Dividends
  Yield: 3.5%
  Payout: 45.4%
Market value ($ mil.): 39,102

	STOCK PRICE ($) FY Close	P/E High/Low		PER SHARE ($) Earnings	Dividends	Book Value
12/19	60.25	17	11	3.97	2.12	51.92
12/18	59.01	16	10	5.28	1.84	51.73
12/17	65.98	10	7	6.70	1.52	28.87
12/16	50.35	23	14	2.21	1.36	25.68
12/15	51.84	20	8	5.26	1.14	24.93
Annual Growth	3.8%	—	—	(6.8%)	16.8%	20.1%

Markel Corp (Holding Co)

Have you ever thought about who insures the manicurist or an antique motorcycle? Specialty insurer Markel takes on the risks other insurers will not touch from amusement parks to thoroughbred horses to summer camps. Coverage is also available for one-time events such as golf tournaments and auto races. The company provides customized direct and facultative placements in the US and abroad as well as treaty reinsurance. Markel International provides specialty insurance internationally from its base in the UK while investment management is provided by Markel CATCo and Nephila Holdings. Subsidiary Markel Ventures invests in non-insurance companies. About 80% of the total premium was generated from the US.

Operations

Markel operates through two primary segments: Insurance (about 85%) and Reinsurance (more than 15%).

The Insurance segment writes commercial risks – primarily excess and surplus lines – which are distributed through a network of wholesale brokers. This segment includes both hard-to-place risks written outside of the standard market on an E&S basis and unique and hard-to-place risks that must be written on an admitted basis due to marketing and regulatory reasons. Markel Assurance writes business for commercial and Fortune 1000 accounts Markel Specialty writes program insurance and other specialty coverage London and Munich-based Markel International writes business worldwide and State National writes collateral protection insurance.

US Insurance also provides specialty insurance to clients that engage in highly specialized activities requiring niche coverage typically not offered by standard insurers. Underwriting entities include FirstComp Insurance Markel Insurance and Markel American Insurance. Excess and surplus insurance is provided by Evanston Insurance.

The Reinsurance segment provides property casualty and specialty treaty reinsurance to other insurers around the world. Key products include structured and whole turnover credit political risk mortgage contract and commercial surety reinsurance programs covering worldwide exposures public entity reinsurance products workers' compensation excess of loss and quota share treaties whole account marine and agriculture reinsurance products.. These are underwritten by the Global Reinsurance and Market International divisions.

Geographic Reach

Headquartered in Richmond Virginia Markel primarily operates in the US market which accounts for roughly 80% of premiums. Its UK unit Markel International writes policies for UK clients as well as on a global basis through the Lloyd's of London market.

Markel operates in 73 offices in 21 countries. Outside of the US the company operates largely in the UK Europe and Bermuda as well as in Canada Latin America Asia Pacific and the Middle East.

Sales and Marketing

Markel distributes its products through independent agents and brokers. Its top three independent brokers represent more than 25% of the group's gross premiums written.

Financial Performance

Markel's revenue has been climbing steadily for the past five years as premium and fee income has grown.

In 2019 revenue increased 39% to $9.5 billion compared with the revenue from the previous year

The company's net income for the year 2019 was $1.8 billion a $1.6 billion increase compared with $128.2 million in 2018. The increase was primarily due to higher operating income partially offset by higher income tax and interest expenses.

Markel ended 2019 with $3.5 billion in net cash compared with $2.4 billion in 2018. Operating activities provided $1.3 billion while investing activities used $535.2 million and financing activities provided another $359.3 million. The company's main cash was primarily used to purchase fixed maturities and equity securities senior long-term debt and other debt and common stock repurchased.

Strategy

Markel's strategy for growth is to leverage its expertise and specialized market knowledge of niche markets to differentiate its business from competitors. It is also looking to diversify into new specialty insurance markets as well as developing innovative products to reach more clients. The firm works at improving its existing policies to provide its customers with the evolving types of coverage they need. For example in 2017 it expanded the professional liability offerings it provides for law firms. Another area Markel is heavily invested in is the insurance linked securities market bolstered by its purchase of Nephila Holdings in 2018.

The group has also been growing other operations through acquisitions. In 2017 it acquired insurance fronting services provider State National Companies for $919 million fresh on the heels of its purchase of commercial surety firm SureTec.

The company is additionally focused on expanding international operations. It plans to establish an insurance provider in Germany ahead of the UK's pending exit from the European Union. (It currently offers insurance in Germany from a branch office in Munich where the new company will eventually be located.) That should help the company as it seeks other opportunities to expand in Europe.

Markel launched Lodgepine Capital Management Limited a new retrocessional Insurance Linked Securities (ILS) platform based in Bermuda.

Mergers and Acquisitions

In late 2019 the company acquired VSC Fire & Security Inc. (VSC) a provider of comprehensive fire protection life safety and low voltage solutions to retailers commercial campuses healthcare facilities and government properties throughout the southeastern United States. Total consideration for the acquisition was $225.0 million which included cash consideration of $204.0 million. The purchase price was preliminarily allocated to the acquired assets and liabilities of VSC based on estimated fair value at the acquisition date.

In mid-2019 The company acquired a minority ownership interest in The Hagerty Group LLC (Hagerty Group) a company that primarily operates as a managing general agent under the names Hagerty Insurance Agency and Hagerty Classic Marine Insurance Agency (collectively Hagerty). Hagerty Group also includes Hagerty Re a Bermuda Class 3 reinsurance company. Hagerty Group is a leading automotive lifestyle brand and provider of specialty insurance to automobile enthusiasts. Total consideration for the Company's investment was $212.5 million. The Company's investment in Hagerty Group is accounted for under the equity method and is included in other assets on the Company's consolidated balance sheet.

Company Background

In the 1920s Sam Markel formed a mutual insurance company for "jitneys" (passenger cars refurbished as public transportation buses). In 1930 he founded Markel Service to expand nationally. To keep up with industry growth the company revamped itself as a managing general agent and independent claims service organization in the late 1950s. In 1978 Markel began covering taverns restaurants and vacant buildings. It created excess and surplus lines underwriter Essex Insurance in 1980.

Markel went public in 1986.

HISTORY

In the 1920s Sam Markel formed a mutual insurance company for "jitneys" (passenger cars refurbished as public transportation buses). In 1930 he founded Markel Service to expand nationally. To keep up with industry growth the company revamped itself as a managing general agent and independent claims service organization in the late 1950s. In 1978 Markel began covering taverns restaurants and vacant buildings. It created excess and surplus lines underwriter Essex Insurance in 1980.

Markel went public in 1986. The next year it invested in Shand Morahan and Evanston Insurance (specialty coverage including architects engineers and lawyers professional liability; officers and directors insurance; errors and omissions; and medical malpractice). It bought summer camp insurer Rhulen Agency in 1989.

In the 1990s Markel began buying insurers with their own offbeat niches. In 1990 it bought the rest of Shand Morahan and Evanston Insurance. In 1995 it bought Lincoln Insurance (excess and surplus lines) from media giant Thomson (now Thomson Reuters). The next year the company bought Investors Insurance Holding (excess and surplus lines). Markel which already owned nearly 10% of Gryphon Holdings (commercial property/casualty) bought the rest in 1999.

Expanding internationally Markel bought Bermuda-based Terra Nova Holdings a reinsurer and a Lloyd's managing agency in 2000. The company experienced heavy losses in 2001 not only related to the events of September 11 but also to

its slumping international business (the company took a $100 million charge).

Unlike standard insurers (whose rates are generally regulated) specialty insurers can charge the rates they consider reasonable. To that end after taking significant losses from the 2005 hurricane season (Katrina Rita Wilma) and additional hits from the 2008 season (Gustav Ike) the company decided to raise the rates on its catastrophe-exposed businesses.

EXECUTIVES

Co-ceo, Thomas S. Gayner, age 58, $807,692 total compensation

Co-ceo, Richard R. Whitt, age 56, $807,692 total compensation

Vice Chairman, F. Michael Crowley, age 68, $793,269 total compensation

Chief Administrative Officer, Britton L. (Britt) Glisson, age 63

Evp And Chief Underwriting Officer, Gerard Albanese, age 67, $615,385 total compensation

Evp And Cfo, Anne G. Waleski, age 53, $578,846 total compensation

Evp And Chief Actuarial Officer, Bradley J. Kiscaden, age 57

Cio, Mike Scyphers

Associate Vice President Of Claims, David Ashley

Senior Vice President, Nessa Goodman

Vice President And Chief Administrative Officer, Robert Blazer

Vice President Investor, Mike Kotlowski

Vice President Marketing, Cara Bowen

Vice President Claims Manager, Rick Raeder

Svp Strategic Management, Linda Schreiner

Vice President Ocean Marine, Karla Scott

Vice President Western Region Marine Underwriting, Philip B Nelson

Vice President Ocean Marine, John Grossenbacher

Vice President Professional Liability, Michael Cunney

Executive Vice President Professional Liability, Daniel Gamble

Vice President, Lyle Mccoy

Senior Vice President Financial Institutions, Bret Hilgart

Senior Vice President, Steven Schreiber

Senior Vice President And Marketing Director, Kip Herring

Vice President Western Region Marine Underwriting, Philip Nelson

Senior Vice President, Steven Dorsey

Senior Vice President Professional Liability, Ben Munro

Assistant Vice President Medical Malpractice And Professional Liability, Amy Gimbel

Vice President North American Property Cat Reinsurance, Miles Staples

Assistant Vice President, Louis Botticelli

Associate Vice President, Terri Ashley

Senior Vice President, Tony Markel

Senior Vice President, Sharon Lynch

Vice President Central Region, Michael Buckley

Vice President, Edward Ellis

Vice President Global Information Technology, Daniela Galli

Vice President Global Information Technology, Daniel Iespa

Assistant Vice President Credit Surety And Political Risk, Margaux Hackett

Senior Vice President, Sally Gibson

Vice President Of Manufacturing Operations, Rick Kreppel

Senior Vice President, Pam Pamela

Assistant Vice President, Tony Nickolson

Vice President, Chris Ventrone

Senior Vice President, Don Meyer

Vice President, Rolf Gesen

Vice President, Ralph Fox

Vice President Sales, David Panish
Vice President And Director Of Contractor
 Support Services, Scott Olson
Vice Chairman, Anthony F. Markel, age 78
Vice Chairman, Steven A. Markel, age 71
Chairman, Alan I. Kirshner, age 84
Board Member, Stewart Kasen
Board Member, Michael Schewel
Board Member, Debora Wilson
Board Member, Lemuel Lewis
Board Member, Michael O'reilly
Board Member, Alfred Broaddus
Board Member, Bruce Connell
Auditors: KPMG LLP

LOCATIONS

HQ: Markel Corp (Holding Co)
 4521 Highwoods Parkway, Glen Allen, VA 23060-6148
Phone: 804 747-0136
Web: www.markel.com

2018 Gross Written Premiums

	% of total
US	79
UK	8
Canada	2
Other	11
Total	**100**

PRODUCTS/OPERATIONS

2018 Sales

	$ mil.	% of total
Earned premiums		
Insurance	3,784	51
Reinsurance	928	13
Other	(0.5)	-
Products	1,497	20
Services & other	635	9
Net investment income	434	6
Net foreign exchange gains	106	1
Adjustments	(437.6)	
Total	**6,947**	**100**

Selected Products

Insurance
 FirstComp - Workers' Comp
 Global Insurance
 Practice Groups
 Specialty Commercial
 Specialty Personal
Reinsurance
 Casualty
 Property
 Public Entity
 Specialty

COMPETITORS

Assurant
CNA Financial
Great American Insurance Company
HCC Insurance
Meadowbrook Insurance
Medical Liability Mutual Insurance
National Indemnity Company
Nationwide
Philadelphia Insurance Companies
ProSight Specialty Insurance Group
RLI
United States Liability Insurance Group
XL Group plc

HISTORICAL FINANCIALS

Company Type: Public

Income Statement

				FYE: December 31
	ASSETS ($ mil.)	NET INCOME ($ mil.)	INCOME AS % OF ASSETS	EMPLOYEES
12/19	37,473	1,790	4.8%	18,600
12/18	33,306	(128)	—	1,700
12/17	32,805	395	1.2%	15,600
12/16	25,875	455	1.8%	10,900
12/15	24,941	582	2.3%	10,600
Annual Growth	**10.7%**	**32.4%**	**—**	**15.1%**

2019 Year-End Financials

Debt ratio: 9.43%
Return on equity: 17.77%
Cash ($ mil.): 3,072
Current ratio: —
Long-term debt ($ mil.): —

No. of shares (mil.): 13
Dividends
 Yield: —
 Payout: —
Market value ($ mil.): 15,769

	STOCK PRICE ($) FY Close	P/E High/Low		PER SHARE ($) Earnings	Dividends	Book Value
12/19	1,143.17	9	7	129.07	0.00	802.58
12/18	1,038.05	—	—	(9.55)	0.00	653.86
12/17	1,139.13	44	34	25.81	0.00	683.58
12/16	904.50	31	26	31.27	0.00	606.30
12/15	883.35	22	16	41.74	0.00	561.23
Annual Growth	**6.7%**	**—**	**—**	**32.6%**	**—**	**9.4%**

Marriott International, Inc.

Marriott International is one of the world's leading hoteliers. The company operates or franchises some 7300 hotel residential and timeshare properties worldwide. Its hotel portfolio which comprises nearly 1.4 million guest rooms includes the premium Delta Hotels and Renaissance Hotels brands and its flagship Marriott Hotels & Resorts as well as the Ritz-Carlton W Hotels The Luxury Collection and JW Marriott luxury brands. Additionally the company operates the select-service and extended-stay brands Courtyard and Fairfield Inn. I North America accounts for about 80% of Marriott International's revenue.

HISTORY

The company began in 1927 as a Washington DC root beer stand operated by John and Alice Marriott. Later they added hot food and named their business the Hot Shoppe. In 1929 the couple incorporated and began building a regional chain.

Hot Shoppes opened its first hotel the Twin Bridges Marriott Motor Hotel in Arlington Virginia in 1957. When the Marriotts' son Bill became president in 1964 (CEO in 1972 chairman in 1985) he focused on expanding the hotel business. The company changed its name to Marriott Corp. in 1967. With the rise in airline travel Marriott built several airport hotels during the 1970s. By 1977 sales had topped $1 billion.

Marriott became the #1 operator of airport food beverage and merchandise facilities in the US with its 1982 acquisition of Host International and it introduced moderately priced Courtyard hotels in 1983. Acquisitions in the 1980s included a timeshare business foodservice companies and com-

petitor Howard Johnson. (Marriott later sold the hotels but kept the restaurants and turnpike units.)

The company entered three new market segments in 1987: Marriott Suites (full-service suites) Residence Inn (moderately priced suites) and Fairfield Inn (economy hotels). It also began developing "life-care" communities which provide apartments meals and limited nursing care to the elderly in 1988.

Marriott split its operations into two companies in 1993: Host Marriott to own hotels and Marriott International primarily to manage them. However Marriott International still owned some of the properties and in 1995 it bought 49% of the Ritz-Carlton luxury hotel group.

In 1996 Marriott purchased the Forum Group (assisted living communities and health care services) and merged it into Marriott Senior Living Services.

Marriott introduced its Marriott Executive Residences in 1997. Also that year the firm expanded overseas operations with its purchase of the 150-unit Hong Kong-based Renaissance Hotel Group a deal that included branding rights to the Ramada chain.

In 1998 after the division of its lodging and food distribution services the new Marriott International then began trading as a separate company. That year Marriott also acquired the rest of Ritz-Carlton and established SpringHill Suites by Marriott.

Marriott entered the corporate housing business in 1999 through its acquisition of ExecuStay Corporation (renamed ExecuStay by Marriott) which provided fully furnished and accessorized apartments for stays of 30 days or more. The following year it joined Italy's Bulgari the world's #3 jeweler in a $140 million venture of luxury hotels sporting the Bulgari name.

Marriott refocused its operations on the lodging market in 2003 when it exited both the senior living and distribution services businesses. It sold Marriott Distribution Services (food and beverage distribution) to Services Group of America and sold Marriott Senior Living Services to Sunrise Assisted Living (the management business) and CNL Retirement Properties (nine communities). The following year Marriott sold the international branding rights to the Ramada and Days Inn chains to Cendant (now Avis Budget Group) for about $200 million.

In 2005 Marriott acquired about 30 properties from CTF Holdings (an affiliate of Hong Kong-based New World Development) for nearly $1.5 billion. It sold 14 properties immediately to Sunstone Hotel Investors and Walton Street Capital. The deal put an end to an ongoing legal battle between Marriott and CTF Holdings which had alleged that the hotelier had pocketed kickbacks and fees from outside vendors.

Marriott invested about $200 million in 2005 to upgrade its hotel beds with higher thread-count sheets and triple-sheeted tops and it renovated and upgraded many of its Courtyard and Residence Inn locations during 2006. A difficult 2009 called for the elimination of more than 1000 jobs. Also that year the company cut costs by modifying menus and restaurant hours adjusting room amenities and relaxing some brand standards.

In 2010 Marriott introduced two new hotel brands into the market: Edtion (a boutique luxury chain) and Autograph Collection (independent luxury properties that each have their own unique identity). The firm spun off its time-share business Marriott Vacations Worldwide in 2011.

EXECUTIVES

Evp Finance, Carl Berquist

Vice President Diversity And Workforce Effectivene, Maruiel Perkins-chavis
Executive Vice President, Geoffrey Garside
President And Ceo, Arne M. Sorenson, age 61, $1,236,000 total compensation
Vice President For Student Life, Marilyn Lasecki
Evp Finance And Global Treasurer, Carolyn B. Handlon
Group President, David J. Grissen, age 62, $725,000 total compensation
Evp And Global Chief Human Resources Officer, David A. Rodriguez, age 61
Svp Global Revenue Management And Reservation Sales, Amy C. McPherson, age 58
Global Chief Communications And Public Affairs Officer, Tricia Primrose
Evp And Global Chief Development Officer, Anthony G. (Tony) Capuano, age 54, $750,000 total compensation
Evp Cfrst Brand Management And Operations, Tim Sheldon
Global Chief Commercial Officer, Stephanie C. Linnartz, age 51, $700,000 total compensation
Global Cio, Bruce Hoffmeister
President And Managing Director Middle East And Africa, Alex Kyriakidis, age 67
Cfo, Kathleen K. (Leeny) Oberg, age 59, $650,000 total compensation
President And Managing Director Asia Pacific, Craig S. Smith, age 57
President Marriott Hotels Of Canada, Don Cleary
Executive Vice President, Pamela Murray
Vice President, Michael Cullen
Svp Canadian Development Ritz Carlton Hotels, Michael Beckley
Evp Taxes, Lester Pulse
Svp Middle East And Africa, Philip Bryson
Vp Design And Project Management, Robert Reinders
Vice President Human Resources Change Management, Heather Powell
Vice President Talent Acquisition And Selection, Steve Bauman
Regional Vice President Central, Teresa Walrath
Vice President Human Resources, Kimberly Reed
Vice President Brand Marketing Courtyard, Gini Gladstone
Vice President, Russell Vereb
Vice President Europe Planning And Transformation, Arielle Quick
Regional Vice President Human Resources, Marisa Milton
Vice President Brand Operations Design And Development, James Addison
Senior Vice President Global Marketing Optimization, Andy Kauffman
Vice President, Julie Sieracki
Vice President Marketing, Amy Mullens
Vice President Business Process Governance, Carol Cernugel
Vice President Sales And Marketing, Chris Greenleaf
Vice President Consumer Insight And Advisory Services Marketing Digital, Cathy Hartman
Vice President, Mitzi Gaskins
Vp Human Resources, Shelly Ahrens
Vice President, Victor Fernandez
Vice President, Michelle Mutton
Vice President Executive Compensation, Thaddeus Shepherd
Regional Vice President Of Sales And Marketing Caribbean And Latin America Region, Alex Fiz
Vice President, Cecilia Lewis
Vice President, Jeff Spilman
Vice President Sales And Group Solutions, Glen Harvell
Vice President Human Resources, Porter Shifflett
Vice President Global Property Systems, Violeta Seidell
Vice President, Steve Stamas

Regional Vice President Sales And Marketing Asia Pacific, Kent Maury
Vice President And Senior Counsel, Taisha Urland
Senior Vice President Lodging Development, Christopher Rose
Senior Vice President Comp And Benefits, Tracey Ballow
Senior Vice President Finance Department, Gary Rosenthal
Vice President, Jennie Benzon
Vice President And Senior Counsel, Linda Miller
Senior Vice President Brand Strategy And Innovation, Julie Moll
Vice President Contract Management, Yvette Young
Vp Customer Experience Insight, Mark Schwartz
Vice President, Brandon Linton
Senior Vice President Reservations Sales And Customer Care, Kaye Dengel
Vice President Marriott.com And Mobile Technology, Todd Nemoir
Senior Vice President And General Counsel, Myron Walker
Vice President, William Holmes
Vice President Marketing, Daniel Vihn
Vice President, Jim O'Hern
Senior Vice President, Jasraj Singh
Vice President, Tushaar Agrawal
Vice President, Judy Fennimore
Vice President Of Human Resources, Debbie Wilson
Vice President Applications Delivery Reservations And Revenue Management, Prashant Lonkar
Vice President Leisure Business Development, Warren Ruello
Vice President Jw Marriott Hotels And Resorts Marriott Hotels And Resorts, Michael Darne
Vice President Sales And Marketing Support, Beth Jones
Executive Vice President Architecture And Construction, Susan Levenson
Vice President New Business Development, Annie Brooks
Executive Vice President Arch And Design, Bradford Bryan
Senior Vice President Global Marketing, Rick Medwedeff
Senior Vice President Mortgage Bankin, Abid Gilani
Vice President Sales And Marketing, David Nostrand
Senior Vice President And Chief Techno, Barry Schuler
Vice President Of Interior Design, Teri Urovsky
Vice President Assistant General Counsel And Corporate Secretary, Bancroft S Gordon
Evp, Jurgen Giesbert
Senior Vice President And Associate General Counsel, Jeffrey A Holdaway
Vice President, Stephen Maselko
Vice President Insurance, Hector Mastrapa
Svp And Deputy General Counsel, Nancy Lee
Vice President And Senior Counsel, Phil Brandt
Vice President Information Technology Infrastructure, Stephanie Carrick
Vice President International Business, Howard Leigh
Senior Vice President Owner And Franchise Services, James Fisher
Vice President Application Development, Dave Rupp
Vice President And Executive Director, Tad Asbury
Vice President Of Finance, Matt Barker
Vice President Application Development Digital Platforms And Reservations, Dave Blankenship
Vice President And Senior Counsel, Brendan Ross
Vice President Hotel Development Latin America And Caribbean, Paul Adan
Vice President Marriott Rewards Partnerships And Global Card Programs, Misha Lapcevic

Vice President And Senior Counsel, Carnot Evans
Vp Ecommerce, Devin Sung
Vice President Global Claims, Stephen Perroots
Vice President Brand Marketing And Communications (asia Pacific), Mike Fulkerson
Vp Brands Marketing And Digital Cala, Diana Plazas
Senior Vice President Human Resources, Carol S Anderson
Vice President Communications Asia Pacific, Alethea Lam
Vice President Information Technology, Delfina Reimers
Vp Accounting, Astrid Burrows
Senior Vice President Information Technology Business Partnership And Planning, Jenifer L Mason
Vice President Asset Management Europe, Laurent Pavageau
Executive Vice President And Chief Financial Officer, Leeny Oberg
Senior Vice President Global Compliance Counsel, William Dempster
Vp Mobile And Digital Guest Services, Todd Strickler
Vice President Global Sales Asia Pacific, John Toomey
Vice President Global Tax Accounting And Compliance, Barbara Young
Vice President Human Resources Europe, Ben Di Benedetto
Vice President And Assistant General Counsel Practice Group Leader, Shazmah Hakim
Global Vice President Infrastructure Engineering And Operations, Lenny Guardino
Vice President Sales And Marketing, Andrew Cymrot
Vice President Workplace And End User Technology, Terry Herring
Vice President Luxury Brand Marketing And Brand Management Middle East And Africa, Candice D'Cruz
Vice President Luxury Brands And Brand Marketing Asia Pacific Marriott International, Bruce Ryde
Vice President Information Technology, Mary Lou Bondel
Vice President Event Production, Patricia Campbell
Vice President Community Footprints, Stewart Ron
Vp Revenue Management Operations, Nancy Bergamini
Senior Vice President And Associate General Counsel For Dispute Resolution, Michael Martinez
Legal Secretary, Karen Greiman
Vice President Of Business Development, Chris Dabi
Vice President, Tom Onken
Vp Brand Marketing And Digital U.s. East, Dennis Skiba
Vice President Labor Relations Marriott International, George Greene
Vice President And Assistant General Counsel, David Manderscheid
Vice President Lodging Development, David Aupied
Vice President Finance, Louis Capone
Vice President Program Evaluation, Katharine Epperson
Vice President Finance At Marriott International, Don Clendenin
Vice President Global Sales Luxury, John Harper
Vice President Global Creative Content Marketing, Scott Weisenthal
Vice President Global Product Development, Deborah Huguely
Area Vice President Luxury Brands United Arab Emirates, Sandeep Walia
Vp Hr Planning And Talent Management, Han-ron Siah

Vice President Brand Marketing And Sales, Pj Rivera
Vp Asset Management, Eric Czech
Vice President And Senior Counsel, Priscilla Saba
Vice President, Bobby Molinary
Vice President Design Management, Rob Reinders
Vice President Andamp; Assistant General Counsel Employment Law Gr, Patricia Cousins
Vice President Sales And Marketing, Elizabeth Green
Auditors: Ernst & Young LLP

LOCATIONS

HQ: Marriott International, Inc.
10400 Fernwood Road, Bethesda, MD 20817
Phone: 301 380-3000
Web: www.marriott.com

PRODUCTS/OPERATIONS

2018 Sales

	$ mil.	% of total
North American Full-Service segment	13,072	63
North American Limited-Service segment	3,217	16
Asia Pacific	1,118	5
Other	3,351	16
Total	**20,758**	**100**

2018 Sales

	$ mil.	% of total
Cost reimbursements	15,543	75
Franchise fees	1,849	9
Owned leased and other revenue	1,635	8
Base management fees	1,140	5
Incentive management fees and other	591	3
Total	**20,758**	**100**

COMPETITORS

Accor	Four Seasons Hotels
Best Western	Hilton Worldwide
Carlson Hotels	Hyatt
Choice Hotels	InterContinental
Club Med	Hotels
Extended Stay America Inc.	LXR Luxury Resorts
	Loews Hotels
FRHI Hotels and Resorts	

HISTORICAL FINANCIALS

Company Type: Public

Income Statement				FYE: December 31
	REVENUE ($ mil.)	NET INCOME ($ mil.)	NET PROFIT MARGIN	EMPLOYEES
12/19	20,972	1,273	6.1%	174,000
12/18	20,758	1,907	9.2%	176,000
12/17	22,894	1,372	6.0%	177,000
12/16	17,072	780	4.6%	226,500
12/15	14,486	859	5.9%	127,500
Annual Growth	**9.7%**	**10.3%**	—	**8.1%**

2019 Year-End Financials

Debt ratio: 43.67%
Return on equity: 86.95%
Cash ($ mil.): 225
Current ratio: 0.47
Long-term debt ($ mil.): 9,963

No. of shares (mil.): 324
Dividends
Yield: 1.2%
Payout: 44.6%
Market value ($ mil.): 49,063

	STOCK PRICE ($) FY Close	P/E High/Low		PER SHARE ($) Earnings	Dividends	Book Value
12/19	151.43	40	27	3.80	1.85	2.17
12/18	108.56	27	19	5.38	1.56	6.56
12/17	135.73	37	22	3.61	1.29	10.39
12/16	82.68	32	22	2.64	1.15	13.87
12/15	67.04	26	20	3.15	0.95	(14.01)
Annual Growth	**22.6%**			—	**4.8%**	**18.1%**

Marsh & McLennan Companies Inc.

One of the world's largest insurance brokers Marsh & McLennan Companies (MMC) is a heavyweight insurance middleman. Through core subsidiary Marsh the company provides a broad array of insurance-related brokerage consulting and risk management services to clients in more than 130 countries. Customers include large and small companies government entities and not-for-profit organizations. MMC's global reinsurance brokerage business is handled by subsidiary Guy Carpenter. The company also owns Mercer which provides human resources and financial consulting services to customers in about 45 countries worldwide; and Oliver Wyman which provides management consulting services. In 2019 MMC acquired Jardine Lloyd Thompson for $5.6 billion. About 55% of total revenue comes from international customers.

Operations

MMC's operations are split into two groups — the Risk and Insurance Services (RIS) segment (consisting of Marsh and Guy Carpenter) and the Consulting segment (Mercer and Oliver Wyman). Both segments help clients assess risks in their businesses and ascertain whether those risks are insurable.

The RIS segment accounts for more than 55% of revenue; insurance subsidiary Marsh alone accounts for about half of MMC's total revenues while Guy Carpenter accounts for about 10%.

The Consulting segment brings in the remaining revenue; its Mercer human resources unit (MMC's second-largest subsidiary) accounts for a third of the group's total revenues. Oliver Wyman brings in another 15%.

Geographic Reach

New York- based MMC provides services in the Americas the Asia/Pacific region and the EMEA (Europe Middle East and Africa) region.

The US contributes more than 45% of annual revenues. The UK and Continental Europe bring in about one-third of total sales while the Asia/Pacific region and other markets each bring in about 10%.

Sales and Marketing

MMC's business customers include small- mid-sized and multinational corporations. Its consulting division serves entities engaged in industries including transportation communication technology energy retail distribution and wholesale and finance.

Financial Performance

MMC has seen relatively steady revenue growth over the last few years. Net income was also rising but took a dip in 2017. In 2019 revenue rose 11% to $16.7 billion.

Revenue in the Risk and Insurance Services segment increased 17%; revenue increased 4% and 5% on an underlying basis at Marsh and Guy Carpenter respectively. The Consulting segment's revenue increased 5%; and Revenue increased 2% and 6% on an underlying basis at Mercer and Oliver Wyman Group respectively as compared with 2018.

Net income rose 6% to $1.7 billion in 2019. That increase was largely due to lower acquisition loss related to derivative contracts.

The company ended 2019 with $1.2 billion in net cash $89 million more than it had at the end of 2018. Operating activities provided $2.4 billion and financing activities added another $3.3 billion to the coffers. Investing activities however used $5.7 billion for acquisitions.

Strategy

MMC has a number of strategic initiatives involving investments in or partnerships with technology companies as well as investments in technology systems and infrastructure to support its growth strategy. It depends in large part on technology systems for conducting business as well as for providing the data and analytics it utilizes to manage its business. As a result it business success is dependent on maintaining the effectiveness of existing technology systems and on continuing to develop and enhance technology systems that support its business processes and strategic initiatives in a cost and resource efficient manner particularly as its business processes become more digital. The company's investments may include direct investments in insurance consulting or other strategically linked companies and investments in private equity funds.

The company also expects that acquisitions will continue to be a key part of its business strategy. Its success in this regard will depend on its ability to identify and compete for appropriate acquisition candidates and to finance and complete the transactions it decides to pursue on favorable terms with positive results.

Citing the rise of economic difficulties natural disasters such as tsunamis and hurricanes international terrorism and other hazards for businesses MMC has been working to expand its role as a risk consultant. Subsidiary Marsh has been steadily branching out from its straight brokerage operations expanding its offerings of risk and insurance-related services including benefits management international risk placement and consumer programs for executives employees and high-net-worth individuals. The Mercer business has also been expanding through acquisitions in recent years especially in the growing field of data solutions. Furthermore Mercer is seeking to expand its investment consulting operations.

Nonetheless like its leading US competitors Marsh's most basic strategy for growth through the years has been to buy up regional brokerages large and small. It has kept up a steady pace of acquisitions of regional commercial brokerage firms especially in the mid-sized business market. The 2019 $6.4 billion acquisition of UK-based Jardine Lloyd Thompson positioned the group for further international expansion.

Because the company is so acquisitive it carries the risk of not being able to successfully integrate new businesses. Related challenges include integrating IT financial reporting human resources and other systems as well as retaining key customers and personnel.

While continuing to pursue an aggressive acquisition strategy — the firm has acquired more than 110 businesses since 2013 — MMC has also been working to de-risk its own operations by enacting some cost-cutting measures in recent years.

Restructuring measures such as divesting underperforming businesses aim to overcome the impact of historical regulatory and litigation issues as well as economic and competitive conditions on its bottom line.

Mergers and Acquisitions

MMC is a very acquisitive group; its Marsh subsidiary makes numerous purchases each year. However it made a big splash in 2019 when it acquired another top 10 broker Jardine Lloyd Thompson (JLT). The deal valued at some $5.6 billion created the world's largest reinsurance broker. The company agreed to sell JLT's aerospace division to Arthur J. Gallagher to gain approval for the merger.

Company Background

Marsh & McLennan was founded in 1905 when Henry W. Marsh and Donald R. McLennan merged their firms to form the world's largest insurance brokerage.

HISTORY

Marsh & McLennan Companies dates back to the Dan H. Bomar Company founded in 1871 after the Great Chicago Fire. In 1885 a plucky Harvard dropout named Henry Marsh joined the company then known as R.A. Waller and Company. When Robert Waller died in 1889 Marsh and fellow employee Herbert Ulmann bought a controlling stake and renamed the company Marsh Ulmann & Co. Marsh pioneered insurance brokering and in 1901 set up U.S. Steel's self-insurance program.

In 1904 different directors at Burlington Northern Railroad promised their account to Marsh Ulmann as well as Manley-McLennan of Duluth (railroad insurance) and D.W. Burrows (a small Chicago-based railroad insurance firm). Rather than fight over it the firms joined forces to form the world's largest insurance brokerage. When Burrows retired in 1906 the firm became Marsh & McLennan.

In the early 20th century Marsh won AT&T's business and McLennan landed the account of Armour Meat Packing.

In 1923 Marsh & McLennan became a closely held corporation. Marsh sold out to McLennan in 1935. The company weathered the Depression without major layoffs by cutting pay and branching into life insurance and employee-benefits consulting after passage of the Social Security Act (1935).

The firm grew through acquisitions in the 1950s went public in 1962 and in 1969 formed a holding company that became Marsh & McLennan Companies. In the 1970s it diversified into investment management employee-benefits consulting and geographically into the UK with C.T. Bowring Reinsurance. As the insurance business slowed in the 1980s the financial and consulting fields grew through acquisitions and organic growth.

With offices in the World Trade Center the company lost some 300 employees in the September 11 terrorist attacks. Following the attacks on the World Trade Center Marsh & McLennan launched a new subsidiary (AXIS Specialty) to deal with the capacity shortage in the insurance industry.

Two major Marsh & McLennan units came under legal fire in probes of the mutual fund and insurance brokerage industries respectively in the early 2000s. In 2003 Putnam agreed to settle securities fraud charges with the SEC and reimburse investors; many of Putnam's top officers were replaced and its compliance procedures were restructured.

The following year Marsh found itself at the center of a price-fixing investigation that involved several insurance companies including AIG and Chubb Limited. At least nine employees of Marsh and AIG pled guilty to criminal charges. Jeffery Greenberg the son of outspoken AIG chairman and CEO Maurice Greenberg who had served as Marsh & McLennan's chairman and CEO since 1999 resigned in 2004 as a result of the price-fixing allegations.

EXECUTIVES

Senior Vice President Chief Compliance Officer, E Scott Gilbert

President And Ceo Mercer, Julio A. Portalatin, age 60, $900,000 total compensation

Cfo, Mark C. McGivney, age 52, $750,000 total compensation

President Ceo And Director, Daniel S. (Dan) Glaser, age 59, $1,400,000 total compensation

Evp And General Counsel, Peter J. Beshar, age 59, $800,000 total compensation

Svp And Cio, E. Scott Gilbert, age 65

President Marsh, John Q. Doyle, age 56

President And Ceo Oliver Wyman Group, Scott McDonald, age 54

Ceo Marsh International, Flavio Piccolomini

Ceo Marsh, John Doyle

Chief Executive Marsh Continental Europe, Siegmund Fahrig

Vice President, Eric Ritter

Vice President Information Technology, Patty Martucci

Vice President, Bradley Morrow

Vice President Of Client Operations, William Walker

Senior Vice President, Lisa Kremer

Systems Director; Vice President It Project Manager, Michael Leyvi

Senior Vice President Regional Premium Finance, Irene Kaminski

Senior Vice President, David Abbene

Senior Vice President, Michelle Pingor

Vice President Budgets, Carlota Vargas

Vice President Risk Consultant, Edward Guzy

Senior Vice President, Cindy L Lusignan

Vice President And Chief Counsel Global Risk And Specialties, Barry Kerschner

Senior Vice President And Western Zone Education, Bruce Bernstein

Senior Vice President And Placement Specialist, Mary Naughton

Senior Vice President Private Equity And M And A Services, Matson Allen

Senior Vice President, Niki Tsalikis

Assistant Vice President, Jean Aguirre

Vice President, Rob Selnes

Senior Vice President Surety Compliance Leader, Pamela Beelman

Vice President Investor Relations, Keith Walsh

Senior Vice President Of The National Construction Practice, Ric Glover

Senior Vice President, Debby Colquhoun

Svp Strategic Solutions Group, Joseph Fusco

Assistant Vice President, Nazrin Zahani

Vice President, Marivel Andreu

Senior Vice President, Ronald Reinartz

Senior Vice President Global Information Technology, Scott Francis

Senior Vice President, Marla Nicholson

Cpcu Vice President And Knowledge Manager, Karen Parker

Vice President Administration, Michael Petrullo

Vice President Risk Consulting, Matthew Blair

Assistant Vice President, Brad Elfman

Senior Vice President, Sean Crnkovich

Senior Vice President, Cindy Hernandez

Vice President, Thomas Fremont

Svp, Robert Welsh

Vice President Finance Director, Brent Donnelly

Senior Vice President, Anna Kohli

Senior Vice President, Eric Peabody

Vice President And Chief Information Officer Middl, Nixon Thomas

Systems Director Vice President Information Techn, Michele Leyvi

Assistant Vice President Client Manager, Martin Goh

Senior Vice President, Eileen Quenell

Assistant Vice President Sales And Business Development, Pepper Periquet

Senior Vice President, Tim Brandt

Vice President, Joan Spiegel

Vice President, Florence Vasquez

Vice President, Patricia Robinson

Senior Vice President, Joseph Asmar

Vice President Finance, Michael Murphy

Senior Vice President Northeast Sales Operations Leader, David Russell

Senior Vice President, Bijesh Jacob

Senior Vice President, Daniel Kelley

Assistant Vice President, Matthew Theriault

Senior Vice President, Randy Dickman

Vice President Business Development, Hallie Beddes

Vice President, Michael Price

Vice President, Romaneo Adams

Vice President In Marsh Risk Consulting's Reputational Risk And Crisis Management Practice Based, Susan Morton

Vice President, Virginia Del Lago

Assistant Vice President, Felix Chung

Vice President, Catherine Ricia

Senior Vice President, Dawn Buelow

Vice President, Jessica Hatch

Assistant Vice President, Thadd Northam

Vice President Environmental Practice, Jack Palis

Senior Vice President, Mark Alderman

Senior Vice President Global Program Manager, Lori Suske

Vice President, Raegan Buckley

Senior Vice President And Global Head Of Operational Services, Gregg Congleton

Senior Vice President, Jeralyn Sorensen

Senior Vice President, Stanley Zimmerman

Senior Vice President, Eugene Charney

Assistant Vice President, Edward Mitchell

Executive Vice President Of Information Technology, Jennifer Adams

Vice President, Louise Casazza

Senior Vice President, Marcy Waterfall

Senior Vice President U S Marine And Energy, John Pallasch

Dip Fs (gen Ins) Qpib Cipvice President Head Of Businessdevelopment Singapore, Andrew Paul

Assistant Vice President, Kristin Will

Sr Vice President Multinational Client S, Janis Thornton

Senior Vice President, Rita Patullo

Vice President, Michael Hargis

Senior Vice President Advanced Risk Solutions, Scott Sanderson

Senior Vice President, James Helm

Vice President Information Technology, Gursharan Sant

Senior Vice President, Mary Berry

Vice President, Thomas Luty

Vice President National Brokerage Property Practice, Natalie Kenny

Senior Vice President, Chris Victorino

Senior Regional Premium Finance Vice President, Natasha Lee

Senior Vice President Strategic Development Officer At Marsh And Mclennan, Leonard Battifarano

Senior Vice President, Brett Gillmon

Assistant Vice President, Jenny Dickson

Assistant Vice President Asia Client Services, Kathleen Schimmenti

Senior Vice President, Michaela Grasshoff

Senior Vice President Global Broking North America, Jason Monteforte

Senior Vice President Global Broking Specialties, Jack Reid

Vice President, David Erdman

Senior Vice President, Natasha Tarasova

Vice President, David Ghilardi

Senior Vice President, Kwabena Akoto

Assistant Vice President, Michael Hourihan

Senior Vice President, Christine Williams

Senior Vice President, Greg Miller

Vice President, Melanie Dunne

Senior Vice President, Tracey Cole

Vice President Private Client Services, Susan Ott

Senior Vice President And Chief Financial Officer For Largest Insurance Broker, Adrian Serge

Assistant Vice President, Lynn Patino

Vice President, Denise Mitchell

Senior Vice President And Chief Compliance Officer, Scott E Gilbert

Vice President Global Tech Srv, Christopher Murphy

Vice President, Rich Cuff

Vice President Information Systems, Sue Denecke
Assistant Vice President, Daniel Kovatich
Vice President, Robert Howe
Senior Vice President At Marsh, Lynda Gammons
Senior Vice President Risk Consulting, Steve Logoyda
Avp It Project Manager, Kelly Lively
Senior Vice President And Compliance Officer, April Bohmler
Vice President Project Manager, Paul Gibaldi
Senior Vice President Forensic Accountant, Brian Hudecek
Vice President, Lucy Mihalik
Vice President, Joseph Hall
Vice President, Blake Maybeck
Senior Vice President Finpro, Jennifer Dowd
Senior Vice President, Ken Kosinski
Vice President, Lisa Jaimovich
Vice President, Tim Wright
Senior Vice President, Larry Gracer
Vice President, Erika Almquist
Assistant Vice President, Jacob Lockard
Vice President, Timothy Tumulty
Vice President, John Lyons
Vice President, Joann Crook
Vice President, Donald W Russell
Senior Vice President, Richard Wyatt
Assistant Vice President, Robert Trumbore
Auditors: Deloitte & Touche LLP

LOCATIONS

HQ: Marsh & McLennan Companies Inc.
1166 Avenue of the Americas, New York, NY 10036-2774
Phone: 212 345-5000   Fax: 212 345-4809
Web: www.mmc.com

2018 Sales

	$ mil.	% of total
US	7,219	48
Continental Europe	2,694	18
UK	2,243	15
Asia/Pacific	1,616	11
Other	1,235	8
Adjustments	(57)	-
Total	14,950	100

PRODUCTS/OPERATIONS

2018 Sales by Segment

	$ mil.	% of total
Risk & Insurance Services		
Marsh	6,877	46
Guy Carpenter	1,286	9
Fiduciary interest income	65	-
Consulting		
Mercer	4,732	31
Oliver Wyman	2,047	14
Adjustments	(57)	-
Total	14,950	100

COMPETITORS

Accenture	Gallagher
AmWINS Group	Hub International
Aon	McKinsey & Company
Bain & Company	National Financial
Booz Allen	Partners
Brown & Brown	USI
FTI Consulting	Willis Towers Watson

HISTORICAL FINANCIALS

Company Type: Public

Income Statement

FYE: December 31

	REVENUE ($ mil.)	NET INCOME ($ mil.)	NET PROFIT MARGIN	EMPLOYEES
12/19	16,652	1,742	10.5%	76,000
12/18	14,950	1,650	11.0%	65,000
12/17	14,024	1,492	10.6%	65,000
12/16	13,211	1,768	13.4%	60,000
12/15	12,893	1,599	12.4%	60,000
Annual Growth	6.6%	2.2%	—	6.1%

2019 Year-End Financials

Debt ratio: 38.13%
Return on equity: 22.77%
Cash ($ mil.): 1,155
Current ratio: 1.06
Long-term debt ($ mil.): 10,741

No. of shares (mil.): 503
Dividends
Yield: 1.5%
Payout: 51.0%
Market value ($ mil.): 56,109

	STOCK PRICE ($) FY Close	P/E High/Low	PER SHARE ($) Earnings	Dividends	Book Value
12/19	111.41	33 23	3.41	1.74	15.47
12/18	79.75	27 23	3.23	1.58	14.91
12/17	81.39	30 23	2.87	1.43	14.47
12/16	67.59	20 15	3.38	1.30	12.04
12/15	55.45	20 17	2.98	1.18	12.48
Annual Growth	19.1%	— —	3.4%	10.2%	5.5%

MASS GENERAL BRIGHAM INCORPORATED

Partners HealthCare operates two large acute-care medical centers — Brigham and Women's Hospital and Massachusetts General Hospital — and about 15 community hospitals in Boston and surrounding communities. The not-for-profit system also provides primary and specialty care through clinics physician offices rehabilitation centers long-term care facilities and home health and hospice agencies. Subsidiary MassHealth provides medical insurance to state residents. Partners HealthCare also provides medical training and research through an affiliation with Harvard. The organization has additional partnerships with health research and educational organizations around the globe.

Financial Performance

Partners Healthcare reported $13.3 billion in revenue in 2018 a less than 1% decline from 2017 results. Patient service revenue which accounts for about 70% of sales increased 10% but insurance premium revenue (10% of sales) decreased 43% due to membership declines (related to the transition of customers from managed care to accountable care programs). Academic and research revenue (15% of sales) increased 4%.

Excess of revenue over expenses increased 25% to $826.6 million due to lower operating costs related to the insurance business.

The organization ended 2018 with $398.4 million in cash down $340.7 million from 2017. Operating activities contributed $899 million while investing activities used $1.4 billion (mostly for acquisitions property and equipment) and financing activities contributed $140.8 million via long-term debt proceeds and investment income.

Strategy

Partners HealthCare has expanded its operations through a stream of acquisitions and construction efforts. It completed construction of a replacement facility for the Nantucket Cottage Hospital in 2018. The company is also adding three new outpatient care buildings (containing primary women's cancer diagnostic orthopedic physical therapy and surgery care centers) to its Wentworth-Douglass Hospital campus.

Partners HealthCare is investing in new IT tools to improve efficiencies enhance quality and lower the cost of care. The company has installed an electronic health record (EHR) system across all of its facilities; it is also adding a digital imaging platform and a centralized credentialing system.

In addition the company regularly updates medical equipment at its facilities to keep pace with medical innovations. For instance it has added a minimally invasive spine surgery program at Brigham and Women's Faulkner Hospital and robotic surgery centers at two of its community hospitals in recent years.

Mergers and Acquisitions

Partners HealthCare has had two failed efforts to expand beyond Massachusetts. The company's agreement to acquire Care New England was canceled in 2019 after Rhode Island's governor objected to the deal. Partners and Care New England had approached Rhode Island-based Lifespan to also join forces in 2018 but that proposal was subsequently dropped. The organization did successfully acquire specialty hospital Massachusetts Eye and Ear in 2018.

Company Background

Partners HealthCare was founded in 1994 through the merger of Brigham and Women's Hospital and Massachusetts General Hospital.

EXECUTIVES

Vice President Public Affairs Partners Community Benefit Programs, Lee Chelminiak
Vice President Of Finance, David Mcguire
Evp Administration And Finance Cfo And Treasurer, Peter K. Markell, age 64
President And Ceo Massachusetts General Hospital, Peter L. Slavin
Cio, James W. (Jim) Noga
President And Ceo North Shore Medical Center, Robert G. (Bob) Norton, age 70
President And Ceo Neighborhood Health Plan, Deborah C. Enos
President And Ceo Partners Continuing Care, David E. Storto
President And Ceo Brigham And Women's Hospital, Elizabeth G. (Betsy) Nabel
President And Chief Executive Officer, David F. Torchiana
President Of Partners Community, Thomas H. Lee
President And Ceo Spaulding Rehabilitation Network, Maureen Banks
President Mclean Hospital, Scott L. Rauch
President And Ceo Brigham And Women's Physicians Organization, Allen L. Smith
President And Ceo Martha's Vineyard Hospital, Timothy J. Walsh
President And Ceo Mgh Institute Of Health Professions, Janis P. Bellack
President And Ceo, David Torchiana
President And Ceo Nantucket Cottage Hospital, Margot Hartmann
President And Ceo Partners Healthcare At Home, Rod Carnifax
Medical Director, Jane Erb
Medical Director Breast Care Center, Katherina Zabicki
Director Of Nursing, Deborah Morrissey

Avp Technical Services (dana Farber Cancer Institute), Rick Williams
Vice President Of Population Health Management, Timothy Ferris
Senior Medical Director, Elizabeth Mort
Nursing Director, Michelle Anastasi
Medical Director Of The Breast And Ovarian Cancer, Paula Ryan
Nursing Director, Elizabeth Mcgrath
Medical Director, David Chen
Vice President Of Partners Innovation, Christopher Coburn
Clinical Director, Karon Konner
Director Of Nursing, Deirdre Greene
Medical Director, William Holgerson
Senior Vice President Of Clinical Services, David Mccready
Medical Director, Richard Kaufman
Project Manager To Senior Vice President Research, Angela Vail
Senior Vice President Human Resources, Jeff Davis
Medical Director, Sharon Bober
Nursing Director, Michele Ohara
Clinical Director, Martha Kane
Clinical Director Department Of Pt Ot; Clinical Content Lead Partners Ecare, James Zachazewski
Vice President Of Operations, Hofmann Erika
Nursing Director, Peggy Settle
Director Of Medical Records, Doherty Linda
Nursing Director, Lisa Wichmann
Nursing Director, Dorothy Parker
Vice President, Anne Fitzgerald
Assistant Vice President Regional Consultant, Viscomi Rudy
Nursing Director, Jennifer Sargent
Director Of Radiology, Dave Marchione
Rsvp Team Leader, Jessica Grajeda
Vice President Of Information Technology, Karl Fitch
Medical Director, Renee Sorrentino
Medical Director, Angelo Volandes
Vice President, Shelly Anderson
Medical Director Emergency Medicine, Patricia Henwood
Senior Vice President Of Communication And Public Affairs, Erin Mcdonough
Senior Vice President Payer Solution Sales, Wilson Caryn
Vice President Of Operations, Ricci Elisabeth
Senior Vice President Research, Richard Bringhurst
Medical Director, Robert Gottlieb
Vice President, Terry Garfinkle
Nursing Director, Kathryn Hall
Senior Vice President Of Finance And Treasurer, Karen Lavoie
Vice President, Eileen Flaherty
Associate Medical Director, R Nicholas Nace Md
Physical Therapy, Tom Rossignoll
Vp Operations, Mary Jo Gagnon
Co Medical Director, Jaime Rivera
Medical Director, James Macon
Nursing Director, Diane Tsitos
Physical Therapy Notetaker, Jaclyn Pontell
Chairman, Edward P. Lawrence, age 78
Vice Chair Of Medicine, Jacob Karas
Secretary, Maria Sanchez
Secretary, Ruth Valdez
Board Member, Warren Foote
Treasurer, Xandra Breakefield
Board Member, Natalia Berry
Board Member, Martha Pitman
Department Secretary, Josephine Freni
Department Secretary, Theresa Crotty
Secretary, Estimable Jerry
Department Secretary, Julie Baratta
Treasurer, Susanne Churchill
Secretary, Rosemary T Jaromin
Treasurer, Peggy Breneus
Board Member, Edgar Robertson

LOCATIONS

HQ: MASS GENERAL BRIGHAM INCORPORATED
800 BOYLSTON ST STE 1150, BOSTON, MA
021998123
Phone: 617 278-1000
Web: WWW.PARTNERS.ORG

PRODUCTS/OPERATIONS

2014 Sales

	$ mil.	% of total
Net patient service revenue	7,042	65
Premium revenue	1,622	15
Direct academic and research	1,225	11
Indirect academic and research	353	3
Other revenue	662	6
Total	**10,906**	**100**

COMPETITORS

Baystate Health
Boston Medical Center
Cambridge Health Alliance
Cape Cod Healthcare
Cape Cod Hospital
Care New England
CareGroup
Children's Hospital Boston
Milford Regional Medical Center
Northeast Health System
Southcoast Hospitals Group
Steward Health Care
Universal Health Services

HISTORICAL FINANCIALS

Company Type: Private

Income Statement				FYE: September 30
	REVENUE ($ mil.)	NET INCOME ($ mil.)	NET PROFIT MARGIN	EMPLOYEES
09/15	11,665	(916)	—	67,000
09/10	8	(0)	—	—
09/08	551	(44)	—	—
Annual Growth	54.7%	—	—	—

MASSACHUSETTS HOUSING FINANCE AGENCY PROPERTY ACQUISITION AND DISPOSITION CORPORATION

EXECUTIVES

Chb, Michael J Dirrane
Chm*, Ronald A Homer
Exec Dir*, Thomas R Gleason
Treas*, Andris J Silins
Prin*, Tom O'Brien
Cfo*, Michael Fitzmaurice
Staff, Tyrone Reed
Real Estate Conultant, Kristin Olsen
Vp-Homeownership Programs, Mounzer M Aylouche

Business Officer E, Angelo Nuby
Officer, Antonio Torres

LOCATIONS

HQ: MASSACHUSETTS HOUSING FINANCE AGENCY PROPERTY ACQUISITION AND DISPOSITION CORPORATION
1 BEACON ST, BOSTON, MA 021083107
Phone: 617 854-1000
Web: WWW.MASSHOUSING.COM

HISTORICAL FINANCIALS

Company Type: Private

Income Statement				FYE: June 30
	ASSETS ($ mil.)	NET INCOME ($ mil.)	INCOME AS % OF ASSETS	EMPLOYEES
06/20	5,948	149	2.5%	325
06/18	5,460	6	0.1%	—
Annual Growth	4.4%	395.9%	—	—

MasTec Inc. (FL)

MasTec goes the last mile – and the first mile and the miles in between – to bring communications and energy to homes offices factories and other places. The company digs the trenches lays the cable and builds the towers that power communications and provide cell service and high-speed internet. The contractor plans and builds pipelines that transport natural gas and oil from wells to processing plants. It provides infrastructure construction to telecom vendors wireless providers cable TV operators and energy and utility companies. MasTec also builds electrical utility transmission and distribution and power generation including renewables; heavy civil; and industrial infrastructure. MasTec is a leading infrastructure construction company operating mainly throughout North America across a range of industries.

Operations

With more than 20000 employees and locations throughout North America MasTec has the size to tackle big projects that require large resources in equipment and people.

MasTec operates in five business units with most focused on a particular industry. The units are: Oil and Gas Communications; Power Generation and Industrial; Electrical Transmission; and Other.

The Oil and Gas segment does engineering construction and maintenance on oil and natural gas pipelines and processing facilities for the energy and utilities industries. It accounts for about 45% of sales.

The Communications segment performs engineering construction and maintenance of communications infrastructure primarily related to wireless and wireline communications and install to the home and infrastructure for electrical utilities. It accounts for more than 35% of sales.

The Power Generation and Industrial segment serves the energy and utility through the installation and construction of power plants wind farms solar farms related electrical transmission infrastructure ethanol plants and other industrial infrastructure. It accounts for less about 15% of sales.

The Electrical Transmission segment primarily serves energy and utility industries through the engineering construction and maintenance of electrical transmission lines and substations. It accounts for about 5% of sales.

The Other segment primarily includes small business units that perform construction services for a variety of end markets in Mexico and in other locations outside the US. It accounts for less than 1% of sales.

Geographic Reach

MasTec headquartered in Coral Gables Florida has approximately 350 locations in the US and Canada and lesser extent to Mexico and Caribbean. Mastec is one of the leading renewables contractors in North America with expertise in wind solar and biomass as well as industrial and other power plant construction and expect to benefit from these market trends.

Sales and Marketing

MasTec sells directly to existing and potential customers for service agreement contracts and individual projects. MasTec's current fortunes are tied to two companies Energy Transfer and AT&T. Pipeline work for Energy Transfer accounts for about 10% of MasTec's revenue. MasTec's communications work revolves around AT&T (including DirecTV) which supplies approximately 20% of revenue. The company's level of business with AT&T has been consistent in recent years but business with Energy Transfer decrease from more than 30% of revenue in 2019.

Financial Performance

MasTec's revenues have steadily risen in the last five years rising 71% between 2015 and 2019. Net income has also increased over the same period despite a slight dip in 2018 profits in 2019 have increased considerably from the net loss in 2015.

Revenue increased 4% to $7.2 billion in 2019 compared with $6.9 billion in 2018 due to revenue increases in its Power Generation and Industrial segment Communications segment and Electrical Transmission segment partially offset by decreases in revenue in Oil and Gas and Other segment.

In 2019 net income was $392.3 million a $132.6 million increase from the year prior due to higher revenues and lower goodwill and intangible asset impairment despite a 4% increase in general and administrative expenses.

Cash at the end of the period was $71.4 million a $44 million increase for the year prior. Cash from operations generated $550.3 million. Investing activities used $261.8 million mainly for acquisitions and capital expenditures. Financing activities used another $244.6 million mostly for repayments of credit facilities and acquisition-related considerations.

Strategy

MasTec's strategy consists of four key elements: focus on operational growth operational excellence maintain conservative capital structure and leverage core performance and expertise through strategic acquisitions and other arrangements. MasTec expects development of wireless and wireline/fiber infrastructure; oil and natural gas pipeline infrastructure; expansion maintenance and upgrades of electrical transmission capacity and the electrical distribution grid; development of power generation infrastructure including renewables; and heavy civil and industrial infrastructure construction projects to be areas of investment and opportunity in the coming years.

MasTec expects development of wireless and wireline/fiber infrastructure; oil and natural gas pipeline infrastructure; expansion maintenance and upgrades of electrical transmission capacity and the electrical distribution grid; development of power generation infrastructure including renewables; and heavy civil and industrial infrastructure construction projects to be areas of investment and opportunity in the coming years.

The company seeks to improve its profit margins and cash flows by focusing on services and projects that have high margin potential. It also strives to identify opportunities for leverage within its business such as deploying resources across multiple customers and projects in order to enhance its operating effectiveness and utilization rates.

In terms of maintaining conservative capital structure MasTec evaluates its capital structure on an ongoing basis and has expanded its financial resources in recent years. The company may consider opportunities to borrow additional funds or to refinance repurchase or retire outstanding debt or repurchase shares as part of its ongoing capital structure evaluation.

Lastly MasTec aims to leverage core performance and expertise through strategic acquisitions and other arrangements. The company has diversified its business and expanded its service offerings and geographic footprint in recent years both organically and through acquisition. In order to maximize its potential the strategy is to integrate acquired businesses into its operations and internal control environment in a timely and efficient manner.

HISTORY

MasTec was formed by the merger of Burnup & Sims (B&S) and Church & Tower (C&T). B&S was founded in 1929 to provide construction and maintenance services to the phone and utilities industries. C&T began in 1968 building phone networks in Miami and Puerto Rico. Jorge Mas Canosa was brought on board in 1969 and given half of the company in exchange for managing it. By 1971 he had succeeded in turning C&T around and had bought the remainder.

In 1994 C&T and B&S merged; B&S became MasTec and C&T became a subsidiary. Mas was named chairman and his son who had been at C&T since 1980 was named president and CEO. The company began a program of acquisitions and started building a presence in Latin America.

MasTec doubled its size in 1996 by acquiring Sintel a telecom infrastructure construction firm operating in South America and Spain from Telefonica. MasTec continued to grow through acquisitions buying 10 more companies the next year. Mas died in 1997 and his son Jorge Jr. succeeded him. It sold a near-bankrupt Sintel and began to refocus on domestic operations.

EXECUTIVES

Ceo And Director, José R. Mas, age 48, $980,000 total compensation
Evp And Cfo, George L. Pita, age 58, $450,000 total compensation
Evp General Counsel And Secretary, Alberto de Cardenas, age 51, $385,000 total compensation
Coo, Robert E. (Bob) Apple, age 70, $585,000 total compensation
Cio, Albert Iturrey
Vice President Business Intelligence, Ben Boyd
Regional Vice President, Clint Grassmick
Vice President Latin America, Jorge Mestre
Vice President And General Manager, Chris Bracken
Vice President Sales And Marketing, Jeff Mock
Senior Vice President Project Planning And Management, Paul Troy
Regional Vice President South Region, Helbert Villa
Senior Vice President And President Mastec Wireless Division, Darrell Mays
Senior Vice President, Rick Gray
Vice President Field Service, Chris Gera
Vice President Of Operations, Fred Mercado
Vice President Southwest Region, Erik Hughes
Assistant Vice President Corporate Operations, Jose Tarafa
Vice President, Ron Martin
Vice President Of Sales, Stephen Guillot
Division Vice President, Carl Basden
Vice President Business Development, Andrei Trach
Vice President Project Management And Support Training, Stephen Daunis
Vp Internal Audit Chief Audit Executive, Gilbert Santiesteban
Senior Vice President, Mark Green
Vice President, Robert Perez
Chairman, Jorge Mas, age 57
Board Member, Jose Sorzano
Board Member, Javier Palomarez
Auditors: BDO USA, LLP

LOCATIONS

HQ: MasTec Inc. (FL)
   800 S. Douglas Road, 12th Floor, Coral Gables, FL 33134
Phone: 305 599-1800
Web: www.mastec.com

PRODUCTS/OPERATIONS

2017 Sales

	$ mil.	% of total
Oil & Gas	3,497	53
Communications	2,424	37
Electrical Transmission	378	6
Power Generation & Industrial	299	4
Other	20	-
Adjustments	(13.5)	-
Total	**6,607**	**100**

Selected Services

Broadband networks
   Aerial and underground construction
   Bonding/grounding
   Engineering and design
   FCC testing
   Modem installation
   Optical fiber splicing activation and testing
   Warehouse and inventory management
Telecommunications
   Aerial construction
   Copper/coaxial cable systems
   Directional drilling
   Engineering
   Fiber-optic cable systems
   Fiber-to-the-premises (FTTP) deployment
   Splicing and testing
   Underground construction
Utilities
   Design and engineering
   Gas distribution construction and maintenance
   Storm restoration
   Submarine cable installation
   Substation construction
   Transmission line construction
   Trench construction

COMPETITORS

Bechtel	MDU Construction
Black & Veatch	Services
Dycom	MYR Group
General Dynamics	Pike Corporation
Goldfield	Primoris
Henkels & McCoy	Quanta Services
Jacobs Engineering	Sirti
M. A. Mortenson	Willbros

HISTORICAL FINANCIALS

Company Type: Public

Income Statement

	REVENUE ($ mil.)	NET INCOME ($ mil.)	NET PROFIT MARGIN	EMPLOYEES
12/19	7,183	392	5.5%	21,000
12/18	6,909	259	3.8%	19,000
12/17	6,606	347	5.3%	17,300
12/16	5,134	131	2.6%	15,400
12/15	4,208	(79)	—	15,900
Annual Growth	14.3%	—	—	7.2%

FYE: December 31

2019 Year-End Financials

Debt ratio: 28.67%
Return on equity: 24.70%
Cash ($ mil.): 71
Current ratio: 1.78
Long-term debt ($ mil.): 1,314

No. of shares (mil.): 76
Dividends
Yield: —
Payout: —
Market value ($ mil.): 4,912

	STOCK PRICE ($) FY Close	P/E High/Low		PER SHARE ($) Earnings	Dividends	Book Value
12/19	64.16	14	8	5.17	0.00	23.34
12/18	40.56	17	11	3.26	0.00	18.29
12/17	48.95	12	8	4.22	0.00	17.28
12/16	38.25	25	8	1.61	0.00	13.28
12/15	17.38	—	—	(0.98)	0.00	11.73
Annual Growth	38.6%	—	—	—	—	18.8%

Mastercard Inc

Mastercard is a technology company in the global payments industry that connects consumers financial institutions merchants governments digital partners businesses and other organizations worldwide enabling them to use electronic forms of payment instead of cash and checks. The company provides a wide range of payment solutions and services using its family of well-known brands including MastercardÂ® MaestroÂ® and CirrusÂ®. The company provides its services in more than 210 countries and territories more than 150 currencies and its branded cards are accepted at millions of locations globally. Mastercard generates over a third of its sales in North America.

HISTORY

A group of bankers formed The Interbank Card Association (ICA) in 1966 to establish authorization clearing and settlement procedures for bank credit card transactions. This was particularly important to banks left out of the rapidly growing BankAmericard (later Visa) network sponsored by Bank of America.

By 1969 ICA was issuing the Master Charge card throughout the US and had formed alliances in Europe and Japan. In the mid-1970s ICA modernized its system replacing telephone transaction authorization with a computerized magnetic strip system. ICA had members in Africa Australia and Europe by 1979. That year the organization changed its name (and the card's) to MasterCard.

In 1980 Russell Hogg became president when John Reynolds resigned after disagreeing with the board over company performance and direction. Hogg made major organizational changes and consolidated data processing in St. Louis. MasterCard began offering debit cards in 1980 and traveler's checks in 1981.

MasterCard issued the first credit cards in China in 1987. The next year it bought Cirrus then the world's largest ATM network. It also secured a pact with Belgium-based card company Eurocard (which later became Europay) to supervise MasterCard's European operations and help build the brand.

Hogg resigned in 1988 after disagreements with the board and was succeeded by Alex Hart. In 1991 the Maestro debit card was unveiled.

The 1990s were marked by trouble in Europe: The pact with Europay hadn't resulted in the boom MasterCard had hoped for customer service was below par and competition was keen. Alex Hart retired in 1994 and was succeeded by Eugene Lockhart who tackled the European woes. Lockhart considered ending the relationship but eventually worked things out with Europay. By the end of the decade Europay was locked in a vicious battle to undercut Visa's market share through lower fees.

MasterCard in 1995 invested in UK-based Mondex International maker of electronic set-value refillable smart cards. But US consumer resistance to cash cards and competition in the more advanced European market delayed growth in this area.

In October 1996 a group of merchants including Wal-Mart and Sears filed class-action lawsuits against both MasterCard and Visa challenging the "honor all cards" rule. Because usage fees are higher merchants balked at accepting consumers' MasterCard- or Visa-branded off-line or signature-based debit cards and claimed the card issuers violated antitrust laws by tying acceptance of debit to that of credit. In a dramatic twist minutes before the trial was set to begin in 2003 MasterCard announced a settlement (the card issuer was required to pay $125 million in 2003 and $100 million annually from 2004 through 2012).

Just months later armed with the lawsuit's settlement which also freed merchants to pick which credit and debit card services they use Wal-Mart (along with a handful of others) stopped accepting signature debit cards issued by MasterCard.

Lockhart resigned in 1997 and was succeeded by former head of overseas operations Robert Selander. Yet another management upheaval began in 1999 as the company moved to streamline its organizational structure and shift away from geographical divisions. It also said member banks could boost visibility by putting their logos on card fronts and moving MasterCard's logo to the back.

In 2002 MasterCard merged with Europay with which it already had close ties. As part of the transaction holding company MasterCard Incorporated was formed; MasterCard International become the company's main subsidiary and MasterCard Europe (formerly Europay) became its European subsidiary.

After some 40 years as a private entity MasterCard went public in 2006 in one of the largest IPOs of its time. Following the offering the approximately 1400 financial institutions that wholly owned MasterCard before the offering retained a stake of more than 40%. Two of the top three US banks (Citigroup and JPMorgan Chase) remained among MasterCard's largest shareholders.

Some of the proceeds from the company's IPO were used to fight antitrust lawsuits from such rivals as American Express and Discover as well as other payment processors. In 2008 the company agreed to a $1.8 billion settlement with American Express which had claimed that MasterCard and others tried to stop financial institutions from issuing its AmEx cards. Later that year MasterCard settled the Discover lawsuit agreeing to pay $862.5 million.

Also in 2008 MasterCard bought Ireland-based software provider Orbiscom. The acquired company's technology was used to create MasterCard inControl a platform for making secure Internet and telephone purchases.

MasterCard promoted president and COO Ajay Banga to CEO in 2010. He succeeded Robert Selander who stepped down after more than a dozen years at the helm.

EXECUTIVES

Evp General Manager National Accounts, Michael Fiore
Cfo, Martina Hund-Mejean, age 60, $691,667 total compensation
President And Ceo, Ajaypal S. (Ajay) Banga, age 60, $1,200,000 total compensation
President Global Products And Solutions, Gary J. Flood, age 62, $650,000 total compensation
President International Markets, Ann Cairns, age 63, $609,427 total compensation
Chief Services Officer, Kevin J. Stanton
President U.s. Issuers, Raj Seshadri
President Europe, Javier Perez
General Counsel And Chief Franchise Officer, Timothy H. (Tim) Murphy, age 53
Chief Product Officer, Michael Miebach
Chief Innovation Officer, Garry Lyons
President Operations And Technology, Edward (Ed) McLaughlin
Vice Chairman And President Center For Inclusive Growth, Walt W. Macnee, age 65
President North America, Craig Vosburg, age 53
President Middle East And Africa, Raghu Malhotra
President Enterprise Security Solutions, Ajay Bhalla
Co-president Asia/pacific, Hai Ling
Co-president Asia/pacific, Ari Sarker
President Latin America And Caribbean Region, Gilberto Caldart
President Processing Services, Andrea Scerch
President Prepaid Management Services, Fabrizio Burlando
Senior Vice President And Group Head, Michael Robichaud
Senior Vice President Chief Admin Officer, Joy Thoma
Vice President Of B2b Marketing, Steven Harrison
Evp Chief Information Governance And Privacy Officer, Joann Stonier
Vice President Financial Analysis, Richard Strauss
Vice President, Ashfaq Kamal
Assistant Vice President Product Marketing, Elaine Tham
Vice President Customer Account Management, Jason Taylor
Vice President, Michael Moutenot
Vice President Worldwide Communications, Naya Larsson
Vice President Prepaid Product Management, Ed Wang
Senior Vice President, Patricia Preston
Senior Vice President, George Zilvetti
Evp Digital Partnerships, Sherri Haymond
Vice President Product Management, Eric Mcilwain
Vice President Senior Business Leader Us Commercial Products, Jennifer Merli
Vice President, Christine Friedlein
Senior Business Leader Vice President Brand Strategy And Design, Chuck Breuel
Vice President Global Marketing And Communications Strategy And Operations, Amy Fuller
Vice President Senior Business Leader, Mathias Lilja
Vice President Merchant Marketing, Luciana Amano
Vice President Caribbean, Mario Perez
Vice President Global Prepaid Solutions, Ryan Bodman
Vice President Emerging Payments Central Lac Region, Ali Aidi

Vice President Senior Business Leader, Laura Mackenzie
Vice President Direct Marketing, George Tellado
Vice President Account Management, Patrick Sulston
Senior Vice President Corporate Philanthropy And Citizenship, Patricia Devereux
Svp Social Networks And Digital Payment Platforms, Raj Dhamodharan
Vice President Finance And Planning Global Prepaid, Prasad Iyer
Senior Vice President Global Talent Acquisition, Charlie Hall
Vice President U.s. Markets Emerging Payments, Brian Northey
Vice President And Counsel, Shira Kaplan
Vice President Account Management, Patricia Costanzo
Senior Vice President Employment Law, Diane Dann
Evp Market Development U.s., Michael Cyr
Regional Vice President Member Relations Northeast, Michael Hannan
Vice President And Business Leader, Regina Ng
Vice President (business Leader) Commercial Product Development Authentication Services, Laurie Nicoletti
Vice President Senior Business Leader Us Market Development, Tor Opedal
Vice President Business Leader Crm Platform Management Global Digital Marketing, Shertina Gillespie
Vice President Senior Account Manager, Heather Gray
Vice President Senior Business Leader, Julie Schanzer
Vice President, Michael Luchinsky
Vice President, Kelly Symons
Vice President Corporate Philanthropy, Leslie Meek-wohl
Vice President Direct Marketing, Linda Paczkowski
Group Head Senior Vice President Senior Engineer, Marie Russo
Vice President Loyalty Solutions, Nick Pifani
Vice President Technology Account Management, Timothy Ware
Business Leader Vice President, Holliday Haynes
Vice President Marketing, Arturo Saldana
Senior Vp Data And Services Strategy And Operations, Elena Carroll
Vice President Managing Consultant, Sharlene Palmgren
Vice President Account Planner, Donna Boyle
Vice President, Dawn Barger
Vice President New Markets, Rich Ciamillo
Vice President Global Commercial Products, Caroline Mcgrath
Vice President Of Global Service Center, Michael Baechle
Vice President, John Perry
Vice President Head Of Product Architecture Digital P, Sanjay Challani
Vice President Global Product And Partnerships Digital Payments, Mark Corritori
Vice President Financial Planning And Analysis, Tania Banens
Vice President Senior Counsel Intellectual Property, Edward Tempesta
Vice President, Wade Plummer
Vice President, Karen Lindsay
Vice President Account Management, Sophie Couteaux
Senior Vice President, Trish Preston
Senior Vice President And Group Head, Greg Boosin
Vice President Mobile Alliances, Jeffrey Allen
Vice President Global Interactive Marketing, Elena D'andrea
Vice President Head Of Strategy Development Core Products, Rachael Jenkinson

Vice President, Kehinde Mendes
Vice President, Melanie Gluck
Account Vice President, Jeff Krogman
Svp Global Business Services Gbs Hr Systems Operations, Lois Miller
Executive Vice President B2b Marketing, Elisa Romm
Vice President Business Leader, Gabe Beltramino
Vice President Mobile Applications Emerging Payments, Subu Musti
Vp Senior Business Director, Todd Healy
Vice President Software Engineering, John Crowley
Vice President Account Management National Accounts, Deb Morrison
Executive Vice President Global Tax, Tim Berger
Senior Vice President Group Head Emerging Verticals And Acceptance, Joel Henckel
Vp Market Development Asia Pacific Middle East Africa (pricing Interchange Strategy), Cindy Koh
Vice President, Steven Jonas
Vice President Data Strategy Lead Digital Payments, John Mwangi
Vice President And Tax Counsel, Millie Chun
Vice President And Business Leader, Lori Singer
Vice President, Joyce Laubert
Vice President Global Consumer Marketing, Alison Giordano
Vice President Corporate Fpanda, Gary Held
Vice President Prepaid Product Management, Jason Tymms
Vice President, Rob Keenan
Vice President, Amy Celento
Vice President Business Leader Emerging Payments, Alex Zerio
Vice President Global Marketing Solutions, Caroline Granville
Vice President, Renee Pirone
Vice President Senior Account Manager, Greg Pastorek
Vice President, Lisa Rief
Vice President, Ellen Stibler
Vice President And Senior Business Leader, Chris Morris
Vice President Corporate Strategy, Gaurav Mittal
Senior Vice President Mobile Product Development, James Anderson
Senior Vice President Finance And Strategic Planning, Eileen Sullivan
Senior Vice President Retail And Commerce Solutions Development, Curtis Villars
Vice President And Senior Counsel, Joe Halprin
Vice President Of Social Media, Greg Weiss
Vice President Sr. Business Leader, Ravi Aurora
Vice President, Ranjita Iyer
Vice President Business Leader, Adam Bell
Vice President Emerging Payments Technology, David Grossman
Vice President Technical Account Manager, Sandra Mackert
Vice President, Michael Mcnamara
Vice President Product Development, Paulo Fernandes
Vice President, Nina Biornstad
Senior Business Leader Vice President, Jennifer Berry
Svp, Paul Musser
Executive Vice President, Jennifer Rademaker
Vice President Of Information Technology, Thomas Cronin
Vice President President Direct Interactive Marketing, Jeff White
Vice President B2b Marketing, Mary Masi
Senior Vice President Sales Excellence, Carlos Cornejo
Vice President U.s. Market Development, Adam Goodman
Executive Vice President Account Management, Ed Glassman
Vice President Us Region Counsel, Natasha Friedrichs

Vice President Digital Product Governance, Patricia Bateson
Senior Vice President, Pilar S Ramos
Vice President Information Services, Michelle Becerra
Vice President Global Key Accounts, Ramon Freire
Auditors: PricewaterhouseCoopers LLP

LOCATIONS

HQ: Mastercard Inc
  2000 Purchase Street, Purchase, NY 10577
Phone: 914 249-2000
Web: www.mastercard.com

2016 Revenue

	% of total
US	38
International	62
Total	100

PRODUCTS/OPERATIONS

2018 Revenue

	$ mil.	% of total
North America	5,311	36
International	9,441	63
Other	198	1
Total	14,950	100

2018 Revenue

	$ mil.	% of total
Transaction processing fees	7,391	34
Domestic assessments	6,138	28
Cross-border volume fees	4,954	23
Other	3,348	15
Adjustments	(6881)	-
Total	14,950	100

COMPETITORS

Alibaba.com	JCB International
Amazon.com	NYCE Payments Network
American Express	PULSE Network
China UnionPay	PayPal
Discover	Total System Services
Fifth Third	Visa Inc
First Data	Visa International

HISTORICAL FINANCIALS

Company Type: Public

Income Statement | | | FYE: December 31

	REVENUE ($ mil.)	NET INCOME ($ mil.)	NET PROFIT MARGIN	EMPLOYEES
12/19	16,883	8,118	48.1%	18,600
12/18	14,950	5,859	39.2%	14,800
12/17	12,497	3,915	31.3%	13,400
12/16	10,776	4,059	37.7%	11,900
12/15	9,667	3,808	39.4%	11,300
Annual Growth	15.0%	20.8%	—	13.3%

2019 Year-End Financials

Debt ratio: 29.17%
Return on equity: 143.83%
Cash ($ mil.): 6,988
Current ratio: 1.42
Long-term debt ($ mil.): 8,527

No. of shares (mil.): 1,007
Dividends
  Yield: 0.4%
  Payout: 19.5%
Market value ($ mil.): 300,680

	STOCK PRICE ($) FY Close	P/E High/Low		PER SHARE ($) Earnings	Dividends	Book Value
12/19	298.59	38	23	7.94	1.32	5.85
12/18	188.65	40	27	5.60	1.00	5.23
12/17	151.36	42	29	3.65	0.88	5.19
12/16	103.25	29	22	3.69	0.76	5.23
12/15	97.36	30	24	3.35	0.64	5.40
Annual Growth	32.3%	—	—	24.1%	19.8%	2.0%

MAYO CLINIC HOSPITAL-ROCHESTER

Multidisciplinary teamwork with coordinated care is Mayo Clinic's secret sauce. The not-for-profit Mayo Clinic provides health care most notably for complex medical conditions through its clinics in Rochester Minnesota Arizona and Florida. The clinics' multidisciplinary approach to care attracts more than a million patients a year from around the globe. For less specialized care the Mayo Clinic Health System operates a regional network of affiliated community hospitals and clinics in Minnesota Iowa and Wisconsin. Mayo Clinic also conducts research and trains physicians nurses and other health professionals. The Mayo Clinic is named for Dr. William Worrall Mayo who settled in Rochester in 1863.

Operations

Mayo Clinic Health System's regional network operates more than a dozen hospitals that combined are home to about 1000 beds and 3800 staff physicians medical scientists and clinical and research associates. The system also includes roughly 70 clinics in northern Iowa western Wisconsin and southeastern Minnesota. To manage its patient load Mayo forms referral alliances with other hospital groups HMOs and other organizations.

The clinic's education programs include the Mayo Medical School Mayo Graduate School and the Mayo School of Health Sciences; some medical training programs are conducted through partnerships with universities including the University of Minnesota. It also provides continuing education programs to medical professionals.

Financial Performance

The Mayo Clinic's revenue increased by nearly 7% in 2011 vs. 2010 while net income declined 18% over the same period. Indeed revenue gains and other support has steadily increased in recent years to nearly $8.5 billion in 2011. Sales of medical services (which account for about 85% of the Mayo Clinic's total) grew by 6% vs. the prior year. The Mayo Clinic list more than $10 billion in total assets.

Strategy

Already a giant in health care in the Midwest the Mayo Clinic continues to grow in other regions. In 2018 it announced plans to invest some $648 million in its Phoenix campus over the next five years. The project will roughly double the size of the campus allowing the system to meet growing demand for complex health care services in the Southwest. Similarly Mayo Clinic is investing some $144 million in its Jacksonville Florida campus.

Mayo Clinic strives to accommodate patients who travel to get to its facilities and will schedule multiple appointments and tests tightly together to make the most of patient's time. Rather than paying physicians based upon the quantity of patients seen the clinic's doctors are paid salaries as an incentive to quality care. These and other innovations have drawn attention to the clinic's patient-centered model of care. It has created a Center for the Science of Health Care Delivery and collaborates with other innovators including Cleveland Clinic and Intermountain Healthcare.

To reach remote areas Mayo Clinic in Arizona pioneered a telemedicine program that places robots in rural hospitals allowing local doctors and hospital staff to communicate with Mayo doctors in real time as they treat patients with such conditions as stroke or collapsed lungs.

EXECUTIVES

Regional Vice President, Annie Sadosty
Vice President, Brian Arendt
Treasurer, Harry N Hoffman
Assistant Treasurer, Paul A Gorman
Medical Secretary, Judy Jerabek
Vice Chair Dermatology, Marian Mcevoy
Medical Secretary, Deborah Stark
Medical Secretary, Mark Wojahn
Medical Secretary, Gina Robertson
Auditors: ERNST & YOUNG LLP MINNEAPOLIS

LOCATIONS

HQ: MAYO CLINIC HOSPITAL-ROCHESTER
200 1ST ST SW, ROCHESTER, MN 559050002
Phone: 507 284-2511
Web: WWW.MAYOCLINIC.ORG

Selected Locations and Affiliates
Direct subsidiaries
  Arizona
    Mayo Clinic Hospital (Phoenix)
    Mayo Clinic Scottsdale
  Florida
    Mayo Clinic Hospital (Jacksonville)
    Mayo Clinic Jacksonville
  Minnesota
    Mayo Clinic Rochester
    Rochester Methodist Hospital
    Saint Marys Hospital (Rochester)
    Mayo Eugenio Litta Children's Hospital
Mayo Health System affiliates
  Iowa
    Armstrong Clinic
    Decorah Clinic
    Lake Mills Clinic
      Franciscan
    Swea City Clinic
  Minnesota
    Fountain Centers in Fairmont
    Fountain Centers in Waseca
      FamilyHeal
    FamilyHealth Medical Clinic - Northfield Hospital
    Franciscan Healthcare in Caledonia
    Franciscan Healthcare La Crescent Clinic
    Mayo Clinic Health System - Albert Lea
      Mayo Clini
      Mayo Clini
      Mayo Clini
      Mayo Clini
  Wisconsin
    Chippewa Valley in Bloomer
    Chippewa Valley in Chippewa Falls
    Chippewa Valley in Colfax
    Eau Claire Home Health & Hospice
    Franciscan Healthcare Arcadia Campus
    Franciscan Healthcare Holmen Clinic
    Franciscan Healthcare Lake Tomah Clinic
    Franciscan Healthcare Onalaska Clinic
    Franciscan Healthcare Prairie du Chien Clinic
    Franciscan Healthcare Sparta Campus
    Northland in Barron
    Red Cedar in Elmwood
    Red Cedar in Glenwood
    Red Cedar in Menomonie

PRODUCTS/OPERATIONS

2015 Revenues

	$ mil.	% of total
Medical services	8,620	84
Grants & contracts	386	4
Investment return	233	2
Contributions	211	2
Premiums	144	1
Other	721	6
Total	**8,476**	**100**

COMPETITORS

Allina Hospitals
Ascension Health
Beth Israel Deaconess Medical Center
CentraCare Health
Children's Hospitals and Clinics of Minnesota

Dana-Farber
Fairview Health
Fox Chase Cancer Center
Gundersen Lutheran
HCA
Henry Ford Health System
Intermountain Health Care
Johns Hopkins Medicine
MD Anderson Cancer Center
Memorial Sloan-Kettering
North Memorial Health Care
Olmsted Medical
Park Nicollet Health Services
Roswell Park Cancer Institute
Scottsdale Healthcare
Tenet Healthcare
The Cleveland Clinic
Wistar Institute

HISTORICAL FINANCIALS

Company Type: Private

Income Statement   FYE: December 31

	REVENUE ($ mil.)	NET INCOME ($ mil.)	NET PROFIT MARGIN	EMPLOYEES
12/17	11,993	856	7.1%	32,271
12/16	10,998	(480)	—	—
Annual Growth	9.0%	—	—	—

MBIA Inc.

MBIA does what it can to make sure that bonds get paid no matter what. The holding company's independent subsidiary National Public Finance Guarantee Corporation is a provider of insurance for municipal bonds and stable corporate bonds (such as utility bonds) in the US. Separately its MBIA Insurance Corporation provides global structured finance products and non-US public financial guarantees. Faced with a significant amount of default activity MBIA is currently not issuing new policies.

Operations

MBIA conducts most of its business through subsidiaries National Public Finance Guarantee and MBIA Insurance Corporation. MBIA. Insurance has issued structured finance and international insurance but MBIA does not expect that unit to write any significant new policies in the foreseeable future either. Today MBIA's primary focus is to keep watch on its existing insured portfolio.

Another subsidiary MBIA Services Corporation provides fee-based support services (surveillance risk management IT etc.) to National and MBIA Insurance.

Nearly 35% of sales were generated from net investment income around 25% came from premiums earned and over 20% were generated from variable interest. The rest were generated from net gains and derivatives.

Geographic Reach

MBIA is headquartered in Purchase New York; it also has offices in New York City San Francisco and Mexico City.

Financial Performance

Revenue of the company since 2015 was fluctuating as it cannot establish growth even for two consecutive years.

Revenue for 2019 increased by 73% to $280 million. The increase in consolidated total revenues was primarily due to favorable changes in revenues of consolidated VIEs realized gains from the sale of uninsured PREPA bonds and the exchange and subsequent sale of COFINA bonds and a favorable net change in the value of insured derivatives.

Net loss totaled $359 million in 2019 versus a loss of $296 million the prior year as expenses increased by 39%.

Cash at the end of fiscal 2019 was $83 million. Net cash used by operating activities was $368 million and cash used in financing activities was $1.1 billion. Investing activities contributed $1.3 billion to the company. Main cash uses were for payments of notes and purchases of investments.

Strategy

MBIA Corp.'s primary objectives are to satisfy all claims by its policyholders and to maximize future recoveries if any for its senior lending and surplus note holders and then its preferred stock holders. MBIA Corp. is executing this strategy by among other things pursuing various actions focused on maximizing the collection of recoveries and reducing and mitigating potential losses on its insurance exposures.

The company's capital management strategies include having the company or National repurchase outstanding MBIA Inc. common shares to enhance shareholder value when management deems such actions are appropriate taking into account the price of the stock anticipated liquidity needs and other relevant factors and retiring its unsecured and MBIA Global Funding LLC ("GFL") debt through calls and repurchases at prices that create economic benefit to the company.

Company Background

That MBIA is still standing is remarkable. As one of the largest providers of insurance to asset- and mortgage-based securities MBIA was among the most vulnerable companies when the US housing market imploded in 2007. The company posted losses of $2.3 billion the last quarter of 2007 a result of its investments in subprime mortgage-backed securities.

MBIA split apart its public structured and asset management businesses to separate the stable from the unstable in early 2009: MBIA split its municipal bond insurance business off into an independent subsidiary named National Public Finance Guarantee Corporation. It receives a credit rating separate from the rest of MBIA's riskier structured-finance businesses.

Following the split some 20 banks grew prickly and sued MBIA with one hand while steadily collecting claims with the other. However by mid-2011 banks began dropping out of the lawsuit; the company settled with the final three in 2013.

EXECUTIVES

Evp Chief Legal Officer And Secretary, Ram D. Wertheim, age 66, $500,000 total compensation
Ceo, William C. (Bill) Fallon, age 60, $812,500 total compensation
Evp And Cfo, Anthony McKiernan, age 50, $500,000 total compensation
Assistant Vice President Financial Reporting, James Brown
Assistant Vice President, Jackie Perez
Assistant Vice President, Emily Johnson
Vice President, Cathleen Murray
Vice President, Greg Wright
Vice President, Donna Soto
Chairman, Charles R. Rinehart, age 73
Board Member, Richard Vaughan
Board Member, Francis Chin
Board Member, Diane Dewbrey
Auditors: PricewaterhouseCoopers LLP

LOCATIONS

HQ: MBIA Inc.
1 Manhattanville Road, Suite 301, Purchase, NY 10577
Phone: 914 273-4545
Web: www.mbia.com

COMPETITORS

Ambac	Primus Guaranty
Assured Guaranty	Radian Group
FGIC	Syncora Holdings

HISTORICAL FINANCIALS

Company Type: Public

Income Statement

FYE: December 31

	ASSETS ($ mil.)	NET INCOME ($ mil.)	INCOME AS % OF ASSETS	EMPLOYEES
12/19	7,284	(359)	—	93
12/18	8,076	(296)	—	96
12/17	9,095	(1,605)	—	103
12/16	11,137	(338)	—	164
12/15	14,855	180	1.2%	170
Annual Growth	(16.3%)	—	—	(14.0%)

2019 Year-End Financials

Debt ratio: 61.05%	No. of shares (mil.): 79
Return on equity: (-36.92%)	Dividends
Cash ($ mil.): 83	Yield: —
Current ratio: —	Payout: —
Long-term debt ($ mil.): —	Market value ($ mil.): 739

	STOCK PRICE ($) FY Close	P/E High/Low	Earnings	PER SHARE ($) Dividends	Book Value
12/19	9.30	— —	(4.43)	0.00	10.40
12/18	8.92	— —	(3.33)	0.00	12.46
12/17	7.32	— —	(13.50)	0.00	15.45
12/16	10.70	— —	(2.54)	0.00	23.87
12/15	6.48	9 5	1.06	0.00	24.61
Annual Growth	9.5%		—	—	(19.4%)

McDonald's Corp

Serving billions of hamburgers has put a shine on these arches. McDonald's has more than 38000 restaurants serving burgers and fries in nearly 115 countries. (There are nearly 14000 Golden Arches locations in the US.) The popular chain is well-known for its Big Macs Quarter Pounders McDonald's Fries McFlurry desserts and Chicken McNuggets. The company's main market includes Australia Canada France Germany Italy the Netherlands Russia Spain and the U.K which generates about 85% of franchised while US being their largest markets accounts for 95% of franchised. More than 90% of the restaurants are run by franchisees or affiliates. More than half of revenues are generated outside the US.

HISTORY

The first McDonald's opened in 1948 in San Bernardino California. In 1954 owners Dick and Mac McDonald signed a franchise agreement with 52-year-old Ray Kroc (a malt machine salesman) and a year later Kroc opened his first restaurant in Des Plaines Illinois. By 1957 Kroc was operating 14 McDonald's restaurants in Illinois Indiana and California. In 1961 Kroc bought out the McDonald brothers for $2.7 million.

In 1962 the now-ubiquitous Golden Arches appeared for the first time and the company sold its billionth burger. Ronald McDonald made his debut the following year and the company introduced its first new menu item — the Filet-O-Fish. Two years later McDonald's went public and ran its first TV ads. The company opened its first stores outside the US (in Canada) in 1967 and the next year it added the Big Mac to the menu and opened its 1000th restaurant.

During the 1970s McDonald's grew at the rate of about 500 restaurants per year and the first Ronald McDonald House (a temporary residence for families of hospitalized children) opened in 1974. The drive-through window appeared in 1975.

McDonald's introduced Chicken McNuggets in 1983. Kroc who had become senior chairman in the 1970s died the next year. Growing competition slowed the company's US sales growth to about 5% per year at the end of the 1980s. In response McDonald's added specially priced "value menu" items.

In 1990 the company made history and headlines when it opened the first McDonald's in Moscow. Two years later the Golden Arches expanded into China. The company stumbled with the pricey Arch Deluxe hamburger in 1996 and its Campaign 55 discount promotion the next year. However the giveaway of Teenie Beanie Babies in 1997 was its most successful promotion ever. McDonald's decentralized US operations that year to bring decision-making closer to local franchises. US division CEO Edward Rensi retired and was replaced by division chairman Jack Greenberg.

The next year Greenberg launched the Made For You food preparation system designed to reduce waste and produce a better tasting burger. He was named CEO later that year. McDonald's also made its first investment in another restaurant concept in 1998 when it bought a stake in Chipotle Mexican Grill a Denver-based chain of Mexican food restaurants. That same year saw the death of co-founder Dick McDonald who died at age 89.

During Greenberg's first year he slowed US expansion and stepped up international growth. In 1999 McDonald's added a third brand to its family when it acquired the Ohio-based Donatos Pizzeria chain. The company's biggest deal though came in 2000 when it purchased the Boston Market chain from struggling Boston Chicken for about $175 million.

Early in 2001 McDonald's unveiled its New Tastes Menu in which local markets could feature up to four regional or seasonal foods out of a 40-item national selection. The company continued its move toward diversification and international expansion purchasing a 33% stake in the UK limited-service sandwich chain Pret A Manger for $40 million. It also spun off its Japanese unit to the public retaining a 50% ownership stake.

But even with all its size and power McDonald's found out it was not immune to economic trouble and corporate blunders. The company suffered from ill-thought product changes less-than-successful marketing plans and the growing public preference for lighter fast-food options such as sub sandwiches and salads. Following three quarters of declining profits in 2001 McDonald's announced a major restructuring of its US operations. It cut about 700 corporate jobs hired five new managers and consolidated its service regions.

Business failed to improve however and in 2002 it laid off approximately 600 corporate employees and closed about 175 underperforming units. At the end of 2002 after the company posted its first quarterly loss in history vice chairman and president Jim Cantalupo a veteran of McDonald's international operation replaced Jack Greenberg as chairman and CEO.

McDonald's business began to improve during 2003 with the introduction of healthier menu fare. Late that year the company sold Donatos Pizza back to its founder Jim Grote and closed all Boston Market locations outside the US in order to focus more attention on its core chains. The company ended a joint venture with Seed Restaurant Group that would have led to the development of new Fazoli's locations. Japan however remained a particularly rough market: McDonald's Holdings (Japan) posted losses for both 2002 and 2003. It also gave up on efforts to establish the Pret A Manger sandwich shops in Japan.

Putting its advertising dollars to work McDonald's introduced a global branding campaign in 2003 to help change its image. Called "I'm Lovin' It" the campaign attempted to up the restaurant chain's hip factor and draw young customers. These efforts showed positive results: McDonald's posted steady sales increases through most of 2003 and into early 2004 and investors were encouraged by the progress.

Cantalupo died in 2004. Director Andrew McKenna was named chairman and president. Charlie Bell became CEO. Diagnosed with cancer and undergoing surgery a month later Bell curtailed his workload but returned to his job full-time later that month. He underwent a second surgery procedure later that year again cancer-related and eventually stepped down near the end of 2004 in order to devote all his time to fighting cancer. (Bell died early the next year.) Vice chairman Jim Skinner assumed the mantle of CEO becoming the company's third chief executive in seven months. Mike Roberts the CEO of McDonald's USA assumed the additional titles of president and COO.

In a David and Goliath scenario the Venezuelan government ordered all 80 of the country's McDonald's restaurants closed for three days in 2005 as punishment for not following the country's tax laws. McDonald's sold a 35% stake in Chipotle through an IPO in 2006 and disposed of its remaining holdings later that year. It sold Boston Market to private equity firm Sun Capital Partners for $250 million the following year and in 2008 McDonald's cashed out its stake in Pret A Manger as part of a $670 million buyout by private equity firm Bridgepoint Capital.

In 2011 McDonald's sold its 50% stake in Hardcastle Restaurants one of two joint ventures operating McDonald's restaurants in India and converted it to a franchisee operation.

EXECUTIVES

Evp And Global Chief Marketing Officer, Silvia Lagnado, $615,000 total compensation

Evp Supply Chain And Development, Douglas M. (Doug) Goare, age 67, $648,750 total compensation

President Mcdonald's Usa, Chris (Chris K) Kempczinski, age 51, $111,538 total compensation

Evp And Chief People Officer, David Fairhurst, age 52

Corporate Evp And Cfo, Kevin M. Ozan, age 57, $683,333 total compensation

President Ceo And Director, Stephen J. (Steve) Easterbrook, age 52, $1,266,667 total compensation

Corporate Evp Operations And Technology Systems, Jim Sappington, age 61

Evp Corporate Relations; Chief Communications Officer, Robert Gibbs

President High Growth Markets, Joe Erlinger

Evp General Counsel And Secretary, Jerry Krulewitch

President Foundational Markets, Ian Borden

Vice President, Gerald Newman

Operations Vice President, Jeff Wilfong

Vice President Supply Chain Management, Bob Stewart

Vice President Of Operations, Marcy Amble

Senior Vice President Menu Innovation Mcdonald 's Usa, Greg Watson

Senior Vice President Marketing Technology, Bob Rupczynski

Vice President Of Restaurant Development, Robert Lancaster

Operations Vice President, William Mckernan

Vice President Sales, Carol Fink

Field Vice President, Ofelia Melendrez-kumpf

Vice President, Domineca Neal

Chairman, Enrique (Rick) Hernandez, age 65

Auditors: Ernst & Young LLP

LOCATIONS

HQ: McDonald's Corp
110 North Carpenter Street, Chicago, IL 60607
Phone: 630 623-3000
Web: www.mcdonalds.com

2017 Sales

	$ mil.	% of total
U.S.	8,000	35
International Lead Markets	7,340	32
High Growth Markets	5,533	24
Foundational Markets & Corporate	1,941	9
Total	**22,820**	**100**

2017 Locations

	No.
US	14,036
International Lead Markets	6,921
High Growth Markets	5,884
Foundational Markets & Corporate	10,400
Total	**37,241**

PRODUCTS/OPERATIONS

2017 Locations

	No.
Franchised	34,108
Company-owned	3
Total	**37,241**

2017 Sales

	$ mil.	% of total
Company-owned restaurants	12,719	56
Franchised restaurants	10,101	44
Total	**22,820**	**100**

Selected Products

Big Mac
Chicken McNuggets
Egg McMuffin
Filet-O-Fish
Happy Meal
Mac Snack Wrap
McCafe
McChicken
McDouble
McFlurry
McGriddle
McRib
Quarter Pounder

COMPETITORS

Burger King	Quiznos
CKE Restaurants	Sonic Corp.
Chick-fil-A	Starbucks
Church's Chicken	Subway
Dairy Queen	Tim Hortons
Jack in the Box	Wendy's
Panda Restaurant Group	YUM!
Popeyes	

HISTORICAL FINANCIALS

Company Type: Public

Income Statement

FYE: December 31

	REVENUE ($ mil.)	NET INCOME ($ mil.)	NET PROFIT MARGIN	EMPLOYEES
12/19	21,076	6,025	28.6%	205,000
12/18	21,025	5,924	28.2%	210,000
12/17	22,820	5,192	22.8%	235,000
12/16	24,621	4,686	19.0%	375,000
12/15	25,413	4,529	17.8%	420,000
Annual Growth	**(4.6%)**	**7.4%**	**—**	**(16.4%)**

2019 Year-End Financials

Debt ratio: 71.94%
Return on equity: —
Cash ($ mil.): 898
Current ratio: 0.98
Long-term debt ($ mil.): 34,118

No. of shares (mil.): 746
Dividends
  Yield: 2.3%
  Payout: 60.0%
Market value ($ mil.): 147,476

	STOCK PRICE ($) FY Close	P/E High/Low		PER SHARE ($) Earnings	Dividends	Book Value
12/19	197.61	28	22	7.88	4.73	(11.00)
12/18	177.57	25	19	7.54	4.19	(8.16)
12/17	172.12	27	19	6.37	3.83	(4.12)
12/16	121.72	24	20	5.44	3.61	(2.69)
12/15	118.14	25	18	4.80	3.44	7.82
Annual Growth	**13.7%**	—	—	**13.2%**	**8.3%**	**—**

McKesson Corp

McKesson is a top global pharmaceuticals distributor. The company delivers prescription and generic drugs as well as health and beauty care products to retail and institutional pharmacies worldwide. The company is also a major medical supplies wholesaler providing medical and surgical equipment to alternate health care sites such as doctors' offices surgery centers and long-term care facilities. In addition to distribution McKesson offers management consulting and technology services that help customers navigate supply chain clinical administrative and financial operations. The US is its largest market by accounting nearly 85% of total sales.

HISTORY

John McKesson opened a Manhattan drugstore in 1833 and Daniel Robbins joined him as a partner in 1840. McKesson-Robbins soon expanded into chemical and drug production and the enterprise grew steadily. In 1926 after differences arose between the McKesson and Robbins heirs the company was sold to Donald Coster.

Coster was actually convicted felon Philip Musica who purchased McKesson-Robbins with fraudulently obtained bank loans. For more than a decade his real identity remained secret from all but one blackmailer. By 1930 McKesson-Robbins had wholesale drug operations in 33 states. The company appeared to be growing but a treasurer discovered a Musica-orchestrated accounting scam and a cash shortfall of $3 million. Faced with exposure Musica killed himself in 1939; company bankruptcy followed. McKesson-Robbins emerged from bankruptcy in 1941.

In a hostile takeover in 1967 San Francisco-based Foremost Dairies bought McKesson-Robbins to form Foremost-McKesson. Over the next 20 years the company bought liquor chemical and software wholesalers as well as several bottled-water companies. It sold Foremost Dairies in 1983 to focus on distribution changed its name to McKesson the next year and continued to build its drug wholesaling business through acquisitions. By 1985 it was the US's largest distributor of drugs and medical equipment wine and liquor bottled water and car waxes and polishes.

In 1986 McKesson narrowed its focus to the health industry by selling its liquor and chemical distributors. It acquired Canadian drug distributor Medis by halves in 1990 and 1991 and a 23% stake in Mexican drug distributor Nadro in 1993.

McKesson sold PCS the US's #1 prescription claims processor (acquired in 1970) to Eli Lilly in 1994. In 1996 the firm bought bankrupt distributor FoxMeyer Drug and sold its stake in Armor All (auto and home cleaning products) to Clorox.

In 1997 the company purchased General Medical the US's largest distributor of medical surgical supplies for about $775 million. McKesson began to focus on health care selling its Millbrook Distribution Services unit (health and beauty products general merchandise and specialty foods).

Under new CEO Mark Pulido it agreed to buy drug wholesaler AmeriSource Health (now AmerisourceBergen) but withdrew the offer in 1998 facing FTC opposition. Instead McKesson moved into information systems paying $14 billion for health care information top dog HBO & Company and forming McKesson HBOC. HBO a high-flyer in the high-growth health information systems segment balanced its rather dowdy drug and medical distribution operations.

But just months after the deal closed accounting inconsistencies at HBO prompted McKesson to re-state fourth-quarter results for fiscal 1999 twice triggering shareholder lawsuits and a housecleaning of top brass. Five ex-HBO executives including McKesson HBOC chairman Charlie McCall (who was later indicted for securities fraud) were canned for using improper accounting methods. McKesson's veteran CEO Pulido and CFO Richard Hawkins were forced to resign for not seeing the problems coming.

The company changed its name to McKesson Corporation in 2001. The National Health Services Information Authority entered into an agreement with McKesson to develop a human resources and payroll system for use at the more than 600 NHS locations throughout the UK.

To catch then #1 pharmaceutical distributor Cardinal Health McKesson built up its core areas in 2003 and 2004 while trimming away some of the dead weight (Abaton.com Amysis Managed Care Systems and ProDental Corp.). The company bought PMO a specialty mail-order prescription business. It also acquired Canadian firm A.L.I. Technologies which provided systems for managing medical images.

In 2007 McKesson acquired Oncology Therapeutics Network a specialty pharmaceuticals distributor for $519 million. McKesson launched a new Plasma and BioLogics division in 2008 to deliver plasma and plasma-related products to hospital pharmacies and it expanded its regional drug distribution network through the purchase of Midwest pharmacy distributor McQueary Brothers for $190 million.

The company grew in the oncology physician practice management realm through the $2.2 billion acquisition of US Oncology in 2010. In 2014 it expanded into European drug distribution and retail pharmacy operations by purchasing Celesio for $8.3 billion.

In buying Vantage Oncology Holdings for $515 million McKesson got an oncology management services business that offers comprehensive cancer treatment in 50 facilities in 13 states. Biologics ac-

quired for $692 million added another oncology-focused US specialty pharmacy.

The firm bolstered its position in Ireland and the UK with the purchase of the pharmaceutical distribution businesses of UDG for $447 million in 2016. McKesson also bought Rexall Health in Canada for C$3 billion.

McKesson bought CoverMyMeds which developed software for the pre-authorization of prescription drugs for pharma manufacturers clinicians and payers for $1.1 billion in 2017.

EXECUTIVES

Chairman President And Ceo, John H. Hammergren, age 61, $1,680,000 total compensation
Evp Human Resources, Jorge L. Figueredo, age 59, $708,167 total compensation
Evp And Cfo, James A. Beer, age 59, $840,167 total compensation
Evp And Group President Domestic And International Distribution Solutions, Paul C. Julian, age 64, $1,148,333 total compensation
Evp Cio And Cto, Kathleen D. (Kathy) McElligott, age 64
Evp General Counsel And Chief Compliance Officer, Lori A. Schechter, age 58
Evp And Group President Mckesson Technology Solutions, Patrick J. (Pat) Blake, age 56, $765,500 total compensation
Evp Corporate Strategy And Business Development, Bansi Nagji, age 55
Vice President Home Care Sales, Jeff Bowman
Assistant Vice President Product Development, Beth Kuzmak
Senior Vice President Retail National Accounts, Michael Gallagher
Senior Vice President Investor Relations, Holly Weiss
Vice President National Accounts, Mark Snodgrass
Vp And Gm Technology Solutions Mckesson Specialty Health, Dan Lodder
Vice President And General Manager, Andrew Moore
Vice President National Accounts, Mike Ferguson
Vice President, Mike Cesarz
Assistant Vice President Software Development Mckesson Corporation, Karen Erickson
Vice President Of Marketing, Andy Burtis
Senior Vice President Distribution Systems, Ronald Bone
Vice President Business Development, Deann Cushman
Vice President Of Sales, Deborah Smith
Vice President Of Sales And Operations, Mauricio Chavez
Vice President Office Product Sales, Kevin Boyle
Vice President Marketing And Sales Program, David Brown
Vice President Laboratory Account Sales, Jerry Morrow
Vice President Software Engineering, Jason Warner
Vice President Of Customer Operations, Kathy McGrath
Executive Vice President And Cio, Zalise Edwards
Vice President Segment Marketing, Chris Garnett
Vice President, Victor Solomon
Svp And Gm Mckesson Rxo, Mark Eastham
Vice President Pharmacy Operations Health Mart, Charles Wilson
Vice President Corporate Strategy And Business Development, Aaron Apodaca
Vice President Research And Development, Binny John
Senior Vice President Compliance Regulatory And Ethics, Erik Sandstedt
Vice President Central Fill Operations, Mark Edwards
Vice President Strategy Rxo, Barbara Giacomelli

Vice President Of Materials Management, John Pildis
Vice President Business Strategy And Industry Relations Supplylogix, Victor Vercammen
Field Vice President Strategic Accounts, Carrie Bays
Senior Vice President Associate General Counsel (litigation It Ip And Employment), Robin Jacobsohn
Vice President Corporate Strategy And Business Development, Fred Montross
Board Member, Lauren Coles
Auditors: DELOITTE & TOUCHE LLP

LOCATIONS

HQ: McKesson Corp
6555 State Highway 161, Irving, TX 75039
Phone: 972 446-4800
Web: www.mckesson.com

2018 Sales

	$ mil.	% of total
US	169,943	82
International	38,414	18
Total	**208,357**	**100**

PRODUCTS/OPERATIONS

2018 Sales

	$ mil.	% of total
Distribution Solutions		
North American pharmaceutical distribution & services	174,186	84
International pharmaceutical distribution & services	27,320	13
Medical-Surgical distribution & services	6,611	3
Technology Solutions — products & services	240	-
Total	**208,357**	**100**

Selected Operations and Services

COMPETITORS

Allscripts	H. D. Smith Wholesale
AmerisourceBergen	Drug
Apothecary Products	Imperial Distributors
BioScrip	Medline Industries
Cardinal Health	Omnicare
CuraScript	Owens & Minor
Diplomat Pharmacy	PharMerica
FFF Enterprises	QK Healthcare
Grifols	Surgical Express

HISTORICAL FINANCIALS

Company Type: Public

Income Statement

FYE: March 31

	REVENUE ($ mil.)	NET INCOME ($ mil.)	NET PROFIT MARGIN	EMPLOYEES
03/20	231,051	900	0.4%	80,000
03/19	214,319	34	0.0%	80,000
03/18	208,357	67	0.0%	78,000
03/17	198,533	5,070	2.6%	78,000
03/16	190,884	2,258	1.2%	68,000
Annual Growth	**4.9%**	**(20.5%)**	—	**4.1%**

2020 Year-End Financials

Debt ratio: 12.06%
Return on equity: 13.61%
Cash ($ mil.): 4,015
Current ratio: 0.99
Long-term debt ($ mil.): 6,335

No. of shares (mil.): 162
Dividends
  Yield: 1.2%
  Payout: 32.5%
Market value ($ mil.): 21,912

STOCK PRICE ($)		P/E		PER SHARE ($)		
	FY Close	High/Low		Earnings	Dividends	Book Value
03/20	135.26	35	23	4.98	1.62	31.43
03/19	117.06	930	637	0.17	1.51	42.60
03/18	140.87	552	422	0.32	1.30	48.53
03/17	148.26	9	5	22.73	1.12	52.58
03/16	157.25	25	15	9.70	1.08	39.66
Annual Growth	(3.7%)	—		(15.4%)	10.7%	(5.6%)

MCLANE COMPANY, INC.

McLane Company is one of the largest wholesale suppliers of grocery and food products in the US serving some 50000 retail locations and 35000 restaurants across all 50 states. It delivers more than 50000 different consumer products to customers such as convenience and discount stores mass merchandisers wholesale clubs drug stores military bases and quick-service and casual dining restaurants. The company also distributes alcoholic beverages in the southeastern US and Colorado through subsidiaries. McLane is owned by Warren Buffett's Berkshire Hathaway and accounts for about a fifth of its revenue.

Operations

McLane operates through three business units: grocery distribution foodservice distribution and beverage distribution.

Its grocery business which accounts for about two-thirds of sales serves convenience stores and other retailers nationwide. The company's foodservice business focuses on restaurants across the country while subsidiaries such as Empire Distributors and Baroness Small Estates provide spirits wine and beer to more than 25000 retail locations in the southeastern US and Colorado. Food and beverage distribution together generates about a third of sales.

Geographic Reach

McLane has an extensive distribution network of some 80 facilities across the country with reach in all 50 US states. Its headquarters and grocery operations are based in Temple Texas while its Foodservice operation is based in Carrollton Texas.

The company supplies alcoholic beverages throughout the southeastern US and in Colorado through distribution centers in Colorado Georgia North Carolina and Tennessee.

Sales and Marketing

McLane is a leading supplier to convenience stores; other customers include discount and drug stores mass merchants wholesale clubs military bases and quick-service and casual dining restaurants.

The company is heavily reliant on former parent Walmart which generates about 20% of its revenue; 7-Eleven and Yum! Brands each account for about 10% of revenue.

Financial Performance

McLane's revenue has grown slightly over the past several years up 4% since 2016 amid intense competition.

The company reported 2018 revenue of about $50 billion up less than a percent from the prior year. A slight rise in grocery sales was mostly offset by a decline in foodservice sales because of a net loss in customers.

Strategy

Although McLane is one of the leaders in grocery and food distribution the business is low-margin and intensely competitive. As the company continues to expand by opening new distribution centers it is focused on technology and automation that can improve service while reducing costs. In late 2017 it opened what was its most technologically advanced distribution center in Findlay Ohio. The facility makes use of automation robotics and artificial intelligence among other technologies. McLane has continued opening distribution centers since then including a 2018 opening in Fort Worth Texas and a 2019 opening in Ocala Florida.

In addition to distribution center technology the company has also introduced a new mobile app (Mobile Virtual Trade Show or Mobile VTS) to simplify the ordering process for convenience store retailers.

Company Background

Starting as a family-owned grocery store in 1894 McLane expanded into wholesale distribution in the early 1900s. The McLane family including former Houston Astros owner Drayton McLane sold the business to Wal-Mart Stores in the 1990s. Conglomerate Berkshire Hathaway acquired McLane Company in 2003 for about $1.5 billion.

EXECUTIVES

President Mclane Grocery, Mike Youngblood
Evp Administration, James L. (Jim) Kent
President And Ceo, W. Grady Rosier
President Southeast Southern And Dothan Divisions, Ron Clark
President Mclane Carolina And Mid-atlantic Divisions, George Bolts
President Southwest And High Plains Divisions, Scott Braden
Svp And Chief Marketing Officer, Tom Sicola
Vice President Of Information Technology, Mona Huffman
Second Vice President Customer Service, Margo Star
Vice President Of Sales, Jimmy Morales
Senior Vice President, Charles Freeman
Senior Vice President, Julie Norris
Vice President National Accounts, Jeff Hayes
Vice President Of Distribution, Jackie Palmer
Vice President Of Logistics, Robbie Wainwright
Division Vice President, John Havel
Region Vice President, Calvin Parker
Vice President, Chris Short
Senior Vice President Midwest Division, Tim Donahoe
Senior Vice President Midwest Division, Matt Bowen

LOCATIONS

HQ: MCLANE COMPANY, INC.
4747 MCLANE PKWY, TEMPLE, TX 765044854
Phone: 254 771-7500
Web: WWW.MCLANECO.COM

COMPETITORS

AMCON Distributing	MAINES
Associated Wholesale Grocers	Performance Food Group
Ben E. Keith	Reinhart FoodService
C&S Wholesale	SUPERVALU
Core-Mark	Southern Glazer's Wine and Spirits
Eby-Brown	Sysco
GSC Enterprises	US Foods
Golden State Foods	United Natural
Gordon Food Service	Wakefern Food
H. T. Hackney	

HISTORICAL FINANCIALS

Company Type: Private

Income Statement — FYE: December 30

	REVENUE ($ mil.)	NET INCOME ($ mil.)	NET PROFIT MARGIN	EMPLOYEES
12/16*	48,016	0	—	20,128
01/16	48,144	0	—	
12/12	37,389	0	—	
01/09	29,800	0	—	
Annual Growth	6.1%	—	—	—

*Fiscal year change

Mercantile Bank Corp.

Mercantile Bank Corporation is the holding company for Mercantile Bank of Michigan (formerly Mercantile Bank of West Michigan) which boasts assets of nearly $3 billion and operates more than 50 branches in central and western Michigan around Grand Rapids Holland and Lansing. The bank targets local consumers and businesses offering standard deposit services such as checking and savings accounts CDs IRAs and health savings accounts. Commercial loans make up more than three-fourths of the bank's loan portfolio. Outside of banking subsidiary Mercantile Insurance Center sells insurance products.

Operations

Mercantile Bank Corp. generated 82% of its total revenue from loan interest (including fees) in 2014 with securities interest contributing another 8% to total revenue. Service charges on deposit and sweep accounts and credit and debit card fees made up another 5% of Mercantile's total revenue while its mortgage banking income generated another 2%.

Sales and Marketing

Mercantile provides its banking services to businesses individuals and government organizations. Its commercial banking services mostly cater to small- to medium-sized businesses.

The company spent $1.315 million on advertising in 2014 compared to $1.113 million and $1.167 million in 2013 and 2012 respectively.

Financial Performance

Mercantile Bank Corp's revenues had been declining for a number of years as its loan business withered while profits have remained mostly flat.

The company had a breakout year in 2014 however after its historic acquisition of FirstBank Corp. The bank's revenue skyrocketed by 53% to $99.15 million (the highest level since 2009) mostly as the acquisition nearly doubled its loan assets and boosted its interest income on loans and securities by significant amounts. The bank's non-interest income also grew by 46% thanks to higher fee income across the board also resulting from the recent acquisition.

Higher revenue and a $3.2 million reduction in loan loss provisions with a stronger credit portfolio in 2014 also pushed the company's net income up by 2% to $17.33 million for the year. Mercantile's operating cash declined by 50% to $14.41 million due to changes in accrued interest and other liabilities during the year.

Strategy

Mercantile Bank Corporation has been growing its loan business and branch network reach through strategic acquisitions of smaller banks and bank branches. Its mid-2014 acquisition of Firstbank Corporation was perhaps the most effective to date as the purchase doubled its assets and boosted the size of its branch network nearly seven-fold from seven branches to a whopping 53.

Mergers and Acquisitions

In June 2014 Mercantile Bank Corp. purchased Firstbank Corp of Alma Michigan for a total purchase price of $173 million adding 46 branches and $1.3 billion in assets. The deal which made Mercantile the third-largest bank based in the state also expanded the bank's service offerings diversified its loan portfolio boosted its loan origination capacity and significantly extended its geographic footprint into Michigan's lower peninsula.

EXECUTIVES

Svp Cfo And Treasurer Mercantile Bank Corporation And Svp And Cfo Mercantile Bank Of Michigan, Charles E. (Chuck) Christmas, age 54, $263,000 total compensation

President And Ceo, Robert B. Kaminski, age 58, $315,000 total compensation

Evp Corporate Finance And Strategic Planning Mercantile Bank Corporation And Mercantile Bank Of Michigan, Samuel G. Stone, age 75, $159,833 total compensation

Vice President Treasury Sales, John Byl

Vice President Electronic Banking, Shannon Tramontin

Senior Vice President Commercial Lending, Kevin Paul

Vice President Security, Paul Wegener

Assistant Vice President Human Resources Specialist, Tina Van Valkenburg

Senior Vice President Business Development Officer, Brian Talbot

Branch Manager Vice President, Andrea Spagnuolo

Assistant Vice President Assistant Commercial Operations Manager, Kitty Kale

Senior Vice President Corporate Banking, Matt Zimmerman

Svp Commercial Lender, Andrew Miedema

Assistant Vice President Human Resources Administrator, Kate Glover

Senior Vice President Information Systems Manager, Allen Smith

Vice President Treasury Sales Officer, Tim Ladd

Vice President, Holly Williams

Vice President Risk Asset Management, Danna Mathiesen

Assistant Vice President Leonard Branch Manager, Daniel Zink

Senior Vice President, Michael Erfourth

Vice President, Jim Kloostra

Assistant Vice President Mortgage Lender, Debra Fuller

Senior Vice President Commercial Lending, Michael Stapleton

Vice President Mortgage Lender, Alice Doherty

Vp. Mortgage Market Manager, Jim Kingsley

Chairman, Michael H. Price, age 63

Auditors: BDO USA, LLP

LOCATIONS

HQ: Mercantile Bank Corp.
310 Leonard Street N.W., Grand Rapids, MI 49504
Phone: 616 406-3000
Web: www.mercbank.com

PRODUCTS/OPERATIONS

2014 Sales

	$ mil.	% of total
Interest income		
Loans and leases including fees	80	82
Securities taxable	6	6
Securities tax-exempt	1	2
Other	0	-
Noninterest income		
Service charges on accounts	2	3
Credit and debit card fees	2	2
Mortgage banking activities	1	2
Other	3	3
Total	99	100

COMPETITORS

Chemical Financial	Flagstar Bancorp
ChoiceOne Financial Services	Huntington Bancshares
Comerica	Independent Bank (MI)
Fifth Third	Macatawa Bank

HISTORICAL FINANCIALS

Company Type: Public

Income Statement				FYE: December 31
	ASSETS ($ mil.)	NET INCOME ($ mil.)	INCOME AS % OF ASSETS	EMPLOYEES
12/19	3,632	49	1.4%	683
12/18	3,363	42	1.2%	693
12/17	3,286	31	1.0%	701
12/16	3,082	31	1.0%	682
12/15	2,903	27	0.9%	701
Annual Growth	5.8%	16.3%	—	(0.6%)

2019 Year-End Financials

Debt ratio: 1.29%
Return on equity: 12.49%
Cash ($ mil.): 233
Current ratio: —
Long-term debt ($ mil.): —
No. of shares (mil.): 16
Dividends
  Yield: 2.9%
  Payout: 36.5%
Market value ($ mil.): 599

	STOCK PRICE ($) FY Close	P/E High/Low		PER SHARE ($) Earnings	Dividends	Book Value
12/19	36.47	12	10	3.01	1.06	25.36
12/18	28.26	15	11	2.53	1.68	22.70
12/17	35.37	20	15	1.90	0.74	22.05
12/16	37.70	19	11	1.96	1.16	20.76
12/15	24.54	16	12	1.62	0.58	20.41
Annual Growth	10.4%	—	—	16.8%	16.3%	5.6%

Merchants Bancorp (Indiana)

Auditors: BKD, LLP

LOCATIONS

HQ: Merchants Bancorp (Indiana)
410 Monon Blvd., Carmel, IN 46032
Phone: 317 569-7420
Web: www.merchantsbankofindiana.com

HISTORICAL FINANCIALS

Company Type: Public

Income Statement				FYE: December 31
	ASSETS ($ mil.)	NET INCOME ($ mil.)	INCOME AS % OF ASSETS	EMPLOYEES
12/19	6,371	77	1.2%	329
12/18	3,884	62	1.6%	259
12/17	3,393	54	1.6%	194
12/16	2,718	33	1.2%	157
12/15	2,269	28	1.3%	—
Annual Growth	29.4%	28.5%		

2019 Year-End Financials

Debt ratio: 0.10%
Return on equity: 14.39%
Cash ($ mil.): 506
Current ratio: —
Long-term debt ($ mil.): —
No. of shares (mil.): 28
Dividends
  Yield: 1.4%
  Payout: 14.3%
Market value ($ mil.): 566

	STOCK PRICE ($) FY Close	P/E High/Low		PER SHARE ($) Earnings	Dividends	Book Value
12/19	19.71	10	6	2.37	0.28	22.77
12/18	19.96	14	9	2.07	0.24	14.68
12/17	19.68	9	7	2.28	0.05	12.81
Annual Growth	0.0%	—	—	1.0%	53.8%	15.5%

Merck & Co Inc

A global drugmaker Merck makes medicines for an array of maladies ranging from hypertension to cancer. The pharmaceutical giant's top products include cancer drug Keytruda diabetes drugs Januvia and Janumet HPV vaccine Gardasil a pediatric combination vaccines ProQuad M-M-R II Varivax. In addition Merck makes childhood and adult vaccines for such diseases as measles mumps rubella and varicella and pneumonia as well as veterinary pharmaceuticals through Merck Animal Health. In addition the company provides analytics and clinical services to the health care sector. The US market accounts for about 45% of sales.

HISTORY

Merck traces its roots to the formation of Schering-Plough in 1851 and the founding of the original Merck entity in 1887. (The two companies merged in 2009.)

Schering-Plough dates back to 1851 when Berlin chemist Ernst Schering began to sell chemicals to apothecary shops. By 1880 Schering's business (which eventually became Bayer Schering Pharma) was exporting pharmaceuticals to the US where a subsidiary (the predecessor to Schering-Plough) was established in 1928.

At the outbreak of WWII the US government seized the US Schering subsidiary severing links with its German parent. The company went on to develop such new drugs as Chlor-Trimeton one of the first antihistamines and the cold medicine Coricidin. The US government sold Schering in 1952 to Merrill Lynch which took it public. Schering bought White Labs (which made Coppertone sunscreen) in 1957. In the 1960s the company introduced Garamycin (antibiotic 1964) Tinactin (antifungal 1965) and Afrin (decongestant 1967).

Schering's 1971 merger with Memphis-based Plough expanded the product line to include such cosmetics and consumer items as Coppertone and

Di-Gel. Plough's founder Abe Plough had borrowed $125 from his father to found the company in 1908. Abe remained chairman at Schering-Plough until 1976. Schering-Plough introduced many products after the merger including Lotrimin AF (antifungal 1975) antibiotic Netromycin (1980) and Drixoral (a cold remedy made nonprescription in 1982).

The company was one of the first drug giants to make significant investments in biotechnology: It bought DNAX Research Institute of Palo Alto California in 1982. Acquisitions in the late 1970s and 1980s included Scholl (foot care 1979) Key Pharmaceuticals (cardiovascular drugs 1986) and Cooper Companies (eye care 1988).

In 1993 Schering-Plough began marketing its non-sedating antihistamine Claritin in the US. (Claritin became an OTC drug in 2002.) The next year it gained FDA approval to market the first colored disposable contact lenses only to sell its contact lens business later in the year. In 1996 Schering-Plough bought Canji to strengthen its gene therapy research program. It strengthened its veterinary medicine segment in 1997 when it bought Mallinckrodt's animal health operations.

The firm bought the marketing rights to Centocor's treatment for Crohn's disease in 1998. In 1999 the FDA approved the company's Temodar a chemotherapy treatment for brain tumors and it bought the US rights to Pfizer's Bain de Soleil sun care product line. In 2000 Schering-Plough formed its first collaboration with Merck. In 2002 the company paid a $500 million fine to the FDA over manufacturing concerns.

As Schering-Plough's revenues started to decline in 2003 the company brought in several executives from Pharmacia including CEO Fred Hassan (who retired following the 2009 merger with Plough) to help streamline its operations and expand its R&D programs and product offerings. The firm gave itself a major boost by acquiring Akzo Nobel's Organon unit in 2007 growing in the areas of women's health care neurology vaccines animal health (Intervet) and third-party biologics manufacturing (through Diosynth).

The original Merck was started in 1887 when German chemist Theodore Weicker came to the US to set up a branch of German firm E. Merck AG (which was founded in 1668 and later became Merck KGaA). George Merck (grandson of the German company's founder) came in 1889 and formed a partnership with Weicker and eventually bought out Weicker's shares. At first the firm imported and sold drugs and chemicals from Germany but in 1903 it began manufacturing its own products. During WWI Merck gave the US government the 80% of the US Merck unit's stock owned by the family in Germany (George kept his shares). After the war the stock was sold to the public.

The firm acquired Powers-Weightman-Rosengarten of Philadelphia (a producer of antimalarial quinine) in 1927. Merck opened its first research lab in 1933; Merck scientists there developed the first steroid cortisone in 1944. Five Merck scientists received Nobel Prizes in the 1940s and 1950s. In 1953 Merck bought drugmaker Sharp & Dohme of Philadelphia which brought with it a strong sales force.

The 1958 introduction of Diuril (antihypertensive) and several other drugs (including the first measles vaccine) in the early 1960s was followed by a dry spell. In the 1970s an accelerated R&D organization created new products including Clinoril (antiarthritic) Flexeril (muscle relaxant) and Timoptic (for glaucoma). Merck introduced 10 major new drugs in the 1980s including Mevacor (high cholesterol) and Vasotec (high blood pressure).

In 1990 the company bought the nonprescription drug segment of ICI Americas; products from the purchase were contributed to a Consumer Pharmaceuticals joint venture with Johnson & Johnson. Merck bought pharmacy benefits manager Medco Containment Services in 1993. New drug launches in 1995 and 1996 included Cozaar (for reducing hypertension) and Pepcid AC (antacid). Also in 1996 Merck expanded its pharmacy benefit management operations with the purchase of Systemed.

In 1997 Merck and Rh "ne-Poulenc (now part of Sanofi-Aventis) merged their animal health units to form Merial. Merck also sold its insecticide and fungicide business to Novartis that year. In 1998 DuPont bought out Merck's 50% stake in a drug-marketing joint venture formed by the two firms in 1991. In 1999 the FDA approved Merck's preservative-free hepatitis B vaccine Recombivax HB.

In 2001 Merck acquired biotech firm Rosetta Inpharmatics. The company spun off its highly successful Medco Health Solutions drug distribution subsidiary in 2003.

In 2004 Merck pulled its blockbuster pain medication Vioxx off the market after studies linked the drug to increased risks of strokes and heart attacks. (Merck settled thousands of class-action and personal-injury lawsuits related to Vioxx in 2007 for $4.85 billion.) The Vioxx safety scandal along with the pending loss of patent protection on some of its biggest sellers like Zocor (which began facing competition in 2006) sent the company into recovery mode. Merck announced restructuring plans to make the company's operations leaner and more cost-effective in 2005 under new CEO Richard (Dick) Clark a longtime Merck executive. Between 2005 and 2008 the company eliminated more than 10000 jobs and closed a handful of manufacturing plants.

From 2006 to 2009 Merck worked aggressively to expand its biotech operations through the acquisition of companies including GlycoFi (biologic drug molecules) Abmaxis (monoclonal antibodies) Sirna Therapeutics (RNA interference or RNAi) and NovaCardia (cardiology drugs) as well as the follow-on (generic) biologic assets of Insmed. New drug launches included HIV drug Isentress and diabetes therapy Janumet in 2007 and blockbuster HPV vaccine Gardasil the world's first anti-cancer vaccine which was approved by the FDA in 2006.

In 2008 Merck sold off the assets of its Rosetta Inpharmatics subsidiary to Covance (gene expression laboratory assets) and Microsoft (expression analysis software assets). It also sold another research lab to PPD and contracted out certain lab functions to the buyer. Merck launched a new product Emend for chemotherapy side-effects that year. New drug launches in 2009 included Saphris a treatment for schizophrenia and bipolar disorder and Simponi the next-generation version of top-selling drug Remicade.

Cholesterol drug Vytorin — a combination of Schering-Plough's Zetia and Merck's Zocor — began facing controversy in 2008 when study results were released questioning the drug's effectiveness compared to Merck's older medication Zocor. Controversy over Vytorin along with some other pipeline setbacks (including the FDA's rejection of a Merck/Schering-Plough combo asthma drug and Merck's Cordaptive cholesterol candidate) led both predecessors Merck and Schering-Plough to announce layoffs and restructuring measures in 2008. Each company reduced its workforce by around 10% that year with their respective US sales teams bearing the brunt of the cuts. The companies' troubles with Vytorin came to a head in 2009 when they agreed to pay about $42 million to settle class-action lawsuits filed by consumers and health plans over Vytorin's efficacy.

Later that year Merck and Schering-Plough decided to merge taking the logical step of marriage to strengthen their defenses against future troubles (especially in light of increasing competitive challenges in the market) as well as to create cost savings opportunities and expanded avenues for revenue growth. The $41 billion transaction was conducted through a reverse-merger transaction in which the legacy Schering-Plough entity acquired the legacy Merck entity and took on the Merck name.

Following the merger Merck began simplifying its global branding under the Merck and MSD names gradually phasing out the Schering-Plough moniker. The purchase expanded Merck's offerings in areas including inflammation allergy and cancer treatment as well as biotech drugs. The acquisition also greatly expanded Merck's operations in the animal health and consumer health arenas.

However to gain Schering-Plough's animal health unit Intervet (later renamed Merck Animal Health) Merck had to sell its stake in veterinary joint venture Merial to partner Sanofi-Aventis for about $4 billion later that year to avoid anti-trust issues. (Merck and Sanofi-Aventis later explored options to strike a fresh veterinary medicine joint venture by combining Merial with Intervet; however after a year of planning the two companies called off the deal in 2011 due to concerns over further anti-trust issues.)

The company experienced a sharp gain in profits in 2009 (reporting net income of $12.9 billion) due to gains on the sale of the Merial stake and on recognized equity from assets previously owned jointly with Schering-Plough.

When the Merck/Schering-Plough merger closed the existing Merck CEO Dick Clark took the helm at the new Merck. Once the dust from the merger settled however Clark retired from the CEO post at the end of 2010 while remaining as chairman. President Kenneth Frazier stepped into the CEO role.

EXECUTIVES

Chairman And Ceo, Kenneth C. (Ken) Frazier, age 65, $1,527,404 total compensation

Evp Strategic Communications Global Public Policy And Population Health And Chief Patient Officer, Julie L. Gerberding, age 65

Evp Global Services And Cfo, Robert M. Davis, age 53, $991,654 total compensation

Evp; President Merck Research Laboratories, Roger M. Perlmutter, age 67, $1,052,288 total compensation

Evp; President Global Human Health, Adam H. Schechter, age 56, $1,003,094 total compensation

Evp Human Resources, Mirian M. Graddick-Weir, age 66

Evp; President Merck Animal Health, Richard R. DeLuca, age 57

Evp And General Counsel, Michael J. Holston, age 57, $761,538 total compensation

Evp And Cio, Clark Golestani, age 53

Evp; President Merck Manufacturing, Sanat Chattopadhyay

Ceo Merck Foundation, Rasha Kelej, age 48

Vice President Human Resources And Global Diversity And Inclusion Center Excellence, Celeste Warren

Vice President, John Mccubbins

Vice President Biotechnology Development, Stephen Farrand

Vice President Manufacturing Division Strategy And Integration, Richard Hofmann

Vice President Global Compensation And Benefits, Jeff Geller

Vice President Global Engineering Services, Arthur Burson

Associate Medical Director, Lana Garafola

Vice President, Natalie Principe

Associate Vice President, Curtis Scott

Legal Pa For Uk Director And Also Pa To The Assistant Vice President For Europe And Canada, Michele Creamer

National Sales Manager (turkey), Alper Alptekin

Senior Vice President Managing Director, Pierluigi Antonelli

Executive Vice President Process Solutions, Andrew Bulpin

Senior Vice President Strategy And Business Development, Galeota James

Associate Vice President, Bernie King

Assistant Vice President Merck Consumer Care Information Technology, Fran Geatens

Vp Supply Chain, Francisco Toste

Avp Mmd Trade Compliance, Joseph Koerwer

Vice President Of Imaging, Jeffrey Evelhoch

Vice President Global Technical Operations Vaccines Biolog, Vijay Yabannavar

Senior Vice President Preclinical Development, Guy Padbury

Svp Global Regulatory Affairs And Clinical Safety, Sandra Milligan

Vice President Business Development And Licensing, Klaus Beck

Senior Vice President Tax, Jerome Mychalowych

Vice President, Pk Yegneswaran

Vice President Oncology, Ravinder Dhawan

National Account Manager, Carrie Westphal

Vice President, Carmen Svillar

Executive Vice President Chief Human Resources Officer Human Resources, Steven Mizell

Medical Director Global Vaccine Medical Affairs, Chimeremma Md

National Account Manager, Brad Vines

Associate Vice President, Gursel Aktan

Vice President Quality Assurance, Deb Driscoll

Assistant Treasurer, Joe Promo

Assistant Treasurer, Joseph Promo

Board Member, Craig Thompson

Auditors: PricewaterhouseCoopers LLP

LOCATIONS

HQ: Merck & Co Inc
2000 Galloping Hill Road, Kenilworth, NJ 07033
Phone: 908 740-4000 **Fax:** 908 735-1500
Web: www.merck.com

2017 Sales

	$ mil.	% of total
US	17,424	43
Europe Middle East & Africa	11,478	29
Asia/Pacific	4,337	11
Japan	3,122	8
Latin America	2,339	6
Other	1,422	3
Total	**40,122**	**100**

PRODUCTS/OPERATIONS

2017 Sales by Segment

	$ mil.	% of total
Pharmaceutical		
Primary care & women's health	10,260	25
Hospital & specialty	7,546	19
Vaccines	6,159	15
Oncology	4,636	12
Diversified brands	2,494	6
Other	4,295	11
Other segments	4,272	11
Other	460	1
Total	**40,122**	**100**

COMPETITORS

Abbott Labs	Johnson & Johnson
Allergan plc	Merck KGaA
Amgen	Mylan
AstraZeneca	Novartis
Bayer AG	Perrigo
Biogen	Pfizer
Boehringer Ingelheim	Roche Holding
Bristol-Myers Squibb	Sandoz International
Eli Lilly	GmbH
Gilead Sciences	Sanofi
GlaxoSmithKline	Teva
Heska	Virbac Corporation

HISTORICAL FINANCIALS

Company Type: Public

Income Statement				FYE: December 31
	REVENUE ($ mil.)	NET INCOME ($ mil.)	NET PROFIT MARGIN	EMPLOYEES
12/19	46,840	9,843	21.0%	71,000
12/18	42,294	6,220	14.7%	69,000
12/17	40,122	2,394	6.0%	69,000
12/16	39,807	3,920	9.8%	68,000
12/15	39,498	4,442	11.2%	68,000
Annual Growth	**4.4%**	**22.0%**	**—**	**1.1%**

2019 Year-End Financials

Debt ratio: 31.22%—
Return on equity: 37.42%
Cash ($ mil.): 9,676
Current ratio: 1.24
Long-term debt ($ mil.): 22,736
Dividends
Yield: 2.4%
Payout: 63.1%
Market value ($ mil.): —

	STOCK PRICE ($) FY Close	P/E High/Low	PER SHARE ($) Earnings	Dividends	Book Value
12/19	90.95	24 19	3.81	2.26	10.20
12/18	76.41	34 23	2.32	1.99	10.30
12/17	56.27	76 61	0.87	1.89	12.73
12/16	58.87	46 34	1.41	1.85	14.58
12/15	52.82	40 31	1.56	1.81	16.06
Annual Growth	**14.6%**	**— —**	**25.0%**	**5.7%**	**(10.7%)**

Mercury General Corp.

Named after the Roman god of commerce and travel Mercury General hopes to combine the two and become the ultimate auto insurance provider. The company is the parent of a group of insurers including Mercury Casualty Company that writes automobile insurance for all risk classifications in about a dozen states. Private passenger automobile insurance accounts for a majority of premiums written. However Mercury General also sells commercial vehicle insurance and a bit of homeowners mechanical property and umbrella insurance. The company is a leader in the California auto market and homeowners.

Operations

Mercury General offers automobile insurance products including comprehensive collision property damage body injury personal injury protection underinsured/uninsured motorist and other hazards. It also provides homeowners' coverage including dwelling liability personal property fire and other hazards.

Private passenger automobile insurance accounts for some 75% of the company's premiums followed by homeowners insurance (around 15%). The rest comes from commercial auto insurance and other products.

Geographic Reach

While Mercury General has ventured out of its California comfort zone the state still accounts for more than 85% of total premiums. The company is headquartered in Los Angeles California and underwrites auto insurance in about a dozen other states including Arizona California Florida Georgia Illinois Nevada New Jersey New York Oklahoma Texas and Virginia.

Sales and Marketing

Mercury General sells policies through approximately 9500 independent agents including around 1870 in California some 1320 in Florida and around 1210 in Texas. It also owns insurance agencies AIS and PolicySeek.

The company uses television radio newspaper direct mail and online campaigns to market its products. Mercury General spent $42.2 million in 2019 $40.9 million in 2018 and $37.4 million in 2017 on advertising.

Financial Performance

The company's revenue increased by 18% to $4.0 billion compared to $3.4 billion in the prior year. Net premiums earned and net premiums written in 2019 increased by 7% each from 2018. The increase in net premiums earned and net premiums written was primarily due to higher average premiums per policy arising from rate increases in the California private passenger automobile and homeowners lines of insurance business and growth in the number of homeowners policies written in California.

The company's net income for the year ended December 31 2019 was $320.1 million compared to net loss of $5.7 million for the same period in 2018. Included in net income loss was $141.3 million of pre-tax net investment income that was generated during 2019 on a portfolio of $4.3 billion at fair value at December 31 2019 compared to $135.8 million of pre-tax net investment income that was generated during 2018 on a portfolio of $3.8 billion at fair value at December 31 2018.

The company ended 2019 with $294.4 million in cash $19.9 million less than it had at the end of 2018. Operating activities provided $519.7 million while investing activities used $401.2 million and financing activities used another $138.4 million.

Strategy

The company's investment strategy emphasizes safety of principal and consistent income generation within a total return framework. The investment strategy has historically focused on maximizing after-tax yield with a primary emphasis on maintaining a well-diversified investment grade fixed income portfolio to support the underlying liabilities and achieve a return on capital and profitable growth. The company believes that investment yield is maximized by selecting assets that perform favorably on a long-term basis and by disposing of certain assets to enhance after-tax yield and minimize the potential effect of downgrades and defaults. The company believes that this strategy maintains the optimal investment performance necessary to sustain investment income over time. The company's portfolio management approach utilizes a market risk and asset allocation strategy as the primary basis for the allocation of interest sensitive liquid and credit assets as well as for monitoring credit exposure and diversification requirements. Within the ranges set by the asset allocation strategy tactical investment decisions are made in consideration of prevailing market conditions.

Company Background

Chairman George Joseph founded Mercury General in Los Angeles in 1962. Joseph formed a subsidiary in 1973 to undertake the underwriting of preferred-risk policies. In 1985 Mercury converted to public ownership in an initial public offering on the NASDAQ exchange. Five years later the company took its first steps outside its home state of California opening operations in Georgia and Illinois.

EXECUTIVES

Vp Underwriting, Kenneth G. Kitzmiller, age 73
President And Ceo, Gabriel Tirador, age 55, $948,931 total compensation
Svp And Cfo, Theodore R. Stalick, age 56, $589,445 total compensation
Vp And Chief Investment Officer, Christopher Graves, age 54, $381,679 total compensation
Vp And Chief Actuary, Charles Toney, age 58
Svp And Cio, Allan Lubitz, age 62, $449,470 total compensation
Vp And Chief Product Officer, Robert Houlihan, age 63, $404,493 total compensation
Vp Marketing, Brandt N. Minnich, age 53
Vice President Corporate Controller, David Yeager
Vp And Chief Human Capital Officer, Heidi Sullivan
Vice President Property Claims, Chris Orourke
Chairman, George Joseph, age 98
Auditors: KPMG LLP

LOCATIONS

HQ: Mercury General Corp.
4484 Wilshire Boulevard, Los Angeles, CA 90010
Phone: 323 937-1060
Web: www.mercuryinsurance.com

PRODUCTS/OPERATIONS

2018 Sales

	$ mil.	% of total
Net premiums earned	3,368	96
Net investment income	135	4
Other	9	-
Net realized investment losses	(133.5)	-
Total	**3,380**	**100**

Selected Products

Auto
  Commercial auto
  Mechanical breakdown (extended warranty coverage)
  Niche commercial
  Personal auto
Condo
  Contents coverage
  Guest medical protection and liability
  Personal liability protection
  Personal property
Homeowners
  Apartments
  Condominiums
  Single-family homes
Personal umbrella
Renter
  Liability protection
  Personal property

Selected Operating Brands and Divisions

AIS Management
American Mercury Insurance
American Mercury Lloyds Insurance
American Mercury MGA
Auto Insurance Specialists
California Automobile Insurance
California General Underwriters Insurance
Mercury Casualty
Mercury County Mutual Insurance
Mercury Group
Mercury Indemnity
Mercury Insurance
Mercury National Insurance
Mercury Select Management
PoliSeek AIS Insurance Solutions

COMPETITORS

21st Century Insurance	GEICO
Allstate	State Farm
Auto Club of Southern California	USAA
CSAA Inter-Insurance Bureau	

HISTORICAL FINANCIALS

Company Type: Public

Income Statement

FYE: December 31

	ASSETS ($ mil.)	NET INCOME ($ mil.)	INCOME AS % OF ASSETS	EMPLOYEES
12/19	5,889	320	5.4%	4,500
12/18	5,433	(5)	—	4,400
12/17	5,101	144	2.8%	4,300
12/16	4,788	73	1.5%	4,200
12/15	4,628	74	1.6%	4,300
Annual Growth	**6.2%**	**44.0%**	**—**	**1.1%**

2019 Year-End Financials

Debt ratio: 6.32%
Return on equity: 18.73%
Cash ($ mil.): 294
Current ratio: —
Long-term debt ($ mil.): —
No. of shares (mil.): 55
Dividends
  Yield: 5.1%
  Payout: 67.5%
Market value ($ mil.): 2,698

	STOCK PRICE ($) FY Close	P/E High/Low		PER SHARE ($) Earnings	Dividends	Book Value
12/19	48.73	11	8	5.78	2.51	32.51
12/18	51.71	—	—	(0.10)	2.50	29.23
12/17	53.44	24	20	2.62	2.49	31.83
12/16	60.21	46	33	1.32	2.48	31.70
12/15	46.57	45	34	1.35	2.47	33.01
Annual Growth	**1.1%**			**43.8%**	**0.4%**	**(0.4%)**

Meridian Bancorp Inc

Meridian Bancorp is the holding company of East Boston Savings Bank which provides standard deposit and lending services to individuals and businesses in the greater Boston area. The bank writes single-family commercial and multi-family mortgages as well as construction and business loans and consumer loans. East Boston Savings operates about 30 branches in eastern Massachusetts. Mutual holding company Meridian Financial Services owns 59% of Meridian Bancorp.

EXECUTIVES

Cfo And Treasurer, Mark L. Abbate, age 65
Svp Consumer And Business Banking, Keith D. Armstrong
Chairman President And Ceo Meridian Interstate Bancorp And East Boston Savings Bank, Richard J. Gavegnano, age 72, $311,400 total compensation
Evp Corporate Banking, Frank Romano
Evp Lending, John Migliozzi
Evp And Coo, John A. Carroll
Svp Electronic Banking, Mary Hagen
Svp Retail Banking, James Morgan
Svp Residential Lending, Joseph Nash
Vice President, Michael Raftery
Auditors: Wolf & Company, P.C.

LOCATIONS

HQ: Meridian Bancorp Inc
67 Prospect Street, Peabody, MA 01960
Phone: 617 567-1500

Selected Locations

Allpoint Locator
Allston
Belmont
Cambridge
Danvers
Dorchester
East Boston
Everett
Jamaica Plain
Lynn
Medford
Melrose
Peabody
Revere
Saugus
Somerville
South Boston
South End
Wakefield
West Roxbury
Winthrop

PRODUCTS/OPERATIONS

2015 Sales

	$ mil.	% of total
Interest & dividend income		
Interest & fees on loans	118	87
Interest on debt securities	1	1
Dividends on equity securities	1	1
Others	1	1
Non-interest income		
Customer service fees	8	6
Gain on sales of securities net	2	2
Income from bank-owned life insurance	1	1
Loan fees	1	1
Mortgage banking gains & other income	0	-
Total	**136**	**100**

Selected Products & Services

Personal
  Deposit Rates
  Investments
  Personal Checking
  Personal Lending
  Personal Online Banking
  Retirement Services
  Savings & CDs
Business
  Business Checking
  Business Lending
  Business Online Banking
  Business Retirement Services
  Business Savings
  Deposit Rates
  Institutional Banking
  Merchant Services
Commercial
  Cash Management
  Commercial Lending
  Corporate Banking
  Deposit Rates

COMPETITORS

Bank of America	Middlesex Savings
Cambridge Financial	Peoples Federal
Citizens Financial Group	Bancshares Inc.
	Sovereign Bank
Eastern Bank	TD Bank USA

HISTORICAL FINANCIALS

Company Type: Public

Income Statement

FYE: December 31

	ASSETS ($ mil.)	NET INCOME ($ mil.)	INCOME AS % OF ASSETS	EMPLOYEES
12/19	6,343	67	1.1%	546
12/18	6,178	55	0.9%	549
12/17	5,299	42	0.8%	538
12/16	4,436	34	0.8%	500
12/15	3,524	24	0.7%	488
Annual Growth	**15.8%**	**28.5%**	**—**	**2.8%**

2019 Year-End Financials

Debt ratio: 10.03%
Return on equity: 9.56%
Cash ($ mil.): 406
Current ratio: —
Long-term debt ($ mil.): —
No. of shares (mil.): 53
Dividends
  Yield: 1.4%
  Payout: 24.1%
Market value ($ mil.): 1,072

	STOCK PRICE ($) FY Close	P/E High/Low	PER SHARE ($) Earnings	Dividends	Book Value
12/19	20.09	16 11	1.30	0.29	13.61
12/18	14.32	20 13	1.06	0.22	12.60
12/17	20.60	25 19	0.82	0.17	11.96
12/16	18.90	29 19	0.65	0.12	11.33
12/15	14.10	31 24	0.46	0.06	10.72
Annual Growth	9.3%	—	29.7%	48.3%	6.2%

Meta Financial Group Inc

Delivering financial products and services to Iowa and South Dakota is the calling of Meta Financial Group. The group's biggest component is MetaBank a 10-branch operation that offers standard banking solutions such as deposit accounts CDs home mortgages and student loans. Other subsidiaries provide prepaid card services insurance and a variety of tax related solutions. It holds a loan portfolio that exceeds $1 billion and deposits that surpass $3 billion.

Operations

Meta Financial Group operates two customer-facing business segments Banking and Payments and a supporting segment that includes corporate services and other sources of revenue. The Banking segment generates the majority of interest income and a small amount of non-interest income. The Payments unit is the opposite where non-interest income accounts for 90% of its overall revenue and interest income is less than 10% of its business.

The Banking unit doing business as MetaBank operates 10 branches in four key geographic markets: Central Iowa Storm Lake Iowa Brookings South Dakota and Sioux Falls South Dakota. It offers standard deposit products and services including checking and savings accounts. Its lending and investment activities are weighted towards real estate and real estate-related assets; commercial and multifamily residential mortgages comprise more than half of the bank's loan portfolio. It also writes single-family residential mortgages and business loans.

Meta Financial's bread and butter however is the bank's Meta Payment Systems (MPS) division which provides prepaid cards consumer credit and ATM sponsorship services nationwide under operating names of MPS Refund Advantage EPS Financial and SCS. The segment has grown primarily through acquisitions.

Geographic Reach

The MetaBank subsidiary of Sioux Falls SD-based Meta Financial Group operates mainly in Iowa and South Dakota. Its Payment segment includes subsidiaries that run business out of Dallas TX Newport Beach CA Louisville KY Easton PA and Hurst TX.

Financial Performance

Non-interest income from the Payments business grew more than 70% in the year to $166 million. Interest income from the Bank segment rose 37% to $52 million. Total revenue for 2017 was $265 million. The stellar growth is the result of acquisitions and organic growth – the Bank unit acquired $134 million of private student loans in late 2016 and a further $73 million portfolio in late 2017. The Payment business grew its tax refund business 13-fold underwriting and originating $1.3 billion of refund advance loans for the 2017 tax season.

Net income in 2017 rose 33% to $45 million thanks to the significant upswing in Payments revenue including big growth in its tax business along with improvements in card fee income.

Strategy

Meta Financial Group is looking to boost is non-interest income business endeavors in the Payments division. It feels constrained in its banking business by the need to raise more capital before it can lend out more money from which it would generate interest income. Without the ability to raise more capital (or to raise it at an advantageous cost) the Group believes its efforts are better directed at growth that is not hindered by insufficient capital.

EXECUTIVES

Chairman And Ceo Meta Financial Group And Metabank, J. Tyler Haahr, age 57, $550,000 total compensation
Evp Sales And Operations Metabank And Director Meta Financial Group (mfg) And Metabank, Troy Moore, age 52, $252,350 total compensation
Evp Secretary Treasurer And Cfo, David W. Leedom, age 66, $215,000 total compensation
President Meta Financial Group Inc. (mfg) And Metabank And Division President Meta Payment System, Bradley C. (Brad) Hanson, age 56, $550,000 total compensation
Evp Meta Payment Systems, Scott Galit, age 50, $235,000 total compensation
Evp And Cfo Meta Financial Group (mfg) And Metabank, Glen W. Herrick, age 57, $255,000 total compensation
Vice Chairman Meta Financial Group (mfg) And Metabank, Frederick V. (Fred) Moore, age 64
Auditors: Crowe LLP

LOCATIONS

HQ: Meta Financial Group Inc
5501 South Broadband Lane, Sioux Falls, SD 57108
Phone: 605 782-1767
Web: www.metabank.com

COMPETITORS

Blackhawk Network	Great Western Bancorp
BofI	Green Dot
Citi Prepaid Services	HF Financial
First National of Nebraska	West Bancorporation

HISTORICAL FINANCIALS

Company Type: Public

Income Statement

FYE: September 30

	ASSETS ($ mil.)	NET INCOME ($ mil.)	INCOME AS % OF ASSETS	EMPLOYEES
09/20	6,092	104	1.7%	1,015
09/19	6,182	97	1.6%	1,186
09/18	5,835	51	0.9%	1,219
09/17	5,228	44	0.9%	827
09/16	4,006	33	0.8%	672
Annual Growth	11.0%	33.2%	—	10.9%

2020 Year-End Financials

Debt ratio: 1.61%	No. of shares (mil.): 34
Return on equity: 12.41%	Dividends
Cash ($ mil.): 427	Yield: 1.0%
Current ratio: —	Payout: 6.8%
Long-term debt ($ mil.): —	Market value ($ mil.): 660

	STOCK PRICE ($) FY Close	P/E High/Low	PER SHARE ($) Earnings	Dividends	Book Value
09/20	19.22	14 5	2.94	0.20	24.55
09/19	32.61	33 7	2.49	0.20	22.22
09/18	82.65	70 46	1.67	0.18	19.00
09/17	78.40	66 39	1.61	0.17	15.05
09/16	60.61	47 28	1.31	0.17	13.10
Annual Growth	(25.0%)	—	22.5%	3.6%	17.0%

MetLife Inc

MetLife is one of the largest institutional investors in the United States. Its underwriting subsidiaries offer life insurance policies accident and health coverage credit insurance and property/casualty coverage. It also provides annuities employee benefits and asset management services. MetLife primarily sells its offerings to individuals and small business owners by independent agents and property and casualty specialists through a direct marketing channel. The company uses a range of proprietary and third-parties to distribute its offerings. More than 50% of its revenue comes from the US.

Operations

MetLife is organized into five primary segments: US; Asia; MetLife Holdings; Latin America; and Europe the Middle East and Africa (EMEA). Certain results are also reported in the operations of the Corporate & Other segment. Insurance premiums account for about 60% of revenue followed by investment income (more than 25%) and Universal life & investment-type product policy fees (nearly 10%).

The US segment accounting for more than 50% of annual revenue provides life (term variable and universal) disability dental and accident and health coverage to employee groups. Its retirement and income solutions include institutional income annuities pension risk transfers tort settlements capital markets investment products and stable value investment options for institutional customers. It also sells property/casualty policies (auto and homeowners) to individuals and businesses.

The Asia segment (more than 15% of sales) provides life accident and health retirement and savings products to individuals and corporations in about 10 Asian countries.

MetLife Holdings (some 15% of revenue) comprises businesses no longer actively promoted in the US including Variable Universal and Term Life Insurance Whole Life Insurance Variable Annuities Fixed and Indexed-Linked Annuities and Long-term Care.

The Latin America segment (more than 5% of revenue) offers businesses and individuals a variety of life accident and health retirement and savings and credit insurance policies.

The EMEA segment (about 5% of sales) offers life accident supplemental health and credit insurance plus retirement products to groups businesses and individuals in many countries across EMEA.

Geographic Reach

Headquartered in New York City MetLife operates in the Americas Asia Japan and the EMEA region (Europe the Middle East and Africa). Its largest market is the US accounting for more than 50% of sales.

The company does business in about 10 countries in Asia with its largest operations in Japan. It also does business in Australia Bangladesh Hong Kong China Korea and Malaysia. It has an innovation center in Singapore and a data analytics center in Malaysia.

Its Latin America segment includes the key markets of Mexico and Chile as well as Argentina Brazil and Colombia.

MetLife is active in many countries across EMEA. The segment's biggest operations are in the Gulf region Poland and Turkey.

Sales and Marketing

MetLife's policies and other products are sold to employer groups corporations institutions and individuals.

In the US the company distributes group benefits and retirement products through direct sales forces while the property/casualty policies are sold directly to employees at their employer's worksite. In Asia it distributes through a range of proprietary and third-party distribution channels including independent agents bancassurance and direct marketing. In Latin America it uses exclusive and captive agents telesales and brokers; and in the EMEA region it uses captive and independent agencies banks and direct sales.

Financial Performance

Except in fiscal 2016 when MetLife's total revenue dipped slightly growth for the last five years have been generally steady and the net income followed the same exact trend.

In 2019 revenue increased 2% to $69.6 billion as improved sales in U.S. Group Benefits business as well as in Latin America and EMEA more than offset lower sales in Japan.

Net income rose 15% to $5.9 billion in 2019 primarily driven by a favorable change in net investment gains and an increase in adjusted earnings which includes benefits from certain tax settlements partially offset by an unfavorable change in net derivative gains.

The company ended 2019 with $16.6 billion in cash up by $777 million from 2018. Operating activities contributed $13.8 billion while investing activities used $17.6 billion (mostly purchases of matured securities). Financing activities provided $4.6 billion to the coffers.

Strategy

MetLife introduced its Next Horizon Strategy which is founded on three pillars: Focus – by generating strong free cash flow by deploying capital and resources to the highest value opportunities; Simplify – by simplifying its business to deliver operational efficiency and an outstanding customer experience and; Differentiate – by driving competitive advantage through its brand scale talent and innovation. The pillars of Next Horizon Strategy are the basis of MetLife's ability to create and deliver optimal shareholder value. The company continues to shift its business mix to protection-oriented and fee-based businesses. As a result it expects results to be less sensitive to interest rates. Assuming interest rates follow the observable forward yield curves as of the year ended December 31 2019 it expects the ratio of free cash flow to adjusted earnings over the two-year period of 2020 and 2021 to be 65% to 75% assuming a 10-year U.S. Treasury rate between 1.5% and 4.5%.

In addition MetLife applies disciplined asset/liability management (ALM) strategies including the use of derivatives and may take management actions such as: Lowering interest crediting rates or adjusting the dividend scale on products; Limiting or closing certain products to new sales to manage exposures; and Shifting sales focus to less interest rate sensitive products. The company expects adjusted earnings will continue to increase over the near term despite the sustained low U.S. interest rate environment.

Mergers and Acquisitions

In late 2019 MetLife Inc. and US-based PetFirst Healthcare LLC a fast-growing pet health insurance administrator have entered into a definitive agreement under which MetLife will acquire PetFirst. The acquisition will leverage MetLife's position as a market leader in U.S. group benefits by enabling the company to offer a new benefit that is growing in popularity. Terms of the transaction were not disclosed.

Also in late 2019 MetLife agreed to acquire Florida-based Willing a digital estate planning company that helps families create legal documents such as wills and trusts. The purchase enhances the digital offerings of its group benefits unit. Terms of the transaction were not disclosed.

Company Background

Metropolitan Life Insurance was established as a stock company in 1868. It became a mutual company (owned by its policyholders) in 1915. Starting off serving mutual assistance societies for German immigrants the company began offering group policies in 1917 and auto and homeowners insurance in 1974. The company entered banking in 2001 but exited the operations in the early 2010s to avoid increased regulatory scrutiny following the financial crisis.

US regulators had designated MetLife one of four non-bank systemically important financial institutions (meaning it would pose a risk to the economy if it should collapse) but MetLife fought the designation winning its case in a federal court in 2016. A federal government appeal of the ruling was dropped in 2018.

The company sold its US retail captive agency distribution channel (MetLife Premier Client Group) and its broker dealer unit (MetLife Securities) in mid-2016 to MassMutual.

MetLife acquired Logan Circle Partners from Fortress Investment Group for some $250 million in 2017 to expand its asset management business for institutional investors.

HISTORY

New York merchant Simeon Draper tried to form National Union Life and Limb Insurance to cover Union soldiers in the Civil War but investors were scared away by heavy casualties. After several reorganizations and name changes the enterprise emerged in 1868 as Metropolitan Life Insurance (MetLife) a stock company.

Sustained at first by business from mutual assistance societies for German immigrants MetLife went into industrial insurance with workers' burial policies. The firm was known for its aggressive sales methods. Agents combed working-class neighborhoods collecting small premiums. If a worker missed one payment the company could cancel the policy and keep all premiums paid a practice outlawed in 1900.

MetLife became a mutual company (owned by its policyholders) in 1915 and began offering group insurance two years later.

After a period of conservative management under the Eckers family from 1929 to 1963 MetLife began to change dropping industrial insurance in 1964. It started offering auto and homeowners insurance in 1974.

To diversify the company bought State Street Research & Management (1983) Century 21 Real Estate (1985 sold 1995) London-based Albany Life Assurance (1985) and Allstate's group life and health business (1988). In 1987 it took over the annuities segment of the failed Baldwin United Co. and expanded into Spain and Taiwan in 1988. During the early 1990s MetLife reemphasized insurance adding such new products as long-term-care insurance.

It entered the banking business in 2001 but exited the bulk of its banking operations in 2013 to avoid the increased scrutiny of banks under Dodd-Frank financial regulations following the 2008 recession. It also stopped writing new residential mortgages and reverse mortgages in 2012 and sold its mortgage servicing unit to JPMorgan Chase. The company surrendered its status as a bank holding company following the divestitures.

Following the financial crisis US regulators designated MetLife one of four non-bank systemically important financial institutions (meaning it would pose a risk to the economy if it should collapse) but MetLife fought the designation winning its case in a federal court in 2016. (A federal government appeal of the ruling was dropped in 2018.)

In mid-2016 MassMutual bought MetLife's US retail captive agency distribution channel MetLife Premier Client Group and broker dealer MetLife Securities.

In 2017 MetLife spun off most of its US retail operations into a new company named Brighthouse Financial in an IPO.

EXECUTIVES

Evp And Global Chief Marketing Officer, Esther Lee

Chairman President And Ceo, Steven A. (Steve) Kandarian, age 68, $1,525,000 total compensation

Evp And Cfo, John C. R. Hele, age 62, $781,250 total compensation

Evp Global Employee Benefits, Maria R. Morris, age 57, $525,000 total compensation

Evp And General Counsel, Ricardo A. Anzaldua

Evp Chief Investment Officer And Interim President Metlife Asia, Steven J. Goulart, age 61, $725,000 total compensation

President Us, Michel Khalaf, $476,313 total compensation

Evp Global Technology And Operations And Metlife Holdings, Martin J. (Marty) Lippert, $756,250 total compensation

Managing Director Institutional Client Group, Thomas Metzler

Ceo Metlife Hong Kong, Lee Wood

Vice President Learning And Development, John Wiltshire

Vp Itg Vendor Mgmt Sourcing, Elizabeth Langone

Svp And Chief Administrative Officer Global Technology And Operations, Mona Moazzaz

Regional Vice President Northeast Region, Joe Heaney

Vice President Human Resources, Doris Jackson

Vice President Information Technology, Annette Fugina

Vice President Risk Management, Richard Barquist

Senior Vice President Marketing Planning, James Valentino

Vice President Information Technology, Marcella Kelly

Vice President Global Information Security Officer, Jesus L Montano

Vice President Of Technology, Linus Makhulo

Vice President, Andrew Aoyama

Vice President And Actuary, Enid Reichert

Vp, Curt Breckon

Vice President, David Mcmichael

Sec Reporting Assistant Vice President, Matt Gominiak

Assistant Vice President, Gary Glacken

Vice President Information Technology, Neil Melleky

Vice President Information Technology, Alvin Sheinheit

Vice President, Peter Pastre

Vice President Information Technology, Tom Kelly

Vice President And Chief Privacy Officer, Joseph Trovato

Distribution Vp, Pam Blalock

Senior Vice President, Liz Forget
Vice President Information Technology, Roderick Pasqualicchio
Assistant Vice President, Robert Lynch
Vice President Actuary, Marian Zeldin
Vice President Group Underwriting, Jim Pabst
Regional Sales Vice President, Scott Safranek
Vice President, Guy Lawrence
Vice President, Randy Stram
Assistant Vice President And Actuary, Jonathan Trend
Vice President, Roberta Rafaloff
Assistant Vice President, John Gilmore
Vice President, Rose Wolf
Evp Global Corporate Services Global Technology And Operations, Joe Sprouls
Senior Vice President And Global Chief Information Security Officer, Zulfi Ahmed
Vice President Information Technology, Dinah Moore
Vice President Of Application Development, Jack Rooney
Vice President Human Resources, Lynne Distasio
Assistant Vice President, Gladys Rosetta
Svp Global Head Of Alm, Bryan Boudreau
Regional Vice President, Brenda Perkins
Vice President Life And Income Funding Solutions, Tim Brown
Vice President, Harry Xiao
Assistant Vice President, Andy Vigar
Assistant Vice President, Robert Bean
Regional Sales Vice President Se Team Lead, Martin Topor
Assistant Vice President Recognition Event Management, Danielle Pratt
Assistant Vice President, Crystal Mcelroy
Vice President Information Technology Infrastructu, Gail Weimer
Regional Sales Vice President, Michael Casimiro
Assistant Vice President, Patricia Wersching
Vice President, Bob Linzey
Vice President Global Operations, Lisa Pang
Vice President Information Technology International Asia Pacific Region, Nancy Perez-Vasquez
Vice President Retirement Plans, Bill Slater
Vice President Corporate Information Technology Security D, Steve Vnuck
Svp Global Talent Processes And Organizational Effectiveness, Rachel Lee
Vice President Of Information Technology, Ron Gillmore
Vice President Disability Claims Coordinator, Sue Avery
Assistant Vice President Shared Service, Shari A Corrigan
Assistant Vice President, Betty Dubuisson
Vice President, Don Anderson Don Anderson
Executive Vice President, Todd Katz
Regional Sales Vice President, Shaun Seales
Vice President, Ignazio Greco
Vice President Global Internal Audit, Carlos Mendez
Vice President Operations Governance Strategy, Pamela Hallagan
Assistant Vice President, Natty Estok
Vice President Actuary, Laura Vazquez
Regional Sales Vice President, Ed Wustefeld
Assistant Vice President, Amie Donahue
Assistant Vice President, Jeremy Davies
Assistant Vice President Enterprise Strategy Group, Kevin Chean
Vice President, Nancy Davenport
Vice President, Robert Klahre
Vice President Capital Strategy Planning, Kevin Mackay
Vice President And Actuary Life Products, Barbara Stroz
Assistant Vice President, Basha Hoffman
Regional Sales Vice President, Stacey Waite

Vice President, Michael Evenzwig
Vice President Finance Principal, John Wiede
Svp And Head Mergers And Acquisitions, Adam Hodes
Senior Vice President Executive And Global Compensation, Kathryn Kessel
Vice President Of Retail Marketing, Matthew Quale
Regional Sales Vice President, Derrik Bullen
Senior Vice President Investments And Br, Anthony Colyandro
Vp Head Of Health And Wellness, Leena Johns
Regional Sales Vice President, Tony Nguyen
Vice President, Emilia Kyff
Regional Sales Vice President, Chris Bunting
Vice President, George Bell
Assistant Vice President And Actuary Financial Research, William Chirolas
Regional Sales Vice President, Michelle Perez
Regional Sales Vice President, Nancy Power
Vice President Investments Controller, David Rooney
Senior Vice President And Associate General Counsel, Lawrence Wolff
Second Vice President, Mark Remington
Svp And Head Investor Relations, John Hall
Vice President, Chris Stern
Assistant Vice President, John Zelinske
Vice President, Lise Hasegawa
Assistant Vice President, Share Winn
Avp Global Talent Acquisition, Erica Langdon
Senior Vice President, Joseph Reali
Vice President Human Resources, Stuart Cook
Vice President, Dale King
Vice President Operations, John Abela
Assistant Vice President Individual Disability Underwriting, Rod Boggs
Regional Sales Vice President, Jan Primmer
Assistant Vice President Information Technology, Paul Mattern
Senior Vice President, Debra Capolarello
Svp Global Shared Services India, Kush Kamra
Avp Global Product, Mira Shastry
Avp Global Strategy, Suresh Gunupure
Vice President, Arthur Bruhmuller
Assistant Vice President, Jai Maxwell
Assisttant Vice President Growth Strategies, Tina Beckwith
Vice President Information Technology, Leonard Kasendorf
Vice President, Marc Cohn
Vice President Sales And Marketing, Suzanne Andrews
Vice President Information Technology Services, Bob Levin
Vice President Global Technology, Ed Evans
Vice President, Melissa Grady
Associate Vice President Enterprise Security, Satin Montano
Vice President, Dennis Gates
Vice President Executive Learning And Development, Mara Jane
Vice President And Associate General Counsel, Margaret Allen
Assistant Vice President Of Enterprise Security, Laz Montano
Vice President Director Fund Administration, Alan Otis
Regional Vice President Agency Asia Pacific, Stephen Zhang
Assistant Vice President And Actuary Actuarial, Simone Chen
Senior Vice President Risk Management, Henry Essert
Assistant Vice President Field Services, Patty Derner
Evp And Chief Risk Officer, Marlene Debel
Vice President, Ingrid Tolentino
Vice President Operations, Robert Scotte
Assistant Application Development Vice President, Kimberly Donica

Assistant Vice President, Rosemary Castillo
Vice President, Brian Bruneau
Auditors: Deloitte & Touche LLP

LOCATIONS

HQ: MetLife Inc
200 Park Avenue, New York, NY 10166-0188
Phone: 212 578-9500
Web: www.metlife.com

2017 Sales by Segment

	$ mil.	% of total
US	31,810	50
Asia	11,875	19
MetLife Holding	11,005	17
Latin America	5,118	8
EMEA	3,729	6
Adjustments	(1229)	-
Total	**62,308**	**100**

PRODUCTS/OPERATIONS

2017 Sales

	$ mil.	% of total
Premiums	38,992	62
Net investment income	17,363	27
Universal life & investment-type product policy fees	5,510	9
Other	1,341	2
Adjustments	898	-
Total	**62,308**	**100**

Selected Subsidiaries and Affiliates

American Life Insurance Co. (ALICO)
General American Life Insurance Company
Hyatt Legal Plans Inc. (prepaid legal plans)
MetLife Funding Inc.
MetLife Insurance Company USA
MetLife Investors Group Inc. (distribution)
Metropolitan Property and Casualty Insurance Company
New England Life Insurance Company

COMPETITORS

AEGON USA	Liberty Mutual
AIG	MassMutual
AXA	Meiji Yasuda Life
Aetna	Mutual of Omaha
Allianz	Nationwide
Allstate	New York Life
American General	Nippon Life Insurance
Aon	Northwestern Mutual
COUNTRY Financial	Pacific Mutual
Genworth Financial	Prudential
Guardian Life	TIAA
ING	The Hartford
John Hancock Financial Services	

HISTORICAL FINANCIALS

Company Type: Public

Income Statement

FYE: December 31

	ASSETS ($ mil.)	NET INCOME ($ mil.)	INCOME AS % OF ASSETS	EMPLOYEES
12/19	740,463	5,899	0.8%	49,000
12/18	687,538	5,123	0.7%	48,000
12/17	719,892	4,010	0.6%	49,000
12/16	898,764	800	0.1%	58,000
12/15	877,933	5,310	0.6%	69,000
Annual Growth	(4.2%)	2.7%	—	(8.2%)

2019 Year-End Financials

Debt ratio: 2.38%	No. of shares (mil.): 915
Return on equity: 9.92%	Dividends
Cash ($ mil.): 16,598	Yield: 3.4%
Current ratio: —	Payout: 23.2%
Long-term debt ($ mil.): —	Market value ($ mil.): 46,655

	STOCK PRICE ($) FY Close	P/E High/Low		PER SHARE ($) Earnings	Dividends	Book Value
12/19	50.97	8	7	6.06	1.74	72.26
12/18	41.06	11	8	4.91	1.66	55.02
12/17	50.56	15	13	3.62	1.60	56.23
12/16	53.89	91	56	0.63	1.58	61.44
12/15	48.21	13	10	4.57	1.48	61.95
Annual Growth	1.4%	—	—	7.3%	4.2%	3.9%

Metropolitan Bank Holding Corp

Auditors: Crowe LLP

LOCATIONS

HQ: Metropolitan Bank Holding Corp
99 Park Avenue, New York, NY 10016
Phone: 212 659-0600
Web: www.mcbankny.com

HISTORICAL FINANCIALS
Company Type: Public

Income Statement   FYE: December 31

	ASSETS ($ mil.)	NET INCOME ($ mil.)	INCOME AS % OF ASSETS	EMPLOYEES
12/19	3,357	30	0.9%	167
12/18	2,182	25	1.2%	153
12/17	1,759	12	0.7%	129
12/16	1,220	5	0.4%	118
12/15	964	4	0.4%	
Annual Growth	36.6%	63.0%	—	—

2019 Year-End Financials

Debt ratio: 2.01%
Return on equity: 10.69%
Cash ($ mil.): 391
Current ratio: —
Long-term debt ($ mil.): —

No. of shares (mil.): 8
Dividends
  Yield: —
  Payout: —
Market value ($ mil.): 401

	STOCK PRICE ($) FY Close	P/E High/Low		PER SHARE ($) Earnings	Dividends	Book Value
12/19	48.23	13	8	3.56	0.00	35.98
12/18	30.85	18	10	3.06	0.00	32.19
12/17	42.10	21	15	2.34	0.00	28.90
Annual Growth	3.5%	—	—	11.1%	—	5.6%

METROPOLITAN TRANSPORTATION AUTHORITY

The largest public transportation system in the US New York City's Metropolitan Transportation Authority (MTA) provides about 2.6 billion passenger trips and sees about 380 million vehicles travel its system annually. The MTA's largest agency the New York City Transit Authority operates about 8700 rail and subway cars that provide service across New York's five boroughs; it also runs a fleet of some 5900 buses. Other MTA units offer bus and rail service to Connecticut and Long Island and operate the Triborough system of toll bridges and tunnels.

Strategy

The government-owned MTA a public-benefit corporation chartered by the New York Legislature in 1965 operates with an annual budget of $12.6 billion. The system has been working to become more self-sufficient in recent years but it has battled persistent operating losses brought on by among other causes high operating costs and the struggling US economy. In an attempt to reduce its expenses the company in 2010 cut payroll by 20% at its headquarters and 15% at other agencies. The MTA has also bolstered its revenue through increased fares and tolls and freed up capital by restructuring its debt at lower interest rates.

While it is making cuts in some areas the MTA is investing in capital improvements to its system including extending the Long Island Rail Road to Grand Central Station and creating a direct link between John F. Kennedy Airport and downtown Manhattan. Other key projects have included the construction of the Second Avenue Subway and renovations at the Fulton Street Transit Center. The MTA also is looking at installing wireless Internet access on its Metro-North and Long Island rail lines' trains.

EXECUTIVES

Cfo, Robert E. (Bob) Foran
Executive Officer Corporate Communications Marketing And Branding, John McKay
Director Security, Raymond Diaz
Coo, Phil Eng
Interim Executive Director, Veronique Hakim
President Mta Bridges And Tunnels, Cedrick Fulton
Chairman, Joseph J. Lhota
Auditors: DELOITTE & TOUCHE LLP NEW YOR

LOCATIONS

HQ: METROPOLITAN TRANSPORTATION AUTHORITY
2 BROADWAY BSMT B, NEW YORK, NY 100043354
Phone: 212 878-7000
Web: WWW.MTA.INFO

PRODUCTS/OPERATIONS

Selected Operations

Bus
  Long Island Bus
  MTA Bus Company
  New York City Transit
Commuter Rail
  Long Island Rail Road
  Metro-North Railroad
  Staten Island Railway

HISTORICAL FINANCIALS
Company Type: Private

Income Statement   FYE: December 31

	REVENUE ($ mil.)	NET INCOME ($ mil.)	NET PROFIT MARGIN	EMPLOYEES
12/19	9,043	502	5.6%	67,457
12/18	8,736	(145)	—	—
12/17	8	(0)	—	—
12/16	8,527	(271)	—	—
Annual Growth	2.0%	—	—	—

MGIC Investment Corp. (WI)

Since a pinkie-promise isn't good enough for most lenders there's MGIC Investment's mortgage insurance to protect lenders from home buyers who don't hold up their end of the bargain. MGIC owns Mortgage Guaranty Insurance Corporation (MGIC) the largest provider of private mortgage insurance in the US Puerto Rico and Guam. Such coverage allows otherwise-qualified buyers who aren't able to scrape up the standard about 20% down payment to get mortgages. MGIC writes primary insurance on individual loans; its customers include banks mortgage brokers credit unions and other residential mortgage lenders. MGIC had about $58 million primary insurance in force covering about 14 million mortgages.

Operations

Historically MGIC has provided two primary types of private mortgage insurance — primary and pool. Primary insurance default protection on individual mortgages and covers unpaid loan principal related delinquent interest and expenses and foreclosure or sale approved by MGIC. Pool insurance is typically an additional credit enhancement for secondary market mortgage transactions. It generally covers the loss on a defaulted loan exceeding the claim payment under the primary coverage (if required) or the total loss on a defaulted loan which did not require primary coverage. Although the company hasn't written any new pool risk it may do so in the future as it weighs the market.

Other offerings include contract underwriting services for lenders and mortgage lead generation for the finance industry.

The company earned about 85% of net premiums at the end of fiscal year 2019.

Geographic Reach

MGIC operates in every US state the District of Columbia Puerto Rico and Guam. Its corporate headquarters is located in Milwaukee Wisconsin.

Sales and Marketing

MGIC's customers include savings institutions commercial banks mortgage brokers credit unions mortgage bankers and other lenders. The company's products are sold by its employees.

Financial Performance

MGIC has achieved year-over-year revenue growth for the last five years recording a 17% increase from 2015 to 2019. Meanwhile net income has achieved year-over-year growth after experiencing a 71% decrease in 2016. Despite the yearly increase after 2016 the 2015 net income is still higher than the 2019 revenue.

Revenue was $1.2 billion 8% higher compared to the previous year due to increased net premiums.

Net income was $673.8 million $3.7 million higher than in the previous year.

Cash and cash equivalents at the end of the year increased from $155 million to $169.1 million in 2019. Cash provided by operating activities was $609.5 million. Investing activities and financing activities used $422.1 million and $173.4 million respectively. Main cash uses were purchases of investments and repurchase of common stock.

Strategy

MGIC's current business strategies are to prudently grow IIF pursue new business opportunities that improve its competitive position in the market preserve and expand its role and that of the PMI industry in housing finance policy manage and deploy capital to maximize the company's long-term value and foster an environment that best positions its people to succeed.

In 2019 MGIC continued to enhance the reputation of the company and the industry relative to changing housing finance policy and a broader role for PMI; successfully launched MiQ its risk-based pricing system that establishes its premium rates based on a borrower's individual risk profile and loan attributes; executed a $316 million insurance linked note transaction the company' second such post-financial crisis transaction which allows the company to better manage its risk profile and provides an alternative source of capital; delivered training workshops designed to build strategic capabilities which enhance performance; and continued to enhance career developments talent analytics and financial health capabilities for employees.

Company Background

Originally formed in 1957 by Milwaukee real estate attorney Max Karl.

EXECUTIVES

Vice President Human Resources, Kurt Thomas
Senior Vice President Information Services And Chief Information Officer Of Mgic, Michael Meade
Senior Vice President, Carla A Gallas
President And Coo, Patrick Sinks, age 63, $524,423 total compensation
Evp General Counsel And Secretary, Jeffrey H. Lane, age 70, $415,385 total compensation
Evp Risk Management, Lawrence J. Pierzchalski, age 67, $449,654 total compensation
Chairman And Ceo, Curt S. Culver, age 67, $898,269 total compensation
Evp And Cfo, Timothy Mattke
Vice President Investments, Paul Spiroff
Vice President Marketing And Customer Experience, Margaret Crowley
Assistant Vice President Regulatory Relations, Chris Burns
Vice President Claims, David Schroeder
Vice President, Lisa Pendergast
Vice President, Julie Sperber
Vice President, John Schroeder
Vice President, Mike Kull
Vice President Field Operations, Jerry Murphy
Executive Vice President Business Strategy And Operations, Sal Miosi
National Accounts Manager, Rick Lewandowski
Vice President Talent Management, Stacey Murphy
Vice President National Accounts Manager, Robert Bates
Vice President Product Development, Geoffrey Cooper
Svp National Sales, Jay Hughes
Vice President Pricing And Credit Policy, Steve Thompson
Auditors: PricewaterhouseCoopers LLP

LOCATIONS

HQ: MGIC Investment Corp. (WI)
250 E. Kilbourn Avenue, Milwaukee, WI 53202
Phone: 414 347-6480
Web: www.mgic.com

PRODUCTS/OPERATIONS

2017 Sales

	$ mil.	% of total
Net premiums earned	934	88
Net investment income	120	11
Net realized investment gains	0	.
Other	10	1
Total	**1,066**	**100**

COMPETITORS

Fannie Mae	Radian Group
Freddie Mac	US Department of
Genworth Mortgage	Veterans Affairs
Insurance	United Guaranty
National Mortgage	
Insurance	

HISTORICAL FINANCIALS

Company Type: Public

Income Statement   FYE: December 31

	ASSETS ($ mil.)	NET INCOME ($ mil.)	INCOME AS % OF ASSETS	EMPLOYEES
12/19	6,229	673	10.8%	724
12/18	5,677	670	11.8%	793
12/17	5,619	355	6.3%	819
12/16	5,734	342	6.0%	823
12/15	5,879	1,172	19.9%	800
Annual Growth	1.5%	(12.9%)	—	(2.5%)

2019 Year-End Financials

Debt ratio: 13.37%	No. of shares (mil.): 347
Return on equity: 17.08%	Dividends
Cash ($ mil.): 161	Yield: 0.8%
Current ratio: —	Payout: 6.4%
Long-term debt ($ mil.): —	Market value ($ mil.): 4,921

	STOCK PRICE ($) FY Close	P/E High/Low		Earnings	PER SHARE ($) Dividends	Book Value
12/19	14.17	8	6	1.85	0.12	12.41
12/18	10.46	9	5	1.78	0.00	10.08
12/17	14.11	16	10	0.95	0.00	8.51
12/16	10.19	11	5	0.86	0.00	7.48
12/15	8.83	3	2	2.60	0.00	6.58
Annual Growth	12.6%	—	—	(8.2%)	—	17.2%

MGM Resorts International

MGM Resorts International is one of the world's largest gaming firms. The company's properties include some of the biggest names on the Las Vegas Strip including MGM Grand The Mirage Park MGM as well as Luxor Bellagio New York-New York Mandalay Bay and the new T-Mobile Arena. MGM Resorts also operates regional properties in a handful of other US states including the MGM Grand Detroit and the Borgata in Atlantic City New Jersey among others. Internationally MGM Resorts operates in Macau an autonomous

Chinese territory famed for gambling. Revenue comes from casino room reservations food and drinks entertainment and retail operations.

Operations

MGM Resorts' hotels boast a combined approximately 45000 rooms. Domestic properties on the Las Vegas strip and other regional locations include nearly 37700 rooms and its CityCenter joint venture a mixed-use development in Las Vegas has another some 5500. Its hotels in Macau have about 1970 rooms. The company's properties altogether host approximately 2.5 million square feet of casino space about 34500 slot machines and more than 2000 gaming tables.

Casino operations generate nearly half the company's total revenue while hotel rooms generate about 20% and food and drink bring in approximately 15%. Other revenue-generators include entertainment and retail holdings.

The company operates and manages its hotels which are owned by MGM Growth Properties an affiliated real-estate investment trust.

Geographic Reach

MGM Resorts' reportable segments are based on the geographic regions in which it operates. Domestic Resorts including Las Vegas strip resorts and regional operations account for nearly 75% of sales while MGM China accounts for about 20%. (A corporate segment occupies the remainder.)

The company has nine properties on the Las Vegas strip. It has another six in the US in Maryland Massachusetts Michigan Mississippi and New Jersey. MGM also owns about 50% of the CityCenter in Las Vegas which it manages for a fee and is expanding in Ohio with MGM Northfield Park and in New York with Empire City.

MGM Resorts' China operations consist of two sites in Macau: MGM Macau resort and casino and MGM Cotai a casino hotel and entertainment resort on the Cotai strip China's. MGM owns approximately 55% of MGM China which owns MGM Grand Paradise.

The company's headquarters is located in Las Vegas Nevada.

Sales and Marketing

MGM Resorts advertises on the radio television internet billboards and in newspapers and magazines in selected cities throughout the US and overseas. MGM Resorts also uses direct mail and social media to target past guests and potential customers. The company advertises through regional marketing offices located in major cities.

The firm encourages customers to keep their total gaming and entertainment spending at its casino resorts through its customer loyalty program M life Rewards. The tiered program allows customers to qualify for benefits across participating resorts in both gaming and non-gaming areas. It also offers the Golden Lion Club for gaming-focused customers in addition to M life Rewards at MGM China.

Advertising expenses were about 255 million in 2019 exceeded $300 million in 2018 and reached nearly $225 million in 2017.

Financial Performance

MGM Resorts International has for the most part grown its revenue year-over-year in recent years. The company's net income during the most recent five-year period ending 2018 has been more sporadic – up one year and down the next. Overall net revenue increased 40% from 2015-2019.

Consolidated net revenues in 2019 increased 10% compared to 2018 due primarily to continued ramp-up of operations at MGM Cotai following its opening in February 2018 a full year of operating results at MGM Springfield which opened in August 2018 the acquisition of Empire City in January 2019 a full year of operating results at MGM Northfield Park which MGP acquired in July 2018 and an increase in revenues as a result of the ramp-up of operations at Park MGM partially offset by a decrease in casino revenues at certain of our other Las Vegas Strip Resorts.

MGM Resorts posted profits of $2.0 in 2019 down from record profits of nearly $467 million in 2018 due to higher revenue.

At the end of 2019 MGM Resorts had $2.3 billion in cash and cash equivalents. Cash from operations was $1.8 billion. Cash provided in investing activities was $3.5 billion primarily for capital expenditures. Cash used by financing activities was $4.5 billion.

Strategy

MGM Resorts International in 2019 announced the implementation of the MGM 2020 plan to reduce costs improve efficiencies and drive revenue growth. The MGM 2020 plan is a company-wide initiative aimed to create a more centralized organizational structure and lay the groundwork for a digital transformation through key investments in technology. As part of MGM 2020 the company cut more than 1000 jobs at its properties in 2019. The plan is expected to boost earnings before interest taxes depreciation and amortization by $200 million by the end of 2020 and another $100 million by the end of 2021.

As part of its transformation MGM Resorts divests its Las Vegas Strip properties including Circus Circus and its flagship MGM Grand. MGM Resorts will enter two attractive markets in New York and Ohio.

As part of the second phase of MGM 2020 Plan MGM plan to invest in its digital transformation to drive customer-centric strategy for revenue growth. In addition MGM Resorts continued to focus on key growth opportunities to develop an integrated resort in Japan and also continued investments in sports betting through its venture Roar Digital LLC.

Mergers and Acquisitions

In 2019 MGM Resorts acquired Empire City Casino's race track and casino in Yonkers New York just 15 miles north of Manhattan's Times Square for approximately $850 million. The purchase gives MGM a fourth property in the Northeast; it previously opened its MGM Springfield resort casino in Massachusetts in 2018. Representatives from MGM say the Empire City deal is designed to tap into the underserved New York market and will complement the MGM Springfield market.

MGM is also in the final stages of buying Hard Rock Rocksino Northfield Park in Ohio for $1.06 billion. It plans to re-brand the property MGM Northfield Park.

Company Background

Billionaire Kirk Kerkorian purchased a stake in famed movie studio Metro-Goldwyn-Mayer (formed 1924) for just over $80 million in 1970. Around the same time he began acquiring property in Las Vegas and started construction on the city's largest hotel.

Financial difficulties led Kerkorian to sell his new hotel but he retained the rights to the MGM Grand name and logo. Kerkorian founded MGM Grand Inc. in 1986 and took the company public in 1987. In 1993 Kerkorian and company unveiled Las Vegas' MGM Grand a $1.1 billion complex featuring a theme park and at the time the largest casino on the planet. The project was a success and spawned plans for expansion.

In a landmark deal MGM Grand bought rival Mirage Resorts for $6.4 billion (including $2 billion in debt) in 2000 and became one of the top gaming companies in the world. The purchase of Mirage Resorts allowed MGM Grand to add a string of opulent casinos to its collection including Las Vegas strip properties Bellagio and The Mirage. After the deal closed MGM Grand changed its name to MGM MIRAGE.

The company opened MGM Grand Macau in China in 2007. In 2010 MGM MIRAGE changed its name to MGM Resorts International to emphasize the brand's global scope.

EXECUTIVES

Coo, Corey I. Sanders, age 56, $1,119,368 total compensation

President And Chief Marketing Officer, William J. Hornbuckle, age 62, $1,269,368 total compensation

Chairman And Ceo, James J. Murren, age 58, $2,000,000 total compensation

Chief Design And Construction Officer And Director, Robert H. Baldwin, age 69, $1,650,000 total compensation

Evp Special Counsel Litigation And Chief Diversity Officer, Phyllis A. James, age 67

Evp Cfo And Treasurer, Daniel J. D'Arrigo, age 51, $875,000 total compensation

Evp And Chief Accounting Officer, Robert C. Selwood, age 64, $439,286 total compensation

Evp General Counsel And Secretary, John M. McManus, age 52

President And Coo Borgata Hotel Casino & Spa, Marcus Glover

Representative Officer And President Mgm Resorts Japan, Jason P. Hyland

President And Coo Gold Strike Casino Resort, Melonie Johnson

Vice President Of Corporate Ticketing, Cynthia Jones

Assistant Vice President Of Marketing, John Lai

Vice President Digital Design, Christopher Hume

Vice President, Vanesa Bui

Senior Vice President And Chief Sales Officer, Michael Dominguez

Vice President Of Global Sports And Events Sales, Daniel Rush

Vice President, Jeff Eisenhart

Vice President Gaming Operations, Todd Haushalter

Vp Field Technology Services, Bill Driver

Senior Vice President Customer Development, Larry Altschul

Corporate Vice President Talent And Organizational Effec, Christopher Henry

Vice President Global Sourcing, Paul Sinowitz

Senior Vice President Of Finance, Yvette Harris

Vice President Of Arena Booking, Sid Greenfeig

Senior Vice President Strategic Initiatives, Jeff Gebben

Executive Vice President, William Scott

Corporate Vice President Of Strategic Operations, David Tsai

Senior Vice President Capital Markets And Strategy, Jim Freeman

Vice President Of Human Resources At Circus Circus Las Vegas, Ashley Eddy

National Sales Manager, Michelle Lizarraga

Senior Vice President Revenue Management And Services, Micah Richins

Senior Vice President International Development, Rishi Kapoor

Svp Entertainment Operations, Mark Prows

Vice President Marketing, Jessie Yee

Assistant Vice President Taxes, Marcie Fleck

Svp Innovation Station Casinos, Thomas Mikulich

Senior Vice President And Chief Compliance Officer, Stephen Martino

Senior Vice President, Cliff Atkinson

Vice President Customer Development, Jodi Myers

Vice President, Jacqueline Goldy

Vice President, Anna Romanova

Vice President Of Accounting Services, Lara Brooks

Senior Vice President Far East Marketing Mgm Grand Mgm Resorts International Marketing, Tracy Tsoi

Svp Hr Operations And Shared Services, Tonia Horton

Vice President Of Legal Affairs, Greg Riches

Svp Global Retail Leasing And Development, Farid Matraki

Senior Vice President Global Gaming Development, Ed Bowers

Senior Vice President Global Security, Steve Martinez

Vice President Construction Finance, Alan Palardy

Vice President Contact Center Operations, Jason Lynch

National Sales Manager, Sarah Abbott

Vp Of Marketing Events And Nightlife, Bryan Bass

Vice President Talent Acquisition Strategy, Randy Goldberg

Vice President Procurement Vice President, Amanda Prochaska

Senior Vice President Engineering, Jay Sreedharan

Vp Entertainment Administration Operations, Nathalie Binette

Senior Vice President Deputy General Counsel And Compliance Officer, Laurie Digrandi

Vice President Aviation, David Cox

Evp Business And Legal Affairs, Michael Minden

Vice President Financial Reporting, Melissa Wargo

Vice President Of Events And Nightlife, James Reyes

Board Member, Daniel Taylor

Board Member, Mary Chris Gay

Auditors: DELOITTE & TOUCHE LLP

LOCATIONS

HQ: MGM Resorts International
3600 Las Vegas Boulevard South, Las Vegas, NV 89109
Phone: 702 693-7120
Web: www.mgmresorts.com

2017 Sales

	$ mil.	% of total
Domestic resorts	8,322	77
MGM China	1,970	18
Corporate & other	481	5
Total	**10,773**	**100**

PRODUCTS/OPERATIONS

2017 Sales

	$ mil.	% of total
Casino	5,984	51
Rooms	2,151	18
Food and beverage	1,790	15
Entertainment	542	5
Retail	214	2
Other	605	5
Reimbursed costs	402	4
Less: Promotional allowances	(917.0)	-
Total	**10,773**	**100**

Selected Properties

Nevada
  Las Vegas
  Bellagio
  Circus Circus
  CityCenter (50%)
  Excalibur
  Luxor
  Mandalay Bay Resort & Casino
  MGM Grand
  The Mirage
  T-Mobile Arena
  Monte Carlo
  New York-New York
Other US
  Beau Rivage (Biloxi MS)
  Borgata (Atlantic City New Jersey)
  Gold Strike (Tunica County MS)
  Grand Victoria (50%; Elgin New Jersey)
  MGM Grand Detroit
  MGM National Harbor (Prince George's Country Maryland)
  MG Springfield
China

MGM Grand Macau (51%; Macau)
MGM Cotai

COMPETITORS

Boyd Gaming	Sands China
Caesars Entertainment	Star City
Galaxy Entertainment	Station Casinos
Las Vegas Sands	Stratosphere
Rio All-Suite Hotel &	Tropicana
Casino	Entertainment
Riviera Holdings	Trump Resorts
SJM	Wynn Resorts

HISTORICAL FINANCIALS

Company Type: Public

Income Statement — FYE: December 31

	REVENUE ($ mil.)	NET INCOME ($ mil.)	NET PROFIT MARGIN	EMPLOYEES
12/19	12,899	2,049	15.9%	70,000
12/18	11,763	466	4.0%	72,000
12/17	10,773	1,960	18.2%	68,000
12/16	9,455	1,101	11.6%	69,000
12/15	9,190	(447)	—	59,500
Annual Growth	8.8%			4.1%

2019 Year-End Financials

Debt ratio: 32.97%
Return on equity: 28.78%
Cash ($ mil.): 2,329
Current ratio: 1.26
Long-term debt ($ mil.): 11,168

No. of shares (mil.): 503
Dividends
Yield: 1.5%
Payout: 13.4%
Market value ($ mil.): 16,740

	STOCK PRICE ($) FY Close	P/E High/Low		PER SHARE ($) Earnings	Dividends	Book Value
12/19	33.27	9	6	3.88	0.52	15.36
12/18	24.26	46	27	0.81	0.48	12.35
12/17	33.39	10	8	3.35	0.44	13.44
12/16	28.83	15	9	1.92	0.00	10.83
12/15	22.72	—	—	(0.82)	0.00	9.06
Annual Growth	10.0%	—	—	—	—	14.1%

Micron Technology Inc.

Micron Technology is one of the largest memory chip makers in the world. It makes DRAM (Dynamic Random Access Memory) NAND Flash and NOR Flash memory and other memory technologies. Its memory and storage solutions enable disruptive trends including artificial intelligence 5G machine learning and autonomous vehicles in key market segments like mobile data center client consumer industrial graphics automotive and networking. Micron's products are offered under the Micron Crucial and Ballistix brands as well as private labels. Micron generates nearly 55% of revenue from US.

Operations

Micron operates through four segments centered on its markets: Compute and Networking Business Unit ("CNBU"); Mobile Business Unit ("MBU"); Storage Business Unit ("SBU"); and Embedded Business Unit ("EBU").

The largest segment accounting for about 45% of sales is the Compute and Networking Business Unit which sells products for the enterprise networking graphics and cloud server markets. Mobile Business Unit generate more than 25% which includes memory for smartphone tablet and other mobile-device markets. The Storage Business Unit

contributes more than 15% of revenue includes includes SSDs and component-level solutions. About 15% of revenue comes from the Embedded Business Unit which makes memory and storage products for the automotive industrial and consumer markets.

About 65% of revenue comes from DRAM products and NAND Flash memory products supply the rest. DRAM and flash are sold throughout each of Micron's segments.

Geographic Reach

Boise Idaho-based Micron generates about 55% of its revenue in US with the rest comes from Taiwan Japan and other Asia/Pacific region countries. The company has fabrication and assembly facilities in China Japan Malaysia Singapore Taiwan and the US. The company makes its own products in a dozen plants throughout the world.

Sales and Marketing

Micron sells to equipment manufacturers and retailers via a direct sales force third-party sales representatives and distributors. The company sells its Crucial-branded products through a web-based customer direct sales channel as well as through channel and distribution partners.

Micron's gets about 10% of sales from Huawei and Kingston.

Financial Performance

Micron's financial results for the past five years were typical of the cyclical semiconductor industry – up and down but trending higher. The last two years however have been straight up delivering record revenue and net income.

In 2019 (ended September) revenue fell 23% to $23.4 billion from $30.4 billion in 2018 primarily due to pricing declines resulting from the challenging memory market environment in 2019.

The company recorded net income of $6.3 million a decline of 55% compared to its $14.1 million in 2018 primarily due to decrease of revenue

Micron's coffers held $7.3 billion in cash and equivalents at the end of 2019 compared to $6.6 billion the year before. Operations generated $13.2 billion and investing activities used $10.1 billion and financing activities used $2.4 billion in 2019. Micron used 2019 main cash in expenditures for property plant and equipment and repayments of debt.

Strategy

Micron expand portfolio of DRAM NAND and NOR solutions to the automotive market as well as its extensive customer support network enable to maintain its strong leadership position in this market. In 2019 the company introduced its UFS 2.1 managed NAND portfolio based on its reliable automotive-grade 64-layer 3D TLC NAND that features ultrafast boot-up time with up to three times the sequential read-performance of e.MMC-based products. It also introduced the industry's first 1TB TLC NVMe automotive SSD.

Mergers and Acquisitions

In 2019 Micron Technology acquired Fwdnxt a maker of hardware and software tools for artificial intelligence deep learning applications. Fwdnxt's technology is to help Micron explore deep learning tools required for data analytics particularly with internet of things and edge computing applications.

In early 2019 Micron gained full control of IM Flash Technologies the company's joint venture with Intel. The IM Flash acquisition will enable Micron to accelerate its R&D and optimize its manufacturing plan for 3D XPoint.

EXECUTIVES

President And Ceo, Sanjay Mehrotra, age 61
Vice President Operations, Jay Hawkins

Vp Finance And Cfo, Ernest E. (Ernie) Maddock, age 62, $550,000 total compensation
Vp Information Technology And Cio, Trevor Schulze
Human Resource Vice President Director Manager, Dan Spangler
Vice President, Matt Elzie
Vice President Nsg Design Engineering, Ramin Ghodsi
Vice President Advanced Storage Solutions, Robert Peglar
Vice President Of Software Engineering, Steve Moyer
Vice President Wsg Marketing, Reynette Au
Vice President Ww Enterprise Sales, Mark Glasgow
Executive Vice President, Michael Sadler
Vice President Worldwide Oem Sales, Mike Bokan
Vice President Procurement, Rodney Morgan
Vp Global Talent Management, Steinar Hjelle
Vice President Director Manager, Brian Kalisek
Vice President Director Manager, Michael Knapp
Vice President Business Planning And Process Management, Karen Metz
Vice President Memory Marketing, Jan duPreez
Vice President Of Compliance, Jeff Moss
Vice President Marketing Cnbu, Malcolm Humphrey
Executive Vice President Sales And Marketing, Brian Klene
Vice President Enigneering, Currie Munce
Corporate Vice President And Gm Embedded Business Unit, Jeffrey Bader
Executive Vice President Global Operations, Manish Bhatia
Corporate Vice President And Gm Storage Business Unit, Derek Dicker
Vice President 3dxp Systems And Solutions Engineering, Samir Mittal
Vp Package Technology Development, Mark Tuttle
Vice President Nvm Quality And Reliability, Hiroaki Fukuto
Vp Technology Strategy And Operations, Linda Somerville
Chairman, Robert E. (Bob) Switz, age 73
Treasurer, Bill Stover
Board Member, Caleb Bailey
Board Member, Pat Byrne
Auditors: PricewaterhouseCoopers LLP

LOCATIONS

HQ: Micron Technology Inc.
8000 S. Federal Way, Boise, ID 83716-9632
Phone: 208 368-4000
Web: www.micron.com

2018 Sales

	$ mil.	% of total
China	17,357	57
United States	3,624	12
Asia Pacific (exclusive China Taiwan and Japan)	2,559	9
Taiwan	2,798	9
Europe	2,128	7
Japan	1,254	4
Other	671	2
Total	**30,391**	**100**

PRODUCTS/OPERATIONS

2018 Sales

	$ mil.	% of total
Compute and Networking Business Unit	15,252	50
Storage Business Unit	5,022	17
Mobile Business unit	6,579	22
Embedded Business Unit	3,479	11
All Other	59	-
Total	**30,391**	**100**

2018 Sales

	$ mil.	% of total
DRAM	21,232	70
Trade NAND	7,843	26
Non-Trade	554	2
Other	578	3
Total	**30,391**	**100**

Semiconductor Products
Dynamic random-access memories (DRAMs)
  Direct Rambus DRAMs (RDRAMs)
  Synchronous DRAMs (SDRAMs)
  Double data rate synchronous DRAMs (DDR SDRAMs)
Flash memory devices
Memory modules
Photomasks

COMPETITORS

Atmel	SMART Modular
Cypress Semiconductor	Technologies
Intel	Samsung Electronics
Kingston Technology	SanDisk
Mosel Vitelic	Toshiba Semiconductor
Nanya	& Storage Products
PNY Technologies	Western Digital
SK Hynix	

HISTORICAL FINANCIALS

Company Type: Public

Income Statement
FYE: September 3

	REVENUE ($ mil.)	NET INCOME ($ mil.)	NET PROFIT MARGIN	EMPLOYEES
09/20*	21,435	2,687	12.5%	40,000
08/19	23,406	6,313	27.0%	37,000
08/18	30,391	14,135	46.5%	36,000
08/17	20,322	5,089	25.0%	34,100
09/16	12,399	(276)	—	31,400
Annual Growth	14.7%	—	—	6.2%

*Fiscal year change

2020 Year-End Financials

Debt ratio: 12.38%	No. of shares (mil.): 1,113
Return on equity: 7.06%	Dividends
Cash ($ mil.): 7,624	Yield: —
Current ratio: 2.71	Payout: —
Long-term debt ($ mil.): 6,373	Market value ($ mil.): 51,565

	STOCK PRICE ($) FY Close	P/E High/Low		PER SHARE ($) Earnings	Dividends	Book Value
09/20*	46.33	25	14	2.37	0.00	35.04
08/19	44.67	9	5	5.51	0.00	32.44
08/18	52.76	5	3	11.51	0.00	27.82
08/17	31.97	7	4	4.41	0.00	16.75
09/16	16.64	—	—	(0.27)	0.00	11.62
Annual Growth	29.2%		—	—	—	31.8%

*Fiscal year change

Microsoft Corporation

Microsoft is one of the world's leading technology companies with products that include the Windows operating system Office productivity applications and Azure cloud services. LinkedIn its business-oriented social network is used by millions to make connections. Outside the office Microsoft's Xbox gaming system is second only to Sony's PlayStation. Microsoft's customers range from consumers and small businesses to the world's biggest companies and government agencies. Geographically Microsoft's revenue is evenly split between the US and the other countries. Microsoft founded in 1975

Operations

Microsoft operates three business segments: More Personal Computing Productivity and Business Processes and Intelligent Cloud.

The More Personal Computing segment generates about 35% of revenue by selling products and services for end users developers and IT managers across devices. Included are Windows operating system products; devices including the Surface tablet phones and PC accessories; gaming such as Xbox hardware and Xbox Live; video games; HoloLens virtual reality technology; and third-party video game royalties; and search advertising.

The Productivity and Business Processes segment about one-third of sales covers productivity communication and information products and services across devices and platforms. Among the products are Office Office 365 (the cloud version) Exchange SharePoint Skype and Skype for Business and the Dynamics ERP and CRM products. Office products and cloud services by themselves account for about a quarter of total revenue. LinkedIn is part of the segment.

The Intelligent Cloud segment about 30% of revenue consists of its public private and hybrid server products and cloud services headlined by the Azure cloud computing service. Other products and services include SQL Server Windows Server Visual Studio and System Center.

Geographic Reach

Based in Redmond Washington Microsoft's sales are split between the US which accounts for about 50% of revenue and other countries which provide the balance of sales.

Internationally Microsoft operates research and development centers in China and India; data centers in Ireland Singapore and the Netherlands; and operations and facilities in Ireland and the UK. The company also has offices in India China Canada Australia Germany Japan and the UK.

Sales and Marketing

Microsoft sells through multiple channels to a wide range of customers as well as conducting sales online and through OEMs distributors and resellers as well as retailers.

Maintaining its brand identity and keeping itself in front-of-mind for potential consumer and commercial buyers is a key strategy to ongoing sales. Customers include consumers small and medium organizations large global enterprises public-sector institutions internet service providers application developers and OEMs.

The company spend $18.2 billion $17.5 billion and $15.5 billion on sales and marketing for the years 2019 2018 and 2017 respectively

Financial Performance

Microsoft's revenue has grown at a 15% clip in each of the past two years fueled by higher sales in each
of its business segments while net income reached a company high in 2019.

Revenue totaled $125.8 billion in 2019 (ended June) up about $15.5 billion from 2018. The Intelligent Cloud segment's revenue rose 21% year-over-year driven by server products and cloud services. Growth in Office and LinkedIn products fueled an increase in Productivity and Business Processes sales while stronger contributions from Surface Gaming and Windows boosted revenue in the Personal Computing segment.

Net income jumped to $39.2 billion in 2019 $22.6 billion more than 2018 due to higher revenue and a tax bill that was about $15.4 million less year-over-year.

Microsoft's coffers held $11.3 billion in cash in 2019 compared to $11.9 billion the year before. In 2019 operations generated $52.2 million in cash while investing activities used $15.7 million and financing activities used $36.8 million.

Strategy

In the past several years Microsoft has reoriented its products to the cloud which has driven sales higher. Microsoft's commercial cloud business which includes Azure Office 365 Commercial the commercial portion of LinkedIn and Dynamics 365 accounted for more than 73% of the company's revenue growth in 2018 and 2019. Revenue from the Azure cloud services business which ranks second in size only to Amazon.com's Amazon Web Services jumped 64% in 2019 from 2018.

The company offers customers subscriptions to cloud-based versions of its familiar Office productivity suite (Word Excel PowerPoint) and other popular programs that fueled robust growth in 2018 and 2019.

In gaming Microsoft is due to offer a new game-streaming service Project xCloud which will begin public trials in late 2019. To furnish new games for its Xbox system Microsoft has about doubled first-party game studios through acquisitions for its subscription services like Xbox Game Pass.

The company might seem invulnerable but Microsoft faces unrelenting competition throughout its portfolio. Amazon IBM Google are top rivals in web services and Apple and Google compete in operating systems and software. Those two companies also have thriving mobile phone businesses which Microsoft lacks. In gaming Electronic Arts Activision-Blizzard and others offer blockbuster games to players.

Mergers and Acquisitions

In 2020 Microsoft acquired Softomotive a world-leading provider of robotic process automation (RPA). By bringing Softomotive's desktop automation together with the existing Microsoft Power Automate capabilities at uniquely affordable pricing Microsoft is further democratizing RPA and enabling everyone to create bots to automate manual business processes.

Also in 2020 Microsoft agreed to acquire Metaswitch Networks a leading provider of virtualized network software and voice data and communications solutions for operators. Microsoft intends to leverage the talent and technology of these two organizations extending the Azure platform to both deploy and grow these capabilities at scale in a way that is secure efficient and creates a sustainable ecosystem.

In early 2020 Microsoft acquired Affirmed Network fully virtualized cloud-native mobile network solutions enable operators to simplify network operations reduce costs and rapidly create and launch new revenue-generating services. With Affirmed

In 2019 Microsoft acquired Movere a developer of software for moving data to cloud computing environments. The deal will help Microsoft migrate customers to its Azure cloud. Movere's technology helps IT administrators figure out the best options when they move data into the public cloud.

Microsoft in 2019 acquired BlueTalon a private company that develops data governance and compliance software. The software lets user run queries on sensitive data while not revealing the underlying information. Microsoft plans to incorporate Blue-Talon into its Azure Data Governance group. In another 2019 transaction Microsoft acquired jClarity a Java support services company. The deal should help Java workloads run more efficiently on Microsoft's Azure cloud services.

Company Background

Bill Gates and Paul Allen founded Microsoft (originally named Micro-soft) in 1975 after Gates dropped out of Harvard at age 19 to sell a version of the programming language BASIC. While Gates was at Harvard the pair wrote the language for Altair the first commercial microcomputer. The company was born in Albuquerque New Mexico and grew by modifying BASIC for other computers.

Gates and Allen moved Microsoft to their native Seattle in 1979 and began developing software that let others write programs. The modern PC era dawned in 1980 when IBM chose Microsoft to write the operating system for its new machines. Although hesitant at first Gates bought QDOS short for "quick and dirty operating system" for $50000 from a Seattle programmer renaming it the Microsoft Disk Operating System (MS-DOS).

Allen fell ill with Hodgkin's disease and left Microsoft in 1983. In the mid-1980s Microsoft introduced Windows a graphics-based version of MS-DOS that borrowed from rival Apple's Macintosh system. The company went public in 1986 and Gates became the industry's first billionaire a year later. Microsoft introduced Windows NT in 1993 to compete with the UNIX operating system popular on mainframes and large networks.

The early 1990s brought monopoly charges from inside and outside the industry. In 1995 antitrust concerns scotched a $1.5 billion acquisition of personal finance software maker Intuit.

EXECUTIVES

Cvp, Yusuf Mehdi
Corporate Vice President Finance Administration And Chief Accounting Officer, Frank Brod
Vice President Enterprise Sales And Partner Group, John Fikany
Evp And President Microsoft Global Sales Marketing And Operations, Jean-Philippe Courtois
Ceo, Satya Nadella, $1,200,000 total compensation
Evp Corporate Strategy And Operations, Kurt DelBene, $638,333 total compensation
President And Chief Legal Officer, Bradford L. (Brad) Smith, $704,167 total compensation
Evp And Chief Marketing Officer, Christopher C. (Chris) Capossela
Ceo Microsoft Uk, Cindy Rose
Evp Applications And Services, Lu Qi
Evp Technology And Research, Harry Shum, $573,939 total compensation
Evp Human Resources, Kathleen T. Hogan
Evp Office Product Group, Rajesh Jha
Corporate Vp And President Middle East And Africa, Ali Faramawy
Evp Microsoft Cloud And Enterprise Group, Scott Guthrie
Evp Worldwide Commercial Business, Judson Althoff
Corporate Vp And President Latin America, Cesar Cernuda
Evp Windows And Devices Group, Terry Myerson
Evp And Cfo, Amy E. Hood, $731,250 total compensation
Cto, J. Kevin Scott
Evp Business Development, Margaret L. (Peggy) Johnson, $704,167 total compensation
Worldwide Svp And President Asia Pacific, Ralph Haupter
Coo Russia, Tomasz Bochenek
Acting Ceo Microsoft Viet Nam, Aung San Maung
President Microsoft Indonesia, Haris Izmee
Corporate Vice President, Will Kennedy
Corporate Vice President Consumer And Device Sales, Nick Parker
Vice President Europe Middle East Africa Public Sector, Joe Macri
Corporate Vice President, Brad Anderson
Corporate Vp Central And Eastern Europe, Philippe Rogge
Corporate Vice President Software Development Core Operating System, Henry Sanders
Vice President, Mark Wilson
National Account Manager, Jason Wright
Vice President Of Human Resources, Chris Williams

Vice President Board Of Directors, Rhetick Sengupta
Corporate Vice President, Dan Roth
Human Resources Director Or Vice President Of Human Resources, Rupert Bader
Assistant Vice President, Patrick Dengler
Corporate Vice President And Deputy General Counsel, Rich Sauer
Vp Research And Technology, Markus Kohler
Vice President Technology Operations Smsg Retail, Terri Jordan
Cvp Engineering, Dayne Sampson
Svp Microsoft Services And It, Richard R Devenuti, age 65
Business Dvpt Manager, Tracye Foy
Vice President, Lili Cheng
Corporate Vice President Gaming Cloud, Kareem Choudhry
Corporate Vice President Commercial Partner Channels And Programs, Gavriella Schuster
Corporate Vice President Windows Marketing, Tony Prophet
Corporate Vice President, Richard Qian
Corporate Vice President Small And Midmarket Solutions And Partners Microsoft Corporation, Eduardo Rosini
Senior Vice President Product Strategy (xbox Entertainment Studios), Randy Ahn
Executive Vice President Operating, Terry Ramsey
Senior Vice President, Chris Caposella
Vice President Research And Development China, Ya-Qin Zhang
Corporate Vice President Office Product Management Group, Takeshi Numoto
Corporate Vice President Onedrive And Sharepoint, Jeff Teper
Corporate Vice President, Rajiv Kumar
Vice President, Carel Maske
Corporate Vice President Outlook Engineering, Gaurav Sareen
Vice President Of Global Agencies, Stephen Kim
Corporate Vice President, Sherman Pierce
Corporate Vp Azure Infrastructure And Management, Mike Neil
Vice President, Jim Alchin
Cvp Wdg Core Quality, Michael Fortin
Vice President Corporate Controller And Chief Accounting Officer At Dynamics Research, Shaun Mccarthy Shaun Mccarthy
Senior Vice President Of Marketing For Phones, Tuula Rytil
Vice President Enterprise Services Public Sector, Catherine Kuenzel
Corporate Vice President And Deputy General Counsel, Julie Brill
Vice President And General Manager Service Enablers And Applications Mobile Phones Microsoft Devices, Rich Bernardo
Corporate Vice President Communications Sector, Austin Mulinder
Vice President Developer And Platform Group, Mary-Ellen Anderson
Vp Of Finance, Mahima Srinivasan
Senior Vice President, Rajesh Nair
Corporate Vice President One Commercial Partner, Ron Huddleston
Corporate Vice President Mixed Reality Marketing (windows And Devices Group), Liz Hamren
Vice President Of Sales And Marketing, Ami Silverman
Vice President Deputy General Counsel, Richard Wallis
Vice President Sales And Marketing, Claus Minet
Senior Vice President, Jada Miranda
Vice President Health Technology And Alliances, Gregory Moore
Vice President Worldwide Financial Services, Janet Lewis
Vp Enterprise Cyber Security Group, Ann Johnson
Vice President, Brad Rowland

Board Member, Nicole Summitt
Secretary Treasurer, Shelby Grieve
Secretary, Sally Carroll
Auditors: DELOITTE & TOUCHE LLP

LOCATIONS

HQ: Microsoft Corporation
  One Microsoft Way, Redmond, WA 98052-6399
Phone: 425 882-8080
Web: www.microsoft.com

2018 Sales

	$ mil.	% of total
US	55,926	51
Other countries	54,434	49
Total	**110,360**	**100**

PRODUCTS/OPERATIONS

2019 Sales

	$ mil.	% of total
More Personal Computing	45,698	36
Productivity and Business Processes	41,160	33
Intelligent Cloud	38,985	31
Total	**125,843**	**100**

2019 Sales

	$ mil.	% of total
Product	66,069	53
Services & other	59,774	47
Total	**125,843**	**100**

2019 Sales

	$ mil.	% of total
Office Products and Cloud Services	31,769	25
Server Products and Cloud Services	32,622	26
Windows	20,395	16
Gaming	11,386	9
Search Advertising	7,628	6
Enterprise Services	6,124	5
Devices	6,095	5
LinkedIn	6,754	5
Other	3,070	3
Total	**125,843**	**100**

Selected Products

Consumer software services and devices
  Xbox (video game console)
Desktop applications
  Access (relational database management)
  Excel (integrated spreadsheet)
  FrontPage (website publishing)
  MS Office (business productivity software suite)
  Outlook (messaging and collaboration)
  PowerPoint (presentation graphics)
  Project (project scheduling and resource allocation)
  Word (word processing)
Enterprise software
  BackOffice (server software suite)
  Content Management Server (content management)
  Exchange Server (messaging server)
  Proxy Server (Internet gateway)
  Site Server (website management)
  SQL Server (database and data analysis management)
  Systems Management Server (centralized management)
  Visio (visualization and diagramming suite)

COMPETITORS

Adobe Systems	IBM
Amazon.com	Logitech
Apple Inc.	Nintendo
BMC Software	Oracle
CA Inc.	Red Hat
Cisco Systems	SAP
Dell	Sage Group
Facebook	Sony
Google	VMware
HP	salesforce.com

HISTORICAL FINANCIALS

Company Type: Public

Income Statement   FYE: June 30

	REVENUE ($ mil.)	NET INCOME ($ mil.)	NET PROFIT MARGIN	EMPLOYEES
06/20	143,015	44,281	31.0%	163,000
06/19	125,843	39,240	31.2%	144,000
06/18	110,360	16,571	15.0%	97,535
06/17	89,950	21,204	23.6%	124,000
06/16	85,320	16,798	19.7%	114,000
Annual Growth	13.8%	27.4%	—	9.4%

2020 Year-End Financials

Debt ratio: 21.02%—
Return on equity: 40.03%
Cash ($ mil.): 13,576
Current ratio: 2.52
Long-term debt ($ mil.): 59,578

Dividends
Yield: 0.9%
Payout: 33.2%
Market value ($ mil.): —

	STOCK PRICE ($) FY Close	P/E High/Low		PER SHARE ($) Earnings	Dividends	Book Value
06/20	203.51	35	23	5.76	1.99	15.63
06/19	133.96	27	18	5.06	1.80	13.39
06/18	98.61	48	32	2.13	1.65	10.77
06/17	68.93	26	19	2.71	1.53	9.39
06/16	51.17	27	19	2.10	1.39	9.22
Annual Growth	41.2%	—	—	28.7%	9.4%	14.1%

HISTORICAL FINANCIALS

Company Type: Public

Income Statement   FYE: December 31

	ASSETS ($ mil.)	NET INCOME ($ mil.)	INCOME AS % OF ASSETS	EMPLOYEES
12/19	2,231	17	0.8%	444
12/18	2,077	10	0.5%	406
12/17	1,170	7	0.6%	277
12/16	1,032	7	0.8%	257
12/15	931	6	0.7%	252
Annual Growth	24.4%	28.3%	—	15.2%

2019 Year-End Financials

Debt ratio: 2.69%
Return on equity: 7.68%
Cash ($ mil.): 30
Current ratio: —
Long-term debt ($ mil.): —

No. of shares (mil.): 8
Dividends
Yield: 2.7%
Payout: 36.5%
Market value ($ mil.): 244

	STOCK PRICE ($) FY Close	P/E High/Low		PER SHARE ($) Earnings	Dividends	Book Value
12/19	28.80	14	10	2.09	0.79	28.05
12/18	23.02	25	15	1.48	0.70	26.38
12/17	33.10	21	14	1.67	0.77	17.85
12/16	23.83	13	8	1.85	0.68	16.65
12/15	16.10	12	10	1.47	0.54	16.58
Annual Growth	15.6%	—	—	9.2%	10.0%	14.1%

Mid Penn Bancorp Inc

Mid Penn Bancorp is the holding company for Mid Penn Bank which operatesÂ more thanÂ a dozen branches in central Pennsylvania's Cumberland Dauphin Northumberland and Schuylkill counties. The bank offers full-service commercial banking insuranceÂ and trust services.Â Its deposit products include checking savings money market and NOWÂ accounts. Commercial real estate construction andÂ land developmentÂ loans account for nearly 80% of the company's loan portfolio; the bank also writes residential mortgages and business agricultural and consumer loans. Mid Penn is a descendant of Millersburg Bank founded in 1868. Trust company CEDE & Co. ownsÂ about aÂ thirdÂ of Mid Penn Bancorp.

EXECUTIVES

Vice President Commercial Loan Officer, Peter Johnson
Auditors: RSM US LLP

LOCATIONS

HQ: Mid Penn Bancorp Inc
349 Union Street, Millersburg, PA 17061
Phone: 866 642-7736
Web: www.midpennbank.com

COMPETITORS

Fulton Financial
PNC Financial
Pennsylvania State Employees Credit Union

Midland States Bancorp Inc

Born in rural Illinois Midland States Bancorp is now discovering banking life in new states. It is the $3 billion-asset holding company for Midland States Bank a community bank that operates more than 35 branches in central and northern Illinois and around 15 branches in the St. Louis metropolitan area. The bank offers traditional consumer and commercial banking products and services as well as merchant card services insurance and financial planning. Subsidiary Midland Wealth Management which boasts $1.2 billion-plus in assets under administration provides wealth management services while Heartland Business Credit offers commercial equipment leasing services. Midland States Bancorp went public in 2016.

IPO

The bank holding company raised $80.1 million in its initial public offering. It plans to contribute some $25 million to Midland States Bank and use the rest for general corporate purposes including possible acquisitions.

Operations

About 57% of Midland States Bancorp's total revenue came from loan interest during 2014 while another 17% came from interest income from investment securities. The rest came from wealth management fees (8% of revenue) deposit account service charges (3%) ATM and interchange revenue (3%) mortgage banking revenue (3%) merchant services revenue (1%) and nonrecurring gains on the sales of assets (around 8%).

Subsidiary Love Funding provides multifamily and healthcare facility FHA financing.

Geographic Reach

Midland has more than 80 branches and offices across the US with around 50 in Illinois and around the St. Louis metro area and the rest in California Colorado Florida Massachusetts North Carolina Ohio Tennessee and Texas.

Financial Performance

Midland States Bancorp's revenue climbed 3% to $93 million despite a decline in loan interest income during 2014 mostly thanks to profitable asset sales and other income.

Despite modest revenue growth in 2014 the bank's net income dove 67% to $3.2 billion as acquisition and integration expenses stemming from its late 2014 acquisition of Heartland ate up any revenue gains it had made. Excluding these nonrecurring items the bank's net income grew modestly.

Strategy

Midland States Bancorp has been pursuing an acquisition and branch expansion growth strategy since 2007 after it replaced its executive management and laid out a plan to expand Midland States Bank's presence in Illinois. Midland States Bank continues to focus on moving into suburban areas and other markets in Illinois and Missouri that have growing populations. During 2015 it opened a new branches in the St. Louis region (in Jennings) downtown Joliet and downtown Effingham areas as well as a wealth management office in downtown Decatur.

The company also planned in 2016 to continue building its fast-growing wealth management business which now makes up nearly 10% of its total revenue. Thanks to Midland's efforts the business' wealth management assets under administration have skyrocketed twelve-fold since 2008 growing from $95 million then to $1.19 billion at the end of 2014.

Mergers and Acquisitions

Midland States Bancorp agreed to acquire HomeStar Financial Group in 2019 in a transaction valued at about $10 million. HomeStar's Manteno Illinois-based HomeStar Bank and Financial Services has about $375 million in assets $220 million in loans and $330 million in deposits. HomeStar has five locations in northern Illinois. The deal expands Midland's presence in the Kankakee Illinois metropolitan area.

In 2017 CEO Leon Holschbach signed a $175 million deal with rival Centrue Bank to merge. The two banks had been treading on each others' toes in Princeton Illinois.

Company Background

Between 2008 and 2010 the bank's branch locations grew from just a half-dozen in central Illinois and St. Louis to nearly 30 around the state and in the St. Louis metropolitan area. During that time the bank acquired the assets of Waterloo Bancshares and WestBridge in St. Louis AMCORE in northern Illinois and Strategic Capital in central Illinois. It also opened new locations in some of its faster-growing markets. As a result of its efforts Midland States Bancorp has watched its revenue and profits trend upward significantly from 2007 levels.

EXECUTIVES

Vice Chairman President And Ceo, Leon J. Holschbach, age 67, $529,389 total compensation
Evp Midland States Bancorp And President Midland States Bank, Jeffrey G. Ludwig, age 48, $367,500 total compensation
Evp Banking, Jeffrey S. Medford
Cfo Midland States Bancorp And Midland States Bank, Kevin L. Thompson
Vice President Commercial Banking, Jan Woodward
Senior Vice President And Corporate Counsel Of The Company And The Bank, Douglas Tucker
Vice President, Deanna Haught

Vice President Mortgage Banking, Mark
  Widdicombe
Senior Vice President, Sharon Schaubert
Vice President Marketing, Jo Ann Luallen
Svp, James Thompson
Vice President, Benjamin Malsch
Chairman, John M. Schultz, age 68
Board Member, Robert Schultz
Board Member, Deborah Golden
Board Member, Jeffrey Mcdonnell
Board Member, Dwight Miller
Board Member, Richard Ramos
Auditors: Crowe LLP

LOCATIONS

HQ: Midland States Bancorp Inc
  1201 Network Centre Drive, Effingham, IL 62401
Phone: 217 342-7321
Web: www.midlandsb.com

PRODUCTS/OPERATIONS

2014 Sales

	$ mil.	% of total
Interest income		
Loans	56	57
Investment Securities & others	16	17
Noninterest income		
Wealth management revenue	7	8
Service charges on deposit accounts	3	3
Mortgage banking revenue	3	3
Gain on sale of other assets	3	3
ATM and interchange revenue	2	3
Impairments	(2.6)	-
Other	4	6
Total	**93**	**100**

Selected Services

Bank By Phone
Bill Paying
Checking
Debit Card
Online Banking
Savings & CDs

COMPETITORS

Bank of America	Harris
Edward D. Jones	Mercantile Bancorp
Fifth Third	PNC Financial
First Mid-Illinois	U.S. Bancorp
Bancshares	

HISTORICAL FINANCIALS

Company Type: Public

Income Statement — FYE: December 31

	ASSETS ($ mil.)	NET INCOME ($ mil.)	INCOME AS % OF ASSETS	EMPLOYEES
12/19	6,087	55	0.9%	1,100
12/18	5,637	39	0.7%	1,100
12/17	4,412	16	0.4%	840
12/16	3,233	31	1.0%	715
12/15	2,884	24	0.8%	700
Annual Growth	**20.5%**	**23.1%**	**—**	**12.0%**

2019 Year-End Financials

Debt ratio: 3.70%
Return on equity: 8.78%
Cash ($ mil.): 392
Current ratio: —
Long-term debt ($ mil.): —

No. of shares (mil.): 24
Dividends
  Yield: 3.3%
  Payout: 39.9%
Market value ($ mil.): 707

	STOCK PRICE ($) FY Close	P/E High/Low		PER SHARE ($) Earnings	Dividends	Book Value
12/19	28.96	13	10	2.26	0.97	27.10
12/18	22.34	21	12	1.66	0.88	25.62
12/17	32.48	40	33	0.87	0.80	23.51
12/16	36.18	17	9	2.17	0.36	20.78
Annual Growth	**(5.4%)**	**—**	**—**	**1.0%**	**28.1%**	**6.9%**

MidWestOne Financial Group, Inc.

MidWestOne Financial Group is the holding company for MidWestOne Bank which operates about 35 branches throughout central and east-central Iowa. The bank offers standard deposit products such as checking and savings accounts CDs and IRAs in addition to trust services private banking home loans and investment services. More than two-thirds of MidWestOne Financial's loan portfolio consists of commercial real estate loans and commercial mortgages and industrial loans. Founded in 1983 MidWestOne has total assets of $4.65 billion.

Operations

MidWestOne Financial Group provides a wide range of commercial and retail lending services to businesses individuals and government agencies. The company's credit activities include commercial and residential real estate loans (approximately 70% of total loan portfolio) commercial and industrial loans (almost 25%) agricultural loans (nearly 5%) and consumer loans (less than 5%).

Overall MidWestOne Financial Group generates roughly 85% of its revenue from interest income more than 75% comes from interest and fees on loans the remaining 10% comes from investment securities the rest of its revenue comes from non-interest income.

Geographic Reach

Headquartered in Iowa City MidWestOne Financial Group's MidWestOne Bank has branch offices and operating facilities in Minnesota Wisconsin Florida and Colorado.

Sales and Marketing

MidWestOne Financial Group market its services to qualified lending customers. Lending officers actively solicit the business of new companies entering their market areas as well as long-standing members of the business communities in which the company operate.

Financial Performance

The company's revenue in 2019 increased by 36% to $174.9 million compared to $128.5 million in the prior year.

MidWestOne's consolidated net income for 2019 was $43.6 million an increase of $13.3 million or 44% compared to $30.4 million for 2018. The increase in net income was due primarily to an increase in net interest income of $38.4 million which was primarily attributable to the increased volume of interest-earning assets as a consequence of the ATBancorp merger.

Cash held by the company at the end of 2019 increased to $73.5 million. Cash provided by operations and investing activities were $47.3 million and $72.7 million respectively. Cash used for financing activities was $92.1 million mainly for short-term borrowings.

Strategy

MidWestOne's operating strategy is based upon a community banking model of delivering a comprehensive suite of financial products and services while following five operating principles: take care of its customers; hire and retain excellent employees; conduct business with the utmost integrity; work as one team; and learn constantly so the company can continually improve. Management believes the depth and breadth of the Company's products and services coupled with the personal and professional delivery of the same provides an appealing alternative to competitors.

Mergers and Acquisitions

In early 2019 MidWestOne Financial Group acquired ATBancorp a bank holding company whose wholly-owned banking subsidiaries were ATSB and ABTW for paid cash in the amount of $34.8 million. The acquisition helps to expand the company's business into new markets and grow the size of the company's business.

EXECUTIVES

President And Ceo, Charles N. Funk, age 66, $422,000 total compensation
Evp And Chief Credit Officer, Kent L. Jehle, age 60, $271,000 total compensation
Vp And Chief Risk Officer, James M. Cantrell, $205,000 total compensation
Coo, Kevin Kramer
Svp And Cfo, Katie A. Lorenson, age 40, $206,231 total compensation
Senior Regional President, Mitchell W. Cook, age 56, $204,400 total compensation
Vice President Information Technology Managing Officer, Allen Schneider
Senior Vice President Loan Sales, Jason Swestka
Vice President Lpl Financial Advisor Located, John Evans
Vice President And Program Manager, Daniel Bailey
Senior Vice President Treasury Management, Kevin Pleasant
Vice President Mortgage Loan Operations, Linda A Nelson
Second Vice President Mortgage Banker, Niki Gysbers
Senior Vice President Small Business Administration, John Kimball
Vice President Commercial Banking, Jeff Schebler
Second Vice President Mortgage Banker, Kerri Higgins
Vice President Commercial Lending, Andrew L Brust
Senior Vice President Credit Administration, Bob Blenkush
Vice President Human Resource Manager, Cathi Weber
Senior Vice President Retail Banking, David Lindstrom
Vice President Commercial Banking, Nick Raffensperger
Chairman, Kevin W. Monson, age 68
Board Member, Michael Hatch
Board Member, Nate Kaeding
Auditors: RSM US LLP

LOCATIONS

HQ: MidWestOne Financial Group, Inc.
  102 South Clinton Street, Iowa City, IA 52240
Phone: 319 356-5800
Web: www.midwestone.com

PRODUCTS/OPERATIONS

2015 Sales

	$ mil.	% of total
Interest Income		
Interest and fees on loans	86	71
Interest on investment securities	13	11
Other	0	1
Non-Interest Income		
Trust investment and insurance fees	6	5
Other service charges commissions and fees	5	5
Service charges and fees on deposit accounts	4	3
Mortgage origination and loan servicing fees	2	2
Other	2	2
Total	121	100

Selected Subsidiaries

MidWestOne Bank
MidWestOne Insurance Services Inc.
MidWestOne Statutory Trust II

COMPETITORS

Bank of the West	U.S. Bancorp
Hills Bancorporation	Wells Fargo
QCR Holdings	West Bancorporation

HISTORICAL FINANCIALS
Company Type: Public

Income Statement
FYE: December 31

	ASSETS ($ mil.)	NET INCOME ($ mil.)	INCOME AS % OF ASSETS	EMPLOYEES
12/19	4,653	43	0.9%	771
12/18	3,291	30	0.9%	597
12/17	3,212	18	0.6%	610
12/16	3,079	20	0.7%	587
12/15	2,979	25	0.8%	648
Annual Growth	11.8%	14.8%	—	4.4%

2019 Year-End Financials

Debt ratio: 4.98%	No. of shares (mil.): 16
Return on equity: 10.08%	Dividends
Cash ($ mil.): 73	Yield: 2.2%
Current ratio: —	Payout: 30.0%
Long-term debt ($ mil.): —	Market value ($ mil.): 586

	STOCK PRICE ($) FY Close	P/E High/Low	PER SHARE ($) Earnings	Dividends	Book Value
12/19	36.23	13 9	2.93	0.81	31.49
12/18	24.83	14 10	2.48	0.78	29.32
12/17	33.53	25 21	1.55	0.67	27.85
12/16	37.60	22 14	1.78	0.64	26.71
12/15	30.41	14 12	2.42	0.60	25.96
Annual Growth	4.5%	— —	4.9%	7.8%	4.9%

MODERN WOODMEN OF AMERICA

No need to pitch a tent to have Modern Woodmen in your camp. One of the largest fraternal benefit societies in the US Modern Woodmen of America provides annuities life insurance and other financial savings products to more than 740000 members through some 1000 agents. The group founded in 1883 is organized into "camps" (or chapters) that provide financial social recreational and service benefits to members. Founder Joseph Cullen Root chose the society's name to compare pioneering woodmen clearing forests to

men using life insurance to remove the financial burdens their families could face upon their deaths.

Operations

The organization claims some approximately 2500 chapters nationwide provide opportunities for members to take part in educational social and volunteer activities; nearly 300 summit chapters offer activities for members age 55 and over; and more than 800 youth service clubs which are led by adult member volunteers.

In addition to financial services the organization offers life insurance for member families include term life insurance plans specifically designed for children and young adults and permanent life insurance plans with a minimum insurance amount of $50000. Its annuities services include Max-Provider for retirement savings variable annuity for multiple investment options and single premium immediate annuity. In addition to life insurance and annuities the company offers retirement accounts including IRAs college savings plans investment assistance and other insurance products. Modern Woodmen has $20.4 million in life insurance in force.

Subsidiary MWA Financial Services offers securities and advisory products. The MWABank (dba Modern Woodmen Bank) division provides retail banking services.

Geographic Reach

Based in Rock Island Illinois the organization has nearly 500 home offices and operates throughout the US. It has agents in more than 45 regions throughout 45 states.

Financial Performance

In 2019 Modern Woodmen had $17.34 billion in assets. This was higher than the $16.5 billion reported in 2018 as bonds and stocks both increased.

Net income for the same year was $89.5 million which was lower than the $109.9 million reported the year prior. The decrease was mainly due to lower realized capital gains.

Cash at the end of the year for the company was $363.4 million. Net cash provided by operating activities was $189.2 million while cash used for investments was $299.9 million.

Strategy

Modern Woodmen manages its assets so that changes in the financial markets – recessions depressions or periods of inflation – have minimal effect. Modern Woodmen is also careful not to follow investment fads. To build its investment portfolio its financial management team follows these principles: High-quality investments; Diversified investments; and Competitive rates of return.

Assets are invested primarily in high-quality low-risk investments. As of December 31 2019 approximately 99.7 percent of bonds were of high or medium quality.

Company Background

Although Modern Woodmen's roots are tangled with Woodmen of the World Life Insurance Society the two fraternal benefit societies are not related. Modern Woodmen of America was founded in 1883.

EXECUTIVES

Vice President, Rob Sevilla
Vice President Of It, Becky Hansen
Vice Pres, Alan Blackmon
Board Of Directors, Gary Medd

LOCATIONS

HQ: MODERN WOODMEN OF AMERICA
1701 1ST AVE, ROCK ISLAND, IL 612018779
Phone: 309 793-5537
Web: WWW.MODERNWOODMEN.ORG

PRODUCTS/OPERATIONS

Selected Products
Annuities (fixed immediate and variable; through MWA Financial Services)
Banking (MWABank)
  Certificates of Deposit
  Checking and savings accounts
  Credit cards and gift cards
  First mortgage and refinancing home loans
  Home equity loans
Insurance (through MWAGIA)
  Dental and vision insurance
  Disability income insurance
  Group employee benefits
  Group voluntary benefits
  Impaired risk life insurance
  International life and health insurance
  Long-term care insurance
  Major medical insurance
  Medicare supplement insurance
Investment (through MWA Financial Services)
  Brokerage services
  College savings plans
  Mutual funds
  Retirement plans
Life Insurance
  Term life insurance
  Term life insurance for children
  Universal life insurance
  Whole life insurance

COMPETITORS

Allstate	Reliance Standard
MassMutual	Royal Neighbors Of
MetLife	America
Nationwide Financial	State Farm
New York Life	Thrivent Financial
Northwestern Mutual	Woodmen of the World
Prudential	Life Insurance

HISTORICAL FINANCIALS
Company Type: Private

Income Statement
FYE: December 31

	ASSETS ($ mil.)	NET INCOME ($ mil.)	INCOME AS % OF ASSETS	EMPLOYEES
12/07	8,318	96	1.2%	480
12/06	7,928	99	1.3%	—
Annual Growth	4.9%	(2.6%)		

Mohawk Industries, Inc.

Mohawk Industries is the world's largest maker of commercial and residential flooring products. The company manufactures carpets and rugs ceramic and stone tile and laminate wood and vinyl flooring. It produces a range of broadloom carpets and rugs under such names as Mohawk Aladdin Durkan Karastan and Leoline. Mohawk's ceramic tile and stone flooring products are marketed under the popular Daltile brand and Unilin and Pergo laminate and wood flooring and other wood products round out Mohawk's operations. The company sells its products worldwide. Most of its revenue is generated in the US (about 60%) and it has a strong market position in Brazil.

Operations

Mohawk works through three business segments: Flooring North America (Flooring NA) Global Ceramic and Flooring Rest of World (Flooring ROW).

The Flooring NA segment generates about 40% of total sales and makes several floor covering products for residential and commercial markets for both remodeling and new construction. This segment includes products such as broadloom carpet carpet tile rugs and mats wood laminate luxury vinyl tile (LVT) and sheet vinyl. In addition to its own Mohawk brands it markets and distributes brands such as Aladdin Commercial Durkan IVC Karastan Pergo Portico and Quick-Step.

The Global Ceramic segment (more than 35%) comprises ceramic porcelain and natural stone tile products used for floors and walls in both residential and commercial applications. It also provides natural stone quartz and porcelain slab countertops and installation materials. Some Global Ceramic segment brands are American Olean Daltile KAI and Marazzi.

The Flooring ROW segment (approximately 25%) designs manufactures and distributes most of the company's products as well as roofing panels insulation boards and chipboards. In addition Flooring ROW licenses certain manufacturers' patents which it sells through retailers and distributors primarily in European market.

On a product level Mohawk generates nearly 40% of revenue from its carpet and resilient product group more than 35% from ceramic and stone and approximately 15% from laminate and wood. Other products represent the remaining 10%.

Geographic Reach

Calhoun Georgia-based Mohawk Industries sells its products to more than 170 countries around the world. It generates around 60% of its revenue in the US. Other significant markets include Europe (about 25%) and Russia (about 5%).

The company has about 95 manufacturing and distribution facilities in about 20 countries. It has more than 25 manufacturing and nearly 20 distribution facilities in North America and nearly 30 manufacturing and roughly 10 distribution facilities in Europe and Russia. The company's operations cover Australia India Canada Brazil Malaysia Mexico Russia USA and New Zealand.

Sales and Marketing

Mohawk exports its products worldwide and is a market leader in North America Brazil Europe Russia and Australasia. For distribution it uses regional distribution centers as well as direct shipping and customer pick-up from manufacturing facilities. Mohawk's truck fleet operates from warehouses and cross-docks that receive products from the company's manufacturing plants.

Through its sales force the company sells its products to more than 25000 customers which include independent floor covering retailers and distributors ceramic specialists home centers wholesalers and mass merchandisers. In 2019 no single customer accounted for more than 10% of the Company's total net sales and the top 10 customers accounted for less than 20% of the Company's total net sales.

Advertising and promotion expenses included in selling general and administrative expenses were $130207 in 2019 $116854 in 2018 and $119560 in 2017 respectively.

Financial Performance

Mohawk Industries has seen a significant upward trend in revenue over the past few years. Between 2015 and 2019 the company's sales increased by 23% to $9.9.

Sales in 2019 amounted to $9.97 billion a slight decrease compared with $9.98 billion in 2018. The decrease was primarily attributable to the unfavorable net impact from foreign exchange rates and by the unfavorable net impact of price and product mix which includes the full year impact on sales from the prior year acquisitions.

Net income however dropped by 13% to $744.2 million in 2019 down from $861.7 the previous year. The decrease in EPS was primarily attributable to higher inflation costs unfavorable net impact of price and product mix impairment charge related to the company's net investment in a manufacturer and distributor of ceramic tile in China. Unfavorable net impact due to lower sales volumes an increase in costs due to lower productivity (offset by lower startup costs) costs due to temporarily reducing production unfavorable net impact from foreign exchange rates costs associated with investments in new product development sales personnel and marketing partially offset by decreased income tax expense were also the reason of this decrease.

Cash at the end of fiscal 2019 was $134.8 million an increase of $15.7 million from the prior year. Cash from operations contributed $1.4 billion to the coffers while investing activities used $616.0 million mainly for additions to property plant and equipment and acquisitions. Financing activities used $789.9 million primarily from Commercial Paper.

Strategy

Mohawk's 2018 acquisitions served to strengthen the company's geographic reach with the purchase of Godfrey Hirst in Australia and New Zealand and with the Eliane ceramic tile company in Brazil. In Australasia Mohawk plans to expand Godfrey Hirst's commercial carpet position and capitalize on New Zealand's wool collections adding those to the US luxury carpet portfolio.

Product innovations such as Mohawk's Reveal Imaging printing technology (replicates the appearance of natural wood and stone) are driving increases in sales and Mohawk's SmartStrand fiber technology was introduced to create softer yet stain-resistant carpets and rugs. In laminates the company has increased the water resistance properties of its products which allow for more kitchen and bath installations. Mohawk has also started making quartz countertops in addition to its existing stone and porcelain countertop slabs.

As luxury vinyl tile (LTV) is becoming more popular it's taking market share from other products and Mohawk is scrambling to catch up with demand. Pressured to increase supply the company will expand its LTV operations specifically in the US and Europe.

Mohawk's Business Strategy is cascaded down through the organization with an emphasis on five key points; optimizing the company's position as the industry's preferred provider by delivering exceptional value to customers; treating employees fairly to retain the best organization; driving innovation in all aspects of the business.

In addition the company is taking reasonable well-considered risks to grow the business and enhancing the communities in which the company operates. These provides continuity for the company's operating principles and ensures a focus on exceeding customer expectations.

Mergers and Acquisitions

During 2019 the Company acquired two businesses in the Flooring ROW segment for hard surface flooring distribution companies based in the Netherlands and Czech Republic for $76237 resulting in a preliminary goodwill allocation of $48008. The results have been included in the Flooring ROW segment and are not material to the Company's consolidated results of operations.

Company Background

The company was founded in 1902 in Amsterdam New York as the Shuttleworth Brothers Company later becoming Mohawk Carpet Mills in 1920. As Mohawk's carpet business grew it merged with other carpet manufacturers and was eventually bought by MHS Holdings in 1988. MHS spun off the carpet business as Mowhawk Industries.

From 1992 (when Mohawk Industries went public) to 2000 the company made twelve soft surface acquisitions and grew to ten times its size. With the acquisition of Dal-Tile in 2002 the company became the largest ceramic provider in North America and added international manufacturing to its operations. It entered the European market in 2005 with the acquisition of Belgium-based laminate manufacturer Unilin and in 2007 the purchase of Columbia Wood Flooring added engineered and solid wood flooring to its product lineup and expanded its presence in Asia with a manufacturing facility in Malaysia.

Mohawk began doing business in Brazil through a joint venture in 2012 that included the company's laminate flooring. A year later it added laminate producer Pergo to its fold and also became the world's largest ceramic tile supplier with the acquisition of Marazzi which added operations in Italy Spain Russia and the US.

To continue to add revenue to its bottom line Mohawk gobbled up several more flooring product companies including IVC Group (sheet vinyl and LVT) Kai Group in Eastern Europe Xtratherm (insulation board) in Europe European ceramic tile maker EmilGroup Godfrey Hirst (carpeting) in Australia and New Zealand and Brazilian tile manufacturer Eliane.

HISTORY

Mohawk traces its origins to the Shuttleworth family who founded the company in Amsterdam New York in 1878 setting up their business with 14 second-hand looms imported from England. The company was incorporated as Shuttleworth Brothers in 1902. It introduced the popular Karnak carpet design in 1908.

EXECUTIVES

Svp Marketing, Karen R. Mendelsohn
Chairman And Ceo, Jeffrey S. Lorberbaum, age 65, $1,142,473 total compensation
President And Coo, W. Christopher (Chris) Wellborn, age 64, $987,186 total compensation
President Ceramic North America, John C. Turner, age 51

President Flooring North America, Brian M.
Carson, age 55, $618,000 total compensation
Vp Finance And Cfo, Frank H. Boykin, age 64,
$615,605 total compensation
President Flooring Rest Of World, Bernard P.
Thiers, age 64, $609,312 total compensation
**Vice President Sales Bigelow And Mohawk
Commercial Brands,** Jeff Davis
**Regional Vice President Strategic And Global
Customers Pacific Northwest,** Lori Edwards
Vp Internal Audit, Carley Ferguson
Vice President Of Flooring Production, Willy
Chandler
Vice President Sales, Craig Trimble
Vice President Sourcing, Jim Mason
Senior Vice President Sales, Randy Gardner
Regional Vice President, Russell Ence
Vice President Sales, Tom Merriman
Vice President Research And Development, David
Earl
**Vice President Of Residential Carpet Product
Development,** Jamie Welborn
National Sales Manager Multi Family, Doug Davis
**Mohawk Commercial Sales Flooring Commercial
Rvp Mountain West,** Ralph Holland
**Vice President Of Design And Product
Development,** Neil Hegwood
National Accounts Manager, Farris Cagle
Mvp, Tonia Morris
Regional Vice President, Mike Stinnette
Senior Vice President Of Produ, Mike Goodall
Vice President, Carl Holdridge
Vice President Marketing, Tom Donoghue
**Vice President Business Development And
International Sales,** Nick Sterghos
Vice President Logistics, Scot Bernstein
Regional Vice President, Frank Abraham
Mvp, Michelle Rhodes
Regional Vice President Sales Southeast, Tracy
Lambeth
Regional Vice President, O'hara Jerry
Regional Vice President, Jim Waters
Regional Vice President Mid Atlantic, Jeff Weaver
Vice President Commercial Marketing, Kevin
Wildes
**Regional Vice President Of Sales Midsouth
Region,** Todd Lomas
Regional Vice President, Cheryl Peale
Senior Vice President Sales, David Dembowitz
**Regional Vice President Builder Multi Family
Division,** Dan Hill
**Vice President Information Technology Chief
Officer Daltile,** Nellson Burns
Vice President, Mark Dye
Auditors: KPMG LLP

LOCATIONS

HQ: Mohawk Industries, Inc.
160 S. Industrial Blvd., Calhoun, GA 30701
Phone: 706 629-7721
Web: www.mohawkind.com

2018 Sales

	$ mil.	% of total
US	6,103	61
Europe	2,582	26
Russia	349	4
All other countries	947	9
Total	**9,983**	**100**

PRODUCTS/OPERATIONS

2018 Sales

	$ mil.	% of total
Carpet and Resilient	3,903	39
Ceramic and Stone	3,621	36
Laminate and wood	1,553	16
Other	905	9
Total	**9,983**	**100**

2018 Sales

	$ mil.	% of total
Flooring NA	4,029	40
Global Ceramic	3,552	36
Flooring ROW	2,401	24
Total	**9,983**	**100**

Products Selected
Residential Carpet
Commercial Carpet
Bath Rugs Area Rugs and Mats
Ceramic Tile & Stone
Laminate Flooring
Hardwood Flooring
Luxury Vinyl Tile (LVT)

Selected Operations

Glazed wall tile
Hardwood flooring
Hardwood flooring
Insulation panels
Laminate flooring
Laminate flooring
Porcelain tile
Quarry tile
Resilient flooring
Roofing systems
Rugs
Stone products

Selected Brand Names

Aladdin
American Olean
Bigelow Commercial
Century Flooring
Columbia Flooring
Dal-Tile
Durkan
Horizon
Karastan
Lees
Merit
Mohawk
Mohawk Home
Quick-Step

COMPETITORS

Armstrong World Industries	Interface Inc.
Beaulieu of America	International Textile Group
Couristan	JJJ Floor Covering
Dixie Group	Mannington Mills
Formica	MasterTile
Guilford Performance Textiles	Perstorp
Hollander Home Fashions	Shaw Industries
	Tarkett Inc.
Interceramic Inc.	Wilsonart International

HISTORICAL FINANCIALS

Company Type: Public

Income Statement

FYE: December 31

	REVENUE ($ mil.)	NET INCOME ($ mil.)	NET PROFIT MARGIN	EMPLOYEES
12/19	9,970	744	7.5%	41,800
12/18	9,983	861	8.6%	42,100
12/17	9,491	971	10.2%	38,800
12/16	8,959	930	10.4%	37,800
12/15	8,071	615	7.6%	34,100
Annual Growth	**5.4%**	**4.9%**	**—**	**5.2%**

2019 Year-End Financials

Debt ratio: 19.20%
Return on equity: 9.57%
Cash ($ mil.): 134
Current ratio: 1.63
Long-term debt ($ mil.): 1,518

No. of shares (mil.): 71
Dividends
  Yield: —
  Payout: —
Market value ($ mil.): 9,769

	STOCK PRICE ($) FY Close	P/E High/Low	PER SHARE ($)		
			Earnings	Dividends	Book Value
12/19	136.38	15 11	10.30	0.00	113.35
12/18	116.96	24 10	11.47	0.00	102.81
12/17	275.90	22 15	12.98	0.00	94.85
12/16	199.68	17 12	12.48	0.00	77.88
12/15	189.39	25 18	8.31	0.00	65.66
Annual Growth	**(7.9%)**	**— —**	**5.5%**	**—**	**14.6%**

Molina Healthcare Inc

Molina Healthcare is dedicated to helping low-income Americans receive health and behavioral health coverage as well as primary care services. The company's Health Plan segment arranges for the delivery of health services to approximately 3.3 million people who receive their care through Medicaid Medicare and other government-funded programs in about 15 states and Puerto Rico. The family of founder C. David Molina controls the company through holdings and trusts.

Operations

Molina operated through two primary segments: Health Plan and the others segment. Altogether the company's operations provide plans or services to approximately 3.3 million individuals in about 15 states. Molina's Health Plans segment accounts for majority of revenues. The company's health plans provide medical services through state networks of contracted hospitals and physicians that accept Molina health plan coverage. The health plans are each licensed as health maintenance organizations (HMOs).

The Other segment includes the historical results of the MMIS and behavioral health subsidiaries that were sold in late 2018 as well as certain corporate amounts not allocated to the Health Plans segment.

Geographic Reach

Molina's health plans primarily operate in Washington California South Carolina Texas Ohio and Michigan as well as in New Mexico and Florida. Its corporate headquarters is located in Long Beach California.

Sales and Marketing

Molina's primary customers include state Medicaid agencies and the federal government. Marketplace members enroll in health plans with the assistance of insurance agents employed like outside brokers vendors direct to consumer marketing and via the Internet.

Financial Performance

The company's revenue decreased by $2.1 billion to $16.8 billion compared to $18.9 billion in the prior year. The fall was due to the decrease on their premium revenue Health insurer fees reimbursed and Service revenue.

Net income amounted to $737 million compared with net income of $707 million in 2018. The year over year comparison for net income is impacted by significantly higher costs in 2018 relating to restructuring activities interest expense debt repayment and the loss on sales of subsidiaries as well as the non-deductible HIF incurred in 2018 and the moratorium of the HIF in 2019.

The cash held by the company at the end of 2019 decreased by $418 million to $2.5 billion compared to $2.9 billion in the prior year. Cash provided by operations was $427 million while investing and financing activities were $293 million and $552 million respectively.

Strategy

In 2019 Molina's entered a new phase in its turnaround strategy by pivoting focus to a disciplined and steady approach to growth. Organic growth which includes leveraging the company's existing health plan portfolio and winning new territories is its highest priority. The strategic initiatives that will drive long-term organic growth include: Increasing market share in the company's Medicaid Medicare and Marketplace programs; Adding adjacent Medicaid geographies; Pursuing Medicaid benefit additions; Increasing market share of other programs within existing Medicaid footprint; and Winning Medicaid bids in new states and in re-procurements in existing states.

In addition to organic growth Molina will consider targeted inorganic growth opportunities that provide a strategic fit leverage operational synergies and lead to incremental earnings accretion. This will include "bolt-on" membership opportunities in its current states and health plans in new states. As noted above the company entered into two acquisition agreements in the fourth quarter of 2019 pursuant to which Molina expects to add Medicaid membership in Illinois and New York in 2020.

Mergers and Acquisitions

In 2020 Molina HealthCare Inc announced that it has completed its acquisition of certain assets of YourCare Health Plan Inc. a not-for-profit subsidiary of Monroe Plan for Medical Care. As a part of the transaction Molina assumed the right to serve approximately 47000 Medicaid members in seven counties in the Western New York and Finger Lakes regions. Monroe and its affiliate MP Care Solutions will provide certain post-closing management and administrative services related to member care and provider relations.

EXECUTIVES

Cfo And Treasurer, Joseph W. White, age 61, $538,000 total compensation

Evp Research And Development, Martha Molina Bernadett, $357,000 total compensation

President Ceo And Director, Joseph M. Zubretsky, age 64

Coo, Terry P. Bayer, age 69, $644,000 total compensation

Svp General Counsel And Secretary, Jeff D. Barlow, age 57, $525,000 total compensation

Cio, Rick Hopfer

Associate Vp State Affairs Policy And Government Advocacy, David Pingree

Associate Vice President, Chang Liu

Associate Vice President Care Management, Kelly Giardina

Regional Vice President Molina Healthcare Ohio And Molina Healthcare Missouri, Kathie Mancini

Medical Director, Lawrence O'Brien

Vice President Enterprise Pmo, Sanjay Bhat

Regional Vice President, Del Bell

Avp Accounting, Fay Adams

Assistant Vice President Rating, Ben Lynam

Vice President Of Accounting, Derek Danley

Associate Vice President Enterprise Infrastructure Services, Bharani Krish

Vice President Healthcare Services, Jeffrey King

Mhu Associate Vice President Government Contracts, Douglas Springmeyer

Director Of Pharmacy, John Vu

Vice President Sales, Ryan Boe

Medical Director, Delores Baker

Vice President, Anne Lee

Vice President Of Call Centre, Randall Fillmore

Associate Vice President Of State Affairs, Cameron Smyth

Senior Vice President Provider And Member Engagement And Operations, Mary Syiek

Medical Director, Raymond Zastrow

Avp Medicare Pharmacy Services, Erin Gordon

Vice President, Douglas Rodgers

Assistant Vice President Of Health Plan Operations, Betty Thomas

Vice President Tax, George Figueroa

Associate Vice President Of Government Contracts, David Vinkler

Vice President Business Innovation, Tom Giedlin

Associate Vice President Of Molina Healthcare Inc., Brian Monsen

Vp Of It, Jasmine Gonzalez

Vice President Network Strategy And Services, Kim Sweers

Vice President Finance And Analytics, Steve Whiting

Vice President Of Finance And Analytics, Dennis Akotia

Medical Director, James Bowerman

Medical Director, Richard Sharon

Associate Vice President, Anita Carter

Vice President, Carolyn Ingram

Vice President Government Contracts, Karen Zeiler

Assistant Vice President, Cheryl Faroughi

Medical Director, David Eibling

Vice President Corporate Development, Eric De Garceau

Medical Director, Terry Fowler

Avp Government Contracts, Barbara Maxwell

Vice President Of Operations, Elizabeth Richardson

Avp Healthplan Operations, Jaime Perikly

Vice President Of Government Contracts, Jeremy Greenfield

Vp And Medical Director, Michael Siegel

Avp Of Healthcare Services, Lorena Moore

Medical Director, Mary Engrav

Medical Director Of Behavioral Health, Ayo Gathing

Assistant Vice President Government Contracts, Nichole Mitchell

Medical Director, Felix Nunez

Vice President, Dave Boim

Associate Vice President, Suma Simcoe

Executive Assistant To Sudhakar Gummadi Vice President, Chandara Toler

Assistant Vice President Of Long Term Care Operations, Robert Kalin

Medical Director, Shyama Gandhi

Associate Vice President Sales, Rick Knickerbocker

Associate Vice President Medicare Sales, Brian Shasha

Medical Director, Latha R Shankar

Associate Vice President, Mario J Garza

Senior Vice President Deputy General Counsel, Ronald D Kurtz

Director Of Pharmacy, Jacqueline Jacobi

Assistant Vice President Health Plan Operations, Kathy Lyall

Medical Director, Arik Olson

Vice President Of Clinical Operations And New Initiatives, Rebecca Wozniak

Avp, Elizabeth Lau

Exec Vp Research And Innovation, Mary Bernadett

Associate Vice President Community Engagement, Babette Honore

Vice President, Debra Enigl

Vice President Of Network And Operations, Matt Wolf

Vice President Behavioral Health Plans, Taft Parsons

Assistant Vice President Community Engagement Enrollment Growth, Ruth Villalonga

Executive Vice President Strategic Planning Corporate Development And Transformation, Mark L Keim

Exec V Pres Health Plan Oprs, Pamela S Sedmak

Associate Vice President Healthcare Services, Deborah Mccormick

Vice President Enterprise Infrastructure Services, Benjamin Gordon

Vice President Senior Assistant General Counsel And Assistant Secretary, Burt Park

Associate Vice President Business Development, Chris Heldman

Avp, Ana Rivera

Medical Director, Ilyse Lifton

Vice President Sandm, Svitek David

Associate Vice President Finance And Analytics, Rossi Gabriel De

Senior Vice President Investor Relations, Julie Trudell

Vice President Provider Network Management And Operations, Bryon Grizzard

Vice President Network Strategy And Services, Carol Dobosh

Vice President Information Technology Business Relationship Management, Jeffrey Cangialosi

Executive Vice President Marketplace, Jason Dees

Chairman, Dale B. Wolf, age 65

Auditors: Ernst & Young LLP

LOCATIONS

HQ: Molina Healthcare Inc
200 Oceangate, Suite 100, Long Beach, CA 90802
Phone: 562 435-3666   **Fax:** 562 437-1335
Web: www.molinahealthcare.com

2017 Membership by Health Plan

	$ mil.	% of total
Washington	777,000	17
California	746,000	17
Florida	625,000	14
Texas	430,000	9
Michigan	398,000	9
Ohio	327,000	7
Puerto Rico	314,000	7
New Mexico	253,000	6
Illinois	165,000	4
Utah	152,000	3
Wisconsin	118,000	3
South Carolina	116,000	3
New York	32,000	1
Total	**4,453,000**	**100**

PRODUCTS/OPERATIONS

2017 Sales

	$ mil.	% of total
Health plans	19,352	97
Medicaid solutions	187	1
Other	344	2
Total	**19,883**	**100**

2017 Sales

	$ mil.	% of total
Premiums	18,884	95
Services	521	3
Premium tax revenue	438	2
Investment income	70	-
Total	**19,883**	**100**

COMPETITORS

AMERIGROUP	Humana
Aetna	Kaiser Foundation
Anthem	Health Plan
CIGNA	L. A. Care Health Plan
Cambia Health	Premera Blue Cross

Solutions
Centene
Community Health Group
HCSC

Priority Health
Total Health Care
UnitedHealth Group
WellCare Health Plans

HISTORICAL FINANCIALS
Company Type: Public

Income Statement
FYE: December 31

	REVENUE ($ mil.)	NET INCOME ($ mil.)	NET PROFIT MARGIN	EMPLOYEES
12/19	16,829	737	4.4%	10,000
12/18	18,890	707	3.7%	11,000
12/17	19,883	(512)	—	20,000
12/16	17,782	52	0.3%	21,000
12/15	14,178	143	1.0%	21,000
Annual Growth	4.4%	50.7%		(16.9%)

2019 Year-End Financials

Debt ratio: 21.89%
Return on equity: 40.86%
Cash ($ mil.): 2,452
Current ratio: 1.83
Long-term debt ($ mil.): 1,468

No. of shares (mil.): 62
Dividends
Yield: —
Payout: —
Market value ($ mil.): 8,413

	STOCK PRICE ($) FY Close	P/E High/Low		PER SHARE ($) Earnings	Dividends	Book Value
12/19	135.69	13	9	11.47	0.00	31.61
12/18	116.22	13	6	10.61	0.00	26.56
12/17	76.68	—	—	(9.07)	0.00	22.28
12/16	54.26	73	49	0.92	0.00	28.93
12/15	60.13	30	18	2.58	0.00	27.80
Annual Growth	22.6%			45.2%		3.3%

Molson Coors Beverage Co

Auditors: PricewaterhouseCoopers LLP

LOCATIONS

HQ: Molson Coors Beverage Co
1555 Notre Dame Street East, Montreal, Quebec H2L 2R5
Phone: 514 521-1786
Web: www.molsoncoors.com

HISTORICAL FINANCIALS
Company Type: Public

Income Statement
FYE: December 31

	REVENUE ($ mil.)	NET INCOME ($ mil.)	NET PROFIT MARGIN	EMPLOYEES
12/19	10,579	241	2.3%	17,700
12/18	10,769	1,116	10.4%	17,750
12/17	11,002	1,414	12.9%	17,200
12/16	4,885	1,975	40.4%	17,400
12/15	3,567	359	10.1%	17,500
Annual Growth	31.2%	(9.4%)	—	0.3%

2019 Year-End Financials

Debt ratio: 31.32%
Return on equity: 1.80%
Cash ($ mil.): 523
Current ratio: 0.59
Long-term debt ($ mil.): 8,109

No. of shares (mil.): 216
Dividends
Yield: 3.6%
Payout: 176.5%
Market value ($ mil.): 11,659

	STOCK PRICE ($) FY Close	P/E High/Low		PER SHARE ($) Earnings	Dividends	Book Value
12/19	53.90	59	45	1.11	1.96	62.04
12/18	56.16	16	11	5.15	1.64	62.51
12/17	82.07	15	12	6.53	1.64	61.40
12/16	97.31	12	9	9.26	1.64	53.13
12/15	93.92	49	34	1.93	1.64	38.17
Annual Growth	(13.0%)	—	—	(12.9%)	4.6%	12.9%

Mondelez International Inc

One of the world's largest snack companies Mondelez International owns a pantry of billion-dollar brands such as Cadbury and Milka chocolates; LU BelVita and Oreo biscuits; Trident gum; and Tang powdered beverages. The company's portfolio includes global national and regional brands many of which are more than 100 years old. Biscuits (cookies crackers and salted snacks) and chocolate account for most of the company's sales. Mondelez which operates in more than 80 countries and sells its products in some 150 countries but generates most of its revenue outside the US.

HISTORY

The Kraft tale began in 1903 when James L. Kraft began delivering cheese to Chicago grocers. His four brothers joined in forming the J.L. Kraft & Bros. Company in 1909. By 1914 the company had opened a cheese factory and was selling cheese across the US. Kraft developed its first blended pasteurized cheese the following year.

Kraft went public in 1924; four years later it merged with Philadelphia cream-cheese maker Phoenix and also created Velveeta cheese spread. In 1930 Kraft was bought by National Dairy but its operations were kept separate. New and notable products included Miracle Whip salad dressing (1933) macaroni and cheese dinners (1937) and Parkay margarine (1940). In the decades that followed Kraft expanded into foreign markets.

National Dairy became Kraftco in 1969 and Kraft in 1976 hoping to benefit from its internationally known trademark. To diversify Kraft merged with Dart Industries in 1980; Dart's subsidiaries (including Duracell batteries) and Kraft kept separate operations. With non-food sales sagging Dart & Kraft split up in 1986. Kraft kept its original lines and added Duracell (sold 1988); the rest became Premark International. Tobacco giant Philip Morris Companies bought Kraft in 1988 for $12.9 billion. The next year Philip Morris joined Kraft with another unit General Foods.

General Foods began when Charles Post who marketed a wheat/bran health beverage established the Postum Cereal Co. in 1896; he expanded the firm with such cereals as Grape-Nuts and Post Toasties. The company went public in 1922. Postum bought the makers of Jell-O (1925) Baker's chocolate (1927) Log Cabin syrup (1927) and Maxwell House coffee (1928) and in 1929 it acquired control of General Foods (owned by frozen vegetable pioneer Clarence Birdseye) and changed its own name to General Foods.

Its later purchases included Perkins Products (Kool-Aid 1953) and Kohner Brothers (toys 1970). Most of its non-food lines proved unsuccessful and were sold throughout the years. General Foods bought Oscar Mayer the US's #1 hot dog maker in 1981. Philip Morris bought General Foods for $5.6 billion in 1985.

The 1989 combination of Kraft and General Foods (the units still ran independently) created the largest US food maker Kraft General Foods. In the 1990s Kraft General Foods lost market share in areas such as frozen vegetables and processed meat. It introduced "light" meat products and stopped making nearly 300 food items. In 1993 it bought RJR Nabisco's cold cereal business (Shredded Wheat) and sold its Breyers ice-cream business to Unilever.

To streamline management Philip Morris integrated Kraft and General Foods in 1995. Newly named Kraft Foods sold off lower-margin businesses including its bakery unit and its North American table spreads business. Kraft bought Del Monte's shelf-stable pudding business (1995) and Taco Bell's grocery line (1996). It also sold its Lender's bagels (1996) and Log Cabin (1997) lines.

Deciding to eat healthy in early 2000 Kraft bought Boca Burger (soy products) for about $100 million and Balance Bar (meal-replacement snack bars drink mixes and beverages) for $268 million.

In 2000 parent Philip Morris (which renamed itself the Altria Group in 2003) outbid Danone and Cadbury Schweppes (later Cadbury) and agreed to buy Nabisco Holdings. It completed the deal that December for $18.9 billion (including $4 billion in debt) and began integrating those operations into Kraft Foods and Kraft Foods International. Then Philip Morris created a holding company for the newly combined food operations under the Kraft Foods Inc. name in 2001. The original Kraft Foods was renamed Kraft Foods North America.

Kraft Foods International CEO Roger Deromedi was appointed co-CEO of the new holding company along with Betsy Holden. Kraft Foods Inc. was spun off by Altria in 2001 in what was the US's second-largest IPO ever at the time (behind AT&T Wireless now AT&T Mobility).

Kraft cut 7500 jobs in 2002 as a result of the integration of Nabisco operations paying out $373 million in cash for severance and related costs. That year Kraft was also part of a $9 million settlement of a federal lawsuit regarding the use of genetically modified corn in its taco shells.

A strategy to shed brands that do not fit with the rest of the company's portfolio led Kraft to sell Farley's and Sathers in 2002 to FS Partners which renamed the company Farley's & Sathers Candy Company. Later that year Kraft sold some of its candy brands (Now and Later Intense Fruit Chews and Mity Bite) to FS Partners.

In a move to combat the population's growing obesity problem Kraft said in 2003 that it intended to reduce the fat and sugar content and cut the portion sizes of its food products as well as cease marketing in schools.

Deromedi shared the CEO slot with co-CEO Betsy Holden until 2003 at which time Deromedi was named sole CEO. (Holden was demoted to a marketing slot in the company and eventually left Kraft in 2005.) During his tenure as CEO Deromide was dogged by Kraft's looming spinoff from Altria and struggled to improve company profits by selling off underperforming and non-core brands.

The company in 2004 formed an alliance with Dr. Arthur Agatston of low-carb South Beach Diet fame to use the South Beach Diet trademark on some of its products including cereal meal replacements cereal bars refrigerated sandwich wraps and frozen entrees and pizza.

As part of Deromedi's plan to refashion Kraft's product lineup in 2005 the company sold its Altoids breath mints LifeSavers and CremeSavers candies brands whose combined sales were at the time estimated to be about $660 million a year. Wm. Wrigley Jr. Company paid about $1.4 billion for the popular brands.

Despite his best efforts to improve the bottom line Deromedi was shown the door in 2006. He was replaced by Frito-Lay's CEO Irene Rosenfeld (a former top Kraft executive who was instrumental in the company's acquisition and integration of Nabisco). She returned to Kraft after being head of Pepsico's Frito-Lay from 2004 to 2006.

Kraft extricated itself from the haze of secondhand tobacco smoke when it was spun off from Altria in 2007. Having edged toward splitting from its former parent for years the separation relieved the food maker of many headaches. It freed Kraft from any tobacco-related liability that Altria may be found guilty of post-spinoff. It also eliminated a significant layer of management which made it easier for Kraft to improve its sluggish sales.

Focusing on sharpening its brand portfolio Kraft sold off its hot cereals business in 2007. The $200 million sale to B&G Foods included two old favorites Cream of Wheat and Cream of Rice. It also sold its Fruit2O and Veryfine juice brands and operations to Sunny Delight Beverages.

As part of its plan to offer new product categories Kraft entered the lucrative and popular premade salad market in 2007 with the introduction of South Beach Living brand chicken-salad kits.

Adding more on the expansion front Kraft bought the Spanish and Portuguese operations of United Biscuits that year; the deal returned to Kraft the rights to Nabisco trademarks such as Oreo Ritz and Chips Ahoy! in Europe the Middle East and Africa.

Kraft further expanded its foreign operations with its 2007 purchase of the cookie/biscuit business of Groupe Danone for some $7.6 billion. The purchase gave the company brands such as LU Petit Ecolier and Cr¨me Roulée and made biscuits (cookies to us Yanks) the company's largest global business. It also added the Tiger and Prince brands to its Egyptian portfolio.

Billionaire Warren Buffett acquired a small percentage of Kraft in 2007 (less than 5% at the time) joining the also famously rich and famous-on-Wall Street corporate raiders Nelson Peltz (whose estimated Kraft holdings are 3%) and

Carl Icahn (who owns about 3%) in ownership of the Velveeta vendor. Peltz and Ichan are typically activist investors making suggestions regarding company operations. Peltz has suggested that Kraft concentrate on its core brands as well as undertake divestitures to fund overseas expansion.

Kraft acquiesced to Peltz on one front agreeing with his investment operations collectively known as Trian Partners by adding two directors (selected by the company and supported by Trian) to its board in 2007. Kraft also signed a "standstill" agreement with Trian agreeing to support the board's full list of nominees at Kraft's next two annual meetings.

Late in 2007 Kraft announced the re-rebranding of its South Beach products from South Beach Diet to South Beach Living saying that it wanted to capture a more positive image for the products. That year the company also sold its Veryfine juice and Fruit2O water brands and operations to the Sunny Delight company.

Kraft's 2008 sale of its slow-growing Post (Shredded Wheat Raisin Bran Honeycomb Grape-Nuts Pebbles and others) to Ralcorp a maker of private-label cereals and other foods is part of Kraft's strategy to pare down its brand offerings and concentrate on high-yield products. Ralcorp paid some $1.6 billion in stock for the acquisition. Post is the #3 US cereal maker by sales after General Millsand Kellogg. Post brought in more than $1 billion for Kraft in both 2006 and 2007.

In February 2010 Kraft acquired Cadbury for about $19 billion of which 60% was cash and 40% was stock. A majority of Cadbury's shareholders (almost 72% according to Kraft) accepted the offer effectively making Cadbury part of Kraft.

EXECUTIVES

Evp Human Resources, Karen J. May, age 61
Evp And Cfo, Brian T. Gladden, age 55, $900,000 total compensation
Ceo And Director, Dirk Van de Put, age 58
Evp And President North America, Glen Walter
Evp Integrated Supply Chain, Daniel Myers, age 65
Evp And President Europe, Hubert Weber, age 57
Evp And General Counsel, Gerhard (Gerd) Pleuhs, age 63
Evp And President Asia Middle East & Africa, Maurizio Brusadelli, age 51
Evp Research Development And Quality, Robin S. (Rob) Hargrove, age 54
Evp And President Latin America, Alejandro R. Lorenzo, age 48
Vice President Sales Channels, David Burns
Vice President Marketing Kraft Singles Natural Cheese And Velveeta, Mary Sagritanti
Senior Vice President And Global Chief Information Officer, Joher Akolawala
Vice President Human Resources Compensation, Dave Pendleton
Vp Information Systems, David Diedrich
Executive Vice President President North America, Roberto Marques
Senior Vice President And Corporate Controller, Kim Jones
Vice President Human Resources Grocery Bu And Kraft University Relations, Ginny Packer
Evp And Chief Growth Officer, Tim Cofer
Vice President Information Technology Group, Ariel Altarriba
Vice President Information Technology Group, Ariel Camacho Perez

Vice President Investor Relations, Shep Dunlap
Chairman, Irene B. Rosenfeld, age 66
Board Member, Debra Crew
Assistant Treasurer, Bill Whisler
Board Member, Fredric Reynolds
Auditors: PricewaterhouseCoopers LLP

LOCATIONS

HQ: Mondelez International Inc
  905 West Fulton Market, Suite 200, Chicago, IL 60607
Phone: 847 943-4000
Web: www.mondelezinternational.com

2018 Sales

	$ mil.	% of total
Europe	10,122	39
North America	6,885	27
AMEA	5,729	22
Latin America	3,202	12
Total	**25,938**	**100**

PRODUCTS/OPERATIONS

2018 Sales

	$ mil.	% of total
Biscuits	11,185	43
Chocolate	8,177	32
Gum & Candy	3,491	13
Cheese & Grocery	1,901	7
Beverages	1,184	5
Total	**25,938**	**100**

COMPETITORS

Associated British Foods	Hershey
Campbell Soup	Kellogg
Coca-Cola	Kerry Group
Dr Pepper Snapple Group	Kraft Heinz
Frito-Lay	Maple Leaf Foods
General Mills	Mars Incorporated
	Nestlé
	Pepperidge Farm

HISTORICAL FINANCIALS

Company Type: Public

Income Statement

FYE: December 31

	REVENUE ($ mil.)	NET INCOME ($ mil.)	NET PROFIT MARGIN	EMPLOYEES
12/20	26,581	3,555	13.4%	79,000
12/19	25,868	3,870	15.0%	80,000
12/18	25,938	3,381	13.0%	80,000
12/17	25,896	2,922	11.3%	90,000
12/16	25,923	1,659	6.4%	90,000
Annual Growth	**0.6%**	**21.0%**	**—**	**(3.2%)**

2020 Year-End Financials

Debt ratio: 29.56%	No. of shares (mil.): 1,419
Return on equity: 12.93%	Dividends
Cash ($ mil.): 3,619	Yield: 2.0%
Current ratio: 0.66	Payout: 55.0%
Long-term debt ($ mil.): 17,276	Market value ($ mil.): 82,979

	STOCK PRICE ($) FY Close	P/E High/Low		PER SHARE ($) Earnings	Dividends	Book Value
12/20	58.47	24	17	2.47	1.20	19.43
12/19	55.08	21	15	2.65	1.09	19.01
12/18	40.03	20	16	2.28	0.96	17.67
12/17	42.80	24	20	1.91	0.82	17.55
12/16	44.33	43	34	1.05	0.72	16.46
Annual Growth	**7.2%**	—	—	**23.8%**	**13.6%**	**4.2%**

Morgan Stanley

One of the world's top investment banks Morgan Stanley serves up a smorgasbord of financial services. It offers everything from advising corporate clients on mergers & acquisitions to raising capital for large companies to managing real estate investments for wealthy individuals. It boasts one of the largest financial advisor networks which works with clients to pursue their investment goals. Morgan Stanley has more than $550 billion of assets under management. The investment bank is a global enterprise with a presence in more than 40 nations serving corporate institutional government and individual clients.

HISTORY

In 1934 the Glass-Steagall Act required the J. P. Morgan bank (now part of JPMorgan Chase & Co.) to sell its securities-related activities. The next year Henry Morgan Harold Stanley and others established Morgan Stanley as an investment bank. Capitalizing on old ties to major corporations the firm handled $1 billion in issues its first year. By 1941 when it joined the NYSE it had managed 25% of all bond issues underwritten since Glass-Steagall took effect.

In the 1950s Morgan Stanley was known for handling large issues alone. Clients included General Motors U.S. Steel General Electric and DuPont. The firm avoided the merger wave of the 1960s but in the early 1970s it formed Wall Street's first mergers and acquisitions (M&A) department. In 1974 Morgan Stanley handled its first hostile takeover International Nickel's (now Vale Inco) buy of ESB the world's #1 battery maker.

Morgan Stanley went public in 1986. It escaped the carnage of the 1987 crash but a lawsuit arising from investor dissatisfaction with its M&A and LBO activities during that period lasted well into the 1990s.

By 1994 it was talking to possible merger mates including Dean Witter and finally merged with Dean Witter Discover in 1997 creating Morgan Stanley Dean Witter & Co. The San Francisco brokerage founded by Dean Witter in 1924 had remained regional for 40 years serving wealthy customers. In 1977 the firm merged with Reynolds Securities another regional retail brokerage started by Richard Reynolds Jr. the son of the founder of Reynolds Metals (now part of Alcoa) and grandnephew of the founder of R.J. Reynolds Tobacco. The new company Dean Witter Reynolds became the #2 US brokerage after Merrill Lynch and one of the top 10 US underwriters.

Dean Witter needed capital in the early 1980s and sold itself to Sears which hoped to turn it into a financial Allstate. Sears put in a retail-oriented management team and tried to shoehorn Dean Witter into in-store brokerages. Sears' indifference to the investment side hobbled operations.

The Discover card introduced by Sears and Dean Witter in 1986 was a hit but by the late 1980s it was obvious Sears would never be a financial giant. The retailer spun off Allstate Insurance and the newly renamed Dean Witter Discover in 1993.

Amazingly all but six of Morgan Stanley's 3700 World Trade Center employees survived the September 11 2001 terrorist attack on the towers. Hoping to capitalize on deregulations and privatizations in Europe as well as the rise of the individual investor Morgan Stanley acquired UK-based private bank Quilter & Co. in 2001 (then later sold it to Citigroup in 2006). Also that year the firm dropped the public use of "Dean Witter" in 2001 for promotional purposes and then dropped it completely in 2002.

When regulatory scrutiny fell on the mutual fund industry Morgan Stanley was charged with failing to adequately disclose the incentives its brokers and managers received for selling certain funds. In 2003 the firm agreed to pay a $50 million fine and adopt a "plain English" approach to informing investors about its product fees and broker compensation.

In mid-2004 the firm agreed to pay $54 million to settle a sex discrimination lawsuit filed on behalf of more than 300 female employees who claimed they were denied promotions and salary raises.

Unhappy with the firm's performance eight former Morgan Stanley executives (dubbed the Group of Eight) publicly called for the ouster of chairman and CEO Philip Purcell in 2005; Purcell was replaced by John Mack. That year a jury ordered Morgan Stanley to pay more than $1.5 billion to Ronald Perelman now the chairman of cosmetics giant Revlon. (Morgan Stanley in 2003 rejected an offer from Perelman to settle the dispute for $20 million.) Perelman contended that Morgan Stanley withheld knowledge of massive accounting fraud at appliance maker Sunbeam when he sold his camping gear firm Coleman to that company for some $1.5 billion in cash and stock in 1998; a Florida appeals court overturned the verdict in 2007.

In 2006 the firm agreed to pay a $15 million fine to settle charges that it was uncooperative and did not produce documents during investigations performed by the Securities and Exchange Commission (SEC). In addition the company settled charges (while not pleading guilty) that it falsely claimed to arbitration claimants and regulators that it lost e-mails on September 11 2001; it agreed to pay $12.5 million in 2007.

Morgan Stanley had been one of the largest credit card issuers through Discover Financial Services. However it spun those operations off in 2007. Discover was the last remnant of company's merger with the venerable Dean Witter at the end of the previous century.

After the company wrote down more than $9 billion in mortgage-related investments in 2007 it was compelled to sell part of itself to an investment arm of the Chinese government China Investment Corp. for some $5 billion in order to raise capital. The equity units included in the deal could be converted to a nearly 10% stake in Morgan Stanley.

As its traditional investment banking business faced hard times Morgan Stanley increasingly focused on private equity investing. In 2008 the company's Infrastructure unit teamed up with Ontario Teachers' Pension Plan to acquire electrical services provider SAESA the Chilean subsidiary of Public Service Enterprise Group. In 2007 Morgan Stanley teamed up with Apax Partners Worldwide to buy insurance brokerage Hub International. The previous year Morgan Stanley acquired TransMontaigne a Denver-based oil and gas transportation company (sold 2014) and Heidmar Group a Connecticut-based marine transportation and logistics firm (it later sold Heidmar's lightering business).

In order to shore up the big banks during the financial crisis the US government invested $250 billion in healthy banks to help them jumpstart their operations; Morgan Stanley received about $10 billion of that. The cash — part of the $700 billion taxpayer-fueled bailout in 2008 — came with several stipulations including restrictions on executive pay and the order to use the funds not hoard them. Deciding it didn't need the money that badly Morgan Stanley repaid the $10 billion in 2009. The company announced in late 2008 that it would cut its staff by 10% in an effort to reduce costs.

Also in 2008 the Federal Reserve mandated that Morgan Stanley and Goldman Sachs (the other remaining independent bulge-bracket US investment bank) convert to a bank holding company structure. The structure subjected them to tighter scrutiny but enabled them to acquire a commercial bank to shore up their balance sheets if need be. The move came after rivals Bear Stearns Merrill Lynch and Lehman Brothers were either acquired or went bankrupt.

In 2009 Morgan Stanley sold its remaining stake in investment analysis and market index firm MSCI to raise capital. The deal brought the company some $625 million.

Morgan Stanley also shook up its top leadership. John Mack stepped down as CEO in early 2010; he remained chairman but stepped down at the end of 2011. James Gorman the firm's co-president succeeded Mack at the helm of the company and as chairman. The change marked a significant shift for Morgan Stanley as it scaled back its operations in riskier proprietary trading.

Morgan Stanley's Asian operations got a boost in 2011 when regulators in China gave the go-ahead for the company to begin establishing operations there. It launched a joint securities venture with China Fortune Securities later that year; Morgan Stanley owns a third of the business the maximum stake allowed. China is a strategic market for growth for the company as are the emerging economies of Brazil and India.

The company in 2012 sold its Quilter wealth management division which serves the UK's mass-wealth market to private equity firm Bridgepoint Capital to focus on its wealthiest clients and institutional investors.

EXECUTIVES

Chairman And Ceo, James P. Gorman, age 62, $1,500,000 total compensation
Global Co-head Investment Banking, Franck Petitgas
President, Colm Kelleher, age 63, $1,666,041 total compensation
Co-head Wealth Management, Andy Saperstein
Global Head Sales And Trading, Ted Pick
Evp And Cfo, Jonathan Pruzan, age 52, $1,000,000 total compensation
Evp And Chief Risk Officer, Keishi Hotsuki, age 57
Global Co-head Investment Banking, Mark Eichorn
Global Co-head Of Fixed Income, Robert Rooney
Coo Institutional Securities, Clare Woodman

Head Investment Management, Daniel A. (Dan) Simkowitz, $1,000,000 total compensation

Senior Vice President Senior Consultant, David Esham

Vice President Data Center Operations, Christopher Mcdermott

Vice President, Desiree Ally

Senior Vice President And Senior Financial Advisor, Lee Corey

Senior Vice President Of Client Services Nationa, Richard French

Vice President Training, Maria Prego

Senior Vice President Portfolio Manager Wealth Advisor, Frank Corrigan

Vice President, Geoffrey Burke

Vice President, Ruben Badar

Vice President, Duncan Fudge

Vice President, Andy Jaglall

National Account Manager, Rosie Bailey

Vice President Information Technology, Anne Egan

First Vice President, Thomas Niles

Senior Vice President And Financial Advisor, Anthony Brock

Vice President Information Technology Department, Francis Rial

Vice President Head Of Engineering, Philip O'Dwyer

Vice President, Thomas Hartl

First Vice President, Ronald Phelps

Vice President Enterprise Infrastructure And Tech And Info Risk And Qapm, Zhenqin Li

Vice President Information Technology, Richard Wong

Vice President Information Technology, Alex Raykis

Vice President, Wendy Lowe

Vice President In Charge Of European Media And Internet, Fausto Zanetton

Vice President, Andrew Mento

Vice President Risk And Margins, Manu Agarwal

Vice President Network, Nathan Alexander

Senior Vice President, Adam Schur

Certified Wealth Strategist Vice President Morgan Stanley Smith Barney, Brian Weinkle

Vice President, Donny Chia

Vice President Of Communications, Jennifer Clark

Senior Vice President Financial Advisor, Thomas Bencosme

Vice President, David Cohen

Vice President, Geoffrey Berman

Senior Vice President Financial Advisor, Byron Hood

Vice President Of Information Technology Vice President Global Pricing Services, Steven Sfiroudis

Vice President, Roxane Rose

Senior Vice President Human Resources, Christine Discola

Vice President Of Human Resources, Toretha Mcguire

First Vice President And Counsel, Mark A Rhodes

Vice President Technical Support, Steve Mase

Vice President, Michael Bebawi

First Vice President Investments, Shereen Lakhani

Assistant Vice President, Charles L Wickham

Vice President Finance, Dominick Gallo

Vice President, Jeffrey Krein

Vice President Of Information Systems, Saba Anvar

Senior Vice President Of The Private Banking And Investment Group, Frank Migliazzo

Vice President Of Technology, Brian McCue

Vice President Desktop Engineering, David Gagliardotto

Vice President Gpc Marketing, Ray Difrancesco

Vice President, Peter C Bernard

Vice President, Jaymie Wetzel

Vice President, Mary Webb

Vice President, Steven Warch

Vice President, Herman Watson

Vice President, Kenneth Weitzman

Executive Vice President, Joseph Grunfeld

Vice President Product Management, Bryan Thistlethwaite

Vice President, Paul Horowitz

Vice President, Jamie Herring

Vice President Governance Risk And Compliance, Bobby Singh

Vice President, Sam Chang

Vice President, Rachel Heidingsfelder

Senior Vice President, James Davis

Vice President Business Operations, David Birnbaum

Vice President Financial Advisor, Steven Ernst

Vice President Portfolio Manager, Edward Ingold

Vice President, Richard Mejzak

Vice President, Phil Green

Vice President, Jason Devlin

Vice President Research And Development, Karen Definis

Senior Vice President, Andrew Gergel

Vice President Value Add And Retirement Marketing, Courtney Golisano

Vice President Investment Knowledge Strategist, Brooke Juniper

Vice President Defined Contribution Consultant, Peter Campagna

Vice President Finance, Jennifer Shoup

Vice President Strategic Initiatives Cash Management Marketing, Katlin Mongelluzzo

Senior Vice President And Counsel, Patricia E Brigantic

Senior Vice President, Theodore Kornobis

Vice President At Nomura, Krishna Natarajan

First Vice President Pia Portfolio Manager Cfm, James Smith

Vice President Senior Financial Advisor, Derek Rogers

Vice President, Eric Neis

Vice President, Faizan Minhas

Vice President Corporate Finance, Thomas Marcot

Vice President Defined Contribution, Jeffrey Kern

Svp Head Of Asian Sales, Lye Tho

Vice President, David Edson

Ishares Governance Vice President, Leah Schoellkopf

Vice President Investor Relations, Samantha Tortora

Vice President, Uri Morris

Product Development Vice President, Stephen Boustouler

Vice President Senior Marketing Manager Marketing Germany And Austria, Karin Emmrich

Vice President And Compensation Consultant, Michael Lebowitz

Vice President, Demitra Liapis

Vice President, Krystle Rudzinski

Associate Vice President Quantitative Analytics, Craig Dana

Vice President, Tim Harsh

Vice President, Justin Wheeler

Vice President, Lisa Kulan

Vice President, Kate Mcgrogan

Vice President Of Content And Brand Strategy, Jim Huffman

Vice President, Kevin Reynolds

Executive Vice President Head Of Us Wealth, Peter Mottek

Vice President Security Engineering, Reed Kelly

Vice President, Barry Bloomfield

Vice President Business Partner Enterprise Transformation Sales Operations And Strategy, Michael Fino

Vice President Trader, Mark Mckenzie

Vice President, Amit Soni

Vice President, John Kent

Vice President Messaging Services Manager, Ian Dobson

Vice President, Carlos Oliveira

Vice President, Sudhakar Bandu

Vice President Senior Financial Advisor, Osama Albibi

Senior Vice President, Paul Weeks

Senior Vice President Wealth Management Wealth Management Advisor Merrill Lynch, Courtney Kwas

Vice President Client Services, Gabriel Helgerson

Vice President Accounting Systems, Jose Berrios

Vice Chairman, Thomas R. (Tom) Nides, age 59

Auditors: Deloitte & Touche LLP

LOCATIONS

HQ: Morgan Stanley
1585 Broadway, New York, NY 10036
Phone: 212 761-4000
Web: www.morganstanley.com

2016 Sales

	% of total
Americas	74
EMEA	14
Asia-Pacific	12
Total	**100**

PRODUCTS/OPERATIONS

2016 Sales

	$ mil.	% of total
Interest income	7,016	19
Non-interest income		
Asset management distribution and administration fees	10,697	28
Trading	10,209	27
Investment banking	4,933	13
Commission and fees	4,109	11
Investments	160	0
Others	825	2
Total	**37,949**	**100**

2016 Sales

	% of total
Institutional Securities	50
Wealth Management	44
Investment Management	6
Total	**100**

COMPETITORS

Brown Brothers Harriman	Lehman Brothers
CIBC	Marsh & McLennan
Charles Schwab	Merrill Lynch
Citigroup	Nomura Securities
Citigroup Global Markets	Oppenheimer Holdings
Deutsche Bank	Raymond James Financial
FMR	State Street
Franklin Templeton	T. Rowe Price
Goldman Sachs	TD Bank
JPMorgan Chase	UBS
	Wells Fargo Securities

HISTORICAL FINANCIALS

Company Type: Public

Income Statement

	ASSETS ($ mil.)	NET INCOME ($ mil.)	INCOME AS % OF ASSETS	EMPLOYEES
12/19	895,429	9,042	1.0%	60,431
12/18	853,531	8,748	1.0%	60,348
12/17	851,733	6,111	0.7%	57,633
12/16	814,949	5,979	0.7%	55,311
12/15	787,465	6,127	0.8%	56,218
Annual Growth	3.3%	10.2%	—	1.8%

FYE: December 31

2019 Year-End Financials

Debt ratio: 21.51%	No. of shares (mil.): 1,593
Return on equity: 11.18%	Dividends
Cash ($ mil.): 82,171	Yield: 2.5%
Current ratio: —	Payout: 25.0%
Long-term debt ($ mil.): —	Market value ($ mil.): 81,484

STOCK PRICE ($)		P/E		PER SHARE ($)		
	FY Close	High/Low		Earnings	Dividends	Book Value
12/19	51.12	10	7	5.19	1.30	51.16
12/18	39.65	12	8	4.73	1.10	47.21
12/17	52.47	17	13	3.07	0.90	43.28
12/16	42.25	15	7	2.92	0.70	41.05
12/15	31.81	14	10	2.90	0.55	39.16
Annual Growth	12.6%	—	—	15.7%	24.0%	6.9%

Mosaic Co (The)

Big pieces of the global agricultural chemical industry come together to form The Mosaic Co. It ranks as one of the world's largest producers of phosphate and potash which are used for crop nutrition and as input to animal feed. In North America Mosaic accounts for about 75% of annual phosphate production and about 35% of potash production. In the rest of the world the company holds significant market share about 15% of phosphate and some 10% of potash production. The raw materials of its products are mined from locations in Canada and the US. About 75% of Mosaic's sales are from international customers.

Operations

Mosaic operates three business segments: Mosaic Fertilizantes Phosphates and Potash.

The Mosaic Fertilizantes segment about 40% of sales owns and operates mines chemical plants crop nutrients blending and bagging facilities port terminals and warehouses in Brazil and Paraguay. The segment produces and sells concentrated phosphates crop nutrients phosphate-based animal feed ingredients and potash fertilizer.

The Phosphates segment which generates about 35% of Mosaic's revenues owns and operates mines and production facilities in Florida and Louisiana. It produces concentrated phosphate crop nutrients and phosphate-based animal feed ingredients. Its animal feed products are sold under brand names Biofos and Nexfos. A key phosphate product is MicroEssentials a fertilizer that is enhanced through a patented process.

The Potash segment nearly 25% of revenue owns and operates potash mines in Canada (Saskatchewan province) and New Mexico. Most of its product is used for crop nutrients and as input for animal feed. Mosaic's annual potash capacity can produce nearly 7.9 million tons or about 10% of world capacity and more than 35% of North American capacity.

Geographic Reach

Mosaic is headquartered in Plymouth Minnesota and has customers in about 40 countries. The company relies on two countries for 65 of its revenue with Brazil supplying about 40% and the US providing about 25%.

The company operates phosphate rock mines in Florida and Brazil and processes the rock into finished phosphate products at facilities in Florida Louisiana and Brazil.

Mosaic owns port facilities in Tampa Florida and Houston Texas as well as warehouse distri-

bution facilities in Savage and Rosemount Minnesota Pekin Illinois and Henderson Kentucky.

Its distribution operations also include leased distribution space or contractual throughput agreements in some 15 states including California Indiana Iowa Kentucky and Missouri. It also lease and own warehouse facilities in Saskatchewan Ontario Quebec and Manitoba in Canada.

Sales and Marketing

Mosaic sells products to wholesale distributors retail chains cooperatives independent retailers and national accounts.

Phosphate crop nutrient products are marketed worldwide to crop nutrient manufacturers distributors retailers and farmers. Potash products are marketed worldwide to crop nutrient manufacturers distributors and retailers and are also used in the manufacturing of mixed crop nutrients and to a lesser extent in animal feed ingredients. It also sells potash to customers for industrial use.

Mosaic markets its Canadian potash outside of the US and Canada through Canpotex an export association.

Financial Performance

Mosaic has struggled to attain meaningful revenue growth in recent years while profits have fluctuated.

In 2019 revenue dropped 7% to $8.9 billion down $681 million from 2018. The decline was due to decrease sales in Phosphates and Potash segment partially offset by Mosaic Fertilizantes.

The company's posted a net loss of $1.1 billion in 2019 from a $470 million profit the year before due to higher expenses and lower in revenue.

Mosaic held $532.3 million in cash in 2019 compared to $871.0 billion in the previous year. In 2019 operations generated $1.1 billion investing activities used $1.4 billion and financing activities used another $82.2 billion.

Strategy

In 2019 Mosaic plan to accelerate development of the Esterhazy K3 potash mine shaft by an additional year with expected completion by mid-2022. As production from the K3 shaft ramps up it plan to cease underground mining at the K1 and K2 mine shafts. Underground operations will be completely transitioned to K3 in 2022 which is expected to eliminate its brine inflow management costs at the K1 and K2 shafts. A total of 1.4 million tonnes of ore was produced from the K3 shaft in 2019.

While it purchased the Pine Bend distribution facility in Rosemount Minnesota near the northern end of the Mississippi River for $55 million. It closed the phosphate facility located in Plant City Florida that was previously idled in late 2017. The cost of the closure were approximately $341 million.

In response to slow market conditions throughout 2019 Mosaic took steps to reduce its fertilizer production until market conditions improve. In late 2019 the company plan to decrease phosphate production at its Central Florida facilities by 150000 tonnes per month in addition to the 500000 tonne reduction it implemented in the second half of 2019 primarily at its Louisiana facility. It also plan to continue to operate at lower rates at its Canadian potash mines.

Company Background

Mosaic was created through the merger of IMC Global and Cargill's former crop nutrition unit in 2004. In 2011 Cargill divested its 64% of Mosaic shares to its shareholders and debtholders in a $24 billion transaction splitting off Mosaic and ending its status as a majority-owned company.

EXECUTIVES

Evp And Cfo, Richard L. (Rich) Mack, age 52, $624,000 total compensation
President And Ceo, James (Joc) O'Rourke, age 59, $893,833 total compensation
Svp Potash Operations, Walter F. (Walt) Precourt, age 55
Svp Potash, Bruce Bodine
Vice President Chief Compliance Officer, Diana Jagiella
Assistant Vice President Business Development, Courtney Mattson
Assistant Vice President, David Jellerson
Vice President Information Technology, Ralph Mills
Vice President Procurement, Chris Martus
Senior Vice President Strategy And Growth, Walt Precourt
Vice President Human Resources, Kerrie Campbell
Vice President Internal Audit, Allen Cooper
Chairman, Robert L. Lumpkins, age 76
Auditors: KPMG LLP

LOCATIONS

HQ: Mosaic Co (The)
101 East Kennedy Blvd, Suite 2500, Tampa, FL 33602
Phone: 800 918-8270 **Fax:** 763 577-2990
Web: www.mosaicco.com

2018 Sales

	% of total
United States	31
Brazil	39
Canpotex	9
Canada	7
India	3
others regions	11
Total	**100**

PRODUCTS/OPERATIONS

2018 Sales

	$ mil.	% of total
Phosphates	3,886	40
Potash	2,173	22
International distribution	3,747	38
Elimination	(220)	-
Total	**9,587**	**100**

Premium Crop Nutrients

Premium Crop Nutrients
MicroEssentials®; SZ;
MicroEssentials®; S15;
MicroEssentials®; S10;
K-Mag®; Granular
K-Mag®; Premium
K-Mag®; Special Standard
K-Mag®; Standard
Pegasus®; Fine
Pegasus®; Granular
Potash
White Standard 0-0-62
Red Granular 0-0-60
Red Standard 0-0-60
Crystal Granular 0-0-60
Crystal Turf 150
Phosphates
Diammonium Phosphate (DAP) 18-46-0
Monoammonium Phosphate (MAP) 11-52-0
Powdered MAP
Feed Ingredients
Biofos®;
Dyna-K®;

Dynamate®;
Dyna-K White®;
Nexfos®;
Industrial Products
FSA Products
Hydrofluorosilicic Acid (FSA or HFS)
Potash Products
White Fine 0-0-62
White Granular 0-0-62
White Industrial High Quality
White Industrial Special
Red Standard 0-0-60

COMPETITORS

Arab Potash	Potash Corp
CF Industries	Sinofert
Israel Chemicals	Uralkali
K+S	

HISTORICAL FINANCIALS

Company Type: Public

Income Statement   FYE: December 31

	REVENUE ($ mil.)	NET INCOME ($ mil.)	NET PROFIT MARGIN	EMPLOYEES
12/19	8,906	(1,067)	—	12,600
12/18	9,587	470	4.9%	12,900
12/17	7,409	(107)	—	8,500
12/16	7,162	297	4.2%	8,700
12/15	8,895	1,000	11.2%	8,900
Annual Growth	0.0%	—	—	9.1%

2019 Year-End Financials

Debt ratio: 23.91%	No. of shares (mil.): 378
Return on equity: (-10.90%)	Dividends
Cash ($ mil.): 519	Yield: 0.8%
Current ratio: 1.43	Payout: —
Long-term debt ($ mil.): 4,525	Market value ($ mil.): 8,196

	STOCK PRICE ($) FY Close	P/E High/Low	PER SHARE ($) Earnings	Dividends	Book Value
12/19	21.64	— —	(2.78)	0.18	24.25
12/18	29.21	30 19	1.22	0.10	26.97
12/17	25.66	— —	(0.31)	0.60	27.40
12/16	29.33	37 26	0.85	1.10	27.37
12/15	27.59	19 10	2.78	1.08	27.04
Annual Growth	(5.9%)	— —	—	(36.5%)	(2.7%)

Motorola Solutions Inc

Do you copy? and "Roger that" might be snippets of conversation heard over two-way radios and other devices made by Motorola Solutions. The company's radios and wireless broadband products are used by government public safety and first-responder agencies for communications and personnel deployment. Commercial and industrial customers use products from Motorola to stay in touch with mobile work forces. Besides two-way radios the company makes vehicle-mounted radios body cameras and other devices and develops software systems to connect them. Some 65% of sales are to customers in the US. Motorola Solutions goes back to the late 1920s when the company made radios for police cars.

Operations

Motorola has two operating segments: Products and Systems Integration and Services and Software.

The Products and Systems Integration segment accounting for about 70% of revenue offers infrastructure devices such as two-way radios and vehicle-mounted radios accessories and video tools as well implementation and integration services. The segment also provides customized radio networks software and applications.

The Services and Software segment over 30% of revenue provides repair technical support and maintenance as well as monitoring and cybersecurity services. Software products include a public safety and enterprise command center software suite unified communications applications and video software delivered on premise and through the cloud.

Geographic Reach

Headquartered in Chicago Illinois Motorola Solutions operates throughout the world but it relies on the US for about 65% of sales. The UK contributes about 10% of sales and Canada provides about 5% with other countries supplying the remaining quater of revenue. Motorola owns three facilities: one manufacturing facility in Europe an office in Europe and an office in the U.S. The company also leases over 230 facilities almost 130 of which are located in the Americas region and over 100 of which were located in other countries.

Sales and Marketing

Motorola Solutions sells through an in-house sales operation that directly approaches its largest accounts and through channel partners for other accounts. Primary customers are government public safety first-responder agencies and municipalities. Other important customers are commercial and industrial companies that operate private communications networks and manage mobile work forces.

Motorola Solutions depends on agencies in the US federal government for about 10% of sales and the Home Office of the UK for about 10% of sales.

Financial Performance

Motorola Solutions posted a fourth-straight year of higher revenue in 2019.

In 2019 Motorola Solutions' sales rose 7% to $7.8 billion up over $500 million from 2018 driven by growth in the Americas.

Net income was $868 million in 2019 compared to a loss of $966 million in 2018.

Motorola Solutions' cash and equivalents dipped at about $1 billion. In 2019 operations generated $1.8 billion while investing and financing activities used $934 million and $1.1 billion respectively.

Strategy

Motorola's strategy for long-term growth and the evolution of its business includes organic and inorganic investments in the following four areas:

Innovation in a standards-based mission critical voice and data solutions market which is made up of LMR and Long-Term Evolution ("LTE") technologies; Service offerings that leverage its large global install base and allow its customers to improve performance across their systems devices and applications for greater safety and productivity; Video analytics network video management software and hardware video cameras and access control solutions for government and commercial customers; and Command center software solutions to support public

safety workflow from calling 9-1-1 and dispatching first responders to communicating with personnel in the field and managing records and evidence.

Acquisitions play an important part in Motorola Solutions' growth plans. It acquired Avigilon Corp. a developer of video security products to enhance offerings that capture and analyze video. The 2019 acquisition of VaaS International Holdings also expanded video capabilities.

Mergers and Acquisitions

In 2019 Motorola Solutions acquired WatchGuard Inc. which designs and makes mobile video systems. The deal adds to Motorola's video security offerings that include fixed cameras and analytics and license plate recognition cameras and software. WatchGuard's products are in-car video systems body-worn cameras evidence management systems and software.

In 2019 Motorola Solutions acquired VaaS International Holdings which develops video analysis-as-a-service technologies for $445 million. VaaS provides data and image analytics for vehicle location. Its subsidiaries include Vigilant Solutions for law enforcement users and Digital Recognition Network for commercial customers. The acquisition expands Motorola Solutions' command center software portfolio.

Also in 2019 Motorola Solutions acquired Avtec Inc. a provider of voice over internet protocol (VoIP) dispatch services for public safety and commercial customers expanding the company's portfolio for those markets.

Company Background

Motorola got its start in 1928 when Paul Galvin then 33 founded Galvin Manufacturing in Chicago to make battery eliminators so early radios could run on household current instead of batteries. The following year Galvin began making car radio receivers and trying to develop a mobile radio for the police. In 1940 the company developed the first handheld two-way radio for the US Army.

In 1947 Galvin renamed the company Motorola after its car radios. In the late 1950s Motorola started making integrated circuits and microprocessors stepping outside its auto industry mainstay. When Galvin died in 1959 his son Robert became CEO. The company's purchase that year of a hospital communications systems maker led it to produce some of the first pagers.

Over the years the company has expanded and contracted evening launching a satellite system to handle its communications.m An early leader in cell phones the company failed to make the transition to smart phone. Eventually the company divested parts of the business to again focus on communications oriented toward public safety applications.

EXECUTIVES

Chairman And Ceo, Gregory Q. (Greg) Brown, age 61, $1,250,000 total compensation

Evp Strategy And Innovation, Eduardo F. Conrado, age 53, $448,750 total compensation

Svp Global Solutions And Services, Bruce W. Brda, age 59, $550,769 total compensation

Evp And Cfo, Gino A. Bonanotte, age 56, $645,385 total compensation

Evp General Counsel And Chief Administrative Officer, Mark S. Hacker, age 49, $526,337 total compensation

Evp Worldwide Sales, John P. (Jack) Malloy, age 49, $497,615 total compensation
Executive Vice President President Global Custo, Joseph M Guglielmi
Territory Vice President, Mark Schmidl
Mssi Vice President, Derek Phipps
Vice President Of Environment Health And Safety, Jodi Shapiro
Senior Vice President, Jonathan Meyer
Vice President Of Sales, Edward Fuerst
Regional Vice President Services Operations User. Western Region, Howard Chercoe
Vice President Astro Subscriber Products, Steve Young
Vice President Of Software Enterprise, Dan Twohig
Svp Sales And Marketing U.s. And Canada, Jim Mears
Vice President, Chris Rapala
Vice President Of Strategic Sales, Patty Holtschneider
Vice President Of Records And Evidence Systems, Alam Ali
Vice President Sales And Services And Territory Director Nola Region, Fernando Bonilla
Msssi Vice President, Mary Wathen
Vice President, Chris Kustor
Board Member, Kenneth Denman
Auditors: PricewaterhouseCoopers LLP

LOCATIONS

HQ: Motorola Solutions Inc
500 West Monroe Street, Chicago, IL 60661
Phone: 847 576-5000   **Fax:** 847 576-3477
Web: www.motorolasolutions.com

2018 Sales

	$ mil.	% of total
US	4,361	59
UK	638	9
Canada	303	4
Other countries	2,097	33
Total	**7,343**	**100**

PRODUCTS/OPERATIONS

2018 Sales

	$ mil.	% of total
Products and Systems Integration	5,100	69
Services and Software	2,243	39
Total	**7,343**	**100**

Selected Products and Services

Devices
 Mobile computers
 Mobile-to-mobile wireless modules
 Public safety LTE infrastructure devices and services (handheld USB modem vehicle modem)
 Radio-frequency identification products (RFID) and accessories
 Two-way radios and pagers
 Two-way radio accessories
Networks
 Mobile broadband (public safety LTE)
 Private broadband networks
 Wireless broadband networks

Services

Enterprise
 Enterprise video solutions
 Integrated enterprise communications
 Managed network infrastructure
 Managed security and compliance
 Supply chain visibility solutions
 Government and Public Safety
 Advanced video security systems
 Complex network design and integration
 Interoperability and unified communications
 Next-generation command and control
 Public safety managed services
Software
 Application development framework
 Mobility software
 Network design software

Public sector applications
 Support and help desk applications
Systems
 Dispatch systems
 Enterprise voice systems
 SCADA Systems (real-time facilities monitoring and control)

COMPETITORS

Airbus Group	Intergraph
Cisco Systems	Intermec
EF Johnson	JVC KENWOOD
Technologies	Sepura
Harris Corp.	Tri-Tech
Honeywell	West Corporation
International	

HISTORICAL FINANCIALS

Company Type: Public

Income Statement

FYE: December 31

	REVENUE ($ mil.)	NET INCOME ($ mil.)	NET PROFIT MARGIN	EMPLOYEES
12/19	7,887	868	11.0%	17,000
12/18	7,343	966	13.2%	16,000
12/17	6,380	(155)	—	15,000
12/16	6,038	560	9.3%	14,000
12/15	5,695	610	10.7%	14,000
Annual Growth	**8.5%**	**9.2%**	**—**	**5.0%**

2019 Year-End Financials

Debt ratio: 48.20%	No. of shares (mil.): 170
Return on equity:—	Dividends
Cash ($ mil.): 1,001	Yield: 1.4%
Current ratio: 1.21	Payout: 39.1%
Long-term debt ($ mil.): 5,113	Market value ($ mil.): 27,474

	STOCK PRICE ($) FY Close	P/E High/Low	PER SHARE ($) Earnings	Dividends	Book Value
12/19	161.14	35 21	4.95	2.35	(4.11)
12/18	115.04	22 15	5.62	2.13	(7.91)
12/17	90.34	— —	(0.95)	1.93	(10.81)
12/16	82.89	25 18	3.24	1.70	(5.85)
12/15	68.45	24 19	3.02	1.43	(0.61)
Annual Growth	**23.9%**	**— —**	**13.1%**	**13.2%**	**—**

MOTT, CHARLES STEWART FOUNDATION INC

EXECUTIVES

Chb-Pres-Ceo, William S White
V Pres-Sec-Treas*, Phillip Peters
V Pres-Invest*, Robert E Swaney Jr
V Pres-Programs*, Maureen Smyth
V Pres-Communications, Marilyn Stein Lefeber
Vce Prsdnt Infrmtn Systms, Gavin T Flint
H Ranalyst, Julie M Flynn
Database Administrator, Karen Poindexter
Communications Officer, Jessica Jones
Hr Administrator, Aria Staffne
Auditors: GRANT THORNTON LLP MILWAUKEE

LOCATIONS

HQ: MOTT, CHARLES STEWART FOUNDATION INC
503 S SAGINAW ST STE 1200, FLINT, MI 485021807
Phone: 810 238-5651
Web: WWW.MOTT.ORG

HISTORICAL FINANCIALS

Company Type: Private

Income Statement

FYE: December 31

	ASSETS ($ mil.)	NET INCOME ($ mil.)	INCOME AS % OF ASSETS	EMPLOYEES
12/17	3,098	42	1.4%	106
12/15	2,720	82	3.0%	
12/09	2,079	0	—	
12/04	2,524	305	12.1%	
Annual Growth	**1.6%**	**(14.1%)**		

MPLX LP

MPLX is a diversified master limited partnership formed in 2012 by Marathon Petroleum Corporation (MPC) to own operate develop and acquire midstream energy infrastructure assets. It gathers processes and transports natural gas; gathers transports fractionates stores and markets natural gas liquids (NGLs); and transports stores and distributes crude oil and refined petroleum products. Headquartered in Findlay Ohio MPLX's assets consist of a network of crude oil and products pipeline assets located in the Midwest and Gulf Coast regions of the United States. It owns and operates light-product terminals an inland marine business storage caverns crude oil and product storage facilities (tank farms) a barge dock facility and gathering and processing assets. MPLX went public in 2012. Marathon Petroleum Corporation and MPLX completed another large drop-down deal in 2017 whereby MPLX paid $8.1 billion to obtain refining logistics assets and fuels distribution services from MPC. The transaction increased by 50% the size of MPLX's balance sheet.

EXECUTIVES

Executive Vice President And Chief Commercial Officer Markwest Assets, Randy Nickerson
Vice President And Controller, C Kristopher Hagedorn
Vice President Tax Of Mplx Gp Llc, Frank Quintana
Board Member, Dan Sandman
Auditors: PricewaterhouseCoopers LLP

LOCATIONS

HQ: MPLX LP
200 E. Hardin Street, Findlay, OH 45840
Phone: 419 421-2414
Web: www.mplx.com

COMPETITORS

American Midstream Partners	Genesis Energy
Blueknight Energy Partners	Holly Energy Partners
Boardwalk Pipeline	Jayhawk Pipeline
Chevron Pipe Line	Kinder Morgan
	Magellan Midstream
	Plains All American

Crestwood Midstream Partners LP | Pipeline
DCP Midstream Partners | Rose Rock Midstream
EQT Midstream | SemGroup
Enterprise Products | Sunoco Logistics
ExxonMobil Pipeline | TransMontaigne
| Williams

HISTORICAL FINANCIALS
Company Type: Public

Income Statement — FYE: December 31

	REVENUE ($ mil.)	NET INCOME ($ mil.)	NET PROFIT MARGIN	EMPLOYEES
12/19	9,041	1,434	15.9%	—
12/18	6,425	1,818	28.3%	—
12/17	3,867	830	21.5%	—
12/16	2,590	256	9.9%	—
12/15	703	156	22.2%	—
Annual Growth	89.4%	74.1%	—	—

2019 Year-End Financials
Debt ratio: 48.74%
Return on equity: 147.76%
Cash ($ mil.): 15
Current ratio: 0.70
Long-term debt ($ mil.): 19,704
No. of shares (mil.): 1,058
Dividends
Yield: 10.4%
Payout: 115.2%
Market value ($ mil.): 26,946

	STOCK PRICE ($) FY Close	P/E High/Low		PER SHARE ($) Earnings	Dividends	Book Value
12/19	25.46	36	23	1.00	2.65	16.38
12/18	30.30	17	13	2.29	2.49	9.71
12/17	35.47	36	29	1.06	2.21	26.06
12/16	34.62	—	—	(0.00)	2.03	30.66
12/15	39.33	67	23	1.22	1.70	29.67
Annual Growth	(10.3%)	—	—	(4.8%)	11.7%	(13.8%)

Mr Cooper Group Inc

EXECUTIVES

Chm, Michael Willingham
Vice President Information Security Officer, Todd Bailey
Auditors: Ernst & Young LLP

LOCATIONS

HQ: Mr Cooper Group Inc
8950 Cypress Waters Blvd., Coppell, TX 75019
Phone: 469 549-2000
Web: www.mrcoopergroup.com

HISTORICAL FINANCIALS
Company Type: Public

Income Statement — FYE: December 31

	ASSETS ($ mil.)	NET INCOME ($ mil.)	INCOME AS % OF ASSETS	EMPLOYEES
12/19	18,305	274	1.5%	9,100
12/18*	16,973	884	5.2%	8,500
07/18	0	154	—	—
12/17	614	25	4.2%	6
12/16	736	201	27.4%	6
Annual Growth	191.9%	10.8%	—	1048.9%
*Fiscal year change

2019 Year-End Financials
Debt ratio: 40.22%
Return on equity: 13.13%
Cash ($ mil.): 329
Current ratio: —
Long-term debt ($ mil.): —
No. of shares (mil.): 91
Dividends
Yield: —
Payout: —
Market value ($ mil.): 1,140

	STOCK PRICE ($) FY Close	P/E High/Low		PER SHARE ($) Earnings	Dividends	Book Value
12/19	12.51	5	2	2.95	0.00	24.50
12/18*	11.67	2	0	9.54	0.00	21.39
07/18	1.36	1	0	1.55	0.00	(0.00)
12/17	0.85	13	5	0.12	0.00	34.67
12/16	1.55	1	0	3.60	0.00	40.49
Annual Growth	100.6%	—	—	(6.4%)	—	(15.4%)
*Fiscal year change

Murphy USA Inc

It may not be the biggest but Murphy USA is flexing its muscles in the US gas station market. Murphy USA (a former operating unit of Murphy Oil) markets refined products through its network of branded gasoline stations and convenience stores customers and unbranded wholesale customers in more than 25 Southeast Southwest and Midwest US states to more than 1.6 million customers. The company's nearly 1500 retail gas stations (almost all of which are in close proximity to Walmart stores) sell gas under the Murphy USA brand. It also operates about 330 Murphy Express locations and sells some 4.4 billion gallons of motor fuel through retail outlets.

Operations

The company markets retail motor fuel products and convenience merchandise through its own chain of retail stations almost all of which are in close proximity to Wal-Mart stores. Its business also includes product supply and wholesale assets such as product distribution terminals and pipelines.

Petroleum product sales account for about 80% of the company's total revenues.

Geographic Reach

Murphy USA has retail stations in more than 25 US states (primarily in the Southeast — Florida and Tennessee) as well as in the Southwest and the Midwest.

Texas Florida Georgia North Carolina and Tennessee together account for nearly 50% of its total retail outlets.

Murphy's headquarters is located in El Dorado Arkansas.

Sales and Marketing

They sell gasoline under the Murphy USA and Murphy Express brands.

Financial Performance

Murphy's revenue has gone down from 419 billion in 2012 to just under $13 billion in 2017. Net income has been more stable staying mostly above $200 million mark each year but decreased to some $155 million in 2019.

2019 revenue decreased $0.3 billion or 2.3% compared to 2018. The decrease was primarily due to a decrease in retail fuel prices of 14 cpg for the 2019 full year which was partially offset by an increase in retail fuel sales volumes of 3.4% due primarily to an increase in the number of stores and improved pricing tactics. Merchandise sales were also higher year-over-year by 8.1%.

Net income fell 28% some to $155 million primarily due to lower settlement proceeds from Deepwater Horizon spill higher expenses and loss on early debt extinguishment.

Murphy's cash holdings increased slightly from $185 million to $280 million. Operating activities brought in $313 million. Investment utilized $203.1 million mostly in purchase of property and plants while a further $14 million went towards financing activities.

Strategy

Murphy intends for its independent growth plan to be a key driver of its organic growth over the next several years. The company expects to build up to 30 NTI locations and up to 25 raze-and-rebuilds per year targeting high-return locations either near Walmart Supercenters other high traffic areas or by strategic infill in its core market areas complemented by its supply chain capabilities. Murphy previously focused on smaller lot sizes the company expected to build more NTI stores that are 2800 square feet. Murphy's real estate development team works to maintain a multi-year pipeline of projects that supports ratable expansion.

Murphy also plan to continuously evaluate its remaining kiosk strategy in an effort to maximize its site economics and return on investment. Complementary to that strategy Murphy continually refining and increasingly constructing its 1200-1400 square foot and 2800 square foot design to create a foundation for increasing higher-margin non-tobacco sales and diversifying our merchandise offerings. Murphy further expands its merchandise revenue and margins through its primary supplier relationship with Core-Mark in addition to optimizing its promotional planning merchandise assortment and pricing effectiveness in order to help boost overall site returns.

The company also focuses on improving its infrastructure to lower overhead costs and on long-term investment. It plans to continue to focus its product supply and wholesale efforts on activities that enhance its ability to be a low-price retail fuel leader by optimizing its fuel supply contracts to capitalize on market dynamics whenever possible and minimizing physical product supply and wholesale asset ownership.

Company Background

Boosting its customer offerings in 2010 the company teamed up with Western Union signing a deal to offer online money transfer services at its Murphy USA gas stations and Murphy Express convenience stores across the country.

As part of its former parent's decision to exit the refining business in 2011 MUSA sold its Superior Wisconsin refinery to Calumet Specialty Products Partners for $475 million. It also sold its refinery in Meraux Louisiana to Valero Energy for $625 million. The divestitures transformed MUSA into a pure gas station/convenience store company.

In 2013 Murphy Oil completed the spin-off of its US retail marketing business into an independent public company — Murphy USA Inc. The spin-off was achieved through the distribution to Murphy Oil's shareholders of one share of Murphy USA common stock for every four shares of Murphy Oil stock. It holds through its subsidiaries the US retail marketing business that was separated from its former parent company plus certain ethanol production facilities and other assets and liabilities of Murphy Oil that supported the activities of the US retail marketing operations.

In an effort to exit non-core businesses in the fall of 2013 the company sold underperforming subsidiary Hankinson Renewable Energy LLC (which owns and operates the Hankinson North Dakota ethanol plant) to Guardian Hankinson LLC for $173 million.

EXECUTIVES

Evp And Cfo, Mindy K. West, age 51, $546,083 total compensation
Svp Retail Operations And Support, Marn K. Cheng, age 54, $382,627 total compensation
President And Ceo, R. Andrew Clyde, age 56, $991,667 total compensation
Svp Marketing, Robert J. (Rob) Chumley, $116,667 total compensation
Vice President And Controller, Donnie Smith
Senior Vice President Human Resources, Terry Hatten
Chairman, R. Madison Murphy, age 62
Treasurer, Jennifer Bridges
Auditors: KPMG LLP

LOCATIONS

HQ: Murphy USA Inc
200 Peach Street, El Dorado, AR 71730-5836
Phone: 870 875-7600
Web: www.murphyusa.com

2016 Stores

States	no. of stores
Texas	294
Florida	120
Georgia	94
Tennessee	92
North Carolina	86
Alabama	76
Louisiana	75
Arkansas	68
Mississippi	55
South Carolina	56
Oklahoma	53
Missouri	48
Kentucky	47
Ohio	44
Indiana	38
Illinois	37
Michigan	27
Iowa	22
Virginia	22
New Mexico	12
Colorado	12
Minnesota	9
Kansas	5
Utah	4
Nebraska	3
Nevada	2
Total	**1,401**

PRODUCTS/OPERATIONS

2016 Sales

	$ mil.	% of total
Petroleum product sales	9,070	78
Merchandise sales	2,338	20
Other operating revenue	185	2
Total	**11,594**	**100**

COMPETITORS

7-Eleven	Hess Corporation
Alon Brands	QuikTrip
Chevron	Racetrac Petroleum
ConocoPhillips	Royal Dutch Shell
Couche-Tard	Valero Energy
Exxon Mobil	

HISTORICAL FINANCIALS
Company Type: Public

Income Statement
FYE: December 31

	REVENUE ($ mil.)	NET INCOME ($ mil.)	NET PROFIT MARGIN	EMPLOYEES
12/19	14,034	154	1.1%	9,900
12/18	14,362	213	1.5%	9,500
12/17	12,826	245	1.9%	9,600
12/16	11,594	221	1.9%	9,100
12/15	12,699	176	1.4%	9,800
Annual Growth	**2.5%**	**(3.2%)**	**—**	**0.3%**

2019 Year-End Financials

Debt ratio: 38.63%
Return on equity: 19.23%
Cash ($ mil.): 280
Current ratio: 1.41
Long-term debt ($ mil.): 999

No. of shares (mil.): 30
Dividends
  Yield: —
  Payout: —
Market value ($ mil.): 3,564

	STOCK PRICE ($) FY Close	P/E High/Low	Earnings	PER SHARE ($) Dividends	Book Value
12/19	117.00	25 15	4.86	0.00	26.36
12/18	76.64	14 10	6.48	0.00	25.02
12/17	80.36	12 9	6.78	0.00	21.66
12/16	61.47	14 10	5.59	0.00	18.87
12/15	60.74	18 12	4.02	0.00	19.01
Annual Growth	**17.8%**	**— —**	**4.9%**	**—**	**8.5%**

NASB Financial Inc

NASB Financial is the holding company for North American Savings Bank which operates about 15 branches and loan offices in the Kansas City and Springfield Missouri areas. Established in 1927 the bank offers standard deposit products to retail and commercial customers including checking and savings accounts and CDs. Mortgages secured by residential or commercial properties make up most of the bank's lending activities; it also originates business consumer and construction loans. Subsidiary Nor-Am sells annuities mutual funds and credit life and disability insurance. Chairman David Hancock and his wife Linda who is also a member of the company's board of directors own about 45% of NASB Financial.

EXECUTIVES

Vice President, Lori West
Vice President, Ron Stafford
Vice President Construction And Development Lending, Christopher Vick
Assistant Vice President, Carmen Cunningham
Executive Vice President Chief Lending Officer, Michael Braman
Executive Vice President And Chief Human Resources Office, Burke Walker
Auditors: BKD, LLP

LOCATIONS

HQ: NASB Financial Inc
12498 South 71 Highway, Grandview, MO 64030
Phone: 816 765-2200
Web: www.nasb.com

COMPETITORS

Bank of America	Guaranty Federal
Commerce Bancshares	U.S. Bancorp
Dickinson Financial	UMB Financial

HISTORICAL FINANCIALS
Company Type: Public

Income Statement
FYE: September 30

	ASSETS ($ mil.)	NET INCOME ($ mil.)	INCOME AS % OF ASSETS	EMPLOYEES
09/20	2,552	103	4.1%	—
09/19	2,605	43	1.7%	—
09/18	2,060	29	1.4%	—
09/17	2,062	29	1.4%	—
09/16	1,949	22	1.1%	—
Annual Growth	**7.0%**	**46.6%**		

2020 Year-End Financials

Debt ratio: 2.31%
Return on equity: 33.70%
Cash ($ mil.): 90
Current ratio: —
Long-term debt ($ mil.): —

No. of shares (mil.): 7
Dividends
  Yield: 3.5%
  Payout: 31.0%
Market value ($ mil.): 443

	STOCK PRICE ($) FY Close	P/E High/Low	Earnings	PER SHARE ($) Dividends	Book Value
09/20	60.00	4 2	14.01	2.15	47.42
09/19	44.20	8 6	5.85	2.00	35.56
09/18	40.60	11 9	3.94	3.82	31.37
09/17	36.11	10 8	3.98	1.22	31.55
09/16	33.75	11 9	3.02	0.98	28.92
Annual Growth	**15.5%**	**— —**	**46.8%**	**21.7%**	**13.2%**

National Bank Holdings Corp

National Bank Holdings is the holding company for NBH Bank which operates nearly 100 branches in four south and central US states under various brands including: Bank Midwest in Kansas and Missouri Community Banks of Colorado in Colorado and Hillcrest Bank in Texas. Targeting small to medium-sized businesses and consumers the banks offer traditional checking and savings accounts as well as commercial and residential mortgages agricultural loans and commercial loans. The bank boasted $4.7 billion in assets at the end of 2015 including $2.6 billion in loans and $3.8 billion in deposits. Over 80% of its total revenue is made up of interest income.

Operations
About 63% of the bank's total revenue came from loan interest (including fees) during 2015 while another 19% came from interest on its investment securities. The rest of its revenue came from service charges (7%) bank card fees (5%) and other miscellaneous income sources.

Geographic Reach
National Bank Holdings had a network of 97 banking centers in four states at the end of 2015 with more than half of those in Colorado a third in Missouri nearly a dozen branches in Kansas and two branches in Texas.

Sales and Marketing

The bank serves small- to medium-sized businesses and consumers via its network of banking locations and through online and mobile banking products. It spent $4.3 million on advertising during 2015 down from $4.6 million and $5.3 million in 2014 and 2013 respectively.

Financial Performance

The group's annual revenues and profits have been trending downward over the past few years as it has been selling off branches and loan business to concentrate on the geographic markets and loan types where it carries the most expertise.

National Bank Holdings' revenue rebounded 5% to $192.86 million during 2015 mostly as it earned $21 million in FDIC-related income related to lower indemnification amortization increased FDIC loss-share income and a $5 million gain on an FDIC loss-share agreement termination.

Despite revenue growth in 2015 the group's net income plummeted 47% to $4.9 million mostly on higher loan loss provisions which climbed more than $6.2 million during the year as it increased its specific reserves on non 310-30 loans. National Bank Holdings' operations used $37.65 million compared to just $2.76 million in cash during 2014 mostly after adjusting its earnings for non-cash items mostly related to a decrease in net amounts due to the FDIC.

Strategy

National Bank Holdings has been trimming its branch count in recent years to focus on serving clients through full-service banking centers across its four chief markets of Colorado Kansas Missouri and Texas as well as through online and mobile banking channels. Toward this end in 2013 the bank began integrating its limited-service retirement center locations into its full-service banking centers while also exiting its limited presence in California (its banks there had operated under the Community Banks of California banner).

Meanwhile the regional community bank continues to selectively acquire smaller banks and complementary financial companies that serve small- and medium-sized businesses to grow its loan and deposit business.

Mergers and Acquisitions

In August 2015 National Bank Holdings bought $142 million-asset Pine River Bank in Colorado along with its $64 million in loans and $130 million in deposits for $9.5 million in cash.

Company Background

Formed in 2009 National Bank Holdings went public in 2012. Prior to its filing National Bank Holdings was minority-owned by a number of private shareholders and corporate entities including Taconic Capital Advisors Wellington Management and Paulson & Co.

EXECUTIVES

Chairman President And Ceo, G. Timothy (Tim) Laney, age 60, $500,000 total compensation
Chief Of Enterprise Technology & Integration And Nbh Bank N.a. Midwest/ Texas Division President, Thomas M. (Tom) Metzger, $300,000 total compensation
Chief Financial Officer, Brian F. Lilly, age 61, $295,705 total compensation
Chief Risk Officer, Richard U. Newfield, age 59, $300,000 total compensation

Vice President Sales, Jim Irisawa
Vice President Commercial Real Estate, Derek Haverkamp
Board Member, Burney Warren
Board Member, Arthur Zeile
Auditors: KPMG LLP

LOCATIONS

HQ: National Bank Holdings Corp
7800 East Orchard Road, Suite 300, Greenwood Village, CO 80111
Phone: 303 892-8715
Web: www.nationalbankholdings.com

PRODUCTS/OPERATIONS

2015 Sales

	$ mil.	% of total
Interest and dividend income:		
Interest and fees on loans	131	63
Interest and dividends on investment securities	38	18
Dividends on non-marketable securities	1	1
Interest on interest-bearing bank deposits	0	-
Total interest and dividend income	171	82
Non-interest income:		
Service charges	14	7
Bank card fees	10	5
Gain on sales of mortgages net	2	1
Bank-owned life insurance income	1	1
Other non-interest income	3	2
Bargain purchase gain	1	1
Gain on previously charged-off acquired loans	0	-
OREO related write-ups and other income	2	1
FDIC indemnification asset amortization net of gain on termination	(15.9)	-
FDIC loss sharing income (expense)	0	-
Total non-interest income	21	18
Total	**192**	**100**

COMPETITORS

BBVA Compass Bancshares	FirstBank Holding Company
Bank of America	JPMorgan Chase
Bank of the West	KeyCorp
Capitol Federal Financial	U.S. Bancorp
Central Bancompany	UMB Financial
Commerce Bancshares	Wells Fargo
Enterprise Financial Services	Zions Bancorporation

HISTORICAL FINANCIALS

Company Type: Public

Income Statement				FYE: December 31
	ASSETS ($ mil.)	NET INCOME ($ mil.)	INCOME AS % OF ASSETS	EMPLOYEES
12/19	5,895	80	1.4%	1,298
12/18	5,676	61	1.1%	1,332
12/17	4,843	14	0.3%	926
12/16	4,573	23	0.5%	1,004
12/15	4,683	4	0.1%	1,042
Annual Growth	5.9%	101.4%	—	5.6%

2019 Year-End Financials

Debt ratio: —
Return on equity: 10.99%
Cash ($ mil.): 110
Current ratio: —
Long-term debt ($ mil.): —

No. of shares (mil.): 31
Dividends
Yield: 2.1%
Payout: 30.3%
Market value ($ mil.): 1,098

	STOCK PRICE ($) FY Close	P/E High/Low	PER SHARE ($) Earnings	Dividends	Book Value
12/19	35.22	15 12	2.55	0.75	24.60
12/18	30.87	21 15	1.95	0.54	22.59
12/17	32.43	68 56	0.53	0.34	19.81
12/16	31.89	40 23	0.79	0.22	20.32
12/15	21.37	166 127	0.14	0.20	20.34
Annual Growth	13.3%	—	—106.6%	39.2%	4.9%

National Western Life Group Inc

Auditors: BKD, LLP

LOCATIONS

HQ: National Western Life Group Inc
10801 N. Mopac Expy Bldg. 3, Austin, TX 78759
Phone: 512 836-1010
Web: www.nwlgi.com

HISTORICAL FINANCIALS

Company Type: Public

Income Statement				FYE: December 31
	ASSETS ($ mil.)	NET INCOME ($ mil.)	INCOME AS % OF ASSETS	EMPLOYEES
12/19	12,553	131	1.0%	287
12/18	11,931	116	1.0%	276
12/17	12,225	110	0.9%	279
12/16	11,894	100	0.8%	265
12/15	11,612	98	0.8%	261
Annual Growth	2.0%	7.5%	—	2.4%

2019 Year-End Financials

Debt ratio: —
Return on equity: 6.53%
Cash ($ mil.): 253
Current ratio: —
Long-term debt ($ mil.): —

No. of shares (mil.): 3
Dividends
Yield: 0.1%
Payout: 1.1%
Market value ($ mil.): 1,058

	STOCK PRICE ($) FY Close	P/E High/Low	PER SHARE ($) Earnings	Dividends	Book Value
12/19	290.88	8 6	37.22	0.36	585.32
12/18	300.70	10 8	33.02	0.36	522.76
12/17	331.02	12 9	31.23	0.36	503.88
12/16	310.80	11 7	28.53	0.36	473.53
12/15	251.94	10 8	27.82	0.36	443.32
Annual Growth	3.7%	—	7.5%	(0.0%)	7.2%

Navient Corp

Navient is a leading provider of education loan management and business processing solutions for education healthcare and government clients at the federal state and local levels. Navient originates and owns $86.8 billion of education loans. In addition to serving indebted former students Navient provides servicing and asset recovery services (collections) on its own loan portfolio federal education loans owned by ED and other intitutions.. Navient manages the largest portfolio of Federal Family Education Loan Program (FFELP) loans as well as the largest portfolio of private education loans). Navient began life as an independent company through a strategic divestiture from Sallie Mae which still exists and continues to provide consumer loans.

Operations

Navient operates three business segments: two that own and collect interest on loans and one that services loans and provides loan processing services. The largest segment the Federal Family Education Loan Program (FFELP) brings in approximately 50% of total revenue. It collects interest income from its about $65 billion portfolio of FFELP loans and adds to its holdings by opportunistically buying FFELP loans from other servicers. FFELP Loans are insured or guaranteed by state or not-for-profit agencies and are protected by contractual rights to recovery from the United States pursuant to guaranty agreements among ED and these agencies. More than 95% of FFELP loans are government guaranteed.

Navient's Consumer Lending segment (nearly 40% of revenue) originates and acquires consumer loans and performs servicing activities on its own education loan portfolio while also collecting interest on more than $20 billion portfolio of such loans.

Business Processing (more than 10% of revenue) performs revenue cycle management and business processing services for over 500 non-education related government and healthcare clients. Its integrated solutions technology and superior data driven approach allows state governments agencies court systems municipalities and toll authorities (Government Services) to reduce their operating expenses while maximizing revenue opportunities.

Broadly Navient makes about 75% of its revenue from interest income on its FFELP and around 25% from its private education loan portfolios.

Geographic Reach

Wilmington Delaware-based Navient operates throughout the US.

Most of the company's properties are loan servicing and collection centers in the New York and Indiana with additional offices in Virginia Florida Texas California New Jersey Wisconsin and Tennessee. Its largest facility in Fishers Indiana houses 450000 sq. ft. of space representing about 35%% of all owned and leased space.

Sales and Marketing

Navient services and performs asset recovery activities on its own portfolio of education loans as well as education loans owned by other institutions the US Department of Education with whom Navient has an existing significant contract through 2019.

The company also sells its services to federal state and local governments; municipal clients public authorities; cand health care organizations.

Financial Performance

The company's revenue increase $99 million or 5% to $1.9 billion during 2019due to the increase on their other income and decrease on provisions for loans losses.

For the year ended 2019 net income was $597 million compared with net income of $395 million in the prior year. The primary contributors to the increase in net income are as follows: Asset recovery and business processing revenue increased by $58 million primarily due to higher account resolution; and net gains on derivative and hedging activities increased $60 million.

Cash and cash equivalents decreased by $1.5 billion to $3.8 billion in 2019. Cash provided by operations and investing activities were $1.0 billion and $7.5 billion respectively. Cash used for financing activities was $10 billion primarily for repaying borrowings collateralized by loans in trusts.

Strategy

Navient's overarching strategy includes both maintenance and growth. It seeks to maintain income streams from its portfolio of loan holdings and from servicing others' loans the latter being heavily dependent on its contracts with the US Department of Education. Keeping default rates low and collecting on delinquent loans are a major focus.

The company strives to maintain an overall strategy that uses derivatives to minimize the economic effect of interest rate and/or foreign currency changes.

Its growth strategy has included making opportunistic acquisitions of or material investments in loan portfolios and complementary businesses and products. All acquisitions of companies operations or loan portfolios involve financial risks as well as operational risks.

EXECUTIVES

President And Ceo, John F. (Jack) Remondi, age 57, $1,000,000 total compensation
Evp And Chief Decision Management Officer, Somsak Chivavibul, age 53, $379,999 total compensation
Evp Chief Legal Officer And Secretary, Mark L. Heleen, age 58, $369,357 total compensation
Evp And Chief Risk And Compliance Officer, Timothy (Tim) Hynes, age 51, $370,000 total compensation
Group President Business Processing Solutions, John Kane, age 51, $449,999 total compensation
Evp And Cio, Pat Lawicki
Group President Asset Management And Servicing, John F. (Jeff) Whorley, age 59, $449,999 total compensation
Evp And Cfo, Christian Lown, age 51
Senior Vice President, Troy Standish
Senior Vice President Human Resources, Jon Kroehler
Vice President Of Corporate Marketing, Deidre Ostrowski
Vice President And Assistant Treasurer, Scott Booher
Senior Vice President Government Relations And Public Policy, Sarah Ducich
Vice President Government Relations And Public Policy, Lucia Lebens
Vice President, Chris Tuten
Vice President Internal Audit, Jennifer Walker
Executive Vice President And Chief Legal Officer, Mark L Heleen
Vice President, Stephen Tinney
Vice President Compliance Suppgovernance, Bill Brooks
Vice President Application Development, Carol Swartz
Senior Vice President, Paul Mayer
Vice President; President, Brian Hill

Senior Vice President And Deputy General Counsel, Andrew G Wachtel
Vice President Instrument Technician Technical Services, Jeff Dierckman
Vice President Real Estate, Joseph Muffler
Vice President Enterprise Architecture, Matt Anderson
Vice President Operational Support Services, Patty Peterson
Senior Vice President Technology Infrastructure And Operations, Jon Jones
Vice President Information Technology Technical Services, Jeffrey Dossman
Chairman, William M. Diefenderfer, age 75
Auditors: KPMG LLP

LOCATIONS

HQ: Navient Corp
123 Justison Street, Wilmington, DE 19801
Phone: 302 283-8000
Web: www.navient.com

PRODUCTS/OPERATIONS

2017 Sales

	$ mil.	% of total
Interest		
FFELP loans	2,693	52
Private education loans	1,634	32
Other loans	13	-
Cash & investments	43	1
Non-interest		
Asset recovery & business processing	475	9
Servicing	290	6
Net gains on derivatives & hedging activities	22	-
Gains on sales of loans & investments	3	-
Other	9	-
Adjustments	(2974)	
Total	**2,208**	**100**

COMPETITORS

Bank of America
Brazos Higher Education Service Corp.
Great Lakes Higher Education
Mohela
Nelnet
Pennsylvania Higher Education Assistance Agency
Sallie Mae
Texas Guaranteed

HISTORICAL FINANCIALS

Company Type: Public

Income Statement

FYE: December 31

	ASSETS ($ mil.)	NET INCOME ($ mil.)	INCOME AS % OF ASSETS	EMPLOYEES
12/19	94,903	597	0.6%	5,800
12/18	104,176	395	0.4%	6,500
12/17	114,991	292	0.3%	6,700
12/16	121,136	681	0.6%	6,773
12/15	134,112	997	0.7%	7,300
Annual Growth	(8.3%)	(12.0%)	—	(5.6%)

2019 Year-End Financials

Debt ratio: 86.10%	No. of shares (mil.): 215
Return on equity: 17.42%	Dividends
Cash ($ mil.): 1,233	Yield: 4.6%
Current ratio: —	Payout: 25.0%
Long-term debt ($ mil.): —	Market value ($ mil.): 2,947

	STOCK PRICE ($) FY Close	P/E High/Low		PER SHARE ($) Earnings	Dividends	Book Value
12/19	13.68	6	4	2.56	0.64	15.48
12/18	8.81	10	6	1.49	0.64	14.22
12/17	13.32	16	11	1.04	0.64	13.13
12/16	16.43	8	4	2.12	0.64	12.72
12/15	11.45	8	4	2.61	0.64	11.42
Annual Growth	4.5%	—.—		(0.5%)	(0.0%)	7.9%

Navistar International Corp.

If you drive in North America chances are you've passed a Navistar vehicle on the road. The company produces school buses (under the IC Bus brand) and heavy-duty trucks (under the International brand) as well as military and defense vehicles and diesel engines. Navistar's parts distribution network one of the largest in the US. The company also supplies engine parts and its financial sector offers sales and lease financing for dealers and customers. Navistar derives most of its sales from North America.

Operations

Navistar operates in four industry segments: Truck Parts Global Operations and Financial Services.

The Truck division which is the company's largest segment (around three quarters of sales) makes class 4 through 8 trucks buses and military vehicles as well as proprietary engines. Its International brand trucks and IC Bus buses are manufactured and distributed primarily in the US Canada and Mexico.

Parts the company's second largest segment which accounts for almost 20% of sales distributes service parts through an extensive dealer network supporting its trucks and engine products. A joint venture with Ford Motor?Blue Diamond Parts LLC (BDP)?also manages the merchandising and distribution of select service parts for Ford vehicles in North America.

Global Operations (less than 5%) operates through its wholly-owned subsidiary IIAA in South America. IIAA manufactures and distributes mid-range diesel engines for the South American market as well as engines for the agriculture marine and light truck markets in that region.

The Financial Services segment provides retail wholesale and lease financing for products sold by the Truck and Parts segments and its dealers within the US and Mexico.

Geographic Reach

Navistar's main product development and engineering facilities reside in Lisle and Melrose Park IL.;New Carlisle IN; and Monterrey Mexico. In North America the company has four manufacturing and assembly facilities. Global Operations segment owns and operates a manufacturing plant in Brazil. The Parts segment also leases seven distribution centers in the US two in Canada one in Mexico and one in South Africa.

The US accounts for over 80% of Navistar's revenues while other major markets include Canada (almost 10%) and Mexico (over 5%)and Brazil(less than 5%).

Sales and Marketing

The company sells its products through its independent dealer network. The Parts segment also distributes goods through about a dozen regional distribution centers in North America or through direct shipment from its suppliers and serves global markets through an export business for customers in Latin America the Middle East northern Africa South Africa Europe Australia Asia and Russia.

The company's advertising expenses were $31 million $31 million and $26 million for the years ended October 31 2019 2018 and 2017 respectively.

Financial Performance

After a big drop in fiscal 2016 (ending October 31) Navistar's revenue elevated for the third consecutive year in 2019 increasing almost 40% to $11.3 billion. The Truck segment from 2018 increased 15% contributing almost $1.1 billion in revenue primarily due to higher volumes in our Core markets the commencement of sales of GM-branded units manufactured for GM partially offset by the impact of the sale of a majority interest in Navistar Defense.

Navistar's profits took a dive in 2019 with $221 million in net income a 35% difference compared to its $340 million net income in 2018.

Navistar ended 2019 with $1.4 billion of consolidated cash cash equivalents and marketable securities. Cash from operations contributed $450 million to the coffers while investing activities used $68 million mainly for purchases of leased equipment. Financing activities used $258 million for payments on non-securitized debt.

Strategy

Navistar has moved from a turnaround phase to a new growth phase. Going forward the company is focusing on further growing its core truck and parts businesses in the US and Canada. With customer segmentation initiatives it aims to better align its development efforts with customer-specific applications. In addition it is adding e-commerce capabilities aligned with an ease-of-doing-business initiative and investing in electrification. The company introduced its first electric medium duty vehicle at the recent North American Commercial Vehicle Show.

It is also continuing its strategic alliance with the TRATON Group a joint venture formed by Volkswagen Truck & Bus that allows Navistar to take advantage of joint procurement activities and licensing and developing new technologies. WithTRATON Navistar expects to have a fully integrated proprietary powertrain with a new connectivity module that allows for feature sharing by 2020.

In 2019 the company made several notable advancements in their strategic visions. Their focus on customer and market segmentation to better align their efforts the #1 choice in their industry. Navistar made improvements to operations as follows: reduce their warranty expense as a percentage of manufacturing revenue from 1.7% in 2018 to 1.4% in 2019; announced investments in their manufacturing footprint expand their capabilities in Huntsville Alabama for an integrated powertrain with TRATON Group

and building a benchmark truck manufacturing facility in San Antonio Texas.

Company Background

Virginia-born inventor Cyrus McCormick perfected the reaper in 1831 and moved west to open a factory in Chicago in 1846. Before his death in 1884 McCormick had implemented such innovations as installment plans written guarantees and factory-trained repairmen. In 1902 with help from banker J. P. Morgan the company merged with Deering Harvester (agricultural machinery) and several smaller companies to form International Harvester (IH); it soon controlled 85% of US harvester production.

IH set up its first overseas plant in 1905 in Sweden. It entered the tractor industry in 1906 and in 1907 it began making the forerunner of the truck — the Auto Buggy. By 1910 IH was making 1300 trucks and 1400 tractors annually and had exceeded $100 million in sales. After several decades the company was renamed Navistar International in 1986.

EXECUTIVES

Evp And Cfo, Walter G. Borst, $742,630 total compensation

Svp And General Counsel, Steven K. (Steve) Covey, $611,455 total compensation

Svp And Cio, Terry S. Kline

President Operations, Phil Christman

Chairman President And Ceo, Troy A. Clarke, $950,000 total compensation

Svp And Chief Procurement Officer, Persio V. Lisboa, $544,688 total compensation

Treasurer; President Financial Services, William V. McMenamin

Vice President Global Product Support, Mark Reiter

Vice President Global Procurement, David McKean

Vice President Global Parts, Michael Lynch

Vice President Finance, Kevin Stack

Chief Sales Officer Service Readiness Manager, Beatrice Borges

Vice President Tax, Kristene Schumacher

Vice President Government Affairs, Jacqueline Gelb

Vice President Engineering And Program Management, Chet Ciesielski

Vice President, Jan Allman

Vice President, Carl Webb

Vice President Tax, Carol Garnant

Vice President Representative Clients Customers, Michael Scribner

Senior Vice President And General Manager Parts Division, Phyllis Cochran

Vice President Engineering, Tony Sutton

National Account Manager, Katie Sundra

National Account Manager, Scott Metroff

Vice President Latin America And The Caribbean, Manuel Barrios

Vice President Dealer Sales, Bob Mann

Vice President, Jim Spangler

Vice President Western Region, Kevin Madigan

National Account Manager, Ken Whitley

National Account Manager, Chris Cummings

National Account Manager, Gio DeVito

Vice President Dealer Operations, Patricia Brault

Vice President Global Engineering, Josef Kory

Group Vp Global Product Development, Dennis denny Mooney

Svp Global Manufacturing, Mark Hernandez

Medical Director, Thomas Ehni

Senior Vice President Enterprise Information Technology, Mike Huntzinger

Svp And Cio, Julie Ragland

Vp Sales Strategy And Market Segmentation, Diane Hames

Senior Vice President Joint Strategy And Planning, Friedrich-w Baumann
National Account Manager, Tarik Green
Assistant Treasurer, Anthony A Aiello
Treasurer, Stephen Gilligan
Auditors: KPMG LLP

LOCATIONS

HQ: Navistar International Corp.
2701 Navistar Drive, Lisle, IL 60532
Phone: 331 332-5000
Web: www.navistar.com

2018 Sales

	$ mil.	% of total
United States	7,223	71
Mexico	933	9
Canada	868	8
Brazil	263	3
Other	963	9
Total	**10,250**	**100**

PRODUCTS/OPERATIONS

2018 Sales

	$ mil.	% of total
Truck	7,490	71
Parts	2,407	23
Global Operations	360	3
Financial services	257	3
Corporate and Eliminations	(264)	-
Total	**10,250**	**100**

Selected Brands Products and Services

Vehicles
  International Trucks
  IC Bus
  Navistar Defense
Engines
  N9
  N10
  N13

Services

OnCommand Connection
Fleetrite Parts
Navistar Financial

COMPETITORS

BAE SYSTEMS	Isuzu
Cummins	MAN
Deere	Mercedes-Benz U.S.
Delphi Automotive	International
Systems	Oshkosh Truck
Freightliner Custom	PACCAR
Chassis	Scania
General Dynamics Land	UD Trucks
Systems	Volvo
Hino Motors	

HISTORICAL FINANCIALS

Company Type: Public

Income Statement

FYE: October 31

	REVENUE ($ mil.)	NET INCOME ($ mil.)	NET PROFIT MARGIN	EMPLOYEES
10/20	7,503	(347)	—	11,000
10/19	11,251	221	2.0%	12,300
10/18	10,250	340	3.3%	13,100
10/17	8,570	30	0.4%	11,400
10/16	8,111	(97)	—	11,300
Annual Growth	**(1.9%)**	**—**	**—**	**(0.7%)**

2020 Year-End Financials

Debt ratio: 80.31%
Return on equity: —
Cash ($ mil.): 1,843
Current ratio: 1.36
Long-term debt ($ mil.): 4,690

No. of shares (mil.): 99
Dividends
Yield: —
Payout: —
Market value ($ mil.): 4,294

Stock Price

	STOCK PRICE ($) FY Close	P/E High/Low	PER SHARE ($) Earnings	Dividends	Book Value
10/20	43.11	—	(3.48)	0.00	(38.41)
10/19	31.28	18 10	2.22	0.00	(37.56)
10/18	33.49	14 9	3.41	0.00	(39.75)
10/17	42.31	140 71	0.32	0.00	(46.48)
10/16	22.30	—	(1.19)	0.00	(64.93)
Annual Growth	**17.9%**	**—**	**—**	**—**	**—**

NBT Bancorp. Inc.

NBT Bancorp is the holding company for NBT Bank which operates about 155 branches mainly in suburban and rural areas of central and northern New York northeastern Pennsylvania western Massachusetts southern New Hampshire and northwestern Vermont. The bank offers traditional deposit accounts and trust services and specializes in making business and commercial real estate loans. NBT also holds two main financial services subsidiaries: the EPIC Advisors unit administers retirement plans while Mang Insurance Agency sells personal and commercial coverage. NBT Capital provides venture funding to growing area businesses.

Operations

Other subsidiaries include property manager Broad Street Property Associates title insurance firm NBT Services real estate investment trusts CNB Realty Trust and Alliance Preferred Funding Corp and and equipment leasing services provider Alliance Leasing.

About 63% of the bank's total revenue came from loan interest (including fees) in 2015 while another 7% came from interest on investment securities. The rest of its revenue came from insurance and other financial services fees (6% of revenue) deposit account service charges (4%) ATM and debit card fees (5%) retirement plan administration fees (4%) trust fees (5%) and other miscellaneous sources.

Sales and Marketing

NBT Bancorp serves individuals businesses and municipalities. The bank spent $2.7 million on advertising during 2015 down from $2.8 million and $3.2 million in 2014 and 2013 respectively.

Financial Performance

NBT Bancorp's annual revenue has risen more than 20% since 2011 mostly as bank acquisitions have buoyed its loan business. Meanwhile its annual profit has grown by one-third.

The bank's revenue dipped 2% to $391.7 million during 2015 however mostly as the low-interest environment continued to squeeze its interest margins on its loans and investment securities. It also collected $15 million less in (non-recurring) gains from the sale of its Springtone investment compared to the prior year.

Despite modest revenue declines in 2015 NBT's net income climbed 2% to $76.43 million primarily because in 2014 it had incurred $17.9 million in non-recurring prepayment penalties as it paid down its long-term debt. The company's operating cash levels jumped 42% to $124.54 million for the year mostly as it collected more

in net proceeds on the sale of its loans held for sale and sold off more of its non-loan assets.

Strategy

New York-based NBT Bancorp has expanded its financial service lines outside of traditional banking on its own and through acquisitions in recent years.

Mergers and Acquisitions

In October 2015 NBT Bancorp beefed up its Wealth Management and 401(k) recordkeeping businesses after purchasing New Hampshire-based Third Party Administrators Inc which provided administrative services for 401(k) profit sharing and defined benefit plans on behalf of 700 businesses and Section 125 administration. The $4.1 million acquisition helped complement services offered by its Wealth Management division and EPIC Advisors affiliate.

In March 2013 NBT purchased Alliance Financial for $233 million which bolstered its presence in central New York by adding 26 branches in Onondaga Cortland Madison Oneida and Oswego counties. The deal also added $1.4 billion in assets including $920 million in net loans held for investment and $1.1 billion in deposits.

Company Background

NBT Bancorp remained profitable through the recession even as real estate values fell and the number of non-performing loans in its portfolio grew. To do this the company increased its loan collection efforts and focused on selling conforming real estate mortgages. It also stopped originating auto leases.

NBT Bancorp was founded in 1986. However NBT Bank traces its roots to 1856.

EXECUTIVES

Vice President, Timothy Handy
Sevp And Cfo, Michael J. Chewens, age 58, $446,610 total compensation
Evp; President Commercial Banking, Jeffrey M. Levy, age 58, $436,000 total compensation
President And Ceo, John H. Watt, age 61
Evp Operations And Retail Banking, Joseph R. Stagliano
Evp Chief Human Resources Officer And Chief Ethics Officer, Catherine M. Scarlett
Evp; President Wealth Management, Timothy L. Brenner, age 63, $331,050 total compensation
Evp General Counsel And Corporate Secretary, F. Sheldon Prentice
Evp; President New England, Matthew K. Durkee
Evp And President Commercial Banking, Sarah A. Halliday
Vice President And Retirement Plan Services Manager, Peter Kain
Senior Vice President Of Sales, Rita Demarko
Assistant Vice President Information Technology Officer Security Officer, Heidi Fisher
Vice President, Karen Sastri
Vice President Systems, Anne Ferguson
Senior Vice President Product Management, Sharon Horning
Vice President Information Processing, Robert Keller
Vice President Market Manager, Lyle Smith
Vice President Business Development, Debra Turner
Senior Vice President Administrator, Jeffrey Lake
Vice President Vice President Systems, Deb Curriere
Vice President Of Information Technology, Robert Hill
Assistant Vice President And Audit Manager, Bryan Green

Director Media Relations, Salvator Arcidiacono
Senior Vice President, Kevin O'hara
Senior Vice President Director Of Operational
Ris, Jim Terry
Vice President Commercial Banking, Bob Vertucci
Senior Vice President, Kurt Edwards
Vice President, David Krupski
Assistant Vice President Security Investigations
Officer, Rebecca Powell
Assistant Vp And Manager Application Support,
Chad Lytle
Vice President Commercial Loan Officer, Tim
Robinson
Vice President, Tom Weingart
Vice President Credit Officer, Jeffrey Rochefort
Vp Retail Special Assets And Collection Manager,
Jason Town
Senior Vp And Regional Commercial Banking
Manager For New Hampshire, Al Romero
Chairman, Martin A. Dietrich, age 64
Board Member, V Daniel Robinson
Auditors: KPMG LLP

LOCATIONS

HQ: NBT Bancorp. Inc.
52 South Broad Street, Norwich, NY 13815
Phone: 607 337-2265   Fax: 607 336-7538
Web: www.nbtbancorp.com

PRODUCTS/OPERATIONS

2015 Sales

	$ mil.	% of total
Interest		
Interest and fees on loans	241	63
Securities available for sale	20	5
Securities held to maturity	9	2
Other	1	-
Non-interest		
Insurance and other financial services revenue	24	6
Service charges on deposit accounts	17	4
Trust	19	5
ATM & debit card fees	18	5
Retirement plan administration fees	14	4
Bank-owned life insurance income	4	1
Gain on the sale of Springtone investment	4	1
Net securities gains	3	-
Other	14	4
Total	**391**	**100**

Selected Subsidiaries

Broad Street Property Associates Inc.
CNB Realty Trust
Colonial Finance Services Inc.
EPIC Advisors Inc.
FNB Financial Services Inc.
Hathaway Agency Inc.
LA Lease Inc.
Mang Insurance Agency LLC
NBT Bank National Association
NBT Capital Corp.
NBT Financial Services Inc.
NBT Holdings Inc.
NBT Services Inc.
Pennstar Bank Services Company
Pennstar Financial Services Inc.

COMPETITORS

Astoria Financial	M&T Bank
Community Bank System	Oneida Financial
HSBC USA	Sovereign Bank
KeyCorp	TrustCo Bank Corp NY

HISTORICAL FINANCIALS

Company Type: Public

Income Statement

FYE: December 31

	ASSETS ($ mil.)	NET INCOME ($ mil.)	INCOME AS % OF ASSETS	EMPLOYEES
12/19	9,715	121	1.2%	1,788
12/18	9,556	112	1.2%	1,791
12/17	9,136	82	0.9%	1,733
12/16	8,867	78	0.9%	1,704
12/15	8,262	76	0.9%	1,721
Annual Growth	4.1%	12.2%	—	1.0%

2019 Year-End Financials

Debt ratio: 1.70%
Return on equity: 11.32%
Cash ($ mil.): 216
Current ratio: —
Long-term debt ($ mil.): —

No. of shares (mil.): 43
Dividends
Yield: 2.5%
Payout: 38.4%
Market value ($ mil.): 1,776

	STOCK PRICE ($) FY Close	P/E High/Low	PER SHARE ($) Earnings	Dividends	Book Value
12/19	40.56	15 12	2.74	1.05	25.58
12/18	34.59	16 13	2.56	0.99	23.31
12/17	36.80	22 17	1.87	0.92	22.01
12/16	41.88	23 13	1.80	0.90	21.11
12/15	27.88	17 13	1.72	0.87	20.31
Annual Growth	9.8%	—	12.3%	4.8%	5.9%

Nelnet Inc

Got Ivy League tastes on a community college budget? Nelnet may be able to help. The education planning and financing company helps students and parents plan and pay for college educations. Nelnet is mostly known for servicing federal student loans. The firm manages about $76 billion in student loan assets most of which are government loans. However in light of regulatory changes to the student lending market Nelnet is increasingly expanding its fee-based education services. It serves the K-12 and higher education marketplace providing long-term payment plans college enrollment services and software and technology services. It acquired in 2018 Great Lakes Educational Loan Services for $150 million. The firm is part of financial holding company Farmers & Merchants Investment.

Operations

Nelnet provides innovative educational services in loan servicing payment processing education planning and asset management for families and educational institutions. The Company's four operating segments offer a broad range of services designed to simplify education planning and financing for students and families and the administrative and financial processes for schools and financial institutions.

The largest is Asset Generation and Management which acquires and manages Nelnet's student loan holdings. The portfolio includes Nelnet's existing loans originated under the now-defunct Federal Family Education Loan Program (FFELP). However in efforts to diversify its fee-based business and lessen its dependence on student loans the company is focused on developing new products and growing in areas

such as tuition payment processing and lead generation products and services such as enrollment management and test prep services.

The three fee-based segments include Student Loan and Guaranty Servicing which services FFELP and other third-party loans writes and services private student loans and provides loan servicing software. (Nelnet is one of four companies providing servicing for the Department of Education.) Tuition Payment Processing and Campus Commerce serves the K-12 market as well as higher education providing financing for families and processing services for schools. Enrollment Services works to connect students with schools by providing marketing for schools and publishing school directories and test preparation study guides for potential students.

Geographic Reach

The company has offices in the US and Canada.

Sales and Marketing

The company's customers include students and families colleges and universities specifically financial aid business and admissions offices K-12 schools lenders state agencies and government entities.

Financial Performance

Nelnet has seen steady growth in revenues in the last few years. In 2013 the company's revenue increased to $1.14 billion (compared to $923.7 million in 2012) primarily due to an increase in Student Loan and Guaranty Servicing (as the result of growth in servicing volume under the company's contract with the Department of Education) and an increase in collection revenues from defaulted FFELP loan assets on behalf of guaranty agencies. Tuition Payment Processing and Campus Commerce revenues grew due to a higher number of managed tuition payment plans as a result of providing more plans at existing schools and obtaining new school customers.

Net income increased to $302.7 million in 2013 (from $117.8 million in 2012) due to higher revenues and lower operating costs (the result of a decrease in depreciation and amortization costs).

In 2013 Nelnet's operating cash flow increased to $387.2 million (compared to $299.3 million in 2012) due to higher net income and proceeds from the termination of one of the company's cross-currency interest rate swaps. The increase in cash provided by operating activities was partially offset by the impacts of changes in non-cash fair value adjustments for derivatives.

Strategy

The company grows organically and through acquisitions.

Mergers and Acquisitions

To strengthen its student loans business Nelnet purchased in 2018 Great Lakes Educational Loan Services for $150 million and in 2014 acquired CIT's student lending business for $1.1 billion.

In 2014 FACTS Management brand a part of Nelnet's Tuition Payment Processing and Campus Commerce segment and the leader in payment plan services for K-12 schools acquired RenWeb School Management Software one of the leading school information systems for private and faith-based schools. RenWeb currently helps over 3000 schools automate administrative processes like admissions scheduling student billing attendance and grade book management. By automating these tasks RenWeb gives teachers more time to shape the lives of students while saving money and resources. FACTS helps over 6500 schools with tuition management billing and financial aid assessment services.

Company Background

Nelnet has been through a turbulent few years as student loan reform and the financial crisis disrupted business and sent revenues down. The company's ability to adapt to the economic pressures and policy changes have helped it land face-up following the recession. Measures taken including laying off staff and tightening lending practices helped boost profits despite lower revenues. Although non-FFELP servicing income and payment processing revenues grew in 2011 FFELP servicing revenues declined as the portfolio further shrunk and school marketing sales decreased as schools cut back on spending. As a result revenues fell that year by 8% to $979 million. Net income increased 8% (to $204 million) in 2011 compared to 2010 when the company had expenses related to restructuring. Also in 2010 Nelnet paid the US government $55 million to settle a lawsuit claiming it had made false statements to receive extra subsidies.

In a blow to the student lending industry President Barack Obama eliminated the FFELP and prohibited private lenders from making federal student loans in 2010. All new federal student loans began going directly through the Department of Education's Direct Loan Program. As a result Nelnet no longer originates new FFELP loans.

But the change didn't put an end to Nelnet. The company was awarded a five-year servicing contract for federally owned student loans including existing FFELP loans. Nelnet also began servicing new loans generated directly under the Federal Direct Loan Program. The contract was a major win for the company. Nelnet expects that its fee-based revenue will increase as the servicing volume for these loans increases (while the FFELP portfolio declines). The company is also focusing on improving its customer service to increase the allotted percentage of new government loans it services.

CEO Michael Dunlap controls the company holding 68% of the voting power for Nelnet. Dunlap and his family also own Farmers & Merchants Investment.

EXECUTIVES

Coo, Terry J. Heimes, age 56, $550,000 total compensation
Ceo, Jeffrey R. (Jeff) Noordhoek, age 54, $550,000 total compensation
President, Timothy A. (Tim) Tewes, age 61, $375,000 total compensation
Cfo, James D. (Jim) Kruger, $375,000 total compensation
Regional Vice President Of Sales K 12 Mi, Mike Spanier
Regional Vice President, Roy Chernikoff
Regional Vice President, Carol Morris
Vice President Campus Solutions, Anne Delplato
Vice President Of Engineering And Chief Technology Officer, Traci Wardman
Executive Chairman, Michael S. (Mike) Dunlap, age 57
Vice Chairman, Stephen F. (Steve) Butterfield, age 68
Auditors: KPMG LLP

LOCATIONS

HQ: Nelnet Inc
  121 South 13th Street, Suite 100, Lincoln, NE 68508
Phone: 402 458-2370
Web: www.nelnetinvestors.com

PRODUCTS/OPERATIONS

2015 Sales

	$ mil.	% of total
Interest		
Loans	726	60
Investments	7	1
Noninterest		
Loan & guaranty servicing	239	20
Enrollment services	70	6
Tuition payment processing & campus commerce revenue	120	10
Gains on sale of loans & debt repurchases net	5	1
Other	32	2
Total	**1,202**	**100**

COMPETITORS

American Student Assistance
Bank of America
Brazos Higher Education Service Corp.
College Loan Corporation
First Marblehead
Great Lakes Higher Education
JPMorgan Chase
Pennsylvania Higher Education Assistance Agency
Sallie Mae
Texas Guaranteed
Wells Fargo

HISTORICAL FINANCIALS

Company Type: Public

Income Statement

FYE: December 31

	ASSETS ($ mil.)	NET INCOME ($ mil.)	INCOME AS % OF ASSETS	EMPLOYEES
12/19	23,708	141	0.6%	6,600
12/18	25,220	227	0.9%	6,200
12/17	23,964	173	0.7%	4,300
12/16	27,180	256	0.9%	3,700
12/15	30,485	267	0.9%	3,400
Annual Growth	(6.1%)	(14.7%)	—	18.0%

2019 Year-End Financials

Debt ratio: 86.59%
Return on equity: 6.05%
Cash ($ mil.): 133
Current ratio: —
Long-term debt ($ mil.): —

No. of shares (mil.): 39
Dividends
Yield: 1.2%
Payout: 24.6%
Market value ($ mil.): 2,314

	STOCK PRICE ($) FY Close	P/E High/Low	PER SHARE ($) Earnings	Dividends	Book Value
12/19	58.24	20 15	3.54	0.74	60.07
12/18	52.34	11 9	5.57	0.66	57.24
12/17	54.78	14 9	4.14	0.58	52.67
12/16	50.75	9 5	6.02	0.50	48.96
12/15	33.57	8 5	5.89	0.42	42.87
Annual Growth	14.8%	—	— (12.0%)	15.2%	8.8%

Netflix Inc

Netflix and chill? More like Netflix and bill the increasing numbers of global viewers who subscribe to the video streaming service. The world's leading internet streaming company distributes movies and TV shows in a variety of genres and languages to with nearly 183 million paid subscribers in more than 190 countries. Netflix creates its own content and strikes deals with other producers for the rights to distribute programming. To keep viewers binging it deploys sophisticated algorithms to predict viewer preferences and make recommendations on what to watch. Netflix still sends DVDs to US customers through the mail though the legacy business gets smaller every year.

Operations

Netflix's business is organized in three operating segments: international streaming (nearly 55% of revenue) domestic streaming (about 45%) and domestic DVD accounts the remainder.

Domestic streaming derives revenues from monthly membership fees to subscribers in the US while the international streaming segment does the same to subscribers outside of the US. The legacy domestic DVD segment charges a monthly membership fee for DVD rental to US customers.

For its streaming services the company offers different subscription plans at various price points based on the quality of streaming (Standard Definition HD or Ultra HD) and the number of internet-connected screens on which a viewer can watch at the same time (one two or four). All plans include unlimited viewing of available TV shows and movies and can be canceled at any time. The company's content is commercial-free giving it a leg up in an increasingly competitive market filled with many advertising-supported rivals.

Geographic Reach

The Los Gatos California-based Netflix has moved beyond the borders of the US to reach more than 190 countries. Netflix has also created and licensed content for local markets across the globe.

To grow overseas Netflix must contend with international rivals that may offer pirated content via bootleg DVDs illegal downloads or unauthorized streaming. The service is not available in China one of the few markets it has yet to penetrate. While the nation presents opportunity for significant subscriber growth Netflix faces rigid restrictions there. As a workaround the company has been spending to acquire and produce Mandarin-language content to court Chinese audiences living elsewhere.

Sales and MarketingNetflix has spent increasing amounts of money on advertising $1879 million $1808 million and $1091 million for the FY 2019 2018 and 2017 respectively. It offers a month-long free trial at sign-up to first-time subscribers a key marketing strategy for the company. Its US streaming plans consists of Basic plan (with a single non-HD stream) is $8.99 per month while for the Standard plan (two HD streams) $12.99 per month at a time with HD available. The Premium plan (up to four Ultra HD streams) from $15.99 per month.

Financial Performance

Netflix' revenue has been rising consistently for the last five years with an overall growth of almost 200%. Its net revenues has been following a similar pattern generating a $1.7 billion improvement between 2015 and 2019.

Consolidated revenues for the year ended December 31 2019 increased 28% as compared to the year ended December 31 2018. The increase in consolidated revenues was due to the 23% growth in average paying memberships and a 5% increase in average monthly revenue per paying membership.

Net income rose $655 million (54%) to $1.9 billion in 2019 compared to $1.2 billion from the previous year.

Cash at the end of 2019 was $5 billion an increase of $1.2 billion from 2018. Cash from operations used $2.9 billion investing activities used $387.1 million while financing activities generated about $4.5 billion.

Strategy

The company's strategy is to grow its streaming membership globally improving its members' experience by making massive investments in content. Netflix is continuously improving its members' experience by expanding streaming content with a focus on a programming mix of content that delights members and attracts new members. In addition The Company is continuously enhancing its user interface and extending its streaming service to more internet-connected screens.

The firm continues to explore strategic agreements with TV networks and pay channels while also producing content in-house. Major Hollywood stars including Brad Pitt and Jane Fonda have developed Netflix-only programs and the company has signed successful TV producers like Shonda Rhimes and Ryan Murphy to exclusive development deals. Netflix lures in audiences with new movie releases such as The Irishman a crime drama from Martin Scorsese and breakout TV hits such as Stranger Things.

Mergers and Acquisitions

In 2020 Netflix Inc. has completed its acquisition of Hollywood's iconic Egyptian Theatre from Los Angeles nonprofit American Cinematheque. "The collaboration will allow the American Cinematheque to expand the scope and diversity of programming while continuing the nonprofit's mission to celebrate the experience of cinema as a moving art form" Netflix said in a statement. Terms of the deal were not disclosed.

In 2019 Netflix to acquire global streaming rights for 'Seinfeld' starting in 2021. It has just scored a major content deal that could help it stem the loss of subscribers as competition among streamers heats up. The company announced it has acquired the global streaming rights to the popular sitcom "Seinfeld" which will bring all 180 episodes of the Emmy winner to Netflix subscribers starting in 2021.

Company Background

Marc Randolph and Reed Hastings founded the DVD-by-mail service in 1997 as a challenge to Blockbuster Video. (Hastings said he got the idea after being hit with a $40 late fee from Blockbuster for failing to return his copy of Apollo 13 which was overdue by about a month.) The company launched its streaming service in 2007 placing a big (and eventually winning) bet on the popularity of accessing entertainment content via subscriptions over the internet.

Netflix released its first original TV series House of Cards in 2013. The critically-acclaimed show was also a hit with audiences putting the streaming company on the map as a producer of high quality content.

EXECUTIVES

Chairman President And Ceo, Reed Hastings, $900,000 total compensation
Chief Product Officer, Neil Hunt, age 59, $1,000,000 total compensation
Chief Content Officer, Ted Sarandos, age 56, $1,000,000 total compensation
International Development Officer, Greg Peters, age 49, $1,000,000 total compensation
Cfo, David Wells, age 48, $2,400,000 total compensation
Vice President Data Engineering And Analytics, Paul Ellwood
Vice President Information Technology, Eric Pallotta
Vice President Talent (human Resources), Barbie Graver
Vice President Marketing Apac, Jerret West
Vice President Consumer Insights, Adrien Lanusse
Vice President Product Innovation, Chris Jaffe
Vice President Marketing Latin America, Vinicius Losacco
Vice President User Interface Engineering, Matt Marenghi
Vice President Content Acquisition, Sean Carey
Vice President Engineering It, Anthony Park
Vice President Consumer Insights, Zoe Friend
Vice President Content Acquisition, Robert Roy
Vice President Of Networks, David Temkin
Vice President, Melissa Cobb
Board Member, Jay Hoag
Board Member, Richard Barton
Board Member, Reed Hasting
Board Member, Anne Sweeney
Auditors: Ernst & Young LLP

LOCATIONS

HQ: Netflix Inc
100 Winchester Circle, Los Gatos, CA 95032
Phone: 408 540-3700
Web: www.netflix.com

PRODUCTS/OPERATIONS

2017 Sales

	$ mil.	% of total
Domestic Streaming	6,153	53
International Streaming	5,089	43
Domestic DVD	450	4
Total	**11,692**	**100**

Selected Netflix Streaming Devices

Apple iPhone
Apple iPad
Apple iPod touch
Apple TV
Blu-ray disc players
Digital video recorders
Google TV
Internet video players
Internet-connected TVs
Home theatre systems
Microsoft Xbox 360 console
Nintendo Wii console
Sony PS3 console

COMPETITORS

AT&T	HBO
Amazon.com	Hastings Entertainment
Apple Inc.	Hulu
Best Buy	Kroger
Charter Communications	Redbox
Columbia House	Showtime Networks
Comcast	Target Corporation
Cox Communications	Time Warner Cable
DIRECTV	Verizon
DISH Network	Wal-Mart
EchoStar	YouTube
Google	

HISTORICAL FINANCIALS

Company Type: Public

Income Statement

FYE: December 31

	REVENUE ($ mil.)	NET INCOME ($ mil.)	NET PROFIT MARGIN	EMPLOYEES
12/20	24,996	2,761	11.0%	9,400
12/19	20,156	1,866	9.3%	8,600
12/18	15,794	1,211	7.7%	7,100
12/17	11,692	558	4.8%	5,500
12/16	8,830	186	2.1%	4,700
Annual Growth	29.7%	96.1%	—	18.9%

2020 Year-End Financials

Debt ratio: 41.52%
Return on equity: 29.54%
Cash ($ mil.): 8,205
Current ratio: 1.25
Long-term debt ($ mil.): 15,809
No. of shares (mil.): 442
Dividends
Yield: —
Payout: —
Market value ($ mil.): 239,487

	STOCK PRICE ($) FY Close	P/E High/Low	PER SHARE ($) Earnings	Dividends	Book Value
12/20	540.73	89 48	6.08	0.00	24.98
12/19	323.57	90 60	4.13	0.00	17.28
12/18	267.66	151 72	2.68	0.00	12.00
12/17	191.96	157 99	1.25	0.00	8.26
12/16	123.80	292188	0.43	0.00	6.23
Annual Growth	44.6%	— —	93.9%	—	41.5%

NEW YORK CITY HEALTH AND HOSPITALS CORPORATION

New York City Health and Hospitals Corporation (NYC H+H) operates health care facilities in all five boroughs of New York City. As one of the largest municipal health service systems in the US HHC serves 1 million New Yorkers including more than 500000 who are uninsured. It operates a network of around 10 acute care hospitals (including Bellevue the nation's oldest public hospital) large diagnostic and treatment centers skilled nursing centers long-term care facilities and a home health care agency. NYC H+H also operates more than 70 community-based clinics and provides medical services to New York City's correctional facilities. In addition it operates MetroPlus a managed health care plan.

Operations

NYC H+H provides health care services including primary and preventive care emergency care long-term care plant-based nutrition guidance school-based health care and services for victims of domestic violence.

Geographic Reach

NYC H+H operates health care facilities in New York's Manhattan Brooklyn Queens Bronx and Staten Island boroughs.

Sales and Marketing

NYC H+H's MetroPlus health plan provides low to no-cost insurance to more than 500000 customers in New York. It insures many New York City government employees.

Financial Performance

NYC H+H's operating revenue fell in fiscal 2017 (ended June) but recovered the following year surpassing that of fiscal 2016. Operating revenue increased 6% to $7.8 billion in 2018 as net patient service revenue and net appropriations from New York City increased. Those gains were partially offset by a decline in grants revenue.

The company has been losing money for years. In fiscal 2018 it had an operating loss of $57.5 million an improvement over the 2017 operating loss of $272.7 million. That improvement was driven by the higher operating revenue plus certain cost-control measures such as lower other-than-personal services and pension expenses. NYC H+H ended fiscal 2018 with a net deficit of $5.5 billion.

Strategy

NYC H+H has been struggling financially facing a projected $1.8 billion budget gap by 2020. In mid-2017 the system cut 476 positions including nearly 400 management positions. It has closed certain clinics and shuttered its Goldwater specialty care hospital and nursing facility. And although the system has received positive care quality reviews from external organizations it is challenged to attract patients with commercial insurance. To further exacerbate matters the health system has a number of older facilities that would benefit from improvements but it has few resources to allocate to those types of projects.

HISTORY

The City of New York in 1929 created a department to manage its hospitals for the poor. During the Depression more than half of the city's residents were eligible for subsidized care and its public hospitals operated at full capacity.

Four new hospitals opened in the 1950s but the city was already having trouble maintaining existing facilities and attracting staff (young doctors preferred private insurance-supported hospitals catering to the middle class). Meanwhile technological advances and increased demand for skilled nurses made hospitals more expensive to operate. The advent of Medicaid in 1965 was a boon for the system because it brought in federal money.

In 1969 the city created the New York City Health and Hospitals Corporation (HHC) to manage its public health care system — and it was hoped to distance it from the political arena. But HHC was still dependent on the city for funds arousing criticism from those who had hoped for more autonomy. A 1973 state report claimed "the people of New York City are not materially better served by the Health and Hospitals Corporation than by its predecessor agencies."

City budget shortfalls in the mid-1970s led to cutbacks at HHC including nearly 20% of staff. Later in the decade several hospitals closed and some services were discontinued. Ed Koch became mayor in 1978 and gained more control over HHC's operations. Struggles between his administration and the system led three HHC presidents to resign by 1981. That year Koch crony Stanley Brezenoff assumed the post and helped transform HHC into a city pseudo-department.

The early 1980s brought greater prosperity to the system. Reimbursement rates and collections procedures improved allowing HHC to upgrade its record-keeping and its ambulatory and psychiatric care programs. In the late 1980s sharp increases in AIDS and crack addiction cases strained the system and a sluggish economy decreased city funding. Criticism mounted in the early 1990s with allegations of wrongful deaths dangerous facilities and lack of Medicaid payment controls. HHC lost patients to managed care providers and revenues plummeted. In 1995 a city panel recommended radically revamping the system.

Faced with declining revenues and criticism from Mayor Rudolph Giuliani that HHC was "a jobs program" the company began cutting jobs and consolidating facilities in 1996. Under Giuliani's direction HHC made plans to sell its Coney Island Elmhurst and Queens hospital centers. In 1997 the New York State Supreme Court struck down Giuliani's privatization efforts saying the city council had a right to review and approve each sale. In 1998 Giuliani continued to seek to restructure HHC and the agency itself contended it was making progress toward its restructuring goals which were aimed at giving HHC more autonomy as well as more fiscal responsibility. In anticipation of a budget shortfall that year the system laid off some 900 support staff employees. In 1999 the state court of appeals ruled HHC could not legally lease or sell its hospitals.

In 2000 HHC launched an effort to improve its physical infrastructure by beginning the rebuilding and renovation of facilities in Brooklyn Manhattan and Queens. The organization also began converting to an electronic (and thus more efficient) clinical information system. In 2001 HHC forged ahead with further restructuring initiatives. It introduced the Open Access plan a cost-cutting measure designed to expedite the processes involved in outpatient visits.

In 2006 Mayor Michael Bloomberg committed $16 million in funds toward the treatment of those affected by exposure to toxic fumes and dust from the 2001 attacks on the World Trade Center. Together with the city HHC established the WTC Environmental Health Center at Bellevue Hospital; treatment was made available at little or no charge to the patient.

EXECUTIVES

Svp And General Counsel, Alan D. Aviles
Svp South Manhattan Health Network; Executive Director Bellevue Hospital Center, Lynda D. Curtis
Svp North Bronx Healthcare Network; Executive Director Jacobi Medical Center, William P. Walsh
Svp Finance And Cfo, Marlene Zurack
Evp And Coo, Antonio Martin
Executive Director Metropolitan Hospital Center, Meryl Weinberg
Executive Director Elmhurst Hospital Center, Chris Constantino
Executive Director And Cfo Gouverneur Healthcare Services, Mendel Hagler
Executive Director And President Metroplus Health Plan, Arnold Saperstein
Executive Director Sea View Hospital Rehabilitation Center And Home, Angelo Mascia
Svp Queens Healthcare Network, Anne Marie Sullivan
Executive Director Hhc Health And Home Care, Ann Frisch

Svp Information Technology And Cio, Norberto (Bert) Robles
Executive Director Dr. Susan Smith Mckinney Nursing And Rehabilitation Center, Michael Tartaglia
Executive Director Coler-goldwater Specialty Hospital And Nursing Facility, Robert K. Hughes
Svp Quality And Corporate Chief Medical Officer, Ross Wilson
Acting Svp Generations Plus Northern Manhattan Healthcare Network; Executive Director Lincoln Medical And Mental Health Center, Denise C. Soares
Executive Director Kings County Hospital Center, Ernest J. Baptiste
Executive Director Queens Hospital Center, Julius Wool
Assistant Vice President Information Technology Services, Michael Keil
Senior Assistant Vice President, Roslyn Weinstein
Senior Assistant Vice President, Caroline Jacobs
Senior Assistant Vice President, Paul Albertson
Senior Vice President, Arthur Wagner
Senior Assistant Vice President, Maxine Katz
Director Of Admissions, Alex Toro
Assistant Vice President Data Science, Vijay Saradhi
Director Of Pharmacy, Danielle Petrocelli
Vice President Of Finance And Chief Fina, Tim Buit
Senior Vice President Of Hospitals, William Foley
Senior Assistant Vice President Onecity Health, Ishmael Carter
Assistant Vice President, Nichola Davis
Head Nurse, Carmentina Silvestre-tan
Senior Assistant Vice President, Kaushal Challa
Assistant Vice President Operations, Grace-ann Weick
Program Medical Director, Natalya Kozlov
Vice President Business Development, Ken Sundaresan
Chairman, Michael A. Stocker
Vice Chair, Diane E. Lacey
Auditors: KPMG LLP NEW YORK NY

LOCATIONS

HQ: NEW YORK CITY HEALTH AND HOSPITALS CORPORATION
125 WORTH ST RM 514, NEW YORK, NY 100134006
Phone: 212 788-3321
Web: WWW.NYCHEALTHANDHOSPITALS.ORG

HHC Networks

Central Brooklyn Family Health Network
  Dr. Susan Smith McKinney Nursing and Rehabilitation Center
  East New York Diagnostic & Treatment Center
  Kings County Hospital Center
Generations Plus Northern Manhattan Health Network
  Harlem Hospital Center
  Lincoln Medical and Mental Health Center
  Metropolitan Hospital Center
  Morrisania Diagnostic & Treatment Center
  Renaissance Health Care Network Diagnostic & Treatment Center
  Segundo Ruiz Belvis Diagnostic & Treatment Center
North Bronx Healthcare Network
  Jacobi Medical Center
  North Central Bronx Hospital
North Brooklyn Health Network
  Cumberland Diagnostic & Treatment Center
  Woodhull Medical and Mental Health Center
Queens Health Network
  Elmhurst Hospital Center
  Queens Health Center
South Brooklyn and Staten Island Health Network
  Coney Island Hospital
  Sea View Hospital Rehabilitation Center & Home
South Manhattan Healthcare Network
  Bellevue Hospital Center
  Gouverneur Healthcare Services

PRODUCTS/OPERATIONS

2018 Sales

	$ mil.	% of total
Net patient services	6,216	80
Net appropriations from City of New York	787	10
Grants	652	9
Other	105	1
Total	**7,761**	**100**

Selected Services

Alcohol and Opioid Use Disorder
Asthma Care
Bariatric Services
Breast Health
Burn Care
Cancer Care
Cardiology
Child Health and Pediatrics
Colon Cancer Screening
Deaf and Hard-of-Hearing
Dental Care
Depression
Diabetes Care
Farmers Market
Flu Vaccination
Geriatric Services
HIV/AIDS Care
HPV Vaccine
Hyptertension
Language/Translation Services
LGBTQ Services
Men's Health
Mental Health
Neonatal Intensive Care
Obstetrics & Gynecology
Palliative Care
Parkinson's Disease
Pediatrics
Quit Smoking
Rehab Services
Victims of Domestic Violence
Sexual Response Assault Teams
Sickle Cell Disease
Sleep Disorder Labs
Stroke Prevention and Care
Telehealth Initiatives
Trauma Centers
Vision Care
Women's Health
WTC Environmental Health Center
Youth Health

COMPETITORS

Beth Israel Medical Center
Catholic Healthcare System
Columbia University
Continuum Health Partners
Cornell University
Lenox Hill Hospital Memorial Sloan-Kettering
Montefiore Medical
NYU
NewYork-Presbyterian Healthcare
Northwell Health

HISTORICAL FINANCIALS

Company Type: Private

Income Statement   FYE: June 30

	REVENUE ($ mil.)	NET INCOME ($ mil.)	NET PROFIT MARGIN	EMPLOYEES
06/17	9,550	(193)	—	35,700
06/02	4,285	(118)	—	—
06/01	4,287	(71)	—	—
06/00	4,083	9	0.2%	—
Annual Growth	5.1%	—	—	—

New York Community Bancorp Inc.

It's big banking in the Big Apple and beyond. New York Community Bancorp is the holding company for one of the largest thrifts in the US New York Community Bank as well as dba Atlantic Bank) and eight other banking divisions. In its home state New York Community Bank operates through Queens County Savings Bank Richmond County Savings Bank Roosevelt Savings Bank and Roslyn Savings Bank. It serves customers in New Jersey through its Garden State Community Bank division. New York Community Bank also does business as AmTrust Bank which operates in Arizona and Florida and Ohio Savings Bank. Altogether New York Community Bancorp has about 240 bank branches in five states.

Operations

The bank generates some 95% of total revenue from interest income and serves consumers and businesses with standard services such as checking and savings accounts CDs IRAs credit cards mortgages and loans. New York Community Bancorp also owns investment advisory firm Peter B. Cannell & Co.

Multifamily mortgage loans (with an emphasis on rent-regulated apartment buildings) are the company's key assets making up nearly 75% of its loan book. New York Community Bancorp prefers rent-regulated properties because they tend to have lower-than-average tenant turnover and can often be expected to bring in steady income during economic downturns. The company also focuses on loans secured by commercial real estate in New York and New Jersey.

Geographic Reach

Westbury New York-based New York Community Bancorp has branches in five states: New York home to about 130 community and commercial bank branches; New Jersey with about 40 locations; Ohio and Florida with more than 25 branches each; and Arizona with nearly 15 locations.

Sales and Marketing

In addition to its branches there are approximately 350 ATM locations including nearly 235 ATM that operate 24 hours a day and 75 that are off-site ATMs. Customers also have 24-hour access to their accounts through bank-by-phone service through mobile banking and online through the website www.myNYCB.com.Certain money market accounts certificates of deposit ("CDs") and checking accounts through a dedicated websitewww.myBankingDirect.com.

In addition to checking and savings accounts Individual Retirement Accounts and CDs for both businesses and consumers by offering a suite of cash management products to address the needs of small and mid-size businesses and professional associations. Complementing broad selection of traditional banking products with an extensive menu of alternative financial services including annuities life and long-term care insurance and mutual funds of various third-party service providers.

Financial Performance

New York Community Bancorp has struggled to attain meaningful growth in the past five years.

In fiscal 2019 sales fell a further 7% to $1 billion due higher interest expense.

Net income was $395.0 in 2019 decreased of $27.4 million incurred in the previous year.

The company's coffers held $741 million in cash and equivalents in 2019 a drop of about $733.1million from the previous year. Cash from operations was $509.8 million in 2019 investing used $2.1 billion and financing activities provided another $816 million.

Strategy

The general investment strategy is to purchase liquid investments with various maturities to ensure that the overall interest rate risk position stays within the required limits of the investment policies. Generally limiting the investments to GSE obligations and U.S. Treasury obligations.

As a financial institution the company is focused on reducing the exposure to interest rate volatility which represents the primary market risk. Changes in market interest rates represent the greatest challenge to financial performance as such changes can have a significant impact on the level of income and expense recorded on a large portion of interest-earning assets and interest-bearing liabilities and on the market value of all interest-earning assets other than those possessing a short term to maturity. To reduce the exposure to changing rates the Board of Directors and management monitor interest rate sensitivity on a regular or as needed basis so that adjustments to the asset and liability mix can be made when deemed appropriate.

Company Background

In 2012 it acquired some $2.2 billion in deposits mainly short-term CDs but also money market accounts from Aurora Bank.

New York Community Bank was founded in 1859. New York Community Bancorp was incorporated in 1993.

EXECUTIVES

Sevp And Coo, Robert Wann, age 65, $1,100,000 total compensation
President And Ceo, Joseph R. Ficalora, age 73, $1,400,000 total compensation
Sevp And Cfo, Thomas R. (Tom) Cangemi, age 51, $850,000 total compensation
Evp Chief Corporate Governance Officer And Corporate Secretary, R. Patrick Quinn
Sevp And Chief Lending Officer, James J. Carpenter, age 59, $775,000 total compensation
Evp And Chief Accounting Officer, John J. Pinto, age 49, $575,000 total compensation
Evp And Cio, Robert Brown
Senior Vice President And Controller, James Speranza
Assistant Vice President Regional Human Resources Director, Patricia King
Vice President Risk Management, Debbie Messina
Executive Vice President, Barbara Ann Tosi-Renna
Second Vice President Staff Attorney, Laura Coleman
Senior Vice President Mortgage, Charles Baker
Senior Vice President, Michael Frain
Vice President Loan Review Officer, Ronald Lehrer
Executive Vice President, Andrew Kaplan
Underwriter Iii Second Vice President, Tiffany Cohen
First Vice President, Deborah Schaum

First Senior Vice President And Branch Coordinator, Louis Riccio
Assistant Vice President Procurement, Susan Pace-Burke
Application Development Manager First Vice President, Sharon Michitsch
Edandt Training Manager Vice President, Susan Weaver
Vice President Asset Manager, Jeff Roe
First Vp Marketing, Donna Winfield
Vice President Commercial Lending, John Adams
Assistant Vice President Manager Of Loan Admin Customer Service, Ken Hsiung
Vice President, Kevin Kaufmann
Vice President Market Manager, Leonard Bosso
Assistant Vice President, Peter Zito
Vice President, Ines Kurtov
Vice President, Jeff Lee
First Vice President, Scott Armstrong
Vice President Audit Manager, Adam Sullivan
Assistant Vice President Lead, Kate Riese
Second Vice President, Crocefissa Grima
Vice President Network Engineering, Michael Mike Gluckman
First Vice President And Sox Compliance Officer, Andrew LaRocca
Assistant Vice President, Cathy Karalis
Vice President, James Drum
Vice President Retail Operations, Jamil Salah
Irst Vice President Team Leader Commercial Real Estate For The Western Pennsylvania West Virginia And Ohio Markets, Michael Warrick
Vice President Premier Banking Business Development Officer Nycb123 Bug.png, Dimitra Difranco
Executive Vice President, Kenneth Scheriff
Assistant Vice President Network Engineering, Anthony Ardezzone
Executive Vice President And Chief Human Resources Officer, Eric Kracov
Vice President Systems Engineering, Craig Preiser
Vp It Core Operations Manager, Perry Kaganis
Vice President Branch Manager, Susan Fisher
Assistanty Vice President, Michael Yetemian
Vice President, Kathy Kowler
Assistant Vice President Branch Manager, Vincent Oyola
Vice President Mortgage Lending Officer, Michael Scarola
Senior Vice President Director Investor Relations, Donna Condiles
Vice President Of Inquiry Management, Kristina Hosea
Vice President Enterprise Risk Asset Liability Management, Tejas Doshi
Assistant Vice President, Beth Gant
Second Vice President, Sarah Artino
Senior Vice President, Frank Macchio
Vp Commercial Lending Officer, Frank Maffei
Assistant Vice President Insurance Risk Analyst, Jacqueline Cox
Assistant Vice President, Angela Gallagher
Vice President Compliance Manager Lending Oversight, Christine Patterson
Vice President And Credit Risk Manager, Jeffrey Roe
Vice President, Daniel Koppelman Mcse
Avp And Credit Risk Manager, Stephen Hasenbein
Chairman, Dominick Ciampa, age 87
Board Member, Ronald Rosenfeld
Board Member, John Tsimbinos
Auditors: KPMG LLP

LOCATIONS

HQ: New York Community Bancorp Inc.
615 Merrick Avenue, Westbury, NY 11590
Phone: 516 683-4100
Web: www.mynycb.com

2016 Locations

	No.
New York Community Bank	
New York	111
New Jersey	45
Ohio	28
Florida	27
Arizona	14
New York Commercial Bank	48
Total	**273**

PRODUCTS/OPERATIONS

2016 Sales

	$ mil.	% of total
Interest		
Mortgage & other loans	1,472	81
Securities & money market investments	202	11
Noninterest		
Fee income	32	2
Bank-owned life insurance	31	2
Mortgage banking income	27	1
Net gain on sale of loans	15	1
Net gain on sales of securities	3	-
Other	41	2
FDIC indemnification expenses	(6.2)	-
Total	**1,820**	**100**

2016 Sales

	% of total
Banking operations	
Interest	89
Non Interest	7
Residential Mortgage banking	
Interest	1
Non Interest	3
Total	**100**

Selected Operations

AmTrust Bank (Arizona Florida)
Atlantic Bank (New York commercial bank)
Garden State Community Bank (New Jersey)
Ohio Savings Bank (Ohio)
Queens County Savings Bank (Queens NY)
Richmond County Savings Bank (Staten Island NY)
Roosevelt Savings Bank (Brooklyn NY)
Roslyn Savings Bank (Long Island NY)

COMPETITORS

Apple Bank for Savings	Provident Financial Services
Astoria Financial	Ridgewood Savings Bank
Bank of America	Safra Bank
Citigroup	TD Bank USA
Emigrant Bank	Valley National Bancorp
Flushing Financial	Wells Fargo
HSBC USA	
Investors Bancorp	
JPMorgan Chase	

HISTORICAL FINANCIALS

Company Type: Public

Income Statement

FYE: December 31

	ASSETS ($ mil.)	NET INCOME ($ mil.)	INCOME AS % OF ASSETS	EMPLOYEES
12/19	53,640	395	0.7%	2,786
12/18	51,899	422	0.8%	2,913
12/17	49,124	466	0.9%	3,096
12/16	48,926	495	1.0%	3,487
12/15	50,317	(47)	—	3,448
Annual Growth	1.6%	—	—	(5.2%)

2019 Year-End Financials

Debt ratio: 1.22%
Return on equity: 5.91%
Cash ($ mil.): 741
Current ratio: —
Long-term debt ($ mil.): —

No. of shares (mil.): 467
Dividends
  Yield: 5.6%
  Payout: 89.4%
Market value ($ mil.): 5,618

	STOCK PRICE ($) FY Close	P/E High/Low	PER SHARE ($) Earnings	Dividends	Book Value
12/19	12.02	18 12	0.77	0.68	14.36
12/18	9.41	18 11	0.79	0.68	14.05
12/17	13.02	18 13	0.90	0.68	13.91
12/16	15.91	17 14	1.01	0.68	12.57
12/15	16.32	—	(0.11)	1.00	12.24
Annual Growth	(7.4%)	— —	—	(9.2%)	4.1%

NEW YORK COMMUNITY TRUST AND COMMUNITY FUNDS INC

EXECUTIVES

Pres-Exec Dir, Lorie A Slutsky
Sr V Pres*, Joyce Bove
V Pres Donor Rltns*, Robert V Edgar
V Pres of ADM*, Mercedes M Leon
Program Officer, Eve A Stotland
Senior Program Officer, Patricia Swann
Vice President, Shawn V Morehead
Director, Eileen P Casey
CIO, Mary Greenebaum
Program Officer, Rachel D Pardoe
Controller, Wen Weng
Auditors: GRANT THORNTON LLP NEW YORK

LOCATIONS

HQ: NEW YORK COMMUNITY TRUST AND COMMUNITY FUNDS INC
909 3RD AVE FL 22, NEW YORK, NY 100224752
Phone: 212 686-0010
Web: WWW.NYCOMMUNITYTRUST.ORG

HISTORICAL FINANCIALS

Company Type: Private

Income Statement

FYE: December 31

	ASSETS ($ mil.)	NET INCOME ($ mil.)	INCOME AS % OF ASSETS	EMPLOYEES
12/17	2,806	(5)	—	65
12/16	2,552	(5)	—	
12/15	2,473	(99)	—	
12/14	2,570	130	5.1%	
Annual Growth	3.0%	—	—	

NEW YORK UNIVERSITY

Higher education is at the core of this Big Apple institution. The setting and heritage of New York University (NYU) make it one of the nation's most popular educational institutions. With more thanÄ 50000 students attending its 18 schools and colleges NYU is among the largest private schools in the US. Its Tisch School of the Arts is well-regarded and its law school and Leonard N. Stern School of Business are among the foremost in the country. NYU occupies five major centers in Manhattan; its Washington Square campus is in the heart of Greenwich Village. The school was founded in 1831. Notable alumni include former Federal Reserve Chairman Alan Greenspan and film producer Oliver Stone.

Operations

NYU reports its financials in two segments — University and NYU Langone Health. The latter segment is composed of the NYU Langone Health System and NYU School of Medicine.

The University includes nearly 20 colleges and divisions including schools of art and sciences law dentistry business mathematical sciences fine arts professional studies public services social work and engineering. NYU also operates NYU Abu Dhabi and NYU Shanghai a joint venture with East China Normal University. The University segment accounts for some 30% of NYU's total revenue.

NYU Langone Health operates two hospitals Kimmel Pavilion and Tisch Hospital which together have some 850 beds. It also operates the 225-bed NYU Langone Orthopedic Hospital the 450-bed NYU Langone Hospital in Brooklyn and several ambulatory care facilities. The segment brings in some 70% of NYU's total revenue.

NYU alumni and faculty boast several prestigious awards including more than a dozen Nobel and Crafoord prizes and another four Pulitzer prizes.

Geographic Reach

Along with its campuses in New York NYU operates degree-granting campuses in Abu Dhabi and Shanghai. It also has more than 10 global academic centers in Africa Asia Europe and the Americas and research programs in more than 25 countries.

Financial Performance

In fiscal 2018 (ended August) NYU's operating revenue increased 17% to $11.6 billion. Driving that gain was an increase in patient care revenue which rose from $5.6 billion to $7 billion that year.

However the university's excess of operating revenue over expenses fell dramatically from $196.8 million to $11.2 million in fiscal 2018. Salaries and medical and pharmaceutical costs rose as did facilities expenses professional services expenses and all other expenses.

NYU ended fiscal 2018 with $1.5 billion in net cash some $217 million more than what it had at the end of 2017. Operating activities provided $941.1 million in net cash financing activities provided another $580.4 million while investing activities used $1.3 billion.

Strategy

In 2018 NYU School of Medicine offered all students full tuition scholarships regardless of merit or financial need. The move was largely designed to promote the training of primary care physicians which is an area of great need in the US. By removing the heavy debt load that medical students typically face the school hopes to encourage students to pursue careers in lower-paying areas such as primary care.

Later that year NYU announced plans to establish a new medical school on Long Island. That campus will also provide full tuition scholarships to students.

HISTORY

New York University was founded by several prominent New Yorkers in 1831. The school held its first classes the following year in rented rooms on the corner of Beekman and Nassau streets then moved to a building in Washington Square in 1835. It established its law school that year. NYU started its school of medicine in 1841 followed by the school of engineering and science (1854). Postgraduate studies in arts and science (its first coeducational program) began in 1886.

NYU's enrollment jumped from fewer than 2000 in 1900 to 28000 in 1930. After a lull during the Depression and WWII the campus boomed again in the postwar years. During the 1950s the university began focusing on improving academics rather than on increasing enrollment. It created a school of the arts in 1965 and in the early 1970s it completed the Elmer Holmes Bobst Library. However a cash crunch during that decade almost forced the school into bankruptcy.

President Jay Oliva took the reins in 1981 and focused on transforming NYU from a largely commuter college into a global university. The school began a campaign to raise $1 billion in 1984 but earmarked the funds for campus improvements rather than swelling its endowment. During the late 1980s NYU opened several new dormitories and conference spaces. In 1994 British historian and collector Sir Harold Acton bequeathed to the school his Tuscany estate — five art-filled villas overlooking Florence Italy.

In 1996 NYU's Medical Center began talks with Mount Sinai Medical Center aimed at merging their hospitals and medical schools. The talks fell apart in early 1997 but the following year the two sides agreed to merge hospitals and keep their medical schools distinct. Also in 1998 NYU formed NYU On-Line Inc. a for-profit subsidiary to develop and sell specialized Internet courses to other schools training centers and students; the venture was subsequently folded in late 2001. During 1999 contributions to the school approached $250 million. That year however two upper-level school officials were fired following allegations of improper use of university money.

Oliva retired as president in 2002 and was replaced by John Sexton former School of Law dean. In 2004 Sexton announced that NYU would give $1 million to New York City towards renovation of Washington Square Park (the school annually gives some $200000 for the park's ongoing maintenance).

EXECUTIVES

Vp Academic And Health Affairs, Robert (Bob) Berne
Vp Information Technology And Chief Information Technology Officer, Marilyn A. McMillan
Provost, David W. McLaughlin
Evp Finance And Information Technology, Martin S. Dorph
Director Global Institute Of Public Health; Dean Of Global Public Health, Cheryl G. Healton
Dean Libraries, Carol A. Mandel
Herman Robert Fox Dean College Of Dentistry, Charles N. Bertolami
Evp Operations, Alison Leary
Director Institute For The Study Of The Ancient World, Roger Bagnall

Director Courant Institute Of Mathematical Sciences, Gérard Ben Arous
Saul J. Farber Dean Nyu School Of Medicine; Ceo Nyu Hospitals Center, Robert I. Grossman
Dean Gallatin School Of Individualized Study, Susanne L. Wofford
Dean Polytechnic School Of Engineering, Katepalli R. (Sreeni) Sreenivasan
Dean Silver School Of Social Work, Lynn Videka
Dean Liberal Studies, Fred Schwarzbach
Judy And Michael Steinhardt Director Institute Of Fine Arts, Patricia Lee Rubin
Dean Leonard N. Stern School Of Business, Peter B. Henry, age 50
Vice Chancellor New York University Abu Dhabi, Alfred H. Bloom
Vp Global Technology And Chief Global Technology Officer, Thomas A. (Tom) Delaney
Dean For Science Faculty Of Arts And Science, Michael D. Purugganan
President, Andrew Hamilton
Gale And Ira Drukier Dean Steinhardt School For Culture Education And Human Development, Dominic Brewer
Anne And Joel Ehrenkranz Dean Faculty Of Arts And Sciences, Thomas J. Carew
Dean For Humanities Faculty Of Arts And Sciences, Joy Connolly
Harvey J. Stedman Dean School Of Professional Studies, Dennis DiLorenzo
Dean Robert F. Wagner Graduate School Of Public Service, Sherry A. Glied
Dean Tisch School Of The Arts, Allyson Green
Dean For Social Sciences Faculty Of Arts And Science, Michael Laver
Vice Chancellor Nyu Shanghai, Jeffrey S. Lehman
Dean Undergraduate College Leonard N. Stern School Of Business, Geeta Menon
Dean School Of Law, Trevor Morrison
Director Marron Institute Of Urban Management, Paul Romer
Seryl Kushner Dean College Of Arts And Science, G. Gabrielle Starr
Dean College Of Nursing, Eileen Sullivan-Marx
Chancellor Nyu Shanghai, Yu Lizhong
Interim Dean Graduate School Of Arts And Science, Anna L. Harvey
Assistant Vice President, Zoe Ragouzeos
Vice President, Marc Wais
Vice Provost, Carol Morrow
Associate Vice President Student Health, Carlo Ciotoli
Vice President Financial Operations And Treasurer, Stephanie Pianka
Assistant Vice President Employee Relations, Barbara Cardeli-Arroyo
Vice President Finance, Harold T Read
Associate Vice President, Deborah Broderick
Assistant Vice President, Allen Mcfarlane
Assistant Vice President, John Beckman
Vice President, Andrew Gordon
Vice President Of Public Relations, Carolynn Choi
Associate Vice President Campus Planning And Design, Lori Mazor
Vice President Chief Information Security Officer, Mehdi Idrissi
Assistant Vice President, Janet Alperstein
Nursing Director, Mary Gribbin
Director Of Government Relations, Steve Heuer
Associate Medical Director, Nathan Bertelsen
Vice President For Enrollment Management, Mj Knoll-finn
Vice President For, Robert Campbell
Associate Vice President For Global Technologies, Heather Stewart
Administrative Aide To The Associate Vice President Of Alumni Relations, Danielle Ohrenberger
Vice President Finance, Pamela Morris
Vice President, Robert Levine

Executive Vice President, Tom Jordan
Vice President General Manager, Laurence F Maslon
Executive Vice President Research And
  Innovation Cross Platform, Lisa Sokolov
Vice President And Special Counsel, Leo L
  Goldsmith
Vice President, Victoria M Mccoy-cosentino
Vice President For Student Affairs, Susan B
  Neuman
Vice President Director Engineering, Chris Pak
Vice President Global Security And Crisis
  Management, Jules Martin
Assistant Vice President External Affairs And
  Protective Services, Carl Barchus
Senior Vice President Manager International
  Banking, Vonetta Moses
Director Of Admissions, Williams Cassandra
Vice President Finance And Administration,
  Charice Washington-warner
Vice President Sales, Joe Harris
Vice President And Manager Raines Perspectives
  Raines International, Jessica Deoliveira
Senior Vice President Deputy General Counsel
  Chief Compliance And Ethics Officer, Genie
  Gavenchak
Vice President For Operations Capital Projects,
  Andy Buonpastore
Executive Vice President, Mandy Hu
Vice President Facilities Management, Debra
  Berger
Vice President Global Campus Safety, Marlon
  Lynch
Medical Director, John Wang
Director Of Pharmacy Director Of Pharmacy
  Services, Jeanie Kantrowitz
Vice President Of Event Planning, Kristyn M
  Curran
Executive Vice President, Linda Tempel
Senior Vice President, Evelyn Alvarez
Executive Vice President, Mia Higgins
Assistant Vice President, De Toro Yadira
Vice President, Laura Schattschneider
Chairman Board Of Trustees, William R. (Bill)
  Berkley, age 74
Board Director, Christine Trump
Honorary Board Member, John Tintori
Treasurer, Peter Rajsingh
Treasurer, Simon Mun
Assistant Treasurer, Elisa Cohen
Medical Secretary, Latia Davis
Secretary, Candice Jarvis
Secretary, Jennifer Neuman
Ward Secretary, Mark Brennan
Ms Global Affairs Candidate Treasurer Energy
  Policy International Club, Jude Buenaseda
Secretary, Lara Maraziti
Treasurer, Daphne Tso
Secretary, Lewis R Stejnberg
Secretary Athletic Development, Raffaela Ianniciello
Secretary And Marketing, August Morar
Secretary, Beverly Wideman
Cab Treasurer, Erin Adams
Secretary, Iris Lam
Secretary, John Milito
Vice Chairman, Allan Feldman
Secretary To The Authority, Thomas Donohue
Auditors: PRICEWATERHOUSECOOPERS LLP NE

LOCATIONS

HQ: NEW YORK UNIVERSITY
  70 WASHINGTON SQ S, NEW YORK, NY 100121019
Phone: 212 998-1212
Web: WWW.NYU.EDU

PRODUCTS/OPERATIONS

2018 Sales

	$ mil.	% of total
Patient care	6,981	60
Tuition & fees	1,852	16
Grants & contracts	1,011	9
Auxiliary enterprises	505	4
Hospital affiliations	342	3
Endowment distribution	169	2
Contributions	168	2
Net assets from restrictions	121	1
Insurance premiums earned	115	1
Return on short-term investments	16	-
Programs & other	272	2
Total	**11,556**	**100**

2018 Sales

	$ mil.	% of total
NYU Langone Health	8,298	72
University	3,267	28
Adjustments	(10.3)	-
Total	**11,556**	**100**

Selected Schools and Colleges

College of Arts and Science (founded 1832)
College of Dentistry (1865)
Courant Institute of Mathematical Sciences (1934)
Gallatin School of Individualized Study (1972)
Graduate School of Arts and Science (1886)
Leonard N. Stern School of Business (1900)
Robert F. Wagner Graduate School of Public Service
  (1938)
School of Continuing and Professional Studies (1934)
School of Law (1835)
School of Medicine (1841)
School of Social Work (1960)
Steinhardt School of Culture Education and Human
  Development (1890)
Tisch School of the Arts (1965)

HISTORICAL FINANCIALS
Company Type: Private

Income Statement
FYE: August 31

	REVENUE ($ mil.)	NET INCOME ($ mil.)	NET PROFIT MARGIN	EMPLOYEES
08/16	8,500	177	2.1%	21,000
08/11	5,172	563	10.9%	—
08/06	2,148	195	9.1%	—
Annual Growth	14.7%	(1.0%)	—	—

Newell Brands Inc

Newell Brands is the company behind such household names as Rubbermaid storage boxes Calphalon cookware Graco pushchairs and Sharpie pens. Newell Brands' customers are mainly mass retailers such as Target and home and office supply stores such as Staples. Newell's footprint spans 55 factories and some 85 warehouses and distribution centers globally. It also has approximately 250 retail stores (490 stores are located in US) primarily related to Yankee Candle. About two-thirds of Newell Brands' sales comes from US operation.

Operations

Newell Brands structures its operations into four main reporting segments: Learning and Development Home and Outdoor Living Food and Commercial and Appliances and Cookware.

Learning and Development accounts for about 30% of total sales and makes pens pencils highlighters and markers glue labels and baby gear and infant care products. Its brands include Aprica Baby Jogger Expo Graco Mr Sketch Parker Sharpie and X-Acto.

The Home and Outdoor Living segment (roughly 30%) makes products for outdoor activities home fragrance products and connected home and security products. Brands include Chespeake Bay Candle Contigo First Alert and Yankee Candle.

Food and Commercial segment (nearly 25%) makes food storage and home storage products vacuum sealing products hygiene systems and material handling solutions. Brands include FoodSaver Rubbermaid Mapa Quickie and Spontex.

Appliances and Cookware (more than 15% of sales) makes household products including kitchen appliances gourmet cookware bakeware and cutlery. Brands include Calphalon Crock-Pot Mr. Coffee Oster and Sunbeam.

Geographic Reach

Based in Atlanta Georgia Newell Brands sells its products in nearly 200 countries and operates in nearly 100 countries around the world.

Roughly two-thirds of sales come from the US while Europe Middle East and Africa (EMEA) region generates about 15% of sales. Latin America and the Asia Pacific regions both generate more than 5% of revenue while Canada brings in the remainder of total sales.

Sales and Marketing

Newell Brands reaches consumers through large mass merchandisers such as discount stores home centers warehouse clubs office superstores specialty retailers and wholesalers commercial distributors and e-commerce companies. It also sells direct-to-consumer online while certain brands such as Yankee Candle have dedicated stores.

Newell Brands' biggest customer is Wal-Mart sales to which account for about 10% to 15% of its net sales each year. Other customers are Amazon Bed Bath & Beyond Costco Lowe's Kroger Office Depot Staples Target and The Home Depot.

The company advertising and promotion costs totalled $389 million $397 million and $485 million in 2019 2018 and 2017 respectively.

Financial Performance

The acquisition of Jarden in 2016 nearly doubled Newell Brands' sales which peaked at $9.6 billion in 2017. However all is not well at Newell as weak cash flow and bankruptcy of key customer Toys "R" Us triggered huge goodwill impairments at the tail end of 2018 and caused the company to accelerate its transformation plan.

In 2019 the company's sales fell 4% to $9.7 billion compared to $10.2 billion in 2018 due to declines across all segments primarily within the Appliances and Cookware Food and Commercial and Home and Outdoor Living segments.

Newell reported a $106.6 billion net income in 2019 compared to its net loss of $6.9 billion in 2018. It booked a $1.2 billion impairment charge which recorded mainly in the Food and Commercial Appliances and Cookware and Home and Outdoor Living segments while Learning and Development at $24.8 million.

Newell's cash on hand fell $124.8 million during 2019 ending the year at $370.9 million. The company's operations generated $1 billion and its investing activities generated $735.4 million while financing activities used $1.9 billion. Newell's main cash uses in 2019 were payment on long-term debt dividends and share repurchases while business divestitures generated $995.7 million.

Strategy

With the brands acquired from Jarden not providing the hoped-for synergies Newell accelerated its transformation plan in 2018. The company plans to sell off big chunks of its portfolio notably its industrial and commercial assets such as Waddington plastic packaging and Rexair vacuum cleaners. It's also selling non-core consumer products such as Rawlings Jostens Pure Fishing among others. The goal is to sell all of them before the end of 2019 and with the capital raised Newell will deleverage its balance sheet strengthen its operations and return cash to shareholders.

The company decided that the Rubbermaid Outdoor Closet Refuse Garage and Cleaning businesses and the Mapa/Spontex and Quickie businesses are no longer held for sales and now reported in the Food and Commercial segment. The decision is to keep this business due to its competitive large and growing category revenue growth and margin expansion.

HISTORY

Businessmen in Ogdensburg New York advanced curtain rod maker W.F. Linton Co. $1000 to relocate from Rhode Island in the early 1900s. Local wholesaler Edgar Newell signed off on the loan; when the company went bankrupt in 1903 he was forced to take over. The company renamed Newell Manufacturing set up plants in Canada and Freeport Illinois to ease shipping costs and speed delivery.

Production expanded into towel racks ice picks and other items; Woolworth's decision to carry Newell's products turned the company into a national supplier. Edgar Newell died in 1920. The company made its first acquisition in 1938 buying window treatment specialist Drapery Hardware.

The Newell companies were consolidated in the mid-1960s into a single corporation. Daniel Ferguson was named president in 1965 and served alongside his CEO father Leonard one of Newell's original employees. During his tenure Daniel hitched the company's future to the growing dominance of large discount stores. Newell went from a $14 million family business to a global multi-line conglomerate by acquiring products that it distributed to these big buyers. The company went public in 1972.

As for Rubbermaid it was originally a balloon maker in the 1920s called Wooster Rubber. By the mid-1930s Ohio's Wooster Rubber had acquired the Rubbermaid product line of rubber housewares. It went public in 1955 and two years later changed its name to Rubbermaid. During the 1980s the company enjoyed a decade of phenomenal growth. Newell's $6 billion purchase of Rubbermaid in 1999 sealed its biggest deal yet and resulted in a name change: Newell Rubbermaid.

Decades later the company changed its name to Newell Brands in 2016 after it purchased consumer goods giant Jarden in a mega-merger valued at around $15.4 billion.

EXECUTIVES

Evp And Cfo, Ralph J. Nicoletti, age 62, $493,845 total compensation

Ceo, Michael B. (Mike) Polk, age 59, $1,312,500 total compensation

Coo, William A. (Bill) Burke, age 59, $796,053 total compensation

Chief Development Officer, Richard Davies

Chief Customer Officer, Joseph W. Cavaliere

President, Mark S. Tarchetti, age 44, $922,212 total compensation

Svp Information Technology And Cio, Dan Gustafson

Chief Transformation Officer, Russ Torres

Vp Global Ecommerce, Jeremy Liebowitz

Vice President Corporate Human Resources, Meredith Soree

Svp Design And Innovation, Nate Young

Vice President Strategy And Analytics, Dan Sedlak

Executive Vice President Chief Human Resources And Communications Officer, Fiona Laird

Svp Investor Relations And Communications, Nancy O'donnell

Vice President Sales, Larry Scarlett

Senior Business Intelligence Developer, Robert Esteves

Vp Hr Service Delivery And Technology, Sam Perkinson

Vice President Sales, Mick Piche

Chairman, Michael T. Cowhig, age 73

Board Member, Steven Strobel

Board Member, Michael Todman

Board Member, Debra Crew

Auditors: PricewaterhouseCoopers LLP

LOCATIONS

HQ: Newell Brands Inc
6655 Peachtree Dunwoody Road, Atlanta, GA 30328
Phone: 770 418-7000
Web: www.newellrubbermaid.com

2018 Sales

	$ mil.	% of total
North America		
United States	5,805	67
Canada	396	5
Europe Middle East and Africa	1,096	13
Asia Pacific	684	8
Latin America	647	8
Total	**8,630**	**100**

PRODUCTS/OPERATIONS

2018 sales

	$ mil.	% of total
Learning and Development	2,981	35
Home and Outdoor Living	2,946	34
Food and Appliances	2,699	31
Other	3	-
Total	**8,630**	**100**

Selected Brands & Trade Names

Cleaning organization and decor
  Brute
  Roughneck
  Rubbermaid
  TakeAlongs
Office products
  Accent
  Berol
  DYMO
  Expo
  Liquid Paper
  Paper Mate
  Parker
  Rotring
  Sharpie
  Uni-Ball (under license)
  Waterman
Home and family
  Aprica
  Avex
  Calphalon
  Calphalon One
  Contigo
  Cooking with Calphalon

Goody
Graco
Katana
Kitchen Essentials
Teutonia

COMPETITORS

ACCO Brands	Knape & Vogt
Acme United	Lancaster Colony
Alticor	Libbey
Avery Dennison	Lifetime Brands
BIC	Myers Industries
Bridgestone	Owens-Illinois
Coleman	Springs Global US
Crayola	Sterilite
Decorator Industries	Tupperware Brands
Dixon Ticonderoga	Uniek
Faber-Castell	WKI Holding
Home Products International	Wilton Brands
	ZAG Industries
Katy Industries	

HISTORICAL FINANCIALS

Company Type: Public

Income Statement

FYE: December 31

	REVENUE ($ mil.)	NET INCOME ($ mil.)	NET PROFIT MARGIN	EMPLOYEES
12/19	9,714	106	1.1%	30,000
12/18	8,630	(6,917)	—	37,000
12/17	14,742	2,748	18.6%	49,000
12/16	13,264	527	4.0%	53,400
12/15	5,915	350	5.9%	17,200
Annual Growth	13.2%	(25.7%)	—	14.9%

2019 Year-End Financials

Debt ratio: 36.59%	No. of shares (mil.): 423
Return on equity: 2.09%	Dividends
Cash ($ mil.): 348	Yield: 4.7%
Current ratio: 1.38	Payout: 368.0%
Long-term debt ($ mil.): 5,391	Market value ($ mil.): 8,140

	STOCK PRICE ($) FY Close	P/E High/Low		PER SHARE ($) Earnings	Dividends	Book Value
12/19	19.22	87	54	0.25	0.92	11.72
12/18	18.59	—	—	(14.60)	0.92	12.40
12/17	30.90	10	5	5.63	0.88	29.15
12/16	44.65	44	27	1.25	0.76	23.52
12/15	44.08	37	28	1.29	0.76	6.82
Annual Growth	(18.7%)	—	—	(33.7%)	4.9%	14.5%

Newmont Corp

Newmont goes for the gold. Producing close to 6.3 million ounces of gold annually Newmont Corporation (formerly Newmont Goldcorp Corporation) is a gold producer that has significant operations in countries such as the US Australia Peru Ghana and Suriname. Its gold reserves are over 100 million ounces spread across around 26400 square miles of its own land. Newmont also produces some copper principally through Boddington in Australia and Phoenix in the US. Although Newmont makes almost all its sales from refined gold the end-product of its operations is doré bars an alloy consisting primarily of gold but also containing silver and other metals. In 2019 Newmont Mining acquired Goldcorp for $10 billion to create the newly rebranded Newmont Goldcorp Corporation which changed its name in 2020 to Newmont Corporation. The company generates most of its revenue in UK.

Operations

Newmont's operations are organized in five geographic regions; North America South America Australia Africa and Nevada. Except for Africa which accounts for around 15% all other segments' revenue account for around or a little over 20%.

The company's North American operations consists primarily of Cripple Creek &Victor ("CC&V") in the United States of America ("U.S." or "USA") Red Lake Musselwhite Porcupine and léonore in Canada and Peñasquito in Mexico.

South America segment consists primarily of Yanacocha in Peru Merian in Suriname and Cerro Negro in Argentina.

Australia segment consists primarily of Boddington Tanami and Kalgoorlie in Australia.

Africa segment consists primarily of Ahafo and Akyem in Ghana.

Nevada segment consists primarily of NGM Carlin Phoenix Twin Creeks and Long Canyon in the USA.

Overall the company generates almost 95% of its revenue from gold followed by silver with almost 5% while the rest is generated by copper lead and zinc.

Geographic Reach

Over 80% of the Colorado-based company's sale comes from the spot market in London UK with over 5% coming from Korea.

Newmont holds mineral rights on around 26400 square miles of land.

Sales and Marketing

Newmont sells almost 6.5 million ounces of gold at the London bullion spot market which is either used as an investment or finds a variety of end uses including jewelry electronics dentistry industrial and decorative uses.

The company also sells around 80 million pounds of copper a year in the form of concentrate that is sold to smelters for further treatment and refining and cathode.

Financial Performance

Sales increased 34% from $7.4 billion in 2018 to $9.7 billion in 2019. This came mostly from gold products. Other products also contributed to the increase with the exception of Copper.

Newmont's net income skyrocketed in 2019 to $2.8 billion compared to $341 million in 2018 primarily due to the gain recognized on the formation of NGM as well as higher production due to the Newmont Goldcorp transaction and higher average realized gold prices.

Operations provided $2.7 billion offset by $1.2 billion going towards investments and a further $2.8 billion used in financing activities. Newmont's cash at the end of the year totaled $2.3 billion.

Strategy

Newport's strategy includes strengthening its portfolio (by building a longer-life lower-cost asset portfolio) and moving on promising exploration project development and inorganic opportunities.

The company assembled a collection of assets in top-tier jurisdictions with the acquisition of Goldcorp and the formation of NGM; successfully delivered four projects on four continents with Tanami Power in Australia the Borden mine in

Canada Ahafo Mill Expansion in Ghana and Quecher Main in Peru; approved Tanami Expansion 2 and Autonomous Haulage at Boddington; formed strategic partnerships in GT Gold Prodigy Gold and Irving Resources to fund exploration activities in Canada Australia and Japan respectively; divested the Nimba iron ore project in Guinea; entered into binding agreements to sell Red Lake in Canada and investment holdings in Continental Gold; completed divestiture of the Company's 50 percent interest in Kalgoorlie Consolidated Gold Mines ("Kalgoorlie") in Australia.

In 2019 Newmont rejected an unsolicited takeover bid from its competitor Barrick Gold and instead proposed a joint venture in Nevada USA. Meanwhile the company is also looking to create a newly rebranded Newmont Goldcorp corporation by taking over Goldcorp to become a top player in the industry.

Mergers and Acquisitions

In early 2019 Newmont Corporation entered into a definitive agreement to acquire all outstanding common shares of Goldcorp Inc. In the same year Newmont closed its acquisition of Goldcorp following receipt of all regulatory approvals and approval by Newmont's and Goldcorp's shareholders of the resolutions at the shareholder meetings on April 11 and April 4 2019 respectively for total cash and non-cash consideration of $9456 in a primarily stock transaction. The combined company is known as Newmont Corporation continuing to be traded on the New York Stock Exchange under the ticker NEM and listed on the Toronto Stock Exchange under the ticker NGT.

Company Background

Colonel William Boyce Thompson a flamboyant trader founded the Newmont Co. in 1916 to trade his various oil and mining stocks. The Newmont name was a combination of New York and Montana where Thompson grew up. The company was renamed Newmont Corporation in 1921 and Newmont Mining Corporation in 1925 when it went public.

In 2019 Newmont Mining became Newmont Goldcorp after its acquisition of Goldcorp Corporation.

HISTORY

The company was founded in 1921 and began publicly trading in 1925. BlackRock Inc. owns 13% of Newmont.

Colonel William Boyce Thompson a flamboyant trader founded the Newmont Co. in 1916 to trade his various oil and mining stocks. The Newmont name was a combination of New York and Montana where Thompson grew up. The company was renamed Newmont Corporation in 1921 and Newmont Mining Corporation in 1925 when it went public. Thompson died five years later. During its first 10 years Newmont focused on investing and trading stocks in promising mineral properties including US copper and gold mines.

Newmont's gold mines bolstered the company throughout the Depression. During the 1940s its focus shifted to copper and Africa. It bought Idarado Mining in 1943 and Newmont Oil in 1944 (sold 1988). The company grew during the 1950s by acquiring stakes in North American companies involved in offshore oil drilling nickel mining and uranium oxide production. It also

bought stakes in copper mines in South Africa and South America.

Newmont started producing gold from the Carlin Trend in Nevada in the mid-1960s. It bought a one-third stake in Foote Mineral (iron alloys and lithium) in 1967; by 1974 it controlled 83% of the company (sold 1987). In 1969 Newmont merged with Magma Copper one of the US's largest copper companies. A Newmont-led consortium bought Peabody Coal the US's largest coal producer from Kennecott Copper in 1977 (sold 1990).

After its 1980 discovery of one of the century's most important gold stakes Gold Quarry in the Carlin Trend Newmont spent a decade fending off takeover attempts. The company began selling off noncore operations to focus on gold. Magma Copper was spun off to stockholders in 1988.

A proposed merger with American Barrick Resources a major stockholder collapsed in 1991. Former Freeport-McMoRan VP Ronald Cambre became CEO in 1993 and that year the company began mining in Peru. A 1994 action by the French government one of Newmont's partners in Peru's Yanacocha Mine kicked off a protracted battle over the property's ownership. The claim was upheld in 1998 raising Newmont's stake to more than 50%. Reflecting its increasing interest in Indonesia in 1996 Newmont and Japan's Sumitomo formed a joint venture to exploit gold reserves on Sumbawa Island. In 1997 the company increased its gold reserves and territory by acquiring Santa Fe Pacific Gold for about $2.1 billion.

For years Newmont and Barrick Gold Corporation operated interlocked mining claims in Nevada's Carlin Trend which prevented optimal exploitation by either company. In 1999 both companies agreed to a mutually advantageous land swap in the region.

In 2000 an Indonesian court ordered the closure of the Minahasa mine over a local tax dispute; the company's joint venture agreed to pay a $500000 penalty to settle the matter. Newmont was fined $500000 after a mercury spill at its Yanacocha mine. That year Newmont settled the lingering ownership dispute over the Yanacocha.

Company president Wayne Murdy became CEO early in 2001 (he replaced Cambre as chairman in 2002). Newmont acquired Battle Mountain Gold in 2001 for nearly $600 million. Late that year Newmont moved to acquire Australia's top gold producer Normandy Mining (setting off a bidding war with AngloGold) as well as Canadian gold miner France-Nevada Mining Corp. AngloGold bowed out of the "battle for Normandy" in early 2002 but later completed a three-way deal in which it acquired Normandy and Franco-Nevada.

In 2003 Newmont reduced its stake in Kinross Gold from 14% to 5% and it considered selling off the Ghanaian interests it had gained in the Normandy merger. However in 2004 Newmont literally discovered a gold mine in Ghana — a major district with some 16 million equity ounces of gold.

Murdy retired in 2007; taking the helm was former CEO Richard O'Brien. In 2007 Newmont spun off its royalty assets acquired in 2002 as Franco-Nevada Corporation. Those assets then operated as Newmont Mining Corporation of Canada now a subsidiary of Newmont.

In 2008 Newmont bought Canadian gold producer Miramar Mining which controls the Hope Bay project for about $1.5 billion. It also acquired in 2009 a 33% stake in Boddington from AngloGold Ashanti for about $1 billion giving Newmont 100% of the Boddington project.

In 2011 Newmont acquired Fronteer Gold a Canadian company with properties in the US Turkey and Peru for $2.3 billion. The deal significantly expands Newmont's holdings in Nevada.

EXECUTIVES

Svp South America, Trent Tempel
Evp Human Resources, William N. (Bill) MacGowan, age 60, $450,000 total compensation
Vp And Cio, James (Jim) Zetwick
Evp And Cfo, Nancy K. Buese, age 51, $90,865 total compensation
Evp Strategic Development, Randy Engel, age 53, $627,196 total compensation
Evp And General Counsel, Stephen P. Gottesfeld, age 52, $512,074 total compensation
Svp Exploration, Grigore Simon
Evp Technical Services, Scott P. Lawson
President And Ceo, Gary J. Goldberg, age 61, $1,270,742 total compensation
Evp Sustainability And External Relations, Elaine Dorward-King, $468,297 total compensation
Svp Africa, Alwyn Pretorius, age 48
Evp And Coo, Thomas (Tom) Palmer, $615,134 total compensation
Vice President External Relations And Social Responsibilty, Nick Cotts
Senior Vice President Projects, Ramzi Fawaz
Vice President Supply Chain, Ramsey Musa
Vice President Total Rewards And Human Resources Systems, David Kristoff
Vice President Investments And Value Management, David McLaren
Senior Vice President African Operations, Jeffrey Huspeni
Vice President Marketing And Sales, Edmond Leblanc
Director Of Government Relations, Tarrah Darenzo
Vice President Investor Relations, Jessica Largent
Regional Vice President Human Resources, David Kern
Vice President Controller And Chief Accounting Officer, John Kitlen
Vice President Finance And Treasurer, Joshua Hallenbeck
Vice President Operations And Finance Planning, Philip Starkle
Senior Vice President Exploration, Marcelo Godoy
Vice President North American Government Relations, Mary Beth Donnelly
Vice President Talent Management, Jennifer Cmil
Vice President Internal Audit, Bryan Teets
Regional Vice President Human Resources, Sabrina Wilson
Vice President Of Supply Chain, Doug Nalbach
Secretary, Lisa Becker
Board Member, Joel Melgar
Board Member, Audrey Nelson
Auditors: PricewaterhouseCoopers LLP

LOCATIONS

HQ: Newmont Corp
6900 E Layton Ave   ?   ?, Denver, CO
80237
Phone: 303 863-7414   **Fax:** 303 837-5837
Web: www.newmont.com

2017 Sales

	$ mil.	% of total
UK	5,490	74
Switzerland	657	9
Korea	384	5
Philippines	310	5
Germany	168	3
Canada	96	1
US	91	1
Japan	87	1
Other	65	1
Total	**7,384**	**100**

PRODUCTS/OPERATIONS

2017 Sales

	$ mil.	% of total
Gold	7,033	96
Copper	315	4
Total	**7,348**	**100**

COMPETITORS

Agnico-Eagle	Goldcorp
AngloGold Ashanti	Kinross Gold
Barrick Gold	Newcrest Mining
Franco-Nevada	

HISTORICAL FINANCIALS

Company Type: Public

Income Statement   FYE: December 31

	REVENUE ($ mil.)	NET INCOME ($ mil.)	NET PROFIT MARGIN	EMPLOYEES
12/19	9,740	2,805	28.8%	31,600
12/18	7,253	341	4.7%	24,200
12/17	7,348	(98)	—	24,658
12/16	6,711	(627)	—	12,400
12/15	7,729	220	2.8%	15,600
Annual Growth	**6.0%**	**89.0%**		**19.3%**

2019 Year-End Financials

Debt ratio: 17.10%
Return on equity: 17.57%
Cash ($ mil.): 2,243
Current ratio: 2.63
Long-term debt ($ mil.): 6,734

No. of shares (mil.): 808
Dividends
  Yield: 3.3%
  Payout: 51.6%
Market value ($ mil.): 35,108

	STOCK PRICE ($) FY Close	P/E High/Low	PER SHARE ($) Earnings	Dividends	Book Value
12/19	43.45	11 8	3.81	1.44	26.51
12/18	34.65	66 46	0.64	0.56	19.70
12/17	37.52	— —	(0.18)	0.25	19.90
12/16	34.07	— —	(1.18)	0.13	20.21
12/15	17.99	64 36	0.43	0.10	21.43
Annual Growth	**24.7%**	**— —**	**72.5%**	**94.8%**	**5.5%**

News Corp (New)

News Corp is a global diversified media and information services company publishing well-known mastheads such as The Wall Street Journal and New York Post Australia's Herald Sun and The Sun and The Times in the UK. The company owns the Dow Jones and Factiva information services as well as book publisher Harper-Collins. In TV News Corp has a majority stake in Foxtel in Australia and owns the Australian News Channel. Other properties are the real estate

websites REA Group and Move. Australia and other countries generate over 40% of sales.

Operations

News Corp divides its operations into six segments — News Media around 30% of revenue; Subscription Video Services more than 20%; Book Publishing about 20% of revenue; Dow Jones nearly 20% of revenue; and Digital Real Estate Services more than 10%. Other segment accounts for the rest.

The News and Media segment includes: News Corp Australia News UK and the New York Post. This segment also includes Wireless Group operator of talkSPORT the leading sports radio network in the UK and Virgin Radio and Storyful a social media content agency that enables the company to source real-time video content through social media platforms.

The Subscription Video Services segment provides sports entertainment and news services to pay-TV subscribers via cable satellite and over the internet. This segment consists of the company's some 65% interest in NXE Australia Pty Limited which is referred to herein as Foxtel (the remaining around 35% interest in Foxtel is held by Telstra Corporation Limited) and Australian News Channel.

In Book Publishing the imprints under Harper Collins owns more than 120 brands including Harper William Morrow Avon Thomas Nelson Christian publishers Zondervan and Harlequin. Among its recent best-sellers have been Hillbilly Elegy and The Woman in the Window.

The company's Dow Jones segment is a global provider of news and business information which distributes its content and data through a variety of media channels including newspapers newswires websites applications or apps for mobile devices tablets and e-book readers newsletters magazines proprietary databases live journalism video and podcasts. This segment consists of the Dow Jones business whose products target individual consumers and enterprise customers and include The Wall Street Journal Factiva Dow Jones Risk & Compliance Dow Jones Newswires Barron's and MarketWatch.

The Digital Real Estate Services segment consists of News Corp's over 60% in REA Group a publicly-traded company based in Australia and its approximately 80% interest in Move. The remaining some 20% interest in Move is held by REA Group. REA lists properties for sale in Australia and Asia and offers financial services. Move operates the realtor.com website in the US.

The Other segment includes the company's general corporate overhead expenses corporate Strategy Group and costs related to the UK Newspaper Matters.

Overall the company generates about 45% of its revenue from circulation and subscription followed by over a quarter of revenue from advertising. Consumer generates about 20% while the remainder comes from real estate and other.

Geographic Reach

News Corp is based in New York City and has subsidiaries elsewhere in the US Australia Asia and the UK. In addition book publisher Harper-Collins has a warehouse in Scotland and Dow Jones runs an office in Hong Kong. Australia and other countries generate over 40% of sales. Followed by the US and Canada account for roughly 40% of sales and Europe (mostly the UK and Ireland) more than 15%.

Sales and Marketing

The company distributes its content and other products and services to consumers and customers across various platforms consisting of traditional print and television as well as an array of digital platforms including websites applications for mobile devices and tablets social media and e-book devices. The Dow Jones segment targets individual consumers and enterprise customers.

Advertising and promotional expenses recognized totaled $525 million $669 million and $663 million for the fiscal years 2020 2019 and 2018 respectively.

Financial Performance

For the year ended 2020 the company had a revenue of $9 billion a 9% decrease compared to the previous year of $10.1 billion. The company had lower sales in all of its segments.

News Corp had a net loss of $1.3 billion for the year ended 2020.

The company's cash for the year ended 2020 was $1.5 billion. Operating activities generated $780 million while investing activities used $427 million primarily for capital expenditures. Financing activities used another $472 million mainly for repayment of borrowings.

Strategy

News Corp believes that the increasing number of media choices and formats will allow it to continue to deliver its content and other products and services in a more engaging timely and personalized manner and provide opportunities for more effective monetization via strong consumer and customer relationships licensing arrangements and more compelling and engaging advertising solutions. The company is pursuing multiple strategies to exploit these opportunities including sharing technologies and practices across geographies and businesses and bundling selected offerings to provide greater value to consumers customers and advertising partners.

Mergers and Acquisitions

In early 2020 Israel-based Tremor International Ltd a global leader in video advertising technologies reached an agreement with News Corp a global diversified media and information services company to acquire Unruly News Corp's programmatic video marketplace for an undisclosed amount. The transaction is expected to be financially beneficial for both Tremor International and News Corp. News Corp is receiving 6.91% of Tremor International stock subject to an 18-month lock up period and to certain adjustments. "The sale of Unruly marks an important step in our strategy of simplification at News Corp while we expect it to yield ongoing financial benefits. We look forward to partnering with Tremor and are grateful to Unruly and its truly talented team who have helped our businesses in the U.K. US and Australia advance their digital advertising expertise." Robert Thomson Chief Executive of News Corp said.

EXECUTIVES

Senior Vice President And Deputy General Counsel, Genie Gavenchak
Ceo Harper Collins, Brian Murray, age 53
Chairman And Ceo News America Marketing, Martin (Marty) Garofalo

Ceo News Uk, Rebekah Brooks, age 52
Cto, Marc Frons, age 62
Ceo Unruly, Sarah Wood
Ceo, Robert Thomson, age 60, $2,038,462 total compensation
Cfo, Susan Panuccio
General Counsel And Chief Compliance Officer, David B. Pitofsky, $968,269 total compensation
Ceo The New York Post, Jesse Angelo
Ceo Dow Jones & Company, William (Will) Lewis
Ceo Storyful, Rahul Chopra
Ceo Move Inc., Ryan OÁ'Hara
Evp And Chief Communications Officer, James E. (Jim) Kennedy
Chairman News Corp Australasia, Michael Miller
Evp And Global Head Government Affairs, Antoinette (Toni) Bush
Vice President, Linden Slaugh
Senior Vice President Head Of Human Resources Coverage Products And Operations, Katie Perdomo
Vice President Telecommunications, Guy Wheaton
Vice President Strategic Sourcing Procurement, Tracey Williamson
Vice President Of Technology, Dan Gould
Vice President Marketing Services At News America Marketing, Marissa Bishop
Senior Vice President, Paula Wardynski, age 64
Senior Vice President Physical Production, Thomas Imperato
Vice President Information Technology, Cindy Schwan
Senior Vice President Strategy And Corporate Development European Television, Marc Heller
Vice President Manager Director, Trista Reiser
Senior Vice President Corporate Affairs, Jim Platt
Vice President Global Transfer Pricing, Kathrin Zoeller
Vice President, Robert Ennis
Executive Vice President Office Of The Chairman, Jeremy Phillips
Svp Platform And Product Delivery, Andy Nichol
Svp And Global Head Programmatic, Christopher Guenther
Vp Information Governance And Ediscovery Operations, Daniel Mandon
Vice President Corporate And Business Development, Amanda Greenfield
Vice President Of Fsi Operations, Michael Solano
Executive Vice President Trade, Marty Garofalo
Information Technology Of Vice President, Laura Richards
Vice President Marketing Services, Mary Mattimore
Senior Vice President Shopper Marketing, Nancy Perkins
Vice President In Sotre Operations, Bill Schulze
Vice President Human Resources, Theresa Enk
Vice President Group Sales Manager, Lauren Marglous
Vice President And Senior Account Director Merchandising Sales, Renee Young
Vice President Shopper Marketing, Amity Cherry
Vice President Group Sales Manager Shopper Marketing, Jenna Nudelman
Division Vice President, Kate Ellis
Executive Vice President Marketing, Jesse Aversano
Vice President, Stefanie Detwiler
Vice President Channel Expansion, Jon Rubin
Vp Of It, Laura Mcpadden
Vice President Information Security, Janice Clauer
Vice President, Jennifer Hayes
Co-chairman News Corp And 21st Century Fox, Lachlan K. Murdoch, age 47
Chairman, K. Rupert Murdoch, age 89
Assistant Treasurer, Stanley Pauzer
Board Member, Joel Klein
Board Member, James Murdoch
Board Member, Jose Aznar
Board Member, Thilo Semmelbauer
Auditors: Ernst & Young LLP

LOCATIONS

HQ: News Corp (New)
1211 Avenue of the Americas, New York, NY 10036
Phone: 212 416-3400
Web: www.newscorp.com

2018 Sales

	$ mil.	% of total
US & Canada	3,998	44
Europe	1,766	20
Australia and others	3,260	36
Total	**9,024**	**100**

PRODUCTS/OPERATIONS

2018 Sales

	$ mil.	% of total
News & information services	5,119	57
Book publishing	1,758	19
Digital real estate services	1,141	13
Subscription Video Services	1,004	11
Other	2	-
Total	**9,024**	**100**

2018 Sales

	$ mil.	% of total
Advertising	2,799	31
Circulation & subscription	3,021	33
Consumer	1,664	18
Real Estate	858	10
Other	682	8
Total	**9,024**	**100**

List of Items

List of Items
Newspapers
Dow Jones
Barron's (magazine)
Dow Jones Newswires
Factiva (online news and business research)
The Wall Street Journal
The Wall Street Journal Digital Network
MarketWatch
WSJ.com
New York Post
News International Limited (UK)
The Sun
The Sunday Times
The Times
The Advertiser (Adelaide)
The Australian (national daily)
The Courier-Mail (Brisbane)
The Daily Telegraph (Sydney)
Herald Sun (Melbourne)
Sunday Herald Sun (Melbourne)
Sunday Mail (Adelaide)
The Sunday Mail (Brisbane)
The Sunday Telegraph (Sydney)
The Sunday Times (Perth)
Book publishing
HarperCollins Publishers
Cable network programming
Foxtel (65% stake0
Digital real estate services
REA (61.6% stake)
Other
Amplify (digital education)

COMPETITORS

Bloomberg L.P.	LexisNexis
Crain Communications	New York Times
Financial Times	Pearson plc
Forbes	Simon & Schuster
Graham Holdings	Thomson Reuters
Hachette Book Group	Valassis
Hearst Corporation	

HISTORICAL FINANCIALS

Company Type: Public

Income Statement

FYE: June 30

	REVENUE ($ mil.)	NET INCOME ($ mil.)	NET PROFIT MARGIN	EMPLOYEES
06/20	9,008	(1,269)	—	23,500
06/19	10,074	155	1.5%	28,000
06/18	9,024	(1,514)	—	28,000
06/17	8,139	(738)	—	26,000
06/16	8,292	179	2.2%	24,000
Annual Growth	2.1%	—	—	(0.5%)

2020 Year-End Financials

Debt ratio: 8.83%
Return on equity: (-15.13%)
Cash ($ mil.): 1,517
Current ratio: 1.29
Long-term debt ($ mil.): 1,183

No. of shares (mil.): 588
Dividends
Yield: 1.6%
Payout: —
Market value ($ mil.): 6,980

	STOCK PRICE ($) FY Close	P/E High/Low		PER SHARE ($) Earnings	Dividends	Book Value
06/20	11.86	—	—	(2.16)	0.20	12.88
06/19	13.49	58	40	0.26	0.20	15.63
06/18	15.50	—	—	(2.60)	0.20	15.97
06/17	13.70	—	—	(1.27)	0.20	18.57
06/16	11.35	52	35	0.30	0.20	19.97
Annual Growth	1.1% (10.4%)	—	—	—	(0.0%)	

NextEra Energy Inc

NextEra Energy (NEE) owns and operates two businesses: Florida Power & Light (FPL) Florida's largest electric company and NextEra Energy Resources (NEER) one of the world's largest generators of renewable energy. FPL generates more than 27000 MW of electricity and delivers it to more than five million mostly residential customers in the state. NEER generates almost 22000 MW of energy via wind and solar sources. NEE operates one of the largest nuclear power fleets in the US with eight commercial nuclear power units in Florida New Hampshire Iowa and Wisconsin. All total the company has assets in more than 35 US states four Canadian provinces and one province in Spain.

HISTORY

During Florida's land boom of the early 1920s new homes and businesses were going up fast. But electric utilities were sparse and no transmission lines linked systems.

In 1925 American Power & Light Company (AP&L) which operated utilities throughout the Americas set up Florida Power & Light (FPL) to consolidate the state's electric assets. AP&L built transmission lines linking 58 communities from Miami to Stuart on the Atlantic Coast and from Arcadia to Punta Gorda on the Gulf.

FPL accumulated many holdings including a limestone quarry streetcars phone companies and water utilities and purchases in 1926 and 1927 nearly doubled its electric properties. In 1927 the company used an electric pump to demonstrate how swamplands could be drained and cultivated.

During the 1940s and 1950s FPL sold its non-electric properties. The Public Utility Holding Company Act of 1935 forced AP&L to spin off FPL in 1950. The company was listed on the NYSE that year.

FPL grew with Florida's booming population. In 1972 its first nuclear plant (Turkey Point south of Miami) went on line. In the 1980s it began to diversify with the purchase of real estate firm W. Flagler Investment in 1981 and FPL Group was created in 1984 as a holding company. It subsequently acquired Telesat Cablevision (1985) Colonial Penn Group (1985 insurance) and Turner Foods (1988 citrus groves). FPL Group formed ESI Energy in 1985 to develop nonutility energy projects.

Diversification efforts didn't pan out and in 1990 the firm wrote off about $750 million. That year sticking to electricity the utility snagged its first out-of-state power plant in Georgia acquiring a 76% stake (over five years). FPL Group sold its ailing Colonial Penn unit in 1991; two years later it sold its real estate holdings and some of its cable TV businesses.

The utility gave environmentalists cause to complain in 1995. First the St. Lucie nuclear plant was fined by the Nuclear Regulatory Commission for a series of problems. FPL also wanted to burn orimulsion a cheap tar-like fuel. (Barred by the governor the utility gave up the plan in 1998.)

In 1997 FPL Group created FPL Energy an independent power producer (IPP) out of its ESI Energy and international operations; FPL Energy teamed up with Belgium-based Tractebel the next year to buy two gas-fired plants in Boston and Newark New Jersey.

FPL Energy built wind-power facilities in Iowa in 1998 and in Wisconsin and Texas in 1999; it also bought 35 generating plants in Maine in 1999. That year FPL Group sold its Turner Foods citrus unit and the rest of its cable TV holdings. By 2000 FPL Energy owned interests in plants in 12 states.

EXECUTIVES

Chairman And Ceo, James L. (Jim) Robo, age 58, $1,300,000 total compensation

Evp And General Counsel, Charles E. Sieving, age 47, $689,000 total compensation

President And Ceo Nextera Energy Resources, Armando Pimentel, age 58, $838,100 total compensation

President And Ceo Florida Power & Light, Eric E. Silagy, $796,100 total compensation

Evp Human Resources And Corporate Sevices, Deborah H. Caplan

Evp Finance And Cfo, John Ketchum, $575,000 total compensation

Vp Hr Nextera Energy Resources, Kevin Suncine

Vice President And Managing Director Str, Mark Palanchian

Vice President Controller And Chief Accounting Officer Nextera Energy Inc., Kirk Crews

Evp Federal Regulatory Affairs Nextera Energy Inc., Joseph Kelliher

Vp And Chief Communications Officer Nextera Energy Inc., Robert Gould

Svp Power Delivery Florida Power And Light Company, Manuel Miranda

Vp Controller And Chief Accounting Officer Florida Power And Light Company, Kimberly Ousdahl

Treas, Mark Sorensen

Treasurer, Paul Cutler

Board Member, William Swanson

Auditors: DELOITTE & TOUCHE LLP

LOCATIONS

HQ: NextEra Energy Inc
700 Universe Boulevard, Juno Beach, FL 33408
Phone: 561 694-4000   **Fax:** 561 694-4620
Web: www.nexteraenergy.com

PRODUCTS/OPERATIONS

2016 sales

	$ mil.	% of total
Florida Power & Light	10,895	68
NextEra Energy Resources	4,893	30
Corporate & other	367	2
Total	**16**	**100**

Selected Subsidiaries and Divisions

Florida Power & Light Company
Energy Marketing and Trading
NextEra Energy Capital Holdings Inc.
NextEra Energy Resources LLC
NextEra Energy Partners
NextEra Energy Transmission

COMPETITORS

AES
Bangor Hydro-Electric
Berkshire Hathaway
 Energy
CMS Energy
Calpine
Chesapeake Utilities
Duke Energy
Entergy
Exelon

Florida Public
 Utilities
JEA
Oglethorpe Power
Progress Energy
Public Service
 Enterprise Group
Seminole Electric
Southern Company
TECO Energy

HISTORICAL FINANCIALS

Company Type: Public

Income Statement

FYE: December 31

	REVENUE ($ mil.)	NET INCOME ($ mil.)	NET PROFIT MARGIN	EMPLOYEES
12/19	19,204	3,769	19.6%	14,800
12/18	16,727	6,638	39.7%	14,200
12/17	17,195	5,378	31.3%	13,900
12/16	16,155	2,912	18.0%	14,200
12/15	17,486	2,762	15.8%	13,800
Annual Growth	2.4%	8.1%	—	1.8%

2019 Year-End Financials

Debt ratio: 36.18%
Return on equity: 10.59%
Cash ($ mil.): 600
Current ratio: 0.53
Long-term debt ($ mil.): 37,543

No. of shares (mil.): 1,956
Dividends
Yield: 2.0%
Payout: 64.4%
Market value ($ mil.): 473,665

	STOCK PRICE ($) FY Close	P/E High/Low		PER SHARE ($) Earnings	Dividends	Book Value
12/19	242.16	124	87	1.94	1.25	18.92
12/18	173.82	52	41	3.47	1.11	17.86
12/17	156.19	56	41	2.85	0.98	14.97
12/16	119.46	83	66	1.56	0.87	13.00
12/15	103.89	73	62	1.52	0.77	12.24
Annual Growth	23.6%	—	—	6.4%	12.9%	11.5%

NGL Energy Partners LP

All hail NGL for providing a secured energy trail. This Master Limited Partnership (MLP) provides transportation storage blending and marketing services for crude oil natural gas refined products and renewables in the US. With the Grand Mesa pipeline six storage terminals and some 5.2 MMbbls of storage capacity to its name NGL buys refined petroleum in the Gulf Coast Southeast and Midwest regions transports them through the Colonial and Plantation pipelines and ultimately sells them to industrial end users or independent retailers and distributors. In addition the company provides water solutions that treats processes and disposes wastewater and solids generated from oil and natural gas production. The company also has a fleet of 170 trucks and about 250 trailers as well as 10 tows and about 20 barges. In 2018 NGL sold its retail propane delivery business.

Operations

NGL Energy reports four major business segments.

Refined Products and Renewables (around 75% of sales) buys refined petroleum in the Gulf Coast Southeast and Midwest regions transports them via the Colonial and Plantation pipelines. In addition in certain storage location the company's Refined Products and Renewables segment may also purchase unfinished gasoline blending components for subsequent blending into finished gasoline to supply their marketing business as well as third parties.

The company's crude oil logistics business (approximately 15%) purchases crude oil from producers and transports it for resale at pipeline injection points storage terminals barge loading facilities rail facilities refineries and other trade hubs and provides storage terminaling trucking marine and pipeline transportation services through its own assets.

The Liquids segment (10% revenue) supplies natural gas liquids to retailers wholesalers refiners and petrochemical plants throughout the US and in Canada and provides NGL terminaling and storage services through more than 25 terminals throughout the US its salt dome storage facility in Utah and its leased storage and railcar transportation services.

Water Solutions segment revenues (some 1%) are derived from the gathering transportation treatment and disposal of wastewater generated from oil and natural gas production operations. The company owns more than 80 water treatment and disposal facilities and more than 135 injection wells.

Geographic ReachNGL Energy has significant operations in the Bakken Shale Basin of North Dakota the DJ Basin in Colorado the Mississippi Lime shale play in Oklahoma the Permian Basin in Texas and New Mexico the Eagle Ford shale play in Texas as well as the Anadarko Basin in Oklahoma and Texas and southern Louisiana. The company also provides Water Solutions near elevated lands with oil and natural gas production such as the Pinedale Anticline Basin in Wyoming the DJ Basin in Colorado the Permian and Eagle Ford Basins in Texas as well as the Delaware Basin in New Mexico. Its liquid natural gas terminals are in Jefferson City Missouri East St. Louis Illinois and in Ontario Canada. Headquartered in Tulsa Oklahoma the company has corporate offices in Denver and Houston.

Sales and Marketing

NGL Energy sells its refined and renewables products to commercial and industrial end users independent retailers distributors marketers government entities and other wholesalers of refined petroleum products. Its liquids business serves national regional and independent retail industrial wholesale petrochemical refiner and natural gas liquids production customers.

Financial Performance

Growth at NGL has skyrocketed over the last decade. The company's revenue increased by $7.1 billion from $16.9 billion to $24 billion.

Sales at NGL has burgeoned from $16.9 billion in 2018 to $24 billion in 2019. Most of it came from NGL's largest segment Refined Products & renewables ($5.9 billion increase) adding pipeline capacity rights purchased during 2019. Crude oil prices and volumes sold went up adding over $875 million more to the coffers.

Net income increased from loss $69.6 million in profits in 2018 to $339.4 million in 2019 mostly due to the increase of income from discontinued operations with $403.1 million and decrease in loss from continuing operations for about $63.7 million.

The company has $22.1 million in cash holdings at the end of 2019. Operations provided $138 million and a further $270.6 million came from investments (mostly from sale of businesses) offset by $394.3 million used in financing activities mostly going towards long-term debt reduction.

Strategy

NGL Energy has an extensive industry and MLP experience with acquiring integrating operating and growing successful businesses. Additionally the company wants to focus on its core businesses?crude logistics and water solutions. An equal emphasis is being given on increasing fee-based business and long-term contracts with high credit quality customers by transitioning a repeatable cash flow model.

NGL Energy is well poised for profits going forward. Its Crude Oil Logistics segment posted exceptional numbers due to increased volumes on Grand Mesa as the pipeline continues to benefit from increased production out of the DJ Basin. Water Solutions business has also continued to benefit from high crude oil prices increased rig counts and increased crude oil production due to price recovery.

Furthermore In the beginning of 2018 NGL and Magnum Liquids formed a joint venture to focus on the storage of natural gas liquids and refined products by combining NGL's Sawtooth Storage Facility with Magnum's refined products rights and adjacent leasehold. NGL will sell an interest in Sawtooth to Magnum for $45 million in cash due at closing.

Mergers and Acquisitions

NGL Energy is focused on expanding its Water Solution business in the Delaware Basin. This included the purchase of 9.6 million barrels of annual fresh water rights from the 36000-acre Beckham Ranch in Lea County New Mexico. The company furthered the strategy late in 2019 when it purchased Hillstone Environmental Partners from Golden Gate capital for about $600 million. Hillstone provides water pipeline services to producers in Eddy and Lea Counties in New Mexico and northern Loving County Texas in the Delaware Basin.

NGL Energy also acquired the McCloy Ranch located in Eddy and Lea Counties which comes with some 87000 acres of land and 2 million barrels of annual water rights. The company now owns 30 million barrels of available freshwater volumes in the Delaware Basin

Company Background

Formed in 2010 by several investors NGL Energy Partners acquired and combined the assets and operations of NGL Supply a wholesale propane and terminalling business founded in 1967 and Hicksgas a retail propane business founded in 1940.

EXECUTIVES

Vice President Wholesale, Stan Bugh
Ceo, H. Michael Krimbill, age 66, $292,500 total compensation
Evp And Cfo, Robert W. (Trey) Karlovich, age 43
President Retail Division, Shawn W. Coady, age 58, $311,250 total compensation
President Eastern Retail Operations, Vincent J. Osterman, age 63, $250,000 total compensation
President Ngl And President And Ceo High Sierra Energy, James J. (Jim) Burke, age 64, $381,750 total compensation
Evp Ngl Crude Logistics, Don Robinson
Evp Ngl Liquids, Jack Eberhardt
Cio, Jennifer Kingham
Executive Vice President Midstream Division, David Eastin
Senior Vice President Legal, Bill Laughlin
Senior Vice President Of Accounting, Patrice Armbruster
Vice President Rocky Mountain Region, Britt Stephenson
Executive Vice President, Gregory Pound
Executive Vice President Ngl Refined Products, Donald Jensen
Svp Accounting And Corporate Controller, Sharra Straight
Vice President, Mark Mcginty
Evp Ngl Water Solutions, Doug White
Vice President Of Tax, Joel Gustafson
Svp Business Development, Greg Blais
Executive Vice President Operations, Greg Pound
Senior Vice President Asset Management, Todd Tanory
Vice President Eagle Ford, Tim Jurco
Vice President Ngl Water Solutions Formerly High Sierra, Doran Oancia
Vice President Business Development Crude Assets, Derek Graham
Vice President Business Development, Carl Peterson
Vice President Finance And Treasurer, Linda Bridges
Vice President Credit And Market Risk Management, Thomas Matthews
Vice President Trucking, Willie Seale
Senior Vice President Of Water, James Winter
Evp Ngl Refined Products, Don Jensen
Svp Ngl Bio Diesel, Grant Vangilder
Executive Vice President, Greg Piper
Vice President, Mark Mcgrath
Vice President Environmental Health And Safety, Garrett Clemons
Vice President West Texas Region, Wes Pearson
Svp Mergers And Acquisitions, Christian Dobrauc
Senior Vice President, Jeff Pinter
Senior Vice President Water Holdings, Joshua Patterson

Vice President Midcontinent Region, Jeff Matthews
Vice President Supply Chain And Logistics, Bryon Beckwith
Auditors: Grant Thornton LLP

LOCATIONS

HQ: NGL Energy Partners LP
 6120 South Yale Avenue, Suite 805, Tulsa, OK 74136
Phone: 918 481-1119
Web: www.nglenergypartners.com

PRODUCTS/OPERATIONS

2017 Sales

	$ mil.	% of total
Refined products and Renewables	12,200	71
Crude oil logistics	2,260	13
Liquids	2,070	12
Retail propane	521	3
Water solutions	229	1
Other	1	-
Total	**17,282**	**100**

COMPETITORS

AmeriGas Partners	Exxon Mobil
Blueknight Energy Partners	Ferrellgas Partners
Crestwood Midstream Partners LP	Holly Energy Partners
Duke Energy	Huntsman International
Energy Transfer	Martin Midstream Partners
Enterprise Products	Occidental Petroleum
Equistar Chemicals	Williams Companies

HISTORICAL FINANCIALS

Company Type: Public

Income Statement
FYE: March 31

	REVENUE ($ mil.)	NET INCOME ($ mil.)	NET PROFIT MARGIN	EMPLOYEES
03/20	7,584	(397)	—	1,400
03/19	24,016	360	1.5%	1,300
03/18	17,282	(70)	—	2,400
03/17	13,022	137	1.1%	2,700
03/16	11,742	(198)	—	3,200
Annual Growth	**(10.4%)**	**—**	**—**	**(18.7%)**

2020 Year-End Financials

Debt ratio: 48.46%
Return on equity: (-115.24%)
Cash ($ mil.): 22
Current ratio: 0.92
Long-term debt ($ mil.): 3,144
No. of shares (mil.): 128
Dividends
 Yield: 60.0%
 Payout: —
Market value ($ mil.): 335

	STOCK PRICE ($) FY Close	P/E High/Low	PER SHARE ($) Earnings	Dividends	Book Value
03/20	2.60	— —	(4.59)	1.56	17.07
03/19	14.03	7 4	2.01	1.56	19.01
03/18	11.00	— —	(1.08)	1.56	17.15
03/17	22.60	26 7	0.95	1.56	18.32
03/16	7.52	— —	(2.35)	2.54	15.88
Annual Growth	**(23.3%)**	**— —**	**—**	**(11.5%)**	**1.8%**

Nicolet Bankshares Inc

EXECUTIVES

Pres-ceo, Robert Atwell
Vice President Commercial Banking, Scott Jandrin
Senior Vice President Private Banking Director, Kristy Maney

Vice President Commercial Banking, Trent Willihnganz
Board Member, Michael Gilson
Auditors: Wipfli LLP

LOCATIONS

HQ: Nicolet Bankshares Inc
 111 North Washington Street, Green Bay, WI 54301
Phone: 920 430-1400
Web: www.nicoletbank.com

HISTORICAL FINANCIALS

Company Type: Public

Income Statement
FYE: December 31

	ASSETS ($ mil.)	NET INCOME ($ mil.)	INCOME AS % OF ASSETS	EMPLOYEES
12/19	3,577	54	1.5%	575
12/18	3,096	41	1.3%	550
12/17	2,932	33	1.1%	535
12/16	2,300	18	0.8%	480
12/15	1,214	11	0.9%	280
Annual Growth	**31.0%**	**47.9%**	**—**	**19.7%**

2019 Year-End Financials

Debt ratio: 1.19%
Return on equity: 12.10%
Cash ($ mil.): 182
Current ratio: —
Long-term debt ($ mil.): —
No. of shares (mil.): 10
Dividends
 Yield: —
 Payout: —
Market value ($ mil.): 782

	STOCK PRICE ($) FY Close	P/E High/Low	PER SHARE ($) Earnings	Dividends	Book Value
12/19	73.85	13 9	5.52	0.00	48.76
12/18	48.80	14 11	4.12	0.00	40.72
12/17	54.74	17 13	3.33	0.00	37.09
12/16	47.69	19 12	2.37	0.00	32.26
12/15	31.79	12 9	2.57	0.00	26.36
Annual Growth	**23.5%**	**— —**	**21.1%**	**—**	**16.6%**

NIKE Inc

NIKE named for the Greek goddess of victory is a shoe and apparel company. It designs develops and sells a variety of products to help in playing basketball and soccer (football) as well as in running men's and women's training and other action sports. Under its namesake brand NIKE also markets sports-inspired products for children and various competitive and recreational activities; it also sells sportswear under the Converse. The company which generates some 60% of sales outside the US sells through more than 1090-owned retail stores worldwide and an e-commerce site and to thousands of retail accounts independent distributors licensees and sales representatives. Customer in North America accounts for about 40% of total revenue.

Operations

NIKE-branded products which account for 95% of total revenue are focused on six key categories: Running NIKE Basketball the Jordan Brand Football (Soccer) Training and Sportswear (sports-inspired lifestyle products).

NIKE footwear is the company's leading product offering bringing in more than 60% of sales and led by the iconic Jordan Brand and other collections. NIKE Apparel accounts for about 30% of sales and NIKE Equipment (bags socks sport balls eyewear timepieces digital devices bats protective equipment and other equipment designed for sports activities) adds about 5%.

Converse and other brands contribute the remainder of revenue.

Geographic Reach

NIKE is based near Beaverton Oregon; it has a 400-acre site with more than 40 buildings. It also has regional headquarters in Hilversum the Netherlands (for the EMEA region) and Shanghai China (for the Greater China region) and branch offices and subsidiaries in more than 50 other countries.

In the US NIKE owns half a dozen significant distribution centers four in Memphis Tennessee one in Dayton Tennessee and one in Indianapolis Indiana. The most significant distribution facilities outside the US are located in Laakdal Belgium; Taicang China; Tomisato Japan; and Incheon Korea.

The company generates nearly 40% of sales in North America (mostly the US) with another quarter in Europe the Middle East and Africa. Greater China account for about 20% of revenue and some 15% for the rest of the Asia-Pacific region and Latin America.

Sales and Marketing

NIKE generates about two-thirds of sales from wholesale customers such as retail accounts (footwear and sporting goods stores; athletic specialty stores; department stores; skate tennis and golf shops) independent distributors licensees and sales representatives. It also sells directly to consumers through a strong global network of company-owned stores and its growing ecommerce site.

NIKE markets its footwear and other products globally through diverse advertising and promotional programs and campaigns including print social media online advertising and endorsement contracts with celebrity athletes. Total advertising and promotion expenseswere $3.6 billion $3.8 billion and $3.6 billion for fiscal years 2020 2019 and 2018 respectively.

Financial Performance

NIKE's revenue has been consistently growing for a few years with the exception of 2020. Despite the minor decline on that year NIKE's revenue has had an overall growth of 16% over the last five years. Its net income has climbed for three years dropped in 2019 but bounced back in 2020.

In fiscal 2020 (ended May) the company reported revenue of $37.4 billion down 4% from the prior year. It saw decline in all segments.

Net income adjusted for non-cash items generated $3.7 billion of operating cash inflow for fiscal 2020 compared to $5.3 billion for fiscal 2019. The decrease primarily reflects lower Net Income resulting from the unfavorable impacts of COVID-19.

Cash at the end of fiscal 2020 was $8.3 billion an increase of $3.9 billion from the prior year. Cash from operations contributed $2.5 billion to the coffers while investing activities used $1 billion mainly for capital expenditures. Financing activities provided another $2.5 billion from proceeds of borrowings.

Strategy

NIKE's strategy is to achieve long-term revenue growth by creating innovative "must-have" products building deep personal consumer connections with its brands and delivering compelling consumer experiences through digital platforms and at retail.

Since fiscal 2018 through the Consumer Direct Offense and NIKE's Triple Double strategy the company has focused on doubling the impact of innovation increasing its speed and agility to market and growing its direct connections with consumers. In June 2020 the company announced a new digitally empowered phase of the Consumer Direct Offense strategy: Consumer Direct Acceleration.

On July 22 2020 management announced a series of leadership and operating model changes to streamline and speed up strategic execution. These changes are expected to lead to a net loss of jobs resulting in pre-tax one-time employee termination costs of approximately $200 million to $250 million which is expected to be incurred primarily during the first half of fiscal 2021 in the form of cash expenditures.

This next phase of NIKE's Consumer Direct Offense is expected to drive sustainable growth and profitability as the company accelerates NIKE to a digital-first company. The company is committed to the execution of this strategy despite the short-term adverse impacts to business from a novel strain of coronavirus (COVID-19). As such its long-term financial goals on average per year remain the same.

Company Background

Phil Knight a good miler and Bill Bowerman a track coach who tinkered with shoe designs met at the University of Oregon in 1957. The two men formed Blue Ribbon Sports in 1962 in an effort to make quality American running shoes. The next year they began selling Tiger shoes manufactured by Japanese shoe manufacturer Onitsuka Tiger. They sold the running shoes out of cars at track meets.

The company rebranded as NIKE in 1972 named for the Greek goddess of victory. The NIKE "Swoosh" logo was designed by a graduate student named Carolyn Davidson who was paid $35. The same year NIKE broke with Onitsuka in a dispute over distribution rights.

It went public in 1980.

EXECUTIVES

Vice President Brand Management Subsidia, Mike Wilskey

Vice President Of Sales And Marketing, Shelley Dewey

Chairman President And Ceo, Mark G. Parker, $1,550,000 total compensation

Coo, Eric D. Sprunk, $990,000 total compensation

President Nike Brand, Trevor A. Edwards, $990,000 total compensation

President Of Geographies And Integrated Marketplace, Elliott J. Hill

President Product And Merchandising, Michael Spillane

Evp Chief Administrative Officer And General Counsel, Hilary K. Krane

President And Ceo Converse, Davide Grasso

Evp Global Sports Marketing, John F. Slusher

Evp Global Human Resources, David J. Ayre

President Dtc, Heidi OA'Neill

Evp And Cfo, Andrew (Andy) Campion, $822,306 total compensation

Global Cio, Jim Scholefield

Vice President Human Resources Business Partner Geographies, Mike Tarbell

Vice President Of Design, Katy Tisch

Vice President North America Supply Chain Operations, Trish Young

Vice President Sports Marketing North America, Jonathan Banks

Vp And General Manager Athletic Specialty, Jim Reynolds

Vice President Creative Director Apparel, Thomas Walker

Vice President And General Manager Global Football, Bert Hoyt

Vp And Gm Global Categories, Amy Montagne

Vice President Global Accounting, Dan Mckenzie

Senior Vice President Of Commercial Banking, Evelyn Gomez

Vice President General Manager Global Womens Training, Heidi ONeill

Vice President Information Technology Infrastructure, Mike Malin

Vice President Creative Director Nike Sportswear, Kurt Parker

Vp Of Innovation Marketing, Paolo Tubito

Vp Manufacturing, Greg Bui

Vp Women's Training Apparel, Helen Boucher

Executive Vice President Of Meth Production, Jim Ford

Vice President In House Manufacturing, Lalit Monteiro

National Account Manager, David Howard

Vice President And Corporate Secretary, Ann Miller

Vice President Young Athletes Sales, Mark Trelease

Global Vp And Gm Greater China, Angela Dong

Vice President Global Apparel And Equipment Materials Nike, Susi Proudman

Vice President Global Digital Commerce, Kristine Rebber

Vice President Footwear Young Athletes, Elisabetta Quaglia

National Account Manager, Joni Kristo

Vice President Glbl Sales Nike Women's, Jason Kirrer

Vice President Creative Director Athletic Training, Janett Nichol

Vice President Global Entertainment Marketing, Pamela McConnell

Vp Of Global Growth Initiatives, Clare Hamill

Vice President Global Running Footwear, Tim Slingsby

Executive Assistant Senior Vice President Government And Public Affairs, Keyanus Jacobo

Global Vice President Sports Apparel, Aaron Heiser

Vice President And Chief Administrative Officer, Ronald McCray

Vice President And General Manager Nike Japan, Christophe Merkel

Vice President Treasure, Bob Woodruff

Vice President Of Marketing, James Johnson

Vice President Human Resources Business Partner E, Karen Weisz

Vice President, Ailsa Gilroy

Vice President Marketing, Todd Jacobs

Vice President Director Manager, Nick Athanasakos

Vice President Director Of Tec, Scott Marien

Vice President Footwear Sportswear Nike Inc., Andrea Correani

Vice President And General Manager Nike Sportswear, Dirk-jan Van Hameren

Vice President Global Operations And Technology, Hans Vanalebeek

Management Vice President, Hubertus Hoyt

Vice President Nike Design, John Hoke

Vice President Emerging Marketing Legal, Colin Graham

Vp And Corporate Controller, Chris Abston

Department Head, ERIC Irby

Vp And General Manager Global Young Athletes, Carl Grebert

Vice President Human Resources Business Partner Emerging Markets, Julie Fuller

Vice President Broad Based Total Rewards, Kimberly Lupo

Vice President Integrated Marketplace Development, Susan Carey

Vice President Treasury And Investor Relations, Nitesh Sharan

Vice President And General Manager Global Dtc Retail Coe, Ravi Thanawala

Vice President Global Intellectual Property Transactions And Licensing, Paul Saraceni

Vice President Diversity And Inclusion, Antoine Andrews

Vice President And Chief Tax Officer, Patti Johnson

Vp Manufacturing, Rich Sayre

Senior Vice President Enterprise Information Technology, Radhika Sharma

Vice President Global Business Planning, Lee Arden

Vice President North America Fulfillment, Sean Halligan

Vice President Global Digital Operations And Geo Expansion, Shannon Glass

Vice President And General Manager Greater China South Territory, Simon Men

Vice President Merchant Global Training, Cedric Fletcher

Vice President Sales Account, Eddie Hu

Vice President Merchandising Global Football, Mary Seabright

Vice President Global Basketball Apparel, Matt Park

Vice President Jordan Cfl, Dave Schechter

Vice President And General Manager Running Emerging Markets, Fabian Tinnirello

Vice President Digital Platforms And Partnerships, Eric Wood

Vice President, Lisa Carter

Senior Business Intelligence Developer, Buvaneswaran Matheswaran

Vice President Logistics, Nicole Montanez

Vice President Senior Human Resources Business Partner, Bernard Bedon

Board Member, Nico Harrison

Board Member, Tim Cook

Board Member, Avery Cook

Auditors: PricewaterhouseCoopers LLP

LOCATIONS

HQ: NIKE Inc
One Bowerman Drive, Beaverton, OR 97005-6453
Phone: 503 671-6453
Web: www.nike.com

2019 Sales

	% of total
NIKE North America	41
NIKE EMEA	25
NIKE Greater China	16
NIKE Asia-Pacific and Latin America	13
Converse	5
Total	**100**

PRODUCTS/OPERATIONS

2019 Sales

	% of total
NIKE Footwear	62
NIKE Apparel	30
NIKE Equipment	4
Converse	4
Total	**100**

Selected Products

Athletic Shoes
  Aquatic
  Auto racing
  Baseball
  Basketball
  Bicycling

Cheerleading
Cross-training
Fitness
Football
Golf
Running
Soccer
Tennis
Volleyball
Wrestling
Athletic Wear and Equipment
  Accessories
  Athletic bags
  Bats
  Caps
  Digital devices
  Eyewear
  Fitness wear
  Gloves
  Golf clubs
  Headwear
  Jackets
  Pants
  Protective equipment
  Running clothes
  Shirts
  Shorts
  Skirts
  Snowboards and snowboard apparel
  Socks
  Sport balls
  Timepieces
  Uniforms

COMPETITORS

ASICS	New Balance
Amer Sports	PUMA SE
Columbia Sportswear	Skechers U.S.A.
Deckers Outdoor	Under Armour
Fila Korea	VF Corporation
K-Swiss	Wolverine World Wide
Li Ning	adidas
Lululemon	

HISTORICAL FINANCIALS

Company Type: Public

Income Statement				FYE: May 31
	REVENUE ($ mil.)	NET INCOME ($ mil.)	NET PROFIT MARGIN	EMPLOYEES
05/20	37,403	2,539	6.8%	75,400
05/19	39,117	4,029	10.3%	76,700
05/18	36,397	1,933	5.3%	73,100
05/17	34,350	4,240	12.3%	74,400
05/16	32,376	3,760	11.6%	70,700
Annual Growth	3.7%	(9.3%)	—	1.6%

2020 Year-End Financials

Debt ratio: 30.81%
Return on equity: 29.62%
Cash ($ mil.): 8,348
Current ratio: 2.48
Long-term debt ($ mil.): 9,406

No. of shares (mil.): 1,558
Dividends
  Yield: 0.0%
  Payout: 59.6%
Market value ($ mil.): 153,588

	STOCK PRICE ($) FY Close	P/E High/Low	PER SHARE ($) Earnings	Dividends	Book Value
05/20	98.58	64 39	1.60	0.96	5.17
05/19	77.14	35 26	2.49	0.86	5.77
05/18	71.80	61 43	1.17	0.76	6.13
05/17	52.99	24 19	2.51	0.68	7.55
05/16	55.22	61 25	2.16	0.76	7.29
Annual Growth	15.6%	— —	(7.2%)	5.9%	(8.2%)

Nordstrom, Inc.

Service with a smile is a part of Nordstrom's corporate culture. One of the nation's largest upscale apparel and shoe retailers Nordstrom sells clothes shoes and accessories through about 110 Nordstrom full-line stores and about 240 off-price outlet stores (Nordstrom Rack) in about 40 states and online. It also operates about 5 full-line and about 5 Rack stores in Canada less than 5 Jeffrey luxury boutiques about 5 Trunk Club personal clothing service clubhouses roughly 5 Nordstrom Local hubs a couple of "Last Chance" clearance stores and online private sale site HauteLook. With its easy-return policy and touches such as thank-you notes from employees Nordstrom has earned a reputation for top-notch customer service. Nordstrom family members who own about 30% of the retailer's stock closely supervise the chain.

Operations

Nordstrom's operates in one business segment the Retail . The Retail segment accounts for all (100%) of Nordstrom's revenue and includes sales from its full-line and Nordstrom Rack stores as well as from its Nordstrom.com nordstrom-rack.com Hautelook.com Trunk Club.com Jeffrey Nordstrom Local Last Chance and Canadian operations.

Nordstrom's Full Price operations (Nordstrom US full-line stores Nordstrom.com Canadian operations Trunk Club Jeffrey and Nordstrom Local) generate over 65% of the retail sales while Off-Price operations (Nordstrom US Rack stores Nordstromrack.com/HauteLook and Last Chance clearance stores) accounts for the remaining sales.

By product the company generates nearly 30% of its net sales from women's apparel while shoe sales make up about 25%. The rest of its net sales came from men's apparel (more than 15%) women's accessories (more than 10%) cosmetics (some 10%) and kid's apparel and other items (some 5% each).

Geographic Reach

Based in Seattle Washington Nordstrom has about380 full-line and Nordstrom Rack stores in approximately 40 US states as well as about a dozen Nordstrom full-line stores and Rack stores in Canada. California is the retailer's largest market with nearly 90 full-line and Rack stores. Other major markets for the chain include Florida Illinois and Texas. The company also operates six distribution centers in California Florida Iowa Maryland and Oregon; three fulfillment centers in California Iowa and Pennsylvania; and four office facilities in California Colorado Illinois and New York.

Sales and Marketing

Nordstrom processes and ships orders directly to customers through fulfillment centers while its distribution centers process and ship merchandise to its stores and other facilities.

The company promotes its products through online marketing magazines store events and other media. Nordstrom's advertising expense totaled $299 million $246 million and $261 million for the years 2019 2018 and 2017 respectively.

Financial Performance

In 2019 total Company net sales decreased 2.2% compared with 2018. While net sales decreased the company successfully executed plans to drive their top-line in the second half of the year due to the company's loyalty digital marketing and merchandising programs. Digital sales increased 7% compared with 2018 and order pickup as a percentage of digital sales increased compared with 2018.

Nordstrom's net sales decrease of 2% started with the first half of the year below expectations while they improved sales trends in the second half across our Full-Price and Off-Price businesses.

The company's cash held at the end of 2019 decreased by $104 million to $853 million compared to $957 million in the prior year. Cash provided by operations was $1.2 billion while cash used for investing and financing activities were $909 million and $431 million respectively.

Strategy

As its Full-Price business evolves the company's market strategy leverages its inventory to serve customers on its terms through investments in digital capabilities and in people product and place. Nordstrom's goal is to gain market share while driving customer engagement and inventory efficiencies. There are two elements to this strategy: first the company provides customers a greater selection of merchandise available for next-day pickup or delivery without increasing inventory levels. Second it increases engagement with customers by offering express services such as order pickup returns and alterations at additional convenient locations. The company accelerated its strategy to five of its top markets ? New York Los Angeles Chicago Dallas and San Francisco ? in 2019 and will expand Nordstrom's strategy into five additional markets in 2020 including Philadelphia Washington D.C. Boston Seattle and Toronto. In addition the company is integrating Trunk Club into Nordstrom full-line stores and Nordstrom.com to create a cohesive styling offering across Nordstrom and to gain efficiencies.

HISTORY

In 1901 John Nordstrom a lumberjack and successful gold miner used his Alaska Gold Rush money to open Wallin & Nordstrom shoe store in Seattle with shoemaker Carl Wallin. Nordstrom retired in 1928 and sold his half of the business which included a second store to his sons Everett and Elmer. Wallin sold his share to the brothers after retiring the following year. A third Nordstrom son Lloyd joined in 1933. The shoe chain thrived and incorporated as Nordstrom's in 1946.

By 1963 Nordstrom's was the largest independent shoe chain in the country. The company diversified by acquiring Best Apparel's stores in Seattle and Portland Oregon. Three years later Nordstrom's bought Portland's Nicholas Ungar a fashion retailer and merged it with one of its shoe stores in Portland under the name Nordstrom Best.

Renaming itself Nordstrom Best in 1966 the company went public in 1971 and changed its name again in 1973 to Nordstrom. The retailer grew steadily throughout the 1970s opening new stores boosting sales in existing stores and diversifying. In 1976 Nordstrom started Place Two featuring apparel and shoes in smaller stores than its traditional department layouts. It moved into Southern California (Orange County) two years later. Buoyed by almost $300 million in new sales Nordstrom executives planned an aggressive expansion.

Nordstrom opened its first store on the East Coast in 1988 in Virginia. The chain continued to expand opening stores in Northern California and in the affluent Washington DC suburbs.

The 1989 San Francisco earthquake along with a national downturn hurt retail sales significantly. Nordstrom's much-touted focus on customer service had a downside: The company was investigated in 1990 for not paying employees for customer services they performed including delivery of merchandise on their own time. (Three years later Nordstrom set aside $15 million to pay back wages to employees who had performed off-the-clock services.)

The company continued to expand in the East and Midwest opening its first store in the New York City area in 1991. In 1993 the retailer opened a men's boutique in New York (Fa Şonnable). Looking for new ways to attract customers Nordstrom introduced a mail-order catalog the next year.

Following the family's business tradition six members of Nordstrom's fourth generation began running the company in 1995. Third-generation members James Nordstrom John Nordstrom Bruce Nordstrom and Jack McMillan retired as co-chairmen and were replaced by non-family members Ray Johnson and John Whitacre. (Johnson retired in 1996.)

Nordstrom created Nordstrom.com a partnership with Benchmark Capital and Madrona Investment Group in 1999 to consolidate its catalog and Internet operations.

In early 2000 amid slumping sales the company dissolved the co-presidency. Less than a year later however the Nordstroms were back in charge. Chairman and CEO Whitacre resigned and Blake Nordstrom took over running the company as president. His father Bruce came out of retirement to take the chairman's role. Later the company bought the French design company Fa Şonnable which supplies the products for its Fa Şonnable boutiques.

In May 2002 the company bought out Benchmark's and Madrona's minority stake in Nordstrom.com.

Nordstrom bought a majority interest in August 2005 in luxury specialty stores Jeffrey New York and Jeffrey Atlanta. Terms of the agreement were not disclosed. The Jeffrey stores had about $35 million in sales in 2004. Also in 2005 the company opened stores in Atlanta; Dallas; Irvine California; and San Antonio.

In late 2007 Nordstrom sold its four US Fa Şonnable boutiques and 37 European locations to Lebanon-based M1 Group for about $210 million. Overall in 2007 Nordstrom opened three full-line department stores and a single Rack store.

Nordstrom opened its first full-line department store in Hawaii in early 2008. That October amid economic gloom the retailer opened a store in Pittsburgh. Overall the retailer opened eight new Nordstrom stores and half a dozen Rack outlets

in 2008. In 2009 it added three full-line Nordstrom locations and 13 Rack outlets.

Nordstrom acquired e-tailer HauteLook for $180 million in stock in March 2011. Based in Los Angeles HauteLook was a leader in online private sales.

EXECUTIVES

Co-president, Blake W. Nordstrom, age 59, $751,152 total compensation

Co-president, Peter E. (Pete) Nordstrom, age 58, $751,152 total compensation

Co-president, Erik B. Nordstrom, age 58, $751,152 total compensation

Evp General Counsel And Secretary, Robert B. Sari, age 64

Evp And Chief Innovation Officer, Geevy S.K. Thomas, age 55

Evp And Cio, Daniel F. (Dan) Little, age 59, $552,806 total compensation

Evp And President Stores, James F. (Jamie) Nordstrom, age 47

Evp And General Merchandise Manager Designer Women's Apparel, Tricia D. Smith, age 49

Evp And Chief Marketing Officer, Scott A. Meden, age 57

Evp Finance And Treasurer, James A. Howell, age 55

Evp And General Merchandise Manager Menâ's And Kids Wear, Paige L. Thomas, age 49

Evp And President Nordstrom.com, Kenneth J. (Ken) Worzel, age 55, $657,417 total compensation

Evp Nordstrom Merchandising Group, Teri Bariquit, age 54

Evp And General Merchandise Manager Accessories At Home And Beauty, Gemma Lionello, age 55

Evp; Chairman And Ceo Nordstrom Fsb; President Nordstrom Credit, Steven C. Mattics, age 51

Evp Supply Chain, Michael Sato

Cfo, Anne L. Bramman, age 52

Evp Online Merchandising, Kirk M. Beardsley

Evp And President Nordstromrack.com Hautelook And Trunk Club, Terence Boyle

Evp Human Resources, Christine F. Deputy, age 54, $319,206 total compensation

Evp Strategy, Lisa C. Luther

Evp And President Nordstrom Product Group, Jennifer Jackson Brown

Evp And General Merchandise Manager Shoe Division, Kristin Frossmo

Evp And President Nordstrom Rack, Karen S. McKibbin, age 60

Evp And General Merchandise Manager Nordstrom Rack, Brian Roberts

Senior Vice President Customer Experience, Shea Jensen

Vice President Marketing, KRISTEN LAMEY

Vice President Divisional Merchandise Manager, Lori Marten

Vice President Merchandising Strategy And Operations, Corinne Copello

Vice President Finance, Mike Bengs

Senior Vice President Chief Accounting Officer, Kelley Hall

Senior Vice President Human Resources, Lisa V Price

Vice President Customer Experience, Shea D Jensen

Vice President Human Resources, Farrell Redwine

Vice President Technology, Joanne Kennedy

Vice President Technology, John Xiao

Vice President Merchandise Planning, Angie L Caldwell

Vice President Operations Finance, Chris Goelkel

Vice President Corporate Affairs And Public Relations, Gigi Ganatra

Vice President Assistant General Counsel And Aco Nfsb, Janine M Weaver

Vice President Nfsb Senior Vice President Strategic Delivery And Support, Jeanne Muenchau

Vice President Divisional Merch Planning And Inventory, Joe Brazell

Executive Vice President Chief Supply Chain Officer, Brent Beabout

Vice President Nmg Strategy And Operations, Corinne E Copello

Vice President Compensation And Leadership Benefits, Dave Anders

Vice President Creative Projects, Olivia Kim

Vice President Engineering, Alan John

Vice President Divisional Merchandise Manager Men 's And Kid 's Shoes, Robert Evans

Senior Vice President Human Resources, Lisa Price

Vice President Innovation, Laura Janney

Vice President Learning And Leadership, Jesse Schlueter

Vice President Human Resources, Kerry Price-duffy

Svp Technology, Brian Gill

Vice President Divisional General Manager Women's Appa, Anita Ortiz

Vice President Strategy, Rebecca Godecke

Vice President Operations, Jason Trusley

Assistant Treasurer, Daniel Fleming

Board Member, Shellye Archambeau

Auditors: DELOITTE & TOUCHE LLP

LOCATIONS

HQ: Nordstrom, Inc.
  1617 Sixth Avenue, Seattle, WA 98101
Phone: 206 628-2111
Web: www.nordstrom.com

PRODUCTS/OPERATIONS

2017 Sales

	$ mil.	% of total
Full-line stores US	7,186	48
Nordstrom.com	2,519	17
Nordstrom Rack	3,809	25
Nordstromrack.com/Hautelook	700	4
Other retail	554	4
Corporate/Other	(270)	0
Credit Card revenues net	259	2
Total	**14,757**	**100**

2017 Sales

	$ mil.	% of total
Retail	14,768	98
Credit	259	2
Corporate/Other	(270)	0
Total	**14,757**	**100**

2017 Products category

	% of total
Women's Apparel	32
Shoes	23
Men's Apparel	17
Women's Accessories	11
Beauty	11
Kids' Apparel	3
Other	3
Total	**100**

2017 sales

	No.
Nordstrom full-line stores - U.S.and Canada	123
Nordstrom Rack and others	226
Total	**349**

PRODUCTS OFFERED: Selected

Dresses
Tops
Jeans
Sweaters
Coats
Jackets
Pants
Suits

Skirts
Swimsuits & Cover-Ups
Active Yoga & Outdoor
Bras Panties & Lingerie
Shapewear
Sleep Lounge & Robes
Hosiery Leggings & Socks
Plus-Size Clothing
Petite-Size Clothing
Maternity Clothing
Shoes
Handbags & Wallets
Watches
Jewelry
Fine Jewelry
Optical Frames & Reading Glasses
Sunglasses
Scarves & Wraps
Hats & Hair Accessories
Winter Accessories
Gloves
Belts
Luggage & Travel
Tech Accessories & Cases
Hosiery & Socks

Selected Retail Operations

HauteLook (private-sale website for apparel and home
  decor)
Jeffrey (boutiques)
Last Chance (clearance store)
Nordstrom (specialty stores selling apparel shoes and
  accessories for women men and children)
Nordstrom Direct (catalogs and online ordering)
Nordstrom Rack (outlets selling merchandise from
  Nordstrom specialty stores and manufacturers)

COMPETITORS

Ann Taylor	J. Crew
Astor & Black	Lands' End
Barneys	Macy's
Benetton	Neiman Marcus
Bloomingdale's	Nine West
Bluefly	Tailored Brands
Brooks Brothers	Talbots
Caleres	The Gap
Dillard's	Tiffany & Co.
Donna Karan	Von Maur
Eddie Bauer LLC	Wayfair

HISTORICAL FINANCIALS

Company Type: Public

Income Statement

FYE: February 1

	REVENUE ($ mil.)	NET INCOME ($ mil.)	NET PROFIT MARGIN	EMPLOYEES
02/20	15,524	496	3.2%	68,000
02/19	15,860	564	3.6%	71,000
02/18*	15,478	437	2.8%	72,500
01/17	14,757	354	2.4%	72,500
01/16	14,437	600	4.2%	72,500
Annual Growth	1.8%	(4.6%)	—	(1.6%)

*Fiscal year change

2020 Year-End Financials

Debt ratio: 27.48%
Return on equity: 53.71%
Cash ($ mil.): 853
Current ratio: 0.92
Long-term debt ($ mil.): 2,676

No. of shares (mil.): 155
Dividends
  Yield: 0.0%
  Payout: 46.5%
Market value ($ mil.): 5,735

	STOCK PRICE ($) FY Close	P/E High/Low		PER SHARE ($) Earnings	Dividends	Book Value
02/20	36.86	15	8	3.18	1.48	6.29
02/19	45.33	20	13	3.32	1.48	5.54
02/18*	47.85	20	15	2.59	1.48	5.85
01/17	42.83	30	18	2.02	1.48	5.12
01/16	49.10	26	14	3.15	6.33	5.02
Annual Growth	(6.9%)	—	—	0.2%	(30.5%)	5.8%

*Fiscal year change

Norfolk Southern Corp

Norfolk Southern Corporation's main subsidiary Norfolk Southern Railway transports freight over a network consisting of about 20000 route miles in 20-plus states (plus DC) in the eastern southeastern and Midwestern US. The rail system is made up of nearly 20000 route miles owned by Norfolk Southern and about 8000 route miles of trackage rights which allow the company to use tracks owned by other railroads. Norfolk Southern transports coal and merchandise including automotive products and chemicals.

Operations

Norfolk Southern operates about 4000 locomotives and more than 50000 freight cars. It reports through three segments: Merchandise (60% of net sales) Intermodal (approximately 25%) and Coal (about 15%).

The Merchandise segment is subdivided into five commodity groups: Agriculture (such commodities and products as soybeans wheat corn fertilizer livestock and poultry feed food products food oils flour sweeteners and ethanol); Chemicals (sulfur petroleum products chlorine and bleaching compounds plastics rubber industrial chemicals and chemical wastes); Metals/Construction (steel aluminum machinery scrap metals cement aggregates sand minerals transportation equipment and items for the U.S. military); Automotive (finished vehicles from and auto parts for such auto OEMs as Ford General Motors and Toyota); and Forest and consumer (lumber and wood products pulp board and paper products wood fibers wood pulp scrap paper clay beverages canned goods and consumer products). The Merchandise segment maintains more than 2.4 million railroad carloads each year.

Intermodal carries about 4 million units for such clients as intermodal marketing companies international steamship lines and truckers.

Coal is Norfolk Southern's single largest commodity group (narrowly ahead of chemicals). The coal segment carries about 100 million tons of coal originating from major coal basins and destined for approximately 60 coal generation plants as well as export metallurgical and industrial facilities.

Geographic Reach

Based in Virginia Norfolk Southern operates in more than 20 US states and Washington DC and transports overseas freight from several Atlantic and Gulf Coast ports. The company serves every major container port in the eastern US.

Sales and Marketing

Norfolk Southern mainly targets the chemical agriculture metals construction automotive and paper sectors.

Financial Performance

Norfolk Southern's revenue fell by $623 million to $9.8 billion in 2016 compared to the company's revenue in 2015. Its sales spiked back since 2017. Norfolk's sales increased by 7% to $11.3 billion in 2019 compared to $10.5 billion in 2015. In 2019 Norfolk Southern's sales fell about 60 million to $11.3 billion compared to $11.4 billion in 2018. Income from railway operations rose in 2019 as a 3% reduction in railway operating expenses more than offset the impact of a 1% decline in railway operating revenues.

Net income in 2019 increased to $2.7 billion compared to $2.6 billion in 2018 primarily because of income from railway operations and income before income taxes.

Norfolk Southern's cash on hand increased by $134 to $580 in 2019 compared to $446 million during 2018. The company's operations generated $3.7 billion offset by $1.8 billion used in its investing activities and $2.0 billion used in its financing activities. Norfolk Southern's main cash uses in 2019 were property additions share repurchases and dividends.

Strategy

The company's goal is to maintain a capital structure with appropriate leverage to support its business strategy and provide flexibility through business cycles.

Norfolk has released a mobile app NS Trax that makes it easier than ever for customers to conduct business with the railroad ? no matter where they are.

Norfolk announced the details of its strategic plan ? focused on increased productivity efficiency and revenue growth and targeting an operating ratio of 60 percent by 2021 ? at its Investor and Financial Analyst Conference in Atlanta. In March 2020 the company held a groundbreaking ceremony to launch construction of its new corporate headquarters building in Atlanta Georgia. Plans call for the building to be completed and occupied by Norfolk Southern in the third quarter of 2021.

HISTORY

Norfolk Southern Corporation resulted from the 1982 merger of two US rail giants — Norfolk & Western Railway Company (N&W) and Southern Railway Company — which had emerged from more than 200 and 150 previous mergers respectively.

N&W dates to 1838 when one track connected Petersburg Virginia to City Point (now Hopewell). This eight-miler became part of the Atlantic Mississippi & Ohio (AM&O) which was created by consolidating three Virginia railways in 1870.

In 1881 Philadelphia banker E.W. Clark bought the AM&O and renamed it the Norfolk & Western. N&W rolled into Ohio by purchasing two other railroads (1892 1901).

The company took over the Virginian Railway a coal carrier with track paralleling much of its own in 1959. In 1964 N&W became a key railroad in the Midwest by acquiring the New York Chicago & St. Louis Railroad and the Pennsylvania Railroad's line between Columbus and Sandusky Ohio. It also leased the Wabash Railroad with lines from Detroit and Chicago to Kansas City and St. Louis.

Southern Railway can be traced back to the South Carolina Canal & Rail Road a nine-mile line chartered in 1827 and built by Horatio Allen to win trade for Charleston's port. It began operating the US's first regularly scheduled passenger train in 1830 and became the world's longest railway when it opened a 136-mile line to Hamburg South Carolina (1833).

Soon other railroads sprang up in the South including the Richmond & Danville (Virginia 1847) and the East Tennessee Virginia & Georgia (1869) which were combined to form the

Southern Railway System in 1894. Southern eventually controlled more than 100 railroads forging a system from Washington DC to St. Louis and New Orleans.

The 1982 merger of Southern and N&W created an extensive rail system throughout the East South and Midwest. Norfolk Southern (a holding company created for the two railroads) also bought North American Van Lines in 1985. Triple Crown Services the company's intermodal subsidiary was started in 1986. The company also made a failed attempt to take over Piedmont Aviation the next year.

Norfolk Southern revived North American Van Lines by selling its refrigerator truck operation Tran-star (1993) and suspending its commercial trucking line. But it later sold the rest of the motor carrier (1998) to focus on rail operations.

When CSX announced its plans to buy Conrail in 1997 Norfolk Southern's counteroffer led to a split of the former Northeastern monopoly between Norfolk Southern (58%) and CSX (42%). Problems with integrating Conrail's assets hurt Norfolk Southern's results. But by 2000 it had regained some of the traffic it had lost to service problems and its intermodal shipping business also gained speed. In 2004 Norfolk Southern and CSX reorganized Conrail to give each parent company direct ownership of the portion of Conrail's assets that it operates. Conrail still operates switching facilities and terminals used by both Norfolk Southern and CSX.

Norfolk Southern got hit in the wallet in 2001: The company agreed to pay $28 million to settle a racial discrimination lawsuit brought by black employees in 1993. Norfolk Southern began rounds of layoffs and closed redundant depots and facilities in 2001.

In 2005 nine people died in South Carolina when chlorine gas leaked from a ruptured car on a Norfolk Southern freight train. The car was breached when the train crashed into a company-owned locomotive and two train cars that were parked on a siding.

Jumping ahead ten years the company in 2015 rejected an unsolicited takeover by Canadian Pacific in a deal worth $37.8 billion.

EXECUTIVES

Evp Cfo And Cio, Cynthia C. (Cindy) Earhart, $600,000 total compensation
Chairman President And Ceo, James A. (Jim) Squires, age 58, $900,000 total compensation
Vp Intermodal Operations, Alan H. Shaw, $500,000 total compensation
Evp And Coo, Michael J. Wheeler, $581,250 total compensation
Vp Business, Robert Martinez
National Account Manager, Rick Lentz
Avp Research And Advanced Technology, Tom Schnautz
National Account Manager, Ty Hildum
Vice President Chief Engineer Design, Dave Becker
National Account Manager, Kevin Fizer
National Account Manager, Brady Daniels
Vice President Inbound Service Ma, Bud Clapp
Group Vice President, Ken Joyner
National Account Manager, Tom Landrum
National Account Manager, Bill Flanagan
Vice President Process Engineering, Terry Evans
Vice President, David Dixon
Assistant Vice President Finance, Chris Neikirk
Group Vice President, James Schaaf
Vp Engrg, Philip Merilli

Evp And Chief Transformation Officer, Ann Adams
Resident Vp Government Relations Pennsylvania And New York, Michael Fesen
Resident Vice President Government Relations, With Gabrielle
National Account Manager, Megan Duperow
National Account Manager, John Reilly
Vp Government Relations, Marque Ledoux
Vice President Human Resources, Annie Adams
Assistant Vice President Corporate Accounting, Jason Zampi
Vice President, Nesmith Amanda
Board Member, Thomas Bell
Secretary, Julie Weil
Treasurer, Rachael Sears
Secretary, Donna Coleman
Secretary 1, Heather Faber
Auditors: KPMG LLP

LOCATIONS

HQ: Norfolk Southern Corp
Three Commercial Place, Norfolk, VA 23510-2191
Phone: 757 629-2680
Web: www.norfolksouthern.com

PRODUCTS/OPERATIONS

2018 Sales

	$ mil.	% of total
Merchandise		
Chemicals	1,808	16
Agriculture consumer government	1,674	14
Metals & construction	1,462	13
Automotive	991	8
Paper clay and forest	809	7
Intermodal	2,893	25
Coal	1,821	16
Total	**11,458**	**100**

Selected Facilities Served

Active coal-loading facilities
Auto assembly plants
Auto distribution facilities
Bulk transfer facilities
Coal and iron ore transload facilities
General warehouses/distribution centers
Intermodal terminals
Just-in-time rail auto parts center
Lumber reload centers
Metals distribution centers
Paper distribution centers
Paper mills
Power generation plants served
Steel mills and processing facilities
Triple Crown Service terminals
Vehicle mixing centers

COMPETITORS

APL Logistics
American Commercial Lines
Burlington Northern Santa Fe
CSX
Canadian National Railway
Canadian Pacific Railway
Genesee & Wyoming
Hub Group
Ingram Industries

J.B. Hunt
Kansas City Southern
Kirby Corporation
Landstar System
PVH
Piedmont Natural Gas
Pier 1 Imports
Pilgrim's Pride
Pinnacle West
Pitney Bowes
Schneider National
Union Pacific
Werner Enterprises

HISTORICAL FINANCIALS

Company Type: Public

Income Statement

FYE: December 31

	REVENUE ($ mil.)	NET INCOME ($ mil.)	NET PROFIT MARGIN	EMPLOYEES
12/20	9,789	2,013	20.6%	20,156
12/19	11,296	2,722	24.1%	24,587
12/18	11,458	2,666	23.3%	26,662
12/17	10,551	5,404	51.2%	27,110
12/16	9,888	1,668	16.9%	28,044
Annual Growth	(0.3%)	4.8%	—	(7.9%)

2020 Year-End Financials

Debt ratio: 33.40%
Return on equity: 13.39%
Cash ($ mil.): 1,115
Current ratio: 1.07
Long-term debt ($ mil.): 12,102

No. of shares (mil.): 252
Dividends
Yield: 1.5%
Payout: 48.3%
Market value ($ mil.): 59,900

	STOCK PRICE ($) FY Close	P/E High/Low		Earnings	PER SHARE ($) Dividends	Book Value
12/20	237.61	31	15	7.84	3.76	58.67
12/19	194.13	20	14	10.25	3.60	58.87
12/18	149.54	19	13	9.51	3.04	57.30
12/17	144.90	8	6	18.61	2.44	57.57
12/16	108.07	20	12	5.62	2.36	42.73
Annual Growth	21.8%	—	—	8.7%	12.3%	8.3%

Northern Trust Corp

Through its flagship subsidiary The Northern Trust Company Northern Trust provides wealth management securities lending asset servicing and management and banking solutions. The firm addresses institutional clients and affluent individuals in some 20 states and more than 20 countries. Operating two main segments?Corporate and Institutional Services (C&IS) and Wealth Management?Northern Trust has approximately $12 trillion in assets under custody/administration roughly $9 trillion under custody and greater than $1 trillion under direct management. About 70% of company's total revenue comes from the US.

Operations

The firm operates through two segments: Corporate and Institutional Services (C&IS) and Wealth Management. A third business unit Asset Management provides asset management and related services to the two main segments.

The C&IS segment provides asset servicing and related services to endowments sovereign wealth funds corporate and public retirement funds fund managers foundations insurance companies and other institutional investors. Its offerings include investment and treasury management securities lending foreign exchange brokerage cash management transition management investment risk and analytical services and banking. It has more thn $915 billion in assets under management nearly $9 trillion in assets under custody and over $11 trillion in assets under custody/administration. The segment accounts for about 60% of Northern Trust's revenue.

The Wealth Management business focuses on high-net-worth individuals and families business owners executives and the like. It provides services such as custody investment and trust management financial and family business consulting estate administration brokerage and banking. The segment has nearly $325 billion in assets under management approximately $735 billion in assets under custody and about $740 billion in assets under custody/administration. It generates the remaining revenue not produced by C&IS.

Trust investment and other servicing fees represent nearly 65% of the company's revenue; about 30% derives from net interest income.

Geographic Reach

Based in Chicago Northern Trust has a presence in some 20 states and more than 20 countries in the Americas Europe the Middle East and the Asia-Pacific region. The US generates roughly 70% of company's total revenue and accounts for approximately 80% its assets.

Sales and Marketing

The firm serves corporations institutions (such as foundations endowments and sovereign wealth funds) and affluent families and individuals. Client relationships are managed through the Bank and the Bank's and the Corporation's other subsidiaries.

Financial Performance

Revenue increased $112.8 million or 2% to $6.1 billion in 2019 from $6.0 billion in the prior year primarily driven by an increase in trust investment and other servicing fees of 3% an increase in net interest income of 3% and an increase in other operating income of 14% partially offset by a decrease in foreign exchange trading income of 18%.

Net income decreased $64.2 million or 4% to $1.5 billion in 2019 from $1.6 billion in 2018. The decrease primarily due to the increase on their noninterest expense and provision for income taxes offsetting the increase on their revenue.

The cash held by the company in 2019 was $4.5 billion $122.4 million less than the cash in the prior year. Cash provided by operations and financing activities were $2.6 billion and $615.9 million respectively while cash used for investing activities was $3.4 billion.

Strategy

Northern Trust's business strategy is to provide quality financial services to targeted market segments in which it believes it has a competitive advantage and favorable growth prospects. As part of this strategy Northern Trust seeks to differentiate itself from its competitors with premier holistic solutions and exceptional experiences tailored to meet clients' needs. In addition Northern Trust emphasizes the development and growth of recurring sources of fee-based income and continual productivity improvements. Northern Trust also seeks to maintain its foundational strength with a strong conservative balance sheet and a globally respected brand.

Capital expenditures in 2019 included continued investments to enhance Northern Trust's software and hardware capabilities the opening of new offices and the expansion and renovation of several existing offices. Capital expenditures for 2019 totaled $599.8 million of which $441.8 million was for software $73.7 million was for computer hardware $77.7 million was for building and leasehold improvements and $6.6 million was for furnishings.

Mergers and Acquisitions

In 2019 Northern Trust Asset Management has completed its acquisition of Poland-based Belvedere Advisors LLC which owns Emotomy an open-architecture digital investment advice platform designed for financial professionals. With the completion of the acquisition Belvedere Advisors is an independent wholly owned subsidiary of Northern Trust Investments Inc. Northern Trust Asset Management's primary SEC registered investment advisor. Terms not disclosed.

Company Background

As part of its international growth plan Northern Trust expanded in Europe with the 2011 purchase of Bank of Ireland's fund administration investment operations outsourcing and custody business. The acquisition was combined with Northern Trust's existing operations in Ireland which is a European hub for cross-border fund administration. The company worked to support European fund managers by expanding its depositary services across multiple fund types asset classes fund locations and investment strategies as well as by implementing the Alternative Investment Fund Managers Directive (AIFMD).

In 2010 Northern Trust expanded its Wealth Management business with the acquisition of Los Angeles-based investment advisory Waterline Partners.

HISTORY

When banker Byron Smith took time off to handle family concerns in 1885 friends turned to him for advice on trust and estate matters. It occurred to him that there was a market for such services within a banking framework.

Smith tested new Illinois banking and trust laws by arranging for state banking authorities to reject his charter application for Northern Trust. As Smith had hoped the charter was upheld by the Illinois Supreme Court.

Northern Trust opened in 1889 in one of Chicago's new skyscrapers the Rookery. With $1 million in capital — about 40% from Smith and the rest from the likes of Marshall Field (retailing) Martin Ryerson (steel) and Philip Armour (meatpacking) — the bank attracted $138000 in deposits its first day.

By 1896 the bank was firmly established; Smith began taking a salary and the company issued its first dividend. Ten years later the firm built its solid granite edifice the "Gray Lady of LaSalle Street" where it still resides.

The bank began buying commercial paper in 1912 joined the Federal Reserve System in 1917 and became a custodian for expropriated German assets during WWI. Byron Smith died in 1914 and was succeeded by his son Solomon.

Northern Trust rejected the get-rich-quick ethos of the 1920s. It was so strong during the Depression that after the 1933 bank holiday people actually clamored to make deposits and the bank administered the Depression-era scholarship fund that helped Ronald Reagan attend college. By 1941 almost half of Northern Trust's commercial deposits originated outside the Chicago area. The bank kept growing during and after WWII.

Solomon Smith retired in 1963; his son Edward took over and launched the company's expansion overseas (Northern Trust International was formed in 1968) and out of state (Florida in 1971 Arizona in 1974). The firm's business was helped by the 1974 passage by Congress of ERISA which required company retirement plans to be overseen by an outside custodian. Edward retired in 1979.

Northern Trust expanded locally when Illinois legalized intrastate branch banking in 1981. In 1987 the company lost money due in part to defaults on loans made to developing countries. It moved into California in 1988 and Texas in 1989.

Northern Trust navigated the early 1990s recession expanded geographically in the mid-1990s and added services through acquisitions. In 1995 the company became the first foreign trust company to operate throughout Canada. That year it bought investment management service RCB International (now Northern Trust Global Advisors). It expanded in the Sun Belt with such acquisitions as Dallas' Metroplex Bancshares and was made first custodian for the Teacher Retirement System of Texas (1997).

In 1998 the company expanded into Michigan and broke into the Cleveland and Seattle markets in 1999. Northern Trust entered cyberspace as well launching a website for its mutual funds. In 2000 the company opened locations in Nevada and Missouri and bought Florida-based investment adviser Carl Domino Associates (renamed Northern Trust Value Investors). Also that year the bank bought Ireland's Ulster Bank Investment Services.

In 2004 Northern Trust bought the fund management custody and trust operations of Baring Asset Management from Amsterdam-based ING Groep.

EXECUTIVES

Vice President, Brian Ovaert
Vice President Of Loans, Jean Sheridan
Vice President, Monique Noblett
Senior Vice President, Donald Berk
Executive Vice President; Head Capital Markets Group Northern Trust Asset Management, Michael Vardas
Evp And President Wealth Management, Steven L. (Steve) Fradkin, age 58, $600,000 total compensation
Evp And President Corporate And Institutional Services, Jeffery D. Cohodes, age 59
Evp And Coo, Jana R. Schreuder, age 61, $693,750 total compensation
Evp And President Asset Management, Stephen N. Potter, age 63, $587,500 total compensation
Evp And Chief Capital Management Officer, Joyce St. Clair, age 60
Evp And President Corporate And Institutional Services, Peter B. Cherecwich, age 55
Evp And Chief Risk Officer, Wilson Leech, age 58
Evp And Cfo, Stephen B. (Biff) Bowman, age 56, $568,750 total compensation
Evp And Chief Investment Officer, Robert P. (Bob) Browne, age 55
Evp And President Corporate And Institutional Services, Michael G. O'Grady, age 54, $606,250 total compensation
Evp And General Counsel, Susan C. Levy, age 62
Evp Human Resources, S. Gillian Pembleton, age 61
Senior Vice President Information Technology Applications, Barry Bonds
Senior Vice President Technology, Ken Bell
Senior Vice President, Paul D'Ouville

Senior Vice President, Kay Vicino

Svp And Director Community Affairs, Deborah Liverett

Senior Vice President Asia Pacific Region, Lawrence Au

Vice President, Jackie Clipper

Vice President Network Services, Peter Poncia

Senior Vice President, Caroline Devlin

Vice President Information Technology, Ken Le Breux

Vice President International Strategy, Jeremy Baskin

Vice President, Thomas Smith

Senior Vice President, Corinne Mcclintic

Second Vice President Event Marketing Manager, Danielle Czyz

Vice President, Robert Potsic

Vice President, David J Peterson

Executive Vice President, James Mitchell

Vice President Portfolio Manager, Chris Fronk

2nd Vp, Annette Daniel

Senior Vice President, Mark Rice

Vice President Information Technology Project Management Office, Gwen Chamberlin

Ex Vice President, Connie Lindsey

Senior Vice President Treasury, Duane Rocheleau

Senior Vice President Northeast Sales Wealth Management Group Northern Trust Company, Ann Zeiler

Vice President, Jon Seele

Vice President Integrated Risk Management, Carolyn M Schiffels

Vice President Management Division, Patrick Quinn

Senior Product Developer Vice President, Rick Clemons

Senior Vice President Relationship Manager, Stephen Kuropas

Vice President Offshore Vendor Manager, Kathryn Furtek

Vice President, Rich Michaels

Senior Vice President, Timothy Geraghty

Vice President Of Marketing, Mark Welch

Vice President Division Head, James Monhart

Senior Vice President, Peter Flood

Vice President, Michael Hunniford

Senior Vice President, Molly Drennan

Senior Vice President, John Freel

Vice President Storage Engineer, Michael Goudes

Vice President Security Architect, Wendy Betts

Senior Vice President And Managing Director, Gene Harvey

Vice President, Sheldon Woldt

Vice President, Janet Schultz

Senior Vice President Of Marketing, Diane Spradlin

Vice President, Doris Schutzbach

Vice President, Bert Saxon

Senior Vice President Mobile Product Manager, Dennis Flowers

Vice President, Felencia Terrell

Vice President, Greg Werra

Vice President, Deiken Maloney

Vice President, David Sullivan

Vice President Investment Systems Quality Assurance, Cheryl Flack

Second Vice President, Judith Wilson

Vice President Business Services, Matt Adams

Senior Vice President, Stephen Brown

Senior Vice President, Kristin Missil

Vice President, Marc Frost

Second Vice President, Yueru Gu

Vice President Human Resources, Denyse Reese

Senior Vice President Chief Banking Officer Pfs Central Region, Paul Theiss

Vice President, Andrew Glick

Senior Vice President Worldwide Technologies, John Burke

Second Vice President, Karen Smilie

Senior Vice President, James Ferguson

Vice President Operations And Technology, Manan Mehta

Vice President Strategic Sourcing, Angela Quates

Vice President Wealth Advisor (southeast Region), Mike Byrne

Vice President Senior Consultant, Mark Maly

Vice President Wealth Management, Al Combs

Senior Vice President Senior Investment Officer, Ann Farrall

Vice President, Steven Santiccioli

Senior Vice President, Jason Tyler

Vice President, Raje Kantamneni

Vice President, Chris Gilbert

Senior Vice President, Chris Carlson

Senior Vice President, Scott Hensley

Second Vice President Global Network, Lawrence Walter

Second Vice President Information Technology, Jim Weatherhead

Vice President, Andrew Lewis

Vice President, Anita Nikolov

Vice President Global Mobility, Susan Kubiesa

Senior Vice President, Tom Eichenberger

Vice President And Portfolio Manager, Jason A Lawit

Second Vice President, Brent Zonyk

Vice President On Line Product Manager, Mary Jackowiak

Senior Vice President Output Facilities, Steve Schneider

Senior Vice President, Thomas James

Senior Vice President, Nancy Lyon

Vice President, Scott Hertzog

Vice President Operations Risk, Monica Steeg

Vice President Infrastructure Project Management O, Nita Cabuso

Second Vice President, Amit Dalal

Senior Vice President, Kaz Sikora

Vice President, John Brady

Second Vice President, Alex Hingston

Second Vice President, Michelle Bergthold

Vice President, Timothy Blair

Senior Vice President Foundation And Institutional, Dave Cyganiak

Vice President Technology, Paul Baldwin

Vice President Wealth Management, Christine Fleming

Vice President Information Technology, Bob Schroeder

Senior Vice President Pfs Client Servicing Solutions, Julie Sausen

Senior Vice President, Michael Furey

Vice President Tax Analyst, Cassandra Miller

Senior Vice President, Mark Hardtke

Senior Vice President, Thomas Kim

Senior Vice President, Richard Burke

Senior Vice President, Phil Maughan

Senior Vice President, Karen Cortese

Information Technology Vice President, Paul Palasek

Vice President Applications, Evans Chang

Senior Vice President, Mark DeVries

Vice President, Lee R Freitag

Vice President Database Engineering, Jason Antonitis

Senior Vice President, Mark Austin

Vice President Corporate Banking Relationship Manager, Mike Fornal

Vice President, Ryan Gagala

Senior Vice President, Sharon Cohen

Second Vice President Manager Fund Operations Support, Gavin Moran

Executive Vice President Foreign Exchange And Cash Management, Patrick Mcdougal

Vice President Applications Manager, Jean Turbyville

Vice President Worldwide Technology, Patricia Toler

Vice President Corporate Banking Group, Jeff Clark

Vice President Wealth Advisory Services, Michelle Tolliver

Vice President, Robert Raimondi

Second Vice President, Mary Cormier

Senior Vice President Data Center Tech, Sandra Bastow

Auditors: KPMG LLP

LOCATIONS

HQ: Northern Trust Corp
50 South LaSalle Street, Chicago, IL 60603
Phone: 312 630-6000
Web: www.northerntrust.com

Selected Operations

US
Arizona
California
Colorado
Connecticut
Delaware
Florida
Georgia
Illinois
Massachusetts
Michigan
Minnesota
Missouri
Nevada
New York
Ohio
Texas
Washington
Wisconsin
International
Africa
Australia
Canada
China
Hong Kong
India
Ireland
Japan
Luxembourg
Middle East
The Netherlands
New Zealand
Saudi Arabia
Singapore
Sweden
UK

PRODUCTS/OPERATIONS

2018 sales

	$ mil.	% of total
US	3,942	66
Non-US	2,018	34
Total	**5,960**	**100**

2018 sales

	$ mil.	% of total
Net interest income	1,622	27
Noninterest expense		
Trust Investment & Other Servicing Fees	3,753	63
Foreign Exchange Trading Income	307	5
Treasury Management Fees	51	1
Security Commissions & Trading Income	98	2
Other Operating Income	127	2
Investment Security Lossesnet	(1)	-
Total	**5,960**	**100**

Selected Subsidiaries

The Northern Trust Company
  MFC Company Inc.
  Norlease Inc.
  The Northern Trust Company Canada
  Northern Trust Holdings Limited
  The Northern Trust International Banking Corporation
    Northern Trust Cayman International Ltd. (Cayman Islands)
    The Northern Trust Company of Hong Kong Limited
    Northern Trust Fund Managers (Ireland) Limited
    Northern Trust (Ireland) Limited
  Northern Trust Fund Services (Ireland) Limited

Northern Trust Management Services Limited (Ireland)
Northern Trust Partners Scotland Limited (UK)
Northern Trust Scottish Limited Partnership (99% UK)
Northern Trust Luxembourg Capital S.A.R.L.
  Northern Trust Investments Inc.
The Northern Trust Company of Delaware
  NT Global Advisors Inc. (Canada)
Northern Trust Global Investments Japan K.K.
Northern Trust Holdings L.L.C.
Northern Trust Securities Inc.
Northern Trust Services Inc.
Nortrust Realty Management Inc.

COMPETITORS

Bank of America	Goldman Sachs
Bank of New York	Harris
Mellon	JPMorgan Chase
Barclays	Morgan Stanley
Citigroup	SEI Investments
Deutsche Bank	State Street
Fifth Third	Wells Fargo

HISTORICAL FINANCIALS

Company Type: Public

Income Statement   FYE: December 31

	ASSETS ($ mil.)	NET INCOME ($ mil.)	INCOME AS % OF ASSETS	EMPLOYEES
12/19	136,828	1,492	1.1%	19,800
12/18	132,212	1,556	1.2%	18,800
12/17	138,590	1,199	0.9%	18,100
12/16	123,926	1,032	0.8%	17,100
12/15	116,749	973	0.8%	16,200
Annual Growth	4.0%	11.3%	—	5.1%

2019 Year-End Financials

Debt ratio: 2.92%	No. of shares (mil.): 209
Return on equity: 13.82%	Dividends
Cash ($ mil.): 43,222	Yield: 2.4%
Current ratio: —	Payout: 38.6%
Long-term debt ($ mil.): —	Market value ($ mil.): 22,279

	STOCK PRICE ($) FY Close	P/E High/Low		PER SHARE ($) Earnings	Dividends	Book Value
12/19	106.24	16	12	6.63	2.60	52.89
12/18	83.59	17	12	6.64	1.94	47.98
12/17	99.89	20	17	4.92	1.60	45.18
12/16	89.05	21	13	4.32	1.48	42.74
12/15	72.09	20	15	3.99	1.41	37.97
Annual Growth	10.2%	—	—	13.5%	16.5%	8.6%

Northfield Bancorp Inc (DE)

Auditors: KPMG LLP

LOCATIONS

HQ: Northfield Bancorp Inc (DE)
  581 Main Street, Woodbridge, NJ 07095
Phone: 732 499-7200
Web: www.eNorthfield.com

HISTORICAL FINANCIALS

Company Type: Public

Income Statement   FYE: December 31

	ASSETS ($ mil.)	NET INCOME ($ mil.)	INCOME AS % OF ASSETS	EMPLOYEES
12/19	5,055	40	0.8%	380
12/18	4,408	40	0.9%	368
12/17	3,991	24	0.6%	352
12/16	3,850	26	0.7%	366
12/15	3,202	19	0.6%	306
Annual Growth	12.1%	19.8%	—	5.6%

2019 Year-End Financials

Debt ratio: 0.12%	No. of shares (mil.): 49
Return on equity: 5.91%	Dividends
Cash ($ mil.): 147	Yield: 2.5%
Current ratio: —	Payout: 50.5%
Long-term debt ($ mil.): —	Market value ($ mil.): 834

	STOCK PRICE ($) FY Close	P/E High/Low		PER SHARE ($) Earnings	Dividends	Book Value
12/19	16.96	20	16	0.85	0.43	14.15
12/18	13.55	20	15	0.85	0.40	13.43
12/17	17.08	37	28	0.53	0.34	13.09
12/16	19.97	35	24	0.57	0.31	12.80
12/15	15.92	36	31	0.45	0.28	12.29
Annual Growth	1.6%	—	—	17.2%	11.3%	3.6%

Northrop Grumman Corp

Northrop Grumman's major military systems include manned and autonomous aircraft such as the Global Hawk drone a next-generation B-21 Raider bomber and fuselage sections for the F-35 Lightening. Other products and services include various command control communications computer intelligence surveillance and reconnaissance (C4ISR) systems that support the military from the ground the air and space. The company also offers software and services in support of national security for the US and its allies. The US government accounts for about 85% of Northrop Grumman's sales.

HISTORY

Huntington Ingalls Industries Jack Northrop co-founded Lockheed Aircraft in 1927 and designed its record-setting Vega monoplane. He founded two more companies — Avion Corporation (formed in 1928 and bought by United Aircraft and Transportation) and Northrop Corporation (formed in 1932 with Douglas Aircraft which absorbed it in 1938) — before founding Northrop Aircraft in California in 1939.

During WWII Northrop produced the P-61 fighter and the famous Flying Wing bomber which failed to win a production contract. In the 1950s Northrop depended heavily on F-89 fighter and Snark missile sales. When Thomas Jones succeeded Jack Northrop as president (1959) he moved the company away from risky prime contracts in favor of numerous subcon-

tracts and bought Page Communications Engineers (telecommunications 1959) and Hallicrafters (electronics 1966) to reduce its dependence on government contracts.

In the early 1970s Northrop was hit with a bribery scandal and the disclosure of illegal payments to Richard Nixon's 1972 campaign fund; Jones was eventually fined for an illegal contribution. As a result a shareholder lawsuit forced Jones to resign as president (he was allowed to remain as chairman). In 1981 the company won the B-2 bomber contract. Jones retired as chairman in late 1990 and under the leadership of Kent Kresa (who became CEO in early 1990 and chairman when Jones retired) Northrop pleaded guilty to 34 counts related to fudging test results on some government projects; it was fined $17 million. In a related shareholders' suit Northrop paid $18 million in damages in 1991.

Northrop and The Carlyle Group bought LTV's Vought Aircraft Industries (now named Triumph Aerostructures - Vought Aircraft Division) in 1992. In 1994 it paid $2.1 billion for Grumman Corporation a premier electronic systems firm and manufacturer of fighter aircraft for the US Navy and changed its name to Northrop Grumman.

In 1929 Roy Grumman Jake Swirbul and Bill Schwendler founded Grumman; within three months it had a contract to design a Navy fighter. Grumman completed its first commercial aircraft (the Grumman Goose) in 1937 and went public in 1938. It soared during WWII on the wings of its Wildcat and Hellcat fighter planes.

Grumman built its first corporate jet (Gulfstream) in 1958 and began work on the Lunar Module for the Apollo space program in 1963. It was near bankruptcy during the 1970s due to costs related to its F-14 Tomcat fighter. Grumman rebuilt its military business in the 1980s and achieved its greatest success in electronic systems.

The UK Ministry of Defence awarded a $279 million contract to Northrop Grumman in 1995 to develop and produce a system to counter infrared missiles. In 1997 Northrop Grumman bought Logicon (information and battle-management systems). It then agreed to an $11.6 billion purchase by Lockheed Martin but the US government citing concerns about increased lack of competition in the defense industry blocked the deal in 1998. As a result Northrop Grumman began a restructuring that cut 10500 defense and aircraft jobs and added 2500 positions to its Logicon subsidiary.

In 1999 Northrop Grumman bought the information systems division of California Microwave for $93 million and Allegheny Teledyne's Ryan Aeronautical (aerial drones) for $140 million. The next year Northrop Grumman sold its underperforming commercial aerostructures business to The Carlyle Group in a $1.2 billion transaction in order to focus on its growing defense electronics and information technology segments. Later in 2000 Northrop Grumman acquired Comptek Research and bought Federal Data (information systems for the US government) from Carlyle in a transaction valued at $302 million. Pension income that year accounted for more than $500 million (about 55%) of the company's pretax profit.

In 2001 the company completed the deal to acquire Litton Industries for $3.8 billion plus $1.3 billion in debt. In the fall Northrop Grumman acquired the electronics and information unit of Aerojet-General Corp. a subsidiary of GenCorp (later renamed Aerojet Rocketdyne) for about $300 million (it became Grumman's Space Systems Division). While its wallet was open the company agreed to match the $2.6 billion that General Dynamics had agreed to pay for submarine and aircraft carrier builder Newport News— a move that the US Defense Department endorsed. In December Honeywell agreed to pay Northrop Grumman $440 million to settle an antitrust and patent infringement lawsuit that Litton had filed against Honeywell in 1990.

The deal to buy Newport News was completed in early 2002. Northrop Grumman then made a hostile $6 billion bid for conglomerate TRW when TRW's stock plunged following the sudden departure of its CEO David Cote to Honeywell. In the wake of Northrop Grumman's spurned initial bid Raytheon General Dynamics and BAE SYSTEMS made offers for TRW's aerospace and defense assets. Finally though TRW accepted a sweetened $7.8 billion offer from Northrop Grumman in July 2002.

The acquisition fortified Northrop Grumman's position in military satellites missile systems and systems integration. In fact Northrop signed a consent decree with the US Justice Department in which the company agreed (under pain of fines) that it wouldn't take unfair advantage of its exclusive position when selling certain components — such as satellite sensors — to competitors.

TRW's Systems unit became Northrop Grumman Mission Systems; TRW's Space and Electronics unit was later known as Northrop Grumman Space Technology. As for TRW's car parts business Northrop sold all but 19.6% of the unit to Blackstone Group for about $4.7 billion to pay down debt; by early 2005 Northrop reduced its stake to 9.9%.

In April 2003 Kresa stepped down as president and CEO and Ronald Sugar took over those roles; Sugar added the chairmanship to his title when Kresa retired in October.

Among Northrop's 2004 contracts were $1.04 billion for X-47B Joint Unmanned Combat Air Systems $1.2 billion (preferred bidder) for E-3D AWACS contract support and $1.4 billion for the CVN 21 generation aircraft carrier. The company also split an $8.4 billion submarine contract with General Dynamics.

Early in 2005 Northrop sold 7.2 million shares of its TRW Automotive stake raising more than $142 million and reducing its stake to 9.9%. It also acquired Integic Corporation an IT company that specialized in business process management and enterprise health applications.

In 2006 Northrop Grumman established Northrop Grumman Technical Services (NGTS) as a separate sector; it was tasked with consolidating Northrop's logistics operations across its various sectors.

Late that same year Northrop Grumman agreed to buy Essex Corporation — a provider of signal image and information processing for defense and intelligence customers in the US. The deal was valued at about $580 million including the assumption of debt. The deal was completed early in 2007 and Essex became a part of Northrop Grumman Mission Systems (now Northrop Grumman Information Systems).

In 2008 the company shed its Electro-Optical Systems business (night vision and applied optics products) to L-3 Communications for $175 million.

In 2009 Northrop Grumman sold its Advisory Services Division comprising subsidiary TASC (engineering and consulting services to the US military and state governments) to private equities General Atlantic LLC and KKR for $1.65 billion. The sale brings Northrop Grumman into compliance with a new federal law that strengthens conflict of interest rules for defense contractors that both sell to and provide consulting for the US military.

Expanding its aerospace and information capabilities the company purchased Sonoma Photonics and assets from Swift Engineering's Killer Bee Unmanned Air Systems lineup for its Aerospace Systems sector (2009). The deal followed its acquisition of 3001 International for $92 million (a nearly three times larger investment) in 2008. The Virginia-based geospatial data collection and analysis provider not only bolstered Northrop Grumman's military offerings but it also reeled in a host of new civilian customers.

Also in 2009 Northrop Grumman settled two decade-old lawsuits with the US government. It agreed to pay $325 million to resolve allegations that it provided defective military satellite parts to the National Reconnaissance Office. The second lawsuit was filed by Northrop Grumman against the US government for uncompensated costs incurred as a result of the cancellation of the Tri-Service Standoff Attack Missile program.

To concentrate more on its core areas Northrop Grumman spun off its shipbuilding business under former subsidiary Huntington Ingalls Industries in 2011. Despite modest increases in year-over-year revenues the shipbuilding sector had struggled to regain profitability after suffering a loss in 2008 attributable to absorbing most of the company's goodwill impairment charge. Also in 2011 the company reduced operations in other segments. It sold its Viper Strike laser-guided bomb operations in Alabama to European consortium MBDA for an undisclosed amount. And it lowered its participation in the National Security Technologies joint venture that manages and operates the Nevada National Security Site.

Focusing on increasing its presence in the Asia/Pacific in 2012 Northrop Grumman purchased M5 Network Security a provider of cyber security and secure mobile communications technology based in Australia.

EXECUTIVES

Chairman President And Ceo, Wesley G. (Wes) Bush, age 58, $1,530,000 total compensation
Vp And Cto, Patrick M. Antkowiak, age 59
Vp And President Technical Services, Christopher T. Jones, age 55
President And Coo, Kathy J. Warden, age 48, $772,500 total compensation
Corporate Vp And President Mission Systems, Mark A. Caylor, age 55
Vp And Cfo, Kenneth L. Bedingfield, age 47, $756,539 total compensation
Chief Executive Northrop Grumman Japan, Stan Crow

General Manager Strategic Systems Aerospace Systems, Janis G. Pamiljans
Corporate Vp And President Enterprise Services, Shawn N. Purvis
Vp And Deputy General Counsel, Kathryn Simpson
Corporate Vp And Secretary, Jennifer Mcgarey
Vice President Human Resources, Heidi Hendrix
Vice President And Chief Information Officer Of Technology Services, Jim Kane
Vp And Chief Information Security Officer, Mike Papay
Vice President Japan, Curtis Orchard
Security Vice President, Jerry Dodd
Vice President Mritime Systems, Todd Leavitt
Vice President Enterprise Communications, Daniel Mcclain
Vice President Of Basic Research, Tom Pieronek
Senior Vice President, Monty Frahm
Vp Of Programs Of Land And Avionics C4isr Division, Robert Fleming
Vice President Business Development Northrop Grumman Space Technology, Jeffrey Grant
Vice President, Bart Lagrone
Vice President Elect Programs, Bull Douglas
Vice President, Robert Snodgrass
Vp Information Technology, Martin Bernet
Vice President Government And Industry R, Ryan Casey
Government Relations, Robert McCaleb
Vice President Business Management, Joseph Nicolaus
Vice President Operations Command And Control, Christina Williams
Vice President Middle East, Samir Narmouq
Vice President Strategic Communications, Tim Paynter
Sector Vice President Global Operations Aerospace System, Kevin Mitchell
Vice President Associate General Counsel And Sector Counsel Technologyservices Sector, Don Chavez
Vice President Mission Solutions Land And Avionics C4isr Division, Carl Smith
Sector Vp Global Logistics And Operational Support Aerospace Systems, Michelle Scarpella
Vice President Business Management And Cfo, Sunil Navale
Vice President Communications Systems, Cyrus Dhalla
Vp And Cio, Sam Abbate
Vp And Cto Electronic Systems Sector, Eric Reinke Iii
Vice President And Assistant General Counsel, John Cox
Vice President, Andrew Reynolds
Corporate Vice President And President Northrop Grumman Innovation Systems, Blake Larson
Sector Vp Of Mission Assurance Of Innovation Systems, Jim Judd
Sector Vp Of Supply Chain Management Of Innovation Systems, Vicky Schumann
Vice President, Simon Mason
Vice President Security, Mary Mccaffrey
Corporate Vice President Communications, Lucy C Ryan
Vice President Intelligence Solutions Business Unit, Ginger Wierzbanowski
Senior Vice President Global Human Resources, Ann Addison
Vice President Business Development And Strategy, Bart Olson
Vice President, Denise Hobson
Vice President, Jerry Brode
Board Member, Mary Brown
Secretary, Karla Parker
Treas, Nam Nguyen
Treasurer, Sam Schreiber
Auditors: DELOITTE & TOUCHE LLP

LOCATIONS

HQ: Northrop Grumman Corp
  2980 Fairview Park Drive, Falls Church, VA 22042
Phone: 703 280-2900
Web: www.northropgrumman.com

PRODUCTS/OPERATIONS

2016 Sales

Segments	$ mil.	% of total
Aerospace Systems	10,828	41
Mission Systems	10,928	41
Technology Services	4,825	18
Intersegment eliminations	(2073)	-
Total	**24,508**	**100**

2016 Sales

	$ mil.	% of total
Product	14,738	60
Service	9,770	40
Total	**24,508**	**100**

2016 Sales

	$ mil.	% of total
U.S. Government	20,573	84
International	3,205	13
Other Customers	730	3
Total	**24,508**	**100**

Selected Capabilities

Unmanned Systems
C4ISR
Cyber
Logistics
Advanced Electronics
Commercial Aviation
Directed Energy
IT & Enterprise Solutions
Manned Aircraft
Military Aviation
Missile Defense
Naval Systems
Navigation Systems

COMPETITORS

BAE SYSTEMS	Leonardo
Boeing	Lockheed Martin
Booz Allen	Meggitt
General Dynamics	Raytheon
L3 Technologies	Thales
Leidos	

HISTORICAL FINANCIALS

Company Type: Public

Income Statement   FYE: December 31

	REVENUE ($ mil.)	NET INCOME ($ mil.)	NET PROFIT MARGIN	EMPLOYEES
12/20	36,799	3,189	8.7%	97,000
12/19	33,841	2,248	6.6%	90,000
12/18	30,095	3,229	10.7%	85,000
12/17	25,803	2,015	7.8%	70,000
12/16	24,508	2,200	9.0%	67,000
Annual Growth	**10.7%**	**9.7%**	**—**	**9.7%**

2020 Year-End Financials

Debt ratio: 32.07%
Return on equity: 32.79%
Cash ($ mil.): 4,907
Current ratio: 1.60
Long-term debt ($ mil.): 14,261
No. of shares (mil.): 166
Dividends
  Yield: 1.8%
  Payout: 38.6%
Market value ($ mil.): 50,802

	STOCK PRICE ($) FY Close	P/E High/Low	PER SHARE ($) Earnings	Dividends	Book Value
12/20	304.72	20 14	19.03	5.67	63.45
12/19	343.97	29 18	13.22	5.16	52.54
12/18	244.90	19 12	18.49	4.70	47.99
12/17	306.91	27 20	11.47	3.90	40.49
12/16	232.58	20 14	12.19	3.50	30.04
Annual Growth	**7.0%**	**— —**	**11.8%**	**12.8%**	**20.6%**

Northwest Bancshares, Inc. (MD)

EXECUTIVES

Chief Executive Officer, Julie McTpavish
Executive Vp, Julia Mctavish
Senior Vice President District Manager, Kara Odom
Senior Vice President Region Manager Commercial Lending, Richard Cefalo
Assistant Vp Information Security, Lance Spencer
Divisional Vice President And Trust Officer, John Zador
Senior Vice President Commercial Lending Team Leader, Douglas Byers
Senior Vice President, Bradley Chovit
Corporate Assistant Vice President Computer Operations Manager, Robert Pope
Vice President Insurance Services, David Winans
Board Member, John Meegan
Auditors: KPMG LLP

LOCATIONS

HQ: Northwest Bancshares, Inc. (MD)
  100 Liberty Street, Warren, PA 16365
Phone: 814 726-2140
Web: www.northwestsavingsbank.com

HISTORICAL FINANCIALS

Company Type: Public

Income Statement   FYE: December 31

	ASSETS ($ mil.)	NET INCOME ($ mil.)	INCOME AS % OF ASSETS	EMPLOYEES
12/19	10,493	110	1.1%	2,333
12/18	9,607	105	1.1%	2,258
12/17	9,363	94	1.0%	2,254
12/16	9,623	49	0.5%	2,466
12/15	8,951	60	0.7%	2,364
Annual Growth	**4.1%**	**16.2%**	**—**	**(0.3%)**

2019 Year-End Financials

Debt ratio: 2.62%
Return on equity: 8.46%
Cash ($ mil.): 60
Current ratio: —
Long-term debt ($ mil.): —
No. of shares (mil.): 106
Dividends
  Yield: 4.3%
  Payout: 69.2%
Market value ($ mil.): 1,777

	STOCK PRICE ($) FY Close	P/E High/Low	PER SHARE ($) Earnings	Dividends	Book Value
12/19	16.63	18 15	1.04	0.72	12.66
12/18	16.94	18 15	1.02	0.68	12.17
12/17	16.73	20 16	0.92	0.64	11.79
12/16	18.03	38 24	0.49	0.60	11.51
12/15	13.39	22 18	0.64	0.56	11.42
Annual Growth	**5.6%**	**— —**	**12.9%**	**6.5%**	**2.6%**

NORTHWEST FARM CREDIT SERVICES

Customer-owned financial cooperative Northwest Farm Credit Services is an agricultural lender that provides financial services to farmers ranchers agribusinesses commercial fishermen timber producers and rural home owners in Alaska Idaho Montana Oregon and Washington. The company has a network of around 45 branches and offers a broad range of flexible loan programs to meet the needs of people in the agriculture business. Northwest Farm Credit also provides leasing services appraisal services and life mortgage disability and crop insurance as well as legal advocacy and assistance to customers in need. It is part of the Farm Credit System a network of lenders serving the US agriculture industry.

Operations

The credit union provides financing and related services to farmers ranchers agribusinesses commercial fishermen timber producers rural homeowners and crop insurance customers. Northwest Farm Credit provides $10.3 billion in loans. Farm Credit System a nationwide network of borrower-owned lending institutions of which it is part provides $205 billion in loans to rural America.

Geographic Reach

Northwest Farm Credit serves customers through 45 offices located in Idaho Alaska Montana Oregon and Washington.

Sales and Marketing

Northwest Farm Credit finances farmers ranchers agribusinesses commercial fishermen timber producers and rural homeowners as well as farm-related businesses agricultural cooperatives and rural utilities.

Financial Performance

In 2015 the company's net revenue increased by 5% due to higher net interest income driven by increased loan volume.

Northwest Farm Credit's net income rose by 12% due to higher net revenues and a decrease in income tax expense.

In 2015 the company's operating cash inflow increased by 19%.

Strategy

The company plans to continue to fund lending operations primarily through its borrowing relationship with CoBank (a fellow Farm Credit System member) and from retained earnings.

Mergers and Acquisitions

In 2014 the company expanded its operations in Montana by buying Culbertson State Agency's crop insurance portfolio.

Company Background

The US Congress created the Farm Credit System in 1916 to meet the financial needs of farmers ranchers and cooperatives who invest as well as borrow from the institutions within the system. All Farm Credit System members are regulated by the Farm Credit Administration.

EXECUTIVES

Evp Financial Services, Fred (Fred) DePell
Evp And General Counsel, Thomas (Tom) Tracy

Evp Corporate Administration And Secretary, Joan E. Haynes

Evp Cfo And Cio, Tom Nakano

Vice President Internal Controls, Don Bellamy

Vice President Market Research And Development, Michael Stolp

Vice President, Carol L Sobson

Vice President Appraisal Services, Joe Moore

Vice President Relationship Manager Iii, Sean Kolb

Svp Policy And Collateral Risk Management, Paul Nelson

Chairman, Drew Eggers

Vice Chairman, Kevin Riel

Auditors: PRICEWATERHOUSECOOPERS LLP S

LOCATIONS

HQ: NORTHWEST FARM CREDIT SERVICES
2001 S FLINT RD, SPOKANE, WA 992249198
Phone: 509 838-2429
Web: WWW.NORTHWESTFCS.COM

PRODUCTS/OPERATIONS

2015 Sales

	$ mil.	% of total
Interest Income	412	82
Patronage income	52	11
Financially Related Services	19	4
loans and other fee	6	1
Other non-interest income	11	2
Total	**502**	**100**

COMPETITORS

Bank of America	U.S. Bancorp
First Interstate	Wells Fargo
Idaho Independent Bank	Zions Bancorporation
KeyCorp	
Northwest Bancorporation	

HISTORICAL FINANCIALS

Company Type: Private

Income Statement				FYE: December 31
	ASSETS ($ mil.)	NET INCOME ($ mil.)	INCOME AS % OF ASSETS	EMPLOYEES
12/13	9,604	236	2.5%	500
12/12	9,471	187	2.0%	—
12/11	8,696	159	1.8%	—
Annual Growth	5.1%	22.0%	—	—

NOV Inc

National Oilwell Varco provides goods and services to exploration and production companies operating in oil fields around the world as well to infrastructure clients. The company makes distributes and services oil and gas drilling equipment for land and offshore drilling rigs. Its mechanical components include jacking systems assembly systems fluid transfer technologies pressure control equipment power transmission systems control systems;. Other products include masts derricks substructures and cranes. It serves oil and gas operators in about 65 countries worldwide and typically has around 2200 drilling rigs in operation. The US accounts for over 35% of sales.

Operations

National Oilwell Varco operates three business segments: Wellbore Technologies Completion & Production Solutions and Rig Technologies.

National Oilwell Varco's Wellbore Technologies segment (more than 35% of sales) provides equipment and technologies used to perform drilling operations and offers services that optimize their performance including solids control and waste management equipment and services portable power generation drill pipe wired pipe drilling optimization and automation services tubular inspection repair and coating services instrumentation measuring and monitoring downhole and fishing tools steerable technologies and drill bits.

The Completion & Production Services segment brings in over 30% of sales and designs manufactures and sells equipment and technologies needed for hydraulic fracture stimulation (including pressure pumping trucks and pumps blenders sanders hydration units injection units flowline manifolds and wellheads); well intervention (coiled tubing units coiled tubing and wireline units and tools); onshore production (composite pipe surface transfer and progressive cavity pumps and artificial lift systems); and offshore production (floating production systems subsea production technologies and connectors for conductor pipe).

The Rig Technologies segment (roughly 30% of sales) designs manufactures and sells land rigs offshore drilling equipment packages including installation and commissioning services and drilling rig components that mechanize and automate the drilling process and rig functionality. It also provides spare parts repairs and rentals as well as comprehensive remote equipment monitoring technical support field service and customer training.

Geographic Reach

Houston Texas-based National Oilwell Varco has significant non-US operations in Canada Europe the Far East the Middle East Africa Russia and Latin America. It operates in almost 650 locations on six continents including a network of about 280 repair and manufacturing facilities; approximately 115 engineering sales and admin facilities; and more than 250 service centers. It has major facilities in Denmark France the Netherlands Norway Canada UK and US and a presence in Singapore Mexico Malaysia Brazil South Korea and the UAE. The company produces about 65% of its total revenues from operations outside of the US.

Sales and Marketing

Substantially all of Rig Systems' capital equipment and Rig Aftermarket's spare parts sales and a large portion of their smaller pumps and parts sales are made through the company's direct sales force and distribution service centers. Sales to foreign oil companies are often made with or through agent or representative arrangements.

The company's Rig Technologies segments' customers include drilling contractors oilfield service companies oilfield rental companies drill oil and gas wells on land and offshore companies.

Wellbore Technologies' customers are mainly oil and gas companies drilling contractors oilfield service companies and oilfield rental companies.

Completion & Production Solutions' customers are predominantly service companies and oil and gas companies.

NOV's products are used in extremely harsh environments and need replacing often generated reliable demand for replacements and aftermarket sales.

Financial Performance

National Oilwell Varco's revenue was halved from $14.8 billion in 2015 to $7.3 billion in 2016. Despite its gradual recovery in the years that followed its revenue has an overall decline of 43% in the last five years. The company has a fluctuating net loss in the last five years from $769 million in 2015 to $6.1 billion in 2019.

The recovery in prices in the years since has lifted the company's sales since but they are yet to reach pre-crash levels. Further National Oilwell has not made a net profit since 2015. In 2019 its sales slightly increased by $26 million to $8.47 billion compared to the previous year $8.45 billion.

National Oilwell reported a net loss of $6.1 billion in 2019 compared to a net loss of $31 million during 2018.

NOV's cash on hand declined by 18% in 2019 to $1.2 billion compared to $1.4 billion in 2018. The company's operations generated $714 million while its investing activities used $315 million and its financing used $647 million

Strategy

National Oilwell's strategy is first and foremost one of survival and once that is assured to position itself for the assumed next surge in oil prices and along with it demand for the company's services. Company remains optimistic regarding improvements in market fundamentals as existing oil and gas fields continue to deplete and investments in major projects to replenish supply remain constrained while global demand continues to grow. NOV remains committed to streamlining its operations and improving organizational efficiencies while continuing to focus on the capital investment strategies of the company's customers to ensure its investments in innovative products and services including environmentally friendly technologies are responsive to their longer-term investment outlook.

NOV continues to develop and introduce technologies that further enhance oilfield economics with particular focus technologies related to drilling automation multistage completions predictive analytics and condition-based maintenance and improved deepwater project economics.

Mergers and Acquisitions

The company completed its acquisition of Denali Incorporated (Denali) (including its brands Belco Ershigs Fabricated Plastics Fibra and Plasti-Fab). Denali is a renowned leader in fiberglass-reinforced plastic (FRP) products and technologies with more than 50 years of providing innovative FRP solutions to the petroleum chemical power generation and water industries.

Company Background

In 2013 it acquired Robbins & Myers a provider of services and equipment to the upstream oil and gas industry in an all-cash transaction for $2.5 billion. Robbins & Myers' complementary products include downhole tools pumps and valves. This was the company's second-largest acquisition since it bought Grant

Prideco for about $7.2 billion in 2008. That year it also bought Canadian equipment distributor CE Franklin for about $240 million.

In 2012 National Oilwell Varco bought parts and supplies provider Wilson International from Schlumberger. Wilson has an extensive supply chain portfolio with which National Oilwell Varco expects to take advantage of new market opportunities. It also bought Denmark-based flexible pipe maker NKT Flexibles (a joint venture between NKT Holding and Subsea 7) for $670 million.

National Oilwell Varco bought 17 companies for $2.9 billion in 2012 and 10 companies for more than $1 billion in 2011. Significant acquisitions included that of oilfield equipment maker and services provider Ameron in a $777 million deal a move that helped to expand National Oilwell Varco's Fiberglass & Composite Tubulars business.

National Oilwell Varco took its current form when National Oilwell and Varco International merged in 2005.

EXECUTIVES

Chairman President And Ceo, Clay C. Williams, $800,000 total compensation

President Nov Wellbore Technologies, Isaac A. Joseph

Svp And Cfo, Jose A. Bayardo, $650,000 total compensation

President Rig Systems And Rig Aftermarket, Joseph W. (Joe) Rovig, $550,000 total compensation

President Completion And Production Solutions, Kirk Shelton

Vp Corporate Controller Chief Accounting Officer, Scott K. Duff, $360,000 total compensation

Cio, Alex Philips

Svp And General Counsel, Craig L. Weinstock, $510,000 total compensation

Vice President Global Corporate Accounts, Tab Tettleton

Group Vice President Global Manufacturing And Sourcing Rig Solutions, Bruce Dawson

Vice President Administration Down Hole Tools Group, Danielle Al-tayar

Vice President Manufacturing, Jeff Stolasz

Corporate Vp And Cto, Hege Kverneland

Vice President Sales, Bob Lepera

Vice President Of Sales And Operations, Todd Lee

Vice President Operations China, Lynn White

Vice President, Larry Engel

Vice President Application Engineering, Randy Lucas

Vice President Finance, Jim Lock

Vice President Corporate Cont, Bob Blanchard

Vice President Southern Us, Bryan Suire

Vice President Regional Sales Asia Pacific, Jason Major

Corporate Vice President And Chief Technology Officer, Hege Kvernland

Senior Vice President, Brad Wood

Vice President Buisness Developement, Frank J Torma

Vice President Intervention And Completion Tools, Blake Hammond

Vice President Automated Drilling Applications, Tony Pink

Vice President Industrial Products And Solutions, Jim Putnam

Vice President Marketing And Sales Services, Nelson F Allen

Vice President Global Offshore Accounts Americas, Cobie Loper

Sr.vice President, Scott Livingston

Vp Manufacturing, Norm Shearer

Vice President Finance, Lewis Cadwallader

Vice President Engineering S E Asia, Bob Donnally

Vice President And Treasurer, Trevor Martin

Vice President, Jerry Givens

Auditors: Ernst & Young LLP

LOCATIONS

HQ: NOV Inc
  7909 Parkwood Circle Drive, Houston, TX 77036-6565
Phone: 713 346-7500
Web: www.nov.com

2018 Sales

	$ mil.	% of total
US	3,480	41
China	231	3
South Korea	169	2
Singapore	321	4
Norway	368	4
United Arab Emirates	248	3
UK	309	4
Saudi Arabia	444	5
Brazil	415	5
Canada	302	4
Other countries	2,166	25
Total	**8,453**	**100**

PRODUCTS/OPERATIONS

2018 Sales

	$ mil.	% of total
Rig Technologies	2,575	29
Wellbore Technologies	3,235	37
Eliminations	(288)	-
Total	**8,453**	**100**

2018 Sales

	$ mil.	% of total
Sales	5,699	67
Services	1,612	19
Rental	1,142	14
Total	**8,453**	**100**

Selected Products and Services

Automation systems
Computer control systems
Derricks
Drawworks
Drilling motors
Electrical power systems
Masts
Mud pumps
Specialized downhole tools (including fishing tools drilling jars shock tools)
Substructures
Supply chain management
Top drives
Well drilling and servicing (drill stem technology)
Technology Solutions
Coiled Tubing Equipment
Coiled Tubing Equipment Services
Coiled Tubing Instrumentation
Coiled Tubing Pressure Control
Coiled Tubing Products and Service
Coiled Tubing Pumping Support
Coiled Tubing Software
CT Equipment Repair Center
Well Service and Completion
All Terrain Vehicles
Cementing
Completion Fluids and Services
Flowline Equipment
Fluid End Expandables
Frac Sand Handling Equipment
Multipurpose Pumps
Nitrogen Equipment
Rigs
Snubbing Equipment
Stimulation Equipment
TCP Products
Wireline
Workover
Tubular and Corrosion Control
Coiled Tubing Products and Service
Conductors and Casing
Corrosion Control
Drill Pipe Services
Drilling Tubulars

Fiber Glass Pipe
Inspection Services
Line Pipe Services
Machining Services
New Pipe Services
Specialty Inspection Services
Sucker Rod Services
Surveillance Services
Tubular Leak Detection
Used Pipe Services
Supply Chain
Artificial Lift
Electrical Products
Integrated Supply
Oilfield Supply
RigPAC
RigStore
ValveAutomation
Production
Artificial Lift
Floating Production Solutions
Fluid King Pump Expendables
Multipurpose Pumps
Process Equipment
Production Pressure Control
Lifting and Handling
AHTS Equipment Packages
Cabelay Systems
Cranes
Marine Vessel Equipment
Mooring Systems
Pipelay Systems
Winches
Industrial
Construction Supply
Fiber Glass Pipe
Fluid End Expendables
Monoflo - Mono
Multipurpose Pumps
Nitrogen Equipment
Power Systems
Protective Lining Products
Solids Control
Water Transmission
Engineering and Project Management
New Technology Development
Project Specific Solutions
Successful Project Execution
Drilling
Aftermarket Services
Control and Advisory Systems
Drill Bits
Drilling Business Solutions
Drilling Expendables Databook
Drilling Fluids
Drilling Fluid Equipment
Drilling Pressure Control
Drilling Tubulars
Flowline Equipment
Fluid End Expendables
Fluid End Modules and Accessories
Fluid Transfer Systems
Handling Tools
Hoisting
Instrumentation Data Acquisition
Iron Roughnecks
Jacking and Skidding
Mining and Minerals
Motion Compensation
Multipurpose Pumps
Pipe Handling
Power Systems
Rigs
Rotating Equipment
Specialty Inspection Services
Structures
Top Drive Systems
Waste Management
Downhole
Advanced Drilling Solutions
Borehole Enlargement
Coring Services
Directional Tools
Downhole Motors
Drill Bits
Drilling Tools
Fishing Tools
Intervention and Completion Tools
Service Equipment
Telemetry Drill Strings

Selected Brands

AmClyde
Ameron
Baylor
Bear Pumps
Best Flow Products
BlackMax - BlackStar
Bowen
Brandt
Continental Emsco
CTES
Fiber Glass Systems
Gaso
HSI
Hydrastab
IntelliServ
Quality Tubing
ReedHycalog
Rolligon
Texas Oil Tools
Wheatley
Wheatley Gaso
XL Systems

COMPETITORS

Aker Solutions	Nabors Industries
Baker Hughes	Schlumberger
Bechtel	Siemens AG
Cameron International	Stewart & Stevenson
Forum Energy	LLC
GE Oil	Superior Energy
Halliburton	Weatherford
McDermott	International

HISTORICAL FINANCIALS

Company Type: Public

Income Statement · FYE: December 31

	REVENUE ($ mil.)	NET INCOME ($ mil.)	NET PROFIT MARGIN	EMPLOYEES
12/19	8,479	(6,095)	—	35,479
12/18	8,453	(31)	—	35,063
12/17	7,304	(237)	—	31,889
12/16	7,251	(2,412)	—	36,627
12/15	14,757	(769)	—	50,197
Annual Growth	(12.9%)	—		(8.3%)

2019 Year-End Financials

Debt ratio: 15.13%	No. of shares (mil.): 385
Return on equity: (-56.44%)	Dividends
Cash ($ mil.): 1,171	Yield: 0.8%
Current ratio: 2.72	Payout: —
Long-term debt ($ mil.): 1,989	Market value ($ mil.): 9,666

	STOCK PRICE ($) FY Close	P/E High/Low	PER SHARE ($) Earnings	Dividends	Book Value
12/19	25.05	— —	(15.96)	0.20	20.16
12/18	25.70	— —	(0.08)	0.20	36.04
12/17	36.02	— —	(0.63)	0.20	37.08
12/16	37.44	— —	(6.41)	0.61	36.82
12/15	33.49	— —	(1.99)	1.84	43.60
Annual Growth	(7.0%)	— —		—(42.6%)	(17.5%)

NOVARTIS PHARMACEUTICALS CORPORATION

EXECUTIVES

Pres, Marie-France Tschudin
Sr V-Pres-Cmo*, Nancy Lurker
Pres*, Andre Wyss
V Pres*, Yves Teirlynck
V Pres*, Julie Kane
Coo*, Alex Gorsky
V-Pres-Cfo*, Gary E Rosenthal
Cfo*, Helen Boudreau
US Country Head, Information T, Ruth Thorpe
Director, Kenneth Wong
Executive Director, Tom Jones
Auditors: PRICEWATERHOUSECOOPERS LLP-BR

LOCATIONS

HQ: NOVARTIS PHARMACEUTICALS CORPORATION
1 HEALTH PLZ, EAST HANOVER, NJ 079361016
Phone: 862 778-8300
Web: WWW.NOVARTIS.COM

HISTORICAL FINANCIALS

Company Type: Private

Income Statement · FYE: December 31

	REVENUE ($ mil.)	NET INCOME ($ mil.)	NET PROFIT MARGIN	EMPLOYEES
12/16	49,436	6,698	13.5%	7,000
12/15	49,440	17,794	36.0%	—
12/13	58,831	9,292	15.8%	—
Annual Growth	(5.6%)	(10.3%)	—	—

NRG Energy Inc

NRG Energy is a leading retail energy marketer and independent power producer in the US market. NRG's retail units (including Reliant Energy and Green Mountain Energy) distribute electricity and natural gas to some 3.7 million customers in competitive markets in about 20 US states and two Canadian provinces. The company has a generating capacity of 23000 MW from its portfolio of about 30 power plants. The vast majority of NRG's business is in Texas where the Company's generation supply is fully integrated with its retail load.

Operations

NRG's operating segments are Retail Generation and Corporate.

NRG's Retail segment accounting for about two-thirds of revenue is one of the largest US retail energy marketers with operations in deregulated utility markets in 20 states plus two Canadian provinces. It provides electricity and natural gas to residential commercial and industrial customers. The segment overlooks several brands that collectively are the largest providers of electricity in Texas. Its Business Solutions group provides demand response commodity sales efficiency consulting and energy management services to commercial customers.

Generation a capital-intensive segment accounting for one-third of sales has about 23000 MW of fossil-fueled nuclear and renewable (wind and solar) generation capacity at some 30 plants.

Geographic Reach

NRG's retail subsidiaries serve customers in some 20 US states and Washington DC and two Canadian provinces.

The company has generation assets in the US and Australia. Its US plants are primarily located in Texas New York Connecticut Arizona Maryland Illinois California and Delaware.

NRG has its corporate headquarters in Princeton New Jersey and an operational base in Houston.

Sales and Marketing

NRG's Retail segment serves residential business commercial and industrial customers. The company's sales are conducted through direct representatives online platforms call centers and brokers.

Financial Performance

NRG reported steadily increase in revenue over the past five years hitting a $10.8 billion in 2015.

Revenue increased 4% in 2019 to some $9.8 billion due to 8% and 11% growth in the Retail segment and Generation segment respectively.

Net income rose to $4.4 billion in 2019 due to income tax benefits.

The company ended 2019 with $385 million in cash down $228 million from 2018. Operating activities contributed $1.4 billion while investing activities provided another $556 million (mostly acquisitions and capital expenditures) and financing activities used $2.2 billion mainly for treasury stock purchases and debt payments.

Strategy

NRG's strategy is to maximize stockholder value through the safe production and sale of reliable power to its customers in the markets it serves while positioning the Company to provide innovative solutions to the end-use energy customer. This strategy is intended to enable the Company to optimize its integrated model to generate stable and predictable cash flow significantly strengthen earnings and cost competitiveness and lower risk and volatility.

To effectuate the Company's strategy NRG is focused on serving the energy needs of end-use residential commercial and industrial customers in competitive markets through multiple brands and channels with a variety of retail energy products and services differentiated by innovative features premium service sustainability and loyalty/affinity programs; offering innovative and renewable energy solutions for customers; excellence in operating performance of its existing assets; optimal hedging of NRG's net retail and generation positions; and engaging in disciplined and transparent capital allocation.

In 2019 NRG announced the acceleration of its science-based GHG emissions reduction goals to align with prevailing climate science limiting warming to a 1.5 degree Celsius scenario. Under its new GHG emissions reduction timeline NRG is targeting to achieve a 50% reduction by 2025 and net-zero emissions by 2050 from a 2014 baseline.

Mergers and Acquisitions

In 2019 NRG acquired the retail electricity and gas business of Stream Energy for $300 million. The deal adds more than 600000 residential customers in Texas Pennsylvania and seven other states plus Washington DC and is aligned with NRG's strategy to focus on its retail energy operations.

Company Background

NRG Energy was founded in 1992 to acquire and operate power generation facilities. A portion of the company was spun off from parent Northern States Power (later Xcel Energy) in an IPO in 2000. NRG became a wholly owned subsidiary of Xcel again in 2002 and filed for chapter 11 bankruptcy in 2003. Upon emerging from bankruptcy later that year NRG became a public entity once again and separated completely from Xcel.

EXECUTIVES

President And Ceo, Mauricio Gutierrez, age 50, $1,125,000 total compensation

Evp And Cfo, Kirkland B. Andrews, age 53, $642,952 total compensation

Evp Nrg Retail, Elizabeth Killinger, age 50, $504,634 total compensation

Evp National Business Development; President West Region, John Chillemi, age 53, $475,001 total compensation

Evp And General Counsel, David R. Hill, age 57, $500,000 total compensation

Svp Operations, Chris Moser

Svp Information Technology, Donna Benefield

Svp Renewables And President Nrg Renewables, Craig Cornelius

Vice President Strategic Marketing, Virginia Kinney

Senior Vice President Asset Management And Development, Howard Taylor

Vice President Internal Audit, Debra Holmes

Vice President Sustainable Solutions, Lynda Clemmons

Vice President Engineering And Project Services, Robert Patrick

Vice President Information Technology, John Redding

Senior Vice President Business Operations, Jim Ingoldsby

Vice President Of Human Resources, Leonard Kluft

Vice President Reliability Solutions, Phil Kairis

Senior Vice President And Treasurer, Gabriel Garcia

Vice President And Deputy General Counsel Regulatory, Abraham Silverman

Vice President Of Engineering And Technical Operations, Logan Granger

Senior Vice President, Daniel Keane

Svp Of Administration And Senior Counsel, John Blomquist

Vice President Electric Vehicle Services, Glen Stancil

Vice President Environment And Assistant General Counsel, Walter Stone

Vice President Regional Plant Operations, Don Poe

Chairman, Lawrence S. Coben, age 61

Board Member, William Hantke

Board Member, Kirbyjon Caldwell

Board Member, Anne Schaumburg

Vice Chairman, Edward Muller

Board Member, Paul Hobby

Auditors: KPMG LLP

LOCATIONS

HQ: NRG Energy Inc
804 Carnegie Center, Princeton, NJ 08540
Phone: 609 524-4500
Web: www.nrgenergy.com

PRODUCTS/OPERATIONS

2016 Sales

	$ mil.	% of total
Retail revenue	6,274	47
Energy revenue	4,469	34
Capacity revenue	1,970	15
Other revenues	558	4
Mark-to-market activities	(865)	-
Contract amortization	(55)	-
Total	**12,351**	**100**

2016 Sales

	$ mil.	% of total
Retail	6,336	47
Generation	5,679	42
NRG Yield	1,021	7
Renewables	417	3
Corporate	77	1
Other	(1179)	-
Total	**12,351**	**100**

2016 Sales

	$ mil.	% of total
Generation	6,927	51
Retail Mass	4,966	37
NRG Yield	1,021	8
Renewable	417	3
Corporate	137	1
Eliminations	(1117)	-
Total	**12,351**	**100**

Selected Subsidiaries

Energy Plus
Green Mountain Energy Company (retail power)
NEO Corporation (distributed generation; landfill gas hydroelectric and other renewable generation)
NRG Power Marketing Inc. (power sales)
NRG Resource Recovery (waste-to-energy facilities)
NRG Texas LLC (power generation)
NRG Thermal Corporation (district heating and cooling combined heat and power facilities)
Reliant Energy Texas Retail LLC
Texas Genco LP (power generation)
West Coast Power LLC (power generation)

Selected Mergers and Acquisitions

COMPETITORS

AEP	FirstEnergy
AES	Gexa Energy
Accent Energy	Integrys Energy
Alliant Energy	Services
Avista	Nicor Gas
Berkshire Hathaway	PG&E Corporation
Energy	PPL Corporation
Calpine	PSEG Power
Cogentrix Energy	Preferred Energy
Community Energy	Services
Direct Energy	SCANA
Duke Energy	Sempra Generation
Edison International	Tenaska
Entergy	

HISTORICAL FINANCIALS

Company Type: Public

Income Statement   FYE: December 31

	REVENUE ($ mil.)	NET INCOME ($ mil.)	NET PROFIT MARGIN	EMPLOYEES
12/19	9,821	4,438	45.2%	4,577
12/18	9,478	268	2.8%	4,862
12/17	10,629	(2,153)	—	5,940
12/16	12,351	(774)	—	8,763
12/15	14,674	(6,382)	—	10,468
Annual Growth	(9.6%)	—	—	(18.7%)

2019 Year-End Financials

Debt ratio: 47.01%
Return on equity: 2,093.40%
Cash ($ mil.): 377
Current ratio: 1.31
Long-term debt ($ mil.): 5,803

No. of shares (mil.): 249
Dividends
  Yield: 0.3%
  Payout: 3.0%
Market value ($ mil.): 9,898

	STOCK PRICE ($) FY Close	P/E High/Low		PER SHARE ($) Earnings	Dividends	Book Value
12/19	39.75	3	2	16.81	0.12	6.66
12/18	39.60	49	27	0.87	0.12	(4.35)
12/17	28.48	—	—	(6.79)	0.12	(1.09)
12/16	12.26	—	—	(2.22)	0.24	6.47
12/15	11.77	—	—	(19.46)	0.58	9.58
Annual Growth	35.6%			—	(32.6%)	(8.7%)

Nucor Corp.

Nucor Corporation is a leading manufacturer trader and seller of steel and steel products in the US. It is also North America's largest recycler of scrap metal and a leading scrap broker. The company produces rolled sheets bars and beams used in the energy automotive transportation and heavy equipment industries. Its other steel products including steel joists electrical conduits and metal building systems are sold to fabricators distributors and metal manufacturers. Subsidiary Harris Steel fabricates rebar for highways and bridges and other construction projects. Another unit the David J. Joseph Company processes and brokers metals pig iron hot briquetted iron and direct reduced iron (DRI).

HISTORY

Nucor started as the second carmaking venture of Ransom Olds who built his first gasoline-powered car in 1897. Two years later Samuel Smith a Detroit copper and lumber magnate put up $199600 to finance Olds Motor Works. A fire destroyed the company's Detroit plant in 1901 so Olds moved production to Lansing Michigan where he built America's first mass-produced car — the Oldsmobile. In 1904 Olds left Olds Motor Works which was bought by General Motors (GM) in 1908 and formed Reo Car Company (renamed Reo Motor Car in 1906). In addition to cars it eventually made trucks and buses.

By the end of the Depression Ford GM and Chrysler commanded over 85% of the US passenger car market. Reo stopped making cars in 1936 and sold its truck manufacturing operations in 1957. Meanwhile it had formed Reo

Holding which in 1955 merged with Nuclear Consultants to form Nuclear Corporation of America. The new company offered services such as radiation studies and made nuclear instruments and electronics.

In 1962 Nuclear bought steel joist maker Vulcraft and gained the services of Kenneth Iverson. The diverse company was unprofitable losing $2 million on $22 million in sales in 1965. That year Iverson took over as CEO moved headquarters to Charlotte North Carolina and shut down or sold about half of the company's businesses. By focusing on its profitable steel joist operations the firm ended 1966 in the black. Because the company depended on imports for 80% of its steel needs Iverson decided to move into steel production. Nuclear Corporation built its first minimill in 1969.

The company was renamed Nucor in 1972. It started making steel deck (1977) and cold-finished steel bars (1979). Production tripled and sales more than doubled between 1974 and 1979.

Nucor began to diversify adding grinding balls (used in the mining industry to process ores 1981); steel bolts steel bearings and machined steel parts (1986); and metal buildings and components (1987). Nucor and Japanese steelmaker Yamato Kogyo formed Nucor-Yamato and built a mill in 1988 to produce wide-flange beams (for heavy construction). The following year Nucor opened a state-of-the-art mill in Crawfordsville Indiana and another mill near Hickman Arkansas in 1992.

Iverson turned over his CEO duties to company veteran John Correnti in 1996. The next year Nucor began building a steel beam mill in South Carolina and added a galvanizing facility to its Hickman mill.

In 1998 Nucor announced plans to build its first steel plate mill which became operational in 2000. The company slashed prices twice in 1998 to compete against low-cost imports from Russia Japan and Brazil. Both sales and earnings declined that year due to low metal prices reduced shipments and start-up costs for new plants. The company raised its prices in 1999 and continued its expansion plans. Differences with the board prompted Correnti to resign in 1999; chairman David Aycock assumed his duties. In September 2000 Aycock resigned from the company and Daniel DiMicco formerly an EVP moved up to the rank of CEO.

Nucor along with Australia's Broken Hill Proprietary Corporation and Japan's Ishikawajima-Harima Heavy Industries began a joint venture in 2000 for its technology strip casting. The new technology allows steel production in smaller cheaper plants. In 2001 Nucor purchased a significant amount of assets of Auburn Steel a producer of merchant steel bar for $115 million.

In 2002 Nucor teamed up with Companhia Vale do Rio Doce (Vale) a Brazilian producer and exporter of iron-ore pellets to develop low-cost iron based products. That year Nucor purchased Alabama-based Trico Steel a steel sheet producer for approximately $116 million. In late 2002 Nucor bought financially troubled Birmingham Steel for $615 million in cash and debt.

Nucor Steel Kingman LLC a subsidiary of Nucor Corporation purchased the Kingman Arizona rebar and wire rod rolling unit of North Star Steel for around $35 million in 2003.

Its Vulcraft unit saw an increase in non-residential building construction in 2004 which boosted sales of joist girders steel deck and steel joists. Nucor bought Nucor Tuscaloosa in mid-2004 a producer of coiled plate with an annual capacity of around 700000 tons. The following year saw the company purchase Ohio's Marion Steel for approximately $110 million. The mill was added to Nucor's bar products line.

Record high prices in the industry (led by high demand throughout the world) led to record high sales in 2004. As a matter of fact Nucor's first half of the year outpaced previous annual highs and the company achieved that feat again in the second half.

The company named CEO DiMicco chairman in 2006.

In the latter half of the last decade it started a program of rapid external growth. It acquired the former Connecticut Steel Verco Manufacturing and Canadian steel products maker Harris Steel which like Connecticut Steel had been a customer and partner of Nucor for years. Harris itself made an acquisition in 2008 when it bought rebar fabricator and distributor Ambassador Steel. Nucor also expanded its downstream operations with the 2007 acquisition of building systems maker MAGNATRAX for $280 million. Its largest acquisition was that of the David J. Joseph Company a scrap metal broker that had supplied Nucor's minimills for 40 years.

The company has always operated primarily in the US but in 2008 it moved into the international market with the formation of a European joint venture with Duferco. The JV produces steel beams and merchant bar products from manufacturing locations in Italy and serves the European and North African markets. Nucor put about $650 million into the new venture called Nucor S.r.l. Duferdofin.

That year it also expanded considerably in the US by spending $1 billion to buy ferrous and nonferrous metals group The David J. Joseph Company.

In 2010 Nucor formed a US-based joint venture with Mitsui & Co. Nucor paid $225 million for its half of the venture named Steel Technologies.

In 2012 Nucor acquired New Jersey-based Skyline Steel and its subsidiaries from ArcelorMittal for about $605 million. Skyline which has served as a distributor of Nucor's products for more than 20 years accelerated Nucor's growth in steel piling and foundation products. Steel sheet piles are long structural sections having a vertical interlocking system that creates a wall. Skyline's flagship products include hot-rolled and cold-formed sheet piles and pipe piling. A steel foundation distributor in North America Skyline serves industries that include marine construction bridge and highway construction heavy civil construction and underground commercial parking.

In 2011 Nucor sold its NuPro Steel subsidiary to Steel Technologies its joint venture with Mitsui & Co. NuPro produces flat-rolled steel at its plant in Crawfordsville Indiana. Nucor also announced that Steel Technologies would build a steel processing plant in Mexico to serve Japanese electronics and auto companies moving into the region.

In early 2011 Nucor and joint venture partners Rio Tinto Group Mitsubishi and Shougang Corp. permanently closed the high-intensity smelt (hismelt) steel plant in Kwinana Western Australia. Nucor had a 25% stake in the joint venture that was terminated.

Continuing its strategy for key acquisitions in 2013 Nucor acquired Gallatin Steel for $780 million. This addition allowed the company to better serve customers by offering them a wider range of products and further enhancing our reliability. Nucor Steel Gallatin has an annual capacity of 1.8 million tons increasing Nucor's total flat-rolled production to 13 million tons annually. The acquisition also strengthens Nucor's position serving flat-rolled customers in the growing pipe and tube segment.

EXECUTIVES

Evp Flat-rolled Products, Ladd R. Hall, age 63, $463,100 total compensation

Vp; General Manager Sheet Mill Group (crawfordsville In), John J. Ferriola, age 67, $1,300,000 total compensation

Vp; General Manager Bar Mill Division (jewett Texas), James R. Darsey, age 64, $463,100 total compensation

Evp Raw Materials And Chief Digital Officer, R. Joseph Stratman, age 63, $473,914 total compensation

Evp Cfo And Treasurer, James D. (Jim) Frias, age 63, $490,350 total compensation

Evp Fabricated Construction Products, Raymond S. Napolitan, age 62

Evp Beam And Plate Products, D. Chad Utermark, age 52

Evp Engineered Bar Products, David A. Sumoski, age 53

Vice President And Gm, K Rex Query

Vice President; General Manager Bar Mill Division Plymouth Utah, David Smith

Vice President And General Manager Vulcraft Division Cold Finish Division, Doyle Hopper

Vice President General Manager, Drew Wilcox

Executive Vice President Beam Plate Products, Chad Utermark

Vp And Gm Nucor Steel Gallatin, John Farris

Vice President; Executive Vice President The David J. Joseph Company, James Goetz

Vice President General Manager Vulcraft Division Fort Payne Alabama, D Ryan

Vp And General Manager Vulcraft Division Cold Finish Division, Doyle Hopper Jr

Evp Engineered Bar Products, Ray Napolitan Jr

Executive Vice President Beam And Plate Products, Douglas Utermark

Board Member, John Walker

Board Member, Laurette Koellner

Board Member, Christopher Kearney

Board Member, Patrick Dempsey

Auditors: PricewaterhouseCoopers LLP

LOCATIONS

HQ: Nucor Corp.
1915 Rexford Road, Charlotte, NC 28211
Phone: 704 366-7000   **Fax:** 704 362-4208
Web: www.nucor.com

PRODUCTS/OPERATIONS

2018 Sales

	$ mil.	% of total
Steel Mills	16,245	65
Steel Products	6,796	27
Raw Materials	2,025	8
Total	**25,067**	**100**

2018 Sales by Product

	$ mil.	% of total
Sheet	7,571	30
Bar	4,709	19
Other Steel products	3,952	16
Plate	2,133	9
Raw Material	2,025	8
Structural	1,830	7
Rebar Fabrication	1,496	6
Tubular products	1,347	5
Total	**25,067**	**100**

Selected Products

Alloy steel
  Cold-drawn steel bars
  Finished hex caps
  Hex-head cap screws
  Locknuts
  Structural bolts and nuts
Carbon steel
  Angles
  Beams
  Channels
  Cold-drawn steel bars
  Finished hex nuts
  Flats
  Floor plate
  Galvanized sheet
  Grinding balls
  Hexagons
  Hot-rolled sheet
  Reinforcing bars
  Structural bolts and nuts
  Wide-range beams
Engineered products
  Composite floor joists
  Floor deck
  Joists
  Joist girders
  Pre-engineered metal buildings
  Roof deck
  Special-profile steel trusses
Stainless steel
  Cold-rolled steel
  Hot-rolled steel
  Pickled sheet

Selected Subsidiaries

Harris Steel Inc.
Harris Steel ULC (Canada)
The David J. Joseph Company
Magnatrax Corporation
Nucor Castrip Arkansas LLC
Nucor Energy Holdings Inc.
Nucor-Yamato Steel Company

COMPETITORS

AK Steel Holding Corporation	Renco
ArcelorMittal USA	Steel Dynamics
Arconic	Tata Europe
	United States Steel

HISTORICAL FINANCIALS

Company Type: Public

Income Statement — FYE: December 31

	REVENUE ($ mil.)	NET INCOME ($ mil.)	NET PROFIT MARGIN	EMPLOYEES
12/19	22,588	1,271	5.6%	26,800
12/18	25,067	2,360	9.4%	26,300
12/17	20,252	1,318	6.5%	25,100
12/16	16,208	796	4.9%	23,900
12/15	16,439	357	2.2%	23,700
Annual Growth	**8.3%**	**37.3%**	**—**	**3.1%**

2019 Year-End Financials

Debt ratio: 23.89%
Return on equity: 12.62%
Cash ($ mil.): 1,534
Current ratio: 3.34
Long-term debt ($ mil.): 4,291
No. of shares (mil.): 301
Dividends
Yield: 2.8%
Payout: 27.3%
Market value ($ mil.): 16,986

	STOCK PRICE ($) FY Close	P/E High/Low		PER SHARE ($) Earnings	Dividends	Book Value
12/19	56.28	15	11	4.14	1.60	34.32
12/18	51.81	9	7	7.42	1.54	32.04
12/17	63.58	16	13	4.10	1.51	27.48
12/16	59.52	27	14	2.48	1.50	24.72
12/15	40.30	45	33	1.11	1.49	23.33
Annual Growth	**8.7%**	**—**		**39.0%**	**1.8%**	**10.1%**

NVIDIA Corp

NVIDIA is racking up points in computer games logging miles in driverless cars and going deep into data centers. The Santa Clara California-based company's graphics processing units (GPUs) are used to generate computer game images in many PCs and game consoles in the gaming market. What's more its GPUs work well in applications for autonomous vehicles and deep learning a branch of artificial intelligence. NVIDIA's GPU brands are GeForce for games Quadro for designers and digital artists and Tesla and DGX for scientists and researchers. Its Tegra line of system-on-a-chip devices is for mobile gaming and entertainment as well as autonomous robots drones and cars. The company generates the most revenue in Taiwan. In 2019 NVIDIA agreed to buy chipmaker Mellanox for $6.9 billion.

Operations

NVIDIA operates in two reportable segments: GPU and Tegra Processor.

GPUs account for more than 85% of the company's revenue while the Tegra brand brings in about 15%. In terms of markets gaming produces over 50% of revenue followed by data centers over 25% visualization over 10% and automotive and intellectual property combined more than 10%.

The GPU products include GeForce for PC gaming and GeForce NOW for cloud-based game-streaming services; Quadro for computer-aided design video editing and special effects; Tesla for AI using deep learning and accelerated computing; GRID for providing NVIDIA graphics capabilities through the cloud and data centers; DGX for AI scientists researchers and developers; and EGX for accelerated AI computing at the edge.

The Tegra line includes DRIVE AGX automotive chip systems that provide self-driving capabilities; Clara AGX for medical instruments; Jetson AGX for robotics and other embedded use; and SHIELD which includes a family of devices and services for cloud-based mobile applications for home entertainment AI and gaming.

The company also develops software and software libraries for virtual reality called VRWorks which allows developers to create fully immersive experiences by enabling physically realistic visuals sound touch interactions and simulated environments.

NVIDIA outsources manufacturing to Taiwan Semiconductor Manufacturing Company Limited and Samsung Electronics Co. Ltd. The assembly testing and packaging work is done by independent subcontractors that include Advanced Semiconductor Engineering Inc. Amkor Technology BYD Auto Co. Hon Hai Precision Industry Co. and JSI Logistics Ltd.

Geographic Reach

NVIDIA based in Santa Clara California has more than 50 offices worldwide in the Americas Asia and Europe.

While almost 80% of NVIDIA's sales are to customers in Asia they are spread out over several countries. Customers in Taiwan generate nearly 30% of NVIDIA's revenue followed by customers in China with about 25% and other Asia/Pacific countries around 25%. The US market accounts for just under 10% of NVIDIA's sales.

Sales and Marketing

NVIDIA's sales and marketing team works with end customers and through partner networks that include original equipment manufacturers original device manufacturers system builders add-in board makers retailers and distributors internet and cloud service providers automotive manufacturers and tier-1 automotive suppliers mapping companies start-ups and other ecosystem participants. As part of its sales and marketing efforts NVIDIA offers rebates to resellers as incentives and it provides marketing development funds to help partners in promoting NVIDIA's products as well as their own.

As NVIDIA products have expanded beyond gaming applications the company has developed more routes to market and a wider more diverse customer roster. No customer accounts for more than 10% or more of sales.

Advertising expenses for fiscal years 2020 2019 and 2018 were $15 million $21 million and $25 million respectively.

Financial Performance

To say NVIDIA has been on a roll would be an understatement. Over the past five years the company's sales have risen 118% and profit has increased 355% driven by sales of chips for artificial intelligence data centers and more complex gaming applications.

In 2020 (ended January) revenue hit $10.9 billion an $800 million decrease from 2019 due to a decrease across all segments.

The Company's net income declined by 32% in 2020 compared to the previous year primarily due to R&D expenses.

Cash and cash equivalents spiked to $10.9 billion in 2020 from $780 million in 2019. Cash used in financing activities was $792 million while cash generated by investing activities was $6.1 billion in 2020. Cash generated by operations was $4.7 billion in 2020 compared to $3.7 billion the previous year.

Strategy

NVIDIA's key strategies consist of advancing the GPU computing platform; extending the company's technology and platform leadership in AI; extending the company's technology and platform leadership in visual computing; advancing the leading autonomous vehicle platform; and leveraging the company's intellectual property.

It takes a lot of computing power to render graphics capable of holding gamers' attention for hours at a time. In providing that power NVIDIA established itself as the dominant player in computer game graphics controlling more than 70% of the market. The company continues to turn out architectures and processors that generate realistic renderings of all kinds of games played on all kinds of platforms. The company sees potential for continued gaming growth in the rise of computer gaming as a spectator sport.

From its gaming base NVIDIA has positioned its GPUs for the artificial intelligence and automotive markets. The high processing power of GPUs enables them to handle the demands of artificial intelligence applications. The biggest cloud infrastructure providers ? Amazon Web Services Microsoft and Google ? use NVIDIA processors in their operations. GPUs also are used to turn analyzed information into graphics through visualization applications.

NVIDIA has plenty of competition with greater overall resources. AMD a long-time player in graphics has released processors recently that rival others in the market. Intel Corp. has used its deep resources to develop and buy technologies to compete in these markets including automotive with its acquisition of Mobileye. Although NVIDIA has grown rapidly over the past five years it cracked the list of Top 10 chipmakers for the first time in 2017.

Mergers and Acquisitions

NVIDIA agreed to buy Mellanox a maker of computer chips and other hardware for data center servers for $6.9 billion in 2019. The companies' say their combined forces will enable them to gain greater market share the growing market for equipping data centers as the use of cloud computing increases. Data center-related products generate about 20% of NVIDIA's sales. The transaction is expected to close by the end of 2019.

Company Background

Taiwan-born and Stanford-trained engineer Jen-Hsun Huang was already a veteran of Advanced Micro Devices and LSI Logic (now just LSI) when he decided to start his own company at age 30. He co-founded NVIDIA in 1992 with fellow engineers and industry veterans Chris Malachowsky (SVP) and Curtis Priem (former CTO). It was incorporated in 1993.

After its first try at a graphics chip failed miserably in 1995 NVIDIA hit the big time in 1997 when it introduced a graphics processor that set a new industry standard for speed. Good product timing and flawless execution kept the company growing: After turning its first profit in 1998 NVIDIA crossed the $100 million $300 million and $700 million sales thresholds in successive years. The company made its IPO in 1999.

EXECUTIVES

Senior Vice President Gpu Engineering, Jonah M Alben

President And Ceo, Jen-Hsun Huang, age 57, $996,216 total compensation

Evp Operations, Debora C. Shoquist, age 65, $695,131 total compensation

Evp Worldwide Field Operations, Ajay K. (Jay) Puri, age 65, $889,573 total compensation

Evp And Cfo, Colette M. Kress, age 52, $769,609 total compensation

Svp Content And Technology, Tony Tamasi

Vice President Supply Chain Projects, Brian Ebbs

Vice President, Alejandro Troccoli

Vice President Hardware Engineering, John Schafer

Vice President, Rajeev Jayavant

Vice President, Jim Vanwelzen

Vice President Software Engineering, Sam Azar

Senior Vice President, Ilyas Elkin

Executive Vice President Business Development, Alban Douillet

Vp Operations, David Miller

Vice President Automotive Software, Kevin Flory

Vice President Engineering, Laurent Coudrelle

Vice President Of Engineering, Luke Durant

Vice President Of The Investment Group, Shantanu Kalchuri

Vice President, Richard Cameron

Senior Vice President, Jizhi Zhang

National Sales Manager, James Reilley

Vp Internal Audit, Bruce Carpenter

Senior Vice President Vlsi Engineering, Joe Grech

Vice President Oem Sales, John Leggio

Vice President Software Security, Daniel Rohrer

Senior Vice President Geforce Business Unit, Jeff Fisher

Vice President Corporate Marketing, Rob Csonger

Vice President Of Engineering Computer Vision, Ashu Rege

Vice President Gpu Asic Engineering, Arjun Prabhu

Vice President, Rev Lebaredian

Evp Worldwide Field Operations, Jay Puri

Vice President Enterprise Sales, Mark Williams

Vice President Emeai, Jaap Zuiderveld

Senior Vice President Appliances, Ashok Almeida

Vice President Software, Richard Clark

Vice President Enterprise Marketing Corporate Communications And Global Events, Laura Fay

Vice President Operations Engineering, Keith Katcher

Vice President Corporate Communications, Robert Sherbin

Vice President Controller, Usman Ahmad

Vice President Of Investor Relations, Simona Jankowski

Vice President Systems Supply Chain, Jeff Whitmer

Area Vice President Enterprise Sales, Rima Alameddine

Vice President Product, John Fanelli

Vice President, Bratin Saha

Vice President Real Estate, Mike Demuro

Vice President And Treasurer, Chris Ginieczki

Consultant And Member Of The Board, James Forman

Board Member, Hyungon Ryu

Board Member, Mark Perry

Auditors: PricewaterhouseCoopers LLP

LOCATIONS

HQ: NVIDIA Corp
  2788 San Tomas Expressway, Santa Clara, CA 95051
Phone: 408 486-2000
Web: www.nvidia.com

2019 Sales

	$ mil.	% of total
Asia/Pacific		
Taiwan	3,360	29
China	2,801	24
Other Asia/Pacific	2,368	20
US	1,506	13
Europe	914	7
Other Countries	767	6
Total	**11,716**	**100**

PRODUCTS/OPERATIONS

2019 Sales

	$ mil.	% of total
GPU	10,175	87
Tegra Processor	1,541	13
Total	**11,716**	**100**

2019 sales by Market

	$ mil.	% of total
Gaming	6,246	53
Datacenter	2,932	25
Professional Visualization	1,130	10
OEM and IP	767	7
Automotive	641	5
Total	**11,716**	**100**

COMPETITORS

AMD	Renesas Electronics
Ambarella	Samsung Electronics
Intel	Texas Instruments
QUALCOMM	Xilinx

HISTORICAL FINANCIALS

Company Type: Public

Income Statement

FYE: January 26

	REVENUE ($ mil.)	NET INCOME ($ mil.)	NET PROFIT MARGIN	EMPLOYEES
01/20	10,918	2,796	25.6%	13,775
01/19	11,716	4,141	35.3%	13,277
01/18	9,714	3,047	31.4%	11,528
01/17	6,910	1,666	24.1%	10,299
01/16	5,010	614	12.3%	6,566
Annual Growth	21.5%	46.1%	—	20.4%

2020 Year-End Financials

Debt ratio: 11.50%
Return on equity: 26.03%
Cash ($ mil.): 10,896
Current ratio: 7.67
Long-term debt ($ mil.): 1,991
No. of shares (mil.): 612
Dividends
  Yield: 0.0%
  Payout: 14.1%
Market value ($ mil.): 153,294

	STOCK PRICE ($) FY Close	P/E High/Low		PER SHARE ($) Earnings	Dividends	Book Value
01/20	250.48	55	29	4.52	0.64	19.94
01/19	160.15	42	19	6.63	0.61	15.42
01/18	243.33	48	19	4.82	0.57	12.33
01/17	111.77	38	8	2.57	0.49	9.90
01/16	29.29	30	17	1.08	0.40	8.45
Annual Growth	71.0%	—	—	43.0%	12.8%	23.9%

NVR Inc.

From finished lot to signed mortgage NVR offers homebuyers everything?including the kitchen sink. The company builds single-family detached homes townhomes and condominiums?mainly for first-time and move-up buyers?primarily in the eastern US. NVR's houses range in size from 1000 sq. ft. to 9500 sq. ft. and sell for an average price of around $367100. The company's brands include Ryan Homes Heartland Homes and NVHomes. Its largest markets are the Washington DC and Baltimore areas; together they account for around 30% of sales. Its subsidiary NVR Mortgage Finance offers mortgage and title services. The builder was founded in 1980 as NVHomes.

Operations

NVR's Ryan Homes brand is primarily marketed to first-time and first-time move-up buyers. Ryan Homes has operations in more than thirty metropolitan areas along the eastern seaboard and in Illinois Indiana Ohio Pennsylvania Tennessee and West Virginia. NVHomes and Heartland Homes cater to move-up and luxury buyers. NVHomes builds primarily in Delaware and the Baltimore Philadelphia and DC metro areas; Heartland Homes operates in the Pittsburg metro. Homes sell for between $140000 and $1.5 million and at an average of roughly $367100. NVR engages independent subcontractors through fixed-price contracts for its home construction.

To support its homebuilding operations the company offers banking and title services through NVR Mortgage Finance.

Homebuilding accounts for substantially all the builder's total sales; its mortgage banking business?which closes more than 13000 loans totaling about $5.2 billion annually.

Geographic Reach

Reston Virginia-based NVR's homebuilding operations serve more than 30 metropolitan areas in some 15 states in the eastern half of the US. Home sales in the Mid-Atlantic (Maryland Virginia West Virginia Delaware and Washington DC) bring in about 55% of the builder's total sales while Mid-East states (New York Ohio Western Pennsylvania Indiana and Illinois) account for around 20%. The Southeast (North Carolina South Carolina Florida and Tennessee) and Northeast (New Jersey and eastern Pennsylvania) generate more than 15% and more than 5% of revenue respectively. Its largest markets are Washington DC?which produces more than 20% of homebuilding sales?and Baltimore?which provides some 10% of revenue.

Sales and Marketing

NVR markets its homes through sales representatives and model homes converted into temporary offices for salespeople to review alternative floor plans facades and designs for other house models with the client. Its houses are aimed at first-time first-time move-up and upscale buyers.

Financial Performance

NVR's sales boomed in recent years with an overall growth of 43% from $5.2 billion in 2015 to $7.4 billion in 2019. Between 2015 and 2019 its net income increased by more than 130%.

Despite a slight decrease in its homes' average selling price the homebuilder's revenue grew 3% to $7.2 billion in 2019 thanks to a 7% increase in units settled. The increase in the number of units settled was primarily attributable to a higher backlog turnover rate year over year.

NVR's net income added a whopping 10% to $878.5 million in 2019 thanks to the strength of its sales performance and a greatly lowered income tax expense slightly offset by a drop in gross profit margin of half a percentage point.

The company added $428.6 million to its cash to end the year with $1.2 billion. Operations provided $866.5 million. The company used only $13.3 million on investments?almost entirely on property plant and equipment. Treasury stock purchases pushed outflows from financing activities to $424.7 million.

Strategy

The company's lot acquisition strategy is predicated upon avoiding the financial requirements and risks associated with direct land ownership and development. They generally do not engage in land development. Instead they typically acquire finished lots at market prices from various third party land developers pursuant to Lot Purchase Agreements. These Lot Purchase Agreements require deposits typically ranging up to 10% of the aggregate purchase price of the finished lots in the form of cash or letters of credit that may be forfeited if they fail to perform under the Lot Purchase Agreement. This strategy has allowed them to maximize inventory turnover which they believe enables them to minimize market risk and to operate with less capital thereby enhancing rates of return on equity and total capital.

Company Background

NVR expanded its portfolio of homebuilding companies in late 2012 when it acquired Heartland Homes the second largest homebuilder in Pittsburgh. NVR continues to use the Heartland Homes name.

HISTORY

NVR got its start when Dwight Schar founded NVHomes Inc. in 1980. Schar had worked for Ryan Homes (founded 1948) since 1969. Like Ryan Homes NVHomes specialized in single-family homes around Washington DC. The strong economy of the 1980s and the deregulation of lending institutions — coupled with favorable partnership and real estate tax laws passed by the Reagan administration — resulted in rapid growth. The company was clearing income of more than $1 million a year by 1983 and soon branched into building townhomes and condominiums.

In 1986 when the company was reorganized as a limited partnership (NVH L.P.) income was up to $14 million. The new entity soon acquired a controlling interest in Ryan Homes; it completed its acquisition of that company in 1987. NVH reorganized as a holding company (NVRyan L.P.) and 1988 profits reached $33.5 million. Over the years the company formed or acquired almost 100 subsidiaries that were involved in all aspects of homebuilding — from land acquisition and construction to home finance and investment advice. It had also branched out into California Florida Indiana Kentucky North Carolina Ohio Pennsylvania and Virginia.

Following an economic recession in 1989 demand for new housing dropped off in the US. The company shortened its name to NVR L.P. and its inventory of unsold land and houses started to grow. The situation was exacerbated by changes in the tax code that made real estate less attractive as an investment; sales from development and construction projects dropped from more than $1 billion in 1988 to about $600 million in 1991. NVR posted a $260 million loss in 1990 as sales and the value of its inventory nose-dived.

NVR reorganized in 1990 and 1991. Focused on eight mid-Atlantic states it put homebuilding under one management structure consolidated its finance activities exited its land-development businesses and offered its mortgage services to customers who weren't NVR homebuyers. It also organized its business into two product lines: upscale (NVHomes) and moderately priced (Ryan Homes) homes. Despite the reorganization and introduction of innovative marketing NVR and several of its subsidiaries filed for Chapter 11 bankruptcy relief in 1992. That year the CFO of NVR's thrift (NVR Savings Bank) went on the lam to Malta after embezzling more than $750000.

The company emerged from bankruptcy as NVR Inc. in 1993 with less debt new owners and a new line of credit; it also had its IPO that year. The next year NVR sold NVR Savings Bank which had four branches in northern Virginia. The robust mid-1990s economy aided NVR; as home sales rose the company entered new markets including the Cleveland and Nashville areas in 1995. To reduce its vulnerability to downturns in the mid-Atlantic area it continued its expansion outside that region buying Fox Ridge Homes (the #2 builder in Nashville) in 1997.

In 1999 it merged its homebuilding subsidiary NVR Homes and mortgage banking holding company NVR Financial Services into NVR. It also acquired Rockville Maryland-based First Republic Mortgage that year but closed the subsidiary's retail operations in 2000 and realigned its mortgage banking business to serve NVR customers exclusively.

From 1994 through 2003 the company benefited from increased housing activity recording steady increases in unit sales backlog and profits for nine years. During the housing downturn that began in 2008 the company performed better than its competitors reporting only one losing quarter in the period.

In late 2012 NVR expanded its portfolio of home-building companies when it acquired Heartland Homes the second-largest homebuilder in Pittsburgh. As part of the purchase NVR planned to continue to use the Heartland Homes name and pair the company with its complementary Ryan Homes.

EXECUTIVES

President Ceo And Director, Paul C. Saville, age 64, $1,566,375 total compensation
President Nvr Mortgage (nvrm), Robert W. Henley, age 53, $460,000 total compensation
Vp Cfo And Treasurer, Daniel D. Malzahn, age 50, $490,000 total compensation
Vp Chief Accounting Officer And Controller, Eugene J. Bredow, $341,250 total compensation
President Homebuilding Operations, Jeffrey D. Martchek, age 55, $539,000 total compensation
Chairman, Dwight C. Schar, age 78
Auditors: KPMG LLP

LOCATIONS

HQ: NVR Inc.
11700 Plaza America Drive, Suite 500, Reston, VA 20190
Phone: 703 956-4000
Web: www.nvrinc.com

O'Reilly Automotive, Inc.

O'Reilly Automotive has its foot on the gas. One of the largest specialty retailers of automotive aftermarket parts (both new and remanufactured) maintenance supplies professional service equipment tools and accessories. It also offers customers a range of services including oil and battery recycling battery testing paint mixing tool rental drum and rotor resurfacing electric and module testing battery wiper and bulb replacement and check engine light code extraction. O'Reilly operates through a fast-growing network of more than 5400 stores across the US more than 20 in Mexico as well as online. The family-founded and -operated company wheels and deals with automotive professionals as well as DIY (do-it-yourself) customers.

Operations

O'Reilly currently operates nearly 30 regional DCs which provide their stores with same-day or overnight access to an average of about 160000 stock keeping units. They also operates more than 355 Hub stores that also provide delivery service and same-day access to an average of approximately 70000 SKUs from a Super Hub or more than 40000 SKUs from a Hub to other stores within the surrounding area.

Its products include nationally-known premium brands such as AC Delco Castrol Pennnzoil Turtle Wax and Valvoline as well as private-label brands such as BrakeBest Murray O'Reilly and Ultima.

Beyond its vast array of products O'Reilly's offers a host of services battery diagnostic testing battery wiper and bulb replacement check engine light code extraction custom hydraulic hoses drum and rotor resurfacing electrical and module testing loaner tool program machine shops professional paint shop mixing used oil oil filter and battery recycling.

Geographic Reach

With its headquarter in Missouri O'Reilly also operate stores in more than 45 US states including Texas California Florida and Georgia that accounts for more than 730 550 230 and 200 stores respectively. O'Reilly also operates in more than 20 stores in Mexico.

The company has nearly 30 distribution centers that are located in more than 25 states. They also acquired six small distribution centers in Mexico from the Mayasa acquisition.

Sales and Marketing

O'Reilly generates more than 50% of sales from DIY (do-it-yourself) customers and more than 40% of sales from professional service providers. It also sells automotive products directly to independently owned parts stores ("jobber stores") in certain markets.

The company maintains a full-time sales staff of more than 800. Marketing their business through national media channels in-store digital and social media activation as well as automotive event sponsorships and on-site appearances throughout the country. They also target Spanish-speaking market through radio print and sports marketing as well as sponsorships of local and regional events.

The company spend nearly $80 million for advertising expenses in fiscal 2019.

Financial Performance

O'Reilly's revenue and net income have both seen strong growth over the past five years. Between 2015 and 2019 O'Reilly's revenue rose by 27% while net income rose by 49%. The company has greatly expanded its store network during that time.

In 2019 the company reported record revenue of $10.1 billion an increase of $614 million or 6% from the prior year. The results were powered by comparable-store sales growth of 4% driven by an increase in average ticket values for both DIY and professional service provider customers.

Net income also rose that year jumping 5% to $1.4 billion. In addition to increased revenue the growth in net income resulted from an increase in gross profit of 7% from the prior year driven by sales from new stores and increase sales in comparable stores.

Cash at the end of 2019 was $40.4 million an increase of $9 million from the prior year. Cash from operations contributed $1.7 billion to the coffers while investing activities used $796.7 million mainly for purchases of property and equipment. Financing activities used another $902.8 million primarily for stock repurchase.

Strategy

O'Reilly adheres to a "dual market" strategy by appealing to both do-it-yourself (DIY) and professional service providers. The company believes that this strategy is a unique competitive advantage as it enables them to compete by targeting a larger base of automotive aftermarket parts consumers capitalized their existing retail and distribution infrastructure operates profitably in both large markets and less densely populated geographic areas and enhanced the service levels they offer to their DIY customers through the offering of a broad inventory and the extensive product knowledge.

More than ever before customers' purchase decisions are informed by a range of interactions whether in-person over the phone or through a variety of digital channels. O'Reilly's Omnichannel growth strategies are focused on offering their customers an enhanced and seamless research and buying experience through their websites including www.OReillyAuto.com and www.FirstCallOnline.com. They believe that the functionality and features of their digital sites complements the outstanding customer service provided in their over 5400 brick and mortar locations.

O'Reilly's aggressive expansion has been a key element of its growth. During 2019 the company opened 200 net new domestic stores as well as 20 net additional stores from the Bennett Auto Supply Inc. acquisition and 21 additional stores from the Mayasa acquisition. In 2020 O'Reilly is planning to open approximately 180 net new stores which will increase their penetration in existing markets and allow for expansion into new contiguous markets.

Mergers and Acquisitions

In 2019 O'Reilly Automotive Inc. completed an acquisition with Mayoreo de Autopartes y Aceites S.A. de C.V. ("Mayasa") a specialty retailer of automotive aftermarket parts headquartered in Guadalajara Jalisco Mexico. At the time of the acquisition Mayasa operated six distribution centers more than 20 Orma Autopartes stores and served over 2000 independent jobber locations in nearly 30 Mexican states.

Company Background

O'Reilly was founded in 1957 by Charles F. O'Reilly and his son "Chub." It opened a second store in 1965.

In 1978 the company introduced its dual strategy of serving both the professional and DIY retail markets. By 1989 it had 100 stores.

The company went public in 1993 and nearly doubled its size with the 1998 purchase of rival Hi/Lo Auto Supply.

O'Reilly opened its 5000th store in 2017.

EXECUTIVES

President And Ceo, Gregory L. (Greg) Henslee, age 59, $1,238,461 total compensation

Co-president, Jeff M. Shaw, age 57, $396,923 total compensation

Evp Finance And Cfo, Thomas G. (Tom) McFall, age 49, $713,846 total compensation

Evp Supply Chain, Gregory D. (Greg) Johnson, age 54, $342,308 total compensation

Svp Information Systems, Jeff Lauro

Svp Finance And Controller, Jeremy Fletcher

Vice President Northern Division, Kenny Martin

Senior Vice President Merchandise And Marketing, Mike Swearengin

Vice Chairman, Lawrence P. (Larry) O'Reilly, age 73

Vice Chairman, Charles H. O'Reilly, age 81

Chairman, David E. O'Reilly, age 71

Auditors: Ernst & Young LLP

LOCATIONS

HQ: O'Reilly Automotive, Inc.
233 South Patterson Avenue, Springfield, MO 65802
Phone: 417 862-6708
Web: www.oreillyauto.com

2018 Stores

	No.
Texas	706
California	553
Missouri	201
Georgia	205
Illinois	203
Ohio	196
Florida	200
Tennessee	176
Michigan	168
North Carolina	173
Washington	156
Arizona	139
Alabama	139
Oklahoma	121
Indiana	137
Minnesota	125
Wisconsin	121
Louisiana	121
Arkansas	112
Colorado	102
South Carolina	108
Other states	1,057
Total	**5,219**

PRODUCTS/OPERATIONS

2018 Sales

	$ mil.	% of total
DIY customers	5,351	56
Professional customers	4,035	42
Other	149	2
Total	**9,536**	**100**

Selected Products

Accessories - Exterior
Accessories - Interior
Air Conditioning
Battery & Accessories
Belts & Hoses
Body & Trim
Brakes
Charging & Starting
Cooling & Heating
Engine Parts & Mounts
Exhaust
Filters & PCV Valves
Fuel & Emissions
Hardware & Fasteners
Ignition & Tune-Up
Lighting & Electrical
Oil Fluids & Chemicals
Performance
Suspension & Steering
Tire & Wheel
Tools & Equipment
Transmission & Transaxle
Truck & Towing
Waxes & Washes
Wipers

COMPETITORS

Advance Auto Parts	Pep Boys
Amazon.com	Replacement Parts
AutoZone	Target Corporation
CARQUEST	U.S. Auto Parts
Genuine Parts	Wal-Mart

HISTORICAL FINANCIALS

Company Type: Public

Income Statement   FYE: December 31

	REVENUE ($ mil.)	NET INCOME ($ mil.)	NET PROFIT MARGIN	EMPLOYEES
12/19	10,149	1,391	13.7%	82,167
12/18	9,536	1,324	13.9%	79,174
12/17	8,977	1,133	12.6%	75,289
12/16	8,593	1,037	12.1%	74,715
12/15	7,966	931	11.7%	71,943
Annual Growth	**6.2%**	**10.6%**	**—**	**3.4%**

2019 Year-End Financials

Debt ratio: 36.30%
Return on equity: 370.45%
Cash ($ mil.): 40
Current ratio: 0.86
Long-term debt ($ mil.): 3,890

No. of shares (mil.): 75
Dividends
  Yield: —
  Payout: —
Market value ($ mil.): 33,141

	STOCK PRICE ($) FY Close	P/E High/Low		PER SHARE ($) Earnings	Dividends	Book Value
12/19	438.26	25	19	17.88	0.00	5.25
12/18	344.33	22	14	16.10	0.00	4.47
12/17	240.54	22	13	12.67	0.00	7.75
12/16	278.41	27	21	10.73	0.00	17.52
12/15	253.42	30	19	9.17	0.00	20.07
Annual Growth	**14.7%**	**—**	**—**	**18.2%**	**—**	**(28.5%)**

Occidental Petroleum Corp

Harnessing its heritage of Western technical know-how Occidental Petroleum engages in oil and gas exploration and production and makes basic chemicals and vinyls.. It boasts proved reserves of around 3.8 billion barrels of oil equivalent primarily from assets in the US the Middle East North Africa and Latin America. Subsidiary Occidental Chemical (OxyChem) produces caustic soda chlorine and chlorinated isocyanurates and ranks in the top three producer of polyvinyl chloride (PVC) resin in the United States. Occidental Petroleum's midstream and marketing units purchase gather process transport store and market crude oil natural gas NGLs condensate and CO_2 and generate and market power. In 2019 it acquired Anadarko for $55 billion.

HISTORY

Founded in 1920 Occidental Petroleum struggled until 1956 when billionaire industrialist Dr. Armand Hammer sank $100000 into the company then worth $34000. It drilled two wells and both came in. Hammer eventually gained control of the company.

Occidental's discovery of California's second-largest gas field (1959) was followed by a concession from Libya's King Idris (1966) and the discovery of a billion-barrel Libyan oil field. In 1968 Occidental bought Signal Oil's European refining and marketing business as an outlet for the Libyan oil. It also diversified buying Island Creek Coal and Hooker Chemical.

In 1969 Occidental sold 51% of its Libyan production to the Libyan government under duress after Idris was ousted. (It suspended operations there in 1986). It soon began oil exploration in Latin America (1971) and in the North Sea (1972-73) where it discovered the lucrative Piper field. Other projects included a 20-year fertilizer-for-ammonia deal with the USSR (1974) and a coal joint venture with China (1985).

During the 1980s Occidental sold some foreign assets and bought US natural gas pipeline firm MidCon (1986). It also bought Iowa Beef Processors (IBP) for stock worth $750 million (1981) and then spun off 49% of it in 1987 for $960 million.

In 1983 Hammer hired Ray Irani to revive Occidental's ailing chemicals business (losses that year: $38 million). Irani integrated operations to ensure higher margins during industry downturns and purchased Diamond Shamrock Chemicals (1986) Shell's vinyl chloride monomer unit (1987) a DuPont chloralkali facility (1987) and Cain Chemical (1988). OxyChem's profits reached almost $1.1 billion by 1989.

Hammer died in 1990 and Irani became CEO. In 1991 to reduce debt Occidental exited the Chinese coal business and sold the North Sea oil properties. Occidental also spun off IBP the largest US red-meat producer to its shareholders.

Occidental paid Irani $95 million in 1997 to buy out his employment contract; instead his compensation (a minimum of $1.2 million a year) was tied to the company's fortunes. That year Occidental's $3.65 billion bid won the US government's auction of its 78% stake in California's Elk Hills petroleum reserve one of the largest in the continental US.

To help pay for Elk Hills the company sold MidCon to K N Energy for $3.1 billion in 1998. Occidental traded its petrochemical operations to Equistar Chemicals a partnership between Lyondell (now LyondellBasell) and Millennium Chemicals for $425 million and a 29.5% stake.

In a venture with The Geon Company Occidental in 1999 formed Oxy Vinyls the #1 producer of polyvinyl chloride (PVC) resin in North America. That year also brought a windfall: Chevron agreed to pay Occidental $775 million to settle a lawsuit stemming from the 1982 withdrawal by Gulf (later acquired by Chevron) of an offer to buy Cities Service (later acquired by Occidental).

In 2000 Occidental sold its 29% stake in Canadian Occidental back to the company for $828 million to help fund the purchase of oil and gas producer Altura Energy a partnership of BP and

Shell Oil for $3.6 billion. Later that year the company sold some Gulf of Mexico properties to Apache for $385 million.

Occidental acquired a new exploration block in Yemen in 2001. The next year it sold its 30% of Equistar Chemicals to Lyondell in exchange for a 21% stake in Lyondell. In 2005 it acquired a stake in a gas and oil production site located in Texas' Permian Basin from ExxonMobil for a reported $972 million. Occidental closed the acquisition of Vintage Petroleum for a reported $3.8 billion in early 2006.

The government of Ecuador seized Occidental Petroleum's Ecuadorian assets in 2006 as part of a nationalization drive. That year Plains Exploration and Production sold non-core oil and gas properties to Occidental for $865 million.

Also in 2006 Occidental reduced its stake in Lyondell from 12% to 8%. The following year Occidental sold its remaining Lyondell shares on the open market.

In North America in 2008 the company bought a 15% stake in the Joslyn Oil Sands project for nearly $500 million. That project is based in Alberta Canada and is operated by Total.

The company re-entered Libya in 2008.

Beefing up its investment vehicles in 2009 the company purchased Citigroup's commodities trading unit (Philbro LLC).

To raise cash to pay down debt in 2011 the company sold its Argentina-based assets to China Petrochemical for $2.45 billion. The deal helped cover some of the costs of Occidental's $3.4 billion acquisition (in late 2010 and early 2011) of safer US-based assets — oil and gas properties in South Texas and North Dakota.

In the US in 2012 Occidental paid $2.3 billion for oil and gas properties in the Permian Basin Williston Basin South Texas and California.

That year Occidental and Magellan Midstream Partners L.P. formed BridgeTex Pipeline Company LLC (BridgeTex) to build the 450-mile-long BridgeTex Pipeline to transport 300000 barrels per day of crude oil between the Permian region and the Gulf Coast refinery markets.

In 2013 OxyChem and Mexichem formed a 50/50 joint venture Ingleside Ethylene LLC to build a 1.2-billion-pound per year capacity ethylene cracker at the OxyChem plant in Ingleside Texas along with pipelines and storage at Markham Texas. As part of a long-term strategic supply relationship between the companies essentially all of the ethylene produced from the cracker will be consumed in the manufacture of vinyl chloride monomer (VCM) utilizing existing VCM capacity. VCM will be delivered to Mexichem to produce polyvinyl chloride (PVC) and PVC piping systems.

Growing it assets in 2013 the company and Qatar Petroleum agreed on the Phase 5 Field Development Plan of the Idd El Shargi North Dome Field offshore Qatar. The project will sustain oil production levels at about 100000 barrels per day through 2019. (In 2011 Occidental also teamed up with ADNOC to develop the major Shah gas field in the UAE).

In 2013 the company paid approximately $500 million to acquire various US-based oil and gas properties.

EXECUTIVES

Svp And Cfo, Cedric W. Burgher, age 60

Svp General Counsel And Chief Compliance Officer, Marcia E. Backus, age 65, $646,970 total compensation

Evp And Group Chairman - Middle East, Edward A. (Sandy) Lowe, age 68, $625,000 total compensation

Svp Marketing And Midstream Operations And Development, Cynthia L. Walker, age 44, $600,000 total compensation

President Ceo And Director, Vicki A. Hollub, age 60, $1,143,314 total compensation

Vp And Cio, Ioannis A. Charalambous

Svp And President Oxy Oil And Gas Domestic, Joseph C. Elliott, age 62

Svp And President Occidental Chemical Corporation, Robert L. Peterson

Medical Director, Jose Cristancho

Vice President U.s. Oil Marketing Permian Basin And Hugoton, Steven Rafferty

Vp And Principal Accounting Officer, Jennifer Kirk

Vice President Business Development, Kevin Pilkington

Vice President Health Environment Safety And Security, Wesley Scott

Vice President Government Relations, Ian Davis

Vice President Exploration And Geoscience, Pedro Romero

Vice President Worldwide Drilling And Completions, Brenda Harris

Vice President Business Analyst, Eric Wynia

Vice President, Sylvia Low

Executive Vice President, Robert Williams

National Sales Manager, Keith Benn

Executive Vp Commodities, Mary Andrews

Chairman, Eugene L. (Gene) Batchelder, age 72

Secretary, Melanie Rome

Secretary Ii, Elvenia Jackson

Auditors: KPMG LLP

LOCATIONS

HQ: Occidental Petroleum Corp
5 Greenway Plaza, Suite 110, Houston, TX 77046
Phone: 713 215-7000
Web: www.oxy.com

2018 Sales

	% of total
US	71
Qatar	9
Oman	9
United Arab Emirates	5
Colombia	4
Other countries	2
Total	**100**

PRODUCTS/OPERATIONS

2018 Sales

	$ mil.	% of total
Oil & gas	10,441	56
Chemicals	4,657	25
Midstream marketing & other	3,656	19
Eliminations	(930)	
Total		100

Selected Subsidiaries

Occidental Chemical Corp. (OxyChem; chemicals polymers and plastics)
   Oxy Vinyls LP (76% polyvinyl chloride)
Occidental Energy Marketing Inc. (energy marketing)
Occidental Exploration and Production Company (exploration and production)

COMPETITORS

Apache	Huntsman International
Ashland	Imperial Oil
BP	J.M. Huber
Chevron	Koch Industries Inc.
ConocoPhillips	Marathon Oil
Devon Energy	Olin
Dow Chemical	PEMEX

Eastman Chemical	Royal Dutch Shell
Exxon Mobil	Sunoco
Hess Corporation	TOTAL

HISTORICAL FINANCIALS

Company Type: Public

Income Statement

FYE: December 31

	REVENUE ($ mil.)	NET INCOME ($ mil.)	NET PROFIT MARGIN	EMPLOYEES
12/19	21,232	(667)	—	14,400
12/18	18,934	4,131	21.8%	11,000
12/17	13,274	1,311	9.9%	11,000
12/16	10,398	(574)	—	11,000
12/15	12,699	(7,829)	—	11,100
Annual Growth	13.7%	—		6.7%

2019 Year-End Financials

Debt ratio: 35.29%
Return on equity: (-2.40%)
Cash ($ mil.): 3,032
Current ratio: 1.25
Long-term debt ($ mil.): 38,537

No. of shares (mil.): 894
Dividends
  Yield: 7.6%
  Payout: —
Market value ($ mil.): 36,846

	STOCK PRICE ($) FY Close	P/E High/Low		PER SHARE ($) Earnings	Dividends	Book Value
12/19	41.21	— —		(1.22)	3.14	38.29
12/18	61.38	16 11		5.39	3.10	28.46
12/17	73.66	43 34		1.70	3.06	26.89
12/16	71.23	— —		(0.75)	3.02	28.13
12/15	67.61	— —		(10.23)	2.97	31.89
Annual Growth	(11.6%)	— —			1.4%	4.7%

OceanFirst Financial Corp

Ask the folks at OceanFirst Bank for a home loan and they might say "shore." The subsidiary of holding company OceanFirst Financial operates 25 branches in the coastal New Jersey counties of Middlesex Monmouth and Ocean. The community-oriented bank caters to individuals and small to midsized businesses in the Jersey Shore area offering standard products such as checking and savings accounts CDs and IRAs. It uses funds from deposits mainly to invest in mortgages loans and securities. One- to four-family residential mortgages make up more than half of OceanFirst Financial's loan portfolio which also includes commercial real estate (about 30%) business construction and consumer loans.

Operations

The Bank's principal business is attracting deposits from the general public in the communities surrounding its branch offices and investing those deposits primarily in single-family owner-occupied residential mortgage loans and commercial real estate loans. It active subsidiaries include OceanFirst Services LLC OceanFirst REIT Holdings Inc. and 975 Holdings LLC.

Geographic Reach

OceanFirst has operations in the New Jersey counties of Middlesex Monmouth and Ocean.

Financial Performance

OceanFirst's revenues dropped by 4% in 2012 due to decrease in loans and mortgage-backed securities partially offset by higher revenues from investment securities and other.

Net income declined by 3% in 2012 due to an increase in provision for loan losses and non-interest expenses (higher professional fees).

Strategy

OceanFirst seeks to grow commercial loans receivable by offering commercial lending services to local businesses; grow core deposits through broader product offerings andbranch expansion; and increase non-interest income by expanding its fee-based products and services.

Part of the company's strategy for growth includes expanding its fee-based offerings. The bank for example offers trust and asset management services. Company subsidiary OceanFirst Services sells mutual funds annuities and insurance products from third-party vendors. OceanFirst is also seeking opportunities to grow by opening new branch locations within its existing markets.

In 2013 the Bank opened a full service Financial Solutions Center in Red Bank New Jersey offering deposit lending and asset management services. It also opened an additional branch office in Jackson New Jersey.

Since 1995 OceanFirst has opened sixteen branch offices (twelve in Ocean County and four in Monmouth County).

Mergers and Acquisitions

In January 2016 OceanFirst Financial agreed to buy Cape Bancorp— along with its 22 branches in central and southern New Jersey counties $1.1 billion in loans and $1.3 billion in deposits — for $208.1 million. The deal would grow OceanFirst's total total assets by over 60% and nearly double the size of its branch network.

Company Background

OceanFirst Bank's employee stock option plan owns more than 10% of OceanFirst Financial's shares. The company's charitable foundation OceanFirst Foundation owns 7%.

The Bank was founded as a state-chartered building and loan association in 1902. It converted to a Federal savings and loan association in 1945 and became a Federally-chartered mutual savings bank in 1989.

EXECUTIVES

Evp And Cfo, Michael J. Fitzpatrick, age 63, $285,577 total compensation

Evp And Chief Administrative Officer, Joseph R. Iantosca, age 58, $284,808 total compensation

Evp And Chief Lending Officer, Joseph J. Lebel, age 56, $284,808 total compensation

First Svp General Counsel And Corporate Secretary, Steven J. Tsimbinos, $252,798 total compensation

Chairman President And Ceo, Christopher D. Maher, age 52, $566,346 total compensation

Vice President It, Elizabeth Alexander

Senior Vice President, Sharon Danielson

Vice President Secondary Marketing Manager, Anthony Cecchetto

Vice President Bank Counsel, Denise Horner

Assistant Vice President Oceanfirst Bank, Karen Rack

Vice President Loan Servicing Operations Manager, Christine Schiess

Assistant Vice President, Barbara Wright

Senior Vice President And Director Human Resources, Anne Johnson

Senior Vice President Director Of Human Resources, Gary Hett

Senior Vice President And Team Leader, Brad Fouss

Assistant Vice President Information Technology Service Manager, Vicki Cannizzaro

Assistant Vice President Project Manager, David Mowder

Assistant Vice President Collections Department, Karen Farrell

Vice President Senior Marketing Officer Strategy, Lisa Natale

Senior Vice President Loan Servicing, Janet Bossi

Auditors: KPMG LLP

LOCATIONS

HQ: OceanFirst Financial Corp
110 West Front Street, Red Bank, NJ 07701
Phone: 732 240-4500
Web: www.oceanfirst.com

PRODUCTS/OPERATIONS

2016 sales

	$ mil.	% of total
Interest Income		
Loans	123	80
Mortgage-backed securities	6	4
Investment securities & other	3	2
Non-interest		
Bankcard services revenue	4	3
Wealth management revenue	2	2
Fees & service charges	10	7
Loan Servicing income	0	-
Net gains on sales of loans	1	1
Net loss from other real estate operations	(0.9)	-
Income from Bank owned Life Insurance	2	1
Other	0	-
Total	153	100

COMPETITORS

Bank of America	PNC Financial
Cape Bancorp	Sovereign Bank
Citibank	TD Bank USA
Hudson City Bancorp	Valley National
Investors Bancorp	Bancorp
JPMorgan Chase	

HISTORICAL FINANCIALS

Company Type: Public

Income Statement				FYE: December 31
	ASSETS ($ mil.)	NET INCOME ($ mil.)	INCOME AS % OF ASSETS	EMPLOYEES
12/19	8,246	88	1.1%	924
12/18	7,516	71	1.0%	892
12/17	5,416	42	0.8%	684
12/16	5,167	23	0.4%	797
12/15	2,593	20	0.8%	393
Annual Growth	33.5%	44.5%	—	23.8%

2019 Year-End Financials

Debt ratio: 1.17%	No. of shares (mil.): 50
Return on equity: 8.08%	Dividends
Cash ($ mil.): 120	Yield: 2.6%
Current ratio: —	Payout: 36.9%
Long-term debt ($ mil.): —	Market value ($ mil.): 1,287

	STOCK PRICE ($) FY Close	P/E High/Low	PER SHARE ($) Earnings	Dividends	Book Value
12/19	25.54	15 12	1.75	0.68	22.88
12/18	22.51	20 14	1.51	0.62	21.68
12/17	26.25	23 18	1.28	0.60	18.47
12/16	30.03	30 16	0.98	0.54	17.80
12/15	20.03	17 13	1.21	0.52	13.79
Annual Growth	6.3%	— —	9.7%	6.9%	13.5%

OCHSNER CLINIC FOUNDATION

EXECUTIVES

Ceo-Pres, Patrick J Quinlan
Exec V Pres-Dir of Fin, B C Brannon
Project Consultant, Sandy Warren
Endocrinology, Anita Richard
Executive Vice President, Bobby Brannon
Pulmonary Critical Care, Stephen Kantrow
Nurse, Bonnie Foto
Director of Supply Chain, Clifford C Harlan
Referral Coordinator, Denise Usand
Rn, Dennis Pfefferle
Coordinator, Natalie Rodriguez
Auditors: ERNST & YOUNG US LLP FORT WOR

LOCATIONS

HQ: OCHSNER CLINIC FOUNDATION
2614 JEFFERSON HWY, JEFFERSON, LA 701213828
Phone: 504 842-3000
Web: WWW.OCHSNER.ORG

HISTORICAL FINANCIALS

Company Type: Private

Income Statement				FYE: December 31
	REVENUE ($ mil.)	NET INCOME ($ mil.)	NET PROFIT MARGIN	EMPLOYEES
12/17	8,405	128	1.5%	10,500
12/14	2,196	(16)		—
12/13	5,550	52	0.9%	—
12/12	4,829	12	0.3%	—
Annual Growth	11.7%	60.1%	—	—

ODP Corp (The)

Paper and pens have made room for PC repair and point-of-sale services at office products giant Office Depot (#3 worldwide behind Amazon and Staples). The office supply chain operates over 1300 retail stores under the Office Depot and OfficeMax names through which it sells a wide selection of office supplies furniture printers and breakroom and cleaning products. It has also moved into IT support and other business-to-business services which it offers through CompuCom and other brands. Office Depot operates entirely in North America.

HISTORY

Pat Scher Stephen Dougherty and Jack Kopkin opened the first Office Depot one of the first office supply superstores in Lauderdale Lakes Florida in 1986. Scher was selected as chairman. By the end of the year the fledgling company had opened two more stores (both in Florida).

Office Depot opened seven more stores in 1987. When Scher died of leukemia that year the company recruited David Fuente former president of Sherwin-Williams' Paint Store Division as chairman and CEO. Office Depot continued its breakneck expansion under Fuente. In 1988 — the year the company went public — it opened 16 stores and broke into new markets in four states.

The chain stepped up its pace and by 1990 it had expanded into several other areas including the South and Midwest. Office Depot also added computers and peripherals and opened its first delivery center.

In 1991 the company became North America's #1 office products retailer and expanded its presence in the West through the acquisition of Office Club another warehouse-type office supply chain with 59 stores (most in California). Fuente remained chairman and CEO while former Office Club CEO Mark Begelman became president and COO. (Begelman who left in 1995 and eventually formed the MARS music chain had founded the first Office Club in 1987 in Concord California; he took it public in 1989.)

The company entered the international market with its 1992 purchase of Canada's H. Q. Office International and through licensing agreements in 1993 (in Colombia and Israel). Office Depot created its business services division by acquiring various contract stationers including Eastman Office Products (the West Coast's #1 contract office supplier) in the mid-1990s and added locations in Mexico and Poland; it established a joint venture in France with retailer Carrefour in 1996.

Also in 1996 Office Depot announced a $3.4 billion agreement to be acquired by Staples which would have created a company with more than 1100 stores. However the government blocked the purchase on antitrust grounds in 1997 and the agreement dissolved. Unfettered by merger distractions Office Depot resumed opening stores at a rapid pace including two in Thailand and took its catalog and delivery services online. It then established a joint venture with Japanese retailer Deo Deo.

In 1998 Office Depot acquired Viking Office Products in a $2.7 billion deal. With more than 60% of its sales coming from outside the US Viking augmented Office Depot's already strong delivery network and international expansion. Office Depot acquired the remaining 50% of its French operations from Carrefour in 1998 and the remaining 50% of its Japanese operations from Deo Deo in 1999.

Office Depot started putting Internet kiosks in its US stores in 2000 allowing customers to browse and shop company Web sites. In July 2000 Bruce Nelson CEO of Viking replaced Fuente as CEO of Office Depot. Citing weak computer sales and high warehouse prices the company closed about 70 stores and cut its workforce. In early 2002 Nelson was named chairman as well as CEO after Fuente stepped down.

Office Depot sold its Australian operations to Officeworks a unit of Coles Myer in January 2003. Office Depot used the proceeds to expand its faster-growing European operations. Also that year the company acquired the retail operations of French office supplier Guilbert from Pinault-Printemps-Redoute a move that doubled the company's business in Europe. (Staples had acquired Guilbert's mail-order business the previous year.)

In 2004 the company acquired about 125 retail locations from troubled toy seller Toys "R" Us converting 50 of those into Office Depot locations and selling off the remainder.

Nelson left the company and Neil Austrian served as interim head. Office Depot named AutoZone leader Steve Odland as CEO and chairman in 2005. That year the company shuttered its Viking Office Products brand in the US consolidating its catalog sales under the Office Depot banner. (It still markets products through Viking in international markets.) The business services division also sells technology products through Tech Depot (formerly 4SURE.com).

The company acquired privately held Allied Office Products (AOP) the largest independent dealer of office products and services in the US in 2006. AOP became part of Office Depot's North American Business Solutions Division.

Office Depot opened 70 new stores in 2007 (vs. 115 the previous year).

In mid-2008 the company acquired 13 stores in Sweden through the acquisition of AGE Kontor & Data AB a contract and retail office supply company operating there.

In 2009 the company closed about 125 stores in North America and exited the Japanese market.

CEO Steve Odland resigned in November 2010. In late 2010 Israeli department store operator New Hamashbir Lazarchan acquired Office Depot's operations in Israel for $50 million. New Hamashbir Lazarchan also agreed to pay royalties on revenues generated by Office Depot Israel which has about 45 stores.

Office Depot appointed new leadership in mid-2011 naming interim leader Neil Austrian as the company's permanent replacement for chief executive and chairman. Austrian has served as a director at Office Depot since 1998. He stepped in to lead the office products retailer on a temporary basis following the resignation of Steve Odland in late 2010. Odland's resignation came soon after Office Depot settled Securities and Exchange Commission charges that the company selectively informed analysts and institutional investors that its earnings would fall short of estimates. Office Depot agreed to pay $1 million while Odland and the firm's former CFO agreed to pay $50000.

EXECUTIVES

Evp And Cfo, Joseph T. (Joe) Lower, age 53
Evp Chief Legal Officer And Corporate Secretary, N. David Bleisch, age 61
Evp And Chief Marketing Officer, Jerri L. DeVard, age 60
Ceo And Director, Gerry P. Smith, age 57
Evp Chief Legal Officer Corporate Secretary And President Business Solutions Division, Steve Calkins, age 49
Evp And Chief Administrative Officer, Michael Allison, age 62, $539,423 total compensation

Evp Transformation And Strategic Sourcing, John W. Gannfors
Svp Ecommerce And Chief Digital Officer, Kevin Moffitt
Svp Retail Division, Marko Ibrahim
Senior Vice President North American Business Development, John Lander
Vice President, Chris Edler
Vice President Enterprise Account Management, Steve Dvorchak
Vice President Transformation Delivery, Sharon McGregor
Vice President, Alex Jaime
Vice President Distribution, Rick DiMaio
Vice President Global Talent Management, Robyn Tyler
Vp Tax, Richard Haas
Vice President Information Technology Shared Services, Tonya Peer
Vp It Application Development, Andrew Parry
Evp And Chief Merchandising And Services Officer, Janet Schijns
National Account Manager, Lindsey Trahan
Svp And Chief Accounting Officer, Scott Kriss
Vice President Financial Operations, Max Hood
Chairman, Joseph S. (Joe) Vassalluzzo, age 72
Vp Finance And Treasurer, Rich Leland
Board Member, David Szymanski
Board Member, Cynthia Jamison
Board Member, Kristin Campbell
Board Member, Nigel Travis
Auditors: DELOITTE & TOUCHE LLP

LOCATIONS

HQ: ODP Corp (The)
  6600 North Military Trail, Boca Raton, FL 33496
Phone: 561 438-4800   **Fax:** 561 265-4406
Web: www.officedepot.com

PRODUCTS/OPERATIONS

2018 Sales

	$ mil.	% of total
Business Solutions	5,282	48
Retail	4,641	42
CompuCom	1,086	10
Other	6	-
Total	**11,015**	**100**

2018 Sales

	$ mil.	% of total
Products	9,322	85
Services	1,693	15
Total	**11,015**	**100**

COMPETITORS

Amazon.com	HP Enterprise Services
BJ's Wholesale Club	IBM Global Services
Best Buy	Insight Enterprises
CDW	Staples
Costco Wholesale	The UPS Store
Dell	Veritiv
Essendant	Wal-Mart
FedEx Office	

HISTORICAL FINANCIALS

Company Type: Public

Income Statement   FYE: December 28

	REVENUE ($ mil.)	NET INCOME ($ mil.)	NET PROFIT MARGIN	EMPLOYEES
12/19	10,647	99	0.9%	40,000
12/18	11,015	104	0.9%	44,000
12/17	10,240	181	1.8%	45,000
12/16	11,021	529	4.8%	38,000
12/15	14,485	8	0.1%	49,000
Annual Growth	(7.4%)	87.6%	—	(4.9%)

Old National Bancorp (Evansville, IN)

Old National Bank is old but it's not quite national. Founded in 1834 the main subsidiary of Old National Bancorp operates about 200 bank centers across Indiana Kentucky Michigan and Illinois. The bank serves consumers and business customers offering standard checking and savings accounts credit cards and loans. Its treasury segment manages investments for bank and commercial clients. Business loans commercial and residential mortgages and consumer loans account for most of Old National's lending activity. The company also sells insurance manages wealth for high-net-worth clients and offers investment and retirement services through third-party provider LPL Financial.

Operations

Old National Bancorp operates two main segments: Banking which generates the bulk of Old National's revenue and provides traditional loan and deposit products as well as wealth management services; and Insurance which provides commercial property and casualty surety loss control services employee benefits consulting and administration as well as personal insurance.

The bank generated 51% of its revenue from loan interest (including fees) in 2014 while another 14% came from interest on investment securities. Insurance premiums and commissions contributed 7% to the company's total revenues that year while wealth management fees made up another 5%.

Geographic Reach

The bank's nearly 200 banking centers are located across four Midwestern states and Kentucky. Most are in the central northern and southern parts of Indiana; while others are in central Illinois; Western Kentucky and Louisville; Grand Rapids Southeastern and Southwestern Michigan; and Ohio.

Sales and Marketing

Old National has identified metropolitan areas within its market including Indianapolis; Louisville Kentucky; and Lafayette Indiana for growth within its core community banking segment.

The company spent $9.59 million on marketing in 2014 up from $7.21 million and $7.45 million in 2013 and 2012 respectively.

Financial Performance

Old National Bancorp's revenues and profits have been on the uptrend for the past several years thanks to new loan business from a series of bank acquisitions and declining loan loss provisions as its loan portfolio's credit quality has improved with the strengthened economy.

The company's revenue rose by 5% to $554.86 million in 2014 mostly thanks to new loan business stemming from the bank's acquisitions of Tower Financial United Bancorp and LSB Financial during the year along with organic loan growth. Higher revenue in 2014 coupled with strong cost controls lower interest on deposits and a continued decline in loan loss provisions drove Old National's net income higher by 3% to $103.62 million for the year.

Old National's operating cash fell by 21% to $199.72 million after adjusting its earnings for non-cash items related to its net sales proceeds from the sale of its residential real estate loans held-for-sale.

Strategy

Old National continues to seek out additional branch and whole bank acquisitions to grow its loan business and expand its geographic reach. Its acquisition of United Bancorp in mid-2014 for example added nearly $1 billion in new loan business and $869 million in wealth management assets under management while doubling Old National's presence in Michigan to 36 total branches.

The company is also pursuing growth by increasing its focus on commercial banking and cross-selling its insurance and wealth management offerings. To this end Old National in 2014 bought the insurance accounts (consisting of mostly commercial property/casualty accounts) serviced by the Evansville branch office of Wells Fargo Insurance.

Meanwhile it is also selectively exiting markets that haven't been profitable. In early 2015 as part of its ongoing efficiency improvement efforts the bank announced that it would sell 17 of its banking centers including all twelve of its branches in Southern Illinois and close or consolidate another 19 branches in other states over the following months.

Mergers and Acquisitions

In December 2014 Old National agreed to acquire Founders Financial Corporation along with its Founders Bank & Trust subsidiary in Grand Rapids Michigan for $91.7 million which would add nearly $460 million in total assets and four branches in Kent County.

In November 2014 the company purchased LSB Financial and its Lafayette Savings Bank subsidiary for $51.8 million adding five branches near Lafayette Indiana.

In July 2014 the company acquired Ann Arbor-based United Bancorp along with United Bank & Trust for a total of $122 million adding 18 branches in Michigan nearly $919 million in total assets a $963 million loan servicing portfolio and $688 million in trust assets under management.

In April 2014 Old National purchased Indiana-based Tower Financial along with its Tower Bank & Trust subsidiary adding seven new branches

and some $556 million in trust assets under management.

In 2013 the bank bolstered its presence in Michigan after acquiring two dozen Bank of America branches in northern Indiana and southwest Michigan. The previous year the bank purchased Indiana Community Bancorp which added 17 branches in the southeastern part of the state. The transaction was valued at nearly $80 million.

EXECUTIVES

Chairman President And Ceo, Robert G. (Bob) Jones, age 63, $668,269 total compensation
Svp And Corporate Secretary, Jeffrey L. (Jeff) Knight, age 60, $321,051 total compensation
Evp And Chief Credit Officer, Daryl D. Moore, age 62, $305,040 total compensation
Ceo North Central Region, Mark D. Bradford, age 62
Evp And Chief Client Services Officer, Annette W. Hudgions, age 62, $250,016 total compensation
President And Ceo Wealth Management, Caroline J. Ellspermann, age 52
Ceo Eastern Region, Dennis P. Heishman
Sevp And Cfo, Christopher A. (Chris) Wolking, age 60, $364,730 total compensation
Evp And Chief Community Relations And Social Responsibility Officer, Kathy A. Schoettlin
Region Ceo Old National Bank, Randall (Randy) Reichmann
Ceo Central And Western Michigan Region, Todd C. Clark, age 50
Evp And Chief Risk Officer, Candice J. Rickard, age 56
Evp And Chief Banking Officer, James Sandgren, $357,673 total compensation
Ceo Central Region, Dan L. Doan
Evp And Director Corporate Strategy, James C. Ryan, age 48
Evp And Cio, John R. Kamin
Evp Associate Engagement And Integrations, Kendra L. Vanzo
Evp Chief Auditing Executive And Chief Ethics Officer, Richard W. (Dick) Dubé
President Onb Investment Services, Kenneth J. Ellspermann
President Old National Insurance, Scott J. Evernham
Ceo Southern Region, Sara L. Miller
President And Coo, Jim Sandgren
President North Central Region, Scott Shishman
Vice President Administration, Gloria Reinhart
Assistant Vice President Mortgage Origination, Lynn Greulich
Vice President Administration, Doug Schuba
Vice President And Client Advisor, Steve Hackman
Senior Vice President Of Marketing, Scott Adams
Senior Vice President, Peggy Rohrman
Vice President Chief Procurement Officer, Kawn Watters
Assistant Vice President, Sandy Keen
Assistant Vice President, Gidget Rowe
Vice President Sarbanes Oxley Analyst, Denise Rexing
Vice President, Randy Lilly
Assistant Vice President, Jenny Clark
Assistant Vice President Mortgage Loan Officer, Debra Fulkerson
Vp Lpl Financial Advisor, Gary Shelton
Vice President Commercial Banking, Rob Snyder
Retail Center Manager Assistant Vice President, Pam Norris
Application Support Analyst Iii Avp, Laurie Holmes
Assistant Vice President Retail Center Manager, Sabrina Mancuso
Assistant Vice President Banking Center Manager, Tami Pitale

Vice President Assistant Treasurer, Mike Loyd
Vice President Commercial Lender, Tim Helber
Senior Vice President Treasurer, Jennifer Guzman
Vice President Commercial Relationship Manager, Sarah Strimmenos
Vice President, Jason Etter
Vice President Corporate Banking, James Tutt
Vice President Mortgage Lending, Steve Anderson
Vice President Of Community Banking And Office V, Tammy Hall
Vice President And Trust Officer, Melanie Newkirk
Assistant Vice President Secondary Marketing, Chris Weiberg
Senior Vice President Commercial Banking, James Barnum
Senior Vice President, Lynell Walton
Human Resources Operations Manager Vice President, Ann Claspell
Svp Mortgage Sales Manager, Joel Van Elderen
Vp Client Advisor Corporate Trust Manager, Shannon Perry
Vice President Technology, Richard Utley
Vice President And Financial Center Manager, Cathy Stidham
Vice President Treasury Management, Dana Lackey
Vice President Commercial Lender, Steve Wells
Vice President Server Systems, John Knight
Senior Vice President, Tommy Elliott
Vice President, Rob Triplett
Private Banker L Vice President, Becky Robledo
Senior Vice President And Commercial Relationship Team Leader, Troy Briggs
Vice President Cash Management, Andrea Solis
Volunteer And Work Life Programs Manager Avp, Amy Mpsa
Senior Vice President, Marty Richardson
Vice President Director Of Deposit Operations, Mike Eddington
Vice President, Jeff Kleinschmidt
Vice President, Jame Tutt
Client Advisor Ll Vice President, Michael Wiederkehr
Client Advanced Senior And Wm Mkt Lead Senior Vice President, Dan Callahan
Client Advisor Ii Vice President, Tamra Inman
Vice President Director And Assistant Controller, Treadweay Todd
Vice President Data Analytics And Loan Acquisition Marketing Manager, Karen Ellison
Executive Vice President And Chief Legal Counsel, Jefferey Knight
Vice President Compliance Audit Manager, Sonja Kriegsmann
Assistant Operations And Underwriting Manager Vice President, Melissa Bunker
Vice President Director Of Information Technology Risk Management, Luke Zeller
Senior Vice President Commercial Real Estate, Carl Hennen
Vice President Commercial Relationship Manager, James Kilsdonk
Senior Vice President Security, Shari Krutulis
Vp Portfolio Manager Iii Commercial Real Estate, Dan Ryan
Senior Vice President Operational Risk Director, Sherry Schneider
Vice President Senior Special Assets Officer, Doug Mitcheson
Vice President And Senior Trust Officer, Desiree Eddington
Svp And Manager Nonprofit Banking And Community Development, Kelly Elkin
Vice President Client Advisor, Rebecca Grasmeyer
Community Relations Manager Vice President, Andrea Marquardt Finck
Vice President, Mary Schilder
Business Banker Ii Vice President, Tim Sery
Cbu Underwriting Manager Assistant Vice President, Sarah Luhman
Assistant Vice President, Judith Starr

Assistant Vice President, Kyle Conapinski
Senior Vice President, Matt Sell
Retail Center Manger Vice President, Mike Lewis
Bank Support Analyst Assistant Vice President, Phil Effinger
Special Assets Officer Ll Vice President, Rob Hanzel
Commercial Rerl Manager Lll Vice President, Susan Johnson
Investment Officer Lll Vice President, Gregory Hunt
Direct Underwriting Team Leader Assistant Vice President, Jewell Frazier
Trust Admin Reg Manager Michgn Vice President, John Logan
Financial Report Anlystseniorassistant Vice President, Julie Jaques
Securities Trading Specialist Assistant Vice President, Amanda Foster
Commercail Rel Mgrm Ii Vice President, Brad Condon
Vice President, Carrie Gutman
Commercial Rel Team Lead Senior Vice President, Cassandra Miller
Real Estate Review Appraiser Vice President, Cyndi Gianneschi
Vice President Special Asset Officer, Charlie Goebel
Avp And Mortgage Loan Originator, Amanda Byers
Vice President Finance, Kathy Reiter
Mortgage Loan Originator Vice President, Shellie Sparks
Board Member, Alan Braun
Board Member, Rebecca Skillman
Board Member, Jerome Henry
Board Member, Katherine White
Auditors: Crowe LLP

LOCATIONS

HQ: Old National Bancorp (Evansville, IN)
One Main Street, Evansville, IN 47708
Phone: 800 731-2265
Web: www.oldnational.com

PRODUCTS/OPERATIONS

2014 Sales

	$ mil.	% of total
Interest		
Loans including fees	306	51
Investment securities	83	14
Noninterest		
Service charges on deposit accounts	47	8
Insurance premiums & commissions	41	7
Wealth management fees	28	5
ATM Fees	25	4
Investment product fees	17	3
Mortgage banking revenue	6	1
Other	41	7
Adjustments	(43.3)	-
Total	**554**	**100**

COMPETITORS

Fifth Third	JPMorgan Chase
First Financial (IN)	PNC Financial
German American Bancorp	Peoples Bancorp (IN)
Huntington Bancshares	U.S. Bancorp

Old Republic International Corp.

Old Republic International also known as Old Republic keeps pace with changing financial times. With about 135 subsidiaries across North America Old Republic's primary operations are conducted through the Old Republic General Insurance division which offers commercial liability and property/casualty insurance (mostly commercial trucking workers' compensation and general liability policies). In addition the company's Title Insurance group specializes in naturally issuing title insurance to property owners and lenders. Its Old Republic National Title subsidiary is one of the US's oldest and largest title insurance companies with offices throughout the US. Craig Smiddy was appointed as the new CEO of the company with effect in late 2019.

Operations

Old Republic's subsidiaries market underwrite and offer risk management services for insurance products including general and title coverage. Property and liability insurance issued by the general insurance segment account for nearly 55% of the company's sales. Meanwhile the title insurance segment accounts for approximately 35% of revenues and the company's Republic Financial Indemnity Group (RFIG comprising mortgage guaranty and consumer credit indemnity runoff operations) brings in less than 5% of sales. The company also maintains a small life and accident insurance business.

Roughly 75% of the company's consolidated title premium and related fee income comes from independent title agents and underwritten title companies. The rest stems from direct operations including branches of its title insurance businesses and wholly owned agency and service subsidiaries.

The company earned about 85% of total revenue from premiums and fees. The remaining revenues are from net investment and other income and investment gains.

Geographic Reach

The company's executive offices are located in Chicago Illinois. Through its subsidiaries Old Republic is licensed to do business throughout the US (including the District of Columbia) Puerto Rico the US Virgin Islands Guam and in all Canadian provinces.

Sales and Marketing

While Old Republic does sell some of its property/casualty and specialty products directly it relies on independent agencies brokers and financial institutions to distribute the majority. The company focuses on certain sectors especially transportation commercial construction health care education forest products energy manufacturing retail and wholesale trade and financial services.

Title insurance and related settlement products are sold through some 280 company offices and through agencies and underwritten title companies throughout the US.

Financial Performance

The company's revenue in 2019 increased by $1.2 billion to $7.2 billion from $6.0 billion in the prior year. The increase was primarily due to higher operating revenues and investment gains of $636.1 million.

Old Republic's net income increased by 185% to $1.1 billion in 2019 from $370.5 million in the prior year. The increase was primarily due to higher revenues and while maintaining a lower operating expenses.

Cash held by the company at the end of 2019 decreased by $21.4 million to $78.8 million from $100.3 million in the prior year. Cash provided by operations was $936.2 million while cash used by investing and financing activities were $424.6 million and $533.1 million respectively.

Strategy

The insurance business is distinguished from most others in that the prices (premiums) charged for various insurance products are set without certainty of the ultimate benefit and claim costs that will emerge often many years after issuance and expiration of a policy. This basic fact casts Old Republic as a risk-taking enterprise managed for the long run. Management therefore conducts the business with a primary focus on achieving favorable underwriting results over cycles and on the maintenance of financial soundness in support of the insurance subsidiaries' long-term obligations to policyholders and their beneficiaries. To achieve these objectives adherence to insurance risk management principles is stressed and asset diversification and quality are emphasized. The underwriting principles encompass: Disciplined risk selection evaluation and pricing to reduce uncertainty and adverse selection; Enhancing the predictability of expected outcomes through insurance of the largest number of homogeneous risks as to each type of coverage; Reducing the insurance portfolio risk profile through: diversification and spread of insured risks; and assimilation of un-

correlated asset and liability exposures across economic sectors that tend to offset or counterbalance one another; and Effective management of gross and net limits of liability through appropriate use of reinsurance.

In addition to income arising from Old Republic's basic underwriting and related services functions significant investment income is earned from invested funds generated by those functions and from capital resources. Investment management aims for stability of income from interest and dividends protection of capital and for sufficiency of liquidity to meet insurance underwriting and other obligations as they become payable in the future. Securities trading and the realization of capital gains are not primary objectives. The investment philosophy is therefore best characterized as emphasizing value credit quality and relatively long-term holding periods. The company's ability to hold both fixed maturity and equity securities for long periods of time is in turn enabled by the scheduling of maturities in contemplation of an appropriate matching of assets and liabilities and by investments in large capitalization highly liquid equity securities.

EXECUTIVES

Chairman And Ceo, Aldo C. (Al) Zucaro, age 81, $895,000 total compensation

President And Coo, R. Scott Rager, age 71, $510,000 total compensation

Chairman And Ceo Old Republic Title Companies, Rande K. Yeager, age 71, $510,000 total compensation

Svp And Cfo, Karl W. Mueller, age 60, $465,000 total compensation

President And Coo Old Republic General Insurance Group Inc. (orgig), Craig R. Smiddy, age 56, $485,000 total compensation

Vice President And Associate General Counsel, Kathleen Kumer

Assistant Vice President Commercial Counsel, Avi A Marcus

Vice Chairman, James Kellogg

Board Member, Charles Titterton

Auditors: KPMG LLP

LOCATIONS

HQ: Old Republic International Corp.
307 North Michigan Avenue, Chicago, IL 60601
Phone: 312 346-8100
Web: www.oldrepublic.com

PRODUCTS/OPERATIONS

2017 Sales

	% of total
General Insurance	57
Title Insurance	37
Realized investment gains	3
RFIG (run-off)	2
Corporate & other	1
Total	**100**

COMPETITORS

AIG	ING
AXA	Progressive
Allianz	Corporation
Berkshire Hathaway	Stewart Information
CNA Financial	Services
Chubb Limited	The Hartford
Farmers Group	Travelers Companies
Fidelity National	Unum Group
Financial	W. R. Berkley
First American	

HISTORICAL FINANCIALS

Company Type: Public

Income Statement

FYE: December 31

	ASSETS ($ mil.)	NET INCOME ($ mil.)	INCOME AS % OF ASSETS	EMPLOYEES
12/19	21,076	1,056	5.0%	9,000
12/18	19,327	370	1.9%	9,000
12/17	19,403	560	2.9%	8,700
12/16	18,591	466	2.5%	8,500
12/15	17,110	422	2.5%	8,200
Annual Growth	**5.3%**	**25.8%**	—	**2.4%**

2019 Year-End Financials

Debt ratio: 4.62%	No. of shares (mil.): 303
Return on equity: 18.96%	Dividends
Cash ($ mil.): 78	Yield: 8.0%
Current ratio: —	Payout: 80.3%
Long-term debt ($ mil.): —	Market value ($ mil.): 6,793

	STOCK PRICE ($) FY Close	P/E High/Low		PER SHARE ($) Earnings	Dividends	Book Value
12/19	22.37	7	6	3.51	1.80	19.76
12/18	20.57	18	16	1.24	1.78	17.00
12/17	21.38	10	8	1.92	0.76	17.58
12/16	19.00	11	9	1.62	0.75	17.02
12/15	18.63	12	9	1.48	0.74	14.81
Annual Growth	**4.7%**	—	—	**24.1%**	**24.9%**	**7.5%**

Old Second Bancorp., Inc. (Aurora, Ill.)

Old Second won't settle for a silver finish when it comes to community banking around Chicago. Old Second Bancorp is the holding company for Old Second National Bank which serves the Chicago metropolitan area through 25 branches in Kane Kendall DeKalb DuPage LaSalle Will and Cook counties. The bank provides standard services such as checking and savings accounts credit and debit cards CDs mortgages loans and trust services to consumers and business clients. Subsidiary River Street Advisors offers investment management and advisory services. Another unit Old Second Affordable Housing Fund provides home-buying assistance to lower-income customers.

Operations

Commercial real estate loans accounted for 53% of Old Second's loan portfolio at the end of 2015 while residential mortgages made up another 31%. The rest was made up of general commercial loans (12% of loan assets) and construction lending (2%).

Roughtly 70% of the bank's revenue comes from interest income. About 54% of its revenue came from loan interest (including fees) during 2015 with another 15% coming from interest on investment securities. The remainder of Old Second's revenue came from deposit account service charges (7%) trust income (6%) mortgage loan sale gains (6%) secondary mortgage fees (1%) and other sources.

Geographic Reach

The bank mostly serves customers in Aurora Illinois (which is 40 miles west of Chicago) and surrounding communities. Its 24 branches are located in the Kane Kendall DeKalb DuPage LaSalle Will and Cook counties of Illinois.

Sales and Marketing

Old Second has been ramping up its advertising spend in recent years. It spent $1.34 million on advertising in 2015 up from $1.28 million and $1.23 million in 2014 and 2013 respectively.

Financial Performance

Old Second's annual revenues have fallen 20% since 2011 as it's had to sell of many of its non-performing loan assets to de-risk its loan portfolio. The company's profits however have been on the mend as its de-risking measures have led to declining loan loss provisions.

The bank's revenue rebounded by less than 1% to $97.46 million during 2015 as its average loans including loans held for sale grew by 2% for the year.

Revenue growth in 2015 combined with lower interest and amortization costs on deposits drove Old Second Bancorp's net income up by over 50% to $15.39 million. The bank's operating cash levels jumped sharply to $21.14 million (operations had used $6.3 million in 2014) partially thanks to earnings growth but mostly thanks to positive working capital changes related to sales proceeds from loans held for sale and changes in accrued interest payable and other liabilities.

Strategy

Old Second Bancorp continued in 2016 to focus on shedding riskier loan assets that led it to deep losses in 2011 while focusing on securing high-quality loans with more creditworthiness. Its efforts began to pay off in 2015 as its average loan balances and revenues began to grow again after years of being in decline.

EXECUTIVES

Assistant Vice President Operations, Brian Bermes
Evp Cfo And Director, J. Douglas Cheatham, age 64, $252,000 total compensation
Ceo And Director Old Second Bancorp Inc. And Old Second National Bank, James L. Eccher, age 55, $325,000 total compensation
Vice President, Jeff Downs
Assistant Vice President, Janet Mutz
Vice President, Robin Hill
Senior Vice President And Treasurer, Stan Faries
Executive Vice President Human Resources, Robert Dicosola
Senior Vice President, Chris Barry
Avp Residential Lender, Terri Hanson
Vice President, Peggy Nelson
Executive Vice President, Don Pilmer
First Vice President Commercial Loan Officer, David Mottet
Vice President, John Annis
Vice President, Jocelyn Retz
Vice President Residential Lending, Michelle Domson
Vice President, Jeri Ott
Vice President Residential Lending, Ana Torres
Vice President Commercial Banking, Ted Koch
Vice President Commercial Banking, Kristin Zell
Vice President Commercial Banker, Vanessa Aguirre
Vice President Regional Retail Manager, Joseph Huml
Vice President, Kim Mason
Senior Vice President Commercial Lending, Mark Fleming
Vice President Residential Lending, Michelle Almond
Avp Operations, Barbara Collette
Assistant Vice President Branch Manager, Nancy Baker
Vice President Mortgage Lending, Phillip Delafuente
Vp Regional Manager, Deborah Foote
First Vice President, Chris Hainey
Assistant Vice President Retail Manager, Julie Fuller
Senior Vice President, Peter Harrison
Assistant Vice President, Joseph Gordon
First Vice President, Jacqueline Volkert
Senior Vice President Commercial Leasing Manager, Tim Jwoodcock
Vice President Loan Administration, Jason Evans
Senior Vice President, Dan Siadak
Senior Vp, Andres Roach
Chairman Old Second Bancorp Inc. And Old Second National Bank, William B. Skoglund, age 70
Vice Chairman, Gary S. Collins, age 62
Board Member, John Ladowicz
Auditors: Plante & Moran PLLC

LOCATIONS

HQ: Old Second Bancorp., Inc. (Aurora, Ill.)
37 South River Street, Aurora, IL 60507
Phone: 630 892-0202
Web: www.oldsecond.com

PRODUCTS/OPERATIONS

2015 sales

	% of total
Interest and dividend income	
Loans including fees	54
Taxable	14
Tax exempt	1
Non-interest income	
Service charges on deposits	7
Trust income	6
Net gain on sales of mortgage loans	6
Debit card interchange income	4
Secondary mortgage fees	1
Increase in cash surrender value of bank-owned life insurance	1
Other income	6
Total	**100**

Products/Services

Personal Banking
Card Services
Checking
Loans
Money Services
Online and Mobile Banking
Prime Time Club
Retirement Services
Savings
Loans
Auto and Personal Loans
Home Equity Loans
Home Loans
Mortgage Lenders
Required Documents
SAFE Act
Business Banking
Commercial Banking
Online and Mobile Banking
Small Business Banking
Wealth Management
Business Plan Options
Real Estate Services
Retirement Services

COMPETITORS

Bank of America	Harris
BankFinancial	MB Financial
Fifth Third	Northern Trust
First Midwest Bancorp	West Suburban Bancorp

HISTORICAL FINANCIALS

Company Type: Public

Income Statement

FYE: December 31

	ASSETS ($ mil.)	NET INCOME ($ mil.)	INCOME AS % OF ASSETS	EMPLOYEES
12/19	2,635	39	1.5%	535
12/18	2,676	34	1.3%	518
12/17	2,383	15	0.6%	450
12/16	2,251	15	0.7%	467
12/15	2,077	15	0.7%	450
Annual Growth	6.1%	26.5%	—	4.4%

2019 Year-End Financials

Debt ratio: 4.12%	No. of shares (mil.): 29
Return on equity: 15.57%	Dividends
Cash ($ mil.): 50	Yield: 0.3%
Current ratio: —	Payout: 3.1%
Long-term debt ($ mil.): —	Market value ($ mil.): 403

	STOCK PRICE ($) FY Close	P/E High/Low		PER SHARE ($) Earnings	Dividends	Book Value
12/19	13.47	11	9	1.30	0.04	9.28
12/18	13.00	14	11	1.12	0.04	7.70
12/17	13.65	28	20	0.50	0.04	6.76
12/16	11.05	22	12	0.53	0.03	5.93
12/15	7.84	18	11	0.46	0.00	5.29
Annual Growth	14.5%	—	—	29.7%	—	15.1%

Omnicom Group, Inc.

Omnicom Group creates advertising that is omnipresent. The company is a leading global marketing and corporate communications company that provides services to over 5000 clients across 100-plus countries. Omnicom's branded networks and numerous specialty firms provide advertising strategic media planning and buying digital and interactive marketing direct and promotional marketing public relations and other specialty communications services. The US accounts for about 55% of sales.

Operations

Omnicom is active in five primary disciplines: Advertising CRM Consumer Experience CRM Execution & Support Public Relations and Healthcare.

Advertising accounts for over 55% of Omnicom's total revenue. It includes creative services as well as strategic planning and data analytics.

CRM Customer Experience and CRM Execution & Support generates over 15% and almost 10% respectively. CRM Consumer Experience includes Omnicom Precision Marketing Group and digital/direct marketing agencies as well as branding shopper marketing and experiential marketing agencies. CRM Execution & Support carries out field marketing sales support merchandising and point of sale as well as other specialized marketing and custom communications services.

Public Relations services including corporate communications and crisis management generate about 10% of sales as well as Healthcare-focused marketing and communications provides about 10%.

Geographic Reach

Omnicom has principal corporate offices in New York Connecticut and Florida while it has international offices in London Shanghai and Singapore. The group's network of agencies serves some 5000 clients in more than 100 countries.

Around 60% of the company's revenue comes from the Americas while EMEA (Europe Middle East and Africa) contributes almost 30%. The remaining 10% or so comes from the Asia-Pacific region.

Sales and Marketing

As a leading global advertising marketing and corporate communications company Omnicom has a large and diverse client base. Often several Omnicom agencies will serve the same client concurrently. None of its clients account for more than 5% of revenue while its top 100 clients account for a little more than 50% of revenue and are served on average by more than 60 Omnicom agencies.

By industry food and beverage companies along with pharmaceutical and healthcare firms account for the largest share of customers with each contributing nearly 15% of the company's total revenue. Omnicom serves other notable industries including consumer products technology financial services and the auto industry each accounting for nearly 10% of sales.

Financial Performance

Omnicom's revenue fluctuated in the last five years. It has an overall decline of 1%.

In 2019 revenue decreased $336.5 million or 2.2% to $15 billion from $15.3 billion in 2018.

Net income increased to $12.7 million or 1.0% to $1.34 billion from $1.33 billion in 2018 due to the decrease in salary and service costs and net interest expense.

Cash at the end of 2019 was $4.3 billion. Cash from operations was $1.9 billion while investing activities used $31 million. Financing activities used $1.2 billion.

Strategy

Omnicom continues to use its virtual client networks to grow business relationships with its largest clients by serving them across its networks disciplines and geographies.

Its acquisition strategy is focused on acquiring the expertise of an assembled workforce in order to continue to build upon the core capabilities of the company's various strategic business platforms and agency brands through the expansion of their geographic reach or their service capabilities to better serve clients.

Mergers and Acquisitions

In late 2019 Omnicom Precision Marketing Group the digital and customer relationship management (CRM) specialist group within Omnicom Group Inc. agreed to acquire a majority stake in Smart Digital GmbH. "Partnering with Smart Digital is not only a strategic move for Omnicom as we grow and leverage proprietary tools like Omni to strengthen our AI and personalization capabilities but moreover it's important for our clients ? for whom we'll be better able to deliver powerful end-to-end customer experience solutions" said Luke Taylor CEO of OPMG.

Company Background

Omnicom Group was created in 1986 to combine three leading ad agencies ? BBDO Worldwide Doyle Dane Bernbach Group (DDB) and Needham Harper Worldwide ? into a single group capable of competing in the worldwide market.

BBDO Worldwide founded in New York in 1928 as Batten Barton Durstine & Osborn had a huge PepsiCo account and developed the Pepsi Generation campaign.

Doyle Dane Bernbach Group (DDB) which had created the fahrvergn gen ads for Volkswagen had strong ties in Europe.

Needham Harper Worldwide which had served up the "You Deserve a Break Today" commercials for McDonald's had connections in Asia.

Omnicom was established as holding company of independent operating units working together to gain scale.

HISTORY

Omnicom Group was created in 1986 to combine three leading ad agencies into a single group capable of competing in the worldwide market. BBDO Worldwide founded in New York in 1928 as Batten Barton Durstine & Osborn had a huge PepsiCo account and developed the Pepsi Generation campaign. Doyle Dane Bernbach Group (DDB) which had created the fahrvergn gen ads for Volkswagen had strong ties in Europe. And Needham Harper Worldwide which had served up the "You Deserve a Break Today" commercials for McDonald's had connections in Asia. BBDO remained separate but DDB and Needham Harper were merged to form DDB Needham Worldwide. The business services units (public relations firms and direct marketers) of each of these companies were tucked under the Diversified Agency Services (DAS) umbrella.

Bruce Crawford a previous chairman of BBDO who had just finished a stint running New York's Metropolitan Opera became chairman and CEO in 1989. He transformed DAS from a chaotic group of shops into an integrated marketing giant and ran Omnicom as a holding company of independent operating units working together through cross-referrals. By keeping costs low especially interest expenses Omnicom survived the 1990-91 recession with little pain. The company acquired Goodby Berlin & Silverstein (now Goodby Silverstein & Partner s) in 1992. The next year TBWA Advertising (founded in Paris in 1970 by American Bill Tragos) was added to Omnicom's roster.

The merger spree continued in 1994 when Omnicom purchased WWAV Group the largest direct-marketing agency in the UK. In 1995 Omnicom fused TBWA with Chiat/Day (founded in 1968 by Jay Chiat and Guy Day) to form TBWA International Network. Omnicom also acquired Michigan-based Ross Roy Communications (later Interone Marketing Group). In 1997 DDB Needham won back its McDonald's account after a 15-year hiatus. That year Crawford stepped down as CEO (though he remained chairman) and John Wren took control of Omnicom.

In 1998 the company acquired PR firm Fleishman-Hillard adding to the PR clout it established with the acquisition of Ketchum Communications (now Ketchum) in 1996. Omnicom also acquired GGT Group of London for $235 million. (GGT's New York office Wells BDDP had lost a large Procter & Gamble account that year.) It merged GGT's BDDP Worldwide with TBWA to form TBWA Worldwide. BBDO landed a $200 million account with PepsiCo's Frito-Lay that year.

Omnicom's position in Europe was boosted in 1999 when it bought the Abbot Mead Vickers (now Abbot Mead Vickers BBDO) shares it didn't already own. That year TBWA founder William Tragos retired from the company (replaced by Lee Clow) and DDB Needham changed its moniker to DDB Worldwide Communications Group. Omnicom also bought market research firm M/A/R/C for about $95 million and invested $20 million in pharmaceutical clinical trials company SCIREX. In 2000 BBDO scored a major coup over rival FCB Worldwide (now part of Interpublic) by landing the $1.8 billion DaimlerChrysler account. The next year it formed Seneca Investments to hold its stakes in several i-services shops including Agency.com and Organic. (Omnicom acquired the interactive agencies outright in 2003.)

After years of acquisitions and fine-tuning its operating structure Omnicom encountered the effects of the global recession in late 2008. Like most players in the media communications and advertising industries Omnicom experienced declines in revenue and net income at the end of 2009. It attributed the crisis within the automotive industry and declines in the demand for its sports and event marketing services as major reasons for the drops.

In 2010 the company acquired seven companies including Sales Power an in-store promotion company catering to South China and Maslov PR a public relations firm based in Moscow. Among the twelve companies it acquired in 2011 was Nancy Bailey & Associates a corporate licensing and consulting firm.

EXECUTIVES

Evp And Cfo, Philip J. Angelastro, age 56, $850,000 total compensation

Treasurer Omnicom Group And President And Ceo Omnicom Capital, Dennis E. Hewitt, age 75, $395,000 total compensation

President And Ceo, John D. Wren, age 68, $1,000,000 total compensation

Vice Chairman; Chairman Asia Pacific, Serge Dumont

Evp, Asit Mehra

Evp And Dean Omnicom University, Janet Riccio

Evp, Rita E. Rodriguez

Evp, Peter Sherman

Ceo Omnicom Digital, Jonathan B. Nelson, age 52, $850,000 total compensation

Svp General Counsel And Secretary, Michael J. O'Brien, age 58, $700,000 total compensation

Vice President Financial Systems, Allen Flissler

Executive Vice President, Thomas Carey

Vice President Finance Operations, Michael Larson

Senior Vice President And Chief Diversity Officer, Tiffany R Warren

Vice President Of Finance Operations, Brian Sullivan

Senior Vice President, Joe Ricciardi

Vice President Financial Planning And Analysis, Daniel Bearison

Senior Vice President Director Of Global Business Strategy, Celine Vita

Vice President Global Travel, Tony Occhipinti

Vice President Strategy And Operations, Josh Tobey

Senior Vice President Director Of Client Services, Deirdre Eliopoulos

Vice President Sports Network, Courtney Leddy

Vice President Account Director, Phil Brolly

Vice President Account Supervisor Ketchum. Passion And Precision In Communication, Stephanie Buttrill

Vice President Director, Tracey Maffeo

Vice President Human Resources Director, Hope MacGregor

Senior Vice President Group Creative Director, Marcia Iacobucci

Vice President Account Director, Amy Hatton

Vice President, Dalya Browne

Vice President Group Account Supervisor, Joseph Bailey

Senior Vice President Director Brand Practice, Becca Leish

Vice President Group Manager, Kim Assalone

Vice President Social Strategy, Melissa Schreiber

Vice President Director Of Strategy, Kim Ryneska

Vice President Account Director, Natalie Connelly

Vice President Account Director, Allen McCormick

Vice President Group Account Supervisor, Jesse Jenkins

Senior Vice President Account Director, Meg Fitzpatrick

Vice President Group Copy Supervisor, Jessica Krause

Vice President, Elizabeth Watters Roberts

Vice President Account Director, Carrie White

Executive Vice President Management Director, Doug Walker

Chairman, Bruce Crawford, age 90

Treasurer, Angie Hickman

Board Member, Debbie Kissire

Auditors: KPMG LLP

LOCATIONS

HQ: Omnicom Group, Inc.
437 Madison Avenue, New York, NY 10022
Phone: 212 415-3600   Fax: 212 415-3393
Web: www.omnicomgroup.com

2017 Sales

	$ mil.	% of total
Americas		
North America	8,686	57
Latin America	494	3
EMEA		
Europe	4,127	27
Middle East and Africa	314	2
Asia Pacific	1,650	11
Total	**15,273**	**100**

PRODUCTS/OPERATIONS

2017 sales

	$ mil.	% of total
Advertising	8,142	53
Customer relationship management	4,819	32
Public relations	1,376	9
Specialty communications	934	6
Total	**15,273**	**100**

Selected Operations

Global advertising networks
  BBDO Worldwide
  DDB Worldwide
  TBWA Worldwide
National advertising agencies
  Goodby Silverstein & Partners (San Francisco)
  GSD&M (Austin TX)
  Martin|Williams (Minneapolis)
  Merkley + Partners (New York City)
  Zimmerman Partners Advertising (Fort Lauderdale FL)
Direct response
  Interbrand (brand identity)
  M/A/R/C Research (market research)
  Rapp (direct marketing)
  Targetbase (direct marketing)
Promotional marketing
  The Beanstalk Group (brand licensing and consulting)
  CPM (field marketing)
  The Integer Group (retail marketing)
  Kaleidoscope (sports and event marketing)

  Millsport (sports and event marketing)
Public relations
  Clark & Weinstock
  Cone
  Fleishman-Hillard
  Gavin Anderson & Company
  GPC International
  Ketchum
  Porter Novelli International
  Smythe Dorward Lambert
Specialty communications
  Adelphi Group (health care)
  Corbett Accel Healthcare (health care)
  Dieste (multicultural marketing)
  Doremus (business-to-business advertising)
  SafirRosetti (security and intelligence)
Media services
  Icon International
  Novus Print Media
  OMD Worldwide
  PHD Network

COMPETITORS

Dentsu	Interpublic Group
Dentsu Aegis	Publicis Groupe
Hakuhodo	WPP
Havas	

HISTORICAL FINANCIALS

Company Type: Public

Income Statement

FYE: December 31

	REVENUE ($ mil.)	NET INCOME ($ mil.)	NET PROFIT MARGIN	EMPLOYEES
12/19	14,953	1,339	9.0%	70,000
12/18	15,290	1,326	8.7%	70,400
12/17	15,273	1,088	7.1%	77,300
12/16	15,416	1,148	7.5%	78,500
12/15	15,134	1,093	7.2%	74,900
Annual Growth	(0.3%)	5.2%		(1.7%)

2019 Year-End Financials

Debt ratio: 19.21%
Return on equity: 49.59%
Cash ($ mil.): 4,305
Current ratio: 0.91
Long-term debt ($ mil.): 4,531

No. of shares (mil.): 217
Dividends
  Yield: 3.2%
  Payout: 43.7%
Market value ($ mil.): 17,589

	STOCK PRICE ($) FY Close	P/E High/Low	PER SHARE ($) Earnings	Dividends	Book Value
12/19	81.02	14 12	6.06	2.60	13.15
12/18	73.24	14 12	5.83	2.40	11.38
12/17	72.83	19 14	4.65	2.25	11.37
12/16	85.11	18 14	4.78	2.15	9.21
12/15	75.66	18 15	4.41	2.00	10.23
Annual Growth	1.7%	— —	8.3%	6.8%	6.5%

OneMain Holdings Inc

With more than $21 billion in total assets consumer finance company OneMain Holdings direct subsidiary was Springleaf Inc. The company offers auto loans and personal loans primarily to non-prime customers who have limited access to credit from banks credit card companies and other lenders through more than 1500 branches in around 44 states. It also provides credit insurance non-credit insurance and related products through subsidiaries AHL and Triton. The Company sold all of the issued and outstanding shares of its former insurance subsidiaries

Yosemite Insurance Company ("Yosemite") and Merit Life Insurance Co. ("Merit"). Tracing its roots back to 1920 Springleaf renamed itself in late 2015 after acquiring OneMain Financial.

Operations

OneMain Holdings' operates through its segment of Consumer and Insurance. Beginning in the fourth quarter of 2019 the company included the Acquisitions and Servicing ("A&S") which was previously presented as a distinct reporting segment in Other.

The Consumer and Insurance originates and services secured and unsecured personal loans and offers optional credit and non-credit insurance and related products through the combined branch network and the centralized operations. Personal loan origination and servicing along with the insurance products form the core of the company's operations (typically ranging from $1500 to $30000). In addition it offers credit insurance (also known as payment protection insurance) an optional add-on for borrowers to ensure repayment if they can't repay the loan. It also offers non-credit insurance policies which are primarily traditional level-term life policies with very limited underwriting. The company has around $18.4 billion in personal loan assets due to about 2.4 million customer accounts.

Geographic Reach

Evansville Indiana-based OneMain Holdings serves customers across the US and has servicing facilities in Mendota Heights Minnesota; Tempe Arizona; London Kentucky; Evansville Indiana; Fort Mill South Carolina; and Fort Worth Texas.

Sales and Marketing

OneMain Holdings is aggressive in targeting high-risk borrowers who might be reluctant to seek financing. It uses direct mail promotions web ads and local marketing to acquire new customers and regain former customers. The customers are primarily considered non-prime and often require significantly higher levels of service than prime customers. As a result the company tends to charge these customers higher interest rates to compensate for the related credit risks and servicing costs.

The company solicits prospective customers as well as current and former customers through a variety of direct mail offers and targeted online advertising. The company's digital platform allows current and prospective customers the ability to apply for a personal loan online at omf.com.

Financial Performance

After suffering almost a 30% revenue reduction in 2015 (caused by predecessor company Springleaf's net gain on sale of its real estate loans in 2014) OneMain Holdings bounced back the next year with a near-doubling of its revenue. Revenue has an overall growth of 158% between 2015 and 2019.

The total revenue increased by almost 13% to $3.8 billion.

Net income increased by 91% to $858 million in 2019. The increase is related to Net interest income after provision for finance receivable losses and other revenues.

Net cash used for investing activities of $3.4 billion for 2019 was primarily due to net principal originations of finance receivables held for investment and held for sale and purchases of available-for-sale securities partially offset by net sales calls and maturities of available-for-sale securities.Net cash provided by financing activities of $1.5 billion for 2019 was primarily due to net issuances of long-term debt offset primarily by the cash dividends paid in 2019. Net cash provided by operations of $2.4 billion for 2019 reflected net income of $855 million the impact of non-cash items and a favorable change in working capital of $67 million. The company's position gained $454 million during 2019 ending the year at $1.6 billion.

Strategy

The company believes that the future success depends on its ability to implement the strategy the key feature of which has been to shift the primary focus to originating personal loans as well as acquiring portfolios of personal loans pursuing acquisitions of companies and/or establishing joint ventures or other strategic alliances. The company has also expanded the digital presence in online lending through centralized operations which may involve additional risks associated with verifying income and customer identities.

The company executes on strategic priorities to strengthen the capital base through the following key initiatives: continuing growth in receivables through enhanced marketing strategies and customer product options; maintaining and enhancing credit performance; leveraging the scale and cost discipline across the company to deliver improved operating leverage; increasing tangible equity and reducing financial leverage; and maintaining a strong liquidity level.

The company intends to support its liquidity position by utilizing some or all of the following strategies: maintaining disciplined underwriting standards and pricing for loans and originate or purchase and managing purchases of finance receivables; pursuing additional debt financings (including new securitizations and new unsecured debt issuances debt refinancing transactions and revolving conduit facilities) or a combination of the foregoing; purchasing portions of the outstanding indebtedness through open market or privately negotiated transactions with third parties or according to one or more tender or exchange offers or otherwise upon such terms and at such prices as well as with such consideration and obtaining new and extending existing secured revolving facilities to provide committed liquidity in case of prolonged market fluctuations with diversified funding sources.

Mergers and Acquisitions

On September 20 2019 SFC (Springleaf Finance Corporation) entered into a merger agreement with its direct parent SFI (Springleaf Finance Inc) to merge SFI with and into SFC with SFC as the surviving entity. The merger was effective in SFC's consolidated financial statements as of July 1 2019. As a result of SFI's merger with and into SFC SFC became a wholly-owned direct subsidiary of OMH.

The net deficiency of SFI included an intercompany note payable plus accrued interest of $166 million from SFI to OMH which SFC assumed through the merger. On September 23 2019 SFC repaid SFI's note to OMH. Concurrently OMH paid $22 million in other payables due to SFC and made an equity contribution of $144 million to SFC. Additionally as a result of the merger the intercompany notes between SFI and SFC were eliminated. The transactions noted above resulted in a net $264 million reduction to SFC's equity. There was no impact on OMH's equity as a result of the merger.

EXECUTIVES

Evp Legal Compliance And Operational Risk, John C. Anderson, age 62, $350,000 total compensation

President And Ceo, Jay N. Levine, age 58, $400,000 total compensation

Evp And Cfo, Scott T. Parker, age 53, $400,000 total compensation

Evp Branch Operations, Bradford D. Borchers, age 56, $350,000 total compensation

Evp Credit And Analytics, David P. Hogan, age 51, $350,000 total compensation

Evp And Coo, Robert A. Hurzeler, age 59, $350,000 total compensation

Evp And Chief Administrative Officer, Lawrence N. Skeats, age 55, $336,539 total compensation

Evp Human Resources, Angela Celestin, age 49, $26,442 total compensation

Vice President Investor Relations, Rohit Dewan

Senior Vice President, Donald Breivogel

Senior Vice President Marketing, Hari Lymon

Vice President Director Marketing, Melody Bateman

Senior Vice President Of Communications, Howard M Schloss

Executive Vice President And Chief Distribution Officer, John B Deremo

Vice President Director Of Operations, Gary Fulk

Regional Vice President, Daniel Ritenour

Chairman, Wesley R. (Wes) Edens, age 58

Auditors: PricewaterhouseCoppers LLP

LOCATIONS

HQ: OneMain Holdings Inc
601 N.W. Second Street, Evansville, IN 47708
Phone: 812 424-8031
Web: www.onemainfinancial.com

PRODUCTS/OPERATIONS

2018 Sales

	$ mil.	% of total
Net Interest Income		
Interest Income	3,658	86
Interest Expense	(875)	-
Non-interest Income		
Insurance	429	10
Investment	66	2
Net gain on sale of SpringCastle interests	18	-
Net gain on sales of personal and real estate loans	70	2
Total	3,366	100

COMPETITORS

Advance America
Atlanticus
Check 'n Go
Check Into Cash
Community Choice Financial
DFC Global
EZCORP
FirstCash
NetSpend
QC Holdings
Regional Management
Security Finance Corporation of Spartanburg
World Acceptance
Xponential

HISTORICAL FINANCIALS

Company Type: Public

Income Statement

FYE: December 31

	ASSETS ($ mil.)	NET INCOME ($ mil.)	INCOME AS % OF ASSETS	EMPLOYEES
12/19	22,817	855	3.7%	9,700
12/18	20,090	447	2.2%	10,200
12/17	19,433	183	0.9%	10,100
12/16	18,123	215	1.2%	10,100
12/15	21,056	(242)	—	11,400
Annual Growth	2.0%	—	—	(4.0%)

2019 Year-End Financials

Debt ratio: 75.43%
Return on equity: 21.04%
Cash ($ mil.): 1,227
Current ratio: —
Long-term debt ($ mil.): —

No. of shares (mil.): 136
Dividends
 Yield: 7.1%
 Payout: 53.6%
Market value ($ mil.): 5,737

	STOCK PRICE ($) FY Close	P/E High/Low		PER SHARE ($) Earnings	Dividends	Book Value
12/19	42.15	7	4	6.27	3.00	31.81
12/18	24.29	11	7	3.29	0.00	27.97
12/17	25.99	24	16	1.35	0.00	24.22
12/16	22.14	26	11	1.59	0.00	22.73
12/15	41.54	—	—	(1.89)	0.00	20.45
Annual Growth	0.4%	—	—	—	—	11.7%

ONEOK Inc

ONEOK ("one oak") is having a gas pursuing its pipeline dreams. ONEOK is an Oklahoma-based midstream service provider that owns one of the nation's premier NGL systems connecting NGL supply in the Rocky Mountain Permian and Mid-Continent regions with key market centers and an extensive network of natural gas gathering processing storage and transportation assets. It serves customers such as petrochemical companies propane distributors heating fuel users ethanol producers refineries and exporters. The company have an ownership interest in FERC-regulated NGL gathering and distribution pipelines in Oklahoma Kansas Texas New Mexico Montana North Dakota Wyoming and Colorado and terminal and storage facilities in Missouri Nebraska Iowa and Illinois.

Operations

ONEOK operates three reportable segments: Natural Gas Liquids Natural Gas Gathering and Processing and Natural Gas Pipelines.

The Natural Gas Liquids segment owns and operates facilities that gather NGLs and then fractionate and treat them separating them into NGL products primarily in Oklahoma Kansas Texas New Mexico and Rocky Mountain regions. The NGL products are then held in storage facilities or distributed to customers such as petrochemical manufacturers heating fuel users ethanol producers refineries exporters and propane distributors.

The Natural Gas Gathering and Processing segment serves producers of natural gas in Kansas Montana North Dakota Oklahoma and Wyoming. Raw natural gas is typically gathered at the wellhead compressed and transported through pipelines to their processing facilities. The NGLs separated from the natural gas are delivered through NGL Pipelines to fractionation facilities for further processing.

The Natural Gas Pipelines segment owns and operates more than 5000 miles of regulated natural gas transmission pipelines and around 55 billion cubic feet of natural gas storage facilities. It provides interstate and intrastate natural gas transportation and storage services (underground natural gas storage facilities in Kansas Oklahoma and Texas). It is also part owner of two additional pipelines Northern Border Pipeline located near the US-Canada border and Roadrunner which runs from West Texas to the Mexican border.

Geographic Reach

Tulsa Oklahoma-based ONEOK operates gathering and treatment facilities in well-known natural gas plays such as Bakken Permian Basin and Powder River Basin. It has pipeline and plants in some 15 US states with much of its infrastructure in Oklahoma Kansas and Texas though its operations stretch as far as Tennessee Montana and Wyoming.

Sales and Marketing

Natural Gas Gathering and Processing and Natural Gas Liquids segments derive services revenue from major and independent crude oil and natural gas producers. Their Natural Gas Liquids segment's customers also include NGL and natural gas gathering and processing companies. The company's downstream commodity sales customers are primarily utilities large industrial companies natural gasoline distributors propane distributors municipalities and petrochemical refining and marketing companies. ONEOK's Natural Gas Pipeline segment's assets primarily serve local natural gas distribution companies electric-generation facilities large industrial companies municipalities producers processors and marketing companies.

Financial Performance

Except in 2019 the company's revenue has been rising for the last five years. It has an overall growth of 31% between 2015 and 2019.

Sales in 2019 decreased 19% to $10.2 billion compared to $12.6 billion in 2018. Decrease in revenue was due to changes in commodity prices and sales volumes affect both revenue and cost of sales and fuel.

Net income increased by about $126.9 million to $1.3 billion in 2019 compared to 2018 mainly due to higher natural gas and NGL volumes in the company's Natural Gas Gathering and Processing and Natural Gas Liquids segments; and higher allowance for equity funds used during construction related to its capital-growth projects offset partially by higher interest expense related to its underwritten public debt offerings in March and August 2019.

Cash at the end of 2019 was $21.0 million an increase of $9.0 million from the prior year. Cash from operations contributed $1.9 billion to the coffers while investing activities used $3.8 billion mainly for capital expenditures. Financing activities provided $1.8 billion primarily in the form of issuance of long-term debt.

Strategy

Oneok's primary business strategy is to maintain prudent financial strength and flexibility while growing its fee-based earnings and dividends per share with a focus on safe reliable environmentally responsible legally compliant and sustainable operations for customers employees contractors and the public through the following:

Operate in a safe reliable environmentally responsible and sustainable manner; Pursue organic investments in existing operating regions to support earnings growth; Manage balance sheet and maintain investment-grade credit ratings; and Attract select develop motivate challenge and retain a diverse group of employees to support strategy execution.

HISTORY

In 1906 Oklahoma Natural Gas (ONG) was founded to pipe natural gas from northeastern Oklahoma to Oklahoma City. A 100-mile pipeline was completed the next year. In 1921 ONG created two oil companies to pump out the oil it found as a result of its natural gas exploration.

ONG changed hands many times in the 1920s ending up with utility financier G. L. Ohrstrom and Company which milked it dry by brokering acquisitions (purchasing gas properties and then selling them to ONG) and collecting fees. Stock sales drove revenues inflating the stock's price and the inflated price triggered more stock sales. The bubble burst on October 29 1929. A series of leadership changes ensued and in 1932 the company was dissolved and reincorporated. Under president Joseph Bowes ONG recovered wooing back dissatisfied customers and upgrading its pipelines.

In the late 1930s the company pioneered a type of underground storage that injected gas into depleted gas reservoirs in the summer and withdrew it during winter's peak use times.

The 1950s and 1960s saw the company expand. In 1962 it created its first subsidiary Oklahoma Natural Gas Gathering Company selling gas out of state and therefore subject to federal regulation.

ONG was not affected in the lean 1970s by federal laws that kept wellhead prices low for gas transported across state lines because its main operations were confined to Oklahoma. Congress deregulated wellhead prices in 1978 spurring exploration but causing great price fluctuations in the 1980s. In 1980 ONG changed its name to ONEOK.

In the 1980s ONEOK signed take-or-pay contracts which forced it to pay for gas offered by its suppliers even if it had no customers. When recession in the 1980s caused demand to drop ONEOK had to pay for high-priced natural gas it couldn't sell. In 1988 the company was ordered to pay some $50 million to supplier Forest Oil of Denver. A year later ONEOK was sued for allegedly failing to tell stockholders about the take-or-pay agreements (settled in 1993 for $5.5 million). It later sold more than half of its oil and gas reserves to Mustang Energy for $52 million to finance the Forest Oil court award. The company was still settling lawsuits over the agreements into the 1990s; it settled the last of the claims by 1998.

ONEOK began buying gas transmission and production facilities in Oklahoma and creating drilling alliances in the 1990s. In 1997 ONEOK bought the natural gas assets of Westar Energy formerly Western Resources for $660 million and ONEOK stock worth $800 million. The acquisition doubled the number of ONEOK's customers and increased its gas marketing gathering and transmission operations.

The company also acquired Southern Union's Texas natural gas distribution business (540000 customers) as well as Southern Union's stake in a Mexican gas utility and its propane distribution gas marketing and gas transmission operations in the southwestern US for $420 million.

ONEOK acquired Northern Plains Natural Gas a general partner of pipeline operator Northern Border Partners (later renamed ONEOK Partners) from CCE Holdings (a joint venture of Southern Union and GE Commercial Finance) for $175 million in 2004. The transaction followed CCE Holdings' acquisition of Enron's CrossCountry Energy unit.

Also in 2004 ONEOK changed the name of its wholesale energy unit from ONEOK Energy Marketing and Trading to ONEOK Energy Services.

The company bought Koch Industries' natural gas liquids assets in 2005 for $1.35 billion.

In 2013 the company announced plans to invest $440 million in the natural gas liquids-rich area in the Powder River Basin in Wyoming to by a 50-million cubic feet per day natural gas processing facility in Wyoming (the Sage Creek plant and related infrastructure) for $305 million. It plans to invest $135 million to upgrade and construct natural gas gathering and processing related infrastructure NGL gathering pipelines and well connections.

In 2017 ONEOK completed its $9.3 billion purchase of ONEOK Partners a subsidiary that has and will for the foreseeable future generate the majority of ONEOK's revenue. Prior to the purchase ONEOK owned about 40% of ONEOK Partners and the investing public owned the remaining shares. With the merger complete ONEOK Partners is a wholly owned subsidiary of ONEOK and its shares no longer trade on public markets. ONEOK funded the acquisition with stock doubling its number of issued shares.

EXECUTIVES

Senior Vice President Administrative Services, David Roth

Evp And Chief Administrative Officer, Robert F. (Rob) Martinovich, age 62, $500,000 total compensation

President And Ceo, Terry K. Spencer, age 60, $700,000 total compensation

Svp Operations, Wesley J. Christensen, age 66, $400,000 total compensation

Svp Cfo And Treasurer, Derek S. Reiners, age 49, $375,000 total compensation

Svp Natural Gas Gathering And Processing, Kevin L. Burdick, age 55

Vp And Cio, Brien H. Brown

Vp Natural Gas Pipelines, J. Phillip (Phill) May

Evp Strategic Planning And Corporate Affairs, Walter S. Hulse, age 56, $500,000 total compensation

Svp Natural Gas Liquids Oneok Partners, Sheridan C. Swords

Vice President Commercial G And P, Michael A Fitzgibbons

Vice President Natural Gas Gathering And Processing Operations Oneok Partners, Geoffrey Sands

Vice President Customer Service, Krystal Parker

Vice President Human Resources, Angela Wells

Vice President Government Relations, Steve Johnson

Vice President, Walter Allen
Vice President Of Marketing, Mike Clark
Vice President Project Development And Business Analysis, Michael Crisman
Vice President Gas Supply, Christy Williamson
Vice President Commercial Natural Gas Pipelines, Hayley Rose
Vp Marketing Oneok Energy Resources, George Drake
Vice President And Chief Accounting Officer, Mike Miers
Vice President, Randy Jordan
Vice President Customer Service And Support, James Fallan
Vice President, Donald Jacobsen
Vice President Of Customer Support, William Eliason
Vice President Rates And Regulatory Affairs, Ron Mucci
Vice President Natural Gas Liquids Gathering And Fand#8230, Michael L Turner
Senior Vice President Operations, Wesley Christenson
Vice President Western Region, Dan Walker
Vice President, David Scharf
Vice President, Jackie Null Witt
Manager Government Relations, Michael Gillaspie
Vice President And Associate General Counsel, Vicky Benedict
Vice President Information Technology, Winsford Spears
Vice President Planning, Mike Christman
Vice President Of Investor Relations And Public Affairs, Dan L Harrison
Svp Natural Gas Pipelines, J Philip May
Vp Commercial Interstate Pipelines Segment, Philip May
Vice President Associate General Counsel, Brandon Watson
Executive Vice President Human Resources, Amber Waid
Vice President Gas Supply (ofs), Greg Lusardi
Chairman Oneok Oneok Partners And One Gas, John W. Gibson, age 67
Board Member, Gary Parker
Board Member, Jim Mogg
Board Member, Randy Larson
Board Member, Brian Derksen
Board Member, Randall Larson
Sec Treas, Kathleen Fricke
Auditors: PricewaterhouseCoopers LLP

LOCATIONS

HQ: ONEOK Inc
100 West Fifth Street, Tulsa, OK 74103
Phone: 918 588-7000   **Fax:** 918 588-7273
Web: www.oneok.com

PRODUCTS/OPERATIONS

2016 Sales

	$ mil.	% of total
Natural Gas Liquids	7,675	76
Natural Gas Gathering and Processing	2,051	20
Natural Gas Pipeline	379	4
Reconciled Intersegment Revenues	(1185.7)	-
Total	**8,920**	**0**

COMPETITORS

BP
DCP Midstream Partners
EQT Corporation
Enable Midstream Partners
Enterprise Products

Exxon Mobil
National Fuel Gas
SemGroup
Southwest Gas
TRII
Williams Companies

HISTORICAL FINANCIALS

Company Type: Public

Income Statement

<span></span>   FYE: December 31

	REVENUE ($ mil.)	NET INCOME ($ mil.)	NET PROFIT MARGIN	EMPLOYEES
12/19	10,164	1,278	12.6%	2,882
12/18	12,593	1,151	9.1%	2,684
12/17	12,173	387	3.2%	2,470
12/16	8,920	352	3.9%	2,384
12/15	7,763	244	3.2%	2,364
Annual Growth	**7.0%**	**51.1%**	**—**	**5.1%**

2019 Year-End Financials

Debt ratio: 58.26%
Return on equity: 19.97%
Cash ($ mil.): 20
Current ratio: 0.73
Long-term debt ($ mil.): 12,479

No. of shares (mil.): 413
Dividends
Yield: 4.6%
Payout: 117.2%
Market value ($ mil.): 31,270

	STOCK PRICE ($) FY Close	P/E High/Low		PER SHARE ($) Earnings	Dividends	Book Value
12/19	75.67	25	18	3.07	3.53	15.07
12/18	53.95	26	18	2.78	3.25	15.99
12/17	53.45	45	36	1.29	2.72	14.22
12/16	57.41	35	12	1.66	2.46	0.90
12/15	24.66	44	16	1.16	2.43	1.60
Annual Growth	**32.4%**	**—**		**27.5%**	**9.8%**	**75.1%**

ONEOK PARTNERS, L.P.

For ONEOK Partners it's OK to have three businesses: natural gas pipelines; gas gathering and processing; and natural gas liquids (NGLs). Its pipelines include Midwestern Gas Transmission Guardian Pipeline Viking Gas Transmission and OkTex Pipeline. The ONEOK affiliate operates 17100 miles of gas-gathering pipeline and 7600 miles of transportation pipeline as well as gas processing plants and storage facilities (with 52 billion cu. ft. of capacity). It also owns one of the US's top natural NGL systems (more than 7200 miles of pipeline). In 2017 41%-owner ONEOK agreed to buy the stock of ONEOK Partners that it did not already own for $9.3 billion in a stock deal. Operations ONEOK Partners operates in three business segments: natural gas gathering and processing; natural gas pipelines; and natural gas liquids. Geographic Reach The company gathers and processes natural gas in the Mid-Continent region which includes the NGL-rich Cana-Woodford Shale and Granite Wash formations the Mississippian Lime formation of Oklahoma and Kansas and the Hugoton and Central Kansas Uplift Basins of Kansas. The Natural Gas Pipelines segment owns and operates regulated natural gas transmission pipelines natural gas storage facilities and natural gas gathering systems for nonprocessed gas. It also provide interstate natural gas transportation and storage service. The company's interstate natural gas pipeline assets transport natural gas through pipelines in North Dakota Minnesota Wisconsin Illinois Indiana Kentucky Tennessee Oklahoma Texas and New Mexico. Its Natural gas liquids assets provide nondiscretionary services to producers that consist of facilities that gather frac-

tionate and treat NGLs and store NGL products primarily in Oklahoma Kansas and Texas. It also owns or has stakes in natural gas liquids gathering and distribution pipelines in Oklahoma Kansas Texas Wyoming and Colorado and terminal and storage facilities in Missouri Nebraska Iowa and Illinois. In addition it owns natural gas liquids distribution and refined petroleum products pipelines in Kansas Missouri Nebraska Iowa Illinois and Indiana that connect the company's Mid-Continent assets with Midwest markets including Chicago.

Financial Performance

Revenues decreased by 10% in 2012 due to lower net realized natural gas and NGL product prices offset partially by higher natural gas and NGL sales volumes from completed capital projects. The increase in natural gas supply resulting from the development of nonconventional resource areas in North America and a warmer than normal winter caused natural gas prices to drop. NGL prices particularly ethane and propane also decreased in 2012 due primarily to increased NGL production and an increase in available supply. Propane prices also were affected by a warmer than normal winter.

ONEOK Partners' net income grew by 7% in 2012 thanks to lower costs of sales and fuels and lower interest expenses.

Strategy

The company pursues a strategy of building up its fee-based earnings coupled with organic growth and complementary acquisitions in both conventional oil and gas and unconventional (shale plays).

It is looking to increase NGL volumes gathered and fractionated in its NGL segment and natural gas volumes processed in its natural gas gathering and processing segment as producers continue to develop NGL-rich resource plays in the Mid-Continent and Rocky Mountain areas.

In 2012 ONEOK Partners announced plans to invest up to $360 million to grow its projects in the Woodford Shale formation.

Company Background

ONEOK Partners was formed in 2006 when ONEOK spun off its gathering and processing NGLs pipelines and storage businesses for $3 billion following that company's acquisition of Northern Border Partners (which was founded in 1993). Building out its assets in 2007 the company acquired an interstate pipeline system from Kinder Morgan Energy Partners for $300 million.

EXECUTIVES

Pres-Ceo, Terry K Spencer
Evp-Cfo, Walter S Hulse III
Svp,naturalgasgathering&procce, Michael A Fitzgibbons
Executive Vice President Opera, Robert F Martinovich

LOCATIONS

HQ: ONEOK PARTNERS, L.P.
100 W 5TH ST STE LL, TULSA, OK 741034298
Phone: 918 588-7000
Web: WWW.ONEOK.COM

PRODUCTS/OPERATIONS

Natural Gas Pipelines
Midwestern Gas Transmission Company
Viking Gas Transmission Company
Guardian Pipeline
OkTex Pipeline Company
ONEOK Gas Transportation
ONEOK Gas Gathering
ONEOK Gas Storage
ONEOK WesTex Transmission
ONEOK Texas Gas Storage
Mid Continent Market Center
ONEOK Transmission Company
Natural Gas Gathering & Processing
Crestone Energy Ventures
ONEOK Field Services
ONEOK Rockies Midstream

COMPETITORS

Enbridge
Kinder Morgan Energy
Partners

Panhandle Eastern Pipe
Line
TransCanada

HISTORICAL FINANCIALS

Company Type: Private

Income Statement   FYE: December 31

	REVENUE ($ mil.)	NET INCOME ($ mil.)	NET PROFIT MARGIN	EMPLOYEES
12/16	8,918	1,072	12.0%	2,364
12/15	7,761	597	7.7%	—
12/14	12,191	911	7.5%	—
Annual Growth	(14.5%)	8.5%	—	—

Oracle Corp

Oracle provides products and services that address enterprise information technology (IT) environments. The enterprise software company offers a range of cloud-based applications and platforms as well as hardware and services to help companies improve their processes. Oracle's applications center on enterprise resource planning data management collaboration content and experience business analytics IT operations management security and emerging technologies. In recent years Oracle has aggressively expanded through acquisitions that have helped build its cloud offerings. The company's mainstay product has been Oracle Database one of the most popular corporate database offerings. More than half its revenue comes from international customers. The company was founded in 1977 and the founder was Larry Ellison.

Operations

The company operates three segments: cloud and license business hardware business and services business.

Oracle's cloud and license businesses generates nearly 85% of its sales. It engages in the sale marketing and delivery of applications and infrastructure technologies through cloud and on-premise deployment models including cloud services and license support offerings; and the cloud license and on-premise license offerings. The company's on-premise software brands are

Siebel PeopleSoft and JD Edwards and the Oracle E-Business Suite.

Oracle is moving its products to cloud computing environments where customers can access programs from multiple locations and devices. The company's cloud applications are Oracle Human Capital Management (HCM) Cloud Oracle Enterprise Resource Planning (ERP) Cloud Oracle Customer Experience (CX) Cloud Oracle Supply Chain Management (SCM) Cloud and Oracle Data Cloud. Its Autonomous Database is cloud software with machine learnings capabilities.

About 10% of Oracle's sales come from its hardware business which includes infrastructure technologies consist of hardware products and certain unique hardware-related software offerings including Oracle Engineered Systems enterprise servers storage solutions industry-specific hardware virtualization software operating systems management software and related hardware services including hardware support at the customer's option.

Oracle also offers helps customers and partners maximize the performance of their investments in Oracle applications and infrastructure technologies. In addition services offerings include consulting services advanced customer services and education services. Those businesses account for less than 10% of Oracle's revenue.

Geographic Reach

Headquartered in Redwood City California Oracle operates facilities in the US including a factory in Hillsboro Oregon and overseas.

Oracle has a wide geographic distribution of customers. Those in the US generate about 45% of sales. The other countries for which the company breaks out sales ? the UK Japan Canada and Germany ? each account for 5% or less. The other 170-some countries with Oracle customers account for more than 35% of the company's sales.

Sales and Marketing

Oracle uses direct and indirect channels including independent distributors and value-added resellers to market and sell its products and services. The companies that comprise Oracle's indirect channel network are members of the Oracle Partner Network. In addition customers include businesses of many sizes government agencies and educational institutions.

The company has customers in a range of industries such as aerospace and defense automotive financial technology manufacturing hospitals oil and gas retail telecommunications and utilities.

Advertising expenses were $178 million $169 million and $138 million in fiscal 2020 2019 and 2018 respectively.

Financial Performance

After several years of uneven revenue Oracle Corp.'s sales rose in the past three years although in 2020 it decreased by 1%.

In 2020 (ended May) Oracle's revenue fell $438 million to about $39.1 billion. The small decrease was primarily to the decrease on their operations in Americas and EMEA by 1% and 2% respectively.

Net income slid down to $10.1 billion in 2020 from $11.1 billion in 2019. The decrease was primarily due to the increase on their provisions

for income taxes and also a decrease on their revenue.

Oracle's coffers held $37.2 billion in cash in 2020 compared to $20.5 billion in 2019. Operating activities generated $13.1 billion in 2020 and investing activities provided $9.8 billion while financing activities used $6.1 billion for payments for repurchases of common stock and repayment of borrowings.

Strategy

Providing choice and flexibility to Oracle customers as to when and how they deploy Oracle applications and infrastructure technologies is an important element of their corporate strategy. The company believe that offering customers broad comprehensive flexible and interoperable deployment models for Oracle applications and infrastructure technologies is important to their growth strategy and better addresses customer needs relative to their competitors many of whom provide fewer offerings more restrictive deployment models and less flexibility for a customer's transition to cloud-based IT environments.

Oracle's investments in and innovation with respect to Oracle products and services that the company offer through their cloud and license hardware and services businesses are another important element of their corporate strategy. In fiscal 2020 2019 and 2018 the company have invested $6.1 billion $6.0 billion and $6.1 billion respectively in research and development to enhance their existing portfolio of offerings and products and to develop new technologies and services.

Mergers and Acquisitions

In 2020 Oracle announced that it has entered into an agreement to acquire LiveData Utilities. The acquisition extends Oracle Utilities' Network Management System by adding a long-standing partner that provides leading operational technology (OT) middleware solutions and SCADA capabilities to monitor and control utility equipment while reducing the complexity of real-time systems. The transaction is now closed and the LiveData Utilities team will join the Oracle Utilities organization.

In 2019 Oracle acquired Brazil-based Oxygen Systems to widen its footprint in Brazil and expand business with small and medium businesses in the country. Oxygen a spinoff of Chile-based IT integrator Sonda localizes Oracle's Netsuite enterprise resource planning software for small and medium businesses.

In late 2019 Oracle agreed to acquire CrowdTwist the leading cloud-native customer loyalty solution to empower brands to offer personalized customer experiences. The CrowdTwist solution offers over 100 out-of-the-box engagement paths providing rapid time-to-value for marketers to develop a more complete view of the customer. CrowdTwist team will join the Oracle Customer Experience (CX) Cloud organization.

Company Background

Larry Ellison Robert Miner Bruce Scott and Edward Oates founded System Development Laboratories in 1977 to create a database management system according to theoretical specifications published by IBM. Ellison had studied physics at the University of Chicago but dropped out in the 1960s to seek his fortune in Silicon Valley. He was part of the team that developed the first IBM-compatible mainframe. Miner an experienced programmer was the main developer of Oracle's database manager which was able to run on many computer brands and was introduced in 1979. The company also changed its name that year to Relational Software.

In 1983 the company changed its name again this time to Oracle in order to more closely align itself with its primary product. Oracle went public in 1986 and within two years had a 36% share of Uncle Sam's PC database market. It also added financial management graphics and human resource management software.

EXECUTIVES

Evp, David A. (Dave) Donatelli
Executive Chairman And Cto, Lawrence J. (Larry) Ellison, $1 total compensation
Evp Oracle Customer Support Services, Charles A. (Chuck) Rozwat, $600,000 total compensation
Ceo, Mark V. Hurd, $950,000 total compensation
Evp Global Business Units, Robert K. (Bob) Weiler
Svp Cloud, Shawn Price
Ceo, Safra A. Catz, $950,000 total compensation
Evp Human Resources, Joyce Westerdahl
President Oracle Product Development, Thomas Kurian, $800,000 total compensation
Evp Oracle Applications Development, Steve Miranda
Svp Oracle Database Server Technologies, Andrew Mendelsohn
Evp Microelectronics Group, Michael E. (Mike) Splain
Svp And Cio, Mark E. Sunday
Evp Systems, John F. Fowler, $700,000 total compensation
Evp General Counsel And Secretary, Dorian E. Daley
Svp And General Manager Financial Services Global Business Unit, Sonny Singh
Evp Chief Of Staff And Head Corporate Development, Douglas Kehring
Svp North American Technology Division, Rich Geraffo
Svp Cloud Development, Peter S. Magnusson
Svp Worldwide Operations, Karl Braitberg
Evp Oracle Fusion Middleware Development, Inderjeet Singh
Svp And Managing Director China, Roger Li
Senior Vice President Oracle Applications Development, Cliff Godwin
Vice President Engineering, George Thomas
Vice President Info Technology, Alain Ozan
Senior Vice President North America Support Services, Juan C Jones
Vice President Consulting Services, Teresa Short
Vice President Global Customer Programs, Carol Sato
Vice President Of Product, Lyle Ekdahl
Senior Vice President, Kevin Walsh
Vice President Of Software Development, Ken Peterka
Vice President Oracle Database Product Management, William Hardie
Vice President, Brent Grech
Vice President Global Hrms Product Development, Rob Watson
Vice President Human Capital Transformation And Thought Leadership Practice, Cara Capretta
Group Vice President, Greg Calhoun
Vice President Customer Loyalty, Joan Smeal
Vice President, Terrance Wampler
Vice President Ebs Practice, Robert Allen
Vice President Applications Development, Paulo Back
Vice President Of Engineering, Ashish Kolli
Vice President Application Development Tools, Paul Hartenstine

Vice President Product Development Information Technology, Campbell Webb
Senior Vice President Global Business Finance, Ivgen Guner
Senior Vice President Global Customer Support, Buffy Ransom
Regional Vice President ??? Consulting, Vishal Singh
Vice President Application Development Tools, Chris Tonas
Vice President Revenue Management Products, Mahadevan Subramanian
Vp Finance, Gary Pola
Regional Vice President, Martin Zabielski
Vice President Database Global Customer Support, Lauren Verno
Consulting Vice President, Deborah Rooney
Svp Investor Relations, Ken Bond
Regional Vice President, Jeff Keplar
Consulting Vice President Jd Edwards, Steven Reeter
Vice President Product Development, Prakash Dodeja
Senior Vice President, Ian Smith
Vice President Develop, Ilan Bensimhon
Vice President Global Information Technology Risk Management, Brennan Baybeck
Vice President Of Information Technology And Compliance, Julie Barton
Consulting Vice President, Ellen Lapriore
Vice President, David Carey
Evp, Luiz Meisler
Vp Global Business Units Pmo, Elizabeth Bell
Vice President, John Emery
Rvp, James Montrie
Regional Vice President, Michael Placido
Hardware Group Vice President Of Business Developm, Avery Collard
Vice President Business Development, Hemanth Vedagarbha
Vice President Software Development, Meeten Bhavsar
Vice President Crm Sales Support, Frank Mouthaan
Regional Vice President, Lupe Noguera
Vice President Global Practices, Ellen Eder
Vice President Finance, Jim English
Group Vice President And Global Head Of Product Consulting, Kishore Kapoor
Vice President International Human Resources, Elizabeth Snyder
Group Vice President, Brendan Logan
Senior Vice President, Douglas Doedens
Vice President Government Relations, Jason Mahler
Vice President Epm Applications, Matthew Bradley
Senior Vice President Of Applications Development, Rick Jewell
Vice President Of Product Marketing, Rex Wang
Vice President Corporate Marketing, Christina Cavanna
Regional Vice President, Kirby Rouser
Vice President, Carol Adams
Vice President Technology Solutions And Channels, Alan Hartwell
Group Vice President, Jim Standard
Vice President, Dave Rose
Senior Vice President Peoplesoft Enterprise Development, Paco Aubrejuan
Vice President Autovue Development, Sami Bannour
Division Vice President, Ryan Feaver
Vice President Of Epm And Bi Marketing, Rich Clayton
Vice President Process, Gopi Tummala
Vice President, Denise Grills
Vice President Marketing, Paul Salinger
Regional Vice President, Scott Carlin
Vice President Professional Services, Brad Kitchin
Vice President Product Strategy, Stephen Johnston

Vice President Customer Services Emea Major Accounts, Nick Harber
Vice President Of Product Support, Paul Martin
Senior Vice President Of Engineering Systems, Ali Alasti
Vice President Operations Tech And System Suppor, Paul Williamson
Vice President, Chuck Jones
Regional Vice President, Jeff Ellington
Sales Vice President Bi Analytics And Epm Latin America, Marvio Portela
Vice President Global Tech, Susan Zwinger
Retail Vice President, William O'Brien
Vice President Finance Europe North, Oliver Schlemper
Vice President Of Technology Marketing, Robert Shimp
Vice President Of Operations, Brett Smith
Vice President Consulting, Heather Graham
Senior Vice President Of Product Development, Angelo Pruscino
Vice President Development, Hannes Sandmeier
Regional Vice President, Brook Crichton
Group Vice President Human Capital Management Strategy, Gretchen Alarcon
Vice President, Giovanna Sangiorgi
Vice President Central Europe, Pawel Piwowar
Regional Vice President, Timothy Tarkinton
Vice President Accounts, Jason Lerman
Vice President Of Supply Chain Applications Market, Maha Muzumdar
Vice President Product Managment, Alex Gleyzer
Vice President Software Development, Ryan Carroll
Vice President Of Product Management And Product Development, Amit Zavery
Vice President Sales Manufacturing Industry, Junichi Iijima
Vice President Signaling Products, Wesley Tilley
Vice President And General Manager, Barry Dyer
Vp Of Cloud Services, Rick Potocki
Area Vice President, Jack Davis
Vice President North American Commercial Hardware Sales Consulting, Chris Hause
Vice President Of Manufacturing, John Barcus
Vice President Of Business Operations, Mitch Codkind
Vice President Engineering Information Technology, Eugene Weinstein
Vice President Technology Consulting Services, Ashok Rajan
Vice President Linux And Infrastructure, Van Okamura
Senior Vice President Oracle Managed Cloud Services, Steve McMillan
Regional Vice President, Jonathan Conwell
Vice President Of Sales For The Americas, Ed Coke
Vice President Business Operations North America Infrastructure Sales, Laurie Birch
Vice President Hcm Sales, Scott Stoll
Vice President, Venkata Subramanian
Vice President Enterprise Accounts, Bob Barrett
Vice President Customer Programs, Bob Schumm
Vice President Casinos, Scott Lampman
Vice President Of Sales Smb, Brendan Caleca
Vice President Tax Planning, Jonathan Grahmann
Vice President, Juana Schurman
Vice President, Tania Weidick
Vice President Marketing Operations And Shared Services, Lori Granville
Vice President, Michael Poplack
Vice President Of Strategic Programs, Patrick Mungovan
Vice President, Michael Miller
Auditors: Ernst & Young LLP

LOCATIONS

HQ: Oracle Corp
  2300 Oracle Way, Austin, TX 78741
Phone: 737 867-1000
Web: www.oracle.com

2018 Sales

	$ mil.	% of total
United States	18,596	47
United Kingdom	2,054	5
Japan	1,848	5
Germany	1,583	4
Canada	1,166	3
Other countries	14,259	36
Total	**39,506**	**100**

Selected Acquisitions

FY 2017
  Moat (SaaS search engine)
  Wercker (cloud infrastructure software)
  Apiary (API development)
FY 2016
  Dyn (managed DNS and cloud infrastructure)
  Palerra (cloud security)
  LogFire (cloud management for retailers)
  NetSuite (cloud-based applications)
  Opower (SaaS energy efficiency)
  Textura (online collaboration for construction)
  Crosswise (cross-device ID mapping)
FY 2013
  Responsys (marketing automation software)
  Nimbula (private cloud infrastructure management
  software)
  Tekelec (data management)
  Acme Packet (data management)
FY 2012
  Collective Intellect (social media monitoring software)
  Vitrue (social media software)
  Eloqua (marketing automation software)
  Skire (project management software)
  SelectMinds (human resources software)
  Xsigo Systems (networking technology)

PRODUCTS/OPERATIONS

2019 Sales

	$ mil.	% of total
Cloud services and license support	26,707	68
Cloud license and on-premise license	5,855	15
Hardware revenue	3,704	9
Services revenues	3,240	8
Total	**39,506**	**100**

2019 Sales

	$ mil.	% of total
Cloud and on-premise software	32,562	83
Hardware	3,704	9
Services	3,240	8
Total	**39,506**	**100**

Selected Products

Software
  Business applications
  Business intelligence
  Customer experience
  Customer relationship
  Enterprise content
  Financial
  Governance risk & compliance
  Human capital
  Supply chain
  Databases
  Enterprise application integration
  Middleware

Services
  Consulting
  Application Development and Integration
  Enterprise architecture
  Infrastructure and Platform
  Education/training
Hardware
  Servers (SPARC servers x86 servers)
  Solaris operating system (hardware-related software)
  Storage & tape

COMPETITORS

AWS	IBM
Accenture	Infor Global
Adobe Systems	Intel
Alphabet Inc.	Microsoft
BMC Software	SAP
CA Inc.	Workday Inc.
Cisco Systems	salesforce.com
Hewlett Packard	
Enterprise	

HISTORICAL FINANCIALS

Company Type: Public

Income Statement

FYE: May 31

	REVENUE ($ mil.)	NET INCOME ($ mil.)	NET PROFIT MARGIN	EMPLOYEES
05/20	39,068	10,135	25.9%	135,000
05/19	39,506	11,083	28.1%	136,000
05/18	39,831	3,825	9.6%	137,000
05/17	37,728	9,335	24.7%	138,000
05/16	37,047	8,901	24.0%	136,000
Annual Growth	1.3%	3.3%	—	(0.2%)

2020 Year-End Financials

Debt ratio: 62.02%—
Return on equity: 59.70%
Cash ($ mil.): 37,239
Current ratio: 3.03
Long-term debt ($ mil.): 69,226

Dividends
  Yield: 0.0%
  Payout: 31.1%
  Market value ($ mil.): —

	STOCK PRICE ($) FY Close	P/E High/Low	PER SHARE ($) Earnings	Dividends	Book Value
05/20	53.77	19 13	3.08	0.96	3.94
05/19	50.60	18 14	2.97	0.81	6.49
05/18	46.72	57 48	0.90	0.76	11.44
05/17	45.39	20 17	2.21	0.64	13.02
05/16	40.20	21 16	2.07	0.60	11.45
Annual Growth	7.5%	— —	10.4%	12.5%	(23.4%)

Orchid Island Capital Inc

No REIT is an island unless your name is Orchid Island Capital. The company which is seeking to become a real estate investment trust invests in residential mortgage-backed securities (RMBS) that are guaranteed by the US government or federally sponsored entities like Fannie Mae Freddie Mac and Ginnie Mae. Its portfolio and principal investment targets consist of pass-through agency RMBS and structured agency RMBS including fixed-rate mortgages adjustable-rate mortgages (ARMs) and hybrid ARMs as well as collateralized mortgage obligations. Formed by mortgage REIT Bimini Capital Management in 2010 Orchid Island Capital filed to go public for the second time in October 2014.

EXECUTIVES

Chairman President And Ceo; Chairman And Ceo Bimini, Robert E. Cauley, age 61
Cfo Chief Investment Officer Secretary And Director; President Cfo And Chief Investment Officer Bimini, G. Hunter Haas, age 44
Auditors: BDO USA, LLP

LOCATIONS

HQ: Orchid Island Capital Inc
  3305 Flamingo Drive, Vero Beach, FL 32963
Phone: 772 231-1400
Web: www.orchidislandcapital.com

COMPETITORS

AG Mortgage Investment Trust	Capstead Mortgage
ARMOUR Residential REIT	Hatteras Financial
	MFA Financial
American Capital Agency Corp.	Provident Mortgage Capital
Annaly Capital Management	Redwood Trust
	TMAC Mortgage
Anworth Mortgage Asset	Two Harbors
Apollo Residential Mortgage	

HISTORICAL FINANCIALS

Company Type: Public

Income Statement

FYE: December 31

	ASSETS ($ mil.)	NET INCOME ($ mil.)	INCOME AS % OF ASSETS	EMPLOYEES
12/19	3,882	24	0.6%	—
12/18	3,395	(44)	—	—
12/17	4,023	2	0.0%	—
12/16	3,138	1	0.1%	—
12/15	2,241	1	0.0%	—
Annual Growth	14.7%	118.2%	—	—

2019 Year-End Financials

Debt ratio: —
Return on equity: 6.63%
Cash ($ mil.): 193
Current ratio: —
Long-term debt ($ mil.): —

No. of shares (mil.): 63
Dividends
  Yield: 16.4%
  Payout: 223.2%
  Market value ($ mil.): 369

	STOCK PRICE ($) FY Close	P/E High/Low	PER SHARE ($) Earnings	Dividends	Book Value
12/19	5.85	17 12	0.43	0.96	6.27
12/18	6.39	— —	(0.85)	1.07	6.84
12/17	9.28	250 184	0.05	1.68	8.71
12/16	10.83	140 103	0.08	1.68	10.10
12/15	9.93	284 155	0.05	1.92	11.64
Annual Growth	(12.4%)	— —	71.2%	(15.9%)	(14.3%)

Origin Bancorp Inc

Auditors: BKD, LLP

LOCATIONS

HQ: Origin Bancorp Inc
  500 South Service Road East, Ruston, LA 71270
Phone: 318 255-2222
Web: www.origin.bank

HISTORICAL FINANCIALS

Company Type: Public

Income Statement

FYE: December 31

	ASSETS ($ mil.)	NET INCOME ($ mil.)	INCOME AS % OF ASSETS	EMPLOYEES
12/19	5,324	53	1.0%	751
12/18	4,821	51	1.1%	761
12/17	4,154	14	0.4%	686
12/16	4,071	12	0.3%	—
Annual Growth	9.4%	61.3%	—	—

2019 Year-End Financials

Debt ratio: 0.70%
Return on equity: 9.38%
Cash ($ mil.): 291
Current ratio: —
Long-term debt ($ mil.): —

No. of shares (mil.): 23
Dividends
  Yield: 0.7%
  Payout: 12.2%
Market value ($ mil.): 889

	STOCK PRICE ($) FY Close	P/E High/Low	PER SHARE ($) Earnings	Dividends	Book Value
12/19	37.84	17 14	2.28	0.28	25.52
12/18	34.08	19 15	2.20	0.10	23.17
12/17	0.00	— —	0.50	0.13	23.33
Annual Growth	—	—	65.8%	29.5%	3.0%

Orrstown Financial Services, Inc.

Orrstown Financial Services keeps both paddles in the money pool. TheÂ institutionÂ is the holding company for Orrstown Bank which operates some 20 branches in Pennsylvania's Cumberland PerryÂ and Franklin counties as well as in Maryland's Washington County. In addition to traditional retail deposit offeringsÂ Orrstown alsoÂ provides investment management services including retirement planning and investment analysis. Real estate mortgages account for about 40% of the bank's lending portfolio followed by commercial construction and consumer loans. Orrstown is growing its mortgage lending capabilities. It launched an online application system in order to increase mortgage origination sales.

EXECUTIVES

Senior Vice President Director Of Commer, Andrew Johnson
Vice President Credit Officer, David Chajkowski
Vp Financial Advisor, Kim Ressler
Board Member, Floyd Stoner
Board Member, Thomas Longenecker
Auditors: Crowe LLP

LOCATIONS

HQ: Orrstown Financial Services, Inc.
  77 East King Street, P.O. Box 250, Shippensburg, PA 17257
Phone: 717 532-6114
Web: www.orrstown.com

COMPETITORS

Citizens Financial Group	M&T Bank
Franklin Financial Services	PNC Financial
	Sovereign Bank

HISTORICAL FINANCIALS

Company Type: Public

Income Statement

FYE: December 31

	ASSETS ($ mil.)	NET INCOME ($ mil.)	INCOME AS % OF ASSETS	EMPLOYEES
12/19	2,383	16	0.7%	460
12/18	1,934	12	0.7%	386
12/17	1,558	8	0.5%	338
12/16	1,414	6	0.5%	327
12/15	1,292	7	0.6%	306
Annual Growth	16.5%	21.1%	—	10.7%

2019 Year-End Financials

Debt ratio: 1.34%
Return on equity: 8.53%
Cash ($ mil.): 56
Current ratio: —
Long-term debt ($ mil.): —

No. of shares (mil.): 11
Dividends
  Yield: 2.6%
  Payout: 46.1%
Market value ($ mil.): 253

	STOCK PRICE ($) FY Close	P/E High/Low	PER SHARE ($) Earnings	Dividends	Book Value
12/19	22.62	14 11	1.61	0.60	19.93
12/18	18.21	18 12	1.50	0.51	18.39
12/17	25.25	27 20	0.98	0.42	17.34
12/16	22.40	29 20	0.81	0.35	16.28
12/15	17.84	19 16	0.97	0.22	16.08
Annual Growth	6.1%	—	13.5%	28.5%	5.5%

Otis Worldwide Corp

EXECUTIVES

Pres-Ceo, Judith F Marks
Exec Chb, Christopher J Kearney
V Pres-Cfo, Rahul Ghai
V Pres-Chro, Laurie P Havanec
V Pres-Gen Counsel-Corp SEC, Nora E Lafreniere
V Pres-Cao, Michael P Ryan
Pres Otis Asia Pacific, Stephane De Montlivault
Pres Otis Emea, Richard M Eubanks
Pres Otis China, Peiming Zheng
Pres, Otis Emea, Bernardo Calleja

LOCATIONS

HQ: Otis Worldwide Corp
  One Carrier Place, Farmington, CT 06032
Phone: 860 233-6847
Web: www.otis.com

HISTORICAL FINANCIALS

Company Type: Public

Income Statement

FYE: December 31

	REVENUE ($ mil.)	NET INCOME ($ mil.)	NET PROFIT MARGIN	EMPLOYEES
12/19	13,118	1,116	8.5%	69,000
12/18	12,915	1,049	8.1%	—
12/17	12,323	636	5.2%	—
Annual Growth	3.2%	32.5%	—	—

2019 Year-End Financials

Debt ratio: 0.35%—
Return on equity: 68.28%
Cash ($ mil.): 1,446
Current ratio: 1.05
Long-term debt ($ mil.): —

Dividends
  Yield: —
  Payout: —
Market value ($ mil.): —

	STOCK PRICE ($) FY Close	P/E High/Low	PER SHARE ($) Earnings	Dividends	Book Value
12/19	0.00	— —	(0.00)	0.00	(0.00)
12/18	0.00	— —	(0.00)	0.00	(0.00)
Annual Growth					

Owens & Minor, Inc.

Owens & Minor (O&M) is a leading distributor of medical and surgical supplies. The company offers nearly 200000 products from third-party manufacturers as well as its own proprietary products. Offerings include sterilization wrap surgical drapes and gowns facial protection protective apparel medical exam gloves custom and minor procedure kits and other medical products. They manufacture and sources medical surgical products through their own production and kitting operations. O&M primarily serves hospitals and health systems and the purchasing organizations that serve them. The US accounts for nearly 95% of the company's sales.

Operations

Owens & Minor (O&M) operates in two segments: Global Solutions and Global Products.

The Global Solutions segment (approximately 85% of sales) offers medical and surgical supplies from third-party manufacturers and well as O&M's proprietary products. The company serves hospitals and health systems through nearly 50 US distribution centers.

Global Solutions also provide logistics and other services to healthcare providers O&M's own suppliers and the pharmaceutical and medical device industries. Healthcare provider services include supplier and inventory management analytics and clinical supply management which helps providers improve their vendor contracting purchasing and inventory processes. The company also provides logistics and marketing services to drive sales growth and market share for its suppliers. The company's significant investment in information technology supports the company's business including warehouse management systems customer service and ordering functions demand forecasting programs electronic commerce data warehousing decision support and supply-chain management.

Global Products segment (about 15% of sales) manufactures and sources medical surgical products through its production and kitting operations including sterilization wrap surgical drapes and gowns facial protection protective apparel medical exam gloves and custom and minor procedure kits and other medical products.

Geographic Reach

Headquartered in Mechanicsville VA Owens & Minor's (O&M) Global Solutions segment operates nearly 50 US distribution centers.

The Global Products division has manufacturing facilities in US Thailand Honduras Mexico and Ireland.

The company has 25 offices in Europe US Canada and Asia. US generates about 95% of the company's total sales while International sales generate the remaining.

Sales and Marketing

The company provides products and services to thousands of healthcare provider customers either directly or indirectly through third-party distributors. Most of Owens & Minor's (O&M) sales are attributed to contracts with acute care hospitals which are often represented by group purchasing organizations (GPOs) or integrated delivery networks (IDNs). GPOs Vizient Premier and HealthTrust Purchasing Group are the company's largest customers. Additional clients include other government agencies and alternate health care locations such as physician clinics nursing homes and surgery centers. In addition O&M provides outsourced distribution services to suppliers of surgical and medical products.

Financial Performance

Owens & Minor's sales have been inconsistent the past five years mostly downward trend. Net income also fluctuated with the last two years suffering losses.

Sales in 2019 decreased 2% to $9.2 billion compared to $9.4 billion in 2018. The decrease in net revenue for the year reflected the impact of lower distribution revenues as a result of customer non-renewals primarily resulting from service issues prior to early 2019 partially offset by revenue growth in other business lines.

O&M reported a net income loss of $62 million in 2019 compared to net income loss of $437 million in 2018.

Cash at the end of 2019 was $84.7 million a decrease of $18.7 million from the prior year. Cash from operations contributed $166.1 million to the coffers while investing activities used $51.9 million mainly for additions to property and equipment. Financing activities provided $130.2 million primarily the issuance of debt and revolving credit facility borrowing.

Strategy

Patents trademarks and other proprietary rights are very important to the growth of O&M's business. It also relies upon trade secrets manufacturing know-how continuing technological innovations and licensing opportunities to maintain and improve its competitive position. In an effort to develop an effective intellectual property strategy avoid infringement of third-party proprietary rights identify licensing opportunities and monitor the intellectual property owned by others the Company review third-party proprietary rights including patents and patent applications.

In connection with O&M's growth strategy the company from time to time acquire other businesses including the Halyard acquisition (Halyard) and Byram Healthcare (Byram) that it believes will expand or complement its existing businesses and operations.

Company Background

George Gilmer Minor Jr.'s great-grandfather was an apothecary and surgeon in colonial Williamsburg Virginia. His grandfather was Thomas Jefferson's personal physician. Minor himself worked as a wholesale drug salesman in Richmond after the Civil War. In 1882 he and rival wholesaler Otho Owens partnered to form the Owens & Minor Drug Company.

During the 1920s the Owens family sold their stake in the firm. George Gilmer Minor III served briefly as the company's president in the early

1940s; his son George Gilmer Minor IV (called Mr. Minor Jr. to differentiate him from his father) became president in 1947.

In 1954 Owens & Minor installed its first computerized order fulfillment system. The following year the firm became Owens Minor & Bodeker when it bought the Bodeker Drug Company which was both older and larger than Owens & Minor.

After 84 years in the drug wholesale business the company entered the medical and surgical distribution business after buying A&J Hospital Supply in 1966 and Powers & Anderson in 1968. In 1971 Owens Minor & Bodeker went public. By the end of the decade the company had operations in 10 states.

The company reverted to its original name on its 100th anniversary in 1982. By 1984 medical supplies supplanted wholesale drugs as its primary source of income. In 1988 Owens & Minor listed on the NYSE.

The company passed the $1 billion revenue mark in 1990 and later sold its wholesale drug business.

HISTORY

George Gilmer Minor Jr.'s great-grandfather was an apothecary and surgeon in colonial Williamsburg Virginia. His grandfather was Thomas Jefferson's personal physician. Minor himself worked as a wholesale drug salesman in Richmond after the Civil War. In 1882 he and rival wholesaler Otho Owens partnered to form the Owens & Minor Drug Company. The company was both a retail and wholesale business with a storefront that filled prescriptions and sold sundries paints oils and window glass. When Owens died in 1906 Minor became the company's president.

During the 1920s the Owens family sold their stake in the firm. George Gilmer Minor III served briefly as the company's president in the early 1940s; his son George Gilmer Minor IV (called Mr. Minor Jr. to differentiate him from his father) became president in 1947.

In 1954 Owens & Minor installed its first computerized order fulfillment system. The following year the firm became Owens Minor & Bodeker when it bought the Bodeker Drug Company which was both older and larger than Owens & Minor.

After 84 years in the drug wholesale business the company entered the medical and surgical distribution business after buying A&J Hospital Supply in 1966 and Powers & Anderson in 1968. In 1971 Owens Minor & Bodeker went public. By the end of the decade the company had operations in 10 states.

The fourth Minor to run the firm G. Gilmer Minor III (Mr. Minor Jr.'s son) was named president in 1981 (he became CEO in 1984). Under his direction Owens Minor & Bodeker would complete the transition from a drug wholesaler to a medical supplies distributor. In 1981 it purchased the Will Ross subsidiary of G.D. Searle (then the country's #2 medical and surgical supplies distributor).

The company reverted to its original name on its 100th anniversary in 1982. By 1984 medical supplies supplanted wholesale drugs as its primary source of income. In 1988 Owens & Minor listed on the NYSE.

The company passed the $1 billion revenue mark in 1990 and later sold its wholesale drug business. It extended its reach with the purchase of Lyons Physician Supply in 1993 and Stuart Medical (the #3 national distributor) in 1994.

EXECUTIVES

Svp And Chief Of Staff, Erika T. Davis, age 57, $513,719 total compensation

Svp Owens & Minor Europe Operations, Charles C. Colpo, age 63, $453,466 total compensation

Vice President Technology, Charles Eismamn

Evp And Cfo; President International, Richard A. (Randy) Meier, age 60, $648,260 total compensation

Chairman President And Ceo, P. Cody Phipps, age 58, $915,577 total compensation

Evp North American Operations, Rony C. Kordahi, age 56, $328,846 total compensation

Evp Global Manufacturer Services, Stuart Morris-Hipkins

Svp Clinical Procedural Solutions, James S. Glasscock

Svp Manufacturer Services, Geoff T. Marlatt

Svp And Cio, Stephen R. Olive

Svp Strategic Supply Management, Javara D. Perrilliat

Svp Commercial Services, Joseph B. Zaluzney

Vice President Global Tax, Chris McGowan

Vice President Emerging Channels, Thomas Mitchell

Board Member, James Rogers

Auditors: KPMG LLP

LOCATIONS

HQ: Owens & Minor, Inc.
9120 Lockwood Boulevard, Mechanicsville, VA 23116
Phone: 804 723-7000   **Fax:** 804 723-7100
Web: www.owens-minor.com

2017 Sales

	$ mil.	% of total
US	8,899	96
UK	175	2
Ireland	57	1
Germany	49	-
France	39	-
Other European countries	98	1
Total	**9,318**	**100**

PRODUCTS/OPERATIONS

2017 Sales by Segment

	$ mil.	% of total
Domestic	8,794	91
International	391	4
Proprietary Products	504	5
Adjustments	(371.8)	-
Total	**9,318**	**100**

Selected Products and Services

Clinical Supply Solutions (inventory and contract management service)
Implant Purchase Manager (utilization contract compliance and billing)
OMDirect (Internet order fulfillment)
OMSolutions (resource management and consulting)
PANDAC system (helps track and control operating room inventories)
QSight (clinical inventory management system)
SurgiTrack (customizable surgical supply service)

COMPETITORS

Alloga UK	FedEx
AmerisourceBergen	Kerma Medical Products
Buffalo Supply	McKesson
Cardinal Health	Medline Industries
Deutsche Post	UPS

HISTORICAL FINANCIALS

Company Type: Public

Income Statement

FYE: December 31

	REVENUE ($ mil.)	NET INCOME ($ mil.)	NET PROFIT MARGIN	EMPLOYEES
12/19	9,210	(62)	—	15,400
12/18	9,838	(437)	—	17,900
12/17	9,318	72	0.8%	6,200
12/16	9,723	108	1.1%	7,900
12/15	9,772	103	1.1%	8,100
Annual Growth	(1.5%)	—	—	17.4%

2019 Year-End Financials

Debt ratio: 41.40%
Return on equity: (-12.72%)
Cash ($ mil.): 67
Current ratio: 1.70
Long-term debt ($ mil.): 1,508

No. of shares (mil.): 62
Dividends
  Yield: 0.1%
  Payout: —
Market value ($ mil.): 325

	STOCK PRICE ($) FY Close	P/E High/Low		PER SHARE ($) Earnings	Dividends	Book Value
12/19	5.17	—	—	(1.03)	0.01	7.35
12/18	6.33	—	—	(7.28)	0.86	8.32
12/17	18.88	31	15	1.20	1.03	16.52
12/16	35.29	23	18	1.76	1.02	15.73
12/15	35.98	24	19	1.65	1.01	15.80
Annual Growth (17.4%)	(38.4%)	—	—	—	(68.5%)	

Owens Corning

Famous for its Pink Panther mascot and its trademarked PINK glass fiber insulation Owens Corning (OC) is one of the top global makers of building and composite material systems. The building materials company makes insulation roofing fiber-based glass reinforcements and other materials for the residential industrial and commercial markets. Its composite products business makes glass fiber reinforcement materials that can be used in 40000-plus products for the transportation industrial infrastructure automotive aviation wind energy and consumer markets. Owens Corning has operations worldwide but generates majority of revenue from the US.

Operations

Owens Corning is organized in three business segments: Insulation Roofing and Composites.

Insulation which generates more than 35% of revenue makes and sells fiberglass insulation for both thermal and acoustical applications. It also sells glass fiber pipe insulation flexible duct media bonded and granulated mineral wool insulation and other materials for a variety of markets.

Over 35% of revenue comes from the Roofing segment which offers residential roofing shingles oxidized asphalt materials roofing components and synthetic packaging materials.

The Composites segment manufactures fabricates and sells glass reinforcements in the form of fiber and sells glass fiber products downstream in the form of fabrics mat and other specialized products. This segment accounts for almost 30% of revenue.

Geographic Reach

Ohio-based Owens Corning has more than 100 manufacturing facilities in almost 30 countries in the Americas Europe and the Asia/Pacific region. The US generates over 65% of its sales while Europe accounts for just more than 15%; the Asia/Pacific region and Canada and other countries contribute to the remaining sales of the company.

Sales and Marketing

Owens Corning sells shingles and roofing accessories primarily through home centers lumberyards retailers distributors and contractors under its well-known brands and trademarks such as: Thermafiber FOAMGLAS and Porac. Other asphalt products are sold to other shingle manufacturers to roofing contractors and to manufacturers of automotive chemical rubber and construction.

The company spent $117 million $120 million and $108 million on advertising for the years 2019 2018 and 2017 respectively.

Financial Performance

Owens Corning has seen its revenue rise over the past five years with sales up 34% since 2015.

In 2019 the company reported revenue of $7.2 billion up 1% from the prior year. The increase was primarily due to the $142 million increase in roofing sales.

Net income was down that year declining 26% to $405 million.

Cash at the end of 2019 was $179 million a decrease of $94 million from the prior year. Cash from operations contributed $1 billion to the coffers while investing activities used $394 million mainly for property plant and equipment. Financing activities used another $573 million from payments on senior revolving credit and receivables securitization facilities.

Strategy

With steady revenue crossing the $7 billion mark in 2018 Owens Corning is looking to expand. With acquisitions of Paroc (in 2018) and Pittsburgh Corning (in 2017) have particularly boosted the company's insulation segment. Its insulation products include the high medium and low temperature products with geographic mix of Canada Europe Asia-Pacific Latin America and the US with market mix or residential commercial industrial and other markets and with channel mix of retailer contractor and distribution.

The composites segment is in the process of closing certain sub-scale manufacturing facilities for expanding its operations in India.

HISTORY

In the 1930s Corning Glass Works and Owens-Illinois Glass independently found that glass fiber has special resilience and strength. Realizing the potential market they formed joint venture Owens-Corning Fiberglas in 1938. The companies expanded rapidly in the 1940s and 1950s establishing several US plants and one in Canada. Their products included fine fibers thermal wool textiles and continuous filaments.

Owens Corning went public on the NYSE in 1952.

EXECUTIVES

Chairman President And Ceo, Michael H. (Mike) Thaman, age 56, $1,140,500 total compensation
President Roofing And Asphalt, Brian D. Chambers, age 51, $450,000 total compensation
Svp Organization And Administration, Daniel T. (Dan) Smith, age 55, $527,500 total compensation
President Composite Solutions, Arnaud P. Genis, age 55, $596,667 total compensation
Svp And Cfo, Michael C. McMurray, age 55, $589,167 total compensation
President Insulation, Julian Francis
Vice President Hr Centers Of Excellence, Suzann Trevisan
Vp Of Network Operations, Tara Silberhorn
Vp Global Strategic Marketing, Teresa May
Vice President Human Resources (composites Solutions Business), Paula Russell
Vice President Investor Relations, Thierry Denis
National Accounts Manager, Chuck Stanislav
Vice President Corporate Affairs, Suzanne Harnett
National Account Manager, Greg Meilinger
Corporate Medical Director, Brian Linder
National Account Manager, Phil Johnson
Treasurer, Victor Defilippis
Auditors: PricewaterhouseCoopers LLP

LOCATIONS

HQ: Owens Corning
  One Owens Corning Parkway, Toledo, OH 43659
Phone: 419 248-8000
Web: www.owenscorning.com

2018 Sales

	$ mil.	% of total
US	4,647	66
Asia Pacific	656	9
Europe	1,209	17
Canada and other	545	8
Total	**7,057**	**100**

PRODUCTS/OPERATIONS

2018 Sales

	$ mil.	% of total
Roofing	2,492	34
Composites	2,041	28
Insulation	2,720	38
Corporate eliminations	(196)	-
Total	**7,057**	**100**

COMPETITORS

CertainTeed	Louisiana-Pacific
China Fiberglass Co. Ltd.	Nippon Electric Glass
	PPG Industries
Dow Chemical	SIG plc
GAF Materials	Saint-Gobain
Johns Manville	TAMKO
Knauf Insulation	USG

HISTORICAL FINANCIALS

Company Type: Public

Income Statement

FYE: December 31

	REVENUE ($ mil.)	NET INCOME ($ mil.)	NET PROFIT MARGIN	EMPLOYEES
12/19	7,160	405	5.7%	19,000
12/18	7,057	545	7.7%	20,000
12/17	6,384	289	4.5%	17,000
12/16	5,677	393	6.9%	16,000
12/15	5,350	330	6.2%	15,000
Annual Growth	7.6%	5.3%	—	6.1%

2019 Year-End Financials

Debt ratio: 29.84%
Return on equity: 9.09%
Cash ($ mil.): 172
Current ratio: 1.55
Long-term debt ($ mil.): 2,986

No. of shares (mil.): 109
Dividends
  Yield: 1.3%
  Payout: 19.3%
Market value ($ mil.): 7,098

	STOCK PRICE ($) FY Close	P/E High/Low	PER SHARE ($) Earnings	Dividends	Book Value
12/19	65.12	18 12	3.68	0.88	42.49
12/18	43.98	20 8	4.89	0.84	39.11
12/17	91.94	36 20	2.55	0.81	37.33
12/16	51.56	16 12	3.41	0.74	34.15
12/15	47.03	17 12	2.79	0.68	32.26
Annual Growth	8.5%	— —	7.2%	6.7%	7.1%

PACCAR Inc.

PACCAR (named for former rail car manufacturer Pacific Car and Foundry Company) is one of the world's leading designers and manufacturers of big rig diesel trucks. Its lineup of light- medium- and heavy-duty trucks includes the Kenworth Peterbilt and DAF nameplates. The company also manufactures and distributes aftermarket truck parts for these brands. PACCAR's other products include Braden Carco and Gearmatic industrial winches. PACCAR typically sells its trucks and parts through independent dealers. Its PACCAR Financial Services arm offers vehicle financing and its PacLease subsidiary handles truck leasing. About 60% of its sales comes from US operations.

Operations

PACCAR divides its business into three primary segments: Trucks Parts and Financial Services. The Truck segment generates more than 75% of total sales and sells trucks under the Kenworth Peterbilt and DAF brands. The company manufactures trucks in the US Europe Australia Brazil Canada and Mexico. In Europe PACCAR subsidiary Leyland assembles DAF trucks in the UK.

Parts (accounting for around 15% of sales) distributes aftermarket parts globally for PACCAR vehicles. PACCAR manufactures its own parts and purchases from suppliers. Financial Services represents about 5% of net revenue and provides financing to independent dealers franchises and directly to customers for trucks and related equipment.

In addition PACCAR's Other business includes the manufacture and marketing of industrial winches; sales in this business are less than 1% of total revenue.

Geographic Reach

PACCAR's headquarters are in Bellevue WA. It operates more than 30 manufacturing plants and distribution centers on four continents including North and South America Europe and Australia. In North America the company operates four US manufacturing plants in Washington Mississippi Texas and Ohio and one each in Canada and Mexico. In Europe PACCAR owns factories in the Netherlands and the UK and it has one plant each in Australia and Brazil. PAC-

CAR Financial Services operates across the globe in 25 countries.

About 60% of PACCAR's revenues are generated ins US with more than 25% coming from Europe.

Sales and Marketing

PACCAR delivers its products and services to customers worldwide in about 100 countries through its dealer network of more than 2200 locations.

Financial Performance

Except for a dip in 2016 PACCAR's revenue has seen steady growth the last five years rising nearly 34% between 2015 and 2019. The company's Trucks segment has been the chief growth driver and helped propel PACCAR's revenue to record levels in both 2018 and 2019.

Sales in 2019 increased 9% to $25.6 billion compared to $23.5 billion in 2018. Growth in 2019 was fueled by PACCAR's Trucks segment which increased 10% over 2018 primarily due to higher truck deliveries in the U.S. and Canada and Latin America.. The company enjoyed robust growth in truck revenue across all its geographic markets but North America led the way with a sales rise of 15%. The Parts and Financial Services segments also grew sales in 2019.

Net income increased 31% to $2.2 billion in 2019 compared to 2018 primarily due to higher truck delivery volumes and increased sales prices.

Cash at the end of 2019 was $4.2 billion an increase of $739.2 million from the prior year. Cash from operations contributed $2.9 billion to the coffers while investing activities used $2.2 billion mainly for originations of retail loans and direct financing leases. Financing activities provided $83.4 million primarily from term borrowing.

Strategy

PACCAR spent nearly $745 million on capital investments in 2019 and more than $325 million on R&D. To achieve growth it regularly expands its vehicle product range and upgrades its manufacturing and parts distribution facilities.

PACCAR opened Global Embedded Software centers in Kirkland Washington and Eindhoven the Netherlands which will accelerate embedded software development and connected vehicle solutions to benefit customers' operating efficiency.

In January 2020 PACCAR exhibited three vehicles with autonomous and alternative powertrain technologies at the CES 2020 show in Las Vegas Nevada: a level 4 autonomous Kenworth T680; a battery-electric Peterbilt Model 520EV; and a battery-electric Kenworth K270E. These trucks are designed for a range of customer applications including over-the-road transportation refuse collection and urban distribution.

Peterbilt Kenworth and DAF are field-testing battery-electric hydrogen fuel cell and hybrid powertrain trucks with customers in North America and Europe. These customer field tests are providing excellent feedback on future truck technologies which will support PACCAR's environmental and engineering leadership with the development of innovative alternative powertrain technologies.

PACCAR continues to add global distribution capacity to deliver industry-leading aftermarket parts availability to customers. PACCAR will open a new 250000 square-foot parts distribution center in Las Vegas Nevada and a new

160000 square-foot parts distribution center in Ponta Grossa Brasil in 2020 to enhance parts availability for customers.

Company Background

William Pigott founded the Seattle Car Manufacturing Company in 1905 to produce railroad cars for timber transport. Finding immediate success Pigott began to make other kinds of railcars in 1906.

In 1917 Seattle Car merged with the Twohy Brothers of Portland. The new company Pacific Car & Foundry was sold to American Car & Foundry in 1924.

Pacific Car was in decline by 1934 when William's son Paul bought it; since then the company has remained under family management. The company entered the truck-making business with the 1945 purchase of Seattle-based Kenworth.

In the 1950s Pacific Car became the industry leader in mechanical refrigerator car production. It began producing off-road heavy trucks and acquired Peterbilt Trucks of Oakland (1958).

The company moved its headquarters to Bellevue Washington in 1969 and changed its name to PACCAR in 1971.

HISTORY

William Pigott founded the Seattle Car Manufacturing Company in 1905 to produce railroad cars for timber transport. Finding immediate success Pigott began to make other kinds of railcars in 1906. When the Seattle plant burned the next year the company moved near Renton Washington. In 1911 Pigott renamed the company Seattle Car & Foundry.

In 1917 Seattle Car merged with the Twohy Brothers of Portland. The new company Pacific Car & Foundry was sold to American Car & Foundry in 1924. Pacific Car then diversified into bus manufacturing structural steel fabrications and metal technology.

Pacific Car was in decline by 1934 when William's son Paul bought it; since then the company has remained under family management. Paul Pigott added Hofius Steel and Equipment and Tricoach a bus manufacturer in 1936. The company entered the truck-making business with the 1945 purchase of Seattle-based Kenworth.

In the 1950s Pacific Car became the industry leader in mechanical refrigerator car production. It began producing off-road heavy trucks and acquired Peterbilt Trucks of Oakland (1958). To augment its winch business Pacific Car bought Canada's Gearmatic in 1963.

The company moved its headquarters to Bellevue Washington in 1969 and changed its name to PACCAR in 1971.

EXECUTIVES

Ceo, Ronald E. (Ron) Armstrong, age 64, $1,210,000 total compensation

Svp And General Manager Peterbilt, T. Kyle Quinn, age 59, $440,000 total compensation

Evp And Cfo, Harrie C.A.M. Schippers, age 58, $396,022 total compensation

Svp Financial Services, Robert A. Bengston, age 64, $449,615 total compensation

Evp, Gary L Moore, age 64, $547,693 total compensation

Vp And General Manager Kw, C. Michael Dozier

Vp Paccar And President Daf Trucks N.v., R. Preston Feight, age 52
Vp And Cio, A. Lily Ley, age 54
Vp; President Paccar Financial Corporation, Todd Hubbard
Executive Vice President, Dan Sobic
Vice President And Controller, Michael Barkley
Vice President, James Cardillo
Vp Manufacturing, George West Jr
Board Member, Alison Carnwath
Executive Chairman, Mark C. Pigott, age 67
Treasurer, Ulrich Kammholz
Auditors: Ernst & Young LLP

LOCATIONS

HQ: PACCAR Inc.
777 - 106th Ave. N.E., Bellevue, WA 98004
Phone: 425 468-7400
Web: www.paccar.com

2017 Sales

	$ mil.	% of total
US	10,530	54
Europe	5,354	28
Other regions	3,571	18
Total	**19,456**	**100**

PRODUCTS/OPERATIONS

2017 Sales

	$ mil.	% of total
Truck	14,774	76
Parts	3,327	17
Financial services	1,268	7
Other	85	
Total	**19,456**	**100**

Selected Divisions and Subsidiaries

DAF trucks
Kenworth Trucks
Peterbilt trucks
Leyland Trucks Limited (UK)
PACCAR Engine Company
PACCAR Financial Corp.
PACCAR Parts
PACCAR Machinery
PACCAR Winch
  Braden winches
  Carco winches
  Gearmatic winches

COMPETITORS

AGCO	Iveco S.p.A.
CNH Industrial	MAN
Caterpillar	Mack Trucks
Cummins	Meritor
Dana	Morris Material
Deere	Handling
Eaton	Navistar International
Fiat Chrysler	Oshkosh Truck
Ford Motor	Scania
General Motors	UD Trucks
Hino Motors	Volvo
Isuzu	

HISTORICAL FINANCIALS
Company Type: Public

Income Statement				FYE: December 31
	REVENUE ($ mil.)	NET INCOME ($ mil.)	NET PROFIT MARGIN	EMPLOYEES
12/19	25,599	2,387	9.3%	27,000
12/18	23,495	2,195	9.3%	28,000
12/17	19,456	1,675	8.6%	25,000
12/16	17,033	521	3.1%	23,000
12/15	19,115	1,604	8.4%	23,000
Annual Growth	**7.6%**	**10.5%**	**—**	**4.1%**

2019 Year-End Financials

Debt ratio: 39.57%
Return on equity: 26.10%
Cash ($ mil.): 4,175
Current ratio: 1.77
Long-term debt ($ mil.): 11,222

No. of shares (mil.): 346
Dividends
  Yield: 4.5%
  Payout: 51.2%
Market value ($ mil.): 27,392

	STOCK PRICE ($) FY Close	P/E High/Low		PER SHARE ($) Earnings	Dividends	Book Value
12/19	79.10	12	8	6.87	3.58	28.03
12/18	57.14	13	9	6.24	3.09	24.79
12/17	71.08	16	13	4.75	2.19	22.88
12/16	63.90	46	30	1.48	1.56	19.33
12/15	47.40	15	10	4.51	2.32	19.76
Annual Growth	**13.7%**	**—**		**11.1%**	**11.5%**	**9.1%**

Pacific Premier Bancorp Inc

EXECUTIVES

Pres-Ceo, Steven R Gardner
Chb*, Jeff C Jones
Sr V Pres-Cfo*, Kent Smith
Sr Exec Vpres-Cfo*, Ronald J Nicolas Jr
Cro*, Michael Karr
Evp-Cco*, Donn Jakosky
Evp-Chief Acctg Officer*, Lori Wright
Senior Vice President Director, Thomas Galindo
Desk Manager, Robert Prater
Vp Information Technology, Dinorah Roggero
Credit Analyst, Carol Hiegl
Auditors: Crowe LLP

LOCATIONS

HQ: Pacific Premier Bancorp Inc
17901 Von Karman Avenue, Suite 1200, Irvine, CA 92614
Phone: 949 864-8000
Web: www.ppbi.com

HISTORICAL FINANCIALS
Company Type: Public

Income Statement				FYE: December 31
	ASSETS ($ mil.)	NET INCOME ($ mil.)	INCOME AS % OF ASSETS	EMPLOYEES
12/19	11,776	159	1.4%	1,006
12/18	11,487	123	1.1%	1,030
12/17	8,024	60	0.7%	846
12/16	4,036	40	1.0%	448
12/15	2,790	25	0.9%	335
Annual Growth	**43.3%**	**58.2%**	**—**	**31.6%**

2019 Year-End Financials

Debt ratio: 6.22%
Return on equity: 8.02%
Cash ($ mil.): 329
Current ratio: —
Long-term debt ($ mil.): —

No. of shares (mil.): 59
Dividends
  Yield: 2.7%
  Payout: 33.8%
Market value ($ mil.): 1,940

	STOCK PRICE ($) FY Close	P/E High/Low		PER SHARE ($) Earnings	Dividends	Book Value
12/19	32.61	13	10	2.60	0.88	33.82
12/18	25.52	20	10	2.26	0.00	31.52
12/17	40.00	26	20	1.56	0.00	26.86
12/16	35.35	24	13	1.46	0.00	16.54
12/15	21.25	20	12	1.19	0.00	13.86
Annual Growth	**11.3%**	**—**		**21.6%**	**—**	**25.0%**

PACIFIC PREMIER BANK

EXECUTIVES

Pres-Ceo, Steven R Gardner
Chb*, Jeff C Jones
Sr V Pres-Cfo*, Kent Smith
Sr Exec Vpres-Cfo*, Ronald J Nicolas Jr
Cro*, Michael Karr
Evp-Cco*, Donn Jakosky
Evp-Chief Acctg Officer*, Lori Wright
Senior Vice President Director, Thomas Galindo
Desk Manager, Robert Prater
Vp Information Technology, Dinorah Roggero
Credit Analyst, Carol Hiegl

LOCATIONS

HQ: PACIFIC PREMIER BANK
17901 VON KARMAN AVE # 1, IRVINE, CA 926146297
Phone: 714 431-4000
Web: WWW.PPBI.COM

HISTORICAL FINANCIALS
Company Type: Private

Income Statement				FYE: December 31
	ASSETS ($ mil.)	NET INCOME ($ mil.)	INCOME AS % OF ASSETS	EMPLOYEES
12/17	8,022	68	0.9%	104
12/16	4,035	44	1.1%	—
12/15	2,782	29	1.1%	—
12/14	2,033	18	0.9%	—
Annual Growth	**58.0%**	**54.0%**	**—**	**—**

Pactiv Evergreen Inc

LOCATIONS

HQ: Pactiv Evergreen Inc
1900 W. Field Court, Lake Forest, IL 60045
Phone: 847 482-2000
Web: www.pactivevergreen.com

HISTORICAL FINANCIALS

Company Type: Public

Income Statement

FYE: December 31

	REVENUE ($ mil.)	NET INCOME ($ mil.)	NET PROFIT MARGIN	EMPLOYEES
12/19	7,115	91	1.3%	15,033
12/18	7,395	279	3.8%	—
12/17	7,439	594	8.0%	—
Annual Growth	(2.2%)	(60.9%)	—	—

2019 Year-End Financials

Debt ratio: 65.72%
Return on equity: 4.72%
Cash ($ mil.): 1,189
Current ratio: 0.76
Long-term debt ($ mil.): 7,043

No. of shares (mil.): 35
Dividends
 Yield: —
 Payout: —
Market value ($ mil.): —

	STOCK PRICE ($) FY Close	P/E High/Low	PER SHARE ($) Earnings	Dividends	Book Value
12/19	0.00	— —	2.55	0.00	58.22
12/18	0.00	— —	7.82	0.00	49.74
Annual Growth		— —	(42.9%)	—	8.2%

PacWest Bancorp

PacWest Bancorp is the holding company for Pacific Western Bank which operates about 80 branches mostly in southern and central California plus an additional branch in Durham North Carolina. The $21 billion-asset bank caters to small and midsized businesses and their owners and employees offering traditional deposit and loan products and services. Commercial real estate mortgages make up more than 30% of its loan portfolio while cash flow- and asset-based business loans make up another 40%. The bank also originates residential mortgage real estate construction and land loans venture capital equipment finance and consumer loans. PacWest offers investment services and international banking through agreements with correspondent banks.

Operations

Like other retail banks PacWest generates the bulk of its revenue from interest income. About 83% of its total revenue came from interest income on loans and leases during 2015 while another 7% came from interest income on investments. The rest of its revenue came from leased equipment income (3% of revenue) deposit account service charges (1%) other commissions and fees (3%) and other miscellaneous income sources.

The bank's Square 1 Bank Division caters to entrepreneurial businesses and their venture capital and private equity investors while its CapitalSource Division provides cash flow asset-based equipment and real estate loans and leases as well as treasury management services to established middle-market businesses across the country.

Geographic Reach

PWB's branches are located across California in Los Angeles Orange Riverside San Bernardino Santa Barbara San Diego San Francisco San Luis Obispo San Mateo and Ventura Counties. It also has a branch in Durham North Carolina.

Financial Performance

PacWest's acquisitions in 2014 and 2015 boosted its interest-earning loan asset balances more than three-fold which sent its revenues and profits soaring during those years.

The bank's revenue jumped 30% to $968.3 million during 2015 mostly as newly acquired loans from its CapitalSource boosted its interest income during the year.

Strong revenue growth coupled with lower acquisition integration and reorganization costs in 2015 drove PacWest's net income up 77% to $300 million. Its operating cash levels spiked 79% to $594 million with the rise in cash-denominated earnings.

Strategy

PacWest has grown its loan and deposit business as well as its branch network through acquisitions of California community banks and specialized financial services companies. It has made 28 acquisitions since 2000 with some of its most recent being the Square 1 acquisition in 2015 and the CapitalSource Inc. acquisition in 2014.

Mergers and Acquisitions

In October 2015 PacWest purchased $4.6 billion-asset Square 1 and its Square 1 Bank subsidiary for $849 million forming the Square 1 Bank Division of the Bank. The deal boosted its core deposits expanded its national lending platform and bolstered its presence in the technology and life-sciences markets.

In April 2014 the bank bought $10.7 billion-asset CapitalSource Inc. and its CapitalSource Bank (CSB) subsidiary.

In May 2013 PacWest acquired $1.7 billion-asset First California Financial Group operator of First California Bank for $237 million. The purchase added six branches (after consolidation) in Los Angeles Orange Riverside San Bernardino San Diego San Luis Obispo and Ventura Counties.

Company Background

During the economic downturn PacWest took advantage of a rash of bank failures through FDIC-assisted transactions. The acquired institutions were merged into Pacific Western Bank. Under the loss-sharing deals the FDIC agreed to reimburse PacWest for future losses tied to the acquisitions. In a 2012 non-FDIC-assisted deal PacWest bought American Perspective Bank adding two branches and a loan office in the Central Coast area.

EXECUTIVES

Evp And Director The Company And Pacific Western Bank, Daniel B. Platt, age 73, $52,500 total compensation
Evp And Chief Risk Officer, Suzanne R. Brennan, age 69, $165,000 total compensation
Ceo, Matthew P. (Matt) Wagner, age 63, $754,167 total compensation
Evp And Cfo Pacific Western Bank, Patrick J. (Pat) Rusnak, age 56
Evp And Chief Accounting Officer, Lynn M. Hopkins, age 52
Evp; Director Human Resources, Christopher D. Blake, age 60, $298,958 total compensation
Evp And Chief Credit Officer, Bryan M. Corsini, age 58, $375,624 total compensation
Evp; President Capitalsource, James J. (Jim) Pieczynski, age 57, $554,539 total compensation
Evp Operations And Systems, Mark Christian
Evp General Counsel And Corporate Secretary, Kori L. Ogrosky
Vice President Senior Credit Analyst, Viet Pham
Senior Vice President Information Systems Manager, Norma Lopez
Senior Vice President, Scott Foote
Vice President Operations Manager, Arbi John
Vice President, Sue Thomas
Vice President Bsa Officer, Sali Tice
Chairman, John M. Eggemeyer, age 74
Treasurer, Victor Santoro
Auditors: KPMG LLP

LOCATIONS

HQ: PacWest Bancorp
9701 Wilshire Blvd., Suite 700, Beverly Hills, CA 90212
Phone: 310 887-8500
Web: www.pacwestbancorp.com

PRODUCTS/OPERATIONS

2015 Sales

	$ mil.	% of total
Interest income		
Loans and leases	819	87
Investment securities & other	64	7
Noninterest income		
Other commissions and fees	31	3
Leased equipment income	24	3
Service charges on deposit accounts	11	1
Other	35	3
FDIC loss sharing expense net	(18.2)	
Total	**968**	**100**

Selected Mergers & Acquisitions

COMPETITORS

Bank of America	Rabobank America
CVB Financial	San Diego County
California Bank &	Credit Union
Trust	U.S. Bancorp
City National	Wells Fargo
JPMorgan Chase	Westamerica
MUFG Americas Holdings	

HISTORICAL FINANCIALS

Company Type: Public

Income Statement

FYE: December 31

	ASSETS ($ mil.)	NET INCOME ($ mil.)	INCOME AS % OF ASSETS	EMPLOYEES
12/19	26,770	468	1.8%	1,835
12/18	25,731	465	1.8%	1,833
12/17	24,994	357	1.4%	1,786
12/16	21,869	352	1.6%	1,669
12/15	21,288	299	1.4%	1,670
Annual Growth	5.9%	11.8%	—	2.4%

2019 Year-End Financials

Debt ratio: 2.83%
Return on equity: 9.58%
Cash ($ mil.): 637
Current ratio: —
Long-term debt ($ mil.): —

No. of shares (mil.): 119
Dividends
 Yield: 6.2%
 Payout: 62.5%
Market value ($ mil.): 4,584

	STOCK PRICE ($) FY Close	P/E High/Low	PER SHARE ($) Earnings	Dividends	Book Value
12/19	38.27	11 8	3.90	2.40	41.36
12/18	33.28	15 8	3.72	2.30	39.17
12/17	50.40	20 15	2.91	2.00	38.65
12/16	54.44	19 10	2.90	2.00	36.93
12/15	43.10	17 14	2.79	2.00	36.22
Annual Growth	(2.9%)	— —	8.7%	4.7%	3.4%

Park National Corp (Newark, OH)

Customers can park their money with Park National. The holding company owns Park National Bank which operates more than 120 branches in Ohio and northern Kentucky through 11 community banking divisions. The banks provide an array of consumer and business banking services including traditional savings and checking accounts and CDs. Business loans including commercial leases and mortgages operating loans and agricultural loans account for about 35% of Park National's loan portfolio. The banks also originate consumer residential real estate and construction loans. Park National's nonbank units include consumer finance outfit Guardian Finance Scope Aircraft Finance and Park Title Agency. In 2018 it acquired Charlotte NC-based NewDominion Bank for some $75 million.

Operations

Each of Park National Corporation's bank affiliates specialize in serving specific geographic locations. It's bank divisions include: Century National Bank; Fairfield National Bank; Farmers Bank; First-Knox National Bank; Park National Bank; Richland Bank; Security National Bank; Second National Bank; Unity National Bank; and United Bank.

Geographic Reach

Park National Corporation and its subsidiaries operate in Ohio and northern Kentucky.

Financial Performance

The company's revenue decreased in fiscal 2013 compared to the previous year. It reported $336.2 million in revenue for fiscal 2013 down from $378.1 million in fiscal 2012.

The company's net income dropped slightly in fiscal 2013 compared to the prior period as well. It reported a net income of $77 million in fiscal 2013 after netting a little more than $78 million the prior year.

Park National Corporation's cash on hand increased by almost $10 million in fiscal 2013 compared to fiscal 2012 levels.

EXECUTIVES

President And Ceo, David L. Trautman, age 58, $775,000 total compensation
Cfo Treasurer And Secretary; Svp And Cfo Park National Bank, Brady T. Burt, age 45, $325,000 total compensation
Vice President Commercial Lender, John MacRitchie
Chairman, C. Daniel (Dan) DeLawder, age 70
Auditors: Crowe LLP

LOCATIONS

HQ: Park National Corp (Newark, OH)
50 North Third Street, P.O. Box 3500, Newark, OH 43058-3500
Phone: 740 349-8451
Web: www.parknationalcorp.com

PRODUCTS/OPERATIONS

2015 Sales

	$ mil.	% of total
Interest and fees on loans	228	66
Interest and dividends	37	10
Income from fiduciary activities	20	7
Service charges on deposit accounts	14	4
Checkcard fee income	14	4
Other service income	11	3
Other	16	6
Total	**342**	**100**

Selected Affiliates

Century National Bank
Fairfield National Bank
Farmers Bank
First-Knox National Bank
Guardian Finance Company
Park National Bank
Richland Bank
Scope Aircraft Finance
Second National Bank
Security National Bank
United bank
Unity National Bank

COMPETITORS

Bank of America
Fifth Third
Huntington Bancshares
JPMorgan Chase
PNC Financial
U.S. Bancorp
Wayne Savings
Bancshares
Wells Fargo

HISTORICAL FINANCIALS

Company Type: Public

Income Statement

FYE: December 31

	ASSETS ($ mil.)	NET INCOME ($ mil.)	INCOME AS % OF ASSETS	EMPLOYEES
12/19	8,558	102	1.2%	1,907
12/18	7,804	110	1.4%	1,782
12/17	7,537	84	1.1%	1,746
12/16	7,467	86	1.2%	1,726
12/15	7,311	81	1.1%	1,793
Annual Growth	4.0%	6.1%	—	1.6%

2019 Year-End Financials

Debt ratio: 0.67%
Return on equity: 11.40%
Cash ($ mil.): 159
Current ratio: —
Long-term debt ($ mil.): —
No. of shares (mil.): 16
Dividends
  Yield: 4.1%
  Payout: 65.2%
Market value ($ mil.): 1,674

	STOCK PRICE ($) FY Close	P/E High/Low		PER SHARE ($) Earnings	Dividends	Book Value
12/19	102.38	17	14	6.29	4.24	59.28
12/18	84.95	17	11	7.07	4.07	53.03
12/17	104.00	22	17	5.47	3.76	49.46
12/16	119.66	22	14	5.59	3.76	48.38
12/15	90.48	19	15	5.26	3.76	46.53
Annual Growth	3.1%	—	—	4.6%	3.0%	6.2%

Parker Hannifin Corp

Parker-Hannifin (Parker) is a leading global manufacturer of motion and control technologies including fluid power systems for the manufacturing and processing industries. Other business lines include the manufacture of hydraulic fuel pneumatic and electromechanical systems and components for the aerospace/defense industry; and motion and control systems for the heating ventilation air conditioning and refrigeration (HVACR) and transportation industries. Parker owns some 320 manufacturing plants and operates through the two business segments of Diversified Industrial and Aerospace. More than 35% of total revenue derived from customers outside the US. The company traces its historical roots back to 1917.

Operations

Parker-Hannifin is a worldwide diversified manufacturer of motion and control technologies and systems. It provides precision engineered technologies products and services for a wide variety of mobile industrial and aerospace markets.

Its largest division Diversified Industrial consists of several divisions: Engineered Materials (seals o-rings interference shielding medial products); Filtration Group (filters and diagnostic solutions to remove contaminants); Fluid Connectors (valves couplings hose and tubing and IoT sensors); Instrumentation (accumulators valves pumps); and Motion Systems (hydraulic actuation pneumatics and electronics). The segment generates about 80% of sales.

The Aerospace segment produces control actuation systems components for engines fluid conveyance and metering fuel systems hydraulics lubrication and pneumatic control as well as wheels and brakes and thermal management products. It supplies commercial and military customers in the OEM and maintenance repair and overhaul end user markets for use in aircraft engines missiles unmanned aerial vehicles and in power generation applications. It accounts for some 20% of revenue.

Geographic Reach

Cleveland-Ohio-based Parker-Hannifin has around 320 factories and maintains distribution centers and sales and administrative offices in nearly 40 states and in roughly 50 other countries worldwide. North America accounts for more than 65% of its sales.

Sales and Marketing

Sales of products under Parker's Diversified Industrial businesses in North American and international markets are made primarily to original equipment manufacturers (OEMs) and their replacement markets in various sectors within the manufacturing processing and transportation industries. They include agriculture alternative energy chemical processing construction machinery food production life sciences material handling and water among many others. This segment's sales are marketed primarily through field sales employees and approximately 16400 independent distributor locations throughout the world.

Aerospace products cater to the commercial and military aerospace markets to both OEMs and to end-users for spares maintenance repair and overhaul.

Approximately 464000 customers who purchase Parker products are found in almost every significant manufacturing transportation and processing industry.

Financial Performance

Parker-Hannifin's growth rates over the past five years varied. Excluding 2020 its revenues and net income have steadily risen year after year. Overall revenue has grown 21% and net income has risen 50% between 2016 and 2020.

In fiscal 2020 (ended June 30) Parker's sales were lower by 4% to $13.7 billion compared to $14.3 billion in the year prior. This was due to lower volume in all segments partially offset by an increase in sales from acquisitions made within the last 12 months of $949 million. The effect of currency rate changes decreased sales by approximately $167 million of which $152 million was attributable to the Diversified Industrial International operations.

Net income fell 20% to $1.2 billion in 2020 compared to %1.5 billion in the year prior. This was due to a 7% increase in selling general and administrative expenses from acquisition-related transactions costs and higher intangible asset amortization expense related to the Lord and Exotic acquisitions.

Parker-Hannifin's cash on hand decreased $2.5 billion in 2020 ending the year at $685.5 million. The company's operations generated $2.1 billion and its financing activities yielded $449.3 million partially offset by the $5 billion used in investing activities. Parker took on $1.7 billion in new borrowing to support its shareholder returns program which included $216 million in share repurchases and $453.8 million in dividends. Capital expenditures were a comparatively low $232.6 million however acquisitions increased to $5.1 billion.

Strategy

Parker-Hannifin is a leading worldwide diversified manufacturer of motion and control technologies and systems providing precision engineered solutions for a wide variety of mobile industrial and aerospace markets. Its long-term strategy aligns with this focusing on business opportunities in the areas of energy water food environment defense life sciences infrastructure and transportation.

It meets these strategic objectives by successfully executing The Win Strategy initiatives; engineering innovative systems and products to provide superior customer value; acquiring strategic businesses; and organizing around targeted regions technologies and markets.

Parker's Win Strategy is built on the established goals of engaged people premier customer experience profitable growth and financial performance and will position the company to achieve financial performance among its diversified industrial proxy peer companies.

Parker also sets out to improve its products. In 2019 it launched a new patent for the metal working industry which is designed to optimize drainage within the SmogHog SHM self-contained media mist collector and provide best in class particulate removal efficiency and long filter life using state of the art coalescing filter media technology. It released another patent this time in 2020 of a connector to be used with pleated filter elements. This product development provides customers more options to better manage their baghouse filtration systems.

Mergers and Acquisitions

Parker Hannifin uses acquisitions as a means of enhancing its product portfolio and growing its global footprint.

In 2019 Parker-Hannifin bought Exotic Metals Forming Company for more than $1.7 billion in cash. Exotic is a manufacturer of air and exhaust management systems for aircraft and engines. The deal expands Parker Hannifin's offerings in a high-growth segment of the aircraft engine market.

Also in 2019 the company bought Lord Corporation for about $3.6 billion. Lord is a privately-held manufacturer of advanced adhesives coatings specialty materials and vibration and motion control technologies. The addition of Lord will grow Parker-Hannifin's material sciences operations that serve key markets including the aerospace and automotive industries.

HISTORY

Entrepreneurial engineer Arthur Parker founded the Parker Appliance Company in 1918 to make pneumatic brake boosters. Its products were designed to help trucks and buses stop more easily. Unfortunately Parker's own truck slid off an icy road and over a cliff in 1919 destroying the company's inventory and ending that line of business.

Undeterred Parker started a hydraulics and pneumatic components business in 1924 to serve automotive and industrial clients. In 1927 the fuel-linkage system the company developed for the Spirit of St. Louis helped Lindbergh cross the Atlantic. The company prospered during the Depression; sales reached $2 million in 1934. Two of Parker's long-term clients were Douglas Aircraft and Lockheed.

The company went public in 1938. It employed 5000 defense workers during WWII. After Parker died in 1945 his wife Helen hired new management to focus on the automation market. The firm bought cylinder maker Hannifin in 1957 and became Parker-Hannifin.

In 1960 Parker-Hannifin formed an international unit in Amsterdam and it set up a German subsidiary in 1962. Overseas acquisitions and increased demand from the space program and the aviation market spurred growth in the 1960s. Patrick Parker the founder's son became president in 1968 and chairman in 1977. Parker-Hannifin expanded its aerospace business in 1978 with the purchase of Bertea (electrohydraulic flight controls). Patrick Parker continued as CEO until 1983 and as chairman until 1999.

In mid-2016 Parker Hannifin acquired J ¤ger Automobil-Technik GmbH and J ¤ger Automotive Polska Sp. z.o.o headquartered in Hannover Germany. The J ¤ger Group is a pioneer in rubber-to-plastic direct bonded sealing systems for automotive markets and a leading developer of two-component (2K) direct injection molding technology. The deal provided Parker with innovative injection molding technology and businesses with a strong reputation in the automotive industry.

EXECUTIVES

Vp Ebusiness Iot And Services, Robert W. (Bob) Bond, age 62, $548,700 total compensation
President And Coo, Lee C. Banks, age 57, $850,000 total compensation
Vp And Cio, William G. (Bill) Eline, age 64
Vp And President Instrumentation Group, John R. Greco, age 66
Vp And Chief Technology And Innovation Officer, M. Craig Maxwell, age 62
Vp And President Aerospace Group, Roger S. Sherrard, age 54

Chairman And Ceo, Thomas L. (Tom) Williams, age 61, $1,000,000 total compensation
Vp Global Supply Chain And Procurement, John G. Dedinsky, age 63
Vp And President Automation Group, Yoon (Michael) Chung, age 57
Vp And President Asia Pacific Group, Kurt A. Keller, age 62
Cfo, Catherine A. (Cathy) Suever, age 62
Vp And President - Fluid Connectors Group, Andrew D. Ross
Vp And President Latin America Group, Candido Lima
Vp And President Filtration Group, Robert W. Malone
Vp And President Europe Middle East And Africa Group (emea), Joachim Guhe
Evp Human Resources And External Affairs, Mark J. Hart
Vp And President Engineered Materials Group, Jennifer A. Parmentier
Vp And President Hydraulics Group, Andrew M. Weeks, $400,956 total compensation
Vp General Counsel And Secretary, Joseph R. Leonti, $410,400 total compensation
Vice President Human Resources, Kevin Ruffer
National Sales Manager, Dan Connolly
Vp Information Technology, Mark Czaja
Vice President Human Resources, Linda Smith
Vice President Of Operations, Jim Rowell
Vice President Of Military And Helicopter Business, Ray Bumpus
Vice President, Malcolm Lewis
Vice President Of Information Technology, Ursula Hartman
Vice President, Timothy Logan
National Account Manager, Deirdre Stinson
Vice President Corporate Strategy, Shawn Horner
Vp And Group Controller, Nick Liberatore
Department Head, Steve Bolanos
Vice President Corporate Business Planning And Development, Paul Vallone
Vice President And President Instrumentation Group, William Bowman
Vice President Strategic Pricing, Richard Braun
Vice President Of Operations North America, Rob Malone
Group Vice President Operations, Colleen Haley
National Accounts Manager, Rachel Hoffman
Vp Sales North America, John Murray
Vp Controller Hydraulics Group, Colin Wilkinson
Vice President Gobal Sales And Marketing, Michael J O'hara
Group Vice President Supply Chain Management Aerospace Group, Dorith Hakim
Vice President, Greg Parker
Board Member, Glenn Crame
Auditors: Deloitte & Touche, LLP

LOCATIONS

HQ: Parker Hannifin Corp
6035 Parkland Boulevard, Cleveland, OH 44124-4141
Phone: 216 896-3000
Web: www.parker.com

2019 Sales

	$ mil.	% of total
North America	9,318	65
International	2,969	21
Asia Pacific	1,855	13
Latin America	177	1
Total	**14,320**	**100**

PRODUCTS/OPERATIONS

2019 Sales

	$ mil.	% of total
Diversified Industrial		
Flow and Process Control	4,293	30
Filtration and Engineered Materials	4,031	28
Motion Systems	3,485	24
Aerospace Systems	2,510	18
Total	**14,320**	**100**

Selected Brand Names

Atlas Cylinders
Balston
Bayside
Bellows
Cabett
Calzoni
Chelsea
Chomerics
Compumotor
croloop
CTC
Ermeto
Fluid Power
Gold Ring
Greer
Gresen
Hiross
IPS
Jet-Pipe
Lucifer
Miller
Ross
Schrader
Sempress
Skinner
Sporlan
STC
Operating Groups and Selected Products
Aerospace
  Aircraft wheels and brakes
  Flight control components
  Fuel systems
  Pneumatic pumps and valves
Climate and industrial controls
  Expansion valves
  Filter-dryers
  Hose assemblies
  Pressure regulators
  Solenoid valves
Industrial
  Automation
  Air preparation units
  Electric actuators
  Human/machine interface hardware and software
  Indexers
  Multi-axis positioning tables
  Pneumatic valves
  Stepper and servo drives
  Structural extrusions
  Vacuum products
  Filtration
  Cabin air filters
  Compressed-air and gas-purification filters
  Fuel conditioning filters
  Fuel filters/water separators
  Gas generators
  Gas generators
  Hydraulic lubrication and coolant filters
  Lube oil and fuel filters
  Monitoring devices
  Nitrogen and hydrogen generators
  Process chemical and microfiltration filters
  Water desalinization and purification
  Fluid Connectors
  Couplers
  Diagnostic equipment
  Hoses and hose fittings
  Tube fittings
  Valves
  Hydraulics
  Accumulators
  Cylinders
  Electrohydraulic systems
  Hydrostatic steering units
  Metering pumps
  Motors and pumps
  Power units
  Rotary actuators

Sensors
Valves
Instrumentation
Ball plug and needle valves
Cylinder connections
Fluoropolymer fittings
Miniature solenoid valves
Multi-solenoid manifolds
Packless ultra-high-purity valves
Quick connects
Regulators
Spray guns
Transducers
Tubing
Ultra-high-purity tube fittings
Seals
Gaskets and packings
Metal and plastic composite seals
Medical devices seals and instruments
O-rings
O-seals
Thermal management products

COMPETITORS

Bosch Rexroth	ITT Corp.
Crane Co.	Moog
Danaher	SMC Corp.
Danfoss	Swagelok
Donaldson Company	Trelleborg
Eaton	Woodward Governor
Emerson Electric	Zodiac Aerospace
Honeywell	
International	

HISTORICAL FINANCIALS

Company Type: Public

Income Statement

FYE: June 30

	REVENUE ($ mil.)	NET INCOME ($ mil.)	NET PROFIT MARGIN	EMPLOYEES
06/20	13,695	1,206	8.8%	50,520
06/19	14,320	1,512	10.6%	55,610
06/18	14,302	1,060	7.4%	57,170
06/17	12,029	983	8.2%	56,690
06/16	11,360	806	7.1%	48,950
Annual Growth	4.8%	10.6%	—	0.8%

2020 Year-End Financials

Debt ratio: 42.87%	No. of shares (mil.): 128
Return on equity: 19.92%	Dividends
Cash ($ mil.): 685	Yield: 1.9%
Current ratio: 1.55	Payout: 37.8%
Long-term debt ($ mil.): 7,652	Market value ($ mil.): 23,560

	STOCK PRICE ($) FY Close	P/E High/Low	Earnings	Dividends	Book Value
06/20	183.27	23 10	9.29	3.52	47.56
06/19	170.01	16 12	11.48	3.16	46.40
06/18	155.85	26 19	7.83	2.74	44.25
06/17	159.82	22 15	7.25	2.58	39.50
06/16	108.05	20 15	5.89	2.52	34.14
Annual Growth	14.1%	— —	12.1%	8.7%	8.6%

PayPal Holdings Inc

PayPal transacts millions of payments at digital speed. The company enables individuals and merchants to electronically transfer money via numerous methods with payments originating from a customer's bank account credit card or PayPal account. PayPal is a giant in the online payments industry with around 280 million active accounts and nearly 25 million merchant accounts across more than 200 markets. It earns fees from payment transactions foreign exchange and withdrawals from foreign bank accounts as well as from interest on customer balances and PayPal-branded credit and debit cards. The firm processes approximately 12.4 billion payment transactions a year. The US accounts for more than half of PayPal's total revenue.

Operations

PayPal depends on transaction fees which account for about 90% of the company's business for revenue. Secondary activities through value-added services generate the other 10%.

PayPal oversees a global technology platform that links its customers ? both merchants and consumers ? so they may digitally exchange payment for goods and services. Customers use computers smartphones bank accounts credit cards and other methods to originate and accept payment through the PayPal platform. In addition to its namesake PayPal service the company's products include Xoom (secure online money transfer) Venmo (digital wallet service) Braintree (digital payment service integration) and iZettle (payment tool for small businesses).

The company provides value-added services with PayPal Credit and gateway services. PayPal Credit functions like a typical credit card though PayPal advances the credit. The gateway services unit includes Payflow and Braintree Gateway services and enables a merchant's website to link to its processing network and merchant account and enables merchants to accept online payments with credit and debit cards.

Geographic Reach

PayPal is based in San Jose California and operates globally. About 55% of the company's revenue comes from the US about 10% from the UK and the remainder from the rest of the world.

The company's Xoom service allows overseas payments and deposits to and from bank accounts mobile phones and other accounts. PayPal customers can send payments in more than 200 markets across the globe and in more than 100 currencies withdraw funds to their bank accounts in 56 currencies and hold balances in their PayPal accounts in 25 currencies.

Sales and Marketing

PayPal aims its digital payment services to both ends of the transaction: consumers and merchants.

Advertising expenses totaled $399 million $484 million and $438 million for the years ended 2019 2018 and 2017 and respectively.

Financial Performance

PayPal has realized strong financial performance over the past several years as consumer enthusiasm for buying things online shows no sign of waning and smartphones fuel growth in mobile payment. Between 2015 and 2019 the company almost doubled its revenue and its net income.

Net revenues increased $2.3 billion or 15% in 2019 as compared to 2018 driven primarily by growth in TPV of 23%. Net revenues from our acquisitions completed in 2018 contributed approximately one percentage point to the growth rate in 2019. These increases were partially offset by a decrease in interest and fee income due to the sale of our U.S. consumer credit receivables portfolio to Synchrony Bank in July 2018 which resulted in a negative impact of approximately four percentage points to the net revenues growth rate in 2019.

Net income increased by $402 million or 20% in 2019 as compared to 2018 due to an increase in operating income of $525 million and an increase in other income (expense) net of $97 million driven primarily by net unrealized gains on strategic investments partially offset by an increase in income tax expense of $220 million.

Cash and cash equivalents at the end of 2019 reached $15.7 billion. Cash from operations provided $4.6 billion while investing activities used $5.7 billion. Financing activities generated another $3.7 billion.

Strategy

PayPal's ability to grow revenue is affected by among other things consumer spending patterns merchant and consumer adoption of digital payment methods the expansion of multiple commerce channels the growth of mobile devices and merchant and consumer applications on those devices the growth of consumers globally with internet and mobile access the pace of transition from cash and checks to digital forms of payment the company's share of the digital payments market and its ability to innovate and introduce new products and services that merchants and consumers value. PayPal's strategy to drive growth in business includes the following:

Growing core business: through expanding our global capabilities customer base and scale increasing customers' use of products and services by better addressing their everyday needs related to accessing managing and moving money and expanding the adoption of the company's solutions by merchants and consumers;

Expanding value proposition for merchants and consumers: by being technology and platform agnostic partnering with merchants to grow and expand their business online and in-store; and providing consumers with simple secure and flexible ways to manage and move money across different markets merchants and platforms;

Forming strategic partnerships: by building new strategic partnerships to provide better experiences for customers offering greater choice and flexibility acquiring new customers and reinforcing PayPal's role in the ecosystem; and

Seeking new areas of growth: organically and through acquisitions and strategic investments in existing and new international markets around the world and focusing on innovation both in the digital and physical world.

Mergers and Acquisitions

Growth through acquisitions is an important element of Paypal's corporate strategy.

In 2020 the completed its acquisition with Honey Science Corp. which helps consumers find shopping discounts online for $4 billion. Honey also helps retailers develop personalized offers for shoppers. Paypal intends to embed Honey into its apps to develop deeper engagement with its customers. The company also hopes to help merchants target new customer segments. After the acquisition closes Honey is to retain its brand and headquarters in Los Angeles.

Company Background

Tech entrepreneurs Max Levchin Elon Musk Peter Thiel Luke Nosek and Ken Howery together founded PayPal in 1998 in Palto Alto California with the idea of enabling consumers to make payments using email.

PayPal went public for the first time in February 2002. eBay acquired the payments network for $1.5 billion in October 2002. Under pressure from activist investor Carl Icahn eBay spun-off PayPal in 2014. The company went public a second time in 2015.

EXECUTIVES

Evp Emea; Ceo Paypal Europe Bank, Rupert G. Keeley

Evp And Cfo, John D. Rainey, $650,000 total compensation

Evp And Chief Commercial Officer, Gary Marino

Svp; Ceo Apac, Rohan Mahadevan

President And Ceo, Daniel H. (Dan) Schulman, $1,000,000 total compensation

Evp And Coo, William (Bill) Ready, $580,000 total compensation

Evp And Chief Enterprise Services Officer, Tomer Barel, $494,149 total compensation

Evp Chief Risk Compliance And Security Officer, Aaron Karczmer

Svp Human Resources People Operations, Peggy Abkemeier Alford

Vice President, Mary Anne Gillespie

Executive Vice President, James Hogan

Vice President, Farhad Irani

Vice President, Don Kingsborough

Vice President, Donald Kingsborough

Executive Vice President, Keith Rabois

Senior Vice President, James Templeton

Vice President Real Estate And Procurement, Tim Ritz

Vp Of Corporate Legal And Secretary, Brian Yamasaki

Svp Global Credit, Mark Britto

Evp Chief Business Affairs And Legal Officer, A Louise Pentland

Vp Head Of Global Core Payments, Jim Magats

Xoom Treasurer, Rick Rohrs

Auditors: PricewaterhouseCoopers LLP

LOCATIONS

HQ: PayPal Holdings Inc
2211 North First Street, San Jose, CA 95131
Phone: 408 967-1000
Web: www.paypal.com

2017 Sales

	$ mil.	% of total
U.S	7,084	54
U.K	1,402	11
Other countries	4,608	35
Total	**13,094**	**100**

PRODUCTS/OPERATIONS

2017 Sales

	$ mil.	% of total
Transaction revenue	11,402	87
Other value added services	1,692	13
Total	**13,094**	**100**

COMPETITORS

Amazon.com	Intuit
American Express	MasterCard
Apple Inc.	MoneyGram
Authorize.Net	International
Chase Paymentech	Nochex
Solutions	Samsung Electronics
Citigroup	Square
CyberSource	US Postal Service
Discover	Visa Inc
First Data	Western Union
Google	iPayment

HISTORICAL FINANCIALS

Company Type: Public

Income Statement

FYE: December 31

	REVENUE ($ mil.)	NET INCOME ($ mil.)	NET PROFIT MARGIN	EMPLOYEES
12/20	21,454	4,202	19.6%	26,500
12/19	17,772	2,459	13.8%	23,200
12/18	15,451	2,057	13.3%	21,800
12/17	13,094	1,795	13.7%	18,700
12/16	10,842	1,401	12.9%	18,100
Annual Growth	**18.6%**	**31.6%**	**—**	**10.0%**

2020 Year-End Financials

Debt ratio: 12.70%
Return on equity: 22.71%
Cash ($ mil.): 4,794
Current ratio: 1.33
Long-term debt ($ mil.): 8,939

No. of shares (mil.): 1,172
Dividends
  Yield: —
  Payout: —
Market value ($ mil.): 274,482

	STOCK PRICE ($) FY Close	P/E High/Low	PER SHARE ($)		
			Earnings	Dividends	Book Value
12/20	234.20	68 24	3.54	0.00	17.08
12/19	108.17	58 39	2.07	0.00	14.39
12/18	84.09	53 41	1.71	0.00	13.11
12/17	73.62	53 26	1.47	0.00	13.33
12/16	39.47	38 27	1.15	0.00	12.19
Annual Growth	**56.1%**	**— —**	**32.5%**	**—**	**8.8%**

PBF Energy Inc

Established US oil refiners meet the new kid on the block. Formed in the first decade of 21st century PBF Energy's five oil refineries are located in California Delaware Louisiana New Jersey and Ohio and have a combined production capacity of about 900000 barrels per day making the company one of the largest refiners in the US. PBF's refineries produce gasoline ultra-low-sulfur diesel heating oil jet fuel lubricants petrochemicals and asphalt for the Midwestern Gulf Coast West Coast and Northeastern US. The company indirectly owns the general partner and approximately 48.2% of the limited partnership interest of PBF Logistics LP. PBF Energy is majority-owned by investment firms The Blackstone Group and First Reserve.

Operations

PBF Energy operates two business segments: Refining which accounts for almost all of its sales and Logistics (through PBF Logistics) which accounts for the remainder.

Refineries in the East Coast (Delaware City and Paulsboro) average total throughput rates of 370000 barrels per day (bpd) and in the Mid-Continent (Toledo) 170000 bpd. Total refined product barrels sold are around 370000 at East Coast refineries; 170000 at Mid-Continent refineries; and 189000 at Gulf Coast refineries.

Gasoline and distillates account for more than 85% of PBF Energy's total sales.

Geographic Reach

New Jersey-based PBF Energy operates refineries in Torrance California; Delaware City Delaware; New Orleans Louisiana; Paulsboro New Jersey; and Toledo Ohio and sells its products in Canada and the US.

Sales and Marketing

The Majority of its refined products are sold through short-term contracts or on the spot market.

Financial Performance

Except in 2019 PBF's revenue has been consistently increasing. Despite its decrease in 2019 the company's revenue has an overall growth of 87%. PBF's net income has been fluctuating. Despite of this net income has an overall growth of 118%.

Revenues totaled $24.5 billion for the year ended December 31 2019 compared to $27.2 billion for the year ended December 31 2018 a decrease of approximately $2.7 billion or 9.9%.

Net income increased 149% to $319.4 million compare to $128.3 million from 2018.

Cash from operations increased 37% to $813.7 million. Cash provided by operating activities totaled $936.9 million. Investing activities used $712.6 million and financing activities used $6.6 million.

Strategy

The Company's investment strategy for its Qualified Plan is to achieve a reasonable return on assets that supports the plan's interest credit rating subject to a moderate level of portfolio risk that provides liquidity.

Mergers and Acquisitions

In early 2020 PBF Energy Inc. completed the acquisition of Martinez refinery and related logistics assets from Equilon Enterprises LLC d/b/a Shell Oil Products US. With the acquisition PBF increased its total throughput capacity to more than one million barrels per day and becomes the most complex independent refiner with a consolidated Nelson Complexity of 12.8 million. The purchase price for the assets was $960.0 million plus the value of hydrocarbon inventory. In conjunction with the transaction PBF has entered into market-based crude oil supply and product offtake agreements with Shell.

Company Background

PBF Energy was created in 2008 by Swiss oil refiner Petroplus to help it establish a foothold in the US. Petroplus and The Blackstone Group each invested $667 million to begin buying oil refineries at the height of the global economic recession when larger companies were looking to sell off assets to drum up cash. PBF first bought the Delaware refinery from Valero in 2010 for $220 million. (The low price tag came because the refinery had been shut down since 2009). Next came the New Jersey refinery again purchased from Valero for $358 million.

In 2011 PBF Energy bought an Ohio refinery from Sunoco for $400 million.

PBF Energy went public in 2012 with an IPO that raised $429 million. The IPO came as a quick turnaround before PBF Energy was able to recognize any significant revenue and the company used the $613 million in proceeds to pay back its principal investors Blackstone and First Reserve.

In 2013 PBF Energy signed a deal with Continental Resources for the oil company to supply PBF Energy with Bakken crude oil. The deal marks a shift for the East Coast refinery market - a market that has historically relied on imports of foreign oil.

EXECUTIVES

Chairman And Ceo, Thomas J. Nimbley, age 68, $1,500,000 total compensation

Svp Commercial, Thomas L. O'Connor, age 47, $500,000 total compensation

President, Matthew C. Lucey, age 46, $600,000 total compensation

Cfo, C. Erik Young, age 44, $523,958 total compensation

Svp Refining, Herman Seedorf, age 68

Svp Commercial Western Region, Timothy Paul Davis

Vice President, Clark Wrigley

Auditors: DELOITTE & TOUCHE LLP

LOCATIONS

HQ: PBF Energy Inc
One Sylvan Way, Second Floor, Parsippany, NJ 07054
Phone: 973 455-7500
Web: www.pbfenergy.com

PRODUCTS/OPERATIONS

Products
Clean Fuels
Lubes
Petrochemicals
LPG

2016 sales by segment

	$ mil.	% of total
Refining	15,908	99
Logistics	187	1
Elimination	(175.4)	-
Total	**15,920**	**100**

2016 sales

	$ mil.	% of total
Gasoline & distillates	14,017	88
Asphalt and blackoils	699	5
Chemicals	554	3
Feedstocks and other	388	2
Lubricants	260	2
Total	**15,920**	**100**

COMPETITORS

Alon USA Energy	Motiva Enterprises
CITGO Refining and Chemicals	Paramount Petroleum
	Placid Refining
Chevron	San Joaquin Refining
ConocoPhillips	Shell Oil Products
Exxon Mobil	Sunoco
Flint Hills	Tauber Oil
HollyFrontier	United Refining
Marathon Petroleum	Valero Energy

HISTORICAL FINANCIALS

Company Type: Public

Income Statement   FYE: December 31

	REVENUE ($ mil.)	NET INCOME ($ mil.)	NET PROFIT MARGIN	EMPLOYEES
12/19	24,508	319	1.3%	3,442
12/18	27,186	128	0.5%	3,266
12/17	21,786	415	1.9%	3,165
12/16	15,920	170	1.1%	3,165
12/15	13,123	146	1.1%	2,270
Annual Growth	**16.9%**	**21.5%**	**—**	**11.0%**

2019 Year-End Financials

Debt ratio: 22.61%
Return on equity: 11.18%
Cash ($ mil.): 814
Current ratio: 1.52
Long-term debt ($ mil.): 2,064

No. of shares (mil.): 119
Dividends
  Yield: 3.8%
  Payout: 45.4%
Market value ($ mil.): 3,758

	STOCK PRICE ($) FY Close	P/E High/Low		PER SHARE ($) Earnings	Dividends	Book Value
12/19	31.37	14	8	2.64	1.20	25.37
12/18	32.67	48	26	1.10	1.20	22.33
12/17	35.45	9	5	3.73	1.20	21.13
12/16	27.88	22	11	1.74	1.20	18.54
12/15	36.81	25	14	1.65	1.20	16.85
Annual Growth	**(3.9%)**	—	—	**12.5%**	**(0.0%)**	**10.8%**

Peapack-Gladstone Financial Corp.

Peapack-Gladstone Financial is the $3.4 billion-asset holding company for the near-century-old Peapack-Gladstone Bank which operates more than 20 branches in New Jersey's Hunterdon Morris Somerset Middlesex and Union counties. Founded in 1921 the bank provides traditional deposit accounts credit cards and loans to individuals and small businesses as well as trust and investment management services through its PGB Trust and Investments unit. Multifamily residential mortgages represent nearly 50% of the company's loan portfolio while commercial mortgages make up around 15%. The bank also originates construction consumer and business loans.

Operations

Peapack-Gladstone Financial operates two main divisions: Banking which offers traditional deposit and loan services merchant card services; and Wealth Management which boasts more than $3.3 billion in assets under administration (as of early 2016) and operates through PGB Trust and Investments which offers asset management services for individuals and institutions as well as personal trust services. More than 80% of the bank's total revenue came from interest income (mostly on its loans) during 2015 while 14% came from its wealth management fee income and 3% came from service charges and fees.

Multifamily residential mortgages represented nearly 50% of the company's loan portfolio at the end of 2015 while commercial mortgages made up another 15%. The rest of its portfolio was made up of construction consumer and business loans.

Geographic Reach

The bank's branches are located across New Jersey in Somerset Morris Hunterdon Middlesex and Union counties Its private banking and wealth management locations are located in Bedminster Morristown Princeton and Teaneck.

Sales and Marketing

The bank's commercial banking business serves business owners professionals retailers contractors and real estate investors. Its wealth management division serves individuals families foundations endowments trusts and estates.

Peapack-Gladstone has been ramping up its advertising spend in recent years. It spent $637000 on advertising during 2015 up from

$594000 and $519000 in 2014 and 2013 respectively.

Financial Performance

Peapack-Gladstone's annual revenues and profits have swelled more than 60% since 2011 as its nearly tripled its loan assets to over $2.9 billion.

The bank's revenue jumped 27% to $122.86 million during 2015 mostly thanks to higher interest income as its loan assets grew by 30% with exceptional increases in its multifamily mortgage and commercial loan volumes. Peapack-Gladstone's wealth management division income grew 20% with increases in securities gains service charges and other non-interest income.

Strong revenue growth in 2015 drove Peapack-Gladstone's net income up 34% to $19.97 million. The bank's operating cash levels climbed 11% to $30.31 million thanks to a rise in cash-based earnings.

Strategy

Peapack-Gladstone Financial continued in 2016 to focus on: enhancing its risk management to keep its loan provisions at a minimum and its profits up; expanding its multi-family loans as well as its commercial real estate loans (to a lesser extent); growing its commercial and industrial (C&I) lending business through its private banking divisions; and expanding its wealth management business which now accounts for 15% of its annual revenue.

Mergers and Acquisitions

In May 2015 Peapack-Gladstone bolstered its wealth management division after buying Morristown-based Wealth Management Consultants LLC for $2.8 million. The deal boosted the bank's assets under advisement and administration to $3.5 billion.

EXECUTIVES

Sevp And Cfo Peapack-gladstone Financial And Peapack-gladstone Bank, Jeffrey J. Carfora, age 62
Evp And Coo, Robert A. (Bob) Plante, age 61
President And Ceo Peapack-gladstone Financial And Peapack-gladstone Bank, Douglas L. Kennedy, age 61
Evp Cio And Head Of Banking Services Peapack-gladstone Bank, Kevin B. Runyon
Sevp Chief Strategy Officer And General Counsel, Finn M.W. Casperson, age 50
Evp And Head Of Retail Banking Peapack-gladstone Bank, Anthony V. Bilotta, age 60
Evp And Head Of Commercial Real Estate Peapack-gladstone Bank, Vincent A. Spero
Sevp And President Private Wealth Management, John P. Babcock
Evp And Chief Credit Officer Peapack-gladstone Bank, Lisa Chalkan
Evp And Director Human Capital Peapack-gladstone Bank, Philip Portantino
Evp And President Wealth Management Consultants Peapack-gladstone Bank, Thomas J. Ross
Evp And Head Of Commercial Banking Peapack-gladstone Bank, Eric H. Waser
Svp And Head Of Residential And Consumer Lending Peapack-gladstone, Glenn R. Straffi
Senior Vice President, Charles Adornetto
Vice President, Sean Martin
Vice President And Trust Officer, Kim Czyzewski
Vice President, Glenn Carroll
Private Banker Vice President, Ryan Beltz
Vice President Portfolio Manager, Sarah Krieger
Vice President, Georgette Barnes

Svp Head Of Asset Management At Peapack Capital, David Santom
Assistant Vice President And Senior Custody Officer, Amanda Pullizzi
Svp Senior Underwriter, Christian Gaudioso
Assistant Vice President And Mortgage Consultant, Stephanie Chu
Vice President Financial Analyst, Renee Skuraton
Vice President, David Oddo
Vp Of Deposit Operations, Carlos Pacheco
Senior Vp Head Of Loan Operations, Lisa Ciampi
Assistant Vice President And Senior Staff Accountant And Technical Support, Jennifer Greenwood
Senior Vice President And Chief Accounting Officer, Frank Rossi
Chairman, F. Duffield (Duff) Meyercord, age 73
Board Treasurer, Denise Wright
Board Member, Susan Cole
Board Member, Richard Daingerfield
Auditors: Crowe LLP

LOCATIONS

HQ: Peapack-Gladstone Financial Corp.
500 Hills Drive, Suite 300, Bedminster, NJ 07921-0700
Phone: 908 234-0700
Web: www.pgbank.com

PRODUCTS/OPERATIONS

2015 Sales

	$ mil.	% of total
Interest Income		
Loans including fees	94	77
Securities available for sale	4	4
Other	0	-
Other Income		
Wealth management fee income	17	14
Service charges and fees	3	3
Bank owned life insurance	1	1
Other Income	1	1
Other	1	-
Total	**122**	**100**

COMPETITORS

Bank of America	PNC Financial
Hudson City Bancorp	TD Bank USA
JPMorgan Chase	Valley National
MSB Financial	Bancorp

HISTORICAL FINANCIALS

Company Type: Public

Income Statement				FYE: December 31
	ASSETS ($ mil.)	NET INCOME ($ mil.)	INCOME AS % OF ASSETS	EMPLOYEES
12/19	5,182	47	0.9%	446
12/18	4,617	44	1.0%	409
12/17	4,260	36	0.9%	384
12/16	3,878	26	0.7%	338
12/15	3,364	19	0.6%	316
Annual Growth	11.4%	24.1%	—	9.0%

2019 Year-End Financials

Debt ratio: 1.76%	No. of shares (mil.): 18
Return on equity: 9.75%	Dividends
Cash ($ mil.): 208	Yield: 0.6%
Current ratio: —	Payout: 8.4%
Long-term debt ($ mil.): —	Market value ($ mil.): 585

	STOCK PRICE ($) FY Close	P/E High/Low	PER SHARE ($) Earnings	Dividends	Book Value
12/19	30.90	13 10	2.44	0.20	26.61
12/18	25.18	16 10	2.31	0.20	24.25
12/17	35.02	18 14	2.03	0.20	21.68
12/16	30.88	20 10	1.60	0.20	18.79
12/15	20.62	18 14	1.29	0.20	17.16
Annual Growth	10.6%	—	17.3%	(0.0%)	11.6%

PENNSYLVANIA HOUSING FINANCE AGENCY

Pennsylvania Housing Finance Agency (PHFA) helps residents of the Keystone State obtain keys to their dream homes. The government-owned agency provides financing for low-income homebuyers including the elderly and disabled and participates in rental housing development initiatives. It generates funding from state and federal grants interest earned on investments and loans and the sale of its own securities to private investors. The agency is run by a board which includes Pennsylvania's secretary of banking secretary of community and economic development secretary of public welfare and the state treasurer. The PHFA has funded more than 130000 houses and 54000 apartment units since its founding in 1972.

EXECUTIVES

Chm, Robin Wiessmann
V Pres*, Thomas B Hagen
Exec Dir*, Craig H Alexander
Human Resources Representative, Arlene Frontz
Finance Manager, John Zapotocky
Financial Officer, Kelly Wilson
Manager, Kevin Wike
Accountant, Laura Wildman
Senior Special Programs Office, Roberta Schwalm
Officer, Theodore Jackson
Engineer, Kris Clymans

LOCATIONS

HQ: PENNSYLVANIA HOUSING FINANCE AGENCY
211 N FRONT ST, HARRISBURG, PA 171011406
Phone: 717 780-3800
Web: WWW.PHFA.ORG

HISTORICAL FINANCIALS

Company Type: Private

Income Statement				FYE: June 30
	ASSETS ($ mil.)	NET INCOME ($ mil.)	INCOME AS % OF ASSETS	EMPLOYEES
06/20	4,542	14	0.3%	250
06/19	4,366	22	0.5%	—
06/18	4,366	20	0.5%	—
06/12	5,593	10	0.2%	—
Annual Growth	(2.6%)	4.3%	—	

PennyMac Financial Services Inc (New)

If you're thinking residential mortgage this company has more than a penny for your thoughts. The parent of investment management loan services and investment trust companies PennyMac Financial Services (PennyMac) focuses on the US residential mortgage market offering loans and investment management services. Through its Private National Mortgage Acceptance Company the company's PennyMac Loan Services (PLS) originates home loans in 45 states and DC and services loans in 49 states DC and the US Virgin Islands. PLS's counterpart PNMAC Capital Management acts as investment manager and advisor. The companies service and advise PennyMac Mortgage Investment Trust (PMT). PennyMac went public in 2013.

IPO

PennyMac hoped to raise $287.5 million in its IPO but investors responded with $199.9 million. The company plans to use the proceeds to fund growth of its mortgage business through Private National Mortgage Acceptance Company. It will also use the funds for general corporate purposes.

Operations

PennyMac's mortgage banking segment includes correspondent lending retail lending and loan servicing. The correspondent line includes conventional residential mortgages acquired by PMT as well as those guaranteed by FreddieMac FannieMae and other government agencies. The company has more than 140 approved sellers; in 2012 it had $13 billion in conventional loans and $8.4 billion in government-insured loans. Retail lending originates new prime residential conventional and government-backed mortgage loans for purchasing or refinancing homes. PennyMac uses the Internet and a call center rather than traditional branch locations for direct-to-consumer approach. The company's loan servicing business includes the back office work of loan administration collection and default activities. It serves PennyMac subsidiaries and other mortgage companies. The unit handles prime credit and distress loans under the prime servicing and special servicing headings respectively.

PennyMac's investment management segment operates as an investment manager through PNMAC Capital Management (PCM). PCM handles the $1.8 billion in combined assets from PMT and PennyMac's other investment funds. PMT is a publicly traded real estate investment trust (REIT).

Geographic Reach

While PennyMac serves nearly the entire US its portfolio is heavily weighted toward California (38%) Florida (5%) and Colorado (5%).

Financial Performance

The company's revenue has increased on the strength of gains in both the loan servicing and management segments. Other operating metrics include net assets under management total mortgage loans serviced and total mortgage loan production; all have increased in the last three years. PennyMac reported lower net income for 2012 due to amortization and impairment charges and

higher spending on compensation. It sold and repurchased loans loans and earned interest on investments to more than double its cash flow for the same period.

Strategy

Since PennyMac was formed during the financial crisis it hasn't had to scramble and adapt like many of its competitors. As many mortgage shoppers turn away from large banks the company believes its poised to take advantage of growth and a lack of stringent regulations imposed on banks. For growth the company intends to focus on expanding its servicing business organically and through acquisitions increasing the number of loan sellers from which it purchases loans and leveraging its servicing portfolio to increase refinance and loan servicing opportunities.

EXECUTIVES

Senior Managing Director And Chief Enterprise Operations Officer, Anne D. McCallion, age 65
President And Ceo, David A. Spector, age 57, $503,370 total compensation
President Pennymac Loan Services, Douglas E. (Doug) Jones, age 63, $325,000 total compensation
Senior Managing Director And Chief Risk Officer, David M. (Dave) Walker, age 64
Senior Managing Director And Chief Mortgage Operations Officer, Steve R. Bailey, age 58
Senior Managing Director And Cfo, Andrew S. Chang, age 42
Senior Managing Director And Chief Capital Markets Officer, Vandad Fartaj, age 45
Senior Managing Director And Chief Administrative And Legal Officer, Jeffrey P. Grogin, age 59
Senior Managing Director And Deputy Cfo, Daniel S. Perotti, age 39
Chairman And Ceo Pennymac Financial Services Inc. And Private National Mortgage Acceptance Company Llc, Stanford L. Kurland, age 67
Auditors: DELOITTE & TOUCHE LLP

LOCATIONS

HQ: PennyMac Financial Services Inc (New)
3043 Townsgate Road, Westlake Village, CA 91361
Phone: 818 224-7442
Web: www.pennymacfinancial.com

2016 Sales

	$ mil.	% of total
Net gains on mortgage loans held for sale	531	56
Net mortgage loan servicing fees	185	19
Loan origination fees	125	13
Fulfillment fees from PennyMac Mortgage Investment Trust	86	9
Management fees and Carried Interest	23	2
Other	4	1
Net interest expense	-25.1 -	
Total	**931**	**0**

COMPETITORS

Bank of America	Quicken Loans
Citigroup	Stonegate Mortgage
JPMorgan Chase	U.S. Bancorp
Nationstar Mortgage	Wells Fargo
Ocwen Financial	

HISTORICAL FINANCIALS

Company Type: Public

Income Statement

FYE: December 31

	ASSETS ($ mil.)	NET INCOME ($ mil.)	INCOME AS % OF ASSETS	EMPLOYEES
12/19	10,204	392	3.9%	4,215
12/18	7,478	87	1.2%	3,460
12/17	7,368	100	1.4%	3,189
12/16	5,133	66	1.3%	3,038
12/15	3,505	47	1.3%	2,509
Annual Growth	30.6%	69.8%	—	13.8%

2019 Year-End Financials

Debt ratio: 12.89%	No. of shares (mil.): 78
Return on equity: 21.15%	Dividends
Cash ($ mil.): 188	Yield: 0.3%
Current ratio: —	Payout: 3.2%
Long-term debt ($ mil.): —	Market value ($ mil.): 2,673

	STOCK PRICE ($) FY Close	P/E High/Low		PER SHARE ($) Earnings	Dividends	Book Value
12/19	34.04	7	4	4.89	0.12	26.26
12/18	21.26	9	7	2.59	0.40	21.34
12/17	22.35	5	4	4.03	0.00	19.95
12/16	16.65	6	4	2.94	0.00	15.49
12/15	15.36	9	7	2.17	0.00	12.32
Annual Growth	22.0%	—	—	22.5%	—	20.8%

Penske Automotive Group Inc

Penske Automotive Group has lots of lots. The US' #2 publicly traded auto dealer behind AutoNation Penske operates about 145 auto franchises from California to New Jersey and Puerto Rico and another 175 franchises abroad mainly in the UK. It sells about 35 car brands. Non-US brands including AUDI BMW Land Rover Mercedez-Benz and Porsche generate more than 70% of sales. Penske also sells used vehicles provides financing and runs more than 35 collision repair centers. UK subsidiary Sytner Group operates more than 130 franchises. Additionally Penske holds a nearly 30% stake in Penske Truck Leasing (PTL) known for commercial leasing and contract maintenance. The company is named after its Chairman Roger Penske.

Operations

Penske operates through four reportable segments: Retail Automotive Retail Commercial Truck Non-Automotive Investments and Other.

The Retail Automotive segment brings in the vast majority of company revenue (over 90%) and consists of its 320 retail automotive franchises in the US and abroad. It sells new and used cars under around 35 auto brands; around 70% of sales are from premium brands particularly Audi BMW and Porsche. The segment sells over 629000 cars each year.

Retail Commercial Truck accounts for about 10% of revenue and consists of the heavy-duty truck dealerships Premier Truck Group. Premier Truck Group has over 25 locations in the US and Canada that offer used trucks servicing and parts. Its service and parts departments are open 24/7.

Other consists of the company's commercial vehicle and power systems distribution operations and other non-automotive consolidated operations.

Geographic Reach

Michigan-based Penske rings up some 55% of its sales in the US. The remainder comes from its overseas franchises which are predominantly found in the UK but also in Germany Canada and Italy. The company also has operations in Australia and New Zealand.

Sales and Marketing

Penske conducts its advertising and marketing at the local level. In recent years it has concentrated on the internet and other digital media including its own websites.

By manufacturer Audi/Volkswagen/Porsche/Bentley franchises brings in about 25% of Penske's total revenue. BMW/MINI brand franchises account for about 25% of revenue Toyota brands (Toyota and Lexus) generate about 15% of revenue and Mercedes-Benz brands (Mercedes-Benz/Sprinter/Smart) generate 10%.

Advertising expenses were $113 million and $115 million in 2019 and 2018 respectively.

Financial Performance

Penske has seen robust revenue growth in recent years. Its annual revenues have risen around 20% since 2015.

Revenue increased to $23.2 billion in 2019 an approximately 2% increase from the year prior. The increase was driven by higher used vehicles sales higher service and parts sales and dealership acquisitions.

Net income was $435.1 million in fiscal year 2019 a drop from $470.3 million in fiscal year 2018. Selling general and administrative expenses grew 2% in fiscal 2019 to $2.7 billion and also income taxes grew 17%.

Cash provided by operating activities was $518.3 million in fiscal 2019 while investing activities used $532.7 million. Financing activities provided $2.6 million. In 2019 cash held by the company decreased by $11.3 million to $28.1 million from the prior year.

Strategy

The company's long-term business strategy focuses on several key areas in an effort to foster long-term relationships with its customers and their associates. The key areas of Penske's long-term strategy are: Attract develop and empower associates to grow business; diversification; offer outstanding brands in premium facilities and superior customer service; expand revenues at existing locations and increase higher-margin businesses; grow through strategic acquisitions; enhance customer satisfaction; leverage scale and implement "best practices"; and embrace digital sales and marketing.

Penske's business benefits from its diversified revenue and gross profit mix including the multiple revenue and gross profit streams in their traditional vehicle and commercial truck dealerships (new vehicles used vehicles finance and insurance and service and parts operations) the company's commercial vehicle distribution and power systems operations and returns relating to its joint venture investments which the company believes help to mitigate the cyclicality that has historically impacted some elements of the automotive sector.

EXECUTIVES

Evp Human Resources, Claude H. (Bud) Denker, age 61, $500,000 total compensation
Chairman And Ceo, Roger S. Penske, age 83, $1,200,000 total compensation
President, Robert H. Kurnick, age 58, $700,000 total compensation
Chairman Sytner Group, Gerard Nieuwenhuys, age 59
Evp Investor Relations And Corporate Development, Anthony R. (Tony) Pordon, age 56
Managing Director Sytner Group, Darren Edwards
Evp West Operations, Bernie Wolfe, age 64
Evp Strategic Development, George Brochick, age 72
Evp Central Operations, R. Whitfield Ramonat, age 59
Evp General Counsel And Secretary, Shane M. Spradlin, age 50, $500,000 total compensation
Evp East Operations, John Cragg
Svp And Corporate Controller, J.D. Carlson, age 50, $475,000 total compensation
Evp Marketing And Business Development, Terri Mulcahey
Svp And Cio, Rich Hook
Vice President, Joe Ziniti
Area Vice President, Robert Miller
Vice President Corporate Marketing, Tracy Cassady
Vice President {, Christian Collins
Executive Vice President Human Resources, Bud Denker
Executive Vice President And General Counsel, Walter P Czarnecki, age 78
Vice President Finance, James Harris
Vice President, Jerry Byrd
Senior Vice President Human Resources, Tim Roop
Senior Vice President Manufacturer Relations, Robert K Wilshaw
Senior Vice President Of Premium Brands, Michael Famiglietti
Senior Vice President Penske Automotive Group, Tony Pordon
Assistant Vice President, Curt Imber
Senior Vice President, Bob Willshaw
Area Vice President, Bob Miller
Vice President, Michael Montri
Vice President, Sally Hillen
Vice President, Niall Hay
Asst. To Area Vice President, Fisher Tena
Area Vice President, Alan Perlin
Vice President Manufacturer Relations, Jason Beidelman
Executive Vice President Corporate Development, Tony Pardon
Executive Vice President Operations, Art Vallely
Area Vice President, John Robben
Vice President, Daniel Morales
Evp Hr, Bud Denker Iii
Board Member, William Lovejoy
Board Member, Alisa Davis
Board Member, Brian Thompson
Board Member, Sandra Pierce
Auditors: DELOITTE & TOUCHE LLP

LOCATIONS

HQ: Penske Automotive Group Inc
   2555 Telegraph Road, Bloomfield Hills, MI 48302-0954
Phone: 248 648-2500   **Fax:** 248 648-2525
Web: www.penskeautomotive.com

2016 Sales

	$ mil.	% of total
U.S	12,005	60
International	8,112	40
Total	**20,118**	**100**

2016 Stores

	No.
U.S	164
U.K	146
Germany	28
Italy	17
Total	**355**

PRODUCTS/OPERATIONS

2016 Sales

	$ mil.	% of total
Retail Automotive	18,673	93
Retail Commercial Truck	1,000	5
Commercial vehicle and Other	448	2
Elimination	(3.9)	
Total	**20,118**	**100**

COMPETITORS

Asbury Automotive	JM Family Enterprises
AutoNation	Jordan Automotive
Autobytel	Larry H. Miller Group
Avis Budget	Lithia Motors
CarMax	Lookers
Ed Morse Auto	Microsoft
Enterprise Group	National Car Rental
Fletcher Jones	Pendragon
Group 1 Automotive	Potamkin Automotive
Hendrick Automotive	Serra Automotive
Holman Enterprises	Sonic Automotive

HISTORICAL FINANCIALS

Company Type: Public

Income Statement

FYE: December 31

	REVENUE ($ mil.)	NET INCOME ($ mil.)	NET PROFIT MARGIN	EMPLOYEES
12/19	23,179	435	1.9%	27,000
12/18	22,785	471	2.1%	27,000
12/17	21,386	613	2.9%	26,000
12/16	20,118	342	1.7%	24,000
12/15	19,284	326	1.7%	22,000
Annual Growth	4.7%	7.5%	—	5.3%

2019 Year-End Financials

Debt ratio: 45.66%	No. of shares (mil.): 81
Return on equity: 16.13%	Dividends
Cash ($ mil.): 28	Yield: 3.1%
Current ratio: 0.98	Payout: 30.4%
Long-term debt ($ mil.): 2,257	Market value ($ mil.): 4,072

	STOCK PRICE ($) FY Close	P/E High/Low		PER SHARE ($) Earnings	Dividends	Book Value
12/19	50.22	10	8	5.28	1.58	34.45
12/18	40.32	10	7	5.53	1.42	30.86
12/17	47.85	8	5	7.14	1.26	27.92
12/16	51.84	14	8	3.99	1.10	20.55
12/15	42.34	15	12	3.63	0.94	20.00
Annual Growth	4.4%		—	9.8%	13.9%	14.6%

People's United Financial Inc

People's United Financial is the holding company for People's United Bank (formerly People's Bank) which boasts more than 400 traditional branches supermarket branches commercial banking offices investment and brokerage offices and equipment leasing offices across New England and eastern New York. In addition to retail and commercial banking services the bank offers trust wealth management brokerage and insurance services. Its lending activities consist mainly of commercial mortgages (more than a third of its loan portfolio) commercial and industrial loans (more than a quarter) residential mortgages equipment financing and home equity loans. Founded in 1842 the bank has $36 billion in assets.

Operations

People's United operates two core business segments Retail Banking and Commercial Banking which both share duties of the bank's now-defunct Wealth Management division. The bank also has a non-core Treasury division that manages the company's securities portfolio and other investments.

Commercial Banking which makes up more than half of the company's total revenue provides business loans equipment financing (through People's Capital and Leasing Corp. or PCLC and People's United Equipment Finance Corp or PUEFC) and municipal banking as well as trust services for corporations and institutions and private banking services for wealthy individuals.

Retail Banking which makes up around 20% of total revenues provides deposit services residential mortgages and home equity loans financial advisory and investment management services as well as life insurance through People's United Insurance Agency.

Overall the bank generated 68% of its total revenue from loan interest in 2014 and 7% from interest on securities. About 10% of total revenues came from bank service charges while investment management fees commercial banking lending fees insurance revenue and brokerage commissions each made up less than 3% of overall revenue for the year.

Geographic Reach

People's United has more than 400 branches across Connecticut southeastern New York Massachusetts Vermont New Hampshire and Maine. Connecticut is its largest lending market with 27% of the bank's loan portfolio being extended to consumers and businesses in the region in 2014. New York and Massachusetts are the bank's next largest markets with a 19% and 18% share of its loan portfolio.

Sales and Marketing

The bank sells its products and services through investment and brokerage offices commercial branches online banking and investment trading and through its 24-hour telephone banking service. The company's PCLC and PUEFC affiliates have a sales presence in 16 states to support equipment financing operations throughout the US.

People's United spent $13 million on advertising in 2014 compared to $15.4 million and $17.7 million in 2013 and 2012 respectively.

Strategy

People's United emphasizes cross-selling financial products by developing client relationships and has increasingly tied employee compensation to this ability. The company is particularly focused on building its small business lending wealth management and insurance business. It

also continues to open new branches and seeks acquisition targets for further growth.

One other key element of its strategy involves boosting its deposit assets through its expanded convenient store reach. In early 2015 the company boasted nearly 150 full-service branches in Stop & Shop supermarkets across Connecticut and southeastern New York which comprised 36% of the bank's total branch network and held 14% of its total deposits. Much of this is attributed to a key acquisition in 2012 when the company purchased nearly 60 branches (many within Stop & Shop supermarkets) in the New York metro area from RBS Citizens. People's United already had more than 80 Stop & Shop branches in Connecticut so the deal strengthened its relationship with the retailer and expanded its presence in the New York market.

Mergers and Acquisitions

In 2019 People's United Financial acquired BSB Bancorp the holding company for Belmont Savings Bank for about $330 million. Belmont Massachusetts-headquartered Bemont Savings Bank holds about $3 billion in assets and has six branches in the Greater Boston area. The acquisition deepens People's United's presence in the area. That year the company also agreed to buy United Financial Bancorp in a transaction valued at around $760 million. United Financial is the holding company for United Bank a Hartford-based community bank with $7.3 billion in assets and roughly 60 branches in central Connecticut and western Massachusetts.

People's United acquired independent leasing and finance company VAR Technology Finance in early 2019. VAR uses its software platform to finance commercial and public sector customers of large technology manufacturers. The company will maintain its brand but become a division of People's United's LEAF Commercial Capital subsidiary. VAR originated $180 million in loans in 2018.

In 2018 People's United agreed to acquire First Connecticut Bancorp in an all-stock transaction valued at $544 million. The acquisition will further enhance People's United's established presence in the northeastern US. First Connecticut Bancorp is the holding company of Farmington Bank which operates nearly 30 community bank locations across Connecticut and in western Massachusetts.

Company Background

One of the main goals of People's United has been to build its presence in the two largest metropolitan areas in its market New York City and Boston. One of the largest in the Boston area Danvers Bancorp added some 30 branches and carried a price tag of approximately $493 million. People's United also acquired LSB Corporation and Butler Bank the latter in an FDIC-assisted transaction that included a loss-sharing agreement with the regulator covering all acquired loans and foreclosed real estate of the failed bank bringing in another 10 branches in the Boston area. In 2010 People's United bought Bank of Smithtown which had about 30 branches primarily on Long Island in New York.

People's United Financial acquired commercial lender Financial Federal Corporation in 2010 (now People's United Equipment Finance) which provides financing and leasing to small and mid-sized business nationwide.

People's United Financial underwent significant transformation in past years. The company demutualized and converted to a stock holding company in 2007 and early the following year acquired multibank holding company Chittenden Corporation. The deal added some 140 branches doubling People's United Bank's branch network and expanding its reach beyond Connecticut and New York and into the rest of New England.

EXECUTIVES

President And Ceo, John P. (Jack) Barnes, age 64, $890,384 total compensation

Sevp Corporate Development And Strategic Planning, Kirk W. Walters, age 65, $468,461 total compensation

Svp And President Merrill Bank, William P. (Bill) Lucy, age 61

Chief Financial Officer, R. David Rosato, age 58

Sevp Retail And Business Banking, Robert R. (Bob) D'Amore, age 67, $429,323 total compensation

President Vermont, Michael L. Seaver

Sevp Wealth Management, Louise T. Sandberg, age 68

Svp And President The Bank Of Western Massachusetts And Flagship Bank, Timothy P. Crimmins

Market Leader New York, Sara M. Longobardi

Svp And President People's United Bank North Connecticut, Michael J. Casparino

Sevp Human Resources, David K. Norton, age 65, $411,231 total compensation

Sevp Commercial Banking, Jeffrey J. (Jeff) Tengel, age 57, $408,654 total compensation

Svp And Division President People's United Bank Southern Connecticut, Armando F. Goncalves

Sevp And General Counsel, Robert E. Trautmann, age 66

Sevp And Chief Administrative Officer, Lee C. Powlus

President New Hampshire, Dianne M. Mercier

President Southern Maine, Daniel P. (Dan) Thornton

Vice President Information Technology, Carol Anderson

Vice President Information Technology, Roy Allison

Vice President, Kon Khongkham

Vice President Information Technology, Albert Sanna

Vice President Financial Services Manager, Cheryl Nickerson

Vice President Sales Aviation Finance, Jim Pulie

First Vice President Retail And Business Banking Human Resources, Doreen Moffat

Vice President Market Research, Craig Noble

Vice President Commercial Lending, Michael Sheridan

First Vice President Wealth Management, John Lescure

Executive Vice President, Candace C Fitzek

Senior Vice President Human Resources, Michelle McNeil

Senior Vice President And Market Development Officer, Brian Shea

Vice President, Peter Martinez

Vp Call Center, David Weber

Divisional Vice President, Peter Brestovan

Assistant Vice President, Patrick Talcott

Vice President Real Estate Services, David Iassogna

Vice President Capital Markets, Russ Hardy

Svp, Doug Smith

Vice President Customer Experience Manager, Thomas Griesing

Vice President Commercial Relationship Manager, Kasi White

Vice President Director Of Tax, Kathleen Jones

Vp Operations Manager Commercial Services, Keara Piscitelli

Market Manager Assistant Vice President, Alice Baird

Vice President Commercial Lending, Edgar Auchincloss

Senior Vice President And Director Marketing, Kathleen Schirling

Vice President Customer Service Manager, Joan Foster

Vice President, Daniel Reilly

Vice President Market Manager, David Conner

Vice President, Melissa Curtis

Vice President Customer Service Manager, Magda Wachel-Florczyk

Vice President, Elaine Khu

Vice President, Patrick Lorent

Vice President Business Banking Portfolio Management, Louis Paffumi

Assistant Vice President Customer Service, Ana Saraiva

Assistant Vice President, Kasey Franzoni

Senior Vice President, Kathleen Lepak

Vice President Financial Analyst, Rita Rivers

Vice President Finance, Brian Connery

Purchasing Vice President, Theresa Knies

Assistant Vice President, David Schalk

Assistant Vice President, Francine Grandmaison

Executive Vice President And Market Mana, John Bundschuh

Vice President, Kurtis Denison

Vice President, Bethany Dubuque

Vice President, Lisa Rollins

Senior Vice President Commercial Lending, Tom Wolcott

Vice President, Michael Ciborowski

Vice President, Steven Wurtz

Vice President Financial Services Manager, Jennifer Lynch

Vice President, Joanne Murgalo

Senior Vice President, Marilyn Hardacre

Vice President, Sheila Moran

Region Manager Senior Vice President Commercial Real Estate Finance, Kathleen Hayes

Vice President Customer Service Manager, Rashiya Thompson

Vice President, James Bucko

Assistant Vice President Financial Services Manager, Angela Gallagher

Senior Vice President Commercial Re Finance, Linda Tremblay

Senior Vice President, Mark Leonardi

Vice President Commercial Banking, Deborah Quirk

Senior Vice President Relationship Manager, Vincent Bergin

Senior Vice President Of Wealth Management, David Dixon

Executive Vice President Mid Corporate, Dexter Freeman

Commercial Portfolio Manager Assistant Vice President, James Davenport

Vice President Customer Service Manager, Scott Zimmerman

Vice President Financial Services Manager, Kristen Keil

Market Manager Vice President, Renee Goupille

Financial Services Manager Assistant Vice President, Cathy Ferreira-Golino

Assistant Vice President Customer Service Manager, Sylvana Chiluisa

Senior Vice President Senior Portfolio Manager, James Witterschein

Vice President Model Validation And Risk Management, Julien Lee

Assistant Vice President Mortgage Account Officer, Richard Klein

Executive Vice President Chief Credit Officer, David Barey

Senior Vice President, Stephanie Wernhoff

Team Leader Vice President Senior Commercial Review Appraiser, Michelle Gamache

Vice President Comm Lending, Frank Cory

Senior Vice President And Senior Relationship Manager, Ellery Perkinson

Senior Vice President, Patrick Lee

Assistant Vice President Customer Service Manager, Krupali Doshi

Vice President Sales And Leasing, Rick Curtiss

Vice President, Tom Emery

Assistant Vice President, Ana Espinal

Assistant Vice President, Miriam James

Regional Vice President, Gary Fisher

Vice President And Sr.market Manager Bridgeport Market, Virgilio Lopez

Senior Vice President Senior Relationship Manager New York Cre, Ted Dalton

Senior Vice President, Lisa Overton

Vice President, Justin Jennings

Vice President Corporate Communications, Steven Bodakowski

Senior Vice President Head Of Wealth Strategy Product And Marketing, Daniel Darst

Vice President Wealth Management Marketing, Sara Sparks

First Vice President Digital Marketing, James Roy

Senior Market Manager Vice President, Raymond DiPresso

Vice President Residential Lending Officer, Cathy Eakins

Avp Bank Manager, Flawer Bardales

Assistant Vice President Customer Service Manager, Danielle Lutz

Vice President, Elizabeth Dougherty

Vice President, Justin Mills

Vice President, Kenneth Vaccaro

Vice President Customer Service Manager, Lacey Bicknell

First Vice President, Maria Kastanis

Vice President Information Technology, Michael Kirven

Senior Vice President, Mark Danie

Senior Vice President, Victor Galati

Vice President, Mick Kirven

Vice President Treasury Management Sales Officer, Elaine Canton

Senior Vice President Commercial Banking, David Estes

Vice President Market Manager, Benish Shah

Senior Vice President, Phil Cohen

Vice President Customer Service Manager, Silveras Sboui

Assistant Vice President Bank Manager, Andrew Matarese

Senior Vice President, Mary McLemore

Senior Vice President Healthcare Financial Services, Walter Unangst

Market Manager Vice President, Tyler Eames

Vice President Senior Private Banker, Sarah Haley

Vice President, Theodore Horan

Assistant Vice President, Rosalind Rubin

Vice President Market Manager, Steven Sessions

Senior Vice President, Greg Batsevitsky

N.a. Vice President, Kimberly Alty

Vice President Senior Market Manager, Dean Debiase

Associate Vice President Documentation, Raquel Harduby

Vice President T Community Development And Clinical Research Associate Officer New York, Elizabeth Custodio

Senior Vice President Regional Manager Massachusetts, Veronica Ctfa

Vice President, Kevin Dougherty

Vice President Business Banking, Michael Tardella

Vice President Financial Services Manager, Jeanie Szostek

Vice President, Timothy Mcmachen

Senior Vice President, Patricia Camelio

Senior Vice President Commercial Relationship Manager, Michael Lavoie

Vice President Private Banking Administration, Katharine Bosley

Vice President Commercial Lending, Matthew Harrison

First Vice President Senior Credit Officer, David Sherrill

Auditors: KPMG LLP

LOCATIONS

HQ: People's United Financial Inc
850 Main Street, Bridgeport, CT 06604
Phone: 203 338-7171   Fax: 203 338-2545
Web: www.peoples.com

PRODUCTS/OPERATIONS

2014 Sales

	$ mil.	% of total
Interest & dividends		
Loans		
Commercial real estate	354	26
Commercial	351	26
Residential mortgage	153	12
Consumer	73	5
Securities	96	7
Other	1	.
Noninterest		
Bank service charges	128	10
Investment management fees	41	3
Operating lease income	41	3
Commercial banking lending fees	33	2
Insurance revenue	29	2
Other	76	4
Adjustment	(0.9)	.
Total	**1,381**	**100**

COMPETITORS

Bank of America	KeyCorp
Citibank	Liberty Bank
Citizens Financial Group	Sovereign Bank
Fairfield County Bank	TD Bank USA
	Webster Financial

HISTORICAL FINANCIALS

Company Type: Public

Income Statement

FYE: December 31

	ASSETS ($ mil.)	NET INCOME ($ mil.)	INCOME AS % OF ASSETS	EMPLOYEES
12/19	58,589	520	0.9%	6,499
12/18	47,877	468	1.0%	5,920
12/17	44,453	337	0.8%	5,584
12/16	40,609	281	0.7%	5,173
12/15	38,877	260	0.7%	5,139
Annual Growth	10.8%	18.9%	—	6.0%

2019 Year-End Financials

Debt ratio: 1.70%
Return on equity: 7.19%
Cash ($ mil.): 703
Current ratio: —
Long-term debt ($ mil.): —

No. of shares (mil.): 443
Dividends
　Yield: 4.1%
　Payout: 54.0%
Market value ($ mil.): 7,497

	STOCK PRICE ($) FY Close	P/E High/Low		PER SHARE ($) Earnings	Dividends	Book Value
12/19	16.90	14	11	1.27	0.71	17.92
12/18	14.43	16	11	1.29	0.70	17.32
12/17	18.70	20	16	0.97	0.69	16.79
12/16	19.36	22	15	0.92	0.68	16.28
12/15	16.15	20	16	0.86	0.67	15.26
Annual Growth	1.1%	—	—	10.2%	1.5%	4.1%

Peoples Bancorp Inc (Marietta, OH)

Peoples Bancorp offers banking for the people by the people and of the people. The holding company owns Peoples Bank which has about 50 branches in rural and small urban markets in Ohio Kentucky and West Virginia. The bank offers traditional services such as checking and savings accounts CDs loans and trust services. Commercial and agricultural loans including those secured by commercial real estate account for the majority of the bank's lending activities. Its Peoples Financial Advisors division offers investment management services while Peoples Insurance sells life health and property/casualty coverage.

Operations

Credit cards and brokerage services are offered through third-party providers.

Financial Performance

The company's revenue increased from $103.7 million in fiscal 2012 up to $104.6 million for fiscal 2013. However despite the slight spike in annual revenue Peoples Bancorp's net income decreased from $29.9 million in fiscal 2012 down to $29 million for fiscal 2013.

The company's cash on hand decreased by about $1 million in fiscal 2013 compared to fiscal 2012 levels.

Strategy

Peoples Bancorp is looking to increase its revenue from service changes and other fees and commissions particularly from insurance and wealth management which are not reliant on fluctuating interest rate margins.

The company is also looking to strengthen its brand and build deeper relationships with its clients.

EXECUTIVES

Evp And Chief Administrative Officer Peoples Bancorp And Evp Chief Administrative Officer And Cashierpeoples Bank N.a., Carol A. Schneeberger, age 63, $233,000 total compensation

Evp And Chief Commercial Lending Officer Peoples Bancorp And Peoples Bank N.a., Daniel K. (Dan) McGill, age 65, $250,000 total compensation

Evp And Chief Credit Officer Peoples Bancorp And Peoples Bank N.a., Timothy H. Kirtley, age 50, $221,500 total compensation

President Ceo And Director Peoples Bancorp And Peoples Bank N.a., Charles W. Sulerzyski, age 62, $500,000 total compensation

Evp Cfo And Treasurer Peoples Bancorp And Peoples Bank N.a., John C. Rogers, age 60, $26,136 total compensation

Vice President, Steven Nulter

Assistant Vice President Branch Market Manager, Candace Frump

Branch Market Manager Assistant Vice President, Peggy Scott-Morgan

Vice President And Controller, Jeffrey Baran

Vice President, Randy Barengo

Chairman Peoples Bancorp And Peoples Bank N.a., David L. Mead, age 65

Auditors: Ernst & Young LLP

LOCATIONS

HQ: Peoples Bancorp Inc (Marietta, OH)
138 Putnam Street, P.O. Box 738, Marietta, OH 45750
Phone: 740 373-3155
Web: www.peoplesbancorp.com

PRODUCTS/OPERATIONS

2016 Sales

	$ mil.	% of total
Interest Income:		
Interest and fees on loans	93	56
Interest and dividends on taxable investment securities	18	11
Interest on tax-exempt investment securities	3	2
Other Income:		
Insurance income	13	8
Deposit account service charges	10	6
Trust and investment income	10	6
Electronic banking income	10	6
Bank owned life insurance income	1	1
Mortgage banking income	1	1
Commercial loan swap fee income	1	1
Net gain on investment securities	0	1
Net loss on asset disposals and other transactions	(1.1)	-
Other	1	1
Total	**166**	**100**

COMPETITORS

1st West Virginia Bancorp	Huntington Bancshares
BB&T	Ohio Valley Banc
Fifth Third	U.S. Bancorp
	United Bankshares

HISTORICAL FINANCIALS

Company Type: Public

Income Statement

FYE: December 31

	ASSETS ($ mil.)	NET INCOME ($ mil.)	INCOME AS % OF ASSETS	EMPLOYEES
12/19	4,354	53	1.2%	900
12/18	3,991	46	1.2%	871
12/17	3,581	38	1.1%	774
12/16	3,432	31	0.9%	782
12/15	3,258	10	0.3%	817
Annual Growth	**7.5%**	**48.8%**	**—**	**2.4%**

2019 Year-End Financials

Debt ratio: 0.17%
Return on equity: 9.64%
Cash ($ mil.): 115
Current ratio: —
Long-term debt ($ mil.): —

No. of shares (mil.): 20
Dividends
　Yield: 3.8%
　Payout: 50.1%
Market value ($ mil.): 716

	STOCK PRICE ($) FY Close	P/E High/Low		PER SHARE ($) Earnings	Dividends	Book Value
12/19	34.66	13	11	2.63	1.32	28.78
12/18	30.10	16	12	2.41	1.12	26.64
12/17	32.62	16	14	2.10	0.84	25.13
12/16	32.46	19	10	1.71	0.64	23.99
12/15	18.84	42	30	0.61	0.60	22.88
Annual Growth	**16.5%**	**—**	**—**	**44.1%**	**21.8%**	**5.9%**

Peoples Financial Services Corp

Power to the Peoples Financial Services. The firm is the holding company for Peoples Security Bank and Trust Company (formerly Peoples National Bank) which operates about 25 branches across northeastern Pennsylvania and neighboring Broome County in New York. Established in 1905 the bank offers standard retail products and services including checking and savings accounts CDs and credit cards to local businesses and individuals. Commercial loans including mortgages construction loans and operating loans make up the greatest portion (40%) of the company's loan book followed by residential mortgages (25%) and consumer loans. The company's Peoples Advisors subsidiary provides investment and brokerage services.

Operations

About 80% of Peoples Financial Services' total revenue came from interest income (mostly on loans) in 2014 while the remainder comes from non-interest income. The bank had a staff of 354 full-time employees at the end of that year.

Geographic Reach

Scranton-based Peoples Security Bank has more than 25 branches across Northeastern Pennsylvania (in the Lackawanna Lehigh Luzerne Monroe Susquehanna Wayne and Wyoming counties) and Broome County in New York state.

Sales and Marketing

The company primarily makes loans to small- and medium-sized businesses. It spent $450 on advertising in 2014 up from $350 and $287 in 2013 and 2012 respectively.

Financial Performance

Peoples has struggled to consistently grow its revenues in recent years due to shrinking interest margins on loans amidst the low-interest environment. Its profits however have been rising thanks to lower interest expenses on deposits and declining loan loss provisions as its loan portfolio's credit quality has improved with higher property valuations in the strengthened economy.

The company enjoyed a breakout year in 2014 however as its revenue jumped 60% to a record $79.21 million mostly as its interest income swelled from new loan business from its 2013 acquisition of Penseco Financial Services. Its service charge fees and commissions merchant services income and commission and fee income from fiduciary services also rose mostly as a result of the significant acquisition.

Higher revenue in 2014 allowed Peoples' net income to more than triple to a record $17.6 million while its operating cash levels more than doubled to $20.6 million on higher cash earnings for the year.

Strategy

Peoples Security Bank occasionally acquires smaller banks to extend its branch network across target markets while adding new loan and deposit business. Its late 2013 acquisition of Penseco Financial Services Corporation for example nearly doubled its loan and deposit business and more than doubled its branch network to 25 branches.

Mergers and Acquisitions

In November 2013 Peoples acquired Penseco Financial Services Corporation along with its Penn Security Bank and Trust subsidiary. The $155 million-deal doubled Peoples' branch network from 12 to 25 branches creating the largest community bank headquartered in Northeastern Pennsylvania.

EXECUTIVES

Ceo And President, Alan W. Dakey, age 68
Evp And Coo Peoples National Bank, Debra E. Dissinger, age 65, $110,000 total compensation
Director, Richard S. Lochen, age 56, $130,000 total compensation
Senior Vice President Chief Financial Officer, Scott Seasock
Chairman, William E. Aubrey, age 57
Auditors: Baker Tilly Virchow Krause, LLP

LOCATIONS

HQ: Peoples Financial Services Corp
150 North Washington Avenue, Scranton, PA 18503
Phone: 570 346-7741

PRODUCTS/OPERATIONS

2014 Sales

	$ mil.	% of total
Interest	64	81
Non-interest	15	19
Total	**79**	**100**

COMPETITORS

Citizens & Northern	HSBC USA
Citizens Financial Services	M&T Bank
	NBT Bancorp
Fidelity D & D	Penns Woods Bancorp
First Keystone	
First National Community Bancorp	

HISTORICAL FINANCIALS

Company Type: Public

Income Statement
FYE: December 31

	ASSETS ($ mil.)	NET INCOME ($ mil.)	INCOME AS % OF ASSETS	EMPLOYEES
12/19	2,475	25	1.0%	408
12/18	2,288	24	1.1%	390
12/17	2,169	18	0.9%	388
12/16	1,999	19	1.0%	364
12/15	1,819	17	1.0%	348
Annual Growth	**8.0%**	**9.8%**	—	**4.1%**

2019 Year-End Financials

Debt ratio: —	No. of shares (mil.): 7
Return on equity: 8.91%	Dividends
Cash ($ mil.): 31	Yield: 2.7%
Current ratio: —	Payout: 37.3%
Long-term debt ($ mil.): —	Market value ($ mil.): 372

	STOCK PRICE ($) FY Close	P/E High/Low	PER SHARE ($) Earnings	Dividends	Book Value
12/19	50.35	15 12	3.48	1.37	40.47
12/18	44.06	15 12	3.37	1.31	37.66
12/17	46.58	20 16	2.50	1.26	35.82
12/16	48.70	19 13	2.65	1.24	34.71
12/15	38.08	21 15	2.36	1.24	33.57
Annual Growth	**7.2%**	— —	**10.2%**	**2.5%**	**4.8%**

PepsiCo Inc

PepsiCo butts heads with its eternal rival The Coca-Cola Company. PepsiCo's beverage brands include Pepsi Mountain Dew Tropicana Gatorade and Aquafina water. The company also owns Frito-Lay-maker with offerings such as Lay's Ruffles Doritos and Cheetos. The Quaker Foods unit makes breakfast cereals (Quaker oatmeal Life) Rice-A-Roni and Near East side dishes. Most of the products are sold to independent distributors and retailers. Pepsi products are available in 200-plus countries although the US accounts for nearly 60% of total sales. The company operates about half of its bottling plants and distribution facilities. The company was incorporated in Delaware in 1919 and reincorporated in North Carolina in 1986.

HISTORY

Pharmacist Caleb Bradham invented Pepsi in 1898 in New Bern North Carolina. He named his new drink Pepsi-Cola (claiming it cured dyspepsia or indigestion) and registered the trademark in 1903. Following The Coca-Cola Company's example Bradham developed a bottling franchise system. By WWI 300 bottlers had signed up. After the war Bradham stockpiled sugar to safeguard against rising costs but in 1920 sugar prices plunged forcing him into bankruptcy in 1923.

Pepsi existed on the brink of ruin under various owners until Loft Candy bought it in 1931. Its fortunes improved in 1933 when in the midst of the Depression it doubled the size of its bottles to 12 ounces without raising the five-cent price. In 1939 Pepsi introduced the world's first radio jingle. Two years later Loft Candy merged with its Pepsi subsidiary and became The Pepsi-Cola Company.

Donald Kendall who became Pepsi-Cola's president in 1963 turned the firm's attention to young people ("The Pepsi Generation"). It acquired Mountain Dew in 1964 and became PepsiCo in 1965 when it acquired Frito-Lay.

In 1972 PepsiCo agreed to distribute Stolichnaya vodka in the US in exchange for being the only Western firm allowed to bottle soft drinks in the USSR. With the purchases of Pizza Hut (1977) Taco Bell (1978) and Kentucky Fried Chicken (1986) it became a major force in the fast-food industry.

When Coca-Cola changed its formula in 1985 Pepsi had a short-lived victory in the cola wars (until the return of Coca-Cola classic the new formula having been a dismal failure). The rivalry was extended to ready-to-drink tea in 1991 when in response to Coca-Cola's Nestea venture with Nestlé PepsiCo teamed up with Lipton.

Between 1991 and 1996 PepsiCo aggressively expanded its overseas bottling operations. However its efforts contrasted markedly with Coca-Cola's well-oiled international distribution machine. The firm then shifted its attention to the organization of its overseas network. Roger Enrico became CEO in 1996.

A year later PepsiCo spun off its $10 billion fast-food unit as TRICON Global Restaurants (now known as YUM! Brands Inc.) putting itself in a better position to sell its soft drinks at other restaurants. Also in 1997 it bought Borden's Cracker Jack snack and Smith's snacks from the UK's United Biscuits.

In 1998 it bought Seagram's market-leading Tropicana juices (rival of Coca-Cola's Minute Maid) for $3.3 billion. The firm sold a 65% stake in its new Pepsi Bottling Group to the public in 1999.

Its more than $13 billion purchase of The Quaker Oats Company in 2001 added the dominant Gatorade sports drink brand to its lineup. To make room for Gatorade PepsiCo sold its competing All Sport energy drink to The Monarch Beverage Company an Atlanta-based soda company later that year.

PepsiCo began a major restructuring of its PepsiCo Beverages & Foods division in 2003. The restructuring resulted in four company divisions: PepsiCo International PepsiCo Beverages North America Frito-Lay North America and Quaker Foods North America.

In 2004 PepsiCo approached juice maker Ocean Spray about a joint venture but was turned away by the cranberry farmers who own the juice manufacturer. The company bought General Mills' stake of their joint venture Snack Ventures Europe (SVE) in 2005 for $750 million. The deal gave Pepsi control of Europe's largest snack food company.

It's also been driving its snack brands to new markets as it bolts on new and more nutritious foods categories through small acquisitions and alliances. In 2013 Muller Quaker Dairy a joint venture between PepsiCo and Theo Muller Group (a Germany-based privately held dairy holding company) opened of its new yogurt manufacturing facility in Batavia New York. It serves as the national production and distribution center for a premium lineup of M ller brand yogurts to US supermarket and club retailers.

EXECUTIVES

Ceo North America, Albert P. (Al) Carey, age 68, $984,615 total compensation
Chairman And Ceo, Indra K. Nooyi, age 64, $1,725,000 total compensation
Evp Human Resources And Chief Human Resources Officer, Cynthia M. Trudell, age 67
Vice Chairman Evp Global Research And Development And Chief Scientific Officer, Mehmood Khan, age 61, $756,731 total compensation
Svp And Cio, Jody R. Davids, age 64
President Essa Category Teams Franchise And Po1 Sub-saharan Africa, Richard D. Evans
Vice Chairman Evp And Cfo, Hugh F. Johnston, age 59, $960,577 total compensation
President Pepsico Russia, Silviu Popovici, age 52
President Global Beverages Group, Brad Jakeman
President Pepsico Mexico, Pedro Padierna
President Latin America Beverages, Luis Montoya
President And Coo Frito-lay North America (flna), Vivek Sankaran, age 58
President Global Snacks Group And Global Insights, Simon Lowden
Evp Corporate Strategy And Chief Venturing Officer, Jim Andrew, age 59
President And Coo North America Beverages (nab), Kirk Tanner, age 52
Ceo Asia Middle East And North Africa, Sanjeev Chadha, age 60, $764,423 total compensation
President Pepsico, Ramon Laguarta, age 56, $748,846 total compensation
Evp Global Categories And Franchise Management, Eugene Willemsen
Evp Communications, Jon Banner
Svp And Chief Procurement Officer, Grace Puma Whiteford
Ceo Pepsico Latin America Foods, Laxman Narasimhan, age 52
Evp Government Affairs General Counsel And Corporate Secretary, Tony West, age 54
Evp Global Operations, Brian Newman
President And Ceo Greater China Region, Mike Spanos

President Global Foodservice, Anne Fink

Senior Vice President Finance And Treasurer, Kenneth Smith

Senior Vice President And Controller, Marie Gallagher

Marketing Vice President, Haston Lewis

Vice President Revenue Strategy And Management, Eric Hanson

Vice President Of Lrb Strategy, Brian Kelly

Vice President Of Finance, Bruce Matzner

Vice President Human Resources, Dave Moncur

Senior Vice President Finance Pepsico, Gary Murtha

Senior Vice President, Jessica Burt

Finance Senior Vice President, Chris Hall

Vice President (division), Steven Williams

National Sales Manager, Jill Griffith

Vice President Global Public Policy, Paul Boykas

Vice President Data Analytics And Analytics, Martha Roos

Vice President Technical Accounting And Policy, Lisa Halper

Regional Vice President, Mark Darrow

Vice President Corporate And Commercial Planning Europe, Claire Stone

Vice President, Huw Gilbert

Vice President Selling And Delivery, Greg Moore

Vice President, Shridhar Kulkarni

Vice President Of Public Relations, Larry Jabbonsky

Sales Vice President, Byron Brooks

Senior Vice President Finance, Nick Dalessandro

Vice President Sales Operations, Kenneth Morgan

Vice President Finance, Ralph Goedderz

Vice President Finance, Corey Gottschalk

Legal Vice President, Thomas P Schur

Vice President Finance, Christy Jacoby

Vice President, Michael McMahon

Vice President Category Leadership, Mike Gervasio

National Sales Manager, Jennifer Caro

Vice President Information Technology Global Development, Subodh Chawla

Vice President Finance, Mark Beach

Senior Vice President Business Development, Hugh Roth

Vice President Global Labor Relations, Carolyn Fisher

Vp Of Tax, Christine Griff

Vice President Purchase, Ashish Karanjkar

National Sales Manager Restaurant Channel, Christian Duperron

Vice President Infrastructure And Engineering, Johnathan Thibodeau

Vice President Consumer Strategy, Tekla Back

National Sales Manager, Tony Huerta

Vice President Foodservice Division, Kathryn Matheson

Vice President Of Regulatory Affairs, Paul Carr

Vice President, Sabrina M Pean

Vice President Strategic Insights, Laura Jones

Vice President Legal India Region, Paul Walton

Vice President, Tarkan Gurkan

Vice President Of Marketing For Atlantic Business Unit, Tammy Sumpter

Vice President Of Consumer Engagement, Anne Howarth

Pepsi Trademark Vice President Of Marketing, Chad Stubbs

Senior Vice President Customer Supply Chain And Global Go To Market, John Phillips

Vice President Sales Operations, Jaime Cardenas

Vice President, Sarina Sposta

Vice President Investor Relations, Ravi Pamnani

Vice President Of Finance, Brent Bracey

Senior Vice President Chief Compliance And Ethics Officer, Debra Torres

Tax Vice President, Jeff Coniaris

Executive Assistant To Robert Mac Kay Vice President And General Auditor, Diana Marra

Vp Supply Chain, Mark Brinker

Regional Vice President, James Simms

National Sales Manager, Jeff Utne

Vice President And Assistant Treasurer, Jay Laramie

Vice President Human Resources, Jam Johnson

Tax Vice President, Tom Salcito

National Account Manager, Terry Thaden

Sc Cntrct Manufacturing Vice President Naf Cntrct, Karl Schraer

National Account Manager, Jose Abarca

Executive Vice President Global Operations, Grace Puma

Svp And Chro Global Functions And Global Category Groups, Janine Waclawski

Vice President, Denise Lefebvre

National Account Manager, William Leonard

Vice President Asia Middle East And Africa Technical Innovation And Head Greater China Research And Development, Vr Basker

National Account Manager, Cindy Armlin

First Vice President Financial Advisor, George Sebastian

Vice President Sales East, Karen Plavsity

Vice President, Willem Kuzee

Legal Vice President, Timothy F Civil

National Account Manager, Jake Fuller

Vice President Scientific And Regulatory Affairs, Shaminder Singh

National Account Manager, Adam Palmer

National Account Manager, Keesje Kort

National Account Manager, Tyler Lewis

Vice President Marketing Advertising, David Phillips

National Account Manager, Tessa McArthur

Svp Head Of Global Ecommerce, Gibu Thomas

Senior Vice President Global E Commerce Marketing And Product, Michal Geller

Senior Vice President Food Safety Quality Assurance And Scientific And Regulatory Affiars, Mike Liewen

National Account Manager, Brenda Ung

Finance Vice President, Mohamed Ahmed

National Account Manager, Megan McCartney

Vice President Global Water And Environmental Solutions, Roberta Barbieri

Senior Vice President Talent Management Training And Development, Kyle Faulconer

Senior Vice President Chief Insights And Analytics Officer, Stephan Gans

Svp And General Manager Global Pepsico Walmart, Chris Turner

National Sales Manager, Tim Berchtold

Vice President Sales, Scott Sheafe

Regional Vice President, Scott Henzi

National Account Manager Target, Suzanne Rupp

Vice President Global Marketing Hydration Portfolio, Olga OSMINKINA-JONES

Vice President Manufacturing And Engineering Amea, Murat Suer

Senior Vice President, Lily Zaidman

Vice President And General Manager, Joe Mchugh

Vice President Sales Asia Middle East And Africa, Paul Tabet

Vice President Operations Western Europe, Chris Daly

Vice President Supply Chain Asia Pacific Region, Bassim Rizk

Vice President Of Sales, Gerard Garcia

Vice President Of Global Product Design And Design Innovation, Martin Broen

Vice President, Jean Belliard

Senior Vice President And General Manager Quaker Oats Company, Robbert Rietbroek

National Account Manager, Molly Link

Svp Head Of Operations Global Ecommerce, Vince Jones

Vice President Of Food Processor, Carl Wilson

Vice President Of Retail Sales, Steve Milonovich

Prod Development Vice President, Kevin Osullivan

Legal Vice President General Cousel, Civil Timothy

National Account Manager, Doug Fowler

Vice President, Gary Ducros

Region Vice President Frito Lay Northern California Hawaii, Dan Luciano

Vp Global Agronomy Solutions, Christine Daugherty

Vice President Supply Chain Execution, Alex Baxter

Senior Vice President And Chief Global Groups And Functions Counsel, Marjorie De La Cruz

Advisory Board Member, Jayne Vetere

Vice President And Assistant Treasurer For International, Noha Topalian

Board Member, Darren Walker

Secretary, Josefa Brito

Board Member, David Page

Auditors: KPMG LLP

LOCATIONS

HQ: PepsiCo Inc
700 Anderson Hill Road, Purchase, NY 10577
Phone: 914 253-2000
Web: www.pepsico.com

2018 Sales

	$ mil.	% of total
US	37,148	57
Mexico	3,878	6
Russia	3,191	5
Canada	2,736	4
UK	1,743	3
Brazil	1,335	2
All other countries	14,630	23
Total	**64,661**	**100**

PRODUCTS/OPERATIONS

2018 Sales

	$ mil.	% of total
NAB	21,072	33
FLNA	16,346	25
ESSA	11,523	18
Latin America	7,354	11
AMENA	5,901	9
QFNA	2,465	4
Total	**64,661**	**100**

COMPETITORS

Campbell Soup	Kellogg
Coca-Cola	Kraft Heinz
ConAgra	Mondelez International
Danone	Monster Beverage
Dr Pepper Snapple	Nestlé
Group	Post Holdings
Hain Celestial	Red Bull

HISTORICAL FINANCIALS

Company Type: Public

Income Statement   FYE: December 28

	REVENUE ($ mil.)	NET INCOME ($ mil.)	NET PROFIT MARGIN	EMPLOYEES
12/19	67,161	7,314	10.9%	267,000
12/18	64,661	12,515	19.4%	267,000
12/17	63,525	4,857	7.6%	263,000
12/16	62,799	6,329	10.1%	264,000
12/15	63,056	5,452	8.6%	263,000
Annual Growth	**1.6%**	**7.6%**	**—**	**0.4%**

2019 Year-End Financials

Debt ratio: 40.83%	No. of shares (mil.): 1,391
Return on equity: 50.06%	Dividends
Cash ($ mil.): 5,509	Yield: 0.0%
Current ratio: 0.86	Payout: 72.9%
Long-term debt ($ mil.): 29,148	Market value ($ mil.): 191,318

STOCK PRICE ($)		P/E		PER SHARE ($)		
	FY Close	High/Low		Earnings	Dividends	Book Value
12/19	137.54	27	21	5.20	3.79	10.63
12/18	110.36	14	11	8.78	3.59	10.30
12/17	119.92	35	30	3.38	3.17	7.67
12/16	104.63	25	21	4.36	2.96	7.77
12/15	100.54	28	24	3.67	2.76	8.23
Annual Growth	8.1%	—	—	9.1%	8.2%	6.6%

Performance Food Group Co

Auditors: DELOITTE & TOUCHE LLP

LOCATIONS

HQ: Performance Food Group Co
12500 West Creek Parkway, Richmond, VA 23238
Phone: 804 484-7700
Web: www.pfgc.com

HISTORICAL FINANCIALS

Company Type: Public

Income Statement   FYE: June 27

	REVENUE ($ mil.)	NET INCOME ($ mil.)	NET PROFIT MARGIN	EMPLOYEES
06/20	25,086	(114)	—	20,000
06/19	19,743	166	0.8%	18,000
06/18*	17,619	198	1.1%	15,000
07/17	16,761	96	0.6%	14,000
07/16	16,104	68	0.4%	13,000
Annual Growth	11.7%	—	—	11.4%

*Fiscal year change

2020 Year-End Financials

Debt ratio: 33.33%
Return on equity: (-6.92%)
Cash ($ mil.): 420
Current ratio: 1.32
Long-term debt ($ mil.): 2,435

No. of shares (mil.): 131
Dividends
    Yield: —
    Payout: —
Market value ($ mil.): 3,661

STOCK PRICE ($)		P/E		PER SHARE ($)		
	FY Close	High/Low		Earnings	Dividends	Book Value
06/20	27.88	—	—	(1.01)	0.00	15.31
06/19	40.03	26	18	1.59	0.00	12.51
06/18*	36.70	19	13	1.90	0.00	11.00
07/17	27.40	30	21	0.93	0.00	9.18
07/16	26.92	39	27	0.70	0.00	8.04
Annual Growth	0.9%	—	—	—	—	17.5%

*Fiscal year change

PETER KIEWIT SONS', INC.

A heavyweight in the heavy construction industry Kiewit is one of North America's largest construction and engineering firms. The company is active in building industrial mining oil gas chemicals power transportation water and wastewater. It builds everything from roads and dams to high-rise office towers and power plants. The company focuses on projects located throughout the US Canada and Mexico. Affiliate Kiewit Mining owns or manages coal mines in Texas and Wyoming and manages a phosphate operation in southeast Idaho. Founded in 1884 Kiewit is owned by employees and Kiewit family members.

Operations

Kiewit's operations are diversified across seven segments: Building; Industrial; Mining; Oil Gas & Chemical; Power; Transportation; and Water/Wastewater.

Kiewit's Transportation segment constructs airport runways bridges marine and port projects rail lines mass transit roads and tunnels. Transportation has completed about 1000 projects which provided nearly $30 billion in revenue over the last 10 years. Kiewit's Power unit is active in gas coal retrofit power delivery renewables nuclear energy and engineering. Over the last 10 years Power has generated almost $20 billion.

Generating $7.5 billion through more than 1100 projects in the last 10 years the company's Building segment builds offices; industrial complexes; education and sports facilities; hotels; hospitals; transportation terminals; science and technology facilities; manufacturing retail and special-use facilities; interior construction; and tenant improvements. Kiewit conducts general construction construction management design-build and -assist and turnkey project development.

The Mining segment (which has generated nearly $3 billion over more than 100 mining projects in the last 10 years) carries out contract mining mine infrastructure ore processing and owned operations. Kiewit's Oil Gas & Chemical business (which completed more than 1200 projects that provides nearly $22 billion in revenue over the last 10 years) includes offshore construction oil sands gas processing compressor and pump stations pipelines and terminals liquefied natural gas and refining.

Through its Industrial division the company processes minerals; builds cement plants; treats water; provides engineering procurement and construction; installs paper production and packaging machines; and constructs food plants and related structures. Water/Wastewater manages dam water supply and wastewater projects.

Kiewit operates a number of subsidiaries. Kiewit Offshore Services fabricates complex offshore oil production platforms at a facility in Texas. Another subsidiary Kiewit Energy US refines petroleum. Kiewit's TIC subsidiary is an industrial construction firm based in Colorado.

Geographic Reach

Based in Omaha Nebraska Kiewit operates across the US (approximately 85 locations) and Canada (more than 10 locations) and Mexico (1 location).

Sales and Marketing

Kiewit's clients include various public and private entities.

Strategy

Data strategy and technology are becoming increasingly important in companies ? and Kiewit is no exception. As these practices develop Kiewit is looking to hire individuals who are excited about working for a company that values their skills and challenges them to learn more in these fields.

The Data Strategy and Transformation team; Danielle Maddux Manager of Strategy and Analytics works on aims to deliver data-driven solutions and augment various business processes to save Kiewit valuable time and money. She hopes for Kiewit to become "an industry leader in data strategy and technology and to promote data literacy across the company."

Company Background

The sons of Dutch immigrants Peter and Andrew Kiewit founded masonry contractor Kiewit Brothers in 1884 in Omaha Nebraska. Following the dissolution of the partnership in 1904 Peter continued as the company's sole proprietor. In 1931 ? 17 years after Peter's death ? his son Peter reorganized the business as Peter Kiewit Sons'.

HISTORY

Born to Dutch immigrants Peter Kiewit and brother Andrew founded Kiewit Brothers a brickyard in 1884 in Omaha Nebraska. By 1912 two of Peter's sons worked at the yard which was named Peter Kiewit & Sons. When Peter Kiewit died in 1914 his son Ralph took over and the firm took the name Peter Kiewit Sons'. Another son Peter joined Ralph at the helm in 1924 after dropping out of Dartmouth and later took over.

During the Depression Kiewit managed huge federal public works projects and in the 1940s it focused on war-related emergency construction projects.

One of the firm's most difficult projects was top-secret Thule Air Force Base in Greenland above the Arctic Circle. For more than two years 5000 men worked around the clock beginning in 1951; the site was in development for 15 years. In 1952 the company won a contract to build a $1.2 billion gas diffusion plant in Portsmouth Ohio. It also became a contractor for the US interstate highway system (begun in 1956).

Peter Kiewit died in 1979 after stipulating that the largely employee-owned company should remain under employee control and that no one employee could own more than 10%. His 40% stake when returned to the company transformed many employees into millionaires. Walter Scott Jr. whose father had been the first graduate engineer to work for Kiewit took charge. Scott made his mark by parlaying money from construction into successful investments.

When the construction industry slumped Kiewit began looking for other investment opportunities and in 1984 it acquired packaging company Continental Can Co. (selling off noncore insurance energy and timber assets). Continental was saddled with a 1983 class action lawsuit alleging that it had plotted to close plants and lay off workers before they were qualified for pensions. In 1991 Kiewit agreed to pay $415 million to settle the lawsuit. In the face of a consolidating packaging industry the company sold Continental in the early 1990s.

In 1986 Kiewit loaned money to a business group to build a fiber-optic loop in Chicago; by 1987 it had launched MFS Communications to build local fiber loops in downtown districts. In 1992 Kiewit split its business into two pieces: the construction group which was strictly employee-owned; and a diversified group to which it added a controlling stake in phone and cable TV company C-TEC in 1993. That year Kiewit took MFS public; by 1995 it had sold all its shares and the next year MFS was bought by telecom giant WorldCom.

In 1996 Kiewit assisted CalEnergy (now MidAmerican Energy) in a hostile $1.3 billion takeover of the UK's Northern Electric. Kiewit got stock in CalEnergy and a 30% stake in the UK electric company all of which it sold to CalEnergy in 1998.

That year Kiewit spun off its telecom and computer services holdings into Level 3 Communications. Scott who had been hospitalized the year before for a blood clot in his lung stepped down as CEO and Ken Stinson CEO of Kiewit Construction Group took over Peter Kiewit Sons'.

In 1999 Kiewit acquired a majority interest in Pacific Rock Products a construction materials firm in Canada. Kiewit spun off its asphalt concrete and aggregates operations in 2000 as Kiewit Materials. Also that year the company created Kiewit Offshore Services to focus on construction for the offshore drilling industry. In 2001 the company acquired marine construction firm General Construction Company (GCC). The next year it expanded its offshore business further by buying a Canadian subsidiary from oil and gas equipment services company Friede Goldman Halter which was trying to emerge from bankruptcy.

Kiewit made history in 2002 for the fastest completion of a project of its type when it completed the rebuilding of Webbers Falls I-40 Bridge in Oklahoma at the end of July. (The bridge had collapsed in May after being hit by a pair of barges resulting in 14 fatalities.)

In 2004 Kiewit greatly increased its coal sales and reserves with the acquisition of the Buckskin Mine in Wyoming from Arch Coal.

Kiewit underwent a changing of the guard at the end of 2004 when 22-year veteran Bruce Grewcock took the reins as the company's fourth CEO since its founding. Stinson stayed on as the company's chairman.

In 2008 the group acquired TIC Holdings a heavy industrial construction and engineering firm.

Through its Kiewit Power Engineers Co. the company was contracted by Plutonic Energy Corporation and GE Energy Financial Services to work on the 235 MW hydroelectric Toba Montrose project one of British Columbia's largest renewable energy projects (completed around 2011).

In 2013 Kiewit entered the Australian market through a joint venture agreement that involves as $247 million engineer-procure-construct contract for a wet front end and ore wash plant situated at the Cloudbreak Mine in Northwest Australia. Fortescue Metals Group is the previous owner of Cloudbreak prior to the handover in early 2013.

EXECUTIVES

Svp And Cfo, Michael J. Piechoski, $236,600 total compensation
Chairman President And Ceo, Bruce E. Grewcock, $750,000 total compensation
Evp Energy, Thomas S. Shelby
Cio, Kris Lappala
Vice President For Development, Gerald Pfeffer
Vp Healthcare Services, Aj Klebba
Senior Vice President District Manager, Matt Swinton
Vice President Finance Canada, Leonardo Morabito
Executive Vice President Operations, Jay Steinmetz
Treasurer, Stephen Thomas
Secretary, Matthew Michler
Auditors: KPMG LLP OMAHA NEBRASKA

LOCATIONS

HQ: PETER KIEWIT SONS', INC.
1550 MIKE FAHEY ST, OMAHA, NE 681024722
Phone: 402 342-2052
Web: WWW.KIEWIT.COM

Selected Locations

US
Alaska
Arizona
Arkansas
California
Colorado
Florida
Georgia
Hawaii
Idaho
Illinois
Iowa
Kansas
Louisiana
Maryland
Massachusetts
Minnesota
Nebraska
Nevada
New Jersey
New York
North Carolina
Oregon
Tennessee
Texas
Utah
Virginia
Washington
Wyoming
Australia
　Western Australia
Canada
Alberta
British Columbia
Manitoba
Newfoundland
New Brunswick
Ontario
Quebec
Saskatchewan

PRODUCTS/OPERATIONS

Selected Locations
US
Alaska
Arizona
California
Colorado
Florida
Georgia
Hawaii
Illinois
Iowa
Kansas
Maryland
Massachusetts
Minnesota
Nebraska
Nevada
New Jersey
New York
North Carolina
Oregon
Texas
Utah
Virginia
Washington
Wyoming
Canada
Alberta
British Columbia
Newfoundland
Ontario
Quebec
Mexico
Mexico City

Selected Subsidiaries and Affiliates
Aero Automatic Sprinkler
Cherne Contracting Corporation
Continental Fire Sprinkler Company
Kiewit Australia
Kiewit Bridge & Marine
Kiewit Building Group
Kiewit Energy Company
Kiewit Engineering Group Inc.
Kiewit Infrastructure Co.
Kiewit Infrastructure South Co.
Kiewit Infrastructure West Co.
Kiewit Mining Group
Dry Valley/No. Rassmussen Ridge Mines
Buckskin Mining Company
San Miguel Mine
Walnut Creek Mining Company
Kiewit Offshore Services Ltd..
Kiewit Power Constructors Co.
Kiewit Power Engineers
Kiewit Texas Construction L.P.

COMPETITORS

ABB	Lane Construction
Ames Construction	PCL Constructors
Balfour Beatty Infrastructure	Parsons Corporation
Bechtel	Raytheon
Black & Veatch	Rio Tinto plc
Fluor	Skanska USA Civil
Granite Construction	Turner Corporation
Halliburton	Tutor Perini
Hubbard Group	Walsh Group
Jacobs Engineering	Whiting-Turner
KBR	Williams Companies

HISTORICAL FINANCIALS

Company Type: Private

Income Statement				FYE: December 29
	REVENUE ($ mil.)	NET INCOME ($ mil.)	NET PROFIT MARGIN	EMPLOYEES
12/12	11,220	515	4.6%	14,700
12/11	10,381	790	7.6%	—
12/10	9,938	789	7.9%	—
Annual Growth	6.3%	(19.2%)	—	—

Pfizer Inc

Pfizer Inc. is one of the world's largest research-based pharmaceuticals firm producing medicines for cardiovascular health metabolism oncology inflammation and immunology and other areas with about 10 products that fetch approximately $1 billion or more in annual revenue. Its top prescription products include cholesterol-lowering Lipitor pain management drugs Celebrex and Lyrica pneumonia vaccine Prevnar and erectile dysfunction treatment Viagra as well as arthritis drug Enbrel antibiotic Zyvox and blood-thinner Eliquis. The company also makes and sells generic drugs and consumer health products. Pfizer operates around the world and gets about 55% of its revenue from international customers.

HISTORY

Charles Pfizer and his cousin confectioner Charles Erhart began making chemicals in Brooklyn in 1849. Products included camphor citric acid and santonin (an early antiparasitic). The company incorporated in 1900 as Chas. Pfizer & Co. was propelled into the modern drug business when it was asked to mass-produce penicillin for the war effort in 1941.

Pfizer discovered Terramycin and introduced it in 1950. Three years later it bought drugmaker Roerig its first major acquisition. In the 1950s the company opened branches in Belgium Canada Cuba Mexico and the UK and began manufacturing in Asia Europe and South America. By the mid-1960s Pfizer had worldwide sales of more than $200 million.

Beginning in the late 1950s Pfizer made Salk and Sabin polio vaccines and added new drugs such as Diabinese (antidiabetic 1958) and Vibramycin (antibiotic 1967). It moved into consumer products in the early 1960s buying Ben-Gay Desitin and cosmetics maker Coty (sold in 1992). It bought hospital products company Howmedica in 1972 (sold in 1998) and heart-valve maker Shiley in 1979. In the 1980s Pfizer expanded its hospital products division buying 18 product lines and companies.

In 1995 Pfizer bought SmithKline Beecham's animal health business and Procter & Gamble's Bain de Soleil skin care line (sold in 1999).

Pfizer made headlines (and lots of men happy) when the company won FDA approval for Viagra in 1998. The little blue pill became a pop icon and made the company a household name.

When Warner-Lambert said in 1999 that it would merge with American Home Products (now Wyeth) Pfizer sued to prevent the union and eventually succeeded with its own hostile bid. The merger with Warner-Lambert was completed and CEO William Steere retired. Pfizer also sold its animal feed additive business.

Pfizer IBM and Microsoft in 2001 formed a joint venture to sell software to automate prescription writing and other administrative procedures in physicians' offices. Determined to narrow its focus on pharmaceuticals the company in 2002 sold its Tetra fish care then sold its Adams confectionery and Schick-Wilkinson Sword shaving products businesses in 2003.

That year Pfizer purchased rival Pharmacia for $54 billion making it the world's largest research-based pharmaceutical company. Following its two giant acquisitions the company trimmed some 20000 people. In 2004 Pfizer acquired the research divisions of QuoreX which develops anti-bacterial drugs targeting hospital infections. It also purchased Esperion Therapeutics a developer of cholesterol drugs headed by Lipitor discoverer Roger Newton for $1.2 billion. (Pfizer eventually spun Esperion back off into a private independent entity in 2008 after its development drugs didn't pan out as planned although Pfizer retained some assets and a minority stake in the spinoff.)

In the wake of revelations that Merck's Vioxx increased the risk for cardiovascular diseases in 2004 Pfizer reviewed its own COX-2 pain medication Celebrex. Preliminary studies showed Celebrex increased the risk of heart attack; Pfizer didn't pull Celebrex off the market but did add a "black box" warning of possible cardiovascular and gastrointestinal risks. (In 2008 Pfizer reached an agreement in principle to settle for $894 million most of its pending patient lawsuits alleging that Celebrex caused heart attacks and strokes.)

Acquisitions in 2005 included the purchase of Angiosyn a private biotech working on an anti-angiogenesis therapy for macular degeneration (which can lead to blindness) and Idun Pharmaceuticals which was developing apoptosis (programmed cell death) inhibitors to treat liver disease cancer and other diseases.

That year the company scooped up research partner Vicuron Pharmaceuticals which had two anti-infective (anidulafungin and dalbavancin) drugs under review by the FDA and Bioren which has developed a technology that helps drugs last longer through antibody optimization. (Pfizer divested Vicuron as part of its cost-cutting efforts in 2009.)

While acquiring new holdings on the pharmaceutical front Pfizer trimmed its non-pharmaceutical businesses between 2003 and 2005 including operations it acquired with Pharmacia and its European generics portfolio. The company's animal health division sold off its diagnostics products division (which manufactured tests for bovine tuberculosis and paratuberculosis) to Swiss firm Prionics.

On the consumer health care front the population's increased germaphobia translated into high dollars for Pfizer following the acquisition of Purell. However Pfizer later unloaded its consumer unit altogether refocusing efforts onto its core pharmaceutical business. Johnson & Johnson in 2006 acquired the whole consumer caboodle including such brands as Benadryl Listerine Nicorette Rolaids and Sudafed for $16.6 billion. To comply with regulatory requirements for the deal the companies sold Zantac marketing rights in the US to Boehringer Ingelheim for $510 million; they sold the Cortizone Kaopectate and Unisom brands to Chattem.

As part of its ongoing acquisition strategy Pfizer bought biotech firm Rinat Neuroscience which was developing drugs for pain Alzheimer's disease and other neurological disorders in 2006. Pfizer also acquired vaccine technology firm PowderMed that year and it spent $1.4 billion acquiring Sanofi's joint rights to inhaled insulin

drug Exubera. (Pfizer dropped Exubera from its product list in late 2007 however due to lukewarm response from physicians and patients. The company took a $2.8 billion charge as a result).

In 2015 Pfizer completed a $17 billion acquisition of Hospira. Two years later Pfizer sold Hospira Infusion Systems (HIS) to ICU Medical for $1 billion. HIS was Pfizer's global infusion therapy business and included IV pumps and devices. Through the deal Pfizer gained a stake of about 17% in ICU Medical.

In 2016 Pfizer and Ireland-based Allergan terminated their planned merger which would have been the largest-ever health care deal. The $160 billion transaction would have created the world's largest drug maker surpassing Johnson & Johnson.

Also in 2016 Pfizer bought Anacor Pharmaceuticals which has a non-steroid ointment for the treatment of eczema in its pipeline for $5.2 billion. It also acquired biopharmaceutical firm Medivation for $14 billion gaining a pipeline of cancer drugs as well as prostate cancer drug Xtandi.

EXECUTIVES

Evp Corporate Affairs, Sally Susman, age 59
Evp Business Operations And Cfo, Frank A. D'Amelio, age 62, $1,324,000 total compensation
Chairman And Ceo, Ian C. Read, age 66, $1,905,250 total compensation
Evp And Chief Medical Officer, Freda C. Lewis-Hall, age 64, $800,000 total compensation
Evp And President Worldwide Research And Development, Mikael Dolsten, age 61, $1,237,500 total compensation
Evp And General Counsel, Douglas M. (Doug) Lankler, age 54
Svp And Head Pharmatherapeutics Research And Development, Alexander R. (Rod) MacKenzie, age 60
Evp Worldwide Human Resources, Charles H. (Chuck) Hill, age 64
Group President Pfizer Innovative Health, John D. Young, age 55, $1,130,000 total compensation
Evp Strategy And Commercial Operations, Laurie J. Olson, age 56
Coo, Albert Bourla, age 58, $1,117,500 total compensation
Evp And Chief Compliance And Risk Officer, Rady A. Johnson, age 58
Vp Innovative Health Product Portfolio Management And Consumer Operations, Kirsten Lund-Jurgensen, age 60
Global President And General Manager For Pfizer Inflammation & Immunology, Angela Hwang
Medical Director Womens And Mens Health Global Innovative Pharma Business, Warachal Faison
Vice President Us Primary Care Marketing, James Sage
Vice President Sales, John Zgombic
Vice President Information Management, Craig Barrila
Vice President Manufacturing, Kevin Nepveux
Medical Director, Michael Wajnrajch
Medical Director, Hernan Valdez
Vice President Medical Affairs Platform Strategy Lead, Edith Eby
Senior Vice President Of Product, Chris Hillebrecht
Vice President Us Trade Group, Lou Dallago
Senior Vice President, Stephen Pennacchio
Vice President Compliance, Jeffrey Liu
Medical Director, Jean Chow
Vice President Of Medical Affairs And, Paul Mensah

Senior Vice President Of Brand, Carey Petersen

National Account Manager, James Dunworth

Senior Vice President Vaccine Clinical Research And Development, William Gruber

Vice President Human Resources, Mario Gagliano

Vice President External Affairs And Worldwide Communications, Elizabeth Golden

Vice President Membership, Steven Hogue

Vice President, Charles Knirsch

Senior Vice President Human Resources Global Human Resources Operations, Tracy Miller

Senior Medical Director, George Sands

National Account Manager, Teri Kittredge

Vice President And Assistant Treasurer, Brian McMahon

Executive Vice President Development, Shaileen English

Vice President Specialty Biotechnology Operating Unit, Mike McDermott

Commercial Vice President, Nanette Cocero

Medical Director, Charles Tressler

Vp Clinical Development Quality, Chris Hilton

Vice President Global Procurement, Mike Hoffman

Vice President Nanomedicines And Bioconjugates, Puja Sapra

Medical Director, Alejandra Nieto

Vice President External Supply, Christina Ayllon

National Account Manager, Mark Desantis

Senior Vice President Fin Biopharma And Cons Hlth, Sajal Mitra

Vice President Cso, John Clark

Senior Vice President And Portfolio Manager, John Goceljak

Vice President Chief Of Staff To The Chairman And Chief Executive Officer, Navin Katyal

National Account Manager, Alan J Hemler

Senior Vice President, Salomon Azoulay

Vice President Finance, George Eder

Senior Vice President, Peter Honig

Global Medical Director, Leslie Amass

Senior Vice President, Kostas Giamouridis

Vice President, Lynne Handanyan

Vice President, Lisa Housianitis

Senior Vice President, Jaume Pons

Medical Director, Seth Woodruff

Medical Director, Judith Hadavi

Vice President Global Commercial Lead Pain And Cns Franchise, Scott Richardson

Vice President Human Resources Global Randd, Sander De Beer

Vice President Emea Logistics And Supply Operations, Danny Hendrikse

Associate Medical Director, Silvina Gallo

Medical Director Oncology, Daniel Kalanovic

Medical Director Oncology, Mahmood Alam

Vice President And Assistant Gc, Edward Nowicki

Associate Medical Director, Barbara Sleight

Senior Vice President Worldwide Business Development, Doug Giordano

Vice President, Nicola Clear

Senior Vice President, Charles Triano

Vice President Commercial Development, Andy Schmeltz

Medical Director, David Grolman

Senior Vice President Human Resources Gep And Compliance, Don Stewart

Senior Vice President, William Carapezzi

Global Vice President And Head Vaccines Medical Development And Medical Scientific Affairs, Luis Jodar

Vice President, Mark Schneyer

Senior Vice President Wrd Development And Strategic Operations, Evan Loh

Executive Vice President, Karine Gravel

Medical Director Psychiatry And Neurology, Brian Klee

National Sales Manager, Gary Ellis

Vice President Finance, Fergus O'sullivan

Senior Medical Director, Dan Sheehan

Vice President And Assistant General Counsel, Lindsay Havern

Vice President Scottsdale Operations, Beatrice Colombo

Vice President Financial Planning And Operations, Toni King

Regional President Emea Pch, Tarek Youssef

Medical Director, Vaibhav Katkade

Vice President And Assistant General Counsel Chief Antit, Marc Brotman

Associate Medical Director, David Witcombe

National Sales Manager, Beatriz Sanchez

Vice President Finance, Serge Roussel

Vice President Established Products Qo, Kevin Jenkins

Vice President, John Hutchison

Executive Vice President And Co Founder, Cathryn Adams

Vice President External Research And Development Innovation, Barbara Sosnowski

Vice President Gfs Global Shared Services, Terry Wright

Vice President Regulatory Affairs Oncology, Ramzi Dagher

Vice President Global Vac Pneumo, Raul Isturiz

Medical Director, Ioana Russ

Vice President Legal Affairs And General Counsel, Darren Noseworthy

National Sales Manager, Tuncay Ekici

National Sales Manager Consumer Healthcare, Jung-tak Shin

Vice President Regional Head Of Medical Affairs North America, Juan Ovalle

Vice President Of Quality Operations, Steve Brooks

Vice President, Rich Hollander

Medical Director Hematology, Krupa Sivamurthy

Medical Director, Carlos Estevez

Vice President Endocrine Care, Jose Cara

Vice President Sales, Dennis Kozak

Senior Medical Director, Manuela Berger

Vice President, Cory Stiff

Vice President, Kevin Filipski

Senior Vice President Of Sales, Mike Byrne

Vice President Payer Accounts, Joseph Kucharski

National Sales Manager Biosimilars, Natalie Bedard

Vice President Training, Nancy Friedman

Vice President Corporate Audit, Jennifer Damico

Medical Director, Judith Hey-Hadavi

Vice President Human Resources Medical Corporate Strategy And Human Resources Business Developme, Janice Beauchamp

Vice President, Tracey Boyden

Executive Vice President And Chief Financial Officer, Alan G Levin

Vice President And Chief Counsel Global Business Development, Arthur Cohn

Senior Medical Director, Birgitta Benda

Vice President Bioprocess Services Group, Roberto Silveira

Medical Director Russia, Kirill Tverskoy

National Sales Manager, Leonore JAcobs

Vp And Assistant General Cousel, David Smith

Senior Vice President Total Rewards, Steve Pennacchio

National Sales Manager, Tolgay Sevimsavur

Senior Medical Director, Diane Martire

Medical Director Risk Management Lead, Vlad Bykoriz

Senior Medical Director Global Medical Affairs, Gorana Dasic

Medical Director, Eme Una-Efiong

Vice President And Assistant General Counsel Vaccines, Jason Smith

Vice President Human Resources, Kristin Papesh

Vice President Finance Japan Asia Area, Gordon Loh

Vice President Us Oncology Commercial, Matthew Shaulis

Government Relations, Ryan Bounsy

Vice President Of Human Resources, Laura Larbalestier

Vice President Vaccine Clinical Research, Dan Scott

Medical Director, Mohamed Harti

Medical Director Us Medical Affairs, Elif Silva

Vice President Finance, Edmund Huver

Medical Director, Rebecca Luk

Senior Vice President And Chief Scientific Officer Oncology Research Unit, Tara Brown

Vice President Rare Disease Clinical Resea, Michael Binks

Auditors: KPMG LLP

LOCATIONS

HQ: Pfizer Inc
235 East 42nd Street, New York, NY 10017
Phone: 212 733-2323
Web: www.pfizer.com

2018 Sales

	$ mil.	% of total
US	25,329	47
Emerging Markets	12,651	24
Developed Europe	9,116	17
Developed Rest of World	6,551	12
Total	**53,647**	**100**

PRODUCTS/OPERATIONS

2018 Sales by Segment

	$ mil.	% of total
Innovative Health	33,426	62
Essential Health	20,221	38
Total	**53,647**	**100**

Selected Products

Pharmaceuticals
Aricept (Alzheimer's disease)
Aromasin (breast cancer)
+Arthrotec (osteoarthritis and rheumatoid arthritis)
BeneFIX (hemophilia)
BMP2 (bone and cartilage development)
Caduet (high cholesterol and blood pressure dual therapy)
Camptosar (colorectal cancer)
Cardura (hypertension and enlarged prostate disease)
Celebrex (arthritis pain)
Chantix/Champix (smoking cessation)
Dalacin/Cleocin (antibiotic for bacterial infections)
Detrol/Detrol LA (overactive bladder)
Diflucan (antifungal)
Effexor (antidepressant and anxiety disorder treatment)
Enbrel (arthritis treatment)
Fragmin (anticoagulant)
Genotropin (growth hormone deficiency)
Geodon/Zeldox (schizophrenia and bipolar disorder)
Inspra (high blood pressure)
Lipitor (cholesterol)
Lyrica (nerve pain)
Medrol (inflammation)
Methotrexate (severe psoriasis)
Neurontin (epilepsy)
Norvasc (hypertension)
Premarin (hormone replacement therapy)
Prevnar (pneumococcus vaccine)
Pristiq (antidepressant)
Protonix (protein pump inhibitor)
Quillivant XR (ADHD)
Rapamune (organ rejection preventative)
Rebif (multiple sclerosis)
ReFacto AF/Xyntha (hemophilia)
Relpax (migraines)
Revatio (hypertension)
Selzentry (HIV)
Skelaxin (muscle relaxant)
Somavert (acromegaly)
Spiriva (chronic obstructive pulmonary disease)
Sulperazon (antibiotic)
Sutent (carcinoma and tumors)
Toviaz (overactive bladder)
Tygacil (anti-infective)
Unasyn (injectable antibacterial)
Vfend (fungal infections)
Viagra (impotence)

Xalatan/Xalacom (glaucoma)
Xanax XR (anti-anxiety treatment)
Zithromax/Zmax (antibiotic)
Zoloft (depression)
Zosyn/Tazocin (anti-infective)
Zyvox (antibiotic)
Animal Health
Cerenia (nausia treatment for canines)
Convenia (canine and feline antibiotics)
Draxxin (cattle antibiotic)
Excede (cattle antibiotic)
Improvac (swine vaccine for boar taint)
Palladia (dog cancer treatment)
Revolution/Stronghold (antiparasitic for dogs and cats)
Rimadyl (canine osteoarthritis treatment)
Suvaxyn (swine vaccine)
Consumer Health
Advil (analgesic)
Anbesol (oral pain relief)
Caltrate (nutritional supplement)
Centrum (vitamins)
ChapStick (lip care)
Dimetapp (cough/cold remedy)
Emergen-C (vitamin C supplement)
FiberCon (laxative)
Nexium (acid reflux)
Preparation H (hemorrhoid treatment)
Robitussin (cough/cold remedy)
ThermaCare (aches and pains)

COMPETITORS

Allergan plc	Merck
AstraZeneca	Mylan
Boehringer Ingelheim	Novartis
Bristol-Myers Squibb	Roche Holding
Eli Lilly	Sanofi
GlaxoSmithKline	Teva
Johnson & Johnson	

HISTORICAL FINANCIALS

Company Type: Public

Income Statement   FYE: December 31

	REVENUE ($ mil.)	NET INCOME ($ mil.)	NET PROFIT MARGIN	EMPLOYEES
12/19	51,750	16,273	31.4%	88,300
12/18	53,647	11,153	20.8%	92,400
12/17	52,546	21,308	40.6%	90,200
12/16	52,824	7,215	13.7%	96,500
12/15	48,851	6,960	14.2%	97,900
Annual Growth	1.5%	23.7%	—	(2.5%)

2019 Year-End Financials

Debt ratio: 31.14%—
Return on equity: 25.72%
Cash ($ mil.): 1,305
Current ratio: 0.88
Long-term debt ($ mil.): 35,955

Dividends
Yield: 3.8%
Payout: 52.8%
Market value ($ mil.): —

	STOCK PRICE ($) FY Close	P/E High/Low	PER SHARE ($) Earnings	Dividends	Book Value
12/19	39.18	15 12	2.87	1.44	11.41
12/18	43.65	24 18	1.87	1.36	11.09
12/17	36.22	10 9	3.52	1.28	11.93
12/16	32.48	32 24	1.17	1.20	9.81
12/15	32.28	32 27	1.11	1.12	10.48
Annual Growth	5.0%	— —	26.8%	6.5%	2.1%

PG&E Corp (Holding Co)

Pacific Gas and Electric Company one of the largest public utility providers in California supplies electricity and natural gas to residential commercial industrial and agricultural customers in northern and central California. It reaches approximately 5.4 million electric customers via approximately 107000 miles of electric distribution lines and some 4.4 million gas customers via some 43100 miles of gas distribution lines. The company sources its electric and natural gas supply from owned generation facilities (some 135 electric plants) and through third-party disposal sites. The utility along with its parent PG&E Corporation filed for Chapter 11 bankruptcy protection in January 2019 as it faced up to $30 billion in damage liabilities related to California wildfires in 2017 and 2018.

Bankruptcy

In January 2019 PG&E filed for Chapter 11 bankruptcy protection as it faces more than $30 billion in liabilities from damages related to massive wildfires that ravaged parts of California in 2017 and 2018. The wildfires killed dozens of people and destroyed thousands of homes. The future of the company is uncertain as it deals with these liability claims from victims bankers and insurance companies.

Operations

Electric Utility the core business of the company consists of 135 generation facilities in California with a net operating capacity of around 7685 MW. This business also includes about 35 electric transmission substations and approximately 18000 circuit miles of transmission lines as well as distribution assets including some 107000 miles of distribution lines about 70 transmission switching substations and around 760 substations. Almost 75% of the company's annual sales comes from its electric business which delivers some 78070 GWh of electricity each year.

The Natural Gas Utility (25% of annual sales) maintains approximately 43300 miles of distribution pipelines more than 6400 miles local transmission pipelines storage facilities and eight natural gas compressor stations. It also owns three underground natural gas storage fields. The company buys around 227620 MMcf of gas from third-party providers under firm transportation agreements (uninterruptible services for the period specified).

Geographic Reach

Pacific Gas and Electric owns approximately 158000 of land in California consisting of its 135 electric power generation facilities three natural gas storage fields and various transmission and distribution properties. It is headquartered in San Francisco.

Sales and Marketing

It reaches approximately 5.4 million electric customers and some 4.4 million gas customers.

Financial Performance

Pacific Gas and Electric has seen fluctuating revenue for the past five years recording a 2% increase from 2015 to 2019.

Revenue increased 2% from $16.8 billion in 2018 to $17.1 billion in 2019 which resulted from an increase in electric and natural gas operating revenues.

Net loss was $7.6 billion a 12% jump from $6.8 billion in the previous year.

Cash and cash equivalents at the end of the year were $1.6 billion $98 million less than in the previous year. Cash provided by operations was $4.8 billion. Investing activities used $6.4 billion primarily for capital expenditures while financing activities provided $1.5 billion from proceeds from debtor-in-possession credit facility.

Strategy

Pacific Gas and Electric's strategy follows its parent company's strategy which is to help its customers rebuild and recover after wildfires.

Having taken a serious hit to its reputation Pacific Gas and Electric has revamped its board with 10 new members (in a 13-member board) and a new CEO (Bill Johnson a former head of Progress Energy) at the helm. It plans to change the current image that the company favors its stockholders over its customers' wellbeing by working closely with the bankruptcy court's judge as well as the state's utilities regulators and the representatives of wildfire victims. This includes cutting back trees near electrical lines submitting to random inspections by the state complying with state environmental laws and improving the company's own fire mitigation plans.

Company Background

Pacific Gas and Electric Company was incorporated in California in 1905. In 1997 the utility company and its subsidiaries started reporting under the holding company PG&E Corporation.

Damage-related liabilities from California wildfires totaling $30 billion forced PG&E Corporation to file for bankruptcy in 2019.

EXECUTIVES

President Electric, Geisha J. Williams, age 58, $634,183 total compensation
Svp And Cio, Karen A. Austin, age 58
Svp Human Resources, Dinyar B. Mistry, age 58, $381,433 total compensation
President Gas, Nickolas (Nick) Stavropoulos, age 61, $613,221 total compensation
Svp Human Resources, John R. Simon, age 56, $424,994 total compensation
Svp Generation And Chief Nuclear Officer, Edward D. (Ed) Halpin, age 58
Vp Cfo And Controller, David S. Thomason, age 45
Vice President Network Services, Jeff Hernandez
Senior Vice President And Chief Supply Officer, Des Bell
Board Member, Allan Smith
Auditors: Deloitte & Touche LLP

LOCATIONS

HQ: PG&E Corp (Holding Co)
77 Beale Street, P.O. Box 770000, San Francisco, CA 94177
Phone: 415 973-1000   **Fax:** 415 267-7265
Web: www.pgecorp.com

PRODUCTS/OPERATIONS

2018 sales

	$ mil.	% of total
Electric	12,713	75
Natural Gas	4,047	25
Total	16,760	100

COMPETITORS

Edison International	Sempra Energy
PacifiCorp	

HISTORICAL FINANCIALS

Company Type: Public

Income Statement

FYE: December 31

	REVENUE ($ mil.)	NET INCOME ($ mil.)	NET PROFIT MARGIN	EMPLOYEES
12/19	17,129	(7,642)	—	23,000
12/18	16,759	(6,837)	—	24,000
12/17	17,135	1,660	9.7%	23,000
12/16	17,666	1,407	8.0%	24,000
12/15	16,833	888	5.3%	23,000
Annual Growth	0.4%	—	—	0.0%

2019 Year-End Financials

Debt ratio: —
Return on equity: (-85.93%)
Cash ($ mil.): 1,570
Current ratio: 1.33
Long-term debt ($ mil.): —

No. of shares (mil.): 529
Dividends
  Yield: —
  Payout: —
Market value ($ mil.): 5,753

	STOCK PRICE ($) FY Close	P/E High/Low		PER SHARE ($) Earnings	Dividends	Book Value
12/19	10.87	—	—	(14.50)	0.00	9.70
12/18	23.75	—	—	(13.25)	0.00	24.31
12/17	44.83	22	14	3.21	1.55	37.34
12/16	60.77	23	18	2.78	1.93	35.39
12/15	53.19	33	26	1.79	1.82	33.69
Annual Growth	(32.8%)	—	—	—	—	(26.7%)

PHILADELPHIA CONSOLIDATED HOLDING CORP.

Because each industry has its own unique set of risks Philadelphia Insurance Companies and its subsidiaries specialize in designing and underwriting commercial property/casualty insurance. Its niche clients include rental car companies (for that insurance they always want to sell you at the counter) not-for-profits health and fitness centers and day-care facilities. Its specialty lines include loss-control policies and liability coverage for such professionals as lawyers doctors accountants dog groomers and even insurance claims adjusters. Philadelphia Insurance Companies is a subsidiary of Tokio Marine Holdings.

Geographic Reach

Philadelphia Insurance Companies' operating subsidiaries Philadelphia Insurance and Philadelphia Indemnity Insurance sell and service policies through a network of independent agents and about 50 regional offices that stretch across the US. With its new-found backing from Tokio Marine the insurer has access to broader distribution avenues in the US and overseas.

Sales and Marketing

In addition to commercial property and casualty insurance the company also sells personal coverage for collectible cars and homeowners flood insurance.

Strategy

Philadelphia Insurance Companies has been enhancing its information technology systems.

The firm is working to upgrade its back-office infrastructure for more efficient handling of billing claims accounting and data management functions.

EXECUTIVES

Regional Vice President, Brent Kruse
Vice President Metro Region, Brian O'reilly
Assistant Vice President, Michael Henk
Vp Marketing, Mike Ricca
Senior Vice President, John Doyle
Regional Vice President, Bill Misita
Assistant Vice President, Liney Kevin
Vice President Commerical Underwriting, Mark Plousis
Avp Contract Surety, Rick Morgan
Vice President, Robert Morgan
Regional Vice President, Daniel Shea
Assistant Vice President Chief Information Security Officer (ciso), Mark Viola
Vice President, Jon Peeples

LOCATIONS

HQ: PHILADELPHIA CONSOLIDATED HOLDING CORP.
1 BALA PLZ STE 100, BALA CYNWYD, PA 190041401
Phone: 610 617-7900
Web: WWW.PHLY.COM

PRODUCTS/OPERATIONS

Selected Products

Commercial and Personal Property/Casualty Insurance
  Adoption agencies
  Adult day care
  Amateur sports
  Antique collector car
  Apartments
  Auto leasing/rental program
  Boat dealers
  Bowling centers
  Builder's exchange
  Builders' risk
  Business auto fleet
  Camp operators
  Child care centers
  Consulting foresters
  Contractor environmental coverage
  Crime protection plus
  Entertainment
  Environmental
  Fairs and fairgrounds
  Festivals
  Film production
  Flood
  Golf and country clubs
  Health fitness and wellness
  Home health care
  Homeowners association
  Hospice
  Hotels
  Life and business coaches
  Loss control
  Medical facilities and hospitals
  Motorsports
  Museums
  Non-profit and social service organizations
  Nursing homes
  Office parks
  Outdoor recreation
  Performing arts
  Pest control services
  Professional sports
  Public entities
  Real rstate dchedules
  Religious organizations
  RV parks and campgrounds
  Schools
  Security services (The Guardian)
  Shopping centers
  Special events
  Substance abuse rehabilitation facilities
  Temporary staffing agencies
  Volunteer fire department
  Zoos
Liability
  Accountants professional liability
  Allied Health professional liability
  Business owners
  Cyber security liability
  Employed lawyers professional liability
  Employment practices stand alone
  Excess liability
  Miscellaneous professional liability (Affinity Pro)

COMPETITORS

AIG	Liberty Mutual
American Financial Group	Markel
	North Pointe
CNA Financial	RLI
Hagerty Insurance	State Farm
Hanover Insurance	Travelers Companies

HISTORICAL FINANCIALS

Company Type: Private

Income Statement

FYE: December 31

	ASSETS ($ mil.)	NET INCOME ($ mil.)	INCOME AS % OF ASSETS	EMPLOYEES
12/16	9,719	347	3.6%	1,374
12/15	9,047	323	3.6%	
Annual Growth	7.4%	7.5%	—	—

Philip Morris International Inc

Philip Morris is quitting smoking: The cigarette company is on the long path to a smoke-free product portfolio. In the meantime however Philip Morris International (PMI) is still one of the world's leading cigarette manufacturers. Despite being US-based its sales presence is entirely non-US. Its biggest brands are Marlboro (the world's #1-selling cigarette) which accounts for over 35% of PMI's total shipment volume L&M and Bond Street. Top local brands include Fortune Sampoerna and Dji Sam Soe..

Operations

Philip Morris International (PMI) operates six segments according to the company's top geographic markets. PMI's European Union segment generates around a third of its total revenue East Asia and Australia account for roughly a fifth the South and Southeast Asia and Middle East and Africa segments both account for over 15% of sales and the Latin America and Canada and the Eastern Europe segments collectively represent some 20% of sales.

PMI's international brands make up almost 80% of its shipment volume while the Marlboro brand accounts for more than 35%. PMI's other tobacco products (OTP) primarily include tobacco for roll-your-own and make-your-own cigarettes pipe tobacco cigars and cigarillos.

Its international brands are premium price brands Marlboro and Parliament; mid-price brands are L&M Lark and Philip Morris; and low-price brands Bond Street and Chesterfield.

Important local brands include Dji Sam Soe and Sampoerna in Indonesia; Fortune and Jackpot in the Philippines.

PMI's smokeless tobacco portfolio includes IQOS HEETS Marlboro HeatSticks and Parliament HeatSticks. These products described as Reduced Risk Products account for nearly 20% of net sales.

Geographic Reach

New York-based Philip Morris International's (PMI) products are sold in more than 180 markets worldwide. PMI operates almost 40 manufacturing facilities across its six operating segments.

Sales and Marketing

PMI's main types of distribution are tailored to the characteristics of each market and are often used simultaneously: Direct sales and distribution (gas stations and other key accounts); distribution through independent distributors; exclusive zonified distribution; distribution through national or regional wholesalers; and its own brand retail and e-commerce infrastructures for RRP products and accessories.

Advertising expenses were $730 million $896 million and $830 million in 2019 2018 and 2017 respectively.

Financial Performance

PMI's total revenue has been gradually increasing except in 2016. It has an overall growth of 11% over the last five years. On the other hand the company's net income over the last five years has been fluctuating.

The company's total revenue for 2019 rose by 1% or 180 million to $29.8 billion from $29.6 billion in 2018. The increase was primarily due to the 6% increase of the company's European Union segment.

PMI's net income in 2019 dipped 9% to $7.2 billion from $7.9 billion in 2018.

PMI's cash on hand rose by $245 million during 2019 ending the year at $6.9 billion. The company's operations generated $10.1 billion offset by $1.8 billion used in its investing and $8.1 billion used in its financing.

Strategy

PMI recognizes that smoking cigarettes cause serious diseases and that the best way to avoid the harms of smoking is never to start or to quit.

The company's key strategic priorities are: to develop and commercialize products that present less risk of harm to adult smokers who switch to those products versus continued smoking; and to convince current adult smokers who would otherwise continue to smoke to switch to those RRPs.

One element of the company's growth strategy is to strengthen its brand portfolio and market positions through selective acquisitions and the development of strategic business relationships.

Company Background

PMI is a result of a spinoff from Altria in 2008. The separation positioned PMI as an independent publicly traded company free from its US branch Philip Morris USA. Altria simultaneously avoided an entanglement in various US legal and regulatory issues.

PMI has made a number of acquisitions to enhance its brand-rich portfolio and geographic presence. In mid-2011 PMI took over a cigarette manufacturer in Jordan. The purchase followed PMI's acquisition of a cigar business comprising trademarks in Australia and New Zealand. During 2011 PMI also revised its joint venture with Vietnam National Tobacco Corp. (Vinataba) in Vietnam opening the door to licensing the Marlboro label as PMI established a local branch to build its brands.

In 2009 PMI acquired the South African tobacco branch of Swedish Match for 1.93 billion ZAR (about $256 million) giving PMI a leg up in producing smokeless tobacco products and builds upon a joint venture between PMI and Swedish Match to market Swedish style snus and other smokeless tobacco lines outside of Scandinavia and the US. (Altria moved to dominate the rapidly rising niche by taking over UST a leader in the US market for smokeless products including the Copenhagen Husky and Skoal brands.) In the same month PMI purchased the Petter es tobacco business for $209 million pocketing fine-cut brands popular in Sweden and Norway.

EXECUTIVES

Ceo, André Calantzopoulos, age 62, $1,501,552 total compensation
Cfo, Martin G. King, age 55, $842,239 total compensation
President External Affairs & General Counsel, Marc S. Firestone, age 61, $1,015,680 total compensation
President Science & Innovation, Miroslaw Zielinski, age 59, $943,738 total compensation
President South & Southeast Asia Region Including Indonesia And The Philippines, Stacey Kennedy
Coo, Jacek Olczak, age 55, $971,563 total compensation
Svp And Cio, Patrick Brunel, age 54
President European Union Region, Frederic de Wilde, age 52
President Eastern Europe Middle East Africa Region And Pmi Duty Free Including North Africa, Drago Azinovic, age 57
President Latin America And Canada Region, Jeanne Poll ̄s, age 55
Svp Commercial, Werner Barth, age 55
President Eastern Europe Region, Marco Mariotti
President Pmi Japan, Paul Riley
Vp Digital Strategy Reduced-risk Products, Jaime Suarez
Vice President Information Systems Management, Siegfried Diesch
Vice President Of Supply Chain, Hafed Belhadj
V Pres Controller, Andreas Kurali
Vice President Compensation Benefits And International Assignments, Ralf Zysk
Chairman, Louis C. Camilleri, age 65
Auditors: PricewaterhouseCoopers SA

LOCATIONS

HQ: Philip Morris International Inc
120 Park Avenue, New York, NY 10017
Phone: 917 663-2000　　**Fax:** 917 663-5372
Web: www.pmi.com

2018 Sales

	$ mil.	% of total
European Union	9,298	31
East Asia & Australasia	5,580	19
South & Southeast Asia	4,656	16
Middle East & Africa	4,114	14
Eastern Europe	2,921	10
Total	**29,625**	**100**

PRODUCTS/OPERATIONS

Selected Brands
Local brands
　Apollo-Soyuz (Russia)
　Assos (Greece)
　Belmont (Canada)
　Best (Serbia)
　Boston (Colombia)
　Canadian Classics (Canada)
　Champion (Philippines)
　Classic (Serbia)
　Delicados (Mexico)
　Diana (Italy)
　Dji Sam Soe (Indonesia)
　f6 (Germany)
　Fortune (Philippines)
　Hope (Philippines)
　Morven Gold (Pakistan)
　Number 7 (Canada)
　Optima (Russia)
　Petra (Czech Republic and Slovakia)
　Sampoerna A (Indonesia)
　Sampoerna Kretek (Indonesia)
Mid-price brands
　L&M
　Chesterfield
Other international brands
　Benson & Hedges
　Bond Street
　Lark
　Muratti
　Next
　Philip Morris
　Red & White
Premium-price
　Marlboro
　Merit
　Parliament
　Virginia Slims
Other tobacco products
　Interval (France)
　Petterøes (Norway and Sweden)
　Swedish Match snus smokefree tobacco

2018 Shipment Volumes

	% of total
Cigarettes	95
Heated Tobacco Units	5
Total	**100**

COMPETITORS

British American Tobacco	Japan Tobacco
Gudang Garam	Reemtsma
Imperial Brands	Cigarettenfabriken

HISTORICAL FINANCIALS

Company Type: Public

Income Statement

FYE: December 31

	REVENUE ($ mil.)	NET INCOME ($ mil.)	NET PROFIT MARGIN	EMPLOYEES
12/19	29,805	7,185	24.1%	73,500
12/18	29,625	7,911	26.7%	77,400
12/17	28,748	6,035	21.0%	80,600
12/16	26,685	6,967	26.1%	79,500
12/15	26,794	6,873	25.7%	80,200
Annual Growth	**2.7%**	**1.1%**	**—**	**(2.2%)**

2019 Year-End Financials

Debt ratio: 72.41%	No. of shares (mil.): 1,555
Return on equity:—	Dividends
Cash ($ mil.): 6,861	Yield: 5.4%
Current ratio: 1.09	Payout: 100.2%
Long-term debt ($ mil.): 26,656	Market value ($ mil.): 132,391

	STOCK PRICE ($) FY Close	P/E High/Low	PER SHARE ($) Earnings	Dividends	Book Value
12/19	85.09	20 14	4.61	4.62	(7.44)
12/18	66.76	22 13	5.08	4.49	(8.01)
12/17	105.65	32 23	3.88	4.22	(7.78)
12/16	91.49	23 19	4.48	4.12	(8.18)
12/15	87.91	20 17	4.42	4.04	(8.55)
Annual Growth	(0.8%)	— —	1.1%	3.4%	—

Phillips 66

Phillips 66 is a leading marketer of gas aviation fuels crude oil and other refined petroleum products as well as specialty products such as oils waxes solvents and lubricants. It markets in the US under the Phillips 66 Conoco and 76 brands and internationally under the JET and Coop brands. One of the largest crude oil refiners the company processes transports and markets natural gas and natural gas liquids as well as liquefied petroleum gas. It produces olefins and polyolefins and other products through CPChem a joint venture with Chevron. Phillips 66 operates primarily in the US and Europe.

Operations

Of the four segments that Phillips 66 reports Marketing and Specialties is the largest contributing about 65% of sales. It purchases for resale and markets refined petroleum products mainly in the United States and Europe. In addition this segment includes the manufacturing and marketing of specialty products such as base oils and lubricants.

The Refining segment which accounts for just roughly 30% of total revenue refines crude oil and other feedstocks into petroleum products (gasoline distillates and aviation fuel) at about a dozen refineries in the United States and Europe.

The Midstream segment of Phillips 66 makes up around 5% of total revenue. Midstream provides crude oil and refined petroleum product transportation terminaling and process services as well as natural gas liquids (NGL) transportation storage fractionation processing and marketing services mainly in the United States. This segment includes their master limited partnership Phillips 66 Partners LP as well as their 50% equity investment in DCP Midstream LLC.

Chemicals segment consists of their 50% equity investment in Chevron Phillips Chemical Company LLC which manufactures and markets petrochemicals and plastics on a worldwide basis.

Overall the company generates over 80% of its revenue from refined products; almost 15% from crude oil resales; and around 5% from NGL; while a small portion comes from services and other.

Geographic Reach

Phillips 66 operates primarily in the US. Its presence in Europe is largely concentrated in the UK with some assets in mainland Europe. The US accounts for more than three-quarters of revenue followed by the UK at about 10%.

CPChem is involved in about 30 global manufacturing facilities in five continents but most significant assets are on the Texas Gulf Coast.

Sales and Marketing

Phillips 66 markets petroleum and specialty products through a network of approximately 7540 marketer-owned or -supplied outlets across the US under brand names 76 Conoco and Phillips 66. It also holds brand-licensing agreements with approximately 1280 sites. Its refined products are marketed on both a branded and unbranded basis.

n Europe Phillips 66 sells retail and wholesale products in Austria Germany and the UK under the JET brand and in Switzerland under the Coop brand (equity interest).

Financial Performance

Phillips 66's revenue is closely tied to oil prices meaning its revenue has fallen and risen again over the last five years along with prices. In 2019 the company's sales continued on their upward trajectory falling 4% to $107.3 billion due to higher prices.

Net income fell 45% to $4.2 billion due to the $2.5 billion decrease on their operating income partially offset by the decrease on their income tax expense.

Phillips 66's cash on hand fell $1.4 billion during 2019 ending the year at $1.6 billion. The company's operations generated 4.8 billion offset by the $3.7 billion used in its investing activities and $2.5 billion used in its financing. Phillips 66's main cash uses in 2018 were capital expenditures share repurchases and dividends.

Strategy

Phillips 66 continue to focus on the following strategic properties: operating excellence growth returns distributions and high-performing organizations.

Their strategy focuses on investing in growth opportunities in the Midstream and Chemical segments. They also plan to enhance Refining returns by increasing throughput of advantaged feedstocks improving yields portfolio optimization and an ongoing commitment to operating excellence.

The company's European marketing strategy is to sell primarily through owned leased or joint venture retail sites using a low-cost high-volume approach.

Company Background

Brothers Frank and L.E. Phillips founded Phillips Petroleum Company headquartered in Bartlesville OK in 1917. In 1981 DuPont acquired Conoco after a heated takeover battle and Conoco became a wholly owned DuPont subsidiary. Conoco and Phillips Petroleum officially merged in 2002 to become Conoco Phillips. ConocoPhillips spun off its midstream and downstream businesses to create a publicly traded company called Phillips 66 that began trading under the symbol PSX on the New York Stock Exchange on May 2012.

EXECUTIVES

Chairman And Ceo, Greg C. Garland, age 63, $1,616,816 total compensation
Evp And Cfo, Kevin J. Mitchell, $688,448 total compensation
Evp Refining, Lawrence M. (Larry) Ziemba, $690,312 total compensation

Evp Midstream, Robert A. (Bob) Herman, age 62, $661,608 total compensation
Vp Technology, Merl R. Lindstrom
Evp Commercial Marketing Transportation And Business Development, Tim G. Taylor, age 66, $1,071,376 total compensation
Evp Legal And Government Affairs General Counsel And Corporate Secretary, Paula A. Johnson, $698,976 total compensation
Evp Marketing And Commercial, Timothy D. (Tim) Roberts
Vice President State Affairs, Jennifer Stettner
Vice President Of Engineering, Christina Andersen
European Treasurer, John Wallace
Auditors: Ernst & Young LLP

LOCATIONS

HQ: Phillips 66
2331 CityWest Blvd., Houston, TX 77042
Phone: 281 293-6600
Web: www.Phillips66.com

2018 Sales

	% of total
US	77
UK	10
Germany	4
Other countries	9
Total	**100**

PRODUCTS/OPERATIONS

2018 Sales

	% of total
Refined products	79
Crude oil resales	15
NGL	5
Services and other	1
Total	**100**

2018 Sales

	$ mil.	% of total
Marketing and Specialties	71,515	64
Refining	33,797	30
Midstream	6,117	6
Chemicals	5	-
Corporate and Other	27	-
Total	**111,461**	**100**

Selected Brands
76
Conoco
Coop
Copylene
JET
Kendall
Phillips 66
Red Line

COMPETITORS

BP	Marathon Petroleum
CITGO	Motiva Enterprises
CVR	NOVA Chemicals
Chevron	National Cooperative
CrossAmerica Partners	Refinery Association
Dow Chemical	Shell Oil Products
Exxon Mobil	Sinclair Oil
Gibson Energy	Sunoco
Hess Corporation	TOTAL
HollyFrontier	Tesoro
LyondellBasell	Valero Energy

HISTORICAL FINANCIALS

Company Type: Public

Income Statement				FYE: December 31
	REVENUE ($ mil.)	NET INCOME ($ mil.)	NET PROFIT MARGIN	EMPLOYEES
12/19	109,559	3,076	2.8%	14,500
12/18	114,217	5,595	4.9%	14,200
12/17	104,622	5,106	4.9%	14,600
12/16	85,777	1,555	1.8%	14,800
12/15	100,949	4,227	4.2%	14,000
Annual Growth	2.1%	(7.6%)	—	0.9%

2019 Year-End Financials

Debt ratio: 20.03%
Return on equity: 12.41%
Cash ($ mil.): 1,614
Current ratio: 1.24
Long-term debt ($ mil.): 11,216

No. of shares (mil.): 441
Dividends
Yield: 3.1%
Payout: 35.3%
Market value ($ mil.): 49,135

	STOCK PRICE ($) FY Close	P/E High/Low		PER SHARE ($) Earnings	Dividends	Book Value
12/19	111.41	18	12	6.77	3.50	56.48
12/18	86.15	10	7	11.80	3.10	54.04
12/17	101.15	10	8	9.85	2.73	49.94
12/16	86.41	31	25	2.92	2.45	43.16
12/15	81.80	12	8	7.73	2.18	43.63
Annual Growth	8.0%	—	—	(3.3%)	12.6%	6.7%

PHILLIPS EDISON - ARC SHOPPING CENTER REIT INC.

EXECUTIVES

Chb- Ceo, Jeffrey S Edison
Co-Chb, Michael C Phillips
Pres, John Bessey
Cfo, Richard J Smith
Coo, R Mark Addy
CIO, Hal Scudder
Cfo-Treas-Sec, Devin I Murphy
Auditors: DELOITTE & TOUCHE LLP CINCINN

LOCATIONS

HQ: PHILLIPS EDISON - ARC SHOPPING CENTER REIT INC.
11501 NORTHLAKE DR FL 1, CINCINNATI, OH 452491667
Phone: 513 554-1110
Web: WWW.PHILLIPSEDISON.COM

HISTORICAL FINANCIALS

Company Type: Private

Income Statement				FYE: December 31
	ASSETS ($ mil.)	NET INCOME ($ mil.)	INCOME AS % OF ASSETS	EMPLOYEES
12/14	2,150	(22)	—	18
12/13	1,721	(12)	—	—
12/12	325	(4)	—	—
12/11	85	(2)	—	—
Annual Growth	193.4%	—	—	—

Pilgrims Pride Corp.

As one of the world's top chicken processors Pilgrim's Pride has a lot to crow about. The company sells fresh frozen and value-added poultry products under a host of brands (Pilgrim's Pride Gold Kist and Moy Park among them) primarily in North America and Europe. Vertically integrated Pilgrim's Pride is involved in breeding hatching raising processing and distributing chicken and pork; it produces more than 13 billion pounds of chicken and approximately 443 million pounds of pork products annually. The company ? which serves more than 6500 grocery store chains wholesale clubs and other retail distributors ? is majority owned by Brazil's JBS.

Operations

Pilgrim's Pride conducts its operations through a huge network of some 5200 growers nearly 40 feed mills some 50 hatcheries about 40 processing plants more than 25 prepared foods cook plants and about 25 distribution centers as well as ten rendering facilities and four pet food plants.

The company's reporting segments are geographic with US Chicken accounting for approximately 65% of sales; UK and European Chicken and Mexican Chicken account for more than 15% and more than 10% UK and Europe pork generates the remaining. Within its largest US segment fresh chicken (refrigerated whole or cut-up chicken marinated or non-marinated) accounts for approximately 55% of revenue. Prepared chicken (breast filets strips nuggets patties deli products) generates more than 5% of revenue and export/other (refrigerated for US distributors or frozen for distribution to export markets) accounts for the rest. Export pork sales accounted for roughly 5% of the company's total UK and Europe pork sales.

Geographic Reach

Customers in the US generate more than 65% of Pilgrim's Pride's total revenue with European customers accounting for nearly 20% and Mexican customers accounting for over 10%. It exports its products to approximately 110 countries worldwide including in the US UK and continental Europe Mexico the Middle East Asia and other international markets.

The company is based in Colorado.

Sales and Marketing

Pilgrim's Pride has over 6500 customers including restaurants and food processors (Chick-fil-A) grocery store chains and wholesale clubs (Kroger Publix Costco Tesco Wal-Mart and Waitrose) and chain restaurants (McDonald's).

The company's foodservice market principally consists of chain restaurants food processors broad-line distributors and certain other institutions. Its retail market consists primarily of grocery store chains wholesale clubs and other retail distributors.

Its two largest customers accounted for approximately 15% of its net sales.

Advertising costs totaled $26.5 million $20.8 million and $18.5 million for 2019 2018 and 2017 respectively.

Financial Performance

Net sales for 2019 increased $471.4 million or 4% from $10.9 billion generated in 2018 to $11.4 billion generated in 2019.

The company reported net income attributable to Pilgrim's Pride Corporation of $455.9 million and profit before tax totaling $617.5 million for 2019.

Cash held by the company in 2019 decreased to $280.6 million compared to $361.6 million in the prior year. Cash provided by operations was $666.5 million while cash used for investing and financing activities were $717.1 million and $34.5 million respectively. Main uses for cash were purchase of acquired business and Payments on revolving line of credit.

Mergers and Acquisitions

In late 2019 Pilgrim's Pride completed the acquisition of Tulip Limited from Danish Crown for around Â 290 million (or approximately $354 million based on a 1.22 exchange rate as of 2019). Tulip is the UK's largest pig rearer with 12 sites around the country and has annual sales of around Â 1 billion from products such as sausages bacon and pre-cooked meats. The transaction solidifies Pilgrim's as a leading European food company creating one of the largest integrated prepared foods businesses in the UK with a portfolio of brands and retail private label solutions.

EXECUTIVES

Evp Operations - Technical Services And Engineering, Walter F. Shafer
Ceo, Don Jackson, age 69
Svp Commodity Risk Management Feed Ingredient Purchasing And Export Sales, Charles Von Der Heyde
Cfo, Fabio Sandri, age 48, $375,000 total compensation
Evp Sales And Operations, Jayson Penn
Evp Sales And Operations - Prepared Foods, Kevin Miller
Senior Vice President Human Resources, Doug Schult
National Sales Manager Fresh Foodservice, Andrew Hays
Senior Vice President Of Research And Development, Phil Hurwitz
Vp Sales, Sidney Prince
Vice President Wal Mart And Sams Sales Team, Leah Harpole
Vice President Corporate Accounts, Stacy Fiedler
Executive Vice President, Walt Shafer
Senior Vice President Operations, Matthew Herman
Vice President Foodservice Marketing, Keith Arnold
Chairman, Wesley Mendon Şa Batista
Board Member, David Bell
Auditors: KPMG LLP

LOCATIONS

HQ: Pilgrims Pride Corp.
1770 Promontory Circle, Greeley, CO 80634-9038
Phone: 970 506-8000
Web: www.pilgrims.com

2018 Sales

	$ mil.	% of total
US	7,173	66
Europe	2,134	20
Mexico	1,411	13
Asia	158	1
Other locations	59	-
Total	10,937	100

PRODUCTS/OPERATIONS

2018 Sales

	$ mil.	% of total
US chicken		
Fresh chicken	5,959	55
Prepared chicken	774	7
Export & other chicken	258	2
UK/Europe chicken		
Fresh chicken	925	9
Prepared chicken	865	8
Export & other chicken	303	3
Mexico chicken		
Fresh chicken	1,252	11
Prepared chicken	76	1
Other products		
US	433	4
UK/Europe	53	.
Mexico	34	-
Total	**10,937**	**0**

Selected Brands

Pilgrim's
Pierce Chicken
Gold Kist Farms
County Post
Country Pride
Moy Park

Selected Products

Fresh chicken
Fully cooked
Ready to cook
Individually frozen

COMPETITORS

Allen Family Foods	Noble Foods
Bachoco	Perdue Incorporated
Coleman Natural Foods	Rose Acre Farms
Eberly Poultry	Sanderson Farms
Farmer's Pride	Tecumseh Poultry
Keystone Foods	Tyson Foods

HISTORICAL FINANCIALS

Company Type: Public

Income Statement

FYE: December 29

	REVENUE ($ mil.)	NET INCOME ($ mil.)	NET PROFIT MARGIN	EMPLOYEES
12/19	11,409	455	4.0%	53,100
12/18	10,937	247	2.3%	52,100
12/17	10,767	718	6.7%	51,300
12/16	7,931	440	5.6%	39,600
12/15	8,180	645	7.9%	38,850
Annual Growth	8.7%	(8.3%)	—	8.1%

2019 Year-End Financials

Debt ratio: 32.42%	No. of shares (mil.): 249
Return on equity: 20.16%	Dividends
Cash ($ mil.): 260	Yield: —
Current ratio: 1.58	Payout: —
Long-term debt ($ mil.): 2,276	Market value ($ mil.): 8,228

	STOCK PRICE ($) FY Close	P/E High/Low		PER SHARE ($) Earnings	Dividends	Book Value
12/19	32.97	18	8	1.83	0.00	10.12
12/18	15.59	31	15	1.00	0.00	8.07
12/17	31.06	14	7	2.79	0.00	7.42
12/16	19.02	16	10	1.73	2.75	3.56
12/15	22.49	15	7	2.50	5.77	4.94
Annual Growth	10.0%	—	—	(7.5%)	—	19.6%

Pinnacle Financial Partners Inc

Pinnacle Financial Partners works to be at the top of the community banking mountain in central Tennessee. It's the holding company for Tennessee-based Pinnacle Bank which has grown to some 40 branches in the Nashville and Knoxville areas since its founding in 2000. Serving consumers and small- to mid-sized business the $9 billion financial institution provides standard services such as checking and savings accounts CDs credit cards and loans and mortgages. The company also offers investment and trust services through Pinnacle Asset Management while its insurance brokerage subsidiary Miller Loughry Beach specializes in property/casualty policies. Pinnacle agreed to merge with North Carolina-based BNC Bancorp in 2017.

Operations

Pinnacle Financial Partners' commercial and industrial loans and commercial real estate loans account for nearly 40% and 20% respectively of its total portfolio of loans.

As part of its primary services to both individual and commercial clients Tennessee-based subsidiary Pinnacle Bank provides core deposits including savings checking interest-bearing checking money market and certificate of deposit accounts.

The bank's lending products include commercial real estate and consumer loans to individuals and small- to medium-sized businesses and professional entities. Pinnacle Bank Partners also offers auto dealer finance services to certain automobile dealers and their customers. Additionally it offers Pinnacle-branded consumer credit cards to select clients.

Its convenience-centered products and services include 24-hour telephone and Internet banking debit and credit cards direct deposit and cash management services.

Geographic Reach

Based in Tennessee Pinnacle Financial Partners has become the second-largest bank holding company in the state with nearly 35 offices in eight Middle Tennessee counties and four Knoxville offices. It boasts locations in Nashville Knoxville Murfreesboro Dickson Ashland City Mt. Juliet Lebanon Franklin Brentwood Hendersonville Goodlettsville Smyrna and Shelbyville.

Sales and Marketing

Pinnacle Bank traditionally has obtained its deposits through personal solicitation by its officers and directors although it has used media advertising more in recent years due to its advertising and banking sponsorship with the Tennessee Titans NFL Football team. While it would prefer its customers to bank in person the institution allows customers to bank remotely.

Its marketing and other business development costs have risen in recent years: $4.13 million $3.639 million and $3.636 million in 2014 2013 and 2012 respectively.

Financial Performance

Pinnacle Financial Partners has enjoyed steady revenue and profit growth for the past several years thanks to positive loan growth. Revenue in 2014 rose by 9% to a record $258.77 million mostly to thanks to 9% growth in interest income from loans as the bank's loan assets grew by double digits. Pinnacle also saw double-digit growth in its fee income from service charges on deposit accounts as deposit balances grew and double-digit growth in its investment services income and trust fees as brokerage and trust account balances grew.

Higher revenue drove net income up by 22% to a record $70.47 million. Operations provided $95.06 million or 25% less cash than in 2013 primarily because the bank collected roughly $30 million less in proceeds from its mortgage loans held for sale than it did the year before.

Strategy

Pinnacle's goal is to become the dominant bank in its home market of the Southeast. In 2016 it acquired Avenue Financial Holdings for $200 million and followed up the acquisition by agreeing to merge with regional rival BNC Bancorp of North Carolina in 2017. Once the merger completes the combined company will be the biggest in the region.

Pinnacle Financial Partners been looking to diversify its revenue streams through strategic investments in recent years. In early 2015 for example Tennessee-based subsidiary Pinnacle Bank purchased a 30% membership interest in Bankers Healthcare Group LLC which makes term loans to healthcare professionals and practices for $75 million.

Primarily serving small- to medium-sized businesses in the Nashville and Knoxville areas the company in 2013 began extending its reach in its primary markets by opening its fourth full-service banking location in the Knoxville market in the Cedar Bluff area.

Mergers and Acquisitions

In 2017 Pinnacle agreed to merge with BNC Bancorp. The combined company will have assets of some $20 billion and a presence in four states and in 12 of the largest metropolitan markets in the Southeast.

In 2016 Pinnacle acquired Avenue Financial Holdings (holding company of Avenue Bank withfive banking locations in Nashville); the transaction was valued at some $201.4 million. Avenue Bank will operate as a division of Pinnacle Bank for a few months after which the companies will combine operations.

EXECUTIVES

President And Ceo, M. Terry Turner, age 64, $784,700 total compensation

Evp And Chief Administrative Officer, Hugh M. Queener, age 64, $376,700 total compensation

Evp And Senior Lending Officer; Manager Client Advisory Group Nashville, J. Edward (Ed) White, age 70, $145,000 total compensation

Evp And Director Assocaite And Client Experience, Joanne B. Jackson, age 63, $117,000 total compensation

Cfo, Harold R. Carpenter, age 61, $376,700 total compensation

Svp And Manager Trust And Investment Advisory, Robert Newman

President Pinnacle Knoxville, Mike DiStefano

Chief Credit Officer; President Pinnacle Knoxville, J. Harvey White, $283,800 total compensation

Evp And Manager Pinnacle Asset Management, Gary Collier

Svp And Senior Credit Officer Real Estate, Mike Hendren

Svp And Senior Credit Officer, Tim Huestis
Svp And Cio, Randy Withrow
President And Ceo Pnfp Capital Markets, Roger Osborne
Svp And Manager Residential Mortgage Services, Ross Kinney
Evp And Area Executive Rutherford County, Bill Jones
Chief Investment Officer, Mac Johnston
Svp Small Business Banking, Chip Higgins
Evp And Financial Advisor, Jerry Hampton
President Pinnacle Memphis, Damon Bell
Senior Vice President And Financial Advisor In Nashville, Lynn Kendrick
Senior Vice President, Scott Mccabe
Senior Vice President, Kay Mcalister
Vice President, Tyane Powell
Senior Vice President, Kevin Marchetti
Senior Vice President Mortgage Advisor, Jeff Anderson
Senior Vice President Financial Advisor, Lynn Lassiter
Senior Vice President, Michael G Lindseth
Senior Vice President, Steve Horn
Senior Vice President, Eric Kruse
Senior Vice President, Gail Outland
Senior Vice President, Larry Trabue
Senior Vice President, Mary Smith
Senior Vice President, Doug Daugherty
Senior Vice President, Steve Uebelhor
Senior Vice President Mortgage Advisor, Chris Maultsby
Senior Vice President, Doug Nall
Senior Vice President, Sarah Teague
Senior Vice President, Kirk Garrett
Senior Vice President Financial Advisor, David Ligon
Senior Vice President, Ken Warren
Senior Vice President, Natalie Readett
Svp And Mortgage Advisor, Laurel Mckenzie
Senior Vice President, Rob Masengill
Credit Advisor Vice President Sba, Pamela Holmes
Sr Vice President, Tina Hoke
Senior Vice President, Pam Pedrick
Senior Vice President, William Diehl
Senior Vice President Financial Advisor, Kim Ciukowski
Vice President Automotive Finance, Jeff Rhodes
Svp Mortgage Advisor, Luciano Scala
Chief People Officer, Rachel West
Vice President, Shelly Donohoo
Senior Vice President, Todd Carter
Srvp; Mortgage Advisor, Scott Ractliffe
Svp Mortgage Advisor, Deon Ducey
Svp And Office Leader, Sherrie Hicks
Vice President Compliance And Community Development, Carla Jarrell
Executive Vice President And Chief Financial Officerand#8230, Alan Haefele
Senior Vice President, Sherry McHaffie
Senior Vice President And Financial Adviser In Commercial Real Estate, Thomas Vester
Senior Vice President, Robert Denovo
Senior Vice President Financial Advisor, Keely Ritchie
Senior Vice President, Allison Jones
Vice President Of Training And Development, Eddie Alford
Senior Vice President Trust And Investment Advisor, Keith B Davis
Senior Vice President Financial Advisor, Stacey Richards
Senior Vice President, Amy Charles
Vice President Treasury Management Advisor, Jondra Settle
Senior Vice President, Bryan Bean
Vice President, Gary Green
Senior Vice President And Financial Advisor, Samuel King
Vice President Financial Advisor, Robert Sutton

Senior Vice President, Chris Rippy
Senior Vice President, Nathan Matheson
Senior Vice President And Portfolio Manager, Christopher Bricker
Senior Vice President And Financial Advisor, Ashley Preskenis
Senior Vice President And Financial Advisor, Nancy Benskin
Senior Vice President Credit Advisor, Stacey Fantom
Svp Credit Advisor, Kendria Northcutt
Svp And Learning And Development Manager, Summer Yeiser
Senior Vice President, Sam King
Senior Vice President, Tom Dozier
Senior Vice President, Gina Scott
Senior Vice President And Trust Officer, Scott Lindsey
Senior Vice President, Ron Stinson
Senior Vice President Financial Advisor, Tim Bewley
Senior Vice President, Jason Reierson
Senior Vice President, Jeffery Mcgruder
Senior Vice President Financial Advisor, Josh Hopkins
Executive Vice President, Kent Cleaver
Senior Vice President, Jodi Scruggs
Senior Vice President, Lisa Baskette
Svp Mortgage Advisor, Bridget Mounger
Vice President, Bob Stimson
Executive Vice President, Phil Stevenson
Sr. Vp Mortgage Advisor, Sharon Church
Senior Vice President, Cooper Samuels
Senior Vice President Financial Advisor, Amy Campbell
Senior Vice President, Diane Jones
Vice President: Treasury Management Advisor, Joy Bowen
Cmb Senior Vice President, Jeff Tucker
Senior Vice President Mortgage Advisor, Clint Porter
Senior Vice President, Andy Wright
Senior Vice President Credit Advisor, Katherine Graham
Senior Vice President, Ryan Murphy
Ctfa Senior Vice President Financial Advisor, Steve Scott
Senior Vice President, Bob Lawhon
Senior Vice President Mortgage Advisor, Becky Fiedler
Senior Vice President, Debbie Morgan
Senior Vice President, Jeff East
Svp And Manager Loan Review, Dianne Porter
Senior Vice President Financial Advisor, Cameron Puckett
Senior Vice President, Jimmy Moncrief
Evp And Music And Entertainment Director, Andy Moats
Senior Vice President, Dan Neumann
Senior Vice President Mortgage Advisor, Todd Flynn
Vice President, Cheryl Plummer
Senior Vice President, Donna Edwards
Senior Vice President, Glenn Layne
Senior Vice President Commercial Banking, Scott Williams
Svp Group Banking Manager, Lucy Daugherty
Svp Financial Advisory, Richard Harris
Senior Vice President Financial Advisor, Debbie Indermuehle
Vp Sba Business Development Officer, Janet Matthew
Vice President, Rick Lalance
Senior Vice President Financial Advisor, Mj Isham
Mortgage Adv Sor Vice President, Debbie Del Corro
Senior Vice President, Jamie Hare
Executive Vice President Director Of Client Services, Andy Boyer
Senior Vice President Financial Advisor, Danny Hester

Svp Fice Leader, Michael Colyer
Credit Advisor Svp, Jana Luellen
Senior Vice President, Rene Jennings
Senior Vice President Financial Advisor, Bob Johnson
Senior Vice President Credit Advisor, Warren Jackson
Senior Vice President Human Resources Manager, Sonja Stanley
Evp And Nc Eastern Region President, Mark Carlton
Vice President Office Leader, Shyrl Wood
Senior Vice President, Regina Jennings
Evp And Banking Operations Manager, Pat Pritchard
Svp Communications Strategist, Alisha Boger
Vice President Financial Advisor, Joe Yochim
Senior Vice President Commercial Banking, Jeff Hendrick
Senior Vice President Credit Advisor, April Heath
Senior Vice President Financial Advisor, Helen Ballentine
Senior Vice President City Executive, Jon Greenlee
Senior Vice President Financial Advisor, Henry Caldwell
Svp Mortgage Advisor, Donna Elliott
Senior Vice President, Larry Davis
Vice President Financial Advisor, Matt Robinson
Senior Vice President Commercial Real Estate, Ryan Jones
Auditors: Crowe LLP

LOCATIONS

HQ: Pinnacle Financial Partners Inc
150 Third Avenue South, Suite 900, Nashville, TN 37201
Phone: 615 744-3700
Web: www.pnfp.com

PRODUCTS/OPERATIONS

2014 Revenue

	% of total
Interest Income	80
Non-interest Income	20
Total	**100**

Selected Subsidiaries

Pinnacle Advisory Services Inc.
Pinnacle Credit Enhancement Holdings Inc.
Pinnacle National Bank
  Miller & Loughry Inc. (dba Miller Loughry Beach)
  PFP Title Company
  Pinnacle Community Development Corporation
  Pinnacle Nashville Real Estate Inc.
  Pinnacle Rutherford Real Estate Inc.
  Pinnacle Rutherford Towers Inc.
  Pinnacle Service Company Inc.
PNFP Insurance Inc.

COMPETITORS

BB&T	Regions Financial
Bank of America	SunTrust
Fifth Third	U.S. Bancorp
First Horizon	

HISTORICAL FINANCIALS

Company Type: Public

Income Statement   FYE: December 31

	ASSETS ($ mil.)	NET INCOME ($ mil.)	INCOME AS % OF ASSETS	EMPLOYEES
12/19	27,805	400	1.4%	2,487
12/18	25,031	359	1.4%	2,297
12/17	22,205	173	0.8%	2,132
12/16	11,194	127	1.1%	1,180
12/15	8,715	95	1.1%	1,065
Annual Growth	**33.6%**	**43.1%**	—	**23.6%**

2019 Year-End Financials

Debt ratio: 2.69%   No. of shares (mil.): 76
Return on equity: 9.63%   Dividends
Cash ($ mil.): 526   Yield: 1.0%
Current ratio: —   Payout: 12.3%
Long-term debt ($ mil.): —   Market value ($ mil.): 4,900

	STOCK PRICE ($) FY Close	P/E High/Low		PER SHARE ($) Earnings	Dividends	Book Value
12/19	64.00	12	9	5.22	0.64	56.89
12/18	46.10	15	9	4.64	0.58	51.18
12/17	66.30	26	21	2.70	0.56	47.70
12/16	69.30	24	15	2.91	0.56	32.28
12/15	51.36	22	14	2.52	0.48	28.25
Annual Growth	5.7%	—	—	20.0%	7.5%	19.1%

Pioneer Natural Resources Co

Pioneer Natural Resources Company explores for and produces oil gas and NGLs in the Permian Basin of West Texas. With some 680000 net acres containing proved reserves of 1136 million barrels of oil equivalent this independent energy company is one the biggest energy producers in the Permian Basin. Pioneer's production comes mostly from its Spraberry/Wolfcamp oil field The company reports around 5961 net producing wells. Additionally the company owns interests in 11 gas processing plants including the related gathering systems.. Its major customers include Sunoco Logistics Partners Occidental Energy Marketing and Plains Marketing.

HISTORY

The 1997 merger of MESA and Parker & Parsley moved quickly to pull itself out of the dry hole created by its own debt and the industry's late-1990s dropoff. Parker & Parsley began in 1962 as a partnership between geologist Howard Parker and engineer Joe Parsley. In 1977 it began drilling wells in West Texas. Southmark a Dallas real estate firm bought the company in 1984; in 1989 management purchased it from Southmark. The company went public in 1991.

T. Boone Pickens founded Petroleum Exploration in 1956. In 1964 Petroleum Exploration and Pickens' Canadian holding Altair Oil and Gas merged as MESA and went public. With gas prices declining in the 1990s MESA began selling assets. Pickens resigned as CEO in 1996.

Richard Rainwater took control of MESA and then merged the firm into Parker & Parsley which became Pioneer Natural Resources. The company moved into Argentina when it paid $1.2 billion for Calgary-based Chauvco Resources in 1997.

To streamline operations and reduce debt Pioneer cut its workforce and in 1999 it sold 400 US properties to Prize Energy.

Pioneer sold oil and gas properties in Texas and Canada in 1999 and moved to consolidate its Permian Basin operations by offering to buy out limited partners. It also drilled its first deepwater well in the Gulf of Mexico and acquired additional properties in Argentina.

In 2000 the company disposed of noncore natural gas assets in Louisiana New Mexico and Oklahoma. At the same time it boosted its deepwater holdings in the Gulf of Mexico. The next year the company announced successful test drilling in its prospects in Argentina and South Africa.

Pioneer also announced an oil discovery in 2001 on its Ozona Deep prospect in the Gulf of Mexico indicating another deepwater production asset for the company. In 2003 Pioneer teamed up with Woodside Energy to conduct a joint exploration program in the shallow-water Texas Shelf region of the Gulf of Mexico.

In 2005 Pioneer sold the Martin Creek Conroy Black and Lookout Butte oil and gas properties in Canada to Ketch Resources for $199 million. That year it acquired oil and gas assets in the Permian Basin and South Texas for a total of $177 million.

Realigning its exploration portfolio the company sold all of its operations in Argentina in 2006 to Apache for $675 million. That year Pioneer sold the bulk of its Gulf of Mexico oil and gas assets to Marubeni Offshore Production for $1.3 billion. In 2007 the company sold its Canadian subsidiary to Abu Dhabi National Energy Company PJSC for $540 million.

In 2009 the company reported a sharp dip in revenues as the result of global recession's impact on lowering commodity prices and weakening demand for oil and gas. Although Pioneer made about $89 million of property acquisitions (primarily in its South Texas shale) in 2009 financial conditions prompted the company to sell non-core assets to pay down debt. It sold its assets in the Spraberry field in West Texas to a subsidiary Pioneer Southwest Energy Partners for $168.2 million. It also sold its Mississippi and shelf properties in the Gulf of Mexico for about $24 million.

To gain capital to develop its US shale properties in 2010 Pioneer entered a joint venture selling a 45% stake in its southern Texas gas field Eagle Ford Shale to the USA subsidiary of India's Reliance Industries for $1.15 billion.

It has exited higher risk foreign ventures. To raise cash and to focus on its core North American assets in 2011 the company sold its Tunisia-based exploration and production units to OMV for $866 million. It also sold its South African business in 2012 for $38 million.

Securing an industrial sands business to support its hydraulic fracturing drilling activities in the Wolfcamp Shale and Barnett Shale plays in Texas in 2012 Pioneer acquired Carmeuse Industrial Sands for $297 million.

In 2013 it sold its Barnett Shale assets in North Texas to an undisclosed private party for cash proceeds of $155 million.

In 2013 Pioneer Natural Resources sold a 40% stake in 207000 net acres leased in Wolfcamp Shale play (Permian Basin) in the southern portion of the Spraberry Trend Area Field to Sinochem for $1.7 billion.

In 2013 Pioneer Natural Resources Company acquired 52%-owned Pioneer Southwest Energy Partners L.P. which then became a wholly-owned subsidiary of Pioneer Natural Resources USA through a stock-for-unit exchange.

EXECUTIVES

Evp Corporate And Operations, Mark S. Berg, age 61, $437,846 total compensation
President Ceo And Director, Timothy L. (Tim) Dove, age 63, $672,808 total compensation
Evp And Cfo, Richard P. (Rich) Dealy, age 53, $555,131 total compensation
Evp Business Development And Geoscience, Chris J. Cheatwood, age 59, $440,615 total compensation
Vp Marketing, John C. Distaso
Evp Permian Operations, J. D. Hall, age 54
Evp Stat Wat And Corporate Engineering, Kenneth H. Sheffield, age 59
Vp And Cio, Stephanie D. Stewart, age 51
Vice President Of Corporate Reserves, Kerry Scott
Vice President Operations Accounting, Teri Pender
Vp Corporate Drilling And Completions, Steve Mamerow
Senior Vice President Operations And Engineering, Ken Sheffield
Executive Vice President Operations, J D Hall
Vice President Information Technology, Glen Paris
Vice President Administration And Risk Management, Larry Paulsen
Vice President Environmental, Bonnie Black
Vice President Communications And Government Relations, Thaddeus Owens
Vice President Legal And Chief Compliance Officer, Ron Schindler
Vice President Permian Land, David Sutter
Vice President Investor Relations, Neal H Shah
Vice President, Neal Shah
Vice President Sales Marketing And Logistics, Michael Siragusa
Chairman, Scott D. Sheffield, age 67
Board Member, Frank Risch
Board Member, Mona Sutphen
Board Member, Larry Grillot
Auditors: Ernst & Young LLP

LOCATIONS

HQ: Pioneer Natural Resources Co
777 Hidden Ridge, Irving, TX 75038
Phone: 972 444-9001   **Fax:** 972 969-3587
Web: www.pxd.com

PRODUCTS/OPERATIONS

2018 sales

	$ mil.	% of total
Oil & gas	4,991	52
Sales of purchased oil & gas	4,388	45
Interest & Other	38	-
Derivative gains	(292)	-
Gain from disposition of assets	290	3
Total	**9,415**	**100**

COMPETITORS

Apache	Energen
Chevron	Exxon Mobil
Concho	Kinder Morgan
EOG	Occidental Chemical
Encana Oil & Gas (USA) Inc.	

HISTORICAL FINANCIALS

Company Type: Public

Income Statement

FYE: December 31

	REVENUE ($ mil.)	NET INCOME ($ mil.)	NET PROFIT MARGIN	EMPLOYEES
12/19	9,304	756	8.1%	2,323
12/18	9,415	978	10.4%	3,177
12/17	5,455	833	15.3%	3,836
12/16	3,824	(556)	—	3,604
12/15	4,825	(273)	—	3,732
Annual Growth	17.8%	—	—	(11.2%)

2019 Year-End Financials

Debt ratio: 12.01%
Return on equity: 6.24%
Cash ($ mil.): 631
Current ratio: 0.88
Long-term debt ($ mil.): 1,839

No. of shares (mil.): 165
Dividends
  Yield: 0.7%
  Payout: 26.6%
Market value ($ mil.): 25,059

	STOCK PRICE ($) FY Close	P/E High/Low	PER SHARE ($) Earnings	Dividends	Book Value
12/19	151.37	39 26	4.50	1.20	73.21
12/18	131.52	37 21	5.70	0.32	71.45
12/17	172.85	41 26	4.85	0.08	66.24
12/16	180.07	— —	(3.34)	0.08	61.30
12/15	125.38	— —	(1.83)	0.08	56.02
Annual Growth	4.8%	— —	—	96.8%	6.9%

Plains All American Pipeline LP

Plains All American Pipeline owns and operates an extensive network of midstream energy infrastructure that provides logistical and transportation services to oil and gas companies in the US and Canada. With some 35 million barrels of active above-ground storage capacity the limited partnership is engaged in the transportation storage terminaling and marketing of crude oil natural gas liquids (NGLs) and natural gas products. Its portfolio includes some 18535 miles of pipelines and a fleet of approximately 825 trailers some 50 barges and around 20 transport tugs. Plains All American Pipeline has a presence in the major energy market hubs in US and Canada. Its prominent customers include Marathon Petroleum ExxonMobil and Phillips 66. Majority of the company's sales were generated in the US.

Operations

Plains All American Pipeline reports in three business segments? Supply and Logistics Transportation and Facilities.

Accounting for some 95% of the company's revenue the Supply and Logistics segment makes its money by purchasing crude oil and NGLs from producers and refiners and transporting and reselling these products downstream in the major energy market hubs or directly to end-users in North America. The segment reports some 16 million barrels of crude oil storage capacity.

The Transportation segment charges fees for transporting energy products through a combination of tariffs and pipeline capacity agreements.

It also invests in transportation assets for equity earnings. Similarly the Facilities business the company's third segment charges fees for the use of its storage terminaling and throughput services. Together these two segments make up the remaining around 5% of the company's revenue.

Geographic Reach

Based in Texas Plains All American Pipeline has an extensive network of transportation terminaling and storage facilities at the major energy market hubs in the US including California Louisiana Oklahoma and Texas as well as in the Alberta and Saskatchewan provinces of Canada.

The US accounted for more than 80% of company's total revenue and Canada accounted for the rest.

Sales and Marketing

Plains All American Pipeline collects around 35% of its annual revenue from just three customers: Marathon Petroleum ExxonMobil and Phillips 66. A loss of the customers may significantly affect the company's revenue.

Financial Performance

In the last five years Plains All American Pipeline saw its revenue achieve inconsistent growth though it increased by 45% since 2015.

In 2019 revenue declined by 1% to $33.7 billion mainly due to a $547 million fall in the Supply and Logistics segment.

Net income for the year of $2.18 billion was relatively flat compared to net income of $2.22 billion recognized for 2018. The significant items impacting income for the comparative period included favorable results from Supply and Logistics Transportation segments offset by the unfavorable impact of the mark-to-market of certain derivative instruments net loss on asset sales and asset impairments of $28 million and higher depreciation and amortization expense.

The company's cash and cash equivalents increased by $16 million ending 2019 with $82 million on hand. Cash from operations generated $2.5 billion while cash used in investing activities was $1.8 billion. Financing activities used a further $720 million. Main cash uses for the year were for additions to property plant and equipment and repayment of senior notes.

Strategy

The company's principal business strategy is to provide competitive and efficient midstream transportation terminalling storage processing fractionation and supply and logistics services to producers refiners and other customers. Toward this end it endeavors to address regional supply and demand imbalances for crude oil and NGL in the United States and Canada by combining the strategic location and capabilities of its transportation terminalling storage processing and fractionation assets with its supply logistics and distribution expertise. It believes the successful execution of this strategy will enable it to generate sustainable earnings and cash flow.

The company intends to execute this strategy by: Focusing on operational excellence continuous improvement and running a safe reliable environmentally and socially responsible operation; Enabling North American production growth and creating access to multiple markets through the development and implementation of timely and competitive solutions that support evolving crude oil and NGL needs in the midstream transporta-

tion and infrastructure sector in North America and are well positioned to benefit from long-term industry trends and opportunities; Using its transportation terminalling storage processing and fractionation assets in conjunction with its commercial capabilities to provide flexibility and deliver value chain solutions to its customers capture market opportunities address physical market imbalances mitigate inherent risks and sustain or increase margins; Optimizing its operations and portfolio of assets by delivering industry leading reliability and efficiency in order to attract business opportunities and enhance returns; and Pursuing a balanced long-term financial strategy that is focused on enhancing financial flexibility by making disciplined capital allocation decisions that sustain or increase distributable cash flow and returns while sustainably increasing cash returned to equity holders over time.

Company Background

Goodyear Tire & Rubber subsidiary Celeron began designing the All American Pipeline in 1983 to bring heavy crude from California to the less-regulated refineries of Texas. It was completed in 1987 at a cost of $1.6 billion but by 1991 only a trickle of oil was dribbling through as it struggled to attract customers. Prospects began to look up in the mid-1990s when Chevron Texaco and Exxon signed contracts to use the pipeline beginning in 1996. Plains Resources bought the pipeline but then sold off a 43% stake in an IPO.

In 2012 to boost its midstream assets the company bought BP's Canadian NGL operations for $1.7 billion.

HISTORY

Goodyear Tire & Rubber subsidiary Celeron began designing the All American Pipeline in 1983 to bring heavy crude from California to the less-regulated refineries of Texas. It was completed in 1987 at a cost of $1.6 billion but by 1991 only a trickle of oil was dribbling through. The pipeline did not post a profit until 1994.

Prospects began to look up in the mid-1990s when Chevron Texaco and Exxon signed contracts to use the pipeline beginning in 1996. Plains Resources bought the pipeline in 1998 for $400 million; the company created Plains All American Pipeline to acquire and operate the pipeline then sold off a 43% stake in an IPO that raised $260 million. The next year Plains All American bought Scurlock Permian (2300 miles of pipeline) from Marathon Ashland Petroleum for $141 million and the West Texas Gathering System from Chevron (450 miles) for $36 million.

Shareholders sued Plains All American in 1999 after it reported that an employee's unauthorized crude-oil trading would cost the company about $160 million. (In 2000 the company agreed to pay $29.5 million plus interest to settle the cases.)

Plains All American announced plans to mothball all but the California section of the All American Pipeline in 1999. The next year El Paso Energy bought the 1088-mile section of the pipeline that was to be deactivated plus the right to run fiber-optic cable over the entire pipeline for $129 million.

Targeting Canada as part of its expansion strategy in 2001 Plains All American bought about 450 miles of oil pipeline and other midstream assets from Murphy Oil and acquired crude oil and LPG marketing firm CANPET Energy. Also that year Plains Resources reduced its stake in Plains All American from 44% to 29%.

In 2002 the company acquired the Wapella Pipeline System located in southeastern Saskatchewan and southwestern Manitoba. It also bought Shell Pipeline's West Texas crude oil pipeline assets for $315 million. Plains All American Pipeline continued its acquisition streak in 2003 with the acquisitions of the South Saskatchewan pipeline system in Canada and the ArkLaTex pipeline system originating in Sabine Texas.

In 2004 Plains All American continued its expansion with the acquisition of interests in the Capline and Capwood pipeline systems from Shell Pipeline Company for about $158 million. It also acquired the crude oil and pipeline operations of Link Energy for about $330 million and the Cal Ven pipeline system from Unocal Canada for about $19 million. Later that year the company continued its system expansion by acquiring the Schaefferstown propane storage facility from Koch Hydrocarbon for about $32 million.

In 2006 the company acquired Andrews Petroleum and Lone Star Trucking for $205 million. It also acquired stakes in a number of Gulf Coast crude oil pipeline systems from BP Oil Pipeline Company for $133.5 million. That year in a major deal the company acquired Pacific Energy Partners for $2.4 billion moving the company beyond crude oil and into the refined products and barging businesses.

In 2007 Plains All American Pipeline acquired LPG storage facilities in Arizona and South Carolina.

In 2008 Occidental Petroleum acquired 10% of the company's general partner boosting the amount of new capital available for Plains All American Pipeline to pay down debt and make further acquisitions. It also boosted its Canadian midstream assets with the acquisition of Rainbow Pipeline (crude oil gathering and pipelines).

In 2012 to boost its midstream assets the company bought BP's Canadian NGL operation.

EXECUTIVES

President And Coo, Harry N. Pefanis, age 63, $300,000 total compensation

Evp, Phillip D. (Phil) Kramer, $250,000 total compensation

Chairman And Ceo, Greg L. Armstrong, age 62, $375,000 total compensation

Evp Operations And Business Development, Mark J. Gorman

Evp General Counsel And Secretary, Richard K. McGee, age 59

Svp Technology Process And Risk Management, Alfred A. (Al) Lindseth

Evp And Cfo, Al Swanson, age 56, $250,000 total compensation

President Plains Midstream Canada, W. David (Dave) Duckett, $276,666 total compensation

Evp Commercial Activities, John P. von Berg, $250,000 total compensation

Evp, John R. Rutherford, $62,500 total compensation

President Pngs, Dean Liollio, age 62

Executive Vice President Commercial Activities, John Berg

Vice President Marketing And Business Development, John Tsouvalas

Vice President West Coast Pipelines, Dominic Ferrari

Svp Operations Plains Midstream Canada, Scott Sill

Vp Pipeline Business Development, Sam Brown

Evp Operations And Engineering, Daniel Nerbonne

Vice President Lease Supply, Robert Sanford

Vp And Treasurer, Sharon Spurlin

Vice President Refinery Supply, Jim Fryfogle

Senior Vice President Commercial Activities, John VonBerg

Vice President Lpg Commercial Plains Midstream Canada, James Shelford

Vice President Commercial, Todd Brown

Evp, Phil Kramer

Executive Vice President Of Operations, Neil Mckellar

Board Member, Christopher Temple

Assistant Treasurer, Michael McLaughlin

Board Member, Gary Petersen

Board Member, Bobby Shackouls

Auditors: PricewaterhouseCoopers LLP

LOCATIONS

HQ: Plains All American Pipeline LP
333 Clay Street, Suite 1600, Houston, TX 77002
Phone: 713 646-4100
Web: www.plainsallamerican.com

2018 Sales

	$ mil.	% of total
US	28,362	83
Canada	5,693	17
Total	**34,055**	**100**

PRODUCTS/OPERATIONS

2018 Sales

	$ mil.	% of total
Supply and logistics	32,819	96
Transportation	648	2
Facilities	588	2
Total	**34,055**	**100**

COMPETITORS

Buckeye Partners	ONEOK
Enbridge	Sunoco Logistics
Enterprise Products	TransMontaigne
NGL Energy Partners	

HISTORICAL FINANCIALS

Company Type: Public

Income Statement — FYE: December 31

	REVENUE ($ mil.)	NET INCOME ($ mil.)	NET PROFIT MARGIN	EMPLOYEES
12/19	33,669	2,171	6.4%	5,000
12/18	34,055	2,216	6.5%	4,900
12/17	26,223	856	3.3%	4,850
12/16	20,182	726	3.6%	5,100
12/15	23,152	903	3.9%	5,400
Annual Growth	9.8%	24.5%	—	(1.9%)

2019 Year-End Financials

Debt ratio: 33.79%
Return on equity: —
Cash ($ mil.): 45
Current ratio: 0.92
Long-term debt ($ mil.): 9,187
No. of shares (mil.): 728
Dividends
Yield: 7.5%
Payout: 52.0%
Market value ($ mil.): 13,388

	STOCK PRICE ($) FY Close	P/E High/Low		PER SHARE ($) Earnings	Dividends	Book Value
12/19	18.39	9	6	2.65	1.38	17.94
12/18	20.04	10	7	2.71	1.20	16.52
12/17	20.64	34	19	0.95	1.95	15.11
12/16	32.29	78	36	0.43	2.65	13.09
12/15	23.10	67	24	0.77	2.76	19.82
Annual Growth	(5.5%)	—		36.2%	(15.9%)	(2.5%)

Plains GP Holdings LP

EXECUTIVES

MBR, Greg L Armstrong
Pres, Harry N Pefanis
Exec V Pres, Phil D Kramer
Dir, Roy I Lamoreaux
Cfo, Al Swanson
Exec V Pres-MBR, Mark J Gorman
Coordinator, Afton Shelton
Compliance Staff, Chrystah Carter
Vice-President Engineering, Dan Nerbonne
Safety Manager, Beckey Evans
Accounting Staff, Jake Ragle
Auditors: PricewaterhouseCoopers LLP

LOCATIONS

HQ: Plains GP Holdings LP
333 Clay Street, Suite 1600, Houston, TX 77002
Phone: 713 646-4100
Web: www.plainsallamerican.com

HISTORICAL FINANCIALS

Company Type: Public

Income Statement — FYE: December 31

	REVENUE ($ mil.)	NET INCOME ($ mil.)	NET PROFIT MARGIN	EMPLOYEES
12/19	33,669	331	1.0%	5,000
12/18	34,055	334	1.0%	4,900
12/17	26,223	(731)	—	4,850
12/16	20,182	94	0.5%	5,100
12/15	23,152	118	0.5%	5,400
Annual Growth	9.8%	29.4%	—	(1.9%)

2019 Year-End Financials

Debt ratio: 32.34%
Return on equity: —
Cash ($ mil.): 47
Current ratio: 0.92
Long-term debt ($ mil.): 9,187
No. of shares (mil.): 797
Dividends
Yield: 7.2%
Payout: 70.4%
Market value ($ mil.): 15,112

	STOCK PRICE ($) FY Close	P/E High/Low		PER SHARE ($) Earnings	Dividends	Book Value
12/19	18.95	13	9	1.96	1.38	2.70
12/18	20.10	13	9	2.11	1.20	2.32
12/17	21.95	—	—	(5.03)	1.95	2.13
12/16	34.68	38	6	0.94	0.00	2.38
12/15	9.45	21	5	1.41	0.00	7.74
Annual Growth	19.0%	—		8.6%	—	(23.1%)

PNC Financial Services Group (The)

The PNC Financial Services Group is one of the country's largest providers of diversified financial services with total assets of more than $410 billion and total deposits exceeding $288 billion. Its flagship PNC Bank subsidiary operates branches across the Mid-Atlantic Midwest and Southeast. In addition to retail and corporate banking which together account for over 80% of total revenue the company offers personal and institutional asset management. PNC Financial Services also has an economic interest of over 20% in BlackRock the world's largest public investment management firm.

Operations

PNC Financial Services operates through four core business segments: Retail Banking Corporate & Institutional Banking Asset Management Group and BlackRock.

It generates over 45% of total revenue from its Retail Banking business which includes traditional deposit and lending products while another 35% comes from its Corporate & Institutional Banking business.

The Asset Management Group segment and the company's investment in money manager BlackRock together account for just more than 10% of revenue.

Broken down further PNC Financial Services generates about 65% of its total revenue from interest income — primarily loan interest — while most of the rest comes from asset management corporate service and consumer service fees (together accounting for over 35% of revenue).

Geographic Reach

Pennsylvania-based PNC Financial Services serves markets in US states across the Mid-Atlantic Midwest and Southeast. Its leading markets for home equity and residential real estate loans include Pennsylvania New Jersey Ohio Maryland and Illinois.

Financial Performance

Excluding 2016 PNC Financial Services' revenue has been on an upward trend.

In 2019 the company reported record revenue of $17.8 billion up 4% from the prior year. All of the company's segments had a hand on the increase.

Net income increased slightly that year rising 1% to $5.4 billion.

Cash at the end of 2019 was $5.1 billion a decrease of $547 million from the prior year. Cash from operations contributed $7.4 billion to the coffers while investing activities used $25 billion mainly for purchases of securities. Financing activities provided another $17.1 billion.

Strategy

PNC is focused on the fundamentals of growing customers loans deposits and revenue and improving profitability while investing for the future and managing risk expenses and capital.

The company's strategic priorities consist of: Expanding its leading banking franchise to new markets and digital platforms; Deepening customer relationships by delivering a superior banking experience and financial solutions; and Leveraging technology to innovate and enhance products services security and processes.

In late 2019 The PNC Financial Services Group and M Financial Group announced the signing of an insurance marketing and service agreement to offer insurance solutions advice and service to PNC's Wealth ManagementÂ® and Hawthorn PNC Family WealthÂ® clients. Through this strategic relationship M Financial will offer differentiated insurance products and support to PNC's clients through a team that is dedicated to PNC. As M Financial's only firmwide relationship PNC will leverage this distribution network by working exclusively with a group of M Member Firms that solely focus on insurance.

Mergers and Acquisitions

In 2019 PNC Financial Services acquired Ambassador Financial Group (now PNC FIG Advisory) which provides balance sheet management investment banking and capital markets services to banks insurance companies and other financial institutions. The group which will integrate into PNC's Capital Markets Financial Institutions Group will expand its advisory services in mergers and acquisitions and capital markets for financial institutions.

Company Background

First National Bank of Pittsburgh (PNC Financial Services' predecessor) opened in 1863. In 1913 the bank consolidated with Second National Bank of Pittsburgh and in 1921 it bought Peoples National. The company changed its name to Pittsburgh National after a long expansion following the Depression and WWII. In 1983 Pittsburgh National merged with Provident National of Philadelphia (founded by Quakers in 1865) to form PNC Corp. The union combined Pittsburgh National's corporate lending strength with Provident's money management and trust operations.

EXECUTIVES

Evp And Chief Credit Officer, Michael J. Hannon
Chairman President And Ceo, William S. (Bill) Demchak, $1,100,000 total compensation
Evp Chief Investment Officer And Treasurer, E. William (Bill) Parsley, $588,462 total compensation
Evp And Cfo, Robert Q. (Rob) Reilly, $500,000 total compensation
Evp And Head Corporate And Institutional Banking, Michael P. Lyons, $700,000 total compensation
Evp And Head Technology And Operations, Steven C. (Steve) Van Wyk, $500,000 total compensation
Evp And Head Asset Management Group, Orlando C. Esposito
Evp; Head Retail Banking, Karen L. Larrimer
Evp And Chief Risk Officer, Joseph E. Rockey
Evp General Counsel And Head Regulatory And Government Affairs, Gregory B. Jordan
Evp And General Auditor, Stacy M. Juchno
Evp And Chief Human Resources Officer, Vicki C. Henn
Evp And Director Investor Relations, Bryan K. Gill
Executive Vice President, James Graham
Vice President Marketing, Richard Kopchinski
Avp And Manager Media Relations, Alan Aldinger
Executive Vice President And Manager Public Finance Group, George Whitmer
Vice President And Executive Client Relation Manager, Mary Taylor
Vice President, Evans S Duncan
Executive Vice President Treasury Management Sales Manager, Lynn Aleksov

Senior Vice President, Glen Siniawski
Data Quality Data Stewart Vice President, Katherine Novak
Vice President Private Banking Team Director Wealth Management, Susan Houlihan
Vice President, Casey Brill
Evp, Lakhbir Lamba
Senior Vice President, Samuel Patterson
Senior Vice President Real Estate Solutions, David Spotts
Senior Vice President Corporate Banking Department, Craig Pinder
Vp And Sr. Manager Corporate Marketing, Catherine Bernard
Vice President Product Development, Mark Vizza
Vice President Marketing, Michael Ball
Vice President Business Banking, Cindy Klingler
Svp Corporate Marketing, Dresdyn Hefferen
Executive Vice President Information Technology, Mary Baker
Senior Vice President Of Corporate Communications, Mike Moll
Assistant Vice President Of Marketing, Tony Morante
Vice President, Graham Coover
Executive Vice President Chief Model Risk Officer, Elizabeth Mays
Vice President Product Delivery Treasury Management, Clayton Keefer
Vice President Branch Manager, April Thompson
Vice President Senior Product Manager, Benjamin Degroot
Vice President Direct Marketing Program Manager, Nancy Oconnor
Vice President, Dirk Elston
Senior Vice President Credit Executive, Tej Panjwani
Executive Vice President And Head Of Retail Distribution Pnc Bank, Todd Barnhart
Vice President Senior Organizational Devel, Vicki Brown
Senior Vice President, Marc D McAndrew
Seniorvp Enterpriseservices, Cheryl Barruso
Vice President Marketing, Andrew Chuba
Vice President, Roderick Hirsch
Chief Vice President Marketing, Brian Gray
Vice President Human Resources, Patty Toney
Vice President Sales And Marketing, Cheryl Kraft
Regional Manager Senior Vice President, Alisa Winslow
Vice President Community Development Banking Consultant, Maria Thompson
Vice President, Deborah Madigan
Senior Vice President Corporate Banking, Troy Brown
Vice President Application Systems Manager, John Mayberry
Vice President Senior Relationship Manager, Moises Almonte
Executive Vice President Business Banking Market Manager, Don Stock
Vice President, Maureen Seskey
Vice President, Mike Hrycenko
Senior Vice President, Hayden Lutz
Executive Vice President, Kim D Mcneil
Senior Vice President Corporate Banking, Bob Spencer
Vice President, Diane Richert
Senior Vice President, Mark Kiskorna
Vice President Finance, William Betty
Vice President Senior Operations Manager, Debbie Hernandez
Senior Vice President, Elena Ray
Vp And Economist, Kurt Rankin
Senior Vice President Of Real Estate Finance, Bill G Lashbrook
Executive Vice President Market Manager, Sandy Zimmerman
Vice President Information Technology Pnc Arcs, Gary Baratta

Avp Lob Risk Specialist Senior, Tyler Moser
Vice President, Sharon Rigsby
Vice President, Chris Goecke
Vice President Commercial Relationship Manager, John Leighton
Assistant Vice President Financial Advisor, Nathan Garcia
Senior Vice President Corporate Banking, Nancy Halwig
Senior Vice President, Lola Kayler
Vice President Business Banking Relationship Manager, Brandon Mooney
Vice President Human Resources, Brenda Thomas
Vice President Retail Banking, Nadeem Khaliq
Vp Senior Portfolio Manager, Judy Zhu
Vice President, Denise Peak
Vice President Branch Manager Iii, Kandace Helbing
Vice President Business Banking, Dan Smith
Assistant Vice President, Shirley Carew
Vice President, Kimberly Jackson
Senior Vice President Southeast Region Manager, Adam Gordon
Vice President, Brent Mathews
Vice President Senior Underwriter, Meredith Heavner
Vice President, Tarek Soubra
Senior Vice President, Maureen Dunne
Assistant Vice President, Marie Rivera
Svp Sales Pnc Investments, Susan Poller-newman
Vice President, Karen Cameron
Business Banker Vice President, Nadira Mohammed
Vice President And Senior Portfolio Manager, William Francis
Vice President Senior Underwriting Manager, Karlie Hubbard
Client Advisor Assistant Vice President, Josh Campbell
Vp Senior Marketing Manager, Chris Trice
Assistant Vice President, Lyndsey Guggenmos
Vice President Pnc Dealer Finance, Susan Pauels
Senior Vice President, Scott Fowler
Senior Account Manager And Vice President, Lori Hinson
Senior Vice President, Ilan Yehros
Senior Vice President, Tim Gleeson
Vice President, Susan Blake
Vice President Application Systems Manager, Andrew Haky
Vp Branch Manager, Merelyn Baczor
Vice President Investment Advisor, Bruce Worthen
Vice President Strategic Sourcing, Robert Boone
Avp Business Banking Officer, Justin Breitenstein
Vice President Analytics And Portfolio Management, Vinod Mandre
Assistant Vice President Investor Reporting Manager, Matt Atwood
Senior Vice President, John Puhatch
Executive Vice President Chief Data Officer, Denise Letcher
Vp Integration, Erica Trnavsky
Svp Strategic Initiatives, James Defoggia
Svp And Chief Procurement Officer, James Vespoli
Vp Solutions Architect, Ravi Annaswamy
Vp Corporate Communications, Kelly Amen
Senior Vice President Business Banking Sales, Marc Huey
Vp And Director Executive Communications, Shawn Bannon
Vp And Senior Manager Media Relations, Zoraya Suarez
Avp; Manager Technology, John Pfirrman
Svp System Director Call Center And Incentive Compensation Technology, Stephen Chauvin
Vp Project Portfolio Business Applications, Tom Nicklas
Senior Vice President Sales Pnc Investments, Georgia Gertz
Svp Business Banking Sales, Todd Olsen

Senior Vice President Market Manager, Joe Krzywicki
Assistant Vice President Finance Technology Software Engineer Lead, Leo Hoopes
Vice President, Tracy Bernstein
Senior Vice President And Market Manager, Mike Pacyna
Vice President Dealer Finance, David Keebler
Vice President Multifamily Finance, Kevin Justh
Vice President Trust Real Estate Advisor, Barbara Roettker
Executive Vice President And Managing Executive Institutional Asset Management Group, Alistair Jessiman
Vice President Asset Resolution Team, Jennifer Callen
Vice President, Elaine Smith
Vp Technology Governance Enterprise Project Management Office, Melanie Maurer Westwood
Avp; Manager Collections System, Andrea ellis Colella
Vice President And Senior Trust Officer, Gary Windmiller
Vice President And Relationship Strategist, Susan Fisher
Senior Vice President Real Estate Credit Officer, Charles Simms
Healthcare Business Banker Vice President, Jerry Hudson
Assistant Vice President Banking Advisor, Heather Wachenheimer
Auditors: PricewaterhouseCoopers LLP

LOCATIONS

HQ: PNC Financial Services Group (The)
The Tower at PNC Plaza, 300 Fifth Avenue, Pittsburgh, PA 15222-2401
Phone: 412 762-2000 **Fax:** 412 762-5798
Web: www.pnc.com

PRODUCTS/OPERATIONS

2018 Sales

	$ mil.	% of total
Retail Banking	7,750	45
Corporate and Institutional Banking	5,957	35
Asset Management group	1,179	7
BlackRock	935	5
Others	1,311	8
Total	**17,132**	**100**

2018 Sales

	$ mil.	% of total
Interest		
Loans	9,580	48
Investment securities	2,261	11
Other	741	4
Expense	(2861)	-
Non-interest		
Asset management	1,825	9
Corporate services	1,849	9
Consumer services	1,502	8
Service charges on deposits	714	3
Residential mortgage	316	2
Other	1,205	6
Total	**17,132**	**100**

COMPETITORS

Bank of America	JPMorgan Chase
Citigroup	KeyCorp
Citizens Financial Group	M&T Bank
	Sovereign Bank
Fifth Third	TD Bank USA
Harris	U.S. Bancorp
Huntington Bancshares	Wells Fargo

HISTORICAL FINANCIALS

Company Type: Public

Income Statement FYE: December 31

	ASSETS ($ mil.)	NET INCOME ($ mil.)	INCOME AS % OF ASSETS	EMPLOYEES
12/19	410,295	5,369	1.3%	51,918
12/18	382,315	5,301	1.4%	53,063
12/17	380,768	5,338	1.4%	52,906
12/16	366,380	3,903	1.1%	52,006
12/15	358,493	4,106	1.1%	52,513
Annual Growth	**3.4%**	**6.9%**	**—**	**(0.3%)**

2019 Year-End Financials

Debt ratio: 10.70%
Return on equity: 11.07%
Cash ($ mil.): 28,474
Current ratio: —
Long-term debt ($ mil.): —
No. of shares (mil.): 433
Dividends
　Yield: 2.6%
　Payout: 36.8%
Market value ($ mil.): 69,120

	STOCK PRICE ($) FY Close	P/E High/Low	PER SHARE ($) Earnings	Dividends	Book Value
12/19	159.63	14 10	11.39	4.20	113.89
12/18	116.91	15 10	10.71	3.40	104.44
12/17	144.29	14 11	10.36	2.60	100.45
12/16	116.96	16 10	7.30	2.12	94.22
12/15	95.31	13 11	7.39	2.01	88.71
Annual Growth	**13.8%**	**— —**	**11.4%**	**20.2%**	**6.4%**

Popular Inc.

Founded in 1893 Popular is the holding company for Banco Popular de Puerto Rico the largest bank in Puerto Rico with about 175 branches and more than 620 ATMs. In addition to commercial and retail banking services Popular owns subsidiaries that offer vehicle financing and leasing (Popular Auto) insurance (Popular Insurance) financial advisory and brokerage services (Popular Securities) and mortgages (Popular Mortgage). Popular serves a mainly Hispanic customer base on the US mainland through subsidiary Popular Bank which has around 50 branches in New York New Jersey and Florida plus about 120 ATMs. Additionally the company has a handful of branches and about 25 ATMs in the US Virgin Islands.

Operations

Popular operates through two segments: Banco Popular de Puerto Rico and Popular US which comprise the company's banking activities in Puerto Rico and the US respectively. The Puerto Rico operations represent more than 80% of sales and US operations about 15%.

Popular generates the bulk of its revenue from interest income. Around 65% of its total revenue comes from interest on about $27.4 billion in loans while about 15% comes from interest on its investment securities.

Commercial real estate loans make up about 45% of Popular's loan portfolio while residential mortgage loans represent more than 25%. Consumer loans make up more than 20% of the portfolio; the rest of the portfolio comprises lease financing and construction loans.

Popular's other financial services include the insurance agency and reinsurance businesses of

Popular Insurance Popular Insurance V.I. Popular Risk Services and Popular Life Re. BPNA also owns E-LOAN Popular Equipment Finance and Popular Insurance Agency USA. E-LOAN's sole purpose is to provide an online platform to raise deposits for BPNA.

Geographic Reach
Popular operates more than 170 branches in Puerto Rico and around 50 Popular Bank branches in the US the majority of which are leased premises. Popular also has around 620 ATMs in Puerto Rico more than 20 in the US Virgin Islands and about 120 in New York New Jersey and Florida.

Popular's headquarters are in Hato Rey Puerto Rico and it generates more than 80% of revenue in its home country and approximately 15% in the US. Others generate the remaining revenue.

Financial Performance
In 2018 the bank's revenue decreased 5% to $2.5 billion primarily due to lower noninterest income.

The Corporation's net income for the Pyear ended December 31 2019 amounted to $671.1 million compared to a net income of $618.2 million for 2018. The results for the year ended December 31 2018 include a pre-tax gain of $94.6 million resulting from the Termination Agreement with the FDIC previously disclosed; a net income tax benefit of $63.9 million resulting from the impact of the Termination Agreement and the related Tax Closing Agreement and $27.7 million non-cash income tax expense as a result of a reduction in the Corporation's net deferred tax asset related to the Puerto Rico operations due to the reduction in tax rates as a result of an amendment to the Puerto Rico Internal Revenue Code.

Cash held by the company at the end of 2019 decreased by $8.9 million to $394.3 million from $403.3 million in the prior year. Cash provided by operations and financing activities were $705.4 million and $3.5 billion respectively. Cash used for investing activities was $4.2 billion primarily for purchases of investment securities.

Strategy
The use of derivatives is incorporated as part of the corporation's overall interest rate risk management strategy to minimize significant unplanned fluctuations in earnings and cash flows that are caused by interest rate volatility. The Corporation's goal is to manage interest rate sensitivity by modifying the repricing or maturity characteristics of certain balance sheet assets and liabilities so that the net interest income is not materially affected by movements in interest rates. The Corporation uses derivatives in its trading activities to facilitate customer transactions and as a means of risk management. As a result of interest rate fluctuations hedged fixed and variable interest rate assets and liabilities will appreciate or depreciate in fair value.

The Corporation's pension fund investment strategy is to invest in a prudent manner for the exclusive purpose of providing benefits to participants. A well-defined internal structure has been established to develop and implement a risk-controlled investment strategy that is targeted to produce a total return that when combined with BPPR contributions to the fund will maintain the fund's ability to meet all required benefit obligations.

Mergers and Acquisitions
In 2018 Popular acquired Wells Fargo's Puerto Rican auto finance business Reliable for $1.7 billion. The purchase comprises $1.5 billion in retail auto loans and $340 million in commercial loans and makes Popular the undisputed auto loan leader in Puerto Rico.

Company Background
To broaden its target audience beyond the Hispanic community Popular rebranded itself in the US switching its name from "Banco Popular" to "Popular Community Bank". The change which was initially begun in pilot markets in 2010 was completed officially in 2012 when the company changed its name in New York City. In 2018 Popular Community Bank became just Popular Bank.

EXECUTIVES

Chairman President And Ceo, Richard L. Carri n, age 67, $1,453,846 total compensation
Evp Financial And Insurance, Juan O. Guerrero, age 60, $375,000 total compensation
Evp Administration, Eduardo J. Negr n, age 55, $385,000 total compensation
Evp And Coo Popular Community Bank, Manuel Chinea, age 54
Evp Retail Banking, Néstor O. Rivera, age 73, $375,000 total compensation
Evp And Cfo, Carlos J. V zquez, age 61, $700,962 total compensation
Evp And Chief Risk Officer, Lidio V. Soriano, age 51, $519,231 total compensation
President And Ceo, Ignacio lvarez, age 61, $742,500 total compensation
Evp Commercial Credit, Eli S. Sep lveda, age 57, $420,000 total compensation
Evp Individual Credit, Gilberto F. Monz n, age 60
Evp And Chief Legal Officer, Javier D. Ferrer, age 58, $571,154 total compensation
Evp Cto And Chief Digital Officer, Camille Burckhart, age 41
First Vice President, Jorge Roig
Vice President, Michelle Cianchini
Vice President Finance, Iris Reyes
Svp Corporate Communications, Teruca Rullan
Executive Vice President, Liesl A Rodriguez
Senior Vice President, Fabio Garcia
Svp Regulatory Affairs, Fred Teed
First Vp Individual Banking Banco Popular Western Region, Olga Morales
Vice President, Franklyn Vargas
First Vice President Banco Popular Fiduciary Services, Javier Rubio
Senior Vice President Corporate Comptroller, Jorge Garcia
Vice President And Legal Counsel, Angelica Lavergne
First Vice President Business Development Popular Auto, Gladys Molina
First Vice President Marketing And Advertising Popular Auto, Edouard Lafontant
Vice President Information Technology Popular Community Bank, Sanjay Shitole
First Vp Individual Banking Banco Popular Rio Piedras Region, Martiza Mendez
Vice President Area Manager, Julian Herradon
Senior Vice President, David Peters
Vice President Corporate Banking Investor Services Hub, Natalie Claudio
Vice President, Nelson Jorge
Senior Vice President And Division Manager, Oran Bowry
Vice President International Private Banking, David Hitt
Executive Vice President Of Retail Banking And Operations, Nestor Obie

Assistant Vice President And Model Risk Operations Supervisor, Betsy Candelario
Senior Vice President And Manager People Services Division, Douglas Hachenburg
Vice President And Manager Cra Compliance, Vannessa Montes
Auditors: PricewaterhouseCoopers LLP

LOCATIONS

HQ: Popular Inc.
Popular Center Building, 209 Munoz Rivera Avenue, Hato Rey, San Juan, PR 00918
Phone: 787 765-9800
Web: www.popular.com

2018 sales

	% of total
Puerto Rico	82
United States	15
Other	3
Total	**100**

PRODUCTS/OPERATIONS

Sales 2018

	$ mil.	% of total
Interest income:		
Loans	1,645	61
Money market investments	111	4
Investment securities	264	10
Interest Expense	(287.0)	-
Non-interest income:		
Mortgage banking activities	52	2
FDIC loss-share income	94	4
Other non-interest income	520	19
Other	(15.3)	-
Total	**2,387**	**100**

Selected Subsidiaries and Affiliates
Banco Popular de Puerto Rico
  BP Sirenusa International LLC (US)
  Popular Auto Inc.
  Popular Mortgage Inc.
Popular Capital Trust I (US)
Popular Insurance Inc.
Popular International Bank Inc.
  Banco Popular North America (US)
  E-LOAN Inc.
  Equity One Inc.
  Popular Insurance V.I. Inc. (US Virgin Islands)
Popular Life RE
Popular Securities Inc.

COMPETITORS

Bank of America	JPMorgan Chase
Bolivar Banco Venezuela	OFG Bancorp
Citigroup	RBC Financial Group
First BanCorp (Puerto Rico)	Santander BanCorp
	Scotiabank

HISTORICAL FINANCIALS
Company Type: Public

Income Statement
FYE: December 31

	ASSETS ($ mil.)	NET INCOME ($ mil.)	INCOME AS % OF ASSETS	EMPLOYEES
12/19	52,115	671	1.3%	8,560
12/18	47,604	618	1.3%	8,474
12/17	44,277	107	0.2%	7,784
12/16	38,661	216	0.6%	7,828
12/15	35,769	895	2.5%	7,810
Annual Growth	**9.9%**	**(7.0%)**	**—**	**2.3%**

2019 Year-End Financials

Debt ratio: 1.31%	No. of shares (mil.): 95
Return on equity: 11.72%	Dividends
Cash ($ mil.): 21,339	Yield: 2.0%
Current ratio: —	Payout: 17.4%
Long-term debt ($ mil.): —	Market value ($ mil.): 5,616

	STOCK PRICE ($)	P/E		PER SHARE ($)		
	FY Close	High/Low	Earnings	Dividends	Book Value	
12/19	58.75	9 7	6.88	1.20	62.94	
12/18	47.22	9 6	6.06	1.00	54.38	
12/17	35.49	45 32	1.02	1.00	50.00	
12/16	43.82	22 11	2.06	0.60	50.08	
12/15	28.34	4 3	8.65	0.30	49.27	
Annual Growth	20.0%	— —	(5.6%)	41.4%	6.3%	

PPG Industries Inc

Thanks to its extensive range of paints and coatings you won't catch PPG Industries painting itself into a corner. The company?s Performance and Industrial coatings offerings include paints stains adhesives and sealants for automotive aerospace marine architectural and industrial applications. Well-known paint brands include Glidden Olympic and PPG Pittsburg Paints. Other products include packaging coatings used for the protection and decoration of metal cans closures and plastic tubes. PPG's specialty coatings are used in lighting and lens materials and label substrates. In recent years the company has shed its fiber glass and flat glass businesses to focus on its core coatings operations.

HISTORY

After the failure of his first two plate-glass manufacturing plants John Ford persuaded former railroad superintendent John Pitcairn to invest $200000 in a third factory in 1883 in Creighton Pennsylvania. The enterprise Pittsburgh Plate Glass (PPG) became the first commercially successful US plate-glass factory.

Ford left in 1896 after Pitcairn established a company distribution system replacing glass jobbers. Ford went on to found a predecessor of competitor Libbey-Owens-Ford (now owned by glassmaker Pilkington).

Pitcairn built a soda ash plant in 1899 bought a Milwaukee paint company the following year and began producing window glass in 1908. Pitcairn died in 1916 leaving his stock to his sons.

Strong automobile and construction markets in the early 20th century increased demand for the company's products. In 1924 PPG revolutionized glass production with the introduction of a straight-line conveyor manufacturing method. In the 1930s and 1940s PPG successfully promoted structural glass for use in the commercial construction industry.

PPG was listed on the NYSE in 1945. In 1952 it started making fiberglass and in 1968 the company adopted its present name.

Vincent Sarni (CEO 1984-93) recognized that 85% of the company's sales were to the maturing construction and automobile industries. Sarni decided to move the company into growing industries such as electronics.

In 1986 PPG spent $154 million on acquisitions including the medical electronics units of Litton Industries and Honeywell. It acquired the medical technology business of Allegheny International in 1987 and bought Casco Nobel a coatings distributor and the Olympic and Lucite paint lines from Clorox in 1989.

The company which owned one-third of Dutch fiberglass producer Silenka BV acquired the rest in 1991. In 1992 PPG acquired a silica plant in the Netherlands its first in Europe. Two years later it acquired the European automotive coatings business of Netherlands-based Akzo Nobel.

In the 1990s PPG backed away from Sarni's earlier strategies for greater diversification and unloaded a number of high-tech businesses. The firm refocused on its core coatings glass and chemicals operations. PPG acquired Matthews Paints a leading maker of paints for outdoor signs and the refinish coating business of Lilly Industries in 1995.

The company bolstered its chemical operations in 1997 with the addition of France's Sipsy Chime Fine. That same year President and COO Raymond LeBoeuf took over as CEO. In 1998 PPG sold its European flat and automotive glass business to Belgium-based Glaverbel. Acquisitions that year included Australia-based Orica's technical coatings unit and the US paint operations (Porter Paints) of Akzo Nobel.

In 1999 PPG expanded its European coatings business with the purchase of Belgium-based Sigma Coatings' commercial transport coatings unit and Akzo Nobel's aircraft coatings and sealants company PRC-DeSoto International. That year PPG also bought Imperial Chemical Industries' Germany-based coatings business for large commercial vehicles and its US-based auto refinish and industrial coatings businesses. PPG's acquisition spree continued in 2000 with architectural coating maker Monarch Paint.

Early in the new decade PPG suffered from flat or declining earnings from existing operations. Amid falling sales and lower prices for chemicals and glass PPG began to cut jobs and closed some facilities. Still the company recorded its first loss in more than 10 years in 2002 and its second straight year of declining sales.

Like many manufacturers in its industry PPG has been exposed to potentially costly asbestos litigation mainly because of its 50% stake in the bankrupt Pittsburgh Corning a joint venture with Corning that made insulation with asbestos. In 2002 PPG and its insurers agreed to pay roughly $2.7 billion to settle its asbestos claims.

LeBoeuf retired in 2005. He was replaced by president and COO Charles Bunch who had joined the company in 1979 and worked up through the ranks of first the finance department and then the coatings operations.

In 2008 PPG acquired SigmaKalon for $3 billion. SigmaKalon was among the top 10 paint manufacturers in the world and did business almost entirely outside the US. The company now operates as PPG's Architectural Coatings segment. That same year PPG sold its auto glass business to private equity group Kohlberg & Company which set the unit up as a stand-alone company called Pittsburgh Glass Works. PPG received $330 million plus a 40% interest in the company.

In 2011 PPG acquired Equa-Chlor a producer of chlorine caustic soda and muriatic acid for $27 million. Equa-Chlor produces about 220 tons of chlorine per day. In addition to its products PPG also bought Equa-Chlor's distribution system which includes a railcar fleet it integrated into its own. The deal for the Washington state-based company bolsters PPG's chlor-alkali business in the Northwest US and expands its overall supply chain.

As part of its push to expand in emerging markets in 2011 PPG formed a joint venture with an India-based company Harsha Exito Engineering Private to produce fiber glass reinforcement products.

It made two foreign acquisitions to expand its international operations in 2011. First it bought the business assets of Ducol Coatings South Africa Ltd. which had served as an importer and distributor of PPG's automotive refinish products in South Africa since 2003. PPG also expanded its joint venture with India-based Asian Paints (India's largest coatings company) and created a second 50-50 JV in 2012. The deals boosts PPG's position in the Chinese and Asian packaging coatings industry part of its global strategy to expand into emerging regions.

During 2012 the company made four acquisitions related to its coatings business for a total of $288 million including US-based Spraylat Corp. Denmark based Dyrup A/S and the coatings business of Ecuador-based Colpisa Colombiana de Pinturas.

Expanding PPG's architectural coatings business in the US Canada and the Caribbean in 2013 it bought Azko Nobel's North American Decorative Paints business for $1.05 billion.

The company divested flat glass and fiber glass operations in transactions in 2016 and 2017. The sale of flat glass and European fiber glass businesses and the company?s ownership in two Asian fiber glass joint ventures brought in more than $1 billion of cash.

EXECUTIVES

Chairman And Ceo, Michael H. McGarry, age 62, $1,100,000 total compensation
Evp, Viktoras R. Sekmakas, age 59, $646,667 total compensation
Svp Architectural Coatings; President Ppg Emea, Jean-Marie Greindl, age 57
Vp Science And Technology And Cto, David S. Bem
President Ppg Asia Pacific And Vp Protective And Marine Coatings Asia Pacific, Michael Horton
Svp Industrial Coatings, Timothy M. Knavish, age 54, $438,333 total compensation
Vp Coatings Services; President Metokote, Jeffrey J. Oravitz
Chief Commercial Officer Ppg Comex, Henrik Bergstr ¶m, age 49
Svp And Cfo, Vincent J. Morales, age 55
Vp Information Technology, Christopher R. Caruso
Svp Protective And Marine Coatings, Ramaparasad (Ram) Vadlamannati, age 57
Vice President Global Supply Management, Radhika Batra
Vice President And Treasurer, John Jankowski
Vice President Fiber Glass, Kevin McDonald
Senior Vice President General Counsel Secretary, Anne Foulkes
Vice President Automotive Refinish Europe Middle East And Asia, Jerome Zamblera
National Account Manager, William Dunster
Global Vice President Aerospace, Daniel Korte
Senior Vice President Automotive Coatings, Rebecca Liebert
Vice President And Chief Digital Officer, Devashish Saxena
Board Member, Martin Richenhagen
Board Member, Gary Heminger
Auditors: PricewaterhouseCoopers LLP

LOCATIONS

HQ: PPG Industries Inc
One PPG Place, Pittsburgh, PA 15272
Phone: 412 434-3131
Web: www.ppg.com

2016 Sales

	$ mil.	% of total
United States and Canada	6,595	45
Europe Middle East and Africa	4,304	29
Asia Pacific	2,431	16
Latin America	1,421	10
Total	**14,751**	**100**

PRODUCTS/OPERATIONS

2016 Sales

	$ mil.	% of total
Performance Coatings	8,580	58
Industrial Coatings	5,690	39
Glass	481	3
Total	**14,751**	**100**

Selected Products

Performance Coatings
  Aerospace coatings
  Architectural coatings (Lucite paints Olympic stains)
  Refinish
Industrial Coatings
  Automotive coatings chemicals adhesives and sealants
  Industrial coatings
  Packaging coatings (food and beverage containers)
Commodity Chemicals
  Calcium hypochlorite
  Caustic soda
  Chlorine
  Chlorine derivatives
  Phosgene derivatives
Optical and Specialty Materials
  Optical products (Transitions variable-tint lenses)
  Silica products
Glass
  Aircraft transparencies
  Coated glass
  Continuous-strand fiberglass
  Flat glass

COMPETITORS

3M	KANSAI PAINT CO. LTD.
Akzo Nobel	Kelly-Moore
Axalta Coating Systems	Nippon Paint
BASF Coatings AG	Nippon Sheet Glass
BEHR	Pilkington Group
Benjamin Moore	RPM International
Dow Chemical	Sherwin-Williams
Ferro	

HISTORICAL FINANCIALS

Company Type: Public

Income Statement

FYE: December 31

	REVENUE ($ mil.)	NET INCOME ($ mil.)	NET PROFIT MARGIN	EMPLOYEES
12/19	15,146	1,243	8.2%	27,700
12/18	15,374	1,341	8.7%	27,800
12/17	14,750	1,591	10.8%	47,200
12/16	14,751	877	5.9%	47,000
12/15	15,330	1,406	9.2%	46,600
Annual Growth	**(0.3%)**	**(3.0%)**	**—**	**(12.2%)**

2019 Year-End Financials

Debt ratio: 28.53%
Return on equity: 25.08%
Cash ($ mil.): 1,216
Current ratio: 1.41
Long-term debt ($ mil.): 4,539

No. of shares (mil.): 235
Dividends
  Yield: 1.4%
  Payout: 38.9%
Market value ($ mil.): 31,461

	STOCK PRICE ($) FY Close	P/E High/Low	PER SHARE ($) Earnings	Dividends	Book Value
12/19	133.49	25 19	5.22	1.98	22.42
12/18	102.23	22 17	5.47	1.86	19.63
12/17	116.82	19 15	6.17	1.70	22.13
12/16	94.76	35 27	3.28	1.56	18.75
12/15	98.82	46 16	5.14	1.42	18.67
Annual Growth	**7.8%**	**—**	**0.4%**	**8.8%**	**4.7%**

PPL Corp

PPL Corporation is one of the largest utility companies in the world delivering electricity to more than 10 million customers through its regulated utility subsidiaries in Kentucky Pennsylvania and Virginia as well as in the UK. It also delivers natural gas to customers in Kentucky Operating as Western Power Distribution in the UK It holds four of the UK's 14 Ofgem power distribution licenses. The company has more than 8000 MW of electric generating capacity about 220000 miles of electric lines and gas transmission mains and storage fields. PPL was incorporated in 1994.

Operations

PPL has three segments: Kentucky Regulated UK Regulated and Pennsylvania Regulated. While the UK and Pennsylvania each bring in about 30% of total revenue Kentucky is the highest earner bringing in about 40%.

The Kentucky segment includes Louisville Gas and Electric which provides electric services to approximately 420000 customers in Louisville and adjacent areas in Kentucky and natural gas service to almost 330000 customers. It also comprises of Kentucky Utility which serves around 560000 customers in Kentucky Virginia and Tennessee.

The UK segment which includes primarily Western Power Distribution's (WPD) regulated electricity distribution operation serves almost 8 million end users in south Wales and southwest and central England. It holds the four of the UK's 14 Ofgem regulated distribution operator network (DNO) licenses.

The Pennsylvania segment (PPL Electric) delivers electricity to 1.4 million customers in eastern and central Pennsylvania.

Geographic Reach

Headquartered in Allentown Pennsylvania PPL delivers electricity to customers in Kentucky Pennsylvania Virginia and the UK and natural gas to customers in Kentucky.

The US accounts for more than 70% of company's revenue; the rest comes from the UK.

Sales and Marketing

PPL Corporation serves more than 10 million customers in the United States and the United Kingdom.

Financial Performance

Operating in a highly regulated sector PPL's revenue has been decreasing since 2015 until 2017. The company's revenue spiked up in 2018 but slightly decreased in 2019. Since 2015 the company's revenue increased by 1% compared to $7.8 billion in 2019.

In fiscal 2019 the company's sales decreased by $16 million to $7.74 billion compared to $7.79 billion in 2018. The decreased was primarily from its UK business which fell its sales 4% while PPL's US operation grew 2%.

Net income dropped by 4% to $1.7 billion due to lower income taxes.

PPL's coffers grew $193 million during 2019 ending the year at $836 million. It generated $2.4 billion from its operations and $836 million from its financing activities. Investing activities used $3.1 billion. PPL's main cash uses in 2019 were capital expenditures dividends and long-term debt repayments.

Strategy

Faced with falling revenue and technological disruptions that are rapidly changing the energy grid PPL Corporation is embarking on a long-term core strategy of sustainable production.

Strong cash flows put PPL in a strong investment position. As the world considers climate change and as PPL looks to the future the company will continue to take steps to minimize its impact on the environment transform the way the company generate electricity and incorporate new lower-emitting technology. It is aiming to cut CO_2 emissions 80% from 2010 levels by 2050.

HISTORY

PPL's wires reach back to Lehigh Coal & Navigation which was formed in 1822 to mine Pennsylvania coal and build a canal to deliver it to Philadelphia. Heavy industry and steel mills flourished in the Lehigh Valley and Thomas Edison formed small electric companies to serve the area in the early 1880s. Rivals soon followed and by 1900 there were 64 companies in what would become PPL's territory.

EXECUTIVES

President And Coo Lg&e And Ku Energy, Paul W. Thompson
Chairman And Ceo Lg&e And Ku Energy, Victor A. Staffieri, age 64, $811,220 total compensation
Chief Executive Western Power Distribution, Robert A. Symons, age 66, $741,127 total compensation
Chairman President And Ceo, William H. Spence, age 62, $1,154,712 total compensation
President Ppl Electric Utilities, Gregory N. Dudkin, age 62, $524,143 total compensation
Svp And Cfo, Vincent (Vince) Sorgi, age 48, $524,134 total compensation
Vice President Administration And Inside Sales And Marketing Coordinator, Barb Sipe
Vice President Transmission And Substations, Stephanie Raymond
Vice President Marketing, Linda Miller
Vice President And Controller, Stephen Breininger
Vice President, John Barbera
Vice President And Chief Human Resources Officer, Thomas Lynch
Vice President, Bill Riebling
Corporate Audit Services Vp, Marty Urban
Vice President Finance And Regulatory Affairs And Controller, Marlene Beers
Treas, Stephen C May
Board Member, Steven G Elliott
Board Member, Venkata Madabhushi
Board Member, John Conway
Board Member, Rodney Adkins
Assistant Treasurer, Tadd J Henninger

Assistant Secretary Board Services, Diane Koch
Board Member, Phoebe Wood
Auditors: DELOITTE & TOUCHE LLP

LOCATIONS

HQ: PPL Corp
Two North Ninth Street, Allentown, PA 18101-1179
Phone: 610 774-5151
Web: www.pplweb.com

2015 Sales

	$ mil.	% of total
US	5,259	68
UK	2,410	32
Total	**7,669**	**100**

PRODUCTS/OPERATIONS

2018 Sales

	$ mil.	% of total
Kentucky Regulated	3,214	42
Pennsylvania Regulated	2,277	29
UK Regulated	2,268	29
Corporate and other	26	-
Total	**7,785**	**100**

Selected Subsidiaries

PPL Development Corporation (acquisition and
   divestiture activities)
PPL Electric Utilities Corporation (electricity
   distribution)
PPL Energy Supply (nonregulated operations)
   PPL EnergyPlus LLC (wholesale and retail energy
   marketing)
   PPL Generation LLC (electricity generation)
   PPL Montana LLC (electricity generation)
   PPL Global LLC (international utility operations)
   Western Power Distribution Holdings Limited
   (formerly WPD Holdings UK electricity distribution)
PPL Services Corporation (shared services for PPL Corp.
   and other subsidiaries)

COMPETITORS

ABB	Green Mountain Energy
AEP	HC Energ a
Avangrid	Maine & Maritimes
Canadian Utilities	Midwest Generation
Centrica	Ontario Power
Con Edison	Generation
Constellation Energy	Orange & Rockland
Group	Utilities
Covanta	Pepco Holdings
Delmarva Power	Public Service
Dominion Energy	Enterprise Group
Duke Energy	Scottish and Southern
Duquesne Light	Energy
Holdings	South Jersey
EnergySolve	Industries
Exelon	Southern Company
FirstEnergy	TransAlta

HISTORICAL FINANCIALS

Company Type: Public

Income Statement

FYE: December 31

	REVENUE ($ mil.)	NET INCOME ($ mil.)	NET PROFIT MARGIN	EMPLOYEES
12/19	7,769	1,746	22.5%	12,280
12/18	7,785	1,827	23.5%	12,444
12/17	7,447	1,128	15.1%	12,512
12/16	7,517	1,902	25.3%	12,689
12/15	7,669	682	8.9%	12,799
Annual Growth	**0.3%**	**26.5%**	**—**	**(1.0%)**

2019 Year-End Financials

Debt ratio: 50.45%
Return on equity: 14.17%
Cash ($ mil.): 815
Current ratio: 0.56
Long-term debt ($ mil.): 20,721

No. of shares (mil.): 767
Dividends
   Yield: 4.6%
   Payout: 67.0%
Market value ($ mil.): 27,528

	STOCK PRICE ($) FY Close	P/E High/Low	PER SHARE ($) Earnings	Dividends	Book Value
12/19	35.88	15 12	2.37	1.65	16.93
12/18	28.33	12 10	2.58	1.64	16.18
12/17	30.95	24 19	1.64	1.58	15.52
12/16	34.05	14 11	2.79	1.52	14.56
12/15	34.13	36 29	1.01	1.50	14.72
Annual Growth	**1.3%**	**— —**	**23.8%**	**2.4%**	**3.6%**

PRECISION CASTPARTS CORP.

Precision Castparts Corp. (PCC) is a maker of investment castings and forged and fastener products that have applications in industries from aerospace and energy markets. Products include metal components for aircraft engines and industrial gas turbines (IGT). The company also makes metal forgings including seamless pipe used in power plants downhole casings and tubing pipe for oil and gas production. PCC is also a leading manufacturer of fasteners and fastening systems used in the aerospace construction and machinery industries. It has locations in North America Europe and Asia. The majority of PCC's sales are from purchase orders. The company is a subsidiary of Berkshire Hathaway.

HISTORY

The history of Precision Castparts Corp. (PCC) is not as precise as its castings. The Oregon Saw Company was founded in 1949 and sold in 1953; its buyer wanted neither the future PCC nor a power tools unit so the two became Omark Industries. In 1956 a buyer purchased the power tool business but wasn't interested in castings; that operation was spun off as Precision Castparts Corp.

In the early 1950s a group of Oregon Saw's casting employees developed a process for producing parts as large as 60 inches by use of investment casting making products that rivaled the strength of forged and machined parts at a fraction of the cost. After a two-year search they landed their first aerospace customer — Air Research Corp. — with many to follow. The higher operating temperatures generated by aircraft engines led the company to buy a vacuum furnace in 1959 to fabricate parts that could tolerate greater heat; two more vacuum furnaces were added and sales vaulted toward $10 million by 1967. PCC went public in 1968 and continued to grow. In 1976 the company acquired Centaur Cast Alloys (small investment castings UK) to make parts for the European aerospace industry. By that time General Electric (GE) and Pratt & Whitney accounted for most of PCC's business. Edward Cooley who had masterminded the company's growth since incorporation forged ahead with plans to double production capacity.

In 1980 the airline industry crashed but PCC's sales held at about $90 million. Structural airplane products soon picked up and in 1984 the company bought two titanium foundries in France. To diversify it added TRW's cast airfoils (used in aircraft engines and industrial gas turbines) division in 1986. That acquisition renamed PCC Airfoils increased PCC's annual sales by about 80%; sales reached $443 million by 1989.

The company broadened its offerings again in 1991 when it acquired Advanced Forming Technology which made small complex metal-injection molded parts used in everything from adding machines to military ordnance. The early 1990s recession hit the airline industry and sales dropped. Cooley retired as chairman in 1994 and GE veteran William McCormick replaced him. The next year PCC acquired Quamco Inc. (industrial tools and machines). In 1996 PCC flowed into the fluid management market with the acquisition of NEWFLO for about $300 million.

In 1997 PCC spent $437 million to acquire seven more companies that helped boost sales 75% from 1996 levels. The next year it purchased four metalworking companies that served industries other than aerospace. Having reduced dependence on sales to the aerospace industry to just over 50% PCC began consolidating operations and closing plants to reduce costs.

The company continued to diversify through acquisitions in 1999 but it also expanded its aerospace operations with the purchase of Wyman-Gordon a leading maker of advanced metal forgings for the aerospace market. PCC's 2000 acquisitions included the aerospace division of United Engineering Forgings and Germany-based Convey Engineering (heavy-duty valves). The next year the company bought the assets of Netherlands-based Wouter Witzel and the US's Drop Dies and Forgings Company (renamed Wyman-Gordon Cleveland). In 2002 PCC bought the rest of Western Australian Specialty Alloys (casting and forging alloys) for $27.6 million in cash and PCC shares.

In 2003 Precision Castparts' PCC Structurals unit reached a $400 million agreement with Rolls-Royce to supply large titanium and steel castings. That year the company acquired SPS Technologies a producer of fasteners and other metal components for the aerospace automotive and industrial markets. In 2004 subsidiary SPS Aerospace Fasteners signed a four-year deal with Airbus worth about $72 million to supply collars nuts studs and titanium pins to Airbus plants across Europe.

PCC acquired Air Industries Corporation in early 2005. In 2006 PCC bought Special Metals Corporation (SMC) a maker of nickel alloys and super alloys for $295 million in cash and the assumption of $245 million in SMC debt. PCC intended to use SMC's product as raw materials for its own aircraft engine components. SMC also served the automotive chemical and power generation industries.

Later in 2006 PCC bought Shur-Lok Corporation a manufacturer of aerospace fasteners for about $110 million. The acquisition combined with the 2005 purchase of Air Industries Corporation helped to further PCC's desire to grow its airframe fasteners business.

Early in 2007 PCC completed the purchase of GSC a leading maker of aluminum and steel structural investment casting for the aerospace energy and medical markets. It also acquired

Cherry Aerospace which expanded its fastener products portfolio.

In 2009 the company acquired Carlton Forge Works which makes aircraft engines for Boeing and Airbus; California-based Arcturus Manufacturing (hammer forging operations) was included in the transaction. PCC also picked up Airdrome Holdings (fluid fittings) Fatigue Technology (cold expansion technology) and Hackney Ladish (forged pipe fittings) in 2009.

In late summer 2011 PPC purchased Primus International a maker of complex metal industrial parts and assemblies. Its products (machined aluminum and titanium components used in aircraft wings fuselages and engine-related assemblies) cater to Boeing Airbus and other aerospace OEMs. The $900 million deal furthered the company's commitment to the global aerospace industry. In a similar vein the company obtained Unison Engine Components (operating as Tru-Form Rings) from GE Aviation in mid-2011. Tru-Form made flash-welded and cold-rolled rings with jet engine as well as gas turbine applications.

PCC also acquired RathGibson which makes tubing for the oil and gas chemical/petrochemical power-generation and other markets in 2012.

To expand both its Fasteners and Forged Products segments PCC acquired the aerostructures and industrial products businesses of Héroux-Devtek for about CAD$300 million (about $295.5 million) in 2012. Among other benefits the acquisition expanded the company's product line for such OEMs as Lockheed Bombardier and Gulfstream. PCC also inked a deal to purchase the Synchronous Aerospace Group business of private investment firm Littlejohn & Co. in late 2012.

EXECUTIVES

Evp And Cfo, Shawn R. Hagel, $687,500 total compensation
Chairman And Ceo, Mark Donegan, $1,585,000 total compensation
Svp And President Airframe Products, Alan J. (Al) Power
Evp And President Wyman-gordon, Andrew V. Masterman, $592,500 total compensation
Vp And Cio, Byron J. Gaddis
Evp, Steven G. (Steve) Hackett, $708,750 total compensation
Svp And General Counsel, Ruth A. Beyer, $569,000 total compensation
President Aerostructures Products, Joseph I. Snowden, $356,347 total compensation
Svp And President Pcc Airfoils, John P. O'Neill
Svp And President Timet And Special Metals, James R. Pieron
Vice President, Mark Ellis
Vice President, Geoffrey Hawkes
Senior Vice President, Russell Gould
Senior Vice President, Ross Lienhart
Executive Vice President, David Norris
Secretary, Russell Pattee
Auditors: DELOITTE & TOUCHE LLP PORTLAN

LOCATIONS

HQ: PRECISION CASTPARTS CORP.
4650 SW MCDAM AVE STE 300, PORTLAND, OR 97239
Phone: 503 946-4800
Web: WWW.PRECAST.COM

PRODUCTS/OPERATIONS

Selected Products and Services

Fasteners
Advanced forming technology
E/One (for the disposal of residential sanitary waste)
J&L fiber services (for pulp and paper industry)
PCC Precision Tool Group
SPS aerospace fasteners (for commercial/military aircraft)
SPS engineered fasteners (high strength for automotive and construction applications)
Forged products
Special Metals Corporation
Wyman-Gordon Forgings
Investment Cast Products
PCC Airfoils (high-temperature blades and vanes)
PCC Structurals (structural investment castings)
Specialty materials and alloys (alloys waxes and metal processing for investment casting)

COMPETITORS

ATI Ladish	Hitachi Metals
Allegheny Technologies	Kennametal
Arconic	LISI
Carpenter Technology	Mettis Aerospace
Chicago Rivet	SOURIAU PA&E
Crane Co.	Swagelok
Curtiss-Wright	Teleflex
ESCO	ThyssenKrupp
Farwest Steel	United Technologies
Corporation	Universal Stainless
Federal Screw Works	V & M Tubes (USA)
Georg Fischer	Volvo Aero
Haynes International	

HISTORICAL FINANCIALS

Company Type: Private

Income Statement   FYE: January 3

	REVENUE ($ mil.)	NET INCOME ($ mil.)	NET PROFIT MARGIN	EMPLOYEES
01/16*	7,002	817	11.7%	30,106
03/15	10,005	1,533	15.3%	—
03/14	9,616	1,784	18.6%	—
03/13	8,377	1,429	17.1%	—
Annual Growth	(5.8%)	(17.0%)	—	—

*Fiscal year change

Preferred Bank (Los Angeles, CA)

Preferred Bank wants to be the bank of choice of Chinese-Americans in Southern California. Employing a multilingual staff the bank provides international banking services to companies doing business in the Asia/Pacific region. It targets middle-market businesses typically manufacturing service distribution and real estate firms as well as entrepreneurs professionals and high-net-worth individuals through about a dozen branches in Los Angeles Orange and San Francisco Counties. Preferred Bank offers standard deposit products such as checking accounts savings money market and NOW accounts. Specialized services include private banking and international trade finance.

Geographic Reach
Preferred Bank markets its services in half a dozen Southern Californian counties: Los Angeles Orange Riverside San Bernardino San Francisco and Ventura.

Financial Performance
In 2013 Preferred Bank reported about $72 million in revenue up just more than 10% from the prior year. The increase was solely from interest income as non-interest income (a very small part of overall revenue anyway) fell more than 40%. The company saw growth in its loan portfolio that year as well as overall deposit growth. Net income fell 20% to $19 million; the decline was primarily related to a boost in net income for 2012 because of a $20 million income tax benefit (compared to income tax expense of $12 million in 2013).

Strategy
Historically the company was focused on the Chinese-American market and although it continues to cater to that clientele most of its current customer base is from the diversified mainstream market.

EXECUTIVES

Evp And Cfo, Edward J. Czajka
President And Coo, Wellington Chen, age 60
Chairman And Ceo, Li Yu, age 79
Senior Vice President, Erika Chi
Senior Vice President, Ted Hsu
Vice President Commercial Real Esate Loan Officer, Sally Chang
Vice President, William Ko
Senior Vice President, Jim Belanic
Senior Vice President, John C Stipanov
Vice President, Debbie White
Vice President, Barbara Gordon
Vice President Real Estate Industries Group, Greg Hahn
Senior Vice President And Corporate Banking Manager, Christina Ching
Vice President, Craig Miller
Avp Senior Bsa Analyst, Joshua Barron
Executive Vice President Norcal, Alice Huang
Senior Vice President, Pamela Lau
Vice President, Sofia Huang
Vice President Financial Reporting, Brandon George
First Vice President, Johnny Hsu
Vice President Lending, Luey Couto
Senior Vice President, Ann Cheung
Vice President, Wayne Chow
Vice President Human Resources Manager, Karen Cangey
Vp Marketing, Louie Couto
Senior Vice President Internal Audit, Jenny Own
Senior Vice President And Controller, Debbie Kong
Vp Internal Audit Manager, Carlo Garcia
Vice President Assistant Compliance Officer, Florence Hsu
Vice President, Joyce Gillette
Vice President, Silvia Espinoza
First Vice President, Philip Wong
Vice President Product Manager, John Wong
Vice President And Portfolio Manager, Welmer Jurado
Senior Vice President, Bill Oberholzer
Executive Vice President Chief Credit Officer, Jonathan Sigal
Assistant Vice President Operations Officer, Patty Artavia
Avp, Xiao Wells
First Vice President, Jean Ou
Vice President Relationship Manager, Eddie Ong

Vice President Financial Intelligence Unit
  Manager, Krishan Sirimane
Vice President Portfolio Manager, Judy Chang
Senior Vice President Head Of International
  Banking And Commercial Industrial Lending,
  Samuel Leung
Vice President, Clara Moore
Vice President, Winny Lo
Senior Vice President, Ann J Cheung
Senior Vice President Operations, Muna Issa
Vice President And Operations Officer, Valerie
  Feng
Vice President Relationship Manager, Julie Orr
Vice President Core Banking And Product
  Development, Jonathan Hover
Board Member, Clark Hsu
Fvp Treasurer, Eric Chen
Auditors: Crowe LLP

LOCATIONS

HQ: Preferred Bank (Los Angeles, CA)
  601 S. Figueroa Street, 48th Floor, Los Angeles, CA
  90017
Phone: 213 891-1188
Web: www.preferredbank.com

PRODUCTS/OPERATIONS

2015 Sales

	mil$ mil.	% of total
Interest income		
Loans and leases	88	90
Investment securities available for sale	6	6
Federal funds sold	0	-
Non-interest income		
Fees and service charges on deposit accounts	1	1
Trade finance income	1	2
BOLI income	0	-
Other income	0	1
Total	**98**	**100**

COMPETITORS

Bank of America	City National
Bank of the West	East West Bancorp
Broadway Financial	Far East National Bank
Cathay General Bancorp	Hanmi Financial
Citigroup	MUFG Americas Holdings

HISTORICAL FINANCIALS

Company Type: Public

Income Statement   FYE: December 31

	ASSETS ($ mil.)	NET INCOME ($ mil.)	INCOME AS % OF ASSETS	EMPLOYEES
12/19	4,628	78	1.7%	279
12/18	4,216	70	1.7%	263
12/17	3,769	43	1.2%	238
12/16	3,221	36	1.1%	218
12/15	2,598	29	1.1%	205
Annual Growth	15.5%	27.4%	—	8.0%

2019 Year-End Financials

Debt ratio: 2.14%
Return on equity: 17.68%
Cash ($ mil.): 498
Current ratio: —
Long-term debt ($ mil.): —

No. of shares (mil.): 14
Dividends
  Yield: 2.0%
  Payout: 24.1%
Market value ($ mil.): 897

	STOCK PRICE ($) FY Close	P/E High/Low	PER SHARE ($) Earnings	Dividends	Book Value
12/19	60.09	12 8	5.16	1.20	31.47
12/18	43.35	15 9	4.64	0.94	27.22
12/17	58.78	22 16	2.96	0.76	23.48
12/16	52.42	20 10	2.56	0.60	20.94
12/15	33.02	17 12	2.14	0.46	19.02
Annual Growth	16.1%	— —	24.6%	27.1%	13.4%

Premier Financial Corp

Named for its hometown not its attitude First Defiance Financial is the holding company for First Federal Bank of the Midwest which operates more than 30 branches serving northwestern Ohio western Indiana and southern Michigan. The thrift offers standard deposit products including checking savings and money market accounts and CDs. Commercial real estate loans account for more than half of the bank's loan portfolio; commercial loans make up another quarter of all loans. The company's insurance agency subsidiary First Insurance Group of the Midwest which accounts for some 7% of the company's revenues provides life insurance property/casualty coverage and investments. In 2019 First Defiance Financial agreed to merge with Ohio-based United Community Financial (the holding company for Home Savings Bank and HSB Insurance) in a deal valued at $473 million.

Strategy

First Defiance Financial has boosted its non-banking product lines via acquisitions. It bought the employee benefits insurance business of another local agency Andres O'Neil & Lowe in 2010; and property/casualty agency Payak-Dubbs Insurance Agency in 2011. Both additions became part of First Insurance Group of the Midwest (formerly named First Insurance & Investments).

In 2016 the company agreed to buy another bank serving northwest Ohio Commercial Bancshares. The deal is valued at some $63 million and adds seven branches and $342 million in assets.

Mergers and Acquisitions

In 2019 First Defiance Financial agreed to merge with Ohio-based United Community Financial (the holding company for Home Savings Bank and HSB Insurance) in a deal valued at $473 million. United Community's Home Savings Bank subsidiary will merge into First Federal to create a bank with more than $6 billion in assets. First Defiance shareholders will have a 52.5% stake in the new company.

EXECUTIVES

Evp Business Banking First Federal Bank, Dennis
E. Rose, age 51, $144,077 total compensation
President And Ceo First Defiance Financial And
First Federal Bank, Donald P. Hileman, age 67,
$400,000 total compensation
Evp General Counsel And Chief Risk Officer First
Defiance Financial Corp And First Federal Bank,
John R. Reisner, age 64, $180,147 total compensation
Evp And Community Banking President Â– First
Federal Bank, Gregory R. Allen, age 56, $200,000
total compensation
Evp And President Western Market Area First
Federal Bank, James R. Williams, age 52
Evp And President Eastern Market Area First
Federal Bank, Timothy K. (Tim) Harris, age 61
Evp And Chief Credit Officer First Federal Bank,
Michael D. Mulford, age 55, $149,387 total
compensation
Evp And President Northern Market Area First
Federal Bank, Marybeth Shunck, age 50
Evp And Cfo First Defiance Financial Corp. And
First Federal Bank, Kent T. Thompson, age 66,
$218,360 total compensation

Evp And Director Human Resources First
  Defiance Financial Corp. And First Federal
  Bank, Sharon L. Davis, age 38
Evp And President Southern Market Area First
  Federal Bank, Amy L. Hackenberg, age 49
Vice President, Gary Verhoff
Assistant Vice President Human Resources, Diane
  Beam
Assistant Vice President, Julie Harris
Senior Vice President, Lisa R Christy
Avp Information Security Analyst, Chad Kaup
Senior Vice President Information Technology,
  Kathy Miller
Vice President Senior Accountant, Steve Giesige
Vice President Business Intelligence And
  Strategic Implementation, Justin Rodemich
Assistant Vp Business And Banker, Darrell Baird
Chairman, William J. (Bill) Small, age 69
Vice Chairman, Stephen L. Boomer, age 69
Board Member, Barbara Mitzel
Auditors: Crowe LLP

LOCATIONS

HQ: Premier Financial Corp
  601 Clinton Street, Defiance, OH 43512
Phone: 419 782-5015
Web: www.fdef.com

PRODUCTS/OPERATIONS

2016 Sales

	$ mil.	% of total
Interest		
Loans	80	66
Investment securities		
Taxable	3	3
Tax-exempt	3	2
Interest-bearing deposits	0	-
FHLB stock dividends	0	1
Non-interest		
Service fees & other charges	10	9
Insurance commissions	10	9
Mortgage banking income	7	6
Trust income	1	1
Gain on sale of non-mortgage loans	0	1
Income from bank owned life insurance	0	1
Gain on sale or call of securities	0	-
Other	1	1
Total	**121**	**100**

COMPETITORS

Farmers National	Huntington Bancshares
Fifth Third	KeyCorp
First Citizens Banc Corp	PNC Financial
First Financial Bancorp	SB Financial Group

HISTORICAL FINANCIALS

Company Type: Public

Income Statement   FYE: December 31

	ASSETS ($ mil.)	NET INCOME ($ mil.)	INCOME AS % OF ASSETS	EMPLOYEES
12/19	3,468	49	1.4%	699
12/18	3,181	46	1.5%	696
12/17	2,993	32	1.1%	674
12/16	2,477	28	1.2%	581
12/15	2,297	26	1.2%	586
Annual Growth	10.8%	16.9%	—	4.5%

2019 Year-End Financials

Debt ratio: 1.04%
Return on equity: 11.96%
Cash ($ mil.): 46
Current ratio: —
Long-term debt ($ mil.): —

No. of shares (mil.): 19
Dividends
  Yield: 2.5%
  Payout: 31.8%
Market value ($ mil.): 621

STOCK PRICE ($) FY Close	P/E High/Low	PER SHARE ($) Earnings	Dividends	Book Value
12/19 31.49	13 10	2.48	0.79	21.60
12/18 24.51	30 10	2.26	0.64	19.81
12/17 51.97	35 29	1.61	0.50	18.38
12/16 50.74	32 22	1.60	0.44	16.31
12/15 37.78	29 21	1.41	0.39	15.39
Annual Growth (4.5%)	—	15.2%	19.5%	8.8%

Primerica Inc

EXECUTIVES

Chb, Rick Williams
Co Chb*, John Addison
Pres*, David T Chadwick
Dir*, Michael K Wells
Coo*, Douglas G Elliott
SEC*, Stacey K Geer
Cfo*, Allison Rand
Vice President, Ron Kennett
Office Manager, Vanessa N Hill
Auditors: KPMG LLP

LOCATIONS

HQ: Primerica Inc
　1 Primerica Parkway, Duluth, GA 30099
Phone: 770 381-1000
Web: www.primerica.com

HISTORICAL FINANCIALS

Company Type: Public

Income Statement　　　　　　　　FYE: December 31

	ASSETS ($ mil.)	NET INCOME ($ mil.)	INCOME AS % OF ASSETS	EMPLOYEES
12/19	13,688	366	2.7%	2,803
12/18	12,595	324	2.6%	2,699
12/17	12,460	350	2.8%	2,718
12/16	11,438	219	1.9%	2,662
12/15	10,612	189	1.8%	2,626
Annual Growth	6.6%	17.9%	—	1.6%

2019 Year-End Financials

Debt ratio: 11.38%
Return on equity: 23.53%
Cash ($ mil.): 256
Current ratio: —
Long-term debt ($ mil.): —

No. of shares (mil.): 41
Dividends
　Yield: 1.0%
　Payout: 16.2%
Market value ($ mil.): 5,380

STOCK PRICE ($) FY Close	P/E High/Low	PER SHARE ($) Earnings	Dividends	Book Value
12/19 130.56	16 11	8.62	1.36	40.10
12/18 97.71	17 12	7.33	1.00	34.23
12/17 101.55	14 9	7.61	0.78	32.07
12/16 69.15	16 9	4.59	0.70	26.71
12/15 47.23	15 11	3.70	0.64	23.72
Annual Growth 28.9%	—	23.5%	20.7%	14.0%

Principal Financial Group Inc

Founded in 1879 Principal Financial Group (Principal) is a top global investment management offering businesses individuals and institutional clients a wide range of financial products and services including retirement asset management and insurance through financial services companies. The company offers a range of capabilities including equity fixed income real estate and other alternative investments as well as fund offerings. Its insurance segment provides group and individual life and disability insurance and group dental and vision coverage. Principal has more than $735 billion in assets under management. Principal operates offices in nearly 25 countries and serves clients in more than 85 countries.

Operations

Principal offers its financial products and services through four business segments: Retirement and Income Solutions US Insurance Solutions Principal International and Principal Global Investors.

The Retirement and Investor Services segment generates some 55% of annual revenue. It provides retirement and other financial products and services such as 401(k) and 403(b) plans Individual Retirement Accounts (IRAs) personal trusts and annuities to individuals and businesses.

The US Insurance Solutions segment (more than 25% of revenue) provides individual life insurance and specialty benefits insurance which includes group dental and vision individual and group disability and group life insurance along with non-medical fee-for-service claims administration services.

The Principal International segment (nearly 10% of revenue) serves retirement and insurance needs to clients in countries with large middle classes and growing long-term savings. The company typically enters a new market through acquisitions joint ventures and sometimes its own start-up operations.

The Principal Global Investors segment (less than 10% of revenue) offers asset management services to the company's internal asset accumulation business and insurance operations along with third-party clients. Almost 50% of the company's revenue were generated from premiums and other consideration. The fees and other accounts for over 25% of sales and the remaining sales came from net investment income.

Geographic Reach

Principal Financial Group operates out of offices in nearly 25 countries and serves clients in more than 85 countries. It is headquartered in Des Moines IA.

Its Principal International segment has operations in the Americas (Brazil Chile Mexico) Asia (China Hong Kong India) and Southeast Asia (Singapore Thailand Malaysia Indonesia). The Principal Global Investors segment has offices in Australia Brazil China France Germany Hong Kong Ireland Italy Japan Luxembourg the Netherlands Portugal Singapore Spain Switzerland the United Arab Emirates the United Kingdom and the United States.

Sales and Marketing

Principal distributes its products and services through institutional and retail sales representatives relationship management and client service professionals who work with consultants and directly with investors to acquire and retain institutional clients retail clients and other investors. The company maintains relationships with independent broker-dealers to distribute its products and services maintaining relationships with over 81000 independent brokers consultants and agents. Principal Global Investors and its focused investment teams had over 750 third party institutional clients in 40 countries.

The Principal International segment focuses on regions with a growing middle class and demographics that are aligned with Principal's target customer criteria as well as where it is common for workers to contribute to defined contribution retirement plans (similar to 401(k) and IRA plans).

Financial Performance

Over the past five years Principal's financial results continued a long-term upward trend. Its annual revenue has risen more than 35% since 2015 mostly thanks to growing premium income from annuity and life insurance sales.

In 2019 revenue rose 14% to $16.2 billion. Premiums increased $1226.8 million for the Retirement and Income Solutions segment primarily due to higher sales of single premium group annuities with life contingencies. Fees and other revenues increased $209.3 million for the Retirement and Income Solutions segment primarily due to the Acquired Business.

Net income attributable to Principal Financial Group Inc. decreased primarily from $1.5 billion in 2018 to $1.4 billion in 2019 due to a $73.9 million favorable impact in 2018 related to the realignment of a real estate investment team and $68.6 million related to actuarial assumption updates and model refinements that had an unfavorable impact in 2019 as compared to a favorable impact in 2018.

Cash at the end of the year was $2.5 billion down by $461.6 million from 2018. Cash from operations added $5.5 billion to the coffers while financing activities contributed $1.7 billion. Investing activities used $7.7 billion.

Strategy

A growing global middle class. Increasingly fiscally constrained governments. The approaching retirement age of US Baby Boomers?and the need for greater asset accumulation among Echo Boomers. The era of personal responsibility has arrived and Principal Financial Group finds itself facing an unprecedented demand for long-term savings solutions.

Principal meets that demand with deliberately diverse expertise across multiple lines of business creating a balanced business model that allows it to be aggressive while minimizing risk.

A highly competitive range of savings and retirement solutions and investment management capabilities helps clients and customers in existing markets and select emerging markets to save for the long term and invest for growth while US insurance solutions help investors to protect their assets.

The company also invests in its people. Through innovative technology and best-in-class collaboration solutions the company empowers its employees financial professionals and partners to do their best work?and positions itself to attract and retain the world's best talent bolstering its continued success.

This inclusive global perspective and dynamic blend of expertise have driven Principal well beyond $600 billion in assets under management pushed its non-GAAP operating earnings to record levels and solidified its competitive edge in an array of global markets.

Mergers and Acquisitions

In 2019 Principal Financial Group acquired the Wells Fargo's retirement plan services business for $1.2 billion. With $827 billion in assets under administration the Wells Fargo business unit expanded Principal Financial's 401(k) savings account business. The company indicated the deal transformed it into one of the largest retirement providers. Principal capitalized on the acquisition of the stunted retirement plan services business as Wells Fargo had been prohibited from growing in size by the Federal Reserve following its customer abuse scandals.

Company Background

Principal Financial was founded as the Bankers Life Association in 1879 by Edward Temple a Civil War veteran and banker. Life insurance became popular after the war but some dishonest insurers canceled customers' policies before they had to pay out benefits. Bankers Life an assessable association (members shared the cost of death benefits as the claims arose) was intended to provide low-cost protection to bankers and their families. The company soon after began offering life insurance to nonbankers.

The Principal Financial Group Inc. is traded on the Nasdaq Global Select Market (Nasdaq) under the ticker symbol PFG.

HISTORY

Principal Financial was founded as the Bankers Life Association in 1879 by Edward Temple a Civil War veteran and banker. Life insurance became popular after the war but some dishonest insurers canceled customers' policies before they had to pay out benefits. Bankers Life an assessable association (members shared the cost of death benefits as the claims arose) was intended to provide low-cost protection to bankers and their families. The company soon began offering life insurance to nonbankers but it refused to insure women because of the high mortality rate among mothers during childbirth.

In October 2012 PFG scooped up First Dental Health a California-based preferred provider organization (PPO) with more than 11000 dentists operating in Arizona California and Nevada. The acquisition bolstered PFG's specialty benefits insurance business.

EXECUTIVES

Evp And Cfo, Deanna Strable
Evp And Cfo, Terrance Lillis
Chairman President And Ceo, Daniel J. (Dan) Houston, age 59, $795,192 total compensation
Evp General Counsel And Secretary, Karen E. Shaff, age 66

President Global Asset Management; Ceo Principal Global Investors, James P. (Jim) McCaughan, age 67, $663,500 total compensation
Evp Cio And Chief Digital Officer, Gary P. Scholten, age 63
President Retirement And Investor Services And Chairman Principal Funds, Nora M. Everett, age 60
Ceo Principal Real Estate Investors, Patrick G. (Pat) Halter
Senior Executive Director And Coo Strategy And Boutique Operations, Barbara A. (Barb) McKenzie
Svp And Controller, Gregory B. (Greg) Elming, age 59
President Principal International, Luis Valdés, age 62, $589,288 total compensation
Chairman Principal Financial Group Asia, Rex Auyeung
Evp Principal Financial Group Inc. And Principal Life And Chief Investment Officer, Timothy M. (Tim) Dunbar, age 62, $483,577 total compensation
Svp; President Principal Financial Group Latin America, Roberto Walker
Svp And Chief Marketing Officer, Elizabeth S. (Beth) Brady
Svp And Chief Investment Officer Principal Life Insurance Company, Dennis Menken
Senior Executive Director And Head Global Fixed Income, David M. Blake
Evp And Cfo, Deanna D. Strable-Soethout, age 51, $488,846 total compensation
President United States Insurance Solutions, Amy C. Friedrich, age 49
Vice President, Debra Stoll
Vice President Sales, Joseph Martin
Vice President, Mihail Dobrinov
Second Vice President, Rajesh Chalamalasetti
Vice President Tax, Rich Wireman
Vice President Executive Benefits Consulting, John Baergen
Second Vice President, Shelly Meighan
Senior Vice President Risk Management, Lou Flori
Senior Vice President Retirement Distrib, Timothy Minard
Vice President Life, Don Cooper
Vice President Of Annuity Distribution, Steven Becker
Regional Vice President Nonqualified Plans, Jack Leavy
Regional Vice President, Ron Giardini
Vice President Of Sales, Tim Hollinger
Regional Vice President Life Sales, Michelle Tish
Regional Vice President, Wayne Mohr
Regional Vice President, Paul Schreiber
Svp And Deputy General Counsel, Mark Lagomarcino
Vice President Consulting, Joseph Marx
Svp And Deputy General Counsel, Leanne Valentine
Vp And Head Government Relations, Chris Payne
Assistant Vice President, Joe Mccarty
Avp It, Lori Smith
Disability Income Regional Vice President, Justin Harrison
Disability Income Regional Vice President, Bob Herman
Assistant Vice President And Actuary, Chris Kinnison
Vp Of Sales, Mike Downing
Medical Director, Frenesa Hall
Vice President, Cui Sufang
Vice President Of Account, Christine Johnson
Senior Vice President And Appointed Actuary, Reed Matthew
Regional Vice President, Donald Schamay
Vice President, Andrea Garrett
Second Vice President, Margot Karlin
Vice President Technology Director, Angie Peters
Auditors: Ernst & Young LLP

LOCATIONS

HQ: Principal Financial Group Inc
711 High Street, Des Moines, IA 50392
Phone: 515 247-5111
Web: www.principal.com

Selected Geographic Locations
Australia
Brazil
Chile
China
Hong Kong
India
Indonesia
Japan
Malaysia
Mexico
Singapore
Thailand
UK
US

PRODUCTS/OPERATIONS

2016 Sales by Segment

	$ mil.	% of total
Retirement & Investor Services	6,150	49
US Insurance Solutions	3,637	29
Principal International	1,252	10
Principal Global Investors	1,387	11
Corporate	(46.3)	-
Net realized capital gains	80	1
Adjustments	(67.6)	-
Total	**12,394**	**100**

2016 Sales

	% of total
Premiums & other considerations	43
Fees and other revenues	29
Net investment income	27
Net realized capital gains	1
Total	**100**

COMPETITORS

AIG
AXA
Aetna
Allianz
BlackRock
FMR
JPMorgan Chase
John Hancock Financial Services
Lincoln Financial Group
MassMutual
MetLife
Morgan Stanley Investment Management
PIMCO
T. Rowe Price
The Vanguard Group
Unum Group
Voya Financial

HISTORICAL FINANCIALS

Company Type: Public

Income Statement   FYE: December 31

	ASSETS ($ mil.)	NET INCOME ($ mil.)	INCOME AS % OF ASSETS	EMPLOYEES
12/19	276,087	1,394	0.5%	17,601
12/18	243,036	1,546	0.6%	16,475
12/17	253,941	2,310	0.9%	15,378
12/16	228,014	1,316	0.6%	14,854
12/15	218,685	1,234	0.6%	14,895
Annual Growth	**6.0%**	**3.1%**	**—**	**4.3%**

2019 Year-End Financials

Debt ratio: 1.35%	No. of shares (mil.): 276
Return on equity: 10.72%	Dividends
Cash ($ mil.): 2,515	Yield: 3.9%
Current ratio: —	Payout: 46.1%
Long-term debt ($ mil.): —	Market value ($ mil.): 15,213

	STOCK PRICE ($)	P/E		PER SHARE ($)		
	FY Close	High/Low	Earnings	Dividends	Book Value
12/19	55.00	12 9	4.96	2.18	52.85
12/18	44.17	14 8	5.36	2.10	40.75
12/17	70.56	9 7	7.88	1.87	44.46
12/16	57.86	13 8	4.50	1.61	35.55
12/15	44.98	14 11	4.06	1.50	31.95
Annual Growth	5.2%	— —	5.1%	9.8%	13.4%

ProAssurance Corp

ProAssurance protects professional health associates — the doctors dentists and nurses of the US. One of the largest medical liability insurance providers in the nation ProAssurance is the holding company for ProAssurance Indemnity ProAssurance Casualty and other subsidiaries that sell liability coverage for health care providers primarily in the South and Midwest. Products liability for medical technology and life sciences is written through Medmarc Casualty Insurance Company and Noetic Specialty Insurance Company. Its customers include healthcare professionals and healthcare entities including hospitals and other healthcare facilities... ProAssurance Casualty also provides some coverage for legal professionals.

Operations

ProAssurance operates through four primary segments: Specialty Property and Casualty (some% of all sales) Workers' Compensation (around 25% of sales) Lloyd's Syndicate (some 10%) Segregated Portfolio Cell Reinsurance (nearly 10%) and Corporate.

Specialty Property & Casualty segment includes the company's professional liability business and medical technology liability business. Professional liability insurance is primarily offered to healthcare providers and institutions and to attorneys and their firms. The Workers' Compensation Insurance segment includes its workers' compensation insurance business which is provided primarily to employers with approximately 1000 or fewer employees. The Lloyd's Syndicate segment includes the operating results from the company's participation in Lloyd's of London Syndicate 1729 and its 100% participation in Syndicate 6131 which is an SPA that underwrites on a quota share basis with Syndicate 1729. The Segregated Portfolio Cell Reinsurance segment includes the operating results (underwriting profit or loss plus investment results) of SPCs at Inova Re and Eastern Re our Cayman Islands SPC operations. The Corporate segment includes the company's investment operations other than those reported in Segregated Portfolio Cell Reinsurance and Lloyd's Syndicates segments interest expense and U.S. income taxes. This segment also includes non-premium revenues generated outside its insurance entities and corporate expenses.

Physician policies make up ProAssurance's largest business accounting for about 70% of annual insurance premiums. Other key product groups include policies covering other health professionals medical facilities and legal profession-als.. ProAssurance is also the majority capital provider to Lloyd's of London Syndicate 1729.

Geographic Reach

Although the company is licensed throughout the US its operations are concentrated in select states in the southern and midwestern US. Its largest markets — Alabama Indiana Michigan Pennsylanvia and Texas — together account for about 40% of the company's premiums.

The company owns office facilities in Alabama Michigan Nevada Tennessee and Wisconsin among others.

Its corporate office is located in Birmingham Alabama.

Sales and Marketing

ProAssurance employs an internal sales force to write its health care professional liability policies. It also utilizes independent agencies and brokerages.

Customers include physicians dentists chiropractors allied health care professionals medical facilities lawyers life science and medical technology entities.

Financial Performance

ProAssurance is able to sustain financial stability during turbulent market conditions through disciplined underwriting prudent pricing and loss reserve practices and conservative investment strategies. Revenues in the last five years were on the upward trend and posted a 29% increase over that span.

Revenue rose 13% to $999.8 million in 2019 as premiums written and earned investment income and realized investment gains all increased for the year.

Net income has been somewhat turbulent over the past five years. In 2019 income dropped to $1 million from $47 million in 2018. The sudden drop was brought about by a $171.56 million increase in operating expenses.

Cash and cash equivalents at the end of the period were $175.4 million. Cash provided by operations was $148.2 million and cash added by investing activities was $50.5 million. Investing activities used $103.8 million for dividends payment.

Strategy

The company's main business objective is to generate an attractive total return for its shareholders. The basic components of its strategy for achieving this objective are: Provide specialized healthcare-centric expertise to meet evolving demands in the healthcare marketplace; Provide superior workers' compensation products and services; Provide superior customer service; Effectively manage capital; Manage claims effectively; Pursue profitable underwriting opportunities; Emphasize risk management; Maintain a conservative investment strategy; Focus on culture and people; and Maintain financial stability.

Its overall investment strategy is to maximize current income from its investment portfolio while maintaining safety liquidity duration targets and portfolio diversification. The portfolio is generally managed by professional third-party asset managers whose results it monitors and evaluates. The asset managers typically have the authority to make investment decisions within the asset classes they are responsible for managing subject to its investment policy and oversight including a requirement that available-for-sale se-curities in a loss position cannot be sold without specific authorization from the company.

Mergers and Acquisitions

In 2020 ProAssurance Corporation and California-based NORCAL Group a company that provides medical professional liability insurance risk management solutions and provider wellness resources to healthcare facilities announced the signing of a definitive agreement under which NORCAL would become a part of ProAssurance in a $450 million transaction following the demutualization of NORCAL Mutual Insurance Company (NORCAL Mutual) NORCAL's ultimate controlling party. The demutualization and the acquisition agreement are mutually contingent and are subject to required regulatory and policyholder approvals. Based on available estimates of premium the combination of these companies is expected to create the nation's third largest specialty writer of liability insurance for healthcare professionals and facilities.

EXECUTIVES

Chairman President And Ceo, W. Stancil (Stan) Starnes, age 71, $854,100 total compensation
President Healthcare Professional Liability Group Chief Underwriting Officer And Chief Actuary, Howard H. Friedman, age 61, $476,325 total compensation
Evp And Cfo, Edward L. (Ned) Rand, age 53, $443,475 total compensation
Svp And Chief Marketing Officer Professional Liability Group, Jeffrey L. Bowlby
President Eastern Insurance, Michael L. Boguski, age 57
Evp Corporate Secretary And General Counsel, Jeffrey P. Lisenby, age 51
Svp And Chief Medical Officer, Hayes V. Whiteside
Group Technology Officer Information Systems, Michael Stoeckert
President And Chief Medical Officer Podiatric Insurance Company Of America (pica), Ross E. Taubman
Vice President Information Systems, David Brown
Regional Vice President Claims, Richard Walter
Regional Vice President Underwriting, Heather Spicer
Vice President Actuarial Services, Randy Chaffinch
Regional Vice President Claims, Scott Hunsberger
Regional Vice President Claims, Hal Mcclelland
Vice President Sales, Greg Wood
Senior Vice President Proassurance Risk Solutions, Gregory Cuzzi
Vice President Sales, David Goss
Vice President Marketing, Marge Maxbauer
Asst Vp Income Taxes, Philip Lewis
Vice President, Vicky Gould
Vice President Of Operations, Sally Gilmore
Vice President, Tom Langan
Assistant Vice President, Sandy Cook
Regional Vice President Sales And Marketing, Kerry Kravik
Assistant Vice President, Tonya Bussey
Regional Vice President Claims, Mark Lightfoot
Board Member, Thomas Wilson
Assistant Secretary, Shelley Grandon
Board Member, Samuel Dipiazza
Auditors: Ernst & Young LLP

LOCATIONS

HQ: ProAssurance Corp
100 Brookwood Place, Birmingham, AL 35209
Phone: 205 877-4400
Web: www.proassurance.com

PRODUCTS/OPERATIONS

2014 Sales by Segment

	$ mil.	% of total
Specialty Property and Casualty	498	58
Workers' Compensation	195	23
Corporate	146	17
Lloyd's Syndicate	13	2
Eliminations	(0.5)	-
Total	**852**	**100**

2014 Sales

	$ mil.	% of total
Net premium earned	699	82
Net investment	129	15
Net realized investment gains	14	2
Other income	8	1
Total	**852**	**100**

COMPETITORS

Berkshire Hathaway
CNA Financial
COPIC
Coverys
Dentists Insurance
  Company
EDIC
Markel
Medical Liability
  Mutual Insurance
Monitor Liability
  Managers Inc.

NCMIC
Physicians' Reciprocal
  Insurers
Princeton Insurance
  Company
State Volunteer Mutual
  Insurance
The Doctors Company
Travelers Companies
White Mountains
  Insurance Group

HISTORICAL FINANCIALS

Company Type: Public

Income Statement

FYE: December 31

	ASSETS ($ mil.)	NET INCOME ($ mil.)	INCOME AS % OF ASSETS	EMPLOYEES
12/19	4,805	1	0.0%	961
12/18	4,600	47	1.0%	991
12/17	4,929	107	2.2%	994
12/16	5,065	151	3.0%	965
12/15	4,908	116	2.4%	938
Annual Growth	(0.5%)	(69.5%)	—	0.6%

2019 Year-End Financials

Debt ratio: 5.95%
Return on equity: 0.07%
Cash ($ mil.): 175
Current ratio: —
Long-term debt ($ mil.): —

No. of shares (mil.): 53
Dividends
Yield: 3.4%
Payout: 185.0%
Market value ($ mil.): 1,944

	STOCK PRICE ($) FY Close	P/E High/Low	PER SHARE ($) Earnings	Dividends	Book Value
12/19	36.14	2268 1731	0.02	1.24	28.11
12/18	40.56	64 40	0.88	1.74	28.39
12/17	57.15	31 26	2.00	5.93	29.83
12/16	56.20	22 16	2.83	5.93	33.78
12/15	48.53	25 21	2.11	2.24	36.88
Annual Growth	(7.1%)	—	(68.8%)	(13.7%)	(6.6%)

Procter & Gamble Company (The)

The Procter & Gamble Company (P&G) boasts billion-dollar brands for home and health. The world's largest maker of consumer packaged goods divides its business into five global seg-ments that comprise its vast portfolio of hair skin and personal oral family feminine fabric care grooming and baby care product lines. Its nearly 35 brands include Bounce Crest Gillette Pampers Pepto Bismol Puffs Old Spice Swiffer and Tide. Fabric and home care is P&G's leading product category accounting for about a third of sales. The company sells products in 180-plus countries although the US is its largest market.

HISTORY

Candle maker William Procter and soap maker James Gamble merged their small Cincinnati businesses in 1837 creating The Procter & Gamble Company (P&G) which incorporated in 1890. By 1859 P&G had become one of the largest companies in Cincinnati with sales of $1 million. It introduced Ivory a floating soap in 1879 and Crisco shortening in 1911.The Ivory campaign was one of the first to advertise directly to the consumer. Other advertising innovations included sponsorship of daytime radio dramas in 1932. P&G's first TV commercial for Ivory aired in 1939.

Family members headed the company until 1930 when William Deupree became president. In the 29 years that Deupree served as president and then chairman P&G became the largest US seller of packaged goods.

After years of researching cleansers for use in hard water P&G introduced Tide detergent in 1947. It began a string of acquisitions when it picked up Spic and Span (1945; sold 2001) Duncan Hines (1956; sold 1998) Charmin Paper Mills (1957) and Folgers Coffee (1963 sold 2008). P&G launched Crest toothpaste in 1955 and Head & Shoulders shampoo and Pampers disposable diapers in 1961.

Rely tampons were pulled from shelves in 1980 when investigators linked them to toxic shock syndrome. In 1985 P&G moved into health care when it purchased Richardson-Vicks (NyQuil Vicks) and G.D. Searle's nonprescription drug division (Metamucil). The acquisitions of Noxell (1989; CoverGirl Noxzema) and Max Factor (1991) made it a top cosmetics company in the US. (It sold Noxzema in 2008.)

P&G began a major restructuring in 1993 cutting 13000 jobs and closing 30 plants. The firm acquired Eagle Snacks from Anheuser-Busch in 1996 and sued rival Amway over rumors connecting P&G and its moon-and-stars logo to Satanism. (The suit was dismissed in 1999.) Also in 1996 the FDA approved the use of olestra a controversial fat substitute developed by P&G.

In 1997 it acquired Tambrands (Tampax tampons) making P&G #1 in feminine sanitary protection. Impatient with progress on its sales goals in 1998 P&G began restructuring to focus on global business units rather than geographic regions. Chairman John Pepper handed over his chairman and CEO title in 1999 to president Durk Jager who promised five new products a year and a shakeup of the corporate culture.

In 1999 the company announced further reorganization plans including 15000 job cuts worldwide by 2005. That same year P&G bought The Iams Company (maker of Eukanuba- and Iams-brand dog and cat foods).

With earnings flat Jager resigned in 2000. P&G insider Alan G. Lafley immediately assumed the president and CEO duties and Pepper returned to succeed Jager as chairman.

In 2001 P&G announced job cuts for 9600 employees to further reduce costs. It also sold its Comet cleaner business. That year P&G completed its purchase of the Clairol hair care company from Bristol-Myers Squibb for nearly $5 billion.

In 2002 P&G closed three Clairol plants one warehouse and one distribution center — eliminating about 750 jobs. Production of Clairol products was moved to existing P&G plants. It also sold its olestra plant in Cincinnati to Twin Rivers Technologies but retained ownership of the Olean brand and technology. Additionally it sold its Jif peanut butter and Crisco shortening brands to J.M. Smucker and several personal care brands (including Sea Breeze and Vitalis) to Helen of Troy.

In 2002 P&G branched out in a joint venture with Clorox to help it improve the Glad-brand plastic bags and wraps. P&G held a 10% stake in the Glad venture until late 2004 when the company invested another $133 million to boost its stake to 20% the limit allowed by the agreement.

Also that year Lafley announced that P&G had completed its multiyear restructuring and would stop reporting two sets of results (one with restructuring charges and one without).

Further expanding its hair care segment and building on its successes with Clairol P&G purchased the first of several stakes in Wella in 2003 (it now owns the entire company). That year P&G also entered the premium pet food market with its purchase of The Iams Company for $2.3 billion. And to secure its foothold in China P&G bought the remaining 20% stake in its joint venture with partner Hutchison Whampoa China Ltd. in 2004 for $1.8 billion.

P&G bought four brands to sell in Southeast Asia in its effort to erode market share from Unilever. In 2005 P&G purchased Fab Trojan Dynamo and Paic laundry brands sold in Hong Kong Singapore Thailand and Malaysia from Colgate-Palmolive.

The company reached its lofty spot as the world's largest consumer products company in 2005 through one of its boldest moves — buying Boston-based The Gillette Company for about $57 billion. Overnight the ambitious deal gave P&G the golden ticket to leapfrog over former #1 supplier Unilever. P&G's purchase of Gillette added well-known complementary brands to its already vast portfolio such as Gillette razors and blades Duracell batteries Oral-B oral care items and Braun appliances.

In 2006 P&G paired up with ARYx Therapeutics to develop that company's gastrointestinal disorder treatment.

In 2007 P&G paired its marketing savvy with the diagnostics expertise of Inverness Medical Innovations to form a joint venture company called SPD Swiss Precision Diagnostics. The joint venture makes and markets in-home diagnostic products including pregnancy tests and ovulation/fertility monitoring products under the Clearblue PERSONA Accu-Clear and other names. P&G paid $325 million for its 50% stake in the venture.

EXECUTIVES

Group President Global Grooming, Charles E. Pierce, age 64

Chairman President And Ceo, David S. Taylor, age 62, $1,393,333 total compensation

Group President North America Selling And Market Operations, Carolyn Tastad, age 57

Group President Global Health Care, Steven D. (Steve) Bishop, age 56, $796,667 total compensation

Vp Uk And Ireland, Giovanni Ciserani, age 58, $845,833 total compensation

Group President Global Family Care, Mary L. Ferguson-McHugh, age 61

President Global Personal Health Care, Thomas M. Finn, age 58

Vice Chairman And Cfo, Jon R. Moeller, age 56, $950,000 total compensation

Global Design Officer, Philip J Duncan, age 55

Cio, Linda W. Clement-Holmes, age 58

Global Product Supply Officer, Yannis Skoufalos, age 62

President Beauty Specialty Businesses, Colleen E. Jay, age 58

President Europe Selling & Market Operations, Gary Coombe

Cto, Kathleen B. (Kathy) Fish

President India Middle East And Africa Selling And Market Operations, Mohamed Samir

President Global Home Care And P&g Professional, George Tsouroupas, age 60

President Global Fabric Care And Brand Building Organization Global Fabric And Home Care, Shailesh G. Jejurikar

President Global Skin And Personal Care, R. Alexandra Keith

President Global Business Services, Julio Nemeth

President Latin America Selling And Market Operations, Juan F. Posada

President Greater China Selling And Market Operations, Matthew S. Price

President Asia/pacific Selling And Market Operations, Magesvaran Suranjan

Vice President Supply Chain And Procurement, Kara Baker

Vice President, Charlene Patten

Vice President Of Human Resources, Rebecca Barrett

Vice President, Jerry Vikara

Vice President Sales, Matthew Zirkle

Chief Sales Officer Reinvention Training Developer, Ryan P Siereveld

Vp And Associate General Counsel, Ken Patel

Vice President Of Communications, Lisa Bartz

Chief Sales Officer Team Operations Leader, Kelly Horton

Vice President, Dicky Kho

Vice President Sales, Frank Craft

Vice President Global Investor Relations, John T Chevalier

Vice President, Patrick Conklin

Call Center Customer Service Director Vice President, Ron Chisholm

Director Managed Care, Debbie Burge

National Sales Manager Canada, David Roberts

Vice President And General Manager Research And Development, Petra Hanke-baier

Chief Sales Officer Manager Romania, Georgeta Parchisanu

Vice President Corporate Solutions, Bob Martindale

Vice President Corporate Development And Strategic Planning, Becky Frayer

Vice President And General Manager Asia Pacific, Omar Channawi

Vice President Of Information Technology Chief Information Offcier, Cindy Schumacher

Vice President Management Systems, Frank Caccamo

Senior Vice President Go To Market China, Henry Karamanoukian

Vice President Finance Asia, Nicolas Defauw

Vice President, Kim Kraus

Vice President, Luis Amaro

Vice President, Denise Crookshanks

Sr V Pres-comptroller-treas, Valarie Sheppard

Board Member, Mike Eftink

Shs Band Booster Treasurer, Lisa Hennessy

Board Member, Bob Kruthaupt

Board Member, BO Passey

Secretary, Jenny Tan

Abm, Christina Morazzani

Assistant Treasurer, Douglas Gerstle

Abm, Marta Roballo

Secretary Treasurer, Dave Seidel

Board Member, John Biscotti

Auditors: Deloitte & Touche LLP

LOCATIONS

HQ: Procter & Gamble Company (The)
One Procter & Gamble Plaza, Cincinnati, OH 45202
Phone: 513 983-1100
Web: www.pg.com

2019 Sales

	% of total
North America	45
Europe	23
Asia Pacific	10
Greater China	9
India Middle East and Africa (IMEA)	7
Latin America	6
Total	**100**

PRODUCTS/OPERATIONS

2019 Sales

	$ mil.	% of total
Fabric & Home Care	22,080	33
Baby Feminine & Family Care	17,806	26
Beauty	12,897	19
Health Care	8,218	12
Grooming	6,199	9
Corporate	484	1
Total	**67,684**	**100**

Selected Segments and Brands

Fabric Care & Home Care
  Ariel
  Dawn
  Downy
  Febreze
  Gain
  Tide
Beauty
  Head & Shoulders
  Olay
  Old Spice
  Pantene
  SK-II
Baby Feminine & Family Care
  Always
  Bounty
  Charmin
  Luvs
  Pampers
  Tampax
Health Care
  Crest
  Oral-B
  Vicks
Grooming
  Braun
  Fusion
  Gillette
  Mach3
  Venus

COMPETITORS

Alticor	Kao
Amway	Kimberly-Clark
Church & Dwight	S.C. Johnson
Clorox	Shiseido
Colgate-Palmolive	Tom's of Maine
Edgewell Personal Care	Unilever NV
Henkel	Unilever PLC
Johnson & Johnson	

HISTORICAL FINANCIALS

Company Type: Public

Income Statement				FYE: June 30
	REVENUE ($ mil.)	NET INCOME ($ mil.)	NET PROFIT MARGIN	EMPLOYEES
06/20	70,950	13,027	18.4%	99,000
06/19	67,684	3,897	5.8%	97,000
06/18	66,832	9,750	14.6%	92,000
06/17	65,058	15,326	23.6%	95,000
06/16	65,299	10,508	16.1%	105,000
Annual Growth	2.1%	5.5%	—	(1.5%)

2020 Year-End Financials

Debt ratio: 28.77%—
Return on equity: 27.73%
Cash ($ mil.): 16,181
Current ratio: 0.85
Long-term debt ($ mil.): 23,537

Dividends
Yield: 2.5%
Payout: 164.5%
Market value ($ mil.): —

	STOCK PRICE ($) FY Close	P/E High/Low		PER SHARE ($)		
			Earnings	Dividends	Book Value
06/20	119.57	25 19		4.96	3.03	18.76
06/19	109.65	77 54		1.43	2.90	18.84
06/18	78.06	25 19		3.67	2.79	20.93
06/17	87.15	16 14		5.59	2.70	21.61
06/16	84.67	22 18		3.69	2.66	21.49
Annual Growth	9.0%	— —		7.7%	3.3%	(3.3%)

Progressive Corp. (OH)

The Progressive Corporation offers personal lines insurance as well as commercial lines and property insurance. Personal auto insurance is Progressive's largest business; it also offers personal-use vehicle policies for motorcycles RVs snowmobiles and other specialty vehicles. The company's commercial policies cover vans and light to heavy trucks. Most of its commercial lines policies are sold to small business owners. The property insurance business writes residential property insurance for homeowners and offers renters insurance. Progressive markets directly to consumers online and by phone and through more than 35000 independent agents.

Operations

Progressive earns revenue through three segments: Personal Lines (the largest segment accounting for some 85% of total revenue) Commercial Lines (about 15%) Property (roughly 5%).

The company primarily offers coverage to auto insurance customers underwritten by third-party insurance carriers. Personal auto insurance accounts for some 95% of its Personal Lines net premiums. Progressive also offers personal umbrella insurance that provides coverage for the extras in life such as personal injury and legal defense.

Geographic Reach
In addition to its Mayfield Village Ohio headquarters Progressive has offices in Colorado Springs Colorado; Tampa and St. Petersburg Florida; and Phoenix Arizona. The company owns approximately 90 buildings throughout US.

Sales and Marketing
Progressive sells its personal lines insurance through more than 35000 independent agencies and through partnerships with other insurance companies financial institutions and national agencies. It also sells directly to customers online and by telephone. Commercial lines are distributed directly and through independent agencies.

The company's popular television ads featuring perky spokesperson "Flo" have been a boon for the company's brand recognition.

Financial Performance
Progressive's revenues for the last five years have been progressive. It has an overall growth of 87% during that period. Net income followed a similar trend except in 2016 when it dipped 19%.Revenue jumped 22% to $39.0 billion in 2019 as net premiums increased across Progressive's business segments.

Net income rose 51% to $3.9 billion a healthy increase driven mostly by the jump in revenue.

Progressive does not hold any cash but has unrestricted access to funds maintained in a non-insurance investment subsidiary to meet its holding company obligations. Cash from operations provided $2.2 billion while investing activities used $411.3 million (additional investments) and financing used $1.8billion primarily due to dividends paid to common shareholders and acquisition of treasury shares for restricted stock tax liabilities.

Strategy
Unlike some insurers who in healthy markets earn more from their investments than their premiums more than 90% of Progressive's revenues have historically come from policy premiums.

The company's insurance operations have remained profitable and have grown as the company has entered into new geographic markets and expanded the online distribution of its personal auto products.

The auto insurance industry is highly competitive with large carriers and regional carriers competing for market share. Because it is easy for customers to switch auto insurers Progressive competes on price and accessibility. The company also find success through advertising to attract and retain customers. Its television ads featuring its perky spokesperson "Flo" have boosted company's brand recognition.

Progressive is looking to reduce its exposure to the competitive auto insurance industry by growing its property insurance business. It promotes its residential products through bundled packages with lower auto rates and has rebranded its majority-owned homeowners insurance carrier American Strategic Insurance to the Progressive name to make it easier to sell auto and home bundles. This cross-selling strategy comes with a retention benefit as well; once a customer has bought a bundled package of home/auto/umbrella coverage they are less likely to switch insurance providers.

The company's strategy is to be a competitively priced provider of a broad range of personal auto and special lines insurance products with distinctive service distributed through whichever channel the customer prefers and combined with property insurance and other products when appropriate to match its customers' needs. Volume potential is driven by Progressive's price competitiveness brand recognition quality service and the actions of the company's competitors among other factors. The company is also focused on efforts to form deeper and longer-term relationships with its customers through its Destination Era strategy.

Progressive launched its business owners policy (BOP) insurance offering general liability and property insurance. This product is geared specifically to small businesses and currently available to agents in eight states with plans to expand to additional states during the remainder of 2020. The company also continue to act as an agent for business customers to place BOP general liability professional liability and workers' compensation coverage through unaffiliated insurance carriers and are compensated through commissions which are reported as service revenues. To further help the company's direct customers Progressive offered BusinessQuote Explorer (BQX) a digital application that allows small business owners to obtain quotes for these products from a select group of unaffiliated carriers.

Company Background
Attorneys Jack Green and Joseph Lewis founded Progressive Mutual Insurance in Cleveland in 1937. Initially offering standard auto insurance the company attracted customers through such innovations as installment plans for premiums (a payment method popularized during the Depression) and drive-in claims services headquartered in a garage. Progressive's early years were uncertain — at one point the founders were even advised to go out of business — but the advent of WWII bolstered business. Car and insurance purchases went up but accidents declined as gas rationing limited driving.

HISTORY

Attorneys Jack Green and Joseph Lewis founded Progressive Mutual Insurance in Cleveland in 1937. Initially offering standard auto insurance the company attracted customers through such innovations as installment plans for premiums (a payment method popularized during the Depression) and drive-in claims services (the company was headquartered in a garage). Progressive's early years were uncertain — at one point the founders were even advised to go out of business — but the advent of WWII bolstered business: Car and insurance purchases were up but accidents were down as gas rationing limited driving.

Then came the suburbs and cars of the 1950s. While most competitors sought low-risk drivers Progressive exploited the high-risk niche through careful underwriting and statistical analysis. Subsidiary Progressive Casualty was founded in 1956 (the year after Joseph Lewis died) to insure the best of the worst. Lewis' son Peter joined the company in 1955 and helped engineer its early-1960s expansion outside Ohio. After Green retired in 1965 Peter gained control of the company through a leveraged buyout and renamed it The Progressive Corporation. Six years later Lewis took it public and formed subsidiary Progressive American in Florida.

In the mid-1970s the industry went into a funk as it was hit by a wave of consolidations and rising interest rates. Lewis set a goal for the company to always earn an underwriting profit instead of depending on investments to make a profit. Progressive achieved stellar results during the 1970s especially after states began requiring drivers to be insured and other insurers began weeding out higher risks.

Competition in nonstandard insurance grew in the 1980s as major insurers such as Allstate and State Farm joined the fray with their larger sales forces and deeper pockets. In 1988 California's Proposition 103 retroactively reduced rates; Progressive fought California's demand for refunds but set aside reserves to pay them.

That year Lewis hired Cleveland financier Alfred Lerner to guide company investments. Lerner invested $75 million in Progressive via a convertible debenture; five years later he converted it to stock half of which he sold for $122 million. Soon after he was asked to resign. In 1993 Progressive settled with California for $51 million and applied to earnings the remaining $100 million in refund reserves. (Company soul-searching related to Proposition 103 led to the launch of Progressive's now-famous "Immediate Response" vehicles which provide 24-hour claims service at accident sites.)

In 1995 Progressive's practice of using consumer credit information to make underwriting decisions drew the attention of Arkansas and Vermont insurance regulators who said the company might be discriminating against people who didn't have the credit cards Progressive used to evaluate creditworthiness. In 1996 insurance regulators in Alaska Maryland and Texas also began probing Progressive's credit information practices.

In 1997 Progressive bought nonstandard auto insurer Midland Financial Group. As competition grew in 1999 the company cut rates and said it would write no new policies in Canada. In 2000 — with underwriting margins dropping industry-wide — the company continued advertising aggressively. Progressive stopped writing new homeowners insurance in 2002 instead concentrating on its core operations. In 2006 the company began offering personal umbrella coverage.

The company took a bold international expansion measure in 2009: Launching personal auto insurance online in Australia. International expansion has not been a key strategy for Progressive but apparently the time was right for such growth. And apparently the company is prepared to give the new operation time to grow which is good considering that it has not yet made significant contributions to overall revenues.

EXECUTIVES
Chief Investment Officer, William M. (Bill) Cody, age 58, $463,269 total compensation
President Of Customer Operations, S. Patricia (Tricia) Griffith, age 56, $616,346 total compensation
President Commercial Lines Group, John A. Barbagallo, age 61, $463,269 total compensation
Cfo, John P. Sauerland, age 56, $546,538 total compensation
Chief Legal Officer, Dan Mascaro

President Personal Lines, Patrick K. (Pat) Callahan, age 49
President Claims, Michael D. (Mike) Sieger, age 58
Cio, Steven A. (Steve) Broz, age 49
Customer Relationship Management President, John Murphy, age 50
National Sales Manager, Eric Brunelle
Vice President Information Technology, Edward Fowler
Vice President, James Kusmer
Vice President Information Technology, Kerry Breitenbach
Vice President Marketing, Carlton Spencer
Chairman, Glenn M. Renwick, age 65
Treasurer, David Krew
Auditors: PricewaterhouseCoopers LLP

LOCATIONS

HQ: Progressive Corp. (OH)
6300 Wilson Mills Road, Mayfield Village, OH 44143
Phone: 440 461-5000   **Fax:** 440 446-7168
Web: www.progressive.com

PRODUCTS/OPERATIONS

2018 Premium Revenue

	% of total
Personal Lines	85
Commercial Lines	10
Property	5
Total	**100**

Selected Insurance Options

Auto Insurance
Local Car Insurance
Motorcycle Insurance
RV Insurance
Commercial Insurance
Snowmobile Insurance
PWC Insurance
Homeowners Insurance
Renters Insurance
ATV Insurance
Life Insurance
Health Insurance
Umbrella Insurance

COMPETITORS

21st Century Insurance	Liberty Mutual
Allstate	Nationwide
American Family Insurance	Old Republic
Cincinnati Financial	State Auto Financial
Farmers Group	State Farm
GEICO	Travelers Companies
Infinity Property & Casualty	USAA

HISTORICAL FINANCIALS
Company Type: Public

Income Statement				FYE: December 31
	ASSETS ($ mil.)	NET INCOME ($ mil.)	INCOME AS % OF ASSETS	EMPLOYEES
12/19	54,895	3,970	7.2%	41,571
12/18	46,575	2,615	5.6%	37,346
12/17	38,701	1,592	4.1%	33,656
12/16	33,427	1,031	3.1%	31,721
12/15	29,819	1,267	4.3%	28,580
Annual Growth	**16.5%**	**33.0%**	**—**	**9.8%**

2019 Year-End Financials

Debt ratio: 8.03%
Return on equity: 32.42%
Cash ($ mil.): 227
Current ratio: —
Long-term debt ($ mil.): —

No. of shares (mil.): 584
Dividends
  Yield: 3.8%
  Payout: 52.6%
Market value ($ mil.): 42,319

	STOCK PRICE ($) FY Close	P/E High/Low		PER SHARE ($) Earnings	Dividends	Book Value
12/19	72.39	13	9	6.72	2.81	23.39
12/18	60.33	17	11	4.42	1.12	18.56
12/17	56.32	21	13	2.72	0.68	15.96
12/16	35.50	20	17	1.76	0.89	13.72
12/15	31.80	16	12	2.15	0.69	12.49
Annual Growth	**22.8%**	**—**	**—**	**33.0%**	**42.3%**	**17.0%**

ProSight Global Inc

Auditors: Ernst & Young LLP

LOCATIONS

HQ: ProSight Global Inc
412 Mt. Kemble Avenue, Suite 300, Morristown, NJ 07960
Phone: 973 532-1900
Web: www.prosightspecialty.com

HISTORICAL FINANCIALS
Company Type: Public

Income Statement				FYE: December 31
	ASSETS ($ mil.)	NET INCOME ($ mil.)	INCOME AS % OF ASSETS	EMPLOYEES
12/19	2,877	38	1.4%	396
12/18	2,577	54	2.1%	392
12/17	2,409	(43)	—	—
12/16	0	(100)	—	—
Annual Growth	**—**	**—**	**—**	**—**

2019 Year-End Financials

Debt ratio: 5.72%
Return on equity: 8.34%
Cash ($ mil.): 17
Current ratio: —
Long-term debt ($ mil.): —

No. of shares (mil.): 43
Dividends
  Yield: —
  Payout: —
Market value ($ mil.): 695

	STOCK PRICE ($) FY Close	P/E High/Low		PER SHARE ($) Earnings	Dividends	Book Value
12/19	16.13	22	16	0.94	0.00	12.61
12/18	0.00	—	—	1.38	0.00	10.03
Annual Growth	**—**	**—**	**—**	**(12.1%)**	**—**	**7.9%**

Prosperity Bancshares Inc.

Prosperity Bancshares reaches banking customers across the Lone Star State. The holding company for Prosperity Bank operates about 230 branches across Texas and about 15 more in Oklahoma. Serving consumers and small to mid-sized businesses the bank offers traditional deposit and loan services in addition to wealth management retail brokerage and mortgage banking investment services. Prosperity Bank focuses on real estate lending: Commercial mortgages make up the largest segment of the company's loan portfolio (33%) followed by residential mortgages (24%). Credit cards business auto consumer home equity loans round out its lending activities.

Operations

About 63% of Prosperity's total revenue came from loan interest (including fees) in 2014 while another 22% came from interest on its investment securities. The rest of its revenue came from non-sufficient fund fees (4%) credit and debit card income (3%) deposit account service charges (2%) trust income (1%) mortgage income (1%) and brokerage income (1%).

Geographic Reach

Prosperity Bancshares operates 230 Texas banking locations across Houston South Texas the Dallas/Fort Worth metroplex East Texas Bryan/College Station Central Texas and West Texas. It also has 15 branch locations in Oklahoma (including Tulsa).

Sales and Marketing

The bank mainly targets consumers and small and medium-sized businesses and tailors its products to the specific needs of a given market.

Financial Performance

Prosperity's revenues and profits have been prospering thanks to loan and deposit business growth from acquisitions and declining loan loss provisions as its loan portfolio's credit quality has improved with higher property valuations in a strengthened economy.

The company's revenue jumped by 32% to $837.7 million in 2014 mostly as its loan interest income swelled by 40% on loan asset growth from its F&M acquisition. The bank's non-interest income rose by 29% as well from new deposit account service fees from the acquisition and additional income from its newly added brokerage and trust business.

Higher revenue and strong operating cost controls in 2014 drove Prosperity's net income higher by 34% to $297.4 million while its operating cash levels rose by 13% to $348.3 million on higher cash earnings.

Strategy

Prosperity Bancshares bases its growth strategy on three key elements: Internal loan and deposit business growth through "individualized customer service" and service line expansion opportunities; cost controls to maximize profitability; and acquisitions.

Toward its internal business growth initiatives Prosperity spent 2012 and 2013 launching its new trust brokerage mortgage lending and credit card products and services to customers for the first time.

With cost-controls in mind the bank tracks its branches "as separate profit centers" noting each branch's interest income efficiency ratio deposit growth loan growth and overall profitability. That way it can reward individual branch managers and presidents accordingly by merit rather than giving higher compensation across the board.

The acquisitive Prosperity Bancshares has been buying up small banks in Texas — and now Oklahoma — as it hopes to hit a sweet spot in the market between the national giants that dominate the Texas banking scene and smaller community banks.

Mergers and Acquisitions

In January 2016 furthering its presence in the Houston market Prosperity Bancshares purchased Tradition Bancshares along with its seven branches in the Houston Area (Bellaire Katy and the Woodlands) $540 million in assets $239 million in loans and $483.8 million in deposits.

In April 2014 toward expansion in the Oklahoma and Dallas markets Prosperity purchased Tulsa-based F&M Bancorporation and its subsidiary The F&M Bank & Trust Company. The deal added 13 branches including nine in Tulsa and surrounding areas three in Dallas and a loan production office in Oklahoma City.

In April 2013 it acquired Coppermark Bank one of Oklahoma City's largest banks with six branches in Oklahoma City and three locations in North Dallas for $194 million. The deal also added the credit card and agent bank merchant processing business from its subsidiary Bankers Credit Card Services.

In January 2013 the company boosted its market share in East Texas after buying East Texas Financial Services and its four First Federal Bank Texas branch locations including three branches in Tyler and one in Gilmer.

Company Background

In early 2012 Prosperity acquired Texas Bankers a three-branch Austin bank with some $72 million in assets. The merger increased Prosperity's number of Central Texas branches to 34 banking locations. It followed that deal with the purchase of The Bank Arlington a single-branch bank operating in the Dallas/Ft. Worth area. It acquired single-branch Community National Bank of Bellaire Texas in late 2012.

Also in 2012 Prosperity expanded into West Texas after it merged American State Financial Corporation and its American State Bank subsidiary into its operations. The deal added $3 billion in assets and 37 West Texas banking offices in Lubbock Midland/Odessa and Abilene.

EXECUTIVES

Executive Vice President Cashier Prosperity Bank, Michael Harris
Evp Cashier Prosperity Bank, Mike Harris
Senior Chairman And Ceo, David Zalman, age 63, $851,567 total compensation
Cfo; Evp And Cfo Prosperity Bank, David Hollaway, age 64, $425,000 total compensation
Vice Chairman; Chairman And Coo Prosperity Bank, H. E. (Tim) Timanus, age 76, $452,400 total compensation
Vice Chairman And Area Chairman Central Texas, Edward Z. (Eddie) Safady
Evp Regulatory And Compliance Prosperity Bank, Rhonda L. Carroll
Chief Lending Officer Prosperity Bank, Randy D. Hester, $325,000 total compensation
Sevp Financial Operations And Administration Prosperity Bank, Mike Epps, $327,625 total compensation
Evp And Cio Prosperity Bank, Gisela Riggan
Chief Risk Oficer, Jennifer Willcoxon
Chief Credit Officer Prosperity Bank, Merle Karnes
President Prosperity Bank, Bob Benter
Evp Prosperity Bancshares And Prosperity Bank, Robert (Bob) Dowdell
Chairman Wealth Management, Russell Marshall
Senior Vice President Retail Banking, Tim Granger
Erm Risk Analyst Vice President, Amy Polasek
Senior Vice President Sba Lending, Beverly Layne
Senior Executive Vice President, Randall Reeves

Assistant Vice President Of Technology Procurement, Lausanne Barrett
Vice President, Rhonda Hamm
Assistant Vice President, Debbie Rodriguez
Senior Vice President Lending, Josie Amejorado
Assistant Vice President Lending Assistant, Flo Carmack
Assistant Vice President, Kim Lankston
Senior Vice President Iso Sponsorship Program, Jamie Bigley
Vice President Manager, Donna Brune
Vice President Commercial Lending, Kevin Deming
Vice President, Adrian Ozuna
Assistant Vice President Lobby Manager, Barbara Wilsher
Vice President Lobby Manager, Jana Rachunek
Assistant Vice President Lobby Manager, Bennie Gallentine
Vice President, Bill Hailey
Senior Vice President, Jamie Lander
Vice President, Candi Biggers
Vice President Lobby Manager, Donna Kraemer
Executive Vice President, Cathy Waller
President, Duncan Mcadoo
Assistant Vice President Lending Area, Betty Kindred
Vice President, Cecil Childers
Senior Vice President, Tim Cardinal
Vice President Marketing And Business Development, Brice Fowler
Senior Vice President, Jim Schroeder
Senior Vice President, Mark Odlis
7 Assistant Vice President, Kimberly Knight
Assistant Vice President, Robyn Totah
Assistant Vice President, Leslie Labrador
Vice President, Susan Rodriguez
Senior Vice President Trust Officer, Wendy Scribner
Vice President Lobby Manager, Bertha Ramos
Assistant Vice President Lending Assistant, Shannon Marshall
Senior Vice President, Charles Stuart
Vice President And Lending Assistant, Laura Wavra
Vice President, James Long
Vice President, Domingo Gonzales
Senior Vice President Backroom Operation, Thomas Petras
Senior Vice President, Kim Love
Senior Vice President, Sally Aman
Vice President And Trust Off Icer, Teal Stargel
Vice President Treasury Management Support, Jackie Bohon
Vice President Commercial Lending, Brandon Kidd
Senior Vice President, Mike Channel
Vice President, Yolanda Cox
Vice President, Melissa Owens
Assistant Vice President Lending, Beverly Allen
Vice President Commerical Lender, Rene Pena
Assistant Vice President Sba Lending, Valerie Alldredge
Assistant Vice President, Bella Molina
Vice President, Brittani Conoley
Vice President, Tess Schroeder
Vice President, Lauri Jefferson
Senior Vice President Prosperityprivate, Marilyn Morris
Senior Vice President, Robert Boone
Senior Vice President Commercial Real Estate, Dave Mccarthy
Senior Vice President And Residential Real Estate Manager, Allison Barlow
Vice President, Trixy Saldivar
Vp Facilities Manager, Todd Taylor
Senior Vice President, Jessica Chu
Board Member, Leah Henderson
Board Member, Stephanie Collier
Board Member, Jack Lord
Auditors: Deloitte and Touche LLP

LOCATIONS

HQ: Prosperity Bancshares Inc.
Prosperity Bank Plaza, 4295 San Felipe, Houston, TX 77027
Phone: 281 269-7199
Web: www.prosperitybankusa.com

PRODUCTS/OPERATIONS

2014 Sales

	$ mil.	% of total
Interest		
Loans including fees	525	63
Securities	188	22
Federal funds sold	0	-
Noninterest		
Non-sufficient funds fees	37	4
Debit card and ATM card income	22	3
Service charges on deposit accounts	16	2
Trust income	8	1
Brokerage income	5	1
Mortgage income	4	1
Other	28	3
Total	**837**	**100**

COMPETITORS

Amegy	JPMorgan Chase
BBVA Compass	North Dallas Bank
Bancshares	Texas Capital
Bank of America	Bancshares
Citibank	Wells Fargo
Comerica	Woodforest Financial
Cullen/Frost Bankers	

HISTORICAL FINANCIALS

Company Type: Public

Income Statement

FYE: December 31

	ASSETS ($ mil.)	NET INCOME ($ mil.)	INCOME AS % OF ASSETS	EMPLOYEES
12/19	32,185	332	1.0%	3,901
12/18	22,693	321	1.4%	3,036
12/17	22,587	272	1.2%	3,035
12/16	22,331	274	1.2%	3,035
12/15	22,037	286	1.3%	3,037
Annual Growth	9.9%	3.8%	—	6.5%

2019 Year-End Financials

Debt ratio: 4.44%	No. of shares (mil.): 94
Return on equity: 6.64%	Dividends
Cash ($ mil.): 573	Yield: 2.3%
Current ratio: —	Payout: 35.6%
Long-term debt ($ mil.): —	Market value ($ mil.): 6,811

	STOCK PRICE ($) FY Close	P/E High/Low	PER SHARE ($) Earnings	Dividends	Book Value
12/19	71.89	17 14	4.52	1.69	63.02
12/18	62.30	17 12	4.61	1.49	58.02
12/17	70.07	20 14	3.92	1.38	55.03
12/16	71.78	19 9	3.94	1.24	52.41
12/15	47.86	14 11	4.09	1.12	49.45
Annual Growth	10.7%	— —	2.5%	10.9%	6.2%

Protective Life Insurance Co

Protective Life & Annuity markets and sells financial security in the form of term and universal life insurance policies and fixed and variable annuity products. Although the company is based in Alabama and licensed to sell insurance throughout the US it exclusively serves clients in New York. Sister companies include West Coast Life Insurance (life insurance and annuities) MONY Life Insurance (ditto) and Lyndon Insurance (specialty coverage). Protective Life & Annuity is a unit of Protective Life Insurance which is part of Dai-Ichi Life Holdings subsidiary Protective Life Corporation.

Operations

Every state has unique requirements that insurance companies must meet in order to gain permission to operate there. New York's insurance code has the stiffest requirements and many small companies simply choose not to operate in that market. However the market is so large and tempting that other companies opt to maintain separate subsidiaries that exclusively serve New York. In this instance parent company Protective Life Insurance Company serves the rest of the US while Protective Life & Annuity is strictly focused on New York.

Protective Life Corporation was acquired by Japanese insurer Dai-ichi Life in early 2015.

Sales and Marketing

Protective Life & Annuity sells coverage through independent agents broker-dealers and financial institutions as well as through partnerships with employer groups and through its own sales division.

EXECUTIVES

Evp Chief Legal Officer Secretary And General Counsel, Deborah J. Long, age 66
Chairman And Ceo, John D. Johns, age 67
Evp And Chief Investment Officer, Carl S. Thigpen, age 63
Evp And Chief Administrative Officer, D. Scott Adams, age 55
President And Coo, Richard J. Bielen
Evp Finance And Risk; Chief Risk Officer, Michael G. (Mike) Temple, age 57
Svp Chief Information And Operations Officer, Mark J. Cyphert
Evp Cfo And Controller, Steven G. Walker
Auditors: KPMG LLP

LOCATIONS

HQ: Protective Life Insurance Co
2801 Highway 280 South, Birmingham, AL 35223
Phone: 205 268-1000
Web: www.protective.com

COMPETITORS

Guardian Insurance and Annuity	Penn Mutual
MetLife	Prudential
New York Life	The Hartford

HISTORICAL FINANCIALS
Company Type: Public

Income Statement
FYE: December 31

	ASSETS ($ mil.)	NET INCOME ($ mil.)	INCOME AS % OF ASSETS	EMPLOYEES
12/19	120,477	552	0.5%	3,096
12/18	89,383	193	0.2%	2,957
12/17	79,113	1,182	1.5%	2,773
12/16	74,465	352	0.5%	2,719
12/15	68,031	179	0.3%	2,541
Annual Growth	15.4%	32.4%	—	5.1%

2019 Year-End Financials

Debt ratio: 2.93%	No. of shares (mil.): 5
Return on equity: 6.06%	Dividends
Cash ($ mil.): 171	Yield: —
Current ratio: —	Payout: —
Long-term debt ($ mil.): —	Market value ($ mil.): —

PROVIDENCE HEALTH & SERVICES

EXECUTIVES

Ceo, Rod Hochman
Pres- Chief Dev Officer, Laurie Kelley
Exec V Pres-Cfo, Todd Hofheins
Technology, Henry Morgan
Coordinator, Mayra Graves
Security Engineering Consultan, Diana Bullion
Admin Assistant, Alex Figueroa
Pharmacy Director, Helen Noonan-Harnsber
Chief Human Resources Officer, Ron Chavira
Executive Director, Terri Warren
Senior Financial Analyst Real, Tuan Nguyen
Auditors: KPMG LLP SEATTLE WA

LOCATIONS

HQ: PROVIDENCE HEALTH & SERVICES
1801 LIND AVE SW, RENTON, WA 980573368
Phone: 425 525-3355
Web: WWW.PROVIDENCE.ORG

HISTORICAL FINANCIALS
Company Type: Private

Income Statement
FYE: December 31

	REVENUE ($ mil.)	NET INCOME ($ mil.)	NET PROFIT MARGIN	EMPLOYEES
12/15	14,433	49	0.3%	130
12/12	280	14	5.3%	—
12/08	7,026	(156)	—	—
12/07	6,348	434	6.8%	—
Annual Growth	10.8%	(23.8%)	—	—

Provident Financial Services Inc

Provident wants to be a prominent force in the New Jersey banking scene. Provident Financial Services owns The Provident Bank which serves individuals businesses and families from 85 branches across more than 10 northern and central New Jersey counties. Founded in 1839 the $8.5 billion-bank offers traditional deposit and lending products as well as wealth management and trust services. About 50% of its revenue comes from real estate loan interest while another 25% comes from interest on commercial and consumer loans. Construction loans round out its lending activities. The company's Provident Investment Services subsidiary sells life and health insurance and investment products.

Operations

Provident which staffed more than 1020 employees boasted some $8.5 billion in total assets loans of $6.1 billion and deposits of $5.8 billion at the end of 2014. Mortgages loans made up 70% of its total loan portfolio that year.

Geographic Reach

The bank's 86 branches are located in northern and central New Jersey as well as in Pennsylvania (in the Bucks Lehigh and Northampton counties). Its administrative offices are in Iselin New Jersey while its satellite loan production offices are in Covent Station Flemington Paramus Princeton and West Orange in New Jersey; and in Bethleham and Newtown Pennsylvania.

Sales and Marketing

Provident targets individuals families and businesses in its primary market areas in New Jersey (which covered a population of 6.9 million or 78% of the state's population) and Pennsylvania (where the bank's primary market covered 10% of that state's population.

Provident's primary markets include a mix of urban and suburban communities. It serves companies in a variety of industries including pharmaceutical and other manufacturing companies network communications insurance and financial services healthcare and retail businesses.

Financial Performance

Provident has struggled to consistently grow its revenues in recent years due to shrinking interest margins on loans amidst the low-interest environment. Its profits however have been rising thanks to declining loan loss provisions as its loan portfolio's credit quality has improved with higher property valuations in a strengthened economy.

The bank's revenue rose by 8% to $320.5 million in 2014 mostly thanks to added interest income from loan asset growth — including a 9% rise in real estate secured loan business and a 24% rise in commercial loan business — stemming from its acquisition of Team Capital Bank.

Higher revenue and a continued decline in loan loss provisions in 2014 drove Provident's net income higher by 4% to $73.6 million. Its operating cash levels dipped by 3% to $96.4 million after adjusting its earnings for non-cash items mostly related to an increase in other assets.

Strategy

Provident Financial continues to look for strategic acquisition opportunities of banks and other financial services providers to grow its loan and deposit business and extend its branch network into more of its primary market areas.

The company also remains focused on its conservative lending practices and is seeking to diversify its portfolio and reduce risk by placing more emphasis on commercial real estate multi-family residential and business loans.

Mergers and Acquisitions

In May 2014 Provident Financial Services purchased Team Capital Bank for $115.1 million effectively extending its reach into Eastern Pennsylvania and the affluent counties of Hunterdon and Somerset. The deal also added $964 million in total assets $631 million in loan assets and $770 million in deposits.

Company Background

In 2011 the company acquired Beacon Trust Company an asset manager for individuals municipalities corporations pension funds and not-for-profit organizations. The deal significantly expanded its wealth management business and boosted its assets under management to some $1.5 billion.

EXECUTIVES

Chairman President And Ceo, Christopher P. Martin, age 64, $608,846 total compensation
Evp And Cfo, Thomas M. Lyons, age 56, $349,308 total compensation
Evp And Director Retail Banking The Provident Bank, Michael A. Raimonde, age 68, $238,370 total compensation
Evp General Counsel And Corporate Secretary The Provident Bank, John F. Kuntz, age 65, $312,700 total compensation
Evp And Chief Lending Officer The Provident Bank, Donald W. Blum, age 64, $314,562 total compensation
Evp And Cio The Provident Bank, Jack Novielli, age 61
Evp And And Chief Human Resources Officer The Provident Bank, Janet D. Krasowski, age 67
Evp And Chief Credit Officer The Provident Bank, Brian Giovinazzi, age 66, $161,138 total compensation
Evp And Chief Wealth Officer The Provident Bank, James D. Nesci, age 48, $274,423 total compensation
Svp And Chief Risk Officer The Provident Bank, James Christy
Executive Vice President Human Resources, John Falco
First Vice President Marketing Director, Robert Capozzoli
Vice President, Brown Small
Assistant Vice President, Joseph Labib
Senior Vice President Director Asset Recovery, Rudolph Nemeth
First Vice President, Diane Conboy
Vice President Commercial Credit Underwriting, Debra Williams
Auditors: KPMG LLP

LOCATIONS

HQ: Provident Financial Services Inc
239 Washington Street, Jersey City, NJ 07302
Phone: 732 590-9200
Web: www.providentnj.com

PRODUCTS/OPERATIONS

2014 Sales

	$ mil.	% of total
Interest		
Real estate secured loans	166	52
Commercial loans	50	16
Consumer loans	23	7
Securities & other	38	12
Non-interest		
Fees	31	10
Other	9	3
Total	**320**	**100**

COMPETITORS

Bank of America	PNC Financial
Capital One	TD Bank USA
Citibank	Valley National
Hudson City Bancorp	Bancorp
JPMorgan Chase	
New York Community Bancorp	

HISTORICAL FINANCIALS

Company Type: Public

Income Statement — FYE: December 31

	ASSETS ($ mil.)	NET INCOME ($ mil.)	INCOME AS % OF ASSETS	EMPLOYEES
12/19	9,808	112	1.1%	1,015
12/18	9,725	118	1.2%	1,044
12/17	9,845	93	1.0%	1,054
12/16	9,500	87	0.9%	1,057
12/15	8,911	83	0.9%	1,064
Annual Growth	2.4%	7.7%	—	(1.2%)

2019 Year-End Financials

Debt ratio: 3.66%
Return on equity: 8.12%
Cash ($ mil.): 186
Current ratio: —
Long-term debt ($ mil.): —
No. of shares (mil.): 65
Dividends
Yield: 4.5%
Payout: 64.3%
Market value ($ mil.): 1,622

	STOCK PRICE ($) FY Close	P/E High/Low	PER SHARE ($) Earnings	Dividends	Book Value
12/19	24.65	16 13	1.74	1.12	21.49
12/18	24.13	16 12	1.82	0.97	20.49
12/17	26.97	20 16	1.45	0.93	19.52
12/16	28.30	21 13	1.38	0.71	18.94
12/15	20.15	16 13	1.33	0.65	18.26
Annual Growth	5.2%	— —	6.9%	14.6%	4.2%

Prudential Annuities Life Assurance Corp

Prudential Annuities Life AssuranceÂ hasÂ a name that fits — the companyÂ is theÂ annuities business unit of life insurance giant Prudential Financial. ItÂ offers variable and fixedÂ annuitiesÂ and other retirement and long-term investment products and services.Â Prudential Annuities Life Assurance's products are distributed through independent financial planners brokers and banks. ItÂ holds the lead position in the US variable annuities market; its variable annuities are distributed by Prudential Annuities Distributors. The company which is part of Prudential

Financial's US Retirement Solutions and Investment Management DivisionÂ targets US residents with a household income level of above $100000.

EXECUTIVES

Pres-Ceo, Robert F O'Donnell
Exec V Pres-Cfo, Yanela C Frias
Vice-President, Gary Palmer
Vice-President, Jan Hoffmeister
Executive of Sales, Lynn Erikson
Chief Operating Officer, Pelle Wahlstrom
Chief Information Officer, Ulf Tingstrom
Database Administrator, Cheryl Stewart
Software Developer, Dave Gianetti
Chief Investment Officer, Michael Long
Public Relations Executive, Scott Hawkins
Auditors: PricewaterhouseCoopers LLP

LOCATIONS

HQ: Prudential Annuities Life Assurance Corp
One Corporate Drive, Shelton, CT 06484
Phone: 203 926-1888
Web: www.investor.prudential.com

COMPETITORS

American Equity Investment Life Holding Company
Genworth Financial
Great American Financial Resources
John Hancock Financial Services
Kansas City Life
Lincoln Financial Group
MassMutual
MetLife
National Western
Northwestern Mutual
Presidential Life

HISTORICAL FINANCIALS

Company Type: Public

Income Statement — FYE: December 31

	ASSETS ($ mil.)	NET INCOME ($ mil.)	INCOME AS % OF ASSETS	EMPLOYEES
12/19	58,835	(989)	—	—
12/18	54,677	1,682	3.1%	—
12/17	59,960	(83)	—	—
12/16	59,822	(1,090)	—	—
12/15	47,254	173	0.4%	—
Annual Growth	5.6%	—	—	—

2019 Year-End Financials

Debt ratio: 0.71%
Return on equity: (-16.13%)
Cash ($ mil.): 3,130
Current ratio: —
Long-term debt ($ mil.): —
No. of shares (mil.): 0
Dividends
Yield: —
Payout: —
Market value ($ mil.): —

Prudential Financial Inc

Prudential Financial wants to make sure its position near the top of the life insurance summit is set in stone. Prudential known for its Rock of Gibraltar logo is one of the top US life insurers and one of the largest life insurance companies worldwide. The firm is perhaps best known for its individual life insurance though it also sells group life and disability insurance as well as annuities. Prudential also offers investment products and services including asset management services mutual funds and retirement planning. Prudential has about $1.5 trillion in assets under management. It generates more than 35% of revenue in the US.

Operations

Prudential operates through five primary divisions.

The second-largest division also at about 35% of revenue is International Insurance. That division provides individual life group insurance and retirement products including certain health policies in Japan Korea Taiwan Brazil Argentina and Mexico.

Its US Workplace Solutions division bringing in more than 30%of revenue ? comprises the Retirement and Group Insurance segments. The Retirement segment provides investment and income products and services to retirement plan sponsors. The Group Insurance segment offers a full range of group life long-term and short-term group disability and group corporate- bank- and trust-owned life insurance in the US. It primarily sells these to institutional clients.

The US Individual Solutions division (more than 15% of revenue) includes the Individual Life and Individual Annuities segments. The division distributes variable life term life and universal life policies as well as individual variable and fixed annuity products largely to middle-class affluent and wealthy clients in the US.

The final two divisions which together account for about 15% of revenue are Closed Block (inforce policies and annuities ? issued prior to the group's demutualization in 2001 ? as well as related assets and liabilities) and PGIM (investment management services).

Overall premiums account for about 50% of revenue followed by investment income (about 25%); fees and gains on investments generate most of the rest.

Geographic Reach

Prudential's US operations account for about 35% of sales. It also offers international products in regions including Asia Latin America and Europe.

Prudential has home offices (and hundreds of field offices) in about 60% Asian countries and about 35% European countries as well as Mexico Brazil Argentina and Australia.

Sales and Marketing

Prudential's group insurance products are marketed through an in-house sales force while its retirement products are primarily sold through third-party financial advisors benefit consultants and brokers. Individual life products are offered through third-party channels including independent brokers banks general agencies investment consultants and producer groups.

Financial Performance

Revenue for Prudential has grown over the last five years ? up 13% since 2015 ? as it continues to benefit from its diverse mix of complementary businesses. Net income has been fluctuating during that time.

In 2019 the company reported revenue of $64.8 billion up 3% from the prior year. The retirement business of the US Workplace segment saw revenue jump nearly $1.3 billion mostly because of new pension risk transfer transactions.

Net income in 2019 rose 3% to $4.2 billion from $4.1 billion the prior year. The $112 million increase reflected favorable variances of $1.6 billion from adjustments to reserves $954 million from unrealized gains from equity securities and $642 million from income in the current period from Divested and Run-off Businesses.

Cash at the end of 2019 was $16.5 billion an increase of $979 million from the prior year. Cash from operations contributed $19.6 billion to the coffers while investing activities used $17 billion. Financing activities used another $1.6 billion. Prudential's primary cash uses in 2019 were short-term investments acquisitions acquisition of common stock and repayments of notes issued by consolidated VIEs.

Strategy

Prudential's strategy centers on its mix of high-quality protection retirement and investment management business which creates growth potential due to earnings diversification and the opportunity to provide customers with integrated cross-business solutions as well as capital benefits from a balanced risk profile.

The company is also investing more in digital data and technology capabilities that is hopes to leverage across all its businesses to improve the customer experience. In 2019 Prudential acquired Assurance IQ a leading consumer solutions platform for health and financial wellness needs. With Assurance IQ it leverages data science and technology to distribute third-party life health Medicare and property and casualty products directly to retail shoppers primarily through its digital and independent agent channels.

Prudential is also selling Prudential of Taiwan to Taishin Financial a leading Taiwan-based financial institution. This transaction is consistent with Prudential's strategic focus internationally on Japan and higher-growth emerging markets around the world. PGIM the asset management business of Prudential Life will remain active in Taiwan.

Additionally PGIM Real Estate has completed its sale of 11 senior housing properties located throughout the Northeast and Mid-Atlantic U.S. PGIM has capitalized on powerful demographic trends driving the senior housing industry nationally which then provides a compelling return for its investors.

Mergers and Acquisitions

A leading consumer platform for health and financial wellness needs. Assurance which will be a subsidiary of the company adds a large and growing direct-to-consumer channel to Prudential's financial wellness businesses.

In 2019 Prudential completed the acquisition of Assurance IQ Inc. ("Assurance IQ") a leading consumer solutions platform that offers a range of solutions that help meet consumers' financial needs.

In 2019 Prudential acquired Administradora de Fondos de Pensiones Colfondos S.A. ("AFP Colfondos") a leading provider of retirement services in Colombia.

Company Background

Prudential traces its roots to 1875 when insurance agent John Fairfield Dryden establishes the Prudential Friendly Society. It was renamed The Prudential Insurance Company of America a decade later and adopted the Rock of Gibraltar as its company logo. It began trading on New York Stock Exchange in 2001.

HISTORY

In 1873 John Dryden founded the Widows and Orphans Friendly Society in New Jersey to sell workers industrial insurance (low-face-value weekly premium life insurance). In 1875 it became The Prudential Friendly Society taking the name from England's Prudential Assurance Co. The next year Dryden visited the English company and copied some of its methods such as recruiting agents from its targeted neighborhoods.

Prudential added ordinary whole life insurance in 1886. By 1900 the firm was selling more than 2000 such policies annually and had 3000 agents in eight states. In 1896 the J. Walter Thompson advertising agency (now the WPP Group) designed Prudential's Rock of Gibraltar logo.

The firm issued its first group life policy in 1916 (Prudential became a major group life insurer in the 1940s). In 1928 it introduced an Accidental Death Benefit which cost it an extra $3 million in benefits the next year alone (death claims rose drastically early in the Depression).

In 1943 Prudential mutualized. The company began decentralizing operations in the 1940s. Later it introduced a Property Investment Separate Account (PRISA) which gave pension plans a real estate investment option. By 1974 the firm was the US's group pension leader.

The insurer bought securities brokerage The Bache Group to form Pru Bache (now Prudential Securities) in 1981. Bache's forte was retail investments an area expected to blend well with Prudential's insurance business. Under George Ball Pru Bache tried to become a major investment banker — but failed. In 1991 Ball resigned leaving losses of almost $260 million and numerous lawsuits involving real estate limited partnerships.

Despite the 1992 settlement of the real estate partnership suits Prudential remained under scrutiny by several states because of "churning" a process in which agents generated commissions by inducing policyholders to trade up to more expensive policies. In 1995 new management led by former Chase Manhattanite Arthur Ryan brought sales under control sold such units as reinsurance and mortgage servicing and put its $6 billion real estate portfolio on the block. (In 1997 it sold its property management unit and Canadian commercial real estate unit; in 1998 it sold its landmark Prudential Center complex in Boston.)

In 1996 regulators from 30 states found that Prudential knew about the churning earlier than it had admitted had not stopped the perpetrators and had even promoted them. A 1997 settlement called for the company to pay restitution but the more than $2 billion estimated cost was thought to be less than the losses customers had suffered.

As the financial services industry continued to restructure Prudential in 1998 announced plans to demutualize. To focus on life insurance the company sold its health care unit to Aetna in 1999. The same year Prudential paid $62 million to resolve more churning claims revamped itself into international institutional and retail divisions and trimmed jobs. Ending its attempts to originate business the company cut 75% of its investment banking staff in 2000.

Demutualized Prudential Financial's 2001 IPO — one of the largest ever in the insurance industry — raised more than $3 billion. Prudential Financial became the holding company name for all operations making Prudential Insurance (the company's former name) a subsidiary and pure life insurer.

EXECUTIVES

Vice President Information Systems, Daniel Galvin
Chairman And Ceo, John R. Strangfeld, age 66, $1,400,000 total compensation
Svp Corporate Human Resources And Chair The Prudential Foundation, Sharon C. Taylor, age 66
Evp And Coo International, Charles F. (Charlie) Lowrey, age 62, $770,000 total compensation
Svp And Cio, Barbara G. Koster, age 65
Evp And Coo Us Businesses, Stephen (Steve) Pelletier, age 66, $770,000 total compensation
Managing Director And Ceo European Business; Head Of Global Merchant Banking Group, Robert M. Falzon, age 60, $759,231 total compensation
Svp And Chief Investment Officer, Scott G. Sleyster, age 60
Svp And Chief Risk Officer, Nicholas C. (Nick) Silitch, age 58
Svp And Chief Actuary, Richard F. Lambert, age 63
President And Ceo Prudential Retirement, Phil Waldeck
Evp And General Counsel, Timothy P. Harris, age 59
Vice President Information Systems, Michael Falzon
Vice President Information Technology, Jim Tonno
Vice President Information Technology, Diana D'Amore
Vice President Human Resources, Suzy Burnham
Vice President, Kevin Prue
Vp And Senior Corporate Counsel, Francine Boucher
Vice President Information Systems, Elaine Forsyth
Vice President Corporate Counselor, Lisa Chow
Vice President, Patrick Busby
Vice President Finance Pricing, Kimberly Plumb
Vice President Marketing Support, Donna Marzo
Senior Vice President Human Resources, Sue Taylor
Vice President Actuarial Talent Management Organization, Michelle Jankowski
Vice President Of International Operations And Systems, Ryugo Toh
Vice President Enterprise Information Security, Carol Haeberle
Regional Sales Vice President, Michael Latour
Vice President Financial Systems, John Toner
Vice President Corporate Development, Gaurav Wadhwa
Vice President, Rushabh Shah
Vice President Chief Information Security Officer, Thomas Doughty
Vice President Issues Management, Greg Loder
Vice President And Account Executive National Accounts, Karen Lehman
Vice President Process Management, Greg Steffe
Vice President Process Management, Michael Fedak
Vice President And Corporate Counsel, Edmond Papantonio
Vice President Corporate Development, Timothy Maroney
Vice President Marketing And Advertising Strategy, Niharika Shah
Vice President Institutional Sales, Kevin McGrory
Vice President Corporate Counsel, Richard Hibbard
M Sales Vice President, Doug Peterson
Vice President National Accounts, David Johnston
Vice President Information Systems, Venkata Natarajan
Svp And Head Global Product And Market Solutions Pension Risk Transfer Business, Rohit Mathur

Vice President Marketing Metrics, Bob Conover
Vice President Corporate Counsel (1997), William H Bulmer
Vice President Information Technology, Nicholas Defeis
Vice President Customer Service, Pauline Rossbauer
Vice President Finance, Jurgen Muhlhauser
Vice President Finance Chief Officer Prudential Group Insurance, Christine Knight
Vp And Controller Individual Life, Jamie Riesterer
Vice President Operational Risk Management, Susanna Davi
Vice President, Barbara Fuchs
Vice President Compensation, Ben Gunderson
Vice President Marketing Operations, William Peters
Vice President And Corporate Counsel, Michael Marchant
Vice President, Joshua Shipley
Vice President Portfolio Advisor, Clark Biggers
Vice President Asset Management, Sarah Downey
Vice President Of Financial Reporting, Stanley Lezon
Territorial Vice President, Mark Sears
Vice President Sales And Strategic Relationships Experience, Anne Thibeault
Vice President Corporate Counsel Enterprise Litigation Group, Susanna Gray
Vice President Of Project Management, Aimara Toledo
Vice President Of Stable Value Markets, Dylan Tyson
Vice President Counsel, Lisa Wolmart
Investment Vice President, Jennifer Riffle
Vice President Corporate Counsel, Richard Hoffman
Vice President Global Communications, Karen Oliver Moore
Vice President Investment Operations, Ralph Vasquez
Vice President Recruiting And Development, Catalina Camoscio
Vice President, Lily Huang
Senior Vice President Client Relations And Business Development, Sean Mclaughlin
Vice President Corporate And Community Engagement, Spring Taylor Lacy
Investment Senior Vice President, Eva Brezin
Vice President Strategic Initiatives, Amy Tedesco
Vice President Talent Partner, Matthew Dreyer
Vice President, Paul Curran
Assistant Vice President Actuary, Hannah Sun
Vice President Emarketing, Eric Philp
Regional Vice President External Wholesaler, Kinga Gawron
Vice President Asset Liability, Thomas Brennan
Regional Sales Vice President, Lawrence Slabosz
Vice President National Accounts, Trish Dedolce
Vice President Enterprise Compliance Training, Alan Greatorex
Investment Senior Vice President, Anne Fifick
Vice President Of Global Communications, Linda Fung
Vice President Strategic Sourcing, Mark Vogt
Senior Vice President Business Development, Marc Pester
Vice President And Assistant Treasurer, Kathleen Hoffman
Vice President, Hansjerg Schlenker
Vice President Human Resources International Hr, Erin Bokina
Vice President, Georgia Kingsley
Senior Vice President, Nick Silitch
Vice President, Steve Ahrens
Vp Human Resources Senior Hr Business Partner, Christina Schelling
Vice President Business Development Executive, Dawn Goldbacher
Vice President Operating Risk Management, Richard Didio

Vice President Data Governance And Solutions, John Adamo
Investment Vice President, Fernando Herrera
Vice President Key Accounts, William Stahl
Vice President Marketing, Theresa Austin
Vice President, Daniel Hess
Executive Vice President Head Of Global Accounts, Kimberly Lapointe
Regional Vice President, Keith Brennan
Vice President Information Systems, Marion Campbell
Vice President Information Systems, Anita Manchandra
Vice President Telecommunications Information Systems, Warren Leary
Vice President Sales, Richard Kinville
Vice President, Jim Street
Vice President Conference And Travel, Joanne Gandolfo
Vice President Information Technology, Joe Corrato
Vice President Chief Compliance Officer, Teresa M Gilbreath
Vice President Risk And Control, Susanna Banic
Vice President, George Haase
Vice President, James Quartuccio
Vice President, Larry Frank
Vice President Marketing And Brokerage Services, Michael Kalen
Vice President Audit, Hai You
Vice President, Brian Cloonan
Vice President Corporate Counsel (2006), Richard E Buckley
Vice President And Actuary, Sharon S Brody
Vice President Corporate Couns, Carlos R Gonzalez
Regional Vice President, Don Lanham
Vice President Corporate Couns, Jeffrey Clott
Vice President Of Strategic Initiatives, Vishal Jain
Investment Sr. Vice President, Husnu Kipcak
Senior Vice President International Inve, Bob Fallon
Vice President Business Solutions Center, Arthur Selverian
Vice President Marketing And Leads, Danielle Elliott
Vice President, Jeff Lee
Regional Vice President Advisor Channel, Matt Welch
Vice President Human Resources, Allison Philhower
Vice President Pbf Strategic Initiatives, Andrea Potts
Vice President Corporate Counsel, Benedict Carmicino
Executive Vice President, Richard Welch
Regional Vice President, George Laventure
Vice President, Craig Schwartzhoff
Vice President Risk Management, Giselle Lim
Senior Vice President, Dawn Richardson
Vice President Internal Audit, Margaret Byrne
Vice Presideni Investment Operations, Glenn Gutiahr
Vice President Marketing, Dawn Reilly
Vice President Corporate Counsel, Andrew French
Vice President Annuities Product Management, Dawn Leblanc
Vice President, Jeffrey Harrington
Vice President, Damian Wach
Investment Vice President, Adam Berkowitz
National Account Manager, Kathy B Thompson
Auditors: PricewaterhouseCoopers LLP

LOCATIONS

HQ: Prudential Financial Inc
751 Broad Street, Newark, NJ 07102
Phone: 973 802-6000
Web: www.investor.prudential.com

2018 Sales

	$ mil.	% of total
Domestic operations	40,603	64
Foreign operations	22,389	36
Total	**62,992**	**100**

PRODUCTS/OPERATIONS

2018 Sales

	$ mil.	% of total
International Insurance	22,234	35
US Workplace Solutions	22,510	35
US Individual Solutions	10,797	17
Closed block business	5,483	8
PGIM	3,294	5
Adjustments	(1326)	-
Total	**62,992**	**100**

2018 Sales

	$ mil.	% of total
Premiums	35,779	56
Net investment income	16,176	25
Policy charges & fee income	6,002	9
Asset management & service fees	4,100	7
Net realized investment gains	1,977	3
Losses	(1042)	-
Total	**62,992**	**100**

COMPETITORS

AEGON	Dai-ichi Life
AIG	ING
AXA	John Hancock Financial
Aetna	Services
Aflac	MetLife
Allianz	Northwestern Mutual
Aviva	Principal Financial
COUNTRY Financial	Zurich Insurance Group

HISTORICAL FINANCIALS

Company Type: Public

Income Statement   FYE: December 31

	ASSETS ($ mil.)	NET INCOME ($ mil.)	INCOME AS % OF ASSETS	EMPLOYEES
12/19	896,552	4,186	0.5%	51,511
12/18	815,078	4,074	0.5%	50,492
12/17	831,921	7,863	0.9%	49,705
12/16	783,962	4,368	0.6%	49,739
12/15	757,388	5,642	0.7%	49,384
Annual Growth	**4.3%**	**(7.2%)**	**—**	**1.1%**

2019 Year-End Financials

Debt ratio: 2.35%	No. of shares (mil.): 398
Return on equity: 7.49%	Dividends
Cash ($ mil.): 16,327	Yield: 4.2%
Current ratio: —	Payout: 42.7%
Long-term debt ($ mil.): —	Market value ($ mil.): 37,387

	STOCK PRICE ($) FY Close	P/E High/Low		PER SHARE ($) Earnings	Dividends	Book Value
12/19	93.74	10	8	10.11	4.00	158.25
12/18	81.55	13	8	9.50	3.60	118.37
12/17	114.98	6	5	17.86	3.00	127.96
12/16	104.06	11	6	9.71	2.80	106.76
12/15	81.41	7	6	12.17	2.44	93.69
Annual Growth	**3.6%**	**—**	**—**	**(4.5%)**	**13.2%**	**14.0%**

PSECU SERVICES, INC.

EXECUTIVES

Pres, Gregory A Smith
Public Relations Manager, Melissa Etshied
Member, John H McNamara
Member, Stephen Hedrick
Network Analyst, Mike Lamartina
Member, Ralph Britt

LOCATIONS

HQ: PSECU SERVICES, INC.
1 CREDIT UNION PL STE 1 # 1, HARRISBURG, PA
171102912
Phone: 800 237-7328
Web: WWW.PSECU.COM

HISTORICAL FINANCIALS

Company Type: Private

Income Statement   FYE: December 31

	ASSETS ($ mil.)	NET INCOME ($ mil.)	INCOME AS % OF ASSETS	EMPLOYEES
12/14	4,201	10	0.3%	5
12/13	4,119	43	1.1%	—
12/12	4,004	31	0.8%	—
12/01	1,736	15	0.9%	—
Annual Growth	**7.0%**	**(2.9%)**	**—**	**—**

Public Service Enterprise Group Inc

In the Garden State Public Service Enterprise Group's (PSEG) diversified business model has it smelling like a rose. Regulated subsidiary Public Service Electric and Gas (PSE&G) transmits and distributes electricity to 2.3 million customers and natural gas to 1.9 million customers in New Jersey. Subsidiary PSEG Power operates power generating plants and sells its energy wholesale to PSE&G and others. PSEG Power also owns and operates nearly 470 MW direct current (dc) of PV solar generation facilities. PSEG Power also has a 50% ownership interest in about 210 MW oil-fired generation facility in Hawaii. The remainder of this section about PSEG Power covers their nuclear and fossil fleet in the Mid-Atlantic and Northeast regions which comprises the vast majority of PSEG Power's operations and financial performance.

HISTORY

Tragedy struck Newark New Jersey in 1903 when a trolley slid down an icy hill and collided with a train killing more than 30 people. While investigating the accident state attorney general Thomas McCarter discovered the mismanagement of the trolley company and many of New Jersey's other transportation gas and electric companies. Planning to buy and consolidate these companies McCarter resigned and estab-

lished the Public Service Corporation in 1903 with several colleagues.

The company formed divisions for gas utilities electric utilities and transportation companies. The trolley company generated almost half of Public Service's sales during its first year.

In 1924 the gas and electric companies consolidated as Public Service Electric and Gas (PSE&G). A new company was formed that year to operate buses and in 1928 it merged with the trolley company to form Public Service Coordinated Transport (later Transport of New Jersey). PSE&G signed interconnection agreements with two Pennsylvania electric companies in 1928 to form the first integrated power pool — later known as the Pennsylvania-New Jersey-Maryland Interconnection. The Public Utility Holding Company Act of 1935 ushered in the era of regulated regional monopolies ensuring PSE&G a captive market.

During the 1960s PSE&G joined Philadelphia Electric to build its first nuclear plant at Peach Bottom Pennsylvania. The company completed a second plant in 1977 at Salem New Jersey. Its third one went on line at Hope Creek New Jersey. However plant mismanagement earned PSE&G a slew of fines in the 1980s and 1990s.

The company sold its transportation system to the State of New Jersey in 1980. Five years later PSE&G formed holding company Public Service Enterprise Group (PSEG) to move into nonutility enterprises and created Community Energy Alternatives (CEA now PSEG Global) to invest in independent power projects. In 1989 Enterprise Diversified Holdings (now PSEG Energy Holdings) was formed to handle activities ranging from real estate to oil and gas production.

CEA and three partners acquired a Buenos Aires power plant in 1993. Taking advantage of overseas privatization in the late 1990s it expanded into Asia and with AES purchased two Argentine electric companies.

PSE&G's nuclear problems resurfaced when the Salem plant was shut down in 1995 to rectify equipment breakdowns. In 1997 PSEG paid Salem partners Delmarva Power & Light and PECO Energy $82 million to settle their lawsuits charging mismanagement of Salem; both units were back on line by 1998.

Continuing to diversify in the late 1990s PSEG formed PSEG Energy Technologies in 1997 to market power and acquired five mechanical services companies in 1998 and 1999.

In 1999 PSEG Global teamed up with Panda Energy International to build three merchant plants in Texas (to be completed by 2001). It also planned plants in India and Venezuela and joined Sempra Energy to buy 90% of Chilquinta Energ a an energy distributor in Chile and Peru. In 2000 it bought 90% of a distributor serving Argentina and Brazil.

New Jersey's electricity markets were deregulated in 1999; a year later the company transferred PSE&G's generation assets to nonregulated unit PSEG Power. PSEG Power also took charge of PSEG Global's plants under development in Illinois Indiana and Ohio; announced plans for new plants in New Jersey; and acquired an Albany New York plant from Niagara Mohawk.

PSEG Global completed a power plant in Texas in 2001. It also bought 94% of generator and distributor Saesa from Chile's largest conglomerate Copec for $460 million; it later acquired the rest of Saesa through a tender offer. It also purchased a Peruvian generation firm ElectroAndes for $227 million.

In 2002 PSEG Power acquired two Connecticut plants from WEC Energy for approximately $270 million.

PSEG had agreed to be acquired by Exelon but both New Jersey and Pennsylvania opposed the merger and the deal fell through in 2006.

In 2006 PSEG Global sold its 32% stake in RGE a Brazilian electric distribution company with approximately 1.1 million customers to Companhia Paulista de For §a e Luz. In 2008 it sold the SAESA Group of Companies (a power distribution group) in southern Chile to a consortium formed by Morgan Stanley Infrastructure and the Ontario Teachers' Pension Plan for $887 million.

In 2013 PSEG Solar Source announced that it purchased two utility-scale solar power plants totaling 4.4 MW from Canadian Solar Inc. The solar installations are the largest in Shasta county California built at more than 3300 feet in elevation.

EXECUTIVES

Vice President Finance (pseandg) Pseg Services Corporation, Scott Jennings
President And Coo Pseg Power Llc, Ralph A. LaRossa, age 57, $684,308 total compensation
Chairman President And Ceo, Ralph Izzo, age 62, $1,298,269 total compensation
Evp And Cfo, Daniel J. (Dan) Cregg, age 56, $520,000 total compensation
Evp And General Counsel, Tamara L. Linde, age 55, $533,789 total compensation
President And Coo Pse&g And Chairman Pseg Long Island Llc, David M. Daly, age 58
President Pseg Services Corporation, Derek M. Di Risio, age 55
Vice President Engineering Pseg Nuclear, Paul J Davison
Vice President Gas Supply Pseg Energy Resources And Trade, David Caffery
Vice President Of Employee Benefits Health And Safety, John Tiberi
Vice President Construction Pseg Power, Kevin Cellars
Vice President Manager Director, Donald Staudt
Vice President Tax, Robert Krueger
Vice President Of Tax, Norman Chadwick
Regional Vice President And Managing Director, Guy Vogt
Vp Finance Corporate Strategy And Planning, Rose Chernick
Vice President Regulatory And Deputy General Counsel, Joseph Accardo
Vice President Of Tax, Jose M Perez
Legal Secretary, June Barnett
Vice President Of Tax, Mark Creely
Legal Secretary, Sandra Mayer
Vice President Procurement Pseg Service Corp., Brian Clark
Vp Transmission And Distribution Pseg Long Island, John O'Connell
Vp Power Markets Pseg Long Island, Paul Napoli
Vp Corporate Communications Pseg Services Corporation, Karen Cleeve
Vice President Of Compliance, David Mannai
Government Relations, Vincent Frigeria
Senior Vice President Design, Thomas Ango

Vice President Strategy And Policy (lipa), John Little
Board Member, Hak Shin
Assistant Treasurer, Lynn Manganaro
Treasurer, Bradford Huntington
Board Member, Michael F Percarpio
Board Member, Willie Deese
Auditors: DELOITTE & TOUCHE LLP

LOCATIONS

HQ: Public Service Enterprise Group Inc
80 Park Plaza, Newark, NJ 07102
Phone: 973 430-7000
Web: www.pseg.com

PRODUCTS/OPERATIONS

2016 Sales

	$ mil.	% of total
PSE&G	6,221	59
Power	4,023	38
Others	370	3
Adjustments	(1553)	-
Total	**9,061**	**100**

Selected Subsidiaries

PSEG Energy Holdings Inc. (nonutility companies)
  PSEG Global Inc. (solar plants and other alternative energy investments)
  PSEG Resources Inc. (energy infrastructure investments)
PSEG Power LLC
  PSEG Fossil LLC (operator of PSEG's fossil fuel plants)
  PSEG Nuclear LLC (operator of PSEG's nuclear plants)
  PSEG Energy Resources and Trade LLC (energy marketing)
PSEG Services Corporation (management and administrative services for PSEG)
Public Service Electric and Gas Company (PSE&G distribution of electricity and gas)

COMPETITORS

AEP	FirstEnergy
CenterPoint Energy	NRG Energy
Con Edison	National Grid USA
Constellation Energy Group	New Jersey Resources
Delmarva Power	NextEra Energy
Eversource Energy	PPL Corporation
Exelon	South Jersey Industries

HISTORICAL FINANCIALS

Company Type: Public

Income Statement

FYE: December 31

	REVENUE ($ mil.)	NET INCOME ($ mil.)	NET PROFIT MARGIN	EMPLOYEES
12/19	10,076	1,693	16.8%	12,992
12/18	9,696	1,438	14.8%	13,145
12/17	9,084	1,574	17.3%	12,945
12/16	9,061	887	9.8%	13,065
12/15	10,415	1,679	16.1%	13,025
Annual Growth	(0.8%)	0.2%	—	(0.1%)

2019 Year-End Financials

Debt ratio: 33.99%
Return on equity: 11.49%
Cash ($ mil.): 147
Current ratio: 0.64
Long-term debt ($ mil.): 13,743
No. of shares (mil.): 504
Dividends
  Yield: 3.1%
  Payout: 65.7%
Market value ($ mil.): 29,761

	STOCK PRICE ($) FY Close	P/E High/Low	PER SHARE ($) Earnings	Dividends	Book Value
12/19	59.05	19 15	3.33	1.88	29.94
12/18	52.05	20 16	2.83	1.80	28.53
12/17	51.50	17 13	3.10	1.72	27.42
12/16	43.88	27 22	1.75	1.64	26.01
12/15	38.69	13 11	3.30	1.56	25.86
Annual Growth	11.1%	— —	0.2%	4.8%	3.7%

Publix Super Markets, Inc.

Publix Super Markets tops the list of privately owned grocery operators in the US. By emphasizing service and a family-friendly image over price Publix has outgrown and outperformed its regional rivals. About 65% of its 1200-plus stores are in Florida but it also operates in half a dozen other southeastern states. Publix makes some of its own bakery deli dairy goods and fresh prepared foods at its own manufacturing plants in Florida and Georgia. Founder George Jenkins began offering stock to Publix employees in 1930; employees own around 45% of the company.

Operations

Publix stores sell grocery products (dairy produce deli baker meat and seafood) health and beauty care products general merchandise pharmacy products flowers and other products and services. Grocery activities account for some 85% of sales and the remaining revenue came from other operations.

Geographic Reach

Lakeland Florida-based Publix has more than 1200 supermarkets in Florida (about 65% of total) and Georgia (about 15% of total) also it has stores in Alabama South Carolina Tennessee North Carolina and Virginia.

It restocks store shelves from nearly ten distribution centers ? more than five in Florida and in Georgia and Alabama. The grocer also operates half a dozen dairy bakery and deli facilities located in Florida Georgia and Atlanta.

Sales and Marketing

The company receives the food and nonfood products it distributes from many sources. These products are delivered to the supermarkets through the company's distribution centers or directly from the suppliers and are generally available in sufficient quantities to enable the company to satisfy its customers. Approximately 75% of the total cost of products purchased is delivered to the supermarkets through the company's distribution centers. Private label items are produced in the company's dairy bakery and deli manufacturing facilities or are manufactured for the company by suppliers.

Advertising costs are expensed as incurred and were $245.4 million in 2019 $249.1 million in 2018 and $251.9 million in 2017 respectively.

Financial Performance

Publix has shown solid sales growth over the past five years as it continues to expand and open new stores across the Southeast. Its revenue has risen nearly 18% since 2015. With profit margins higher than many (if not all) of its grocery competitors the company has also seen increases in its net income in recent years.

In 2019 Publix reported revenue of $38.1 billion up 6% from the prior year. This was primarily due to new supermarket sales and a 4% increase in comparable store sales. These comparable store sales increased primarily due to increased product costs.

Net income in 2019 was $3 billion compared with $2.4 billion in 2018. The increase in earnings was primarily due to an increase in investment income.

Cash at the end of 2019 was $763.4 million an increase of $164.1 million from the prior year. Cash from operations contributed $4 billion to the coffers. Investing activities used $2.3 billion mainly for investments and capital expenditures. Financing activities used another $1.6 billion mostly for acquisition of common stock and dividends paid.

Strategy

Publix's growth strategy is based on investing in its stores and enhancing its customer service. Its core strategies include customer service product quality shopping environment competitive pricing and convenient locations. The company has implemented several strategic business and technology initiatives as part of the execution of these core strategies.

The company opened 31 stores in 2019 which included five replacement supermarkets and 177 supermarkets were remodeled. Seven supermarkets were closed during the period. The replacement supermarkets that opened in 2019 replaced one supermarket closed in 2019 and four supermarkets closed in a previous period.

Publix expects its capital expenditures for 2020 to be approximately $1.6 billion primarily related to new supermarkets remodeling existing supermarkets new or enhanced information technology hardware and software and the acquisition of shopping centers with the company as the anchor tenant.

Company Background

George Jenkins former manager of the Piggly Wiggly grocery in Winter Haven Florida opened his own store Publix in 1930. The chain expanded organically and through acquisitions and included 100 stores by 1964.

In 1991 Publix opened its first store outside Florida in Georgia as part of its plan to become a major player in the Southeast.

George Jenkins died in 1996 but Publix has continued to thrive as a family- and employee-owned company.

EXECUTIVES

Evp And Cfo, David P. Phillips, age 60, $1,051,090 total compensation

Svp General Counsel And Secretary, John A. Attaway, age 61, $690,310 total compensation

Svp, David E. Bornmann, age 62, $488,300 total compensation

President Ceo And Director, Randall T. (Todd) Jones, age 57, $1,688,750 total compensation

Svp And Cio, Laurie Z. Douglas, age 56, $890,255 total compensation

Manager Government Relations, Shane Kunze

Vice Chairman, Hoyt R. (Barney) Barnett, age 77

President And Director, William E. (Ed) Crenshaw, age 69

Auditors: KPMG LLP

LOCATIONS

HQ: Publix Super Markets, Inc.
3300 Publix Corporate Parkway, Lakeland, FL 33811
Phone: 863 688-1188
Web: www.publix.com

2018 Supermarkets

	No.
Florida	798
Georgia	186
Alabama	71
South Carolina	59
Tennessee	44
North Carolina	41
Virginia	12
Total	**1,211**

PRODUCTS/OPERATIONS

2018 Sales

	% of total
Grocery	84
Other	16
Total	**100**

Selected Supermarket Departments

Bakery
Dairy
Deli
Floral
Groceries
Health and beauty care
Meat
Pharmacy
Produce
Seafood
Foods Processed
Baked goods
Dairy products
Deli items

COMPETITORS

ALDI	Piggly Wiggly Carolina
CVS	Rite Aid
Costco Wholesale	Sedano's
Food Lion	Southeastern Grocers
IGA	Wal-Mart
Ingles Markets	Walgreen
Kmart	Whole Foods
Kroger	

HISTORICAL FINANCIALS

Company Type: Public

Income Statement

FYE: December 28

	REVENUE ($ mil.)	NET INCOME ($ mil.)	NET PROFIT MARGIN	EMPLOYEES
12/19	38,462	3,005	7.8%	207,000
12/18	36,395	2,381	6.5%	202,000
12/17	34,836	2,291	6.6%	193,000
12/16	34,274	2,025	5.9%	191,000
12/15	32,618	1,965	6.0%	180,000
Annual Growth	**4.2%**	**11.2%**	**—**	**3.6%**

2019 Year-End Financials

Debt ratio: 0.70%	No. of shares (mil.): 706
Return on equity: 23.70%	Dividends
Cash ($ mil.): 763	Yield: —
Current ratio: 1.06	Payout: 27.5%
Long-term debt ($ mil.): 132	Market value ($ mil.): —

PulteGroup Inc

PulteGroup targets a cross-section of home buyers nationwide by buying or optioning land to build single-family houses duplexes townhouses and condominiums. Its Centex brand is marketed to entry-level buyers while Pulte Homes aims to capture customers looking to trade up. PulteGroup also builds Del Webb retiree communities for the growing number of buyers in the 55-plus age range. The company sells its homes in more than 40 markets across roughly 25 states. Its homes go for an average price of $427000. PulteGroup became one of the top homebuilders in the US by buying rivals John Wieland Homes and Centex Homes.

HISTORY

William Pulte built his first home in Detroit in 1950 and incorporated his business in 1956 as William J. Pulte Inc.

In 1961 the company built its first subdivision in Detroit. During that decade Pulte moved into Washington DC (1964) Chicago (1966) and Atlanta (1968). In 1969 Pulte merged with Colorado's American Builders to form the Pulte Home Corporation a publicly traded company.

Originally a builder of high-priced single-family homes Pulte began expanding into affordable and midrange housing markets. To lower costs it pioneered modular designs and prebuilt components. Pulte architects designed the Quadrominium a large structure with four separate two-bedroom units each with its own entrance and garage (priced at a mere $20000 per unit in the 1970s).

Pulte formed Intercontinental Mortgage (later renamed ICM Mortgage) and began making home loans in 1972. The company ran into trouble in 1988 when it was accused of forcing Pulte homebuyers in Baltimore to use ICM financing instead of cheaper loans from the county. Pulte settled by repaying the difference in loan costs.

By the mid-1980s Pulte was one of the US's largest on-site homebuilders. PHM Corporation was created in 1987 as a holding company for the Pulte group of companies. That year PHM entered the thrift business by assisting the Federal Savings and Loan Insurance Corp.'s S&L bailout. It acquired five Texas S&Ls (with assets of $1.3 billion) for $45 million and eventually combined them to form First Heights (finally discontinuing the business in 1994).

Pulte Homes' Quality Leadership customer satisfaction program introduced in the early 1990s paid off in 1991 as Pulte enjoyed record sales despite a depressed home market. Renamed Pulte Corporation in 1993 the company soon faced rising interest rates which dampened the US housing market and affected the Mexican peso. Pulte recorded a $2 million foreign-currency loss on an affordable-housing venture in Mexico in 1994. Nonetheless it began a second joint venture in that country in 1995 and helped form mortgage bank Su Casita with nine Mexican homebuilders to finance home construction on its border. That year it also started developing retirement communities when it bought the Ponds at Clearbrook in New Jersey.

In 1996 its Mexican joint venture Condake-Pulte began building thousands of affordable homes for General Motors and Sony employees in maquiladora residential areas near the US-Mexico border. The company also bought Rhode Island's top homebuilder LeBlanc.

Pulte restructured in 1997 and a year later shed its manufactured housing and building supply business. It also acquired DiVosta one of Florida's largest homebuilders and Tennessee-based Radnor Homes.

The company's 1988 foray into S&Ls came back to haunt it in 1998: The Federal Deposit Insurance Corp. won a lawsuit that accused the builder of abusing tax benefits associated with the S&Ls. (Pulte settled the case in 2001 by paying $41.5 million.) In 1999 Pulte bought the interest held by investment firm Blackstone Group its partner in active-adult homebuilding.

The next year Pulte joined other builders in an Internet-based building materials cooperative. Also in 2000 the company began dealings to expand its homebuilding operations into Argentina.

The company changed its name to Pulte Homes in 2001. That year Mark O'Brien became the company's CEO. He directed Pulte through the major acquisition of retirement community developer Del Webb for about $800 million in stock and $950 million in assumed debt. The combined company became the largest US homebuilder. In 2002 Pulte reorganized the structure of its operations in Mexico and created Pulte Mexico S. de R.L. de C.V. one of the largest builders in that country.

Adding to its portfolio of accolades Pulte was named 2002 "Builder of the Year" by Professional Builder magazine and in 2003 Pulte ranked 19th among the "Top 50 Best-Performing Companies" in Business Week's performance rankings of the Standard & Poor's 500-stock index.

Pulte expanded its operations in the fast-growing San Diego area in 2003 by purchasing assets of ColRich Communities which included about 500 entitled lots in five communities in the South Bay and Coastal North areas of San Diego. It boosted its presence in the Albuquerque Phoenix and Tucson markets by acquiring Sivage-Thomas Homes (Albuquerque) with about 7000 lots in the region and Del Webb entered the Reno Nevada market with its Sierra Canyon active adult community. O'Brien left the company in June 2003 after having served in senior management positions for six years (and 21 total years) within the company. EVP and COO Richard Dugas stepped up to become the company's president and CEO at that time.

In September 2003 the US Court of Federal Claims awarded Pulte and related parties $48.7 million as a result of a breach of contract by the US government related to Pulte's acquisition of five savings and loans in 1988.

J.D. Power and Associates recognized Pulte as a top performer for its fifth consecutive year in its "2004 New Home Builder Customer Satisfaction Study." Out of the 25 markets it surveyed Pulte ranked highest in 14 markets #2 in nine markets and #3 in six markets.

At the close of 2004 Pulte sold some operations in Argentina to real estate developer Grupo Farallon. The next year it sold its Mexican and remaining Argentine homebuilding enterprises to focus exclusively on US operations.

The downturn in the US housing market — due to a toxic cocktail of higher home prices increased foreclosures high unemployment and constraints on mortgage lending — led to weakened demand for new homes and higher cancellation rates. For Pulte this trend meant decreased profitability and a decline in homebuilding activity. Pulte responded to the downturn and adjusted its operations by cutting jobs and shuttering plants to meet lower demand levels.

The company bought rival Centex in 2009. The acquisition made Pulte the largest homebuilder in the US and also strengthened Pulte's offerings in the lower-priced home segment.

A year following the Centex merger founder William Pulte retired from the company and from its board of directors. He was named chairman emeritus.

EXECUTIVES

Evp And Coo, Harmon D. Smith, age 56, $688,462 total compensation
Vp And Cio, Joseph L. Drouin
Evp Human Resources, James R. (Jim) Ellinghausen, age 62, $546,154 total compensation
Evp And Cfo, Robert T. (Bob) O'Shaughnessy, age 54, $742,307 total compensation
President Ceo And Director, Ryan R. Marshall, age 45, $738,462 total compensation
Evp General Counsel And Corporate Secretary, Todd N. Sheldon
Vp And Chief Marketing Officer, Manish M. Shrivastava
Area Vice President Of Finance, Rick Wiles
Vice President Marketing Communications, James VanKirk
Sales Vice President, Sean Clancy
Senior Vice President Human Resources, Michelle Hairston
Svp Finance, James Ossowski
Vice President Of Procurement, Ryan Rossiter
Vice President Finance, Michael Hyland
Vice President Information Security And Chief Information Security Officer, Alex Wood
Senior Vice President Operations Pulte Mortgage, Wyvetter Livingston
Vice President Tax And Assistant Secretary, Kimberly Hill
Vice President Investor Relations And Corporate Communications, Jim Zeumer
Vice President Of Construction Operations, Chris Edwards
Vice President Land Acquisition, Brad Piroli
Vice President Finance, John Evans
Division Vice President Of Land Acquisition, Matt Callahan
Vice President Construction Operations Middle Atlantic Division, Brad Nicholas
Senior Vice President Capital Markets, Jeff Moran
Vice President Human Resources, Sharyn Torrisi-Cartwright
Vice President And Treasurer, D Bryce Bryce Langen
Vice President, David Demarco
Senior Vice President Field Operations, Marc Rego
Sr.vice President Operations, Leslie Devera-duncan
Vice President Regional Service Manager, Paul Harris
Vice President Sales And Marketing, Matt Roesch
Vice President And Area General Counsel, Scott V Williams
Area Vice President Southeast, Paul Johnson
Division Vice President Construction Operations, Rick Kyle
Board Member, Andre Hawaux

Board Member, Scott Powers
Board Member, Cheryl Grise
Board Member, Thomas Folliard
Board Member, Richard Dreiling
Board Member, John Peshkin
Auditors: Ernst & Young LLP

LOCATIONS

HQ: PulteGroup Inc
  3350 Peachtree Road N.E., Suite 150, Atlanta, GA 30326
Phone: 404 978-6400
Web: www.pultegroupinc.com

Selected Homebuilding Regions

Florida
North (IL IN MI MN MO Northern CA OH OR WA)
Northeast (CT DE MD MA NJ NY PA RI VA)
Southeast (GA NC SC TN)
Southwest (AZ CO HI NV NM Southern CA)
Texas

PRODUCTS/OPERATIONS

2018 Sales

	$ mil.	% of total
West	2,654	26
Florida	1,944	19
Southeast	1,746	17
Midwest	1,497	15
Texas	1,301	13
Northeast	839	8
Financial Services	205	2
Total	**10,188**	**100**

2018 Sales

	$ mil.	% of total
Home building		
Home Sales	9818.4	96
Land Sales	164.5	2
Financial Services	205	2
Total	**10,188**	**100**

Selected Brands

Centex (entry-level buyers)
Del Webb (active-adult buyers)
DiVosta (Florida)
Pulte Homes (move-up buyers)

COMPETITORS

Beazer Homes	M.D.C.
CalAtlantic	Meritage Homes
D.R. Horton	NVR
Hovnanian Enterprises	Pardee Homes
KB Home	Toll Brothers
Lennar	

HISTORICAL FINANCIALS

Company Type: Public

Income Statement   FYE: December 31

	REVENUE ($ mil.)	NET INCOME ($ mil.)	NET PROFIT MARGIN	EMPLOYEES
12/20	11,036	1,406	12.7%	5,249
12/19	10,212	1,016	10.0%	5,245
12/18	10,188	1,022	10.0%	5,086
12/17	8,573	447	5.2%	4,810
12/16	7,668	602	7.9%	4,623
Annual Growth	9.5%	23.6%	—	3.2%

2020 Year-End Financials

Debt ratio: 25.92%	No. of shares (mil.): 266
Return on equity: 23.33%	Dividends
Cash ($ mil.): 2,582	Yield: 1.1%
Current ratio: 8.89	Payout: 10.4%
Long-term debt ($ mil.): 3,164	Market value ($ mil.): 11,490

	STOCK PRICE ($) FY Close	P/E High/Low	PER SHARE ($) Earnings	Dividends	Book Value
12/20	43.12	10 3	5.18	0.50	24.66
12/19	38.80	11 7	3.66	0.45	20.20
12/18	25.99	10 6	3.55	0.38	17.39
12/17	33.25	24 13	1.44	0.36	14.49
12/16	18.38	13 9	1.75	0.36	14.60
Annual Growth	23.8%	— —	31.2%	8.6%	14.0%

PVH Corp

PVH has the buttoned-up look down. A top global apparel player PVH is the world's largest dress shirt and neckwear company. The company owns three titans of the apparel industry: Calvin Klein Tommy Hilfiger and Heritage Brands. The former two are multi-billion-dollar global lifestyle brands while Heritage Brands is a luxury apparel wholesaler that owns the brands Van Heusen IZOD ARROW Warner's Olga and True & Co. PVH is also has licenses for third-party brands such as DKNY Speedo Kenneth Cole Reaction Michael Kors Collection and others. The company generates sales from multiple channels including more than 1800 company-operated retail stores and approximately 1500 concession stands retail partners and licensees. It also charges royalty and advertising fees. Nearly 45% of sales were generated in the US.

Operations

PVH organizes its business into three main areas: Tommy Hilfiger Calvin Klein and Heritage Brands.

Tommy Hilfiger split into Tommy Hilfiger North America and Tommy Hilfiger International contributes nearly 50% to PVH's revenue. The brand makes every day and formalwear for the upper-middle class characterized by its classic American preppy stylings. It runs a number of sub-brands such as Hilfiger Collection Tommy Hilfiger Tailored Tommy Hilfiger Tommy Jeans and Tommy Sport. It sells its products wholesale to third party retailers and at retail via a network of owned outlets and has around 25 license agreements with third parties in Brazil India and Mexico among other countries.

Calvin Klein accounts for more than 35% of revenue and runs a number of sub-brands alongside its Calvin Klein "master" brand: Calvin Klein Calvin Klein Jeans Calvin Klein Performance CK Calvin Klein and Calvin Klein Underwear. Together they fill various price points through multiple distribution channels and to different consumer groups. As with Tommy Hilfiger Calvin Klein has around 45 licensing and other arrangements across its brands including JVs in India and Mexico.

Heritage Brands accounts for around 15% of revenue and makes shirts neckwear sportswear swimwear intimates underwear and accessories through a range of owned brands and licensed brands. Its licensed brands are DKNY Speedo Kenneth Cole New York Kenneth Cole Reaction MICHAEL Kors Michael Kors Collection and Chaps. It sells wholesale and through Heritage Brands retail outlets across the United States and Canada. Some of its stores stock IZOD Golf Warner's and Speedo products. Heritage Brands has licensing agreements with around 80 US and international companies.

Geographic Reach

PVH's products are made in more 1200 factories in some 50 countries worldwide. PVH maintains wholesale and retail warehousing and distribution centers in the US China South Korea Brazil Australia Canada Japan and the Netherlands. The centers inspect sort pack and ship goods to customers.

The company sells products in the US Canada Europe Asia Mexico and Brazil. Its US business accounts for about 45% of sales and Europe accounts for more than 35%. Asia Canada and others bring in the rest.

The company is headquartered in New York.

Sales and Marketing

PVH has a relatively concentrated customer base. Its five largest customers including Macy's J. C. Penney account for about 20% each of sales.

PVH targets the marketing of its brands at distinct consumer demographics. The company advertises its brands through digital media (including its e-commerce and social media sites) national print media television outdoor signage special events promotions and store locations. It also advertises through product tie-ins and sport sponsorships . The Tommy Hilfiger marketing team also coordinates appearances by the designer himself Tommy Hilfiger at runway shows special events and flagship store openings.

The company's advertising expenses totaled $509.7 million $526.0 million and $501.3 million in 20192018 and 2017 respectively.

Financial Performance

PVH's sales have been rising for the last five years with an overall growth of 24%. Revenue in 2019 was $9.9 billion.

The increase in revenue of $252 million or 3% in 2019 as compared to 2018 was due principally to the net effect of the net addition of an aggregate $367 million of revenue or an 8% increase over the prior year attributable to its Tommy Hilfiger International and Tommy Hilfiger North America segments which included a negative impact of $129 million or 3% related to foreign currency translation.

Net income was reduced 44% to $417.3 million in 2019.

PVH's cash on hand rose $51.4 million during fiscal 2019 standing at $503.4 million at year's end. The company's operations generated $1 billion offset by $505.9 million used in investing activities and $451.6 million used in financing activities. PVH's main cash uses in fiscal 2019 were capital expenditures debt repayments and share repurchases.

Strategy

PVH sees opportunities for long-term growth as it employs its strategic priorities across the organization. Its global growth strategies include:

Driving consumer engagement through innovative designs and personalized brand and shopping experiences that capture the heart of the consumer;

Leveraging data driven marketing to deepen the relationships with consumers through segmented product assortments and personalized content;

Expanding its worldwide reach through organic growth and acquisitions;

Investing in and evolving how it operates by leveraging technology and data to be dynamic nimble and forward-thinking;

Evolving its supply chain to adapt more quickly to change and reduce lead times;

Developing a talented and skilled workforce that embodies its core values and an entrepreneurial spirit while empowering its associates to design its future;

And delivering sustainable profitable growth and generating free cash flow to create long-term stockholder value.

Mergers and Acquisitions

Bringing some of its international businesses under direct control in 2019 PVH spent about $90 million on acquiring the remaining about 80% of Gazal Corporation PVH's long-term Australian partner that it did not already own. PVH also paid approximately $75 million to acquire the Tommy Hilfiger business in Hong Kong Macau Taiwan Singapore and Malaysia. The transaction is intended to allow the company to capitalize on the significant growth opportunity in the region.

HISTORY

Moses Phillips came to America from Poland in 1881. While living in a one-room apartment in Pottsville Pennsylvania he sold flannel shirts (which his wife sewed) to coal miners from a pushcart. He soon brought the rest of his family to the US and upgraded the pushcart to a horse and buggy. Business continued to grow and the Phillips-Jones Corporation was formed in 1907.

The company moved to New York in 1914 and control passed from father to son for four generations. Isaac followed Moses then Seymour took over in 1941 until he handed the reins to Lawrence who joined the company in 1948 and became president and CEO in 1969. Ads in the 1950s featured such actors as Anthony Quinn Burt Lancaster and Ronald Reagan in Van Heusen shirts. In 1957 the company received its new name Phillips-Van Heusen (PVH). It grew via acquisitions throughout the 1970s and began selling its merchandise at its own outlet stores in 1979 but it didn't want its products sold at the off-price outlets that became popular in the early 1980s. The company stopped doing business with stores and distributors that allowed PVH merchandise to reach cut-price vendors.

In 1987 PVH bought back more than 5 million shares of stock in order to fend off an acquisition bid by the Hunt family of Texas. Lawrence stepped down in 1993 ending the unbroken chain of Phillipses at the helm. In 1995 the Phillips family sold its stake in the business. In June 2011 the company renamed itself PVH Corp. officially dropping the Phillips-Van Heusen moniker to emphasize its diversified portfolio of brands.

EXECUTIVES

President Geoffrey Beene Retail, Margaret P. (Meg) Lachance
Executive Vice President Finance And Risk, Bruce Goldstein
Chairman And Ceo, Emanuel (Manny) Chirico, age 63, $1,350,000 total compensation

Evp Chief Operating And Financial Officer, Michael A. (Mike) Shaffer, age 58, $891,667 total compensation

Ceo Heritage Brands And North America Wholesale, Francis K. (Ken) Duane, age 64, $1,091,667 total compensation

President Licensing, Kenneth L. (Ken) Wyse

Ceo Tommy Hilfiger And Pvh Europe, Daniel Grieder, age 58, $937,209 total compensation

Evp The Marketing Group, Michael (Mike) Kelly

Ceo Tommy Hilfiger Americas, Gary Sheinbaum

Ceo Calvin Klein, Steven B. (Steve) Shiffman, age 62, $908,333 total compensation

President Heritage Sportswear, Geoffrey (Geoff) Barrett

Evp Logistics Services, Kevin J. Urban

President Calvin Klein Retail, Barrie Scardina, age 56

President Calvin Klein 205w39nyc And Calvin Klein By Appointment, Michelle Kessler-Sanders

President Calvin Klein North America Design And Product Development, Alexander (Alex) Cannon

Svp And Chief Risk Officer, Melanie Steiner

President Neckwear, David Sirkin

President Core Intimates, Leslie (Les) Hall

President The Underwear Group, Cheryl Abel-Hodges

President Calvin Klein Retail, Nicholas (Nick) Strange

Regional President Pvh Asia Pacific, Frank Cancelloni

Evp General Counsel And Secretary, Mark D. Fischer, age 58

Evp And Chief Human Resources Officer, David F. (Dave) Kozel, age 64

Evp And Cio, Eileen Mahoney

Chief Supply Chain Officer, William (Bill) McRaith

Evp Wholesale Canada, Richard Deck

President Calvin Klein Europe Brand Management, Marcela Wartenbergh

Country Manager Calvin Klein Brazil, F bio Vasconcellos

Svp Sales Speedo, John Graham

President Pvh Japan, Tom Chu

Managing Director Calvin Klein Asia Pacific Korea, You Hyun-Ko

Managing Director Calvin Klein Asia Pacific China, Hanson Gu

Managing Director Calvin Klein Asia Pacific Commercial, Annie Wong

Managing Director France, Laurent Albouy

Managing Director Turkey, Hakan Atalay

Managing Director Russia, Georg Faisst

Managing Director Middle East Africa And The Netherlands, Maela Mandelli

Managing Director Uk And Ireland, David Pyne

Managing Director Nordic, Jesper Waerum

Svp And Controller, James Holmes

Vice President, Tom Whitmer

Vice President, Akiko Inui

Group Vice President Womens Sourcing, Susan Parson

Vp Purchasing, Jason Zuckerman

Group Vice President Human Resources, Danielle Korins

Vice President Of Mens Design Van Heusen Retail, Jeanne Clarke

Vice President Regional Sales Manager, John Karwacki

Senior Vice President Planning, Steve Leibow

Executive Vice President Pvh Supply, Matthew Wallace

Vice President Merchandising, Gladys Yu

Vice President Planning Process And Technology Integration, Jennifer Taras

Vice President Information Technology, Camille Szczecina

Vice President Of Planning And Analysis Calvin Klein, Pamela Silverstein

Svp Real Estate And Leasing, Natalie Turpan

Executive Vice President Sales And Marketing, Jarratt John

Vp Human Resources, Danielle Bernier

Vice President Distribution, Richard Vuich

Vice President Investor Relations, Nicole Shevins

Vice President Of Planning Calvin Klein, Milena Schaefer

Vice President Human Rights, Roopa Nair

Assistant Vice President Human Resources Learning And Development, Brian Paich

Vice President And Assistant General Counsel, Jeffrey Hellman

Vice President Marketing Operations, Kathleen Livingston

Dvp Core Brands, Dan Bowe

Group Vice President Ii Logistics Systems, Lamont Wharton

Vice President Of Creative Design For Warner's Olga Core Brands, Don Allen

Vice President Treasury, Christian Kochan

Vice President Of Design, Kevin Michales

Senior Vice President, Jillian Zino

Vice President Of Design For Timberland Apparel, Michael Flynn

Vice President Finance Global Supply Chain, John Benz

Evp Integrated Global Marketing, Michael Delellis

Vice President Finance And Operations, Guilford Robinson

Vice President Real Estate, Lauren Kinder

Group Vice President Wholesale Information Technology, Debbie Beer-christensen

Vice President Marketing And Communications, Leslie Davenport

Vice President Creative Services, Andrea Murray

Senior Vice President Of Communications, Tiffin Jernstedt

Vice President, Marissa Pagnani

Vice President, Laura Feinsinger

Svp Accounting, Erik Graf

Vice President Construction X 6306, Susan Pierce

Vp International Transportation, Dennis O'connor

Vice President, Larry Meltzer

Vice President Sales, Rebecca Lucas

Executive Vice President, Franck Belochi

National Sales Manager, Ray Hennessy

Vice President Communications, Lauren Mcclain

Vice President Dmm Sportswear And Accessories, Judith Colaiacovo

Vice President Technical Sevices, Mark Charlton

Vice President Distribution And Cs, Douglas Christian

Vice President, Marion Stienemeier

Senior Vice President Retail Planning And Analysis, Thomas Whitmer

Vice President Human Resources, MaryAnn Vale

Vice President Global Financial Systems And Sap, Raj Varughese

Vice President Ecommerce (tommy Hilfiger), Sean Reynolds

Vice President Communications North America (tommy Hilfiger), Pearl Lee

Executive Vice President Ecommerce (calvin Klein), Mike Dupuis

Senior Vice President Marketing And Communications (tommy Hilfiger), Abdel Hamri

Vice President Of Merchandising Sportswear, Thomas Chanthaphasouk

Executive Vice President Operations And Chief Financial Officer Calvin Klein, Gene Gosselin

Divisional Vice President Store Operations, David Herridge

Grp Vice President Infrastructure Services, Dan Quigley

Vice President Global Supply Chain, Sanjeev Shrivastava

Vice President Strategy And Business Development, Candice Baseden

Senior Vice President Infrastructure And Operations, Joe Melfi

Senior Vice President Marketing, Jill Krizelman

Vice President Ecommerce (dmm Calvin Klein), Jimmy Carter

Vice President Of Business Development, Jay Fitzgerald

Senior Vice President Technical Design And Quality Assurance, Michael Collinson

Group Vice President International Information Technology, Fabrizio Zanardo

Vice President Of Communications, Timothy Robertson

Vice President Sales And Mark, Bill Kluber

Vice President Technical Accounting, Mark Green

Vice President Business Planning Store Planning And Analytics, Kathleen Tobi

Vice President Retail Marketing (tommy Hilfiger), Rich Lampmann

Svp Planning And Allocation, James Buehler

Senior Vice President Finance, Dan Raimondo

Vice President Planning And Operations, Lisa Kilgallon

Svp For Global Community Relations, Ronnie Guy Vickers

Vice President Corporate Treasury, Lisa Wu

Senior Vice President Business Process And Project Portfolio Management, Scott Lamb

Grp Vice President Business Development, Lina Yoo

Vice President Retail Development, Sean Osullivan

Vice President, Shawn Ricker

Vice President, Linda Davidson

Vice President Of Human Resources, Mark Couch

Vice President, Yvonne Anderson

Vice President Of Finance, Ricky Heep

Senior Vice President Controller, Jim Holmes

Senior Vice President Customer Service, Judith Widicus

Vice President It Global Financial Systems, Howard Dubin

Vice President Corporate Benefits, Tammie Palchanes

Vice President Of Sales Calvin Klein, Jason Ckerman

Vice President Human Resources Latin America, Nica Canto

Vice President, Christopher Depalma

Assistant Secretary, Michelle Odonnell

Auditors: Ernst & Young LLP

LOCATIONS

HQ: PVH Corp
200 Madison Avenue, New York, NY 10016
Phone: 212 381-3500
Web: www.pvh.com

2019 Sales

	$ mil.	% of total
U.S.	4,481	46
Canada	528	6
Europe	3	35
Asia	1,163	12
Other	120	3
Total	**9,656**	**100**

PRODUCTS/OPERATIONS

2019 Sales

	$ mil.	% of total
Calvin Klein North America	1,793	18
Calvin Klein International	1,937	20
Tommy Hilfiger North America	1,669	17
Tommy Hilfiger International	26,753	28
Heritage Brands Wholesale	1,317	14
Heritage Brands Retail	263	3
Total	**9,656**	**100**

2019 Sales

	$ mil.	% of total
Wholesale	4,969	52
Retail	4,184	43
Royalty	375	4
Advertising and other	126	1
Total	**9,656**	**100**

Selected Brands

Owned
  ARROW
  Bass
  Calvin Klein
  Eagle
  IZOD
  Tommy Hilfiger
  Van Heusen
Licensed
  Chaps
  Claiborne
  DKNY
  Kenneth Cole New York
  Kenneth Cole Reaction
  MICHAEL Michael Kors
  Michael Kors Collection
  Robert Graham
  Sean John

COMPETITORS

Allen-Edmonds	Kellwood
Armani	Kenneth Cole
Caleres	Levi Strauss
Capital Mercury	Nine West
Apparel	Oxford Industries
Donna Karan	Perry Ellis
Eddie Bauer LLC	International
Genesco	Prada
Gucci	Ralph Lauren
Haggar	Reebok
Hugo Boss	The Gap
J. Crew	Timberland
Kate Spade	VF Corporation

HISTORICAL FINANCIALS

Company Type: Public

Income Statement   FYE: February 2

	REVENUE ($ mil.)	NET INCOME ($ mil.)	NET PROFIT MARGIN	EMPLOYEES
02/20	9,909	417	4.2%	40,000
02/19	9,656	746	7.7%	38,000
02/18*	8,914	537	6.0%	36,500
01/17	8,203	549	6.7%	44,500
01/16	8,020	572	7.1%	34,200
Annual Growth	**5.4%**	**(7.6%)**	—	**4.0%**

*Fiscal year change

2020 Year-End Financials

Debt ratio: 20.23%
Return on equity: 7.19%
Cash ($ mil.): 503
Current ratio: 1.44
Long-term debt ($ mil.): 2,693
No. of shares (mil.): 72
Dividends
  Yield: 0.0%
  Payout: 2.6%
Market value ($ mil.): 6,302

	STOCK PRICE ($) FY Close	P/E High/Low	Earnings	PER SHARE ($) Dividends	Book Value
02/20	87.17	24 12	5.60	0.15	80.39
02/19	108.76	17 9	9.65	0.15	77.29
02/18*	151.07	23 12	6.84	0.15	71.73
01/17	90.30	17 10	6.79	0.15	61.16
01/16	73.38	17 10	6.89	0.15	55.86
Annual Growth	**4.4%**	— —	**(5.1%)**	**(0.0%)**	**9.5%**

*Fiscal year change

QCR Holdings Inc

Quad City is muscling in on the community banking scene in the Midwest. QCR Holdings is the holding company for Quad City Bank & Trust Cedar Rapids Bank & Trust Rockford Bank & Trust and Community State Bank. Together the banks have about 20 offices serving the Quad City area of Illinois and Iowa as well as the communities of Cedar Rapids Iowa; Rockford Illinois; and Milwaukee. The banks offer traditional deposit products and services and concentrate their lending activities on local businesses: Commercial real estate loans make up about half of the loan portfolio; commercial loans and leases make up another third.

Operations

QCR Holdings' Bancard subsidiary provides credit card processing services; its majority-owned M2 Lease Funds leases machinery and equipment to commercial and industrial businesses.

Strategy

QCR Holdings has grown by launching operations in new geographic markets and then building upon them. It also expands through acquisitions. In mid-2016 the company acquired Iowa-based Community State Bank which operates some 10 branches in the Des Moines area.

EXECUTIVES

Senior Vice President And Director Dep, Kathleen M Francque
President And Ceo, Douglas M. (Doug) Hultquist, age 65, $290,000 total compensation
Director; President And Ceo Cedar Rapids Bank And Trust, Larry J. Helling, age 64, $251,899 total compensation
Evp And Chief Credit Officer, Dana L. Nichols
Evp Coo And Cfo, Todd A. Gipple, age 57, $251,899 total compensation
Evp Corporate Strategy Human Resources And Branding, Cathie Whiteside, $162,000 total compensation
President And Ceo Rockford Bank And Trust, Thomas D. Budd, $172,000 total compensation
President And Ceo Quad City Bank And Trust, John H. Anderson, $200,000 total compensation
Evp Deposit Operations And Information Services, John A. Rodriguez
Svp And Cio, Michael J. Wyffels
Evp And Chief Operations Officer, John R. McEvoy
President And Ceo Community Bank And Trust, Stacey Bentley
President M2 Lease Funds, Richard W. Couch
Chairman And Ceo M2 Lease Funds, John R. Engelbrecht
Evp And Chief Investment Officer, M. Randolph (Rand) Westlund
Vice President Operations Manager, Sherrie L Larson
Senior Vice President Marketing And Co, Cathy Whiteside
Vice President Controller, Jeri Vandervinne
Vice President And Controller, Nick Anderson
Vice President, Rick Jennings
Assistant Vice President Compliance, Thomas King
Vp Of Marketing, Karon Schladetzky
Vice President Product, Gregory Braid
Senior Vice President Treasury Management, Lori Diaz
Assistant Vice President Marketing And Public Relations Officer, Stacey L Keller
Assistant Vice President Marketing And Public Relations Officer, Stacey Keller
Executive Vice President Corporate Strategy And Branding, S Whiteside
Chairman, Patrick S. (Pat) Baird, age 67
Auditors: RSM US LLP

LOCATIONS

HQ: QCR Holdings Inc
3551 7th Street, Moline, IL 61265
Phone: 309 736-3580
Web: www.qcrh.com

PRODUCTS/OPERATIONS

2015 Sales

	$ mil.	% of total
Quad City Bank & Trust	52	46
Cedar Rapids Bank & Trust	37	32
Rockford Bank & Trust	14	13
Wealth Management	9	8
All other	0	1
Inter-company Eliminations	(0.4)	—
Total	**114**	**100**

COMPETITORS

Bank of America	First National of
Blackhawk Bancorp	Nebraska
First Business	MidWestOne
Financial	U.S. Bancorp
First Midwest Bancorp	

HISTORICAL FINANCIALS

Company Type: Public

Income Statement   FYE: December 31

	ASSETS ($ mil.)	NET INCOME ($ mil.)	INCOME AS % OF ASSETS	EMPLOYEES
12/19	4,909	57	1.2%	697
12/18	4,949	43	0.9%	755
12/17	3,982	35	0.9%	641
12/16	3,301	27	0.8%	572
12/15	2,593	16	0.7%	406
Annual Growth	**17.3%**	**35.7%**	—	**14.5%**

2019 Year-End Financials

Debt ratio: 2.16%
Return on equity: 11.38%
Cash ($ mil.): 224
Current ratio: —
Long-term debt ($ mil.): —
No. of shares (mil.): 15
Dividends
  Yield: 0.5%
  Payout: 6.9%
Market value ($ mil.): 694

	STOCK PRICE ($) FY Close	P/E High/Low	Earnings	PER SHARE ($) Dividends	Book Value
12/19	43.86	12 9	3.60	0.24	33.82
12/18	32.09	17 10	2.86	0.24	30.10
12/17	42.85	18 15	2.61	0.20	25.38
12/16	43.30	20 10	2.17	0.16	21.82
12/15	24.29	15 11	1.61	0.08	19.21
Annual Growth	**15.9%**	— —	**22.3%**	**31.6%**	**15.2%**

Qualcomm Inc

QUALCOMM is a leading designer and supplier of computer chips that mobile phone and wireless carriers depend on to get signals straight. The company pioneered the commercialization of the code-division multiple access (CDMA) technology used in digital wireless communications equipment and satellite ground stations mainly in North America. It generates most of its sales through the development and marketing of semiconductor chips such as its Snapdragon line and system software based on CDMA and other technologies. Its biggest customers have been suppliers to mobile phone makers Samsung and Apple.

Operations

The company operates through three reportable segments: QCT QTL and QSI.

QCT develops and supplies integrated circuits and system software based on CDMA OFDMA and other technologies for use in mobile devices wireless networks broadband gateway equipment consumer electronic devices devices used in IoT and automotive telematics and infotainment systems. The segment accounts for around 60% of revenue.

QTL grants licenses grants licenses to use portions of their intellectual property portfolio which includes certain patent rights essential to and/or useful in the manufacture and sale of certain wireless products. The segment accounts for 20% of revenue.

QSI reportable segment makes strategic investments.

Geographic Reach

QUALCOMM based in San Diego California gets about half of its revenue from customers based in China (including Hong Kong) while customers based in Ireland U.S. and South Korea supplies about 10% of revenue each.

QCT segment's non-United States headquarters is located in Singapore. The segment also operates manufacturing facilities in Germany China and Singapore and also sales and administrative offices and research and development centers primarily in the United States and India.

Sales and Marketing

Revenues from Apple Inc. and its contract manufacturers (Hon Hai Precision Industry Co. Ltd./Foxconn its affiliates and other suppliers to Apple) Samsung Electronics and combined revenues from GuangDong OPPO Mobile Telecommunications and vivo Communication Technology and their respective affiliates (including BBK) each comprised 10% or more of consolidated revenues. Revenues from Xiaomi also comprised 10% or more of consolidated revenues.

Financial Performance

QUALCOMM halted a three-year string of falling revenue in 2018 (ended September) and the company recovered from their loss thanks to lower operating cost and expenses.

Sales edged 7% higher to $24.3 billion in 2019 from $22.6 billion in 2018 due to $4.7 billion on their reconciling items even though with the decrease of QCT and QTL segments fell.

In 2019 the company's net income increased by $9.4 billion resulting to $4.4 billion compared to net loss of $5.0 billion in fiscal 2018. The recovery was due to the increase on company's revenue and a lesser operating cost and expense.

The company's cash and equivalent balance grew by $62 million maintaining the cash with $11.8 billion in 2019. In 2019 operations generated $7.3 billion while investment activities used $806 million and investing activities used $6.4 billion.

Strategy

Qualcomm engage in strategic acquisitions and other transactions including joint ventures and make investments which they believe are important to the future of the company's business with the goal of maximizing stockholder value. From time to time they acquire businesses and other assets including patents technology wireless spectrum and other intangible assets enter into joint ventures or other strategic transactions and purchase minority equity interests in or make loans to companies including those that may be private and early-stage. Qualcomm's strategic activities are generally focused on opening or expanding opportunities for their products and technologies and supporting the design and introduction of new products and services (or enhancing existing products or services) for voice and data communications and new industry segments.

From time to time companies initiate various strategies to attempt to negotiate renegotiate reduce and/or eliminate their need to pay royalties to us for the use of their intellectual property.

Mergers and Acquisitions

QUALCOMM acquired Scyfer B.V. a company that developed artificial intelligence technologies in 2017. Qualcomm added Scyfer's applications to end-use devices such as smartphones cars and robotics to ensure that processing can be done with or without a network

QUALCOMM and TDK formed a joint venture in 2017 to provide chips for mobile devices and internet of things applications. The entity called RF360 Holdings combines QUALCOMM's chip expertise with that of TDK in filters. Application areas are mobile devices automotive and drones. The ownership of the joint venture is split 51% by QUALCOMM and 49% by TDK.

Company Background

Professors Irwin Mark Jacobs and Andrew Viterbi founded digital signal processing equipment company Linkabit in 1968. M/A-COM acquired the company in 1980. Led by Jacobs Viterbi and five other executives left M/A-COM Linkabit in 1985 to start engineer-focused QUALCOMM (for "quality communications") to provide contract R&D services. The company's first home was located above a strip mall pizza parlor in San Diego. CEO Jacobs dreamed of modifying code-division multiple access (CDMA) — a secure wireless transmission system developed during WWII — for commercial use.

In 1988 QUALCOMM introduced OmniTRACS a satellite-based system that tracks the location of long-haul truckers. By 1989 when QUALCOMM unveiled its version of CDMA the company was working on military contracts worth $15 million.

In 1990 the company interrupted the Cellular Telecommunications Industry Association's (CTIA) plans to adopt a rival technology called time-division multiple access when communications service providers NYNEX (now part of Verizon) and Ameritech (later part of SBC Communications and now part of AT&T) adopted QUALCOMM's maverick technology. QUALCOMM initiated a CDMA public relations blitz and by 1991 Motorola AT&T Clarion and Nokia had signed product development and testing agreements.

The company went public in 1991 and introduced the Eudora e-mail software program (named for "Why I Live at the P.O." author Eudora Welty) which it licensed from the University of Illinois. That year QUALCOMM and Loral Corporation unveiled plans for Globalstar a satellite telecommunications system similar to the Iridium system. The CTIA adopted CDMA as a North American standard for wireless communications in 1993.

EXECUTIVES

Vice President Compensation And Benefits, Michelle Mckinney

Vice President Engineering, King-chung Lai

Vice President Of Technology, Sherman Gregory

Vice President And Treasurer, Dick Grannis

Vice President Engineering, Vladimir Aparin

Vice President 2net Business Qualcomm Life, Chris Talbot

Vice President Learning And Development, Tamar Elkeles

Executive Vice President Learning And Development, David Whittaker

Vice President Engineering, Brian K Harms

Senior Vice President Strategy And Corporate Development, Matt Eichenberger

Vice President Engineering, Gene Mcallister

Executive Vice President Of The Americas And India, Peggy L Johnson

Vice President Marketing, Jenny Beneke

Vice President Of Technology, Rob Gilmore

Vice President And Division Counsel, Marc Sands

Vice President Government Affairs, Steve Crout

Senior Vice President And General Manager, Rick Valencia

Vice President Product Management, Francesco Grilli

Vice President Patent Counsel, Timothy Loomis

Executive Vice President, Andrew Gilbert

Vice President Finance, Akash Palkhiwala

Vice President, Cliff Ficke

Senior Vice President Engineering, Ron Tessitore

Vp Engineering; Head Of Product Security, Alex Gantman

Vice President Engineering, Andrew Hunter

Vice President Legal Counsel, Chris Longman

Vice President Business Development, Salvador Blasco

Vice President Engineering, Dan Waldburger

Vice President Engineering, Ajay Bawale

Vice President Of Technology, Geoffrey Yeap

Vice President Global Security, Stewart Roberts

Vice President Engineering, Eric Tallet

Vice President Sales, Curt Thornton

Vice President Engineering, Benny Malekkhosravi

Vice President Business Development, Jeffery Torrance

Vice President Engineering, Husnu Masaracioglu

Senior Vice President Engineering, Christopher Patrick

Vice President Engineering Qct Software, Tony Schwarz

Vice President Engineering, Samir Kapoor

Vice President Technology, Lennart Mathe

Executive Vice President And President Qualcomm Technology Licensing, Alex Rogers

Vice President, Jeremiah Golston

Vice President Technology, Walid Ali-Ahmad

Vice President Hardware Engineering Group Corpor, Ernie Ozaki

Svp Finance, Sanjay Mehta

Vice President Engineering, Andre Izotov

Senior Vice President, Chuck Wheatley

Svp Engineering, Bill Earnshaw

Vice President Modem Senior Writer Engineering, Vanitha Kumar

Vice President Software Product Management, Nancy Fares

Vice President Package Engineering, Raj Pendse

Vice President Engineering, Mike Leary

Vice President Business Operations, Laura Hart

Vice President Technology, Ken Wiseman

Vice President Engineering, Prakash Suvarna

Vp Strategic Programs, Edward Charbonneau

Vice President Global Technical Education, Sei Seung Yoon

Vice President Of Engineering, Jose Corleto-mena

Vice President Of Engineering, William Miller

Executive Vice President Fin Office, Tony Thornley

Assistant To Don Rosenberg Executive Vice President And General Counsel, Sylvie Julian

Senior Vice President, John Han

Vice President Product Management, Raj Talluri

Vice President And President Of Qualcomm Korea Yh, Oh Hyung Kwon

Vice President Engineering, Frederic Darguesse

Vice President, Alejandro Holcman

Vice President, Hsi Hsu

Vice President Business Develo, Jim Bennette

Executive Chairman, Paul E. Jacobs, age 58

Secretary, Maria Terris

Secretary Executive, Laurie Mee

Secretary Senior, Joann Carter

Senior Secretary, Kathleen Jayne

Board Member, Barbara Alexander

Secretary Executive, Cynthia Almazan

Secretary Executive, Gloria Holmes

Secretary Executive, Wendy Walsh

Senior Secretary, Lori Freeman

Secretary Executive, Maria Mackinnon

Secretary Senior, Katy Martin

Board Member, Aurora Fields

Secretary Senior, Heather Gallegos

Secretary Executive, Robin Frampton

Senior Secretary, Jan Harris

Board Member, Anthony Vinciquerra

Board Member, Clark Randt

Board Member, Harish Manwani

Board Member, Francisco Ros

Secretary Executive, Jill Wolf

Secretary Executive, Linda Chinn

Auditors: PricewaterhouseCoopers LLP

LOCATIONS

HQ: Qualcomm Inc
5775 Morehouse Dr., San Diego, CA 92121-1714
Phone: 858 587-1121
Web: www.qualcomm.com

2018 Sales

	$ mil.	% of total
China (including Hong Kong)	15,149	67
South Korea	3,173	14
United States	603	2
Other foreign	3,805	17
Total	22,732	100

PRODUCTS/OPERATIONS

2018 Sales

	$ mil.	% of total
QCT (Qualcomm CDMA Technologies)	17,282	76
QTL (Qualcomm Technology Licensing)	5,163	23
QSI (Qualcomm Strategic Initiatives)	100	-
Adjustments	187	1
Total	22,732	100

2018 Sales

	$ mil.	% of total
Equipment & services	17,400	77
Licensing	5,332	23
Total	22,732	100

Selected Operations and Products

Code-Division Multiple Access (CDMA) Technologies Group
  Integrated circuits
  Baseband
  Intermediate-frequency
  Power management
  Radio-frequency
  Systems software
Engineering Services Group
Enterprise Services
Firethorn Holdings
Flarion Technologies
Government Technologies
Innovation Center
Internet Services
MediaFLO Technologies
MEMS Technologies
Qualcomm Ventures
Strategic Initiatives
Technology Licensing Group

CDMA technologies and patents (cdmaOne CDMA2000 WCDMA TD-SCDMA)
  Royalties from products incorporating CDMA technology
Wireless and Internet Group
  Digital Media
  Digital motion picture delivery systems (under development)
  Government systems (development and analysis services; wireless base stations and phones)
  Internet Services
  Applications development software for wireless devices (BREW)
  Wireless Systems
  Low-Earth-orbit satellite-based telecommunications system (Globalstar)

COMPETITORS

Broadcom	REALTEK
SEMICONDUCTOR	
Cirrus Logic	CORP.
InterDigital	Renesas Electronics
Marvell Technology	STMicroelectronics
Maxim Integrated	Samsung Electronics
Products	Sequans Communications
MediaTek	Spreadtrum
Murata Manufacturing	Texas Instruments
NVIDIA	

HISTORICAL FINANCIALS

Company Type: Public

Income Statement

FYE: September 27

	REVENUE ($ mil.)	NET INCOME ($ mil.)	NET PROFIT MARGIN	EMPLOYEES
09/20	23,531	5,198	22.1%	41,000
09/19	24,273	4,386	18.1%	37,000
09/18	22,732	(4,864)	—	35,400
09/17	22,291	2,466	11.1%	33,800
09/16	23,554	5,705	24.2%	30,500
Annual Growth	(0.0%)	(2.3%)	—	7.7%

2020 Year-End Financials

Debt ratio: 44.18%
Return on equity: 94.89%
Cash ($ mil.): 6,707
Current ratio: 2.14
Long-term debt ($ mil.): 15,226
No. of shares (mil.): 1,131
Dividends
  Yield: 0.0%
  Payout: 56.1%
Market value ($ mil.): 129,500

	STOCK PRICE ($) FY Close	P/E High/Low	PER SHARE ($) Earnings	Dividends	Book Value
09/20	114.50	27 13	4.52	2.54	5.37
09/19	76.63	25 14	3.59	2.48	4.29
09/18	72.03	— —	(3.32)	2.38	0.76
09/17	52.09	42 30	1.65	2.20	20.86
09/16	62.75	17 11	3.81	2.02	21.53
Annual Growth	16.2%	— —	4.4%	5.9%	(29.3%)

Quanta Services, Inc.

Quanta Services is a specialty contractor that designs installs repairs and maintains network infrastructure across North America and abroad. The company serves the electric power pipeline oil and natural gas and communication industries. Capabilities include pylon construction distribution infrastructure emergency response and its pipeline and industrial business offers offshore services. Quanta also handles energized installation electric power infrastructure maintenance and upgrade installation of smart grid technologies on electric power networks and building wind and solar power facilities. Quanta gets nearly 85% of its revenue from customers in the US.

Operations

Quanta operates through two primary segments: Electric Power Infrastructure which generates about 60% of revenue and Pipeline and Industrial Infrastructure Services more than 40% of revenue.

The Electric Power Infrastructure segment offers a comprehensive network solutions to customers in the electric power industry including transmission construction distribution construction communications infrastructure service power generation emergency response EPC (engineering procurement and construction) services training for electrical workers and more.

The Pipeline and Industrial Infrastructure Services segment designs installs upgrade repair and maintains pipelines and has directional boring trenching and mechanized welding capabilities. It serves the offshore sector with services including fueling system water and sewer installation integrity testing pipeline protection repair and rehabilitation of pipeline supports and fabrication.

Geographic Reach

Houston-based Quanta Services generates around 85% of its revenue in the US. Its next largest market is Canada which accounts for about 15% of its business followed by Australia. The company has more than 60 facilities in the US Canada Latin America and Australia.

Sales and Marketing

Quanta mostly serves companies in the electric power energy and communications markets though it also serves commercial industrial and governmental organizations.

Quanta relies on its 10 largest customers for about 35% of its revenue. The loss of one or more customers could have a significant impact of the company's revenue. That said Quanta's roster of customers includes notable utility and energy companies such as American Electric Power Duke Energy PG&E Corp. TC energy Corp. Valero Energy Corp. and Exelon Corp. among others.

Financial Performance

The company's revenue in 2019 increased by $940.7 million to $12.1 billion compared to $11.2 billion in the prior year. Contributing to the increase were incremental revenues of $706.3 million from electric power infrastructure services and $234.5 million from pipeline and industrial infrastructure services.

Net income in 2019 increased by $110.8 million to $406.8 million compared to $296.0 million in the prior year. The change was due to the increase/recovery on their other income with about $130.6 million.

Cash held by the company at the end of 2019 increased by $86.5 million to $169.7 million compared to $83.3 million in the prior year. Cash provided by operations and financing activities were $526.6 million and $177.7 million respectively. Cash used for investing activities was $617.6 million primarily for Cash paid for acquisitions net of cash cash equivalents and restricted cash acquired.

Strategy

Quanta's strategies of expanding its portfolio of service offerings for existing and potential customers increasing the company's geographic technological and training capabilities promoting best practices and cross-selling services to existing customers as well as continuing to maintain financial strength place them in the position to capitalize on opportunities and trends in the industries it serves and expand its operations to select new markets. The company continues to evaluate potential strategic acquisitions and investments to broaden its customer base expand geographic area of operations grow the company's portfolio of services and increase opportunities across its operations.

Although the company has a centralized marketing and business development strategy management at each of its operating units is responsible for developing and maintaining successful long-term relationships with customers.

Mergers and Acquisitions

In 2019 Quanta announced that it has completed the acquisition of The Hallen Construction Co. Inc. (Hallen) a leading and sizeable gas utility contractor serving key strategic markets in the northeast United States.Hallen has strong customer relationships with leading utilities in its markets primarily providing gas distribution and transmission services and to a lesser extent underground electric distribution and transmission services. Over the past several years Hallen has achieved solid organic revenue and profit growth by leveraging its operational excellence and working collaboratively with its customers. Additionally Quanta recently completed the acquisition of two specialty utility foundation and pole-setting contractors serving the southeast United States. The aggregate consideration paid for these companies was approximately $330 million consisting of approximately $328 million in cash subject to working capital adjustments and approximately $2 million in stock.

EXECUTIVES

Cfo, Derrick A. Jensen, age 49, $600,000 total compensation
President Ceo And Coo, Earl C. (Duke) Austin, age 50, $979,924 total compensation
Evp Corporate Development And President Infrastructure Solutions, Jesse E. Morris, age 52, $466,900 total compensation
Evp Operations And Health/safety And Environmental, Randall C. Wisenbaker, age 55, $475,625 total compensation
President Electric Power, Dale L. Querrey, age 56, $595,880 total compensation
President Oil And Gas Division And Chief Strategy Officer, Paul C. Gregory, age 56
Senior Vice President, Bengt Jarlsjo
Vice President Of Operations, Dan Govin
Vp Business Development, Jack Dwyer
Corporate Vice President Human Resource, Mary St Michael
Vp Sales, Vivek Arora
Vice President Business Development, Rob Schleider
Vice President, Fred Hogman
Senior Vice President Operations Integration, Jim O'Neil
Executive Vice President, Ron Tagliapietra
Senior Vice President Business Development, Lonnie Hamilton
Quanta Vice President, Jody Shea

Vice President Project Development, Richard Vaughan
Executive Vice President, Mike Kemper
Vice President Health Safety And Environmental, Matt Compher
Vice President Telecom Operations, Greg Edmoundson
Executive Vice President Operations, David Meisel
Vice President Executive Pastry Chef, Kevin Cater
Chairman, Bruce E. Ranck
Assistant Treasurer, Jeff Walker
Treasurer, Nick Grindstaff
Auditors: PricewaterhouseCoopers LLP

LOCATIONS

HQ: Quanta Services, Inc.
2800 Post Oak Boulevard, Suite 2600, Houston, TX 77056
Phone: 713 629-7600
Web: www.quantaservices.com

2018 Sales

	$ mil.	% of total
United States	8,575	77
Canada	1,984	18
Australia	377	3
Latin America and other	234	2
Total	**11,171**	**100**

PRODUCTS/OPERATIONS

2017 sales

	$ mil.	% of total
Electric power infrastructure	6,415	57
Pipeline and industrial infrastructure	4,755	43
Total	**11,171**	**100**

COMPETITORS

Cable Com	MDU Construction
Comm-Works	Services
Dycom	MYR Group
EMCOR	MasTec
Goldfield	Mass Electric
Henkels & McCoy	Pike Corporation
IES Holdings	Tetra Tech

HISTORICAL FINANCIALS

Company Type: Public

Income Statement

	REVENUE ($ mil.)	NET INCOME ($ mil.)	NET PROFIT MARGIN	EMPLOYEES
12/19	12,112	402	3.3%	40,300
12/18	11,171	293	2.6%	39,200
12/17	9,466	314	3.3%	32,800
12/16	7,651	198	2.6%	28,100
12/15	7,572	310	4.1%	24,500
Annual Growth	**12.5%**	**6.6%**	**—**	**13.2%**

FYE: December 31

2019 Year-End Financials

Debt ratio: 16.62%
Return on equity: 10.50%
Cash ($ mil.): 164
Current ratio: 1.69
Long-term debt ($ mil.): 1,292

No. of shares (mil.): 142
Dividends
  Yield: 0.4%
  Payout: 7.3%
Market value ($ mil.): 5,795

	STOCK PRICE ($) FY Close	P/E High/Low		PER SHARE ($) Earnings	Dividends	Book Value
12/19	40.71	16	11	2.73	0.17	28.45
12/18	30.10	21	15	1.90	0.04	25.45
12/17	39.11	20	15	2.00	0.00	24.65
12/16	34.85	28	14	1.26	0.00	22.08
12/15	20.25	19	12	1.59	0.00	19.31
Annual Growth	**19.1%**	**—**	**—**	**14.5%**	**—**	**10.2%**

Quest Diagnostics, Inc.

Quest Diagnostics is one of the largest clinical labs in the US. The company's services are used by physicians across dozens of clinical areas including cancer cardiovascular disease prescription drug monitoring health and wellness infectious disease neurology and women's health. Quest Diagnostics also performs esoteric testing (such as genetic screening) and anatomic pathology testing (such as tissue biopsies for cancer testing). In all the company serves about half of the physicians and half of the hospitals in the US per year. Quest Diagnostics has about 2275 patient service centers where samples are collected.

Operations

Quest Diagnostics operates through two primary segments — Diagnostic Information Services (DIS) and Diagnostic Solutions.

More than 95% of Quest's revenue comes from its DIS segment develops and delivers diagnostic information services providing insights that empower and enable a broad range of customers including patients clinicians hospitals IDNs health plans employers and ACOs. Routine tests account for about 55% of Quest's total sales; gene-based and esoteric tests account for about 35% and pathology tests account for nearly 10%.

The Diagnostic Solutions segment includes their risk assessment services business which offers solutions for insurers and their healthcare information technology businesses which offers solutions for healthcare providers. The segment accounts for about 5% of revenue.

Their services primarily are provided under the Quest Diagnostics brand but they also provide services under other brands including AmeriPath Dermpath Diagnostics Athena Diagnostics ExamOne and Quanum.

Quest's logistics holdings include approximately 4000 vehicles and some 25 aircraft that combined make approximately 76000 stops daily.

Geographic Reach

Quest Diagnostics has labs in California (3) Florida Georgia Illinois (2) Kansas Maryland Massachusetts New Jersey North Carolina Ohio Pennsylvania Texas (2) and Virginia. It also has labs in Mexico and Puerto Rico as well as a majority interest in a drug testing venture in Brazil.

The company is headquartered at Secaucus New Jersey.

Sales and Marketing

Quest's customers include health plans and other insurers physicians hospitals accountable care organizations employers individual patients retail health care providers government agencies pharmaceuticals and other commercial laboratories.

Financial Performance

In 2019 total net revenues of $7.7 billion were up 3% from the prior year. In DIS: Revenues of $7.4 billion increased by 3% compared to the prior year driven by organic volume growth (growth excluding the impact of acquisitions) and the impact of recent acquisitions partially offset by a decline in revenue per requisition. DS revenues of $321 million decreased by 2% compared to the prior year.

Net income grew 17% to $858 million in 2019. Operating income increased while non-operating expense decreased for almost $20 million.

The company ended 2019 with $1.2 billion in net cash $1.1 billion more than it had at the end of 2018. Operating activities provided $1.2 billion that year while investing activities used $411 million and financing activities provided $225 million.

Strategy

The company continuously strives to strengthen their organizational capabilities to support their two-point strategy enable growth and productivity better focus on customers speed decision-making and empower employees. Highlights include:

Align for Growth Execution and Efficiency. The company's organization is designed to align around future growth opportunities coordinate business units for seamless execution and leverage their company-wide infrastructure to gain more capability value and efficiency. The value creation side of their business includes product and commercial marketing and is organized by clinical franchise and focuses on customer solutions for the marketplace including new test development and diagnostic insights. The value delivery side includes sales laboratory operations field operations logistics and client services.

Quest Management System. This system provides a foundation for day-to-day management and includes best-in-class business performance tools to help develop new capabilities to improve their Company. The system enables them to run the Company with a common language approach and philosophy and supports our efforts as they build a high-performance culture with employees focused on behaviors to make them more agile transparent customer-focused collaborative and performance oriented.

Everyday Excellence Program. This program includes guiding principles for their entire organization to support a superior customer experience and inspire employees to be their best every day with every person and with every customer interaction. It is integrated into performance assessments and frontline employee behavioral standards.

Leading Quest Academy. The Academy is designed to strengthen their more senior employee leaders through a highly experiential leadership development program to create a high-performance culture and sharpen the capabilities needed to lead their organization. The company also offer leadership training programs for other employees.

Code of Ethics. Their Code reinforces our commitment to integrity and aligns with their vision values goals and brand.

The Company's strategy includes generating growth through value-creating strategically-aligned acquisitions using disciplined investment criteria.

Mergers and Acquisitions

In 2020 Quest Diagnostics announced that it has acquired Blueprint Genetics in an all-cash equity transaction. Blueprint Genetics is a leading specialty genetic testing company with deep expertise in gene variant interpretation based on next generation sequencing (NGS) and proprietary bioinformatics. Together Quest and Blueprint Genetics will broaden access to actionable insights in genetic and rare diseases improving patient care and pharmaceutical drug research and development. Financial terms of the transaction were not disclosed.

In 2019 announced that it has acquired certain assets of the clinical laboratory services business of Boston Clinical Laboratories (BCL) a Waltham-based regional provider of laboratory services. BCL's patients and providers now have access to Quest's broader range of diagnostic services a larger network of patient service centers and access to unique tools such as the company's Quanum? suite of healthcare information technologies and data analytics. BCL services will transition to the Quest Diagnostics state-of-the-art laboratory in Marlborough Mass. Financial terms were not disclosed.

Company Background

Quest Diagnostics was incorporated in 1990 but its predecessors date their history back to 1967.

HISTORY

Quest Diagnostics began as one man's quest to make clinical tests more affordable. Pathologist Paul Brown started Metropolitan Pathological Laboratory (MetPath) in his Manhattan apartment in 1967. To help his business take off in 1969 he bought two $55000 blood analyzers that could automatically perform a dozen common tests; the machines allowed him to charge patients $5.50 while hospitals and other labs were charging upwards of $40. Investments in emerging lab technology helped MetPath continue to beat competitors' prices and grow its business. It made its first profit in 1971 and eventually attracted the attention of Corning Glass Works which bought 10% of the company in 1973.

MetPath's growth was due in part to investments in technology. The company built a state-of-the-art central lab in New Jersey in 1978 that could process some 30000 specimens daily; it also went on an acquisition spree to expand across the US. These investments left the firm swamped with debt and Corning bought the company in 1982.

An autonomous unit of Corning MetPath continued to grow as Medicare reimbursement for lab tests went up and more doctors ordered more tests to catch and prevent disease before it happened. To cut costs in the mid-1980s the company reorganized its facilities to create a regional lab network. A reorganization in 1990 at its parent placed MetPath in the Corning Lab Services subsidiary.

Corning Lab Services strengthened its operations in the early 1990s by buying labs from regional operators. In 1994 MetPath became Corning Clinical Laboratories. Around the same time the company found itself besieged with demands from HMOs and other managed care providers to lower its costs. Also during this time the company settled a handful of federal suits accusing it of fraudulent Medicare billing. In the face of increasing pressure parent Corning spun off its lab testing business to the public as Quest Diagnostics in 1996.

On its own Quest aimed to grow through acquisitions. In 1999 it bought rival SmithKline Beecham Clinical Laboratories from GlaxoSmithKline. (GSK gained a minority stake in

Quest through the deal; it gradually sold off all shares in Quest by 2011.) Continuing its growth strategy in the 21st century it bought American Medical Laboratories to expand its esoteric testing operations in 2002. The company was finally able to close its acquisition of Unilab in early 2003 after the deal ran into delays with the FTC. Quest sold some labs and service contracts in northern California to LabCorp to appease FTC regulators.

To expand internationally the company began providing testing services in India in 2008 including esoteric testing for hospitals tests for the life insurance industry and diagnostics for global clinical trials.

EXECUTIVES

Chairman President And Ceo, Stephen H. (Steve) Rusckowski, age 62, $1,100,000 total compensation

Svp And Group Executive Diagnostic Solutions, Jon R. Cohen, age 65, $575,000 total compensation

Svp And Group Executive Clinical Franchise Solutions And Marketing, Catherine T. Doherty, age 57, $575,000 total compensation

Svp Commercial, Everett V. Cunningham, age 53

Vp Global Markets And Chairman Q2 Solutions, John B. Haydon

Evp And Cfo, Mark J. Guinan, age 58, $586,538 total compensation

Evp General Diagnostics, James E. Davis, age 57, $586,538 total compensation

Svp Research And Development And Medical And Chief Medical Officer, Jay G. Wohlgemuth

Svp And Cio, Lidia Fonseca

Vp And Treasurer, Tracy Cinco-abela

Vice President Clinical Trials, Christopher Fikry

Svp Strategy Mergers And Acquisitions And Ventures, Dermot Shorten

Regional Vice President Commercial, Geoffrey Albrecht

Auditors: PricewaterhouseCoopers LLP

LOCATIONS

HQ: Quest Diagnostics, Inc.
500 Plaza Drive, Secaucus, NJ 07094
Phone: 973 520-2700
Web: www.QuestDiagnostics.com

PRODUCTS/OPERATIONS

2018 Sales

	$ mil.	% of total
Diagnostic Information Services		
Routine clinical testing services	4,217	56
Gene-based & esoteric testing services	2,409	32
Anatomic pathology testing services	578	8
Other	327	4
Total	**7,531**	**100**

Selected Products and Services

Clincial laboratory testing
    Routine clinical testing (body fluid testing)
    Alcohol and other substance-abuse tests
    Allergy tests (ImmunoCap)
    Blood cholesterol
    Complete blood cell counts
    Pap smears
    Pregnancy testing
    Urinalyses
    Gene-based and esoteric testing
    Endocrinology
    Cancer monitoring (gene-based)
    Cellular immunology
    Genetics
    Hematology
    Microbiology
    Molecular diagnostics
    Oncology
    Protein chemistry
    Serology
    Toxicology
    Anatomic pathology testing (AmeriPath Dermpath Diagnostics and Quest Diagnostics brands)
    Cancer biopsies
    Tissue and cell testing
Other products and services
    Clinical trials testing
    Diagnostic products
    Medical data management systems
    Life insurance risk assessment services

Selected Subsidiaries

American Medical Laboratories Incorporated
AmeriPath Inc.
Celera Corporation
Enterix Inc.
Focus Diagnostics Inc.
HemoCue Inc.
LabOne Inc.
MedPlus Inc.
OralDNA Labs Inc.
Quest Diagnostics Nichols Institute

COMPETITORS

Arup Laboratories	Pathology Associates
Bio-Reference Labs	Medical Laboratories
Genomic Health	Psychemedics
LabCorp	Solstas
Medtox Scientific	Sonic Healthcare
Oncolab	

HISTORICAL FINANCIALS

Company Type: Public

Income Statement

FYE: December 31

	REVENUE ($ mil.)	NET INCOME ($ mil.)	NET PROFIT MARGIN	EMPLOYEES
12/19	7,726	858	11.1%	47,000
12/18	7,531	736	9.8%	46,000
12/17	7,709	772	10.0%	45,000
12/16	7,515	645	8.6%	43,000
12/15	7,493	709	9.5%	44,000
Annual Growth	**0.8%**	**4.9%**	**—**	**1.7%**

2019 Year-End Financials

Debt ratio: 37.14%
Return on equity: 15.81%
Cash ($ mil.): 1,192
Current ratio: 1.25
Long-term debt ($ mil.): 3,966

No. of shares (mil.): 133
Dividends
    Yield: 1.9%
    Payout: 39.7%
Market value ($ mil.): 14,203

	STOCK PRICE ($) FY Close	P/E High/Low	PER SHARE ($) Earnings	Dividends	Book Value
12/19	106.79	17 13	6.28	2.12	42.41
12/18	83.27	21 15	5.29	1.95	38.64
12/17	98.49	20 16	5.50	1.80	36.45
12/16	91.90	20 13	4.51	1.58	33.78
12/15	71.14	16 12	4.87	1.47	32.76
Annual Growth	**10.7%**	**— —**	**6.6%**	**9.6%**	**6.7%**

Qurate Retail Inc

Qurate Retail stands by your right to shop at home and online. The company owns and operates market-leading home shopping channel QVC which sells an average 710 products each week across the home apparel beauty and accessories jewelry and electronics categories. QVC also sells online. Qurate Retail also runs online businesses including Zulily and online invitation site Evite. It also holds equity stakes in FTD Companies HSN and LendingTree among others. Liberty Interactive acquired the long-standing rival of its QVC business HSN Inc. for around $2.1 billion in 2017. Liberty Interactive Corp. was formed in 2011 when its predecessor restructured and split off its Liberty Capital and Liberty Starz businesses as Liberty Media which changed its name to Qurate Retail Inc. in early 2018. The US accounts for majority of sales.

Operations

Qurate Retail operates through QxH QVC International Zulily and Corporate and other.

QxH accounts more than 60% of the company's total sales. It includes QVC US and HSN which market and sell a wide variety of consumer products in the US primarily by means of their televised shopping programs and via the Internet through their websites and mobile applications.

QVC International which accounts for approximately 20% of sales markets and sells a wide variety of consumer products in several foreign countries primarily by means of its televised shopping programs and via the Internet through its international websites and mobile applications.

Zulily brings in over 10% of sales and sells products in the US and elsewhere online through flash sales events primarily through its desktop and mobile websites and mobile applications.

Qurate Retail viewed LendingTree Evite and Liberty Broadband as separate components and evaluated them separately for discontinued operations presentation.

The company's home products generates about 40% of total sales followed by apparel for almost 20%. The remaining revenues are produced by beauty accessories electronics jewelry and other products.

Geographic Reach

Headquartered in Colorado Qurate Retail rings up almost 80% of its sales in the US. Japan accounts about 10% and Germany produces more than 5% of sales. Other foreign countries generate roughly 5% of sales. QxH unit owns its corporate headquarters and operations center in West Chester Pennsylvania. QxH also owns call centers and distribution centers in Texas Chesapeake Pennsylvania Tennessee and Virginia while QVC International owns call centers distribution centers and multi-functional buildings in Germany Chiba-Shi Japan Italy and the UK. Zulily leases its corporate headquarters in Seattle Washington; fulfillment centers in Lockbourne Ohio McCarran Nevada Bethlehem and Pennsylvania; and corporate offices in Gahanna Ohio and Shenzhen China. Cornerstone owns an office and storage facility in Franconia New Hampshire. Cornerstone also leases its fulfillment centers in Butler and Warren Counties in Ohio and Phoenix Arizona.

Sales and Marketing

Flagship subsidiary QVC distributes its television programs through satellite and optical fiber to cable and satellite system providers in the US Germany Japan the UK and neighboring countries. It also transmits programs via digital terrestrial broadcast television to viewers in Italy the UK and certain parts of the US and Germany. Additionally QVC offers a web-based catalog for retailers.

Some of QVC's clients include Comcast Cox Dish Network DirecTV Verizon and AT&T.

Financial Performance

The company's consolidated revenue decreased 4% to $13.5 billion for the year ended December 31 2019. QxH Zulily and QVC International revenue decreased $267 million $246 million and $29 million respectively during the year ended December 31 2019 as compared to the same period in the prior year.

Net income incurred a loss of $405 million from $964 million in the prior year.

Cash at the end of 2019 increased by $21 million to $681 million from $660 million in 2018. Cash provided by was $1.3 billion while cash used for investing and financing activities were $600 million and $661 million respectively.

Strategy

QVC's operating strategies are to Curate special products at compelling values; Extend video reach and relevance; Reimagine daily digital discovery; Expand and engage its passionate community; and Deliver joyful customer service. In addition QVC is exploring opportunities to evolve the International operating model to pursue growth opportunities in a more leveraged way across markets.

To preserve the tax-free treatment of the GCI Liberty Split-Off the company may determine to forgo certain transactions that might have otherwise been advantageous to their company including certain asset dispositions or other strategic transactions for some period of time following the GCI Liberty Split-Off. In addition their potential tax liabilities related to the GCI Liberty Split-Off might discourage delay or prevent a change of control transaction for some period of time following the GCI Liberty Split-Off.

HISTORY

The man who would be king of cable programming got his start on the hardware end of the business. In 1970 John Malone became president of General Instrument's Jerrold Communications subsidiary which supplied equipment to the then-new cable TV industry. One of Jerrold's customers was Bob Magness a former Texas rancher who in the 1950s started the company that eventually became Denver-based cable operator Tele-Communications Inc. (TCI). In the early 1970s TCI struggled in need of leadership. In 1973 the 32-year-old Malone was named CEO of TCI.

Malone restructured TCI's debt in 1977 paving the way for expansion into bigger cable markets after deregulation in 1984. He also acquired programming buying stakes in Black Entertainment Television (33% 1979 sold to Viacom in 2001) the Discovery Channel (14% 1986) and American Movie Classics (50% 1986). In 1987 TCI helped save debt-plagued Turner Broadcasting and came away with 12% of Turner Broadcasting's stock.

Due in part to antitrust pressure from government regulators in 1991 TCI spun off much of its programming assets along with interests in 14 cable systems as Liberty Media. Malone became chairman and principal shareholder. In its first year the company launched Court TV in a joint venture and introduced film channel Encore. The next year it bought an interest in the Home Shopping Network (which became USA Networks in 1998 and later changed names to USA

Interactive in 2002 InterActiveCorp in 2003 and finally IAC/InterActiveCorp in 2004).

In 1994 TCI reacquired Liberty Media; it issued a tracking stock the next year to reflect the value of Liberty's program assets. Also in 1995 Liberty Media and News Corp. joined forces to create FOX/Liberty Networks a national sports network designed to compete with Disney's ESPN.

In 2011 Liberty Media Corp. changed its name to Liberty Interactive Corp. following the split-off of its Liberty Capital and Liberty Starz tracking stocks.

EXECUTIVES

President And Ceo, Gregory B. (Greg) Maffei, age 59, $1,045,739 total compensation
Chief Corporate Development Officer, Albert E. Rosenthaler, age 60, $336,031 total compensation
Chief Legal Officer, Richard N. (Rich) Baer, age 63, $327,307 total compensation
Cfo Liberty Media Corporation Liberty Interactive Corporation And Liberty Broadband Corporation, Mark D. Carleton, age 59, $127,147 total compensation
Chairman, John C. Malone, age 79
Auditors: KPMG LLP

LOCATIONS

HQ: Qurate Retail Inc
  12300 Liberty Boulevard, Englewood, CO 80112
Phone: 720 875-5300
Web: www.qurateretail.com

2016 Sales

	$ mil.	% of total
US	7,979	75
Japan	900	8
Germany	866	8
Other countries	902	9
Total	**10,647**	**100**

PRODUCTS/OPERATIONS

2016 Sales

	$ mil.	% of total
QVC	8,682	81
zulily	1,547	15
Ventures Group	428	4
eliminations	(10)	-
Total	**10,647**	**100**

2016 Sales

	% of total
Home	33
Apparel	19
Beauty	17
Accessories	13
Jewelry	9
Electronics	9
Total	**100**

COMPETITORS

Access TV	Orbitz Worldwide
Amazon.com	Priceline
American Express	Travelocity
EVINE Live	Wal-Mart
IAC	

HISTORICAL FINANCIALS

Company Type: Public

Income Statement

FYE: December 31

	REVENUE ($ mil.)	NET INCOME ($ mil.)	NET PROFIT MARGIN	EMPLOYEES
12/19	13,458	(456)	—	25,228
12/18	14,070	916	6.5%	27,226
12/17	10,404	2,441	23.5%	28,255
12/16	10,647	1,235	11.6%	21,080
12/15	9,989	869	8.7%	22,080
Annual Growth	**7.7%**	**—**		**3.4%**

2019 Year-End Financials

Debt ratio: 42.83%
Return on equity: (-8.72%)
Cash ($ mil.): 673
Current ratio: 1.14
Long-term debt ($ mil.): 5,855

No. of shares (mil.): 415
Dividends
  Yield: —
  Payout: —
Market value ($ mil.): 3,507

	STOCK PRICE ($) FY Close	P/E High/Low		PER SHARE ($) Earnings	Dividends	Book Value
12/19	8.43	—	—	(1.08)	0.00	11.64
12/18	19.52	20	13	1.45	0.00	12.81
12/17	24.42	10	7	2.70	0.00	17.68
12/16	19.98	28	18	0.98	0.00	12.45
12/15	27.32	10	9	2.93	0.00	10.73
Annual Growth	**(25.5%)**	—	—			**2.1%**

Qwest Corp

EXECUTIVES

Exec V Pres-cao-contrl, David D Cole
Executive Vice President Product Management, Shaun Andrews
Vice President And General Manager, Alison Greenwood
Senior Business Intelligence Developer, Scott Reames
Auditors: KPMG LLP

LOCATIONS

HQ: Qwest Corp
  100 CenturyLink Drive, Monroe, LA 71203
Phone: 318 388-9000
Web: www.centurylink.com

HISTORICAL FINANCIALS

Company Type: Public

Income Statement

FYE: December 31

	REVENUE ($ mil.)	NET INCOME ($ mil.)	NET PROFIT MARGIN	EMPLOYEES
12/19	8,157	1,827	22.4%	17,700
12/18	8,493	1,665	19.6%	19,000
12/17	8,550	1,657	19.4%	22,000
12/16	8,910	1,085	12.2%	22,000
12/15	8,964	1,074	12.0%	22,000
Annual Growth	**(2.3%)**	**14.2%**	**—**	**(5.3%)**

2019 Year-End Financials

Debt ratio: 33.43%
Return on equity: 18.28%
Cash ($ mil.): 2
Current ratio: 0.73
Long-term debt ($ mil.): 4,846

No. of shares (mil.): 0
Dividends
  Yield: 0.0%
  Payout: 87.5%
Market value ($ mil.): 0

	STOCK PRICE ($)	P/E	PER SHARE ($)		
	FY Close	High/Low	Earnings	Dividends	Book Value
12/19	25.63	— —	(0.00)	1.69	**
12/18	18.98	— —	(0.00)	1.69	**
12/17	22.88	— —	(0.00)	1.07	**
Annual Growth	2.9%	—	—	12.1%	2.0%

R. DIRECTIONAL DRILLING & UNDERGROUND TECHNOLOGY, INC.

EXECUTIVES

Pres-Ceo, Jose M Ruiz
V Pres of Oprs*, Aurelio Ruiz
V Pres of Sls*, Derek Reeve
Office Manager, Colleen Hale
Job Coordinator, Denise Lenz
Fleet Manager, Tim Howe
Auditors: KEN DUSSEAU PC

LOCATIONS

HQ: R. DIRECTIONAL DRILLING & UNDERGROUND TECHNOLOGY, INC.
8560 N 77TH DR, PEORIA, AZ 853457969
Phone: 602 374-3173
Web: WWW.DRILLRDD.COM

HISTORICAL FINANCIALS

Company Type: Private

Income Statement   FYE: December 31

	REVENUE ($ mil.)	NET INCOME ($ mil.)	NET PROFIT MARGIN	EMPLOYEES
12/12	7,667	(1,040)	—	61
12/11*	7	2	29.9%	—
09/10	2	0	27.4%	—
Annual Growth	5174.7%	—	—	—

*Fiscal year change

Radian Group, Inc.

Radian Group is glowing from a conflagration of private mortgage insurance claims. Through subsidiaries Radian Guaranty Radian Mortgage Assurance and Radian Insurance Radian Group provides traditional private mortgage insurance coverage to protect lenders from defaults by borrowers who put down a deposit of less than 20% when buying a home. Such coverage provides protection on individual loans and covers unpaid loan principal and delinquent intere st. Its pool insurance covers limited exposure on groups of loans. Radian still insures municipal bonds written before 2008 through its financial guaranty business . Radian Group's customers include mortgage bankers commercial banks and savings institutions.

Operations

Radian operates in two segments: The Mortgage insurance (accounts for about 85% of revenue) division offers credit-related insurance coverage primarily private mortgage insurance as well as risk services for lending agencies. These operations are primarily conducted through the Radian Guaranty subsidiary. The company also provides mortgage and real estate services through its principal services subsidiary Clayton which were sold on 2020 as well as Red Bell Real Estate and ValuAmerica.

Meanwhile the services segment (about 10%) — primarily a fee-for-service business that offers a broad array of real estate title and mortgage services to market participants across the mortgage and real estate value chain. Its Mortgage services account for nearly 50% of sales Real estate services generate more than 40% and Title service account for the rest.

The company generates three-fourths of its sales from net premiums earned while services revenue and gains from investment and other account for the rest.

Geographic Reach

Headquartered in Philadelphia Radian has offices across the US as well as in Ohio Colorado and Utah.

Its top ten countries with the highest mortgage insurance RIF include California Texas Florida Illinois Georgia Virginia Maryland Arizona North Carolina and Washington with a total of more than 50%.

Sales and Marketing

The principal customers of Radian's mortgage insurance business are mortgage originators such as mortgage bankers mortgage brokers commercial banks savings institutions credit unions and community banks.

Financial Performance

For the last five years the company revenue continued an upward trend with an overall growth of 28% since 2015.

In fiscal 2019 Radian's revenue climbed 20% to $1.5 billion due mainly to a 13% increase in premiums earned a 7% increase in the Services segment 13% increase in investment income and $51.7 million gain on investments and other financial instruments.

Net income increased by 11% to $672.3 million due to higher revenue and lower interest expense.

Cash and restricted cash at the end of 2019 was $96.3 million. Net cash provided by operating activities was $694.4 million while investing and financing activities each used $302 million and $403.1 million respectively. Main cash uses for the year were for purchases of fixed maturities repayments of senior notes and repurchases of common stocks.

Strategy

Radian is focused on supporting the American dream of homeownership by delivering new levels of service and innovation to its customers across the residential mortgage and real estate spectrum through the combination of its mortgage insurance and risk services business and its comprehensive suite of real estate title and mortgage services. Its objectives include driving strong growth increasing value creation and providing attractive stockholder returns. Consistent with these objectives the company business strategy is focused on growing its businesses and diversifying its revenue sources while at the same time leveraging its operational excellence and the strength of its "One Radian" brand.

The company's long-term strategic objectives are: Maximizing the long-term economic value of its insured portfolio to drive future earnings by writing profitable NIW and effectively maintaining the portfolio's health balance and profitability including by using risk distribution strategies to manage its retained exposure; Leveraging the strength of its One Radian brand and core competencies and increase its competitive differentiation; and Managing its capital to build strategic financial flexibility and increase stockholder value.

Mergers and Acquisitions

In 2019 Radian announced that it has acquired Five Bridges Advisors LLC a renowned developer of proprietary software data analytics and predictive models leveraging artificial intelligence machine learning and traditional econometric techniques based in Bethesda Maryland.The acquisition is consistent with Radian's growth and diversification strategy as well as its focus on the core product offerings of its Title Mortgage and Real Estate Services. Terms were not disclosed.

HISTORY

Radian Group was born from the ashes of the 1987 stock crash and the rubble of the natural disasters of the early 1990s. Parent insurance company Reliance Group was deep in debt and desperately in need of cash. To raise money Reliance separated CMAC Investment (and operating subsidiary Commonwealth Mortgage Assurance) from subsidiary Commonwealth Land Title and took the company public in 1992.

In 1994 after two years of lackluster stock performance the board promoted CFO Frank Filipps (an American International Group veteran) to CEO. Filipps limited commissions to new policies rather than retained business. The pokey stock nosed up with some help from low interest rates and high numbers of new mortgage loans. Despite a raise in interest rates in 1995 the company continued to expand its market share.

In 1996 the company launched Prophet Score a new risk-assessment model that allowed CMAC to expand its coverage to include subprime loans. These measures jump-started sales to new highs in 1997 and 1998. Nevertheless CMAC (and its competitors) suffered in the market because of negative publicity: private mortgage (PMI) insurers were slammed for keeping quiet when borrowers' equity rose to 20% the point when PMI is usually considered unnecessary. In 1999 CMAC bought former rival Amerin and changed the name of the combined company to Radian Group.

Radian diversified its operations through the 2001 acquisition of credit-based insurance and financial services provider Enhance Financial (renamed Radian Reinsurance and later merged into Radian Asset Assurance Inc.) In 2002 Radian sold off the Enhance Consumer Services subsidiary.

In 2005 Filipps departed to join Clayton Holdings. Sanford Ibrahim was then named CEO.

The company expanded into Asia in 2005 through a partnership with Standard Chartered Bank (Hong Kong) with Radian as the exclusive provider of residential mortgage insurance to the lender. However the deal did not take root and Standard Chartered Bank yanked their contract in early 2008.

As the credit markets went into meltdown that year the company began pulling back on the riskiest of bonds (such as second-liens) by mid-2007 but by early 2008 its ratings had been lowered.

In response to the market troubles Radian stopped insuring certain types of higher-risk home loans and began working with existing mortgage services to help distressed borrowers modify their loan terms. The company's Radian Asset Assurance operations in the US and UK also stopped accepting new business as part of its general hunkering down to ride out the storm and in 2010 it put the UK unit into liquidation.

EXECUTIVES

Ceo, Richard G. (Rick) Thornberry
President Radian Guaranty, Teresa A. Bryce Bazemore, age 60, $550,000 total compensation
Evp And Cfo, J. Franklin (Frank) Hall, age 52, $400,000 total compensation
Evp And Cio, Richard I. (Rick) Altman, age 53
Evp And Chief Risk Officer, Derek V. Brummer, $415,000 total compensation
President Clayton Holdings, Jeff Tennyson
Assistant Vice President Manager Information Technology Administration, Nicole Phillipine
Vice President Mirs Business Transformation, Robert Miller
Senior Vice President, Robert Quigley
Vice President Secondary Marketing, John A Castiello
Vice President Information Technology, David Krause
Divisional Vice President, Matt Rohl
Vice President National Account Manager, Todd Ebert
Assistant Vice President Accounting, Julie Jones
Senior Vice President And Deputy General Counsel, Glenn Davis
Vice President Business Development, Shelley Duffy
Assistant Vice President Corporate Accounting, Abigail Rodriguez
Vice President E Commerce, Lora Wasson
Senior Vice President Corporate Planning, Rick Altman
Senior Vice President, Michael Dziuba
Assistant Vice President Client Connectivity, Siv Anantuni
Vp Security Assurance, Lucas Burke
Assistant Vice President Quality Assurance, Christine Harney
Executive Vice President, Shawn Murphy
Avp Security Assurance, Brad Bowers
Vp Operations Training, Matthew Carroll
Vice President Enterprise Information Management, Karen Stine
Vice President Compensation, Steve Lensing
Director, Herbert Wender, age 83
Board Member, Howard Culang
Board Member, Dave Carney
Auditors: PricewaterhouseCoopers LLP

LOCATIONS

HQ: Radian Group, Inc.
1500 Market Street, Philadelphia, PA 19102
Phone: 215 231-1000
Web: www.radian.biz

PRODUCTS/OPERATIONS

2016 Revenues

	$ mil.	% of total
Net premiums earned;insurance	921	74
Services revenue	168	14
Net investment income	113	9
Net gains (losses) on investments and other financial instruments	30	3
Other income	3	-
Total	**1,238**	**100**

COMPETITORS

Assured Guaranty	Old Republic
Genworth Financial	Triad Guaranty
MGIC Investment	US Department of
National Mortgage	Veterans Affairs
Insurance	United Guaranty

HISTORICAL FINANCIALS

Company Type: Public

Income Statement

FYE: December 31

	ASSETS ($ mil.)	NET INCOME ($ mil.)	INCOME AS % OF ASSETS	EMPLOYEES
12/19	6,808	672	9.9%	2,000
12/18	6,314	606	9.6%	1,942
12/17	5,900	121	2.1%	1,887
12/16	5,863	308	5.3%	1,971
12/15	5,642	286	5.1%	1,881
Annual Growth	4.8%	23.7%	—	1.5%

2019 Year-End Financials

Debt ratio: 15.01%	No. of shares (mil.): 201
Return on equity: 17.84%	Dividends
Cash ($ mil.): 92	Yield: 0.0%
Current ratio: —	Payout: 0.3%
Long-term debt ($ mil.):	Market value ($ mil.): 5,061

	STOCK PRICE ($) FY Close	P/E High/Low		PER SHARE ($) Earnings	Dividends	Book Value
12/19	25.16	8	5	3.20	0.01	20.13
12/18	16.36	8	5	2.77	0.01	16.34
12/17	20.61	40	28	0.55	0.01	13.90
12/16	17.98	13	6	1.37	0.01	13.39
12/15	13.39	13	9	1.22	0.01	12.07
Annual Growth	17.1%			27.3%	(0.0%)	13.6%

RAYMOND JAMES & ASSOCIATES INC

Does everybody love Raymond James & Associates (RJA)? Raymond James Financial hopes so. RJA is that company's primary subsidiary and one of the largest retail brokerages in the US. The unit provides brokerage financial planning investments and related services to consumers. It performs equity and fixed income sales trading and research for institutional clients in North America and Europe. Its investment banking group provides corporate and public finance debt underwriting and mergers and acquisitions advice. RJA also makes markets for approximately 1000 stocks including thinly traded issues. Planning Corporation of America a wholly-owned subsidiary of RJA sells insurance and annuities.

Operations
RJA is engaged in most aspects of securities distribution and investment banking.

Geographic Reach
The company has more than 200 branches and satellite offices concentrated in the Mid-Atlantic Midwest Southeast and Southwest portions of the US in addition to ten institutional sales offices in Europe.

Sales and Marketing
RJA has many big name clients across dozens of industries. In 2013 Titan Medical announced that it has retained RJA to provide advisory services and present options which could include a possible sale.

Strategy
In 2012 the company's parent completed its acquisition of Morgan Keegan & Co. and MK Holding Inc. from Regions Financial Corporation. Some of the equity capital markets and fixed income operations of were integrated into RJA.

EXECUTIVES

Senior Vice President, Charles Stubbs
Vice President, William Wallace
Vice President, Scott Cutliff
Vice President Investments Financial Advisor, Aamsa Zuniga
Vice President Investments, Hall Sumner
Senior Vice President Corporate Risk Management New Products, Tarek Helal
Auditors: KPMG LLP TAMPA FL

LOCATIONS

HQ: RAYMOND JAMES & ASSOCIATES INC
880 CARILLON PKWY, SAINT PETERSBURG, FL 337161100
Phone: 727 567-1000
Web: WWW.RAYMONDJAMES.COM

COMPETITORS

Ameriprise	Janney Montgomery
Charles Schwab	Scott
E*TRADE Financial	Merrill Lynch
Edward D. Jones	Scottrade
Edward Jones	TD Ameritrade
FMR	Wells Fargo Advisors

HISTORICAL FINANCIALS

Company Type: Private

Income Statement

FYE: September 30

	ASSETS ($ mil.)	NET INCOME ($ mil.)	INCOME AS % OF ASSETS	EMPLOYEES
09/17	9,917	198	2.0%	10,000
09/16	10,689	145	1.4%	—
09/15	7,893	167	2.1%	—
09/14	6,955	182	2.6%	—
Annual Growth	12.6%	2.8%		—

Raymond James Financial, Inc.

Diversified financial services company Raymond James Financial offers financial advice to retail clients and corporations alike. The brokerage house has approximately 8200 advisors and about $930 billion in total client assets held. Raymond James offers investment and asset management services for retail and institutional clients; underwriting distribution trading and brokerage of equity and debt securities; sale of mutual funds and other investment products; corporate and retail banking services; and trust services. The company primarily earns its revenue from its domestic operations with approximately 95% of the total revenue.

Operations

Raymond James Financial operates through five core business segments: Private Client Group (PCG) Capital Markets the RJ Bank Asset Management and Other.

The PCG unit generates more than 65% of the company's net revenue through investment advisory securities transaction and financial planning services. The segment's assets under administration is approximately $883.3 billion. PCG segment provides services through their branch office network throughout the US Canada and the UK.

Raymond James' Capital Markets unit (about 15% of net revenue) provides services for investment banking public finance institutional sales and trading equity research and syndication and management of tax credit-qualifying investments primarily in the US Canada and Europe.

RJ Bank segment provides around 10% of the company's revenue and offers corporate SBL tax-exempt and residential loans. The bank also offers deposit services to Raymond James' broker-dealer clients and the public. Corporate and tax-exempt loans account for more than 55% of the bank's loan portfolio.

The Asset Management segment provides investment advisory and related administrative services to Raymond James' PCG clients and investment advisory and asset management services to individual and institutional investors including third-party broker-dealers. The segment accounts for nearly 10% of net revenue.

Asset management and related administrative fees generate more than 45% of total revenue while nearly 20% came from securities commissions and more than 10% came from interest income.

Geographic Reach

Headquartered in St. Petersburg Florida Raymond James Financial generates about 95% of its revenue from US operations. Canadian customers contribute about 5% to revenue; European clients contribute the remainder.

The company has operations in the US Canada and Europe but substantially all of its long-lived assets are in the US. Its information technology data center is located in the Denver Colorado area.

Sales and Marketing

Raymond James Financial markets and sells to clients mainly through its network of approximately 8200 financial advisors at branch locations mostly in the US Canada and UK and through its website.

The company directly employs more than 4800 independently contracted financial advisors.

Raymond James markets its products to individual corporations municipalities retail and institutional clients.

Financial Performance

Net revenues of $8.0 billion for the company's fiscal year 2020 (ended September) increased by $250 million or 3%.

Raymond James Financial's net income of $818 million decreased by $216 million or 21%.

Cash held by the company at the end of 2020 increased to $9.6 billion compared to $6.0 billion in the prior year. Cash provided by operations and financing activities were $4.1 billion and $4.6 billion respectively. Cash used for investing activities was $5.0 billion mainly for purchases of available-for-sale securities.

Strategy

RJ Bank's strategy for credit risk management includes well-defined credit policies uniform underwriting criteria and ongoing risk monitoring and review processes for all corporate tax-exempt residential SBL and other credit exposures. The strategy also includes diversification on a geographic industry and customer level regular credit examinations and management reviews of all corporate and tax-exempt loans as well as individual delinquent residential loans.

Mergers and Acquisitions

In 2020 Raymond James Financial agreed to acquire Financo a boutique investment bank focused on the consumer sector with offices in New York and London. With the acquisition of Financo Raymond James Investment Banking's new and enhanced sub-sectors of coverage within Consumer & Retail will include apparel and accessories beauty and personal care consumer services direct-to-consumer/e-commerce enthusiast brands and active lifestyle fitness and healthy living footwear food and beverage home furnishings and décor restaurants and specialty retail. The acquisition of Financo continues the firm's strategic growth in its Investment Banking capabilities both domestically and internationally.

In late 2020 Raymond James Financial agreed to acquire NWPS Holdings Inc. doing business as NWPS and Northwest Plan Services an independent provider of retirement plan administration consulting actuarial and administration services based in Seattle Washington. The addition of NWPS allows Raymond James to expand its retirement services offerings including retirement plan administration services to advisors and clients.

Company Background

Raymond James Financial was formed from the combination of financial services company Robert A. James Investments and Raymond and Associates. James' brother Roy James joined the company in 1965 to establish its marketing department. Bob James' son Tom James was named the company's Chairman and CEO in 1970. Raymond James went public in 1983.

Robert James often called the "founder of financial planning" first started a construction business in Ohio after his WWII service in the US Navy and then began a Florida home-building company. He got into the financial services business in 1954 with Florida Mutual Fund a company he and Gerard Jobin formed that eventually became American National Growth Fund. But when most companies were selling just stocks or mutual funds James saw a need for a more comprehensive approach to investing. He decided to focus on helping individual clients learning about their financial needs and goals and then working with them on everything from investments to taxes. To that end he began offering seminars for retirees.

In 1960 those seminars had turned into a new company James and Associates which two years later became Robert A. James Investments. In 1964 James acquired Raymond and Associates a firm started by Edward Raymond in 1962; the newly merged firm was renamed Raymond James & Associates (RJA).

James' son Thomas joined the firm in 1966 the year the company's revenues first surpassed $1 million. Over the next several years the company expanded its investment offerings and set up new divisions. It added Investment Management & Research as an affiliate broker/dealer in 1967 and Planning Corporation of America as a general insurance agency in 1968.

Raymond James Financial incorporated as a holding company in 1969 and Thomas James became CEO the next year. RJA formed Eagle Asset Management in 1975 RJ Oil & Gas (subsidiary for oil and gas limited partnerships) in 1977 securities and real estate subsidiaries in 1980 (Robert Thomas Securities and RJ Properties respectively) and an equipment leasing subsidiary (RJ Leasing) in 1982.

Raymond James Financial went public in 1983 the year Robert James died. Two years later the company organized its Heritage Family of Funds. RJA became an international company in the late 1980s opening an office in Paris in 1987 and in Geneva the next year. It also began offering a cash management program in 1988 and began its Stock Loan Department. Trust and banking subsidiaries were begun in 1992 and 1994 respectively followed by the creation of Equity Capital Markets Group in 1996.

In 2000 Raymond James Financial crossed the billion-dollar-mark hitting $1.7 billion in sales. That year it acquired Canadian investment firm Goepel McDermid (renamed Raymond James Ltd.) to offer individual and institutional investment services to the Canadian market and it launched Raymond James Killik a UK joint venture that became Raymond James Investment Services in 2002.

In 2006 Raymond James Financial reduced front-end commissions with variations of variable annuity products; the next year it kicked off its Wealth Solutions department a unit designed to help high-net-worth clients and their advisors. Also that year Raymond James Financial extended its deal to attach its name to the home stadium of the NFL's Tampa Bay Buccaneers through 2015.

In 2012 to build its capital markets business in one of its largest purchases to date the company bought the investment banking and brokerage business of Morgan Keegan from Regions Financial for $1.2 billion and integrated the Morgan Keegan platform into its RJ&A platform. Raymond James Financial previously purchased boutique investment bank Lane Berry & Co. International in Boston in 2009 and Chicago-based investment bank and brokerage Howe Barnes Hoefer & Arnett in 2011.

To boost its large-cap investments the firm in 2012 acquired a 45% interest in ClariVest Asset Management.

RJ Bank acquired the Canadian operations of Allied Irish Banks in 2012 adding a portfolio of approximately $430 million in loan commitments. In conjunction with the deal RJ Bank launched a new finance company in Canada which will help the company grow its corporate and real estate banking business. It's part of Raymond James Financial's strategy of expanding its corporate lending business to additional markets.

EXECUTIVES

President Global Equities And Investment Banking Raymond James & Associates, Jeffrey E. (Jeff) Trocin, age 60, $305,000 total compensation

Evp Finance Cfo And Treasurer, Jeffrey P. (Jeff) Julien, age 63, $280,000 total compensation

Coo Raymond James Financial And Ceo Raymond James & Associates, Dennis W. Zank, age 65, $330,000 total compensation

Vice President Human Resources Executive, Michael Girolamo

President Raymond James Financial And Fixed Income Capital Markets, John C. Carson, age 63, $300,000 total compensation

President Raymond James Financial Services, Scott A. Curtis, age 57

Chairman And Ceo, Paul C. Reilly, age 65, $445,000 total compensation

President And Ceo Raymond James Bank, Steven M. (Steve) Raney, age 54

Chairman And Ceo Raymond James Ltd., Paul D. Allison, age 63

President Raymond James & Associates Private Client Group, Tashtego S. (Tash) Elwyn, age 48

Evp Technology And Operations, Bella Loykhter Allaire, age 66

Evp And President Asset Management Group, Jeffrey A. (Jeff) Dowdle, age 55

Evp General Counsel And Secretary, Jonathan N. Santelli, age 48

Senior Vice President; Director European Equities, Mark Abbott

Senior Vice President Communications, Tracey Bustamante

Vice President Investments, Greg Williams

Senior Vice President Fixed Income Sales, Gerard Buquicchio

Vice President And Managing Director Acquisitions Northeast Raymond James Tax Credit Funds, Darryl Seavey

Vice President Corporate Client Services, Hunt James

Vice President And Managing Director Acquisitions West Raymond James Tax Credit Funds, Kevin Kilbane

Senior Vice President, Mark Mchugh

Vice President, Charlie Williams

Senior Vice President Financial Planning Raymond James And Associates, Charles J Bauder

Vice President, David Thomas

Vice President Investments, Don Minton

Vice President Institutional Equity Sales, Rob Mills

First Vice President Investments, Scott Newmann

Senior Vice President, Helen Rice-devlin

Vice President Agency Trader Ii, James Nielsen

Vice President, Neil Deakin

Vice President Client Communications Technology, Randy McGlothin

Associate Vice President Investments, Ryan Rothermund

Vice President Investments, Josh Rajewski

Vice President, Mark Matheson

Vice President, Ed Cashman

Vice President Deposit Operations, Barbara Shore

Senior Vice President Healthcare Public Finance Dallas, Peter H Delaney

Senior Vice President, David Schaffer

Senior Vice President, Michael Gibbs

Vice President Investments, Sandy Martin

First Vice President, Beth Smith

Vice President Of Investments Programs And Services Committee Chair, Linda Larkin Smith

Senior Vice President, Bill Specht

Senior Vice President, Scott Brinner

Senior Vice President, Sandy Webb

Senior Vice President. Investments, Albert Fregosi

Vice President Operations, Steve Bartalo

First Vice President Investments, Rachel Gammerman

Vice President Variable Annuity Sales, Vanessa Marcos

Vice President Investments, Sandy Russell

Senior Vice President, Steve Shapiro

Senior Vice President Investments, John Reuter

Vice President Information Technology, Frank Bugh

Senior Vice President Loan Operations, Sheryl Williams

Senior Vice President, John Abington

Senior Vice President, Andrea Tihal

Vice President Investments, Ron Bailey

Senior Vice President And Head Corporate Development, Alexandra Band

Vice President, Zach Berg

Vice President Of Investments, James Heinen

National Sales Manager, Peter Delahunt

Vice President Sales Trader International, Sharon Agudio

Vice President, Christine Holder

Assistant Vice President Of Information Technology, Brian Miller

Vice President, Ann M Hensler

Vice President Regulatory Reporting, Marshall Ollia

Senior Vice President Of Operations, Denise Samson

First Vice President Investments, Robert Hodgson

Vice President Investments, Sonya Choeff

Senior Vice President, Roxanne Post

Vice President Syndicate Operations, Andrea Borum

Vice President Investments, Ladd Bednar

Senior Vice President Institutional Equity Sales, Zachary Taylor

Vice President, Robert Goff

Senior Vice President Healthcare Public Finance New York, Vasanta B Pundarika

Vice President Acquisitions Southeast, John Colvin

Senior Vice President Office Services, Raymond Lacour

Vice President Agency Trader Team Lead, Allen Spence

Vice President For Investments, Brian Rimel

Senior Vice President Equity Research Infrastruct, Michael Turits

Senior Vice President Institute Equity Sales Trader, Mike Christian

Vice President Investment Banking, Justin Cadman

Vice President Sales Trader, Marilyn Hiner

Associate Vice President, Nick Roederer

Senior Vice President, Justin Roman

Vice President, Stacy W Houston

Senior Vice President Fi Trading, Randall Hawkins

Vice President Investments, Mark Mazman

Senior Vice President, Fred Coble

Senior Vice President, Tom Donegan

Vice President Regional Manager, Angela Nye

Vice President Fi Trading, Chad Runnels

Associate Vice President, Daniel Allen

Vice President, Christine Pedrick

Corporate Bond Trader And Vice President, Mark Schreiner

Vice President Investments, Brent Carlton

Assistant Vice President, Ruth Quinlan

First Vice President, Kenny Mcclain

Fvp Fi Trading, Edward Wildrick

Senior Vice President Investments, Michael Mccall

Senior Vice President Investments, Dianne Townsend

Vice President Investments, Tim Kelley

Senior Vice President Investments, Mark Williams

Vice President Fi Strategies, Emilio Garma-Fernandez

Assistant Vice President Lending Solutions Consultant, Dino Martinbianco

Senior Vice President Fi Trading, Stephen Lewis

Senior Vice President Investments, Philip L Evans

Senior Vice President, Jeanna Bryan

First Vice President, Allison Willingham

Senior Vice President, Jeff Harring

Vice President, Michael Mobley

Assistant Vice President Internal Sales, Samantha Fernandez

First Vice President Investments, Tom Mahoney

Vice President Of Operations, Jesus Cruz

Senior Vice President Fi Trading, BEN LAPOINTE

Vice President, Al Caudullo

Senior Vp Investments, Jason Pucci

Vice President Investments, Christy Cornell

Assistant Vice President Corporate Loan Operations, Tonia Armes

Executive Vice President And Senior Corporate And Real Estate Banking Executive Raymond James Bank, Tom Macina

Vice President, Scott Englehardt

Vice President, Lee Morthland

Senior Vice President Healthcare Public Finance New York, Dean Scarano

Vice President, Sasha Stipanovich

Senior Vice President Financial Advisor, Chip Lee

Senior Vice President Controller, Ken Ginel

First Vice President, Tom Owens

Senior Vice President Investments, Tom Ross

Vice President, Chris Cowing

Assistant Vice President Application Development, John D'Agostino

Vice President Client Reporting, Salit Nagy-todd

Associate Vice President Investments, Michael Lowe

Senior Vice President Investments Branch Manager, Matt Quigley

Vice President Compliance, Brad Cole

Senior Vice President Investments, Bob Taylor

Senior Vice President Fixed Income Sales, Geoffrey Waters

Senior Vice President Fi Trading, Gail Tyler

Vice President, Bob Jones

Senior Vice President Of Investments, Todd Tindall

Vice President Public Finance, Ogden Kniffin

Senior Vice President Real Estate Investment Banking St. Petersburg, Jozsi Popper

Vice President, Holly Hayes

Senior Vice President Listed And Otc And International Trading, Terri Stewart

Vice President, Paul Shoukry

Certified Financial Planner??? Senior Vice President Investments, Frank Maurno

Associate Vp Wealth Management, Mark Canavesio

Senior Vice President, Chad Puryear

Associate Vice President, Kristin Smith

First Vice President, Eduardo Bonilla

Associate Vice President Investments Sim, Lynn T Shaw

Senior Vice President, Matthew Crosby
Auditors: KPMG LLP

LOCATIONS

HQ: Raymond James Financial, Inc.
880 Carillon Parkway, St. Petersburg, FL 33716
Phone: 727 567-1000
Web: www.raymondjames.com

2018 Sales

	$ mil.	% of total
US	6,914	92
Canada	422	6
Europe	139	2
Other	- -	
Total	**7,475**	**100**

PRODUCTS/OPERATIONS

2018 Sales By Segment

	$ mil.	% of total
Private Client Group	5,120	67
Capital Markets	991	13
RJ Bank	654	8
Asset Management	815	11
Other	60	1
Eliminations	(166.3)	-
Total	**7,475**	**100**

2018 Sales by Revenue Type

	$ mil.	% of total
Securities commissions & fees	4,483	60
Investment banking	440	6
Investment advisory and related administrative fees	605	8
Interest income	1,044	14
Account and service fees	771	10
Net trading profit	56	1
Other	74	1
Total	**7,475**	**100**

Selected Subsidiaries

Alex. Brown
Eagle Asset Management Inc.
Eagle Boston Investment Management Inc.
Eagle Fund Distributors Inc.
Howe Barnes Hoefer & Arnett Inc.
Lane Berry & Co. International
Planning Corporation of America
Raymond James & Associates
Raymond James Asset Management International S.A.
  (France)
Raymond James Bank FSB (dba RJ Bank)
Raymond James Canada LLC
Raymond James Capital Partners L.P.
Raymond James European Holdings Inc.
Raymond James Financial Services Inc.
Raymond James Financial Services Advisors
Raymond James Investment Services Limited (UK 75%)
Raymond James Ltd. (Canada)
Raymond James Tax Credit Funds Inc.
Raymond James Trust N.A.
Reams Asset Management
Scout Investments

COMPETITORS

Charles Schwab	National Financial
E*TRADE Financial	Partners
Edward Jones	Oppenheimer Holdings
FMR	Piper Jaffray
LPL Financial	Stifel Financial
Legg Mason	TD Ameritrade
Merrill Lynch	Wells Fargo Advisors
Morgan Stanley	

HISTORICAL FINANCIALS

Company Type: Public

Income Statement   FYE: September 30

	REVENUE ($ mil.)	NET INCOME ($ mil.)	NET PROFIT MARGIN	EMPLOYEES
09/20	8,168	818	10.0%	19,635
09/19	8,023	1,034	12.9%	18,910
09/18	7,475	856	11.5%	18,550
09/17	6,524	636	9.8%	17,000
09/16	5,520	529	9.6%	15,900
Annual Growth	**10.3%**	**11.5%**	**—**	**5.4%**

2020 Year-End Financials

Debt ratio: 6.70%
Return on equity: 11.91%
Cash ($ mil.): 9,634
Current ratio: 0.39
Long-term debt ($ mil.): 2,933

No. of shares (mil.): 136
Dividends
  Yield: 2.0%
  Payout: 23.9%
Market value ($ mil.): 9,936

	STOCK PRICE ($) FY Close	P/E High/Low		PER SHARE ($) Earnings	Dividends	Book Value
09/20	72.76	17	9	5.83	1.48	52.10
09/19	82.46	13	10	7.17	1.36	47.74
09/18	92.05	17	14	5.75	1.10	43.73
09/17	84.33	19	13	4.33	0.88	38.74
09/16	58.21	16	11	3.65	0.80	34.72
Annual Growth	**5.7%**	**—**	**—**	**12.4%**	**16.6%**	**10.7%**

Raytheon Technologies Corp

Raytheon technologies provides high-tech products and services for the aerospace and commercial building industries. It operates through engine aircraft manufacturer Pratt & Whitney; Carrier its former climate controls and security business; Collins Aerospace Systems maker of engine controls and flight systems for military and commercial aircraft; and Otis the world's largest elevator and escalator manufacturer. The company generates the majority of its revenue in the US. In 2020 Raytheon Technologies Corporation completed the all-stock merger of equal transaction with United Technologies Corporation following the completion by United Technologies of its previously announced spin-offs of its Carrier and Otis businesses.

Operations

Raytheon Technologies operates through four segments: Pratt & Whitney Carrier Collins Aerospace Systems and Otis.

Pratt & Whitney (over 25% of total sales) makes and sells aircraft engines for the commercial military business jet and general aviation markets. It also provides fleet management and aftermarket maintenance services. Its Pratt & Whitney Canada is among the world's leading suppliers of engines for the general and business aviation markets and also supplies products for regional airlines utility airplanes and helicopters.

The Carrier segment (nearly 25%) makes HVAC refrigeration fire security and building automation products for the commercial industrial smart cold chain and residential sectors. It also provides a wide range of residential and building systems including air conditioners heating systems and controls refrigeration fire flame gas smoke and carbon monoxide detection portable fire extinguishers fire suppression intruder alarms access control systems video management systems and electronic controls.. Many of Carrier's security and fire safety products are marketed under the Chubb and Kidde brand names.

Collins Aerospace Systems (almost 35%) provides aerospace products and aftermarket services for aircraft manufacturers airlines regional business and general aviation markets the military and space operations. Products include power generation and management and distribution aircraft sensing and engine control systems and surveillance and reconnaissance systems among several others. It also provides information management services through voice and data communication networks worldwide.

The company's Otis segment (generating over 15% of revenue) is the world's largest elevator and escalator manufacturer. It designs installs and services a wide range of passenger and freight elevators as well as escalators and moving walkways. Otis also makes modernization products that improve the safety reliability and aesthetics of existing installations.

Overall product sales generate around 70% of revenue while the remainder comes from service sales.

Geographic Reach

Headquartered in Farmington CT Raytheon operates more than 650 major properties in almost 100 countries.

The US generates over 60% of the company's total sales followed by Europe (over 15%) and the Asia Pacific region (over 10%).

Sales and Marketing

Customers in the commercial and industrial sectors contribute around 40% of Raytheon's total revenue. The commercial aerospace market generates almost 45% and the military aerospace and space sectors over 15%. Carrier sells its products directly to customers and through joint ventures distributors dealers and through retail channels. Otis sells directly to customers and through sales reps and distributors. Collins Aerospace Systems sells aerospace products and services to aircraft manufacturers airlines and other aircraft operators the U.S. and foreign governments maintenance repair and overhaul providers and independent distributors.

Financial Performance

Revenue in 2019 spiked up by 16% to $77 billion compared with $66.5 billion the previous year. The increase in revenue was primarily driven by higher sales in Collins Aerospace Systems.

Net income reached $5.5 billion up 5% over $5.2 billion in 2018 mainly from increased sales.

Cash at the end of fiscal 2019 was $7.4 billion an increase of $1.2 billion from the prior year. Cash from operations contributed $8.8 billion to the coffers while investing activities used $3.1 billion mainly for capital expenditures. Financing activities used $4.6 billion primarily from repayment of long-term debt.

Strategy

As part of the company's globalization strategy it have invested in certain countries including

Argentina Brazil China India Indonesia Mexico Poland Russia South Africa Turkey Ukraine and countries in the Middle East and Central Asia that carry high levels of currency political compliance and economic risk. Raytheon Technologies expects that sales to these and other emerging markets will continue to account for a significant portion of its sales as the company's businesses evolve and as these and other developing nations and regions around the world increase its demand for Raytheon's products.

Raytheon Technologies seeks to grow through strategic acquisitions in addition to internal growth. In the past several years the company made various acquisitions including the acquisition of Rockwell Collins in November 2018 and have entered into joint ventures intended to complement and expand its businesses. The company expects to continue to undertake such transactions in the future.

Mergers and Acquisitions

In early 2020 Raytheon Technologies Corporation a Waltham Massachussets-based aerospace and defense company completed the all-stock merger of equals transaction with United Technologies Corporation following the completion by United Technologies of its previously announced spin-offs of its Carrier and Otis businesses.

Company Background

United Technologies dates back to 1929 when William Boeing of Boeing Firms and Frederick Rentschler of Pratt & Whitney formed the United Aircraft and Transport Corporation. United Aircraft soon bought aviation companies Hamilton Aero Standard Steel Propeller and Sikorsky.

United Aircraft split in 1934 into three independent entities: United Airlines Boeing Airplane Company and United Aircraft. United Aircraft retained Pratt & Whitney and several other manufacturing interests. In 1975 the company changed its name to United Technologies Corporation representing the intent to diversify into other fields in addition to the aerospace industry.

HISTORY

In 1925 Frederick Rentschler and George Mead founded Pratt & Whitney Aircraft (P&W) to develop aircraft engines. P&W merged with Seattle-based Boeing Airplane Company and Chance Vought Corporation in 1929 to form United Aircraft & Transport. United Aircraft soon bought aviation companies Hamilton Aero Standard Steel Propeller and Sikorsky.

After congressional investigations led to new antitrust laws United Aircraft split in 1934 into three independent entities: United Airlines Boeing Airplane Company and United Aircraft. United Aircraft retained P&W and several other manufacturing interests.

A design flaw in engines produced for Boeing 747s sent P&W on an expensive trip back to the drawing board in the late 1960s. A concerned board of directors appointed Harry Gray a 17-year veteran of Litton Industries as president in 1971. Gray transformed the company into a conglomerate; it adopted its present name in 1975.

The company entered into a new stage of development with the milestone 2012 acquisitions of Goodrich and Rolls-Royce's share in the International Aero Engines (IAE) joint venture. The $16.5 billion acquisition of Goodrich an aircraft components manufacturer was one of UTC's largest. Through the transaction UTC absorbed $1.9 billion in assumed debt but it also sizably boosted its services to the commercial aerospace/defense industry and increased its revenues. Goodrich was combined with the former Hamilton Sundstrand operations and now form its UTC Aerospace Systems segment.

UTC in early 2013 sold its UTC Power unit to Oregon-based ClearEdge Power. In late 2015 it also sold its former Sikorsky helicopter subsidiary to Lockheed Martin for $9 billion.

EXECUTIVES

President Pratt & Whitney, Robert F. Leduc, age 64, $665,057 total compensation
Coo Americas Utc Building And Industrial Systems, Robert J. (Bob) McDonough, age 60, $806,250 total compensation
Chairman President And Ceo, Gregory J. Hayes, age 59, $1,450,000 total compensation
President Otis Elevator, Judy F. Marks
Vp General Counsel And Secretary Carrier, Charles D. Gill, age 56, $715,000 total compensation
Evp Operations And Strategy, Michael R. (Mike) Dumais, age 53
President Utc Aerospace Systems, David L. Gitlin, age 50
Evp And Chief Human Resources Officer, Elizabeth B. Amato, age 63
Svp And Cfo, Akhil Johri, age 59, $766,667 total compensation
Svp Digital And Cio, Vince Campisi
Svp And Cto, Paul Eremenko
Vice President Engineering And Technology Hamilton Sundstrand, Dave Carter
Vice President Actuation Systems, Rishi Grover
Vice President Finance, Rory Richardson
Senior Vice President And Chief Communications Officer, Kelli Parsons
Vice President Engineering Pratt And Whitney Military Engines, Thomas Prete
Vice President Engineering And Technology, Stephane Dion
Vice President Global Talent Acquisition, Yvette Stortz
Vice President Interiors, Cheryl Gorman
Vice President Compliance, William Erickson
Vp Supply Chain, Edward Dunn
National Accounts Manager, Jim Stewart
Board Member, Marshall Larsen
Auditors: PricewaterhouseCoopers LLP

LOCATIONS

HQ: Raytheon Technologies Corp
870 Winter Street, Waltham, MA 02451
Phone: 781 522-3000
Web: www.rtx.com

2018 Sales

	$ mil.	% of total
US	39,481	58
Europe	12,857	19
Asia/Pacific	8,847	13
Other	6,672	10
Eliminations and other	(1356)	-
Total	**66,501**	**100**

PRODUCTS/OPERATIONS

2018 Sales

	$ mil.	% of total
Carrier	18,922	28
Pratt & Whitney	19,397	29
Collins Aerospace Systems	16,634	24
Otis	12,904	19
Eliminations	(1356)	
Total	**66,501**	**100**

2018 Sales by Market

	$ mil.	% of total
Commercial & industrial	31,941	47
Commercial aerospace	26,591	39
Military aerospace & space	9,325	14
Eliminations and other	(1356)	
Total	**66,501**	**100**

2018 Sales

	$ mil.	% of total
Product sales	46,643	69
Service sales	21,214	31
Eliminations	(1356)	
Total	**66,501**	**100**

Products & Brands Selected

Actuation & Propeller Systems
Air Management Systems
Carrier
Carrier Transicold
Chubb
Chubb eConnect Monitoring Solution
Delta Security Solutions

Selected Operations

Otis (elevators escalators moving walkways and service)
Pratt & Whitney (commercial military business jet and general aviation aircraft engines auxiliary power units and parts and services)
Collins Aerospace Systems (aerospace products and aftermarket services)
Carrier (heating ventilating air conditioning and refrigeration systems and security systems)

COMPETITORS

CFM International SA	Lockheed Martin
GE Aviation	Parker-Hannifin
General Dynamics	Raytheon
Hitachi	SAFRAN
Honeywell	Siemens AG
International	ThyssenKrupp
Kaman	Trane Inc.
L3 Technologies	

HISTORICAL FINANCIALS

Company Type: Public

Income Statement

FYE: December 31

	REVENUE ($ mil.)	NET INCOME ($ mil.)	NET PROFIT MARGIN	EMPLOYEES
12/19	77,046	5,537	7.2%	243,200
12/18	66,501	5,269	7.9%	240,200
12/17	59,837	4,552	7.6%	205,000
12/16	57,244	5,055	8.8%	201,600
12/15	56,098	7,608	13.6%	197,200
Annual Growth	**8.3%**	**(7.6%)**	**—**	**5.4%**

2019 Year-End Financials

Debt ratio: 31.24%
Return on equity: 13.80%
Cash ($ mil.): 7,378
Current ratio: 1.08
Long-term debt ($ mil.): 37,788

No. of shares (mil.): 864
Dividends
  Yield: 3.3%
  Payout: 77.7%
Market value ($ mil.): 129,447

	STOCK PRICE ($) FY Close	P/E High/Low		PER SHARE ($) Earnings	Dividends	Book Value
12/19	149.76	23	16	6.41	2.94	48.33
12/18	106.48	22	16	6.50	2.84	44.63
12/17	127.57	22	19	5.70	2.72	37.05
12/16	109.62	18	14	6.12	2.62	34.10
12/15	96.07	14	10	8.61	2.56	32.63
Annual Growth	11.7%	—	—	(7.1%)	3.5%	10.3%

RBB Bancorp

Auditors: Eide Bailly LLP

LOCATIONS

HQ: RBB Bancorp
1055 Wilshire Blvd., Suite 1200, Los Angeles, CA 90017
Phone: 213 627-9888
Web: www.royalbusinessbankusa.com

HISTORICAL FINANCIALS

Company Type: Public

Income Statement   FYE: December 31

	ASSETS ($ mil.)	NET INCOME ($ mil.)	INCOME AS % OF ASSETS	EMPLOYEES
12/19	2,788	39	1.4%	355
12/18	2,974	36	1.2%	365
12/17	1,691	25	1.5%	203
12/16	1,395	19	1.4%	177
12/15	1,023	12	1.3%	—
Annual Growth	28.5%	31.9%	—	—

2019 Year-End Financials

Debt ratio: 4.08%
Return on equity: 10.03%
Cash ($ mil.): 182
Current ratio: —
Long-term debt ($ mil.): —

No. of shares (mil.): 20
Dividends
Yield: 1.8%
Payout: 21.3%
Market value ($ mil.): 424

	STOCK PRICE ($) FY Close	P/E High/Low		PER SHARE ($) Earnings	Dividends	Book Value
12/19	21.17	11	9	1.92	0.40	20.35
12/18	17.57	16	8	2.01	0.43	18.73
12/17	27.37	15	12	1.68	0.08	16.67
Annual Growth	(6.2%)	—	—	3.4%	49.5%	5.1%

RECKSON OPERATING PARTNERSHIP, L.P.

EXECUTIVES

Pres-Ceo, Marc Holliday
Cfo-Cao-Treas, Matthew J Diliberto
Gen Ptnr, Wyoming Acquisition GP LLC

LOCATIONS

HQ: RECKSON OPERATING PARTNERSHIP, L.P.
420 LEXINGTON AVE, NEW YORK, NY 101700002
Phone: 212 594-2700
Web: WWW.SLGREEN.COM

HISTORICAL FINANCIALS

Company Type: Private

Income Statement   FYE: December 31

	ASSETS ($ mil.)	NET INCOME ($ mil.)	INCOME AS % OF ASSETS	EMPLOYEES
12/18	7,009	199	2.8%	279
12/17	8,541	198	2.3%	—
12/16	8,754	313	3.6%	—
12/15	8,858	362	4.1%	—
Annual Growth	(7.5%)	(18.1%)	—	—

REDWOOD CREDIT UNION

EXECUTIVES

Pres-Ceo, Brett Martinez
Loan Officer, Carrie Bruce
Assistant Manager, Earl Chavez
Branch Manager, Stephen Hazard
Information Specialist, Jonathan Busch
Assistant Manager, Amy Murphy
Accountant, Catharine Lyne
Branch Manager, Robin Ashford
Accountant I, Raul Yanez
Electronic Manager, Skye Woodward
Programmer I, Todd Cook
Auditors: CLIFTONLARSONALLEN LLP PHOENI

LOCATIONS

HQ: REDWOOD CREDIT UNION
3033 CLEVELAND AVE # 100, SANTA ROSA, CA 954032126
Phone: 707 545-4000
Web: WWW.REDWOODCU.ORG

HISTORICAL FINANCIALS

Company Type: Private

Income Statement   FYE: December 31

	ASSETS ($ mil.)	NET INCOME ($ mil.)	INCOME AS % OF ASSETS	EMPLOYEES
12/17	4,046	67	1.7%	390
12/16	3,287	57	1.7%	—
12/14	2,468	47	1.9%	—
12/13	2,271	48	2.1%	—
Annual Growth	15.5%	8.6%	—	—

Redwood Trust Inc

Redwood Trust is cultivating a forest of real estate mortgage assets. The real estate investment trust (REIT) finances manages and invests in residential real estate mortgages and securities backed by such loans. It also invests in commercial real estate loans and securities. Redwood acquires assets throughout the US but has a concentration of credit risk in California Texas New Jersey Florida Georgia and Arizona which hold some of the US' most active real estate markets. Redwood Trust slowed loan origination acquisition and securitization during the most recent recession but has picked up those activities as the economy has recovered.

Operations

Redwood Trust invests in real estate related assets that have the potential to provide attractive cash flows over a long time period and distribute attractive levels of dividends to stockholders. The mortgage-backed securities the company typically invests in include senior securities. Redwood Trust also invests in other assets securities and instruments that are related to residential and commercial real estate.

About 10% of Redwood's total revenue came from interest income on its real estate securities in 2019 while interest income on its residential loans and multifamily loans made up of about 40% and more than 15% of total revenue that year respectively. The rest of its revenue (more than 10%) came from its mortgage banking activities which involves buying and selling mortgage loans. The bank had a staff of more than 370 people at the end of 2019.

Geographic Reach

California-based Redwood primarily concentrates on supplying loans to the markets of California Texas New Jersey Georgia Florida and Arizona — which held about 50% of its credit held for sale and about 50% of its credit held-for-investment in 2019. The REIT has offices in California Colorado and New York.

Financial Performance

The company's revenue in 2019 was $308.3 million higher than $219.7 million in the prior year. The increase was primarily due to higher interest income and investment fair value changes.

Net income increased by $45.9 million to $176.6 million in 2019 compared from $130.7 million in the prior year.

Cash held by the company at the end of 2019 increased by $85.8 million to $290.8 million compared from the prior year with $205.1 million. Cash used for operations was $1.2 billion while cash provided by investing and financing activities were $1.0 billion and $225.5 million respectively.

Strategy

During 2019 the company completed the acquisitions of two business-purpose real estate loan origination platforms 5 Arches and CoreVest through which the company now originates business-purpose loans. Prior to the completion of these two acquisitions Redwood had not previously acquired an operating company and it had not been engaged in directly originating mortgage loans since 2016 when the company ceased its commercial origination and mortgage banking activities.

During 2019 the company made significant progress on its strategic priorities. Enabled in part by two acquisitions it was a historic year for Redwood' business that set a new foundation for its participation in several distinct areas of housing credit and allowed its consolidated portfolio of investments to evolve to incorporate a diverse mix of residential business purpose and multi-family investments. The company now operates out of four principal geographic locations across the United States and its earnings power is supported by organically created investments and the associated platforms that produce them.

Mergers and Acquisitions

In 2019 Redwood announced it has entered into a definitive agreement to acquire CoreVest American Finance Lender LLC a leading nationwide originator and portfolio manager of business-purpose residential loans (BPLs) and several of its affiliates ("CoreVest") from certain affiliates of Fortress Investment Group's credit funds business ("Fortress Sellers") and CoreVest Management Partners LLC ("Management Seller" and together with the Fortress Sellers "Sellers").

Under the terms of the agreement Redwood will acquire CoreVest's operating platform and assets ? including its business-purpose loan portfolio and subordinate bonds from CoreVest-sponsored securitizations ? from the Sellers. Consideration for the acquisition is approximately $490 million net of in-place financing on the financial assets. Redwood plans to fund this transaction with a mix of cash on hand and shares of Redwood stock.

EXECUTIVES

Ceo, Martin S. (Marty) Hughes, age 62, $750,000 total compensation
President, Christopher J. Abate, age 40, $425,000 total compensation
Evp General Counsel And Secretary, Andrew P. Stone, age 49, $375,000 total compensation
Cfo, Collin Cochrane, age 44
Evp Commercial Investments And Finance, Fred J. Matera, age 56, $500,000 total compensation
Evp, Dashiell Robinson
Vice President Treasury, Vada Battaglia
Vice President, Fred Ty
Associate Vice President, Jennifer Wolff
Vice President Infrastructure, Jason Newman
Vice Chairman, Douglas B. Hansen, age 62
Chairman, Richard D. Baum, age 73
Auditors: Grant Thornton LLP

LOCATIONS

HQ: Redwood Trust Inc
One Belvedere Place, Suite 300, Mill Valley, CA 94941
Phone: 415 389-7373
Web: www.redwoodtrust.com

PRODUCTS/OPERATIONS

2014 Sales

	$ mil.	% of total
Interest income		
Real estate securities	125	43
Residential loans	68	24
Commercial loans	47	16
Others	0	.
Non-interest income		
Mortgage banking activities	34	12
Realized Gains	15	5
Adjustments	(14.4)	.
Total	**278**	**100**

COMPETITORS

Annaly Capital Management	MFA Financial
Bank of America	Main Street Capital
	NewStar Financial

Capstead Mortgage	Starwood Property
Duff & Phelps	Triangle Capital
Dynex Capital	iStar Financial Inc
Hercules Technology	

HISTORICAL FINANCIALS

Company Type: Public

Income Statement   FYE: December 31

	ASSETS ($ mil.)	NET INCOME ($ mil.)	INCOME AS % OF ASSETS	EMPLOYEES
12/19	17,995	169	0.9%	372
12/18	11,937	119	1.0%	149
12/17	7,039	140	2.0%	120
12/16	5,483	131	2.4%	125
12/15	6,231	102	1.6%	211
Annual Growth	30.4%	13.5%	—	15.2%

2019 Year-End Financials

Debt ratio: 16.41%
Return on equity: 10.65%
Cash ($ mil.): 196
Current ratio: —
Long-term debt ($ mil.): —
No. of shares (mil.): 114
Dividends
  Yield: 7.2%
  Payout: 105.2%
Market value ($ mil.): 1,891

	STOCK PRICE ($) FY Close	P/E High/Low		PER SHARE ($) Earnings	Dividends	Book Value
12/19	16.54	11	9	1.46	1.20	15.98
12/18	15.07	12	10	1.34	1.18	15.89
12/17	14.82	10	8	1.60	1.12	15.83
12/16	15.21	10	6	1.54	1.12	14.96
12/15	13.20	17	10	1.18	1.12	14.67
Annual Growth	5.8%	—	—	5.5%	1.7%	2.2%

Regeneron Pharmaceuticals, Inc.

Regeneron is fighting some serious enemies. Regeneron Pharmaceuticals develops protein-based drugs used to battle a variety of diseases and conditions including cancer high cholesterol inflammatory ailments cardiovascular and metabolic diseases infectious disease rare diseases and eye diseases. The biotechnology company has a handful of products on the market including macular degeneration treatment EYLEA (aflibercept) cholesterol-lowering drug Praluent rare inflammatory disease treatment ARCALYST rheumatoid arthritis drug Kevzara and cancer treatment ZALTRAP. Research-focused Regeneron has more than 20 candidates in clinical development. The US accounts for about 60% of Regeneron's sales.

Operations

Regeneron operates in one business segment which includes all activities from discovery and development through commercialization of its pharmaceutical products. Most of the segment's revenue comes from EYLEA sales followed by Libtayo and ARCALYST. The company also has development candidates in areas including hypercholesterolemia oncology rheumatoid arthritis asthma and atopic dermatitis. The segment brings in more than 60% of the company's revenue.

The rest of the company's revenue comes from development collaborations. Regeneron has collaborations with Sanofi and Bayer HealthCare to develop aflibercept for additional indications including cancerous tumors as well as obtain approvals outside of the US. The Sanofi accounts for nearly 20% of revenue and Bayer collaborations account for about 15% of revenue and others account for about 5% of revenue.

Geographic Reach

Regeneron has its corporate and R&D headquarters in Tarrytown New York and a clinical and biostats office in Basking Ridge New Jersey. It manufactures bulk drug materials in Renssalaer New York.

Internationally Regeneron is headquartered in Dublin Ireland and has a manufacturing facility in Limerick Ireland as well as an office in London.

Nearly 60% of Regeneron's sales are in the US. Sales outside the US account for about 20% as do sales from the Sanofi collaboration and the remaining sales from Bayer and other accounts (which Regeneron counts as international revenue).

Sales and Marketing

Regeneron uses distributors and specialty pharmacies to sell its products directly to health care providers. ARCALYST is sold directly to patients through the specialty pharmacies.

The company's largest customers are AmerisourceBergen subsidiary Besse Medical and McKesson which each account for more than 10% of sales. Regeneron also collaborates with Bayer and Sanofi for global sales of EYLEA Dupixent Praluent and Keyzara.

Financial Performance

In 2019 the company's revenue increased by about $1.2 billion to $7.9 billion compared to $6.7 billion in the prior year. Net product sales of EYLEA in the United States increased in 2019 compared to 2018 due to higher sales volume partly offset by an increase in sales-related deductions primarily due to higher rebates and discounts.

Regeneron's net income decreased by $328.6 million to $2.1 billion compared to $2.4 billion in the prior year. The decrease was due to the increase on their operating expenses and income tax expenses by $1.5 billion and $204.2 million offsetting the $1.2 billion increase on their revenue.

The cash held by the company at the end of 2019 increased by $150 million to $1.6 billion compared to the prior year with cash held of about $1.5 billion. The cash provided by operations was $2.4 billion while cash used by investing and financing activities were $2.0 billion and $252.1 million respectively.

Strategy

Regeneron's core business strategy is to maintain a strong foundation in basic scientific research and discovery-enabling technologies and to build on that foundation with our clinical development manufacturing and commercial capabilities. The company's objective is to continue to be an integrated multi-product biotechnology company that provides patients and medical professionals with important options for preventing and treating human diseases.

In December 2019 the company and Sanofi announced their intent to restructure the antibody collaboration for Kevzara and Praluent; completion of the proposed arrangement is expected to be finalized in the first quarter of 2020. Under their collaboration agreement Sanofi records product sales for commercialized products and Regeneron has the right to co-commercialize such products on a country-by-country basis.

Company Background

Regeneron was founded in New York City in 1988.

ARCALYST (rilonacept) was approved by the FDA in 2008 and subsequently became the company's first market-stage product.

EXECUTIVES

Evp Research And Development, Neil Stahl, age 63, $619,300 total compensation

Chief Scientific Officer; President Regeneron Laboratories, George D. Yancopoulos, age 60, $1,055,700 total compensation

President And Ceo, Leonard S. Schleifer, age 67, $1,242,000 total compensation

Evp Commercial, Robert J. Terifay, age 60, $550,700 total compensation

Svp Finance And Cfo, Robert E. Landry, $585,600 total compensation

Evp; General Manager Industrial Operations And Product Supply, Daniel P. Van Plew, age 47, $349,200 total compensation

Medical Director Medical Affairs, Andrew Korotzer

Medical Director, Gregory John

Medical Director, Mark Ballard

Vice President Strategic Program Direction Oncology, Robert Charnas

Medical Director, Brad Shumel

Svp And Head Of Commercial, Marion Mccourt

Vice President Early Clinical Development, Olivier Harari

Vice President Strategic Program Direction Cardiovasc, Andrew Rankin

Medical Director Oncology, Jigar Desai

Chairman, P. Roy Vagelos, age 90

Board Member, Bonnie Bassler

Board Member, Huda Zoghbi

Auditors: PricewaterhouseCoopers LLP

LOCATIONS

HQ: Regeneron Pharmaceuticals, Inc.
777 Old Saw Mill River Road, Tarrytown, NY 10591-6707
Phone: 914 847-7000
Web: www.regeneron.com

2018 Sales

	$ mil.	% of total
United States	4,106	61
Outside US	1,076	16
Sanofi collaboration	1,111	17
Other	416	6
Total	**6,710**	**100**

PRODUCTS/OPERATIONS

2018 Sales

	$ mil.	% of total
Net product sales		
EYLEA	4,076	61
Libtayo	14	-
ARCALYST	14	-
Bayer collaboration	1,111	17
Sanofi collaboration	416	16
Other	338	6
Total	**6,710**	**100**

COMPETITORS

Alimera	Novartis
Allergan Limited	Pfizer
AstraZeneca	REGENXBIO
Bristol-Myers Squibb	Roche Holding
Genentech	

HISTORICAL FINANCIALS

Company Type: Public

Income Statement   FYE: December 31

	REVENUE ($ mil.)	NET INCOME ($ mil.)	NET PROFIT MARGIN	EMPLOYEES
12/19	7,863	2,115	26.9%	8,100
12/18	6,710	2,444	36.4%	7,400
12/17	5,872	1,198	20.4%	6,200
12/16	4,860	895	18.4%	5,400
12/15	4,103	636	15.5%	4,300
Annual Growth	17.7%	35.1%	—	17.2%

2019 Year-End Financials

Debt ratio: 4.82%
Return on equity: 21.32%
Cash ($ mil.): 1,617
Current ratio: 3.67
Long-term debt ($ mil.): 713

No. of shares (mil.): 110
Dividends
Yield: —
Payout: —
Market value ($ mil.): 41,407

	STOCK PRICE ($) FY Close	P/E High/Low	Earnings	PER SHARE ($) Dividends	Book Value
12/19	375.48	23 14	18.46	0.00	100.56
12/18	373.50	18 13	21.29	0.00	80.34
12/17	375.96	47 30	10.34	0.00	57.09
12/16	367.09	63 39	7.70	0.00	41.97
12/15	542.87	96 64	5.52	0.00	34.92
Annual Growth	(8.8%)	— —	35.2%	—	30.3%

REGENTS OF THE UNIVERSITY OF MICHIGAN

Ranking among the top US public universities Regents of the University of Michigan (or simply University of Michigan) boasts more than 64580 students in southeast Michigan. Its three campuses in Ann Arbor Dearborn and Flint offer more than 275 undergraduate and graduate degree programs in fields including architecture education law medicine music and social work. The university has a student to faculty ratio of 15:1. The University of Michigan Health System includes three hospitals and more than 125 health clinics/centers. The university is supported by $12.5 billion endowment.

Operations

The university's about 15 undergraduate schools and colleges offer architecture & urban planning; art & design; business; dental hygiene; education; engineering; information; kinesiology; literature science and the arts (LSA); music theatre & dance; nursing; pharmacy; public health; and public policy. Its seven academic units accept first-year applications: LSA; engineering; architecture & urban planning; art & design; kinesiology; music theatre & dance; and nursing. Its graduate programs include certificate doctoral and master's in the areas of anthropology architecture biophysics business chemical biology and criminal study among others.

Geographic Reach

From its primary campuses in southeast Michigan the university attracts students from more than 80 Michigan counties nearly 50 states and about 140 countries.

Financial Performance

University of Michigan's revenue increased 7% to $8 billion in 2019 from $7.5 billion in 2018. Student tuition and fees sponsored programs patient care revenues and others increased that year.

Cash and cash equivalents at the end of the year were $397.3 million $263.9 million higher from the year prior. Operating activities used $317.9 million in 2019 while investing activities provided $411.3 million from sales and maturities of investments.

Strategy

The University of Michigan aims to serve the people of Michigan and the world through preeminence in creating communicating preserving and applying knowledge art and academic values and in developing leaders and citizens who will change the present and enrich the future.

In late 2020 UM launched a record 31 startups in the fiscal year 2020 a 40% increase during a period that included a pandemic and temporarily shuttered labs. U-M inventors went to market with a wide range of discoveries including those from a company using machine learning predictive modeling to help cities like Flint replace their lead-tainted water pipes to another that pivoted from prostate cancer screening to rapid COVID-19 testing during a global health crisis.

The University of Michigan School of Music Theatre & Dance and Grammy Award-winning baritone Thomas Hamson's Hampsong Foundation formed a new partnership to strengthen the work of both organizations in song research vocal performance and education at all levels. This new collaboration strengthened previous work allowing both organizations to amplify the preservation study and practice of song more broadly and in new contexts.

EXECUTIVES

Vp Government Relations, Cynthia H. Wilbanks

Vp Development, Jerry A. May

Chancellor University Of Michigan-dearborn, Daniel Little

Evp And Cfo, Kevin P. Hegarty, age 64

Chairman Victors For Michigan, Stephen M. Ross

President, Mark S. Schlissel

Dean School Of Public Health, Martin Philbert

Vp Information Technology And Cio, Kelli Trosvig

Dean Stamps School Of Art And Design, Gunalan Nadarajan

Dean School Of Dentistry, Laurie McCauley

Dean Law School, Mark D. West

Chancellor University Of Michigan-flint, Susan E. Borrego

Interim Provost And Evp Academic Affairs, Paul N. Courant

Evp Medical Affairs; Dean Medical School; Ceo Michigan Medicine, Marschall S. Runge

Vp And General Counsel, Timothy G. Lynch

Vp Research, S. Jack Hu

Interim Dean Taubman College Of Architecture And Urban Planning, Robert Fishman

Edward J. Frey Dean Ross School Of Business, Scott DeRue

Dean School Of Education, Elizabeth Birr Moje

Dean School Of Engineering, Alec D. Gallimore

Dean School Of Information, Thomas A. Finholt

Dean School Of Kinesiology, Lori Ploutz-Snyder

Dean College Of Literature Science And The Arts, Andrew D. Martin

Dean College Of Music Theatre And Dance, Aaron Dworkin

Interim Dean School Of Natural Resources And Environment, Dan Brown

Dean School Of Nursing, Patricia D. Hurn

Dean College Of Pharmacy, James T. Dalton

Dean School Of Social Work, Lynn Videka

Dean Rackham Graduate School; Vice Provost Academic Affairs Graduate Studies, Carol A. Fierke

Vice President Research, Stephen Forrest

Associate Vice President And Executive Director For Research Administration, Marvin Parnes

Associate Vice President Development, Julie Sparkman

Vice President Marketing, Rachelle Caoagas

Assistant Vice President Estate, Diane Tracy

Associate Vice President Facilities And Operations, Henry D Baier

Vice President Marketing, Fred Howard

Vice President Client Team Leader, Andrew Crawford

Associate Vice President For Research Douvan Collegiate Professor Of Psychology Research Professor, Toni Antonucci

Vice President Of Technology, Trung Nguyen

Vice President Technology, Jamila Power

Vice President Technology, Mehra Rohit

Clinical Director, Donn Hilker

First Vice President, Rob Geer

Vice President Of Administration, Andy White

Vice President For Finance, Kelli Pape

Vice President Student Government Budget Allocations Committee, Mackenzie Swart

Director Of Admissions And Orientation, Deb Peffer

Vice President Of Sales, Bill Bobrowsky

Vice President Finance Technology, William Hausman

Vice President For Research University Administration, Linda Wilson

Associate Vice President And Deputy General Counsel, Kara Morgenstern

Int Assistant Vice President Academic Human Resources, Donna Lartigue

Vice President, Erik J Rebbe

Vice President In Operations, William Chan

Vice President Finance, Kevin Kuo

Interim Vp Information Technology And Cio, Andrew Rosenberg

Director Of Clinical Services And Research; Assistant Professor Of Psychiatry, Renee Hoste

Vice President Program Delivery, Dave Schueler

Interim Vice President For Communications, Kate Michael

Vice President Of Finance, Morgan Slaff

Uofm Emba Vice President, Eric James Forster

Vice President, Mohammed Islam

Vice President Finance, Dennis Diebolt

Dsp Xi Vice President Of Alumni Relations, Moynawk Gangopadhyay

Vice President, Amani Echols

Vice President Beta Alpha Psi, Emily Wolney

Vice President Of Projects Net Impact Advanced Fellow, Charlene Franke

Medical Director, Darrell Campbell

Vice President, Olivia Herron

Vice President And Corporate Counsel, Gael Tisack

Vice President, Shiuh Lee

Vice President, Beatrice Thaman

Vp Of Women In Mathematics, Vijita Kamath

Vice President, Margaret Perrett

Vice President, Robert Carter

External Vice President, Erika Chow

Investment Banking Vice President, Vikram Chandrasekaran

Vice President, Seth Kaufman

Vice President, Andrew Odesky

Vice President, Faye Racovitis

Vice President, Yervant Demirjian

Medical Director, William Kennedy

Vice President, Debra Thomas-darke

Vice President: Finance, Caroline Kelly

Vice President, Adam Oakley

Vice President Of Communications, Ally Reis

Vice President Of Social Responsibility, Alexander Krupiak

Vice President For Global Communications And Strategic Initiatives, Debbie Serwach

Vice President Of Finance, Nizamuddin Alavi

Vice President, Martha McKinnon

Vice President, Georga Armstrong

Vice President Sales, Chris Wallbank

Director Of Pharmacy, Mike Dabaja

Vice President, Colleen Crouch

Vice President Finance, Chris Winkelmann

Vice President Internal Operations, Ethan Tubbs

Vice President Public Relations, Ashton Russo

Vice President Of Membership, Stav Nachum

Vice President, Adam Greer

Vice President, Kyra Fleming

Vice President Strategy, Elif Sagsen-ercel

Vice Chairman, Michael J. Behm

Chairman, Mark J. Bernstein

Program Secretary, Frances Liao

Senior Business Analyst Treasurers Office Department, Kristopher Covietz

Secretary, Jeff Evans

Secretary Iv Law School Department, LauraA Shiltz

Secretary Iii Department Of Family Medicine Department, SophiaS Scoma

Board Member, Shary Balius

Board Member, Neil Elkin

Secretary Office Of Early Childhood Education And Family Services, Martin Stroud

Secretary, Mary Burton

Secretary Iii, Qiana London

Treasurer, Eleonore Edgell

Senior Secretary, Andrew Mcintyre

Secretary Iv, Allisssa Ebenhoeh

Secretary B Temp Flint Ecdc, Kristina Russo

Secretary Of The University Office Of, Roberta Ruth Palmer

Secretary Senior, Debra Most

Lead Secretary, Amber French

Board Member, Ellen Toronto

Assistant Secretary Of The University, Erin Katz

Secretary Office Of The Vice President For Government Relations, Jill Crane

Board Member, John White

Secretary, Sara VanLooy

Treasurer, Kathleen Ropella

Theta Delta Chi Treasurer And Executive Board, Brandon Goethals

Treasurer, Theodore Zimbo

Treasurer, Chris Attar

Treasurer, Gabrielle Zimbler

Secretary, Jill Katic

Secretary, Alison Bradley

Board Member, Andrew Noh

Auditors: PRICEWATERHOUSECOOPERS LLP DE

LOCATIONS

HQ: REGENTS OF THE UNIVERSITY OF MICHIGAN
503 THOMPSON ST, ANN ARBOR, MI 481091340
Phone: 734 764-1817
Web: WWW.UMICH.EDU

PRODUCTS/OPERATIONS

Selected Academic Units
Architecture and urban planning
Art and design
Business administration
Dentistry
Education
Engineering
Kinesiology
Law
Literature science and the arts
Medicine
Music
Natural resources and environment
Nursing
Pharmacy
Public health
Public policy
Social work

HISTORICAL FINANCIALS

Company Type: Private

Income Statement | | | | FYE: June 30

	REVENUE ($ mil.)	NET INCOME ($ mil.)	NET PROFIT MARGIN	EMPLOYEES
06/20	7,955	(276)	—	34,624
06/19	7,989	522	6.5%	—
06/18	7,466	920	12.3%	—
06/17	7,079	1,275	18.0%	—
Annual Growth	4.0%	—	—	—

Regions Financial Corp (New)

The holding company for Alabama-chartered Regions Bank Regions Financial boasts around $144 billion in total assets. With more than 1400 branches and more than 2000 ATMs across the South Midwest and Texas Regions offers banking services for large corporations middle market companies and commercial real estate developers and investors on top of its main business of standard banking products for retail customers and small businesses. The company's smaller wealth and asset management operations target affluent private individuals businesses governmental institutions and non-profit entities. Formed in 1971 as First Alabama Bancshares Regions was Alabama's first multibank holding company.

HISTORY

Regions Financial was created out of three venerable Alabama banks. The oldest First National Bank of Huntsville was founded in 1855. When 10 years later the bank was besieged by Union troops a loyal cashier hid securities in the chimney and refused to tell the soldiers where they were. A few years later it was robbed by Jesse James (for years the bank kept in its vaults a gun purported to belong to a James gang member). First National Bank of Montgomery was founded in 1871 and Exchange Security Bank in 1928.

Banking veteran Frank Plummer consolidated the three banks to form Alabama's first multibank holding company First Alabama Bancshares in 1971. The combined firm then became the bank that ate Alabama. But even as it gobbled up other banks its diet remained bland: Its lending programs were modest and focused on a narrow range of business.

The bank's growth in the 1980s was solid if unexciting as it picked up community banks in Alabama (Anniston National Bank and South Baldwin Bank among others) and Georgia (Georgia Co. a mortgage subsidiary of Columbus Bank and Trust). Before he died in 1987 Plummer brought in Willard Hurley as chairman. Hurley put the brakes on acquisitions when they overloaded the bank's data-processing systems. He also put the company up for sale igniting its stock price for a while but there were no serious suitors.

When Hurley passed the baton to Stanley Mackin in 1990 the bank was still rumored to be for sale. But Mackin had other ideas. He put the bank back on its acquisition track and raised the bar on profitability expectations for each department. In 1993 Mackin orchestrated First Alabama's purchase of Secor a failed New Orleans thrift outbidding rival AmSouth Bancorporation. The Secor purchase raised eyebrows but First Alabama sold some branches and folded other operations into its organization.

In 1994 First Alabama changed its name to Regions Financial in order to reflect its out-of-state operations. The next year Regions rolled into Georgia in a big way leaping from a few banks to holdings with approximately $4 billion in assets. Rumors of a merger with either Wachovia or SunTrust Banks popped up in 1996 but the bank continued on its independent course. The next year the company's tank-like progress was halted when it was outbid for Mississippi's Deposit Guaranty Corp. by First American.

By way of consolation Regions in 1998 bought First Commercial Corp. of Little Rock paying a premium price for its 26 banks mortgage company and investment company. Regions also acquired 13 other companies that year and began a major overhaul of its systems concurrently with the assimilation of these operations. This effort included the consolidation of the back-office aspects of its retail and indirect lending operations.

Mackin retired in 1998 and banking veteran Carl Jones Jr. became CEO. Under his direction the bank continued its geographic infill strategy with acquisitions of banks and branches in Arkansas Florida Louisiana Tennessee and Texas in 1999 and 2000. The company also sold its credit card portfolio to MBNA (since acquired by Bank of America) and in 2001 acquired Memphis-based investment bank Morgan Keegan.

Regions Financial has looked for acquisitions in order to grow geographically and diversify its product and services mix. It fortified its foothold in the South and expanded into the Midwest with its blockbuster merger with Union Planters in 2004. Roughly two years later the company acquired fellow Birmingham-based bank AmSouth for nearly $10 billion in stock. The latter deal created one of the 10 largest banks in the US and helped Regions Financial keep pace with other megabanks in its markets such as Bank of America and SunTrust. The deals also helped entrench the company in states such as Alabama Arkansas Mississippi and Tennessee where it is a market leader.

EXECUTIVES

President Chief Executive Officer Regions Bank And Regions Financial Corporation Director, John M. Turner, age 60

Sevp Coo, John B. Owen, $659,816 total compensation

Sevp General Counsel And Corporate Secretary, Fournier J. (Boots) Gale, $570,554 total compensation

Sevp Head Of Corporate Banking Group, Ronald G. (Ronnie) Smith

Sevp Head Of Commercial Banking, William E. (Bill) Horton

Sevp Head Of Corporate Responsibility And Community Engagement, C. Keith Herron

Sevp Head Of Corporate Real Estate And Procurement, Brett D. Couch

Sevp And Head Of Consumer Banking Group, Scott M. Peters

Sevp And Head Of Wealth Management, William D. (Bill) Ritter

Sevp And Cfo Regions Bank And Regions Financial Corporation, David J. Turner, $644,062 total compensation

Sevp Chro, David R. (Dave) Keenan

Sevp And Chief Risk Officer, C. Matthew Lusco, $566,308 total compensation

Sevp Head Of Strategic Performance And Alignment, Ellen S. Jones

Senior Vice President Senior Credit Officer Commercial Real Estate, Aubrey Martin

Vice President Information Technology Manager, Kristopher Bridges

Senior Vice President Direct Marketing Manager, Jim Screws

Vp Firewall, Jeff Green

Senior Vice President And Head Consumer Collections And Asset Recovery, Brent Pyatt

Evp Stategic And Corporate Planning, Houston Cook

Vice President, Mark Senter

Vice President And Technology Contract Manager, Mike Ritchie

Vice President, Stephanie Slade

Senior Vice President, Keith Pressley

Vice President Commercial Real Estate, Todd Harris

Senior Vice President Consumer Sales Manager, Ken Knapp Ken Knapp

Vice President, Brandon Pettagrue

Senior Vice President, Donald Sinclair

Vice President Information Technology Risk Manager, Rusk Feltman

Assistant Vice President, Laura Durbin

Senior Vice President Of Mortg, Ginger Ricchetti

Assistant Vice President Business Systems Analyst, Tim Boles

Vice President Secondary Marketing, Jonathan Loukotka

Vice President Branch Sales Manager, Cathy Cosey

Senior Vice President Mortgage Division Controller, Rita Young

Senior Vice President Consumer Sales Manager Regions Bank, Cedric Oliver

Vice President, Robert Shaw

Vice President, William Laenger

Vice President Business Banking, Keith Boling

Vice President, Kenneth Bizzard

Vice President Relationship Manager, Cory Guillory

Executive Vice President Of Commercial Banking, Tammi Sanchez

Vice President, Kathy Patterson

Assistant Vice President And Branch Manager And Small Business Lender, Bryan Furlong

Vice President North Central Alabama Marketing And Event, Joy Parker

Assistant Vice President Branch Manager, Linda Barton

Vice President Global Trade Finance, Chuck Youngerman

Vice President Florida Market, Lisa Fulghum

Regulatory Operations Vp, Rodney Ford

Svp Business Risk Management, Florence Morris

Senior Vice President Corporate Financial Planning And Analysis, Becky Crain

Senior Vice President And Texas Market Manager, Wendel Pardue

Senior Vice President, Tom Bohrer

Vice President, Tina Wiggins

Senior Vice President Texas Area Wealth Executive, Craig Kennington

Senior Vice President Program Development Manager, David Fron

Senior Vice President Information Security, John Ballew

Vice President Of Information Technology, Adrian Castanon

Senior Vice President Private Wealth Executive Middle Tn, Lee Blank

Vice President Relationship Manager, Franklin Reyes

Vice President Mortgage Loan Officer, Mary Ethridge

Vice President, John Fuller

Vice President Manager Of Special Projects And Incentive Compensation Modeling, Matthew Bledsoe

Assistant Vice President Of In, Don Turrentine

Vice President Mortgage Production Manager, Alan Noe

Vice President Escrow Manager, Kathy Schwartz

Evp Corporate Security, William Burch

Evp Of Delivery, Denise Canfield

Executive Assistant To Bill Askew Senior Executive Vice President And Chris Ewing Executive Vice President, Pamela Ashley

Vice President Business Banking, Brian Brooks

Vice President, Barrett Vawter

Vice President, Tanya Noletto

Senior Vice President Treasury Management, Sean Payne

Vice President, Stan Gist

Evp Corporate Hr, Janet Parker

Senior Vice President, Jorge Goris

Senior Executive Vice President And Chief Credit Officer, Barb Godin

Assistant Vice President Branch Manager, Patrick Cayson

Vice President Information Technology Manager, Kris Bridges

Senior Vice President Corporate Banking Regions Bank, JP Hickey

Vice President Wealth Management, Leslie G Stricklin

Senior Vice President, Jeff Taylor

Vice President And Trust Advisor, Conor Duggan

Vice President Human Resources, Ellie Long

Vice President Private Wealth Management, Patty Franco

Vice President, Raghunandan Gorur

Svp And Assistant General Counsel, Bradley Blair

Senior Vice President, Jim Phillips

Senior Vice President, Matt Morrow

Assistant Vice President Sba Underwriter, Erica Bivins

Senior Vice President Wealth Management Compliance, Aneidre Amerson-Allman

Vice President, Jennifer Jackson

Senior Vice President Regional Manager, Jeff Bradley

Senior Vice President Wealth Management, Lisa Harless

Executive Vice President Human Resources Regions Bank, Anthony Hernandez

Executive Vice President Human Resources Operations Regions Bank, Todd Godwin

Executive Vice President And Chief Audit Executive, Michael Balbirnie

Senior Vice President, James Watkins

Vice President And Mortgage Operations Manager Regions Bank, Matthew Knueven
Vice President, Michael Harrington
Vice President Enterprise Risk Management, James Madden
Vice President Credit Portfolio Manager Regions Bank, Suresh Nair
Vice President Of Business Banking, Gene Columbus
Senior Vice President, Wade Parker
Executive Vice President, Pam Davis
Senior Vice President, Bill Robertson
Vice President, Mauricio Cardenas
Senior Vice President, Angie Llaca
Vice President And Commercial Relationship Manager, Pat Brandenburg
Vice President Estate Administration, Judi Wurm
Vice President Trust Advisor, Andrew Colgan
Vice President Trust Advisor, Natalie Mann
Senior Vice President, Barry Musselman
Senior Vice President, Edward Ryrie
Vice President, Carl Taube
Vice President Commercial And Industrial, Philip Ugalde
Senior Vice President Mergers And Acquisitions, Marc Bromstad
Vice President Rewards And Loyalty Program Management, Bryan Shimko
Senior Vice President And Head Of Model Validation, Jacob Kosoff
Vice President Business Banking, Sandy Salyers
Senior Vice President, Redmond Taylor
Vice President, Mary Willis
Senior Vice President Special Assets Division Regions Bank, Gray Ives
Senior Vice President Commercial Banking, Alicia McCory
Vice President, Kristine Prall
Vice President Consumer Lending, Kandy Shirley
Senior Vice President Ebusiness, Joe Jordan
Assistant Vice President, Ella Shakeel
Senior Vice President, Philip Bittel
Assistant Vice President, Zachary Dark
Avp Manager Of Security Analytics And Orchestration, Sean Maher
Vice President Global Trade Finance, Al Li
Vice President Branch Manager, Cathy Haywood
Vice President, Adriana Martinez
Vice President Of Mortgage Lending, Javier Mozca
Senior Vice President, Dewitt King
Vp Branch Manager, Juanita Shope
Senior Vice President, Rob Stivers
Vice President Senior Commercial Portfolio Manager (restaurants), Kelly B Nyquist
Evp And Head Of Diversity And Inclusion Of Regions Bank, Clara Green
Vice President, Chris Fitz
Vice President, Brent Goers
Vice President Regional Portfolio Manager, Sue Schmidt
Senior Vice President, Shawn Coard
Senior Vice President, Fernanda Hailey
Vice President, Rick Saenz
Vp Branch Manager, Miles Victor
Executive Vice President And Treasurer, M Deron Smithy
Vice President Trust Advisor, Marlin Evans
Auditors: Ernst & Young LLP

LOCATIONS

HQ: Regions Financial Corp (New)
1900 Fifth Avenue North, Birmingham, AL 35203
Phone: 205 581-7890
Web: www.regions.com

2018 Branch Locations

	No.
Florida	307
Tennessee	220
Alabama	211
Mississippi	126
Georgia	116
Louisiana	99
Arkansas	82
Texas	80
Missouri	64
Indiana	52
Illinois	48
South Carolina	23
Kentucky	11
Iowa	8
North Carolina	7
Total	**1,454**

PRODUCTS/OPERATIONS

2018 Sales

	$ mil.	% of total
Interest income		
Loans including fees	3,613	56
Debt securities - taxable	625	10
Operating lease assets	70	1
Loans held for sale	15	-
Other earning assets	70	1
Interest Expense	(658.0)	-
Non-interest income		
Service charges on deposits	710	11
Card and ATM fees	438	7
Investment management and trust fee income	235	4
Capital markets income	202	3
Mortgage income	137	2
Securities gains (losses) net	1	-
Others	296	5
Total	**5,754**	**100**

2018 Sales

	$ mil.	% of total
Consumer Bank	3,405	58
Corporate Bank	1,931	33
Wealth Management	510	9
Other	(92.0)	-
Total		**100**

Selected Products

Banking
  Checking
  Money Market
  Savings
  CDs
  Regions Visa CheckCard
  Business Checking
  Business Savings
  Merchant Services
  Treasury Management
  Payroll
  Audit Confirmations
Commercial Banking
  Deposit Services
  Treasury Management
  Online Services
  Merchant Services
  Global Trade Finance
  Corporate Trust
Private Wealth Management
  Solutions for Individuals
  Credit and Risk Management
  Wealth Management
  Solutions for Professionals

COMPETITORS

Arvest Bank	First Horizon
BB&T	Investar
BBVA Compass Bancshares	JPMorgan Chase
Bank of America	SunTrust
Capital One	Synovus
Citigroup	Trustmark
First Citizens BancShares	Wells Fargo
	Woodforest Financial

HISTORICAL FINANCIALS

Company Type: Public

Income Statement

FYE: December 31

	ASSETS ($ mil.)	NET INCOME ($ mil.)	INCOME AS % OF ASSETS	EMPLOYEES
12/19	126,240	1,582	1.3%	19,564
12/18	125,688	1,759	1.4%	19,969
12/17	124,294	1,263	1.0%	21,714
12/16	125,968	1,163	0.9%	22,166
12/15	126,050	1,062	0.8%	23,916
Annual Growth	0.0%	10.5%	—	(4.9%)

2019 Year-End Financials

Debt ratio: 4.26%
Return on equity: 10.08%
Cash ($ mil.): 4,114
Current ratio: —
Long-term debt ($ mil.): —

No. of shares (mil.): 957
Dividends
  Yield: 3.4%
  Payout: 39.0%
Market value ($ mil.): 16,426

	STOCK PRICE ($) FY Close	P/E High/Low	Earnings	PER SHARE ($) Dividends	Book Value
12/19	17.16	12 9	1.50	0.59	17.02
12/18	13.38	13 8	1.54	0.46	14.72
12/17	17.28	17 13	1.00	0.32	14.28
12/16	14.36	17 8	0.87	0.26	13.72
12/15	9.60	14 12	0.75	0.23	12.98
Annual Growth	15.6%	— —	18.9%	26.6%	7.0%

Reinsurance Group of America, Inc.

Just what is reinsurance? Here hold this pile of insurance risk while we explain that holding company Reinsurance Group of America (RGA) is one of the largest life reinsurers in the US. RGA provides traditional life and health reinsurance and financial solutions. Traditional reinsurance includes individual and group life and health disability long-term care and critical illness coverage while Financial Solutions includes longevity capital solutions stable value and asset-intensive products. RGA operates in more than 25 countries in Canada Latin Americas Asia/Pacific region Europe Middle East and Africa. The US and Latin America account for some 55% of RGA's total sales.

Operations

RGA's operations are organized into two large groups: Traditional and Financial Solutions.

RGA's Traditional group which accounts for almost 85% of its total sales provides both traditional life reinsurance and reinsurance on investment assets such as annuities and corporate-owned life insurance policies. In addition to its traditional mortality-risk and asset reinsurance the group offers financial reinsurance to help its customers meet regulatory requirements.

The Financial Solutions unit (nearly 15% of total sales) consists of four businesses: asset-intensive reinsurance (full-risk coinsurance of annuities or reinsurance with a large investment component) financial reinsurance (involving ceding companies) stable value products (guaranteed investment contracts) and longevity reinsurance (employee retirement benefits).

RGA has life reinsurance in force valued at about $3.5 trillion and about $76.7 billion in consolidated assets. Its net premiums account for almost 80% of total revenue.

Geographic Reach

RGA organizes its operating segments by geographic region: US and Latin America; Asia/Pacific; Europe Middle East and Africa; and Canada. The US and Latin America segment accounts for almost55% of total sales.

The company has offices in Australia Barbados Bermuda Brazil Canada China France Germany Hong Kong India Ireland the US the UK and about 15 other countries.

Sales and Marketing

RGA primarily provides reinsurance to the largest insurance companies in the world. Its top five customers generate some $2.6 billion representing about 20% of its gross premiums. In addition 29 other clients each generated annual gross premiums and other revenues of $100 million or more and the aggregate gross premiums and other revenues from these clients represented approximately 45% of the company's gross premiums and other revenues.

Financial Performance

RGA's revenue has been trending upward over the past five years. Net income has also been rising although 2017 was an outlier year in which the company netted $1.8 billion — about triple what it typically nets.

In 2019 revenue increased 11% to $14.3 billion. Consolidated net premiums increased $753 million or 7% in 2019 primarily due to growth in life reinsurance in force.

In 2019 net income rose 22% to $870 million compared to the prior year.

The company ended 2019 with $1.4 billion in net cash about $441 million less than it had at the end of 2018. Operating activities provided $2.3 billion while investing activities used $2.6 billion and financing activities used $121 million.

Strategy

A significant portion of RGA's net premiums come from its operations outside of the US. One of its strategies is to grow these international operations.

As part of its efforts to diversify RGA has been seeking new longevity risk contracts. (Longevity risk refers to the risk of having to make payments to a retiree for a longer period than planned for if the person lives longer than expected.) For example in 2019 the company signed a deal with Manulife to reinsure longevity risk from an in-force block of Canadian annuities.

Company Background

General American Life Insurance launched a life reinsurance division in 1973. General American Re became a top 10 US reinsurer by the 1980s and it started doing business in Canada and Europe in 1989. It went public as Reinsurance Group of America in 1993.

EXECUTIVES

Evp General Counsel And Secretary, William L. Hutton

Sevp And Cfo, Todd C. Larson, age 57, $472,428 total compensation

Evp And Chief Of Staff, Robert M. Musen

Evp Global Financial Solutions; President Rga Financial Group, John P. Laughlin

Interim Ceo Rgax Americas And Chief Solutions Officer Rgax, Mark E. Showers

Evp And Chief Human Resources Officer, Gay Burns

President And Ceo, Anna Manning, $750,000 total compensation

Evp Global Acquisitions, Scott D. Cochran

Sevp And Coo, Alain P. Néemeh, $563,750 total compensation

Evp And Chief Investment Officer, Timothy (Tim) Matson

Evp And Cio, Suzy Scanlon

Evp And Global Chief Risk Officer, Jonathan Porter

Senior Vice President Long Term Care And U.s. Individual Health, Wayne Adams

Vice President Global Human Resources Business Partner, Marcia Bequette

Vice President Deputy Compliance Counsel, Robert Jett

Regional Vice President, Joseph Klimchak

Vice President Information Management And Analytics Services, Mike Foster

Vice President And Actuary Financial M, Christopher Clark

Senior Vice President Public Relations, Yuko Oshima

Vice President Actuary, Julie Decker

Senior Vice President, Brian Haynes

Vice President Finance, John Hayden

Senior Vice President Valuation And Financial Analysis, James Kellett

Evp International Business Development, Brendan Galligan

Senior Vice President Global Acquisitions, Richard Leblanc

Vice President Aura Client Services, Mike Casale

Vice President And Assistant General Counsel, Christopher Rickey

Vice President Life Product Services, David Burgoon

Sales Vice President U S Individual Health, Winona Berdine

Vice President Business Development, Quentin Marsh

Senior Vice President And Director Global Tax, Kent Zimmerman

Vice President Global Underwriting Quality And Risk Assurance, Stephanie Williams

Senior Vice President Of The Latin American Division, Jaime Correa

Vice President Underwriting, Kim Lancaster

Vice President Valuation And Financial Analysis, Chris Murphy

Vice President For Financial Markets, Mark M Hopfinger

Senior Vice President Heathcare, Steven Abood

Vice President And Director, Keiko Imuro

Senior Vice President Of Quota Share Healthcare Reinsurance, David Vnenchak

Vice President Information Technology Infrastructure, Ron Hollowell

Vice President Business Development, Lisa Renetzky

Vice President And Actuary, Dustin Hetzler

Vice President Of Operations, Anne Riley

Vice President Corporate Underwriting Auditor, Pat Bradley

Senior Vice President, Dave Fischer

Vice President Credit Research And Risk Management, Scott Stone

Senior Vice President And Associate Gc, Dana Wiele

Vice President, Doris Jackson

Vice President And Managing Actuary, Alden Skar

Vice President Global Compensation And Benefits, Ray Stengel

Svp And Chief Actuary U.s. Group Reinsurance, Dean Abbott

Vp Stable Value Marketing, Kara Marr

Vice President And Assistant General Counsel Corporate, Cliff Jenks

Vp And Sr. Actuary Rgax, Derek Kueker

Vice President Business Development, Mike Choate

Senior Vice President Global Acquisitions, Matthew Easley

Vice President Underwriting, Scott Grandmont

Vice President Risk Management, Sarah Maune

Vice President Director Of Investment Strategy And Research, Amy Gibson

Vice President Data Strategy Global Research And Development, Brad Lipic

Vice President Global Marketing, Sue Carrillo

Vice President And Actuary Head Of Global Experience Analytics, Michael Lane

Senior Vice President Business Operations Program Lead Tom Program, Jeff Birkholz

Vice President And Medical Director, Valerie Kaufman

Vice President Corporate Communications, Lynn Phillips

Vice President Business Initiatives, Peter Schindler

Svp Group Life Accident And Disability Reinsurance U.s. Group Reinsurance, Jim Rathbum

Vice Pr, Alka Gautam

Svp Investor Relations, Jeffrey Hopson

Vice President Global Tax, Bridget Linde

Vice President Aura Product Management, Brad Butler

Vice President, Joe Korosec

Svp And Chief Risk Officer Global Financial Solutions, Jeff Nordstrom

Svp And Chief Medical Director Of U.s. Mortality Markets, Holowaty Carl

Senior Vice President Head Of Asset Liability Management, Brad Barks

Vice President Ehr Initiatives, Susan Wehrman

Regional Vice President And Underwriting Manager, Brent Hoehne

Vice President Regional Manager, Rance Nakama

Vp Valuation And Financial Analysis, Eric Walta

Vice President Business Initiatives, Daniel Lyons

Assistant Vice President International Treaties, Diane Hare

Vice President Derivatives Manager, Mark Tabor

Vice President Corporate Modeling, Steve Pummer

Vice President Investments Planning And Operations, David Clayton

Vice President, Paul Thakadiyil

Vp Head Of U.s. Portfolio Management, Christopher Quallen

Senior Vice President Erm, Robert Lamarche

Vice President And Senior Actuary Business Initiatives, Stephanie Grass

Global Business Initiatives Lead Data Solution Vice President, Carolyn Balfany

Chairman, J. Cliff Eason

Board Member, Stanley Tulin

Assistant Treasurer, Jeffrey Boyer

Board Member, Tricia Guinn

Auditors: DELOITTE & TOUCHE LLP

LOCATIONS

HQ: Reinsurance Group of America, Inc.
16600 Swingley Ridge Road, Chesterfield, MO 63017
Phone: 636 736-7000
Web: www.rgare.com

2018 Sales

	$ mil.	% of total
US & Latin America	7,203	56
Asia/Pacific	2,471	19
Europe Middle East and Africa	1,844	14
Canada	273	10
Corporate & other	83	1
Total	**12,875**	**100**

Selected Countries of Operation

Australia
Barbados
Bermuda
Canada
China
France
Germany
Hong Kong
India
Ireland
Italy
Japan
Malaysia
Mexico
Netherlands
New Zealand
Poland
Singapore
South Africa
South Korea
Spain
Taiwan
Turkey
United Arab Emirates
UK
US

PRODUCTS/OPERATIONS

2018 Sales by Segment

	$ mil.	% of total
Traditional	11,431	89
Financial Solutions	1,360	10
Corporate & other	83	1
Total	**12,875**	**100**

2018 Sales

	$ mil.	% of total
Net premiums	10,543	81
Investment income	2,138	16
Other	363	3
Adjustments	(505.1)	-
Total	**12,875**	**100**

Selected Products and Services

e-Underwriting solutions
Facultative and underwriting expertise
Financial solutions
Group reinsurance
Individual life reinsurance
Individual living benefits reinsurance
Product development

Selected Subsidiaries

Reinsurance Company of Missouri Incorporated (RCM)
RGA Americas Reinsurance Company Ltd. (RGA Americas)
RGA Atlantic Reinsurance Company Ltd. (RGA Atlantic)
RGA International Reinsurance Company (RGA International)
RGA Life Reinsurance Company of Canada (RGA Canada)
RGA Reinsurance Company (Barbados) Ltd. (RGA Barbados)
RGA Reinsurance Company (RGA Reinsurance)
RGA Reinsurance Company of Australia Limited (RGA Australia)

COMPETITORS

General Re	Prudential
Hannover Re	SCOR Reinsurance
Munich Re Group	Swiss Re
Pacific Life	XL Group plc

HISTORICAL FINANCIALS

Company Type: Public

Income Statement

FYE: December 31

	ASSETS ($ mil.)	NET INCOME ($ mil.)	INCOME AS % OF ASSETS	EMPLOYEES
12/19	76,731	870	1.1%	3,188
12/18	64,535	715	1.1%	2,767
12/17	60,514	1,822	3.0%	2,640
12/16	53,097	701	1.3%	2,482
12/15	50,383	502	1.0%	2,201
Annual Growth	**11.1%**	**14.7%**	—	**9.7%**

2019 Year-End Financials

Debt ratio: 4.66%
Return on equity: 8.68%
Cash ($ mil.): 1,449
Current ratio: —
Long-term debt ($ mil.): —

No. of shares (mil.): 62
Dividends
  Yield: 1.5%
  Payout: 19.0%
Market value ($ mil.): 10,217

	STOCK PRICE ($) FY Close	P/E High/Low	PER SHARE ($) Earnings	Dividends	Book Value
12/19	163.06	12 10	13.62	2.60	185.15
12/18	140.23	15 11	11.00	2.20	134.53
12/17	155.93	6 4	27.71	1.82	148.48
12/16	125.83	12 7	10.79	1.56	110.31
12/15	85.55	13 11	7.46	1.40	94.09
Annual Growth	**17.5%**	— —	**16.2%**	**16.7%**	**18.4%**

Reliance Steel & Aluminum Co.

Reliance Steel & Aluminum shows its mettle as North America's largest metals service center company. Operating in the US (about 300 service centers in 40 states) and a dozen other countries it processes and distributes more than 100000 metal products (bars beams pipes tubes plates coils etc.) to 125000-plus customers in industries like aerospace energy construction manufacturing semiconductor and electronics and transportation. Carbon steel is its top product; Reliance also markets alloy stainless and specialty steel as well as aluminum brass copper and titanium products. The company's trade names include Earle M. Jorgensen Metals USA and Precision Strip.

Operations

Reliance operates under several brand names including Earle M. Jorgensen Metals USA Precision Strip Phoenix Metals Reliance Metalcenter and Yarde Metals.

Although Reliance has only one reportable operating segment Metal Service Centers it earns revenue through six products and services. Carbon steel is its highest revenue earner accounting for more than 50% of total sales followed by Aluminum at 20% and Stainless Steel with about 15% of revenue. The rest (Alloy Toll processing and Logistics and Other) make up just some 15% of company revenues.

Geographic Reach

Based in Los Angeles California Reliance operates in about 40 US states and Australia Belgium Canada China France India Malaysia Mex-

ico Singapore South Korea Turkey the UAE and the UK.

The company purchases inventory from US metals producer and some international suppliers.

The US is by far Reliance's largest market accounting for more than 90% of revenue. Sales mostly arise from the Midwest (more than 30%) and Southeast.

Sales and Marketing

Reliance has some 125000 customers active in a wide range of industries including general manufacturing non-residential construction (including infrastructure) transportation (rail truck trailer and shipbuilding) aerospace and defense energy (oil and natural gas) electronics and semiconductor fabrication and heavy industry (agricultural construction and mining equipment). The company also service the auto industry primarily through its toll processing operations where it process the metal for a fee without taking ownership of the metal.

Reliance focuses on smaller customers and order sizes with quick turnarounds although it serves large original equipment manufacturers as well. About 95% are repeat customers. Products are delivered via a fleet of approximately 1750 trucks. The company has around 2100 sales personnel in about 40 states and a dozen other countries.

Financial Performance

Reliance Steel's sales and general health fluctuate with steel prices. Its recent history has been characterized by declining sales for several years up to 2016 after which an uptick in the global price of steel has lifted sales once more.

In fiscal 2019 the company's sales declined less than 5% to $11 billion due to lower tons sold and lower average selling price per ton sold.

Net income grew about 6% to $701 million was mainly due to higher operating income (higher gross profit and decreased impairment charges) and operating income margin (higher gross profit margin and decreased impairment charges).

Reliance's cash position increase $46.1 million in 2019 ending the year $174.3 million. The company generated $1.3 billion from its operating activities while investing activities used $419.1 million and financing activities used $840.6 million. The company's main cash uses in 2019 were debt repayments share repurchases and capital expenditures.

Strategy

Reliance's strategic priorities are building up high-margin specialty businesses and growing its product and geographic base including abroad. It pursues these goals via internal investment and numerous acquisitions.

Reliance primary business strategy is to provide the highest levels of quality and service to its customer in the most efficient operational manner allowing to maximize its financial results.

The growth strategy is based on increasing its operating results through organic growth activities and strategic acquisitions that enhance its product customer and geographic diversification with a focus on higher margin specialty products and value-added processing services. Reliance focus on improving the operating performance at acquired locations by integrating them into its operational model and providing them access to capital and other resources to promote growth and efficiencies.

Reliance maintained its focus on internal growth in 2019 by opening new facilities building or expanding existing facilities adding processing equipment improving the safety of its operations and enhancing the working environments of its employees.

Additionally Reliance focused on servicing customers with small order sizes and quick turnaround by expanding its service network to ensure the proximity of its metal service centers to its customers.

Mergers and Acquisitions

Reliance has been prolific in acquiring companies?almost 70 since 1994.

In 2020 the company acquired California-based Fry Steel Company a general line and long bar distributor. Fry also offers cutting services for its line of more than 8000 types of long bar in brass stainless steel aluminum alloys carbon steel and bronze. The deal furthers Reliance's strategy of expanding through acquisitions and diversifying its customer and product mix.

Company Background

The company was founded in 1939 by Thomas Neilan as Reliance Steel Products Company a distributor of steel reinforcing bar in Los Angeles California. In 1956 the company is renamed for a second time to reflect its expanding product lines assuming the name it holds today: Reliance Steel & Aluminum Co.

EXECUTIVES

President Ccc Steel, Brian M. Tenenbaum

Sevp And Cfo, Karla R. Lewis, age 55, $604,250 total compensation

Vp Non-ferrous Operations, William K. Sales, age 63, $550,000 total compensation

President And Ceo, Gregg J. Mollins, age 65, $1,025,000 total compensation

Managing Director All Metal Services, David L. Potts

President Ami Metals, Scott A. Smith

Executive Svp Operations, James D. Hoffman, age 61, $577,500 total compensation

President Allegheny Steel Distributors, Bernie J. Herrmann

President Aluminum And Stainless, Joseph B. Wolf

President Pacific Metal, John S. Nosler

President Infra-metals, Mark A Haight, age 61

President Earle M. Jorgensen Co., James Desmond

Svp Operations, Stephen P. (Steve) Koch, age 53, $486,250 total compensation

President Siskin Steel & Supply, Paul J. Loftin

President Yarde Metals, Matthew L. (Matt) Smith

President Sugar Steel, Robert J. Sugar

President Chapel Steel, Stanley J. (Stan) Altman

President Clayton Metals, Brian K. Cleveland

Cio, Susan C. Borchers, age 59

President Feralloy, Carlos Rodriguez-Borjas

President American Metals, Nicole Heater

President Crest Steel, Kristofer M. Farris

President Delta Steel, Eric J. Offenberger

President Diamond Manufacturing, David L. Simpson

President National Specialty Alloys, Mark Russ

President Service Steel Aerospace, Douglas Nesbitt

President Viking Materials, Michael E. Allen

President Chatham Steel, Jerome Rooney

President Precision Strip, Joseph P. Wolf

President Continental Alloys & Services, Randall C. (Randy) Zajicek

President Liebovich Bros., David Corirossi

President Northern Illinois Steel Supply, Michael J. Ruth

President Pdm Steel Service Centers, Sean Mollins

President Phoenix Metals, Barry L. Epps

President Best Manufacturing, James Best

President Precision Flamecutting And Steel, Susan McKay

President Valex, Steve Simon

Managing Director Metalweb Limited, Karl Weston

Vice President Tax, Silva Yeghyayan

Senior Vice President Operations, Steve Koch

Vice President Finance, Judy Bennett

Vice President Health Safety And Human Resources, Don Prebola

Svp General Counsel And Corporate Secretary, William Smith Ii

Chairman, Mark V. Kaminski, age 65

Secretary, Yvette M Schiotis

Board Member, John Figueroa

Auditors: KPMG LLP

LOCATIONS

HQ: Reliance Steel & Aluminum Co.
350 South Grand Avenue, Suite 5100, Los Angeles, CA 90071
Phone: 213 687-7700
Web: www.rsac.com

2018 Sales

	$ mil.	% of total
United States	10,638	92
Foreign Countries	896	8
Total	**11,534**	**100**

2018 Sales

	% of total
Midwest	32
West/Southwest	22
Southeast	18
International	8
Mid-Atlantic	6
Northeast	6
Pacific Northwest	5
Mountain	3
Total	**100**

PRODUCTS/OPERATIONS

2018 Sales

	% of total
Carbon steel	54
Aluminum	19
Stainless steel	14
Alloy	6
Toll processing	4
Other	3
Total	**100**

PRODUCTS
Alloy Steel
Aluminum
Brass & Copper
Carbon Steel
Stainless Steel
Titanium

COMPETITORS

A. M. Castle	Ryerson
O'Neal Steel	Steel Technologies
Olympic Steel	Ternium Mexico
Russel Metals	Worthington Industries

HISTORICAL FINANCIALS

Company Type: Public

Income Statement

FYE: December 31

	REVENUE ($ mil.)	NET INCOME ($ mil.)	NET PROFIT MARGIN	EMPLOYEES
12/19	10,973	701	6.4%	15,300
12/18	11,534	633	5.5%	15,600
12/17	9,721	613	6.3%	14,900
12/16	8,613	304	3.5%	14,500
12/15	9,350	311	3.3%	14,000
Annual Growth	**4.1%**	**22.5%**	**—**	**2.2%**

2019 Year-End Financials

Debt ratio: 19.54%	No. of shares (mil.): 66
Return on equity: 14.20%	Dividends
Cash ($ mil.): 174	Yield: 1.8%
Current ratio: 4.46	Payout: 24.0%
Long-term debt ($ mil.): 1,523	Market value ($ mil.): 8,006

	STOCK PRICE ($) FY Close	P/E High/Low		PER SHARE ($) Earnings	Dividends	Book Value
12/19	119.76	12	7	10.34	2.20	77.88
12/18	71.17	11	8	8.75	2.00	69.85
12/17	85.79	10	8	8.34	1.80	64.28
12/16	79.54	21	12	4.16	1.65	57.08
12/15	57.91	16	12	4.16	1.60	54.56
Annual Growth	**19.9%**	**—**	**—**	**25.6%**	**8.3%**	**9.3%**

Renasant Corp

Those who are cognizant of their finances may want to do business with Renasant Corporation. The holding company owns Renasant Bank which serves consumers and local business through about 80 locations in Alabama Georgia Mississippi and Tennessee. The bank offers standard products such as checking and savings accounts CDs credit cards and loans and mortgages as well as trust retail brokerage and retirement plan services. Its loan portfolio is dominated by residential and commercial real estate loans. The bank also offers agricultural business construction and consumer loans and lease financing. Subsidiary Renasant Insurance sells personal and business coverage.Shareholders approved a merger with Metropolitan Bank in mid-2017.

Financial Performance

The company's revenue increased in fiscal 2013 compared to the prior year. It reported revenue of $252.6 million for fiscal 2013 up from $228 million in revenue for fiscal 2012.

Renasant's net income also went up in fiscal 2013 compared to the previous fiscal period. It reported net income of about $33.5 million for fiscal 2013 up from net income of $26.6 million in fiscal 2012.

The company's cash on hand decreased by about $24 million in fiscal 2013 compared to fiscal 2012 levels.

Strategy

Renasant has looked to diversify its loan portfolio. The bank has reduced its amount of loans for construction and land development — a sector that has been hit particularly hard — by tightening its underwriting standards.

It's also been growing through acquistions. In late 2014 for example Renasant purchased Heritage Financial Group in an all stock merger deal that amounted to $258 million. The move added $1.9 billion in assets $1.2 billion in loan assets and $1.3 billion in deposit assets to Renasant's collection. In addition the move significantly expanded the bank's geographic reach adding 48 banking mortgage and investment offices in Alabama Florida and Georgia. All told the deal made Renasant one of the largest community banks in the Southeast region of the United States.

Mergers and Acquisitions

In 2017 Renasant agreed to a $190 million merger with Metropolitan Bank.

EXECUTIVES

Evp, Stuart R. Johnson, age 67, $250,000 total compensation

Chairman President And Ceo, E. Robinson (Robin) McGraw, age 73, $750,000 total compensation

Evp, James W. Gray, age 64, $230,000 total compensation

Evp And Director Of Retail Banking Renasant Bank, C. Mitchell (Mitch) Waycaster, age 62, $450,000 total compensation

Evp, Mary J. Witt, age 61

Evp, W. Mark Williams, age 57

Evp, R. Rick Hart, age 72, $496,000 total compensation

Evp And General Counsel, Stephen M. Corban, age 65, $75,000 total compensation

Evp; President Eastern Region Renasant Bank, O. Leonard (Len) Dorminey, age 67, $213,285 total compensation

Evp And Cfo, Kevin D. Chapman, age 45, $375,000 total compensation

Evp; President Western Region Renasant Bank, J. Scott Cochran, age 57

First Vice President Director Of Corporate Communication And Ir Contact, John Oxford

Executive Vice President, Danny Gladney

Vice President And Trust Officer, Allison Youngblood

Executive Vice President, Craig Gardella

Senior Vice President Corporate Banking, Will Smithhart

Assistant Vice President Account Executive, Brian Gagel

Senior Vice President Of Information Systems, Jerry Iverson

Senior Vice President, Robert Hankins

Senior Vice President And Business Development Officer, Bobby Harper

Vice President Commercial Banker, Larry Finkel

Executive Vice President Credit Administration, Stuart Weise

Senior Vice President, Scott Rossman

Vice President, Jack Stuart

Vice President Relationship Officer, Danny Crabtree

Senior Vice President Commercial Banking, David Harwell

Senior Vice President, Jason McClimans

Division President Executive Vice President, Raymond Vannorman

Vice President Appraisal Officer Card, Lisa Wells

Central Monitoring Department Manager Vice President, Tracey Aldridge

Assistant Vice President Operations, Stephen Flynn

Senior Vice President Director Of Senior Business Analyst Lending, John Daly

Vice President, Raakhi Phillips

Vice President, Brian Porter

Assistant Vice President Senior Business Analyst Portfolio Manager, Kathy Davis

Senior Vice President, Phil Smith

Executive Vice President, Mark Jeanfreau

Senior Vice President Commercial Banking, Noble Jones

Assistant Vice President Senior Accounting Officer, Jennifer Flanagan

Vice President Commercial Lending, Al Manry

Senior Vice President Commercial Banking, Scott Freese

Senior Vice President, Melanie Kurn

Assistant Vice President, Debra Prosba

Assistant Vice President Treasury Management Specialist, Chrissy Aubin

Vice President Special Assets Officer, Scott Williams

Senior Executive Vice President, David Durland

Board Member, Richard Heyer

Auditors: HORNE LLP

LOCATIONS

HQ: Renasant Corp
209 Troy Street, Tupelo, MS 38804-4827
Phone: 662 680-1001
Web: www.renasant.com

PRODUCTS/OPERATIONS

2015 Sales

	$ mil.	% of total
Interest income		
Loans	236	64
Securities	26	7
Other	0	-
Non-interest income		
Mortgage banking income	35	10
Service charges on deposit accounts	29	8
Fees and commissions	16	4
Wealth management	9	3
Other	17	4
Total	371	100

COMPETITORS

BBVA Compass Bancshares
BancorpSouth
Citizens Holding
Citizens National Bank of Meridian
First Horizon
Hancock Holding
Regions Financial
Trustmark

HISTORICAL FINANCIALS

Company Type: Public

Income Statement				FYE: December 31
	ASSETS ($ mil.)	NET INCOME ($ mil.)	INCOME AS % OF ASSETS	EMPLOYEES
12/19	13,400	167	1.3%	2,527
12/18	12,934	146	1.1%	2,359
12/17	9,829	92	0.9%	2,102
12/16	8,699	90	1.0%	1,965
12/15	7,926	68	0.9%	1,996
Annual Growth	14.0%	25.3%	—	6.1%

2019 Year-End Financials

Debt ratio: 1.67%
Return on equity: 8.04%
Cash ($ mil.): 414
Current ratio: —
Long-term debt ($ mil.): —

No. of shares (mil.): 56
Dividends
Yield: 2.4%
Payout: 30.2%
Market value ($ mil.): 2,014

	STOCK PRICE ($) FY Close	P/E High/Low		PER SHARE ($) Earnings	Dividends	Book Value
12/19	35.42	13	11	2.88	0.87	37.39
12/18	30.18	18	10	2.79	0.80	34.91
12/17	40.89	23	19	1.96	0.73	30.72
12/16	42.22	20	14	2.17	0.71	27.81
12/15	34.41	20	14	1.88	0.68	25.73
Annual Growth	0.7%	—	—	11.3%	6.4%	9.8%

Republic Bancorp, Inc. (KY)

As one of the top five bank holding companies based in Kentucky $4 billion-asset Republic Bancorp is the parent of Republic Bank & Trust (formerly First Commercial Bank) which offers deposit accounts loans and mortgages credit cards private banking and trust services through more than 30 branches in across Kentucky and around 10 more in southern Indiana Nashville Tampa and Cincinnati Ohio. About one-third of the bank's $3 billion-loan portfolio is tied to residential real estate while another 25% is made up of commercial real estate loans. Warehouse lines of credit home equity loans and commercial and industrial loans make up most of the rest. The company also offers short-term consumer loans and tax refund loans.

Operations

Republic Bancorp operates three "core banking" segments: Traditional Banking which generated more than 80% of the company's total profit during 2015; Warehouse (almost 20% of profit) and Mortgage Banking (less than 1%). Its Warehouse lending business offers short-term credit facilities secured by single-family residences to mortgage bankers nationwide. Its Republic Processing Group segment offers short-term consumer loans prepaid debit cards and tax refund loans.

The bank made 75% of its total revenue from interest income almost entirely from loans during 2015 though a small percentage came from taxed investments and Federal Home Loan Bank stock. The rest of its revenue came from net refund transfer fees from its Republic Processing Group segment (9% of revenue) deposit account service charges (7%) interchange fee income (4%) mortgage banking income (2%) and other miscellaneous income sources.

Subsidiary Republic Insurance Services (also known as the Captive) provides property and casualty insurance coverage to the company and eight other third-party insurance captives for which insurance may not be available or cost effective.

Geographic Reach

The company had 40 RB&T branches at the end of 2015 including 32 in Kentucky mostly in the Louisville Metro area and others in the Central Western and Northern parts of the state. It had 3 branches in southern Indiana (in Floyds Knobs Jeffersonville and New Albany); two branches in the Tampa Florida metro area; two branches in the Nashville Tennessee metro area; and one more in the Cincinnati Ohio metro area.

Sales and Marketing

Republic spent $3.16 million on marketing and development expenses during 2015 compared to $3.26 million and $3.11 million in 2014 and 2013 respectively.

Financial Performance

Republic Bancorp's revenues and profits have been trending higher since 2013 as its loan assets have risen more than 30% over the period.

The company's revenue climbed 9% to $190 million during 2015 mostly thanks to higher interest income as its loan assets grew by 9% to

$3.33 billion with commercial loans (real estate and business loans) and residential mortgage loans and lines of credit driving most of the growth.

Strong revenue growth in 2015 drove Republic's net income up 22% to $35 million for the year. The company's operating cash levels nearly doubled to $50 million after adjusting its earnings for non-cash items related to mortgage loan sales and thanks to favorable working capital changes related to changes in other liabilities.

Strategy

Republic Bancorp is moving toward building its commercial loans business launching a Corporate Banking division in 2015 to originate commercial loans with amounts ranging from $2.5 million to $25 million to borrowers with the highest credit ratings in its existing geographic markets. It also acquires smaller community banks to expand into new geographic markets while building its loan and deposit business.

Additionally Republic Bancorp has been moving into other revolving credit lines while also looking to take advantage of the rapidly growing prepaid card market. During 2015 for example it partnered with netSpend to become a pilot issuer of netSpend-branded prepaid cards; and partnered with ClearBalance to originate revolving lines of credit nationally for hospital receivables.

Mergers and Acquisitions

In October 2015 Republic Bancorp expanded its presence in Florida and grew its loan business after agreeing to buy $250 million-asset Cornerstone Bancorp along its four Cornerstone Community Bank branches in the Tampa Florida metro area $190 million in loans and $200 million in deposits. The deal was expected to be completed in the first half of 2016.

Company Background

In 2012 Republic Bancorp entered the Nashville and Minneapolis market through the FDIC-assisted acquisitions of the failed Tennessee Commerce Bank and First Commercial Bank respectively.

EXECUTIVES

Vice Chairman; President Republic Bank & Trust, A. Scott Trager, age 67, $350,000 total compensation
President And Ceo; Ceo Republic Bank & Trust, Steven E. (Steve) Trager, age 59, $353,000 total compensation
Evp Cfo And Chief Accounting Officer Republic Bancorp And Republic Bank & Trust, Kevin Sipes, age 48, $281,500 total compensation
Vice President And Risk Manager, Bryan Hendrick
Svp And Managing Director Mortgage Warehouse Lending, Kevin Rost
Senior Vice President Director Of Operations, Steve Pieragowski
Assistant Vice President, Mike Long
Vice President, Susan Smith
Assistant Vice President Accounting Supervisor, Denise Witten
Senior Vice President, Lisa Butcher
Assistant Vice President Technology Services Managerand#8230, Scott Estes
Assistant Vice President Finance Project Manager, Tim Wheatley
Vice President Project Services Manager, Michelle Cunningham
Vice President Commercial Credit, Bill Thomas
Vice President Retail Collections, Lori Forbes
Avp Banking Center Supervisor, Robin Verenna

Assistant Vice President, Marie Daniels
Senior Vice President, David Buchanon
Vice President Director Of Business Intelligence, Deb Reese
Assistant Vice President, Philip Thomas
Senior Vice President, Doug Burgess
Vice President, Karen McGee
Vice President Senior Manager Of Technology Services, Sean O'Mahoney
Assistant Vice President Managing Director, Brad Savko
Assistant Vice President, Amy Quinn
Vice President Mortgage Warehouse Lending, Tim Poole
Vice President Senior Private Banking Officer, Steven Sharp
Senior Vice President Regional Sales Director, James Roberts
Vice President Business Banking, Ryan Paxton
Executive Vice President Chief Lending Officer, Andy Powell
Vice President Treasury Management, Tamara McCain
Vice President, Scott Lee
Vice President Mortgage Warehouse Lending, Scott Davis
Assistant Vice President Business Development Manager, Wende Cosby
Vice President Cra Officer, Kenneth Webb
Vice President Relationship Manager, Steven Shields
Vice President Treasury Management, Chris Cahill
Vice President Loan Review Manager, Elizabeth Frame
Vice President Loan Operations, Donna Blincoe
Senior Vice President And Chief Compliance Officer, Scott Nardi
Vice President Contact Center Director Of Client Experience, Damion Robinson
Chairman, Bernard M. Trager, age 91
Secretary, Madhurie Nagir
Auditors: Crowe LLP

LOCATIONS

HQ: Republic Bancorp, Inc. (KY)
601 West Market Street, Louisville, KY 40202
Phone: 502 584-3600
Web: www.republicbank.com

PRODUCTS/OPERATIONS

2015 Sales

	$ mil.	% of total
Interest		
Loans including fees	134	70
Taxable investment securities	7	4
Other	1	1
Noninterest		
Net refund transfer fees	17	9
Service charges on deposit accounts	13	7
Interchange fee income	8	4
Mortgage banking	4	2
Other	5	3
Adjustments	(0.3)	-
Total	**190**	**100**

Selected Services

Checking
Credit & Debit Cards
Internet & Mobile Banking
Lending
Private Banking & Wealth Management
Savings & Investing

COMPETITORS

BB&T	KeyCorp
Bank of America	PNC Financial
Community Trust	Stock Yards Bancorp
Fifth Third	U.S. Bancorp
Home Federal	

HISTORICAL FINANCIALS

Company Type: Public

Income Statement

FYE: December 31

	ASSETS ($ mil.)	NET INCOME ($ mil.)	INCOME AS % OF ASSETS	EMPLOYEES
12/19	5,620	91	1.6%	1,092
12/18	5,240	77	1.5%	1,064
12/17	5,085	45	0.9%	1,009
12/16	4,816	45	1.0%	954
12/15	4,230	35	0.8%	799
Annual Growth	7.4%	27.1%	—	8.1%

2019 Year-End Financials

Debt ratio: 0.73%
Return on equity: 12.61%
Cash ($ mil.): 385
Current ratio: —
Long-term debt ($ mil.): —

No. of shares (mil.): 20
Dividends
  Yield: 2.2%
  Payout: 26.4%
Market value ($ mil.): 980

	STOCK PRICE ($) FY Close	P/E High/Low		PER SHARE ($) Earnings	Dividends	Book Value
12/19	46.80	6	5	8.38	1.06	36.49
12/18	38.72	7	5	7.14	0.97	33.03
12/17	38.02	19	15	2.20	0.87	30.33
12/16	39.54	18	11	2.22	0.83	28.97
12/15	26.41	16	13	1.70	0.78	27.59
Annual Growth	15.4%	—	—	49.0%	7.8%	7.2%

Republic First Bancorp, Inc.

Republic First Bancorp is the holding company for Republic Bank which serves the Greater Philadelphia area and southern New Jersey from more than 15 branches. Boasting over $1 billion in assets the bank targets individuals and small to midsized businesses offering standard deposit products including checking and savings accounts money market accounts IRAs and CDs. Commercial mortgages account for more than 70% of the company's loan portfolio which also includes consumer loans business loans and residential mortgages. Republic has been transitioning from a commercial bank into a major regional retail and commercial bank.

Operations

The bank's loan portfolio is made up of mostly commercial loans including commercial real estate loans construction and land development loans commercial and industrial loans as well as owner occupied real estate loans consumer-related loans and residential mortgages. As of 2015 each its commercial loans typically ranged from $250000 to $5 million though it sometimes lent up to its legal limit of $19.9 million.

About 72% of Republic First Bancorp's total revenue came from loan interest (including fees) in 2014 while another 11% came from interest and dividends on its taxable and tax-exempt investment securities. The rest of its revenue came from gains on sales of SBA loans (10%) loan advisory and servicing fees (3%) service fees on deposit accounts (3%) and other miscellaneous income sources. The bank had a staff of 235 full-time employees at the end of 2014.

Geographic Reach

Republic First boasts more than 15 branch offices in Pennsylvania (in Abington Ardmore Bala Cynwyd Plymout Meeting Media and Philadelphia) and New Jersey (in Berlin Cherry Hill Glassboro Haddonfield Marlton and Voorhees).

Sales and Marketing

The bank's commercial loans are mostly made to small and medium-sized businesses as well as professionals who need working capital financing for asset acquisitions or other financial services.

Republic First has been ramping up its advertising spend in recent years. It spent $597 thousand on advertising in 2014 compared to $447 thousand and $307 thousand in 2013 and 2012 respectively.

Financial Performance

The company has struggled to consistently grow its revenues in recent years due to shrinking interest margins on loans amidst the low-interest environment. Republic First has been steadily climbing out from prior years of losses (2013 2011 2010) however thanks to declining interest expenses and lower loan loss provisions as its loan portfolio's credit quality has improved with higher property valuations in the strengthened economy.

Republic First's revenue rose by 4% to $48.4 million in 2014 mostly thanks to an 8% jump in interest income as loan balances increased during the year. The bank's non-interest income fell on lower sales of SBA loans with fewer SBA loan originations which offset some of its top-line growth.

The company shot back into the black with a $2.4 million profit in 2014 (compared to a net loss of $3.5 million in 2013) mostly because in 2013 it had suffered a non-recurring $3.6 million loan loss on a bad loan as well as a non-recurring $1.9 million charge related to a legal settlement. Republic First's operating cash levels also skyrocketed to $9.7 million mostly on higher cash earnings.

Strategy

Republic Bank which had historically been known for its business and commercial lending has been focused on retail banking in the past few years and is working to become a major regional retail and commercial bank. As part of this strategy the bank has restructured its loan portfolio to reduce its emphasis on commercial real estate loans and has pursued a "retail-focused" strategy by offering customers "extended store hours absolutely free checking and coin counting more than 55000 surcharge ATMs and free VISA gift cards" according to the company's CEO letter included in the 2014 annual report.

The company has been expanding organically through new branch openings in recent years. In 2015 for example Republic Bank opened three new branches in South New Jersey in Berlin Marlton and Glassboro. In April of that year the company also sold $45 million in common stock through a private placement offering to cover its "aggressive expansion plans in 2015 and beyond."

EXECUTIVES

Vice President, John Lavin
Regional Vice President, Matt Moresco

Assistant Vice President Network Engineer, John Rudolph
Marketing Regional Manager Senior Vice President, Robert Worley
Vice President, Tom Waller
Svp Human Resources Director, Janine Zangrilli
Assistant Vice President, Jared Kushner
Senior Vice President Chief Risk Officer, Tracie Young
Vice President And Marketing Manager, Katie Michaleski
Senior Vice President Compliance Officer, Robert A Dobie
Vice President Store Manager, Nikkia Warlow
Senior Vice President And Retail Market Manager, Leslie DiLuigi
Vice President Senior Business Development Officer, Judy Rosner
Vice President, Krista Collings
Vice President, Amy Osborn
Svp Senior Relationship Manager Commercial Real Estate, Mark Kane
Senior Vice President, Brennan Charlene
Assistant Vice President Loan Closer Sba Division, Camille Oldenburg
Vice President Compliance Manager, Anne Paglia
Senior Vice President Sba Division, Kelly Gengoult
Assistant Vice President, Eric Blankenship
Executive Vice President And Chief Risk Officer Of Republic Bank And Trust Company, John Rippy
Senior Vice President, Chip Hancock
Vice President Senior Business Banker, Greg Bromley
Auditors: BDO USA, LLP

LOCATIONS

HQ: Republic First Bancorp, Inc.
50 South 16th Street, Philadelphia, PA 19102
Phone: 215 735-4422
Web: www.myrepublicbank.com

PRODUCTS/OPERATIONS

2014 Sales

	$ mil.	% of total
Interest income		
Interest and fees on taxable loans	34	71
Interest and dividends on taxable investment securities	5	10
Interest and fees on tax-exempt loans	0	1
Interest and dividends on tax-exempt investment securities	0	1
Interest on federal funds sold and other interest-earning assets	0	0
Non interest		
Gain on sales of SBA loans	4	10
Loan advisory and servicing fees	1	3
Service fees on deposit accounts	1	3
Gain on sale of investment securities	0	1
Legal settlements	0	0
Other-than-temporary impairment	0	0
Portion recognized in other comprehensive income (before taxes)	(0.03)	0
Net impairment loss on investment securities	0	0
Bank owned life insurance income	0	0
Other non-interest income	0	0
Total	**48**	**100**

COMPETITORS

Bank of America	Sovereign Bank
Citizens Financial Group	Sun Bancorp (NJ)
	TD Bank USA
PNC Financial	TF Financial
Prudential Bancorp	Wells Fargo
Royal Bancshares	

HISTORICAL FINANCIALS

Company Type: Public

Income Statement

FYE: December 31

	ASSETS ($ mil.)	NET INCOME ($ mil.)	INCOME AS % OF ASSETS	EMPLOYEES
12/19	3,341	(3)	—	599
12/18	2,753	8	0.3%	531
12/17	2,322	8	0.4%	448
12/16	1,923	4	0.3%	306
12/15	1,439	2	0.2%	277
Annual Growth	23.4%	—	—	21.3%

2019 Year-End Financials

Debt ratio: 0.34%
Return on equity: (-1.42%)
Cash ($ mil.): 168
Current ratio: —
Long-term debt ($ mil.): —

No. of shares (mil.): 58
Dividends
  Yield: —
  Payout: —
Market value ($ mil.): 246

	STOCK PRICE ($) FY Close	P/E High/Low		PER SHARE ($) Earnings	Dividends	Book Value
12/19	4.18	—	—	(0.06)	0.00	4.23
12/18	5.97	62	39	0.15	0.00	4.17
12/17	8.45	62	47	0.15	0.00	3.97
12/16	8.35	69	29	0.12	0.00	3.79
12/15	4.33	77	55	0.06	0.00	3.00
Annual Growth	(0.9%)	—	—	—	—	9.0%

Republic Services Inc

Republic Services is the second-largest non-hazardous waste management provider in the US behind leader Waste Management in terms of revenue and geographic coverage. Republic provides waste disposal services for commercial industrial municipal and residential customers through its network of 340 collection firms. It owns or operates some 190 solid waste landfills more than 210 transfer stations and about 80 recycling centers. Other assets include seven treatment recovery and disposal facilities and 15 salt water disposal wells. It also has about 75 landfill-to-gas and a handful of other renewable energy projects.

Operations

Republic Services divides its operations into two broad geographic categories Group 1 and Group 2. Group 1 covers the western US and parts of the Midwest. Group 2 covers the remaining portion of the Midwest the eastern US and Texas. Group 2 accounts for more than 50% of revenue.

Solid waste collection operations is Republic Services' largest revenue generator. Small-container collection brings in 30% of revenue while residential and large containers account for more than one-fifth each. Its landfill disposal services generate 15% of revenue.

Geographic Reach

Phoenix Arizona-based Republic Services operates throughout the US. The company has collection businesses transfer stations active solid waste landfills and recycling centers in about 40 US states and Puerto Rico. Its active solid waste landfills total 109150 acres including nearly 38500 permitted acres.

Sales and Marketing

Republic Services employs municipal marketing representatives responsible for working with municipalities or communities seeking Republic's residential services. It also employs a National Accounts selling organization.

Financial Performance

In the past five years Republic Services' revenue has trended upwards.

Revenue for the year ended December 31 2019 increased by 2.6% to $10299.4 million compared to $10040.9 million for the same period in 2018. This change in revenue is due to increases in total price including fuel recovery fees of 2.8% and acquisitions net of divestitures of 0.8% partially offset by the impact of decreased volumes of (0.4)% environmental services of (0.3)% and recycling processing and commodity sales of (0.3)%.

Republic Services' net income increased by 4% to $1.1 billion from 2018 results of $1.0 billion due in large part to higher income taxes than in the prior period.

Total cash on hand at the end of 2019 increased $44.1 million to $177.4 million. Cash from operations contributed $2.4 billion while investing activities used $1.7 billion for capital expenditures and other investments. Financing used $589 million to repay debt repurchase stock and pay dividends.

Strategy

The company believe that their products and services are valuable and that by developing a superior team and delivering superior products they can differentiate ourselves from their competitors. Differentiation allows them to attract and retain the best talent win more customers increase customer loyalty and ultimately drive higher revenue and profits. Their strategy of Profitable Growth through Differentiation is built on five key pillars including market position operating model people and talent agenda customer zeal and digital platform.

Company Background

Republic Services began in 1980 as Republic Resources an oil exploration and production company. In 1989 after a stockholder group tried to force Republic into liquidation Browning-Ferris (BFI) founder Thomas Fatjo stepped in gained control of Republic Resources and refocused it on a field he knew well — solid waste. Renamed Republic Waste the company began making acquisitions.

In 1990 Michael DeGroote founder of BFI competitor Laidlaw bought into Republic Waste. In 1995 Wayne Huizenga — who co-founded Waste Management in 1971 and was beginning to develop a national auto sales organization in the mid-1990s after his tenure as chairman and CEO of Blockbuster Entertainment — approached DeGroote about a deal. They rejected an immediate merger of the waste and auto businesses because the latter was not well-enough developed and would drag down Republic's numbers. Instead they agreed to merge Republic and the Hudson Companies (a trash business owned by Huizenga's brother-in-law Harris Hudson) to sell Huizenga a large interest in Republic through a private offering and to give him control of the board (in 1995). The company became Republic Industries.

Republic Industries spun off about 30% of its waste business as Republic Services in 1998; the IPO raised $1.3 billion. Republic's acquisition trend continued as it agreed to buy 16 landfills 136 commercial collection routes and 11 transfer stations from Waste Management for $500 million. Later that year Waste Management veteran James O'Connor succeeded Huizenga as CEO although Huizenga continued as chairman.

HISTORY

Republic Services began in 1980 as Republic Resources an oil exploration and production company. In 1989 after a stockholder group tried to force Republic into liquidation Browning-Ferris (BFI) founder Thomas Fatjo stepped in gained control of Republic Resources and refocused it on a field he knew well — solid waste. Renamed Republic Waste the company began making acquisitions.

In 1990 Michael DeGroote founder of BFI competitor Laidlaw bought into Republic Waste. In 1995 Wayne Huizenga — who co-founded Waste Management in 1971 and was beginning to develop a national auto sales organization in the mid-1990s after his tenure as chairman and CEO of Blockbuster Entertainment — approached DeGroote about a deal. They rejected an immediate merger of the waste and auto businesses because the latter was not well-enough developed and would drag down Republic's numbers. Instead they agreed to merge Republic and the Hudson Companies (a trash business owned by Huizenga's brother-in-law Harris Hudson) to sell Huizenga a large interest in Republic through a private offering and to give him control of the board (in 1995). The company became Republic Industries.

Huizenga's investment brought a flood of new investors. With new resources Republic Industries became a driving force in the garbage industry's consolidation binge and the company bought more than 100 smaller waste haulers between 1995 and 1998. Republic Industries spun off about 30% of its waste business as Republic Services in 1998; the IPO raised $1.3 billion. Republic's acquisition trend continued as it agreed to buy 16 landfills 136 commercial collection routes and 11 transfer stations from Waste Management for $500 million. Later that year Waste Management veteran James O'Connor succeeded Huizenga as CEO although Huizenga continued as chairman.

Investors filed class-action lawsuits against Republic in 1999 claiming the Waste Management purchases held far more integration problems than the company admitted. In 2000 Republic swapped nine of its solid-waste operations for eight Allied Waste businesses which Allied needed to divest in order to gain federal approval for its merger with BFI.

While many firms in the industry were selling off assets in 2001 Republic was expanding its operations in the Northern California market by acquiring Richmond Sanitary Services. Huizenga retired as chairman at the end of 2002 and was once again succeeded by O'Connor. Huizenga stayed on the board as a director until May 2004.

In 2007 the company sold Living Earth Technology Company (a noncore stand-alone business in Texas) for about $37 million. In 2008 prior to its megadeal with Allied Waste Republic rebuffed a takeover bid by industry leader Waste Management.

In late 2008 Republic Services the once #3 industry player acquired #2 company Allied Waste for $6 billion to place it closer to industry leader Waste Management in terms of revenues and geographic coverage. Following the acquisition Republic divested assets in seven markets (six municipal solid waste landfills six collection businesses and three transfer stations) in order to meet US antitrust regulations.

During 2012 the company invested $76 million on five recycling centers and plans to continue to look for opportunities to expand its recycling capabilities.

In 2013 the company dedicated a 2037 acre state-of-the-art landfill and transfer station in Texas to meet the Rio Grande Valley's waste needs for the next 100 years. The new La Gloria landfill replaced Republic's Rio Grande Valley Landfill in Donna Texas that had reached full capacity.

EXECUTIVES

President And Ceo, Donald W. (Don) Slager, age 58, $1,100,000 total compensation

Evp And Chief Development Officer, Brian A. Bales

Evp Chief Legal Officer Chief Ethics And Compliance Officer And Corporate Secretary, Catharine D. Ellingsen, age 56, $395,107 total compensation

Evp And Chief Administrative Officer, Jeffrey A. (Jeff) Hughes, age 64, $482,061 total compensation

Evp Operations, Jon Vander Ark

Evp Operations, Tim Stuart

Svp And Cio, Bill Halnon

Svp And Chief Accounting Officer, Charles F. (Chuck) Serianni, age 58, $511,779 total compensation

Evp Operations Support, Nathan Cabbil

Evp And Chief Transformation Officer, Stuart Levy

Evp And Chief Customer Officer, Tom Lynch

Evp And Chief Marketing Officer, Sue Klug

Senior Vice President Treasurer, Edward A Lang

Executive Vice President General Counsel And Corporate Secretary, Michael Rissman

Chairman, Manuel Kadre, age 54

Auditors: Ernst & Young LLP

LOCATIONS

HQ: Republic Services Inc
18500 North Allied Way, Phoenix, AZ 85054
Phone: 480 627-2700
Web: www.republicservices.com

2018 Sales

	$ mil.	% of total
Group2	5,071	50
Group1	4,811	48
Corporate entities	158	2
Total	**10,040**	**100**

PRODUCTS/OPERATIONS

2018 Sales

	$ mil.	% of total
Small-container	3,057	31
Residential	2,235	22
Large-container	2	22
Other	43	0
Transfer	537	5
Landfill	1	13
Energy services	194	2
Other	520	5
Total	**10,040**	**100**

HISTORICAL FINANCIALS

Company Type: Public

Income Statement
FYE: December 31

	REVENUE ($ mil.)	NET INCOME ($ mil.)	NET PROFIT MARGIN	EMPLOYEES
12/19	10,299	1,073	10.4%	36,000
12/18	10,040	1,036	10.3%	36,000
12/17	10,041	1,278	12.7%	35,000
12/16	9,387	612	6.5%	33,000
12/15	9,115	749	8.2%	33,000
Annual Growth	3.1%	9.4%	—	2.2%

2019 Year-End Financials

Debt ratio: 38.30%	No. of shares (mil.): 318
Return on equity: 13.38%	Dividends
Cash ($ mil.): 47	Yield: 1.7%
Current ratio: 0.52	Payout: 46.4%
Long-term debt ($ mil.): 7,758	Market value ($ mil.): 28,574

	STOCK PRICE ($) FY Close	P/E High/Low	PER SHARE ($) Earnings	Dividends	Book Value
12/19	89.63	27 21	3.33	1.56	25.46
12/18	72.09	24 20	3.16	1.44	24.58
12/17	67.61	18 15	3.77	1.33	23.99
12/16	57.05	32 24	1.78	1.24	22.66
12/15	43.99	21 18	2.13	1.16	22.49
Annual Growth	19.5%	— —	11.8%	7.7%	3.1%

Rite Aid Corp

While Rite Aid ranks 7th (behind Walgreen and CVS) in the US retail drugstore business it nevertheless boasts a formidable presence with over 2400 drugstores in almost 20 states and the District of Columbia. Rite Aid stores generate roughly 70% of their sales from filling prescriptions while the rest comes from selling health and beauty aids convenience foods greeting cards and more including Rite Aid brand private-label products. Some 60% of all Rite Aid stores are freestanding about 55% have drive-through pharmacies and more than 65% have a GNC store within them.

HISTORY

Wholesale grocer Alex Grass founded Rack Rite Distributors in Harrisburg Pennsylvania in 1958 to provide health and beauty aids and other sundries to grocery stores. He offered the same products at his first discount drugstore Thrif D Discount Center opened in 1962 in Scranton Pennsylvania. Four years later the company began placing pharmacies in its 36 stores. Rite Aid went public and adopted its current name in 1968 and the next year it made the first of many diverse acquisitions: Daw Drug Blue Ridge Nursing Homes and plasma suppliers Immuno Serums and Sero Genics.

Purchases in the 1970s included Sera-Tec Biologicals of New Jersey (blood plasma) and nearly 300 stores. By 1981 Rite Aid was the #3 drugstore chain and sales exceeded $1 billion. In 1984 it bought the American Discount Auto Parts chain and Encore Books discount chain and spun off its wholesale grocery operation in 1984 as Super Rite retaining a 47% stake (sold 1989).

Acquisitions added almost 900 stores during the 1980s. Expansion costs eroded Rite Aid's profit margins and the company focused on integrating its buys in 1990.

As part of a major restructuring in 1994 the company began selling its non-drugstore assets. Also in 1994 Rite Aid acquired Pharmacy Card and Intell-Rx and merged the two to form Eagle Managed Care.

Martin Grass took Rite Aid's reins from his dad in 1995. That year the company agreed to buy Revco at the time the #2 drugstore operator but the deal was derailed by FTC and Department of Justice objections in 1996. Rite Aid bounced back and acquired Thrifty PayLess (with more than 1000 stores) for about $2.3 billion in 1996. The deal gave the company more than 3600 stores and a presence in the western US. Also in 1996 Rite Aid exited several markets. In 1998 it closed many smaller stores and bought PCS Health Systems (the #1 US pharmacy benefits manager) from drug maker Eli Lilly and merged its Eagle Managed Care division into PCS.

In 1999 after a Wall Street Journal investigation Rite Aid revealed that Martin Grass Alex Grass and other family members held stakes in several suppliers and real estate interests doing business with the company. That year Rite Aid partnered with General Nutrition Companies Inc. (GNC) and took a 25% stake in the Internet retailer drugstore.com. Later in 1999 Rite Aid began slashing its $5.1 billion debt by cutting corporate staff and selling off some stores in California and the Pacific Northwest. CEO Martin Grass resigned and a team of former Fred Meyer officers — led by Robert Miller — took over.

In 2000 the company secured $1 billion from Citibank to reduce debt and provide capital. In July 2000 the company announced it would restate profits that over the past two years had been inflated in excess of $1 billion. Later that year Rite Aid sold PCS Health Systems to pharmacy benefits manager Advance Paradigm for more than $1 billion (about $500 million less than what Rite Aid originally paid for it). Rite Aid announced plans in 2001 to expand GNC concessions to additional stores.

To raise cash Rite Aid sold large blocks of its drugstore.com stock trimming its original 25% stake to less than 10% by April 2002. Former chairman and CEO Martin Grass former general counsel and vice chairman Franklin Brown and former CFO Frank Bergonzi among others were indicted in June 2002 for allegedly falsifying Rite Aid's books.

In April 2003 former chairman and CEO Martin Grass agreed to pay nearly $1.5 million to settle a lawsuit in which shareholders alleged that Rite Aid's books were falsified inflating the stock's value. In June Grass and former CFO Franklyn Bergonzi both pleaded guilty to conspiracy to defraud shareholders. Eric Sorkin Rite

Aid's former VP of pharmacy services pleaded guilty to conspiring to obstruct justice. The following month Rite Aid began mailing checks totaling nearly $140 million to thousands of its current and former shareholders damaged by the accounting scandal at the company. In October former chief counsel Franklin Brown was convicted of conspiracy and lying to the Securities and Exchange Commission among other charges.

Despite its high debt load Rite Aid reportedly made a $4 billion cash-and-stock offer for struggling rival Eckerd but lost out to CVS and Canada's Jean Coutu Group who divvied up Eckerd in mid-2004.

In May 2004 Grass whose father founded Rite Aid struck a plea deal with prosecutors under which he was sentenced to eight years in prison. Also in May several other former company executives including Sorkin and ex-CFO Frank Bergonzi were sentenced in the accounting scandal. In June Rite Aid agreed to pay the US government $5.6 million (plus another $1.4 million to more than 20 states) to settle a federal lawsuit alleging the drugstore chain submitted false prescription claims to government insurance programs. In October former vice chairman Brown was sentenced to 10 years in prison the longest sentence of six Rite Aid officials charged in the accounting scandal.

CFO John Standley resigned in 2005 to join supermarket operator Pathmark Stores as its CEO. Standley joined Rite Aid as its CFO in 1999.

In April 2007 the company agreed to a store swap with California-based Longs Drug Stores. Under the terms of the agreement Rite Aid acquired six Longs stores in Northern California Oregon and Washington in exchange for giving Longs six of its stores in Nevada.

In its first major deal since its brush with bankruptcy in 1999 Rite Aid acquired more than 1850 Brooks and Eckerd drugstores and six distribution centers from Canada's Jean Coutu Group in a cash-and-stock deal valued at about $4 billion in June 2007.

Rite Aid exited the Las Vegas market in 2008 saying it was not a core market and had not contributed to overall results. It sold 27 of its Las Vegas stores to Walgreens. It March 2009 Rite Aid made a similar disposal of all seven of its stores in San Francisco and five locations in eastern Idaho when it sold them to Walgreen. Rite Aid said the stores were in areas with too light a store presence to operate efficiently. In July Rite Aid agreed to pay $500000 in consumer refunds to settle charges by the FTC that the company falsely advertised its Germ Defense line of cold-and-flu remedies as preventing illness or reducing the severity and duration of symptoms. The FTC said Rite Aid did not have evidence to support its Germ Defense product claims. Rite Aid founder Alex Grass died in August 2009 at the age of 82.

President and CEO John Standley added the title of chairman in mid-2012.

EXECUTIVES

Chairman And Ceo, John T. Standley, age 57, $1,184,500 total compensation

Svp Ny Metro Division, Mark Kramer, age 70

Sevp Cfo And Chief Administrative Officer, Darren W. Karst, age 60, $809,751 total compensation
Evp Merchandising And Distribution, Enio A. (Tony) Montini, age 68, $471,500 total compensation
President And Coo, Kermit R. Crawford, age 61
Coo Rite Aid Stores, Bryan Everett, age 47, $461,250 total compensation
Evp Marketing, David Abelman, age 61
Svp Mid-atlantic Division, Scott Bernard
Svp Western Division, Bill Romine
Svp Northeast Division, Derek Griffith
Svp And Cio, Steve Rempel
Evp Pharmacy, Jocelyn Konrad, age 50
Svp Southern Division, Bill Jackson
Svp General Counsel And Secretary, Jim Comitale
Svp And Chief Human Resources Officer, Ken Black
Pharmacy Manager, John Stanbrough
Rph, Rajesh Kumar
Vice President And Chief Information Security Officer, Robert Lautsch
Pharmacy Manager, Ana Miladinovic
Pharmacy Manager, Kari McCabe
Pharmacy Manager, Ngozi Onumonu
Pharmacy Manager, Mark Hanna
Regional Vice President, Sri Pinninti
Vice President Pharmacy Operations, Scott Jacobson
Pharmacy Manager, Sameh Shenoodah
Pharmacist Manager, Mandy Hoysan
Director Of Pharmacy Acquisitions, Todd Rossi
Vice President Category Management Support And Front End Analysis, Nate Newcomer
Vice President, Robert Palmer
Regional Pharmacy Vice President, Bill Cropper
Pharmacy Manager, Viljan Kristollari
Senior Vice President Pharmacy Regulatory Affairs, Daniel Miller
Pharmacy Manager, Fiona Richardson
Vp Operations, Brian Dein
Pharmacy Manager, Donald Brensinger
Pharmacy Manager, Nilay Parikh
Pharmacy Manager, Farnaz Heidari
Pharmacy Manager, Vickie-hanh Le
Pharmacy Manager, Katerina Stefanou
Pharmacy Manager, Kristina Mironichenko
Pharmd, Van M Mar
Pharmacy Manager, Diane Brown
Senior Vice President And Chief Communications Officer, Susan Henderson
Regional Vice President Administration, Nancy Wight-Tally
Vice President Federal Affairs And Public Policy, Yong Choe
Pharmacy Manager, Helen Rey
Pharmacy Manager, Tina-shai Quallis
Pharmacy Manager, Dante Lanzillo
Pharmacy Manager, Jugraj Johl
Pharmacist Manager, Denise Mercuri
Pharmacy Manager, Laksana Kik
Pharmacy Manager, Andre Leandro
Pharmacy Manager, Joshua Maher
Regional Vice President, Kirt Patel
Group Vice President Category Management Consumables General Merchandise And Seasonal, Ted Williams
Vice President Private Brand Development, Bob Himler
Vp Human Resources, Michael Atcovitz
Pharmacy Manager, Bhaveer Dhanjee
Pharmacy Manager, Anand Mangu
Pharmacy Manager, Soheila Zahedpour
Director Of Pharmacy Operations, Stefan Wyk
Pharmacy Manager, Marina Gerr
Pharmacy Manager, Jill Watters
Pharmacy Manager, Rakesh Trivedi
Pharmacy Manager, Toan Bui
Pharmacy Manager, Avneet Vats
Director Of Pharmacy, Abdolreza Kossarian
Secretary And Clerk, Cindy Kelley

Board Member, David Jessick
Board Member, Joseph Anderson
Board Member, Myrtle Potter
Treasurer, Robin Sarro
Auditors: DELOITTE & TOUCHE LLP

LOCATIONS

HQ: Rite Aid Corp
30 Hunter Lane, Camp Hill, PA 17011
Phone: 717 761-2633   **Fax:** 717 975-5905
Web: www.riteaid.com

2016 Stores

	No.
New York	604
California	580
Pennsylvania	537
Michigan	275
New Jersey	257
North Carolina	225
Ohio	224
Virginia	190
Georgia	179
Massachusetts	146
Maryland	140
Washington	139
Kentucky	116
West Virginia	104
Alabama	93
South Carolina	91
Tennessee	81
Maine	79
Connecticut	77
Oregon	72
New Hampshire	68
Louisiana	62
Rhode Island	44
Delaware	42
Vermont	37
Mississippi	26
Utah	22
Colorado	20
Idaho	13
Indiana	10
District of Columbia	7
Nevada	1
Total	**4,561**

PRODUCTS/OPERATIONS

2019 Sales

	$ mil.	% of total
Retail Pharmacy	15,757	72
Pharmacy Services	6,093	28
Inter-segment elimination	(211.3)	-
Total	**21,639**	**100**

2019 Sales

	% of total
Prescription drugs	66
General merchandise & other	18
Over-the-counter medications & personal care	11
Health & beauty aids	5
Total	**100**

Selected Merchandise and Services

Beverages
Convenience foods
Cosmetics
Designer fragrances
Greeting cards
Health and personal care products
Household items
Over-the-counter drugs
Photo processing
Prescription drugs
Private-label products
Seasonal merchandise
Vitamins and minerals

COMPETITORS

A&P	Kroger
BJ's Wholesale Club	Marc Glassman
CVS	Medicine Shoppe
Costco Wholesale	Publix

Dollar General	Safeway
Family Dollar Stores	Target Corporation
Kinney Drugs Inc.	Wal-Mart
Kmart	Walgreen

HISTORICAL FINANCIALS
Company Type: Public

Income Statement

	REVENUE ($ mil.)	NET INCOME ($ mil.)	NET PROFIT MARGIN	EMPLOYEES
02/20*	21,928	(452)	—	50,000
03/19	21,639	(422)	—	53,100
03/18	21,528	943	4.4%	59,000
03/17	32,845	4	0.0%	87,000
02/16	30,736	165	0.5%	88,000
Annual Growth	(8.1%)	—		(13.2%)

FYE: February 29
*Fiscal year change

2020 Year-End Financials

Debt ratio: 32.85%
Return on equity: (-48.72%)
Cash ($ mil.): 218
Current ratio: 1.34
Long-term debt ($ mil.): 3,096
No. of shares (mil.): 54
Dividends
Yield: —
Payout: —
Market value ($ mil.): 745

	STOCK PRICE ($) FY Close	P/E High/Low	Earnings	Dividends	Book Value
02/20*	13.62	— —	(8.50)	0.00	12.33
03/19	0.73	— —	(7.99)	0.00	21.97
03/18	1.91	0 0	18.00	0.00	30.00
03/17	5.45	— —	(0.00)	0.00	11.66
02/16	7.96	3 2	3.20	0.00	11.10
Annual Growth	14.4%	— —	—	—	2.7%

*Fiscal year change

RiverSource Life Insurance Co

EXECUTIVES

Chb-pres, John R Worner
Executive Vice President Human Resources, Kelli Hunter
Auditors: PricewaterhouseCoopers LLP

LOCATIONS

HQ: RiverSource Life Insurance Co
1099 Ameriprise Financial Center, Minneapolis, MN 55474
Phone: 612 671-3131
Web: www.riversource.com

HISTORICAL FINANCIALS
Company Type: Public

Income Statement

	ASSETS ($ mil.)	NET INCOME ($ mil.)	INCOME AS % OF ASSETS	EMPLOYEES
12/19	121,943	587	0.5%	—
12/18	110,073	905	0.8%	—
12/17	120,440	741	0.6%	—
12/16	114,053	686	0.6%	—
12/15	113,356	895	0.8%	—
Annual Growth	1.8%	(10.0%)	—	—

FYE: December 31

Debt ratio: 0.04%
Return on equity: 16.99%
Cash ($ mil.): 1,275
Current ratio: —
Long-term debt ($ mil.): —

No. of shares (mil.): 0
Dividends
Yield: —
Payout: 229.9%
Market value ($ mil.): —

RLI Corp

You might wonder what folks in Illinois know about earthquake insurance but as a specialty property/casualty insurer Peoria-based RLI knows how to write such policies. Through its subsidiaries the company mainly offers coverage for US niche markets — risks that are hard to place in the standard market and are otherwise underserved. It focuses on public and private companies as well as non-profit organizations. RLI's commercial property/casualty lines include products liability property damage marine cargo directors and officers liability medical malpractice and general liability. It also writes commercial surety bonds and a smattering of specialty personal insurance.

Operations

RLI operates into three segments; Casualty Property and Surety. Casualty segment accounts for about 55% of revenue followed by property (more than 15%) and surety (about 10%).

RLI's specialty commercial property/casualty operations are conducted through its RLI Insurance Mt. Hawley Insurance Contractors Bonding and Insurance Company and RLI Indemnity subsidiaries. Personal offerings account for small portion of RLI's revenues and include homeowners insurance in Hawaii home business coverage and personal umbrella (supplemental property/casualty) policies.

The company's net premium earns generated nearly 85% of sales while net investment income and net realized gains account for the rest.

Geographic Reach

While the company operates in all 50 US states the District of Columbia the Virgin Islands Guam and Puerto Rico California is RLI's largest market accounting for more than 15% of the company's premiums.

Its corporate headquarters is located in Peoria Illinois.

Sales and Marketing

RLI markets its products to brokers and independent agents through branch offices scattered across the US.

Financial Performance

The company posted revenue growth for the last five years despite a slight drop in 2017. Net income continued its drop from 2015 to 2018 until the company arrested its decline.

Consolidated revenue totaled $1.0 billion in 2019 compared to $0.8 billion in 2018. Increased levels of earned premium and net investment income as well as unrealized gains on equity securities led to increased consolidated revenue in 2019.

Net earnings for 2019 totaled $191.6 million up from $64.2 million in 2018. Improved underwriting income net investment income and equity in earnings of unconsolidated investees con-

tributed to the overall increase. Additionally 2019 experienced a larger benefit from increased gains on equity securities.

Cash at the end of the year was $46.2 million. Net cash provided by operating activities was $276.9 million while cash used by investing and financing activities were $184.8 million and $76.1 million respectively.

Strategy

RLI's investment portfolio serves as the primary resource for loss payments and secondly as a source of income to support operations. Its investment strategy is based on the preservation of capital as the priority with a secondary focus on growing book value through total return. Investments of the highest quality and marketability are critical for preserving its claims-paying ability.

Its portfolio contains no derivatives or off-balance sheet structured investments. In addition it has a diversified investment portfolio that distributes credit risk across many issuers and a policy that limits aggregate credit exposure. Despite periodic fluctuations in market value its equity portfolio is part of a long-term asset allocation strategy and has contributed significantly to its growth in book value.

Company Background

Gerald Stephens founded the company in 1961 and served as its chairman from 2001 until his retirement in 2011.

EXECUTIVES

Vice President, Paul Dietrich
Chairman And Ceo, Jonathan E. Michael, age 66, $775,000 total compensation
President And Coo, Craig W. Kliethermes, age 55, $473,269 total compensation
Vp And Chief Investment Officer, Aaron P. Diefenthaler, age 46
Svp And Cfo, Thomas L. Brown, age 63, $417,308 total compensation
President Rli Transportation Division, Dan Meyer
Svp Operations Rli Product Divisions, Jennifer L. Klobnak, age 48, $298,462 total compensation
Vice President Information Technology, Murali Natarajan
Vice President, Martha Weissbaum
Vice President, Brent Flanigan
Avp Internal Audit Services, Patrick Ferrell
Assistant Vice President Specialty Markets, Paul V Harris
Vice President Ocean Marine, Lenny Pekola
Assistant Vice President Fidelity Group, Thomas Huber
Vice President Passenger Transportation, Tim Hathy
Vice President, Chris D Randall
Vice President Contract Surety, Bart Davis
Senior Vice President, Blake Ahrens
Assistant Vice President Claims, Andrea Dean
Vice President General Counsel Corporate Secretary, Aniel O Kennedy
Assistant Vice President, Brian Combs
Assistant Vice President Executive Products Group, Kerrick Porter
Assistant Vice President And Product Manager, Victor Garcia
Vice President Communications, Greg Tiemeier
Vice President Finance, Jonathan Micheal
Vice President Underwriting, Carol Denzer
Assistant Vice President Specialty Products Client Solutions, Barbara Sable
Assistant Vice President, Ted McGrath
Assistant Vice President Ocean Marine Underwriter, Sue Whittington

Assistant Vice President, Philip Abellera
Assistant Vice President, Don Johnson
Vice President And Healthcare Product Leader, Scott Ducey
Assistant Vice President Underwriting And Senior Business Analyst, Steven Cave
Assistant Vice President And Director Surety And Surety Automation, Sandy Swinford
Assistant Vice President Underwriting, Brian Schick
Assistant Vice President Risk Services, Tim O'bryan
Vice President, William J Irish
Vice President National Fidelity Practice Leader, Tom Huber
Vp Energy Casualty, Jeff Foering
Assistant Vice President Claims Operations, Scott Ostericher
Vice President Environmental Eands, Will Bell
Avp, Pat Wishman
Board Member, Barbara Allen
Board Member, Kaj Ahlmann
Board Member, Robert Viets
Board Member, Michael Angelina
Board Member, Charles Link
Member Board Of Directors, Bob Restrepo
Auditors: KPMG LLP

LOCATIONS

HQ: RLI Corp
9025 North Lindbergh Drive, Peoria, IL 61615
Phone: 309 692-1000   **Fax:** 309 692-1068
Web: www.rlicorp.com

PRODUCTS/OPERATIONS

2016 Revenues

	$ mil.	% of total
Net premiums earned		
Casualty	454	56
Property	152	19
Surety	121	15
Net investment income	53	6
Net realized gains	34	4
Total	**816**	**100**

Selected Products

Commercial
  Casualty
  Contractors bonding and insurance
  Executive products liability
  Marine
  Professional services
  Property
  Reinsurance
  Specialty programs
  Transportation
Personal
  Homeowners (Hawaii)
  Home business owners
  Personal umbrella
Surety Bonds

COMPETITORS

Arch Insurance Group
Baldwin & Lyons
CNA Financial
Chubb Limited
Crum & Forster
Great American Insurance Company
Great West Casualty
HCC Insurance
James River Group
Lancer Insurance
Lexington Insurance
Markel
Meadowbrook Insurance
Navigators
Philadelphia Insurance Companies
Safeco
Sompo International
The Hartford

HISTORICAL FINANCIALS

Company Type: Public

Income Statement   FYE: December 31

	ASSETS ($ mil.)	NET INCOME ($ mil.)	INCOME AS % OF ASSETS	EMPLOYEES
12/19	3,545	191	5.4%	905
12/18	3,105	64	2.1%	912
12/17	2,947	105	3.6%	902
12/16	2,777	114	4.1%	943
12/15	2,736	137	5.0%	902
Annual Growth	6.7%	8.6%	—	0.1%

2019 Year-End Financials

Debt ratio: 4.21%
Return on equity: 21.27%
Cash ($ mil.): 46
Current ratio: —
Long-term debt ($ mil.): —

No. of shares (mil.): 44
Dividends
Yield: 2.1%
Payout: 73.7%
Market value ($ mil.): 4,039

	STOCK PRICE ($) FY Close	P/E High/Low	PER SHARE ($) Earnings	Dividends	Book Value
12/19	90.02	23 15	4.23	1.91	22.18
12/18	68.99	55 40	1.43	1.87	18.13
12/17	60.66	26 21	2.36	2.58	19.33
12/16	63.13	27 21	2.59	2.79	18.74
12/15	61.75	20 15	3.12	2.75	18.91
Annual Growth	9.9%	— —	7.9%	(8.7%)	4.1%

ROBERT BOSCH LLC

Robert Bosch LLC is your one-stop shop for German-engineered auto parts appliances and power tools. The North American subsidiary of German giant Robert Bosch GmbH Bosch LLC makes and markets automotive original equipment and aftermarket products industrial drive and control technology packaging technology power tools home appliances security and communication systems thermotechnology and software solutions. Robert Bosch LLC's biggest area Mobility Solutions makes products aimed at the next generation of automobiles particularly around connectivity automation and electrification. Active since 1906 Bosch LLC has grown to around 70 primary North American locations.

Operations

Robert Bosch LLC comprises four reporting segments Mobility Solutions Industrial Technology Consumer Goods and Energy and Building Technology.

The Mobility Solutions segment represents two-thirds of sales and is active in injection technology and powertrain peripherals for internal-combustion engines powertrain electrification steering systems safety and driver-assistance systems car multimedia vehicle-to-vehicle and vehicle-to-infrastructure communication repair-shop concepts and technology and services.

The Industrial Control segment produces drive and control products and packaging technology and generates around 10% of sales. The Consumer Goods segment accounts for around a fifth of sales and consists of Robert Bosch's US power tools home appliances business. Energy and Building Technology segment (5% of sales) outfits buildings with heating ventilation and lighting infrastructure.

Geographic Reach

Robert Bosch LLC accounts for 15% of global sales. It has around 70 primary facilities in the US Canada and Mexico

Financial Performance

Robert Bosch LLC's sales grew 6% to $14.5 billion in 2018.

Strategy

One of Robert Bosch's major markets North America continues to receive substantial investment. It has expanded Mobility Solutions plants in Charleston and Anderson South Carolina and a dishwasher factory and central distribution center in New Bern North Carolina. It has also broke earth in the construction of a $120 million plant in Celaya Mexico. The 225000 sq. ft. factory will produce electronic control units which are used in connected mobility for the American market. Most recently Bosch opened a technology and innovation hub in Guadalajara Mexico.

EXECUTIVES

President Bosch Security Systems, Christopher P. Gerace
Cfo; Evp Controlling Finance And Administration, Maximiliane Straub
President And Ceo Bosch Rexroth Corporation, Berend Bracht
Regional President Gasoline Systems North America, Sujit Jain
Regional President Chassis Systems Control, D. Scott Winchip
Regional President Car Multimedia North America, Juergen Peters
Evp Original Equipment Sales Ford, Manfred Mueller
President And Ceo Bsh Home Appliances, Michael Traub
Regional President Automotive Electronics North America, Timothy (Tim) Frasier
Regional President Diesel Systems North America, Bernd Boisten
President, Mike Mansuetti
Regional President Robert Bosch Automotive Aftermarket Division, Odd Joergenrud
Evp Original Equipment Sales General Motors, Clesio Honma
Regional President Electrical Drives, Peter Denk
Regional President Starter Motors And Generators North America, Pres Lawhon
Regional President Bosch Engineering Group North America, Wayne (Keith) Andrews
President Robert Bosch Healthcare Systems Inc., Micha Kirchhoff
Vp Original Equipment Sales Chrysler, Paul Thomas
Vice President Business Development, Michael Barhaug
Vice President Purchasing, Scott Schafer
Vice President, Tim Williams
Vice President, Christine Zimmerman
Executive Vice President Finance And Administ, Cara Reynolds
Vice President Sales, George Kostopoulos
Senior Vice President, Martin Kueper
Vice President, Heiko Weller
Vice President Of Sales, Doug Arnold
Vice President Automotive Aftermarket, Karen Folger
Vice President Of Information Technology, James Puttick
National Sales Manager, Robert Dono
Vice President Of Sales, Rajesh Darji
Vice President Marketing And Business Strategy, Andreas Sambel
Vice President Sales Marketing And Aftermarket, Ross Long
Vice President Mergers And Acquisitions, Marcia Medendorp
Senior Vice President Sales, Stefan Thiel
Vice President And General Manager, Erwin Wieckowski
Chairman, Werner Struth

LOCATIONS

HQ: ROBERT BOSCH LLC
38000 HILLS TECH DR, FARMINGTON HILLS, MI 483313418
Phone: 248 876-1000
Web: WWW.BOSCH.US

PRODUCTS/OPERATIONS

2019 Sales

	% of total
Mobility Solutions	66
Consumer Goods	18
Industrial Technology	10
Energy and Building Technology	6
Other	3
Total	**100**

Selected Products

Automotive Technology
  Aftermarket
  Alternators
  Brake pads
  Car audio products
  Diesel parts
  Filters
  Fuel pumps
  Ignition products
  Oxygen sensors
  Spark plugs
  Spark plug wire sets
  Starters
  Wiper blades
  Original equipment
  Actuators
  Braking and chassis systems
  Car multimedia
  Electrical systems
  Electronic systems
  Powertrain systems - diesel
  Powertrain systems - gasoline
Consumer Goods and Building Technology
  Household appliances
  Cooktops
  Dishwashers
  Ovens
  Washers and dryers
  Power tools
  Angle grinders
  Belt sanders
  Circular saws
  Drill bits
  Drills
  Drywall drivers
  Impact wrenches
  Jigsaws
  Orbit sanders/polishers
  Planers
  Reciprocating saws
  Rotary hammers
  Routers
  Screwdriver bits and accessories
  Wet/dry vacuums
  Security Systems
  Access control
  Communications
  Fire detection
  Security management
  Video surveillance
  Thermotechnology
  Indoor climate control (heating and cooling and hot water production)
Industrial Technology
  Drive and control

Assembly
Electric drives and controls
Gears
Hydraulics
Linear motion
Pneumatics
Packaging
Confectionary cosmetics and chemicals
Packaging machines
Packaging services
Pharmaceuticals
Production tools
Air assembly tools
Cordless assembly tools
DC electric assembly tools
Electric assembly tools
Solar Energy
Crystalline PV modules
Solar cells
Thin-film modules
Wafers

COMPETITORS

AISIN World Corp.	LG Electronics
Advanced Security & Controls	Makita
	Molins
DENSO America	Motorcar Parts
Dana	NGK Spark Plugs
Delphi Automotive Systems	Neaton Auto Products
	Stanley Black and Decker
GE	Visteon
Hitachi Automotive Systems Americas	Whirlpool

HISTORICAL FINANCIALS

Company Type: Private

Income Statement   FYE: December 31

	REVENUE ($ mil.)	NET INCOME ($ mil.)	NET PROFIT MARGIN	EMPLOYEES
12/14	10,474	181	1.7%	12
12/10	6,810	326	4.8%	—
12/09	5,464	59	1.1%	—
Annual Growth	13.9%	25.1%	—	—

ROBERT W. BAIRD & CO. INCORPORATED

Employee-owned Robert W. Baird & Co. brings midwestern sensibility to the high-flying world of investment banking. The company offers brokerage asset management and investment banking services to middle-market corporations institutional clients and wealthy individuals and families. Its investment banking activities include underwriting and distributing corporate securities mergers and acquisition advisory and institutional sales and trading. The company also conducts equity research on more than 600 US firms. Baird manages more than $97 billion in client assets.

Operations

The company manages about 10 bond and equity mutual funds: Baird Advisors manages fixed income investments while Baird Investment Management handles the equities side. Baird also invests in private equity and venture capital.

Geographic Reach

The firm has more than 100 offices in North America Asia and Europe where it owns 48% of Baird UK. More than half of Baird's locations are wealth management offices in the US.

Sales and Marketing

Baird is the marketing name for Robert W. Baird & Co. Incorporated and its subsidiaries and affiliates worldwide.

Financial Performance

The company's revenues increased by 9% in 2011 and net income grew by 2%.

Strategy

The driving forces for the company's growth have been its wealth management and investment banking operations. Unlike many financial services firms Baird has been adding staff and opening new offices in the US.

The company has also turned to the East for its fortunes. Its private equity group recently has an office in Shanghai hoping to capitalize on China's increasingly business-friendly environment. The outpost focuses on small high-growth businesses that have been overlooked by other venture capitalists. Baird has also expanded its investment banking operations in the region.

In 2012 Baird formed a strategic alliance with Axis Capital the investment banking subsidiary of Axis Bank with an initial focus on cross-border mergers and acquisitions between India and Europe and India and the US.

Company Background

Founded in 1919 Baird had been majority-owned by Northwestern Mutual since 1982. However employees bought back the company's stock in a series of purchases that culminated in 2004.

EXECUTIVES

Coo, Russell P. (Russ) Schwei
Chief Investment Officer, Mary Ellen Stanek
Cfo, Terrance P. (Terry) Maxwell
President Private Wealth Management, Michael J. (Mike) Schroeder
Director Fixed Income Capital Markets, Patrick S. (Pat) Lawton
Managing Director And Director Institutional Equity Services, William W. (Bill) Mahler
Co-head Global Investment Banking, Brian S. Doyal
President And Coo, Steven G. (Steve) Booth
Co-head Global Investment Banking, Brian McDonagh
Director Risk Management, Mark A. Roble
Managing Partner Baird Capital, Gordon G. Pan
Head Global Equities And Director Equity Research, Jon A. Langenfeld
Cio, Timothy (Tim) Byrne
Senior Vice President, Jay Schwister
Vice President, Mark Zalewski
Vice President, Peter Klode
Vice President Vice President Administration, Thomas Seidcheck
Vice President, Joseph G Verdi
Senior Vice President, Dustin Hutter
Senior Vice President, Karen Heintz
Vice President Technology Product Manager, Lesley Augustine
Vice President, Tom Coburn
Senior Vice President Of Wealth Management Office, Paul McWane
Senior Vice President Supervisory Analyst, Keith Dorris

Vice President Information Technology Architect, Jim Cornelius
Vice President, Charles Galarza
Vice President, Robert Ferriman
Senior Vice President, Peter Hammond
Vice President Financial Analyst, Lori Jackson
Senior Vice President Investments, Cory Davis
Senior Vice President, Jayson C Bales
Senior Vice President And Senior Portfolio Manager, Daniel Tranchita
Senior Vice President, Michael Chorley
First Vice President, Trish M Young
Vice President, Janet Holsclaw
Vice President, Marla Regan
First Vice President Purchase And Sales, Dean Markofski
Vice President, Jonathan Dekker
Vice President, Dalena Welkomer
Vice President, Adrianne Limjoco
Vice President, Ryan Unthank
First Vice President, Eileen Wingenter
Assistant Vice President, Tonia G Morris
Senior Vice President, Richard Palm
Vice President, Dale Rudow
Assistant Vice President Compliance Officer, Heidi Mclemore
Compliance Officer Vice President, Edgar Sturkey
Assistant Vice President Private Asset Management, Robert Filetti
Vice President, Mike Monfeli
Vice President Financial Advisor, Dan Koth
Vice President Private Wealth Management, Rebecca Ross
Senior Vice President Private Wealth Management, Matthew H Schmitt
Senior Vice President, Shawn B Smith
Senior Vice President Public Relations, Angela Pittman Taylor
Assistant Vice President, Dominic Burrescia
Vice President, Abhishek Pulakanti
Senior Vice President, Douglas Stencel
First Vice President Tech And Systems, Dennis Weishan
Vice President Financial Advisor, Jeff Pedersen
Vice President And Art Director, Virginia Sunu
Vice President, Mike Malone
Vice President Wealth Management, Theresa Rynaski
Vice President Information Technology Project Services, Jim Whittet
Senior Vice President, Chuck Cairns
Vice President, Frank Downey
Vice President Financial Advisor, Blaine Gibson
Assistant Vice President And Marketing Specialist, Karen Sweeney
First Vice President, Bryan Fiene
Vice President, Mary E Levar
Vice President, Michael Halloran
Assistant Vice President, Genise Brandt
Senior Vice President, Baron Becker
Senior Vice President, Rob Zwiebel
Assistant Vice President, Heather Melzer
Assistant Vice President, Kathy Cobb
Senior Vice President Private Wealth Management, Bryan Sampson
Senior Vice President Internal Audit Director, David Cook
Vice President Investments, Thomas Olson
Senior Vice President Director Of Application Development, Jason Montague
Vice President Quantitative Analyst, Jordan Masnica
Vice President Investment Banking, Christopher Hildreth
Vice President, Alex Ballantine
Vice President Portfolio Analyst, Aaron Benson
Vice President, Suzanne King
Senior Vice President, Gail Bivens-rose
First Vice President, Terry Lineberger
Vice President And Financial Advisor, Jon Bolton

Vice President, Rich Nigro
Senior Vice President Investments, Ronald Christian
Vice President, Marcy Finley
Senior Vice President, Mike Parrott
Senior Vice President, David Schwarz
Vice President, Greg Pauly
Vice President Senior Research Associate, Luke Junk
Vice President, Chase Hinderstein
Vice President, Joe Vruwink
Vice President, Brian Ellenbecker
Assistant Vice President, Stacey Leigh
Assistant Vice President, Deanne Soetenga
Vice President, Frederick Jetter
Vice President Private Wealth Management, Robert King
Assistant Vice President, Bernadette Ross
Vice President, Ryan Cox
Vice President, Ralph Cefalu
Senior Vice President, Douglas Crandall
Vice President, Randall McLaughlin
Vice President, Richard Roesch
Senior Vice President, Orlando C Montesino
First Vice President Research, Ron Freisleben
Vice President Private Wealth Management, Phyllis Lovrien
Vice President Investment Banking, John Sun
Vice President, Brian Kelso
Vice President Investments, John Barnefield
Vice President, Tyson Eubanks
Vice President, Gavin Amato
Vice President Private Wealth Management, Larry Magid
Vice President Senior Estate Planner, Rick Holman
Vice President, Alex Lawhorn
Vice President, Jay Bitter
Vice President Investments, Frances D Bobbie
Assistant Vice President, Ginny Moye
Vice President, Peter Philpott
Senior Vice President, Mary Howard
Vice President, James Cain
Vice President Private Wealth Management, Wes Oliver
Assistant Vice President, Dale Jacques
Senior Vice President, Gerald Jarzabek
Senior Vice President, Jan Bayle
Assistant Vice President, Mary Zavaglia
Assistant Vice President, Judie Meriweather
Vice President Pwm, Clay Ryan
Assistant Vice President, Mary Walters
Senior Vice President And Associate General Counsel, Andrew Ketter
Vice President Resources Consultant Business Partner Human Capital, Lynn Rudolph
Senior Vice President Investments, Lewis Krinsky
Assistant Vice President, Michelle Hernandez
Vice President, Alice Ambrowiak
First Vice President, Kelly Kontowski
Vice President, Phillip Banta
Vice President And Senior Investment Consultant, Penny Cruse
Assistant Vice President, Robert Schultz
Senior Vice President, Joyce Linker
Vice President Pwm, George Gamez
Assistant Vice President Registered Client Relationship Specialist, Shawn Zoltak
Vice President Public Finance, Andrew Arndt
Senior Vice President, Robert Slater
Senior Vice President And Wealth Managaement, Brian Mcgrath
Financial Adviser Senior Vice President, Cliff Henrickson
Vice President Information Technology, Steve Acton
Senior Vice President Regional Director Private Wealth Management, William T Johnson
Vice President, Matthew Anderson

LOCATIONS

HQ: ROBERT W. BAIRD & CO. INCORPORATED
777 E WISCONSIN AVE FL 29, MILWAUKEE, WI 532025391
Phone: 414 765-3500
Web: WWW.BAIRDFINANCIALADVISOR.COM

PRODUCTS/OPERATIONS

Business Groups
Asset Management
Equity Capital Markets
Fixed Income Capital Markets
Private Equity
Private Wealth Management

COMPETITORS

Citigroup Global Markets	Piper Jaffray
Cowen Group	Raymond James Financial
Goldman Sachs	Stephens
Greenhill	Stifel Financial
Jefferies Group	Thomas Weisel Partners
Morgan Stanley	William Blair

HISTORICAL FINANCIALS

Company Type: Private

Income Statement				FYE: December 31
	ASSETS ($ mil.)	NET INCOME ($ mil.)	INCOME AS % OF ASSETS	EMPLOYEES
12/09	2,063	41	2.0%	2,298
12/08	1,080	36	3.4%	—
12/07	1,712	50	2.9%	—
Annual Growth	9.8%	(8.6%)	—	—

Robinson (C.H.) Worldwide, Inc.

C.H. Robinson Worldwide (CHRW) is a third-party logistics (3PL) provider. The company contracts with more than 78000 carriers including trucks trains ships and airplanes to arrange freight transportation for its 119000-plus customers in the food and beverage manufacturing and retail industries. Using its proprietary Navisphere platform the company handles about 18 million shipments annually. Besides transportation C.H. Robinson also offers logistics supply chain management and transportation management services. It operates worldwide but generates almost all of its revenue in the US.

HISTORY

In the early 1900s Charles H. Robinson began a produce brokerage in Grand Forks North Dakota. Robinson entered a partnership in 1905 with Nash Brothers the leading wholesaler in North Dakota and the company C.H. Robinson was born.

Robinson became president but soon relinquished control under mysterious circumstances (rumor had it he ran off with Annie Oakley). H. B. Finch took charge and by 1913 a new company Nash Finch became C.H. Robinson's sole owner.

As a subsidiary C.H. Robinson primarily procured produce for Nash Finch which helped it expand into Illinois Minnesota Texas and Wisconsin. To avoid FTC scrutiny over preferential treatment Nash Finch split CHR in two: C.H. Robinson Co. owned by C.H. Robinson employees which sold produce to Nash Finch warehouses; and C.H. Robinson Inc. owned by Nash Finch.

After WWII the interstate highway system and refrigerated trucks changed the industry. No longer dependent on railroads C.H. Robinson began charging for truck brokerage of perishables. The two companies formed by the 1940s split reunited under the C.H. Robinson name in the mid-1960s; Nash Finch kept a 25% stake in the company and sold the rest to employees. Not surprisingly Nash Finch wanted to divert C.H. Robinson profits to its other businesses so in 1976 C.H. Robinson employees bought out Nash Finch.

The next year D. R. "Sid" Verdoorn was named president and Looe Baker became chairman. They focused on increasing C.H. Robinson's data-processing capability and adding branch offices. In 1980 the Motor Carrier Act deregulated the transportation industry and C.H. Robinson entered the freight-contracting business acting as a middleman for all types of goods. The company grew rapidly from about 30 offices in 1980 to more than 60 in 1990.

As part of its overall effort to become a full-service provider C.H. Robinson formed its Intermodal Division (more than one mode of transport) in 1988. It also established an information services division (1991) and bought fruit juice concentrate distributor Daystar International (1993). By this time the company was working with more than 14000 shippers and moving more than 500000 shipments a year.

Meanwhile C.H. Robinson had ventured overseas with the launch of its international division in 1989. It entered Mexico in 1990 and added airfreight operations and international freight forwarding through the 1992 purchase of C.S. Green International. In 1993 C.H. Robinson picked up a 30% stake in French motor carrier Transeco (acquiring the rest later) and opened offices in Mexico Chile and Venezuela.

The company went public in 1997 and became C.H. Robinson Worldwide (CHRW). The next year Verdoorn who was CEO assumed the additional role of chairman. The following year the company acquired Argentina's Comexter transportation group to gain market share in South America and it expanded its European operation in 1999 through the purchase of Norminter a French third-party logistics provider. Much closer to home CHRW bought Eden Prairie-based Preferred Translocation Systems a logistics provider to LTL carriers and Chicago-based transportation provider American Backhaulers.

In 2000 CHRW partnered with PaperExchange.com Inc. the global e-business marketplace for the pulp and paper industry to provide an exclusive logistics service to PaperExchange.com members. CHRW continued to expand in 2002 with the purchase of Miami-based Smith Terminal Transportation Services. Verdoorn stepped down as CEO that year and company president John Wiehoff was promoted to replace him. Verdoorn retired at the end of 2006 and Wiehoff succeeded him as chairman.

The company acquired three US-based produce sourcing and marketing companies — FoodSource Inc. FoodSource Procurement and Epic Roots — in 2004 for a reported $270 million. That year CHRW added seven offices in China by acquiring a Dalian-based freight forwarder and in 2005 it gained operations in Germany Italy and the US by buying two freight forwarding companies Hirdes Group Worldwide and Bussini Transport. Also in 2005 CHRW bought US-based freight broker Payne Lynch & Associates as well as an India-based freight forwarder Triune. The following year (2006) the company acquired US-based LXSI Services a specialist in domestic airfreight and expedited ground transportation management that had gross revenue of about $25 million.

In mid-2008 CHRW acquired Transera International Holdings a project forwarding business based in Canada. Transera has office locations in Canada Dubai Singapore and the US and has annual revenues of about $125 million.

In 2009 the company purchased London-based Walker Logistics Overseas an international freight forwarder serving primarily the electronics telecommunications medical sporting goods and military industries. The acquisition expanded its capabilities in Asia-to-Europe trade and brought two key distribution gateways — London and Amsterdam. CHRW then expanded its produce distribution business even further in 2009 by opening a European-based produce sourcing company in France which will focus on bringing fresh produce from France Italy and Spain to North and South America Europe Asia and Middle Eastern countries. That same year CHRW acquired certain assets of International Trade & Commerce (ITC) a US customs brokerage company that specializes in warehousing distribution and services between the US and Mexico. Also in 2009 the company bought Rosemont Farms as well as Quality Logistics which provides logistics for produce transportation; both companies are based in Florida.

In 2010 CHRW expanded its transportation management services to India by building a new facility and control tower operations. The India-based facility was established to serve customers in South and Southeast Asia as well as in Pakistan and the Middle East.

CHRW divested its former payment services segment T-Chek (only 1% of total sales in 2012) in October 2012 to Electronic Funds Source LLC for $303 million in cash. The T-Chek unit provided such services as funds transfer and fuel purchasing management and CHRW made the deal to focus on its core transportation and logistics services.

In late 2012 CHRW acquired Phoenix International a provider of international ocean air and customs brokerage freight forwarding services. CHRW bought Phoenix for nearly $572 million in cash and roughly $63.5 million in newly-issued CHRW stock in a deal that sizably enhanced its international freight forwarding capabilities.

During that same time period CHRW swallowed up Apreo Logistics S.A. a freight forwarding firm based in Poland. The acquisition

strengthened the company's toehold in Europe and further diversified its modal offering.

EXECUTIVES

Cio, Chad M. Lindbloom, $590,000 total compensation
Chairman President And Ceo, John P. Wiehoff, $1,167,000 total compensation
Cfo, Andrew C. Clarke, $525,000 total compensation
President Robinson Fresh, James P. (Jim) Lemke, $210,000 total compensation
Chief Commercial Officer, Christopher J. (Chris) O'Brien, $500,000 total compensation
President Asia, Andy Wang
President Global Freight Forwarding, Michael J. (Mike) Short, $500,000 total compensation
President Managed Services, Jordan T. Kass
President North American Surface Transportation, Robert C. Biesterfeld
President Europe, Jeroen Eijsink
Vice President Global Forwarding Sales, Matt Mcinerney
Vice President Global Accounts, Richard Kapsner
National Account Manager, Jen Theisen
Vice President, Terry Bigaouette
Vice President Information Technology, Steve Enberg
National Account Manager, Andy Hutson
National Account Manager, Matt Lapolice
National Account Manager, Michelle Clayton
Vice President Asia Global Forwarding, John Chen
Vice President Global Sales, Brian Tonn
Vice President Investor Relations And Treasury, Robert Houghton
Vice President Oceana, Andrew Coldrey
Vice President Tax And Risk Management, Nathan Zietlow
Vice President Corporate Business Development, Francisco Guzman
Vice President Technology, Kollen Glynn
Treasurer, Troy A Renner, age 56
Board Member, Trey Bullard
Board Member, James Stake
Board Member, Scott Anderson
Auditors: DELOITTE & TOUCHE LLP

LOCATIONS

HQ: Robinson (C.H.) Worldwide, Inc.
14701 Charlson Road, Eden Prairie, MN 55347
Phone: 952 937-8500   **Fax:** 952 937-6714
Web: www.chrobinson.com

2018 Sales

	$ mil.	% of total
United States	4,370	86
Other locations	2,260	14
Total	**16,631**	**100**

PRODUCTS/OPERATIONS

2018 Sales

By Segment	$ mil.	% of total
NAST	11,793	68
Robinson Fresh	2,480	14
Global Forwarding	2,536	14
All Other & Corporate	647	4
Eliminations	(825.8)	-
Total	**16,631**	**100**

2018 Sales

By Product	$ mil.	% of total
Transportation	15,515	93
Sourcing	1,115	7
Total	**16,631**	**100**

Selected Services

Air
Intermodal
Less-than-truckload
Logistics
Customs brokerage
Transportation management services
Warehousing services
Ocean
Truckload

COMPETITORS

APL Logistics	J.B. Hunt
CEVA Logistics	Kuehne + Nagel
Cass Information	International
Systems	Landstar Inway
DHL	Penske Truck Leasing
Expeditors	Ryder System
Fresh Del Monte	Schneider Logistics
Produce	UPS Supply Chain
Hub Group	Solutions

HISTORICAL FINANCIALS

Company Type: Public

Income Statement				FYE: December 31
	REVENUE ($ mil.)	NET INCOME ($ mil.)	NET PROFIT MARGIN	EMPLOYEES
12/19	15,309	576	3.8%	15,427
12/18	16,631	664	4.0%	15,262
12/17	14,869	504	3.4%	15,074
12/16	13,144	513	3.9%	14,125
12/15	13,476	509	3.8%	13,159
Annual Growth	3.2%	3.1%	—	4.1%

2019 Year-End Financials

Debt ratio: 26.62%
Return on equity: 35.33%
Cash ($ mil.): 447
Current ratio: 1.70
Long-term debt ($ mil.): 1,092

No. of shares (mil.): 134
Dividends
  Yield: 2.5%
  Payout: 41.9%
Market value ($ mil.): 10,549

	STOCK PRICE ($) FY Close	P/E High/Low		PER SHARE ($)		
				Earnings	Dividends	Book Value
12/19	78.20	22	18	4.19	2.01	12.39
12/18	84.09	21	17	4.73	1.88	11.62
12/17	89.09	25	18	3.57	1.81	10.22
12/16	73.26	22	17	3.59	1.74	8.90
12/15	62.02	22	17	3.51	1.57	8.02
Annual Growth	6.0%		—	4.5%	6.4%	11.5%

Ross Stores Inc

Ross wants you to dress for less. An off-price apparel retailer (along with TJX Cos. and Kohl's) and home fashion chain Ross operates more than 1545 Ross Dress for Less and nearly 260 dd's Discounts stores that sell closeout merchandise including men's women's and children's clothing at prices well below those of department and specialty stores. While apparel accounts for more than half of sales the company also sells small furnishings home accents bed and bath beauty toys and games luggage gourmet food cookware and accessories. Featuring the Ross "Dress for Less" trademark the chain targets 18- to 54-year-old white-collar shoppers from primarily middle-income households. Ross and dd's stores are located in strip malls in about 60 states and mostly in the western US and Guam.

Operations

Ross Stores operates two brands of off-price retail apparel and home fashion stores: Ross

Dress for Less and dd's DISCOUNTS. Ross does a roaring trade in off-price apparel and home fashion chain offering first-quality in-season name-brand and designer apparel as well as accessories footwear and home decor at between 20%-60% off department and specialty store regular prices.

dd's DISCOUNTS offers brand-name apparel at a 20%-70% discount.

The company generates a little over a quarter of its revenue from its Ladies' products. Home Accents and Bed & Bath products combined account for another 25%. Men's apparel accessories lingerie fine jewelry and fragrances and shoes collectively generate 40% of the company's revenue. The rest is generated from children's apparel.

Ross Stores has one reportable segment. The Company's operations include only activities related to off-price retailing in stores throughout the United States.

Geographic Reach

Almost half of California-based Ross' stores are located in the states of California Texas and Florida. The company's distribution centers and warehouses are in Pennsylvania South Carolina California and Texas. Aside from the territory of Guam Ross does not have an international presence.Almost half of California-based Ross' stores are located in the states of California Texas and Florida. The company's distribution centers and warehouses are in Pennsylvania South Carolina California and Texas. Aside from the territory of Guam Ross does not have an international presence.

dd's DISCOUNTS has about 260 locations in about 20 states are located in strip shopping centers in urban and suburban neighborhoods.

The retailer operates six distribution processing facilities: three in California two in South Carolina and one in Pennsylvania. These distribution centers are the sole source of its stores merchandise. Additionally the discounter owns four and leases five other warehouse facilities for packaway storage. To distribute merchandise to stores on a regular basis Ross Stores enlists the help of third-party cross docks. Shipments are made by contract carriers to stores between three and six times per week depending on the location.

Sales and Marketing

Ross Stores relies primarily on television as a medium to share the Ross Dress for Less value proposition with its current and potential customers. The company believes that television advertising is the most efficient and cost-effective medium while it continues to use additional channels to build brand awareness. Advertising for its dd's DISCOUNTS stores is focused on new store grand openings and on radio. The company also employs social media to communicate its brand position.

Advertising costs for fiscal 2019 2018 and 2017 were $74 million $79.9 million and $76.4 million respectively.

Financial Performance

Ross Stores' annual sales have steadily risen since 2015 thanks to rapid store expansion and steady same-store sale growth. Its net income has also risen in the same period peaking this year at $1.7 billion.

Revenue increased to $16 billion in fiscal 2019 an almost 7% increase from the year prior driven primarily by continued store growth. Comparable store sales also increased by a solid 3%.

Net income was $1.7 billion in 2019 an increase from $1.6 billion in 2018 primarily due to higher cost of goods sold partially offset by lower SG&A expenses and higher interest income.

Cash provided by operating activities was $2.2 billion in 2020 while investing activities used $555 million mostly for property and equipment. Financing activities used another $1.7 billion mainly due to repurchase of common stock and dividends. The company ended 2020 with $1.4 billion in cash and cash equivalents.

Strategy

Ross Stores' growth strategy is based on successfully expanding their off-price model in current markets and in new geographic regions.

Ross Stores' real estate strategy in 2020 is to primarily open stores in states where they currently operate to increase their market penetration and leverage overhead and advertising expenses as a percentage of sales in each market. The company also expect to continue store expansion in newer markets in 2020. Important considerations in evaluating a new store location in both newer and more established markets are the availability and quality of potential sites demographic characteristics competition and population density of the local trade area.

The company's expansion strategy is to open additional stores based on market penetration local demographic characteristics competition expected store profitability and the ability to leverage overhead expenses. They continually evaluate opportunistic real estate acquisitions and opportunities for potential new store locations.

Company Background

Ross Stores origins date back to the 1950s when the Ross family founded the company in the San Francisco area. In 1982 two retailing veterans Stuart Moldaw (founder of Country Casuals and The Athletic Shoe Factory) and Donald Rowlett (creator of Woolworth's off-price subsidiary J. Brannam) led the acquisition of the company with the goal of creating an off-price chain. The chain's first non-California store in Reno Nevada (much of the chain's expansion came through the acquisition of existing strip mall stores) was added in 1983. Another 40 stores were added in 1984. The company went public in 1985 to help fund its expansion and extended its reach to include Colorado Florida Georgia New Mexico and Oregon; that year it opened 41 stores. In 2004 Ross opened its first three dd's Discounts stores in Vallejo San Leandro and Fresno California.

HISTORY

In 1957 the Ross family founded Ross Stores and opened its first junior department store; by 1982 there were six of the stores in the San Francisco area. That year two retailing veterans Stuart Moldaw (founder of Country Casuals and The Athletic Shoe Factory) and Donald Rowlett (creator of Woolworth's off-price subsidiary J. Brannam) led the acquisition of the company. Moldaw (chairman) and Rowlett (president) wanted to create an off-price chain in California where — despite the success such endeavors were having in the rest of the country — such

stores were largely absent. The duo intended to establish a foothold by saturating California markets before competitors muddied the waters.

They restocked the stores with brand-name men's women's and children's apparel shoes accessories and domestics merchandise at reduced prices. Before the end of 1982 they opened two more Ross "Dress for Less" stores; the next year 18 more were added including the chain's first non-California store in Reno Nevada (much of the chain's expansion came through the acquisition of existing strip mall stores). Another 40 stores were added in 1984.

The company went public in 1985 to help fund its expansion and extended its reach to include Colorado Florida Georgia New Mexico and Oregon; that year it opened 41 stores.

In August 2004 Ross opened its first three dd's DISCOUNTS stores in Vallejo San Leandro and Fresno California. The retailer moved its headquarters from Newark California to Pleasanton in mid-2004 and then sold the Newark property for about $17 million.

EXECUTIVES

HQ: Ross Stores Inc
   5130 Hacienda Drive, Dublin, CA 94568-7579
Phone: 925 965-4400
Web: www.rossstores.com

2017 Stores

	No.
California	364
Texas	222
Florida	185
Arizona	74
Illinois	62
Georgia	56
North Carolina	45
Pennsylvania	44
Washington	42
Virginia	38
Colorado	33
Nevada	33
Tennessee	31
Oregon	30
Maryland	24
Oklahoma	23
South Carolina	23
Alabama	23
Missouri	21
Louisiana	18
Hawaii	17
Utah	17
New Jersey	13
Wisconsin	13
New Mexico	12
Idaho	11
Kansas	10
Kentucky	9
Indiana	9
Mississippi	8
Arkansas	8
Montana	6
Wyoming	3
Delaware	2
District of Columbia	1
Guam	1
North Dakota	1
South Dakota	1
Total	**1,533**

PRODUCTS/OPERATIONS

2017 Sales

	% of total
Women's apparel	28
Home accents bed & bath	25
Accessories lingerie fine jewelry & fragrances	13
Men's apparel	13
Shoes	13
Children's apparel	8
Total	**100**

2017 Stores

	No.
Ross Dress for Less	1,340
dd's DISCOUNTS	193
Total	**1,533**

Selected Merchandise

Bed and bath
Children's apparel
Cookware
Educational toys
Fine jewelry
Fragrances
Gourmet foods
Home accents
Ladies' apparel
   Accessories
   Dresses
   Junior
   Lingerie
   Maternity
   Misses sportswear
   Petites
   Women's World
Luggage
Men's apparel
   Traditional men's
   Young men's

Shoes
Small electronics
Small furnishings
Sporting goods and exercise equipment

COMPETITORS

Ascena Retail	Fred's
Big Lots	Kmart
Burlington Coat	Kohl's
Factory	TJX Companies
Cato	Tailored Brands
Charming Shoppes	Target Corporation
Family Dollar Stores	Wal-Mart

HISTORICAL FINANCIALS

Company Type: Public

Income Statement

FYE: February 1

	REVENUE ($ mil.)	NET INCOME ($ mil.)	NET PROFIT MARGIN	EMPLOYEES
02/20	16,039	1,660	10.4%	92,500
02/19	14,983	1,587	10.6%	88,100
02/18*	14,134	1,362	9.6%	82,700
01/17	12,866	1,117	8.7%	78,600
01/16	11,940	1,020	8.5%	77,800
Annual Growth	**7.7%**	**12.9%**	**—**	**4.4%**

*Fiscal year change

2020 Year-End Financials

Debt ratio: 3.35%
Return on equity: 49.98%
Cash ($ mil.): 1,351
Current ratio: 1.27
Long-term debt ($ mil.): 312

No. of shares (mil.): 356
Dividends
   Yield: 0.0%
   Payout: 22.1%
Market value ($ mil.): 40,027

	STOCK PRICE ($) FY Close	P/E High/Low		PER SHARE ($) Earnings	Dividends	Book Value
02/20	112.19	26	19	4.60	1.02	9.42
02/19	91.73	24	17	4.26	0.90	8.98
02/18*	79.08	24	15	3.55	0.64	8.03
01/17	65.33	24	18	2.83	0.54	7.01
01/16	56.26	42	18	2.51	0.47	6.14
Annual Growth	**18.8%**			**16.4%**	**21.4%**	**11.3%**

*Fiscal year change

Ryder System, Inc.

When it comes to commercial vehicles and distribution Ryder System wants to be the designated driver. The company's Fleet Management Solutions (FMS) segment acquires manages and maintains fleet vehicles for commercial customers. Similarly the Supply Chain Solutions (SCS) segment provides logistics and supply chain services from industrial start to finish?raw material supply to product distribution. SCS also offers dedicated contract carriage service by supplying trucks drivers and management and administrative services to customers on a contract basis. Ryder's worldwide fleet of more than 200000 vehicles ranges from tractor-trailers to light-duty trucks and more recently electric trucks. The majority of its revenue comes from the US.

Operations

Ryder operates through three main divisions: Fleet Management Solutions (FMS) Supply Chain Solutions (SCS) and Dedicated Transportation Solutions (DTS).

Fleet Management Solutions provides full-service leasing contract maintenance and contract-related maintenance for commercial truck fleets as well as commercial truck tractor and trailer rentals. FMS accounts for nearly 60% of revenue and operates in North America and the UK.

Supply Chain Solutions offers integrated logistics solutions including distribution management dedicated transportation and professional services primarily in North America. It accounts for more than 25% of revenue.

Dedicated Transportation Solutions accounts for some 15% of sales and provides vehicles and drivers as part of a dedicated transportation solution in the US.

Overall revenue from services represents around 50% of Ryder's total sales; lease and rental revenue accounts for more than 40%; and the remaining revenue comes from fuel services sales.

Geographic Reach

Based in Miami FL Ryder operates in North America (the US Canada Mexico and Puerto Rico) Europe (Germany and the UK) and Asia (Singapore). The US accounts for around 90% of its revenue.

Sales and Marketing

Ryder's Fleet Management Services customers in the US range from small businesses to large national enterprises operating in a wide variety of industries the most significant of which are food and beverage industrial transportation and warehousing and business and personal services.

Financial Performance

Ryder System has grown significantly over the last several years with a 36% increase in sales since 2015. On the other hand the company's net income has fluctuated and suffered an overall decrease of over 300%. In 2019 total revenue increased 6% to $8.9 billion and operating revenue increased 8% to $7.2 billion.

Total revenue and operating revenue increased due to new business and higher volumes in all segments. Total and operating revenue growth also reflects the acquisition of MXD in the second quarter of 2018.

The company posted a net loss of $24.4 million a $260.2 million loss from the previous year mainly due to the increase of their operating expenses by $943.6 million to about $9.0 billion.

Cash at the end of fiscal 2019 was $73.6 million an increase of $5.5 million from the prior year. Cash from operations contributed $2.1 billion to the coffers while investing activities used $3.2 billion mainly for purchases of property plant and equipment and acquisitions. Financing activities provided $1.1 billion from borrowings offset by dividends paid to stockholders and the company's stock repurchase program.

Strategy

Ryder's mission is to provide innovative fleet management and supply chain solutions that are reliable safe and efficient enabling its customers to deliver on their promises.

The company seeks to deliver valuable solutions that will compel customers to outsource their fleet management and supply chain needs to them. Their primary strategy is to grow their fleet management and supply chain outsourcing services by targeting those companies not currently outsourcing their fleet-related and logistics services as well as companies who have outsourced to other providers by offering innovative solutions operational excellence best in class talent and information technology.

This strategy is supported by offering innovative products solutions and support services that will create and strengthen customer relationships; delivering operational excellence through continuous productivity and process improvements; attracting developing and retaining the best talent; and deploying technology that will enable growth while improving operational efficiencies.

Company Background

Ryder Truck Rental was founded in Miami by Jim Ryder in 1933. It was the first truck leasing company in the US with operations in four southern states until 1952 when it bought Great Southern Trucking (renamed Ryder Truck Lines) and doubled its size. In 1955 the year it went public as Ryder System Ryder bought South Carolina-based Carolina Fleets and Yellow Rental (a leasing service operating in the Northeast). More acquisitions over the next decade extended Ryder's truck rental business across the US and into Canada. Ryder Truck Lines was sold to International Utilities in 1965.

HISTORY

Ryder Truck Rental founded in Miami by Jim Ryder in 1933 was the first truck leasing company in the US. It rented trucks in four southern states until 1952 when it bought Great Southern Trucking (renamed Ryder Truck Lines) doubling its size. In 1955 the year it went public as Ryder System Ryder bought Carolina Fleets (a South Carolina trucking company) and Yellow Rental (a northeastern leasing service). More purchases over the next decade extended its truck rental business across the US and into Canada. Ryder Truck Lines was sold to International Utilities in 1965.

EXECUTIVES

Evp And Cfo, Art A. Garcia, age 58, $479,783 total compensation
Chairman And Ceo, Robert E. Sanchez, age 54, $785,225 total compensation
Evp And Chief Marketing Officer, Karen M. Jones, age 57
Evp Chief Legal Officer And Secretary, Robert D. Fatovic, age 54, $392,650 total compensation
President Global Fleet Management Solutions, Dennis C. Cooke, age 55, $543,750 total compensation
Evp And Chief Sales Officer, John J. Gleason, age 64
President Dedicated Transport Solutions, John J. Diez, $411,000 total compensation
President Global Supply Chain Solutions, J. Steven (Steve) Sensing
Svp And Cio, Melvin (Mel) Kirk
Vice President Technical Services And Operations, Michael Pivowar
Vice President Audit Services, Clifford Zoller
Vice President Information Technology, Greg Knott
Senior Vice President And Treasurer, Daniel Susik
Vice President Compensation And Benefits, Boon Ooi
Vice President Sales Hci, Dave Sims
Vice President Chief Compliance Officer, Pilar Caballero

Assistant Vice President Accounting, Maria Milian
Vice President Sales And Marketing, Doug Wilkinson
Vice President Talent Management And Human Resources, Amparo Bared
Vice President And General Manager Global Transportation Management, Todd Carter
Vice President Asset Management, Eugene Tangney
Vice President Business Development, Mark Swenson
Vice President Business Development, Ron Mullowney
Vice President Of Tax, Ben Schmoyer
Vice President Information Technology, Mike Parvor
Vice President Business Development, Tim Sweeney
Vice President Information Technology, Stephen Hitchings
Vice President Business Development, Paul Skinner
Executive Vice President Chief Human Resources Officer, Gregory Greene
Vice President Automotive, Dick Jennings
Vice President Of Global Talent Management, Amparo Bared-Dukenik
Senior Vice President National Sales, John Deris
Vice President Compensation And Benefits, Charles R Patton
Vice President Of Sales, Chris Fairey
Vice President National Sales, William Toerpe
Senior Vice President Sales And Solutions, Todd Skiles
Vice President National Sales, Norm Veilleux
Vice President Business Development And Marketing, Jeffrey Boudreau
Vice President, Eugenio Sevilla-Sacasa
Vice President Supply Chain Excellence, Gary Allen
Vice President Supply Chain Solutions, Steve Thoke
Vp Operations, Bryce Kinsley
Vice President Of Business Development, Dave Walby
Vice President Sales And Marketing, Chuck Lounsbury
Senior Vice President And General Manager Supply Chains Solutions, Tom Jones
Vice President International Supply Chain Solutions, Gene Sevilla
Vice President Information Technology Strategic Operations, Jonathan Mish
Vice President And General Manager, Gerald Brown
Director Of Government Relations, Joshua Grodin
Vice President Audit Services, Sanjay Singh
Vice President Finance, Bret Alger
Vice President Technical Services And Operations, Mike Pivower
Vice President And Controller, Frank Mullen
Vice President Corporate Strategy And Investor Relations, Bob Brunn
Vice President Global Marketing, Samuel H Johnson
Vice President Director Of Business Development Lease Finance, Scott M Mishoe
Senior Vice President And Chief Information Officer, Rajeev Ravindran
Vice President And Managing Director Latin America, Eugene Sevilla-Sacasa
National Account Manager, David Gifford
Vice President Compensation And Benefits, Nicole Turner
Executive Vice President, Patrick Floyd
Vice President Finance, Lee Simmerman
Vice President Corporate Communications, Amy Federman
Board Member, Robert Eck
Board Member, Luis Nieto
Board Member, Abbie Smith
Board Member, Tamara Lundgren
Assistant Treasurer, Mary Aderholdt

Board Member, Hansel Tookes
Board Member, John Berra
Board Member, Robert Hagemann
Board Member, Follin E Smith
Member Board Of Directors, Dmitri Stockton
Vice Chairman Of The Board And U Box Project Manager, Sam Shoen
Auditors: PricewaterhouseCoopers LLP

LOCATIONS

HQ: Ryder System, Inc.
  11690 N.W., 105th Street, Miami, FL 33178
Phone: 305 500-3726
Web: www.ryder.com

2018 Sales

	$ mil.	% of total
US	7,387	88
Canada	464	5
Europe	335	4
Mexico	198	3
Singapore	23	-
Total	**8,409**	**100**

PRODUCTS/OPERATIONS

2018 Sales

	$ mil.	% of total
Fleet Management Solutions	5,255	58
Supply Chain Solutions	2,398	27
Dedicated Transportation Solutions	1,333	15
Eliminations	(577.5)	-
Total	**8,409**	**100**

2017 Sales

	$ mil.	% of total
Services revenue	4,280	51
Lease and rental revenue	3	42
Fuel services revenue	620	7
Total	**8,409**	**100**

Selected Services

Fleet Management Solutions
  Commercial rental
  Contract maintenance
  Full service leasing
  Used vehicles
Supply Chain Solutions
  Distribution management
  Transportation management
Dedicated Contract Carriage

COMPETITORS

ArcBest	Penske Truck Leasing
Barloworld Handling	Schenker Inc.
C.H. Robinson	Schneider National
Worldwide	UPS
FedEx	UniGroup
J.B. Hunt	YRC Worldwide
Landstar System	

HISTORICAL FINANCIALS

Company Type: Public

Income Statement				FYE: December 31
	REVENUE ($ mil.)	NET INCOME ($ mil.)	NET PROFIT MARGIN	EMPLOYEES
12/19	8,925	(24)	—	39,900
12/18	8,409	273	3.3%	39,600
12/17	7,329	790	10.8%	36,100
12/16	6,786	262	3.9%	34,500
12/15	6,571	304	4.6%	33,100
Annual Growth	**8.0%**	**—**	**—**	**4.8%**

2019 Year-End Financials

Debt ratio: 54.75%
Return on equity: (-0.91%)
Cash ($ mil.): 73
Current ratio: 0.59
Long-term debt ($ mil.): 6,770

No. of shares (mil.): 53
Dividends
  Yield: 4.0%
  Payout: 84.6%
Market value ($ mil.): 2,894

STOCK PRICE ($)	P/E		PER SHARE ($)		
FY Close	High/Low		Earnings	Dividends	Book Value
12/19	54.31	—	—	(0.47)	2.20	46.48
12/18	48.15	17	9	5.17	2.12	54.79
12/17	84.17	6	4	14.87	1.80	53.54
12/16	74.44	17	10	4.90	1.70	38.39
12/15	56.83	17	9	5.71	1.56	37.15
Annual Growth	(1.1%)	—	—	—	9.0%	5.8%

RYMAN HOSPITALITY PROPERTIES, INC.

Ryman Hospitality Properties (formerly Gaylord Entertainment) may be hollerin' for attention in the hospitality game but it's no corporate hayseed. Its properties consist of resort hotels tethered closely to attractions that appeal to the meetings and conventions market. They include the Gaylord Opryland Resort & Convention Center in Nashville the Gaylord Palms Resort in Florida (close to Disney World) the Gaylord Texan Resort near Dallas and the Gaylord National Resort and Convention Center in the Washington DC area. Ryman's hotels are managed by hotel giant Marriott.

HISTORY

The origins of Gaylord Entertainment can be traced back to the Oklahoma Publishing Co. a newspaper publishing company founded by Edward K. Gaylord Ray Dickinson and Roy McClintock in 1903. The publisher of The Daily Oklahoman Oklahoma Publishing branched into radio in 1928 with the purchase of Oklahoma City radio station WKY. With its 1949 creation of Oklahoma City television station WKY-TV Oklahoma Publishing made the leap into television.

Edward K. Gaylord died in 1974 at the age of 101 and his son Edward L. Gaylord was appointed CEO. Under his leadership the company purchased Opryland USA in 1983 — an acquisition that netted it the Grand Ole Opry Opryland Themepark and the Opryland Hotel. Opryland USA also launched country music cable network The Nashville Network that year.

In 1991 the increasingly diverse Oklahoma Publishing spun off its entertainment and broadcast holdings in the form of public company Gaylord Entertainment which established its headquarters in Nashville Tennessee. Gaylord Entertainment acquired a majority interest in cable music network Country Music Television (CMT) the same year. It later expanded CMT into Latin America Asia and the Pacific Rim. CMT also made a brief foray into Europe but that initiative was ended in 1998.

Facing a consolidating entertainment and media landscape Gaylord sold The Nashville Network and the US operations of CMT to Westinghouse (now CBS) in 1997. It also sold television station KSTW that year. The company expanded its reach into Christian music with the purchase of Word Entertainment and its 1997 acquisition of Blanton Harrell Entertainment gave Gaylord a presence in artist management. Terry London was appointed CEO in 1997.

The company closed its Opryland theme park in 1998 in the face of declining attendance and broke ground at the same site for the Opry Mills entertainment shopping and restaurant complex (opened 2000). Gaylord also purchased a Nashville Ramada Inn in 1998 (later renaming it Radisson Hotel at Opryland). With its 1998 acquisition of Paris-based Pandora Investment Gaylord branched into film distribution.

In 1999 the company formed Opryland Hospitality Group to oversee expansion of the Opryland hotel concept across the US. It also sold its last television station KTVT in Dallas/Fort Worth to CBS. Edward K. Gaylord II succeeded his father as chairman in 1999. That year the company launched its Internet division GETdigitalmedia (later renamed Gaylord Digital) and moved online with the purchase of Christian Web sites Musicforce.com and Lightsource.com. Later the same year the company expanded its Internet presence with the purchase of Songs.com a music Web site focused on independent artists. But in late 2000 the company announced it would close its Internet unit. Also in 2000 the company bought Corporate Magic a firm focused on producing entertainment events for corporate audiences.

At the end of 2000 Gaylord sold Musicforce.com to Christian Book Distributors. Following that sale it sold Lightsource.com to LifeAudio.com in early 2001. That year the company sold its film and television production units and announced a restructuring in order to cut costs. It also renamed Opryland Hotels to Gaylord Opryland while expanding into Texas and Florida. Colin Reed was appointed CEO in 2001.

Between 2001 and 2003 Gaylord Entertainment sold Word Entertainment to Warner Music Group the Opry Mills shopping and restaurant complex to The Mills Corporation the Acuff-Rose Music Publishing business to Sony/ATV two of its Nashville radio stations to Cumulus Media and its majority interest in the Oklahoma City Redhawks minor league baseball team.

Edward L. Gaylord officially retired from the company in 2003 at age 83. Also that year the company significantly expanded its hospitality business with the purchase of ResortQuest a vacation and condominium property management firm. In 2004 the Gaylord family sold more than half its shares in the company making Gabelli Funds the majority owner.

In 2005 Gaylord acquired 50% of Corporate Magic a Dallas-based provider of production support for corporate meetings and events. It did so to support its meeting and convention facilities.

The company unloaded its minority interest in minor league hockey team the Nashville Predators in 2005. Two years later it sold ResortQuest to a subsidiary of Leucadia National Corp. for $35 million. Also in 2007 it sold its interest in sporting goods store operator Bass Pro Group. In 2008 the company opened the Gaylord National Resort and Convention Center in the Washington DC area. The property has some 2000 rooms and approximately 450000 square feet of meeting space.

Also in 2008 Gaylord terminated plans to acquire the Westin La Cantera Resort in San Antonio for about $253 million citing a tough economic environment. In addition the 2008 sale of its ResortQuest subsidiary an online booking service in vacation rentals property management and resort real estate sales fit the company's strategy of selling off assets that aren't related to its Grand Ole Opry or its operations in the meetings and convention market.

In 2009 the company responded to weak earnings by cutting approximately 500 jobs across all areas of the business. Gaylord reported steep dip in profits in 2010 primarily due to harsh flooding in Nashville when the Cumberland River rose to historic levels flowing over protective levees. The flood resulted in property damage and temporary closures at its properties in Nashville causing lost revenues and an increase in expenses. Also in 2010 Gaylord sold its 50% stake in Corporate Magic back to that company's CEO.

The company changed its name to Ryman Hospitality Properties in 2012. It also converted to an REIT and sold the Gaylord brand to Marriott which now manages Ryman's hotel properties and certain other entertainment holdings.

EXECUTIVES

Evp Ryman Hospitality Properties; President Opry Entertainment Group, Stephen G. (Steve) Buchanan
Chairman And Ceo, Colin V. Reed, age 72, $782,830 total compensation
Svp Investments Design And Construction, Bennett D. Westbrook, age 53, $318,447 total compensation
President And Cfo, Mark Fioravanti, age 58, $469,407 total compensation
Svp Asset Management, Patrick Chaffin, age 46, $274,975 total compensation
Svp General Counsel And Secretary, Scott J. Lynn, age 46, $364,876 total compensation
Senior Vice President And Corporate Controller, Jennifer Hutcheson
Vice President Information Technology, Sharon Asmus
Vice President, James Chamblin
Vice President Human Resources, Shawn Smith
Svp Of Marketing, Laura Hollingsworth
Board Member, Michael J Bender
Board Member, Patrick Moore
Member Board Of Directors, Fazal Merchant
Auditors: ERNST & YOUNG LLP NASHVILLE

LOCATIONS

HQ: RYMAN HOSPITALITY PROPERTIES, INC. 1 GAYLORD DR, NASHVILLE, TN 372141207
Phone: 615 316-6000
Web: WWW.RYMANHP.COM

PRODUCTS/OPERATIONS

2015 Sales

	$ mil.	% of total
Hospitality	994	91
Entertainment (previously Opry and Attractions)	97	9
Total	1,092	100

2015 Sales

	$ mil.	% of total
Food and beverage	461	42
Rooms	404	37
Other hotel revenue	129	12
Entertainment (previously Opry and Attractions)	97	9
Total	1,092	100

Select Operations

Hospitality
Gaylord Opryland Resort & Convention Center (Tennessee)
Gaylord Palms Resort & Convention Center (Florida)

Gaylord Texan Resort & Convention Center
Radisson Hotel at Opryland (Tennessee)
Attractions
Gaylord Springs Golf Links (golf club Tennessee)
General Jackson Showboat
Grand Ole Opry
Ryman Auditorium
Wildhorse Saloon
WSM-AM

COMPETITORS

CKX
Caesars Entertainment
Disney Parks & Resorts
Elvis Presley Enterprises
Herschend Entertainment
Hershey Entertainment
Hilton Worldwide
Kennywood
Las Vegas Sands
Live Nation Entertainment
MGM Resorts
Marriott
New York Convention Center Operating Corporation
SeaWorld
Welk Group

HISTORICAL FINANCIALS

Company Type: Private

Income Statement				FYE: December 31
	ASSETS ($ mil.)	NET INCOME ($ mil.)	INCOME AS % OF ASSETS	EMPLOYEES
12/16	2,405	159	6.6%	177,000
12/15	2,331	111	4.8%	—
12/14	2,413	126	5.2%	—
12/13	2,424	113	4.7%	—
Annual Growth	(0.3%)	12.0%	—	—

S & T Bancorp Inc (Indiana, PA)

S&T Bancorp is the bank holding company for S&T Bank which boasts nearly $5 billion in assets and serves customers from some 60 branch offices in western Pennsylvania. Targeting individuals and local businesses the bank offers such standard retail products as checking savings and money market accounts CDs and credit cards. Business loans including commercial mortgages make up more than 80% of the company's loan portfolio. The bank also originates residential mortgages construction loans and consumer loans. Through subsidiaries S&T Bank sells life disability and commercial property/casualty insurance provides investment management services and advises the Stewart Capital Mid Cap Fund.

Operations

S&T Bancorp operates through three main business segments: Community Banking which offers traditional banking services and commercial and consumer loans; Wealth Management which boasts $2 billion in assets under management and administration and provides brokerage services trust and custodial services and investment advisory for affluent individuals and insti-

tutions; and Insurance which offers commercial property and casualty insurance group life and health coverage employee benefit services and personal insurance products through S&T Insurance Group LLC.

Its S&T Bancholding subsidiary provides investment services in the Wealth Management segment while its Stewart Capital Advisors subsidiary provides investment advisory services in the segment.

Overall S&T Bancorp generated 72% of its total revenue from loan interest (including fees) in 2014 plus another 6% from interest on its investment securities. About 10% of its total revenue came from debit and credit card fees and deposit account service charges while wealth management fees and insurance fees made up 6% and 3% of total revenue that year respectively.

Geographic Reach

Headquartered in Indiana Pennsylvania S&T Bancorp boasts branches in a dozen counties in the state including: Allegheny Armstrong Blair Butler Cambria Centre Clarion Clearfield Indiana Jefferson Washington and Westmoreland counties. It also has loan production offices in northeast and central Ohio and in western New York.

Sales and Marketing

Targeting both individuals and local businesses S&T Bancorp spent $3.32 million on marketing in 2014 up from the $2.93 million and $3.21 million it spent in 2013 and 2012 respectively.

Financial Performance

S&T Bancorp's revenue has slowly declined in recent years due to shrinking interest margins on loans amidst the low-interest environment. The firm's profits however have been rising thanks to declining loan loss provisions as its loan portfolio's credit quality has improved with the strengthened economy.

Following several years of top-line declines the bank's revenue inched up by nearly 1% to $206.86 million in 2014. The rise was mostly thanks to higher interest income as overall earning-asset balances grew by nearly 7% during the year reflecting the bank's growing loan business and increased investment securities assets. Wealth Management fees also continued to grow rising by 6% during the year.

Higher revenue coupled with lower interest expenses on deposits and a $6.6 million reduction in loan loss provisions in 2014 drove S&T Bancorp's net income higher by 15% to $57.91 million. S&T's operating cash levels fell by 9% to $78.1 million for the year after adjusting its earnings for non-cash items mostly related to its net proceeds from sales of its mortgage loans originated-for-sale.

Strategy

S&T Bancorp reiterated in 2015 that its growth strategy is centered around organic growth in existing and new markets and growth through strategic acquisitions that introduce new lines of business. Its 2015 acquisition of Integrity Bancshares for example expanded S&T's footprint eastward across four counties in Pennsylvania and added millions of dollars worth of new loan business. Also that year the bank entered the western part of New York for the first time with the opening of a new loan production office in the region.

In late 2012 the bank extended its operations into its neighbor Ohio when it opened a handful of branches in Akron. That same year the bank acquired Mainline Bancorp and Gateway Bank of Pennsylvania bolstering its presence in its core western Pennsylvania market.

Mergers and Acquisitions

In March 2015 S&T Bancorp purchased Camp Hill-based Integrity Bancshares for $155 million adding $860 million in assets and eight branches expanding S&T's geographic footprint eastward into Cumberland Dauphin Lancaster and York counties in Pennsylvania. S&T added that the acquisition positioned the bank in high-growth markets within the state and added experienced members to the bank's loan team.

In 2012 the bank acquired Mainline Bancorp and Gateway Bank of Pennsylvania. Both transactions served to expand S&T's presence in western Pennsylvania.

EXECUTIVES

Sevp And Coo, David P. Ruddock, age 58, $265,000 total compensation
President And Ceo S&t And S&t Bank, Todd D. Brice, age 57, $525,000 total compensation
Evp And Retail Banking Division Manager, Richard A. (Rich) Fiscus
Svp And Treasurer, Mark Kochvar, age 59, $278,000 total compensation
Sevp And Chief Lending Officer, David G. Antolik, age 53, $302,000 total compensation
Evp And Chief Investment Officer Wealth Management, Malcolm E. Polley, age 57
Svp And Risk Management Officer S&t Bank, Ernest J. Draganza
Evp And Deputy Chief Credit Officer, William (Bill) Kametz
Sevp And Chief Credit Officer, Patrick Haberfield
Sevp And Chief Banking Officer, Rebecca Stapleton
Evp And Commercial Loan Officer, Steve Drahnak
Evp And Chief Audit Executive, LaDawn D. Yesho
Evp, David Richards
Evp Marketing Division Manager, Rob Jorgenson
Evp And Cio, Jim Mill
Evp And Manager, Robert Jogrenson
Sevp And Market Executive, Thomas J. Sposito
Market President Central Pennsylvania, Jordan Space
Market President Northeast Ohio, Steve Hendricks
Vice President Mortgage Underwriting Manager, Christine Rumbaugh
Vice President Marketing, Kelly Thomas
Vice President Credit Analysis Operation Manager, Dennis Scott
Senior Vice President Banking Operations, Robert Coleman
Vice President Network Operations Manager, Ron Todd
Evp And Chief Risk Officer, Ernie Draganza
Vice President Of Information Technology, Ron Rodman
Vice President Regional Manager, Megan White
Assistant Vice President Sba Commercial Loan, Becky Oldenski
Evp And Chief Security Officer, Kevin Dodds
Svp Regional Busines Banking Sandt Bank, Sean Dockery
Svp Commercial Banker Sandt Bank, Jeffrey Bierlein
Svp Commercial Banker Sandt Bank, David D'angelo
Vice President Financial Reporting Manager, Ron Schibner
Vice President Special Assets Officer, Peter Talarovich

Vice President Business Banker, Cathleen
Campriani-square
Senior Vice President Commercial Banker, Paul
Kelly
Vice President Platforms Support Manager, Debbie
Silveri
Vice President Commercial Banking, Randy
Patterson
Chairman S&t And S&t Bank, Charles G. Urtin
Vice Chairman S&t And S&t Bank, Christine J.
Toretti, age 63
Board Member, Jeffrey D Grube
Auditors: Ernst & Young LLP

LOCATIONS

HQ: S & T Bancorp Inc (Indiana, PA)
  800 Philadelphia Street, Indiana, PA 15701
Phone: 800 325-2265
Web: www.stbancorp.com

PRODUCTS/OPERATIONS

2014 Sales

	$ mil.	% of total
Interest		
Loans including fees	147	72
Investment securities & other	13	6
Noninterest		
Wealth management fees	11	6
Debit and credit card fees	10	5
Service charges on deposit accounts	10	5
Insurance fees	6	3
Others	7	3
Total	**206**	**100**

Selected Subsidiaries

9th Street Holdings Inc.
Commonwealth Trust Credit Life Insurance Company
  (50%)
S&T Bank
  S&T Insurance Group LLC
  S&T-Evergreen Insurance LLC
  S&T Bancholdings Inc.
  S&T Professional Resources Group LLC
  S&T Settlement Services LLC
  Stewart Capital Advisors LLC

COMPETITORS

AmeriServ Financial	First Commonwealth
Citizens Financial	Financial
Group	Northwest Bancshares
F.N.B. (PA)	PNC Financial
Fidelity Bancorp (PA)	

HISTORICAL FINANCIALS

Company Type: Public

Income Statement				FYE: December 31
	ASSETS ($ mil.)	NET INCOME ($ mil.)	INCOME AS % OF ASSETS	EMPLOYEES
12/19	8,764	98	1.1%	1,201
12/18	7,252	105	1.5%	1,040
12/17	7,060	72	1.0%	1,080
12/16	6,943	71	1.0%	1,080
12/14	4,964	57	1.2%	945
Annual Growth	12.0%	11.1%	—	4.9%

2019 Year-End Financials

Debt ratio: 1.31%	No. of shares (mil.): 39
Return on equity: 9.23%	Dividends
Cash ($ mil.): 197	Yield: 2.7%
Current ratio: —	Payout: 36.5%
Long-term debt ($ mil.): —	Market value ($ mil.): 1,594

	STOCK PRICE ($)	P/E	PER SHARE ($)		
	FY Close	High/Low	Earnings	Dividends	Book Value
12/19	40.29	15 12	2.82	1.09	30.13
12/18	37.84	16 12	3.01	0.99	26.98
12/17	39.81	21 16	2.09	0.82	25.28
12/16	39.04	19 11	2.05	0.77	24.12
12/14	29.81	16 11	1.95	0.68	20.42
Annual Growth	6.2%	—	7.7%	9.9%	8.1%

Safety Insurance Group, Inc.

Buckle up Bostonians car safety first! Safety Insurance Group through subsidiaries Safety Insurance Safety Indemnity Insurance and Safety Property and Casualty sells property/casualty insurance exclusively in Massachusetts Maine and New Hampshire. It is one of the top private passenger automobile and commercial automobile insurers in the region controlling about 10% of the markets in its home state. Safety Insurance also provides homeowners dwelling fire personal umbrella and business-owner policies; it cross-sells its non-auto property/casualty products to increase its share of the market. The firm sells its products through more than 890 independent agents and about 1120 offices.

Operations

The company comprises one business segment: property and casualty insurance operations. Management organizes the business around private passenger automobile insurance in Massachusetts sold exclusively through independent agents and offers other personal and commercial insurance as complementary products. About 90% of its revenues came from net premiums earned the remaining accounts for the rest.

Geographic Reach

Safety Insurance operates in Massachusetts Maine and New Hampshire. The company headquarters is located in Boston Massachusetts.

Sales and Marketing

The company distributes its policies through more than 890 independent agents in some 1120 offices.

Auto insurance makes up the lion's share of the group's written premiums with private passenger auto insurance contributing of about 55% of its direct written premiums Homeowners insurance accounts for more than 20% of written premiums while commercial automobile insurance accounts for more than 15%.

Total advertising costs were $2182 $2500 and $2216 for the years ended December 31 2019 2018 and 2017 respectively.

Financial Performance

Revenue has been rising for the past five years. It posted a growth of about 10% over the same span.

It grew 5% to $877.8 million in 2019 thanks to growth in its net investment income and an increase in unrealized gains on equity investments.

Net income for 2019 increased by 20% to $99.6 million on the back of higher revenue reported by the company.

Cash and cash equivalents at the end of the period were $44.4 million. Net cash provided by operating activities was $112.5 million while investing and financing activities used $53 million each. Main cash uses were for purchases of securities and dividends payment.

Strategy

To achieve its goal of increasing shareholder value the company strategy is to maintain and develop strong independent agent relationships by providing its agents with a full package of insurance products and information technology services.

The company believes this strategy will allow it to: further penetrate the Massachusetts New Hampshire and Maine markets in all lines of business; implement rates forms and billing options that allows it to cross-sell private passenger automobile homeowners dwelling fire and personal umbrella policies in the personal lines market and commercial automobile business owner policies commercial property package and commercial umbrella policies in the commercial lines market in order to capture a larger share of the total Massachusetts New Hampshire and Maine property and casualty insurance business written by each of its independent agents; and continue to expand its technology to enable independent agents to more easily serve their customers and conduct business with them thereby strengthening their relationships with the company.

EXECUTIVES

Vp Cfo And Secretary, William J. Begley, age 65,
$400,000 total compensation
Vp Property Claims, David E. Krupa, age 59,
$210,796 total compensation
Vp Underwriting, James D. Berry, age 60, $263,682
total compensation
President And Ceo, George M. Murphy, age 53,
$350,000 total compensation
Vp Insurance Operations, Ann M. McKeown
Vp Casualty Claims, Paul J. Narciso, age 56
Vp Management Information Systems, Stephen A.
Varga, age 52
Vp Marketing, John P. Drago
Board Member, Peter Manning
Auditors: PricewaterhouseCoopers LLP

LOCATIONS

HQ: Safety Insurance Group, Inc.
  20 Custom House Street, Boston, MA 02110
Phone: 617 951-0600   **Fax:** 617 603-4837
Web: www.safetyinsurance.com

PRODUCTS/OPERATIONS

2015 Sales

	$ mil.	% of total
Net earned premiums	738	92
Net investment income	40	5
Finance & other service income	18	2
Earnings from partnership investments	2	1
Adjustments	(1.2)	-
Total	**798**	**100**

COMPETITORS

AIG	Plymouth Rock
Allstate	Assurance
Ameriprise	Preferred Mutual
Arbella Insurance	Progressive

Electric Insurance   Corporation
Foremost Insurance   Quincy Mutual
GEICO   Travelers of
Liberty Mutual   Massachusetts
MAPFRE USA   Vermont Mutual
OneBeacon

HISTORICAL FINANCIALS
Company Type: Public

Income Statement				FYE: December 31
	ASSETS ($ mil.)	NET INCOME ($ mil.)	INCOME AS % OF ASSETS	EMPLOYEES
12/19	2,022	99	4.9%	609
12/18	1,856	83	4.5%	627
12/17	1,807	62	3.5%	623
12/16	1,758	64	3.7%	643
12/15	1,703	(13)	—	622
Annual Growth	4.4%	—	—	(0.5%)

2019 Year-End Financials

Debt ratio: —	No. of shares (mil.): 15
Return on equity: 13.04%	Dividends
Cash ($ mil.): 44	Yield: 3.6%
Current ratio: —	Payout: 58.3%
Long-term debt ($ mil.): —	Market value ($ mil.): 1,423

	STOCK PRICE ($) FY Close	P/E High/Low		PER SHARE ($) Earnings	Dividends	Book Value
12/19	92.53	16	12	6.46	3.40	52.55
12/18	81.81	18	13	5.43	3.20	47.01
12/17	80.40	20	16	4.10	3.00	46.06
12/16	73.70	17	12	4.27	2.80	44.27
12/15	56.38	—	—	(0.93)	2.80	42.70
Annual Growth	13.2%	—	—	—	5.0%	5.3%

Salesforce.Com Inc

Salesforce.com Inc. is the top developer and seller of customer relationship management software with more than 150000 users. The company offers cloud-based applications that manage customer relationships including Sales Cloud Marketing and Commerce Cloud and Service Cloud (for customer support) as well as the Salesforce Platform. Other products offer e-Commerce analytics and social media tools through cloud-based applications. Salesforce's customers come from a variety of industries including financial services telecommunications manufacturing entertainment and government. It generates most of its revenue in Americas. Salesforce bought Tableau for about $15 billion in mid-2019.

Operations

Besides its big three cloud products ? Sales Cloud Service Cloud and Marketing and Commerce Cloud Salesforce offers several others that help companies manage their relationships with customers. They include: Community Cloud which helps companies create and manage branded digital destinations for customers partners and employees; IoT (Internet of Things) Cloud which helps companies collect information from connected devices products sensors and apps; Analytics Cloud which helps an employee explore business data from any device; and Salesforce Quip a productivity tool designed for teams.

Salesforce also offers consulting services for deployment training and design and integration.

Most of the company's revenue comes from its subscription and support segment which accounts for nearly 95% while the rest comes from professional and other services.

Geographic Reach

Salesforce relies on customers in the US for more than 70% of its revenue while customers in Europe account for about 20% of revenue and those in the Asia/Pacific region generate almost 10%. Salesforce is headquartered in San Francisco California.

Sales and Marketing

Salesforce.com counts more than 150000 users from small businesses with one subscription to large enterprises with thousands. With such a large customer base.

The company uses a direct sales force made up of telephone sales reps based in regional hubs and field sales reps in territories close to their customers. It also works with consulting firms systems integrators and others to find customers. For successful sales Salesforce pays a fee based on the first-year subscription revenue generated by the referred customers.

Salesforce's marketing and sales expenses were $7.9 billion $6.1 billion and $4.7 billion for the years 2020 2019 and 2018 respectively.

Financial Performance

Salesforce has turned in a fast-growing revenue line for the past five years averaging almost 30% annual increase as the company has added more applications to its basic customer relationship management offerings.

In 2020 (ended January) revenue hit about $17.1 billion up some $3.8 billion and a 29% increase from 2019. The growth was driven by higher revenues from Salesforce.org and Tableau.

Salesforce's net income dipped to $126 million in 2020 from $1.1 billion in 2019 due to higher operating expenses incurred during the period.

Salesforce has cash and equivalents of $4.1 billion in 2020 compared to $2.7 billion in 2019. The company's operations generated $4.3 billion while investing activities used $3 billion. Financing activities provided another $164 million.

Strategy

Salesforce orient its business strategy and invest for future growth by focusing on the following key priorities:

Expanding relationships with existing customers by aiming to upgrade the customer experience with new products premium editions and additional subscriptions by targeting new functional areas and business units and expanding all editions of its service offerings with new features functions and increased security through its own development acquisitions and partnerships;

International expansion by continuing to increase investment in its international go-to-market resources operations and infrastructure to deliver the highest quality service to its customers around the world;

Extending go-to-market capabilities by pursuing businesses of all sizes in major regions globally primarily through its direct sales force and have steadily increased and plan to continue to increase the number of direct sales professionals it employs. The company will also continue to

develop indirect distribution channels for its solutions around the globe and new go-to-market strategies such as self-service for Essentials;

Targeting vertical industries by providing solutions specifically built for customers in certain industries such as financial services healthcare and life sciences government manufacturing consumer goods and philanthropy. These solutions help to expand its potential customer base and help to attract new customers;

Expanding into new categories by delivering innovative solutions in new categories including analytics e-commerce Internet of Things ("IoT") and integration and expect to continue this type of category expansion in the future;

Expanding and strengthening our partner ecosystem by continuing to work with and invest in its partner ecosystem including these ISVs and system integrators ("SIs") to accelerate our reach into new markets and industries offer a variety of solutions natively and through the AppExchange and address the business requirements of both current and future customers;

And promoting strong customer adoption and reducing customer attrition by strive to reduce attrition and secure renewals of existing customer subscriptions prior to the end of their contractual terms.

Mergers and Acquisitions

In early 2020 Salesforce acquired Vlocity for $1.3 billion. Vlocity is a leading provider of industry-specific cloud and mobile software based in San Francisco California. The acquisition enhances and complements Salesforce's industry capabilities built on its platform.

In addition to the company's early 2020 transaction Salesforce acquired Evergage based in Massachusetts. Evergage's real-time personalization and customer data platform enables the company to transform 1-to-1 engagement across channels. The transaction accelerates Salesforce efforts to offer enhanced personalization solutions to its customers.

In late 2019 Salesforce in its biggest deal acquired Tableau Software which develops applications for analyzing and presenting data based in Washington for $15.7 billion. With Tableau's products in its software arsenal Salesforce offers customers a more comprehensive package for data collection and analysis.

In another 2019 deal Salesforce acquired ClickSoftware a developer of field service management software based in Massachusetts for $1.35 billion in cash and shares to speed growth of its cloud-based products for customer service operations. ClickSoftware's offerings would become part of Salesforce's Service Cloud.

In early 2019 Salesforce acquired privately held Bonobo AI which develops artificial intelligence software to gather insight on customers by analyzing phone calls texts and chats based in Israel for $45 million. Salesforce is to add the Bonobo software to its Salesforce Sales Cloud.

EXECUTIVES

Chairman And Ceo, Marc Benioff, age 55, $1,550,000 total compensation
President And Chief Strategy Officer, Alexandre (Alex) Dayon, age 52, $900,000 total compensation
Vice Chairman President And Coo, Keith G. Block, age 58, $1,150,000 total compensation

President Global Customer Success And Salesforce Latin America, Maria Martinez, age 62

President And Cfo, Mark J. Hawkins, age 60, $750,000 total compensation

Svp Marketing, Elizabeth Pinkham

President And Chief Product Officer, Bret Taylor

President Legal And General Counsel, Amy E. Weaver, age 52

Evp Corporate Relations And Chief Philanthropy Officer, Suzanne DiBianca

President And Chief People Officer, Cindy Robbins, age 47

Senior Vice President Product Marketing, Eric Stahl

Svp Office Of The Chairman And Ceo, Jim Cavalieri

Regional Vice President Sales Salesforce. Experience Success, Julie Hall

Regional Vice President Sales Cloud, Bhavin Shah

Vice President Partner Marketing, Leslie Tom

Vice President Technology Services, Andrea Leszek

Evp And Cio, Ross Meyercord

Svp Engineering Cloud Services, Arvind Seshan

Executive Vice President Operations And Mobility, Todd Pierce

Vice President Global Operations Salesforce University, Shane Anastasi

Area Vice President Northeast, Evans Killeen

Vice President Platform Amer, Christopher Culp

Senior Vice President App Cloud And Pardot Marketing, Shannon Duffy

Vice President Sales Engineering, Mike Booth

Area Vice President, Philip Klebba

Area Vice President Automotive And Manufacturing, Paul Culpepper

Evp Chief Accounting Officer And Corporate Controller, Joe Allanson

Vice President Software Engineering, Ritu Bhargava

Senior Vice President Customer Success, Manjula Talreja

Senior Vice President And Associate General Counsel, Todd Machtmes

Vice President, Anil Dindigal

Senior Vice President, Jon Sigler

Vice President Enterprise Sales, Dallas Stonhaus

Vice President Of Engineering At Salesforce, Ramesh Ragineni

Vice President Of Sales, Tom Richards

Evp And Chief Marketing Officer, Stephanie Buscemi

Regional Vice President Enterprise Sales, Stacy Parker

Senior Vice President Employee Marketing And Engag, Jody Kohner

Vice President Commercial Sales, Dean Tobe

Senior Vice President Manufacturing And Consumer Goods Industries Salesforce.com, Cynthia Bolt

Svp Communities Engineering, Stephen Ayers

Area Vice President Federal Sales, Dan Davis

Regional Vice President Enterprise Sales, Charlie Rapier

Regional Vice President, Jeffrey Pope

Vice President Salesforce, Dan Whalen

Vice President, Mary Heston

Regional Vice President Health Care And Life Sciences, Aaron Stine

Regional Vice President Customer Success, Israel Forst

Regional Vice President, Craig Lashmet

Regional Vice President, Sheldon Buytenhuys

Regional Vice President Enterprise Accounts, Dick Cotter

Vice President Customer Intelligence, Ashfaq Mohiuddin

Regional Vice President Public Sector Customers For Life, Tom Gardner

Area Vice President, Steve Moroski

Regional Vice President, David Rubinstein

Regional Vice President, Joe Haney

Regional Vice President Success Services, Jon Lokay

Regional Vice President, Tim Murdoch

Regional Vice President Commercial Sales, David Jeffrey

Regional Vice President Of Enterprise Sales, Michael Green

Senior Vice President Strategic Planning, Peter Schwartz

Regional Vice President Enterprise Sales, Scott Duval

Vp Product Management, Amruta Moktali

Vice President Platform And Iot, Keith Fortson

Area Vice President Marketing Cloud, Joe Stojkov

Senior Vice President Chief Creative Officer, Colin Fleming

Svp Chief Procurement Officer, Lisa Null Edwards

Svp Enterprise Americas, John Vitalie

Regional Vice President Marketing Cloud, Garner White

Senior Vice President Vice President Corporate Planning Finance And Strategy, Evan Goldstein

Vice President Northern Europe, Renzo Taal

Regional Vice President, Yasuhide Inoue

Svp And Gm Salesforce Marketing Cloud Japac, Lee Hawksley

Regional Vice President Middle East And Africa, Richard McGuinness

Regional Vice President Asia Pacific Platform Analytics Service Cloud, Robert Wickham

Regional Vice President Commercial Sales Latam, Fernando Bertolla

Vp Revenue Operations Products And Enablement, Heather Atkinson

Regional Vice President Enterprise Sales Salesforce Marketing Cloud, Michael Huffines

Vice President Marketing Cloud Experience, Mike Kaplan

Area Vice President Partner Sales, Julia Fare

Senior Vice President Communications Field Marketing, Bill Taylor

Svp Gm Messaging, Joanna Milliken

Regional Vice President Enterprise Sales, Reed Overby

Senior Vice President Infrastructure, Vijay Gill

Regional Vice President Enterprise Sales, Jerry Schorn

Regional Vice President Marketing Cloud, James Bishop

Regional Vice President Salesforce Marketing Cloud, Roman Howe

Vice President, Johnny Khoury

Regional Vice President Uk Commercial Sales, Conor O'malley

Vice President Sales Financial Services, John Messina

Regional Vice President, Mark Niemiec

Regional Vice President Sales, Jeremy Watson

Regional Vice President Enterprise Sales, Greg Rakauskas

Regional Vice President Enterprise Sales, David Chatterton

Regional Vice President Alliances And Channels Southern Europe, Pascal Voirand

Senior Avp North America Platform Cloud Sales, Mark Desrosiers

Vice President Business Development, Brian Remmel

Regional Vp Salesforce Commerce Cloud, Charles Ellis

Vice President Platform User Experience, Guy Jenkins

Regional Vice President Of Commercial Sales, Daisuke Yasuda

Regional Vice President Sales Italy, Ezio Russo

Regional Vice President Social Sales, Sheehan Murphy

Regional Vice President Marketing Cloud, David Mcnally

Vice President Associate General Counsel Emea, Adam Burrows

Regional Vice President Platform Sales, Joe Lanier

Regional Vice President Alliances And Channels Gtm Asia, Francis Chong

Vice President Marketing, Sara Varni

Regional Vice President Commercial Sales, Laurent Malpeli

Rvp Sales Data And Audiences, Frederick Stanichev

Vice President Area, Markus Ehrle

Area Vice President Of Sales, Christina Meitus

Regional Vice President Sales, Federico Casa

Senior Vice President Government Affairs And Public Policy, Jim Green

Regional Vice President, Christopher Moore

Vice President Compliance, Perez Art

Svp Total Rewards And Mobility, Stan Dunlap

Vice President And Associate General Counsel Corporate And Securities, Sarah Dods

Vice President Client Relationship Manager Infrastructure Engineering, Brad Cameron

Vice President Head Of Digital And Interactive, Mark Yolton

Vice President And Associate General Counsel (global Labor And Employment), Rachel Courtney

Vice President Data Science Apps, Robin Glinton

Vice President Sales Development (marketing Cloud), Vik Naik

Vice President Data Science And Software Engineering (salesforce Commerce Cloud), Bharath Krishnan

Regional Vice President Strategic Sales, Sebastien Zins

Vice President Gtm Alliances Apac, Charles Woodall

Regional Vice President Platform, Biliouris Mike

Vice President Program Executive, Natalie Petouhoff

Regional Vice President West, John Danahy

Vice President Employee Success, Mark Gundacker

Vice President Global Sales Strategy And Planning, Ozlem Yuksel

Vp Product Infrastructure, Kartik Chandrayana

Vice President Sales, Alison Childers

Vice President Global Controller At Salesforce.org And Foundation, Anne Kroger

Area Vice President Sales, Jeremy Thies

Regional Vice President, Jake Upton

Regional Vice President, Tripp Murphy

Vice President Enterprise Retail, Christian Conway

Svp Product Gm Einstein, John Ball

Regional Vice President Enterprise Sales, Lobdell Chris

Regional Vice President Enterprise Sales, Shannon Nesbit

Vice President Global Recruiting Futureforce, Dellisanti Suzana

Vice President Voting Systems, Bill Pessin

Senior Vice President Product Management, Liam Doyle

Regional Vice President, Scott Kirtland

Senior Vice President, Kori Obrien

Regional Vice President Strategic Partners, Elizabeth Greco

Vp Of Sales And Marketing, Mark Caruso

Regional Vice President Marketing Cloud, Mike Hinker

Vice President Enterprise Sales, Pam Campisano

Vice President East, John Colson

Regional Vice President Marketing Cloud, Janine Dinkel

Auditors: Ernst & Young LLP

LOCATIONS

HQ: Salesforce.Com Inc
  Salesforce Tower, 415 Mission Street, 3rd Fl, San Francisco, CA 94105
Phone: 415 901-7000
Web: www.salesforce.com

2019 Sales

	$ mil.	% of total
Americas	9,445	71
Europe	2,553	19
Asia/Pacific	1,284	10
Total	**13,282**	**100**

PRODUCTS/OPERATIONS

2019 Sales

	$ mil.	% of total
Subscription & support	12,413	93
Professional services & other	869	7
Total	**13,282**	**100**

COMPETITORS

CDC Software	Microsoft Dynamics
Google	NetSuite
Hewlett Packard Enterprise	Oracle
	SAP
IBM	Sage Software
Infor Global	ServiceNow
KANA	SugarCRM

HISTORICAL FINANCIALS

Company Type: Public

Income Statement

FYE: January 31

	REVENUE ($ mil.)	NET INCOME ($ mil.)	NET PROFIT MARGIN	EMPLOYEES
01/20	17,098	126	0.7%	49,000
01/19	13,282	1,110	8.4%	35,000
01/18	10,480	127	1.2%	29,000
01/17	8,391	179	2.1%	25,000
01/16	6,667	(47)	—	19,000
Annual Growth	26.5%			26.7%

2020 Year-End Financials

Debt ratio: 4.85%
Return on equity: 0.51%
Cash ($ mil.): 4,145
Current ratio: 1.08
Long-term debt ($ mil.): 2,673

No. of shares (mil.): 893
Dividends
Yield: —
Payout: —
Market value ($ mil.): 162,803

	STOCK PRICE ($) FY Close	P/E High/Low	PER SHARE ($) Earnings	Dividends	Book Value
01/20	182.31	1238931	0.15	0.00	37.95
01/19	151.97	108 70	1.43	0.00	20.27
01/18	113.91	632437	0.17	0.00	12.87
01/17	79.10	322208	0.26	0.00	10.60
01/16	68.06	— —	(0.07)	0.00	7.46
Annual Growth	27.9%	— —	—	—	50.2%

Sandy Spring Bancorp Inc

Sandy Spring Bancorp is the holding company for Sandy Spring Bank which operates around 50 branches in the Baltimore and Washington DC metropolitan areas. Founded in 1868 the bank is one of the largest and oldest headquartered in Maryland. It provides standard deposit services including checking and savings accounts money market accounts and CDs. Commercial and residential real estate loans account for nearly three-quarters of the company's loan portfolio; the remainder is a mix of consumer loans business loans and equipment leases. The company also offers personal investing services wealth management trust services insurance and retirement planning.

Operations

Sandy Spring Bancorp's nonbank subsidiaries include money manager West Financial Services and Sandy Spring Insurance which sells annuities and operates insurance agencies Chesapeake Insurance Group and Neff & Associates.

Financial Performance

The company's revenue increased in fiscal 2013 compared to the previous year. It reported $196.9 million in revenue for fiscal 2013 after bringing in revenue of $190.8 million in fiscal 2012.

The company's net income also went up in fiscal 2013 compared to the prior period. It claimed a profit of about $44 million in fiscal 2013 after netting a little more than $36 million in fiscal 2012.

Sandy Spring Bancorp's cash on hand increased by about $43 million in fiscal 2013 compared to fiscal 2012 levels.

Mergers and Acquisitions

In 2012 Sandy Spring Bancorp acquired CommerceFirst Bancorp a small Maryland bank with a strong Small Business Administration lending practice. The $25.4 million transaction added five branches to Sandy Spring Bank's network.

EXECUTIVES

Evp General Counsel And Secretary, Ronald E. Kuykendall, age 67, $279,039 total compensation
Evp Wealth Management Insurance Mortgage, R. Louis (Lou) Caceres, age 57, $333,865 total compensation
President And Ceo Bancorp And Bank, Daniel J. (Dan) Schrider, age 55, $600,692 total compensation
Evp And Cfo Bancorp And Bank, Philip J. Mantua, age 61, $333,192 total compensation
Evp And Cio, John D. Sadowski, age 56
Evp Commercial And Retail Banking, Joseph O'Brien, $355,038 total compensation
Evp And Chief Credit Officer, Ronda M. McDowell
Vice President, Brian Schott
Vice President Private Banking Relationship Manager, Victor Emeogo
Vice President, Christopher Huang
Senior Vice President, Todd Ellis
Senior Business Analyst Assistant Vice President, Stephen Marsico
Vice President Marketing Communications Manager, Jennifer Schell
Assistant Vice President Team Leader, Tamika Daniels
Vice President, Denise Kratz
Vice President Hris Project Administrator, Patti Boyle
Vice President, Isaac Sterbenz
Assistant Vice President Public Relations Specialist, Amanda Walsh
Senior Vice President, Scott Sims
Vice President, William Grahe
Assistant Vice President And Portfolio Manager, Brian Lopes
Senior Vice President Commercial Relatio, Wendy Lance
Vice President, Larry Arch
Senior Vice President, Glen Buco
Vice President Ecommerce, Lisa Johnson
Senior Portfolio Manager Vice President, Christy Powell
Assistant Vice President Branch Manager, Phil Hicks
Vice President And Underwriter, Jacqueline Gerhart
Vice President And Fiduciary Officer, Barbara Mulitz
Senior Vice President And Division Manager, Fred Burke
Vice President, James Holochuk
Vice President Facilities, Thomas Gemmell
Senior Vice President Alternative Delivery, Don Haasen
Vice President, Eba Elorza
Vice President Debit And Credit Card Product Manager, Ron Waters
Vice President, Michael Mckeon
Vice President Commercial Relationship Manager, James Bear
Senior Vice President, Laurie Kramer
Assistant Vice President Loan Support, Barbara Nixon
Vice President Private Banking Division, Ann Conger
Vice President, Cave Katie
Vice President And Insurance And Surety Bonding, Fred Hildebrand
Senior Vice President Director Of Regulatory Management, Diane Slack
Senior Vice President Marketing, Amalia G Kastberg
Assistant Vice President, Alexis Vining
Vice President, Todd Levine
Vice President Mortgage Banker, Jeff Starcher
Senior Vice President Marketing, Amalia Kastberg
Card Systems And Operations Manager Vice President, Rebecca Kruse
Senior Vice President, Michael Acton
Vice President, Philip Fish
Vice President, Asma Iqbal
Assistant Vice President, Joe Malazo
Vice President, Dushanti Peiris
Vice President And Relationship Manager Commercial Banking, Timothy Kelley
Assistant Vice President Human Resources Business Partner, Jayme Dungan
Senior Vice President, Michelle Levenson
Business Development Vice President And Branch Manager, Anna Massey
Chairman, Robert L. Orndorff, age 64
Auditors: Ernst & Young

LOCATIONS

HQ: Sandy Spring Bancorp Inc
17801 Georgia Avenue, Olney, MD 20832
Phone: 301 774-6400
Web: www.sandyspringbank.com

PRODUCTS/OPERATIONS

2015 Sales

	$ mil.	% of total
Interest Income:		
Interest and fees on loans and leases	135	65
Interest and dividends on investment securities	22	11
Other	0	-
Non-interest Income:		
Wealth management income	19	10
Service charges on deposit accounts	7	4
Insurance agency commissions	5	2
Bank card fees	4	2
Mortgage banking activities	3	2
Other Income	9	4
Total	**208**	**100**

COMPETITORS

BB&T	Fulton Financial
Bank of America	OBA Financial Services
Bay Bancorp	PNC Financial
Capital One	SunTrust

HISTORICAL FINANCIALS

Company Type: Public

Income Statement
FYE: December 31

	ASSETS ($ mil.)	NET INCOME ($ mil.)	INCOME AS % OF ASSETS	EMPLOYEES
12/19	8,629	116	1.3%	932
12/18	8,243	100	1.2%	932
12/17	5,446	53	1.0%	754
12/16	5,091	48	0.9%	752
12/15	4,655	45	1.0%	737
Annual Growth	16.7%	26.6%	—	6.0%

2019 Year-End Financials

Debt ratio: 2.43%
Return on equity: 10.58%
Cash ($ mil.): 145
Current ratio: —
Long-term debt ($ mil.): —

No. of shares (mil.): 34
Dividends
Yield: 3.1%
Payout: 36.3%
Market value ($ mil.): 1,325

	STOCK PRICE ($) FY Close	P/E High/Low		PER SHARE ($) Earnings	Dividends	Book Value
12/19	37.88	12	9	3.25	1.18	32.40
12/18	31.34	15	11	2.82	1.10	30.06
12/17	39.02	21	17	2.20	1.04	23.50
12/16	39.99	20	12	2.00	0.98	22.32
12/15	26.96	16	13	1.84	0.90	21.58
Annual Growth	8.9%	—	—	15.3%	7.0%	10.7%

Santander Consumer USA Holdings Inc

This auto finance company aims to put credit-impaired car buyers in the driver's seat. Santander Consumer USA (SCUSA) makes subprime new and used vehicle loans to buyers at more than 14000 Chrysler Ford GM and Toyota dealerships throughout the US. The technology-driven company also originates loans through independent dealers such as CarMax banks and its direct-to-consumer website Roadloans.com. SCUSA also provides refinancing and cash-back refinancing services. While subprime loans make up more than 80% of its loan portfolio the company is looking to increase its prime loan business. Founded in 1995 SCUSA is owned by Spanish banking giant Banco Santander SA. The company went public in 2014.

IPO

Santander Consumer USA (SCUSA) went public in January 2014 with an offering valued at $1.5 billion. The IPO capitalizes on the rebound in auto sales as credit-impaired borrowers return to the car market. Post IPO Banco Santander owns 61% of SCUSA.

Financial Performance

The auto lender reported more than $2.9 billion in finance and other interest income in 2012 a 14% increase versus 2011.

Strategy

SCUSA is looking to expand its portfolio of prime loans through partnerships with automakers. To that end in February 2013 SCUSA entered into a 10-year agreement with Chrysler whereby it originates private-label loans and leases under the Chrysler Capital brand. The company relies on third-party banks and parent company Banco Santander for approximately $12 billion and $5 billion respectively in committed financing. It also has agreements with Bank of America and Sovereign to fund the Chrysler Capital business.

Company Background

In 2006 Banco Santander acquired a 90% stake in Drive Financial from HBOS and the company's founding partners for $651 million. Drive changed its name to Santander Consumer USA in 2008.

EXECUTIVES

Board Member, Edith Holiday
Auditors: PricewaterhouseCoopers LLP

LOCATIONS

HQ: Santander Consumer USA Holdings Inc
1601 Elm Street, Suite 800, Dallas, TX 75201
Phone: 214 634-1110
Web: www.santanderconsumerusa.com

COMPETITORS

Ally Bank	Credit Acceptance
Bank of America	Ford Motor Credit
Capital One Auto Finance	GM Financial
	Toyota Motor Credit

HISTORICAL FINANCIALS

Company Type: Public

Income Statement
FYE: December 31

	ASSETS ($ mil.)	NET INCOME ($ mil.)	INCOME AS % OF ASSETS	EMPLOYEES
12/19	48,933	994	2.0%	5,175
12/18	43,959	915	2.1%	4,952
12/17	39,422	1,187	3.0%	5,076
12/16	38,539	766	2.0%	5,100
12/15	36,570	827	2.3%	5,100
Annual Growth	7.6%	4.7%	—	0.4%

2019 Year-End Financials

Debt ratio: 80.10%
Return on equity: 13.87%
Cash ($ mil.): 81
Current ratio: —
Long-term debt ($ mil.): —

No. of shares (mil.): 339
Dividends
Yield: 3.5%
Payout: 30.8%
Market value ($ mil.): 7,927

	STOCK PRICE ($) FY Close	P/E High/Low		PER SHARE ($) Earnings	Dividends	Book Value
12/19	23.37	10	6	2.86	0.84	21.58
12/18	17.59	9	6	2.54	0.50	19.92
12/17	18.62	6	3	3.30	0.03	17.98
12/16	13.50	7	4	2.13	0.00	14.60
12/15	15.85	11	7	2.31	0.00	12.36
Annual Growth	10.2%	—	—	5.5%	—	14.9%

Santander Holdings USA Inc.

Santander Holdings USA is the parent company of Sovereign Bank which reigns in the Northeast with more than 700 branch locations. TheÂ bankÂ caters to individuals and small to midsized businesses offeringÂ deposits creditÂ cards insurance and investmentsÂ as well as commercial loans and mortgages (which together account for nearlyÂ half of its total portfolio) and residential mortgages and home equity loansÂ (more than a quarter).Â Santander Holdings also owns a majority of Santander Consumer USA which purchases and services subprime car loans made byÂ auto dealerships and other companies.Â Spain-based banking giant Banco Santander acquired the rest of Sovereign BancorpÂ it didn't already own in 2009.

EXECUTIVES

Vice President Off Lease Remarketing Title Manager, Annemarie Brusseler
Vice President, Matthew Bartlett
Avp Sbrm, Ijaz Mughal
Evp Head Of Consumer Lending And Deposit Products, Jason Hardgrave
Auditors: PricewaterhouseCoopers LLP

LOCATIONS

HQ: Santander Holdings USA Inc.
75 State Street, Boston, MA 02109
Phone: 617 346-7200
Web:
www.santanderus.com/us/investorshareholderrelations

Selected Locations
Connecticut
Delaware
Maryland
Massachusetts
New Hampshire
New Jersey
New York
Pennsylvania
Rhode Island

PRODUCTS/OPERATIONS

2013 Sales

	$ mil.	% of total
Interest		
Loans	1,958	58
Investment securities	330	10
Deposits	6	.
Noninterest		
Equity method investment	426	12
Consumer banking fees	228	7
Commercial banking fees	199	6
Mortgage bankin revenue	122	4
Bank owned life insurance	57	3
Others	54	.
Total	**3,384**	**100**

COMPETITORS

Bank of America	M&T Bank
Citibank	PNC Financial
Citizens Financial Group	People's United Financial
Fulton Financial	TD Bank USA
HSBC USA	Webster Financial
JPMorgan Chase	Wells Fargo
KeyCorp	

HISTORICAL FINANCIALS

Company Type: Public

Income Statement

FYE: December 31

	REVENUE ($ mil.)	NET INCOME ($ mil.)	NET PROFIT MARGIN	EMPLOYEES
12/19	12,379	753	6.1%	16,900
12/18	11,313	707	6.3%	16,700
12/17	10,715	561	5.2%	17,000
12/16	10,745	362	3.4%	16,500
12/15	10,473	(1,454)	—	15,150
Annual Growth	4.3%	—	—	2.8%

2019 Year-End Financials

Debt ratio: 33.88%
Return on equity: 3.48%
Cash ($ mil.): 7,644
Current ratio: 0.18
Long-term debt ($ mil.): 50,654

No. of shares (mil.): 530
Dividends
Yield: —
Payout: 53.1%
Market value ($ mil.): —

	STOCK PRICE ($) FY Close	P/E High/Low	PER SHARE ($) Earnings	Dividends	Book Value
12/19	0.00	— —	(0.00)	0.00	41.52
12/18	0.00	— —	(0.00)	1.37	40.20
12/17	25.68	— —	(0.00)	1.83	39.94
Annual Growth	—	— —	—	—	1.0%

Schein (Henry) Inc

From Poughkeepsie to Prague Henry Schein outfits dental offices around the world with everything they need. The company is a leading global distributor of health care products and services primarily to office-based dental and medical practitioners. Henry Schein provides everything from infection-control products handpieces preventatives impression materials composites anesthetics and dental implants to vaccines surgical products diagnostic tests infection-control products and X-ray products. Other offerings include practice management software repair services and financing. The US accounts for about 70% of revenue.

Operations

Henry Schein's health care distribution segment accounts for almost 95% of the company's sales and is divided into two smaller divisions: global dental (accounting for around 70% of sales) medical (around 30%). This segment distributes consumable products small equipment laboratory products large equipment equipment repair services branded and generic pharmaceuticals vaccines surgical products diagnostic tests infection-control products and vitamins. Altogether Henry Schein offers more than 120000 branded and private-label products as well as 180000 special order offerings.

The company spun off its animal health business in 2019.

Henry Schein also has a health care technology and value-added services segment which provides practice management software hardware and other technology systems as well as e-commerce and financial services.

Geographic Reach

Henry Schein is headquartered in Melville New York and has locations across the US. It also has dental and medical distribution operations or af-filiates in more than 30 countries in the Asia/Pacific region Europe the Americas and Africa.

The company generates almost 70% of its revenue domestically.

Sales and Marketing

Henry Schein markets health care products to office-based dentists and physicians as well as dental labs surgery centers government and community clinics and other alternative care locations. The company's field sales force of almost 3700 sales consultants (including equipment sales specialists) and around 2000 telesales representatives primarily serve the North American and European markets as well as other select international regions. The firm also sells through social media and e-commerce platforms.

Henry Schein's advertising and promotional expenses were $25.2 million $12.9 million and $0.8 million for the years 2019 2018 and 2017 respectively.

Financial Performance

Henry Schein's revenue has been rising consistently for the last five years. It has an overall growth of 31%. Its net income has been fluctuating but has an overall growth of 45%.

In 2019 sales rose about 6% to $10 billion from 2018 boosted by higher revenue in each segment.

The company's net income jumped $158 million to $694.7 million in 2019 from 2018 due to increase in sales.

Henry Schein's coffers held $106.1 million in cash and equivalents in 2019 some $49 million more than in 2018. Operations generated about $654.1 million in 2019 while investing and financing activities used $424.4 million and $216.0 million respectively.

Strategy

Henry Schein's strategy consists of:

Increasing penetration of existing customer base ? Henry Schein has over one million customers worldwide and it intends to increase sales to its existing customer base and enhance its position as its primary supplier.

Second increase the number of customers it serves ? this strategy includes increasing the number and productivity of field sales consultants as well as using its customer database to focus its marketing efforts in all of its operating segments. In the dental business Henry Schein provides products and services to traditional dental practices as well as new emerging segments such as dental service organizations and community health centers. Leveraging its broad array of assets and capabilities Henry Schein offers solutions to address these new markets. In the medical business the company have expanded to serve customers located in settings outside of the traditional office such as urgent care clinics retail and occupational health settings.

Third leverage its value-added products and services ? Henry Schein continues to increase cross-selling efforts for key product lines utilizing a consultative selling process. In the dental business it has significant cross-selling opportunities between its dental practice management software users and its dental distribution customers. In the medical business Henry Schein have opportunities to expand its vaccine injectables and other pharmaceuticals sales to health care practitioners as well as cross-selling core products and electronic health record and practice man-agement software. Its strategy extends to providing health systems integrated delivery networks and other large group and multi-site health care organizations that include physician clinics these same value added products and services. As physicians and health systems closely align the company increased access to opportunities for cross-marketing and selling its product and service portfolios.

Lastly pursue strategic acquisitions and joint ventures - acquisition strategy includes acquiring businesses and entering into joint ventures complementary that will provide among other things additional sales to be channeled through its existing distribution infrastructure access to additional product lines and field sales consultants and an opportunity to further expand into new geographic markets.

In 2019 Henry Schein spun off its animal health business into a separate company Covetrus allowing each company to focus on its key markets. Henry Schein received $1.1 billion cash distribution from the transaction that it used to pay down debt.

Mergers and Acquisitions

In mid-2019 Henry Schein Inc. acquired a majority equity stake in Cliniclands an innovative distributor serving dental practices throughout Sweden Denmark and Norway. Based in Trelleborg Sweden Cliniclands represents the first presence of Henry Schein Dental in Scandinavia and offers a wide range of dental consumables implants prosthetic and orthodontic solutions as well as small and office equipment. With the addition of Cliniclands Henry Schein now has operations in 32 countries around the world.

In the same year the company acquired Utah-based Elite Computer Italia S.r.L. (Elite) a full-service software company that delivers state-of-the-art practice management solutions to dental practices and dental laboratories in Italy. The addition of Elite complements Henry Schein One's strategy to deliver integrated technology platforms that help dental teams become more productive and improve each stage of the patient experience and marks Henry Schein's entry into the Italian dental practice management software market. Financial terms were not disclosed.

In 2019 Henry Schein acquired Lighthouse 360 through its Henry Schein One joint venture with Internet Brands. Lighthouse 360 provides dental practice management and patient communication software that will expand Lighthouse 360's offerings.

In early 2019 Henry Schein acquired North American Rescue which supplies medical products used by first responders. The purchase expanded its domestic and foreign military businesses.

Company Background

For more than 50 years Henry Schein distributed drugs made by Schein Pharmaceuticals. In 1992 management spun off the drug business and led by former accountant Stanley Bergman began acquiring other dental supply companies at a terrific rate: 34 between 1994 and 1996 alone.

The company went public in 1995 and bought more than a dozen businesses. These purchases which included product marketer Vertex Corp.'s distribution unit moved Henry Schein into the medical and veterinary supply fields. The purchase of Schein Dental Equipment (founded by Marvin Schein) boosted per-customer sales by adding big-ticket merchandise to the product mix.

HISTORY

For more than 50 years Henry Schein distributed drugs made by Schein Pharmaceuticals. In 1992 management spun off the drug business and led by former accountant Stanley Bergman began acquiring other dental supply companies at a terrific rate: 34 between 1994 and 1996 alone.

The company went public in 1995 and bought more than a dozen businesses. These purchases which included product marketer Vertex Corporation's distribution unit moved Henry Schein into the medical and veterinary supply fields. The purchase of Schein Dental Equipment (founded by Marvin Schein) boosted per-customer sales by adding big-ticket merchandise to the product mix.

Acquisitions continued hot and heavy as the company boosted operations abroad. The purchases hit the bottom line; Schein avoided bloat by restructuring operations closing facilities and developing new systems. The company consolidated 13 distribution centers into five in 1997. The following year the firm expanded into Canada and bought a controlling stake in UK direct marketer Porter Nash.

To boost profits the company announced in 2000 that it would cut 5% of its workforce. It also shut down some facilities and sold its software development business as part of its overall restructuring plan. In 2001 the firm resumed its acquisitions when it bought the dental supply business of drug maker Zila. Over the next few years it expanded internationally when it bought up firms in the Czech Republic Germany Italy New Zealand and the UK.

Choosing to focus on supplying office-based health care practitioners in 2006 it sold its hospital supply business for $36.5 million. Other dispositions have included the sale of its oncology and specialty pharmaceutical businesses (2007) and a dental products wholesaler (2009). In 2009 Henry Schein acquired a majority stake in Butler Animal Health tripling the size of its domestic animal health operations; the unit was renamed Butler Schein Animal Health following the deal. (The company increased its stake in Butler Schein Animal Health to about 72% in 2012.)

Henry Schein expanded its health care technology segment in 2010 through the acquisition of majority ownership of ImproMed and McAllister Software Systems both developers of veterinary practice management systems in the US. In 2011 the company entered the veterinary market in Australia and New Zealand with the $92 million buy of Provet Holdings. The purchase helped Henry Schein cement its strategy to expand its international health care distribution unit.

EXECUTIVES

Evp And Chief Strategic Officer, Mark E. Mlotek, age 64, $555,962 total compensation
Evp And Chief Administrative Officer, Gerald A. Benjamin, age 67, $551,308 total compensation
President; Ceo Global Dental Group, James P. Breslawski, age 66, $698,769 total compensation

Evp And Cfo, Steven Paladino, age 63, $551,308 total compensation
Chairman And Ceo, Stanley M. Bergman, age 71, $1,342,385 total compensation
Svp And Chief Merchandising Officer, Michael Racioppi, age 65, $340,275 total compensation
President Henry Schein Europe, Robert (Bob) Minowitz, age 61
Chief Commercial Officer; President Corporate Commercial Development Group, David C. (Dave) McKinley, age 67
Svp And Cto, James A. (Jim) Harding, age 64
Evp; Ceo Global Animal Health Medical And Dental Surgical Group, Karen Prange, age 56, $410,000 total compensation
President Global Animal Health Group, Peter McCarthy
President Global Medical Group, Bridget A. Ross, age 55
Vice President Global E Commerce, Robert Lamb
Vice President Corporate Finance, Ronald South
Vice President Investor Relations, Carolynne Borders
Vice President Finance, Charles Crawford
Vice President, Patrick Allen
Vice President And General Manager, Lou Ferraro
Sales Vice President, Gerard Metselaar
Vice President Product Merchandising, Marguerite Walsh
Vice President Business Planning And Development, Rich Miranda
Vice President Of Technology Sales, John Cox
Vice President, Marie Woods
Vice President Regulatory Affairs, Jeff Peacock
Vice President, Keith Drayer
Vice President North American Distribution, Michael Richardson
Vice President Marketing Canada, Peter Jugoon
Vice President Sales Midwest, Cy Elborne
Vice President Business Development, Edward L Mohr
Vice President Business Development, Richard Miranda
National Sales Manager, Deanna Evans
Vice President National Telesales Operations, Jim Loiacono
National Sales Manager, Bill Nixon
Vice President Corporate Business Development, Scott Sanders
Vice President Director Of Operations, Ravi Bhir
Vice President, Jesse Garringer
Vp And General Auditor, James Patterson
Senior Vice President International Group, Michael Zack
Vice President Of Communications, Susan Vassallo
Vice President, Gene Heller
National Sales Manager, Deanna Wright
Vice President Dental Marketing, Joachim Feldmer
Vice President Global Marketing, Shirley Stanley
Vice President Technology Global Prosthetic Solutions, Patrick Thurm
Vp Safety, Shirley Taylor
Vice President Supply Chain Services, Jurgen Debrier
Vice President Of Technology Sales, Tommy Maguire
Vice President Data And Business Analytics, Diana Friedman
Vice President Financial Reporting Taxation, Reid Arstark
Vice President Corporate Business Development An, John Kristich
National Sales Manager, Christian Marsolais
National Account Manager, John Ballarin
Vice President Global Supply Chain Europe, Axel Pfitzenreiter
Vice President, Brian Peterson
Senior Vice President And Chief Executive Officer Global Dental Group, Jonathan Koch
Vice President, Howard Tapler

Vice President North America Digital Dental Marketing, Leigh Benowitz
National Account Manager, Richard Lapsley
Vice President Global Compensation And Benefits, Jonathan Lee
Executive Vice President Of Sales, Ann Gothard
Vpt Customer Service Representative And Ed Hs Cares Fdn, Jennifer Field
Vice President Corporate Media Relations, Annmarie Gothard
Auditors: BDO USA, LLP

LOCATIONS

HQ: Schein (Henry) Inc
135 Duryea Road, Melville, NY 11747
Phone: 631 843-5500
Web: www.henryschein.com

2018 Sales

	$ mil.	% of total
US	8,348	63
Other countries	4,853	37
Total	**13,202**	**100**

PRODUCTS/OPERATIONS

2018 Sales by Segment

	$ mil.	% of total
Health Care Distribution		
Dental	6,349	48
Animal health	3,682	28
Medical	2,661	20
Technology and Value-Added Services	509	4
Total	**13,202**	**100**

COMPETITORS

Allscripts	McKesson
Benco Dental	Medline Industries
Burkhart Dental	NextGen
Cardinal Health	Patterson Companies
Carestream Health	Sybron Dental
Darby Dental	athenahealth
IDEXX Labs	eClinicalWorks
MWI Veterinary Supply	

HISTORICAL FINANCIALS

Company Type: Public

Income Statement

FYE: December 28

	REVENUE ($ mil.)	NET INCOME ($ mil.)	NET PROFIT MARGIN	EMPLOYEES
12/19	9,985	694	7.0%	19,000
12/18	13,202	535	4.1%	18,000
12/17	12,461	406	3.3%	22,000
12/16	11,571	506	4.4%	21,000
12/15	10,629	479	4.5%	19,000
Annual Growth	(1.6%)	9.7%	—	0.0%

2019 Year-End Financials

Debt ratio: 10.58%
Return on equity: 23.38%
Cash ($ mil.): 106
Current ratio: 1.58
Long-term debt ($ mil.): 622

No. of shares (mil.): 143
Dividends
  Yield: —
  Payout: —
Market value ($ mil.): 9,544

	STOCK PRICE ($) FY Close	P/E High/Low		PER SHARE ($) Earnings	Dividends	Book Value
12/19	66.58	17	12	4.65	0.00	20.91
12/18	77.92	26	18	3.49	0.00	19.56
12/17	69.88	72	26	2.57	0.00	18.29
12/16	151.71	58	46	3.10	0.00	17.59
12/15	157.09	55	44	2.85	0.00	17.50
Annual Growth	(19.3%)	—	—	13.1%	—	4.6%

Schwab (Charles) Corp (The)

The once-rebellious Charles Schwab is all grown up: the discount broker now offers the same traditional brokerage services it shunned over three decades ago. Schwab manages more than $4 trillion in assets for some 15.5 million individual investors and institutional clients. Traders can access its services via telephone the internet-enabled devices and through approximately 360 offices in about 50-plus states as well as United Kingdom Hong Kong Singapore and Australia. Besides discount brokerage the firm offers financial research advice and planning investment management and retirement and employee compensation plans. It also operates a federal savings bank and an investment advisory firm. In 2019 Schwab agreed to buy competitor TD Ameritrade for about $26 billion.

Operations

Charles Schwab firm operates through two business segments. Its Investor Services segment generates some 70% of company revenue and offers retail brokerage and banking services to individual investors as well as retirement plan and corporate brokerage services. Its Advisor Services segment generating nearly 30% of revenue provides custodial trading and support services to institutional investors.

More than 60% of Charles Schwab's revenue comes from interest income on cash investment securities brokerage-related receivables and loans to banking clients. Approximately 30% of its revenue comes from asset management and administration fees which consist of mostly mutual fund service fees proprietary and third-party mutual funds and exchange-traded funds (ETFs) and fee-based advisory solutions. Trading revenue makes about 5% of its total revenue and consists of commission and principal transaction income. Other revenue generates the remaining sales includes order flow revenue other service fees software fees from our portfolio management solutions exchange processing fees and non-recurring gains.

Geographic Reach

San Francisco-based Charles Schwab has more than 360 branch offices in about 50 US states as well as offices in United Kingdom Hong Kong Singapore Australia and Puerto Rico.

Sales and Marketing

Charles Schwab provides financial services to both individuals and institutional clients. Its Advisor Services segment provides custodial trading and support services to independent investment advisors and retirement business services to independent retirement plan advisors and record keepers with assets plans held at Schwab Bank. Its Investor Services provides retail brokerage and banking services to individual investor and retirement plan services as well as other corporate brokerage services to businesses and employees.

Charles Schwab has around $4 trillion in client assets across about 12.5 million active brokerage accounts about 1.5 million banking accounts and nearly 1.5 million corporate retirement plan participants.

Advertising and market development expense for 2019 was $307 million.

Financial Performance

Charles Schwab's revenue had been steadily increasing in five consecutive years rising about 68% between 2015 and 2019.

Charles Schwab had a very good 2019. The company's revenue increased about 6% to $10.7 billion compared to $10.1 billion in 2018. Driven by higher average investment yields and also by an increase in client cash balances held at our bank and broker-dealer subsidiaries.

Net income increased about 6% to $3.7 billion compared to $3.5 billion in 2018 driven by higher taxes on income.

Cash at the end of 2019 was $2.8 billion increased about 36% compared to $2.1 billion in 2018. Operating activities provided $5.0 billion while investing used $1.7 billion primarily from increase in investment in subsidiaries and purchases of available for sale securities. Financing activities used $2.6 billion mainly used for dividends and repurchases of common stocks.

Strategy

The company's strategy emphasizes placing clients' perspectives needs and desires at the forefront. Because investing plays a fundamental role in building financial security the company strives to deliver ? a better investing experience for its clients ? individual investors and the people and institutions who serve them ? by disrupting longstanding industry practices on their behalf and providing superior service. The company also aims to offer a broad range of products and solutions to meet client needs with a focus on transparency value and trust. In addition the management works to couple Schwab's scale and resources with ongoing expense discipline to keep costs low and ensure that products and solutions are affordable as well as responsive to client needs. In combination these are the key elements of our "no trade-offs" approach to serving investors. The company believes that following this strategy is the best way to maximize its market valuation and stockholder returns over time.

The company's strategy is based on the principle that developing trusted relationships will translate into more assets from both new and existing clients ultimately driving more revenue and along with expense discipline and thoughtful capital management will generate earnings growth and build long-term stockholder value.

HISTORY

During the 1960s Stanford graduate Charles Schwab founded First Commander Corp. which managed investments and published a newsletter. But he failed to properly register with the SEC and after a hiatus he returned to the business under the name Charles Schwab & Co. in 1971. Initially a full-service broker Schwab moved into discount brokerage after the SEC outlawed fixed commissions in 1975. While most brokers defiantly raised commissions Schwab cut its rates steeply.

From 1977 to 1983 Schwab's client list increased thirtyfold and revenues grew from $4.6 million to $126.5 million enabling the firm to automate its operations and develop cash-management account systems. To gain capital Charles sold the company to BankAmerica (now Bank of America) in 1983. Schwab grew but federal

regulations prevented expansion into such services as mutual funds and telephone trading. Charles bought his company back in 1987 and took it public. When the stock market crashed later that year trading volume fell by nearly half from 17900 per day. Stung Schwab diversified further offering new fee-based services. Commission revenues fell from 64% of sales in 1987 to 39% in 1990 but by 1995 the long bull market had pushed commissions to more than 50%.

In 1989 Schwab introduced TeleBroker a 24-hour Touch-Tone telephone trading service available in English Spanish Mandarin or Cantonese.

Schwab continued to diversify courting independent financial advisors. Other buys included Mayer & Schweitzer (1991 now Schwab Capital Markets) an OTC market maker that accounted for about 7% of all NASDAQ trades. In 1993 the firm opened its first overseas office in London but traded only in dollar-denominated stocks until it bought Share-Link (later Charles Schwab Europe) the UK's largest discount brokerage in 1995. It subsequently sold the British pound sterling brokerage business to Barclays PLC although it has maintained its US dollar business in the UK.

During the next year Schwab made a concerted effort to build its retirement services by creating a 401(k) administration and investment services unit. In 1997 Schwab allied with J.P. Morgan Hambrecht & Quist and Credit Suisse First Boston (CSFB) to give its customers access to IPOs; the next year the relationship with CSFB deepened to give Schwab access to debt offerings. In late 1997 and early 1998 Schwab reorganized to reflect its new business lines. The firm also began recruiting talent rather than promoting from within.

Expansion was key at the turn of the century. In 1999 Schwab moved toward more broker-advised investing: It inked a deal (geared toward its retirement products customers) with online financial advice firm Financial Engines and introduced Velocity a desktop system designed to make trading easier for fiscally endowed investors. In 2000 Schwab bought online broker CyBerCorp (later CyberTrader) as well as U.S. Trust which markets to affluent clients.

While Schwab's World Trade Center offices were destroyed by the September 11 terrorist attacks the company did not lose any of its New York staff.

To pare expenses Schwab reduced its workforce by about 35% between 2000 and 2003. Founder and chairman Charles Schwab relinquished his role of co-CEO in early 2003 only to move back into the driver's seat in mid-2004 when former CEO David Pottruck was asked to step down by the company's board.

One of Schwab's first orders of business was to reexamine the company's 2004 acquisition of SoundView Technology Group which was combined with its Capital Markets operations to form Schwab SoundView Capital Markets. While the purchase was intended to help the company beef up its services for institutional investors Schwab said that SoundView lacked "synergy" with the company's tradition of supporting the individual investor and sold the business to Swiss bank UBS.

Schwab acquired The 401(k) Companies from Nationwide Financial Services in 2007. The addition became part of the company's existing Charles Schwab Trust subsidiary which serves as a trustee for employee benefit plans. Also that year Schwab sold U.S. Trust to Bank of America for some $3.3 billion in cash and shut down its CyberTrader day trading arm merging the direct-access brokerage's business with its own.

In 2011 Charles Schwab acquired retail brokerage optionsXpress. The $1 billion deal expanded its client base and online equity options and futures trading business and it has already boosted the company's trading revenues.

In another 2011 transaction Charles Schwab acquired Compliance11 which allowed the company to offer compliance monitoring and reporting services.

In December 2012 the firm purchased Massachusetts-based ThomasPartners a dividend income-focused asset management firm with some $2.3 billion in assets under management for $85 million in cash.

EXECUTIVES

Cfo, Peter Crawford, age 52
President And Ceo, Walter W. (Walt) Bettinger, age 59, $1,041,667 total compensation
President And Ceo Charles Schwab Bank, Paul V. Woolway
Evp Client Solutions, G. Andrew (Andy) Gill, age 57
Evp Corporate Initiatives, James D. McCool, age 61, $550,000 total compensation
President And Ceo Charles Schwab Investment Management, Marie A. Chandoha, age 59, $572,500 total compensation
Evp International Services And Special Business Development, Lisa Kidd Hunt
Evp Advisor Services, Bernard J. Clark, age 61, $525,000 total compensation
Evp Operational Services, Ron Carter
Evp And Chief Marketing Officer, Jonathan M. Craig
Evp Corporate Risk, Nigel J. Murtagh, age 57
Evp Retirement Plan Services, Steven H. (Steve) Anderson
Evp Technology Services, Jim McGuire
Evp General Counsel And Corporate Secretary, David R. Garfield, age 64
Evp Investor Services, Terri R. Kallsen, age 52, $450,000 total compensation
Evp Investor Services Strategy Segments And Platforms, Neesha Hathi
Evp And Cto, Timothy C. Heier
Evp And Cio, Dennis Howard
Evp Internal Audit, Mitch Mantua
Vice President Managing Director Relationship Management New York Metro Region, Tom Cantillon
Vice President Financial Consultant, Rich Kahan
Vice President Financial Consultant, Martin Kurtz
Vice President Senior Financial Consultant, Jerry Santoro
Vice President Financial Consultant, John Curren
Vice President Financial Consultant, Shelley Chidley
Vice President Plan Sponsor Services, Ben Sheppard
Vice President Financial Consultant, Tyler Amos
Vice President Financial Consultant, David Bernstein
Vice President Financial Consultant, Ari Strait
Vice President Financial Consultant, Jane Gudgel
Vice President, Dana Ecker
Vice President Internal Audit, Shayne Zundel
Vice President Financial Consultant, Eric Flynn
Vice President Financial Consultant, Robert Brouthers
Vp Financial Consultant, Justin White

Vice President Financial Consultant, Michael Castro
Senior Vice President Analytics Insight And Loyalty, John Carter
Vice President Financial Consultant, James Kukurin
Vice President Financial Consultant, Tim Thomas
Vice President Financial Consultant, Jonathan Harel
Vice President Senior Financial Consultant, Douglas Kaminski
Vice President Financial Consultant, Tatum Schuler
Vice President Financial, James Riefe
Vice President And Financial Consultant, Scott S DePiazza
Vice President, John Gutierrez
Vice President Financial Consultant, Hans Raymond
Senior Vice President Financial Consultant, Sean Reeves
Vice President, William Parrott
Vice President Financial Consultant, Selene Argao
Vice President Financial Consultant, Bill Schwind
Vice President Financial Consultant, Stuart Evans
Vice President, Matthew Heck
Vice President Financial Consultant, Rick Fine
Vice President Senior Financial Consultant, John Khoury
Vice President Finance Transformation, Brian Godfrey
Vice President Sales Retirement Plan Services, Jen Papay
Vice President Financial Consultant, Christian Beck
Vice President Financial Consultant Dallas Tx Park Cities, Jason Dugdale
Vice President Financial Consultant, Tristyn Eames
Vp Sr Financial Consultant, Jason Burke
Vice President Financial Consultant Schwab Private Client, Jess Ramos
Vice President And Branch Manager International Schwab International Orlando, Cynthia Paul
Senior Vice President Financial Consultant, Michael Maniscalco
Vice President Financial Consultant, Patrick Means
Vp Financial Consultant, Teb Yu
Vice President Financial Consultant, Robert Freddino
Vice President Financial Consultant, Jennifer Depriest
Vice President Financial Consultant, Brandon Lilley
Vice President Financial Consultant, German Ramirez
Vice President Financial Consultant, Drake Beck
Vice President, Jake King
Vice President Financial Consultant Ca Insurance License #0b27845, Cynthia Leal
Vice President Financial Consultant, Denise Patridge
Vice President Financial Consultant Carlsbad Branch, Ron Scherdorf
Vice President Financial Consultant, Carter Taylor
Vice President Financial Consultant, Garrett Sloan
Vice President Ibs Compliance, Gary Wachs
Executive Vice President Retirement Plan Services, Steve Anderson
Vice President Financial Consultant, Giancarlo Mateus
Vice President Financial Consultant, Andrew Thompson
Vice President Financial Consultant, Michael Murray
Vice President Financial Consultant, Travis Nelson
Vice President Financial Consultant, Michael Cook
Vice President, Deborah Pritchard
Vice President And Branch Manager, Francisco J Vivas
Vice President, Lisa Quartarone
Vice President Financial Consultant, Mark Findling

Vice President Financial Consultant, Trent Fifield
Vice President Financial Consultant, Angie Krylo
Vice President Talent Acquisition, Robert Mundell
Vice President Associate General Counsel, Steve Johnson
Svp Financial Consultant, Aaron Olson
Vice President Distributor And Business Oversight Regulatory Communications, Jennifer Hafner
Vice President Financial Consultant, Linda Tarbet
Vice President Financial Consultant, Sue Cheung
Vice President Financial Consultant, Grant Seaton
Vice President Financial Consultant, Kathy Khuu
Vice President Branch Manager, Whitney Fletcher
Vice President Branch Manager, Joe Benvenuto
Vice President Financial Consultant, John Moriarty
Vice President Financial Consultant, Kenneth Jorgenson
Vice President Financial Consultant, Brian Mitchell
Vice President Financial Consultant, Gary Hettler
Vice President Financial Consultant, Jeff Han
Senior Vice President And Head Office Legislative And Regulatory Affairs, Jeff Brown
Vice President Financial Consultant, Karl Michael Lulu
Vice President Financial Consultant, Phillip Thanawiwat
Vice President Financial Consultant, David Bubb
Vice President Financial Consultant, Anthony Khavarani
Senior Vice President Infrastructure, Dustin Yates
Senior Vice President Compensation And Benefits, David Callahan
Vice President Human Resources, Sarah Stanson
Executive Vice President Human Resources, Katie Casey
Vice President Financial Consultant, Mevlan Mata
Vice President Financial Consultant, Scott Jeamel
Vice President Financial Consultant, Stella Hui
Vice President Finacial Consultant, Dan Weisman
Vice President Financial Consultant, Scott Kleinbaum
Vice President Senior Financial Consultant, Ryan Kaplan
Vice President Senior Financial Consultant, Paul Dunk
Vice President Financial Consultant, William Lang
Svp Treasurer, Bill Quinn
Vice President Financial Consultant, Brian Moriarty
Vice President Brokerage Accounting And Trading Technology, Rama Bokka
Vice President Investor Relations, Michael Canady
Auditors: DELOITTE & TOUCHE LLP

LOCATIONS

HQ: Schwab (Charles) Corp (The)
211 Main Street, San Francisco, CA 94105
Phone: 415 667-7000 **Fax:** 415 627-8894
Web: www.aboutschwab.com

PRODUCTS/OPERATIONS

2017 Sales

	$ mil.	% of total
Investor Services	6,200	72
Advisor Services	2,418	28
Total	**8,618**	**100**

2017 Sales

	$ mil.	% of total
Interest	4,282	50
Asset management & administration fees	3,392	39
Trading	654	8
Provision for loan losses	- -	
Other	290	4
Total	**8,618**	**100**

Selected Subsidiaries
Charles Schwab Bank

Charles Schwab Investment Management Inc. (mutual fund investment adviser)
Schwab Holdings Inc.
Charles Schwab & Co. Inc. (securities broker-dealer)

COMPETITORS

Ameriprise	Morgan Stanley
Bank of America	Principal Financial
E*TRADE Financial	Raymond James
Edward Jones	Financial
FMR	Scottrade
Franklin Templeton	ShareBuilder
John Hancock Financial	T. Rowe Price
Services	TD Ameritrade
Legg Mason	The Vanguard Group

HISTORICAL FINANCIALS

Company Type: Public

Income Statement

FYE: December 31

	REVENUE ($ mil.)	NET INCOME ($ mil.)	NET PROFIT MARGIN	EMPLOYEES
12/19	11,785	3,704	31.4%	19,700
12/18	10,989	3,507	31.9%	19,500
12/17	8,960	2,354	26.3%	17,600
12/16	7,649	1,889	24.7%	16,200
12/15	6,512	1,447	22.2%	15,300
Annual Growth	16.0%	26.5%	—	6.5%

2019 Year-End Financials

Debt ratio: 2.53%	No. of shares (mil.): 1,285
Return on equity: 17.47%	Dividends
Cash ($ mil.): 29,345	Yield: 1.4%
Current ratio: 0.28	Payout: 25.4%
Long-term debt ($ mil.): 7,430	Market value ($ mil.): 61,149

	STOCK PRICE ($) FY Close	P/E High/Low		PER SHARE ($) Earnings	Dividends	Book Value
12/19	47.56	19	13	2.67	0.68	16.91
12/18	41.53	24	15	2.45	0.46	15.51
12/17	51.37	32	23	1.61	0.32	13.77
12/16	39.47	31	17	1.31	0.27	12.32
12/15	32.93	34	25	1.03	0.24	10.15
Annual Growth	9.6%	—	—	26.9%	29.7%	13.6%

Seacoast Banking Corp. of Florida

Seacoast Banking Corporation is the holding company for Seacoast National Bank. It operates some 50 branches in Florida with a concentration in four large city markets. Serving individuals and businesses the bank offers a range of financial products and services including deposit accounts credit cards trust services and private banking. Commercial and residential real estate loans make up most of the bank's lending activities; to a lesser extent it also originates business and consumer loans.

Operations

Seacoast Bank offers traditional banking products such as deposit accounts checking & savings accounts CDs business loans home mortgages and the like. It also makes available to its customers brokerage and annuity services along with insurance products. A division of the bank

Seacoast Marine Finance specializes in boat loans which it typically originates itself and then sells into the secondary market.

Geographic Reach

Seacoast National Bank has some 50 branches in 14 counties across Florida stretching from Broward County north through the Treasure Coast and into Orlando and west to Okeechobee and surrounding counties. Its primary markets are Tampa Orlando Port St. Lucie and West Palm Beach/Ft. Lauderdale.

Financial Performance

Seacoast Banking Corporation has done well in recent years steadily growing interest income to nearly $200 million in 2017 up from a low of $70 million just four years prior. The bank registered positive earnings from 2013 forward albeit the results fluctuated wildly.

In 2017 interest income grew 30% to $192 million and non-interest income improved by 25% to $170 million. Its loan portfolio grew ? through organic means as well as via acquisitions ? by almost 30% against which it earned additional interest income. The bank's average net interest margin rose 10 basis points to 3.73%.

Net income also lodged an excellent year increasing 48% from the prior year to $43 million. Although the company incurred an $8.6 million impairment of its deferred tax assets due to the change in US Federal tax law the increase in revenue along with a $15 million gain on the sale an investment it made in Visa company stock pushed up yearly earnings.

Cash at the end of the year was $109 million unchanged from 2016. Financing activities contributed $196 million mostly from an increase in deposits from acquisitions. Investing activities used $246 million in the process of buying and selling securities and originating new loans. Operating activities added $49 million.

Strategy

Seacoast Bank has grown mostly through acquisitions in recent years. Since 2014 it opened one new office and acquired 49 branches (19 of which were subsequently shuttered). Orlando has been a hot destination for it as it transformed its presence there just a few branches to the largest Florida-based bank in the market by 2017. The bank anticipates continued geographic growth in Florida through organic means but also through acquisition if the right opportunity arises as with the 2017 purchases of NorthStar Banking and Palm Beach Community Bank.

Although it caters to personal customers as well as business clients the focus on businesses has sparked significant growth in the associated loan portfolio. The company tends to commercial clients with revenues exceeding $5 million in specific industry verticals. It takes a comprehensive relationship approach by providing business treasury lending and wealth management services. The commercial loan portfolio grew nearly 300% between year-end 2013 and year-end 2017 from $632 million to $2.5 billion.

The bank significantly expanded its banking technology platform by introducing digital deposit capture on smartphones updating its mobile platforms for consumer and business customers and enhancing its ATM capabilities. Customers have taken to the online functionality and in 2017 the bank processed more digital

transactions than it did through its physical branch network.

Mergers and Acquisitions

In 2017 Seacoast purchased NorthStar Banking Corporation adding more than $200 million in assets $170 million in deposits and nearly $140 million in loans to Seacoast's balance sheet. In the same year it acquired Palm Beach Community Bank for some $70 million adding $270 million in loans and four bank branches to Seacoast's operations.

EXECUTIVES

Chairman And Ceo, Dennis S. (Denny) Hudson, age 64, $537,852 total compensation
Evp And Residential Lending Executive, Michael J. (Mike) Sonego
Evp And Commercial Banking Executive, Charles K. Cross, age 62, $273,333 total compensation
Evp And Chief Risk And Credit Officer, David D. Houdeshell, age 59, $262,500 total compensation
Evp Enterprise Services And Initiatives, Kathleen (Kathy) Cavicchioli
Evp And Chief Marketing Officer, Jeffery (Jeff) Lee
Evp Service And Operations, Jeffery (Jeff) Bray
Evp And Chief Human Resources Officer, Daniel G. (Dan) Chappell
Cfo And Head Of Strategy, Charles M. (Chuck) Shaffer, age 46, $248,333 total compensation
Evp Community Banking, Julie Kleffel
Senior Vice President Marketing Director, Susan Bergstrom
Senior Vice President Human Resources Director, Charles Olsson
Vp Sba Portfolio Manager, Maureen Swierkowski
Executive Vice President, William Hahl
Assistant Vice President And Call Center Manager, Joni Wyszkowski
Vice President Financial Advisor, Carl Newton
Executive Vice President, Tom Hall
Vice President Business Banking Manager, Theresa Vazquez
Svp Senior Fiduciary And Risk Officer Cfp Clu, Peter Lowery
Avp Banking Center Manager, Amber Shirk
Senior Vice President Commercial Banking, Thomas Dargan
Assistant Vice President Corporate Finance, Zev Zaretsky
Vice President Commercial Banking, David Beckey
Vice President Cra Officer, Iris Jones
Vice President Leadership Development Manager, Angel Birch
Evp Small Business Banking Leader, Juliette Kleffel
Vice President Market Manager, Hart Donovan
Vice President, Travis Engebretsen
Vice President Business Banker, Stephen Markham
Senior Market Manager Vice President, Monika Krumbock
Vice President Collection And Recovery Manager, Gary Albert
Vice President Residential Lending, Steve Bilbo
Vp Of Seacoast Bank Commercial Banking, Greg Peters
Vice President Commercial Banking, Daniel Lightfritz
Vice President And Market Manager, Lee Jeff
Senior Vice President Of Retail Banking, Mathew Kennedy
Vice President Mortgage Banking Officer, Grace Monforte
Vice President Mortgage Lending Area Manager, Megan Martinez
Assistant Vice President Commercial Loan Officer, Ronnie Houck
Vice President Business Banker, Joe Ritchie
Vp Small Business Banking And Commercial Banking, Gilbert Russell

Vp Regional Business Banking Manager, Phil Fitzpatrick
Senior Vice President Commercial Banker, Jennifer Potter
Vice President Commercial Banker, Shane McCutchen
Senior Vice President, Toni Diaz
Senior Vice President Regional Community Banking Director, Vance Rea
Senior Vice President Commercial Relationship Manager, Jennifer Murphy
Vice President Banking Center Manager, Patricia Hill
Board Member, Herbert Lurie
Board Member, Jacqueline Bradley
Board Member, Tim Huval
Auditors: Crowe LLP

LOCATIONS

HQ: Seacoast Banking Corp. of Florida
815 Colorado Avenue, Stuart, FL 34994
Phone: 772 287-4000
Web: www.seacoastbanking.com

PRODUCTS/OPERATIONS

Selected Services
Commercial and retail banking
Mortgage services
Wealth management

COMPETITORS

BB&T	PNC Financial
BBX Capital	Regions Financial
Bank of America	SunTrust
BankUnited	Suncoast Schools FCU
CenterState Banks	Wells Fargo
EverBank Financial	

HISTORICAL FINANCIALS
Company Type: Public

Income Statement   FYE: December 31

	ASSETS ($ mil.)	NET INCOME ($ mil.)	INCOME AS % OF ASSETS	EMPLOYEES
12/19	7,108	98	1.4%	867
12/18	6,747	67	1.0%	902
12/17	5,810	42	0.7%	805
12/16	4,680	29	0.6%	725
12/15	3,534	22	0.6%	665
Annual Growth	19.1%	45.3%	—	6.9%

2019 Year-End Financials

Debt ratio: 1.00%	No. of shares (mil.): 51
Return on equity: 10.68%	Dividends
Cash ($ mil.): 124	Yield: —
Current ratio: —	Payout: —
Long-term debt ($ mil.): —	Market value ($ mil.): 1,575

	STOCK PRICE ($) FY Close	P/E High/Low	PER SHARE ($) Earnings	Dividends	Book Value
12/19	30.57	16 12	1.90	0.00	19.13
12/18	26.02	24 17	1.38	0.00	16.83
12/17	25.21	26 21	0.99	0.00	14.70
12/16	22.06	29 17	0.78	0.00	11.45
12/15	14.98	25 18	0.66	0.00	10.29
Annual Growth	19.5%	— —	30.3%	—	16.8%

SECURITIES INVESTOR PROTECTION CORPORATION

EXECUTIVES

Vice President Operations, Karen Saperstein
Assistant Vice President Information Technology, Bob Ferry
Auditors: GRANT THORNTON MCLEAN VA

LOCATIONS

HQ: SECURITIES INVESTOR PROTECTION CORPORATION
1667 K ST NW STE 1000, WASHINGTON, DC 200061620
Phone: 202 371-8300
Web: WWW.SIPC.ORG

HISTORICAL FINANCIALS
Company Type: Private

Income Statement   FYE: December 31

	ASSETS ($ mil.)	NET INCOME ($ mil.)	INCOME AS % OF ASSETS	EMPLOYEES
12/16	2,944	362	12.3%	39
12/15	2,652	169	6.4%	—
12/14	2,362	307	13.0%	—
12/11	1,606	131	8.2%	—
Annual Growth	12.9%	22.4%	—	—

Selective Insurance Group Inc

Property/casualty insurance holding company Selective Insurance Group's reach primarily covers the entire eastern US seaboard and much of the Midwest. Commercial policies include workers' compensation and commercial automobile property and liability insurance. Personal lines include homeowners and automobile insurance. The company also offers federal flood insurance administration services throughout the US and some excess and surplus (E&S nonstandard) insurance. Selective Insurance Group operates through four reportable segments: Standard Commercial Lines Standard Personal Lines E&S Lines and Investments.

Operations

Selective's Standard Commercial Lines segment which serves business not-for-profit organizations and government agencies accounts for about three-fourths of Selective's total revenue. Standard Personal Lines ? including flood insurance coverage ? follows representing more than 10% of total revenue. The E&S Lines segment which covers more unusual risks than standard insurance accounts for nearly 10% of total revenue. Investments (less than 10% of total revenue) which invests the premiums collected by

our insurance operations and amounts generated through our capital management strategies which include the issuance of debt and equity securities.

The company's flood insurance is sold to businesses· and individuals through the National Flood Insurance Program.

Geographic Reach

Selective primarily writes commercial policies in more than 25 eastern midwestern and southwestern states plus Washington DC. Personal policies are primarily sold in nearly 15 states in the East and Midwest. The company also offers flood and E&S insurance policies in all 50 states plus Washington DC.

While its native New Jersey market still accounts for about 20% of Selective's net written premiums the company has successfully become a "super-regional" insurer. By doing business in a wider geographic range Selective is better able to spread out its catastrophic risk exposure. It maintains its headquarters in New Jersey and regional branch offices in New Jersey Indiana Maryland North Carolina Pennsylvania and Arizona.

Sales and Marketing

Some 1350 independent retail agents sell Selective's Standard Commercial Lines products with a focus on providing policies to small and mid-sized businesses and government entities. The company's nationwide flood protection products are sold by a network of some 6000 retail agents while E&S policies are sold through about 90 wholesale agencies and brokers.

Target clients include manufacturing and wholesale contractor community and public services and mercantile and services customers.

Financial Performance

Selective Insurance's revenue has been rising since 2015 and in general net income has also been rising. These gains have largely been driven by growth in the core commercial lines segment as well as solid retention rates. Revenue grew 34% between 2015 and 2019 while net income grew 64% over the same period.

Revenue increased 10% to $2.8 billion in 2019 compared to $2.6 billion in 2018. Net premiums earned and investment income both grew that year and the company realized net gains of $14.4 million versus net realized losses of $54.9 million in 2018.

With a higher revenue net income rose 52% to $271.6 million in 2019 despite a corresponding increase in expenses for the year.

The company ended 2019 with $8 million in net cash an $8.9 million decrease from 2018. Operating activities provided $477.5 million in cash that year. Investing activities used $543.6 million while financing activities provided $57.2 million. Selective's primary cash uses in 2019 were purchase of fixed income securities purchase of short-term investments and purchase of property and equipment. Proceeds from borrowings contributed the majority of cash to the company's financing activities.

Strategy

Selective's three primary areas of interest are improving its overall customer experience refining its underwriting tools and enhancing its technological capabilities.

As part of its digital strategy Selective provides customers with a mobile application and a web-based portal that provides its customers with on-demand self-service access to account information and the ability to electrically pay the bills and report claims. It also provides value-added services such as proactive messaging about vehicle and product recalls adverse weather activity and claim status updates.

In mid-2020 Selective announced the launch of Smart Secure an all-in-one smart home and security program that gives Selective's customers new levels of control over their home protection. The new Smart Secure incorporates years of customer insights into a unique offering centered on giving customers the power of choice to design a system to meet their needs. This development enhances Selective's technological capabilities even further.

The company works with what it refers to as "ivy league" distribution partners who have a strong presence in Selective's key markets. A product of one of these partnerships is Selective's new Recall Alert System which works to alert consumers of potentially dangerous recalls affecting their vehicles and personal safety through proactive notifications.

Company Background

In the 1920s Daniel L.B. Smith was a general store operator in Sussex County New Jersey. Almost by accident he began selling insurance out of one of his store locations and he decided that the area needed a local insurance company. With an initial investment of $20000 Smith and several partners opened Selected Risks Insurance Company. The company expanded beyond its New Jersey origins over the next several decades.

EXECUTIVES

Vice President, Eric Thiessen
Assistant Vp And Regional Safety Operations Manager, Alan Null Costa
Chairman And Ceo, Gregory E. Murphy, age 65, $946,923 total compensation
Vice President Operations, Yanina Hupka
Evp And Chief Actuary, Ronald J. Zaleski, age 66, $437,692 total compensation
Evp General Counsel And Chief Compliance Officer, Michael H. Lanza, age 59, $536,923 total compensation
President And Coo, John J. Marchioni, age 50, $793,846 total compensation
Evp And Cfo, Mark A. Wilcox, age 52
Evp And Chief Claims Officer, George A. Neale
Evp And Chief Human Resources Officer, Angelique Carbo
Evp And Cio, Gordon J. Gaudet
Svp And Chief Marketing Officer, Rohit Mull
Vice President, Dennis L Barger
Assistant Vice President Bond Underwriting Manager, Debra Paziora
Assistant Vice President, Robert Mitchell
Commercial Auto Underwriting Assistant Vice President, Stan Willey
Vice President Application Development, Richard Agresta
Assistant Vice President, Jack Ribeiro
Vice President, Christopher Nickol
Vice President Office Automation, Kathy Koval
Legal Secretary, Maria Rodriguez
Assistant Vice President Business Case Manger, Sue Insalaco
Vice President Field Operations Manager, Tony Miller
Vice President, Jim Klotz
Assistant Vice President, Deborah Dickens-hunter
Vice President Personal Lines Pricing, Mindy Oosten

Assistant Vice President Application Architecture, Kevin Vieten
Assistant Vice President Property Line, Scott Crump
Assistant Vice President Assistant Controller, Angelo Mastrolia
Assistant Vice President Workers Compensation, Joe Greco
Vice President Government Affairs And Compliance, Jeff Beck
Assistant Vice President Northeast Regional Manager Claims, Vincent Disimone
Assistant Vice President, Haide Krygoski
Vice President Specialty Programs, Lorraine Miller
Vice President Field Operations, Steven Bennett
Assistant Vice President, Robert L Redden
Assistant Vice President Claims Service Center, Susan L Brown
Vice President Of Flood Operat, Cassie Masone
Vice President Commercial Lines Underwriting Line Of Business And Product Development, Vere Bryan
Vice President Bonds East Hanover Nj, Timothy Marchio
Executive Vice President And Chief Actuary, Vincent Senia
Senior Vice President Deputy General Counsel, Maria Orecchio
Assistant Vice President Director Of Communications, Jamie Morgan
Assistant Vice President Property, Matt Caton
Vice President And Director Communications, Jamie Beal
Assistant Vice President Corporate Systems Applica, Gary Beumee
Vice President Information Technology, Harikrishna Raghumandala
Vp Underwriting, John Rhodes
Vice President Underwriting, Mike Lucas
Legal Secretary, Lori Coyle
Senior Vice President, Martin Hollander
Assistant Vice President Quality Assuran, Daksha Kantaria
Assistant Vice President Contractors Strategic Business Unit Leader, Nicole Hayes
Avp Property Claims, Christopher Carpenter
Avp Claims Application Delivery, Kevin Forrey
Vice President, Darryl Holmes
Vp Underwriting Nj Region, Jason Raider
Senior Vice President, Charles M Adams
Vp And Regional Manager, Deneen Dallago-Iohan
Svp Actuarial Reserving, Christopher Cunniff
Vice President, Ryan Bradley
Assistant Vice President Regional Claim Manager, Stephen Bartholomew
Executive Vice President, Chuck Chapman
Assistant Vice President Corporate Claims, Peyton Artz
Auditors: KPMG LLP

LOCATIONS

HQ: Selective Insurance Group Inc
40 Wantage Avenue, Branchville, NJ 07890
Phone: 973 948-3000   **Fax:** 973 948-0282
Web: www.selective.com

PRODUCTS/OPERATIONS

2017 Sales by Segment

	$ mil.	% of total
Standard Commercial Lines	1,798	73
Standard Personal Lines	290	12
E&S Lines	212	8
Investments	168	7
Total	**2,470**	**100**

2017 Sales

	$ mil.	% of total
Net premiums earned	2,291	93
Net investment income earned	161	7
Other	10	-
Net realized gains	6	-
Total	**2,470**	**100**

COMPETITORS

Allstate	Progressive
Chubb Limited	Corporation
Cincinnati Financial	State Farm
Erie Indemnity	The Hartford
GEICO	Travelers Companies
Hanover Insurance	United Fire
Company	W. R. Berkley
Liberty Mutual	Zurich Insurance Group
Nationwide	

HISTORICAL FINANCIALS

Company Type: Public

Income Statement
FYE: December 31

	ASSETS ($ mil.)	NET INCOME ($ mil.)	INCOME AS % OF ASSETS	EMPLOYEES
12/19	8,797	271	3.1%	2,400
12/18	7,952	178	2.3%	2,290
12/17	7,686	168	2.2%	2,260
12/16	7,355	158	2.2%	2,250
12/15	6,904	165	2.4%	2,200
Annual Growth	**6.2%**	**13.1%**	—	**2.2%**

2019 Year-End Financials

Debt ratio: 6.26%
Return on equity: 13.63%
Cash ($ mil.): 0
Current ratio: —
Long-term debt ($ mil.): —

No. of shares (mil.): 59
Dividends
  Yield: 1.2%
  Payout: 21.1%
Market value ($ mil.): 3,876

	STOCK PRICE ($) FY Close	P/E High/Low	PER SHARE ($) Earnings	Dividends	Book Value
12/19	65.19	18 13	4.53	0.83	36.91
12/18	60.94	22 18	3.00	0.74	30.40
12/17	58.70	21 14	2.84	0.66	29.28
12/16	43.05	16 11	2.70	0.61	26.42
12/15	33.58	13 9	2.85	0.57	24.37
Annual Growth	**18.0%**	—	**12.3%**	**9.9%**	**10.9%**

Sempra Energy

Sempra Energy's mission is to be North America's premier energy infrastructure company. The company delivers energy to over 35 million consumers through its subsidiaries. SoCalGas is the nation's largest gas distribution company and operates nearly 100000 miles of distribution pipelines and more than 3000 miles of transmission pipelines. SDG&E operates over 25000 miles of electric transmission and distribution lines and over 15700 miles of combined pipeline. Oncor is the largest energy delivery company in Texas and IEnova is one of the largest infrastructure companies in Mexico. Sempra LNG develops and builds natural gas liquefaction facilities and the Cameron LNG liquefaction facility is fully operational with a projected export of about 12 million tonnes per annum of LNG.

HISTORY

Sempra Energy is the latest incarnation of some of California's leading lights. Formed by the $6.2 billion merger between Enova and Pacific Enterprises the company traces its roots back to the 1880s.

Enova began as San Diego Gas which lit its first gaslights in 1881 and added electricity in 1887 (when it became San Diego Gas & Electric Light). Massive utility holding company Standard Gas & Electric bought the company in 1905 and renamed it San Diego Consolidated Gas & Electric. Over the next few decades San Diego Consolidated expanded through acquisitions and even stayed profitable during the Depression. But the 1935 Public Utilities Holding Company Act forced Standard to divest many of its widespread utilities and in 1940 San Diego Consolidated went public as San Diego Gas & Electric (SDG&E).

SDG&E grew quickly until the 1970s when new environmental laws slowed plans to build more power plants and rates soared because the company had to purchase power. The company finally added more generating capacity in the 1980s and the state of California allowed SDG&E to diversify into real estate software and oil and gas distribution. In 1995 it created Enova to serve as its holding company.

Meanwhile up the coast in San Francisco Pacific Enterprises began as gas lamp rental firm Pacific Lighting in 1886; it quickly moved into gas distribution to defend its market against electricity. The firm bought three Los Angeles gas and electric utilities in 1889 and continued to grow through acquisitions; it consolidated all of its utilities in the 1920s. Pacific Lighting sold its electric properties to the city of Los Angeles in 1937 in exchange for a long-term gas franchise.

The company entered oil and gas exploration in 1960. A decade later it merged its gas utility operations into Southern California Gas (SoCalGas). Pacific Lighting continued to diversify in the 1980s buying two oil and gas companies and three drugstore chains. Renamed Pacific Enterprises in 1988 the company launched an unsuccessful diversification effort that cost it $88 million in 1991. Over the next two years it sold off noncore businesses to focus on SoCalGas and in the mid-1990s it began moving into South and Central America. This included a joint venture with Enova and Mexico's Proxima SA to build and operate Mexico's first private utility.

Pacific Enterprises and Enova agreed in 1997 to a $6.2 billion merger; Sempra Energy was born in 1998. That year California began deregulating its retail power market. In response Sempra sold SDG&E's non-nuclear power plants (1900 MW) in 1999. It used the proceeds to eliminate its competitive transition charge and in turn lowered its electric rates.

But under deregulation rates tripled by mid-2000; that summer the California Public Utilities Commission (CPUC) implemented a rate freeze for electric customers. Wholesale power prices soared and rolling blackouts occurred in 2000 and 2001 as a result of the state's inadequate energy supply. In 2001 the CPUC began allowing utilities to increase their rates and SDG&E agreed to sell its transmission assets to the state for about $1 billion.

Sempra sold its 72.5% share in power marketing firm Energy America to British energy company Centrica in 2001. In 2002 the company purchased bankrupt utility Enron's London-based metals trading unit for about $145 million; later that year it purchased Enron's metals concentrates and metals warehousing businesses.

The company restructured its competitive energy business units in 2005 renaming several divisions and dividing the former Sempra Energy Solutions operations (retail energy marketing and services for commercial and industrial customers) under the Commodities and Generation divisions. That year Sempra sold one of its gas storage units to Vulcan's investment company for a reported $250 million.

In 2006 the company settled class-action litigation that claimed that two of its subsidiaries Southern California Gas and San Diego Gas & Electric had helped to create the 2000-2001 energy crises in California by restricting the supply of natural gas to the state.

In 2007 Sempra was awarded a $172 million settlement arising from a 2002 dispute over the company's minority stakes in two Argentine natural gas holding companies.

In 2008 Sempra Energy formed a commodities marketing joint venture with The Royal Bank of Scotland RBS Sempra Commodities.

In a move to expand its midstream and distribution assets in the southeastern US in 2008 the company acquired EnergySouth for $510 million.

The company reported a jump in its revenues in 2010 thanks to a recovering global economy that drove up energy demand along with higher oil and gas prices and increased rates. Losses related to winding down its commodities unit trimmed Sempra Energy's net income for the year.

In 2013 Sempra U.S. Gas & Power acquired the Broken Bow 2 wind project in Nebraska. When Broken Bow 2 is completed Sempra U.S. Gas & Power will have joint-venture projects totaling more than 1000 MW of wind generating capacity. Sempra U.S. Gas & Power also agreed to purchase 43 1.7-MW General Electric wind turbines to power the 75-MW wind farm. Located in Custer County the wind farm will generate enough renewable power for 30000 Nebraska homes.

Building its midstream portfolio in 2010 the company acquired El Paso's Mexico-based pipeline and compression assets for $300 million.

In 2010 and 2011 Sempra Energy exited the commodities trading business. (In 2008 Sempra Energy had formed a partnership with The Royal Bank of Scotland to operate RBS Sempra Commodities including Sempra Energy Trading which traded and markets wholesale energy commodities in Asia Europe and North America. However to refocus its operations around its more financially reliable North American businesses to pay down debt and to meet EU antitrust requirements in 2010 the company sold the European and Asian segments of this partnership to JP Morgan Chase for about $1.6 billion. It also sold that unit's retail commodity operations to Noble Group for $318 million and eventually wound down its joint venture with The Royal Bank of Scotland).

In early 2012 the company consolidated Sempra Generation Sempra Pipelines & Storage and Sempra LNG (together formerly Sempra Global) into Sempra International and Sempra US Gas & Power to improve its management and pursue strategic initiatives. Sempra US Gas & Power includes natural gas and renewables while Sempra International includes subsidiaries Sempra Mexico and Sempra South American Utilities.

Taking advantage of abundant natural gas supply from US shale plays In 2013 Sempra Energy teamed up with GDF SUEZ Mitsubishi and Mitsui & Co. to design and build an LNG export facility at the Cameron LNG receipt terminal in Hackberry Louisiana capable of processing 13.5 million tons per year.

To raise cash to fund its growth initiative the company sold one 625-MW block of Sempra U.S. Gas & Power's 1250-MW Mesquite Power natural gas-fired power plant to Salt River Project Agricultural Improvement and Power District for $371 million.

In 2012 BP Wind Energy and Sempra U.S. Gas & Power expand their strategic relationship by agreeing to jointly develop the Mehoopany Wind Farm in Pennsylvania and the Flat Ridge 2 Wind Farm in Kansas (a combined investment of more than $1 billion).

Growing its natural gas footprint in the Southeast US in 2012 Sempra U.S. Gas & Power agreed to buy Hattiesburg Mississippi-based Willmut Gas & Oil Company a natural gas utility which provides service to about 20000 customers in Hattiesburg and the surrounding area.

EXECUTIVES

Evp And General Counsel, Martha B. Wyrsch, age 62, $577,900 total compensation
Chairman President And Ceo, Debra L. (Debbie) Reed, age 63, $1,391,900 total compensation
Evp Corporate Strategy And External Affairs, Dennis V. Arriola, age 59
Corporate Group President Infrastructure, Joseph A. (Joe) Householder, age 64, $700,000 total compensation
Chairman And Ceo Infraestructura Energética Nova (ienova), Carlos Ruiz Sacrist`n, age 70
President Coo And Director Socalgas, J. Bret Lane, age 61
Ceo Southern California Gas Company (socalgas), Patricia K. (Patti) Wagner, age 58
Svp Human Resources, G. Joyce Rowland, age 65, $405,000 total compensation
Corporate Group President Of Utilities, Steven D. Davis, age 64, $541,400 total compensation
Evp And Cfo, Jeffrey W. Martin, age 58
President San Diego Gas & Electric (sdg&e), Scott D. Drury, age 54
Cio, P. Kevin Chase, age 51
Regional Vice President Commercial Development Sempra U.s. Gas And Power, Sue Bradham
Vice President Business Origination, Michael Sliwowski
Senior Vice President Regulatory And Finance, Schavrien Lee
Vice President Federal Government Affairs, Maryam Brown
Board Member, William Jones
Board Member, Mike Harriel
Board Member, Bethany Mayer
Auditors: DELOITTE & TOUCHE LLP

HQ: Sempra Energy
    488 8th Avenue, San Diego, CA 92101
Phone: 619 696-2000
Web: www.sempra.com

2018 Sales

	$ mil.	% of total
US	8,840	76
South America	1,585	13
Mexico	1,262	11
Total	**11,687**	**100**

PRODUCTS/OPERATIONS

2018 Sales

	$ mil.	% of total
SDG&E	4,568	38
SoCalGas	3,962	33
Sempra South American Utilities	1,585	13
Sempra Mexico	1,376	11
Sempra LNG & Midstream	472	4
Sempra Renewables	124	1
Adjustments and eliminations	(400)	-
Total	**11,687**	**100**

2018 Sales

	$ mil.	% of total
Utilities:		
Electric	5,506	47
Natural gas	4,540	39
Energy-related businesses	1,641	14
Total	**11,687**	**100**

COMPETITORS

AEP	IBERDROLA
AES	Los Angeles Water and
AT&T	Power
Avista	NRG Energy
CMS Energy	NV Energy
Calpine	PG&E Corporation
CenterPoint Energy	PacifiCorp
Constellation Energy	Public Service
Group	Enterprise Group
Dominion Energy	Sacramento Municipal
Duke Energy	Utility
Edison International	Southern Company
Endesa S.A.	Southwest Gas
Entergy	Tenaska
Exelon Energy	Williams Companies
FirstEnergy	

HISTORICAL FINANCIALS

Company Type: Public

Income Statement				FYE: December 31
	REVENUE ($ mil.)	NET INCOME ($ mil.)	NET PROFIT MARGIN	EMPLOYEES
12/19	10,829	2,198	20.3%	13,969
12/18	11,687	1,050	9.0%	4,015
12/17	11,207	257	2.3%	16,046
12/16	10,183	1,371	13.5%	16,575
12/15	10,231	1,350	13.2%	17,387
Annual Growth	**1.4%**	**13.0%**	**—**	**(5.3%)**

2019 Year-End Financials

Debt ratio: 39.31%
Return on equity: 11.86%
Cash ($ mil.): 108
Current ratio: 0.36
Long-term debt ($ mil.): 20,785

No. of shares (mil.): 291
Dividends
    Yield: 2.5%
    Payout: 53.0%
Market value ($ mil.): 44,189

	STOCK PRICE ($) FY Close	P/E High/Low		PER SHARE ($) Earnings	Dividends	Book Value
12/19	151.48	21	14	7.29	3.87	68.32
12/18	108.19	34	29	3.42	3.58	62.60
12/17	106.92	120	99	1.01	3.29	50.41
12/16	100.64	21	16	5.46	3.02	51.77
12/15	94.01	21	17	5.37	2.80	47.56
Annual Growth	**12.7%**	**—**	**—**	**7.9%**	**8.4%**	**9.5%**

ServisFirst Bancshares Inc

ServisFirst Bancshares is a bank holding company for ServisFirst Bank a regional commercial bank with about a dozen branches located in Alabama and the Florida panhandle. The bank also has a loan office in Nashville. ServisFirst Bank targets privately-held businesses with $2 million to $250 million in annual sales as well as professionals and affluent customers. The bank focuses on traditional commercial banking services including loan origination deposits and electronic banking services such as online and mobile banking. Founded in 2005 by its chairman and CEO Thomas Broughton III the bank went public in 2014 with an offering valued at nearly $57 million.

IPO
ServisFirst Bancshares sold 625000 shares priced at $91 per share. Proceeds from the May 2014 IPO will be used to support the bank's growth plans both in Alabama and in other states.

Geographic Reach
Birmingham-based ServisFirst Bank has branches in Birmingham Huntsville Montgomery Mobile Dothan Pensacola and Nashville.

Financial Performance
The bank reported net income of $41.2 million in 2013 compared with $34 million in 2012. The increase was primarily due to an increase in net interest income which rose nearly 20% to $112.5 million. Noninterest income increased 4% to $10 million in 2013.

As of March 2014 the bank had total assets of approximately $3.6 billion total loans of $2.9 billion and total deposits of about $3.0 billion.

EXECUTIVES

President And Ceo Servisfirst Bancshares And Servisfirst Bank, Thomas A. (Tom) Broughton, age 64, $350,000 total compensation
Evp And Coo Servisfirst Bancshares And Servisfirst Bank, Clarence C. Pouncey, age 63, $263,000 total compensation
Evp Cfo Treasurer And Secretary Servisfirst Bancshares And Servisfirst Bank, William M. Foshee, age 65, $230,000 total compensation
Evp Servisfirst Bancshares And President And Ceo Servisfirst Bank Of Huntsville, Andrew N. (Andy) Kattos, age 50
President And Ceo Servisfirst Bank Of Mobile, William (Bibb) Lamar, age 76

Evp Servisfirst Bancshares And President And Ceo Servisfirst Bank Of Montgomery, G. Carlton (Carl) Barker, age 65
Evp Servisfirst Bancshares And President And Ceo Servisfirst Bank Of Pensacola, Rex D. McKinney, age 57
Evp Correspondent Banking Servisfirst Bancshares And Servisfirst Bank, Rodney E. Rushing, age 62, $245,000 total compensation
Svp And Chief Credit Officer Servisfirst Bancshares And Servisfirst Bank, Don G. Owens, age 68, $187,200 total compensation
President And Ceo Servisfirst Bank Of Atlanta, Ken Barber
Evp And Chief Lending Officer, Doug Rehm
Ceo Servisfirst Bank Dothan, B. Harrison Morris, age 43
First Vice President, Lee McKinnon
Senior Vice President Commercial Lending, Chad Thomason
Senior Vice President Of Commerical Banking, David Hearne
Senior Vice President Commercial Banking, Jeff Johnson
Vice President, John Peacock
Senior Vice President Commercial Banking Team Lead, Lawson Kirkland
Vice President Retail Banking Center Manager, Crystal Lee
Senior Vice President Commercial Relationship Manager, Jim Gardner
Senior Vice President, Justin Fontenot
Vice President, Kiley Elmore
Senior Vice President Of Commercial Banking, Walter Brand
Senior Vice President Private Banking, Patricia Griner
Assistant Vice President, Debbie Crook
Vice President Portfolio Manager, Gary Allen
Fvp Commercial Banking, Cheryl Dunn
Senior Vice President Commercial And Healthcare Banking At Servisfirst Bank, Clif Tant
Executive Vice President, Brad Armagost
Vice President, Barry Devane
Vice President, Bart Mcbride
Assistant Vice President Branch Manager, Ron Leddon
Vice President And Commercial Lender, Max Coblentz
Senior Vice President, Samantha S Curd
Vice President Credit Officer, Stacy B Suddeth
Vice President, Sam Scott
Senior Vice President, Hill Womble
Senior Vice President Commercial Banking, Will Clay
Vice President Credit Officer, Stacy Suddeth
Senior Vice President, Bryan Neth
Vice President Portfolio Manager, Jill Alvarez
Executive Vice President Commercial Banking, Bruce Finley
Vice President Of Cash Management, Delbert Madison
Chairman Servisfirst Bancshares And Servisfirst Bank, Stanley M. (Skip) Brock, age 69
Auditors: Dixon Hughes Goodman LLP

LOCATIONS

HQ: ServisFirst Bancshares Inc
    2500 Woodcrest Place, Birmingham, AL 35209
Phone: 205 949-0302
Web: www.servisfirstbank.com

2013 Branches

	No.
Alabama	10
Florida	2
Total	**12**

Bank of America   Wells Fargo
Bank of the Ozarks

HISTORICAL FINANCIALS
Company Type: Public

Income Statement
FYE: December 31

	ASSETS ($ mil.)	NET INCOME ($ mil.)	INCOME AS % OF ASSETS	EMPLOYEES
12/19	8,947	149	1.7%	505
12/18	8,007	136	1.7%	473
12/17	7,082	93	1.3%	434
12/16	6,370	81	1.3%	420
12/15	5,095	63	1.2%	371
Annual Growth	15.1%	23.8%	—	8.0%

2019 Year-End Financials

Debt ratio: 0.72%
Return on equity: 19.17%
Cash ($ mil.): 530
Current ratio: —
Long-term debt ($ mil.): —

No. of shares (mil.): 53
Dividends
  Yield: 1.6%
  Payout: 23.4%
Market value ($ mil.): 2,021

	STOCK PRICE ($) FY Close	P/E High/Low	PER SHARE ($) Earnings	Dividends	Book Value
12/19	37.68	14 10	2.76	0.63	15.71
12/18	31.87	17 12	2.53	0.48	13.39
12/17	41.50	25 19	1.72	0.20	11.46
12/16	37.44	48 23	1.52	0.19	9.93
12/15	47.53	40 24	1.20	0.12	8.64
Annual Growth	(5.6%)	— —	23.3%	52.7%	16.1%

Sherwin-Williams Co (The)

For roughly 150 years Sherwin-Williams has maintained its position as one of the world's top paint manufacturers (along with Akzo Nobel PPG Industries and Henkel). Sherwin-Williams' products include a variety of paints finishes coatings applicators and varnishes sold under brands such as Dutch Boy Krylon Sherwin-Williams and Valspar The company operates mostly in the US Canada Latin America and the Caribbean through more than 4700 paint stores and sells automotive finishing and refinishing products through wholesale branches. Its other outlets include home centers independent dealers and automotive retailers. More than 90% of US residents live within 50 miles of one of the company's retail locations.

HISTORY

In 1870 Henry Sherwin bought out paint materials distributor Truman Dunham and joined Edward Williams and A. T. Osborn to form Sherwin Williams & Company in Cleveland. The business began making paints in 1871 and became the industry leader after improving the paint-grinding mill in the mid-1870s patenting a reclosable can in 1877 and improving liquid paint in 1880.

In 1874 Sherwin-Williams introduced a special paint for carriages beginning the concept of specific-purpose paint. (By 1900 the company had paints for floors roofs barns metal bridges railroad cars and automobiles.) Sherwin-Williams incorporated in 1884 and opened a dealership in Massachusetts in 1891 that was the forerunner of its company-run retail stores. The company obtained its "Cover the Earth" trademark in 1895.

Before the Depression Sherwin-Williams bought a number of smaller paint makers: Detroit White Lead (1910) Martin-Senour (1917) Acme Quality Paints (1920) and The Lowe Brothers (1929). Responding to wartime restrictions the company developed a fast-drying and water-reducible paint called Kem-Tone and the forerunner of the paint roller the Roller-Koater.

Sales doubled during the 1960s as the company made acquisitions including Sprayon (aerosol paint 1966) but rising expenses kept earnings flat. In 1972 the company expanded its stores to include carpeting draperies and other decorating items. But long-term debt ballooned from $80 million in 1974 to $196 million by 1977 when the company lost $8.2 million and suspended dividends for the first time since 1885.

John Breen became CEO in 1979 reinstated the dividend purged over half of the top management positions and closed inefficient plants. He also focused stores on paint and wallpaper merchandise and purchased Dutch Boy (1980).

In 1990 Sherwin-Williams began selling Dutch Boy in Sears stores and Kem-Tone in Wal-Marts. Acquisitions that year included Borden's Krylon and Illinois Bronze aerosol operations and DeSoto's architectural coatings segment which made private-label paints for Sears and Home Depot. In 1991 Sherwin-Williams bought two coatings business units from Cook Paint and Varnish and the Cuprinol brand of coatings.

Sherwin-Williams purchased paint manufacturer Pratt & Lambert in 1996. That year it introduced several new products including Low Temp 35 a paint for low temperatures; Healthspec a low-odor paint; and Ralph Lauren designer paints. Prep-Rite do-it-yourself interior primers debuted in 1997. Also that year Sherwin-Williams bought Thompson Minwax (Thompson's Water Seal Minwax Wood Products) from Forstmann Little and Chile-based Marson Chilena a spray paint maker.

The company streamlined some of its business segments and trimmed jobs in 1998. Christopher Connor president of the Paint Stores group replaced Breen as CEO in 1999 and chairman in 2000. Also in 2000 Sherwin-Williams moved into the European automotive coatings market by acquiring Italy-based ScottWarren.

In late 2001 the company acquired Wisconsin-based Mautz Paint Company.

After a rough but still profitable 2001 the company grew revenues and profits for its consumer units (consumer paints and paint stores) in 2002 thanks largely to a healthy do-it-yourself market. Sales for its automotive finishes and international units however were down because of a slow collision-repair market and currency-exchange effects.

In 2010 Sherwin-Williams bought Arch Chemicals' Sayerlack a leading Italian wood care coating company and acquired Becker Acroma In-

dustrial Wood Coatings a Swedish manufacturer of industrial wood coatings. It also acquired all shares of AlSher Titania (a joint venture with Altair Nanotechnologies) it did not already own giving it a 100% stake in the technology company. AlSher Titania is developing a promising titanium dioxide technology that Sherwin-Williams plans to commercialize.

That same year the company also acquired Pinturas C "ndor an Ecuadorian diversified coatings supplier with $60 million in annual sales bolstering its market share in architectural paint in Latin America.

Among its acquisitions in 2011 was UK-based Leighs Paints a leader in fire-protectant (intumescent) coatings. (Because the intumescent technology prolongs the structural integrity of steel and concrete in a catastrophic fire more people are able to evacuate.)

In 2012 Sherwin-Williams made a significant purchase in the buyout of Jiangsu Pulanna Coating Co. headquartered in Changzhou China. Pulanna is an automotive refinishes coatings manufacturer and the deal improved Sherwin-Williams' presence in the most populous country in the world.

Also in 2012 Sherwin-Williams picked up Geocel Holdings a maker of caulks sealants and adhesives serving construction and repair applications. Geocel has locations in the US and the UK and the deal strengthened Sherwin-Williams' Consumer Group segment.

In a major geographic expansion in late 2012 the company agreed to acquire Grupo Comex a leader in the paint and coatings market in Mexico for $2.34 billion. However Mexico's antitrust regulator blocked the deal in mid-2013 stating the new company could artificially set higher prices at its discretion. Sherwin-Williams subsequently terminated the proposed deal.

However in 2013 the company acquired the US/Canada business of Comex. Sherwin-Williams paid $90 million in cash and assumed liabilities in the range of $75 million. Comex operations in the US and Canada consist of 314 company operated stores (234 in the US and 80 in Canada) and 8 manufacturing sites (5 in the US and 3 in Canada). In addition Comex supplies paint and coatings products to 1500 external retail locations.

2013 product launches included Sherwin-Williams Protective & Marine Coatings' Magnalux 404 FF the first styrene-free vinyl ester for use with steel and concrete substrates in the oil and gas market; Fast Clad 105ER a 100% solids tank lining for crude oil and ethanol storage; and Nova-Plate 325 an extended lifecycle 100% solids tank lining for high-temperature crude oil produced water and frac tank applications.

In 2013 Sherwin-Williams teamed up with Williams-Sonoma to create seasonal palettes of Sherwin-Williams paint colors that coordinate with the Pottery Barn Pottery Barn Kids PBteen and West Elm collections.

EXECUTIVES

Chairman President And Ceo, John G. Morikis, age 57, $1,095,795 total compensation
President And General Manager Latin America Division The Americas Group, Paul R. Clifford
Cio, Thomas J. (Tom) Lucas

President The Americas Group, Robert J. Davisson, age 60, $611,936 total compensation

President And General Manager South Western Division The Americas Group, Monty J. Griffin, age 60

President And General Manager Diversified Brands Division Consumer Group, Cheri M. Phyfer, age 49

President And General Manager Automotive Division Global Finishes Group, Thomas C. Hablitzel, age 58

President And General Manager Global Supply Chain Division Consumer Group, Joel D. Baxter, age 60

President And General Manager Mid Western Division The Americas Group, Peter J. Ippolito, age 56

President And General Manager Protective And Marine Coatings Division Global Finishes Group, Ronald B. Rossetto

President Global Finishes Group, David B. Sewell, age 52

President Southeastern Division Paint Stores Group, Todd V. Wipf

President And General Manager Product Finishes Division Global Finishes Group, Bruce G. Irussi

Svp Finance And Cfo, Allen J. Mistysyn, age 51

President And General Manager Eastern Division The Americas Group, Justin T. Binns

Vice President Sales, Brian Padden

National Sales Manager, Craig Mackay

Senior Vice President Of Human Resources For Gsc, Matt Schupp

National Account Manager, Vincent Barone

Vice President Of Sales, Jim Sinko

National Account Manager, Pat Busch

National Account Manager, Frank Anderson

National Accounts Manager, Harvey Kulkin

National Sales Manager, Christopher Olden

Vice President Human Resources, Scott Gradert

Vice President Finance And Controller Diversified Brands Division, Dan Scalabrino

National Account Manager, Richard May

Vice President Taxes And Assistant Secretary Sherwin Williams Company, Michael Cummins

Vice President Global Sourcing, David Ash

Corporate Medical Director, Gregory Ornella

Vp Of Human Resources, Susan – Keough

Vice President Of Sales, Cj Dibattista

Senior Vice President Of Sales, Todd Stephenson

Vice President Sales, Doug Henson

Vice President Executive Compensation, Greg Sofish

National Sales Manager, Murray Shanks

National Account Manager, John Hackett

Vice President, Brett White

Vice President Human Resources Paint Stores Group, Thomas Gilligan

Vice President Human Resources, Lonnie McGowen

Vice President Of Information Security, Karen Gabel

Svp Corporate Communications And Public Affairs, Robert Wells

National Account Manager, Randy Scott

National Accounts Manager, Zach Wechter

Vice President Of Regional Operations, Phil Matisak

Vice President Global Sourcing, Jose Aravena

Vice President Merchandising, Kevin Madigan

Vice President Ecommerce, Peter Rein

Board Member, Joseph Banks

Treasurer, Scott McVeigh

Board Member, Chris Pluta

Treasurer, Isaac Blaylock

Auditors: Ernst & Young LLP

LOCATIONS

HQ: Sherwin-Williams Co (The)
101 West Prospect Avenue, Cleveland, OH 44115-1075
Phone: 216 566-2000   **Fax:** 216 566-3310
Web: www.sherwin.com

PRODUCTS/OPERATIONS

2018 sales

	$ mil.	% of total
The Americas Group	9,625	55
Performance Coatings Group	5,166	29
Consumer Brands Group	2,739	16
Administrative	3	-
Total	**11,855**	**100**

Operations

Operations
Paint Stores
  Products
  Architectural coatings
  Industrial maintenance
  Marine products
  Brands
  ArmorSeal
  Brod-Dugan
  Con-Lux
  FlexBon Paints
  Hi-Temp
  Kem
  Mautz
  Mercury
  Old Quaker
  Powdura
  Pro-Line
  SeaGuard
  Sherwin-Williams
Consumer
  Products
  Architectural paints
  Industrial maintenance
  Paints
  Private-label coatings
  Stains
  Wood finishings
  Varnishes
  Brands
  Cabot
  Cuprinol
  Dupli-color
  Dura Clad
  Dutch Boy
  EverLast
  Formby's
  H&C
  Krylon
  Martin Senour
  Maxwood Latex Stains
  Minwax
  Plastic Kote
  Pratt & Lambert
  Red Devil
  Rubberset
  Signature Select
  Thompson's WaterSeal
  Valspar
  White Lightning
Automotive Finishes
  Products
  Finishing refinishing and touch-up products for motor vehicles
  Brands
  Baco
  Excelo
  Lazzuril
  Martin Senour
  ScottWarren
  Sherwin-Williams
  Western
International Coatings
  Products
  Architectural paints
  Industrial maintenance products
  Stains
  Varnishes
  Wood finishing products
  Brands
  Andina

Colorgin
Dutch Boy
Globo
Kem-Tone
Krylon
Marson
Martin Senour
Minwax
Pratt & Lambert
Pulverlack
Ronseal
Sherwin-Williams
Sumare

COMPETITORS

Akzo Nobel	Dunn-Edwards
BASF SE	Ferro
Benjamin Moore	H.B. Fuller
California Products	Kelly-Moore
Comex Group	Masco
Coronado Paint	PPG Industries
Diamond Vogel Paint	RPM International

HISTORICAL FINANCIALS

Company Type: Public

Income Statement

FYE: December 31

	REVENUE ($ mil.)	NET INCOME ($ mil.)	NET PROFIT MARGIN	EMPLOYEES
12/19	17,900	1,541	8.6%	61,111
12/18	17,534	1,108	6.3%	53,368
12/17	14,983	1,772	11.8%	52,695
12/16	11,855	1,132	9.6%	42,550
12/15	11,339	1,053	9.3%	40,706
Annual Growth	12.1%	10.0%	—	10.7%

2019 Year-End Financials

Debt ratio: 42.37%	No. of shares (mil.): 92
Return on equity: 39.25%	Dividends
Cash ($ mil.): 161	Yield: 0.7%
Current ratio: 1.02	Payout: 27.4%
Long-term debt ($ mil.): 8,050	Market value ($ mil.): 53,770

	STOCK PRICE ($) FY Close	P/E High/Low		PER SHARE ($) Earnings	Dividends	Book Value
12/19	583.54	35	23	16.49	4.52	44.75
12/18	393.46	40	31	11.67	3.44	40.07
12/17	410.04	22	14	18.67	3.40	39.33
12/16	268.74	25	19	11.99	3.36	20.20
12/15	259.60	26	19	11.16	2.68	9.41
Annual Growth	22.4%	—	—	10.3%	14.0%	47.7%

SHI INTERNATIONAL CORP.

Businesses that need more than boxes of hardware and software can call SHI International. The company distributes scores of computer hardware and software products from suppliers such as Adobe Cisco Microsoft VMware Symantec and Lenovo. It resells PCs networking products data storage systems printers software and keyboards among other items. SHI offers a range of professional services including software licensing asset management managed desktop services systems integration and vocational training. The company serves corporate government and health care customers from approximately 35 offices across the US Canada the UK Germany

France and Hong Kong. SHI was founded in 1989 by Chairman Koguan Leo.

Operations

SHI serves several sectors and verticals. The company specializes in software and hardware procurement deployment planning configuration data center optimization IT asset management and cloud computing as well as custom IT solutions.

The company's popular product categories include laptops desktop tablets printers and monitors. Featured brands include Acer Citrix Samsung LG Nvidia and HP among others.

Geographic Reach

Based in Somerset New Jersey SHI has a global reach through approximately 35 offices worldwide including its five international offices in Canada France Hong Kong Ireland Singapore and in the UK.

Sales and Marketing

SHI has some 5000 experts from every area of IT operations from volume licensing to security data center to mobility and collaboration supporting approximately 10 million end-users.

Strategy

SHI International made a strategic investment in mLogica a developer of technologies for migrating on-premises databases and applications to the cloud.

With the agreement SHI will have full access to mLogica's technologies and will be authorized to deliver services based on that technology alone or in partnership with mLogica.

mLogica has three focus areas that are of strategic importance to SHI. The first is an automated migration suite for migrating databases and applications to the cloud in an expedited fashion. The second is mLogica's MCAP big data and analytics platform for real-time ingesting and processing of data. The third is mLogica's managed services that dovetail into SHI's own managed services.

EXECUTIVES

Vice President Finance, Paul Ng
President And Co-ceo, Thai Lee, age 63
Vp And General Manager, Hal Jagger
Vice President Internal Audit And Finance Operations, Kevin Boyles
Vice President, Melissa Graham
Chairman, Koguan Leo
Auditors: COHN REZNICK LLP WHITE PLAINS

LOCATIONS

HQ: SHI INTERNATIONAL CORP.
   290 DAVIDSON AVE., SOMERSET, NJ 088734145
Phone: 732 764-8888
Web: WWW.SHI.COM

PRODUCTS/OPERATIONS

Selected Products
Accessories
Peripherals
Hardware
Memory
Software

Selected Services
Cloud services
Computer vocational training services
Data center services
Events
Hardware services
Networking
POLARIS Software asset management

Storage
Strategic consulting
Webinars

COMPETITORS

ASI Computer Technologies	Computacenter
Agilysys	Ingram Micro
Arrow Electronics	Insight Enterprises
Avnet	PC Mall
CDW	Softchoice
CompuCom	Tech Data

HISTORICAL FINANCIALS

Company Type: Private

Income Statement   FYE: December 31

	REVENUE ($ mil.)	NET INCOME ($ mil.)	NET PROFIT MARGIN	EMPLOYEES
12/19	10,372	253	2.4%	5,000
12/18	9,767	245	2.5%	—
12/17	8,243	197	2.4%	—
12/16	7,268	104	1.4%	—
Annual Growth	12.6%	34.3%	—	—

Sierra Bancorp

Sierra Bancorp is the holding company for the nearly $2 billion-asset Bank of the Sierra which operates approximately 30 branches in Central California's San Joaquin Valley between (and including) Bakersfield and Fresno. The bank offers traditional deposit products and loans to individuals and small and mid-size businesses. About 70% of its loan portfolio is made up of real estate loans while another 15% is made up of mortgage warehouse loans and a further 10% is tied to commercial and industrial loans (including SBA loans and direct finance leases). The bank also issues agricultural loans and consumer loans.

Operations

Bank of the Sierra makes almost 80% of its revenue from interest income. About 64% of its total revenue came from interest income on loans and leases (including fees) during 2015 while another 14% came from interest income on taxed and tax-exempt securities. The rest of its revenue came from deposit account service charges (12% of revenue) checkcard fees (5%) and other non-interest income sources.

Geographic Reach

The Porterville California-based bank operates branches and offices mostly in the San Joaquin Valley in Porterville Arroyo Grande Atascadero Bakersfield California City Clovis Delano Dinuba Exeter Farmersville Fillmore Fresno Hanford Lindsay Oxnard Paso Robles Reedley San Luis Obispo Santa Clarita Santa Paula Selma Tehachapi Three Rivers Visalia and Tulare.

Sales and Marketing

Bank of the Sierra has been gradually increasing its advertising spend in recent years. It spent $2.3 million on advertising and promotion in 2015 up from $2.2 million and $1.9 million in 2014 and 2013 respectively.

Financial Performance

The bank's revenue has been steadily rising over the past few years mostly as bank acquisitions and organic loan business growth has spurred higher interest income. Meanwhile its profits have more than doubled since 2011 thanks to declining loan loss provisions as its loan portfolio's credit quality has improved with higher property valuations in the strengthened economy.

Sierra Bancorp's revenue jumped 13% to $80.4 million during 2015 thanks to higher interest income from continued double-digit loan asset growth led by a jump in mortgage warehouse lines from increased line utilization a first-quarter purchase of residential mortgage loans and strong organic growth in non-farm real estate and agricultural production loans. Deposit account service fees also grew thanks to organic deposit client growth.

Strong revenue growth and lower acquisition costs in 2015 drove the bank's net income up 19% to $18 million. Sierra's operating cash levels rose 4% to $29.78 million during the year as its cash-based earnings increased.

Strategy

While the Bank of Sierra has traditionally grown organically by opening around one new branch per year in the Central Valley it has more recently acquired small area banks and individual branches to bolster its deposit and loan business while expanding into untapped markets such as further south into the Santa Clara Valley.

Mergers and Acquisitions

In July 2016 the bank bought $145 million-asset Coast Bancorp and its Coast National Bank branches in San Luis Obispo Paso Robles Arroyo Grande and Atascadero California.

In November 2014 Sierra Bancorp bought $129 million-asset Santa Clara Valley Bank N.A. and its branches in Santa Paula Santa Clarita and Fillmore in California for $15 million. the deal expanded Sierra's reach outside of its traditional market for the first time more south into the Santa Clara Valley of California.

EXECUTIVES

Evp And Cfo, Kenneth R. (Ken) Taylor, age 60, $242,500 total compensation
Evp And Chief Credit Officer, James F. (Jim) Gardunio, age 69, $197,600 total compensation
President And Ceo, Kevin J. McPhaill, age 47, $185,000 total compensation
Senior Vp, Matthew Hessler
Senior Vice President Of Tulare County And Manager Of Tulare County, David Soares
Vice President Assistant Risk Manager, Cyndi Carmichael
Chairman, Morris A. Tharp, age 80
Auditors: Eide Bailly LLP

LOCATIONS

HQ: Sierra Bancorp
   86 North Main Street, Porterville, CA 93257
Phone: 559 782-4900
Web: www.bankofthesierra.com

COMPETITORS

Bank of America	MUFG Americas Holdings
Bank of the West	United Security
Central Valley Community Bancorp	Bancshares
	Wells Fargo
Citibank	Westamerica

Comerica
JPMorgan Chase Zions Bancorporation

HISTORICAL FINANCIALS

Company Type: Public

Income Statement

FYE: December 31

	ASSETS ($ mil.)	NET INCOME ($ mil.)	INCOME AS % OF ASSETS	EMPLOYEES
12/19	2,593	35	1.4%	513
12/18	2,522	29	1.2%	556
12/17	2,340	19	0.8%	576
12/16	2,032	17	0.9%	497
12/15	1,796	18	1.0%	431
Annual Growth	9.6%	18.8%	—	4.5%

2019 Year-End Financials

Debt ratio: 1.35%
Return on equity: 12.35%
Cash ($ mil.): 80
Current ratio: —
Long-term debt ($ mil.): —

No. of shares (mil.): 15
Dividends
  Yield: 2.5%
  Payout: 33.0%
Market value ($ mil.): 445

	STOCK PRICE ($) FY Close	P/E High/Low		PER SHARE ($) Earnings	Dividends	Book Value
12/19	29.12	13	10	2.33	0.74	20.24
12/18	24.03	16	12	1.92	0.64	17.84
12/17	26.56	21	17	1.36	0.56	16.81
12/16	26.59	20	12	1.29	0.48	14.94
12/15	17.65	14	11	1.33	0.42	14.36
Annual Growth	13.3%	—	—	15.0%	15.2%	9.0%

Signature Bank (New York, NY)

Signature Bank marks the spot where some professional New Yorkers bank. The institution provides customized banking and financial services to smaller private businesses their owners and their top executives through 30 branches across the New York metropolitan area including all five boroughs Long Island and affluent Westchester County. The bank's lending activities mainly entail real estate and business loans. Subsidiary Signature Securities offers wealth management financial planning brokerage services asset management and insurance while its Signature Financial subsidiary offers equipment financing and leasing. Founded in 2001 the bank now boasts assets of roughly $29 billion.

Operations

Mortgage loans including commercial real estate loans multifamily residential mortgages home loans and lines of credit and construction and land loans comprise the bulk of Signature Bank's loan portfolio (and much of its asset base as well).

The bank which staffed some 1010 employees at the end of 2014 generated 68% of its revenue from interest on loans and leases that year while 20% came from interest on its securities available-for-sale and 7% came from securities held-to-maturity. The remainder of its revenue came from fees and service charges (2%) and various other miscellaneous sources.

Geographic Reach

The bank's nearly 30 branch offices are mostly in the New York metropolitan area which includes Manhattan Brooklyn Westchester Long Island Queens the Bronx Staten Island and Connecticut.

Sales and Marketing

Signature Bank mostly serves privately-owned businesses their owners and senior managers (typically with a net worth between $500000 and $20 million).

Financial Performance

The company's revenues and profits have risen in recent years thanks to strong organic loan business growth and declining loan loss provisions as its loan portfolio's credit quality has improved with higher property valuations in the strengthened economy.

Signature's revenue jumped by 22% to a record $959.3 million in 2014 mostly as loan interest (on commercial loans mortgages and leases) and security interest income continued to grow as the bank built up its interest-earning assets during the year.

Higher revenue and a continued decline and loan loss provisions in 2014 boosted the bank's net income by 30% to a record $296.7 million. Signature's operating cash levels more than doubled to $421 million on higher cash earnings.

Strategy

Signature Bank has long targeted privately-held businesses that have fewer than 1000 employees and revenues of less than $200 million. Some of its target clients include real estate owners/companies law firms accounting firms entertainment business managers medical professionals retail establishments money management firms and non-profit foundations.

The bank continues to expand its service lines particularly focusing on specialty financing to grow its business organically. In 2015 it planned to offer direct commercial vehicle financing through a network of approved commercial vehicle dealerships in New York's Tri-State area with loans targeting small and mid-size business borrowers looking to acquire commercial vehicles and fleets. Also that year it formed its Maryland-based Signature Public Funding Corp subsidiary to provide municipal finance and tax-exempt lending and leasing products to local state and federal government agencies nationwide.

Company Background

The bank's emphasis on personal service helped it to grow its deposit base and loan portfolio in 2011. During a time when many other banks struggled under the weight of bad loans in a bad economy Signature Bank achieved record earnings for the fourth consecutive year.

Founded in 2001 as an alternative to megabanks Signature Bank was spun off from Bank Hapoalim in 2004.

EXECUTIVES

President Ceo And Director, Joseph J. DePaolo, $577,500 total compensation
Svp And Cfo, Vito Susca
President Ceo And Director, Michael G. O'Rourke
Evp, Kevin P. Bastuga
Evp, Bryan D. Duncan
Vp Retail Operations Manager, Ella Riordan-Pacheco
Vice President, John C Spagnuolo

Vice President, Joseph Fingerman
Group Director Senior Vice President, Kevin Hardiman
Vice President Commercial Banking, Ross Thomson
Vice President, Ann Buzzo
Senior Vice President Group Director, Salvatore Costa
Svp, Maria Hegi
Assistant Vice President, Nathan Dinger
Chairman And Director, Leonard S. Caronia
Auditors: KPMG LLP

LOCATIONS

HQ: Signature Bank (New York, NY)
  565 Fifth Avenue, New York, NY 10017
Phone: 646 822-1500
Web: www.signatureny.com

PRODUCTS/OPERATIONS

2014 Sales

	$ mil.	% of total
Interest		
Loans net	655	68
Securities available for sale	193	20
Securities held to maturity	69	7
Other	5	1
Noninterest		
Fees & service charges	19	2
Commissions	10	1
Net gains on sales of loans	5	1
Net gains on sales of securities	5	—
Other	2	—
Adjustments	(7.8)	—
Total	**959**	**100**

COMPETITORS

Apple Bank for Savings
Astoria Financial
Bank Leumi USA
Capital One
Citigroup
HSBC USA

Herald National Bank
JPMorgan Chase
New York Community Bancorp
Safra Bank
TD Bank USA

HISTORICAL FINANCIALS

Company Type: Public

Income Statement

FYE: December 31

	ASSETS ($ mil.)	NET INCOME ($ mil.)	INCOME AS % OF ASSETS	EMPLOYEES
12/19	50,616	588	1.2%	1,472
12/18	47,364	505	1.1%	1,393
12/17	43,117	387	0.9%	1,305
12/16	39,047	396	1.0%	1,218
12/15	33,450	373	1.1%	1,122
Annual Growth	10.9%	12.1%	—	7.0%

2019 Year-End Financials

Debt ratio: 0.90%
Return on equity: 12.83%
Cash ($ mil.): 789
Current ratio: —
Long-term debt ($ mil.): —

No. of shares (mil.): 53
Dividends
  Yield: 1.6%
  Payout: 20.2%
Market value ($ mil.): 7,311

	STOCK PRICE ($) FY Close	P/E High/Low		PER SHARE ($) Earnings	Dividends	Book Value
12/19	136.61	13	10	10.87	2.24	89.12
12/18	102.81	17	11	9.23	1.12	80.07
12/17	137.26	23	17	7.12	0.00	73.33
12/16	150.20	21	15	7.37	0.00	66.15
12/15	153.37	22	16	7.27	0.00	56.81
Annual Growth	(2.9%)	—	—	10.6%	—	11.9%

SIGNATURE FINANCIAL LLC

EXECUTIVES

Ceo-MBR, Joseph J Depaolo
MBR, Eric Howell
Senior Vice President, Ann Buzzo
Senior Vice President, Anne Doligale
Senior Vice President, Lisa Wente
Senior Vice President, Marietta Mullane
Vice President, Brandon Tran
Vice President, Jason Chess
Senior Vice President, John Mangan
Senior Vice President, Tim Moran
Vice President, Brad Kranich

LOCATIONS

HQ: SIGNATURE FINANCIAL LLC
565 5TH AVE AT46TH, NEW YORK, NY 100172413
Phone: 646 865-0767
Web: WWW.SIGNATURENY.COM

HISTORICAL FINANCIALS
Company Type: Private

Income Statement   FYE: December 31

	ASSETS ($ mil.)	NET INCOME ($ mil.)	INCOME AS % OF ASSETS	EMPLOYEES
12/18	47,364	505	1.1%	10
12/17	43,119	387	0.9%	—
12/16	39,047	396	1.0%	—
12/15	33,450	373	1.1%	—
Annual Growth	12.3%	10.6%	—	—

Silvergate Capital Corp

Auditors: Crowe LLP

LOCATIONS

HQ: Silvergate Capital Corp
4250 Executive Square, Suite 300, La Jolla, CA 92037
Phone: 858 362-6300
Web: www.silvergatebank.com

HISTORICAL FINANCIALS
Company Type: Public

Income Statement   FYE: December 31

	ASSETS ($ mil.)	NET INCOME ($ mil.)	INCOME AS % OF ASSETS	EMPLOYEES
12/19	2,128	24	1.2%	215
12/18	2,004	22	1.1%	209
12/17	1,891	7	0.4%	—
Annual Growth	6.1%	80.3%	—	—

2019 Year-End Financials

Debt ratio: 0.92%
Return on equity: 11.77%
Cash ($ mil.): 133
Current ratio: —
Long-term debt ($ mil.): —

No. of shares (mil.): 18
Dividends
Yield: —
Payout: —
Market value ($ mil.): 297

STOCK PRICE ($) FY Close	P/E High/Low		PER SHARE ($) Earnings	Dividends	Book Value
12/19	15.91	12	9	1.35	0.00	12.38
12/18	0.00	—	—	1.31	0.00	10.73
12/17	0.00	—	—	0.79	0.00	8.00
Annual Growth	—	—	—	30.7%	—	24.4%

Simmons First National Corp

Simmons First National thinks it's only natural it should be one of the largest financial institutions in The Natural State. The $8.1 billion-asset holding company owns Simmons First National Bank and seven other community banks that bear the Simmons First Bank name and maintain local identities; together they operate around 150 branches throughout Arkansas and in Kansas Tennessee and Missouri. Serving consumers and area businesses the banks offer standard deposit products like checking and savings accounts IRAs and CDs. Lending activities mainly consist of commercial real estate loans single-family mortgages and consumer loans such as credit card and student loans.

Operations

In addition to Simmons First National Bank the company owns Simmons First Bank of Jonesboro Simmons First Bank of South Arkansas Simmons First Bank of Northwest Arkansas Simmons First Bank of Russellville Simmons First Bank of Searcy Simmons First Bank of El Dorado and Simmons First Bank of Hot Springs. Simmons First Trust Company a subsidiary of Simmons First National Bank provides trust and fiduciary services; Simmons First Investment Group offers broker-dealer services.

Like other retail banks Simmons makes the bulk of its money from interest income. About 65% of its total revenue came from loan interest during 2015 while another 8% came from interest on investment securities. The rest of its revenue came from service charges on deposit accounts (8% of revenue) debit and credit card fees (6%) mortgage lending income (3%) trust income (2%) investment banking income (1%) and other non-interest income sources.

Geographic Reach

The bank has around 150 branches mostly in Arkansas but also in Kansas Missouri and Tennessee.

Financial Performance

Simmons First National Bank's annual revenues and profits have been rising mostly thanks to new loan business from rapid bank expansion (mostly stemming from acquisitions).

The bank's revenue jumped 60% to $396.8 million during 2015 mostly thanks to 58% growth in legacy loans and growth in acquired loan business from the acquisitions of Liberty and Community First. Non-interest income grew 54% thanks to rising trust service charges deposit fees mortgage lending income all also tied to its recent acquisitions.

Revenue growth in 2015 more than doubled Simmons' net income to $74.36 million. The bank's operating cash levels spiked eight-fold to $88.7 million for the year thanks to a rise in cash-based earnings and favorable changes in working capital.

Strategy

Simmons tries to differentiate itself from smaller competitors by offering a wider array of products while striving to provide more personalized service than larger regional banks. The company also likes to acquire banks to grow its loan and deposit business while expanding into new geographic markets. Between 1990 and 2015 Simmons made 11 whole bank acquisitions and a handful of branch deals with other banks adding some 125 branches to its total branch network.

Mergers and Acquisitions

In 2019 Simmons First National acquired Reliance Bancshares a bank holding company with more than 20 branches in the St. Louis Missouri metropolitan area. The acquisition brings Simmons total assets to $17.6 billion and its total number of branches to more than 200 across Arkansas Colorado Illinois Kansas Missouri Oklahoma Tennessee and Texas. That year the company also purchased The Landrum Company the parent of Landmark Bank. Landrum brings with it approximately $3.3 billion in assets $2.1 billion in loans $3 billion in deposits and 40 branches in Missouri Oklahoma and Texas.

EXECUTIVES

Evp Organizational Development, Stephen C. Massanelli, age 64
Chairman And Ceo, George A. Makris, age 63, $502,500 total compensation
Sevp Cfo And Treasurer, Robert A. Fehlman, age 55, $306,614 total compensation
Evp And Central And Northeast Arkansas Regional Chairman Simmons First National Bank, Barry K. Ledbetter
President And Chief Credit Officer Simmons First National Bank, N. Craig Hunt
Evp And South Arkansas Regional Chairman Simmons First National Bank, Freddie G. Black
Evp Corporate Strategy And Performance And Secretary, Susan F. Smith, age 58
President Chief Banking Officer And Director, David L. Bartlett, age 68, $376,142 total compensation
Evp, Marty D. Casteel, age 68, $304,180 total compensation
Evp Controller Chief Accounting Officer And Investment Relations Officer, David W. Garner, age 50
Evp Of Marketing, Robert C. Dill, age 77, $179,393 total compensation
Evp And Chief Risk Officer, Tina M. Groves, age 50
Evp Technology And Operations Simmons First National Bank, Lisa W. Hunter
Svp And Marketing Director Simmons First National Bank, Amy W. Johnson
President El Dorado Community Bank, Robert L. Robinson
Chairman Russellville Community Chairman, Ronald B. (Ron) Jackson
President Hot Springs Community Bank, Steven W. (Steve) Trusty
President Conway Community Bank, Jason Culpepper
Evp And General Counsel, Patrick A. Burrow, age 66
Evp Specialty Lending Simmons First National Bank, Larry L. Bates

Evp And Tennessee Regional Chairman Simmons
First National Bank, John C. Clark
Evp And Kansas And Missouri Regional Chairman
Simmons First National Bank, Gary E. Metsger
Vice President, Clint Parton
Vice President And Personnel Manager, Leigh
Cockrum
Vice President, Pam Lawshe
Assistant Vice President, Donna Kriner
Vp Of Mortgage, Deana Powell
Vice President, Josh Caldwell
Assistant Vice President Branch Manager, Emily
Ferguson
Assistant Vice President Loans, Esther Chapman
Vice President, Chad Pittillo
Vice President Loan Review Manager, David
Coleman
Executive Vice President Operations, Glenda
Tolson
Vice President Regional Manager, Zilpha Wilson
Senior Vice President, Adam Mitchell
Senior Vice President Regulatory And Consumer
Affairs, Kevin Archer
Vice President Market Manager, Dorvan Wiley
Vice President And Trust Officer, Robin Thornton
Svp Assistant Controller, Kevin Pletcher
Senior Vice President Of Commercial Lending,
Issac Wood
Senior Vice President, Tommie Jones
Assistant Vice President And Trust Officer, Karen
Cash
Vice President Mortgage Lending Manager, Justin
Moore
Vice President Regional Manager, Michael Ramsey
Vice President, Diane Wilson
Vice President Commercial Banking, Scott Clark
Commercial Lender Vice President, Channing
Powers
Senior Vice President, Matthew Riley
Senior Vice President, David Peer
Vice President, Roland Getchell
Vice President Commercial Lending, Wayne Wilson
Assistant Vice President And Investment Officer,
Kelton Harrison
Vice President Andamp; Trust Officer, Catherine
Roper
Senior Vice President Commercial Lending
Manager, Karen Marine
Senior Vice President, Steve Landry
Vice President Of Retail Operations, Daphne
Stallings
Assistant Vice President, Chris Rittelmeyer
Vice President Commercial Lending, Vernon Scott
Assistant Vice President Atm Operations, Karla
Dial
Vice President Facilities Management, Anita
Murrell
Executive Vice President Financial Services,
Phillip Tappan
Svp Dtr Of Community Dev, Martie North
Vice President, William Murray
Senior Vice President, Kris K Nau
Senior Vice President Commercial Loan Officer,
Robert Gephardt
Senior Vice President Commerical Lending, Scott
Tumlin
Senior Vice President Commercial Manager,
Marlene Bown
Vice President Community Banker, Jim Wyatt
Senior Vice President Special Assets, David W
Scobee
Vice President Financial Advisor, James Watkins
Senior Vice President And Senior Credit Officer,
Stephen Landry
Executive Vp, Tina Graves
Senior Vice President Commercial Lending, Shane
Strahl
Senior Vice President, Andra Dillard
Senior Vice Presidnet, Ron McDaniel
Vice President General Manager, Mark Simpson

Vice President Franchise Finance, Turner Gaw
Vice President Commercial Banking, Clarence Boyd
Board Member, Edward Drilling
Board Member, Eugene Hunt
Board Member, Brandy West
Board Member, Christopher Kirkland
Board Member, Mark Doramus
Board Member, Jay Burchfield
Board Member, Scott Mcgeorge
Auditors: BKD, LLP

LOCATIONS

HQ: Simmons First National Corp
501 Main Street, Pine Bluff, AR 71601
Phone: 870 541-1000
Web: www.simmonsbank.com

PRODUCTS/OPERATIONS

2015 Sales

	$ mil.	% of total
Interest Income		
Loans	268	65
Investment securities	30	8
Others	2	
Non-interest income		
Service charges on deposit accounts	31	8
Debit and credit card fees	26	6
Mortgage lending income	11	3
Trust income	9	2
Other service charges and fees	9	2
others	22	6
Net (loss) gain on assets covered by FDIC loss share agreements	(14.8)	-
Total	**396**	**100**

COMPETITORS

Arvest Bank	Bear State Financial
BOK Financial	Home BancShares
BancorpSouth	IBERIABANK
Bank of America	Regions Financial
Bank of the Ozarks	U.S. Bancorp

HISTORICAL FINANCIALS

Company Type: Public

Income Statement

FYE: December 31

	ASSETS ($ mil.)	NET INCOME ($ mil.)	INCOME AS % OF ASSETS	EMPLOYEES
12/19	21,259	238	1.1%	3,270
12/18	16,543	215	1.3%	2,654
12/17	15,055	92	0.6%	2,640
12/16	8,400	96	1.2%	1,875
12/15	7,559	74	1.0%	1,946
Annual Growth	**29.5%**	**33.8%**	**—**	**13.9%**

2019 Year-End Financials

Debt ratio: 1.99%
Return on equity: 9.10%
Cash ($ mil.): 996
Current ratio: —
Long-term debt ($ mil.): —

No. of shares (mil.): 113
Dividends
  Yield: 2.3%
  Payout: 25.3%
Market value ($ mil.): 3,044

	STOCK PRICE ($) FY Close	P/E High/Low		PER SHARE ($) Earnings	Dividends	Book Value
12/19	26.79	11	9	2.41	0.64	26.30
12/18	24.13	26	10	2.32	0.60	24.33
12/17	57.10	47	37	1.33	0.50	22.65
12/16	62.15	42	25	1.57	0.48	18.40
12/15	51.36	44	27	1.32	0.46	17.78
Annual Growth	**(15.0%)**	**—**	**—**	**16.4%**	**8.6%**	**10.3%**

Sirius XM Holdings Inc

Sirius XM Holdings operates Sirius XM Radio which transmits music sports entertainment comedy talk news traffic and weather channels to some 35 million subscribers in the US and more than 2.5 million subscribers in Canada. The home of Howard Stern offers two proprietary satellite radio systems; a streaming service accessible via desktop mobile apps smart speakers and other consumer electronic devices; and connected vehicle services. The company has equipment alliances with several automakers; it also sells satellite radio equipment through its website and through retail outlets such as Amazon. In 2019 SiriusXM acquired music streaming service Pandora for $3.5 billion. Liberty Media owns a majority of the company.

Operations

More than 70% of Sirius XM's revenue comes from subscription fees. The remainder comes from advertising equipment and ancillary revenue.

Subscription revenue includes self-pay and paid promotional subscriptions and other fees for its programming line-up of commercial-free content. Advertising revenue includes the sale of advertising on certain non-music channels. Equipment revenue includes revenue and royalties from the sale of satellite radios components and accessories.

Geographic Reach

Based in New York Sirius XM has more than a of dozen properties — including offices and studio/production/engineering facilities as well as a data center a call center and a warehouse — in several states. These include New Jersey Florida Minnesota Tennessee Georgia Virginia California Texas and Washington DC.

The company also has approximately 540 locations for use in connection with the terrestrial repeater networks that support its satellite radio services. In general these leases and licenses are for space on building rooftops and communications towers.

Sales and Marketing

Sirius XM's sales and marketing activities include advertising promotional events and sponsorships along with direct mail outbound telemarketing email communication campaigns and digital performance media.

The company has two primary subscription categories: self-pay (from consumers) and paid promotion (bundled with a car purchase/lease). In 2019 Sirius had approximately 30 million self-pay subscribers and approximately 5 million paid promotional subscribers. The company works to grow self-pay subscribers through converting trial promotional subscriptions.

During 2019 2018 and 2017 the company recorded advertising costs of $392 million $267million and $263 million respectively.

Financial Performance

SiriusXM has experienced year-over-year revenue growth over the most recent five-year period with an overall growth of 75% from 2015 to 2019. Meanwhile its net income has struggled to gain steady growth but overall increased 79% from 2015 to 2019.

The company's fiscal 2019 revenue increased 35% to $7.8 billion up from $5.8 billion in 2018. Revenue in all operation segments grew: subscriber by 7% advertising by 9% equipment by 12% and other by less than 1%.

SiriusXM saw its net income fall to $914 million in 2019 down 22% from prior year. The decrease was due to higher operating expenses.

Cash at the end of 2019 was $120 million. Cash provided by operations was $2 billion while investing activities used $3 million primarily for additions to property and equipment. Financing activities used $2 billion primarily for repurchased of common stock and dividends paid.

Strategy

In 2020 Sirius XM made an investment and an acquisition to provide a better customer offering as well as reach a larger audience.

Sirius XM invested $75 million in SoundCloud. The agreement enables advertisers and brands to purchase SoundCloud's US ad inventory directly through Pandora leveraging the company's direct sales capabilities targeting data and audio programmatic platform.

To attract podcasters of any size the company acquired Simplecast a leading podcast management platform that enables podcasters to publish manage and measure their content and paired it with AdsWizz to create an end-to-end solution that enables creators to publish and generate revenue from their podcasts all in one place.

Mergers and Acquisitions

Sirius XM completed the acquisition of Pandora for $3.5 billion in an all-stock deal in early 2019 to become the world's largest audio media company. Pandora is the largest US streaming music provider with a personalized free ad-supported service and the combination caters to more than 100 million listeners in North America. These two brands are positioned to lead a new era of audio entertainment by delivering the most compelling subscription-based and ad-supported audio experiences to millions of listeners. The combined companies will drive long-term growth and value for its stockholders.

Company Background

XM and Sirius launched as competitors in 2001 and 2002 respectively. Howard Stern gave Sirius Satellite Radio a big boost when he left terrestrial radio for the company in 2004. The two companies merged in 2008 figuring joining forces would help them better contend in the premium audio space.

EXECUTIVES

Evp And Cfo, David J. Frear, age 64, $850,000 total compensation
Evp And General Counsel, Patrick L. Donnelly, age 58, $575,000 total compensation
Evp Sales And Automotive, Stephen R. (Steve) Cook, age 64, $518,583 total compensation
Svp And Cio, William C. (Bill) Pratt
Ceo, James E. (Jim) Meyer, age 66, $1,468,590 total compensation
President And Chief Content Officer, Scott A. Greenstein, age 61, $1,224,520 total compensation
Evp And Chief Administrative Officer, Dara F. Altman, age 62, $500,000 total compensation
Evp Operations And Products, Enrique Rodriguez, $531,827 total compensation
Group Vp And Gm Infotainment Telematics And Audio Services, Larry Pesce

Senior Vice President Promotions Event Marketing And Talent Relations, Ross Zapin
Vice President Of Application Development, Daniel Eccles
Vice President Purchasing And Procurement, Larry Simon
Corporate Vice President And Chief Engineering Officer, Terry Smith
Vice President, Denise Stevens
Executive Vice President Sales And Development, Joseph A Verbrugge
Vice President Business Solutions Management, Mike Leary
Svp And General Manager Music Programming, Steve Blatter
Vice President Information Technology And Corporate Solutions, Moshe Pridan
Corporate Vice President And Chief Innovation Officer, Stell Patsiokas
Senior Vice President Sports Programming, Steve Cohen
Vice President Marine And Aviation, Craig Correa
Vice President Human Resources, Walt Sanderson
Vice President Interactive, Patrick Fitzgerald
Senior Vice President Advertising Sales, Bette Rockmore
Vice President Information Security And Compliance, Patricia Edfors
Vice President Market Research, Kathie Mahoney
Vice President Process And Information Management, Evelyn Sasmor
Senior Vice President Automotive Partnerships, Rodney Pickett
Vice President Marketing Operations, James Dunn
Vice President And General Manager Talk Prgrmg, Dave Gorab
Chairman, Gregory B. (Greg) Maffei, age 59
Auditors: KPMG LLP

LOCATIONS

HQ: Sirius XM Holdings Inc
1221 Avenue of the Americas, 35th Floor, New York, NY 10020
Phone: 212 584-5100
Web: www.siriusxm.com

COMPETITORS

CBS Radio	Saga Communications
Cox Radio	Spanish Broadcasting
Cumulus Media	Townsquare Media
Emmis Communications	Univision Radio
Entercom	WestwoodOne
Entravision	iHeartCommunications
Radio One Inc.	

HISTORICAL FINANCIALS
Company Type: Public

Income Statement
FYE: December 31

	REVENUE ($ mil.)	NET INCOME ($ mil.)	NET PROFIT MARGIN	EMPLOYEES
12/20	8,040	131	1.6%	5,726
12/19	7,794	914	11.7%	4,534
12/18	5,770	1,175	20.4%	2,699
12/17	5,425	647	11.9%	2,575
12/16	5,017	745	14.9%	2,402
Annual Growth	12.5%	(35.3%)		24.3%

2020 Year-End Financials
Debt ratio: 82.26%—
Return on equity:—
Cash ($ mil.): 71
Current ratio: 0.31
Long-term debt ($ mil.): 8,499

Dividends
Yield: 0.8%
Payout: 23.7%
Market value ($ mil.): —

	STOCK PRICE ($) FY Close	P/E High/Low	PER SHARE ($) Earnings	Dividends	Book Value
12/20	6.37	245 148	0.03	0.05	(0.55)
12/19	7.15	36 26	0.20	0.05	(0.17)
12/18	5.71	29 20	0.26	0.05	(0.42)
12/17	5.36	42 32	0.14	0.04	(0.34)
12/16	4.45	31 22	0.15	0.01	(0.17)
Annual Growth	9.4%	—	— (33.1%)	52.8%	

Sixth Street Specialty Lending Inc

Auditors: KPMG LLP

LOCATIONS

HQ: Sixth Street Specialty Lending Inc
2100 McKinney Avenue, Suite 1500, Dallas, TX 75201
Phone: 469 621-3001
Web: www.tpgspecialtylending.com

HISTORICAL FINANCIALS
Company Type: Public

Income Statement
FYE: December 31

	ASSETS ($ mil.)	NET INCOME ($ mil.)	INCOME AS % OF ASSETS	EMPLOYEES
12/19	2,280	128	5.6%	—
12/18	1,730	143	8.3%	—
12/17	1,720	120	7.0%	—
12/16	1,675	107	6.4%	—
12/15	1,516	95	6.3%	—
Annual Growth	10.7%	7.7%		

2019 Year-End Financials
Debt ratio: 47.98%
Return on equity: 11.76%
Cash ($ mil.): 14
Current ratio: —
Long-term debt ($ mil.): —

No. of shares (mil.): 66
Dividends
Yield: 8.4%
Payout: 93.3%
Market value ($ mil.): 1,428

	STOCK PRICE ($) FY Close	P/E High/Low	PER SHARE ($) Earnings	Dividends	Book Value
12/19	21.47	11 10	1.94	1.81	16.83
12/18	18.09	9 8	2.25	1.78	16.25
12/17	19.80	11 9	2.00	1.75	16.09
12/16	18.68	10 8	1.83	1.56	15.95
12/15	16.22	11 9	1.76	1.56	15.15
Annual Growth	7.3%	—	— 2.5%	3.8%	2.7%

SLM Corp.

If SLM doesn't seem familiar perhaps you know it by its more common moniker Sallie Mae. Holding some $22.9 billion in private education Loans SLM's main subsidiary Sallie Mae Bank is one of the nation's largest education loan providers and specializes in originating acquiring financing and servicing private student loans which are not guaranteed by the government. The company also earns fees for its processing and administrative offerings through various subsidiaries.

HISTORY

The Student Loan Marketing Association was chartered in 1972 as a response to problems in the Guaranteed Student Loan Program of 1965. For years the GSL program had tinkered with rates to induce banks to make loans but servicing the small loans was expensive and troublesome. Sallie Mae began operations in 1973 buying loans from their originators; its size provided economies of scale in loan servicing.

Originally only institutions making educational or student loans were allowed to own stock in Sallie Mae. This was later changed so that anyone could buy nonvoting stock. In 1993 voting stock was listed on the NYSE.

Sallie Mae was always a political football altered again and again to reflect the education policies of the party in power. When it was founded during the Nixon administration its loans were restricted by a needs test which was repealed during the Carter years. The Reagan administration reimposed the needs test and at the same time sped up the schedule under which the company was to become self-supporting which it did by late 1981.

Forced to rely on its own resources Sallie Mae turned to creative financing. One of its traditional advantages was that its loan interest rates were linked to Treasury bills traditionally about 3% above the T-bill rate. The company became a master at riding the spread between its cost of funds and the interest rates it charged.

Between 1983 and 1992 Sallie Mae's assets swelled by more than 400% and its income rose by almost 500%. As the firm grew management became more visible with high pay and extravagant perks. Although salaries were not inconsistent with those of executives at comparable private corporations the remuneration level and perks irked Congress. But Sallie Mae kept growing — in 1992 it expanded its facilities and added 900 new staff members.

The 1993 Omnibus Budget Reconciliation Act with its transfer of the student loan program directly to the government and its surcharge on Sallie Mae began to adversely affect earnings in 1994. While awaiting permission to alter its charter the company stepped up its marketing efforts especially to school loan officers who advised students on loan options.

In 1995 then-COO Albert Lord led a group of stockholders in a push to cut operating expenses and repackage student loans as securities   la Freddie Mac and Fannie Mae. Lord and some of his supporters won seats on the board (as well as the enmity of Lawrence Hough who resigned as CEO in the midst of the melee). That year Sallie Mae bought HICA Holding one of two private insurers of education loans. In 1996 Congress passed legislation forcing Sallie Mae's privatization.

Despite SLM's rising stock shareholders were unhappy with chairman William Arceneaux's status quo business plan. Lord gained control in 1997.

In 1998 the organization became SLM Holding. Assets and earnings were muted that year when unfavorable market conditions prevented Sallie Mae from securitizing its loans.

The firm the next year expanded its lending operations by buying Nellie Mae. Also in 1999 Sallie Mae teamed with Answer Financial to sell insurance. Growth continued in 2000 when the company bought loan servicer Student Loan Funding Resources as well as the marketing student loan servicing and administrative operations of USA Group; the company changed its name to USA Education following the acquisition. The company also cut some 1700 jobs approximately 25% of its workforce.

The following year Sallie Mae teamed with Intuit allowing the financial software company access to Sallie Mae's 7 million customers. It also launched online recruiting service TrueCareers that year.

In 2002 it bought Pioneer Credit Recovery and General Revenue Corporation two of the nation's largest student loan collection agencies. It also reverted to the SLM moniker to reconnect with the name by which it has so long been known.

The privatization plan put into place in the mid-'90s (orchestrated in large part by then-CEO Lord) came to fruition nearly four years ahead of schedule when SLM transitioned to a private organization in December 2004.

In 2007 SLM saw its stock values plummet to their lowest levels in about a decade. A number of industry-wide factors figured into the losses not the least of which was the downturn in the credit market. Also affecting the company was the signing into law of the College Cost Reduction and Access Act (CCRAA). Intended to reform student lending and cut costs for borrowers the act slashed subsidies for lenders participating in the Federal Family Education Loan Program (FFELP). The reform cut into the company's interest-earning operations. As a result SLM increased its focus on higher-yielding private education loans which carry a lower risk.

Additionally SLM that year became ensnared in a student-lending industry probe led by New York attorney general Andrew Cuomo. The company agreed to a $2 million settlement and to abide by a code of conduct regarding its dealings with college employees.

One of the most dramatic results of the troubles was the collapse of a planned acquisition by a consortium of investment firms. The planned $8.8 billion deal included buyers J.C. Flowers (which was to own about a half of SLM) Bank of America and JPMorgan Chase. In the midst of the industry probe J.C. Flowers sought a change in SLM's leadership in an effort to secure regulatory approval for the acquisition; Thomas J. (Tim) Fitzpatrick was ousted as CEO. Ultimately the buyers canceled the deal citing the reduced potential value of SLM. The student lender filed a lawsuit to challenge the termination but eventually dropped the suit. It later cut more than 10% of its workforce.

EXECUTIVES

Vice President Finance And Information Research, Brian Burgess
Senior Vice President Loan Operations, Michael Maier

Chairman And Ceo, Raymond J. Quinlan, $600,000 total compensation
Evp And General Counsel, Laurent C. Lutz, $525,000 total compensation
Evp And Cfo, Steven J. McGarry, $375,000 total compensation
Svp And Chief Risk Officer, Jeffery F. Dale, age 58, $400,000 total compensation
Evp And Chief Marketing Officer, Charles P. Rocha, $375,000 total compensation
Svp And Chief Compliance Officer, Jim Truitt
Vice President West Region Head, Robin Famiglietti
Vice President Financial Planning And Analysis, Steve Kirkpatrick
Svp Corporate Development, Paul Mayer
Svp And Chief Risk Officer, Jeffrey Dale
Vice President Of Tax, Tina Vogel
Assistant Vice President Network Services, Peter Tropf
Vice President, Jonathan Boyles
Senior Vice President General Counsel, Nicolas Jafarieh
Vice President Finance Other Credit, Doug Maurer
Vice President Operations Contingency Services, Jeff Mersmann
Vice President And Associate General Counsel, Anne Milem
Vice President, Lynn M Langdon
Vice President Information Technology Credit Origination, Michael Migliore
Senior Executive Administrative Assistant For Senior Vice President Corporate Finance, Kathleen Mullaney
Vice President Information Technology Risk And Compliance, Karen Delozier
Svp And Chief Security Officer, Jerry Archer
Vice President Product Development, John Lazzati
Senior Vice President Chief Regulatory Counsel And Assistant Corporate Secretary, Rick Nelson
Senior Vice President Corporate Financ, Lance Franke
Vice President, Tom Linton
Vice President, Brenda Hymes
Vice President Finance, Donald Walden
Auditors: KPMG LLP

LOCATIONS

HQ: SLM Corp.
  300 Continental Drive, Newark, DE 19713
Phone: 302 451-0200
Web: www.salliemae.com

PRODUCTS/OPERATIONS

2016 Sales

	$ mil.	% of total
Interest		
Lons	1,060	79
Investments	9	1
Cash & cash equivalents	7	1
Non-Interest income		
Gain on sale of loans	0	14
(Losses) gains on derivatives and hedging activities net	(0.9)	5
Other income	69	-
Total	1,146	100

Selected Subsidiaries

HICA Holding
Sallie Mae Bank
Sallie Mae Inc.
SLM Education Credit Finance Corporation
  Bull Run I LLC
  SLM Education Credit Funding LLC
SLM Investment Corporation
Southwest Student Services Corporation

COMPETITORS

Bank of America
Brazos Higher Education Service Corp.
Citizens Financial Group

Discover
Educational Funding of The South
First Marblehead
FirstCity Financial
Great Lakes Higher Education
KeyCorp
Mohela
Nelnet
PNC Financial
Pennsylvania Higher Education Assistance Agency
SunTrust
Texas Guaranteed

HISTORICAL FINANCIALS
Company Type: Public

Income Statement				FYE: December 31
	ASSETS ($ mil.)	NET INCOME ($ mil.)	INCOME AS % OF ASSETS	EMPLOYEES
12/19	32,686	578	1.8%	1,900
12/18	26,638	487	1.8%	1,700
12/17	21,779	288	1.3%	1,500
12/16	18,533	250	1.4%	1,300
12/15	15,214	274	1.8%	1,200
Annual Growth	21.1%	20.5%	—	12.2%

2019 Year-End Financials

Debt ratio: 13.32%
Return on equity: 18.40%
Cash ($ mil.): 5,563
Current ratio: —
Long-term debt ($ mil.): —

No. of shares (mil.): 421
Dividends
  Yield: 1.3%
  Payout: 9.2%
Market value ($ mil.): 3,752

	STOCK PRICE ($) FY Close	P/E High/Low		PER SHARE ($) Earnings	Dividends	Book Value
12/19	8.91	9	6	1.30	0.12	7.86
12/18	8.31	11	8	1.07	0.00	6.82
12/17	11.30	20	16	0.62	0.00	5.72
12/16	11.02	21	10	0.53	0.00	5.47
12/15	6.52	18	11	0.59	0.00	4.92
Annual Growth	8.1%	—	—	21.8%	—	12.5%

SmartFinancial Inc

Cornerstone Bancshares is theÂ holding company for Cornerstone Community Bank which operates about five locations in Chattanooga Tennessee and surrounding communities in addition to two loan production offices in Knoxville Tennessee and Dalton Georgia. The bank offers standard retail and commercial services including checking and savings accounts money market accounts and CDs. Its lending activities primarily consist of commercial real estate loans residential mortgages real estate construction loans and business and agricultural loans. Another subsidiary of Cornerstone Bancshares Eagle Financial purchases accounts receivable and acts as a conduit lender.

EXECUTIVES

Senior Vice President Knoxville Area Market Executive, Mike Honeycutt
Auditors: Dixon Hughes Goodman LLP

LOCATIONS

HQ: SmartFinancial Inc
  5401 Kingston Pike, Suite 600, Knoxville, TN 37919
Phone: 865 437-5700
Web: www.smartfinancialinc.com

COMPETITORS

Bank of America	Regions Financial
First Horizon	SunTrust
First Security Group	Tennessee Valley
Home Federal Bank (TN)	Financial Holdings

HISTORICAL FINANCIALS
Company Type: Public

Income Statement				FYE: December 31
	ASSETS ($ mil.)	NET INCOME ($ mil.)	INCOME AS % OF ASSETS	EMPLOYEES
12/19	2,449	26	1.1%	399
12/18	2,274	18	0.8%	387
12/17	1,720	5	0.3%	343
12/16	1,062	5	0.5%	222
12/15	1,023	1	0.1%	225
Annual Growth	24.4%	104.8%	—	15.4%

2019 Year-End Financials

Debt ratio: 2.64%
Return on equity: 8.91%
Cash ($ mil.): 160
Current ratio: —
Long-term debt ($ mil.): —

No. of shares (mil.): 14
Dividends
  Yield: 0.2%
  Payout: 2.6%
Market value ($ mil.): 331

	STOCK PRICE ($) FY Close	P/E High/Low		PER SHARE ($) Earnings	Dividends	Book Value
12/19	23.65	13	9	1.89	0.05	22.33
12/18	18.27	19	12	1.45	0.00	20.31
12/17	21.70	47	33	0.55	0.00	18.46
12/16	18.56	24	18	0.78	0.00	17.85
12/15	16.09	46	9	0.32	0.00	17.25
Annual Growth	10.1%	—	—	55.9%	—	6.7%

Smucker (J.M.) Co.

The J. M. Smucker Company operates principally in one industry the manufacturing and marketing of branded food and beverage products on a worldwide basis although the majority of the sales are in the U.S The principal products are coffee dog food cat food pet snacks peanut butter fruit spreads frozen handheld products shortening and oils portion control products juices and beverages and baking mixes and ingredients The products are has an extended product portfolio that includes Folgers coffee jif and Milk-Bone plus new favorites like Café Bustelo Smucker's Uncrustables and Rachael Ray Nutrish and other products among its 40-plus brands include shortening and oils frozen sandwiches juices and baking mixes and ingredient. It generates the most revenue from pet foods followed by coffee and consumer foods. Smucker's generates nearly 95% of its sales in the US. It was established in 1897 and incorporated in Ohio in 1921.

Operations

Smucker's operations are divided among four business segments: US Retail Pet Foods (more than 35% of revenue) US Retail Coffee (more than 25%) US Retail Consumer Foods (more than 20%) and International/Away from Home (about 15%).

The U.S. Retail Pet Foods' mainstream pet foods brands includes Meow Mix 9Lives Rachael Ray Nutrish Nature's Recipe premium pet food Natural Balance and pet snacks Milk-Bone and Pup-Peroni. Its coffee operations include mainstream ground single-serve and premium coffee (Folgers Dunkin Donuts Cafe Bustelo) and its consumer foods operations include peanut butter (Jif) fruit spreads (Smucker's) and shortening and oils (Crisco).

Smucker's international segment primarily includes coffee for Canadian and other non-US markets as well as Canadian flour (Robin Hood Five Roses).Overall coffee is the company's leading product category generating about a third of sales; dog food accounts for more than 15% with cat food pet snacks and peanut butter each bringing in about 10%.

Geographic Reach

Unlike many of its major competitors Ohio-based Smucker counts the US as its largest market by far accounting for nearly 95% of revenue; Canada generates about 5%.

The company has eight sales and administrative offices in the U.S. and one in Canada. Canadian headquarters is located in Markham Ontario.

Sales and Marketing

In the US retail market segments Smucker's products are primarily sold through direct sales and brokers to food retailers supermarkets food wholesalers drug stores club stores mass merchandisers discount and dollar stores military commissaries natural foods stores and distributors pet specialty stores and online retailers. The International products are distributed through retail channels foodservice distributors and operators (e.g. restaurants lodging schools and universities health care operators).

Walmart Inc. and subsidiaries amounted to more than 30% of net sales in 2020 2019 and 2018. These sales are primarily included in the U.S. retail market segments. No other customer exceeded 10 percent of net sales during 2020 2019 or 2018.

Advertising expense were $198.6 million $237.5 million and $194.2 million in 2020 2019 and 2018 respectively.

Financial Performance

After two years of declining revenue Smucker's saw sales rise in the past five years peaking with revenues in fiscal 2019. Net income over the past five years has been sporadic.

In fiscal 2020 (ended April 2020) the company reported revenue of $7.8 billion down $37 million from the prior year. This was due to declines for private label dog food and the Natural Balance brand. Lower net price realization impacted net sales due to lower net pricing for coffee and peanut butter.

Net income rose that year increasing 52% to $779.5 million as compared to fiscal 2019 due to decreases in intangible asset impairment charges special project costs and in selling distribution and administrative expenses.

Cash at the end of fiscal 2020 was $391.1 million an increase of $289.8 million from the prior year. Cash from operations contributed $1.3 billion to the coffers while investing activities used $271.5 million mainly for property plant and equipment additions. Financing activities used another $688.7 million for repayments on both short-term and long-term debt.

Strategy

Smucker's strategy focuses on growth through owning and marketing the #1 brand name food products (both people and pet) in North America with potential for worldwide appeal. New product innovation and acquisitions underpin these ends.

It introduced new products in 2020 such as its Jif Squeeze Creamy Peanut Butter Santa Cruz Organic Creamy Dark Roasted Almond Butter and four new Organic Juice Beverage Shots. As a result of this focus on top brands particularly pet food and snacks and coffee the company in fiscal 2019 divested its US baking business (Pillsbury Martha White Hungry Jack and other brands) to investment firms for $375 million.

With the late fiscal 2015 acquisition of Big Heart Pet Brands the company instantly became a player in the growing pet food and snacks market (now Smucker's largest segment); it further strengthened that segment with the fiscal 2019 purchase of Ainsworth Pet Nutrition.

Mergers and Acquisitions

In 2018 Smucker's paid nearly $2 billion for premium pet food company Ainsworth Pet Nutrition. The deal adds a handful of pet food and snack brands including fast-growing Rachel Ray Nutrish to Smucker's pet food division which already includes Meow Mix Milk-Bone and 9Lives among other brands.

Company Background

Jerome Smucker began operating a steam-powered cider mill in 1897 for farmers in Orrville Ohio but he found that his biggest business was selling apple butter made using a secret Smucker family recipe. By the 1920s The J. M. Smucker Company had begun producing a full line of preserves and jellies.

HISTORY

Jerome Smucker began operating a steam-powered cider mill in 1897 for farmers in Orrville Ohio but he found that his biggest business was selling apple butter made using a secret Smucker family recipe. By the 1920s The J. M. Smucker Company had begun producing a full line of preserves and jellies and in 1935 it acquired its first fruit-processing operations.

Under Jerome's grandson Paul Smucker the company gained widespread national distribution by the mid-1960s. Tim Smucker succeeded his father Paul as president in 1981 then as chairman in 1987 when his brother Richard became president.

The company's growth has been enhanced through the development of its industrial fruit fillings business and acquisitions of domestic natural juice and peanut butter companies including Knudsen & Sons (1984) After the Fall (1994) and Laura Scudder's (from National Grape Co-op 1994). It has gradually expanded internationally through acquisitions. In 1993 it acquired the jam preserves and pie-filling unit of Canada's Culinar. In a 1998 deal Smucker purchased Australia's Allowrie jam and Lackersteens marmalade lines.

Smucker sold its flagging Mrs. Smith's frozen pie business to Flowers in 1997 less than two

years after buying the unit from Kellogg. It bought Kraft's domestic fruit spread unit in 1997 and in 1999 purchased the northwestern Adams peanut butter business from Pro-Fac Cooperative. Smucker kept the Adams name but shifted packaging to its Pennsylvania peanut butter plant.

Spreading into retail the company opened a store in 1999 in its hometown of Orrville and then launched online and catalog sales. Also that year Smucker bought a fruit filling plant in Brazil from Groupe Danone a major customer. During 2000 the company's Henry Jones Foods subsidiary (Australia) purchased Taylor Foods (sauces marinades).

Smucker acquired International Flavors & Fragrances' formulated fruit and vegetable preparation businesses in 2001. Moving beyond its stronghold in natural peanut butter brands the next year Smucker purchased the Jif peanut butter and Crisco cooking oil and shortening brands from Procter & Gamble. The $670 million purchase price for Jif and Crisco included shifting 53% of Smucker stock into the hands of P&G shareholders.

A decision to concentrate on North America led to the $37 million sale of Australian subsidiary Henry Jones Foods in 2004. Also that year Smucker sold its operations in Brazil to Cargill and closed down two fruit processing plants in California and Oregon. Its purchase of International Multifoods that year added an array of US brands to the Smucker family including Pillsbury flour baking mixes and ready-to-spread frostings; Hungry Jack pancake mixes syrup and potato side dishes; Martha White baking mixes and ingredients; and PET evaporated milk brands. Canadian brands included Robin Hood flour and baking mixes Bick's pickles and condiments and Golden Temple flour and rice.

To further its strategy of concentrating on its core retail brands in 2005 Smucker sold its US foodservice and bakery business and the Canadian operations of Gourmet Baker (all part of its International Multifoods acquisition) to Value Creation Partners. The following year the company sold its Canadian grain-based foodservice operations and industrial businesses to Cargill and CHS Inc. The operations were integrated into leading US flour miller Horizon Milling (which is jointly owned by Cargill and CHS). Adding to its name-brand offerings in 2006 Smucker acquired the White Lily brand of flours baking mixes and frozen biscuits from C.H. Guenther.

The company extended its baking offerings with the 2007 acquisition of sweetened condensed and evaporated milk producer Eagle Family Foods Holdings. Smucker paid $133 million in cash and $115 million in assumed debt for it. Eagle is a good fit with Smucker's PET milk products. Given Smucker's size and subsequent bargaining power with food retailers (including Wal-Mart the giant in US food retailing) and Eagle's domination of the North American canned-milk sector (it is the largest producer of evaporated and sweetened condensed milk in the US and Canada) the pairing of the two companies was a sensible move for both.

EXECUTIVES

Vice Chairman And Cfo, Mark R. Belgya, age 59, $545,962 total compensation

Senior Vp, Chris Resweber

Vice Chairman; President U.s. Food And Beverage, Steven T. Oakland, age 59, $623,077 total compensation

President Pet Food And Pet Snacks, Barry C. Dunaway, age 57, $330,000 total compensation

President And Ceo, Mark T. Smucker, age 51, $355,000 total compensation

President Canada And International, David J. Lemmon

Vp Marketing Services, Tamara J. Fynan

Svp Operations, J. Randal Day

Vice President Of Marketing, Kent Wadsworth

Vice President, Sonal Robinson

Senior Vice President Human Resources And Corporate Communications, Jill Penrose

Svp General Counsel And Secretary, Jeannette Knudsen

Vice President Sales And Trade Marketing, Stephen Kouri

Vice President Finance, Mark Draa

Vice President Market Research, Jill Boyce

Vice President Customer Logistics, Rob Fox

Vp Sales And Marketing, John Hall

Vice President Of Supply Chain And Operations, Todd Campbell

Vice President Sales And Support, Chantel Meza

National Account Manager, Matt Kleinhenz

National Account Manager, Scott Dacus

Svp Operations, J Randal Day

National Account Manager, Mike Freitas

Vice President Green Coffee, Roger Larsh

National Account Manager, Erik Corbett

National Account Manager, Adrienne Brown

Vice President Ecommerce, Daniel Cooke

Chairman, Richard K. Smucker, age 72

Board Member, Dan Russell

Auditors: Ernst & Young LLP

LOCATIONS

HQ: Smucker (J.M.) Co.
One Strawberry Lane, Orrville, OH 44667-0280
Phone: 330 682-3000
Web: www.jmsmucker.com

2019 Sales

	$ mil.	% of total
US	7,298	93
International		
Canada	421	5
Other countries	118	2
Total	**7,838**	**100**

PRODUCTS/OPERATIONS

2019 Sales

	$ mil.	% of total
US Retail Pet Foods	2,879	37
US Retail Coffee	2,122	27
US Retail Consumer Foods	1,761	22
International and Away From Home	1,074	14
Total	**7,838**	**100**

2019 Sales

	% of total
Coffee	32
Dog food	17
Pet snacks	10
Cat food	10
Peanut butter	10
Fruit spreads	4
Frozen handheld	4
Shortening and oils	3
Baking mixes and ingredients	2
Portion control	2
Juices and beverages	2
Other	4
Total	**100**

Selected Products

Coffee
Frozen sandwiches
Fruit spreads
Juices and beverages
Peanut butter
Pet food
Pet snacks
Pickles and condiments
Shortening and oils
Syrups
Toppings

Selected Brands

Canadian brands
Adams
Bick's
Carnation (under license)
Double Fruit
Five Roses
Golden Temple
Robin Hood
Smucker's
Coffee
Café; Bustelo
Café; Pilon
Dunkin' Donuts (under license)
Folgers
kava
Medaglia D'oro
Consumer and natural foods
Adams
Crisco
Dickinson's
Jif
Knott's Berry Farm
Laura Scudder's
Smucker's
Pet food and snacks
9Lives
Dad's
Gravy Train
Kibbles 'n Bits
Meow Mix
Milk-Bone
Natural Balance
Nature's Recipe
Rachel Ray Nutrish
Snausages

COMPETITORS

Caribou Coffee	Mars Incorporated
Community Coffee	National Grape
ConAgra	Cooperative
Ferrero	Nestlé Purina PetCare
General Mills	Pinnacle Foods
Hill's Pet Nutrition	Starbucks
Hormel	Tata Global Beverages
Kraft Heinz	Welch's

HISTORICAL FINANCIALS

Company Type: Public

Income Statement   FYE: April 30

	REVENUE ($ mil.)	NET INCOME ($ mil.)	NET PROFIT MARGIN	EMPLOYEES
04/20	7,801	779	10.0%	7,300
04/19	7,838	514	6.6%	7,400
04/18	7,357	1,338	18.2%	7,000
04/17	7,392	592	8.0%	7,140
04/16	7,811	688	8.8%	6,910
Annual Growth	(0.0%)	3.1%	—	1.4%

2020 Year-End Financials

Debt ratio: 33.12%	No. of shares (mil.): 114
Return on equity: 9.62%	Dividends
Cash ($ mil.): 391	Yield: 3.0%
Current ratio: 1.24	Payout: 63.6%
Long-term debt ($ mil.): 5,373	Market value ($ mil.): 13,108

	STOCK PRICE ($) FY Close	P/E High/Low		PER SHARE ($)		
				Earnings	Dividends	Book Value
04/20	114.91	19	14	6.84	3.49	71.80
04/19	122.63	27	21	4.52	3.33	70.08
04/18	114.08	11	8	11.78	3.09	69.48
04/17	126.72	31	24	5.10	2.92	60.39
04/16	126.98	23	18	5.76	2.65	60.26
Annual Growth	(2.5%)	—	—	4.4%	7.1%	4.5%

SOLSTICE HOLDINGS INC.

EXECUTIVES

Pres, Mr Doug L Devos
Chm, Stephen Van Andel
Exec V Pres-Cfo, Russ Evans
Exec V Pres-Coo, Alvin Koop
V Pres, Mr Michael Mohr
Cntrl, Mr Craig V Witcher
Senior Software Developer, Carolyn Knott

LOCATIONS

HQ: SOLSTICE HOLDINGS INC.
7575 FULTON ST E, ADA, MI 493550001
Phone: 616 787-1000

HISTORICAL FINANCIALS

Company Type: Private

Income Statement   FYE: December 31

	REVENUE ($ mil.)	NET INCOME ($ mil.)	NET PROFIT MARGIN	EMPLOYEES
12/08	8,235	0	—	14,000
12/07	7,168	0	—	—
12/06	6,387	0	—	—
Annual Growth	13.5%	—	—	—

Sonic Automotive, Inc.

Sonic Automotive is one of the leading US auto dealers with more than 85 stores in its franchised dealerships and about 10 stores in echopark segment. Sonic operates about 100 new and used vehicle franchises and about 15 collision repair centers in major markets in more than 10 states including California Texas the Carolinas Alabama and Tennessee. The company sells about 25 brands of cars and light trucks including Honda Ford and Subaru and offers extended aftermarket services. Chairman O. Bruton Smith is also the majority owner of Speedway Motorsports which operates eight NASCAR auto racetracks.

Operations

Sonic Automotive sells new vehicles including luxury cars (BMW Mercedes Audi Lexus Land Rover Porsche and Cadillac) mid-line imports (Honda Hyundai Volkswagen and Toyota) and domestic brands (Ford and General Motors). Luxury brands account for more than 60% of new vehicle sales mid-line brands bring in about 30% of new vehicle sales and domestic brands of nearly 10%.

Sonic operates in two segments: Franchised Dealership segment and EchoPark segment.

The Franchised Dealership segment operate more than 85 stores and accounts for nearly 90% of the company's sales. This segment comprised on retail automotive franchises that sell new vehicles and buy and sell used vehicles sell replacement parts perform vehicle maintenance warranty and repair services arrange finance and insurance products.

EchoPark segment which accounts for more than 10% of sales operates about eight stores that buy and sell pre-owned vehicles and arrange finance and insurance products.

Geographic Reach

Sonic is headquartered in Charlotte North Carolina. California is Sonic's #1 market accounting for nearly 30% of sales followed closely by Texas at more than a quarter of total sales. EchoPark's retail units are clustered in Colorado Texas North Carolina and California.

Sales and Marketing

Sonic's advertising expenses were $60.8 million $63.1 million and $61.6 million for 2019 2018 and 2017 respectively.

Financial Performance

Sonic Automotive has seen healthy revenue growth in recent years through a strategy of new stores and acquisitions. Its annual revenues have risen close to 10% since 2015.

Revenue increased to $10.5 billion in 2019 from $9.9 billion in 2018 driven by the increase of sales in both the Franchised Dealerships and Echopark segments.

Net income was $144 million in 2019 an increase of 180% from $52 million in 2018 primarily due to the decrease of Selling general and administrative expenses by 4% from the prior year.

Cash at the end of 2019 was $29.1 million an increase of $23.2 million from the prior year. Cash provided by operating activities was $171 million in fiscal 2019 while investing activities provided another $136.8 million. Financing activities used $284.4 million primarily for the borrowings on revolving credit facilities.

Strategy

As part of the company's strategic plans Sonic is primarily focused on growing its operations in large metropolitan markets in the Southeast Texas and California. The company plans to grow its new-vehicle franchise business both organically and opportunistically through acquisitions. The company also aims to achieve its long-term growth strategy of targeting luxury or mid-line import brands in regions where it already operates. Approximately 90% of total new vehicle revenue was generated by luxury and mid-line import dealerships which usually have higher operating margins lower associate turnover and lower inventory levels.

The company have been operating their business through dealership primarily on property financed through long-term operating leases. The company is aiming to purchase existing properties or relocating dealership operations to owned real estate as they believe that owning properties will over the long term strengthen their balance sheet and reduce overall cost of operating and financing facilities.

Sonic have augmented their manufacturer-franchised dealership operations with EchoPark pre-owned vehicle specialty retail locations. Their EchoPark business operates independently from their franchised dealerships business. The company seeks to execute its EchoPark expansion plan by opening three additional Echopark store in 2020. As of 2019 They have been operating three EchoPark stores in Colorado four in Texas one in North Carolina and California.

Company Background

O. Bruton Smith and his son Scott control the company through their ownership of about 40% of Sonic Automotive's voting stock.

EXECUTIVES

President And Ceo, B. Scott Smith, age 52, $1,085,438 total compensation

Evp Operations, Frank J. (Jeff) Dyke, age 53, $969,179 total compensation

Vp And Chief Marketing Officer, Rachel M. Richards

Evp And Cfo, Heath R. Byrd, age 53, $677,327 total compensation

Vp Information Technology, Christopher (Chris) Maritato

Vice President Of Finance And Insurance, Richard O'Connor

Vice President, John Russ

Vice President, William Sullivan

Senior Regional Vice President, Karen McKemie

Vice President Manufacturer Relations, Raymond Valentine

Regional Vice President Tn Dc, Kevin Gaither

Senior Business Intelligence Developer, Jonathan Henin

Vice President, James Brannon

Chairman, O. Bruton Smith, age 92

Vice Chairman, David B. Smith, age 45

Board Member, William Belk

Assistant Treasurer, Chris Cellini

Auditors: KPMG LLP

LOCATIONS

HQ: Sonic Automotive, Inc.
4401 Colwick Road, Charlotte, NC 28211
Phone: 704 566-2400   **Fax:** 704 536-5116
Web: www.sonicautomotive.com

PRODUCTS/OPERATIONS

2016 sales

	$ mil.	% of total
Franchised Dealerships	9,602	99
EchoPark	129	1
Total	**9,731**	**100**

2016 sales

	$ mil.	% of total
New vehicles	5,234	54
Used vehicles	2,533	26
Wholesale vehicles	211	2
Parts service and collision repair	1,409	14
Finance insurance and other	343	4
Total	**9,731**	**100**

Services Center List-Selected:
Acura of Serramonte Service Center
Audi West Houston Service Center
BMW of Birmingham Service Center
Cadillac of Las Vegas Service Center
Capitol Chevrolet of Columbia Service Center
Fort Mill Ford Service Center
Honda of Santa Monica Service Center
Momentum Volkswagen Service Center
North Central Ford Service Center

Toyota of Fort Worth Service Center
Volkswagen of Fort Myers Service Center
Brands
BMW
Mercedes
Lexus
Audi
Land Rover
Cadillac
Porsche
Honda
Toyota
Volkswagen
Hyundai
Ford
General Motors

COMPETITORS

Asbury Automotive	Enterprise Rent-A-Car
AutoNation	Group 1 Automotive
AutoTrader	Gunn Automotive
Autobytel	Internet Brands
CarMax	JM Family Enterprises
Darcars	Penske Automotive
David McDavid Auto	Group
Group	Sewell Automotive
DriveTime Automotive	

HISTORICAL FINANCIALS

Company Type: Public

Income Statement			FYE: December 31

	REVENUE ($ mil.)	NET INCOME ($ mil.)	NET PROFIT MARGIN	EMPLOYEES
12/19	10,454	144	1.4%	9,300
12/18	9,951	51	0.5%	9,700
12/17	9,867	92	0.9%	9,750
12/16	9,731	93	1.0%	9,800
12/15	9,624	86	0.9%	9,800
Annual Growth	**2.1%**	**13.7%**	—	**(1.3%)**

2019 Year-End Financials

Debt ratio: 56.10%
Return on equity: 16.31%
Cash ($ mil.): 29
Current ratio: 0.98
Long-term debt ($ mil.): 673

No. of shares (mil.): 43
Dividends
Yield: 1.2%
Payout: 14.4%
Market value ($ mil.): 1,337

	STOCK PRICE ($) FY Close	P/E High/Low		PER SHARE ($) Earnings	Dividends	Book Value
12/19	31.00	10	4	3.30	0.40	21.90
12/18	13.76	19	11	1.20	0.24	19.25
12/17	18.45	12	8	2.09	0.20	18.21
12/16	22.90	12	8	2.04	0.20	16.21
12/15	22.76	16	12	1.70	0.11	14.60
Annual Growth	**8.0%**	—	—	**18.0%**	**37.3%**	**10.7%**

South Plains Financial Inc

Auditors: Weaver and Tidwell, L.L.P

LOCATIONS

HQ: South Plains Financial Inc
5219 City Bank Parkway, Lubbock, TX 79407
Phone: 806 792-7101
Web: www.spfi.bank

HISTORICAL FINANCIALS

Company Type: Public

Income Statement			FYE: December 31

	ASSETS ($ mil.)	NET INCOME ($ mil.)	INCOME AS % OF ASSETS	EMPLOYEES
12/19	3,237	29	0.9%	679
12/18	2,712	29	1.1%	684
12/17	2,573	23	0.9%	—
Annual Growth	**12.2%**	**11.2%**	—	—

2019 Year-End Financials

Debt ratio: 5.19%
Return on equity: 11.26%
Cash ($ mil.): 158
Current ratio: —
Long-term debt ($ mil.): —

No. of shares (mil.): 18
Dividends
Yield: 0.2%
Payout: 3.9%
Market value ($ mil.): 376

	STOCK PRICE ($) FY Close	P/E High/Low		PER SHARE ($) Earnings	Dividends	Book Value
12/19	20.87	12	9	1.71	0.06	16.98
12/18	0.00	—	—	1.98	2.03	14.40
12/17	0.00	—	—	1.60	0.53	14.58
Annual Growth	—	—	—	**3.4%**	**(66.4%)**	**7.9%**

South State Corp

South State Corporation (formerly First Financial Holdings) is the holding company for South State Bank (formerly South Carolina Bank and Trust and South Carolina Bank and Trust of the Piedmont both known as SCBT). The bank operates branches throughout the Palmetto state as well as in select counties in Georgia and North Carolina. Serving retail and business customers the banks provide deposit accounts loans and mortgages as well as trust and investment planning services. More than half of the firm's loan portfolio is devoted to commercial mortgages while consumer real estate loans make up more than a quarter. South State plans to merge with Southeastern Bank Financial parent of Georgia Bank & Trust.

Operations

Beyond its retail and commercial banking mortgage lending consumer finance and trust and investment businesses the bank operates registered investment advisors Minis & Co. and First Southeast 401K Fiduciaries as well as limited-purpose broker-dealer First Southeast Investor Services.

South State Corporation generated 70% of its total revenue from loan interest (including fees) in 2014 while another 4% came from interest income on investment securities. Service charges and Bankcard services income made up another 14% of total revenue while trust and investment services income and mortgage banking income each contributed roughly 4% during the year.

Geographic Reach

South State Corporation boasts nearly 130 branches across nearly 20 counties in South Carolina a handful of counties in North Carolina and about a dozen counties in the northeast and coastal regions of Georgia.

Financial Performance

South State Corporation's revenues and profits have been on the rise over the past few years mostly thanks to continued growth of its loan business and declining loan loss provisions as its loan portfolio's credit quality has improved with the strengthened economy.

The company's revenue jumped by 28% to $436.72 million in 2014 which was mostly driven by 20% growth in its loan interest income as its average loan asset balances swelled by a similar percentage. South State's non-interest income also swelled by 76% thanks to higher deposit account service charge bankcard service trust and investment service and mortgage banking fees from overall growth in the business through acquisitions and organic initiatives.

Higher revenue and controlled operating costs in 2014 drove the bank's net income higher by 53% to $75.44 million. South State's operating cash levels declined by 51% to $118.65 million for the year after adjusting its earnings for non-cash net sales proceeds from its mortgage loans held-for-sale and as the bank spent more cash toward its accrued income taxes.

Strategy

Though it does sometimes expand or relocate its existing branches to better position its locations for more growth South State Corporation has been mostly growing its loan business and branch network through strategic bank and branch acquisitions. Its 2015 acquisition of 13 branch locations from Bank of America for example extended South State's reach into six new markets and three existing markets while adding millions of dollars worth of new loan business. Then in mid-2016 South State Corporation agreed to buy Southeastern Bank Financial the holding company of Georgia Bank & Trust (which also operates in South Carolina as Southern Bank & Trust). The combined company will operate more than 130 branches in Georgia and the Carolinas.

Mergers and Acquisitions

In 2015 South State Corporation agreed to purchase 12 South Carolina branches and one Georgia branch from Bank of America expanding its reach into six new markets. The acquired branches were located in Hartwell Georgia; as well as Florence Greenwood Orangeburg Sumter Newberry Batesburg-Leesville Abbeville and Hartsville in South Carolina.

Company Background

South State Corporation and South State Bank changed their names from First Financial Holdings and South Carolina Bank and Trust respectively in 2014. The change was designed to better promote the South State brand with customers.

EXECUTIVES

Ceo, Robert R. Hill, age 53, $645,000 total compensation
Vice President Of Public Relations, Donna Pullen
Cfo And Coo, John C. Pollok, age 54, $442,000 total compensation
Regional President Upstate, John F. Windley, age 68, $315,000 total compensation
Chief Credit Officer And Chief Risk Officer, Joseph Burns, $295,000 total compensation
President, R. Wayne Hall, $203,405 total compensation
Vice President, Reid Davis
Senior Vice President Technology, Ross Bagley
Senior Executive Vice President, Dane H Murray
Vice President, Stacy Cannon
Avp, Sandy Elvington

Senior Vice President Corporate Counsel, Nici Comer
Vice President Consumer Loan Administration, Suzanne Frierson
Senior Vice President Chief Compliance Officer, Lora Jex
Chairman, Robert R. Horger, age 69
Vice Chairman, Paula Harper Bethea
Board Member, Jimmy Addison
Auditors: Dixon Hughes Goodman LLP

LOCATIONS

HQ: South State Corp
1101 First Street South, Suite 202, Winter Haven, FL 33880
Phone: 863 293-4710
Web: www.southstatebank.com

PRODUCTS/OPERATIONS

2011 Sales

	$ mil.	% of total
Interest		
Loans including fees	319	70
Investment securities	20	4
Other	1	-
Noninterest		
Service charges on deposit accounts	36	10
Bankcard services income	29	6
Trust and investment services income	18	4
Mortgage banking	16	4
Securities gains net	-	0
Amortization of FDIC indemnification asset	(21.9)	0
Other	16	4
Total	**436**	**100**

COMPETITORS

BB&T
Bank of America
Bank of South Carolina
First Citizens
Bancorporation

Regions Financial
Security Federal

HISTORICAL FINANCIALS

Company Type: Public

Income Statement

FYE: December 31

	ASSETS ($ mil.)	NET INCOME ($ mil.)	INCOME AS % OF ASSETS	EMPLOYEES
12/19	15,921	186	1.2%	2,547
12/18	14,676	178	1.2%	2,602
12/17	14,466	87	0.6%	2,719
12/16	8,900	101	1.1%	2,055
12/15	8,557	99	1.2%	2,058
Annual Growth	16.8%	17.0%	—	5.5%

2019 Year-End Financials

Debt ratio: 0.73%
Return on equity: 7.87%
Cash ($ mil.): 688
Current ratio: —
Long-term debt ($ mil.): —

No. of shares (mil.): 33
Dividends
Yield: 1.9%
Payout: 31.1%
Market value ($ mil.): 2,927

	STOCK PRICE ($) FY Close	P/E High/Low	PER SHARE ($) Earnings	Dividends	Book Value
12/19	86.75	16 11	5.36	1.67	70.32
12/18	59.95	19 12	4.86	1.38	66.04
12/17	87.15	32 27	2.93	1.32	62.81
12/16	87.40	22 14	4.18	1.21	46.83
12/15	71.95	19 14	4.11	0.98	43.84
Annual Growth	4.8%	—	6.9%	14.3%	12.5%

Southern California Edison Co.

One of the Golden State's largest utilities Southern California Edison (SCE) distributes power to more than 5 million customers in central coastal and southern California (excluding Los Angeles and some other cities). The utility's system consists of some 12635 miles of transmission lines and some 91375 miles of distribution lines. SCE has about 7000 MW of generating capacity from stakes in nuclear hydroelectric fossil-fueled and solar power plants. The utility also has power purchase agreements and sells excess power to wholesale customers. SCE is a unit of utility and competitive power holding company Edison International.

Operations

SCE's results of operations are derived mainly through two sources: Earning activities (about 55% of sales) and Cost-recovery activities (around 45%).

Earning activities represent revenue authorized by the CPUC and the FERC which is intended to provide SCE a reasonable opportunity to recover its costs and earn a return on its net investment in generation transmission and distribution assets. Also included in earnings activities are revenue or penalties related to incentive mechanisms other operating revenue and regulatory charges or disallowances.

The Cost-recovery activities represent CPUC- and FERC-authorized balancing accounts which allow for recovery of specific project or program costs subject to reasonableness review or compliance with upfront standards. Cost-recovery activities include rates which provide recovery subject to reasonableness review of among other things fuel costs purchased power costs public purpose related-program costs (including energy efficiency and demand-side management programs) and certain operation and maintenance expenses. SCE earns no return on these activities.

Geographic Reach

Headquartered in Rosemead California SCE supplies and delivers electricity through its electrical infrastructure to an approximately 50000 square-mile area of Southern California. This service area contains a population of nearly 15 million people.

Sales and Marketing

SCE generates about 45% of its revenues from commercial customers and about 40% from residential customers. Other revenue comes from agricultural industrial customers and public authorities. SCE serves the population via more than 5 million customer accounts.

Financial Performance

SCE's revenue decreased from $12.6 billion in 2018 to $12.3 billion in 2019 because of a decrease in cost-recovery activities revenue.

The company reported a net income of $1.5 billion as opposed to a net loss of $189 million in the previous year

Cash and cash equivalents at the end of the year were $24 million. Cash used by operating activities was $91 million. Financing activities provided $4.8 billion primarily from Capital contributions from Edison International Parent while investing activities used $4.7 billion primarily for capital expenditures and funding of nuclear decommissioning trusts.

Strategy

SCE has a two-tier residential rate structure with a separate High Usage Charge ("HUC") for customers consuming more than 400% of average usage. The first tier is priced at below-average cost and is intended to cover the customer's essential electricity needs. The second tier is priced at 25% more than the first tier and the HUC rate is set at more than twice the rate of the first tier. The CPUC has ordered a transition from tiered to TOU rates for most residential customers unless they opt to stay on the tiered rate structure. SCE anticipates starting that transition in the fourth quarter of 2020. To recover a portion of the fixed costs of serving no- or low-usage residential customers SCE assesses both fixed charges of less than $1 per month and a minimum charge of $10 per month ($5 for low-income customers).

SCE obtains the power energy and local grid support needed to serve its customers primarily from purchases from external parties. Approximately 19% of the needed power in 2019 was provided by SCE's own generating facilities.

SCE requires natural gas to meet contractual obligations for power tolling agreements (power contracts in which SCE has agreed to provide or pay for the natural gas used to generate electricity). SCE also requires natural gas to fuel its Mountainview and peaker plants which are generation units that operate in response to wholesale market signals related to power prices and reliability needs.

Company Background

Southern California Edison was founded in 1896 as West Side Lighting. It later merged with Los Angeles Edison Electric and became Southern California Edison in 1909. Holding company SCEcorp was formed in 1987 and was renamed Edison International in 1996.

EXECUTIVES

Svp And Cio, Todd L. Inlander
Ceo, Kevin M. Payne, age 59
Svp Customer And Operational Services, Stuart R. Hemphill
Vp Operational Services And Chief Procurement Officer, Douglas R. Bauder
Svp Transmission And Distribution, Peter T. Dietrich
Vp Distribution, Gregory M. Ferree
Vp Transmission Substations And Operations, Paul J. Grigaux
President, Ronald O. (R.O.) Nichols, age 66
Vp Decommissioning And Chief Nuclear Officer San Onofre Nuclear Generating Station, Thomas J. (Tom) Palmisano
Svp And Cfo, William (Tres) Petmecky, age 51
Vice President And Treasurer, Robert C Boada
Senior Vice President Regulatory Affairs, Caroline Choi
Vice President, Anthony Blakemore
Vice President, Debbie Rodgers
Government Relations, Karen Cadavona
Vice President, Dawn Anaiscourt
Vice President General, Robert Baldwin
Vice President And Treasurer Sce, Daniel Wood
Senior Vice President, So Edison
Vice President Distribution Sce, Greg Ferree
Vice President, Mark Carter

Senior Vice President Power Supply Sce, Kevin Walker
Vice President, Jill Anderson
Secretary, Darin Hester
Auditors: PricewaterhouseCoopers LLP

LOCATIONS

HQ: Southern California Edison Co.
2244 Walnut Grove Avenue, P.O. Box 800, Rosemead, CA 91770
Phone: 626 302-1212
Web: www.sce.com

PRODUCTS/OPERATIONS

2015 Sales

	% of total
Commercial customers	43
Residential customers	38
Industrial customers	5
Public authorities	5
Agriculture & other operating revenue	9
Total	**100**

2015 Sales

	$ mil.	% of total
Utility Earning Activities	6,305	55
Utility Cost- Recovery Activities	5,180	45
Total	**11,485**	**100**

COMPETITORS

American States Water	Portland General
Avista	Electric
Bonneville Power	Sacramento Municipal
Calpine	Utility
Imperial Irrigation	San Diego Gas &
District	Electric
NV Energy	SoCalGas
PacifiCorp	
Pacific Gas and	
Electric	

HISTORICAL FINANCIALS

Company Type: Public

Income Statement FYE: December 31

	REVENUE ($ mil.)	NET INCOME ($ mil.)	NET PROFIT MARGIN	EMPLOYEES
12/19	12,306	1,530	12.4%	12,720
12/18	12,611	(189)	—	12,219
12/17	12,254	1,136	9.3%	12,234
12/16	11,830	1,499	12.7%	11,947
12/15	11,485	1,111	9.7%	12,678
Annual Growth	**1.7%**	**8.3%**	**—**	**0.1%**

2019 Year-End Financials

Debt ratio: 24.52%
Return on equity: 9.68%
Cash ($ mil.): 24
Current ratio: 0.70
Long-term debt ($ mil.): 15,132

No. of shares (mil.): 434
Dividends
Yield: 4.8%
Payout: 42.5%
Market value ($ mil.): 10,690

	STOCK PRICE ($) FY Close	P/E High/Low	PER SHARE ($) Earnings	Dividends	Book Value
12/19	24.58	— —	(0.00)	1.20	40.99
12/18	20.44	— —	(0.00)	1.20	31.70
12/17	25.42	— —	(0.00)	1.20	33.74
12/16	25.15	— —	(0.00)	1.20	33.30
12/15	24.85	— —	(0.00)	1.20	31.44
Annual Growth	**(0.3%)**		**—**	**(0.0%)**	**6.9%**

Southern Company (The)

Southern Power provides power for the burgeoning population in the South. The company owns builds acquires and markets energy in the competitive wholesale supply business. It develops and operates independent power plants in the southeastern US. The company which is part of Southern Company's generation and energy marketing operations has more than 10500 MW of primarily fossil-fueled facilities generating capacity operating or under construction in Alabama California Florida Georgia Nevada North Carolina Texas and New Mexico. Southern Power's electricity output is marketed to wholesale customers in the region. It is growing by acquiring and developing solar power facilities.

Operations

The company is a wholesale energy provider serving electricity needs of municipalities electric cooperatives and investor-owned utilities. Southern Power and its subsidiaries owns and/or operates 35 facilities in nine states. Its renewable assets include biomass and solar.

Thanks to solar facilities under construction and the acquisitions of Calipatria Solar and Grant Wind as well as other capacity and energy contracts the Southern Power has an average of 75% of its available demonstrated capacity covered through 2020 and an average of 70% of its available demonstrated capacity covered through 2025.

Geographic Reach

Southern Power has operations Alabama California Florida Georgia Nevada New Mexico North Carolina Oklahoma and Texas.

Financial Performance

In fiscal 2015 Southern Power's net sales decreased by $111 million compared to 2014. Power purchase agreements (PPA) energy revenues declined due to lower energy prices driven by a drop in natural gas prices which was passed through in fuel revenues.

Wholesale revenues and non-affiliates revenues declined due to lower energy and capacity revenues.

In 2015 net income increased by 25% due to lower fuel expenses and purchased power partially offset by decreased sales.

Fuel expense decreased due to lower natural gas generation costs.

Purchased power expenses decreased primarily due to a drop in volume of KWhs purchased as well as a decrease associated with the average cost of purchased power.

Net cash provided by the operating activities increased by 66% due to higher income tax benefits received and higher revenues from new PPAs including solar PPAs.

Strategy

The company is expanding its regional generation portfolio (primarily with solar power plants) in order to boost its overall generating capacity to almost 10000 MW.

Mergers and Acquisitions

Growing its solar power assets in 2016 Southern Power acquired the 120-MW East Pecos solar facility (Southern Power's second solar project in Texas).

That year Southern Power and Turner Renewable Energy jointly bought the 20-MW Calipatria solar facility from Solar Frontier Americas. (Southern Power's 10th solar facility in California).

In 2015 Southern Power acquired a controlling interest in the 200-MW Garland solar facility under construction in California from Recurrent Energy a subsidiary of Canadian Solar Inc.

In 2014 Southern Power and Turner Renewable Energy acquired the largest solar facility in New Mexico the 50-MW Macho Springs Solar Facility. The Southern Power-Turner Renewable Energy partnership's seventh solar project and its second-largest overall the plant is expected to generate enough electricity to power more than 18000 homes.

EXECUTIVES

Svp Commercial Operations And Planning Southern Company Services, John G. Trawick
Vice President Of Construction, Keith Russell
Senior Vice President Compliance Officer, Thomas Bishop
Board Member, Larry Thompson
Auditors: DELOITTE & TOUCHE LLP

LOCATIONS

HQ: Southern Company (The)
30 Ivan Allen Jr. Boulevard, N.W., Atlanta, GA 30308
Phone: 404 506-5000   **Fax:** 404 506-0455
Web: www.southerncompany.com

PRODUCTS/OPERATIONS

2015 Sales

	$ mil.	% of total
Wholesale revenues non-affiliates	964	69
Wholesale revenues affiliates	417	30
Other revenues	9	1
Total	**1,390**	**100**

COMPETITORS

AEP	Duke Energy
AES	Entergy
Calpine	NextEra Energy

HISTORICAL FINANCIALS

Company Type: Public

Income Statement   FYE: December 31

	REVENUE ($ mil.)	NET INCOME ($ mil.)	NET PROFIT MARGIN	EMPLOYEES
12/19	21,419	4,754	22.2%	27,943
12/18	23,495	2,242	9.5%	29,192
12/17	23,031	880	3.8%	31,344
12/16	19,896	2,493	12.5%	32,020
12/15	17,489	2,421	13.8%	26,703
Annual Growth	**5.2%**	**18.4%**	**—**	**1.1%**

2019 Year-End Financials

Debt ratio: 37.73%	No. of shares (mil.): 1,053
Return on equity: 18.00%	Dividends
Cash ($ mil.): 1,975	Yield: 3.8%
Current ratio: 0.78	Payout: 56.5%
Long-term debt ($ mil.): 41,798	Market value ($ mil.): 67,092

	STOCK PRICE ($) FY Close	P/E High/Low	PER SHARE ($) Earnings	Dividends	Book Value
12/19	63.70	14 10	4.50	2.46	26.39
12/18	43.92	23 20	2.17	2.38	24.20
12/17	48.09	63 56	0.84	2.30	24.31
12/16	49.19	21 18	2.55	2.22	25.73
12/15	46.79	20 16	2.59	2.15	23.38
Annual Growth	**8.0%**	**— —**	**14.8%**	**3.4%**	**3.1%**

Southern Copper Corp

EXECUTIVES

Pres-Ceo, Oscar Gonzalez Rocha
Chb, German Larrea Mota-Velasco
V Pres Fin-Cfo-Treas, Raul Jacob Ruisanchez
General Counsel, Andres Carlos Ferrero Ghislier
Comptroller, Lina Vingerhoets Vilca
SEC, Julian Jorge Lazalde Psihas
V Pres Exploration, Edgard Corrales Aguilar
Gen Auditor, Rafael Lopez Abad
Secretary, Julian Lazalde Psihas
Board Member, Carlos Sacristan
Board Member, Gilberto Cifuentes
Auditors: Galaz, Yamazaki, Ruiz Urquiza, S.C.

LOCATIONS

HQ: Southern Copper Corp
1440 East Missouri Avenue, Suite 160, Phoenix, AZ 85014
Phone: 602 264-1375   **Fax:** 602 264-1397
Web: www.southerncoppercorp.com

HISTORICAL FINANCIALS

Company Type: Public

Income Statement   FYE: December 31

	REVENUE ($ mil.)	NET INCOME ($ mil.)	NET PROFIT MARGIN	EMPLOYEES
12/19	7,285	1,485	20.4%	14,301
12/18	7,096	1,543	21.7%	13,899
12/17	6,654	728	10.9%	13,140
12/16	5,379	776	14.4%	13,414
12/15	5,045	736	14.6%	13,024
Annual Growth	**9.6%**	**19.2%**	**—**	**2.4%**

2019 Year-End Financials

Debt ratio: 42.30%	No. of shares (mil.): 773
Return on equity: 22.21%	Dividends
Cash ($ mil.): 1,925	Yield: 4.8%
Current ratio: 2.83	Payout: 107.5%
Long-term debt ($ mil.): 6,541	Market value ($ mil.): 32,840

	STOCK PRICE ($) FY Close	P/E High/Low	PER SHARE ($) Earnings	Dividends	Book Value
12/19	42.48	22 15	1.92	2.04	8.81
12/18	30.77	29 15	2.00	1.40	8.50
12/17	47.45	51 34	0.94	0.59	7.90
12/16	31.94	35 22	1.00	0.18	7.54
12/15	26.12	36 26	0.93	0.34	6.80
Annual Growth	**12.9%**	**— —**	**19.9%**	**56.6%**	**6.7%**

Southern First Bancshares, Inc.

Southern First Bancshares operates in two markets: Greenville South Carolina where it operates under the Greenville First BankÂ moniker and in Columbia South CarolinaÂ as Southern First Bank.Â Selling itself as a local alternative to larger institutions theÂ company which has more than fiveÂ bank branchesÂ targets individuals and small to midsized businesses. It offers traditional deposit services and products including checking accounts savings accounts and CDs. The banks use funds from deposits mainlyÂ to write commercial mortgages residential mortgages andÂ commercial business loans.

EXECUTIVES

Senior Vice President, Shannon Smoak
Vice President Team Leader, Fielding Troutman
Board Member, Rudolph Johnstone
Board Member, Fred Gilmer
Auditors: Elliott Davis, LLC

LOCATIONS

HQ: Southern First Bancshares, Inc.
100 Verdae Boulevard, Suite 100, Greenville, SC 29607
Phone: 864 679-9000
Web: www.southernfirst.com

COMPETITORS

BB&T	Regions Financial
Bank of America	
First Citizens Bancorporation	

HISTORICAL FINANCIALS

Company Type: Public

Income Statement   FYE: December 31

	ASSETS ($ mil.)	NET INCOME ($ mil.)	INCOME AS % OF ASSETS	EMPLOYEES
12/19	2,267	27	1.2%	242
12/18	1,900	22	1.2%	229
12/17	1,624	13	0.8%	198
12/16	1,340	13	1.0%	179
12/15	1,217	10	0.8%	167
Annual Growth	**16.8%**	**28.7%**	**—**	**9.7%**

2019 Year-End Financials

Debt ratio: 6.43%	No. of shares (mil.): 7
Return on equity: 14.67%	Dividends
Cash ($ mil.): 38	Yield: —
Current ratio: —	Payout: —
Long-term debt ($ mil.): —	Market value ($ mil.): 326

	STOCK PRICE ($) FY Close	P/E High/Low	PER SHARE ($) Earnings	Dividends	Book Value
12/19	42.49	12 9	3.58	0.00	26.83
12/18	32.07	16 10	2.88	0.00	23.29
12/17	41.25	23 17	1.76	0.00	20.37
12/16	36.00	18 11	1.94	0.00	17.00
12/15	22.70	14 10	1.55	0.00	14.98
Annual Growth	**17.0%**	**— —**	**23.3%**	**—**	**15.7%**

Southern Missouri Bancorp, Inc.

Southern Missouri Bancorp isÂ the holding company for Southern Bank (formerly Southern Missouri Bank and Trust) which serves localÂ residents and businesses in southeastern Missouri and northeastern ArkansasÂ through more than 10 branches.Â Residential mortgages account for the largest percentage of the bank's loan portfolio followed by commercial mortgages and business loans. Construction and consumer loans round out its lending activities. Deposit products include checking savings andÂ money market accounts CDs and IRAs. The bankÂ also offers financial planning and investment services. Originally chartered in 1887 Southern Bank acquired Arkansas-based Southern Bank of Commerce in 2009.

EXECUTIVES

Vice President Of Deposit Operations, Tiffany Beaton
Auditors: BKD, LLP

LOCATIONS

HQ: Southern Missouri Bancorp, Inc.
2991 Oak Grove Road, Poplar Bluff, MO 63901
Phone: 573 778-1800
Web: www.bankwithsouthern.com

COMPETITORS

Bank of America	Regions Financial
Commerce Bancshares	U.S. Bancorp
IBERIABANK	UMB Financial

HISTORICAL FINANCIALS
Company Type: Public

Income Statement				FYE: June 30
	ASSETS ($ mil.)	NET INCOME ($ mil.)	INCOME AS % OF ASSETS	EMPLOYEES
06/20	2,542	27	1.1%	492
06/19	2,214	28	1.3%	470
06/18	1,886	20	1.1%	415
06/17	1,707	15	0.9%	390
06/16	1,403	14	1.1%	342
Annual Growth	16.0%	16.7%	—	9.5%

2020 Year-End Financials

Debt ratio: 0.60%	No. of shares (mil.): 9
Return on equity: 11.06%	Dividends
Cash ($ mil.): 55	Yield: 2.4%
Current ratio: —	Payout: 19.6%
Long-term debt ($ mil.): —	Market value ($ mil.): 222

	STOCK PRICE ($) FY Close	P/E High/Low		PER SHARE ($) Earnings	Dividends	Book Value
06/20	24.30	13	7	2.99	0.60	28.30
06/19	34.83	13	10	3.14	0.52	25.66
06/18	39.02	17	13	2.39	0.44	22.31
06/17	32.26	18	11	2.07	0.40	20.15
06/16	23.53	12	9	1.98	0.36	16.94
Annual Growth	0.8%	—	—	10.9%	13.6%	13.7%

Southern National Bancorp Of Virginia Inc

Southern National Bancorp of Virginia isÂ the holding company forÂ Sonabank which hasÂ some 20 locations inÂ central and northern Virginia and southern Maryland. Founded in 2005 the bank servesÂ small and midsized businesses their owners andÂ retail consumers. It offers standard deposit products includingÂ checking savings and money market accounts and CDs.Â TheÂ bank'sÂ lending is focused on commercial real estate single-family residential construction and single-family homes as well asÂ other types of consumer and commercial loans.Â In 2009 Southern National Bancorp acquired the failed Greater Atlantic Bank in an FDIC-assisted transaction; in 2012 it acquired the loans and deposits of HarVest Bank of Maryland.

EXECUTIVES

Senior Vice President, Linda Sandridge
Vice President Human Resources, Bertie Gibson
Vice President Senior Lending Officer, Marie Leibson
Senior Vice President And Chief Credit Officer Of The Company And The Bank, Tom Baker
Assistant Vice President, Sharon Tyson
Auditors: Dixon Hughes Goodman LLP

LOCATIONS

HQ: Southern National Bancorp Of Virginia Inc
6830 Old Dominion Drive, McLean, VA 22101
Phone: 703 893-7400
Web: www.sonabank.com

COMPETITORS

BB&T	SunTrust
Bank of America	Virginia Commerce
Burke & Herbert Bank	Bancorp
Capital One	Wells Fargo
PNC Financial	

HISTORICAL FINANCIALS
Company Type: Public

Income Statement				FYE: December 31
	ASSETS ($ mil.)	NET INCOME ($ mil.)	INCOME AS % OF ASSETS	EMPLOYEES
12/19	2,722	33	1.2%	350
12/18	2,701	33	1.2%	348
12/17	2,614	2	0.1%	393
12/16	1,142	10	0.9%	162
12/15	1,036	9	0.9%	181
Annual Growth	27.3%	37.5%	—	17.9%

2019 Year-End Financials

Debt ratio: 2.08%	No. of shares (mil.): 24
Return on equity: 9.14%	Dividends
Cash ($ mil.): 31	Yield: 2.2%
Current ratio: —	Payout: 27.4%
Long-term debt ($ mil.): —	Market value ($ mil.): 395

	STOCK PRICE ($) FY Close	P/E High/Low		PER SHARE ($) Earnings	Dividends	Book Value
12/19	16.35	12	10	1.36	0.36	15.60
12/18	13.22	13	9	1.39	0.32	14.48
12/17	16.03	142	118	0.13	0.32	13.48
12/16	16.34	20	14	0.83	0.32	10.30
12/15	13.06	17	15	0.75	0.52	9.78
Annual Growth	5.8%	—	—	16.0%	(8.8%)	12.4%

Southside Bancshares, Inc.

Southside Bancshares is the holding company for Southside Bank which boasts nearly 65 branches across East North and Central Texas with many around the cities of Tyler and Longview. About one-third of its branches are located in supermarkets (including Albertsons and Brookshire stores) and 40% are motor bank facilities. The bank provides traditional services such as savings money market and checking accounts CDs and other deposit products as well as trust and wealth management services. Real estate loans primarily residential mortgages make up about half of the company's loan portfolio which also includes business consumer and municipal loans. The bank has total assets exceeding $4.8 billion.

Operations
Southside generated 48% of its total revenue from loan interest in 2014 while interest income on taxable investment securities and mortgage-backed securities made up 16% and 19% respectively. About 9% of its revenue came from deposit service fees and another 2% came from trust income.

Geographic Reach
The bank's branches are located in East North and Central Texas. Its main markets are in East Texas the greater Fort Worth area and the greater Austin area. It is also an affiliate with more than 55000 foreign ATMs worldwide.

Sales and Marketing
Southside which staffed 813 employees at 2014's end serves individuals businesses municipal entities and non-profit organizations in local communities.

Financial Performance
Southside Bancshares' revenues and profits have been falling over the past several years despite consistent growth in loan and investment interest income mostly because the bank's gains on securities held-for-sale have declined.

The company's revenue dipped by 4% to $148.3 million in 2014 mostly due to a $5.6 million decline in gains on the sale of its AFS securities and a $2.8 million impairment of equity related to its investment in SFG Finance stemming from the sale of loans purchased by SFG and the repossessed assets.

Lower revenue and an uptick in loan loss provisions in 2014 caused Southside's net income to tumble 49% to $20.8 million for the year while its operating cash levels dipped by 6% to $56 million on lower cash earnings.

Strategy

Southside looks to acquire financial institutions to grow its loan business and expand its geographic reach outside of its existing markets. Its 2014 acquisition of OmniAmerican Bank alone helped boost its loan assets by more than 60% to $2.17 billion while adding 14 branches in a new market (Dallas/Fort Worth).

To grow its deposits and deepen its presence in the markets it serves the company has also been expanding its network of banking locations — both in-store and full-service branches.

Mergers and Acquisitions

In December 2014 the company acquired OmniAmerican Bank to boost its loan business and expand its footprint to the Dallas area. The deal added 14 full-service branches in the 12-county Dallas/Fort Worth metroplex and more than $763 million in new loan business.

EXECUTIVES

Senior Executive Vice President, Jeryl Story
President And Ceo Southside Bancshares And Southside Bank, Lee R. Gibson, age 63, $493,325 total compensation
Regional President North Texas Southside Bank, Tim Carter, age 65
Regional President Central Texas Southside Bank, Peter M. Boyd, age 64, $435,510 total compensation
Evp And Chief Credit Officer Southside Bank, Earl W. (Bill) Clawater, age 66, $265,000 total compensation
Evp And Chief Analytics Officer Southside Bank And Company Secretary, Brian K. McCabe, age 59, $228,385 total compensation
Regional President East Texas Southside Bank, Tim Alexander, age 63
Evp And Cfo, Julie N. Shamburger, age 57
Assistant Vice President Marketing, Jill Payne
Assistant Vice President, Julie A Brown
Vice President, Jeff Quesenberry
Vice President, Cindy Davis
Senior Vice President, Michael Custer
Senior Vice President, Kim Partin
Executive Vice President, Debra Rutledge
Vp Of Information Technology, Gina Heppel
Senior Vice President, Zelton Harvey
Senior Vice President, Doug Cassidy
Vice President, Julie Hunter
Assistant Vice President, Tanya Merritt
Senior Vice President, Mary Mclarry
Vice President Business Services, Grant Williams
Senior Vice President, Landon Brim
Senior Vice President Loan Operations, Krystyna Alexander
Vp Sr. Credit Analyst, Ken Hetherington
Vp Commercial Lending, Ryan Reeve
Executive Vice President, Brad Browder
Vice President Special Assets, Ginger Hines
Vice President Mortgage Loan Officer, Martha Hernandez
Vice President, Bradan Myrick
Vice Chairman, John R. (Bob) Garrett, age 67
Chairman, W.D. (Joe) Norton, age 83
Board Member, Elaine Anderson
Auditors: Ernst & Young LLP

LOCATIONS

HQ: Southside Bancshares, Inc.
1201 S. Beckham Avenue, Tyler, TX 75701
Phone: 903 531-7111
Web: www.southside.com

PRODUCTS/OPERATIONS

2014 Sales

	$ mil.	% of total
Interest		
Loans	70	48
Mortgage-backed & related securities	28	19
Investment securities	24	16
Other	0	-
Non-interest		
Deposit services	15	9
Gain on sale of securities	2	2
Trust income	3	2
Back owned life insurance income	1	1
Gain on sale of loans	0	-
Other	4	3
Adjustments	(2.8)	
Total	148	100

COMPETITORS

Bank of America
Capital One
East Texas Financial
Jacksonville Bancorp of Illinois
Regions Financial

HISTORICAL FINANCIALS

Company Type: Public

Income Statement   FYE: December 31

	ASSETS ($ mil.)	NET INCOME ($ mil.)	INCOME AS % OF ASSETS	EMPLOYEES
12/19	6,748	74	1.1%	845
12/18	6,123	74	1.2%	820
12/17	6,498	54	0.8%	855
12/16	5,563	49	0.9%	679
12/15	5,162	44	0.9%	683
Annual Growth	6.9%	14.1%	—	5.5%

2019 Year-End Financials

Debt ratio: 2.35%
Return on equity: 9.71%
Cash ($ mil.): 110
Current ratio: —
Long-term debt ($ mil.): —

No. of shares (mil.): 33
Dividends
Yield: 3.3%
Payout: 57.5%
Market value ($ mil.): 1,256

	STOCK PRICE ($) FY Close	P/E High/Low	PER SHARE ($) Earnings	Dividends	Book Value
12/19	37.14	17 14	2.20	1.26	23.79
12/18	31.75	17 14	2.11	1.20	21.68
12/17	33.68	21 17	1.81	1.10	21.55
12/16	37.67	21 11	1.81	0.96	17.71
12/15	24.02	19 15	1.61	0.92	16.25
Annual Growth	11.5%	— —	8.2%	8.2%	10.0%

Southwest Airlines Co

Southwest Airlines is the largest carrier of US domestic passengers and has enjoyed almost half a century of straight profitable years amid the airline industry's ups and downs. The airline employs a single aircraft type?the Boeing 737?and offers first-come first-served seating. Sticking with what has worked the company has expanded its low-cost no-frills and no-reserved-seats approach to air travel throughout North America Mexico and the Caribbean to serve more than 100 destinations. Southwest's fleet numbers around 745 Boeing 737s.

Operations

Southwest offers point-to-point service (rather than a hub-and-spoke system which concentrates on a limited number of central hub cities) allowing the airline to offer more direct nonstop flights. More than three-quarters of the company's customers fly nonstop between about 720 city pairs. Schedules include 20 weekday flights between Dallas and Houston and around 15 weekday flights between cities such as Burbank and Oakland CA; San Diego and San Jose CA; and Los Angeles CA and Las Vegas NE. It also offers near-international service to about 15 destinations as well as freight services. In 2019 the company hopes to begin service to Hawaii.

The company has three major categories of fares: Wanna Get Away Anytime and Business Select. Fare prices vary depending on the refund policy and reward points earned on its Rapid Rewards loyalty program. All flights include two free checked bags complimentary soft drinks and snacks and free movies and TV on WiFi-enabled aircraft. And unlike most of its competitors Southwest does not charge fees for changes to flight reservations.

The company's fleet of aircraft consists of more than 745 Boeing 737 aircraft?over 505 737-700s more than 205 737-800s and some 35 737 MAX 8s. It continues to add the Boeing 737 MAX 8 and 737-800 aircraft to its fleet offering more seating capacity and improved fuel economy.

Geographic Reach

Headquartered in Dallas TX Southwest serves more than 100 destinations in some 40 US states and ten near-international countries including Mexico Jamaica Dominican Republic Costa Rica and Cuba.

Southwest leases or pays usage fees for terminal passenger services at each of the airports it serves. It leases land and structures for its aircraft maintenance centers located at Dallas Love Field Houston Hobby Phoenix Sky Harbor Chicago Midway Hartsfield-Jackson Atlanta International and Orlando International airports. It is also committed to paying for various airport improvement projects for new facilities and the rebuilding or modernization of existing facilities.

The company owns a main headquarters building in Dallas as well as two additional headquarters buildings?an energy-efficient modern building called TOPS which houses operational and training functions; and the Wings Complex which consists of a Leadership Education and Aircrew Development (LEAD) Center as well as simulator classrooms and office facilities.

Sales and Marketing

Southwest Airlines' Rapid Rewards loyalty program is designed to retain engage and acquire customers. Rapid Rewards enables program members to earn points for every dollar spent on Southwest fares.

Expenses for advertising and promotions have decreased recently with $212 million spent for marketing in fiscal 2019 versus $215 million in 2018 and $224 million in 2017.

Financial Performance

Southwest has grown steadily over the last several years. Its revenue grew 2% from $22 billion in 2018 to $22.4 billion in 2019. The growth in 2019 was driven by a 2% bump in passenger revenue fueled by increased capacity and strong demand.

Net income dropped 7% to $2.3 billion in 2019 compared with $2.4 billion in 2018 but was in line with previous levels. The decrease was primarily due to the $249 million increase in the company's operating expense.

Cash at the end of fiscal 2019 was $2.5 billion an increase of $694 million from the prior year. Cash from operations contributed $4.0 billion to the coffers while investing activities used $303 million mainly for capital expenditures related to ongoing technology projects airport and other facility construction projects and progress payments related to new aircraft to be delivered to the company. Financing activities used another $3 billion for dividends to stockholders and the company's stock repurchase program.

Strategy

The company's low-cost strategy includes among other elements the use of an aircraft type the Boeing 737 the company's operationally efficient point-to-point route structure and it highly productive employees. The Company's focus on controlling costs also includes a continued commitment to pursuing implementing and enhancing initiatives to reduce fuel consumption and improve fuel efficiency. Although Fuel and oil expense for 2019 decreased compared with 2018 primarily due to lower market jet fuel prices it nonetheless remained the Company's second largest operating cost for 2019.

These conveniently located airports are typically less congested than other airlines' hub airports which has contributed to Southwest's ability to achieve high asset utilization because aircraft can be scheduled to minimize the amount of time they are on the ground. This in turn has reduced the number of aircraft and gate facilities that would otherwise be required and allows for high Employee productivity (lower headcount per aircraft).

Company Background

Texas businessman Rollin King and lawyer Herb Kelleher founded Air Southwest in 1967 as an intrastate airline linking Dallas Houston and San Antonio. In 1971 the company renamed Southwest Airlines made its first scheduled flight. By 1979 Southwest was flying between eleven Texas cities; it added its first out-of-state destination from Houston to New Orleans that year. It later expanded to Oklahoma Kansas Arizona Nevada and California in 1980.

In 2014 Southwest first started offering international service outside the US beginning with Aruba Jamaica and the Bahamas. Its route map now includes over one hundred cities and destinations.

EXECUTIVES

Evp Corporate Services, Robert E. (Bob) Jordan, $470,000 total compensation
Chairman And Ceo, Gary C. Kelly, $10,084 total compensation
Evp Daily Operations, Gregory D. (Greg) Wells
Evp And Cfo, Tammy Romo, $460,000 total compensation
Vp And Chief Technology Architect, Stan Alexander
Coo, Michael G. (Mike) Van de Ven, $474,373 total compensation
Vp And Chief Communications Officer, Linda B. Rutherford
Svp And Cio, Kathleen Wayton
Evp And Chief Revenue Officer, Andrew Watterson
Vp And Chief Marketing Officer, Ryan Green

President, Thomas M. (Tom) Nealon
Vice President Strategy And Planning, Reid Grandle
Vice Chairman, Ron Ricks
Board Member, Nancy Loeffler
Board Member, David Biegler
Auditors: Ernst & Young LLP

LOCATIONS

HQ: Southwest Airlines Co
 P.O. Box 36611, Dallas, TX 75235-1611
Phone: 214 792-4000   **Fax:** 214 792-5015
Web: www.southwest.com

PRODUCTS/OPERATIONS

2018 Sales

	$ mil.	% of total
Passenger	20,455	93
Freight	175	1
Other	1,335	6
Total	**21,965**	**100**

Selected Products

Wanna Get Away fare
Anytime fare
Business Select fare
Rapid Rewards loyalty program
EarlyBird Check-in
Express Bag Drop
Southwest Gift Card
Inairtainment
Community Coffee
Self-Tagging

COMPETITORS

Alaska Air	Hawaiian Holdings
American Airlines Group	JetBlue
Delta Air Lines	Spirit Airlines
Frontier Airlines	United Continental

HISTORICAL FINANCIALS

Company Type: Public

Income Statement

FYE: December 31

	REVENUE ($ mil.)	NET INCOME ($ mil.)	NET PROFIT MARGIN	EMPLOYEES
12/19	22,428	2,300	10.3%	60,800
12/18	21,965	2,465	11.2%	58,800
12/17	21,171	3,488	16.5%	56,100
12/16	20,425	2,244	11.0%	53,500
12/15	19,820	2,181	11.0%	49,583
Annual Growth	3.1%	1.3%	—	5.2%

2019 Year-End Financials

Debt ratio: 10.29%
Return on equity: 23.37%
Cash ($ mil.): 2,548
Current ratio: 0.67
Long-term debt ($ mil.): 1,846

No. of shares (mil.): 519
Dividends
 Yield: 1.3%
 Payout: 15.7%
Market value ($ mil.): 28,019

	STOCK PRICE ($) FY Close	P/E High/Low		PER SHARE ($) Earnings	Dividends	Book Value
12/19	53.98	14	11	4.27	0.70	18.94
12/18	46.48	15	10	4.29	0.61	17.83
12/17	65.45	11	9	5.79	0.48	17.72
12/16	49.84	14	10	3.55	0.38	13.72
12/15	43.06	15	10	3.27	0.29	11.36
Annual Growth	5.8%			6.9%	25.2%	13.6%

SpartanNash Co.

Grocery wholesaler and retailer SpartanNash distributes some 52000 stock-keeping units (SKUs) of nationally branded and private-label products to more than 2100 independent grocery retail locations across all 50 US states through some 20 distribution centers. It also services national retailers such as Dollar General. In addition the company distributes goods to 560 US military commissaries and exchanges in the US and several other countries. On the retail side SpartanNash operates more than 155 supermarkets under the Family Fare Supermarkets D&W Fresh Market VG's Grocery Martin's and Sun Mart Foods among others. The company traces its roots to 1917.

HISTORY

Making dinner in the early 1900s often required several shopping stops: the grocer for canned goods a butcher for meat and yet another place for produce. Eventually the big grocery chains began offering one-stop shopping not to mention better prices due to greater buying power. Worrying about how to compete in 1917 approximately 100 small grocers met in Grand Rapids Michigan to discuss organizing a cooperative; almost half of those formed the Grand Rapids Wholesale Grocery Co. The stores remained independent operating under different names but achieving economies of scale and volume buying through the co-op. They also began developing a variety of services for member stores. Sales topped $1 million in 1934.

Over the years the company expanded beyond its Grand Rapids origins. In 1950 it formed subsidiary United Wholesale which served independent grocers on a cash-and-carry basis. It acquired the Grand Rapids Coffee Company in 1953. The next year the co-op launched its first private-label item Spartan Coffee with a green Spartan logo reminiscent of the Michigan State University mascot. The company changed its name to Spartan Stores in 1957.

Spartan Stores entered retailing in the early 1970s when it bought 19 Harding's stores. It became a for-profit company in 1973 but continued to provide rebates to customers based on their purchases. Spartan Stores began offering insurance to its customers in 1979.

Concerned about the direction of the company customers named Patrick Quinn formerly a VP at a small chain of grocery stores as president and CEO in 1985. To focus on the wholesale business and to avoid any appearance of conflict of interest in both supplying member stores and operating competing stores Spartan Stores sold its 23 retail stores between 1987 and 1994 giving customer stores the first option on them. It entered the convenience store wholesale business with its 1987 acquisition of L&L/Jiroch. Two years later the co-op acquired Associated Grocers of Michigan (later known as Capistar closed in 1996).

Sales topped $2 billion in 1991. Spartan Stores expanded its convenience store operations in 1993 by buying wholesaler J.F. Walker. Despite record sales in 1996 a $46 million restructuring charge that included extensive technological improvements led to a $21.7 million loss the largest in the company's history. The following year Jim Meyer who had joined Spartan Stores in 1973 replaced the retiring Quinn as president and CEO. Also in 1997 the company stopped giving its customers rebates finally doing away with the last remnants of its co-op years.

To keep Michigan customers out of the clutches of its wholesaling rivals Spartan Stores re-entered retailing in 1999 by acquiring eight Ashcraft's Markets. It bought 13 Family Fare stores and 23 Glen's grocery stores that year. In early 2000 the company sold off its insurance business. Later that year Spartan Stores acquired food and drug chain Seaway Food Town (Michigan and Ohio) for about $180 million and began publicly trading.

In 2001 the company purchased longtime customer Prevo's Family Markets a supermarket chain with 10 stores in western Michigan. In an effort to reduce debt and improve profitability in mid-2002 the company announced plans to close its Food Town stores which suffered from competitors such as Meier Kroger and Farmer Jack's. (By mid-2003 Spartan had sold the last of its 26 Food Town stores. Spartan Stores' retail operations had accounted for about 40% of the company's sales.)

In 2003 Spartan Stores sold seven shopping centers in Michigan for $46 million as part of its strategy to sell noncore properties and focus on its retail and distributions businesses. That year James Meyer retired as president and CEO of Spartan Stores and was succeeded by Craig Sturken a former executive of the Great Atlantic & Pacific Tea Company. Later the company sold convenience store suppliers L&L/Jiroch and J.F. Walker to Knoxville Tennessee-based distributor H.T. Hackney Co.

Spartan Stores sold the assets of United Wholesale Grocery Co. a privately held firm in Michigan for about $10 million in 2004. The sale marked Spartan's exit from the convenience store distribution business. The company also closed or sold all of its Food Town stores for $42.1 million.

In 2005 the company opened three fuel centers in Michigan under the Family Fare Quick Stops and Glen's Quick Stop banners. The company acquired D&W Food Centers the following year and purchased about 20 stores from G&R Felpausch in 2007. Spartan Stores' retail expansion continued in 2008 when it acquired more than 15 stores from V.G.'s Food Center. Sturken stepped down as CEO that year and was replaced by Dennis Eidson. In early 2011 Sturken took a less responsible role as chairman and advisor as he looked to transition out of the business.

EXECUTIVES

Vp Information Technology And Cio, David deS. (Dave) Couch, age 69, $205,920 total compensation
President And Ceo, David M. (Dave) Staples, age 57, $600,000 total compensation
Evp Retail Operations, Theodore C. (Ted) Adornato, age 66, $369,308 total compensation
Evp And Cfo, Mark E. Shamber, age 52
Evp Merchandising And Marketing, Larry Pierce, age 65
Evp Chief Legal Officer And President Mdv, Kathleen M. (Kathy) Mahoney, age 65, $415,000 total compensation
Evp; Ceo Caito Foods, Bob Kirch

Vice President Sales Great Lakes Region, Jim Gohsman
Vice President Corporate Affairs, Jeanne Norcross
Divisional Vice President Of West, Bruce Emery
Vice President South Heartland Regions, Joe Hermes
Vice President Logistics Military And National Accounts Logistics, Mitch Cadlo
Vice President Private Brands, John Paul
Vice President Of Inventory Management, Jason Burnett
Senior Vice President And General Manager, Pat Weslow
Vice President Of Marketing, Brian Holt
Senior Vice President Supply Chain, Tom Lee
Chairman, Dennis Eidson, age 66
Treasurer, Bill Jacobs
Auditors: Deloitte & Touche LLP

LOCATIONS

HQ: SpartanNash Co.
850 76th Street, S.W., P.O. Box 8700, Grand Rapids, MI 49518
Phone: 616 878-2000
Web: www.spartannash.com

COMPETITORS

Alex Lee	IGA
Associated Wholesale Grocers	Kroger
	McLane
C&S Wholesale	Meijer
Coastal Pacific Food Distributors Inc.	Miner's
	S. Abraham & Sons
Core-Mark	SUPERVALU
Costco Wholesale	Wal-Mart

HISTORICAL FINANCIALS

Company Type: Public

Income Statement   FYE: December 28

	REVENUE ($ mil.)	NET INCOME ($ mil.)	NET PROFIT MARGIN	EMPLOYEES
12/19	8,536	5	0.1%	17,200
12/18	8,064	33	0.4%	14,000
12/17	8,128	(52)	—	14,800
12/16*	7,734	56	0.7%	14,700
01/16	7,651	62	0.8%	15,200
Annual Growth	2.8%	(45.0%)	—	3.1%

*Fiscal year change

2019 Year-End Financials

Debt ratio: 30.26%	No. of shares (mil.): 36
Return on equity: 0.82%	Dividends
Cash ($ mil.): 24	Yield: 0.0%
Current ratio: 1.76	Payout: 475.0%
Long-term debt ($ mil.): 682	Market value ($ mil.): 513

	STOCK PRICE ($) FY Close	P/E High/Low		PER SHARE ($) Earnings	Dividends	Book Value
12/19	14.12	139	56	0.16	0.76	18.91
12/18	16.89	29	18	0.93	0.72	19.91
12/17	26.68	—	—	(1.41)	0.66	19.80
12/16*	39.54	26	12	1.51	0.60	21.99
01/16	21.64	20	13	1.66	0.54	21.03
Annual Growth	(10.1%)	—	—	(44.3%)	8.9%	(2.6%)

*Fiscal year change

Spirit AeroSystems Holdings Inc

Spirit AeroSystems Holdings is one of the largest independent non-OEM makers of commercial and military airplane components such as fuselages propulsion systems wings and wing components. It designs and builds aerostructures for every Boeing aircraft currently in production (including the majority of aerostructures for Boeing's 737) as well as for Boeing's chief rival Airbus. It is a key supplier of wing parts for Airbus' A320 aircraft. Sales from Boeing and Airbus represent 95% of the company's business. Spirit AeroSystems also provides maintenance repair and overhaul (MRO) services. The company maintains operations in the US the UK and Asia; however the US is its largest market.

Operations

Spirit AeroSystems' operations are divided among three segments. Fuselage Systems is its largest generating about 55% of total sales. Propulsion Systems accounts for about a 25% and Wing Systems earns around 20% of revenue.

The Fuselage Systems segment manufactures forward mid and rear fuselage sections and systems. The forward section houses the flight deck passenger cabin and cargo area. This segment also manufactures the floor beams for the fuselage and provides maintenance repair and overhaul (MRO) services.

The Propulsion Systems segment produces nacelles the aerodynamic structure surrounding the aircraft engine and struts and pylons that connect the engine to the wing. It also makes related engine structural components and provides MRO services. Wing Systems makes aircraft wings including the spars ribs stringers and fixed leading edges and trailing edges of wings. It also makes wing components such as flaps and slats (flight control surfaces) and other miscellaneous structural parts.

In addition the company also offers engineering tooling and measurement services.

Geographic Reach

Spirit AeroSystems' headquarters facilities in Wichita Kansas also includes a manufacturing facility. The US is the company's largest market accounting for nearly 85% of total sales while the UK generates about 10%.

In addition to its manufacturing plant in Wichita Spirit AeroSystems maintains seven other manufacturing facilities in the US Scotland France and Malaysia. It also operates through an international network of suppliers in more than 25 countries.

Sales and Marketing

About 80% of the company's revenue comes from Boeing since Spirit AeroSystems started out as an internal supplier for Boeing aircraft. Airbus accounts for around 15%. This may seem risky but the company is the only source for most of its products and its contracts give Sprit supplier rights for the life of the aircraft program for most models. Other customers include Lockheed Martin Northrop Grumman Sikorsky Rolls-Royce and Mitsubishi Aircraft Corporation as well as the US government and major defense contractors.

Financial Performance

Spirit AeroSystems has seen a general upward trend in revenue over the last several years. Net sales in 2019 amounted to $7.9 billion up 9% from $7.2 billion the previous year. The uptick in 2019 is attributed to production increases in B777 B787 A220 and A350 XWB programs offset by lower production on the B737.

Net income was $530.1 million compared with $617 million in 2018. The decrease in profit is generally due to increased sales and cost of sales.

Cash at the end of fiscal 2019 was $2.4 billion an increase of $1.6 billion from the prior year. Cash from operations contributed $922.7 million to the coffers while investing activities used $239.9 million mainly for the purchase of property plant and equipment. Financing activities provided $884.4 million.

Strategy

The company continue to focus on business growth through the application of key strengths including design for manufacturability materials utilization expertise targeted automation advanced tooling and testing concepts and determinate assembly to enable cost-effective highly efficient production. It also invest in new technology to bring the most advanced techniques manufacturing and automation to our customers.

Spirit recently launched an automated factory and digitization initiative that uses digital factory tools and simulators to cut down on the time needed to ramp up production on new projects. To improve production efficiencies and inventory management the company is building a new 50000 square foot logistics center in Malaysia and a new Global Digital Logistics Center in Wichita KS.

The company is investing in research and development to boost product sales and increase its margins. It's building an Aerospace Innovation Center in Prestwick Scotland (scheduled for completion in late September 2020) where Spirit will focus on infusion processes for composite materials part handling assembly automation rapid prototyping and virtual and augmented reality technology. In Wichita the company partnered with Norsk Titanium to create additive-manufactured titanium components which allow for parts to be built to a "near-net" shape before being finished. The process reduces waste as well as product costs.

Spirit AeroSystems initiates workforce actions due to expected lower levels of 737 MAX productions. In early 2020 the company issued a notice under the Worker Adjustment and Retraining Notification Act of layoffs affecting approximately 2800 employees at its Wichita Kansas facility. Spirit has taken steps to lessen the impact of expected layoffs transferring some 737 MAX employees to other programs where possible. Additionally Spirit plans to facilitate job fairs with other aerospace companies to help laid-off employees transition to new jobs.

Mergers and Acquisitions

Late in 2019 Spirit AeroSystems said it would buy the aerostructures business of Canada-based Bombardier for a total consideration of about $500 million. The deal includes Bombardier's aerostructures and aftermarket services operations in Belfast Northern Ireland; Casablanca Morocco; and Dallas. The acquisition will also give Spirit Aerosystems the ability to supply composite wings for the Airbus A220 while growing the company's low-cost country footprint and boosting its aftermarket business.

Earlier in 2019 the company agreed to acquire S.R.I.F. N.V. the parent company of Asco Industries for $420 million. Asco makes high lift wing structures mechanical assemblies and functional components for OEMs and Tier-1 suppliers in the commercial aerospace and military markets. The acquisition will add more capabilities to its Airbus and F-35 aircraft and expands the company's fabrication business.

Company Background

The company was founded in 2005 when Boeing spun off its Wichita Division and Oklahoma operations as a new entity Spirit AeroSystems. Spirit grew into a global supplier with multiple customers and platforms acquiring the aerostructures business from BAE Systems (now operating as Spirit AeroSystems (Europe) Limited).

The company later acquired other aerospace companies expanding globally with manufacturing facilities in Malaysia and France and with additional facilities in North Carolina in the US.

EXECUTIVES

Svp And Cto, John Pilla, $334,618 total compensation
Svp And Chief Administration Officer, Samantha (Sam) Marnick, $460,465 total compensation
Svp And General Manager Boeing Defense And Regional Jet Programs, Duane F. Hawkins, $497,684 total compensation
Svp And Cfo, Sanjay Kapoor, $624,229 total compensation
President And Ceo, Thomas C. (Tom) Gentile, $770,773 total compensation
Svp And General Manager Airbus Programs, Michelle J. Lohmeier, $472,125 total compensation
Svp Business Development, Krisstie Kondrotis, $424,840 total compensation
Svp Operations, Ron Rabe
Senior Vice President Global Fabrication, Kevin Matthies
Vice President M And A And Strategy, Kailash Krishnaswamy
Auditors: Ernst & Young LLP

LOCATIONS

HQ: Spirit AeroSystems Holdings Inc
3801 South Oliver, Wichita, KS 67210
Phone: 316 526-9000
Web: www.spiritaero.com

2018 Sales

	$ mil.	% of total
US	5,967	83
UK	763	10
Other	491	7
Total	**7,222**	**100**

PRODUCTS/OPERATIONS

2018 Sales by Customers

	$ mil.	% of total
Boeing	5,677	79
Airbus	1,180	16
Other	363	5
Total	**7,222**	**100**

2018 Sales

	$ mil.	% of total
Fuselage Systems	4,000	55
Propulsion Systems	1,702	24
Wing Systems	1,513	21
All Other	5	—
Total	**7,222**	**100**

COMPETITORS

Embraer
GKN
Kawasaki Heavy Industries
Latecoere
Leonardo
Mitsubishi Heavy Industries
SAFRAN
Subaru
Triumph Aerostructures - Vought Aircraft Division
Triumph Group
United Technologies

HISTORICAL FINANCIALS

Company Type: Public

Income Statement

FYE: December 31

	REVENUE ($ mil.)	NET INCOME ($ mil.)	NET PROFIT MARGIN	EMPLOYEES
12/19	7,863	530	6.7%	18,200
12/18	7,222	617	8.5%	17,000
12/17	6,983	354	5.1%	15,500
12/16	6,792	469	6.9%	14,400
12/15	6,643	788	11.9%	15,200
Annual Growth	**4.3%**	**(9.5%)**	**—**	**4.6%**

2019 Year-End Financials

Debt ratio: 39.89%
Return on equity: 35.35%
Cash ($ mil.): 2,350
Current ratio: 2.64
Long-term debt ($ mil.): 2,984
No. of shares (mil.): 104
Dividends
Yield: 0.6%
Payout: 7.8%
Market value ($ mil.): 7,644

	STOCK PRICE ($) FY Close	P/E High/Low	PER SHARE ($) Earnings	Dividends	Book Value
12/19	72.88	19 14	5.06	0.48	16.79
12/18	72.09	18 12	5.65	0.46	11.74
12/17	87.25	29 17	3.01	0.40	15.74
12/16	58.35	16 11	3.70	0.10	15.85
12/15	50.07	10 7	5.66	0.00	15.63
Annual Growth	**9.8%**	**— —**	**(2.8%)**	**—**	**1.8%**

Spirit of Texas Bancshares Inc

Auditors: BDO USA, LLP

LOCATIONS

HQ: Spirit of Texas Bancshares Inc
1836 Spirit of Texas Way, Conroe, TX 77301
Phone: 936 521-1836
Web: www.sotb.com

Stanley Black & Decker Inc

Income Statement				FYE: December 31
	ASSETS ($ mil.)	NET INCOME ($ mil.)	INCOME AS % OF ASSETS	EMPLOYEES
12/19	2,384	21	0.9%	409
12/18	1,466	9	0.7%	289
12/17	1,030	4	0.5%	195
12/16	980	3	0.4%	—
Annual Growth	34.5%	78.5%	—	—

2019 Year-End Financials

Debt ratio: 0.62%
Return on equity: 7.76%
Cash ($ mil.): 325
Current ratio: —
Long-term debt ($ mil.): —

No. of shares (mil.): 18
Dividends
  Yield: —
  Payout: —
Market value ($ mil.): 420

	STOCK PRICE ($) FY Close	P/E High/Low	PER SHARE ($) Earnings	Dividends	Book Value
12/19	23.00	16 14	1.40	0.00	18.93
12/18	22.78	21 17	1.03	0.00	16.42
12/17	0.00	— —	0.63	0.00	13.62
Annual Growth	—	— —	30.5%	—	11.6%

SPIRIT REALTY CAPITAL, INC.

EXECUTIVES

Pres-Ceo, Jackson Hsieh
Exec V Pres-Cfo, Phillip D Joseph Jr
Exec V Pres-Chief Acquisitions, Boyd Messmann
Exec V Pres Asset Management, Mark L Manheimer
Sr V Pres-Chief Hr Officer, Michelle M Greenstreet
Sr V Pres-Cao, Prakash J Parag
Chb, Richard I Gilchrist
Evp-Cfo, Michael Hughes
Asset Management Analyst, Charlie Bernet
Information Technology Directo, Colin Lane
Commercial Risk Mana, Gayle Hazlett
Auditors: ERNST & YOUNG LLP DALLAS TEX

LOCATIONS

HQ: SPIRIT REALTY CAPITAL, INC.
  2727 N HARWOOD ST STE 300, DALLAS, TX
  752012407
Phone: 480 606-0820
Web: WWW.SPIRITREALTY.COM

HISTORICAL FINANCIALS
Company Type: Private

Income Statement				FYE: December 31
	ASSETS ($ mil.)	NET INCOME ($ mil.)	INCOME AS % OF ASSETS	EMPLOYEES
12/17	7,263	77	1.1%	85
12/16	7,677	97	1.3%	—
12/14	8,017	(33)	—	—
12/13	7,231	1	0.0%	—
Annual Growth	0.1%	160.4%	—	—

Stanley Black & Decker has all the tools of the trade. A leading global toolmaker the company sells power tools and equipment (electric power tools pneumatic tools and lawn and garden products) and hand tools power tool accessories and storage products. In addition to its well-known namesake brands it sells other top brands such as Bostitch Mac Tools DEWALT and Craftsman directly to consumers as well as through distributors home centers and mass-merchant distributors. Stanley Black & Decker also sells engineered fastening and infrastructure products to customers in the automotive manufacturing and oil and gas industries among others and designs and installs electronic security systems and automatic doors to commercial customers. It generates about 60% of its sales in the US.

Operations

Stanley Black & Decker operates its business through three segments: Tools & Storage (which generates about 70% of sales) Industrial (more than 15%) and Security (about 15%).

The Tools & Storage segment includes professional and consumer power tools (saws drills grinders nail guns lawn mowers vacuums and cleaning tools) and accessories hand tools and storage products such as tool boxes and sawhorses. The products are mostly available via home centers hardware stores mass merchants and other retailers.

The industrial segment includes engineered fastening and infrastructure business that sells rivets inserts weld studs and other fastening products through its Industrial segment. The segment also includes infrastructure equipment used by the oil and gas industry and hydraulic tools and accessories.

The company's Security segment includes Convergent Security Solutions which designs and installs electronic security systems and provides monitoring surveillance and other services and Mechanical Access Solutions which sells automatic doors. These products are primarily sold directly to commercial customers.

Geographic Reach

Stanley Black & Decker operates primarily in the Americas Europe and Asia. The US is its largest market accounting for almost 60% of sales followed by Europe including France for nearly 25% of sales. Asia brings in nearly 10% and Canada accounts for almost 5%.

Headquartered in New Britain CT the company has major facilities for manufacturing distribution and sales in more than 15 countries including locations in about 20 US states.

Sales and Marketing

The Tools & Storage segment sells its products to professional end users industrial users distributors and retail consumers. The majority of sales are distributed through retailers including home centers mass merchants hardware stores and retail lumber yards. US and international mass merchants and home centers collectively account for about 40% of sales; home improvement giant Lowe's accounts for just about 15% while the home depot accounts for approximately 10%.

Stanley Black & Decker markets its other products and services directly and through third-party distributors to customers in a host of industries including automotive manufacturing oil and gas electronics and aerospace.

Advertising cost was $323.2 million in 2019 $315.8 million in 2018 and $297.4 million in 2017.

Financial Performance

Stanley Black & Decker has seen solid revenue growth over the past five years as the company has pursued acquisitions and manufacturing and supply chain efficiencies. Revenue is up over 29% since 2015.

In 2019 the company reported a record-high revenue of $14.4 billion up 3% from $14 billion in 2018 representing an increase of 3% driven by organic growth of 3% including a 2% increase in volume and 1% increase in price.

Net income have increased 58% in 2019 to $956 million mainly as a result of higher revenue.

Cash at the end of fiscal 2019 was $314.6 million an increase of $3.2 million from the prior year. Cash from operations contributed to the coffers was $1.5 billion while investing activities used $1.2 billion mainly for acquisitions and software expenditures. Financing activities used another $292.5 million for payments of long-term debt and cash dividends.

Strategy

Stanley Black & Decker's overarching strategy is based on its next-generation Stanley Fulfillment System SFS 2.0. The SFS operating model which the company has used for several years is being adapted for the digital age with process improvements encompassing digital tools to increase sales and efficiency and leverage the growing e-commerce market.

The company also continues to pursue a growth and acquisition strategy which involves industry geographic and customer diversification to foster sustainable revenue earnings and cash flow growth and employ the following strategic framework in pursuit of its vision to deliver top-quartile financial performance become known as one of the world's leading innovators and elevate its commitment to social responsibility: Continuing organic growth momentum by leveraging the SBD Operating Model to drive innovation and commercial excellence while diversifying toward higher-growth higher-margin businesses; Be selective and operate in markets where brand is meaningful the value proposition is definable and sustainable through innovation and global cost leadership is achievable; and Pursuing acquisitive growth on multiple fronts by building upon its existing global tools platform expanding the Industrial platform in Engineered Fastening and Infrastructure.

Execution of the above strategy has resulted in approximately $10.1 billion of acquisitions since 2002 a 20 percent investment in MTD Holdings Inc. ("MTD") several divestitures improved efficiency in the supply chain and manufacturing operations and enhanced investments in organic growth enabled by cash flow generation and increased debt capacity. In addition the company's continued focus on diversification and organic growth has resulted in improved financial results and an increase in its global presence.

Mergers and Acquisitions

In 2019 Stanley Black & Decker acquired a 20% interest in outdoor power equipment maker MTD Products for $234 million. The deal which included the option of purchasing the rest of MTD beginning in July 2021 strengthens the company's presence in the growing lawn and garden market.

Company Background

Stanley Black & Decker traces its roots back to 1843 when Frederick Stanley opened a bolt shop in a converted early-19th-century armory in New Britain Connecticut. In 1852 he teamed with his brother and five friends to form The Stanley Works to cast form and manufacture various types of metal. In 2010 it merged with The Black & Decker Corporation a company founded by S. Duncan Black and Alonzo G. Decker and incorporated in Maryland in 1910 and changed its name to Stanley Black & Decker.

EXECUTIVES

President And Ceo, James M. (Jim) Loree, age 61, $992,500 total compensation
Vp And Cio, Rhonda O. Gass, age 56
Svp And Group Executive Global Tools And Storage, Jeffery D. (Jeff) Ansell, age 53, $660,833 total compensation
Svp And Cfo, Donald (Don) Allan, age 55, $671,667 total compensation
Svp And President Global Emerging Markets, Jaime A. Ramirez, age 52, $425,000 total compensation
President Sales And Marketing Global Tools And Storage, John H. A. Wyatt, age 61, $541,667 total compensation
President Hand Tools Accessories And Storage, Lee B. McChesney, age 48
Cto, Mark T Maybury
President Stanley Security Europe, Aru Bala
President Stanley Oil And Gas, Pete Morris
President Asia, Yingli (Christine) Yan
President Power Tools And Equipment Global Tools And Storage, Frank A. Mannarino
President Emerging Markets Group, Bart Muller
President Sales And Marketing Global Tools And Storage, James P. OÀ'Sullivan
President Hydraulics, J. Douglas Redpath
National Account Manager, Allison Lawrence
Vice President, Debi Geyer
Vice President Compensation Benefits And Hris, Michele Webster
Vice President Manufatura Latin America, Domingos Dragone
Vp Sales, Kirk Starr
Vice President Brand Marketing, Scott Bannell
Vice President And Managing Director Europe And Asia, Ned Urschel
Vp Of Global Consumer Power Tool Manufacturing, Qin Zou
Vice President Real Estate, Gregory Smulski
National Account Manager, Dennis Kellagher
Senior Vice President, Don Allan
Vice President Digital Product Innovation And Marketing, Robert Ross
Vice President Of North American Sales, Martin Guay
National Account Manager, Dan Costanzo
Vp Operations Global Tools And Storage And Emerging Markets, Steven Stafstrom
Senior Vice President General Counsel, Janet M Link
Vice President And General Manager, Jim Gillis
National Sales Manager, Dan Miller
National Sales Manager, Jevri Christanto

Vice President Of Human Resources, Rodney Hobbs
National Account Manager, Greg Glenn
Vice President Engineering, Colin Dyke
Vice President Global Operations And Integrated Supply Chain Spectrum Brands, David Booher
Vice President Finance, Frank Walker
Vice President Engineering At Black And Decker, Roby Bailey
Chairman, George W. Buckley, age 73
Secretary, Don Riccitelli
Board Member, Carlos Cardoso
Executive Board Member, Stanley Doors
Auditors: Ernst & Young LLP

LOCATIONS

HQ: Stanley Black & Decker Inc
1000 Stanley Drive, New Britain, CT 06053
Phone: 860 225-5111 **Fax:** 860 827-3895
Web: www.stanleyblackanddecker.com

2018 Sales

	$ mil.	% of total
Americas		
US	7,700	55
Canada	628	5
Other	801	6
Europe		
France	627	4
Other	2,989	21
Asia	1,234	9
Total	**13,982**	**100**

PRODUCTS/OPERATIONS

2018 Sales

	$ mil.	% of total
Tools & Storage	9,814	70
Industrial	2,187	16
Security	1,980	14
Total	**13,982**	**100**

Product and Services

Commercial Security
Fastening Solutions
Hospital & Healthcare Services
Infrastructure Products
Pipeline Services
Tools & Storage

Selected Brand Names

Black & Decker
Bostitch
Craftsman
DEWALT
FatMax
LaBounty
Mac Tools
Proto
Stanley
Vidmar

COMPETITORS

3M	IRWIN Industrial Tool
ASSA ABLOY	Illinois Tool Works
Apex Tool Group	Klein Tools
Atlas Copco	Makita
Fortune Brands Home & Security	Robert Bosch Tool
	Snap-on
Hilti Corp.	Techtronic
Husqvarna	

HISTORICAL FINANCIALS

Company Type: Public

Income Statement

FYE: December 28

	REVENUE ($ mil.)	NET INCOME ($ mil.)	NET PROFIT MARGIN	EMPLOYEES
12/19	14,442	955	6.6%	59,438
12/18	13,982	605	4.3%	60,767
12/17	12,747	1,226	9.6%	57,765
12/16*	11,406	965	8.5%	54,023
01/16	11,171	883	7.9%	51,250
Annual Growth	**6.6%**	**2.0%**	**—**	**3.8%**

*Fiscal year change

2019 Year-End Financials

Debt ratio: 17.07%
Return on equity: 11.29%
Cash ($ mil.): 297
Current ratio: 1.01
Long-term debt ($ mil.): 3,176
No. of shares (mil.): 153
Dividends
Yield: 0.0%
Payout: 42.5%
Market value ($ mil.): 25,467

	STOCK PRICE ($) FY Close	P/E High/Low	PER SHARE ($) Earnings	Dividends	Book Value
12/19	165.90	26 18	6.35	2.70	59.52
12/18	118.83	43 27	3.99	2.58	51.79
12/17	169.69	21 14	8.04	2.42	53.86
12/16*	114.69	19 14	6.51	2.26	41.73
01/16	106.73	18 15	5.79	2.14	37.75
Annual Growth	**11.7%**	**— —**	**2.3%**	**6.0%**	**12.1%**

*Fiscal year change

Starbucks Corp.

Wake up and smell the coffee — Starbucks is everywhere. The world's #1 specialty coffee retailer Starbucks has some 32660 coffee shops. The shops offer coffee drinks and food items as well as roasted beans coffee accessories and teas. Starbucks operates more than 16635 of its own shops which are located mostly in the US while licensees and franchisees operate roughly 16025 units worldwide (including many locations in shopping centers and airports). In addition Starbucks markets its coffee through grocery stores food service customers and licenses its brand for other food and beverage products. The US accounts for the majority of Starbucks' revenue.

HISTORY

Starbucks was founded in 1971 in Seattle by coffee aficionados Gordon Bowker Jerry Baldwin and Ziv Siegl who named the company for the coffee-loving first mate in Moby Dick and created its famous two-tailed siren logo. They aimed to sell the finest-quality whole bean and ground coffees. By 1982 Starbucks had five retail stores and was selling coffee to restaurants and espresso stands in Seattle. That year Howard Schultz joined Starbucks to manage retail sales and marketing. In 1983 Schultz traveled to Italy and was struck by the popularity of coffee bars. He convinced Starbucks' owners to open a downtown Seattle coffee bar in 1984. It was a success; Schultz left the company the following year to open his own coffee bar Il Giornale which served Starbucks coffee.

Frustrated by its inability to control quality Starbucks sold off its wholesale business in 1987. Later that year Il Giornale acquired Starbucks' retail operations for $4 million. (Starbucks' founders held on to their other coffee business Peet's Coffee & Tea.) Il Giornale changed its name to Starbucks Corporation prepared to expand nationally and opened locations in Chicago and Vancouver. In 1988 the company published its first mail-order catalog.

Starbucks lost money in the late 1980s as it focused on expansion (it tripled its number of stores to 55 between 1987 and 1989). Schultz brought in experienced managers to run Starbucks' stores. In 1991 it became the nation's first privately owned company to offer stock options to all employees.

In 1992 Starbucks went public and set up shops in Nordstrom's department stores. The following year it began operating cafes in Barnes & Noble bookstores. The company had nearly 275 locations by the end of 1993. Starbucks inked a deal in 1994 to provide coffee to ITT/Sheraton hotels (later acquired by Starwood Hotels & Resorts). The next year it capitalized on its popular in-house music selections by selling compact discs. Also in 1995 Starbucks joined with PepsiCo to develop a bottled coffee drink and agreed to produce a line of premium coffee ice cream with Dreyer's.

Starbucks expanded into Japan and Singapore in 1996. Also that year the company created Caffe Starbucks an online store located on AOL's marketplace. In 1997 Starbucks began testing sales of whole-bean and ground coffees in Chicago supermarkets.

In 1998 Starbucks expanded into the UK when it acquired that country's Seattle Coffee Company chain (founded in 1995) for about $86 million and converted its stores into Starbucks locations. It also announced plans to sell coffee in supermarkets nationwide through an agreement with Kraft Foods. In 1999 Starbucks bought Tazo an Oregon-based tea company as well as music retailer Hear Music and opened its first store in China. Schultz toned down his Internet plans in late 1999 after investors and analysts voiced skepticism.

In 2000 Schultz ceded the CEO post to president Orin Smith remaining chairman but focusing primarily on the company's global strategy. Starbucks jumpstarted its worldwide expansion the next year opening about 1100 stores worldwide including locations in a handful of new European countries such as Austria and Switzerland. It also spun off its Japanese operations as a public company. The following year the company opened its first shop in Spain and went on to open Starbucks locations in Greece and Germany. Later in 2002 it announced large-scale expansion plans in Mexico and Latin America.

The next year Starbucks acquired Seattle Coffee Company (and its Seattle's Best Coffee brand) from Popeyes for $72 million. The deal gave Starbucks an additional 150 coffee shops (as if it needed them) but more importantly it gave the coffee giant the Seattle's Best Coffee brand and wholesale coffee business. It also got something new out of the deal: franchised locations.

Starbucks was one of the first national retailers to jump on the Wi-Fi bandwagon teaming with Hewlett-Packard and Deutsche Telekom's T-Mobile unit to offer high-speed wireless Internet access at 1200 of its locations in the US London and Berlin. In 2004 Starbucks and Hewlett-Packard unveiled their Hear Music service which allows Starbucks customers to create custom music CDs in some locations. It later premiered the Hear Music channel on XM Satellite Radio (later SIRIUS XM Radio) and launched a new Hear Music CD-burning media bar (co-developed with HP) in selected stores.

In 2005 the company began offering a hot chocolate in its US and Canada markets and in conjunction with Jim Beam Brands (now Beam) it introduced Starbucks Coffee Liqueur and Starbucks Cream Liqueur. That year Starbucks signed agreements with Suntory in Japan and Uni-President in Taiwan to sell its ready-to-drink coffees in those countries. Additionally Smith retired as president and CEO in 2005; he was replaced by Starbucks' North American president Jim Donald.

The company acquired full ownership of joint ventures Coffee Partners Hawaii and Cafe del Caribe (Puerto Rican outlets) in 2006. While Starbucks continued to dominate the coffee business traffic at its stores began to decline in 2007. The company brought Schultz back as CEO in 2008 replacing Donald.

Starbucks acquired fruit and vegetable juice maker Evolution Fresh in 2011 for $30 million in cash. In December 2012 the company purchased Teavana Holdings Inc. for $620 million in cash. Teavana operates some 300 Heaven of Tea retail stores.

In 2012 Starbucks agreed to acquire San Francisco-based Bay Bread LLC and its La Boulange bakery brand. It made the purchase to try its hand in the French bakery market. The previous year Starbucks acquired fruit and vegetable juice maker Evolution Fresh for $30 million as part of an effort to push itself as a healthy lifestyle brand.

EXECUTIVES

Evp And Cto, Gerri Martin-Flickinger
President And Coo, Kevin R. Johnson, age 59, $576,923 total compensation
Group President Us And Americas, Clifford (Cliff) Burrows, age 61, $796,300 total compensation
Group President China And Asia/pacific Channel Development And Emerging Brands, John Culver, age 59, $633,300 total compensation
Svp And President Europe Middle East And Africa (emea), Martin Brok
Evp Us Retail Store Operations, Cosimo LaPorta
Evp And Global Chief Marketing Officer, Sharon Rothstein
Svp; President Teavana, Bernard Acoca
Chief Creative Officer; President Global Innovation, Arthur Rubinfeld, age 66, $484,058 total compensation
Evp Licensed Stores Us And Americas, Chris Carr
Evp Law And Corporate Affairs General Counsel And Secretary, Lucy Lee Helm, $493,172 total compensation
Evp Public Affairs, Vivek Varma
Evp And Chief Partner Resources Officer, Scott Pitasky
Evp And Cfo, Scott H. Maw, $632,500 total compensation
Evp Global Coffee, Craig Russell
Svp; President Starbucks Canada, Rossann Williams
President Starbucks Global Channel Development, Michael Conway
Evp And Chief Digital Officer, Adam Brotman
Evp And Global Chief Strategy Officer, Matthew Ryan
President Starbucks Europe Middle East And Africa, Kris Engskov
President Starbucks China, Belinda Wong
Senior Vice President Chief Design Officer, Liz Muller
Vice President And Assistant General Counsel, Mark Fordham
Regional Vice President, Dennis Brockman
Vice President Global Sourcing And Supplier Relations, Jonathan Gardner
Senior Business Intelligence Application Developer, Eric Espinal
Vice President Of Partner Resources, Angel Yu
Senior Vice President Operations Services And U.s. Alignment, Denise Nelsen
Vice President Global Store Development, Badger Godwin
Senior Vice President Food Evenings And Licensed Stores, Christine Barone
Vice President Global Creative Studios, Jennifer Berger
Senior Vice President Customer Relationship Management, Aimee Johnson
Vp Assistant General Counsel Global Commercial Marcom And Regulatory, Kenneth Wan
Vice President Operations Implementation, Steve Figliola
Vice President Global Operations Innovation, Dennis Mcgrath
Senior Vice President Partner Resources Global Retail, Angela Lis
Vice President, Pablo Arizmendi
Vice President Manager Director, Lesley Blyth
Senior Vice President Chief Procurement Officer Global Sourcing, Kelly Bengston
Vice President Software Engineering, Marianne Marck
Vice President, John Boline
Vice President Global Coffee, Andrew Linnemann
National Account Manager, Hamilton Seale
Vice President, William Mcnichols
Senior Vice President Gbl Design And Construction Execution, Bill Transue
Senior Vice President Research And Development Qandr, Mary Wagner
Vp Of Operations, Miguel Lozano
Vice President And Treasurer, Drew Wolff
Vice President, Terry Holshouser
Vice President Corp. Social Responsibility, Sue Mecklenburg
Senior Vice President Store Development And Design, Scott Keller
Vice President Zone Licensed Stores East, Lisa Compton
Senior Vice President Finance, David Chichester
Svp Siren Retail Operations, Katie Seawell
Vice President Of Global Public Affairs, Cathy Heseltine
Regional Vice President, Suzanne Dechant
Vice President Field Information Technology, Lisa Orchard
Vice President It Channel Development B2b Technology, Brad Jones
Vice President, James Koster
Vice President Global Learning, Stephen Krempl
Vice President, Doug Wayles
Senior Vice President Southeast Plains, Paul Twohig
Vice President Global Digital Marketing, Alexandra Wheeler
Vice President, Sophie Hume
Senior Vice President Partner Resources U.s. And Americas, Marissa Andrada
Vice President Information Technology, George Eglinton
Vp Channel Brand Management, Bruce Katsman
Svp Global Strategy Insights And Analytics, Pam Greer

Senior Vice President Public Affairs, Rajiv Chandrasekaran

Vice President Retail Technology, Courtney Kissler

Senior Vice President Infrastructure And Enablement, Jeff Wile

Senior Vice President Partner Resources And Human Resources, Lucy Hur

Senior Vice President Executive Creative Director Starbucks Global Creative, Leanne Fremar

Executive Vice President Global Supply Chain, Hans Melotte

Senior Vice President Global Integrated Logistics, Ash Walia

Divisional Senior Vice President East Division, Zeta Smith

Senior Vice President Engineering And Architecture Starbucks Technololgy, Tal Saraf

Senior Vice President Entrepreneur In Residence, Richard Tait

Senior Vice President Corporate Development And Business Alliances, Bill McNichols

Svp Global Coffee And Tea, Michelle Burns

Vice President Finance, Robert Dilworth

Vice President Global Engineering, Jeff Juneau

Senior Vice President Logistics And Us Retail Supply Chain, Carl Mount

Vp Global Security And Resilience, Garrett Petraia

Senior Vice President Sirenideas, Mesh Gelman

Vp Partnerships, Maria Smith

Vice President Information Technology, Tammy Green

Vice President Information Technology, Georg Gorostiza

Co Managing Director At Starbucks, Matthew Courtney

Vice President Store Development Support Services, Ray Silverstein

Senior Vice President Global Supply Chain Finance And Shared Services, Sena M Kwawu

Vice President Food Safety And Quality, Stephen P Graham

Vice President Category Brand Management Americas, Christopher Tebben

Senior Vice President Supply Chain Finance And Shared Services, Sena Kwawu

Vice President Business Systems Development, Wouleta Ayele

Vp Digital Experiences, Shawn Sweeney

Vice President Marketing, Rebekah Lyle

Vp Hr, Steve Bennet

Vice President Marketing Technology, Tony Kippen

Senior Vice President U.s. Marketing, Emily Chang

Senior Vice President Global Total Rewards, Holly May

Senior Vice President Deputy General Counsel And Chief Ethics And Compliance Officer, Ashish Mishra

Vice President Total Rewards, Julie Ann Overcash

Senior Vice President Logistics Manufacturing, John Dicecco

Director Of Pharmacy, Susan Kang

Vice President Of Sales, Jerry Cravens

Pharmacy Manager, Toni Doster

Pharmacy Manager, Jerry Szczybura

Pharmacy Manager, Erik Sundet

Pharmacy Manager, Winnie Pedro

Pharmacy Manager, Patrick Bakken

Pharmacy Manager, Vijay Kaza

Vice President, Susan Warner

Director Of Pharmacy, Alan Dalsing

Chairman And Ceo, Howard D. Schultz, age 67

Treasurer, Melanie Canto

Board Member, Mary Dillon

Vice Chairman Of The Board, Mellody Hobson

Board Member, Jorgen Knudstorp

Treasurer, Gregory Biggs

Auditors: DELOITTE & TOUCHE LLP

LOCATIONS

HQ: Starbucks Corp.
2401 Utah Avenue South, Seattle, WA 98134
Phone: 206 447-1575
Web: www.starbucks.com

2018 Sales

	% of total
Americas	68
China/Asia Pacific	18
EMEA	4
Channel Development	9
Corporate and Other	1
Total	**100**

PRODUCTS/OPERATIONS

2018 Sales

	$ mil.	% of total
Company-owned stores	19,690	80
Licensed stores	2,652	11
Other	2,377	9
Total	**24,719**	**100**

2018 Sales

	% of total
Beverage	59
Food	18
Package and single-serve coffees and teas	11
Other	12
Total	**100**

Brand Portfolio

Brand Portfolio
Starbucks Coffee
Seattle's Best Coffee
Teavana
Evolution Fresh
La Boulange
Ethos Water
Torrefazione Italia Coffee

Selected Products

Coffee
Handcrafted Beverages
Merchandise
Fresh Food

COMPETITORS

Cinnabon	Nestlé
Community Coffee	Panera Bread
Dunkin	The Coffee Bean
Einstein Noah	Tim Hortons
Restaurant Group	Whitbread
Farmer Bros.	illy
McDonald's	

HISTORICAL FINANCIALS

Company Type: Public

Income Statement   FYE: September 27

	REVENUE ($ mil.)	NET INCOME ($ mil.)	NET PROFIT MARGIN	EMPLOYEES
09/20	23,518	928	3.9%	349,000
09/19	26,508	3,599	13.6%	346,000
09/18*	24,719	4,518	18.3%	291,000
10/17	22,386	2,884	12.9%	277,000
10/16	21,315	2,817	13.2%	254,000
Annual Growth	**2.5%**	**(24.2%)**	**—**	**8.3%**

*Fiscal year change

2020 Year-End Financials

Debt ratio: 55.65%
Return on equity:—
Cash ($ mil.): 4,350
Current ratio: 1.06
Long-term debt ($ mil.): 14,659
No. of shares (mil.): 1,173
Dividends
  Yield: 0.0%
  Payout: 207.5%
Market value ($ mil.): 98,909

	STOCK PRICE ($) FY Close	P/E High/Low	PER SHARE ($) Earnings	Dividends	Book Value
09/20	84.30	119 71	0.79	1.64	(6.65)
09/19	88.37	34 19	2.92	1.44	(5.26)
09/18*	56.84	19 15	3.24	1.26	0.89
10/17	53.71	32 26	1.97	1.00	3.81
10/16	54.14	33 28	1.90	0.80	4.03
Annual Growth	**.11.7%**	**—**	**—(19.7%)**	**19.7%**	**—**

*Fiscal year change

Starwood Property Trust Inc.

Starwood Property Trust hopes to shine brightly in the world of mortgages. A real estate investment trust (REIT) the company originates finances and manages US commercial and residential mortgage loans commercial mortgage-backed securities and other commercial real estate debt investments. It acquires discounted loans from failed banks and financial institutions some through the FDIC which typically auctions off large pools of loan portfolios. Starwood Property Trust is externally managed by SPT Management LLC an affiliate of Starwood Capital Group. As a REIT the trust is exempt from paying federal income tax so long as it distributes quarterly dividends to shareholders.

Financial Performance

Overall revenues grew 63% in 2012 to $327 million up from $201 million in 2011. The trust primarily earns money on interest income from mortgage-backed securities and loans.

Mergers and Acquisitions

In 2013 Starwood Property Trust bought LNR Property LLC a real estate investment finance management and development firm. The trust paid $862 million for LNR's US special servicer the US investment securities portfolio Archetype Mortgage Capital (now Starwood Mortgage Capital) Archetype Financial Institution Services LNR Europe and 50% of LNR's interest in Auction.com.

Later that year it moved to spin off its single-family residential business as a new REIT named Starwood Waypoint Residential Trust. The trust which will be affiliated with Waypoint Homes will invest own and operate single-family rental homes and non-performing residential mortgage loans in the US.

EXECUTIVES

Vice President, Daniel Yih
Auditors: DELOITTE & TOUCHE LLP

LOCATIONS

HQ: Starwood Property Trust Inc.
591 West Putnam Avenue, Greenwich, CT 06830
Phone: 203 422-7700
Web: www.starwoodpropertytrust.com

COMPETITORS

American Capital Agency Corp.	JER Investors Trust
Annaly Capital Management	MFA Financial
	PennyMac Mortgage
Arbor Realty Trust	Petra Real Estate
Colony Northstar	RAIT Financial Trust
Drive Shack	Realty Finance Corporation
Hatteras Financial	Redwood Trust
Invesco Mortgage Capital	Two Harbors
	iStar Financial Inc

HISTORICAL FINANCIALS

Company Type: Public

Income Statement — FYE: December 31

	ASSETS ($ mil.)	NET INCOME ($ mil.)	INCOME AS % OF ASSETS	EMPLOYEES
12/19	78,042	509	0.7%	296
12/18	68,262	385	0.6%	290
12/17	62,941	400	0.6%	312
12/16	77,256	365	0.5%	340
12/15	85,738	450	0.5%	450
Annual Growth	(2.3%)	3.1%	—	(9.9%)

2019 Year-End Financials

Debt ratio: 15.07%
Return on equity: 10.96%
Cash ($ mil.): 478
Current ratio: —
Long-term debt ($ mil.): —

No. of shares (mil.): 282
Dividends
Yield: 7.7%
Payout: 126.3%
Market value ($ mil.): 7,016

	STOCK PRICE ($) FY Close	P/E High/Low	PER SHARE ($) Earnings	Dividends	Book Value
12/19	24.86	14 11	1.79	1.92	16.66
12/18	19.71	16 13	1.42	1.92	16.70
12/17	21.35	15 14	1.52	1.92	17.13
12/16	21.95	15 11	1.50	1.92	17.44
12/15	20.56	13 10	1.91	1.92	17.43
Annual Growth	4.9%	— —	(1.6%)	(0.0%)	(1.1%)

State Auto Financial Corp.

Thanks to State Auto Financial the state of auto insurance is healthy in the Midwest. The company sells property/casualty policies through several subsidiaries writing personal and commercial including automobile homeowners multiperil and workers' compensation insurance. It also participates in an insurance pool through its parent company State Auto Mutual Insurance which owns about 35% of State Auto Financial and provides the offices for its headquarters. Subsidiary Stateco Financial Services manages the company's invested assets.

Operations

State Auto Financial has three reportable segments: personal insurance commercial insurance and investment operations.

The personal insurance segment provides primarily personal automobile and homeowners to the personal insurance market. It brings in some 55% of State Auto's total revenue.

The commercial insurance segment provides commercial automobile commercial multi-peril

property data compromise and risk control insurance covering small-to-medium sized commercial exposures in the business insurance market. That segment accounts for about 35% of total revenue.

The investment operations segment managed by subsidiary Stateco provides investment services. It represents some 10% of total revenue.

The specialty insurance segment is no longer a reportable segment and is disclosed as specialty run-off.

Overall about 90% of the company's sales were generated from earned premiums and the rest were generated from net investment income and net investment gains.

Geographic Reach

Ohio Kentucky and Texas are its biggest markets accounting for more than 25% of its annual premiums.Its corporate headquarters is located in Columbus Ohio.

Sales and Marketing

Through the mutual pool State Auto Financial and its sister companies known collectively as State Auto Group market products through retail agents and wholesale brokers. It works with some 3200 retail agencies. The company focuses its business insurance sales on small-to-medium-sized companies.

Financial Performance

State Auto Financial's revenue has been experiencing slow growth over the past five years while net income has been falling since 2015 but started to recover the last two years.

Revenue increased 1% to $1.3 billion in 2019 thanks to increases in earned premiums and Other investment gain. That was partially offset by a decline in net investment income.

The company had an $87.4 million in net income that year after netting $12.8 million in 2018. Higher revenues contributed mainly to the increase in net income.

State Auto ended 2019 with $78 million in net cash some $20 million more than it had at the end of 2018. Operating activities used $43.9 million and financing activities used $12 million while investing activities contributed $74.1 million to the company. Main cash uses were for dividends payment and purchases of fixtures.

Strategy

The primary objectives of its investment strategy are to maintain adequate liquidity and capital to meet its responsibilities to policyholders; grow surplus long term to support the growth of the company; provide a consistent level of income; and manage investment risk.

As part of its technology strategy in developing and enhancing its controls processes and practices designed to protect its systems computers software data and networks from attack damage or unauthorized access the company utilizes the US off-shore and cloud vendors.

EXECUTIVES

Svp And Chief Risk Officer, Cynthia A. Powell, age 59

President And Ceo, Michael E. (Mike) LaRocco, age 63

Svp And Cfo, Steven E. English, age 59, $447,231 total compensation

Svp And Director Operations, Lyle D. Rhodebeck, age 62

Svp Secretary And General Counsel, James A. (Jay) Yano, age 69, $357,692 total compensation

Svp Standard Lines, Joel E. Brown, age 62

Svp And Director Specialty Lines, Jessica E. Buss, age 48, $372,692 total compensation

Svp And Chief Claims Officer, Stephen P. Hunckler, age 61

Senior Vice President General Counsel Secretary, Melissa Centers

Vice President Chief Risk Officer, Bill Cody Bill Cody

Rvp Personal Underwriting, Amy L Skaggs

Vice President Specialty Claims, Jay Carleton

Senior Vice President And Chief Information And Strategy Officer Of Stfc And State Auto Mutual, Greg Tacchetti

Vice President Specialty Programs, Greg Scullans

Assistant Vice President Reinsurance, Cpcu Olmstead

Senior Vice President Personal Lines, Jason E Berkeu

Director Of Government Relations, Elise Spriggs

Vice President Legal, Perry Fioravanti

Senior Vice President Chief Information And Strategy Officer, Gregory Tacchetti

Evp, Ryan Helon

Evp, Wayne Embree

Chairman, Robert P. (Bob) Restrepo, age 69

Board Member, Kym Hubbard

Auditors: PricewaterhouseCoopers LLP

LOCATIONS

HQ: State Auto Financial Corp.
518 East Broad Street, Columbus, OH 43215-3976
Phone: 614 464-5000
Web: www.stateauto.com

2017 Direct Written Premiums

	% of total
Ohio	9
Texas	9
Kentucky	6
California	5
Minnesota	4
Tennessee	4
Georgia	4
Indiana	4
Mississippi	4
South Carolina	4
Illinois	3
Maryland	3
Pennsylvania	3
North Carolina	3
Other	36
Total	**100**

PRODUCTS/OPERATIONS

2017 Sales

	$ mil.	% of total
Personal insurance premiums	580	41
Commercial insurance premiums	455	32
Specialty insurance premiums	239	17
Investment income & other	146	10
Total	**1,421**	**100**

COMPETITORS

AIG	National General Holdings
Allstate	
American Family Insurance	Nationwide
	Progressive Corporation
American Southern	
GEICO	State Farm
Kentucky Employers' Mutual	The Hartford
	Travelers Companies

HISTORICAL FINANCIALS

Company Type: Public

Income Statement   FYE: December 31

	ASSETS ($ mil.)	NET INCOME ($ mil.)	INCOME AS % OF ASSETS	EMPLOYEES
12/19	2,985	87	2.9%	1,978
12/18	2,895	12	0.4%	1,854
12/17	3,014	(10)	—	1,962
12/16	2,959	21	0.7%	2,020
12/15	2,828	51	1.8%	2,065
Annual Growth	1.4%	14.3%	—	(1.1%)

2019 Year-End Financials

Debt ratio: 4.09%
Return on equity: 9.83%
Cash ($ mil.): 78
Current ratio: —
Long-term debt ($ mil.): —

No. of shares (mil.): 43
Dividends
  Yield: 1.2%
  Payout: 60.6%
Market value ($ mil.): 1,349

	STOCK PRICE ($) FY Close	P/E High/Low	PER SHARE ($) Earnings	Dividends	Book Value
12/19	31.02	18 15	1.96	0.40	22.07
12/18	34.04	117 92	0.29	0.40	18.95
12/17	29.12	— —	(0.25)	0.40	20.78
12/16	26.81	54 37	0.50	0.40	21.32
12/15	20.59	22 16	1.23	0.40	21.42
Annual Growth	10.8%	— —	12.4%	(0.0%)	0.7%

STATE OF ALABAMA

EXECUTIVES

Governor, Kay Ivey
Comptroller*, Kathleen D Baxter
Atty Gen, Troy King
Cmptlr, Robert Childree
Director and State Law Librari, Timothy Lewis
Associate Justice, Tom Parker
Chief of Staff, Jo Bonner
Program Manager, Donna Jordan
Donor Relations Coordinator, Cherie H Smith
Information Technology Operati, Janice Majors
Web Resources Librarian, Myra Sabel
Auditors: RONALD L JONES MONTGOMERY A

LOCATIONS

HQ: STATE OF ALABAMA
  300 DEXTER AVE, MONTGOMERY, AL 361043741
Phone: 334 242-7100
Web: WWW.ALABAMA.GOV

HISTORICAL FINANCIALS

Company Type: Private

Income Statement   FYE: September 30

	REVENUE ($ mil.)	NET INCOME ($ mil.)	NET PROFIT MARGIN	EMPLOYEES
09/19	23,698	677	2.9%	37,659
09/18	22,258	(34)	—	—
09/17	21,740	1,393	6.4%	—
09/16	21,126	349	1.7%	—
Annual Growth	3.9%	24.6%	—	—

STATE OF ALASKA

EXECUTIVES

Governor, Michael Dunleavy
Lt. Governor, Kevin Meyer
Accounting Staff, Nove Barril
Coordinator, Sara Chambers
Accounting Staff, Christine Spence
Accounting Staff, Amy Johnson
Accounting Staff, Caroline Byford
Coordinator, Heidi Hedberg
Coordinator, Katie Reilly
Employee, Dinah Aquino
Senior Adviser On Fish and Gam, Ephraim Froehlich
Auditors: KRIS CURTIS CPA CISA JUNEAU

LOCATIONS

HQ: STATE OF ALASKA
  120 4TH ST, JUNEAU, AK 998011162
Phone: 907 465-3500
Web: WWW.ALASKA.GOV

HISTORICAL FINANCIALS

Company Type: Private

Income Statement   FYE: June 30

	REVENUE ($ mil.)	NET INCOME ($ mil.)	NET PROFIT MARGIN	EMPLOYEES
06/19	12,421	2,275	18.3%	4,300
06/18	12,318	2,779	22.6%	—
06/17	12,693	3,224	25.4%	—
Annual Growth	(1.1%)	(16.0%)	—	—

STATE OF ARIZONA

EXECUTIVES

Governor, Doug Ducey
Attor Gen*, Terry Goddard
Treas*, David Petersen
Acctng Mgr, Jean Bell
Sergeant, Joe Kubacki
Chief Information Security Off, Mike Lettman
U.S. District Court Judge, Susan Brnovich
Member, Nancy Barto
Member, Frank Pratt
Manager, Ted Hale
Information Technology Infrast, Allan Gazza
Auditors: LINDSEY PERRY CPA CFE PHOENI

LOCATIONS

HQ: STATE OF ARIZONA
  1700 W WASHINGTON ST FL 7, PHOENIX, AZ
  850072808
Phone: 602 542-4331
Web: WWW.AZ.GOV

HISTORICAL FINANCIALS

Company Type: Private

Income Statement   FYE: June 30

	REVENUE ($ mil.)	NET INCOME ($ mil.)	NET PROFIT MARGIN	EMPLOYEES
06/19	34,554	1,496	4.3%	34,161
06/18	32,354	539	1.7%	—
06/17	31,295	385	1.2%	—
06/16	871	4	0.6%	—
Annual Growth	241.0%	570.6%	—	—

STATE OF ARKANSAS

EXECUTIVES

Governor, Asa Hutchinson
Lt Gov*, Tim Griffin
Chief of Staff*, Morril Harriman
Acting Manager, Tom Smith
State Chief Security Officer, Franklin Andrews
Coordinator, Carla Jordan
Information Specialist, Justin Villines
Information Specialist, Ken Giesbrecht
Coordinator, Randall Anderson
Coordinator, Randie Jones
Dhhs Division of Administrativ, Gail Boykins
Auditors: ROGER A NORMAN JD CPA CFE

LOCATIONS

HQ: STATE OF ARKANSAS
  4 CAPITOL MALL RM 403A, LITTLE ROCK, AR
  722011013
Phone: 501 682-2345
Web: WWW.ARKANSAS.GOV

HISTORICAL FINANCIALS

Company Type: Private

Income Statement   FYE: June 30

	REVENUE ($ mil.)	NET INCOME ($ mil.)	NET PROFIT MARGIN	EMPLOYEES
06/19	13,821	997	7.2%	28,272
06/18	17,966	40	0.2%	—
06/17	17,915	(91)	—	—
06/16	17,333	161	0.9%	—
Annual Growth	(7.3%)	83.5%	—	—

STATE OF CALIFORNIA

EXECUTIVES

Governor, Gavin Newsom
Lt. Governor*, Eleni Kounalakis
Consultant, A Kirk McKenzie
Chief Licensing/Information Te, Brian Desmarais
Chief Information Security Off, Carol Kelly
Budgets and Fiscal STA, Caroline McNeil
Computer Support Staff Represe, Cheryl Drefs
Budgets and Fiscal STA, Diane Herteg
Chief Technology Support Servi, Jim Rengstorff
AG Technician II, Jose Antonio Diaz
Analyst, Karen Bianchi Walsh
Auditors: MICHAEL S TILDEN CPA SACRAM

LOCATIONS

HQ: STATE OF CALIFORNIA
STATE CAPITAL, SACRAMENTO, CA 95814
Phone: 916 445-2864
Web: WWW.CA.GOV

HISTORICAL FINANCIALS

Company Type: Private

Income Statement — FYE: June 30

	REVENUE ($ mil.)	NET INCOME ($ mil.)	NET PROFIT MARGIN	EMPLOYEES
06/16	255,725	4,798	1.9%	208,580
06/15	249,923	6,252	2.5%	—
06/14	219,871	8,082	3.7%	—
06/13	204	8	3.9%	—
Annual Growth	976.7%	742.3%	—	—

STATE OF COLORADO

EXECUTIVES

Governor, Jared Polis
Lt Gov*, Dianne Primavera
Treasurer*, Dave Young
Sergeant, Ron Watkins
Information Technology Special, Martin Pullam
Acting Communications Director, Holly Shrewsbury
Staff, Jessika Shipley
Director, John Penn
Press Secretary, Jacque Montgomery
Vice-President Research and Te, Gert Thygesen
Staff, Ron Kirk
Auditors: DIANNE E RAY CPA DENVER CO

LOCATIONS

HQ: STATE OF COLORADO
200 E COLFAX AVE STE 91, DENVER, CO 802031716
Phone: 303 866-5000
Web: WWW.COLORADO.GOV

HISTORICAL FINANCIALS

Company Type: Private

Income Statement — FYE: June 30

	REVENUE ($ mil.)	NET INCOME ($ mil.)	NET PROFIT MARGIN	EMPLOYEES
06/17	22,949	(240)	—	81,349
06/16	23,139	(295)	—	—
06/13	18,658	788	4.2%	—
06/12	17,586	472	2.7%	—
Annual Growth	5.5%	—	—	—

STATE OF DELAWARE

EXECUTIVES

Governor, John Carney
Lt Gov, Bethany Hall-Long
Prin, Beau Biden
Treas, Chip Flowers
Prin, Thomas Wagner Jr

Comm, Karen Weldin Stewart
Information Specialist, Tim LI
Information Technology Custome, John Trabaudo
Information Technology Custome, Dorothy Kope
Adjutant General, Michael Berry
Team Leader, Colleen Gause
Auditors: KPMG LLP PHILADELPHIA PENNSY

LOCATIONS

HQ: STATE OF DELAWARE
860 SILVER LAKE BLVD # 1, DOVER, DE 199042402
Phone: 302 744-4101
Web: WWW.DELAWARE.GOV

HISTORICAL FINANCIALS

Company Type: Private

Income Statement — FYE: June 30

	REVENUE ($ mil.)	NET INCOME ($ mil.)	NET PROFIT MARGIN	EMPLOYEES
06/19	8,124	371	4.6%	25
06/17	7,368	(351)	—	—
06/16	7,106	(347)	—	—
06/15	6,955	62	0.9%	—
Annual Growth	4.0%	55.9%	—	—

STATE OF GEORGIA

EXECUTIVES

Governor, Brian Kemp
Lt Governor*, Geoff Duncan
Treas*, Lynnette Riley
Microbiologist, Amanda Balish
Director, Andrew Dent
Microbiologist, Anne Whitney
Officer, Catherine McLean
Supreme Court Judge, Charlie Bethel
Information Technology Special, Cheri Gatland-Lightne
Court of Appeals Judge, Christian A Coomer
Public Affairs Specialist, Courtney Lenard
Auditors: GREG S GRIFFIN STATE AUDITOR

LOCATIONS

HQ: STATE OF GEORGIA
206 WSHNGTON ST 111 STATE, ATLANTA, GA 30334
Phone: 404 656-1776
Web: WWW.GEORGIA.GOV

HISTORICAL FINANCIALS

Company Type: Private

Income Statement — FYE: June 30

	REVENUE ($ mil.)	NET INCOME ($ mil.)	NET PROFIT MARGIN	EMPLOYEES
06/19	45,109	1,235	2.7%	67,139
06/17	42,410	1,167	2.8%	—
06/16	40,422	1,513	3.7%	—
06/15	38,901	512	1.3%	—
Annual Growth	3.8%	24.6%	—	—

STATE OF HAWAII

EXECUTIVES

Gov, David Ige
Lt. Gov*, Josh Green
Chief Information Security Off*, Vincent Hoang
Director of Operations, Jing Xu
Supervisor, Kristine Shimogawa
Director, Hawaii Officer of PI, Mary Alice Evans
Hawaii Attorney General, Russell Suzuki
Deputy Admin Director, Walter Ozawa
Director, Zheng Fang
Information Specialist, Andrew Jackson
Executive Officer, Charlene Tamanaha
Auditors: ACCUITY LLP HONOLULU HAWAII

LOCATIONS

HQ: STATE OF HAWAII
201 MERCHANT ST STE 1805, HONOLULU, HI 968132963
Phone: 808 695-4620
Web: WWW.PORTAL.EHAWAII.GOV

HISTORICAL FINANCIALS

Company Type: Private

Income Statement — FYE: June 30

	REVENUE ($ mil.)	NET INCOME ($ mil.)	NET PROFIT MARGIN	EMPLOYEES
06/19	11,744	57	0.5%	44,201
06/18	11,316	(39)	—	—
06/17	10,516	435	4.1%	—
06/16	10,309	574	5.6%	—
Annual Growth	4.4%	(53.5%)	—	—

STATE OF IDAHO

EXECUTIVES

Governor, Brad Little
Lt Governor*, Janice McGeachin
Cmsnr*, Tom Katsilometes
Cmsnr*, Rich Jackson
Cmsnr*, Elliot Werk
Information Specialist, Cory Woodbury
Admin Idaho Div Veterans Serv, Marv Hagedorn
Project Coordinator, Elizabeth Ultis
Executive Director, Laura Wilder
Supervisor, Lisa Tordjman
Senior Project Manager, Margie Kennedy
Auditors: APRIL RENFRO CPA MANAGER BO

LOCATIONS

HQ: STATE OF IDAHO
700 W JEFFERSON ST, BOISE, ID 837200001
Phone: 208 334-2100
Web: WWW.IDAHO.GOV

HISTORICAL FINANCIALS
Company Type: Private

Income Statement				FYE: June 30
	REVENUE ($ mil.)	NET INCOME ($ mil.)	NET PROFIT MARGIN	EMPLOYEES
06/19	8,615	157	1.8%	429
06/18	8,403	542	6.5%	—
06/17	7,788	473	6.1%	—
06/15	7,219	426	5.9%	—
Annual Growth	4.5%	(22.0%)	—	—

STATE OF ILLINOIS

EXECUTIVES

Governor, J B Pritzker
Lt Gov, Julianna Stratton
SEC of State, Jesse White
Treasurer, Michael Frerichs
Deputy Governor, Sol Flores
General Counsel, Roma Larson
Director, Pamela Simon
Deputy Director, Ryan Prehn
Quality Assurance Director, Scott Hughes
Executive Director, Scott McFarland
Accounting Manager, Tracy McGee
Auditors: WILLIAM G HOLLAND

LOCATIONS

HQ: STATE OF ILLINOIS
207 STATE HOUSE, SPRINGFIELD, IL 627060001
Phone: 217 782-6830

HISTORICAL FINANCIALS
Company Type: Private

Income Statement				FYE: June 30
	REVENUE ($ mil.)	NET INCOME ($ mil.)	NET PROFIT MARGIN	EMPLOYEES
06/13	62,451	1,596	2.6%	59,659
06/12	58,747	(522)	—	—
06/11	55,157	869	1.6%	—
Annual Growth	6.4%	35.5%	—	—

STATE OF INDIANA

EXECUTIVES

Lt Gov*, Suzanne Crouch
Director of Finance, Carl Zapfe
Public Relations Executive, Carlos Pettiford
Commissioner, Christine Klika
Manager-Geo-Spatial Is, Chuck Carufel
Mis, Ron Bolander
Marketing Director, Stephanie Genrich
SEC, Stephene Reeve
Superintendent, Suellen Reed
Data, Anthony Barker
Auditors: PAUL D JOYCE CPA INDIANAPOL

LOCATIONS

HQ: STATE OF INDIANA
200 W WA ST STE 201, INDIANAPOLIS, IN 462042731
Phone: 317 232-4567
Web: WWW.STATE.IN.US

HISTORICAL FINANCIALS
Company Type: Private

Income Statement				FYE: June 30
	REVENUE ($ mil.)	NET INCOME ($ mil.)	NET PROFIT MARGIN	EMPLOYEES
06/19	36,469	986	2.7%	33,000
06/18	33,877	408	1.2%	—
06/17	32,576	(78)	—	—
Annual Growth	5.8%	—	—	—

STATE OF IOWA

EXECUTIVES

Governor, Kim Reynolds
Lt Governor, Adam Gregg
Consultants, Jillian Dotson
Indexing Supervisor, Kristin Wentz
Performance Investigation Divi, Annette Campbell
Deputy Medicaid Director, Julie Lovelady
Assistant Aud 6, Michelle Meyer
Teacher Visually Impair, Michelle Tauke
Phys Supervisor Human, Mohammad Rehman
Ddm Contractor, Balaji Punukula
Administrative Law Judge, Jeanene Elder
Auditors: MARY MOSIMAN CPA DES MOINES

LOCATIONS

HQ: STATE OF IOWA
1007 E GRAND AVE RM 105, DES MOINES, IA 503199003
Phone: 515 281-5211
Web: WWW.IOWA.GOV

HISTORICAL FINANCIALS
Company Type: Private

Income Statement				FYE: June 30
	REVENUE ($ mil.)	NET INCOME ($ mil.)	NET PROFIT MARGIN	EMPLOYEES
06/19	18,006	471	2.6%	24,304
06/18	17,093	(79)	—	—
06/17	16,806	(130)	—	—
06/16	16,563	(297)	—	—
Annual Growth	2.8%	—	—	—

STATE OF KANSAS

EXECUTIVES

Governor, Laura Kelly
Treasurer*, Jake Laturner
Chief Information Technology O*, Lee Allen
City Clark, Adam Moore
Staff, Marc Galbraith
Staff, Stan Frownfelter

Communications Director, Kara Zeyer
Member, Elaine Bowers
Director of Program Finance, Adam Proffitt
Accountant, Becky Bahr
Program Director, Bryna Stacey
Auditors: CLIFFTONLARSONALLEN LLP BROOM

LOCATIONS

HQ: STATE OF KANSAS
534 S KANSAS AVE STE 1210, TOPEKA, KS 666033434
Phone: 785 354-1388
Web: WWW.KANSAS.GOV

HISTORICAL FINANCIALS
Company Type: Private

Income Statement				FYE: June 30
	REVENUE ($ mil.)	NET INCOME ($ mil.)	NET PROFIT MARGIN	EMPLOYEES
06/19	14,988	794	5.3%	22,375
06/18	14,322	895	6.3%	—
06/17	12,935	(187)	—	—
06/16	12,563	(240)	—	—
Annual Growth	6.1%	—	—	—

STATE OF LOUISIANA

EXECUTIVES

Governor, Bobby Jindal
Lt Gov, Jay Dardenne
Director, Margaret Gehdauer
Treasurer, John Schroder
Compensation Division Administ, Brandy Malatesta
Finance, Marella Houghton
Sphr Human Resources Director, Sophia Pipsair
Vice President Management, Joseph Livingston
Information Technology Technic, Mike Cavell
Senior, Alden Clement
Specialist, Brooke Guidry
Auditors: DARYL G PURPERA CPA CFE BA

LOCATIONS

HQ: STATE OF LOUISIANA
900 N 3RD ST FL 4, BATON ROUGE, LA 708025236
Phone: 225 342-0991
Web: WWW.LOUISIANA.GOV

HISTORICAL FINANCIALS
Company Type: Private

Income Statement				FYE: June 30
	REVENUE ($ mil.)	NET INCOME ($ mil.)	NET PROFIT MARGIN	EMPLOYEES
06/19	30,034	1,386	4.6%	47,937
06/18	28,849	829	2.9%	—
Annual Growth	4.1%	67.2%	—	—

STATE OF MAINE

EXECUTIVES

Governor, Janet Mills
Senior Health Policy Adviser, Nick Adolphsen
Senior Policy Adviser, Sean Ingram
Legislative Policy Coordinator, Andrew Bracy
Information Specialist, Dale Irish
Sergeant, Jonathan Shapiro
Accounting Staff, Laura Larrabee
Procurement Staff, Marie Malloy
Sergeant, Mark Tibbetts
Coordinator, Michael Laberge
Coordinator, Michael Mayo
Auditors: POLA A BUCKLEY CPA CISA/MAR

LOCATIONS

HQ: STATE OF MAINE
1 STATE HOUSE STA, AUGUSTA, ME 043330001
Phone: 207 287-3531
Web: WWW.MAINE.GOV

HISTORICAL FINANCIALS
Company Type: Private

Income Statement				FYE: June 30
	REVENUE ($ mil.)	NET INCOME ($ mil.)	NET PROFIT MARGIN	EMPLOYEES
06/19	8,155	357	4.4%	12,000
06/18	7,798	110	1.4%	—
06/17	7,623	146	1.9%	—
06/16	7,389	179	2.4%	—
Annual Growth	3.3%	25.9%	—	—

STATE OF MICHIGAN

EXECUTIVES

Governor, Gretchen Whitmer
Lt Governor*, Garlin Gilchrist
SEC*, Joseph Gordon
Chief Deputy Treasurer*, Jeff Guilfoyle
Member Advisor, Alyssa Vanhyfte
Accounting Staff, Anita Westry
Senior Management Analyst, Bill Bartels
Trade Developmen, Chris Bosio
Business Capital Relationship, Chris Cook
Scientist, Clarence Jones
Director, Eric Dean
Auditors: DOUG A RINGLER CPA CIA LAN

LOCATIONS

HQ: STATE OF MICHIGAN
111 S CAPITOL AVE, LANSING, MI 489331555
Phone: 517 373-7910
Web: WWW.MICHIGAN.GOV

HISTORICAL FINANCIALS
Company Type: Private

Income Statement				FYE: September 30
	REVENUE ($ mil.)	NET INCOME ($ mil.)	NET PROFIT MARGIN	EMPLOYEES
09/18	54,684	832	1.5%	55,416
09/17	52,459	702	1.3%	—
09/16	52,181	168	0.3%	—
Annual Growth	2.4%	122.5%	—	—

STATE OF MINNESOTA

EXECUTIVES

Governor, Tim Walz
Lt Governor, Peggy Flanagan
ATT Gen, Mike Hatch
St Treas, Carol C Johnson
SEC of State, Mary Kiffmeyer
Security Staff, William Fowler
Coordinator, Evie Wold
Minnesota Adjutant General, Jon A Jensen
Supreme Court Judge, Paul Thissen
Court of Appeals Judge, Randall J Slieter
Court of Appeals Judge For Six, Jeanne M Cochran
Auditors: JAMES R NOBLES/CECILE M FERK

LOCATIONS

HQ: STATE OF MINNESOTA
116 VETERAN SERVICE BLD, SAINT PAUL, MN 551550001
Phone: 218 828-2400
Web: WWW.STATE.MN.US

HISTORICAL FINANCIALS
Company Type: Private

Income Statement				FYE: June 30
	REVENUE ($ mil.)	NET INCOME ($ mil.)	NET PROFIT MARGIN	EMPLOYEES
06/19	41,741	1,040	2.5%	35,217
06/17	37,751	793	2.1%	—
06/16	36,717	479	1.3%	—
06/15	35,721	812	2.3%	—
Annual Growth	4.0%	6.4%	—	—

STATE OF MISSISSIPPI

EXECUTIVES

Governor, Phil Bryant
Lieutenant Governor*, Tate Reeves
Executive Director*, Kevin J Upchurch
Executive Assistant, Dorthy Kuykendall
Administrator, Dana Kidd
Scientist, Kerwin Cuevas
Procurement Staff, Vicki Brown
Special Projects Officer IV, Kenneth Judie
Staff, Susanne Merchant
U.S. Marshal, Southern Distric, Mark B Shepherd
Communications Director, Kathy Waterbury
Auditors: STEPHANIE C PALMERTREE CPA

LOCATIONS

HQ: STATE OF MISSISSIPPI
501 NW ST STE 1301 WLFOL, JACKSON, MS 39201
Phone: 601 359-3100
Web: WWW.MISSISSIPPI.GOV

HISTORICAL FINANCIALS
Company Type: Private

Income Statement				FYE: June 30
	REVENUE ($ mil.)	NET INCOME ($ mil.)	NET PROFIT MARGIN	EMPLOYEES
06/19	16,887	773	4.6%	27,775
06/18	16,518	(9)	—	—
06/17	16,436	156	0.9%	—
06/16	16,438	158	1.0%	—
Annual Growth	0.9%	69.8%	—	—

STATE OF MISSOURI

EXECUTIVES

Governor, Mike Parson
Lt Gov, Mike Kehoe
Comm, Doug Nelson
Security Staff, Scotty Allen
Scientist, Alica Alexander
Coordinator, Karen Cassmeyer
Scientist, Tracey Mason
Server Administrator, Billy Sarver
Actuary, David Cox
Director, Dean Linneman
Alcohol and Tobacco Enforcemen, Keith Hendrickson
Auditors: THOMAS A SCHWEICH JEFFERSON

LOCATIONS

HQ: STATE OF MISSOURI
301 W HIGH ST RM 570, JEFFERSON CITY, MO 651011517
Phone: 573 751-4013
Web: WWW.MO.GOV

HISTORICAL FINANCIALS
Company Type: Private

Income Statement				FYE: June 30
	REVENUE ($ mil.)	NET INCOME ($ mil.)	NET PROFIT MARGIN	EMPLOYEES
06/19	25,748	309	1.2%	51,488
06/18	25,326	110	0.4%	—
06/17	24,769	(153)	—	—
06/16	24,115	267	1.1%	—
Annual Growth	2.2%	5.0%	—	—

STATE OF NEBRASKA

EXECUTIVES

Governor, Pete Ricketts
Lt. Gov*, Mike Foley
Staff, Traci Cooney

Acting Superintendent, Russ Stanczyk
Coordinator, John Rockenbach
Fire Marshal, Christopher Cantrell
Information Technology Infrast, Garry Kapperman
Operations Consultant, Jesse Cushman
Legal Counsel, Ron Theis
Law Enforcement Officer, Scott Eveland
Government Official, Steve Burns
Auditors: PHILIP J OLSEN CPA CISA LI

LOCATIONS

HQ: STATE OF NEBRASKA
  521 S 14TH ST STE 400, LINCOLN, NE 685082707
Phone: 402 471-2311
Web: WWW.NEBRASKA.GOV

HISTORICAL FINANCIALS
Company Type: Private

Income Statement				FYE: June 30
	REVENUE ($ mil.)	NET INCOME ($ mil.)	NET PROFIT MARGIN	EMPLOYEES
06/19	9,322	401	4.3%	18,653
06/18	8,643	(108)	—	—
06/17	8,449	(266)	—	—
Annual Growth	5.0%	—	—	—

STATE OF NEVADA

EXECUTIVES

Governor, Steve Sisolak
Lt. Governor, Kate Marshall
Attorney General, Catherine Cortez Masto
Chief of Staff, Gerald Gardner
State Contrl, Kim Wallin
SEC of State, Ross Miller
Dir, Jim Groth
General Counsel, Kathryn Reynolds
Chief Information Security Off, Brian Wilcox
Communications Director, Mari St Martin
Chief Manager, Robert Dehnhardt
Auditors: EIDE BAILLY LLP RENO NEVADA

LOCATIONS

HQ: STATE OF NEVADA
  101 N CARSON ST STE 1, CARSON CITY, NV
  897017011
Phone: 775 684-5670
Web: WWW.NV.GOV

HISTORICAL FINANCIALS
Company Type: Private

Income Statement				FYE: June 30
	REVENUE ($ mil.)	NET INCOME ($ mil.)	NET PROFIT MARGIN	EMPLOYEES
06/16	10,436	301	2.9%	14,790
06/15	9,446	(144)	—	—
06/14	8,131	161	2.0%	—
06/13	7,965	171	2.2%	—
Annual Growth	9.4%	20.6%	—	—

STATE OF NEW MEXICO

EXECUTIVES

Governor, Michelle Lujan Grisham
Lt. Governor*, Howie Morales
Dep Chief of Staff*, Scott Darnell
Auditor*, Wayne Johnson
Coordinator, Laura Dalemarre
Court of Appeals Judge, Zachary A Ives
Chief of Police, Tim Johnson
Deputy Chief, Robert O Thornton III
Deputy Chief, Nick Aragon
Deputy Chief, Carolyn N Huynh
Member, Deborah A Armstrong
Auditors: CLIFTONLARSONALLEN LLP ALBUQU

LOCATIONS

HQ: STATE OF NEW MEXICO
  237 DON GASPAR AVE, SANTA FE, NM 875012178
Phone: 505 827-3000
Web: WWW.NEWMEXICO.GOV

HISTORICAL FINANCIALS
Company Type: Private

Income Statement				FYE: June 30
	REVENUE ($ mil.)	NET INCOME ($ mil.)	NET PROFIT MARGIN	EMPLOYEES
06/19	18,370	3,033	16.5%	22,217
06/18	17,364	2,968	17.1%	—
06/17	32	1	3.6%	—
06/16	14,929	(828)	—	—
Annual Growth	7.2%	—	—	—

STATE OF NEW YORK MORTGAGE AGENCY

The State of New York Mortgage Agency (SONYMA pronounced "Sony Mae") is a public benefit corporation of the State of New York that makes homebuying more affordable for low- and moderate-income residents of the state. SONYMA has two program divisions: Its single-family programs and financing division provides low-interest rate mortgages to first-time home-buyers with low and moderate incomes through the issuance of mortgage revenue bonds while its mortgage insurance fund provides mortgage insurance and credit support for multi-family affordable residential projects and special care facilities throughout the state.

EXECUTIVES

Vice President, Daniel Murphy
Assistant Vice President, Robert Rosado
Vice President Special Projects, Mark Flescher
Assistant Vice President Senior Underwriter, Maria Lasorsa
Vice President Internal Audit, Stephen Chopey
Senior Vice President, Michael Friedman
Assistant Vice President, Olivia Jervis
Auditors: ERNST & YOUNG LLP NEW YORK N

LOCATIONS

HQ: STATE OF NEW YORK MORTGAGE AGENCY
  641 LEXINGTON AVE FL 4, NEW YORK, NY
  100224503
Phone: 212 688-4000
Web: WWW.HCR.NY.GOV

HISTORICAL FINANCIALS
Company Type: Private

Income Statement				FYE: October 31
	ASSETS ($ mil.)	NET INCOME ($ mil.)	INCOME AS % OF ASSETS	EMPLOYEES
10/19	5,936	392	6.6%	221
10/18	5,324	147	2.8%	—
10/17	5,228	34	0.7%	—
10/16	5,187	63	1.2%	—
Annual Growth	4.6%	83.2%	—	—

STATE OF NORTH CAROLINA

EXECUTIVES

Governor, Roy Cooper
Lt Gov*, Dan Forest
Chief of Staff*, Thomas Stith
Controller*, Linda M Combs
District Court Judge, Judicial, Annette Turik
Staff, Barry Anderson
Staff, Beth P Mills
Staff, Betty M Jones
Coordinator, Bill Davis
Dep Adv-Jobs & Economy, Blannie Cheng
Cdsa Manager, Brian Deese
Auditors: BETH A WOOD CPA RALEIGH NO

LOCATIONS

HQ: STATE OF NORTH CAROLINA
  20301 MAIL SERVICE CTR, RALEIGH, NC 276990300
Phone: 919 715-1411
Web: WWW.NC.GOV

HISTORICAL FINANCIALS
Company Type: Private

Income Statement				FYE: June 30
	REVENUE ($ mil.)	NET INCOME ($ mil.)	NET PROFIT MARGIN	EMPLOYEES
06/19	48,977	836	1.7%	69,869
06/18	46,551	208	0.4%	—
06/17	45,371	1,172	2.6%	—
06/16	44,395	1,501	3.4%	—
Annual Growth	3.3%	(17.7%)	—	—

STATE OF NORTH DAKOTA

EXECUTIVES

Governor, Doug Burgum
Lt Gov*, Brent Sanford
Auditor*, Bob Peterson
Coo*, Jodi Uecker
Cao*, Jodee Hanson
Chief People Officer*, Kelsey Roth
Information Technology/Interne, Jason Bryhn
Dept of Agriculture Livestoc, Becky Gietzen
Dept of Agriculture Exec Srv, Bonnie Sunby
Instructional Special, Cheryl Thompson
Dept of Agriculture Plant In, Elaine Sayley
Auditors: JOSHUA C GALLION BISMARCK N

LOCATIONS

HQ: STATE OF NORTH DAKOTA
600 E BOULEVARD AVE # 101, BISMARCK, ND
585050601
Phone: 701 328-4905
Web: WWW.ND.GOV

HISTORICAL FINANCIALS
Company Type: Private

Income Statement				FYE: June 30
	REVENUE ($ mil.)	NET INCOME ($ mil.)	NET PROFIT MARGIN	EMPLOYEES
06/19	7,860	1,955	24.9%	8,800
06/17	6,408	172	2.7%	—
06/16	5,667	(1,080)	—	—
06/15	7,902	1,203	15.2%	—
Annual Growth	(0.1%)	12.9%	—	—

STATE OF OHIO

EXECUTIVES

Governor, Mike Dewine
Lt Govnr*, Jon Husted
Chief of Staff, AVI Zaffini
Communications Director, Joshua Eck
Dpty Communications Director, Eve Mueller
Press Secretary, Dan Tierney
Minority Affairs Liaison, Ronald C Todd
Chief of Staff, Laurel Dawson
Director, Washington DC Office, Nikki Guilford
Vice Chair, Chris Widener
Manager, Angela Albrecht
Auditors: KEITH FABER COLUMBUS OHIO

LOCATIONS

HQ: STATE OF OHIO
30 E BROAD ST FL 40, COLUMBUS, OH 432153414
Phone: 614 466-3455
Web: WWW.OHIO.GOV

HISTORICAL FINANCIALS
Company Type: Private

Income Statement				FYE: June 30
	REVENUE ($ mil.)	NET INCOME ($ mil.)	NET PROFIT MARGIN	EMPLOYEES
06/19	60,384	1,717	2.8%	57,631
06/17	56,959	(267)	—	—
Annual Growth	3.0%	—	—	—

STATE OF OKLAHOMA

EXECUTIVES

Governor, Kevin Stitt
Lt Gov*, Matt Pinnell
General Counsel-Sec*, James Williamson
Sec, Science and Innovation, Kayse Shrum
Sec, Health and Mental Health, Jerome Loughridge
Contracting Andamp, Kathy Hallum
Coordinator Mark, Barbara Charlet
Senior Screening Consultant, Dane Libart
Editor, Donna Bruce
DOT Public Works Director, Ernestine Mbroh
Board of Trustees Member, James Hixon
Auditors: GARY A JONES CPA CFE OKLAH

LOCATIONS

HQ: STATE OF OKLAHOMA
421 NW 13TH ST STE 220, OKLAHOMA CITY, OK
731033784
Phone: 405 521-2342
Web: WWW.OK.GOV

HISTORICAL FINANCIALS
Company Type: Private

Income Statement				FYE: June 30
	REVENUE ($ mil.)	NET INCOME ($ mil.)	NET PROFIT MARGIN	EMPLOYEES
06/19	19,784	1,636	8.3%	37,613
06/18	17,805	602	3.4%	—
06/17	17,175	48	0.3%	—
06/16	16,789	(1,025)	—	—
Annual Growth	5.6%	—	—	—

STATE OF OREGON

EXECUTIVES

Governor, Kate Brown
State SEC, Bev Clarno
Staff, Caroline Zavitkovski
Public Safety Policy Adviser, Constantin Severe
Human Resources Administration, Donna Minor
Deputy Health Care Policy Advi, Jackie Yerby
North Coast Regional, Jennifer Purcell
Coordinator, Jessica Guerrero
Communications Specialist, Jessica Sall
Dhs Human, Larry Nicholson
Security Staff, Mike Meza
Auditors: OFFICE OF THE ACCOUNTANCY OF S

LOCATIONS

HQ: STATE OF OREGON
900 COURT ST NE STE 160, SALEM, OR 973014046
Phone: 503 378-3111
Web: WWW.STATE.OR.US

HISTORICAL FINANCIALS
Company Type: Private

Income Statement				FYE: June 30
	REVENUE ($ mil.)	NET INCOME ($ mil.)	NET PROFIT MARGIN	EMPLOYEES
06/19	28,230	2,142	7.6%	36,176
06/18	26,037	874	3.4%	—
06/17	24,296	1,536	6.3%	—
06/16	23,578	1,568	6.7%	—
Annual Growth	6.2%	10.9%	—	—

STATE OF RHODE ISLAND AND PROVIDENCE PLANTATIONS

EXECUTIVES

Gov, Gina M Raimondo
Lt Gov, Daniel J McKee
State Controller, Lawrence C Franklin Jr
Research Scientist, Adam Miller
Grant Manager, Andrea Creach
Research Technician, Caitlin Oconnor
Human Resources Manager, Cecille Antonelli
Associate Director, Cheryl Burrell
Human Resources Rep, Crystine Marandola
Labor, Diane Buerger
Communications Director, Evan England
Auditors: DENNIS E HOYLE CPA PROVIDEN

LOCATIONS

HQ: STATE OF RHODE ISLAND AND PROVIDENCE
PLANTATIONS
82 SMITH ST STE 102, PROVIDENCE, RI 029031121
Phone: 401 222-2080
Web: WWW.RI.GOV

HISTORICAL FINANCIALS
Company Type: Private

Income Statement				FYE: June 30
	REVENUE ($ mil.)	NET INCOME ($ mil.)	NET PROFIT MARGIN	EMPLOYEES
06/19	7,547	(49)	—	13,535
06/17	7,012	215	3.1%	—
06/16	6,860	(10)	—	—
06/15	6,787	160	2.4%	—
Annual Growth	2.7%	—	—	—

STATE OF SOUTH CAROLINA

EXECUTIVES

Gov, Henry Dargan McMaster
Lt Gov*, Pamela S Evette
Exec Asst*, Kara Smoak
Atty Gen, Henry McMaster
Governors Aid, Susane Cooper
Director of Information Techno, Andrew Blais
Branch Manager, Robert Liming
Adjutant General, R Van McCarty
Professional Responsibility, Kenneth Phelps
Administrative Coordinator, Bonnie Brooks
Assistant District Maintenance, Dusty S Turner
Auditors: GEORGE L KENNEDY III COLUMB

LOCATIONS

HQ: STATE OF SOUTH CAROLINA
  1205 PENDLETON ST, COLUMBIA, SC 292013756
Phone: 803 734-2100
Web: WWW.SC.GOV

HISTORICAL FINANCIALS

Company Type: Private

Income Statement — FYE: June 30

	REVENUE ($ mil.)	NET INCOME ($ mil.)	NET PROFIT MARGIN	EMPLOYEES
06/19	24,767	1,774	7.2%	67,816
06/15	21,191	224	1.1%	—
06/14	20,459	613	3.0%	—
06/13	19,706	944	4.8%	—
Annual Growth	3.9%	11.1%	—	—

STATE OF TENNESSEE

EXECUTIVES

Governor-Prin, Bill Haslam
Lt Gov*, Ron Ramsey
Speaker - House, James O Naifeh
Speaker - Senate, John S Wilder
East TN Field Dr, Harlow Sumerford
Staff, Amanda Carter
Assistant Chief, Glenn Moates
Coordinator, Steve Cross
Director - Communications, Jennifer Donnals
Staff Assistant To Treasur, Ashley Humphrey
Specialist, Barry Bryant
Auditors: DEBORAH V LOVELESS CPA DIRE

LOCATIONS

HQ: STATE OF TENNESSEE
  312 ROSA L PARKS AVE, NASHVILLE, TN 372431102
Phone: 615 741-2001
Web: WWW.TN.GOV

HISTORICAL FINANCIALS

Company Type: Private

Income Statement — FYE: June 30

	REVENUE ($ mil.)	NET INCOME ($ mil.)	NET PROFIT MARGIN	EMPLOYEES
06/19	32,779	754	2.3%	37,737
06/18	32,194	902	2.8%	—
06/17	31,145	981	3.2%	—
06/16	30,452	1,162	3.8%	—
Annual Growth	2.5%	(13.4%)	—	—

STATE OF TEXAS

EXECUTIVES

Governor, Greg Abbott
Chief of Staff*, Luis Saenz
Deputy Chief of Staff*, David Whitley
Chief Operating Officer*, Reed Clay
Deputy Chief of Staff*, Jordan Hale
Senior Adviser For State Opera, Steven Albright
Texas District Attorney, Andria Bender
Senior Adviser, Sarah Hicks
Chief of Staff, Amy Bruno
Shift Coordinator, Darrell Taylor
Administrator, David Carter
Auditors: LISA R COLLIER CPA CFE CID

LOCATIONS

HQ: STATE OF TEXAS
  1100 SAN JACINTO BLVD, AUSTIN, TX 787011935
Phone: 512 463-2000
Web: WWW.TEXAS.GOV

HISTORICAL FINANCIALS

Company Type: Private

Income Statement — FYE: August 31

	REVENUE ($ mil.)	NET INCOME ($ mil.)	NET PROFIT MARGIN	EMPLOYEES
08/17	115,336	1,882	1.6%	144,175
08/15	107,350	1,993	1.9%	—
08/14	109,860	8,184	7.4%	—
08/13	0	0	—	—
Annual Growth	—	—	—	—

STATE OF UTAH

EXECUTIVES

Governor, Gary Herbert
Gov, Gary R Herbert
Lt Gov, Spencer J Cox
Exec-Dir, Q Val Hale
General Counsel, Ron Gordon
Accounting Staff, Susan Lundquist
Local Area Network Administrat, Cindy Talboe
Senior Information Tea, Dan Cox
Department of Workforce Servic, Elizabeth Thorpe
Specialist, Jill Grimm
Department of Workforce Servic, Julie Thurston
Auditors: OFFICE OF THE STATE AUDITOR

LOCATIONS

HQ: STATE OF UTAH
  350 N STATE ST STE 200, SALT LAKE CITY, UT
  841140002
Phone: 801 538-1000
Web: WWW.UTAH.GOV

HISTORICAL FINANCIALS

Company Type: Private

Income Statement — FYE: June 30

	REVENUE ($ mil.)	NET INCOME ($ mil.)	NET PROFIT MARGIN	EMPLOYEES
06/19	14,316	696	4.9%	29,821
06/18	13,582	986	7.3%	—
06/17	12,668	199	1.6%	—
06/16	11,723	55	0.5%	—
Annual Growth	6.9%	132.2%	—	—

STATE OF WASHINGTON

EXECUTIVES

Governor, Jay Inslee
Lt Govnr*, Brad Owen
SEC State*, Sam Reed
Treas*, Michael Murphy
Pub Inst*, Terry Bergeson
Exec SEC*, Sue Martin
Chief of Staff*, Mary Alice Heuschel
Senior Adviser, Joby Shimomura
Manager, Linda Garland
Deputy Chief Information Offic, Debbie Hoxit
Manager, Ginny Schenck
Auditors: PAT MCCARTHY OLYMPIA WA

LOCATIONS

HQ: STATE OF WASHINGTON
  106 LEGISLATIVE BUILDING, OLYMPIA, WA
  985040001
Phone: 360 902-4111
Web: WWW.ACCESS.WA.GOV

HISTORICAL FINANCIALS

Company Type: Private

Income Statement — FYE: June 30

	REVENUE ($ mil.)	NET INCOME ($ mil.)	NET PROFIT MARGIN	EMPLOYEES
06/19	50,993	264	0.5%	57,659
06/18	49,114	2,692	5.5%	—
06/17	46,269	1,100	2.4%	—
06/16	43,294	1,096	2.5%	—
Annual Growth	5.6%	(37.8%)	—	—

STATE OF WEST VIRGINIA

EXECUTIVES

Governor, Jim Justice
State Auditor*, Glen Gainer III
Chief of Staff*, Chris Stadelman
Chief of Staff*, Nick Casey
Member, L W Linger
Assistant Treasurer, Josh Stowers
Director Participant Accountin, Diane Holcomb
Supreme Court of Judge, John Hutchison
Debt Manager, Bryan Archer
Web Designer, Jeff Takarsh
Local Government Dire, Ora Ash
Auditors: ERNST & YOUNG LLP CHARLESTON

LOCATIONS

HQ: STATE OF WEST VIRGINIA
1900 KANAWHA BLVD E, CHARLESTON, WV
253050009
Phone: 304 558-2000
Web: WWW.WV.GOV

HISTORICAL FINANCIALS
Company Type: Private

Income Statement				FYE: June 30
	REVENUE ($ mil.)	NET INCOME ($ mil.)	NET PROFIT MARGIN	EMPLOYEES
06/19	12,469	649	5.2%	19,357
06/17	11,650	(2)	—	—
06/16	11,147	(231)	—	—
06/15	11,175	(159)	—	—
Annual Growth	2.8%	—	—	—

STATE OF WISCONSIN

EXECUTIVES

Governor, Tony Evers
Lt. Governor*, Mandela Barnes
Coordinator, Lisa Jorgensen
Project Coordinator, Cynthia Moore
Office Press Secretary, Amy Hasenberg
Deputy Chief of Staff, Jack Jablonski
Chief of Staff, Eric Schutt
Specialist, Erika Ryerson
Civil Engineering Supervisor, David Castleberg
Revenue Section Chief, Dawn Wenzel
Accountant, Doug Meek
Auditors: JOE CHRISMAN MADISON WI

LOCATIONS

HQ: STATE OF WISCONSIN
115 E CAPITOL, MADISON, WI 537020015
Phone: 608 266-1212
Web: WWW.WISCONSIN.GOV

HISTORICAL FINANCIALS
Company Type: Private

Income Statement				FYE: June 30
	REVENUE ($ mil.)	NET INCOME ($ mil.)	NET PROFIT MARGIN	EMPLOYEES
06/19	31,683	693	2.2%	35,522
06/17	28,874	474	1.6%	—
06/16	28,533	357	1.3%	—
06/15	28,158	(537)	—	—
Annual Growth	3.0%	—	—	—

State Street Corp.

Through its flagship State Street Bank and other subsidiaries State Street provides investment servicing (including clearing settlement payment brokerage and trading and risk and compliance analytics) and investment management services (which include core and enhanced indexing multi-asset strategies environment and social investing and ETFs). The holding company's primary clientele comprises investment managers mutual funds corporate and public retirement plans collective investment funds and other investment pools foundations endowments and insurance companies. Founded in 1792 as Union Bank State Street has some $34.4 trillion in assets under custody and administration and roughly $3.1 trillion in assets under management.

Operations
State Street has two lines of business.

The company's Investment Servicing segment represents about 85% of its total revenue and comprises a wide breadth of offerings. Among the line's services are custody; accounting; cash and financial data management; and trading (including foreign exchange and brokerage). State Street's other business Investment Management — conducted through its State Street Global Advisors (SSGA) subsidiary — provides passive and active investment management strategies. The company's assets under management are weighted primarily toward indexed strategies (which are designed to match not beat a market). Investment Management (which accounts for more than 15% of total sales).

State Street makes more than 75% of its revenue from fees; about 45% of its total revenue comes from servicing fees. Management fees provide roughly 15% and foreign exchange trading services fees contribute approximately 10% to the total. Securities finance fees generate about 5% and software and processing fees comprise just over 5%. The remainder derives from net interest income from investment securities interest-bearing bank deposits resale agreements and loans and leases

Geographic Reach
Based in Boston State Street is active in more than 100 geographic markets including the US Canada Europe the Middle East Africa and the Asia-Pacific region.

About 70% of State Street's assets under custody and/or administration (AUC/A) are in North America. It has offices in nearly a dozen states (including California Florida Georgia Illinois Massachusetts Missouri New Jersey New York North Carolina Pennsylvania and Texas). More than 15% of the holding company's AUC/A come from the EMEA region; the remaining 15% comes from the Asia-Pacific region.

Sales and Marketing
State Street's clients include mutual funds collective investment funds and other investment pools corporate and public retirement plans insurance companies foundations endowments and investment managers.

State Street spent $114 million in 2019 $115 million in 2018 and $67 million in 2017 on advertising and public relations.

Financial Performance
State Street's revenue has been fluctuating for the last five years with an overall growth of 12% between 2015 and 2019. Net income was rising consistently but dropped in 2019.

State Street's revenue increased to $11.8 billion in 2019 compared to the previous year.

Net income dipped 14% to $2.2 billion in the same period. The fall was primarily due to the decrease on their revenue.

Cash held by the company at the end of 2019 was $90 million higher than the prior year with $3.3 billion. The Company has $2.7 billion generated from operating activities. It used $783 million on investing activities with an additional $1.9 billion used in financing activities.

Strategy
State Street's strategy focuses on building on its strong core achieving a digital enterprise investing in opportunities and optimizing capital. The Company maintains close relationships with analysts and investors to make sure they understand State Street's goals how the Company plans to get there and its progress along the way. By transparently sharing developments on its strategic progress and financial results State Street keeps lines of communication open so that all stakeholders can make informed decisions on their investments.

Company Background
Established in 1792 State Street predecessor Union Bank formed to service investment in maritime and China trade. Union Bank received its national banking charter in 1891. In 1924 it became the custodian for the first-ever mutual fund. State Street Bank and Trust formed in 1961 through the merger of 13 predecessor banks.

HISTORY

The US's chaotic post-revolutionary era gave birth to the first ancestor of State Street Corporation. Union Bank was founded in 1792 by Boston businessmen breaking the eight-year monopoly held on Boston banking by Massachusetts Bank (a forerunner of FleetBoston which was acquired by Bank of America in 2004). Governor John Hancock's distinctive signature graced Union's charter; the bank set up shop at 40 State Street near the port and enjoyed the glory days of New England's shipping trade.

In the mid-19th century Boston's financial eminence faded as New York flexed its economic muscle. In 1865 the bank was nationally chartered and changed its name to National Union Bank of Boston. It got a new neighbor in 1891:

nancial advisors with established client relationships and continuing to selectively consider acquisition opportunities as they may arise.

Further expand institutional business both domestically and internationally. Stifel's institutional equity business is built upon the premise that high-quality fundamental research is not a commodity. The company's goal is to further monetize its research platform by adding additional institutional sales and trading teams and by placing a greater emphasis on client management.

Grow the investment banking business. By leveraging the industry expertise product knowledge research platform experienced associates capital markets strength middle-market focus and private client network the company intends to grow investment banking business.

Focus on asset generation within Stifel Bancorp by offering banking services to the clients. Stifel believes the banking services provided through Stifel Bancorp strengthens the existing client relationships and helps recruit financial advisors seeking to provide a full range of services to their private clients. The company intends to continue focusing on the sale of banking products and services to private and corporate clients.

Approach acquisition opportunities with discipline. Over the course of the company's operating history Stifel has demonstrated its ability to identify effect and integrate attractive acquisition opportunities. The company believes the current environment and market dislocation will continue to provide the ability to thoughtfully consider acquisitions on an opportunistic basis.

Mergers and Acquisitions

Stifel Financial has achieved historic revenue growth over the years by using acquisitions primarily to fortify its wealth management business.

In late 2019 tifel Nicolaus Europe Limited a wholly owned subsidiary of Stifel Financial Corp. has completed its previously announced merger with MainFirst Bank AG an independent European investment bank offering equity brokerage and equity capital markets services to institutions and corporations in key European markets. The combined entity will employ more than 400 professionals operating out of nine offices in Frankfurt Geneva London Madrid Milan Munich New York Paris and Zurich. Terms not disclosed.

Stifel Financial Corp. announced that it has completed the acquisition of certain assets of Kansas-based George K. Baum & Company a recognized industry leader in the structuring underwriting and marketing of taxable and tax-exempt municipal securities in 2019 with an undisclosed terms. This transaction brings GKB's nationally recognized municipal securities business to Stifel and further strengthens Stifel's ability to provide top tier service to municipal issuer clients and non-profit borrowers.

On the same year Stifel Financial Corp. also completed the acquisition of B&F Capital Markets Inc. headquartered in Ohio an industry leader in providing regional and community banks with extensive interest rate swap capabilities. Terms of the transaction were not disclosed

Stifel acquired mergers and acquisitions and private capital advisory firm Mooreland Partners also in 2019. The company serves the technology industry through its offices in New York Silicon Valley London and Frankfurt. It has completed more than 250 M&A and capital raising transactions for mid-market companies primarily in North America and Europe.

EXECUTIVES

Vice Chairman Svp And Director Stifel Financial Corp. And Evp Investment Banking Stifel Nicolaus & Co., Richard J. Himelfarb, age 79, $250,000 total compensation

Chairman President And Ceo, Ronald J. (Ron) Kruszewski, age 61, $200,000 total compensation

President Cfo And Director, James M. Zemlyak, age 60, $250,000 total compensation

Evp; President And Co-director Institutional Group, Thomas P. Mulroy, age 58, $250,000 total compensation

Svp And Director Stifel Financial Corp. And President And Ceo Keefe Bruyette And Woods, Thomas B. (Tom) Michaud, age 55, $250,000 total compensation

Evp; President And Co-director Institutional Group, Victor J. Nesi, age 60, $250,000 total compensation

Vice President Mortgage Banker, Dan Bayer

Vice President Investments Sarasota, Brad Wilson

Senior Vice President Investments Charleston, Park Smith

Senior Vice President Investments Walnut Creek, Chris Thompson

Assistant Vice President, David Odria

Associate Vice President And Trust Officer, Andrea Cosmano

Senior Vice President, Jay E Harker

Vice President And Portfolio Manager, Tom Marcrander

Vice President, Suhaill R Garavi

Svp And Sr Mortgage Loan Officer, Kent Hackstadt

Vice Chairman; Evp Stifel Nicolaus & Co., Ben A. Plotkin, age 64

Co-chairman, Thomas W. (Thom) Weisel, age 78

Auditors: Ernst & Young LLP

LOCATIONS

HQ: Stifel Financial Corp
501 North Broadway, St. Louis, MO 63102-2188
Phone: 314 342-2000
Web: www.stifel.com

2016 Sales

	% of total
US	94
UK	5
Other European countries	1
Total	**100**

PRODUCTS/OPERATIONS

2016 Sales

	$ mil.	% of total
Commissions	730	28
Asset management and service fees	582	22
Investment banking	513	19
Principal transactions	475	18
Interest	294	11
Others	46	2
Total	**2,642**	**100**

Selected Services

Individual
Bonds
Corporate Executive Services
Estate Planning
Exchange Traded Funds
Financial And Wealth Planning
Insurance
Investment Advisory Services
Market News
Mutual Funds
Options
Portfolio Tracker
Prospectus
Retirement Plans

Stifel Bank & Trust
Stifel Cash Management Accounts
Stifel Mobile Announcement
Stifel Trust
Institutions
Asset Management
Conferences & Events
Equity Capital Markets
Equity Sales & Trading
Fixed Income Sales & Trading
Investment Banking
Public Finance
Research
Senior Management

Selected Subsidiaries

Broadway Air Corp.
  CSA Insurance Agency Incorporated
Choice Financial Partners Inc.
  Stifel Bank & Trust
Stifel Nicolaus Limited (UK)
Stifel Nicolaus & Company Incorporated
  Ryan Beck Holdings LLC
Thomas Weisel Partners Group Inc.

COMPETITORS

Edward Jones	Oppenheimer Holdings
FBR	Piper Jaffray
Goldman Sachs	Raymond James
JMP Group	Financial
Lazard	Wells Fargo Advisors
Morgan Stanley	

HISTORICAL FINANCIALS

Company Type: Public

Income Statement

FYE: December 31

	ASSETS ($ mil.)	NET INCOME ($ mil.)	INCOME AS % OF ASSETS	EMPLOYEES
12/19	24,610	448	1.8%	8,300
12/18	24,519	393	1.6%	7,500
12/17	21,383	182	0.9%	7,100
12/16	19,129	81	0.4%	7,100
12/15	13,335	92	0.7%	7,100
Annual Growth	16.6%	48.4%	—	4.0%

2019 Year-End Financials

Debt ratio: 4.38%
Return on equity: 13.22%
Cash ($ mil.): 1,273
Current ratio: —
Long-term debt ($ mil.): —

No. of shares (mil.): 102
Dividends
  Yield: 1.4%
  Payout: 16.3%
Market value ($ mil.): 6,216

	STOCK PRICE ($) FY Close	P/E High/Low		PER SHARE ($) Earnings	Dividends	Book Value
12/19	60.65	16	10	3.66	0.60	35.27
12/18	41.42	19	11	3.15	0.48	29.83
12/17	59.56	36	25	1.43	0.20	26.92
12/16	49.95	68	35	0.67	0.00	27.39
12/15	42.36	66	45	0.79	0.00	24.79
Annual Growth	9.4%	—	—	46.9%	—	9.2%

Stock Yards Bancorp Inc

Stock Yards Bancorp is the holding company of Stock Yards Bank & Trust which operates about 35 branches mostly in Louisville Kentucky but also in Indianapolis and Cincinnati. Founded in 1904 the $3 billion-asset bank targets individuals and regional business customers offering standard retail services such as checking and savings accounts credit cards certificates of deposit and IRAs. It also provides trust services while brokerage and credit card services are offered through agreements with other banks. Commercial real estate mortgages make up 40% of the bank's loan portfolio which also includes commercial and industrial loans (30%) residential mortgages (15%) construction loans and consumer loans.

Operations

Stock Yards Bank & Trust operates two main business lines: Commercial Banking which provides loans and deposits to individual consumers and businesses as well as mortgage origination and company brokerage activity; and Investment Management and Trust which provides wealth management services such as investment management trust estate administration and retirement plan services.

About 63% of the company's total revenue came from loan interest during 2015 while another 7% came from interest income on its securities. The rest came from its investment management and trust services (13% of revenue) deposit account service charges (7%) bankcard transaction revenue (4%) mortgage banking revenue (3%) brokerage commissions and fees (1%) and other non-interest sources.

Geographic Reach

Kentucky-based Stock Yards Bancorp had 37 branches at the end of 2015 including 28 branches in the Louisville Kentucky metro area and the rest in the Indianapolis Indiana and Cincinnati Ohio metro areas.

Financial Performance

Stock Yards' annual revenues have risen 11% since 2011 thanks to a combination of mostly organic loan growth and investment management and trust services fee growth. Meanwhile its annual profits have grown more than 55% on declining loan loss provisions as its loan portfolio's credit quality has improved with higher property valuations in the strengthened economy.

The bank's revenue climbed 4% to a record $133.12 million during 2015 on higher interest income mostly as its loan assets grew 9% to $2 billion with record loan production.

Revenue growth and a decline in interest expense on deposits in 2015 drove Stock Yard's net income up 7% to a record $34.82 million. The bank's operating cash levels jumped 8% to $43.17 million mostly thanks to the increase in cash-based earnings.

Strategy

Stock Yards outlined its plans for 2016 and beyond to maintain stable net interest margins achieve near-double digit loan growth manage credit quality to keep loan loss provisions down and increasing its regulatory readiness.

Mergers and Acquisitions

In 2013 the bank extended the reach of its operations into Oldham County through its purchase of $146 million-asset The BANcorp Inc. and its five THE BANK branches in the region for $19.9 million.

EXECUTIVES

Sevp, Kathy C. Thompson, age 58, $345,000 total compensation

Chairman And Ceo, David P. Heintzman, age 60, $535,000 total compensation

Evp Secretary Treasurer And Cfo, Nancy B. Davis, age 64, $232,000 total compensation

Evp And Chief Lending Officer, Philip S. Poindexter, age 54, $270,000 total compensation

President, James A. (Ja) Hillebrand, age 51, $375,000 total compensation

Evp And Chief Risk Officer, William M. Dishman, age 58

Evp And Chief Strategic Officer, Clay Stinnett

Evp Retail Banking Brokerage And Business Banking, Michael J. Croce

Assistant Vice President Deposit Operations, Marcia Sweat

Vice President Private Banking, Dan Thacker

Vice President Commercial Lending, Kevin Mccullough

Assistant Vice President, Crystal Fryer

Assistant Vice President, June Schenk

Vice President Commerical Lending, Jason Morgan

Vice President Investment Advisor, Damon Massey

Board Member, Richard Northern

Auditors: BKD LLP

LOCATIONS

HQ: Stock Yards Bancorp Inc
1040 East Main Street, Louisville, KY 40206
Phone: 502 582-2571
Web: www.syb.com

PRODUCTS/OPERATIONS

2015 Revenues by Category

	$ mil.	% of total
Interest income	93	70
Non-interest income	40	30
Total	**133**	**100**

Selected Products & Services

Personal Banking
  Banking
  Personal Lending
  Personal Investing & Wealth Management Services
Business Banking
  Credit Loans & Leasing
  Deposit Services
  Treasury Management
  Business Retirement Plans
Wealth Management Services
  Investment Management
  Financial Planning
  Trust & Estate Services
  Brokerage Service

COMPETITORS

Fifth Third	Porter Bancorp
First Capital	Republic Bancorp
Home Federal	U.S. Bancorp
PNC Financial	

HISTORICAL FINANCIALS

Company Type: Public

Income Statement   FYE: December 31

	ASSETS ($ mil.)	NET INCOME ($ mil.)	INCOME AS % OF ASSETS	EMPLOYEES
12/19	3,724	66	1.8%	615
12/18	3,302	55	1.7%	591
12/17	3,239	38	1.2%	580
12/16	3,039	41	1.3%	578
12/15	2,816	37	1.3%	555
Annual Growth	**7.2%**	**15.5%**	**—**	**2.6%**

2019 Year-End Financials

Debt ratio: —
Return on equity: 17.10%
Cash ($ mil.): 249
Current ratio: —
Long-term debt ($ mil.): —

No. of shares (mil.): 22
Dividends
  Yield: 2.5%
  Payout: 37.1%
Market value ($ mil.): 928

	STOCK PRICE ($) FY Close	P/E High/Low	PER SHARE ($) Earnings	Dividends	Book Value
12/19	41.06	15 11	2.89	1.04	17.97
12/18	32.80	17 12	2.42	0.96	16.11
12/17	37.70	28 19	1.66	0.80	14.71
12/16	46.95	26 15	1.80	0.72	13.88
12/15	37.79	24 18	1.65	0.64	12.80
Annual Growth	**2.1%**	**— —**	**15.0%**	**12.9%**	**8.9%**

StoneX Group Inc

Going global is the name of the game for commodities broker StoneX Group Inc. (formerly known as INTL FCStone Inc.). The company specializes in the physical trade of commodities such as corn gold renewable fuels and livestock though its primary activities are hedging securities trading and clearing. It offers clearing and execution services of listed futures and options on futures and serves as a market-maker for some 5000 foreign securities. Its global platform provides execution market intelligence and post-trade services across all its asset classes and markets. It operates in international markets offering commodity risk management consulting asset management and commodity financing. Its client base includes financial institutions corporations and charitable organizations in the US and abroad. Most of its revenue comes from outside of US.

Operations

StoneX Group garners a diverse revenue stream across five operating segments ? Physical Commodities; Clearing & Execution Services; Commercial Hedging; Securities and Global Payments.

Although the Physical Commodities segment accounts for the vast majority of revenue the segment provides trading and hedging capabilities for precious metals and physical agricultural and energy commodities and commits its own capital for buying and selling on a spot and forward basis.

The CES segment matches customer trades with the relevant commodity or stock exchange collects and manages customer margin deposits and accounts for and reports on transactions for all major futures and securities exchanges globally.

The Commercial Hedging segment provides assesses risk and designs and executes hedging strategies particularly for agricultural and energy commodities and base metals.

Global Payments provides cross-border money movement services to banks businesses charities and non-government and government organizations in approximately 170 countries and 140 currencies.

Geographic Reach

New York City-headquartered StoneX serves in more than 130 countries around the world. The company operates through a network of approximately 25 offices in the US. The company also has offices throughout the South America (Brazil Argentina Paraguay and Colombia) Europe (Ireland and the UK) Middle East (the UAE) and Asia (India China and Singapore).

Middle East and Asia represents about 95% of the company's total revenue. The US provides about 5% of StoneX's total revenue.

Sales and Marketing

With more than 20000 customers StoneX utilizes a direct sales force of risk management consultants who are organized by commodity verticals such as agriculture energy metals and livestock.

Its clients include commercial customers asset managers broker-dealers insurance companies brokers institutional and professional investors commercial and investment banks and governmental and non-governmental organizations.

Financial Performance

While StoneX produces eye-popping revenue numbers ? almost $33 billion in its fiscal 2019 ? its preferred performance metric is operating revenue as it removes dramatic multi-year price swings in commodities. Operating revenue has risen year after year since 2015 from roughly $624.3 million in FY2015 to about $1.1 billion in FY2017.

For 2019 revenue was $32.9 billion; operating revenue was $1.1 billion. Operating revenue grew 13% from the prior year owing to record performance in all five of the company's segments. The growth was spurred by periods of increased market volatility that bolstered client activity and widened spreads as well as higher short-term interest rates and average client balances.

The company's net income increased $29.6 million to $85.1 million in fiscal 2019 compared to $55.5 million in fiscal 2018.

Cash at the end of the year was $471.3 million an increase of $129 million from the prior year. Operations used $195.6 million and financing activities added $9.6 million. Investing activities used $40.8 million for property and equipment purchases and net acquisitions.

Strategy

The company engage in direct sales efforts to seek new clients with a strategy of extending their services to potential clients that are similar in size and operations to their existing client base. In executing this strategy the company intend to both target new geographic locations and expand the services offered in geographic locations in which they currently operate where there is an unmet demand for our services. In addition StoneX selectively pursue small- to medium-sized acquisitions focusing primarily on targets that satisfy specified criteria including client-centric organizations that may help us expand into new asset classes client segments and geographies where we currently have a small or limited market presence.

The company's strategy is to utilize a centralized and disciplined process for capital allocation risk management and cost control while delegating the execution of strategic objectives and day-to-day management to experienced individuals. This requires high quality managers a clear communication of performance objectives and strong financial and compliance controls. StoneX believe this strategy will enable them to build a more scalable and significantly larger organization that embraces an entrepreneurial approach to business supported and underpinned by strong centralized financial and compliance controls.

Mergers and Acquisitions

In 2020 StoneX announced that it has entered into definitive agreement to acquire GAIN Capital Holdings Inc. (NYSE: GCAP) ("GAIN") which has been approved by the Board of Directors of both StoneX and GAIN. The company has agreed to acquire GAIN for an all-cash transaction representing approximately $236 million in equity value. The acquisition is expected to increase StoneX's transaction flows and raise client float by ~$1 billion. The acquisition of GAIN's digital assets and expertise will also accelerate the digitization of StoneX Group's platform.

In early 2020 the company agreed to acquire IFCM Commodities provides commodity price risk management solutions for base metals serving clients across Germany and continental Europe. This purchase is part of INTL FCStone's overall strategic plan to expand the company's footprint in Germany and continental Europe in order to handle European clients and regional metals business post-Brexit.

Also in 2020 the Company London-based subsidiary INTL FCStone Ltd. agreed to acquire Europe- based GIROXX provides online payment and foreign exchange hedging services to small and medium sized enterprises in Germany Austria and Switzerland. This purchase completes a series of acquisitions and company restructuring to ensure that all clients of INTL FCStone Ltd are secure with their continuity of service and market access and are 100% unaffected by Brexit.

In 2019 INTL FCStone acquired online precious metal providers CoinInvest and European Precious Metal Trading. Through their websites coininvest.com and silver-to-go.com the companies provide gold silver platinum and palladium to private individuals institutional investors and financial advisors. The deal extends INTL's Precious Metals Division allowing customers to purchase the metals in multiple forms and denominations.

INTL bought the US-based broker-dealer GMP Securities a subsidiary of GMP International Holdings in 2019. The purchase expanded INTL's fixed income product portfolio to include high yield convertible and emerging market debt gave the company more than 2400 institutional customers.

Company Background

INTL FCStone which traces its roots to 1924 was created after the 2009 merger of FCStone Group and International Assets Holding. In mid-2020 the company announced that is rebranding the firm as StoneX Group Inc. ("StoneX").

EXECUTIVES

President And Ceo, Sean M. O'Connor, age 58, $400,000 total compensation
Cfo, William J. (Bill) Dunaway, age 49, $275,000 total compensation
Coo, Xuong Nguyen, age 52, $325,000 total compensation
Chief Risk Officer, Tricia Harrod, age 61
Ceo Europe Middle East Africa And Asia, Philip A. Smith, age 48, $324,105 total compensation
Executive Chairman Europe Middle East Africa And Asia, Malcolm Wilde, age 69
Ceo Intl Fcstone Markets, Mark Maurer, age 44
Vice President, Thiago Vieira
Svp Global Payments, Byard Bridge
Vice President Equity Trading, Thomas Moore
Assistant Vice President Financial Operations, Marcelo Taborda
Vice President Equity Trading, Al Barbella
Senior Vice President Base Metals Lead, Tom Gramlich
Vice President Equity Trading, Erich Huggler
Vice President Energy, Jonathan Kist
Vice President Technology, David Leung
Vice President Latin America Payments Division, Fernando Mazzanti
Vice President Digital Marketing, Monica Schmidt
Vice President Business And Legal Affairs, Ryan Mcnearney
Vice President Of Institutional Sales, Daniel D'avila
Senior Vice President Energy, John Best
Chairman, John Radziwill
Board Member, Bruce Krehbiel
Board Member, Eric Parthemore
Board Member, Brent Bunte
Board Member, Daryl Henze
Group Treasurer, Bruce Fields
Auditors: KPMG LLP

LOCATIONS

HQ: StoneX Group Inc
155 East 44th Street, Suite 900, New York, NY 10017
Phone: 212 485-3500
Web: www.intlfcstone.com

2018 Sales

	% of total
US	6
Asia	93
Europe	1
South America	0
Other	0
Total	**100**

PRODUCTS/OPERATIONS

2018 Total Revenue

	% of total
Commercial Hedging	1
Global Payments	0
Securities	1
Clearing & Execution Services	1
Physical Commodities	97
Corporate unallocated	0
Total	**100**

Selected Subsidiaries

FCC Futures Inc.
INTL Asia Pte. Ltd.
INTL FCStone Pte. Ltd.
FCStone do Brazil Ltda.
FCStone Financial Inc.
FCStone Group
FCStone Merchant Services LLC
FCStone Paraguary S.R.L.
FCStone LLC
Gainvest Asset Management Ltd.
Gainvest S.A.
Gainvest Uruguay Asset Management S.A.
Gletir S.A.
INTL Capital S.A. (Argentina)
INTL CIBSA Sociedad de Bolsa S.A.
INTL Commodities DMCC
INTL Custody & Clearing Solutions Inc.
INTL FCStone (Europe) Ltd.
INTL FCStone Financial
INTL FCStone (Netherlands) B.V.
INTL Netherlands B.V.
INTL Participacoes Ltda.
SA Stone Investment Advisors Inc.
Westown Commodities LLC

HISTORICAL FINANCIALS

Company Type: Public

Income Statement				FYE: September 30
	REVENUE ($ mil.)	NET INCOME ($ mil.)	NET PROFIT MARGIN	EMPLOYEES
09/20	54,035	169	0.3%	2,950
09/19	32,742	85	0.3%	2,012
09/18	27,542	55	0.2%	1,701
09/17	29,381	6	0.0%	1,607
09/16	14,726	54	0.4%	1,464
Annual Growth	38.4%	32.7%	—	19.1%

2020 Year-End Financials

Debt ratio: 5.82%
Return on equity: 24.84%
Cash ($ mil.): 2,648
Current ratio: 0.82
Long-term debt ($ mil.): 515

No. of shares (mil.): 19
Dividends
Yield: —
Payout: —
Market value ($ mil.): 991

	STOCK PRICE ($) FY Close	P/E High/Low		PER SHARE ($) Earnings	Dividends	Book Value
09/20	51.16	7	3	8.61	0.00	39.61
09/19	41.06	11	8	4.39	0.00	31.15
09/18	48.32	19	13	2.87	0.00	26.72
09/17	38.32	138	107	0.31	0.00	24.02
09/16	38.85	13	8	2.90	0.00	23.53
Annual Growth	7.1%	—	—	31.3%	—	13.9%

Stryker Corp

Is this an operating room or Dad's workshop? Stryker's surgical products include such instruments as drills saws and even cement mixers. The company operates through three primary segments ? MedSurg Orthopaedic and Neurotechnology and Spine. MedSurg's products include instruments endoscopy medical products sustainability and other medical specialties. The Orthopaedic segment makes artificial hip and knee joints trauma implants and other orthopedic supplies. The Neurotechnology and Spine segment provides neurosurgical neurovascular and spinal implant devices. Stryker's products are marketed globally to doctors hospitals and other health care facilities via direct sales personnel and distributors. The US generates about 75% of total sales.

Operations

Stryker's MedSurg and Surgical segment is the largest unit bringing in about 45% of total revenues. Its MedSurg Equipment division provides surgical navigation systems endoscopic systems emergency medical equipment and other medical devices.

Stryker's Orthopaedic segment is nearly as large accounting for about 35% of annual revenues. The division's products consist primarily of implants used in hip and knee joint replacements and trauma and extremities surgeries. Its Mako System currently offers three applications supporting Partial Knee Total Hip and Total Knee procedures. Mako is the only robotic-arm assisted technology enabled by 3D CT-based preoperative planning and with AccuStop haptic technology it provides surgeons intra-operative haptic guidance for bone preparation and implant placement.

The company's smallest segment ? Neurotechnology & Spine ? accounts for some 20% of sales. It provides both neurosurgical and neurovascular devices for minimally invasive surgical procedures. Spinal implant products include cervical thoracolumbar and interbody systems used in various therapies.

Geographic Reach

The company's smallest segment ? Neurotechnology & Spine ? accounts for some 20% of sales. It provides both neurosurgical and neurovascular devices for minimally invasive surgical procedures. Spinal implant products include cervical thoracolumbar and interbody systems used in various therapies.

Sales and Marketing

In the US most of Stryker's products are marketed directly to doctors hospitals and other healthcare facilities.. By allowing for specialization each team can provide expertise and guidance directed specifically to customers in each of the medical specialties Stryker serves. In over 75 countries its products are sold through company-owned subsidiaries and branches as well as third-party dealers and distributors.

Financial Performance

Stryker's revenues have increased steadily over the last five years rising about 50% between 2015 and 2019. Net income fluctuated for the same period

In 2019 revenue grew 9% to $14.9 billion compared to $13.6 billion in 2018.

Net income in 2019 fell 41% to $2.1 billion compared to $3.6 billion in 2018. The decrease was driven by higher operating expenses and income taxes.

Stryker ended 2019 with $4.3 billion in cash and cash equivalents an increase of 20% compared to $3.6 billion in 2018. Cash provided by operations declined by 16% to $2.2 billion and cash used in investing activities was $1.5 billion. Financing activities provided $3 million.

Strategy

Stryker's strategy for growth centers around strengthening its position at the high-end of the medical technology industry by prioritizing acquisitions dividends and share repurchases. The company continued its capital allocation strategy by investing $802 million in acquisitions paying $778 million in dividends to its shareholders and using $307 million for share repurchases.

Mergers and Acquisitions

Purchases in recent years have brought Stryker new software and manufacturing technologies and entered it into new lines of business such as surgical imaging and minimally invasive devices for treatment of stroke and brain conditions.

Purchases in recent years have brought Stryker new software and manufacturing technologies and entered it into new lines of business such as surgical imaging and minimally invasive devices for treatment of stroke and brain conditions. In late 2019 the company completed the acquisition of Mobius Imaging and Cardan Robotics for net cash consideration of about $360 million and future regulatory and commercial milestone payments of approximately $130 million. Mobius Imaging is a leader in point-of-care imaging technology focused on integrating advanced imaging technologies into medical workflow. Its Cardan Robotics is working to develop innovative robotics and navigation technology systems for surgical and interventional radiology procedures.

In a separate transaction Stryker acquired TSO3 which develops sterilization technology for medical devices for about $52 million. TSOP3 makes the STERIZONE VP4 a low-temperature sterilizer that is cleared for use in the US Canada and Europe.

In March 2019 the company acquired Israel-based OrthoSpace for $110 million plus up to $110 million in milestone payments. OrthoSpace makes balloons that prevent friction during minimally invasive bone procedures; it is approved in Europe and being tested in the US.

In early 2019 the company completed the acquisition of a medical device company headquartered in Menlo Park California that has developed ClariFix a novel cryoablation technology for the treatment of chronic rhinitis the Arrinex Inc.

Company Background

Stryker was founded in 1941 by Dr. Homer Stryker.

HISTORY

Stryker was founded in 1941 by Dr. Homer Stryker an orthopedic surgeon who had invented several orthopedic devices. It was incorporated in 1946 as a Michigan company. The company expanded through organic measures and occasional acquisitions over the following decades while the Stryker family kept a hand in its operations.

Beginning in 2009 Stryker set out to further diversify its operations through acquisitions. In 2010 Stryker purchased supportive surface maker (think: beds and tables) Gaymar Industries for approximately $150 million in cash. The two companies were already well-acquainted through a longstanding supply and sales agreement in the US.

Its $1.5 billion acquisition of Boston Scientific's neurovascular division in 2011 added minimally invasive devices (such as coils stents and balloon catheters) for the treatment of cerebral conditions such as brain aneurysms and hemorrhagic and ischemic strokes.

Stryker further boosted its neurovascular operations later that year when it acquired Concentric Medical a maker of clot removal products for use in ischemic stroke procedures for some $135 million. Following these acquisitions Stryker rearranged its operating structure from two divisions into three: Reconstructive MedSurg Equipment and Neurotechnology and Spine.

The company's OP-1 bone growth product was so successful that in 2011 the company sold the product franchise to Olympus for $60 million. During 2011 Stryker acquired synthetic bone graft material maker Orthovita for some $304 million in cash. It also spent $150 million to purchase France's Memometal Technologies for its in hand and foot device products.

EXECUTIVES

Vp Regulatory Affairs Quality, Elizabeth Staub
Vice President, Bronwen Taylor
Group President Orthopaedics, David K. Floyd, $575,000 total compensation
Chairman President And Ceo, Kevin A. Lobo, $1,129,167 total compensation
Group President Global Quality And Operations, Lonny J. Carpenter, $497,500 total compensation
Group President Medsurg And Neurotechnology, Timothy J. Scannell, $610,333 total compensation
Vp And Cio, Bijoy Sagar
Vp Communications Public Affairs And Strategic Marketing, Yin C. Becker
Group Cfo Medsurg & Neurotechnology (msnt), Glenn Boehnlein, $517,333 total compensation
President Asia Pacific, Graham A. McLean
Vice President Information Technology, Justin Ritchie
Marketing Vice President, Stewart Simpson
Vice President Information Technology Infrastructure And Security, Alan Douville
Vice President Healthcare Systems, Lara Latham
Area Vice President Stryker Orthopaedics, Eric Tamweber
Mvp Manager, Nicole Westin
Vice President Human Resources, Art Hartman
National Accounts Manager, Mark Axe
Vice President Vendor Consolidation, Lee Petrides
Vice President Operations, Mike Vanvleet
Vice President, Bill Cymbaluk
Area Vice President, William Fain
Area Vp Of Spine Sales, Christopher Hambrick
Vice President Global Infrastructure Services, Michael Doyle
Vp Hr Joint Replacement, Karen Bick
Regional Vice President, Jonathan Lehmann
Vice President And General Manager, Ryan Landon
Vice President Strategic Growth Stryker Spine, Roy Ward
Vice President Spine, Tony Troncale
Board Of Director, Louise Francesconi
Board Of Director, Ronda Stryker
Board Director, Srikant Datar
Vp Finance And Treasurer, Jeanne Blondia
Board Member, Andrew Silvernail
Board Member, Mary Brainerd
Secretary, Carrie Johnson
Auditors: Ernst & Young LLP

LOCATIONS

HQ: Stryker Corp
2825 Airview Boulevard, Kalamazoo, MI 49002
Phone: 269 385-2600   **Fax:** 269 385-1062
Web: www.stryker.com

2017 Sales

	$ mil.	% of total
US	9,059	73
Europe Middle East & Africa	1,567	13
Asia/Pacific	1,413	11
Other	405	3
Total	**12,444**	**100**

PRODUCTS/OPERATIONS

2017 Sales by Segment

	$ mil.	% of total
MedSurg		
Medical	1,969	16
Instruments	1,678	14
Endoscopy	1,652	13
Sustainability	258	2
Orthopaedics		
Knees	1,595	13
Trauma & Extremities	1,478	12
Hips	1,303	10
Other	337	3
Neurotechnology & Spine		
Neurotechnology	1,423	11
Spine	751	6
Total	**12,444**	**100**

COMPETITORS

Arthrex	Olympus
CONMED Corporation	Penumbra
DePuy	Philips Electronics
DePuy Spine	STERIS
Globus Medical	Smith & Nephew
Hill-Rom Holdings	Synthes
Medline Industries	Terumo Medical
Medtronic	Corporation
Medtronic Sofamor	ZOLL
Danek	Zimmer Biomet
NuVasive	

HISTORICAL FINANCIALS

Company Type: Public

Income Statement   FYE: December 31

	REVENUE ($ mil.)	NET INCOME ($ mil.)	NET PROFIT MARGIN	EMPLOYEES
12/19	14,884	2,083	14.0%	40,000
12/18	13,601	3,553	26.1%	36,000
12/17	12,444	1,020	8.2%	33,000
12/16	11,325	1,647	14.5%	33,000
12/15	9,946	1,439	14.5%	27,000
Annual Growth	10.6%	9.7%		10.3%

2019 Year-End Financials

Debt ratio: 36.76%
Return on equity: 16.98%
Cash ($ mil.): 4,337
Current ratio: 2.58
Long-term debt ($ mil.): 10,231

No. of shares (mil.): 374
Dividends
 Yield: 1.0%
 Payout: 38.9%
Market value ($ mil.): 78,623

	STOCK PRICE ($) FY Close	P/E High/Low	PER SHARE ($) Earnings	Dividends	Book Value
12/19	209.94	40 27	5.48	2.14	34.20
12/18	156.75	19 15	9.34	1.93	31.33
12/17	154.84	59 43	2.68	1.75	26.62
12/16	119.81	28 20	4.35	1.57	25.47
12/15	92.94	27 24	3.78	1.42	22.82
Annual Growth	22.6%	— —	9.7%	10.8%	10.6%

Summit Financial Group Inc

Summit Financial Group is at the peak of community banking in West Virginia and northern Virginia. The company owns Summit Community Bank which operates about 20 branches that offer standard retail banking fare such as deposit accounts loans and cash management services. Commercial real estate loans including land development and construction loans account for about 40% of Summit Financial Group's loan portfolio which also includes residential mortgages and a smaller percentage of business and consumer loans. The bank's Summit Insurance Services unit sells both commercial and personal coverage.

EXECUTIVES

Senior Vice President And Chief Banking, Doug Mitchell
Senior Vice President Chief Banking Offi, Patty Owens
Senior Vice President Commercial Lending, Jason Hicks
Senior Vice President Commercial Lending, Lisa Dennison
Senior Vice President, Tony Ward
Executive Vice President Of Business Development, Jack Rossi
Senior Vice President And Trust Officer, Julie H Johnson
Vice President Commerical Loans, Anna B Abbey
Vice President Of Mortgage Originations, Oguz Sengul
Vice President Commerical Loans, Anna Abbey
Senior Vice President And Trust Officer, Julie Johnson
Secretary Independent Director, Phoebe Heishman
Board Member, Scott Bridgeforth
Auditors: Yount, Hyde & Barbour, P.C.

LOCATIONS

HQ: Summit Financial Group Inc
 300 North Main Street, Moorefield, WV 26836
Phone: 304 530-1000
Web: www.summitfgi.com

COMPETITORS

Allegheny Bancshares	Highlands Bankshares
BB&T	Inc.
F & M Bank	SunTrust
Fauquier Bankshares	

HISTORICAL FINANCIALS

Company Type: Public

Income Statement   FYE: December 31

	ASSETS ($ mil.)	NET INCOME ($ mil.)	INCOME AS % OF ASSETS	EMPLOYEES
12/19	2,403	31	1.3%	383
12/18	2,200	28	1.3%	371
12/17	2,134	11	0.6%	349
12/16	1,758	17	1.0%	251
12/15	1,492	16	1.1%	231
Annual Growth	12.7%	18.6%	—	13.5%

2019 Year-End Financials

Debt ratio: 0.82%
Return on equity: 13.63%
Cash ($ mil.): 61
Current ratio: —
Long-term debt ($ mil.): —

No. of shares (mil.): 12
Dividends
 Yield: 2.1%
 Payout: 23.6%
Market value ($ mil.): 336

	STOCK PRICE ($) FY Close	P/E High/Low	PER SHARE ($) Earnings	Dividends	Book Value
12/19	27.09	11 8	2.53	0.59	19.97
12/18	19.31	12 8	2.26	0.53	17.85
12/17	26.32	28 19	1.00	0.44	16.30
12/16	27.53	18 7	1.61	0.40	14.47
12/15	11.88	8 7	1.50	0.32	13.47
Annual Growth	22.9%	— —	14.0%	16.5%	10.3%

Sunoco LP

Sunoco LP (formerly Susser Petroleum Partners) pairs with its parent to proffer petroleum. It operates about 900 convenience stores and retail fuel sites and distributes motor fuel to convenience stores independent dealers commercial customers and distributors in more than 30 US states at 6800 sites both directly and through its 32% stake in in Sunoco LLC owned in partnership with Energy Transfer Partners (ETP). Energy Transfer Equity owns 's general partner and incentive distribution rights. ETP owns a 38.4% limited partner interest in the company. In 2016 Sunoco LP bought the fuels business of Emerge Energy Services LP for $167.7 million.In 2017 Japan-based Seven & i Holdings agreed to buy 1100 convenience stores and gas stations from Sunoco LP for about $3.3 billion.

EXECUTIVES

Vp Retail Company Operations, Paul A Brzezicki
Vice President Manufacturing Executive, Norbert E Mitchell
Board Member, Thomas Long
Board Member, James Bryant
Treasurer, Janet M Hoyt
Auditors: Grant Thornton LLP

LOCATIONS

HQ: Sunoco LP
  8111 Westchester Drive, Suite 400, Dallas, TX 75225
Phone: 214 981-0700
Web: www.sunocolp.com

COMPETITORS

CITGO	Shell Oil Products
Chevron	Sinclair Oil
ConocoPhillips	Sunoco
Exxon Mobil	TOTAL
Hess Corporation	Valero Energy
Royal Dutch Shell	

HISTORICAL FINANCIALS

Company Type: Public

Income Statement   FYE: December 31

	REVENUE ($ mil.)	NET INCOME ($ mil.)	NET PROFIT MARGIN	EMPLOYEES
12/19	16,596	313	1.9%	2,909
12/18	16,994	(207)	—	3,622
12/17	11,723	149	1.3%	—
12/16	15,698	(406)	—	—
12/15	16,935	237	1.4%	—
Annual Growth	(0.5%)	7.2%		

2019 Year-End Financials

Debt ratio: 56.47%	No. of shares (mil.): 99
Return on equity: 40.60%	Dividends
Cash ($ mil.): 21	Yield: 10.7%
Current ratio: 1.24	Payout: 340.4%
Long-term debt ($ mil.): 3,060	Market value ($ mil.): 3,042

	STOCK PRICE ($) FY Close	P/E High/Low	Earnings	PER SHARE ($) Dividends	Book Value
12/19	30.60	12 10	2.82	3.30	7.63
12/18	27.19	— —	(3.39)	3.30	7.91
12/17	28.40	93 67	0.34	3.30	19.36
12/16	26.89	— —	(5.26)	3.27	19.16
12/15	39.61	48 28	1.11	2.68	31.25
Annual Growth	(6.2%)	— —	26.3%	5.3%	(29.7%)

SVB Financial Group

SVB Financial Group is the holding company for Silicon Valley Bank which serves emerging and established companies involved in technology life sciences and private equity and provides customized financing to entrepreneurs executives and investors in those industries. It also offers deposit accounts loans and international banking and plays matchmaker for young firms and private investors. SVB also provides investment advisory brokerage and asset management services and markets credit and banking services to wealthy individuals. Founded in 1983 SVB has $60 billion in assets and holds $29 billion in deposits.

Operations

SVB Financial Group has four reporting segments: Global Commercial Bank SVB Leerink SVB Capital and SVB Private Bank.

SVB's revenue derives heavily from its Global Commercial Bank segment; it accounts for about 85% of the total. The division comprises five subunits: Commercial Bank Private Equity Division SVB Wine SVB Analytics and Debt Fund Investments. The Commercial Bank provides financial services including credit treasury management and foreign exchange to commercial clients in the technology venture capital and private equity life science and healthcare industries. SVB Analytics offers research to innovation economy investors and companies while Debt Fund Investments houses SVB's investments debt fund investments.

Healthcare- and life science-focused investment bank SVB Leerink offers biotechs pharmas and medical device and diagnostic companies capital raising and sales and trading services merger and acquisition advisory and equity research. It also sponsors private investment funds. The segment generates roughly 10% of SVB's revenue.

SVB Capital and SVB Private Bank each bring in less than 5% of the company's revenue. The former manages third parties' venture capital funds. The latter markets banking products to the private equity and venture capital community.

Roughly 85% SVB's $29 billion loan portfolio is dedicated to commercial loans; about 50% of the total portfolio is allocated to private equity and venture capital entities and some 25% of the total is to software and internet companies. Loans to life science and healthcare companies make up about 10%.

Geographic Reach

Santa Clara California-based SVB Financial has more than 25 regional offices in California Arizona Colorado Georgia Illinois Massachusetts New York North Carolina Oregon Pennsylvania Texas Utah Virginia and Washington. It has international offices in Hong Kong China Germany India Israel and England.

Sales and Marketing

Clients to SVB Financial Group's Global Commercial Bank primarily encompass technology life science healthcare private equity and venture capital entities. The company's technology clients typically include semiconductor data and storage companies; software and internet companies;

and innovators in energy and resources. SVB Leerink's customers include biotechs pharmas medical device and diagnostic makers healthcare services and digital health firms and life science tool companies.

Financial Performance

Against the backdrop of the Silicon Valley tech boom SVB Financial Group's asset and loan base has grown steadily over the last five years as has its revenue?which posted overall growth of some 85%. The company's net income fared even better soaring about 270% in that time.

SVB's revenue jumped 34% to $2.6 billion in 2018. Increased average loan balances and yields and fixed income investment balances and securities yield drove a net interest income gain of $479.7 million. Fee income rose $136.9 on additions across all of SVB's fee sources particularly client investments.

The company's net income shot up 99% to $974 million that year on the strength of its revenue.

SVB infused its cash stores with $648.5 million in 2018 to end the year with $3.6 billion. Operations provided $933.6 million. It used $4.8 billion on investments (mostly increased net loans and held-to-maturity securities) and received $4.5 billion from its investing activities (stemming from net increased deposits).

Strategy

SVB Financial Group adjusts its business strategy according to each of its client niches including life science healthcare and technology companies; private equity and venture capital firms; premium wine producers; and private bank and wealth management customers.

The holding company's most robust strategy is centered on technology and life science companies. SVB seeks to develop relationships with such clients early in their development and continually offer them expanded services as they mature. Its SVB Accelerator offers banking and financial services to pre-revenue or low-revenue (less than $5 million annually) startups primarily performing research and development that have brought few if any products to market. SVB Growth addresses mid- and late-stage companies?mostly private entities dependent on venture capital that may be poised for an IPO. They typically have yearly revenue of between $5 and $75 million. SVB Corporate Finance serves established large corporations with advanced products or services and annual revenue of more than $75 million.

In a move to expand its operations in the growing life science and healthcare industries in 2019 SVB purchased Leerink Partners?an investment bank serving biotechs pharmas and other healthcare-centric companies. Leerink's operations remain largely unchanged under the SVB Leerink banner.

SVB relies on strong relationships with the private equity and venture capital communities cultivated over its three decades of existence to maintain its client base in those sectors.

Mergers and Acquisitions

In January 2019 SVB Financial Group acquired Boston-based Leerink Holdings the parent company of healthcare and life science investment bank Leerink Partners. SVB paid $280 million up front and created a retention pool for employees of $60 million to be paid over five years. The deal greatly expanded its operations and client base among biotechs pharmas and medical device and diagnostic companies.

Company Background

Established in 1983 SVB Financial Group went public on Nasdaq five years later. By 1996 it had expanded to 15 US states.

HISTORY

Silicon Valley Bank was founded in 1983 by Roger Smith to provide banking services to tech startups in San Jose. The bank boomed along with tech companies during the 1980s lending to the likes of Cisco Systems.

In 1990 the bank spread east to Boston's burgeoning technology alley. It also expanded into residential and commercial real estate lending. The recession of 1989 to 1991 found Silicon Valley Bancshares with an overextended loan portfolio and in 1992 the bank booked a loss due to nonperforming loans; the next year it was put under federal supervision.

To rally stockholder confidence the company brought in new management and demoted Smith from chairman to vice chairman; he left the in 1995. The bank reduced its real estate lending and diversified into factoring foreign exchange and executive banking for venture capitalists and clients' upper management.

The 1995 IPO frenzy aided the company's turnaround. Silicon Valley cashed in on warrants it had taken as collateral from young companies. Regulatory supervision was lifted in 1996 and the bank soon opened offices in the Atlanta; Austin Texas; Boulder Colorado; Phoenix; and Seattle areas.

In 1999 Silicon Valley Bancshares created a website targeted at technology firms in need of financing employees office space and equipment. However nonperforming loans began to dog the bank once again affecting profits and bringing a regulatory request to boost capital reserves.

In 2000 despite being hammered by the high-tech stock selloff the company continued to expand opening offices in West Palm Beach Florida and North Carolina's Research Triangle and successfully capitalizing its first venture fund. The following year it bought tech-focused investment bank Alliant Partners (later renamed SVB Alliant) to broaden its service offerings.

Still licking its wounds from the tech bust the company ceased lending to the entertainment industry and to churches in 2002. Silicon Valley Bancshares changed its name to SVB Financial Services in 2005.

SVB Alliant struggled with losses for years and SVB Financial explored its options including spinning the unit off to management. It ultimately decided to shut down the division which ceased operations in 2008.

EXECUTIVES

Coo, Michael L. Dreyer, age 56
Chief Digital Officer, Bruce E. Wallace, age 55, $398,113 total compensation
President And Ceo Svb Financial Group And Silicon Valley Bank, Gregory W. (Greg) Becker, age 53, $925,904 total compensation
President Silicon Valley Bank, Michael R. (Mike) Descheneaux, age 53, $602,308 total compensation
Head Of Technology Banking, John D. China, $498,385 total compensation

Head Of Europe Middle East And Africa (emea) And President Uk Branch, Philip C. Cox, age 53
Chief Credit Officer Silicon Valley Bank, Marc C. Cadieux, age 53, $447,308 total compensation
Cfo, Daniel Beck
Chief Risk Officer, Laura Izurieta, age 59
Cio, Roger E. Leone, age 66
Vice President, Vincent Vallejos
Senior Vice President, Dave Bhagat
Vice President Relationship Manager, Don Chandler
Vice President, Jocelyn Hartmann
Vice President, Suzann Russell
Vice President Manager Of Sales And Business Product Management, Dennis Corbett
Vice President Relationship Manager Corporate Technology, Phil Silvia
Vice President, Damarie Rodriguez
Vice President, Sam Subilia
Vice President And Relationship Managersouth Bay Region, Jacob Moseley
Vice President And Foreign Exchange Trader, Patrick Chin
Senior Vice President, Li Song
Vice President, Julia Bobrovich
Vice President Regional Director, Carmella Montesdeoca
Vice President Early Stage Banking, Ricky Khamphoumy
Vice President, Lauren Cole
Vice President Corporate Finance, Andrea Jones
Vice President, Ryan Ficks
Vice President, Ann Kim
Vice President Product Management, Susan Merrill
Vice President, Patrick Haggerty
Vice President, Austin Badger
Vice President Software, Alex Choy
Vice President, Bailey Morrow
Vice President, Jigar Patel
Senior Vice President, Andy Tsao
Vice President Relationship Manager, John Peck
Vice President, Benjermin Colombo
Vice President, Patrick Scheper
Senior Vice President, Michael Tramack
Senior Vice President, Chris Stoecker
Executive Vice President And Founder, Rob Mcmillan
Vice President Relationship Manager Cleantech, Jordan Kanis
Vice President Leveraged Finance, Jordan Samiljan
Vice President, Ellen Ayoub
Vice President Life Science And Healthcare, Ryan Roller
Vice President Ii, Ryan Kirschling
Vice President, Cody Nenadal
Vice President, Max Lautmann
Vice President Corporate Finance, Will Deevy
Vice President, Tom Gordon
Vice President, Paula Sen
Vice President, Kyle Swan
Vice President I, Russell Follansbee
Vice President, Dennis He
Vice President, Chelsea Hakso
Vice President, Ashlee Gomes
Vice President Private Equity Services, Sara Cohn
Vice President Structured Finance, James Caron
Vice President Relationship Manager, Glenn Marasigan
Vice President, Brandon Pollock
Vice President, Matt Kelty
Vice President, Marc Neri
Vice President I Sponsor Finance, Stan Skimina
Vice President, Kelly Belcher
Vice President, Steve Lyons
Vice President Structured Finance, Derek Almeida
Vice President, Erin Angerer
Vice President, Tyler Dietrich
Vice President, Karen Sperling
Vice President Early Stage Banking, Navid Shahrestani
Vice President Global Fund Banking, Robert Pyke

Vice President, Jordan Parcell
Vice President Partnerships, George Hotarek
Vice President Wine Division, Dave Morrison
Vice President, Carly Kiser
Vice President, AJ Fang
Vice President, Donna Karraz
Vice President, Frank O'brien
Vice President, Lindsey Guinn
Vice President Life Sciences, Kristina Peralta
Vice President Ii Cfd, Claudia Canales
Vice President Leveraged Finance, Andrew Merget
Vice President Corporate Finance, Ted Bell
Vice President Technology Banking, Patrick Johnson
Vice President, Janice Ahn
Senior Loan Officer Vice President, Sandra Bifolchi
Chairman Svb Financial Group And Silicon Valley Bank, Roger F. Dunbar, age 74
Treasurer, Shawn Street
Assistant Secretary And Treasurer, Lori De Leon
Board Member, Mary Miller
Auditors: KPMG LLP

LOCATIONS

HQ: SVB Financial Group
   3003 Tasman Drive, Santa Clara, CA 95054-1191
Phone: 408 654-7400
Web: www.svb.com

Selected Offices

US
   Atlanta
   Austin TX
   Broomfield CO
   Chicago
   Dallas
   Irvine CA
   Menlo Park CA
   Minnetonka MN
   New York
   Newton MA
   Palo Alto CA
   Philadelphia
   Phoenix
   Pleasanton CA
   Portland OR
   Raleigh NC
   Salt Lake City
   San Diego
   San Francisco
   Santa Rosa CA
   Seattle
   St. Helena CA
   Tysons Corner VA
International
   Bangalore India
   Beijing
   Herzliya Pituach Israel
   London
   Mumbai India
   Shanghai

PRODUCTS/OPERATIONS

2016 Sales

	$ mil.	% of total
Interest		
Loans	834	51
Investment securities	359	22
Noninterest		
Net gains on investment securities	51	3
Net gains on derivative instruments	48	3
Foreign exchange fees	104	6
Credit card fees	68	4
Deposit service charges	52	3
Lending related fees	33	2
Letters of credit	25	2
Client investment fees	32	2
Other	40	2
Total	**1,649**	**100**

Selected Subsidiaries and Affiliates

Silicon Valley Bank
SVB Analytics Inc.
SVB Asset Management
SVB Business Partners (Beijing) Co. Ltd.
SVB Business Partners (Shanghai) Co. Ltd.
SVB Global Financial Inc.
SVB Global Investors LLC
SVB Growth Investors LLC
SVB India Advisors Pvt. Ltd.
SVB Israel Advisors Ltd.
SVB Qualified Investors Fund LLC
SVB Real Estate Investment Trust
SVB Securities
SVB Strategic Investors LLC
SVB Strategic Investors Fund L.P.
Venture Investment Managers L.P.

COMPETITORS

Bank of America	Heritage Commerce
Citigroup	MUFG Americas Holdings
City National	U.S. Bancorp
Comerica	

HISTORICAL FINANCIALS

Company Type: Public

Income Statement

FYE: December 31

	ASSETS ($ mil.)	NET INCOME ($ mil.)	INCOME AS % OF ASSETS	EMPLOYEES
12/19	71,004	1,136	1.6%	3,564
12/18	56,927	973	1.7%	2,900
12/17	51,214	490	1.0%	2,438
12/16	44,683	382	0.9%	2,311
12/15	44,686	343	0.8%	2,089
Annual Growth	12.3%	34.8%	—	14.3%

2019 Year-End Financials

Debt ratio: 0.49%	No. of shares (mil.): 51
Return on equity: 19.62%	Dividends
Cash ($ mil.): 6,492	Yield: —
Current ratio: —	Payout: —
Long-term debt ($ mil.): —	Market value ($ mil.): 12,968

	STOCK PRICE ($) FY Close	P/E High/Low		PER SHARE ($) Earnings	Dividends	Book Value
12/19	251.04	12	8	21.73	0.00	125.26
12/18	189.92	18	10	18.11	0.00	97.29
12/17	233.77	26	17	9.20	0.00	79.11
12/16	171.66	24	11	7.31	0.00	69.71
12/15	118.90	22	15	6.62	0.00	61.97
Annual Growth	20.5%	—	—	34.6%	—	19.2%

Synchrony Financial

Synchrony Financial is a premier consumer financial services company in the US (based on purchase volume and receivables). The company works with a wide range of partners including national and regional retailers local merchants manufacturers buying groups industry associations and healthcare service providers. It counts many of America's major retailers as partners such as Walmart Lowe's JCPenney and Sam's Club. Through its partners' over 410000 locations across the United States and Canada and their websites and mobile applications we offer their customers a variety of credit products to finance the purchase of goods and services. It professes some $87.2 billion of loan receivables and

75.5 million active accounts. The company also offers retail banking services through Synchrony Bank.

Operations

Synchrony operates through three sales platforms: Retail Card Payment Solutions and Care-Credit.

Retail Card generates some 75% of revenue and provides private label credit cards Dual Cards (Dual cards are private label credit cards used to purchase goods and services from partner companies or for general purposes when used elsewhere.) and products for small- and medium-sized businesses. The business runs programs with 25 national and regional retailers accounting for some 10000 locations including department stores (such as JCPenney) specialty retailers (The Gap) mass merchandisers (Sam's Club).

Payment Solutions accounts for around 15% of sales and offers primarily private label credit cards and installment loans. The segment's partners cover 160000 retail locations.

CareCredit brings in more than 10% of sales and provides promotional financing to consumers for health and personal care procedures and products such as dental veterinary cosmetic vision and hearing. The business's products are accepted at more than 240000 locations.

Geographic Reach

Connecticut-based Synchrony operates solely in the US and Canada. California accounts for more than 10% of total outstanding loans followed by Texas (just around 10%) Florida (8%) New York (6%) and Pennsylvania (4%).

Sales and Marketing

Synchrony has an omni-channel (in-store online and mobile) technology and marketing capabilities which allows it to offer and deliver its credit products instantly to customers across multiple channels.

In its Retail Card and Payment Solutions platforms the company works directly with its partners using their distribution network communication channels and customer interactions to market products to their existing and potential customers

Financial Performance

Over the last five years Synchrony's revenue has trended upwards increasing 38% from 2015 to 2019. Net income has increased despite its drop in 2017 with an overall growth of 69% in the last five years.

In fiscal 2019 revenue increased 5% to $17.2 billion from $16.4 billion in 2018 most of which was driven by 6% increase in interest income and partially offset by higher interest expense (on deposits and long-term debt).

Net income increased 34% to $3.7 billion from $2.7 billion.

Cash on hand at the end of 2019 stood at $12.6 billion up by $2.3 billion from the end of the previous period. Cash from operating activities provided $9 billion while investing activities used $261 million mostly in the form of increased loan receivables and purchases of debt securities. Financing activities used $6.5 billion primarily from maturities and repayment of securitized debt.

Strategy

Synchrony's business benefits from longstanding and collaborative relationships with partners which include leading US retailers and other

companies with well-known brands such as Lowes Wal-mart Amazon and PayPal. Its partners promote Synchrony's credit products to consumers looking for instant access to credit to purchase partners' products and services. The symbiotic relationship between Synchrony and its consumer-facing partners secures sales of both Synchrony credit products and partner products.

The company also seeks to differentiate itself through deep partner integration and extensive marketing activity. It has omni-channel (in-store online and mobile) technology and marketing capabilities which allow Synchrony to offer and deliver its credit products instantly to customers across multiple channels.

Through Synchrony Bank the company offers to retail and commercial customers a range of FDIC-insured deposit products including CDs IRAs and money market and savings accounts. It has some $65 billion in deposits.

Mergers and Acquisitions

In 2019 Synchrony Financial acquired pet health insurance company Pets Best which operates through Synchrony's CareCredit platform. CareCredit provides health wellness and personal care credit products. Pets Best has more than 125000 pet health insurance policies in force greater than one million processed claims and $200 million in claims payouts.

Company Background

Synchrony Financial traces its roots back to 1932 when it was founded as GE Capital Retail bank. The company separated from GE in 2015 and became Synchrony Financial.

EXECUTIVES

Evp And Ceo Retail Card, Thomas M. (Tom) Quindlen, $782,825 total compensation
President Ceo And Director, Margaret M. Keane, $933,893 total compensation
Evp Compliance And Regulatory, Paul D. Whynott
Evp And Chief Audit Executive, Mark Martinelli
Evp Cfo And Treasurer, Brian D. Doubles, $631,394 total compensation
Evp And Chief Risk Officer, Henry F. Greig
Evp General Counsel And Secretary, Jonathan S. Mothner, $660,447 total compensation
Evp Ceo Payment Solutions And Chief Commercial Officer, Glenn P. Marino, $712,077 total compensation
Evp And Ceo Carecredit, David Fasoli
Evp And Human Resources Leader, Mark Chini
Evp Coo And President Synchrony Bank, Kurt Grossheim
Evp And Cio, Carol Juel
Evp Business Strategy And Development, Neeraj Mehta
Evp And Chief Credit Officer, Steve Min
Evp And Chief Marketing Officer, Bart Schaller
Vice President Compliance Audit, Deborah Carroll
Vice President, Kim Lankie
Vice President Customer Service, Byron Curry
Vice President Compliance Operations, Mescal Powell
Senior Vice President Digital Engineering, Daniel Murphy
Svp Chief Security Officer, William Reiner
Vice President Talent Acquisition, Claudine Hoverson
Senior Vice President, Max Axler
Assistant Vice President Credit Infrastructure, Scott Stewart
Vice President, Angie Allen
Vice President, Shelby Marshall

Vice President Marketing Home, Nicole Kulchar
Assistant Vice President, Justin Stocker
Assistant Vice President Client Marketing Cosmetic And Dermatology, Hasha Zangana
Vice President Sales, Brian Copps
Sr Vice President Sales Operations, Todd Rodden
Vice President Payables Systems, Julie Seguin
Industry Vice President, John Huffman
Vice President Risk Management, Misael Mauricio
Vice President, Sean Xu
Vice President Product Technology And Channel Management, Matthew Muscolo
Vp Marketing, Joseph Lyons
Assistant Vice President Marketing, Margaret Fertig
Assistant Vice President User Experience Interaction Designer, Jeffrey Amorello
Vice President Strategic Initiatives, Sue Mckee
Vp Hris, Eric Burgess
Vice President Client Development, Lisa Miller
Vp Finance, Kevin Egan
Vice President, Brian Kelly
Senior Vice President Operational Risk, Konrad Sobolewski
Vice President Supplier Risk Management, Geoffrey Magley
Vice President Human Resources, Paula Shook
Vice President Controller And Compliance Risk, Ryan Bond
Vice President Bi Dw Design And Big Data Platform Delivery, Shub Rakshit
Assistant Vice President Lead Big Data Engineer, Nikhat Farha
Svp Treasury Operations, Mary Gilvin
Svp Internal Audit, Vicky Zhang
Vice President Portfolio Risk Management, Gene Thorncroft
Assistant Vice President Sec Reporting, Anna Kwok
Assistant Vice President Marketing, Geoff Northup
Assistant Vice President Service Delivery, Jerad Paolino
Vice President Senior Internal Audit Manager, Jeremy Ashby
Vice President Internal Audit, Lisa Pollock
Vice President Operations Audit, Supriya Namboodiri
Senior Vice President Marketing, Michael Walberg
Vice President Compliance Audit, L Shane Weekes
Vice President Business Development, Daniel Miller
Svp Client Marketing, Jennifer Showalter
Assistant Vice President Small Business Marketing, Jennifer Robinson
Vice President Marketing Governance, Kevin Clark
Senior Vice President, Robert Moore
Vice President Strategic Initiatives, Thomas Stevenson
Account Vice President Marketing, Jonathan Ball
Vice President Client Initiatives, Alba Pasqua
Vice President Purchasing Systems, Rekha Pata
Senior Vice President Carecredit Provider Experience, Nicole Keller
Assistant Vice President Operations, Kibwe Ali
Assistant Vice President Credit Analyst, Matthew Biehl
Vp Fraud Operations, Scott Briggs
Senior Vice President, Ricky Davis
Vp Human Resources, Shannel Sykes
Vice President Client Marketing, Matthew Coughlin
Vice President Client Marketing, Amy Sharp
Vice President Of Financial Planning And, Andres Ocariz
Vice President And Counsel, Bernadette Savage
Assistant Vice President Advertising, Renee Gilmore
Vice President Marketing Analytics, Brad Mischler
Vice President Sales Operations, Jeff Loch
Svp Risk Management, Michael Smith
Senior Vice President And Senior Regulatory Counsel, Daniel Loskove

Vice President Customer Experience, Valerie Foxman
Vp Finance, Philip Pitonyak
Vice President National Sales Leader, Christian Hansen
Vice President Client Marketing, Ameeta Patel
Vp Program Development, Kelly Heller
Vp Information Technology Pr, Joy Bowling
Vp Regulatory Reporting, Dimple Makhijani
Vice President Cloud Architecture, Robert Morel
Vice President General Manager P66, Eric Fatkin
Avp Learning Services, Loreen Clinton
Vice President Enterprise Operations, Andrew Navran
Assistant Vice President Process Control, John Somerfield
Assistant Vice President Credit Infrastructure, Tracy Harriss
Vice President Operations Facilities, Lisa Branum
Svp Financial Reporting, Steven Crossling
Avp, Mark Fahey
Vice President Marketing, Jason Dahl
Assistant Vice President Marketing, Nyoki Johnson
Asst. Vice President, Kavita Parwal
Svp And Chief Credit Risk Officer, Reda Supe
Vice President It Program Manager, Frederick Day
Senior Vice President Strategic Initiatives, Mary Giffels
Vice President Supplier Management, Greg Meyer
Vp Cra Investment, Syd Peacock
Vice President Senior Investigator, Michelle Minor
Senior Vice President Marketing, Gautam Borooah
Senior Vice President And Cra Officer, Alan Urie
Avp It Vendor Manager, Curtis Allison
Senior Vice President Consumer Banking Operations Leader, Kevin Button
Senior Vice President Retail Card Fp And A, Joseph Ressa
Vice President Technology Audits, Rajiv Virdy
Vice President Partner Experience, Brian Hoover
Senior Vice President And Chief Credit Officer Carecredit, Jonathan Smith
Vice President Srategic Sourcing Operations, Ralph Passarelli
Vice President Social Media, Nicole Johnson
Assistant Vice President Fraud Tactical Operations, Matthew Broughton
Vice President Of Sales, Frank Davis
Senior Vice President Business Development Leader Retail Card, Brian Abry
Vice President Credit Portfolio Management, Scott Savoy
Assistant Vice President Issue Analysis And Resolution, Barbara Kline
Assistant Vice President Operations, Cassandra Cruz
Vice President Enterprise Architecture, David Chau
Avp Enterprise Integration Services, Sree Gunturi
Vice President Information Technology Innovation And Mobile, Timothy Christensen
Svp And Gm Carecredit, Doug Hammond
Vice President Information Security, Raymond Lai
Senior Vice President Marketing, Kelli Nesseth
Vice President Senior Information Technology Project Manager, Gregg Peters
Vice President Information Technology Enterprise Operations, Sanjay Khatri
Vice President Hris, Jamie Rubin
Vice President Information Technology Service Delivery, David Gill
Senior Vice President Information Technology Client Relationships, Annemarie Jonsson
Vice President Marketing (digital Consumer Servicing), Bijayta Berger
Assistant Vice President Strategic Initiatives Controls And Countermeasures, Mark Underwood
Assistant Vice President B2b Digital Commerce, Robert Dornbusch

Vice President Collaboration And Technology Services, Scott Cicciari
Assistant Vice President Information Technology Supplier Management, Diane Autore
Assistant Vice President Information Technology Remediation, Pam Thomas
Vice President Technology Learning Leader, Nicholas Anaya
Vice President Information Technology Transformation And Strategic Initiatives, Michael Biron
Vice President Information Technology Infrastructure Transformation, JD Miller
Vice President Fpanda Information Technology, Russ Hunger
Assistant Vice President Information Technology Qa, Shravan Vemula
Vice President Cloud And Virtualization Architecture, Jeffrey Hoyt
Vice President Client Leader, Diane Hortman
Evp And Chief Customer Engagement Officer, Alberto Casellas
Auditors: KPMG LLP

LOCATIONS

HQ: Synchrony Financial
777 Long Ridge Road, Stamford, CT 06902
Phone: 203 585-2400
Web: www.synchronyfinancial.com

PRODUCTS/OPERATIONS

Selected Products
Credit Products
Commercial Credit Products
Credit Cards
Installment Loans

COMPETITORS

Alliance Data Systems	JPMorgan Chase
American Express	MasterCard
Bank of America	USAA
Capital One	Visa Inc
Citibank	Wells Fargo
Discover	

HISTORICAL FINANCIALS

Company Type: Public

Income Statement   FYE: December 31

	ASSETS ($ mil.)	NET INCOME ($ mil.)	INCOME AS % OF ASSETS	EMPLOYEES
12/19	104,826	3,747	3.6%	16,500
12/18	106,792	2,790	2.6%	16,500
12/17	95,808	1,935	2.0%	16,000
12/16	90,207	2,251	2.5%	15,000
12/15	84,135	2,214	2.6%	12,000
Annual Growth	5.7%	14.1%	—	8.3%

2019 Year-End Financials

Debt ratio: 18.95%	No. of shares (mil.): 615
Return on equity: 25.18%	Dividends
Cash ($ mil.): 12,147	Yield: 2.3%
Current ratio: —	Payout: 15.6%
Long-term debt ($ mil.): —	Market value ($ mil.): 22,179

	STOCK PRICE ($) FY Close	P/E High/Low		PER SHARE ($) Earnings	Dividends	Book Value
12/19	36.01	7	4	5.56	0.86	24.50
12/18	23.46	11	6	3.74	0.72	20.42
12/17	38.61	16	11	2.42	0.56	18.47
12/16	36.27	14	9	2.71	0.26	17.37
12/15	30.41	14	11	2.65	0.00	15.12
Annual Growth	4.3%	—	—	20.4%	—	12.8%

SYNNEX Corp

SYNNEX connects technology sellers with buyers and helps with customer service after the sale. The company distributes PCs peripherals software and consumer electronics from manufacturers that include HP Inc. Hewlett-Packard Enterprise Google Panasonic Lenovo Asus and Microsoft. Its Concentrix segment offers customer support services using phone chat web e-mail and digital print. In addition the company offers contract design and assembly build-to-order and configure-to-order services for manufacturers and systems integrators. SYNNEX depends on the US for about 65% of sales. In 2020 the company plans to separate its Concentrix segment into an independently publicly-traded company.

Operations

SYNNEX operates through two segments: Technology Solutions (TS) and Concentrix.

The TS segment which accounts for about 80% of the company's revenue distributes IT systems peripherals system components software networking equipment consumer electronics (CE) and complementary products. It also offers data center server and storage. In addition it provide systems design and integration solutions.

Concentrix accounting for the remaining sales offers a range of business process outsourcing (BPO) services such as technical support renewals management lead management direct sales customer service back office processing and IT outsourcing. HP Inc. is its biggest OEM supplier providing an eighth of revenue.

Geographic Reach

SYNNEX headquartered in Fremont California gets two-thirds of sales from the US and about 35% from other countries.

The company has about 65 distribution and administrative facilities in the US US Canada Japan Mexico China and Central and South America. Concentrix operates more than 275 delivery centers and administrative facilities in 40 countries throughout the world.

Sales and Marketing

SYNNEX sells to its large commercial government reseller and retail customers through its own sales force. SYNNEX markets its products and services to smaller resellers and OEMs through regional sales teams. The company also employs product management and business development specialists who focus on selling and promoting the products and services of selected suppliers or for specific end-market verticals.

The customer accounts for nearly 20% of SYNNEX's revenue

Financial Performance

SYNNEX has achieved unprecedented growth over the past four years with revenue reaching a company high of $23 billion in 2019 a 20% increase from 2018 boosted by contributions from acquisitions.

The Technology Solutions segment's revenue rose about 10% in 2019 from 2018 swathe increase was due to the strength in sales of peripherals IT systems software and networking products in the US. The Concentrix segment's revenue jumped about 20% in 2019 from 2018 primarily due to the impact of the acquisition of Convergys in October 2018 which was partially offset by the translation effect of the foreign currencies.

Net income increased to $500.7 million in 2019 from $300 million in 2018. The company had higher interest expense and finance charges in 2019 from 2017 because of borrowing money to pay for acquisitions and support growth of the Technology Solutions business.

SYNNEX had $231.1 million in cash and equivalents in 2019 compared to $462.0 million in 2018. In 2019 cash from operations stood at $550.0 million while investing activities used $146.8 million and financing activities used about $631.7 million.

Strategy

SYNNEX has made acquisitions in the past few years to strengthen the Technology Solutions and the Concentrix segments. The deals for Westcon-Comstor Americas' distribution business for $526.7 million in 2017 and Convergys for $2.3 billion in 2018 helped push SYNNEX over the $20 billion revenue mark in 2018. The deals also bolstered the company as competitors like Avnet and Tech Data also made acquisitions to expand.

SYNNEX end market strategy for its Technology Solutions business while focused on the Americas is expanding internationally on a selective basis in order to provide its distribution capabilities to OEMs in locations that meet their regional requirements.

SYNNEX has invested in making its operations more efficient increasing the amount of automation and adding more digital practices with higher margins.

SYNNEX's Hyve data center business hasn't performed to expectations and the company continues to work to diversify Hyve's customers and improve its profitability.

Company Background

Robert Huang founded SYNNEX in 1980. The company has grown with the help of acquisitions; it bought about 25 companies from 1997-2018. The company's name comes from the combination of synergy and nexus.

EXECUTIVES

President And Ceo, Kevin M. Murai, age 57, $633,794 total compensation
President Hyve Solutions, Stephen Ichinaga, age 59
President North American Technology Solutions, Peter Larocque, age 59, $459,499 total compensation
President Synnex Canada, Mitchell P. Martin, age 57
Svp And Cio, Gary Gulmon, age 59
Svp Marketing North America, Robert L. (Bob) Stegner
Coo, Dennis Polk, age 54, $459,499 total compensation
Cfo, Marshall Witt, $437,986 total compensation
President New Age Electronics, Fred Towns
Evp; President Concentrix, Christopher (Chris) Caldwell, $441,670 total compensation
Corporate Vice President Business Operations, Gina Rugani
Vice President, Steve Heslop
Vice President Of Procurement, Cynthia Su
Senior Vice President Information Technology, Robert Sturycz
Vice President Sales, Willa Flemate
Assistant Vice President Product Management, Sarah Lin
Vice President Internal Audit, Dana Aghai-Yazdi
Vice President Hp Enterprise Sales, Peter Montana
National Account Manager, Keith Cox
Assistant Vice President Commercial Sales Smb, John Phillips
Senior Vice President Sales New Age Electronics, Eric Kirkendall
Senior Vice President Systems Integration, Steve Ichinaga
Vice President Marketing Technology Solutions Divi, Denna Mensch
Vice President Of Enterprise Products, Doug Bone
Senior Vice President Operations, Tim Rush
Executive Vice President And President Of Concentrix Corporation, Chris Caldwell
Senior Vice President Marketing North America, Bob Stegner
Senior Counsel (vice President, Daniel Brennan
Senior Vice President Sales And Account Management Concetrix Corporation, Rick Rosso
Senior Vice President Europe Global Applications Development Solutions Pricing And Strategic Pro, Philip Cassidy
Senior Vice President Operations And Delivery Concentrix Corporation, Winnie Sun
Senior Vice President Information Systems And Infosec Security Concentrix Corporation, Guy Brosseau
Vice President Finance, Charlie Spano
Vice President Of Enterprise Sales, Synnex Hpenterprise
Vice President Corporate Controller, Lee Adair
Vice President Cloud And Emerging Services, Darren Harbaugh
Vice President Retail Product Management, Pierre Montminy
Svp Concetrix Insurance Solutions, Marc Fedor
Svp High Value Services Concentrix Corporation, Kathy Juve
Board Member, Andrea Zulberti
Chairman, Dwight Steffensen, age 77
Vice Chairman, Calvin Currie
Auditors: KPMG LLP

LOCATIONS

HQ: SYNNEX Corp
44201 Nobel Drive, Fremont, CA 94538
Phone: 510 656-3333
Web: www.synnex.com

2018 Sales

	$ mil.	% of total
United States	14,352	72
Canada	1,801	9
Other	3,898	19
Total	**20,054**	**100**

PRODUCTS/OPERATIONS

2018 Sales

	$ mil.	% of total
Technology solutions	17,609	88
Concentrix	2,463	12
Inter-segment	(18.4)	-
Total	**20,054**	**100**

2018 Sales

	$ mil.	% of total
Products	17,609	88
Services	2,445	12
Total	**20,054**	**100**

Selected Subsidiaries

Concentrix Technologies
ComputerLand Corporation
Concentrix Technologies (India) Private Limited
Concentrix Corporation
Concentrix Costa Rica S.A.
Concentrix Free Trade Zone S.A.
Concentrix HK Limited
Concentrix Nicaragua S.A
Sennex Enterprises Limited
SIT Funding Corporation
SYNNEX Canada Limited

SYNNEX Information Technologies (Beijing) Ltd
SYNNEX Information Technologies (Chengdu) Ltd
SYNNEX Information Technologies (China) Ltd
SYNNEX Infotec Corporation
SYNNEX de Mé:xico S.A. de C.V
SYNNEX Software Technologies (HK) Limited
SYNNEX-Concentrix Corporation
SYNNEX-Concentrix UK Limited

Selected Services

Distribution
  Contract assembly
  Distribution services
  Logistics services
Global Business Services
  Automated service renewals software
  Customer services
  Hosted renewals services software in Europe
  (RenewalsManager)
  Financing services
  Marketing services
  Outsourced back-office services
  Technical support services

COMPETITORS

Accenture	Plexus
Arrow Electronics	Premier Farnell
Avnet	Sanmina
Benchmark Electronics	ScanSource
Conduent	Tech Data
Hon Hai	Teleperformance
Ingram Micro	Wistron
Jabil	

HISTORICAL FINANCIALS

Company Type: Public

Income Statement

FYE: November 30

	REVENUE ($ mil.)	NET INCOME ($ mil.)	NET PROFIT MARGIN	EMPLOYEES
11/20	24,675	529	2.1%	277,900
11/19	23,757	500	2.1%	240,900
11/18	20,053	300	1.5%	231,600
11/17	17,045	301	1.8%	113,600
11/16	14,061	234	1.7%	110,000
Annual Growth	15.1%	22.5%	—	26.1%

2020 Year-End Financials

Debt ratio: 20.54%
Return on equity: 12.99%
Cash ($ mil.): 1,564
Current ratio: 1.56
Long-term debt ($ mil.): 2,608

No. of shares (mil.): 51
Dividends
Yield: 1.7%
Payout: 29.7%
Market value ($ mil.): 8,197

	STOCK PRICE ($) FY Close	P/E High/Low		PER SHARE ($) Earnings	Dividends	Book Value
11/20	160.31	16	6	10.21	1.15	84.85
11/19	122.81	13	8	9.74	1.50	74.64
11/18	80.74	19	10	7.19	1.40	67.70
11/17	136.20	18	14	7.51	1.05	57.56
11/16	116.91	20	13	5.88	0.85	50.05
Annual Growth	8.2%		—	14.8%	7.8%	14.1%

Synovus Financial Corp

Synovus Financial has a nose for community banking. The holding company owns flagship subsidiary Synovus Bank and more than 25 locally branded banking divisions that offer deposit accounts and consumer and business loans in Alabama Florida Georgia South Carolina and Tennessee. Through more than 280 branches the bank provides checking and savings accounts loans and mortgages and credit cards. Other divisions offer insurance private banking wealth and asset management and other financial services. Nonbank subsidiaries include Synovus Mortgage Synovus Trust investment bank and brokerage Synovus Securities and GLOBALT which provides asset management and financial planning services.

Geographic Reach

Georgia-based Synovus Financial has about 130 bank branches in Georgia. Florida is the bank's second largest market with nearly 50 branches while Alabama and South Carolina are home to more than 40 each.

Financial Performance

While the bank reported a 10% decline in revenue in 2013 versus 2012 to $1.18 billion and an 81% plunge in net income (to $159.4 million) it did make some progress on the long road to recovery. Significantly the bank redeemed its obligations under TARP (troubled asset relief program) in July 2013 funding more than two-thirds of the TARP redemption with internally available funds. The firm redeemed the remainder with proceeds from offerings of its common and preferred stock. Its loan portfolio grew by about $516 million up nearly 3% versus 2012. Credit quality also continued to improve while the bank lowered expenses.

Synovus blamed its continuing revenue slide on lower interest and non-interest income in 2013 versus 2012. Interest income fell on lower income on loans and investment securities. Non-interest income suffered relative to 2012 when the bank experienced higher levels of investment securities gains and gains on private equity investments as well as a decline in income from mortgage banking.

Strategy

Synovus has been cutting costs raising capital and improving efficiency in the aftermath of the residential and commercial real estate bust that hit the southeastern US particularly hard. During the dark days of the banking crisis (2008 to 2009) the company slashed about 10% of its workforce and it cut approximately 10% more in 2010 and 2011. It also closed nearly 40 branches and consolidated others.

Also Synovus which has traditionally maintained separate charters and local boards of directors for its subsidiary banks consolidated all of its charters into one in 2010 in order to reduce complexity and improve efficiency. Synovus also consolidated by merging some of its banks in Georgia and Florida; two of its Florida banking subsidiaries (one de novo and the other formed in the merger of three subsidiaries' banking charters) have taken the Synovus Bank brand a new strategy for the company.

The company returned to profitability in 2012 and remained profitable (although considerably less so) in 2013. To right itself Synovus has deemphasized commercial real estate lending and increased its focus on commercial and industrial banking including specialized services such as asset-based lending international banking and treasury management in an effort to increase revenue. The company is courting large corporate clients in the health care manufacturing distribution financial services natural resources and transportation sectors. Among smaller enterprises it targets professional practices such as physicians attorneys and accountants particularly for its private banking business.

Mergers and Acquisitions

In May 2013 Synovus assumed $56.8 million in deposits that belonged to failed Sunrise Bank from its receiver the FDIC. As part of the deal the bank acquired $492000 in loans.

The company bought specialty finance firm Entaire Global in October 2016. Entaire a private life insurance premium finance lender primarily serves small businesses. Synovus which is aiming to diversify its loan portfolio with the purchase paid an initial $30 million; it will pay extra earnings-based payments over a period of up to five years.

EXECUTIVES

Evp And Coo, Allen J. Gula, age 65, $434,192 total compensation
Evp And Chief Risk Officer, Mark G. Holladay, age 64, $428,454 total compensation
Evp And Chief Retail Banking Officer, D. Wayne Akins, age 57
Chairman And Ceo, Kessel D. Stelling, age 64, $962,269 total compensation
Evp Financial Management Services, J. Barton Singleton, age 56, $390,606 total compensation
Evp And Chief Credit Officer, Kevin J. Howard, age 55
Evp And Chief Community Banking Officer, R. Dallis (Roy) Copeland, age 51, $412,336 total compensation
Evp And Chief Corporate Banking Officer, Curtis J. Perry, age 57
Evp And Cfo, Kevin S. Blair
Cio, Renee S. Roth
Cto, Santosh Kokate
Evp General Counsel And Secretary, Allan E. Kamensky, age 59, $417,229 total compensation
Chief Information Security Officer, Kevin P. Gowen
Vice President Of Regional Sales, Ron Ward
Executive Vice President Corporate Affairs, Calvin Smyre
Vice President Senior Credit Analyst, Lisa McCurdy
Senior Vice President Asset Liability Management, Joseph M Lowery
Senior Vice President Deputy General Counsel, Michael Smith
Senior Vice President Diversity And Career Resources, Audrey Hollingsworth
Senior Vice President Private Wealth Advisor, Michelle Mcclellan
Executive Vice President Risk And Compliance, John Latimer
Vice President, Susan Pitts
Vice President Product Management, Lynn White
Executive Vice President Retail Branches Columbus Band And Trust, Carolynn Obleton
Senior Vice President And Chief Audit Executive, Stephen Sawyer
Vice President Accounting Manager, Liz Gobbel
Vice President Tax Compliance Manager, Jim Buchs
Vice President And Director Compliance, Deborah Kent-Cochran
Senior Vice President, Brick F Luke
Senior Vice President, Jason Ninas
Senior Vice President Facility Management Division, Mike Webb
Vice President Commercial Banking, Michael Harley
Vice President Retail Market Manager, Stephan Hollis
Vice President, Joseph Sumner
Vice President Finance Account Manager, Richard Pettit

Vice President Senior Business Analyst Lender, Alvena Pareja
Senior Vice President, Dan Summers
Vice President Commercial Real Estate, Mark Mathews
Senior Vice President Director Of Correspondent Banking, Richard Lane
Senior Vice President And Director Lcbg East, Michael Sawicki
Vice President, Phyllis Lyons
Group Vice President, Pam Wall
Vice President, Sandy Gowan
Senior Vice President, Jeff Cox
Evp Commercial Real Estate Division, Paige Collier
Vice President Commercial Banking, Patrick Ahern
Senior Vice President Market Executive, Jennifer Mulligan
Senior Vice President, Daniel Bass
Senior Vice President Capital Markets, Bobby Dillon
Senior Vice President, David O'rear
Vice President Of Marketing, Judith Dearborn
Evp And President Florida, Kent Ellert
Assistant Vice President Retail Market Manager, Leteria Waters
Senior Vice President, Wayne Gray
Vp And Commercial Banker, Gregory Alt
Senior Vice President Corporate Banking, Brad Beard
Vice President Retail Market Manager, Pamela Stith
Assistant Vice President Branch Manager, Eileen Burton
Senior Vice President, Rod Payton
Senior Vice President Market President, Patrick Murphy
Assistant Vice President, Janice Vagner
Vice President Investments, Robert Duncan
Vice President And Commercial Banker, Marc Powell
Vice President, Stephen Taylor
Senior Vice President Market Manager, Joseph Levi
Vice President Commercial Banking, Joseph Berardi
Vice President, Tim Thompson
Board Member, Jennifer Brooke
Auditors: KPMG LLP

LOCATIONS

HQ: Synovus Financial Corp
1111 Bay Avenue, Suite 500, Columbus, GA 31901
Phone: 706 6415-6500
Web: www.synovus.com

Bank Branch Locations

	No.
Georgia	114
Florida	48
South Carolina	38
Alabama	37
Tennessee	11
Total	**248**

PRODUCTS/OPERATIONS

2016 Sales

	$ mil.	% of total
Interest income:		
Loans including fees	944	73
Investment securities available for sale	67	5
Trading account assets	0	-
Mortgage loans held for sale	2	-
Federal Reserve Bank balances	4	-
Other earning assets	4	-
Non-interest income:		
Service charges on deposit accounts	81	6
Fiduciary and asset management fees	46	4
Bankcard fees	33	3
Other non-interest income	34	3
Brokerage revenue	27	2
Mortgage banking income	24	2
Other fee income	20	2
Investment securities gains net	6	-
Total	**1,296**	**100**

COMPETITORS

BB&T	First Citizens
BBVA Compass Bancshares	BancShares
	First Horizon
BBX Capital	Regions Financial
BancorpSouth	SunTrust
Bank of America	Trustmark
Citigroup	Wells Fargo

HISTORICAL FINANCIALS

Company Type: Public

Income Statement — FYE: December 31

	ASSETS ($ mil.)	NET INCOME ($ mil.)	INCOME AS % OF ASSETS	EMPLOYEES
12/19	48,203	563	1.2%	5,389
12/18	32,669	428	1.3%	4,651
12/17	31,221	275	0.9%	4,541
12/16	30,104	246	0.8%	4,436
12/15	28,792	226	0.8%	4,452
Annual Growth	**13.7%**	**25.7%**	**—**	**4.9%**

2019 Year-End Financials

Debt ratio: 1.77%
Return on equity: 13.96%
Cash ($ mil.): 556
Current ratio: —
Long-term debt ($ mil.): —

No. of shares (mil.): 147
Dividends
  Yield: 3.0%
  Payout: 35.5%
Market value ($ mil.): 5,769

	STOCK PRICE ($) FY Close	P/E High/Low		PER SHARE ($) Earnings	Dividends	Book Value
12/19	39.20	11	9	3.47	1.20	33.58
12/18	31.99	16	9	3.47	1.00	27.05
12/17	47.94	23	18	2.17	0.60	24.91
12/16	41.08	22	14	1.89	0.48	23.95
12/15	32.38	21	15	1.62	0.42	23.16
Annual Growth	**4.9%**	**—**	**—**	**21.0%**	**30.0%**	**9.7%**

Sysco Corp

Sysco is one of the top food distributor in the US. The company serves more than 625000 customer locations in the US and internationally in the restaurant (standalone and chain) healthcare and education and hotel industries among others. Its 325-plus distribution centers and some 14000 delivery vehicles deliver branded and private-label food — including fresh frozen and canned foods and specialty and meat products — as well as non-food items such as silverware and utensils. The SYGMA Network focuses on supplying specific chain restaurants. The US accounts for more than 80% of sales. The company acquired Armstrong Produce Kula Produce and J. Kings Food Service Professionals in late 2019.

Operations

Sysco operates through three primary segments: US Foodservice International Foodservice and SYGMA.

The US Foodservice business generates some 70% of total sales and consists of its food and non-food delivery operations in the US including its custom-cut meat and seafood companies specialty produce business and specialty imports. The International Foodservice segment which generates about 20% of sales delivers similar product lines to its customers in Canada Europe (primarily the UK France Ireland and Sweden) the Bahamas Mexico Costa Rica and Panama.

The SYGMA segment accounts for roughly 10% of sales and consists of Sysco's customized distribution to select chain restaurants.

Overall the fresh and frozen meats category accounts for about 20% of sales with the canned and dry products and frozen products each accounts for more than 15% bakery other categories each bringing in about 10%.

Geographic Reach

Houston-based Sysco operates more than 170 US distribution facilities more than half its total; the country accounts for more than 80% of sales.

Its other facilities are found in about a dozen other countries notably Canada (more than 30 sites and nearly 10% of sales) the UK (around 65 sites and some 5% of sales) and France (nearly 30 sites and less than 5% of sales).

Sales and Marketing

Sysco has a huge client base with more than 625000 customer locations including restaurants (more than 60% of revenue) hospitals nursing homes schools hotels and motels industrial caterers and other foodservice providers.

It claims to serve more than 15% of approximately $310 billion foodservice market.

Financial Performance

Except in 2020 the company's revenue has been rising in the last five years with an overall growth of 5% between 2016 and 2020. Net earnings has been climbing in the same period.

Sysco's revenue declined 12% from $60.1 billion in 2019 to $52.9 billion in 2020. All of the company's segments decline in 2020.

Net income in 2020 was $215.5 billion an 87% decrease from the previous year. Sysco had lower gross profit and higher operating expenses.

Cash at the end of 2020 totaled $6.1 billion. Operating activities generated $1.6 billion while investing activities used $756.3 million. Financing activities used another $4.7 billion mainly for debt repayments.

Strategy

An element of the company's strategy includes further expansion of operations into international markets and the establishment of international procurement organizations. Another element of its strategy includes the possibility of expansion into businesses that are closely related or complementary to but not currently part of its core foodservice distribution business.

Mergers and Acquisitions

Sysco is an acquisitive company using purchases to bolster its market strength add to its product portfolio and expand geographically.

In late 2019 Sysco acquired Armstrong Produce and Kula Produce Hawaii-based broadline fresh produce wholesalers and distributors with approximately $155 million in combined annual revenue. The acquired companies operate as part of FreshPoint Sysco's specialty produce company.

In addition to late 2019 acquisition Sysco also acquired J. Kings Food Service Professionals a New York broadline distributor with approximately $150 million in annual sales. J. Kings' strong local presence combined with Sysco's scale and depth provides its customers with even more of what they need to be successful in the competitive New York area market. The company paid a total of $142.8 million for all acquisitions in late 2019.

In early 2019 Sysco acquired J & M Wholesale Meats and Imperio Foods Inc. leading California distributors with approximately $44 million in combined annual sales. The acquisition of businesses is a complementary adjacency to Sysco's existing California area business and provides Sysco with the opportunity to further extend its reach into the Hispanic customer segment.

Company Background

Sysco was founded in 1969 when John Baugh a Houston wholesale food distributor formed a national distribution company with the owners of eight other US wholesalers. The company went public in 1970 and has grown organically as well as through major acquisitions.

HISTORY

Sysco was founded in 1969 when John Baugh a Houston wholesale food distributor formed a national distribution company with the owners of eight other US wholesalers. Joining Baugh's Zero Foods of Houston to form Sysco were Frost-Pack Distributing (Grand Rapids Michigan) Louisville Grocery (Louisville Kentucky) Plantation Foods (Miami) Thomas Foods and its Justrite subsidiary (Cincinnati) Wicker (Dallas) Food Service Company (Houston) Global Frozen Foods (New York) and Texas Wholesale Grocery (Dallas). The company went public in 1970. Sysco which derives its name from Systems and Services Company benefited from Baugh's recognition of the trend toward dining out. Until Sysco was formed small independent operators almost exclusively provided food distribution to restaurants hotels and other non-grocers.

In the 2000s Sysco acquired smaller competitors who hadn't fared quite as well during the downturn. In 2013 the company acquired food-service operations in Nassau Bahamas; San Francisco California; San Jose California; Stockton California; Ontario Canada; Quebec Canada; Orlando Florida; Dublin Ireland; St. Cloud Minnesota; Co. Down Northern Ireland; Greenville Ohio; and Houston Texas.

Its 2012 acquisition of European Imports Ltd. helped it expand into the specialty import products segment. Purchasing Crossgar a leading privately owned foodservice supplier in Northern Ireland strengthened Sysco's presence on the island and complemented its 2009 acquisition of Pallas Foods. Other 2012 conquests include Appert's Foodservice Buchy Food Service Central Seafood Company and Metro Richelieu's Distagro. Their combined annual revenues were about $520 million.

In a sweeping move for the foodservice industry Sysco in late 2013 attempted to acquire its rival U.S. Foods for $3.5 billion. The deal would have boosted its share of the US market to about 25% from about 18%. By combining Sysco and US Foods the company expected to achieve annual synergies of at least $600 million and estimated annual sales of approximately $65 billion. The deal was pushed back due to delays in talks with anti-trust regulators and the parties terminated to planned transaction in 2015 after failing to obtain regulator approvals.

EXECUTIVES

Assistant Vp Of Hr, Susan Billiot
Vice President Personnel, David Seaver
Svp Marketing, William W. (Bill) Goetz
Vice President, Charles Staes
Vice President Sysco President Specialtymeatco, Louis Nasir
Vp Corporate Social Responsibility, Catherine Kayser
Vice President, Kirk Drummond
Vp Financial Reporting, Bob Culak
Vice President Supply Chain, Robert Howell
Senior Vice President Canadian Foodservi, G Humphries
Evp Merchandising And Sysco Business Services, William B. (Bill) Day, age 63, $508,333 total compensation
Evp Supply Chain, R. Scott Charlton, age 61
Svp International Foodservice Operations Americas, Scott A. Sonnemaker
President And Ceo Sysco Food Services Of Charlotte, William J. (Bill) DeLaney, age 64, $1,245,833 total compensation
President And Coo, Thomas L. (Tom) Bené, age 58, $770,833 total compensation
Evp Human Resources, Paul T. Moskowitz, age 56
Svp U.s. Foodservice Operations, Greg D. Bertrand, age 56
Evp Administration And Corporate Secretary, Russell T. Libby, age 54, $590,125 total compensation
Svp Market Segment Strategy And President Sysco Ventures (cake), Brian C. Beach
Evp And Cfo, Joel T. Grade, age 50, $605,833 total compensation
Evp And Cto, Wayne Shurts, age 61, $621,602 total compensation
Vice President, Loren Gausman
Vice President Human Resources Search, Mark Wisnoski
Vice President Merchandising, Brian Smith
Vice President Information Systems, Ira Wilson
Southwest Market Vice President Of Merchandising, Bobby Rose
Vice President Agreement Services, David L Valentine
Vice President National Accounts, Justin Hiraki
Vice President Associate General Counsel Transactions, Carmen Ng
Vp Human Resources, Tony Watson
Vice President Of Sales, Troy Willis
Vice President Merchandising, David Haberkorn
Vice President Merchandising Services, Robert Thurber
Vice President Of Marketing, Chad Lombardo
Vice President Systems, Kristin Lindsay
Executive Vice President, Stephen Smith
Vice President Business Development, Gregory Keller
Senior Vice President Sourcing, Joseph Barton
Assistant Vice President Of Customer Services, Rita Kolberg
Vp Business Resources, Paul Hudson
Senior Vice President Of Operations Western Region, Arthur Swenka
Vice President, Dennis Hernandez
Regional Vice President, Gary Hammer
Vice President Of Merchandising, Jeff Hartley
Sr Vp Operations, Chuck Fraser
Vice President Corporate Business Development, Greg Keller
Assistant Vice President Merchandising Center Of The Plate Supply Chain Manager, Jeff Kimmich
Vice President Business Development National Accounts, Amy Davis-Smith
Vice President Of Operations, William Mastrosimone
Vice President Merchandising, Gail Mccoy

Executive Vice President Sysco Food Services, Timothy Peterzen
Vice President Of Marketing, Sharon Armentrout
Vice President Of Merchandising, Dale Kahn
Vice President Of Information Technology, Lucas Wagner
Vice President Finance, Gregory Lee
Vice President Accounts Payable, Alison Peterman
Vice President Of Finance, Alma Vega
Vp Multi Unit Accounts, Skip Fauber
Vice President, Daniel Gentry
Vice President, Julie Swan
Senior Vice President Sales And Marketing, Jim Hope
Assistant Vice President Of Marketing, Tracey Mills
Vice President Call Center, Alena Galsnte
Vice President Of Merchandising, Richard Ashlock
National Account Manager, Cindy Rankin
Vice President Supply Chain Management, Masao Nishi
Vice President Human Resources, Michele Giordano
Vice President Sales, John Counts
Vice President Sales Marketing, John Miko
Vice President, Bruce Briggs
Vice President Human Resources, Sabrina Knouse
Vice President Marketing, Barry Ivy
Vice President Brand Executive, David Montpetit
Senior Vice President Marketing, Bill Goetz
Vice President Sales, Eric Kane
Senior Vice President Merchandising, Brian R Todd
Principal Vice President Of Finance And Administ
Vice President Finance And Administration, Erica Koranda
Executive Vice President, Thaire Bryant
Vice President Customer Service, Jackie Mack
Vice President Sales And Marketing, Keith Lusk
Vice President Merchandising, John Riczo
Senior Vice President, Ken Beckwith
Senior Vice President Of Finance, Ajoy Karna
Vice President Warehouse And Logistics Operations, George Moses
Senior Vice President Contract Sales Executive Officer, Kent Humphries
Vice President, Navin Advani
Vice President Of Human Resources, Sue Billiot
Senior Vice President, Scott Charlton
Vice President Of Operations, Rudy Villanueva
Vice President Merchandising, David Passaro
National Account Manager, Kristin Smith
Vp Merchandising, Brian Mathers
Vice President Sales, John Woolery
National Sales Manager, Hugh Morgan
National Account Manager, Carol Vogt
Vice President Merchandising And Marketing, Christopher Flint
Vice President, Heike Gillman
Vice President Finance, Enrique Becerra
National Account Manager, Martin Escatel
National Account Manager, Clay Steadham
Market Vp Of Merchandising Northeast, Eric Zeilor
Vice President Field Transformation, Matt Whitney
Sr.vp Operations, Arvid Klein
Vp Of Finance And Cfo Of Spokane, Jeff Kolcum
Sr Vp Merchandising And Marketing, Debbie Morey
National Account Manager, Tracy Jones
Vice President Human Resources, Sharon Parker
Vice President Human Resources, Brett Appleberg
Vice President Of Sales, Melissa White
Vice President Of Merchandising, Raymond Gambow
Vice President Merchandising, Kathleen Griego
Vice President Of Human Resources, Jessica Mihal
Senior Vice President Operations, Ray Nicholas
Vice President Total Rewards, Erin Packwood
Vp Compliance, Jose Colondres
Vp Government Relations, Gerald Kunde
Vice President Government Relations, Chip Kunde
Vice President Marketing, Maureen Quirk
Vice President And Treasurer, Gregory Keyes

Vp Sysco Business Services, Chris Davis
Vice President Operations, Justin Dalton
Vp Operations, Grady Metoyer
Vp Of Finance And Cfo Of Sysco San Diego, Jim Harlan
Vice President National Sales, Sean O'shea
Government Relations, Brad Christie
Vice President Operations, John Petrossian
Regional Vice President Multi Unit Healthcare Hospitality Sales, Victoria Gardner
Vp Operations, Kevin Proulx
Vice President Of Sales, Troy S Willis
Regional Vice President Healthcare, Greg Mcculloch
National Sales Manager, Hugh G Morgan
Vice President Marketing, Maureen M Quirk
Vice President Human Resources Business Partner, Douangchan Steele
Vice President And Human Resources Business Partner, Terri L Clark
Vice President Of Purchasing, Robert C Thurber
National Account Manager, Kelly P Garcia
Vice President Of Human Resources, John J Fraser
Vice President And General Manager, Joe Napoli
Vice President And Treasurer, Gregory S Keyes
Vice President Finance, Enrique X Becerra
Regional Vice President Human Resources, Bettina Brayshaw
National Account Manager, Sonnie Broxton
Vice President Of Operations, Michael R Caldwell
Market Vice President Merchandising, Ruth Warthen
Vice President National Accounts Restaurant, Cary T Nelms
Market Vice President Operations, Michael Oller
Vice President Facilities Construction Real Estate, Theodore W Speas
Vice President National Accounts Foodservice Management, Ryan Dewitt
Vice President, Chris Shepardson
Vice President Sales And Marketing, Thomas Lessaris
National Account Manager, Kelly Garcia
Auditors: Ernst & Young LLP

LOCATIONS

HQ: Sysco Corp
  1390 Enclave Parkway, Houston, TX 77077-2099
Phone: 281 584-1390   **Fax:** 281 584-2880
Web: www.sysco.com

2019 Sales

	$ mil.	% of total
US	48,257	80
Canada	4,660	8
UK	3,134	5
France	1,582	3
Other	2,481	4
Total	**60,114**	**100**

PRODUCTS/OPERATIONS

2019 Sales

	$ mil.	% of total
US Foodservice	41,288	69
International Foodservice	11,493	19
SYGMA	6,244	10
Other	1,089	2
Total	**60,114**	**100**

2019 Sales

	$ mil.	% of total
Fresh & frozen meats	11,570	19
Canned & dry food	9,941	16
Frozen fruits vegetables bakery & other	8,978	15
Dairy products	6,114	10
Poultry	5,848	10
Fresh produce	5,066	8
Paper & disposables	3,960	7
Seafood	3,382	6
Beverage products	2,309	4
Other	2,946	5
Total	**60,114**	**100**

COMPETITORS

Ben E. Keith	Performance Food Group
Edward Don	Reinhart FoodService
Golden State Foods	Shamrock Foods
Gordon Food Service	US Foods
MAINES	UniPro Foodservice
McLane Foodservice	
Meadowbrook Meat Company	

HISTORICAL FINANCIALS

Company Type: Public

Income Statement

FYE: June 27

	REVENUE ($ mil.)	NET INCOME ($ mil.)	NET PROFIT MARGIN	EMPLOYEES
06/20	52,893	215	0.4%	57,000
06/19	60,113	1,674	2.8%	69,000
06/18*	58,727	1,430	2.4%	67,000
07/17	55,371	1,142	2.1%	66,500
07/16	50,366	949	1.9%	51,900
Annual Growth	**1.2%**	**(31.0%)**	**—**	**2.4%**

*Fiscal year change

2020 Year-End Financials

Debt ratio: 63.83%
Return on equity: 11.80%
Cash ($ mil.): 6,059
Current ratio: 1.84
Long-term debt ($ mil.): 12,902

No. of shares (mil.): 508
Dividends
  Yield: 0.0%
  Payout: 400.0%
Market value ($ mil.): 26,582

	STOCK PRICE ($) FY Close	P/E High/Low	PER SHARE ($) Earnings	Dividends	Book Value
06/20	52.30	204 74	0.42	1.68	2.28
06/19	70.72	23 19	3.20	1.50	4.88
06/18*	68.29	25 18	2.70	1.38	4.82
07/17	50.33	27 23	2.08	0.97	4.49
07/16	50.73	31 21	1.64	1.23	6.22
Annual Growth	**0.8%**	**—**	**(28.9%)**	**8.1%**	**(22.2%)**

*Fiscal year change

T-Mobile US Inc

T-Mobile US is one of the largest providers of wireless voice and data communications services in the US with more than 81 million customers. The company's T-Mobile and Metro by T-Mobile (formerly MetroPCS) subscribers use its networks domestically and can connect to the compatible network of Deutsche Telekom which owns 30% of T-Mobile when in Europe. In addition T-Mobile sells phones tablets and accessories from such vendors as Apple Samsung and Google. It has about 2200 T-Mobile and MetroPCS branded retail sites (ranging from kiosks to stores). In 2018 T-Mobile and Sprint agreed to combine in a $26.5 billion deal. US regulators are studying the proposed transaction.

Operations

T-Mobile provides wireless communications and equipment sales including branded postpaid branded prepaid wholesale and equipment sales.

Branded postpaid generally provides wireless communication services for phones mobile broadband devices such as tablets and wearables. The business accounts for about 50% of the total revenue.

Branded prepaid generally provides wireless communication services but the customers will pay in advance. The company offers prepaid service through the T-Mobile and Metro by T-Mobile brands. The business accounts for more than 20% of revenue.

Equipment sales include the sales of phones tablets wearables and accessories. Equipment sales account for about 25% of the total revenue.

The Wholesale business includes sales to machine-to-machine and Mobile Virtual Network Operator customers that operate on the T-Mobile network but are managed by wholesale partners. The business accounts for about 5% of revenue.

Geographic Reach

T-Mobile US based in Bellevue Washington gets all of its revenue from the US including Puerto Rico and the US Virgin Islands. The company has more than 100 facilities including switch centers data centers call centers and warehouses around the country. It also has some 64000 macro towers and 21000 distributed antenna systems and small cell sites in the US.

Sales and Marketing

T-Mobile US has about 2200 T-Mobile and Metro by T-Mobile stores and kiosks around the US.

The company's largest customer segment is postpaid which accounts for more than half of its customers and generates around 65% sales. The prepaid segment includes about a quarter of customers and accounts for about 30% of revenue; wholesale clients roaming charges and other services account for the remaining revenue.

Financial Performance

T-Mobile's revenue has grown at a 9% a year clip over five years rising from $29.5 billion in 2015 to $43.3 billion in 2018. Net income rose even faster reaching $4.5 billion in 2017 (due to a tax benefit) from $247 million in 2014.

In 2018 sales rose 7% from $40.6 billion in 2017 driven by higher service and equipment revenue. Service revenue was up 6% year-to-year on growth in existing and new markets which included the T-Mobile ONE Unlimited 55+ and T-Mobile ONE Military plans. Other factors were lower customer turnover growth in connected devices and contributions from Metro by T-Mobile brand. Equipment revenue increased 7% due to a higher average revenue per device sold. That more than offset a decrease in the number of devices sold.

T-Mobile reported $2.9 billion in 2018 net income a 36% decrease from 2017 mainly because of higher taxes in 2018 after a tax benefit in 2017.

The company's cash on hand totaled $1.2 billion in 2018 about even with 2017's cash. In 2018 operations generated $3.9 billion in cash while investing activities used $579 million and financing activities used $3.3 billion.

T-Mobile has significant long-term debt $26.7 billion which could limit flexibility in reacting to business changes or pursuing growth opportunities. In 2018 however interest expense was $835 million compared to more than $1 billion in each of the previous two years.

Strategy

T-Mobile calls itself the Un-carrier because of its strategy upending the wireless market by offering unlimited data at lower cost and doing away with annual service plans among other changes. As other carriers such as Verizon and AT&T followed suit T-Mobile offered more "un-carrier" programs such as unlimited streaming of Netflix. Such offerings have helped increase the number of subscribers has risen by more than 5 million a year for five straight years before dropping to just more than 4 million new customers in 2018. Further the costs associated with the Netflix offering reduced average revenue per user by 32 cents in 2018 from 2017.

T-Mobile is putting its Layer3 acquisition to work in offering a Pay-TV service called TVision. Rolled out in the 2019 second quarter the service offers local channels sports and traditional pay channels. The cost $100 a month is on par with competitor offerings but T-Mobile vows not to raise prices.

T-Mobile is building out 5G across the US including in six of the top 10 markets with plans to have a nationwide standards-based network in place in 2020. The capability of a built-out 5G network is one of T-Mobile's selling points for its merger with Sprint.

Despite its growth T-Mobile is still much smaller than Verizon and AT&T. Even the combination of T-Mobile the third biggest provider and Sprint the fourth biggest would make the combined company a bigger third place competitor. Verizon and AT&T have more resources and they've added other capabilities such as content that gives them a broader reach.

Mergers and Acquisitions
For the third time Sprint and T-Mobile majority-owned by Deutsche Telekom agreed to team up in a $26.5 billion deal that would form the third largest wireless carrier after Verizon Communications and AT&T Inc. Previous attempts were scuttled by regulators' antitrust concerns. Sprint and T-Mobile hope that a new regulatory environment gives them a better chance this time. They promised to keep prices low for consumers while using their assets to build a robust 5G network the next generation of wireless technology. The merged company would take the T-Mobile name. The deal came together once Softbank Sprint's majority owner agreed to give Deutsche Telekom control of the combined company. Many of the antitrust issues that ended the previous merger attempts remain. T-Mobile and Sprint must overcome concerns that so much of the US's wireless service would be provided by just three companies.

In 2018 T-Mobile acquired Layer3 TV. T-Mobile rolled out a TV service TVision built on Layer3 technology in 2019.

EXECUTIVES

Evp And Cio, Gary A. King, $488,462 total compensation
Vice President Controller, Patricia L Miller
President And Ceo, John J. Legere, $1,250,000 total compensation
Coo, G. Michael (Mike) Sievert, $550,000 total compensation
Evp And Cfo, J. Braxton Carter, $650,000 total compensation
Evp Corporate Services, David R. (Dave) Carey
Evp General Counsel And Secretary, David A. (Dave) Miller
President T-mobile Indirect Channels, Thomas C. Keys
Svp And Chief People Officer, Larry L. Myers

Evp Corporate Strategy, Peter A. Ewens
Evp And Cto, Neville R. Ray
Evp T-mobile Retail And Direct Channels, Jon A. Freier
Evp And Chief Marketing Officer, J. Andrew Sherrard
National Account Manager, Vance Reyes
Senior Vice President Customer Service, Brian Brueckman
Senior Vice President Corporate Development And Wholesale Roaming, Dirk Mosa
Vice President Engineering Services And Quality Assurance, Grant Castle
Evp Communications And Community Engagement, Janice Kapner
Vice President System Integrity And Reporting, Terri Smith
Vice President Of Legal Affairs, Andrew Fisher
National Account Manager, Michael Murray
Vice President Information Systems, Leanne Prince
Senior Vice President Legal Affairs, Andrew Sacks
Senior Vice President Human Resources, Elizabeth Sullivan
Vice President Strategic Development And Investments, Michael Goo
Vice President Sales, Kevin Glassman
Vice President Product Management, Andrew Morrison
National Account Manager, Diego Andrade
Vice President Legal Affairs Technology Transactions, Dan Menser
Vice President Business Sales, Andrew Rainone
Vice President Business Sales, Rebecca Jensen
Vice President Sales Operations, Sara Nicholson
Vice President Engineering Finance, Dave Mayo
Vice President Information Technology, Chuck Knostman
Vice President And Corporate Information Security Officer, Bill Boni
Vice President Legal Affairs, Stephen Leptich
Vice President And Project Director, Heidi Monahan
Vp Marketing Strategy And Digital Innovation, Lincoln Lopez
Vice President Of Communications, Catherine Captain
Senior Vice President Marketing Strategy And Insights, Wolfgang Sixl
Vp Legal Affairs Sales And Distribution, Susan Hacker
Vice President And Chief Compliance Officer, Steve Cochran
Vice President Public Relations, Clint Patterson
National Sales Manager, Julieanna Gild
Executive Vice President Human Resources, Elizabeth McAuliffe
Vice President Legal Affairs, Craig Codlin
Vice President Handset Insurance And Financing, Roger Brown
Vp Corporate Real Estate And Facilities, Darcey Estes
Vice President, Ann Guske
Chairman, Timotheus (Tim) H ¶ttges
Board Member, Lawrence Guffey
Board Member, Srikant Datar
Treas, Sergio Horta
Auditors: PricewaterhouseCoopers LLP

LOCATIONS

HQ: T-Mobile US Inc
  12920 SE 38th Street, Bellevue, WA 98006-1350
Phone: 425 378-4000
Web: www.T-Mobile.com

PRODUCTS/OPERATIONS

2018 Sales

	$ mil.	% of total
Branded postpaid	20,862	48
Branded Prepaid	9,598	22
Equipment Sales	10,009	23
Wholesale	1,183	3
Roaming and other services	349	1
Other	1,309	3
Total	**43,310**	**100**

2018 Customers

	$ mil.	% of total
Branded postpaid		42
Branded prepaid		21
Wholesale		16
Total	**0**	**79**

COMPETITORS

AT&T Mobility	Sprint Communications
Boost Mobile	TracFone
CenturyLink	U.S. Cellular
Comcast	Verizon Wireless Inc.
Cricket	Virgin Mobile USA

HISTORICAL FINANCIALS
Company Type: Public

Income Statement				FYE: December 31
	REVENUE ($ mil.)	NET INCOME ($ mil.)	NET PROFIT MARGIN	EMPLOYEES
12/19	44,998	3,468	7.7%	53,000
12/18	43,310	2,888	6.7%	52,000
12/17	40,604	4,536	11.2%	51,000
12/16	37,242	1,460	3.9%	50,000
12/15	32,053	733	2.3%	50,000
Annual Growth	8.9%	47.5%	—	1.5%

2019 Year-End Financials

Debt ratio: 33.95%	No. of shares (mil.): 856
Return on equity: 12.96%	Dividends
Cash ($ mil.): 1,528	Yield: —
Current ratio: 0.74	Payout: —
Long-term debt ($ mil.): 28,526	Market value ($ mil.): 67,199

	STOCK PRICE ($) FY Close	P/E High/Low		PER SHARE ($) Earnings	Dividends	Book Value
12/19	78.42	21	16	4.02	0.00	33.60
12/18	63.61	21	16	3.36	0.00	29.07
12/17	63.51	13	10	5.20	0.00	26.25
12/16	57.51	34	20	1.69	0.00	22.07
12/15	39.12	52	32	0.82	0.00	20.23
Annual Growth	19.0%	—	—	48.8%	—	13.5%

Targa Resources Corp

Targa Resources Corp. has the energy to deliver natural gas throughout its service territory of Texas Oklahoma and neighboring states. Through its Targa Resources Partners entity it gathers processes transports and sells natural gas natural gas liquids (NGLs) crude oil and refined petroleum products. It owns or operates nearly 30000 miles of natural gas gathering pipelines and more than 45 processing plants. It has a presence in many shale basins including the Permian Eagle Ford Barnett Anadarko Arkoma and Williston. In early 2016 Targa Resources Corp purchased all unowned shares of Targa Resources Partners securing complete control of its previously majority-owned subsidiary.

Operations

Targa Resources operates two segments: Gathering and Processing and Logistics and Transportation..

The Logistics and Transportation segment accounting for nearly 80% of total revenue is Targa's downstream business. It converts mixed NGLs into NGL products and provides certain value-added services such as transporting storing fractionating terminaling and marketing NGLs and NGL products.. It performs marketing activities in support of Targa's other businesses including services to LPG exporters. Assets owned by this segment are generally connected to and supplied in part by the Gathering and Processing segment. The segment also includes Grand Prix Pipeline and equity interest in Gulf Coast Express Pipeline LLC. It also owns and leases out almost 700 railcars and nearly 140 transport tractors to move products.

The Gathering and Processing segment generates more than 20% of total revenue. It gathers natural gas produced from oil and gas wells and processes this raw natural gas into sellable natural gas by extracting NGLs and removing impurities. It also gathers and terminals crude oil. The segment has a gross processing capacity of more than 10 billion cubic feet of natural gas per day.

Overall the company generates about 85% of revenue from sales of commodities and roughly 15% from Fees from midstream services.

Geographic Reach

Targa Resources is headquartered in Houston TX. The assets owned by the Logistics and Transportation segment are predominantly located in Mont Belvieu and Galena Park Texas and in Lake Charles Louisiana. The Gathering and Processing segment's assets are located in the Permian Basin of West Texas and Southeast New Mexico; the Eagle Ford Shale in South Texas; the Barnett Shale in North Texas; the Anadarko Ardmore and Arkoma Basins in Oklahoma and South Central Kansas; the Williston Basin in North Dakota and in the onshore and near offshore regions of the Louisiana Gulf Coast and the Gulf of Mexico.

Sales and Marketing

Targa sells its products to petrochemical companies refineries export companies large commercial and industrial customers as well as to natural gas and electric utilities that serve individual consumers. Targa also earns revenue by purchasing and reselling NGL products in the spot and forward physical markets.

Targa Resources' wholesale propane marketing operations primarily sell propane and related logistics services to major multi-state retailers independent retailers and other end-users.

Financial Performance

In 2019 after rising in the last four years Targa's net revenue declined. Even so the company's revenue has an overall growth of 30% in the last five years. On the other hand the company's profits have been fluctuating for the last five years and went deeper in losses in 2019.

For the year 2018 revenue declined 17% to $8.7 billion coming entirely from the 20% decrease of sale of commodities.

In 2019 the company suffered losses of almost $210 million.

Targa's cash holdings increased from $232.1 million in 2018 to $331.1 million in 2019. Operations contributed $1.4 billion followed by an even great contribution of $1.8 billion from financing activities coming from. By contrast investment utilized $3.1 billion mostly in purchase of property plant and equipment.

Strategy

Targa's gathering and processing businesses are strategically located in attractive oil and gas producing basins and are well positioned within each of those basins. Activity in the shale resource plays underlying the company's gathering assets is driven by the economics of oil condensate gas and NGL production from the particular reservoirs in each play. Activity levels for most of its gathering and processing assets are driven by commodity prices primarily crude oil prices. If drilling and production activities in these areas continue the volumes of natural gas and crude oil available to our gathering and processing systems will likely increase.

Additionally the company continues to invest capital in its businesses to enhance its competitive advantage as an integrated midstream services provider. Targa has invested approximately $8.4 billion in growth capital expenditures since 2015 including approximately $2.6 billion in 2019 (approximately $2.3 billion of net growth capital). These expansion investments are distributed across the company's businesses with 52% to Gathering and Processing and 48% related to Logistics and Transportation. Targa expects to continue to invest in both large and small organic growth projects in 2020 and currently estimates that it will invest approximately $1.2 to $1.3 billion in net organic growth capital expenditures in 2020.

Company Background

Targa Resources Inc. was formed in 2003 by Warburg Pincus and its Management Team. The company conducted its IPO in 2010 under the NYSE. In 2012 Targa acquired Saddle Butte Pipeline LLC's crude oil gathering pipeline and terminal system and natural gas gathering and processing that expanded the company's operations. Targa acquired Atlas Pipeline Partners L.P. and Atlas Energy L.P. in 2015.

EXECUTIVES

Ceo, Joe Bob Perkins, age 59
President Administration, Jeffrey J. (Jeff) McParland, age 65, $500,000 total compensation
Evp Southern Field Gathering And Processing, Patrick J. (Pat) McDonie, age 60
Evp General Counsel And Secretary, Paul W. Chung, age 59, $490,000 total compensation
Evp And Cfo, Mattthew J. (Matt) Meloy, age 42, $450,000 total compensation
Evp Logistics And Marketing, D. Scott Pryor, age 58
Evp Northern Field Gathering And Processing, Dan C. Middlebrooks, age 64
Evp Engineering And Operations, Clark White, age 61
Evp Commercial, Robert Muraro, age 44
Vice President Finance, Howard M Tate
Svp Natural Gas Marketing, Stacey Duke
Vice President Comm Svs And Downstream Acctg, Janet Sullivan
Chairman, James W. Whalen, age 79
Vice Chairman, Michael A. Heim, age 72
Auditors: PricewaterhouseCoopers LLP

LOCATIONS

HQ: Targa Resources Corp
811 Louisiana St., Suite 2100, Houston, TX 77002
Phone: 713 584-1000　　**Fax:** 713 584-1100
Web: www.targaresources.com

PRODUCTS/OPERATIONS

2016 sales

	$ mil.	% of total
Logistics and Marketing	5,519	82
Gathering and Processing	1,108	17
Other	62	1
Total	**6,690**	**100**

COMPETITORS

DCP Midstream Partners	Enterprise Products
Devon Energy	Kinder Morgan
EnLink Midstream Partners	Magellan Midstream
Enbridge	ONEOK Partners
Energy Transfer	Summit Midstream Partners LP

HISTORICAL FINANCIALS

Company Type: Public

Income Statement　　　　　　　　　　　　FYE: December 31

	REVENUE ($ mil.)	NET INCOME ($ mil.)	NET PROFIT MARGIN	EMPLOYEES
12/19	8,671	(209)	—	2,680
12/18	10,484	1	0.0%	2,460
12/17	8,814	54	0.6%	2,130
12/16	6,690	(187)	—	1,970
12/15	6,658	58	0.9%	1,870
Annual Growth	**6.8%**	**—**	**—**	**9.4%**

2019 Year-End Financials

Debt ratio: 41.58%	No. of shares (mil.): 232
Return on equity: (-3.63%)	Dividends
Cash ($ mil.): 331	Yield: 8.9%
Current ratio: 0.89	Payout: —
Long-term debt ($ mil.): 7,440	Market value ($ mil.): 9,507

	STOCK PRICE ($) FY Close	P/E High/Low	PER SHARE ($) Earnings	Dividends	Book Value
12/19	40.83	— —	(1.44)	3.64	22.33
12/18	36.02	— —	(0.53)	3.64	27.29
12/17	48.42	— —	(0.31)	3.64	29.31
12/16	56.07	— —	(1.80)	3.64	29.45
12/15	27.06	98 24	1.09	3.39	26.09
Annual Growth	**10.8%**	**— —**	**—**	**1.8%**	**(3.8%)**

Target Corp

Cheap-but-chic Target is the US's #2 discount chain (behind Wal-Mart). The fashion-forward discounter operates 1800-plus Target stores across the US as well as an online business at Target.com. It sells a broad range of household goods food and pet supplies apparel and accessories electronics decor and other items under national brands as well as owned and exclusive brands. Target also sell merchandise through periodic exclusive design and creative partnerships and generate revenue from in-store amenities such as Target Café and leased or licensed departments such as Target Optical Starbucks and other food service offerings. The company also offers pharmacy and clinic services in its stores through an operating agreement with CVS Pharmacy

HISTORY

The panic of 1873 left Joseph Hudson bankrupt. After he paid his debts at 60 cents on the dollar he saved enough by 1881 to open a men's clothing store in Detroit. Among his innovations were merchandise-return privileges and price marking in place of bargaining. By 1891 Hudson's was the largest retailer of men's clothing in the US. Hudson repaid his creditors from 1873 in full with interest. When Hudson died in 1912 four nephews expanded the business.

Former banker George Dayton established a dry-goods store in 1902 in Minneapolis. Like Hudson he offered return privileges and liberal credit. His store grew to a 12-story full-line department store.

After WWII both companies saw that the future lay in the suburbs. In 1954 Hudson's built Northland in Detroit then the largest US shopping center. Dayton's built the world's first fully enclosed shopping mall in Edina a Minneapolis suburb in 1956. In 1962 Dayton's opened its first discount store in Roseville (naming the store Target to distinguish the discounter from its higher-end department stores).

Dayton's went public in 1966 the same year it began the B. Dalton bookstore chain. Three years later it merged with the family-owned Hudson's forming Dayton Hudson. Dayton Hudson purchased more malls and invested in such specialty areas as consumer electronics and hard goods. Target had 24 stores by 1970.

The Target chain became the company's top moneymaker in 1977. The next year Dayton Hudson bought California-based Mervyn's (later Mervyns). In the late 1970s and 1980s it sold nine regional malls and several other businesses including the 800-store B. Dalton chain to Barnes & Noble. The Target stores division purchased Indianapolis-based Ayr-Way (1980) and Southern California-based Fedmart stores (1983). In the late 1980s Dayton Hudson took Target to Los Angeles and the Northwest. Robert Ulrich who began with the company as a merchandise trainee in 1967 became president and CEO of the Target stores division in 1987 and chairman and CEO of Dayton Hudson in 1994.

Dayton Hudson opened the first Target Greatland store in 1990. By this time it had 420 Target stores. Also that year Dayton Hudson bought the Marshall Field's chain of 24 department stores from B.A.T Industries. Marshall Field's began as a dry-goods business that Marshall Field bought in 1865 and subsequently built into Chicago's premier upscale retailer.

SuperTarget stores were introduced in 1995. The Target stores division opened stores in the Mid-Atlantic and Northeast the next year while the department store division began selling off its Marshall Field's locations in Texas.

In 1998 Dayton Hudson boosted its Internet presence by purchasing direct-marketing company Rivertown Trading; it also bought apparel supplier Associated Merchandising that year. In 2000 Dayton Hudson renamed itself Target Corporation. In early 2001 the company renamed its Dayton's and Hudson's chains Marshall Field's. Also that year Target acquired the rights to 35 former Montgomery Wards stores from the bankrupt retailer.

The nation's #2 discounter was #1 when it came to corporate giving in 2001. Target topped the Forbes list of America's Most Philanthropic Companies that year donating 2.5% of its 2000 income (nearly $86 million). By comparison Wal-Mart gave away $116.5 million in 2001 less than 1% of its income in 2000.

In 2002 the company reopened 30 of the former Montgomery Ward stores as Target outlets. Net of closings 94 Target stores opened in 2002 while neither Mervyns nor Marshall Field's added to their store counts. In March 2003 three new SuperTarget stores opened in the Dallas/Fort Worth area.

2004 was a year of divestments for Target. In January the discounter announced it was exiting the catalog business. To that end in April Target sold its Signals and Wireless gifts catalogs to Universal Screen Arts for an undisclosed sum. In July Target sold its Marshall Field's business to The May Department Stores Co. for about $3.2 billion in cash. In September Target completed the sale of 257 Mervyns stores in 13 states to an investment group that includes Cerberus Capital Management Lubert-Adler/Klaff and Partners and Sun Capital Partners as well as its Mervyns credit card receivables to GE Consumer Finance for a combined sum of approximately $1.65 billion in cash. (Later Mervyns filed for bankruptcy and closed the last of its stores by the end of 2008.)

In October 2005 vice chairman Gerald Storch resigned unexpectedly after more than a dozen years with the company. No reason was given for his departure. In the largest mass opening in Target's history the retailer opened 60 new stores on October 9.

In July 2006 Target.com extended its partnership with Amazon Enterprise Solutions a unit of online retailer Amazon.com through August 2010. Amazon provides e-commerce technology to the discount chain.

In May 2008 Ulrich who served as chairman and CEO since 1994 handed his CEO title to president Gregg Steinhafel. (Steinhafel joined the retailer in 1979 and worked his way up the executive ranks.) Also in May Target closed on the sale of a 47% stake in its credit-card receivable to JPMorgan Chase for $3.6 billion. The five-year deal allows Target to buy back the stake at the end of the term. In October the company opened a pair of stores in Alaska thereby expanding its retail presence to 48 states. In November Target said no thanks to a plan Ackman had proposed for Target to spin off its real estate holdings in a bid to increase shareholder value citing uncertainty about valuation assumptions and the potential reduction in financial flexibility as a result of spin off.

Ulrich retired from the board in January 2009 and Steinhafel added the chairman's title to his job description.

In April 2010 Target stopped offering new credit card applicants its co-branded Visa credit card.

Chairman president and CEO Steinhafel resigned in May 2014 five months after a massive data breach at the company. In July 2014 the company named retail veteran Brian Cornell as chairman and CEO. Cornell 55 joined Target from PepsiCo Americas Foods where he served as CEO and oversaw the global food business. Before joining PepsiCo Cornell served as president and CEO of Sam's Club a division of Wal-Mart Stores.

EXECUTIVES

Evp Chief Legal Officer And Corporate Secretary, Don H. Liu, age 59, $275,000 total compensation

Evp Merchandising Product Group, Patricia (Trish) Adams

Director Community Relations, Laysha L. Ward, age 52

Chairman And Ceo, Brian C. Cornell, age 61, $1,300,000 total compensation

Evp And Coo, John J. Mulligan, age 54, $1,000,000 total compensation

Evp And Chief Merchandising Officer, Mark J. Tritton, age 56, $396,635 total compensation

Evp And Chief Stores Officer, Janna A. Potts, age 52

Evp And Cio, Michael E. (Mike) McNamara, age 55, $468,462 total compensation

Evp And Cfo, Catherine R. (Cathy) Smith, age 56, $798,558 total compensation

President Target Sourcing Services, Kelly Caruso

Evp And Chief Human Resources Officer, Stephanie A. Lundquist, age 44

Evp And Chief Risk And Compliance Officer, Jacqueline Hourigan Rice, age 48

Evp And Chief Marketing Officer, Rick H. Gomez, age 50

Svp Grocery Fresh Food And Beverage, Jeff Burt

President Target Financial And Retail Services, Scott Kennedy

President Target India, Tammy Redpath

Svp Global Sourcing, Cynthia Ho

Senior Vice President Risk And Government Affairs, Matt Zabel

Pharmacy Manager, Mikel Gilbert

Vice President Technology Services, Tim Milne

Pharmacy Manager, Joseph Legrand

Vice President Assistant, Dana Winkler

Senior Vice President Region Ii, Robert Thompson

Vice President Administration Property Dvlpt Department, Katy DeLaTorre

Vice President And General Manager, Steve Mattson

Senior Vice President Distribution, Carson Landsgard

Vice President Of Marketing, William White

Senior Vice President Enterprise Data Analytics And Business Intelligence, Paritosh Desai

Senior Vice President Administrative Assistant, Nadean Mueller

Senior Vice President, Manojkumar Shah

Vice President Cyber Security, Jodie Kautt

Pharmacy Manager, Jacqueline Jansen

Vice President, Sarah Arrell

Senior Vice President Talent And Organizational Effectiveness, Tim Curoe

Vice President Of Store Operations, Sergio Villar

Vice President Of Communications, Dustee T Jenkins

Vice President Supply Chain Technology, Rachel Whitcomb

Pharmacy Manager, David Cathcart

Senior Vice President Assistant, Amanda Dale

Vice President Human Resources, Ann Florell

Executive Vice President Executive Assistant, Kari Meiller

Vice President Finance, Scott Brill
Senior Vice President Business Development, Aaron Alt
Executive Vice President And Chief Human Resources Officer, Melissa Kremer
Senior Vp Vp Technical Architect, Subbarao Gudipalli
Vice President Healthcare Operations, John Holcomb
Senior Vice President Owned Brand Management And Product Design, Julie Guggemos
Vice President Of Distribution Operations, Diane Closs
Executive Vice President Merchandising Apparel And Home, Trish Adams
Vice President Assistant, Rhonda Broyles
Senior Vice President Gc Sec'y, TimothyR Baer
Vice President Assistant, Christina Hayes
Senior Vice President Home, Cara Sylvester
Vp Engineering And System Operations, Valerie Blihovde
Executive Vice President Chief Legal Officer And Corporate Secretary, Tim Baer
Vp Admin, Lorene Laubach
Vice President, Catherine Helm
Pharmacy Manager, Kari Ratkevich
Senior Vice President Infrastructure And Operations, Tom Kadlec
Vice President Architecture, Joel Crabb
Senior Vice President Operational Excellence, Anu Gupta
Senior Vp Vp Technical Architect, Dean Mclain
Vp Enterprise Risk Mgmt, Soraya Wright
Senior Vice President Fulfillment Operations, Preston Mosier
Senior Vice President Global Logistics Inventory Allocation And Replenishment, Ben Cook
Senior Vice President Network Planning And Operational Design, Shekar Natarajan
Senior Vice President, Samir Shah
Svp Chief Accounting Officer And Controller, Robert Harrison
Senior Vice President And Chief Information Security Officer, Rich Agostino
Vice President Internal Innovation And Operations, West Stringfellow
Group Vice President, Amanda Vela
Vice President Divisional Meat And Fresh Prepared Food, Mark Kenny
Senior Vice President Marketing, Michelle Messenberg
Vice President Property Management, John Leisen
Senior Vice President Merchandising Apparel And Accessories, Michelle Wlazlo
Senior Vice President Merchandising And Supply Chain Portfolio Solutions, Brett Craig
Evp And Chief Supply Chain And Logistics Officer, Arthur Valdez
Vp Corporate Responsibilty, Jennifer Silberman
Vice President Merchandise Manager, Scott Bradley
Pharmacy Manager, Samantha Schrempp
Vice President Store Planning And Engineering, Curt Ulrich
Vice President, Sumesh George
Vice President, Aaron Allen
Svp Global Supply Chain And Logistics, Tim Hotze
Group Vice President Stores, Lydia Stroup
Svp Assistant, Melissa Scanlon
Vice President Divisional Planning, Moore Brandon
Vice President Of Planning, Joe Shillings
Senior Vice President Food And Beverage Supply Chain, Frank Bruni
Senior Vice President Food And Beverage Supply Chain, Frank Brunl
Senior Vice President Target Properties, Mark Schlndele
Senior Vice President Enterprise Data Analytics And Business Intelligence, Parltosh Desal
Senior Vice President Supply Chain Field Operations, Preston Mosler

Vp Womens Apparel Merchandising, Jenna Renfrew
Vice President Assurance, Matt Ladegaard
Vice President;prin, Rick Harris
Vp Of Product Design And Development For Home And Hardlines, Greg Van Bellinger
Senior Vice President Treasurer, Corey L Haaland
Assistant Treasurer, Sara Ross
Board Member, Rakesh Mishra
Vice Chairman, Mollie McCarty
Board Member, Robert Edwards
Board Member, Megan Healey
Auditors: Ernst & Young LLP

LOCATIONS

HQ: Target Corp
1000 Nicollet Mall, Minneapolis, MN 55403
Phone: 612 304-6073
Web: www.target.com

2018 Locations

	No.
California	287
Texas	150
Florida	123
Illinois	94
New York	82
Minnesota	73
Pennsylvania	75
Ohio	63
Virginia	59
Michigan	53
North Carolina	51
Georgia	50
Other	684
Total	**1,844**

PRODUCTS/OPERATIONS

2018 Sales

	$ mil.	% of total
Beauty & household essentials	17,726	24
Apparel & accessories	15,004	20
Food & beverage	14,585	19
Home furnishings & dé;cor	14,298	19
Hardlines	12,709	17
Credit card profit sharing	673	1
Other	250	-
Total	**75,356**	**100**

Selected Exclusive Brands
DENIZEN from Levi's
Genuine Kids from OshKosh
Isabel Maternity by Ingrid & Isabel
Nate Berkus for Target
Oh Joy! for Target

Selected Private Labels
Archer Farms (food)
Cat & Jack (children's apparel)
Market Pantry
Smith & Hawken (garden & outdoor)
Xhilaration (apparel)

COMPETITORS

Amazon.com	Home Depot
BJ's Wholesale Club	J. C. Penney Company
Bed Bath & Beyond	Kohl's
Best Buy	Kroger
Costco Wholesale	Lowe's
Dollar General	Sears Holdings
Dollar Tree	Wal-Mart
Euromarket Designs	

HISTORICAL FINANCIALS
Company Type: Public

Income Statement   FYE: February 1

	REVENUE ($ mil.)	NET INCOME ($ mil.)	NET PROFIT MARGIN	EMPLOYEES
02/20	78,112	3,281	4.2%	368,000
02/19	75,356	2,937	3.9%	360,000
02/18*	71,879	2,934	4.1%	345,000
01/17	69,495	2,737	3.9%	323,000
01/16	73,785	3,363	4.6%	341,000
Annual Growth	**1.4%**	**(0.6%)**	**—**	**1.9%**

*Fiscal year change

2020 Year-End Financials

Debt ratio: 26.88%
Return on equity: 28.45%
Cash ($ mil.): 2,577
Current ratio: 0.89
Long-term debt ($ mil.): 11,338

No. of shares (mil.): 504
Dividends
  Yield: 0.0%
  Payout: 40.8%
Market value ($ mil.): 55,835

	STOCK PRICE ($) FY Close	P/E High/Low		PER SHARE ($) Earnings	Dividends	Book Value
02/20	110.74	20	11	6.36	2.60	23.47
02/19	71.17	16	11	5.51	2.52	21.82
02/18*	72.95	15	9	5.33	2.44	21.62
01/17	63.70	18	13	4.70	2.32	19.69
01/16	72.42	16	13	5.31	2.16	21.52
Annual Growth	**11.2%**	**—**	**—**	**4.6%**	**4.7%**	**2.2%**

*Fiscal year change

TCF Financial Corp (New)

Chemical Financial has banking down to a science. It's the holding company for Chemical Bank which provides standard services such as checking and savings accounts CDs and IRAs credit and debit cards and loans and mortgages to individuals and businesses through nearly 190 branches in the lower peninsula of Michigan. The majority of the bank's loan portfolio is made up of commercial loans while consumer loans make up the remainder. Boasting assets of $9 billion Chemical is the second largest bank in Michigan. The company also offers trust investment management brokerage and title insurance services through subsidiaries.

Operations

Its Wealth Management division which has some $4 billion in assets under custody offers trust services estate planning investment management and employee benefit programs. Chemical Financial Advisors offers mutual funds and marketable securities while CFC Title Services issues title insurance for mortgage properties. CFC Capital manages the company's municipal investment securities portfolio.

About 72% of Chemical Financial's total revenue came from loan interest (including fees) in 2014 while another 6% came from interest on its investment securities. The rest of its revenue came from deposit account service charges and fees (8%) wealth management revenue (6%)

mortgage banking income (2%) and other miscellaneous sources of income.

Sales and Marketing
Chemical Financial spent $3.45 million on advertising in 2014 up from $2.97 million and $3.11 million in 2013 and 2012 respectively.

Financial Performance
Chemical Financial's revenues and profits have been rising over the past few years thanks growing loan and deposit business from acquisitions lower interest expenses on deposits and declining loan loss provisions as its loan portfolio's credit quality has improved with higher property valuations in the strengthened economy.

The bank's revenue rose by 6% to $290.4 million in 2014 as the bank as its acquisition of Northwestern Bancorp boosted its loan business during the year. Higher revenue lower interest expenses and a continued decline in loan loss provisions drove the bank's net income up by 9% to a record $62.1 million. The bank's operating cash levels inched higher to $89.9 million on higher cash earnings.

Strategy
The bank follows an aggressive acquisition strategy to boost its loan and deposit business while expanding its branch network into key parts of Michigan. Indeed its acquisitions in 2015 and 2014 boosted the bank's presence in northwestern Michigan and along the Michigan-Indiana border. By the end of 2014 the bank had acquired some 21 community banks and 36 branch bank offices.

Mergers and Acquisitions
Chemical Financial agreed in January 2019 to merge with Minnesota-based TCF Financial to form a Midwest bank with about $45 billion in assets $34 billion in total deposits and more than 500 branches in nine states. TCF's large deposit base and national wholesale lending business will complement Chemical's commercial lending and wealth management activities. The combined company which is to retain the TCF brand will have a more diversified deposit mix between retail and commercial lines and a more balanced loan portfolio across geographies asset classes and industries. Following the merger TCF shareholders will have a controlling interest in the combined company.

Company Background
In late 2012 the company acquired 21 branches in northeastern Michigan and Battle Creek from Independent Bank. That more than $8-million transaction further expands Chemical Bank's presence geographically. Additional acquisitions including FDIC-assisted takeovers of failed banks are possible.

EXECUTIVES

Svp Cfo And Treasurer, Lori A. Gwizdala, age 62, $344,720 total compensation
Vice Chairman And President Chemical Bank, Thomas C. (Tom) Shafer, age 61
Evp And Senior Credit Officer Chemical Bank, James E. Tomczyk, age 68, $225,504 total compensation
Vice Chairman Chemical Bank And Ceo Insite Capital Llc, Thomas W. Kohn, age 66, $329,174 total compensation
Evp Commercial Lending Chemical Bank, Daniel W. Terpsma, age 66

Evp And Cfo Chemical Financial And Chemical Bank, Dennis L. Klaeser, age 62, $183,483 total compensation
President And Ceo, David T. Provost
Director Chemical Financial And Chairman Chemical Bank, Franklin C. Wheatlake, age 72
Evp And Coo Business Operations Chemical Bank, Leonardo Amat, age 51, $309,477 total compensation
Evp And Chief Risk Officer Chemical Bank, Lynn M. Kerber, age 51
Evp General Counsel And Secretary, William C. Collins, age 67
Evp And Coo Customer Experience Chemical Bank, Robert S. Rathbun, age 56, $309,477 total compensation
Svp And Cio, Greg Meidt
Executive Vice President, John Kessler
Vice President Of Customer Service, Sue Lynde
Senior Vice President, Laura Yockey
Vice President, Robert O Burgess
Assistant Vice President Product Development, Jim Hubinger
Vice President Commercial Loan Officer, Jeff Hyde
Executive Vice President Chief Operating Officer, James Milroy
Vice President, Carl Ahearn
Vice President Information Systems, Laurie Soren
Senior Vice President And Trust Officer, Jude Patnaude
First Vice President, David Vermilye
Vice President, Robin Grove
Mortgage Officer Assistant Vice President, Sue Moody
Vice President Information Technology, Annette Rus
Executive Vice President, Diane M Schweigert
Assistant Vice President And Audit Manager, Tom Vanhoof
Vice President, John Laman
Vice President Trust Investment Officer, Duane Carpenter
Vice President Treasury Management And Business Development, Marc Cesere
Vice President Mortgage Originator, Krista Martiny
Assistant Vice President Electronic Banking Services, Mary Green
Vice President First, Michael Debo
Vice President Secretary, Michelle Pilaske
Vice President, Daniel Plumert
Vice President Director Application Services, John Vander Velde
Vice President, Angela Gonino
Assistant Vice President Treasury Management Sales Advisor, Julie Kuchnicki
Vice President, Jon Harrison
Executive Vice President Chief Delivery Officer, Gregory Bixby
Vice President Associate Legal Counsel, Bill Garchow
Vice President And Loan Services Manager, Heather Daughenbaugh
Vice President Commercial Lending Officer, Thomas Roddy
Vice President And Trust Officer, Pamela Dolezan
Assistant Vice President Branch Manager, Sharon Langenberg
Senior Vice President Business Banking Credit Director, Nita Cohen
Vice President And Personal Trust Officer, Joanna Keenan
Vice President, Daniel Zinser
Senior Vice President, Jennifer Dakoske
Chairman, Gary H. Torgow, age 62
Treasurer, Cheryl Whitman
Board Member, James Fitterling
Auditors: KPMG LLP

LOCATIONS

HQ: TCF Financial Corp (New)
333 W. Fort Street, Suite 1800, Detroit, MI 48226
Phone: 800 867-9757
Web: www.tcfbank.com

PRODUCTS/OPERATIONS

2014 Sales

	$ mil.	% of total
Interest		
Loans including fees	209	72
Investment securities	17	6
Other	0	-
Non-interest		
Service charges on deposit accounts	22	8
Wealth management revenue	16	6
Other customer service charges & fees	18	6
Other	6	2
Total	290	100

COMPETITORS

1st Source Corporation	Flagstar Bancorp
Bank of America	Huntington Bancshares
Comerica	Independent Bank (MI)
Fifth Third	Mercantile Bank
Firstbank	

HISTORICAL FINANCIALS

Company Type: Public

Income Statement
FYE: December 31

	ASSETS ($ mil.)	NET INCOME ($ mil.)	INCOME AS % OF ASSETS	EMPLOYEES
12/19	46,651	295	0.6%	8,209
12/18	21,498	284	1.3%	3,100
12/17	19,280	149	0.8%	3,000
12/16	17,355	108	0.6%	3,300
12/15	9,188	86	0.9%	2,100
Annual Growth	50.1%	35.8%	—	40.6%

2019 Year-End Financials

Debt ratio: 1.14%	No. of shares (mil.): 152
Return on equity: 6.92%	Dividends
Cash ($ mil.): 1,228	Yield: 3.6%
Current ratio: —	Payout: 57.5%
Long-term debt ($ mil.): —	Market value ($ mil.): 7,159

	STOCK PRICE ($) FY Close	P/E High/Low		PER SHARE ($) Earnings	Dividends	Book Value
12/19	46.80	19	14	2.55	1.72	37.31
12/18	36.61	15	9	3.94	1.24	39.69
12/17	53.47	27	21	2.08	1.10	37.48
12/16	54.17	25	13	2.17	1.06	36.57
12/15	34.27	15	12	2.39	1.00	26.62
Annual Growth	8.1%	—	—	1.6%	14.5%	8.8%

Tenet Healthcare Corp.

Tenet Healthcare is a diversified healthcare services company headquartered in Dallas Texas. Its operations include 65 hospitals and over 500 other healthcare facilities including ambulatory surgery centers urgent care centers imaging centers surgical hospitals off-campus emergency departments and micro-hospitals in about 10 US states including Alabama Arizona California Florida Massachusetts Michigan Missouri Tennessee and Texas. Its United Surgical Partners

International (USPI) division operates ambulatory surgery centers urgent care centers imaging centers and surgical hospitals. Tenet is spinning off its Conifer unit which provides healthcare business process services in the areas of hospital and physician revenue cycle management and value-based care solutions to healthcare systems and other entities.

HISTORY

Hospital attorney Richard Eamer along with attorneys Leonard Cohen and John Bedrosian founded National Medical Enterprises (NME) in 1969. After its IPO NME bought 10 hospitals nursing homes an office building and land in California. Within six years the company owned operated and managed 23 hospitals and a home health care business. It sold medical equipment and bottled oxygen and provided vocational training for nurses.

In the 1970s NME expanded into hospital construction and bought five Florida hospitals. By 1981 NME was the #3 health care concern in the US owning or managing 193 hospitals and nursing homes. In the 1980s NME diversified further buying nursing homes and mental health centers. By the end of the decade the company's Specialty Hospital Group brought in more than 50% of revenues. NME was the second-largest publicly owned health care company in the US (after HCA) by 1985.

In 1990 NME reversed course spinning off most of its long-term-care businesses but kept 19 UK nursing facilities operated by its Westminster Health Care subsidiary (sold 1996). In 1992 the company acquired an Australian hospital management firm.

That year several insurance companies sued NME alleging fraudulent psychiatric claims; NME settled the suits in 1993. Federal agents later raided company headquarters seizing papers related to the suspected fraud. That year investment banker Jeff Barbakow took over as CEO forcing out Eamer and Cohen.

In 1993 and 1994 NME dumped most of its psychiatric and rehabilitation facilities using the proceeds to help pay penalties stemming from the federal investigation into alleged insurance fraud kickbacks and patient abuse at its psychiatric units. NME paid another $16 million in related state fines. (Related civil lawsuits were settled in 1997.)

The company's name change to Tenet Healthcare coincided with new purchases throughout the South in 1995 and 1996.

The next few years were mixed for Tenet. On the upside it bought OrNda HealthCorp which complemented Tenet's existing networks. Tenet and MedPartners (now Caremark Rx) then the #1 practice management firm formed a Southern California hospital-doctor network in 1997 that gave both companies heft in dealing with HMOs (the partnership crumbled in 1999 when MedPartners exited practice management to focus on pharmacy benefits management and ceased operations in California). Merger discussions began with embattled market leader Columbia/HCA (now HCA) but fizzled.

In 1998 Tenet bought eight Philadelphia hospitals owned by the bankrupt Allegheny Health Education & Research Foundation. The company was dogged by another investigation this time by the Health and Human Services Inspector General's office over allegations the company paid more than fair market value for a physician practice in return for kickbacks. Tenet in 2004 agreed to pay about $31 million to settle two lawsuits stemming from these allegations.

Like many companies in the industry in 1999 Tenet began feeling the effects of the Balanced Budget Act of 1997 which mandated more scrutiny of Medicare expenditures to health care providers. In response the company began divesting some of its hospitals; it also shed its practice management business and reorganized its corporate structure.

Tenet rebounded and acquired hospitals in 2001 and 2002 but the next year proved not so kind. Federal investigations into the company's billing practices particularly those related to Medicare began late in 2002. In 2003 the company settled claims brought by the Department of Justice that doctors performed unnecessary cardiac surgeries at its Redding Medical Center (now Shasta Regional Medical Center) in California; the settlement cost Tenet $54 million (plus millions more to settle patients' claims). Tenet sold the facility in 2004 and also disposed of more than a dozen other facilities cutting its holdings from 115 to 100.

An even larger sell-off began in 2004 and included nearly 20 hospitals in California and others in Louisiana Massachusetts (all three were sold to Vanguard Health Systems in early 2005) Missouri and Texas. The company also exited the Nevada market when it sold Lake Mead Hospital Medical Center in Las Vegas in early 2004. Additionally the company ended some operating leases and joint ventures primarily in California; sold its Barcelona Spain hospital; and sold about a dozen home health agencies and hospice providers to Amedisys.

Tenet Healthcare moved its headquarters from Santa Barbara California to Dallas in 2005. The move was intended to streamline operations and save money.

Tenet saw some hard times in 2005 and spent years struggling to emerge from several subsequent years of investigations lawsuits and bad publicity. Its New Orleans and Mississippi facilities were hit hard by Hurricane Katrina in 2005 and its Memorial Medical Hospital in New Orleans became a symbol of the city's devastation after several dozen bodies were found there in the aftermath of the storm. The company has since sold both locations.

In 2006 it resolved multiple federal investigations regarding its billing practices by agreeing to a $900 million deal with the Justice Department. Its sale of hospitals post-Katrina was part of a larger plan announced in 2006 to sell off about a dozen facilities ridding itself of some low-performing operations partly to pay its $900 million bill to government investigators and partly so it could invest in equipment upgrades at its remaining hospitals. (The sales followed a larger-scale divestiture of about 25 facilities begun earlier.) In 2009 Tenet sold the USC University Hospital and Kenneth Norris Jr. Cancer Hospital to the University of Southern California for $275 million.

In 2010 Tenet sold its stake in supply chain and clinical workforce management firm Broadlane to MedAssets for some $159 million.

In late 2010 fellow hospital operator and rival Community Health Systems(CHS) made an unsolicited bid to acquire Tenet in a deal worth some $7.3 billion ($3.3 billion in cash and stock plus the assumption of $4 billion in debt). Tenet responded with a resounding "thanks but no thanks" saying the bid undervalued the company. CHS remained persistent despite a "poison pill" plan Tenet adopted and a volley of lawsuits. After Tenet's board rejected a plumped up offer of $4.1 billion in cash CHS formally withdrew all offers in 2011.

EXECUTIVES

Chairman And Ceo, Ronald A. (Ron) Rittenmeyer, age 73
Ceo Doctors Medical Center, Warren J. Kirk
Ceo San Antonio Market, Trip Pilgrim
Ceo Western Region, Jeffrey (Jeff) Koury
Vp Patient Financial Services, Stephen M. (Steve) Mooney
Svp And Chief Managed Care Officer, Clint Hailey
Cfo, Daniel J. (Dan) Cancelmi, age 57, $618,000 total compensation
Ceo Desert Market, Michele Finney
Ceo Eastern Region Â– Central Division, Garry Gause
Ceo Philadelphia Market, Michael P. (Mike) Halter
Ceo Texas Region, Tim Adams
Ceo Eastern Region Â– Coastal Division, Marsha Powers
President Hospital Operations, J. Eric Evans, age 42, $626,538 total compensation
Svp Applied Informatics And Cio, Paul T. Browne
Ceo South Texas Market, Manuel R. (Manny) Vela
Ceo Memphis Market, Audrey Gregory
Ceo United Surgical Partners International, William H. (Bill) Wilcox
Ceo El Paso Market, Sally Deitch
Ceo Detroit Market, Anthony Tedeschi
Svp And Chief Compliance Officer, Howard Hacker
Vp Patient Care Services And Chief Nursing Officer, Dian Adams
Chief Medical Officer, Octavio J. (Tavi) Diaz
Ceo Phoenix Market, Frank Molinaro
Ceo Birmingham Market, Keith Parrott
Vice President Construction And Design, Kenneth Sutherland
Regional Vice President Chief Financial Officer, Bill Durham
Vice President Chief Financial Officer Central Region At Tenet Healthcare, Kathryn Engstrom
Blood Bank Director, Melanie Orourke
Vice President Government Relations, Corey Davison
Vice President Financial Information Systems, Michael Hongola
Vice President And Chief Of Staff Executive Office, Katy Black
Svp Of Chief Human Resources Officer, Robb Webb
Vp And Cio Of Conifer Health Solution, Chris Tyler
Svp And Cfo Of Conifer Health Solutions, Daniel Karnuta
Svp And Chief Compliance Officer Of Conifer Health Solutions, Dan Feldman
Senior Vp Reimbursement, Carol Bailey
Senior Vice President Global Services, Rod Fomby
Vice President Financial Planning And Analysis, Michael B Rice
Radiology Director, RICHARD COBOS
Board Member, Tammy Romo
Unit Secretary, Erica Roche
Board Member, Richard Mark
Board Member, James Bierman
Board Member, Richard Fisher
Auditors: DELOITTE & TOUCHE LLP

LOCATIONS

HQ: Tenet Healthcare Corp.
14201 Dallas Parkway, Dallas, TX 75254
Phone: 469 893-2200
Web: www.tenethealth.com

Selected Hospitals

Alabama
  Brookwood Medical Center (Birmingham)
California
  Desert Regional Medical Center (Palm Springs)
  Doctors Hospital of Manteca
  Doctors Medical Center (Modesto)
  Emanuel Medical Center (Turlock)
  Fountain Valley Regional Hospital and Medical Center
  John F. Kennedy Memorial Hospital (Indio)
  Lakewood Regional Medical Center
  Los Alamitos Medical Center
  Placentia Linda Hospital
  San Ramon Regional Medical Center
  Sierra Vista Regional Medical Center (San Luis Obispo)
  Twin Cities Community Hospital (Templeton)
Florida
  Coral Gables Hospital
  Delray Medical Center (Delray Beach)
  Good Samaritan Medical Center (West Palm Beach)
  Hialeah Hospital
  North Shore Medical Center (Miami)
  Palm Beach Gardens Medical Center
  Palmetto General Hospital (Hialeah)
  St. Mary's Medical Center (West Palm Beach)
  West Boca Medical Center (Boca Raton)
Missouri
  Des Peres Hospital (St. Louis)
South Carolina
  Coastal Carolina Hospital (Hardeeville)
  East Cooper Regional Medical Center (Mt. Pleasant)
  Hilton Head Hospital
  Piedmont Medical Center (Rock Hill)
Tennessee
  Saint Francis Hospital (Memphis)
  Saint Francis Hospital-Bartlett
Texas
  Centennial Medical Center (Frisco)
  Cypress Fairbanks Medical Center (Houston)
  Doctors Hospital at White Rock Lake (Dallas)
  Houston Northwest Medical Center
  Lake Pointe Medical Center (Rowlett)
  Nacogdoches Medical Center
  Park Plaza Hospital (Houston)
  The Hospitals of Providence Memorial Campus (El Paso)
  Texas Regional Medical Center (Sunnyvale)

PRODUCTS/OPERATIONS

2017 Sales by Segment

	$ mil.	% of total
Hospital Operations	16,260	82
Ambulatory Care	1,940	10
Conifer		
Tenet	618	3
Other customers	979	5
Adjustments	(618)	-
Total	**19,179**	**100**

COMPETITORS

Adventist Health System Sunbelt Healthcare
Ascension Health
Banner Health
CHRISTUS Health
Carolinas HealthCare System
Catholic Health Initiatives
Community Health Systems
Dignity Health
Encompass Health
HCA
LifePoint Health
Memorial Health Services
Mercy Health
SSM Health Care
Sutter Health
Texas Health Resources
Universal Health Services
University Health Services

HISTORICAL FINANCIALS

Company Type: Public

Income Statement   FYE: December 31

	REVENUE ($ mil.)	NET INCOME ($ mil.)	NET PROFIT MARGIN	EMPLOYEES
12/19	18,479	(232)	—	113,600
12/18	18,313	111	0.6%	115,500
12/17	19,179	(704)	—	125,820
12/16	19,621	(192)	—	130,000
12/15	18,634	(140)	—	134,630
Annual Growth	**(0.2%)**	**—**		**(4.2%)**

2019 Year-End Financials

Debt ratio: 63.17%
Return on equity:—
Cash ($ mil.): 262
Current ratio: 1.21
Long-term debt ($ mil.): 14,580

No. of shares (mil.): 104
Dividends
  Yield: —
  Payout: —
Market value ($ mil.): 3,963

	STOCK PRICE ($) FY Close	P/E High/Low	PER SHARE ($) Earnings	Dividends	Book Value
12/19	38.03	— —	(2.24)	0.00	(3.56)
12/18	17.14	36 14	1.07	0.00	(1.16)
12/17	15.16	— —	(7.00)	0.00	(1.46)
12/16	14.84	— —	(1.93)	0.00	4.18
12/15	30.30	— —	(1.41)	0.00	7.02
Annual Growth	**5.8%**		**—**	**—**	**—**

Tenneco Inc

Tenneco is a global auto parts manufacturer of innovative clean air powertrain and ride performance products and systems and serve both original equipment manufacturers (OEM) and replacement markets. It makes ride control equipment such as shock absorbers struts and dampers under brands like Monroe and Quick-Strut and emissions-control systems including catalytic converters exhaust pipes and mufflers under the Walker Tru-Fit Fonos and DynoMax brands. It also makes Clevite elastomer products (bushings mounts and exhaust isolators) for vibration control in cars and heavy trucks. It supplies both the original equipment (OE) and replacement markets worldwide. Major customers Ford Motor and General Motors each accounts for more about 10% of sales. Tenneco operates worldwide on six continents.

Operations

Tenneco divides its operations across four segments. These are Clean Air Powertrain Ride Performance and Motorparts.

Clean Air products and systems generate roughly 40% of the company's revenue designs manufactures markets and distributes a variety of clean air products and systems. Precise engineering of the exhaust system - which extends from the manifold that connects an engine's exhaust ports to an exhaust pipe to the catalytic converter that eliminates pollutants from the exhaust and to the muffler that modulates noise emissions - leads to a pleasantly tuned engine sound reduced pollutants and optimized engine performance.

The Ride Performance segment represents more than 15% of revenue designs manufactures

markets and distributes a variety of ride performance solutions and systems to a global OE customer base including NVH performance materials advanced suspension technologies ride control and braking. In addition to automotive light vehicles and commercial vehicles Ride Performance also services a wide range of other mobility markets such as rail two-wheelers such as motorcycles and mountain bikes and motorsports.

Powertrain segment generates approximately 25% of revenue. Powertrain offers its customers a diverse array of market-leading products for OE applications including pistons piston rings piston pins cylinder liners valvetrain products valve seats and guides ignition products dynamic seals bonded piston seals combustion and exhaust gaskets static gaskets and seals rigid heat shields engine bearings industrial bearings bushings and washers systems protection sleeves acoustic shielding and flexible heat shields.

The Motorparts segment accounts for about 20% plus of the company's revenue. Designs manufactures markets and distributes leading brand-name products to a diversified and global aftermarket customer base. Within the business Motorparts has many of the most recognized brand-name products in the automotive industry including Monroe Champion –hlins MOOG Walker Fel-Pro and others.

Geographic Reach

In addition to key alliances and joint ventures Tenneco operates in about 200 manufacturing facilities on six continents throughout the world including Argentina Brazil India China and Thailand.

The Clean Air segment operates about 60 manufacturing facilities worldwide some of which are joint ventures. About 15 are in North and South America approximately 20 are in Europe and close to 25 are in Asia Pacific. Ride Performance has 40 manufacturing facilities with about 15 in North and South America roughly 15 in Europe and about 10 in Asia Pacific.

Tenneco's major geographic segments are the US which represents about 35% of its total sales followed by China and Germany with almost 15% each.

Sales and Marketing

Tenneco has separate sales and marketing staffs for original equipment (OE) and aftermarket customers. For OE the sales team includes engineers and program managers and are organized by customer business unit and product type (ride performance clean air and powertrain).

For aftermarket sales the sales force is organized by region and covers multiple product lines. It sells aftermarket products through a combination of full-line warehouse distributors direct sales to retailers and service providers and direct sales through online channels.

GM and Ford each account for about 10% of Tenneco's total revenue. Other customers include Nissan BMW Navistar PSA Peugeot FAW Toyota and Jaguar among others. In addition to the motor vehicle industry the company also serves the agricultural (John Deere and Caterpillar) marine railroad aerospace power generation and industrial markets.

Financial Performance

Tenneco has seen a general upward trend in sales over the last several years. Since 2015 the company's revenue increased by $9.3 billion to $17.5 billion in 2019.

Tenneco's revenues were $17450 million an increase of $5687 million or 48% for the year 2019. The acquisitions increased revenues by $5600 million or 48%. The net favorable effects of organic growth primarily drove the remaining increase in revenues from higher sales volume. This was partially offset by the unfavorable effects of foreign currency exchange.

The company's profits jumped to $334 million in 2019 compared with $55 million the prior year.

Cash at the end of fiscal 2018 was $566 million a decreased of $136 million from the prior year. Cash from operations contributed $444 million to the coffers while investing activities used $606 million mainly for the acquisition and cash payments for plant property and equipment. Financing activities provided $3 million from the proceeds from term loans to finance the acquisition.

Strategy

The company focuses on growth addressing the evolving needs of its OE and aftermarket customers around the world to drive growth. The company seeks to continue optimizing its performance through enhanced efficiencies in order to meet the world-class delivery performance its customers increasingly require. The company has made and will continue to make investments in its global distribution network to maximize its manufacturing footprint and manage complexities of its supply chain.

As stricter environmental standards are enacted Tenneco finds itself well positioned as a supplier of emission control systems. The company has developed diesel particulate filters (DPFs) for passenger cars and medium-duty trucks both in Europe and North America. The filters when used with converters can reduce emissions of particulates by up to 90% and of nitrogen oxide by up to 85%.

Another trend in the automotive industry that is building Tenneco's business is OEMs simplify their assembly process thus reducing costs and development times. To achieve this they are outsourcing more of the design and manufacturing of vehicle parts as well as fully-integrated systems that support emission control anti-lock braking roll-control and powertrains. This trend has given rise to Tier 1 systems integrators in addition to Tier 1 suppliers. Tenneco fits the bill for both roles. To boost its position even further the company offers just-in-time (JIT) systems for its emission control operations and has built JIT facilities close to customers' plants for quick delivery of product components.

Mergers and Acquisitions

In 2019 Tenneco completed the acquisition of a 90.5% ownership interest in –hlins Intressenter AB (the –hlins Acquisition) a Swedish technology company that develops premium suspension systems and components for the automotive and motorsport industries which is part of its Ride Performance operating segment. The purchase price was $162 million.

HISTORY

Tennessee Gas and Transmission began in 1943 as a division of the Chicago Corporation headed by Gardiner Symonds and authorized to build a pipeline from West Virginia to the Gulf of Mexico. With the US facing WWII fuel shortages the group finished the project in 11 months.

After WWII Tennessee Gas went public with Symonds as president. It merged its oil and gas exploration interests into Tennessee Production Company (1954) which with Bay Petroleum (bought 1955) became Tenneco Oil in 1961. Symonds acquired complementary firms and entered the chemical industry by buying 50% of Petro-Tex Chemical in 1955.

Tenneco Oil moved its headquarters to Houston in 1963 to better ship natural gas from the Texas Gulf Coast. Symonds bought Packaging Corporation of America a maker of shipping containers pulp and paperboard products in 1965. A year later the company which had become a conglomerate adopted the Tenneco name.

EXECUTIVES

Vice President Human Resources, Mike Schneider

Evp And Cfo, Kenneth R. (Ken) Trammell, age 59, $625,000 total compensation

Vp And Cio, H. William Haser, age 59

Ceo, Brian Kesseler, age 54, $895,000 total compensation

Evp And President Asia/pacific, Peng (Patrick) Guo, age 54

Svp And General Manager Global Aftermarket, Joseph A. (Joe) Pomaranski, age 64

Vp And General Manager North America Aftermarket, Jeff Koviak

Vp And General Manager North America Clean Air, Michael Seurynck

Vp And General Manager North America Ride Performance, Jack Hall

Vp And General Manager Europe Aftermarket, Bruce Ronning

Vp And General Manager China Clean Air, Yih Sng

Vp And General Manager China Aftermarket, Edward Hang

Vp And General Manager Global Elastomers, Steve Pohlman

Managing Director India, Sagar Hemade

General Manager Japan, Yasuhara Shimonishi

Vp Clean Air Global Research And Development And Systems Integration, Ben Patel

Evp And President Ride Performance, Martin Hendricks, age 57

Vp And General Manager Europe Ride Performance, Jean-Luc Desire

Vp And General Manager Europe Clean Air, Traci Melville

Vp And General Manager China Ride Performance, Yi Ren

Vice President General Manager, Alex Gelbcke

Vp Global Communications, Jane Ostrander

Svp, Gregg Bolt

Vice President, Richard Wambold

Vice President Finance, Leo Waner

Vp And Gm Aftermarket Europe, Maurits Binnendijk

Vp Business Management Systems, Steve Vielmetti

Vice President Of Human Resources, Brian Boukalik

Senior Vice President Strategy And Corporate Development, Elizabeth Williams

Vice President Finance Global Clean Air Division, Steven Darwin

Vice President, Kaled Awada

Vice President Of South America Aftermarket, Antonio Teodoro

Vice President Of Investor Relations, Richard Kwas

Chairman, Gregg M. Sherrill, age 67

Auditors: PricewaterhouseCoopers LLP

LOCATIONS

HQ: Tenneco Inc
500 North Field Drive, Lake Forest, IL 60045
Phone: 847 482-5000
Web: www.tenneco.com

2018 Sales

	$ mil.	% of total
US	4,488	38
China	1,553	13
Germany	1,212	10
Poland	731	6
Mexico	543	5
United Kingdom	499	4
India	316	3
Turkey	7	-
Other Foreign	2,414	21
Total	**11,763**	**100**

PRODUCTS/OPERATIONS

2018 Sales

	$ mil.	% of total
Clean Air Products & Systems	6,707	57
Ride Performance	1,949	17
Aftermarket	1,221	10
Powertrain	1,112	9
Motorparts	774	7
Total	**11,763**	**100**

Selected Brands and Products

Emission control systems (DynoMax Fonos Thrush and Walker)
  Aftertreatment control units
  Burner systems
  Catalytic converters and diesel oxidation catalysts
  Diesel particulate filters (DPFs)
  Exhaust manifolds
  Hangers and isolators
  High-frequency turbo decoupler
  Hydrocarbon vaporizers and injectors
  Lean NOx traps
  Mufflers
  Pipes
  Resonators
  Selective catalytic reduction (SCR)
Ride control systems (Fric-Rot Monroe and Rancho)
  Coil and leaf springs
  Computerized electronic suspension (CES)
  Corner and full axle modules
  Heavy duty truck and train shocks
  Kinetic suspension technology
  Shock absorbers and struts
  Suspension systems
  Top mounts
  Vibration control components (Clevite Elastomers)
  Engine and body mounts
  Exhaust isolators
  Leaf and coil springs
  Spring seats
  Suspension control arm link and stabilizer bar bushings

COMPETITORS

Benteler Automotive
Cooper-Standard Automotive
Edelbrock
Faurecia Exhaust Systems
Kolbenschmidt Pierburg
Letts Industries
Meritor
Wescast Industries
ZF Group NAO

Income Statement				FYE: December 31
	REVENUE ($ mil.)	NET INCOME ($ mil.)	NET PROFIT MARGIN	EMPLOYEES
12/19	17,450	(334)	—	78,000
12/18	11,763	55	0.5%	81,000
12/17	9,274	207	2.2%	32,000
12/16	8,599	363	4.2%	31,000
12/15	8,209	247	3.0%	30,000
Annual Growth	20.7%	—	—	27.0%

2019 Year-End Financials

Debt ratio: 41.99%	No. of shares (mil.): 80
Return on equity: (-21.20%)	Dividends
Cash ($ mil.): 564	Yield: 7.6%
Current ratio: 1.33	Payout: —
Long-term debt ($ mil.): 5,371	Market value ($ mil.): 1,060

	STOCK PRICE ($) FY Close	P/E High/Low		PER SHARE ($) Earnings	Dividends	Book Value
12/19	13.10	—	—	(4.12)	1.00	17.61
12/18	27.39	70	28	0.93	1.00	21.34
12/17	58.54	17	13	3.91	1.00	13.53
12/16	62.47	10	5	6.44	0.00	10.84
12/15	45.91	15	10	4.11	0.00	7.52
Annual Growth	(26.9%)	—	—	—	—	23.7%

Tennessee Valley Authority

Tennessee Valley Authority (TVA) is a US government-owned corporation and the largest public power producer in the country. It sells wholesale electricity to more than 150 municipal and cooperative power distributors which serve nearly 10 million people in Tennessee and parts of Alabama Georgia Kentucky Mississippi North Carolina and Virginia. It also sells power directly to large industrial customers and federal agencies. In addition TVA provides flood control and land management for the Tennessee River system and assists utilities and state and local governments with economic development.

Operations

Tennessee Valley Authority operates six fossil plants three nuclear plants more than 15 natural gas or oil-fired plants and about 30 hydroelectric plants. TVA provides electric power through a network of nearly 20000 miles of transmission line which delivers more than 160 billion kWh of electricity annually. While most of its power comes from traditional generation sources it also operates nearly 15 solar energy sites. Other facilities include a diesel generator plant digester gas co-firing capacity at one coal-fired plant and biomass co-firing potential located at its coal-fired sites.

TVA's power generation mix includes nuclear (about 40% of sales) coal and natural gas (about 20% each) hydro (10%) and the rest from purchased renewable and non-renewable power.

TVA also has an agreement with the US Department of Energy (DOE) to produce tritium a radioactive gas that boosts the power of nuclear weapons at its Watts Bar TN nuclear plant.

Geographic Reach

TVA supplies power in large parts of Tennessee Alabama Mississippi and Kentucky and in portions of Georgia North Carolina and Virginia. Tennessee accounts for 65% of the company's revenue Alabama around 15% and Mississippi about 10%.

Sales and Marketing

Tennessee Valley Authority provides electricity to large industrial customers federal agencies and local power companies (LPCs) serving nearly 10 million people in parts of seven southeastern states. Two of the largest LPCs served by TVA are the Memphis Light Gas and Water Division and Nashville Electric Service.

Financial Performance

TVA has seen fluctuations in revenue over the last several years as the company is dependent on the weather for both demand for electricity as well as the price for that power.

Revenue for TVA increased 5% in 2018 primarily due to colder than normal temperatures and an increase in total degree days (measured by how many degrees the temperature fluctuates from 65Å F in the five largest cities in its service area).

Net income almost doubled to $1.1 billion in 2018 compared with $685 million the previous year. This was primarily due to increased sales and lower operating and fuel costs. Operating costs in 2017 included a one-time $500 million contribution to the TVA's pension plan.

Cash at the end of fiscal 2018 was $299 million a decrease of $1 million from the prior year. Cash from operations contributed $4.0 billion to the coffers while investing activities used $2.3 billion mainly for construction and nuclear fuel expenditures. Financing activities used another $1.7 billion for bond repurchases.

Strategy

TVA is changing its power generation mix to become a cleaner producer of energy. It has closed or is closing several older less efficient coal-generated power units while putting more natural gas-fired units online as well as increasing nuclear generation capabilities. The authority is working toward obtaining 50% of its power supply from low- or zero-carbon-emitting or renewable sources by 2020.

In 2019 the company released a draft of its Integrated Resource Plan (IRP). The document outlines the company's long-term operational and financial plan to provide reliable electric power and support environmental stewardship while creating a flexible operating model that takes into account increasing amounts of renewable energy sources and distributed energy resources (DER).

HISTORY

TVA was established by Congress in 1933 primarily to reduce flood damage improve navigation on the Tennessee River and promote agricultural and industrial development in the region. In 1999 government appropriations for the authority ceased.

In 1924 the Army Corps of Engineers finished building the Wilson Dam on the Tennessee River in Alabama to provide power for two WWI-era nitrate plants. With the war over the question of what to do with the plants became a political football.

An act of Congress created the Tennessee Valley Authority (TVA) in 1933 to manage the plants and Tennessee Valley waterways. New Dealers saw TVA as a way to revitalize the local economy through improved navigation and power generation. Power companies claimed the agency was unconstitutional but by 1939 when a federal court ruled against them TVA had five operating hydroelectric plants and five under construction.

During the 1940s TVA supplied power for the war effort including the Manhattan Project in Tennessee. During the postwar boom between 1945 and 1950 power usage in the Tennessee Valley nearly doubled. Despite adding dams TVA couldn't keep up with demand so in 1949 it began building a coal-fired unit. Because coal-fired plants weren't part of TVA's original mission in 1955 a Congressional panel recommended the authority be dissolved.

Though TVA survived its funding was cut. In 1959 it was allowed to sell bonds but it no longer received direct government appropriations for power operations. In addition it had to pay back the government for past appropriations.

TVA began to build the first unit of an ambitious 17-plant nuclear power program in Alabama in 1967. However skyrocketing costs forced it to raise rates and cut maintenance on its coal-fired plants which led to breakdowns. In 1985 five reactors had to be shut down because of safety concerns.

In 1988 former auto industry executive Marvin Runyon was appointed chairman of the agency. "Carvin' Marvin" cut management sold three airplanes and got rid of peripheral businesses saving $400 million a year. In 1992 Runyon left to go to the postal service and was replaced by Craven Crowell who began preparing TVA for competition in the retail power market.

TVA ended its nuclear construction program in 1996 after bringing two nuclear units on line within three months a first for a US utility. The next year it raised rates for the first time in 10 years planning to reduce its debt. In response to a lawsuit filed by neighboring utilities it agreed to stop "laundering" power by using third parties to sell outside the agency's legally authorized area.

In 1999 the authority finished installing almost $2 billion in scrubbers and other equipment at its coal-fired plants so that it could buy Kentucky coal along with cleaner Wyoming coal. That year however the EPA charged TVA with violating the Clean Air Act by making major overhauls on some of its older coal-fired plants without getting permits or installing updated pollution-control equipment. It ordered TVA to bring most of its coal-fired plants into compliance with more current pollution standards. The next year TVA contested the order in court stating compliance would jack up electricity rates.

TVA was fined by the US Nuclear Regulatory Commission in 2000 for laying off a nuclear plant whistleblower.

In 2008 a holding pond at TVA's coal-burning Kingston Fossil Plant failed and dumped some 5.4 million cu. yd. of fly ash over 400 acres in eastern Tennessee's Roane County. The slide knocked down utility poles and trees and damaged at least a dozen homes (some beyond repair). Although no one was hurt some residents were cut off by the spill prompting officials to build a new road. The flooding was the pond's third reported incident in six years. The cleanup will likely cost more than $1 billion. Some 14 lawsuits were filed against the TVA as a result of the incident.

William D. Johnson former chairman president and CEO of Progress Energy was named president and CEO of TVA in 2013.

EXECUTIVES

Evp And Cfo, John M. Thomas, age 57, $577,212 total compensation

Evp And Chief Nuclear Officer, Joseph P. (Joe) Grimes, age 63, $557,135 total compensation

Svp Distributed Energy Resources, Jay C. Stowe

Evp And Coo, Charles G. (Chip) Pardee, age 60, $647,481 total compensation

Evp External Relations, Van M. Wardlaw, age 60

Svp Watts Bar Operations And Construction, Michael D. (Mike) Skaggs, $446,712 total compensation

President Ceo And Director, William D. (Bill) Johnson, age 65, $998,827 total compensation

Svp Chief Communications And Marketing Officer, Janet J. Brewer

Evp And General Counsel, Sherry A. Quirk, age 65

Senior Vice President Human Resources And Communication, Katherine Black

Executive Vice President And Chief Nuclear Officer, Joe Grimes

Chair, V. Lynn Evans

Auditors: Ernst & Young LLP

LOCATIONS

HQ: Tennessee Valley Authority
400 W. Summit Hill Drive, Knoxville, TN 37902
Phone: 865 632-2101
Web: www.tva.gov

2018 Sales

	$ mil.	% of total
Tennessee	7,350	65
Alabama	1,600	14
Mississippi	1,052	9
Kentucky	696	6
Georgia	267	2
North Carolina	66	1
Virginia	48	1
Off-system sales	7	—
Other revenues	158	2
Revenue capitalized during pre-commercial plant operations	(11)	-
Total	**11,233**	**100**

PRODUCTS/OPERATIONS

2018 Sales

	$ mil.	% of total
Electricity sales:		
Local power companies	10,262	91
Industries directly served	695	6
Federal agencies and other	129	1
Other revenues	158	2
Revenue capitalized during per-commercial plant operations	(11)	-
Total	**11,233**	**100**

HISTORICAL FINANCIALS
Company Type: Public

Income Statement   FYE: September 30

	REVENUE ($ mil.)	NET INCOME ($ mil.)	NET PROFIT MARGIN	EMPLOYEES
09/20	10,249	1,352	13.2%	9,989
09/19	11,318	1,417	12.5%	10,009
09/18	11,233	1,119	10.0%	10,023
09/17	10,739	685	6.4%	10,092
09/16	10,616	1,233	11.6%	10,691
Annual Growth	**(0.9%)**	**2.3%**	**—**	**(1.7%)**

2020 Year-End Financials

Debt ratio: 39.54%—
Return on equity: 10.98%
Cash ($ mil.): 500
Current ratio: 0.69
Long-term debt ($ mil.): 19,004

Dividends
Yield: 2.9%
Payout: —
Market value ($ mil.): —

	STOCK PRICE ($) FY Close	P/E High/Low	PER SHARE ($) Earnings	Dividends	Book Value
09/20	27.53	— —	(0.00)	0.80	(0.00)
09/19	25.11	— —	(0.00)	0.89	(0.00)
09/18	24.65	— —	(0.00)	0.84	(0.00)
09/17	25.18	— —	(0.00)	0.84	(0.00)
09/16	25.91	— —	(0.00)	0.89	(0.00)
Annual Growth	**1.5%**	**— —**	**—**	**(2.6%)**	

Territorial Bancorp Inc

Territorial Bancorp serves its customers island-style. It is the financial holding company for Territorial Savings Bank which provides standard products and services such as checking and savings accounts money market accounts CDs IRAs and loans from its nearly 30 branch locations across Hawaii. Its Territorial Financial Services subsidiary sells insurance while LPL Financial offers Mutual funds and annuities. Territorial Savings Bank targets the territorial nature of its customers — one- to four-family residential mortgages account for 95% of its loan portfolio. Multifamily and commercial mortgages and construction and home equity loans round out its lending activities.

Operations

Territorial Bancorp generated 61% of its total revenue from loan interest in 2014 with another 31% coming from interest on its investment securities. About 3% of its revenue came from service fees on loan and deposit accounts while 2% came from gains on its investment security sales.

Sales and Marketing

The bank provides financial services to individuals families and small- to medium-sized businesses from its 28 branches spread across the state of Hawaii.

Financial Performance

Territorial's revenues and profits have been slowly declining in recent years mostly as its margins have been squeezed in the low-interest environment and as its gains on its held-for-sale loans have been shrinking.

The company's revenue ended mostly flat around $64.8 million in 2014 with mixed results. The bank's loan and investment security interest grew by 7% thanks to asset growth though these improvements were offset by lower gains on in-

---

vestment securities and loans compared to the year before.

Lower revenue in 2014 coupled with a slight uptick in loan loss provisions and equipment investment costs caused Territorial Bancorp's net income to tumble by 4% to $14.1 million. Its operating cash levels also fell by 19% to $14.1 million after adjusting its earnings for non-cash items mostly related to its net proceeds on its held-for-sale loans.

Strategy

Territorial Bancorp relies on its competitive rates and pricing to grow its loan and deposit business. During 2014 its deposit business grew organically by nearly 6% mostly as the bank promoted its higher-than-market rates for its passbook and statement savings accounts.

Company Background

Founded in 1921 Territorial Savings was mutually owned until 2009 when its former parent Territorial Mutual Holding Company converted to a stock form of ownership and sold shares in itself to the public. The move allowed the company to offer other financial services in addition to banking.

EXECUTIVES

Chairman President And Ceo Territorial Bancorp Inc. And Territorial Savings Bank, Allan S. Kitagawa, age 74, $766,080 total compensation

Vice Chairman Co-coo General Counsel And Corporate Secretary Territorial Bancorp Inc. And Territorial Savings Bank, Vernon Hirata, age 67, $269,100 total compensation

Svp Business Development And Marketing, Denise Takashima

Svp Branch Administration, Robert Costa

Vice Chairman And Co-coo Territorial Bancorp Inc. And Territorial Savings Bank, Ralph Y. Nakatsuka, age 64, $269,100 total compensation

Assistant Vice President Branch Manager Loan Officer, Geoffrey Baricaua

Board Of Directors, David Murakami

Auditors: Moss Adams LLP

LOCATIONS

HQ: Territorial Bancorp Inc
1132 Bishop Street, Suite 2200, Honolulu, HI 96813
Phone: 808 946-1400
Web: www.territorialsavings.net

PRODUCTS/OPERATIONS

2014 Sales

	$ mil.	% of total
Interest and dividend income		
Loans	39	61
Investment securities	19	31
Others	0	-
Non-interest income		
Service fees on loan and deposits	2	3
Income on bank owned life insurance	1	2
Others	2	3
Total	**64**	**100**

COMPETITORS

American Savings Bank	Central Pacific
Bank of Hawaii	Financial

HISTORICAL FINANCIALS

Company Type: Public

Income Statement

FYE: December 31

	ASSETS ($ mil.)	NET INCOME ($ mil.)	INCOME AS % OF ASSETS	EMPLOYEES
12/19	2,086	22	1.1%	281
12/18	2,069	19	0.9%	285
12/17	2,003	14	0.7%	283
12/16	1,877	16	0.9%	276
12/15	1,821	14	0.8%	280
Annual Growth	3.5%	10.5%	—	0.1%

2019 Year-End Financials

Debt ratio: —
Return on equity: 9.18%
Cash ($ mil.): 44
Current ratio: —
Long-term debt ($ mil.): —

No. of shares (mil.): 9
Dividends
Yield: 4.8%
Payout: 64.7%
Market value ($ mil.): 300

	STOCK PRICE ($) FY Close	P/E High/Low	PER SHARE ($) Earnings	Dividends	Book Value
12/19	30.94	14 11	2.34	1.49	25.19
12/18	25.98	15 12	2.03	1.14	24.37
12/17	30.87	21 18	1.57	1.20	23.69
12/16	32.84	18 14	1.76	0.92	23.50
12/15	27.74	18 13	1.59	0.76	22.74
Annual Growth	2.8%	— —	10.1%	18.3%	2.6%

Tesla Inc

Founded in 2003 the company designs develops manufactures and markets high-performance technologically advanced electric cars and solar energy generation and energy storage products. Tesla sells more than five fully electric cars among others the Model S sedan and the Model X SUV and the Model 3 sedan which is among the world's top-selling electric cars. The fuel-efficient fully electric vehicles recharge their lithium-ion batteries from an outlet. Tesla's Autopilot self-driving technology hardware has been available on all Tesla models since late 2016. US customers generate more than half of Tesla's sales. CEO Elon Musk cofounded PayPal and also runs SpaceX.

Operations

Tesla operates in two repotable segments: Automotive and Energy generation and storage.

The automotive segment generates about 85% of sales. The segment includes sales and leasing of electric vehicles as well as sales of automotive regulatory credits. Its other electric vehicles are: Model Y Cybertruck Tesla Roadster and Tesla Semi. Additionally the segment is also comprised of services and others. It accounts almost 10% of sales and includes non-warranty after-sales vehicle services sales of used vehicles retail merchandise sales by the acquired subsidiaries to third party customers and vehicle insurance revenue.

The company's energy generation and storage segment (just over 5% of revenue) makes and sells stationary energy storage products and solar energy systems to residential and small commercial customers. Its Powerwall lithium-ion battery with integrated inverter system is designed to store energy at a home or small commercial facility. Tesla's commercial industrial and utility offering Powerpack and Megapack is an energy storage system that can also be combined with renewable energy generation sources to create microgrids. Megapack also offers feature like grouping multiple units to form a larger installations capable of reaching gigawatt hours or greater. Tesla's solar energy systems include solar panels inverters and rack systems. The company's Solar Roof gathers solar energy from glass tiles that aim to be more architecturally pleasing than traditional roof-mounted solar panels.

Geographic Reach

Tesla headquartered in Palo Alto California operates manufacturing facilities in Fremont and Lathrop California; Tilburg the Netherlands; and its Gigafactories near Reno Nevada Buffalo New York Berlin Germany and Shanghai China. Energy storage products are manufactured at its Gigafactory Nevada. Solar products are made primarily at Tesla's Gigafactory in Buffalo New York. The US accounts for more than 50% of sales. Other markets for which the company breaks out sales include China (over 10% of sales) Netherlands (more than 5%) and Norway (about 5%). The remainder is generated by other countries for about 25% of sales.

Sales and Marketing

Tesla markets and sells cars directly to consumers through website and an international network of company-owned stores and galleries. Tesla is notable in that it does not use dealerships (due in some states to legal restrictions). The company also offers used vehicle business that supports new vehicle sales by integrating sales of new Tesla vehicle with customer's trade-in needs for their vehicle. The company continuously builds networks of Supercharger and Destination Charging stations in Australia Canada China France Germany Italy Japan Russia South Korea U.A.E. U.K. U.S. and in approximately more than 40 countries that provides fast convenient charging locations for Tesla owners to recharge their vehicles.

The company's solar energy and storage products are typically sold directly to residential customers through the company's stores and galleries and through channel partners domestically. An international sales organizations and network of channel partners market and sell Powerwall directly to utilities Powerpack and Megapack systems to commercial and utility customers.

Tesla's advertising costs were $27 million $32 million and $37 million for the years 2019 2018 and 2017 respectively.

Financial Performance

Tesla's revenue growth has accelerated like its first car the Roadster sportscar (0-60 in 1.9 seconds) driven by the rising number of vehicles sold each year. Between 2015 and 2019 sales have grown a whopping 507%. The company however has posted a string of net losses as it pours money into research and development and manufacturing.

Tesla's revenue jumped 15% to $24.6 billion in 2019 driven by an 87% increase in automotive revenue. This was primarily due to the increase of automotive sales revenue by $2.32 billion or 13% in the year ended December 31 2019 as compared to the year ended December 31 2018.

The company lost about $862 million in 2019 which was an improvement over the $976 million lost in 2018.

Cash at the end of 2019 was $6.8 billion an increase of about $2.5 billion from the prior year. Cash from operations contributed $2.4 billion to the coffers while investing activities used $1.4 billion mainly for capital expenditures. Financing activities generated $1.5 billion primarily in the form proceeds from issuances of convertible and other debt.

Strategy

To help meet that goal and ramp up sales in overseas markets Tesla's Gigafactory 3 in Shanghai China began building cars in late 2019. Model 3s rolling out of Gigafactory 3 is pivotal to Tesla's play in the world's largest electric car market and will help it gain ground in China while avoiding import tariffs. Shortly after the opening of Gigafactory 3 Tesla announced it would build its next Gigafactory in Germany outside Berlin. A manufacturing base in Germany is expected to avoid the complications of exporting cars to Europe.

Tesla is also busy advancing its autonomous car technology. The company's Autopilot driver assist system includes auto-steering traffic-aware cruise control automated lane changing and other features that together offer a complete self-driving experience while keeping the driver in ultimate control of the car.

Mergers and Acquisitions

In late 2019 Tesla acquired Canada-based Hibar Systems Ltd. a manufacturer of battery systems for electric automobiles laptops and other products. Industry watchers believe the deal is part of Tesla's strategy to establish its own battery cell manufacturing capacity.

In late 2019 Tesla bought computer vision start-up DeepScale based in Mount View California. DeepScale's technology helps automakers use low-wattage processors to power very accurate computer vision. The purchase of DeepScale is expected to accelerate Tesla's autonomous driving technology efforts.

In early 2019 Tesla acquired energy technology company Maxwell Technologies Inc. in an all-stock deal valued at more than $200 million. Maxwell based in San Diego California develops and makes ultracapacitors devices that can store and quickly deliver surges of energy. Tesla would use Maxwell's dry electrode technology that will have a very big impact to the company.

Company Background

Tesla Motors is named for Nikola Tesla (1856-1943) the renowned Serbian-American engineer and inventor. Tesla Motors was incorporated in July 2003.

EXECUTIVES

Chairman Ceo And Product Architect, Elon Musk, age 49, $45,936 total compensation
Cfo, Deepak Ahuja, age 57, $338,000 total compensation
Cto, Jeffrey B. (JB) Straubel, age 44, $250,560 total compensation
Vice President Power Electronics, Nick Kalayjian
Vice President Global Investor Relations, Jeff Evanson
National Sales Manager, Christine Moore
Vice President Production, Peter Hochholdinger
Chief People Officer, Gaby Toledano
Vice President Ir And Strategy, Jeff K Evanson

LOCATIONS

HQ: Tesla Inc
  3500 Deer Creek Road, Palo Alto, CA 94304
Phone: 650 681-5000
Web: www.teslamotors.com

2017 Sales

	$ mil.	% of total
US	6,221	53
China	2,027	17
Norway	823	7
Other	2,687	23
Total	**11,758**	**100**

PRODUCTS/OPERATIONS

2017 Sales

	$ mil.	% of total
Automotive	10,624	91
Energy generation & storage	1,116	9
Total	**11,758**	**100**

COMPETITORS

AES	Mitsubishi Motors
BMW	Nissan
BYD	Samsung Electronics
Daimler	Siemens Energy
FCA US	Subaru of America
Ford Motor	SunPower
General Motors	Sunrun
Honda	Suzuki Motor
Hyundai Motor	Toyota
Isuzu	Vivint Solar Inc.
Kia Motors	Volkswagen
LG Chem	VydroTech

HISTORICAL FINANCIALS

Company Type: Public

Income Statement   FYE: December 31

	REVENUE ($ mil.)	NET INCOME ($ mil.)	NET PROFIT MARGIN	EMPLOYEES
12/19	24,578	(862)	—	48,016
12/18	21,461	(976)	—	48,817
12/17	11,758	(1,961)	—	37,543
12/16	7,000	(674)	—	30,025
12/15	4,046	(888)	—	13,058
Annual Growth	**57.0%**	—	—	**38.5%**

2019 Year-End Financials

Debt ratio: 39.11%
Return on equity: (-14.94%)
Cash ($ mil.): 6,268
Current ratio: 1.13
Long-term debt ($ mil.): 11,634

No. of shares (mil.): 905
Dividends
  Yield: —
  Payout: —
Market value ($ mil.): 378,589

	STOCK PRICE ($) FY Close	P/E High/Low	PER SHARE ($) Earnings	Dividends	Book Value
12/19	418.33	— —	(0.98)	0.00	7.31
12/18	332.80	— —	(1.14)	0.00	5.70
12/17	311.35	— —	(2.37)	0.00	5.02
12/16	213.69	— —	(0.94)	0.00	5.88
12/15	240.01	— —	(1.39)	0.00	1.66
Annual Growth	**14.9%**	— —	—	—	**44.9%**

Texas Capital Bancshares Inc

Texas Capital Bancshares is the parent company of Texas Capital Bank with more than 10 branches in Austin Dallas Fort Worth Houston and San Antonio. The bank targets high-net-worth individuals and Texas-based businesses with more than $5 million in annual revenue with a focus on the real estate financial services transportation communications petrochemicals and mining sectors. Striving for personalized services for its clients the bank offers deposit accounts Visa credit cards commercial loans and mortgages equipment leasing wealth management and trust services. Its BankDirect division provides online banking services. Founded in 1998 Texas Capital Bancshares has about $11.7 billion in assets.

Financial Performance
The bank reported $488.6 million in revenue in 2013 an nearly 11% increase versus 2012. Net income was flat at about $121 million after posting three consecutive years of gains. Cash flow from operations continued its steep three year decline. The bank's total assets increased 11% from about $10.5 billion in 2012 to $11.7 billion in 2013. Total deposits increased 24% year over year to about $9.3 billion.

Strategy
Headquartered in Dallas Texas Capital Bank (TCB) believes that its Texas roots give it a competitive advantage over larger competitors that are headquartered out of state. Indeed TCB is gaining market share and is expanding by hiring experienced bankers and support staff. The bank is looking to grow within its main metropolitan markets but has also branched out beyond the borders of its home state. The bank has an Cayman Islands branch to offer offshore cash management and deposit products to it core clientele.

EXECUTIVES

President And Ceo Texas Capital Bancshares Inc. President And Ceo Texas Capital Bank, C. Keith Cargill, age 67, $825,000 total compensation
President Texas And Chief Lending Officer Texas Capital Bank, Vince A. Ackerson, age 63, $454,166 total compensation
Managing Director Regional And Specialty Banking Texas Capital Bank Austin Fort Worth And San Antonio And Commercial Real Estate And Builder Finance, Mark M. Johnson
Evp Austin Region Texas Capital Bank, Kerry L. Hall
Regional President Texas Capital Bank Dallas, Russell Hartsfield
Chief Risk Officer Texas Capital Bancshares Inc. And Texas Capital Bank, John D. Hudgens, age 64, $455,833 total compensation
Managing Director Specialty And Regional Banking Texas Capital Bank Dallas And Syndicated Finance Lender Finance Leasing And Financial Institutions, James D. (Jim) Recer
Regional Chairman Texas Capital Bank Houston, Bill Wilson
Regional President Texas Capital Bank San Antonio, David Pope
Managing Director Regional And Specialty Banking Texas Capital Bank Houston, John C. Sarvadi
Cfo, Julie L. Anderson, age 51, $355,000 total compensation
Regional Chairman Texas Capital Bank San Antonio, Shaun Kennedy
Regional Chairman Texas Capital Bank Fort Worth, Robin Hamilton
Regional President Texas Capital Bank Fort Worth, David Williams
Evp Builder Finance, Melissa Abel
Evp Asset Based Lending, Chris Capriotti
Evp Commercial Real Estate, Rob Delph
Evp Lender Finance, David Fricke
Evp Energy/oil And Gas Syndicated Finance And Financial Institutions, Lester Keliher
Evp Financial Institutions, Peter Stringer
President Mortgage Finance, Gary Ort
Evp Technology Operations Enterprise Planning And Information Security Texas Capital Bank, Kirk Coleman
Evp Sba Lending, John Gannon
Evp Public Finance, Paul Howell
Evp Strategic Sales And Marketing, Greg Lewis
President Private Wealth Advisors, Alan L. Miller
Senior Vice President Compensation Director, Chris Gullo
Vice President, Raul Cantu
Vice President Electronic Funds Transfer Texas Capital Bank, Leslie Marsh
Vice President Of Information Technology Infrastructure, Randy Tiegs
Senior Vice President And Deposit Operation, Connie Couch
Vice President, Jenny Downey
Vice President Corp Security And Investigations, Cary Wicker
Vice President Fraud Investigator, Jamie Burud
Vice President Security, Neal Baker
Vice President Planning, Prasad Varma
Executive Vice President Director Of Operations, James White
Senior Vice President And Cra Manager, Phil Aslin
Chairman, Larry L. Helm, age 72
Board Member, Elysia Ragusa
Board Member, James Browning
Board Member, Robert Stallings
Board Member, Steven Rosenberg
Auditors: Ernst & Young LLP

LOCATIONS

HQ: Texas Capital Bancshares Inc
  2000 McKinney Avenue, Suite 700, Dallas, TX 75201
Phone: 214 932-6600
Web: www.texascapitalbank.com

PRODUCTS/OPERATIONS

2015 Sales

	$ mil.	% of total
Interest income		
Interest and fees on loans	594	92
Other	8	1
Non-interest income		
Brokered loan fees	18	3
Service charges on deposit accounts	8	1
Trust fee income	5	1
Swap fees	4	1
Other	11	1
Total	**650**	**100**

Selected Services

Association capital bank
Bankdirect
Business services
Mortgage business finance
Online services
Personal banking
Private wealth advisors
Treasury and liquidity

COMPETITORS

Amegy	Comerica
BBVA Compass	Cullen/Frost Bankers
Bancshares	JPMorgan Chase
BOK Financial	Prosperity Bancshares
Bank of America	Wells Fargo

HISTORICAL FINANCIALS

Company Type: Public

Income Statement

FYE: December 31

	ASSETS ($ mil.)	NET INCOME ($ mil.)	INCOME AS % OF ASSETS	EMPLOYEES
12/19	32,548	322	1.0%	1,738
12/18	28,257	300	1.1%	1,641
12/17	25,075	197	0.8%	1,564
12/16	21,697	155	0.7%	1,442
12/15	18,909	144	0.8%	1,329
Annual Growth	14.5%	22.2%	—	6.9%

2019 Year-End Financials

Debt ratio: 8.59%	No. of shares (mil.): 50
Return on equity: 12.11%	Dividends
Cash ($ mil.): 4,395	Yield: —
Current ratio: —	Payout: —
Long-term debt ($ mil.): —	Market value ($ mil.): 2,858

	STOCK PRICE ($) FY Close	P/E High/Low		PER SHARE ($) Earnings	Dividends	Book Value
12/19	56.77	11	8	6.21	0.00	56.27
12/18	51.09	18	8	5.79	0.00	49.81
12/17	88.90	25	19	3.73	0.00	44.37
12/16	78.40	26	10	3.11	0.00	40.59
12/15	49.42	21	14	2.91	0.00	35.39
Annual Growth	3.5%	—	—	20.9%	—	12.3%

TEXAS COUNTY AND DISTRICT RETIREMENT SYSTEM

EXECUTIVES

Exec Dir, Gene Glass
Cao*, Ray Smith
Deputy Dir*, Amy Bishop
Staff, Brad Eddins
Network Analyst, Brad Watkins
Contrl, Vincent Prendergast
Hedge Associate, Derek Bergquist
Investment Executive Assistant, Rachel Epstein
Accounting Manager, Tom Shephard
Investment Administrator, Vickie Dodson
Employer Plan Management Analy, Allison Coffey
Auditors: KPMG LLP AUSTIN TX

LOCATIONS

HQ: TEXAS COUNTY AND DISTRICT RETIREMENT SYSTEM
901 S MO PAC EXPY STE V50, AUSTIN, TX 787465776
Phone: 512 328-8889
Web: WWW.TCDRS.ORG

HISTORICAL FINANCIALS

Company Type: Private

Income Statement

FYE: December 31

	ASSETS ($ mil.)	NET INCOME ($ mil.)	INCOME AS % OF ASSETS	EMPLOYEES
12/16	26,387	1,761	6.7%	108
12/15	24,654	(182)	—	—
12/14	24,832	0	—	—
12/10	18,116	2,178	12.0%	—
Annual Growth	6.5%	(3.5%)	—	—

TEXAS DEPARTMENT OF TRANSPORTATION

Bob Wills saw Miles and Miles of Texas and the Texas Department of Transportation (TxDOT) makes sure that we do too. TxDOT builds and maintains interstate US and state highways as well as farm-to-market roads throughout the state. It also oversees public transportation systems in the state. The aviation division helps local governments manage funds for airport development. In 2009 the agency transferred some its responsibilities including issuing license plates and vehicle titles to the newly created Texas Department of Motor Vehicles. The governor-appointed five-member Texas Transportation Commission oversees TxDOT's work. The agency dates back to the Texas Highway Department created in 1917.

Operations

The Texas Department of Transportation is divided into 25 districts that each supervise the construction and maintenance of state highways in their jurisdictions. These districts are further divided into four administrative regions that provide such services as information technology purchasing accounting and project management support for the districts. A major Texas city is included in each of the four regions.

Current TxDOT projects include widening Interstate 35 to six lanes throughout Central Texas and reconstructing the State Loop 12/State Highway 114 interchange to improve traffic conditions in the Dallas/Fort Worth area.

EXECUTIVES

Exec Dir, James M Bass
P.e, Deputy Exec Dir*, Marc D Williams
Chief of Staff*, Richard McMonagle
Chief Planning and Project Off, Russell Zapalac
Chief Strategy and Innovation, Darran Anderson
Revenue Accounting, Nigel Lewis
Chief Audit & Compliance Ofcr, Benito Ybarra
Chief Procurement Off, Lauren Garduno Pe
Chief Engineer, Bill Hale
Supervisor Judge Roy Bean Tic, Miguel Zuniga
Purchaser, Keith Reiss

LOCATIONS

HQ: TEXAS DEPARTMENT OF TRANSPORTATION
150 E RIVERSIDE DR, AUSTIN, TX 787041202
Phone: 512 463-8588
Web: WWW.TXDOT.GOV

HISTORICAL FINANCIALS

Company Type: Private

Income Statement

FYE: August 31

	REVENUE ($ mil.)	NET INCOME ($ mil.)	NET PROFIT MARGIN	EMPLOYEES
08/19	12,069	1,107	9.2%	14,720
08/18	10,993	1,123	10.2%	—
08/17	8,143	1,526	18.8%	—
08/16	8,699	332	3.8%	—
Annual Growth	11.5%	49.3%	—	—

Texas Instruments Inc.

Texas Instruments sticks to basics — producing analog and embedded processors the workhorses of the industry. The company's analog chips manage power in electronic equipment and its embedded processors handle specific tasks in electronic devices. TI's customers which number about 100000 use the company's chips for applications that include autos industrial machinery consumer electronics communications devices and calculators. The company also sticks to basics in production operating its own manufacturing plants which it places around the world. International customers generate about 85% of revenue. Another TI basic: TI engineer Jack Kilby was credited as co-inventor of the integrated circuit in the late 1950s.

Operations

Texas Instruments operates through two segments: Analog and Embedded Processing.

The Analog business which accounts for about 70% of sales includes high-volume analog and logic products power management semiconductors and amplifiers and data converters. The company's analog products are used in the personal electronics automotive and industrial markets as well as others.

The Embedded Processing segment which generates about 20% of sales makes digital signal processors (DSPs) and microcontrollers. TI's embedded processors range from low-cost microcontrollers used in products such as electric toothbrushes to complex devices used in automotive applications such as infotainment and advanced driver assistance systems.

The remaining revenue comes from the Other segment which includes digital light processors (DLP) used in projectors to create high-definition images calculators application specific integrated circuits (ASICs) and custom semiconductors.

Geographic Reach

China is the biggest single market for Texas Instruments accounting for about 50% of revenue with other Asia/Pacific countries (including Japan) accounting for some 10% of revenue. The US generates nearly 15% of TI's sales. Headquartered in Dallas Texas the company designs manufactures and has sales operations in more than 30 countries.

Sales and Marketing

Texas Instruments market and sell its products through direct sales channels including its broad sales force and website as well as through its distributors. About 65% of the company's revenue comes through distributors who keep inventory of TI products on hand. As for customers its 100 biggest account for about one-third of TI's sales.

In terms of markets TI gets about 35% of revenue from industrial about 25% from personal electronics about a fifth from automotive and more than 10% from communications with enterprise systems and calculators accounting for the remaining revenue.

Texas Instruments' advertising costs was $30 million $34 million and $39 million in 2019 2018 and 2017 respectively.

Financial Performance

After several years of fluctuating revenue TI has posted three straight years of solid gains.

In 2019 TI's revenue down 9% to $14.4 billion compared to $15.8 billion in 2018. Analog revenue decrease due to Power High Volume and to a lesser extent Signal Chain while Embedded Processing revenue decreased in both product lines led by Processors. Other revenue was 15% lower in 2019 from 2018.

Net income fell to $5 billion in 2019 from $5.6 billion in 2018.

The company's coffers held $2.4 billion in cash and equivalents in 2019 compared to its previous year. TI's operations generated $6.6 billion in 2019 while investing activities used $1.9 billion and financing activities used $4.7 billion.

Strategy

Texas Instruments' focus on its Analog and Embedded Processing units is paying off. They combined to produce 90% of the company's revenue. The company believes that analog and embedded processors offer diversity of applications long product life cycles and lower-cost manufacturing processes.

More narrowly TI has identified two markets where analog and embedded processes can generate growing sales over time: industrial and automotive. In 2019 automotive and industrial combined to provide about 55% of TI's revenue. TI believe these markets represent the best growth opportunities over the next decade or longer due to increasing semiconductor content.

On the manufacturing end TI is moving to produce more chips on 300-millimeter wafers which have a 40% cost advantage over standard 200-millimeter wafers. To strengthen this advantage TI is moving forward with its plan to build its new 300- millimetre wafer facility in Richardson Texas as 300-millimeter wafers will continue to support the majority of its Analog growth.

TI faces strong competition around the world from other chipmakers. The industry consolidation that TI has avoided has created bigger competitors with wider ranges of products and deeper resources. On the other side of the spectrum small companies with innovative products are capable of snatching market share away.

Company Background

Clarence "Doc" Karcher and Eugene McDermott founded Geophysical Service Inc. (GSI) in Newark New Jersey in 1930 to develop reflective seismology a new technology for oil and gas exploration. In 1934 GSI moved to Dallas. The company produced military electronics during WWII including submarine detectors for the US Navy. GSI changed its name to Texas Instruments (TI) in 1951.

TI began making transistors in 1952 after buying a license from Western Electric. The company went public on the New York Stock Exchange in 1953. In 1954 it introduced the Regency Radio the first pocket-sized transistor radio. (That year TI also produced the first commercial silicon transistor.)

TI engineer Jack Kilby invented the integrated circuit (IC) in 1958. Working independently Intel co-founder Robert Noyce developed an IC at the same time while working at Fairchild Semiconductor; the two men are credited as co-inventors. In 2000 Kilby was awarded the Nobel Prize in Physics for his work.

EXECUTIVES

Chairman President And Ceo, Richard K. (Rich) Templeton, age 61, $1,164,083 total compensation

Svp High-volume Analog And Logic Central Analog Services Dlpâ® Products And Education Technology, Stephen A. (Steve) Anderson, age 58, $616,500 total compensation

Svp Analog Power Products, Niels Anderskouv, age 50

Svp Technology And Manufacturing, Kevin J. Ritchie, age 64, $688,333 total compensation

Svp Embedded Processing, R. Gregory (Greg) Delagi, age 57, $622,917 total compensation

Evp And Coo, Brian T. Crutcher, age 47, $822,917 total compensation

Svp Information Technology Services And Cio, Ellen L. Barker, age 57

Svp Worldwide Sales And Applications, Bing Xie, age 52

Svp Cfo And Chief Accounting Officer Finance And Operations, Rafael R. Lizardi, age 47

Svp Analog Signal Chain, Haviv Ilan, age 51

Vice President Connected Microcontrollers, Ray Upton

High Power Controllers Hpc High Voltage Power Hvp, Ramanan Natarajan

Vice President Internet Marketing, Dave Youngblood

National Sales Manager, Dennis Smith

Vice President Digital Signal Processing Systems, Greg Delagi

Senior Vice President Communications And Investor Relations, Teresa West

Senior Vice President High Volume Analog And Logic Central Analog Services Dlp Products And Educ, Hagop Kozanian

Vice President Human Resources, Shanon Leonard

Vice President, Eugene Charles Vallow

Board Member, Carrie Cox

Board Member, Robert Sanchez

Board Member, David Deleon

Auditors: Ernst & Young LLP

LOCATIONS

HQ: Texas Instruments Inc.
12500 TI Boulevard, Dallas, TX 75243
Phone: 214 479-3773
Web: www.ti.com

2018 Sales

	$ mil.	% of total
US	2,288	14
Asia	9,240	59
EMEA	3,047	19
Japan	869	6
Rest of World	340	2
Total	**15,784**	**100**

PRODUCTS/OPERATIONS

2018 Sales

	$ mil.	% of total
Analog	10,801	68
Embedded processing	3,554	23
Other	1,429	9
Total	**15,784**	**100**

2018 Sales by Market

	% of total
Industrial	36
Personal electronics	23
Automotive	20
Communications equipment	11
Enterprise sytems	7
Calculators	3
Total	**100**

Selected Products

Semiconductors
  Analog and mixed-signal
  Amplifiers and comparators
  Clocks and timers
  Data converters
  Power management chips
  Radio-frequency (RF) chips
  Application-specific integrated circuits (ASICs)
  Digital light processors (DLPs micro-mirror-based devices for video displays)
  Digital signal processors (DSPs)
  Microcontrollers
  Microprocessors
  Standard logic
Educational Technology
  Calculators (including graphing handheld and printing models)

COMPETITORS

AMD	Maxim Integrated
ARM Holdings	Products
Analog Devices	Microchip Technology
Atmel	Microsemi
CASIO COMPUTER	NVIDIA
Canon	NXP Semiconductors
Fairchild	ON Semiconductor
Semiconductor	QUALCOMM
Infineon Technologies	Renesas Electronics
Intel	STMicroelectronics
Intersil	Samsung Electronics
Marvell Technology	

HISTORICAL FINANCIALS

Company Type: Public

Income Statement				FYE: December 31
	REVENUE ($ mil.)	NET INCOME ($ mil.)	NET PROFIT MARGIN	EMPLOYEES
12/20	14,461	5,595	38.7%	30,000
12/19	14,383	5,017	34.9%	29,768
12/18	15,784	5,580	35.4%	29,888
12/17	14,961	3,682	24.6%	29,714
12/16	13,370	3,595	26.9%	29,865
Annual Growth	2.0%	11.7%	—	0.1%

2020 Year-End Financials

Debt ratio: 35.13%	No. of shares (mil.): 919
Return on equity: 61.67%	Dividends
Cash ($ mil.): 3,107	Yield: 2.2%
Current ratio: 4.28	Payout: 70.3%
Long-term debt ($ mil.): 6,248	Market value ($ mil.): 150,894

	STOCK PRICE ($)	P/E		PER SHARE ($)		
	FY Close	High/Low	Earnings	Dividends	Book Value
12/20	164.13	28 15	5.97	3.72	9.99
12/19	128.29	25 17	5.24	3.21	9.56
12/18	94.50	21 15	5.59	2.63	9.52
12/17	104.44	28 20	3.61	2.12	10.51
12/16	72.97	21 14	3.48	1.64	10.52
Annual Growth	22.5%	— —	14.4%	22.7%	(1.3%)

Textron Inc

Texton's products help customers across the globe get on the move — by air land or sea. The company is known for its Beechcraft and Cessna aircraft and Bell military and commercial helicopters. It also services Hawker business jets. In addition Textron provides parts repair and other aftermarket services. The company also makes specialty vehicles (E-Z-GO golf carts Arctic Cat ATVs) fuel systems land and marine systems unmanned aerial vehicles and simulation and training products. Textron which generates about two-thirds of revenue from the US serves government industrial and commercial clients.

Operations

The company operates through five segments: Textron Aviation Industrial Bell Textron Systems and Finance.

Textron Aviation (nearly 40% of company revenue) manufactures and services Beechcraft and Cessna aircraft and provides service for Hawker brand business jets. Aircraft offerings include business jets and turboprop piston engine military trainer and defense airplanes. Textron Aviation also sells aircraft parts and offers maintenance inspection and repair services through a global network of some 20 service centers. Through subsidiary Able Aerospace Services Textron Aviation provides maintenance repair and overhaul (MRO) services to military and commercial aircraft.

The Industrial segment (nearly 30% of sales) operates two products lines: fuel systems and functional components (sold through its German-based Kautex subsidiary) and specialized vehicles (such as E-Z-GO golf carts and recently-acquired Arctic Cat snowmobiles and ATVs).

The Bell segment (about 25% of sales) supplies the US military with the V-22 tilt rotor aircraft which can operate with the features of both a fixed-wing craft and a helicopter and the H-1 helicopter. Bell produces and supports the V-22 program through a partnership with Boeing. Bell also manufacturers a range of commercial helicopters. Through six service centers four parts distribution centers and some 100 independent dealers Bell provides repair and overhaul and customizing services for an installed base of 13000 helicopters.

Textron Systems (some 10% of sales) provides unmanned systems marine and land systems and simulation and training solutions. It serves markets that include aerospace defense and general aviation. Besides the US military the segment sells to foreign military organizations approved by the US government.

Finance consists of Textron Financial Corporation (TFC) and offers financing mainly for new and used Textron Aviation aircraft and Bell helicopters.

Geographic Reach

Rhode Island- based Textron operates about 55 plants in the US and another 50 outside the US. The US account for more than 65% of sales. Other major markets include Europe (about 15%) and Asia Pacific (nearly 10%). Other international sales account for about 15% of sales.

Sales and Marketing

Textron Aviation sells through its own sales force as well as through a network of authorized independent sales representatives. Post-sale support and service is offered though global service and parts distribution centers.

It sells to US government customers (about 25% of consolidated revenues results from US government contracts) to customers outside the US through foreign military sales sponsored by the US government and directly through commercial sales channels.

The Industrial segment sells through a combination of factory direct resources and a worldwide network of independent distributors and dealers.

Financial Performance

Textron's revenue has been uneven the last five years rising about 2% between 2015 and 2019.

Sales in 2019 decreased 2% to $13.6 billion compared to $14 billion in 2018. The dip in 2019 was primarily due to the decrease in sales in Industrial and Textron System partially offset by Textron Aviation and Bell segment revenue.

Net income decreased about 33% to $815 million in 2019 compared to 2018 primarily due to the decrease in its revenues.

Cash at the end of 2019 was $1.4 billion an increase of $250 million from the prior year. Cash from operations contributed $1.0 billion to the coffers while investing activities used $266 million mainly for capital expenditures. Financing activities used $502 million primarily for repurchases of common stock.

Strategy

Textron is focused on innovation and developing new products to expand its customer base. The first Citation Longitude jets a new large-cabin business aircraft were delivered to customers in late 2019. Other projects in Textron Aviation's pipeline include a cargo version of the Cessna SkyCourier (a twin-engine large-utility turboprop aircraft) and the Cessna Denali a new single-engine turboprop.

Bell's new V-280 Valor which the company is developing for the US military contains a new vertical lift technology that it expects to define the future of tiltrotor vertical lift aircraft. Bell has also made strides in the development of the V-247 an unmanned aerial tiltrotor aircraft.

Textron is revamping its Industrial division. In 2018 it sold its tools and test equipment businesses to Emerson for $810 million. The company used the proceeds to fund additional share repurchases. The following year Textron announced it was exploring strategic alternatives for its Kautex business unit. Germany-based Kautex is a maker of blow-molded plastic fuel systems sold to automotive OEMs. Other products include automotive catalytic reduction systems and engine components.

Through its strategic alliance with Boeing Bell produces and supports the V-22 tiltrotor aircraft for the U.S. Department of Defense (DoD) and also for Japan under the U.S. Government-sponsored foreign military sales program.

Mergers and Acquisitions

The company occasionally beefs up its segments through acquisitions. In early 2019 Textron completed the acquisition of Howe & Howe Technologies Inc. of Waterboro Maine. Howe & Howe makes robotic land vehicles built for the most extreme conditions in the world. This includes the small and mobile Ripsaw Super Tank chosen by the U.S. Army as its first platoon load-carrying robot and the world's first and only purpose-built robotic firefighting solution its Thermite firefighting robot.

HISTORY

Pioneer conglomerate builder Royal Little founded Special Yarns Corporation a Boston textile business in 1923 and merged it with the Franklin Rayon Dyeing Company in 1928. The result Franklin Rayon Corporation moved its headquarters to Providence Rhode Island in 1930 and changed its name to Atlantic Rayon in 1938.

The company expanded during WWII to make parachutes and in 1944 adopted the name Textron to reflect the use of synthetics in its textiles. Between 1953 and 1960 Textron bought more than 40 businesses including Bell Helicopter before banker Rupe Thompson took over in 1960.

Thompson sold weak businesses such as Amerotron Textron's last textile business (1963) but also bought 20 companies between 1960 and 1965. By 1968 when former Wall Street attorney William Miller replaced Thompson as CEO Textron made products ranging from chain saws to watchbands. Miller sold several companies and bought Jacobsen Manufacturers (lawn care equipment 1978) before leaving Textron in 1978 to head the Federal Reserve and become treasury secretary under President Jimmy Carter.

EXECUTIVES

Vp And Cio, Diane K. Schwarz

Chairman President And Ceo, Scott C. Donnelly, age 58, $1,146,500 total compensation

Evp General Counsel Secretary And Chief Compliance Officer, E. Robert Lupone, age 60, $695,192 total compensation

President And Ceo Textron Aviation, Scott A. Ernest

Evp Human Resources, Cheryl H. Johnson, age 59, $445,192 total compensation

President And Ceo Textron Specialized Vehicles, Kevin P. Holleran

President And Ceo Textron Systems, Ellen Lord

Evp And Cfo, Frank T. Connor, age 60, $940,385 total compensation

President And Ceo Tru Simulation + Training, Ian K. Walsh

President And Ceo Textron Airborne Solutions, Russ Bartlett

President And Ceo Textron Financial, R. Danny Maldonado

President And Ceo Bell Helicopter, Mitch Snyder

President And Ceo Greenlee Textron Inc. Sherman + Reilly Inc. And Hd Electric Company, Jason Butchko

President And Ceo Kautex, J ¶rg Rautenstrauch
Vice President And Investor Relations, Eric Salander
Vice President, James Runstadler
Vice President Of Tax, Dana Goldberg
Vice President Audit Services, Thomas Nichipor
Vice President Engineering, Chris Spencer
Vice President Business Development.a.99, Byron Green
Vice President, Thomas Tyson
Board Member, Kerry Clark
Auditors: Ernst & Young LLP

LOCATIONS

HQ: Textron Inc
40 Westminster Street, Providence, RI 02903
Phone: 401 421-2800
Web: www.textron.com

2017 Sales

	$ mil.	% of total
United States	8,786	62
Europe	1,962	14
Asia and Australia	1,206	9
Canada	913	6
Latin and South America	883	6
Middle East and Africa	448	3
Total	**14,198**	**100**

PRODUCTS/OPERATIONS

2017 Sales

	$ mil.	% of total
Textron Aviation	4,686	33
Bell	3,317	23
Textron Systems	1,840	13
Industrial	4,286	30
Finance	69	1
Total	**14,198**	**100**

Selected Products

Textron Aviation
  Beechcraft
  Cessna
  Hawker
  Citation
  Business jets
  Turboprop aircraft
  Piston engine aircraft
  Military trainer and defense aircraft
Bell
  Commercial helicopters
  Military helicopters
  Tiltrotor aircraft
Industrial
  Fuel Systems and Functional Components (Kautex)
  Blow-molded plastic fuel systems
  Clear vision systems
  Catalytic reduction systems
  Plastic bottles and containers
  Specialized Vehicles
  E-Z-GO golf cars
  Textron Off Road
  Arctic Cat
  UG Technologies
  Douglas Equipment
  Jacobsen turf maintenance equipment
  Tools and Test Equipment
  Greenlee
  Greenlee Communications
  Greenlee Utility
  HD Electric
  Klauke
  Sherman+Reilly
  Endura
Textron Systems
  Unmanned systems and support solutions
  Marine and land systems
  Simulation and training systems
  TRU Simulation + Training
  Textron Airborne Solutions
  Electronic systems
  Lycoming
  Weapons and sensors
Finance (primarily for new and used aircraft and helicopters)

COMPETITORS

AgustaWestland	Lockheed Martin
Airbus Group	Magna International
Boeing	Moog
Bombardier	Northrop Grumman
Deere	Northstar Aerospace
Embraer	Piper Aircraft
GE	Raytheon
General Dynamics	Rockwell Collins
Gulfstream Aerospace	Rolls-Royce
Honda	SAFRAN
Honeywell	Spirit AeroSystems
International	Sun Hydraulics
Illinois Tool Works	Terex
Ingersoll-Rand	Thales Aerospace
Israel Aerospace	Toro Company
Industries	United Technologies
Kaman	
Kawasaki Heavy	
Industries	

HISTORICAL FINANCIALS

Company Type: Public

Income Statement
FYE: January 4

	REVENUE ($ mil.)	NET INCOME ($ mil.)	NET PROFIT MARGIN	EMPLOYEES
01/20*	13,630	815	6.0%	35,000
12/18	13,972	1,222	8.7%	35,000
12/17	14,198	307	2.2%	37,000
12/16	13,788	962	7.0%	36,000
01/16	13,423	697	5.2%	35,000
Annual Growth	**0.4%**	**4.0%**	**—**	**0.0%**

*Fiscal year change

2020 Year-End Financials

Debt ratio: 25.37%
Return on equity: 14.97%
Cash ($ mil.): 1,181
Current ratio: 1.84
Long-term debt ($ mil.): 3,249

No. of shares (mil.): 227
Dividends
 Yield: 0.0%
 Payout: 2.2%
Market value ($ mil.): 10,199

	STOCK PRICE ($) FY Close	P/E High/Low		PER SHARE ($) Earnings	Dividends	Book Value
01/20*	44.74	16	12	3.50	0.08	24.21
12/18	45.65	15	9	4.83	0.08	22.04
12/17	56.59	50	39	1.14	0.08	21.60
12/16	48.56	14	9	3.53	0.08	20.62
01/16	42.01	19	15	2.50	0.08	18.10
Annual Growth	**1.6%**	—	—	**8.8%**	**(0.0%)**	**7.5%**

*Fiscal year change

TFS Financial Corp

TFS Financial is the holding company for Third Federal Savings and Loan a thrift with some 45 branches and loan production offices in Ohio and southern Florida. The bank offers such deposit products as checking savings and retirement accounts and CDs. It uses funds from deposits to originate a variety of consumer loans primarily residential mortgages. Third Federal also offers IRAs annuities and mutual funds as well as retirement and college savings plans. TFS subsidiary Third Capital owns stakes in commercial real estate private equity funds and other investments. Mutual holding company Third Federal Savings and Loan Association of Cleveland owns nearly three-quarters of TFS Financial.

EXECUTIVES

Vice President Information Technology Group, Anthony Cefaratti
Board Member, William C Mulligan
Board Member, John P Ringenbach
Auditors: Deloitte & Touche LLP

LOCATIONS

HQ: TFS Financial Corp
7007 Broadway Avenue, Cleveland, OH 44105
Phone: 216 441-6000
Web: www.thirdfederal.com

COMPETITORS

Bank of America	KeyCorp
Citigroup	PNC Financial
Fifth Third	U.S. Bancorp
Huntington Bancshares	Wells Fargo
JPMorgan Chase	

HISTORICAL FINANCIALS

Company Type: Public

Income Statement
FYE: September 30

	ASSETS ($ mil.)	NET INCOME ($ mil.)	INCOME AS % OF ASSETS	EMPLOYEES
09/20	14,642	83	0.6%	—
09/19	14,542	80	0.6%	—
09/18	14,137	85	0.6%	—
09/17	13,692	88	0.6%	—
09/16	12,906	80	0.6%	—
Annual Growth	**3.2%**	**0.8%**	**—**	**—**

2020 Year-End Financials

Debt ratio: —
Return on equity: 4.93%
Cash ($ mil.): 498
Current ratio: —
Long-term debt ($ mil.): —

No. of shares (mil.): 280
Dividends
 Yield: 7.5%
 Payout: 346.8%
Market value ($ mil.): 4,115

	STOCK PRICE ($) FY Close	P/E High/Low		PER SHARE ($) Earnings	Dividends	Book Value
09/20	14.69	75	43	0.29	1.11	5.97
09/19	18.02	64	49	0.28	1.02	6.06
09/18	15.01	53	46	0.30	0.76	6.27
09/17	16.13	62	46	0.32	0.55	6.01
09/16	17.81	69	56	0.28	0.43	5.84
Annual Growth	**(4.7%)**	—	—	**0.9%**	**27.1%**	**0.5%**

The Bancorp Inc

The Bancorp is — what else? — the holding company for The Bancorp Bank which provides financial services in the virtual world. Targeting non-bank financial service companies across the US and Europe from start-ups to small and mid-sized businesses underserved by larger banks in the market The Bancorp Bank provides private-label online banking to 200 affinity groups; offers specialty lending; issues prepaid debit cards; and processes ACH and merchant credit card transactions. Its specialty lending products include securities backed lines of credit (SBLOC) auto fleet and equipment leasing SBA loans and commercial mortgage loans for sale in capital markets.

Operations

The Bancorp and The Bancorp Bank operate three business segments: Payments which made up 45% of the bank's total revenue in 2015 and provides prepaid cards card payments and ACH processing services; Specialty Finance (31% of revenue) which consists of commercial mortgage loan sales small business administration (SBA) loans leasing and security backed lines of credit and related deposit business; and Corporate (24% of revenue) which includes the company's investment portfolio.

Unlike other banks which rely on interest income The Bancorp makes more than 60% of its revenue from fee-based income. About 38% of its total revenue came from loan interest (including fees) during 2015 while another 14% came from interest income on investment securities. The rest of its revenue came from prepaid card fees (22% of revenue) service fees on deposit accounts (3%) card payment and ACH processing fees (3%) leasing income (1%) debit card income (1%) affinity fees (2%) and non-recurring gains from the sale of its loans investment securities and health savings portfolio (27%).

Geographic Reach

Wilmington Delaware-based The Bancorp serves customers in the US and Europe from 16 offices in the two regions and Southeast Asia.

Sales and Marketing

The company targets non-bank financial services companies including start-ups small and medium businesses underserved by large banks and Fortune 500 companies. It spent $387000 on advertising during 2015 down from $621000 and $706000 in 2014 and 2013 respectively.

Financial Performance

The Bancorp's annual revenues and profits have nearly doubled since 2011 mostly as its Payments business income has nearly quadrupled over the period. Its loan assets have also nearly tripled spurring additional interest income growth.

The company's revenue jumped 39% to $216.5 million during 2015 thanks largely to a $33.5 million gain on the sale of the majority of its health savings business and a $14.4 million gain on the sale of its tax-exempt municipal bonds portfolio. The Bancorp's loan interest revenue was also up 37% as its specialty lending balances continued to grow with new SBLOC SBA leasing and loans-for-sale business.

Despite strong revenue growth in 2015 The Bancorp's net income plunged more than 75% to $13.43 million mostly as its discontinued operations (its discontinued Philadelphia commercial loan business) generated $27 million less in revenue than the year before and because in 2014 it had collected a $14.5 million income tax benefit from a reversal of valuation allowances. The company's operations used $234.8 million or more than four times more cash than in 2014 mainly on a steep decline cash-based earnings especially after accounting for net proceeds from sales of its loans-originated-for-resale.

Strategy

The Bancorp and The Bancorp Bank has been winding down its non-core operations in recent years to concentrate more in its national specialty lending business. In October 2015 the bank sold its $400 million-HSA portfolio to HealthEquity for $34..4 million after selling its regional Commercial Lending business in 2014. As a result the bank noted that its discontinued operations were reduced by 50% at the end of 2015 and expected its discontinued loan portfolio to shrink from there through loan repayments and opportunistic loan sales.

On the growth side The Bancorp continues to buy specialty financing assets from other financial companies to bolster its loan assets and extend its geographic reach. In December 2015 it expanded its commercial fleet leasing presence in the West Coast with a new California office after buying the commercial leasing assets of Ellis Brooks Leasing Inc.

EXECUTIVES

Evp Strategy Cfo And Secretary, Paul Frenkiel, age 68, $312,200 total compensation

President And Ceo, Damian Kozlowski, age 53

Evp And Chief Credit Officer The Bancorp Inc. And The Bancorp Bank, Donald F. (Don) McGraw, age 63, $317,500 total compensation

Evp Commercial Fleet Leasing And Chief Lending Officer, Scott R. Megargee, age 68, $202,541 total compensation

Svp Network And Security, Peter (Pete) Chiccino

Svp; Managing Director Payment Solutions, Jeremy L. Kuiper, $458,060 total compensation

Svp And General Counsel, Thomas G. Pareigat, $347,500 total compensation

Evp And Coo, Gail S. Ball

Evp And Chief Risk Officer, Steven Turowski

Evp Commercial Mortgage Securitization, Ron Wechsler

First Vp Loan Committee, Genevieve Johnson

Senior Vice President Chief Information Security Officer, Anthony Meholic

Vice President Information Security Officer, Darin Wipf

Vice President Database Administration Manager, David Heisel

First Vice President And Bro, Michael Terroni

Vice President Credit Risk, Dennis Day

Vice President, Carole Turansky

Vice President Key Account Manager, Brian Doman

Vp And Sba Business Development Officer, Jeffrey Fulcher

Vp Sba Business Development Officer, Ashley Olejnik

Vp Vendor Manager Ii, Michael Meiskey

Vice President Business Development Officer, Thomas Hurdman

Assistant Vice President Senior Risk Analyst, Craig Tabun

Vice President Threat And Vulnerability Management Officer, Peter Iancic

Vice President Credit Sponsorship, Adriana Ramon

Chairman The Bancorp Inc. And The Bancorp Bank, Daniel G. Cohen, age 50

Board Member, John Chrystal

Auditors: Grant Thornton LLP

LOCATIONS

HQ: The Bancorp Inc
409 Silverside Road, Wilmington, DE 19809
Phone: 302 385-5000
Web: www.thebancorp.com

PRODUCTS/OPERATIONS

2015 sales

	$ mil.	% of total
Payments	98	45
Specialty finance	67	31
Corporate	51	24
Total	**216**	**100**

2015 Sales

	$ mil.	% of total
Interest income		
Loans including fees	49	23
Interest on investment securities:	30	14
Federal funds sold/securities purchased under agreements to resell	0	-
Interest earning deposits	2	1
Non-interest income		
Prepaid card fees	47	22
Gain on sale of health savings portfolio	33	15
Gain on sale of investment securities	14	7
Gain on sale of loans	10	5
Service fees on deposit accounts	7	3
Card payment and ACH processing fees	5	3
Affinity fees	3	2
Other	5	2
Change in value of investment in unconsolidated entity	1	1
Leasing income	2	1
Debit card income	1	1
Total	**216**	**100**

COMPETITORS

Citizens Financial Group	Royal Bancshares
E*TRADE Bank	Sovereign Bank
M&T Bank	Sun Bancorp (NJ)
PNC Financial	TD Bank USA
Republic First Bank	WSFS Financial

HISTORICAL FINANCIALS

Company Type: Public

Income Statement

FYE: December 31

	ASSETS ($ mil.)	NET INCOME ($ mil.)	INCOME AS % OF ASSETS	EMPLOYEES
12/19	5,656	51	0.9%	612
12/18	4,437	88	2.0%	589
12/17	4,708	21	0.5%	538
12/16	4,858	(96)	—	589
12/15	4,765	13	0.3%	762
Annual Growth	**4.4%**	**40.0%**	**—**	**(5.3%)**

2019 Year-End Financials

Debt ratio: 0.96%	No. of shares (mil.): 56
Return on equity: 11.57%	Dividends
Cash ($ mil.): 944	Yield: —
Current ratio: —	Payout: —
Long-term debt ($ mil.): —	Market value ($ mil.): 739

	STOCK PRICE ($) FY Close	P/E High/Low		PER SHARE ($) Earnings	Dividends	Book Value
12/19	12.97	15	9	0.90	0.00	8.51
12/18	7.96	7	5	1.55	0.00	7.22
12/17	9.88	26	12	0.39	0.00	5.81
12/16	7.86	—	—	(2.17)	0.00	5.40
12/15	6.37	31	18	0.35	0.00	8.47
Annual Growth	**19.5%**			**26.6%**	**—**	**0.1%**

THE CLEVELAND CLINIC FOUNDATION

The not-for-profit Cleveland Clinic Foundation operates about 20 hospitals in Ohio Florida Abu Dhabi Toronto and soon in London. Combined the foundation's hospitals have more than 6000 beds. Its flagship location is its namesake Cleveland Clinic an academic medical center in Cleveland Ohio. The campus specializes in cardiac care digestive disease treatment and urological and kidney care along with education and research opportunities. It has an international care center children's hospital and an outpatient center; it also contains research and educational institutes covering clinical drug research ophthalmic studies and cancer research as well as physician and scientist training programs.

Operations

The Cleveland Clinic operates approximately 220 outpatient facilities in northern Ohio. These include outpatient family health centers ambulatory surgery centers physician offices specialized cancer centers and wellness centers.

The foundation operates the Lerner College of Medicine and the Lerner Research Institute through a partnership with Case Western Reserve University and it has continuing education nursing and residency programs. It also operates Cleveland Clinic Innovations a unit that oversees collaborative research and technology commercialization programs with partners including MedStar Health and the University of Notre Dame. Cleveland Clinic educates about 1975 residents and fellows and receives more than $305 million in research funding (from grants contracts and federal support) each year.

Altogether the medical centers known as the Cleveland Clinic Health System include more than 6000 beds and employ more than 4500 full-time physicians. The group handles almost 308770 hospital admissions and more than 9.5 million outpatient visits each year. In 2019 it had more than 255000 surgical cases.

Geographic Reach

In addition to its primary campus Cleveland Clinic operates regional hospitals and numerous family and specialty health centers in northeastern Ohio. It operates a handful of facilities in Florida and several brain clinics in Nevada.

Internationally it operates a health and wellness center in Canada and manages health centers in the United Arab Emirates.

Its corporate headquarters is located in Cleveland Ohio.

Strategy

In late 2019 Cleveland Clinic and American Well are partnering on a first-of-its-kind initiative to provide broad access to comprehensive and high-acuity care services via telehealth. Together the organizations will form a Cleveland-based joint venture company named The Clinic which will offer virtual care from Cleveland Clinic's highly specialized experts through American Well's well-established digital health technology platform.

Mergers and Acquisitions

In early 2019 Cleveland Clinic expanded its operations in the Sunshine State when it acquired Martin Health System and its three hospitals (with more than 520 beds) in Southeast Florida. It also acquired Indian River Medical Center which has more than 330 beds and is located on Florida's Treasure Coast. The system plans to invest millions in the newly added operations over the next few years.

Company Background

Cleveland Clinic Foundation traces its roots to 1921 when a group of Cleveland doctors teamed up to improve medical care and education. Its main campus has conducted breakthrough medical innovations through its history such as the first face transplant in 2008 and it is regularly named to the US News & World Report's list of America's Best Hospitals.

EXECUTIVES

Cio, C. Martin Harris
Chairman And Ceo, Delos M. (Toby) Cosgrove
Ceo Cleveland Clinic Regional Hospitals, David L. Bronson
Controller And Chief Accounting Officer, Steven C. Glass
Ceo Cleveland Clinic Abu Dhabi, A. Marc Harrison
Chief Medical Operations Officer, Robert Wyllie
Chief Of Operations, William (Bill) Peacock
Interim Ceo Sheikh Khalifa Medical City, Ben Frank
Interim Executive Chief Nursing Officer, K. Kelly Hancock
Chair Department Of Palm Ccm, Herbert Wiedemann
Vice President, Sanford Timen
Medical Director, Kevin Hopkins
Director Of Health Information, Bryan Holtz
Vice President Of Medical Operations, William Riebel
Medical Director, Cheryl Hubbard
Vice President Of Operations, Kris Bennett
Vice President, Toribio Flores
Medical Director, Damon Kralovic
Medical Director, Michael Machuzak
Assistant Vice President Operations, Janet Gulley
Medical Director, John Donohue
Medical Director, Hany Aziz
Associate Medical Director, Faith Factora
Medical Director, Purva Grover
Vice President Oncology Services West, Susan Dunson
Pharmacy Manager Transitions Of Care, Erick Sokn
Regional Vice President Cv Services East, Dan Sutton
Vice President Market Leader, Grace Jen
Senior Vice President System Operations, Steve Abdenour
Chairman, Robert E. (Bob) Rich
Vice Chairman, Joseph M. (Joe) Scaminace
Medical Secretary, Brenda Hammond
Surgical Operations Secretary, Denise Slovan
Secretary, Lynn Meyers
Medical Secretary, Lisa Yospur
Medical Secretary, Mattie Dalton
Medical Secretary, Judith Burdett
Medical Secretary, Sally Cooper
Secretary, Pam Staub
Medical Secretary, Joyce Velazquez
Board Member, Donna Munic-Miller
Unit Secretary, Karen Ginley
Medical Secretary, Heather Karn
Appt Secretary, Robin Allen
Secretary, Joye Grebb
Department Secretary, Chris Morchak
Secretary, Marianne Simon
Medical Secretary, Charylie Rivers
Medical Secretary, Lucy Bufkin
Medical Secretary, Linda Rosa
Ap Secretary, Patricia Lichtenfeld
Secretary Medical Education, Barb Salak
Auditors: ERNST & YOUNG LLP CLEVELAND

LOCATIONS

HQ: THE CLEVELAND CLINIC FOUNDATION
9500 EUCLID AVE. CLEVELAND, OH 441950002
Phone: 216 636-8335
Web: WWW.CLEVELANDCLINIC.ORG

Selected Facilities

Ashtabula County Medical Center (Ashtabula Ohio; management contract)
The Cleveland Clinic (Cleveland Ohio)
Cleveland Clinic Children's Hospital
Cleveland Clinic International Center
Cleveland Clinic Canada (Toronto)
Cleveland Clinic Children's Hospital for Rehabilitation (Shaker Campus in Cleveland Ohio)
Cleveland Clinic Family Health Centers (multiple locations in northeast Ohio)
Cleveland Clinic Florida (Weston Florida)
Cleveland Clinic Florida (West Palm Beach Florida)
Cleveland Clinic Lou Ruvo Center for Brain Health (Elko Nevada)
Cleveland Clinic Lou Ruvo Center for Brain Health (Las Vegas Nevada)
Cleveland Clinic Lou Ruvo Center for Brain Health (Reno Nevada)
Euclid Hospital (Euclid Ohio)
Fairview Hospital (Cleveland Ohio)
Hillcrest Hospital (Mayfield Heights Ohio)
Lakewood Hospital (Lakewood Ohio)
Lutheran Hospital (Cleveland Ohio)
Marymount Hospital (Garfield Heights Ohio)
Medina Hospital (Medina Ohio)
Richard E. Jacobs Health Center (Avon Ohio)
South Pointe Hospital (Warrensville Heights Ohio)

Selected Institutes

Cleveland Clinic Institutes
Anesthesiology and Pain Management
Bariatric and Metabolic
Cancer Center/Taussig Cancer Institute
Cleveland Clinic Children's and Pediatric
Dermatology and Plastic Surgery
Digestive Disease and Surgery
Emergency Services
Endocrinology and Metabolism
Genomics
Head and Neck
Heart and Vascular
Imaging
Medicine
Neurological
Nursing
Orthopaedic and Rheumatologic
Pathology and Laboratory Medicine
Respiratory
Urology and Kidney
Wellness
Special Expertise Institutes
Arts and Medicine
Body Donation
Patient Experience
Philanthropy
Professional Staff Affairs
Quality and Patient Safety
Research

PRODUCTS/OPERATIONS

2018 Sales

	$ mil.	% of total
Net patient service revenue		
Self-pay	4,465	50
Managed care & commercial	2,871	32
Medicare	649	7
Medicaid	45	1
Other	895	10
Total	**8,927**	**100**

COMPETITORS

Akron Children's Hospital
Catholic Health Initiatives
Deaconess Associations
Kettering Health Network
Lake Health
Mayo Clinic
Memorial Sloan-Kettering
MetroHealth System
OhioHealth
Parma Community General Hospital
Premier Health Partners
Robinson Memorial Hospital
Shriners Hospitals For Children
Summa Health System
University Hospitals Health System

HISTORICAL FINANCIALS

Company Type: Private

Income Statement

FYE: December 31

	REVENUE ($ mil.)	NET INCOME ($ mil.)	NET PROFIT MARGIN	EMPLOYEES
12/19	10,559	2,239	21.2%	44,000
12/18	8,927	176	2.0%	—
12/17	8,407	1,150	13.7%	—
12/16	8,037	513	6.4%	—
Annual Growth	9.5%	63.4%	—	—

THE FORD FOUNDATION

As one of the nation's largest philanthropic organizations the Ford Foundation can afford to be generous. The foundation offers grants to individuals and institutions worldwide that work to meet its goals of strengthening democratic values reducing poverty and injustice promoting international cooperation and advancing human achievement. The Ford Foundation's charitable giving has run the gamut from A (Association for Asian Studies) to Z (Zanzibar International Film Festival). The foundation has an endowment of about $10 billion. Established in 1936 by Edsel Ford whose father founded the Ford Motor Company the foundation no longer owns stock in the automaker or has ties to the founding family.

Operations

The foundation which is governed by an international board of trustees makes grants in all 50 US states and supports programs in more than 50 countries.

It boasts about 10 regional offices in Latin America Africa the Middle East and Asia.

Geographic Reach

Based in New York the Ford Foundation is a grantmaking foundation that primarily serves the US but also global programs.

Strategy

The Ford Foundation's programs address several social justice issues including democratic and accountable government freedom of expression access to education economic fairness and opportunity sexuality and reproductive rights sustainable development social justice metropolitan opportunity and human rights.

A small portion of its endowment is set aside for social investing. The foundation's funds typically finance critical projects set new business models and develop sustainable organizations. By investing $1 million or more in initiatives the Ford Foundation's investment strategy aims to make a noteworthy impact and encourage other investors to also fund projects.

EXECUTIVES

Secretary, Karen Mcburnie

LOCATIONS

HQ: THE FORD FOUNDATION
320 E 43RD ST FL 4, NEW YORK, NY 100174890
Phone: 212 573-5370
Web: WWW.FORDFOUNDATION.ORG

PRODUCTS/OPERATIONS

Selected Core Issues

Democratic and accountable government
Economic fairness
Education opportunity and scholarship
Freedom of expression
Human rights
Metropolitan opportunity
Sexuality and reproductive health rights
Social justice philanthropy
Sustainable development

HISTORICAL FINANCIALS

Company Type: Private

Income Statement

FYE: December 31

	ASSETS ($ mil.)	NET INCOME ($ mil.)	INCOME AS % OF ASSETS	EMPLOYEES
12/15	12,114	(270)	—	556
12/14*	12,400	(7)	—	—
09/11	10,344	(5)	—	—
09/09	10,234	0	—	—
Annual Growth	2.8%	—	—	—

*Fiscal year change

The Gap Inc

The ubiquitous clothing retailer Gap has been filling closets with jeans and khakis T-shirts button-downs and poplin for some 50 years. The company which operates more than 3900 owned and franchised stores worldwide built its iconic casual brand on basics for men women and children. Over the years it has extended its namesake brand to include GapBody GapKids and babyGap (among others) and has added brands such as the urban chic Banana Republic family budgeteer Old Navy women's activewear chain Athleta designer-focused Intermix and men's clothier Hill City. The company generates more than 80% of its revenue from the US.

HISTORY

Donald Fisher and his wife Doris opened a small store in 1969 near what is now San Francisco State University. The couple named their store The Gap (after "the generation gap") and concentrated on selling Levi's jeans. The couple opened a second store in San Jose California eight months later and by the end of 1970 there were six Gap stores. The Gap went public six years later.

In the beginning the Fishers catered almost exclusively to teenagers but in the 1970s they expanded into activewear that would appeal to a larger spectrum of customers. Nevertheless by the early 1980s The Gap — which had grown to about 500 stores — was still dependent upon its largely teenage customer base. However it was less dependent on Levi's (about 35% of sales) thanks to its growing stable of private labels.

In a 1983 effort to revamp the company's image Donald hired Mickey Drexler a former president of AnnTaylor with a spotless apparel industry track record as The Gap's new president. Drexler immediately overhauled the motley clothing lines to concentrate on sturdy brightly colored cotton clothing. He also consolidated the stores' many private clothing labels into the Gap brand. As a final touch Drexler replaced circular clothing racks with white shelving so clothes could be neatly stacked and displayed.

Also in 1983 The Gap bought Banana Republic a unique chain of jungle-themed stores that sold safari clothing. The company expanded the chain which enjoyed tremendous success in the mid-1980s but slumped after the novelty of the stores wore off late in the decade. In response Drexler introduced a broader range of clothes (including higher-priced leather items) and dumped the safari lines in 1988. By 1990 Banana Republic was again profitable.

The first GapKids opened in 1985 after Drexler couldn't find clothing that he liked for his son. During the late 1980s and early 1990s the company grew rapidly opening its first stores in Canada and the UK. In 1990 it introduced babyGap in 25 GapKids stores featuring miniature versions of its GapKids line. The Gap announced in 1991 it would no longer sell Levi's (which had fallen to less than 2% of total sales) and would sell nothing but private-label items.

Earnings fell in fiscal 1993 because of Gap division losses brought on by low margins and high rents. The company shuffled management positions and titles as part of a streamlining effort. It rebounded in 1994 by concentrating on improving profit margins rather than sales and by launching Old Navy Clothing Co. named after a bar Drexler saw in Paris. Banana Republic opened its first two stores outside the US both in Canada in 1995.

Robert Fisher (the founders' son) became the new president of the Gap division (including babyGap and GapKids) in 1997 and was charged with reversing the segment's sales decline. The company refocused its Gap chain on basics (jeans T-shirts and khakis) and helped boost its performance with a high-profile advertising campaign focusing on those wares. Later in 1997 the Gap opened an online Gap store. In 1998 it began opening Torpedo Joe submarine-themed shops in select Old Navy flagships.

Also in 1998 the retailer opened its first GapBody stores and introduced its only catalog (for Banana Republic). In late 1999 amid sluggish Gap division sales Robert Fisher resigned and Drexler took over his duties. Gap misjudged fashion trends in 2000 which resulted in two years of disappointing earnings. After a 10% reduction in its workforce the company returned to a more conservative fashion approach.

The company split Gap and Gap International into two separate units in early 2002 to improve performance in the flagship brand. In September Drexler retired and was replaced by Paul Pressler a veteran of The Walt Disney Company.

Gap sold its 10 stores in Germany to Swedish retailer H&M in 2004 taking a $14 million write-down related to the sale.

The next year the retailer launched Forth & Towne its first new chain in a decade with the new stores catering to women over the age of 35. Also Gap dipped its toes into personal care products by signing an agreement with Inter Parfums in mid-2005. As part of the deal Inter Parfums develops formulates manufactures and packages the products which are branded under the Gap and Banana Republic names. The Gap markets and sells them in its GapBody stores.

In January 2006 Gap entered into a 10-year non-exclusive services agreement with International Business Machines valued at $1.1 billion. As a result IBM took over certain information technology functions from the retailer; up to 400 Gap employees joined IBM as a result of the deal. Gap Direct launched an online footwear business called Piperlime in November.

CEO Pressler left the company and the board in January 2007 after four years in the top job. He was succeeded as CEO on an interim basis by Robert Fisher previously the non-executive chairman of the retailer. In June the company shut down its Forth & Towne retail format after less than two years in business. In July Gap named a new chairman and CEO Glenn Murphy. Murphy joined the company from Canadian drugstore chain Shoppers Drug Mart where he had retired as chairman and CEO in March. Stung by allegations in the British press of forced child labor in India being used in the manufacture of apparel for its Gap Kids chain Gap in November announced a package of measures intended to strengthen its commitment to eradicating the exploitation of children in the garment industry. Actions include a $200000 grant to improve working conditions and an upcoming conference dedicated to finding solutions to issues related to child labor.

In October 2008 Gap acquired Athleta a direct-marketer of women's active wear for about $150 million. Gap purchased Athleta as part of its strategy to diversify its brand offerings. The company also opened its first Banana Republic and Gap brand factory stores in Canada in late October extending its outlet busuiness launched in 1994 to Canada. The retailer opened 101 new stores and shuttered 119 locations in 2008.

Don Fisher Gap co-founder died in September 2009 at the age of 81. Also in 2009 Gap began opening stores inside Mexico's leading department store chain Distribuidora Liverpool via a franchise agreement.

In November 2010 Gap entered Italy with a store in Milan.

EXECUTIVES

President And General Manager Athleta, Nancy Green, age 58
President Growth Innovation And Digital, Arthur (Art) Peck, age 64, $1,330,288 total compensation
President And General Manager Intermix, Jyothi Rao
Global President Old Navy, Sonia Syngal, age 50, $850,000 total compensation
Head Of Gap China, Jeff Kirwan, age 54, $893,269 total compensation
Evp And Cfo, Teri L. List-Stoll, $30,288 total compensation
Evp; General Manager Greater China, Abinta Malik
Evp Global General Counsel Corporate Secretary And Chief Compliance Officer, Julie Gruber

Evp Strategy And Chief Customer Officer, Sebastian DiGrande, $505,385 total compensation
Evp And Cio, Paul Chapman
Evp Global Supply Chain Sourcing And Production, Michael Yee
Evp Global Supply Chain Logistics And Product Operations, Shawn Curran
Vp P.a.c.e., Kindley Lawlor
Vice President Brand Creative, Stephanie Nahrgang
Vice President Deputy General Counsel, Delli Mireskandari
Vice President Ocm, Rita Martell
Vice President, Chris Baer
Vice President, Paul Adams
Executive Vice President Product Design And Development, Wendi Goldman
Vice President Customer Experience Acquisition, Mark Goblirsch
Senior Vice President Store Operations, Steve Peters
Senior Vice President Human Resources And Communications, Brent Hyder
Executive Vice President Global Sourcing, Christophe Roussel
Vice President Of Women's Design, Sarah Holme
Vice President Visual Merchandising Design, Kristi Argo
Chairman, Robert J. (Bob) Fisher, age 65
Board Member, Bill Fisher
Auditors: DELOITTE & TOUCHE LLP

LOCATIONS

HQ: The Gap Inc
  Two Folsom Street, San Francisco, CA 94105
Phone: 415 427-0100
Web: www.gapinc.com

2018 Sales

	$ mil.	% of total
US	13,340	81
Asia	1,233	7
Canada	1,193	7
Europe	603	4
Other regions	211	1
Total	**16,580**	**100**

PRODUCTS/OPERATIONS

2018 Sales

	$ mil.	% of total
Old Navy Global	7,840	47
Gap	5,160	31
Banana Republic Global	2,456	15
Other	1,124	7
Total	**16,580**	**100**

2018 Stores

	No.
Company-operated	
Gap	1,242
Old Navy	1,154
Banana Republic	601
Athleta	161
Intermix	36
Franchise	472
Total	**3,666**

Selected Stores and Brands

Athleta (women's activewear)
babyGap (clothing for infants and toddlers)
Banana Republic (upscale clothing and accessories)
Gap (casual and active clothing and body care products)
GapBody (intimate apparel)
GapKids (clothing for children)
Intermix (designer clothing for women)
Old Navy (lower-priced family clothing)

COMPETITORS

Abercrombie & Fitch	Kohl's
American Eagle Outfitters	L Brands
Dillard's	Lululemon
	Macy's
Express	Nordstrom
H&M	Ralph Lauren
Inditex	TJX Companies
J. Crew	Urban Outfitters

HISTORICAL FINANCIALS

Company Type: Public

Income Statement
FYE: February 1

	REVENUE ($ mil.)	NET INCOME ($ mil.)	NET PROFIT MARGIN	EMPLOYEES
02/20	16,383	351	2.1%	129,000
02/19	16,580	1,003	6.0%	135,000
02/18*	15,855	848	5.3%	135,000
01/17	15,516	676	4.4%	135,000
01/16	15,797	920	5.8%	141,000
Annual Growth	**0.9%**	**(21.4%)**	**—**	**(2.2%)**

*Fiscal year change

2020 Year-End Financials

Debt ratio: 9.13%	No. of shares (mil.): 371
Return on equity: 10.25%	Dividends
Cash ($ mil.): 1,364	Yield: 0.0%
Current ratio: 1.41	Payout: 104.3%
Long-term debt ($ mil.): 1,249	Market value ($ mil.): 6,459

	STOCK PRICE ($) FY Close	P/E High/Low		Earnings	PER SHARE ($) Dividends	Book Value
02/20	17.41	32	17	0.93	0.97	8.94
02/19	25.00	13	9	2.59	0.97	9.40
02/18*	32.09	16	10	2.14	0.92	8.08
01/17	22.58	18	10	1.69	0.92	7.28
01/16	24.72	19	10	2.23	0.92	6.41
Annual Growth	**(8.4%)**	**—**	**—**	**(19.6%)**	**1.3%**	**8.7%**

*Fiscal year change

THE HERTZ CORPORATION

EXECUTIVES

Ceo-Pres, Paul E Stone
Non Exec Chb*, Henry R Keizer
Exec V Pres-Cfo, Jamere Jackson
Exec V Pres-Cmo, Jodi J Allen
Exec V Pres-General Counsel-SE, M David Galainena
Sr V Pres-Cao, Richard E Esper
Manager, Al Greene
Associate, Alexander Mejia
Project Manager, Andrew Roberson
Human Resources Programs Speci, Annasuela Fritz
Business Transformation Manage, Ben Wylie
Auditors: PRICEWATERHOUSECOOPERS LLP FO

LOCATIONS

HQ: THE HERTZ CORPORATION
  8501 WILLIAMS RD, ESTERO, FL 339283325
Phone: 239 301-7000
Web: WWW.HERTZ.COM

HISTORICAL FINANCIALS

Company Type: Private

Income Statement				FYE: December 31
	REVENUE ($ mil.)	NET INCOME ($ mil.)	NET PROFIT MARGIN	EMPLOYEES
12/17	8,803	332	3.8%	38,000
12/16	8,803	(488)	—	—
12/15	10,535	276	2.6%	—
Annual Growth	(8.6%)	9.7%	—	—

THE IRVINE JAMES FOUNDATION

EXECUTIVES

Pres-Ceo, Donald Howard
Director of Finance, Casey Budesilich
Director of Impact Assessment, Kim Howard
Senior Communications Officer, Leslie Payne
Communications Officer, Mike Smith
Program Officer, April Yee
Senior Program Officer, Christina Garcia
Director of Finance, Eric Broque
Leadership Awards Officer, Jessica Kaczmarek
Director of Grants Administrat, Kelly Martin
Arts Program Associate, Jason Blackwell

LOCATIONS

HQ: THE IRVINE JAMES FOUNDATION
1 BUSH ST STE 800, SAN FRANCISCO, CA 941044494
Phone: 415 777-2244
Web: WWW.IRVINE.ORG

HISTORICAL FINANCIALS

Company Type: Private

Income Statement				FYE: December 31
	ASSETS ($ mil.)	NET INCOME ($ mil.)	INCOME AS % OF ASSETS	EMPLOYEES
12/17	2,371	9	0.4%	36
12/15	2,185	38	1.8%	—
12/14	1,611	44	2.7%	—
12/09	1,507	(57)	—	—
Annual Growth	5.8%	—	—	—

THE JOHNS HOPKINS HEALTH SYSTEM CORPORATION

Named after philanthropist Johns Hopkins the Johns Hopkins Health System (JHHS) gifts Baltimore residents with an array of health care services. The health system is an affiliate of world-renowned Johns Hopkins Medicine and oversees six hospitals: All Children's Hospital Johns Hopkins Hospital Bayview Medical Center Howard County General Hospital Sibley Memorial Hospital and Suburban Hospital. The not-for-profit teaching hospitals offer inpatient and outpatient health services that include general medicine emergency/trauma care pediatrics maternity care senior care and numerous specialized areas of medicine. JHHS also operates community health and satellite care facilities.

Operations

JHHS facilities handle 2.8 million patient encounters each year including 115000 inpatient admissions and 350000 emergency room visits. In addition to the six Johns Hopkins Medicine hospitals (which combined house more than 2600 beds) the JHHS organization includes four surgery centers two dozen primary care clinics associated with the Johns Hopkins Community Physicians practice organization and a home health care services agency. JHHS offers unified shared services to its members including advertising purchasing finance legal and other administrative functions.

The Johns Hopkins name is well-known for health care but is probably equally as well-known for its medical education and research initiatives. The health system's hospitals are affiliated with Johns Hopkins University offering physicians-in-training a whole host of residency options.

Geographic Reach

The JHHS inpatient and outpatient facilities are located throughout Maryland and the Washington DC-area as well as in Florida. The system operates a handful of outpatient surgery and imaging centers as well. The group's hospitals serve visitors from all over the world.

Strategy

The organization regularly expands through small to large construction efforts as well as through acquisitions. For example it has acquired two hospitals (All Children's Hospital in Florida and Sibley Memorial Hospital in Washington DC) since 2010.

EXECUTIVES

Pres, Ronald R Peterson
Chb*, C Micheal Amstrong
V Pres Fin-Cfo*, Ronald J Werthman
V Pres-Medical Affairs*, Beryl Rosenstein
Corp SEC*, Hannah Jones
Manager, Bridget Carver
Coordinator, Matthew Trojanowski
Senior Vice-President, Bertrand M Emerson
Scientist, Edina Avdic
Assistant Professor, Ming-Hsien Wang
Coordinator, Tiesha Mobley
Auditors: PRICEWATERHOUSECOOPERS LLP BA

LOCATIONS

HQ: THE JOHNS HOPKINS HEALTH SYSTEM CORPORATION
600 N WOLFE ST, BALTIMORE, MD 212870005
Phone: 410 955-5000
Web: WWW.HOPKINSMEDICINE.ORG

PRODUCTS/OPERATIONS

Selected Facilities
All Children's Hospital (St. Petersburg FL)
Bayview Medical Center (Baltimore MD)
Howard County General Hospital (Columbia MD)
Johns Hopkins at Cedar Lane (Columbia MD)
Johns Hopkins at Greenspring Station (Lutherville MD)
Johns Hopkins at Odenton (Odenton MD)
Johns Hopkins at White Marsh (White Marsh MD)
Johns Hopkins Hospital (Baltimore MD)
Johns Hopkins Outpatient Center (Baltimore MD)
Sibley Memorial Hospital (Washington DC)
Suburban Hospital (Bethesda MD)

COMPETITORS

Anne Arundel Medical Center
Ascension Health
Bon Secours Health
Carilion Clinic
Christiana Care
Dimensions Healthcare
Franklin Square Hospital Center
GBMC
Good Samaritan Hospital of Maryland
Harbor Hospital
Levindale Hospital
LifeBridge Health
MedStar Health
MedStar Union Memorial Hospital
Sinai Hospital of Baltimore
St. Agnes HealthCare
St. Joseph Medical Center
University of Maryland Medical System
Upper Chesapeake Health

HISTORICAL FINANCIALS

Company Type: Private

Income Statement				FYE: June 30
	REVENUE ($ mil.)	NET INCOME ($ mil.)	NET PROFIT MARGIN	EMPLOYEES
06/20	7,110	(306)	—	13,000
06/19	6,826	(59)	—	—
06/18	6,558	308	4.7%	—
Annual Growth	4.1%	—	—	—

THE NEW YORK AND PRESBYTERIAN HOSPITAL

The New York and Presbyterian Hospital is a learned institution: The not-for-profit hospital is affiliated with both the Columbia University College of Physicians & Surgeons and the Weill Cornell Medical College of Cornell University. Known as NewYork-Presbyterian Hospital the organization includes two major medical centers Columbia University Medical Center and Weill Cornell Medical Center which conduct educational and research programs in partnership with the universities. The two facilities combined have about 2600 beds and offer specialized programs for burns digestive diseases pediatrics women's health and other conditions. NewYork-Presbyterian Hospital is part of the NewYork-Presbyterian Healthcare System.

Operations

Altogether the NewYork-Presbyterian Hospital campuses handle some 2 million patient visits each year (both on an inpatient and outpatient basis) including inpatient admissions and more than 310000 emergency room visits and about 15000 births. The facilities employ a total of more than 6500 physicians including residents and fellows. NewYork-Presbyterian Hospital provides more than $108 million in charity and community care services each year.

Geographic Reach

In addition to its flagship campuses NewYork-Presbyterian/Columbia and NewYork-Presbyterian/Weill Cornell NewYork-Presbyterian Hospital operates two small community hospitals in Manhattan — the Allen Hospital and the Lower Manhattan Hospital — and an inpatient mental health facility (the Westchester Division). The broader NewYork-Presbyterian Healthcare System operates facilities in other areas of New York as well as in New Jersey and Connecticut. The NewYork-Presbyterian Hospital/Columbia campus houses the Morgan Stanley Children's Hospital as well as other specialist units.

Sales and Marketing

Medicare and Medicaid recipients account for more than 60% of NewYork-Presbyterian Hospital's patients. Commercial managed care organizations and insurance firms as well as self-pay customers account for the rest.

Financial Performance

NewYork-Presbyterian Hospital's revenue in fiscal 2015 totaled $4.8 billion.

Strategy

As the health care landscape has become increasingly complex and competitive especially with changing regulations and the push to provide more integrated patient care NewYork-Presbyterian Hospital has made some major organizational changes. Chief among its goals is to provide a patient-centered model of care creating a system that can easily be accessed by its patient consumers. It recently established its Community and Population Health division which includes community programs and initiatives ambulatory care network sites and the management of its new Accountable Care Organization.

It has also expanded beyond its former base of Manhattan in order to provide a regional system of care. For example the system took ownership of former affiliate Brooklyn Methodist in early 2017 with the intention of investing in the hospital's development; the move falls in line with its strategy of providing integrated care for communities particularly in light of a number of recent hospital failures in the borough.

Mergers and Acquisitions

New York Methodist Hospital (now NewYork-Presbyterian Brooklyn Methodist Hospital) was added to the organization in early 2017. Brooklyn Methodist will gain funds for a new $400 million ambulatory care building as part of the new relationship.

Company Background

NewYork-Presbyterian Hospital was formed through the 1998 merger of the New York Hospital (founded in 1771) and the Presbyterian Hospital (founded in 1868). New York Hospital was known for advancing care in areas including women's health and surgery while the Presbyterian Hospital was known for its pediatric division and its cancer center.

EXECUTIVES

Vice President Risk Management And Associate General Counsel, John Campano
Vice President, Valerie Punnett
Vice President Medical Director, Philip Wilner
Svp Cfo And Treasurer, Phyllis R. Lantos
President And Ceo, Steven J. (Steve) Corwin

Chief Nursing Officer; Vp Patient Services Newyork-presbyterian/columbia, Wilhelmina Manzano
Evp And Coo, Laura L. Forese
Vp Medical Affairs And Associate Chief Medical Officer, Richard S. Liebowitz
Cio, William Lee
Evp Chief Legal Officer And General Counsel, Maxine Frank
Finance Vice President, Ana Arroyo
Director Of Health Information, Deborah Forde
Vice President Compensation Benefits And Hris, Mary Falkowitz
Vice President Nursing, Michaelle Williams
Vice President Human Resources, Lorraine Orlando
Vice President Finance, William Farrell
Finance Vice President, Salvatore Logiudice
Senior Vice President And Chief Quality, Henry Ting
Vice President Of Human Resources, April Rodgers
Vice President Public Affairs, Karen Sodomick
Clinical Director, Gina A Rivera
Vice President Finance, Lugeion Y Carter
Vice President, Tanya Clark
Senior Vice President Chief Information Officer, Daniel Barchi
Vice President And Chief Administrative Officer, Kim Roldan-sanchez
Vice President Support Services East Campus, Mila Henn
Vice President Legal Affairs, Fred Title
Assistant Vice President Patient Financial Services, Elizabeth Carnevale
Vp Operations And Engagement, Keren Rozenfeld
Asst Vp, Jennifer Donovan
Vice President, Diego Rodriguez
Medical Director, Robert H Birkhahn
Director Of Medical Records, Alexandra Velnik
Director Of Pharmacy, Alexander Melchert
Director Of Radiology, Joseph Cianci
Group Senior Vice President Facilities And Real Estate, Joe Ienuso
Vice President Patient Flow And Capacity Management, Mary Godfrey
Vice President Quality And Patient Safety, Mary Kincart
Vice Chairman, Frank A. Bennack, age 87
Executive Vice Chair, Herbert Pardes, age 86
Treasurer, Karen Turi
Assistant Treasurer, Sedare Coradine
Surgical Secretary, Eileen Chavez
Assistant Secretary, Mary Braunsdorf

LOCATIONS

HQ: THE NEW YORK AND PRESBYTERIAN HOSPITAL
525 E 68TH ST, NEW YORK, NY 100654870
Phone: 212 746-5454
Web: WWW.NYP.ORG

PRODUCTS/OPERATIONS

2016 Patient Mix

	% of total
Medicare Managed	9
Medicare FFS	22
Medicaid Managed	23
Medicaid FFS	7
Managed Care and Other	37
Self-Pay	1
Workers Comp	1
Total	**100**

Selected Services

Cancer
Children's Health
Digestive
Geriatrics
Heart
Mens Health
Neuroscience
Orthopedic
Psychiatry
Rehabilitation Medicine
Transplant
Vascular
Womens Health

COMPETITORS

Ascension Health
Beth Israel Medical Center
Bronx-Lebanon Hospital
Catholic Healthcare System
Continuum Health Partners
Lenox Hill Hospital
Lutheran HealthCare
Maimonides Medical Center

MediSys Health Network
Memorial Sloan-Kettering
Montefiore Medical
New York City Health and Hospitals
Northwell Health
Winthrop-University Hospital
Yale New Haven Health System

HISTORICAL FINANCIALS

Company Type: Private

Income Statement

FYE: December 31

	REVENUE ($ mil.)	NET INCOME ($ mil.)	NET PROFIT MARGIN	EMPLOYEES
12/18	8,483	526	6.2%	23,709
12/17	5,616	762	13.6%	—
12/16	4,935	496	10.1%	—
12/14	4,206	197	4.7%	—
Annual Growth	**19.2%**	**27.8%**	—	—

THE PRIDDY FOUNDATION

EXECUTIVES

President, David Wolverton
Director, Debbie White

LOCATIONS

HQ: THE PRIDDY FOUNDATION
807 8TH ST STE 1010, WICHITA FALLS, TX
763013310
Phone: 940 723-8720
Web: WWW.PRIDDYFDN.ORG

HISTORICAL FINANCIALS

Company Type: Private

Income Statement

FYE: December 31

	REVENUE ($ mil.)	NET INCOME ($ mil.)	NET PROFIT MARGIN	EMPLOYEES
12/13	8,791	3	0.0%	4
12/12	3	(4)	—	
12/10	32	27	86.7%	
12/09	0	0		
Annual Growth				

THE TURNER CORPORATION

The Turner Corporation a subsidiary of German construction giant HOCHTIEF is the leading general building and construction management firm in the US (as ranked by Engineering News-Record) ahead of rivals Bechtel and Fluor. The firm operates primarily through subsidiary Turner Construction and has worked on notable projects such as Madison Square Garden the UN headquarters Yankee Stadium the Taipei 101 Tower and the 68000-seat open-air stadium for the San Francisco 49ers. Known for its large projects also offers services for midsized and smaller projects and provides interior construction and renovation services.

Operations

Turner works on more than 1500 projects in a year totaling $8 billion in volume. The group has divisions dedicated to serving the aviation health care biotechnology public assembly sports education justice and industrial sectors. Its homeland security group was established in order handle a growing demand for security systems and protection. The unit installed detection equipment in some 450 airports throughout the US. Turner Corporation also has an arm specializing in green building with a focus on Leadership in Energy and Environmental Design (LEED) -certified projects. Turner Green Building has more than 400 LEED projects and green projects either completed or in progress.

Turner Corporation has subsidiaries providing auxiliary operations. Turner's risk management department offers contract review project safety and claims handling. Turner Logistics handles procurement and supply chain management for projects and Turner Facilities Management Solutions offers ongoing operations services. Also the Turner School of Construction Management provides training for local subcontractors.

Geographic Reach

Dallas-based Turner Corporation boasts a network of offices across the US (with most in California and Ohio) and Canada (Vancouver and Toronto) with an global presence in 20 countries in Europe Africa East Asia India Latin America and the Caribbean.

Sales and Marketing

Turner works on variety of projects from several sectors. It's known for its work in the categories of healthcare education offices commercial properties cultural facilities sports facilities and hotels. The company is also a leader in the green building category.

Strategy

With the construction market rebounding from the economic downturn Turner is looking to high-growth markets in the US and overseas. As of early 2015 it was working on more than 1900 projects 80% of which were Education Commercial or Interior project-related. Some of these projects included the 17000 sq. ft- interior remodel for Salesforce's Vancouver office; the 325000 sq. ft- construction of the LEED-Certified RAND Corporation Headquarters in Santa Monica California; and the 25000-seat Charlotte Coliseum event arena for the City of Charlotte North Carolina.

The company has also been making moves to expand its business abroad in recent years. In 2012 for example Turner partnered with one of India's largest real estate developers Sahara Prime City Ltd. to form Sahara Turner which would lead the development and construction of multiple townships across the country with an approximate value of $2.5 billion by 2017. It also purchased a majority stake in Clark Builders Canada to capitalize on the country's growing construction market.

Turner often partners with fellow US-based HOCHTIEF subsidiary Flatiron which specializes in civil engineering. Examples of the teamwork are the expansions of airports in San Diego and Sacramento.

HISTORY

At the turn of the century an engineer and devout Quaker named Henry Chandlee Turner was convinced that a new type of steel-reinforced concrete (called the Ransome system) would change the construction industry. With this conviction and with the help of his partner D. H. Dixon Turner bought the rights to the technology for $25000 and in 1902 founded Turner Construction Company.

One of the company's early projects was building the stairways for New York's first subway stations. As the Ransome method proved to be successful Turner's reputation grew. Defense contracts during WWI raised Turner's take to $35 million in 1918.

Before the Depression Turner was building high-rises hotels and stadiums. During the economic crash that started in 1929 the company survived by building retail stores churches and public buildings a strategy it would employ successfully in later recessions.

Henry Turner retired in 1941. His brother Archer Turner managed the company during most of the war effort. As WWII raged more than 80% of the company's work was defense-related. Projects included building and managing a submarine base in Oak Ridge Tennessee during the development of the atomic bomb.

In 1947 Henry C. Turner Jr. the founder's son became president and within four years he had led the company to more than $100 million in sales. By the time he stepped down as chairman in 1970 the firm had built skyscrapers futuristic airports and such landmarks as Madison Square Garden and the United Nations Secretariat and Plaza in New York City. Turner went public in 1969.

Howard S. Turner (the final family member to head the business) led the company during the 1970s. The company extended its global presence opening offices in more countries including Iran Pakistan and the United Arab Emirates. Turner also developed construction management services.

In 1984 The Turner Corporation was formed as a holding company for the construction company and the subsidiaries created or acquired as a result of diversification. Property development was one of these activities but by 1987 Turner had begun to dispose of its real estate holdings. It did not move quickly enough however and when the real estate market crashed Turner was caught with a large portfolio.

As commercial projects slowed Turner sought work in more sectors including public works and amusement projects (aquariums arenas hospitals and universities). By 1994 these areas accounted for 70% of business. In 1993 as the building slump continued Turner began a cost-cutting plan which included laying off workers and closing offices. That year the company set up an $8.5 million restructuring reserve and as the real estate market eased into recovery Turner sold more of its real estate holdings.

In 1996 Turner won a contract to build a 10000-seat arena in Salt Lake City to be used for the 2002 Winter Olympics. In 1997 Turner contracted to renovate 811 schools and build two campuses in California's San Fernando Valley and in 1998 it was chosen to manage the construction of the Kansas City Motor Speedway.

Profits were recovering quickly. Nonetheless in 1999 the company agreed to be acquired by German construction giant HOCHTIEF in a $370 million deal that ended Turner's joint venture with Switzerland's Karl Steiner. The company also relocated its corporate headquarters to Dallas that year to take advantage of the construction boom in the US Southwest.

In 2000 Turner created three new business groups to serve the aviation pharmaceutical and sports sectors. By the next year Turner's sports group was working on 17 projects. In 2001 the company was a member of the construction team that responded to the September 11 devastation at Ground Zero in New York City.

The next year the company celebrated its 100th anniversary with an exhibit at the National Building Museum in Washington DC; the exhibit featured drawings and photos of some of Turner's notable projects during the past century. In 2003 Turner Construction acquired the assets of Tompkins Builders the third-largest construction company in the Washington DC area from former rival J.A. Jones Construction Co.

Turner Construction which celebrated its 100th anniversary in 2002 has ranked among the leading general builders in the US since WWI. For 80 of the 100 years the group had a Turner among its senior executives. Howard S. Turner was the last member of the family to serve in the company's senior ranks. The company's appointment of Peter Davoren in 2003 as president of Turner Construction reflected the rise of a new generation of leaders for the unit. Davoren was additionally appointed chairman and CEO in 2007.

Turner Construction announced in 2008 that it had signed the contract on its 15000th major project.

EXECUTIVES

Pres-Chb-Ceo, Peter J Davoren
Sr V Pres-Cfo & Treas, Karen Gould
V Pres-Finance & Asst Treas, Don Oshiro
Attrny, Richard L Smith Jr
Svp, Turner, Thomas B Gerlach Jr
Project Engineer, Bernardo Lomeli
Procurement Agent, Paul Dempsey
Superintendent, Austin Armstrong
Purchasing Agent, Jared Posvistak
Superintendent, Michael Depoortere
Project Engineer, Sam Padovano

LOCATIONS

HQ: THE TURNER CORPORATION
375 HUDSON ST RM 700, NEW YORK, NY 100143667
Phone: 212 229-6000
Web: WWW.TURNERCONSTRUCTION.COM

PRODUCTS/OPERATIONS

Selected Related Companies
E. E. Cruz (infrastructure)
Flatiron Construction Corp. (transportation
   construction civil engineering)
Clark Builders (51% Canada)

Selected Markets Served
Aviation
Commercial
Cultural and entertainment
Data center
Education
Government
Green building
Health care
Infrastructure
Industrial
Interiors
Pharmaceutical
Public Assembly
Religious
Research and development
Residential/hotel
Sports

Selected Services
Building information modeling
Building maintenance
Construction management
Design-build
Design-build/finance
Facilities management
General construction
Lean construction
Logistics
Medical planning and procurement
Preconstruction consulting
Program management
Project management

COMPETITORS

Balfour Beatty	Hunt Construction
Construction	Imperial Construction
Bechtel	Group
Clark Construction	Jacobs Engineering
Group	Parsons Corporation
Fluor	Peter Kiewit Sons'
Gilbane Building	Skanska
Company	Structure Tone

HISTORICAL FINANCIALS

Company Type: Private

Income Statement   FYE: December 31

	REVENUE ($ mil.)	NET INCOME ($ mil.)	NET PROFIT MARGIN	EMPLOYEES
12/15	10,523	107	1.0%	5,000
12/14	10,560	95	0.9%	—
12/13	9,522	80	0.8%	—
12/12	8,575	74	0.9%	—
Annual Growth	7.1%	12.9%	—	—

THE UCLA FOUNDATION

Helping to make La-La Land a little more erudite The UCLA Foundation raises manages and disperses funds to help support the tripartite education research and service mission of UCLA. With more than $1 billion in assets the organization funds the aforementioned purposes as well as campus improvements and special programs. About half of the foundation's gifts received are provided by foundations; corporations and alumni each account for some 15% of gifts. The UCLA Progress Fund predecessor of the foundation was established in 1945 by the school's alumni association.

EXECUTIVES

Secretary To Ucla Fund, Wendy Lohman
Auditors: PRICEWATERHOUSECOOPERS LLP LO

LOCATIONS

HQ: THE UCLA FOUNDATION
10920 WILSHIRE BLVD # 200, LOS ANGELES, CA
900246502
Phone: 310 794-3193
Web: WWW.UCLAFOUNDATION.ORG

HISTORICAL FINANCIALS

Company Type: Private

Income Statement   FYE: June 30

	ASSETS ($ mil.)	NET INCOME ($ mil.)	INCOME AS % OF ASSETS	EMPLOYEES
06/18	3,539	336	9.5%	317
06/17	3,050	346	11.4%	—
Annual Growth	16.0%	(3.1%)	—	—

THE WILLIAM PENN FOUNDATION

EXECUTIVES

President, Helen Davis Picher
Director of Investments, Jeffrey Jackman
Investment Analyst, Christine Chien
Information Technology Manager, Edward Wagner
Ms Program Officer, Kellie Brown
Program Officer, Cara Ferrentino
Director of Evaluation, Hilary Rhodes
Senior Program Officer, Hillary Murray
Program Officer, Jennifer Stavrakos
Planning, Jessica Richards
Staff Accountant, Joanne Sabasino
Auditors: KPMG LLP

LOCATIONS

HQ: THE WILLIAM PENN FOUNDATION
2 LOGAN SQ FL 11, PHILADELPHIA, PA 191032763
Phone: 215 988-1830
Web: WWW.WILLIAMPENNFOUNDATION.ORG

HISTORICAL FINANCIALS

Company Type: Private

Income Statement   FYE: December 31

	ASSETS ($ mil.)	NET INCOME ($ mil.)	INCOME AS % OF ASSETS	EMPLOYEES
12/13	2,283	40	1.8%	27
12/00	1,170	(21)	—	—
12/99	1,202	129	10.7%	—
12/98	904	77	8.6%	—
Annual Growth	6.4%	(4.3%)	—	—

Thermo Fisher Scientific Inc

Thermo Fisher Scientific preps the laboratory for research analysis discovery or diagnostics. The company makes and distributes analytical instruments scientific equipment consumables and other laboratory supplies. Products range from chromatographs and spectrometers to Erlenmeyer flasks and fume hoods to gene-sequencers. Moving into other areas it offers testing and manufacturing of drugs including biologicals. Thermo Fisher also provides specialty diagnostic testing products as well as clinical analytical tools. The company tallies more than 400000 customers worldwide. Its key markets are pharmaceutical and biotech diagnostics and health care academic and government and industrial and applied research. Nearly half of the company's sales were generated in the US.

Operations

Thermo Fisher Scientific operates in four segments.

The Laboratory Product and Services unit which generates some 40% of revenue provides basics for the lab. It sells equipment (refrigerators ovens filtration systems) consumables (slides dishes flasks) and chemicals (solvents and reagents). It also includes the Research and Safety Market Channel (catalogs and access to more than 1.5 million products) and Pharma Services (clinical trials).

Life Sciences Solutions about 25% of revenue provides reagents instruments and consumables used in biological and medical research drug discovery and drug production. The unit's businesses are Biosciences Genetic Sciences Clinical Next-Generation Sequencing and BioProduction.

Analytical Instruments more than 20% of revenue supplies instruments consumables software and services. Its businesses are Chromatography and Mass Spectrometry Chemical Analysis and Materials and Structural Analysis.

Specialty Diagnostics about 15% of revenue offers diagnostic test kits reagents culture media and instruments. Its businesses are Clinical Diagnostics ImmunoDiagnostics Anatomical Pathology Microbiology Transplant Diagnostics and the Healthcare Market Channel.

Products from those operational units are sold under Thermo Fisher's five main brands: Thermo

Scientific Applied Biosystems Invitrogen Fisher Scientific and Unity Lab Services.

Overall sales to its products accounts for about three-fourth of total revenue and the rest comes from services.

Geographic Reach

About half of Massachusetts-based Thermo Fisher's revenue comes from its US customers. China is the second biggest single-country market accounting for about 10% of revenue.

The country has office engineering laboratory and productions facilities worldwide from 50 countries.

Sales and Marketing

Thermo Fisher's sales channels include direct sales e-commerce distributors and catalogs. Its sales staff numbers about 13000. The company also offers supply chain management services.

Financial Performance

Thermo Fisher's revenue has risen 51% from 2015-2019 lifted by the company's penchant for acquisitions. Net income have enjoyed growth too for the same period.

Revenue in 2019 were $25.5 billion an increase of $1.2 billion from 2018. Sales increased $153 million due to acquisitions net of a divestiture.

Thermo Fisher posted a profit of $3.7 billion in 2019 $758 million above the 2018 profit primarily due to higher sales the gain on the sale of the Anatomical Pathology business and to a lesser extent productivity improvements net of inflationary cost increases.

Cash and equivalents in Thermo Fisher's coffers totaled $2.4 billion in 2019 compared to $2.1 billion in 2018. In 2019 operations generated $5 billion while investing and financing activities used $1.5 billion and $3.1 billion respectively.

Strategy

Thermo Fisher's growth strategy includes significant investment in and expenditures for product development. It sells its products in several industries that are characterized by rapid and significant technological changes frequent new product and service introductions and enhancements and evolving industry standards. Competitive factors include technological innovation price service and delivery breadth of product line customer support e-business capabilities and the ability to meet the special requirements of customers. Its competitors may adapt more quickly to new technologies and changes in customers' requirements than it can. Without the timely introduction of new products services and enhancements our products and services will likely become technologically obsolete over time in which case our revenue and operating results would suffer.

The Company's growth depends in part on the growth of the markets which it serves. Any decline or lower than expected growth in its served markets could diminish demand for its products and services which would adversely affect its results of operations and financial condition. To address this issue it is pursuing a number of strategies to improve its internal growth including: strengthening our presence in selected geographic markets; allocating research and development funding to products with higher growth prospects; developing new applications for our technologies; expanding our service offerings;

continuing key customer initiatives; combining sales and marketing operations in appropriate markets to compete more effectively; finding new markets for our products; and continuing the development of commercial tools and infrastructure to increase and support cross-selling opportunities of products and services to take advantage of our depth in product offerings.

If the Company may not be able to successfully implement these strategies it may not result in the expected growth of its business.

Mergers and Acquisitions

Thermo Fisher bought HighChem Ltd. a developer of mass spectrometry software based in Bratislava Slovakia in 2019. HighChem's software products are used to analyze complex data and identify small molecules in pharmaceutical and metabolomics research. The acquisition becomes part of Thermo Fisher's chromatography and mass spectrometry business in its Analytical Instruments segment.

In 2019 Thermo Fisher acquired Brammer Bio a viral vector manufacturer for gene and cell therapies for $1.7 billion. Brammer's technologies help Thermo Fisher's biopharma customers deliver medicines based on gene therapies and gene-modified cell therapies.

Company Background

Predating the acquiring company Thermo Electron Fisher Scientific dates back to 1902 when 20-year-old Chester Fisher bought the stockroom of Pittsburgh Testing Laboratories (established 1884) and formed Scientific Materials Co. The company's earliest products supplied from Europe included simple tools such as microscopes balances and calorimeters. It published its first catalog in 1904.

When the outbreak of WWI disrupted supplies from Europe Scientific Materials established its own R&D and manufacturing facilities. It acquired Montreal-based Scientific Supplies in 1925 and the following year changed its name to Fisher Scientific Company. By 1935 Fisher had doubled its size adding glass-blowing operations and an instrument shop.

During the German occupation of Greece in WWII George Hatsopoulos part of a well-to-do family packed with politicians and engineering professors made radios for the Greek resistance. After the war he came to the US and became a professor of mechanical engineering at MIT. With a $50000 loan Hatsopoulos founded Thermo Electron in 1956 to identify emerging technology needs and create solutions for them.

In 2006 Thermo Electron merged with Fisher Scientific International in a stock-swap transaction valued at nearly $11 billion.

HISTORY

Predating the acquiring company Thermo Electron Fisher Scientific dates back to 1902 when 20-year-old Chester Fisher bought the stockroom of Pittsburgh Testing Laboratories (established 1884) and formed Scientific Materials Co. The company's earliest products supplied from Europe included simple tools such as microscopes balances and calorimeters. It published its first catalog in 1904.

When the outbreak of WWI disrupted supplies from Europe Scientific Materials established its own R&D and manufacturing facilities. It acquired Montreal-based Scientific Supplies in

1925 and the following year changed its name to Fisher Scientific Company. By 1935 Fisher had doubled its size adding glass-blowing operations and an instrument shop.

During the German occupation of Greece in WWII George Hatsopoulos part of a well-to-do family packed with politicians and engineering professors made radios for the Greek resistance. After the war he came to the US and became a professor of mechanical engineering at MIT. With a $50000 loan Hatsopoulos founded Thermo Electron in 1956 to identify emerging technology needs and create solutions for them.

In 2006 Thermo Electron merged with Fisher Scientific International in a stock-swap transaction valued at nearly $11 billion.

EXECUTIVES

Vice President Corporate Communications, Karen Kirkwood

President And Ceo, Marc N. Casper, age 52, $1,407,471 total compensation

Evp And President Life Sciences Solutions, Mark P. Stevenson, age 57, $850,301 total compensation

Vp Financial Operations, Stephen Williamson, age 54, $597,031 total compensation

Svp And Chief Commercial Officer, Thomas W. (Tom) Loewald, age 56, $610,115 total compensation

Svp And President Europe The Middle East And Africa (emea), Andrew J. (Andy) Thomson, age 55

Svp And President Asia-pacific And Emerging Markets, Syed A. Jafry

Svp And President Customer Channels, Gregory J. (Greg) Herrema

Svp; President Laboratory Products, Frederick M. (Fred) Lowery

Svp And Cio, Joseph C. (Joe) Beery

Svp And President Specialty Diagnostics, Patrick M. Durbin, age 54

Svp; President Analytical Instruments, Daniel P. (Dan) Shine, age 52

Vice President Commercial Idd Us, Michele Zwickl

Vice President Sales And Marketing, Keith Whittlinger

Vice President Sales, Carlo Bertorelli

Vice President Marketing, Valerie Elliott

Vice President Human Resources, Michael Jewett

Vice President Global Operations, Bret Johnson

Vice President, Charles Lincoln

Vice President Corporate Sales, Mark Covington

Vice President And General Manager, Mitchell Kennedy

Vice President, Elizabeth Woo

National Sales Manager, Michael Bartlett

Vice President Information Technology, Krish Kumar

Vice President Of Engineering, Jerry Welch

Vice President Commercial And Corporate Finance, Marni Kirousis

Executive Vice President Marketing, Andrew Bennison

Vice President Corporate Accounts, Susan Riley

Vice President World Wide Finance, Andy Long

Vice President Inside Sales, Kimberly Brown

Vice President Regional Sales, Greg Lauritzen

Vice President Of Sales, Samantha Wexler

Vice President Sales, Tami Janus

Vice President Commercial Operations Scientific Instruments, Herb Kenny

Vice President, Peter Lee

Vice President Of Sales, Tammy Starr

Vice President Information Technology, Liberino Martino

National Sales Manager, Todd Baker

Vice President Human Resources Biosciences, Fiona Walker

Management Vice President, Andy Thomson

Vice President Human Resources Laboratory
  Products Group, Joseph Baiunco
Vice President Sales, Michael Fuchs
Vice President Employee Benefits, David Reirden
Vice President And General Manager, Christopher
  Budde
Vice President Human Resources, Ali Wilders
Vice President Talent Acquisition, Ronita Griffin
Vice President Human Resources, Derek Mikuriya
Vice President Information Technology, Manoj
  Prasad
Vice President E Business And Vertical Markets,
  Matthew Yoshikawa
Vice President Communications, Tyler Gronbach
Senior Vice President And President Pharma
  Services, Michel Lagarde
Vp Human Resources, Karen Wilson
Vice President Corporate Global Security Please
  Note Our Office Address Has Changed, Lisa
  Quinn
Vice President And General Manager Cell Biology,
  Amy Butler
Vice President Engineering, Richard Duffy
Vice President, Steve Fox
Executive Vice President Global Marketing,
  Christopher Tama
Vice President Strategic Partnerships, Joe Principe
Executive Assistant To Helge Bastian Vp And Gm
  Synthetic Biology And Ole Dahlberg Vp And Gm
  Sample Prep, Gabriela Ramirez
Vice President Diversity And Inclusion, Rueben
  Stokes
Vice President Information Technology Human
  Resources Services, Sean Murphy
Vice President And General Manager Of Fisher
  Bioservices, Dennis Barger
Vice President And General Manager Thermo
  Fisher Scientific Life Science Solutions Group,
  Dara Wright
Senior Vice President Commercial Operationsus,
  Bob Lozano
Vice President, Don Arii
Assistant Treasurer, Stacy Cordier
Treasurer, Tony Smith
Board Director, Thomas Lynch
Board Member, Tyler Jacks
Assistant Treasurer, Danielle Pierre
Auditors: PricewaterhouseCoopers LLP

LOCATIONS

HQ: Thermo Fisher Scientific Inc
  168 Third Avenue, Waltham, MA 02451
Phone: 781 622-1000   Fax: 781 933-4476
Web: www.thermofisher.com

2017 Sales

	$ mil.	% of total
US	10,177	49
China	2,058	10
Other countries	8,683	41
Total	20,918	100

PRODUCTS/OPERATIONS

2018 Sales

	$ mil.	% of total
Laboratory Products & Services	10,035	39
Life Sciences Solutions	6,269	25
Analytical Instruments	5,469	21
Specialty Diagnostics	3,724	15
Adjustments	(1139)	-
Total	24,358	100

2018 Sales

	$ mil.	% of total
Products	18,868	77
Services	5,490	23
Total	24,358	100

Selected Services

Custom Services

Instrument & Qualification Services
Out-Licensing and OEM Sales
Most Popular Products
TaqMan Real-Time PCR Assays
Oligos Primers Probes & Nucleotides
Lipofectamine Reagents
TRIzol Reagents
SuperScript Reverse Transcriptase
eSolutions
eProcurement
Supply Center
Instrument Management

Selected Products

Analytical Instruments
Life Science Research consumables
Chemicals
Consumables
Custom Products
Diagnostics
Equipment
Software

Selected Brands

Thermo Scientific
Applied Biosystems
Invitrogen
Fisher Scientific
Unity Lab Services

COMPETITORS

Abbott Labs	IDEXX Labs
Agilent Technologies	Johnson & Johnson
Beckman Coulter	Life Technologies
Becton Dickinson	Corporation
Bio-Rad Labs	Mettler-Toledo
Danaher	PerkinElmer
Emerson Electric	Shimadzu
Harvard Bioscience	Waters Corp.
Hitachi	
Honeywell	
International	

HISTORICAL FINANCIALS

Company Type: Public

Income Statement   FYE: December 31

	REVENUE ($ mil.)	NET INCOME ($ mil.)	NET PROFIT MARGIN	EMPLOYEES
12/19	25,542	3,696	14.5%	75,000
12/18	24,358	2,938	12.1%	70,000
12/17	20,918	2,225	10.6%	70,000
12/16	18,274	2,021	11.1%	55,000
12/15	16,965	1,975	11.6%	52,000
Annual Growth	10.8%	17.0%	—	9.6%

2019 Year-End Financials

Debt ratio: 30.41%   No. of shares (mil.): 398
Return on equity: 12.91%   Dividends
Cash ($ mil.): 2,399   Yield: 0.2%
Current ratio: 1.92   Payout: 8.5%
Long-term debt ($ mil.): 17,076   Market value ($ mil.): 129,539

	STOCK PRICE ($) FY Close	P/E High/Low		PER SHARE ($) Earnings	Dividends	Book Value
12/19	324.87	36	23	9.17	0.76	74.42
12/18	223.79	34	26	7.24	0.68	68.60
12/17	189.88	36	25	5.59	0.60	63.32
12/16	141.10	31	24	5.09	0.60	54.74
12/15	141.85	29	24	4.92	0.60	53.42
Annual Growth	23.0%	—	—	16.8%	6.1%	8.6%

Thor Industries, Inc.

Thor Industries is a recreation vehicle builder that makes and sells a range of RVs from motor homes to travel trailers as well as related parts. Brands include Airstream Thor Motor Coach Compass Sunlight and Dutchmen. The company's RV manufacturing plants generally produce vehicles to dealer order. Thor sells through some 3300 independent dealers throughout the US Canada and Europe. The company has domestic facilities in Idaho Indiana Michigan Ohio and Oregon. The US is its largest market accounting for 65% of total sales. In 2019 Thor completed the acquisition of Germany-based RV manufacturer Erwin Hymer Group (EHG) in a cash and stock deal valued at about $9.7 billion.

Operations

Thor operates through three segments: North American Towable Recreational Vehicles North American Motorized Recreational Vehicles and European Recreational Vehicles.

The North American Towable Recreational Vehicle segment accounts for around half of total sales and includes towable Airstream products Heartland (Bison Cruiser RV and DRV) Jayco (Jayco towable Starcraft and Highland Ridge) Keystone (CrossRoads and Dutchmen) and KZ (Venture RV).

The North American Motorized Recreational Vehicle segment (more than 15% of sales) includes Airstream (motorized) Jayco (Jayco motorized and Entegra Coach) and Thor Motor Coach.

The European Recreational Vehicle segment offers numerous types of towable and motorized recreational vehicles including motorcaravans caravans and campervans. Brands include Hymer Eriba Carado LMC Xplore and Elddis. The segment generates 30% of company's total sales.

Geographic Reach

Thor's US facilities are in Idaho Indiana Michigan Ohio and Oregon. The company also has facilities in France Germany Italy and the UK. The US accounts for 65% of sales. Other key markets include Europe (about 30% of sales) and Canada (some 5%).

Thor is headquartered in Indiana.

Sales and Marketing

The company's products are sold through some 2300 independent dealerships in the US and Canada and about 1000 dealerships in Europe. One of the company's independent dealers FreedomRoads accounts for 15% of its revenue.

While each of Thor's operating subsidiaries has an independent sales force the most significant sales events are RV trade shows throughout the US Canada and Europe. The company also benefits from marketing activities by the RV Industry Association (RVIA) a trade group that promotes the RV lifestyle.

Thor's advertising costs were $67019 $38643 and $26874 in fiscal 2020 2019 and 2018 respectively.

Financial Performance

Thor has seen rising revenue from 2016 to 2018 a drop in revenue in 2019 then rise again in 2020 even though it has not surpassed the 2018 value. The same trend has been observed in the company's net income. Overall revenue increased by 78% for the past five years while net income decreased by 13%.

Revenue in 2020 amounted to $8.2 billion 4% more than in the previous year. This resulted from an increase in total recreational vehicles' revenue as well as a decrease in intercompany eliminations offset by a decrease in other revenue sources.

Net income was $223 million $89.7 million less than in 2019.

Cash and cash equivalents at the end of the year were $538.5 million 27% more compared to the previous year. Cash provided by operating activities was $540.9 million. Investing activities used $84.2 million and financing activities used $392.9 million. Main cash uses were purchases of property plant and equipment and payments on revolving credit facilities and term-loan credit facilities.

Strategy

Thor spent most of its 2020 capital expenditures for land and production building additions and improvements and replacing machinery and equipment used in the ordinary course of business.

Mergers and Acquisitions

In early 2019 Thor completed the acquisition of Germany-based RV manufacturer Erwin Hymer Group (EHG) in a cash and stock deal valued at about $9.7 billion. The acquisition consists of EHG's European operations which represent the vast majority and core of EHG's historical operations and are the driving strategic rationale for the acquisition. The transaction also provides attractive growth opportunities for the combined company both in the near and long term through EHG's leading position in the growing European RV market.

Company Background

Mergers and acquisitions specialist Wade Thompson and investment banker Peter Orthwein saw the potential of the RV market after buying Hi-Lo Trailer in 1977. Thor Industries was formed when they bought the troubled Airstream Trailers unit (founded in 1931) from Beatrice Foods in 1980. Named after the mythical Norse god of thunder and containing the first two letters of the founders' last names Thor Industries went public in 1984.

HISTORY

Mergers and acquisitions specialist Wade Thompson and investment banker Peter Orthwein saw the potential of the RV market after buying Hi-Lo Trailer in 1977. Thor Industries was formed when they bought the troubled Airstream Trailers unit (founded in 1931) from Beatrice Foods in 1980. Named after the mythical Norse god of thunder and containing the first two letters of the founders' last names Thor Industries went public in 1984.

EXECUTIVES

President Thor Motor Coach, Jeffery L. (Jeff) Kime
Cfo, Colleen A. Zuhl, age 53, $500,000 total compensation
President Airstream, Robert H. Wheeler
President And Ceo, Robert W. Martin, age 50, $750,000 total compensation
Vp Administration And Human Resources, Kenneth D. Julian, age 52, $500,000 total compensation

Director Information Technology, John Stukenborg
President Heartland, Christopher J. Hermon
President Keystone, Matthew T. Zimmerman
Svp General Counsel And Corporate Secretary, W. Todd Woelfer, age 52, $600,000 total compensation
Coo Kz, Aram Koltookian
President Crossroads Rv, Ryan Juday
Vice President Of Operational Improvement, John Rhymer
Senior Vice President, Todd Woelfer
Vice President Purchasing Thor Motor Coach, Sara Jessup
Vp Of Investor Relations, Mark Trinske
National Sales Manager, Darin Elswick
Executive Chairman, Peter B. Orthwein, age 74
Board Member, Wilson Jones
Auditors: DELOITTE & TOUCHE LLP

LOCATIONS

HQ: Thor Industries, Inc.
601 East Beardsley Ave., Elkhart, IN 46514-3305
Phone: 574 970-7460
Web: www.thorindustries.com

PRODUCTS/OPERATIONS

2017 Sales

	% of total
Recreation vehicles	
Towables	71
Motorized	27
Other	2
Intercompany elimination	-
Total	**100**

COMPETITORS

All American Group	Prevost Car
Collins Industries	Rexhall Industries
Featherlite	Skyline
Forest River	Supreme Industries
Motor Coach Industries	Winnebago

HISTORICAL FINANCIALS

Company Type: Public

Income Statement   FYE: July 31

	REVENUE ($ mil.)	NET INCOME ($ mil.)	NET PROFIT MARGIN	EMPLOYEES
07/20	8,167	222	2.7%	22,250
07/19	7,864	133	1.7%	21,750
07/18	8,328	430	5.2%	17,500
07/17	7,246	374	5.2%	17,800
07/16	4,582	256	5.6%	14,900
Annual Growth	**15.5%**	**(3.4%)**	—	**10.5%**

2020 Year-End Financials

Debt ratio: 28.88%	No. of shares (mil.): 55
Return on equity: 10.10%	Dividends
Cash ($ mil.): 538	Yield: 1.4%
Current ratio: 1.39	Payout: 44.8%
Long-term debt ($ mil.): 1,652	Market value ($ mil.): 6,292

	STOCK PRICE ($) FY Close	P/E High/Low	PER SHARE ($) Earnings	Dividends	Book Value
07/20	113.99	29 9	4.02	1.60	42.03
07/19	59.60	43 20	2.47	1.56	37.85
07/18	94.85	19 11	8.14	1.48	36.77
07/17	105.35	16 10	7.09	1.32	29.98
07/16	76.54	16 10	4.88	1.20	24.11
Annual Growth	**10.5%**	— —	**(4.7%)**	**7.5%**	**14.9%**

TJX Companies, Inc.

The TJX Companies operates about 4500 stores worldwide under half a dozen retail brand names including the two largest off-price clothing retailers in the US: T.J. Maxx and Marshalls which operate more than 2400 stores nationwide. T.J. Maxx sells brand-name family apparel accessories shoes domestics giftware and jewelry at discount prices while Marshalls offers similar items plus a broader selection of shoes and menswear through more than 1200 stores worldwide. Its HomeGoods chain of 800-plus US stores focuses exclusively on home furnishings. It trades as T.K. Maxx in Europe with 600-plus stores in the UK Ireland Austria Germany Poland and the Netherlands. TJX keeps prices low by scooping up excess stock from manufacturers and department stores. The US generates the largest revenue amounting more than 60%.

HISTORY

Cousins Stanley and Sumner Feldberg opened the first Zayre (Yiddish for "very good") store in Hyannis Massachusetts in 1956. During the next 15 years the number of stores grew to nearly 200.

Zayre purchased the Hit or Miss chain which sold upscale women's clothing at discounted prices in 1969. When the recession of the early 1970s hit superb results at Hit or Miss prompted Zayre to look for further opportunities in the off-price apparel marketplace. Zayre hired Ben Cammarata to create a new store concept and in March 1977 he opened the first T.J. Maxx in Auburn Massachusetts to market discounted upscale family clothing. Six years later Zayre formed the catalog retailer Chadwick's of Boston to sell Hit or Miss apparel by mail.

The company came to rely increasingly on its specialty operations to provide consistent sales and income as its flagship general merchandise stores often struggled. By 1983 the specialty chains were producing almost half of Zayre's sales.

In the second half of the 1980s Zayre's upscale (yet still off-priced) retailers' sales rose while its general merchandise stores (targeting lower-income customers) dropped. To keep its specialty stores unhindered by its flagging Zayre stores it established The TJX Companies as a public company in 1987. Zayre sold about 17% of its new subsidiary to the public with Cammarata as CEO.

Zayre sold its 400 general merchandise stores in 1988 to Ames for about $430 million in cash $140 million in Ames stock and a receivable note. The next year the company spun off its warehouse club operations as Waban (the warehouse component eventually became BJ's Wholesale) and merged with its subsidiary The TJX Companies taking that name.

TJX acquired Winners Apparel a Toronto-based five-store apparel chain in 1990. That year in the same month that Ames declared bankruptcy TJX established a $185 million reserve against losses it might suffer through its ownership of Ames' stock. Ames emerged from bankruptcy two years later and TJX was left with 4% of Ames' voting shares and over 100 empty Ames stores. TJX sold or leased most of them.

Also in 1992 TJX opened HomeGoods gift and houseware outlets in three of its remaining Ames stores and closed about 70 Hit or Miss stores. That year the company paid off about $128 million of its long-term debt. Encouraged by the success of its off-price operations in Canada in 1994 TJX opened five T.K. Maxx stores (similar to T.J. Maxx and Winners Apparel) in the UK.

A year later TJX paid $550 million for Melville's ailing chain of 450 Marshalls clothing stores. In addition the company sold its Hit or Miss apparel chain.

To help pay for Marshalls TJX sold the Chadwick's of Boston catalog in 1996 to retailer Brylane for about $325 million. Two years later the company opened two T.K. Maxx stores in the Netherlands and said it planned to have 75 stores in Europe in three years. It also debuted the A.J. Wright discount chain in New England in 1998.

In 1999 TJX elected Cammarata to the additional post of chairman and elevated Ted English to president and COO. In 2000 Cammarata relinquished his CEO post to English but remained chairman. Citing the successes of its new stores the company announced in early 2001 it expected to increase its total number of stores 12% annually for the next several years. Also that year the company shuttered its T.K. Maxx stores in the Netherlands. Seven TJX employees perished on September 11 2001 when their flight bound for Los Angeles crashed into the World Trade Center during the worst terrorist attack in US history.

In 2002 the company opened HomeSense a new Canadian home furnishings chain fashioned after its US counterpart HomeGoods. In December 2003 TJX finalized its acquisition of Bob's Stores a Connecticut-based discount retail chain with 31 stores in the Northeast.

In September 2005 English resigned abruptly after five years as the company's CEO. In October the company closed down its tjmaxx.com and homegoods.com Web sites citing poor sales.

In March 2006 TJX cut about 250 jobs in its corporate and divisional offices and reduced the salaries of a dozen senior executives including its chairman and acting CEO and its president by 10% in an effort to increase profits.

A year after the abrupt resignation of CEO Edmond English in September 2005 TJX named company president Carol Meyrowitz to the post effective January 2007. (Cammarata had been acting CEO of the company in the interim.) Also in January 34 A.J. Wright stores were closed.

In November 2007 TJX reached a settlement with Visa and Fifth Third Bancorp stemming from a breach of its computer systems in which customer data was stolen. Under the terms of the agreement TJX will fund up to $40.9 million for recovery payments for US Visa issuers. Also in the fall of 2007 the retailer's European arm T.K. Maxx entered the German market with five stores there.

In 2008 TJX sold money-losing Bob's Stores which has about 35 locations in the Northeast to the private equity firms Versa Capital Management and Crystal Capital for an undisclosed amount.

EXECUTIVES

President Ceo And Director, Ernie Herrman, age 59, $1,525,001 total compensation

Sevp And Group President, Richard Sherr, age 62, $921,232 total compensation

Sevp Finance And Cfo, Scott Goldenberg, age 66, $813,462 total compensation

Svp Corporate Controller, Ken Canestrari, age 59

President The Marmaxx Group, Michael MacMillan, age 63, $1,052,309 total compensation

Executive Vice President Merchandise Coaching And Development, Louis Luciano

Executive Vice President Secretary And General Counsel, Alicia Kelly

Vice President Merchandising, Joseph Domenick

Assistant Vice President Corporate Internal Audit, John Caban

Avp Total Rewards, Cindy Hillman

Assistant Vice President E Marketing, Melanie Campbell

Vice President Tax Audits Director, Joan Korzec-Brown

Senior Vice President And General Counsel, Beverly Kennedy

Divisional Vp, Mark Azar

Senior Vice President And Chief Technology Officer, John Reichelt

Vice President Merchandising, Paula Bingham

Assistant Vice President Loss Prevention, Steve Forgette

Assistant Vice President Merchandise Planning, Doreen Keville

Senior Vice President Store Operations A J Wright, Mike McGrath

Assistant Vice President, Brett Amosson

Assistant Vice President Director Store Operations, Kim Smith

Assistant Vice President Loss Prevention, Mike Marquis

Assistant Vice President Merchandise Planning, Debra Duprez

Vice President Gmm Ecommerce Merchandising And Planning, Mark Deoliveira

Vice President, Timothy Lippold

Assistant Vice President Merchandise Planning, Rose Riggieri

Vice President General Merchandise Manager, Shade Jennifer

Regional Vice President, David Wiese

Assistant Vice President Merchandise Manager Sheets Deco, Corina Roth

Vice President Human Resources, Kelli McNary

Dvp Merchandise Manager, Jeff Nesbit

Dvp Merchandise Manager, Paul Bibbo

Vice President Finance, Peter Daniels

Assistant Vice President Corporate Benefits Director, Lauren Mullin

Vice President Data Centers, George Stephatos

Vp Ecommerce Labs, Enzo Micali

Vice President End User Services, Sandra Rossetsky

Divisional Vice President Merchandise Manager, Kyle Garry

Vice President Gmm Mens, Ken Shuler

Assistant Vice President Loss Prevention, Kate Hughes

Assistant Vice President Merchandise Planning, Nancy Atchue

Assistant Vice President Loss Prevention, Kevin Taparausky

Assistant Vice President, Ken Downey

Vice President, Anand Devendran

Assistant Vice President, Lisa Pratico

Senior Vice President Total Rewards, Julio Mantilla

Assistant Vice President Workplace Services Director, Kathleen LaShoto

Divisional Vice President Market Manager, Narges Castillo

Avp Stores Business Solutions, Christina Oster

Assistant Vice President Director Loss Prevention, Frederick L Mullen

Vice President Of Merchandising, Tim Miner

Senior Vice President Gmm And Director Ladies Sportswear, Nancy Carpenter

Regional Vice President, Guy Reda

Senior Vice President Information Technology, Dave Spooner

Assistant Vice President, Joanne Wolfe

Vice President Office Services Director, Mike Brogan

Assistant Vice President, Jeff Botte

Assistant Vice President Mens Specialty Merchandise Manager, Geno Chiavelli

Divisional Vice President Merchandise Manager Ecommerce, Roland Webber

Assistant Vice President Talent Acquisition, Doug Corcoran

Assistant Vice President, Pam Richards

Dvp Dmm E Commerce, Inna Leipzig

Vice President, David Federico

Vice President Store Systems Director, Martin Whitmore

Assistant Vice President, Tom Sgammato

Assistant Vice President Corporate Communications, Colleen Beauregard

Assistant Vice President Human Resources Marshalls, Steve Dellazoppa

Sr Vice President, Peter Benjamin

Assistant Vice President Construction, John Cox

Senior Vice President, Richard Peck

Assistant Vice President Merchandise Manager Home Accent, Marni Jones

Assistant Vice President, Matthew Garvey

Vice President, Cheryl Oldfield

Assistant Vice President Human Resources, Michelle Okimoto

Vice President, Charlotte Arnold

Vice President The Marmaxx Group, Celine Lewis

Vice President Of Planning And Allocation, Nancy Mendis

Vice President The Marmaxx Group, Manuela Millington

Vice President Human Resources Business Partner, Sharon Simons

Assistant Vice President Store Operations Home Goods, Mike Farrell

Vice President Marketing Director, Katherine Beede

Assistant Vice President Loss Prevention, Kevin Kurtz

Executive Vice President And Chro, Amy Fardella

Avp, Kevin Tubridy

Vice President Of Global Talent Development, Carolyn Fischer

Vice President, Lou Luciano

Avp Supply Chain Business Services, Richard Oppenheimer

Senior Vice President Corporate Human Resources Business Partner, Nancy Maher

Assistant Vice President, Genevieve Barrett

Associate Vice President, Keith Schantz

Assistant Vice President Compensation, April Fontaine

Assistant Vice President Product Development, Kathy Batson

Avp Merchandise Operations, Susan Arapoff

Vp Of It Finance, Scott Tomsik

Vice President Director Of Real Estate, Denise Downing

Senior Vice President And Treasurer, Mary Reynolds

Vice President End User Services, Sandy Rossetsky

Vice President, Beverly Edgehill

Vice President, Scott Garozzo

Vice President General Merchandise Manager, Tom Hayes

Vice President Human Resources Operations, Daniel Finacchio

Assistant Vice President Property Tax Director, Bradford Dunn

National Vice President Of Financial Affairs, Gautam Madineedi

Dvp Merchandise Manager, Jill Rodgers

Divisional Vice President Market Manager, Guido Galli

Senior Vice President Merchandise Planning Allocation And Analysis, Mark Heitin

Regional Vice President Administrative Assistant, Steven Lipasek

Assistant Vice President And Director Store Operations Engineering, Antoinette Wallace

Senior Vice President Transportation And Logistics, Jeff Tawney

Assistant Vice President And Director Corporate Communications, Erika Tower

Rvp, Sheri Gaal

Avp Director Of Human Resources, Michael Doto

Assistant Vice President Marketing Services, Stephanie Games

Assistant Vice President Organizational Development, Cindy Cercone

Associate Vice President Product Development, Carla Bossone

Vp Executive Development, Kelly Ricciardelli

Vice President Financial Accounting, Mike Russo

Senior Vice President Infrasturcutre And Operations, Larry Foster

Assistant Vice President, Glen Brenner

Avp Ctc Data Center, Jeremy Anderson

Avp Network Operations, Tim Kearney

Divisional Vice President Merchandise Manager, Jennifer Shade

Vice President Transportation Network Operations, Carol Beaumont

Avp Digital Marketing, Steve Dow

Divisional Vice President Market Manager, Lindsay Snell

Assistant Vice President Of Mens Furnishings, Deschene Steven

Avp Supply Chain It Solution Delivery, Adam Kaufman

Vice President Fulfillment Operations, Craig O'connor

Regional Vice President, Terrell Davis

Vice President Human Resources, Laura Johnson

Vice President Product Development, Chris Bourget

Vice President Global Sourcing Procurement Us, Brian Richard

Assistant Vice President Director, Patrick Flavin

Area Vice President Merchandising Tk Maxx, Alicia Garfield

Vice President, Sue Flynn

Assistant Vice President Cybersecurity Technology, Gregory Haufe

Avp Of Business Development, Julie Henly

Chairman, Carol M. Meyrowitz, age 66

Assistant Treasurer, Nancy Hendrickson

District Secretary, Cheryl Rowell

Auditors: PricewaterhouseCoopers LLP

LOCATIONS

HQ: TJX Companies, Inc.
770 Cochituate Road, Framingham, MA 01701
Phone: 508 390-1000   **Fax:** 508 390-2091
Web: www.tjx.com

2019 Stores

	No.
US	
T.J. Maxx	1,252
Marshalls	1,091
HomeGoods	749
Sierra Trading Post	35
HomeSense	16
Canada	
Winners	271
HomeSense	125
Marshalls	88
Europe	
T.K. Maxx	567
HomeSense	68
Australia	
T.K. Maxx	44
Total	**4,306**

2019 Sales

	$ mil.	% of total
US		
Marmaxx	24,058	62
HomeGoods	5,787	15
TJX Canada	3,869	10
TJX International	5,257	13
Total	**38,972**	**100**

PRODUCTS/OPERATIONS

Selected Stores

HomeGoods (off-price home fashion chain)
HomeSense (off-price home fashion chain Canada and UK)
Marshalls (off-price retailer of apparel shoes home fashions)
Marshalls Mega-Stores (combination Marshalls and HomeGoods stores)
Sierra Trading Post (off-price online retailer of outdoor gear and apparel)
T.J. Maxx (off-price retailer of apparel shoes home fashions)
T.J. Maxx 'N More (combination T.J. Maxx and HomeGoods stores)
T.K. Maxx (off-price retailer of apparel shoes home fashions Europe)
Winners Apparel (off-price family apparel chain Canada)

2019 Sales

	% of total
Clothing & footwear	52
Home fashions	33
Jewelry & accessories	15
Total	**100**

COMPETITORS

ASDA	Kmart
Amazon.com	Kohl's
Bed Bath & Beyond	Liberty Interactive
Belk	Macy's
Big Lots	Primark
Burlington Coat Factory	Ross Stores
Caleres	Sports Authority
Cato	Stage Stores
Charming Shoppes	Stein Mart
Children's Place	Tailored Brands
Claire's Stores	Target Corporation
Dillard's	Tesco
Dollar General	The Gap
Eddie Bauer LLC	Tuesday Morning Corporation
Foot Locker	Wal-Mart
Inditex	

HISTORICAL FINANCIALS

Company Type: Public

Income Statement

FYE: February 1

	REVENUE ($ mil.)	NET INCOME ($ mil.)	NET PROFIT MARGIN	EMPLOYEES
02/20	41,716	3,272	7.8%	286,000
02/19	38,972	3,059	7.9%	270,000
02/18*	35,864	2,607	7.3%	249,000
01/17	33,183	2,298	6.9%	235,000
01/16	30,944	2,277	7.4%	216,000
Annual Growth	**7.8%**	**9.5%**	**—**	**7.3%**

*Fiscal year change

2020 Year-End Financials

Debt ratio: 9.26%
Return on equity: 59.68%
Cash ($ mil.): 3,216
Current ratio: 1.24
Long-term debt ($ mil.): 2,236
No. of shares (mil.): 1,199
Dividends
Yield: 0.0%
Payout: 33.1%
Market value ($ mil.): 70,795

	STOCK PRICE ($) FY Close	P/E High/Low		PER SHARE ($) Earnings	Dividends	Book Value
02/20	59.04	23	18	2.67	0.89	4.96
02/19	48.90	45	17	2.43	0.74	4.15
02/18*	78.47	39	33	2.02	0.60	4.10
01/17	74.26	47	39	1.73	0.50	3.49
01/16	71.24	45	38	1.67	0.40	3.25
Annual Growth	**(4.6%)**	**—**	**—**	**12.5%**	**21.8%**	**11.2%**

*Fiscal year change

TMV CORP.

EXECUTIVES

Ceo, Mark J Whitt
Chm, Howard L Hawks
Ceo, Fred R Hunzeker
Chief Marketing Officer, Lori A Bruck
Evp-Cfo, John Obermiller
Svp-Bus Devt, Martin E Titus
Svp-Gen Counsel, Mark A McQuade
Vice President, Corey S Kopiasz
Vice President, Gaye L Schaffart
Vice President, Michael H Crabb
Vice President, Todd M Litjen

LOCATIONS

HQ: TMV CORP.
14302 FNB PKWY, OMAHA, NE 681545212
Phone: 402 691-9500
Web: WWW.TENASKA.COM

HISTORICAL FINANCIALS

Company Type: Private

Income Statement

FYE: December 31

	REVENUE ($ mil.)	NET INCOME ($ mil.)	NET PROFIT MARGIN	EMPLOYEES
12/07	10,309	0	—	91
12/05	9,470	0	—	—
12/04	0	0	—	—
12/03	4,940	0	—	—
Annual Growth	**20.2%**	**—**	**—**	**—**

Toll Brothers Inc.

Toll Brothers builds luxury homes in the US targeted at move-up empty nester and second-home buyers. Toll Brothers operates its own security TBI Smart Home which provides homeowners with home automation and technology options. The company also develops communities for active adults and operates country club communities. Subsidiaries offer related services and products including architectural and engineering services title and mortgage services and landscaping. Toll Brothers has operations in around 25 states. Traditionally a suburban developer Toll Brothers has branched out to mid- and high-rise condominiums in urban markets and luxury rentals.

Operations

Toll Brothers' two segments are Traditional Home Building and City Living. Traditional Home Building accounts for almost all company revenue.

The firm operates a slew of subsidiaries that handle architecture engineering mortgage title land development insurance and landscaping. It also has its own lumber distribution house component assembly and manufacturing operations.

The company also develops rental apartments?mainly via joint ventures. The company and its partners have controlling interests in around 65 land parcels for rental projects totaling about 20800 units that it runs or will run under the brand names Toll Brothers Apartment Living and Toll Brothers Campus Living.

Furthermore Toll Brothers' Gibraltar Capital and Asset Management subsidiary offers builders and developers with land banking and venture capital and owns foreclosed real estate through joint ventures.

Geographic Reach

Fort Washington Pennsylvania-based Toll Brother's largest market Pacific (California Oregon and Washington) generates around 30% of sales; it also builds houses in the Mountain (Arizona Colorado Idaho Nevada Oregon Utah; about 20% of sales) North (Connecticut Delaware Illinois Massachusetts Michigan Pennsylvania New Jersey New York; nearly 20%) South (Florida South Carolina Texas; about 15%) and Mid-Atlantic (Georgia North Carolina Maryland Tennessee Virginia; more than 10%) regions of the US. It has development operations in the Salt Lake City Utah and Portland Oregon.

Toll Brothers' City Living builds in urban markets including Hoboken and Jersey City New Jersey and New York City New York and also has planned developments in New York City New York; Northern New Jersey; Philadelphia Pennsylvania; a suburb of Washington D.C.; Los Angeles California; and Seattle Washington.

Sales and Marketing

The homebuilder's marketing strategy for its Traditional Home Building Products has enhanced its reputation as a builder and developer of high-quality luxury living spaces. It includes attractive décor in its less expensive homes to enhance its marketing and sales efforts.

Toll Brothers advertises its homes online through www.TollBrothers.com and via its own sales office and personnel. It also markets through newspapers local publications and billboards.

Advertising costs were $37.1 million $38.5 million and $28.5 million for the years ended October 31 2020 2019 and 2018 respectively.

Financial Performance

Toll Brothers has seen exceptional growth in the past years until 2019 before declining in subsequent years. Overall revenues rose 34% between 2016 and 2020. The company's net income rose 17% over the same five-year period. During the five-year period the company delivered more than 35000 homes from 780 countries.

Toll Brothers' revenue declined 2% to $7.1 billion in 2020 from $7.2 billion the year prior. The company's home sales revenue declined due to a 7% decrease in the average price of the homes

delivered offset by a 5% increase in the number of homes delivered.

Net income fell 24% to $446.6 million in 2020 mainly due to the decline in revenue even as the company's SG&A expenses decreased for the year.

Toll Brothers added $77 million to its cash in 2020 to end the year with $1.4 billion. Operations contributed $1 billion to the coffers. Investments used $177.8 million mainly for purchases of property construction and office equipment as well as business acquisitions. The company used $753.3 million in its financing activities primarily for principle loan payments and treasury stock purchases.

Strategy

Toll Brothers continues to pursue its strategy of broadening its product lines price points and geographic footprint. As part of its strategy to continue expanding its geographic footprint and product offerings in fiscal 2020 the company acquired substantially all of the assets and operations of The Thrive Group LLC an urban infill builder with operations in Atlanta Georgia and Nashville Tennessee. The company also acquired Keller Homes Inc. a builder with operations in Colorado Springs Colorado.

In addition Toll Brothers has acquired control of a number of land parcels as for-rent apartment projects over the years as part of its strategy to diversify product lines. By late 2020 the company had an aggregate of $246 million of investments in 26 Rental Property Joint Ventures.

Company Background

Bob and Bruce Toll founded Toll Brothers in 1967 in southeastern Pennsylvania. In 1982 the company built its first home in the neighboring state of New Jersey. The company went public in 1986 with a listing on the New York Stock Exchange.

HISTORY

Homebuilder Albert Toll's two sons Robert and Bruce Toll founded their own business in 1967. The duo began by building starter homes in the Philadelphia suburbs of Elkins Park and Yardley. As Philadelphia's population began to sprawl beyond these older suburban areas the company grew and in 1982 it moved beyond Pennsylvania to build houses in New Jersey. The young firm also began to distinguish itself by catering to upmarket customers.

Toll Brothers Inc. went public in 1986 and later expanded around New York City north to the Boston area and south to the suburbs of Washington DC. The firm survived the late 1980s real estate recession in the Northeast because unlike many builders it did not overextend itself.

Until the 1990s Toll Brothers operated primarily in the northeastern US but it expanded as the housing market began an upward cycle. It entered California and North Carolina in 1994 and Arizona Florida and Texas in 1995. Toll Brothers began work in Nashville Tennessee and Las Vegas in 1997. The next year the company entered the active adult market building its first two age-qualified communities in New Jersey. Also in 1998 the company joined other investors including the Pennsylvania State Employees Retirement System and formed the Toll Brothers

Realty Trust to acquire and develop commercial property.

In 1999 Toll Brothers acquired Silverman Companies a leading homebuilder and developer of luxury apartments with more than 80 years of experience in Detroit. The company also began building homes in the Chicago San Diego and San Francisco markets that year and it teamed with Marriott International to begin developing an assisted-living community in Reston Virginia.

It also set up its cable and broadband subsidiary Advanced Broadband that year to provide its communities with Internet connectivity. Toll Brothers sold those operations to Comcast in 2007.

The company began operating in Rhode Island and New Hampshire in 2000 and the next year entered Colorado. In 2002 the company entered South Carolina in the Hilton Head area to develop Hampton Hall a luxury country club community with a master-planned golf course.

In 2003 Toll Brothers acquired Jacksonville Florida-based homebuilder Richard R. Dostie Inc. for an undisclosed cash amount. The company also expanded its luxury urban in-fill market operations by acquiring The Manhattan Building Company a developer of luxury mid- and high-rise condos on northern New Jersey's waterfront. The next year Toll Brothers and Pinnacle Ltd. jointly began development of an 832-home luxury condominium community (Maxwell Place on the Hudson) on the waterfront of Hoboken New Jersey overlooking Manhattan.

For its 12th consecutive year Toll Brothers produced record fiscal-year-end results for earnings revenues contracts and backlog in 2004. The company's net income grew 57% over the previous year's earnings and it operated in more communities and offered more product lines than it had in previous years. Another record was set in 2005; revenue from home sales increased 50% and net income increased 97%. That year Toll Brothers began operations in West Virginia but stopped selling homes in Ohio.

Toll correctly predicted an industry slowdown in 2006 and for both 2006 and 2007 the number of homes it built dropped from 8600 to around 6700. As numbers continued to sink it sold land holdings reduced its backlog and divested its cable Internet and home security businesses.

CEO and co-founder Robert Toll stepped down as CEO in 2010. He was succeeded by Douglas Yearley.

EXECUTIVES

President And Coo, Richard T. (Rick) Hartman, age 62, $1,000,000 total compensation
Svp Operations, Douglas C. (Doug) Yearley, age 59, $1,000,000 total compensation
Cfo, Martin P. (Marty) Connor, age 55, $970,833 total compensation
Svp And Chief Marketing Officer, Kira Sterling
Vice President Land Acquisition Land D, Edward Oliu
Vice President, Donald Barnes
Senior Vice President And Chief Audit Officer, Daniel Kennedy
Central Florida Division Vice President, Andre Vidrine
Assistant Vice President Marketing, Michael Klouda
Vice President Central Florida Division, Brock Fanning

Other Contacts Finance Assistant Vice President Fina, Andy Lawhorn

Executive Vice President Ld, Joe Palka

Division Vice President, Kevin Rosinski

Senior Vice President, John Mccullough

Division Vice President, Joshua M Rubinich

Assistant Vice President Benefits, Barbara Colaizzi

Vice President Of Land Acquistions, David Hutcheson

Division Vice President, Mark Nosal

Vice President And Regional Controller, Richard Hoelzle

Vice President, Kathy Gaffney

Senior Vice President, Brian Thierrin

Assistant Vice President, Joe Ogletree

Vice President, Brad Hare

Divison Assistant Vice President, Matt Markovich

Senior Vice President, Gregory Lagreca

Vice President Accounting, Michael Grubb

Assistant Vice President Land Development, Greg Leygraaf

Vice President Land Acqusition, David Ernst

Vice President Land Acquisition Land D, Terry Hodge

Senior Vice President Finance International Development And Ir, Frederick Cooper

Division Vice President, Brian Wulfestieg

Division Vice President, Daniel Wright

Division Vice President, Craig Cherry

Sr. Vice President, Jim Majewski

Senior Vice President, Pete Alles

Division Assistant Vice President, Ch Brittingham

Assistant Vice President And Counsel, Marsha Martin

Vice President Of Process Improvement Hr, Jay Lehman

Assistant Vice President Purchasing, Ron Zega

Division Assistant Vice President, Dan Walton

Assistant Vice President, Tony Casapulla

Assistant Vice President, Steve Savage

Senior Vice President And Controller, Kevin Mcmaster

Assistant Vice President, Glenn Phillips

Division Assistant Vice President, Christopher Kopitsky

Division President Home Building Operations, David Bauer

Vice President Marketing, Christine Sciarrolta

Vice President Land Entitlement, Aaron Hollingbery

Vice President, David Shea

Chro And Senior Vice President Hr, Joy Roman

Senior Business Intelligence Developer, Christopher Arndt

Division Assistant Vice President, Scott Boegner

Vice President Safety, William Meyers

Division Vice President, Scott Tressler

Chairman, Robert I. Toll, age 78

Board Member, Richard Braemer

Board Member, John Mclean

Auditors: Ernst & Young LLP

LOCATIONS

HQ: Toll Brothers Inc.
1140 Virginia Drive, Fort Washington, PA 19034
Phone: 215 938-8000   **Fax:** 215 938-8023
Web: www.tollbrothers.com

2018 Number of Delivered Homes by Region

	No.
Mid-Atlantic	1,800
West	2,130
North	1,453
South	1,391
California	1,322
City Living	169
Total	**8,265**

2018 Sales

	$ mil.	% of total
Traditional Home Building		
California	2,208	31
West	1,451	20
Mid-Atlantic	1,141	16
South	1,045	15
North	975	14
City Living	321	4
Total	**7,143**	**100**

PRODUCTS/OPERATIONS

Selected Operations

Architectural design services
Golf course development and operation
Engineering services
House component assembly
Land development
Landscape services
Lumber distribution
Mortgage lending
Title insurance

COMPETITORS

D.R. Horton	Lennar
David Weekley Homes	PulteGroup
Hovnanian Enterprises	William Lyon Homes
KB Home	

HISTORICAL FINANCIALS

Company Type: Public

Income Statement   FYE: October 31

	REVENUE ($ mil.)	NET INCOME ($ mil.)	NET PROFIT MARGIN	EMPLOYEES
10/20	7,077	446	6.3%	4,500
10/19	7,223	590	8.2%	5,100
10/18	7,143	748	10.5%	4,900
10/17	5,815	535	9.2%	4,500
10/16	5,169	382	7.4%	4,200
Annual Growth	8.2%	4.0%	—	1.7%

2020 Year-End Financials

Debt ratio: 35.77%
Return on equity: 8.96%
Cash ($ mil.): 1,370
Current ratio: 4.41
Long-term debt ($ mil.): 3,958

No. of shares (mil.): 126
Dividends
 Yield: 0.0%
 Payout: 12.9%
Market value ($ mil.): 5,350

	STOCK PRICE ($) FY Close	P/E High/Low		PER SHARE ($) Earnings	Dividends	Book Value
10/20	42.28	15	4	3.40	0.44	38.53
10/19	39.77	10	7	4.03	0.44	35.99
10/18	33.66	11	6	4.85	0.41	32.57
10/17	46.04	14	8	3.17	0.24	28.82
10/16	27.44	17	11	2.18	0.00	26.14
Annual Growth	11.4%	—	—	11.8%	—	10.2%

Tompkins Financial Corp

Tompkins Financial is the holding company for Tompkins Trust Company The Bank of Castile and Mahopac Bank which offer traditional banking services through some 45 offices in upstate New York. It also owns the 20-branch Pennsylvania-based VIST Bank. Funds from de-posit products such as checking savings and money market accounts are mainly used to originate real estate loans and mortgages as well as commercial and consumer loans. Tompkins also offers trust and estate financial and tax planning and investment management services through Tompkins Financial Advisors. Tompkins Insurance Agencies sells property/casualty coverage in central and western New York and Pennsylvania.

Operations

Tompkins Financial operates in three segments: banking insurance and wealth management. Banking represents most of its revenue — more than 80%. About 70% of the banks' loan portfolios is made up of commercial and commercial real estate loans.

Tompkins' Insurance and Wealth Management divisions operate through subsidiaries and make up roughly 10% and 5% of sales respectively. Its subsidiary Tompkins Insurance Agencies Inc. offers property and casualty insurance services and employee benefit consulting services. The firm's trust company Tompkins Financial Advisors offers trust financial planning and wealth management services.

Geographic Reach

Between its four bank subsidiaries the Tompkins operates 66 branches in the US with more than two thirds of the branches in New York and around 20 branches in Pennsylvania.

Sales and Marketing

The company's banks target individual and small business customers for its financial services. Tompkins spent $4.94 million on its marketing expenses in 2014 or slightly less than the $4.96 million spent in 2013 but 22% more than what it spent in 2012.

Financial Performance

Tompkin's revenue rose for a second straight year growing by less than 1% to $255.26 million in 2014 most thanks to growth in the company's non-interest fee income from an increase in deposit account service charges card services income and growth in personal health and benefit insurance sales.

The company's net income ended higher for a second year as well thanks to higher revenue lower interest expense on deposits and lower provisions for loan losses as its loan portfolio's credit improved. Operations provided $77.36 million or 8% less cash than in 2013 mostly because in 2013 the company was able to use more funds from its prepaid accounts to pay for FDIC insurance.

Strategy

The company's strategy for growth includes making inroads into new markets and new business areas through acquisitions. It entered the southeastern Pennsylvania market with its 2012 acquisition of VIST Financial parent of VIST Bank (which continues to operate under a separate charter under existing management) VIST Insurance and VIST Capital Management. The deal added about 20 branches to Tompkins' network along with $889 million in new loan business and $1.2 billion in new deposits.

Mergers and Acquisitions

In August 2012 Tompkins Financial purchased VIST Financial Corp in an all stock transaction valued at $86 million. The deal added all 20 VIST Bank branches (and VIST Bank's assets) in Pennsylvania the VIST Capital Management business and the VIST Insurance business which doubled Tompkin's annual insurance revenue; all of which were folded into Tompkins' banking operations Tompkins Financial Advisors and Tompkins Insurance Agencies operations respectively.

EXECUTIVES

Evp President And Ceo Vist Bank, Robert D. (Bob) Davis, age 72
Director; Vice Chairman Tompkins Insurance Agencies, James R. Hardie, age 76
Executive Vice President Chief Operations Officer Chief Financial Officer & Treasurer, Francis M. Fetsko, age 55, $281,877 total compensation
President Ceo And Director, Stephen S. Romaine, age 56, $474,898 total compensation
Executive Vice President, David S. Boyce, age 53, $185,000 total compensation
Executive Vice-president, Gregory J. Hartz, age 59, $237,107 total compensation
Executive Vice-president, Gerald J. Klein, age 61, $238,369 total compensation
Executive Vice President; President & Coo Of Vist Bank, Scott L. Gruber, age 64
Evp Corporate Marketing, Susan M. Valenti
Svp - Chief Technology Officer, Bradley G. James
Vice President, Bill Steinmetz
Vp Credit Administration Division Manager, Elisa Hogan
Vice President, Frank Christello
Vice President Controller, David Kershaw
Senior Vice President, David DeMilia
Vice President Commercial Relationship Manager, Thomas Evans
Executive Vice President, Greg Hartz
Senior Vice President, Brian Bisaccio
Vice President, Mark Deyoung
Senior Vice President Regional, James Whitton
Vice President, Peter Hin
Assistant Vice President, Susan Herendeen
Senior Vice President, Kara Taylor
Senior Vice President Cash Management, Gerhard Voggel
Senior Vice President Chief Risk Officer, Steven Cribbs
Sr. Vice President, Kara Pass
Vice President, Lynn Carleton
Assistant Vice President, Joe Monteleone
Chairman Tompkins Financial Corporation And Tompkins Trust Company, James J. Byrnes, age 77
Vice Chairman, James W. (Jim) Fulmer, age 68
Board Member, Michael Spain
Board Member, John Alexander
Recording Secretary, Janet Hewitt
Auditors: KPMG LLP

LOCATIONS

HQ: Tompkins Financial Corp
 118 E. Seneca Street, P.O. Box 460, Ithaca, NY 14851
Phone: 607 274-7299
Web: www.tompkinsfinancial.com

PRODUCTS/OPERATIONS

2016 Sales

	$ mil.	% of total
Interest		
Loans	169	63
Available-for-sale securities	27	10
Held-to-maturity securities	3	1
Federal Home Loan Bank stock and Federal Reserve Bank stock	1	1
Trading securities	0	-
Due from banks		
Non-interest		
Insurance commissions & fees	29	11
Investment services	15	6
Service charges on deposit accounts	8	3
Card services income	8	3
Mark-to-market gain on liabilities held at fair value	0	-
Net gain on securities transactions	0	-
Other	6	2
Mark-to-market loss on trading securities	(0.2)	-
Total	**271**	**100**

2016 Sales

	$ mil.	% of total
Banking	227	84
Insurance	29	11
Wealth Management	15	5
Others	(1.2)	-
Total	**271**	**100**

COMPETITORS

Bank of America	Community Bank System
Chemung Financial	Elmira Savings Bank
Citigroup	HSBC USA
Citizens Financial Group	JPMorgan Chase
	M&T Bank

HISTORICAL FINANCIALS

Company Type: Public

Income Statement
FYE: December 31

	ASSETS ($ mil.)	NET INCOME ($ mil.)	INCOME AS % OF ASSETS	EMPLOYEES
12/19	6,725	81	1.2%	1,048
12/18	6,758	82	1.2%	1,035
12/17	6,648	52	0.8%	1,041
12/16	6,236	59	1.0%	1,046
12/15	5,690	58	1.0%	1,038
Annual Growth	**4.3%**	**8.8%**	**—**	**0.2%**

2019 Year-End Financials

Debt ratio: 0.31%	No. of shares (mil.): 14
Return on equity: 12.76%	Dividends
Cash ($ mil.): 137	Yield: 2.2%
Current ratio: —	Payout: 38.7%
Long-term debt ($ mil.): —	Market value ($ mil.): 1,362

	STOCK PRICE ($) FY Close	P/E High/Low	PER SHARE ($) Earnings	Dividends	Book Value
12/19	91.50	17 14	5.37	2.02	44.43
12/18	75.01	17 13	5.35	1.94	40.68
12/17	81.35	28 21	3.43	1.82	37.86
12/16	94.54	24 13	3.91	1.77	36.40
12/15	56.16	16 13	3.87	1.70	34.57
Annual Growth	**13.0%**	**— —**	**8.5%**	**4.4%**	**6.5%**

TOMPKINS TRUST COMPANY

EXECUTIVES

Chb, James Byrnes
Prin, Steven Garner
Vice President, Bill Steinmetz
Wealth Management Associate, Dimitrios Alissandratos
Vice President Information TEC, James Frey
Assistant Vice President of Co, Jason Moore
Vice President, Scott Pronti
Vp Com Banking Rel Manager, John Bauda
Small Business Lending Manager, Brad Totman
Vice President, Karen Parks
Corporate Secretary, Kathy Manley

LOCATIONS

HQ: TOMPKINS TRUST COMPANY
 110 N TIOGA ST, ITHACA, NY 148504320
Phone: 607 273-3210
Web: WWW.TOMPKINSTRUST.COM

HISTORICAL FINANCIALS

Company Type: Private

Income Statement
FYE: December 31

	ASSETS ($ mil.)	NET INCOME ($ mil.)	INCOME AS % OF ASSETS	EMPLOYEES
12/17	2,118	21	1.0%	1
12/16	1,962	23	1.2%	—
12/15	1,805	24	1.3%	—
12/14	1,682	22	1.3%	—
Annual Growth	**8.0%**	**(0.7%)**	**—**	**—**

TowneBank

EXECUTIVES

BR Mgr, Becky Zambas
Executive Officer, Anne Conner
Administrative Officer, Teresa Plummer
Board Member, Douglas Ellis
Board Member, Thomas Broyles
Manager, Ashlee Diehl
Executive, Aston Robert
Senior Vice President, Joseph Johann
Auditors: Dixon Hughes Goodman LLP

LOCATIONS

HQ: TowneBank
 5716 High Street, Portsmouth, VA 23703
Phone: 757 638-7500
Web: www.townebank.com

HISTORICAL FINANCIALS

Company Type: Public

Income Statement				FYE: December 31
	ASSETS ($ mil.)	NET INCOME ($ mil.)	INCOME AS % OF ASSETS	EMPLOYEES
12/19	11,947	138	1.2%	2,853
12/18	11,163	133	1.2%	2,897
12/17	8,522	87	1.0%	2,727
12/16	7,973	67	0.8%	2,529
12/15	6,296	62	1.0%	1,903
Annual Growth	17.4%	22.1%	—	10.7%

2019 Year-End Financials

Debt ratio: 2.52%
Return on equity: 8.77%
Cash ($ mil.): 442
Current ratio: —
Long-term debt ($ mil.): —

No. of shares (mil.): 72
Dividends
  Yield: 2.5%
  Payout: 35.9%
Market value ($ mil.): 2,021

	STOCK PRICE ($) FY Close	P/E High/Low	PER SHARE ($) Earnings	Dividends	Book Value
12/19	27.82	15 12	1.92	0.70	22.58
12/18	23.95	18 12	1.88	0.62	21.05
12/17	30.75	25 21	1.41	0.55	18.06
12/16	33.25	29 14	1.18	0.51	17.20
12/15	20.87	18 12	1.22	0.47	15.71
Annual Growth	7.5%	— —	12.0%	10.5%	9.5%

Toyota Motor Credit Corp.

Toyota Motor Credit (TMCC) is the US financing arm of Toyota Financial Services which is a subsidiary of Toyota Motor Corporation the world's largest carmaker. TMCC provides retail leasing retail and wholesale sales financing and other financial services to Toyota and Lexus dealers and their customers for the purchase of new and used cars and trucks. It offers similar services to Toyota industrial equipment dealers. TMCC which underwrites and services the finance contracts operates three regional customer service centers and some 30 dealer sales and service branches across the US and Puerto Rico.

Operations

TMCC organizes its business around two product categories: Finance and Insurance.

Its Finance segment which generates more than 90% of the company's total sales acquires a variety of retail finance products such as consumer and commercial installment sales contracts in the US and Puerto Rico as well as leasing contracts — either direct finance leases or operating leases from US vehicle or industrial equipment dealers. The segment also provides dealer financing (including wholesale financing revolving credit lines and working capital loans) and real estate financing for vehicle and industrial equipment dealers in the US and Puerto Rico.

The Insurance division operates through subsidiary Toyota Motor Insurance Services which underwrites and sells insurance products such as extended service coverage total loss protection and prepaid maintenance protection. It also pro-

vides marketing and claims administration services related to covering select risks of vehicle dealers and their customers in the US.

Broken down TMCC generated 67% of its total revenue from operating leases in fiscal 2015 (ended March) and another 20% from retail financing income. Its Insurance premium and contract revenue brought in 7% of total revenue while dealer financing revenue (4%) and investment income (2%) brought in the rest.

Geographic Reach

The California-based company serves dealers and their customers across the US. About 21% of TMCC's vehicle retail and lease contracts were based in California in fiscal 2015 while 10% were from Texas 8% were from New York and 6% came from New Jersey.

Financial Performance

TMCC has seen its revenues and profits trend downward for most of the past several years. However the company's revenue has been recovering since 2014.

TMCC's revenue inched up by more than 1% to $8.10 billion in fiscal 2015 (ended March) mostly as its Operating Lease business grew by 21% thanks to higher average outstanding earning asset balances as Toyota Motor Sales USA (the primary US distributor of Toyota Lexus and Scion vehicles) focused more on pushing lease subvention during the year. The company's Insurance business also grew thanks to higher premiums and contract revenues resulting from an increase in the average number of agreements in force during the year.

Higher revenue in fiscal 2015 allowed TMCC's profit to rebound sharply with net income jumping by 40% to $1.20 billion. Cash from operations declined by 23% to $3.77 billion as the company collected less in cash earnings after foreign exchange currency adjustments.

EXECUTIVES

President And Ceo; Cfo, Michael R. (Mike) Groff, age 65
Auditors: PricewaterhouseCoopers LLP

LOCATIONS

HQ: Toyota Motor Credit Corp.
6565 Headquarters Drive, Plano, TX 75024
Phone: 469 486-9300
Web: www.toyotafinancial.com

PRODUCTS/OPERATIONS

2016 Sales

	$ mil.	% of total
Financing		
Operating leases	7,141	68
Retail	1,859	18
Dealer	403	4
Insurance premiums earned & contract revenues	719	7
Investment & other	164	1
Gain on sale of commercial finance business	197	2
Total	**10,483**	**100**

2016 Sales

	$ mil.	% of total
Financing revenues	9,403	90
Insurance earned premiums and contract revenues	719	7
Investment and other income net	164	1
Gain on sale of commercial finance business	197	2
Total	**10,483**	**100**

COMPETITORS

Ally Financial	Ford Motor Credit
American Honda Finance	GM Financial
AutoNation	Mercedes-Benz Credit
Capital One Auto Finance	Volkswagen Financial Services
Daimler Financial Services	Volvo Car Finance

HISTORICAL FINANCIALS

Company Type: Public

Income Statement				FYE: March 31
	REVENUE ($ mil.)	NET INCOME ($ mil.)	NET PROFIT MARGIN	EMPLOYEES
03/20	13,284	913	6.9%	3,300
03/19	12,836	795	6.2%	3,200
03/18	11,856	3,410	28.8%	3,300
03/17	11,246	267	2.4%	3,185
03/16	10,483	932	8.9%	3,140
Annual Growth	6.1%	(0.5%)	—	1.3%

2020 Year-End Financials

Debt ratio: 77.85%
Return on equity: 6.48%
Cash ($ mil.): 6,790
Current ratio: —
Long-term debt ($ mil.): 97,740

No. of shares (mil.): 0
Dividends
  Yield: —
  Payout: —
Market value ($ mil.): —

Tractor Supply Co.

Tractor Supply Company (TSC) does a lot more than its name suggests. Besides providing agricultural machine parts TSC offers animal feed fencing power tools riding mowers work clothing and pet supplies as well as tools for gardening irrigation welding and towing. It is the nation's leading rural lifestyle retail chain. TSC offers both name-brand merchandise and its own crop of private-label goods. It has nationwide scope operating more than 2000 stores across the US under the Tractor Supply Company Del's Feed & Farm Supply and Petsense banners. Stores are concentrated in rural areas and near large cities to cater to full- and part-time farmers ranchers and contractors. TSC also sells online.

Operations

TSC operates more than 1800 Tractor Supply and Del's Feed & Farm Supply stores and about 180 Petsense stores. It breaks its operations into product categories.

Livestock and pet products account for more than 45% of total sales with hardware tools and truck products and seasonal gift and toy products each contributing about 20%. The remaining 15% of company sales is generated from clothing and footwear and agricultural products.

Proprietary brands — Countyline Producer's Pride Jobsmart TSC Tractor Supply Co. Huskee Red Shed Bit & Brindle and Redstone among them — represent nearly a third of TSC's sales.

The company's products are sourced through both US and international vendors. It purchases merchandise from a group of roughly 975 vendors some 375 of which supply 90% of TSC's products.

Geographic Reach

TSC based in Brentwood Tennessee operates stores in some 50 US states. Its largest market is Texas home to about 220 stores followed by

Pennsylvania Tennessee and North Carolina (nearly 100 each) and Ohio Georgia Michigan and New York (more than 90 each).

The company has distribution facilities in Arizona Georgia Indiana Kentucky Maryland Nebraska New York Texas and Washington.

Sales and Marketing

TSC's customers are home and landowners and pet and livestock owners in rural areas and the outskirts of major metropolitan areas. While its customers are often recreational farmers i.e. those that enjoy the outdoor lifestyle but are non-professionals it also serves tradesmen and small businesses.

The company's advertising strategy is based on merchandise its website newspaper circulars direct mail and email and digital and social media. Advertising expenses were $86.6 million $83.4 million and $81.3 million for fiscal 2019 2018 and 2017 respectively.

Financial Performance

TSC's revenue has grown steadily over the past five years as the company continues to add locations; sales are up 34% since 2015 and net income is up 37%.

In 2019 the company reported a 6% increase in revenue valued at $8.4 billion compared to $7.9 billion in 2018. This was driven by an increase in comparable store sales growth as well as sales from stores opened less than one year.

Net income in fiscal 2019 was $562.4 million a 6% increase compared to $532.4 million in fiscal 2018.

Cash and cash equivalents at the end of 2019 amounted to $84 million a 2% decrease from the prior year. Cash from operations contributed $812 million to the coffers while investing activities used $215 million primarily for capital expenditures. Financing activities used $599 million primarily for repurchase of the company's common stock and cash dividends paid to stockholders.

Strategy

Tractor Supply Company believes the business can grow by being the most dependable supplier of relevant products and services for the "Out Here" lifestyle creating customer loyalty through personalized experiences and providing convenience customers expect at anytime anywhere and in any way they choose. The company's long-term growth strategy is to: drive profitable growth through new store openings and by expanding omni-channel capabilities thus tying together its website product content social media digital and online shopping experience attracting new customers and driving loyalty; build customer-centric engagement by leveraging analytics to deliver legendary customer service seasoned advice and personalized experiences; offer relevant assortments and services across all channels through exclusive and national brands and continue to introduce new products and services through its test and learn strategy; enhance its core and foundational capabilities by investing in infrastructure and process improvements which will support growth scale and agility while improving the customer experience; and expand through selective acquisitions as such opportunities arise to add complementary businesses and to enhance penetration into new and existing markets to supplement organic growth.

Achieving this strategy will require a foundational focus on organizing optimizing and empowering TSC's team members for growth by developing skills talent and leadership across the organization and implementing operational efficiency initiatives including leverage of technology and automation to align the company's cost structure to support new business capabilities for margin improvement and cost reductions.

The company plans to open approximately 80 new Tractor Supply and 10 to 15 new Petsense stores in fiscal 2020 a selling square footage increase of approximately 4.5%. In fiscal 2019 it opened 80 new Tractor Supply stores and 8 new Petsense stores. In fiscal 2018 it opened 80 new Tractor Supply stores and 18 new Petsense stores.

Company Background

TSC was founded in 1938 by Charles Schmidt as a mail-order tractor parts business.

EXECUTIVES

Evp Real Estate And Construction General Counsel And Corporate Secretary, Benjamin F. (Ben) Parrish, age 64, $522,615 total compensation

Vice President Of Logistics And Transportation, Les Gardner

Ceo, Gregory A. (Greg) Sandfort, age 65, $1,033,846 total compensation

President And Chief Merchandising Officer, Steve K. Barbarick, age 52, $607,885 total compensation

Svp And Cio, Robert D. Mills, age 47, $397,692 total compensation

Svp Cfo And Treasurer, Kurt Barton

Vice President Information Technology, Jessica Cornelius

Vp And Manager Merchandise, Karl Olsen

Regional Vice President, John Logan

Vice President Information Technology, George Argodale

Vice President Merchandising, Greg Sanford

Regional Vice President, Pat Coulter

Svp Distribution And Logistics, Colin Yankee

Regional Vice President, Jason Brooks

Vice President Tax, Blake Snider

Vp Customer Engagement Loyalty And Insights, Michael Cooper

Vice President Information Technology Manager, Andy Reed

Vp Of Gasoline Marketing, Lloyd Sanford

Chairman, Cynthia T. Jamison, age 60

Board Member, Edna Morris

Board Member, Peter Bewley

Member Board Of Directors, Denise Jackson

Auditors: Ernst & Young LLP

LOCATIONS

HQ: Tractor Supply Co.
5401 Virginia Way, Brentwood, TN 37027
Phone: 615 440-4000
Web: www.tractorsupply.com

2018 Stores

	No.
Texas	212
North Carolina	99
Pennsylvania	97
Tennessee	96
Ohio	92
Michigan	87
Georgia	86
New York	82
Kentucky	70
California	66
Other states	953
Total	**1,940**

PRODUCTS/OPERATIONS

2018 Sales

	% of total
Livestock and Pet	47
Hardware Tools and Truck	22
Seasonal Gift and Toy Products	19
Clothing and Footwear	8
Agriculture	4
Total	**100**

Selected Products

Farm & Ranch
Poultry
Pets & Livestock
Lawn & Garden
Truck & Trailer
Hardware & Tools
Heating & Cooling
Outdoors
Home & Decor
Footwear
Clothing
Big & Tall
Plus Sizes
Gift Cards
Selected Brands
4health (pet foods and supplies)
Bit & Bridle (apparel and fo

COMPETITORS

Ace Hardware	Northern Tool
Amazon.com	Southern States
Farm King	Tennessee Farmers
Home Depot	Co-op
Lowe's	True Value
Menard	Wal-Mart
Miles Enterprises	Wilbur-Ellis

HISTORICAL FINANCIALS

Company Type: Public

Income Statement

FYE: December 28

	REVENUE ($ mil.)	NET INCOME ($ mil.)	NET PROFIT MARGIN	EMPLOYEES
12/19	8,351	562	6.7%	32,000
12/18	7,911	532	6.7%	29,000
12/17	7,256	422	5.8%	28,000
12/16	6,779	437	6.4%	26,000
12/15	6,226	410	6.6%	23,000
Annual Growth	**7.6%**	**8.2%**	**—**	**8.6%**

2019 Year-End Financials

Debt ratio: 8.15%	No. of shares (mil.): 118
Return on equity: 36.04%	Dividends
Cash ($ mil.): 84	Yield: 0.0%
Current ratio: 1.43	Payout: 29.1%
Long-term debt ($ mil.): 396	Market value ($ mil.): 10,907

	STOCK PRICE ($) FY Close	P/E High/Low		PER SHARE ($) Earnings	Dividends	Book Value
12/19	92.30	24	17	4.66	1.36	13.26
12/18	83.21	22	13	4.31	1.20	12.82
12/17	74.75	23	15	3.30	1.05	11.32
12/16	75.81	29	19	3.27	0.92	11.11
12/15	85.67	32	25	3.00	0.76	10.38
Annual Growth	**1.9%**	**—**	**—**	**11.6%**	**15.7%**	**6.3%**

Travelers Companies Inc (The)

Running a business is a risk The Travelers Companies will insure. While it does offer personal insurance the company's largest segment is commercial property/casualty insurance for businesses big and small. Travelers is one of the largest business insurers in the US providing commercial auto property workers' compensation and general liability coverage to companies. Personal insurance offerings include auto and homeowners policies. The company also offers surety and fidelity bonds as well as professional and management liability coverage. The US accounts for a majority of sales though the company has international operations.

Operations

Travelers operates in three segments — Business Insurance Personal Insurance and Bond & Specialty Insurance.

The Business Insurance segment (which accounts for nearly 50% of revenue) offers property/casualty insurance and related services to large midsized and small companies primarily in the US. It also operates in Canada the UK Ireland and throughout other parts of the world as a corporate member of Lloyd's. Products include commercial auto property liability workers' compensation and multi-peril coverage.

The Personal Insurance segment (nearly 35% of sales) offers auto homeowners flood marine property and umbrella (liability fraud and events) policies. It operates in the US and Canada.

The Bond & Specialty Insurance segment (nearly 10% of sales) provides fidelity coverage surety bonds and management and professional liability policies in the US. It also writes property general liability auto and workers' compensation coverage for financial institutions and provides select specialty policies in overseas markets. The remainder accounts for other revenue.

The company operates through underwriting subsidiaries including Travelers Property Casualty Standard Fire Travelers Casualty and Surety Travelers Indemnity Travelers Insurance (UK) and Travelers Syndicate Management (a UK Lloyd's of London syndicate). Travelers also offers reinsurance.

Geographic Reach

The vast majority (about 95%) of Travelers' business is in the US. Its largest markets are California New York and Texas. The firm is headquartered in New York City and has executive offices in Hartford Connecticut and St. Paul Minnesota. The company also has about 15 claims management centers and around 50 satellite claims offices in some 45 states.

Additionally Travelers has modest operations in Canada the UK Ireland Brazil and Colombia.

Sales and Marketing

Travelers' customers include commercial businesses associations government agencies and individuals.

The company's offerings are distributed through independent agents and brokers across the US. In the Business Insurance segment some 9400 agents are supported by customer service centers and about 100 field offices. The unit also writes business abroad where its products are distributed through independent brokers and via Lloyd's wholesale and retail brokers.

Personal products are distributed through about 9900 independent agents and select employee and affinity groups. Meanwhile the Bond & Specialty Insurance segment distributes products through some 5000 independent agents and brokers.

Financial Performance

Travelers' revenue has maintained a slow-but-steady growth rate over the past five years. Overall sales increased 18% between 2015 and 2019.

In 2019 revenue increased 4% to some $31.6 billion. This was primarily due to the $1.2 billion increase in premiums.

Net income of $2.6 billion in 2019 increased by 4% over net income of $2.5 billion in 2018. The higher rate of increase in diluted net income per share reflected the impact of share repurchases in recent periods.

The company ended 2019 with $494 million in cash up $121 million from 2018. Operating activities contributed $5.2 billion while investing activities used $2.9 billion (mostly purchases of fixed maturities) and financing activities used $2.2 billion via treasury stock purchases and dividends.

Strategy

Travelers targets long-term growth in returns on equity with the notion that economic cycles weather patterns and other factors can impact its business in the short term. Like all property/casualty insurers the company is especially vulnerable to severe weather and natural disasters. Recent challenges have also come from increasing injury costs in commercial auto policies.

To mitigate these types of losses companies must have accurate pricing mechanisms and maintain sufficient loss reserves. The company follows disciplined underwriting and investment strategies and maintains a diverse product portfolio to help it stay immune to market and interest rate fluctuations.

From time to time to protect and grow market share and/or improve the company's efficiency it invests in strategic initiatives to: Improve business processes and workflow to increase efficiencies and productivity and to enhance the experience of its customers and distributors; Change its underwriting processes; Develop products that insure risks it has not previously insured contain new coverages or change coverage terms; Expand distribution channels; Change commission terms; and Enter geographic markets within or outside of the United States where it has had relatively little or no market share.

Company Background

The company was formed in 2004 through the merger of The St. Paul Companies and Travelers Property Casualty creating The St. Paul Travelers Companies. The firm changed its name to The Travelers Companies in 2007.

St. Paul Mutual Insurance was founded in 1853 by a group of Minnesota investors led by George and John Farrington and Alexander Wilkin. It changed its name to St. Paul Fire and Marine Insurance in 1865 when it halted mutual policy sales and expanded throughout the Midwest. The company operated nationwide by the turn of the century and it changed its name to The St. Paul Companies in 1968.

Travelers Property Casualty was founded in 1864 in Hartford Connecticut by businessman James Batterson banker James Bolter and other area businessmen. The firm provided travel and accident insurance; it later added auto workers' compensation life property and liability policies. It divested its travel accident and life operations in the 1990s and 2000s.

HISTORY

The Travelers Companies was formed in 2004 through the merger of The St. Paul Companies and Travelers Property Casualty creating The St. Paul Travelers Companies. The firm changed its name to The Travelers Companies in 2007.

St. Paul Minnesota was a boomtown in 1852 thanks to traffic on the Mississippi. Settlers knew fire insurance was a must in their wooden town but there were no local insurers. Buying policies from eastern companies and getting claims processed was difficult — especially in the winter when river traffic stopped.

In 1853 a group of local investors led by George and John Farrington and Alexander Wilkin formed St. Paul Mutual Insurance a mixed stock and mutual company (mutual members shared in the firm's profits and losses while stockholders could benefit by selling if the company's value rose). St. Paul Mutual sold its first policy the following year.

The company changed its name in 1865 to St. Paul Fire and Marine Insurance stopped offering mutual policies and expanded throughout the Midwest. Claims from the Chicago Fire in 1871 nearly sank the company which assessed its shareholders $15 for each share of stock but prompt and full payment of claims resulted in more business. By the turn of the century St. Paul Fire and Marine was operating nationwide.

Although the company was hard hit by shipping losses in WWI it continued expanding joining other US insurers in the American Foreign Insurance Association to market insurance in Europe.

In 1926 St. Paul Fire and Marine organized its first subsidiary St. Paul Mercury Indemnity to write liability insurance policies. Other additions included coverage for automobiles aircraft burglary and robbery and in 1940 turkey farming.

During WWII St. Paul Fire and Marine joined the War Damage Corp. a government-financed consortium that paid claims for war damage. The St. Paul Companies was formed in 1968 as the umbrella organization for the various subsidiaries and the firm grew through purchases.

Lines of business blossomed during the 1970s including life and title insurance leasing a mail-order consumer finance company oil and gas and real estate. Many of these were sold during the 1980s but one The John Nuveen Co. (1974) became the nucleus of St. Paul's financial services operations.

Travelers Property Casualty was founded in 1864 in Hartford Connecticut by businessman James Batterson banker James Bolter and other area businessmen. The firm provided travel and accident insurance; it later added auto workers' compensation life property and liability policies.

Travelers sold its travel and accident operations to Crum and Forster in the 1990s. It was acquired by Primerica (later Citigroup) in 1993 and purchased Aetna's property/casualty operations and went public in 1996. Citigroup spun off its remaining shares in Travelers in 2002. The life insurance operation were sold to MetLife in 2005.

In 2004 The St. Paul Companies merged with Travelers Property Casualty creating The St. Paul Travelers Companies a top US commercial property/casualty insurer. The firm changed its name to The Travelers Companies in 2007 and reacquired rights to the red umbrella logo from Citigroup in 2008.

Travelers entered the Brazilian market in 2011 and the Colombian market in 2015. It purchased The Dominion of Canada General Insurance in 2013 and it acquired Simply Business a UK-based online business insurance broker for $490 million in 2017.

EXECUTIVES

Evp And Chief Administrative Officer, Andy F. Bessette, age 67
President And Coo, Brian W. MacLean, age 67, $962,548 total compensation
Vice Chairman And Cfo, Jay S. Benet, age 68, $1,000,000 total compensation
Evp And Chief Human Resources Officer, John P. Clifford, age 64
Evp Strategic Development And Corporate Treasurer, Maria Olivo, age 55
Evp And General Counsel, Kenneth F. (Ken) Spence, age 65
Evp Marketing And Communications, Lisa M. Caputo, age 56
Evp Enterprise Risk Management, Fred R. Donner, age 63
Chairman And Ceo, Alan D. Schnitzer, age 55, $1,000,000 total compensation
President Field Management, Patrick J. Kinney
Evp Middle Market, Michael F. Klein
Evp Public Policy; President The Travelers Institute, Joan Kois Woodward
Evp; President Bond And Specialty Insurance, Thomas M. (Tom) Kunkel
Evp; President Business Insurance, Greg C Toczydlowski
Evp; President International, Kevin C. Smith
Evp And Cio, Madelyn Lankton
Evp Claim Services And Specialty Liability, Robert C. (Bob) Brody
Evp And Chief Underwriting Officer, Marlyss J. Gage
Evp And Chief Risk Officer, Bruce R. Jones
Evp President National Accounts And First Party, William C Malugen
Evp And President Small Commercial, Behram M. Dinshaw
Evp And President Middle Market, Scott F. Higgins
Evp Management Liability, Jeffrey P. (Jeff) Klenk
Vp Finance And Workforce Analytic, Todd Clements
Claim Center Vice President, Claude Howard
Senior Vice President Human Resources, Jason Angilan
Vice President Of Finance, Sheila Brown
Vice President Product Strategy, Patty Koziol
Vp And Cio Bond And Fp Information Systems, Dave Condren
Regional Vice President Construction, Carol Matthys
Second Vice President Corporate Audit, Debra Barlow
Vice President Public Sector Services, David Hyde
Senior Vice President, Len Mariani
2vp Complex Claim Specialist, Milena Ivanis

Regional Vice President Select Group, Sean Ramalho
Vice President, John Komidar
Second Vice President Finance And Governance, Jeffrey Longo
Second Vice President, Pamela Latty
Vice President, Ken Chapman
Division President, Maureen Bass
Second Vice President Product Ocean Marine, James Thompson
Second Vice President Credit Risk Management, Charles Chamberlain
Senior Vice President Operations, Pete Collins
Corporate Vice President, Jim Stevenson
Regional Vice President Select Accounts Kansas City, Bryan Whipple
Vice President Product Management, Ken Surian
Vice President, Melissa Ohara
Regional Vice President, Mark Lear
Vice President Finance And Investment, Robert Nelson
Second Vice President General Liability, Donald Nichols
Senior Vice President, Scott Belden
Underwriting Vice President, Anthony Gadaleta
Field Product Line Manager 2vp Auto Claims, Trevor Engels
2vp, Carla Schirm
2vp And Actuary, Dan Carr
Second Vp Information Systems, Vincent Bryan
Evp And President Business Insurance, Gregory Toczydlowski
Second Vp Bond And Financial Products; Enterprise Lead Cyber Insurance, Timothy Francis
Svp Auto Property And Catastrophe Claim, Patrick Gee
2vp And Senior Counsel, Lori Dube
Regional Vice President, Joseph Coffey
Claim Center Vice President, Kelly Hopper
Regional Vice President, Tad Cluff
Second Vice President, Seeta Hilton
Regional Vice President, Jim Jarvis
Vice President Human Resources, Janette Suffern
Vice President Finance, Carl Cavaliere
Svp And Group General Counsel Corporate Litigation, Peter Schwartz
2vp Pl Actuarial At Travelers, Patrick Wang
Vice President Practice Leader Boiler And Machinery, Chris Magendantz
Second Vice President Wc Product Group, Julie Morgan
Vice President Of Compensation, Stacy Morris-carter
Regional Vice President, Angela Reilley
Vice President, Alan Wirkman
Vice President, John Coyne
2vp, Arleen Desmond
Vice President Southeast Region Select Accounts, James Albert
2vp Finance, Andy Smith
2nd Vice President, David Roy
Vice President Innovation, Lee Ng
Rc Field Director, Tim Howe
Svp Chief Human Resource Officer, Axel Freudmann
National Accounts Vice President, Peter Heard
Second Vice President, Darrell Evans
Senior Vice President And Corporate Ac, Rich Schug
Second Vice President, Cynthia Mims
Regional Vice President Commercial Accounts Midwest Region, Genus Dalton
Regional Vice President Personal Insurance South Central Region, Doug Purcell
Second Vice President And Actuary, David Lesieur
Second Vice President Business Project Center, Michael Figulski
Second Vice President Pi Platform And Experience, Bill Zielinski
Zone Vice President, John Liptak

Second Vice President Business Insurance Technology, Nancy Moran
Assistant Vice President, Jose Flores
Claim Vice President, Keith Andersen
Second Vice President Of Business Intelligence, Pranay Mittal
Senior Vice President Of Business Insurance Claims, Vincent J Armentano
Vice President Product Management Personal Insurance, Sigurd Peterson
2vp Claim Experience And Strategic Communications, Miles Wickless
Senior Vice President Product Management, Eric Nordquist
Second Vice President, Jeff Lamo
Senior Vice President Administration Services, Jim Scannell
Vice President Reinsurance, Bill Lewis
Vice President And Controller, Robert Gold
Vice President And Actuary, Davis Renee
Vice Chairman And Chief Investment Officer, William H. (Bill) Heyman, age 72
Vice Chairman And Chief Legal Officer, Avrohom J. Kess
Board Member, Janet Dolan
Auditors: KPMG LLP

LOCATIONS

HQ: Travelers Companies Inc (The)
  485 Lexington Avenue, New York, NY 10017
Phone: 917 778-6000
Web: www.travelers.com

2017 Sales

	$ mil.	% of total
US	27,253	94
Canada	1,232	4
Other	417	2
Total	**28,902**	**100**

PRODUCTS/OPERATIONS

2017 Sales

	$ mil.	% of total
Premiums	25,683	89
Net investment income	2,397	8
Fees	447	1
Investment gains	216	1
Other	159	1
Total	**28,902**	**100**

Selected Products

Business
Commercial Automobile
Commercial Multi-Peril
Commercial Property
General Liability
Workers' Compensation
Individual
Affinity Auto and Home Program
Auto Insurance
Boat and Yacht Insurance
Condo Insurance
Flood Insurance
Homeowners Insurance
Identity Fraud Protection
Renters Insurance
Umbrella Insurance
Valuable Items Coverage
Wedding and Private Events Insurance

Selected Subsidiaries and Divisions

J. Malucelli Participacoes em Seguros e Resseguros S.A. (49.5% Brazil)
St. Paul Fire and Marine Insurance Company
Travelers Property Casualty Corp.
  The Standard Fire Insurance Company
  Travelers Casualty and Surety Company
  Travelers Casualty and Surety Company of America
  The Travelers Indemnity Company
  First Floridian Auto and Home Insurance Company
  The Premier Insurance Co. of Massachusetts
Travelers Insurance Company Limited (UK)
Travelers Syndicate Management Limited (UK)

COMPETITORS

AIG	Chubb Limited
AXA	Liberty Mutual Agency
Allianz	Markel
Allstate	Nationwide
American Financial Group	The Hartford
	W. R. Berkley
CNA Financial	Zurich Insurance Group

HISTORICAL FINANCIALS

Company Type: Public

Income Statement				FYE: December 31
	ASSETS ($ mil.)	NET INCOME ($ mil.)	INCOME AS % OF ASSETS	EMPLOYEES
12/19	110,122	2,622	2.4%	30,800
12/18	104,233	2,523	2.4%	30,400
12/17	103,483	2,056	2.0%	30,800
12/16	100,245	3,014	3.0%	30,900
12/15	100,184	3,439	3.4%	30,900
Annual Growth	2.4%	(6.6%)	—	(0.1%)

2019 Year-End Financials

Debt ratio: 5.86%
Return on equity: 10.74%
Cash ($ mil.): 494
Current ratio: —
Long-term debt ($ mil.): —

No. of shares (mil.): 255
Dividends
  Yield: 2.3%
  Payout: 36.2%
Market value ($ mil.): 34,991

	STOCK PRICE ($) FY Close	P/E High/Low	PER SHARE ($) Earnings	Dividends	Book Value
12/19	136.95	15 12	9.92	3.23	101.54
12/18	119.75	16 12	9.28	3.03	86.85
12/17	135.64	18 16	7.33	2.83	87.44
12/16	122.42	12 10	10.28	2.62	83.05
12/15	112.86	11 9	10.88	2.38	79.75
Annual Growth	5.0%	— —	(2.3%)	7.9%	6.2%

TriCo Bancshares (Chico, CA)

People looking for a community bank in California's Sacramento Valley can try TriCo. TriCo Bancshares is the holding company for Tri Counties Bank which serves customers through some 65 traditional and in-store branches in 23 counties in Northern and Central California. Founded in 1974 Tri Counties Bank provides a variety of deposit services including checking and savings accounts money market accounts and CDs. Most patrons are retail customers and small to mid-sized businesses. The bank primarily originates real estate mortgages which account for about 65% of its loan portfolio; consumer loans contribute about 25%. TriCo has agreed to acquire rival North Valley Bancorp.

Operations

In addition to its retail banking products and services the company provides wholesale banking and investment services; TriCo offers brokerage services through an arrangement with Raymond James Financial. The company does not provide trust or international banking services.

Geographic Reach

Based in Chico California Tri Counties Bank operates 66 branches (41 traditional branches and 25 in-store branches) in 23 counties in Northern and central California including Fresno Kern Mendocino Napa Sacramento and Yuba counties.

Financial Performance

In 2013 net interest income the company's primary source of revenue rose 0.6% compared with 2012 to $102.2 million. The slight increase in net interest income was mainly due to a decrease in average balance of other borrowings a shift in deposit balances from relatively high interest rate earning time deposits to noninterest-earning demand and savings deposits an increase in the average balance of investments securities and an increase in the average balance of loans; all of which were substantially offset by a decrease in the average yield on loans.

Strategy

The bank's growth has been fueled by acquisitions and the opening of new branches; it frequently opens branches within grocery stores or other retailers including Wal-Mart. TriCo in 2010 acquired the three branches of Granite Community Bank which had been seized by regulators. The transaction which also included most of the failed bank's assets and deposits was facilitated by the FDIC and includes a loss-sharing agreement with the agency. The following year TriCo acquired Citizens Bank of Northern California. The FDIC-assisted deal included seven branches. The acquisitions are part of TriCo's strategy of adding new customers.

Mergers and Acquisitions

TriCo in January 2014 announced plans to buy its rival in Northern California North Valley Bancorp (NVB) for about $178.4 million. NVB is the parent company of North Valley Bank which had about $918 million in assets and 22 commercial banking offices across eight Northern California counties at the end of 2013. At closing which is expected in the second or third quarter of 2014 NVB will be merged into Tri Counties Bank. The combined bank would have about $3.6 billion in assets.

EXECUTIVES

Evp And Cfo Trico Bancshares And Tri Counties Bank, Thomas J. (Tom) Reddish, age 60, $309,601 total compensation
Evp And Chief Credit Officer, Craig B. Carney, age 61, $274,932 total compensation
Evp Wholesale Banking, Richard B. O'Sullivan, age 63, $260,890 total compensation
President And Ceo, Richard P. Smith, age 62, $549,846 total compensation
Evp And Coo, John S. Fleshood, age 58
Evp And Chief Retail Banking Officer, Daniel K. (Dan) Bailey, age 51, $268,335 total compensation
Svp And Cio, Bruce Barnett
Vice President Facilities Expansion Ma, Chimene Sonsteng
Vice President Marketing, Dan Herbert
Senior Vice President Special Assets Manager, Steve Macrae
Vice President Direct Banking Manager, Kay Armstrong
Senior Vice President, Gretchen Hritz
Senior Vice President, Mark Davis
Senior Vice President, Brent Mcclure
Chairman, William J. Casey, age 75
Vice Chairman, Michael W. Koehnen, age 59

Board Member, Virginia Walker
Auditors: Moss Adams LLP

LOCATIONS

HQ: TriCo Bancshares (Chico, CA)
  63 Constitution Drive, Chico, CA 95973
Phone: 530 898-0300
Web: www.tcbk.com

PRODUCTS/OPERATIONS

2015 Sales

	$ mil.	% of total
Interest		
Loans including fees	131	64
Debt securities	26	13
Dividends	2	1
Other	0	
Noninterest		
Service charges & fees	31	16
Commissions	3	2
Gain on sale of loans	3	1
Other	7	3
Total	206	100

Selected Services

Business debit cards
Business online banking
Business workshops
Cash management
Education savings and CDs
Loans and credits
Merchant services
Order checks
Overdraft services
Pension and retirement
Personal certificates of deposit
Personal checking
Personal savings and money market
Retirement savings and CDs

COMPETITORS

Bank of America	MUFG Americas Holdings
Bank of the West	PremierWest
Central Valley	Wells Fargo
Community Bancorp	Westamerica

HISTORICAL FINANCIALS

Company Type: Public

Income Statement				FYE: December 31
	ASSETS ($ mil.)	NET INCOME ($ mil.)	INCOME AS % OF ASSETS	EMPLOYEES
12/19	6,471	92	1.4%	1,184
12/18	6,352	68	1.1%	1,174
12/17	4,761	40	0.9%	1,023
12/16	4,517	44	1.0%	1,063
12/15	4,220	43	1.0%	1,011
Annual Growth	11.3%	20.4%	—	4.0%

2019 Year-End Financials

Debt ratio: 1.17%
Return on equity: 10.62%
Cash ($ mil.): 276
Current ratio: —
Long-term debt ($ mil.): —

No. of shares (mil.): 30
Dividends
  Yield: 2.0%
  Payout: 27.0%
Market value ($ mil.): 1,246

	STOCK PRICE ($) FY Close	P/E High/Low	PER SHARE ($) Earnings	Dividends	Book Value
12/19	40.81	14 11	3.00	0.82	29.70
12/18	33.79	16 12	2.54	0.70	27.20
12/17	37.86	25 19	1.74	0.66	22.03
12/16	34.18	18 12	1.94	0.60	20.87
12/15	27.44	15 12	1.91	0.52	19.85
Annual Growth	10.4%	— —	11.9%	12.1%	10.6%

TRINITY HEALTH CORPORATION

Hospitals health centers and nursing homes make up Trinity Health. One of the largest Catholic health care systems in the US Trinity Health runs about 90 hospitals and more than 100 continuing care facilities more than 20 states across the country. In addition to acute care services include behavioral health pediatrics oncology neurology senior housing and home health and hospice care. It also provides senior service management supply chain management research and international consulting services. The company employs more than 7800 physicians and clinicians.

Operations
Trinity Health gets its revenue from acute care inpatient services (about 40% of revenue) outpatient acute care (more than 30%) physician services (10%) long-term and home health (5%) health insurance (5%) and other sources.

Geographic Reach
Based in Livonia Michigan Trinity Health has locations in Alabama California Connecticut Delaware Florida Georgia Idaho Illinois Indiana Iowa Maryland Massachusetts Michigan Nebraska New Jersey New York North Carolina Ohio Oregon Pennsylvania and South Dakota.

Sales and Marketing
Medicare accounts for about 40% of net patient service revenues; Blue Cross accounts for 20% Medicaid for 15% while commercial and other represents about 25%.

Financial Performance
Trinity Health reported some $19.3 billion in revenue in fiscal 2019 (ending June 30) a 5% increase over 2018 results. The growth was attributed to hospital acquisitions volume growth rate increases case mix improvements higher retail pharmacy revenue and other gains. Growth was offset by increased payment denials unfavorable patient mix shifts and reduced health plan earnings.

Excess of revenue over expenses attributable to Trinity Health declined 13% to $786 million in 2019 due to lower investment earnings and affiliate earnings and a change in interest rate swap values.

The company ended 2018 with $474.3 million in cash down $497.4 million from 2017. Operating activities contributed $919.6 million while investing activities used $1.5 billion (mostly property equipment and investment purchases) and financing activities contributed $102.4 million via an expanded credit line.

Trinity Health has net assets of $13.8 billion and a community benefit ministry of $1.2 billion.

Strategy
To meet federal health reform guidelines improve quality of care and lower medical costs Trinity Health is working to coordinate patient care across all regional facilities and upgrade its infrastructure with new information technology systems. The company is shifting its facilities to a common electronic health record (EHR) and revenue cycle platform and it announced plans to create three centralized patient billing service centers in 2019.

Trinity Health expands its network through construction efforts and by acquiring facilities such as the purchase of MacNeal Hospital in Illinois in 2018. The company also grows by forming collaborations with other area providers. In 2018 the company sold a 49% stake in St. Joseph Mercy Chelsea Hospital to the Regents of the University of Michigan to establish a partnership with the university and improve delivery of care in the area.

The company also occasionally divests underperforming or noncore assets. In 2019 it sold its Lourdes Health System unit (Camden New Jersey) to Virtua Health.

In 2018 Trinity Health joined a consortium of health care providers to form a not-for-profit generic drug company Civica Rx which aims to address the excessive costs and shortages of essential medicines that often plague hospitals in the US.

As a not-for-profit health system and a sponsored organization of the Catholic Health Ministries Trinity Health carries out a number of ministry programs including investing in community housing and child care resources and providing health outreach services.

Mergers and Acquisitions
Trinity Health acquired the 370-bed MacNeal Hospital in Berwyn Illinois along with related health entities from Tenet Healthcare in 2018. The hospital was added to the Loyola University Health System subsidiary.

Company Background
Trinity Health was established in 2013 from the merger of Catholic Health East and the former Trinity Health organization.

The predecessor Trinity Health organization was formed through the 2000 merger of Mercy Health Services and Holy Cross Health System. Holy Cross was founded in 1979 but traces its roots to the founding of the Congregation of the Sisters of the Holy Cross in 1841; Mercy Health was founded in 1976 but originates with the Sisters of Mercy establishing operations in Iowa and Michigan in the 1860s and 1870s.

Catholic Health East was formed through the 1998 merger of three health ministries: Franciscan Sisters of Allegany Health System (tracing its roots to 1883 in Boston) Eastern Mercy Health System (1847 Pittsburgh) and Sisters of Providence Health System (1892; Holyoke Massachusetts).

In 2015 New York-based St. Joseph's Hospital Health Center joined the Trinity hospital system.

EXECUTIVES

Executive Vice President Eastern Division, Michael A Slubowski

Evp Governance And Sponsorship, Catherine DeClercq

Svp Treasurer And Chief Investment Officer, James W. Bosscher

Svp And General Counsel, Daniel G. (Dan) Hale

Evp And Cfo, Benjamin R. (Ben) Carter

President And Ceo, Richard J. (Rick) Gilfillan

Evp And Chief Clinical Officer, P. Terrence (Terry) O'Rourke

Evp And Chief Culture And Talent Effectiveness Officer, Debra A. (Deb) Canales

Evp And President East Group, Richard (Rick) O'Connell

Evp And General Counsel, Paul G. Neumann

Evp West/midwest Group, Sally E. Jeffcoat

Evp Continuing Care Group, John Capasso

Evp System Services And Chief Human Resources Officer, Clayton Fitzhugh

Svp And Chief Medical Officer, Donald Bignotti

Svp And Cio, Marcus B. Shipley

Evp Growth Strategy And Innovation, Scott Nordlund

President Saint Francis Hospital And Medical Center, John F. Rodis

Evp And Chief Clinical Officer, Mark I. Froimson

Evp Mission Integration, Mary Persico

Evp And Chief Population Health Officer, Barbara A. Walters

Vice President Labor Relations And Human Resources Operations, Martha Murphy

Vice President Supply Chain Operations, Clay Johnson

Vice President Reimbursement And Revenue Integrity, Lisa Wille

Vice President Clinical Integration, Thomas Anderson

Vice President Patient Financial Services, Linda Schaeffer

Vice President Client Services And Transformation, Chuck Lund

Vice President Clinical Quality Analytics And Improvement, Shanna Johnson

Vice President Asset Management, Beverly Erickson

Medical Records Director, Janice Walsh

Senior Vice President, Dina Richard

Senior Vice President, Paul Marceau

Vice President, Kathy Connor

Vice President Audit Services, Heidi Crosby

Vice President Of Ancillary, Rebekah Smith

Vice President Finance, Lori Shively

Vice President Service Management, Julie Moran

Vice President Technology Services, Frank Abate

Vice President Of Operational Excellence, Jonathan Maner

Vice President, Anna Butrie

Evp Chief Clinical Officer, Dan Roth

Vice President Operations, Anne Lewis

Evp Chief Medical Officer, Jeff Komins

Senior Vice President And Chief Nursing Officer, Nora Triola

Senior Vice President Ma And Partnership Development, Sheri Shapiro

Executive Vice President And Chief Human Resources Officer, Edmund Hodge

Executive Vice President And Chief Clinical Officer, Daniel Roth

Senior Vice President Insurance And Risk Management Services, Ruth Goodell

Vice President, Darren Vianueva

Vice President Advocacy And Government Relations, Daniel Keenan

Vice President Financial Operations And Budget, Kathy Ralston

Vice President, Katherine Zbanek

Vice President Executive Development, Anita Jensen

Vice President Mission Formation, Stephen Surprenant

Vice President Human Resources Strategy And Services, Mark Story

Vice President Provider Contracting And Reimbursement, Rick O'donnell

Vice President Sales And Marketing, Christopher Caserta

Senior Vice President Chief Medical Officer, Tammy Lundstrom

Vice President Finance, Lannie Checketts

Vice President, Brendan Dunnigan

Vice President, Maria Martinico

Vice President Human Resources, Karyn Doran

Operating Room Dir, DAWN PETERS

Director Of Medical Records, Kim Dudich

Senior Vice President Mission Integration Ethics, Philip Boyle

Vice President Performance Leadership, Sara Schmanske
Senior Vice President Chief Mission Officer, Bartholomew Rodrigues
Medical Records Director, Katie Wilson
Chair, Melanie C. Dreher
Assistant Treasurer Th Director Debt, Marianne Cunningham
Auditors: DELOITTE & TOUCHE LLP DETROIT

LOCATIONS

HQ: TRINITY HEALTH CORPORATION
20555 VICTOR PKWY, LIVONIA, MI 481527031
Phone: 734 343-1000
Web: WWW.TRINITY-HEALTH.ORG

Selected Facilities

California
  Saint Agnes Medical Center (Fresno)
Idaho and Oregon
  Saint Alphonsus Medical Center - Baker City
                              Saint Alph
                              Saint Alph
  Saint Alphonsus Regional Medical Center (Boise)
Indiana
  Saint Joseph Regional Medical Center (South Bend)
  Saint Joseph Regional Medical Center (Plymouth)
Illinois
  Loyola University Health System (Chicago)
  Loyola University Medical Center
  Loyola Gottlieb Memorial Hospital
  Mercy Hospital & Medical Center (Chicago)
Iowa and Nebraska
  Mercy Health Network (Clinton Des Moines Dubuque Dyersville Mason City New Hampton and Sioux City Iowa; Oakland Nebraska)
Maryland
  Holy Cross Hospital (Silver Spring)
Michigan
  Mercy Health Partners (Muskegon)
  Mercy Hospital (Cadillac)
  Mercy Hospital (Grayling)
  Saint Joseph Mercy Health System (Ann Arbor)
  Saint Mary's Health Care (Grand Rapids)
Ohio
  Mount Carmel Health System (Columbus)

PRODUCTS/OPERATIONS

2014 Net Patient Revnue

	% of total
Medicare	38
Blue Cross	20
Medicaid	13
Uninsured	4
Commercial and other	25
Total	**100**

2014 Sales

	% of total
Net patient service revenuel less provision for bad debts	87
Capitation and premium revenue	5
Other revenue	8
Total	**100**

COMPETITORS

Advocate Health Care	MedStar Health
Amedisys	Memorial Hospital &
Ascension Health	Health System
Beaumont Health System	OhioHealth
Community Health	St. Luke's Health
Systems	System
Encompass Health	Tenet Healthcare
HCA	Universal Health
Henry Ford Health	Services
System	University of Chicago
Hospice of Michigan	Medical Center
Johns Hopkins Medicine	VITAS Healthcare
Kindred Healthcare	Wheaton Franciscan
Mayo Clinic	Services

HISTORICAL FINANCIALS

Company Type: Private

Income Statement   FYE: June 30

	REVENUE ($ mil.)	NET INCOME ($ mil.)	NET PROFIT MARGIN	EMPLOYEES
06/18	18,345	1,358	7.4%	51,100
06/15	1,375	19	1.4%	—
Annual Growth	137.1%	314.2%	—	—

TriState Capital Holdings Inc

TriState Capital Holdings has found its niche right in the middle of the banking industry. The holding company owns TriState Capital Bank a regional business bank that caters to middle-market businesses executives and high-net-worth individuals. TriState Capital has three wholly owned subsidiaries: TriState Capital Bank Chartwell Investment Partners LLC and Chartwell TSC Securities Corp. Its loan portfolio consists of less than 50% for middle-market banking loans less than 30% commercial real estate loans and more than 50% for private banking loans. The bank serves clients from branches in Cleveland; New Jersey; New York City Philadelphia and Pittsburgh. Altogether it has $7.6 billion in assets.

Operations

The company operates two reportable segments: Bank and Investment Management.

The Bank segment provides commercial banking products and services to middle-market businesses and private banking products and services to high-net-worth individuals through the Bank. The Investment Management segment provides investment management services primarily to institutional investors mutual funds and individual investors through Chartwell and also supports marketing efforts for Chartwell's proprietary investment products through CTSC Securities.

Geographic Reach

Headquartered in Pittsburgh Pennsylvania the company also leases office space for each of the four representative bank offices in the metropolitan areas of Philadelphia Pennsylvania; Cleveland Ohio; Edison New Jersey; and New York New York; and it leases office space for Chartwell Investment Partners LLC in Berwyn Pennsylvania.

Sales and Marketing

The company caters to middle-market businesses. Its primary markets and private banking business also serve high-net-worth individuals on a national basis. It primarily sources this business through referral relationships with independent broker/dealers wealth managers family offices trust companies and other financial intermediaries. In addition its distribution channels pursue and create deposit relationships including treasury management relationships with customers in its primary markets and throughout the US.

Financial Performance

In 2019 total revenue increased $18.0 million or 11% to $179.4 million from $161.4 million in 2018 driven largely by higher net interest income and swap fees for the Bank.

In 2019 the company's net was $54.4 million compared to $52.3 million in 2018 an increase of $2.1 million or 4%. This increase was primarily due to the net impact of a $13.7 million or 12% increase in its net interest income; an increase in the credit to provision for loan and lease losses of $0.8 million; an increase of $4.9 million or 10% in non-interest income; offset by an increase of $11.0 million or 11% in our non-interest expense; a $2.5 million increase in income taxes; and an increase in preferred stock dividends of $3.6 million.

Cash held by the company at the end of 2019 increased to $403.9 million compared to the prior year with $213.9 million. Cash provided by operations and financing activities were $68.2 million and $1.6 billion respectively. Cash used for investing activities was $1.5 billion mainly for net increase in loans and leases.

Strategy

Tristate Capital's success has been built upon the vision and focus of its executive management team to combine the sophisticated products services and risk management efforts of a large financial institution with the personalized service of a community bank. The company believe that a results-based culture combined with a well-managed middle-market and private banking business and its targeted investment management business will continue to grow and generate attractive returns for shareholders. The following are the key components of the company's business strategies: Sales and Distribution Culture; Disciplined Risk Management; Experienced Professionals; Lending Strategy; Deposit Funding Strategy; and Investment Management Strategy.

Company Background

TriState Capital was founded in 2007 by two banking industry executives — chairman and CEO James Getz who spent 20 years at Federated Investors and vice chairman William Schenck the former secretary of banking for Pennsylvania.

EXECUTIVES

Chairman President And Ceo, James F. (Jim) Getz, $1,500,000 total compensation
President Commercial Banking, David A. Molnar
Vice Chairman And Cfo, Mark L. Sullivan, $425,000 total compensation
Regional President New Jersey, Kenneth R. Orchard
Regional President New York, Thomas N. Gilmartin
Regional President Ohio, John D. Barrett
Regional President Eastern Pennsylvania, Joseph M. Finley
Regional President Western Pennsylvania, Vince Locher
President Private Bank Team, Charles C. Fawcett
President And Ceo Tristate Capital Bank, Brian S. Fetterolf
Senior Vice President Relationship Manager, Michael Blasko
Senior Vice President, David Hurtuk
Senior Vice President, Sheila Roberts
Senior Vice President, Robert Gambitsky
Senior Vice President, John Buglione
Senior Vice President Commercial Real Estate Finance, David Segal

Senior Vice President Relationship Manager, Joe Pascarella
Senior Vice President, Tim Moriarity
Svp Treasury And Liquidity Manager, Matthew Fisher
Vice Chairman, A. William (Bill) Schenck
Auditors: KPMG LLP

LOCATIONS

HQ: TriState Capital Holdings Inc
One Oxford Centre, 301 Grant Street, Suite 2700, Pittsburgh, PA 15219
Phone: 412 304-0304   **Fax:** 412 304-0391
Web: www.tristatecapitalbank.com

PRODUCTS/OPERATIONS

2015 Sales

	$ mil.	% of total
Interest income		
Loans	79	67
Investments	3	3
Interest-earning deposits	0	
Noninterest income		
Investment management fees	29	25
Commitment and other fees	2	2
Other income	4	3
Total	119	100

COMPETITORS

Bank of America	HSBC Private Bank
Bank of New York Mellon	Herald National Bank
	JPMorgan Private Bank
Boston Private	Julius Baer
Brown Brothers Harriman	Lakeland Bancorp
	M&T Bank
Citigroup	Safra Bank
Citigroup Private Bank	U.S. Trust
First Republic (CA)	

HISTORICAL FINANCIALS

Company Type: Public

Income Statement   FYE: December 31

	ASSETS ($ mil.)	NET INCOME ($ mil.)	INCOME AS % OF ASSETS	EMPLOYEES
12/19	7,765	60	0.8%	276
12/18	6,035	54	0.9%	257
12/17	4,777	37	0.8%	230
12/16	3,930	28	0.7%	224
12/15	3,302	22	0.7%	192
Annual Growth	23.8%	27.9%	—	9.5%

2019 Year-End Financials

Debt ratio: 4.57%	No. of shares (mil.): 29
Return on equity: 10.94%	Dividends
Cash ($ mil.): 396	Yield: —
Current ratio: —	Payout: —
Long-term debt ($ mil.): —	Market value ($ mil.): 767

	STOCK PRICE ($) FY Close	P/E High/Low	PER SHARE ($) Earnings	Dividends	Book Value
12/19	26.12	13 10	1.89	0.00	21.16
12/18	19.46	16 10	1.81	0.00	16.60
12/17	23.00	18 15	1.32	0.00	13.61
12/16	22.10	22 11	1.01	0.00	12.38
12/15	13.99	18 12	0.80	0.00	11.62
Annual Growth	16.9%	— —	24.0%	—	16.2%

Triumph Bancorp Inc

Auditors: Crowe LLP

LOCATIONS

HQ: Triumph Bancorp Inc
12700 Park Central Drive, Suite 1700, Dallas, TX 75251
Phone: 214 365-6900
Web: www.triumphbancorp.com

HISTORICAL FINANCIALS

Company Type: Public

Income Statement   FYE: December 31

	ASSETS ($ mil.)	NET INCOME ($ mil.)	INCOME AS % OF ASSETS	EMPLOYEES
12/19	5,060	58	1.2%	1,107
12/18	4,559	51	1.1%	1,121
12/17	3,499	36	1.0%	820
12/16	2,641	20	0.8%	705
12/15	1,691	29	1.7%	500
Annual Growth	31.5%	19.1%	—	22.0%

2019 Year-End Financials

Debt ratio: 2.51%	No. of shares (mil.): 24
Return on equity: 9.20%	Dividends
Cash ($ mil.): 197	Yield: —
Current ratio: —	Payout: —
Long-term debt ($ mil.): —	Market value ($ mil.): 949

	STOCK PRICE ($) FY Close	P/E High/Low	PER SHARE ($) Earnings	Dividends	Book Value
12/19	38.02	17 12	2.25	0.00	25.50
12/18	29.70	22 13	2.03	0.00	23.62
12/17	31.50	19 11	1.81	0.00	18.81
12/16	26.15	24 12	1.10	0.00	16.01
12/15	16.50	11 8	1.57	0.00	14.88
Annual Growth	23.2%	— —	9.4%	—	14.4%

Truist Financial Corp

BB&T is now Truist. Truist Financial Corporation is a purpose-driven financial services company committed to inspire and build better lives and communities. With 275 years of combined BB&T and SunTrust history Truist serves approximately 12 million households with market share in many high-growth markets in the country. The company offers a wide range of services including retail small business and commercial banking; asset management; capital markets; commercial real estate; corporate and institutional banking; insurance; mortgage; payments; specialized lending and wealth management. Truist conducts its business operations primarily through its bank subsidiary Truist Bank and other nonbank subsidiaries.

Change in Company Type

The Company was formed by the merger of BB&T and SunTrust in 2019. Truist anticipates further integration of systems operations and personnel of BB&T and SunTrust over the next several years.

Operations

Truist operates and measures business activity across three segments: Consumer Banking and Wealth Corporate and Commercial Banking and Insurance Holdings with functional activities included in Other Treasury and Corporate.

Consumer Banking and Wealth creates about 45% of the total revenue. The CB&W segment is made up of five primary businesses: Retail Community Banking; NCF&P; Wealth; Mortgage Banking; and Dealer Retail Services.

Corporate and Commercial Banking segment made nearly 50% of company's revenue. The C&CB segment is made up of four primary businesses and the Treasury Solutions product group: Corporate and Investment Banking; Commercial Community Banking; Commercial Real Estate; and Grandbridge Real Estate Capital LLC.

Insurance Holdings segment some 10% of revenue. Truist's IH segment provides property and casualty employee benefits and life insurance to businesses and individuals. This segment also provides small business and corporate services such as workers compensation and professional liability as well as surety coverage and title insurance. IH also includes Prime Rate Premium Finance Corporation which includes AFCO Credit Corporation and CAFO Holding Company insurance premium finance subsidiaries that provide funding to businesses in the United States and Canada.

Geographic Reach

Charlotte North Carolina-based Truist operates in various locations in the Southeastern and Mid-Atlantic United States. Its largest markets are Florida where it has more than 670 bank branches; Virginia with around 445 branches; and North Carolina with over 400 branches.

Sales and Marketing

Truist operates in markets covering numerous industries. The company has made significant investments in recent years to develop its digital platform.

The Company also offers selling and distribution services and earns commissions through the sale of annuity and mutual fund products acting as agent in these transactions and recognizing revenue at a point in time when the client enters into an agreement with the product carrier.

Financial Performance

BB&T has consistently grown its revenue each year since 2015 to yield an overall expansion of about 30%; net income added some 50% in that time despite the volatility for the past five years.

The holding company's revenue ticked up almost 10% to $12.7 billion in 2019 spurred by larger loan and lease portfolios and interest rates.

BB&T's net income fell slightly of one percent to $3.2 billion in 2019 due to high net loss in other treasury & corporate segment.

The company added $15.2 billion to its cash in 2019 to end the year at $19.1 billion. Operations provided $1.5 billion and financing activities?mainly proceeds from issuance of long-term debt?contributed $5.4 billion. Proceeds from sales of AFS securities drove investment supplied of $8.3 billion.

Strategy

Truist seeks to satisfy all of its clients' needs enabling the Company to grow and diversify its sources of revenue and profitability. Truist's long-term strategy encompasses both organic growth and mergers or acquisitions of complimentary banks and financial institutions.

Truist's merger and acquisition strategy focuses on meeting the following criteria: the organization must be a good fit with Truist's culture; the merger or acquisition must be strategically attractive; any risks must be identified and mitigation plans put in place to ensure any residual risks fall within Truist's risk appetite; and the transaction must meet Truist's financial criteria.

Truist's business is dynamic and complex. Consequently management annually evaluates and as necessary adjusts the Company's business strategy in the context of the current operating environment. During this process management considers the current financial condition and performance of the Company and its expectations for future economic activity from both a national and local market perspective. Achieving key strategic objectives and established long-term financial goals is subject to many uncertainties and challenges. In the opinion of management the following challenges are the most likely to impact Truist's near to medium term performance: Achieving the potential benefits from the Merger including anticipated synergies and cost savings; Managing the integration of systems and operations while safeguarding the Company against external threats; Executing the Company's "T3 strategy" by focusing on personal touch and technology to engender trust and provide distinctive secure and successful client experiences; Driving innovation and remaining attuned to evolving client preferences to succeed in an intensely competitive environment; Retaining key personnel and activating the Company's culture of striving to make things better for its clients teammates and stakeholders; and Navigating global economic and geopolitical risks and ensuring that the Company is well positioned for changes in the credit cycle.

In 2019 BB&T and SunTrust merged with the expectation that the Merger would result in various synergies including benefits relating to enhanced revenues a strengthened and expanded market position for the combined organization technology efficiencies cost savings and operating efficiencies. Achieving the anticipated benefits of the merger is subject to a number of uncertainties including whether the Company integrates the institutions in an efficient and effective manner as well as general competitive factors in the marketplace.

Mergers and Acquisitions

In late-2019 Truist completed its previously announced Merger with SunTrust a company that offers a full line of financial services for consumers businesses corporations institutions and not-for-profit entities both through branches and through other digital and national delivery channels. In connection with the Merger the Company changed its name from BB&T Corporation to Truist Financial Corporation. Following the Merger in late-2019 SunTrust Bank a wholly-owned subsidiary of SunTrust merged with and into Branch Bank with Branch Bank continuing as the surviving bank. In connection with the Merger Branch Bank changed its name to Truist Bank.

HISTORY

In 1872 Alpheus Branch son of a wealthy planter founded Branch and Company a mercantile business in Wilson North Carolina. He and Thomas Jefferson Hadley who was organizing a public school system created the Branch and Hadley bank later that same year. The private bank helped rebuild farms and small businesses after the Civil War.

In 1887 Branch bought out Hadley and changed the bank's name to Branch and Company Bankers. Two years later Branch secured a state trust charter for the Wilson Banking and Trust Company. He never got the business running however and died in 1893. The trust charter was amended to change the name to Branch Banking and Company and Branch and Company Bankers was folded into it in 1900.

In 1907 the bank finally got its trust operations running and began calling itself Branch Banking and Trust Company. In 1922 it opened its first insurance department; the next year it started its mortgage loan activities.

BB&T survived the 1929 stock market crash with the help of the Post Office. Nervous customers withdrew their funds from BB&T and other banks and deposited them in postal savings accounts unaware that BB&T was the local Post Office's bank and the withdrawn funds went right back to the bank. BB&T opened six more branches between 1929 and 1933.

After WWII consumerism skyrocketed resulting in more car loans and mortgages. During the 1960s and 1970s the bank embarked on a series of mergers and acquisitions forming the thin end of a buying wedge that would widen significantly in the coming decades.

By 1994 BB&T was the fourth-largest bank in North Carolina. In 1995 it merged with North Carolina's fifth-largest bank Southern National Corp. founded in 1897.

With banking regulations loosening to allow different types of operations BB&T in 1997 made several acquisitions including banks thrifts and securities brokerage Craigie.

BB&T's 1998 activities included three bank acquisitions that pushed it into metro Washington DC. The company also increased holdings in fields such as insurance sales venture capital for Southern businesses and investment banking (through its acquisition of Scott & Stringfellow Financial the South's oldest NYSE member).

In 1999 Craigie was melded into Scott & Stringfellow. That year BB&T bought several insurance companies and small banks. The company continued its march through the South the following year buying several Georgia banks and Tennessee's BankFirst. In 2001 BB&T purchased South Carolina's FirstSpartan Financial multibank holding company Century South Banks Maryland-based FCNB Corporation and western Georgia's Community First Banking Company. To bolster its presence in the Washington DC market it bought Virginia Capital Bancshares and F&M National.

BB&T purchased Alabama-based Cooney Rikard & Curtin a wholesale insurance broker active in 45 states in 2002. Also that year it added about 100 branches in Kentucky after buying MidAmerica Bancorp and AREA Bancshares and entered the coveted Florida market

following its purchase of Regional Financial the privately held parent of First South Bank.

Acquisitions continued the following three years as the bank swallowed First Virginia Banks among other targets. It took a break in 2005 to assimilate its holdings before joining the acquisition hunt in 2006 with deals for banks in Georgia (Main Street Banks) and Tennessee (First Citizens Bancorp) and in South Carolina (Coastal Financial) in 2007.

EXECUTIVES

Chairman And Ceo, Kelly S. King, age 71, $1,075,000 total compensation

Atlanta Regional President, Christopher L. (Chris) Henson, age 58, $700,000 total compensation

Sevp And Cio, Barbara F. Duck, age 53, $507,083 total compensation

Sevp And Deposit Services Manager, Donna C. Goodrich, age 57, $507,083 total compensation

Sevp And Chief Risk Officer, Clarke R. Starnes, age 61, $582,500 total compensation

Sevp And Cfo, Daryl N. Bible, age 58, $590,000 total compensation

Sevp And President Community Banking, David H. Weaver, age 54

Sevp General Counsel Secretary And Chief Corporate Governance Officer, Robert J. Johnson, age 47

Sevp President And Ceo Bb&t Securities Llc And Capital Markets Manager, W. Rufus Yates, age 62

President West Florida Region, Jim Daly, age 59

Sevp And Chief Digital Officer, W. Bennett Bradley, age 58

Sevp And Lending Group Manager, Brant J. Standridge, age 44

Sevp And Chief Client Experience Officer, Dont L. Wilson, age 43

Sevp And Deputy Chief Risk Officer, Jim D. Godwin, age 51

Vice President, Cindy Powell

Senior Vice President, Ann Hardison

Senior Vice President Strategic Planning Manager Bbandt Corporation, James Anthos

Vice President, Debrah More

Vice President, Sharon Silvermintz

Senior Vice President, Kimberly E Moore

Assistant Vice President Cf Operations Manager, Karen Cruise

Senior Vice President Associate General Counsel, Kevin Brekka

Vice President Production Control Manager, Gasford Brown

Wealth Advisor Assistant Vice President, Tommy Rhyne

Vice President, Jay Hall

Vice President Technology Manager Bank Of America, Stuart Jones

Vice President Benefits Administration Manager, Andrea Branscome

Senior Vice President, Chip Falk

Vice President Business Development, Aimee Creamer

Msr Valaution Manager Vice President Funds Management, Shiv Bansal

Senior Vice President, Greg Tawes

Vice President Bbandt Insurance, Ben Manning

Assistant Vice President Comme, Deborah Masley

Vice President, Rosie Blackburn

Assistant Vice President And Team Lead Ediscovery, James Guziak

Senior Vice President, Craig Pascal

Vice President Technology Innovation, Sajid Khan

Vice President, Meredith Camp

Assistant Vice President, Ken Zeller

Vice President, Jo Lynn Burgess

Vice President, Gregg Yanok

Vice President, Brett Walser

Assistant Vice President Financial Center Leader Hablo Espaiiol, Gil Rolon
Executive Vice President Chief Market And Liquidity Risk Officer, Steve Buisson
Assistant Vice President, Bonnie Edwards
Vice President Portfolio Risk Officer, Matt Wagner
Vice President, Duncan Moseley
Vice President, Michael Walter
Assistant Vice President, Jason Matthews
Assistant Vice President, Scott Parks
Vice President, Lisa Allen
Vice President, Karen Starnes
Vice President Personal Trust Specialist, Kim Lamm
Assistant Vice President, Timothy Watson
Assistant Vice President, Tisha Flowers
Assistant Vice President Business Lendin, David Paske
Assistant Vice President And Underwriting Section Manager, Ana Restrepo
Svp Enterprise Information Management Strategy And Architecture, Michael Vaughan
Senior Vice President Corporate Bankin, Troy Weaver
Senior Vice President Credit Risk Review Team Leader, Nancy Ortkiese
Assistant Vice President Operations Division Production Manager, Rick Marino
Assistant Vice President Large, Cathy Lyons
Vice President, Michael Clevenger
Vice President, Scott Fisher
Senior Vice President Comm'l Fin Loan Admin Manager, John Davis
Vice President, Mark Grunder
Vice President Business Services Officer, Linda Shirley
Vice President Senior Service Delivery Manager, Ray Cline
Senior Vice President, Beth Sterner
Vice President, Susan Tittl
Client Information Analyst Vice President, Terri-beth Heffernan
Senior Vice President, Barry Maness
Senior Vice President, Tom Butsch
Senior Vice President, Kelly Sain
Senior Vice President Commerci, Gus Phillips
Executive Search Consultant; Vice President, Chris Kuhn
Vice President, Rick Canipe
Assistant Vice President, Steve Eng
Vice President, Angela Britt
Vice President Network Support Manager, Cherie Otten
Svp And Market President Greensboro Winston Salem North Carolina Area, Jack Lynch
Vice President It Marketing And Communication, Neil Middlemiss
Vice President Of Real Estate Acquisition, Brenda Shamloo
Vice President, Jill Angulo
Vice President, Shelley Travis
Senior Vice President And Senior Credit Officer, Scott Carpenter
Assistant Vice President, Shawn Mercer
Svp Energy Group Denver, Ryan Michael
Vice President Strategic Planning Analyst, Donna Garcia
Vice President, Mary Burns
Vice President, Kenneth Gorham
Assistant Vice President, Terry Donahue
Vice President Commercial Cards, Melanie Epp
Vice President Comm Development, Marlo Scruggs
Vice President, Brian Westcott
Vice President, Lorie Garland
Assistant Vice President Supplier Diversity Coordinator, Lakeisha Lawton
Vice President, David Wesley
Vice President, Jamie Humphrey
Regional Manager Vice President, Julie Simpson
Senior Vice President, Masoud Shahri

Senior Vice President, Bo Wayne
Vice President, Scott Snow
Assistant Vice President, Kevin Barrett
N L Eevp Of Marketing, Carol Bond
Vice President, Al James
Vice President Of Deposit Access, Catherine Kauffman
Senior Vice President It Services Manager Project Office, Gail Fuller
Assistant Vice President Information Technology Team Leader, Bill Cherry
Assistant Vice President, Paul McManus
Senior Vice President, Eric Lowman
Avp It Vendor Management, Patrick Cleary
Vice President, Abdul Labi
Residential Real Estate Lending Vice President, Keri Jackson
Financial Center Leader Assistant Vice President, Matthew Brown
Wealth Management Vice President, Cole Benoit
Senior Vice President, Len Lewan
Vice President Customer Credit Manager, Michael Catapano
Executive Vice President, Tol Broome
Vice President Employee Benefits Agent, Will Stewart
Senior Executive Vice President, Leon Wilson
Senior Vice President, Robert Searson
Vice President, Christopher Pearce
Vice President Financial Center Leader, Michelle Haines
Senior Vice President, Mildred Henry
Vice President, John Kincaid
Vice President, Theresa Arrighi
Vice President, Mark Caspero
Vice President, Kelly Fallen
Vice President, Jennifer Weaver
Vice President, Steve Jordan
Information Technology Infrastructure Engineer Client Server Engineer Cs Iv Assistant Vice President, Rufus Bynum
Vice President Surety, Peter Holley
Senior Vice President Corporate Banker Capital Markets, Eric Searls
Senior Vice President Bb And T Information Technology Risk Management, Charlie Hinnant
Vice President, Vanessa Hampton
Vice President, Mike Chou
Assistant Vice President It Problem Management Team Lead, Bobby Davenport
Vice President, Charles Peden
Vice President, Ken Powell
Vice President, Lynn Williams
Electronic Delivery Channel Strategist Vice President, Ken Nixon
Vice President Mortgage Loan Officer, Vincent Spadea
Assistant Vice President Information Technology Resource, Jill Deanhardt
Assistant Vice President Project Manager, Sharon McMichael
Team Lead Vice President, Monte Wheeler
Senior Vice President Operations, Robert Davis
Vice President, Barbara McAllister
Vice President Enterprise Data Governance Bbandt Corporation, Jan England
Vice President, David Samuel
Senior Vice President, Stan Crawford
Auditors: PricewaterhouseCoopers LLP

LOCATIONS

HQ: Truist Financial Corp
214 North Tryon Street, Charlotte, NC 28202
Phone: 336 733-2000   **Fax:** 336 671-2399
Web: www.bbt.com

2018 sales

	No.
North Carolina	304
Virginia	291
Florida	272
Pennsylvania	221
Maryland	144
Georgia	137
Texas	110
South Carolina	97
Kentucky	86
Alabama	73
West Virginia	59
Tennessee	40
New Jersey	28
Washington D.C.	12
Ohio	3
Indiana	2
Total	**1,879**

PRODUCTS/OPERATIONS

2018 Sales

	$ mil.	% of total
Interest Income:		
Interest & fees on loans & leases	6,894	53
Interest & dividends on securities	1,160	9
Interest on other earning assets	66	1
Non-interest income:		
Insurance income	1,852	14
Service charges on deposits	712	5
Mortgage banking income	477	4
Investment banking & brokerage fees & commissions	358	3
Trust & investment advisory	285	2
Bankcard fees & merchant discounts	287	2
Checkcard fees	221	2
Operating lease income	145	1
Income from bank-owned life insurance	116	1
Other income	420	3
Securities gains (losses) net	3	-
Total	**11,558**	**100**

2018 Sales

	% of total
Community Banking Retail and Consumer Finance	42
Community Banking Commercial	34
Financial Services and Commercial Finance	17
Insurance Holdings	7
Total	**100**

Selected Services

Commercial
  Asset management
  Association services
  Capital markets services
  Commercial deposit and treasury services
  Commercial finance
  Commercial middle market lending
  Commercial mortgage lending
  Institutional trust services
  Insurance
  Insurance premium finance
  International banking services
  Leasing
  Merchant services
  Payment solutions
  Private equity investments
  Real estate lending
  Supply chain management
Retail
  Asset management
  Automobile lending
  Bankcard lending
  Consumer finance
  Home equity lending
  Insurance
  Investment brokerage services
  Mobile/online banking
  Payment solutions
  Retail deposit services
  Sales finance
  Small business lending
  Wealth management/private banking

Selected Subsidiaries & Affiliates

American Coastal Insurance Company
BB&T Equipment Finance Corporation
BB&T Financial FSB
  Sheffield Financial

BB&T Insurance Services Inc.
BB&T Investment Services Inc.
BB&T Securities LLC
Branch Banking and Trust Company
Clearview Correspondent Services
CRC Insurance Services
Grandbridge Real Estate Capital LLC
Lendmark Financial Services Inc.
McGriff Seibels & Williams Inc.
MidAmerica Gift Certificate Company
Prime Rate Premium Finance Corporation Inc.
  AFCO Credit Corporation
Regional Acceptance Corporation
Stanley Hunt DuPree & Rhine Inc.
Sterling Capital Management LLC

COMPETITORS

Bank of America	PNC Financial
Capital One	Regions Financial
Fifth Third	SunTrust
First Citizens	Synovus
BancShares	United Bankshares
First Horizon	Wells Fargo
JPMorgan Chase	

HISTORICAL FINANCIALS

Company Type: Public

Income Statement   FYE: December 31

	ASSETS ($ mil.)	NET INCOME ($ mil.)	INCOME AS % OF ASSETS	EMPLOYEES
12/19	473,078	3,224	0.7%	59,000
12/18	225,697	3,237	1.4%	35,852
12/17	221,642	2,394	1.1%	36,484
12/16	219,276	2,426	1.1%	37,500
12/15	209,947	2,084	1.0%	37,200
Annual Growth	22.5%	11.5%	—	12.2%

2019 Year-End Financials

Debt ratio: 7.86%	No. of shares (mil.): 1,342
Return on equity: 6.68%	Dividends
Cash ($ mil.): 19,065	Yield: 3.0%
Current ratio: —	Payout: 42.9%
Long-term debt ($ mil.): —	Market value ($ mil.): 75,591

	STOCK PRICE ($) FY Close	P/E High/Low	PER SHARE ($) Earnings	Dividends	Book Value
12/19	56.32	15 12	3.71	1.71	49.46
12/18	43.32	14 10	3.91	1.56	39.46
12/17	49.72	18 15	2.74	1.26	37.91
12/16	47.02	17 11	2.77	1.15	36.91
12/15	37.81	16 13	2.56	1.05	34.99
Annual Growth	10.5%	— —	9.7%	13.0%	9.0%

Trustco Bank Corp. (N.Y.)

In Banking They Trust. TrustCo Bank Corp is the holding company for Trustco Bank which boasts more than 140 branches across eastern New York central and western Florida and parts of Vermont Massachusetts and New Jersey. The bank offers personal and business customers a variety of deposit products loans and mortgages and trust and investment services. It primarily originates residential and commercial mortgages which account for more than three-quarters of its loan portfolio. It also writes business construc-

tion and installment loans and home equity lines of credit.

Operations

TrustCo Bank Corp generated 77% of its total revenue from interest and fees on loans in 2014 while interest on its securities available for sale (which were mostly residential mortgage-backed securities and collateralized mortgage obligations but also its GSE SBA-backed securities) made up another 16% of the bank's revenue. Customer service fees and Trustco Financial Services income made up 6% and 3% of total revenue in 2014 respectively.

Sales and Marketing

Trustco provides personal and business banking services to individuals partnerships and corporations among other kinds of business and organizations. It spent $2.49 million on advertising in 2014 compared to $2.83 million and $3.84 million in 2013 and 2012 respectively.

Financial Performance

Trustco has struggled to grow its revenue in recent years though its profits have been rising at a healthy clip mostly because its loan loss provisions have dissipated with an improving credit portfolio amidst the strengthening economy.

TrustCo's revenue rose by nearly 4% to $176.85 million in 2014 mostly as new branch openings during the year added nearly double-digit loan business growth. The bank also collected more interest income from its securities as it invested more and made a gain on the sale of its Florida regional headquarters property.

Higher revenue and a decline in interest expense on deposits in the low-interest environment also drove the bank's net income up by 11% to $4.38 million. A continuing decline in loan loss provisions buoyed by improving economic conditions (especially in Florida) also helped boost the bank's bottom line.

Despite higher earnings in 2014 TrustCo's operating cash fell by 21% to $49.54 million during the year as it spent more toward acquiring additional assets.

Strategy

TrustCo has focused on building its loan business through new branch additions as well as through growth from its existing offices in recent years. Using this strategy in 2014 the bank added five new branches and successfully boosted its deposit business by 2.7% to $4.03 billion while loan balances swelled by 8.6% to $3.16 billion as the bank aggressively pushed its loan business during the year.

The bank underwent a major branch expansion from 2002 through 2009 and more than doubled its branch network in New York and Florida by opening new locations (more than 75 of them). It continues to open new branches albeit not as rapidly.

EXECUTIVES

President And Ceo, Robert J. McCormick, age 57, $880,000 total compensation

Administrative Vp Branch Administration/marketing Trustco Bank, Scot R. Salvador, age 54, $510,000 total compensation

Vp Branch Administration/marketing Trustco Bank, Robert M. Leonard, age 58, $260,000 total compensation

Vp Commercial Lending Trustco Bank, Eric W. Schreck, age 53, $255,000 total compensation

Svp And Cfo Trustco Bank Corp Ny And Trustco Bank, Michael M. Ozimek, $142,500 total compensation

Senior Vice President, Kevin Curley

Vice President Commercial Lending, Pat Canavan

Vice President Mortgage Loans Trustco, Michael Lofrumento

Chairman, Thomas O. Maggs, age 76

Auditors: Crowe LLP

LOCATIONS

HQ: Trustco Bank Corp. (N.Y.)
  5 Sarnowski Drive, Glenville, NY 12302
Phone: 518 377-3311   **Fax:** 518 381-3668
Web: www.trustcobank.com

PRODUCTS/OPERATIONS

2011 Sales

	$ mil.	% of total
Interest		
Loans including fees	129	73
Securities	30	17
Other	1	1
Noninterest		
Fees for services to customers	8	5
Trustco Financial Services	5	3
Other	2	1
Total	177	100

COMPETITORS

Arrow Financial	HSBC USA
Ballston Spa Bancorp	Hudson Valley FCU
Bank of America	KeyCorp
Citizens Financial	M&T Bank
Group	NBT Bancorp

HISTORICAL FINANCIALS

Company Type: Public

Income Statement   FYE: December 31

	ASSETS ($ mil.)	NET INCOME ($ mil.)	INCOME AS % OF ASSETS	EMPLOYEES
12/19	5,221	57	1.1%	814
12/18	4,958	61	1.2%	854
12/17	4,908	43	0.9%	846
12/16	4,868	42	0.9%	808
12/15	4,734	42	0.9%	787
Annual Growth	2.5%	8.2%	—	0.8%

2019 Year-End Financials

Debt ratio: —	No. of shares (mil.): 96
Return on equity: 11.25%	Dividends
Cash ($ mil.): 456	Yield: 3.1%
Current ratio: —	Payout: 44.0%
Long-term debt ($ mil.): —	Market value ($ mil.): 840

	STOCK PRICE ($) FY Close	P/E High/Low	PER SHARE ($) Earnings	Dividends	Book Value
12/19	8.67	15 12	0.60	0.27	5.55
12/18	6.86	15 10	0.64	0.27	5.07
12/17	9.20	22 16	0.45	0.26	4.76
12/16	8.75	20 12	0.45	0.26	4.52
12/15	6.14	16 13	0.44	0.26	4.34
Annual Growth	9.0%	— —	7.7%	0.9%	6.4%

Trustmark Corp

Trustmark Corporation is the holding company for Trustmark National Bank which has 208 locations mainly in Mississippi but also in East Texas the Florida panhandle and Tennessee where it also operates its Somerville Bank & Trust subsidiary in the Memphis area. Focusing on individuals and small businesses Trustmark offers a range of financial products and services such as checking and savings accounts certificates of deposit credit cards insurance investments and trust services. The diversified financial services firm has about $11.7 billion in assets.

Operations

Trustmark operates through three operating segments: General Banking Insurance and Wealth Management.

The General Banking Division is responsible for all traditional banking products and services including a full range of commercial and consumer banking services such as checking accounts savings programs overdraft facilities commercial installment and real estate loans home equity loans and lines of credit drive-in and night deposit services and safe deposit facilities offered through 208 offices in Alabama Florida Mississippi Tennessee and Texas.

The Wealth Management Division serve Trustmark's customers as a financial partner providing reliable guidance and sound practical advice for accumulating preserving and transferring wealth.

Trustmark's Insurance Division provides a full range of retail insurance products including commercial risk management products bonding group benefits and personal lines coverage through Trustmark National Bank subsidiary FBBI a Mississippi corporation.

Subsidiary Fisher Brown Bottrell sells insurance while Trustmark Investment Advisors provides wealth management products and services including the proprietary Performance Fund family of mutual funds. The latter unit has approximately $9 billion of assets under management.

Geographic Reach

Mississippi by far is Trustmark's largest market accounting for 63% of 2013 revenues. Tennessee Texas and Florida contributed about 9% 7% and 10% respectively.

Financial Performance

After experiencing a revenue dip in 2012 due to decrease in interest income in 2013 Trustmark's revenues increased by 8% thanks to an increase in the net interest income due to a significant increase in interest and fees on acquired loans related to the BancTrust acquisition as well as modest declines in the cost of interest-bearing deposits. These gains were partially offset by downward repricing of loans and securities. After experiencing sizable growth over the last few years in 2013 Trustmark's net income decreased to $117.1 million (from $117.2 million in 2012) due to an increase in the noninterest expenses as a result of BancTrust non-routine merger expenses and increases in salaries and employee benefits services and fees and ORE/foreclosure expenses.

In 2013 the company's operating cash inflow increased to $155.4 million (compared to $92.1 million in 2012) was due to a major increase in net assets and liabilities and a decline in purchases and originations of loans held for sale.

Strategy

Trustmark is growing its branch network by opening or acquiring new offices with a focus on the Houston and Memphis markets.

In 2013 Trustmark opened a new 12000-sq.-ft. office location on the first and second floors of the Nexen Building in Bunker Hill. Trustmark operates 15 locations in the Houston market with loans outstanding of approximately $835 million and deposits of approximately $425 million.

Mergers and Acquisitions

In 2013 the company purchased two branches in Oxford Mississippi from SOUTHBank F.S.B. That year it also bought Mobile Alabama-based BancTrust Financial Group for $55 million providing Trustmark entry into more than 15 markets in Alabama and enhancing the Trustmark franchise in the Florida Panhandle.

Company Background

Trustmark grew in 2011 with the FDIC-assisted acquisition of Heritage Banking Group. It took over the failed bank's assets and deposits after the institution was closed by regulators. The transaction added four bank branches in Mississippi (four other locations were consolidated due to their proximity to existing Trustmark branches).

BlackRock Inc. owns more than 11% of Trustmark Corp's. shares.

Trustmark National Bank traces its roots to 1889 when it was first chartered in Mississippi.

EXECUTIVES

Treasurer And Director; President And Coo Financial Services Group Trustmark National Bank, Gerard R. (Jerry) Host, age 65, $730,000 total compensation
President Corporate Banking Trustmark National Bank, Duane A. Dewey, age 61, $348,840 total compensation
Treasurer And Principal Financial Officertrustmark Corporation And Evp And Cfo Trustmark National Bank, Louis E. Greer, age 65, $360,000 total compensation
President Mortgage Services Trustmark National Bank, Breck W. Tyler, age 62, $306,000 total compensation
President Wealth Management Trustmark National Bank, W. Arthur Stevens, age 55, $333,540 total compensation
Vice President Recovery Department, Terry Collins
First Vice President Corporate Planning, Joseph Rein
Vice President Human Resources, David Kenney
First Vice President, Ronnie Bethay
Vice President And Trust Officer In The Trust Department, Agnes Tribble
Assistant Vice President, Marian Alderman
Senior Vice President Trustmark National Bank, Murray Fincher
Senior Vice President And Sco, Tommy Lyle
Vice President Investments, Andy Leslie
Senior Vice President And Assistant Controller, Donnie Tynes
First Vice President, John Yow
Vice President Advertising, Kristine Jacobs
Senior Vice President, Kim Holley
Vice President, Vincent Powell
Senior Vice President And Employee Services Manager And Of Human Resources, Janice Brown
Vice President Payroll And Compensatio, Mike Oconnell

Vice President And Portfolio Manager, Ben Edwards
Vice President Sales, Kristi Bradley
Executive Vice President, Kirk Whitehouse
Vice President Commercial Banking, Colby Calcote
Assistant Vice President, Sue Hancock
Senior Vice President And Corporate Private Banking Manager, Mark Lewis
Executive Vice President Commercial Banking Manager, Mark Hope
Assistant Vice President, Laura Ryan
Senior Vice President, Mitchell Campbell
First Vice President, Bethany L Smith
Assistant Vice President And Strategic Sourcing, Matt Noland
Vice President Corporate Treasury Services, Tiffany Hancock
Vice President Sugar Land Commercial Banking, John Martinez
Vice President Mortgage Loan Originator, Jason Hebert
Senior Vice President Commercial Banking, Scott Killman
Vice President Commercial Relationship Manager, Lee Webb
Svp, Allen Hart
Assistant Vice President And Hr Business Unit Manager, Stephanie Valentine
First Vice President, Bethany Smith
Vice President, Gloria Craig
Vice President, Bard Shirley
Vice President, Audrey Sylvester
First Vice President, Sherry Lawrence
Evp Treasurer, Tom Owens
Vice President, Randy Taylor
Mortgage Loan Originator And Assistant Vice President, Bobbie Mccowan
Chairman, R. Michael Summerford, age 71
Assistant Secretary, Melanie Morgan
Board Member, Calvin Brown
Auditors: Crowe LLP

LOCATIONS

HQ: Trustmark Corp
248 East Capitol Street, Jackson, MS 39201
Phone: 601 208-5111   **Fax:** 601 354-5053
Web: www.trustmark.com

2016 Sales

	% of total
Mississippi	65
Alabama	12
Florida	8
Texas	8
Tennessee	7
Total	100

PRODUCTS/OPERATIONS

2016 Sales

	% of total
General Banking	91
Insurance	5
Wealth Management	4
Total	100

2016 Sales

	$ mil.	% of total
Interest Income:		
Interest and fees on LHFS & LHFI	299	51
Interest on securities	81	14
Interest and fees on acquired loans	30	5
Other interest income	1	-
Noninterest Income:		
Service charges on deposit accounts	45	8
Insurance commissions	36	6
Bank card and other fees	27	5
Mortgage banking net	28	5
Wealth management	30	5
Other net	5	1
Securities (losses) gains net	(0.3)	-
Total	**586**	**100**

COMPETITORS

BancorpSouth	Hancock Holding
Capital One	Regions Financial
Citizens Holding	Renasant
First Horizon	Wells Fargo
Great Southern Bancorp	

HISTORICAL FINANCIALS

Company Type: Public

Income Statement
FYE: December 31

	ASSETS ($ mil.)	NET INCOME ($ mil.)	INCOME AS % OF ASSETS	EMPLOYEES
12/19	13,497	150	1.1%	2,844
12/18	13,286	149	1.1%	2,856
12/17	13,797	105	0.8%	2,893
12/16	13,352	108	0.8%	2,788
12/15	12,678	116	0.9%	2,941
Annual Growth	1.6%	6.7%	—	(0.8%)

2019 Year-End Financials

Debt ratio: 0.46%	No. of shares (mil.): 64
Return on equity: 9.25%	Dividends
Cash ($ mil.): 358	Yield: 2.6%
Current ratio: —	Payout: 39.3%
Long-term debt ($ mil.): —	Market value ($ mil.): 2,216

	STOCK PRICE ($) FY Close	P/E High/Low	PER SHARE ($) Earnings	Dividends	Book Value
12/19	34.51	16 12	2.32	0.92	25.87
12/18	28.43	16 12	2.21	0.92	24.17
12/17	31.86	23 18	1.56	0.92	23.20
12/16	35.65	23 12	1.60	0.92	22.48
12/15	23.04	15 12	1.71	0.92	21.80
Annual Growth	10.6%	—	7.9%	(0.0%)	4.4%

TURNER CONSTRUCTION COMPANY INC

Turner Construction has been the mastermind for scores of head-turning projects for more than a century. The company that built Madison Square Garden has ranked among the leading general builders in the US since the early 1900s. Turner provides construction and project management services for commercial and multifamily buildings airports and stadiums as well as correctional educational entertainment and manufacturing facilities. The company is also a leader in sustainable or green building practices. Founded in 1902 by Henry Turner the company is the main operating unit of The Turner Corporation which is a subsidiary of German construction group HOCHTIEF.

Operations

Turner Construction works on some 1500 projects each year. For decades Turner has kept tabs on construction prices with its quarterly Building Cost Index which forecasts construction costs by considering labor rates productivity and material prices.

The index is used by federal and state governments to track building costs and pricing trends.

As part of HOCHTIEF's Americas division Turner works alongside other contractors in the US and Canada such as Flatiron its subsidiary E.E. Cruz and Clark Builders.

Geographic Reach

Headquartered in New York Turner Construction has offices across North America and with a presence in about 20 countries. It has operations in Latin America and the Caribbean India Europe Southeast Asia and the Middle East.

Sales and Marketing

Turner Construction works on projects in industries including aviation transportation commercial entertainment government green building manufacturing pharmaceutical research & development retail and sports.

Company Background

Notable projects in Turner Construction's history include the World War II Memorial in Washington DC the John F. Kennedy Memorial Library in Boston and the Rock and Roll Hall of Fame. Turner also built the new Yankee Stadium in New York. The company reached a milestone in 2008 by inking its 15000th major contract.

EXECUTIVES

President, Peter J. Davoren
Vp, Stephen W. Fort
Evp (new York New Jersey Maryland Pennsylvania Connecticut And New England), Pasquale A. (Pat) Di Filippo
Svp, Michael J. (Mike) Kuntz
Svp, Mark A. Boyle
Evp (ohio Nashville Huntsville Atlanta Florida And The Carolinas), Richard P. Homan
Vp, Thomas J. (Tom) Manahan
Svp; President And Ceo Turner International, Abrar Sheriff
Svp And Cfo, Karen O. Gould
Svp (mid-atlantic And Southeast), Tom Reilly
President The Lathrop Company, Steve Johnson
Vp And Construction Executive, Robert Hubner
Vice President, Neil D Jensen
Vice President, Phillip Parker
Senior Vice President, Christa Andresky
Vice President, Christoph Verbeek
Vice President Business Integration, Travis Cole
Vp And Operations Manager Of Central Texas, Jeremiah Hudson
Vice President Operations Manager, Dan VonKossovsky
Vice President And General Manager, Tom Stachowiak
Vice President And Financial Manager, Sarah Garner
Vice President And Construction Executive, Bob Grace
Vp And Operations Manager Of Connecticut, Tom Dutchyshyn
Vice President, Dave Welber
Executive Vice President Operational Services, David Benton
Vice President, Stephen J Spaulding
Vice President, Carlo A Disilvestro
Vice President And Construction Executive Middle Atlantic, Derek Brown
Vice President, Peter S Ramstedt
Vice President, Davey Mass
Vp Of Special Projects Division Of Dallas, Nick Barker
Vice President, Douglas W Cooper
Vice President, Charles Egbert
Vice President, Maureen Kirkpatrick
Vice President, Filippo Restivo
Auditors: DELOITTE & TOUCHE LLP PRINCET

LOCATIONS

HQ: TURNER CONSTRUCTION COMPANY INC
375 HUDSON ST FL 6, NEW YORK, NY 100143667
Phone: 212 229-6000
Web: WWW.TURNERCONSTRUCTION.COM

PRODUCTS/OPERATIONS

Selected Services
Turner Engineering Group
Design+Build
Turner Logistics: Procurement Services
Medical Planning and Procurement
Building Information Modeling (BIM)
Lean Construction

COMPETITORS

Bechtel	Hunt Construction
C. G. Schmidt	Jacobs Engineering
Catamount Constructors	PCL Employees Holdings
Dimeo Construction	Parsons Corporation
DooleyMack	Peter Kiewit Sons'
English Construction Company	Shook National
F.A. Wilhelm	Skanska USA Building
Fluor	Structure Tone
Gilbane Building Company	Tully Construction
Hensel Phelps Construction	Tutor Perini
	Winter Construction

HISTORICAL FINANCIALS

Company Type: Private

Income Statement
FYE: December 31

	REVENUE ($ mil.)	NET INCOME ($ mil.)	NET PROFIT MARGIN	EMPLOYEES
12/14	10,516	96	0.9%	5,000
12/13	9,488	76	0.8%	—
12/12	8,552	70	0.8%	—
Annual Growth	10.9%	17.2%	—	—

Two Harbors Investment Corp

Two Harbors Investment Corp. is ready to double its money. The real estate investment trust (REIT) is managed and advised by (and was founded by) PRCM Advisers a subsidiary of Pine River Capital Management. The trust primarily invests in agency residential mortgage-backed securities (RMBS) with fixed or adjustable interest rates that are backed by government-supported enterprises Fannie Mae Freddie Mac or Ginnie Mae. About a quarter of its mortgage portfolio is made up of non-agency RMBS such as subprime mortgages which carry more risk than federally-backed securities but offer higher yields.

EXECUTIVES

Vice President Data Management, Sree Kunduru
Assistant Vice President Data Analytics, Billy Raleigh
Assistant Vice President Human Resources, Beth Petersen

LOCATIONS

HQ: Two Harbors Investment Corp
601 Carlson Parkway, Suite 1400, Minnetonka, MN
55305
Phone: 612 453-4100
Web: www.twoharborsinvestment.com

COMPETITORS

American Capital	Invesco Mortgage
Agency Corp.	Capital
Annaly Capital	MFA Financial
Management	New York Mortgage
Capstead Mortgage	Trust
Chimera	Putnam Mortgage
Drive Shack	Redwood Trust
Gramercy	iStar Financial Inc

HISTORICAL FINANCIALS

Company Type: Public

Income Statement   FYE: December 31

	ASSETS ($ mil.)	NET INCOME ($ mil.)	INCOME AS % OF ASSETS	EMPLOYEES
12/19	35,921	323	0.9%	—
12/18	30,132	(44)	—	—
12/17	24,789	348	1.4%	—
12/16	20,112	353	1.8%	—
12/15	14,575	492	3.4%	—
Annual Growth	25.3%	(9.9%)	—	—

2019 Year-End Financials

Debt ratio: 2.73%	No. of shares (mil.): 272
Return on equity: 7.02%	Dividends
Cash ($ mil.): 1,616	Yield: 11.4%
Current ratio: —	Payout: 179.5%
Long-term debt ($ mil.): —	Market value ($ mil.): 3,990

	STOCK PRICE ($) FY Close	P/E High/Low		PER SHARE ($) Earnings	Dividends	Book Value
12/19	14.62	16	13	0.93	1.67	18.21
12/18	12.84	—	—	(0.53)	1.88	17.15
12/17	16.26	9	5	1.81	0.47	20.47
12/16	8.72	5	4	2.02	1.86	19.57
12/15	8.10	4	3	2.70	2.08	20.21
Annual Growth	15.9%	—	—	(23.4%)	(5.3%)	(2.6%)

Tyson Foods Inc

Tyson Foods spreads its wings beyond the chicken coop. While it is one of the largest US chicken producers (with processing capacity of some 45 million a week) Tyson's Fresh Meats division makes it a giant in the beef and pork sectors as well. The company also offers value-added processed and pre-cooked meats and re-frigerated and frozen prepared foods. Its chicken operations are vertically integrated — the company hatches the eggs supplies contract growers with the chicks and feed and brings them back for processing when ready. Tyson's brands include Tyson Jimmy Dean Hillshire Farm Ball Park Wright ibp Aidells and State Fair. Its customers include retail wholesale and food service companies worldwide although the US accounts for most sales.

HISTORY

During the Great Depression Arkansas poultry farmer John Tyson supported his family by selling vegetables and poultry. In 1935 after developing a method for transporting live poultry (he installed a food-and-water trough and nailed small feed cups on a trailer) he bought 500 chickens in Arkansas and sold them in Chicago.

For the next decade Tyson bought sold and transported chickens. By 1947 the year he incorporated the company as Tyson Feed & Hatchery he was raising the chickens himself. He emphasized chicken production opening his first processing plant in 1958 in Springdale where he implemented an ice-packing system that allowed the company to send its products greater distances.

John's son Don took over as manager in 1960 and in 1963 it went public as Tyson Foods. Tyson Country Fresh Chicken (packaged chicken that would become the company's mainstay) was introduced in 1967.

Rapid expansion included a new egg-processing building (1970) a new plant and computerized feed mill (1971) and the acquisitions of Prospect Farms (1969 precooked chicken) and the Ocoma Foods Division (1972 poultry) as well as hog operations.

Health-conscious consumers increasingly turned from red meats to poultry during the 1980s. Tyson became the industry leader with several key acquisitions of poultry operations including the Tastybird division of Valmac (1985) Lane Processing (1986) and Heritage Valley (1986). Its 1989 purchase of Holly Farms added beef and pork processing.

Don Tyson relinquished the CEO position to Leland Tollett in 1991. The company increased its presence in Mexico the next year through a joint venture with poultry producer Trasgo. Also in 1992 the firm plunged into seafood with the purchase of Arctic Alaska Fisheries and Louis Kemp Seafood.

Tyson bought Culinary Foods (frozen foods) and Trasgo in 1994 and the seafood division of International Multifoods in 1995. High feed costs and an oversupply of chickens brought down company earnings the next year. In 1997 the company pleaded guilty to charges that it illegally gave former Agriculture Secretary Mike Espy thousands of dollars' worth of gifts; the settlement included $6 million in fines and fees.

Tyson bought embattled Hudson Foods' poultry operations in 1998. The company said it would take a charge that year of $196 million to restructure. It also sold turkey processor Willow Brook Foods (now part of Cargill Meat Solutions) to Willow Brook management in 1998. That year John H. Tyson grandson of the founder was elected chairman.

In 1999 Tyson sold its seafood business for about $180 million in a two-part transaction to International Home Foods and Trident Seafoods. John Tyson became CEO in 2000.

As the winner in a bidding war with Smithfield Foods in 2001 Tyson agreed to buy IBP Inc. the #1 beef processor and #2 pork processor in the US for nearly $3.2 billion. Tyson tried to back away from the table after accounting irregularities were discovered at an IBP subsidiary but a Delaware judge ordered Tyson to sit down and finish dinner. The deal was made final in September and Tyson changed the beef processor's name to IBP Fresh Meats.

In late 2001 Tyson Foods and six managers were indicted for conspiring to smuggle illegal immigrants from Mexico and Central America to work for lower than legal wages in 15 of its US poultry processing plants. Two managers made plea bargains and testified for the government; another manager committed suicide. Tyson and the remaining three managers were acquitted of the conspiracy charges in 2003.

Suffering from mild indigestion after the merger in 2002 Tyson announced a restructuring to trim some fat from its fresh pork operations and agreed to sell its Specialty Brands (frozen foods) subsidiary. In early 2003 sold off its frozen appetizer business DFG Foods.

Following the discovery of bird flu on a Texas chicken farm in 2004 and the subsequent banning of the importation of US chicken products by other countries Tyson consolidated and automated its poultry operations resulting in hundreds of layoffs at the company.

Tyson announced in 2004 it was being formally investigated by the SEC regarding perquisites given to executives including retired senior chairman Don Tyson and then-current chairman and CEO John Tyson. By August the SEC recommended civil action against the company for its failure to disclose $1.7 million in corporate perks given to Don Tyson without authorization from Tyson's compensation committee. Although Don Tyson had already reimbursed the company $1.53 million for then-unspecified benefits the SEC also announced plans to recommend civil action be taken against him. With neither the company nor Tyson admitting any guilt the case was settled in 2005 with Tyson paying the SEC $700000 in fines and the company $1.5 million. Many of the perks were not disclosed because Don Tyson did not fill out SEC-required questionnaires; however disclosed perks included having the company pay for his housekeeping and lawn maintenance and routine non-business use of the corporate jet by his family and friends.

In 2005 the company opened its largest case-ready meat plant in Sherman Texas. However that January and February it suspended operations at four of its other beef plants and cut back at a fifth due to a shortage of cattle and the loss of beef exports due to the US's 2003 case of BSE (Bovine spongiform encephalopathy or "mad cow" disease).

Growing concern over the role of trans-fatty acids (from hydrogenated vegetable oils) in diet and health led Tyson to begin removing them from its processed foods such as breaded chicken nuggets and chicken tenders. The company announced the removal of trans-fats from all its retail poultry and school foodservice products in 2005.

Recognizing the growing market for alternative and renewable fuels and recognizing its unending supply of meat by-products (in this case such lovelies as fat tallow lard and grease) Tyson decided to get into the alternative fuel market in

2007 with the formation of a 50-50 joint venture with fuel refiner Syntroleum called Dynamic Fuels. The joint venture was set up to explore the possibility of producing synthetic fuel from Tyson's waste products for the diesel- jet- and military-fuel markets. In conjunction with this joint venture Tyson created a new business unit Tyson Renewable Products.

EXECUTIVES

Evp And General Counsel, David L. Van Bebber, age 64

Evp And Chief Human Resources Officer, Mary A. Oleksiuk, age 58

Coo, Noel White, age 62, $777,716 total compensation

Cfo, Stewart F. Glendinning, age 54

President North American Foodservice And International, Andrew P. (Andy) Callahan, age 53

President North American Retail, Sally Grimes, age 48

Evp Operations Services, Howell P. (Hal) Carper, age 65

President Ceo And Director, Thomas P. (Tom) Hayes, age 54, $712,954 total compensation

Chief Growth Officer, Monica McGurk, age 49

President Poultry Operations, Doug Ramsey

Cto, Scott Spradley

Executive Vice President Business Process And Continuous Improvement, Russell Tooley

Vice President Of Food Safety And Quality Assurance, Dean Danilson

Vice President Customer Development Account Manager Executive Officer, John Conklin

Vice President Engineering, Jeff Sandorf

Vice President Foodservice Sales, Joel Sappenfield

Senior Vice President Chief Accounting O, Jerry Hartfield

Vice President Of Direct Materials, Lindsay Piepho

Svp Procurement, Melanie Russell

Senior Vp, Mike Collins

National Account Manager, Sally Kumasaki

Senior Vice President Operations, Steve Taylor

Vice President Of Marketing, Wendy Bruce

Executive Vice President Alternative Protein, Justin Whitmore

Vice President Human Resources, Cindy Goats

Vice President, Brandy Bilderack

Vice President Marketing, Bill Welsh

National Account Manager, Ken Mcallister

National Accounts Manager, Peter Chesna

Senior Vice President Operations, Roy Slaughter

Senior Vice President Raw Value Added, Ray McGaugh

Svp Foodservice Sales, Johnny Hughes

Vice President Marketing Services, Susan Quillin

Vice President Of Purchasing, Mike Wetzel

Vice President Finance Growth And Sales, Kirk Wardlow

Vice President Marketing, Kim Cupelli

Vice President Operations, Richard Irvin

Rsm West Coast Cvp, Kristopher Duckworth

Evp And Chief Customer Officer, Scott Rouse

Senior Vice President Grocery Sales, David Bray

Vice President Government Relations, Chuck Penry

Vice President Food Safety And Quality Assurance, Scott Stillwell

Sls Deli Vice President, Brent Schmiegelow

Vice President Food Service Sales East, Mike Curtin

Senior Vice President Tax, Mark Elser

Senior Vice President And Marketing Manager, Jeff Sandore

National Account Manager, Rich Markich

Senior Vice President, Craig Hart

Svp Fresh Meats Pork Division, Shane Miller

National Account Manager, Steve Maher

National Accounts Manager, Jared Mitchell

Vice President Associate General Counsel And Asst. Secretary, Nate Hodne

Senior Vice President Wal Mart Operations, Jason Nichol

Senior Vice President Foodservice, Kristin Bird

Vice President Laboratory Services, Dan Zelenka

Vice President National Accounts, Brian Roberts

Executive Vice President And General Counsel, Amy Tu

Vice President Of Live Operations, Chip Miller

Vice President Of Network Strategy, Michael Ahmed

Vice President, Lee Slezak

Vp Fresh Meats Marketing And Premium Programs, Kent Harrison

Senior Vice President Chief Accounting Officer Controller, Steve Gibbs

Vice President Public Relations And Media Communications, Steve Eisler

Executive Vice President, Leroy Zachow

Vice President Corporate Accounts, Shawn Huxley

Chairman, John H. Tyson, age 67

Board Member, Brad Sauer

Treasurer, Matt Ellis

Board Member, Samuel Banks

Board Member, Gaurdie E Banister

Secretary, Lori Donnelly

Secretary, Vicky Harp

Secretary Iv, Bobbie Meredith

Secretary, Connie Owens

Board Treasurer Secretary, Robert Anderson

Auditors: PricewaterhouseCoopers LLP

LOCATIONS

HQ: Tyson Foods Inc
2200 West Don Tyson Parkway, Springdale, AR 72762-6999

Phone: 479 290-4000   **Fax:** 479 290-7984
Web: www.tyson.com

PRODUCTS/OPERATIONS

2018 Sales

	$ mil.	% of total
Beef	15,473	38
Chicken	12,044	29
Prepared foods	8,668	21
Pork	4,879	12
Other	305	-
Inter segment Sales	(1317)	-
Total	**40,052**	**100**

COMPETITORS

Cargill	Pilgrim's Pride
ConAgra	Rosen's Diversified
Foster Farms	Sanderson Farms
Hormel	Smithfield Foods
JBS	U.S. Premium Beef
Koch Foods	WH Group
Kraft Heinz	Wayne Farms
Perdue Incorporated	

HISTORICAL FINANCIALS

Company Type: Public

Income Statement   FYE: October 3

	REVENUE ($ mil.)	NET INCOME ($ mil.)	NET PROFIT MARGIN	EMPLOYEES
10/20*	43,185	2,140	5.0%	139,000
09/19	42,405	2,022	4.8%	141,000
09/18	40,052	3,024	7.6%	121,000
09/17	38,260	1,774	4.6%	122,000
10/16	36,881	1,768	4.8%	114,000
Annual Growth	**4.0%**	**4.9%**	**—**	**5.1%**

*Fiscal year change

2020 Year-End Financials

Debt ratio: 32.64%	No. of shares (mil.): 365
Return on equity: 14.25%	Dividends
Cash ($ mil.): 1,420	Yield: 0.0%
Current ratio: 1.86	Payout: 28.6%
Long-term debt ($ mil.): 10,791	Market value ($ mil.): 21,648

	STOCK PRICE ($) FY Close	P/E High/Low		PER SHARE ($) Earnings	Dividends	Book Value
10/20*	59.31	16	7	5.86	1.68	42.37
09/19	85.20	16	9	5.52	1.50	38.48
09/18	59.53	5	4	8.19	1.20	34.98
09/17	70.45	15	11	4.79	0.90	28.64
10/16	74.67	16	9	4.53	0.60	26.61
Annual Growth	(5.6%)	—	—	6.6%	29.4%	12.3%

*Fiscal year change

U.S. GENERAL SERVICES ADMINISTRATION

The U.S. General Services Administration (GSA) manages the rental of more than 370 million square feet of real estate in US government-owned properties. In addition to acting as the government's landlord in obtaining office space for over a million federal workers the GSA also manages properties and supplies equipment telecommunications and information technology products to its customer agencies. It spends some $55 billion annually for goods and services supporting about 8700 buildings and more than 250000 vehicles. The agency operates through divisions including the Federal Acquisition Service and Public Buildings Service. The GSA was established in 1949 to streamline the administrative work of the federal government.

Operations

GSA comprises the Federal Acquisition Service (FAS) the Public Buildings Service (PBS) and the Office of Government-wide Policy (OGP). In addition it operates about 10 staff offices and a handful of independent offices. FAS and PBS each generate about half of the agency's revenue; the OGP does not contribute to overall revenue.

Through a network of service providers FAS delivers information technology products and services telecommunications services travel and transportation management motor vehicles and fleet services and issues more than 35 million charge cards.

PBS operates within two divisions?workspace acquisition and property management. It acquires space for the federal government through new construction and leasing and leases almost 370 million square feet of workspace in more than 8700 buildings about 500 of which are on the National Register of Historic Places. PBS also manages the disposal of unused properties. In 2018 it disposed of 140 assets generating more than $123 million in proceeds.

The OGP develops government policy and performance standards and provides data analysis and transparent reporting to drive efficiency across key administrative areas including travel and transportation acquisition fleet management information technology modernization and real estate management.

Geographic Reach

Headquartered in Washington DC the U.S. General Services Administration provides services and support to more than 60 Federal departments and agencies. It delivers goods and services across the country and overseas through more than 10 regional offices located in major US cities.

Strategy

The GSA has been working to streamline access to its Federal marketplace by implementing more efficient systems and processes with a focus on IT modernization data analytics and change management. In 2018 it made data from the government's real property inventory available to the public for the first time making it easier to identify and dispose of underused property. Also in 2018 it introduced its IT Modernization Centers of Excellence (CoE) where the agency is assessing IT resources and technology needs at the US Department of Agriculture and US Department of Housing and Urban Development in hopes of reducing redundancies. GSA also administers the Technology Modernization Fund (TMF) a lending vehicle through which Federal agencies can borrow money to invest in modernizing aging technologies.

In 2019 the agency is working on a shared services initiative to create the infrastructure necessary to centralize administrative functions and systems such as hiring payroll finance and contract processing. There are currently more than 100 systems that track time and attendance for government employees.

Company Background

The U.S. General Services Administration was established by President Harry Truman in 1949 to streamline the administrative work of the federal government. It consolidated the National Archives Establishment the Federal Works Agency the Public Buildings Administration the Bureau of Federal Supply the Office of Contract Settlement and the War Assets Administration into one federal agency delivering and managing supplies and providing workplaces for federal employees.

GSA's original mission was to dispose of war surplus goods manage and store government records handle emergency preparedness and stockpile strategic supplies for wartime.

EXECUTIVES

Commissioner Federal Acquisition Service, James A. Williams
Cfo, Kathleen M. Turco
Acting Associate Administrator Office Of Citizen Services And Communications, Martha Dorris
Acting Administrator, Paul F. Prouty
Acting Commissioner Public Buildings Service, Anthony E. Costa
Acting Associate Administrator Office Of Governmentwide Policy, Stanley F. Kaczmarczyk
Acting Associate Administrator Office Of Small Business Utilization, Mary Parks
Acting Associate Administrator Office Of Performance Improvement, Steven D. McPeek
Acting Chief Office Of Emergency Response And Recovery, Joshua B. (Josh) Sawislak
Director Office Of Management Services, Elizabeth I. Kelley

Chairman Civilian Board Of Contract Appeals, Stephen M. Daniels
Chief Information Officer, Diane Merriett

LOCATIONS

HQ: U.S. GENERAL SERVICES ADMINISTRATION 1800 F ST NW RM 6100, WASHINGTON, DC 204050001
Phone: 202 501-0450
Web: WWW.GSA.GOV

PRODUCTS/OPERATIONS

2018 Sales

	$ mil.	% of total
Federal Buildings Fund		
Building Operations-Leased	6,420	26
Building Operations-Government Owned	5,261	21
Acquisition Services Fund		
Assisted Acquisition Services	7,043	29
Travel Transportation and Logistics	2,060	8
Information Technology	1,786	7
General Supplies and Services	1,300	5
Professional Services and Human Capital	87	-
Other Programs	113	1
Other Funds		
Working Capital Fund	657	3
Other General	37	-
Eliminations	(921)	-
Total	**23,843**	**100**

Selected Products and Services

Facilities & Construction
Construction Related Materials
Facility Related Materials
Facility Related Services
Human Capital
Administrative Services
Human Capital and Training Solutions
Human Resources System
General Support Services

HISTORICAL FINANCIALS

Company Type: Private

Income Statement   FYE: September 30

	REVENUE ($ mil.)	NET INCOME ($ mil.)	NET PROFIT MARGIN	EMPLOYEES
09/19	11,785	536	4.5%	13,000
09/16	20,457	290	1.4%	—
09/15*	38,976	486	1.2%	—
12/05	0	0	—	—
Annual Growth	—	—	—	—

*Fiscal year change

U.S. VENTURE, INC.

Privately held US Venture Inc is a North American leader in the distribution of fuel and transportation products. US Oil its division transports more than 2 billion gallons of fuel annually via pipelines rail light oil-barges and trucks. The division maintains over 7.5 million BOE in storage capacity and has access to nearly 200 terminals. Through US AutoForce the company is also a top distributor of tires and car parts to independent tire retailers auto repair shops and dealerships. The company's Lubricants division maintains a competitive business as well set up to blend and market chemical products to automotive industrial and metalworking industries.

Through the GAIN Clean Fuel brand US Venture also sells clean biofuels.

Operations

US Venture has six business divisions.

US Oil is a leading distributor of branded and unbranded refined products in the US and Canada. It transports more than 2 billion gallons of energy products annually. US Oil also engages in energy trading.

Tires car parts and lubricants are distributed through the US AutoForce division another industry leader. Its portfolio includes more than 35 tire brands beyond 15 lubricant brands and many branded car parts (mostly brakes chassis repair equipment and exhausts).

US Lubricants blends and distributes lubricants under its THRIVE brand for automotive industrial and metalworking needs. It also provides support services like mobile filtration systems oil analysis lab services and fluids storage and handling systems.

US Venture is also developing and building alternative fuel transportation networks and filling stations in the US. Headed by the US GAIN division the company supplies compressed natural gas (CNG) and renewable natural gas (RNG) to more than 50 fueling stations.

Breakthrough provides innovative transportation and supply chain strategies for the world's leading shippers. IGEN build excise tax software that meets the needs of the motor fuel industry.

Geographic Reach

Headquartered in Appleton Wisconsin US Venture operates throughout North America. US Oil handles fuel supply in the Midwest with 25 terminals and nearly 200 third-party terminal partners. The company has a concentration of fuel tires car parts and convenience store services in the Midwest. It distributes fuels car parts and lubricants in North America.

Sales and Marketing

The US Oil division distributes products from a-dozen major oil brands including BP Shell Exxon Mobil Marathon Citgo Sunoco Clark and Phillips 66. It offers flexible pricing and fixed-fuel contracts and commodity trading. Traded products include gasoline ethanol biodiesel jet fuels propane and butane. In the Midwest the company also owns the Express chain of convenience stores.

US AutoForce offers more than 35 tire brands including Michelin Bridgestone Dunlop Firestone and Goodyear. Together with US Lubricants it serve the agricultural construction forestry marine and mining industries. US Lubricants also supplies its products to automotive dealerships repair shops lube shops and tire centers and customers in commercial transportation as well as industrial and metalworking lubricants.

US Venture is a major sponsor of the USA Luge team.

Company Background

U.S. Oil was established in 1951 as Schmidt Oil by the sons of local fuel distributor Albert Schmidt. The company changed its name to U.S. Venture in 2010 to reflect the company's increasingly diverse portfolio of entrepreneurial businesses. It has remained family-owned since its inception and today it is one of the largest privately held companies in Wisconsin.

EXECUTIVES

President And Ceo, John Schmidt
Vp Marketing And Strategy, Jeff Van Brunt
President U.s. Gain, Mike Koel
Vice President Treasurer Assistant Secretary, Lori Karls
Vp Of Sales And Operations, Kevin Olson
Senior Vice President Merchandise Planning And Allocation, Mark Duenig
Vp Insight And Analytics, Gary Cao
Secretary, Raymond Schmidt
Treasurer, Martin Tomczyk
Secretary And Treasurer, Ray Schmidt
Treasurer, Judy Engen-pazdera
Auditors: DELOITTE & TOUCHE LLP MILWAU

LOCATIONS

HQ: U.S. VENTURE, INC.
425 BETTER WAY, APPLETON, WI 549156192
Phone: 920 739-6101
Web: WWW.USVENTURE.COM

PRODUCTS/OPERATIONS

Selected Operations

U.S. AutoForce (exhaust pipe manufacturing and autoparts distribution)
U.S. Lubricants (motor oil and related products)
U.S. Oil (gasoline fuel oil and natural gas)
U.S Gain (compressed natural gas)

COMPETITORS

American Tire Distributors
Guttman Oil
Petroleum Traders Corporation

HISTORICAL FINANCIALS

Company Type: Private

Income Statement — FYE: July 31

	REVENUE ($ mil.)	NET INCOME ($ mil.)	NET PROFIT MARGIN	EMPLOYEES
07/15	8,076	173	2.1%	1,673
07/14	9,088	49	0.5%	—
07/13	7,346	47	0.6%	—
Annual Growth	4.9%	91.7%	—	—

UAW RETIREE MEDICAL BENEFITS TRUST

EXECUTIVES

Head of Trustees, Robert Naftaly
Prin, Rober Naftaly
Senior Manager Human Resources, Karen Blair
Director Communications, Matthew Wood
Strategy Consultant, Vince Ferri
Senior Managing Director, Benjamin Cotton
Corporate Governance Analyst, Ryan Droze
Manager Strategic Opportunitie, Adrian Ohmer
Senior Accountant, Amy Hawkins
Director, Brian Gimotty
Vice President, Cindy Estrada
Auditors: DELOITTE TAX LLP DETROIT MI

LOCATIONS

HQ: UAW RETIREE MEDICAL BENEFITS TRUST
200 WALKER ST STE 400, DETROIT, MI 482074229
Phone: 313 324-5900
Web: WWW.RHAC.COM

HISTORICAL FINANCIALS

Company Type: Private

Income Statement — FYE: December 31

	ASSETS ($ mil.)	NET INCOME ($ mil.)	INCOME AS % OF ASSETS	EMPLOYEES
12/18	60,352	1,176	1.9%	94
12/17	63,225	88	0.1%	—
12/16	58,966	(1,839)		—
Annual Growth	1.2%	—	—	—

Uber Technologies Inc

Auditors: PricewaterhouseCoopers LLP

LOCATIONS

HQ: Uber Technologies Inc
1455 Market Street, 4th Floor, San Francisco, CA 94103
Phone: 415 612-8582
Web: www.uber.com

HISTORICAL FINANCIALS

Company Type: Public

Income Statement — FYE: December 31

	REVENUE ($ mil.)	NET INCOME ($ mil.)	NET PROFIT MARGIN	EMPLOYEES
12/19	14,147	(8,506)		26,900
12/18	11,270	997	8.8%	22,263
12/17	7,932	(4,033)		—
12/16	3,845	(370)		—
Annual Growth	54.4%	—	—	—

2019 Year-End Financials

Debt ratio: 18.49%
Return on equity: (-81.08%)
Cash ($ mil.): 10,972
Current ratio: 2.47
Long-term debt ($ mil.): 5,707

No. of shares (mil.): 1,716
Dividends
　Yield: —
　Payout: —
Market value ($ mil.): 51,054

	STOCK PRICE ($) FY Close	P/E High/Low	PER SHARE ($) Earnings	Dividends	Book Value
12/19	29.74	— —	(6.81)	0.00	8.27
12/18	0.00	— —	(0.00)	0.00	14.86
Annual Growth	—	— —	—	—	(17.8%)

Ulta Beauty Inc

EXECUTIVES

Ceo, Mary N Dillon
Non-Exec Chb*, Charles J Philippin
Cfo-Treas-Asst SEC, Scott M Settersten
Chief Hr Officer, Jeffrey J Childs
Chief Merchandising & Mkt Offi, David C Kimbell
General Counsel-Corp SEC, Jodi J Caro
Beauty Advisor, Alexa Neri
Beauty Advisor, Amanda Jones
Prestige Manager, Amber Krause
Prestige Market Trainer Genera, Ashley Robles
Associate Operations Manager, Audrey Breecher
Auditors: Ernst & Young LLP

LOCATIONS

HQ: Ulta Beauty Inc
1000 Remington Blvd., Suite 120, Bolingbrook, IL 60440
Phone: 630 410-4800
Web: www.ulta.com

COMPETITORS

Bath & Body Works	Nordstrom
Bed Bath & Beyond	Premier Salons
Body Shop	Regis Corporation
CVS Caremark	Sally Beauty
Dillard's	Sephora USA
J. C. Penney	Supercuts
L'Oreal USA	Target Corporation
Lush Ltd.	Wal-Mart
Macy's	Walgreen
Merle Norman	

HISTORICAL FINANCIALS

Company Type: Public

Income Statement — FYE: February 1

	REVENUE ($ mil.)	NET INCOME ($ mil.)	NET PROFIT MARGIN	EMPLOYEES
02/20	7,398	705	9.5%	44,000
02/19	6,716	658	9.8%	44,000
02/18*	5,884	555	9.4%	34,700
01/17	4,854	409	8.4%	31,800
01/16	3,924	320	8.2%	26,500
Annual Growth	17.2%	21.9%	—	13.5%

*Fiscal year change

2020 Year-End Financials

Debt ratio: —
Return on equity: 38.03%
Cash ($ mil.): 392
Current ratio: 1.81
Long-term debt ($ mil.): —

No. of shares (mil.): 56
Dividends
　Yield: —
　Payout: —
Market value ($ mil.): 15,166

	STOCK PRICE ($) FY Close	P/E High/Low	PER SHARE ($) Earnings	Dividends	Book Value
02/20	267.91	30 18	12.15	0.00	33.60
02/19	291.36	29 18	10.94	0.00	31.07
02/18*	219.47	35 21	8.96	0.00	29.17
01/17	271.44	42 23	6.52	0.00	24.95
01/16	181.17	37 26	4.98	0.00	22.71
Annual Growth	10.3%	— —	25.0%	—	10.3%

*Fiscal year change

UMB Financial Corp

UMB Financial is the holding company for four UMB-branded commercial banks serving Arizona Colorado Illinois Kansas Nebraska Oklahoma and Missouri. Through some 110 branches the banks offer standard services such as checking and savings accounts credit and debit cards and trust and investment services. Commercial loans account for more than 50% of UMB's loan portfolio. Beyond its banking business it offers insurance brokerage services leasing treasury management health savings accounts and proprietary mutual funds through its more than 20 subsidiaries. Founded in 1913 the bank ranks first in the Kansas City market (based on deposits).

Operations

It operates through four business segments: Bank Payment Solutions Institutional Investment Management and Asset Servicing.

Its Bank segment focuses on traditional commercial and consumer banking treasury management leasing foreign exchange merchant bankcards wealth management brokerage insurance capital markets investment banking corporate trust and correspondent banking.

The Payment Solutions segment offers consumer and commercial credit and debit cards prepaid debit card solutions healthcare services and institutional cash management.

UMB Financial's Institutional Investment Management segment serves the intermediary and institutional markets through mutual funds traditional separate accounts and sub-advisory relationships using private equity and fixed income investment strategies.

The Asset Servicing segment caters to the asset management industry and supports investment products such as mutual funds alternative investments and managed accounts.

Geographic Reach

UMB Financial's four commercial banks are located in Arizona Colorado Kansas and Missouri. Its principal subsidiary bank Missouri-based UMB Bank n.a. also has branches in Illinois Kansas Nebraska and Oklahoma. In Texas the firm operates a loan production office.

Sales and Marketing

UMB Financial serves commercial retail government and correspondent bank customers through its branch locations call center Internet banking and network of ATMs.

The company spent $24.15 million toward marketing and business development expenses in 2014; up from $22.7 million in 2013 but down from the $24.6 million it spent in 2012.

Financial Performance

UMB Financial has enjoyed rising revenue and profit in recent years thanks to loan asset growth and . Revenue in 2014 grew by more than 2% to $862.56 million thanks to 8% growth in trust and securities processing fee income and thanks to higher loan interest income from another year of double-digit growth in average loan balances.

Following several years of profit growth net income in 2014 fell by 10% to $120.66 million mostly because the bank spent more toward salary raises and incurred higher benefit costs but also because it spent more on equipment and a contingency reserve it established in 2014

related to a settlement agreement involving the sellers and employees of PCM.

Cash from operations fell by 21% to $243.78 million partially from lower cash earnings but also because it adjusted for fewer non-cash items such as accrued expenses and taxes than it did in 2013.

The company's loan assets grew by 14% to $7.47 billion in 2014 while its total deposits increased slightly to $13.62 billion.

Strategy

UMB Financial is focused on four main strategies for growth. The first is to grow its fee-based business through acquisitions or organically as fee-based services are typically non-credit related and are not generally affected by fluctuations in interest rates. Accordingly the bank has boosted its non-interest income by 20% over the past three years from $414 million in 2011 to $498.7 million in 2014. In mid-2014 to add fuel to this growth UMB Bank purchased the Oklahoma Corporate Trust Business from RCB Bank to be incorporated into its own business in the region expanding the company's reach into the Oklahoma Corporate Trust Market.

The second strategy is to focus on net interest income through loan and deposit growth. In 2014 for example the bank grew its loan assets by a whopping 14% adding $16.8 million in net interest income (5% more than in 2013) to the bank's top line.

Thirdly UMB Financial aims to improve operating efficiencies by offering more services through its existing branch network which helped it grow its loan and deposit business greatly in 2014.

Fourth the firm is focused on managing its capital to promote investor confidence and acquisition opportunities.

Mergers and Acquisitions

In late 2014 UMB agreed to buy commercial finance firm Marquette Financial from longtime owners the Pohlad family for $182 million. The acquisition would increase UMB's presence in key growth markets Arizona and Texas — where Marquette operated Meridian Bank. As part of the deal the Pohlad family gained a 7% stake in UMB (the second-largest stake behind chairman Mariner Kemper who holds 12%).

Company Background

To grow its fee-based business and diversify its business model UMB has made several acquisitions in its past. The company built up its investment advisory and corporate trust business through several 2009 purchases. In 2010 UMB made 10 acquisitions including Prairie Capital Management and Indiana-based Reams Asset Management. The deals more than doubled UMB's Scout Investment Advisors' assets under management to more than $27 billion.

EXECUTIVES

Senior Vice President And Corporate Controller, Bryan Walker

Chairman President And Ceo, J. Mariner Kemper, age 47, $862,110 total compensation

Vice Chairman Umb Financial Corporation And President And Ceo Umb Bank, Michael D. (Mike) Hagedorn, age 54, $444,986 total compensation

Ceo Scout Investments, Andrew J. (Andy) Iseman, age 56, $6,047 total compensation

President Umb Fund Services Inc., Anthony J. (Tony) Fischer, age 61, $281,154 total compensation

Evp And Chief Credit Officer, Christian R. (Chris) Swett, age 64

Evp And Chief Lending Officer, Thomas S. (Tom) Terry, age 56

Cfo, Ram Shankar, age 47

Evp And Chief Human Resources Officer, Shannon A. Johnson, age 40

Evp And Director Of Operations Bank, Kevin M. Macke, age 47

Evp And Chief Risk Officer, Jennifer M. Payne, age 43

Vice President Of Commercial Underwriting, Rebecca A Lang

Vice President Marketing, Kelli Christman

Vice President Quality Assurance And Risk Management, Mark Kitchin

Vp Loan Review Team Lead, Christopher Nelson

Senior Vice President, Dan Dennis

Assistant Vice President And Financial Center Manager Ii, Jenna Harris

Assistant Vice President And Information Technology Manager And Data Architecture, Bob Eber

Vice President Banking Services Compliance Directo, Stephanie Boryla

Assistant Vice President Financial Center Manager, Chad Treacy

Vice President Of Commercial Banking, Mark Winker

Vice President, Pam Ungashick

Vice President Senior Loan Review, James Engelhart

Vice President Private Banking Client Manager, Chad Roberts

Senior Vice President, Phil Richter

Executive Vice President And Managing Director, Andre Trudell

Vice President Commercial Banking, Jess Adams

Vp Retail Operations Officer, Michele Mcreynolds

Senior Vice President Loan Operations, Linda Gallagher

Vp Fraud Strategy Manager, Clayton Wariner

Senior Vice President Credit Risk Director, Jim Caniglia

Avp Financial Center Manager Ii, Dustin Smith

Executive Vice President Director Bank Strategy And Administration, Rekha Patnaik

Senior Vice President Commercial Banking, Drue Thomas

Avp And Senior Benefits Administrator, Rebecca Moodie

Senior Vice President, Gordon Gendler

Vice President Debit Product Manager, Hugh Meadows

Vice President, Sandy Battas

Senior Vice President, Kathryn Anastasio

Vice President Financial Center Manager, Casey Kudrna

Senior Vice President, Gavin Wilkinson

Vice President Trust Custody Operations Manager, Melvin Porter

Vice President Enterprise Data Operations, Sara Rock

Executive Vice President Regional Credit Officer, Kurt Kastendick

Commercial Development Officer Vice President, Edin Salkic

Assistant Vice President Commercial Underwriting Officer, Brad Boeshaar

Vice President, Mark Volkmer

Vice President Corporate Trust, Laura Roberson

Vice President Corporate Trust, Brian Krippner

Senior Vice President, Ann Porter

Vice President And Program Operations Management Lssbb, Renee Taylor

Vice President Product Development And Marketing, Bruce Parker

Vice President Senior Loan Review Officer, Chris Landry

Vice President Of Commercial Underwriting, Rebecca Lang

Senior Vice President, Mark Hannah

Vice President Investment And Wealth Management, Kelley Lauer

Vice President Finance, Debbie Johnson

Assistant Vice President, Steve Collins

Executive Vice President Chief Lending Officer, Tom Terry

Vice President, Lee Speir

Executive Vice President, Thomas Hof

Vice President Commercial Banking, William Thomasjr

Assistant Vice President Trust Advisor, Karin Behnk

Senior Vice President, Rick Bennett

Senior Vice President Treasury Management, David Pucci

Vice President And Director Healthcare Services Risk And Compliance, Stacy King

Vice President, Beth Ewert

Vice President Private Banking Client Manager, Chris Herwig

Financial Center Manager Assistant Vice President, Nicholas Foreman

Vp Agribusiness Banking, Michael Laplant

Vice President Business Banking, Randall Rodgers

Vice President Treasury Solutions Officer, Shannon Toney

Senior Vice President Commerci, Cydney Gurgens

Vp Financial Center Manager Ii, Benjamin Marx

Vice President, Laurie Box

Vice President, Rick Beaver

Assistant Vice President Financial Center Manager, Douglas Empson

Vice President Administration, Ann Maurer

Vice President Trust Operations Manager, Pete Bergman

Vice President, Jack Curtis

Senior Vice President, Janet Clements

Avp Commercial Technical Support, Elaine Wadehra

Senior Vice President And Counsel, Paul Scheuerman

Healthcare Services Vp Product Management, Scott Joling

Assistant Vice President Marketing Activation, Jeff Bowers

Svp Customer Experience Strategy, Amy Mendenhall

Vp Third Party Risk Management, Jeff Hovious

Vice President Commercial Relationship Manager, Shawn Harbour

Vice President Treasury Management, Lanie Sedlacek

Assistant Vice President Loss Mitigation, Sarah Read

Vice President Implementation Manager, Lori Lamanno

Vice President Private Banker, Shelly Parker

Senior Vice President Commercial Lending, Aaron Emel

Vice President Capital Markets, Nick Arthachinda

Sr Treasury Management Fulfillment Analyst Avp, Lynn Hornberg

Vice President, Michael Scholten

Vice President Portfolio Manager, Jason Harrison

Vice President Trust Administration, Brian Thurston

Assistant Vice President Treasury Analyst, Mike Groff

Senior Vice President And Director, Jennifer Matney

Senior Vice President Chief Information Security Officer, Sara Flores

Vice President And Corporate Legal Counsel, Megan Mercer

Senior Vice President, John Misiewicz

Vice President Commercial Banking, Evan Weishar

Vice President And Private Banking Client Manager, Ellen Burris

Senior Vice President Public Finance, Chip Schultz

Vice President, Nancy Mogelnicki

Vice President And Senior Financial Planner, Dan Weeks

Executive Vice President And Chief Information Officer, Sarah Mannix

Vice President Financial Center Manager, Karen Hanson

Vice President Commercial Banking, Bryson Bowden

Vice President, Clay Phillips

Senior Vice President Commercial Lending, Valerie Kroiss

Senior Vice President Commercial Team Lead, Dennis Wright

Senior Vice President Financial Advisor, Peter Braun

Vice President Senior Trust Advisor, James Gilmour

Vice President, Marcia Matthews

Vice President Legal Counsel, Terri Munsell

Senior Vice President, Clinton Patterson

Vice President Organizational Effecitveness Business Partner, Diane Epley

Senior Vice President, Marion De Barros

Senior Vice President Compliance, Jeff Maxwell

Vice President, Julius Zamora

Vp Business Aviation Finance, Morgan Littell

Vprelationship Manager, Madelyn Wallace

Vice President Business Development, Richard Tailey

Vice President Energy Division, Erica Spencer

Fund Accounting Manager Assistant Vice President, Brian Schmidt

Vice President, Karen Kohl

Vice President Business Banking, Randy Rodgers

Assistant Vice President Information Technology Help Desk And Olbs Manager, Michael Meredith

Vice President Investment Banking, Sheri Catlett

Vice President Global Relationship Manager, Bart Woodson

Assistant Vice President, Pam Sudduth

Senior Vice President, Chris Orlowski

Vice President Commercial Card Sales Manager Payment Solutions, Cherie Figge

Vice President Credit Analysis Manager, Lisa Smith

Vice President And Aml Investigations Supervisor, Venus Griswold

Vice President And Tax Senior Manager, Megan Kimzey

Assistant Vice President Instutional Asset Management Iam Support Division Manager, Sarah Johnson

Assistant Vice President Control Group Manager, John Effenheim

Executive Vice President, Frank Gorman

Assistant Vice President, Liz Angotti

Vice President Commercial Relationship Specialist, Christy Thomas

Vice President Construction Loan Manager, Sheila Larkey

Senior Vice President, Jay R Boster

Avp And Senior Benefits Plan Administrator, Chris Li-owens

Senior Vice President, Eric Crane

Senior Vice President Business Banking, Adam Donahue

Vp Private Banking Client Manager, Susan Beasley

Assistant Vice President Healthcare Services, Kelly Boreas

Auditors: KPMG LLP

LOCATIONS

HQ: UMB Financial Corp
1010 Grand Boulevard, Kansas City, MO 64106
Phone: 816 860-7000   Fax: 816 860-7143
Web: www.umb.com

PRODUCTS/OPERATIONS

2016 Sales

	$ mil.	% of total
Interest income		
Loans	386	29
Securities	131	13
Federal funds and resell agreements	2	
Interest-bearing due from banks	2.4	
Trading securities	0.6	
Non-interest income		
Trust and securities processing	239	24
Trading and investment banking	21	2
Service charges on deposit accounts	86	9
Insurance fees and commissions	4	-
Brokerage fees	17	2
Bankcard fees	68	7
Gains on sales of securities available for sale net	8	1
Equity earnings (losses) on alternative investments	2	-
Other	26	3
Total	**999**	**100**

Selected Subsidiaries & Affiliates

Grand Distribution Services LLC
J.D. Clark & Company
Kansas City Financial Corporation
Kansas City Realty Company
Prairie Capital Management LLC
Scout Distributors LLC
Scout Investment Advisors Inc.
UMB Banc Leasing Corp.
UMB Bank and Trust n.a.
UMB Bank Arizona n.a.
UMB Bank Colorado n.a.
UMB Capital Corporation
UMB Community Development Corporation
UMB Distribution Services LLC
UMB Financial Services Inc.
UMB Fund Services Inc.
UMB Insurance Inc.
UMB National Bank of America
UMB Realty Company LLC
UMB Redevelopment Corporation
UMB Trust Company of South Dakota
United Missouri Insurance Company

COMPETITORS

BOK Financial	Great Southern Bancorp
Bank of America	Guaranty Bancorp
Capitol Federal Financial	TCF Financial
Commerce Bancshares	U.S. Bancorp
Dickinson Financial	Zions Bancorporation
First National of Nebraska	

HISTORICAL FINANCIALS

Company Type: Public

Income Statement
FYE: December 31

	ASSETS ($ mil.)	NET INCOME ($ mil.)	INCOME AS % OF ASSETS	EMPLOYEES
12/19	26,561	243	0.9%	3,670
12/18	23,351	195	0.8%	3,573
12/17	21,771	247	1.1%	3,570
12/16	20,682	158	0.8%	3,688
12/15	19,094	116	0.6%	3,830
Annual Growth	8.6%	20.4%	—	(1.1%)

2019 Year-End Financials

Debt ratio: 0.37%	No. of shares (mil.): 49
Return on equity: 10.08%	Dividends
Cash ($ mil.): 1,744	Yield: 1.7%
Current ratio: —	Payout: 29.2%
Long-term debt ($ mil.): —	Market value ($ mil.): 3,370

	STOCK PRICE ($)	P/E	PER SHARE ($)		
	FY Close	High/Low	Earnings	Dividends	Book Value
12/19	68.64	14 12	4.96	1.21	53.09
12/18	60.97	20 15	3.93	1.17	45.37
12/17	71.92	16 13	4.96	1.04	43.72
12/16	77.12	25 13	3.22	0.99	39.51
12/15	46.55	24 19	2.44	0.95	38.34
Annual Growth	10.2%	— —	19.4%	6.2%	8.5%

Umpqua Holdings Corp

Umpqua Holdings thinks of itself not so much as a bank but rather a retailer that sells financial products. Consequently many of the company's 380-plus Umpqua Bank "stores" in northern California northern Nevada Idaho Oregon and Washington feature coffee bars and computer cafes. While customers sip Umpqua-branded coffee pay bills online attend a financial seminar catch a poetry reading or check out wares from local merchants staff members pitch deposit accounts mortgages loans life insurance investments and more. Subsidiary Umpqua Investments (formerly Strand Atkinson Williams & York) provides retail brokerage services through more than a dozen locations mostly inside Umpqua Bank branches.

Operations

Umpqua operates two business segments: Community Banking which made up 79% of the company's total revenue during 2015 and provides traditional banking services as well as wealth management and private banking services for wealthier individuals; and Home Lending (21% of revenue) which originates and sells residential mortgage loans.

The company makes more than 75% of its revenue from interest income. About 72% of its revenue came from loan interest (including fees) during 2015 with another 5% coming from interest on investment securities. The rest of its revenue came from residential mortgage banking revenue (9% of revenue) deposit account service charges (5%) brokerage revenue (2%) and other miscellaneous income streams.

Geographic Reach

Oregon-based Umpqua Bank has branches in Idaho Washington Oregon California and Northern Nevada. Umpqua Investments has offices in Portland Lake Oswego and Medford Oregon as well as Santa Rosa California.

Sales and Marketing

Umpqua Holdings promotes its brand through customer-facing channels public relations social media and community-based events. It spent $11.4 million on marketing to promote its brand during 2015 up from $9.5 million and $6.1 million in 2014 and 2013 respectively.

Financial Performance

The bank's annual revenues have doubled since 2011 as its loan and lease assets have tripled to $16.85 billion which has resulted in strong interest income growth. Exceptional revenue growth and effective cost controls have helped the bank's net income triple over the same period.

Umpqua Holdings' revenue jumped 20% to $1.21 billion during 2015 mostly as its earning assets (including loans investments and loans held for sale) swelled by 20% which led to higher interest income. The bank's non-interest income also rose 52% for the year mostly thanks to the 2014 acquisition of Sterling Financial with residential mortgage banking revenue brokerage commissions and deposit service charges all growing during the year.

Strong revenue growth in 2015 drove the bank's net income up 51% to $222.54 million for the year. Umpqua's operating cash levels climbed 5% to $376.74 million as earnings rose.

Strategy

Umpqua Bank's primary mission is to become the top community-oriented financial services firm in the Western US by strategically acquiring banks in new markets and building its brand by offering unique personal experience for customers entering its "store" branches. Its mid-2014 acquisition of Sterling Financial — the largest ever acquisition in Umpqua's history — successfully extended the bank's presence in Southern California Eastern Washington Eastern Oregon and Idaho.

The bank differentiates itself by encouraging clients to come into its stores instead of using impersonal interfaces like ATMs and electronic banking more cost-effective methods preferred by many of its competitors. The bank's "Next Generation" stores feature interactive touchscreen walls fresh fruit and cold drinks. It hopes the comfortable environment will inspire customers to use more of the bank's financial services.

Hoping to build upon its one-of-a-kind branch experiences Umpqua Bank in 2015 launched its Silicon Valley-based Pivotus Ventures Inc subsidiary to explore disruptive new bank technologies.

In 2016 Umpqua launched its corporate banking division which is dedicated to providing companies with access to such offerings as treasury management international banking debt capital markets and others.

Mergers and Acquisitions

In April 2014 Umpqua Bank acquired $10-billion-in-assets Sterling Financial Corp. headquartered in Spokane Washington. The largest merger in Umpqua's history created the West Coast's largest community bank with some $22 billion in assets and 394 stores across five states. The Sterling branches were rebranded as part of the $1.9 billion deal.

Company Background

Traditionally consumer focused Umpqua Bank established a business banking division in 2011 to court small and mid-sized business clients. That year it pursued deposit growth assembled new lending teams and added new stores in key metropolitan areas like Portland Oregon; Seattle; San Francisco; and California's Silicon Valley.

Umpqua Holdings established a wealth management division in 2009 and launched a trust services group the following year. It provided asset management services through an agreement with independent firm Ferguson Wellman Capital Management.

EXECUTIVES

Evp Wealth Management Umpqua Holdings And Umpqua Bank, Kelly Johnson
Evp Creative Strategies Group Umpqua Bank, Lani Hayward, age 53
Evp And Chief Lending Officer Umpqua Holdings Corp And Umpqua Bank, David F. (Dave) Shotwell, age 61
Evp Cfo And Principal Financial Officer Umpqua Holdings And Umpqua Bank, Ronald L. (Ron) Farnsworth, age 50, $425,000 total compensation
Evp Treasurer And Principal Accounting Officer Umpqua Holdings And Umpqua Bank, Neal T. McLaughlin, age 52
Evp Corporate Communications Umpqua Bank, Eve Callahan, age 46
President Ceo And Director, Cort O'Haver, age 57, $565,000 total compensation
Evp And Chief Auditor Umpqua Bank, Joel Brandenburg, age 57
Evp Enterprise Risk Management Umpqua Holdings Corp And Umpqua Bank, Gary F. Neal, age 65
Evp Associate Relations Umpqua Holdings Corp And Umpqua Bank, Sheri T. Burns, age 52
Evp Cultural Enhancement And Government Relations Umpqua Bank, Marty J. Dickinson, age 50
Evp General Counsel And Corporate Secretary Umpqua Holdings Corp And Umpqua Bank, Andrew H. Ognall, age 48, $300,000 total compensation
Senior Vice President Data Processing, Bo Harrison
Vice President Rewards And Recognition, Sandy Hunt
Vice President Enterprise Risk Manager, Aretina Trepczyk
Assistant Vice President Store Systems Architect, Richard Silvas
Vice President Systems Administrator, Sherri Kittilstved
Assistant Vice President Technical Business Systems Analyst Supervisor, Erika Martin
Assistant Vice President Technical Business Systems Analyst, Nicole Jett
Vice President Commercial Banking Center Manager, Jamie Hudson
Senior Executive Vice President Chief Banking Officer, Torran Nixon
Senior Vice President Director Of Investor Relations, Drew Anderson
Vice President And Relationship Manager, Maria Talavera
Vice President Investments, Tinh Nguyen
Senior Vice President Investments, Keith Morgan
Senior Vice President, Bob Jondall
Vp Cyber Security Operations Center, Joshua Lewis
Vice President Manager, Ken Ries
Chairman, Raymond P. (Ray) Davis, age 71
Vice Chairman, Bryan L. Timm, age 56
Board Member, Maria Pope
Board Member, John Schultz
Auditors: Moss Adams LLP

LOCATIONS

HQ: Umpqua Holdings Corp
One S.W. Columbia Street, Suite 1200, Portland, OR 97258
Phone: 503 727-4100
Web: www.umpquaholdingscorp.com

PRODUCTS/OPERATIONS

2015 Sales

	$ mil.	% of total
Interest		
Interest and fees on loans and leases	869	72
Taxable Interest and dividends investment securities	58	5

Other	2	.
Non-interest		
Mortgage banking	124	9
Service charges on deposit accounts	59	5
Brokerage	18	2
Gain on loan sales net	22	2
BOLI income	8	1
Gain on investment securities net	2	.
Other	46	4
Adjustments	(7.2)	-
Total	**1,205**	**100**

2015 Sales

	$ mil.	% of total
Community Banking	954	79
Home Lending	250	21
Total	**1,205**	**100**

COMPETITORS

Bank of America	KeyCorp
Bank of the West	U.S. Bancorp
Banner Corp	Washington Federal
Cascade Bancorp	Wells Fargo
Columbia Banking	

HISTORICAL FINANCIALS
Company Type: Public

Income Statement
FYE: December 31

	ASSETS ($ mil.)	NET INCOME ($ mil.)	INCOME AS % OF ASSETS	EMPLOYEES
12/19	28,846	354	1.2%	3,943
12/18	26,939	316	1.2%	3,928
12/17	25,741	246	1.0%	4,380
12/16	24,813	232	0.9%	4,295
12/15	23,387	222	1.0%	4,491
Annual Growth	5.4%	12.3%	—	(3.2%)

2019 Year-End Financials

Debt ratio: 4.40%	No. of shares (mil.): 220
Return on equity: 8.46%	Dividends
Cash ($ mil.): 1,362	Yield: 4.7%
Current ratio: —	Payout: 52.8%
Long-term debt ($ mil.): —	Market value ($ mil.): 3,898

	STOCK PRICE ($) FY Close	P/E High/Low		PER SHARE ($) Earnings	Dividends	Book Value
12/19	17.70	12	9	1.60	0.84	19.59
12/18	15.90	17	11	1.43	0.82	18.42
12/17	20.80	20	15	1.11	0.68	18.24
12/16	18.78	18	13	1.05	0.64	17.79
12/15	15.90	19	15	1.01	0.62	17.48
Annual Growth	2.7%	—	—	12.2%	7.9%	2.9%

UNION BANK AND TRUST COMPANY

Union Bank & Trust a subsidiary of financial services holding company Farmers & Merchants Investment operates more than 35 branches throughout Nebraska and in Kansas. As Nebraska's third-largest privately-owned bank it offers traditional deposit and trust services as well as insurance equipment finance and investment management services. Consumer loans account for the largest portion of the bank's portfolio followed by commercial real estate and farmland loans. Union Bank also originates business loans

and residential mortgages. Affiliate company Union Investment Advisors manages the Stratus family of mutual funds. Another Farmers & Merchants unit Nelnet Capital offers brokerage services.

Operations
Union Bank has grown to become one of Nebraska's largest privately-owned banks. As of mid-2013 it boasted bank assets of $2.6 billion and trust assets of $11.8 billion.

Aside from its branches in Nebraska and Kansas Union Bank offers banking products and services through its online mobile and electronic banking services.

Geographic Reach
Union Bank operates mostly in Nebraska but also in Kansas.

Sales and Marketing
The bank primarily serves customers in Lincoln and Omaha as well as the Kansas City metropolitan area.

Strategy
Union Bank continues to expand its footprint in existing markets. The financial institution will have added three new Nebraska branches to its portfolio by 2014.

Company Background
The bank was originally founded in 1917 as Farmer's State Bank. It took on the Union Bank name in 1935 and became Union Bank & Trust in 1959.

EXECUTIVES

Vice President Small Business Banking, Stephanie Dinger
Vice President And Business Development Officer, Michael G Kulas
Vice President Financial Reporting And Controller, Kimberly Keller
Executive Vice President And Commercial Banking Group Executive, David V Ring
Vice President, Raymond Grace
Vice President And Trust Services Advisor, Douglas J Koenig
Assistant Vice President, Nick Nash
Vice President, Malinie Staben

LOCATIONS

HQ: UNION BANK AND TRUST COMPANY
3643 S 48TH ST, LINCOLN, NE 685064390
Phone: 402 323-1235
Web: WWW.UBT.COM

PRODUCTS/OPERATIONS

Selected Services
Business banking
Investment & retirement
Personal banking
Wealth management

Selected Affiliates
InfoVisa
Nelnet Capital LLC
Nelnet Inc.
Union Agency Inc.
Union Equipment Finance LLC
Union Investment Advisors
Union Title Company LLC
Zelle

COMPETITORS

Bank of America	Great Western Bancorp
Bank of the West	JPMorgan Chase
Citigroup	Pinnacle Bancorp

First National of Nebraska	U.S. Bancorp
	Wells Fargo

HISTORICAL FINANCIALS
Company Type: Private

Income Statement
FYE: December 31

	ASSETS ($ mil.)	NET INCOME ($ mil.)	INCOME AS % OF ASSETS	EMPLOYEES
12/18	4,149	68	1.7%	800
12/17	3,836	45	1.2%	—
12/16	3,595	40	1.1%	—
12/15	3,351	32	1.0%	—
Annual Growth	7.4%	28.7%	—	—

Union Pacific Corp

Venerable Union Pacific Railroad (UP) has been chugging down the track since the 19th century. Owned by Union Pacific Corporation (UPC) UP is one of the nation's leading rail carriers operating about 56875 freight cars and about 7690 locomotives. UP transports automobiles chemicals energy and industrial agricultural and other bulk freight over a system of some 32340 rail miles in about 25 states in the western two-thirds of the US. UP owns more than 26000 route miles of its rail network; leases and trackage rights which allow it to use other railroads' tracks account for the rest.

HISTORY

In 1862 the US Congress chartered the Union Pacific Railroad (UP) to build part of the first transcontinental railway. The driving of the Golden Spike at Promontory Utah in 1869 marked the linking of the East and West coasts as UP's rails met those of Central Pacific Railroad (predecessor of Southern Pacific or SP) which had been built east from Sacramento California.

In 1872 the New York Sun revealed the Credit Mobilier scandal: UP officials had pocketed excess profits during the railroad's construction. Debt and lingering effects of the scandal forced UP into bankruptcy in 1893.

A syndicate headed by E. H. Harriman bought UP in 1897. After reacquiring the Oregon branches it lost in the bankruptcy UP gained control of SP (1901) and Chicago & Alton (1904). The Supreme Court ordered UP to sell its SP holdings in 1913 on antitrust grounds. In the 1930s UP diversified into trucking and in the 1970s and 1980s it moved into oil and gas production.

UP bought trucking firm Overnite Transportation in 1986. During the 1980s UP also built up its rail operations acquiring the Missouri Pacific and Western Pacific railroads in 1982 and the Missouri-Kansas-Texas Railroad in 1988. It joined Chicago and North Western (CNW) Railway managers in an investment group led by Blackstone Capital Partners that bought CNW in 1989.

CNW traced its roots to the Galena & Chicago Union Railroad which was founded by Chicago's first mayor W. B. Ogden in 1836 and merged with CNW in 1864. By 1925 the North Western (as it was then known) had tracks throughout the Midwest. In 1995 UP completed its purchase of CNW and made a bid for SP.

SP was founded in 1865 but its history dates to 1861 when four Sacramento merchants founded Central Pacific. By building new track and buying other railroads (including SP in 1868) Central Pacific had expanded throughout California Texas and Oregon by 1887. The two railroads merged in 1885 under the SP name. In 1983 SP was sold to a holding company controlled by Philip Anschutz which in 1995 agreed to sell the company to UP.

UP completed its SP acquisition in 1996 but assimilation of the purchase led to widespread rail traffic jams. UP also sold its remaining interest in Union Pacific Resources an oil company it had spun off the year before. In 1997 UP moved from Bethlehem Pennsylvania to Dallas and joined a consortium led by mining company Grupo México that won a bid to run two major Mexican rail lines. In the US however fatal collisions led to a federal review of UP which found a breakdown in rail safety such as overworked employees and widespread train defects. Meanwhile regulators seeking to resolve UP's massive freight backlog ordered the railroad to open its Houston lines to competitors.

The company decentralized its management into three regions (north south and west) in 1998 to improve traffic flow. It also hired more workers added new trains and realigned routes while selling Skyway Freight Systems its logistics services unit.

In 1999 UP moved its headquarters from Dallas to Omaha Nebraska where Union Pacific Railroad offices already were located. In 2000 it formed Fenix a holding company charged with developing and expanding the company's telecommunications and technology assets. (By 2003 however UP had reabsorbed Fenix and scaled back its support for its remaining technology subsidiaries.)

The company expanded its less-than-truckload operations into the western US in 2001 by buying Motor Cargo Industries. Also that year it completed the integration of Southern Pacific's operations.

UP sold its trucking unit Overnite Corporation (a holding company for Overnite Transportation and Motor Cargo Industries) in an IPO in 2003. (Overnite Corporation was acquired by United Parcel Service in 2005 and renamed UPS Freight the next year.) UP sold its Timera subsidiary (workforce management software) in 2004.

Traffic congestion in the UP system brought on by a shortage of train crews caused some freight from UPS and other customers to be rerouted onto trucks in 2004. The crew shortage was attributed in part to a greater-than-expected number of retirements in 2003. UP accelerated its hiring and training efforts but the company still had to restrict freight volume in an effort to minimize bottlenecks.

In 2006 Union Pacific Railroad reorganized its operating structure going from four regions to three: northern southern and western. Service units of the company's central region were reassigned to the northern and southern regions.

The company added 45 miles of double track to its Sunset Corridor in 2008.

In the midst of the Great Recession UPC's 2009 freight volumes decreased 16% from 2008's numbers. The company was forced to raise its rates by about 6%; it also parked approximately 26% of its locomotives 18% of its freight car stock and furloughed about 3000 employees.

As the nation slowly recovered economically UPC realized a 13% increase in volume in 2010 over 2009 with automotive intermodal and industrial product shipments showing the strongest growth. Even with 2010 fuel prices more than 30% higher than 2009 the company's freight revenues increased 20% in 2010. UPC cited economic improvement across the majority of its market sectors as the reason for the recovery.

In mid-2012 UPC subsidiary PS Technology (PST) acquired the Yard Control Systems division of Ansaldo STS USA. The acquisition boosted PST's enterprise management capabilities by adding rail yard process control and automation technology.

EXECUTIVES

Evp And Cfo, Robert M. Knight, age 63, $575,000 total compensation
Svp And Cio, Lynden L. Tennison
Chairman President And Ceo, Lance M. Fritz, age 57, $1,000,000 total compensation
Evp And Chief Administration Officer, Eric L. Butler, age 59, $485,000 total compensation
Evp And Chief Legal Officer, Rhonda S. Ferguson, age 51, $200,000 total compensation
Evp And Chief Marketing Officer, Elizabeth F. (Beth) Whited, age 55
Evp And Coo, Cameron A. Scott, age 57, $457,500 total compensation
President Shipcarsnow Inc., Peter Decher
Vp; General Manager Chemicals, Kari Kirchhoefer
Assistant Vice President Federal Tax, Bryan Clark
Vice President Energy, Linda Brandl
Assistant Vice President Information Technology, Ashok Fichadia
National Account Manager, Rachael Molinelli
Assistant Vice President Strategic Planning, Grant Janke
Avp Chemicals, Kim Hess
Senior Assistant Vice President Chemicals, Robert G Worrell
Vice President Engineering, Greg Workman
Assistant Vice President Health And Medical Services, Chandra Henley
Secretary Ii, Patty Cuppernull
Board Member, Annie Mccarthy
Auditors: DELOITTE & TOUCHE LLP

LOCATIONS

HQ: Union Pacific Corp
1400 Douglas Street, Omaha, NE 68179
Phone: 402 544-5000
Web: www.up.com

PRODUCTS/OPERATIONS

2017 Sales

	$ mil.	% of total
Freight	19,837	93
Other	1,403	7
Total	**21,240**	**100**

2017 Sales

	$ mil.	% of total
Freight revenues		
Intermodal	3,835	18
Agricultural Products	3,685	17
Chemicals	3,596	17
Industrial Products	4,078	19
Coal	2,645	13
Automotive	1,998	9
Other revenues	1,403	7
Total	**21,240**	**100**

COMPETITORS

American Commercial Lines	Ingram Industries
Burlington Northern Santa Fe	J.B. Hunt
	Kansas City Southern
CSX	Kirby Corporation
Canadian National Railway	Landstar System
	Norfolk Southern
Canadian Pacific Railway	Schneider National
	Werner Enterprises

HISTORICAL FINANCIALS

Company Type: Public

Income Statement				FYE: December 31
	REVENUE ($ mil.)	NET INCOME ($ mil.)	NET PROFIT MARGIN	EMPLOYEES
12/20	19,533	5,349	27.4%	30,960
12/19	21,708	5,919	27.3%	37,483
12/18	22,832	5,966	26.1%	41,967
12/17	21,240	10,712	50.4%	41,992
12/16	19,941	4,233	21.2%	42,919
Annual Growth	(0.5%)	6.0%	—	(7.8%)

2020 Year-End Financials

Debt ratio: 42.84%	No. of shares (mil.): 671
Return on equity: 30.41%	Dividends
Cash ($ mil.): 1,799	Yield: 1.8%
Current ratio: 1.01	Payout: 49.4%
Long-term debt ($ mil.): 25,660	Market value ($ mil.): 139,789

	STOCK PRICE ($) FY Close	P/E High/Low		PER SHARE ($) Earnings	Dividends	Book Value
12/20	208.22	27	14	7.88	3.88	25.26
12/19	180.79	22	16	8.38	3.70	26.19
12/18	138.23	21	16	7.91	3.06	28.17
12/17	134.10	10	8	13.36	2.48	31.83
12/16	103.68	21	14	5.07	2.26	24.43
Annual Growth	19.0%	—	—	11.7%	14.5%	0.8%

United Airlines Holdings Inc

United Airlines Holdings (formerly United Continental Holdings) operates through its primary United Air Lines subsidiary. United Airlines is a leading passenger and cargo airline operating more than 4900 flights a day to more than 360 airports. It serves destinations across five continents from US hubs in Newark Chicago Denver Houston Los Angeles San Francisco Washington DC and the US island of Guam. In addition United is a member of the Star Alliance a marketing and code-sharing group (the largest in the world) that includes several international airlines. In

2019 the company changed its name to United Airlines Holdings Inc.

Operations

United Airlines reports its earnings in three segments: passenger revenue cargo revenue and other operating revenue. Passenger revenue generates more than 90% of sales and other operating revenue (includes loyalty program MileagePlus miles sales) about 5%. Cargo revenue accounts for less than 5% of total sales.

United's mainline operations are managed through a hub and spoke system which allows for the addition of new destinations from numerous cities using a limited number of aircraft. Its regional operations connect the hubs and allow for flights to smaller cities. This service is conducted through regional carriers branded as United Express some of which include Republic Commuter Air ExpressJet GoJet and Sky West.

United is a member of the Star Alliance airline network which provides reciprocal earnings sharing of frequent flyer miles access to airport lounges and code sharing of flight operations (flights marketed under another carrier's brand name). It also has joint business arrangements with Air Canada Lufthansa Air New Zealand and Avianca and Copa Airlines which provide United the ability to integrate schedules and fares with those airlines.

The company runs a loyalty program MileagePlus which offers awards benefits and services to program members. MileagePlus members can earn travel rewards on United United Express and Star Alliance member airlines. It also offers a MileagePlus credit card through Chase Bank.

Geographic Reach

The company serves destinations across North America as well as in Asia Europe the Middle East and Latin America. United leases airport facilities gates hangar sites terminal buildings and other facilities at destination airports. It has major terminal facility leases at its hubs at Newark Liberty International Airport Chicago O'Hare Denver International Houston Bush LAX (Los Angeles) SFO (San Francisco) Washington Dulles and A.B. Won Pat International Airport in Guam.

Domestic flights (the US and Canada) generate more than 60% of United Airline's global revenue Atlantic with more than 15% and Pacific routes with for more than 10% and Latin America about 10%.

United Airlines headquarter is located at Chicago Illinois.

Sales and Marketing

United Airlines fares are sold through its direct sales website?www.united.com the company's mobile applications and through traditional and online travel agencies.

Its advertising expenses are more than $200 million annually.

Financial Performance

United's operating revenue has seen an upward climb in recent years. Sales in 2019 reached $43.3 billion up 5% from $41.3 billion the previous year. Passenger revenue increased $1.9 billion or 5% in 2019 as compared to 2018 primarily due to a 4.0% increase in traffic continuing strong domestic demand improvements in average fares in the Latin and Domestic markets and increases in ancillary fees driven by improved product offerings. Cargo revenue decreased $58 million or 5% in 2019 as compared to 2018 pri-

marily due to an approximately 3% decrease in cargo ton miles and a 2% decline in cargo ton mile yield.

Net income remained relatively at $3 billion in 2019 increased by $887 million compared with 2018. The increase was due to higher revenue by $2 billion with slight increase on their operating expense.

Cash at the end of fiscal 2019 was $2.9 billion an increase of $1.1 billion from the prior year. Cash from operations contributed $6.9 billion to the coffers while investing activities used $4.6 billion mainly for purchases of aircraft and aircraft improvements facility and fleet-related costs and purchases of information technology assets. Financing activities used another $1.3 billion for the company's stock repurchase program.

Strategy

United Airlines have announced several strategic plans in recent years including several revenue-generating initiatives and plans to optimize their revenue such as to add capacity including international expansion and new or increased service to mid-size airports and initiatives and plans to optimize and control their costs. The company also continue to explore opportunities to enhance its segmentation including the introduction of Polaris Basic Economy and United Premium Plus and are implementing many programs and policies to improve the customer experience at all points in air travel. In developing their strategic operating plan they make certain assumptions including but not limited to those related to customer demand competition market consolidation the availability of aircraft and the global economy. Actual economic market and other conditions may be different from their assumptions.

In 2019 United Airlines' capacity growth was lower than planned due to the grounding of Boeing 737 MAX aircraft among other factors which adversely impacted their ability to execute their strategic operating plans. If they do not successfully execute their strategic operating plan or if actual results vary significantly from their assumptions their business operating results and financial condition could be materially and adversely impacted.

Company Background

In 1929 aircraft designer Bill Boeing and engine designer Fred Rentschler of Pratt & Whitney joined forces to form United Aircraft and Transport. Renamed United Air Lines in 1931 the New York-based company offered one of the first coast-to-coast airline services. In 1934 United's manufacturing and transportation divisions split. Former banker Bill Patterson became president of the latter United Air Lines and moved it to the Chicago area. In 1969 UAL Corp. was formed as a holding company.

A subsidiary of UAL Corporation merged with and into Continental in October 2010 with Continental surviving as a wholly-owned subsidiary of UAL. Upon closing of the merger UAL became the parent company of both Continental and United Air Lines and UAL Corporation's name was changed to United Continental Holdings. The transaction created the world's largest airline. In 2013 United Air Lines Inc. was merged into Continental to form one legal entity and Continental's name and brand were changed to United Airlines Inc. In 2019 the company

changed its name to United Airlines Holdings dropping all reference to Continental Airlines.

HISTORY

United Airlines traces its roots back to 1931 after the United Aircraft and Transport Corporation a partnership between Boeing Airplane Company and Pratt & Whitney established an operating division known as United Air Lines then one of the world's largest airlines flying coast-to-coast from New York to San Francisco and Los Angeles.

The company began its cargo service in 1940 flying freight between New York and Chicago and during World War II began service to Alaska and across the Pacific Ocean transporting men and materials over 21 million miles.

By the 1960s United had the highest number of passenger miles of any US airline ahead of American Eastern and TWA. It remained the largest domestic airline in the US for much of the 1970s until the Deregulation Act of 1978 forced the airline to cut back on its operations where it was no longer profitable. The recession in the 1990s followed and the company sold off some of its travel subsidiaries and canceled orders for new aircraft but United survived as one of the "Big Three" airlines along with Delta and American that still dominate US market.In 1997 United expanded into international markets by partnering with other carriers forming the Star Alliance network of airlines.

EXECUTIVES

Svp Finance And Procurement And Treasurer, Gerald (Gerry) Laderman, age 62, $500,000 total compensation

President, J. Scott Kirby, age 52, $301,763 total compensation

Evp And Chief Revenue Officer, Andrew P. Nocella

Ceo, Oscar Munoz, age 62, $1,193,909 total compensation

Evp And Cio, Linda P. Jojo, age 54

Svp Technical Operations, Kris B. Bauer, age 56

Evp And Cfo, Andrew C. Levy, age 50, $243,750 total compensation

Evp And General Counsel, Brett J. Hart, age 50, $715,000 total compensation

Evp And Coo, Gregory L. (Greg) Hart, age 54, $850,000 total compensation

Evp Human Resources And Labor Relations, Michael P. (Mike) Bonds, age 58, $650,000 total compensation

Svp And Chief Customer Officer, Toby J Enqvist

Vp And Corporate Secretary, Jennifer Kraft

Senior Vice President Airport And Catering Operations, Jonathan Roitman

Evp Hr And Labor Relations, Kate Gebo

Senior Vice President United Express, Brad Rich

Vice President United Cargo Sales Asia Pacific, Mirco Renfer

Vice President United Cargo Sales Emeia, Jacques Leijssenaar

Vp And Cfo Of Operations, Tom Doxey

Senior Vice President Flight Operations, Howard W Attarian

Vice President Marketing, Mark Krolick

Vice President Loyalty And Business Development, Praveen Sharma

Senior Vice President Government Affairs, Teri Fariello

Senior Vice President Government Affairs, Terri Fariello

Svp Of Labor Relations, P Douglas Mckeen

Svp Of United Express, Tracy Lee

Vice President Operations Technology, Jason Birnbaum
Svp And Chief Communications Officer, Josh Earnest
Chairman, Robert A. Milton, age 60
Board Member, William Nuti
Auditors: Ernst & Young LLP

LOCATIONS

HQ: United Airlines Holdings Inc
233 South Wacker Drive, Chicago, IL 60606
Phone: 872 825-4000
Web: www.united.com

2018 Sales

	$ mil.	% of total
Domestic (US & Canada)	25,552	62
Atlantic	7,103	17
Pacific	5,188	13
Latin America	3,460	8
Total	**41,303**	**100**

PRODUCTS/OPERATIONS

2018 Sales

	$ mil.	% of total
Passenger Revenue	37,706	91
Cargo Revenue	1,237	3
Other Operating Revenue	2,360	6
Total	**41,303**	**100**

COMPETITORS

Air France-KLM	Japan Airlines
AirTran Airways	JetBlue
Alaska Air	Qantas
Alitalia	SkyWest
American Airlines	Southwest Airlines
Group	UPS
Delta Air Lines	Virgin Atlantic
FedEx	Airways
Frontier Airlines	

HISTORICAL FINANCIALS

Company Type: Public

Income Statement
FYE: December 31

	REVENUE ($ mil.)	NET INCOME ($ mil.)	NET PROFIT MARGIN	EMPLOYEES
12/19	43,259	3,009	7.0%	96,000
12/18	41,303	2,129	5.2%	92,000
12/17	37,736	2,131	5.6%	89,800
12/16	36,556	2,263	6.2%	88,000
12/15	37,864	7,340	19.4%	84,000
Annual Growth	**3.4%**	**(20.0%)**	**—**	**3.4%**

2019 Year-End Financials

Debt ratio: 28.17%	No. of shares (mil.): 251
Return on equity: 27.96%	Dividends
Cash ($ mil.): 4,944	Yield: —
Current ratio: 0.55	Payout: —
Long-term debt ($ mil.): 13,365	Market value ($ mil.): 22,130

	STOCK PRICE ($) FY Close	P/E High/Low		PER SHARE ($) Earnings	Dividends	Book Value
12/19	88.09	8	7	11.58	0.00	45.90
12/18	83.73	13	8	7.70	0.00	37.03
12/17	67.40	12	8	7.02	0.00	30.69
12/16	72.88	11	6	6.85	0.00	27.52
12/15	57.30	4	3	19.47	0.00	24.59
Annual Growth	**11.4%**	—	—	**(12.2%)**	—	**16.9%**

United Bankshares Inc

United Bankshares (no relation to Ohio's United Bancshares) keeps it together as the holding company for two subsidiaries doing business as United Bank (WV) and United Bank (VA). Combined the banks boast some $12 billion in assets and operate roughly 130 branches that serve West Virginia Virginia and Washington DC as well as nearby portions of Maryland Pennsylvania and Ohio. The branches offer traditional deposit trust and lending services with a focus on residential mortgages and commercial loans. United Bankshares also owns United Brokerage Services which provides investments asset management and financial planning in addition to brokerage services.

Operations

The company's loan portfolio is made up of commercial and construction commercial and residential real estate and consumer loans (including credit card and home equity loans).

United Bankshares generated 75% of its total revenue from interest and fees on loans in 2014 plus an additional 7% from interest and dividends on its investment securities. The company generated about 9% of its total revenue from deposit services fees and another 4% from trust and brokerage services fees.

Geographic Reach

United Bankshares boasts some 130 full-service branches including more than 55 across the state of West Virginia nearly 70 in the Shenendoah Valley region of Virginia and the Northern Virginia Maryland and Washington DC metro area and a handful of branches split between southwestern Pennsylvania and southeastern Ohio.

Sales and Marketing

The company spent $4.76 million on advertising in 2014 up from $3.78 million and $4.27 million spent in 2013 and 2012 respectively.

Financial Performance

United Bankshares' revenues and profits have trended higher over the past few years thanks to growth in its loan business from acquisitions increased trust and brokerage services fee income and declining interest expense on deposits amidst the low-interest environment.

The company's revenue jumped by nearly 34% to a record $499.50 million in 2014 mostly as its interest income spiked by 37% after its Virginia Commerce acquisition added new interest-earning assets and increased the average yields on its loans investments and security assets. United Bankshare's non-interest income also swelled by 22% thanks to higher income from fees from trust and brokerage services bankcard fees and merchant discounts and net gains on investment securities.

Higher revenue in 2014 boosted the company's profits by 52% to a record $129.89 million while the company's operating cash grew by 2% thanks to higher cash earnings.

Strategy

United Bankshares has historically expanded through small bank and branch acquisitions closing nearly 30 bank purchases in the past quarter-century. Its growth strategy has mainly been focused in on the Washington DC/suburban

Maryland/northern Virginia market though its also expanded into Pennsylvania in recent years as well. In 2014 for example the company extended its reach into Washington DC while boosting its loan business by $2 billion after completing its largest-ever acquisition of Virginia Commerce Bancorp.

In 2016 the company agreed to buy Cardinal Financial which has some $4.2 billion in assets and operates 30 branches in Virginia Maryland and Washington DC.

Mergers and Acquisitions

In January 2014 United Bankshares acquired Arlington-based Virginia Commerce Bancorp for a total cost of $585.53 million. The deal expanded United's reach into the Washington DC metropolitan area and added $2.07 billion in new loan business and $2.02 billion in deposits.

Company Background

The 2011 acquisition of West Virginia-based Centra Financial Holdings gave United Bankshares its first branches in Pennsylvania and entry into the Pittsburgh market.

EXECUTIVES

Evp The Company And United Bank And Wv, James B. Hayhurst, age 74, $225,000 total compensation
President, Richard M. Adams, age 52, $328,846 total compensation
Coo, James J. Consagra, age 60, $334,462 total compensation
Evp And Coo United Bank (va), Craige L. Smith, age 68, $243,750 total compensation
Evp And Cfo, W. Mark Tatterson, age 45
Evp, Darren K. Williams
Assistant Vice President Information Technology Audit Manager, Jason Moore
Senior Vice President, Dale Homan
Vice President Internal Audit Manager, Steve Hizak
Assistant Vice President Corporate Security Officer, Rachel Wilson
Assistant Vice President And C, Erica Fowler
Executive Vice President, Mark Null Tatterson
Vp Financial Advisor, Cameron Stewart
Assistant Vp Branch Administration, Ricardo Carmenates
Board Member, Peter Converse
Auditors: Ernst & Young LLP

LOCATIONS

HQ: United Bankshares Inc
300 United Center, 500 Virginia Street, East, Charleston, WV 25301
Phone: 304 424-8716
Web: www.ubsi-inc.com

PRODUCTS/OPERATIONS

2014 Sales

	$ mil.	% of total
Interest		
Loans including fees	383	75
Interest and dividends on securities	33	7
Other	0	-
Noninterest		
Fees from deposit services	42	9
Fees from trust & brokerage services	18	4
Other	28	5
Adjustment (losses)	(8.4)	-
Total	**499**	**100**

COMPETITORS

BB&T	JPMorgan Chase
Bank of America	M&T Bank
Burke & Herbert Bank	PNC Financial

Cardinal Financial
City Holding
Fifth Third
Fulton Financial
Huntington Bancshares

SunTrust
United Bancorp
Virginia Commerce
Bancorp
WesBanco

HISTORICAL FINANCIALS

Company Type: Public

Income Statement

FYE: December 31

	ASSETS ($ mil.)	NET INCOME ($ mil.)	INCOME AS % OF ASSETS	EMPLOYEES
12/19	19,662	260	1.3%	2,204
12/18	19,250	256	1.3%	2,230
12/17	19,058	150	0.8%	2,381
12/16	14,508	147	1.0%	1,701
12/15	12,577	137	1.1%	1,701
Annual Growth	11.8%	17.2%	—	6.7%

2019 Year-End Financials

Debt ratio: 1.20%
Return on equity: 7.86%
Cash ($ mil.): 836
Current ratio: —
Long-term debt ($ mil.): —

No. of shares (mil.): 101
Dividends
Yield: 3.5%
Payout: 53.7%
Market value ($ mil.): 3,926

	STOCK PRICE ($) FY Close	P/E High/Low	PER SHARE ($) Earnings	Dividends	Book Value
12/19	38.66	16 12	2.55	1.37	33.12
12/18	31.11	16 12	2.45	1.36	31.78
12/17	34.75	30 21	1.54	1.33	30.85
12/16	46.25	25 16	1.99	1.32	27.59
12/15	36.99	22 17	1.98	1.29	24.61
Annual Growth	1.1%	— —	6.5%	1.5%	7.7%

United Community Banks Inc (Blairsville, GA)

United Community Banks is the holding company for United Community Bank (UCB). UCB provides consumer and business banking products and services through nearly 150 branches across Georgia North Carolina Tennessee and South Carolina. Commercial loans including construction loans and mortgages account for the largest portion of UCB's loan portfolio (more than 50%); residential mortgages make up 30%. The company which boasts roughly $10 billion in assets also has a mortgage lending division and provides insurance through its United Community Insurance Services subsidiary (aka United Community Advisory Services).

Operations

The bank's retail mortgage lending division United Community Mortgage Services (UCMS) sells and services mortgages for Fannie Mae and Freddie Mac and provides fixed and adjustable-rate home mortgages. It also offers retail brokerage services through an affiliation with a third-party broker/dealer.

About 65% of UCB's total revenue came from loan interest (including fees) in 2014 while another 16% came from taxable investments. The rest of its revenue came from service charges and fees (10%) mortgage loan fees (2%) and brokerage fees (2%) among other sources.

Geographic Reach

UCB's nearly 105 branches are located in Georgia (in the north the Atlanta-Sandy Springs-Roswell metro area Gainsville metro area and coastal areas); western North Carolina; eastern and central Tennessee; and South Carolina (in the Greenville-Anderson-Mauldin metro area).

Sales and Marketing

The bank provides community banking services for individuals small businesses and corporations.

Financial Performance

UCB has struggled to consistently grow its revenues in recent years due to shrinking interest margins on loans amidst the low-interest environment. Its profits however have been rising thanks to declining loan loss provisions as its loan portfolio's credit quality has improved with higher property valuations in the strengthened economy.

The bank's revenue inched higher by 1% to $304 million in 2014 thanks to an increase in interest income stemming from strategic business growth initiatives designed to add new business lines and expand into new markets as well as balance sheet management and restructuring actions taken in the second quarter of the year.

Despite higher revenue in 2014 UCB's net income dove 75% to $67.6 million mostly because in 2013 it had received a non-recurring income tax benefit of $238 million stemming from reversal of a deferred tax valuation allowance. Not counting this item however the bank's profit before taxes nearly tripled during the year. UCB's operating cash levels dropped by 47% to $101.9 million in 2014 due to lower cash earnings.

Strategy

UCB has been concentrating on growing its small business lending business in recent years. In 2014 it made "significant investments" in its SBA business after acquiring Business Carolina which specialized in SBA and USDA lending.

It also continues to pursue bank acquisitions to expand its reach in its existing core markets and boost its loan and deposit business. Its acquisitions in 2015 and 2014 alone have added over $1 billion in new loan business and $1.3 billion in new deposits.

Mergers and Acquisitions

In 2016 United Community Banks expanded into key markets in coastal South Carolina after buying Mt. Pleasant-based Tidelands and its seven Tidelands Bank branches in the Charleston Myrtle Beach and Hilton Head areas.

In 2015 UCB bought Tennessee-based MoneyTree Corporation and its 10 First National Bank branches in east Tennessee. The deal added $425 million in assets $354 million in deposits and $253 million in new loan business to UCB's books.

In 2014 the company purchased Palmetto Bancshares and its Palmetto Bank branches expanding its footprint into "major" southeastern metro markets in Greenville and the Upstate South Carolina area. The deal also added $1.2 billion in assets $832 million in loans and $967 million in deposits.

Also in 2014 UCB purchased Columbia-based Business Carolina a commercial lender that specialized in SBA and USDA loans for $31.3 million in cash. The deal included $25 million in loans $6 million in other assets and substantially all of the company's employees.

EXECUTIVES

President Of Specialized Lending, Richard W. Bradshaw, age 58
Chairman And Ceo, Jimmy C. Tallent, age 67, $750,000 total compensation
President Community Banking, William M. (Bill) Gilbert, age 67, $308,334 total compensation
President And Director United Community Banks Inc. And President Ceo And Director United Community Bank, H. Lynn Harton, age 58, $575,000 total compensation
Evp General Counsel And Chief Risk Officer, Bradley J. (Brad) Miller, age 49
Evp And Chief Credit Officer, Robert A. (Rob) Edwards, age 55, $305,000 total compensation
Evp And Cfo United Community Banks Inc. And United Community Bank, Jefferson L. Harralson
Senior Vice President, Robert Head
Vice President Mortgage Origination, Lisa Mericle
Vice President, Casey Brogdon
Senior Vice President Commercial Lending, Don Fowler
Senior Vice President Commercial Banking, Jay Roper
Executive Vice President, Rick Rowland
Assistant Vice President Branch Manager, Brandon Grimsley
Vice President, Ronney Dixon
Avp Mortgage Loan Officer, Tabitha Helms
Senior Vice President, David Shelnutt
Assistant Vice President Incentive Marketing Manager, Diana White
Senior Vice President, Ron Altman
Vice President, David Henry
Senior Vice President, Rebecca Munteanu
Assistant Vice President, Wendy Cawthon
Chief Accounting Officer Senior Vice President And Controller, Alan Kumler
Vice President Mortgage Banker, Angie Abston
Vice President, Sandy Worley
Senior Vice President Commercial Lending, Sam Churchill
Senior Vice President, Donald Harris
Senior Vice President Corporate Services Support, Jeanette Garrett
Vice President, Keith Brady
Vp Marketing, Greg Stephens
Avp Mortgage Loan Originator, Sharon Eisenbeil
Assistant Vice President Controller, Jason Boskey
Vice President, Jane Callihan
Assistant Vice President Business Banking Underwriting, Eric Rivenbark
Vice President, Nick Harty
Senior Vice President Commercial Banking, Ben Walker
Senior Vice President, Phil Beaudette
Assistant Vice President, Rob Andrews
Executive Vice President, Wayne Lowrey
Vice President Commercial Banking, Michael Emigh
Senior Vice President Builder Finance, Scott Ernest
Vice President, Darryl Meadows
Vice President, Tyler White
Vp Lending, Julie Plattner
Executive Vice President Sales Marketing, Eddie Wayne
Vice President, Anne Wade
Vice President And Private Banker, Terra Winter
Senior Vice President Commercial Lending, Fred Faulkner
Vice President Relationship Manager, Jeff Tanner
Senior Vice President, Jessie Marolis
Vice President Branch Manager, Wendy Martin

Senior Vice President Secondary Marketing, Jim Mcevoy

Vice President Commercial Lender, Donna Clark

Vice President, David Brindley

Senior Vice President, Christie Manning

Vice President Craft Beverage Lending, Ken Jernigan

Vice President Treasury Management, Victor Cordone

Senior Vice President United Community Bank, Dennis McBride

Senior Vice President, Sheila Stolorena

Vice President, David Ball

Vice President Commercial Relationship Manager, Beth Lemke

Senior Vice President And Corporate Controller, Alan H Kumler

Vice President Branch Manager, Liz Bowen

Senior Vice President, Will Ferguson

Vice President Commercial Relationship Manager, William Marcus

Vice President Commercial Relationship Manager, Laura Hodge

Vice President Underwriting, Linda Durden

Assistant Vice President Branch Manager, Michelle Galarza

Assistant Vice President And Mortgage Processing Manager, Nalann Moss

Vice President, Frank Scott

Vice President Customer Contact Center Team Manager Sc, Jeanie Roberts

Vice President, Kirby Butler

Vice President And Mortgage Origination Support Manager, Darin Scheidly

Senior Vice President Commercial Relationship Manager, Lynn Kornita

Market Vice President Business Development, Ryan Clayton

Vice President Relationship Management, Nate Rohler

Senior Vice President, Nancy Halwig

Vice President, Rick Sayward

Vice President Commercial Relationship Manager, Matt Babb

Vice President Indirect Lending Department, Scott Tollison

Assistant Treasurer, Mitchell Bleske

Board Member, Kenneth Daniels

Board Member, David Wilkins

Board Member, David Shaver

Secretary, Ashley Matthews

Auditors: PricewaterhouseCoopers LLP

LOCATIONS

HQ: United Community Banks Inc (Blairsville, GA)
125 Highway 515 East, Blairsville, GA 30512
Phone: 706 781-2265
Web: www.ucbi.com

PRODUCTS/OPERATIONS

2011 Sales

	$ mil.	% of total
Interest		
Loans including fees	239	69
Taxable investment securities	55	16
Other	3	1
Noninterest		
Service charges & fees	29	8
Mortgage loans & related fees	5	2
Brokerage fees	3	1
Net securities gains	0	-
Other	12	3
Adjustment	(0.7)	-
Total	**347**	**100**

COMPETITORS

Atlantic Coast Financial	Peoples Bancorp (NC)
BB&T	Regions Financial
	Southeastern Bank

Bank of America
Bank of Oak Ridge
First Citizens BancShares
Georgia Bancshares
Georgia-Carolina Bancshares

Financial
Southeastern Banking
SunTrust
Synovus
WGNB

HISTORICAL FINANCIALS

Company Type: Public

Income Statement				FYE: December 31
	ASSETS ($ mil.)	NET INCOME ($ mil.)	INCOME AS % OF ASSETS	EMPLOYEES
12/19	12,916	185	1.4%	2,309
12/18	12,573	166	1.3%	2,312
12/17	11,915	67	0.6%	2,137
12/16	10,708	100	0.9%	1,916
12/15	9,626	71	0.7%	1,883
Annual Growth	**7.6%**	**26.9%**	**—**	**5.2%**

2019 Year-End Financials

Debt ratio: 1.65%	No. of shares (mil.): 79
Return on equity: 12.01%	Dividends
Cash ($ mil.): 515	Yield: 2.2%
Current ratio: —	Payout: 29.4%
Long-term debt ($ mil.): —	Market value ($ mil.): 2,440

	STOCK PRICE ($) FY Close	P/E High/Low	PER SHARE ($) Earnings	Dividends	Book Value
12/19	30.88	14 9	2.31	0.68	20.70
12/18	21.46	16 10	2.07	0.58	18.40
12/17	28.14	33 27	0.92	0.38	16.80
12/16	29.62	21 11	1.40	0.30	15.17
12/15	19.49	20 15	1.09	0.22	14.24
Annual Growth	**12.2%**	**— —**	**20.7%**	**32.6%**	**9.8%**

United Fire Group, Inc.

The United Fire Group (UFG) companies join together to offer a range of property/casualty products. The group operates through its United Fire & Casualty subsidiary which in turn holds entities that carry a variety of property/casualty offerings including fidelity and surety bonds and fire auto employee liability homeowners and workers' compensation lines. Some 1200 independent agencies in around 45 states sell its property/casualty products to businesses and individuals.

Operations

UFG's property/casualty offerings accounted for more than 90% of its annual insurance premiums with a majority of those policies being written to commercial group customers. The company also offers certain personal policies to individual customers.

Geographic Reach

UFG markets its products from its headquarters in Iowa and from five regional offices in Arizona California Colorado New Jersey and Texas. Its three largest geographic concentration is Texas California and Iowa with a total of more than 35%.

Sales and Marketing

To increase policy placement in its existing markets UFG offers profit-sharing and commission programs to its independent agents. It also

seeks to provide modern technological tools to best serve both its agents and its policyholders.

The company is represented by some 1200-independent property/casualty agencies.

Financial Performance

UFG's revenue has been growing year-over-year. Net income has been more volatile rising and falling from year to year.

In 2019 revenue increased 12% to $1.2 billion . Direct premiums written increased $31.7 million in 2019 due to rate increases premium audits and endorsements assumed premiums written also increased $11.1 million due to an increase in client premium growth and additional program placements.

Net income declined 46% to $14.8 million in 2019 from $27.7 million in 2018. Despite the increase in revenue the company's benefits losses and expenses also increased that year. In addition the company recorded a $27.3 million gain on sale of discontinued operations for the prior year

.

UFG ended 2019 with $120.7 million in net cash some $56.3 million more than it had at the end of 2018. Operating activities provided $93.8 million while investing activities provided another $4.5 million from maturities. Financing activities used $42 million for cash dividends and repurchases of common stock .

Strategy

In early 2020 UFG entered into a renewal rights agreement for its personal lines business providing its independent insurance agents with the opportunity to transfer their personal lines policies to Nationwide Mutual Insurance Company beginning in the third quarter of 2020. UFG's entry into a renewal rights agreement with Nationwide was completed as part of its long-term strategic planning allowing the company to focus on the success of its core commercial lines business which currently represents 94% of its business mix. UFG's decision to exit the personal lines market was purely a strategic one was it concentrates its efforts on the growth and profitability of its core commercial lines business including commercial insurance excess and surplus lines insurance and surety bonds.

Company Background

UFG originally known as United Casualty Company were established in 1946 in Cedar Rapids Iowa by Scott McIntyre Sr.

EXECUTIVES

Vp General Counsel And Secretary, Neal R. Scharmer, age 64, $250,000 total compensation

Coo, Michael T. Wilkins, age 57, $388,600 total compensation

Vp And Chief Investment Officer, Barrie W. Ernst, age 66, $305,000 total compensation

President And Ceo, Randy A. Ramlo, age 59, $595,000 total compensation

Vp And Chief Claims Officer, David E. Conner, age 62

Cfo, Dawn M. Jaffray, age 55

Vp Information Services, Scott A. Minkel, age 59

Vp Corporate Marketing, Colleen R. Sova, age 67

Assistant Vice President Midwest Regional Office, Corey J. Ruehle

Vp And Coo United Life Insurance Company, Michael J. Sheeley

Cto, Brian Frese

Assistant Vice President And Midwest Regional Claims Manager, Dean Walstrom

Assistant Vice President Personal Lines, Victoria Hefel
Vice President Of Accounting, Sue Haupert
Asst. Vice Presdient And Senior Portfolio Manager, Bob Cataldo
Vice President, Douglas Penn
Assistant Vice President And Great Lakes Reg. Marketing Manager, Patrick P Kane
Vice President, Kathy Booher
Assistant Vice President And Marketing Manager, Miguel Diaz
Vice President, Joseph Johnson
Vice President Surety, Dennis Richmann
Vice Chairman, John A. Rife, age 78
Chairman, Jack B. Evans, age 72
Auditors: Ernst & Young LLP

LOCATIONS

HQ: United Fire Group, Inc.
118 Second Avenue SE, Cedar Rapids, IA 52401
Phone: 319 399-5700
Web: www.ufginsurance.com

PRODUCTS/OPERATIONS

2017 Sales

	$ mil.	% of total
Net premiums earned	997	95
Net investment income	51	5
Net realized investment gains	4	.
Total	**1,052**	**100**

Selected Subsidiaries

United Fire & Casualty Company
Addison Insurance Company
American Indemnity Financial Corporation
Texas General Indemnity Company
Lafayette Insurance Company
Mercer Insurance Group Inc.
Financial Pacific Insurance Company
Mercer Insurance Company
Franklin Insurance Company
Mercer Insurance Company of New Jersey Inc.
United Fire & Indemnity Company
United Fire Lloyds

COMPETITORS

AIG	John Hancock Financial
Allstate	Services
American Family	Liberty Mutual
Insurance	Progressive
American Financial	Corporation
Group	Prudential
CNA Surety	State Farm
Farmers Group	The Hartford
GEICO	Travelers Companies
Hanover Insurance	

HISTORICAL FINANCIALS

Company Type: Public

Income Statement — FYE: December 31

	ASSETS ($ mil.)	NET INCOME ($ mil.)	INCOME AS % OF ASSETS	EMPLOYEES
12/19	3,013	14	0.5%	1,185
12/18	2,816	27	1.0%	1,183
12/17	4,183	51	1.2%	1,180
12/16	4,054	49	1.2%	1,112
12/15	3,890	89	2.3%	1,070
Annual Growth	**(6.2%)**	**(36.1%)**	**—**	**2.6%**

2019 Year-End Financials

Debt ratio: —
Return on equity: 1.65%
Cash ($ mil.): 120
Current ratio: —
Long-term debt ($ mil.): —
No. of shares (mil.): 25
Dividends
Yield: 2.9%
Payout: 393.9%
Market value ($ mil.): 1,094

STOCK PRICE ($) / P/E / PER SHARE ($)

	FY Close	High/Low	Earnings	Dividends	Book Value
12/19	43.73	94 71	0.58	1.30	36.40
12/18	55.45	55 37	1.08	4.21	35.40
12/17	45.58	24 19	1.99	1.09	39.06
12/16	49.17	26 18	1.93	0.97	37.04
12/15	38.31	11 8	3.53	0.86	34.94
Annual Growth	**3.4%**	**— —**	**(36.3%)**	**10.9%**	**1.0%**

United Insurance Holdings Corp

United Insurance Holdings insures homeowners in the Sunshine State throughout the seasons even hurricane season. The company is a holding company primarily engaged in the residential personal and commercial property and casualty insurance business in the United States. It distributes its products through approximately 11500 independent agents. United Insurance was founded in 1999 then underwent a reverse merger in 2008 when it bought the OTC-listed FMG Acquisition Corp. for $95 million ($25 million in cash and 8.75 million shares of stock.) The newly merged company has listed on the NASDAQ exchange.

EXECUTIVES

Chief Underwriting Officer, Paul DiFrancesco
Ceo, John L. Forney, $800,000 total compensation
Cfo, B. Bradford Martz, $300,000 total compensation
Cio, Andrew D. (Andy) Swenson, $210,000 total compensation
General Counsel And Chief Legal Officer, Kimberly Salmon
Board Member, Kern Davis
Chairman, Gregory C. Branch
Board Member, Alec Poitevint
Board Member, Patrick Maroney
Auditors: DELOITTE & TOUCHE LLP

LOCATIONS

HQ: United Insurance Holdings Corp
800 2nd Avenue S, St. Petersburg, FL 33701
Phone: 727 895-7737
Web: www.upcinsurance.com

PRODUCTS/OPERATIONS

2015 Sales

	$ mil.	% of total
Net premiums earned	336	94
Investment income	9	3
Net realized gains	0	.
Other revenue	11	3
Total	**357**	**100**

COMPETITORS

AAA Auto Club South	Federated National
Allstate	Holding
American National	HCI Group
Insurance	Liberty Mutual
Bankers Financial	State Farm
Citizens Property	Universal Insurance
Insurance	Holdings

HISTORICAL FINANCIALS

Company Type: Public

Income Statement — FYE: December 31

	ASSETS ($ mil.)	NET INCOME ($ mil.)	INCOME AS % OF ASSETS	EMPLOYEES
12/19	2,467	(29)	—	363
12/18	2,321	0	0.0%	293
12/17	2,059	10	0.5%	210
12/16	999	5	0.6%	167
12/15	740	27	3.7%	120
Annual Growth	**35.1%**	**—**	**—**	**31.9%**

2019 Year-End Financials

Debt ratio: 6.44%
Return on equity: (-5.84%)
Cash ($ mil.): 215
Current ratio: —
Long-term debt ($ mil.): —
No. of shares (mil.): 43
Dividends
Yield: 1.9%
Payout: —
Market value ($ mil.): 543

STOCK PRICE ($) / P/E / PER SHARE ($)

	FY Close	High/Low	Earnings	Dividends	Book Value
12/19	12.61	— —	(0.70)	0.24	11.69
12/18	16.62	2238 1580	0.01	0.24	12.10
12/17	17.25	65 49	0.27	0.24	12.56
12/16	15.14	73 40	0.26	0.23	11.15
12/15	17.10	22 10	1.28	0.20	11.11
Annual Growth	**(7.3%)**	**— —**	**—**	**4.7%**	**1.3%**

United Natural Foods Inc.

United Natural Foods Inc. (UNFI) is one of the top wholesale distributors of natural organic and specialty foods in the US and Canada. It maintains around 55 distribution centers that supply more than 275000 items to 30000 unique customer locations including independently-owned retailers supernatural chain Whole Foods (its #1 customer) and conventional supermarkets. The company offers groceries supplements produce frozen foods and ethnic as well as foodservice products and personal care items. UNFI also produces roasted nuts dried fruits and other snack items through subsidiary Woodstock Farms.

Operations

UNFI's operations are comprised of two principal divisions: Wholesale and Retail; and also includes a manufacturing division and a branded product line division.

The company's wholesale division generates more than 90% of its sales and operates through four US regions: Atlantic South Central and Pacific; each of which is led by separate region presidents responsible for product and service strategy execution and financial results; and Canada Wholesale which is operated separately from the US Wholesale business. Product and service categories include grocery fresh wellness private brands e-commerce food service and multi-cultural.

Retail Division (about 10% of sales) provides an extensive grocery offering and depending on size a variety of additional products including general merchandise home health and beauty care and pharmacy. It offers national and regional brands as well as the company's own private label products.

In addition UNFI's offers six main product categories: grocery and general merchandise; produce; perishables and frozen foods; nutritional supplements and sports nutrition; bulk and food-service products; and personal care items. The company's private-label products include: Culinary Circle and Wild Harvest and Field Day. Its core brands are Essential Everyday Equaline Springfield and category-specific brands Arctic Shores Seafood Company Baby Basics Stone Ridge Creamery and Super Chill as well as the value brand Shoppers Value.

Geographic Reach

Rhode Island-based UNFI maintains about 55 distribution centers in US and Canada. It also has smaller administrative offices across the US including an executive office in Eden Prairie Minnesota.

The company serves customers in the US Canada and other countries but the US and Canada accounts for all of the company's revenue.

Sales and Marketing

UNFI is heavily reliant on Amazon subsidiary Whole Foods Market its largest wholesale customer representing about 20% of net sales. The company divides its sales in five customer channels: Chains (approximately 40% of total sales) which consists of customer accounts that typically have more than 10 operating stores and exclude stores; Independent retailers (some 25%) which include smaller size accounts and include single store and multiple store locations; Super-natural (about 20%) which consists of chain accounts that are national in scope and carry primarily natural products and currently consists solely of Whole Foods Market; Retail (almost 10%) which includes the company's Retail segment including the Cub Foods business and the majority of the remaining Shoppers locations; and Other (nearly 10%) which includes international customers outside of Canada foodservice e-commerce conventional military business and other sales. Wholesale customers include Kroger Publix and Wegman's among others. In addition the company's international net sales primarily reflect UNFI Canada Inc.

Financial Performance

UNFI has shown exponential revenue growth since 2016 recording a 213% increase from 2016 to 2020. The same trend was seen in net income recording a 2014% increase from 2016 to 2020.

Revenue increased from $22.3 billion in 2019 to $26.5 billion in 2020. Its wholesale segment which comprised 96% of the company's 2020 revenue increased by 18% from $21.5 billion in 2019.

Net income was $3.9 billion 21% higher than in the previous year.

Cash and cash equivalents at the end of the year increased 6% to $47.0 million compared to the previous year. Cash provided by operating activities was $456.5 million. Investing activities used $1.5 million primarily for capital expenditures while financing activities used $453.1 million primarily for repayments of borrowings under revolving credit line.

Strategy

UNFI has increased its sales to existing and new customers through the acquisition of natural and specialty products distributors and most recently the previously largest publicly traded conventional distributor Supervalu; the continued growth of the natural and organic products industry in general; increased market share as a result of its high quality service and broader product selection including specialty products; the expansion of its existing distribution centers; the construction of new distribution centers; and the introduction of new products and the development of its own line of natural organic and conventional branded products.

The company's strategic plan also includes increasing the type of products and services it provides to its customers including perishable products and conventional produce to "build out the store" and cover center store as well as perimeter offerings and private brands products and providing services to additional customers including marketing and e-commerce solutions.

A primary component of the synergy aspect of the integration is workstream simplification. Dubbed Thrive2 the initiative is focused on an efficient standardized operating model that provides better experiences for customers suppliers and employees.

Company Background

Rhode Island retailer Norman Cloutier founded Cornucopia Natural Foods in 1978 and soon focused on distribution. During the 1980s Cornucopia grew by acquiring other natural foods distributors. It bought suppliers Natural Food Systems (seafood) and BGS Distributing (vitamins) in 1987 and 1990 respectively. Cornucopia expanded into the Southeast in 1991 when it opened a distribution center in Georgia.

In 1996 Cornucopia merged with the leading natural foods distributor in the western US Sacramento-based Mountain People's and became United Natural Foods; it went public later that year.

The company continued to grow organically and through acquisitions over the decades. In 2018 it made the $2.3 billion purchase of rival SUPERVALU which more than doubled its size.

HISTORY

Rhode Island retailer Norman Cloutier founded Cornucopia Natural Foods in 1978 and soon focused on distribution. During the 1980s Cornucopia grew by acquiring other natural foods distributors. It bought suppliers Natural Food Systems (seafood) and BGS Distributing (vitamins) in 1987 and 1990 respectively. Cornucopia expanded into the Southeast in 1991 when it opened a distribution center in Georgia.

Reviving its interest in retailing Cornucopia formed Natural Retail Group in 1993 to buy and run natural foods stores. During the next two years it acquired several retailers. The company expanded its distribution operations in the West in 1995 adding Denver-based Rainbow Distributors.

In 1996 Cornucopia merged with the leading natural foods distributor in the western US Sacramento-based Mountain People's which Michael Funk had founded 20 years earlier. The combined company became United Natural Foods with Cloutier as chairman and CEO and

Funk as president and vice chairman; it went public later that year.

United Natural Foods became the largest natural foods distributor when it bought New Hampshire-based Stow Mills in 1997. The next year it added Hershey Imports an importer and processor of nuts seeds and snacks and Albert's a distributor of organic produce. With the purchase of Mother Earth Markets in 1998 the company's retailing operations had grown to 16 stores but by mid-1999 it had sold four stores. That year United Natural Foods' East Coast consolidation problems became so profound that top customer Whole Foods announced it was finding backup distribution sources.

Funk replaced Cloutier as CEO and the company handed the chairman's post to board member Thomas Simone in 1999. In 2000 after the resignation of Cloutier from the board of directors United Natural Foods adopted a poison-pill plan to block potential takeovers. The company leased a distribution center in the Los Angeles area in 2001 to increase market share in the Southwest. It also acquired Florida's Palm Harbor Natural Foods.

In mid-2002 United Natural Foods lost one of its two largest customers — Wild Oats Markets— when that company defected to rival specialty foods distributor Tree of Life. However United Natural Foods soon won that business back. In October the company completed the acquisition of privately held Blooming Prairie Cooperative for approximately $31 million. In late 2002 the company merged with Northeast Cooperatives a natural foods distributor in the Midwest and Northeast.

That year United Natural Foods discontinued the management sales and support operations at its Hershey Imports subsidiary but continued to manufacture and distribute products from the Edison New Jersey plant.

In 2004 the company renewed its distribution agreement with Wild Oats with a five-year pact. United Natural Foods later announced a new three-year distribution agreement with Whole Foods which it renewed in 2006. Whole Foods later acquired Wild Oats in 2007. That year United Natural Foods acquired ethnic and specialty food distributor Millbrook Distribution Services for about $85 million.

EXECUTIVES

LOCATIONS

HQ: United Natural Foods Inc.
313 Iron Horse Way, Providence, RI 02908
Phone: 401 528-8634
Web: www.unfi.com

PRODUCTS/OPERATIONS

2019 Sales

	$ mil.	% of total
Supermarkets	12,505	58
Supernatural	4,393	21
Independents	3,179	15
Other	1,310	6
Total	**21,387**	**100**

2019 Sales

	$ mil.	% of total
Wholesale	21,325	99
Other	228	1
Adjustments	(166)	-
Total	**21,387**	**100**

COMPETITORS

Associated Wholesale Grocers	McLane
C&S Wholesale	Performance Food Group
DPI Specialty Foods	SpartanNash
KeHE Distributors	Sysco
	US Foods

HISTORICAL FINANCIALS

Company Type: Public

Income Statement

FYE: August 1

	REVENUE ($ mil.)	NET INCOME ($ mil.)	NET PROFIT MARGIN	EMPLOYEES
08/20	26,514	(274)	—	28,300
08/19*	21,387	(284)	—	19,000
07/18	10,226	165	1.6%	10,000
07/17	9,274	130	1.4%	9,700
07/16	8,470	125	1.5%	9,554
Annual Growth	**33.0%**	—	—	**31.2%**

*Fiscal year change

2020 Year-End Financials

Debt ratio: 34.98%
Return on equity: (-20.68%)
Cash ($ mil.): 46
Current ratio: 1.56
Long-term debt ($ mil.): 2,570

No. of shares (mil.): 54
Dividends
Yield: —
Payout: —
Market value ($ mil.): 1,086

	STOCK PRICE ($) FY Close	P/E High/Low		PER SHARE ($) Earnings	Dividends	Book Value
08/20	19.85	—	—	(5.10)	0.00	20.93
08/19*	8.42	—	—	(5.56)	0.00	28.62
07/18	32.51	16	10	3.26	0.00	36.62
07/17	37.88	19	13	2.56	0.00	33.23
07/16	49.98	22	12	2.50	0.00	30.16
Annual Growth	**(20.6%)**	—	—	—	—	**(8.7%)**

*Fiscal year change

United Parcel Service Inc

UPS is the world's largest package deliverer transporting nearly 22 million packages and documents per business day (more than 55 billion a year) throughout the US and in over 220 countries and territories. It deploys a fleet of approximately 125000 cars vans tractors and motorcycles and roughly 600 aircraft for pickups and deliveries. In addition to package delivery the company offers logistics and freight forwarding through UPS Supply Chain Solutions and less-than-truckload (LTL) and truckload (TL) freight transportation through UPS Freight. Nearly 80% of its revenue comes from the US.

Operations

UPS has three business segments: US Domestic Package International Package and Supply Chain & Freight.

US Domestic Package is the company's largest business segment accounting for more than 60% of sales. This division includes UPS SurePost an economy residential ground service for customers with non-urgent lightweight residential shipments. It acts as a contractual residential ground service that partners its UPS Ground network with final delivery often provided by the US Postal Service.

International Package delivers more than 20% of UPS' sales. It offers guaranteed time-definite express options through its Express Plus Express and Express Saver services. The company's Supply Chain & Freight segment which generates close to 20% of sales includes forwarding logistics truckload brokerage UPS Freight and financial services through UPS Capital.

Geographic Reach

UPS is headquartered in Atlanta GA (Its UPS Supply Chain Solutions group is based in Alpharetta.) and has over 1000 package operating facilities. Its US transportation hub called Worldport is in Louisville KY. It also has US regional air hubs located in Texas California Philadelphia Pennsylvania and Illinois. Its European air hub is in Cologne Germany and it maintains Asia-Pacific air hubs in Shanghai and Shenzhen China and in Hong Kong. A facility in Ontario is the regional air hub in Canada and UPS' Miami FL hub covers Latin America and the Caribbean.

Almost 80% of the company's revenue is generated in the US.

Sales and Marketing

In addition to package delivery to consumers UPS targets B2B customers for its logistics services in industries such as health care life sciences government retail automotive industrial manufacturing and aerospace.

Financial Performance

UPS has enjoyed several years of steady revenue growth and solid profits. Its sales have increased 25% since 2015.

Revenue in 2019 reached a record $74.1 billion a 3% increase compared with $71.9 billion in 2018. The increase was due to average daily package volume increased 5.8% primarily driven by our U.S. Domestic Package segment which experienced growth from SMBs as well as several large customers led by our largest customer Amazon.

Profit was $4.4 billion in 2019 down 7% from the previous year as a result of higher operating expenses including higher pension expenses and the cost of transformation initiatives in the US (new facility and technology projects).

Cash at the end of fiscal 2019 was $5.2 billion an increase of $871 million from the prior year. Cash from operations contributed $8.6 billion to the coffers while investing activities used $6.1 billion mainly for capital expenditures on buildings facilities and plant equipment decreased in 2019 compared to 2018 in their U.S. and international package businesses as the company completed several facility automation and capacity expansion projects in 2018. Financing activities used another $1.7 billion for loan payments dividends to stockholders and the company's stock repurchase program.

Strategy

The company's strategy is to provide advanced logistics solutions made possible by a broad portfolio of differentiated services and capabilities integrated into their customers' businesses. This strategy supported by their efficient global multimodal network enables them to deliver value to and build lasting relationships with their customers.

UPS offer a full range of industry-leading products services and capabilities across a growing geographical and industry footprint. Achieving their objectives has required new methods and innovative approaches to develop and implement logistics services that address customer needs for speed to market visibility reliability and greater control. Recent examples include: the acquisition or creation of platform-based offerings such as UPS e-fulfillment and Ware2Go; specialized healthcare solutions such as UPS Premier which offers prioritized handling and visibility for critical healthcare shipments; a full range of global customs brokerage and shipment insurance services; and offerings such as UPS My Choice for business that give small- and medium-sized businesses ("SMBs") greater control visibility and data access to improve their customer service.

The company's strategic investments are primarily focused in areas they believe will drive growth and lasting profit potential: services and solutions for SMBs; international growth markets; global Business to Consumer ("B2C") and Business to Business ("B2B") e-commerce; healthcare and life-sciences logistics; and operational improvements to drive greater productivity and the use of automation to enhance the efficiency of our network.

Company Background

Seattle teens Jim Casey and Claude Ryan started American Messenger Company a delivery and errand service in 1907. They were soon making small-parcel deliveries for local department stores and in 1913 changed the company's name to Merchants Parcel Delivery. Casey who led the company for 50 years established a policy of manager ownership best service and lowest rates. In 1916 new employee Charlie Soderstrom chose the brown paint still used on the company's vehicles. Service expanded outside Seattle in 1919 when Merchants Parcel bought Oakland California-based Motor Parcel Delivery later changing its name to United Parcel Service (UPS).

In 1930 the year after the stock market crash UPS moved its corporate headquarters to New York City where it remained for 45 years until a move to Greenwich Connecticut in 1975. By the 1990s the high-cost Connecticut housing market was making it difficult for the company to attract and retain employees so in 1991 it moved again to Atlanta to leverage its large airport and available labor market.

HISTORY

Seattle teens Jim Casey and Claude Ryan started American Messenger Company a delivery and errand service in 1907. They were soon making small-parcel deliveries for local department stores and in 1913 changed the company's name to Merchants Parcel Delivery. Casey who led the company for 50 years established a policy of manager ownership best service and lowest rates. In 1916 new employee Charlie Soderstrom chose the brown paint still used on the company's vehicles. Service expanded outside Seattle in 1919 when Merchants Parcel bought Oakland California-based Motor Parcel Delivery later changing its name to United Parcel Service (UPS).

EXECUTIVES

Vice President Of Customer Technology Marketing, Jordan Colletta
Coo, James J. (Jim) Barber, age 59, $500,706 total compensation
Evp And Chief Commercial Officer, Alan Gershenhorn, age 62, $565,956 total compensation
Chairman And Ceo, David P. Abney, age 65, $1,082,421 total compensation
President Us Operations, Myron A. Gray, age 63, $514,509 total compensation
Svp Cfo And Treasurer, Richard N. Peretz, age 58, $485,070 total compensation
Svp Global Engineering And Sustainability, Mark R. Wallace, age 57
Svp Chief Marketing And Business Services Officer, Teresa M. Finley, age 59
Svp And Cio, Juan R. Perez
President Operations Ups Latin America, Jose Maria (Chema) Odriozola
President Ups China, Harld Peters
Vice President Marketing Healthcare Logistics, John Menna
Vice President Administration, Charlie Covert
Vice President Of Sales And Marketing, Norm Brothers
Vice President Finance, John Colino
Vice President Of Marketing, Jerome Roberts
Vice President Enterprise Accounts Sales, Michael Tannian
Vice President, Rick Rufolo
Vice President, Beth Breihan
Vice President, Angela Jack
Vice President Enterprise Accounts Retail, Nola Wood
Vice President Of Engineering, Gregory Loppatto
Vice President; Sales And Marketing, Joe Racanelli
Vice President Administration, Michael Francesconi
Vice President Retail Sales, Michael Arias
Vice President Global Customs Policy And Public Affairs, Norm Schenk
Senior Vice President Marketing And Sales, James Thome
Vice President Administration, Nick Basford
Vice President, Steven Gaut
Vice President, Carlos Cubias
Vp Business Development, Annie Outlaw
Vice President Strategic Sales, Frank Cole
Vice President Chicago Area Consolidation Hub Cach, Robert Latchford
Vice President, Ken Torok
Vice President Operations Europe, Dominic Porporino
Vice President Of Operations, George Willis
Vice President, Kathleen Parrish
Vice President, Bill Kruger

Vice President, Scott Heck
Vice President East Central Region, Joseph Zito
National Account Manager, Robert Musca
Vp Human Resources, Regina Hartley
Vice President Sales Global Accounts, Jerry Felton
Vice President Of Human Resources, Tom Upton
Vice President Corporate Public Affairs, Nicole Clifton
Vice President, Susan Ward
Vice Prespident Of Sales Americas, Pedro Anaya
Vice President Enterprise Sales, Sheila Dunn
Regional Vice President, Keith Hall
Vice President, Stefond Harris
Vice President Global Solutions Implemen, Brian Carrier
Vice President, Allen Hill
Vice President Human Resources Benefits Director, Deborah Hyman
Vice President Of Human Resources, David Cole
Vice President Enterprise Accounts, David Canning
Vice President State Government Affairs, Raymond Drake
Vice President Administration, Dave Mace
Vice President State Government Affairs, Kimberly Johnson-bonhart
Vice President Us Engineering, Mark Susor
Vice President Strategy And Innovation Europe, Yannick Mooijman
National Account Manager, Mike Buffon
Vice President Of Human Resources, Debra Harding
Vice President State Government Affairs, Mark Giuffre
Vice President Finance Services, Todd St John
Vice President Chief Operating Officer Eastern Operations, Joe Picone
Vice President Strategy, Anthony Poselenzny
Vice President Plant Engineering, Steven Carter
National Account Manager, Rick Higginson
Vice President, Keith Kellison
Vice President, David Lee
Vice President, David Birkmeyer
Senior Vice President International Public Policy, Leslie Griffin
Vice President Europe Ups Capital Uk, Jorge Navarro
Senior Vice President And Chief Transformation Officer, Scott Price
Vp Global Compensation And Benefits, Justine Turpin
Senior Vice President Global Trade Finance, Mike Bryant
Vice President, Arnold Wellman
Vice President Of Human Resources, Yvonne Mchenry
Vice President Finance, Joseph Tillman
Vp Of Hr, Dave Lovely
Senior Vice President, Jim Bruce
Vice President Ups Ocean, Steve Mcmichael
Senior Vice President General Counsel Secretary, Norman Brothers
Senior Vice President Chief Information Officer, Dj Johnson
Vice President, Doug Moon
National Account Manager, Brendan Reilly
Senior Vice President Chief Sales And Solutions Officer, Kathleen Gutmann
Vice President, Helen B Scott
Vice President, Brandon Hightower
Vice Chairman Of The Board, John Alden
Board Member, Candace Kendle
Assistant Treasurer, Ned Winsor
Board Member, Wayne Powell
Board Member, Kevin Warsh
Board Member, Rodney Adkins
Board Member, Franck Moison
Board Member, John Stankey
Board Member, Willie Johnson
Board Member, Carol Tome
Board Member, Clark Randt

Board Member, Anna Burns
Secretary, Nancy M Cherwek
Auditors: Deloitte & Touche LLP

LOCATIONS

HQ: United Parcel Service Inc
55 Glenlake Parkway N.E., Atlanta, GA 30328
Phone: 404 828-6000
Web: www.ups.com

PRODUCTS/OPERATIONS

2018 Sales

	$ mil.	% of total
US Domestic Package	43,593	61
International Package	14,442	20
Supply Chain & Freight	13,826	19
Total	**71,861**	**100**

2018 Sales

	$ mil.	% of total
US Domestic Package		
Ground	31,223	43
Next day air	7,618	11
Deferred	4,752	7
International Package		
Export	10,973	15
Domestic	2,874	4
Cargo and other	595	1
Supply Chain & Freight		
Forwarding	6,580	9
Logistic	3,234	5
Freight	3,218	4
Other	794	1
Total	**71,861**	**100**

COMPETITORS

American Airlines Group
Canada Post
Deutsche Post
FedEx
Japan Post
Lufthansa
Nippon Express
Panalpina
Royal Mail
Ryder System
TNT Express
US Postal Service
United Continental
XPO logistics
YRC Worldwide

HISTORICAL FINANCIALS

Company Type: Public

Income Statement

	REVENUE ($ mil.)	NET INCOME ($ mil.)	NET PROFIT MARGIN	EMPLOYEES
12/19	74,094	4,440	6.0%	495,000
12/18	71,861	4,791	6.7%	481,000
12/17	65,872	4,910	7.5%	280,000
12/16	60,906	3,431	5.6%	434,000
12/15	58,363	4,844	8.3%	444,000
Annual Growth	6.1%	(2.2%)	—	2.8%

FYE: December 31

2019 Year-End Financials

Debt ratio: 42.76%
Return on equity: 141.22%
Cash ($ mil.): 5,238
Current ratio: 1.11
Long-term debt ($ mil.): 21,320
No. of shares (mil.): 856
Dividends
Yield: 3.2%
Payout: 75.1%
Market value ($ mil.): 100,274

	STOCK PRICE ($) FY Close	P/E High/Low		PER SHARE ($) Earnings	Dividends	Book Value
12/19	117.06	24	18	5.11	3.84	3.81
12/18	97.53	24	16	5.51	3.64	3.52
12/17	119.15	22	18	5.61	3.32	1.16
12/16	114.64	31	23	3.87	3.12	0.47
12/15	96.23	21	18	5.35	2.92	2.79
Annual Growth	5.0%		—	(1.1%)	7.1%	8.2%

United Rentals Inc

United Rentals considers itself the largest commercial and construction equipment renter in the world serving customers in the commercial infrastructure industrial and residential sectors. It operates through a network of nearly 1200 locations in the US Canada and Europe and provides about 4000 equipment items ? everything from general to heavy construction and industrial equipment to hand tools special-event items (such as aerial towers) power (diesel generators) and HVAC equipment and trench-safety equipment. It also sells new and used equipment as well as contractor supplies and parts. United Rentals' original equipment cost (the initial purchase value of all rental equipment) is $14 billion. The US accounts for more than 90% of total sales. Mr. Flannery succeeded Michael Kneeland as CEO in mid- 2019 at which time Mr. Kneeland became Chairman of the Board.

Operations

United Rentals operates two business segments: General Rental and the Trench Power and Fluid Solutions.

General Rental generates around 80% of sales and rents out construction aerial and industrial equipment general tools and light equipment and related services.

The Trench Power and Fluid Solutions segment rents out specialty construction products. It offers trench safety equipment such as trench shields aluminum hydraulic shoring systems and construction lasers; power and HVAC equipment such as portable generators heating and cooling equipment and electric distribution equipment; and fluid solutions equipment for fluid containment transfer and treatment. The segment accounts for the remaining 20% of revenue.

Equipment rentals make up about 85% of revenue. Across both segments the company sells new and used rental equipment which accounts for about 10% of total revenue. It also sells construction consumables tools small equipment and safety supplies and offers maintenance services and parts for customer-owned equipment.

Geographic Reach

Headquartered in Stamford Connecticut United Rentals' nearly 1200 rental locations more than 1000 are in the US approximately 140 are in Canada and about 10 are in Europe.

United Rentals' General Rentals division comprises 11 US geographic regions: Carolinas Gulf South Industrial (which serves the geographic Gulf region and has a strong industrial presence) Mid-Atlantic Mid Central Midwest Northeast Pacific West South Southeast and Western Canada.

Approximately 90% of the company's total sales is generated domestically.

Sales and Marketing

United Rentals' customers include construction and industrial companies manufacturers utilities municipalities and homeowners. The Trench Power and Fluid Solutions segment serves primarily construction companies active in infrastructure projects municipalities and industrial companies.

United Rentals markets its products and services through sales staff at the company's branches and customer care centers; account managers dedicated to large customer accounts; its online rental platform; and advertising (trade publications yellow pages the internet radio and direct mail).

The amounts of qualified advertising reimbursements that reduced advertising expense were $49 $41 and $35 for the years ended 2019 2018 and 2017 respectively.

Financial Performance

Except for a slight dip in 2016 United Rental's revenue has seen steady growth the last two years rising about 61% between 2015 and 2019.

Sales in 2019 increased 16% to $9.4 billion compared to $8.0 billion in 2018. Growth in 2019 was driven by a roughly 15% in equipment rentals.

Net income increased 7% to $1.2 billion in 2019 compared to 2018 driven by selling general and administrative expenses.

Cash at the end of 2019 was $52 million an increase of $9 million from the prior year. Cash from operations contributed $3.0 billion to the coffers while investing activities used $1.7 billion mainly for purchases of rental equipment. Financing activities used $1.3 billion primarily for payments of debt.

Strategy

For the past several years the company have executed a strategy focused on improving the profitability of its core equipment rental business through revenue growth margin expansion and operational efficiencies. In particular the company has focused on customer segmentation customer service differentiation rate management fleet management and operational efficiency.

The company will continue to enhance its performance in serving its current customer base and to focus on the accounts and customer types that are best suited to its strategy for profitable growth. The company believes these efforts will lead to even better service of its target accounts primarily large construction and industrial customers as well as select local contractors.

The company continues to implement Lean kaizen processes across its branch network with the objectives of: reducing the cycle time associated with renting its equipment to customers; improving invoice accuracy and service quality; reducing the elapsed time for equipment pickup and delivery; and improving the effectiveness and efficiency of the company's repair and maintenance operations.

The company continue to focus on Project XL which is a set of eight specific work streams focused on driving profitable growth through revenue opportunities and generating incremental profitability through cost savings across its business. The company plans to open at least 25 specialty rental branches/tool hubs/onsite services locations in 2020 and continues to invest in specialty rental fleet to further position United Rentals as a single source provider of total jobsite solutions through its extensive product and service resources and technology offerings.

Company Background

Bradley Jacobs had made a fortune in the garbage business having used United Waste Systems as a roll-up company to buy small trash-hauling firms in that fragmented industry. Flush with cash after he sold United Waste Systems in 1997 to USA Waste Services (now Waste Management) Jacobs launched the same roll-up strategy to consolidate the equipment-rental industry. He and his management team bought six leasing companies and started United Rentals. The company which went public in 1997 had acquired 38 rental companies in 20 states by mid-1998.

HISTORY

Bradley Jacobs had made a fortune in the garbage business having used United Waste Systems as a roll-up company to buy small trash-hauling firms in that fragmented industry. Flush with cash after he sold United Waste Systems in 1997 to USA Waste Services (now Waste Management) Jacobs launched the same roll-up strategy to consolidate the equipment-rental industry. He and his management team bought six leasing companies and started United Rentals. The company which went public in 1997 had acquired 38 rental companies in 20 states by mid-1998.

EXECUTIVES

Vice President Business Development, Ned Graham

Svp Performance Analytics, Kenneth Mettel

Regional Vice President, Robert Krause

Vice President, Jonathan M Gottsegen

Vice President, Mark Tapia

Evp And Cfo, William B. Plummer, age 61, $595,504 total compensation

President And Ceo, Michael J. Kneeland, age 66, $950,000 total compensation

Evp And Coo, Matthew J. Flannery, age 55, $595,504 total compensation

Svp Business Services And Cio, Dale A. Asplund, age 52, $519,807 total compensation

Evp Chief Administrative And Legal Officer, Craig A. Pintoff, age 50, $473,046 total compensation

Vp Midwest Region, Chris Burlog

Vp Mid-central Region, Kevin M. OBrien

Svp And Chief Marketing Officer, Chris Hummel

Vp Pacific West Region, Robert C. Bower

Vp Southeast Region, Michael G. Cloer

Vp Western Canada Region, John (Scott) Fisher

Region Vp Tools And Industrial Solutions, Joshuah P. Flores

Vp Trench Safety Region, Todd M. Hayes

Vp Mid-atlantic Region, John J. Humphrey

Vp Pump Solutions, William A. (Bill) Kiker

Vp Industrial Region, Donald (Chad) Matter

Vp South Region, Jeffrey S. (Jeff) McGinnis

Vp Northeast Region, Craig Schmidt

Vp Power And Hvac Region, David C. Scott

Vp Gulf South Region, Larry (Don) Irwin

National Account Manager, John Bebout

Vice President Finance Operations, Joseph Pledger

National Account Manager, Jackie Volk

National Account Manager, Reggie Hall

National Account Manager, Frank Branca

National Account Manager, Robert Zupo

Vice President Investor Relations, Fred Bratman

Executive Vice President Corporate Services, Kurtis Barker

National Account Manager, Bill Kenyon

National Account Manager, Shelley Miles

National Account Manager, SHAWNA ERMOLD

Vice President Customer Service Operations, Kenneth Perkins

National Account Manager Oil And Gas, Brian Nagel

National Accounts Manager, Stephen Hedrick

National Account Manager, Greg Littler

Svp Operations West, Michael Durand

National Account Manager, Ray Cruz

National Account Manager, Rick Clinaz

Region Vice President, Bill Kiker

National Account Manager, Valerie Wheatstine

National Account Manager, Christopher Shoemaker
National Account Manager, Jed Rasmussen
Senior Vice President And Chief Marketing
 Officer, Christopher K Hummel
Board Member, Filippo Passerini
Chairman, Jenne K. Britell, age 77
Auditors: Ernst & Young LLP

LOCATIONS

HQ: United Rentals Inc
 100 First Stamford Place, Suite 700, Stamford, CT
 06902
Phone: 203 622-3131
Web: www.unitedrentals.com

2017 Sales

	$ mil.	% of total
Domestic	6,076	91
Foreign	565	9
Total	**6,641**	**100**

PRODUCTS/OPERATIONS

2017 Sales

	$ mil.	% of total
General Rental	5,565	84
Trench power and pump	1,076	16
Total	**6,641**	**100**

2017 Sales

	$ mil.	% of total
Equipment rentals	5,715	86
Sales of rental equipment	550	8
Sales of new equipment	178	3
Contractor supplies sales	80	1
Service & other revenues	118	2
Total	**6,641**	**100**

Selected Products

Aerial lifts
Backhoes
Barricades
Compressors
Concrete & Masonry
Cones
Contractor supplies
Ditching equipment
Earth-moving equipment
Forklifts
Generators
Hand tools
Heaters
HVAC
Lawn & Landscape
Light towers
Material-handling equipment
Message boards
Pavement-marking systems
Portable power units
Power washers
Pumps
Skid-steer loaders
Trench shields
Trucks & Trailers
Warning lights
Water pumps
Welders & Accessories

COMPETITORS

AMECO
Atlas Lift Truck
 Rentals
Case Power & Equipment
Herc Holdings

Maxim Crane Works
RDO Equipment
Sunbelt Rentals
Ziegler inc

HISTORICAL FINANCIALS
Company Type: Public

Income Statement   FYE: December 31

	REVENUE ($ mil.)	NET INCOME ($ mil.)	NET PROFIT MARGIN	EMPLOYEES
12/20	8,530	890	10.4%	18,250
12/19	9,351	1,174	12.6%	19,100
12/18	8,047	1,096	13.6%	18,500
12/17	6,641	1,346	20.3%	14,800
12/16	5,762	566	9.8%	12,500
Annual Growth	**10.3%**	**12.0%**	**—**	**9.9%**

2020 Year-End Financials

Debt ratio: 54.19%
Return on equity: 21.20%
Cash ($ mil.): 202
Current ratio: 1.07
Long-term debt ($ mil.): 8,978

No. of shares (mil.): 72
Dividends
 Yield: —
 Payout: —
Market value ($ mil.): 16,743

	STOCK PRICE ($) FY Close	P/E High/Low		PER SHARE ($) Earnings	Dividends	Book Value
12/20	231.91	20	6	12.20	0.00	62.95
12/19	166.77	11	7	15.11	0.00	51.50
12/18	102.53	14	7	13.12	0.00	42.61
12/17	171.91	11	6	15.73	0.00	36.77
12/16	105.58	17	7	6.45	0.00	19.57
Annual Growth	**21.7%**	**—**	**—**	**17.3%**	**—**	**33.9%**

United States Steel Corp.

United States Steel (U.S. Steel) is one of the world's largest integrated steelmaker. The company operates mills throughout the US Midwest and in Slovakia. U.S. Steel makes a wide range of flat-rolled and tubular steel products and has annual production capacity of approximately 22 million net tons of raw steel. Its customers are primarily in the automotive consumer (packaging and appliance) construction electrical industrial equipment energy (oil country tubular goods and line pipe) markets gas and petrochemical industries. In addition U.S. Steel mines iron ore and procures coke which provide the primary raw materials used in steel making. It is also engaged in railroad and barge operations and real estate. The North America accounts for around 80% of its revenue.

Operations
U.S. Steel divides its operations into three reportable segments: Flat-Rolled Products which represents more than 70% of revenue; US Steel Europe (USSE) about 20% of revenue; and Tubular Products which accounts for the rest of revenue.

The company's North American operations produce about 17 million tons of flat rolled products including slabs rounds strip mill plates sheets and tin mill products. It also has ore and coke production facilities in the US.

Its European operations produce and sell slabs sheet strip mill plate tin mill products and spiral welded pipe as well as heating radiators and refractory ceramic materials. U.S. Steel Kosice in

Slovakia produces sheet steel. Its plant in Kosice has an annual capacity of approximately 5 million tons.

U.S. Steel's tubular steel operation (about 1.9 million tons per year) serves the energy industry primarily providing both seamless and electric resistance welded products commonly called oil country tubular goods.

The company also participates in joint ventures with a number of its industry competitors. They include the world's #1 steelmaker ArcelorMittal Japanese producer Kobe Steel South Korean giant POSCO and US steel service center Worthington Industries.

The company's other businesses include railroad services and real estate operations.

Geographic Reach
In the US U.S. Steel holds integrated steel plants including Gary Works East Chicago Tin and Midwest Plant all in Indiana. It also holds the Great Lakes Works in Michigan Mon Valley Works and Fairless Plant in Pennsylvania and Granite City Works in Illinois. U.S. Steel also has a steel mill and related facilities in Slovakia. North America accounts some 75% of the company's total sales.

The company has a research center and headquarter in Pittsburgh Pennsylvania. It also has an automotive center in Troy Michigan and Research and Development Laboratory and Test Facility for Tubular Products in Houston Texas.

Sales and Marketing
U.S. Steel's integrated steel business serves North American customers in the service center conversion transportation construction container and appliance and electrical markets and European customers in the construction service center conversion container transportation appliance and electrical and oil gas and petrochemical markets.

Financial Performance
Over the last ten years U.S. Steel's revenue declined from a peak of about $24 billion to a low of just over $10 billion in 2016 with a few years of growth since. The company has struggled to remain consistently profitable usually recording either weak profits or net losses through the period.

In 2019 U.S. Steel's revenue fell 9% to $12.9 billion. The decrease in 2019 sales for the Flat-Rolled segment primarily reflects lower average realized prices (decrease of $58 per ton) and a less favorable product mix. While The decrease in 2019 sales for the USSE segment was primarily due to decreased shipments (decrease of 867 thousand net tons) and lower average realized prices (decrease of $41 per net ton) in most product categories due to increased import competition flat to declining demand and the weakening of the Euro versus the U.S. dollar. The decrease in 2019 sales for the Tubular segment resulted from lower average realized prices (decrease of $33 per net ton) and decreased net shipments (decrease of 11 thousand net tons) from lower demand for tubular products.

The company reported a net loss of $630 billion in 2019 compared to its net income of $1.1 billion the year before largely due to lower sales as well as higher restructuring and other expenses.

U.S. Steel's cash balance fell $101 million to $939 million during 2019. Operating activities generated $682 million while investing activities used roughly $2 billion and financing provided another $1.2 billion. The company's main cash uses were capital expenditures and debt repayments.

Strategy

The company's strategy is informed by its critical success factors which are the bedrock of the "best of both" strategy: Move Down the Cost Curve; Win in Strategic Markets; and Move Up the Talent Curve. Several of the strategic projects they are undertaking are expected to result in operational improvements. Additionally the enhanced operating model and organizational structure they implemented beginning in 2020 will also position U. S. Steel to lower its structural fixed costs.

In 2019 U.S. Steel announced several transformation initiatives key to its strategy. On October 31 2019 U. S. Steel acquired about 49.9% ownership interest in Big River Steel at a purchase price of approximately $683 million in cash with a call option to acquire the remaining 50.1% within the next four years. Its investment in Big River Steel will add sustainable steel making technology to their footprint and improve their competitive positioning. Big River Steel is a technological leader combining mini mill technology with aspects of the integrated model to achieve the benefits of each. In December 2019 the company announced their intention to indefinitely idle a significant portion of their Great Lakes Works operation near Detroit Michigan. The company expects to begin idling the iron and steelmaking facilities on or around April 1 2020 and the hot strip mill rolling facility before the end of 2020. This action will transition its footprint to focus on facilities and assets that are differentiated by cost and/or capability.

Mergers and Acquisitions

In 2020 U. S. Steel has closed on the purchase of POSCO-California Corporation (POSCAL)'s 50% partnership interest in USS-POSCO Industries (UPI). UPI headquartered in Pittsburg California markets sheet and tin mill products principally in the western United States. UPI produces cold-rolled sheets galvanized sheets and tin mill products made from hot bands principally provided by U. S. Steel. Terms not disclosed.

In 2019 US Steel took a 49.9% stake in US-based Big River Steel for about $700 million in cash. The deal includes a call option for US Steel to buy the remaining 50.1% of Big River steel within the next four years. The investment in Big River increases US Steel's presence in the mini mill industry (smaller mills that make steel from steel scrap) and complements its existing integrated steel making capabilities (making new steel from iron ore in blast furnaces).

HISTORY

U.S. Steel was conceived through a 1901 merger of 10 steel companies that combined their furnaces ore deposits railroad companies and shipping lines. The deal involved industrial pioneers Andrew Carnegie Charles Schwab Elbert Gary and J. P. Morgan. Morgan had helped organize the Federal Steel Company in 1898 and he then wanted to create a centralized trust to dominate the soaring steel market. Carnegie owned the largest US steel company at the time Carnegie Steel but wanted to retire.

In 1900 Schwab Carnegie Steel's president outlined the idea of the steel trust based on a merger of the Carnegie and Federal steel companies. Morgan asked Schwab to persuade Carnegie to sell his steel mills and name his price. Morgan didn't haggle when Carnegie responded that he would sell for almost half a billion dollars.

The Carnegie-Morgan combination created the world's first billion-dollar company.

EXECUTIVES

President Ceo And Director, David B. (Dave) Burritt, age 64, $800,000 total compensation
Svp Consumer Solutions, Sara A. Greenstein, age 45
Svp Industrial Service Center And Mining Solutions, Douglas R. Matthews, age 55, $541,000 total compensation
Vp European Solutions And President Us Steel Koâšice, Scott D. Buckiso, age 53
Vp And Cio, Charles G. Balawajder, age 64
Svp Government Affairs General Counsel And Chief Compliance Officer, Suzanne R. Folsom, age 58, $700,000 total compensation
Svp Automotive Solutions, James E. Bruno, age 54, $403,500 total compensation
Vp And Chief Supply Chain Officer, Christine S. Breves
Evp And Cfo, Kevin P. Bradley
Senior Vice President And Chief Risk Officer, Larry Brockway
Executive Vice President And Chief Financial Officer, Joseph Stinnett
Vice President Marketing, Kent Harvey
Vice President Commercial Tubular, Craig Horan
Vice President Finance, Pipasu Soni
Vice President, Pat Mullarkey
Senior Vice President And Treasurer, Albert Ferrara
Vice President Global Product Development Andengineering, Bernhard Hoffmann
Vice President Strategic Planning And Corporate Development, Richard Fruehauf
Vice President, Leonard Chuderewicz
Svp General Counsel Chief Compliance Officer And Corporate Secretary, Duane D Holloway
Vice President Workplace Campaign, Linda Jones
Chairman, David S. (Dave) Sutherland, age 70
Board Member, Dan Dinges
Board Member, Patricia Tracey
Board Member, Patricia Dennis
Board Member, John Engel
Auditors: PricewaterhouseCoopers LLP

LOCATIONS

HQ: United States Steel Corp.
600 Grant Street, Pittsburgh, PA 15219-2800
Phone: 412 433-1121   **Fax:** 412 433-4818
Web: www.ussteel.com

2018 Sales

	$ mil.	% of total
North America	10,973	77
Europe	3,205	23
Total	**14,178**	**100**

PRODUCTS/OPERATIONS

2018 Sales

	$ mil.	% of total
Flat-rolled	9,681	68
US Steel Europe	3,205	23
Tubular products	1,231	9
Other	61	-
Total	**14,178**	**100**

Selected Products

Steel
Tin
Tubular

Selected Subsidiaries

Acero Prime S. R. L de CV (44% steel processing and warehousing)
Delray Connecting Railroad Company (transportation)
Double Eagle Steel Coating Company (50% with Severstal; steel processing)
PRO-TEC Coating Co. (50% with Kobe Steel; steel processing)
Transtar Inc. (transportation)
U. S. Steel Kosice sro (steelmaking Slovakia)
USS-POSCO Industries (50% with Pohang Iron & Steel; steel processing)
Worthington Specialty Processing (50% with Worthington Industries; steel processing)

COMPETITORS

AK Steel Holding Corporation
Allegheny Technologies
ArcelorMittal
Baosteel
BlueScope Steel
B –HLER-UDDEHOLM
Carpenter Technology
Gerdau Ameristeel
JFE Holdings
Kobe Steel
Nippon Steel & Sumitomo Metal Corporation
Nucor
POSCO
SSAB North America
SSAB Svenskt
Salzgitter
Simec
Steel Dynamics
Tata Steel
Ternium
ThyssenKrupp Steel
Wuhan Iron & Steel

HISTORICAL FINANCIALS

Company Type: Public

Income Statement

FYE: December 31

	REVENUE ($ mil.)	NET INCOME ($ mil.)	NET PROFIT MARGIN	EMPLOYEES
12/19	12,937	(630)	—	27,500
12/18	14,178	1,115	7.9%	29,000
12/17	12,250	387	3.2%	29,200
12/16	10,261	(440)	—	29,800
12/15	11,574	(1,642)	—	33,200
Annual Growth	**2.8%**	**—**	**—**	**(4.6%)**

2019 Year-End Financials

Debt ratio: 31.37%	No. of shares (mil.): 170
Return on equity: (-15.19%)	Dividends
Cash ($ mil.) 749	Yield: 1.7%
Current ratio: 1.45	Payout: 5.6%
Long-term debt ($ mil.): 3,627	Market value ($ mil.): 1,940

	STOCK PRICE ($) FY Close	P/E High/Low		PER SHARE ($) Earnings	Dividends	Book Value
12/19	11.41	—	—	(3.67)	0.20	24.06
12/18	18.24	7	3	6.25	0.20	24.08
12/17	35.19	19	9	2.19	0.20	18.95
12/16	33.01	—	—	(2.81)	0.20	13.08
12/15	7.98	—	—	(11.24)	0.20	16.65
Annual Growth	**9.4%**	**—**	**—**	**—**	**(0.0%)**	**9.6%**

UnitedHealth Group Inc

UnitedHealth Group is a leading US health insurer offering a variety of plans and services to group and individual customers nationwide. Its UnitedHealthcare health benefits segment manages health maintenance organization (HMO) preferred provider organization (PPO) and point-of-service (POS) plans as well as Medicare Medicaid state-funded and supplemental vision and dental options. In addition UnitedHealth's Optum health services units ? OptumHealth OptumInsight and OptumRx ? provide wellness and care management programs financial services information technology solutions and pharmacy benefit management (PBM) services to individuals and the health care industry.

HISTORY

Dr. Paul Ellwood became known as the "Father of the HMO" for his role as an early champion of the health care concept. As a neurology student in the 1950s Ellwood recognized that applying business principles to medicine could minimize costs and make health care more affordable. Although the HMO was considered a radical approach to health care reform Ellwood got Congress and the Nixon administration to approve his HMO model in 1970; the next year he hired Richard Burke to put the model into action. Burke established United HealthCare (UHC) in 1974 to manage the not-for-profit Physicians Health Plan of Minnesota (PHP). UHC incorporated in 1977.

The company bought HMOs and began managing others operating 11 HMOs in 10 states by 1984 the year it went public. Its expansion continued with the purchases of HMOs Share Development (1985) and Peak Health Care (1986). Unfortunately acquisitions and startups began to eat away at UHC's financial health. Meanwhile Burke CEO of both UHC and PHP was accused by PHP doctors of having a conflict of interest after a change in the HMO's Medicare policy threatened to cut off patients from some member hospitals. Burke resigned in 1987 and was replaced by Kennett Simmons formerly president of Peak.

That year investment firm Warburg Pincus bought nearly 40% of UHC providing it with much-needed cash. UHC lost nearly $16 million in 1987 largely from a restructuring that axed the company's Phoenix HMO as well as startups in six other markets. The next year UHC sold its share of Peak Health Care.

In the late 1980s UHC adopted a new strategy of acquiring specialty companies that provided fee income. It also continued building its HMO network through acquisitions hoping to gain critical mass in such varied markets as the Midwest and New England.

Physician William (Bill) McGuire another former Peak president was named UHC's chairman and CEO in 1991. That year PHP and Share merged into Medica. Warburg Pincus distributed its UHC shares to several pension funds and financial institutions.

The company's expansion accelerated in the 1990s with a string of purchases in the Midwest but there were also divestitures. In 1994 UHC

sold subsidiary Diversified Pharmaceutical Services providing cash for still more purchases including GenCare (St. Louis) Group Sales and Service of Puerto Rico and MetraHealth a former joint venture of Travelers Group and Metropolitan Life. UHC's interest in fee-based businesses continued with the 1997 purchase of Medicode a major provider of health care information products.

In 1998 the firm planned to buy rival Humana. However bloated UHC decided it should slim down to prepare to consummate the agreement; when UHC announced that it would charge $900 million in costs against earnings its plummeting stock price devalued the primary currency of the deal which quickly collapsed. That year it began offering MediGap and other supplements to AARP members.

The company changed its name to UnitedHealth Group in 2000. It also added UK-based contract research organization ClinPharm International to Ingenix that year and it announced it would let doctors — not administrators — choose what treatment patients would get partially because it was spending more on care scrutiny than the practice saved. Nevertheless many doctors claimed the process was still restrictive.

In 2000 the American Medical Association (AMA) and other parties sued the company claiming it used faulty Ingenix data to reduce payments to member doctors. (UnitedHealth settled the AMA lawsuit in 2009 for $350 million without admitting any wrongdoing as well as some state lawsuits related to the database.)

UnitedHealth's strategy for expansion in the early 21st century concentrated on acquisitions and joint ventures. To expand its Medicaid services business the firm bought AmeriChoice in 2002. The company also bought Mid Atlantic Medical Services because its HMOs and specialty health care operations complemented UnitedHealth's core operations. Golden Rule was acquired in late 2003 so UnitedHealth could enter the individual health insurance market by providing medical savings accounts. UnitedHealth also bought individual health care reimbursement account provider Definity Health in late 2004 for the same purpose. To increase its market share in the northeastern US the company bought Oxford Health Plans that year.

UnitedHealth spent $8.8 billion to acquire and integrate PacifiCare in 2005. Adding 3 million customers the acquisition gave UnitedHealth a leading position in the California and West Coast markets but it also prompted a landslide of complaints from customers alleging mishandled claims. The California Insurance Commissioner and other state agencies sought fines of more than $1 billion. While PacifiCare continued to exist as a health plan brand of UnitedHealth the PacifiCare administrative operations were integrated into other UnitedHealth units including UnitedHealthcare. The PacifiCare Prescription Benefits unit became separate operating division of UnitedHealth.

Chairman and CEO McGuire became the focus of inquiry in 2006 over a scandal involving the back-dating of stock options awarded to him and other company executives. Following a board inquiry McGuire was shown the door and was replaced by Stephen Hemsley formerly the company's president and COO. The back-dating

brouhaha continued to be a distraction for UnitedHealth and in 2008 it opted to settle several related shareholder lawsuits by agreeing to pay more than $900 million.

Continuing the acquisitive strategy it laid out after the turn of the millennium the company in 2006 bought Deere & Company's employee health plan as well as Student Resources the student insurance division of HealthMarkets' MEGA Life subsidiary.

The company changed the name of its supplemental health division from Specialized Care Service to OptumHealth in 2007. As part of the restructuring a number of other UnitedHealth businesses were merged into OptumHealth including ACN Group United Resources Networks United Behavioral Health PacifiCare Behavioral Health Exante Bank and Exante Financial Services.

UnitedHealth completed several large acquisitions in 2008 spending $730 million to purchase Fiserv's health-related businesses including Fiserv Health (benefits administration for 2 million members) Avidyn Health (care facilitation) Fiserv Health Specialty Solutions (administration) and Innoviant Pharmacy Benefits Management. UnitedHealth also paid $980 million to acquire Unison Health Plans and used it to expand its AmeriChoice unit.

UnitedHealth completed its controversial purchase of Nevada insurance provider Sierra Health Services for approximately $2.6 billion in 2008 gaining some 600000 health plan members in the state and boosting its position in the growing Southwest market. The acquisition took nearly a year to receive approval from the Department of Justice due to competition concerns. Approval was finally gained on the contingency that UnitedHealth sell its Las Vegas Medicare Advantage program representing some 27000 customers to Humana for $185 million. Sierra Health's operating units including Health Plan of Nevada and Sierra Health and Life became part the UnitedHealthcare Nevada division following the acquisition.

EXECUTIVES

Executive Vice President, Simon Stevens
Evp, Jeannine M. Rivet, $465,000 total compensation
Vice Chairman And Ceo Optum, Larry C. Renfro, age 66, $1,100,000 total compensation
Evp Medical Affairs And Chief Medical Officer, Richard Migliori
Ceo, David S. Wichmann, age 58, $1,100,000 total compensation
Ceo Community Plan Of Kansas, Kevin P. Sparks
Evp Human Capital, D. Ellen Wilson, age 62, $701,923 total compensation
Evp And Chief Legal Officer, Marianne D. Short, age 68, $800,000 total compensation
Evp External Affairs, Cory B. Alexander
Ceo Employer And Individual Iowa-kansas-nebraska, Robert Broomfield
Evp And Cfo, John Rex, $721,923 total compensation
Svp And Chief Marketing Officer, Terry M. Clark
Vice President Network Management, Mark Dicello
Vice President Goverment Programs West Region, Jeanine Donahue
Vice President Finance, Adam Koering
Vice President E Solutions, John O'Neil
Vice President Of Finance, Matthew Pioske
Vice President Technology, Mouli Venkatesan
Vice President Network Management, Camille Kendrick

Vice President Marketing Ovations, Ellen Sexton

Vice President Provider Experience And Nps Programs, Deborah Cooledge

Senior Director Vice President, Tom Brandt

Vp And Chief Information Security Officer, Robert Booker

Vice President, Gayle Adams

Vice President Sales, Philip Brun

Senior Vice President Human Capital, Chris Coleman

Vice President Relationship Office Solutions Group, Brent Muilenburg

Vice President Consumer Strategy, Nancy Brock

Vice President Enterprise Sourcing And Procurement, Brent Shaback

Vice President Empire Plan, Carl Mattson

Senior Vice President Business Platforms And Operations Optuminsight, Steven Mueller

Senior Vice President Strategic Solutions, Deborah Sundal

Vice President Information Technology, Robert Dufek

Vice President Innovation And Randd, Robert Plourde

Senior Vice President Regulatory Affairs, Nick Thompson

Vice President, Brennan Mcnally

Vice President Information Technology Chief Architect, Tom Zielinski

Regional Vice President Sales And Account Management, Steven Beecy

Vice President Computer Services, Thomas Busse

Vice President Clinical Solutions, Kelley Nolan-maccione

Executive Vice President Of Human Capital, Ellen Wilson

Vice President Digital Product, Cara Sjodin

Vice President Operations Advocacy, Mary Higgins

Vice President, Laurie Paidosh

Sr. Vice President Strategic Initiatives, Alison Richards

Svp Finance And Controller, Jeff Putnam

Vice President Product Management, Todd Spaulding

Vice President, Jeff Todd

Vice President Regional Sales, Gliknis Ortiz

Executive Vice President, Chris Ritchie

Medical Director, Daniel Clute

Medical Director, Helene Goldsman

Medical Director, Edward Koza

Senior Vice President Of Risk Management, Michele Nielsen

Vice President Shared Services, Kim Farner

Vice President Sales And Service, Tammy Ohare

Vice President Peo Sales, Elry Falkenstein

Medical Director, Ralph Naftaly

Market Vice President Product Development, John Apuzzio

Vice President Network Programs Se Region, Patricio Cobos

Regional Vice President Account Manager, Kelli Lowery

Avp Network Integration Services, Rossana Salvadori

Vice President Market Development Optum Local Care Delivery, Kathy Winans

Vice President Optum Operations, Karen Mariska

Vice President Marketing, Heidi Svendsen

Senior Medical Director Community And State, Lewis Gregory

Vice President Public Sector Business Development, Kenneth Anderson

Medical Director, Denise Callari

Market Vice President Underwriting, Karl Hermonat

National Account Manager, Beth Beamer

Vp Client Services, Kimberly Burkhart

Vice President Employee Communication, Carla Nuzzo

Vice President Solutions Sales Payer Channel Optum, Laura Cahill

Vice President General Management, Susan Tonkin

Vice President Operations And Client Management Shared Services Public And Labor Markets, Stephen Pronio

Vice President Client Relations, Kelly Mcdevitt

Senior Apps Devpr, Kalyn Shenefelt

Vice President Information Technology, Kevin Kantola

Vice President Executive Assistant Finance, Dan Cummings

Vice President Finance, Kevin Carlson

Vice President Sales, Danielle Peacock

Medical Director, Tony Sun

Vice President Information Technology, Oren Hermel

Vice President Application Development, Guy Grindberg

Vice President Risk Management, Randy Jacob

Vice President Finance, Lisa Iverson

Vice President Small Business, Doug Metzger

Vice President Market Strategy And Marketing, Christi Kruse

Vice President Assistant Treasurer, Paul Runice

Vice President Regulatory Affairs (federal), Deborah Schreiber

Director Of Pharmacy Management, Susan Maddux

National Vice President Consulting Relations, Michael Finn

Vice President Clinical Strategy, Karen Keown

Vice President Sales, Kim Lewis

Vice President Sales, Geoff Buro

Vice President National Alliances, Randy Spicer

Vice President Business Development, Matthew Aaefedt

Vice President Quality Solutions, Peter Naumann

Vp Public Relations, Tyler Mason

Vice President Tax, John Kelly

Vice President Marketing Services, Richard Osberg

Vice President Marketing Operations, Jordana Costello

Medical Director, Todd Johnson

Vice President Client Development, Denise Lindeen

Vice President Information Technology Customer Integration Behavioral Solutions Optumhealth, Adrian Sale

Senior Medical Director, Bethany Reeves

Vice President Strategic Insight And Innovation, Meredith Baratz

Vice President Of State Affairs, Michelle Marto

Vice President Of Financial Planning And Analysis, Robert Schweitzer

Vice President Client Development, Steven Zucker

Vice President Finance, Darren C Moquist

Vice President Of Contracting, Rebecca Bausch

Vice President Client Management, David Twardy

Senior Vice President, Gayle Coyle-ikemoto

Vice President Government Relations, Leah Rummel

Vice President And Actuary, Drew Girton

Vice President Finance, Scott Taylor

National Vice President Appeals And Grievances, Mark Friedman

National Vice President Risk Adjustment Operations, Ovais Jalil

Senior Vice President Sales, Craig Lafiandra

Vice President Healthcare Economics, Tyner Wilson

Medical Director, Barry Stone

Vice President Product Optum Consumer Solutions Group, Glen Kvadus

Vice President Of Government Programs Central Region, Keely Gladieux

Regional Vice President Clinical Quality, Michelle Francisco

Senior Vice President And Chief Accounting Officer, Tom Roos

Vice President Client Relations National Accounts, Scott Roberge

Account Vice President, Christopher Chadbourne

Vice President Total Rewards (optum Compensation), Brad Fagerstrom

Associate Vice President Of Outpatient Behavioral Programs, Michael Brendzal

Vice President External Communications, Lisa Hawks

Vice President Medicare Operations Performance United Healthcare Benefit Operations, Chelsey Berstler

Vice President National Accounts At Optumrx, Kristin Rubino

Vice President, Lalit Lopez

Vice President Internal Audit And Advisory Services, Kendall Bishop

Vice President National Ancillary Contracting And Strategy, Dosedel Greg

Medical Director, Olabisi Kuye

Medical Director, Ola Medhat

Medical Director Community And State, Sara Rinck

Senior Medical Director, Michael Haberman

Vice President Of Financial Planning And Analysis, Shingai Mavengere

Vice President Compliance Exam Management, Joseph Keen

Vice President Government Program Administration, Anthony Dapp

Vp And Deputy General Counsel Unitedhealthcare, Jill Mitchell

National Vice President Of Broker Relations, Kathleen Parks

Evp Operations Unitedhealthcare, Brian Brueckman

Vice President Regional Tpa Sales, Gregory Pavlic

Vice President Of Business Development, Warner Roberts

Vice President Network Contracting, Brian Ward

Vice President Innovation And Strategy, Matt Grimes

Vice President Enterprise Solutions Optum, Mary Joiner

Auditors: Deloitte & Touche LLP

LOCATIONS

HQ: UnitedHealth Group Inc
UnitedHealth Group Center, 9900 Bren Road East, Minnetonka, MN 55343
Phone: 952 936-1300
Web: www.unitedhealthgroup.com

PRODUCTS/OPERATIONS

2018 Sales

	$ mil.	% of total
UnitedHealthcare	184,476	65
Optum		
OptumRx	69,536	24
OptumHealth	24,145	8
OptumInsight	9,008	3
Adjustments	(59918)	-
Total	**226,247**	**100**

2018 Sales

	$ mil.	% of total
Premiums	178,087	79
Products	29,601	13
Services	17,183	8
Investment & other income	1,376	-
Total	**266,247**	**100**

Selected Operations

Optum (Health Services division)
  OptumHealth (specialty benefits)
  OptumInsight (formerly Ingenix information technology and consulting services)
  OptumRx (formerly Prescription Solutions pharmacy benefit management)
UnitedHealthcare (Health Plans division)
  UnitedHealthcare Community & State (former operations of AmeriChoice public-sector programs)
  UnitedHealthcare Employer & Individual (health plans for individuals businesses employers)

UnitedHealthcare International (expatriate coverage for global accounts)
UnitedHealthcare Medicare & Retirement (former operations of Ovations benefits for people age 50 and older)
UnitedHealthcare Military & Veterans (TRICARE West Region contract)

COMPETITORS

Aetna	Humana
Anthem	Kaiser Foundation
Blue Cross	Health Plan
CIGNA	Molina Healthcare
Centene	Prime Therapeutics
Express Scripts	WellCare Health Plans

HISTORICAL FINANCIALS
Company Type: Public

Income Statement   FYE: December 31

	REVENUE ($ mil.)	NET INCOME ($ mil.)	NET PROFIT MARGIN	EMPLOYEES
12/19	242,155	13,839	5.7%	325,000
12/18	226,247	11,986	5.3%	300,000
12/17	201,159	10,558	5.2%	260,800
12/16	184,840	7,017	3.8%	230,000
12/15	157,107	5,813	3.7%	200,000
Annual Growth	11.4%	24.2%	—	12.9%

2019 Year-End Financials

Debt ratio: 23.39%
Return on equity: 25.32%
Cash ($ mil.): 10,985
Current ratio: 0.69
Long-term debt ($ mil.): 36,808

No. of shares (mil.): 948
Dividends
  Yield: 1.4%
  Payout: 30.1%
Market value ($ mil.): 278,693

	STOCK PRICE ($) FY Close	P/E High/Low	Earnings	PER SHARE ($) Dividends	Book Value
12/19	293.98	20 15	14.33	4.14	60.78
12/18	249.12	23 17	12.19	3.45	53.85
12/17	220.46	21 14	10.72	2.88	49.30
12/16	160.04	22 15	7.25	2.38	40.20
12/15	117.64	21 16	6.01	1.88	35.50
Annual Growth	25.7%	— —	24.3%	21.9%	14.4%

Univar Solutions Inc

Auditors: Ernst & Young LLP

LOCATIONS

HQ: Univar Solutions Inc
3075 Highland Parkway, Suite 200, Downers Grove, IL 60515
Phone: 331 777-6000
Web: www.univar.com

HISTORICAL FINANCIALS
Company Type: Public

Income Statement   FYE: December 31

	REVENUE ($ mil.)	NET INCOME ($ mil.)	NET PROFIT MARGIN	EMPLOYEES
12/19	9,286	(100)	—	10,300
12/18	8,632	172	2.0%	8,500
12/17	8,253	119	1.5%	8,600
12/16	8,073	(68)	—	8,700
12/15	8,981	16	0.2%	9,200
Annual Growth	0.8%	—	—	2.9%

2019 Year-End Financials

Debt ratio: 41.79%
Return on equity: (-6.85%)
Cash ($ mil.): 330
Current ratio: 1.69
Long-term debt ($ mil.): 2,688

No. of shares (mil.): 168
Dividends
  Yield: —
  Payout: —
Market value ($ mil.): 4,089

	STOCK PRICE ($) FY Close	P/E High/Low	Earnings	PER SHARE ($) Dividends	Book Value
12/19	24.24	— —	(0.61)	0.00	10.27
12/18	17.74	26 13	1.21	0.00	8.41
12/17	30.96	39 32	0.85	0.00	7.73
12/16	28.37	— —	(0.50)	0.00	5.84
12/15	17.01	195 116	0.14	0.00	5.92
Annual Growth	9.3%	— —	—	—	14.8%

Universal Health Services, Inc.

With dozens of health care facilities in nearly every state Universal Health Services (UHS) isn't quite ubiquitous but it's working on it. One of the nation's largest for-profit hospital operators UHS owns or leases about 25 acute care hospitals with a total of more than 6000 beds primarily in rural and suburban communities. The system also operates outpatient centers and behavioral health treatment facilities most located near its acute care hospitals. In addition UHS' behavioral health division operates approximately 475 psychiatric and substance abuse hospitals with a combined capacity of more than 23000 beds; its UK-based Cygnet unit operates about 20 more facilities. UHS is controlled by founder and CEO Alan Miller.

Operations

UHS receives slightly more than half of its annual revenues from its acute care segment which includes medical hospitals surgical outpatient facilities and radiation oncology centers. The remainder of the company's revenue comes from its portfolio of behavioral health hospitals which include residential facilities for teens adult psychiatric hospitals substance abuse facilities and special education schools for students with emotional problems.

UHS provides central resources to its network of facilities including purchasing information services finance facilities planning administrative personnel marketing public relations and physician recruitment.

Geographic Reach

UHS' acute care facilities are located in about 10 states and are situated mostly in smaller towns and cities with limited competition though the division does have facilities in a few larger markets (such as Las Vegas and Washington DC). UHS' behavioral health hospitals are scattered across about 40 US states as well as Puerto Rico the Washington D.C and the UK. The company's biggest markets for both segments are Nevada (about 20%) Texas (nearly 15%) and California (about 10%).

Headquartered in King of Prussia Pennsylvania UHS also has offices in Wayne Pennsylvania; Brentwood Tennessee; Denton Texas; and Reno Nevada.

Sales and Marketing

Both of UHS' operating segments (Acute Care Hospital Services and Behavioral Health Services) earn more than half of revenues from managed care providers (HMOs PPOs) with the remainder of revenues coming from traditional Medicare and Medicaid plans and other sources.

Financial Performance

UHS' revenue has been consistently growing for the last five years with a 26% growth between 2015 and 2019. It's net income follows the same pattern with a 20% growth in the same period.

Net revenues increased 5.6% or $606 million to $11.38 billion during 2019 as compared to $10.77 billion during 2018. The increase was primarily attributable to the $583 million or 5.5% increase in net revenues generated from the company's acute care and behavioral health care operations owned during both periods (which we refer to as "same facility") and the $23 million of other combined net revenue increases due primarily to the revenues generated at 25 behavioral health facilities located in the U.K. acquired during the third quarter of 2018 in connection with UHS' acquisition of The Danshell Group.

Net income attributable to UHS increased $35 million to $815 million during 2019 as compared to $780 million during 2018.

The system ended 2019 with $105.7 million in cash down by some $94 million from 2018. Operating activities contributed $1.4 billion but investing activities used $688.4 million (primarily for property and equipment additions) and financing activities (largely share repurchases) used another $845 million.

Strategy

UHS believes community-based hospitals will remain the focal point of the healthcare delivery network and it is committed to a philosophy of self-determination for both the company and its hospitals.

Acquisition of Additional Hospitals. The company selectively seeks opportunities to expand its base of operations by acquiring constructing or leasing additional hospital facilities. It is committed to a program of rational growth around core businesses while retaining the missions of the hospitals it manages and the communities it serves. Such expansion may provide us with access to new markets and new healthcare delivery capabilities.

Improvement of Operations of Existing Hospitals and Services. UHS also seeks to increase the operating revenues and profitability of owned hospitals by the introduction of new services improvement of existing services physician recruitment and the application of financial and operational controls.

Quality and Efficiency of Services. Pressures to contain healthcare costs and technological developments allowing more procedures to be performed on an outpatient basis have led payers to demand a shift to ambulatory or outpatient care wherever possible.

In addition The company's aggressive recruiting of highly qualified physicians and developing provider networks help to establish facilities as an important source of quality healthcare in their respective communities.

EXECUTIVES

Evp And Cfo, Steve G. Filton, age 62, $584,606 total compensation

Chairman And Ceo, Alan B. Miller, age 82, $1,600,061 total compensation

Evp; President Behavioral Health, Debra K. Osteen, age 64, $638,025 total compensation

Evp; President Acute Care, Marvin G. Pember, age 66, $618,502 total compensation

President, Marc D. Miller, age 49, $720,861 total compensation

Svp Information Services And Business Solutions, Michael S. Nelson

Vice President And Director, Gayle Bowman

Vice President And Director, Michelle Greenup

Vice President And Director, Sue Wildgoose

Vice President Center Applications, Lorraine Castro

Executive Vice President Of Finance, Debbie Onofrey

Assistant Vice President Clinical Trg An, Bill Lightfoot

Director Of Health, Emily Macko

Executive Vice President Of Finance, Eileen Vido

Vice President E Health Financial Advisor, Andrew Ganti

Vice President Of Hawaii Division, Donna Murray

Chief Medical Director, Kristi Whittaker

Vice President And Director, Jerilin Cummings

Vice President Of Pfs, John Goss

Director Of Radiology Services, Jeff Otto

Vice President And Director, Frank Pizzuto

Regional Vice President, Frank Lopez

Executive Vice President Of Finance, Andy Belen

Director Of Pharmacy, Kristen Palasthy

Executive Vice President Of Finance, Stephanie Hill

Senior Vice President And Treasurer, Cheryl Ramagano

Vice President Financial Operations, Chris Recon

Regional Vp The Valley Health System, Karla Perez

Vice President, Pj Moraci

Director Of Clinical Services, Kate McBride

Director Of Pharmacy, John Luther

Director Of Clinical Services, Becky Mcdonough

Vice President Of Operations, Cori Cole

Nursing Director, Vicki Gant

Director Of Nursing, Miranda Blajszczak

Medical Records Director, Sarah Hoffman

Vice President Acute Finance, Thomas Machozzi

Medical Director, Michael Vines

Vice President Supply Chain Operations, Raymond Davis

Director Of Radiology, Mark Lerner

Vice President Hospital Finance Bh, Lawrence Harrod

Staff Vice President Reimbursement, Bob Halinski

Radiology Director, Beth Louton

Director Of Nursing, Catherine Wright

Director Of Pharmacy, George Morton

Vice President Cno Acute, Jacalyn Liebowitz

Medical Records Director, Melanie Fowler

Svp Finance Behavioral Health, Laurence Harrod

Director Of Him And Risk Management, Gayle Leonard

Medical Director Of Emergency Services, James Rhee

Director Of Nursing, Zachary Love

Director Physical Therapy, Julie Fernie

Regional Vice President Bh, Diane Henneman

Medical Records Director, Sarah Holmes

Director Of Clinical Services, Jeremy Wagoner

Executive Vice President Sales And Marketing, Sandra Rivera

Director Of Pharmacy, Shabnam Bcpp

Svp Hr, Geraldine Johnson Geckle

Director Of Admissions, Fred Knox

Director Of Nursing, Bridgette Bishop

Vice President Of Information Technology, Eric Rasmussen

Nursing Director, Randy Rios

Medical Records Director, Michael Beck

Information Technology Vice President, Clint Jaschen

Medical Records Director, Susan Easterling

Medical Director, Benjamin Nimmo

Nursing Director, Sheila Maraan

Director Of Admissions, Meghan Trice

Occupational Therapy Dir, Jody Chandler

Medical Director, Muhammad Sajid

Respiratory Therapy Director, Michael Mygrants

Nursing Director, Kellie Holland

Occupational Therapy Dir, Christine Bagwell

Nursing Director, Michella Harris

Medical Records Director, Michele Mendel

Secretary, Terry Shaw

Treasurer, Esther Rubin

Auditors: PricewaterhouseCoopers LLP

LOCATIONS

HQ: Universal Health Services, Inc.
Universal Corporate Center, 367 South Gulph Road, King of Prussia, PA 19406-0958
Phone: 610 768-3300
Web: www.uhsinc.com

Selected Facilities

California
Corona Regional Medical Center (Corona)
Palmdale Regional Medical Center (Palmdale)
Southwest Healthcare System — Inland Valley Campus (Wildomar)
Southwest Healthcare System — Rancho Springs Campus (Murrieta)
Temecula Valley Day Surgery and Pain Therapy Center (Murrieta)
Florida
Lakewood Ranch Medical Center (Bradenton)
Manatee Memorial Hospital (Bradenton)
Palms Westside Clinic ASC (50% Royal Palm Beach)
Wellington Regional Medical Center (West Palm Beach)
Nevada
Centennial Hills Hospital Medical Center (Las Vegas)
Desert Springs Hospital (72% Las Vegas)
Northern Nevada Medical Center (Sparks)
Spring Valley Hospital Medical Center (72% Las Vegas)
Summerlin Hospital Medical Center (72% Las Vegas)
Valley Hospital Medical Center (72% Las Vegas)
South Carolina
Aiken Regional Medical Centers (Aiken)
Aurora Pavilion (Aiken)
Cancer Care Institute of Carolina (Aiken)
Oklahoma
St. Mary's Regional Medical Center (Enid)
Puerto Rico
First Hospital Panamericano (Cidra)
First Hospital Panamericano (Ponce)
First Hospital Panamericano (San Juan)
Texas
Cornerstone Regional Hospital (50% Edinburg)
Doctors' Hospital of Laredo (Laredo)
Fort Duncan Regional Medical Center (Eagle Pass)
Northwest Texas Healthcare System (Amarillo)
Northwest Texas Surgery Center (majority owned Amarillo)
The Pavilion at Northwest Texas Healthcare System (Amarillo)
South Texas Health System (Edinburg)

Edinburg Regional Medical Center (Edinburg)
Edinburg Children's Hospital (Edinburg)
McAllen Medical Center (McAllen)
McAllen Heart Hospital (McAllen)
South Texas Behavioral Health System (Edinburg)
Texoma Medical Center (Denison)
TMC Behavioral Health Center (Denison)
Washington D.C.
The George Washington University Hospital (80%)

PRODUCTS/OPERATIONS

2017 Sales by Segment

	$ mil.	% of total
Acute Care Hospital Services	5	53
Behavioral Health Services	4,906	47
Other	18	-
Total	**10,409**	**100**

COMPETITORS

Adventist Health System Sunbelt Healthcare
Adventist Health System West
Ascension Health
Banner Health
CHRISTUS Health
CRC Health
Community Health Systems
Devereux Foundation
HCA
Hazelden Betty Ford
LifePoint Health
Mercy Health
Northwestern Human Services
Sutter Health
Tenet Healthcare
Texas Health Resources
UBH
United Surgical Partners

HISTORICAL FINANCIALS

Company Type: Public

Income Statement

	REVENUE ($ mil.)	NET INCOME ($ mil.)	NET PROFIT MARGIN	EMPLOYEES
12/19	11,378	814	7.2%	90,400
12/18	10,772	779	7.2%	87,100
12/17	10,409	752	7.2%	76,600
12/16	9,766	702	7.2%	75,325
12/15	9,043	680	7.5%	74,600
Annual Growth	**5.9%**	**4.6%**	**—**	**4.9%**

FYE: December 31

2019 Year-End Financials

Debt ratio: 34.15%
Return on equity: 14.96%
Cash ($ mil.): 61
Current ratio: 1.23
Long-term debt ($ mil.): 3,896

No. of shares (mil.): 86
Dividends
  Yield: 0.4%
  Payout: 6.5%
Market value ($ mil.): 12,439

	STOCK PRICE ($) FY Close	P/E High/Low		PER SHARE ($) Earnings	Dividends	Book Value
12/19	143.46	17	13	9.13	0.60	63.48
12/18	116.56	17	13	8.31	0.40	59.00
12/17	113.35	16	12	7.81	0.40	52.95
12/16	106.38	19	14	7.14	0.40	46.91
12/15	119.49	21	15	6.76	0.40	43.23
Annual Growth	**4.7%**	**—**	**—**	**7.8%**	**10.7%**	**10.1%**

UNIVERSITY OF PENNSYLVANIA

EXECUTIVES

Pres, Amy Gutmann
Market Researcher, Market Rese, Jane Anderson
Coordinator, Karen Stevenson
College and Career Programs Co, Laurie Engleman
Lsoca Coordinator, Mark Bardsley
University Recruiting Coordina, Marlene Williams
Administrative Coordinator, Patricia Kozak
Computer Analyst, Dan Bachovin Sr
Information Specialist, Caroline Elizabeth
Financial Support Spec, Janice Brown
Assistant Professor, Benjamin Backus
Auditors: PRICEWATERHOUSECOOPERS LLP PH

LOCATIONS

HQ: UNIVERSITY OF PENNSYLVANIA
3451 WALNUT ST RM 100, PHILADELPHIA, PA
191046243
Phone: 215 898-5000
Web: WWW.UPENN.EDU

HISTORICAL FINANCIALS

Company Type: Private

Income Statement — FYE: June 30

	REVENUE ($ mil.)	NET INCOME ($ mil.)	NET PROFIT MARGIN	EMPLOYEES
06/18	10,093	2,326	23.0%	70
06/16	8,576	1,021	11.9%	—
06/15	0	0	—	—
Annual Growth	—	—	—	—

Univest Financial Corp

Univest Corporation of Pennsylvania will keep your money close to its vest. The holding company owns $3 billion-asset Univest Bank and Trust which serves the southeastern part of the Keystone State and the broader Mid-Atlantic region online and though 30 branches and provides standard retail and commercial banking services such as checking and savings accounts CDs IRAs and credit cards. Subsidiary Univest Capital provides small-ticket commercial financing while Univest Insurance offers personal and commercial coverage. Univest Investments which boasts some $3 billion in assets under management offers brokerage and investment advisory services.

Operations

Univest operates three main business segments: Banking which accounted for 79% of the company's total revenue during 2015 and provides traditional banking services to consumers businesses and government entities through Univest Bank and Trust; Wealth Management (12% of revenue) which offers investment advisory retirement plan trust municipal pension and broker/dealer services through Univest Investments; and Insurance (9% of revenue) which offers commercial and personal insurance lines as well as benefits and human resources consulting through Univest Insurance.

Broadly speaking Univest Corporation gets more than 60% of its revenue from interest income. About 61% of its total revenue came from loan interest (including fees on loans and leases) during 2015 while another 5% came from interest on its investment securities. The rest of its revenue came from insurance commissions and fees (8% of revenue) investment advisory commission and fee income (7%) trust fee income (5%) deposit account service charges (3%) mortgage banking sales (3%) and other miscellaneous income sources.

More than 40% of the company's loan portfolio was made up of commercial real estate loans at the end of 2015 while another 23% of loan assets were made up of commercial loans that were financial or agricultural-related. The remainder of the portfolio was made up of loans tied to residential properties secured for business purposes (10% of loan assets) residential properties for personal purposes (8%) lease financings (7%) construction real estate loans (4%) and loans to individuals (less than 2%).

Geographic Reach

Souderton Pennsylvania-based Univest Corporation and its subsidiaries serve clients across the Mid-Atlantic region. The company has around 30 bank branches and nearly 20 offices in the Montgomery Bucks Philadelphia Chester Berks Lehigh and Delaware counties of Pennsylvania as well as in Calvert County in Maryland Camden County in New Jersey and Lee County in Florida.

Sales and Marketing

Univest Corporation serves individuals businesses municipalities and non-profit organizations. It spent $2.25 million on marketing and advertising during 2015 to reach these clients up from $1.88 million and $1.95 million in 2014 and 2013 respectively.

Financial Performance

The bank's revenues and profits have been trending higher over the past several years thanks to 50% loan asset growth and 50% non-interest revenue growth since 2011 along with a continued reduction in loan loss provisions as its loan portfolio's credit quality has improved with higher property valuations in the strengthened economy.

Univest Corporation's revenue jumped 24% to a record $154.41 million during 2015 mostly as 35% loan asset growth (loan balances swelled to $2.16 billion) stemming from its Valley Green Bank acquisition helped boost interest income. The company's non-interest income also rose 9% as its mortgage banking gains doubled during the year on higher volumes and as its insurance commissions and fee income rose 20% after acquiring Sterner Insurance in mid-2014.

Strong revenue growth in 2015 drove the company's net income up 23% to $27.27 million for the year. Univest Corporation's operating cash levels climbed 12% to $35.63 thanks to the rise in earnings.

Strategy

Univest Corporation has been expanding its service lines and building its loan and deposit businesses by strategically acquiring other banks and investment or insurance-related financial firms.

Mergers and Acquisitions

In December 2015 Univest Corporation agreed to buy Fox Chase Bancorp along with its $1.1 billion in assets $768 million in loans $765 million in deposits and several Fox Chase Bank branches in Pennsylvania and New Jersey for a price exceeding $240 million. The deal would also expand Univest's presence in Bucks Chester Philadelphia and Montgomery counties in Pennsylvania as well as into Atlantic and Cape May counties in New Jersey.

In January 2015 the company purchased Valley Green Bank as well as its three branches and two loan production offices in the greater Philadelphia market for $77 million.

In July 2014 Univest bolstered its Univest Insurance subsidiary after acquiring Sterner Insurance Associates a full-service insurance and consultative risk management firm that served individuals and businesses across the Lehigh Valley Berks Bucks and Montgomery counties.

In January 2014 flagship subsidiary Univest Bank and Trust Co. bought registered investment advisory firm Girard Partners Ltd. as well as its $500 million in assets under management. The deal boosted Univest's assets under management by 20% to a total of $3 billion after the acquisition.

EXECUTIVES

President Corporate Banking, Philip C. (Phil) Jackson, $250,000 total compensation
Evp And Chief Credit Officer Univest Corporation And Univest National Bank, Duane J. Brobst, $200,000 total compensation
President And Ceo, Jeffrey M Schweitzer, $450,000 total compensation
Sevp And Cfo, Michael S Keim, $270,000 total compensation
Executive Vice President, John Duerksen
Senior Vice President, Matt Holland
Vice President, Barry Keck
Vp Operations Services, Mary Schulberger
Senior Vice President In Credit Administration, Tami Garber
Vice President, Lisa Hartley
Vice President Information Technology, Lisa M Perry
Vice President Account Executive, Chip Schofield
Executive Vice President Chief Experience Officer And Director Corporate Planning, Annette Szygiel
Senior Vice President, Richard Swartley
Senior Vice President Team Leader, Jeff Southworth
Senior Vice President, Leanne Hayes
Senior Vice President, Richard Pearce
Senior Vice President Senior Credit Officer, Christine Fox
Vice President Relationship Manager Corporate Banking, Randall Beaman
Vice President Area Manager, Gregory Taber
Senior Vice President Employee Benefits Practice Leader, Dennis Boyle
Vice President, Crystal Smith
Vice President, Barton Skurbe
Vice President And Operations Manager, Roxanne Tornetta
Senior Vice President Director Of Commercial Lending, Bryan Moyer
Vice President Business Banking, Patrick Mullen
National Accounts Manager, Kyle Hirsch
Vice President Commercial Real Estate Lending, Robert Castro
Vice President And Senior Benefits Consultant, Rick Mack

Vice President, Joe Panepresso
Vice President Commercial Lending, Andrew Leaman
Vice President Business Banking, Nan Kelly
Executive Vice President General Counsel And Chief Risk Officer Of The Corporation And The Bank, Megan Santana
Assistant Vice President Finance Business Unit Analytics, Mary Beth Osbeck
Vice President, Brian Lawrence
Senior Vice President Relationship Manager, John Thomas
Vice President, David Henrich
Senior Vice President Finance, Denise Joyce
Vice President Relationship Manager, Samantha Arland
Vice President Asset Recovery, Kevin Boyer
Vice President Commercial Lending, Ramzi Dagher
Vice President Commercial Lending, John P Hogan
Vice President Relationship Manager Commercial Real Estate, Tim Slizofski
Senior Vice President Commerical Lending, Joseph Gennett
Vp Sba Program Director, Jeff Pugh
Executive Vice President Chief Information Officer Of The Corporation And Of The Bank, Eric Deacon
Senior Vice President Phone Icon, Linda La Vay
Chairman, William S. Aichele, age 69
Board Member, Mark Schlosser
Treasurer, Bill Shelley
Board Member, Glenn Moyer
Auditors: KPMG LLP

LOCATIONS

HQ: Univest Financial Corp
14 North Main Street, Souderton, PA 18964
Phone: 215 721-2400
Web: www.univest.net

PRODUCTS/OPERATIONS

2015 sales

	$ mil.	% of total
Banking	120	79
Wealth Management	18	12
Insurance	14	9
Other	0	-
Total	**154**	**100**

COMPETITORS

Citizens Financial Group	PNC Financial
Fulton Financial	QNB Corp.
Harleysville Savings	Royal Bancshares
M&T Bank	Sovereign Bank

HISTORICAL FINANCIALS

Company Type: Public

Income Statement

FYE: December 31

	ASSETS ($ mil.)	NET INCOME ($ mil.)	INCOME AS % OF ASSETS	EMPLOYEES
12/19	5,380	65	1.2%	873
12/18	4,984	50	1.0%	841
12/17	4,554	44	1.0%	855
12/16	4,230	19	0.5%	840
12/15	2,879	27	0.9%	717
Annual Growth	**16.9%**	**24.6%**	**—**	**5.0%**

2019 Year-End Financials

Debt ratio: 4.55%	No. of shares (mil.): 29
Return on equity: 10.12%	Dividends
Cash ($ mil.): 125	Yield: 2.9%
Current ratio: —	Payout: 34.1%
Long-term debt ($ mil.): —	Market value ($ mil.): 786

	STOCK PRICE ($) FY Close	P/E High/Low	PER SHARE ($) Earnings	Dividends	Book Value
12/19	26.78	12 10	2.24	0.80	23.01
12/18	21.57	17 12	1.72	0.80	21.32
12/17	28.05	20 16	1.64	0.80	20.57
12/16	30.90	37 22	0.84	0.80	19.00
12/15	20.86	15 13	1.39	0.80	18.51
Annual Growth	**6.4%**	**— —**	**12.7%**	**(0.0%)**	**5.6%**

Unum Group

Through injury or illness Unum works to keep employees employed. A disability insurer in the US the UK and Poland it offers short-term and long-term disability insurance supplemental health coverage and life and accidental death and dismemberment insurance to individuals and groups. Its Colonial Life unit offers expanded cancer critical illness vision products and dental insurance. Additional subsidiaries include Unum Life Insurance Company of America Provident Life and Accident First Unum Life Colonial Life & Accident Paul Revere Life Insurance Starmount Life Insurance and Unum Poland. The company operates as Unum Limited in the UK. Unum's products are sold through field sales agents and independent brokers.

Operations

Unum reporting segments are comprised of the following: Unum US Unum International Colonial Life Closed Block and Corporate.

More than 55% of Unum's revenue come from the Unum US segment which offers group of group long-term and short-term disability insurance group life and accidental death and dismemberment products as well as supplemental and voluntary lines of business which are comprised of individual disability voluntary benefits and dental and vision products.Unum also generates revenue from its Closed Block segment (more than 20% of sales) which services policies in the long-term care individual disability and other insurance products no longer actively marketed.

The group's Colonial Life segment — which offers accident sickness and disability products which includes our dental and vision products life products and cancer and critical illness products. It accounts around 15% of company's total sales.

The Unum International segment produced more than 5% of revenue operates in the United Kingdom and Poland. Unum UK's business includes insurance for group long-term disability group life and supplemental lines of business which include dental individual disability and critical illness products. Unum Poland's business primarily includes insurance for individual and group life with accident and health riders.

The company covers roughly 39 million people worldwide and counts 182000 businesses in the US and UK among its customers (including a third of the Fortune 500).

Premium income accounts for about 80% of Unum's total revenue.

Geographic Reach

The US market contributes more than 55% of Unum's annual revenue. The company runs five primary operating centers in Tennessee Maine Louisiana South Carolina and the United Kingdom. In addition the company has an office space in Worcester Massachusetts and in various other locations throughout the United States the United Kingdom Ireland and Poland. Its Unum Limited office in Dorking is the headquarters for the smaller Unum UK operations which include Ireland.

Sales and Marketing

Unum uses its own sales force as well as independent agents consultants and brokers to market its products to employers.

Financial Performance

Unum's revenue has inched steadily upward for the past five years thanks to increases in net premiums written. Net income was also on the rise but took a steep dive in 2018.

Revenue rose 3% to $12 billion in 2019 because of increases in Premiums and Other incomes.

Net income increased by 110% to $1.1 billion in 2019 due to higher revenue.

The company ended 2019 with $84.1 million in net cash about $10 million less than it had at the end of 2018. Operating activities provided $1.7 billion in cash while investing activities used $1.4 billion and financing activities used another $358 million.

Strategy

Unum is committed not only to meeting the needs of their customers who depend on them but also to operating with integrity and being accountable for their actions through sound and consistent business practices a strong internal compliance program and a comprehensive risk management strategy. Their strategy is centered on growing their existing business expanding their reach and investing in their operations and technology to anticipate and respond to new market demands to meet the changing needs of their customers.

Although the low interest rate environment continues to place pressure on their profit margins the company continues to analyze and employ strategies that they believe will help them navigate this environment and allows them to maintain solid operating margins and significant financial flexibility to support the needs of their businesses while also continuing to return capital to their shareholders and exploring merger and acquisition opportunities to enhance their business lines. The continued strong labor market in the U.S. and the high level of consumer confidence will have positive impacts on their business. Unum have substantial leverage to rising interest rates and an improving economy which generates payroll growth and wage inflation. The company believes that consistent operating results combined with the implementation of strategic initiatives and the effective deployment of capital will allow them to meet their long-term financial objectives.

Unum's overall investment philosophy is to invest in a portfolio of high quality assets that provide investment returns consistent with that assumed in the pricing of its insurance products. Assets are invested predominantly in fixed maturity securities. Investment strategy for their portfolios is to match the effective asset cash flows and durations with related expected liability cash flows and durations to consistently meet the liability funding requirements of its businesses. The company seeks to earn investment income while assuming credit risk in a prudent and selective manner subject to constraints of quality liquidity diversification and regulatory considerations.

Company Background

Unum traces its roots back to the 1870s when Provident Life & Accident Insurance was established to provide medical insurance to coal miners.

HISTORY

Coal was discovered in eastern Tennessee in the 1870s; in 1887 several Chattanooga professional men formed the Provident Life & Accident Insurance Co. to provide medical insurance to miners. But it was a case of the inexperienced serving the uninsurable and by 1892 the company was on the brink of ruin. The founders sold half the company for $1000 to Thomas Maclellan and John McMaster two Scotsmen who had failed at banking in Canada.

The partners bought the rest of the company in 1895. After a period of strained relations Maclellan bought out McMaster in 1900. Provident which by then operated nationally entered Canada in 1948.

The company began a major move into disability insurance in 1997. It sold its annuity business to American General (now a subsidiary of AIG) the following year.

In 1998 with both Provident and Unum Corporation looking for ways to enhance business the companies commenced merger negotiations and completed the transaction the next year. But the merger was more expensive than anticipated and problems in integrating the companies' sales forces slowed policy sales.

Company operations began melding more smoothly and UnumProvident began addressing the problems with its sales force as well as adding customer service staff in 2000. It pulled money out of reserves by reinsuring several blocks of acquisition-related businesses and sold an inactive shell subsidiary licensed to sell annuities in most states to Allstate.

EXECUTIVES

Evp And General Counsel, Lisa G. Iglesias, age 54, $492,692 total compensation

Vice President The Benefits Center, Rob Hecker

Svp Corporate Marketing And Public Relations, Joseph R. (Joe) Foley

President Ceo And Director, Richard P. (Rick) McKenney, age 52, $994,231 total compensation

President And Ceo Unum Us, Michael Q. Simonds, age 46, $594,231 total compensation

Evp And Cfo, John F. (Jack) McGarry, age 62, $588,461 total compensation

Evp Global Services, Christopher J. (Chris) Jerome, age 58

Evp And Chief Investment Officer, Breege A. Farrell, age 60, $451,500 total compensation

President And Ceo Colonial Life, Timothy G. (Tim) Arnold, age 57

President And Ceo Unum Uk, Peter G. O'Donnell, age 53

Svp And Global Cio, Katherine M. (Kate) Miller

Assistant Vice President And Special Counsel At Unum, Michael Parker

Vice President And Chief Information Security Officer, Lynda Fleury

Assistant Vice President Benefit Operations Finl Svcs, John Howard

Vice President Acquisitions, Steven Cudd

Vice President, John Labrie

Vice President Internal Controls, Rick Patton

Vice President Project Delivery Sfdc, Tim Harper

National Account Manager, Andrew Sapiente

Assistant Vice President, Ken Barber

Vice President Business Analysis, Marylou Murphy

Assistant Vice President Actuary, Paul Lavallee

Assistant Vice President, Chris Castleberry

Assistant Vice President Digital Marketing, Bethany Branon

Avp And Managing Counsel, Pamela Castrucci

Assistant Vice President Consumerism, Jocelyn Grega

National Account Manager, Douglas Burnip

Vice President Distribution Partner Strategy, Benjamin Kahn

Assistant Vice President, Denise Houser

Vice President Customer Service, Stephanie Dyhrberg

Vice President Information Technology Application Managed Services, Randy Robinson

Vice President Compensation Human Resources, Rhonda Rigsby

Assistant Vice President Information Tec, Roy Shelton

Assistant Vice President Contact Center, Cj Jackson

Assistant Vice President Idi Benefits, Laura Chillo

Assistant Vice President Hris, Tina West

Assistant Vice President Financial Reporting, Jonathan Sanford

National Account Manager, Donna Hewes

Vice President, William Stutts

Assistant Vice President, Pat Grossman

Senior Vice President Finance Closed Block Operations, Jeff Condit

Assistant Vice President And Senior Co, Ann Courtney

Vice President Client Service And Support, Michelle Boucher

Avp And Sr. Counsel, Betsy Stivers

Vice President And Chief Litigation Counsel, Doug Baker

Assistant Vice President Senior Human Resources Business Partner, Kristen Prophater

Assistant Vice President Retirement Programs, Carl Gagnon

Assistant Vice President Ltd Benefits, Ahmad Sadaqatmal

Assistant Vice President Ltd Benefits, Joseph Pratico

Vice President And Managing Director Midwest Region, John Stibal

Legal Secretary, Alexa Grassi

Assistant Vice President, Matthew Purington

Vice President, Najla Frayha

Vice President And Director Of External Affairs, Mark Pare

Assistant Vice President Customer Experience, Susan Hoffman

Assistant Vice President And Senior Counsel, Brent Williams

Vice President And Chief Regulatory Counsel, Michelle Lafond

Assistant Vice President And Managing Counsel, Lisa Montelongo-connor

National Account Manager, Brooks Geiger

Senior Vice President Corporate Commercial And Business Banking Manager, Jennifer Jacobs

Avp Sr. Hr Business Partner, Jennifer Watkins

Avp Shared Technology, Joanne McInnis

Assistant Vice President Corporate Social Responsibility, Cary Olson-Cartwright

Senior Vice President Investor Relations, Tom White

Vice President Inclusion And Diversity, Wade Hinton

Vice President Global Delivery Center, Goslant Tammy

Assistant Vice President Government Affairs, Warren Wells

Assistant Vice President Global Human Resources Systems And Solutions, Denise Ferguson

Avp Sr. Human Resources Business Partner, Kristina Walker

Vice President Distribution Channel Expan, Chris Quinn

Vice President, James Cofield

Assistant Vice President Advanced Underwriting, Ron Mobley

National Account Manager, Cassandra Johnston

Assistant Vice President Products And Service Solutions, Andrew Molloy

Vice President Managing Counsel, Dave Canarie

Chairman, Kevin T. Kabat, age 63

Secretary, Priscilla Fairbrother

Auditors: Ernst & Young LLP

LOCATIONS

HQ: Unum Group
1 Fountain Square, Chattanooga, TN 37402
Phone: 423 294-1011
Web: www.unum.com

PRODUCTS/OPERATIONS

2018 Sales

	$ mil.	% of total
Premiums	8,986	77
Net investment income	2,453	21
Other	198	2
Adjustments	(39.5)	-
Total	**11,598**	**500**

2018 Sales by Segment

	$ mil.	% of total
Unum US	5,736	64
Colonial Life	1,603	18
Closed Block	1,077	12
Unum UK	568	6
Total	**11,598**	**100**

Selected Products and Services

Accidental death and dismemberment
Dental insurance
Disability (long-term and short-term)
Life insurance
Supplemental health
Vision products
Voluntary benefits

Selected Subsidiaries and Brands

Colonial Life & Accident Insurance
First Unum Life Insurance
Provident Life and Accident Insurance
Provident Life and Casualty Insurance
Starmount Life Insurance Company
The Paul Revere Life Insurance
Unum Life Insurance Company of America
Unum Limited (UK)

COMPETITORS

AEGON	MetLife
Aflac	Mutual of Omaha
American General	Northwestern Mutual
CIGNA	Principal Financial
Guardian Life	Prudential
Liberty Mutual	Torchmark
Lincoln Financial Group	

HISTORICAL FINANCIALS

Company Type: Public

Income Statement   FYE: December 31

	ASSETS ($ mil.)	NET INCOME ($ mil.)	INCOME AS % OF ASSETS	EMPLOYEES
12/19	67,013	1,100	1.6%	10,300
12/18	61,875	523	0.8%	9,600
12/17	64,013	994	1.6%	9,400
12/16	61,941	931	1.5%	9,400
12/15	60,589	867	1.4%	9,400
Annual Growth	2.6%	6.1%	—	2.3%

2019 Year-End Financials

Debt ratio: 4.37%
Return on equity: 11.84%
Cash ($ mil.): 84
Current ratio: —
Long-term debt ($ mil.): —

No. of shares (mil.): 202
Dividends
 Yield: 3.7%
 Payout: 22.0%
Market value ($ mil.): 5,918

	STOCK PRICE ($) FY Close	P/E High/Low		PER SHARE ($) Earnings	Dividends	Book Value
12/19	29.16	7	5	5.24	1.09	49.10
12/18	29.38	25	11	2.38	0.98	40.18
12/17	54.89	13	10	4.37	0.86	43.02
12/16	43.93	11	6	3.95	0.77	39.02
12/15	33.29	11	9	3.50	0.70	35.96
Annual Growth	(3.3%)	—	—	10.6%	11.7%	8.1%

UPMC

For University of Pittsburgh students and area residents medical care is spelled UPMC. University of Pittsburgh Medical Center (UPMC) is a leading not-for-profit health care delivery system in western Pennsylvania. The organization operates more than 40 hospitals including campuses in the Pittsburgh area regional and community hospitals and specialty facilities such as Children's Hospital of Pittsburgh. Altogether UPMC has about 8400 inpatient beds. In addition the system provides care through hundreds of physician practices outpatient clinics cancer treatment facilities and rehab centers; it also offers health insurance home health care and long-term care through about 25 senior living facilities.

Operations

UPMC is organized into four primary operating divisions: Provider Services Insurance Services UPMC International and UPMC Enterprises.

Provider Service which includes a comprehensive array of tertiary community and regional hospitals; specialty service lines such as transplantation women's health behavioral health pediatrics UPMC Hillman Cancer Center and rehabilitation; in-home care and retirement living options; contract services including pharmacy and clinical laboratories; and nearly 3400 employed physicians and associated practices.

Insurance Services offers health insurance to employers and employees workers' compensation and disability services and behavioral health coverage to Medical Assistance beneficiaries. The division's health plans include UPMC for You UPMC Health Plan UPMC for Kids and UPMC for Life; altogether it serves some 3.8 million members.

UPMC Enterprises functions as the innovation and commercialization arm of UPMC.

UPMC International provides hands on health care and management services with partners around the world.

As an academic medical center affiliated with the University of Pittsburgh's Schools of Health Sciences UPMC also focuses on medical research in a wide range of areas including the fields of regenerative medicine and biosecurity some of which is funded by the National Institutes of Health. The system is also renowned for its organ transplantation programs as well as for its cancer care psychiatric pediatric and neurosurgery.

Geographic Reach

UPMC's primary operating territory is the Pittsburgh area and western and central Pennsylvania. Outside the US UPMC operates health care facilities in Ireland Italy Kazakhstan and China.

Its headquarters is located in Pittsburgh Pennsylvania.

Sales and Marketing

The majority of UPMC's hospital services are rendered to patients under Medicare Highmark Blue Cross Blue Shield (a major area insurer) and medical assistance programs. It also provides management and consulting services partly through partnerships with health equipment and technology firms.

Strategy

The UPMC network of facilities has grown over the years through acquisitions partnerships and the construction of new facilities. For example to address the increasing number of patients seeking high-quality emergency care at UPMC East the hospital has expanded its emergency department more than doubling its capacity in mid-2020.

Also in March 2019 the system broke ground on a new vision and rehabilitation tower at UPMC Mercy as part of its $2 billion investment in specialty care.

Mergers and Acquisitions

In early 2019 Somerset Hospital in Somerset Pennsylvania became an affiliate of UPMC. The hospital is now operating as UPMC Somerset. UPMC plans to invest at least $45 million in the facility over a 10-year period.

Also in 2019 UPMC acquired Clane General Hospital in County Kildare in partnership with the Institute of Eye Surgery (IOES) and is renaming the facility UPMC Kildare Hospital. UPMC will also work with IOES to create a national Ophthalmology Network of Excellence while adding or expanding other needed medical specialties for patients in the region. Terms were not disclosed.

Company Background

UPMC traces its roots to 1893 when Louise Lyle the wife of a Presbyterian minister founded its predecessor. The hospital was incorporated as Presbyterian Hospital of Pittsburgh two years later. In 1930 the hospital joined forces with the University of Pittsburgh and broke ground on a new location which opened its doors in 1938.

EXECUTIVES

President And Ceo, Jeffrey A. Romoff
Evp And Chief Administrative Officer, Gregory Peaslee
Evp And Cfo, Robert A. DeMichiei

Evp President Insurance Services Division And President And Ceo Upmc Health Plan, Diane P. Holder
Evp; President Hospital And Community Services Division, Elizabeth B. Concordia
President Magee Women's Hospital, Leslie C. Davis
Evp And Chief Legal Officer, W. Thomas (Tom) McGough
Evp And President International Commercial Services Division And President Upmc Cancercenter, Charles E. (Chuck) Bogosta
Svp And Chief Of Staff Office Of The President, David M. Farner
Evp Treasurer And President Upmc Enterprises, C. Talbot Heppenstall
Evp Chief Medical And Scientific Officer And President Health Services Division, Steven D. Shapiro
Vice President Information Security And Privacy; Associate General Counsel, John Houston
Vice President Talent Acquisition Human Resources Innovation, Matt Rimer
Svp And Cio, Edward Mccallister
Senior Vice President And Chro, John Galley
Vice President International Technology, Deb Salava
Clinical Director, Debra Frank
Executive Vice President Treasurer And President Upmc Enterprises, C Talbot Heppenstall
Executive Vice President Upmc Enterprises Technology Development, Mark Stabingas
Vice President International Clinical Operations And Quality, Cheryl Brill
Clinical Director, Angela Scolieri
Vice President Of Medical Affairs, Gregory Beard
Cno Vice President Patient Care Services, Sandy Rader
Vice President Strategic Planning, David Russell
Director Of Pharmacy, Jennifer Belavic
Medical Director, Syed Hyder
Clinical Director, Susan Killmeyer
Medical Director Corporate Care Management, Roy Jacobson
Vice President For Medicaid Services For The Insurance Services Division, John Lovelace
Clinical Director, Sharon Hanchett
Director Of Nursing, Donna D Cochran
Senior Vice President Chief Risk Compliance And Ethics Officer, Kc Turan
Associate Medical Director, Richard Ambrosino
Vice President Upmc Imaging Services, Laura Moul
Vice President Government Programs Chief Engineer Ne Pa, Brendan Harris
Medical Secretary, Fay Reed
Secretary, Aleesa Foltz
Vice Chair Clinical Services, Dwight Heron
Auditors: ERNST & YOUNG LLP

LOCATIONS

HQ: UPMC
200 LOTHROP ST, PITTSBURGH, PA 152132536
Phone: 412 647-8762
Web: WWW.UPMC.COM

Selected Pennsylvania Facilities

Children's Hospital of Pittsburgh of UPMC
Magee-Womens Hospital of UPMC (Pittsburgh)
UPMC Bedford Memorial (Everett)
UPMC East (Pittsburgh)
UPMC Hamlot (Erie)
UPMC Horizon (Greenville and Shenango Valley)
UPMC McKeesport (McKeesport)
UPMC Mercy (Pittsburgh)
UPMC Montefiore (Pittsburgh)
UPMC Northwest (Seneca and Oil City)
UPMC Passavant (McCandless and Cranberry)
UPMC Presbyterian (Pittsburgh)
UPMC Shadyside (Pittsburgh)
UPMC St. Margaret (Pittsburgh)
UPMC Western Psychiatric Institute and Clinic (Pittsburgh)

PRODUCTS/OPERATIONS

2018 Sales

	$ mil.	% of total
Net patient services	8,823	47
Insurance enrollment	8,492	45
Other	1,462	8
Total	**18,777**	**100**

2018 Sales by Segment

	$ mil.	% of total
Health Services	11,881	57
Insurance Services	9,005	43
Adjustments	(2109)	.
Total	**18,777**	**100**

Selected Services

Behavioral and Mental Health Services
Cancer
COPD and Emphysema Center
Dermatology
Diabetes and Endocrinology
Ear Nose and Throat
Emergency Medicine
Family/Primary Care Medicine
Gastroenterology
Geriatrics
Heart and Vascular
Imaging Services
Kidney Disease
Liver
Neurology
Ophthalmology
Pain Medicine
Pathology
Pediatrics
Pulmonology and Respiratory
Rehabilitation
Rheumatology
Sports Medicine
Stroke Care
Thyroid
Urology
Women's Health
Wound Healing Services

COMPETITORS

AmeriHealth Mercy Health Plan
Butler Health System
Capital BlueCross
Conemaugh Health System
Excela Health
Geisinger Health System
HealthAmerica
Heritage Valley Health
Highmark
Independence Blue Cross
Jefferson Regional Medical Center of Pennsylvania
Ohio Valley General
St. Clair Health
Universal Health Services
West Penn Allegheny Health System

HISTORICAL FINANCIALS

Company Type: Private

Income Statement

FYE: December 31

	REVENUE ($ mil.)	NET INCOME ($ mil.)	NET PROFIT MARGIN	EMPLOYEES
12/19*	20,609	462	2.2%	80,000
06/15	614	326	53.1%	—
06/13	10,188	441	4.3%	—
12/11	4,758	(2)	—	—
Annual Growth	**20.1%**	—	—	—

*Fiscal year change

UPMC PRESBYTERIAN SHADYSIDE

EXECUTIVES

Pres, John Innocenti
Cfo, Eileen Simmons
Nurse Practitioner, Kristen Baileys
Nurse Practitioner, Kristin Ermine-Baer
Director of Operations, Melanie Houston
Nurse Practitioner, Patti Gigliotti
Nurse Practitioner, Timothy Coleman
Manager, Vicki Bedel
Member, William S Dietrich II
Managing Partner, William Pietragallo II
Member, John Pelusi Jr
Auditors: ERNST & YOUNG LLP PITTSBURGH

LOCATIONS

HQ: UPMC PRESBYTERIAN SHADYSIDE
200 LOTHROP ST MH-N739, PITTSBURGH, PA
152132536
Phone: 412 647-2345
Web: WWW.UPMC.COM

HISTORICAL FINANCIALS

Company Type: Private

Income Statement

FYE: June 30

	REVENUE ($ mil.)	NET INCOME ($ mil.)	NET PROFIT MARGIN	EMPLOYEES
06/10	8,046	276	3.4%	8,200
06/09	1,723	83	4.8%	—
06/06	1,627	0	—	—
Annual Growth	**49.1%**	—	—	—

US Bancorp (DE)

Boasting more than $475 billion in assets U.S. Bancorp is the holding company for U.S. Bank (the US's fifth largest commercial bank). Through that and other subsidiaries the company provides financial services including lending and depository services cash management capital markets and trust and investment management services. It also engages in credit cards services as well as merchant processing mortgage banking trust and investment management brokerage insurance and corporate payments. The bank has about 3000 branches and some 4700 ATMs in more than 30 states (primarily in the Midwest and West).

Operations

U.S. Bancorp's major lines of business are: Consumer and Business Banking Payment Services Corporate and Commercial Banking Wealth Management and Investment Services and Treasury and Corporate Support. It also generates fee income through its Elavon subsidiary?a leading processor of merchant credit card transactions in the US Canada Mexico and Europe.

Consumer and Business Banking is the holding company's largest earner raking in more than 35% of revenue. Through that segment U.S. Bancorp markets standard banking products and services in community and metropolitan settings through physical locations telephone online ATMs and mobile devices. It encompasses community banking metropolitan banking and indirect lending as well as mortgage banking.

Payment Services covers the company's business activities in cards such as consumer and business credit debit corporate stored-value cards government cards and merchant processing. It is responsible for more than 25% of revenue.

The Corporate and Commercial Banking segment generates more than 15% of the revenue focuses on depository services treasury management capital markets services international trade services and other financial services to middle market large corporate commercial real estate financial institution non-profit and public sector clients.

Wealth Management and Investment Services segment bring in about 15% of U.S. Bancorp's revenue from offering private banking financial advisory services investment management retail brokerage services insurance trust custody and fund servicing through four businesses: Wealth Management Global Corporate Trust & Custody U.S. Bancorp Asset Management and Fund Services. Treasury and Corporate Support accounts for more than 5% of revenue and houses U.S. Bancorp's investment portfolios and capital and interest rate risk management.

Commercial loans account for about 35% of the holding company's loan portfolio; residential mortgages represent about 25% of the total.

Geographic Reach

With its headquarter in Minneapolis Minnesota U.S. Bancorp runs a network of about 3000 branches and nearly 4700 ATMs in more than 30 states mainly in the West and Midwest. It is also active in Canada Mexico and Europe. The company has operations centers in about 10 US states.

Sales and Marketing

U.S. Bancorp provides an array of commercial and retail banking products and services to businesses governmental clients other financial institutions and individual customers. For 2019 the company spends more than $425 million on marketing and business development.

Financial Performance

U.S. Bancorp's revenue has expanded reliably each year since 2015 to yield overall growth of more than 15% as increased interest rates and loan volume bolstered the company's performance. Net Income on the other hand had been continuously increasing since 2015 it had its peak in 2018 when U.S. Bancorp sold its ATM servicing business and most of its FDIC-covered loans. However due to the impacts of changes in the yield curve in addition to changes in deposit and funding mix the net income for 2019 decreased by 2%.

The holding company's revenue for 2019 was $23.0 billion or 2% higher than 2018 driven by growth in mortgage banking revenue payment services revenue trust and investment management fees and commercial products revenue partially offset by a decrease in deposit service charges driven by the sale of the Company's ATM third-party processing business in late 2018.

U.S. Bancorp's net income decreased by 2% to end the year at $6.9 billion primarily due to lower noninterest-bearing deposit balances from 2018 and lower rates on loans partially offset by growth in payment services revenue trust and investment management fees and mortgage banking revenue.

The company grew its cash by $952 million to $22.4 billion in 2019. About $4.9 and $17.6 billion were garnered from operations and financing activities respectively. Investments used $21.6 billion primarily for purchases of held-to-maturity and available-for-sale investment securities and increased loans outstanding.

Strategy

Since many remote workers don't have company credit card and are often asked to pay for expenses the traditional way U.S Bank has launched a new corporate card (U.S Bank Instant Card) to help companies support their employees working from home. This will be used for expenses such as remote staff or simply as a means for replacing petty cash.

In 2019 the company completely rebuilt its mobile app based on customer feedback to include face ID enhanced mobile banking and easier account opening. That year it also launched its U.S. Bank Expense Wizard in partnership with Chrome River. The mobile app uses AI-driven chatbots to help employees make payments and report expenses associated with company-arranged travel.

Despite generally seeking to limit its physical location openings as customer banking preferences move increasingly toward online channels U.S. Bancorp does still open new branches in regions where demand exists. The company opened its first retail branch in North Carolina in 2019; it expects to have opened about 10 branches in the state by the end of 2020. Through a broader re-investment initiative U.S. Bancorp expects also to develop between 60 and 80 new relocated or redesigned branches by that target date with an eye toward regional markets in Florida Georgia and Texas.

The Company remains deeply committed to value creation for shareholders. In 2019 the Company increased its dividend rate per common share and expanded its common share repurchase program. This expanded capital distribution reflects the Company's ability to prudently manage capital as it responds to changes in the regulatory landscape while continuing to invest for the future.

Company Background

U.S. Bancorp predecessor bank First National Bank of Cincinnati opened in 1863. U.S. Bank the holding company's bank subsidiary is now the US's fifth largest bank.

HISTORY

When Farmers and Millers Bank was founded in 1853 it operated out of a strongbox in a rented storefront. After surviving a panic in the 1850s the bank became part of the national banking system in 1863 as First National Bank of Milwaukee. The bank grew and in 1894 it merged with Merchants Exchange Bank (founded 1870).

In 1919 the bank merged again with Wisconsin National Bank (founded 1892) to form First Wisconsin National Bank of Milwaukee a leading financial institution in the area from the 1920s on.

First Wisconsin grew through purchases over the next decade though the number of banks fell after the 1929 stock market crash; by the end of WWII it had 11 banks. State and federal legislation particularly the 1956 Bank Holding Company Act (which proscribed acquisitions and branching) constrained postwar growth. In the 1970s Wisconsin eased restrictions on intrastate branching and the bank began to grow again.

Growth accelerated in the late 1980s after Wisconsin and surrounding states legalized interstate banking in adjoining states in 1987. That year First Wisconsin bought seven Minnesota banks and then moved into Illinois. The company focused on strong well-run institutions. Also that year it sold its headquarters and used the proceeds to fund more buys. In 1988 in its first foray outside the Midwest the company bought Metro Bancorp in Phoenix targeting midwestern retirees moving to Arizona.

In 1989 First Wisconsin changed its name to Firstar. The early 1990s saw the company move into Iowa (Banks of Iowa 1990) buy in-state rivals (Federated Bank Geneva Capital Corporation 1992) and roll into Illinois (DSB Corporation 1993). The next year it bought First Southeast Banking Corp. (of Wisconsin) and merged it along with Firstar Bank Racine and Firstar Bank Milwaukee into one bank.

To strengthen its position against larger competitors Firstar continued its buying spree in 1995 (Chicago bank First Colonial Bankshares and Investors Bank Corp. of Minneapolis/St. Paul) and 1996 (Jacob Schmidt Company). The acquisitions left the company bloated: In 1996 Firstar began a restructuring designed to cut costs and increase margins. The restructuring project ended in 1997 but by then its performance lagged behind other midwestern banks considerably. In an effort to diversify it allied with EVEREN Securities to offer debt underwriting and sales fixed income products and public finance advisory services. But it was too little too late; under pressure from major stockholders to seek a partner Firstar began looking for a buyer.

It found Star Banc. Established in 1863 as The First National Bank of Cincinnati under a bank charter signed by Abraham Lincoln Star Banc over the years added branches and bought other banks. The company renamed all of its subsidiary banks Star Bank in 1988 and took the name Star Banc in 1989.

In 1998 Star Banc chairman Jerry Grundhofer approached Firstar about a combination. Negotiations proceeded quickly and a new Firstar was born.

The next year Firstar bought Mercantile Bancorporation. The purchase enabled the bank to expand its international banking services into such markets as Kansas Nebraska and Missouri. In 2000 the company made arrangements to buy U.S. Bancorp a Minneapolis-based bank with roots dating back to 1929. Under the terms of the acquisition Firstar would shed its own name in favor of the more appropriate U.S. Bancorp moniker. U.S. Bancorp completed the conversion of Firstar Bank branches to the U.S. Bank moniker during 2002.

EXECUTIVES

Vice Chairman Wholesale Banking, Leslie V. Godridge, age 64

Vice Chairman And Cfo, Terrance R. (Terry) Dolan, age 58, $545,833 total compensation

Senior Vice President National Sales Manager Small Business Specialty Finance, Erik Daniels

Vice President, Teri Charest

Evp Human Resources, Jennie P. Carlson, age 59

Regional President, Ward Wilson

President Ceo And Director, Andrew Cecere, age 59, $800,000 total compensation

Evp And General Counsel, James L. Chosy, age 56

Vice Chairman Wealth Management And Securities Services, Gunjan Kedia, age 49

Vice Chairman Community Banking And Branch Delivery, John R. Elmore, age 64

Vice Chairman And Chief Risk Officer, P. William (Bill) Parker, age 63, $625,000 total compensation

Vice Chairman Technology And Operations Services, Jeffry H. (Jeff) von Gillern, age 54, $575,000 total compensation

Vice Chairman Consumer Banking Sales And Support, Kent V. Stone, age 62

Evp And Chief Credit Officer, Mark G. Runkel, age 44

Vice Chairman Payment Services, Shailesh M. Kotwal, age 55

Evp And Chief Strategy And Reputation Officer, Katherine B. Quinn, age 55

Vice Chairman Wholesale Banking, James B. Kelligrew, age 54

Executive Vp, Dominic Venturo

Senior Vice President, Patricia Gnetz

Vice President Of Information Technology Security, Coni Pasch

Senior Vice President Dealer Services Regional Manager North Central Region, Dave Donarski

Senior Vice President Risk Infrastructure, Jim Putman

Assistant Vice President Application Consultant Commercial Leasing, Krishna Devarajulu

Vice President Procurement Operations Manager, Michael Lori

Senior Vice President Customer Solutions, Mary Ellen Carney

Vice President, Carol Rossman

Vice President, Scott Miller

Vice President Director Of Marketing And Communications Wealth Management, Mark Iverson

Senior Vice President Risk Analytics, Jacob Seljan

Vice President Program And Project Management, David Staloch

Senior Vice President Rmbs Risk Management, Edward Frere

Vp Credit Risk Assessment, Jennifer Briglia

Vice President, Chris Rodewald

Senior Vice President, Scott Farrell

Vice President Corporate Credit Risk Manager, Brian Richter

Vice President, Karmel Mizrahi

Svp Portfolio Marketing, Tim Stanton

Vice President Finance, Dan Christian

Vice President Information Technology Service Managment, Jim Berghs

Executive Vice President, Lisa Glover

Vice President In Commercial Banking, Alphonso Hawkins

Senior Vice President, Mehrasa Raygani

Vice President Technology Finance Group, Gregory Giannone

Vice President Senior Property Manager, Andrew McGlenon

Vp And Sr. Manager Marketing, Jeff Pick

Vice President Commercial Operations Manager, Victor Kapusinski

Vp And Project Manager, Cory Patrick

Vice President, Steve Kramer

Vice President, William Bayer
Vice President, Spencer Goldsmith
Senior Vice President, Terry Neher
Senior Vice President Utilities Division, Felicia LaForgia
Assistant Vice President Call Center Analytics, Maureen Splettstaszer
Vice President, Jeff Sutherland
Senior Vice President National Corporate Banking, Barry Litwin
Senior Vice President, Donna Fletcher
Vice President Portfolio Manager, Magnus Mcdowell Magnus Mcdowell
Vice President, Marty Barnett
Vice President, Roger Gross
Assistant Vice President, Adam Henderson
Senior Vice President And Deputy General Counsel, Chris Lenhart
Vice President Technology Services, Paul Ylonen
Vice President Commercial Real Estate Lender, Howard Goldberg
Senior Vice President, John Bradley
Vice President Information Services, Brian Mckeown
Vice President Of Marketing, Becky Hill
Assistant Vice President Finance Manager, Wendy Brock
Vice President And Site Manager, Elizabeth Thuning
Assistant Vice President Data Center Design And Planning, David Fortuna
Vice President, Suzanne Bedros
Executive Vice President Kansas City, Tim Petty
Senior Of Vice President, David Albanesi
Assistant Vice President Commercial Relationship Manager, Scott Gruenke
Vice President Of Information Technology, Erik Lindell
Vice President Corporate Credit Risk Management, Gregory Gay
Vice President Loan Administration, Cheryl Dingess
Vice President, Courtney Dowling
Vice President Ecrm Business Capabilities Team, Diane Morse
Vice President, John Pearson
Vice President, David Smith
Vice President Quality Management, Richard McCarthy
Senior Vice President, Douglas Boe
Vice President, Karen Bolton
Senior Vice President Of Finance, Kurt Swiecichowski
Assistant Vice President Real Estate Asset Manager, Karen Thomas
Vice President, Anthony Messina
Vice President And Senior Corporate Counsel, Benjamin Carpenter
Vice President Regional Sales Manager International Banking Group, Brian Cobb
Vice President Personal Trust Relationship Manager, Patrick Grewe
Senior Vice President, David Draxler
Senior Vice President Risk Management Strategy Execution, Michael Leary
Assistant Vice President Voice Implementation Projects, Joy Abts
Vice President, Brian Miner
Vice President Information Technology, Alfonso Gonzalez
Senior Vice President Quality Assurance, AnnMarie Janke
Senior Vice President, Jeff Pape
Senior Vice President, Bill Mulvihill
Vice President National Sales Manager, Richard Struck
Assistant Vice President Application Architect, David Brus
Vice President And Director, Suzanne Galvin
Vice President, Jack Ellerin
Vice President Regional Manager, Chad Laipple

Senior Vice President, Brian Reisenauer
Vice President, Regan Leon
Senior Vice President Relationship Manager, Karen Weathers
Vice President, Rod Swenson
Svp And Head Loan Capital Markets, Jeanne Rudelius
Vice President Commercial Relationship Manager, Corey Hansen
Vice President Business Banking, Brent Blume
Senior Vice President, Curt Steiner
Vice President, Kent Inman
Senior Vice President California Region Manager, Stephen Johnson
Assistant Vice President, Becky Burton
Vice President, Greg Hargis
Vice President Technology Group Manager, Genie Strachan-smith
Assistant Vice President, Lorra Donnelly
Vice President Public Sector Sales, Scott Hesse
Vice President Prm, Robert Hickman
Vice President Managing Director The Private Client Group, Troy Smith
Senior Corporate Counsel And Vice President, Daniel Sundell
Vice President, Cindy Hallberg
Assistant Vice President And Assistant, Stacey Dennehy
Assistant Vice President, Cregg Rogers
Vice President Foreign Exchange, Judy Loretta
Assistant Vice President, Lindsey Poker
Assistant Vice President, Ryan Frank
Vice President Credit Risk Management, Olivier Haise
Senior Vice President, Kevin Miller
Vice President, Peter LaMontagna
Vice President, David Rowe
Assistant Vice President And Branch Manager, Chrissy Kolakowski
Vice President, David Johnson
Senior Vice President Of Consumer Products And Services, Steve Saloutos
Vice President Information Technology, Patrick Ryan
Vice President Credit Risk Assessment, Trina Johnson
Vice President, Richard Clemmerson
Vice President And Government Banking Relationship Manager, Kim Mays
V. P, Bruce Turner
Vice President Institional Risk Management, Sean Devillers
Vice President Regional Ops Manager, Angela Davidson
Vice President Customer Care, Scott Tostengard
Vice President Customer Service, Kevin Donahue
Avp Business Banking Officer, Rhonda Waltenburg
Assistant Vice President, Kimberly McDonough
Vice President, Craig Knott
Senior Vice President, Kurt Imerman
Trust Officer Vice President, Keith Butler
Assistant Vice President, Robin Stoker
Senior Vice President, David Caspar
Senior Vice President, Arif Ahmed
Auditors: Ernst & Young LLP

LOCATIONS

HQ: US Bancorp (DE)
800 Nicollet Mall, Minneapolis, MN 55402
Phone: 651 466-3000
Web: www.usbank.com

Selected Locations
Arizona
Arkansas
California
Colorado
Florida
Idaho
Illinois
Indiana

Iowa
Kansas
Kentucky
Minnesota
Missouri
Michigan
Montana
Nebraska
Nevada
New Mexico
New York
North Dakota
Ohio
Oregon
South Dakota
Tennessee
Utah
Washington
Wisconsin
Wyoming

PRODUCTS/OPERATIONS

2018 Sales

	$ mil.	% of total
Interest		
Loans	13,120	51
Investment securities	2,616	10
Loans held for sale	165	1
Other	272	1
Taxable-equivalent adjustment	116	—
Interest Expense	(3254)	—
Non-interest Income	— —	
Merchant processing services	1,531	6
Trust & investment management fees	1,619	6
Credit & debit card revenue	1,401	5
Mortgage banking	720	3
Commercial products	895	3
Corporate payment products	644	3
Deposit service charges	762	3
Treasury management fees	594	2
ATM processing services	308	1
Investment products fees	188	1
Securities gains (losses) net	30	—
Other	910	4
Total	**22,637**	**100**

2018 sales

	$ mil.	% of total
Consumer and Business Banking	8,466	34
Payment Services	6,046	27
Corporate and Commercial Banking	3,782	15
Treasury and Corporate Support	1,473	14
Wealth Management and Securities Services	2,870	10
Total	**22,637**	**100**

2018 Loan Portfolio

	% of total
Commercial	36
Commercial Real Estate	14
Residential Mortgages	22
Credit Card	8
Other Retail	20
Covered Loans	—
Total	**100**

Selected Subsidiaries
111 Tower Investors Inc. (Minnesota)
Access Mortgage Solutions LLC (Delaware)
AIS Europe Limited (UK)
AIS Fund Administration Ltd. (Cayman Islands)
CF Title Co. (Delaware)
Daimler Title Co. (Delaware)
DSL Service Company (California)
Eclipse Funding LLC (Delaware)
Elan Life Insurance Company Inc. (Arizona)

COMPETITORS

Bank of America	Huntington Bancshares
Capital One	JPMorgan Chase
Citigroup	KeyCorp
Fifth Third	MUFG Americas Holdings
First National of	TCF Financial
Nebraska	Wells Fargo
Great Western Bancorp	Zions Bancorporation

HISTORICAL FINANCIALS

Company Type: Public

Income Statement   FYE: December 31

	ASSETS ($ mil.)	NET INCOME ($ mil.)	INCOME AS % OF ASSETS	EMPLOYEES
12/19	495,426	6,914	1.4%	69,651
12/18	467,374	7,096	1.5%	73,333
12/17	462,040	6,218	1.3%	72,402
12/16	445,964	5,888	1.3%	71,191
12/15	421,853	5,879	1.4%	65,433
Annual Growth	4.1%	4.1%	—	1.6%

2019 Year-End Financials

Debt ratio: 7.22%
Return on equity: 13.44%
Cash ($ mil.): 22,405
Current ratio: —
Long-term debt ($ mil.): —
No. of shares (mil.): 1,534
Dividends
Yield: 2.6%
Payout: 37.9%
Market value ($ mil.): 90,960

	STOCK PRICE ($) FY Close	P/E High/Low	PER SHARE ($) Earnings	Dividends	Book Value
12/19	59.29	15 11	4.16	1.58	33.80
12/18	45.70	14 11	4.14	1.34	31.73
12/17	53.58	16 14	3.51	1.16	29.62
12/16	51.37	16 12	3.24	1.07	27.87
12/15	42.67	14 13	3.16	1.01	26.43
Annual Growth	8.6%	—	7.1%	11.8%	6.3%

	STOCK PRICE ($) FY Close	P/E High/Low	PER SHARE ($) Earnings	Dividends	Book Value
12/19	41.77	24 18	1.75	0.00	16.86
12/18	31.18	22 15	1.87	0.00	14.88
12/17	31.93	16 13	1.97	0.00	12.80
12/16*	27.48	26 21	1.03	0.00	11.49
Annual Growth	11.0%	—	14.2%	—	10.1%

*Fiscal year change

US Foods Holding Corp

Auditors: DELOITTE & TOUCHE LLP

LOCATIONS

HQ: US Foods Holding Corp
9399 W. Higgins Road, Suite 100, Rosemont, IL 60018
Phone: 847 720-8000
Web: www.usfoods.com

HISTORICAL FINANCIALS

Company Type: Public

Income Statement   FYE: December 28

	REVENUE ($ mil.)	NET INCOME ($ mil.)	NET PROFIT MARGIN	EMPLOYEES
12/19	25,939	385	1.5%	28,000
12/18	24,175	407	1.7%	25,000
12/17	24,147	444	1.8%	25,053
12/16*	22,918	209	0.9%	25,000
01/16	23,127	167	0.7%	25,000
Annual Growth	2.9%	23.1%	—	2.9%

*Fiscal year change

2019 Year-End Financials

Debt ratio: 43.92%
Return on equity: 11.13%
Cash ($ mil.): 90
Current ratio: 1.38
Long-term debt ($ mil.): 4,594
No. of shares (mil.): 220
Dividends
Yield: —
Payout: —
Market value ($ mil.): 9,189

UTAH HOUSING CORPORATION

EXECUTIVES

Ceo, Grant Whitaker
Cfo*, Cleon Butterfield
Sr V Pres*, Jonathan Hanks
Compliance Auditor, Susan Schow
Conventional Loan Administrato, Howard Tolley
Information Technology, John Webber
Executive Assistant, Susan Larsen
Loan Document Coordinator, Thomas Wendy
Auditors: DELOITTE & TOUCHE LLP SALT L

LOCATIONS

HQ: UTAH HOUSING CORPORATION
2479 S LAKE PARK BLVD, WEST VALLEY CITY, UT 841208217
Phone: 801 902-8200
Web: WWW.UTAHHOUSINGCORP.ORG

HISTORICAL FINANCIALS

Company Type: Private

Income Statement   FYE: June 30

	ASSETS ($ mil.)	NET INCOME ($ mil.)	INCOME AS % OF ASSETS	EMPLOYEES
06/20	2,073	66	3.2%	90
06/19	2,100	84	4.0%	—
06/18	1,934	36	1.9%	—
06/17	2,002	40	2.0%	—
Annual Growth	1.2%	18.3%	—	—

Valero Energy Corp

Valero Energy was not only named after a mission (the Mission San Antonio de Valero) it is on a mission to be the largest independent refiner in the US. Valero churns out more than 3 million barrels per day refining conventional and premium gasoline diesel low-cost diesel ultra-low-sulfur diesel and other refined petroleum products.. It operates 15 refineries in the US Canada and the UK. It also has about 15 ethanol plants with a combined production capacity of about 1.7 billion gallons per year. Once a more diversified company Valero has exited the retail business in order to focus on its oil refining and ethanol operations. The US accounts for 70% of sales.

HISTORY

Valero Energy was created as a result of the sins of its father Houston-based Coastal States Gas Corporation. Led by flamboyant entrepreneur Oscar Wyatt energy giant Coastal had established Lo-Vaca Gathering Company as a gas marketing subsidiary. Bound by long-term contracts to several Texas cities Coastal was not able to meet its contractual obligations when gas prices rose in the early 1970s and major litigation against the company resulted. The Texas Railroad Commission (the energy-regulating authority) ordered Coastal to refund customers $1.6 billion.

To meet the requirements 55% of Lo-Vaca was spun off to disgruntled former customers as Valero Energy at the end of 1979. The new company was born fully grown — as the largest intrastate pipeline in Texas — with accountant-cum-CEO Bill Greehey the court-appointed chief of Lo-Vaca at its head. Greehey relocated the company to San Antonio where it took its Valero name (from the Alamo or Mission San Antonio de Valero) and put some distance between itself and its discredited former parent. Under Greehey's direction Valero developed a squeaky-clean image by giving to charities stressing a dress code and keeping facilities clean.

Greehey diversified the company into refining unleaded gasoline. Valero bought residual fuel oil from Saudi Arabian refiners and in 1981 built a refinery in Corpus Christi Texas which went on line two years later. But in 1984 a glut of unleaded gasoline on the US market from European refiners undercut Valero's profits. To stay afloat Valero sold pipeline assets including 50% of its West Texas Pipeline in 1985 and 51% of its major pipeline operations in 1987. Refining margins finally began to improve in 1988. With one of the most modern refineries in the US Valero did not have to spend a bundle to upgrade its refining processes to meet the tougher EPA requirements of the 1990s.

In 1992 Valero expanded its refinery's production capacity and acquired two gas processing plants and several hundred miles of gas pipelines from struggling oil firm Oryx Energy (acquired by Kerr-McGee in 1999). That year Valero became the first non-Mexican business engaged in Mexican gasoline production when it signed a deal with state oil company Petr leos Mexicanos S.A. to build a gasoline additive plant there.

To expand its natural gas business substantially in 1994 Valero bought back the 51% of Valero Natural Gas Partners it didn't own. Valero also teamed up with regional oil company Swift Energy in a transportation marketing and processing agreement. As part of that arrangement Valero agreed to build a pipeline linking Swift's Texas gas field with a Valero plant.

In 1997 the company sold Valero Natural Gas to California electric utility PG&E gaining $1.5 billion for expansion. It then purchased Salomon's oil refining unit Basis Petroleum (two refineries in Texas and one in Louisiana) and the next year picked up Mobil's refinery in Paulsboro New Jersey.

With low crude oil prices hurting its bottom line in 1999 Valero explored partnerships with other refiners as a way to cut operating costs. In 2000 the company bought Exxon Mobil's 130000-barrel-per-day Benicia California refinery along with 340 retail outlets for about $1 billion.

In 2001 Valero gained two small refineries when it bought Huntway Refining a leading supplier of asphalt in California. Dwarfing that deal Valero also bought Ultramar Diamond Shamrock for $4 billion in cash and stock (it assumed about $2.1 billion of debt in the deal). As part of the deal and to comply with the demands of regulators in 2002 Valero sold the Golden Eagle (San Francisco-area) refinery and 70 retail service stations in Northern California to Tesoro for $945 million.

In 2003 the company acquired Orion Refining's Louisiana refinery for about $530 million and the next year it acquired an Aruba refinery from asset-shedding El Paso Corp. for $640 million. Suncor Energy bought a Colorado-based refinery from Valero for a reported $30 million in 2005.

The 2005 acquisition of Premcor made Valero the largest independent refiner on the Gulf Coast a major national player.

Greehey turned over the leadership reins to another company veteran Bill Klesse in early 2006. The following year the company sold its Lima Ohio refinery to Husky Energy.

In 2008 the company sold its Krotz Springs Louisiana refinery to Alon USA Energy for $333 million.

In 2009 Valero had an opportunity for international refinery expansion and a foothold in Europe when it agreed to acquire Dow Chemical's 45% interest in Dutch refinery Total Raffinaderij Nederland N.V. However the deal fell through and the stake was sold to LUKOIL.

That year it bought seven ethanol production facilities from VeraSun Energy for $475 million.

To cut costs in 2010 it sold its Delaware City refinery. It also sold its Paulsboro New Jersey refinery that year to PBF Holding for $340 million. It also sold its 50% stake in a pipeline that brings deepwater crude oil from the Gulf of Mexico to the US to Genesis Energy for $330 million.

Expanding its global footprint in 2011 Valero bought Chevron's Pembroke refinery and marketing and logistics assets across the UK for $1.7 billion. It also boosted its US assets that year buying Murphy Oil's refinery outside New Orleans for $585 million to complement its St. Charles facility. Valero also bought Chevron USA Inc.'s Louisville and Lexington Kentucky product terminals expanding its wholesale marketing presence in eastern Kentucky with product supplied primarily from the Valero Memphis Refinery.

It made its first foray into ethanol production in 2009 buying seven ethanol production facilities from VeraSun Energy which was operating under Chapter 11 bankruptcy protection. Valero paid about $475 million for the facilities.

In 2013 the new hydrocracker unit at the Valero St. Charles Refinery began operations.

To better control costs in 2014 the company abandoned our Aruba Refinery except for the associated crude oil and refined products terminal assets that it continues to operate. It also sold its Texas Crude Systems Business to VLP for $154 million.

To get better shareholder returns in 2013 the company spun off its retail business as an independent public company CST Brands. This unit held Valero's company-operated convenience stores in the US and Canada; and filling stations cardlock facilities and heating oil operations in Canada. Valero continues to supply fuel to CST Brands' retail sites through long-term supply agreements. (Valero subsequently sold its remaining 20% stake in the company.)

In 2013 the company's Valero Terminaling and Distribution unit formed a joint venture with TGS Development to start construction on a new marine terminal on the lower Sabine-Neches Waterway near Port Arthur Texas to support the expansion of oil receipts and the marine movements of other commodities at that strategic port.

Growing its foothold in the petrochemical segment that year Valero also announced plans to build a major methanol plant at its 270000 barrel per day St. Charles refinery near New Orleans. Scheduled to commence operating in 2016 the $700 million plant will yield 1.6 million tons of methanol per year.

EXECUTIVES

Vice President Internal Audit, Lee Bailey

Evp And General Counsel, Jay D. Browning, age 61, $595,000 total compensation

Senior Vice President, Anthony Jones

Vp And Cio, Cheryl Thomas

Evp And Cfo, Michael S. (Mike) Ciskowski, age 62, $890,000 total compensation

Vp Wholesale Marketing And International Commercial Operations, Eric Fisher

Chairman President And Ceo, Joseph W. (Joe) Gorder, age 62, $1,450,000 total compensation

Evp Refining Operations And Engineering, Lane Riggs, age 54, $640,000 total compensation

Svp Supply International Operations And Systems Optimization, Gary Simmons, $565,000 total compensation

Vice President Of Strategic, Craig Schnupp

Board Of Director And Vice President, Corey Stewart

Vice President Cost Analysis Transportation, Mark Swensen

Vice President Austin Technology Center, Mike Long

Vice President Accounting, Kevin Hager

Vice President Of Sales And Marketing, Richard Garrett

Vice President Enterprise Architecture, Benjamin Salter

Vice President Of Marketing, Curt Lundquist

Board Of Director And Vice President, Tammy Fulgham

Board Of Director And Vice President, Michael Mazzei

Board Of Director And Vice President, Robert Duffy

Vice President Supply Chain Optimization, Greg Bram

Vice President Products Trading, Scott Lively

Board Of Director And Vice President, Srinivasa Papineni

Senior Vice President, John Roach

Vice President Event Marketing, John Hill

Svp Alternative Fuels, Martin Parrish

Vice President And General Manager, Don Wilson

Board Of Director And Vice President, Brad Mulsow

Vice President Product Supply, Daniel Collier

Vice President Of Human Resour, Nancy Stone

Svp Corporate Development, Ashley Smith

Vice President Risk Management, Joe Van Horn

Regional Vice President, Mark Skobel

Vice President Market Analysis, Anthony Rouse

Vice President Retail Marketing, Steve Motz

Vice President Sales, Mike Whyte

Vice President Project Execution, Tony Jones

Vice President Finance, Kenneth Sparks

Senior Vice President Wholesale Marketing, Gary Arthur

Legal Secretary, Bertha Vasquez

Vp And Gm, Jack Merrill

Vice President Federal Affairs And Counsel, Salo Zelermyer

Svp And Chief Accounting Officer, Mark Schmeltekopf

Vice President And Deputy General Counsel, Rich Walsh

Vp And Treasurer, Christopher Quinn

Vice President Risk Management, Joseph Vanhorn

Vice President Tax, Stephanie A Davis

Treasurer, Dan Stanush

Board Member, Patrick Porter

Board Member, Kirstin Silberschlag

Board Member, Grace Batres

Treasurer, Richard Johnston

Auditors: KPMG LLP

LOCATIONS

HQ: Valero Energy Corp
One Valero Way, San Antonio, TX 78249
Phone: 210 345-2000   **Fax:** 210 246-2646
Web: www.valero.com

2018 Sales

	$ mil.	% of total
US	82,992	71
UK and Ireland	15,208	13
Canada	9,211	8
Other countries	9,622	8
Total	**117,033**	**100**

PRODUCTS/OPERATIONS

2018 Sales

	$ mil.	% of total
Refining	113,615	96
Ethanol	3	3
VLP	546	1
Elimination	(766)	-
Total	**117,033**	**100**

Selected Products

Asphalt
Bunker oils
CARB Phase II gasoline
Clean-burning oxygenates
Conventional gasoline
Crude mineral spirits
Customized clean-burning gasoline blends for export markets
Ethanol
Gasoline blendstocks
Home heating oil
Jet fuel
Kerosene
Low-sulfur diesel
Lube oils
Petrochemical feedstocks
Petroleum coke
Premium reformulated and conventional gasolines
Reformulated gasoline
Sulfur

COMPETITORS

ADM	Motiva Enterprises
BP	National Cooperative
CITGO	Refinery Association
CVR	Phillips 66
Chevron	Sinclair Oil
Exxon Mobil	Sunoco
Green Brick Partners	TOTAL
HollyFrontier	TPC Group
Marathon Petroleum	Tesoro

Company Type: Public

Income Statement				FYE: December 31
	REVENUE ($ mil.)	NET INCOME ($ mil.)	NET PROFIT MARGIN	EMPLOYEES
12/19	108,324	2,422	2.2%	10,222
12/18	117,033	3,122	2.7%	10,261
12/17	93,980	4,065	4.3%	10,015
12/16	75,659	2,289	3.0%	9,996
12/15	87,804	3,990	4.5%	10,103
Annual Growth	5.4%	(11.7%)	—	0.3%

2019 Year-End Financials

Debt ratio: 17.96%
Return on equity: 11.14%
Cash ($ mil.): 2,583
Current ratio: 1.44
Long-term debt ($ mil.): 9,178

No. of shares (mil.): 409
Dividends
Yield: 3.8%
Payout: 65.1%
Market value ($ mil.): 38,330

	STOCK PRICE ($) FY Close	P/E High/Low		PER SHARE ($) Earnings	Dividends	Book Value
12/19	93.65	17	12	5.84	3.60	53.27
12/18	74.97	17	9	7.29	3.20	51.89
12/17	91.91	10	7	9.16	2.80	50.68
12/16	68.32	15	10	4.94	2.40	44.35
12/15	70.71	9	6	7.99	1.70	43.39
Annual Growth	7.3%	—	—	(7.5%)	20.6%	5.3%

Valley National Bancorp (NJ)

Valley National Bancorp is high on New Jersey and New York. The holding company owns Valley National Bank which serves commercial and retail clients through more than 200 branches in northern and central New Jersey and in the New York City boroughs of Manhattan Brooklyn and Queens as well as on Long Island. The bank provides standard services like checking and savings accounts loans and mortgages credit cards and trust services. Subsidiaries offer asset management mortgage and auto loan servicing title insurance asset-based lending and property/casualty life and health insurance. Founded as The Passaic Park Trust Company in 1927 Valley National is looking to expand in Florida.

Operations

In addition to its commercial and retail banking operations Valley National Bancorp through its subsidiaries operates: an all-line insurance agency that offers property and casualty life and health insurance; a wealth management advisory business; title insurance agencies in New York and New Jersey. It also specializes in general aviation financing commercial equipment leasing and custom financing for health care professionals and law firms.

Financial Performance

Valley National reported revenue of $744.7 million in 2013 a decline of 6% versus 2012 on lower interest income caused by lower yields on average interest earning assets as a result of low long-term market interest rates. Net income fell 8% over the same period to about $132 million

on lower revenue and an increase in non-interest expenses.

Strategy

One of the leading commercial banks in the New York and New Jersey metro areas Valley National has set its sights on Florida with its proposed acquisition of Boca Raton-based 1st United Bankcorp the largest commercial bank in Palm Beach County. The deal which is valued at $312 million would add a 21 branch network covering urban banking markets in Florida and approximately $1.7 billion in assets. Combined the two companies will have about $18.1 billion in assets nearly $13 billion in loans and $12.7 billion in deposits. The deal is expected to close in late 2014.

Commercial real estate and construction loans account for the largest portion of Valley's loan portfolio (47%). However the bank has ramped up its residential lending and has been actively marketing its home loan refinancing products amid continued low interest rates.

Mergers and Acquisitions

Valley National completed its approximately $222 million acquisition of New York-based bank holding company State Bancorp at the beginning of 2012. The deal which brought in 17 branches is part of Valley's overall strategy to expand its presence throughout New York City metropolitan area. It marked the company's first foray in Long Island and added locations in Manhattan and Queens as well. It also provides an opportunity to build retail relationships in new markets as State Bancorp focused more on commercial clients. Valley typically targets consumers disillusioned with larger banks.

In 2010 the company acquired the branches and most of the assets and deposits of failed Manhattan-based financial institutions Liberty-Pointe Bank and Park Avenue Bank in FDIC-assisted transactions. It also opened a loan production office in Bethlehem Pennsylvania to offer residential mortgages and title insurance. Valley continues to look for additional expansion opportunities.

EXECUTIVES

President And Chief Banking Officer Valley National Bank, Rudy E. Schupp, age 69, $425,000 total compensation
Sevp And Cfo, Alan D. Eskow, age 72, $545,750 total compensation
Chairman President And Ceo, Gerald H. Lipkin, age 80, $1,123,500 total compensation
Evp And Chief Retail Lending Officer, Albert L. Engel, age 72, $440,000 total compensation
Evp And Director Sales Retail Banking Marketing And Customer Service, Dianne M. Grenz
Evp And Senior Community Reinvestment Act Officer, Bernadette M. Mueller, age 61
Sevp And Treasurer, Ira Robbins, age 45, $425,000 total compensation
Evp And Chief Administrative Officer, Andrea Onorato
Evp And Cio, Robert J. Bardusch
Evp And Chief Risk Officer, Melissa Scofield
Executive Vice President, Eric Gould
Assistant Vice President Commercial Loans, John Kenny
Vice President, Peter Alvarez
Assistant Vice President, Tony Dibenedetto
Vice President, Dave Denoya
Vice President, Timothy Tierney
Assistant Vice President Branch Sales Manager, Marie Castro
Assistant Vice President Business Development Commercial Loans, Kristen Upadek
Vice President Sales Manager, Veronica Valentine
Vice President Community Lending, Angela Brauer
Vice President Territory Sales Manager, Melvin Madera
Senior Vice President Commercial Lending, John Murphy
Vice President Retail Training, Mary Black
Senior Vice President, Chip Woodbury
Vice President, Mark Stanek
Vice President, Karen Conway
Assistant Vice President, Paul Cronen
Vice President, Janet Knipfing
Vice President, Jennifer Yager
Vice President, Ruth A Finn
Senior Corporate Management Vice President Gm, Ralph Passafiume
First Vice President, Ana Mauriello
Senior Vice President, Elizabeth Delaney
Vice President, John Cina
Senior Vice President, Eileen Sackman
Vice President, Tony Zeleszko
Senior Vice President; Regional Manager, Steven Vitale
Vice President, Geriann Smith
Vice President, Luba Gelman
Vice President Senior Marketing Manager, Jeffery Doberman
Vice President Of Sales, John Siberio
Vice President Commercial Lender, Janice Brunson
Vice President, Mark Sabow
Vice President Commercial Lending, Catherine Keller
Executive Vice President Chief Financial Officer And Chief Operating Officer, Stan Pinkham
Avp Branch Sales Manager, Robert Grasso
Vice President Commercial Middle Market Banking, Dan Smith
Vice President Territory Sales Manager, Mary Beltz
Senior Executive Vice President; Chief Lending Officer Of Valley National Bank, Thomas Iadanza
Regional Vice President, Drita Kukic
Vice President Information Technology, Phil Direnzo
Vice President Territory Sales Manager, Nancy Shaulis
Senior Vice President Market Executive, Ivete Pinheiro
Vice President, Mikel Sharpe
First Vice President, Michael Warrington
First Vice President, Ann Kursar
Vice President, Timothy Pewegr
Vice President Territory Sales Manager, Eddie Beylin
Vice President, Linda Diaz
Vp Aml Bsa Compliance, Rahsan Mumcuoglu
Vice President, Alan Gilman
Vice President, Daniel Maes
Vice President Director Of Sales, Amanda Miller
Vice President Regional Facilities Manager, Janice Sloat
Vice President New Business Underwriting, Joseph Klapkowski
Senior Vice President New York Commercial Real Estate, Declan Meagher
Vice President Commercial Lending, William Landers
Vice President Commercial Lender, Fatima Pearn
Vice President, David Beil
Senior Vice President, Linda Casey
Assistant Vice President Training, Jim Hatcher
Vice President Network Operations, Kenneth Aul
Vp Territory Sales Manager, Ijaz Mughal
Senior Executive Vice President; Chief Operating Officer Of Valley National Bank, Bob Bardusch
Cfsa And Senior Auditor And Assistant Vice President, Colleen Moriarty

First Vice President Commercial Loan Team Leader, Dan Sorrell
First Vice President, Ron Fraser
First Senior Vice President, Dorothy Kahlau
First Senior Vice President, Russ Murawski
Assistant Vice President, Ayesha Cevallos
Director Of Clinical Services, Rose Marie Ranuro
Board Member, Marc Lenner
Board Member, Peter Baum
Auditors: KPMG LLP

LOCATIONS

HQ: Valley National Bancorp (NJ)
 One Penn Plaza, New York, NY 10119
Phone: 973 305-8800
Web: www.valleynationalbank.com

PRODUCTS/OPERATIONS

2016 Sales

	$ mil.	% of total
Interest Income		
Interest and fees on loans	685	79
Interest and dividends on investment securities	79	9
Interest on federal funds sold and other short-term investments	1	0
Non-Interest Income		
Gains on sales of loans net	22	3
Service charges on deposit accounts	20	2
Insurance commissions	19	2
Trust and investment services	10	1
Bank owned life insurance	6	1
Fees from loan servicing	6	1
Gains on sales of assets net	1	0
Gains on securities transactions net	0	0
Change in FDIC loss-share receivable	(1.3)	0
Other	16	2
Total	**870**	**100**

COMPETITORS

Bank of America	JPMorgan Chase
Capital One	New York Community
Citigroup	Bancorp
Dime Community	PNC Financial
Bancshares	TD Bank USA
Hudson City Bancorp	Wells Fargo

HISTORICAL FINANCIALS

Company Type: Public

Income Statement				FYE: December 31
	ASSETS ($ mil.)	NET INCOME ($ mil.)	INCOME AS % OF ASSETS	EMPLOYEES
12/19	37,436	309	0.8%	3,174
12/18	31,863	261	0.8%	3,192
12/17	24,002	161	0.7%	2,842
12/16	22,864	168	0.7%	2,828
12/15	21,612	102	0.5%	2,929
Annual Growth	14.7%	31.7%	—	2.0%

2019 Year-End Financials

Debt ratio: 1.86%
Return on equity: 8.01%
Cash ($ mil.): 434
Current ratio: —
Long-term debt ($ mil.): —

No. of shares (mil.): 403
Dividends
 Yield: 3.8%
 Payout: 43.5%
Market value ($ mil.): 4,618

	STOCK PRICE ($) FY Close	P/E High/Low		PER SHARE ($) Earnings	Dividends	Book Value
12/19	11.45	14	10	0.87	0.44	10.87
12/18	8.88	18	11	0.75	0.44	10.11
12/17	11.22	22	18	0.58	0.44	9.58
12/16	11.64	19	13	0.63	0.44	9.02
12/15	9.85	27	22	0.42	0.44	8.70
Annual Growth	3.8%	—	—	20.0%	(0.0%)	5.7%

Veritex Holdings Inc

Auditors: Grant Thornton LLP

LOCATIONS

HQ: Veritex Holdings Inc
 8214 Westchester Drive, Suite 800, Dallas, TX 75225
Phone: 972 349-6200
Web: www.veritexbank.com

HISTORICAL FINANCIALS

Company Type: Public

Income Statement				FYE: December 31
	ASSETS ($ mil.)	NET INCOME ($ mil.)	INCOME AS % OF ASSETS	EMPLOYEES
12/19	7,954	90	1.1%	679
12/18	3,208	39	1.2%	330
12/17	2,945	15	0.5%	324
12/16	1,408	12	0.9%	171
12/15	1,039	8	0.8%	149
Annual Growth	66.3%	79.2%	—	46.1%

2019 Year-End Financials

Debt ratio: 1.83%
Return on equity: 10.54%
Cash ($ mil.): 251
Current ratio: —
Long-term debt ($ mil.): —

No. of shares (mil.): 51
Dividends
 Yield: 1.7%
 Payout: 32.6%
Market value ($ mil.): 1,487

	STOCK PRICE ($) FY Close	P/E High/Low		PER SHARE ($) Earnings	Dividends	Book Value
12/19	29.13	17	13	1.68	0.50	23.32
12/18	21.38	20	13	1.60	0.00	21.88
12/17	27.59	36	30	0.80	0.00	20.28
12/16	26.71	23	11	1.13	0.00	15.73
12/15	16.21	20	15	0.84	0.00	12.33
Annual Growth	15.8%	—	—	18.9%	—	17.3%

Veritiv Corp

Auditors: DELOITTE & TOUCHE LLP

LOCATIONS

HQ: Veritiv Corp
 1000 Abernathy Road N.E., Building 400, Suite 1700, Atlanta, GA 30328
Phone: 770 391-8200
Web: www.veritivcorp.com

HISTORICAL FINANCIALS

Company Type: Public

Income Statement				FYE: December 31
	REVENUE ($ mil.)	NET INCOME ($ mil.)	NET PROFIT MARGIN	EMPLOYEES
12/19	7,659	(29)	—	8,000
12/18	8,696	(15)	—	8,700
12/17	8,364	(13)	—	8,900
12/16	8,326	21	0.3%	8,700
12/15	8,717	26	0.3%	8,800
Annual Growth	(3.2%)	—	—	(2.4%)

2019 Year-End Financials

Debt ratio: 30.07%
Return on equity: (-5.47%)
Cash ($ mil.): 38
Current ratio: 2.23
Long-term debt ($ mil.): 742

No. of shares (mil.): 16
Dividends
 Yield: —
 Payout: —
Market value ($ mil.): 317

	STOCK PRICE ($) FY Close	P/E High/Low		PER SHARE ($) Earnings	Dividends	Book Value
12/19	19.67	—	—	(1.84)	0.00	33.30
12/18	24.97	—	—	(0.99)	0.00	34.16
12/17	28.90	—	—	(0.85)	0.00	35.01
12/16	53.75	43	21	1.30	0.00	34.51
12/15	36.22	32	20	1.67	0.00	33.13
Annual Growth	(14.2%)	—	—	—	—	0.1%

Verizon Communications Inc

Verizon Communications is a provider of communications information and entertainment products and services to consumers businesses and government entities. The company serves approximately 95 million retail connections 6 million broadband connections and 4 million Fios video connections. Verizon's wireline unit provides local telephone long-distance internet access corporate networking and digital TV services. In addition Verizon offers a wide range of telecom managed network security and IT services to commercial and government clients in more than 150 countries. The company also sells devices such as smartphones tablets laptop computers and netbooks and other wireless-enabled connected devices such as smartwatches and other wearables. Verizon has expanded its video and advertising capabilities with the acquisitions of AOL and Yahoo assets. Formerly known as Bell Atlantic Corporation (Bell Atlantic) The company was incorporated in 1983 under the laws of the State of Delaware.

Bankruptcy

The company's consolidated asset-backed debt bankruptcy remote legal entities (each an ABS Entity or collectively the ABS Entities) issue the debt or otherwise a party to the transaction documentation in connection with the asset-backed debt transactions. Under the terms of the asset-backed debt Cellco Partnership (Cellco) and certain other affiliates of Verizon (collectively the Originators) transfer device payment plan agreement receivables to one of the ABS Entities which in turn transfers such receivables to another ABS Entity that issues the debt. Verizon entities retain the equity interests in the ABS Entities which represent the rights to all funds not needed to make required payments on the asset-backed debt and other related payments and expenses.

Operations

Verizon has two reportable segments. These are Verizon Consumer Group (approximately 70% of the sales) and Verizon Business Group (about 25% of the sales) Small portions of the sales come from corporate and other. The consumer segment provides consumer-focused wireless and wireline communications services and products. The wireless services are provided across one of the most extensive wireless networks in the United States (U.S.) under the Verizon brand and through wholesale and other arrangements. The customers can obtain our wireless services on a postpaid or prepaid basis. The Consumer segment's operating revenues for the year ended December 31 2019 totaled $91.1 billion.

The business segment provides wireless and wireline communications services and products video and data services corporate networking solutions security and managed network services local and long-distance voice services and network access to deliver various Internet of Things (IoT) services and products including solutions that support fleet tracking management compliance management field service management asset tracking and other types of mobile resource management. The Consumer segment's operating revenues for the year ended December 31 2019 totaled $91.1 billion.

Corporate and other includes the results of the media business Verizon Media and other businesses investments in unconsolidated businesses insurance captives unallocated corporate expenses certain pension and other employee benefit-related costs and interest and financing expenses.

Geographic Reach

Verizon based in New York City has operations throughout the US. It also has representation in countries around the world.

Sales and Marketing

Verizon sells its prepaid and postpaid wireless phone services through its website its stores omnichannel and national retailers. It also has a dedicated telemarketing sales force. The average retail customer account pays about $134 a month.

The company is a major advertiser. Verizon Media provides consumers with owned and operated and third-party search properties as well as mail news finance sports and entertainment offerings and provides other businesses and partners access to consumers through digital advertising content delivery video streaming platforms. and point-of-sale media promotions.

Selling general and administrative expenses increased $499 million or 6.5% during 2019 compared to 2018 due to increases in advertising expenses and sales commission expense. Advertising expense cost for $3.0 billion.

Financial Performance

Verizon's revenue has risen in the past years after the company hit a sales peak of about $131

billion in 2015 before dropping in 2016. In 2019 the revenue was almost the same in 2016.

Sales were $131.9 billion in 2019 about a one percent increase from 2018 driven by higher consumer revenue from higher-value accounts and overall account growth. Business revenue had a slight decline of $91.0 million since 2018. Verizon's net income increased by almost 25% in 2019 to $19.2 billion.

In 2019 Verizon had about $1 million more in cash and equivalents $3.9 billion compared to the previous year. Operations generated $35.7 billion in cash while investing and financing activities used $17.6 billion and $18.2 billion respectively.

Strategy

The company continues to lead in 4G LTE performance while building momentum for the 5G network. The strategy lays the foundation for the future through investments in Intelligent Edge Network that enable efficiencies throughout the core infrastructure and deliver flexibility to meet customer requirements.

Verizon will continue to offer business and government customers more robust IP products and services and advance IoT strategies by leveraging business models that monetize usage on our networks at the connectivity platform and solution layers.

The Company's overall investment strategy is to achieve a mix of assets that allows the company to meet projected benefit payments while taking into consideration risk and return. In an effort to reduce the risk of portfolio strategy and better align assets with liabilities The company adopted a liability-driven pension strategy that seeks to better match cash flows from investments with projected benefit payments.

In 2020 Verizon collaborated with Riot Games regarding the 5G network for the League of Legends Championship. The three-year partnership will permit Verizon to cooperate with Riot Games and the LCS to reconstruct the overall gaming experience for programmers gamers and fans. Despite the pandemic Verizon exhibits its devotion to gamers and fans by providing weekly music and gaming streaming through Pay It Forward LIVE.

Mergers and Acquisitions

In early 2019 Verizon closed its acquisition of ProtectWise a provider of cloud-delivered Network Detection and Response. This acquisition expands Verizon's security offerings.

In May 2019 Verizon acquired BlueJeans Network. The products of BlueJeans fit Verizon's mobile business solutions particularly to the new development of the 5G product roadmap.

EXECUTIVES

Evp And Chief Strategy Officer, Roy H. Chestnutt, age 61
Chairman And Ceo, Lowell C. McAdam, age 66, $1,600,000 total compensation
Evp Wireless Network Operations, David Small
Evp And Chief Information And Technology Architect, Roger Gurnani, age 59
Evp And Chief Administrative Officer, Marc C. Reed, age 61, $792,307 total compensation
Evp And President Network And Technology, Hans Vestberg, age 55
Evp And President Customer And Product Operations, John G. Stratton, age 59, $896,154 total compensation

Evp And President Product Innovation And New Businesses, Marni M. Walden, age 52, $896,154 total compensation
Svp And Group President Verizon Enterprise Solutions, George J. Fischer, age 57
Svp And Group President Consumer Sales And Service, Kenneth (Ken) Dixon
Evp And Group President Verizon Wireless, Ronan Dunne
Evp Public Policy And General Counsel, Craig L. Silliman, age 52
Svp And Group President Verizon Business Markets (vbm), Martin Burvill
Evp Wireless Operations, Tami Erwin
Svp And Cfo Operations Finance, Matthew D. (Matt) Ellis, age 48, $488,462 total compensation
President Verizon Partner Solutions, Eric Cevis
Evp Solutions And Sales Channels, Joe Chuisano
Senior Vice President And Deputy General Counsel Public Policy And Government Affairs, Kathleen Grillo
Senior Vice President Business Development, Gregory Seiler
Vice President, Christopher Kimm
National Account Manager, Fran Morris
Senior Vice President Public Sector Verizon Enterprise Solutions, Michael Maiorana
Vice President Associate General Counsel, David Wheeler
Vice President Telematics, Shane Scoville
Regional Vice President Public Policy, Karen Campbell
Executive Director Network Operations Vps, Sam Luxton
Vice President, Roland Hicks
Vice President Of Marketing And Sales For Middle Atlantic Region, Mary Yarbrough
National Account Manager, Rob Parker
Vice President Federal Government Relations, Marcela Zamora
Vice President Of Sales, Philip Burroughs
Vice President Global Planning Director, Atul Suri
Vice President, Cesar Gamarra
Vp And Associate General Counsel, Gregory Romano
Senior Vice President Global Real Estate, John Vazquez
National Account Manager, Shirley Bily
Manager Vps Marketing And Sales, Janice Crandall
Executive Assistant To Brian Mecum Vice President Network, Carri Vogl
Vice President, James Franke
Vice President Marketing, Mary Crocker
National Account Manager, Lauren Williams
Vice President Global Planning Director, Wesley Sullivan
Vice President, Lizette Lizardi
Vice President Customer Service Verizon Wireless, Joan Bowyer
Senior Vice President Financial Planning And Analysis, Shane Sanders
Vice President, Tara Mooar
Senior Vice President Investor Relations, Mike Stefanski
Vice President And Assistant General Counsel, Michael Woods
Vp Finance, Brendan Connelly
Svp It, Vivek Gurumurthy
Vice President Communications Verizon Wireless, Mariana Agathoklis Schlock
Senior Vice President, Matt Ellis
Vice President Technology Planning, Adam Koeppe
Vice President Communications Marketing And Public Relations, Chris Ellmore
Vice President Of Mobile And Internet Services, Che Phillip
Vice President Digital Operations, Dustin Humphreys
Board Member, Beryl Thompson

Secretary Manager Network Operations, Salvatore Buttice

Auditors: Ernst & Young LLP

LOCATIONS

HQ: Verizon Communications Inc
1095 Avenue of the Americas, New York, NY 10036
Phone: 212 395-1000
Web: www.verizon.com

PRODUCTS/OPERATIONS

2018 Sales

	$ mil.	% of total
Wireless	91,734	69
Wireline	29,760	23
Corporate and Other	10,942	8
Eliminations	(1573)	0
Total	**130,863**	**100**

2018 Sales

	$ mil.	% of total
Service revenues and other	108,605	83
Wireless equipment revenues	22,258	17
Total	**130,863**	**100**

COMPETITORS

AT&T	Frontier
Altice USA	Communications
CenturyLink	Netflix
Charter Communications	Sprint Communications
Comcast	T-Mobile USA
Cox Communications	Time Warner Cable
Cricket	U.S. Cellular
DIRECTV	Windstream

HISTORICAL FINANCIALS

Company Type: Public

Income Statement				FYE: December 31
	REVENUE ($ mil.)	NET INCOME ($ mil.)	NET PROFIT MARGIN	EMPLOYEES
12/19	131,868	19,265	14.6%	135,000
12/18	130,863	15,528	11.9%	144,500
12/17	126,034	30,101	23.9%	155,400
12/16	125,980	13,127	10.4%	160,900
12/15	131,620	17,879	13.6%	177,700
Annual Growth	0.0%	1.9%		(6.6%)

2019 Year-End Financials

Debt ratio: 38.22%—
Return on equity: 33.64%
Cash ($ mil.): 2,594
Current ratio: 0.84
Long-term debt ($ mil.): 100,712

Dividends
  Yield: 3.9%
  Payout: 62.2%
Market value ($ mil.): —

	STOCK PRICE ($) FY Close	P/E High/Low	PER SHARE ($) Earnings	Dividends	Book Value
12/19	61.40	13 11	4.65	2.42	14.84
12/18	56.22	16 12	3.76	2.37	12.86
12/17	52.93	7 6	7.36	2.32	10.56
12/16	53.38	18 14	3.21	2.27	5.53
12/15	46.22	12 10	4.37	2.22	4.03
Annual Growth	7.4%	— —	1.6%	2.3%	38.5%

VF Corp.

VF Corp. has stitched together a lineup of apparel brands that range from denim to Northface. The company is a leading manufacturer and retailer in the outdoor and action sports apparel industry owning brands in specialist product categories: Timberland and The North Face (outdoor-oriented brands) and Vans (skateboard-inspired footwear). VF also makes the jeans scene owning the Lee Wrangler and Rock & Republic brands. The company sells directly to consumers online and through more than 1375 VF-operated retail stores worldwide. It also sells wholesale to department and specialty stores and mass merchants. As such both the Jeans business subject to the spin-off completed May 22 2019 and the Occupational Workwear business that met the held-for-sale and discontinued operations criteria during the three months ended March 28 2020 have been excluded.

Operations

VF operates three main business segments: Active is the largest at more than 45% of total sales followed by Outdoor (about 45%) and Work (about 10%).

Outdoor segment is a group of authentic outdoor-based lifestyle brands. Product offerings include performance-based and outdoor apparel footwear and equipment. The segment includes brand names such as North Face Timberland Icebreaker Smartwool and Altra.

Active segment is a group of activity-based lifestyle brands. Product offerings include active apparel footwear and accessories. Brands included were Vans Kipling Napapijri Eastpak Jansport and Eagle Creek.

Work Segment consists of work and work-inspired lifestyle brands with product offerings that include apparel footwear and accessories. Brands under the segment Dickies Timberland and Timberland PRO.

Geographic Reach

VF Corp. rings up about 55% of its sales in the US while the remainder mostly comes from Europe. The company's products were obtained from approximately 300 independent contractor manufacturing facilities in approximately 40 countries and from four VF-operated manufacturing facilities. The company's largest distribution centers are located in Visalia California and Prague Czech Republic. Additionally they operate about 25 distribution centers primarily in the U.S. but also in Argentina Belgium Canada Chile China Mexico the Netherlands and the United Kingdom. VF operates four manufacturing facilities in Mexico Honduras and the Dominican Republic.

The company's global headquarters are located at Denver Colorado.

Sales and Marketing

VF makes sales through specialty stores department stores national chains mass merchants and its direct-to-consumer (DTC) operations. The company makes direct-to-customer sales about 40% of revenue through owned-operated stores concession retail stores and online. It generates a significant chunk of its sales through third-party retail chains. V.F.'s 10 largest customers account for more than 15% of sales.

The apparel maker advertises in trade publications and on radio and television. Its digital initiatives include social media mobile platforms and the internet.

Financial Performance

The company's revenue fell two times in the years 2017 and 2018 and recovered in the following years reaching $10.5 billion mark in the year 2020.

Year ended March 2020 revenues increased 2% to $10.5 billion compared to the year ended March 2019 primarily due to the $462.4 million contribution from organic growth including a 2% unfavorable impact from foreign currency. Active segment revenues increased 4% to $4.9 billion compared to the year ended March 2019 including a 2% unfavorable impact from foreign currency. Outdoor segment revenues remained flat at $4.6 billion over the year ended March 2019 including a 1% unfavorable impact from foreign currency.

The company's net income fell by about $580.3 million to $679.4 million from $1.3 billion from the prior year. The decrease was due to $484.0 million increase on their operating costs and expense.

The company's cash by the end of 2019 increased by $854.7 million to $1.4 billion from $556.6 million from the prior year. Cash generated by operations and financing activities were $874.5 million and $309.7 million respectively. Cash used by investing activities was $302 million.

Strategy

The company's long-term growth strategy is focused on four strategic choices: Driving and optimizing its portfolio Investing in its brands to realize its full potential while ensuring the composition of its portfolio positions to win in evolving market conditions; Distorting investments to Asia. Investing in and scaling the company's business across the Asia-Pacific region especially China to unlock growth opportunities for brands in this fast-growing region; Elevating direct channels. Investing in their direct-to-consumer business to make it the pinnacle expression of V.F.'s brands and prioritizing serving consumers through e-commerce and digitally enabled transactions; and accelerate their consumer-minded retail-centric hyper-digital business model transformation. Becoming consumer- and retail-centric to meet and exceed consumers' needs across all channels and operate their business differently - from the design studio to the factory floor to the point of sale - by thinking and acting more like a vertical retailer.

Company Background

The gear-and-apparel maker has invested heavily in acquisitions to further build its outdoor and action sports business which has grown to account for more than 50% of sales. V.F. in September 2011 acquired global footwear maker Timberland for $2 billion. Marking the biggest acquisition in the company's history V.F. was enticed by Timberland's overseas presence and its strong growth during the past decade.

In 2010 on the wholesaling side V.F. took control of its Vans-branded products marketing venture in Mexico. The roughly $30 million purchase also put V.F. in charge of Vans retail stores.

V.F. founded in 1899 is controlled in part by trusts established by its late founder John Barbey.

HISTORY

In 1899 six partners including banker John Barbey started the Reading Glove and Mitten Manufacturing Company. Barbey bought out his five partners in 1911 and changed the name of the Reading Pennsylvania company to Schuylkill Silk Mills in 1913. Barbey expanded the mills' production to include underwear and changed the mills' name to Vanity Fair Silk Mills (after a contest with a $25 prize in 1919).

Barbey (who banned the word "underwear") and his son J. E. led their lingerie company to national prominence. The mills made only silk garments until the 1920s when synthetics were developed. In response to the US embargo on silk in 1941 Vanity Fair changed to rayon finally converting to the new wonder fabric nylon tricot in 1948. Vanity Fair was then manufacturing all stages of its nylon products from filament to finished garment. It won awards for its innovative advertising with photographs of live models in Vanity Fair lingerie.

J. E. owned all of Vanity Fair's stock until 1951 when he sold one-third of his holdings to the public. In 1966 the stock previously traded over the counter was listed on the NYSE.V.F. Corp. is not afraid to cut brands that aren't profitable to free up resources. In 2012 for example it sold its majority stake in upscale men's designer brand John Varvatos to private equity Lion Capital.

In 2013 V.F. Corp. was hoping to boost its outdoor business and its bottom line further through its 2013 bid to take over Australia's boardwear maker Billabong but the Aussie company wanted more than the 526.8 million Australian dollars (US $556 million) V.F. was willing to pay.

EXECUTIVES

Assistant Vice President, Joseph Dzialo
Vice President Supply Chain, Tom Glaser
Vp And Group President International, Karl Heinz Salzburger, age 62, $798,324 total compensation
President Asia/pacific Region, Kevin D. Bailey
Vp; Group President Outdoor And Action Sports Americas, Scott H. Baxter, age 55, $659,200 total compensation
President Workwear Jeans And Sportswear Brands, Curt Holtz
Vp And Cfo, Scott A. Roe, age 55, $675,000 total compensation
Vp Global Business Technology, Sandra Harris
Vp; Group President Vf International, Aidan O'Meara, age 71
Vp And Cio, Martin Schneider
President Europe Middle East And Africa, Martino Scabbia Guerrini, age 56
Brand President Smartwool, Travis Campbell
Vp; President Supply Chain, Thomas A. Glaser
Chairman President And Ceo, Steven E. (Steve) Rendle, age 60, $945,000 total compensation
President Sportswear, Brendan Sullivan
Vice President Of Marketing Communications Western, Allen Montgomery
Human Resources Vice President, Ronald Lawrence
Vice President Investor Relations And Financial Planning And Analysis, Joseph Alkire
Vice President, Kishore Patwa
Senior Vice President, Terri Miller
Vice President Sourcing Lee Jeans, Steve Miller
Vice President Of Retail, Kurt Kleespies
Vice President Global Procurement And Material Supply, Tom Conneen
Vice President Us Sales, Brett Barthel
Vice President General Manager, Doug Mathison
Vice President, Ryan Smith
Vice President Global Strategy And Brand Management, Iain Douglas
Vice President, Sam Tucker
Vice President General Manager, Richard Blaya
Vice President Sales, Ken Wood
Vice President Human Resources Supply Chain, Rod Hewitt

Vice President General Manager Vans North America, Mitchell Whitaker
Vice President Information Systems, Mary Robbins
Vice President, Ellen Blake
Vice President Gmm, Bill Lynch
Vice President Design Research And Development, Paul Herron
Vice President Operations Supply Chain Sportswear Coalition, Karen Smith
Vice President Of Sales Nautica Women's Wear, Eden Richman
Vice President Operation, Martin Duff
Vice President Retail Marketing, Jeff Sharp
Vice President, Robyn Flint
Vice President And Human Resources Business Partner Jeanswear North America, Fran Mellette
Vice President, Jon E Anthony
Vice President Finance, Chastity Black
Vice President Of Merchandising, Dave Theiss
Vice President, Christopher Fuentes
Vice President Finance, Mark Thoma
Vice President Of Marketing Nautica U, Nina Flood
Vice President Operations, Rick Ott
Management Vice President, Rick Wood
Vice President Gm, Hector Torres
Vice President Sales Wrangler, Don Adamic
Chief Accounting Officer Vice President Controller, Bryan Mcneill
Vice President And Managing Director Timberland And Sportswear Vf Asia Pacific, John Gearing
Vp And General Manager Vf (majestic) Overseeing The Nfl Nhl Harley Davidson And International, Rob Brodersen
Vice President Direct To Consumer Jeanswear, Todd Starcevich
Vice President Global Corporate Sustainability, Letitia Webster
Vp Marketing (imagewear), David Crace
Vice President Human Resources Vf International, Monica Valsechini
Vice President, Scott Moore
Vice President Sales, Scott Bowers
Vice President Apparel, Vicki Redding
Vice President Retail And Digital Commer, Ryan Shadrin
Vp It, Deborah Rivera
Vice President Sales Tnf, Tony Erlick
Vp And General Manager Kodiak Group, Katherine Cousins
Executive Vice President Chief Digital And Technology Officer, Velia Carboni
Vice President Mass Operations, Julie Morgan
Vice President Global Innovation, Steve Zades
National Accounts Manager, Matt Hirsch
Vice President Chief Human Resources Officer, Scott Shoener
Vp Manufacturing Workwear Imagewear And Williamson Dickie, Carlos Zavala
Vice President Information Technology, Patrick Skelton
Vice President Director Of Information Technology Risk Management, Marissa Pardini
Vice President Customer Experience, Terence Fong
Named Vice President General Counsel And Corporate Secretary, Laurel Krueger
Vice President Global Marketing (vans), Fara Howard
Vice President Sales (reef), David Schultz
Vice President Global Benefits, Jessica Muhlenberg
Vp Sales, Jeff Green
Board Member, Garrett Chapman
Board Member, Sandy Mcmullen
Board Member, Juan De Bedout
Board Member, Richard Carucci
Board Member, W Alan Mccollough
Secretary, Rebecca Donehew
Auditors: PricewaterhouseCoopers LLP

LOCATIONS

HQ: VF Corp.
1551 Wewatta Street, Denver, CO 80202
Phone: 720 778-4000
Web: www.vfc.com

2017 Sales

	$ mil.	% of total
US	6,785	57
Foreign primarily Europe	5,026	43
Total	**11,811**	**100**

PRODUCTS/OPERATIONS

2017 Sales

	$ mil.	% of total
Net sales	11,735	99
Royalty income	75	1
Total	**11,811**	**100**

2017 Sales

	$ mil.	% of total
Outdoor & action sports	8,212	70
Jeanswear	2,655	23
Imagewear	830	7
Other	113	-
Total	**11,811**	**100**

Selected Brands

Imagewear
  Bulwark
  Horace Small
  Majestic
  Red Kap
  MLB (licensed)
  NFL (licensed)
  Harley-Davidson (licensed)
Jeanswear
  Lee
  Riders
  Rock & Republic
  Rustler
  Timber Creek by Wrangler
  Wrangler
Sportswear
  Kipling
  Nautica
Outdoor and action sports
  Eagle Creek
  Eastpak
  JanSport
  Kipling
  lucy
  Napapijri
  Reef
  SmartWool
  The North Face
  Timberland
  Vans

Selected Licenses

Harley-Davidson Motor Company
Major League Baseball
MLB Players Association
National Basketball Association
National Football League
National Hockey League

COMPETITORS

Abercrombie & Fitch	Lululemon
American Eagle	NIKE
Outfitters	OshKosh B'Gosh
Calvin Klein	Patagonia Inc.
Columbia Sportswear	REI
Diesel SpA	Reebok
Gildan Activewear	Rocky Brands
Guess?	Russell Brands
Joe's Jeans	Sears Holdings
Johnson Outdoors	The Gap
Kate Spade	Tommy Hilfiger
Kellwood	True Religion Apparel
Koos Manufacturing	Under Armour
L Brands	Williamson-Dickie
L.L. Bean	Manufacturing
Levi Strauss	adidas

HISTORICAL FINANCIALS

Company Type: Public

Income Statement

FYE: March 28

	REVENUE ($ mil.)	NET INCOME ($ mil.)	NET PROFIT MARGIN	EMPLOYEES
03/20	10,488	679	6.5%	48,000
03/19	13,848	1,259	9.1%	75,000
03/18*	3,045	252	8.3%	—
12/17	11,811	614	5.2%	69,000
12/16	12,019	1,074	8.9%	69,000
Annual Growth	(4.4%)	(14.2%)	—	(11.4%)

*Fiscal year change

2020 Year-End Financials

Debt ratio: 34.47%	No. of shares (mil.): 388
Return on equity: 17.80%	Dividends
Cash ($ mil.): 1,369	Yield: 0.0%
Current ratio: 1.66	Payout: 111.7%
Long-term debt ($ mil.): 2,608	Market value ($ mil.): 22,469

	STOCK PRICE ($) FY Close	P/E High/Low	PER SHARE ($) Earnings	Dividends	Book Value
03/20	57.79	58 27	1.70	1.90	8.63
03/19	86.91	30 21	3.15	1.94	10.83
03/18*	74.12	131 113	0.63	0.46	9.35
12/17	74.00	48 31	1.52	1.72	9.40
12/16	53.35	26 21	2.54	1.53	11.93
Annual Growth	2.7%	—	(12.5%)	7.5%	(10.2%)

*Fiscal year change

ViacomCBS Inc

ViacomCBS is a leading global media and entertainment company that creates content and experiences for audiences worldwide through TV entertainment cable networks filmed entertainment and publishing. ViacomCBS owns cable network Showtime and produces and distributes TV programming through CBS Television Studios and CBS Television Distribution. Other operations include CBS Interactive and book publisher Simon & Schuster. Chairman Emeritus Sumner Redstone controls NAI Corporation through National Amusements Trust. CBS combined with Viacom its National Amusements sibling in 2019.

HISTORY

The company that would eventually become CBS Corporation began as Viacom in 1970. It was the result of numerous mergers and acquisitions dating back nearly 90 years combining everything from a movie studio to a company that made car bumpers. CBS launched Viacom after the FCC ruled that TV networks could not own cable systems and TV stations in the same market. Viacom took over CBS's program syndication division and bought TV and radio stations in the late 1970s and early 1980s. In 1978 it co-founded pay-TV network Showtime. Viacom became full owner in 1982 and combined Showtime with The Movie Channel the following year to form Showtime Networks. Viacom also began producing TV series and bought MTV Networks in 1986.

After a bidding war with renowned financier Carl Icahn and a Viacom management group Sumner Redstone's National Amusements bought 83% of Viacom in 1987. Viacom bought King's Entertainment (theme parks) shortly thereafter and followed that with two mega-deals in 1994: it bought Paramount Communications for about $10 billion (which included Simon & Schuster) and Blockbuster for $8.4 billion (which included Spelling Entertainment). The next year along with Chris-Craft Viacom launched UPN (United Paramount Network) the fifth commercial-broadcast TV network in the US.

Chiseling away at a mountain of debt Viacom dumped its radio stations and sold its share in USA Networks (now named IAC/InterActiveCorp) to Universal for $1.7 billion in 1997. In 1998 it sold the reference and education publishing divisions of Simon & Schuster to Pearson for $4.6 billion and unloaded the unprofitable Blockbuster Music chain to Wherehouse Entertainment for $115 million.

Viacom created an Internet division (MTV Networks Online) in 1999 to house its MTV VH1 and Nickelodeon Web sites (later decentralized into The MTVi Group and Nickelodeon Online). Later that year it sold 18% of Blockbuster in an IPO and sold 10% of MTVi to TCI Music (later Liberty Digital) in exchange for the SonicNet websites.

Viacom bought Chris-Craft's 50%-stake in the struggling UPN Network for a paltry $5 million in 2000 by exercising a buy-sell clause in the contract. BHC Communications (Chris-Craft's 80%-owned subsidiary that actually owned the stake in UPN) filed suit to block Viacom's merger with CBS claiming that it violated a non-compete clause in the contract but the New York Supreme Court ruled in Viacom's favor. Its $45 billion merger with CBS went through (reuniting two companies split apart by the government 30 years ago) and Viacom was given one year to sell UPN. However a federal law prohibiting ownership of more than one TV network was overturned in 2001 allowing Viacom to keep the network.

Later that year Viacom's victory over Chris-Craft turned to sour grapes when News Corp. agreed to buy Chris-Craft. The deal could have forced UPN to fold if News Corp. had turned Chris-Craft's large-market UPN stations into FOX affiliates (a new pact later signed with Chris-Craft keeps UPN as the stations' network).

In 2001 Viacom bought the rest of Infinity Broadcasting that it didn't already own as well as Black Entertainment Television (the media company targeting African-Americans) for $3 billion. It also folded MTVi back into parent MTV Networks. Other cost cutting measures in 2002 included combining the business operations of UPN and CBS and placing Simon & Schuster under the same division as its film and TV production holdings.

Two years later Viacom finally sold its majority stake in Blockbuster which never really fit in with Viacom's other media properties. The media firm also didn't want to deal with the new challenges facing Blockbuster such as stiff competition from video on demand services the cheap DVD market and mail order video rental company Netflix.

In a move designed to simplify the firm's operations and re-focus the company on its core assets in late 2005 Viacom split into two separately traded firms — one called CBS Corporation consisting of traditional television and radio broadcasting operations and headed by former co-COO Les Moonves; and the other called the "new" Viacom made up of cable television and film operations and headed by former co-COO Tom Freston. (Freston resigned in 2006.) Redstone retained his title as chairman of both firms as well as his majority control.

Shortly after the split CBS Corp. sold Paramount Parks to Cedar Fair for $1.2 billion. A newly formed network called The CW a combination of UPN and The WB debuted in 2006. The following TV season the CBS network fell from first place in the ratings for the first time in six years. CBS Corp. expanded its online publishing operations in 2008 with the $1.8 billion acquisition of CNET Networks.

In 2011 production on the eighth season of its hit comedy Two and a Half Men ceased as a result of the erratic behavior of actor Charlie Sheen. CBS fired Sheen and has put the show on hiatus for an undetermined period of time.

In 2014 the company spun off its CBS Outdoor Americas advertising business.

EXECUTIVES

Chairman President And Ceo, Leslie (Les) Moonves, age 70, $3,500,000 total compensation
Sevp And Chief Communications Officer, Gil Schwartz, age 69, $896,923 total compensation
Sevp Chief Administrative Officer And Chief Human Resources Officer, Anthony G. Ambrosio, age 60, $964,423 total compensation
Sevp And Chief Legal Officer, Lawrence P. (Larry) Tu, age 65, $1,200,000 total compensation
Evp Government Affairs, John Orlando
Evp Investor Relations, Adam Townsend
Evp Deputy General Counsel And Secretary, Jonathan H. Anschell
Coo, Joseph R. Ianniello, age 53, $2,500,000 total compensation
Evp General Tax Counsel And Chief Veteran Officer, Richard M. Jones, age 55
Evp Controller And Chief Accounting Officer, Lawrence (Larry) Liding, age 51
Executive Vice President Cbs Marketing Group, Anne O'grady
Evp And Chief Communications Officer, Dana Mcclintock
Vice President Government Relations, Bryce Harlow
Vice President Advertising And Promotion Finance, Tracey Kimball
Vice President Production, Al Kennedy
Senior Vice President And Creative Director Print Advertising, Lesli Lawrence
Vice President Advertising And Promotion, Michael Pollack
Vice President Of Sales, Betty E Berlamino
Vice President Of Federal Tax, Jim Smolen
Vice President, Robert Noethiger
Senior Vice President Current Programs, Jeanne Mau
Vice President, David Strouse
Senior Vice President, Jonathan Sarrow
Vice President Diversity, Barbara Matos
Vice President Programming, Greg Trager
Vice President Human Resources Specialty Services, Michelle Martin
Evp Corporate Development, Bryon Rubin
Senior Vice President Western Regional Manager, Greg Guenther
Vice President Program Practices, Kingsley Wood

Senior Vice President Information Systems Director, Brelinda Snoddy

Executive Vice President Sales, Dean Kaplan

Senior Vice President Talent Acquisition, Richard Monastersky

Vice President Of Sales And Marketing, Glenn Higgins

Svp Deputy General Tax Counsel, Kenneth Koen

Vice President Creative Director, Chris Cranner

Vice President Of Web Development, Allan Bressler

Vice President Programming, Emilie Deutsch

Vice President Human Resources, Robin Bona

Senior Vice President And General Manager Cbs Mobile, Rob Gelick

Vice President Assistant General Co, Andrew Siegel

Vice President Of Detroit Sales, Joe Butkovich

Vice President Finance, Steve Grosso

Vice President Research, Patti Cohen

Senior Vice President And Director Of Sales Analysis Operations, Bob Kaplan

Vice President And Assistant General Counsel, Mary Tischler

Vice President Of Sales, Kevin Barth

Vice President And News Director, Jeff Kiernan

Vice President, George Lewis

Vice President Distribution, Ken Hinshaw

Senior Vice President Communications, Lauri Metrose

Senior Vice President Sales, Marty Daly

Vice President Drama Development, Bryan Seabury

Vice President Executive Creative Director, James Shefcik

Vice President Of Business Affairs, Alison Choi

Vice President, Rich Cervini

Vice President On Air Promotion, Paul Friedman

Vice President Broadcast And Cable Research, Frank Oneill

Vice President Business Development, Adam London

Senior Vice President And Associate General Counsel, Mark Engstrom

Senior Vice President Associate General Counsel, Rebecca Borden

Senior Vice President And Chief Procurement Officer, Tom Hogan

Vice President Primary Research, Marc Scheer

Vice President Of Sales, Matt Flewelling

Vice President Corporate Finance, Chad Diacont

Vice President Of Program, Pamela Soper

Vice President Client Services, Christoph Hesterbrink

Svp And Associate General Counsel Litigation, Anthony Bongiorno

Vice President Corporate Communications, Judy Dehaven

Vice President Group Sales, Brian Murphy

Senior Vice President For Standards And Special Projects, Linda Mason

Assistant Vice President, Per Wingerup

Vice President Senior Tax Counsel, Mindy Greene

Executive Vice President Business Affairs And Legal, Bruce Pottash

Vice President Payroll Services, Bill Condon

Senior Vice President, Gary Silver

Vice President Travel Services, Hal Rudy

Vice President Finance, Susan Varo

Vice President Senior Counsel, Alissa Makower

Vice President Creative Director, Sam Williams

Vice President, Jay Barnett

National Sales Manager, Vince Mccarthy

Senior Vice President Human Resources Cbs Radio, Mark Zulli

Senior Vice President Executive Search, Conway Shui

Senior Vice President Labor Relations, Edgar Yergeau

Vice President Associate General Counsel, Gigi Davis

Vice President Senior Counsel, Maria Charon

Vice President Advanced Services, Mike Pannacciulli

Svp Cbs Sports Sales And Marketing And Director, Chris Simko

Senior Vice President Communications, Phil Gonzales

Executive Vice President Affiliate Relations, Kurt Davis

Vice President, Randall Lewis

Svp Tax Reporting And Operations, Richard Ciraulo

Senior Vice President Communications Cbs Interactive, Chris Castro

Executive Vice President Communications Cbs Television Distribution, SScott Grogin

Senior Vice President Market Manager, Lauren Morris

Vice President Accounting, Janice Kruk

Svp Associate General Counsel Corporate And Securities, Kim Pittman

Vice President And Associate General Counsel, Ethan Tyer

Evp Business Affairs Cbs Television Studios, Dan Kupetz

Vice President Marketing, Jack Schuster

Senior Vice President Investor Relations, David Bank

Vice President Captioning And Video Description, Mark Turits

Vice President Creative Services, Betsy Siciliano

Vice President Business Affairs And Legal, Charles Gardner

Evp And General Counsel Tv Stations Sports And Broadcast Operations, David Hillman

Senior Vice President, Chris Leanza

Vice President Labor Relations, David Silberman

Executive Vice President Consumer Products, Liz Kalonder

Senior Vice President Sports Sales, Tony Taranto

Vice President Finance, Steven Haft

Senior Vice President Information Technology, Elizabeth Gilmore

Senior Vice President And Deputy General Counsel, Andrea Simon

Vice President Human Resources, Jessica Hurst

Senior Vice President And Deputy General Counsel, Michael Ward

Vice President And Counsel, Mark Maher

Senior Vice President Corporate Communications (showtime Networks), Erin Calhoun

Senior Vice President Digital Sales, Andi Poch

Senior Vice President Business Affairs And Legal, Peter Kane

Senior Vice President Communications, Laurie Metrose

Senior Vice President, Roni Mueller

Vice President Compensation, Julia Ambrose

Senior Vice President Business Development, Jeff Shultz

Senior Vice President, Kim Metcalf

Vice President Current Programs, Marci Cooperstein

Vice President Artist Partnerships And Experiences, Noel Grey

Senior Vice President Specials, Courtney Conroy

Senior Vice President And Associate General Counsel, Naomi Waltman

Vice President Strategic Sourcing, Mike Smyklo

Executive Vice President Digital, JD Crowley

Vice President, Gene Mellevold

Vice President Post Production, Jeff Henry

Vice President Strategic Partnerships, Michael Gulbin

Vice President Financial Reporting, Keith Moeller

Vice President Business Affairs, Allison Brightman

Executive Vice President Development, Elaine Brooks

Executive Vice President Theatrical Distribution, Steven Friedlander

Vice President Director Sales, Chris Ruggeri

Executive Vice President Entertainment Diversity Inclusion And Communications Cbs Entertainment, Tiffany Smith-anoa'i

Senior Vice President Television, Tiffany Grant

Senior Vice President, Paul Gilbert

Vice President Marketing (westinghouse), Kathleen Katz

Vice President Communications Cbs Television Distribution East Coast, Lauren Nowell

Executive Vice President Digital Sales And Sales Strategy, David Lawenda

Vice President Financial Planning And Analysis, Vincent Degeorges

Vice President Digital Sales, Trevor Frederickson

Vice President, Ross Molloy

Executive Vice President Operations And Engineering, Glenn Oakley

Vice President Of Legal Affairs, Josh Deutsch

Vice President Latenight Programs East Coast, Vincent Favale

Vice President Short Term Capital Markets, Ken Woltersdorf

Senior Vice President Business And Legal Affairs, Christine Hagan

Auditors: PricewaterhouseCoopers LLP

LOCATIONS

HQ: ViacomCBS Inc
1515 Broadway, New York, NY 10036
Phone: 212 258-6000
Web: www.viacbs.com

2017 Sales

	$ mil.	% of total
United States	11,675	85
International	2,017	15
Total	**13,692**	**100**

PRODUCTS/OPERATIONS

2017 Sales

	$ mil.	% of total
Entertainment	9,164	66
Cable Networks	2,501	18
Local Media	1,668	12
Publishing	830	4
Corporate/Eliminations	(471)	—
Total	**13,692**	**100**

2017 Sales

	$ mil.	% of total
Advertising	5,753	42
Content licensing & distribution	3,952	29
Affiliate & subscription fees	3,758	27
Other	229	2
Total	**13,692**	**100**

Selected Operations

CBS Television Network
CBS Entertainment
CBS News
CBS Sports
CBS Television Stations
CBS Television Studios
CBS Studios International
CBS Television Distribution
CBS Home Entertainment
CBS Consumer Products
CBS Films
The CW
Showtime
Smithsonian Channel
CBS Sports Network
CBS Interactive
Simon & Schuster
CBS Scene
Watch! Magazine
EcoMedia
Pop
CBS VISION

COMPETITORS

21st Century Fox
AOL
Cumulus Media
Disney
Penguin Random House
SIRIUS XM
Sony Pictures
Entertainment

JCDecaux   Time Warner
Lamar Advertising   Yahoo!
NBCUniversal   iHeartCommunications
Netflix

HISTORICAL FINANCIALS
Company Type: Public

Income Statement
FYE: December 31

	REVENUE ($ mil.)	NET INCOME ($ mil.)	NET PROFIT MARGIN	EMPLOYEES
12/19	27,812	3,308	11.9%	28,570
12/18	14,514	1,960	13.5%	16,730
12/17	13,692	357	2.6%	16,730
12/16	13,166	1,261	9.6%	21,270
12/15	13,886	1,413	10.2%	16,260
Annual Growth	19.0%	23.7%	—	15.1%

2019 Year-End Financials

Debt ratio: 37.80%	No. of shares (mil.): 615
Return on equity: 41.32%	Dividends
Cash ($ mil.): 632	Yield: 1.8%
Current ratio: 1.32	Payout: 14.5%
Long-term debt ($ mil.): 18,002	Market value ($ mil.): 25,812

	STOCK PRICE ($) FY Close	P/E High/Low		PER SHARE ($) Earnings	Dividends	Book Value
12/19	41.97	10	7	5.36	0.78	21.47
12/18	43.72	12	8	5.14	0.72	7.52
12/17	59.00	78	61	0.88	0.72	5.16
12/16	63.62	23	15	2.81	0.66	8.95
12/15	47.13	22	13	2.89	0.60	12.02
Annual Growth	(2.9%)	—	—	16.7%	6.8%	15.6%

Viatris Inc

LOCATIONS

HQ: Viatris Inc
  1000 Mylan Blvd., Canonsburg, PA 15317
Phone: 724 514-1968
Web: www.viatris.com

HISTORICAL FINANCIALS
Company Type: Public

Income Statement
FYE: December 31

	REVENUE ($ mil.)	NET INCOME ($ mil.)	NET PROFIT MARGIN	EMPLOYEES
12/19	10,244	4,917	48.0%	12,300
12/18	12,431	6,128	49.3%	—
12/17	13,359	10,199	76.3%	—
Annual Growth	(12.4%)	(30.6%)	—	—

2019 Year-End Financials

Debt ratio: ——	
Return on equity: 67.78%	Dividends
Cash ($ mil.): 184	Yield: —
Current ratio: 1.28	Payout: —
Long-term debt ($ mil.): —	Market value ($ mil.): —

	STOCK PRICE ($) FY Close	P/E High/Low		PER SHARE ($) Earnings	Dividends	Book Value
12/19	0.00	—	—	(0.00)	0.00	(0.00)
12/18	0.00	—	—	(0.00)	0.00	(0.00)
Annual Growth	—			—	—	—

VIRGINIA COLLEGE BUILDING AUTHORITY

EXECUTIVES

Prin, Robert F McDonnell

LOCATIONS

HQ: VIRGINIA COLLEGE BUILDING AUTHORITY
  101 N 14TH ST FL 3, RICHMOND, VA 232193665
Phone: 804 225-2142
Web: WWW.VIRGINIA.GOV

HISTORICAL FINANCIALS
Company Type: Private

Income Statement
FYE: June 30

	ASSETS ($ mil.)	NET INCOME ($ mil.)	INCOME AS % OF ASSETS	EMPLOYEES
06/19	2,339	(209)	—	2
06/18	2,141	(145)	—	—
06/17	1,754	(98)	—	—
06/16	2,199	(327)	—	—
Annual Growth	2.1%	—	—	—

Virginia Electric & Power Co.

Virginia Electric and Power Company (Virginia Power) operates under the Dominion Virginia Power and Dominion North Carolina Power brands and provides regulated electric delivery services to about 2.4 million homes and businesses. Power generation is derived by means of coal gas oil hydro and nuclear plants. The utility's power plants (with 24300 MW of generating capacity) are managed by the Dominion Generation unit of parent Dominion Energy. Control of Virginia Power's transmission facilities is maintained by PJM Interconnection. Dominion Virginia Power also sells wholesale power to other users.

Geographic Reach

Virginia Power generates transmits and distributes electricity for sale in Virginia and North Carolina.

Sales and Marketing

Virginia Power primarily serves retail customers. It sells electricity at wholesale prices to rural electric cooperatives municipalities and wholesale electricity markets.

Strategy

Virginia Power is trying to beef up its green energy profile. In addition to exploring wind farm options to help produce alternative energy the company is pushing energy conservation programs with the aim of cutting peak demand by electric consumers in Virginia by 650 MW.

In 2016 the company announced plans to invest nearly $2 billion per year through 2020 to add cleaner generation to its infrastructure including solar energy. It also plans to expand secure and upgrade its electric grid in Virginia and northeastern North Carolina.

EXECUTIVES

President Dominion Virginia Power, Robert M. Blue
Auditors: DELOITTE & TOUCHE LLP

LOCATIONS

HQ: Virginia Electric & Power Co.
  120 Tredegar Street, Richmond, VA 23219
Phone: 804 819-2000

COMPETITORS

Appalachian Power	Pepco Holdings
Columbia Gas of Virginia	Rappahannock Electric Cooperative
Duke Energy Carolinas	SCANA
Duke Energy Progress Inc.	South Carolina Electric & Gas

HISTORICAL FINANCIALS
Company Type: Public

Income Statement
FYE: December 31

	REVENUE ($ mil.)	NET INCOME ($ mil.)	NET PROFIT MARGIN	EMPLOYEES
12/19	8,108	1,149	14.2%	6,000
12/18	7,619	1,282	16.8%	6,800
12/17	7,556	1,540	20.4%	6,900
12/16	7,588	1,218	16.1%	6,800
12/15	7,622	1,087	14.3%	6,800
Annual Growth	1.6%	1.4%	—	(3.1%)

2019 Year-End Financials

Debt ratio: 30.39%	No. of shares (mil.): 0
Return on equity: 8.50%	Dividends
Cash ($ mil.): 17	Yield: —
Current ratio: 1.08	Payout: —
Long-term debt ($ mil.): 12,341	Market value ($ mil.): —

VIRGINIA HOUSING DEVELOPMENT AUTHORITY

Though Virginia is famous for its Civil War-era plantations these historic estates represent a lifestyle out of reach for most. For Virginians seeking a more modest homestead there's the Virginia Housing Development Authority (VHDA). The not-for-profit quasi-government agency founded by the Virginia General Assembly in 1972 provides developers of rentalÂ propertiesÂ and low- to moderate-income borrowers with low interest rate loans to renovate or purchase houses and apartments across the state. Its loan products are offered by more than 140 authorized lenders throughout Virginia. The VHDA is self-supporting issuing bonds to raise capital.

EXECUTIVES

Executive Director, Susan F. Dewey

Managing Director Rental Housing, Arthur N. (Art) Bowen

Managing Director Community Outreach, J. Michael Hawkins

Managing Director Executive Services, Llewellyn C. Anderson

Managing Director Homeownership, Janet Wiglesworth

Managing Director Internal Audit And Risk Management, Julie Camus

Managing Director Finance, Pat Carey

Acting Managing Director Information Technology Services, J. Kyle Howard

Vice President Of Operation, Jackie Gibbs

Vice President Of Operation, Sherry Estridge

Executive Vice President Claims And Customer Service Operations, Dyson Darrell

Chairman, Timothy M. Chapman

Vice Chairman, Sarah B. Stedfast

Treasurer, Gary Murray

Auditors: KPMG LLP RICHMOND VIRGINIA

LOCATIONS

HQ: VIRGINIA HOUSING DEVELOPMENT AUTHORITY
601 S BELVIDERE ST, RICHMOND, VA 232206504
Phone: 804 780-0789
Web: WWW.VHDA.COM

HISTORICAL FINANCIALS

Company Type: Private

Income Statement FYE: June 30

	ASSETS ($ mil.)	NET INCOME ($ mil.)	INCOME AS % OF ASSETS	EMPLOYEES
06/18	7,292	132	1.8%	300
06/16	8,024	171	2.1%	—
06/15	8,070	176	2.2%	—
06/14	8,014	132	1.7%	—
Annual Growth	(2.3%)	(0.1%)	—	—

VIRTU FINANCIAL LLC

Auditors: DELOITTE & TOUCHE LLP NEW YOR

LOCATIONS

HQ: VIRTU FINANCIAL LLC
1 LIBERTY PLZ, NEW YORK, NY 100061404
Phone: 212 418-0100
Web: WWW.VIRTU.COM

HISTORICAL FINANCIALS

Company Type: Private

Income Statement FYE: December 31

	ASSETS ($ mil.)	NET INCOME ($ mil.)	INCOME AS % OF ASSETS	EMPLOYEES
12/14	3,324	190	5.7%	18
12/13	3,963	182	4.6%	—
Annual Growth	(16.1%)	4.3%	—	—

Visa Inc

Paper or plastic? Visa hopes you choose the latter. Visa operates the world's largest global consumer payment system (ahead of rivals MasterCard and American Express) and boasts more than 3.4 billion credit and other payment cards in circulation across more than 200 countries. As part of its business the company licenses the Visa name to member institutions which issue and market their own Visa products and participate in the VisaNet payment system that provides authorization processing and settlement services. The company also offers debit cards internet payment systems value-storing smart cards and traveler's checks. Visa's network connects thousands of financial institutions worldwide.

HISTORY

Although the first charge card was issued by Western Union in 1914 it wasn't until 1958 that Bank of America (BofA) issued its BankAmericard which combined the convenience of a charge account with credit privileges. When BofA extended its customer base outside California the interchange system controlling payments began to falter because of design problems and fraud.

In 1968 Dee Hock manager of the BankAmericard operations of the National Bank of Commerce in Seattle convinced member banks that a more reliable system was needed. Two years later National BankAmericard Inc. (NBI) was created as an independent corporation (owned by 243 banks) to buy the BankAmericard system from BofA.

With its initial ad slogan "Think of it as Money" the Hock-led NBI developed BankAmericard into a widely used form of payment in the US. A multinational corporation IBANCO was formed in 1974 to carry the operations into other countries. People outside the US resisted BankAmericard's nominal association with BofA and in 1977 Hock changed the card's name to Visa. NBI became Visa USA and IBANCO became Visa International.

By 1980 Visa had debuted debit cards begun issuing traveler's checks and created an electromagnetic point-of-sale authorization system. Visa developed a global network of ATMs in 1983; it was expanded in 1987 by the purchase of a 33% stake in the Plus System of ATMs then the US's second-largest system. Hock retired in 1984 with the company well on its way to realizing his vision of a universal payment system.

The company built the Visa brand image with aggressive advertising such as sponsorship of the 1988 and 1992 Olympics and by co-branding (issuing cards through other organizations with strong brand names such as Blockbuster and Ford).

In 1994 Visa teamed up with Microsoft and others to develop home banking services and software. Visa Cash was introduced during the 1996 Olympics. Visa pushed its debit cards in 1996 and 1997 with humorous ads featuring presidential also-ran Bob Dole and showbiz success story Daffy Duck.

Visa expanded its smart card infrastructure in 1997. It published with MasterCard encryption and security software for online transactions. The gloves came off the next year as the companies vied to convince the world to rally around their respective e-purse technology standards.

During the 1990s Visa fought American Express' attempts to introduce a bank credit card of its own by forbidding Visa members in the US from issuing the product; the Justice Department responded with an antitrust suit against Visa and MasterCard. The case went to trial in 2000 with the government claiming that Visa and MasterCard stifle competition and enjoy an exclusive cross-ownership structure. Visa eventually agreed to pay American Express $2.25 billion to settle the case.

Also in 2000 the company made a deal with Gemplus the French smart card company to enable payments over wireless networks. Visa then inked e-commerce agreements with telecommunications companies Nokia and Ericsson. The company continued its technology push with a deal with Financial Services Technology Consortium to test biometrics — the use of fingerprints irises and voice recognition to identify cardholders. The company also launched a prepaid card Visa Buxx targeted at teenagers.

The European Union in 2000 launched an investigation into the firm's transaction fees alleging that the fees could restrict competition. The following year Visa International agreed to drop its fee to 0.7% of the transaction value over five years.

Led by retail giant Wal-Mart some 4 million merchants claimed Visa and MasterCard violated antitrust laws and attempted to monopolize a legally defined market for debit cards. The plaintiffs sought up to $200 billion in damages in their class-action suit. Just as the 1996 lawsuit was to go to trial in early 2003 Visa settled agreeing to pay $2 billion (twice that of co-defendant MasterCard) over the next decade. Both agreed to pay $25 million immediately as well as reduce the fee merchants pay for signature-based debit cards.

Visa settled a similar case with Discover Financial in 2008. Visa's net share of the deal totaled some $1.8 billion; MasterCard which was also named agreed to pay $862.5 million.

The group restructured in 2007 in order to offer a more seamless international payments processing platform and to take itself public. Visa International Visa Canada Visa U.S.A. and several other regional organizations merged to create Visa Inc. which became the new parent of the group. It raised about $17 billion in a 2008 IPO.

Visa dedicated some of the funds raised to exploring new payment-related technologies and expanding into more regions. It established joint ventures with payment processors and banks to strengthen its global payment network. Other funds were set aside to cover costs resulting from legal settlements with American Express and Discover Financial totaling more than $4 billion.

EXECUTIVES

Ceo, Alfred F. (Al) Kelly, age 62

Vice Chairman Risk And Public Policy, Ellen Richey, age 71, $600,023 total compensation

Evp And Cfo, Vasant M. Prabhu, age 59, $547,616 total compensation

Evp And Ceo European Operations, Charlotte M. Hogg, age 49

Evp Strategy Mergers And Acquisitions And Government Relations, William M. (Bill) Sheedy, age 53, $525,020 total compensation

Evp And General Counsel, Kelly M. Tullier, age 54

Evp Technology, Rajat Taneja, age 55, $750,029 total compensation

President, Ryan McInerney, age 45, $750,029 total compensation

Vice President, Brian Wood

Vp Strategic Technology Partnerships, Lloyd Cato

Senior Vice President, Elizabeth Hurvitz

Vice President Processing Solutions, Manny Fernandez

Vice President Of Management, James Williams

Vice President Healthcare, Stacy Pourfallah

Vice President, Michael Lemberger

Vice President, Seth Friedman

Vice President Data Center Engineering And Operations, Brian Green

Vice President, Jeff Allison

Vice President, Andrew Carpenter

Vice President Product Technology, Mark Rigby

Vice President, Julie Miller

Senior Vice President And Chief Information Security Officer, Sunil Seshadri

Senior Vice President, Mark Nelsen

Senior Vice President Innovation And Strategic Partnerships, Matt Dill

Vice President Marketing Planning, Stacey Taylor

Senior Vice President Global Government Affairs, Demetrios Marantis

Vice President, Joanna Gill

Vice President Of Product, Alan Johnson

Vice President, Biju Abraham

Vice President Digital Marketing, David Purcell

Vice President Global Product, Gourab Basu

Vice President Financial Institution Sales, Brent Vaughan

Vice President Digital Solutions, Todd Wade

Vice President, Manoj Marathe

Vice President, Kyle Mandry

Vice President Corporate Strategy, Saurabh Chopra

Senior Vice President Chief Corporate Counsel, Tracey Heaton

Senior Vice President Chief Audit Executive, Adrian Kilcoyne

Vice President Intellectual Property Strategy, Tim Bedard

Vice President Infrastructure Project Management Office, Amy Gradnik

Vice President Enterprise Workforce Transformation And Planning, Manish Asnani

Svp Developer Platform India, Nitin Chandel

Senior Vice President Visa Research Labs, Min Wang

Vice President, Margaret Fitzpatrick

Vice President. Consumer, Daniel Sanford

Vice President, Sang Lee

Vice President Strategic Initiatives, Jeff Kim

Vice President Business Development And Strategy, Robert Steinmetz

Senior Vice President Investor Relations, Michael Milotich

Vice President Head Of Global Infrastructure Network Services, Justin Dustzadeh

Vice President Europe Information Security Integration And Global Identity And Access Management, Shirish Puranik

Vice President Marketing, Kevin Skirde

Vice President Information Security Architecture, Subra Kumaraswamy

Vice President Data Architecture, Dirk Reinshagen

Senior Vice President Global Operations, Elizabeth Rector

Vice President Innovation And Strategic Partnerships (visa Innovation Center), Kellie Goodwin

Vice President Marketing Strategy And Operations (north America), Sheila Parmar

Vice President Associate General Counsel Global Litigation And Competition, Ryan Takemoto

Vice President Specialized Product Sales Prepaid, Patrick Williams

Vice President Of Technology, Deepak Bapna

Vice President Global Tax, Carl Andersen

Vp Global Technology Fpanda, Gilbert Niwa

Vice President Risk And Authentication Product Development, Zijian Zheng

Senior Vice President Chief Compliance Officer, Leonard Shen

Vp Global Merchant Support, Noel Pedroza

Vice President Global Regulatory Affairs, Rabia Sheikh

Vice President Of Risk, Rosetta Jones

Vice President Of Communications Latin America And The Caribbean, Dario Cutin

Senior Vice President, Kirk Stuart

Vice President, Chackan Lai

Vp Global Data Science, David Trounce

Senior Vice President Of Marketing, Paulina Hoke

Vice President, Kevin Jacques

Evp General Counsel And Corporate Secretary, Kelly Mahon Tullier

Vice President, Richard Korn

Senior Vice President Platform Strategy And Innovation, Paul Walsh

Vp Global Business Operations Product And Sales Learning Solutions, Lamont Boykins

Chairman, Robert W. Matschullat, age 73

Auditors: KPMG LLP

LOCATIONS

HQ: Visa Inc
  P.O. Box 8999, San Francisco, CA 94128-8999
Phone: 650 432-3200
Web: www.corporate.visa.com

2018 Sales

	$ mil.	% of total
United States	9,332	45
International	11,277	55
Total	20,609	100

PRODUCTS/OPERATIONS

2018 Sales

	$ mil.	% of total
Service Revenues	8,918	34
Data Processing Revenues	9,027	34
International Transaction Revenues	7,211	28
Other Revenues	944	4
Client Incentives	(5491)	-
Total	20,609	100

Selected Products and Services

Commercial and government
  Visa Business Credit Card (small business)
  Visa Business Debit Card (small business)
  Visa Business Electron (international)
  Visa Business Line of Credit
  Visa Commercial One Card
  Visa Corporate Card (travel and entertainment)
  Visa Gift Card
  Visa Incentive Card
  Visa Purchasing Card
  Visa Signature Business Card
Consumer credit
  Visa Classic
  Visa Gold
  Visa Infinite
  Visa Platinum
Consumer deposit
  Interlink Debit (POS debit network)
  Prepaid
  Visa Debit
  Visa Classic
  Visa Gold
  Visa Infinite
  Visa Platinum
  Visa Electron Debit

COMPETITORS

American Express	MasterCard
Apple Inc.	NYCE Payments Network
China UnionPay	PULSE Network
Citigroup	PayPal
Discover	Rewards Network
JCB International	

HISTORICAL FINANCIALS

Company Type: Public

Income Statement
FYE: September 30

	REVENUE ($ mil.)	NET INCOME ($ mil.)	NET PROFIT MARGIN	EMPLOYEES
09/20	21,846	10,866	49.7%	20,500
09/19	22,977	12,080	52.6%	19,500
09/18	20,609	10,301	50.0%	17,000
09/17	18,358	6,699	36.5%	15,000
09/16	15,082	5,991	39.7%	—
Annual Growth	9.7%	16.0%		

2020 Year-End Financials

Debt ratio: 29.75%
Return on equity: 30.57%
Cash ($ mil.): 16,289
Current ratio: 1.91
Long-term debt ($ mil.): 21,071

No. of shares (mil.): 1,939
Dividends
  Yield: 0.6%
  Payout: 9.2%
Market value ($ mil.): 387,742

	STOCK PRICE ($) FY Close	P/E High/Low		PER SHARE ($) Earnings	Dividends	Book Value
09/20	199.97	44	28	4.89	1.20	18.67
09/19	172.01	35	23	5.32	1.00	17.57
09/18	150.09	34	24	4.42	0.83	16.79
09/17	105.24	38	27	2.80	0.66	15.78
09/16	82.70	33	27	2.48	0.56	15.43
Annual Growth	24.7%	—	—	18.5%	21.0%	4.9%

Vistra Corp

Auditors: DELOITTE & TOUCHE LLP

LOCATIONS

HQ: Vistra Corp
  6555 Sierra Drive, Irving, TX 75039
Phone: 214 812-4600
Web: www.vistraenergy.com

HISTORICAL FINANCIALS

Company Type: Public

Income Statement
FYE: December 31

	REVENUE ($ mil.)	NET INCOME ($ mil.)	NET PROFIT MARGIN	EMPLOYEES
12/19	11,809	928	7.9%	5,475
12/18	9,144	(54)	—	5,275
12/17	5,430	(254)	—	4,150
12/16*	1,191	(163)	—	4,435
10/16	4,255	22,851	537.0%	—
Annual Growth	40.5%	(65.6%)	—	—

*Fiscal year change

2019 Year-End Financials

Debt ratio: 40.31%
Return on equity: 11.73%
Cash ($ mil.): 300
Current ratio: 0.90
Long-term debt ($ mil.): 10,102

No. of shares (mil.): 487
Dividends
 Yield: 2.1%
 Payout: 50.0%
Market value ($ mil.): 11,212

	STOCK PRICE ($) FY Close	P/E High/Low		PER SHARE ($) Earnings	Dividends	Book Value
12/19	22.99	15	2	1.86	0.50	16.32
12/18	22.89	—	—	(0.11)	0.00	15.94
12/17	18.32	—	—	(0.59)	0.00	14.80
12/16*	8.43	—	—	(0.38)	2.32	15.43
10/16	8.54	—	—	(0.00)	0.00	(0.00)
Annual Growth	39.1%	—	—	—	—	—

*Fiscal year change

VMware Inc

VMware develops software used to create and manage virtual machines — computer functions spread across multiple systems. Companies use its cloud-based and on-premise applications to more efficiently integrate and manage server storage and networking functions which reduces their IT costs. VMware also offers software maintenance and support training consulting services and hosted services. The company has marketing relationships with top computer hardware vendors including Hewlett Packard Enterprise IBM and Cisco Systems. VMware has strong geographic distribution with international customers accounting for more than half of its sales. Dell Technologies holds a controlling stake in VMware through its acquisition of EMC.

Financial Performance

VMware's virtualization products produce real money driving revenue some $2.4 billion higher from 2015 to 2019 (ended February). The company's net income fluctuated over the same time but leaped in 2019 from 2018.

In 2019 VMware posted a 14% revenue increase to reach $8.9 billion up about $1.1 billion from 2018. License revenue (40% of overall sales) rose 18% year over year with help from the company's Hybrid Cloud Computing and SaaS offerings. Service revenue was 11% higher in 2019 from 2018 due to existing contracts and contracts added though license sales during the year.

VMware recorded net income of $2.2 billion in 2019 compared to $659 million in 2018. The 2019 profit was lifted by higher revenue income from the company's interest in Pivotal Software (which had an IPO in fiscal 2019) and lower income taxes.

Cash in VMware's coffers totaled $2.9 billion in 2019 compared to $6 billion the year before. Operations generated $3.6 billion in 2018 investing activities provided $4.4 billion and financing activities used $11.1 billion (due to payment of a special dividend).

VMware has about $4 billion in debt which could require the company to devote cash flow to debt service instead of investments related to growth. A lack of cash could limit VMware's flexibility in responding to opportunities and crises.

The company has a $1 billion unsecured revolving credit facility that it has yet to use.

Strategy

Although VMware is part of Dell Technologies that hasn't stopped the company from doing deals with Dell competitors. The company has agreements with IBM and Amazon Web Services (AWS) that help customers manage their private clouds and public clouds (running on IBM or AWS) using VMware software. The arrangements provide customers more flexibility with their cloud environments.

For products to run on those systems VMware has assembled a group of software-as-a-service and cloud technologies through in-house R&D and acquisitions including Heptio CloudHealth Technologies Inc. and VeloCloud Networks Inc.

Sales of VMware's network virtualization product NSX have continued to grow since it was introduced in 2013. Sold as part of other VMware products NSX allows networking hardware like routers and switches to be reconfigured and managed by software. NSX has been a hit for the company producing about $1.3 billion in revenue in 2019 (it's used by about 10000 customers).

Part of VMware's strategy is to pack its customers with as many of its products as it can. An increasing number of customers have gone with the company's full VMware Cloud Foundation or its full VMware Cloud on AWS offering generating bigger deals.

VMware relies on sales to distributors Arrow Electronics and Tech Data Corp. for more than 25% of sales. Sales to parent Dell Technologies accounts for another 25% of revenue.

Mergers and Acquisitions

In 2019 VMware agreed to spend about $4.8 billion to buy companies that broaden its cloud offerings and strengthen its security capabilities. The company said it would buy Pivotal Software for about $2.7 billion to build out its software for cloud computing environments and buy CarbonBlack for about $2.1 billion to beef up security throughout its products. The deals are to close by the end of VMware's 2020 fiscal year in January 2020. Like VMware Pivotal is partly owned by Dell Technologies.

VMware in 2019 acquired Intrinsic a cybersecurity company as part of its focus on the public cloud. Intrinsic's products allow software developers to securely access serverless computing by setting policies on how the systems work when certain conditions are met. The deal contributes to the expansion of VMware's AppDefense platform into the public cloud.

In 2019 VMware agreed to acquire Uhana which develops technology to help telecom carriers automate and improve network operations amid carriers' transition from 4G to 5G networks and the increasing need for reduced latency. Uhana's real-time deep learning engine operates in the operator private cloud or public cloud infrastructure. VMware intends to add Uhana's to its Telco Cloud and Edge Cloud portfolio and provide intelligence and analytics for VMware Smart Assurance and VMware Smart Experience products.

VMware agreed to buy Bitfusion which develops technology to make cloud computing workloads more efficient using artificial intelligence in 2019. VMware intends to integrate Bitfusion's tools into its vSphere platform. Bitfusion's technology allows cloud software to access computing power on individual CPUs no matter what server they're sitting on.

In another 2019 deal VMware agreed to buy Avi Networks a developer of multi-cloud application delivery services. Avi's technology is to help VMware to bring benefits of a public cloud experience to the entire data center making the process automated scalable and more secure for its customers. The deal was expected to close bu August 2020.

Also in 2019 VMware agreed to acquire Bitnami a developer of application packaging for cloud and Kubernetes environments. With Bitnami's technologies VMware customers would be able to deploy application packages on any cloud in the appropriate format. The deal is expected to close by the end of the 2019 second quarter.

Company Background

Founded in 1998 VMware was acquired by EMC for about $625 million in cash in 2004. Looking to unlock some of the value in its subsidiary EMC sold some of its stake in VMware in a 2007 IPO. In 2016 Dell bought EMC including VMware for more than $60 billion.

EXECUTIVES

Corporate Senior Vice President And Chief People Officer, Betsy Sutter

Ceo And Director, Patrick P. (Pat) Gelsinger, age 59, $1,000,000 total compensation

Coo Customer Operations, Sanjay Poonen, age 50, $605,000 total compensation

Evp Worldwide Sales, Maurizio Carli

Evp And Cfo, Zane C. Rowe, age 49

Co-coo Products And Cloud Services, Rajiv Ramaswami, age 54

Svp And Cio, Bask Iyer

Evp And General Manager Hybrid Cloud Services Business Unit, Bill Fathers

Co-coo Products And Cloud Services, Rangarajan (Raghu) Raghuram, age 57, $605,000 total compensation

Svp Strategy And Corporate Development And General Manager Telco Nfv Group, Shekar Ayyar

Corporate Svp Software-defined Data Center Division, Ray O'Farrell

Svp General Counsel Chief Compliance Officer And Secretary, S. Dawn Smith, age 56

Senior Vice President Finance And Chief Accounting Officer, Kevan Krysler

Vice President Americas End User Computmg, Robert Ruelas

Vice President U.s. Enterprise Sales, Corey Hutchison

Svp Worldwide Commercial And Channel Sales, Brandon Sweeney

Vice President Product Management Cloud Apps And Desktops, Pat Lee

Vice President And Deputy General Counsel, Laurie Hane

Vice President Ww Federation Sales And Gtm, John Sellers

Vice President Cloud Services Development And Operations, Velchamy Sankarlingam

Vice President Chief Information Security Officer, Alex Tosheff

Vice President Worldwide Sales Operations, Pradeep Vancheeswaran

Vice President And General Manager Japan, Jon Robertson

Vice President Global Technical Support, John Dolan

Global Vice President Strategic Systems Integrators And Outsourcers, David M Parsons
Vice President Corporate Controller, Andrew Munk
Senior Product Manager Mvp, Debapriya Ray
Vice President Field Automation Services And Global Marketing Operations, Mia Leondakis
Vice President And Deputy General Counsel, Brooks Beard
Quality Engineer For Mvp, Bryan Bozzi
Vice President Latin America Sales, Fernando Mollon
Vice President Products, Mark Lohmeyer
Vice President And Deputy General Counsel Corporate Securities And Mergers And Acquisitions, Craig Norris
Vice President End User Computing, Jason Conyard
Vice President Product Management, Paul Fazzone
Vice President Customer Operations Finance, Stephanie Joe
Vice President Research And Development Networking And Security Bu, Umesh Mahajan
Svp Worldwide Partners And Alliances, Ross Brown
Vice President Products, Lee Caswell
Vice President And Chief Open Source Officer, Dirk Hohndel
Vice President Partners And General Business Asia Pacific And Japan, Sharat Sinha
Senior Vice President And General Manager Americas, Brett Shirk
Vice President Cloud Management Business Unit, Jon Herlocker
Vice President Channel And Alliances And General Business In Emea, Jean-Phillipe Barleaza
Svp And Gm Cloud Management Business Unit, Ajay Singh
Vice President Americas Systems Engineering, Dave Gregory
Vice President Cloud Operations, Peter Weideling
Vice President Airwatch Siso Sales, Jeff Baum
Svp Product Development Cloud Services, Ajay Patel
Vice President Cloud Management Product Marketing, Rob Smoot
Vice President Cloud Customer Success, Susan Aoki
Vice President Internal Audit, Gus Shea
Chairman, Michael S. Dell
Board Member, Karen Dykstra
Board Member, Don Carty
Auditors: PricewaterhouseCoopers LLP

LOCATIONS

HQ: VMware Inc
  3401 Hillview Avenue, Palo Alto, CA 94304
Phone: 650 427-5000
Web: www.vmware.com

2019 Sales

	$ mil.	% of total
US	4,205	47
Other countries	4,769	53
Total	**6,571**	**100**

PRODUCTS/OPERATIONS

2019 Sales

	$ mil.	% of total
Services	5,186	58
License	3,788	42
Total	**8,974**	**100**

COMPETITORS

AWS	IBM
CA Inc.	Microsoft
Cisco Systems	Nutanix
Google	Oracle
Hewlett Packard	

Enterprise

HISTORICAL FINANCIALS
Company Type: Public

Income Statement
FYE: January 31

	REVENUE ($ mil.)	NET INCOME ($ mil.)	NET PROFIT MARGIN	EMPLOYEES
01/20*	10,811	6,412	59.3%	31,000
02/19	8,974	2,422	27.0%	24,200
02/18	7,922	570	7.2%	21,700
02/17	496	(8)		
12/16	7,093	1,186	16.7%	19,900
Annual Growth	**15.1%**	**75.5%**	**—**	**15.9%**

*Fiscal year change

2020 Year-End Financials

Debt ratio: 21.86%	No. of shares (mil.): 417
Return on equity: 170.10%	Dividends
Cash ($ mil.): 2,915	Yield: —
Current ratio: 0.65	Payout: —
Long-term debt ($ mil.): 3,001	Market value ($ mil.): 61,846

	STOCK PRICE ($) FY Close	P/E High/Low		PER SHARE ($) Earnings	Dividends	Book Value
01/20*	148.06	13	8	15.08	0.00	16.78
02/19	150.51	28	18	5.85	26.81	1.34
02/18	122.72	107	61	1.38	0.00	19.26
02/17	88.95	—	—	(0.02)	0.00	20.04
12/16	78.73	29	16	2.78	0.00	19.83
Annual Growth	**23.4%**	**—**	**—**	**75.7%**	**—**	**(5.4%)**

*Fiscal year change

Voya Financial Inc

Auditors: Ernst & Young LLP

LOCATIONS

HQ: Voya Financial Inc
  230 Park Avenue, New York, NY 10169
Phone: 212 309-8200
Web: www.ing.us

HISTORICAL FINANCIALS
Company Type: Public

Income Statement
FYE: December 31

	ASSETS ($ mil.)	NET INCOME ($ mil.)	INCOME AS % OF ASSETS	EMPLOYEES
12/19	169,051	(351)	—	6,000
12/18	154,682	875	0.6%	6,000
12/17	222,532	(2,992)	—	6,300
12/16	214,235	(428)	—	6,700
12/15	218,249	408	0.2%	7,000
Annual Growth	**(6.2%)**	**—**	**—**	**(3.8%)**

2019 Year-End Financials

Debt ratio: 1.80%	No. of shares (mil.): 132
Return on equity: (-3.98%)	Dividends
Cash ($ mil.): 1,181	Yield: 0.5%
Current ratio: —	Payout: 9.2%
Long-term debt ($ mil.): —	Market value ($ mil.): 8,069

	STOCK PRICE ($) FY Close	P/E High/Low		PER SHARE ($) Earnings	Dividends	Book Value
12/19	60.98	—	—	(2.58)	0.32	71.10
12/18	40.14	10	7	5.20	0.04	54.40
12/17	49.47	—	—	(16.25)	0.04	58.20
12/16	39.22	—	—	(2.13)	0.04	66.76
12/15	36.91	27	20	1.80	0.04	64.26
Annual Growth	**13.4%**	**—**	**—**	**—**	**68.2%**	**2.6%**

Wabtec Corp

EXECUTIVES

Pres-Ceo, Rafael Santana
Exec V-Pres, Robert J Brooks
Exec V-Pres, John M Meister
Sr V-Pres, Charles F Kovac
Sr V-Pres, R Mark Cox
Sr V-Pres, Patrick D Dugan
Evp-Chro, Nicole Theophilus
National Sales, Tony Ward
Manufacturing Executive, William Rimmer
Facility Maintenence, Joe Carter
Process Engineer, Bill Clanahan
Auditors: Ernst & Young LLP

LOCATIONS

HQ: Wabtec Corp
  30 Isabella Street, Pittsburgh, PA 15212
Phone: 412 825-1000   **Fax:** 412 825-1019
Web: www.wabteccorp.com

HISTORICAL FINANCIALS
Company Type: Public

Income Statement
FYE: December 31

	REVENUE ($ mil.)	NET INCOME ($ mil.)	NET PROFIT MARGIN	EMPLOYEES
12/19	8,200	326	4.0%	27,500
12/18	4,363	294	6.8%	18,000
12/17	3,881	262	6.8%	18,000
12/16	2,931	304	10.4%	20,000
12/15	3,308	398	12.1%	13,000
Annual Growth	**25.5%**	**(4.9%)**	**—**	**20.6%**

2019 Year-End Financials

Debt ratio: 23.38%	No. of shares (mil.): 191
Return on equity: 5.10%	Dividends
Cash ($ mil.): 604	Yield: 0.6%
Current ratio: 1.29	Payout: 26.0%
Long-term debt ($ mil.): 4,333	Market value ($ mil.): 14,914

	STOCK PRICE ($) FY Close	P/E High/Low		PER SHARE ($) Earnings	Dividends	Book Value
12/19	77.80	42	33	1.84	0.48	51.94
12/18	70.25	37	22	3.05	0.48	29.66
12/17	81.43	34	25	2.72	0.44	29.25
12/16	83.02	26	18	3.34	0.36	23.12
12/15	71.12	25	17	4.10	0.28	18.51
Annual Growth	**2.3%**	**—**	**—**	**(18.2%)**	**14.4%**	**29.4%**

WAKEFERN FOOD CORP.

Wakefern Food Corp. is the largest retailer-owned cooperative in the nation with its nearly 50 members owning some 355 supermarkets across the northeastern US. The cooperative offers some $10 billion in purchasing power and provides a host of support services including private label brand development development store layout and design and advertising and marketing as well as technology finance and human resources services. The members' stores operate under the ShopRite The Fresh Grocer Price Rite Marketplace Gourmet Garage and Dearborn Market banners. Wakefern also provides merchandise and services to non-member customers through its wholesale division. It was founded by eight grocers in 1946.

Operations

Wakefern operates its wholesale business with integrity focusing on and consistently meeting the unique needs of its retail customers. From supplying produce and frozen foods to meats and dairy Wakefern is continuously scaling its business and emphasizing teamwork to provide outstanding services. In addition to a milk processing and distribution facility and a seafood processing plant wholesale customers can benefit from a wide range of capabilities offered through Wakefern including transportation quality assurance category management technical support financial support development and store development.

The cooperative's unique brand offerings include Wholesome Pantry Bowl & Basket and Paperbird.

Geographic Reach

Based in Keasbey New Jersey Wakefern's member retailers own and operate about 355 grocery stores across the northeastern US. Markets include Connecticut Delaware Maryland Massachusetts New Jersey New York Pennsylvania Rhode Island and Virginia.

Sales and Marketing

With more than 70000 associates Wakefern's ShopRite serves approximately 7 million customers each week with unprecedented variety and customer service.

Strategy

Wakefern Food Corp. in November announced that Madison Foods a third-generation family grocery business has joined the Wakefern cooperative with plans to convert three Save A Lot stores to Price Rite Marketplace stores in Massachusetts.

Owned and operated by the Slawsby family Madison Foods is a successful local business in the Boston area. The family company will begin converting their Save A Lot stores to Price Rite Marketplace ? a registered trademark and banner of Wakefern Food Corp.

The new Price Rite Marketplace locations will also offer several Wakefern Own Brand products including the new popular Bowl & Basket and Paperbird lines. Shoppers will also be able to purchase Wakefern's award-winning Wholesome Pantry brands which include the Wholesome Pantry Organic line as well as a range of products free from artificial additives and preservatives.

Technology to improve internal efficiency as well as customer experience is also a key element of Wakefern's strategy. In mid-2020 the cooperative partnered with Solutions for Retail Brands (S4RB) a global consulting-led software business to provide new information sharing software for Wakefern and its Own Brand vendors.

S4RB's Affinity platform for Wakefern will allow the retailer to use a proprietary online portal and database to provide real-time data and analytics enabling Wakefern to collaborate with new and existing vendor partners and continue to grow its Own Brand portfolio. The platform will integrate with existing Wakefern systems through all stages of its private brand process from development and launch of new products to product sales and post-purchase review.

Company Background

In 1946 in an effort to assist struggling independent grocers a sales representative from Del Monte Foods introduced cooperative buying to eight independent grocers from Newark New Jersey. By the end of that year each grocer having invested $1000 Wakefern Food Corp. was officially founded.

HISTORY

Wakefern Food was founded in 1946 by seven New York- and New Jersey-based grocers: Louis Weiss Sam and Al Aidekman Abe Kesselman Dave Fern Sam Garb and Albert Goldberg. The company got its name by taking the first letters of the last names of five of the original founders (Weiss Sam and Al Aidekman Kesselman and Fern). Like many cooperatives the association sought to lower costs by increasing its buying power as a group.

They each put in $1000 and began operating a 5000-sq.-ft. warehouse often putting in double time to keep both their stores and the warehouse running. The shopkeepers' collective buying power proved valuable enabling the grocers to stock many items at the same prices as their larger competitors.

In 1951 Wakefern members began pooling their resources to buy advertising space. A common store name — ShopRite — was chosen and each week co-op members met to decide which items would be sale priced. Within a year membership had grown to over 50. Expansion became a priority and in the mid-1950s co-op members united in small groups to take over failed supermarkets. One such group called the Supermarkets Operating Co. (SOC) was formed in 1956. Within 10 years it had acquired a number of failed stores remodeled them and given them the ShopRite name.

During the late 1950s sales at ShopRite stores slumped after Wakefern decided to buck the supermarket trend of offering trading stamps (which could then be exchanged for gifts) figuring that offering the stamps would ultimately lead to higher food prices. The move initially drove away customers but Wakefern cut grocery prices across the board and sales returned. The company did embrace another supermarket trend: stocking stores with nonfood items.

The co-op was severely shaken in 1966 when SOC merged with General Supermarkets a similar small group within Wakefern becoming Supermarkets General Corp. (SGC). SGC was a powerful entity with 71 supermarkets 10 drug-

stores six gas stations a wholesale bakery and a discount department store. Many Wakefern members opposed the merger and attempted to block the action with a court order. By 1968 SGC had beefed up its operations to include department store chains as well as its grocery stores. In a move that threatened to break Wakefern SGC broke away from the co-op and its stores were renamed Pathmark.

Wakefern not only weathered the storm it grew under the direction of chairman and CEO Thomas Infusino elected shortly after the split. The co-op focused on asserting its position as a seller of low-priced products. Wakefern developed private-label brands including the ShopRite brand. In the 1980s members began operating larger stores and adding more nonfood items to the ShopRite product mix. With its number of superstores on the rise and facing increased competition from club stores in 1992 Wakefern opened a centralized nonfood distribution center in New Jersey.

In 1995 30-year Wakefern veteran Dean Janeway was elected president of the co-op. The company debuted its ShopRite MasterCard co-branded with New Jersey's Valley National Bank in 1996. The following year the co-op purchased two of its customers' stores in Pennsylvania then threatened to close them when contract talks with the local union deteriorated. In 1998 Wakefern settled the dispute then sold the stores.

The company partnered with Internet bidding site Priceline in 1999 offering customers an opportunity to bid on groceries and then pick them up at ShopRite stores. Big V Wakefern's biggest customer filed for Chapter 11 bankruptcy protection in 2000 and said it was ending its distribution agreement with the co-op. In July 2002 however Wakefern's ShopRite Supermarkets subsidiary acquired all of Big V's assets for approximately $185 million in cash and assumed liabilities.

Infusino retired in May 2005 after 35 years with Wakefern Food. He was succeeded by former vice chairman Joseph Colalillo. The cooperative added to its footprint in 2007 when it acquired about 10 underperforming retail locations from Stop & Shop. The stores located mostly in South Jersey were rebranded under the ShopRite banner.

EXECUTIVES

Vice President Pharmacy, Jeffrey Mondelli
Vice President Quality Assurance Food Safety, Michael Ambrosio
Auditors: KPMG LLP SHORT HILLS NJ

LOCATIONS

HQ: WAKEFERN FOOD CORP.
  5000 RIVERSIDE DR, KEASBEY, NJ 088321209
Phone: 908 527-3300
Web: WWW.WAKEFERN.COM

COMPETITORS

A&P	IGA
Acme Markets	Krasdale Foods
Bozzuto's	SUPERVALU
C&S Wholesale	Stop & Shop
CVS	Wal-Mart
Hannaford Bros.	Wawa Inc.

HISTORICAL FINANCIALS

Company Type: Private

Income Statement   FYE: September 27

	REVENUE ($ mil.)	NET INCOME ($ mil.)	NET PROFIT MARGIN	EMPLOYEES
09/14	11,871	5	0.0%	3,500
09/13	11,455	0	0.0%	—
09/12	11,010	5	0.0%	—
Annual Growth	3.8%	(0.0%)		

Walgreens Boots Alliance Inc

Whether you get your drugs from the pharmacist or the chemist Walgreens Boots Alliance has you covered. The company formed when US-based Walgreen Co. bought its European counterpart Alliance Boots includes more than 21000 retail and wholesale pharmacies in about a dozen countries selling prescription and many other health and wellbeing products. Walgreens Boots Alliance also includes wholesale operations serving more than 250000 pharmacies hospitals health centers and doctors in upwards of 20 countries. Its retail and business brands include Walgreens Duane Reade Boots and Alliance Health care as well as health and beauty product brands such as No7 Soap & Glory and Liz Earle Botanics Sleek MakeUP and YourGoodSkin. More than three quarters of its revenue comes from the US. Walgreens Alliance Boots was formed in 2014.

Operations

Walgreens Boots Alliance operates three core segments: Retail Pharmacy USA Pharmaceutical Wholesale and
Retail Pharmacy International.

The Retail Pharmacy USA segment generates around 75% of revenue and sells pharmacy and beauty and other items through some 9020 retail stores under the Walgreens and Duane Reade banners. It sells third party and own-brand products in store and online. It also allows customer to refill prescriptions through scan technology using Walgreens mobile application. The pharmacy arm accounts for around 75% of the segment's sales and its retail arm (healthcare beauty products toiletries and general merchandise) the remainder.

The Pharmaceutical Wholesale segment (more than 15% of revenue) flies the Alliance Healthcare banner and delivers drugs and other healthcare products and services from around 305 distribution centers to more than 115000 pharmacies doctors health centers and hospitals primarily in Europe; it's one of the continent's largest pharmaceutical distributor. Its Alphega Pharmacy is a membership group for independent pharmacies. In addition it also provides prewholesale and contract logistics direct deliveries and other services to pharmaceutical manufacturers.

Retail Pharmacy International generates over 5% of revenue and consists mainly of the Boots pharmacy network across the UK Norway Ireland the Netherlands and Thailand. The segment operates about 4430 stores across the Boots brand as well as Benavides in Mexico and Ahumada in Chile. Boots stocks over 33000 products and offers optical markets with around 550 practices of which 165 operated on a franchise basis. Approximately 30% of these optical practices are located in Boots stores with the balance being standalone optical practices.

Geographic Reach

Walgreens Boots Alliance is headquartered in the US (Illinois) and has stores in all 50 US states the District of Columbia Puerto Rico the US Virgin Islands Mexico Chile the UK Thailand Norway Ireland the Netherlands and Lithuania.

In total the company operates over 20 retail distribution centers. In addition it uses public warehouses and third-party distributors to handle certain retail distribution needs. The Retail Pharmacy USA division also operates one prescription mail service facility.

Walgreens Boots Alliance operates some 305 pharmaceutical distribution centers located outside of the United States operated by the Pharmaceutical Wholesale division. It also operates about 30 principal office facilities.

Altogether the company generates more than 75% of its sales in the US while more than 10% comes from Europe (excluding the UK) and about 10% of revenues were tied to business in the UK.

Sales and Marketing

Walgreens Boots Alliance sells in physical stores and online. It offers various loyalty programs such as Balance Rewards and the Boots Advantage Card. It delivers to more than 250000 pharmacies doctors health centers and hospitals each year.

Advertising expenses were $534 million in 2020 $585 million in 2019 or $665 million in 2018 respectively.

Financial Performance

Walgreens Boots Alliance has seen revenue growth in the last five years. Its annual revenues have risen more than 19% since 2016.

Revenue increased to $139.5 billion in 2020 an approximately 2% uptick from the year prior. The increase was driven by higher sales in the Retail Pharmacy USA and Pharmaceutical Wholesale divisions partially offset by lower sales in the Retail Pharmacy International division.

Fiscal 2020 net earnings attributable to Walgreens Boots Alliance decreased 89% to $456 million. The decrease primarily reflects third quarter non-cash impairment charges adverse COVID-19 impacts lower U.S. pharmacy gross profit and year on year bonus changes partially offset by savings from Transformational Cost Management Program. Cash on hand at the end of fiscal 2020 was $746 billion. Cash provided by operating activities was $5.5 billion in 2020 while investing activities used $1.3 billion and financing activities used another $4.6 billion. Main cash uses were for additions to property and equipment and payments of debt.

Strategy

A significant element of its growth strategy is to identify pursue and successfully complete and integrate acquisitions joint ventures and other strategic partnerships and alliances that either expand or complement its existing operations. It has grown significantly through acquisitions in recent years and expects to continue to acquire partner with or invest in businesses that build on or are deemed complementary to its existing businesses or further our strategic objectives.

For example in July 2020 the company announced that it plans to invest $1.0 billion in equity and convertible debt in VillageMD over the next three years including a $250 million equity investment completed in July 2020 subject to the terms of the agreement. The company and VillageMD also announced plans to open 500 to 700 "Village Medical at Walgreens" physician-led primary care clinics in more than 30 US markets in the next five years. Due in part to consolidation in the industries in which we compete there is significant competition for attractive targets and opportunities when available. There can be no assurance that attractive acquisition or other strategic relationship opportunities will be available that we will be successful in identifying negotiating and consummating favorable transaction opportunities or that any such transactions we complete will be successful and justify its investment of financial and other resources.

Company Background

In 1849 John Boot opens first Boots store selling herbal remedies in Goose Gate Nottingham UK and in 1909 Walgreen Co. is formed. Walgreen the largest drugstore company in the US bought 45% of Alliance Boots Europe's largest pharmacy retailer and wholesaler in 2012. The two got along well enough that in 2014 Walgreen exercised its option to purchase the rest of Alliance Boots. It formed Walgreens Boots Alliance and became a subsidiary of the parent along with Alliance Boots.

In 2015 the company entered into a 20-year fulfillment agreement with Valeant Pharmaceuticals that includes reduced pricing on Valeant products. In 2017 Walgreens Boots Alliance entered into long-term global supply chain agreement with Fareva. It also received regulatory clearance to purchase 1932 Rite Aid drugstores in the US in the same year.

EXECUTIVES

Co-coo, Ornella Barra, age 66, $946,897 total compensation
Executive Vice Chairman And Ceo, Stefano Pessina, age 79
Evp And Global Cfo, George R. Fairweather, age 63, $977,118 total compensation
Co-coo, Alexander W. (Alex) Gourlay, age 59, $937,076 total compensation
Evp Global Chief Administrative Officer And General Counsel, Marco Pagni, age 57
Evp And Global Chief Human Resources Officer, Kathleen Wilson-Thompson, age 62, $627,000 total compensation
Evp And Chief Commercial Officer And President Global Brands, Ken Murphy, age 54
President Operations, Richard M. Ashworth
Cio, Steve Turner
Vice President And Director Global Accounts, Ruth Spencer
Vice President Global Enterprise Architecture, Brian DeMay
Pharmacy Manager, Jason Wood
Pharmacy Manager, Damon Grill
Pharmacy Manager, Nisha Soung
Pharmacy Manager, Franklyn Osakwe

Pharmacy Manager, Denise Rhone
Pharmacy Manager, Anthony Silva
Pharmacy Manager, Pratik Shah
Pharmacy Manager, Pramod Allani
Vice President Global Executive Compensation And Stock Programs, Martha Peterson
Vice President Europe And Americas Sourcing, John Miller
Pharmacy Manager, Merykokeb Beyene
Pharmacy Manager, Hugh Zuengler
Pharmacy Manager, Jerry Huff
Pharmacy Manager, Joseph Rancour
Pharmacy Manager, Adel Shamseddine
Pharmacy Manager, Candice Reed
Pharmacy Manager, Ken Emelonye
Pharmacy Manager, Phuong Luc
Pharmacy Manager, Tamara Cisneros
Pharmacy Manager, Heather Rosenblum
Pharmacy Manager, Parnaz Najimi
Pharmacy Manager, Shenjin Orr
Pharmacy Manager, Dustin Hutmacher
Senior Vice President And Managing Director Boots, Elizabeth Fagan
Senior Vice President And Global Chief Public Affairs Officer, Charles Greener
Vice President Store Operations, Charles W Bernard
Senior Vice President Business Development And Strategy, Sue Ewing
Division Vp Marketing Insights And Loyalty, Todd Vang
Divisional Vice President And General Merchandise Manager Beauty And Personal Care, Shannon Petree
Divisional Vp Executive Communications And Events, Liz Roch
Group Vice President Global Sourcing, Moe Alkemade
Senior Vice President Supply Chain Retail And Pharmacy Renewal, Reuben Slone
Senior Vice President Director Global Consumer Brands, Andy Gibson
Market Vice President, Mike Arnoult
Group Vp Supply Chain Global, Dov Shenkman
Pharmacy Manager, Joel Neal
Pharmacy Manager, Eleni Mastromihalis
Pharmacy Manager, Brooke Bailey
Pharmacy Manager, Hugh Tobias
Vice President Global Financial Controls, Bill Zaman
Pharmacy Manager, Mike Corvino
Pharmacy Manager, Jennifer Iwegbue
National Account Manager, Christina Gabriel
Pharmacy Manager, Veronica Zavala
Director Of Pharmacy And Retail Operations, Vince Wilkinson
Pharmacy Manager, Gopal Pillai
Pharmacy Manager, Sofia Betancourt
Pharmacy Manager, Alejandra Russo
Group Vice President Walgreens Retail Brands, Helayna Minsk
Pharmacy Manager, Thomas Dabney
Vice President Global Internal Audit, Troy Kelly
Pharmacy Manager, Audra Hainer
Vice President International Human Resources Support, Hillary Leisten
Senior Vice President Global Controller And Chief Accounting Officer, Heather Dixon
Chairman, James A. (Jim) Skinner, age 75
BBoard Member, Janice Babiak
Board Member, Dominic Murphy
Auditors: Deloitte & Touche LLP

LOCATIONS

HQ: Walgreens Boots Alliance Inc
 108 Wilmot Road, Deerfield, IL 60015
Phone: 847 315-3700
Web: www.walgreensbootsalliance.com

PRODUCTS/OPERATIONS

2016 Sales

	$ mil.	% of total
Retail Pharmacy USA	83,802	72
Pharmaceutical Wholesale	20,293	17
Retail Pharmacy International	13,256	11
Total	**117,351**	**100**

2016 Sales

	$ mil.	% of total
United States	83,802	72
Europe (excluding the United Kingdom)	16,793	14
United Kingdom	14,081	12
Other	2,675	2
Total	**117,351**	**100**

COMPETITORS

BioScrip	OptumRx
Body Shop	Rite Aid
CVS	Sigma Pharmaceuticals
Costco Wholesale	Superdrug
H-E-B	Target Corporation
Kroger	UDG Healthcare
McKesson	Wal-Mart
Medicine Shoppe	

HISTORICAL FINANCIALS

Company Type: Public

Income Statement

FYE: August 31

	REVENUE ($ mil.)	NET INCOME ($ mil.)	NET PROFIT MARGIN	EMPLOYEES
08/20	139,537	456	0.3%	331,000
08/19	136,866	3,982	2.9%	342,000
08/18	131,537	5,024	3.8%	354,000
08/17	118,214	4,078	3.4%	345,000
08/16	117,351	4,173	3.6%	360,000
Annual Growth	**4.4%**	**(42.5%)**	**—**	**(2.1%)**

2020 Year-End Financials

Debt ratio: 18.06%
Return on equity: 2.06%
Cash ($ mil.): 516
Current ratio: 0.67
Long-term debt ($ mil.): 12,203

No. of shares (mil.): 865
Dividends
 Yield: 4.8%
 Payout: 221.6%
Market value ($ mil.): 32,910

	STOCK PRICE ($) FY Close	P/E High/Low		PER SHARE ($) Earnings	Dividends	Book Value
08/20	38.02	121	74	0.52	1.84	23.84
08/19	51.19	20	11	4.31	1.78	26.26
08/18	68.56	16	12	5.05	1.64	27.31
08/17	81.50	23	20	3.78	1.53	26.83
08/16	80.71	25	19	3.82	1.46	27.59
Annual Growth	**(17.2%)**			**(39.3%)**	**6.0%**	**(3.6%)**

Walmart Inc

Walmart is an unstoppable retail force that has yet to meet any immovable object. It is the world's #1 retailer as well as the world's largest company by revenue and largest employer with 2.2 million associates. Walmart sells groceries and general merchandise operating some 5400 stores in the US including about 4800 Walmart stores and 600 Sam's Club membership-only warehouse clubs. Walmart's international division numbers about 6000 locations; operating through regional subsidiaries it's the #1 retailer in Canada and Mexico and has operations in Asia Africa Europe and Latin America. Some 265 million customers visit Walmart's stores and websites each week.

HISTORY

Sam Walton began his retail career as a J. C. Penney management trainee and later leased a Ben Franklin-franchised dime store in Newport Arkansas in 1945. In 1950 he relocated to Bentonville Arkansas and opened a Walton 5 & 10. By 1962 Walton owned 15 Ben Franklin stores under the Walton 5 & 10 name.

After Ben Franklin management rejected his suggestion to open discount stores in small towns Walton with his brother James "Bud" Walton opened the first Wal-Mart Discount City in Rogers Arkansas in 1962. Wal-Mart Stores went public in 1970 with 18 stores and sales of $44 million.

Avoiding regional retailers Walton opened stores in small and midsized towns in the 1970s. The company sold its Ben Franklin stores in 1976. By 1980 Wal-Mart's 276 stores had sales of $1.2 billion.

In 1983 Wal-Mart opened SAM'S Wholesale Club a concept based on the successful cash-and-carry membership-only warehouse format pioneered by the Price Company of California (now Costco Wholesale Corp.).

The company started Hypermart*USA in 1987 as a joint venture with Dallas-based supermarket chain Cullum Companies (now Randall's Food Markets). The 200000-sq.-ft. discount store/supermarket hybrid was later retooled as Wal-Mart Supercenters. Sam stepped down as CEO in 1988 and president David Glass was appointed CEO. Wal-Mart bought out Cullum the next year.

Wal-Mart acquired wholesale distributor McLane Company in 1990. In 1992 the year Sam died the company expanded into Mexico through a joint venture to open SAM'S CLUBS with Mexico's largest retailer Cifra (renamed Wal-Mart de México in 2000). Wal-Mart acquired 122 former Woolco stores in Canada in 1994. Co-founder Bud died a year later.

More international expansion included entering China in 1996; the acquisition of German hypermarket chain Wertkauf in 1997; the purchase of Brazilian retailer Lojas Americanas' 40% interest in a joint venture (1998); and the addition of four stores and other sites in South Korea. Also in 1998 the company began testing the Neighborhood Market format a 40000-sq.-ft. grocery and drug combination store. In 1999 Wal-Mart bought 74 German-based Interspar hypermarkets and acquired ASDA Group the UK's third-largest supermarket chain.

COO Lee Scott succeeded Glass as CEO in 2000; Glass stayed on as chairman of the executive committee. Wal-Mart later began testing its customers' demand for appliances by selling household appliances in selected stores.

Following the bankruptcy and closure of the Montgomery Ward department store chain in 2001 Wal-Mart offered to replace Ward's customers' credit cards with Wal-Mart branded cards. Wal-Mart also formed an alliance with America Online to offer Internet access and later launched its No Boundaries private-label cosmetics for pre-teens and teenagers. In June 2001 a group of six current and former female Wal-Mart employees filed a sex-discrimination lawsuit (seeking to represent up to 500000 current and former Wal-Mart workers) against the company. The next month Wal-Mart said it would acquire all the minority interests in Walmart.com and integrate its online operations with its store operations. It also laid off 100 employees at its corporate headquarters and eliminated 300 unfilled positions. In August it said it was testing the sale of Sealy and private-label mattresses in some of its superstores and it began offering college textbooks discounted up to 30% at its online College Bookstore.

2002 was a huge year for Wal-Mart both at home and abroad. In April the company was crowned America's largest corporation by FORTUNE magazine. In March Wal-Mart gained a foothold in Japan taking a 6% stake in one of Japan's top retailers SEIYU. That December it increased its SEIYU stake to 36% and retains the option to up that to nearly 67% by 2007. In a rare defeat Wal-Mart in July closed its first store in Germany and 2000 workers there went on a two-day strike over wages. (In 2001 Wal-Mart scrapped plans to open 50 more Supercenters there by 2003.) Also in 2002 Wal-Mart Puerto Rico acquired Supermercados Amigo the #1 supermarket chain on the island. (Wal-Mart opened its first Supercenter there in April 2001.)

Overall in 2002 Wal-Mart opened 178 supercenters 33 discount stores and 25 SAM'S CLUB stores. It opened 107 international units with two in Brazil 22 in Canada eight in China two in Germany three in South Korea 59 in Mexico two in Puerto Rico and nine in the UK. The company's attempt to open a state industrial bank in California in 2002 failed however after legislators barred retailers.

In May 2003 Wal-Mart sold its McLane grocery distribution business to Berkshire Hathaway; a rare divestment for the world's largest retailer. In July it opened its first store in Beijing.

In February 2004 a federal judge ruled that Wal-Mart should pay workers for overtime hours. The complaint which was brought by plaintiffs who said they were forced to work unpaid overtime between 1994 and 1999 came at a time when working conditions at the company were being scrutinized. Also that month Wal-Mart acquired the 118-store Bompre o chain of Brazilian supermarkets and hypermarkets from troubled Dutch retailer Royal Ahold for $300 million advancing the world's largest retailer from fifth to third place in the Brazilian market. In March Wal-Mart opened its online music store which sells digital downloads for 11 cents less than major competitors (including Apple's iTunes and Napster). In April voters in Inglewood California overwhelmingly rejected Wal-Mart's proposal to build a supercenter there over the objections of local officials. Wal-Mart had sought to bypass local development and environmental regulations by spending more than $1 million to take its case directly to the voters. Also in April Wal-Mart's Japanese partner Seiyu opened its first Wal-Mart-style supercenter in Numazu.

In May 2004 Wal-Mart agreed to pay $3.1 million in fines for violating the Clean Water Act at 24 sites in nine states. (The retailer was fined $1 million in 2001 for similar violations involving its failure to manage storm-water runoff.)

Vice chairman Tom Coughlin retired in January 2005 after 25 years with Wal-Mart. Coughlin remained on the company's board until March 25 2005 when he resigned prematurely following an internal investigation related to "the alleged unauthorized use of corporate-owned gift cards and personal reimbursements." He was due to retire from the board on June 3 2005. In June the company rescinded Coughlin's retirement agreement including stock awards and incentive payments which may total as much as $12 million.

Also in January Wal-Mart agreed to pay $135540 to settle federal charges that it violated child labor laws. The 24 violations which the retailer denied involved teenage workers in three states using hazardous equipment such as chain saws paper balers and fork lifts. Soon after Wal-Mart was ordered to pay $7.5 million in damages to a disabled former employee who claimed the retailer unfairly reassigned him. In March the retailer settled a high-profile lawsuit by agreeing to pay $11 million to the US government to close an investigation into the use of illegal immigrants by Wal-Mart contractors to clean its stores. In May Wal-Mart increased its stake in SEIYU to 42% (up from 37%).

In August 2005 Wal-Mart signed Garth Brooks to a multiyear exclusive contract under which the country star's music will only be sold in Wal-Mart-owned stores. The deal marks the first time an artist has contracted himself and his entire catalog of music with a single chain. In October the company launched its Metro 7 line of urban women's apparel in 500 stores in and around urban areas. In December Wal-Mart opened its third superstore in the downtown Xuanwu District of Beijing. Also in December Wal-Mart acquired some 140 stores in Brazil from Portuguese retailer Sonae for about $757 million increasing the number of outlets it operates in Brazil to nearly 300.

In January 2006 Wal-Mart opened a supercenter in Santa Clarita California its second in Los Angeles County. In February the company acquired an additional 17.7% interest in CARHCO from Royal Ahold increasing its stake in the Central America supermarket operator to 51%. Wal-Mart's former vice chairman Thomas Coughlin who was accused of misusing more than $500000 in company funds pleaded guilty to fraud and tax charges in January 2006. In August he was sentenced to 27 months of house arrest and ordered to pay $400000 in restitution to his former employer. Wal-Mart itself was ordered by a Pennsylvania jury to pay more than $78 million in damages in a class-action suit brought by employees alleging that they were forced to work during breaks and off the clock. In October Wal-Mart disposed of its retail operations in Germany and South Korea. It sold the last of its 85 stores in Germany to rival METRO AG and sold 16 stores in South Korea to Shinsegae Co. for about $882 million.

In early 2007 Wal-Mart agreed to pay $33.5 million in back wages and interest to settle a federal lawsuit that accused the company of violating ovetime laws involving more than 86000 employees. In February the company announced an agreement with all six major Hollywood studios to sell digital movies and TV shows on walmart.com becoming the first traditional retail chain to do so. In April Helen Robson Walton wife of Wal-Mart founder Sam Walton died at the age of 87. Wal-Mart and Bharti Enterprises formed a 50:50 joint venture in August to jointly build wholesale outlets that will buy goods from farmers and small manufacturers and sell to retailers through a nationwide supply chain. True to form Wal-Mart again cut prices of toys and some 15000 more items such as apparel home and food products for the 2007 holiday selling season.

In May 2008 the retailer revised its $4 prescription program launched in 2006 to cover 90-day prescriptions for $10. In November Mike Duke was named to Wal-Mart's board of directors in preparation for his elevation to president and CEO of the company in February 2009. Also in November Eduardo Castro-Wright president and CEO of Walmart US was promoted to vice chairman of Wal-Mart Stores. He assumed responsibility for the firm's global procurement operation.

The management shuffle continued in 2009 with Lee Scott retiring as CEO in February. Scott was succeeded by Duke who had headed the international arm of the company. In January Wal-Mart acquired a majority stake in Chile's largest food retailer Distribuci "n y Servicio through a tender offer. In May of that year it opened its first location in India via a joint venture with Bharti Enterprises.

In February 2010 the company opened its new Latin America regional headquarters in Miami Florida.

In June 2011 Walmart International acquired a 51% stake in South African retailer Massmart which operates 288 stores in 13 countries in sub-Saharan Africa in a deal valued at about $2.4 billion. Massmart operates stores under the Makro Game Dion Wired Builders Warehouse Builders Express Builders Trade Depot CBW Jumbo Cash and Carry and the Shield buying group. On the day of the Massmart closing the company scored a huge win when the US Supreme Court threw out a massive employment discrimination class-action lawsuit (Dukes vs. Wal-Mart) brought filed back in 2001. While the court did not rule on whether or not Wal-Mart discriminated against women it said they could not proceed as a class.

EXECUTIVES

Executive Vice President Membership Marketing And E Commerce Sam's Club, Cindy Davis
President And Ceo Walmart U.s., Gregory S. (Greg) Foran, age 58, $1,006,424 total compensation
President And Ceo, C. Douglas (Doug) McMillon, age 54, $1,278,989 total compensation
Chief Merchandising Officer Walmart U.s., Steve Bratspies
Evp And President And Ceo International, David Cheesewright, age 57, $1,071,743 total compensation
Evp And Cfo Walmart U.s., Michael P. Dastugue, age 56
Evp And Chief Administrative Officer Walmart International, Scott Price, age 59
Evp And President And Ceo Walmart Ecommerce U.s., Marc Lore, age 48, $346,154 total compensation
Evp Softlines And General Merchandise Walmart U.s., James A. (Andy) Barron
Evp Supply Chain Walmart U.s., Gregory L. (Greg) Smith, age 57
Evp Food Walmart U.s., Charles Redfield

Evp And Cfo Walmart International, Richard Mayfield

Evp Global Governance And Corporate Secretary, Jeffrey J. (Jeff) Gearhart, age 55

Evp Corporate Affairs, Daniel J. (Dan) Bartlett, age 48

Evp Consumables And Health And Wellness, Scott Huff

Evp And President Supercenters Walmart U.s., Michael S. (Mike) Moore

Evp And Cfo, M. Brett Biggs, age 51, $854,670 total compensation

Evp Membership And Technology And Ceo Samsclub.com, Jamie Iannone, age 47

Evp Operations Sam's Club, Gisel Ruiz, age 49

Evp And General Counsel, Karen Roberts

Evp And President And Ceo Walmart Latin America India And Africa And Chairman Walmart Mexico And Central America, Enrique Ostalé

Evp And Coo Walmart U.s., Judith McKenna

Svp And President Jet.com, Liza K. Landsman

Svp New England Division Walmart U.s., Julie Murphy

Evp And Global Chief Ethics And Compliance Officer, Jay T. Jorgensen

Svp And Chief Marketing Officer Walmart U.s., Tony Rogers

Evp Global People Division, Jacqueline P. (Jacqui) Canney, age 52

Evp And President And Ceo Sam's Club, John Furner, age 46

Evp Central Operations Walmart U.s., Mark Ibbotson

Svp And Cto, Jeremy King

Evp And Enterprise Chief Information Officer, Clay Johnson

Evp And Chief Merchandising Officer Sam's Club, Ashley Buchanan

Svp Chief Sustainability Officer And President Walmart Foundation, Kathleen McLaughlin

Evp Walmart Realty, JP Suarez

Vice President And Assistant Treasurer, Mike Cook

Senior Vice President Chief Information Security Officer, Kerry Kilker

Senior Vice President Operations, Don Frieson

Senior Vice President Pharmacy Merchandising And Support, Paul Beahm

Vice President Corporate Affairs, Lee Culpepper

Senior Vice President International Supply Chain (omnichannel), Ramesh Chikkala

Vice President Intl Merchandise Development, Ronald F Virta

Pharmacy Manager, Sharon Lynch

Senior Vice President Global Ecommerce Strategy, Gibu Thomas

Pharmacy Manager, Lydia Orr

Pharmacy Manager, Joby Young

Vice President Entertainment Property Merchandising, Chris Nagelson

Exec Vp-sams Club Operations, Greg Johnston

Vice President Investor Relations, Carol Schumacher

Vice President Manager Director, Judith Sunderland

Vice President, Mehrdad Akbar

Pharmacy Manager, Terry Bennett

Vice President Facilities Management, Cassie Clark

Vice President Of Human Resources, Janet Palmer

Vice President Global Sourcing, Ashish Bharara

Vice President Regional General Manager, Michael Collischan

Pharmacy Manager, Tara Green

Senior Vice President Associate Experience, Drew Holler

Vice President, Sam Dunn

Senior Vice President Assistant Health And Wellness Operations, Michelle Hunsaker

Vice President Global Sourcing, John Mcdowell

Svp Us Chief Ethics And Compliance Officer, Cindy Moehring

Vice President Multi Channel And Merchant Innovations, Shannon Letts

Executive Vice President, Celia Swanson

Senior Vice President Of Brand Merchandising, Andrea Thomas

Vice President Of Food Safety, Frank Yiannas

Vice President Of Information Systems, Chrys Tarvin

Vice President Marketing, Marty Esarte

Vice President Health And Wellness Transformation, Marcus Osborne

Vice President Marketing Assistant, Rosalyn Harris

Vice President Human Resources, Edward Mckissic

Vice President, Amy Terjak

Vice President Of Human Resources, Anne Thomas

Vice President Dmm, Kristen Stevens

Senior Vice President Technology, Cory Gundberg

Vice President Strategic Planning, Anne Marie Kehoe

Vice President Finance And Strategy Services, Jonathan Hall

Vice President Assistant Adult Beverage, Lorraine Spencer

Vice President Of Global Branded Imports, Fernando Serpa

Vice President Assistant To Manolo Reyes Produce And Floral, Philip Bentley

Vice President New Market Entry, Shawn Sederholm

Senior Vice President Global Compensation, Jackie Telfair

Vp Merchandising And Us Manufacturing, Cindi Marsiglio

Vice President Merchandise Finance, Scott Pleiman

Assistant To Kerry Kilker Vice President Information Systems, Eileen Smith

Vice President Assistant, Sheila Musteen

Pharmacy Manager, Teresa Compton

Rph, Susan Long

Pharmacy Manager, Victor Hernandez

Pharmacy Manager, Dan Rafferty

Vice President Global Talent For International, Lisa George

Vice President Of Finance, Alex Aguila

Vice President, Daniel Williams

Human Resources Director And Vice President, Erica Henson

Vp Cross Border Ecommerce, Robert Posey

Vice President Risk Management, William Newberg

Senior Vice President Assistant, Regina Mize

Vice President Regional General Manager, Ben Hassing

Rvp 16, Ken Reese

Vice President Assistant, Cheryl Creighton

Vice President Stragetic Real Estate Finance, Scott Carroll

Vice President Marketing, Demetrio Moysen

Vice President Jewelry, Chris Callahan

Vice President Brand Merchandising Active Classics And Shoes, Jimmy Olsson

Evp Logistics, Chris Sultemeier

Divisional Vice President Logisitics, Joel Marpe

P.e. Vice President Construction, Patrick Hamilton

National Accounts Manager, Matt Cockrell

Vice President, Robert Fusillo

Vice President Merchandising, Rick Mangrum

Senior Vice President And Cont, James Walker

Vice President Of Finance, Par Stanfield

Vice President Head Of Global Ecommerce, Soren Mills

Pharmacy Manager, Ziad Labban

Pharmacy Manager, Will Hart

Pharmacy Manager, Denise Clevenger

Vice President Of Finance, Christine Brick

Executive Vice President Supply Chain, Catherine Smith

Vice President Construction, Wayne Cox

Vice President Logistics, Mike Gray

Vice President Finance, Sherry Taylor

Pharmacy Manager, Lisa Nichols

Vice President Of Engineering, Manu Thapar

Vice President International Strategy, Christine Allen

Senior Vice President Next Generation Supply Chain, Ami Spivey

Vice President Regional General Manager, Steve Schrobilgen

Pharmacy Manager, Shane Fox

Svp International People, Jane Ewing

Pharmacy Manager, Lisa Morris

Vice President Corporate Strategy, Matthew Kistler

Vice President Finance And Global Treasury, Matt Allen

Vice President, Sherry Adams

Pharmacy Manager, Genie Crouch

Vp Apparel Product Development, Paul Burke

Vice President Innovation, John Welling

Pharmacy Manager, Joe Bradac

Senior Vice President International Finance, Ken Plunk

Vice President And Gc Information Syst, Tim Cheatham

Vice President Technology And Product Global Ecommerce, Sriram Samu

Senior Vice President And Controller, Steve Whatley

Vice President Marketing Assistant, Alisa Goulet

Vice President, Diane Bruer

Pharmacy Manager, Jill Harman

Pharmacist Manager, Keith Kleman

Senior Vice President And Chief Audit Executive Global Audit, Stuart Campbell

Vice President Human Resources, Becky Anderson

Executive Vice President Global People Division, Jacqui Canney

Executive Vice President Walmart U.s. People, Linda Simon

Pharmacy Manager, Camelia Ciurbe

Svp Operations Global Sourcing, Ignacio Lopez

Pharmacy Manager, Ian Pak

Pharmacy Manager, John Nguyen

Auditors: Ernst & Young LLP

LOCATIONS

HQ: Walmart Inc
702 S.W. 8th Street, Bentonville, AR 72716
Phone: 479 273-4000
Web: www.stock.walmart.com

2019 Sales

	$ mil.	% of total
US	392,265	76
Non-US	122,140	24
Total	**514,405**	**100**

PRODUCTS/OPERATIONS

2019 Sales

	$ mil.	% of total
Net sales	510,329	99
Membership and other income	4,076	1
Total	**514,405**	**100**

2019 Sales

	% of total
Wal-Mart US	65
International	24
SAM'S CLUB	11
Total	**100**

Selected Private Labels and Licensed Brands

Athletic Works
Better Homes & Gardens (licensed)
Black & Decker (licensed)
Canopy
Danskin Now (licensed)
Disney (licensed)
Equate (health and beauty aids)
Everstart
Faded Glory (jeans licensed)

General Electric (licensed)
George
Great Value (dairy dry grocery meat and produce)
Home Trends
Just My Size (licensed)
Mainstays
Marketside
No Boundaries
Oak Leaf
Ol' Roy (dog food)
OP (licensed)
Ozark Trail
Parent's Choice
Prima Della
Puritan
Rival (licensed)
Sam's Choice (grocery items)
Secret Treasures
Spring Valley
Starter
White Stag

COMPETITORS

Amazon.com	Home Depot
BJ's Wholesale Club	Kohl's
Best Buy	Kroger
Big Lots	Lowe's
CVS	Office Depot
Carrefour	Staples
Costco Wholesale	Target Corporation
Dollar General	

HISTORICAL FINANCIALS

Company Type: Public

Income Statement

FYE: January 31

	REVENUE ($ mil.)	NET INCOME ($ mil.)	NET PROFIT MARGIN	EMPLOYEES
01/20	523,964	14,881	2.8%	2,200,000
01/19	514,405	6,670	1.3%	2,200,000
01/18	500,343	9,862	2.0%	2,300,000
01/17	485,873	13,643	2.8%	2,300,000
01/16	482,130	14,694	3.0%	2,200,000
Annual Growth	2.1%	0.3%	—	0.0%

2020 Year-End Financials

Debt ratio: 23.03%—
Return on equity: 20.22%
Cash ($ mil.): 9,465
Current ratio: 0.79
Long-term debt ($ mil.): 48,021

Dividends
Yield: 1.8%
Payout: 42.4%
Market value ($ mil.): —

	STOCK PRICE ($) FY Close	P/E High/Low	PER SHARE ($) Earnings	Dividends	Book Value
01/20	114.49	23 18	5.19	2.12	26.37
01/19	95.83	46 36	2.26	2.08	25.19
01/18	106.60	33 20	3.28	2.04	26.38
01/17	66.74	17 14	4.38	2.00	25.52
01/16	66.36	19 12	4.57	1.96	25.47
Annual Growth	14.6%	— —	3.2%	2.0%	0.9%

Washington Federal Inc

Washington Federal is the holding company for Washington Federal Savings which operates about 190 branches in eight western states. The thrift which was founded in 1917 collects deposits from consumers and business by offering standard products such as CDs IRAs and checking savings and money market accounts. With these funds the bank mainly originates single-family residential mortgages which account for nearly three-quarters of its loan portfolio. The bank also writes business consumer construction land and multifamily residential loans. Washington Federal sells life home and auto coverage to individuals and businesses through its First Insurance Agency subsidiary.

Operations

In addition to its consumer and commercial banking operations Washington Federal has four wholly-owned subsidiaries: First Insurance Agency which offers a full line of individual and business insurance products to its customers and others; Statewide Mortgage Services Co. which holds about $18.6 million of real estate held for investment (REHI); Washington Services which also holds and markets REHI; and First Mutual Sales Finance a servicer of consumer loans.

Geographic Reach

As its name suggests Washington State is Washington Federal's largest market. Oregon and Arizona are other major markets for the bank.

Financial Performance

Washington Federal's fiscal 2012 (ends September) revenue fell by about 9.5% vs. the previous year due to a decrease both interest and non-interest income. Total interest income which accounts for about 97% of WF's total revenue declined 8% on fewer loans mortgage-backed securities and investment securities and cash equivalents. Other income fell 36%. With the exception of fiscal 2010 which saw a slight gain in revenue WF's revenue has been declining for several years. Net income increased 24% in fiscal 2012 vs. the prior year due to overall lower credit costs.

Strategy

Small relative to its national bank competitors Washington Federal has been building its business through acquisitions adding new markets and growing in established ones. Acquisitions have included both healthy smaller rivals and failed banks seized by regulators. In a bid to unify its brand and increase its name recognition WF rebrands acquired banks under its own moniker.

The bank is also working through its portfolio of nonperforming loans which peaked during the height of the recession in 2009 but now are on the decline.

Mergers and Acquisitions

In 2017 Washington Federal agreed to acquire Anchor Bancorp for $63.9 million. The combined company will have 248 offices in eight states in the Western US and total assets of $15.3 billion.

EXECUTIVES

Chairman, Roy M. Whitehead, age 67, $765,179 total compensation
President And Ceo, Brent J. Beardall, age 48, $390,925 total compensation
Svp And Cfo, Vincent L. Beatty, age 61
Evp And Chief Credit Officer, Mark A. Schoonover, age 61, $335,259 total compensation
Utah And Nevada Regional President, Marlise G. Fisher
Southern Oregon Regional President, Peggy L. Hobin
Evp And Cio, Angela D. Veksler, age 58
Northern Washington Regional President, Tom Kenney
Western Idaho Regional President, Tom Van Hemelryck
Northern Oregon Regional President, Gary Haines
Arizona Regional President, Mike Brown
New Mexico Regional President, Bill Synnamon
Southern Washington Regional President, Greg Toso
Texas Regional President, Tony Barnard
Executive Vice President, Jack Jacobson
Vice President, Patrick Wilson
Vice President, John Iasonides
Vice President, Jeff Birkelo
Assistant Vice President Branch Manager, Gail Vitale
Avp And Treasury Management Officer, Derrick Williams
Vice President Division Manager N Wa Commericial Real Estate, Grace Peschek
Executive Vice President And Commercial Banking Group Manager, Bob Peters
Vice President Relationship Manager Cre, Jon Little
Vice President, Bryan Churchill
Vp Commercial Relationship Manager, Eric Seidenberger
Vice President, Delbert Hague
Branch Manager Andamp; Vice President, Chris Hooper
Assistant Vice President Manager, Sheila DeGuise
Executive Vice President And Commercial Banking Group Manager, Robert Peters
Vice President Mortgage Loan Production, Mark Hatate
Svp Chief Information Officer, Jim Motz
Vice President And Manager, Mary Fling
Avp Branch Manager, Eric Madsen
Senior Vice President And Regional President Mexico, Michelle Coons
Senior Vice President And Manager Seattle Commercial Real Estate, Thomas Pozarycki
Vice President Commercial Lending, Rafa Valiente
Vice President Relationship Manager, Ed Thompson
Senior Vice President Manager Of Internal Audit, Paul Lee
Vice President Commercial Real Estate, Steve West
Vp Finance Officer, Loren Lawrie
Board Member, Barbara Smith
Board Member, Boualoy Smith
Auditors: DELOITTE & TOUCHE LLP

LOCATIONS

HQ: Washington Federal Inc
425 Pike Street, Seattle, WA 98101
Phone: 206 624-7930
Web: www.wafdbank.com
Selected Markets
Arizona
Idaho
Nevada
New Mexico
Oregon
Texas
Utah
Washington

PRODUCTS/OPERATIONS

2013 Sales

	$ mil.	% of total
Interest		
Loans	430	73
Mortgage-backed securities	80	14
Investment securities	22	4
Other income		
Deposit fee income	14	3
Loan fee income	7	1
Others	8	2
Total	564	100

COMPETITORS

Bank of America
Banner Corp
KeyCorp
U.S. Bancorp

Washington Banking
Wells Fargo
Zions Bancorporation

HISTORICAL FINANCIALS

Company Type: Public

Income Statement

FYE: September 30

	ASSETS ($ mil.)	NET INCOME ($ mil.)	INCOME AS % OF ASSETS	EMPLOYEES
09/20	18,794	173	0.9%	2,080
09/19	16,474	210	1.3%	1,971
09/18	15,865	203	1.3%	1,877
09/17	15,253	173	1.1%	1,818
09/16	14,888	164	1.1%	1,806
Annual Growth	6.0%	1.4%	—	3.6%

2020 Year-End Financials

Debt ratio: —
Return on equity: 8.55%
Cash ($ mil.): 1,702
Current ratio: —
Long-term debt ($ mil.): —

No. of shares (mil.): 75
Dividends
Yield: 0.0%
Payout: 38.5%
Market value ($ mil.): 1,579

	STOCK PRICE ($) FY Close	P/E High/Low	PER SHARE ($) Earnings	Dividends	Book Value
09/20	20.86	17 9	2.26	0.87	26.61
09/19	36.99	15 10	2.61	0.79	25.79
09/18	32.00	16 13	2.40	0.67	24.14
09/17	33.65	18 14	1.94	0.84	23.00
09/16	26.68	15 11	1.78	0.55	22.03
Annual Growth	(6.0%)	— —	6.2%	12.1%	4.8%

Washington Trust Bancorp, Inc.

Without seeming naive Washington Trust Bancorp can utter Washington and trust in the same breath. The holding company owns The Washington Trust Company one of the oldest and largest banks in Rhode Island and one of the oldest banks in the entire US. Chartered in 1800 the bank boasts over $3.5 billion in assets and operates nearly 20 branches in the state and one in southeastern Connecticut. Washington Trust offers standard services such as deposit accounts CDs and credit cards. The company's commercial mortgages and loans account for more than half of its loan portfolio while residential mortgages and consumer loans make up most of the rest. The bank also offers wealth management services.

Operations

Around one-third of the bank's loan portfolio was made up of commercial real estate loans in 2014 while business loans made up another 21%.

About 60% of Washington Trust's total revenue came from loan interest (including fees) in 2014 while another 7% came from interest on its taxable and tax-exempt investment securities. The rest of its revenue came from wealth management income (18%) deposit account charges (2%) card interchange fees (2%) merchant processing fees (1%) and other miscellaneous income sources. The bank had a staff of 590 employees at the end of 2014.

Washington Trust's wealth management division includes Washington Trust Investors Weston Financial and 1800 Asset Management. The division offers financial planning investment management and trust services and has more than $4 billion of assets under administration.

Geographic Reach

Of its nearly 20 branches 10 of its branches are located in Southern Rhode Island (Washington County) nearly 10 branches are in the greater Providence area and one branch is in southeastern Connecticut. The company's commercial lending office in Providence and six residential mortgage lending offices in eastern Massachusetts (Sharon Burlington and Braintree); Glastonbury and Darien Connecticut; and Warwick Rhode Island.

Financial Performance

Washington Trust has struggled to consistently grow its revenues in recent years due to shrinking interest margins on loans amidst the low-interest environment. Its profits however have been rising thanks to declining interest expenses and falling loan loss provisions as its loan portfolio's credit quality has improved with higher property valuations in the strengthened economy.

The bank's revenue inched higher by 1% to $180 million in 2014 mostly as its interest income grew with higher average loan balances.

Higher revenue in 2014 combined with lower interest expenses on deposits lower loan loss provisions and lower non-interest expenses boosted Washington Trust's net income higher by 13% to $40.8 million for the year. The company's operating cash levels fell to half the levels of the prior year to $2.7 million after adjusting its earnings for non-cash items mostly related to its mortgage banking net loan proceeds.

Strategy

Washington Trust Bank has been growing its loan and deposit business organically by opening new branches and loan production offices in its target markets. In early 2015 it opened a new branch in Rumford making it the bank's second location in East Providence. In 2014 it opened a branch in Johnston Rhode Island and furthered its expansion into Connecticut with the opening of a new mortgage office in Glastonbury Connecticut.

The company also pursues acquisitions to expand its service offerings extend its reach into new geographic markets and bolster its existing business lines.

Mergers and Acquisitions

In 2015 Washington Trust purchased SEC-registered investment advisory firm Halsey Associates which added more than $850 million in assets under management to its Wealth Management business' books. Acquiring the New Haven Connecticut-based firm also expanded its reach in the Connecticut and metropolitan New York region.

EXECUTIVES

Vice President And Retail Lending Officer The Washington Trust Company, Linda S Smith

Vice Chair Secretary And Cfo, David V. Devault, age 66, $299,731 total compensation
Chairman And Ceo, Joseph J. (Joe) MarcAurele, $514,596 total compensation
Evp And Chief Lending Officer Of The Bank, James Hagerty
President And Coo, Edward O. (Ned) Handy, $385,000 total compensation
Evp Wealth Management And Treasurer, Mark K. W. Gim, $239,462 total compensation
Senior Vice President, Scott Ostrowski
Executive Vice President Chief Retail Lending Officer Senior Management, Mary E Noons
Executive Vice President Of Retail Lending Of The Bank, Stephen Bessette
Executive Vice President And Controller Senior Management, Maria N Janes
Senior Vice President Chief Marketing And Corporate Communications Officer Senior Management, Elizabeth B Eckel
Senior Vice President Chief Audit Executive Senior Management, C Scott Ostrowski
Board Member, John J Bowen
Board Member, Kathleen E McKeough
Board Member, Edwin Santos
Board Member, Robert Dimuccio
Board Member, Katherine Hoxsie
Auditors: KPMG LLP

LOCATIONS

HQ: Washington Trust Bancorp, Inc.
23 Broad Street, Westerly, RI 02891
Phone: 401 348-1200
Web: www.washtrust.com

PRODUCTS/OPERATIONS

2014 Sales

	$ mil.	% of total
Interest		
Loans including fees	107	60
Securities	12	7
Other	0	-
Non-interest		
Wealth management services	33	18
Loan sales & commissions		6.8 4
Gain on sale of business line	6	3
Service charges on deposit accounts	3	2
Other	9	6
Total	180	100

COMPETITORS

Bank of America
Citizens Financial Group
Liberty Bank

People's United Financial
Sovereign Bank
Webster Financial

HISTORICAL FINANCIALS

Company Type: Public

Income Statement

FYE: December 31

	ASSETS ($ mil.)	NET INCOME ($ mil.)	INCOME AS % OF ASSETS	EMPLOYEES
12/19	5,292	69	1.3%	619
12/18	5,010	68	1.4%	623
12/17	4,529	45	1.0%	600
12/16	4,381	46	1.1%	596
12/15	3,771	43	1.2%	582
Annual Growth	8.8%	12.3%	—	1.6%

2019 Year-End Financials

Debt ratio: 0.43%
Return on equity: 14.53%
Cash ($ mil.): 132
Current ratio: —
Long-term debt ($ mil.): —

No. of shares (mil.): 17
Dividends
Yield: 3.7%
Payout: 49.3%
Market value ($ mil.): 934

	STOCK PRICE ($)	P/E	PER SHARE ($)		
	FY Close	High/Low	Earnings	Dividends	Book Value
12/19	53.79	14 11	3.96	2.00	29.00
12/18	47.53	16 12	3.93	1.76	25.90
12/17	53.25	22 18	2.64	1.54	23.99
12/16	56.05	21 13	2.70	1.46	22.76
12/15	39.52	16 14	2.54	1.36	22.06
Annual Growth	8.0%	— —	11.7%	10.1%	7.1%

Waste Management, Inc. (DE)

Holding company Waste Management tops the heap in the US solid-waste industry. Through subsidiaries the company serves millions of residential industrial municipal and commercial customers in the US and Canada. Waste Management provides waste collection transfer recycling and resource recovery and disposal services. Its sites include some 250 owned or operated landfills (the industry's largest network) more than 300 transfer stations and around 100 material recovery facilities. Collection services account for about 55% of sales.

HISTORY

In 1956 Dean Buntrock joined his in-laws' business Ace Scavenger Service an Illinois company that Buntrock expanded into Wisconsin.

Waste Management Inc. was formed in 1971 when Buntrock joined forces with his cousin Wayne Huizenga who had purchased two waste routes in Florida in 1962. In the 1970s Waste Management bought companies in Michigan New York Ohio Pennsylvania and Canada. By 1975 it had an international subsidiary.

The company divided into specialty areas by forming Chemical Waste Management (1975) and offering site-cleanup services (ENRAC 1980) and low-level nuclear-waste disposal (Chem-Nuclear Systems 1982).

USA Waste was founded in 1987 to run disposal and collection operations in Oklahoma. It went public in 1988 and in 1990 Don Moorehead a founder and former CEO of Mid-American Waste Systems bought a controlling interest (most of which he later sold). Moorehead moved the business to Dallas and began buying companies in the fragmented industry. John Drury a former president of Browning-Ferris joined USA Waste in 1994 as CEO.

As USA Waste gathered steam Waste Management got off track. It diversified and Buntrock renamed the company WMX Technologies in 1993 to de-emphasize its waste operations. In 1997 however the company reverted to the Waste Management name and pressured by disappointed investor George Soros CEO Phillip Rooney resigned. After more management changes turnaround specialist Steve Miller became CEO the fourth one in eight months and Buntrock retired.

USA Waste picked up market share with large acquisitions including Envirofill (1994) Chambers Development Corporation (1995) and Western Waste Industries and Sanifill (1996). In 1996 the company moved to Houston. During the next two years it bought United Waste Systems Mid-American Waste the Canadian operations of Allied Waste and Waste Management and TransAmerican Waste Industries .

1998 saw the $20 billion merger between USA Waste and Waste Management. The new company bearing the Waste Management name and led by Drury and other former USA Waste executives controlled nearly a quarter of North America's waste business. The company finished the year by agreeing to pay shareholders $220 million in a suit over overstated earnings.

The new Waste Management bought Eastern Environmental Services for $1.3 billion in 1999. (A legal battle over negotiations between Eastern and Waste Management executives was settled out of court in 2000.) Drury took leave in 1999 because of an illness that would claim his life and director Ralph Whitworth known as a shareholder activist stepped in as acting chairman.

The company faced shareholder lawsuits after it was reported that executives had sold shares before a second-quarter earnings shortfall was announced. Waste Management said it would investigate the sales; later so did the SEC. (By 2001 the company had settled with both the SEC and shareholders.) In the fallout president and COO Rodney Proto who had sold shares before the earnings announcement was fired. Later that year the company tapped Maury Myers CEO of trucking company Yellow Corp. to take over as chairman and CEO.

In 2000 to concentrate on its core business in North America Waste Management sold operations in Europe Asia and South America in a series of transactions that raised about $2.5 billion. The next year the company established a pulp and paper trading group.

Waste Management announced plans in early 2002 to restructure the company by reorganizing its operating areas and cutting its workforce of 57000 by about 3.5%. Also that year the SEC sued six former Waste Management executives charging that they had enriched themselves through accounting fraud between 1992 and 1997.

The company formed a new recycling unit Recycle America Alliance in 2003 after acquiring Milwaukee-based The Peltz Group the largest privately held recycler in the US. The company also acquired 75 complementary collection businesses for about $337 million and divested some operations for about $18 million. That year two former executives of Waste Management Proto and CFO Earl DeFrates agreed to a settlement with the SEC on allegations that they had profited from insider trading in 1999.

In a bid to consolidate its leadership position in the US waste market in 2008 the company made a bid to acquire Republic Services but was rebuffed.

In 2009 the company acquired PharmEcology Associates a national pharmaceutical waste management consulting services firm and Mountain High Medical Disposal Services. In 2010 it added some medical waste assets from MedServe following that company's acquisition by Stericycle.

It also acquired a medical waste processing facility and other assets from Milum Textile Services in Phoenix.

In 2010 it invested in Canadian waste-to-biofuels company Enerkem. Further expanding its "green" businesses the company acquired control of Garick LLC a leading maker and distributor of organic lawn and garden products. The deal helped grow Waste Management's organics recycling services business.

In 2011 it bought Access Computer Products a leading provider of cell phone ink and toner cartridge and consumer electronics reverse logistics remarketing and recycling services and acquired three recycling facilities in Maryland and Virginia in a separate deal.

Also that year Waste Management picked up Connecticut-based Oakleaf Global Holdings and its operations for $425 million. The unit manages a North American network of some 2500 operators who provide hauling disposal waste diversion and recycling services.

In 2012 the company removed a management layer in its four geographic groups consolidated and reduced its geographic areas from 22 to 17 and eliminated some 700 positions.

Expanding its recycling portfolio and supporting its efforts to manage 20 million tons of recyclable material in 2013 Waste Management acquired Greenstar LLC from NTR plc for $170 million. Greenstar manages some 1.5 million tons of material through a dozen material recovery facilities.

That year the company acquired Summit Energy Services and Liquid Logistics two Williston North Dakota-based energy services companies. The acquisitions enhance Waste Management's environmental service offerings to oil and gas industry customers working in the Bakken Shale.

EXECUTIVES

Evp And Coo, James E. Trevathan, age 67, $676,885 total compensation
Svp Field Operations, Jeff M. Harris, age 66, $608,846 total compensation
Evp Corporate Operations; President Recycling, Puneet Bhasin, age 57
President And Ceo, James C. (Jim) Fish, age 58, $705,996 total compensation
Svp Field Operations, John J. Morris, age 50, $593,462 total compensation
Svp Cfo And Treasurer, Devina A. Rankin
Vice President Information Technology, Mark Madsen
Senior Vice President, Don Carpenter
Vice President Business Development And Sports Marketing, Steve Ness
Vice President Strategic Business Solutions, Paul Foody
Vice President Information Technology, Gail Trafton
Vice President Business Development, Joe Cassin
Vice President Commercial Lines Underwriting, Mary Fisher
Vice President Of Business Development, Brian Bauman
Vice President Customer Service, Katy Lydon
Vice President Shared Services And Fleet, David Logsdon
Vice President Market Area, Pittman Alec
Svp Corporate Affairs And Chief People Officer, Barry Caldwell
Area Vice President, Chris Desantis
Vice President Legal Corporate And Securities, John Tsai

Vice President, Ronald Jones
**Svp Operations Safety And Environmental
 Compliance,** Tara Hemmer
Government Relations Director, Henry Sori
Vice President, Eddie Lopez
Vice President, Frank Labarba
Director Of Government Relations, John Wohlrab
Area Vice President, Steve Batchelor
Vice President Commodity Sales, Don Majka
Vice President Public Affairs, Chuck Dees
Vice President Business Partner Operations,
 Buddy West
Svp, Jim Trevathan
Senior Vice President, James Little
Vice President, George Padgett
Chairman, Bradbury H. (Brad) Anderson, age 69
Secretary To The Vice President, Robert Longo
Board Of Directors, Christine Chisholm-krosnicki
Board Member, Michael Parrent
Board Member, Melinda Holt
Secretary, Michael Rich
Auditors: Ernst & Young LLP

LOCATIONS

HQ: Waste Management, Inc. (DE)
 1001 Fannin Street, Houston, TX 77002
Phone: 713 512-6200
Web: www.wm.com

2018 Sales

	$ mil.	% of total
US & Puerto Rico	14,167	95
Canada	747	5
Total	**14,914**	**100**

PRODUCTS/OPERATIONS

2018 sales

	$ mil.	% of total
Collection	9,724	54
Landfill	3,560	20
Transfer	1,711	9
Recycling	1,293	7
Other	1,736	10
Adjustments	(3110)	.
Total	**14,914**	**100**

Selected Services
Collection
Disposal
Hazardous waste management
Landfill management
Portable sanitation services
Recycling
Transfer stations
Treatment

COMPETITORS

Casella Waste Systems	WCA Waste
Republic Services	Waste Connections
Rumpke	Waste Connections US
Safety-Kleen	

HISTORICAL FINANCIALS
Company Type: Public

Income Statement | | | | FYE: December 31

	REVENUE ($ mil.)	NET INCOME ($ mil.)	NET PROFIT MARGIN	EMPLOYEES
12/19	15,455	1,670	10.8%	44,900
12/18	14,914	1,925	12.9%	43,700
12/17	14,485	1,949	13.5%	42,300
12/16	13,609	1,182	8.7%	41,200
12/15	12,961	753	5.8%	40,600
Annual Growth	4.5%	22.0%	—	2.5%

2019 Year-End Financials

Debt ratio: 48.65%
Return on equity: 25.03%
Cash ($ mil.): 3,561
Current ratio: 1.97
Long-term debt ($ mil.): 13,280

No. of shares (mil.): 424
Dividends
 Yield: 1.8%
 Payout: 52.4%
Market value ($ mil.): 48,356

	STOCK PRICE ($) FY Close	P/E High/Low	Earnings	Dividends	Book Value
12/19	113.96	31 23	3.91	2.05	16.66
12/18	88.99	21 18	4.45	1.86	14.80
12/17	86.30	19 16	4.41	1.70	13.89
12/16	70.91	27 19	2.65	1.64	12.06
12/15	53.37	33 28	1.65	1.54	11.95
Annual Growth	20.9%	— —	24.1%	7.4%	8.7%

Wayfair Inc

Auditors: Ernst & Young LLP

LOCATIONS

HQ: Wayfair Inc
 4 Copley Place, Boston, MA 02116
Phone: 617 532-6100
Web: www.wayfair.com

HISTORICAL FINANCIALS
Company Type: Public

Income Statement | | | FYE: December 31

	REVENUE ($ mil.)	NET INCOME ($ mil.)	NET PROFIT MARGIN	EMPLOYEES
12/19	9,127	(984)	—	16,985
12/18	6,779	(504)	—	12,124
12/17	4,720	(244)	—	7,751
12/16	3,380	(194)	—	5,637
12/15	2,249	(77)	—	3,809
Annual Growth	41.9%	—		45.3%

2019 Year-End Financials

Debt ratio: 49.31%
Return on equity:—
Cash ($ mil.): 582
Current ratio: 0.85
Long-term debt ($ mil.): 1,456

No. of shares (mil.): 93
Dividends
 Yield: —
 Payout: —
Market value ($ mil.): 8,459

	STOCK PRICE ($) FY Close	P/E High/Low	Earnings	Dividends	Book Value
12/19	90.37	— —	(10.68)	0.00	(10.09)
12/18	90.08	— —	(5.63)	0.00	(3.64)
12/17	80.27	— —	(2.81)	0.00	(0.55)
12/16	35.05	— —	(2.29)	0.00	0.92
12/15	47.62	— —	(0.92)	0.00	2.88
Annual Growth	17.4%	— —			

Webster Financial Corp (Waterbury, Conn)

Webster Financial is the holding company for Webster Bank which operates about 170 branches in southern New England primarily in Connecticut but also in Massachusetts New York and Rhode Island. The bank provides commercial and retail services such as deposit accounts loans and mortgages and consumer finance as well as government and institutional banking services. It performs asset-based lending through its Webster Business Credit subsidiary and equipment financing through Webster Capital Finance. The company's HSA Bank division offers health savings accounts nationwide. Webster Bank provides brokerage and investment services through an agreement with UVEST a division of LPL Financial.

Operations
Webster Financial operates in three segments: Commercial Banking HSA Bank and Community Banking.

Commercial Banking provides lending deposit and treasury and payment services.

Community Banking services consist of personal and business banking. It operates about 170 banking centers more than 330 ATMs a customer care center and web and mobile banking services.

HSA Bank is focused on health savings accounts as well as providing health reimbursement arrangements flexible spending and commuter benefit account administration services to employers and individuals in all 50 states.

Geographic Reach
Webster's largest market is Connecticut with about 115 branches. Massachusetts has about 35 branches; Rhode Island about 10; and New York fewer than 10. Customers can conduct transactions at some 330 ATMs across throughout New England.

Financial Performance
Webster Financial's revenue and net income have appreciated in recent years. In 2017 the bank's revenue rose to $1.05 billion from $983 million in 2016 while net income rose to $255 million from $207 million.

Webster credited strong loan growth funded with growth in low-cost long-duration HSA deposits for achieving higher net interest margin in 2017. Net interest income increased about $78 million while provision for loan and lease losses dropped about $15 million. The bank reported that non-interest expense rose about $38 million and that it had one-time gain of about $7 million on the sale of an asset in 2016.

Strategy
Webster focuses on building its community banking and health savings account businesses. Tthe community banking unit is expansion in several metro areas led by Boston where the bank is on pace to meet its goal of $1 billion in new deposits and $500 million in loans over five years. While it faces fierce pricing competition in the Boston market it sees steady deposit growth in the core franchise there.

In the HSA Bank business Webster has invested in sales staff which helped drive compensation costs about $27 million higher in 2017 from 2016 and relationship management to gather new clients. The investment seems to be paying off with growth in clients and deposits and some $6 billion under administration. Webster uses deposits made in the HSA Bank to fund lending in its other businesses.

EXECUTIVES

Vice President Association Financial Services, Jordan Arovas

Chairman And Ceo Webster Financial Corporation And Webster Bank N.a., James C. (Jim) Smith, age 70, $882,435 total compensation

Evp General Counsel And Corporate Secretary Webster Financial Corporation And Webster Bank N.a., Harriet M. Wolfe, age 66

President And Coo Webster Business Credit Corporation (wbcc), Warren K. Mino

Regional President Boston Webster Bank N.a., Paul F. Mollica

Evp And Chief Human Resources Officer Webster Financial Corporation And Webster Bank N.a., Bernard M. Garrigues, age 61

Evp And Chief Marketing Officer Webster Financial Corporation And Webster Bank N.a., Dawn C. Morris, age 52

Regional President New Haven Conn. Webster Bank N.a., Jeffrey A. (Jeff) Klaus

Evp Commercial Banking; Chairman Of Regional Presidents' Council, John R. Ciulla, age 54, $363,479 total compensation

Evp And Head Of Community Banking, Nitin J. Mhatre, age 49, $358,521 total compensation

Evp And Cfo Webster Financial Corporation And Webster Bank N.a., Glenn I. MacInnes, age 58, $453,310 total compensation

Evp And Cio Webster Financial Corporation And Webster Bank N.a., Colin D. Eccles, age 61

Evp Consumer Deposits Investments And Network Management Webster Bank N.a., David D. Miree

Evp And Chief Risk Officer Webster Financial Corporation And Webster Bank N.a., Daniel H. Bley, age 51

Evp And Head Of Private Banking Webster Financial Corporation And Webster Bank N.a., Daniel M. (Dan) FitzPatrick, age 61, $300,000 total compensation

Evp Commercial Real Estate, William E. Wrang

Evp Webster Financial Corporation And Webster Bank N.a. And Head Of Hsa Bank, Charles L. (Chad) Wilkins, age 58

Regional President Metro New York, Abby Parsonnet

Regional President Southern Massachusetts And Rhode Island Webster Bank N.a., Douglas E. (Doug) Scala

Regional President Waterbury Conn. Webster Bank N.a., Michael L. (Mike) O'Connor

Regional President For Pennsylvania Webster Bank N.a., Scott C. Meves

Regional President Hartford Conn. Webster Bank N.a., Timothy D. Bergstrom

Evp Middle Market Banking Webster Bank N.a., Christopher J. (Chris) Motl

Vice President Information Technology, Tom Clark

Vice President Human Resources Technology, Chris Muller

Vice President Corporate Facilities Operations, Mark Nisbett

Senior Vice President Director Of Corporate Security, Michael Wolf

Vice President Loan Operations, Terri O'sullivan

Vice President Marketing, Joanne Renna

Vice President Ebanking, Chris Barlow

Vice President External Communications, Sarah Barr

Vice President Database, Jennifer Zbell

Vice President Finance, Shelly Abdella

Senior Vice President Middle Market Commercial Banking Webster Bank, Stephen Corcoran

Executive Vice President Chief Marketing Officer Of The Company And Webster Bank, Michelle Crecca

Senior Vice President Compensation Benefits And Hris, Carole Hynes

Senior Vice President, Torres Gilbert

Vice President Network Services, Philip Campbell

Vice President Business Banking, Gene Marinelli

Vice Chairman Webster Financial Corporation And Webster Bank N.a., Joseph J. (Joe) Savage, age 67

Treasurer And Vice President, Bruce Wandelmaier

Board Member, Mark Pettie

Board Member, Lauren States

Board Member, Elizabeth Flynn

Board Member, William Atwell

Auditors: KPMG LLP

LOCATIONS

HQ: Webster Financial Corp (Waterbury, Conn)
145 Bank Street, Waterbury, CT 06702
Phone: 203 578-2202
Web: www.websterbank.com

2017 Bank Branches

	No.
Connecticut	115
Massachusetts	35
Rhode Island	10
New York	7
Total	**167**

PRODUCTS/OPERATIONS

2017 Sales

	$ mil.	% of total
Interest		
Interest and fees on loans and leases	708	57
Taxable interest and dividends on securities	181	17
Non-taxable interest on securities	22	2
Loans held for sale	1	-
Non-interest		
Deposit service fees	151	13
Loan and lease related fees	26	3
Wealth and investment services	31	3
Mortgage banking activities	9	1
Increase in cash surrender value of life insurance policies	14	1
Gain on sale of investment securities net	—	-
Impairment loss on securities recognized in earnings	(0.13)	-
Other income	26	3
Total	**1,055**	**100**

COMPETITORS

Bank of America	New England Bancshares
Citibank	Patriot National
Citizens Financial	Bancorp
Group	People's United
Fairfield County Bank	Financial
First Connecticut	SBT Bancorp Inc.
Bancorp	SI Financial
JPMorgan Chase	TD Bank USA
KeyCorp	Washington Trust
Liberty Bank	Bancorp

HISTORICAL FINANCIALS

Company Type: Public

Income Statement

FYE: December 31

	ASSETS ($ mil.)	NET INCOME ($ mil.)	INCOME AS % OF ASSETS	EMPLOYEES
12/19	30,389	382	1.3%	3,298
12/18	27,610	360	1.3%	3,265
12/17	26,487	255	1.0%	3,302
12/16	26,072	207	0.8%	3,168
12/15	24,677	206	0.8%	2,946
Annual Growth	**5.3%**	**16.7%**	**—**	**2.9%**

2019 Year-End Financials

Debt ratio: 2.35%
Return on equity: 12.56%
Cash ($ mil.): 257
Current ratio: —
Long-term debt ($ mil.): —

No. of shares (mil.): 92
Dividends
  Yield: 2.8%
  Payout: 36.8%
Market value ($ mil.): 4,911

	STOCK PRICE ($) FY Close	P/E High/Low	PER SHARE ($) Earnings	Dividends	Book Value
12/19	53.36	14 10	4.06	1.53	34.86
12/18	49.29	18 12	3.81	1.25	31.31
12/17	56.16	22 17	2.67	1.03	29.36
12/16	54.28	25 14	2.16	0.98	27.54
12/15	37.19	19 13	2.15	0.89	26.38
Annual Growth	**9.4%**	**— —**	**17.2%**	**14.5%**	**7.2%**

WEC Energy Group Inc

WEC Energy Group keeps the lights illuminated and the gas fires burning for 4.5 million customers in Wisconsin Illinois Michigan and Minnesota. The utility holding company serves energy through its eight regulated utilities which together own more than 7100 MW of electric generation capacity and thousands of miles of natural gas distribution. It also provides Milwaukee with steam for use in processing hot water and humidification. Its generation capacity includes four coal-fired and a dozen gas-fired plants as well as solar wind hydro and biomass plants. WEC is the largest electric utility company in Wisconsin serving residential customers as well as industries such as paper metals manufacturing food retail health services and education on a retail or wholesale basis.

Operations

WEC Energy Group operates six reportable segments: Wisconsin Illinois Other States Electric Transmission Non-Utility Energy Infrastructure and Corporate and Other.

The Wisconsin segment accounts for about 70% of total revenue and includes the electric and natural gas utility operations of Wisconsin Electric (WE) Wisconsin Gas (WG) Wisconsin Public Service Corporation (WPS) and UMERC.

The Illinois segment produces more than 15% of WEC's revenue and includes the natural gas utility and non-utility operations of The Peoples Gas Light and Coke Company (PGL) and North Shore Gas Company (NSG). PGL and NSG provide energy to Chicago and its northern suburbs. PGL also owns and operates a about 39 Bcf natural gas storage facility in central Illinois.

The Other States segment (about 5%) includes the natural gas utility and non-utility operations of Minnesota Energy Resources Corporation (MERC) and Michigan Gas Utilities Corporation (MGU).

The for-profit Non-Utility Energy Infrastructure segment includes We Power which owns and leases generating facilities; underground natural gas storage unit Bluewater; and WEC's majority interests in the Bishop Hill III Coyote Ridge and Upstream wind generating facilities. The segment generates over 5% of revenue.

The Electric Transmission comprises a 60% stake in American Transmission Company LLC

(ATC) which owns maintains monitors and operates electric transmission systems throughout WEC's service territory. It generates revenue on an equity basis. The Corporate and Other segment contains immaterial miscellaneous other units.

WEC owns more than 70600 miles of electric distribution lines and about 50700 miles of n natural gas distribution and transmission lines. The company generates 70% of its energy needs and purchases the rest through power purchase agreements. Of its owned plants about 35% of energy is sourced from coal nearly 30% from natural gas and less than 5% from renewables. Most of the purchased power is nuclear sourced.

Geographic Reach

Most of Milwaukee-based WEC Energy Group's customers are in Wisconsin particularly in the eastern portion of the state. It also has customers in southern Michigan including its Upper Peninsula; Chicago; and in various bits of Minnesota.

Sales and Marketing

WEC provide electric utility service to a diversified base of customers in industries such as metals and other manufacturing paper governmental food products health services education and retail. It serves more than 4.5 million customers in total.

Financial Performance

For the last five years WEC's revenue generally increased except for 2019 which saw a $156.4 million decrease from prior year. Net income registered the same trend except in 2018 when it had a 12% dip in profit.

In 2019 the company's sales fell by 2% to $7.5 billion due to decrease sales across all segment.

Net income grew 7% to $1.1 billion due to increase in operating income at the Wisconsin segment. The increase was driven by lower operation and maintenance expense related to our power plants which primarily resulted from lower maintenance and labor costs.

WEC's cash on hand fell $63.8 million during 2019 ending the year at $82.3 million. The company's operations generated $2.3 billion and its financing produced $85.6 million partially offset by the $2.5 billion used in its investing activities. WEC's main cash uses in 2019 were capital expenditures acquisitions and dividends.

Strategy

The Company's main corporate strategy is to continue to build and sustain long-term value for its shareholders and customers by focusing on the fundamentals of its business: reliability; operating efficiency; financial discipline; customer care; and safety.

Mergers and Acquisitions

In 2020 WEC agreed to increase its ownership interest from 80% to 90% in three Midwest windfarms: Blooming Grove Wind Farm Thunderhead Wind Energy Center and the Upstream Wind Energy Center. The total investment is $118 million for an additional 75 megawatts of capacity.

In early 2020 WEC agreed to acquire 80% ownership interest in Blooming Grove Wind Farm. The project is being developed in McLean County Illinois by Invenergy — a leading developer and operator of sustainable energy solutions. Commercial operation is expected to begin by the end of 2020. The Blooming Grove site

will consist of 94 GE wind turbines with a combined capacity of 250 megawatts. WEC Energy Group's investment will total $345 million for the 80% ownership interest.

In late 2019 WEC agreed to acquire 80% ownership interest in Thunderhead Wind Energy Center. The project is being developed in Antelope and Wheeler counties Nebraska by Invenergy — a leading developer and operator of sustainable energy solutions. Commercial operation is expected to begin by the end of 2020. The Thunderhead site will consist of 108 GE wind turbines with a combined capacity of 300 megawatts. WEC Energy Group's investment will total $338 million for the 80% ownership interest.

Also in early 2019 the company acquired an 80 percent ownership interest in Coyote Ridge Wind Farm under construction in Brookings County South Dakota. The Coyote Ridge site consists of 39 GE wind turbines with a combined capacity of 97 megawatts. WEC Energy Group's investment will total $145 million for the 80% ownership interest.

EXECUTIVES

Chairman Wec Energy Group Inc. And Wisconsin Electric Power Company, Gale E. Klappa, age 70, $589,043 total compensation

President Ceo And Director, Allen L. Leverett, age 54, $941,667 total compensation

Evp General Counsel And Corporate Secretary Wisconsin Energy Corp And We Energies, Susan H. Martin, age 67, $515,000 total compensation

Evp External Affairs, Robert M. (Bert) Garvin, age 53, $416,120 total compensation

Evp And President Michigan Gas Utilities Minnesota Energy Resources Corp. Wec Business Services Llc, J. Patrick Keyes, age 54, $546,400 total compensation

Evp And Cfo, Scott J. Lauber, age 54, $351,784 total compensation

President Â– We Energies And Wisconsin Public Service, J. Kevin Fletcher, age 61, $411,345 total compensation

President And Ceo Peoples Gas And North Shore Gas, Charles R. Matthews, age 63

President Wispark Llc, Jerold P. Franke

Evp Human Resources And Organizational Effectiveness And Compliance Officer, Joan M. Shafer, age 66

Vp And Cio, Molly Mulroy

Evp We Energies And Wisconsin Public Service, Tom Metcalfe, age 52

Vice President Chief Administrative Officer, Kristine Rappe

Senior Vice President Corporate Communications And Investor Relations, Mary Straka

Board Member, Mary Stanek

Board Member, Kevin Fletcher

Auditors: DELOITTE & TOUCHE LLP

LOCATIONS

HQ: WEC Energy Group Inc
231 West Michigan Street, P.O. Box 1331, Milwaukee, WI 53201
Phone: 414 221-2345   **Fax:** 414 221-2172
Web: www.wecenergygroup.com

PRODUCTS/OPERATIONS

2018 sales

	$ mil.	% of total
Wisconsin	5,794	72
Illinois	1,400	17
Other States	438	5

	$ mil.	% of total
Non-Utility Energy Infrastructure	468	6
Corporate and others	8	-
Eliminations	(430.5)	-
Total	**7,679**	**100**

2018 sales

	$ mil.	% of total
Electric	4,432	58
Natural Gas	3,194	41
Other Non-Utility revenue	53	1
Other	(0.8)	-
Total	**7,679**	**100**

Selected Subsidiaries

American Transmission Company LLC (partial ownership)
Michigan Gas utilities Corporation
Minnesota Energy Resources Corporation
North Shore Gas Company
The Peoples Gas Light and Coke Company
Upper Michigan Energy Resources
W.E. Power LLC (We Power regulated power plant construction)
Wisconsin Electric Power Company (operates as We Energies electric gas and steam utility)
Wisconsin Gas LLC (operates as We Energies gas and water utility)
Wisconsin Public Service Corporation
Wispark LLC (real estate development)

COMPETITORS

AEP	MGE Energy
ALLETE	Minnesota Power
Alliant Energy	SEMCO ENERGY
CMS Energy	Wisconsin Power &
Commonwealth Edison	Light
DTE	Xcel Energy
Dairyland Power	

HISTORICAL FINANCIALS

Company Type: Public

Income Statement

FYE: December 31

	REVENUE ($ mil.)	NET INCOME ($ mil.)	NET PROFIT MARGIN	EMPLOYEES
12/19	7,523	1,135	15.1%	7,509
12/18	7,679	1,060	13.8%	7,878
12/17	7,648	1,204	15.8%	8,129
12/16	7,472	940	12.6%	8,164
12/15	5,926	640	10.8%	8,443
Annual Growth	6.1%	15.4%	—	(2.9%)

2019 Year-End Financials

Debt ratio: 36.44%	No. of shares (mil.): 315
Return on equity: 11.37%	Dividends
Cash ($ mil.): 37	Yield: 2.5%
Current ratio: 0.66	Payout: 68.4%
Long-term debt ($ mil.): 11,211	Market value ($ mil.): 29,093

	STOCK PRICE ($) FY Close	P/E High/Low		PER SHARE ($) Earnings	Dividends	Book Value
12/19	92.23	27	19	3.58	2.36	32.16
12/18	69.26	22	17	3.34	2.21	31.12
12/17	66.43	18	15	3.79	2.08	30.08
12/16	58.65	22	17	2.96	1.98	28.39
12/15	51.31	24	19	2.34	1.74	27.51
Annual Growth	15.8%	—	—	11.2%	7.9%	4.0%

Wells Fargo & Co (New)

Auditors: KPMG LLP

LOCATIONS

HQ: Wells Fargo & Co (New)
420 Montgomery Street, San Francisco, CA 94104
Phone: 866 249-3302
Web: www.wellsfargo.com

HISTORICAL FINANCIALS

Company Type: Public

Income Statement

FYE: December 31

	ASSETS ($ mil.)	NET INCOME ($ mil.)	INCOME AS % OF ASSETS	EMPLOYEES
12/19	1,927,555	19,549	1.0%	260,000
12/18	1,895,883	22,393	1.2%	259,000
12/17	1,951,757	22,183	1.1%	262,700
12/16	1,930,115	21,938	1.1%	269,100
12/15	1,787,632	22,894	1.3%	264,700
Annual Growth	1.9%	(3.9%)	—	(0.4%)

2019 Year-End Financials

Debt ratio: 11.84%—
Return on equity: 10.20%
Cash ($ mil.): 141,250
Current ratio: —
Long-term debt ($ mil.): —

Dividends
Yield: 3.5%
Payout: 41.4%
Market value ($ mil.): —

	STOCK PRICE ($) FY Close	P/E High/Low	PER SHARE ($) Earnings	Dividends	Book Value
12/19	53.80	13 11	4.05	1.92	45.27
12/18	46.08	15 10	4.28	1.64	42.82
12/17	60.67	15 12	4.10	1.54	42.30
12/16	55.11	14 11	3.99	1.52	39.79
12/15	54.36	14 12	4.12	1.48	37.90
Annual Growth	(0.3%)	— —	(0.4%)	6.8%	4.5%

WesBanco Inc

WesBanco wants to be the "BesBanco" for its customers. The holding company owns WesBanco Bank which has about 210 branches in Indiana Kentucky Ohio Pennsylvania and West Virginia. In addition to providing traditional services such as deposits and loans the bank operates a wealth management department with offices in West Virginia and Ohio and some $4.7 billion of assets under management and custody including the company's proprietary WesMark mutual funds. Other units include brokerage firm WesBanco Securities and multi-line insurance provider WesBanco Insurance Services.

Operations

Commercial loans including real estate and operating loans account for more than half of of WesBanco's loan portfolio. Its retail portfolio mainly consists of home equity loans and deposit overdraft limits. The bank usually sells new residential mortgages that it originates into the secondary market. It plans to continue to grow its portfolio of commercial and industrial loans.

Strategy

WesBanco likes to purchase smaller banks to expand its reach into new geographic markets while bolstering its loan and deposit business. It's acquired more than 50 banks and financial services firms in the past 25 years.

Mergers and Acquisitions

The company agreed in 2019 to acquire Old Line Bancshares for $500 million. The combined company will have about $15.6 billion in total assets and about 235 branches in more than five states. The deal give WesBanco more than 35 new offices primarily in Baltimore and Washington DC.

In 2018 WesBanco acquired Kentucky-based Farmers Capital Bank Corporation for $429.8 million and West Virginia-based First Sentry Bancshares for $107.5 million.

EXECUTIVES

Evp Treasury And Strategic Planning, Brent E. Richmond, age 57
Evp And Chief Credit Officer, Peter W. Jaworski, age 65, $212,101 total compensation
Evp And Cfo, Robert H. Young, age 64, $269,363 total compensation
President And Ceo, Todd F. Clossin, age 58, $466,923 total compensation
Svp Risk Management, Michael L. Perkins
President East Region Wesbanco Bank, Lynn D. Asensio
Evp And Senior Operations Officer, Gregory A. Dugan
Evp Wealth Management, Jonathan D. Dargusch, age 62, $230,270 total compensation
Evp Human Resources Management, Anthony F. Pietranton
Evp And Chief Lending Officer, Jayson M. Zatta
Market President Kanawha Region, David L. Sayre
Vice President District Sales Manager, Nick Taylor
Vice President Corporate Marketing, Jenny Kimpel
Senior Vice President Human Resources, Lee Blundon
Senior Vice President And Senior Credit Officer, Michael Schwarz
Vice President Risk Management Security Officer, James Thompson
Senior Vice President, Howard Bertram
Vice President Commercial Real Estate, Traci Boeing
Assistant Vice President, Bruce Bandi
Vice President, Allen Retton
Vice President, Tom Medovic
Senior Vice President Credit Risk Management, Edward Polli
Vice President Electronic Banking Manager, Jason Plotner
Assistant Vice President Information Technology Services, W Terrance Naughton
Vice President Of Information Technology, Mike Robbins
Vice President Investments, Steve Kellas
Senior Vice President, Robert Booth
Executive Vice President Commercial Banking, Jay Zatta
Vice President Retail Operations, Lisa Copley
Assistant Vice President Branch Manager, Joseph Kronenberger
Banking Center Manager Assistant Vice President, Jodi McKnight
Senior Vice President Senior Lender, Bob Friend
Vice President And Loan Review Officer, Diane Todd
Vice President Business Development Officer, Neal Jackson
Senior Vice President Investments, Michael Klick

Assistant Vice President Commercial Banking Officer, Randall Trickett
Assistant Vice President Information Technology Services, Terry Naughton
Senior Vice President And Senior Credit Officer, David Knuth
Assistant Vice President Private Banker, Kerrie Smith
Vice President Of Commercial Banking, Michael Mistovich
Vice President And Business Banking Officer, Nathan Mcvicker
Assistant Vice President Branch Manager, Tom Wiggershaus
Vice President Commercial Banker, Lisa Dillon
Banking Center Manager Assistant Vice President, Nicholas Beresh
Vice President Secondary Marketing Manager, Ryan Freimark
Senior Vice President Corporate Banking, Charles Wharton
Vice President, Sabra Thomas Kershaw
Svp And Director Enterprise Services, Jan Pattishall
Vice President Business Banking, John Mcdonough
Assistant Vice President Financial Advisor, Josh Schmalz
Vice President Commercial Lending, Kurt Bevan
Vice President Credit Risk Management, Ryan Potts
Vice President, James Bish
Assistant Vice President, Anthony Habbit
Senior Vice President, Jeff Ferry
Assistant Vice President Information Technology, John Busack
Assistant Vice President Bcm Business Development, Jason Lucarelli
Vice President Corporate Banking, Harry Silvis
Vice President And Manger, Mary Bryson
Senior Vice President, Thomas Ziacik
Assistant Vice President Senior Underwriter, Tim Robinson
Assistant Vice President, Dan Baxter
Vice President, Brent Dapper
Assistant Vice President Banking Center Manager, Linda Yon
Vice President, Michael Puzausky
Vice President, Nathan Schoetz
Vice President Business Banking, Maher-dickerson Stephanie
Vice President Quality Assurance Manager, Pamela Jones
Vice President Corporate Banking, Jack Green
Vice President Private Banker, Leslie D Witzel
Vice President And Commercial Banker, Michael Epperley
Senior Vice President And Senior Commercial Banker, Michael T Misich
Vice President Commercial Lender, Robert E Krzeminski
Vice President Treasury Management Sales, Stacy Graf
Vice President Senior Trust Officer, Thomas D Barsody
Vice President Commercial Lending, Kurt C Bevan
Vice President Commercial Banker, Camde Skidmore
Senior Vice President, Ed Hensley
Vice President And Technology Services Coordinator, Stephanie Skivington
Vice President Commercial Banking, Daniel Hindman
Vice President Commercial Lender, Robert Krzeminski
Vice President Senior Trust Officer, Thomas Barsody
Vice President Private Banker, Leslie Witzel
Senior Vice President And Senior Commercial Banker, Michael Misich

**Assistant Vice President And Appraisal Review
  Officer,** Ann Scranton
Vice President And Credit Resolution Officer,
  Matthew Perks
Senior Vice President, Gregory J Agresta
Vice President, John Mattern
Svp Financial Advisor Crc, Sherri Libersat
Vice President, Jeff Davis
Evp, David Ellwood Cfa
Assistant Vice President Commercial Lender,
  Shelly Thomas
Evp Senior Operations Officer, Greg Dugan
Vice President Private Banker, Angela Smethwick
**Assistant Vice President And Manager Banking
  Center,** Cheryl Landry
Chairman, James C. (Jim) Gardill, age 74
Secretary, Cindy Dailer
Auditors: Ernst & Young LLP

LOCATIONS

HQ: WesBanco Inc
  1 Bank Plaza, Wheeling, WV 26003
Phone: 304 234-9000
Web: www.wesbanco.com

PRODUCTS/OPERATIONS

2016 Sales

	$ mil.	% of total
Interest and Dividend Income		
Loans including fees	227	61
Interest and dividends on securities	56	15
Other interest income	2	1
Non-Interest Income		
Trust fees	21	6
Service charges on deposits	18	5
Electronic banking fees	15	4
Net securities brokerage	6	2
Bank-owned life insurance	4	1
Net gains on sales of mortgage loans	2	1
Net securities gains	2	1
Net gain / (loss) on other real estate owned and other assets	0	-
others	9	3
Total	**367**	**100**

Selected Products and Services

Personal Banking
Internet Banking
Checking
Savings
Time Deposits
Debit Cards
Credit Cards
Loans
Mortgage Lending
Other Services
Business
Internet Banking
Checking
Savings
Time Deposits
Credit Cards
Loans
Treasury Management
Insurance Services
Wealth Management

COMPETITORS

1st West Virginia Bancorp	Huntington Bancshares
BB&T	Ohio Valley Banc
Bank of America	PNC Financial
Cheviot Financial	United Bancorp
City Holding	United Bankshares
First Community Bancshares	

HISTORICAL FINANCIALS

Company Type: Public

Income Statement   FYE: December 31

	ASSETS ($ mil.)	NET INCOME ($ mil.)	INCOME AS % OF ASSETS	EMPLOYEES
12/19	15,720	158	1.0%	2,705
12/18	12,458	143	1.1%	2,383
12/17	9,816	94	1.0%	1,940
12/16	9,790	86	0.9%	1,928
12/15	8,470	80	1.0%	1,633
Annual Growth	**16.7%**	**18.4%**	**—**	**13.4%**

2019 Year-End Financials

Debt ratio: 1.27%	No. of shares (mil.): 67
Return on equity: 6.95%	Dividends
Cash ($ mil.): 234	Yield: 3.2%
Current ratio: —	Payout: 40.6%
Long-term debt ($ mil.): —	Market value ($ mil.): 2,563

	STOCK PRICE ($) FY Close	P/E High/Low	Earnings	PER SHARE ($) Dividends	Book Value
12/19	37.79	15 12	2.83	1.24	38.24
12/18	36.69	17 12	2.92	1.16	36.24
12/17	40.65	20 16	2.14	1.04	31.68
12/16	43.06	20 13	2.16	0.96	30.53
12/15	30.02	17 14	2.15	0.92	29.18
Annual Growth	**5.9%**	**— —**	**7.1%**	**7.7%**	**7.0%**

Wesco International, Inc.

When contractors and manufacturers need parts it's WESCO to the rescue. The company distributes general and electrical supplies (fuses terminals connectors boxes enclosures circuit breakers transformers switchboards tools abrasives filters safety equipment) lighting (lamps fixtures ballasts) wire and conduit materials (wire cable raceway metallic and non-metallic conduit) and automation controls and motors (relays timers and interconnects). WESCO offers more than a million products from some 30000 suppliers with about 70000 customers worldwide. The company generates almost 75% of its sales in the US.

Operations

WESCO products offering include general supplies (about 40% of sales); communications and security (about 15%); wire cable and conduit (nearly 15%); electrical distribution and controls (about 10%); lighting and sustainability (about 10%); and automation controls and motions (nearly 10%).

Company's largest supplier Eaton Corporation accounts for about 10% of purchase while ten largest supplier accounted for about a third of its purchase.

Geographic Reach

Headquartered in Pittsburgh Pennsylvania WESCO operates more than 500 branches of which some 340 are located in the US. Outside of the US about 130 are located in Canada seven are located in Mexico and the remainder are in other countries located in Africa Asia Europe and South America. International markets serviced by its over 10 distribution centers located in the US and Canada. The US accounts for almost 75% of sales and the remaining sales comes from International primarily in Canada.

Sales and Marketing

WESCO caters to 70000 customers. Sales to industrial customers (more than 35%) range from major industrial commercial and data communication projects to small residential contractors. Construction customers (about one-third of sales) include contractors and engineering procurement and constructional firms for commercial and data and broadband communications projects. Utilities and specialty utility contractors (some 15%) include large and rural electric cooperatives and municipal power authorities which maintain transmission distribution lines and power plants.

Commercial institutional and governmental customers (accounting for about 15% of sales) include schools hospitals property management firms retailers and government agencies of all types.

Financial Performance

WESCO has seen limited revenue growth in recent years. Its annual revenues have risen about 11% since 2015.

Revenue increased to $8.4 billion in 2019 an approximately 2% increase from the year prior. The increase was driven by record sales with growth in all end markets and geographies.

Net income was $223.3 million in fiscal year 2019 a decrease from $227.4 million in fiscal year 2018.

Cash provided by operating activities was $224.3 million in fiscal 2019 while investing activities used $60.8 million. Financing activities used another $109.8 million. Cash and cash equivalents at the end of period totaled $1509 million

Strategy

WESCO has been building its business through acquisitions and organic growth. As part of this effort the company's working to develop new end markets broaden its product and service offerings expand its geographic footprint and enhance its sales and customer service.

The company's strategies align around the following six planks: digital solutions; commercial excellence; operational excellence; technology platform; organization talent and culture; and portfolio and strategic M&A.

WESCO is boosting its lighting division through acquisitions. In 2019 its Wesco Services division acquired Sylvania Lighting Solutions (SLS) the lighting business of OSRAM Sylvania. The acquisition adds SLS's customer base an expanded geographic footprint and project management capabilities to WESCO's offerings.

Mergers and Acquisitions

In 2020 WESCO International Inc. a leading provider of electrical industrial and communications MRO and OEM products and Anixter International Inc. a leading global distributor of Network & Security Solutions Electrical & Electronic Solutions and Utility Power Solutions announced that their boards of directors have unanimously approved a definitive merger agreement under which WESCO will acquire Anixter in a transaction valued at approximately $4.5 billion. Anixter's prior agreement to be acquired by

Clayton Dubilier & Rice LLC ("CD&R") has been terminated following CD&R's waiver of its matching rights under the agreement. "The transformational combination of WESCO and Anixter will create a premier electrical and data communications distribution and supply chain services company." Said Mr. John J. Engel WESCO's Chairman President and Chief Executive Officer.

In recent years WESCO has been buying up distributors and other firms to extend its reach and capabilities. In 2019 its Wesco Services division acquired Sylvania Lighting Solutions (SLS) the lighting business of OSRAM Sylvania. The acquisition adds SLS's customer base expanded geographic footprint and project management capabilities to WESCO's offerings.

Company Background

In 1922 Westinghouse Electric formed Westinghouse Electric Supply company to help sell and distribute their products. In 1994 Westinghouse divested their electrical manufacturing division. This opened the door for WESCO management along with a private investment company ? Clayton Dubilier & Rice (CD&R) ? to purchase Westinghouse Electric Supply Company and create WESCO Distribution Inc. WESCO traded on New York Stock Exchange in 1999

HISTORY

WESCO International got its start as a subsidiary of electrical power pioneer Westinghouse Electric Company. George Westinghouse founded the company bearing his name in Pittsburgh in 1886. The company installed the nation's first alternating current power system in Telluride Colorado in 1891. Two years later Westinghouse built the generating system that powered the Chicago World's Fair. The company also was chosen to provide generators for the hydroelectric power station at Niagara Falls.

George Westinghouse was ousted in 1910 after the company was unable to meet its debt obligations. He died four years later at the age of 67. During the next decade the company added the burgeoning radio and appliance markets to its portfolio of electrical distribution and production operations.

In 1922 the firm established Westinghouse Electric Supply Company (WESCO) to distribute power products and appliances. Westinghouse had its share of troubles over the years many of which were caused by ill-advised diversification attempts. These included forays into uranium supply financial services and real estate.

By the 1990s Westinghouse was buried under nearly $10 billion in debt and too busy putting out fires to tend to day-to-day operations properly. Not surprisingly WESCO was caught up in Westinghouse's problems: Sales declined four years in a row and employee turnover was around 25% a year.

Westinghouse embarked on a divestiture program and sold WESCO to investment firm Clayton Dubilier & Rice (CD&R) in 1994 for about $340 million. At the time WESCO had about 250 branch locations. The new owners brought in Roy Haley a veteran insurance and finance executive to turn the ailing business around. Haley tied pay and bonuses to performance and emphasized multisite customers such as contractors and companies with multiple retail industrial

or administrative locations. WESCO grew through acquisitions and in 1995 sales reached $2 billion.

By 1996 the company had added 1000 employees; it operated about 300 distribution branches throughout the world. Sales reached $2.6 billion in 1997 as WESCO continued acquiring complementary companies and formed an alliance with Australian mining and steel company BHP (now BHP Billiton). Managers led a $1.1 billion buyout of the company in 1998 increasing their stake in WESCO from 15% to 33%. Costs related to acquisitions and the buyout caused WESCO to post a loss even though 1998 sales passed the $3 billion mark. The company opened sales offices in the UK Singapore and Mexico.

As it geared up for its IPO in 1999 WESCO bought distributors Industrial Electric Supply Company and Statewide Electrical Supply. The company continued to shop during 2000 adding electrical distributors Orton Utility Supply (Tennessee) Control Corporation of America (Virginia) and KVA Supply Company (Colorado and California).

In 2001 WESCO acquired two distributors (Herning Underground Supply and Alliance Utility Products) that supplied contractors who install gas lighting and communication utility infrastructure in Arizona California Utah and Washington.

The Cypress Group the private-equity firm that helped lead the $1.1 billion management buyout in 1998 sold most of its shares in WESCO in 2004 and 2005. Cypress owned nearly half of WESCO prior to those sales.

WESCO acquired fastener distributor Fastec Industrial and electronics distributor Carlton-Bates in 2005. The following year it bought Communications Supply Corporation (CSC) a distributor of low-voltage network infrastructure and industrial wire and cable products for about $525 million in cash.

In 2007 WESCO acquired J-Mark a supplier of building products which strengthened the company's position in the manufactured housing industry. It also acquired the assets of Monti Electric Supply which provides electricity and furnishes lighting. The purchase gave WESCO a broader market position in the reconstruction of the Gulf Coast region. The company sold a 60% stake in LADD which is a distributor of industrial electrical connectors and accessories to Deutsch Engineered Connecting Devices for approximately $75 million. Proceeds were earmarked to purchase shares of WESCO's common stock.

In 2008 WESCO offered to purchase Industrial Distribution Group (IDG) for about $130 million in cash topping a bid for IDG by Platinum Equity.

Roy Haley stepped aside as CEO in 2009 becoming WESCO's executive chairman. SVP/COO John Engel was promoted to president and CEO as a result.

WESCO acquired TVC Communications for about $246 million in late 2010. The deal expanded WESCO's broadband and telecom distribution network in the Americas and its ties to manufacturers.

EXECUTIVES

Chairman President And Ceo, John J. Engel, age 58, $974,519 total compensation

Svp And Chief Human Resources Officer, Kimberly G. Windrow, age 62, $399,615 total compensation

Svp And Cfo, David S (Dave) Schulz, age 54, $109,375 total compensation

Svp And General Counsel, Diane E. Lazzaris, age 53, $435,096 total compensation

Vice President Of Evening Operations, Joseph Astroth

Vice President, Judy Spicer

Corporate Services Svpr, Michael Wilson

Vice President Information Systems, John Conte

National Sales Manager, Bryan Devito

Sales Vice President, James Blumhardt

Vice President Sales And Marketing, Frank LaPlante

Vice President E Commerce, Dale Kendall

Vice President Tax, Domenic Macioce

Vice President Global Supply Chain And Operations, Hemant Porwal

National Accounts Manager, Angie Rhen

Regional Vice President, Mark Giessing

Vice President Information Technology, Christopher Berardinelli

Vice President Sales And Marketing (broadcast And Entertainment), Mike Vivian

Vice President Information Technology, Anna Vance

Vice President Information Technology Infrastructure, Ken Hawk

Vice President Of Operations And Supply Chains, Ed Jankowski

Vice President And General Manager Utility Group, James Cameron

Board Member, James Singleton

Treasurer, Brian Begg

Board Member, John Morgan

Secretary, Terry Eaton

Auditors: PricewaterhouseCoopers LLP

LOCATIONS

HQ: Wesco International, Inc.
225 West Station Square Drive, Suite 700, Pittsburgh, PA 15219
Phone: 412 454-2200
Web: www.wesco.com

2016 Sales

	$ mil.	% of total
US	5,635	77
Canada	1,394	19
Mexico	62	1
Other countries	243	3
Total	**7,336**	**100**

PRODUCTS/OPERATIONS

2016 Sales

	% of total
Industrial customers	36
Construction	34
Utility	16
Commercial institutional & governmental customers	14
Total	**100**

Selected Services

Collaborative cross-functional cost savings teams;
Consultation on energy-efficient product upgrades
Dedicated on-site support personnel;
Inventory optimization programs including just-in-time delivery and vendor managed inventory;
Safety and product training for customer employee
Technical support for operational and transactional process improvements;

Selected Products

Automation equipment
Ballasts
Boxes
Busways
Cable
Circuit breakers
Connectors
Data communications products
Drives
Electrical products
Fittings
Fixtures
Fuses
Industrial supplies
Light bulbs
Lighting
Lugs
Metallic and nonmetallic conduits
Motor control devices
MRO supplies
Operator interfaces
Panelboards
Patch panels
Premise wiring
Programmable logic controllers
Pushbuttons
Switchboards
Tape
Terminals
Tools
Transformers
Wire
Wire and conduit products

COMPETITORS

Anixter International	HWC
Bearing Distributors	McNaughton-McKay
Border States Electric	Premier Farnell
Consolidated	Rexel Inc.
Electrical	Richardson Electronics
Electro-Wire	SUMMIT Electric Supply
Electrocomponents	Sonepar USA
Graybar Electric	W.W. Grainger

HISTORICAL FINANCIALS

Company Type: Public

Income Statement				FYE: December 31
	REVENUE ($ mil.)	NET INCOME ($ mil.)	NET PROFIT MARGIN	EMPLOYEES
12/19	8,358	223	2.7%	9,500
12/18	8,176	227	2.8%	9,100
12/17	7,679	163	2.1%	9,100
12/16	7,336	101	1.4%	9,000
12/15	7,518	210	2.8%	9,300
Annual Growth	2.7%	1.5%	—	0.5%

2019 Year-End Financials

Debt ratio: 25.58%
Return on equity: 10.15%
Cash ($ mil.): 150
Current ratio: 2.34
Long-term debt ($ mil.): 1,257
No. of shares (mil.): 41
Dividends
Yield: —
Payout: —
Market value ($ mil.): 2,482

	STOCK PRICE ($) FY Close	P/E High/Low		PER SHARE ($) Earnings	Dividends	Book Value
12/19	59.39	12	8	5.14	0.00	54.20
12/18	48.00	14	9	4.82	0.00	47.34
12/17	68.15	22	15	3.38	0.00	45.09
12/16	66.55	31	16	2.10	0.00	41.42
12/15	43.68	16	8	4.18	0.00	42.13
Annual Growth	8.0%	—	—	5.3%	—	6.5%

West Bancorporation, Inc.

West Bancorporation is the holding company for West Bank which serves individuals and small to midsized businesses through about a dozen branches mainly in the Des Moines and Iowa City Iowa areas. Founded in 1893 the bank offers checking savings and money market accounts CDs Visa credit cards and trust services. The bank's lending activities primarily consist of commercial mortgages; construction land and land development loans; and business loans such as revolving lines of credit inventory and accounts receivable financing equipment financing and capital expenditure loans to borrowers in Iowa.

Sales and Marketing

West Bank focuses on small to medium-sized businesses in its local markets. The thinking is that smaller local firms want to develop an exclusive relationship with a single bank.

Financial Performance

The company's revenue has been remarkably consistent year-over-year. It reported $61.2 million in annual revenue for fiscal 2013 after claiming $61.7 million in fiscal 2012 and $64.1 million in fiscal 2011.

Net income has also remained very consistent in recent years. The bank reported net income of $16.8 million for fiscal 2013 after clearing $16 million in fiscal 2012 and $15.27 million in fiscal 2011.

The company's net cash on hand has decreased dramatically in recent fiscal years however mostly as a result of property investments.

Strategy

West Bank has slowly but surely been expanding its territory. The company is working on building a new headquarters building and expanding into Minnesota.

EXECUTIVES

Evp; President West Bank, Brad L. Winterbottom, age 64, $275,000 total compensation
Evp Cfo And Treasurer, Douglas R. (Doug) Gulling, age 67, $275,000 total compensation
President And Ceo, David D. (Dave) Nelson, age 60, $400,000 total compensation
Evp And Chief Risk Officer, Harlee N. Olafson, age 63, $275,000 total compensation
Vice President, Donavon Paulson
Vice President, Nancy Behmer
Senior Vice President, Keith Kurth
Chairman, David R. Milligan
Board Member, Steven Gaer
Board Member, Kaye Lozier
Board Member, Lou Ann Sandburg
Member Board Of Directors, Sean McMurray
Auditors: RSM US LLP

LOCATIONS

HQ: West Bancorporation, Inc.
1601 22nd Street, West Des Moines, IA 50266
Phone: 515 222-2300
Web: www.westbankstrong.com

PRODUCTS/OPERATIONS

2015 Sales

	$ mil.	% of total
Interest		
Loans including fees	52	77
Taxable investment Securities	4	6
Tax-exempt investment Securities	3	5
Federal funds sold	0	-
Noninterest		
Service charges on deposit accounts	2	4
Debit card usage fees	1	3
Trust services	1	2
Revenue from residential mortgage banking	0	-
Increase in cash value of bank-owned life insurance	0	1
Realized investment securities gains net	0	-
Other income	1	2
Total	**68**	**100**

COMPETITORS

BTC Financial	Regions Financial
Bank of America	U.S. Bancorp
Bank of the West	Wells Fargo
MidWestOne	

HISTORICAL FINANCIALS

Company Type: Public

Income Statement				FYE: December 31
	ASSETS ($ mil.)	NET INCOME ($ mil.)	INCOME AS % OF ASSETS	EMPLOYEES
12/19	2,473	28	1.2%	171
12/18	2,296	28	1.2%	163
12/17	2,114	23	1.1%	162
12/16	1,854	23	1.2%	165
12/15	1,748	21	1.2%	174
Annual Growth	9.1%	7.2%	—	(0.4%)

2019 Year-End Financials

Debt ratio: 1.75%
Return on equity: 14.24%
Cash ($ mil.): 37
Current ratio: —
Long-term debt ($ mil.): —
No. of shares (mil.): 16
Dividends
Yield: 3.2%
Payout: 47.9%
Market value ($ mil.): 420

	STOCK PRICE ($) FY Close	P/E High/Low		PER SHARE ($) Earnings	Dividends	Book Value
12/19	25.63	15	11	1.74	0.83	12.93
12/18	19.09	15	10	1.74	0.78	11.72
12/17	25.15	20	15	1.41	0.71	10.98
12/16	24.70	17	11	1.42	0.67	10.25
12/15	19.75	15	12	1.35	0.62	9.49
Annual Growth	6.7%	—	—	6.6%	7.6%	8.1%

WestAmerica Bancorporation

Annie get your checkbook? Maybe not as wild as Buffalo Bill's West but Westamerica Bancorporation still shoots high with its subsidiary Westamerica Bank. The bank operates through 80 branches in Northern and Central California. It offers individuals and businesses such standard fare as checking and savings accounts as well as online banking loans and credits and credit cards. It focuses on the banking needs of small businesses; business loans and commercial mortgages together account for more than three-quarters of the company's loan portfolio. Westamerica Bank was chartered in 1884

Operations

Westamerica Bancorporation provides a full range of banking services to individual and corporate customers through its subsidiary bank Westamerica Bank. The bank's subsidiary Community Banker Services Corporation provides the company and its other subsidiaries with data processing and various support services. Its loan portfolio is composed of commercial real estate (over 50% of total) consumer installment and other (around 25%) commercial (approximately 20%) and residential real estate (about 5%).

Overall Westamerica generate more than 75% of its revenue from interest income roughly 45% from debt securities and about 30% from loans. The rest of the company's revenue comes from non-interest income.

Geographic Reach

California-based Westamerica has around 80 branches in more than 20 Northern and Central California counties. Westamerica owns 30 branch office locations and one administrative facility and leases more than 55 facilities.

Financial Performance

The company's net income was $80.4 million comparing to 2019 with 2018 net income increased by $8.8 million. Net interest and loan fee (FTE) income increased $6.0 million due to a higher net yield on earning assets and higher average balances of investments partially offset by lower average balances of interest-bearing cash and loans.

Cash held by the company at the end of 2019 was $373.4 million. Cash provided by operations was $80.7 million while cash used for investing and financing activities were $22.3 million and $105.3 million respectively. Main uses for cash were purchases of debt securities available for sale and net change in deposits.

Strategy

The company's long-term strategy includes maximizing checking and savings deposits as these types of deposits are lower-cost and less sensitive to changes in interest rates compared to time deposits. The average 2019 volume of checking and savings deposits were 96 % of average total deposits. The company's strategy includes building the value of its deposit base by building balances of lower-costing deposits and avoiding reliance on higher-costing time deposits.

EXECUTIVES

Svp Operations And Systems, Dennis R. Hansen, $130,008 total compensation
Chairman President And Ceo, David L. Payne, $371,000 total compensation
Svp And Cfo, Robert A. Thorson, $149,000 total compensation
Svp Banking Division, David L. Robinson, $150,000 total compensation
Svp Credit Administrator, Russell Rizzardi, $120,960 total compensation
Vice President Accounting Manager, Glen Yasaki
Assistant Vice President And Commercial Loan Adjustment Officer, Christie Marriott
Vice President Risk Management, Marcie Lewis
Senior Vice President, Joseph Dietzen
Executive Vice President Strategy And Development, Jennifer Finger
Vice President Of Sales, Scott Tucker

Vice President And Manager Community Relations, Debbie Friesen
Regional Vice President, Chad Means
Board Member, Catherine Macmillan
Board Of Directors, Patrick Lynch
Board Member, Etta Allen
Auditors: Crowe LLP

LOCATIONS

HQ: WestAmerica Bancorporation
1108 Fifth Avenue, San Rafael, CA 94901
Phone: 707 863-6000
Web: www.westamerica.com

PRODUCTS/OPERATIONS

2016 Sales

	$ mil.	% of total
Interest and Fee Income:		
Loans	69	38
Investment securities available for sale	34	19
Investment securities held to maturity	30	17
Noninterest Income:		
Service charges on deposit accounts	20	12
Merchant processing services	6	4
Debit card fees	6	4
Other service fees	2	1
Trust fees	2	1
ATM processing fees	2	1
Financial services commissions	0	-
Other	4	3
Total	**180**	**100**

COMPETITORS

Bank of America	MUFG Americas Holdings
Citigroup	Mechanics Bank
Comerica	U.S. Bancorp
First Republic (CA)	Wells Fargo
JPMorgan Chase	Western Alliance

HISTORICAL FINANCIALS

Company Type: Public

Income Statement · FYE: December 31

	ASSETS ($ mil.)	NET INCOME ($ mil.)	INCOME AS % OF ASSETS	EMPLOYEES
12/19	5,619	80	1.4%	737
12/18	5,568	71	1.3%	762
12/17	5,513	50	0.9%	785
12/16	5,366	58	1.1%	783
12/15	5,168	58	1.1%	813
Annual Growth	2.1%	8.2%	—	(2.4%)

2019 Year-End Financials

Debt ratio: —	No. of shares (mil.): 27
Return on equity: 11.94%	Dividends
Cash ($ mil.): 373	Yield: 2.4%
Current ratio: —	Payout: 55.8%
Long-term debt ($ mil.): —	Market value ($ mil.): 1,834

	STOCK PRICE ($) FY Close	P/E High/Low	PER SHARE ($) Earnings	Dividends	Book Value
12/19	67.77	23 19	2.98	1.63	27.03
12/18	55.68	24 20	2.67	1.60	23.03
12/17	59.55	34 26	1.89	1.57	22.34
12/16	62.93	28 18	2.29	1.56	21.67
12/15	46.75	23 18	2.30	1.53	20.85
Annual Growth	9.7%	— —	6.7%	1.6%	6.7%

Western Alliance Bancorporation

Western Alliance Bancorporation and its flagship Western Alliance Bank (WAB) have an alliance with several bank brands in the West operating as the Alliance Bank of Arizona; Bank of Nevada; First Independent Bank (Nevada); as well as Bridge Bank and Torrey Pines Bank which are both located across California. Combined the banks operate nearly 50 branches that provide standard consumer and business deposit and loan products. About half of the Western Alliance's loan portfolio is made up of commercial and industrial loans while another 40% is made up of commercial real estate loans. It also makes land development loans and consumer residential mortgages and other lines of credit.

Operations

Western Alliance focuses on commercial lending. About 46% of the bank's loan portfolio consisted of commercial and industrial loans at the end of 2015 while another 39% was made up of commercial real estate loans. The bank also had construction and land development loans (10% of loan assets) residential mortgages (3%) commercial leases (1%) and consumer loans (less than 1%).

More than 90% of the bank's revenue comes from interest income. About 86% of its total revenue came from loan interest during 2015 while another 9% came from interest or dividends on investment securities. The remainder of its revenue came from service charges and fees (2% of revenue) card income (1%) and other miscellaneous sources.

Geographic Reach

Western Alliance's 40 branches and seven loan offices are spread across Arizona Nevada and California as well as Boston Dallas and Reston Virginia. At the end of 2015 its loan business was concentrated in the Los Angeles San Francisco San Jose Phoenix Tuscon Reno and Las Vegas metropolitan areas.

Sales and Marketing

The bank serves local businesses real estate developers and investors not-for-profit organizations and consumers. It specializes in lending to such customers operating in the healthcare professional services manufacturing and distribution resorts and timeshares technology and startups municipalities and local governments non-profit and renewable energy markets. Some of its clients (as of early 2016) include Cutter Aviation FNF Construction Hollenbeck Palms New American Funding and Signature Healthcare Services.

Western Alliance spent $2.89 million on marketing in 2015 up from $2.30 million and $2.58 million in 2014 and 2013 respectively.

Financial Performance

Western Alliance's annual revenues have risen nearly 70% since 2011 as its loan business has swelled. Meanwhile the bank's annual profits have ballooned more than five-fold as its credit portfolio's credit quality has improved with higher property valuations in the strengthened economy.

The group's revenue jumped 26% to $555 million during 2015 mostly thanks to new loan business more than half of which was obtained from the Bridge Bank acquisition which spurred more interest income for the year. Non-interest income especially service charges and lending-related fees grew by double digits during the year also thanks to the acquisition as well as from more organic deposit business growth.

Strong revenue growth and a continued decline in credit loss provisions in 2015 drove Western Alliance's net income up by 31% to $194 million for the year. The company's operating cash levels climbed 30% to $213 million mostly thanks to the rise in cash earnings.

Strategy

Western Alliance Bancorporation looks to expand its branch network and selectively acquire other banks to boost its loan and deposit business and extend its geographic reach. The bank may also buy other financial services businesses to bolster its line of service offerings.

Mergers and Acquisitions

In June 2015 Western Alliance bought $13 billion-asset Bridge Capital Holdings along with its 48 Bridge Bank branches in California Arizona and Nevada in a deal worth about $425 million. The purchase brought expertise in technology and international banking among other areas and expands Western Alliance's market into Northern California.

EXECUTIVES

Evp And Chief Credit Officer, Robert R. (Bob) McAuslan, age 67

Chairman And Ceo, Robert G. Sarver, age 59, $830,000 total compensation

Evp And Cfo, Dale M. Gibbons, age 59, $400,000 total compensation

Evp Northern California Administration And President And Ceo Bridge Bank Division, Daniel P. (Dan) Myers, age 59, $212,885 total compensation

Evp Southern Nevada Administration And Ceo Bank Of Nevada Division, John Guedry

Evp And Cio, John P. Peckham

Evp California Administration And President Torrey Pines Bank, Gerald A. (Gary) Cady, age 65, $360,000 total compensation

Evp And Chief Risk Officer, Patricia A. Taylor

Evp And General Counsel, Randall S. Theisen

Evp And Coo, Jim Haught

Evp Arizona Administration And Ceo Alliance Bank Of Arizona, Don Garner

Senior Vice President, Seth Davis

Vice President, Jennifer Holyoak

Senior Credit Analyst Vice President Warehouse Lending, Bryan Brooks

Chief Human Resource Officer Executive Vice President, Barbara Kennedy

Vp Of Relationship Manager Of Bank Of Nevada, Melanie Maviglia

Evp Bank Of Nevada, Bill Oakley

Board Member, Cary Mack

Board Member, Sung Sohn

Board Member, Donald Snyder

Board Member, Marianne Johnson

Board Member, William Boyd

Auditors: RSM US LLP

LOCATIONS

HQ: Western Alliance Bancorporation
One E. Washington Street, Suite 1400, Phoenix, AZ 85004
Phone: 602 389-3500
Web: www.westernalliancebancorporation.com

PRODUCTS/OPERATIONS

2015 Sales

	$ mil.	% of total
Interest income		
Loans including fees	476	86
Investment securities	37	7
Dividends	10	2
Other	0	-
Non-interest income		
Service charges and fees	14	2
Income from bank owned life insurance	3	1
Card income	3	1
Other	7	1
Total	**554**	**100**

Selected Services

Business Checking & Savings
Business Loans & Credit
Card Services
International Banking
Personal Banking
Treasury Management

COMPETITORS

Bank of America	PacWest Bancorp
Bank of the West	U.S. Bancorp
Desert Schools FCU	Wells Fargo
First Banks	Westamerica
MUFG Americas Holdings	Zions Bancorporation

HISTORICAL FINANCIALS

Company Type: Public

Income Statement   FYE: December 31

	ASSETS ($ mil.)	NET INCOME ($ mil.)	INCOME AS % OF ASSETS	EMPLOYEES
12/19	26,821	499	1.9%	1,835
12/18	23,109	435	1.9%	1,787
12/17	20,329	325	1.6%	1,725
12/16	17,200	259	1.5%	1,557
12/15	14,275	194	1.4%	1,446
Annual Growth	17.1%	26.6%	—	6.1%

2019 Year-End Financials

Debt ratio: 1.47%	No. of shares (mil.): 102
Return on equity: 17.73%	Dividends
Cash ($ mil.): 434	Yield: 0.8%
Current ratio: —	Payout: 10.5%
Long-term debt ($ mil.): —	Market value ($ mil.): 5,844

	STOCK PRICE ($) FY Close	P/E High/Low	Earnings	PER SHARE ($) Dividends	Book Value
12/19	57.00	12 8	4.84	0.50	29.42
12/18	39.49	15 9	4.14	0.00	24.90
12/17	56.62	19 14	3.10	0.00	21.14
12/16	48.71	20 11	2.50	0.00	18.00
12/15	35.86	19 12	2.03	0.00	15.44
Annual Growth	12.3%	— —	24.3%	—	17.5%

Western Asset Mortgage Capital Corp

Auditors: PricewaterhouseCoopers, LLP

LOCATIONS

HQ: Western Asset Mortgage Capital Corp
385 East Colorado Boulevard, Pasadena, CA 91101
Phone: 626 844-9400
Web: www.westernassetmcc.com

HISTORICAL FINANCIALS

Company Type: Public

Income Statement   FYE: December 31

	ASSETS ($ mil.)	NET INCOME ($ mil.)	INCOME AS % OF ASSETS	EMPLOYEES
12/19	5,160	70	1.4%	—
12/18	4,497	26	0.6%	—
12/17	3,886	85	2.2%	—
12/16	3,156	(25)	—	—
12/15	3,414	(9)	—	—
Annual Growth	10.9%	—	—	—

2019 Year-End Financials

Debt ratio: 32.45%	No. of shares (mil.): 53
Return on equity: 13.25%	Dividends
Cash ($ mil.): 31	Yield: 12.0%
Current ratio: —	Payout: 172.2%
Long-term debt ($ mil.): —	Market value ($ mil.): 553

	STOCK PRICE ($) FY Close	P/E High/Low	Earnings	PER SHARE ($) Dividends	Book Value
12/19	10.33	8 6	1.37	1.24	10.55
12/18	8.34	19 14	0.61	1.24	10.45
12/17	9.95	5 5	2.03	1.24	11.15
12/16	10.07	— —	(0.61)	1.38	10.27
12/15	10.22	— —	(0.25)	2.49	12.21
Annual Growth	0.3%		—	(16.0%)	(3.6%)

Western Digital Corp

Western Digital is a leading developer manufacturer and provider of data storage devices and solutions that address the evolving needs of information technology ("IT") and the infrastructure that enables the proliferation of data in virtually every industry. The company makes hard-disk drives (HDDs) which record store and recall volumes of data and fast-growing solid-state drives (SSDs) known as flash drives used in many mobile devices. Drives for PCs account for a major portion of Western Digital's sales although the company also makes devices used in servers cloud computing data centers and home entertainment products such as set-top boxes and video game consoles as well as mobile phones. The company sells to manufacturers retailers and distributors and generates around half of sales from the Asia/Pacific region.

Operations

Western Digital reports its sales in terms of end markets. The company's biggest market nearly 45% of sales is client devices such as PCs smartphones gaming gadgets and security equipment. Data center devices capacity and performance enterprise HDDs enterprise SSDs data center software and systems account for more than 35% of sales and client solutions which are removable products hard drive content devices and flash content devices generate about 20% of sales.

The company markets its products primarily under the Western Digital G-Technology San-Disk and WD brands.

Sales of HDD products account for about 55% of revenue and flash-based products account for the rest.

Geographic Reach

Headquartered in San Jose California Western Digital's largest market is Asia where most electronics are produced. China alone accounts for about a quarter of sales and Hong Kong accounts for around 15%. The US supplies nearly 30% of revenue while the EMEA region accounts for over 15%.

Western Digital has manufacturing facilities in the US as well as in China Japan Malaysia the Philippines and Thailand; it has sales offices worldwide. The company's research and development facilities are in the US Malaysia Thailand India and Israel.

Sales and Marketing

Western Digital sells to OEMs as well as through distributors and retailers. The company's 10 biggest customers account for more than 40% of revenue. The company relies heavily on one customer: Kingston Technology Company which accounts for some 10% of Western Digital's accounts receivable.

The company's advertising costs were $93 million $107 million and $112 million in 2020 2019 and 2018 respectively.

Financial Performance

Western Digital's revenue has had a bumpy path over the past five years capped by a steep decline in 2019 from 2018.

The company's sales rose about 1% from $16.6 billion in 2019 to $16.7 billion in 2020. The increase was primarily due to lower sales volume in client devices and client solutions segments.

The company suffered another net loss ($250 million) in 2020 but it has undoubtedly improved from the previous year ($754 million). This was primarily due to a higher operating income and lower income tax.

Western Digital posted a loss of $724 million in 2019 compared to a profit of $675 million in 2018. While the company had lower costs in 2018 they were higher as a percentage of revenue than in 2018 resulting in the net loss.

The company had about $3 billion in cash and equivalents in 2020 compared to $3.5 billion the year before. In 2020 cash from operations generated $824 million and investing activities provided $278 million. Financing activities used $1.5 billion. Main cash uses in 2020 were for dividends paid debt repayment.

Western Digital has over $10.2 billion in debt in 2020 an amount that could have a negative impact on its liquidity restrict its operations and ability to react to business changes and increase its vulnerability to industry and economic slowdowns.

Strategy

Western Digital's overall strategy is to leverage its technology innovation and execution capabilities to be an industry-leading and broad-based developer manufacturer and provider of storage devices and solutions that support the infrastructure that has enabled the unabated proliferation of data. The company believes that it is the only company in the world with large-scale capabilities to develop and manufacture a portfolio of integrated data storage solutions that are based on both rotating magnetic and flash memory technologies. Western Digital strives to successfully execute its strategy through the following foundational elements to deliver the best outcome for customers partners investors and employees:

Technology Leadership: The company continues to innovate and develop advanced technologies across platforms for both HDD and flash to deliver timely new products and solutions to meet growing demands for scale performance and cost - efficiency in the market.

Broad Product Portfolio: Western Digital leverages its capabilities in firmware software and systems in both HDD and flash to deliver compelling and differentiated integrated storage solutions to customers that offer the best combinations of performance cost power consumption form factor quality and reliability while creating new use cases for solutions in emerging markets.

Operational Excellence: It is focused on delivering the best value for its customers in the data center client and consumer markets through a relentless focus on appropriately scaling its operations across both HDD and flash technologies to efficiently support business growth achieving best in class cost quality and cycle-time maintaining industry leading manufacturing capabilities and having a competitive advantage in supply-chain management.

Mergers and Acquisitions

Western Digital has long used acquisitions to add new product lines and extend its geographic reach.

In late 2019 Western Digital acquired Kazan Networks a provider of technology for data centers to expand its data infrastructure offerings. Kazan's technologies widened Western Digital's products for disaggregated data infrastructure and helped speed its use of non-volatile memory express (NVMe) platforms. The purchase price of this acquisition was $22 million in cash with net assets acquired primarily consisting of IPR&D of $8 million and $14 million allocated to Goodwill.

EXECUTIVES

Evp Memory Technology, Siva Sivaram

Cto, Martin Fink, age 55

President And Ceo, Stephen D. (Steve) Milligan, age 57, $1,050,000 total compensation

Evp Silicon Operations, Manish Bhatia

President And Coo, Michael D. Cordano, age 56, $725,000 total compensation

Evp And Cfo, Mark P. Long, age 53, $500,000 total compensation

Evp And Chief Human Resources Officer, Jacqueline M. DeMaria, age 58

Evp Chief Legal Officer And Secretary, Michael C. Ray, age 53, $500,000 total compensation

Vice President Facilities Asia, Shahzad Mahmud

Vice President Gm Of Manufacturing Head Operations, Norm Armour

Executive Vice President Andchief Technology Officer, Steven Campbell

Senior Vice President And General Manager Data Center Systems, Phil Bullinger

Vice President Engineering Director Engineering, Gerardo Bertero

Vice President Information Technology, Terry Dembitz

Vice President Platform Engineering, Kurt Chan

Svp And Cto (fio) Vp And Senior Fellow (sndk)(wdc), Pankaj Mehra

Engineering Vice President Development, Taro Oike

Engineering Vice President Development, Kris Schouterden

Chairman, Matthew E. (Matt) Massengill, age 59

Board Member, Paula Price

Board Member, Kathleen Cote

Auditors: KPMG LLP

LOCATIONS

HQ: Western Digital Corp
5601 Great Oaks Parkway, San Jose, CA 95119
Phone: 408 717-6000
Web: www.westerndigital.com

2019 Sales

	$ mil.	% of total
Asia		
China	3,861	23
Hong Kong	3,122	19
Rest of Asia	2,116	13
US	3,602	22
Europe Middle East & Africa	3,109	19
Other	759	4
Total	**16,569**	**100**

PRODUCTS/OPERATIONS

2019 Sales by Market

	$ mil.	% of total
Client Devices	8,095	49
Data Center Devices and Solutions	5,038	30
Client Solutions	3,436	21
Total	**15,569**	**100**

2019 Sales by Form Factor

	$ mil.	% of total
HDD	8,746	53
Flash-based	7,823	47
Total	**16,569**	**100**

Selected Products

Portable Storage
Personal Cloud Storage
External Storage
Internal Hard Drive Storage
Internal SSD Storage
Network Attached Storage
Internal Hard Drives for Business
Surveillance Storage

COMPETITORS

Dell	Samsung Electronics
Fujitsu	Sanmina
Intel	Seagate Technology
Micron Technology	TEAC
SK Hynix	Toshiba
SMART Modular Technologies	

HISTORICAL FINANCIALS

Company Type: Public

Income Statement
FYE: July 3

	REVENUE ($ mil.)	NET INCOME ($ mil.)	NET PROFIT MARGIN	EMPLOYEES
07/20*	16,736	(250)	—	63,800
06/19	16,569	(754)	—	61,800
06/18	20,647	675	3.3%	71,600
06/17	19,093	397	2.1%	68,000
07/16	12,994	242	1.9%	72,878
Annual Growth	6.5%	—	—	(3.3%)

*Fiscal year change

2020 Year-End Financials

Debt ratio: 37.31%
Return on equity: (-2.52%)
Cash ($ mil.): 3,048
Current ratio: 2.05
Long-term debt ($ mil.): 9,289
No. of shares (mil.): 302
Dividends
  Yield: 0.0%
  Payout: —
Market value ($ mil.): 12,817

	STOCK PRICE ($) FY Close	P/E High/Low	PER SHARE ($) Earnings	Dividends	Book Value
07/20*	42.44	— —	(0.84)	1.50	31.63
06/19	47.55	— —	(2.58)	2.00	33.79
06/18	77.41	47 34	2.20	2.00	38.96
06/17	88.60	68 31	1.34	2.00	38.84
07/16	46.47	86 35	1.00	2.00	39.24
Annual Growth	(2.2%)	— —	—	(6.9%)	(5.3%)

*Fiscal year change

Western New England Bancorp Inc

Westfield Financial is the holding company for Westfield Bank which serves western Massachusetts' Hampden County and surrounding areas from more than 20 branch locations. Founded in 1853 the bank has traditionally been a community-oriented provider of retail deposit accounts and loans but it is placing more emphasis on serving commercial and industrial clients. Commercial real estate loans account for approximately 45% of the company's loan portfolio and business loans are more than 25%. The bank also makes a smaller number of consumer and home equity loans. In 2016 Westfield Financial merged with Chicopee Bancorp the holding company of Chicopee Savings Bank (another bank serving Hampden County).

EXECUTIVES

Chief Risk Officer And Senior Vice President Of The Company And The Bank, Leo R Sagan
Avp Residential Lending, Michael Laga
Assistant Vice President Financial Services, Libiszewski Darlene
Auditors: Wolf & Company, P.C.

LOCATIONS

HQ: Western New England Bancorp Inc
141 Elm Street, Westfield, MA 01085
Phone: 413 568-1911
Web: www.westfieldbank.com

COMPETITORS

Bank of America
Citizens Financial Group
Sovereign Bank
TD Bank USA

HISTORICAL FINANCIALS

Company Type: Public

Income Statement
FYE: December 31

	ASSETS ($ mil.)	NET INCOME ($ mil.)	INCOME AS % OF ASSETS	EMPLOYEES
12/19	2,181	13	0.6%	340
12/18	2,118	16	0.8%	320
12/17	2,083	12	0.6%	317
12/16	2,076	4	0.2%	310
12/15	1,339	5	0.4%	195
Annual Growth	13.0%	23.6%	—	14.9%

2019 Year-End Financials

Debt ratio: 9.42%
Return on equity: 5.69%
Cash ($ mil.): 23
Current ratio: —
Long-term debt ($ mil.): —
No. of shares (mil.): 26
Dividends
  Yield: 2.0%
  Payout: 39.2%
Market value ($ mil.): 256

	STOCK PRICE ($) FY Close	P/E High/Low	PER SHARE ($) Earnings	Dividends	Book Value
12/19	9.63	20 17	0.51	0.20	8.74
12/18	10.04	20 16	0.57	0.16	8.35
12/17	10.90	27 22	0.41	0.12	8.11
12/16	9.35	38 30	0.24	0.03	7.85
12/15	8.40	25 22	0.33	0.12	7.63
Annual Growth	3.5%	— —	11.5%	13.6%	3.4%

Westlake Chemical Corp

Westlake Chemical produces petrochemicals and plastics. Its plastics offerings include polyvinyl chloride (PVC) and polyethylene both of which are common in packaging products and grocery bags. Its PVC pipe products are sold under the NAPCO Pipe & Fittings and Royal Building Products brands. Westlake also produces the chlorine used in PVC as well as caustic soda. Its petrochemicals include ethylene ethyl benzene and styrene?which are building blocks in plastics. Westlake produces about 40 billion pounds of product each year and is the second largest producer of both PVC and chlor-alkali in the world. TTWF which is controlled by the Chao family (Westlake's founders) owns around 80% of Westlake. The US accounts for about 70% of company's total sales.

Operations

Westlake Chemical operates in two business segments: Vinyls and Olefins.

Westlake's Vinyls segment produces polyvinyl chloride (PVC) vinyl chloride monomer (VCM) ethylene dichloride (EDC) chlor-alkali (chlorine and caustic soda) and ethylene. The company is the second largest chlor-alkali producer in the world and can produce 2.3 billion pounds of chlorinated derivative products and 7.6 billion pounds of VCM each year. Its PVC products are

fabricated into automotive sealants cable sheathing pipe house components and film and sheet products. Caustic soda is used in pulp and paper manufacturing chemicals and neutralization.

The company's Vinyls segment accounts for nearly 80% of sales. The Olefins segment makes polyethylene styrene monomer and ethylene co-products used in the company's polyethylene styrene and VCM operations. The company's primary ethylene co-products are chemical grade propylene crude butadiene pyrolysis gasoline and hydrogen. Olefins generate more than 20% of Westlake's revenue.

Geographic Reach

Houston Texas-based Westlake Chemical has more than 50 manufacturing facilities: roughly 30 are in the US; six in each of Canada and Germany; two each in China and France; and one each in India Italy Japan Mexico Spain Taiwan and Vietnam. The US accounts for around 70% of revenue while Canada and Germany each provide more than 5%. The remainder is garnered from China Italy and Taiwan.

Westlake's olefin production activity is clustered around Lake Charles Louisiana. Westlake's sites in Lake Charles include two Westlake Chemical OpCo-owned ethylene plants two polyethylene plants and a styrene monomer plant. The company also has three polyethylene plants and a specialty polyethylene wax plant at its Longview Site. Westlake has a 22.8% limited partner interest in ethylene production and pipeline company OpCo which spun off from Westlake following the latter's IPO.

Sales and Marketing

Westlake Chemical's products are sold directly to polyethylene customers (some of the largest producers of film and flexible packaging in the US). It also sells ethylene and ethylene co-products to external customers.

The company has the capacity to use all its chlorine internally to produce vinyl chloride monomer (VCM) and ethylene dichloride (EDC) most of which is used in turn to produce polyvinyl chloride (PVC). It sells substantially all its caustic soda production to external customers. Most of its North American and Asian-produced PVC is used internally in the production of building products. The remainder of Westlake's PVC including the PVC produced at its European facilities is sold to downstream fabricators and the international markets.

No single customer accounts for more than 10% of the company's sales.

Financial Performance

Westlake Chemical has nearly doubled its revenue since 2014 thanks largely to its 2016 acquisition of North American chemical and building products manufacturer Axiall which greatly bolstered sales volume in 2017 and made Westlake the world's third largest chlor-alkali and PVC producer. The company's net earnings have seen five-year growth of about 50% owing to the Axiall acquisition and a hefty income tax benefit in 2017 caused by US tax reform. Net income declined every other year since 2014.

Westlake's revenue declined 6% in 2019 to end the year at $8.1 billion primarily due to lower sales prices for lower sales prices for its major products and lower sales volumes for PVC resin partially offset by higher sales volumes for polyethylene styrene and PVC compounds.

Net income fell 55% to $462 million compared to its previous year primarily due to lower sales prices for our major products resulting from international trade uncertainties and slower global economic growth partially offset by lower purchased ethylene feedstock and fuel costs and a lower effective income tax rate.

The company's cash fell $750 million to $775 million in 2018. Operations provided $1.3 billion. Financing activities contributed $630 million?primarily for dividends paid. Investing activities used $2 billion primarily for capital expenditures.

Strategy

Westlake Chemical has adopted a two-pronged growth strategy involving both organic and acquisitive expansion. Since 2013 the company has invested more than $7.4 billion in capital projects and acquisitions.

The company focuses on plant acquisitions new construction and internal expansion. It evaluate each expansion project on the basis of its ability to produce sustained returns in excess of its cost of capital and its ability to improve efficiency or reduce operating costs.

In 2019 the company acquired NAKAN for $249 million; the compounding company's offerings are used in the automotive building and medical industries. The deal expanded Westlake's compounding capabilities through NAKAN's eight production facilities in China France Germany Italy Japan Mexico Spain Vietnam and the US.

Mergers and Acquisitions

In 2019 Westlake Chemical acquired NAKAN a global compounding solution business for about $249 million. NAKAN's products are used in a wide-variety of applications including in the automotive building and construction and medical industries. With this combination Westlake's compounding business now has facilities worldwide in China France Germany Italy Japan Mexico Spain the United States and Vietnam as well as a world-class research facility in France and several application laboratories.

HISTORY

Westlake came into being in 1986 when T.T. Chao bought a polyethylene plant near Lake Charles Louisiana from Occidental Petroleum. Over the years the company has acquired or constructed about 20 more. The founding Chao family took Westlake Chemical public in 2004 with the hope of paying down some of the debt accumulated from those acquisitions

In 2008 a joint venture between Westlake and Chinese chemical company INEOS began producing some 33 million pounds of PVC film each year. Westlake owns 59% of the Suzhou Huasu Plastics.

Westlake made several changes to its PVC production in 2009. Early in the year the company acquired a PVC pipe plant in Janesville Wisconsin and opened its new PVC plant in Yucca Arizona to expand its operations. However to reduce costs Westlake closed its facilities in Bristol Indiana later that year and moved that production to its other PVC operations.

In 2010 Westlake purchased a 50% stake in Cypress Interstate Pipeline LLC from Kinder Morgan Energy Partners. The 104-mile pipeline supplies natural gas liquid feedstocks to Westlake's Lake Charles Louisiana petrochemical complex. The pipeline will continue to be operated by Kinder Morgan under a contract.

Westlake also made a move in 2012 to strengthen its presence in Asia by opening a Singapore office. Its operations there will focus on serving its existing customers and seeking new opportunities for growth in the region.

In early 2012 the company made an all cash offer for Atlanta-based Georgia Gulf one of North America's largest manufacturers of vinyl construction products. However Georgia Gulf rejected the $1.03 billion takeover bid as being financially inadequate and adopted a stockholder rights plan also called a poison pill that allows existing shareholders to buy stock at a discount when a suitor acquires more than 10% of outstanding shares. Westlake wanted to combine its resin and pipe production with Georgia Gulf's chemicals and vinyl products but later that year withdrew its proposal to buy the company.

The company has expanded capacity to meet growing demand. In 2013 it opened a new chloralkali plant in Greismar Louisiana that doubles Westlake's chlor-alkali production capacity. It also beefed up the ethylene capacity at its Lake Charles facility in 2013 (increasing the ethane-based ethylene capacity of the unit and its conversion to 100% ethane feedstock capability). It is also upgrading ethylene production facilities at Calvert City Kentucky.

In 2013 Westlake bought CertainTeed's Pipe and Foundation Group a leading producer of PVC pipe and fittings for municipal water well mining agriculture and irrigation applications for $175 million. It also acquired technologies and intellectual property for the production of a number of specialized products including Certa-Lok restrained joint pipe and Yelomine branded products.

EXECUTIVES

President And Ceo, Albert Chao, age 70, $979,667 total compensation
Svp Cfo And Treasurer, M. Steven (Steve) Bender, age 63, $520,833 total compensation
Vp Manufacturing, Andrew Kenner, age 55, $377,167 total compensation
Svp Vinyls, Robert F. Buesinger, age 63, $406,333 total compensation
Svp Olefins, Lawrence E. (Skip) Teel, age 62
Senior Vice President Global Learning, Randy Richard
Vice President Logistics Information Technology And Business Process Improvement, Tom Janssens
Vice President Human Resources, M Joel Gray
Vice President Matrix Offshore Services, Subhakar Reddy
Chairman, James Y. Chao, age 72
Vice President And Treasurer, Jeff Holy
Auditors: PricewaterhouseCoopers LLP

LOCATIONS

HQ: Westlake Chemical Corp
2801 Post Oak Boulevard, Suite 600, Houston, TX 77056
Phone: 713 960-9111
Web: www.westlake.com

2018 Sales

	$ mil.	% of total
US	6,114	71
Germany	500	6
Canada	649	7
China	155	2
Italy	105	1
Taiwan	102	1
Other countries	1,010	12
Total	**8,635**	**100**

PRODUCTS/OPERATIONS

2018 Sales

	$ mil.	% of total
Olefins		
Polyethylene	1,519	18
Feedstock styrene & other	500	6
Vinyls		
PVC caustic soda & other	5,359	62
Building products	1,257	14
Total	**8,635**	**100**

Selected Products

Olefins
　Ethylene
　Polyethylene
　Styrene
Vinyls
　Caustic soda
　Chlorine
　PVC
　VCM

COMPETITORS

BASF SE	J-M Manufacturing
Chevron Phillips Chemical	LyondellBasell
	Mexichem
Diamond Plastics	NOVA Chemicals
Dow Chemical	Occidental Chemical
ExxonMobil Chemical	Oxy Vinyls
Formosa Plastics	Shell Chemicals
Formosa Plastics USA	Shintech

HISTORICAL FINANCIALS

Company Type: Public

Income Statement

FYE: December 31

	REVENUE ($ mil.)	NET INCOME ($ mil.)	NET PROFIT MARGIN	EMPLOYEES
12/19	8,118	421	5.2%	9,430
12/18	8,635	996	11.5%	8,870
12/17	8,041	1,304	16.2%	8,800
12/16	5,075	398	7.9%	8,870
12/15	4,463	646	14.5%	4,225
Annual Growth	**16.1%**	**(10.2%)**	**—**	**22.2%**

2019 Year-End Financials

Debt ratio: 25.98%
Return on equity: 7.35%
Cash ($ mil.): 728
Current ratio: 2.21
Long-term debt ($ mil.): 3,445

No. of shares (mil.): 128
Dividends
　Yield: 1.4%
　Payout: 31.5%
Market value ($ mil.): 9,006

	STOCK PRICE ($) FY Close	P/E High/Low		PER SHARE ($) Earnings	Dividends	Book Value
12/19	70.15	25	17	3.25	1.03	45.64
12/18	66.17	16	8	7.62	0.92	43.51
12/17	106.53	11	6	10.05	0.80	37.66
12/16	55.99	19	13	3.06	0.74	27.33
12/15	54.32	16	10	4.86	0.69	25.08
Annual Growth	**6.6%**	**—**	**—**	**(9.6%)**	**10.3%**	**16.1%**

WestRock Co

WestRock Co (WestRock) is one of the leading providers of paper and packaging solutions. It manufactures and distributes containerboard and paperboard products such as folding cartons coated paperboard bleached paperboard coated recycled paperboard retail displays partitions and protective packaging and pulp products. It also provides kraft paper and pulp recycled linerboard coated white top linerboard and corrugated containers. The company's products find their applications in various industries such as retail food healthcare beverage commercial printing tobacco home and garden. Its operations are spread across North America South America Europe Asia and Australia.

Operations

WestRock operates through three segments: Corrugated Packaging Consumer Packaging and Land and Development.

Through its Corrugated Packaging Segment (generates about 65% of the company's revenue) operates an integrated corrugated packaging system that manufactures primarily containerboard corrugated sheets corrugated packaging and preprinted linerboard for sale to consumer and industrial products manufacturers and corrugated box manufacturers. The company produces a full range of high-quality corrugated containers designed to protect ship store promote and display products made to customers' merchandising and distribution specifications.

Through its Consumer Packaging segment (generates over 35% of the company's revenue) the company operates integrated virgin and recycled fiber paperboard mills and consumer packaging converting operations which convert items such as folding and beverage cartons interior partitions inserts and labels.

Through its Land and Development Segment the company maximizes the value of the various real estate holdings it owns that are concentrated in the Charleston South Carolina region.

Geographic Reach

The Georgia-based WestRock operate locations in North America including the majority of U.S. states South America Europe Asia and Australia.

Vast majority of WestRock's total sales comes from North America.

Sales and Marketing

The company serves over 15000 customers including over 150 customers that buy at least $1 million from each of the company's segments.

The company markets its products primarily through its own sales force. WestRock also markets a number of our products through independent sales representatives independent distributors or both.

Financial Performance

In 2019 the company had a revenue of around $18.4 billion a 12% increase compared to its revenue in 2018. The increase primarily came from the 22% increase in the Corrugated Packaging segment.

Net Income for 2019 had an increase of 1% primarily from net sales.

Cash and cash equivalents were $151.6 million at the end of 2019 (ended September) compared to $636.8 million from the previous year. Cash from operating activities amounts to $2.3 billion. The company used $4.6 billion for investing activities mainly for acquisitions and capital expenditures. Cash from financing activities amounts to $1.8 billion.

Strategy

In fiscal 2019 WestRock continued to pursue its strategy of offering differentiated paper and packaging solutions.

Mergers and Acquisitions

In 2019 WestRock is expanding its capabilities to support the beauty & personal care nutraceutical and media industries with the acquisition of UBS Printing Group a California- based specialty printing and packaging company that manufactures high impact cartons as well as related literature products. The acquisition further extends the company's geographical footprint on the U.S. West Coast and will become a part of WestRock's Multi Packaging Solutions business.

Also in 2019 the company acquired Linx specializes in automated packaging machinery ranging from single order dispatch systems to fully integrated automation. Its BoxSizer technology platform complements WestRocks' existing automated packaging systems portfolio including its Box on Demand solutions.

Company Background

WestRock was formed in 2015 following the merger of the two paper and packaging companies MeadWestvaco Corporation and Rock-Tenn Company. Rock-Tenn had acquired paperboard giant Smurfit-Stone Container in 2011 already making it North America's second largest producer of containerboard behind International Paper. The MeadWestVaco and Rock-Tenn merger allowed WestRock to effectively compete with International Paper.

EXECUTIVES

President Corrugated Packaging And Recycling, James B. (Jim) Porter, $746,219 total compensation
Ceo, Steven C. (Steve) Voorhees, $1,012,603 total compensation
Evp General Counsel And Secretary, Robert B. (Bob) McIntosh, $433,630 total compensation
Evp Home Health And Beauty Packaging Solutions, Kevin G. Clark
Evp Merchandising Displays And Folding Carton Packaging Solutions, Craig A. Gunckel
Evp Beverage Packaging Solutions, R. Zack Smith
Ceo Ingevity, D. Michael Wilson
Evp Corrugated Container Packaging Solutions, Jeffrey W. (Jeff) Chalovich
Evp And Cfo, Ward H. Dickson, $564,959 total compensation
Evp Corrugated Paper Solutions Paper Solutions, Thomas M. (Tom) Stigers
President Packaging Solutions, Robert K. (Bob) Beckler, $144,932 total compensation
President Land And Development, Ken Seeger
Svp Treasurer, John Stakel
Vice President Real Estate Development Nexton Westrock Land And Development, John Grab
Vice President Westrock Land And Development, James Hill
Vice President Enterprise Information Technology, Todd Campbell
Area Vice President, Dwight Morris
Chairman, John A. Luke
Auditors: Ernst & Young LLP

LOCATIONS

HQ: WestRock Co
1000 Abernathy Road N.E., Atlanta, GA 30328
Phone: 770 448-2193
Web: www.westrock.com

2018 Sales

	% of total
United States	80
International	20
Total	**100**

PRODUCTS/OPERATIONS

2018 Sales

	$ mil.	% of total
Corrugated Packaging	8,941	55
Consumer Packaging	7,200	44
Land and Development	142	1
Total	**16,285**	**0**

Selected Products43 Corrugated containers

Containerboard
Folding cartons
Paperboard
Displays
Kraft paper
Pulp
Partitions and protective packaging
Recycling

Selected Markets   Beverage

Commercial printing
Food
Foodservice
Healthcare
Home and garden
Retail

COMPETITORS

Avery Dennison	International Paper
Bemis	Longview Fibre
Caraustar	Packaging Corp. of
Clearwater Paper	America
Georgia-Pacific	Shorewood Packaging
Graphic Packaging	Sonoco Products
Holding	Stora Enso
Green Bay Packaging	

HISTORICAL FINANCIALS

Company Type: Public

Income Statement

FYE: September 30

	REVENUE ($ mil.)	NET INCOME ($ mil.)	NET PROFIT MARGIN	EMPLOYEES
09/20	17,578	(690)	—	49,300
09/19	18,289	862	4.7%	51,100
09/18	16,285	1,906	11.7%	45,100
09/17	14,859	708	4.8%	44,800
09/16	14,171	(396)	—	39,000
Annual Growth	**5.5%**	**—**		**6.0%**

2020 Year-End Financials

Debt ratio: 32.77%	No. of shares (mil.): 260
Return on equity: (-6.18%)	Dividends
Cash ($ mil.): 251	Yield: 3.8%
Current ratio: 1.69	Payout: 44.4%
Long-term debt ($ mil.): 9,207	Market value ($ mil.): 9,046

	STOCK PRICE ($) FY Close	P/E High/Low		PER SHARE ($) Earnings	Dividends	Book Value
09/20	34.74	—	—	(2.67)	1.33	40.82
09/19	36.45	16	10	3.33	1.82	45.27
09/18	53.44	9	7	7.34	1.72	45.24
09/17	56.73	21	16	2.77	1.60	40.64
09/16	48.48	—	—	(1.54)	1.50	38.76
Annual Growth	**(8.0%)**			**—**	**(3.0%)**	**1.3%**

WHEATLAND UNION HIGH SCHOOL DISTRICT

EXECUTIVES

Supt, Glenn Sewll
Manager, Johnny Anderson
Auditors: DENNIS COOPER & ASSOCIATES CPA

LOCATIONS

HQ: WHEATLAND UNION HIGH SCHOOL DISTRICT
1010 WHEATLAND RD, WHEATLAND, CA 956929798
Phone: 530 633-3100
Web: WWW.WHEATLANDHIGH.ORG

HISTORICAL FINANCIALS

Company Type: Private

Income Statement   FYE: June 30

	REVENUE ($ mil.)	NET INCOME ($ mil.)	NET PROFIT MARGIN	EMPLOYEES
06/19	11,464	788	6.9%	76
06/18	9	0	7.3%	—
06/17	9,186	(1,399)	—	—
06/16	8,941	94	1.1%	—
Annual Growth	8.6%	103.0%	—	—

Whirlpool Corp

With brand names recognized by just about anyone who has ever separated dark colors from light Whirlpool is the world's top home appliance maker. It sells around 67 million laundry appliances refrigerators and freezers cooking appliances dishwashers and compressors each year under a bevy of brand names including Whirlpool Amana KitchenAid Maytag Jenn-Air and Roper. The company markets and distributes these major home appliances in North America Latin America EMEA (Europe the Middle East and Africa) and Asia. It has manufacturing operations in more than a dozen countries. Major customer include retailer Lowe's.

HISTORY

Brothers Fred and Lou Upton and their uncle Emory Upton founded the Upton Machine Company manufacturer of electric motor-driven washing machines in 1911 in St. Joseph Michigan. Sears Roebuck and Co. began buying their products five years later and by 1925 the company was supplying all of Sears' washers. The Uptons combined their company with the Nineteen Hundred Washer Company in 1929 to form the Nineteen Hundred Corporation the world's largest washing machine company.

Sears and Nineteen Hundred prospered during the Great Depression and during WWII Nineteen Hundred's factories produced war materials. In 1948 it began selling its first automatic washing machine (introduced a year earlier) under the Whirlpool brand. In 1950 the company changed its name to Whirlpool following the success of the product and introduced its first automatic dryer.

During the 1950s and 1960s Whirlpool became a full-line appliance manufacturer while continuing as Sears' principal Kenmore appliance supplier. In 1955 the company bought Seeger Refrigerator Company and the stove and air-conditioning interests of RCA. Three years later it made its first investment in Multibras Eletrodom sticos an appliance maker in Brazil. (It has increased that investment over the years.) Other purchases included the gas refrigeration and ice-maker manufacturing facilities of Servel (1958); a majority interest in Heil-Quaker makers of central heaters and space heaters (1964); Sears' major television set supplier Warwick Electronics (1966); and 33% of Canadian appliance maker John Inglis Company (1969). It made a deal with Sony in 1973 for the distribution of Whirlpool-brand products in Japan. Whirlpool sold its TV manufacturing business to SANYO of Japan three years later.

Between 1981 and 1991 despite a static US market Whirlpool's sales tripled to almost $6.6 billion. In 1986 the firm bought top-end appliance manufacturer KitchenAid (from Dart and Kraft) and 65% of Italian cooling compressor manufacturer Aspera. Also that year it sold its Heil-Quaker central heating business. David Whitwam was appointed CEO in 1987. Whirlpool took over total ownership of Inglis in 1990.

The company formed Whirlpool Europe a joint venture with Philips Electronics in 1989; in 1991 it bought out Philips. Two years later Whirlpool took control of appliance marketer SAGAD of Argentina and entered a joint venture with Slovakia's Tatramat (which it bought out in 1994).

Whirlpool acquired control of Kelvinator of India in 1994 and formed a joint venture in China with Shenzhen Petrochemical Holdings in 1995 to produce air conditioners. The following year Whirlpool merged its Whirlpool Washing Machines and Kelvinator of India companies to form Whirlpool of India. The company's European division plunged into the red when competition and a recession kept consumers away from its higher-priced appliances.

In 1997 Whirlpool initiated a restructuring (due to losses from its foreign operations) that included plant closures and substantial layoffs (as much as 10% of its workforce). The next year Whirlpool sold its appliance financing subsidiary to Transamerica. The company also began using a new more efficient product development model in 1998 similar to one used in the auto industry. In 2000 Whirlpool launched the Cielo Bath line of jetted tubs and in 2001 it introduced the Calypso dishwasher and the Duet washer and dryer.

Another global restructuring plan swept through the company in 2000 resulting in significant pretax charges ($373 million incurred in 2001 and 2002) and the elimination of about 6000 employees by October 2003.

In February 2002 Whirlpool bought the remaining 51% of Vitromatic it didn't already own. (Vitromatic — the second-largest appliance manufacturer in Mexico — is now called Whirlpool Mexico.) In March the company purchased 95% of Polar Poland's second-largest appliance maker.

Whirlpool introduced Gladiator GarageWorks (modular storage systems for the garage) and Polara (the first electric range with cooking and refrigeration capabilities) in 2002.

Whirlpool acquired Maytag in early 2006 for about $1.9 billion. The deal added several top brands to its already bulging portfolio including Admiral Amana Jenn-Air Magic Chef and of course the eponymous Maytag. Once the dust settled Whirlpool sold several businesses including Dixie-Narco the Amana commercial business its Hoover unit to Techtronic Industries and its Jade unit to Middleby Corporation. Buying Maytag also spurred Whirlpool to streamline operations and purge staff. In 2006 it laid off some 4500 employees consolidated duplicate functions related to administration and manufacturing and shuttered some offices including a Maytag research and development center based in Newton Illinois. Whirlpool shuttered Maytag's Iowa-based administrative offices and moved them to Michigan and other locations. The company cut 700 jobs at several Tennessee plants the following year.

In 2007 Whirlpool acquired a minority stake in Elica Group in its effort to extend its reach into the global air ventilation market.

The company formed a 50-50 joint venture in 2008 with China's Hisense-Kelon Electrical Holdings to make and sell home appliances there.

In June 2010 Whirlpool closed its refrigerator factory in Evansville Indiana; some 1100 US jobs were lost as a result of the move.

EXECUTIVES

Executive Vice President And Chief Finan, Roy Templin
Vice President Of Sales, Sam Abdelnour
Vice President Human Resources, Michael Todman
Vice President, Chris Hubbuch
Executive Vice President And President Of Whirlpool Europe Middle East And Africa, Esther Galindo
Ceo And Director, Marc R. Bitzer, age 55, $1,000,000 total compensation
Evp Global Product Organization, David T. (Dave) Szczupak, age 64, $746,667 total compensation
Evp And President Of Whirlpool Europe Middle East And Africa (emea), Esther Berrozpe Galindo, age 50, $659,041 total compensation
Evp And President Latin America, Jo o Carlos Brega, age 56, $498,901 total compensation
President Whirlpool North America, Joseph T. Liotine, age 47
Evp And Cfo, James W. (Jim) Peters, age 50, $456,667 total compensation
President Whirlpool Asia, Shengpo (Samuel) Wu
Vice President Global Procurement, Tom Egan
Vice President Marketing, Andrew Batson
Vice President Human Resources Whirlpool S A, Natalie Tessier
National Account Manager, Paula Saul
Vice President Sales Whirlpool Canada, Mark Williams
Vice President And General Manager Integrated Business Units, Brett Dibkey
Vp Human Resources, Kimberly Thompson
Vice President Product Marketing North America, Ludovic Beaufils
Vice President Sales And Marketing, Daniel Clifford
National Sales Manager, Jason Wade
Vice President And Of General Manager Of Emerging Categories, Timothy Kee

Vice President Human Resources Global Pr, Tomas Linden
Vice President Information Services, Nancy Berendsen
National Sales Manager, Christine Lobins
Division Vice President, Brian Gahr
Vice President Corporate Innovation And Information Systems, Jay Michael Berendsen
National Sales Manager, Erin Brown
Vice President Manufacturing Laundry And Dishwashers, Dale Laws
Vice President Product Development, David Klein
National Sales Manager, Jonathan Hodges
Executive Vice President President Whirlpool Emea, Esther Berrozpe, age 50
Executive Vice President Global Product Organizati, Dave Szczupak
Information Technology Management: Executive Vice President Senior Vice President, Mrutyunjaya Rao
Vice President Manager Director, Sandra Coons
Vice President Global Quality, Ken Kleinhample
Vice President Human Resources Business, Cintia Bincoletto
Vice President Human Resources, Carey Martin
Division Vice President, Kenny D Thompson
Vice President For Human Resources Solutions, Abby Luersman
Vice President Quality, J D Rapp
Vice President, Alice Bomar
Vice President Sales, Tamal Saha
National Sales Manager, Carlos Gomez
National Sales Manager, Nic Miller
Vice President Human Resources And Ehs, Levern Kelley
Vice President And General Manager Integ, Brett Dibky
Global Vice President Internal Audit, Sidnei Sanches
Vice President And Associate General Counsel, Robert Kenagy
Vice President, Yongshou Luo
National Sales Manager, Randy Karn
National Sales Manager Kitchenaid Commercial, Susan Azadian
Vp And Cfo North American Region, Christopher Bealer
Vice President Internal Audit, Brian Sarchett
Vice President Information Technology, Dave Langendonk
Vice President Treasurer, Tammy Wiles
Vp And Chief Design Officer, J Mays
Senior Vice President Global Product Organization, Pamela Klyn
Vice President, Michael Stubbs
Vice President, Patricia Martin
Chairman, Jeff M. Fettig, age 63
Board Member, Harish Manwani
Assistant Treasurer, John F Geddes
Board Member, Larry Spencer
Board Member, Greg Creed
Board Member, James Loree
Secretary And Treasurer, Chris Roth
Auditors: Ernst & Young LLP

LOCATIONS

HQ: Whirlpool Corp
2000 North M-63, Benton Harbor, MI 49022-2692
Phone: 269 923-5000
Web: www.whirlpoolcorp.com

2018 Sales

	$ mil.	% of total
North America	11,374	54
Europe the Middle East & Africa	4,536	21
Latin America	3,618	17
Asia	1,587	8
Other/eliminations	(78)	—
Total	**21,037**	**100**

PRODUCTS/OPERATIONS

2018 Sales

	$ mil.	% of total
Laundry	6,200	29
Refrigeration	6,051	29
Cooking	4,821	23
Dishwashing	1,645	8
Compressors	1,135	5
Spare parts and warranties	1,030	5
Other	155	1
Total	**21,037**	**100**

COMPETITORS

BSH Bosch und Siemens Hausger ote
Candy Group
Daewoo Electronics
Electrolux
Electrolux Home Appliances China
Fisher & Paykel Appliances Holdings
Gree Electrical Appliances
GuangDong Midea
Haier Group
Hitachi
LG Electronics
Panasonic Corp
SANYO
Samsung Electronics America
Sears Holdings
Sharp Corp.
Sub-Zero
Viking Range

HISTORICAL FINANCIALS

Company Type: Public

Income Statement

FYE: December 31

	REVENUE ($ mil.)	NET INCOME ($ mil.)	NET PROFIT MARGIN	EMPLOYEES
12/19	20,419	1,184	5.8%	77,000
12/18	21,037	(183)	—	92,000
12/17	21,253	350	1.6%	92,000
12/16	20,718	888	4.3%	93,000
12/15	20,891	783	3.7%	97,000
Annual Growth	**(0.6%)**	**10.9%**	**—**	**(5.6%)**

2019 Year-End Financials

Debt ratio: 26.44%
Return on equity: 43.16%
Cash ($ mil.): 1,952
Current ratio: 0.88
Long-term debt ($ mil.): 4,140

No. of shares (mil.): 63
Dividends
Yield: 3.2%
Payout: 29.0%
Market value ($ mil.): 9,294

	STOCK PRICE ($) FY Close	P/E High/Low		Earnings	Dividends	Book Value
12/19	147.53	9	6	18.45	4.75	50.71
12/18	106.87	—	—	(2.72)	4.55	35.80
12/17	168.64	41	34	4.70	4.30	59.13
12/16	181.77	16	11	11.50	3.90	64.10
12/15	146.87	22	14	9.83	3.45	61.42
Annual Growth	**0.1%**			**17.0%**	**8.3%**	**(4.7%)**

WHOLE FOODS MARKET, INC.

Whole Foods Market is the world's largest natural foods grocery chain. Founded in 1980 it pioneered the supermarket concept in natural and organic foods retailing. The company operates more than 500 stores throughout the US Canada and the UK. It sells private-label items through its 365 Organic Everyday Value and Allegro Coffee lines among others and offers a variety of non-GMO vegan and gluten-free foods.

HISTORY

With a $10000 loan from his father John Mackey started SaferWay Natural Foods in Austin Texas in 1978. Despite struggling Mackey dreamed of opening a larger supermarket-sized natural foods store. Two years later SaferWay merged with Clarksville Natural Grocery and Whole Foods Market was born. Led by Mackey that year it opened an 11000-sq.-ft. supermarket in the counterculture hotbed of Austin. The store was an instant success and a second store was added 18 months later in suburban Austin.

The company slowly expanded in Texas opening or buying stores in Houston in 1984 and Dallas in 1986. Whole Foods expanded into Louisiana in 1988 with the purchase of like-named Whole Food Co. a single New Orleans store owned by Peter Roy (who served as the company's president from 1993 to 1998). Sticking to university towns Whole Foods added another store in California the next year and acquired Wellspring Grocery (two stores North Carolina) in 1991. In 1992 it debuted its first private-label products under the Whole Foods name. Seeking capital to expand even more the company raised $23 million by going public in early 1992 with 12 stores.

Every competitor in the fragmented health foods industry became a potential acquisition and the chain began growing rapidly. In 1992 Whole Foods bought the six-store Bread & Circus chain in New England. The next year it added Mrs. Gooch's Natural Foods Markets (seven stores in the Los Angeles area). Its biggest acquisition came in 1996 when it bought Fresh Fields the second-largest US natural foods chain (22 stores on the East Coast and in Chicago). Although the purchase hurt profits in 1996 sales surpassed $1 billion for the first time in fiscal 1997 as Whole Foods neared 70 stores. In 1997 it introduced the less-expensive 365 private label and acquired the Granary Market (Monterey California) and Bread of Life (two stores South Florida) natural foods supermarkets.

Capitalizing on the growing popularity of nutraceuticals (natural supplements with benefits similar to pharmaceuticals) the company paid $146 million in 1997 for Amrion a maker of nutraceuticals and other nutritional supplements (merged with subsidiary WholePeople.com in 2000). It capped the year by buying coffee roaster Allegro Coffee. (Both companies are based in Boulder Colorado home of its former main rival the smaller Wild Oats.) Also in 1997 Whole Foods acquired the six-store Merchant of Vino natural foods and wine shop chain to foster the development of its wine departments.

In 1998 Whole Foods opened its first store in Boulder — a 39000-sq.-ft. superstore with amenities such as a juice bar and a prepared foods section. At year's end Roy resigned as president and was replaced by Chris Hitt. In 1999 Whole Foods bought four-store Boston-area chain Nature's Heartland.

In 2000 Whole Foods merged its online operations (wholefoods.com) with its direct marketing and nutritional supplement unit (Amrion) to form Wholepeople.com. Later that year the company merged Wholepeople.com with lifestyle marketing firm Gaiam; Whole Foods received a minority stake in Gaiam and started selling food online through Gaiam.com.

Hitt resigned in mid-2001 and Mackey took over his duties. Later that year Whole Foods acquired the three upscale Harry's Farmers Market stores in Atlanta; the sale did not include the Harry's In A Hurry stores which later shut down.

In 2002 Whole Foods crossed the border into Canada. Its first foreign store opened in downtown Toronto that May.

Mackey was named Entrepreneur of the Year in 2003 by consulting firm Ernst & Young. That year Whole Foods acquired Select Fish a Seattle-based seafood processor and distributor and opened a seafood distribution facility in Atlanta.

In 2004 Whole Foods opened a 59000-sq.-ft. store in the new Time Warner Center in Manhattan. The new store which includes a 248-seat cafe sushi bar wine shop and gourmet bakery is the largest supermarket in New York City. That year the company acquired the UK organic-food retailer Fresh & Wild for $38 million.

To support its rapid growth in 2004 Whole Foods Market expanded its number of operating regions from eight to 10 by separating the Southwest region into the Southwest and Rocky Mountain regions and the Northern Pacific region into the Northern California and Pacific Northwest region. The company announced the opening of its first Gluten-Free Bakehouse a dedicated gluten-free baking facility located outside Raleigh North Carolina. Overall the company opened 12 new stores in 2004.

In January 2005 Whole Foods launched the Animal Compassion Foundation an independent non-profit organization dedicated to the compassionate treatment of livestock. The company moved that month to its new corporate headquarters across the street from its old location in downtown Austin. Its new flagship store opened its doors in March at the same location. In October Whole Foods increased its number of operating regions from 10 to 11 by separating the North Atlantic region into the North Atlantic and Tri-State regions. Overall in fiscal 2005 the company opened a dozen new stores including its first in Nebraska and Ohio. In 2006 the company acquired a store in Portland Maine and converted it to the Whole Foods Market banner.

In August 2007 Whole Foods acquired its main competitor — Boulder Colorado-based Wild Oats Markets — in a deal valued at about $565 million (plus $106 million in debt). In early October the company sold 35 Henry's Farmers Market and Sun Harvest stores to a subsidiary of Los Angeles-based Smart & Final for about $166 million. The stores in California and Texas were acquired with Wild Oats.

The company launched a bi-monthly magazine called Whole Foods Market Magazine at its midwestern stores in 2008. On the heels of its disappointing third-quarter results in August 2008 shares of the company's stock fell to a six-year low and Whole Foods suspended its dividend. Blaming the poor economy the company announced the layoffs of some 50 employees at its Austin headquarters in August 2008. Overall in fiscal 2008 the company introduced about 300 new private-label items.

For the first time in its 29-year history Whole Foods reported negative same-store sales in the quarter ended December 2008 as traffic in its stores fell.

In March 2009 the company reached a settlement in its long-running dispute with the FTC over its acquisition of Wild Oats in 2007. Whole Foods agreed to sell 32 stores including 19 Wild Oats locations that had already been closed. In exchange the FTC dropped its crusade to undo the merger. In December 2009 John Elstrott was named chairman of Whole Foods Market after Mackey voluntarily relinquished the chairmanship which he had held since 1980. In May 2010 Walter Robb formerly co-president of the company was promoted to co-CEO of Whole Foods a title he now shares with Mackey.

EXECUTIVES

Ceo, John P. Mackey, $1 total compensation
President And Coo, A. C. Gallo, $501,110 total compensation
President Florida Region, Juan Nuñez
Chairman Whole Kids Foundation And Whole Cities Foundation, Walter E. Robb, $501,110 total compensation
Evp Operations U.s. And Whole Foods 365, David Lannon, $501,110 total compensation
Vp Purchasing Midwest Division, Jeff Turnas
Evp Operations, Christina Minardi
President Southern Pacific Region, Patrick Bradley
President Mid-atlantic Region, Scott Allshouse
President Rocky Mountain Region, Bill Jordan
President Midwest Region, Michael Bashaw
President North Atlantic Region, Laura Derba
Evp And Cio, Jason Buechel, $501,110 total compensation
President South Region, Omar Gaye
President Northern California Region, Rob Twyman
Evp Operations U.s. And The U.k., Kenneth (Ken) Meyer, $486,510 total compensation
Evp Growth And Business Development, James (Jim) Sud, $486,510 total compensation
Evp And Cfo, Keith Manbeck
President Pacific Northwest Region, Angela Lorenzen
Global Vp Marketing, Sonya Gafsi Oblisk
President Northeast Region, Nicole Wescoe
Global Vice President, Bart Beilman
Global Vice President, Lee Matecko
Executive Vice President Operations, Kenny Meyer
Vice President And Marketing Manager, Desa Abbamondi
Vice President Vendor Manager, Ray Hudson
Global Vice President Commmunications, Brooke Buchanan
Vice President And Loan Officer And Branch Manager, Francisco Ibarra
Assistant Vice President Product Manager Marketing, Merijoy Rucker
Regional Vice President, Scott Saulsberry
Regional Vice President, Tim Gates
Vice President Of Information Technology, Shawn Williams
Vice President Digital Marketing Crm Loyalty And Ecommerce, Ryan Linders
Vice President Brand, Madhavi Reese
Chairman, John B. Elstrott
Auditors: ERNST & YOUNG LLP AUSTIN TEX

LOCATIONS

HQ: WHOLE FOODS MARKET, INC.
550 BOWIE ST. AUSTIN, TX 787034644
Phone: 512 477-4455
Web: WWW.WHOLEFOODSMARKET.COM

PRODUCTS/OPERATIONS

Selected Product Categories

Bakery
Body care
Educational products
Floral
Grocery
Household products
Meat and poultry
Nutritional supplements
Pet products
Prepared foods
Produce
Seafood
Specialty (beer wine cheese)
Textiles

COMPETITORS

ALDI	Natural Grocers by
Albertsons	Vitamin Cottage
Costco Wholesale	Publix
Fiesta Mart	Safeway
GNC	Sprouts
H-E-B	Tesco
Kroger	Trader Joe's
Loblaw	Wal-Mart

HISTORICAL FINANCIALS
Company Type: Private

Income Statement				FYE: September 24
	REVENUE ($ mil.)	NET INCOME ($ mil.)	NET PROFIT MARGIN	EMPLOYEES
09/17	16,030	245	1.5%	95,000
09/16	15,724	507	3.2%	—
09/15	15,389	536	3.5%	—
09/14	14,194	579	4.1%	—
Annual Growth	4.1%	(24.9%)	—	—

Williams Cos Inc (The)

EXECUTIVES

MBR-Ceo, Steven J Malcolm
MBR, Joseph Williams
Senior Vice President Northeas, Frank E Billings
Vice President Business Develo, Frank Billings
Auditors: Ernst & Young LLP

LOCATIONS

HQ: Williams Cos Inc (The)
One Williams Center, Tulsa, OK 74172-0172
Phone: 918 573-2000
Web: www.williams.com

HISTORICAL FINANCIALS
Company Type: Public

Income Statement				FYE: December 31
	REVENUE ($ mil.)	NET INCOME ($ mil.)	NET PROFIT MARGIN	EMPLOYEES
12/19	8,201	850	10.4%	4,812
12/18	8,686	(155)	—	5,322
12/17	8,031	2,174	27.1%	5,425
12/16	7,499	(424)	—	5,604
12/15	7,360	(571)	—	6,578
Annual Growth	2.7%	—	—	(7.5%)

WILMINGTON TRUST COMPANY

EXECUTIVES

Chief Executive Officer, Robert Harra
Vice President, Eric Cheung
Assistant Vice President, David Cuocolo
Group Vice President, Richard Marsh
Vice President, Joseph Brooks
Vice President, Mary Pupillo
Vice President, Peter Finkel
Assistant Vice President, Donald Haverstick
Vice President, Steven Cimalore
Vice President Global Capital Markets, Vito Iacovazzi
Vice President Private Banking, Heather Ford
Vp And Manager Business Application Support, Gary Powers
Assistant Vice President, Yvette Howell
Vice President Inv. Management Support Services, Edward Moon
Vice President, Michael Orendorf
Vice President Global Capital Markets, Nicholas Adams
Vice President, Mary Avery
Vice President, Jeanne Oller
Vice President, Margaret Pulgini
Vice President, Sergio Godinho
Assistant Vice President Corporate Trust Custody, Erik Saville
Vice President, Jennifer Matz
Training Manager Vice President, Lynn Dibonaventura
Vice President, Charles Hicks
Assistant Vice President, Steve Barone
Vice President, Lisa Fricke
Vice President Wilmington Trust Fsb, Josh Stump
Vice President, Wendy White
Vice President, Sandra Plowinske
Vice President, Janice Cirillo
Vice President, George Chen
Assistant Vice President Talen, Kathryn Spencer
Assistant Vice President, Adam Vogelsong
Vice President Of Data Center, Ed Olkowski
Vice President, Thomas Raymond
Vice President Corporate Client Services, Christie Longo
Vice President Client Development, Rob Barnett
Vice President, Jeanette Madaya
Vice President, Kevin Bruggeman
Assistant Vice President, Michael Oller
Vice President, Jeffrey Wolken
Vice President, Nadine Black

Vice President Risk Manager, Holly Stiefel
Assistant Vice President, Laura Barone
Vice President Director, Bette Francis
Assistant Vice President, William Morris
Vice President Director Of Wisd Vendor Management, Bill Cunnion
Vice President, Arlene Moyer
Vice President, Karen Touchstone
Assistant Vice President, Liz Hudgens
Vice President, Virginia Machamer
Vice President Network And Desktop Computing, Rob Averbach
Assistant Vice President, Beth Power
Vice President Director Client Services Institu, Amy Roe
Vice President, Robert Quinn
Vice President, Jane Snyder
Assistant Vice President, Greg Cherewko
Vice President And Portfolio Manager, Luke Betterly
Vice President, Joe Fahey
Vice President Wealth Advisory Senior Private Client Fiduciary Advisor, Latonya Hubbard
Vice President, Steven Kochie
Vice President Marketing Manager, Andrea Spahr
Vice President, Thomas Herring
Vice President And Senior Private Client Fiduciary Advisor, Cindy White
Vice President Esop Services, Kristy Britsch
Vice President, Kara Partin
Assistant Vice President, Ryan Thompson
Vice President, Jason Johnson
Executive Vice President, Bill Farrell
Regional Vice President, John Breda
Assistant Vice President, Rachel Simpson
Vice President And Senior Client Development Officer For Wtris, Robert Barnett
Vice President Senior Fiduciary Advisor, Lori Brodbeck
Vice President, Chris Slaybaugh
Assistant Vice President, Thomas Kalafut
Assistant Vice President, Elizabeth Bothner
Vice President Senior Investment Advisor, Mark Stevenson
Assistant Vice President Of Lending, Mary Fisher
Vice President, Rebecca Rogers
Vice President, Glenn Best
Vice President, Clay Weisenberg
Assistant Vice President Loan Agency Group, Jennifer Anderson
Executive Vice President Of The Company Mandt Bank And Wilmington Trust Investment Advisors, Doris Meister
Vice President, John Kelley
Vice President Equity Management, Mark Horst
Vice President Corporate Capital Markets, Aaron Soper
Assistant Vice President, Michael Moorehead
Assistant Vice President, Barry Butina
Vice President, Robert Reynolds
Assistant Vice President, Bonnie Metcalfe
Vice President, Carl Robinson
Assistant Vice President, Chad May
Vice President And Private Client Fiduciary Advisor, Karen Kiley
Vice President, Robert Collins
Assistant Vice President Global Capital Markets, Clarice Wright
Group Vice President, Laura Havranek
Assistant Vice President, Melissa Jalace-vasold
Vice President Senior Private Client Advisor, Sandra Besso Plowinske
Vice President, Ann Harris-johnson
Vice President, Christopher Guardino
Vice President Director Of Sales, Gregory Hasty
Vice President, Mark Gerstenschlager
Vice President Regional Marketing Director, Laura Cleveland
Assistant Vice President, Joann Petry
Avp, Lisa Lewis

Assistant Vice President, Carleen Terranova
Vice President Wealth Advisory Services, Paul Bartkowski
Assistant Vice President Commercial Real Estate, Rachel Skrabak
Vice President Channel Management, John J Hurley
Assistant Vice President, Greg Golden
Assistant Vice President, Melissa Marion
Vice President, Karen Bonn
Vice President And Senior Private Client Investment Advisor, Sue Schnaars
Vice President Private Banking, Julia Odonnell
Assistant Vice President, Brenda Parker
Vice President, Al Miller
Vice President, Barbara Obrien
Vice President, Charlie Buehler
Vice President And Senior Investment Advisor, Andrew Cloud
Assistant Vice President, Andrea Rybczynski
Vice President, Joseph Odonnell
Vice President, Renee Buchner
Assistant Vice President, Nancy Hagner
Assistant Vice President, Catherine Chandler
Vice President, Kyle Barry
Assistant Vice President, Maureen Auld
Vice President, Denise Sbraccia
Assistant Vice President, Sophie Pendolino
Assistant Vice President, Christopher Hickok
Assistant Vice President, Ruth Ann Mcmillen
Assistant Vice President, Jose Paredes
Vice President, Howard Gordon
Vice President, David Bagley
Vice President Private Client Advisor, Ed Barone
Vice President, Jeffrey Ritchie
Vice President, Kaye Crouch
Assistant Vice President, Kevin Ebert
Vice President, Nickole Garrison
Vice President Senior Private Banker, Nicholas Macechko
Assistant Vice President, Russell Whitley
Assistant Vice President, Matthew Lyndaker
Vice President And Investment Advisor, Darren Jordan
Vice President, Erin Miller
Vice President, William Gering
Vice President, Joseph Baker
Vice President, Stephen Seivold
Vice President, Theresa Drew
Assistant Vice President, Tammy Krawczyk
Vice President, Todd Bemiller
Vice President, Brooks Von Arx Jr
Vice President And Team Leader, Donald Hargadon

LOCATIONS

HQ: WILMINGTON TRUST COMPANY
1100 N MARKET ST, WILMINGTON, DE 198900001
Phone: 302 651-1000
Web: WWW.WILMINGTONTRUST.COM

HISTORICAL FINANCIALS

Company Type: Private

Income Statement — FYE: December 31

	ASSETS ($ mil.)	NET INCOME ($ mil.)	INCOME AS % OF ASSETS	EMPLOYEES
12/17	4,960	30	0.6%	1,818
12/16	3,685	17	0.5%	—
12/15	1,928	36	1.9%	—
Annual Growth	60.4%	(9.0%)	—	—

Wilson Bank Holding Co.

EXECUTIVES

Chairman; Chairman Of The Board, John Freeman
Senior Vice President, Mac Griffin
Vice President And Loan Officer Carthage, Lisa Gregory
Vice President And Marketing Director Main Office, Rebecca Jennings
Auditors: Maggart & Associates, P.C.

LOCATIONS

HQ: Wilson Bank Holding Co.
623 West Main Street, Lebanon, TN 37087
Phone: 615 444-2265
Web: www.wilsonbank.com

HISTORICAL FINANCIALS

Company Type: Public

Income Statement

FYE: December 31

	ASSETS ($ mil.)	NET INCOME ($ mil.)	INCOME AS % OF ASSETS	EMPLOYEES
12/19	2,794	36	1.3%	530
12/18	2,543	32	1.3%	487
12/17	2,317	23	1.0%	471
12/16	2,198	25	1.2%	444
12/15	2,021	23	1.2%	446
Annual Growth	8.4%	10.9%	—	4.4%

2019 Year-End Financials

Debt ratio: —
Return on equity: 11.39%
Cash ($ mil.): 139
Current ratio: —
Long-term debt ($ mil.): —
No. of shares (mil.): 10
Dividends
Yield: —
Payout: 32.8%
Market value ($ mil.): —

Wintrust Financial Corp (IL)

Wintrust Financial is a holding company for 15 subsidiary banks (mostly named after the individual communities they serve) with more than 150 branches primarily in the metropolitan Chicago and southern Wisconsin (including Milwaukee) markets. Boasting assets of more than $23 billion the banks offer personal and commercial banking wealth management and specialty lending services with business and commercial real estate loans making up 60% of the company's loan portfolio. Wintrust's banks target small business customers though some of Wintrust's banks also provide niche lending for homeowners associations medical practices franchisees and municipalities.

Operations

Wintrust operates three business segments: Community Banking which accounted for 77% of total revenue in 2015 and serves individuals and small businesses; Specialty Finance (13% of revenue) operating through First Insurance Funding and First Insurance Funding of Canada which provide financing for commercial insurance and life insurance premiums in the US and Canada respectively; and Wealth Management (10% of revenue) which offers financial planning and brokerage services through The Chicago Trust Company N.A. Wayne Hummer Investments LLC and Great Lakes Advisors LLC.

Wintrust makes more than 70% of its revenue from interest income. About 66% of its total revenue came from loan interest (including fees) during 2015 while another 6% came from interest on investment securities. The rest of its revenue came from mortgage banking (12%) wealth management services (7%) deposit account service charges (3%) and other miscellaneous income sources.

Geographic Reach

Wintrust's banks operate more than 150 branches and 220-plus automatic teller machines mostly located in communities throughout the Chicago metropolitan area and southern Wisconsin. Its wealth management offices are in Chicago; Appleton Wisconsin; and Safety Harbor Florida. Its Wintrust Mortgage subsidiary has 55 locations in a dozen states while its insurance subsidiaries have locations in Northbrook Illinois; Jersey City; Long Island New York; Toronto; Mississauga Ontario; and Vancouver.

Sales and Marketing

The bank's customers include individuals small to mid-sized businesses local governmental units and institutional clients residing primarily in the banks' local service areas.

Wintrust has been ramping up its advertising spend in recent years. It spent $21.9 million on advertising during 2015 up from $13.6 million and $11.1 million in 2014 and 2013 respectively.

Financial Performance

Wintrust Financial's annual revenues have risen more than 40% since 2011 as its loan assets have swelled by nearly 70% with rapid branch expansion. Its annual profits have doubled over the same period.

The banking group's revenue jumped 12% to $990.1 million during 2015 mostly as its average loan balances grew by 15% for the year. Mortgage banking revenue increased 26% for the year thanks to higher origination volumes and purchases on a more favorable mortgage banking environment also helping buoy the company's top-line growth.

Strong revenue growth in 2015 drove Wintrust's net income up 4% to $156.75 million despite a rise in acquisition-related professional and legal fees. The group's operating cash levels fell 82% to $37.95 million due to unfavorable working capital changes mainly tied to an increase in accrued interest receivable and other assets.

Strategy

Wintrust has developed its community-based banking franchise through rapid branch expansion stemming from either through new openings or small bank acquisitions. Indeed the bank's branch count has flourished by more than 50% since 2011 from 99 back then to 152 branches at the end of 2015.

Beyond branch expansion the company remains focused on making new loans especially of the commercial and commercial real estate type where opportunities that meet its underwriting standards exist.

Mergers and Acquisitions

In January 2016 Wintrust Financial expanded into Pewaukee Wisconsin after agreeing to buy Generations Bancorp and its Foundations Bank subsidiary. Later that year the company finalized the $33.5 million purchase of First Community Financial Corporation the holding company of First Community Bank (which operates two branches in Elgin Illinois).

In July 2015 the company purchased Community Financial Shares Inc. and its four Community Bank of Wheaton/Glen Ellyn bank branches in the respective communities they serve in Illinois for a total of $42.4 million.

Also in July 2015 the company bought $118 million-asset North Bank and its two branches in Chicago.

In April 2015 Wintrust acquired Suburban Illinois Bancorp and its 10 Suburban Bank & Trust Company (SBT) branches in Chicago and surrounding suburbs for $12.5 million. The SBT locations would operate under Wintrust's Hinsdale Bank & Trust Company subsidiary.

In January 2015 the bank group purchased $224 million-asset Delavan Bancshares Inc. and its Community Bank CBD subsidiary.

Company Background

In 2012 Wintrust expanded its premium funding business into Canada with the acquisition of Macquarie Premium Funding Inc which was a subsidiary of Macquarie Group. The deal marked Wintrust's first international venture.

EXECUTIVES

Evp Technology; President Wintrust Information Technology Services, Lloyd M. Bowden, age 67, $167,333 total compensation
Sevp Coo And Treasurer, David A. Dykstra, age 60, $759,167 total compensation
President Ceo And Director, Edward J. Wehmer, age 65, $1,100,000 total compensation
Evp And Regional Market Head, Frank J. Burke
Evp And Chief Credit Officer, Richard B. Murphy, age 61, $509,167 total compensation
Evp And Chief Administration Officer, Leona A. Gleason
Evp And Cfo, David L. Stoehr, age 61, $419,167 total compensation
Evp And Regional Market Head, Timothy S. (Tim) Crane, age 58
Evp And Market Head Wealth Management Services, Thomas P. (Tom) Zidar
Evp General Counsel And Secretary, Lisa J. Pattis, $446,167 total compensation
Evp And Regional Market Head, David L. Larson
Evp And Coo Wintrust Commercial Finance (wcf), Joseph F. Thompson
Vice President Compliance, Kellie Oostendorp
Group Vp; Treasury Management Sales, Sarah Grooms
Svp Mortgage Lending, Michael Gamble
Executive Vice President, Ursula Moncau
Vice President Bsa Officer, Kathleen Franklin
Vice President Managed Assets Division, Sandy Durek
Vice President Loan Operations, Sharon Hiller
Executive Vice President, Braden R Smith
Vice President Managed Assets Division, Irene Calzadilla
Vice President, Philip Sheridan
Senior Vice President Finance Credit Reporting, Mario Nudo
Senior Vice President Commercial Lender, Gregory Pinter
Avp Treasury Management, Judy Majon

Assistant Vice President Financial System
  Management, Marty Lavin
Avp Middle Market Treasury Management Sales,
  Lauren Hess
Vice President, Mary Koehler
Senior Vice President, Rhonda Pokoj
Vice President Marketing, Todd Younger
Vice President Treasury Management, Linda Bishop
Vice President Compliance, Christine Wujek
Vice President, Sarah Withrow
Vice President Real Estate Services, Trey Meers
Senior Vice President, Darragh Griffin
Senior Vice President Planning, Scott Ernsteen
Senior Vice President Business Development,
  Matt Gambs
Senior Vice President Commercial Real Estate,
  Nick Cannon
Vice President, Joseph Ach
Senior Vice President Commercial Banking, Sean
  Dunn
Vice President, Sara Staniszewski
Vice President Commercial Banking, Michael
  Roman
Senior Vice President, Ronald Pesenko
Senior Vice President, Ryan Witte
Senior Vice President, William Robin
Vice President, Jon Swanson
Assistant Vice President Investments, Scott
  Weichle
Vice President Regulatory Reporting, Anita
  Chakravarthy
Assistant Vice President Commercial Real Estate,
  Kim Curschman
Senior Vice President Investments, David Galvan
Vice President Fair Lending Officer, Teresa
  Handley
Assistant Vice President Branch Management,
  Rick Butterly
Vice President, Caroline Gonos
Vice President Commercial Real Estate, Zornitsa
  Titova
Assistant Vice President, Todd Shifrin
Vice President Managed Assets Division, Hany
  Morsy
Vice President Compliance Officer, Norma
  Ahlstrand
Senior Vice President Personal Banking, Ursula
  Schuebel
Vice President Human Resources, Janet Huffman
Vice President Compliance, Christine Cain
Vice President Assistant Counsel Litigation, Cindy
  Stuyvesant
Vice President Finance Regulatory Reporting,
  James Oranga
Executive Vice President And Chief Credit
  Officer, Paul Hallauer
Vice President Operations Manager Private
  Banker, Nicole Cox
Executive Vice President, Matthew Doucet
Vice President, Paul Varga
Executive Vice President, Christine Smith
Senior Vice President, Anish Saran
Senior Vice President Commercial Loan Review
  Manager, Cindy Bauer
Vice President, Nick Koricanac
Vice President Assistant Controller, Dana French
Senior Vice President Sales, Steve Cusick
Vice President Executive, Sharon Moeller
Assistant Vice President Commercial Product
  Manager, Karon Gater
Assistant Vice President Retail Digital Product
  Manager, Natalie Fedus
Vice President, Jeffery Wolinski
Vice President Credit, Juan Cabrera
Senior Vice President Information Services, Mike
  Nathan
Vice President Finance, Derek Ramsden
Vice President Branch Manager, Joel Rodarte
Assistant Vice President, Katie Cagney

Assistant Vice President Branch Manager, Anthony
  Scott
Senior Vice President, Joe Gensor
Senior Vice President Sales, Tom Forbes
Vice President, Kim Endsley
Vice President, Sharon Sagert
Vice President Risk, Tim Doran
Senior Vice President Treasury Management, Chris
  Lantman
Senior Vice President, Brian de la Houssaye
Assistant Vice President, Edward Semik
Vice President Of Operations Wintrust
  Commercial Finance, Lisa McNeme
Vice President Business Banking, Chris Dana
Senior Vice President Commercial Real Estate,
  Daniel Lawlor
Assistant Vice President, Richard Eber
Vice President Construction And Engineering
  Division, Chris Vantassel
Vice President Infrastructure, Bill Eisenstot
Senior Vice President Commercial Real Estate,
  Joe Nitti
Senior Vice President Risk, Evan Bossard
Vice President Government Nonprofit Healthcare
  Lender, Erinn Siegel
Vp Eft Services, Crystal Tabar
Vice President Commercial Banking, Christopher
  Sobey
Assistant Vice President, Dhaval Gandhi
Vice President, Tara Fedorko
Vice President, Rafiq Harris
Senior Vice President, Dawn Mase
Vice President Business Lending, Katie Moore
Senior Vice President, Tom Carlson
Vice President Senior Commercial Underwriter,
  Sean Little
Vice President Of Marketing, Jennifer Bohnen
Senior Vice President Of Operations, Anna
  Jimenez
Senior Vice President Operations, Stephen Milota
Assistant Vice President Bsa Compliance, Amber
  Schoenauer
Senior Vice President Of Commercial Banking,
  Lena Dawson
Vice President, Timmer John
Vice President Capital Markets, Clark Brian
Assistant Vice President Financial Analyst, Scott
  Gurke
Avp Eeo Compliance, Mary Rivers
Svp, Joseph Gregoire
Assistant Vice President Business Lending, Ryan
  Bauroth
Vp Senior Manager, Joseph White
Vice President, Rob Lewis
Vp Credit Risk Management; Cecl
  Implementation, Ashwin Bhalla
Assistant Vice President Learning And
  Development, Douglas Campbell
Assistant Vice President Marketing Commercial
  Banking, Kim Nagy
Assistant Vice President Loan Administration,
  Judy Nering
Vice President, Laura Sepulveda
Vice President Risk, Thomas Benkoske
Senior Vice President Commercial Banking, Vishal
  Patel
Vice President, Patrice Louis
Vice President Risk Management, Shipra Sethi
Vice President And Audit Manager, Paul Beierwaltes
Assistant Vice President Consumer Loan
  Documentation Manager, Christy Niemietz
Vice President And Assistant General Counsel,
  Erik Hsu
Senior Vice President, Brent Scott
Vice President, Michelle Lezotte
Assistant Vice President Commercial Banker, Nick
  Karalis
Vice President Information Technology Project
  Management, Susan Kucera

Assistant Vice President Default Servicing, Paul
  Hennessy
Senior Vice President, Ezra Jaffe
Senior Vice President, Ronald Calandra
Senior Vice President Of Finance, Daniel Tuerk
Senior Vice President Wealth Services, Kendra L
  Castelloni
Avp Fair Lending, Matt Sabatino
Senior Vice President, Brad Schotanus
Group Senior Vice President, Glenn Margraff
Vice President Audit Manager, Jackie Dragisic
Svp Loan Sales And Syndications, Pat Hennelly
Vice President Loan Collateral, Christina Gersy
Vice President Lending Operations, Patricia Bielat
Vice President Vice Retail Branch Manager, Agnes
  Lyko
Senior Vice President, Nicholas Begley
Auditors: Ernst & Young LLP

LOCATIONS

HQ: Wintrust Financial Corp (IL)
  9700 W. Higgins Road, Suite 800, Rosemont, IL 60018
Phone: 847 939-9000
Web: www.wintrust.com

PRODUCTS/OPERATIONS

2015 Sales

	$ mil.	% of total
Interest		
Loans including fees	651	66
Securities	61	6
Other	5	-
Non-interest		
Mortgage banking	115	12
Wealth management	73	7
Service charges on deposit accounts	27	3
Fees from covered call options	15	2
Other	40	4
Trading (losses) gains net	(0.2)	-
Total	**990**	**100**

Selected Subsidiaries and Affiliates

Banking
  Barrington Bank & Trust Company N.A.
  Beverly Bank & Trust Company N.A.
  Crystal Lake Bank & Trust Company N.A.
  Hinsdale Bank & Trust Company
  Lake Forest Bank & Trust Company
  Libertyville Bank & Trust Company
  North Shore Community Bank & Trust Company
  Northbrook Bank & Trust Company
  Old Plank Trail Community Bank N.A.
  Schaumburg Bank & Trust Company N.A.
  St. Charles Bank & Trust
  State Bank of The Lakes
  Town Bank
  Village Bank & Trust
  Wheaton Bank and Trust Company
Non-banking
  Chicago Trust Company N.A.
  First Insurance Funding Corporation
  Great Lakes Advisors LLC
  Tricom Inc. of Milwaukee
  Wayne Hummer Asset Management Company
  Wayne Hummer Investments LLC
  Wayne Hummer Trust Company N.A.
  Wintrust Information Technology Services Company
  Wintrust Mortgage Corporation (formerly
  WestAmerica Mortgage Company)

COMPETITORS

Associated Banc-Corp	Harris
Bank of America	JPMorgan Chase
Citigroup	MB Financial
Citizens Financial	Northern Trust
Group	PrivateBank
Fifth Third	U.S. Bancorp
First Midwest Bancorp	

HISTORICAL FINANCIALS

Company Type: Public

Income Statement

FYE: December 31

	ASSETS ($ mil.)	NET INCOME ($ mil.)	INCOME AS % OF ASSETS	EMPLOYEES
12/19	36,620	355	1.0%	5,057
12/18	31,244	343	1.1%	4,727
12/17	27,915	257	0.9%	4,075
12/16	25,668	206	0.8%	3,878
12/15	22,917	156	0.7%	3,770
Annual Growth	12.4%	22.7%	—	7.6%

2019 Year-End Financials

Debt ratio: 2.97%
Return on equity: 10.22%
Cash ($ mil.): 2,450
Current ratio: —
Long-term debt ($ mil.): —

No. of shares (mil.): 57
Dividends
  Yield: 1.4%
  Payout: 16.8%
Market value ($ mil.): 4,100

	STOCK PRICE ($) FY Close	P/E High/Low	PER SHARE ($) Earnings	Dividends	Book Value
12/19	70.90	13 10	6.03	1.00	63.84
12/18	66.49	16 11	5.86	0.76	57.93
12/17	82.37	19 14	4.40	0.56	53.19
12/16	72.57	19 10	3.66	0.48	51.96
12/15	48.52	18 14	2.93	0.44	48.62
Annual Growth	9.9%	— —	19.8%	22.8%	7.0%

WISCONSIN HOUSING AND ECONOMIC DEVELOPMENT AUTHORITY

EXECUTIVES

Exec Dir, Wyman B Winston
Chairman*, Ivan Gamboa
Exec Dir*, Joaquin Altoro
Coo*, Kim Plache
Chairman of The Board*, Brad Guse
Real Estate Conultant, David Sheperd
Financial Officer, Dan Besteman
Senior Business, George Petak
Assistant Manager, Scott Phillips
Manager, Connie Martin
Loan Advisor, Donna Lazenby

LOCATIONS

HQ: WISCONSIN HOUSING AND ECONOMIC DEVELOPMENT AUTHORITY
201 W WASHINGTON AVE # 700, MADISON, WI 537032760
Phone: 608 266-7884
Web: WWW.WHEDA.COM

HISTORICAL FINANCIALS

Company Type: Private

Income Statement

FYE: June 30

	ASSETS ($ mil.)	NET INCOME ($ mil.)	INCOME AS % OF ASSETS	EMPLOYEES
06/20	3,213	91	2.8%	171
06/19	2,919	87	3.0%	—
06/18	2,475	33	1.4%	—
06/17	2,201	23	1.1%	—
Annual Growth	13.4%	57.8%	—	—

World Fuel Services Corp.

World Fuel Services is a leading fuel and fuel handling services company selling to air carriers cargo and charter carriers and private aircraft operators around the world. It is also a marine fuel reseller on hand to deliver marine fuel to the shipping industry and commercial vessels and it supplies land transport markets via hundreds of terminals. World Fuel's other services include flight planning weather reports and card payment services. The company which services more than 8000 locations in about 200 countries and territories gets more than 50% of its revenue from the US. World Fuel sells about 15 billion gallons of fuel a year.

Operations

World Fuel Services operates three fueling segments: Aviation Land and Marine. It also offers a range of support services (such as fuel market analysis flight planning ground-handling services and weather reports) to its aviation and marine customers.

The Aviation segment generates about 50% of sales and markets fuel and related products and services to major commercial airlines second and third tier airlines cargo carriers regional and low-cost carriers airports fixed based operators corporate fleets fractional operators private aircraft military fleets and to the US and foreign governments. It purchases fuel from suppliers worldwide and can deliver directly into aircraft or to a storage facility.

The Land segment less than 30% of sales offers fuel and related services to petroleum distributors retail petroleum operators and other fuel users. It also engages in crude oil marketing activities.

The Marine fueling services business about 20% of sales markets fuel lubricants and related products and services. It arranges fueling for ships on a brokered basis and extends credit to a global customer base which includes container and tanker lines cruise ships yachts and time-charter operators.

Geographic Reach

Florida-based World Fuel Services has operations in Brazil Canada Denmark France Germany the UK and the UAE.

The company depends on the US for more than half of its revenue followed by EMEA (Europe Middle East and Africa) around 25% the Asia/Pacific region nearly 15% and the Americas (not including the US) about 10%.

Sales and Marketing

World Fuel purchases inventory at airports or has it shipped via pipelines and held at multiple locations. The company sells fuel via supply contracts where customers commit to purchasing fuel over the contract term. It also conducts spot sales (or non-contract) sales. World Fuel's fuel prices are tied to market-based formulas or are government controlled. The majority of its marine segment activity consists of spot sales. The company also contracts with third parties to provide various services for to customers including fueling of vessels in ports and at sea and transportation and delivery of fuel and fuel-related products.

Financial Performance

World Fuel has a fluctuating revenue in the last five years. 2019 revenue is 7% higher compared to 2015.

The company's revenue for 2019 was $36.8 billion a decrease of $2.9 billion or 7.4% as compared to 2018. Revenues in the marine segment were $8.1 billion for the year ended 2019 a decrease of $1.2 billion or 12.9% as compared to 2018.

The decrease in revenues was driven primarily by lower volume sold in 2019. Net income is improved 40% from $127.7 million in 2018 to $178.9 million in 2019.

World Fuel had $186.1 million in cash and equivalents in 2019 compared to $211.7 million in 2018. Operating activities generated $228.8 million to the coffers. Investing activities used $50.5 million and financing activities used $204.9 million in 2019.

Strategy

A key element of the company's business strategy has been the growth of its business through acquisitions and strategic investments and divestitures. It have been pursuing acquisition opportunities complementary to its business portfolio. Furthermore it is continually assess the strategic fit of its existing businesses and seek the most cost-effective means and efficient structure to serve its customers and suppliers and respond to changes in the markets in which the company operate.

World Fuel rely heavily on its computer systems information technology and network infrastructure across its operations particularly as the company seek to grow technology offerings digitize its business and drive internal efficiencies.

Mergers and Acquisitions

In 2020 World Fuel completes its acquisition with Universal's Aviation and Weather's UVair fuel business for about $170 million. UVair headquartered in Houston Texas serves business and general aviation customers at more than 5000 locations worldwide. While Universal will maintain its international trip planning services business as part of the purchase of the UVair fuel business Universal will now be working exclusively with World Fuel Services to provide fuel supply to their customers. This acquisition complements World Fuel's organic growth initiatives and will provide additional momentum for the advancement of the global aviation platform.

Company Background

Neighbors Ralph Weiser and Jerrold Blair founded International Oil Recovery an oil recycling company in Florida in 1984. The company moved into aviation fueling by acquiring Advance Petroleum in 1986. Two years later International Oil Recovery diversified further entering the hazardous waste market by buying Resource Recovery of America a soil remediation company. In 1989 the firm acquired JCo Energy Partners an aviation fuel company and subsequently renamed its aviation fueling division World Fuel Services.

World Fuels has maintained a steady drumbeat of acquisitions to fuel growth.

HISTORY

Neighbors Ralph Weiser and Jerrold Blair founded International Oil Recovery an oil recycling company in Florida in 1984. The company moved into aviation fueling by acquiring Advance Petroleum in 1986. Two years later International Oil Recovery diversified further entering the hazardous waste market by buying Resource Recovery of America a soil remediation company. In 1989 the firm acquired JCo Energy Partners an aviation fuel company and subsequently renamed its aviation fueling division World Fuel Services. The company set up International Petroleum in 1993 to operate a Delaware used-oil and water-recycling plant.

The company changed its name to World Fuel Services Corp. in 1995 to reflect its expanded range of operations. Also that year it nearly doubled its revenue base with the purchase of Trans-Tec the world's #1 independent marine fuel services company. World Fuel also exited the environmental services business in 1995 to focus on its fuel services and oil recycling businesses.

The following year the company formed World Fuel International a subsidiary based in Costa Rica that serves World Fuel's aviation customers in South and Central America Canada and the Caribbean. In 1998 it acquired corporate jet fuel provider Baseops International which has offices in the UK and Texas.

In 1999 the company expanded its share of the marine fuel market with the acquisition of the Bunkerfuels group of companies one of the world's top marine fuel brokerages.

To focus on its marine and aviation fueling businesses World Fuel exited the oil recycling segment in 2000 when it sold its International Petroleum unit to waste services company Earth-Care for about $33 million.

The company expanded into the United Arab Emirates with its 2001 acquisition of fuel services provider Marine Energy of Dubai. World Fuel acquired Rotterdam-based marine fuel reseller Oil Shipping Group in 2002.

In 2004 World Fuel Services acquired UK-based marine fuel reseller Tramp Holdings for $83 million.

The company diversified further in 2007 acquiring AVCARD a leading provider of contract fuel sales and charge card services to the aviation industry for $55 million.

In 2009 it bought wholesale motor fuel distributor TGS Petroleum. The company combined TGS with Texor to expand World Fuel Services' presence as the largest independent wholesale motor fuel distributor in Illinois.

Expanding its UK market share in 2009 the company acquired the Henty Oil Group of Companies a leading independent provider of marine and land fuels in the UK.

In 2010 it beefed up its position in the branded onshore wholesale market to 1 billion gallons a year by acquiring Lakeside Oil Company based in Milwaukee. It also boosted its market position through the acquisition of leading independent petroleum marketing company Western Petroleum for $95 million.

Boosting its aviation fuel segment in 2011 (for an undisclosed amount) World Fuel Services acquired The Hiller Group an aviation fuel supplier to more than 600 fixed base operators. It also bought Ascent Aviation a national branded reseller of aviation fuel for ConocoPhillips and deicing fluid for Dow Chemical and which supplies more than 450 airports and fixed base operators and NATO aviation fuel and logistics supplier Nordic Camp Supply (for $68.5 million.)

In 2012 the company acquired CarterEnergy's wholesale motor fuel distribution business. Kansas-based CarterEnergy with an annual volume of more than of 500 million gallons distributes branded fuel to more than 700 retail operators and is a supplier to industrial commercial and government customers in more than a dozen states. The deal boosted World Fuel Services' land fuel volume to more than 3.5 billion gallons.

In 2013 to improve its payment processing operations it also bought certain assets from Multi Service Corporation (which specializes in fleet government and commercial payment programs) for $137 million. The Multi Service acquisition expands World Fuel Services' presence in the payment processing industry.

EXECUTIVES

President Coo And Director; Chairman And Ceo Marine Fueling Services, Michael J. Kasbar, age 64, $875,100 total compensation

Evp And Cfo, Ira M. Birns, age 58, $583,400 total compensation

Evp; Regional Managing Director Asia, Francis L Boon Meng

Evp And Coo, Jeff S. Smith

Evp; Regional Managing Director Emea, Wade N. DeClaris

Svp And Cio, Massoud Sedigh, age 65

Evp Global Aviation And Marine, John P. Rau, $475,100 total compensation

Evp Global Land, Michael J. Crosby, $487,550 total compensation

Vice President People And Performance Development, Marcia Morales-jaffe

Senior Vice President, Carlos Cuervo

Vice President Business Development And Strategy, Alexander Garcia

Vice President Of Taxation, Kathy Rossi

Vice President Application Development, Russ Sabbag

Vice President Assistant Treasurer, Glenn Klevitz

Vice President Application Development, Scott DeLoach

Senior Vice President Land North America, Kerry Oliver

Vice President Human Resources, Sue Rider

Vice President, Rebecca Hing

Vice President, Steve Drzymalla

Vice President Information Security, Timothy Ramsay

Vice President Supply And Trading, Steven Fiedler

Vice President Retail Channel Development, Ken Wootton

Senior Vice President Global Trip Support, Joel Purdom

Vice President Business Development, Michael Brown

Vice President Sales, Kevin Macmillan

Vice President Global Head Of Back Office Operations, Fatima Bentoumi

Executive Vice President And Chief Financial Officer, Guru Acharya

Vice President, Kohli Gurinder

Vice President Finance North America Land, Beth Johnson

Auditors: PricewaterhouseCoopers LLP

LOCATIONS

HQ: World Fuel Services Corp.
9800 Northwest 41st Street, Miami, FL 33178
Phone: 305 428-8000   **Fax:** 305 392-5621
Web: www.wfscorp.com

2018 sales

	$ mil.	% of total
United States	20,555	52
Europe & Middle East & Africa	9,721	24
Asia/Pacific	5,537	14
Americas (excluding the US)	3,935	14
Total	**39,705**	**100**

PRODUCTS/OPERATIONS

2018 sales

	$ mil.	% of total
Aviation	19,119	48
Land	11,381	29
Marine	9,249	23
Total	**39,750**	**100**

Selected Subsidiaries

Ascent Aviation Group Inc.
Baseops Europe Ltd. (UK)
Baseops International Inc.
Casa Petro S.R.L. (Costa Rica)
Henty Oil Limited (UK)
Marine Energy Arabia Co. (L.L.C.) (United Arab Emirates)
Nordic Camp Supply ApS (Denmark)
PetroServicios de Costa Rica S.R.L.
TGS Petroleum
The Hiller Group Incorporated
Tramp Holdings Limited (UK)
Trans-Tec International S.R.L. (Costa Rica)
Western Petroleum Company
World Fuel International S.R.L. (Costa Rica)
World Fuel Services Inc.
World Fuel Services Ltd. (UK)
World Fuel Services (Singapore) Pte. Ltd.

Selected products and services

Selected Products and Services

Aviation
Business and General Aviation
Request an Authorization
Validate a Card
Report a Lost Card
Commercial Aviation
Deicing Services
Export Supply
Fuel Management
Risk Management
Tax Information
Marine
Marine Fuels
Lubricants
Operations
Consulting
Yacht Services
Quality Assurance
Physical Supply
Risk Management

BBA Aviation
BP Marine
Exxon Mobil
Fuchs Lubricants

Mercury Air Group
Shell Aviation
Sun Coast Resources

HISTORICAL FINANCIALS

Company Type: Public

Income Statement				FYE: December 31
	REVENUE ($ mil.)	NET INCOME ($ mil.)	NET PROFIT MARGIN	EMPLOYEES
12/19	36,819	178	0.5%	5,500
12/18	39,750	127	0.3%	5,000
12/17	33,695	(170)	—	5,000
12/16	27,015	126	0.5%	5,000
12/15	30,379	186	0.6%	4,700
Annual Growth	4.9%	(1.1%)	—	4.0%

2019 Year-End Financials

Debt ratio: 10.49%
Return on equity: 9.66%
Cash ($ mil.): 186
Current ratio: 1.32
Long-term debt ($ mil.): 574

No. of shares (mil.): 65
Dividends
Yield: 0.8%
Payout: 15.8%
Market value ($ mil.): 2,831

	STOCK PRICE ($) FY Close	P/E High/Low		PER SHARE ($) Earnings	Dividends	Book Value
12/19	43.42	16	8	2.69	0.36	28.99
12/18	21.41	17	11	1.89	0.24	27.10
12/17	28.14	—	—	(2.50)	0.24	25.44
12/16	45.91	28	20	1.81	0.24	27.54
12/15	38.46	22	13	2.64	0.24	27.00
Annual Growth	3.1%	—	—	0.5%	10.7%	1.8%

WSFS Financial Corp

WSFS isn't a radio station but it is tuned to the banking needs of Delaware. WSFS Financial is the holding company for Wilmington Savings Fund Society (WSFS Bank) a thrift with nearly $5 billion in assets and more than 75 branches mostly in Delaware and Pennsylvania. Founded in 1832 WSFS Bank attracts deposits from individuals and local businesses by offering standard products like checking and savings accounts CDs and IRAs. The bank uses funds primarily to lend to businesses: Commercial loans and mortgages account for about 85% of its loan portfolio. Bank subsidiaries Christiana Trust Cypress Capital Management and WSFS Wealth Investment provide trust and investment advisory services to wealthy clients and institutional investors.

Operations

Its Christiana Trust division boasts nearly $9 billion in assets under administration and provides investment fiduciary agency bankruptcy and commercial domicile services from offices in Delaware and Nevada.

The company's Cash Connect division operates more than 450 ATMs for WSFS Bank which boasts the largest branded ATM network in Delaware. The division also manages some $490 million of vault cash in approximately 15000 ATMs nationwide and provides online reporting and ATM cash management predictive cash or-

dering armored carrier management and ATM processing and equipment sales.

Overall the bank generated roughly 57% of its total revenue from interest and fees on loans in 2014 plus an additional 10% from interest on its mortgage-back and other investment securities. About 7% of its total revenue came from wealth management income while mortgage banking income contributed another 2%. The majority of the remaining revenue came from credit/debit card and ATM income and deposit service charges.

Geographic Reach

WSFS Bank has 45 branches throughout Delaware nearly 10 branches in Pennsylvania one branch in Nevada and one in Virginia.

Financial Performance

WSFS Financial's revenues and profits have been trending higher in recent years thanks to sustained growth in its lending business organically and through acquisitions and thanks to declining loan loss provisions as its loan portfolio's credit quality has improved with the strengthened economy.

The company's revenue rose by 5% to $238.62 million in 2014 thanks to interest income growth mostly driven by increased loan business and higher securities interest; which stemmed from a combination of the bank's First Wyoming Financial Corporation acquisition improvements in its balance sheet mix and additional income from its reverse mortgage-related assets.

Higher revenue and a continued decline in loan loss provisions in 2014 pushed WSFS Financial's net income up by 15% to $53.73 million during the year while the company's operating cash levels jumped by 17% to $67.06 million thanks to higher cash earnings.

Strategy

WSFS Financial reiterated its long-term growth strategy in 2015 which included growing the bank's lending business boosting its Trust and Wealth Management group's assets under administration and expanding Cash Connect's ATM customer base and customer cross-sell.

Beyond utilizing its community-oriented and local commercial lending teams the company has been growing its loan business and its branch reach through strategic acquisitions of banks and bank branches in target markets with preference toward markets in southeastern Pennsylvania. Its 2014 acquisition of First Wyoming Financial Corp for example bolstered WSFS' presence in Kent county while strengthening its position as the one of Delaware's top independent community banks.

Mergers and Acquisitions

In mid-2018 WSFS Financial agreed to purchase Philadelphia-based Beneficial Bancorp in a deal worth $1.5 billion. The transaction will create the largest locally headquartered community bank in the Greater Delaware Valley region with about $13 billion in assets.

EXECUTIVES

Chairman President And Ceo, Mark A. Turner, age 57, $639,336 total compensation
Svp And Corporate Auditor Wsfs Financial And Wsfs Bank, Thomas W. Kearney
Evp And Chief Retail Banking Officer, Richard M. (Rick) Wright, age 67, $337,173 total compensation
Evp And Coo, Rodger Levenson, age 58, $348,721 total compensation
Evp And Chief Human Capital Officer, Peggy H. Eddens, age 64
Evp And Chief Wealth Officer, Paul D. Geraghty, $310,671 total compensation
Evp And Cto, S. James (Jim) Mazarakis, $337,173 total compensation
President Cash Connect, Tom Stevenson
Cfo, Dominic Canuso
Vice President Retail Banking, Adrienne Hawes
Assistant Vice President Information Technology Network Services Manager, Peter Ghosh
Senior Vice President, Dennis Matarangas
Vp Division Controller, Ruth Mcdevitt
Assistant Vice President Network Services Director, Jason Berkowitz
Vice President Audit Manager, Rene Lopez
Executive Vice President, Cynthia Cole
Executive Vice President Chief Commercial Banking Officer, Steve Clark
Assistant Vice President Small Business Lender Retail Office Manager, Carol Brindle
Senior Vice President Commercial R E Lending, Joseph C Walker
Executive Vice President And Chief Commercial Banking Officer, Stephen Null Clark
Vice President Financial Advisor, Nick Frake
Evp Pennsylvania Market President, Patrick Ward
Vice President, Joseph Murphy
Assistant Vice President, Paul Roughton
Avp Facilities Manager, Bill Hornung
Senior Vice President And Director, Steven G Kochie
Assistant Vice President Digital Banking And Payments Solutions Manager, Chris Zupko
Assistant Vice President T, Nicole Monroe-cole
Avp Asset Recovery Relationship Manager, William Madgey
Svp, Michael Jordan
Vice President Credit Card Product Management, Paul Brutsche
Vice President And Small Business Relationship Manager, Ronald Miller
Vp Directorgovernment Guaranteed Lending, Candice Caruso
Vice President Small Business Relationship Manager, Amy Flynn
Vice President Sba Lending, Tom Dowling
Avp Retail Office Manager, Chris Graham
Avp Retail Office Manager, Christina Adams
Vice President Regional Manager, Jeremy Shackleford
Vp Middle Market Lending, Yogesh Kantharia
Vice President Commercial Lending, Jessica Straghan
Board Member, Marvin Schoenhals
Vice Chairman, Charles G. Cheleden, age 76
Board Member, David Turner
Board Member, Jennifer Davis
Board Member, Eleuthere Du Pont
Board Member, Christopher Ghysens
Auditors: KPMG LLP

LOCATIONS

HQ: WSFS Financial Corp
500 Delaware Avenue, Wilmington, DE 19801
Phone: 302 792-6000
Web: www.wsfsbank.com

2012 Branches

	No.
Delaware	42
Pennsylvania	7
Nevada	1
Virginia	1
Total	**51**

PRODUCTS/OPERATIONS

2014 Sales

	$ mil.	% of total
Interest		
Loans including fees	137	57
Mortgage-backed securities	13	6
Investment securities	9	4
Noninterest		
Credit/debit card & ATM income	24	11
Deposit service charges	17	7
Wealth management income	17	7
Mortgage baning activities	4	2
Other	15	6
Total	**238**	**100**

COMPETITORS

Bank of America	M&T Bank
Citizens Financial	PNC Financial
Group	Sovereign Bank
Fulton Financial	TD Bank USA
JPMorgan Chase	The Bancorp

HISTORICAL FINANCIALS

Company Type: Public

Income Statement

FYE: December 31

	ASSETS ($ mil.)	NET INCOME ($ mil.)	INCOME AS % OF ASSETS	EMPLOYEES
12/19	12,256	148	1.2%	1,782
12/18	7,248	134	1.9%	1,177
12/17	6,999	50	0.7%	1,159
12/16	6,765	64	0.9%	1,116
12/15	5,585	53	1.0%	947
Annual Growth	21.7%	29.1%	—	17.1%

2019 Year-End Financials

Debt ratio: 1.35%
Return on equity: 11.14%
Cash ($ mil.): 571
Current ratio: —
Long-term debt ($ mil.): —

No. of shares (mil.): 51
Dividends
Yield: 1.0%
Payout: 15.8%
Market value ($ mil.): 2,268

	STOCK PRICE ($) FY Close	P/E High/Low	PER SHARE ($) Earnings	Dividends	Book Value
12/19	43.99	15 12	3.00	0.47	35.88
12/18	37.91	13 9	4.19	0.42	26.17
12/17	47.85	33 27	1.56	0.30	23.05
12/16	46.35	22 13	2.06	0.25	21.90
12/15	32.36	42 13	1.85	0.31	19.50
Annual Growth	8.0%	— —	12.8%	11.0%	16.5%

Xcel Energy Inc

Xcel Energy is a utility holding company distributing electricity to 3.7 million customers and natural gas to 2.1 million customers in eight states through its four regulated utilities: Northern States Power Minnesota Northern States Power Wisconsin the Public Service Company of Colorado and Southwestern Public Service. Colorado and Minnesota account for most of the company's customers. Xcel owns power plants that have combined capacity of more than 18700 MW of electricity. It also owns transmission and distribution lines as well as natural gas assets. It is investing in wind power and operates wind farms in Colorado Minnesota and other states. The company traces its roots back to 1881.

Operations

Xcel Energy's reportable segments are Regulated Electric Utility Regulated Gas Utility and Other.

Regulated Electric is the largest segment producing about 85% of total revenue through the generation purchase transmission and distribution of electricity. Regulated Natural Gas transports stores and distributes natural gas to generate most of the remaining revenue.

The two power segments achieve their objectives through several subsidiaries: Northern States Power Minnesota (NSP-M) Northern States Power Wisconsin (NSP-W) the Public Service Company of Colorado (PSCo) and Southwestern Public Service (SPS).

Xcel owns and operates roughly 18700 MW of electric generating capacity and purchases additional power from third parties through long-term power purchase agreements. Generally Xcel's power plants produce about two-thirds of its needs and the company purchases the other third. Of its generated electricity a third comes from coal another third comes from natural gas about 15% comes from nuclear and the rest is generated from wind hydroelectric and other sources.

The Regulated Natural Gas segment purchases the natural gas from producers and contracts with transmission pipeline companies to move it to Xcel's distributions facilities. From there the company sends natural gas to customers.

Xcel's Other segment generates about 1% of the company's revenue and includes steam revenue appliance repair services and non-utility real estate activities.

Geographic Reach

Minneapolis Minnesota-based Xcel Energy serves eight mid-western and western states including portions of Colorado Michigan Minnesota New Mexico North Dakota South Dakota Texas and Wisconsin. Its Northern States Power Minnesota serves customers in North and South Dakota and in Minnesota. Northern States Power Wisconsin delivers energy to customers in Wisconsin and Michigan. Public Service Company of Colorado provides energy to customers throughout the state while Southwestern Public Service Company serves in New Mexico and Texas.

Sales and Marketing

Xcel Energy's major commercial and industrial electric sales are to customers in the petroleum coal and food products industries. The company also serves small commercial and industrial customers. Commercial and industrial customers account for more than 30% of the company's total revenue.

Residential customers account for about 60% of Xcel's revenue.

Financial Performance

As is true with electric service companies Xcel Energy's revenue has remained essentially unchanged over the past five years.

In 2019 revenue fell by $8 million to $11.5 billion due to decrease in electric segment partially offset by natural gas segment.

Net income in 2019 rose to $1.4 billion up $111 million from the previous year. While operating expenses were lower in 2019 the company paid less in income taxes than it did in the previous period which resulted in the modest bottom line increase.

Cash at the end of the year was $248 million up $101 million from the previous period. Operating activities provided $3.3 billion investing activities (mostly capital expenditures) used $4.3 billion and financing activities provided $1.2 billion largely through issuance of additional debt.

Strategy

Through Xcel's strategic planning process the board of directors and executive leadership team identified three strategic priorities that represent the keys to the company's continued success in achieving its vision to be the preferred and trusted provider of the energy customers need. These priorities include: leading the clean energy transition; enhancing the customer experience; and keeping bills low.

Company Background

The Minnesota Electric Light & Electric Motive Power Company was founded in 1881 and changed its name to Minnesota Brush Electric the next year. In the 1890s it provided street lighting and power for trolleys and became Minneapolis General Electric.

In 1909 Henry Byllesby formed rival firm Washington County Light and Power Co. (soon renamed Consumers Power Company) then created holding company Northern States Power Company of Delaware (NSPD). In 1910 he founded Standard Gas and Electric a holding company overseeing NSPD and many other US utilities.

The company took on its most recent incarnation as Xcel Energy in August 2000 following the merger of Northern States Power Company and New Century Energies Inc.

HISTORY

The Minnesota Electric Light & Electric Motive Power Company was founded in 1881 and changed its name to Minnesota Brush Electric the next year. In the 1890s it provided street lighting and power for trolleys and became Minneapolis General Electric.

In 1909 Henry Byllesby formed rival firm Washington County Light and Power Co. (soon renamed Consumers Power Company) then created holding company Northern States Power Company of Delaware (NSPD). In 1910 he founded Standard Gas and Electric a holding company overseeing NSPD and many other US utilities.

NSPD bought Minneapolis General Electric in 1912 and Consumers Power was renamed the Northern States Power Company (NSP) in 1916. During the 1920s NSPD connected its subsidiaries via transmission lines. Byllesby died in 1924.

In 1931 NSP was placed under NSPD but the Public Utility Holding Company Act of 1935 dissolved Standard and NSPD. NSP became independent in the 1940s and spent $335 million on new facilities after WWII.

During the 1960s NSP moved into Michigan South Dakota and Wisconsin and brought its first nuclear power plant on line in 1964 (converted to natural gas in 1968). It began operating the Monticello and Prairie Island nukes in the early 1970s.

Company sales nearly doubled in the 1980s. In 1989 NSP created NRG Energy (incorporated

1992) to invest in independent power projects. The Federal Energy Policy Act allowed wholesale power competition in 1992 and NSP lost nine of its 19 municipal customers.

NSP acquired Viking Gas Transmission which owned an interstate pipeline in 1993. It also began developing affordable housing. In 1995 NSP and Wisconsin Electric planned to merge but dropped the deal amid antitrust concerns. NSP continued to diversify forming telecommunications provider Seren Innovations in 1996 and starting its cable-testing business in 1997. The next year NSP formed a power marketing unit.

NRG Energy began a shopping spree abroad in 1994 buying interests in plants in Germany and Australia. In 1996 it bought a 48% stake in Bolivia's COBEE (increased to 99% in 2001). Also that year it acquired PacifiCorp's Pacific Generating unit which owned stakes in a dozen geographically scattered plants.

In 1999 NRG Energy gained nearly 7600 MW of capacity through power plant acquisitions in California Connecticut Massachusetts and New York. The next year NRG Energy picked up another 1700 MW in Louisiana and it agreed to buy fossil-fueled plants (1875 MW) from Delaware's Conectiv for $800 million (half of the deal was completed in 2001 the other half was canceled the following year). NSP spun off part of NRG in 2000 in an IPO.

Meanwhile as the utility-merger trend gathered steam in 1999 NSP agreed to acquire Denver-based New Century Engines in a $4.9 billion deal. The acquisition was completed in 2000 and the expanded company changed its name to Xcel Energy.

The next year Xcel sold nearly all of its stake in UK-based Yorkshire Power Group which had been held by New Century Energies to Innogy (now RWE npower). It sold its remaining 5% stake in Yorkshire Power in 2002. NRG purchased several Latin American projects from Swedish utility Vattenfall in 2001. NRG also agreed to purchase four coal-fired plants (2500 MW) in Ohio from FirstEnergy for $1.5 billion; however the deal was later canceled.

In 2002 Xcel repurchased the 26% stake in NRG that it sold to the public in 2000-01.

EXECUTIVES

Evp And Group President Operations, Kent T. Larson, age 60, $550,000 total compensation
Chairman President And Ceo, Benjamin G. S. (Ben) Fowke, age 62, $1,200,000 total compensation
President Xcel Energy - Colorado, David L. Eves, age 62
Svp And Cio, David C. Harkness
Evp And Group President Utilities And Chief Administrative Officer, Marvin E. McDaniel, age 60, $550,000 total compensation
President Xcel Energy Michigan Wisconsin, Mark E. Stoering, age 59
Svp And Chief Nuclear Officer, Timothy (Tim) O'Connor, age 60
President Xcel Energy New Mexico Texas, David T. Hudson, age 59
President Xcel Energy Minnesota South Dakota North Dakota, Christopher B. (Chris) Clark, age 53
Evp And General Counsel, Scott M. Willensky, age 63, $505,000 total compensation
Evp And Cfo, Robert C. (Bob) Frenzel, age 49, $397,500 total compensation
Chief Sales Officer, Candace Morse

Vice President And Treasurer, Brian Van Abel
Vice President Gas Operations, Luke Litteken
Vice President Of Operations, Julie Pippenger
Vice President Construction Operations And Maintenance, Tim Brossart
Vice President, Sarah Soong
Auditors: DELOITTE & TOUCHE LLP

LOCATIONS

HQ: Xcel Energy Inc
   414 Nicollet Mall, Minneapolis, MN 55401
Phone: 612 330-5500
Web: www.xcelenergy.com

PRODUCTS/OPERATIONS

2018 Sales

	$ mil.	% of total
Electric	9,719	84
Natural Gas	1,739	15
Other	79	1
Total	**11,537**	**100**

COMPETITORS

AEP	CenterPoint Energy
ALLETE	DTE
Alliant Energy	FirstEnergy
Ameren	NextEra Energy
Atmos Energy	OGE Energy
Basin Electric Power	PPL Corporation
Black Hills Power	WEC Energy
CMS Energy	

HISTORICAL FINANCIALS

Company Type: Public

Income Statement   FYE: December 31

	REVENUE ($ mil.)	NET INCOME ($ mil.)	NET PROFIT MARGIN	EMPLOYEES
12/19	11,529	1,372	11.9%	11,317
12/18	11,537	1,261	10.9%	11,092
12/17	11,404	1,148	10.1%	11,134
12/16	11,106	1,123	10.1%	11,512
12/15	11,024	984	8.9%	11,687
Annual Growth	1.1%	8.7%	—	(0.8%)

2019 Year-End Financials

Debt ratio: 37.08%	No. of shares (mil.): 524
Return on equity: 10.78%	Dividends
Cash ($ mil.): 248	Yield: 2.5%
Current ratio: 0.68	Payout: 64.8%
Long-term debt ($ mil.): 17,407	Market value ($ mil.): 33,303

	STOCK PRICE ($) FY Close	P/E High/Low	PER SHARE ($) Earnings	Dividends	Book Value
12/19	63.49	25 18	2.64	1.62	25.24
12/18	49.27	22 17	2.47	1.52	23.78
12/17	48.11	23 18	2.25	1.44	22.56
12/16	40.70	21 16	2.21	1.36	21.73
12/15	35.91	20 16	1.94	1.28	20.89
Annual Growth	15.3%	— —	8.0%	6.1%	4.8%

Xerox Holdings Corp

Xerox Corp. is not a copy of its former self. The company whose name has been a synonym for "to copy" remains a leading seller of copiers and printers from basic black-and-white output to high-end color systems. These days Xerox makes most of its revenue from its post-sale services such as document management maintenance supplies and paper and financing. Xerox also sells software for automating and integrating print jobs from start to finish. Its products are used in offices of large and small- and medium-sized businesses and in production plants of commercial printing companies. US customers account for about 60% of revenue.

Operations

Xerox makes machines that make copies print send faxes scan documents and more as well as the ink paper and support that keeps the equipment running. The company charges from a few hundred to thousands of dollars for its equipment but it makes more than 75% of its revenue from those post-sale products and services.

Xerox manages its offerings in three segments: Xerox Services Workplace Solutions and Graphic Communications and Production Solutions.

Xerox Services includes Intelligent Workplace Services (IWS) and a range of Digital Services that leverage its software capabilities in Workflow Automation Personalization and Communication Software Content Management Solutions and Digitization Services.

Workplace Solutions consists of Xerox's Entry and Mid-Range equipment products which share common technology manufacturing and product platforms.

Graphic Communication and Production Solutions are designed for customers in the graphic communications in-plant and production print environment with high-volume printing requirements. Its broad portfolio of presses and solutions provides full-color on-demand printing of wide range of applications.

Geographic Reach

Although Xerox Corp. operates in more than 160 countries about 60% of sales are from customers in the US. About 25% of sales are from Europe with the rest of the world accounting for the rest.

Based in Norwalk Connecticut Xerox has principal manufacturing and engineering facilities located in New York California Oklahoma Oregon Canada the United Kingdom Ireland and a leased site in the Netherlands. It also ha principal research facilities located in California New York and Canada.

Sales and Marketing

Xerox complements its global sales team and sales website with a network of third-party sales channels such as independent agents dealers value-added resellers and systems integrators. In addition its wholly-owned subsidiary XBS an office technology organization comprised of regional core companies in the U.S. sells document management and IT services.

The Xerox brand is well-known and its customers are ranging from small- medium businesses to printing production (including graphic communications) companies government entities educational institutions and Fortune 1000 corporations.

Financial Performance

Xerox's revenue remained on a years-long slide in 2019 falling to $9.1 billion down 6% from 2018 as the company's equipment business continued to lose ground. The company has shed about $2.8 billion of revenue since 2014.

In 2019 equipment sales were 5% lower than in 2018 due to the decrease of sales of entry and mid-level machines. Sales of higher-end higher margin equipment however dropped 4% for color systems and 14% for black-and-white systems. Revenue from the post-sale segment slipped 6% in 2019 from 2018 because of fewer signings and installations.

Xerox's profit popped 275% higher to $1.4 billion in 2019 up $361 million from 2018 boosted by cost reductions that offset revenue declines.

The company's cash and equivalents stood at $2.8 billion in 2019 compared to $1.1 billion in 2018. Operations generated $1.3 billion in 2019 while investing activities provided $2.2 billion and financing activities used $1.8 billion primarily for payments on long-term debt and company's stock repurchase.

Strategy

Xerox is a well-known name in corporate America but it might not carry the gleam of innovation that the company would like. Its sales have declined over the past five years as its copiers and printers have elicited little excitement in the market. The company is moving to change that with new technologies and increased efficiency.

Xerox prioritizes technology development in four areas: Digital packaging and print 3D printing and digital manufacturing artificial intelligence capabilities and sensors and services for the Internet of Things. One of the company's recent offerings was its ConnectKey software that allows Xerox devices to integrate into digital workflows.

The company is also taking steps to make its operations more efficient by increasing use of shared service centers consolidating its IT infrastructure and real estate footprint and speeding up its supply chain. It plans to get $640 million of cost savings in 2019 as part of $1.5 billion in savings between 2019 and 2021. In a related matter Xerox plans to merge into a holding company which it said would eliminate duplicate administrative requirements and costs. The move was approved by shareholders but needs regulatory approval.

Xerox agreed to end its 58-year joint venture called Fuji Xerox with Fujifilm by selling its 25% stake in the venture to its partner for about $2.3 billion. The agreement came about a year after a proposed merger between Xerox and Fujifilm was called off. The companies created Fuji Xerox in 1962 to sell printers and copiers in the Asia/Pacific region. As part of the agreement Fujifilm will drop its lawsuit against Xerox over the soured merger. The agreement will allow each company to pursue new product and geographic markets.

To improve its overall sales structure Xerox reorganized its geographic units into two the Americas and Europe the Middle East and Africa (EMEA). The Americas region combines the US Canada Mexico Central and South America while India becomes part of the EMEA region.

Mergers and Acquisitions

In 2020 Xerox has acquired two services and technology providers Altodigital and ITEC Connect in the U.K. "We're supporting small and midsize businesses seeking a modern work experience through two acquisitions in the U.K."

said Xavier Heiss EVP and president of EMEA Operations Xerox. "Altodigital and ITEC are both leaders in managed print services and specialists in IT services an area into which Xerox is rapidly expanding with new offerings."

In 2019 Xerox acquired two new multi-brand dealers Rabbit Office Automation (ROA) and Heritage Business Systems (HBS) to grow its presence in key markets: the San Francisco Bay Area and the Delaware Valley respectively. Xerox will focus on penetrating the small-to-medium sized business market through organic and inorganic growth which includes making investment in dealers like ROA and HBS. Integrating ROA and HBS into Xerox Business Solutions (XBS) will expand Xerox's local footprint and clients will now have access to the industry's most comprehensive offering portfolio.

Company Background

The Haloid Co. was incorporated in 1906 to make and sell photographic paper. In 1935 it bought photocopier company Rectigraph which led Haloid to buy a license for a process called electrophotography (renamed xerography from the ancient Greek words for "dry" and "writing") from the Battelle Memorial Institute in 1947.

Haloid commercialized xerography with the Model A copier in 1949 and the Xerox Copyflo in 1955 and by 1956 xerographic products represented 40% of sales. The company changed its name to Haloid Xerox in 1958 (Haloid was dropped from the name in 1961) and in 1959 it introduced the first simplified office copier. That machine took the world by storm beating out such competing technologies as mimeograph (A.B.Dick) thermal paper (3M) and damp copy (Kodak). Sales soared to nearly $270 million in 1965.

EXECUTIVES

Evp And Chief Commercial Officer, Kevin M. Warren, age 57
Ceo, Jeffrey (Jeff) Jacobson, age 60, $812,500 total compensation
President Xerox Canada, John Corley
Evp; President International Operations, Hervé Tessler, age 56
Svp And Chief Strategy And Marketing Officer, Farooq Muzaffar, age 45
Evp; President North America Operations, Michael (Mike) Feldman, age 53
Evp And Chief Human Resources Officer, Darrell L. Ford, age 55
Svp And Chief Delivery Officer, Yehia Maaty
Evp And Cfo, William F. (Bill) Osbourn, age 55
Svp And Cto, Stephen (Steve) Hoover, age 59
President Northern Southern And Central European Operations, Al Varney
Evp General Counsel And Corporate Secretary, Sarah Hlavinka McConnell, age 55
Assistant Vice President Information Technology Vendor Management, James Burnell
Vice President And Center Manager, Monica Beltrametti
Senior Vice President Of Technology, Stephen Garner
Senior Vice President And Managing Director Xerox Healthcare Provider Solutions, Justin Lanning
Vice President And Center Manager, Hadi Mahabadi
Svp Sales - It Outsourcing, George Love
Vice President And General Manager, Jack Lafferty
Vice President, Ajay Dhingra
Vice President Sales, Peter Reynolds
Vice President, Ivy McKinney

Vice President Of Engineering And Product Development, Doug Jenkins
Executive Vice President And President Americas Operations, Mike Feldman
Senior Vice President Northeast Etc, Thomas Dorazio
Corporate Vice President And Chief Financial Officer Xerox Technology Business, Grant Fitz
Vice President Of Strategy And Alliances, Tom Kavassalis
Vice President Global Advertising, Barbara Basney
Vice President Client Support Services, Linda Harrison
Vice President Client Services, Michael Sheridan
Vice President Industry Marketing, Dale Sedgwick
Vice President Information Technology Program Services, Tracy Johnson
Vice President, Michael Weldon
Vice President Operations North Dakota, Greg Bryant
National Sales Manager, David Stahler
Vice President Strategy And Workplace Services, David Nappi
Vice President Global Delivery Im Group, Robert Lyubomirsky
Vice President National Field Controller, Nate Loomis
Vice President, Shreve Bill
Vice President, Dick Jennings
Vice President Of Business Development, Matt Bologna
Xsbg Vice President Of Finance, Enos Steve
Vice President, Terence Oi
National Account Manager, Friedman Karen
Vice President Of Operations, Jeff Dalrymple
Vice President Service, Betty Mitchell
Vice President Finance Us Solutions Group, Dave Aquilla
Vpse, Jules Roche
Vice President Mps Business Operations, Robert Coward
National Account Manager, Amanda Carmichael
Vice President, Eric West
Vice President, Carl R Bothner
Senior Vice President, Joe Valenti
Division Vice President, Rebecca Taylor
Senior Vice President, Nicola Posa
Vice President, Gavin Jordan-smith
Vice President Of Operations Travel And Retail, Patrick White
Vice President, Bob Tisone
Vice President Operations, Tom Hinds
Assistant Vice President Recruiting Operations, Craig Deaton
Vice President Human Resources And Administration, George Dourlias
Sr.vice President And General Manager, Douglas J Helmink
Assistant Vice President Talent Acquisition And Staffing, Darrin Johnson
Vice President Sales, Dennis Antishin
Assistant Vice President Talent Leader Executive And Corporate Talent, James Munson
Vice President Business Development, Gloria D'Arezzo
Vice President Human Resources, Jamie Son
Vice President Of Sales Commercial Health Plans, Robert Levy
Vice President Of Sales, Tami Angelo
Vice President Applications And Project Management Office, Kim Ringold
Sbu Director And Vice President, Tom Boyle
Vice President And Senior Corporate Counsel Legal, Don Delorenz
Senior Vice President Southwest Operations, Mary Nelson
Vice President Midrange Hosting, Martin Webb
Senior Vice President Global Service Operations An, Jimmy Brown

**Senior Vice President Managing Director Hro
Services,** Esther Laspisa
Assistant Vice President, Daneen Muto
Vice President Corporate Counsel, Priscilla K Park
Vice President And Chief Accounting Officer,
Joseph Mancini
Senior Vice President Chief Innovation Officer,
Rg Conlee
Vice President Contracts, Bruce Eddy
**Vice President Of Finance For The Us Channels
Group,** Jason Barnecut-Kearns
**Vp And Gm Marketing Communications Channel
Group Operations Uk And Director,** Mark Duffelen
Vice President Epic Solutions, Bradford Grow
Vice President Production Inkjet Sales, Steve
Welkley
**Pa To Bertrand Cerisier Vice President Global
Marketing Office Solutions Business Group,**
Tracy Styles
Vice President Corporate Communications, Kevin
Lightfoot
Vice President Quality, John Lawerence
**Svp Acquisitions Corporate Services And
Marketing Global Imaging Systems,** Michael
Pietrunti
Senior Vice President And Chief Delivery Officer,
Mary Mchugh
**Senior Vice President Chief Communications And
Brand Officer,** Anne Marie Squeo
Vice President, Tim McAuley
Chairman, Robert J. (Bob) Keegan, age 73
Secretary, Jonathan Verna
Secretary, Habiba Soares
Board Member, Greg Brown
Member Board Of Directors, Joe Echevarria
Auditors: PricewaterhouseCoopers LLP

LOCATIONS

HQ: Xerox Holdings Corp
P.O. Box 4505, 201 Merritt 7, Norwalk, CT 06851-1056
Phone: 203 968-3000
Web: www.xerox.com

2018 Sales

	$ mil.	% of total
US	5,778	58
Europe	2,625	27
Canada	569	6
Other	858	9
Total	**10,265**	**100**

PRODUCTS/OPERATIONS

2018 Sales

	$ mil.	% of total
Post-sales		2200
78		
Equipment sales	7,630	22
Total	**9,830**	**100**

2018 Sales

	$ mil.	% of total
Sales	3,972	40
Services	5,590	57
Financing	268	3
Total	**9,830**	**100**

2018

	$ mil.	% of total
Equipment	2,200	22
Supplies paper and other	1,772	18
Maintenance agreements	2,469	25
Service arrangements	2,426	25
Rental and other	695	7
Financing	268	3
Total	**9,830**	**100**

Selected Services

Banking Industry Solutions
Communication & Marketing
Document Management Landing
Document Transaction Processing Services

Education Solutions
Enterprise Content Management
Government Solutions
Healthcare Industry Solutions
Managed Print Services
Manufacturing Industry Solutions
Retail Industry Solutions
Workflow Automation

Selected Products

Office (commercial government and education sectors)
  Copiers
  Displays
  Multifunction devices (copy fax print scan)
  Printers
  Projectors
  Scanners
Production (graphics communications industry and
large corporations)
  Digital presses
  High-volume printers
  Software
Other
  Services
  Wide-format printers

COMPETITORS

Brother Industries	Lexmark
Canon	NEC
Epson	Océ
FUJIFILM	Oki Data
Fujitsu	Panasonic Corp
HP	Pitney Bowes
Heidelberger	Ricoh Company
Druckmaschinen	Sharp Corp.
Hitachi	Toshiba
Konica Minolta	
Kyocera Document	
Solutions	

HISTORICAL FINANCIALS

Company Type: Public

Income Statement

FYE: December 31

	REVENUE ($ mil.)	NET INCOME ($ mil.)	NET PROFIT MARGIN	EMPLOYEES
12/19	9,066	1,353	14.9%	27,000
12/18	9,830	361	3.7%	32,400
12/17	10,265	195	1.9%	35,300
12/16	10,771	(477)	—	37,600
12/15	18,045	474	2.6%	143,600
Annual Growth	**(15.8%)**	**30.0%**	**—**	**(34.2%)**

2019 Year-End Financials

Debt ratio: 28.46%	No. of shares (mil.): 212
Return on equity: 24.56%	Dividends
Cash ($ mil.): 2,740	Yield: 1.3%
Current ratio: 1.79	Payout: 8.6%
Long-term debt ($ mil.): 3,233	Market value ($ mil.): 7,838

	STOCK PRICE ($) FY Close	P/E High/Low		PER SHARE ($) Earnings	Dividends	Book Value
12/19	36.87	7	3	5.80	0.50	27.29
12/18	19.76	24	14	1.38	1.00	22.73
12/17	29.15	48	10	0.71	1.00	21.48
12/16	8.73	—	—	(1.96)	1.24	19.78
12/15	10.63	8	6	1.68	1.12	37.21
Annual Growth	**36.5%**	—	—	**36.3%**	**(18.3%)**	**(7.5%)**

XPO Logistics, Inc.

XPO Logistics is a global provider of transportation and supply chain solutions. It is one of the top five providers of freight brokerage and managed transportation services in the world. It also provides less-than-truckload (LTL) services where carriers consolidate freight from multiple shippers into a single truckload. Through its Logistics segment XPO offers services such as warehousing and distribution e-commerce fulfillment and reverse logistics (moving goods backward from their final destination for the purpose of reuse or disposal). Its customers include companies in the retail and e-commerce food and beverage consumer packaged goods and industrial markets. XPO operates more than 1500 locations in over 30 countries primarily in North America and Europe. The US is its largest market generating almost 60% of revenue.

Operations

XPO Logistics operates through two business segments ? Transportation and Logistics.

Transportation generates about 65% of sales and provides services through six divisions. Freight brokerage operations match shippers' freight with trucking companies; last mile specializes in heavy goods such as appliances furniture and large electronics; and less-than-truckload (LTL) comprises regional and transcontinental freight services using company tractors and trailers and employee drivers. Full truckload functions as dedicated contract carrier providing truckload capacity by its tractors trailers and drivers. Global forwarding includes logistics services using a network of ground air and ocean carriers and managed transportation serves customers who want to outsource their transportation needs.

The Logistics segment (about 35%) provides services such as warehousing and distribution e-fulfillment cold chain solutions reverse logistics packaging and labeling and inventory management. In addition Logistics provides customized supply chain optimization services such as volume flow management predictive analytics and advanced automation.

Geographic Reach

XPO Logistics is based in Greenwich CT. It operates through over 1500 locations across North America Europe and Asia. The US is its largest market accounting for about 60% of its revenue with France and the UK each accounting for more than 10%.

Sales and Marketing

XPO Logistics has approximately 10000 independent carriers and owner-operators under contract to provide drayage expedite last mile and LTL services to customers. It also has more than 50000 independent brokered carriers representing more than 1 million trucks on the road.

The company has more than 50000 customers in a wide range of industries including retail e-commerce consumer packaged goods industrial and food and beverage.

Financial Performance

XPO Logistics has experienced monumental growth over the years due to a flurry of acquisitions. Revenue has increased 118% since 2015.

Sales in 2019 fell to $16.6 billion compared to $17.3 billion in 2018. The decrease was primarily impacted by a reduction in business from the company's largest customers and foreign currency movement reduced.

XPO's profits have decreased by 3% to $419 million compared with $422 million the previous year

Cash at the end of fiscal 2019 was $387 million an increase of $127 million from the prior year. Cash from operations contributed $791 million to the coffers while investing activities used $161 million mainly for purchases of property and equipment. Financing activities used another $759 million for repayment of borrowing debt and finance leases repayment and the company's stock repurchase program.

Strategy

XPO Logistics is growing each of its divisions by expanding networks and increasing the use of technology to beef up sales and service. The company's 2019 investment in technology was among the highest in its industry at approximately $550 million. It is making investments in things like autonomous devices robotics virtual operations and intelligent warehouse management.

XPO Direct was designed to capitalize on the strengths of the company's Logistics and Transportation segments in combination. XPO's technology links strategically located logistics sites and last mile hubs giving customers the flexibility to reposition inventory close to demand as geographic patterns change. Its facilities serve as stockholding sites and cross-docks that can be utilized by multiple customers at the same time. In the Transportation segment XPO is increasing automation with enhancements to its XPO Connect digital platform and XPO Smart labor productivity tools. It is adding analytics and algorithms to the application that improve margins and increase efficiency in its warehouses and synthesizes data science digital automation and real-time visibility for a superior shipper-carrier-consumer experience.

In the Logistics segment the company developed an additional business in verticals where the company already have deep logistics expertise and a strong track record of successful relationships and market the advantages of the company's proprietary WMx technology suite to manage advanced automation robotics labor productivity safety and changes in demand in complex warehouse environments.The company signed a long-term partnership agreement with Mercedes-Benz Parts Logistics to manage UK parts distribution through an integrated digitally-managed transportation network. As part of this partnership XPO has committed to investing in 42 new trucks that will be dedicated to serving the Mercedes-Benz passenger and commercial vehicle dealer networks.

Mergers and Acquisitions

XPO announced to acquire Kuehne + Nagel's UK contract logistics unit. The acquisition includes Kuehne + Nagel's operations that provide inbound and outbound distribution reverse logistics management and inventory management. Revenue in these operations are derived from the beverage technology and e-commerce sectors and totaled approximately GBP 500 million ($656.4 million) in 2019 ($1 equals 0.76 GBP).

EXECUTIVES

Chairman And Ceo, Bradley S. Jacobs, age 63, $607,000 total compensation
Managing Director Logisticsâ–europe, Malcolm Wilson
President Less-than-truckload (ltl), Tony Brooks
Cio, Mario A. Harik, age 39
President Of Transportation North America, Christopher R. Synek
President Intermodal, Paul V. Smith
Cfo, John J. Hardig, age 55, $498,385 total compensation
Chief Strategy Officer, Scott B. Malat, age 43, $472,308 total compensation
Coo And Ceo Europe, Troy A. Cooper, age 50, $511,539 total compensation
Chief Human Resources Officer, Meghan A. Henson
Managing Director Transportâ–europe, Luis-Angel Gomez Izaguirre
President Supply Chain Americas And Asia Pacific, Ashfaque Chowdhury
President Last Mile, Charles Hitt
Vice President Global Information Technology Strategic Projects, Nicole White
Vice President Of Transportation, Don Ingersoll
Vice President Of Strategic Initiatives, Christopher Duffell
National Account Manager, David Hannegan
Vp Strategic Accounts, Tom Ford
National Account Manager, Ed Skarda
Vice President Strategic Accounts, Michael Doumas
Vice President Strategic Accounts, Keith Weaver
Vice President, Dennis McCaffrey
Regional Vice President, David Coker
Vice President Operations, Roger Lekberg
Senior Vice President Operation Last Mile, Fernando Rabel
Vice President Strategic Accounts, Greg DiPalma
Vp Strategic Accounts, Kevin Hollenbush
Vice President Transportation, Nick Caragher
Region Vice President Sales, Anthony Hoereth
Region Vice President, Jeff Groat
Vice President Procurement, Mitch Plaat
National Account Manager, Craig Robertson
Senior Vice President Financial Planning And Analysis, Liam Harrington
Senior Vice President Development Supply Chain Europe, Jean-Luc Declas
Vice President Client Solutions, Jennifer Williams
Vice President Strategic Accounts, Jay Lambert
Vice President Information Technology Client Support, Tim Merritt
Senior Vice President And Treasurer, Ravi Tulsyan
Senior Vice President Sales Supply Chain Europe, Mark Wilkinson
Svp Global It Infrastructure, Grant Richard
Svp Sales Transport Europe, Christophe Haviland
Senior Vice President Communications, Erin Kurtz
Senior Vice President Global Information Technology Infrastructure, Patrick Petersen
Vice President Information Technology Global Vendor Management, Ronald Durham
Senior Vice President Global Talent Acquisition, Bertrand Dussert
National Account Manager, Brad Rouse
Freight Brokerage Regional Vice President, Drew Wilkerson
Senior Vice President Client Services, Jared Baker
Vice President Strategic Account, Joseph Slamons
Svp Business Development, Ritchie Paik
Vice President Strategic Accounts, Drew Paxton
Vice President Operations, Shawn Getchell
Vice President Business Development, Richard Reed
Vice President Strategic Accounts, Rick Mathews
Vice President Strategic Accounts, Terence McCarthy
Vice President Strategic Accounts, Eric Thompson
Vice President Strategic Accounts, Garrett Lutgen
Vice President Strategic Accounts, George Holland
Vice President Of Strategic Accounts, Randall Cason
Vice President And General Counsel, Richard Valitutto
Senior Vice President Corporate Real Estate, Russ Marzen
Vice President Business Development, Errol Keel
Vice President Business Development, Paul Palmieri
Senior Vice President Sales :ess Than Truckload (ltl) North America, Russell Hoch
Vice President Midwest Region, Anthony Graham
Less Than Truckload Vice President Human Resources, Matt Hladki
Vice President Market, Eddie Jones
Vice President Of Operations, Triccia Barrera
Senior Vice President Corporate Counsel, Karlis P Kirsis
Senior Vice President Strategic Sales Europe, Patrick Oestreich
Senior Vice President Global Sales Operations, Michele Chapman
Senior Vice President Transportation Sales, Katrina Liddell
Senior Vice President Human Resources, Jacopo Mazzolin
Vice President Engineering Solutions, Bill Twickler
Board Member, Michael Jesselson
Treasurer And Assistant Controller, Tammy Chupa
Auditors: KPMG LLP

LOCATIONS

HQ: XPO Logistics, Inc.
Five American Lane, Greenwich, CT 06831
Phone: 855 976-6951
Web: www.xpo.com

2018 Sales

	$ mil.	% of total
United States	10,232	59
North America (excluding US)	341	2
France	2,165	12
United Kingdom	2,070	12
Europe (excluding France and UK)	2,359	14
Other	112	1
Total	**17,279**	**100**

PRODUCTS/OPERATIONS

2018 Sales

	$ mil.	% of total
Transportation	11,343	65
Logistics	6,065	35
Eliminations	(129)	-
Total	**17,279**	**100**

Service

Service
Full Truckload
Less-Than-Truckload (LTL)
Drayage
Last Mile
Intermodal
Global Forwarding
Managed Transportation
Expedite
Freight Brokerage

COMPETITORS

C.H. Robinson Worldwide	Forward Air
	J.B. Hunt
CSX	Norfolk Southern
DHL	Ryder System
Daylight Transport	Schneider National
Deutsche Post	UPS
Expeditors	Union Pacific
FedEx	YRC Worldwide

HISTORICAL FINANCIALS

Company Type: Public

Income Statement
FYE: December 31

	REVENUE ($ mil.)	NET INCOME ($ mil.)	NET PROFIT MARGIN	EMPLOYEES
12/19	16,648	419	2.5%	100,000
12/18	17,279	422	2.4%	100,000
12/17	15,380	340	2.2%	95,000
12/16	14,619	69	0.5%	87,000
12/15	7,623	(191)	—	89,000
Annual Growth	21.6%	—	—	3.0%

2019 Year-End Financials

Debt ratio: 37.27%
Return on equity: 13.26%
Cash ($ mil.): 377
Current ratio: 1.03
Long-term debt ($ mil.): 5,182

No. of shares (mil.): 92
Dividends
 Yield: —
 Payout: —
Market value ($ mil.): 7,360

	STOCK PRICE ($) FY Close	P/E High/Low		PER SHARE ($) Earnings	Dividends	Book Value
12/19	79.70	22	12	3.57	0.00	29.70
12/18	57.04	36	14	2.88	0.00	30.90
12/17	91.59	34	16	2.45	0.00	30.06
12/16	43.16	87	34	0.53	0.00	24.31
12/15	27.25	—	—	(2.65)	0.00	24.81
Annual Growth	30.8%	—	—	—	—	4.6%

Yum China Holdings Inc

Auditors: KPMG Huazhen LLP

LOCATIONS

HQ: Yum China Holdings Inc
 7100 Corporate Drive, Plano, TX 75024
Phone: 469 980-2898
Web: www.yumchina.com

HISTORICAL FINANCIALS

Company Type: Public

Income Statement
FYE: December 31

	REVENUE ($ mil.)	NET INCOME ($ mil.)	NET PROFIT MARGIN	EMPLOYEES
12/19	8,776	713	8.1%	450,000
12/18	8,415	708	8.4%	450,000
12/17	7,144	403	5.6%	450,000
12/16	6,752	502	7.4%	420,000
12/15	6,909	323	4.7%	400,000
Annual Growth	6.2%	21.9%	—	3.0%

2019 Year-End Financials

Debt ratio: 0.37%
Return on equity: 23.97%
Cash ($ mil.): 1,046
Current ratio: 1.30
Long-term debt ($ mil.): 26

No. of shares (mil.): 376
Dividends
 Yield: 1.0%
 Payout: 26.0%
Market value ($ mil.): 18,052

	STOCK PRICE ($) FY Close	P/E High/Low		PER SHARE ($) Earnings	Dividends	Book Value
12/19	48.01	26	17	1.84	0.48	8.18
12/18	33.53	26	17	1.79	0.42	7.58
12/17	40.02	41	25	1.01	0.10	7.23
12/16	26.12	22	19	1.36	0.00	6.21
Annual Growth	16.4%	—	—	7.8%	—	7.1%

Zimmer Biomet Holdings Inc

Zimmer Biomet is the top global manufacturer of reconstructive implants used in knee or hip replacement surgery. It makes a variety of other orthopedic devices including shoulder implants bone and tissue grafting materials sports medicine products dental implant systems spinal implants and trauma products for broken bones (such as screws). Additionally Zimmer Biomet makes medical equipment used in orthopedic surgeries and related surgical products. The firm's products are sold around the globe primarily in the Americas (generates about 60%).

Operations

Zimmer Biomet makes most of its money from sales of knee and hip replacement products (around 35% and 25% of revenue respectively). Some of its lead offerings are the Persona and NexGen knee systems Zimmer M/L taper hip prosthesis and Taperloc hip system. In addition to knee and hip replacements the company makes partial replacement early intervention and joint preservation products.

The SET category of products accounting for more than 20% of sales includes the surgical extremities and trauma (SET) offerings and the sports medicine foot and ankle and biologics lines. These products support surgical procedures and treat soft tissue injuries fractures arthritic conditions and broken bones. Products include the JuggerKnot Soft Anchor System ATS Tourniquets and the Zimmer Trabecular Metal Reverse Shoulder System.

The Spine and CMF product groups which together bring in almost 10% of the company's revenue include devices and instruments that treat back and neck injuries and craniomaxillofacial and thoracic (CMF) injuries. Offerings include the Polaris Spinal System SternaLock Blu Closure System and face skull and chest reconstruction items.

The dental products division (which bring in about 5% of sales) makes or distributes implants prosthetics and regenerative products including the Tapered Screw-Vent Implant system and the 3i T3 Implant.

Other products (generates about 5% of sales) include Zimmer Biomet's bone cement and office based technology products.

Geographic Reach

Zimmer Biomet's operations are managed through three major geographic segments: Americas; Europe Middle East and Africa (EMEA) and Asia/Pacific.

The Americas segment (largely consisting of US operations) accounts for more than 60% of annual revenue. The EMEA segment including sales in France Germany Italy and Spain accounts for more than 20% of revenue. The Asia/Pacific region which includes such markets as Australia China India and Japan has grown to account for more than 15% of sales. The company owns or leases approximately 340 different facilities worldwide. Approximately 30 manufacturing facilities are located in the US. The company maintains sales administrative offices and warehouse and distribution facilities in more over 40 countries worldwide.

The company's corporate headquarters are located in Warsaw Indiana and it has regional headquarters in Singapore and Switzerland. Zimmer Biomet's primary manufacturing facilities are located in the US Switzerland Ireland the U.K. China and Puerto Rico.

Sales and Marketing

Zimmer Biomet sells its orthopedic products directly to health care providers such as hospitals surgery centers and surgeons. It also sells to purchasing organizations distributors and health care dealers. Its dental products are sold directly to dental practices and laboratories.

The US sales force consists of a combination of employees and independent sales agents. Direct sales associates commissioned agents independent distributors and sales support personnel handle European sales while Asia/Pacific sales are handled through a network of dealers and associates. Direct channels account for about 80% of the company's net sales.

Financial Performance

Zimmer Biomet's revenue has seen steady upward growth in recent years including a sharp increase in 2016 due to its acquisition of Biomet. For five-year period starting in 2015 net income increased the first three years but decreased the following two years including a loss in 2018.

The company reported a 1% sales increase to $8 billion in 2019 helped by higher sales growth in the second half of the year compared to the first half of the year primarily due to various product launches in its Knees product category which drove improved commercial execution.

The company reported a net increase in earnings by $1.5 billion in 2019 compared in 2018. Higher sales lower interest expense and the recognition of a deferred tax benefit related to Switzerland tax reform resulted in the significant increase in earnings in 2019.

Zimmer Biomet ended 2019 with $618 million in cash up $75.1 million from 2018. Operating activities contributed $1.6 billion while investing activities used $729 million (mostly from spending on instrument property plant and equipment additions as well as for the acquisition of intellectual property rights). Financing activities used another $780 million for loan payments and redemption of senior notes).

Strategy

The rapid commercialization of innovative new materials biologics products implant and instrument designs and surgical techniques remains one of Zimmer Biomet's core strategies and continues to be an important driver of sales growth. The company is broadening its offerings in certain product categories and exploring new technologies with possible applications in multiple areas. It expects to continue to identify innovative technologies which may include acquiring complementary products or businesses establishing technology licensing arrangements or strategic alliances.

Outsourcing manufacturing operations to qualified suppliers who are highly capable of producing components is also one of company strategies.

Company Background

Zimmer Biomet's history can be traced to the 1927 founding of orthopedic splint maker Zimmer Manufacturing in Warsaw Indiana. The company expanded its product offerings over time and was acquired by Bristol-Myers (now Bristol-Myers Squibb) in 1972. Zimmer Holdings was spun off into an independent operation in 2001.

In mid-2015 Zimmer acquired fellow implant maker Biomet for $14 billion. The deal made the combined company the #2 orthopedics seller worldwide behind Johnson & Johnson. It also doubled Zimmer's knee and dental lines and gave it entry into the lucrative sports medicine business. Upon completion of the transaction Zimmer took on the Zimmer Biomet name.

In 2016 Zimmer Biomet completed a number of acquisitions to expand its product portfolio including LDR Holding (spinal products $1 billion) Cayenne Medical (sports medicine) Clinical Graphics (hip preservation) and Ortho Transmission (skeletal implants for amputees).

EXECUTIVES

Executive Vice President Finance And Chief Financial Officer, James T Crines
Group President Joint Reconstruction, Daniel E. (Dan) Williamson, age 54, $224,329 total compensation
Group President Biologics Extremities Sports Medicine Surgical Trauma Foot Ankle And Bone Healing, David A. Nolan
Svp General Counsel And Secretary, Chad F. Phipps, age 49, $470,615 total compensation
Svp Cfo And Interim Ceo And Director, Daniel P. (Dan) Florin, age 56, $562,692 total compensation
President Europe Middle East And Africa, Katarzyna Mazur-Hofsaess, age 56, $612,644 total compensation
Group President Spine Dental Cmf And Thoracic, Adam R. Johnson, age 43
President Asia/pacific, Sang Yi, $459,156 total compensation
President Americas, Robert D. (Rob) Delp
Svp Global Operations And Logistics, Adrian Furey
Vice President, Russell Fleeger
Vpoperations, Brian Mcnicholas
Vp Global Integration, Derek Davis
Vice President, Angela Main
Vice President Manager Director, Randy Verberkmoes
Vice President Us Sales, Mark Bezjak
Vice President Business Development, Indraneel Kanaglekar
Vice President Human Resources (global Corporate), Jack Heeter
Vice President Information Technology (emea), Erik Wijnoogst
Senior Vice President Strategy, Rachel Ellingson
Chairman, Larry C. Glasscock, age 71
Auditors: PricewaterhouseCoopers LLP

LOCATIONS

HQ: Zimmer Biomet Holdings Inc
345 East Main Street, Warsaw, IN 46580
Phone: 574 267-6131
Web: www.zimmer.com

2017 Sales

	$ mil.	% of total
Americas	4,865	62
EMEA	1,745	22
Asia/Pacific	1,213	16
Total	**7,824**	**100**

PRODUCTS/OPERATIONS

2017 Sales

	$ mil.	% of total
Knees	2,737	35
Hips	1,879	24
SET	1,709	22
Spine & CMF	759	10
Dental	418	5
Other	320	4
Total	**7,824**	**100**

Selected Products

Reconstructive implants
  Alloclassic hip system
  Anatomical shoulder implants
  Bigliani/Flatow shoulder implants
  MIS 2-Incision Total Hip Replacement
  MIS Mini-Incision Total Knee Procedure
  NexGen knee replacement
  Trabecular Metal Primary Hip Prosthesis
  VerSys Hip System
  Zimmer Collagen Repair Patch (rotator cuff repair)
Trauma products
  I.T.S.T. Nail System (hip and proximal femur fractures)
  M/DN Intramedullary Fixation (for long bone fractures)
  NCB Locking Plate System (complex long bone fractures)
  Sirus Intramedullary Nail System (for long bone fractures)
Dental products
  AdVent dental implant system
  Tapered screw-vent implant system
Spine products
  CopiOs Bone Void Filler
  Dynesys Dynamic Stabilization System
  Optima ZD Spinal Fixation System
  Puros allografts
  ST360 Spinal Fixation System
Surgical products
  A.T.S. Tourniquet Systems
  Brasseler USA surgical power tools (for long bones)
  Pneumicro surgical power tools (for small bones)
  Pulsavac Plus (wound cleaning)
  Zimmer Ambulatory Pump (pain management)

COMPETITORS

Corin Group	Nobel Biocare
DJO Global	NuVasive
DePuy	Orthofix
Dentsply Sirona	ReGen Biologics
Exactech	Smith & Nephew
Genzyme Biosurgery	Straumann
Globus Medical	Stryker
JRI Orthopaedics	Synthes
MAKO Surgical	

HISTORICAL FINANCIALS

Company Type: Public

Income Statement   FYE: December 31

	REVENUE ($ mil.)	NET INCOME ($ mil.)	NET PROFIT MARGIN	EMPLOYEES
12/19	7,982	1,131	14.2%	19,900
12/18	7,932	(379)	—	19,000
12/17	7,824	1,813	23.2%	18,200
12/16	7,683	305	4.0%	18,500
12/15	5,997	147	2.5%	17,500
Annual Growth	**7.4%**	**66.6%**	**—**	**3.3%**

2019 Year-End Financials

Debt ratio: 33.37%
Return on equity: 9.57%
Cash ($ mil.): 617
Current ratio: 1.37
Long-term debt ($ mil.): 6,721
No. of shares (mil.): 206
Dividends
  Yield: 0.6%
  Payout: 17.5%
Market value ($ mil.): 30,834

	STOCK PRICE ($) FY Close	P/E High/Low	PER SHARE ($) Earnings	Dividends	Book Value
12/19	149.68	27 18	5.47	0.96	60.14
12/18	103.72	—	(1.86)	0.96	55.25
12/17	120.67	15 12	8.90	0.96	57.93
12/16	103.20	87 60	1.51	0.96	48.20
12/15	102.59	156 118	0.77	0.88	48.78
Annual Growth	**9.9%**	**—**	**63.3%**	**2.2%**	**5.4%**

Zions Bancorporation, N.A.

Zions Bancorporation operates about 435 banking branches at year-end 2019 and is currently planning to close 12 branches during 2020. The Bank provides a full range of banking and related services primarily in Arizona California Colorado Idaho Nevada New Mexico Oregon Texas Utah Washington and Wyoming. The Bank focuses on providing community banking services by continuously strengthening its core business lines of small- and medium-sized business and corporate banking; commercial and residential development construction and term lending; retail banking; treasury cash management and related products and services; residential mortgage lending and servicing; trust and wealth management; capital markets activities including municipal finance advisory and underwriting; and investment activities. It operates primarily through seven geographic regions each with its own local branding chief executive officer and management team. Still headquartered in Salt Lake City Zions Bank was founded in 1873 as Utah's first bank by Mormon leader Brigham Young.

Operations

Zions Bancorporation operates under local management teams under the following banking divisions: Amegy Bank California Bank & Trust National Bank of Arizona Nevada State Bank The Commerce Bank of Washington Vectra Bank Colorado and Zions bank.

In addition to providing a wide variety of commercial products and services the Bank provides a range of personal banking services to individuals including home mortgages bankcard other installment loans home equity lines of credit checking accounts savings accounts certificates of deposit of various types and maturities trust services safe deposit facilities and internet and mobile banking. The Bank provides services to key market segments through its Private Client Services and Executive Banking groups.It offers self-directed brokerage services through Zions Direct and also offers comprehensive and personalized wealth management and investment services.

Geographic Reach

Zions Bancorporation National Association and its subsidiaries (collectively "Zions Bancorporation N.A.) is a national commercial bank headquartered in Salt Lake City Utah. The Bank owns and operates about 435 branches at year-end 2019 and is currently planning to close more than 10 branches during 2020. The Bank provides a full range of banking and related services primarily in Arizona California Colorado Idaho Nevada New Mexico Oregon Texas Utah Washington and Wyoming.

Sales and Marketing

Zions Bancorporation is focused on the communities in itsfootprint and banking businesses and itsowners and executives in those communities where relationships are particularly important. The company's experienced bankers develop long-lasting relationships with customers by providing valuable advice and award-winning service; such relationships are further enhanced by digital products the customers desire. Building such relationships is essential to maintaining deposit franchise which currently provides Zion with one of the lowest costs of deposits in the industry and to maintaining an overall high customer satisfaction relative to peers. The company is a consistent national and state-wide leader of customer survey awards in small and middle-market banking as well as a national leader in SBA lending and public finance advisory services.

Advertising expense decreased by $7 million to $19 million for 2019. This decrease was mainly due to lower sponsorships.

Financial Performance

Zions Bancorporation's revenue were steadily growing for the past five years. While net income fell about 10% in 2019 despite the continuous increase in 2015 to 2018.

The company's revenue rose two percent to $2.8 billion in 2019 from prior year. This is primarily due to high interest income.

Net income decreased 10% to $816 million in 2019 compared to $884 million in 2018 due to lower noninterest expense.

Cash and due from banks at end of year 2019 increased 15% to $705 million from the prior year. Cash provided by operating activities fell of more than 40% to $697 million in 2019 compared in 2018 primarily due to change in other assets. Investing activities also delivered $375 million while financing activities used $981 million.

Strategy

The Bank's growth strategy is driven by key factors while adhering to defined risk parameters. The key elements of the Bank's strategy reflect its prudent risk-taking philosophy. The Bank generates revenue by taking prudent and appropriately priced risks. These factors are outlined in the Bank's Risk Appetite Framework.

While the company serves several important customer segments in its markets its strategy is especially focused on four key areas: Small Business Commercial Affluent and Capital Markets. Small Business and Commercial are segments where the company's local operating model is very impactful and valued by customers and Zions continues to invest in the capabilities that differentiate it from its competitors. Zions is making strategic investments in Affluent and Capital Markets to deepen relationships with core customers while also improving noninterest income contribution.

To enable the execution of its strategy the company is investing in five key areas: employees and building their capabilities; Technologies that customers value most and that will make the company efficient; Simplifying how Zions do business at all levels of the company; Maintaining effective risk management practices to ensure judicious risk taking; and Advanced enterprise data and analytics to support local execution.

The company's strategic objectives include: Achieving revenue growth that is competitive with the industry without incurring excessive risk while maintaining a cost structure that results in an efficiency ratio that is competitive with its peers. This includes improving profitability ratios relative to peers and over the long term driving superior PPNR growth; Competing effectively against the largest banks with a combination of technology and service; Zions believes that its long-term success depends upon the success of the local communities it serves; The company strives to make significant long-term business and philanthropic investments that will benefit its communities; and it strives to maintain a strong risk management profile to be a positive outlier (i.e. superior performance relative to peers) in the event of an economic downturn.

Company Background

Zions which built its business through acquisitions strategically managed to extend its reach during the economic downturn in part by helping the FDIC clean up failed banks and it continues to search for acquisition opportunities. It is also building its business by growing its wealth management and advisory services organically.

HISTORY

Zions' history is entwined with that of the Mormon Church. Founded by the church in 1873 to take over the savings department of the Bank of Deseret when it obtained a national charter the new bank was headed by Brigham Young and other church leaders. The church kept control of the bank until 1960 when it sold its interest to a group of investors led by Roy Simmons who moved it into the holding company that became Zions Bancorporation. It went public in 1966.

It has grown over the years by picking up struggling or failing banks during various financial crises. It almost bought fellow Utah bank First Security in 2000 and would have dropped the Zions name to further distance itself from the Mormon Church. But the deal fell through and the name remains.

EXECUTIVES

Executive Vice President Marketing And Communications, Rob Brough

Evp; President And Ceo Zions First National Bank, A. Scott (Scott) Anderson, age 73, $548,000 total compensation

Chairman And Ceo, Harris H. Simmons, age 65, $940,000 total compensation

Evp; President And Ceo Vectra Bank Colorado, Bruce K. Alexander, age 67

Evp; President And Ceo The Commerce Bank Of Washington, Stanley D. Savage, age 74, $312,000 total compensation

Evp; President And Ceo California Bank & Trust, David E. Blackford, age 71, $510,000 total compensation

President And Coo, Scott J. McLean, age 63, $644,000 total compensation

President And Coo National Bank Of Arizona, Keith D. Maio, age 62

Evp Retail Banking, LeeAnne B. Linderman, age 65

Evp And General Counsel, Thomas E. Laursen, age 69

Evp And Chief Risk Officer, Edward P. (Ed) Schreiber, age 62, $518,000 total compensation

Evp And Chief Human Resources Officer, Dianne R. James, age 67

Evp And Cio, Jennifer A. Smith, age 48

Evp; Ceo Amegy Bank Of Texas, Steven D. Stephens, age 61

Evp And Chief Technology Strategist, Joe Reilly, age 67

Evp And Chief Credit Officer, Michael J. Morris, age 62

Evp; President And Ceo National Bank Of Arizona, Mark R. Young, age 61

Cfo, Paul E. Burdiss, age 55, $550,000 total compensation

Evp And Director Wealth Management, Rebecca K. Robinson, age 46

Vice President, Matt Millis

Vice President And Relationship Manager, Adam Whitefield

Senior Vice President Compliance, Norman Merritt

Vice President And Relationship Manager, Cheryl Ginn

Vice President, Steve Earley

Senior Vice President And Chief Credit Administrator C And I Lending, Dennis Spencer

Assistant Vice President Capital Markets, Karen Keeley

Vice President Sales Manager, Howard Anderson

Vice President, Jennifer Jolley

Vice President Technology, Deva Annamalai

Vp And Business Analyst, Kazi Suzuki

Vice President Commercial Loans, David Kohler

Senior Vice President Corporate Procuremen And Vendor Management, Kelly Foreman

First Vice President, James Grether

Applications Developers Vice President Applications, Brent Briggs

Vice President Treasury Management Sales Manager, Jesse Ronnow Jesse Ronnow

Vice President, Zac Nelson

Vice President Business Development Officer, Mark Petrasso

Vice President Financial Analyst, Ian Spencer

Senior Vice President Information Technology Support Services, Lorilee Stoddard

Vice President, Ryan Theriault

Svp Credit Risk Management, Mark Medina

Senior Vice President, Tom Etzel

Auditors: Ernst & Young LLP

LOCATIONS

HQ: Zions Bancorporation, N.A.
One South Main, Salt Lake City, UT 84133-1109
Phone: 801 844-7637
Web: www.zionsbancorporation.com

PRODUCTS/OPERATIONS

Selected Subsidiaries

Amegy Corporation
California Bank & Trust
National Bank of Arizona
Nevada State Bank
The Commerce Bank of Washington
Vectra Bank Colorado
ZB National Association

2017 Sales

	$ mil.	% of total
Interest income		
Interest and fees on loans	1,847	68
Interest on securities	19	1
Interest on money market investment	326	12
Non-interest income		
Other service charges commission and fees	217	8
Service charges and fees on deposit accounts	171	6
Wealth management income	42	2
Loan sales and servicing income 1		**25**
Dividends and other investment income	40	1
Capital markets and foreign Exchange	30	1
Equity securities gains net	14	-
Others	5	-
Total	**2,736**	**100**

COMPETITORS

BOK Financial	Great Western Bancorp
Bank of America	JPMorgan Chase
Bank of the West	MUFG Americas Holdings
Capital One	Prosperity Bancshares
Citigroup	U.S. Bancorp
Cullen/Frost Bankers	Washington Federal
First National of Nebraska	Wells Fargo

HISTORICAL FINANCIALS

Company Type: Public

Income Statement

FYE: December 31

	ASSETS ($ mil.)	NET INCOME ($ mil.)	INCOME AS % OF ASSETS	EMPLOYEES
12/19	69,172	816	1.2%	9,873
12/18	68,746	884	1.3%	10,201
12/17	66,288	592	0.9%	10,083
12/16	63,239	469	0.7%	10,057
12/15	59,669	309	0.5%	10,200
Annual Growth	3.8%	27.4%	—	(0.8%)

2019 Year-End Financials

Debt ratio: 2.49%
Return on equity: 10.93%
Cash ($ mil.): 1,448
Current ratio: —
Long-term debt ($ mil.): —

No. of shares (mil.): 165
Dividends
  Yield: 2.4%
  Payout: 54.9%
Market value ($ mil.): 8,570

	STOCK PRICE ($) FY Close	P/E High/Low		PER SHARE ($) Earnings	Dividends	Book Value
12/19	51.92	12	9	4.16	1.28	44.55
12/18	40.74	13	9	4.08	0.30	40.40
12/17	50.83	19	14	2.60	0.44	38.87
12/16	43.04	22	10	1.99	0.28	37.59
12/15	27.30	27	20	1.20	0.22	36.73
Annual Growth	17.4%	—	—	36.5%	55.3%	4.9%

Hoover's Handbook of

American Business

The Indexes

Index by Headquarters

Deerfield
Walgreens Boots Alliance Inc 848
Caterpillar Inc. 157
Baxter International Inc 106

Downers Grove
Univar Solutions Inc 824
Dover Corp 254

Effingham
Midland States Bancorp Inc 526

Glenview
Illinois Tool Works, Inc. 419

Lake Forest
Tenneco Inc 763
Grainger (W.W.) Inc. 368
Pactiv Evergreen Inc 599

Lincolnshire
CDW Corp 161

Lisle
Navistar International Corp. 543

Mattoon
First Mid Bancshares Inc 324

Moline
Deere & Co. 239
QCR Holdings Inc 654

North Chicago
AbbVie Inc 5

Northbrook
Allstate Corp 26

Peoria
RLI Corp 682

Riverwoods
Discover Financial Services 246

ROCK ISLAND
MODERN WOODMEN OF AMERICA 528

Rolling Meadows
Gallagher (Arthur J.) & Co. 345

Rosemont
US Foods Holding Corp 833
Wintrust Financial Corp (IL) 872

Springfield
Horace Mann Educators Corp. 402
STATE OF ILLINOIS 733

IN

Carmel
CNO Financial Group Inc 188
Merchants Bancorp (Indiana) 513

Columbus
Cummins, Inc. 224

Elkhart
Thor Industries, Inc. 782

Evansville
Berry Global Group Inc 114
OneMain Holdings Inc 588
Old National Bancorp (Evansville, IN) 583

Fishers
First Internet Bancorp 322

Fort Wayne
Steel Dynamics Inc. 740

Indianapolis
Anthem Inc 58
Lilly (Eli) & Co 478
STATE OF INDIANA 733

Jasper
German American Bancorp Inc 358

Michigan City
Horizon Bancorp Inc 403

Muncie
First Merchants Corp 323

South Bend
1st Source Corp 1

Terre Haute
First Financial Corp. (IN) 319

Warsaw
Zimmer Biomet Holdings Inc 882
Lakeland Financial Corp 469

KS

KANSAS CITY
DAIRY FARMERS OF AMERICA, INC. 230
ASSOCIATED WHOLESALE GROCERS, INC. 72

Leawood
CrossFirst Bankshares Inc 220

Topeka
Capitol Federal Financial Inc 149
STATE OF KANSAS 733

Wichita
Spirit AeroSystems Holdings Inc 724
Equity Bancshares Inc 280

KY

FRANKFORT
COMMONWEALTH OF KENTUCKY 204

Louisville
Humana Inc. 410
Republic Bancorp, Inc. (KY) 676
Stock Yards Bancorp Inc 743

Pikeville
Community Trust Bancorp, Inc. 208

LA

Baton Rouge
Business First Bancshares Inc 142
Investar Holding Corp 436
STATE OF LOUISIANA 733

Hammond
First Guaranty Bancshares, Inc. 320

JEFFERSON
OCHSNER CLINIC FOUNDATION 581

Lafayette
Home Bancorp Inc 395

Monroe
Lumen Technologies Inc 490
Qwest Corp 660

New Orleans
Entergy Corp 274

Ruston
Origin Bancorp Inc 594

MA

BEDFORD
ICE DATA SERVICES, INC. 419

Boston
General Electric Co 349
State Street Corp. 738
Santander Holdings USA Inc. 696
Wayfair Inc 855
American Tower Corp (New) 48
Safety Insurance Group, Inc. 692
Berkshire Hills Bancorp Inc 114
Boston Private Financial Holdings, Inc. 132
Brookline Bancorp Inc (DE) 138
COMMONWEALTH OF MASSACHUSETTS 204
MASS GENERAL BRIGHAM INCORPORATED 503
MASSACHUSETTS HOUSING FINANCE AGENCY PROPERTY ACQUISITION AND DISPOSITION CORPORATION 504

Brockton
HarborOne Bancorp Inc (New) 379

Burlington
Keurig Dr Pepper Inc 453

Cambridge
Biogen Inc 117
Cambridge Bancorp 143

Framingham
TJX Companies, Inc. 783

Hanover
Independent Bank Corp (MA) 420

Hingham
Hingham Institution for Savings 393

Lowell
Enterprise Bancorp, Inc. (MA) 275

Marlborough
Boston Scientific Corp. 133

Medford
Century Bancorp, Inc. 165

Peabody
Meridian Bancorp Inc 516

Springfield
Eversource Energy 281

Waltham
Raytheon Technologies Corp 665
Thermo Fisher Scientific Inc 780
Global Partners LP 362

Westborough
BJ's Wholesale Club Holdings Inc 119

Westfield
Western New England Bancorp Inc 865

Worcester
Hanover Insurance Group Inc 377

MD

Baltimore
Howard Bancorp Inc 406
THE JOHNS HOPKINS HEALTH SYSTEM CORPORATION 777

Bethesda
Lockheed Martin Corp 486
Marriott International, Inc. 499
AGNC Investment Corp 19
Eagle Bancorp Inc (MD) 260

HANOVER
ALLEGIS GROUP, INC. 25

Olney
Sandy Spring Bancorp Inc 695

Silver Spring
Discovery Inc 247

ME

AUGUSTA
STATE OF MAINE 734
MAINE MUNICIPAL BOND BANK 495

Bar Harbor
Bar Harbor Bankshares 105

Camden
Camden National Corp. (ME) 144

Damariscotta
First Bancorp Inc (ME) 311

MI

ADA
ALTICOR INC. 31
SOLSTICE HOLDINGS INC. 716

ANN ARBOR
REGENTS OF THE UNIVERSITY OF MICHIGAN 669

Auburn Hills
BorgWarner Inc 130

Battle Creek
Kellogg Co 450

Benton Harbor
Whirlpool Corp 868

Bloomfield Hills
Penske Automotive Group Inc 607

Dearborn
Ford Motor Co. (DE) 338

Detroit
General Motors Co 353
DTE Energy Co 256
Ally Financial Inc 29
TCF Financial Corp (New) 760
UAW RETIREE MEDICAL BENEFITS TRUST 805

EAST LANSING
GREENSTONE FARM CREDIT SERVICES ACA 371

FARMINGTON HILLS
ROBERT BOSCH LLC 683

FLINT
MOTT, CHARLES STEWART FOUNDATION INC 538

Grand Rapids
SpartanNash Co. 723
Independent Bank Corporation (Ionia, MI) 421
Mercantile Bank Corp. 512

Holland
Macatawa Bank Corp. 493

Kalamazoo
Stryker Corp 746

LANSING
STATE OF MICHIGAN 734

LIVONIA
TRINITY HEALTH CORPORATION 794

Midland
Dow Inc 256

Southfield
Lear Corp. 471

Citigroup Inc 180
Macy's Inc 494
MetLife Inc 517
Federal Reserve Bank of New York, Dist. No. 2 298
StoneX Group Inc 744
Goldman Sachs Group Inc 364
Morgan Stanley 534
Pfizer Inc 616
American International Group Inc 45
American Express Co. 41
Travelers Companies Inc (The) 791
Philip Morris International Inc 619
ViacomCBS Inc 840
Bristol Myers Squibb Co. 135
Bank of New York Mellon Corp 99
Marsh & McLennan Companies Inc. 501
Colgate-Palmolive Co. 194
Omnicom Group, Inc. 586
Loews Corp. 486
BlackRock Inc 119
Lauder (Estee) Cos., Inc. (The) 470
Consolidated Edison Inc 213
Fox Corp 340
Consolidated Edison Co. of New York, Inc. 212
Interpublic Group of Companies Inc. 433
Assurant Inc 73
PVH Corp 652
Equitable Holdings Inc 280
Alleghany Corp. 24
News Corp (New) 555
Sirius XM Holdings Inc 711
Foot Locker, Inc. 337
Voya Financial Inc 846
Blackstone Group Inc (The) 121
HSBC USA, Inc. 409
Federal Home Loan Bank New York 296
CIT Group Inc (New) 178
Signature Bank (New York, NY) 709
Valley National Bancorp (NJ) 835
Sterling Bancorp (DE) 741
Chimera Investment Corp 171
Annaly Capital Management Inc 57
Ladder Capital Corp 468
Ambac Financial Group, Inc. 35
Granite Point Mortgage Trust Inc 369
AG Mortgage Investment Trust Inc 16
Metropolitan Bank Holding Corp 520
THE TURNER CORPORATION 779
TURNER CONSTRUCTION COMPANY INC 801
NEW YORK CITY HEALTH AND HOSPITALS CORPORATION* 547
METROPOLITAN TRANSPORTATION AUTHORITY 520
NEW YORK UNIVERSITY 550
THE NEW YORK AND PRESBYTERIAN HOSPITAL 777
SIGNATURE FINANCIAL LLC 710
RECKSON OPERATING PARTNERSHIP, L.P. 667
VIRTU FINANCIAL LLC 843
THE FORD FOUNDATION 775
BRIXMOR LLC 136
NEW YORK COMMUNITY TRUST AND COMMUNITY FUNDS INC 550
STATE OF NEW YORK MORTGAGE AGENCY 735

Norwich
NBT Bancorp. Inc. 544

Purchase
PepsiCo Inc 612
Mastercard Inc 506
MBIA Inc. 508

ROCHESTER
HOME PROPERTIES, LIMITED PARTNERSHIP 398

Tarrytown
Regeneron Pharmaceuticals, Inc. 668

Uniondale
Flushing Financial Corp. 335

Victor
Constellation Brands Inc 215

Warsaw
Financial Institutions Inc. 308

Westbury
New York Community Bancorp Inc. 549

OH

Akron
Goodyear Tire & Rubber Co. 366
FirstEnergy Corp 329

Canfield
Farmers National Banc Corp. (Canfield,OH) 293

Cincinnati
Kroger Co (The) 462
Procter & Gamble Company (The) 639
Fifth Third Bancorp (Cincinnati, OH) 306
American Financial Group Inc 43
Cintas Corporation 175
Federal Home Loan Bank Of Cincinnati 297
First Financial Bancorp (OH) 318
GENERAL ELECTRIC INTERNATIONAL, INC. 350
BON SECOURS MERCY HEALTH, INC. 126
PHILLIPS EDISON - ARC SHOPPING CENTER REIT INC. 622

Cleveland
Sherwin-Williams Co (The) 706
Parker Hannifin Corp 601
KeyCorp 454
TFS Financial Corp 772
THE CLEVELAND CLINIC FOUNDATION 773

Columbus
American Electric Power Co Inc 39
L Brands, Inc 464
Huntington Bancshares Inc 413
State Auto Financial Corp. 730
STATE OF OHIO 736

Defiance
Premier Financial Corp 635

Dublin
Cardinal Health, Inc. 151

Fairfield
Cincinnati Financial Corp. 173

Findlay
Marathon Petroleum Corp. 496
MPLX LP 538

Marietta
Peoples Bancorp Inc (Marietta, OH) 611

Maumee
Dana Inc 231
Andersons Inc 57

Mayfield Village
Progressive Corp. (OH) 640

Newark
Park National Corp (Newark, OH) 601

Orrville
Smucker (J.M.) Co. 714

Sandusky
Civista Bancshares Inc 186

Toledo
Owens Corning 597

OK

Oklahoma City
Chesapeake Energy Corp. 167
BancFirst Corp. (Oklahoma City, Okla) 92
CANDID COLOR SYSTEMS, INC. 147
STATE OF OKLAHOMA 736

Tulsa
ONEOK Inc 589
Williams Cos Inc (The) 870
NGL Energy Partners LP 558
BOK Financial Corp 125
ONEOK PARTNERS, L.P. 591

OR

Beaverton
NIKE Inc 559

Medford
Lithia Motors Inc 482

Portland
Umpqua Holdings Corp 808
PRECISION CASTPARTS CORP. 633

SALEM
STATE OF OREGON 736

PA

Allentown
Air Products & Chemicals Inc 19
PPL Corp 632

BALA CYNWYD
PHILADELPHIA CONSOLIDATED HOLDING CORP. 619

Bryn Mawr
Bryn Mawr Bank Corp 138

Camp Hill
Rite Aid Corp 680

Canonsburg
Viatris Inc 842

Chesterbrook
AmerisourceBergen Corp. 52

Clearfield
CNB Financial Corp. (Clearfield, PA) 187

Coraopolis
Dick's Sporting Goods, Inc 243

DANVILLE
GEISINGER HEALTH. 346

Erie
Erie Indemnity Co. 280

Fort Washington
Toll Brothers Inc. 785

HARRISBURG
COMMONWEALTH OF PENNSYLVANIA 205

PENNSYLVANIA HOUSING FINANCE AGENCY 606
PSECU SERVICES, INC. 648

Hershey
Hershey Company (The) 386

Indiana
First Commonwealth Financial Corp (Indiana, PA) 316
S & T Bancorp Inc (Indiana, PA) 691

Kennett Square
Exelon Generation Co LLC 285

King of Prussia
Universal Health Services, Inc. 824

Lancaster
Fulton Financial Corp. (PA) 343

Millersburg
Mid Penn Bancorp Inc 526

Philadelphia
Comcast Corp 197
Aramark 64
Radian Group, Inc. 661
Republic First Bancorp, Inc. 677
UNIVERSITY OF PENNSYLVANIA 826
THE WILLIAM PENN FOUNDATION 780

Pittsburgh
Kraft Heinz Co (The) 461
PNC Financial Services Group (The) 628
PPG Industries Inc 631
Howmet Aerospace Inc 407
United States Steel Corp. 820
Alcoa Corporation 23
Wesco International, Inc. 859
Wabtec Corp 846
Arconic Corp 67
FNB Corp 336
TriState Capital Holdings Inc 795
UPMC 829
UPMC PRESBYTERIAN SHADYSIDE 830

Radnor
Lincoln National Corp. 480

Scranton
Peoples Financial Services Corp 611

Shippensburg
Orrstown Financial Services, Inc. 595

Souderton
Univest Financial Corp 826

Warren
Northwest Bancshares, Inc. (MD) 569

West Reading
Customers Bancorp Inc 225

Yardley
Crown Holdings Inc 220

PR

San Juan
Popular Inc. 629

QUEBEC

Montreal
Molson Coors Beverage Co 532

RI

Providence
United Natural Foods Inc. 815
Textron Inc 771
Citizens Financial Group Inc (New)
182
STATE OF RHODE ISLAND AND
PROVIDENCE PLANTATIONS 736

Westerly
Washington Trust Bancorp, Inc. 853

Woonsocket
CVS Health Corporation 228

SC

COLUMBIA
STATE OF SOUTH CAROLINA 737
AGFIRST FARM CREDIT BANK 18

Greenville
Southern First Bancshares, Inc. 720
ATHENE ANNUITY & LIFE
ASSURANCE COMPANY 76

SD

Aberdeen
Dacotah Banks Inc. 229

Sioux Falls
Meta Financial Group Inc 517
Great Western Bancorp Inc 371

TN

Brentwood
Delek US Holdings Inc (New) 240
Tractor Supply Co. 789

Chattanooga
Unum Group 827

FARRAGUT
EDUCATIONAL FUNDING OF THE
SOUTH, INC. 267

Franklin
Community Health Systems, Inc. 206

Goodlettsville
Dollar General Corp 250

Kingsport
Eastman Chemical Co 262

Knoxville
Tennessee Valley Authority 765
SmartFinancial Inc 714
CFJ PROPERTIES LLC 166

Lebanon
Wilson Bank Holding Co. 872

Memphis
FedEx Corp 301
International Paper Co 432
AutoZone, Inc. 82
First Horizon Corp 321

Nashville
HCA Healthcare Inc 381
Pinnacle Financial Partners Inc 623
FB Financial Corp 294
CapStar Financial Holdings Inc 150
STATE OF TENNESSEE 737
RYMAN HOSPITALITY PROPERTIES,
INC. 690

TX

Abilene
First Financial Bankshares, Inc. 319

Addison
Guaranty Bancshares Inc 374

Arlington
Horton (DR) Inc 405

Austin
Oracle Corp 592
National Western Life Group Inc 541
STATE OF TEXAS 737
WHOLE FOODS MARKET, INC. 869
TEXAS DEPARTMENT OF
TRANSPORTATION 769
TEXAS COUNTY AND DISTRICT
RETIREMENT SYSTEM 769
FARM CREDIT BANK OF TEXAS 292

BEAUMONT
COMMUNITYBANK OF TEXAS, N.A.
209

Conroe
Spirit of Texas Bancshares Inc 725

Coppell
Mr Cooper Group Inc 539

Dallas
AT&T Inc 74
Energy Transfer LP 272
Energy Transfer Operating LP 273
CBRE Group Inc 159
Southwest Airlines Co 722
Tenet Healthcare Corp. 761
Kimberly-Clark Corp. 457
HollyFrontier Corp 394
Sunoco LP 748
Texas Instruments Inc. 769
Jacobs Engineering Group, Inc. 440
Santander Consumer USA Holdings
Inc 696
Dean Foods Co. 237
Builders FirstSource Inc. 140
Comerica, Inc. 199
Hilltop Holdings, Inc. 390
Texas Capital Bancshares Inc 768
Veritex Holdings Inc 836
Triumph Bancorp Inc 796
Capstead Mortgage Corp. 150
Sixth Street Specialty Lending Inc
712
GWG Holdings Inc 374
BAYLOR SCOTT & WHITE
HOLDINGS 107
SPIRIT REALTY CAPITAL, INC. 726

Fort Worth
American Airlines Group Inc 36
BNSF RAILWAY COMPANY 122

Galveston
American National Group Inc 47

Houston
Phillips 66 621
Sysco Corp 754
ConocoPhillips 212
Plains GP Holdings LP 627
Plains All American Pipeline LP 626
Enterprise Products Partners L.P. 277
Hewlett Packard Enterprise Co 389
Baker Hughes Company 89
Occidental Petroleum Corp 579
EOG Resources, Inc. 278
Waste Management, Inc. (DE) 854
Halliburton Company 374
CenterPoint Energy, Inc 163
Quanta Services, Inc. 656
Group 1 Automotive, Inc. 372
Kinder Morgan Inc. 458

Cheniere Energy Inc. 166
Targa Resources Corp 757
NOV Inc 570
Westlake Chemical Corp 865
Cadence Bancorporation 143
Prosperity Bancshares Inc. 642
Allegiance Bancshares Inc 25
CBTX Inc 161
CAMERON INTERNATIONAL
CORPORATION 145

Irving
Exxon Mobil Corp 288
McKesson Corp 510
Fluor Corp. 333
Vistra Corp 844
Pioneer Natural Resources Co 625
Federal Home Loan Bank Of Dallas
297

Laredo
International Bancshares Corp. 429

Lubbock
South Plains Financial Inc 717

McKinney
Globe Life Inc 363
Independent Bank Group Inc. 422

Plano
Toyota Motor Credit Corp. 789
Yum China Holdings Inc 882

Round Rock
Dell Technologies Inc 241

San Antonio
Valero Energy Corp 833
Cullen/Frost Bankers, Inc. 223

TEMPLE
MCLANE COMPANY, INC. 512

THE WOODLANDS
CHEVRON PHILLIPS CHEMICAL
COMPANY LLC 170
CHEVRON PHILLIPS CHEMICAL
COMPANY LP 171

Tyler
Southside Bancshares, Inc. 721

Westlake
Core Mark Holding Co Inc 216

WICHITA FALLS
THE PRIDDY FOUNDATION 778

UT

American Fork
Altabancorp 31

DRAPER
COMENITY BANK 199

MIDVALE
ALLY BANK 28

Salt Lake City
Zions Bancorporation, N.A. 883
STATE OF UTAH 737
INTERMOUNTAIN HEALTH CARE INC
428

WEST VALLEY CITY
UTAH HOUSING CORPORATION 833

VA

Arlington
AES Corp. 13

Bluefield
First Community Bankshares Inc (VA)
317

Chesapeake
Dollar Tree Inc 252

Danville
American National Bankshares, Inc.
(Danville, VA) 46

Falls Church
Northrop Grumman Corp 567

Glen Allen
Markel Corp (Holding Co) 497

Martinsville
Carter Bankshares Inc 155

McLean
Freddie Mac 340
Capital One Financial Corp 148
Hilton Worldwide Holdings Inc 391
Booz Allen Hamilton Holding Corp.
128
Southern National Bancorp Of
Virginia Inc 721

Mechanicsville
Owens & Minor, Inc. 595

Newport News
Huntington Ingalls Industries, Inc.
416

Norfolk
Norfolk Southern Corp 563

Portsmouth
TowneBank 788

Reston
General Dynamics Corp 347
Leidos Holdings Inc 472
NVR Inc. 576

Richmond
Altria Group Inc 32
Performance Food Group Co 614
Carmax Inc. 153
Dominion Energy Inc (New) 253
Virginia Electric & Power Co. 842
Genworth Financial, Inc. (Holding Co)
356
Atlantic Union Bankshares Corp 77
COMMONWEALTH OF VIRGINIA 205
VIRGINIA COLLEGE BUILDING
AUTHORITY 842
VIRGINIA HOUSING DEVELOPMENT
AUTHORITY 842

Tysons
DXC Technology Co 260
COMPUTER SCIENCES
CORPORATION 209

VI

CHRISTIANSTED
LIMETREE BAY TERMINALS LLC
480

WA

Bellevue
PACCAR Inc. 598
T-Mobile US Inc 756

Everett
Fortive Corp 340

Issaquah
Costco Wholesale Corp 219

Index of Executives

A

Aaefedt, Matthew 823
Aaholm, Sherry A. 225
Aakre, Scott 404
Aaron, Thomas J. (Tom) 207
Aaron, Susan 403
Aase, Rune 279
Abad, Rafael Lopez 720
Abadir, Jeffrey 219
Abadir, Jeff 219
Abanishe, Atinuke 289
Abarca, Jose 613
Abate, Victor (Vic) 349
Abate, Christopher J. 668
Abate, Frank 794
Abbamondi, Desa 870
Abbasi, Azher 298
Abbate, Mark L. 516
Abbate, Sam 568
Abbene, David 502
Abbey, Jared 112
Abbey, Anna B 747
Abbey, Anna 747
Abbott, Lynn 50
Abbott, Sarah 522
Abbott, Mark 664
Abbott, Dean 673
Abbott, Greg 737
Abboud, Ali El 739
Abdella, Shelly 856
Abdelnour, Sam 868
Abdenour, Steve 774
Abdullah, Rao 375
Abel, Greg 113
Abel, Donna 226
Abel, Brandi 406
Abel, Melissa 768
Abel, Brian Van 878
Abel-Hodges, Cheryl 653
Abela, John 519
Abellera, Philip 682
Abelli, Donna L. 421
Abello, Marc P 200
Abelman, David 681
Abeln, Jeur 198
Abhishek, Shukla 240
Abington, John 664
Abiteboul, Jean 167
Abkin, Kimberly 303
Abler, Bill 275
Abney, David P. 818
Aboaf, Eric 739
Abood, Steven 673
Aboulafia, Joseph 100

Abraham, Jai 219
Abraham, JJ 476
Abraham, Frank 530
Abraham, Biju 844
Abrahamson, Laura 12
Abramczyk, Andrew 281
Abramowicz, Daniel A. 221
Abrams, Michael 174
Abrams, Edward 193
Abrams, Gary 481
Abreu, Christopher 380
Abry, Brian 751
Absher, Hall 74
Abston, Chris 560
Abston, Angie 813
Abts, Brad 71
Abts, Joy 832
Accardo, Joseph 649
Accogli, Giuseppe 107
Ace, Brian 206
Ach, J. Wickliffe 318
Ach, J 318
Ach, Joseph 873
Achary, Michael M. 376
Acharya, Guru 875
Achenbach, Mark 473
Achkire, Debra 328
Acito, Paiul 3
Acito, Joe 307
Ackerman, Joel 235
Ackerman, Brian 446
Ackerman, Dean M 471
Ackermann, Peter 96
Ackermann, Dan 270
Ackerson, Vince A. 768
Acoca, Bernard 728
Acton, Steve 685
Acton, Michael 695
Acuna, Francine 92
Adair, Charles 364
Adair, Bryan 431
Adair, Lee 752
Adam, Rolf 423
Adamczyk, Darius 400
Adamic, Don 839
Adamo, Terri 303
Adamo, John 647
Adams, John 72
Adams, Brian 77
Adams, Douglas 88
Adams, Cindy 162
Adams, Ian 176
Adams, Matthew 184
Adams, Kraig 191
Adams, Bruce 227

Adams, Lesley 250
Adams, Marc 266
Adams, Craig L. 284
Adams, Kim 315
Adams, John 315
Adams, Sally 357
Adams, Lisan 384
Adams, Thomas 389
Adams, Michael 415
Adams, David 428
Adams, Gregory A. 449
Adams, Amy 487
Adams, Calvin 489
Adams, Romaneo 502
Adams, Jennifer 502
Adams, Fay 531
Adams, John 550
Adams, Erin 552
Adams, Ann 564
Adams, Annie 564
Adams, Matt 566
Adams, Scott 583
Adams, Carol 593
Adams, Cathryn 617
Adams, D. Scott 644
Adams, Wayne 673
Adams, Charles M 703
Adams, Patricia (Trish) 759
Adams, Trish 760
Adams, Tim 762
Adams, Dian 762
Adams, Paul 776
Adams, Jess 806
Adams, Richard M. 812
Adams, Gayle 823
Adams, Sherry 851
Adams, Nicholas 871
Adams, Christina 876
Adamson, Adam 118
Adan, Paul 500
Adcock, Beth 357
Adcock, Robert H. 396
Adcock, Mary 463
Addiego, Gino 63
Addison, Linda 364
Addison, Ann M. 472
Addison, James 500
Addison, Ann 568
Addison, John 636
Addison, Jimmy 718
Addy, R Mark 622
Ade, Jude 126
Adefioye, Elizabeth 443
Adelman, Marty 13
Adelson, Sarah 299

Aderholdt, Mary 689
Adger, Ellis 333
Adkerson, Richard C. 342
Adkins, Dan 207
Adkins, Chuck 419
Adkins, Rodney 632
Adkins, Rodney 818
Adkison, Jeffrey 446
Adler, Dean S 111
Adler, Paul F. 176
Adolphsen, Nick 734
Adornato, Theodore C. (Ted) 724
Adornetto, Charles 606
Adreani, Lou 739
Advani, Navin 755
Adyniec, Rick 315
Aertker, Gayle 142
Agarwal, Anil 42
Agarwal, Pankaj 182
Agarwal, Achal 457
Agarwal, Manu 535
Agee, Andy 46
Aggarwal, Lokesh 740
Aghai-Yazdy, Dana 752
Aghdami, Amanda 148
Aghili, Aziz S. 231
Agostino, Rich 760
Agrawal, Ajay 154
Agrawal, Tushaar 500
Agresta, Richard 703
Agresta, Gregory J 859
Agroskin, Daniel 140
Agudio, Sharon 664
Aguila, Alex 851
Aguilar, Alfredo 196
Aguilar, Douglas 298
Aguilar, Edgard Corrales 720
Aguinaga, Liz 487
Aguirre, Pascal 193
Aguirre, Ada 270
Aguirre, Edward 453
Aguirre, Jean 502
Aguirre, Vanessa 586
Agulnek, Barbara 381
Agusti, Sandra 96
Agyen, George 378
Ahearn, Tracey 489
Ahearn, Carl 761
Ahee, Joseph 415
Ahern, Lisa 198
Ahern, Michael 365
Ahern, Patrick 754
Aherne, Sean 134
Ahlmann, Kaj 682
Ahlstrand, Norma 873

Arizmendi, Pablo 728
Ark, Jon Vander 679
Arkin, Brad 7
Arko, John 481
Arland, Samantha 827
Armagost, Brad 705
Armbruster, Patrice 558
Armentano, Vincent J 792
Armentrout, Sharon 755
Armes, Tonia 664
Armitage, Courtney 147
Armlin, Cindy 613
Armour, Norm 864
Armstrong, Tim 128
Armstrong, Dean 172
Armstrong, Peter 198
Armstrong, Paula 298
Armstrong, Christopher 299
Armstrong, Steven 339
Armstrong, Kim 413
Armstrong, Keith D. 516
Armstrong, Scott 550
Armstrong, Ronald E. (Ron) 598
Armstrong, Greg L. 627
Armstrong, Greg L 627
Armstrong, Susie 655
Armstrong, Georga 670
Armstrong, Deborah A 735
Armstrong, Austin 779
Armstrong, Kay 793
Arndt, Kenneth A. 343
Arndt, Andrew 685
Arndt, Christopher 787
Arnett, Gevan 189
Arnold, Sarah 50
Arnold, Greg 53
Arnold, Steve 73
Arnold, Scott 82
Arnold, Ken 87
Arnold, Colleen 153
Arnold, Shelly P 203
Arnold, Michael J. 342
Arnold, Christy 423
Arnold, Jeffrey 451
Arnold, Sonia 479
Arnold, Michael 481
Arnold, Keith 622
Arnold, Doug 683
Arnold, Charlotte 784
Arnold, Timothy G. (Tim) 828
Arnoult, Mike 849
Aromando, Nicholas 101
Aronin, Jeffrey 247
Aronoff, Susan 687
Aronowitz, Scott 303
Aronzon, Nicole 434
Arora, Deepak 42
Arora, Vivek 657
Arous, Gérard Ben 551
Arovas, Jordan 856
Arrata, Philippe 116
Arredondo, Fabiola 146
Arrell, Sarah 759
Arrese, Manuel 195
Arriaga, Rene 429
Arrighi, Theresa 798
Arrington, Leslie 291
Arriola, Dennis V. 704
Arronte, Melissa 183
Arrowsmith, Andrea 111
Arroyo, F. Thaddeus 75
Arroyo, Ana 778

Arstark, Reid 698
Art, Perez 694
Artavia, Patty 634
Arters, Doug 433
Arthachinda, Nick 807
Arthur, Sarbah 36
Arthur, Sarah 443
Arthur, Gary 834
Artino, Sarah 550
Artz, Peyton 703
Artz, Eric 816
Arvin, Ann Margaret 474
Asai, Eriko 350
Asbury, John C. 77
Asbury, Stephanie 96
Asbury, Tad 500
Asensio, Lynn D. 858
Ash, Bruce 251
Ash, David 707
Ash, Ora 738
Ashby, Andrew 395
Ashby, Jeremy 751
Ashenbrenner, Fred 216
Asher, Linda 129
Ashford, Robin 667
Ashley, Richard W 5
Ashley, Dennis 45
Ashley, David 178
Ashley, Cathleen 178
Ashley, Andrew 456
Ashley, Anthony 458
Ashley, David 498
Ashley, Terri 498
Ashley, Pamela 671
Ashlock, Richard 755
Ashokkumar, Aashitha 179
Ashton, Martin 10
Ashton, Joseph 354
Ashton, Martin 426
Ashworth, Richard M. 848
Askey, Daniel 355
Asleson, Brett 404
Aslin, Phil 768
Asmar, Joseph 502
Asmus, Sharon 690
Asnani, Manish 844
Aspinwall, Glenn 446
Asplund, Frank 481
Asplund, Dale A. 819
Assalone, Kim 588
Asta, Melanie 114
Astroth, Joseph 860
Asuncion-yacapin, Lee 98
Atalay, Hakan 653
Atchue, Nancy 784
Atcovitz, Michael 681
Aten, Derek 201
Athanasakos, Nick 560
Athanasia, Dean C. 95
Atherton, Patricia 162
Atkins, Margaret 234
Atkins, Brett 337
Atkins, Bruce 362
Atkins, Damien 387
Atkinson, Jonathan 298
Atkinson, Ralph 385
Atkinson, Luanne 446
Atkinson, Cliff 522
Atkinson, Heather 694
Atkinson, Tracy 739
Attal, Jeremy 211
Attar, Chris 670

Attarian, Howard W 811
Attaway, David 76
Attaway, John A. 650
Atteberry, Dean 28
Attig, Kelley A 492
Attili, Srinivas 431
Attwood, Dorothy 250
Atwell, Robert 559
Atwell, William 856
Atwood, Matt 629
Au, Joseph 261
Au, Reynette 523
Au, Lawrence 566
Aubin, Chrissy 676
Aubrejuan, Paco 593
Aubrey, Bob 28
Aubrey, William E. 612
Aubry, Olivier 221
Aubuchon, Michael 224
Auchincloss, Edgar 610
Aufiero, Matt 80
Auger, Stephen 332
Aughenbaugh, Geoffrey 222
August-deWilde, Katherine 328
Augustine, Michael 450
Augustine, Lesley 684
Augustsson, Tommy 348
Aul, Kenneth 835
Auld, David V. 406
Auld, Maureen 871
Aulph, Karen 313
Aument, Tonya 344
Aunan, Erik 3
Aupied, David 500
Aurora, Dana 120
Aurora, Ravi 507
Ausberry, Sheila 200
Ausman, Sara 24
Austin, Roxanne 5
Austin, Danielle 88
Austin, Renea 103
Austin, Mark 566
Austin, Karen A. 618
Austin, Theresa 647
Austin, Earl C. (Duke) 657
Austing, Kimberly 493
Autenried, Paul von 135
Autore, Diane 751
Auvil, Adam 189
Auyeung, Kinwa 226
Auyeung, Rex 637
Avdic, Edina 777
Averbach, Rob 871
Aversano, Jesse 556
Avery, Linda 365
Avery, Sue 519
Avery, Mary 871
Avila, Erin De 96
Avila, Julio 185
Avila, Rene 429
Aviles, Alan D. 548
Avvari, Shyam 491
Awad, Greg 291
Awad, Anwar 425
Awada, Hassan 219
Awada, Kaled 764
Awadallah, Ehab 148
Awbrey, Rick 417
Axe, Mark 747
Axenson, Tanya 26
Axler, Max 750
Ayala, John C. 80

Aycock, Robert 160
Aycock, Angela W 200
Ayele, Wouleta 729
Ayers, Donovan 162
Ayers, Stephen 694
Ayllon, Christina 617
Aylouche, Mounzer M 504
Ayotte, Eric 493
Ayoub, Johnny 130
Ayoub, Ellen 749
Ayre, David J. 560
Ayres, Maria 9
Ayyar, Shekar 845
Azadian, Susan 869
Azar, Larry 460
Azar, Sam 576
Azar, Mark 784
Azinovic, Drago 620
Aziz, Hany 774
Aznar, Jose 556
Azoulay, Salomon 617
Azuara, Katherine 107
Azzarita, Corrado 462
Azzi, Shane 457
Azzinaro, James 88

B

Babb, Ralph W. 200
Babb, Ovid 305
Babb, Matt 814
Babcock, John P. 606
Babiak, Janice 849
Babik, Amber 415
Babikian, Jeffrey C 159
Babineau, Thomas 131
Babinski, Steve 325
Babou, Stephanie 740
Babu, Santhosh 182
Bach, Tommy 304
Bacha, Beth 198
Bachaalani, Issam 195
Bachelder, Stuart 235
Bachman, Theresa 344
Bachmann, John 12
Bachmann, Steve 123
Bachmeyer, Christy 224
Bacigalupo, George F. 114
Back, Paulo 593
Back, Tekla 613
Backer, Chris 80
Backman, Mats 79
Backus, Marcia E. 580
Backus, Benjamin 826
Bacon, Gwen 21
Bacon, Chris 80
Bacon, Graham W. 278
Bacon, Ashley 447
Bacon, Jennie 456
Bacus, Lisa 173
Baczor, Merelyn 629
Badalament, Michael 472
Badam, Ramulu 360
Badar, Ruben 535
Badders, Matt 223
Bader, Jeffrey 523
Bader, Rupert 525
Baderschneider, Jean 289
Badger, Austin 749
Badi, Mohammed 42
Baechle, Michael 507

Bean, Bryan 624
Bear, James 695
Beard, Brad 754
Beard, Gregory 829
Beard, Brooks 846
Beardall, Brent J. 852
Beardi, James 492
Beardsley, Bruce 346
Beardsley, Kirk M. 562
Bearison, Daniel 587
Beasley, Susan 807
Beaton, Mark 454
Beaton, Tiffany 721
Beatty, Mark 118
Beatty, Donald 195
Beatty, Michael 497
Beatty, Vincent L. 852
Beaty, Brian 160
Beaty, Lyn 375
Beauchamp, Janice 617
Beaudette, Phil 813
Beaudoin, Marc Phillipe 355
Beaudry, Vicki 52
Beaufils, Ludovic 868
Beaumont, Simon 431
Beaumont, Carol 785
Beauregard, Colleen 784
Beaver, Steven 16
Beaver, Rick 807
Bebawi, Michael 535
Bebber, David L. Van 803
Bebout, John 819
Becerra, Michelle 507
Becerra, Enrique 755
Becerra, Enrique X 756
Bech, Douglas 395
Bechard, Armond 28
Becherer, Hans 240
Bechtolsheim, Andy 177
Beck, Andrew H. (Andy) 17
Beck, Gary L. 21
Beck, Christophe 266
Beck, Lita 326
Beck, Constance 344
Beck, Connie 344
Beck, Joe 387
Beck, Amy 415
Beck, Elisabeth 438
Beck, Kate 460
Beck, Klaus 515
Beck, Christian 700
Beck, Drake 700
Beck, Jeff 703
Beck, Daniel 749
Beck, Michael 825
Becker, Neil 149
Becker, Jen 305
Becker, Donna 326
Becker, Christopher 327
Becker, Lisa 555
Becker, Dave 564
Becker, Steven 637
Becker, Baron 684
Becker, Yin C. 747
Becker, Gregory W. (Greg) 749
Beckerle, Mary 444
Becketti, Sean 341
Beckey, David 701
Beckham, William 18
Beckler, Robert K. (Bob) 867
Beckley, Michael 500
Beckman, John 551

Beckmann, Stacey 149
Beckmann, Barbara 335
Beckwith, Patricia 289
Beckwith, Tina 519
Beckwith, Bryon 559
Beckwith, Ken 755
Beckwitt, Richard (Rick) 476
Bedard, Natalie 617
Bedard, Tim 844
Beddes, Hallie 502
Bedeau, Theresa 148
Bedel, Vicki 830
Bedi, Virender 366
Bedingfield, Kenneth L. 568
Bednar, Ladd 664
Bednarski, Teresa A 96
Bedon, Bernard 560
Bedout, Juan De 839
Bedros, Suzanne 832
Beebe, Robert 178
Beebe, Brian 273
Beebe, Mike 396
Beecy, Steven 823
Beede, Katherine 784
Beelman, Pamela 502
Beer, Lori A. 447
Beer, James A. 511
Beer, Sander De 617
Beer-christensen, Debbie 653
Beers, Marlene 632
Beery, Joseph C. (Joe) 781
Begam, Thomas 308
Begg, Brian 860
Beggs, Curtis 337
Begle, Curt L. 115
Begley, Jody L. 33
Begley, William J. 692
Begley, Nicholas 873
Behan, Mark 69
Behm, Michael J. 670
Behmer, Nancy 861
Behnk, Karin 807
Behrens, David A. 47
Behrens, Michael 303
Behring, Alexandre (Alex) 462
Beidelman, Jason 608
Beierwaltes, Paul 873
Beil, David 835
Beilman, Bart 870
Beirne, Nazli 448
Belanger, Dennis 270
Belanic, Jim 634
Belardi, James R 76
Belasco, Kent S. 325
Belavic, Jennifer 829
Belcher, Patricia 120
Belcher, Samuel L. 329
Belcher, Brian 465
Belcher, Kelly 749
Belden, Scott 792
Belekewicz, William D. 331
Belen, Andy 825
Beletti, Chris 216
Belgya, Mark R. 715
Belhadj, Hafed 620
Belinske, Joe 160
Belitsky, Lee J. 243
Beliveau-dunn, Jeanne 178
Belk, Deanna 336
Belk, William 717
Bell, Patricia A 16
Bell, Bernice E 19

Bell, Thomas 124
Bell, Gretchen 135
Bell, Brad 200
Bell, Mike 218
Bell, Teri 446
Bell, Steve 453
Bell, Mark 481
Bell, Adam 507
Bell, George 519
Bell, Del 531
Bell, Thomas 564
Bell, Ken 565
Bell, Elizabeth 593
Bell, Des 618
Bell, David 622
Bell, Damon 624
Bell, Will 682
Bell, Jean 731
Bell, Ted 749
Bellack, Janis P. 503
Bellamy, Don 570
Bellanti, Tim 73
Belliard, Jean 613
Bellinger, Greg Van 760
Bellino, Nick 336
Belliot, Laura 305
Belloma, Kevin 202
Belochi, Franck 653
Belous, Scott 42
Below, Ellen 381
Beltrametti, Monica 879
Beltramino, Gabe 507
Beltran, Christina 92
Beltre, Milca 121
Beltz, Ryan 606
Beltz, Mary 835
Bem, David S. 631
Bemiller, Todd 871
Bemis, Mark A. 66
Benavides, David 293
Benchoff, Nancy 365
Bencosme, Thomas 535
Benda, Birgitta 617
Bender, Jim 82
Bender, Danelle 230
Bender, Jason C. 328
Bender, Jeremy 360
Bender, Michael J 690
Bender, Andria 737
Bender, M. Steven (Steve) 866
Beneby, Doyle N 285
Benedetto, Ben Di 500
Benedict, John 491
Benedict, Vicky 591
Benefield, Donna 573
Benegal, Jay 184
Beneke, Jim 88
Beneke, Jenny 656
Benelli, David 120
Benet, Jay S. 792
Benett, Halle J 92
Beneventano, David 366
Bengs, Mike 562
Bengston, Robert A. 598
Bengston, Kelly 728
Benioff, Marc 693
Benito, Michael E. 385
Benjamin, Rachel 179
Benjamin, Andre 365
Benjamin, Gerald A. 698
Benjamin, Peter 784
Benko, Brittany 168

Benkoske, Thomas 873
Benkovich, Nick 419
Benn, Markham 429
Benn, Keith 580
Bennack, Frank A. 778
Benner, David 439
Bennet, Steve 729
Bennett, Rick 3
Bennett, Chap 52
Bennett, Bruce 53
Bennett, Chuck 60
Bennett, Shayne 63
Bennett, Douglas M. 104
Bennett, Brian 216
Bennett, John 309
Bennett, Charles 316
Bennett, Jonathan R. 380
Bennett, Robert 409
Bennett, Stephen 435
Bennett, Judy 675
Bennett, Steven 703
Bennett, Kris 774
Bennett, Rick 807
Bennett, Terry 851
Bennette, Jim 656
Bennington, Todd 131
Bennion, Richard W. H. (Rich) 399
Bennison, Andrew 781
Benns, Norris 162
Benoit, Cole 798
Benowitz, Leigh 698
Benschneider, Angel 160
Bensignor, Laurence E. 260
Bensimhon, Ilan 593
Bension, Ronald (Ron) 484
Benskin, Nancy 624
Benson, Don 118
Benson, Mike 223
Benson, Taylor 224
Benson, Mark 242
Benson, David C. 291
Benson, Ed 292
Benson, Jodi 352
Benson, Aaron 684
Benter, Bob 643
Bentley, Elizabeth M. 77
Bentley, Ashley 107
Bentley, Stacey 654
Bentley, Philip 851
Benton, Antonio 316
Benton, David 801
Bentoumi, Fatima 875
Benvenuto, Joe 700
Benz, John 653
Benzon, Jennie 500
Bené, Thomas L. (Tom) 755
Bequette, Marcia 673
Beranek, Becky 10
Berard, Sarah 380
Berardi, Joseph 754
Berardinelli, Christopher 860
Berberian, Lance V. 467
Berce, Daniel E. (Dan) 353
Berchtold, Joe 484
Berchtold, Tim 613
Bercovici, Nancy 299
Berdine, Winona 673
Berend, Anne 431
Berendsen, Nancy 869
Berendsen, Jay Michael 869
Berensen, Nannette 428
Berenson, Harris 378

Binnie, Bob 180
Binnie, Lisa 378
Binns, Justin T. 707
Binzer, Ann 174
Bion, Joel 174
Bion, Joel 177
Biondi, Paul 135
Biornstad, Nina 507
Biraghi, Sonna 267
Birch, Robert F. 396
Birch, Laurie 593
Birch, Angel 701
Birchmeier, Cindy 371
Bird, Roger M. 4
Bird, Kim 130
Bird, Stephen 181
Bird, Kristin 803
Birdwell, Cameron 365
Birk, Michael 140
Birkelo, Jeff 852
Birkenholtz, Brad 96
Birkhahn, Robert H 778
Birkholz, Shelly 380
Birkholz, Jeff 673
Birkmeyer, David 818
Birla, Nita 366
Birling, Melissa 72
Birmingham, Jessica 160
Birmingham, Martin K. 309
Birmingham-Byrd, Melody 258
Birnbaum, David 535
Birnbaum, Jason 812
Birnbrich, Pamela 415
Birns, Ira M. 875
Biron, Michael 751
Bisaccia, Lisa 229
Bisaccio, Brian 788
Bischof, Tim 189
Bischofberger, Norbert W. 360
Biscotti, John 640
Bisegna, Anthony C. 739
Bish, James 858
Bishop, Daniel 72
Bishop, Russell 237
Bishop, Adam 417
Bishop, John 476
Bishop, Marissa 556
Bishop, Steven D. (Steve) 640
Bishop, James 694
Bishop, Thomas 720
Bishop, Amy 769
Bishop, Kendall 823
Bishop, Bridgette 825
Bishop, Linda 873
Bittarelli, Jason 740
Bittel, Philip 672
Bitter, Jay 685
Bitzer, Marc R. 868
Bivens-rose, Gail 684
Bivins, Erica 671
Bixby, R. Philip 450
Bixby, Walter E. (Web) 450
Bixby, James 450
Bixby, Gregory 761
Bizzard, Kenneth 671
Bjornstad, Geir 279
Black, Krystl 74
Black, Maria 80
Black, David F 143
Black, Willa 177
Black, Dennis 201
Black, Brent 226

Black, Alan 315
Black, Bonnie 625
Black, Peter 655
Black, Ken 681
Black, Freddie G. 710
Black, Katy 762
Black, Katherine 766
Black, Mary 835
Black, Chastity 839
Black, Nadine 871
Blackburn, Fred K. 129
Blackburn, Andy 178
Blackburn, Patrick 311
Blackburn, Stella 438
Blackburn, Randy 460
Blackburn, Rosie 797
Blackford, David E. 884
Blackhurst, Eric 403
Blackley, R. Scott 148
Blackman, Scott 201
Blackmon, Kate 411
Blackmon, Alan 528
Blackwelder, John 148
Blackwell, Tina 302
Blackwell, Jason 777
Blackwood, Hank 218
Blackwood, Elizabeth 444
Blagg, Richard 12
Blain, Robert (Rob) 159
Blair, Ingrid 3
Blair, Jeffrey C. 57
Blair, Rainer M. 232
Blair, Gavin 378
Blair, David G 395
Blair, Matthew 502
Blair, Timothy 566
Blair, Bradley 671
Blair, Kevin S. 753
Blair, Karen 805
Blais, Greg 558
Blais, Andrew 737
Blaise, Timothy 234
Blaising, Rachel 162
Blajszczak, Miranda 825
Blake, Nancy 200
Blake, Francis S. (Frank) 242
Blake, Patrick J. (Pat) 511
Blake, Christopher D. 600
Blake, Susan 629
Blake, David M. 637
Blake, Lynn S. 739
Blake, Ellen 839
Blakemore, Jim 211
Blakemore, Anthony 719
Blakewood, Benjamin F. 18
Blalock, Pam 518
Blanchard, Dan 242
Blanchard, Brent 479
Blanchard, Diane 492
Blanchard, Bob 571
Blanco, Alex 266
Bland, Jim 137
Bland, Alicia 319
Bland, Christine 322
Bland, Mickey 423
Bland, Trabue 427
Blank, Lee 671
Blankenship, Charles P. (Chip) 407
Blankenship, Dave 500
Blankenship, Eric 678
Blankfein, Lloyd C. 365
Blankush, Johanna 251

Blanton, Brice 121
Blanton, Hamilton 148
Blasco, Salvador 656
Blase, William A. (Bill) 75
Blaser, Brian J. 4
Blasini, David P 148
Blaske, Stephen 50
Blasko, Michael 795
Blatcher, Kevin 146
Blatter, Steve 712
Blaug, Suzanne 54
Blaya, Richard 839
Blaylock, Isaac 707
Blazejewski, Steve 152
Blazer, Robert 498
Bledsoe, Vallerie M 302
Bledsoe, Steve 374
Bledsoe, Matthew 671
Bleiman, Aap 89
Bleisch, N. David 582
Blendick, Jeff 415
Blenkush, Bob 527
Bleske, Mitchell 814
Bless, Michael 187
Blestowe, James 49
Blevins, Tim 88
Blevins, P. Rodney 254
Blew, Clinton J. (C.J.) 172
Bley, Daniel H. 856
Bleyl, Steven 428
Blick, Bryan 120
Blihovde, Valerie 760
Blincoe, Donna 677
Blinkiewicz, John 75
Blissett, Julian 353
Blitzer, David S. 121
Blivice, Marni 121
Blixt, Mary 240
Bloch, Jeremy 163
Block, Louis Mark 10
Block, Robert 27
Block, Arthur R. 197
Block, Keith G. 693
Blocker, Jeff 489
Blockhus, Gregory 50
Blomquist, John 573
Blondia, Jeanne 747
Bloom, Leah 6
Bloom, Brent 63
Bloom, Richard S 190
Bloom, William A. (Bill) 380
Bloom, Alfred H. 551
Bloomfield, Barry 535
Blose, James 742
Blount, Sally 5
Bloxam, Richard 445
Bludau, Laurence 207
Bludworth, Jed 62
Blue, Robert M. (Bob) 254
Blue, Robert M. 842
Blum, Jeffrey 249
Blum, Donald W. 645
Blume, Brent 832
Blumenfeld, Stephen 366
Blumer, David J. 120
Blumeyer, Greg 192
Blumhardt, James 860
Blundell, Alan 489
Blundon, Lee 858
Blunt, Chris 121
Blunt, Andy 160
Bluso, Samual 184

Bluth, Thomas J. (Tom) 157
Blutman, Gary 470
Blye, Jeffrey C 299
Blyth, Lesley 728
Blyze, Scott 243
Boada, Robert C 719
Bob, Archuleta 126
Bobb, Stevan B. 122
Bobbie, Frances D 685
Bober, Sharon 504
Bobitz, Ward E. 356
Bobrovich, Julia 749
Bobrowsky, Bill 670
Bochenek, Tomasz 525
Bockhorst, Cheri 181
Bodakowski, Steven 610
Bodapati, Ramesh 178
Boddie, Paul 13
Bodenhafer, Scott 481
Bodi, Attila 233
Bodine, Bruce 536
Bodisch, Laurie 344
Bodman, Ryan 506
Bodnar, Vincent 357
Boe, Ryan 531
Boe, Douglas 832
Boedeker, Kenneth W. 279
Boegner, Scott 787
Boehn, Michael 202
Boehnke, David 229
Boehnlein, Glenn 747
Boeing, Traci 858
Boersma, Brad 307
Boeshaar, Brad 806
Bogan, Gary 415
Bogart, Clinton 160
Boger, Alisha 624
Boggess, Michael 96
Boggetto, Brian 284
Boggs, Gregory 153
Boggs, Rod 519
Bogle, Reese 247
Bogler, John A. 92
Bogosta, Charles E. (Chuck) 829
Boguski, Michael L. 638
Bohaboy, Scott 107
Bohannon, Jason 413
Bohanon, Chris 296
Bohaty, Brian R. 27
Bohbrink, Marshall 374
Bohlinger, Thomas 160
Bohlman, Dave 433
Bohm, David 299
Bohmler, April 503
Bohn, Karen 24
Bohn, William M. 71
Bohn, Don 444
Bohnen, Jennifer 873
Bohon, Jackie 643
Bohrer, Scott 397
Bohrer, Tom 671
Boigegrain, Barbara 326
Boike, Brian D.J. 331
Boim, Dave 531
Boisier, Pierre 109
Boisten, Bernd 683
Boitano, Robert 305
Bojdak, Robert J. 492
Bok, Cathleen 182
Bokan, Mike 523
Bokina, Erin 647
Bokka, Rama 700

Boyes, John C 292
Boyette, Gaye 493
Boykas, Paul 613
Boyken, James W 431
Boykin, Frank H. 530
Boykins, Lamont 50
Boykins, Gail 731
Boykins, Lamont 844
Boyland, Gloria 302
Boyle, Amy 50
Boyle, Hugh F. 92
Boyle, Jim 248
Boyle, Chris 341
Boyle, Jack 460
Boyle, Karen 492
Boyle, Donna 507
Boyle, Kevin 511
Boyle, Terence 562
Boyle, Patti 695
Boyle, Philip 794
Boyle, Mark A. 801
Boyle, Dennis 826
Boyle, Tom 879
Boyles, Andrew 97
Boyles, Kevin 708
Boyles, Jonathan 713
Boza, Xavier 146
Bozek, Kathy 72
Bozzi, Bryan 846
Bozzolo, Albert 335
Brabant, Steven 159
Brabson, Charles 278
Brace, George 399
Bracey, Brent 613
Bracher, Paul H. 223
Bracht, Berend 683
Bracken, Chris 505
Bracy, Kevin 413
Bracy, Andrew 734
Bradac, Joe 851
Braden, Scott 512
Bradford, Douglas 91
Bradford, Mark D. 583
Bradham, Sue 704
Bradish, Bob 40
Bradley, Mike 88
Bradley, Bill 94
Bradley, Myles 147
Bradley, Jen 202
Bradley, Nancy 322
Bradley, John 447
Bradley, William E. (Bill) 490
Bradley, Paul 493
Bradley, Matthew 593
Bradley, Alison 670
Bradley, Jeff 671
Bradley, Pat 673
Bradley, Jacqueline 702
Bradley, Ryan 703
Bradley, Scott 760
Bradley, W. Bennett 797
Bradley, Kristi 800
Bradley, Kevin P. 821
Bradley, John 832
Bradley, Patrick 870
Bradshaw, Steven G. (Steve) 125
Bradshaw, Beverly 160
Bradshaw, Mike 198
Bradshaw, Jim 463
Bradshaw, Richard W. 813
Bradvica, Michael 12
Bradway, Robert A. (Bob) 54

Brady, Sean 1
Brady, Kevin 39
Brady, James 149
Brady, Tim 381
Brady, Deanna T. 404
Brady, Amy G. 455
Brady, Christopher 456
Brady, John 566
Brady, Elizabeth S. (Beth) 637
Brady, Keith 813
Braemer, Richard 787
Brager, David A. 227
Bragg, Chris 102
Bragg, Dorry 304
Brahm, Joerg 270
Braid, Gregory 654
Brainerd, Mary 383
Brainerd, Mary 747
Braitberg, Karl 593
Braithwaite, Jamila 148
Bram, Greg 834
Braman, Michael 540
Bramlage, Stephen P. (Steve) 64
Bramman, Anne L. 562
Branca, Frank 819
Branch, Gregory C. 815
Brand, Meir 30
Brand, Dennis L. 93
Brand, Walter 705
Brandel, Daniel 160
Brandenburg, Pat 672
Brandenburg, Joel 808
Brandl, Linda 810
Brandolini, Nuno 167
Brandon, Joseph P. 25
Brandon, Rush 341
Brandon, Moore 760
Brandt, Kathleen 222
Brandt, Kristi 383
Brandt, James A. 489
Brandt, Phil 500
Brandt, Tim 502
Brandt, Genise 684
Brandt, Tom 823
Branigin, John 298
Brannan, Joseph 481
Brannen, James P. (Jim) 295
Brannon, Jeff 152
Brannon, Jill 302
Brannon, B C 581
Brannon, Bobby 581
Brannon, James 717
Branon, Bethany 828
Branscome, Andrea 797
Brant, Tim 95
Brant, Kevin 445
Brantley, Todd 328
Branum, Lisa 751
Branz, Sandra 380
Branzburg, Paul 740
Braselton, Michele 93
Braskamp, Steve 149
Bratman, Fred 819
Bratspies, Steve 850
Bratt, Mikael 79
Braud, Ken 375
Brauer, Mark 417
Brauer, Angela 835
Brault, Patricia 543
Braun, Dennis 152
Braun, Randall L. 359
Braun, Alan 584

Braun, Richard 602
Braun, Peter 807
Braun-Kolbe, Karl 492
Braunsdorf, Mary 778
Braunstein, Louis 299
Brause, Kenneth 179
Brautigan, Bernard (Bernie) 687
Brautlacht, Gerald 492
Braverman, Alan N 250
Brawner, Eric 201
Bray, Jeffrey 181
Bray, Jeffery (Jeff) 701
Bray, David 803
Brayer, Frank 484
Brayshaw, Bettina 756
Brazell, Joe 562
Brda, Bruce W. 537
Bready, Bruce 469
Breakefield, Xandra 504
Breakey, Mark D. 188
Brearton, David 460
Breaux, John 222
Breaux, Randall 355
Breber, Pierre R. 169
Brecher, Mark 467
Brecker, Nicholas L. 59
Breckon, Steven 273
Breckon, Curt 518
Breda, John 871
Bredow, Eugene J. 577
Breecher, Audrey 805
Breeden, Gregory 413
Breeman, Steven 469
Breen, Edward D. (Ed) 259
Breen, Timothy P. (Tim) 355
Breen, Chuck 357
Brega, Jo-- o Carlos 868
Breight, Matthew 200
Breihan, Beth 818
Breininger, Stephen 632
Breitenbach, Kerry 642
Breitenstein, Justin 629
Breitling, John 415
Breivogel, Donald 589
Brekka, Kevin 797
Brell, Mark 223
Bremser, Brett 417
Brenda, Huff 126
Brenda, Montgomery 422
Brendis, Janet 346
Brendle, Jim 110
Brendzal, Michael 823
Breneus, Peggy 504
Brennan, Daniel J. (Dan) 133
Brennan, Troyen A. 229
Brennan, Thomas 325
Brennan, Matthew 325
Brennan, Kevin F. 346
Brennan, James 434
Brennan, Mark 552
Brennan, Suzanne R. 600
Brennan, Thomas 647
Brennan, Keith 647
Brennan, Daniel 752
Brennen, Robert 305
Brenner, Christina 184
Brenner, Timothy L. 544
Brenner, Dean 655
Brenner, Glen 785
Brensinger, Donald 681
Brent, Thompson 284
Brent, Jacques 339

Brenton, Flint 177
Breshears, Eric 328
Breslauer, Jacque 179
Breslawski, James P. 698
Breslin, David 328
Bresnan, Debra 350
Bress, Tracy 488
Bressler, Allan 841
Brestovan, Peter 609
Brethour, Tom 58
Breuel, Chuck 506
Breux, Ken Le 566
Breves, Christine S. 821
Brewer, Allen M. 335
Brewer, Russell 474
Brewer, Dominic 551
Brewer, Janet J. 766
Brewers, Doug 50
Brezin, Eva 647
Brian, Clark 873
Brice, Todd D. 691
Brick, Christine 851
Bricker, Christopher 624
Brickley, Liam 139
Brickman, David M. 341
Bridarolli, Shelley 131
Bridenbaugh, Carl 329
Bridge, Tracy B. 163
Bridge, Byard 745
Bridgeforth, Scott 747
Bridges, David 18
Bridges, Kimberly 203
Bridges, Jennifer 540
Bridges, Linda 558
Bridges, Kristopher 671
Bridges, Kris 671
Bridwell, Tucker 318
Brier, Jeff 12
Brigantic, Patricia E 535
Brigden, John 177
Briggs, Tammy 16
Briggs, Ashlea 93
Briggs, Michael 355
Briggs, Troy 584
Briggs, Scott 751
Briggs, Bruce 755
Briggs, Brent 884
Brigham, F Gorham 183
Bright, Brian 48
Bright, Tobias 124
Brightman, Allison 841
Brightwell, Jeff 273
Brigiotta, Maria 242
Briglia, Jennifer 831
Brigman, Vince 470
Brill, Casey 184
Brill, Matthew 190
Brill, Julie 525
Brill, Casey 628
Brill, Scott 760
Brill, Cheryl 829
Brim, Landon 722
Brimberry, Jared 22
Brinch, Brian 296
Brindle, Carol 876
Brindley, David 814
Bringhurst, Richard 504
Brink, Evert Van Den 740
Brinker, Mark 613
Brinkerhoff, Joris W 391
Brinkley, Cynthia J. (Cindy) 162
Brinkley, Ruth W. 204

Bruzzano, Marco 257
Bryan, Kathleen 97
Bryan, Cary 178
Bryan, Glynis A. 423
Bryan, Bradford 500
Bryan, Jeanna 664
Bryan, Vere 703
Bryan, Vincent 792
Bryant, Matt 223
Bryant, Steve 270
Bryant, Diane M. 425
Bryant, Andy D. 426
Bryant, John A. 451
Bryant, Phil 734
Bryant, Barry 737
Bryant, James 748
Bryant, Thaire 755
Bryant, Mike 818
Bryant, Greg 879
Bryce, Maria 322
Brycz, Kim 353
Brycz, Kimberly kim 353
Bryhn, Jason 736
Brynelsen, Chuck 5
Bryson, Philip 500
Bryson, Mary 858
Brzezicki, Paul A 748
Brzezinski, Robert 455
Bubb, David 700
Bucci, Don 446
Buchanan, Travis 150
Buchanan, John D. 200
Buchanan, Stephen G. (Steve) 690
Buchanan, Ashley 851
Buchanan, Brooke 870
Buchanon, Kent 466
Buchanon, David 677
Bucher, Jennifer 431
Buchmeier, Peter 178
Buchner, Renee 871
Buchs, Jim 753
Buck, Michele G. 387
Buck, Thomas 415
Buckalew, Steve 374
Buckbee, Kevin 6
Buckheit, Scott 144
Buckingham, Andrew 192
Buckingham, David C 204
Buckingham, Lisa M. 481
Buckiso, David 316
Buckiso, Scott D. 821
Bucklee, Andrew 481
Buckley, Bob 80
Buckley, Brad 165
Buckley, Bradford J 165
Buckley, Leslie 198
Buckley, John 229
Buckley, John 355
Buckley, Michael 498
Buckley, Raegan 502
Buckley, Richard E 647
Buckley, George W. 727
Buckminster, Douglas E. 42
Bucko, James 610
Buco, Glen 695
Buday, Ernie 305
Budd, Thomas D. 654
Budde, Christopher 782
Budesilich, Casey 777
Budraitis, Alyssa A. 20
Budzinski, Jeff 269
Buechel, Jason 870

Buechler, Mark 72
Buechse, Oliver 71
Buehler, James 653
Buehler, Charlie 871
Buelow, Dawn 502
Buenaseda, Jude 552
Buendia, Robin 453
Buerger, Diane 736
Buese, Nancy K. 555
Buesinger, Robert F. 866
Bueter, Brian 40
Buffa, Damiano 121
Buffett, Warren E. 113
Buffie, Craig A. 455
Buffon, Mike 818
Buffoni, Chris 473
Bufkin, Lucy 774
Buford, Mark 207
Bugaj, Rick 308
Bugala, Julie 162
Bugatto, David J. 24
Bugh, Stan 558
Bugh, Frank 664
Buglione, John 795
Buhay, Rene 350
Buhler, Marlene 52
Buhr, Jeffrey L. 1
Buhse, Tom 299
Bui, Vanesa 522
Bui, Greg 560
Bui, Toan 681
Buisson, Steve 798
Buit, Ron 494
Buit, Tim 548
Buitrago, Gus 335
Bulaich, Nick 391
Bulanda, Mark J. 270
Bulandr, Peter 71
Bulawa, Bryan F. 278
Bullard, James B. 300
Bullard, Trey 686
Bullen, Derrik 519
Buller, Katja 118
Bullinger, Phil 864
Bullion, Diana 644
Bullock, Brian H. 276
Bulmer, William H 647
Bulpin, Andrew 515
Bultman, Gary 470
Bulusu, Bhaskar 453
Bumgarner, David L. 185
Bumpus, Ray 602
Bunch, Jimm A. 11
Bunch, Charles 497
Bundschuh, John 610
Bunker, Melissa 584
Bunn, Mike 139
Bunte, Brent 745
Bunting, Theodore H. (Theo) 275
Bunting, Chris 519
Bunyard, Heather 350
Buonforte, Jeffrey J. 469
Buonpastore, Andy 552
Buquicchio, Gerard 664
Burak, Mark 98
Buran, John R. 335
Burba, Melissa M 316
Burch, Monica 183
Burch, William 671
Burchfield, Carol 163
Burchfield, Jay 711
Burchinow, Naran 57

Burckhart, Camille 630
Burd, Travis 130
Burdell, Fred 270
Burdett, Judith 774
Burdick, Don 219
Burdick, Kevin L. 590
Burdiss, Paul E. 884
Burer, Dan 358
Burgdoerfer, Stuart B. 465
Burge, Debbie 640
Burgess, David 58
Burgess, John 355
Burgess, Doug 677
Burgess, Brian 713
Burgess, Eric 751
Burgess, Robert O 761
Burgess, Jo Lynn 797
Burgher, Cedric W. 580
Burgoon, David 673
Burgum, Doug 736
Burik, Jeff 202
Burke, Michael S. (Mike) 12
Burke, Jeffrey 28
Burke, James T. 99
Burke, Sean 132
Burke, Rosaleen 133
Burke, Stephen B. (Steve) 197
Burke, George J 206
Burke, Kevin 213
Burke, Joan A. 314
Burke, Brian 325
Burke, Ken 341
Burke, Susan 341
Burke, Patrick J. (Pat) 410
Burke, Sean 437
Burke, Edward J. (E.J.) 455
Burke, Geoffrey 535
Burke, William A. (Bill) 553
Burke, James J. (Jim) 558
Burke, John 566
Burke, Richard 566
Burke, Lucas 662
Burke, Fred 695
Burke, Jason 700
Burke, Jane 739
Burke, Anthony 742
Burke, Paul 851
Burke, Frank J. 872
Burkhart, Megan D. 200
Burkhart, Kimberly 823
Burlage, David P. 190
Burlando, Fabrizio 506
Burleigh, Clarence 100
Burlog, Chris 819
Burlowski, John 308
Burman, Darryl M. 372
Burmeister, James 57
Burnell, Lawrence 403
Burnell, James 879
Burnett, Janice 126
Burnett, Mike 198
Burnett, Jason 724
Burnette, Dana 78
Burnham, Ellen 306
Burnham, Suzy 647
Burnip, Douglas 828
Burns, Nisha 6
Burns, Shawn 28
Burns, Ward 104
Burns, Ned 160
Burns, Haydon 160
Burns, John 235

Burns, Shira 303
Burns, Matthew 325
Burns, Jean 328
Burns, Larry 334
Burns, Mark L. 348
Burns, Mary 385
Burns, Nellson D. 395
Burns, Stephanie 451
Burns, Chris 521
Burns, Nellson 530
Burns, David 533
Burns, Gay 673
Burns, Joseph 718
Burns, Michelle 729
Burns, Steve 735
Burns, Mary 798
Burns, Sheri T. 808
Burns, Anna 818
Burnside, John 18
Buro, Geoff 823
Burrell, Brian 415
Burrell, Cheryl 736
Burrescia, Dominic 684
Burris, Lee 46
Burris, Alex 476
Burris, Ellen 807
Burritt, David B. (Dave) 821
Burroughs, Margaret 6
Burroughs, Michael 358
Burroughs, Phil 466
Burroughs, Philip 837
Burrow, Lynne M. 143
Burrow, Patrick A. 710
Burrowes, Todd 234
Burrows, Matthew R 174
Burrows, Astrid 500
Burrows, Adam 694
Burrows, Clifford (Cliff) 728
Burson, Arthur 514
Burt, Brady T. 601
Burt, Jessica 613
Burt, Jeff 759
Burtis, Andy 511
Burton, Angel 86
Burton, Brian 100
Burton, Drew 120
Burton, Craig 309
Burton, Vincent 443
Burton, Mary 670
Burton, Eileen 754
Burton, Becky 832
Burtt, Susan 489
Burud, Jamie 768
Burvill, Martin 837
Busa, Theresa 226
Busack, John 858
Busannagari, Chandra 739
Busby, Todd 39
Busby, Patrick 647
Buscaglia, Nick 492
Buscemi, Stephanie 694
Busch, Eric 350
Busch, Tina 457
Busch, Jonathan 667
Busch, Pat 707
Buseman, Michael D. (Mike) 87
Buser, Darin 107
Bush, Julie 42
Bush, Richard 50
Bush, Phil 225
Bush, Mary 247
Bush, James 344

Chandler, Jimmy 318
Chandler, Amber 481
Chandler, Willy 530
Chandler, Don 749
Chandler, Jody 825
Chandler, Catherine 871
Chandoha, Marie A. 700
Chandra, Sumeer 409
Chandrani, Mic 42
Chandrasekaran, Ramakrishnan 193
Chandrasekaran, Vikram 670
Chandrasekaran, Rajiv 729
Chandrasekhar, Arun 425
Chandrashekar, Sriram (Ram) 496
Chandrayana, Kartik 694
Chandwani, Manesh 179
Chaney, Glynn 467
Chang, Annabel 21
Chang, Shen 42
Chang, Helen 98
Chang, Mike 112
Chang, Daniel 121
Chang, Jennifer 121
Chang, Herman 164
Chang, Chris 234
Chang, Christopher 234
Chang, Sam 535
Chang, Evans 566
Chang, Andrew S. 607
Chang, Sally 634
Chang, Judy 635
Chang, Eddie 655
Chang, Emily 729
Chang-diaz, Franklin 225
Channawi, Omar 640
Channel, Mike 643
Chanter, Keith 269
Chanthaphasouk, Thomas 653
Chantzis, Christos 443
Chao, Bo 479
Chao, Albert 866
Chao, James Y. 866
Chapanar, Marilyn 367
Chapel, Lash 415
Chapin, Arthur 286
Chapin, Libby 307
Chapin, David 446
Chapman, Justin 71
Chapman, Ryan 121
Chapman, Robert 136
Chapman, Keith 211
Chapman, Steven M. (Steve) 225
Chapman, Rhonda 315
Chapman, Brent 328
Chapman, Kevin D. 676
Chapman, Chuck 703
Chapman, Esther 711
Chapman, Paul 776
Chapman, Ken 792
Chapman, Garrett 839
Chapman, Timothy M. 843
Chapman, Michele 881
Chappell, Daniel G. (Dan) 701
Chaput, Paul 160
Charalambous, Ioannis A. 580
Charbonneau, Tracy 381
Charbonneau, Ed 655
Charbonneau, Edward 656
Charest, Laurie 183
Charest, Teri 831
Charity, Alicia 50

Charlene, Brennan 678
Charles, Victor 16
Charles, Ronald 162
Charles, Anthony St 208
Charles, Robert 319
Charles, Audrey 470
Charles, Doug 473
Charles, R Lynn 487
Charles, Amy 624
Charlet, Barbara 736
Charlton, Mark 653
Charlton, R. Scott 755
Charlton, Scott 755
Charmatz, Jeff 100
Charnas, Robert 669
Charneski, Brian S. 386
Charney, Eugene 502
Charon, Maria 841
Charri, Ali 234
Charter, Robert B. (Rob) 157
Charton, Daryl 3
Chase, William 4
Chase, William J. 6
Chase, Jonathan 309
Chase, Wendy 481
Chase, P. Kevin 704
Chastain, Megan 365
Chastain, Stephen 446
Chatterton, David 694
Chattopadhyay, Sanat 514
Chau, Celia 120
Chau, David 751
Chaubal, Mahesh 107
Chaubal, Prasad 448
Chauhan, Abhishek 242
Chauvin, Stephen 629
Chavez, R. Martin 365
Chavez, Mauricio 511
Chavez, Don 568
Chavez, Earl 667
Chavez, Eileen 778
Chavira, Isaac 315
Chavira, Ron 644
Chavis, Eva 303
Chawla, Manish 431
Chawla, Sona 460
Chawla, Subodh 613
Chazen, Stephen 266
Chazin, Steve 177
Chea, Jun 456
Chean, Kevin 519
Cheap, Richard A. 414
Cheatham, J. Douglas 586
Cheatham, Tim 851
Cheatwood, Chris J. 625
Checketts, John 442
Checketts, Lannie 794
Checki, Terrence J. 299
Chee, Adrian 164
Chee, Kit 425
Cheek, Richelle 11
Cheek, Bruce D. 41
Cheeseborough, Pamela 184
Cheeseman, Michael 375
Cheesewright, David 850
Cheleden, Charles G. 876
Chelin, Julie 195
Chelminiak, Lee 503
Chen, Lei 42
Chen, Lucy 62
Chen, Wei 62
Chen, Donald 66

Chen, Alexander 107
Chen, Kuohsin 121
Chen, Qihua 157
Chen, Heng W. 158
Chen, Ronald 158
Chen, Jennifer 181
Chen, Kelvin 300
Chen, Nevin 426
Chen, David 504
Chen, Simone 519
Chen, Wellington 634
Chen, Eric 635
Chen, John 686
Chen, George 871
Cheney, Andrew B. (Andy) 51
Cheney, John 476
Cheng, Johnny 261
Cheng, Al 261
Cheng, Andrew 360
Cheng, Rebecca 465
Cheng, Henry 481
Cheng, Lili 525
Cheng, Marn K. 540
Cheng, Blannie 735
Chennakeshu, Sandeep 10
Chenore, Elizabeth 324
Chercoe, Howard 538
Cherecwich, Peter B. 565
Cherewko, Greg 871
Cherland, Angela 60
Chernick, Rose 649
Chernikoff, Roy 546
Cherry, Kimberley C. (Kim) 321
Cherry, Jessica 332
Cherry, Pedro 358
Cherry, Don J. 361
Cherry, Amity 556
Cherry, Craig 787
Cherry, Bill 798
Cherukuri, Ravikrishna 177
Cherwek, Nancy M 818
Chery, Sulexan 36
Cheryl, Lasneske 48
Cheryl, Cossette 198
Chesler, Randall M. (Randy) 361
Chesley, Bruce 124
Chesley, Yonnie 382
Chesna, Peter 803
Chess, Jason 710
Chester, Iris 27
Chestnut, Randy 493
Chestnutt, Roy H. 837
Cheung, Nina 101
Cheung, Annie 431
Cheung, Ann 634
Cheung, Ann J 635
Cheung, Sue 700
Cheung, Eric 871
Chevalier, John T 640
Chew, Lee Fang 63
Chewens, Michael J. 544
ChFC, Brooke 48
Chi, Cindy 401
Chi, Erika 634
Chia, Curtis 247
Chia, Donny 535
Chiang, David 28
Chiang, Lidia 242
Chiang, Ellen 261
Chiang, Hwai Hai (HH) 439
Chiappone, Charles 448
Chiarella, Sharon 34

Chiaromonte, Jeannie 96
Chiavelli, Geno 784
Chiccino, Peter (Pete) 773
Chichester, David 728
Chicoine, Gerry 75
Chicoine, Jerry L. 295
Chidley, Shelley 700
Chien, Christine 780
Chiesa, John 365
Chikkala, Ramesh 851
Childers, Cecil 643
Childers, Alison 694
Childree, Robert 731
Childs, Torrance 132
Childs, Austin 270
Childs, Jeffrey J 805
Chillemi, John 573
Chillo, Laura 828
Chilson, Greg 97
Chilton, Mike 14
Chilton, Jim 123
Chiluisa, Sylvana 610
Chin, Jenny 365
Chin, Francis 509
Chin, Patrick 749
China, John D. 749
Chinea, Manuel 630
Ching, K.C. (Glenn) 164
Ching, Diane 180
Ching, Christina 634
Chini, Mark 750
Chinn, Linda 656
Chintamaneni, Ramakrishna Prasad 193
Chion, Verona 227
Chirachanakul, Prasert 366
Chirico, Emanuel (Manny) 652
Chirillo, Sarah 441
Chirolas, William 519
Chisholm, Jessica 315
Chisholm, Hugh 365
Chisholm, Moody L. 428
Chisholm, Ron 640
Chisholm-krosnicki, Christine 855
Chithambaram, Kalimuthu 493
Chiu, Andrew 655
Chivavibul, Somsak 542
Chivinski, Beth Ann L. 344
Chlebicki, Marilee 339
Cho, Brandie 304
Cho, Alex 401
Cho, Alex 409
Cho, SungHwan 418
Choate, Mike 673
Chodak, Paul 39
Choe, Hyelim 401
Choe, Yong 681
Choeff, Sonya 664
Choi, Sonia 360
Choi, Gina 401
Choi, Carolynn 551
Choi, Caroline 719
Choi, Alison 841
Chojnowski, Tammy 740
Chokron, Jeni 102
Chomienne, Kathleen 350
Chong, Jack 16
Chong, Tze Siong 137
Chong, James 401
Chong, Francis 694
Chopey, Stephen 735
Chopra, Rahul 556

Coward, Robert 879
Cowgill, Dan 304
Cowhig, Michael T. 553
Cowie, Frederick 355
Cowing, Chris 664
Cowles, James C. 181
Cowman, Craig 152
Cox, Frank 52
Cox, Daniel 103
Cox, Ed 150
Cox, Kevin 154
Cox, Rob 162
Cox, Donna 177
Cox, Michael 198
Cox, Shirley 223
Cox, Brian 249
Cox, Shawn 260
Cox, Mark K. 263
Cox, Christopher K. (Chris) 290
Cox, Mark 302
Cox, B. Guille 320
Cox, James W. 330
Cox, Laura J 332
Cox, Rhydian H. 410
Cox, Clay 413
Cox, David 522
Cox, Jacqueline 550
Cox, John 568
Cox, Yolanda 643
Cox, Ryan 685
Cox, John 698
Cox, David 734
Cox, Spencer J 737
Cox, Dan 737
Cox, Philip C. 749
Cox, Keith 752
Cox, Jeff 754
Cox, Carrie 770
Cox, John 784
Cox, R Mark 846
Cox, Wayne 851
Cox, Nicole 873
Coy, Kim 22
Coyle, John 32
Coyle, Kevin 378
Coyle, Michael J. 384
Coyle, Lori 703
Coyle-ikemoto, Gayle 823
Coyne, Patrick 299
Coyne, Brian 495
Coyne, John 792
Coyner, Sheri 59
Cozza, Keith 418
Cozzone, Robert D. 421
Crabb, Joel 760
Crabb, Michael H 785
Crabbe, Amy 326
Crabtree, Thomas 130
Crabtree, Jennifer 223
Crabtree, Danny 676
Cracchiolo, James M. (Jim) 50
Crace, David 839
Crady, Marc 307
Craft, Deborah 43
Craft, Frank 640
Crafter, Lochiel 739
Cragg, Christopher 278
Cragg, John 608
Crahan, Peter 15
Craig, Sean 222
Craig, Pommels 234
Craig, Hamish 305

Craig, Kim 372
Craig, Marian 489
Craig, Jonathan M. 700
Craig, Brett 760
Craig, Gloria 800
Crain, Robert B. 17
Crain, Becky 671
Craine, Barry 50
Craine, Randy 140
Cralle, Chris 182
Crame, Glenn 602
Cramer, Denise 493
Crandall, Brett 121
Crandall, Taylor 391
Crandall, Douglas 685
Crandall, Janice 837
Crandell, Sarah 65
Crane, David L. 11
Crane, Christopher M. (Chris) 284
Crane, Christopher M 285
Crane, Jill 670
Crane, Eric 807
Crane, Timothy S. (Tim) 872
Cranmer, Mark 223
Cranner, Chris 841
Crary, Chris 315
Crater, Ann 179
Cravens, Jerry 729
Craver, Theodore 258
Crawford, Frederick J. (Fred) 15
Crawford, Gordon 36
Crawford, Victor L. 64
Crawford, Matthew 103
Crawford, Tim 144
Crawford, Stephen S. (Steve) 148
Crawford, Gary 196
Crawford, Caroline 222
Crawford, Rhonda 242
Crawford, Carolyn 249
Crawford, Stephen G. (Steve) 263
Crawford, Colleen 266
Crawford, Cree 290
Crawford, Anne 293
Crawford, James C. 311
Crawford, Earl 328
Crawford, Noelle 380
Crawford, Bruce 588
Crawford, Andrew 670
Crawford, Kermit R. 681
Crawford, Charles 698
Crawford, Peter 700
Crawford, David 739
Crawford, Joe 741
Crawford, Stan 798
Crawford-Rosso, Sophie 126
Crcm, Jean Prazecky 317
Creach, Andrea 736
Creamer, Michele 515
Creamer, Aimee 797
Creamons, Joe 325
Creatura, Nick 187
Crecca, Michelle 856
Credle, Eric P. 311
Creech, Matt 481
Creed, Cindy 267
Creed, Greg 869
Creedon, Michael 9
Creely, Mark 649
Creery, Thomas G. 395
Creery, Tom 395
Cregg, Daniel J. (Dan) 649
Creighton, Cheryl 851

Cremin, Mary C 45
Crenshaw, William E. (Ed) 650
Creque, Jeanette 180
Crespo, Frank J. 157
Creviston, Sarah 107
Crew, Matt 93
Crew, Debra A 441
Crew, Debra 533
Crew, Debra 553
Crews, Terrell 66
Crews, Terrell 404
Crews, Kirk 557
Cribb, Gary 687
Cribbs, Kyle 55
Cribbs, Kevin 316
Cribbs, Steven 788
Crichton, Brook 593
Crigler, Forest 344
Crim, Dave 1
Crimmins, John 142
Crimmins, Timothy P. 609
Crines, James T 883
Crisanti, Tom 453
Criscione, David 34
Crisman, Michael 591
Crisp, Stanley 299
Criss, Mike 334
Cristal, Michael 463
Cristancho, Jose 580
Cristoforo, Albert J. (Jerry) 739
Crnkovich, Sean 502
Crocco, M. Scott 20
Croce, Dan 23
Croce, Michael J. 744
Crocker, Janet 417
Crocker, Mary 837
Crockett, Joan 27
Crockett, Kyle 154
Croft, Thomas 365
Crofts, Sharon M. 97
Crone, Michael 434
Cronen, Paul 835
Croney, Steven 198
Cronin, John 50
Cronin, Douglas 134
Cronin, Thomas 507
Cronk, Trent 93
Crook, Joann 503
Crook, Debbie 705
Crooke, Robert B. 425
Crooks, Pam 201
Crookshanks, Denise 640
Crookston, Jesse 79
Croom, Marshall A. 489
Cropper, Bill 681
Crosby, Sarah 72
Crosby, William 434
Crosby, Matthew 665
Crosby, Heidi 794
Crosby, Michael J. 875
Croslen, Rodney 13
Cross, Jeffrey 40
Cross, Karen 52
Cross, Don 72
Cross, Nicholas 103
Cross, Charles K. 701
Cross, Steve 737
Crossen, Laura 111
Crossling, Steven 751
Crossman, Stephen 391
Crosthwaite, Kevin 33
Crotteau, Patrick 134

Crotty, Marty 14
Crotty, Theresa 504
Crouch, M. Andrew (Drew) 91
Crouch, Tami 313
Crouch, Colleen 670
Crouch, Suzanne 733
Crouch, Genie 851
Crouch, Kaye 871
Crouse, Michael 461
Crout, Steve 656
Crow, M. Chad 140
Crow, John 174
Crow, Timothy M. (Tim) 397
Crow, Stan 568
Crowe, Terence 80
Crowe, Richard 130
Crowe, Mike 194
Crowe, Maria 479
Crowell, Wyatt E 410
Crowley, Jennifer 80
Crowley, Larry 103
Crowley, Dennis 107
Crowley, John 198
Crowley, F. Michael 498
Crowley, John 507
Crowley, Margaret 521
Crowley, JD 841
Crown, Timothy A. (Tim) 423
Crowther, David 86
Croxall, Clifford 299
Croxton, Kristen 149
Cruce, Andrea 162
Cruikshank, J. David 100
Cruise, Karen 797
Crum, Bill 415
Crump, Darin 202
Crump, Julie 422
Crump, Scott 703
Cruse, Penny 685
Crutcher, Brian T. 770
Crutchfield, Lisa 344
Crutchfield, Steven 486
Cruz, Edia 181
Cruz, Julie 219
Cruz, Sergio 457
Cruz, Marjorie De La 613
Cruz, Jesus 664
Cruz, Cassandra 751
Cruz, Ray 819
Csonger, Rob 576
Ctfa, Veronica 610
Cubbage, Gary C. 129
Cubias, Carlos 818
Cuccias, Brian 416
Cucco, Wayne 47
Cudd, Steven 828
Cuddihy, Robert 55
Cuddy, Christopher M. (Chris) 66
Cue, Eduardo H. (Eddy) 62
Cuellar, William 429
Cuervo, Larry 376
Cuervo, Carlos 875
Cuevas, Jason 358
Cuevas, Kerwin 734
Cuff, Rich 502
Cuffe, Michael S. 382
Cugini, Dominic 455
Cui, Ted 62
Culak, Bob 755
Culang, Howard 662
Culbertson, Leslie S. 425
Culbreth, John 251

Dastugue, Michael P. 850
Datar, Srikant 747
Datar, Srikant 757
Datoo, Zafer 80
Dattilo, Thomas 466
Daubert, Jon K 224
Daughenbaugh, Heather 761
Daugherty, Wayne 391
Daugherty, Doug 471
Daugherty, Christine 613
Daugherty, Doug 624
Daugherty, Lucy 624
Daughetee, Jessica 88
Daulton, Howard 283
Daunis, Stephen 505
Davenport, Nancy 519
Davenport, James 610
Davenport, Leslie 653
Davenport, Bobby 798
Davey, Deirdre 50
Davey, James E. (Jim) 380
Davi, Susanna 647
David, Doerr 107
David, Rose Marie 399
David, Harmon 466
David, Svitek 531
Davidoni, Giorgio 479
Davids, Jody R. 612
Davidson, Deanna 302
Davidson, Cindy 337
Davidson, Jay 413
Davidson, Wendy 451
Davidson, Linda 653
Davidson, Angela 832
Davies, Erik Null 21
Davies, Jeremy 519
Davies, Richard 553
Davis, Kevin M 7
Davis, Julia K. 15
Davis, James C. (Jim) 26
Davis, Robert 61
Davis, Robert 63
Davis, Ed 80
Davis, Susan 96
Davis, Helene B 98
Davis, Cindy 111
Davis, Joe 120
Davis, Darryl W. 123
Davis, Tim 126
Davis, J. Kimbrough (Kim) 147
Davis, Shelby 149
Davis, Angela 152
Davis, John 174
Davis, Patrick 182
Davis, Patricia 185
Davis, Pat 185
Davis, Laronda 204
Davis, Will 208
Davis, Shantel 222
Davis, Betty 223
Davis, Mike 223
Davis, Amy 225
Davis, Joni 258
Davis, Bob 258
Davis, Robert 258
Davis, Heath 292
Davis, Debby 302
Davis, Chad 305
Davis, Kathie 308
Davis, Lou J. 315
Davis, Bonita 315
Davis, C William 317

Davis, Claude E. 318
Davis, Darlisa E 323
Davis, Michael 352
Davis, Alicia Boler 353
Davis, Kirby 357
Davis, Jana J. 382
Davis, Joe 385
Davis, Douglas L. (Doug) 425
Davis, Doug 426
Davis, Lisa 443
Davis, Alan 444
Davis, Reginald 460
Davis, Martina Del Raso 462
Davis, Ryan 465
Davis, Jeff 481
Davis, Patrick 496
Davis, Audrey 497
Davis, Jeff 504
Davis, Robert M. 514
Davis, Jeff 530
Davis, Doug 530
Davis, James 535
Davis, Nichola 548
Davis, Latia 552
Davis, Ian 580
Davis, Jack 593
Davis, Erika T. 596
Davis, Timothy Paul 605
Davis, Alisa 608
Davis, Keith B 624
Davis, Larry 624
Davis, Sharon L. 635
Davis, George S. 655
Davis, James E. 659
Davis, Glenn 662
Davis, Pam 672
Davis, Kathy 676
Davis, Scott 677
Davis, Bart 682
Davis, Cory 684
Davis, Dan 694
Davis, Steven D. 704
Davis, Reid 718
Davis, Cindy 722
Davis, Bill 735
Davis, Nancy B. 744
Davis, Ricky 751
Davis, Frank 751
Davis, Chris 756
Davis, Terrell 785
Davis, Robert D. (Bob) 788
Davis, Mark 793
Davis, John 798
Davis, Robert 798
Davis, Raymond P. (Ray) 808
Davis, Kern 815
Davis, Raymond 825
Davis, Leslie C. 829
Davis, Stephanie A 834
Davis, Gigi 841
Davis, Kurt 841
Davis, Cindy 850
Davis, Jeff 859
Davis, Seth 863
Davis, Jennifer 876
Davis, Derek 883
Davis-Smith, Amy 755
Davison, Brian 211
Davison, Paul J 649
Davison, Corey 762
Davisson, Robert J. 707
Davoren, Peter J 779

Davoren, Peter J. 801
Dawes, Leah 285
Dawes, Christopher 474
Dawkins, Linda 260
Dawson, Robert 100
Dawson, Mike 341
Dawson, Bruce 571
Dawson, Laurel 736
Dawson, Lena 873
Day, Jason K 154
Day, Mike 190
Day, Kevin 337
Day, Ray 339
Day, Thomas R. 404
Day, Zane 463
Day, J. Randal 715
Day, J Randal 715
Day, Frederick 751
Day, William B. (Bill) 755
Day, Dennis 773
Dayon, Alexandre (Alex) 693
Dayton, Samantha 312
Dayton, Stefani 422
DC, Sister Bernice Coreil 70
DC, Sister Maureen McGuire 71
De, Rossi Gabriel 531
Deacon, Mary Ann 469
Deacon, Eric 827
Deakin, Neil 664
Deal, Stanley A. (Stan) 123
Dealy, Richard P. (Rich) 625
Dean, Aaron 87
Dean, Kim 148
Dean, Robert 160
Dean, John C. 164
Dean, Lloyd H. 245
Dean, Roger 252
Dean, Clay 324
Dean, Andrea 682
Dean, Eric 734
Deane, Stephen 380
Deangelis, Yamynn 227
Deangelo, Lucia 226
Deanhardt, Jill 798
Dearborn, Judith 754
Deardorff, Kevin L. 469
Dearduff, Robert 332
Dearman, Paul 120
Deason, Richard 473
Deaton, Craig 879
Deaver, W. Scott 86
Deaver, Scott 86
Debel, Marlene 519
Debertin, Jay D. 172
Debiase, Dean 610
Deblock, Andrew 413
Debnam, Henry 466
Debo, Michael 761
DeBoer, Bryan B. 482
DeBoer, Sidney B. (Sid) 482
Debrier, Jurgen 698
Decaria, Amanda 139
Dechant, Suzanne 728
Decher, Peter 810
Dechiara, Michael 75
Deck, Richard 653
Decker, Rhonda 28
Decker, Molly 152
Decker, Susan 219
Decker, Sue 219
Decker, Casey 295
Decker, T Blair 348

Decker, Edward P. (Ted) 397
Decker, Julie 673
DeClaris, Wade N. 875
Declas, Jean-Luc 881
DeClercq, Catherine 794
Decolli, Chris 3
Decosta, Lori 283
Decraene, Dave 323
Dedicoat, Chris 177
Dedinsky, John G. 602
Dedolce, Trish 647
Dedovesh, Joseph 305
Dees, Jason 531
Dees, Chuck 855
Deese, Willie 649
Deese, Brian 735
Deevy, Will 749
Defauw, Nicolas 640
Defazio, Gary M 109
Defeciani, Patrick 182
Defeis, Nicholas 647
Defilippis, Victor 597
Definis, Karen 535
Defoggia, James 629
Defontnouvelle, Patrick 300
DeFranco, James (Jim) 249
Defranco, Jim 249
DeFreitas, Shannie 103
Degeorges, Vincent 841
DeGiorgio, Kenneth D. 310
Deglopper, Julie 493
Degraff, Cheryl 200
DeGregorio, Ronald J. (Ron) 284
Degroot, Scott 457
Degroot, Benjamin 628
Deguia, Edgar 238
DeGuise, Sheila 852
Dehaven, Judy 841
Dehner, Craig 120
Dehnhardt, Robert 735
Deigl, Jeffrey 27
Dein, Brian 681
Deisinger, Jennifer 96
Deitch, Sally 762
Deitz, Robert 65
DeJong, Nick 60
Dekay, Sam 100
DeKenipp, Patrick 742
Dekker, Karen 50
Dekker, Hans 334
Dekker, Jonathan 684
Delacruz, Cedric 380
Delafuente, Laura 446
Delafuente, Phillip 586
Delagi, R. Gregory (Greg) 770
Delagi, Greg 770
Delahunt, Susan 165
Delahunt, Peter 664
Delaney, Michael 124
Delaney, John 132
Delaney, Steve 160
Delaney, BradleyBrad 174
Delaney, Brad 174
Delaney, Bradley 174
Delaney, Chris 367
Delaney, Thomas A. (Tom) 551
Delaney, Peter H 664
DeLaney, William J. (Bill) 755
Delaney, Elizabeth 835
DeLaTorre, Katy 759
DeLawder, C. Daniel (Dan) 601
Delbene, Rob 431

Dungan, Jayme 695
Dunigan-wernke, Jennifer 307
Dunk, Paul 700
Dunlap, Kevin 15
Dunlap, James E. (Jim) 414
Dunlap, Shep 533
Dunlap, Michael S. (Mike) 546
Dunlap, Stan 694
Dunleavy, Michael 731
Dunn, Ann 51
Dunn, Rory 72
Dunn, Gary S. 92
Dunn, Colleen 116
Dunn, Tony 174
Dunn, Dan 200
Dunn, Joe 225
Dunn, Ryan 276
Dunn, Kenneth E. 279
Dunn, Marc 346
Dunn, Cind M 411
Dunn, Cind 411
Dunn, Kenneth 491
Dunn, Edward 666
Dunn, Cheryl 705
Dunn, James 712
Dunn, Bradford 784
Dunn, Sheila 818
Dunn, Sam 851
Dunn, Sean 873
Dunne, Melanie 502
Dunne, Maureen 629
Dunne, Ronan 837
Dunnigan, Brendan 794
Dunphy, Paula 183
Dunphy, Keven 270
Dunson, Tom 323
Dunson, Susan 774
Dunster, William 631
Dunton, James K 46
Dunworth, James 617
Duong, Julie 92
Duperow, Megan 564
Duperron, Christian 613
Dupler, Scott 415
Duprat, Pierre-Christophe 66
duPreez, Jan 523
Duprey, Lauren 118
Duprez, Debra 784
Dupuis, Marie Claire 355
Dupuis, Mike 653
Dupuy, Carolyn 302
Duran, Joe 471
Duran, George 484
Durand, Bob 73
Durand, Michael 819
Durant, Luke 576
Durbin, Bill 461
Durbin, Laura 671
Durbin, Patrick M. 781
Durburg, Jack 159
Durden, Linda 814
Durek, Sandy 872
Durfee, Thomas 202
Durfey, Jim 38
Durham, Freeman 44
Durham, Bill 762
Durham, Ronald 881
Durkee, Matthew K. 544
Durkin, Brian 6
Durkin, James W. (Jim) 346
Durkin, Sam 446
Durland, David 676

Durn, Daniel (Dan) 63
Durocher, Philip 194
Durrans, Jan 89
Durre, Edmond 375
Dussert, Bertrand 881
Dustzadeh, Justin 844
Dutchyshyn, Tom 801
Dutertre, Jey 488
Dutt, Shilpa 298
Duval, Scott 694
Duvvur, Amarendra 6
Duvvuru, Niranjan 201
Dvorchak, Steve 582
Dwarka, Swaran 245
Dwight, Craig M. 403
Dworkin, James 403
Dworkin, Aaron 670
Dwyer, Anita 325
Dwyer, Jack 657
Dwyer, Maria F. 739
Dyar, Patricia 240
Dycus, Chris 162
Dye, Justin 23
Dye, Mark 530
Dyer, Jay 152
Dyer, Gary 456
Dyer, Tracy L 481
Dyer, Barry 593
Dyhrberg, Stephanie 828
Dyke, Concetta Van 111
Dyke, Frank J. (Jeff) 717
Dyke, Colin 727
Dykstra, Scott 283
Dykstra, Karen 846
Dykstra, David A. 872
Dymally, Alice 182
Dymtrow, Brice 187
Dyslin, Bradley E. 15
Dyson, Sam 181
Dziadzio, Richard S. 74
Dzialo, Joseph 839
Dziegielewski, Greg 131
Dzielak, Robert 286
Dziuba, Michael 662
Dziuk, David A 383
D'Agostino, John 664
D'aiutolo, Michael 77
D'Alessandro, Carl 466
D'Amelio, Frank A. 616
D'Amore, Robert R. (Bob) 609
D'Amore, Diana 647
D'andrea, Elena 507
D'angelico, Leslie 69
D'angelo, David 691
d'Archirafi, Francesco Vanni 181
D'Arezzo, Gloria 879
D'Arrigo, Daniel J. 522
D'auria, Jay 179
D'avila, Daniel 745
D'Cruz, Candice 500
D'egidio, Robb 198
D'Lugos, Steve 75
D'ornellas, Inigo 221
D'Ouville, Paul 565
D'Souza, Francisco 193

E

Eades, Darren 446
Eagles, Michael 198
Eakins, Cathy 610

Ealet, Isabelle 365
Ealy, Carleton 433
Eames, Tyler 610
Eames, Tristyn 700
Earhart, Cynthia C. (Cindy) 564
Earl, David 530
Earley, Jim 13
Earley, Steve 884
Earnest, Josh 812
Earnshaw, Bill 656
Easley, Matthew 76
Easley, Ed 476
Easley, Matthew 673
Eason, J. Cliff 673
East, Jeff 624
Easterbrook, Stephen J. (Steve) 510
Easterling, Susan 825
Eastham, Mark 511
Eastin, David 558
Easton, Diane 206
Easton, Mark 431
Eaton, Belinda 96
Eaton, Mary Jo 159
Eaton, David 307
Eaton, Bob 339
Eaton, Danny 484
Eaton, Terry 860
Eatroff, Bob 198
Eatroff, Robert 198
Eazor, Joseph 247
Ebbs, Brian 576
Ebenhoeh, Allisssa 670
Eber, Bob 806
Eber, Richard 873
Eberhard, Michael C 80
Eberhardt, Jack 558
Ebermann, Wolfgang 423
Ebers, Kevin H 112
Ebert, Todd 662
Ebert, Kevin 871
Eberts, F. Samuel 467
Eberwein, Elise R. 37
Ebner, R. M. 289
Eby, Edith 616
Eccard, Bryan 465
Eccell, Julius 223
Eccher, James L. 586
Eccles, Daniel 712
Eccles, Colin D. 856
Eccleston, Amber 81
Echevarria, Joe 880
Echols, Matthew T 192
Echols, Amani 670
Eck, Robert 689
Eck, Joshua 736
Eckel, Ryan 243
Eckel, Elizabeth B 853
Ecker, Dana 700
Eckerle, Wayne 225
Eckert, Joseph R 28
Eckert, Steve 426
Eddens, Peggy H. 876
Eddington, Mike 584
Eddington, Desiree 584
Eddins, Brad 769
Eddy, Janet 126
Eddy, Jodi 134
Eddy, Ashley 522
Eddy, Bruce 880
Edeker, Randy 417
Edel, John 179

Edelman, Deane 130
Edelson, David B. 487
Edens, Wesley R. (Wes) 589
Eder, Ellen 593
Eder, George 617
Edfors, Patricia 712
Edgar, Robert V 550
Edge, Judy 302
Edgehill, Beverly 784
Edgell, Eleonore 670
Edgerton, Kevin 11
Edgett, Paul W. 204
Edgmond, Wanda 202
Edicola, Mike 107
Edison, Darrick 80
Edison, Jeffrey S 622
Edison, So 719
Edita, Ramic 284
Edler, Chris 582
Edmonds, Ron 259
Edmondson, Valarie 251
Edmondson, Rhonda 302
Edmoundson, Greg 657
Edmunds, Coleman 82
Edney, Jerry 73
Edris, Warren 456
Edson, David 120
Edson, Kent 229
Edson, David 535
Edwards, Jon S. 51
Edwards, Nate 76
Edwards, Bill 83
Edwards, Rob 96
Edwards, Lisa M 195
Edwards, Angela 226
Edwards, Jon 250
Edwards, Patricia L. 279
Edwards, Jennifer 303
Edwards, Wade 308
Edwards, Murray 318
Edwards, Thomas H. 403
Edwards, Ben 431
Edwards, Tom 431
Edwards, Nick 456
Edwards, William 489
Edwards, Zalise 511
Edwards, Mark 511
Edwards, Lori 530
Edwards, Kurt 545
Edwards, Trevor A. 560
Edwards, Darren 608
Edwards, Donna 624
Edwards, Chris 651
Edwards, Lisa Null 694
Edwards, Robert 760
Edwards, Bonnie 798
Edwards, Ben 800
Edwards, Robert A. (Rob) 813
Effenheim, John 807
Effinger, Phil 584
Eftink, Mike 640
Egan, Anne 535
Egan, Kevin 751
Egan, Tom 868
Egbert, Charles 801
Egbujor, Michael 385
Egeland, Juli 417
Eggemeier, Tom 352
Eggemeyer, John M. 600
Eggers, Daniel 284
Eggers, Drew 570
Eggert, Mark 162

Erickson, Beverly 794
Ericson, Brady D. 131
Ericson, Brent 374
Erika, Hofmann 504
Eriksen, Jim 493
Erikson, Lynn 645
Eriksson, Al 476
Erkan, Hafize Gaye (Gaye) 328
Erlandson, Daniel 415
Erlick, Tony 839
Erlinger, James H. (Jim) 438
Erlinger, Joe 510
Erman, Tim 270
Ermatinger, William R. (Bill) 416
Ermine-Baer, Kristin 830
ERMOLD, SHAWNA 819
Ernest, Scott A. 771
Ernest, Scott 813
Ernst, Mark A. 330
Ernst, Steven 535
Ernst, David 787
Ernst, Barrie W. 814
Ernsteen, Scott 873
Erny, Michelle 448
Errico, Mike 179
Ertel, Elizabeth 174
Ervin, Chuck 375
Erwin, Tami 837
Erzen, Rob 346
Esamann, Douglas F. (Doug) 258
Esarte, Marty 851
Escalera, Elizabeth 33
Escatel, Martin 755
Escobar, Amanda 337
Escossi, Julio 17
Esfarjani, Keyvan 425
Esham, David 535
Eskow, Alan D. 835
Eskue, Kyle 467
Eslick, Rob 417
Espeland, Curtis E. (Curt) 262
Esper, Eric 388
Esper, Richard E 776
Espinal, Ana 610
Espinal, Eric 728
Espindola, Bill 283
Espinosa, Wanda 150
Espinoza, Silvia 634
Esposito, Maria 183
Esposito, Joe 242
Esposito, Chris 325
Esposito, Mike 365
Esposito, Orlando C. 628
Essawi, Tarik 149
Esselman, Tom 50
Essert, Henry 519
Essex, Susan 224
Essig, Marshall 190
Estabrook, David 328
Estabrook, James B. 376
Esteban, Carmen 399
Estep, Julie 318
Estepe, Pablo 103
Estes, Matthew 120
Estes, William 298
Estes, David 610
Estes, Scott 677
Estes, Darcey 757
Esteves, Robert 553
Estevez, Carlos 617
Esther, Chet 374
Estok, Natty 519

Estrada, Ricardo 28
Estrada, Cindy 805
Estrella, Kristen 310
Estridge, Sherry 843
Etchemendy, John W. 474
Ethridge, Mary 671
Etshied, Melissa 648
Etter, Jason 584
Etzel, Tom 884
Eubanks, Russell 298
Eubanks, Brent 484
Eubanks, Richard M 595
Eubanks, Tyson 685
Eugley, Alan 331
Eulacio, Ramon 14
Euler, Jeff 302
Eulich, John S. 277
Eureste, Ralph 28
Eusden, Alan 218
Eusterbrock, Matt 277
Evan, Griffith 284
Evangel, Lori M. 356
Evangelista, Guy 125
Evangelista, Paul A. 165
Evangelista, W. Scott 438
Evans, Michael 1
Evans, David W. 11
Evans, Joseph W 143
Evans, Steve 168
Evans, Mike 173
Evans, Laurence 182
Evans, Michael 196
Evans, Dan 200
Evans, Janice 208
Evans, Mark 211
Evans, Charles L. (Charlie) 300
Evans, Morris 304
Evans, Jill 304
Evans, Mark 317
Evans, Jay 319
Evans, Charles 337
Evans, Janel 376
Evans, Godfrey B. 399
Evans, Aicha S. 425
Evans, Dorothy 428
Evans, Katrina M. (Trina) 455
Evans, Carnot 500
Evans, Ed 519
Evans, John 527
Evans, Robert 562
Evans, Terry 564
Evans, Jason 586
Evans, Richard D. 612
Evans, Beckey 627
Evans, John 651
Evans, Philip L 664
Evans, Jeff 670
Evans, Marlin 672
Evans, Deanna 698
Evans, Stuart 700
Evans, Russ 716
Evans, Mary Alice 732
Evans, Maura 740
Evans, J. Eric 762
Evans, V. Lynn 766
Evans, Thomas 788
Evans, Darrell 792
Evans, Jack B. 815
Evanson, Jeff 767
Evanson, Jeff K 767
Eveland, Scott 735
Evelhoch, Jeffrey 515

Evelyn, Glen H 346
Evenzwig, Michael 519
Everett, Nora M. 637
Everett, Bryan 681
Everling, Jeffrey 463
Evernham, Scott J. 583
Evers, Tony 738
Eversman, Paul 71
Everson, Carolyn 290
Eves, David L. 878
Evett, Todd 92
Evette, Pamela S 737
Evitts, Aaron 171
Ewald, Linda 53
Ewald, Andrew 160
Ewald, Thad 225
Ewald, Thaddeaus 225
Ewens, Peter A. 757
Ewert, Beth 807
Ewig, Randall G. 377
Ewing, Justin 23
Ewing, William 100
Ewing, Gregory 152
Ewing, Clay W. 359
Ewing, Sue 849
Ewing, Jane 851
Exnicios, Joseph S. 376
Exton, Martha 162
Ey, Nick 336
Eyre, Brik V. 107
ez, 870

F

Fabara, Paul D. 42
Faber, Timothy 465
Faber, Heather 564
Fabian, Bruce 179
Fabrini, Alessandro 465
Fabyonic, Jon 337
Facktor, Debra D 91
Factora, Faith 774
Fad, Thomas 198
Fadahunsi, Ajibola 493
Fadden, Thomas Mc 465
Fadool, Joseph F. 131
Fafoglia, Nick 202
Fagan, Stephen 120
Fagan, Elizabeth 849
Fagerstrom, Brad 823
Faggard, Steve 170
Faggard, Steve 170
Fagundes, Henrique 289
Faherty, Sean 380
Fahey, Mike 160
Fahey, Mark 751
Fahey, Joe 871
Fahrig, Siegmund 502
Fain, Eric S. 4
Fain, Daniel 264
Fain, William 747
Faintuch, Amir 425
Fairbairn, Robert W. (Rob) 120
Fairbank, Richard D. (Rich) 148
Fairbrother, Priscilla 828
Fairchild, Mark 308
Faircloth, David 431
Fairey, Chris 689
Fairfax, Justin E 205
Fairhurst, David 510
Fairweather, George R. 848

Faison, Warachal 616
Faisst, Georg 653
Faith, John 77
Fajardo, Jose 305
Fakult, James V. 329
Falb, Mark C. 385
Falco, John 645
Faliszek, David 304
Falk, Thomas J. (Tom) 457
Falk, Christian 476
Falk, Chip 797
Falkenstein, Elry 823
Falkin, Bruce 100
Falkowitz, Mary 778
Falkowski, David 229
Fallan, James 591
Fallen, Kelly 798
Fallon, Katie 392
Fallon, William C. (Bill) 509
Fallon, Bob 647
Falotico, Joy 339
Falzon, Robert M. 647
Falzon, Michael 647
Famiglietti, Michael 608
Famiglietti, Robin 713
Fancher, Geoff 177
Fanelli, Arcangelo 177
Fanelli, John 576
Faneuil, Jesse 112
Faneuil, Edward J. 362
Fang, Zheng 732
Fang, AJ 749
Fanning, Thomas A. (Tom) 298
Fanning, Chris 347
Fanning, Brock 786
Fant, Christopher 307
Fantom, Stacey 624
Fanucchi, Nancy 139
Faraci, John V 154
Faramawy, Ali 525
Farber, Jeffrey M. (Jeff) 378
Fardella, Amy 784
Fare, Julia 694
Fares, Nancy 656
Faresich, Leo 212
Fargnoli, Rich 481
Fargo, Thomas B. 416
Farha, Nikhat 751
Farhat, Jerry 13
Farhi, David 80
Farias, Gil 97
Fariello, Teri 811
Fariello, Terri 811
Faries, Stan 586
Farineau, Don 291
Farland, Jay 226
Farley, Shannon 121
Farley, Ryan 134
Farley, Jack 258
Farley, James D. (Jim) 339
Farley, Thomas W. (Tom) 427
Farley, Dan 739
Farmer, Scott 115
Farmer, Scott D. 176
Farmer, Curtis C. 200
Farmer, Marc 200
Farnan, Patrick 307
Farner, Kim 823
Farner, David M. 829
Farney, Tim 231
Farnin, Paul 152
Farnstrom, Amy 328

Frent, Marty 142
Frenzel, Robert C. (Bob) 878
Frere, Edward 831
Frerichs, Michael 733
Frese, Calvin W. (Cal) 159
Frese, Brian 814
Freudenberg, Kurt 86
Freudmann, Axel 792
Frey, Charles 273
Frey, Chuck 273
Frey, James 788
Freyling, Sylvia 303
Freyou, Jason P 395
Freytas, Denise 101
Frias, Cristina 103
Frias, James D. (Jim) 574
Frias, Yanela C 645
Fricke, Kathleen 591
Fricke, David 768
Fricke, Lisa 871
Frickle, T 361
Frickle, T J 361
Fried, David 470
Friedlander, Steven 841
Friedlein, Christine 506
Friedman, Richard A. 365
Friedman, Farley 366
Friedman, Mark 425
Friedman, Dan 431
Friedman, Leonard 448
Friedman, Howard 461
Friedman, Nancy 617
Friedman, Howard H. 638
Friedman, Diana 698
Friedman, Michael 735
Friedman, Mark 823
Friedman, Paul 841
Friedman, Seth 844
Friedrich, Amy C. 637
Friedrichs, Natasha 507
Friel, Emily 488
Friend, Keith 107
Friend, Carol 196
Friend, Mark 341
Friend, Grant 415
Friend, Michelle 415
Friend, Zoe 547
Friend, Bob 858
Frierson, Suzanne 718
Friesen, Debbie 862
Frieson, Don 851
Friess, Robert 63
Frigeria, Vincent 649
Frimpong, Stephen 457
Frisch, Ann 548
Friske, Rena 149
Fritts, William 189
Fritz, Jake 270
Fritz, Timothy 404
Fritz, Kelly 427
Fritz, Annasuela 776
Fritz, Lance M. 810
Froehlich, Ephraim 731
Frogameni, James 343
Froggatt, Tom 388
Froimson, Mark I. 794
Fromknecht, Greg 270
Fron, David 671
Fronduti, John 44
Fronheiser, Jason 308
Fronk, Chris 566
Frons, Marc 556

Frontz, Marilyn 6
Frontz, Arlene 606
Fronzaglio, Joseph 395
Frooman, Thomas E. 176
Frossmo, Kristin 562
Frost, Christopher 98
Frost, Robert 206
Frost, Patrick B. (Pat) 223
Frost, Marc 566
Frownfelter, Stan 733
Fruehauf, Richard 821
Frulla, Robert 222
Frump, Candace 611
Fry, Earl 164
Fry, John 207
Frye, Andrew 107
Frye, Dawn 305
Frye, Arthur 446
Fryer, Crystal 744
Fryfogle, Jim 627
Frymoyer, Valarry 316
Fu, Frederick 87
Fuchs, Rainer 118
Fuchs, Rob 249
Fuchs, Robert 249
Fuchs, Jim 298
Fuchs, Rick 431
Fuchs, Barbara 647
Fuchs, Michael 782
Fudge, Duncan 535
Fuentes, Antonia 62
Fuentes, Christopher 839
Fuerst, Edward 538
Fugina, Annette 518
Fuguitt, Gayle 352
Fukuto, Hiroaki 523
Fukuzawa, Toshihiko 16
Fulcher, Jeffrey 773
Fulchi, Anthony 103
Fulgham, Tammy 834
Fulghum, Lisa 671
Fulk, Sue 421
Fulk, Gary 589
Fulkerson, Sonny 431
Fulkerson, Mike 500
Fulkerson, Debra 583
Fuller, Charlotte 42
Fuller, Jeff 223
Fuller, Scott 245
Fuller, Gregory 298
Fuller, David 308
Fuller, Lynn B. 384
Fuller, Gary 395
Fuller, Melissa 467
Fuller, Wilford H. (Will) 481
Fuller, Amy 506
Fuller, Debra 513
Fuller, Julie 560
Fuller, Julie 586
Fuller, Jake 613
Fuller, John 671
Fuller, Gail 798
Fullmer, Travis 428
Fulmer, Vicki 116
Fulmer, James W. (Jim) 788
Fulton, Howard 42
Fulton, Marshall 103
Fulton, Cedrick 520
Fund, Steven L. 425
Fung, Linda 647
Funk, Dan 73
Funk, Charles N. 527

Fuoss, Salena 326
Fuqua, Barbara 448
Furey, Shawn 162
Furey, Michael 566
Furey, Adrian 883
Furlong, Mark 132
Furlong, Fred 299
Furlong, Frederick T 299
Furlong, Bryan 671
Furman, David 481
Furner, John 851
Furr, William B. 391
Furtek, Kathryn 566
Fusco, Frank 80
Fusco, Jeff 103
Fusco, Jack A. 167
Fusco, Gary 492
Fusco, Joseph 502
Fusillo, Robert 851
Fussell, Stephen R. (Steve) 4
Fussell, Tara 10
Fusz, Philip 28
Futch, Brenton 179
Fynan, Tamara J. 715

G

Gaal, Sheri 785
Gabbard, Brian 65
Gabbard, Brian 91
Gabel, Garrett 85
Gabel, Barry 484
Gabel, Karen 707
Gable, Deborah 50
Gable, Steve 343
Gabriel, Jamie 276
Gabriel, Gerry 289
Gabriel, Christina 849
Gabriele, Jim 443
Gabrielle, With 564
Gabrielson, Rick 489
Gack, Bruce 463
Gadaleta, Anthony 792
Gadd, Philip 137
Gaddes, Kathy H. 53
Gaddis, Byron J. 634
Gadgil, Beena 112
Gaer, Steven 861
Gaffin, Shawn 315
Gaffney, Dan 100
Gaffney, Paul J. 243
Gaffney, Michael 355
Gaffney, Kathy 787
Gafner, Ivy 493
Gagala, Ryan 566
Gage, Michelle 48
Gage, Douglas 240
Gage, Marlyss J. 792
Gagel, Brian 676
Gagliano, Joe 42
Gagliano, Mario 617
Gagliardi, Frank 168
Gagliardotto, David 535
GAGNON, BRENDA 174
Gagnon, Mary Jo 504
Gagnon, Carl 828
Gahagan, Cole 484
Gaherty, John B. 219
Gahr, Brian 869
Gaiennie, Liz 275
Gainer, Glen 738

Gaines, Floyd 273
Gaines, Bennett L. 329
Gainor, Sue 124
Gaither, Kevin 717
Gaiti, Anthony 160
Gajaria, Rajan 259
Galainena, M David 776
Galanti, Richard A. 219
Galarza, Charles 684
Galarza, Michelle 814
Galati, Victor 610
Galbraith, Marc 733
Gale, Janelle 290
Gale, Samuel 352
Gale, Fournier J. (Boots) 671
Galega, Wakuna 474
Gales, Amy H. 190
Galhotra, A. Kumar 339
Galin, Tomi 207
Galindo, Thomas 599
Galindo, Thomas 599
Galindo, Esther 868
Galindo, Esther Berrozpe 868
Galit, Scott 517
Galiuk, Andrey 255
Gallagher, Patricia 100
Gallagher, John 109
Gallagher, Patrick 160
Gallagher, Kathryn 183
Gallagher, Jerry 269
Gallagher, Kevin 304
Gallagher, J. Patrick (Pat) 346
Gallagher, Thomas J. (Tom) 346
Gallagher, Sheila 352
Gallagher, Thomas C. (Tom) 355
Gallagher, Michael 511
Gallagher, Angela 550
Gallagher, Angela 610
Gallagher, Marie 613
Gallagher, Linda 806
Gallas, Carla A 521
Gallaway, Mike 451
Gallegos, Heather 656
Gallentine, Bennie 643
Gallett, Scott D. 131
Galley, John 829
Galli, Daniela 498
Galli, Guido 785
Galligan, Matthew E. (Matt) 179
Galligan, Peter 183
Galligan, Brendan 673
Gallimore, Alec D. 670
Gallina, John E. 59
Gallino, Matthew 448
Gallo, Laurene (Laurie) 129
Gallo, Pasquale 183
Gallo, Horst 431
Gallo, Dominick 535
Gallo, Silvina 617
Gallo, A. C. 870
Galloway, Ian 45
Galloway, Shannon 429
Galsnte, Alena 755
Galst, Sandra 75
Galuppi, Barb 346
Galuppo, Gail A. 15
Galusha, Rachel 456
Galvan, David 873
Galvanek, Suzanne 75
Galvez, Jean-Marc 115
Galvin, Dana 226
Galvin, Daniel 647

Gunupure, Suresh 519
Guo, Peng (Patrick) 764
Gupta, Sanjay 27
Gupta, Suren 27
Gupta, Anchal 42
Gupta, Vishad 305
Gupta, Sanjiv 353
Gupta, Rocky 353
Gupta, Rohit 356
Gupta, Rajneesh 435
Gupta, Ayan Das 492
Gupta, Anu 760
Gurgens, Cydney 807
Gurgovits, Stephen J. (Steve) 337
Gurin, Steve 105
Gurinder, Kohli 875
Gurkan, Tarkan 613
Gurke, Scott 873
Gurley, Jan 184
Gurnani, Roger 837
Gurumurthy, Vivek 837
Gurvitz, Howard 27
Guse, Brad 874
Gushie, Steve 9
Guske, Ann 757
Gustafson, Paul 200
Gustafson, Todd 409
Gustafson, Thomas 444
Gustafson, Dan 553
Gustafson, Joel 558
Guthery, Christopher 249
Guthneck, Griffin 446
Guthrie, Jeremy 152
Guthrie, A 388
Guthrie, Steve 413
Guthrie, Scott 525
Gutiahr, Glenn 647
Gutierrez, Harvey 223
Gutierrez, Mauricio 573
Gutierrez, John 700
Gutman, Carrie 584
Gutmann, Kathleen 818
Gutmann, Amy 826
Gutt, Jack 299
Guttery, John 266
Gutting, Gregory J. (Greg) 281
Guttman, Tim G. 53
Guy, Jennifer 162
Guy, Jerry 346
Guyaux, Joseph 132
Guyett, Gregory L. 261
Guyot, Pierre 240
Guyse, Clyde 94
Guziak, James 797
Guzman, Jennifer 584
Guzman, Francisco 686
Guzy, Edward 502
Guzzi, Anthony J. (Tony) 269
Guzzie-peck, Peggy 444
Gwalani, Sanjay 42
Gwebster, Richard 284
Gwin, Andrew 71
Gwin, Marie 112
Gwizdala, Lori A. 761
Gyarmaty, Mike 404
Gysbers, Niki 527

H

Haag, Natalie 150
Haahr, J. Tyler 517

Haaland, Corey L 760
Haan, Taco de 334
Haan, Patti 492
Haas, Tracie 6
Haas, Bernard 240
Haas, Bernhard 240
Haas, Richard 582
Haas, G. Hunter 594
Haase, Joseph 382
Haase, George 647
Haasen, Don 695
Haave, Carol 484
Habak, Charles 130
Habbit, Anthony 858
Haber, Jack 195
Haberfield, Patrick 691
Haberkamp, Dean 307
Haberkorn, David 755
Haberman, Michael 823
Hablitzel, Thomas C. 707
Hachenburg, Douglas 630
Hackenberg, Amy L. 635
Hackenson, Elizabeth 14
Hacker, Mark S. 537
Hacker, Susan 757
Hacker, Howard 762
Hackett, William F. (Bill) 216
Hackett, Jim 339
Hackett, Margaux 498
Hackett, Steven G. (Steve) 634
Hackett, John 707
Hackman, Steve 583
Hackney, William 83
Hackstadt, Kent 743
Hadad, Henry 135
Hadavi, Judith 617
Haddad, Michael 53
Haddad, Gabriel 365
Hadley, Lisa 60
Hadsell, Charlie 269
Haeberle, Carol 647
Haeberlein, Samantha 118
Haefele, Alan 624
Haefner, Larry A. 187
Haelsig, Claus-Peter 334
Haensch, Thomas 91
Haessler, Laura 249
Haeussler, Mark 86
Hafer, Kurt 474
Hafertepen, Eric 456
Haffenreffer, Joan 182
Haffner, Jon E 200
Hafner, Steve 128
Hafner, Jennifer 700
Haft, Ian 36
Haft, Steven 841
Hafter, Jeffrey M. (Jeff) 112
Hagan, Howard 233
Hagan, Michael 397
Hagan, Roland 431
Hagan, Christine 841
Hageboeck, Charles R. (Skip) 185
Hagedorn, C Kristopher 497
Hagedorn, C Kristopher 538
Hagedorn, Marv 732
Hagedorn, Michael D. (Mike) 806
Hagekyriakou, Luke 62
Hagel, Shawn R. 634
Hagelin, Carl 100
Hagemann, Robert 689
Hagen, Jonathan Hirt 281
Hagen, Thomas B. 281

Hagen, Terence D. 441
Hagen, Mary 516
Hagen, Thomas B 606
Hager, Kevin 834
Hagerty, James 853
Haggerty, Kathleen 42
Haggerty, Patrick 749
Haggy, Bret 415
Hagler, Mendel 548
Haglund, Matt 50
Hagner, Nancy 871
Hague, Delbert 852
Hahl, William 701
Hahn, Terrence S. 400
Hahn, Greg 634
Haidar, Wael 126
Haidu, James 27
Haight, Mark A 675
Haigney, Stacy 142
Hailey, Bill 643
Hailey, Fernanda 672
Hailey, Clint 762
Hainer, Audra 849
Haines, Ann 489
Haines, Michelle 798
Haines, Gary 852
Hainey, Chris 586
Hairston, John M. 376
Hairston, Michelle 651
Haise, Olivier 832
Hake, Sharon 344
Hakim, Shazmah 500
Hakim, Veronique 520
Hakim, Dorith 602
Hakso, Chelsea 749
Haky, Andrew 629
Halberg, Richard 206
Halberg, Phil 418
Halberstadt, Geoffrey L. 139
Haldeman, Frances 344
Halderman, Robert R 324
Hale, Karen 6
Hale, Edward 75
Hale, Jean R. 208
Hale, Betty 107
Hale, Stephen 421
Hale, Colleen 661
Hale, Ted 731
Hale, Jordan 737
Hale, Q Val 737
Hale, Bill 769
Hale, Daniel G. (Dan) 794
Halechko, John 71
Haley, Jeffrey V. 46
Haley, Michael 46
Haley, Mary 226
Haley, Chris 298
Haley, Colleen 303
Haley, Colleen 602
Haley, Sarah 610
Halinski, Bob 825
Hall, William (Bill) 29
Hall, Mary C 36
Hall, Mary C 46
Hall, Mary 46
Hall, Derwin 46
Hall, Marcus 50
Hall, Elizabeth P 60
Hall, Prentiss 65
Hall, Bob 91
Hall, Jill 125
Hall, Stephanie 162

Hall, Michael 177
Hall, Mark 179
Hall, Ryan 181
Hall, Michael 183
Hall, David 222
Hall, Thomas 234
Hall, Adam 246
Hall, Chris 282
Hall, Tammy 323
Hall, Duncan 357
Hall, Leslie 361
Hall, Charles J. (Chuck) 382
Hall, Neil 488
Hall, Patricia Hemingway 496
Hall, Joseph 503
Hall, Kathryn 504
Hall, Charlie 507
Hall, John 519
Hall, Kelley 562
Hall, Ladd R. 574
Hall, Tammy 584
Hall, Chris 613
Hall, J. D. 625
Hall, J D 625
Hall, Frenesa 637
Hall, Leslie (Les) 653
Hall, J. Franklin (Frank) 662
Hall, Julie 694
Hall, Tom 701
Hall, John 715
Hall, R. Wayne 718
Hall, Jack 764
Hall, Kerry L. 768
Hall, Jay 797
Hall, Keith 818
Hall, Reggie 819
Hall, Jonathan 851
Hall-Long, Bethany 732
Hallagan, Pamela 519
Hallauer, Paul 873
Hallberg, Cindy 832
Hallee, Christopher 184
Hallenbeck, Joshua 555
Halliburton, Shirley 275
Halliday, Sarah A. 544
Halligan, Sean 560
Hallman, Dwayne D. 402
Hallmark, Steve 27
Halloran, Michael 684
Hallowell, Curtis 225
Hallum, Kathy 736
Halmy, Christopher A. 29
Halnon, Bill 679
Halper, John 434
Halper, Lisa 613
Halpin, Edward D. (Ed) 618
Halprin, Joe 507
Halstrom, Danielle 136
Halter, Bob 27
Halter, Patrick G. (Pat) 637
Halter, Michael P. (Mike) 762
Halverson, Bradley M. (Brad) 157
Halverson, Thomas 190
Halverson, Steve 222
Halwig, Nancy 629
Halwig, Nancy 814
Haly, Gregg 159
Ham, Ning 448
Hamalainen, Jim 50
Hamano, Wayne Y. 97
Hamberlin, Mark 232
Hambrick, Thomas 380

Hazard, Stephen 667
Hazboun, Alex 484
Hazen, Samuel N. (Sam) 382
Hazinski, Rich 53
Hazlett, Gayle 726
Hazlin, John 195
He, Dennis 749
Heacock, David A. 254
Head, Minnie 207
Head, Robert 813
Headrick, Chris 456
Heady, Christopher (Chris) 121
Healey, Melanie 393
Healey, Megan 760
Healton, Cheryl G. 551
Healy, Denis 335
Healy, Tom 365
Healy, Mark 397
Healy, Mark G 397
Healy, James 418
Healy, Todd 507
Healy, Colm 655
Heaney, Joe 518
Heard, Mike 189
Heard, Peter 792
Hearn, David 332
Hearne, David 705
Heasley, Teena 456
Heater, Nicole 675
Heath, April 624
Heaton, Gregory L. (Greg) 336
Heaton, Tracey 844
Heavner, Meredith 629
Hebert, Jason 800
Hechtner, Mike 190
Heck, Christopher B. (Chris) 258
Heck, Matthew 700
Heck, Scott 818
Heckenlaible, Charlie 201
Hecker, Rob 828
Heckman, Pam 446
Hecox, Penny 163
Heda, Bhushan 435
Hedberg, Heidi 731
Hedderich, Michael 418
Hedges, Barbara 198
Hedman, Britt 474
Hedrick, Tracy 247
Hedrick, Stephen 648
Hedrick, Stephen 819
Heenan, Palmer T. 331
Heep, Ricky 653
Hees, Bernardo V. 461
Heeter, Jack 883
Hefel, Victoria 815
Hefferen, Dresdyn 628
Hefferle, Brian 299
Heffernan, Dana 104
Heffernan, Terri-beth 798
Heffler, Mava K. 269
Hefflinger, Jeffrey 76
Hefter, Marcia Z. 246
Hegarty, Kevin P. 669
Hegi, Maria 709
Hegwood, Neil 530
Hehn, Christian 118
Heiba, Ibrahim 263
Heidari, Farnaz 681
Heidenreich, Julia 395
Heidenthal, Ryan 81
Heidingsfelder, Rachel 535
Heidrick, Richard 206

Heidt, Alex 466
Heier, Timothy C. 700
Heikkila, Seth 446
Heil, Tim 238
Heim, Michael A. 758
Heiman, Scott 469
Heimes, Terry J. 546
Hein, Jon 71
Heine, Uwe 467
Heine, Robert 479
Heinen, James 664
Heinicke, John 13
Heinrich, Daniel 91
Heinrich, Dan 91
Heintz, Ginger 304
Heintz, Karen 684
Heintzman, David P. 744
Heinz, Karl 326
Heinzelmann, Nick 481
Heise, Arthur G. (Art) 71
Heise, Richard 203
Heise, Angela L. 472
Heisel, David 773
Heiser, Weylon 240
Heiser, Aaron 560
Heishman, Dennis P. 583
Heishman, Phoebe 747
Heisler, Tom 229
Heitin, Mark 785
Hejl, Jeremy 308
Hejmadi, Daaman 426
Helal, Tarek 662
Helber, Tim 584
Helbing, Kandace 629
Held, Gary 507
Helding, Erik M. 189
Heldman, Chris 531
Hele, John C. R. 518
Heleen, Mark L. 542
Heleen, Mark L 542
Helfgott, Alan 493
Helgerson, Gabriel 535
Hellem, Bob 211
Heller, Stacie 53
Heller, Jordan 111
Heller, Adam 111
Heller, Stephanie 299
Heller, Paul G. 415
Heller, Marc 556
Heller, Gene 698
Heller, Kelly 751
Helliker, Carol 163
Helling, Larry J. 654
Hellman, Peter S 107
Hellman, Lisa 460
Hellman, Jeffrey 653
Hellmann, Chris 192
Helm, Bob 348
Helm, Ariel 406
Helm, James 502
Helm, Lucy Lee 728
Helm, Catherine 760
Helm, Larry L. 768
Helmin, Jon C 492
Helminiak, Deanna 71
Helmink, Douglas J 879
Helms, Lloyd W. (Bill) 279
Helms, Cory 279
Helms, Todd 355
Helms, Christopher 497
Helms, Tabitha 813
Helon, Ryan 730

Helow, Ronald 402
Helsel, Christopher 367
Helt, Peter 100
Helterbrand, Scott 3
Helton, Kenneth 34
Helton, Cary 222
Hem, Pannah 104
Hemade, Sagar 764
Hemann, G 334
Hembry, Daryl 455
Hemdev, Vivek 120
Hemelryck, Tom Van 852
Hemesath, Scott 240
Heminger, Gary R. 497
Heminger, Gary 631
Hemker, David J. (Dave) 470
Hemler, Alan J 617
Hemmer, Tara 855
Hempen, Rande 152
Hemphill, Stuart R. 719
Hempton, Sue 327
Henckel, Joel 507
Henderson, Chris 118
Henderson, Mark 139
Henderson, Brantley 147
Henderson, Louis 162
Henderson, Theodore 249
Henderson, Douglas 308
Henderson, Angie 318
Henderson, Paula 492
Henderson, Leah 643
Henderson, Susan 681
Henderson, Adam 832
Hendon, Terry 207
Hendren, Bradley 103
Hendren, Mike 623
Hendrick, John 481
Hendrick, Jeff 624
Hendrick, Bryan 677
Hendricks, Mike 336
Hendricks, Thomas 433
Hendricks, Steve 691
Hendricks, Martin 764
Hendricksen, Matthew 271
Hendrickson, Wray 225
Hendrickson, Keith 734
Hendrickson, Nancy 785
Hendrikse, Pieter 445
Hendrikse, Danny 617
Hendrix, Heidi 568
Hendry, Andrew 195
Hendry, Carol 207
Heneberry, Richard 27
Heneghan, Daniel 466
Hengst, Dean 284
Henigin, Susan 316
Henin, Jonathan 717
Henk, Michael 619
Henke, Daniel F 174
Henkel, Herbert 3
Henkel, Robert J 71
Henley, Travis 389
Henley, Robert W. 577
Henley, Chandra 810
Henly, Julie 785
Henn, Anthony 174
Henn, Tony 174
Henn, Vicki C. 628
Henn, Mila 778
Hennelly, Pat 873
Henneman, Diane 825
Hennen, Carl 584

Hennenfent, Paul 5
Hennerberg, Craig 305
Hennessy, Patricia 179
Hennessy, John L. 474
Hennessy, John 487
Hennessy, Lisa 640
Hennessy, Ray 653
Hennessy, Paul 873
Hennigan, Nathan 92
Hennigan, Mike 497
Henning, Molly 120
Henning, James P. (Jim) 258
Henninger, Tadd J 632
Henningfield, Nancy 325
Hennings, Kristine 417
Henningsen, Dan 458
Henrich, David 827
Henrichsen, Kim 428
Henrickson, Cliff 685
Henrikson, Tracy 479
Henry, Maurice 73
Henry, Kimberley 125
Henry, Kelly 273
Henry, Nicholas 310
Henry, Goscinskit 355
Henry, Brian 429
Henry, Maria G. 457
Henry, Christopher 522
Henry, Peter B. 551
Henry, Jerome 584
Henry, Mildred 798
Henry, David 813
Henry, Jeff 841
Hensel, Robert 179
Hensey, Bernard 123
Henshaw, Carrie 292
Henslee, Gregory L. (Greg) 579
Hensler, Ann M 664
Hensley, Pat 417
Hensley, Dan 433
Hensley, Scott 566
Hensley, Ed 858
Henson, Robert 202
Henson, Doug 707
Henson, Christopher L. (Chris) 797
Henson, Erica 851
Henson, Meghan A. 881
Henthorne, Tamara 225
Henwood, Patricia 504
Henze, Daryl 745
Henzi, Scott 613
Hepburn, Cc 463
Heppel, Gina 722
Heppenstall, C. Talbot 829
Heppenstall, C Talbot 829
Herbein, Andrew 226
Herbel, Vern D. 364
Herbert, Toni 248
Herbert, James H. 328
Herbert, Gary 737
Herbert, Gary R 737
Herbert, Dan 793
Herena, Monique R. 100
Herendeen, Susan 788
Herington, Dave 3
Herlan, Greg 443
Herlocker, Jon 846
Herman, Martin 179
Herman, Mark I. 186
Herman, Robert A. (Bob) 621
Herman, Matthew 622

Homem, Manuel 111
Homer, David P. (Dave) 351
Homer, Ronald A 504
Honda, Amy 98
Hondlik, Carol 50
Hone, Dennis 53
Honeycutt, John 248
Honeycutt, Mike 714
Hong, Peter 407
Hongola, Michael 762
Honig, Peter 617
Honma, Clesio 683
Honore, Babette 531
Honour, Linda 27
Hood, Chris 451
Hood, Amy E. 525
Hood, Byron 535
Hood, Max 582
Hooda, Renu 434
Hoofard, Ron 212
Hoog, Greg 93
Hoogenboom, Jeff 137
Hook, Rich 608
Hooker, Thomas 178
Hooks, Brenda 190
Hooley, Joseph L. (Jay) 739
Hooper, Anthony C. (Tony) 54
Hooper, Tony 55
Hooper, Justin 152
Hooper, Ana 234
Hooper, Chris 852
Hoopes, Leo 629
Hoops, Fred 200
Hooven, Kimberly 80
Hoover, David R 91
Hoover, Sheila 316
Hoover, Travis 417
Hoover, Craig 484
Hoover, Brian 751
Hoover, Stephen (Steve) 879
Hope, Jim 755
Hope, Mark 800
Hopfer, Rick 531
Hopfinger, Mark M 673
Hopkins, Christopher 96
Hopkins, Tim 125
Hopkins, Linda 223
Hopkins, Teresa 481
Hopkins, Lynn M. 600
Hopkins, Josh 624
Hopkins, Kevin 774
Hopmans, John 484
Hopp, Daniel 403
Hoppasted, Curt 240
Hopper, Carolyn 11
Hopper, Sidney 23
Hopper, Doyle 574
Hopper, Kelly 792
Hopson, Benjamin 120
Hopson, Jeffrey 673
Hopwood, Alex 286
Horan, Michael 77
Horan, Cindy Horan 203
Horan, Theodore 610
Horan, Craig 821
Horber, Patrick 6
Horgan, Kathryn M. (Kathy) 739
Horger, Robert R. 718
Horiszny, Laurene 131
Horn, Greg 198
Horn, Lindsay 206
Horn, Paul 431

Horn, Steve 624
Horn, Joe Van 834
Hornberg, Lynn 807
Hornbuckle, William J. 522
Hornby, William P. 165
Horne, Lewis 159
Horner, Ken 180
Horner, Leigh E 387
Horner, Mike 446
Horner, Denise 581
Horner, Shawn 602
Horning, Sharon 544
Hornung, Bill 876
Horowitz, Paul 535
Horst, Mark 871
Horstman, Gregory 148
Horstmann, Douglas J. 384
Horstmann, David L. 384
Horta, Sergio 757
Hortman, Edwin W. (Ed) 51
Hortman, Diane 751
Horton, Rick 406
Horton, Donald R. 406
Horton, Tonia 522
Horton, Michael 631
Horton, Kelly 640
Horton, William E. (Bill) 671
Horvath, Elizabeth 380
Horvath, Lori 446
Horwitz, Alex 198
Hosch, Pete 417
Hosea, Kristina 550
Hosfield, Rick 352
Hoskin, Brett 28
Hoskins, Walter 147
Hossack, Michael 308
Hossain, Taurat 261
Hossle, Dwight 229
Host, Gerard R. (Jerry) 800
Hoste, Renee 670
Hostetler, Matt 360
Hostetter, David 344
Hosty, Neil J. 492
Hotaling, Michael 289
Hotaling, Michael 380
Hotarek, George 749
Hotchkiss, James P. 325
Hotsuki, Keishi 534
Hotze, Tim 760
Houck, Ronnie 701
Houdek, Ritch 460
Houdeshell, David D. 701
Houghton, Nicole 428
Houghton, Robert 686
Houghton, Marella 733
Houlihan, Robert 516
Houlihan, Susan 628
Houmann, Lars D. 11
Hounsell, Randall 198
Hourigan, John 68
Hourigan, Tim 397
Hourihan, Michael 502
House, Michael 13
House, Dan 323
Houseal, Alex 13
Householder, Thomas 39
Householder, Joseph A. (Joe) 704
Houser, Denise 828
Housh, Debbie 202
Housianitis, Lisa 617
Houska, Mark 178
Houssaye, Brian de la 873

Houston, Monica 319
Houston, Helga S. 414
Houston, Daniel J. (Dan) 637
Houston, Stacy W 664
Houston, John 829
Houston, Melanie 830
Houten, Matthew Van 75
Houweling, Tara Van 150
Hove, Kalyn 198
Hover, Jonathan 635
Hoverson, Claudine 750
Hovious, Jeff 807
Howard, June 16
Howard, Cheryl 139
Howard, Paul 183
Howard, Gary 350
Howard, John L. 369
Howard, David 560
Howard, Fred 670
Howard, Mary 685
Howard, Dennis 700
Howard, Kevin J. 753
Howard, Donald 777
Howard, Kim 777
Howard, Claude 792
Howard, John 828
Howard, Fara 839
Howard, J. Kyle 843
Howarth, Anne 613
Howat, Dan 448
Howe, Dave 183
Howe, Margaret 337
Howe, Robert 503
Howe, Tim 661
Howe, Roman 694
Howe, Tim 792
Howell, Peyton R. 53
Howell, Lloyd W. 129
Howell, John 162
Howell, Susie 223
Howell, Kevin 258
Howell, Douglas K. (Doug) 346
Howell, Melissa 451
Howell, James A. 562
Howell, Eric 710
Howell, Robert 755
Howell, Paul 768
Howell, Yvette 871
Howson, David 179
Howze, Marc A. 240
Hoxit, Debbie 737
Hoxsie, Katherine 853
Hoy, Thomas L. 69
Hoy, William 324
Hoysan, Mandy 681
Hoyt, Bert 560
Hoyt, Hubertus 560
Hoyt, Janet M 748
Hoyt, Jeffrey 751
Hoytal, Joseph 150
Hpenterprise, Synnex 752
Hrenko, John 120
Hritz, Gretchen 793
Hrycenko, Mike 628
Hsieh, John 431
Hsieh, Jackson 726
Hsiung, Ken 550
Hsu, Amy 28
Hsu, Christopher P. (Chris) 389
Hsu, Michael D. 457
Hsu, Ted 634
Hsu, Johnny 634

Hsu, Florence 634
Hsu, Clark 635
Hsu, Hsi 656
Hsu, Erik 873
Hu, Kathryn 148
Hu, Anna 164
Hu, Bradford 181
Hu, Hao 182
Hu, Soomin 365
Hu, Mandy 552
Hu, Eddie 560
Hu, S. Jack 669
Huang, Pamela 11
Huang, Stanley 124
Huang, Scott 171
Huang, Beth 283
Huang, Victor 352
Huang, Gene 448
Huang, Jen-Hsun 576
Huang, Alice 634
Huang, Sofia 634
Huang, Lily 647
Huang, Christopher 695
Huang, Jim 740
Hubbard, Richard 125
Hubbard, Skip 126
Hubbard, Todd 599
Hubbard, Karlie 629
Hubbard, Kym 730
Hubbard, Cheryl 774
Hubbard, Latonya 871
Hubbuch, Chris 868
Huber, Marie Oh 264
Huber, John 307
Huber, Michael 365
Huber, J. Kendall 378
Huber, Thomas 682
Huber, Tom 682
Huberty, John 3
Huberty, Sean 286
Hubinger, Jim 761
Hubner, Robert 801
Huch, Jamie 202
Huckabay, Evan 200
Huckabay, David 484
Hudak, James L. (Jim) 179
Hudak, John 325
Huddleston, Ron 525
Hudecek, Brian 503
Hudgens, John D. 768
Hudgens, Liz 871
Hudgions, Annette W. 583
Hudnall, Matt 378
Hudson, David W. 164
Hudson, Jennifer 211
Hudson, Thomas 264
Hudson, Jody 310
Hudson, Scott R. 346
Hudson, Brenda 423
Hudson, Jerry 629
Hudson, Dennis S. (Denny) 701
Hudson, Paul 755
Hudson, Jeremiah 801
Hudson, Jamie 808
Hudson, Ray 870
Hudson, David T. 878
Huerta, Dave 45
Huerta, Liliana 72
Huerta, Tony 613
Huestis, Tim 624
Huey, Louis 32
Huey, Cindy 107

Inscho, Bill 326
Inserra, Andrea 129
Inserra, Lawrence 469
Inslee, Jay 737
Insley, Patricia 481
Intemann, Chris 308
Inui, Akiko 653
Ioriatti, Roberto 242
Ippolito, Peter J. 707
Iqbal, Farhan 72
Iqbal, Asma 695
Irani, Farhad 604
Irby, ERIC 560
Ireland, Jay W. 349
Ireton, John 448
Iris, Krug 162
Irisawa, Jim 541
Irish, Stephen J. 276
Irish, William J 682
Irish, Dale 734
Irizarry, Laurens 214
Irmen, Michael S. 57
Irussi, Bruce G. 707
Irvin, Vernon L. 490
Irvin, Richard 803
Irvine, Jeffrey 42
Irwin, James 180
Irwin, John 415
Irwin, Mike 740
Irwin, Larry (Don) 819
Isaia, Mone 234
Isbell, Ashley 150
Isbell, Ken 203
Isbell, Jeri 240
Isberg, Thomas 3
Iseman, Jay C. 399
Iseman, Andrew J. (Andy) 806
Iserman, Lance 82
Isham, Mj 624
Ishikawa, Brian 98
Ishizu, Wesley 13
Islam, Munib 107
Islam, Mohammed 670
Isom, Robert D. 37
Isom, Kevin 80
Isom, Matt 278
Isom, Wendell 470
Isono, Denis K. 164
Israel, Leonard (Len) 331
Issa, Muna 635
Istas, Frederic 157
Isturiz, Raul 617
Ito, Craig 97
Ito, Val 98
Iturrey, Albert 505
Iturrios, Karina 149
Iuorio, Alex 87
IV, R H Holmes 143
Ivanis, Milena 792
Ivanov, Stanislav (Stan) 427
Ivanova, Detelina 148
Ive, Jonathan 62
Ive, Jony 62
Iverson, Jerry 676
Iverson, Lisa 823
Iverson, Mark 831
Ives, Gray 672
Ives, Zachary A 735
Ivey, Craig S. 213
Ivey, Brian 358
Ivey, Kay 731
Ivry, David 124

Ivy, Barry 755
Iwegbue, Jennifer 849
Iyengar, Narayan 23
Iyer, Sethu 96
Iyer, Chandresh 100
Iyer, Gopal 193
Iyer, Subrmanian 328
Iyer, Prasad 507
Iyer, Ranjita 507
Iyer, Bask 845
Izaguirre, Luis-Angel Gomez 881
Izmee, Haris 525
Izotov, Andre 656
Izurieta, Laura 749
Izzo, Ralph 649

J

Jabal, Kim 302
Jabbar, Omar 264
Jabbonsky, Larry 613
Jabbour, Anthony M. 305
Jablonski, Jack 738
Jack, Angela 818
Jackey, Chris 111
Jacklin, Charles 189
Jackman, Randy 80
Jackman, Earl 411
Jackman, Jeffrey 780
Jackowiak, Mary 566
Jackowski, Julia L. (Julie) 156
Jacks, Tyler 782
Jackson, Jennifer 11
Jackson, James 59
Jackson, Michael J. (Mike) 82
Jackson, Peter 140
Jackson, Rick C. 150
Jackson, Doug 160
Jackson, Delu 211
Jackson, Brian 229
Jackson, Clifton 242
Jackson, Michael J. (Mike) 298
Jackson, Mitchell 302
Jackson, Paul 304
Jackson, Lisa 310
Jackson, Kelly 324
Jackson, Allen 326
Jackson, Kevin 362
Jackson, Brian 385
Jackson, Jamere 388
Jackson, Brian 396
Jackson, Matt 423
Jackson, Benjamin R. (Ben) 427
Jackson, Monique 429
Jackson, Doris 518
Jackson, Elvenia 580
Jackson, Theodore 606
Jackson, Don 622
Jackson, Joanne B. 623
Jackson, Warren 624
Jackson, Kimberly 629
Jackson, Jennifer 671
Jackson, Doris 673
Jackson, Bill 681
Jackson, Lori 684
Jackson, Ronald B. (Ron) 710
Jackson, Andrew 732
Jackson, Rich 732
Jackson, Jamere 776
Jackson, Denise 790
Jackson, Keri 798

Jackson, Philip C. (Phil) 826
Jackson, Cj 828
Jackson, Neal 858
Jacob, Bobby 223
Jacob, Ovadiah 365
Jacob, Bijesh 502
Jacob, Randy 823
Jacobi, Jacqueline 531
Jacobo, Keyanus 560
Jacobs, Kerry J. 25
Jacobs, Sybrena 52
Jacobs, Bonnie 59
Jacobs, Robert 223
Jacobs, Donna 275
Jacobs, Shirley 277
Jacobs, Stephen D. (Jake) 338
Jacobs, Kevin J. 392
Jacobs, Rachel 481
Jacobs, Caroline 548
Jacobs, Todd 560
JAcobs, Leonore 617
Jacobs, Paul E. 656
Jacobs, Bill 724
Jacobs, Kristine 800
Jacobs, Jennifer 828
Jacobs, Bradley S. 881
Jacobsen, Donald 591
Jacobsohn, Robin 511
Jacobson, Angela 11
Jacobson, Paul A. 242
Jacobson, Steve 251
Jacobson, Jeff A. 445
Jacobson, Scott 681
Jacobson, Roy 829
Jacobson, Jack 852
Jacobson, Jeffrey (Jeff) 879
Jacoby, Rebecca J. 177
Jacoby, Christy 613
Jacques, Dale 685
Jacques, Kevin 844
Jadin, Ronald L. 369
Jafarieh, Nicolas 713
Jafarzadeh, Shaun 184
Jaffe, Jonathan M. (Jon) 476
Jaffe, Chris 547
Jaffe, Ezra 873
Jaffery, Farhan 448
Jaffray, Dawn M. 814
Jafry, Syed A. 781
Jagger, Hal 708
Jagiella, Diana 536
Jaglall, Andy 535
Jahn, Andrew 11
Jaime, Alex 582
Jaimovich, Lisa 503
Jain, Ajit 113
Jain, Nitin 162
Jain, Vishal 346
Jain, Vishal 647
Jain, Vikas 655
Jain, Sujit 683
Jakeman, Kelly 53
Jakeman, Brad 612
Jakobsen, Henning 194
Jakosky, Donn 599
Jakosky, Donn 599
Jakubik, Chris 461
Jalace-vasold, Melissa 871
Jalil, Ovais 823
Jambor, Joan 75
Jamerson, Carlene 11
James, Karen 93

James, Gillian 112
James, Hamilton E. (Tony) 121
James, David 190
James, Catherine 258
James, Austin 304
James, Robert 399
James, Schlosser 415
James, Donna 465
James, Galeota 515
James, Phyllis A. 522
James, Thomas 566
James, Miriam 610
James, Hunt 664
James, Bradley G. 788
James, Al 798
James, Dianne R. 884
Jameson, Steven E. (Steve) 208
Jamieson, Robert 1
Jamil, Dhiaa M. 258
Jamison, Gary 404
Jamison, Cynthia 582
Jamison, Cynthia T. 790
Jamrog, Stephanie 201
Jan, Couturier 415
Janatsch, Adam 251
Jandacek, Ed 284
Jandrin, Scott 559
Jandrue, Patricia 304
Jane, Mara 519
Janes, Maria N 853
Janiga, Kathy 234
Janke, Harry 11
Janke, Kenneth S. (Ken) 15
Janke, Kenneth S 16
Janke, Grant 810
Janke, AnnMarie 832
Janki, Daniel 349
Janki, Daniel 350
Jankowski, Simona 576
Jankowski, John 631
Jankowski, Michelle 647
Jankowski, Ed 860
Jannah, Shekar G. 453
Janney, Bill 484
Janney, Laura 562
Jansen, Laura 81
Jansen, Kevin 298
Jansen, Jacqueline 759
Janson, Julie S. 258
Janssen, Gwendolyn 5
Janssen, Ann 279
Janssen, Jerimiah 314
Janssens, Tom 866
Jansson, Verity 42
Jansson, Helena 302
Jante, Adam 317
Jantsch, Paul 176
Jantz, Robert 270
Jantzen, Rebecca 474
Janus, Tami 781
Japlit, Christine 121
Jaquay, Joseph 98
Jaques, Julie 584
Jaramillo, Rafael 270
Jaramillo, Chris 303
Jarlsjo, Bengt 657
Jaromin, Rosemary T 504
Jaroszewski, J Rosow 224
Jarrell, Blake 53
Jarrell, Carla 624
Jarrett, Barry 46

Johnson, Nicole 751
Johnson, William D. (Bill) 766
Johnson, Mark M. 768
Johnson, Cheryl H. 771
Johnson, Genevieve 773
Johnson, Bret 781
Johnson, Laura 785
Johnson, Clay 794
Johnson, Shanna 794
Johnson, Robert J. 797
Johnson, Steve 801
Johnson, Shannon A. 806
Johnson, Debbie 807
Johnson, Sarah 807
Johnson, Kelly 808
Johnson, Joseph 815
Johnson, Dj 818
Johnson, Willie 818
Johnson, Todd 823
Johnson, Stephen 832
Johnson, David 832
Johnson, Trina 832
Johnson, Alan 844
Johnson, Clay 851
Johnson, Marianne 863
Johnson, Jason 871
Johnson, Beth 875
Johnson, Tracy 879
Johnson, Darrin 879
Johnson, Adam R. 883
Johnson-bonhart, Kimberly 818
Johnston, Mary 93
Johnston, Steve 96
Johnston, Linda A. 114
Johnston, Daniel 154
Johnston, Steven J. 174
Johnston, Bryan L 200
Johnston, Andy 211
Johnston, Michael F. (Mike) 255
Johnston, Gregory 298
Johnston, Kelly 328
Johnston, James J. (Jim) 454
Johnston, William 492
Johnston, Stephen 593
Johnston, Hugh F. 612
Johnston, Mac 624
Johnston, David 647
Johnston, Amy 740
Johnston, Cassandra 828
Johnston, Richard 834
Johnston, Greg 851
Johnstone, William O. 93
Johnstone, Robert 124
Johnstone, Rudolph 720
Johnstun, Paul 384
Johri, Akhil 666
Joia, Eduardo 431
Joiner, Brad 298
Joiner, Mary 823
Jois, Ganesh 365
Jojo, Linda P. 811
Jolin, Joanne 226
Joling, Scott 807
Jolley, Jennifer 884
Jolly, Summer 120
Jolly, Ed 331
Joly, Hubert 116
Jonas, David 427
Jonas, Steven 507
Jonathan, Williams 202
Jondall, Bob 808
Jones, Steve 26

Jones, Katie R 28
Jones, Gregg 44
Jones, Brian 53
Jones, Wesley 53
Jones, Bob 62
Jones, Cary 100
Jones, Lacey 124
Jones, Ken 128
Jones, Mike 134
Jones, Nicole 173
Jones, Rosalyn 179
Jones, Thomas 200
Jones, Anthony 204
Jones, Rickee 205
Jones, Larry W. 208
Jones, D. Andrew 208
Jones, David 208
Jones, Bill 219
Jones, Clay 223
Jones, Summara 234
Jones, Tim 238
Jones, Mary 240
Jones, Shane 242
Jones, Paul R 242
Jones, Paul 242
Jones, Keri 243
Jones, Griff 258
Jones, Henry 258
Jones, Jane 258
Jones, Wendy 264
Jones, Karla 275
Jones, Jeanne 284
Jones, Katrina 291
Jones, Evette 298
Jones, Jeffrey A 307
Jones, Alex 323
Jones, Charles E. (Chuck) 329
Jones, Randy 341
Jones, Travis 371
Jones, Bruce 389
Jones, Katrina 392
Jones, Adrienne F 411
Jones, David 411
Jones, Kevin 415
Jones, Carolyn 415
Jones, Sheri 428
Jones, Buff 431
Jones, Raymond 431
Jones, Mamie 435
Jones, Dave 451
Jones, Suzan 456
Jones, Steve 463
Jones, Paul 465
Jones, David 474
Jones, René F. 492
Jones, Beth 500
Jones, Cynthia 522
Jones, Kim 533
Jones, Jessica 538
Jones, Jon 542
Jones, Christopher T. 568
Jones, Tom 572
Jones, Robert G. (Bob) 583
Jones, Juan C 593
Jones, Chuck 593
Jones, Jeff C 599
Jones, Jeff C 599
Jones, Douglas E. (Doug) 607
Jones, Kathleen 609
Jones, Laura 613
Jones, Vince 613
Jones, Bill 624

Jones, Allison 624
Jones, Diane 624
Jones, Ryan 624
Jones, Randall T. (Todd) 650
Jones, Julie 662
Jones, Bob 664
Jones, Ellen S. 671
Jones, Noble 676
Jones, Karen M. 689
Jones, Tom 689
Jones, Iris 701
Jones, William 704
Jones, Tommie 711
Jones, Brad 728
Jones, Randie 731
Jones, Clarence 734
Jones, Betty M 735
Jones, Andrea 749
Jones, Tracy 755
Jones, Hannah 777
Jones, Wilson 783
Jones, Marni 784
Jones, Bruce R. 792
Jones, Stuart 797
Jones, Amanda 805
Jones, Linda 821
Jones, Anthony 834
Jones, Tony 834
Jones, Richard M. 840
Jones, Rosetta 844
Jones, Ronald 855
Jones, Pamela 858
Jones, Eddie 881
Jonsson, Joanna F 46
Jonsson, Annemarie 751
Jord, Scar 299
Jordan, Michael 50
Jordan, Suzanne 100
Jordan, Simon 118
Jordan, Deborah A. 144
Jordan, Rusty 154
Jordan, Whit 160
Jordan, Cedric 200
Jordan, D. Bryan 321
Jordan, Chris 357
Jordan, Terri 525
Jordan, Tom 552
Jordan, Randy 591
Jordan, Gregory B. 628
Jordan, Joe 672
Jordan, Robert E. (Bob) 723
Jordan, Donna 731
Jordan, Carla 731
Jordan, Steve 798
Jordan, Bill 870
Jordan, Darren 871
Jordan, Michael 876
Jordan-smith, Gavin 879
Jorge, Nelson 630
Jorgensen, Ben 9
Jorgensen, Jeff 417
Jorgensen, Leslie 433
Jorgensen, Lisa 738
Jorgensen, Jay T. 851
Jorgenson, Corbett J. (Corey) 57
Jorgenson, James 404
Jorgenson, Rob 691
Jorgenson, Kenneth 700
Josan, Jose Luis 266
Jose, Fran 142
Joseph, Robert 12
Joseph, Gregory 44

Joseph, Loretta 55
Joseph, Oliver 243
Joseph, Tommy S. 433
Joseph, George 516
Joseph, Isaac A. 571
Joshi, Abhay 425
Joshua, Eto 357
Josowitz, Barry 446
Jotwani, Juhi 431
Jover, Angelines 448
Joyce, Rhonda 46
Joyce, Thomas P. 232
Joyce, Teresa 328
Joyce, David L. 349
Joyce, Robert J. (Bob) 453
Joyce, Denise 827
Joyner, J. David 229
Joyner, John 229
Joyner, Andre 465
Joyner, Ken 564
Joysizemore, Dian 93
Jr, Paul G Haaga 36
Jr, Paul G Haaga 38
Jr, George Pierce 44
Jr, Jonathan B Lovelace 46
Jr, Paul B Murphy 143
Jr, Jack E Counts 147
Jr, Domenic Dell'osso 168
Jr, Bruce L Castor 205
Jr, James Spellings 289
Jr, Alton B Lewis 320
Jr, Frank Grese 372
Jr, Robert L Carpenter 406
Jr, Robert D Kunisch 406
Jr, W Michael Amick 433
Jr, C Thomas Evans 453
Jr, Robert E Swaney 538
Jr, Doyle Hopper 574
Jr, Ray Napolitan 574
Jr, George West 599
Jr, Ronald J Nicolas 599
Jr, Ronald J Nicolas 599
Jr, Phillip D Joseph 726
Jr, Thomas Wagner 732
Jr, Lawrence C Franklin 736
Jr, Richard L Smith 779
Jr, Thomas B Gerlach 779
Jr, John Pelusi 830
Jr, Brooks Von Arx 871
Juby, Alyce 456
Juchno, Stacy M. 628
Juday, Mark 28
Juday, Ryan 783
Judd, Jim 568
Jude, Peggy 80
Jude, Justin L. 486
Judge, James J. (Jim) 282
Judge, Kenan 417
Judie, Kenneth 734
Judy, Ryan 59
Jue, Don 431
Juel, Carol 750
Juergensen, Colleen 463
Jugo, Rita 97
Jugoon, Peter 698
Jula, Peg 307
Julian, Paul C. 511
Julian, Sylvie 656
Julian, Kenneth D. 783
Juliane, Jeffrey 149
Juliano, Timothy 742
Julien, Jeffrey P. (Jeff) 664

Jump, Ron 240
Jump, Belinda 360
Juneau, Jeff 729
Junglas, Steve 371
Juniper, Brooke 535
Junk, Luke 685
Junkins, Lowell L. 296
Jurado, Welmer 634
Jurco, Tim 558
Jurgens, Michael 417
Jurrens, Erika 152
Jurrjens, George 365
Jurs, Peter 307
Justh, Kevin 629
Justice, Jim 738
Jutze, Roy 305
Juve, Kathy 752
Jwanier, Tracey 142
Jwoodcock, Tim 586

K

Kaalund, Sekou H 448
Kabat, Kevin T. 828
Kablawi, Hani 100
Kacewicz, Marek 169
Kachel, Vic 339
Kachurka, Matt 226
Kaczmarczyk, Stanley F. 804
Kaczmarek, Larry 378
Kaczmarek, Walter T. (Walt) 385
Kaczmarek, Jessica 777
Kaczynski, Thomas 497
Kaddoura, Maher 307
Kaden, Ellen O 146
Kadien, Thomas G. (Tom) 433
Kadlec, Tom 760
Kadnar, Julie 44
Kadre, Manuel 679
Kaeding, Nate 527
Kaese, Torben 407
Kaeser, Richard 444
Kagan, Amber 350
Kaganis, Perry 550
Kagitcibasi, Elif 85
Kahan, Rich 700
Kahlau, Dorothy 836
Kahn, Cheryl 152
Kahn, Gene 352
Kahn, Dale 755
Kahn, Benjamin 828
Kahne, Michael 323
Kain, Gary D 19
Kain, Peter 544
Kairis, Phil 573
Kaiser, George B. 125
Kaiser, Laura S. 428
Kaiser, Jim 492
Kaiserman, David J. 476
Kajioka, Jenny 97
Kajueter, Henrik 85
Kalafut, Thomas 871
Kalakkad, Dinesh 470
Kalamaras, Paul 437
Kalanovic, Daniel 617
Kalaria, Brij 121
Kalathur, Rajesh (Raj) 239
Kalayjian, Nick 767
Kalchik, Mona 102
Kalchuri, Shantanu 576
Kale, Kitty 513

Kalen, Michael 647
Kalil-Lennon, Theresa 206
Kalin, Robert 531
Kalis, David 431
Kalisek, Brian 523
Kallas, Daniel 120
Kallmerten, Erin 415
Kallsen, Terri R. 700
Kalonder, Liz 841
Kaloustian, Maral 139
Kalscheur, Trisha 240
Kalstein, Michele 299
Kaluzna, Brad 80
Kam, Priscilla 42
Kamal, Mostafa M. 495
Kamal, Ashfaq 506
Kamara, Abdul 152
Kamath, Vijita 670
Kamenash, Tracey 381
Kamensky, Allan E. 753
Kametz, William (Bill) 691
Kamford, Peter 112
Kamin, John R. 583
Kaminski, Jennifer 72
Kaminski, Dale 348
Kaminski, Tom 467
Kaminski, Irene 502
Kaminski, Robert B. 513
Kaminski, Mark V. 675
Kaminski, Douglas 700
Kamitaki, Wayne 164
Kamm, Terry 124
Kammholz, Ulrich 599
Kamminga, Duane 324
Kamra, Kush 519
Kamsickas, James K. (Jim) 231
Kamykowski, Greg 107
Kanaglekar, Indraneel 883
Kanbur, Charu 36
Kanda, Neal 164
Kandarian, Steven A. (Steve) 518
Kane, Courtney 100
Kane, Thomas M. (Tom) 216
Kane, Thomas 304
Kane, Stephen 305
Kane, Brian A. 411
Kane, Edward 414
Kane, Terri 428
Kane, Martha 504
Kane, John 542
Kane, Jim 568
Kane, Julie 572
Kane, Mark 678
Kane, Eric 755
Kane, Patrick P 815
Kane, Peter 841
Kanefsky, Andrea 112
Kanevsky, Dario 270
Kang, Byung 207
Kang, Katelyn 401
Kang, Kyu 427
Kang, Susan 729
Kanigicherla, Balaji 426
Kanis, Jordan 749
Kantamneni, Raje 566
Kantaria, Daksha 703
Kanter, Maurissa 326
Kantharia, Yogesh 876
Kantola, Kevin 823
Kantor, Jonathan D. (Jon) 186
Kantrow, Stephen 581
Kantrowitz, Jeanie 552

Kao, Connie 687
Kaohi, Cheryl 98
Kap, Kim 457
Kapales, Kevin 413
Kapani, Mayur V. 427
Kapcheck, Jeff 160
Kapito, Robert S. (Rob) 120
Kapla, Bob 72
Kaplan, Joel 290
Kaplan, Robert S. (Rob) 300
Kaplan, Shira 507
Kaplan, Andrew 549
Kaplan, Mike 694
Kaplan, Ryan 700
Kaplan, Robert 739
Kaplan, Dean 841
Kaplan, Bob 841
Kaplin, Leo 96
Kapner, Janice 757
Kapoor, Amit 484
Kapoor, Rishi 522
Kapoor, Kishore 593
Kapoor, Samir 656
Kapoor, Sanjay 725
Kapperman, Garry 735
Kapsner, Richard 686
Kapur, Anuj 178
Kapusinski, Victor 831
Karalis, Cathy 550
Karalis, Nick 873
Karamanoukian, Henry 640
Karami, Ladan 149
Karanam, Raj 233
Karanjkar, Ashish 613
Karas, Donald 391
Karas, Jacob 504
Karasiak, Stephanie 80
Karasick, Michael 431
Karatha, Padmanabhan 200
Karczmer, Aaron 604
Karen, Friedman 879
Karich, Joe 6
Karl, James 13
Karlin, Margot 637
Karlovich, Robert W. (Trey) 558
Karls, Lori 805
Karlson, Doug 80
Karn, Alice 455
Karn, Heather 774
Karn, Randy 869
Karna, Ajoy 755
Karnes, Merle 643
Karnuta, Daniel 762
Karolis, George C. 70
Karp, Caroline 107
Karp, Peter 132
Karpik, Mike 739
Karr, Dorothy 325
Karr, Kathi 402
Karr, Michael 599
Karr, Michael 599
Karras, Athanasios 401
Karraz, Donna 749
Karrip, Brian 316
Karros, Kirt 389
Karsner, Alexander 63
Karst, Darren W. 681
Karstens, Kevin 104
Kartson, Marianne 415
Karu, Zoher 264
Karwacki, John 653
Kasanoff, Howard 223

Kasbar, Michael J. 875
Kasch, Adam 225
Kasen, Stewart 499
Kasendorf, Leonard 519
Kashkari, Neel T. 300
Kasinec, Kathryn 415
Kaska, Tony 417
Kasner, Ken 380
Kasper, Michael 28
Kasprowicz, Michael 142
Kass, Jordan T. 686
Kassab, Leanne D. 188
Kassatly, Fady 129
Kassinos, Debbie 318
Kast, Peter 160
Kastanis, Maria 610
Kastberg, Amalia G 695
Kastberg, Amalia 695
Kastendick, Kurt 806
Kaster, Chris 134
Kastner, Evelyn 237
Kastner, Kevin 358
Kastner, Christopher D. 416
Kastriner, Jared 107
Kasturia, Sanjay 655
Katanick, Ron 460
Katcher, Keith 576
Kateman, Amanda 179
Kathryn, Conde 444
Kathy, Schneider 249
Katic, Jill 670
Katie, Cave 695
Katims, Susan 142
Katkade, Vaibhav 617
Katrib, Tony 488
Katsilometes, Tom 732
Katsman, Bruce 728
Katsoudas, Francine 177
Katt, Faye 107
Kattos, Andrew N. (Andy) 705
Katyal, Navin 617
Katz, Richard 48
Katz, Heidi 55
Katz, Marc D. 142
Katz, Jerome 177
Katz, Mark 391
Katz, Robert L. (Bobby) 439
Katz, Todd 519
Katz, Maxine 548
Katz, Erin 670
Katz, Kathleen 841
Kauchak, Lara 270
Kauffman, Holly C 329
Kauffman, Andy 500
Kauffman, Catherine 798
Kaufman, Brian 184
Kaufman, Victor A. 286
Kaufman, Jordan 365
Kaufman, Nick 463
Kaufman, Al 476
Kaufman, Richard 504
Kaufman, Seth 670
Kaufman, Valerie 673
Kaufman, Adam 785
Kaufmann, Michael C. (Mike) 152
Kaufmann, Kevin 550
Kauk, Zachary A. (Zach) 157
Kaul, John 369
Kaup, Chad 635
Kaur, Primal 55
Kaus, Kim 24
Kautt, Jodie 759

Kirkwood, Karen 781
Kirousis, Marni 781
Kirrane, Joseph 86
Kirrer, Jason 560
Kirsch, Eric M. 15
Kirschling, Ryan 749
Kirschner, Randy 12
Kirschner, David 366
Kirshner, Alan I. 499
Kirsis, Karlis P 881
Kirtland, Scott 694
Kirtley, Timothy H. 611
Kirven, Michael 610
Kirven, Mick 610
Kirwan, Jeff 776
Kisber, Michael E. 322
Kiscaden, Bradley J. 498
Kiser, Carly 749
Kish, Donald 341
Kishor, Seetharaman 493
Kiskorna, Mark 628
Kissire, Debbie 588
Kissler, Courtney 729
Kissling, Lou 224
Kist, Jonathan 745
Kistler, Matthew 851
Kistner, Dominic 288
Kitagawa, Allan S. 766
Kitamura, Ryan 98
Kitamura, Sam 304
Kitchin, Brad 593
Kitchin, Mark 806
Kitlen, John 555
Kittilstved, Sherri 808
Kittredge, Mickey 184
Kittredge, Teri 617
Kitzmann, Jessica 149
Kitzmiller, Kenneth G. 516
Kiyono, Jolene 164
Kjellberg, Henrik V. 286
Klaassens, Michael 36
Klaczak, Robert 481
Klaeser, Dennis L. 761
Klahre, Robert 519
Klammer, Thoma P 411
Klapkowski, Joseph 835
Klappa, Gale E. 857
Klaus, Jeffrey A. (Jeff) 856
Klebba, Aj 615
Klebba, Philip 694
Klee, Brian 617
Kleefisch, Brett 466
Kleespies, Kurt 839
Kleffel, Julie 701
Kleffel, Juliette 701
Kleiman, Mitch 80
Klein, Bruce 174
Klein, Bruce 177
Klein, Stacy 179
Klein, John E. 193
Klein, David 216
Klein, Steven A 223
Klein, Kelly 270
Klein, John 304
Klein, Michele 310
Klein, Aaron 456
Klein, Joel 556
Klein, Richard 610
Klein, Arvid 755
Klein, Gerald J. 788
Klein, Michael F. 792
Klein, David 869

Kleinbaum, Scott 700
Kleinhample, Ken 869
Kleinhaut, Mark 455
Kleinhenz, Matt 715
Kleinschmidt, Jeff 584
Kleman, Keith 851
Klene, Brian 523
Klenk, Craig 47
Klenk, Jeffrey P. (Jeff) 792
Klenz, Eric 456
Kleski, Vickie 126
Klett, Kim 306
Kletter, David 129
Klevitz, Glenn 875
Klevorn, Marcy 339
Kleyle, Tom 189
Klick, Michael 858
Kliethermes, Craig W. 682
Klika, Christine 733
Klimchak, Joseph 673
Klimschot, Jeanne 103
Kline, Betsy 65
Kline, Gary J 174
Kline, Linda 315
Kline, Clayton 445
Kline, Terry S. 543
Kline, Barbara 751
Klinger, David 347
Klingler, Cindy 628
Klinkner, Kim 71
Klobnak, Jennifer L. 682
Klocke, Jill 361
Klode, Peter 684
Kloecker, Edward 183
Klokis, Wayne 443
Kloostra, Jim 513
Kloska, Ronald 318
Klotz, Jim 703
Klotzbach, Kevin B. 309
Klouda, Michael 786
Kluber, Bill 653
Kluemper, Steve 371
Kluft, Leonard 573
Klug, Loren C. 410
Klug, Sue 679
Klyce, Harvey 448
Klyn, Pamela 869
Knapke, Murph 318
Knapp, David 134
Knapp, Donald 325
Knapp, Tracy W. 450
Knapp, Gary 456
Knapp, Michael 523
Knapp, Ken Knapp Ken 671
Knaub, Scott 198
Knavish, Timothy M. 631
Kneeland, Michael J. 819
Kneesel, Thomas 71
Kneidinger, Michael (Mike) 234
Kneipp, Carla 163
Knickerbocker, Rick 531
Knieriem, Tim 357
Knies, Theresa 610
Kniffin, Ogden 664
Knight, Angela 200
Knight, Andrea 223
Knight, Nathan 249
Knight, Mike 275
Knight, Michelle 307
Knight, William 355
Knight, M Keith 355
Knight, Michael 448

Knight, Jeffrey L. (Jeff) 583
Knight, John 584
Knight, Jefferey 584
Knight, Kimberly 643
Knight, Christine 647
Knight, Robert M. 810
Knightly, Kevin C. 438
Knipfing, Janet 835
Knirsch, Charles 617
Knoll, Thomas 239
Knoll-finn, Mj 551
Knopf, Claude 107
Knopf, Matthew 242
Knopf, David 461
Knostman, Chuck 757
Knott, Timothy 450
Knott, Greg 689
Knott, Carolyn 716
Knott, Craig 832
Knouse, Sabrina 755
Knowles, Debie 47
Knowles, Leo A 211
Knox, Bradley 16
Knox, Shontell 96
Knox, Fred 825
Knoy, Shane 460
Knuckles, Beth 465
Knudsen, Mary 355
Knudsen, Coby 428
Knudsen, Jeannette 715
Knudstorp, Jorgen 729
Knue, Gregory 98
Knueven, Matthew 672
Knuth, Harlan 72
Knuth, David 858
Knutson, Brian 307
Ko, Al 435
Ko, William 634
Koban, Mark 448
Kobayashi, Edison 97
Koble, Keith 100
Koch, Daniel 73
Koch, Tracy 372
Koch, Johannes 389
Koch, Ted 586
Koch, Diane 633
Koch, Stephen P. (Steve) 675
Koch, Steve 675
Koch, Jonathan 698
Kochan, Christian 653
Kochanov, Oleg 103
Kochie, Steven 871
Kochie, Steven G 876
Kochvar, Mark 691
Kodish, Joel 88
Kody, Michael 53
Koehler, Lisa 247
Koehler, Mike 284
Koehler, Mary 873
Koehly, Hank 202
Koehnen, Michael W. 793
Koel, Mike 805
Koellmann, Stefan 278
Koellner, Meliss A 411
Koellner, Laurette 574
Koen, Kenneth 841
Koenig, Paul 74
Koenig, Jim 160
Koenig, Karl 355
Koenig, Bill 369
Koenig, Douglas J 809
Koening, John 466

Koepke, Ashley 72
Koeppe, Adam 837
Koering, Adam 822
Koerner, Ted 190
Koerner, Michael 446
Koerwer, Joseph 515
Koffer, Danielle 195
Koga, Cristiano 302
Kogan, Allan 411
Koh, Peter 401
Koh, Cindy 507
Kohl, Richard 460
Kohl, Karen 807
Kohler, Kayleen 104
Kohler, Markus 525
Kohler, David 884
Kohlheim, Kevin 415
Kohli, Vimal 243
Kohli, Anna 502
Kohn, Thomas W. 761
Kohner, Jody 694
Kohr, Jeff 71
Kohring, Darlene 455
Kokate, Bhupesh 181
Kokate, Santosh 753
Kola, Nina 136
Kolakowski, Chrissy 832
Kolb, Sean 570
Kolberg, Rita 755
Kolbus, Timothy 68
Kolcum, Jeff 755
Kolcz, Crystal 307
Kolesha, Kurt 226
Kollat, David 465
Kollatz, Christoph 407
Kolli, Ashish 593
Kolluri, Rama 16
Kolsky, Shifra 247
Koltookian, Aram 783
Kolytiris, Valerie 310
Komata, Lillian 185
Komer, Rick 450
Komidar, John 792
Komine, Francine 164
Komins, Jeff 794
Kommala, Dheerendra 107
Kondap, Kedar 655
Kondrotis, Krisstie 725
Konecke, Mark 80
Kong, Debbie 634
Konings, Frank 443
Konner, Karon 504
Konort, Phil 42
Konrad, Jocelyn 681
Konstantinovsky, Irina 107
Kontowski, Kelly 685
Kontul, Dean 455
Konzen, Jerry 92
Kooda-chizek, Kristin 50
Koonce, Paul D. 254
Koons, Michael 178
Koontz, Charles 266
Koontz, Robert 341
Koontz, Dan 476
Koop, Alvin 716
Kopchinski, Richard 628
Kope, Dorothy 732
Kopelman, Donna 448
Kopfensteiner, Thomas R. 204
Kopiasz, Corey S 785
Kopil, Edward 111
Kopitsky, Christopher 787

Kundurthy, Praveen 425
Kunduru, Sree 801
Kuney, Terry 415
Kunk, James E. 414
Kunkel, Ted 103
Kunkel, Heidi 392
Kunkel, Jay K. 471
Kunkel, Thomas M. (Tom) 792
Kunneman, Dale 395
Kunst, Jeff 218
Kuntz, William 160
Kuntz, Jett 355
Kuntz, John F. 645
Kuntz, Michael J. (Mike) 801
Kunze, Shane 650
Kunzelman, Lori 492
Kuo, Jim 389
Kuo, Kevin 670
Kupbens, Bob 264
Kuper, Debra 17
Kupetz, Dan 841
Kupper, Randy 50
Kuppler, Karen 326
Kuppuswamy, Murali 388
Kurali, Andreas 620
Kurek, Robert 455
Kurey, Tammy 71
Kurian, Thomas 593
Kuritzkes, Andrew 739
Kurizaki, Sheryl 164
Kurland, Stanford L. 607
Kurn, Melanie 676
Kurnick, Robert H. 608
Kuropas, Stephen 566
Kurow, Dave 325
Kurowski, Laura 422
Kursar, Ann 835
Kurth, Keith 861
Kurtis, Wilkerson 202
Kurtov, Ines 550
Kurtz, Aaron 206
Kurtz, Ronald D 531
Kurtz, Martin 700
Kurtz, Kevin 784
Kurtz, Erin 881
Kusch, Brooke 71
Kuschel, Kurt 72
Kushel, J. Richard (Rich) 120
Kushner, Jared 678
Kuslits, Thomas R. 332
Kusmer, James 642
Kuster, Robson J. (Rob) 436
Kuster, Kristin 687
Kustor, Chris 538
Kutac, Mary-Katherine 162
Kutchera, Kris 21
Kuye, Olabisi 823
Kuykendall, Debbie 93
Kuykendall, Ronald E. 695
Kuykendall, Dorthy 734
Kuypers, Tom 111
Kuzbel, Jeffrey 148
Kuzee, Willem 613
Kuzmak, Beth 511
Kuznetsov, Sergey 170
Kuzniasz, Stacey 226
Kvadus, Glen 823
Kverneland, Hege 571
Kvernland, Hege 571
Kwan, Irene E B 97
Kwas, Courtney 535
Kwas, Richard 764

Kwasnica, Christina 245
Kwawu, Sena M 729
Kwawu, Sena 729
Kwok, John 96
Kwok, Andrew 149
Kwok, Anna 751
Kwon, Mea 328
Kwon, Oh Hyung 656
Kyff, Emilia 519
Kylberg, Richard 68
Kyle, Rex 102
Kyle, Rick 651
Kymes, Stacy C. 125
Kyre, Erik 415
Kyriakidis, Alex 500
Kyrios, Helen 174
Kyse, Julie 286

L

Laan, Ron Van Der 100
Labar, Frank 216
Labarba, Frank 855
LaBarge, Jeffrey 216
Labban, Ziad 851
Labbett, Bob 270
Laben, Nancy J. 129
Laberge, Michael 734
Labi, Abdul 798
Labian, Paula C 399
Labib, Joseph 645
Labovich, Gary D. 129
Labrador, Leslie 643
Labrie, John 828
Labrique, Steve 59
Labrosse, Derek 102
Lacaille, Rick 739
Lacey, Diane E. 548
Lachance, Margaret P. (Meg) 652
Lacher, Joseph P. (Joe) 453
Lack, Andrew R. (Andy) 197
Lacker, Jeffrey M. (Jeff) 300
Lackey, Michael 334
Lackey, Dana 584
Lackhouse, Gary 75
Lacour, Raymond 664
Lacroix, Richard 193
Lacroix, Rick 193
Lacroix, Chris 226
Lacy, Kris 323
Lacy, Spring Taylor 647
Ladas, Peter 446
Ladd, Tim 513
Ladegaard, Matt 760
Laderman, Gerald (Gerry) 811
Ladner, John 21
Ladouceur, Jacinthe 42
Ladowicz, John 586
Laduke, David 445
Laenger, William 671
Laferle, Michael 397
Lafferty, Jack 879
Laffoon, Chris 484
Lafiandra, Craig 823
Lafitte, Michael J. (Mike) 159
LaFollette, Christopher 60
Lafond, Michelle 828
Lafontant, Edouard 630
LaForgia, Felicia 832
Lafrance, Dan 461
Lafreniere, Nora E 595

Laga, Michael 865
Lagacy, Julie A. 157
Lagarde, Michel 782
LaGatta, Loreen A. 77
Lager, Jeffrey T 38
Laginess, Meredith 243
Lagioia, Andrea 194
Lagnado, Silvia 510
Lago, Virginia Del 502
Lagomarcino, Mark 637
Lagomasino, Maria 192
Lagreca, Gregory 787
Lagrone, Bart 568
Lagrow, Alli 495
Laguarta, Ramon 612
LaHaise, James A. 51
Lahey, Patricia 1
Lai, Nathan 179
Lai, John 522
Lai, King-chung 656
Lai, Raymond 751
Lai, Chackan 844
Lainchbury, David 454
Laine, Jim 322
Laing, Sheila 417
Laipple, Chad 832
Lair, David 395
Laird, Bruce 177
Laird, Tina 491
Laird, Fiona 553
Lake, Charles D. 15
Lake, Robert 243
Lake, Marianne 447
Lake, Frederick 494
Lake, Jeffrey 544
Lakhani, Shereen 535
Lalance, Rick 624
Lalime, Yvonne 139
Lalithakumar, Ananth 162
Lally, James B. 277
Lalor, Angela S. 232
Lalwani, Ellen 469
Lam, Jennifer 97
Lam, Michael 100
Lam, Samsonz 261
Lam, Margaret 407
Lam, Josiah 448
Lam, Alethea 500
Lam, Iris 552
Lam, Winnie 740
Laman, John 761
Lamanno, Lori 807
Lamar, William (Bibb) 705
Lamarche, Robert 673
Lamartina, Mike 648
Lamb, Todd 152
Lamb, Brian 307
Lamb, Gerry 348
Lamb, Scott 653
Lamb, Robert 698
Lamba, Lakhbir 628
Lambert, Michael 325
Lambert, Richard F. 647
Lambert, Jay 881
Lambeth, Tracy 530
Lamboy, Allen 183
LAMEY, KRISTEN 562
Laming, Michael S. 356
Lamkin, Bryan 7
Lamm, Kim 798
Lammers, John 83
Lammers, David 243

Lammers, Dave 243
Lammers, James 299
Lammers, Kent 371
Lamneck, Kenneth T. (Ken) 423
Lamo, Jeff 792
LaMontagna, Peter 832
Lamoreaux, Roy I 627
Lamotte, Cheri 63
Lamotte, Joseph 370
Lamparski, Jerry 27
Lampier, Carol 223
Lampley, Marcus 44
Lampman, Rusty 292
Lampman, Scott 593
Lammpann, Rich 653
Lampo, Craig A. 56
Lanahan, Judith 303
Lancaster, David 216
Lancaster, Tim 318
Lancaster, Christopher 381
Lancaster, Robert 510
Lancaster, Kim 673
Lance, Ryan M 212
Lance, Wendy 695
Lancia, Pete 655
Lanctot, Chris 152
Landa, Jon 484
Landau, Glenn R. 433
Lander, John 582
Lander, Jamie 643
Landers, Richard 146
Landers, Linda K 201
Landers, William 835
Landon, Ryan 747
Landroche, Jeff 103
Landrum, Michael 357
Landrum, Tom 564
Landry, Mark 334
Landry, Robert E. 669
Landry, Steve 711
Landry, Stephen 711
Landry, Chris 806
Landry, Cheryl 859
Landsbaum, Brad 203
Landschulz, Mark 331
Landsgard, Carson 759
Landsman, Liza K. 851
Landy, Nancy 385
Lane, Andrew H. 4
Lane, Danny 73
Lane, Esther 184
Lane, Janet 224
Lane, Brian 306
Lane, Eric S. 365
Lane, Jeffrey H. 521
Lane, Michael 673
Lane, J. Bret 704
Lane, Colin 726
Lane, Richard 754
Lanell, Jacobs 11
Lanesey, Rob 435
Laney, G. Timothy (Tim) 541
Lang, Rick 53
Lang, Robert 235
Lang, Michael (Mike) 248
Lang, Rick 325
Lang, Richard 341
Lang, Greg 458
Lang, Edward A 679
Lang, William 700
Lang, Rebecca A 806
Lang, Rebecca 807

Langan, John 204
Langan, Tom 638
Langdale, Paul 422
Langdon, Erica 519
Langdon, Lynn M 713
Lange, Wade 38
Lange, Bob De 157
Langella, Steve 153
Langen, D Bryce Bryce 651
Langenberg, Sharon 761
Langendonk, Dave 869
Langenfeld, Jon A. 684
Langenus, John 59
Langhoff, Peter 160
Langone, Elizabeth 518
Langston, Danny 240
Lanham, Don 647
Lanier, Lawrence 302
Lanier, Joe 694
Lankie, Kim 750
Lankler, Douglas M. (Doug) 616
Lankston, Kim 643
Lankton, Madelyn 792
Lanning, Justin 879
Lannon, David 870
Lansbury, Stephen 341
Lanter, Greg 323
Lantman, Chris 873
Lantos, Phyllis R. 778
Lantrip, Reese T. 279
Lantz, Tina 152
Lantzsch, Thomas P. (Tom) 425
Lanusse, Adrien 547
Lanza, Michael H. 703
Lanzer, Kris 310
Lanzetta, Keri 740
Lanzillo, Dante 681
Lanzoni, Nancy 103
Lapcevic, Misha 500
Lapierre, Steve 133
Laplant, Michael 807
LaPlante, Frank 860
Lapoint, Shelly 71
Lapoint, Aaron 249
Lapointe, Johanne 105
Lapointe, Kimberly 647
LAPOINTE, BEN 664
Lapolice, Matt 686
LaPorta, Cosimo 728
Lappala, Kris 615
LaPrade, Frank G. 148
Laprade, Ken 466
Lapriore, Ellen 593
Lapsley, Richard 698
Laramie, Jay 613
Larbalestier, Laura 617
Larch, Amy 96
Larchrid, Jim 72
Largent, Jessica 555
Larkey, Sheila 807
Larkin, Terrence B. (Terry) 471
Larkins, Thomas F. 63
Larkins, Kerry 306
Larner, Jeffrey 66
Larocca, Prue B 19
LaRocca, Andrew 550
LaRocco, Michael E. (Mike) 730
Larochelle, Steven R. 276
Larocque, Jim 249
Larocque, Brett 304
Larocque, Peter 752
LaRossa, Ralph A. 649

Laroyia, Varun 486
Larrabee, Laura 734
Larrimer, Karen L. 628
Larrimore, Randall 146
Larsen, Kenneth A. (Ken) 104
Larsen, Jill 178
Larsen, Andrea 240
Larsen, Michael M. 420
Larsen, Marshall 489
Larsen, Marshall 666
Larsen, Susan 833
Larsh, Roger 715
Larson, Kurtis 50
Larson, Jan 62
Larson, Erik 102
Larson, Gloria 132
Larson, Paul 187
Larson, Maxwell 235
Larson, Greg 366
Larson, Blake 568
Larson, Michael 587
Larson, Randy 591
Larson, Randall 591
Larson, Sherrie L 654
Larson, Todd C. 673
Larson, Roma 733
Larson, David L. 872
Larson, Kent T. 878
Larsson, Naya 506
Lartigue, Donna 670
Lasarre, Al 346
Lascari, Scott 304
Laschinger, Mary 451
Lasecki, Marilyn 500
Lash, James H. (Jim) 329
Lash, Keith 476
Lashbrook, Bill G 628
Lashier, Mark E. 170
Lashier, Mark 171
Lashley, Joseph 355
Lashmet, Craig 694
LaShoto, Kathleen 784
Laskawy, Philip 488
Lasky, Charles 329
Lasorsa, Maria 735
Laspisa, Jerry 493
Laspisa, Esther 880
Lass, John J. 343
Lassise, Noel 104
Lassiter, Margaret 120
Lassiter, Lynn 624
Latchford, Robert 818
Latella, Robert N. 309
Latham, Lara 747
Latimer, John 753
Latona, Scott 270
Latour, Michael 647
Latty, Pamela 792
Laturner, Jake 733
Lau, Timothy J. 71
Lau, Malcom 97
Lau, Cindy 149
Lau, Stephen 195
Lau, Jacky 439
Lau, Catherine 443
Lau, James 474
Lau, Elizabeth 531
Lau, Pamela 634
Laub, Jeff 142
Laubach, Lorene 760
Lauber, Ernie 233
Lauber, Scott J. 857

Laubert, Joyce 507
Lauer, Trevor F. 256
Lauer, Kelley 807
Laughbaum, John 16
Laughlin, Terence P. (Terry) 95
Laughlin, Bill 558
Laughlin, John P. 673
Launer, Justin 328
Laureano, Karen 55
Laurence, Scott 442
Lauria, Kristen 431
Laurie, Bob 88
Laurin, Sean 336
Lauritzen, Greg 781
Lauro, Carolyn 100
Lauro, Jeff 579
Laursen, Thomas E. 884
Lautmann, Max 749
Lautsch, Robert 681
Lavallee, Paul 828
Lavelle, Matt 133
Lavenberg, Stephanie 344
Lavender, Shelley K. 123
Lavender, Greg — 177
Laventure, George 647
Laver, Michael 551
Laverdi, Barb 216
Lavergne, Angelica 630
Laverne, Heather 393
Lavers, Jeffrey 3
Lavey, Bob 13
Lavey, Richard W. (Dick) 378
Lavigne, Joe 132
Lavin, John 678
Lavin, Marty 873
Lavoie, Karen 504
Lavoie, Michael 610
Lavu, Ratnakar 460
Law, Beth 96
Law, Philip 247
Law, Christina 351
Lawenda, David 841
Lawerence, John 880
Lawhead, Brian 456
Lawhon, Bob 624
Lawhon, Pres 683
Lawhorn, Alex 685
Lawhorn, Andy 787
Lawicki, Pat 542
Lawing, Douglas 458
Lawit, Jason A 566
Lawler, Robert D. (Doug) 168
Lawler, Chris 198
Lawler, Keith 381
Lawless-Munro, Terri 184
Lawlor, Denis 270
Lawlor, Kindley 776
Lawlor, Daniel 873
Lawrence, Doug 50
Lawrence, Kevin 93
Lawrence, Ralph 129
Lawrence, Tim 130
Lawrence, Steve 152
Lawrence, Jeff 225
Lawrence, Larry 270
Lawrence, Gerry 270
Lawrence, Brett 312
Lawrence, James 351
Lawrence, Ryan 446
Lawrence, Donna 474
Lawrence, Edward P. 504
Lawrence, Guy 519

Lawrence, Allison 727
Lawrence, Sherry 800
Lawrence, Brian 827
Lawrence, Ronald 839
Lawrence, Lesli 840
Lawrence-tarr, Cheryl 6
Lawrie, Loren 852
Laws, Tim 318
Laws, John 350
Laws, Dale 869
Lawshe, Pam 711
Lawson, Linda 73
Lawson, David C. (Dave) 196
Lawson, Mark 277
Lawson, Deb 389
Lawson, Scott P. 555
Lawton, Harry A. (Hal) 264
Lawton, Patrick S. (Pat) 684
Lawton, Lakeisha 798
Laxer, Richard A. (Rich) 349
Laxton, Gregory 124
Lay, Garry 13
Lay, Linda 275
Lay, Jeri 428
Laycock, Debbie 203
Layne, Glenn 624
Layne, Beverly 643
Layton, Donald H. (Don) 341
Lazar, Paula 328
Lazaridis, Nick 409
Lazarus, Mark H. 197
Lazarus, Franz E. 219
Lazenby, Donna 874
Lazzaris, Diane E. 860
Lazzati, John 713
Le, Tammy 3
Le, Hung 45
Le, Vickie-hanh 681
Leach, Andrew 28
Leach, Cliff 381
Leach, Dana 395
Leackfeldt, Stephen M. 105
Leadbeater, Seth M. 203
Leahy, John 50
Leahy, Tim 75
Leahy, Mary 126
Leal, Danny 223
Leal, Cynthia 700
Leaman, Andrew 827
Leandre, Liza 444
Leandro, Andre 681
Leanza, Chris 841
Lear, Mark 792
Leary, Alison 551
Leary, Warren 647
Leary, Mike 656
Leary, Mike 712
Leary, Michael 832
Leatherman, Janelle 41
Leavell, Christopher M. 310
Leavell, Bill E. 364
Leavenworth, Elaine R. 4
Leavitt, Todd 568
Leavy, David C. 248
Leavy, Jack 637
Lebaredian, Rev 576
Lebeau, Christina 359
Lebel, Joseph J. 581
Lebens, Lucia 542
LeBlanc, Claude L. 35
LeBlanc, Nina 163
Leblanc, Jeff 183

LeBlanc, Jeffrey 183
LeBlanc, Robert J. 431
Leblanc, Edmond 555
Leblanc, Dawn 647
Leblanc, Richard 673
Lebold, Suzanne 6
Lebowitz, Peter 444
Lebowitz, Michael 535
Lechleider, Michael 742
Lechleiter, John C. 479
Lechner, Kim 238
Leckman, Linda C. 428
LeClaire, Brian P. 411
Lecoz, Abbie 162
Ledbetter, David H. 347
Ledbetter, Barry K. 710
Leddon, Ron 705
Leddy, Kim 275
Leddy, Courtney 587
Lederman, Ira S. 112
Ledermann, Brian 92
Ledford, Randall D. 270
Ledford-Crissey, Lisa 60
Ledoux, Marque 564
Leduc, Sylvain 299
Leduc, Robert F. 666
Lee, Alan 10
Lee, Jamie 15
Lee, Daniel 40
Lee, Terrance 63
Lee, Lori M. 75
Lee, Alison 98
Lee, Mona 120
Lee, Ned 139
Lee, Sherry 143
Lee, Diane 149
Lee, Jeff 149
Lee, Josephine 171
Lee, Emmelene 179
Lee, Dennis 181
Lee, Melinda 218
Lee, Eugene I. (Gene) 234
Lee, Shreve 242
Lee, John M. 261
Lee, Jay 264
Lee, Bruce 291
Lee, Virginia 315
Lee, Helen 328
Lee, Thomas 341
Lee, Alice 352
Lee, E Chadwick 355
Lee, William A. 360
Lee, Bonita I. (Bonnie) 377
Lee, Nancy 377
Lee, Yusin 377
Lee, Mike 378
Lee, Bruce K. 384
Lee, Lisa 401
Lee, Eric 401
Lee, Sam 431
Lee, Michele 443
Lee, Charlotte 450
Lee, Yong 455
Lee, Al 476
Lee, Melanie 488
Lee, Lara L. 489
Lee, David 492
Lee, Peter 495
Lee, Nancy 500
Lee, Natasha 502
Lee, Thomas H. 503
Lee, Esther 518

Lee, Rachel 519
Lee, Anne 531
Lee, Jeff 550
Lee, Todd 571
Lee, Julien 610
Lee, Patrick 610
Lee, Jeff 647
Lee, Pearl 653
Lee, Chip 664
Lee, Shiuh 670
Lee, Scott 677
Lee, Jonathan 698
Lee, Jeffery (Jeff) 701
Lee, Schavrien 704
Lee, Crystal 705
Lee, Thai 708
Lee, Tom 724
Lee, Gregory 755
Lee, William 778
Lee, Peter 781
Lee, Tracy 811
Lee, David 818
Lee, Sang 844
Lee, Pat 845
Lee, Paul 852
Leech, Wilson 565
Leedom, David W. 517
Lees, Susan L. 27
Lefeber, Marilyn Stein 538
Lefebvre, Denise 613
Leff, Mike 76
Lefferson, C. Douglas (Doug) 318
Lefkowitz, David 484
LeFort, Alan 425
Leganza, Nannette 347
Legere, John J. 757
Legge, Jeffrey D. (Jeff) 185
Legge, Jeff 185
Leggett, Robert 365
Leggett, Pat 433
Leggio, John 576
Legin, Joel 88
Lego, Catherine 470
Legrand, Thomas 48
Legrand, Joseph 759
Legters, Robert 305
Lehman, Daniel 150
Lehman, Gary 324
Lehman, Laura 360
Lehman, Jeffrey S. 551
Lehman, Karen 647
Lehman, Jay 787
Lehmann, Hans 17
Lehmann, Mary 55
Lehmann, Jonathan 747
Lehner, Jon 739
Lehrer, Ronald 549
Leib, Mallory 366
Leibman, Maya 37
Leibman, Christopher 118
Leibow, Steve 653
Leibowitz, Elliot 103
Leibson, Marie 721
Leidesdorf, William 418
Leidwinger, Kevin 187
Leigh, Howard 500
Leigh, Stacey 685
Leighton, Russell 423
Leighton, John 629
Leijssenaar, Jacques 811
Leinenbach, Keith A. 359
Leinroth, Peter 434

Leipzig, Inna 784
Leisen, Tammy 742
Leisen, John 760
Leish, Becca 588
Leisle, Dan 303
Leissring, Kevin 415
Leisten, Hillary 849
Leitch, Kari 33
Leitch, Glenn R. 404
Leite, Adriana 195
Leithauser, Jeffrey 307
Lekberg, Roger 881
Lelah, Larry 75
Leland, Todd 365
Leland, Rich 582
Lelonek, Susan 415
Lemann, Jorge 462
Lemberger, Michael 844
Lembo, Philip J. (Phil) 282
Lembo, Phillip 282
Lemchak, Joseph J. 206
Lemelin, Tracey 481
Lemert, Jennifer 303
Lemire, Anne 47
Lemire, James R 204
Lemire, John 481
Lemkau, Gregg R. 365
Lemke, Kevin 24
Lemke, Jude 218
Lemke, James P. (Jim) 686
Lemke, Beth 814
Lemly, Chris 140
Lemmer, Jeff 339
Lemmer, Peter 371
Lemmerman, Bryan 168
Lemmon, David J. 715
Lemon, Paulette 399
Lemonius, John 42
Lemons, Cynthia 162
Lemson, Steve 42
Lenahan, Kelly 120
Lenahan, Dennis 489
Lenard, Courtney 732
Lenckos, John 96
Lengel, John 291
Lenhardt, David 156
Lenhart, Tom 495
Lenhart, Chris 832
Lenkevich, Ellen 11
Lenna, Robert 495
Lenner, Marc 836
Lennie, William G. (Bill) 397
Lennon, Peter 305
Lennon, William P 348
Lensing, Steve 662
Lentz, Rick 564
Lenz, Rob 55
Lenz, Denise 661
Leo, Sheri 344
Leo, Bruno V. Di 431
Leo, Koguan 708
Leon, Sonny 73
Leon, Heidi Null 428
Leon, Mercedes M 550
Leon, Lori De 749
Leon, Regan 832
Leonard, David E. (Dave) 25
Leonard, Jonathan 192
Leonard, Joeseph 299
Leonard, Tim 302
Leonard, James C. 307
Leonard, Dennis 350

Leonard, William 613
Leonard, Shanon 770
Leonard, Robert M. 799
Leonard, Gayle 825
Leonardi, Mark 610
Leonardis, Jim 112
Leondakis, Mia 846
Leone, Anthony 337
Leone, Roger E. 749
Leong, Jamie 298
Leonti, Joseph R. 602
Leopold, Diane G. 254
Lepak, Kathleen 610
LePenske, Amy 493
Lepera, Bob 571
LeProhon, Scott 355
Leptich, Stephen 757
Lequin, Stan 423
Lerman, Jason 593
Lerner, Arnold S. 276
Lerner, Richard 365
Lerner, Mark 825
Lerose, Frank 302
Lesar, David J. (Dave) 375
Lescure, John 609
Leshe, Lynn 100
Leshovsky, Dave 81
Lesiak, Peg 381
Lesieur, David 792
Lesjak, Catherine A. (Cathie) 409
Lesko, Dirk 348
Leskowitz, Mark 40
Leslie, Claudia 100
Leslie, Dara 198
Leslie, Naomi 365
Leslie, Andy 800
Lessaris, Thomas 756
Lesser, Brian 75
Lessing, Brent 388
Lessmann, Russ 422
Lestourgeon, Paul 174
Leszek, Andrea 694
Letcher, Denise 629
Lete, Laura 476
LeTexier, Matthew 355
Leto, Francis J. 139
Letoumeau, Jerry 203
Lettman, Mike 731
Letts, Shannon 851
Leuhmann, John 415
Leung, Sandra 135
Leung, Juo 164
Leung, Samuel 635
Leung, David 745
Levar, Mary E 684
Levasseur, Dennis B 139
Leveille, Tim D. 170
Leveille, Mark 200
Levenick, Stuart 275
Levenick, Stuart 369
Levenson, Susan 500
Levenson, Michelle 695
Levenson, Rodger 876
Leverett, Allen L. 857
Levey, Caryn 72
Levi, Joseph 754
Levielle, Eric 355
Levin, Greg 120
Levin, Bob 519
Levin, Alan G 617
Levine, Jonathan M. 112
Levine, Jeff 365

Little, Daniel 669
Little, Brad 732
Little, Jon 852
Little, James 855
Little, Sean 873
Littlefair, Andrew 391
Littlefield, Mark D 292
Littlefield, Jerod 302
Littleford, Frankie 442
Littler, Greg 819
Litton, Byran 6
Litton, Jerry 174
Littrell, Wesley 207
Littzi, John 112
Litwin, Barry 832
Litzinger, Ronald L. 267
Liu, Chang 92
Liu, Yanfang 136
Liu, Stanley 149
Liu, Manni 261
Liu, Kelly 302
Liu, Chang 531
Liu, Jeffrey 616
Liu, Don H. 759
Lively, Kelly 503
Lively, Scott 834
Liverett, Deborah 566
Liveris, Andrew N. 259
Livermore, Karen 316
Livesay, Bruce A. 322
Livingston, John T. 12
Livingston, Wendy 124
Livingston, Nathan 240
Livingston, Robert A. (Bob) 255
Livingston, Julie 357
Livingston, Randall S. (Randy) 474
Livingston, Scott 571
Livingston, Wyvetter 651
Livingston, Kathleen 653
Livingston, Joseph 733
Livingstone, Jennifer 187
Livne, Omer 425
Lizardi, Rafael R. 770
Lizardi, Lizette 837
Lizarraga, Michelle 522
Lizarrago, Lisa 426
Lizhong, Yu 551
Llaca, Angie 672
Llanes, Raul 103
LLC, Wyoming Acquisition GP 667
Llopart, Fernando 270
Llope, Richard 418
Lloyd, Gary 10
Lloyd, Scott 235
Lloyd, Dave 355
Lloyd, Steve 361
Lloyd, Don 361
Lloyd, Jack 384
Lo, Winny 635
Lobins, Christine 869
Lobo, Kevin A. 747
Loch, Jeff 751
Lochen, Richard S. 612
Locher, Vince 795
Lochner, David 415
Lochocki, Sharon 456
Lock, Kendall 431
Lock, Jim 571
Lockard, Jacob 503
Locke, Pat 42
Locke, Cory 389
Locker, David 423

Locker, Brad 484
Lockery, Michael 148
Lockhart, Gerald 52
Lockhart, Andy 177
Lockhart, Dennis P. 300
Locklear, Samuel 334
Lockwood, Kenneth 258
Loconsolo, Mike 179
Lodder, Dan 511
Loder, Greg 647
Loeber, Gary 229
Loeffler, Martin H. 56
Loeffler, Nancy 723
Loeger, Julie A. 247
Loehr, Steve 431
Loewald, Thomas W. (Tom) 781
Lofland, Irene G 237
Lofrumento, Michael 799
Loftin, Paul J. 675
Loftis, William 174
Lofton, Kevin E. 204
Logan, Jonathan B. 190
Logan, Jason 200
Logan, Erik 248
Logan, Stephanie 315
Logan, John 584
Logan, Brendan 593
Logan, Timothy 602
Logan, John 790
Loge, Jim 270
Logiudice, Salvatore 778
Logothetis, Peter 27
Logoyda, Steve 503
Logsdon, John 292
Logsdon, David 854
Logue, Greg 57
Logue, Joseph (Joe) 129
Loh, Evan 617
Loh, Gordon 617
Lohman, Wendy 780
Lohmar, Rachel 124
Lohmeier, Michelle J. 725
Lohmeyer, Mark 846
Lohrer, Joe 121
Loiacono, Jim 698
Loiseau, Sharon 120
Lokay, Jon 694
Lomas, Terry 96
Lomas, Todd 530
Lomax, Manning 355
Lombardi, Anthony 57
Lombardi, Todd 243
Lombardi, Leonard V. 316
Lombardi, Len 316
Lombardi, Bill 380
Lombardo, Monica 431
Lombardo, Chad 755
Lomboy, Sheila 326
Lomeli, Bernardo 779
Loncar, Patrick 299
London, Qiana 670
London, Adam 841
Lonegro, Frank A. 222
Lonergan, Robert A. 74
Loney, Andrew 22
Long, Ann 5
Long, Michael J. (Mike) 68
Long, Steve 121
Long, William 126
Long, Suzette M. 157
Long, Tony 159
Long, Rodney 162

Long, Jeffrey R. 219
Long, Brett 226
Long, Brett V 226
Long, Thomas E. (Tom) 273
Long, James 643
Long, Deborah J. 644
Long, Michael 645
Long, Ellie 671
Long, Mike 677
Long, Ross 683
Long, Thomas 748
Long, Andy 781
Long, Mike 834
Long, Susan 851
Long, Mark P. 864
Longe, Thomas 396
Longenecker, Thomas 595
Longhofer, T. Luke 319
Longhurst, Sherri 428
Longman, Chris 656
Longmier, Mark 238
Longmore, Mike 446
Longo, Jeffrey 792
Longo, Robert 855
Longo, Christie 871
Longobardi, Sara M. 609
Longood, Ross 154
Longshore, Rob 80
Lonkar, Prashant 500
Lonsk, Seth 365
Look, Chuck 177
Loomis, Timothy 656
Loomis, Nate 879
Looney, Stephen 273
Loparco, Michael J. 439
Loparrino, Rosemarie 103
Loper, D. Shane 376
Loper, Cobie 571
Lopes, Brian 695
Lopez, John 26
Lopez, Christian 28
Lopez, Angela 89
Lopez, Emilia 148
Lopez, Gabby 179
Lopez, Samuel 224
Lopez, Randolph 448
Lopez, Patricia 457
Lopez, Tom 461
Lopez, Norma 600
Lopez, Virgilio 610
Lopez, Lincoln 757
Lopez, Lalit 823
Lopez, Frank 825
Lopez, Ignacio 851
Lopez, Eddie 855
Lopez, Rene 876
Lopez-Hodoyan, Mauricio 655
Loppatto, Gregory 818
Lorbeck, Jeff 655
Lorberbaum, Jeffrey S. 529
Lord, Pat 470
Lord, Jack 643
Lord, Ellen 771
Lore, Marc 850
Loree, James M. (Jim) 727
Loree, James 869
Lorence, Laurie 383
Lorenson, Donna 444
Lorenson, Katie A. 527
Lorent, Patrick 610
Lorentson, Jeff 323
Lorentson, Jeffery B. 323

Lorentson, Jeffrey 323
Lorenz, Donald 100
Lorenz, Franz 162
Lorenzen, Jeffrey D. (Jeff) 41
Lorenzen, Angela 870
Lorenzo, Alejandro R. 533
Lores, Enrique 409
Loretta, Judy 832
Lorge, Timothy J. (Tim) 221
Lori, William E. 459
Lori, Michael 831
Lorsson, Devin 467
Lortz, Andre 166
Losacco, Vinicius 547
Losch, William C. (BJ) 322
Losenegger, Michael J. 314
Losik, Dennis 87
Loskove, Daniel 751
Lostaglio, Anthony 431
Lotte, Evelina 100
Lotvin, Alan M. 229
Lotzer, John 72
Loucks, Andrew 451
Loudermilk, Robert 355
Loughridge, Jerome 736
Louie, Kevin 182
Louie, Michael 360
Louis, David 316
Louis, Patrice 873
Loukotka, Jonathan 671
Lounsbury, Chuck 689
Louton, Beth 825
Love, Talvis 152
Love, Kelli 152
Love, Marcella 170
Love, Judith S. 200
Love, Joe 319
Love, Kim 643
Love, Zachary 825
Love, George 879
Lovejoy, Madeline 303
Lovejoy, William 608
Lovelace, John 829
Lovelady, Julie 733
Lovely, Dave 818
Lovins, Gregory S. (Greg) 85
Lovrien, Phyllis 685
Lovvorn, Lindsay 487
Low, Sylvia 580
Lowden, Cynthia 74
Lowden, Simon 612
Lowe, Heather 6
Lowe, Meg 248
Lowe, Rich 382
Lowe, John 382
Lowe, Chad 415
Lowe, Bill 484
Lowe, Wendy 535
Lowe, Edward A. (Sandy) 580
Lowe, Michael 664
Lowenfeld, Ed 472
Lower, Joseph T. (Joe) 582
Lowery, Richard M. 112
Lowery, Jason 154
Lowery, Norman D. 320
Lowery, Peter 701
Lowery, Joseph M 753
Lowery, Frederick M. (Fred) 781
Lowery, Kelli 823
Lowman, Amy 46
Lowman, David B. (Dave) 341
Lowman, Eric 798

Macmillan, Kevin 875
Macnee, Walt W. 506
Maco, Marylou 177
Macon, Mary 302
Macon, James 504
Macpherson, Donald G. (D.G.) 369
MacQuarrie, Dennis 229
MacQuillan, Sandra J. 457
Macrae, Bruce 229
Macrae, Steve 793
Macri, Joe 525
Macrie, Sari 27
Macrillo, Sam 179
MacRitchie, John 601
Macwilliams, Robert 13
Macy, Mike 114
Macy, David 271
Madabhushi, Venkata 632
Madalin, Diane 223
Madaya, Jeanette 871
Madden, John F. 92
Madden, James 672
Maddie, John 303
Maddock, Dennis 439
Maddock, Ernest E. (Ernie) 523
Maddox, Willie A 344
Maddox, Willie 344
Maddux, Susan 823
Madeira, Harry R. 139
Mader, Anthony 60
Madera, Melvin 835
Madgey, William 876
Madi, Dani 456
Madia, William 474
Madia, Bill 474
Madigan, Kevin 543
Madigan, Deborah 628
Madigan, Kevin 707
Madineedi, Gautam 784
Madison, Delbert 705
Madonna, John 234
Madra, Sundeep 339
Madrid, Bethany 409
Madsen, C. Fred 112
Madsen, C 112
Madsen, Laurie 136
Madsen, Canen 196
Madsen, Tammy 428
Madsen, Eric 852
Madsen, Mark 854
Maduri, John 343
Maes, Phil 130
Maes, Betty 202
Maes, Daniel 835
Maestas, Karen 13
Maestas, Samantha 304
Maestri, Luca 62
Maestri, Jackie 444
Maffei, Gregory B. (Greg) 484
Maffei, Frank 550
Maffei, Gregory B. (Greg) 660
Maffei, Gregory B. (Greg) 712
Maffeo, Vincent A. (Vince) 472
Maffeo, Tracey 588
Maffettone, Biagio 183
Magann, Rita 42
Magats, Jim 604
Magazachi, Wissam 42
Magendantz, Chris 792
Mager, Bruce 142
Maggelet, Crystal Call 166
Maggio, Michael 443

Maggs, Michelle 434
Maggs, Thomas O. 799
Magid, Larry 685
Magill, M. Elizabeth 474
Magistro, Luca 28
Maglaque, Neal 50
Magleby, Curt 339
Magley, Geoffrey 751
Magnuson, Michele 403
Magnusson, Peter S. 593
Mago, Vikram 182
Mago, Angela G. 455
Magrini, Joyce Manning 142
Maguire, William 275
Maguire, Tim 328
Maguire, Bevin 431
Maguire, Tommy 698
Mahabadi, Hadi 879
Mahadevan, Rohan 604
Mahaffee, Joseph W. (Joe) 129
Mahajan, Umesh 846
Mahan, Chip 485
Mahan, James 485
Maharajan, Suthakar 80
Maher, Helen 286
Maher, Lee A. 355
Maher, Christopher D. 581
Maher, Sean 672
Maher, Joshua 681
Maher, Nancy 784
Maher, Steve 803
Maher, Mark 841
Mahlen, Jennifer 326
Mahler, Jason 593
Mahler, William W. (Bill) 684
Mahlich, Ben 372
Mahon, James 299
Mahoney, Ryan 12
Mahoney, Michael 107
Mahoney, Michael F. (Mike) 133
Mahoney, John 142
Mahoney, Dennis 171
Mahoney, Jon 179
Mahoney, Timothy O. (Tim) 400
Mahoney, Adeline 434
Mahoney, Brendan 492
Mahoney, Eileen 653
Mahoney, Tom 664
Mahoney, Kathie 712
Mahoney, Kathleen M. (Kathy) 724
Mahony, Colin 389
Mahony, Susan (Sue) 479
Mahtaney, Andrew 149
Maier, Al 270
Maier, Henry J. 302
Maier, Richard 476
Maier, Michael 713
Main, Richard W. (Dick) 276
Main, Timothy L. (Tim) 439
Main, Angela 883
Maio, Mike 100
Maio, Keith D. 884
Maiorana, Michael 837
Mair, Nancy 142
Maiuri, Lou 739
Majeski, Carl 27
Majewski, Jim 787
Majka, Don 855
Majon, Judy 872
Majoo, Sanjeev 136
Major, Paul 50

Major, Jason 571
Majors, Teresa 10
Majors, Charles H. (Charlie) 46
Majors, Michael C. 364
Majors, Janice 731
Majumdar, Anurita 479
Majzoub, Jason 13
Mak, Derek 177
Makhijani, Dimple 751
Makhulo, Linus 518
Maki, Jamey 83
Makower, Alissa 841
Makowski, John 160
Makowski, Carla 374
Makris, George A. 710
Malaeb, Rabih 160
Malat, Scott B. 881
Malatesta, Brandy 733
Malazo, Joe 695
Malcolm, Gregory 195
Malcolm, Mark 348
Malcolm, Steven J 870
Maldonado, Diana 220
Maldonado, R. Danny 771
Male, Timothy 222
Malekkhosravi, Benny 656
Maley, Ernie 329
Maley, David 460
Malhotra, Raghu 506
Malik, Abinta 776
Malin, Mike 560
Malizia, Vince 350
Mallard, Ty 54
Mallard, Ben 413
Malley, Chris 740
Malliwal, Mahendra 426
Mallon, Ed 120
Mallory, Don 125
Malloy, Luke 50
Malloy, Demetria 60
Malloy, John P. (Jack) 538
Malloy, Marie 734
Malone, Mary 146
Malone, Kevin 248
Malone, Alicia 302
Malone, Jessica 344
Malone, Robert W. 602
Malone, Rob 602
Malone, John C. 660
Malone, Mike 684
Maloney, Dan 28
Maloney, Robert 96
Maloney, Michael 112
Maloney, Mike 181
Maloney, Deiken 566
Malpeli, Laurent 694
Malsch, Benjamin 527
Maltsbarger, Richard D. 489
Maltz, Richard B. 105
Malugen, William C 792
Maly, Mark 566
Malzahn, Daniel D. 577
Mamerow, Steve 625
Mammadov, Emin 461
Mampetta, Anoop 225
Manahan, Thomas J. (Tom) 801
Manahan-smith, Suzanne 289
Manazir, Mike 124
Manbeck, Keith 870
Manby, Jeff 460
Manchandra, Anita 647
Manchester, Paula 234

Manchester, Eric 463
Mancini, Michael 18
Mancini, Robert 98
Mancini, Kathie 531
Mancini, Joseph 880
Mancl, Dave 431
Mancuso, Sabrina 583
Mandable, Terence 130
Mandala, Rocco 159
Mandapaty, Shashi 443
Mandel, Joseph G. 441
Mandel, Carol A. 551
Mandelli, Maela 653
Manderscheid, David 500
Mandir, Amber 92
Mandon, Daniel 556
Mandraccia, Crocifissa 66
Mandre, Vinod 629
Mandrell, Matthew 344
Mandry, Kyle 844
Manelis, Tatyana 77
Maner, Jonathan 794
Maness, Barry 798
Maney, Kristy 559
Manfredonia, Donald L. 327
Mang, Mark 433
Mangan, John 710
Manganaro, Lynn 649
Manganaro, Mike 740
Mangiaracina, Brian 53
Manginelli, John 456
Mangini, Charles 460
Mango, John 316
Mangrum, Thomas 302
Mangrum, Rick 851
Mangu, Anand 681
Mangum, Jesse 446
Manheimer, Mark L 726
Maniaci, Nick 80
Manire, Ross 57
Maniscalco, Michael 700
Manley, Joe 204
Manley, Kathy 788
Mann, Sara 201
Mann, Bob 543
Mann, Natalie 672
Manna, Heidi 146
Mannai, David 649
Mannan, Sabra 42
Mannarino, Frank A. 727
Manning, Joseph (Joe) 4
Manning, Karen 100
Manning, Joyce 142
Manning, Carolyn 474
Manning, Anna 673
Manning, Peter 692
Manning, Ben 797
Manning, Christie 814
Mannion, Melissa 303
Mannix, Sarah 807
Manno, Federico 344
Manolovic, Michelle 229
Manry, Al 676
Manseau, James J. 246
Mansell, Kevin B. 460
Manser, Marlene 465
Mansfield, Bob 62
Mansfield, William P. 370
Mansuetti, Mike 683
Mansur, Carla 456
Mantilla, Julio 784
Mantua, Philip J. 695

Mcgeorge, Scott 711
Mcgeough, Paul 304
McGettrick, Mark F. 254
Mcgill, Dean 50
Mcgill, Tom 131
Mcgill, Terrance 278
Mcgill, Donald 307
McGill, Bradley 446
McGill, Daniel K. (Dan) 611
Mcgillicuddy, Sherry 224
McGinn, Denise 443
McGinn, Mickey 467
Mcginn, Tammy 481
Mcginness, Shannon 81
McGinnis, Donna 258
McGinnis, John T. (Jack) 496
McGinnis, Jeffrey S. (Jeff) 819
Mcginty, Mark 558
McGinty-polito, Janice 431
McGivney, Mark C. 502
McGlenon, Andrew 831
McGlothin, Randy 664
Mcglynn, Pam 292
McGough, Thomas M. (Tom) 211
McGough, W. Thomas (Tom) 829
Mcgovern, Gail 265
McGovern, Lawrence D. 385
McGowan, Tim 80
Mcgowan, Patt 139
Mcgowan, Bill 315
McGowan, David 316
McGowan, Chris 596
McGowen, Lonnie 707
McGranahan, Devin B. 330
McGrane, Brian N 50
McGrath, Marlene 3
McGrath, Helen 76
McGrath, Robert L. (Bob) 333
McGrath, John 399
Mcgrath, Elizabeth 504
Mcgrath, Caroline 507
Mcgrath, Kathy 511
Mcgrath, Mark 558
McGrath, Ted 682
Mcgrath, Brian 685
Mcgrath, Dennis 728
McGrath, Mike 784
McGraw, Deirdre D. 50
McGraw, E. Robinson (Robin) 676
McGraw, Donald F. (Don) 773
Mcgreevy, David 316
Mcgregor, Thomas 103
Mcgregor, Laura 144
McGregor, Gaylyn 202
Mcgregor, Mark 378
McGregor, Sharon 582
McGrew, Michael 216
Mcgrogan, Kate 535
McGrory, Kevin 647
Mcgruder, Jeffery 624
McGuff, Greg 476
McGuffin, Colleen 152
McGuigan, Gary 66
McGuigan, Charles C. (Charlie) 465
Mcguinness, Bernard 192
McGuinness, Richard 694
Mcguire, Chris 12
McGuire, Jim 76
McGuire, Michael 229
Mcguire, David 503
Mcguire, Toretha 535

McGuire, Jim 700
McGurk, Monica 803
McGurn, David 346
McHaffie, Sherry 624
Mchenry, Yvonne 818
McHugh, Philip R. 307
Mchugh, Joe 613
Mchugh, Mark 664
Mchugh, Mary 880
McHutchison, John G. 360
Mcilwain, Eric 506
McInerney, Thomas J. (Tom) 356
Mcinerney, Matt 686
McInerney, Ryan 844
McInnis, Joanne 828
Mcintosh, Ellen 107
McIntosh, Robert B. (Bob) 867
McIntyre, Bonnie 369
Mcintyre, Andrew 670
Mciver, William 105
Mciver, Tim 222
Mckalvey, Steve 489
McKay, Erik 201
Mckay, Gerald 202
McKay, John D. 219
Mckay, Jennifer 226
McKay, Scott J. 356
McKay, John 520
McKay, Susan 675
McKeag, Bryan R. 384
McKean, David 543
McKeand, Kevin 76
McKee, Lynn B. 64
Mckee, John 200
Mckee, Marie 258
Mckee, Austin 258
McKee, Daniel J 736
Mckee, Sue 751
Mckeen, P Douglas 811
Mckellar, Neil 627
McKemie, Karen 717
McKenna, Judith 851
McKenney, Josh 323
McKenney, Richard P. (Rick) 828
McKenzie, Paul 118
Mckenzie, Mark 120
Mckenzie, Vanessa 270
Mckenzie, Gary 484
Mckenzie, Mark 535
Mckenzie, Dan 560
Mckenzie, Laurel 624
McKenzie, Barbara A. (Barb) 637
McKenzie, A Kirk 731
McKeon, Brian M. 129
Mckeon, Timothy 375
Mckeon, Michael 695
McKeough, Kathleen E 853
McKeown, Ann M. 692
Mckeown, Brian 832
McKernan, John 131
Mckernan, Chris 314
Mckernan, William 510
Mckibbin, Frederick 184
Mckibbin, Karen S. 562
McKiernan, Anthony 509
McKillip, Dean 192
McKim, Anoopa 307
McKim, Tony C. 312
McKinley, Gordon 200
McKinley, David C. (Dave) 698
Mckinney, Robert 40
McKinney, Greg 102

McKinney, Deborah 135
Mckinney, David 174
McKinney, James J. 453
Mckinney, Steve 463
McKinney, Michelle 656
McKinney, Rex D. 705
McKinney, Ivy 879
McKinnon, Paul 183
Mckinnon, Murray 443
McKinnon, Martha 670
McKinnon, Lee 705
Mckissack, John 11
Mckissic, Edward 851
Mcknight, Gary 223
Mcknight, Erin 488
McKnight, Jodi 858
Mckown, David 362
McKoy, Margot 125
Mckuin, John 413
Mclain, Dean 760
McLaren, William 481
McLaren, David 555
Mclarry, Mary 722
Mclauchlin, Chris 271
Mclaughlin, Walter 104
Mclaughlin, Joshua 135
McLaughlin, Robert 139
Mclaughlin, James 183
Mclaughlin, Mary 198
McLaughlin, Lynn 202
McLaughlin, Sean J. 281
McLaughlin, R 309
Mclaughlin, Carl 341
Mclaughlin, Linda 369
McLaughlin, Kellie 443
McLaughlin, Edward (Ed) 506
McLaughlin, David W. 551
McLaughlin, Michael 627
Mclaughlin, Sean 647
McLaughlin, Randall 685
McLaughlin, Neal T. 808
McLaughlin, Kathleen 851
Mclaurim, Greg 411
Mclean, Scott 163
McLean, Catherine 732
McLean, Graham A. 747
Mclean, John 787
McLean, Scott J. 884
McLellan, Heather 435
Mclelland, Alistair 17
McLelland, Dave 328
McLemore, Mary 610
Mclemore, Heidi 684
Mclennan, Kevin 160
McLevish, Timothy 154
Mcloughlin, Karen 116
McLoughlin, Karen 193
Mcmachen, Timothy 610
McMahon, John 68
Mcmahon, Andrea 303
McMahon, Michael 613
McMahon, Brian 617
Mcmannus, Connie 283
McManus, John M. 522
McManus, Paul 798
McMaster, Henry Dargan 737
McMaster, Henry 737
Mcmaster, Kevin 787
McMenamin, William V. 543
Mcmichael, David 518
McMichael, Sharon 798
Mcmichael, Steve 818

Mcmillan, Carrie 315
McMillan, Marilyn A. 551
McMillan, Steve 593
Mcmillan, Rob 749
Mcmillen, Ruth Ann 871
Mcmillen-gore, Sarah 367
McMillon, C. Douglas (Doug) 850
McMonagle, Richard 769
McMullen, W. Rodney 463
Mcmullen, Sandy 839
Mcmurran, Carol 292
Mcmurray, Darin 476
McMurray, Michael C. 597
McMurray, Sean 861
Mcmurry, Fred 312
McMurtrie, M Todd 355
McNab, Paul 177
Mcnair, Brian 174
Mcnally, Sean 152
Mcnally, Michael 177
Mcnally, Maureen 328
McNally, Gerry 443
Mcnally, David 694
Mcnally, Brennan 823
McNamara, Stephen 75
McNamara, Jim 308
McNamara, Daniel R. (Dan) 425
Mcnamara, Michael 507
McNamara, John H 648
McNamara, Michael E. (Mike) 759
McNamee, Brian M. 54
Mcnamee, Joseph 184
McNamee, Sean 302
Mcnamee, Sean S 302
McNary, Kelli 784
Mcnealis, Anne 449
Mcnearney, Ryan 745
McNeely, Joseph E. 57
McNeil, Dan 124
Mcneil, Kurt 353
McNeil, Michelle 609
Mcneil, Kim D 628
McNeil, Caroline 731
Mcneill, Bryan 839
McNeme, Lisa 873
Mcnicholas, Brian 883
Mcnichols, William 728
McNichols, Bill 729
McNiff, Greg 23
Mcnorton, Terri 126
McNulty, Kelly 59
McNulty, Pauline 443
McNulty, Dave 471
Mcpadden, Laura 556
McParland, Jeffrey 258
McParland, Jeffrey J. (Jeff) 758
Mcpartland, Gerry 103
McPartland, James E. (Bo) 364
McPeek, Steven D. 804
Mcphail, Kennth 179
McPhaill, Kevin J. 708
McPherson, Robert 112
Mcpherson, Julie 129
McPherson, Scott E. 217
McPherson, John 222
Mcpherson, Kevin J 302
Mcpherson, Kevin 302
McPherson, Amy C. 500
McQuade, Daniel P. 12
McQuade, Mark A 785
McQueen, Jason 93
Mcqueeney, David 431

Montone, John 381
Montoya, Jessica 88
Montoya, Isabel 319
Montoya, Valerie 425
Montoya, Luis 612
Montpetit, David 755
Montri, Michael 608
Montrie, James 593
Montross, Fred 511
Montz, Renee D. 41
Monusky, Gerard 86
Monz--n, Gilberto F. 630
Moo, Jason 365
Mooar, Tara 837
Moodey, J. Tucker 286
Moodie, Rebecca 806
Moody, Patrick 183
Moody, Todd 304
Moody, Sue 761
Mooijman, Yannick 818
Moon, George 3
Moon, Eric 182
Moon, Dallas 460
Moon, Doug 818
Moon, Edward 871
Mooney, Jim 87
Mooney, Niall 203
Mooney, Randy 230
Mooney, Howard F. 313
Mooney, Kathleen 322
Mooney, Beth E. 455
Mooney, Dennis denny 543
Mooney, Brandon 629
Mooney, Stephen M. (Steve) 762
Moonves, Leslie (Les) 840
Moor, Bill 147
Moore, Steven 1
Moore, Pennie 10
Moore, Jocelyn 37
Moore, Scott 39
Moore, Colin 50
Moore, Andrew 54
Moore, Patrick 66
Moore, Kevin 75
Moore, Thomas 77
Moore, John 100
Moore, Bob 102
Moore, Steve 130
Moore, Kevin 150
Moore, Becky 150
Moore, Annah 160
Moore, Christine 200
Moore, Michael 206
Moore, Elizabeth D. 214
Moore, Peter 216
Moore, Cindy 225
Moore, Tonya 234
Moore, Steve 270
Moore, Terry 293
Moore, Paul 307
Moore, Richard H. 311
Moore, Kelly 347
Moore, Nicholas G 360
Moore, Christopher 364
Moore, A. Bruce 382
Moore, Robert 388
Moore, Jessica 391
Moore, Mikelle 428
Moore, Patrick 434
Moore, Brad 444
Moore, Brian 458
Moore, Jimmy 487

Moore, Andrew 511
Moore, Troy 517
Moore, Frederick V. (Fred) 517
Moore, Dinah 519
Moore, Gregory 525
Moore, Lorena 531
Moore, Joe 570
Moore, Daryl D. 583
Moore, Gary L 598
Moore, Greg 613
Moore, Clara 635
Moore, Karen Oliver 647
Moore, Patrick 690
Moore, Christopher 694
Moore, Justin 711
Moore, Adam 733
Moore, Cynthia 738
Moore, Thomas 745
Moore, Robert 751
Moore, Christine 767
Moore, Jason 788
Moore, Kimberly E 797
Moore, Jason 812
Moore, Scott 839
Moore, Michael S. (Mike) 851
Moore, Katie 873
Moorehead, Michael 871
Moorehouse, David 225
Moorer, Susan 465
Moorjani, Shail 148
Moorman, Charles 258
Moquin, Kelli 303
Moquist, Darren C 823
Mora, Diego 120
Morabito, Leonardo 615
Moraci, Pj 825
Morack, Sarah J 371
Moraes, Roberto 192
Morais, Diane E 28
Morais, Diane 29
Moral-Niles, Christopher J. Del 71
Morales, Wendy 96
Morales, Elisa 350
Morales, Jimmy 512
Morales, Daniel 608
Morales, Olga 630
Morales, Vincent J. 631
Morales, Howie 735
Morales-jaffe, Marcia 875
Moran, Patrick 3
Moran, Patrick 14
Moran, Rob 15
Moran, Edward 50
Moran, Michael 159
Moran, Jim 255
Moran, James 255
Moran, Karina 401
Moran, Tim 484
Moran, Gavin 566
Moran, Sheila 610
Moran, Jeff 651
Moran, Tim 710
Moran, Nancy 792
Moran, Julie 794
Morano, Susan 444
Morante, Tony 628
Morar, August 552
Morasutti, Joseph 229
Morazzani, Christina 640
Morbi, Farzana 366
Morchak, Chris 774
Morche, Ed 490

Morde, Vishal 106
More, Debrah 797
Moreau, Maxine L. 490
Morehead, Bruce 196
Morehead, Shawn V 550
Morel, Robert 751
Moreland, Mary 5
Moreland, Jeffrey 122
Morelli, Kris 254
Morency, Herbert 26
Moreno, Raul E. 16
Moreno, Elisabeth 409
Morera, Santiago 409
Moresco, Matt 678
Moreth, Cary 420
Morey, Debbie 755
Morford, Craig S. 152
Morford, Gerry 204
Morgan, David 170
Morgan, Cindy 200
Morgan, John 243
Morgan, Charlie 270
Morgan, Liz 273
Morgan, Becky 283
Morgan, Michele 325
Morgan, Maria 352
Morgan, Lisa 381
Morgan, William 398
Morgan, Jeff 448
Morgan, Molly 448
Morgan, Mary 458
Morgan, Michael 458
Morgan, Karen 476
Morgan, Bruce 486
Morgan, James 489
Morgan, James 516
Morgan, Rodney 523
Morgan, Kenneth 613
Morgan, Rick 619
Morgan, Robert 619
Morgan, Debbie 624
Morgan, Henry 644
Morgan, Jamie 703
Morgan, Jason 744
Morgan, Hugh 755
Morgan, Hugh G 756
Morgan, Julie 792
Morgan, Melanie 800
Morgan, Keith 808
Morgan, Julie 839
Morgan, John 860
Morgano, Scott 304
Morganthall, Frederick J. (Fred) 463
Morge, Kenneth 242
Morgenlender, Mark 182
Morgenstern, Kara 670
Morgioni, Mike 65
Morgo, Joseph 182
Moriarity, Tim 796
Moriarty, Linda 50
Moriarty, Thomas M. 229
Moriarty, Michael 302
Moriarty, Brad 417
Moriarty, Selina 456
Moriarty, John 700
Moriarty, Brian 700
Moriarty, Colleen 835
Morikis, John G. 706
Morimoto, David S. 164
Morin, Carlos 3
Morin, Jeff 476

Morissette, Daniel J. 245
Moriwaki, Lee Y. 164
Morken, CeCe 435
Moro, Gisele 473
Moroski, Steve 694
Morosov, Anatoly 448
Morrell, Kelley 179
Morris, Donna 7
Morris, Mark 13
Morris, Susan 23
Morris, Leslie 42
Morris, Gregory A. (Greg) 66
Morris, M. Catherine (Cathy) 68
Morris, M Catherine 68
Morris, Mary 96
Morris, Uri 120
Morris, Jim 124
Morris, James 150
Morris, Tim 174
Morris, Kelda — 177
Morris, James 183
Morris, Joe 202
Morris, James 267
Morris, Susan 275
Morris, Rodney 324
Morris, Gerald 352
Morris, Jerry 352
Morris, Ken 353
Morris, James 365
Morris, Janet 389
Morris, Tanya 448
Morris, Chris 507
Morris, Maria R. 518
Morris, Tonia 530
Morris, Uri 535
Morris, Carol 546
Morris, Pamela 551
Morris, Marilyn 643
Morris, Jesse E. 657
Morris, Florence 671
Morris, Tonia G 684
Morris, B. Harrison 705
Morris, Pete 727
Morris, Gene 740
Morris, John 741
Morris, Edna 790
Morris, Fran 837
Morris, Lauren 841
Morris, Lisa 851
Morris, John J. 854
Morris, Dawn C. 856
Morris, Dwight 867
Morris, William 871
Morris, Michael J. 884
Morris-carter, Stacy 792
Morris-gettings, Juanita 481
Morris-Hipkins, Stuart 596
Morrison, Christina 64
Morrison, Scott C. 91
Morrison, Victoria 111
Morrison, Denise M. 146
Morrison, Patricia B. (Patty) 152
Morrison, Richard 282
Morrison, Elizabeth 484
Morrison, Deb 507
Morrison, Trevor 551
Morrison, Dave 749
Morrison, Andrew 757
Morriss, Steve 12
Morriss, John 481
Morrissey, Art 91
Morrissey, Deborah 503

Murray, Renee 397
Murray, Michael 406
Murray, Pam 422
Murray, Pamela 500
Murray, Cathleen 509
Murray, Brian 556
Murray, John 602
Murray, Andrea 653
Murray, Michael 700
Murray, William 711
Murray, Dane H 718
Murray, Michael 757
Murray, Hillary 780
Murray, Donna 825
Murray, Gary 843
Murrell, Anita 711
Murren, James J. 522
Murtagh, Nigel J. 700
Murter, Jeffrey 473
Murtha, Mark G. 384
Murtha, Gary 613
Murtos, Ryan 96
Musa, Ramsey 555
Musca, Robert 818
Muscolo, Matthew 751
Musen, Robert M. 673
Musk, Elon 767
Mussatt, Lynn 154
Musselman, Kerri 126
Musselman, Barry 672
Musser, Eric S. 218
Musser, Jeffrey S. 288
Musser, Paul 507
Musteen, Sheila 851
Musti, Subu 507
Mutch, Marcy D. 323
Mutchler, Rebecca 495
Muth, Ora 185
Muth, Mark 415
Muthler, Craig 336
Muto, Daneen 880
Mutti, Joe 234
Mutton, Michelle 500
Mutz, Janet 586
Muzaffar, Farooq 879
Muzumdar, Maha 593
Mwangi, John 507
Myara, Alicia 341
Mychalowych, Jerome 515
Myers, Denise 1
Myers, Kenneth 13
Myers, Kirstie 42
Myers, Jason 91
Myers, Shirley 93
Myers, Timothy D. (Tim) 99
Myers, Timothy 123
Myers, Tony 162
Myers, Christopher D. (Chris) 227
Myers, Carol 320
Myers, Cynthia M. 332
Myers, Curtis J. 344
Myers, Theresa 357
Myers, Tim D. 407
Myers, Thomas D. 453
Myers, Bradley 493
Myers, Jodi 522
Myers, Daniel 533
Myers, Larry L. 757
Myers, Daniel P. (Dan) 863
Myerson, Terry 525
Mygrants, Michael 825
Myler, Jerold 456

Mylu, Sasikiran 182
Myrick, Ruth 52
Myrick, Bradan 722
Myron, Paul 407

N

Nabel, Elizabeth G. (Betsy) 503
Nachmann, Marc 365
Nachum, Stav 670
Nadarajan, Gunalan 669
Nadeau, Gerard F. 421
Nadella, Satya 525
Nader, Elizabeth 103
Nadkarni, Pranay 36
Nafshi, Elad 198
Naftaly, Robert 805
Naftaly, Rober 805
Naftaly, Ralph 823
Nagaishi, Robert 44
Nagarajan, Sundaram (Naga) 420
Nagata, Ron 382
Nagel, Paul 240
Nagel, Sherri 247
Nagel, David 352
Nagel, Troy 380
Nagel, Brian 819
Nagelson, Chris 851
Nagir, Madhurie 677
Nagji, Bansi 511
Nagle, Margaret 74
Nagy, Michael 172
Nagy, Richard 226
Nagy, Kate 307
Nagy, Kim 873
Nagy-todd, Salit 664
Nahrgang, Stephanie 776
Nahrup, Steve 270
Naifeh, James O 737
Naik, Sangeeta 42
Naik, Vik 694
Nair, Raj 339
Nair, Vas 407
Nair, Mahesh 467
Nair, Rajesh 525
Nair, Roopa 653
Nair, Suresh 672
Najimi, Parnaz 849
Najjar, Fred 245
Najjar, Ted 365
Nakama, Rance 673
Nakamura, Galen 97
Nakano, Tom 570
Nakasone, Norman 164
Nakatsuka, Ralph Y. 766
Nalamasu, Omkaram (Om) 63
Nalbach, Doug 555
Naljayan, Mihran 235
Nall, Doug 624
Nallappan, Andy 137
Nambiar, Vinod 194
Namboodiri, Supriya 751
Namboothiry, Rajesh 496
Nanavaty, Maulik 133
Nandakumar, Anita 366
Nangia, Nikhil 96
Nantz, Mark S. 126
Napier, Lindsey 495
Naples, Richard J. 109
Napol, Marcello 3
Napoli, Frank 53

Napoli, Paul 649
Napoli, Joe 756
Napolitan, Raymond S. 574
Napolitano, Glen 308
Napolitano, Melanie 687
Nappi, David 879
Naquin, Robbie 148
Narang, Manu 42
Narasimhan, Laxman 612
Narayan, Sandeep 310
Narayanan, Lakshmi 193
Narayanan, Krishnan 365
Narayen, Shantanu 7
Narciso, Paul J. 692
Nardi, Scott 677
Nardis, Ronald J 316
Nardone, Mary Kaye 469
Narmouq, Samir 568
Narula, Veru 179
Nash, Nata 72
Nash, William D. (Bill) 154
Nash, Alexis 411
Nash, Calvin 453
Nash, Joseph 516
Nash, Nick 809
Nasir, Louis 755
Nassetta, Christopher J. (Chris) 392
Nasta, David 310
Natale, J 109
Natale, Lisa 581
Natarajan, Sanjay 63
Natarajan, Krishna 535
Natarajan, Venkata 647
Natarajan, Murali 682
Natarajan, Shekar 760
Natarajan, Ramanan 770
Nath, Deepak 4
Nathan, Scott 103
Nathan, Mike 873
Natoli, Jerry 435
Natsis, Elaine 153
Nau, Kris K 711
Naughton, Duncan C. Mac 252
Naughton, Kathy 396
Naughton, Mary 502
Naughton, W Terrance 858
Naughton, Terry 858
Naughton-Gerdes, Joan 28
Nauman, Jeffrey 120
Naumann, Peter 823
Nava, Carmen P 76
Navale, Sunil 568
Navarra, Eric 114
Navarro, Jen 348
Navarro, Mary W. 414
Navarro, Imelda 429
Navarro, Jorge 818
Navia, Frank 140
Navran, Andrew 751
Naylor, Katie 42
Naylor, Lisa 207
Nazak, Keith 336
Nazzaro, Stephen F. (Steve) 739
Ndumele, Mary 152
Neal, Michelle M. 100
Neal, Annmarie 177
Neal, Krista 179
Neal, Domineca 510
Neal, Gary F. 808
Neal, Joel 849
Neale, Donna 489

Neale, George A. 703
Nealon, Gerald 80
Nealon, Thomas M. (Tom) 723
Nearhood, William 308
Neas, Dana 114
Nebreda, Julian 14
Necastro, Daniel Butch 27
NeCastro, Timothy G. 281
Nedder, Michael 335
Needham, Wendy 355
Neely, Eric 453
Neff, Clay 169
Neff, Doug 203
Neff, Lorraine 223
Negr--n, Eduardo J. 630
Negus, Brooke 176
Neher, Terry 832
Neidorff, Michael F. 162
Neikirk, Chris 564
Neil, Mike 525
Neill, James R. (Jim) 355
Neill, Jim R 355
Neis, Eric 120
Neis, Eric 535
Nell, Steven E. 125
Nelms, David W. 247
Nelms, Cary T 756
Nelsen, Keith J. 116
Nelsen, Denise 728
Nelsen, Mark 844
Nelso, Nelson 395
Nelson, Joseph 26
Nelson, Ronald L. (Ron) 86
Nelson, Roy 91
Nelson, Nicole 116
Nelson, Kevin 150
Nelson, Christopher 154
Nelson, Julie 167
Nelson, Joan 190
Nelson, Rosemary 195
Nelson, Rick 237
Nelson, Andy 242
Nelson, Faye A. 256
Nelson, Lisa 270
Nelson, Ann W. 271
Nelson, John P. 271
Nelson, Scott 325
Nelson, Christian 328
Nelson, Paul 346
Nelson, Kimberly A. (Kim) 351
Nelson, Rick 374
Nelson, Mike 433
Nelson, Steven 487
Nelson, Philip B 498
Nelson, Philip 498
Nelson, Linda A 527
Nelson, Audrey 555
Nelson, Paul 570
Nelson, Peggy 586
Nelson, Jonathan B. 587
Nelson, Travis 700
Nelson, Rick 713
Nelson, Doug 734
Nelson, Robert 792
Nelson, Christopher 806
Nelson, Michael S. 825
Nelson, David D. (Dave) 861
Nelson, Mary 879
Nelson, Zac 884
Nemecek, Donna 100
Nemeth, Jeffery 339
Nemeth, Julio 640

Nemeth, Rudolph 645
Nemoir, Todd 500
Nemphos, Ann 380
Nenadal, Cody 749
Nentwig, Robert J. 132
Nepveux, Kevin 616
Nerbonne, Daniel 627
Nerbonne, Dan 627
Neri, Antonio 389
Neri, Marc 749
Neri, Alexa 805
Nering, Judy 873
Nerurkar, Kshitij 193
Nesbit, Shannon 694
NESBIT, JONATHAN 740
Nesbit, Jeff 784
Nesbitt, Stephen R. 410
Nesbitt, Douglas 675
Nesci, James D. 645
Nesemeyer, Ron 202
Nesi, Victor J. 743
Ness, Steve 854
Nessel, Christopher 443
Nesseth, Kelli 751
Neth, Bryan 705
Netherton, Linda 305
Neto, Paulo 476
Nettesheim, Susan 443
Nettles, Richard 444
Neuman, Susan B 552
Neuman, Jennifer 552
Neumann, Karl-Thomas 353
Neumann, Dan 624
Neumann, Paul G. 794
Neumeyer, Daniel J. 415
Neviaser, Robin 42
Neville, Brian 40
Neville, Robert M. 93
Neville, Bob 93
Nevins, Andrew 183
Newallis, David 45
Newberg, William 851
Newbern, Thomas B. 83
Newberry, Stephen G. (Steve) 470
Newbery, Michelle M. 489
Newcom, Jeff 325
Newcomb, Carrie 126
Newcomb, Richard 198
Newcomb, Jorey 216
Newcomer, Mark 284
Newcomer, John 359
Newcomer, Patti 435
Newcomer, Nate 681
Newfield, Richard U. 541
Newhouse, Marie 171
Newhouse, Greg 455
Newkirk, Christopher T. 148
Newkirk, Jesse 325
Newkirk, Melanie 584
Newlands, William A. (Bill) 215
Newlin, Karl 258
Newman, Randy 24
Newman, Kenneth Kenneth
  Newman 100
Newman, Rebecca 100
Newman, Sallie 224
Newman, Dennis 249
Newman, Jenifer 285
Newman, John 330
Newman, Deon 431
Newman, Rainer 443
Newman, Mark 446

Newman, Gerald 510
Newman, Brian 612
Newman, Robert 623
Newman, Jason 668
Newmann, Scott 664
Newsom, Brittany 48
Newsom, Richard W. (Rick) 208
Newsom, Rick 208
Newsom, Gavin 731
Newton, Wayne 21
Newton, Vera 339
Newton, Carl 701
Neylon, Brian V. 249
Ng, Alan 55
Ng, Dominic 261
Ng, Frances 261
Ng, Donna 443
Ng, Stella 448
Ng, Regina 507
Ng, Paul 708
Ng, Carmen 755
Ng, Lee 792
Ngai, Henry 103
Ngo, A. Catherine 164
Nguyen, Timothy 92
Nguyen, Thong M. 95
Nguyen, Kim 229
Nguyen, Troy 267
Nguyen, Thao 312
Nguyen, Chao 383
Nguyen, Joann 385
Nguyen, Tony 519
Nguyen, Nam 568
Nguyen, Tuan 644
Nguyen, Trung 670
Nguyen, Xuong 745
Nguyen, Tinh 808
Nguyen, John 851
Niall, Oconnor 62
Niblock, Robert A. 489
Nichipor, Thomas 772
Nichol, Andy 556
Nichol, Janett 560
Nichol, Jason 803
Nicholas, Georgette C. 356
Nicholas, George 446
Nicholas, Jim 448
Nicholas, Brad 651
Nicholas, Ray 755
Nicholls, Timothy S. (Tim) 433
Nichols, Robbie 52
NICHOLS, ROB 98
Nichols, Victor 98
Nichols, Todd 118
Nichols, Lee 147
Nichols, Holli 258
Nichols, Ronald O. 267
Nichols, Jim 318
Nichols, Aaron 328
Nichols, Nancy 434
Nichols, Russell 479
Nichols, Rob 492
Nichols, Rodney P. 497
Nichols, Dana L. 654
Nichols, Ronald O. (R.O.) 719
Nichols, Donald 792
Nichols, Lisa 851
Nicholson, Glenn 174
Nicholson, E. Allen 227
Nicholson, Allen 227
Nicholson, Darryl 443
Nicholson, Marla 502

Nicholson, Sharon 687
Nicholson, Larry 736
Nicholson, Sara 757
Nickele, Christopher J. (Chris) 189
Nickels, Jeff 320
Nickerson, Richard 144
Nickerson, Randy 538
Nickerson, Cheryl 609
Nicki, David 355
Nicklas, Tom 629
Nickles, Jenny 415
Nickman, Gene 152
Nickol, Christopher 703
Nickolson, Tony 498
Nicolaus, Joseph 568
Nicoletti, Laurie 507
Nicoletti, Ralph J. 553
Nides, Thomas R. (Tom) 535
Nieden, Paul Zur 305
Niehaus, James 44
Nielsen, Dan 162
Nielsen, Joel 339
Nielsen, Mark D. 343
Nielsen, Stan 374
Nielsen, Rob 446
Nielsen, James 664
Nielsen, Michele 823
Niem, Eddie 195
Niemann, Tammy 72
Niemczyk, Todd 303
Niemiec, Mark 694
Niemietz, Christy 873
Nierenberg, Gregg 86
Niermann, Mark 238
Nies, Sharon 316
Nieto, Alejandra 617
Nieto, Luis 689
Nieuwenhuys, Gerard 608
Nieves, Evelyn 326
Niezgodski, Michael 1
Nightingale, Timothy P. 144
Nigro, David 42
Nigro, Joseph (Joe) 284
Nigro, Stephen (Steve) 409
Nigro, James M. 469
Nigro, Rich 685
Nikolov, Anita 566
Niles, Thomas 535
Nimbley, Thomas J. 605
Nimmo, Benjamin 825
Ninas, Jason 753
Nisbett, Mark 856
Nisenson, Allen R. 235
Niswonger, Scott 322
Nitti, Joe 873
Nitzberg, Suzanne 28
Niwa, Gilbert 844
Nix, Craig L. 315
Nixon, Randy 80
Nixon, Michael 286
Nixon, Dennis E. 429
Nixon, Barbara 695
Nixon, Bill 698
Nixon, Ken 798
Nixon, Torran 808
Njonjo, Peter 192
Nober, Roger 122
Noble, Quintin 5

Noble, Mark 198
Noble, Jeff 317
Noble, Jen 431
Noble, Craig 609
Noblett, Monique 565
Nocella, Andrew P. 811
Nodar, Aaron 493
Noe, Alan 671
Noelle, Boudler 741
Noethiger, Robert 840
Noga, James W. (Jim) 503
Nogalski, John 450
Nogles, Thomas 381
Noguera, Lupe 593
Noh, Andrew 670
Nojiri, Scott 164
Nolan, Rebecca 13
Nolan, John 75
Nolan, Bob 211
Nolan, Joseph R. (Joe) 282
Nolan, Robert 289
Nolan, Michael J. (Mike) 303
Nolan, James 366
Nolan, Gary 459
Nolan, Elizabeth 739
Nolan, David A. 883
Nolan-maccione, Kelley 823
Noland, William M 292
Noland, Matt 800
Nolasco, Teresa 200
Nolden, Casey 3
Nolen, Steve 491
Noletto, Tanya 671
Noll, Kelly 27
Nollen, Margaret 258
Noller, Rick 263
Nomura, Stephanie 98
Nomura, Timothy 201
Noonan, Mike 179
Noonan, James R. 469
Noonan-Harnsber, Helen 644
Noons, Mary E 853
Noordhoek, Jeffrey R. (Jeff) 546
Nooyi, Indra K. 612
Nopka, Jacqueline 176
Noppenberger, Louis 183
Norcia, Gerardo (Jerry) 256
Norcross, Gary A. 305
Norcross, Anna 455
Norcross, Jeanne 724
Nordell, Scott 303
Nordlie, Elizabeth M. 351
Nordlund, Scott 794
Nordmeyer, Greg 50
Nordquist, Jeff 54
Nordquist, Eric 792
Nordstrom, Mike 351
Nordstrom, Blake W. 562
Nordstrom, Peter E. (Pete) 562
Nordstrom, Erik B. 562
Nordstrom, James F. (Jamie) 562
Nordstrom, Jeff 673
Noren, Per 124
Norgren, Jim 443
Norick, Ronald 93
Noriega, Erica 223
Nork, Edward 206
Norman, Todd 289
Norman, Kenneth 344
Norman, Brad 415
Norman, Paul T. 451
Normandin, Donna 223

Normington, Debbie 178
Norrington, Lorrie 195
Norris, Derek J. 97
Norris, Brian 369
Norris, Brian 427
Norris, Josephine 448
Norris, Betty 485
Norris, Julie 512
Norris, Pam 583
Norris, David 634
Norris, Craig 846
Norrod, Forrest E. 10
North, Paul 466
North, John F. 482
North, Martie 711
Northam, Ralph 205
Northam, Thadd 502
Northcutt, Kendria 624
Northern, Richard 744
Northey, Brian 507
Northrop, Annie 328
Northup, Geoff 751
Norton, Rita 53
Norton, Todd 203
Norton, Bill 240
Norton, Susan A. 312
Norton, Michael F 456
Norton, Johna 479
Norton, Robert G. (Bob) 503
Norton, David K. 609
Norton, W.D. (Joe) 722
Norwitt, Richard A. (Adam) 56
Nosal, Mark 787
Noseworthy, Darren 617
Nosler, John S. 675
Nostrand, David 500
Novaes, Djalma 221
Novak, Ryan 48
Novak, Katherine 628
Novakovic, Phebe 5
Novakovic, Phebe N. 348
Novich, Neil 369
Novielli, Jack 645
Novo, Guillermo 20
Novosel, John 324
Novotny, Cece 171
Nowell, Lauren 841
Nowicki, Edward 617
Noyes, Mark 214
Nthunzi, Godfrey 195
Nuby, Angelo 504
Nuchims, Fran 149
Nuckols, Jeff 223
Nudelman, Jenna 556
Nudi, Jonathon J. (Jon) 351
Nudo, Mario 872
Nulter, Steven 611
Numoto, Takeshi 525
Nunes, Jack 471
Nunez, Rosie 180
Nunez, Rachel 376
Nunez, Felix 531
Nunnari, Nicholas 179
Nussdorf, Lawrence 473
Nusterer, Norbert 225
Nuti, William 812
Nutter, Michael 223
Nuytten, Jeffrey A 404
Nuzzo, Carla 823
Nwamadi, Tresia 211
Nwele, Kenneth 179
Nwokeji, Linda 147

Nye, Angela 664
Nyeholt, Ron 304
Nyen, Jake 71
Nygren, Elisabeth 120
Nykiel, Alan 125
Nyquist, Kelly B 672
Nysschen, Carel Johannes de 353
Néemeh, Alain P. 673

O

Oake-libow, Eli 481
Oakes, John 55
Oakland, Steven T. 715
Oakley, Christopher 298
Oakley, Adam 670
Oakley, Glenn 841
Oakley, Bill 863
Oancia, Doran 558
Oates, Joseph P. 214
Oates, Michael P. 305
Obando, Glenn 100
Obella, Carlos 270
Oberg, Kathleen K. (Leeny) 500
Oberg, Leeny 500
Oberhaus, Michael 293
Oberholzer, Bill 634
Obering, Henry A. (Trey) 129
Oberman, Stacy 415
Obermeyer, Paul R. 200
Obermiller, John 785
Oberry, Greg 399
Obert, William 481
Obie, Nestor 630
Obleton, Carolynn 753
Oblisk, Sonya Gafsi 870
Obrian, Diana 378
Obrian, Tom 415
Obrien, James J 50
Obrien, James 50
OBrien, Laura 159
Obrien, Sharon 493
Obrien, Kori 694
OBrien, Kevin M. 819
Obrien, Barbara 871
Obzud, John 304
Ocampo, Christopher 6
Ocariz, Andres 751
Ocasio-Fant, Diana 434
Occhipinti, Tony 587
Ochoa, Vanessa 201
Ochoa, Omar 474
OConnell, Dan 380
Oconnell, Mike 800
Oconnor, Nancy 111
Oconnor, Cristina 147
OConnor, Kevin 246
Oconnor, Nancy 628
Oconnor, Caitlin 736
Oda, Calla 98
Oddleifson, Christopher (Chris) 421
Oddo, David 606
Odell, David 456
Odesky, Andrew 670
Odinet, Bertrand (Bert) 342
Odisho, Walter 124
Odle, Roger 27
Odlis, Mark 643
Odom, Ronald 60
Odom, James 198

Odom, Kara 569
Odonnell, Holly 303
Odonnell, Jim 448
Odonnell, Michelle 653
Odonnell, Julia 871
Odonnell, Joseph 871
Odria, David 743
Odriozola, Jose Maria (Chema) 818
Oelke, Dawn 384
Oelke, Les 385
Oestreich, Patrick 881
Oexle, Edward 309
Offenberger, Eric J. 675
Offereins, Diane E. 247
Oftedal, Siv 279
Ogania, Milagros 383
Ogden, Stasia L 107
Ogden, Kylie 188
Ogden, Bob 371
Ogle, Bailey 240
Oglesby, Rodney 222
Ogletree, Joe 787
Ognall, Andrew H. 808
Ogrady, Shawn P 352
Ogrosky, Kori L. 600
Oh, Irene H. 261
Oh, David 446
Ohanian, David 200
OHara, Brooks 372
Ohara, Ruth 474
Ohara, Michele 504
Ohara, Melissa 792
Ohare, Tammy 823
Ohelo, Doree J 97
Ohlsson, Sandy 352
Ohmer, Adrian 805
Ohrenberger, Danielle 551
Oi, Terence 879
Oike, Taro 864
Okada, Terri 97
Okai, Lilian 96
Okamoto, Ron 62
Okamoto, David 98
Okamura, Cindy 97
Okamura, Van 593
Okazaki, Jason 360
Okerlund, Janis 304
Okerstrom, Mark D. 286
Okeson, Todd 308
Okimoto, Michelle 784
Okray, Thomas B. (Tom) 9
Okray, Thomas B 369
Olafson, Harlee N. 861
Olczak, Jacek 620
Olden, Christopher 707
Oldenburg, Camille 678
Oldenski, Becky 691
Oldfield, Cheryl 784
Oldham, Jon 149
Olds, Greg 453
Olejer, Leigh 223
Olejnik, Ashley 773
Oleksiak, Peter B. 256
Oleksiuk, Mary A. 803
Oleon, John 305
Olinsky, Michael 308
Oliu, Edward 786
Oliva, Eugene 179
Olivan, Javier 290
Olive, Stephen R. 596
Oliveira, Marcelo 343
Oliveira, Rafael 461

Oliveira, Carlos 535
Oliver, Gary 75
Oliver, Joel 150
Oliver, Joe 243
Oliver, Joseph 243
Oliver, Sean 305
Oliver, Timothy 333
Oliver, George R 444
Oliver, Cedric 671
Oliver, Wes 685
Oliver, Kerry 875
Olivera, Armando 334
Olivier, Leon J. (Lee) 282
Olivo, Maria 792
Olkowski, Ed 871
Oller, Colleen 283
Oller, Michael 756
Oller, Jeanne 871
Oller, Michael 871
Ollia, Marshall 664
Olmstead, Traci 270
Olmstead, Cpcu 730
Olnick, Bryan 333
Olsavsky, Brian T. 34
Olsen, Rob 203
Olsen, Neil 292
Olsen, Kelly 339
Olsen, Erica 366
Olsen, Richard 451
Olsen, Kristin 504
Olsen, Todd 629
Olsen, Karl 790
Olson, Lisa 6
Olson, Knute A 75
Olson, Chris 80
Olson, Marissa 80
Olson, John 91
Olson, Tiffany P. 152
Olson, Robert 242
Olson, Scott-h 270
Olson, Steven 325
Olson, Eric 346
Olson, Dallas 367
Olson, Scott 499
Olson, Arik 531
Olson, Bart 568
Olson, Laurie J. 616
Olson, Thomas 684
Olson, Aaron 700
Olson, Kevin 805
Olson-Cartwright, Cary 828
Olsson, Charles 701
Olsson, Jimmy 851
Omalley, Sean 299
Oman, Mark 310
Omanakuttan, Sudheer 96
Omberg, Rob 198
Omidfar, Bahr 488
Omidyar, Pierre M 265
Omohundro, Paige 195
Omoss, Mario 219
Ondecker, Marilyn 481
Onders, Mike 455
ONeill, Heidi 560
Oneill, Frank 841
Ong, Eddie 634
Onisick, Bill 96
Onken, Tom 500
Onksen, Bill 111
Onofrey, Debbie 825
Onorato, Andrea 835
Onumonu, Ngozi 681

O'Shaughnessy, Robert T. (Bob) 651
O'Shea, Daniel 380
O'shea, Sean 756
O'Sullivan, Juliann 121
O'sullivan, Fergus 617
O'Sullivan, Michael B. 687
O'Sullivan, Richard B. 793
O'sullivan, Terri 856
O'Tero, Ilene 149
OÂ'Brien, Raymond V. 228
OÂ'Brien, Sean P. 237
OÂ'Brien, Denis P. 284
OÂ'Connell, Brian 183
OÂ'Hara, Ryan 556
OÂ'Leary, David 356
OÂ'Neill, Michael J. 42
OÂ'Neill, Heidi 560
OÂ'Sullivan, James P. 727

P

Paar, David 136
Pabst, Jim 519
Pace, Philip 144
Pace, Paul 455
Pace-Burke, Susan 550
Pacheco, Mike 195
Pacheco, Fernando 441
Pacheco, Carlos 606
Pacicco, Daniel 74
Pacicco, Robert 120
Pacilio, Michael J. 284
Pack, Mike 9
Packee, Jon 446
Packer, Ginny 533
Packwood, Erin 755
Pacula, Joseph 409
Pacyna, Mike 629
Paczkowski, Linda 507
Padbury, Guy 515
Padden, Brian 707
Paddy, Rao 249
Padgett, Pamela 341
Padgett, George 855
Padgitt, Laura 152
Padierna, Pedro 612
Padilla, Maria 227
Padilla, Hector 397
Padmanabhan, Srikanth 225
Padovano, Sam 779
Padron, Angelica 429
Padula, Rich 325
Pady, Stefani 80
Paez, Warren 92
Paffumi, Louis 610
Pagano, Christopher J. 74
Pagano, William 96
Pagano, Dawn 229
Page, Gregory 3
Page, Andrew 9
Page, John 86
Page, Gregory 240
Page, Mark 284
Page, Ed 413
Page, Jack 413
Page, David 613
Paglia, Anne 678
Pagnani, Marissa 653
Pagni, Marco 848
Paiano, Robert 381

Paich, Keith 344
Paich, Brian 653
Paidosh, Laurie 823
Paik, Elaine 195
Paik, Ritchie 881
Paine, Ed 313
Paine, Andrew J. (Randy) 455
Paine, Amy 455
Painter, Corning F. 20
Painter, Robert 193
Pairitz, Peter 403
Pais, Paula 226
Paisley, James A. (Andy) 9
Pak, Nancy 195
Pak, Gene 401
Pak, Chris 552
Pak, Ian 851
Pala, Amy 292
Palacio, Alex 43
Paladino, Steven 698
Palafox, Jose 429
Palanchian, Mark 557
Palardy, Alan 522
Palasek, Paul 566
Palasthy, Kristen 825
Palazzese, Susan 388
Palazzo, Frank 491
Palazzolo, Joseph 325
Palchanes, Tammie 653
Paldy, Szabolcs 247
Paletta, Nilton 438
Palframan, Jessica 249
Palinkos, Michael 183
Palis, Jack 502
Palka, Joe 787
Palkhiwala, Akash 656
Palla, Wayne 230
Pallasch, John 502
Pallone, Philip 366
Pallotta, Eric 547
Palm, Erik 222
Palm, Gregory K. 365
Palm, Richard 684
Palma, Bryan 177
Palmer, Annette 96
Palmer, Johnathan 118
Palmer, Paul 144
Palmer, Eric 173
Palmer, Henry 182
Palmer, April 303
Palmer, Mercy 303
Palmer, Gregory 344
Palmer, Kari 381
Palmer, Anthony J. (Tony) 457
Palmer, C. Michael 497
Palmer, C Michael 497
Palmer, Jackie 512
Palmer, Thomas (Tom) 555
Palmer, Adam 613
Palmer, Gary 645
Palmer, Roberta Ruth 670
Palmer, Robert 681
Palmer, Janet 851
Palmgren, Sharlene 507
Palmieri, Paul 881
Palmisano, Thomas J. (Tom) 719
Palmore, Roderick 352
Palomarez, Javier 505
Paluch, Michael 28
Paluck, Eric 50
Pam, Murray 422
Pamela, Pam 498

Pamiljans, Janis G. 568
Pamnani, Ravi 613
Pamulo, Pj 328
Pan, Gordon G. 684
Panagos, Costa 438
Panas, George 266
Pande, Saumitra 183
Pande, Ravi 443
Pandita, Sunil 389
Panepresso, Joe 827
Panfely, Liz 279
Pang, Laurinda Y. 490
Pang, Lisa 519
Pangan, Aileen 6
Panish, David 499
Panjwani, Tej 628
Pankowski, Jason 111
Pann, Stuart C. 409
Pannacciulli, Mike 841
Panno, Enrico 149
Panno, Corrado 495
Panuccio, Susan 556
Panzarino, James V. 247
Panzer, David 491
Paolini, Bruce 252
Paolino, Jerad 751
Papa, Athony Tony 418
Papadopoulos, Stelios 118
Papageorge, Lisa 454
Papamarkou, Irene 739
Papantonio, Edmond 647
Papay, Mike 568
Papay, Jen 700
Papazis, Petros 169
Pape, Giovanna 448
Pape, Kelli 670
Pape, Jeff 832
Papermaster, Mark D. 10
Papesh, Kristin 617
Papillo, Carol 13
Papineni, Srinivasa 834
Papkoff, Jackie 444
Pappagallo, Michael 136
Pappagallo, Andrea 418
Pappas, Stephen 219
Paquette, Michael S. 271
Parag, Prakash J 726
Param, Melina 216
Parameswaran, Prabha 195
Parasnis, Abhay 7
Parcell, Jordan 749
Parcella, Mike 63
Parcella, Michael 63
Parcher, Dave 146
Parchisanu, Georgeta 640
Pardee, Charles G. (Chip) 766
Pardes, Herbert 778
Pardini, Marissa 839
Pardoe, Rachel D 550
Pardon, Tony 608
Pardue, Wendel 671
Pare, Roger 378
Pare, Mark 828
Paredes, Jose 871
Pareigat, Thomas G. 773
Pareja, Alvena 754
Parent, June B. 144
Parente, Michael Null 339
Parikh, Nilay 681
Parimbelli, Alessandro 439
Paris, Glen 625
Paris, John 816

Parish, Michelle 391
Parisi, Ella 198
Parisi, Mike 420
Park, Ernie 3
Park, David 36
Park, Sun 53
Park, David 92
Park, Danny 180
Park, Joy 198
Park, Jay 290
Park, Anthony J. (Tony) 303
Park, Dave 366
Park, Aekyung 401
Park, Ellie 401
Park, Joon 470
Park, Jae 481
Park, Burt 531
Park, Anthony 547
Park, Matt 560
Park, Priscilla K 880
Parker, Debbie 28
Parker, W. Douglas (Doug) 37
Parker, Karen 65
Parker, Alex 75
Parker, Stephen 124
Parker, Donald T. 125
Parker, Erik 160
Parker, Phil 216
Parker, Greg 223
Parker, Allison 247
Parker, M Jayne 250
Parker, Ted 312
Parker, Karen 502
Parker, Dorothy 504
Parker, Calvin 512
Parker, Nick 525
Parker, Mark G. 560
Parker, Kurt 560
Parker, Karla 568
Parker, Scott T. 589
Parker, Krystal 590
Parker, Gary 591
Parker, Greg 602
Parker, Joy 671
Parker, Janet 671
Parker, Wade 672
Parker, Stacy 694
Parker, Tom 731
Parker, Sharon 755
Parker, Phillip 801
Parker, Bruce 806
Parker, Shelly 807
Parker, Michael 828
Parker, P. William (Bill) 831
Parker, Rob 837
Parker, Brenda 871
Parkinson, Mike 442
Parks, Jon 304
Parks, Lisa 376
Parks, Karen 788
Parks, Scott 798
Parks, Mary 804
Parks, Kathleen 823
Parlapiano, Donna 82
Parmar, Sheila 844
Parmenter, Darren E. 391
Parmentier, Jennifer A. 602
Parnes, Jane 55
Parnes, Marvin 670
Parr, Gregory L 378
Parrent, Michael 855
Parrish, Jeff 152

Poncia, Peter 566
Pond, Randy 177
Pond, Randall 177
Ponnekanti, Hari 63
Pons, Matt 481
Pons, Jaume 617
Ponselle, Cherie 34
Ponsonby, Craig 331
Pont, Eleuthere Du 876
Pontell, Jaclyn 504
Pontzer, Deborah 188
Pool, Kelly 160
Pool, Taylor 391
Poole, Thomas 196
Poole, Mandy 306
Poole, Tim 677
Poole-yaeger, Amy 162
Poonen, Sanjay 845
Pope, Gene 34
Pope, Lawrence J. 375
Pope, Robert 569
Pope, Jeffrey 694
Pope, David 768
Pope, Maria 808
Popham, Matthew 473
Popielarski, Laurie 492
Poplack, Michael 593
Popovici, Silviu 612
Poppell, Jim 332
Popper, Susan 389
Popper, Jozsi 664
Popwell, David T. 321
Porat, Ruth M. 30
Pordon, Anthony R. (Tony) 608
Pordon, Tony 608
Poroch, David 358
Porporino, Dominic 818
Porras, Edward 223
Porta, Megan 205
Porta, Matt 431
Portacci, Michael T. 207
Portalatin, Julio A. 502
Portantino, Philip 606
Portela, Marvio 593
Porter, Darlene 15
Porter, Lisa Porter Lisa 125
Porter, Candace 126
Porter, Cynthia V 200
Porter, Pamela G 200
Porter, Robert 240
Porter, Pam 325
Porter, Biggs C. 334
Porter, David E. 385
Porter, John 431
Porter, Clint 624
Porter, Dianne 624
Porter, Jonathan 673
Porter, Brian 676
Porter, Kerrick 682
Porter, Melvin 806
Porter, Ann 806
Porter, Patrick 834
Porter, James B. (Jim) 867
Portera, Joseph P. (Joe) 219
Porwal, Hemant 860
Posa, Nicola 879
Posada, Juan F. 640
Poselenzny, Anthony 818
Posey, Robert 851
Post, Glen F. 490
Post, Roxanne 664
Postema, Bradley G. 281

Postol, Sean 152
Posvistak, Jared 779
Poteete, Ron 343
Potocki, Rick 593
Potsic, Robert 566
Pottash, Bruce 841
Potter, John 75
Potter, Von 136
Potter, Simon M. 299
Potter, Mary 481
Potter, Stephen N. 565
Potter, Myrtle 681
Potter, Jennifer 702
Potts, Andrea 647
Potts, David L. 675
Potts, Janna A. 759
Potts, Ryan 858
Poulakos, Greg 59
Poulsen, Greg 428
Pouncey, Clarence C. 705
Pound, Theodore 163
Pound, Gregory 558
Pound, Greg 558
Pourfallah, Stacy 844
Povenmire, Rex 249
Povolny, Denise 456
Povse, Mat 116
Powell, Sarah 9
Powell, Ann 136
Powell, Jerry W 143
Powell, Jeffrey 188
Powell, Kellie 200
Powell, Bradley S. (Brad) 288
Powell, Jon 308
Powell, Kendall J. (Ken) 352
Powell, Bill 353
Powell, Christine 355
Powell, Teresa 385
Powell, Heather 500
Powell, Rebecca 545
Powell, Tyane 624
Powell, Andy 677
Powell, Christy 695
Powell, Deana 711
Powell, Cynthia A. 730
Powell, Mescal 750
Powell, Marc 754
Powell, Cindy 797
Powell, Ken 798
Powell, Vincent 800
Powell, Wayne 818
Power, Nancy 519
Power, Alan J. (Al) 634
Power, Jamila 670
Power, Beth 871
Powers, John 39
Powers, Robert P. (Bob) 39
Powers, John 226
Powers, John J. 313
Powers, Scott 651
Powers, Channing 711
Powers, Marsha 762
Powers, Gary 871
Powlus, Lee C. 609
Pozarycki, Thomas 852
Pozez, Norman 260
Pozotrigo, Albert 441
Pozzi, James E. 47
Pozzi, Joseph 366
Prabhu, Arjun 576
Prabhu, Vasant M. 843
Pradyot, Behera 341

Pragada, Robert V. (Bob) 441
Prager, Richard L. (Richie) 120
Prall, Kristine 672
Pralle, Lauren 120
Pramaggiore, Anne R. 284
Prange, Karen 698
Prasad, Veronica 36
Prasad, Krishna 182
Prasad, Manoj 782
Prashanth, Cannanbilla 337
Prater, Robert 599
Prater, Robert 599
Pratico, Lisa 784
Pratico, Joseph 828
Pratka, Hampton 223
Pratka, Robert 302
Prato, Patrick 415
Pratt, Timothy A. (Tim) 133
Pratt, Danielle 519
Pratt, William C. (Bill) 712
Pratt, Frank 731
Pray, Kevin 378
Prebola, Don 675
Precourt, Walter F. (Walt) 536
Precourt, Walt 536
Prego, Maria 535
Prehn, Ryan 733
Preiser, Douglas 455
Preiser, Craig 550
Prejean, Joshua 149
Prendergast, David 27
Prendergast, Michael 149
Prendergast, Neil 326
Prendergast, Vincent 769
Prentice, Bill 237
Prentice, F. Sheldon 544
Prescott, Sidney 101
Present, Randall C. (Randy) 406
Preskenis, Donald 315
Preskenis, Ashley 624
Pressley, Mandell 242
Pressley, W. Michael 364
Pressley, Keith 671
Presson, Michael 434
Presti, Linda 42
Preston, Terry 5
Preston, Steve 160
Preston, James 200
Preston, Patricia 292
Preston, Bryan 308
Preston, Patricia 506
Preston, Trish 507
Prestopine, Hillarie 425
Prete, Thomas 666
Pretorius, Alwyn 555
Preuster, Christopher 448
Previn, Fletcher 431
Prezzano, David N 409
Price, Kevin 54
Price, Zoila 92
Price, Milton 103
Price, Mitch 167
Price, Deb 216
Price, Frank 229
Price, Aaron 286
Price, Thomas Michael (Mike) 316
Price, Harold 332
Price, Greg 413
Price, Michael 415
Price, Jeanine 428
Price, Michael 502
Price, Michael H. 513

Price, Lisa V 562
Price, Lisa 562
Price, Shawn 593
Price, Matthew S. 640
Price, Scott 818
Price, Scott 850
Price, Paula 864
Price-duffy, Kerry 562
Pridan, Moshe 712
Priddle, Justin 114
Pride, Jason 417
Priest, Stephen J. (Steve) 442
Prill, Gina 223
Primavera, Dianne 732
Primmer, Jan 519
Primrose, Tricia 500
Prince, Scott 96
Prince, Mike 142
Prince, Charles 444
Prince, Sidney 622
Prince, Leanne 757
Principe, Natalie 515
Principe, Joe 782
Prinz, Corey 103
Prisco, Dale 174
Prising, Jonas 460
Prising, Jonas 496
Pritchard, Kelly 304
Pritchard, Pat 624
Pritchard, Deborah 700
Pritchett, Wanda 481
Priti, Desai 310
Priti, Desai 318
Pritzker, J B 733
Prizner, John S 12
Probst, Marc 428
Prochaska, Amanda 522
Prochazka, Scott M. 163
Prochnow, Stephen 140
Procida, Thomas 121
Procopio, Russell 53
Proffitt, Julie 417
Proffitt, Adam 733
Proia, Gina M. 179
Prole, Melanie 132
Promo, Joe 515
Promo, Joseph 515
Pronio, Stephen 823
Pronti, Scott 788
Prophater, Kristen 828
Prophet, Tony 525
Propst, Beverly L. 370
Prosba, Debra 676
Proudman, Susi 560
Proulx, Kevin 756
Prout, Mark 331
Prouty, Paul F. 804
Provost, David T. 761
Prows, Mark 522
Prowse, Maureen 60
Pruden, Gary 443
PrudÂ'homme, Sylvain 489
Prue, Kevin 647
Pruitt, Warren 195
Pruitt, Kristin L. 469
Prunesti, Jim 211
Prupas, Annie 160
Pruscino, Angelo 593
Pruss-Jones, Catherine J 124
Pruzan, Jonathan 534
Pryor, David B 71
Pryor, Felecia 131

Scott, William 522
Scott, J. Kevin 525
Scott, Wesley 580
Scott, Dan 617
Scott, Gina 624
Scott, Steve 624
Scott, Kerry 625
Scott, Dennis 691
Scott, Sam 705
Scott, Randy 707
Scott, Vernon 711
Scott, Cameron A. 810
Scott, Frank 814
Scott, Helen B 818
Scott, David C. 819
Scott, Anthony 873

Scott, Brent 873
Scott-Morgan, Peggy 611
Scotte, Robert 519
Scotto, Vince 80
Scoville, Shane 837
Scozzafava, Ralph P. 238
SCRANTON, BRIAN 434
Scranton, Ann 859
Screnar, Ryan T 361
Screws, Jim 671
Scribner, Michael 543
Scribner, Wendy 643
Scrivens, Michael 328
Scruggs, Jodi 624
Scruggs, Marlo 798
Scudder, Michael L. 325
Scudder, Hal 622
Scullans, Greg 730
Scully, Mary Ann 406
Scyphers, Mike 498
Seabaugh, Greg 52
Seabold, Jeffrey T. 92
Seabright, Jefferson 192
Seabright, Mary 560
Seabury, Bryan 841
Seagroatt, Terri 243
Seale, Willie 558
Seale, Hamilton 728
Seales, Shaun 519
Sealey, Stephanie 201
Sealock, Brendy 211
Sealy, Rawle 448
Seaman, Chuck 417
Sear, Steve 242
Searby, Gary 283
Seargent, Jennifer 93
Searle, Nigel 289
Searles, Erin 153
Searls, Eric 798
Sears, Karl 211
Sears, Steven 328
Sears, James A. 329
Sears, Rachael 564
Sears, Mark 647
Searson, Robert 798
Seasock, Scott 612
Seastone, Bj 50
Seat, David M. 93
Seaton, Timothy 182
Seaton, Mark E. 310
Seaton, Charlee 313
Seaton, David T. 334
Seaton, Grant 700
Seaver, Michael L. 609
Seaver, David 755

Seavey, Darryl 664
Seawell, Katie 728
Sebastian, George 613
Seceleanu, Ioan 453
Seck, Wai Kwong 739
Seckinger, Carolyn 198
Secor, Mark E. 403
Secrest, Brent 278
Sederholm, Shawn 851
Sedgwick, Dale 879
Sedigh, Massoud 875
Sedlacek, Lanie 807
Sedlak, Dan 553
Sedmak, Pamela S 531
Seeberger, Mark 223
Seedorf, Herman 605
Seeger, Laureen E. 42
Seeger, Rick 142
Seeger, Ken 867
Seele, Jon 566
Sefcik, James 162
Sefzik, Peter L. 200
Segal, David 3
Segal, David 795
Segars, Debi 183
Segredo, John 346
Segreto, Antionette 109
Seguin, Julie 751
Segura, Michael 375
Seibel, Donald J. (Don) 295
Seiboldt, Jay 295
Seidcheck, Thomas 684
Seidel, Dave 640
Seidell, Violeta 500
Seidenberger, Eric 852
Seifert, James J. (Jim) 266
Seifriz, Jennifer 50
Seigler, Gloria 25
Seiler, David R. 314
Seiler, Gregory 837
Seip, Tom 242
Seitz, James R. 1
Seitze, David 223
Seivold, Stephen 871
Sekmakas, Viktoras R. 631
Selchan, Benjamin 378
Seldon, Eric B. 15
Selfridge, Michael D. (Mike) 328
Selian, Paul J. 739
Selich, Amy 80
Seljan, Jacob 831
Selk, Nate 72
Sell, Bernhard 426
Sell, Matt 584
Sellers, Mary E. 97
Sellers, Ronnie 292
Sellers, Angie 332
Sellers, Nancy 344
Sellers, Karl 488
Sellers, John 845
Sellinger, Howard L 399
Sellitto, Gayle 96
Sells, Jennifer 74
Selnes, Rob 502
Selnick, Allie 120
Selsor, Darlene 223
Selverian, Arthur 647
Selwood, Robert C. 522
Semaan, Fouad 120
Semer, Kelly 415
Semet, Gardner 103
Semik, Edward 873

Semmelbauer, Thilo 556
Semmens, Mark 361
Semo, Michael 481
Semple, Matt 303
Semple, Heather 456
Sen, Paula 749
Sen-Gupta, Prabir 107
Sence, John 346
Sendler, Robert 333
Senger, Joe 229
Sengul, Oguz 747
Sengupta, Rhetick 525
Senia, Vincent 703
Sennott, John L. (Jack) 25
Senroy, Sid 118
Sensing, J. Steven (Steve) 689
Senske, Thomas 92
Senter, Mark 671
Sepe, Louis 111
Sepulveda, Laura 873
Sep--Iveda, Eli S. 630
Serafini, Hester 427
Serbun, Joseph 206
Serck-hanssen, Sverre 279
Serge, Adrian 502
Serianni, Charles F. (Chuck) 679
Serlenga, Louis 389
Serna, Camilo 257
Serpa, Fernando 851
SERRANO, SHERRY 98
Serrano, Jose Fernando 195
Serrano, Jose Fernando Fernando 195
Serrano, Michael 310
Serven, Neal 466
Servodidio, Mark J. 86
Serwach, Debbie 670
Sery, Tim 584
Serzon, Jeffrey 181
Seshadri, Raj 506
Seshadri, Sunil 844
Seshan, Arvind 694
Seskey, Maureen 628
Session, Tracy 72
Sessions, Steven 610
Seth, Ajay 395
Sethi, Rajeev 50
Sethi, Parvesh 178
Sethi, Rahul 491
Sethi, Shipra 873
Setliff, William 460
Setliff, Will 460
Setlur, Varun 426
Settersten, Scott M 805
Settino, Tom 297
Settle, Tom 417
Settle, Peggy 504
Settle, Jondra 624
Seuferer, Kevin 41
Seurynck, Michael 764
Sever, Susan 304
Severe, Constantin 736
Severino, Michael E. 6
Severino, Vittorio M. 410
Sevesind, Elizabeth 92
Sevilla, Rob 528
Sevilla, Gene 689
Sevilla-Sacasa, Eugenio 689
Sevilla-Sacasa, Eugene 689
Sevimsavur, Tolgay 617
Seward, Phil 484
Sewell, D. Bruce 62

Sewell, Leigh 126
Sewell, Michael J. (Mike) 174
Sewell, David 322
Sewell, David B. 707
Sewll, Glenn 868
Sexton, Ellen 823
Seymour, Kim 42
Seymour, Tim 80
Sferrazza, Bob 148
Sferruzza, Maria 350
Sfiroudis, Steven 535
Sgaglione, Lucille T. 112
Sgammato, Tom 784
Shaback, Brent 823
Shabshab, Nabil 109
Shackell, Daniel 221
Shackleford, Jeremy 876
Shackouls, Bobby 627
Shacochis, David 491
Shaddox, Trey 273
Shade, Jennifer 785
Shadid, Sean 93
Shadrin, Ryan 839
Shae, Kate 289
Shafer, Ronald 207
Shafer, Craig 352
Shafer, Walter F. 622
Shafer, Walt 622
Shafer, Thomas C. (Tom) 761
Shafer, Joan M. 857
Shaff, Karen E. 637
Shaffer, Keith 305
Shaffer, Richard 322
Shaffer, Elizabeth 353
Shaffer, Michael A. (Mike) 653
Shaffer, Charles M. (Chuck) 701
Shagoury, Antoine 739
Shah, Samir 5
Shah, Manan 59
Shah, Anish 120
Shah, Ken 149
Shah, Mayank 181
Shah, Manish 207
Shah, Milan 350
Shah, Niyant 353
Shah, Raheel A 426
Shah, Aarti 479
Shah, Benish 610
Shah, Neal H 625
Shah, Neal 625
Shah, Rushabh 647
Shah, Niharika 647
Shah, Bhavin 694
Shah, Rajen 739
Shah, Manojkumar 759
Shah, Samir 760
Shah, Sanjay 768
Shah, Pratik 849
Shaheen, Daniel 352
Shaheen, Gabriel L. 402
Shahrestani, Navid 749
Shahri, Masoud 798
Shaik, Hussain 100
Shakeel, Ella 672
Shallcross, Joanne 139
Shallow, Andrew 72
Shamber, Mark E. 724
Shamburger, Julie N. 722
Shamloo, Brenda 798
Shamseddine, Adel 849
Shan, Jia 365
Shanahan, Patrick M. (Pat) 123

Shanahan, Julie 385
Shand, Yvonne 742
Shankar, Shashi 493
Shankar, Latha R 531
Shankar, Ram 806
Shanks, Robert L. (Bob) 339
Shanks, Murray 707
Shannon, Robert 109
Shannon, John 146
Shannon, John 176
Shannon, Albert 224
Shannon, Sean C 286
Shannon, Angela 292
Shao, Lei 425
Shaper, Darryl 68
Shapira, Adrianne 460
Shapiro, Glenn T. 27
Shapiro, Nancy 444
Shapiro, Marc 487
Shapiro, Jodi 538
Shapiro, Steve 664
Shapiro, Jonathan 734
Shapiro, Sheri 794
Shapiro, Steven D. 829
Shappee, Dave 243
Shara, Thomas J. 469
Sharan, Nitesh 560
Sharin, Meghan 120
Sharkey, Jeff 53
Sharkey, John 218
Sharma, Amit 49
Sharma, Poonam 182
Sharma, Vishal 266
Sharma, Mayank 366
Sharma, Radhika 560
Sharma, Manoj 740
Sharma, Praveen 811
Sharon, Richard 531
Sharp, Pamela 28
Sharp, M. S. (Scott) 170
Sharp, Robert T. (Bob) 270
Sharp, Reid 319
Sharp, Erin S. 463
Sharp, Ken 473
Sharp, Steven 677
Sharp, Amy 751
Sharp, Jeff 839
Sharpe, Stacy 27
Sharpe, Matthew P. 402
Sharpe, Mikel 835
Sharr, Michael 378
Shasha, Brian 531
Shashua, Amnon 426
Shastry, Mira 519
Shattuck, Mayo A. 284
Shattuck, Mayo A 285
Shatzer, Warren 9
Shaukat, Tariq M. 30
Shaulis, Matthew 617
Shaulis, Nancy 835
Shaver, David 814
Shaw, Terry 10
Shaw, Angie 66
Shaw, John 72
Shaw, G W 75
Shaw, Paula 102
Shaw, Kenneth 124
Shaw, Chris 320
Shaw, Todd 344
Shaw, Carl 375
Shaw, Michael 448
Shaw, David 448

Shaw, William 455
Shaw, Christi 479
Shaw, Alan H. 564
Shaw, Jeff M. 579
Shaw, Lynn T 664
Shaw, Robert 671
Shaw, Terry 825
Shea, Ann 152
Shea, Katherine 153
Shea, Colleen 277
Shea, Phil 304
Shea, Brian 609
Shea, Daniel 619
Shea, Jody 657
Shea, Dennis 739
Shea, David 787
Shea, Gus 846
Sheafe, Scott 613
Sheahan, Denis K. 143
Shealy, Aaron 28
Shear, Neal A. 167
Shearer, Bruce 415
Shearer, Norm 571
Shearer-adams, Jackie 162
Shebik, Steven E. (Steve) 27
Shedlin, Gary S. 120
Sheedy, William M. (Bill) 844
Sheehan, John 74
Sheehan, Bill 121
Sheehan, Rory 184
Sheehan, Tom 270
Sheehan, Dennis 338
Sheehan, Daniel J. (Dan) 356
Sheehan, James N. 404
Sheehan, Greg 446
Sheehan, Dan 617
Sheehy, John 81
Sheeley, Michael J. 814
Sheer, Julie 229
Shefcik, James 841
Sheffield, Ivan 225
Sheffield, Tamara 428
Sheffield, Kenneth H. 625
Sheffield, Ken 625
Sheffield, Scott D. 625
Sheftic, Jeff 481
Shehadi, Ramez 129
Sheikh, Rabia 844
Sheinbaum, Gary 653
Sheinheit, Alvin 518
Shelby, Thomas S. 615
Shelby, Laurie 768
Sheldon, Tina 283
Sheldon, Tim 500
Sheldon, Todd N. 651
Shelford, James 627
Sheline, Douglas 492
Shell, Jeff 198
Shell, Yvonne 411
Shelley, Bill 827
Shelnutt, David 813
Shelton, Kirk 571
Shelton, Gary 583
Shelton, Afton 627
Shelton, Roy 828
Shen, Henry 120
Shen, Sam 474
Shen, Leonard 844
Shenefelt, Kalyn 823
Shenkin, Kerri 100
Shenkman, Dov 849
Shenoodah, Sameh 681

Shenoy, Navin 425
Shepard, Andy 12
Shepard, Ernest 107
Shepard, Andrew 195
Shepard, Rob 303
Shepard, Chip 309
Shepardson, Chris 756
Sheperd, David 874
Shephard, Tom 769
Shepherd, Joel 46
Shepherd, Joe 304
Shepherd, Lonna 391
Shepherd, Thaddeus 500
Shepherd, Mark B 734
Sheppard, Charles 279
Sheppard, Charlie 279
Sheppard, Valarie 640
Sheppard, Ben 700
Shepperly, David 135
Shera, Gina 448
Sherbin, Robert 576
Sherer, Jay 174
Sheridan, William 179
Sheridan, Jason 417
Sheridan, Jean 565
Sheridan, Michael 609
Sheridan, Philip 872
Sheridan, Michael 879
Sheriff, Abrar 801
Sherlock, Kevin 417
Sherman, Dale 27
Sherman, Ronald 76
Sherman, Jeffrey S. 109
Sherman, Floyd F 140
Sherman, Catherine 147
Sherman, Patrick 324
Sherman, Matthew 331
Sherman, Arthur 391
Sherman, Peter 587
Shern, Lauren 120
Sherr, Richard 784
Sherrard, Roger S. 602
Sherrard, J. Andrew 757
Sherrer, Kendell 152
Sherrill, David 610
Sherrill, Gregg M. 764
Sherrod, Melissa 284
Sherwood-Wetherwax, Joan 493
Shetti, Victor 96
Shetty, Prajwal Shetty Prajwal 96
Shetty, Rajesh 177
Shevchek, James 375
Shevins, Nicole 653
Shevsky, David 29
Shibata, Michael 164
Shieh, Brian 63
Shiel, James G. 112
Shields, Stephanie 16
Shields, John 121
Shields, Steven 677
Shifflett, Porter 500
Shiffman, Steven B. (Steve) 653
Shifrin, Todd 873
Shigemura, Dean Y. 97
Shih, Elizabeth 245
Shikany, Charlie 216
Shilling, Judy 202
Shillings, Joe 760
Shiltz, LauraA 670
Shimabuku, Corey 98
Shimanski, Janette 3
Shimick, Debby 234

Shimko, Bryan 672
Shimogawa, Kristine 732
Shimomura, Joby 737
Shimonishi, Yasuhara 764
Shimp, Robert 593
Shin, Hak Cheol (H.C.) 3
Shin, Sookyoung 204
Shin, Joonhyok 401
Shin, Jung-tak 617
Shin, Hak 649
Shine, Daniel P. (Dan) 781
Shinkle, Kevin 459
Shinn, Stephanie 107
Shinn, David 429
Shipley, Susan Baker 183
Shipley, Susan (Susie) Baker 415
Shipley, Joshua 647
Shipley, Jessika 732
Shipley, Marcus B. 794
Shirey, Lonnie 75
Shirinian, Jola 100
Shirk, Amber 701
Shirk, Brett 846
Shirley, Ryan 103
Shirley, Kandy 672
Shirley, Linda 798
Shirley, Bard 800
Shishman, Scott 583
Shitole, Sanjay 630
Shively, Lori 794
Shiver, Kim 484
Shivers, William C. 415
Shoback, Jacqueline S. 132
Shockley, Harold 429
Shoeling, Lanny 458
Shoemaker, Christopher 820
Shoeman, Rosalie 86
Shoen, Sam 689
Shoener, Scott 839
Shogren, Steve 3
Shokes, Brad 445
Sholy, George 12
Shomette, Tom 171
Shon, Larry D. De 86
Shon, Harim 182
Shontere, Daniel 50
Shook, John 53
Shook, Paula 751
Shope, Juanita 672
Shoquist, Debora C. 576
Shore, Barbara 664
Short, Andrea G. 1
Short, Joe 53
Short, Sandra 131
Short, Chris 512
Short, Teresa 593
Short, Michael J. (Mike) 686
Short, Marianne D. 822
Shorten, Dermot 659
Shortt, Thomas 397
Shotts, Philip 194
Shotwell, David F. (Dave) 808
Shoukry, Paul 664
Shoup, Jennifer 120
Shoup, Jennifer 535
Shover, Michael 160
Showalter, Jennifer 751
Showers, Mark E. 673
Shows, Susan 477
Shrader, Ralph W. 130
Shrader, Kelly 448
Shrestha, Rasu 78

Shrewsbury, Holly 732
Shriber, Ryan 120
Shrimpton, Sean 5
Shrivastava, Siddharth 365
Shrivastava, Manish M. 651
Shrivastava, Sanjeev 653
Shrock, Jason 135
Shroff, Hiten 110
Shroyer, Christopher M. (Chris) 313
Shrum, Kayse 736
Shryack, Christopher 295
Shryne, Michael 492
Shudtz, Peter 222
Shue, Russell E 124
Shugrue, Vincent 348
Shui, Conway 841
Shukla, Anand 162
Shuler, Brandon R 139
Shuler, Ken 784
Shulick, Brett 103
Shull, Greg 154
Shulman, Doug 100
Shultz, Patti 448
Shultz, Jeff 841
Shum, Harry 525
Shumaker, Dan 13
Shumard, Candy 323
Shumate, Michael 47
Shumel, Brad 669
Shunck, Marybeth 635
Shunnarah, Salem 59
Shurts, Wayne 755
Shustak, Michael 160
Shute, Sarah 150
Shuttleworth, Edward L. 329
Shuyama, Andres 305
Siadak, Dan 586
Siah, Han-ron 500
Siak, Stacey 199
Siao, Susan 195
Siarkowski, Tracey 307
Siatis, Perry 6
Siberio, John 835
Sibley, James M 477
Sica, Frank V. 442
Sica, Frank 460
Sichak, Stephen (Steve) 109
Sichel, Hobart (Bart) 142
Siciliano, Betsy 841
Sickel, Seth Van 249
Sickinger, Lauren 433
Sicola, Tom 512
Siddhu, Vivek 493
Siddiqi, Sajid 200
Sideris, Harry K. 258
Sidhu, Preety 153
Sidhu, Inder 174
Sidhu, Jay S. 226
Sidhu, Roger 360
Sidney, Robert 3
Siebenborn, Bill 230
Siedel, Jay 85
Siedlecki, Sandy 494
Sieg, Andy 95
Siegel, Charles J. 61
Siegel, James 126
Siegel, Steven F 136
Siegel, Steven 136
Siegel, Richard 245
Siegel, Kenneth I. 487
Siegel, Michael 531

Siegel, Andrew 841
Siegel, Erinn 873
Sieger, Michael D. (Mike) 642
Siegmund, Jan 80
Siegrist, Robert N. 144
Sienkiewicz, Mark 444
Sieracki, Julie 500
Siereveld, Ryan P 640
Sierra, Joseph 100
Sievert, G. Michael (Mike) 757
Sieving, Charles E. 333
Sieving, Charles E. 557
Siewert, Patrick 85
Sifer, Joseph F. (Joe) 129
Sifer, Joe 129
Sigal, Jonathan 634
Sigler, Jon 694
Sigman, Brian C. 16
Sigmon, William L 39
Sigmon, Vaughn 154
Sigmund, William 109
Signorino, Charles 162
Sih, Gil 655
Siino, Joseph 86
Sikora, Justin 234
Sikora, Kaz 566
Silagy, Eric E. 333
Silagy, Eric E. 557
Silbaugh, Jason 448
Silberhorn, Tara 597
Silberman, Jennifer 760
Silberman, David 841
Silberschlag, Kirstin 834
Silbert, Mark 50
Silcock, Chris 392
Silcock, Christopher 392
Silfa, Betty 181
Silfee, Keith 344
Silins, Andris J 504
Silitch, Nicholas C. (Nick) 647
Silitch, Nick 647
Sill, Scott 627
Silliman, Craig L. 837
Sills, Stephen J. 24
Silos, Richard 12
Silva, Nicole 124
Silva, Stephen 177
Silva, Francisco A. Aristeguieta 181
Silva, Marc 182
Silva, Marc 196
Silva, Mona 219
Silva, Rodrigo 331
Silva, Rebecca 481
Silva, Elif 617
Silva, Anthony 849
Silvas, Richard 808
Silveira, Roberto 617
Silver, Allison 42
Silver, Noah 185
Silver, Gary 841
Silveri, Debbie 692
Silverman, Rob 129
Silverman, Ami 525
Silverman, Abraham 573
Silvermintz, Sharon 797
Silvernail, Andrew 747
Silvers, David 1
Silverstein, Martin B. 360
Silverstein, Pamela 653
Silverstein, Ray 729
Silvestre-tan, Carmentina 548

Silvia, Tim 198
Silvia, Phil 749
Silvis, Harry 858
Sim, Chris 456
Simard, Curtis C. 105
Simcoe, Suma 531
Simeone, Giovanni 96
Simeone, Robert 484
Simermeyer, Elizabeth A. (Beth) 266
Simes, Sarah 134
Simko, Chris 841
Simkonis, John 316
Simkowitz, Daniel A. (Dan) 535
Simmerman, Lee 689
Simmons, Bob 72
Simmons, Paul 92
Simmons, Angela 234
Simmons, Jodi 428
Simmons, Jeffrey N. (Jeff) 479
Simmons, Eileen 830
Simmons, Gary 834
Simmons, Harris H. 884
Simms, Constance 326
Simms, David 431
Simms, James 613
Simms, Charles 629
Simon, Jon 195
Simon, Lynn T. 207
Simon, Mindy 211
Simon, Kurt 249
Simon, Douglas 493
Simon, Grigore 555
Simon, John R. 618
Simon, Steve 675
Simon, Larry 712
Simon, Pamela 733
Simon, Marianne 774
Simon, Andrea 841
Simon, Linda 851
Simonds, John 494
Simonds, Michael Q. 828
Simonelli, Lorenzo 349
Simons, Christopher 100
Simons, Doyle 331
Simons, Sharon 784
Simpson, Tom 3
Simpson, Dean 12
Simpson, Austin 102
Simpson, Vincent 130
Simpson, Barry N. 191
Simpson, Laurie 240
Simpson, Shelley 413
Simpson, Kristina 455
Simpson, Sue 493
Simpson, Kathryn 568
Simpson, David L. 675
Simpson, Mark 711
Simpson, Stewart 747
Simpson, Julie 798
Simpson, Rachel 871
Sims, Colleen 96
Sims, Sean 270
Sims, C. Randall (Randy) 396
Sims, Heidi 415
Sims, John V. 433
Sims, Dave 689
Sims, Scott 695
Simson, Marck 72
Simson, Thomas H. 246
Sinclair, Stephen 177
Sinclair, Donald 671

Sindoni, James 303
Sinesi, Polly 465
Singer, David 109
Singer, Gadi 425
Singer, Lori 507
Singh, Rajinder P. (Raj) 103
Singh, Kavitha 103
Singh, Jaskiran 111
Singh, Munjeet 130
Singh, Zorawar Biri 177
Singh, Inder 178
Singh, Charan 181
Singh, Dk 211
Singh, Harmeet 470
Singh, Urvashi 481
Singh, Vikram 489
Singh, Jasraj 500
Singh, Bobby 535
Singh, Sonny 593
Singh, Inderjeet 593
Singh, Vishal 593
Singh, Shaminder 613
Singh, Sanjay 689
Singh, Ajay 846
Singhal, Anupam 474
Singler, Craig 431
Singleton, J. Barton 753
Singleton, James 860
Sinha, Santosh 183
Sinha, Dharmendra Kumar 193
Sinha, Sharat 846
Siniawski, Glen 628
Sinko, Christopher 136
Sinko, Jim 707
Sinks, Patrick 521
Sinnard, Pat 44
Sinnott, Eamonn 425
Sinowitz, Paul 522
Sinz, Eric 211
Sipe, Barb 632
Sipes, Kevin 677
Siragusa, Michael 625
Sirakos, William 223
Sirbu, Pete 50
Sireyjol, Nicolas 43
Sirimane, Krishan 635
Sirkin, Clive 451
Sirkin, David 653
Sirmon, Gary L. 104
Sirota, Gennady 177
Sirota, Marc 198
Sirota, Bruce 446
Sirridge, Susan 150
Siry, Marc 198
Siskind, Wendy 142
Sisolak, Steve 735
Sistine, Teriann Van 72
Sivamurthy, Krupa 617
Sivaram, Siva 864
Siverling, Anders 26
Siwek, Janusz 395
Sixl, Wolfgang 757
Sjodin, Cara 823
Sjulin, Susie 237
Skaggs, Amy L 730
Skaggs, Michael D. (Mike) 766
Skains, Tom 258
Skala, Joe 28
Skala, Cathy 107
Skala, P. Justin 194
Skala, Justin 195
Skala, Peter 195

Stecher, Esta E. 365
Stedfast, Sarah B. 843
Stedronsky, Gregg 352
Steeg, Monica 566
Steele, Sally A. 206
Steele, Delaney 687
Steele, Douangchan 756
Steensen, Erik 492
Steer, Michael 13
Steers, Paige 445
Stefanich, Andrew 160
Stefanou, Katerina 681
Stefanski, Mike 837
Steffe, Greg 647
Steffen, Julie 445
Steffensen, Mark 410
Steffensen, Dwight 752
Stegeman, Jeff 455
Stegen, Andrew 488
Steger, Darcy 326
Steger, Troy 385
Stegman, Melissa 308
Stegner, Robert L. (Bob) 752
Stegner, Bob 752
Steigerwalt, Eric T 135
Steigman, Liz 380
Steimer, Richard 307
Stein, Gary 36
Stein, Jeffrey S. 36
Stein, David L. 71
Stein, Derek K. 120
Stein, Clint E. 196
Stein, William G. 217
Stein, Andrew 261
Stein, Rona 299
Stein, Richard 307
Stein, Trudy 438
Steinbach, Justin 224
Steinberg, Chase 149
Steinberg, Jimmy 153
Steinberg, Stephen 446
Steinberg, Lewis R 552
Steinberg, Jesse 802
Steiner, Judy 104
Steiner, Tim 138
Steiner, Troy 142
Steiner, David 302
Steiner, Rachel 385
Steiner, Melanie 653
Steiner, Curt 832
Steinhaus, Tom 385
Steinke, Connie 325
Steinmetz, Jay 615
Steinmetz, Bill 788
Steinmetz, Bill 788
Steinmetz, Robert 844
Steinour, Stephen D. (Steve) 414
Steinwert, Kent A 292
Steinwolf, Chad 181
Stella, John 50
Stelling, James 47
Stelling, Kessel D. 753
Stelman, Randee 5
Stelman, Randee 6
Stemper, William R. (Bill) 197
Stencel, Douglas 684
Stengel, Ray 673
Stenz, John 227
Stenzel, Christopher (Chris) 215
Stepanski, Robert 448
Stephanie, Maher-dickerson 858
Stephatos, George 784

Stephen, Lomsdalen 50
Stephen, Chris 270
Stephens, John J. 75
Stephens, Greg 813
Stephens, Steven D. 884
Stephenson, Randall L. 75
Stephenson, Jacqueline 123
Stephenson, Britt 558
Stephenson, Todd 707
Sterbenz, James 146
Sterbenz, Jim 146
Sterbenz, Isaac 695
Sterghos, Nick 530
Sterling, Jill 80
Sterling, Christine 305
Sterling, Courtney 380
Sterling, Michelle 655
Sterling, Kira 786
Stern, Walter 36
Stern, Peter 62
Stern, Brian 100
Stern, Sonny 242
Stern, Jonathan 335
Stern, Michele 431
Stern, Chris 519
Sterner, Beth 798
Stettner, Jennifer 621
Steve, Davidsen 6
Steve, Harman 491
Steve, Enos 879
Steven, Deschene 785
Stevens, Jim 3
Stevens, Timothy (Chip) 15
Stevens, Kelly 42
Stevens, Michael 72
Stevens, Mark 103
Stevens, Brian 107
Stevens, Craig 206
Stevens, Craig 350
Stevens, Charles K. (Chuck) 353
Stevens, Keith 413
Stevens, Cheryl 465
Stevens, Maureen 492
Stevens, Denise 712
Stevens, Tara 740
Stevens, W. Arthur 800
Stevens, Simon 822
Stevens, Kristen 851
Stevenson, Kimberly 132
Stevenson, Kathie 201
Stevenson, Michael 313
Stevenson, Mark 323
Stevenson, Emily 391
Stevenson, Phil 624
Stevenson, Thomas 751
Stevenson, Mark P. 781
Stevenson, Jim 792
Stevenson, Karen 826
Stevenson, Mark 871
Stevenson, Tom 876
Stewart, Jeffrey R 6
Stewart, Julia 85
Stewart, William (Bill) 129
Stewart, Janie 147
Stewart, Greg 154
Stewart, Steele 162
Stewart, Alice 162
Stewart, Dave 251
Stewart, Jan 256
Stewart, Jamie B 299
Stewart, Debra 315
Stewart, Kevin 318

Stewart, Cecelia 322
Stewart, Michael J. (Mike) 323
Stewart, John F. 335
Stewart, Sheila 337
Stewart, Carol 451
Stewart, Marlene 463
Stewart, Bob 510
Stewart, Heather 551
Stewart, Don 617
Stewart, Stephanie D. 625
Stewart, Cheryl 645
Stewart, Terri 664
Stewart, Jim 666
Stewart, Karen Weldin 732
Stewart, Scott 750
Stewart, Will 798
Stewart, Cameron 812
Stewart, Corey 834
Stibal, John 828
Stibler, Ellen 507
Stibolt, Robert 278
Stichnoth, Roseann 299
Stickels, Eric 206
Stickland, Davina 120
Stickney, Tim 481
Stidham, Cathy 584
Stief, Brian 444
Stiefel, Lester 97
Stiefel, Holly 871
Stienemeier, Marion 653
Stiers, Mark W. 256
Stiff, Cory 617
Stifferclaus, Vanessa 240
Stigers, Thomas M. (Tom) 867
Still, Kevin A. 190
Stilla, John 304
Stille, Randy 72
Stille, Charles 355
Stiller, David 415
Stillwell, Scott 803
Stilwell, Craig G. 185
Stimson, Bob 624
Stine, Karen 662
Stine, Aaron 694
Stingily, Karl 302
Stingl, Jennifer 130
Stinnett, Clay 744
Stinnett, Joseph 821
Stinnette, Mike 530
Stinson, Deirdre 602
Stinson, Ron 624
Stipanov, John C 634
Stipanovich, Sasha 664
Stipek, Deborah 474
Stippig, Julian 182
Stirnkorb, Jed 160
Stith, Melvin 16
Stith, Thomas 735
Stith, Pamela 754
Stitt, Kimberly 318
Stitt, Kevin 736
Stivers, Rob 672
Stivers, Betsy 828
Stjames, Joanne 381
Stlaurent, Janice 96
Stober, Renee L 124
Stock, Don 628
Stockdale, Barry 50
Stocker, Michael A. 548
Stocker, Justin 751
Stockman, Jim 451
Stockmeister, Aaron 307

Stocksdale, Thomas 293
Stockton, Dmitri 240
Stockton, Jed 240
Stockton, Dmitri L. 349
Stockton, Dmitri 689
Stoddard, Daniel G 254
Stoddard, Lorilee 884
Stoecker, Chris 749
Stoeckert, Michael 638
Stoehr, David L. 872
Stoering, Mark E. 878
Stoffels, Paulus (Paul) 443
Stoffels, Paul 444
Stoffers, Brian F. 159
Stoffregen, Lynn 385
Stojanovski, Igor 292
Stojkov, Joe 694
Stoker, Robin 832
Stokes, Russell 349
Stokes, Bobby 382
Stokes, Rueben 782
Stolasz, Jeff 571
Stolfi, Carl 362
Stolhanske, Ruth 304
Stolicker, Melissa 371
Stoll, Scott 593
Stoll, Debra 637
Stollings, Anthony M. (Tony) 318
Stolorena, Sheila 814
Stolp, Michael 570
Stoltman, Gary 460
Stoltmann, Gary 460
Stoltz, Michael 263
Stone, Brenda 100
Stone, Carol 109
Stone, Robert D. 112
Stone, Michelle 182
Stone, Aaron 202
Stone, John 240
Stone, Richard 242
Stone, Jeffrey 258
Stone, Neil 365
Stone, Paul 388
Stone, Denise 415
Stone, Scott 422
Stone, Steven M. 465
Stone, Samuel G. 513
Stone, Walter 573
Stone, Claire 613
Stone, Andrew P. 668
Stone, Scott 673
Stone, Paul E 776
Stone, Barry 823
Stone, Kent V. 831
Stone, Nancy 834
Stonehill, Robyn Price 74
Stoner, Floyd 595
Stonesifer, Timothy C. (Tim) 389
Stoness, Scott 458
Stonestreet, Dana L 399
Stonhaus, Dallas 694
Stonier, Joann 506
Stoop, Peggy 314
Stoothoff, Anthony 28
Storbeck, Robert 415
Storer, Carrie 248
Storey, Marie 305
Storey, Jeffrey K. (Jeff) 490
Storie, Rockey 278
Stork, Ryan D. 120
Storto, David E. 503
Stortz, Yvette 666

Wadhera, Shilpa 247
Wadhwa, Gaurav 647
Wadsworth, Kent 715
Waerum, Jesper 653
Wagers, Gary W. 104
Waghray, Ajay 74
Wagler, Theresa E. 741
Wagner, Jason 60
Wagner, Elizabeth 100
Wagner, Hank 142
Wagner, Janette 147
Wagner, Jody 205
Wagner, Scott 207
Wagner, Lisa 212
Wagner, James 240
Wagner, Stephen 255
Wagner, Darla 304
Wagner, Kevin 324
Wagner, Jim 344
Wagner, Dave 352
Wagner, Arthur 548
Wagner, Matthew P. (Matt) 600
Wagner, Patricia K. (Patti) 704
Wagner, Mary 728
Wagner, Lucas 755
Wagner, Edward 780
Wagner, Matt 798
Wagoner, Amy 1
Wagoner, Jeremy 825
Wagstaff, Craig C. 254
Wahlin, Mary 96
Wahlstrom, Pelle 645
Waid, Amber 591
Wainscott, Jody 174
Wainwright, Brenda 316
Wainwright, Robbie 512
Wais, Marc 551
Waite, Barbara 298
Waite, Stacey 519
Wajner, Matthew F. 310
Wajnrajch, Michael 616
Wakerly, John 178
Walberg, Michael 751
Walby, Dave 689
Waldbaum, Brian 388
Waldburger, Dan 656
Waldeck, Phil 647
Walden, Joshua M. (Josh) 425
Walden, Donald 713
Walden, Marni M. 837
Waldheim, William 237
Waldman, Mitchell B. (Mitch) 416
Waldman, Tom 481
Waldorf, Emily 146
Waldron, John 365
Waldron, John 400
Waldrop, Gabe 413
Walecki, Kurt 435
Walesiewicz, Patricia 109
Waleski, Anne G. 498
Walford, Christopher 96
Walia, Sandeep 500
Walia, Ash 729
Walker, Kevin 14
Walker, Newton 16
Walker, Mark 47
Walker, Sara 71
Walker, Marvonia 75
Walker, Clay 96
Walker, Jeanne 104
Walker, Trish 116
Walker, Lisa 136

Walker, John 148
Walker, Jason 149
Walker, Kevin 152
Walker, Chad 152
Walker, Karen 177
Walker, Mark 183
Walker, David 200
Walker, Marlene 206
Walker, Terry 324
Walker, Sean N. 351
Walker, J Marvin Marvin 355
Walker, Steve 359
Walker, Kathryn 395
Walker, Kellye L. 416
Walker, Christopher 426
Walker, Sandra 449
Walker, Amy 492
Walker, Myron 500
Walker, William 502
Walker, Burke 540
Walker, Jennifer 542
Walker, Thomas 560
Walker, John 574
Walker, Cynthia L. 580
Walker, Doug 588
Walker, Dan 591
Walker, David M. (Dave) 607
Walker, Darren 613
Walker, Roberto 637
Walker, Steven G. 644
Walker, Jeff 657
Walker, Richard 687
Walker, Kevin 719
Walker, Frank 727
Walker, Fiona 781
Walker, Virginia 793
Walker, Bryan 806
Walker, Ben 813
Walker, Kristina 828
Walker, James 851
Walker, Joseph C 876
Wall, Preston 77
Wall, David J 147
Wall, Michael P 160
Wall, Daniel R. 288
Wall, Shane D. 409
Wall, Aileen 441
Wall, Pam 754
Wallace, Grisel 96
Wallace, Kim Roll 107
Wallace, Steve 124
Wallace, Jeff 149
Wallace, Marcus 162
Wallace, Diane 192
Wallace, Noel R. 194
Wallace, Mark K. 222
Wallace, Mark E. 231
Wallace, Akmar 261
Wallace, John 307
Wallace, Kristina 382
Wallace, Brent E. 428
Wallace, Henry D. G. 472
Wallace, John 621
Wallace, Matthew 653
Wallace, William 662
Wallace, Bruce E. 749
Wallace, Antoinette 785
Wallace, Madelyn 807
Wallace, Mark R. 818
Wallach, Russell 484
Wallbank, Chris 670
Wallenta, Craig 50

Waller, Rayne 55
Waller, Kathy N. 191
Waller, Cathy 643
Waller, Tom 678
Walles, Rob 160
Wallfred, Teresa 211
Wallin, Kim 735
Wallington, Michael 80
Wallis, Julie 96
Wallis, James 431
Wallis, Richard 525
Walljasper, William J. (Bill) 156
Walno, Vicki 174
Walrath, Teresa 500
Walser, Brett 797
Walsh, Lambert 7
Walsh, Brian 28
Walsh, David 45
Walsh, Timothy A. 47
Walsh, Tim 75
Walsh, Mike 77
Walsh, Steven 112
Walsh, Joseph 112
Walsh, David 146
Walsh, John 148
Walsh, Bernadette 182
Walsh, Kelly 187
Walsh, Caitlin 365
Walsh, Andrea 383
Walsh, Michael 427
Walsh, Joe 428
Walsh, Brian 446
Walsh, Kate 484
Walsh, Keith 502
Walsh, Timothy J. 503
Walsh, William P. 548
Walsh, Kevin 593
Walsh, Wendy 656
Walsh, Amanda 695
Walsh, Marguerite 698
Walsh, Karen Bianchi 731
Walsh, Despina 742
Walsh, Ian K. 771
Walsh, Janice 794
Walsh, Rich 834
Walsh, Paul 844
Walstrom, Jan 441
Walstrom, Dean 814
Walta, Eric 673
Waltenburg, Rhonda 832
Walter, Luc 56
Walter, Tim 182
Walter, Pati 304
Walter, Frank E. 384
Walter, Glen 533
Walter, Lawrence 566
Walter, Richard 638
Walter, Michael 798
Walters, Brad 80
Walters, Cynthia 200
Walters, Edward 481
Walters, Kirk W. 609
Walters, Mary 685
Walters, Barbara A. 794
Walther, Leanna 6
Waltman, Naomi 841
Walton, Carlyle 11
Walton, Edward 50
Walton, John 75
Walton, David T. (Dave) 157
Walton, Demetra 302
Walton, Karen 473

Walton, Lynell 584
Walton, Paul 613
Walton, Dan 787
Waltz, Mike 72
Waltz, Diana 153
Walz, James 381
Walz, Tim 734
Wambold, Richard 764
Wampler, Kevin S. 252
Wampler, Terrance 593
Wamser, Chris 275
Wan, Kenneth 728
Wanchik, Marry 96
Wandeler, Roland 55
Wandell, Keith E. 231
Wandell, Keith 255
Wandelmaier, Bruce 856
Wander, John 121
Wandschneider, Robin 202
Waner, Leo 764
Wang, David 124
Wang, Xiaoman 179
Wang, Pei 182
Wang, Bill 330
Wang, Gloria 401
Wang, Kai 426
Wang, Li 479
Wang, Ed 506
Wang, John 552
Wang, Rex 593
Wang, Andy 686
Wang, Ming-Hsien 777
Wang, Patrick 792
Wang, Min 844
Wanless, Benjamin 202
Wann, Robert 549
Wanta, Gregory T. 433
Waraksy, Jacqueline 120
Warbinton, Craig 75
Warch, Steven 535
Ward, Chris 13
Ward, Victor 95
Ward, Anita 152
Ward, Jason 203
Ward, Paul J. 206
Ward, Patrick J. (Pat) 225
Ward, Maria 225
Ward, F. Stephen 312
Ward, David 322
Ward, Bill 328
Ward, Steven E. 384
Ward, John 486
Ward, Roy 747
Ward, Tony 747
Ward, Ron 753
Ward, Laysha L. 759
Ward, Susan 818
Ward, Brian 823
Ward, Michael 841
Ward, Tony 846
Ward, Patrick 876
Warden, Kathy J. 568
Wardlaw, Van M. 766
Wardlow, Kirk 803
Wardman, Traci 546
Wardrup, James 15
Wardwell, Myra 96
Wardynski, Paula 556
Ware, Stacey 96
Ware, Timothy 507
Wareheim, Laura 310
Wareing, Peter 163

Ziniti, Joe 608
Zink, Daniel 513
Zino, Jillian 653
Zins, Sebastien 694
Zinser, Daniel 761
Zipter, Rudi 258
Zirkle, Matthew 640
Zito, Peter 550
Zito, Joseph 818
Zitterkopf, Brian 448
Zitting, Shaun 401
Zivelonghi, G. Larry 227
Zkri, Adel 240
Zlateva, Vesela 247
Zoeller, Kathrin 556
Zogg, Jack 346
Zoghbi, Huda 669
Zoiss, Edward J. (Ed) 466
Zoller, Clifford 689
Zolnowski, David 492
Zolotov, Vladimir 431
Zoltak, Shawn 685
Zonyk, Brent 566
Zook, Dennis R. 219
Zorn, Tom 160
Zou, Peter 341
Zou, Qin 727
Zuber, Gregory 240
Zuberi, Faheem 411
Zubretsky, Joseph M. 531
Zucaro, Aldo C. (Al) 585
Zucker, Steven 823
Zuckerberg, Mark 290
Zuckerman, Jason 653
Zuengler, Hugh 849
Zufall, David 249
Zuhl, Colleen A. 783
Zuhlke, Dan 428
Zuhone, Laura 324
Zuiderveld, Jaap 576
Zulberti, Andrea 752
Zulli, Mark 841
Zulueta, Alfonso G. (Chito) 479
Zumbahlen, Therese 315
Zumwalt, LeAnne M. 235
Zundel, Shayne 700
Zuniga, Gaspar 444
Zuniga, Aamsa 662
Zuniga, Miguel 769
Zupko, Chris 876
Zupo, Robert 819
Zurack, Marlene 548
Zuraitis, Marita 402
Zuro, Matthew 316
Zurovitch, John 481
Zwach, Jennifer 50
Zwickl, Michele 781
Zwiebel, Rob 684
Zwinger, Susan 593
Zygiel, Kenneth 380
Zyl, Adriaan Van 88
Zysk, Ralf 620

Directors of Third National Bank set up State Street Deposit & Trust to engage in the newfangled business of trusts.

In 1925 National Union Bank merged with State Street and inherited its custodial business. The bank grew through the 1950s; acquisitions included the Second National Bank and the Rockland-Atlas National Bank.

In 1970 State Street converted to a holding company — the State Street Boston Financial Corp. (State Street Boston Corp. as of 1977). The company also went international that decade opening an office in Munich Germany.

Soaring inflation and the recession of the 1970s forced the company to radically rethink its mission. The 1974 passage of the Employee Retirement Income Security Act changed the laws governing the management of pension funds and created an opportunity. State Street was one of the first banks to move aggressively into high-tech information processing and affiliate Boston Financial Data Services began servicing pension assets in 1974.

Encouraged by that success in 1975 new CEO William Edgerly (who served until 1992) steered State Street away from branch banking and into investments trusts and securities processing. An early achievement was designing PepsiCo's retirement plan. Fee-based sales approached 50% of revenues; the company could now quit focusing on lending. In the 1980s and 1990s the company built its administration and investment management businesses overseas and moved into software.

Evolving in the late 1990s State Street left noncore businesses but expanded globally. In 1997 it formed European Direct Capital Management to invest in eastern and central Europe. State Street Global Advisors opened a London office in 1998 to serve wealthy individuals outside the US.

The company sold its commercial banking business to Royal Bank of Scotland in 1999 signaling an exit from that business and narrowing State Street's scope to the asset and investment management businesses. The company also bought Wachovia's custody and institutional trust business and teamed with Citigroup to sell 401(k) retirement products.

In 2000 State Street created FX Connect an electronic foreign exchange trading system. Also that year David Spina took over as CEO from the retiring Marshall Carter.

The firm bought Bel Air Investment Advisors and its broker/dealer affiliate Bel Air Securities in 2001 to cater to the ultrawealthy. In 2003 State Street sold its corporate trust business to U.S. Bancorp and its private asset management business to Charles Schwab's U.S. Trust. Spina retired in 2004; his prot g Ron Logue stepped in as chairman and CEO.

In 2007 State Street added bulk by acquiring another Boston-based fund accounting and servicing provider Investors Financial Services. The company boosted its foreign exchange offerings with the acquisition of Currenex. The following year State Street and Citigroup sold their CitiStreet retirement and pension plan management joint venture to ING Groep for some $900 million.

The US Treasury invested some $2 billion in the company in 2008 as part of a broader bailout plan to restore confidence and increase liquidity. State Street was among eight other top banks that received a combined $250 billion; the company repaid the full amount within months.

In the distressed economic climate State Street's servicing and management revenues declined due to lower equity market valuations and lending volumes and an increase in bankruptcies. The company hit its nadir in 2009 when it reported more than $2 billion in losses.

EXECUTIVES

President And Coo, Ronald P. (Ron) O'Hanley, age 63, $784,615 total compensation

Evp And Global Head State Street Alternative Investment Solutions, George E. Sullivan

Chairman And Ceo, Joseph L. (Jay) Hooley, age 63, $980,769 total compensation

Evp And Head Of Regulatory Industry And Government Affairs, Stefan M. Gavell

Evp And Head Global Markets And Global Services Asia Pacific, Wai Kwong Seck, age 64

Evp And Chief Legal Officer, Jeffrey N. Carp, age 63, $675,000 total compensation

Evp, Maria F. Dwyer

Evp And Head Securities Finance And Portfolio Solutions, Nicholas T. (Nick) Bonn

Evp And Global Cio, Antoine Shagoury

Evp And Chief Administrative Officer State Street Global Advisors, Marc P. Brown

Evp Corporate Advisory Services, James C. Caccivio

Global Head Of Operations Infrastructure And Business Transformation, Jeffrey D. Conway, age 54

Evp And Cto, Albert J. (Jerry) Cristoforo

Evp, Sharon E. Donovan Hart

President And Ceo State Street Global Advisors, Cyrus Taraporevala

Evp And Head State Street Global Exchange, Lou Maiuri

Evp And Head Global Operations, Robert Kaplan

Evp And Head Sector Solutions Sales Emea, Stefan Gmuer

Evp And Head Tax And Tax Advantaged Investments, Dennis E. Ross

Evp Chief Human Resources And Corporate Citizenship Officer, Kathryn M. (Kathy) Horgan

Evp, Richard G. Taggart, age 60

Evp And General Counsel, David C. Phelan

Evp Trading And Clearing, Martine Bond

Evp, Tracy Atkinson

Evp And Chief Investment Officer, Paul J. Selian

Evp And Chief Marketing Officer, Hannah Grove

Evp And General Counsel, Phillip S. Gillespie

Evp And Chief Risk Officer, Andrew Kuritzkes, age 59

Evp Alternative Asset Managers Solutions, Maria Cantillon

Evp And Coo State Street Global Services Emea, Anthony Carey

Global Chief Investment Officer, Rick Lacaille

Evp And Chief Compliance Officer, Cuan Coulter

Evp, David Crawford

Evp And Head Application Development And Maintenance, Ali El Abboud

Evp And Chief Data Officer, James Hardy

Evp And Head Specialized Products Group State Street Global Services Investment Services Americas, Brenda Lyons

Evp Head Of Institutional Investor Services, Stephen F. (Steve) Nazzaro

Evp And International Chief Risk Officer, David Suetens

Evp And Cfo, Eric Aboaf, age 55

Evp And Managing Director State Street Bank Gmbh, Jorg Ambrosius

Evp Global Markets Sales And Trading And Research, Anthony C. Bisegna

Evp State Street Global Advisors And Cio Global Equity Beta Solutions, Lynn S. Blake

Evp And Head State Street Global Services Ireland, Susan Dargan

Evp Chief Innovation Officer And Head Advisory And Information Solutions, Jessica Donohue

Evp And Head Of Global Services, Andrew Erickson

Evp And Head Sector Solutions Americas And Global Alternatives, Scott R. FitzGerald

Evp And Head Global Total Rewards And Human Resources, Todd Gershkowitz

Evp And Head Derivatives Securities Valuation And Internal Recon Centers Of Excellence, John Griffin

Evp And Head Emea State Street Global Advisors, Mike Karpik

Evp International Finance And Treasury, Mark R. Keating

Evp State Street Global Markets, Karen D. Keenan

Evp State Street Global Markets, Ian Martin

Evp, Ivan Matviak

Evp And General Auditor, Michael Richards

Evp Ssga And Global Head Spdr Exchange Traded Funds Business And Head Intermediary Distribution United States; Chairman Ssga Funds Management Inc., James E. (Jim) Ross

Evp And Head Global Markets Emea, Rajen Shah

Evp State Street Global Advisors And Cio Investment Solutions Group, Dan Farley

Evp And Global Head Of State Street Securities Finance, Paul Fleming

Evp State Street Global Services Investment Services Americas, Michael Fontaine

Evp Legal State Street Global Markets State Street Global Exchange State Street Global Operations And Credit Service, R. Bryan Woodard

Evp, Aunoy Banerjee

Evp And Head Asia Pacific Ssga, Lochiel Crafter

Evp, Pinar Kip

Evp, Jon Lehner

Evp And Head State Street Global Exchange, John Plansky

Evp, Liz Roaldsen

Evp And Treasurer, John Slyconish

Evp And Co-head State Street Global Services Emea, Elizabeth Nolan

Senior Vice President, Martin Sullivan

Vice President Of Information Technology, Phil Pengeroth

Vice President Information Technology, Chandra Busannagari

Vice President Information Technology, Siddharth Jeevan

Executive Vice President, Bernard Reilly

Executive Vice President, Gunjan Kedia

Assistant Vice President (business Analyst), Jane Burke

Vice President Director, Lou Adreani

Vice President It Business Project Analysis, Michael Tarpey

Vice President, Mark Massaro

Vice President, Stephen Farrell

Assistant Vice President, Christina Daniels

Application Developer Consultant Assistant Vice President, Sumitra Kothandaraman

Vice President Product Manager Etf Operations, Adam Hicks

Assistant Vice President, Joanne Farrington

Assistant Vice President, Irene Papamarkou

Assistant Vice President, Dennis Shea

Vice President, Kevin Miley

Senior Vice President, Susan Luo

Senior Vice President, Mark Schafer

Vice President, Hiroshi Saito

Assistant Vice President, Diane Matusic

Senior Vice President, Peter Thurmond

Vice President Of Creative, John Mcclain

Vice President Information Technology, Srihari Valiveti

Vice President, Allan Lewis

Assistant Vice President Mutual Fund Tax, Adriana Grossi
Assistant Vice President, Ed Alter
Senior Vice President And Chief Applications Architect, Chris Mccarthy
Vice President, Jason Salter
Vice President Derivatives Program Manager, Michael Derr
Vice President Investor Services, Dori J Samia
Senior Vice President Information Technology Architect, Maura Evans
Vice President, Travis Calabio
Avp Gcs, Andrew Cammorata
Assistant Vice President, Mike Manganaro
Vice President Financial Reporting, Winnie Lam
Vice President, Paul Branzburg
Senior Counselvice President, Veronica Greenbaum
Senior Vice President, Chris Malley
Vice President Adm Testing, Irina Reznikova
Vice President, Amy Johnston
Senior Vice President And Chief Scientist, David Saul
Senior Vice President, Paul Connolly
Vice President Human Resources Business Partner, Tammy Chojnowski
Senior Vice President Corporate Audit Chief Administrative Officer, Shannon Groppi
Avp, Raquel Ellis
Vice President, Diane Webber
Vice President, Ravi Bandaru
Assistant Vice President Ta Operations, Stephanie Babou
Vice President Information Systems, Scott Wheeler
Assistant Vice President Relationship Management, Tara Stevens
Vice President, Mike Irwin
Open Systems Analyst Vice President (senior Unix System Administrator), James Woest
Vice President, Jason Bittarelli
Senior Vice President Global Business Reporting, Marcy Barker
Vice President, Uma Gorantla
Vice President Application Development Software Design Architect, Manoj Sharma
Vice President, Mary Phillips
Assistant Vice President, Keri Lanzetta
Vice President, Michelle Griffiths
Vice President Strategy Consultant, JONATHAN NESBIT
Vice President, Michelle Hayward
Vice President Fx Trading And Sales, Conor Keane
Assistant Vice President, Lokesh Aggarwal
Vice President, Kevin Moss
Assistant Vice President, Gregory Mullen
Vice President, Daniel Mazza
Vice President And Senior Counsel, Francine Hayes
Senior Vice President Privacy Officer, Gerald Spada
Vice President, James Callahan
Vice President, Gopal Balasubramanian
Vice President, Jim Huang
Avp, Nicole Souza
Vice President Project Team Manager, Karen Rodeo
Vice President, Michael Mccarthy
Vice President Lead Generation Program, Julie Hermann
Assistant Vice President, Renee Hickey
Assistant Vice President, Bimal Patel
Vice President Corporate Citizenship, Wayne Young
Vice President Vdi Infrastructure Architecture, Bruce Lyons
Senior Vice President State Street Bank Gmbh, Evert Van Den Brink
Vice President, Gene Morris
Auditors: Ernst & Young LLP

LOCATIONS

HQ: State Street Corp.
One Lincoln Street, Boston, MA 02111
Phone: 617 786-3000
Web: www.statestreet.com

2016 Assets Mix

	% of total
North America	75
Europe/Middle East/Africa	20
Asia/Pacific	5
Total	**100**

PRODUCTS/OPERATIONS

2018 Assets Mix

	% of total
North America	73
Europe/Middle East/Africa	21
Asia/Pacific	6
Total	**100**

2018 Revenue

	$ mil.	% of total
Fees:		
Servicing fees	5,421	45
Management fees	1,851	16
Foreign exchange trading services	1,201	10
Securities finance	543	5
Processing fees and other	289	2
Net interest revenue	2,671	22
Gains (losses) related to investment securities net	6	-
Total	**11**	**100**

2018 Sales

	$ mil.	% of total
Investment Servicing	10,034	84
Investment Management	1,956	16
Elimination	(8.0)	-
Total	**11,982**	**100**

Selected Capabilities

Data and Analytic
Investment Management
Investment Research and Trading
Investment Servicing

COMPETITORS

Bank of New York Mellon	JPMorgan Chase
Citigroup	Morgan Stanley
Credit Suisse (USA)	Northern Trust
Deutsche Bank	Principal Financial
First Data	SEI Investments
Fiserv	UBS Financial Services

HISTORICAL FINANCIALS

Company Type: Public

Income Statement
FYE: December 31

	ASSETS ($ mil.)	NET INCOME ($ mil.)	INCOME AS % OF ASSETS	EMPLOYEES
12/19	245,610	2,242	0.9%	39,103
12/18	244,626	2,599	1.1%	40,142
12/17	238,425	2,177	0.9%	36,643
12/16	242,698	2,143	0.9%	33,783
12/15	245,192	1,980	0.8%	32,356
Annual Growth	**0.0%**	**3.2%**	**—**	**4.8%**

2019 Year-End Financials

Debt ratio: 5.09%
Return on equity: 9.11%
Cash ($ mil.): 73,181
Current ratio: —
Long-term debt ($ mil.): —

No. of shares (mil.): 357
Dividends
  Yield: 2.5%
  Payout: 39.2%
Market value ($ mil.): 28,270

	STOCK PRICE ($) FY Close	P/E High/Low		PER SHARE ($) Earnings	Dividends	Book Value
12/19	79.10	15	9	5.38	1.98	68.36
12/18	63.07	17	9	6.40	1.78	65.25
12/17	97.61	19	14	5.24	1.60	60.70
12/16	77.72	16	10	4.97	1.44	55.56
12/15	66.36	18	14	4.47	1.32	52.80
Annual Growth	**4.5%**	**—**	**—**	**4.7%**	**10.7%**	**6.7%**

Steel Dynamics Inc.

Steel Dynamics may operate mini-mills but it produces steel on a large scale. Steel Dynamics operates liquid iron-making facilities ferrous and nonferrous steel scrap processing and steel fabrication facilities. The company sells to companies in the automotive construction and manufacturing industries as well as to steel processors and service centers primarily eastern US. Among its mini-mill output are beams rails and other products used in the construction industrial machinery and transportation industries.

Operations

Steel Dynamics has three reporting segments: Steel Metals Recycling and Steel Fabrication.

Its Steel operations have six electric-arc furnace mini-mills producing steel from steel scrap and scrap substitutes utilizing continuous casting automated rolling mills and numerous steel coating and processing lines and IDI. Its Flat Roll Division sheet steel products such as hot rolled cold rolled and coated steel products are used by automakers and other industries. The Long Products Division sells structural steel beams and pilings for the construction industry and industrial quality grade rail for the railroad industry. The Steel operations account for nearly 70%of sales.

The Metals Recycling operations (about 15% of revenue) consist solely of OmniSource which includes ferrous and nonferrous scrap metal processing transportation marketing brokerage and consulting services. In addition OmniSource designs installs and manages customized scrap management programs for industrial manufacturing companies.

The company's Steel Fabrication operations (about 10% of revenue) include seven New Millennium Building Systems plants which fabricate steel joists trusses girders and decking used by the non-residential construction industry.

All told Steel Dynamics operates six electric-arc-furnace steel mills steel coating lines a downstream engineered bar (SBQ) processing facility an iron production facility multiple metals recycling operations and seven steel fabrication plants.

Geographic Reach

Steel Dynamics has operations in Indiana (Butler Columbia City Jeffersonville and Pittsboro) Mississippi (Columbus) Pennsylvania (Pittsburgh) Virginia (Roanoke) and West Virginia (Huntington). It also serves the Southern US Canada and Mexico.

Steel Dynamics' headquarters is located in Fort Wayne Indiana.

Sales and Marketing

Steel Dynamics' primary customers for structural steel products are steel service centers steel fabricators and a range of other manufacturers including metal building firms general construction contractors developers brokers agriculture consumer goods and governmental entities.

Financial Performance

Over the past five years Steel Dynamics hit $11.8 billion in 2018 and decreased to $10.5 billion in 2019. Overall revenue increased by 38%.

Revenue decreased 11% to 10.5 billion compared to $11.8 billion in 2018. The decreased was due to lower sales across all segment.

Steel Dynamics profits in 2019 declined about 47% primarily due to lower sales and higher expenses.

Company's cash holdings increased by $552 million ending the year at $1.4 billion in 2019. Operations generated $1.4 billion. Investment activities took up some $576.9 million while financing activities utilized $266.6 million majority of which went towards long-term debt reduction. CAPEX in 2019 was $425 million.

Strategy

Its entrepreneurial culture fosters a team of energetic positive driven and innovative individuals by utilizing open communication and meaningful performance-based compensation aligned to our strategic focus. This results in safe low-cost and highly efficient operations which drive "best-in-class" operating and financial performance.

Strategic Growth Intentional Margin Expansion and Consistency "Through the Cycle" ? Its intentional value-driven growth has propelled our diversification in both end markets and product offerings to sustain continued higher volume and profitability throughout both strong and weak market environments. The company is focused on continued strategic and responsible growth.

Mergers and Acquisitions

In 2020 Steel Dynamics entered a definitive agreement to acquire 100% of the equity interest of Zimmer headquartered in Monterrey Mexico and operates a ferrous and nonferrous scrap metals recycling business. Zimmer provides a platform to grow Steel Dynamics' metals recycling presence in Mexico representing a meaningful achievement in its raw material sourcing strategy for our Texas steel mill which is currently under construction and expected to begin operations mid-year 2021.

In 2019 the Company acquired a majority of the equity interests of United Steel Supply headquartered in Austin Texas and is a leading distributor of painted Galvalume flat roll steel used for roofing and siding applications. Steel Dynamics purchased 75 percent of the equity interests of United Steel Supply for $134 million. Additionally Steel Dynamics has an option to purchase the remaining 25 percent equity interests of United Steel Supply in the future. The partnership provides an exciting opportunity to expand its painted Galvalume distribution network.

Company Background

Growing its share of the rail market in 2012 Steel Dynamics announced plans to install a heat-treating system (capable of producing up to 350000 tons of standard strength and head hardened plain carbon steel rails for North Amer-

ica's railroad industry) at its Columbia City Indiana Structural and Rail Division.

Steel Dynamics entered a joint venture in 2011 with Spain's Lafarga Group to construct a $39 million facility which will produce copper wire rod from recycled copper.

Steel Dynamics was incorporated in 1993.

EXECUTIVES

Vice President Human Resources, Benjamin Eisbart
President And Ceo, Mark D. Millett, age 61, $1,010,000 total compensation
Evp Metals Recycling And President And Coo Omnisource, Russell B. (Russ) Rinn, age 63, $510,000 total compensation
Svp Long Products Steel Group, Glenn A. Pushis, age 54, $393,750 total compensation
Manager Information Technology, Robert E. (Bob) Francis
Controller, Theresa E. Wagler, age 50, $580,000 total compensation
Vp And General Manager Engineered Bar Products Division, Barry T. Schneider, age 51, $363,750 total compensation
Vp And President Steel Of West Virginia, Timothy R. (Tim) Duke
Svp Downstream Manufacturing Group, Christopher A. (Chris) Graham, age 57, $322,500 total compensation
Vp And Corporate Controller, Brent Ritenour
Vice President Finance, John Morris
Vice President And General Manager Roanoke Bar Division, Joe Crawford
Vice President Business Development, Alex Hoffman
Vice President, Boudler Noelle
Chairman, Keith E. Busse, age 78
Vice President Treasurer And Risk Manager, Richard Poinsatte
Board Member, Richard T Teets
First Secretary Of Desi, Antoniak Renee
Treasurer Chapter, Bob Barrick
Auditors: Ernst & Young LLP

LOCATIONS

HQ: Steel Dynamics Inc.
7575 West Jefferson Blvd., Fort Wayne, IN 46804
Phone: 260 969-3500
Web: www.steeldynamics.com

PRODUCTS/OPERATIONS

2016 sales

	$ mil.	% of total
Steel	5,870	65
Metals Recycling	2,171	24
Steel Fabrication	703	8
Other	276	3
Eliminations	(1246.1)	-
Total	**7,777**	**100**

Selected Products
Cold-rolled galvannealed
Cold-rolled hot-dipped galvanized
Direct reduced iron
Fully processed cold-rolled sheet
Hot-rolled galvannealed
Hot-rolled hot-dipped galvanized
Hot-rolled pickled and oiled
Liquid pig iron
Structural products (steel joists trusses)
Steel Operations
Sheet Products
 Hot rolled Products
 Cold Rolled Products
Long Products
 Structural
 Wide flange American Standard and miscellaneous beams
 H piling

Channel sections
Rail Products
 Engineered Bar Products
 Merchant Bar Products
 Specialty Shapes
Metals Recycling   No. 2 shredded
 No. 1 bundles
 Plate and structural
 No. 1 busheling
 Turnings
 Heavy melt
 Briquettes
 Copper granules
 Stainless steel bundles
Steel Fabrication Operations   Joists
 Decking
 Castellated beams
 Cambered beams

COMPETITORS

AK Steel Holding	Evraz
Corporation	Gerdau Ameristeel
ArcelorMittal USA	Nucor
Canam Steel	Timken
Corporation	United States Steel
Commercial Metals	Wheeling Corrugating

HISTORICAL FINANCIALS

Company Type: Public

Income Statement

FYE: December 31

	REVENUE ($ mil.)	NET INCOME ($ mil.)	NET PROFIT MARGIN	EMPLOYEES
12/19	10,464	671	6.4%	8,385
12/18	11,821	1,258	10.6%	8,200
12/17	9,538	812	8.5%	7,635
12/16	7,777	382	4.9%	7,695
12/15	7,594	(130)	—	7,500
Annual Growth	8.3%	—	—	2.8%

2019 Year-End Financials

Debt ratio: 33.04%
Return on equity: 16.75%
Cash ($ mil.): 1,381
Current ratio: 4.22
Long-term debt ($ mil.): 2,644

No. of shares (mil.): 214
Dividends
 Yield: 2.8%
 Payout: 26.3%
Market value ($ mil.): 7,302

	STOCK PRICE ($) FY Close	P/E High/Low		PER SHARE ($) Earnings	Dividends	Book Value
12/19	34.04	13	8	3.04	0.96	19.00
12/18	30.04	10	5	5.35	0.75	17.47
12/17	43.13	13	10	3.36	0.62	14.12
12/16	35.58	25	10	1.56	0.56	12.01
12/15	17.87	—	—	(0.54)	0.55	11.02
Annual Growth	17.5%	—	—	—	14.9%	14.6%

Sterling Bancorp (DE)

Sterling Bancorp is the holding company for Sterling National Bank a community-based thrift operating dozens of offices in New York's Hudson Valley region and Greater New York City area. Founded in 1888 the bank attracts consumers and business clients by offering traditional deposit products such as checking and savings accounts and CDs. It uses funds from deposits to originate primarily real estate loans and mortgages. Sterling Bancorp which has assets of more than $7 billion was formerly Provident New York Bancorp; Provident acquired the former Sterling Bancorp in late 2013 and changed its name as well as the name of its banking subsidiary to Sterling. In 2017 the bank agreed to acquire Astoria Financial for $2.2 billion.

EXECUTIVES

Chief Administrative Officer Senior Executive Vice President, Rodney Whitwell
Senior Vice President Business Intelligence, Patrick DeKenipp
Executive Vice President General Counsel Chief Legal Officer, James Blose
Executive Vice President Marketing, Anthony Burke
First Vice President, Yvonne Shand
Senior Managing Director And Svp, Tammy Leisen
First Vp Managing Director, Moira Kiernan
Vice President Managing Director, Michael Gogitidze
Assistant Vice President Client Service Manager, Jason Solow
Senior Vice President Managing Director, Laura Greatsinger
Vice President Managing Director, Lisa Congemi-doutney
Vice President Managing Director, Nicole Sarno
Vp Director Facilities Procurement And Vendor Management, Michele Miuta
Senior Vice President And Senior Managing Director, Kevin King
Svp Director Consumer Banking Network, James Griffin
Vice President Senior Counsel, Despina Walsh
Svp Director Consumer Banking Administration, Michael Lechleider
Svp And Sr Managing Director, Timothy Juliano
Operations Workflow Integration Leader Vp, Krista Gulalo
Avp Enterprise Data, Albert Deluca
Auditors: Crowe LLP

LOCATIONS

HQ: Sterling Bancorp (DE)
Two Blue Hill Plaza, 2nd Floor, Pearl River, New York, NY 10965
Phone: 845 369-8040
Web: www.sterlingbancorp.com

COMPETITORS

Capital One	JPMorgan Chase
Citibank	KeyCorp
HSBC USA	M&T Bank

HISTORICAL FINANCIALS

Company Type: Public

Income Statement | | | | FYE: December 31

	ASSETS ($ mil.)	NET INCOME ($ mil.)	INCOME AS % OF ASSETS	EMPLOYEES
12/19	30,586	427	1.4%	1,639
12/18	31,383	447	1.4%	1,907
12/17	30,359	93	0.3%	2,076
12/16	14,178	139	1.0%	970
12/15	11,955	66	0.6%	1,089
Annual Growth	26.5%	59.4%	—	10.8%

2019 Year-End Financials

Debt ratio: 2.09%	No. of shares (mil.): 198
Return on equity: 9.53%	Dividends
Cash ($ mil.): 329	Yield: 1.3%
Current ratio: —	Payout: 13.8%
Long-term debt ($ mil.): —	Market value ($ mil.): 4,183

	STOCK PRICE ($) FY Close	P/E High/Low		PER SHARE ($) Earnings	Dividends	Book Value
12/19	21.08	11	8	2.03	0.28	22.83
12/18	16.51	13	8	1.95	0.28	20.48
12/17	24.60	45	36	0.58	0.28	18.86
12/16	23.40	23	13	1.07	0.28	13.72
12/15	16.22	29	22	0.60	0.28	12.81
Annual Growth	6.8%	—	—	35.6%	(0.0%)	15.5%

Sterling Bancorp Inc (MI)

Auditors: Crowe LLP

LOCATIONS

HQ: Sterling Bancorp Inc (MI)
One Towne Square, Suite 1900, Southfield, MI 48076
Phone: 248 355-2400
Web: www.sterlingbank.com

HISTORICAL FINANCIALS

Company Type: Public

Income Statement | | | | FYE: December 31

	ASSETS ($ mil.)	NET INCOME ($ mil.)	INCOME AS % OF ASSETS	EMPLOYEES
12/19	3,244	29	0.9%	311
12/18	3,196	63	2.0%	352
12/17	2,961	37	1.3%	308
12/16	2,163	33	1.5%	294
12/15	1,712	22	1.3%	—
Annual Growth	17.3%	6.8%		

2019 Year-End Financials

Debt ratio: 2.01%	No. of shares (mil.): 49
Return on equity: 8.76%	Dividends
Cash ($ mil.): 78	Yield: 0.4%
Current ratio: —	Payout: 3.5%
Long-term debt ($ mil.): —	Market value ($ mil.): 405

	STOCK PRICE ($) FY Close	P/E High/Low		PER SHARE ($) Earnings	Dividends	Book Value
12/19	8.10	18	12	0.57	0.04	6.66
12/18	6.95	12	6	1.20	0.04	6.32
12/17	12.70	16	15	0.82	0.21	5.16
Annual Growth	(10.6%)	—	—	(8.7%)	(33.9%)	6.6%

Stifel Financial Corp

Through subsidiaries Stifel Nicolaus (founded 1890) Thomas Weisel Century Securities Associates Stifel Bank & Trust and others Stifel Financial provides asset management financial advice and banking services for private clients investment banking clients and institutional investors in the US. Stifel also offers brokerage and mergers and acquisitions advisory services for corporate clients underwrites debt and equity. The firm boasts around 445 US offices and certain foreign countries.

Operations

Stifel Financial operates three business segments: Global Wealth Management Institutional Group and various corporate activities combined in the Other segment.

The Global Wealth Management segment which generates around 60% of the firm's total revenue consists of two businesses: Stifel Bank which provides traditional banking products and services and the Private Client Group which is made up of offices across the US that provide securities brokerage services and Stifel Bancorp.

The Institutional Group segment (about 40% of revenue) provides securities brokerage trading and research services to institutions and specializes in the sale of equity and fixed-income products.

The Other segment includes interest income from stock borrow activities unallocated interest expense interest income and gains and losses from investments held amortization of stock-based awards and all unallocated overhead cost.

Geographic Reach

The company is headquartered in Missouri with about 445 leased offices and more than 380 private client offices mostly across the US as well as in certain foreign countries. About 95% of its revenue stems from the US.

Sales and Marketing

With its over 2000 financial advisors and approximately 95 independent contractors Stifel serves individuals corporations municipalities and institutions.

Financial Performance

For the year ended December 31 2019 net revenues increased 10% to a record $3.3 billion compared to $3.0 billion during the comparable period in 2018. The increase is primarily attributable to an increase in investment banking revenues higher net interest income as a result of an increase in interest-earning assets at Stifel Bancorp an increase in brokerage revenues and the growth in asset management and service fees as a result of increased assets under management.

The company's net income increased by $56 million to $450 million compared to $394 million in the prior year. The increase was due to the increase on their revenue with less increase on their expenses.

Stifel's cash at the end of 2019 was $1.3 billion which was $795 million less than the prior year. Cash provided by operations was $626.9 million while cash used for investing and financing activities were $350 million and $1.1 billion respectively.

Strategy

Stifel's strategy for growth will allow it to increase revenues and to expand its role with clients as a valued partner. In executing its growth strategy Stifel takes advantage of the consolidation among mid-tier firms which provides opportunities in global wealth and institutional group segments. Stifel intends to pursue the following strategies with discipline:

Further expand private client footprint in the U.S. The company plans to further expand its domestic private client footprint. Stifel plans on achieving this through recruiting experienced fi-